S:COTT®

2003

STANDARD POSTAGE STAMP CATALOGUE

ONE HUNDRED AND FIFTY-NINTH EDITION IN SIX VOLUMES

VOLUME 1
UNITED STATES
and Affiliated Territories
UNITED NATIONS
COUNTRIES OF THE WORLD

A-B

EDITOR	James E. Kloetzel
ASSOCIATE EDITOR	William A. Jones
ASSISTANT EDITOR /NEW ISSUES & VALUING	Martin J. Frankevicz
VALUING ANALYSTS	Leonard J. Gellman
	Rich Wolff
EDITORIAL ASSISTANT	Beth Brown
DESIGN MANAGER	Teresa M. Wenrick
IMAGE COORDINATOR	Nancy S. Martin
ELECTRONIC MEDIA MANAGER	Mark Kaufman
MARKETING/SALES DIRECTOR	William Fay
ADVERTISING	Renee Davis
CIRCULATION / PRODUCT PROMOTION MANAGER	Tim Wagner
EDITORIAL DIRECTOR/AMOS PRESS INC.	Michael Laurence

Scott Publishing Co.

911 Vandemark Road, Sidney, OH 45365-0828

A division of AMOS PRESS, INC., publishers of *Linn's Stamp News, Coin World* and *Cars & Parts* magazine.

Copyright© 2002 by

Released April 2002

Includes New Stamp Listings through the March, 2002 *Scott Stamp Monthly* Catalogue Update

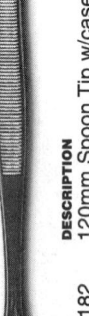

Table of Contents

On the Cover: This year's theme for the catalogue
covers is the Centennial of Powered Flight.
A special thank you to Eric Kindig for allowing us to
photograph his 1941 North American • T-6 "TEXAN"

See Volumes 2 through 6 for Countries of the World, C-Z

Scott Publishing Mission Statement

The Scott Publishing Team exists to serve the recreational,
educational and commercial hobby needs of stamp collectors and dealers.

We strive to set the industry standard for philatelic information and products by developing and
providing goods that help collectors identify, value, organize and present their collections.

Quality customer service is, and will continue to be, our highest priority.
We aspire toward achieving total customer satisfaction.

Scott Publishing Co.

SCOTT   911 VANDEMARK ROAD, SIDNEY, OHIO 45365   937-498-0802

Dear Scott Catalogue User:

Volume 1 of the new 2003 *Scott Standard Postage Stamp Catalogue* continues the image-scanning project that was the most visually obvious change in last year's catalogs. Using the magnificent collection of unused stamps loaned to Scott by an Ohio gentleman, we are now able to scan and print the images of the early stamps from Volumes 1-3 that were missed last year when we were only able to provide actual stamp images for the more modern stamps. We think you will enjoy the difference in the images for 2003.

What about the value changes for 2003?

There are almost 14,000 value changes in Volume 1, which covers the United States, U.S. Possessions, the United Nations, and countries of the world A-B. As expected, the stamps of the United States lead the way with almost 2,800 value changes. Australia and its states have more than 1,600 value changes. However, this is only a fraction of the total value changes for the countries of the British Commonwealth. The others show almost 3,600 adjustments. Additional countries that also record large numbers of value changes are the United Nations, Albania, Afghanistan and the Azores.

What's happening with U.S. stamp values?

Values for very fine and better United States stamps, and especially values for scarce to rare stamps and stamp varieties, are quite solid, and catalog values for such items generally are continuing to rise.

Collectors and dealers need to keep in mind that large numbers of value changes and some editorial changes that were made first in the 2002 *United States Specialized Catalogue* have been brought forward and incorporated into the 2003 Volume 1, and additional value and editorial changes have been added to those. Occasionally we hear from folks who are under the impression that all United States values in a single year's catalogs are the same, but that is not true. United States values are reviewed and changed where necessary twice each year, once in Volume 1 (issued in April) and again in the *United States Specialized* (issued in October).

The values for many 1875 Special Printings increase, such as those of the 1873 1¢-90¢ Banknotes, Scott 167-177, and others. Some of the increases are quite large. There are exceptions to every rule, however, and the 1875 5¢ and 10¢ Reproductions of the 1847 first issue drop slightly to $750 and $950, respectively, from $800 and $1,000 in the 2002 *United States Specialized Catalogue.*

Values for classic issues generally rise in the 5 to 10 percent range, especially unused. Some rise even more, such as the 1863 5¢ brown, Scott 76, which jumps unused to $1,300 from $1,100 in the 2002 Volume 1 and $1,200 in the 2002 *U.S. Specialized.* Some movement is evident in values for used stamps as well, such as Scott 76 again, which rises to $120 from $110. The 1866 15¢ black Lincoln, Scott 77, moves to $160 from $150.

Large value increases are seen for some United States varieties, such as the 1869 1¢ buff without grill, Scott 112b, which leaps to $6,000 unused from $4,250. The double impression variety of the 1873 3¢ green, Scott 158j, doubles in value to $2,500 used from $1,250.

Values for dollar-denomination Columbians of 1893 drop slightly in unused condition, but the values for the same stamps mint, never hinged hold steady. For example, the $5 black, Scott 245, drops to $3,250 unused from $3,500 last year, but remains at $8,250 mint, never hinged.

The 1934 part-perf error varieties of the 1¢ to 7¢ National Parks issue, Scott 739a-746a, increase in value again in 2003, on top of their upward movement in the 2002 *U.S. Specialized.* More modern errors, however, show signs of softening.

In Air Post, a modest correction downward by about 5 to 10 percent affects the $1.30 and $2.60 1930 Zeppelins, Scott C14 and C15, bringing the set to $1,475 unused from $1,550, and to $2,160 mint, never hinged from $2,235.

Most 1919-22 Offices in China stamps, Scott K1-K18, rise in value slightly both unused and mint, never hinged. Huge numbers of upward adjustments are evident in Postal Stationery. In Revenues, higher value dated Documentary stamps and Stock Transfer stamps (the "Reds" and the "Greens") generally rise in value significantly.

Where's the action in the A-B countries?

The continuing strength of the U.S. dollar in the international marketplace against other world currencies has led to some lowering of values in various countries or to the appearance of a flat market. Actually, this reflects the dollar's strength more than it does a weakening in demand for stamps. This situation continues to offer collectors in the United States attractive buying opportunities.

For the stamps of New South Wales, the Australian state with the most value changes, a number of adjustments are quite large in both directions. On balance, a strong upward trend is evident, especially in used material. An example of this trend is the 1854-55 hexagonal Queen Victoria 6-pence gray, Scott 29, which soars to $400 unused and $50 used this year, from $325 unused and $32.50 used in the 2002 catalogue. In the material of Australia proper from 1945-1975, there appears to be a downward trend, although minor error varieties frequently show major increases. A startling example is the 1965 5-pence Christmas Nativity scene with gold omitted, Scott 393a, which skyrockets to $1,000 mint, never hinged in the 2003 catalogue from $300 last year.

Values for the stamps of the Azores have been completely reviewed, resulting in almost 550 changes for this small country. The general trend is downward, although there are enough stamps in the opposite direction to warrant a detailed review. The 1910 King Manuel II definitives, Scott 112-125, and the three sets of overprints that follow are some of the issues that show upward value changes. For many error varieties, such as inverted and double overprints, the editors have noted that little data exists to accurately identify values. As a result, many current values have been replaced with dashes.

Almost 3,600 stamps of the British Commonwealth (not counting the Australian area) show value changes. These changes are spread out over 30 different stamp-issuing entities. More than 340 value changes occur in the Bahamas, where most of the changes are in the 1960-1975 period. Stamps of the earlier portion of this period show upward movement in values, but the later portion show significant value decreases.

Where are the editorial enhancements?

In addition to all the new issue listings, a huge number of listings for United States major errors that appeared for the first time in the 2002 U.S. Specialized have been brought forward to the 2003 Volume 1, and these have been augmented by many newly discovered errors that are listed for the first time.

Values for never-hinged stamps have been added for many United States minor varieties, and some new explanatory or grading notes have been added at various points throughout the catalog. In several countries, minor varieties have been added to identify bisects, double overprints and perf varieties.

In Albania, Scott 1899-1904 has been renumbered and split into two separate sets, one for Alexander Moissi and one for Shanto and Stafa. For Spanish Andorra, a new value, the 1-peseta slate, has been added as a major number, Scott 34A, to the 1936-43 definitive set without control numbers. In the Australian state of Queensland, two new major numbers appear in the perforation varieties of the 1876-78 issues. These new 1¢ and 2¢ perf 12½x11 stamps become Scott 49G and 49H. In Barbados, the major number Scott 12B has been added to designate a previously unlisted 14 x 12½ pin-perf variety.

Happy collecting,

James E. Kloetzel

James E. Kloetzel/Catalogue Editor

Acknowledgments

Our appreciation and gratitude go to the following individuals who have assisted us in preparing information included in the 2003 Scott Catalogues. Some helpers prefer anonymity. These individuals have generously shared their stamp knowledge with others through the medium of the Scott Catalogue.

Those who follow provided information that is in addition to the hundreds of dealer price lists and advertisements and scores of auction catalogues and realizations that were used in producing the catalogue values. It is from those noted here that we have been able to obtain information on items not normally seen in published lists and advertisements. Support from these people goes beyond data leading to catalogue values, for they also are key to editorial changes.

A special acknowledgment to Liane and Sergio Sismondo of The Classic Collector for their extraordinary assistance and knowledge sharing that has aided in the preparation of this year's Standard and Classic Specialized Catalogues.

Dr. Karl Agre
Donald R. Alexander (China Stamp Society)
A. R. Allison (Orange Free State Study Circle)
B. J. Ammel (The Nile Post)
Robert Ausubel (Great Britain Collectors Club)
John Barone (Stamptracks)
Jack Hagop Barsoumian (International Stamp Co.)
William Batty-Smith (Sarawak Specialists' Society)
Jules K. Beck (Latin American Philatelic Society)
John D. Bowman (Carriers and Locals Society)
Chris Brainard (B&S Stamp Bourse)
Jeff Brasor (Honduras Coll. Club, Associated Coll. of El Salvador)
Roger S. Brody
Keith & Margie Brown
Mike Bush (Joseph V. Bush, Inc.)
Peter Bylen
Nathan Carlin
Henry Chlanda
Bob Coale
Laurie Conrad
Leo Constantinides
Frank D. Correl
Andrew Cronin (Canadian Society of Russian Philately)
William T. Crowe (The Philatelic Foundation)
Tony L. Crumbley (Carolina Coin & Stamp, Inc.)
Norman S. Davis
Tom Derbyshire (University Stamp Co.)
John DeStefanis (Matthew Bennett, Inc.)
Bob Dumaine (Sam Houston Duck Co.)
William S. Dunn
Paul G. Eckman
Peter R. Feltus
Karol Fercák (Karol Fercák International)
Leon Finik (Loral Stamps)
Joseph E. Foley (Eire Philatelic Association)
Robert S. Freeman
Richard Friedberg
Bob Genisol (Sultan Stamp Center)
Daniel E. Grau
Michael H. Grollnek (Mid South Stamp Co.)
Harry Hagendorf
Erich E. Hamm (Philactica)
Jerone Hart (Aden & Somaliland Study Group)
Bruce Hecht (Bruce L. Hecht Co.)
Clifford O. Herrick (Fidelity Trading Co.)
Lee H. Hill, Jr.
Wilson Hulme
Kalman V. Illyefalvi (Society for Hungarian Philately)
Eric Jackson

John I. Jamieson (Saskatoon Stamp Centre)
Peter C. Jeannopoulos
Richard A. Johnson
Allan Katz (Ventura Stamp Company)
Stanford M. Katz
Lewis Kaufman
Patricia A. Kaufmann
Dr. James W. Kerr
Charles F. Kezbers
Dr. Thomas C. Kingsley
Juri Kirsimagi
Janet Klug
William V. Kriebel
William Langs
Frederick P. Lawrence
John R. Lewis (The William Henry Stamp Co.)
Ulf Lindahl (Ethiopian Philatelic Society)
William A. Litle
Gary B. Little (Luxembourg Collectors Club)
Pedro Llach (Filatelia Llach S.L.)
William Thomas Lockard (Liberian Philatelic Society)
Dennis Lynch
Larry Lyons (Carriers and Locals Society)
David MacDonnell
Nick Markov (Italia Stamp Co.)
Marilyn R. Mattke
Mark S. Miller
Allen Mintz (United Postal Stationery Society)
Jack E. Molesworth (Jack E. Molesworth, Inc.)
Chuck Q. Moo
Gary M. Morris (Pacific Midwest Co.)
Peter Mosiondz, Jr.
Bruce M. Moyer (Moyer Stamps & Collectibles)
Richard H. Muller (Richard's Stamps)
Naya Nicolins (Indigo)
Robert Odenweller
Victor Ostolaza
Dr. Everett L. Parker (St. Helena, Ascension & Tristan da Cunha Philatelic Society)
John E. Pearson (Pittwater Philatelic Service)
John Pedneault
Donald J. Peterson (International Philippine Philatelic Society)
Stanley M. Piller (Stanley M. Piller & Associates)
Todor Drumev Popov
Peter W. W. Powell
Stephen Radin (Albany Stamp Co.)
Siddique Mahmudur Rahman (Bangladesh Institute of Philatelic Studies)
Ghassan D. Riachi
Michael Rogers (Michael Rogers, Inc.)
Jon W. Rose
Michael Ruggiero

Frans H.A. Rummens (American Society for Netherlands Philately)
Theodosios Sampson
Jacques C. Schiff, Jr. (Jacques C. Schiff, Jr., Inc.)
Bernard Seckler (Fine Arts Philatelists)
F. Burton Sellers
J. Randall Shoemaker (Professional Stamp Experts, Inc.)
Charles F. Shreve (Shreves Philatelic Galleries, Inc.)
Sergio & Liane Sismondo (The Classic Collector)
Richard Stambaugh
Frank J. Stanley, III
Philip & Henry Stevens (postalstationery.com)
Mark Stucker
A. John Ultee (Iran Philatelic Study Circle)
Xavier Verbeck (American Belgian Philatelic Society)
Hal Vogel (American Society of Polar Philatelists)
Philip T. Wall
Daniel C. Warren
Richard A. Washburn
Giana Wayman (Asociacion Filatélica de Costa Rica)
William R. Weiss, Jr. (Weiss Philatelics)
Ed Wener (Indigo)
Hans Westphal
Don White (Dunedin Stamp Centre)
Kirk Wolford
David Wood (Premier Philately Auctions)
Ralph Yorio
Alfonso G. Zulueta, Jr.

Addresses, Telephone Numbers, Web Sites, E-Mail Addresses of General & Specialized Philatelic Societies

Collectors can contact the following groups for information about the philately of the areas within the scope of these societies, or inquire about membership in these groups. Aside from the general societies, we limit this list to groups that specialize in particular fields of philately, particular areas covered by the Scott Standard Postage Stamp Catalogue, and topical groups. Many more specialized philatelic societies exist than those listed below. These addresses were compiled in January 2002, and are, to the best of our knowledge, correct and current. Groups should inform the editors of address changes whenever they occur. The editors also want to hear from other such specialized groups not listed.

Unless otherwise noted all website addresses begin with http://

American Philatelic Society
PO Box 8000
State College PA 16803
Ph: (814) 237-3803
www.stamps.org
E-mail: relamb@stamps.org

American Stamp Dealers'
Association
Joseph Savarese
3 School St.
Glen Cove NY 11542
Ph: (516) 759-7000
www.asdaonline.com
E-mail: asda@erols.com

International Society of Worldwide
Stamp Collectors
Anthony Zollo
PO Box 150407
Lufkin TX 75915-0407
www.iswsc.org
E-mail: stamptmf@frontiernet.net

Junior Philatelists of America
Jennifer Arnold
PO Box 2625
Albany OR 97321
www.jpastamps.org
E-mail: exec.sec@jpastamps.org

Royal Philatelic Society
41 Devonshire Place
London, United Kingdom W1G 6JY

Royal Philatelic Society of Canada
PO Box 929, Station Q
Toronto, ON, Canada M4T 2P1
Ph: (888) 285-4143
www.rpsc.org
E-mail: info@rpsc.org

Groups focusing on fields or aspects found in world-wide philately (some may cover U.S. area only)

American Air Mail Society
Stephen Reinhard
PO Box 110
Mineola NY 11501
ourworld.compuserve.com/homepages/
aams/
E-mail: sr1501@aol.com

American First Day Cover Society
Douglas Kelsey
PO Box 65960
Tucson AZ 85728-5960
Ph: (520) 321-0880
www.afdcs.org
E-mail: afdcs@aol.com

American Revenue Association
Eric Jackson
PO Box 728
Leesport PA 19533-0728
Ph: (610) 926-6200
www.revenuer.org
E-mail: eric@revenuer.com

American Topical Association
Paul E. Tyler
PO Box 50820
Albuquerque NM 87181-0820
Ph: (505) 323-8595
home.prcn.org/~pauld/ata/
E-mail: ATAStamps@juno.com

Errors, Freaks and Oddities
Collectors Club
Jim McDevitt
PO Box 1126
Kingsland GA 31548
Ph: (912) 729-1573
E-mail: cwouscg@aol.com

Fakes and Forgeries Study Group
Anthony Torres
107 Hoover Rd.
Rochester NY 14617-3611
E-mail: ajtorres@rochester.rr.com

First Issues Collectors Club
Kurt Streepy
608 Whitethorn Way
Bloomington IN 47403
Ph: (812) 339-6229
E-mail: kstreepy@msn.com

International Philatelic Society of
Joint Stamp Issues Collectors
Richard Zimmermann
124, Avenue Guy de Coubertin
Saint Remy Les Chevreuse, France
F-78470
perso.clubinternet.fr/rzimmerm/index.
htm
E-mail: rzimmerm@club-internet.fr

National Duck Stamp Collectors
Society
Anthony J. Monico
PO Box 43
Harleysville PA 19438-0043
www.hwcn.org/link/ndscs
E-mail: ndscs@hwcn.org

No Value Identified Club
Albert Sauvanet
Le Clos Royal B, Boulevard des Pas
Enchantes
St. Sebastien-sur Loire, France 44230
E-mail: alain.vailly@irin.univ_nantes.fr

The Perfins Club
Kurt Ottenheimer
462 West Walnut St.
Long Beach NY 11561
Ph: (516) 431-3412
E-mail: oak462@juno.com

Post Mark Collectors Club
David Proulx
7629 Homestead Drive
Baldwinsville NY 13027
E-mail: stampdance@baldcom.net

Postal History Society
Kalman V. Illyefalvi
8207 Daren Court
Pikesville MD 21208-2211
Ph: (410) 653-0665

Precancel Stamp Society
176 Bent Pine Hill
North Wales PA 19454
Ph: (215) 368-6082
E-mail: abentpine1@aol.com

United Postal Stationery Society
Cora Collins
PO Box 1792
Norfolk VA 23501-1792
Ph: (757) 420-3487
www.upss.org
E-mail: poststat@juno.com

Groups focusing on U.S. area philately as covered in the Standard Catalogue

Canal Zone Study Group
Richard H. Salz
60 27th Ave.
San Francisco CA 94121

Carriers and Locals Society
John D. Bowman
PO Box 382436
Birmingham AL 35238-2436
Ph: (205) 967-6200
www.pennypost.org
E-mail: jdbowman@premierhome.net

Confederate Stamp Alliance
Richard L. Calhoun
PO Box 581
Mt. Prospect IL 60056-0581

Hawaiian Philatelic Society
Kay H. Hoke
PO Box 10115
Honolulu HI 96816-0115
Ph: (808) 521-5721
E-mail: bannan@pixi.com

Plate Number Coil Collectors Club
Gene C. Trinks
3603 Bellows Court
Troy MI 48083
www.pnc3.org
E-mail: gctrinks@sprynet.com

United Nations Philatelists
Blanton Clement, Jr.
292 Springdale Terrace
Yardley PA 19067-3421
www.unpi.org
E-mail: bclemjr@aol.com

United States Stamp Society
Executive Secretary
PO Box 6634
Katy TX 77491-6631
www.usstamps.org

U.S. Cancellation Club
Roger Rhoads
3 Ruthana Way
Hockessin DE 19707
www.geocities.com/athens/2088/
usschome.htm
E-mail:rrrhoads@aol.com

U.S. Philatelic Classics Society
Mark D. Rogers
PO Box 80708
Austin TX 78708-0708
www.uspcs.org
E-mail: mrogers23@austin.rr.com

Groups focusing on philately of foreign countries or regions

Aden & Somaliland Study Group
Gary Brown
PO Box 106
Briar Hill, Victoria, Australia 3088
E-mail:
garyjohn951@optushome.com.au

American Society of Polar
Philatelists (Antarctic areas)
Alan Warren
PO Box 39
Exton PA 19341-0039
south-pole.com/aspp.htm
E-mail: alanwar@att.net

Albania Study Circle
Paul Eckman
PO Box 39880
Los Angeles CA 90039
members.netscapeonline.co.uk/johns
phipps/index.html
E-mail: peckman797@earthlink.net

Andorran Philatelic Study Circle
D. Hope
17 Hawthorn Dr.
Stalybridge, Cheshire, United Kingdom
SK15 1UE
www.chy-an-piran.demon.co.uk/
E-mail: apsc@chy-an-piran.demon.co.uk

Australian States Study Circle
Ben Palmer
GPO 1751
Sydney, N.S.W., Australia 1043

Austria Philatelic Society
Ralph Schneider
PO Box 23049
Belleville IL 62223
Ph: (618) 277-6152
www.apsus.esmartweb.com
E-mail: rsstamps@aol.com

American Belgian Philatelic
Society
Kenneth L. Costilow
621 Virginius Dr.
Virginia Beach VA 23452-4417
Ph: (757) 463-6081
groups.hamptonroads.com/ABPS
E-mail: kcos32@home.com

Bechuanalands and Botswana Society
Neville Midwood
69 Porlock Lane
Furzton, Milton Keynes, United Kingdom MK4 1JY
www.netcomuk.co.uk/~midsoft/bbsoc.html
E-mail: runnerpo@netcomuk.co.uk

Bermuda Collectors Society
Thomas J. McMahon
PO Box 1949
Stuart FL 34995

Brazil Philatelic Association
Kurt Ottenheimer
462 West Walnut St.
Long Beach NY 11561
Ph: (516) 431-3412
E-mail: oak462@juno.com

British Caribbean Philatelic Study Group
Dr. Reuben A. Ramkissoon
3011 White Oak Lane
Oak Brook IL 60523-2513

British North America Philatelic Society (Canada & Provinces)
H. P. Jacobi
5295 Moncton St.
Richmond, B.C., Canada V7E 3B2
www.bnaps.org
E-mail: beaver@telus.net

British West Indies Study Circle
W. Clary Holt
PO Drawer 59
Burlington NC 27216
Ph: (336) 227-7461

Burma Philatelic Study Circle
A. Meech
7208 91st Ave.
Edmonton, AB, Canada T6B 0R8
E-mail: ameech@telusplanet.net

Ceylon Study Group
R. W. P. Frost
42 Lonsdale Road, Cannington
Bridgewater, Somerset, United Kingdom TA5 2JS

China Stamp Society
Paul H. Gault
PO Box 20711
Columbus OH 43220
www.chinastampsociety.org
E-mail: secretary@chinastampsociety.org

Colombia/Panama Philatelic Study Group
PO Box 2245
El Cajon CA 92021
E-mail: jimacross@juno.com

Society for Costa Rica Collectors
Dr. Hector R. Mena
PO Box 14831
Baton Rouge LA 70808
www.socorico.org
E-mail: hrmena@aol.com

Croatian Philatelic Society (Croatia & other Balkan areas)
Ekrem Spahich
502 Romero, PO Box 696
Fritch TX 79036-0696
(806) 857-0129
croatianmall.com/cps/
812@arn.net

Cuban Philatelic Society of America
Ernesto Cuesta
PO Box 34434
Bethesda MD 20827
www.philat.com/cpsa

Cyprus Study Circle
Jim Wigmore
19 Riversmeet, Appledore
Bideford, N. Devon, United Kingdom EX39 1RE
www.geocities.com/cyprusstudycircle
E-mail: istug@aol.com

Society for Czechoslovak Philately
Robert T. Cossaboom
PO Box 25332
Scott AFB IL 62225-0332
www.czechoslovakphilately.com
E-mail: klfck1@aol.com

Danish West Indies Study Unit of the Scandinavian Collectors Club
John L. Dubois
Thermalogic Corp.
22 Kane Industrial Drive
Hudson MA 01749
Ph: (800) 343-4492
dwi.thlogic.com
E-mail: jld@thlogic.com

East Africa Study Circle
Ken Hewitt
16 Ashleigh Road
Solihull, United Kingdom B91 1AE
E-mail: 106602.2410@compuserve.com

Egypt Study Circle
Mike Murphy
109 Chadwick Road
London, United Kingdom SE15 4PY
E-mail: egyptstudycircle@hotmail.com

Estonian Philatelic Society
Juri Kirsimagi
29 Clifford Ave.
Pelham NY 10803

Ethiopian Philatelic Society
Ulf Lindahl
640 S. Pine Creek Rd.
Fairfield CT 06430
Ph: (203) 255-8005
members.home.net/fbheiser/ethiopia5.htm
E-mail: ulindahl@optonline.net

Falkland Islands Philatelic Study Group
Carl J. Faulkner
Williams Inn, On-the-Green
Williamstown MA 01267-2620
Ph: (413) 458-9371

Faroe Islands Study Circle
Norman Hudson
28 Enfield Road
Ellesmere Port, Cheshire, United Kingdom CH65 8BY
www.pherber.com/fisc/fisc.html
E-mail: jntropics@hotmail.com

Former French Colonies Specialist Society
BP 628
75367 Paris Cedex 08, France
www.ifrance.com/colfra
E-mail: clubcolfra@aol.com

France & Colonies Philatelic Society
Walter Parshall
103 Spruce St.
Bloomfield NJ 07003-3514

Germany Philatelic Society
PO Box 779
Arnold MD 21012-4779
www.gps.nu
E-mail: germanyphilatelic@starpower.net

German Democratic Republic Study Group of the German Philatelic Society
Ken Lawrence
PO Box 8040
State College PA 16803-8040
Ph: (814) 237-3803
E-mail: apsken@aol.com

Gibraltar Study Circle
D. Brook
80 Farm Road
Weston Super Mare, Avon, United Kingdom BS22 8BD
www.abel.co.uk/~stirrups/GSC.HTM
E-mail: drstirrups@dundee.ac.uk

Great Britain Collectors Club
Parker A. Bailey, Jr.
PO Box 773
Merrimack NH 03054-0773
www.gbstamps.com/gbcc
E-mail: pbaileyjr@worldnet.att.net

Hellenic Philatelic Society of America (Greece and related areas)
Dr. Nicholas Asimakopulos
541 Cedar Hill Ave.
Wyckoff NJ 07481
Ph: (201) 447-6262

International Society of Guatemala Collectors
Mrs. Mae Vignola
105 22nd Ave.
San Francisco CA 94121

Haiti Philatelic Society
Ubaldo Del Toro
5709 Marble Archway
Alexandria VA 22315
E-mail: u007ubi@aol.com

Honduras Collectors Club
Jeff Brasor
PO Box 143383
Irving TX 75014

Hong Kong Stamp Society
Dr. An-Min Chung
3300 Darby Rd. Cottage 503
Haverford PA 19041-1064

Society for Hungarian Philately
Robert Morgan
2201 Roscomare Rd.
Los Angeles CA 90077-2222
www.hungarianphilately.org
E-mail: h.alanhoover@lycosemail.com

India Study Circle
John Warren
PO Box 7326
Washington DC 20044
Ph: (202) 564-6876
E-mail: warren.john@epa.gov

Indian Ocean Study Circle
K. B. Fitton
50 Firlands
Weybridge, Surrey, United Kingdom KT13 0HR
www.stampdomain.com/iosc
E-mail: keithfitton@intonet.co.uk

Society of Indo-China Philatelists
Norman S. Davis
PO Box 290406
Brooklyn NY 11229

Iran Philatelic Study Circle
Darrell R. Hill
1410 Broadway
Bethlehem PA 18015-4025
www.iranphilatelic.org
E-mail: d.r.hill@att.net

Eire Philatelic Association (Ireland)
Myron G. Hill III
PO Box 1210
College Park MD 20741-1210
eirephilatelicassoc.org
E-mail: mhill@radix.net

Society of Israel Philatelists
Paul S. Aufrichtig
300 East 42nd St.
New York NY 10017

Italy and Colonies Study Circle
Andrew D'Anneo
1085 Dunweal Lane
Calistoga CA 94515
E-mail: audanneo@napanet.net

International Society for Japanese Philately
Kenneth Kamholz
PO Box 1283
Haddonfield NJ 08033
www.isjp.org
E-mail: isjp@home.com

Korea Stamp Society
John E. Talmage
PO Box 6889
Oak Ridge TN 37831
www.pennfamily.org/KSS-USA
E-mail: jtalmage@usit.net

Latin American Philatelic Society
Piet Steen
197 Pembina Ave.
Hinton, AB, Canada T7V 2B2

Latvian Philatelic Society
Aris Birze
569 Rougemount Dr.
Pickering, ON, Canada L1W 2C1

Liberian Philatelic Society
William Thomas Lockard
PO Box 106
Wellston OH 45692
Ph: (740) 384-2020
E-mail: tlockard@zoomnet.net

Liechtenstudy USA (Liechtenstein)
Ralph Schneider
PO Box 23049
Belleville IL 62223
Ph: (618) 277-6152
www.rschneiderstamps.com/Liechtenstudy.htm
E-mail: rsstamps@aol.com

Lithuania Philatelic Society
John Variakojis
3715 W. 68th St.
Chicago IL 60629
Ph: (773) 585-8649
www.filatelija.lt/lps/
E-mail: variakojis@earthlink.net

Luxembourg Collectors Club
Gary B. Little
3304 Plateau Dr.
Belmont CA 94002-1312
www.luxcentral.com/stamps/LCC
E-mail: lcc@luxcentral.com

Malaya Study Group
Joe Robertson
12 Lisa Court
Downsland Road
Basingstoke, Hampshire, United
Kingdom RG21 8TU
home.freeuk.net/johnmorgan/msg.htm

Malta Study Circle
Alec Webster
50 Worcester Road
Sutton, Surrey, United Kingdom SM2
6QB
E-mail: alecwebster50@hotmail.com

Mexico-Elmhurst Philatelic Society
International
David Pietsch
PO Box 50997
Irvine CA 92619-0997
E-mail: mepsi@msn.com

Society for Moroccan and Tunisian
Philately
206, bld. Pereire
75017 Paris, France
members.aol.com/Jhaik5814
E-mail: jhaik5814@aol.com

Nepal & Tibet Philatelic Study
Group
Roger D. Skinner
1020 Covington Road
Los Altos CA 94024-5003
Ph: (650) 968-4163
fuchs-online.com/ntpsc/

American Society of Netherlands
Philately
Jan Enthoven
221 Coachlite Ct. S.
Onalaska WI 54650
Ph: (608) 781-8612
www.cs.cornell.edu/Info/People/aswin
/NL/neth
E-mail: jenthoven@centurytel.net

New Zealand Society of Great
Britain
Keith C. Collins
13 Briton Crescent
Sanderstead, Surrey, United Kingdom
CR2 0JN
www.cs.stir.ac.uk/~rgc/nzsgb
E-mail: rgc@cs.stir.ac.uk

Nicaragua Study Group
Erick Rodriguez
11817 S.W. 11th St.
Miami FL 33184-2501
clubs.yahoo.com/clubs/nicaraguastudy
group
E-mail: nsgsec@yahoo.com

Society of Australasian Specialists/
Oceania
Henry Bateman
PO Box 4862
Monroe LA 71211-4862
Ph: (800) 571-0293
members.aol.com/stampsho/saso.html
E-mail: hbateman@jam.rr.com

Orange Free State Study Circle
J. R. Stroud
28 Oxford St.
Burnham-on-sea, Somerset, United
Kingdom TA8 1LQ
www.ofssc.org
E-mail: jrstroud@classicfm.net

Pacific Islands Study Group
John Ray
24 Woodvale Avenue
London, United Kingdom SE25 4AE
www.pisc.org.uk
E-mail: john.ray@bigfoot.com

Pakistan Philatelic Study Circle
Jeff Siddiqui
PO Box 7002
Lynnwood WA 98046
E-mail: jeffsiddiqui@msn.com

Papuan Philatelic Society
Steven Zirinsky
PO Box 49, Ansonia Station
New York NY 10023
E-mail: szirinsky@compuserve.com

International Philippine Philatelic
Society
Robert F. Yacano
PO Box 100
Toast NC 27049
Ph: (336) 783-0768
E-mail: yacano@advi.net

Pitcairn Islands Study Group
Nelson A. L. Weller
2940 Wesleyan Lane
Winston-Salem NC 27106
Ph: (336) 724-6384
E-mail: nalweller@aol.com

Plebiscite-Memel-Saar Study
Group of the German Philatelic
Society
Clay Wallace
100 Lark Court
Alamo CA 94507
E-mail: wallacec@earthlink.net

Polonus Philatelic Society (Poland)
Art Walinski
7414 Lincoln Ave. - D
Skokie IL 60076-3898

International Society for
Portuguese Philately
Clyde Homen
1491 Bonnie View Rd.
Hollister CA 95023-5117
www.portugalstamps.com
E-mail: cjh@hollinet.com

Rhodesian Study Circle
William R. Wallace
PO Box 16381
San Francisco CA 94116
www.rhodesianstudycircle.org.uk
E-mail: bwall8rscr@earthlink.net

Canadian Society of Russian
Philately
Andrew Cronin
PO Box 5722, Station A
Toronto, ON, Canada M5W 1P2
Ph: (905) 764-8968
www3.sympatico.ca/postrider/postrider
E-mail: postrider@sympatico.ca

Rossica Society of Russian Philately
Gerald D. Seiflow
27 N. Wacker Drive #167
Chicago IL 60606-3203
www.rossica.org
E-mail: ged.seiflow@rossica.org

Ryukyu Philatelic Specialist Society
Carmine J. DiVincenzo
PO Box 381
Clayton CA 94517-0381

St. Helena, Ascension & Tristan Da
Cunha Philatelic Society
Dr. Everett L. Parker

HC 76, Box 32
Greenville ME 04441-9727
Ph: (207) 695-3163
ourworld.compuserve.com/home-
pages/ ST_HELENA_ASCEN_TDC
E-mail: eparker@prexar.com

St. Pierre & Miquelon Philatelic
Society
David Salovey
320 Knights Corner
Stony Point NY 10980
E-mail: jamestaylor@wavehome.com

Associated Collectors of El
Salvador
Jeff Brasor
PO Box 143383
Irving TX 75014

Fellowship of Samoa Specialists
Jack R. Hughes
PO Box 1260
Boston MA 02117-1260
members.aol.com/tongaJan/foss.html

Sarawak Specialists' Society
Stu Leven
4031 Samson Way
San Jose CA 95124-3733
Ph: (408) 978-0193
www.britborneostamps.org.uk
E-mail: stulev@ix.netcom.com

Scandinavian Collectors Club
Donald B. Brent
PO Box 13196
El Cajon CA 92020
www.scc-online.org
E-mail: dbrent47@sprynet.com

Slovakia Stamp Society
Jack Benchik
PO Box 555
Notre Dame IN 46556

Philatelic Society for Greater
Southern Africa
William C. Brooks VI
PO Box 4158
Cucamonga CA 91729-4158
Ph: (909) 484-2806
www.homestead.com/psgsa/index.html
E-mail: bbrooks@hss.co.sbcounty.gov

Spanish Philatelic Society
Robert H. Penn
1108 Walnut Drive
Danielsville PA 18038
Ph: (610) 767-6793

Sudan Study Group
Charles Hass
PO Box 3435
Nashua NH 03061-3435
Ph: (603) 888-4160
E-mail: hassstamps@aol.com

American Helvetia Philatelic
Society (Switzerland,
Liechtenstein)
Richard T. Hall
PO Box 15053
Asheville NC 28813-0053
www.swiss-stamps.org
E-mail: secretary@swiss-stamps.org

Tannu Tuva Collectors Society
Ken Simon
513 Sixth Ave. So.
Lake Worth FL 33460-4507
Ph: (561) 588-5954
www.seflin.org/tuva
E-mail: p003115b@pb.seflin.org

Society for Thai Philately
H. R. Blakeney
PO Box 25644
Oklahoma City OK 73125
E-mail:HRBlakeney@aol.com

Transvaal Study Circle
J. Woolgar
132 Dale Street
Chatham, Kent ME4 6QH, United
Kingdom
www.transvaalsc.org

Ottoman and Near East Philatelic
Society (Turkey and related
areas)
Bob Stuchell
193 Valley Stream Lane
Wayne PA 19087
E-mail: president@oneps.org

Ukrainian Philatelic & Numismatic
Society
George Slusarczuk
PO Box 303
Southfields NY 10975-0303
www.upns.org
E-mail: Yurko@warwick.net

Vatican Philatelic Society
Sal Quinonez
2 Aldersgate, Apt. 119
Riverhead NY 11901
Ph: (516) 727-6426

British Virgin Islands Philatelic
Society
Roger Downing
PO Box 11156
St. Thomas VI 00801-1156
Ph: (284) 494-2762
www.islandsun.com/FEATURES/bviph
il9198.html
E-mail: issun@candwbvi.net

West Africa Study Circle
Dr. Peter Newroth
33-520 Marsett Place
Victoria, BC, Canada V8Z 7J1
ourworld.compuserve.com/homepages/
FrankWalton

Western Australia Study Group
Brian Pope
PO Box 423
Claremont, Western Australia,
Australia 6910

Yugoslavia Study Group of the
Croatian Philatelic Society
Michael Lenard
1514 North 3rd Ave.
Wausau WI 54401
Ph: (715) 675-2833
E-mail: mjlenard@aol.com

Topical Groups

Americana Unit
Dennis Dengel
17 Peckham Rd.
Poughkeepsie NY 12603-2018
www.americanaunit.org
E-mail: info@americanaunit.org

Astronomy Study Unit
George Young
PO Box 632
Tewksbury MA 01876-0632
Ph: (978) 851-8283
www.fandm.edu/departments/
astronomy/miscell/astunit.html
E-mail: george-young@msn.com

Bicycle Stamp Club
Norman Batho
358 Iverson Place
East Windsor NJ 08520
Ph: (609) 448-9547
members.tripod.com/~bicyclestamps
E-mail: normbatho@worldnet.att.net

Biology Unit
Alan Hanks
34 Seaton Dr.
Aurora, ON, Canada L4G 2K1
Ph: (905) 727-6993

Bird Stamp Society
G. P. Horsman
9 Cowley Drive, Worthy Down
Winchester, Hants., United Kingdom
SO21 2OW

Canadiana Study Unit
John Peebles
PO Box 3262, Station "A"
London, ON, Canada N6A 4K3
E-mail: john.peebles@odyssey.on.ca

Captain Cook Study Unit
Brian P. Sandford
173 Minuteman Dr.
Concord MA 01742-1923
www.captaincookstudyunit.com/
E-mail: USagent@captaincookstudyunit.com/

Casey Jones Railroad Unit
Oliver C. Atchison
PO Box 31631
San Francisco CA 94131-0631
Ph: (415) 648-8057
www.uqp.de/cjr/index.htm
E-mail: cjrrunit@aol.com

Cats on Stamps Study Unit
Mary Ann Brown
3006 Wade Rd.
Durham NC 27705

Chemistry & Physics on Stamps
   Study Unit
Dr. Roland Hirsch
20458 Water Point Lane
Germantown MD 20874
www.cpossu.org
E-mail: rfhirsch@cpossu.org

Chess on Stamps Study Unit
Anne Kasonic
7625 County Road #153
Interlaken NY 14847
www.iglobal.net/home/reott/stamps1.htm#cossu
E-mail: akasonic@epix.net

Christmas Philatelic Club
Linda Lawrence
312 Northwood Drive
Lexington KY 40505
Ph: (606) 293-0151
www.hwcn.org/link/cpc
E-mail: stamplinda@aol.com

Christopher Columbus Philatelic
   Society
Donald R. Ager
PO Box 71
Hillsboro NH 03244-0071
Ph: (603) 464-5379
E-mail: meganddon@conknet.com

Collectors of Religion on Stamps
Verna Shackleton
425 North Linwood Avenue #110
Appleton WI 54914
Ph: (920) 734-2417
www.powernetonline.com/~corosec/coros1.htm
E-mail: corosec@powernetonline.com

Dogs on Stamps Study Unit
Morris Raskin
202A Newport Rd.
Monroe Township NJ 08831
Ph: (609) 655-7411
www.dossu.org
E-mail: mraskin@nerc.com

Earth's Physical Features Study
   Group
Fred Klein
515 Magdalena Ave.
Los Altos CA 94024
www.philately.com/society_news/earths_physical.htm

Ebony Society of Philatelic Events
   and Reflections (African-
   American topicals)
Sanford L. Byrd
PO Box 8888
Corpus Christi, TX 78468-8888
www.slsabyrd.com/esper.htm
E-mail: esper@ibm.net

Embroidery, Stitchery, Textile Unit
Helen N. Cushman
1001 Genter St., Apt. 9H
La Jolla CA 92037
Ph: (619) 459-1194

Europa Study Unit
Hank Klos
PO Box 611
Bensenville IL 60106
E-mail: eunity@aol.com

Fine & Performing Arts
Ruth Richards
10393 Derby Dr.
Laurel MD 20723
www.philately.com/society_news/fap.htm
E-mail: bersec@aol.com

Fire Service in Philately
Brian R. Engler, Sr.
726 1/2 W. Tilghman St.
Allentown PA 18102-2324
Ph: (610) 433-2782
E-mail: brenglersr@enter.net

Gay & Lesbian History on Stamps
   Club
Joe Petronie
PO Box 190842
Dallas TX 75219-0842
www.glhsc.org
E-mail: glhsc@aol.com

Gems, Minerals & Jewelry Study
   Group
George Young
PO Box 632
Tewksbury MA 01876-0632
Ph: (978) 851-8283
www.rockhounds.com/rockshop/gmjsuapp.txt
E-mail: george-young@msn.com

Graphics Philately Association
Mark Winnegrad
PO Box 380
Bronx NY 10462-0380

Journalists, Authors & Poets on
   Stamps
Sol Baltimore
28742 Blackstone Dr.
Lathrup Village MI 48076

Lighthouse Stamp Society
Dalene Thomas
8612 West Warren Lane
Lakewood CO 80227-2352
Ph: (303) 986-6620
www.lighthousestampsociety.org
E-mail: dalene1@wideopenwest.com

Lions International Stamp Club
John Bargus
304-2777 Barry Rd. RR 2
Mill Bay, BC, Canada V0R 2P0
Ph: (250) 743-5782

Mahatma Gandhi On Stamps
   Study Circle
Pramod Shivagunde
Pratik Clinic, Akluj
Solapur, Maharashtra, India 413101
E-mail: drnanda@bom6.vsnl.net.in

Mask Study Unit
Helen N. Cushman
1001 Genter St. Apt. 9H
La Jolla CA 92037
www.philately.com/philately/masks.htm
E-mail: kencar@vlnk.net

Masonic Study Unit
Stanley R. Longenecker
930 Wood St.
Mount Joy PA 17552-1926
E-mail: natsco@usa.net

Mathematical Study Unit
Estelle Buccino
5615 Glenwood Rd.
Bethesda MD 20817-6727
Ph: (301) 718-8898
www.math.ttu.edu/msu/
E-mail: m.strauss@ttu.edu

Medical Subjects Unit
Dr. Frederick C. Skvara
PO Box 6228
Bridgewater NJ 08807
E-mail: fcskvara@bellatlantic.net

Mesoamerican Archeology Study
   Unit
Chris Moser
PO Box 1442
Riverside CA 92502
www.masu.homestead.com/info.html
E-mail:cmoser@ci.riverside.ca.us

Napoleonic Age Philatelists
Ken Berry
7513 Clayton Dr.
Oklahoma City OK 73132-5636
Ph: (405) 721-0044
E-mail: krb2@earthlink.net

Old World Archeological Study Unit
Eileen Meier
PO Box 369
Palmyra VA 22963

Parachute Study Group
Bill Wickert
3348 Clubhouse Road
Virginia Beach VA 23452-5339
Ph: (757) 486-3614
E-mail: bw47psg@worldnet.att.net

Petroleum Philatelic Society
   International
Linda W. Corwin
5427 Pine Springs Court
Conroe TX 77304
Ph: (936) 441-0216
E-mail: corwin@pdq.net

Philatelic Computing Study Group
Robert de Violini
PO Box 5025
Oxnard CA 93031-5025
www.pcsg.org
E-mail: dviolini@west.net

Philatelic Lepidopterists'
   Association
Alan Hanks
34 Seaton Dr.
Aurora, ON, Canada L4G 2K1
Ph: (905) 727-6933

Philatelic Music Circle
Cathleen Osborne
PO Box 1781
Sequim WA 98382
Ph: (360) 683-6373
www.stampshows.com/pmc.html

Rainbow Study Unit
Shirley Sutton
PO Box 37
Lone Pine, AB, Canada T0G 1M0
Ph: (780) 584-2268
E-mail: george-young@msn.com

Rotary on Stamps Unit
Donald Fiery
PO Box 333
Hanover PA 17331
Ph: (717) 632-8921

Scouts on Stamps Society
   International
Carl Schauer
PO Box 526
Belen NM 87002
Ph: (505) 864-0098
www.sossi.org
E-mail: rfrank@sossi.org

Ships on Stamps Unit
Robert Stuckert
2750 Highway 21 East
Paint Lick KY 40461
Ph: (859) 925-4901
www.shipsonstamps.org

Space Unit
Carmine Torrisi
PO Box 780241
Maspeth NY 11378
Ph: (718) 386-7882
stargate.1usa.com/stamps/
E-mail: ctorrisi1@juno.com

Sports Philatelists International
Margaret Jones
5310 Lindenwood Ave.
St. Louis MO 63109-1758
www.geocities.com/colosseum/track/6279

Stamps on Stamps Collectors Club
William Critzer
1360 Trinity Drive
Menlo Park CA 94025
Ph: (650) 234-1136
www.stampsonstamps.org
E-mail: wllmcritz@aol.com

Windmill Study Unit
Walter J. Hollien
PO Box 346
Long Valley NJ 07853-0346

Wine on Stamps Study Unit
James D. Crum
816 Kingsbury Ct.
Arroyo Grande CA 93420-4517
Ph: (805) 489-3559
E-mail: jdakcrum@aol.com

Women on Stamps Study Unit
Hugh Gottfried
2232 26th St.
Santa Monica CA 90405-1902
Ph: (310) 452-1442
E-mail: hgottfri@lausd.k12.ca.us

Zeppelin Collectors Club
Cheryl Ganz
PO Box A3843
Chicago IL 60690-3843

Expertizing Services

The following organizations will, for a fee, provide expert opinions about stamps submitted to them. Collectors should contact these organizations to find out about their fees and requirements before submitting philatelic material to them. The listing of these groups here is not intended as an endorsement by Scott Publishing Co.

General Expertizing Services

American Philatelic Expertizing Service (a service of the American Philatelic Society)
PO Box 8000
State College PA 16803
Ph: (814) 237-3808
Fax: (814) 237-6128
www.stamps.org
E-mail: ambristo@stamps.org
Areas of Expertise: Worldwide

B. P. A. Expertising, Ltd.
PO Box 137
Leatherhead, Surrey, United Kingdom
KT22 0RG
E-mail: sec.bpa@tcom.co.uk
Areas of Expertise: British Commonwealth, Great Britain, Classics of Europe, South America and the Far East

Philatelic Foundation
501 Fifth Ave., Rm. 1901
New York NY 10017
Areas of Expertise: U.S. & Worldwide

Professional Stamp Experts
PO Box 6170
Newport Beach CA 92658
Ph: (877) STAMP-88
Fax: (949) 833-7955
www.collectors.com/pse
E-mail: pseinfo@collectors.com
Areas of Expertise: Stamps and covers of U.S., U.S. Possessions, British Commonwealth

Royal Philatelic Society Expert Committee
41 Devonshire Place
London, United Kingdom W1N 1PE
www.rpsl.org.uk/experts.html
E-mail: experts@rpsl.org.uk
Areas of Expertise: All

Expertizing Services Covering Specific Fields Or Countries

Canadian Society of Russian Philately Expertizing Service
PO Box 5722, Station A
Toronto, ON, Canada M5W 1P2
Fax: (416)932-0853
Areas of Expertise: Russian areas

China Stamp Society Expertizing Service
1050 West Blue Ridge Blvd
Kansas City MO 64145
Ph: (816) 942-6300
E-mail: hjmesq@aol.com
Areas of Expertise: China

Confederate Stamp Alliance Authentication Service
c/o Patricia A. Kaufmann
10194 N. Old State Road
Lincoln DE 19960-9797
Ph: (302) 422-2656
Fax: (302) 424-1990
www.webuystamps.com/csaauth.htm
E-mail: trish@ce.net
Areas of Expertise: Confederate stamps and postal history

Croatian Philatelic Society Expertizing Service
PO Box 696
Fritch TX 79036-0696
Ph: (806) 857-0129
E-mail: ou812@arn.net
Areas of Expertise: Croatia and other Balkan areas

Errors, Freaks and Oddities Collectors Club Expertizing Service
138 East Lakemont Dr.
Kingsland GA 31548
Ph: (912) 729-1573
Areas of Expertise: U.S. errors, freaks and oddities

Estonian Philatelic Society Expertizing Service
39 Clafford Lane
Melville NY 11747
Ph: (516) 421-2078
E-mail: esto4@aol.com
Areas of Expertise: Estonia

Hawaiian Philatelic Society Expertizing Service
PO Box 10115
Honolulu HI 96816-0115
Areas of Expertise: Hawaii

Hong Kong Stamp Society Expertizing Service
PO Box 206
Glenside PA 19038
Fax: (215) 576-6850
Areas of Expertise: Hong Kong

International Association of Philatelics Experts
United States Associate members:
Paul Buchsbayew
119 W. 57th St.
New York NY 10019
Ph: (212) 977-7734
Fax: (212) 977-8653
Areas of Expertise: Russia, Soviet Union

William T. Crowe
(see Philatelic Foundation)

John Lievsay
(see American Philatelic Expertizing Service and Philatelic Foundation)
Areas of Expertise: France

Robert W. Lyman
P.O. Box 348
Irvington on Hudson NY 10533
Ph and Fax: (914) 591-6937
Areas of Expertise: British North America, New Zealand

Robert Odenweller
P.O. Box 401
Bernardsville, NJ 07924-0401
Ph and Fax: (908) 766-5460
Areas of Expertise: New Zealand, Samoa to 1900

Alex Rendon
P.O. Box 323
Massapequa NY 11762
Ph and Fax: (516) 795-0464
Areas of Expertise: Bolivia, Colombia, Colombian States

Sergio Sismondo
10035 Carousel Center Dr.
Syracuse NY 13290-0001
Ph: (315) 422-2331
Fax: (315) 422-2956
Areas of Expertise: Cape of Good Hope, Canada, British North America

International Society for Japanese Philately Expertizing Committee
32 King James Court
Staten Island NY 10308-2910
Ph: (718) 227-5229
Areas of Expertise: Japan and related areas, except WWII Japanese Occupation issues

International Society for Portuguese Philately Exertizing Service
PO Box 43146
Philadelphia PA 19129-3146
Ph: (215) 843-2106
Fax: (215) 843-2106
E-mail: s.s.washburne@worldnet.att.net
Areas of Expertise: Portugal and colonies

Mexico-Elmhurst Philatelic Society International Expert Committee
PO Box 1133
West Covina CA 91793
Areas of Expertise: Mexico

Philatelic Society for Greater Southern Africa Expert Panel
13955 W. 30th Ave.
Golden CO 80401
Areas of expertise: Entire South and South West Africa area, Bechuanalands, Basutoland, Swaziland

Ryukyu Philatelic Specialist Society Expertizing Service
1710 Buena Vista Ave.
Spring Valley CA 91977-4458
Ph: (619) 697-3205

Areas of Expertise: Ryukyu Islands

Ukrainian Philatelic & Numismatic Society Expertizing Service
30552 Dell Lane
Warren MI 48092-1862
Ph: (810) 751-5754
Areas of Expertise: Ukraine, Western Ukraine

V. G. Greene Philatelic Research Foundation
Box 100, First Canadian Place
Toronto, ON, Canada M5X 1B2
Ph: (416) 863-4593
Fax: (416) 863-4592
Areas of Expertise: British North America

Information on Catalogue Values, Grade and Condition

Catalogue Value

The Scott Catalogue value is a retail value; that is, an amount you could expect to pay for a stamp in the grade of Very Fine with no faults. Any exceptions to the grade valued will be noted in the text. The general introduction on the following pages and the individual section introductions further explain the type of material that is valued. The value listed for any given stamp is a reference that reflects recent actual dealer selling prices for that item.

Dealer retail price lists, public auction results, published prices in advertising and individual solicitation of retail prices from dealers, collectors and specialty organizations have been used in establishing the values found in this catalogue. Scott Publishing Co. values stamps, but Scott is not a company engaged in the business of buying and selling stamps as a dealer.

Use this catalogue as a guide for buying and selling. The actual price you pay for a stamp may be higher or lower than the catalogue value because of many different factors, including the amount of personal service a dealer offers, or increased or decreased interest in the country or topic represented by a stamp or set. An item may occasionally be offered at a lower price as a "loss leader," or as part of a special sale. You also may obtain an item inexpensively at public auction because of little interest at that time or as part of a large lot.

Stamps that are of a lesser grade than Very Fine, or those with condition problems, generally trade at lower prices than those given in this catalogue. Stamps of exceptional quality in both grade and condition often command higher prices than those listed.

Values for pre-1900 unused issues are for stamps with approximately half or more of their original gum. Stamps with most or all of their original gum may be expected to sell for more, and stamps with less than half of their original gum may be expected to sell for somewhat less than the values listed. On rarer stamps, it may be expected that the original gum will be somewhat more disturbed than it will be on more common issues. Post-1900 unused issues are assumed to have full original gum. From breakpoints in most countries' listings, stamps are valued as never hinged, due to the wide availability of stamps in that condition. These notations are prominently placed in the listings and in the country information preceding the listings. Some countries also feature listings with dual values for hinged and never-hinged stamps.

Grade

A stamp's grade and condition are crucial to its value. The accompanying illustrations show examples of Very Fine stamps from different time periods, along with examples of stamps in Fine to Very Fine and Extremely Fine grades as points of reference.

FINE stamps (illustrations not shown) have designs that are noticeably off center on two sides. Imperforate stamps may have small margins, and earlier issues may show the design touching one edge of the stamp design. For perforated stamps, perfs may barely clear the design on one side, and very early issues normally will have the perforations slightly cutting into the design. Used stamps may have heavier than usual cancellations.

FINE-VERY FINE stamps may be somewhat off center on one side, or slightly off center on two sides. Imperforate stamps will have two margins of at least normal size, and the design will not touch any edge. For perforated stamps, the perfs are well clear of the design, but are still noticeably off center. *However, early issues of a country may be printed in such a way that the design naturally is very close to the edges. In these cases, the perforations may cut into the design very slightly.* Used stamps will not have a cancellation that detracts from the design.

VERY FINE stamps may be slightly off center on one side, but the design will be well clear of the edge. The stamp will present a nice, balanced appearance. Imperforate stamps will have three normal-sized margins. *However, early issues of many countries may be printed in*

such a way that the perforations may touch the design on one or more sides. Where this is the case, a boxed note will be found defining the centering and margins of the stamps being valued. Used stamps will have light or otherwise neat cancellations. This is the grade used to establish Scott Catalogue values.

EXTREMELY FINE stamps are close to being perfectly centered. Imperforate stamps will have even margins that are larger than normal. Even the earliest perforated issues will have perforations clear of the design on all sides.

Scott Publishing Co. recognizes that there is no formally enforced grading scheme for postage stamps, and that the final price you pay or obtain for a stamp will be determined by individual agreement at the time of transaction.

Condition

Grade addresses only centering and (for used stamps) cancellation. *Condition* refers to factors other than grade that affect a stamp's desirability.

Factors that can increase the value of a stamp include exceptionally wide margins, particularly fresh color, the presence of selvage, and plate or die varieties. Unusual cancels on used stamps (particularly those of the 19th century) can greatly enhance their value as well.

Factors other than faults that decrease the value of a stamp include loss of original gum, regumming, a hinge remnant or foreign object adhering to the gum, natural inclusions, straight edges, and markings or notations applied by collectors or dealers.

Faults include missing pieces, tears, pin or other holes, surface scuffs, thin spots, creases, toning, short or pulled perforations, clipped perforations, oxidation or other forms of color changelings, soiling, stains, and such man-made changes as reperforations or the chemical removal or lightening of a cancellation.

Grading Illustrations

On the following two pages are illustrations of various stamps from countries appearing in this volume. These stamps are arranged by country, and they represent early or important issues that are often found in widely different grades in the marketplace. The editors believe the illustrations will prove useful in showing the margin size and centering that will be seen on the various issues.

In addition to the matters of margin size and centering, collectors are reminded that the very fine stamps valued in the Scott catalogues also will possess fresh color and intact perforations, and they will be free from defects.

Most examples shown are computer-manipulated images made from single digitized master illustrations.

Stamp Illustrations Used in the Catalogue

It is important to note that the stamp images used for identification purposes in this catlaogue may not be indicative of the grade of stamp being valued. Refer to the written discussion of grades on this page and to the grading illustrations on the following two pages for grading information.

Fine-Very Fine

SCOTT CATALOGUES VALUE STAMPS IN THIS GRADE

Very Fine

Extremely Fine

Fine-Very Fine

SCOTT CATALOGUES VALUE STAMPS IN THIS GRADE

Very Fine

Extremely Fine

For purposes of helping to determine the gum condition and value of an unused stamp, Scott Publishing Co. presents the following chart which details different gum conditions and indicates how the conditions correlate with the Scott values for unused stamps. Used together, the Illustrated Grading Chart on the previous pages and this Illustrated Gum Chart should allow catalogue users to better understand the grade and gum condition of stamps valued in the Scott catalogues.

Gum Categories:	MINT N.H.	ORIGINAL GUM (O.G.)				NO GUM
	Mint Never Hinged *Free from any disturbance*	**Lightly Hinged** *Faint impression of a removed hinge over a small area*	**Hinge Mark or Remnant** *Prominent hinged spot with part or all of the hinge remaining*	**Large part o.g.** *Approximately half or more of the gum intact*	**Small part o.g.** *Approximately less than half of the gum intact*	**No gum** *Only if issued with gum*
Commonly Used Symbol:	★★	★	★	★	★	(★)
Pre-1900 Issues (Pre-1890 for U.S.)	*Very fine pre-1900 stamps in these categories trade at a premium over Scott value*			Scott Value for "Unused"		Scott "No Gum" listings for selected unused classic stamps
From 1900 to break-points for listings of never-hinged stamps	Scott "Never Hinged" listings for selected unused stamps	Scott Value for "Unused" (Actual value will be affected by the degree of hinging of the full o.g.)				
From breakpoints noted for many countries	Scott Value for "Unused"					

Never Hinged (NH; ★★): A never-hinged stamp will have full original gum that will have no hinge mark or disturbance. The presence of an expertizer's mark does not disqualify a stamp from this designation.

Original Gum (OG; ★): Pre-1900 stamps should have approximately half or more of their original gum. On rarer stamps, it may be expected that the original gum will be somewhat more disturbed that it will be on more common issues. Post-1900 stamps should have full original gum. Original gum will show some disturbance caused by a previous hinge(s) which may be present or entirely removed. The actual value of a post-1900 stamp will be affected by the degree of hinging of the full original gum.

Disturbed Original Gum: Gum showing noticeable effects of humidity, climate or hinging over more than half of the gum. The significance of gum disturbance in valuing a stamp in any of the Original Gum categories depends on the degree of disturbance, the rarity and normal gum condition of the issue and other variables affecting quality.

Regummed (RG; (★)): A regummed stamp is a stamp without gum that has had some type of gum privately applied at a time after it was issued. This normally is done to deceive collectors and/or dealers into thinking that the stamp has original gum and therefore has a higher value. A regummed stamp is considered the same as a stamp with none of its original gum for purposes of grading.

SUBSCRIBE TODAY!

Linn's Stamp News is the **indispensable** reading and entertainment guide for all the stamps you **want** and all the news you **need**. Each issue is jam packed with:

- All the latest-breaking news from our exclusive national and international sources.

- In-depth analysis from top authorities on all aspects of collecting, new issues, forgeries, security and more.

- Regular features you always looked forward to - *Stamp Market Tips* and *Tip of the Week, Collectors' Forum, Editor's Choice, Readers' Opinions, Postmark Pursuit, Collectors' Workshop, Refresher Course* and much more.

- The world's largest stamp market place. Listings of events, auctions and sales. Classified ads and readers' notices for buying, selling and trading.

(Offer valid only for U.S. subscribers.
Canadian subscribers add $22.50 for postage.
International subscribers add $37.50 for postage.)

Order online at:

www.linns.com

or Call toll-free:
1-800-448-7293

or write:
**P.O. Box 4315,
Sidney, OH 45365**

**Subscribe Today
and take
advantage
of Linn's get
acquainted offer:**

6 months – 26 issues - $23.95!

AMOS
HOBBY PUBLISHING

Catalogue Listing Policy

It is the intent of Scott Publishing Co. to list all postage stamps of the world in the *Scott Standard Postage Stamp Catalogue*. The only strict criteria for listing is that stamps be decreed legal for postage by the issuing country and that the issuing country actually have an operating postal system. Whether the primary intent of issuing a given stamp or set was for sale to postal patrons or to stamp collectors is not part of our listing criteria. Scott's role is to provide basic comprehensive postage stamp information. It is up to each stamp collector to choose which items to include in a collection.

It is Scott's objective to seek reasons why a stamp should be listed, rather than why it should not. Nevertheless, there are certain types of items that will not be listed. These include the following:

1. Unissued items that are not officially distributed or released by the issuing postal authority. Even if such a stamp is "accidentally" distributed to the philatelic or even postal market, it remains unissued. If such items are officially issued at a later date by the country, they will be listed. Unissued items consist of those that have been printed and then held from sale for reasons such as change in government, errors found on stamps or something deemed objectionable about a stamp subject or design.

2. Stamps "issued" by non-existent postal entities or fantasy countries, such as Nagaland, Occusi-Ambeno, Staffa, Sedang, Torres Straits and others.

3. Semi-official or unofficial items not required for postage. Examples include items issued by private agencies for their own express services. When such items are required for delivery, or are valid as prepayment of postage, they are listed.

4. Local stamps issued for local use only. Postage stamps issued by governments specifically for "domestic" use, such as Haiti Scott 219-228, or the United States non-denominated stamps, are not considered to be locals, since they are valid for postage throughout the country of origin.

5. Items not valid for postal use. For example, a few countries have issued souvenir sheets that are not valid for postage. This area also includes a number of worldwide charity labels (some denominated) that do not pay postage.

6. Intentional varieties, such as imperforate stamps that look like their perforated counterparts and are issued in very small quantities. These are often controlled issues intended for speculation.

7. Items distributed by the issuing government only to a limited group, such as a stamp club, philatelic exhibition or a single stamp dealer, and later brought to market at inflated prices. These items normally will be included in a footnote.

The fact that a stamp has been used successfully as postage, even on international mail, is not in itself sufficient proof that it was legitimately issued. Numerous examples of so-called stamps from non-existent countries are known to have been used to post letters that have successfully passed through the international mail system.

There are certain items that are subject to interpretation. When a stamp falls outside our specifications, it may be listed along with a cautionary footnote.

A number of factors are considered in our approach to analyzing how a stamp is listed. The following list of factors is presented to share with you, the catalogue user, the complexity of the listing process.

Additional printings — "Additional printings" of a previously issued stamp may range from an item that is totally different to cases where it is impossible to differentiate from the original. At least a minor number (a small-letter suffix) is assigned if there is a distinct change in stamp shade, noticeably redrawn design, or a significantly different perforation measurement. A major number (numeral or numeral and capital-letter combination) is assigned if the editors feel the "additional printing" is sufficiently different from the original that it constitutes a different issue.

Commemoratives — Where practical, commemoratives with the same theme are placed in a set. For example, the U.S. Civil War Centennial set of 1961-65 and the Constitution Bicentennial series of 1989-90 appear as sets. Countries such as Japan and Korea issue such material on a regular basis, with an announced, or at least predictable, number of stamps known in advance. Occasionally, however, stamp sets that were released over a period of years have been separated. Appropriately placed footnotes will guide you to each set's continuation.

Definitive sets — Blocks of numbers generally have been reserved for definitive sets, based on previous experience with any given country. If a few more stamps were issued in a set than originally expected, they often have been inserted into the original set with a capital-letter suffix, such as U.S. Scott 1059A. If it appears that many more stamps than the originally allotted block will be released before the set is completed, a new block of numbers will be reserved, with the original one being closed off. In some cases, such as the British Machin Head series or the U.S. Transportation and Great Americans series, several blocks of numbers exist. Appropriately placed footnotes will guide you to each set's continuation.

New country — Membership in the Universal Postal Union is not a consideration for listing status or order of placement within the catalogue. The index will tell you in what volume or page number the listings begin.

"No release date" items — The amount of information available for any given stamp issue varies greatly from country to country and even from time to time. Extremely comprehensive information about new stamps is available from some countries well before the stamps are released. By contrast some countries do not provide information about stamps or release dates. Most countries, however, fall between these extremes. A country may provide denominations or subjects of stamps from upcoming issues that are not issued as planned. Sometimes, philatelic agencies, those private firms hired to represent countries, add these later-issued items to sets well after the formal release date. This time period can range from weeks to years. If these items were officially released by the country, they will be added to the appropriate spot in the set. In many cases, the specific release date of a stamp or set of stamps may never be known.

Overprints — The color of an overprint is always noted if it is other than black. Where more than one color of ink has been used on overprints of a single set, the color used is noted. Early overprint and surcharge illustrations were altered to prevent their use by forgers.

Se-tenants — Connected stamps of differing features (se-tenants) will be listed in the format most commonly collected. This includes pairs, blocks or larger multiples. Se-tenant units are not always symmetrical. An example is Australia Scott 508, which is a block of seven stamps. If the stamps are primarily collected as a unit, the major number may be assigned to the multiple, with minors going to each component stamp. In cases where continuous-design or other unit se-tenants will receive significant postal use, each stamp is given a major Scott number listing. This includes issues from the United States, Canada, Germany and Great Britain, for example.

Understanding the Listings

On the opposite page is an enlarged "typical" listing from this catalogue. Below are detailed explanations of each of the highlighted parts of the listing.

1 **Scott number** — Scott catalogue numbers are used to identify specific items when buying, selling or trading stamps. Each listed postage stamp from every country has a unique Scott catalogue number. Therefore, Germany Scott 99, for example, can only refer to a single stamp. Although the Scott catalogue usually lists stamps in chronological order by date of issue, there are exceptions. When a country has issued a set of stamps over a period of time, those stamps within the set are kept together without regard to date of issue. This follows the normal collecting approach of keeping stamps in their natural sets.

When a country issues a set of stamps over a period of time, a group of consecutive catalogue numbers is reserved for the stamps in that set, as issued. If that group of numbers proves to be too few, capital-letter suffixes, such as "A" or "B," may be added to existing numbers to create enough catalogue numbers to cover all items in the set. A capital-letter suffix indicates a major Scott catalogue number listing. Scott uses a suffix letter only once. Therefore, a catalogue number listing with a capital-letter suffix will not also be found with the same letter (lower case) used as a minor-letter listing. If there is a Scott 16A in a set, for example, there will not also be a Scott 16a. However, a minor-letter "a" listing may be added to a major number containing an "A" suffix (Scott 16Aa, for example).

Suffix letters are cumulative. A minor "b" variety of Scott 16A would be Scott 16Ab, not Scott 16b.

There are times when a reserved block of Scott catalogue numbers is too large for a set, leaving some numbers unused. Such gaps in the numbering sequence also occur when the catalogue editors move an item's listing elsewhere or have removed it entirely from the catalogue. Scott does not attempt to account for every possible number, but rather attempts to assure that each stamp is assigned its own number.

Scott numbers designating regular postage normally are only numerals. Scott numbers for other types of stamps, such as air post, semipostal, postal tax, postage due, occupation and others have a prefix consisting of one or more capital letters or a combination of numerals and capital letters.

2 **Illustration number** — Illustration or design-type numbers are used to identify each catalogue illustration. For most sets, the lowest face-value stamp is shown. It then serves as an example of the basic design approach for other stamps not illustrated. Where more than one stamp use the same illustration number, but have differences in design, the design paragraph or the description line clearly indicates the design on each stamp not illustrated. Where there are both vertical and horizontal designs in a set, a single illustration may be used, with the exceptions noted in the design paragraph or description line.

When an illustration is followed by a lower-case letter in parentheses, such as "A2(b)," the trailing letter indicates which overprint or surcharge illustration applies.

Illustrations normally are 70 percent of the original size of the stamp. An effort has been made to note all illustrations not illustrated at that percentage. Virtually all souvenir sheet illustrations are reduced even more. Overprints and surcharges are shown at 100 percent of their original size if shown alone, but are 70 percent of original size if shown on stamps. In some cases, the illustration will be placed above the set, between listings or omitted completely. Overprint and surcharge illustrations are not placed in this catalogue for purposes of expertizing stamps.

3 **Paper color** — The color of a stamp's paper is noted in italic type when the paper used is not white.

4 **Listing styles** — There are two principal types of catalogue listings: major and minor.

Major listings are in a larger type style than minor listings. The catalogue number is a numeral that can be found with or without a capital-letter suffix, and with or without a prefix.

Minor listings are in a smaller type style and have a small-letter suffix or (if the listing immediately follows that of the major number) may show only the letter. These listings identify a variety of the major item. Examples include perforation, color, watermark or printing method differences, multiples (some souvenir sheets, booklet panes and se-tenant combinations), and singles of multiples.

Examples of major number listings include 16, 28A, B97, C13A, 10N5, and 10N6A. Examples of minor numbers are 16a and C13Ab.

5 **Basic information about a stamp or set** — Introducing each stamp issue is a small section (usually a line listing) of basic information about a stamp or set. This section normally includes the date of issue, method of printing, perforation, watermark and, sometimes, some additional information of note. *Printing method, perforation and watermark apply to the following sets until a change is noted.* Stamps created by overprinting or surcharging previous issues are assumed to have the same perforation, watermark and printing method as the original. Dates of issue are as precise as Scott is able to confirm and often reflect the dates on first-day covers, rather than the actual date of release.

6 **Denomination** — This normally refers to the face value of the stamp; that is, the cost of the unused stamp at the post office at the time of issue. When a denomination is shown in parentheses, it does not appear on the stamp. This includes the non-denominated stamps of the United States, Brazil and Great Britain, for example.

7 **Color or other description** — This area provides information to solidify identification of a stamp. In many recent cases, a description of the stamp design appears in this space, rather than a listing of colors.

8 **Year of issue** — In stamp sets that have been released in a period that spans more than a year, the number shown in parentheses is the year that stamp first appeared. Stamps without a date appeared during the first year of the issue. Dates are not always given for minor varieties.

9 **Value unused and Value used** — The Scott catalogue values are based on stamps that are in a grade of Very Fine unless stated otherwise. Unused values refer to items that have not seen postal, revenue or any other duty for which they were intended. Pre-1900 unused stamps that were issued with gum must have at least most of their original gum. Later issues are assumed to have full original gum. From breakpoints specified in most countries' listings, stamps are valued as never hinged. Stamps issued without gum are noted. Modern issues with PVA or other synthetic adhesives may appear ungummed. Self-adhesive stamps are valued as appearing undisturbed on their original backing paper. For a more detailed explanation of these values, please see the "Catalogue Value," "Condition" and "Understanding Valuing Notations" sections elsewhere in this introduction.

In some cases, where used stamps are more valuable than unused stamps, the value is for an example with a contemporaneous cancel, rather than a modern cancel or a smudge or other unclear marking. For those stamps that were released for postal and fiscal purposes, the used value represents a postally used stamp. Stamps with revenue cancels generally sell for less. Scott values for used self-adhesive stamps are for examples either on piece or off piece.

10 **Changes in basic set information** — Bold type is used to show any changes in the basic data given for a set of stamps. This includes perforation differences from one stamp to the next or a different paper, printing method or watermark.

11 **Total value of a set** — The total value of sets of three or more stamps issued after 1900 are shown. The set line also notes the range of Scott numbers and total number of stamps included in the grouping. The actual value of a set consisting predominantly of stamps having the minimum value of twenty cents may be less than the total value shown. Similary, the actual value or catalogue value of se-tenant pairs or of blocks consisting of stamps having the minimum value of twenty cents may be less than the catalogue values of the component parts.

SCOTT NUMBER ①

ILLUS. NUMBER ②

PAPER COLOR ③

LISTING STYLES ④

MAJORS

MINORS

King George VI and Leopard – A6

King George VI A7

BASIC INFORMATION ON STAMP OR SET ⑤

DENOMINATION ⑥

COLOR OR OTHER DESCRIPTION ⑦

YEAR OF ISSUE ⑧

CATALOGUE VALUES ⑨
UNUSED
USED

CHANGES IN BASIC SET INFORMATION ⑩

TOTAL VALUE OF SET ⑪

1938-44			Engr.	Perf. 12½	
54	A6	½p	green	.20	.30
54A	A6	½p	dk brown ('42)	.20	.40
55	A6	1p	dark brown	.20	.20
55A	A6	1p	green ('42)	.20	.20
56	A6	1½p	dark carmine	.65	*1.90*
56A	A6	1½p	gray ('42)	.20	*1.25*
57	A6	2p	gray	1.25	.40
57A	A6	2p	dark car ('42)	.20	.30
58	A6	3p	blue	.30	.20
59	A6	4p	rose lilac	.80	.30
60	A6	6p	dark violet	.85	.25
61	A6	9p	olive bister	1.40	1.40
62	A6	1sh	orange & blk	1.40	.55

Typo.
Perf. 14
Chalky Paper

63	A7	2sh	ultra & dl vio, *bl*	5.50	4.50
64	A7	2sh6p	red & blk, *bl*	6.50	4.50
65	A7	5sh	red & grn, *yel*	22.50	11.00
a.		5sh dk red & dp grn, *yel* ('44)		50.00	37.50
66	A7	10sh	red & grn, *grn*	32.50	14.00

Wmk. 3

67	A7	£1	blk & vio, *red*	16.00	15.00
			Nos. 54-67 (18)	90.85	56.65

Special Notices

Classification of stamps

The *Scott Standard Postage Stamp Catalogue* lists stamps by country of issue. The next level of organization is a listing by section on the basis of the function of the stamps. The principal sections cover regular postage, semi-postal, air post, special delivery, registration, postage due and other categories. Except for regular postage, catalogue numbers for all sections include a prefix letter (or number-letter combination) denoting the class to which a given stamp belongs. When some countries issue sets containing stamps from more than one category, the catalogue will at times list all of the stamps in one category (such as air post stamps listed as part of a postage set).

The following is a listing of the most commonly used catalogue prefixes.

Prefix...Category

C ....Air Post
M...........Military
P.............Newspaper
N ....Occupation - Regular Issues
O ....Official
Q...........Parcel Post
J..............Postage Due
RA ....Postal Tax
B.............Semi-Postal
E...........Special Delivery
MR ....War Tax

Other prefixes used by more than one country include the following:

H ....Acknowledgment of Receipt
I..............Late Fee
CO.........Air Post Official
CQ.........Air Post Parcel Post
RAC.......Air Post Postal Tax
CF..........Air Post Registration
CB ....Air Post Semi-Postal
CBO.......Air Post Semi-Postal Official
CE ....Air Post Special Delivery
EY..........Authorized Delivery
S ....Franchise
G ....Insured Letter
GY ....Marine Insurance
MC ....Military Air Post
MQ........Military Parcel Post
NC.........Occupation - Air Post
NO.........Occupation - Official
NJ ....Occupation - Postage Due
NRA.......Occupation - Postal Tax
NB ....Occupation - Semi-Postal
NE ....Occupation - Special Delivery
QY ....Parcel Post Authorized Delivery
AR ....Postal-fiscal
RAJ ....Postal Tax Due
RAB ......Postal Tax Semi-Postal
F.............Registration
EB..........Semi-Postal Special Delivery
EO ....Special Delivery Official
QE ....Special Handling

New issue listings

Updates to this catalogue appear each month in the *Scott Stamp Monthly* magazine. Included in this update are additions to the listings of countries found in the *Scott Standard Postage Stamp Catalogue* and the *Specialized Catalogue of United States Stamps*, as well as corrections and updates to current editions of this catalogue.

From time to time there will be changes in the final listings of stamps from the *Scott Stamp Monthly* to the next edition of the catalogue. This occurs as more information about certain stamps or sets becomes available.

The catalogue update section of the *Scott Stamp Monthly* is the most timely presentation of this material available. Annual subscriptions to the *Scott Stamp Monthly* are available from Scott Publishing Co., Box 828, Sidney, OH 45365-0828.

Number additions, deletions & changes

A listing of catalogue number additions, deletions and changes from the previous edition of the catalogue appears in each volume. See Catalogue Number Additions, Deletions & Changes in the table of contents for the location of this list.

Understanding valuing notations

The *minimum catalogue value* of an individual stamp or set is 20 cents. This represents a portion of the cost incurred by a dealer when he prepares an individual stamp for resale. As a point of philatelic-economic fact, the lower the value shown for an item in this catalogue, the greater the percentage of that value is attributed to dealer mark up and profit margin. In many cases, such as the 20-cent minimum value, that price does not cover the labor or other costs involved with stocking it as an individual stamp. The sum of minimum values in a set does not properly represent the value of a complete set primarily composed of a number of minimum-value stamps, nor does the sum represent the actual value of a packet made up of minimum-value stamps. Thus a packet of 1,000 different common stamps — each of which has a catalogue value of 20-cents — normally sells for considerably less than 200 dollars!

The *absence of a retail value* for a stamp does not necessarily suggest that a stamp is scarce or rare. A dash in the value column means that the stamp is known in a stated form or variety, but information is either lacking or insufficient for purposes of establishing a usable catalogue value.

Stamp values in *italics* generally refer to items that are difficult to value accurately. For expensive items, such as those priced at $1,000 or higher, a value in italics indicates that the affected item trades very seldom. For inexpensive items, a value in italics represents a warning. One example is a "blocked" issue where the issuing postal administration may have controlled one stamp in a set in an attempt to make the whole set more valuable. Another example is an item that sold at an extreme multiple of face value in the marketplace at the time of its issue.

One type of warning to collectors that appears in the catalogue is illustrated by a stamp that is valued considerably higher in used condition than it is as unused. In this case, collectors are cautioned to be certain the used version has a genuine and contemporaneous cancellation. The type of cancellation on a stamp can be an important factor in determining its sale price. Catalogue values do not apply to fiscal, telegraph or non-contemporaneous postal cancels, unless otherwise noted.

Some countries have released back issues of stamps in canceled-to-order form, sometimes covering as much as a 10-year period. The Scott Catalogue values for used stamps reflect canceled-to-order material when such stamps are found to predominate in the marketplace for the issue involved. Notes frequently appear in the stamp listings to specify which items are valued as canceled-to-order, or if there is a premium for postally used examples.

Many countries sell canceled-to-order stamps at a marked reduction of face value. Countries that sell or have sold canceled-to-order stamps at *full* face value include Australia, Netherlands, France and Switzerland. It may be almost impossible to identify such stamps if the gum has been removed, because official government canceling devices are used. Postally used copies of these items on cover, however, are usually worth more than the canceled-to-order stamps with original gum.

Abbreviations

Scott Publishing Co. uses a consistent set of abbreviations throughout this catalogue to conserve space, while still providing necessary information.

COLOR ABBREVIATIONS

amb .....amber	crim.....crimson	ol.........olive
anil ......aniline	cr.........cream	olvn .....olivine
ap ....apple	dk........dark	org.......orange
aqua.....aquamarine	dl.........dull	pck ......peacock
az ....azure	dp........deep	pnksh...pinkish
bis........bister	db........drab	Prus.....Prussian
bl.........blue	emer ....emerald	pur.......purple
bld ....blood	gldn .....golden	redsh ...reddish
blk ....black	grysh....grayish	res ....reseda
bril.......brilliant	grn.......green	ros ....rosine
brn.......brown	grnsh ...greenish	ryl........royal
brnsh ...brownish	hel ....heliotrope	sal........salmon
brnz.....bronze	hn........henna	saph.....sapphire
brt ......bright	ind.......indigo	scar......scarlet
brnt .....burnt	int........intense	sep.......sepia
car ......carmine	lav ......lavender	sien.....sienna
cer ....cerise	lem ......lemon	sil ....silver
chlky...chalky	lil.........lilac	sl ....slate
cham ...chamois	lt..........light	stl ....steel
chnt.....chestnut	mag .....magenta	turq .....turquoise
choc.....chocolate	man .....manila	ultra.....ultramarine
chr.......chrome	mar......maroon	Ven ......Venetian
cit........citron	mv.......mauve	ver.......vermilion
cl ....claret	multi ....multicolored	vio ....violet
cob ......cobalt	mlky .....milky	yel ....yellow
cop ......copper	myr.....myrtle	yelsh ....yellowish

When no color is given for an overprint or surcharge, black is the color used. Abbreviations for colors used for overprints and surcharges include: "(B)" or "(Blk)," black; "(Bl)," blue; "(R)," red; and "(G)," green.

Additional abbreviations in this catalogue are shown below:

Adm. ....Administration
AFL ....American Federation of Labor
Anniv...............Anniversary
APS ....American Philatelic Society
Assoc...............Association
ASSR. ....Autonomous Soviet Socialist Republic
b......................Born
BEP ....Bureau of Engraving and Printing
Bicent. ....Bicentennial
Bklt..................Booklet
Brit. ....British
btwn................Between
Bur...................Bureau
c. or ca. ....Circa
Cat. ....Catalogue
Cent. ....Centennial, century, centenary
CIO ....Congress of Industrial Organizations
Conf. ....Conference
Cong................Congress
Cpl. ....Corporal
CTO ....Canceled to order
d......................Died
Dbl. ....Double
EKU.................Earliest known use
Engr. ....Engraved
Exhib...............Exhibition
Expo................Exposition
Fed. ....Federation
GB...................Great Britain
Gen. ....General
GPO ....General post office
Horiz................Horizontal
Imperf..............Imperforate
Impt. ....Imprint

Intl. ....International
Invtd.................Inverted
L.......................Left
Lieut., lt..........Lieutenant
Litho................Lithographed
LL....................Lower left
LR ....Lower right
mm...................Millimeter
Ms....................Manuscript
Natl. ....National
No. ....Number
NY....................New York
NYC ....New York City
Ovpt.................Overprint
Ovptd...............Overprinted
P.......................Plate number
Perf..................Perforated, perforation
Phil...................Philatelic
Photo................Photogravure
PO....................Post office
Pr......................Pair
P.R. ....Puerto Rico
Prec.................Precancel, precanceled
Pres. ....President
PTT ....Post, Telephone and Telegraph
Rio....................Rio de Janeiro
Sgt....................Sergeant
Soc. ....Society
Souv. ....Souvenir
SSR...................Soviet Socialist Republic, see ASSR
St......................Saint, street
Surch................Surcharge
Typo. ....Typographed
UL....................Upper left
Unwmkd. ....Unwatermarked
UPU ....Universal Postal Union
UR....................Upper Right
US....................United States
USPOD...........United States Post Office Department
USSR ....Union of Soviet Socialist Republics
Vert. ....Vertical
VP....................Vice president
Wmk. ....Watermark
Wmkd. ....Watermarked
WWI ....World War I
WWII ....World War II

Examination

Scott Publishing Co. will not comment upon the genuineness, grade or condition of stamps, because of the time and responsibility involved. Rather, there are several expertizing groups that undertake this work for both collectors and dealers. Neither will Scott Publishing Co. appraise or identify philatelic material. The company cannot take responsibility for unsolicited stamps or covers sent by individuals.

How to order from your dealer

When ordering stamps from a dealer, it is not necessary to write the full description of a stamp as listed in this catalogue. All you need is the name of the country, the Scott catalogue number and whether the desired item is unused or used. For example, "Japan Scott 422 unused" is sufficient to identify the unused stamp of Japan listed as "422 A206 5y brown."

Basic Stamp Information

A stamp collector's knowledge of the combined elements that make a given stamp issue unique determines his or her ability to identify stamps. These elements include paper, watermark, method of separation, printing, design and gum. On the following pages each of these important areas is briefly described.

Paper

Paper is an organic material composed of a compacted weave of cellulose fibers and generally formed into sheets. Paper used to print stamps may be manufactured in sheets, or it may have been part of a large roll (called a web) before being cut to size. The fibers most often used to create paper on which stamps are printed include bark, wood, straw and certain grasses. In many cases, linen or cotton rags have been added for greater strength and durability. Grinding, bleaching, cooking and rinsing these raw fibers reduces them to a slushy pulp, referred to by paper makers as "stuff." Sizing and, sometimes, coloring matter is added to the pulp to make different types of finished paper.

After the stuff is prepared, it is poured onto sieve-like frames that allow the water to run off, while retaining the matted pulp. As fibers fall onto the screen and are held by gravity, they form a natural weave that will later hold the paper together. If the screen has metal bits that are formed into letters or images attached, it leaves slightly thinned areas on the paper. These are called watermarks.

When the stuff is almost dry, it is passed under pressure through smooth or engraved rollers - dandy rolls - or placed between cloth in a press to be flattened and dried.

Stamp paper falls broadly into two types: wove and laid. The nature of the surface of the frame onto which the pulp is first deposited causes the differences in appearance between the two. If the surface is smooth and even, the paper will be of fairly uniform texture throughout. This is known as *wove paper*. Early papermaking machines poured the pulp onto a continuously circulating web of felt, but modern machines feed the pulp onto a cloth-like screen made of closely interwoven fine wires. This paper, when held to a light, will show little dots or points very close together. The proper name for this is "wire wove," but the type is still considered wove. Any U.S. or British stamp printed after 1880 will serve as an example of wire wove paper.

Closely spaced parallel wires, with cross wires at wider intervals, make up the frames used for what is known as *laid paper*. A greater thickness of the pulp will settle between the wires. The paper, when held to a light, will show alternate light and dark lines. The spacing and the thickness of the lines may vary, but on any one sheet of paper they are all alike. See Russia Scott 31-38 for examples of laid paper.

Batonne, from the French word meaning "a staff," is a term used if the lines in the paper are spaced quite far apart, like the printed ruling on a writing tablet. Batonne paper may be either wove or laid. If laid, fine laid lines can be seen between the batons. The laid lines, which are a form of watermark, may be geometrical figures such as squares, diamonds, rectangles or wavy lines.

Quadrille is the term used when the lines in the paper form little squares. *Oblong quadrille* is the term used when rectangles, rather than squares, are formed. See Mexico-Guadalajara Scott 35-37 for examples of oblong quadrille paper.

Paper also is classified as thick or thin, hard or soft, and by color if dye is added during manufacture. Such colors may include yellowish, greenish, bluish and reddish.

Brief explanations of other types of paper used for printing stamps, as well as examples, follow.

Pelure — Pelure paper is a very thin, hard and often brittle paper that is sometimes bluish or grayish in appearance. See Serbia Scott 169-170.

Native — This is a term applied to handmade papers used to produce some of the early stamps of the Indian states. Stamps printed on native paper may be expected to display various natural inclusions that are normal and do not negatively affect value. Japanese paper, originally made of mulberry fibers and rice flour, is part of this group. See Japan Scott 1-18.

Manila — This type of paper is often used to make stamped envelopes and wrappers. It is a coarse-textured stock, usually smooth on one side and rough on the other. A variety of colors of manila paper exist, but the most common range is yellowish-brown.

Silk — Introduced by the British in 1847 as a safeguard against counterfeiting, silk paper contains bits of colored silk thread scattered throughout. The density of these fibers varies greatly and can include as few as one fiber per stamp or hundreds. U.S. revenue Scott R152 is a good example of an easy-to-identify silk paper stamp.

Silk-thread paper has uninterrupted threads of colored silk arranged so that one or more threads run through the stamp or postal stationery. See Great Britain Scott 5-6 and Switzerland Scott 14-19.

Granite — Filled with minute cloth or colored paper fibers of various colors and lengths, granite paper should not be confused with either type of silk paper. Austria Scott 172-175 and a number of Swiss stamps are examples of granite paper.

Chalky — A chalk-like substance coats the surface of chalky paper to discourage the cleaning and reuse of canceled stamps, as well as to provide a smoother, more acceptable printing surface. Because the designs of stamps printed on chalky paper are imprinted on what is often a water-soluble coating, any attempt to remove a cancellation will destroy the stamp. *Do not soak these stamps in any fluid.* To remove a stamp printed on chalky paper from an envelope, wet the paper from underneath the stamp until the gum dissolves enough to release the stamp from the paper. See St. Kitts-Nevis Scott 89-90 for examples of stamps printed on this type of chalky paper.

India — Another name for this paper, originally introduced from China about 1750, is "China Paper." It is a thin, opaque paper often used for plate and die proofs by many countries.

Double — In philately, the term double paper has two distinct meanings. The first is a two-ply paper, usually a combination of a thick and a thin sheet, joined during manufacture. This type was used experimentally as a means to discourage the reuse of stamps.

The design is printed on the thin paper. Any attempt to remove a cancellation would destroy the design. U.S. Scott 158 and other Banknote-era stamps exist on this form of double paper.

The second type of double paper occurs on a rotary press, when the end of one paper roll, or web, is affixed to the next roll to save time feeding the paper through the press. Stamp designs are printed over the joined paper and, if overlooked by inspectors, may get into post office stocks.

Goldbeater's Skin — This type of paper was used for the 1866 issue of Prussia, and was a tough, translucent paper. The design was printed in reverse on the back of the stamp, and the gum applied over the printing. It is impossible to remove stamps printed on this type of paper from the paper to which they are affixed without destroying the design.

Ribbed — Ribbed paper has an uneven, corrugated surface made by passing the paper through ridged rollers. This type exists on some copies of U.S. Scott 156-165.

Various other substances, or substrates, have been used for stamp manufacture, including wood, aluminum, copper, silver and gold foil, plastic, and silk and cotton fabrics.

Wove   Laid   Granite

Quadrille   Oblong Quadrille   Batonne

Watermarks

Watermarks are an integral part of some papers. They are formed in the process of paper manufacture. Watermarks consist of small designs, formed of wire or cut from metal and soldered to the surface of the mold or, sometimes, on the dandy roll. The designs may be in the form of crowns, stars, anchors, letters or other characters or symbols. These pieces of metal - known in the paper-making industry as "bits" - impress a design into the paper. The design sometimes may be seen by holding the stamp to the light. Some are more easily seen with a watermark detector. This important tool is a small black tray into which a stamp is placed face down and dampened with a fast-evaporating watermark detection fluid that brings up the watermark image in the form of dark lines against a lighter background. These dark lines are the thinner areas of the paper known as the watermark. Some watermarks are extremely difficult to locate, due to either a faint impression, watermark location or the color of the stamp. There also are electric watermark detectors that come with plastic filter disks of various colors. The disks neutralize the color of the stamp, permitting the watermark to be seen more easily.

Multiple watermarks of Crown Agents and Burma

Watermarks of Uruguay, Vatican City and Jamaica

WARNING: Some inks used in the photogravure process dissolve in watermark fluids (Please see the section on Soluble Printing Inks). Also, see "chalky paper."

Watermarks may be found normal, reversed, inverted, reversed and inverted, sideways or diagonal, as seen from the back of the stamp. The relationship of watermark to stamp design depends on the position of the printing plates or how paper is fed through the press. On machine-made paper, watermarks normally are read from right to left. The design is repeated closely throughout the sheet in a "multiple-watermark design." In a "sheet watermark," the design appears only once on the sheet, but extends over many stamps. Individual stamps may carry only a small fraction or none of the watermark.

"Marginal watermarks" occur in the margins of sheets or panes of stamps. They occur on the outside border of paper (ostensibly outside the area where stamps are to be printed). A large row of letters may spell the name of the country or the manufacturer of the paper, or a border of lines may appear. Careless press feeding may cause parts of these letters and/or lines to show on stamps of the outer row of a pane.

Soluble Printing Inks

WARNING: Most stamp colors are permanent; that is, they are not seriously affected by short-term exposure to light or water. Many colors, especially of modern inks, fade from excessive exposure to light. There are stamps printed with inks that dissolve easily in water or in fluids used to detect watermarks. Use of these inks was intentional to prevent the removal of cancellations. Water affects all aniline inks, those on so-called safety paper and some photogravure printings - all such inks are known as *fugitive colors. Removal from paper of such stamps requires care and alternatives to traditional soaking.*

Separation

"Separation" is the general term used to describe methods used to separate stamps. The three standard forms currently in use are perforating, rouletting and die-cutting. These methods are done during the stamp production process, after printing. Sometimes these methods are done on-press or sometimes as a separate step. The earliest issues, such as the 1840 Penny Black of Great Britain (Scott 1), did not have any means provided for separation. It was expected the stamps would be cut apart with scissors or folded and torn. These are examples of imperforate stamps. Many stamps were first issued in imperforate formats and were later issued with perforations. Therefore, care must be observed in buying single imperforate stamps to be certain they were issued imperforate and are not perforated copies that have been altered by having the perforations trimmed away. Stamps issued imperforate usually are valued as singles. However, imperforate varieties of normally perforated stamps should be collected in pairs or larger pieces as indisputable evidence of their imperforate character.

PERFORATION

The chief style of separation of stamps, and the one that is in almost universal use today, is perforating. By this process, paper between the stamps is cut away in a line of holes, usually round, leaving little bridges of paper between the stamps to hold them together. Some types of perforation, such as hyphen-hole perfs, can be confused with roulettes, but a close visual inspection reveals that paper has been removed. The little perforation bridges, which project from the stamp when it is torn from the pane, are called the teeth of the perforation.

As the size of the perforation is sometimes the only way to differentiate between two otherwise identical stamps, it is necessary to be able to accurately measure and describe them. This is done with a perforation gauge, usually a ruler-like device that has dots or graduated lines to show how many perforations may be counted in the space of two centimeters. Two centimeters is the space universally adopted in which to measure perforations.

Perforation gauge

perce en arc   perce en lignes

perce en points   oblique roulette

perce en scie   perce serpentin

To measure a stamp, run it along the gauge until the dots on it fit exactly into the perforations of the stamp. If you are using a graduated-line perforation gauge, simply slide the stamp along the surface until the lines on the gauge perfectly project from the center of the bridges or holes. The number to the side of the line of dots or lines that fit the stamp's perforation is the measurement. For example, an "11" means that 11 perforations fit between two centimeters. The description of the stamp therefore is "perf. 11." If the gauge of the perforations on the top and bottom of a stamp differs from that on the sides, the result is what is known as *compound perforations.* In measuring compound perforations, the gauge at top and bottom is always given first, then the sides. Thus, a stamp that measures 11 at top and bottom and 10 1/2 at the sides is "perf. 11 x 10 1/2." See U.S. Scott 632-642 for examples of compound perforations.

Stamps also are known with perforations different on three or all four sides. Descriptions of such items are clockwise, beginning with the top of the stamp.

A perforation with small holes and teeth close together is a "fine perforation." One with large holes and teeth far apart is a "coarse perforation." Holes that are jagged, rather than clean-cut, are "rough perforations." *Blind perforations* are the slight impressions left by the perforating pins if they fail to puncture the paper. Multiples of stamps showing blind perforations may command a slight premium over normally perforated stamps.

The term *syncopated perfs* describes intentional irregularities in the perforations. The earliest form was used by the Netherlands from 1925-33, where holes were omitted to create distinctive patterns. Beginning in 1992, Great Britain has used an oval perforation to help prevent counterfeiting. Several other countries have started using the oval perfs or other syncopated perf patterns.

A new type of perforation, still primarily used for postal stationery, is known as microperfs. Microperfs are tiny perforations (in some cases hundreds of holes per two centimeters) that allows items to be intentionally separated very easily, while not accidentally breaking apart as easily as standard perforations. These are not currently measured or differentiated by size, as are standard perforations.

ROULETTING

In rouletting, the stamp paper is cut partly or wholly through, with no paper removed. In perforating, some paper is removed. Rouletting derives its name from the French roulette, a spur-like wheel. As the wheel is rolled over the paper, each point makes a small cut. The number of cuts made in a two-centimeter space determines the gauge of the roulette, just as the number of perforations in two centimeters determines the gauge of the perforation.

The shape and arrangement of the teeth on the wheels varies. Various roulette types generally carry French names:

Perce en lignes - rouletted in lines. The paper receives short, straight cuts in lines. This is the most common type of rouletting. See Mexico Scott 500.

Perce en points - pin-rouletted. This differs from a small perforation because no paper is removed, although round, equidistant holes are pricked through the paper. See Mexico Scott 242-256.

Perce en arc and *perce en scie* - pierced in an arc or saw-toothed designs, forming half circles or small triangles. See Hanover (German States) Scott 25-29.

Perce en serpentin - serpentine roulettes. The cuts form a serpentine or wavy line. See Brunswick (German States) Scott 13-18.

Once again, no paper is removed by these processes, leaving the stamps easily separated, but closely attached.

DIE-CUTTING

The third major form of stamp separation is die-cutting. This is a method where a die in the pattern of separation is created that later cuts the stamp paper in a stroke motion. Although some standard stamps bear die-cut perforations, this process is primarily used for self-adhesive postage stamps. Die-cutting can appear in straight lines, such as U.S. Scott 2522, shapes, such as U.S. Scott 1551, or imitating the appearance of perforations, such as New Zealand Scott 935A and 935B.

Printing Processes

ENGRAVING (Intaglio, Line-engraving, Etching)

Master die — The initial operation in the process of line engraving is making the master die. The die is a small, flat block of softened steel upon which the stamp design is recess engraved in reverse.

Master die

Photographic reduction of the original art is made to the appropriate size. It then serves as a tracing guide for the initial outline of the design. The engraver lightly traces the design on the steel with his graver, then slowly works the design until it is completed. At various points during the engraving process, the engraver hand-inks the die and makes an impression to check his progress. These are known as progressive die proofs. After completion of the engraving, the die is hardened to withstand the stress and pressures of later transfer operations.

Transfer roll

Transfer roll — Next is production of the transfer roll that, as the name implies, is the medium used to transfer the subject from the master die to the printing plate. A blank roll of soft steel, mounted on a mandrel, is placed under the bearers of the transfer press to allow it to roll freely on its axis. The hardened die is placed on the bed of the press and the face of the transfer roll is applied to the die, under pressure. The bed or the roll is then rocked back and forth under increasing pressure, until the soft steel of the roll is forced into every engraved line of the die. The resulting impression on the roll is known as a "relief" or a "relief transfer." The engraved image is now positive in appearance and stands out from the steel. After the required number of reliefs are "rocked in," the soft steel transfer roll is hardened.

Different flaws may occur during the relief process. A defective relief may occur during the rocking in process because of a minute piece of foreign material lodging on the die, or some other cause. Imperfections in the steel of the transfer roll may result in a breaking away of parts of the design. This is known as a relief break, which will show up on finished stamps as small, unprinted areas. If a damaged relief remains in use, it will transfer a repeating defect to the plate. Deliberate alterations of reliefs sometimes occur. "Altered reliefs" designate these changed conditions.

Plate — The final step in pre-printing production is the making of the printing plate. A flat piece of soft steel replaces the die on the bed of the transfer press. One of the reliefs on the transfer roll is positioned over this soft steel. Position, or layout, dots determine the correct position on the plate. The dots have been lightly marked on

the plate in advance. After the correct position of the relief is determined, the design is rocked in by following the same method used in making the transfer roll. The difference is that this time the image is being transferred from the transfer roll, rather than to it. Once the design is entered on the plate, it appears in reverse and is recessed. There are as many transfers entered on the plate as there are subjects printed on the sheet of stamps. It is during this process that double and shifted transfers occur, as well as re-entries. These are the result of improperly entered images that have not been properly burnished out prior to rocking in a new image.

Modern siderography processes, such as those used by the U.S. Bureau of Engraving and Printing, involve an automated form of rocking designs in on preformed cylindrical printing sleeves. The same process also allows for easier removal and re-entry of worn images right on the sleeve.

Transferring the design to the plate

Following the entering of the required transfers on the plate, the position dots, layout dots and lines, scratches and other markings generally are burnished out. Added at this time by the siderographer are any required *guide lines, plate numbers* or other *marginal markings.* The plate is then hand-inked and a proof impression is taken. This is known as a plate proof. If the impression is approved, the plate is machined for fitting onto the press, is hardened and sent to the plate vault ready for use.

On press, the plate is inked and the surface is automatically wiped clean, leaving ink only in the recessed lines. Paper is then forced under pressure into the engraved recessed lines, thereby receiving the ink. Thus, the ink lines on engraved stamps are slightly raised, and slight depressions (debossing) occur on the back of the stamp. Prior to the advent of modern high-speed presses and more advanced ink formulations, paper had to be dampened before receiving the ink. This sometimes led to uneven shrinkage by the time the stamps were perforated, resulting in improperly perforated stamps, or misperfs. Newer presses use drier paper, thus both *wet* and *dry printings* exist on some stamps.

Rotary Press — Until 1914, only flat plates were used to print engraved stamps. Rotary press printing was introduced in 1914, and slowly spread. Some countries still use flat-plate printing.

After approval of the plate proof, older *rotary press plates* require additional machining. They are curved to fit the press cylinder. "Gripper slots" are cut into the back of each plate to receive the "grippers," which hold the plate securely on the press. The plate is then hardened. Stamps printed from these bent rotary press plates are longer or wider than the same stamps printed from flat-plate presses. The stretching of the plate during the curving process is what causes this distortion.

Re-entry — To execute a re-entry on a flat plate, the transfer roll is re-applied to the plate, often at some time after its first use on the press. Worn-out designs can be resharpened by carefully burnishing out the original image and re-entering it from the transfer roll. If the original impression has not been sufficiently removed and the transfer roll is not precisely in line with the remaining impression, the resulting double transfer will make the re-entry obvious. If the registration is true, a re-entry may be difficult or impossible to distinguish. Sometimes a stamp printed from a successful re-entry is identified by having a much sharper and clearer impression than its neighbors. With the advent of rotary presses, post-press re-entries were not possible. After a plate was curved for the rotary press, it was impossible to make a re-entry. This is because the plate had already been bent once (with the design distorted).

However, with the introduction of the previously mentioned modern-style siderography machines, entries are made to the preformed cylindrical printing sleeve. Such sleeves are dechromed and softened. This allows individual images to be burnished out and re-entered on the curved sleeve. The sleeve is then rechromed, resulting in longer press life.

Double Transfer — This is a description of the condition of a transfer on a plate that shows evidence of a duplication of all, or a portion of the design. It usually is the result of the changing of the registration between the transfer roll and the plate during the rocking in of the original entry. Double transfers also occur when only a portion of the design has been rocked in and improper positioning is noted. If the worker elected not to burnish out the partial or completed design, a strong double transfer will occur for part or all of the design.

It sometimes is necessary to remove the original transfer from a plate and repeat the process a second time. If the finished re-worked image shows traces of the original impression, attributable to incomplete burnishing, the result is a partial double transfer.

With the modern automatic machines mentioned previously, double transfers are all but impossible to create. Those partially doubled images on stamps printed from such sleeves are more than likely re-entries, rather than true double transfers.

Re-engraved — Alterations to a stamp design are sometimes necessary after some stamps have been printed. In some cases, either the original die or the actual printing plate may have its "temper" drawn (softened), and the design will be re-cut. The resulting impressions from such a re-engraved die or plate may differ slightly from the original issue, and are known as "re-engraved." If the alteration was made to the master die, all future printings will be consistently different from the original. If alterations were made to the printing plate, each altered stamp on the plate will be slightly different from each other, allowing specialists to reconstruct a complete printing plate.

Dropped Transfers — If an impression from the transfer roll has not been properly placed, a dropped transfer may occur. The final stamp image will appear obviously out of line with its neighbors.

Short Transfer — Sometimes a transfer roll is not rocked its entire length when entering a transfer onto a plate. As a result, the finished transfer on the plate fails to show the complete design, and the finished stamp will have an incomplete design printed. This is known as a "short transfer." U.S. Scott No. 8 is a good example of a short transfer.

TYPOGRAPHY (Letterpress, Surface Printing, Flexography, Dry Offset, High Etch)

Although the word "Typography" is obsolete as a term describing a printing method, it was the accepted term throughout the first century of postage stamps. Therefore, appropriate Scott listings in this catalogue refer to typographed stamps. The current term for this form of printing, however, is "letterpress."

As it relates to the production of postage stamps, letterpress printing is the reverse of engraving. Rather than having recessed areas trap the ink and deposit it on paper, only the raised areas of the design are inked. This is comparable to the type of printing seen by inking and using an ordinary rubber stamp. Letterpress includes all printing where the design is above the surface area, whether it is wood, metal or, in some instances, hardened rubber or polymer plastic.

For most letterpress-printed stamps, the engraved master is made in much the same manner as for engraved stamps. In this instance, however, an additional step is needed. The design is transferred to another surface before being transferred to the transfer roll. In this way, the transfer roll has a recessed stamp design, rather than one done in relief. This makes the printing areas on the final plate raised, or relief areas.

For less-detailed stamps of the 19th century, the area on the die not used as a printing surface was cut away, leaving the surface area raised. The original die was then reproduced by stereotyping or electrotyping. The resulting electrotypes were assembled in the required number and format of the desired sheet of stamps. The plate used in printing the stamps was an electroplate of these assembled electrotypes.

Once the final letterpress plates are created, ink is applied to the raised surface and the pressure of the press transfers the ink impression to the paper. In contrast to engraving, the fine lines of letterpress are impressed on the surface of the stamp, leaving a debossed surface. When viewed from the back (as on a typewritten page), the corresponding line work on the stamp will be raised slightly (embossed) above the surface.

PHOTOGRAVURE (Gravure, Rotogravure, Heliogravure)

In this process, the basic principles of photography are applied to a chemically sensitized metal plate, rather than photographic paper. The design is transferred photographically to the plate through a halftone, or dot-matrix screen, breaking the reproduction into tiny dots. The plate is treated chemically and the dots form depressions, called cells, of varying depths and diameters, depending on the degrees of shade in the design. Then, like engraving, ink is applied to the plate and the surface is wiped clean. This leaves ink in the tiny cells that is lifted out and deposited on the paper when it is pressed against the plate.

Gravure is most often used for multicolored stamps, generally using the three primary colors (red, yellow and blue) and black. By varying the dot matrix pattern and density of these colors, virtually any color can be reproduced. A typical full-color gravure stamp will be created from four printing cylinders (one for each color). The original multicolored image will have been photographically separated into its component colors.

Modern gravure printing may use computer-generated dot-matrix screens, and modern plates may be of various types including metal-coated plastic. The catalogue designation of Photogravure (or "Photo") covers any of these older and more modern gravure methods of printing.

For examples of the first photogravure stamps printed (1914), see Bavaria Scott 94-114.

LITHOGRAPHY (Offset Lithography, Stone Lithography, Dilitho, Planography, Collotype)

The principle that oil and water do not mix is the basis for lithography. The stamp design is drawn by hand or transferred from engraving to the surface of a lithographic stone or metal plate in a greasy (oily) substance. This oily substance holds the ink, which will later be transferred to the paper. The stone (or plate) is wet with an acid fluid, causing it to repel the printing ink in all areas not covered by the greasy substance.

Transfer paper is used to transfer the design from the original stone or plate. A series of duplicate transfers are grouped and, in turn, transferred to the final printing plate.

Photolithography — The application of photographic processes to lithography. This process allows greater flexibility of design, related to use of halftone screens combined with line work. Unlike photogravure or engraving, this process can allow large, solid areas to be printed.

Offset — A refinement of the lithographic process. A rubber-covered blanket cylinder takes the impression from the inked lithographic plate. From the "blanket" the impression is *offset* or transferred to the paper. Greater flexibility and speed are the principal reasons offset printing has largely displaced lithography. The term "lithography" covers both processes, and results are almost identical.

EMBOSSED (Relief) Printing
Embossing, not considered one of the four main printing types, is a method in which the design first is sunk into the metal of the die. Printing is done against a yielding platen, such as leather or linoleum. The platen is forced into the depression of the die, thus forming the design on the paper in relief. This process is often used for metallic inks.

Embossing may be done without color (see Sardinia Scott 4-6); with color printed around the embossed area (see Great Britain Scott 5 and most U.S. envelopes); and with color in exact registration with the embossed subject (see Canada Scott 656-657).

HOLOGRAMS
For objects to appear as holograms on stamps, a model exactly the same size as it is to appear on the hologram must be created. Rather than using photographic film to capture the image, holography records an image on a photoresist material. In processing, chemicals eat away at certain exposed areas, leaving a pattern of constructive and destructive interference. When the phororesist is developed, the result is a pattern of uneven ridges that acts as a mold. This mold is then coated with metal, and the resulting form is used to press copies in much the same way phonograph records are produced.

A typical reflective hologram used for stamps consists of a reproduction of the uneven patterns on a plastic film that is applied to a reflective background, usually a silver or gold foil. Light is reflected off the background through the film, making the pattern present on the film visible. Because of the uneven pattern of the film, the viewer will perceive the objects in their proper three-dimensional relationships with appropriate brightness.

The first hologram on a stamp was produced by Austria in 1988 (Scott 1441).

FOIL APPLICATION
A modern tecnique of applying color to stamps involves the application of metallic foil to the stamp paper. A pattern of foil is applied to the stamp paper by use of a stamping die. The foil usually is flat, but it may be textured. Canada Scott 1735 has three different foil applications in pearl, bronze and gold. The gold foil was textured using a chemical-etch copper embossing die. The printing of this stamp also involved two-color offset lithography plus embossing.

COMBINATION PRINTINGS
Sometimes two or even three printing methods are combined in producing stamps. In these cases, such as Austria Scott 933 or Canada 1735 (described in the preceding paragraph), the multiple-printing technique can be determined by studing the individual characteristics of each printing type. A few stamps, such as Singapore Scott 684-684A, combine as many as three of the four major printing types (lithography, engraving and typography). When this is done it often indicates the incorporation of security devices against counterfeiting.

INK COLORS
Inks or colored papers used in stamp printing often are of mineral origin, although there are numerous examples of organic-based pigments. As a general rule, organic-based pigments are far more subject to varieties and change than those of mineral-based origin.

The appearance of any given color on a stamp may be affected by many aspects, including printing variations, light, color of paper, aging and chemical alterations.

Numerous printing variations may be observed. Heavier pressure or inking will cause a more intense color, while slight interruptions in the ink feed or lighter impressions will cause a lighter appearance. Stamps printed in the same color by water-based and solvent-based inks can differ significantly in appearance. This affects several stamps in the U.S. Prominent Americans series. Hand-mixed ink formulas (primarily from the 19th century) produced under different conditions (humidity and temperature) account for notable color variations in early printings of the same stamp (see U.S. Scott 248-250, 279B, for example). Different sources of pigment can also result in significant differences in color.

Light exposure and aging are closely related in the way they affect stamp color. Both eventually break down the ink and fade colors, so that a carefully kept stamp may differ significantly in color from an identical copy that has been exposed to light. If stamps are exposed to light either intentionally or accidentally, their colors can be faded or completely changed in some cases.

Papers of different quality and consistency used for the same stamp printing may affect color appearance. Most pelure papers, for example, show a richer color when compared with wove or laid papers. See Russia Scott 181a, for an example of this effect.

The very nature of the printing processes can cause a variety of differences in shades or hues of the same stamp. Some of these shades are scarcer than others, and are of particular interest to the advanced collector.

Luminescence
All forms of tagged stamps fall under the general category of luminescence. Within this broad category is fluorescence, dealing with forms of tagging visible under longwave ultraviolet light, and phosphorescence, which deals with tagging visible only under shortwave light. Phosphorescence leaves an afterglow and fluorescence does not. These treated stamps show up in a range of different colors when exposed to UV light. The differing wavelengths of the light activates the tagging material, making it glow in various colors that usually serve different mail processing purposes.

Intentional tagging is a post-World War II phenomenon, brought about by the increased literacy rate and rapidly growing mail volume. It was one of several answers to the problem of the need for more automated mail processes. Early tagged stamps served the purpose of triggering machines to separate different types of mail. A natural outgrowth was to also use the signal to trigger machines that faced all envelopes the same way and canceled them.

Tagged stamps come in many different forms. Some tagged stamps have luminescent shapes or images imprinted on them as a form of security device. Others have blocks (United States), stripes, frames (South Africa and Canada), overall coatings (United States), bars (Great Britain and Canada) and many other types. Some types of tagging are even mixed in with the pigmented printing ink (Australia Scott 366, Netherlands Scott 478 and U.S. Scott 1359 and 2443).

The means of applying taggant to stamps differs as much as the intended purposes for the stamps. The most common form of tagging is a coating applied to the surface of the printed stamp. Since the taggant ink is frequently invisible except under UV light, it does not interfere with the appearance of the stamp. Another common application is the use of phosphored papers. In this case the paper itself either has a coating of taggant applied before the stamp is printed, has taggant applied during the papermaking process (incorporating it into the fibers), or has the taggant mixed into the coating of the paper. The latter method, among others, is currently in use in the United States.

Many countries now use tagging in various forms to either expedite mail handling or to serve as a printing security device against counterfeiting. Following the introduction of tagged stamps for public use in 1959 by Great Britain, other countries have steadily joined the parade. Among those are Germany (1961); Canada and Denmark (1962); United States, Australia, France and Switzerland (1963); Belgium and Japan (1966); Sweden and Norway (1967); Italy (1968); and Russia (1969). Since then, many other countries have begun using forms of tagging, including Brazil, China, Czechoslovakia, Hong Kong, Guatemala, Indonesia, Israel, Lithuania, Luxembourg, Netherlands, Penrhyn Islands, Portugal, St. Vincent, Singapore, South Africa, Spain and Sweden to name a few.

In some cases, including United States, Canada, Great Britain and Switzerland, stamps were released both with and without tagging. Many of these were released during each country's experimental period. Tagged and untagged versions are listed for the aforementioned countries and are noted in some other countries' listings. For at least a few stamps, the experimentally tagged version is worth far more than its untagged counterpart, such as the 1963 experimental tagged version of France Scott 1024.

In some cases, luminescent varieties of stamps were inadvertently created. Several Russian stamps, for example, sport highly fluorescent ink that was not intended as a form of tagging. Older stamps, such as early U.S. postage dues, can be positively identified by the use of UV light, since the organic ink used has become slightly fluorescent over time. Other stamps, such as Austria Scott 70a-82a (varnish bars) and Obock Scott 46-64 (printed quadrille lines), have become fluorescent over time.

Various fluorescent substances have been added to paper to make it appear brighter. These optical brightners, as they are known, greatly affect the appearance of the stamp under UV light. The brightest of these is known as Hi-Brite paper. These paper varieties are beyond the scope of the Scott Catalogue.

Shortwave UV light also is used extensively in expertizing, since each form of paper has its own fluorescent characteristics that are impossible to perfectly match. It is therefore a simple matter to detect filled thins, added perforation teeth and other alterations that involve the addition of paper. UV light also is used to examine stamps that have had cancels chemically removed and for other purposes as well.

Gum

The Illustrated Gum Chart in the first part of this introduction shows and defines various types of gum condition. Because gum condition has an important impact on the value of unused stamps, we recommend studying this chart and the accompanying text carefully.

The gum on the back of a stamp may be shiny, dull, smooth, rough, dark, white, colored or tinted. Most stamp gumming adhesives use gum arabic or dextrine as a base. Certain polymers such as polyvinyl alcohol (PVA) have been used extensively since World War II.

The *Scott Standard Postage Stamp Catalogue* does not list items by types of gum. The *Scott Specialized Catalogue of United States Stamps* does differentiate among some types of gum for certain issues.

Reprints of stamps may have gum differing from the original issues. In addition, some countries have used different gum formulas for different seasons. These adhesives have different properties that may become more apparent over time.

Many stamps have been issued without gum, and the catalogue will note this fact. See, for example, United States Scott 40-47. Sometimes, gum may have been removed to preserve the stamp. Germany Scott B68, for example, has a highly acidic gum that eventually destroys the stamps. This item is valued in the catalogue with gum removed.

Reprints and Reissues

These are impressions of stamps (usually obsolete) made from the original plates or stones. If they are valid for postage and reproduce obsolete issues (such as U.S. Scott 102-111), the stamps are *reissues*. If they are from current issues, they are designated as *second, third,* etc., *printing*. If designated for a particular purpose, they are called *special printings*.

When special printings are not valid for postage, but are made from original dies and plates by authorized persons, they are *official reprints*. *Private reprints* are made from the original plates and dies by private hands. An example of a private reprint is that of the 1871-1932 reprints made from the original die of the 1845 New Haven, Conn., postmaster's provisional. *Official reproductions* or imitations are made from new dies and plates by government authorization. Scott will list those reissues that are valid for postage if they differ significantly from the original printing.

The U.S. government made special printings of its first postage stamps in 1875. Produced were official imitations of the first two stamps (listed as Scott 3-4), reprints of the demonetized pre-1861 issues (Scott 40-47) and reissues of the 1861 stamps, the 1869 stamps and the then-current 1875 denominations. Even though the official imitations and the reprints were not valid for postage, Scott lists all of these U.S. special printings.

Most reprints or reissues differ slightly from the original stamp in some characteristic, such as gum, paper, perforation, color or watermark. Sometimes the details are followed so meticulously that only a student of that specific stamp is able to distinguish the reprint or reissue from the original.

Remainders and Canceled to Order

Some countries sell their stock of old stamps when a new issue replaces them. To avoid postal use, the *remainders* usually are canceled with a punch hole, a heavy line or bar, or a more-or-less regular-looking cancellation. The most famous merchant of remainders was Nicholas F. Seebeck. In the 1880s and 1890s, he arranged printing contracts between the Hamilton Bank Note Co., of which he was a director, and several Central and South American countries. The contracts provided that the plates and all remainders of the yearly issues became the property of Hamilton. Seebeck saw to it that ample stock remained. The "Seebecks," both remainders and reprints, were standard packet fillers for decades.

Some countries also issue stamps *canceled-to-order (CTO)*, either in sheets with original gum or stuck onto pieces of paper or envelopes and canceled. Such CTO items generally are worth less than postally used stamps. In cases where the CTO material is far more prevalent in the marketplace than postally used examples, the catalogue value relates to the CTO examples, with postally used examples noted as premium items. Most CTOs can be detected by the presence of gum. However, as the CTO practice goes back at least to 1885, the gum inevitably has been soaked off some stamps so they could pass as postally used. The normally applied postmarks usually differ slightly from standard postmarks, and specialists are able to tell the difference. When applied individually to envelopes by philatelically minded persons, CTO material is known as *favor canceled* and generally sells at large discounts.

Cinderellas and Facsimiles

Cinderella is a catch-all term used by stamp collectors to describe phantoms, fantasies, bogus items, municipal issues, exhibition seals, local revenues, transportation stamps, labels, poster stamps and many other types of items. Some cinderella collectors include in their collections local postage issues, telegraph stamps, essays and proofs, forgeries and counterfeits.

A *fantasy* is an adhesive created for a nonexistent stamp-issuing authority. Fantasy items range from imaginary countries (Occusi-Ambeno, Kingdom of Sedang, Principality of Trinidad or Torres Straits), to non-existent locals (Winans City Post), or nonexistent transportation lines (McRobish & Co.'s Acapulco-San Francisco Line).

On the other hand, if the entity exists and could have issued stamps (but did not) or was known to have issued other stamps, the items are considered *bogus* stamps. These would include the Mormon postage stamps of Utah, S. Allan Taylor's Guatemala and Paraguay inventions, the propaganda issues for the South Moluccas and the adhesives of the Page & Keyes local post of Boston.

Phantoms is another term for both fantasy and bogus issues.

Facsimiles are copies or imitations made to represent original stamps, but which do not pretend to be originals. A catalogue illustration is such a facsimile. Illustrations from the Moens catalogue of the last century were occasionally colored and passed off as stamps. Since the beginning of stamp collecting, facsimiles have been made for collectors as space fillers or for reference. They often carry the word "facsimile," "falsch" (German), "sanko" or "mozo" (Japanese), or "faux" (French) overprinted on the face or stamped on the back. Unfortunately, over the years a number of these items have had fake cancels applied over the facsimile notation and have been passed off as genuine.

Forgeries and Counterfeits

Forgeries and counterfeits have been with philately virtually from the beginning of stamp production. Over time, the terminology for the two has been used interchangeably. Although both forgeries and counterfeits are reproductions of stamps, the purposes behind their creation differ considerably.

Among specialists there is an increasing movement to more specifically define such items. Although there is no universally accepted terminology, we feel the following definitions most closely mirror the items and their purposes as they are currently defined.

Forgeries (also often referred to as *Counterfeits*) are reproductions of genuine stamps that have been created to defraud collectors. Such spurious items first appeared on the market around 1860, and most old-time collections contain one or more. Many are crude and easily spotted, but some can deceive experts.

An important supplier of these early philatelic forgeries was the Hamburg printer Gebruder Spiro. Many others with reputations in this craft included S. Allan Taylor, George Hussey, James Chute, George Forune, Benjamin & Sarpy, Julius Goldner, E. Oneglia and L.H. Mercier. Among the noted 20th-century forgers were Francois Fournier, Jean Sperati and the prolific Raoul DeThuin.

Forgeries may be complete replications, or they may be genuine stamps altered to resemble a scarcer (and more valuable) type. Most forgeries, particularly those of rare stamps, are worth only a small fraction of the value of a genuine example, but a few types, created by some of the most notable forgers, such as Sperati, can be worth as much or more than the genuine. Fraudulently produced copies are known of most classic rarities and many medium-priced stamps.

In addition to rare stamps, large numbers of common 19th- and early 20th-century stamps were forged to supply stamps to the early packet trade. Many can still be easily found. Few new philatelic forgeries have appeared in recent decades. Successful imitation of well-engraved work is virtually impossible. It has proven far easier to produce a fake by altering a genuine stamp than to duplicate a stamp completely.

Counterfeit (also often referred to as *Postal Counterfeit* or *Postal Forgery*) is the term generally applied to reproductions of stamps that have been created to defraud the government of revenue. Such items usually are created at the time a stamp is current and, in some cases, are hard to detect. Because most counterfeits are seized when the perpetrator is captured, postal counterfeits, particularly used on cover, are usually worth much more than a genuine example to spe-

cialists. The first postal counterfeit was of Spain's 4-cuarto carmine of 1854 (the real one is Scott 25). Apparently, the counterfeiters were not satisfied with their first version, which is now very scarce, and they soon created an engraved counterfeit, which is common. Postal counterfeits quickly followed in Austria, Naples, Sardinia and the Roman States. They have since been created in many other countries as well, including the United States.

An infamous counterfeit to defraud the government is the 1-shilling Great Britain "Stock Exchange" forgery of 1872, used on telegraph forms at the exchange that year. The stamp escaped detection until a stamp dealer noticed it in 1898.

Fakes

Fakes are genuine stamps altered in some way to make them more desirable. One student of this part of stamp collecting has estimated that by the 1950s more than 30,000 varieties of fakes were known. That number has grown greatly since then. The widespread existence of fakes makes it important for stamp collectors to study their philatelic holdings and use relevant literature. Likewise, collectors should buy from reputable dealers who guarantee their stamps and make full and prompt refunds should a purchased item be declared faked or altered by some mutually agreed-upon authority. Because fakes always have some genuine characteristics, it is not always possible to obtain unanimous agreement among experts regarding specific items. These students may change their opinions as philatelic knowledge increases. More than 80 percent of all fakes on the philatelic market today are regummed, reperforated (or perforated for the first time), or bear forged overprints, surcharges or cancellations.

Stamps can be chemically treated to alter or eliminate colors. For example, a pale rose stamp can be re-colored to resemble a blue shade of high market value. In other cases, treated stamps can be made to resemble missing color varieties. Designs may be changed by painting, or a stroke or a dot added or bleached out to turn an ordinary variety into a seemingly scarcer stamp. Part of a stamp can be bleached and reprinted in a different version, achieving an inverted center or frame. Margins can be added or repairs done so deceptively that the stamps move from the "repaired" into the "fake" category.

Fakers have not left the backs of the stamps untouched either. They may create false watermarks, add fake grills or press out genuine grills. A thin India paper proof may be glued onto a thicker backing to create the appearance an issued stamp, or a proof printed on cardboard may be shaved down and perforated to resemble a stamp. Silk threads are impressed into paper and stamps have been split so that a rare paper variety is added to an otherwise inexpensive stamp. The most common treatment to the back of a stamp, however, is regumming.

Some in the business of faking stamps have openly advertised foolproof application of "original gum" to stamps that lack it, although most publications now ban such ads from their pages. It is believed that very few early stamps have survived without being hinged. The large number of never-hinged examples of such earlier material offered for sale thus suggests the widespread extent of regumming activity. Regumming also may be used to hide repairs or thin spots. Dipping the stamp into watermark fluid, or examining it under longwave ultraviolet light often will reveal these flaws.

Fakers also tamper with separations. Ingenious ways to add margins are known. Perforated wide-margin stamps may be falsely represented as imperforate when trimmed. Reperforating is commonly done to create scarce coil or perforation varieties, and to eliminate the naturally occurring straight-edge stamps found in sheet margin positions of many earlier issues. Custom has made straight-edged stamps less desirable. Fakers have obliged by perforating straight-edged stamps so that many are now uncommon, if not rare.

Another fertile field for the faker is that of overprints, surcharges and cancellations. The forging of rare surcharges or overprints began in the 1880s or 1890s. These forgeries are sometimes difficult to detect, but experts have identified almost all. Occasionally, overprints or cancellations are removed to create non-overprinted stamps or seemingly unused items. This is most commonly done by removing a manuscript cancel to make a stamp resemble an unused example. "SPECIMEN" overprints may be removed by scraping and repainting to create non-overprinted varieties. Fakers use inexpensive revenues or pen-canceled stamps to generate unused stamps for further faking by adding other markings. The quartz lamp or UV lamp and a high-powered magnifying glass help to easily detect removed cancellations.

The bigger problem, however, is the addition of overprints, surcharges or cancellations - many with such precision that they are very difficult to ascertain. Plating of the stamps or the overprint can be an important method of detection.

Fake postmarks may range from many spurious fancy cancellations to a host of markings applied to transatlantic covers, to adding normally appearing postmarks to definitives of some countries with stamps that are valued far higher used than unused. With the increased popularity of cover collecting, and the widespread interest in postal history, a fertile new field for fakers has come about. Some have tried to create entire covers. Others specialize in adding stamps, tied by fake cancellations, to genuine stampless covers, or replacing less expensive or damaged stamps with more valuable ones. Detailed study of postal rates in effect at the time a cover in question was mailed, including the analysis of each handstamp used during the period, ink analysis and similar techniques, usually will unmask the fraud.

Restoration and Repairs

Scott Publishing Co. bases its catalogue values on stamps that are free of defects and otherwise meet the standards set forth earlier in this introduction. Most stamp collectors desire to have the finest copy of an item possible. Even within given grading categories there are variances. This leads to a controversial practice that is not defined in any universal manner: stamp *restoration*.

There are broad differences of opinion about what is permissible when it comes to restoration. Carefully applying a soft eraser to a stamp or cover to remove light soiling is one form of restoration, as is washing a stamp in mild soap and water to clean it. These are fairly accepted forms of restoration. More severe forms of restoration include pressing out creases or removing stains caused by tape. To what degree each of these is acceptable is dependent upon the individual situation. Further along the spectrum is the freshening of a stamp's color by removing oxide build-up or the effects of wax paper left next to stamps shipped to the tropics.

At some point in this spectrum the concept of *repair* replaces that of restoration. Repairs include filling thin spots, mending tears by reweaving or adding a missing perforation tooth. Regumming stamps may have been acceptable as a restoration or repair technique many decades ago, but today it is considered a form of fakery.

Restored stamps may or may not sell at a discount, and it is possible that the value of individual restored items may be enhanced over that of their pre-restoration state. Specific situations dictate the resultant value of such an item. Repaired stamps sell at substantial discounts from the value of sound stamps.

Terminology

Booklets — Many countries have issued stamps in small booklets for the convenience of users. This idea continues to become increasingly popular in many countries. Booklets have been issued in many sizes and forms, often with advertising on the covers, the panes of stamps or on the interleaving.

The panes used in booklets may be printed from special plates or made from regular sheets. All panes from booklets issued by the United States and many from those of other countries contain stamps that are straight edged on the sides, but perforated between. Others are distinguished by orientation of watermark or other identifying features. Any stamp-like unit in the pane, either printed or blank, that is not a postage stamp, is considered to be a *label* in the catalogue listings.

Scott lists and values booklet panes only. Complete booklets are listed and valued in only a few cases, such as Grenada Scott 1055 and some forms of British prestige booklets. Individual booklet panes are listed only when they are not fashioned from existing sheet stamps and, therefore, are identifiable from their sheet stamp counterparts.

Panes usually do not have a used value assigned to them because there is little market activity for used booklet panes, even though many exist used and there is some demand for them.

Cancellations — The marks or obliterations put on stamps by postal authorities to show that they have performed service and to prevent their reuse are known as cancellations. If the marking is made with a pen, it is considered a "pen cancel." When the location of the post office appears in the marking, it is a "town cancellation."

A "postmark" is technically any postal marking, but in practice the term generally is applied to a town cancellation with a date. When calling attention to a cause or celebration, the marking is known as a "slogan cancellation." Many other types and styles of cancellations exist, such as duplex, numerals, targets, fancy and others. See also "precancels," below.

Coil Stamps — These are stamps that are issued in rolls for use in dispensers, affixing and vending machines. Those coils of the United States, Canada, Sweden and some other countries are perforated horizontally or vertically only, with the outer edges imperforate. Coil stamps of some countries, such as Great Britain and Germany, are perforated on all four sides and may in some cases be distinguished from their sheet stamp counterparts by watermarks, counting numbers on the reverse or other means.

Covers — Entire envelopes, with or without adhesive postage stamps, that have passed through the mail and bear postal or other markings of philatelic interest are known as covers. Before the introduction of envelopes in about 1840, people folded letters and wrote the address on the outside. Some people covered their letters with an extra sheet of paper on the outside for the address, producing the term "cover." Used airletter sheets, stamped envelopes and other items of postal stationery also are considered covers.

Errors — Stamps that have some major, consistent, unintentional deviation from the normal are considered errors. Errors include, but are not limited to, missing or wrong colors, wrong paper, wrong watermarks, inverted centers or frames on multicolor printing, inverted or missing surcharges or overprints, double impressions, missing perforations and others. Factually wrong or misspelled information, if it appears on all examples of a stamp, are not considered errors in the true sense of the word. They are errors of design. Inconsistent or randomly appearing items, such as misperfs or color shifts, are classified as freaks.

Overprints and Surcharges — Overprinting involves applying wording or design elements over an already existing stamp. Overprints can be used to alter the place of use (such as "Canal Zone" on U.S. stamps), to adapt them for a special purpose ("Porto" on Denmark's 1913-20 regular issues for use as postage due stamps, Scott J1-J7) or to commemorate a special occasion (United States Scott 647-648).

A *surcharge* is a form of overprint that changes or restates the face value of a stamp or piece of postal stationery.

Surcharges and overprints may be handstamped, typeset or, occasionally, lithographed or engraved. A few hand-written overprints and surcharges are known.

Precancels — Stamps that are canceled before they are placed in the mail are known as precancels. Precanceling usually is done to expedite the handling of large mailings and generally allow the affected mail pieces to skip certain phases of mail handling.

In the United States, precancellations generally identified the point of origin; that is, the city and state. This information appeared across the face of the stamp, usually centered between parallel lines. More recently, bureau precancels retained the parallel lines, but the city and state designations were dropped. Recent coils have a service inscription that is present on the original printing plate. These show the mail service paid for by the stamp. Since these stamps are not intended to receive further cancellations when used as intended, they are considered precancels. Such items often do not have parallel lines as part of the precancellation.

In France, the abbreviation *Affranchts* in a semicircle together with the word *Postes* is the general form of precancel in use. Belgian precancellations usually appear in a box in which the name of the city appears. Netherlands precancels have the name of the city enclosed between concentric circles, sometimes called a "lifesaver." Precancellations of other countries usually follow these patterns, but may be any arrangement of bars, boxes and city names.

Precancels are listed in the Scott catalogues only if the precancel changes the denomination (Belgium Scott 477-478); if the precanceled stamp is different from the non-precanceled version (such as untagged U.S. precancels); or if the stamp exists only precanceled (France Scott 1096-1099, U.S. Scott 2265).

Proofs and Essays — Proofs are impressions taken from an approved die, plate or stone in which the design and color are the same as the stamp issued to the public. Trial color proofs are impressions taken from approved dies, plates or stones in colors that vary from the final version. An essay is the impression of a design that differs in some way from the issued stamp. "Progressive die proofs" generally are considered to be essays.

Provisionals — These are stamps that are issued on short notice and intended for temporary use pending the arrival of regular issues. They usually are issued to meet such contingencies as changes in government or currency, shortage of necessary postage values or military occupation.

During the 1840s, postmasters in certain American cities issued stamps that were valid only at specific post offices. In 1861, postmasters of the Confederate States also issued stamps with limited validity. Both of these examples are known as "postmaster's provisionals."

Se-tenant — This term refers to an unsevered pair, strip or block of stamps that differ in design, denomination or overprint.

Unless the se-tenant item has a continuous design (see U.S. Scott 1451a, 1694a) the stamps do not have to be in the same order as shown in the catalogue (see U.S. Scott 2158a).

Specimens — The Universal Postal Union required member nations to send samples of all stamps they released into service to the International Bureau in Switzerland. Member nations of the UPU received these specimens as samples of what stamps were valid for postage. Many are overprinted, handstamped or initial-perforated "Specimen," "Canceled" or "Muestra." Some are marked with bars across the denominations (China-Taiwan), punched holes (Czechoslovakia) or back inscriptions (Mongolia).

Stamps distributed to government officials or for publicity purposes, and stamps submitted by private security printers for official approval, also may receive such defacements.

The previously described defacement markings prevent postal use, and all such items generally are known as "specimens."

Tete Beche — This term describes a pair of stamps in which one is upside down in relation to the other. Some of these are the result of intentional sheet arrangements, such as Morocco Scott B10-B11. Others occurred when one or more electrotypes accidentally were placed upside down on the plate, such as Colombia Scott 57a. Separation of the tete-beche stamps, of course, destroys the tete beche variety.

Currency Conversion

Country	Dollar	Pound	S Franc	Yen	HK Dollar	Euro	Cdn Dollar	Aus Dollar
Australia	1.9214	2.7768	1.1624	0.0147	0.2464	1.7192	1.2039	-----
Canada	1.5960	2.3065	0.9656	0.0122	0.2047	1.4281	-----	0.8306
European Union	1.1176	1.6152	0.6761	0.0085	0.1433	-----	0.7003	0.5817
Hong Kong	7.7986	11.271	4.7181	0.0596	-----	6.9780	4.8863	4.0588
Japan	130.95	189.25	79.224	-----	16.791	117.17	82.049	68.153
Switzerland	1.6529	2.3888	-----	0.0126	0.2119	1.4790	1.0357	0.8603
United Kingdom	0.6919	-----	0.4186	0.0053	0.0887	0.6191	0.4335	0.3601
United States	-----	1.4452	0.6050	0.0076	0.1282	0.8948	0.6266	0.5205

Country	Currency	U.S. $ Equiv.
Afghanistan	afghani	.0002
Aitutaki	New Zealand dollar	.4301
Albania	lek	.0073
Algeria	dinar	.0131
Andorra (French)	euro	.8948
Andorra (Spanish)	euro	.8948
Angola	kwanza	.0548
Anguilla	East Caribbean dollar	.3745
Antigua	East Caribbean dollar	.3745
Argentina	peso	1.00
Armenia	dram	.0018
Aruba	guilder	.5587
Ascension	British pound	1.4452
Australia	dollar	.5205
Australian Antarctic Territory	dollar	.5205
Austria	euro	.8948
Azerbaijan	manat	.00021
Bahamas	dollar	1.00
Bahrain	dinar	2.652
Bangladesh	taka	.0176
Barbados	dollar	.5025
Barbuda	East Caribbean dollar	.3745
Belarus	ruble	.0006
Belgium	euro	.8948
Belize	dollar	.5076
Benin	Community of French Africa (CFA) franc	.00137
Bermuda	dollar	1.02
Bhutan	ngultrum	.0207
Bolivia	boliviano	.1461
Bosnia & Herzegovina	convertible mark	.4576
Botswana	pula	.1429
Brazil	real	.4290
British Antarctic Territory	British pound	1.4452
British Indian Ocean Territory	British pound	1.4452
Brunei	dollar	.5415
Bulgaria	lev	.4583
Burkina Faso	CFA franc	.00137
Burma	kyat	.1482
Burundi	franc	.0012
United Nations-New York	U.S. dollar	1.00
United Nations-Geneva	Swiss franc	.6050
United Nations-Vienna	euro	.8948
United States	dollar	1.00

Source: *Wall Street Journal* Jan. 7, 2002. Figures reflect values as of Jan. 4, 2002.

Common Design Types

Pictured in this section are issues where one illustration has been used for a number of countries in the Catalogue. Not included in this section are overprinted stamps or those issues which are illustrated in each country.

EUROPA

Europa, 1956

The design symbolizing the cooperation among the six countries comprising the Coal and Steel Community is illustrated in each country.

Belgium	496-497
France	805-806
Germany	748-749
Italy	715-716
Luxembourg	318-320
Netherlands	368-369

Europa, 1958

"E" and Dove CD1

European Postal Union at the service of European integration.

1958, Sept. 13

Belgium	527-528
France	889-890
Germany	790-791
Italy	750-751
Luxembourg	341-343
Netherlands	375-376
Saar	317-318

Europa, 1959

6-Link Endless Chain – CD2

1959, Sept. 19

Belgium	536-537
France	929-930
Germany	805-806
Italy	791-792
Luxembourg	354-355
Netherlands	379-380

Europa, 1960

19-Spoke Wheel – CD3

First anniverary of the establishment of C.E.P.T. (Conference Europeenne des Administrations des Postes et des Telecommunications.)

The spokes symbolize the 19 founding members of the Conference.

1960, Sept.

Belgium	553-554
Denmark	379
Finland	376-377
France	970-971
Germany	818-820
Great Britain	377-378

Greece	688
Iceland	327-328
Ireland	175-176
Italy	809-810
Luxembourg	374-375
Netherlands	385-386
Norway	387
Portugal	866-867
Spain	941-942
Sweden	562-563
Switzerland	400-401
Turkey	1493-1494

Europa, 1961

19 Doves Flying as One – CD4

The 19 doves represent the 19 members of the Conference of European Postal and Telecommunications Administrations C.E.P.T.

1961-62

Belgium	572-573
Cyprus	201-203
France	1005-1006
Germany	844-845
Great Britain	383-384
Greece	718-719
Iceland	340-341
Italy	845-846
Luxembourg	382-383
Netherlands	387-388
Spain	1010-1011
Switzerland	410-411
Turkey	1518-1520

Europa, 1962

Young Tree with 19 Leaves CD5

The 19 leaves represent the 19 original members of C.E.P.T.

1962-63

Belgium	582-583
Cyprus	219-221
France	1045-1046
Germany	852-853
Greece	739-740
Iceland	348-349
Ireland	184-185
Italy	860-861
Luxembourg	386-387
Netherlands	394-395
Norway	414-415
Switzerland	416-417
Turkey	1553-1555

Europa, 1963

Stylized Links, Symbolizing Unity – CD6

1963, Sept.

Belgium	598-599
Cyprus	229-231
Finland	419
France	1074-1075
Germany	867-868
Greece	768-769
Iceland	357-358
Ireland	188-189
Italy	880-881
Luxembourg	403-404
Netherlands	416-417
Norway	441-442
Switzerland	429
Turkey	1602-1603

Europa, 1964

Symbolic Daisy CD7

5th anniversary of the establishment of C.E.P.T. The 22 petals of the flower symbolize the 22 members of the Conference.

1964, Sept.

Austria	738
Belgium	614-615
Cyprus	244-246
France	1109-1110
Germany	897-898
Greece	801-802
Iceland	367-368
Ireland	196-197
Italy	894-895
Luxembourg	411-412
Monaco	590-591
Netherlands	428-429
Norway	458
Portugal	931-933
Spain	1262-1263
Switzerland	438-439
Turkey	1628-1629

Europa, 1965

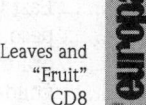

Leaves and "Fruit" CD8

1965

Belgium	636-637
Cyprus	262-264
Finland	437
France	1131-1132
Germany	934-935
Greece	833-834
Iceland	375-376
Ireland	204-205
Italy	915-916
Luxembourg	432-433
Monaco	616-617
Netherlands	438-439
Norway	475-476
Portugal	958-960
Switzerland	469
Turkey	1665-1666

Europa, 1966

Symbolic Sailboat CD9

1966, Sept.

Andorra, French	172
Belgium	675-676
Cyprus	275-277
France	1163-1164
Germany	963-964
Greece	862-863
Iceland	384-385
Ireland	216-217
Italy	942-943
Liechtenstein	415
Luxembourg	440-441
Monaco	639-640
Netherlands	441-442
Norway	496-497
Portugal	980-982
Switzerland	477-478
Turkey	1718-1719

Europa, 1967

Cogwheels CD10

1967

Andorra, French	174-175
Belgium	688-689
Cyprus	297-299
France	1178-1179
Germany	969-970
Greece	891-892
Iceland	389-390
Ireland	232-233
Italy	951-952
Liechtenstein	420
Luxembourg	449-450
Monaco	669-670
Netherlands	444-447
Norway	504-505
Portugal	994-996
Spain	1465-1466
Switzerland	482
Turkey	B120-B121

Europa, 1968

Golden Key with C.E.P.T. Emblem CD11

1968

Andorra, French	182-183
Belgium	705-706
Cyprus	314-316
France	1209-1210
Germany	983-984
Greece	916-917
Iceland	395-396
Ireland	242-243
Italy	979-980
Liechtenstein	442
Luxembourg	466-467
Monaco	689-691
Netherlands	452-453
Portugal	1019-1021
San Marino	687
Spain	1526
Turkey	1775-1776

Europa, 1969

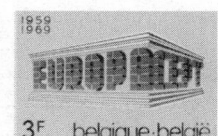

"EUROPA" and "CEPT" – CD12

Tenth anniversary of C.E.P.T.

1969

Andorra, French	188-189
Austria	837
Belgium	718-719
Cyprus	326-328
Denmark	458
Finland	483
France	1245-1246
Germany	996-997
Great Britain	585
Greece	947-948
Iceland	406-407
Ireland	270-271
Italy	1000-1001
Liechtenstein	453
Luxembourg	474-475
Monaco	722-724
Netherlands	475-476
Norway	533-534
Portugal	1038-1040
San Marino	701-702
Spain	1567

Sweden 814-816
Switzerland 500-501
Turkey 1799-1800
Vatican 470-472
Yugoslavia.................................1003-1004

Europa, 1970

Interwoven
Threads
CD13

1970
Andorra, French 196-197
Belgium 741-742
Cyprus 340-342
France 1271-1272
Germany 1018-1019
Greece 985, 987
Iceland 420-421
Ireland 279-281
Italy 1013-1014
Liechtenstein 470
Luxembourg 489-490
Monaco 768-770
Netherlands 483-484
Portugal 1060-1062
San Marino 729-730
Spain 1607
Switzerland 515-516
Turkey 1848-1849
Yugoslavia..................................1024-1025

Europa, 1971

"Fraternity, Cooperation,
Common Effort" – CD14

1971
Andorra, French 205-206
Belgium 803-804
Cyprus 365-367
Finland 504
France 1304
Germany 1064-1065
Greece 1029-1030
Iceland 429-430
Ireland 305-306
Italy 1038-1039
Liechtenstein 485
Luxembourg 500-501
Malta 425-427
Monaco 797-799
Netherlands 488-489
Portugal 1094-1096
San Marino 749-750
Spain 1675-1676
Switzerland 531-532
Turkey 1876-1877
Yugoslavia..................................1052-1053

Europa, 1972

Sparkles,
Symbolic of
Communications
CD15

1972
Andorra, French 210-211
Andorra, Spanish 62
Belgium 825-826
Cyprus 380-382
Finland 512-513
France 1341
Germany 1089-1090
Greece 1049-1050
Iceland 439-440
Ireland 316-317
Italy 1065-1066
Liechtenstein 504
Luxembourg 512-513
Malta 450-453
Monaco 831-832
Netherlands 494-495
Portugal 1141-1143
San Marino 771-772
Spain 1718

Switzerland 544-545
Turkey 1907-1908
Yugoslavia..................................1100-1101

Europa, 1973

Post Horn
and Arrows
CD16

1973
Andorra, French 319-320
Andorra, Spanish 76
Belgium 839-840
Cyprus 396-398
Finland 526
France 1367
Germany 1114-1115
Greece 1090-1092
Iceland 447-448
Ireland 329-330
Italy 1108-1109
Liechtenstein 528-529
Luxembourg 523-524
Malta 469-471
Monaco 866-867
Netherlands 504-505
Norway 604-605
Portugal 1170-1172
San Marino 802-803
Spain 1753
Switzerland 580-581
Turkey 1935-1936
Yugoslavia..................................1138-1139

PORTUGAL & COLONIES
Vasco da Gama

Fleet Departing
CD20

Fleet Arriving
at Calicut
CD21

Embarking
at Rastello
CD22

Muse of   San Gabriel, da Gama
History – CD23   and Camoens – CD24

Archangel Gabriel,   Flagship
the Patron Saint   San Gabriel
CD25   CD26

Vasco da
Gama
CD27

Fourth centenary of Vasco da Gama's discovery of the route to India.
1898
Azores 93-100
Macao 67-74
Madeira 37-44
Portugal 147-154
Port. Africa 1-8
Port. Congo 75-98
Port. India 189-196
St. Thomas & Prince Islands 170-193
Timor 45-52

Pombal
POSTAL TAX
POSTAL TAX DUES

Marquis   Planning
de   Reconstruction
Pombal   of Lisbon,1755
CD28   CD29

Pombal
Monument,
Lisbon
CD30

Sebastiao Jose de Carvalho e Mello, Marquis de Pombal (1699-1782), statesman, rebuilt Lisbon after earthquake of 1755. Tax was for the erection of Pombal monument. Obligatory on all mail on certain days throughout the year.
Postal Tax Dues are inscribed "Multa."
1925
Angola RA1-RA3, RAJ1-RAJ3
Azores..........................RA9-RA11, RAJ2-RAJ4
Cape Verde...................RA1-RA3, RAJ1-RAJ3
Macao RA1-RA3, RAJ1-RAJ3
Madeira RA1-RA3, RAJ1-RAJ3
Mozambique RA1-RA3, RAJ1-RAJ3
Nyassa RA1-RA3, RAJ1-RAJ3
Portugal RA11-RA13, RAJ2-RAJ4
Port. Guinea.................RA1-RA3, RAJ1-RAJ3
Port. India RA1-RA3, RAJ1-RAJ3
St. Thomas & Prince
  Islands RA1-RA3, RAJ1-RAJ3
Timor RA1-RA3, RAJ1-RAJ3

Vasco   Mousinho de
da Gama   Albuquerque
CD34   CD35

Dam   Prince Henry the
CD36   Navigator – CD37

Affonso de   Plane over
Albuquerque   Globe
CD38   CD39

1938-39
Angola...274-291, C1-C9
Cape Verde..................................234-251, C1-C9
Macao 289-305, C7-C15
Mozambique 270-287, C1-C9
Port. Guinea................................233-250, C1-C9
Port. India 439-453, C1-C8
St. Thomas & Prince
  Islands.........302-319, 323-340, C1-C18
Timor 223-239, C1-C9

Lady of Fatima

Our Lady of
the Rosary,
Fatima,
Portugal
CD40

1948-49
Angola...315-318
Cape Verde..................................266
Macao 336
Mozambique 325-328
Port. Guinea................................271
Port. India 480
St. Thomas & Prince Islands.........351
Timor 254

A souvenir sheet of 9 stamps was issued in 1951 to mark the extension of the 1950 Holy Year. The sheet contains: Angola No. 316, Cape Verde No. 266, Macao No. 336, Mozambique No. 325, Portuguese Guinea No. 271, Portugese India Nos. 480, 485, St. Thomas & Prince Islands No. 351, Timor No. 254.

The sheet also contains a portrait of Pope Pius XII and is inscribed "Encerramento do Ano Santo, Fatima 1951." It was sold for 11 escudos.

Holy Year

Church Bells   Angel Holding
and Dove   Candelabra
CD41   CD42

Holy Year, 1950.
1950-51
Angola...331-332
Cape Verde..................................268-269
Macao 339-340
Mozambique 330-331
Port. Guinea................................273-274
Port. India 490-491, 496-503
St. Thomas & Prince Islands..........353-354
Timor 258-259

A souvenir sheet of 8 stamps was issued in 1951 to mark the extension of the Holy Year. The sheet contains: Angola No. 331, Cape Verde No. 269, Macao No. 340, Mozambique No. 331, Portuguese Guinea No. 275, Portuguese India No. 490, St. Thomas & Prince Islands No. 354, Timor No. 258, some with colors changed. The sheet contains doves and is inscribed "Encerramento do Ano Santo, Fatima 1951." It was sold for 17 escudos.

Holy Year Conclusion

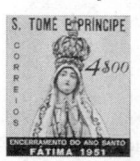

Our Lady
of Fatima
CD43

Conclusion of Holy Year. Sheets contain alternate vertical rows of stamps and labels bearing quotation from Pope Pius XII, different for each colony.

1951

Angola	357
Cape Verde	270
Macao	352
Mozambique	356
Port. Guinea	275
Port. India	506
St. Thomas & Prince Islands	355
Timor	270

Medical Congress

CD44

First National Congress of Tropical Medicine, Lisbon, 1952.

Each stamp has a different design.

1952

Angola	358
Cape Verde	287
Macao	364
Mozambique	359
Port. Guinea	276
Port. India	516
St. Thomas & Prince Islands	356
Timor	271

POSTAGE DUE STAMPS

CD45

1952

Angola	J37-J42
Cape Verde	J31-J36
Macao	J53-J58
Mozambique	J51-J56
Port. Guinea	J40-J45
Port. India	J47-J52
St. Thomas & Prince Islands	J52-J57
Timor	J31-J36

Sao Paulo

Father Manuel
de Nobrega and
View of
Sao Paulo
CD46

Founding of Sao Paulo, Brazil, 400th anniv.

1954

Angola	385
Cape Verde	297
Macao	382
Mozambique	395
Port. Guinea	291
Port. India	530
St. Thomas & Prince Islands	369
Timor	279

Tropical Medicine Congress

CD47

Sixth International Congress for Tropical Medicine and Malaria, Lisbon, Sept. 1958. Each stamp shows a different plant.

1958

Angola	409
Cape Verde	303
Macao	392
Mozambique	404
Port. Guinea	295
Port. India	569
St. Thomas & Prince Islands	371
Timor	289

Sports

CD48

Each stamp shows a different sport.

1962

Angola	433-438
Cape Verde	320-325
Macao	394-399
Mozambique	424-429
Port. Guinea	299-304
St. Thomas & Prince Islands	374-379
Timor	313-318

Anti-Malaria

Anopheles Funestus
and
Malaria Eradication
Symbol
CD49

World Health Organization drive to eradicate malaria.

1962

Angola	439
Cape Verde	326
Macao	400
Mozambique	430
Port. Guinea	305
St. Thomas & Prince Islands	380
Timor	319

Airline Anniversary

Map of Africa,
Super Constellation
and Jet Liner CD50

Tenth anniversary of Transportes Aereos Portugueses (TAP).

1963

Angola	490
Cape Verde	327
Mozambique	434
Port. Guinea	318
St. Thomas & Prince Islands	381

National Overseas Bank

Antonio Teixeira
de Sousa
CD51

Centenary of the National Overseas Bank of Portugal.

1964, May 16

Angola	509
Cape Verde	328
Port. Guinea	319
St. Thomas & Prince Islands	382
Timor	320

ITU

ITU Emblem
and the
archangel
Gabriel
CD52

International Communications Union, Cent.

1965, May 17

Angola	511
Cape Verde	329
Macao	402
Mozambique	464
Port. Guinea	320
St. Thomas & Prince Islands	383
Timor	321

National Revolution

CD53

40th anniv. of the National Revolution. Different buildings on each stamp.

1966, May 28

Angola	525
Cape Verde	338
Macao	403
Mozambique	465
Port. Guinea	329
St. Thomas & Prince Islands	392
Timor	322

Navy Club

CD54

Centenary of Portugal's Navy Club. Each stamp has a different design.

1967, Jan. 31

Angola	527-528
Cape Verde	339-340
Macao	412-413
Mozambique	478-479
Port. Guinea	330-331
St. Thomas & Prince Islands	393-394
Timor	323-324

Admiral Coutinho

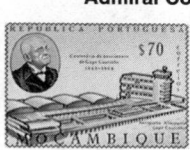

CD55

Centenary of the birth of Admiral Carlos Viegas Gago Coutinho (1869-1959), explorer and aviation pioneer.

Each stamp has a different design.

1969, Feb. 17

Angola	547
Cape Verde	355
Macao	417
Mozambique	484
Port. Guinea	335
St. Thomas & Prince Islands	397
Timor	335

Administration Reform

Luiz Augusto
Rebello da Silva
CD 56

Centenary of the administration reforms of the overseas territories.

1969, Sept. 25

Angola	549
Cape Verde	357
Macao	419
Mozambique	491
Port. Guinea	337
St. Thomas & Prince Islands	399
Timor	338

Marshal Carmona

CD57

Birth centenary of Marshal Antonio Oscar Carmona de Fragoso (1869-1951), President of Portugal.

Each stamp has a different design.

1970, Nov. 15

Angola	563
Cape Verde	359
Macao	422
Mozambique	493
Port. Guinea	340
St. Thomas & Prince Islands	403
Timor	341

Olympic Games

CD59

20th Olympic Games, Munich, Aug. 26-Sept. 11.

Each stamp shows a different sport.

1972, June 20

Angola	569
Cape Verde	361
Macao	426
Mozambique	504
Port. Guinea	342
St. Thomas & Prince Islands	408
Timor	343

Lisbon-Rio de Janeiro Flight

CD60

50th anniversary of the Lisbon to Rio de Janeiro flight by Arturo de Sacadura and Coutinho, March 30-June 5, 1922.

Each stamp shows a different stage of the flight.

1972, Sept. 20

Angola	570
Cape Verde	362
Macao	427
Mozambique	505
Port. Guinea	343
St. Thomas & Prince Islands	409
Timor	344

WMO Centenary

WMO Emblem
CD61

Centenary of international meterological cooperation.

1973, Dec. 15

Angola	571
Cape Verde	363
Macao	429
Mozambique	509
Port. Guinea	344
St. Thomas & Prince Islands	410
Timor	345

FRENCH COMMUNITY

Upper Volta can be found under Burkina Faso in Vol. 1

Madagascar can be found under Malagasy in Vol. 3

Colonial Exposition

People of French Empire CD70

Women's Heads CD71

France Showing Way to Civilization CD72

"Colonial Commerce" CD73

International Colonial Exposition, Paris.

1931

Cameroun	213-216
Chad	60-63
Dahomey	97-100
Fr. Guiana	152-155
Fr. Guinea	116-119
Fr. India	100-103
Fr. Polynesia	76-79
Fr. Sudan	102-105
Gabon	120-123
Guadeloupe	138-141
Indo-China	140-142
Ivory Coast	92-95
Madagascar	169-172
Martinique	129-132
Mauritania	65-68
Middle Congo	61-64
New Caledonia	176-179
Niger	73-76
Reunion	122-125
St. Pierre & Miquelon	132-135
Senegal	138-141
Somali Coast	135-138
Togo	254-257
Ubangi-Shari	82-85
Upper Volta	66-69
Wallis & Futuna Isls.	85-88

Paris International Exposition
Colonial Arts Exposition

"Colonial Resources"
CD74   CD77

Overseas Commerce – CD75

Exposition Building and Women CD76

"France and the Empire" CD78

Cultural Treasures of the Colonies CD79

Souvenir sheets contain one imperf. stamp.

1937

Cameroun	217-222A
Dahomey	101-107
Fr. Equatorial Africa	27-32, 73
Fr. Guiana	162-168
Fr. Guinea	120-126
Fr. India	104-110
Fr. Polynesia	117-123
Fr. Sudan	106-112
Guadeloupe	148-154
Indo-China	193-199
Inini	41
Ivory Coast	152-158
Kwangchowan	132
Madagascar	191-197
Martinique	179-185
Mauritania	69-75
New Caledonia	208-214
Niger	72-83
Reunion	167-173
St. Pierre & Miquelon	165-171
Senegal	172-178
Somali Coast	139-145
Togo	258-264
Wallis & Futuna Isls.	89

Curie

Pierre and Marie Curie CD80

40th anniversary of the discovery of radium. The surtax was for the benefit of the Intl. Union for the Control of Cancer.

1938

Cameroun	B1
Cuba	B1-B2
Dahomey	B2
France	B76
Fr. Equatorial Africa	B1
Fr. Guiana	B3
Fr. Guinea	B2
Fr. India	B6
Fr. Polynesia	B5
Fr. Sudan	B1
Guadeloupe	B3
Indo-China	B14
Ivory Coast	B2
Madagascar	B2
Martinique	B2
Mauritania	B3
New Caledonia	B4
Niger	B1
Reunion	B4
St. Pierre & Miquelon	B3
Senegal	B3
Somali Coast	B2
Togo	B1

Caillie

Rene Caille and Map of Northwestern Africa - CD81

Death centenary of Rene Caillie (1799-1838), French explorer.

All three denominations exist with colony name omitted.

1939

Dahomey	108-110
Fr. Guinea	161-163

Fr. Sudan	113-115
Ivory Coast	160-162
Mauritania	109-111
Niger	84-86
Senegal	188-190
Togo	265-267

New York World's Fair

Natives and New York Skyline CD82

1939

Cameroun	223-224
Dahomey	111-112
Fr. Equatorial Africa	78-79
Fr. Guiana	169-170
Fr. Guinea	164-165
Fr. India	111-112
Fr. Polynesia	124-125
Fr. Sudan	116-117
Guadeloupe	155-156
Indo-China	203-204
Inini	42-43
Ivory Coast	163-164
Kwangchowan	121-122
Madagascar	209-210
Martinique	186-187
Mauritania	112-113
New Caledonia	215-216
Niger	87-88
Reunion	174-175
St. Pierre & Miquelon	205-206
Senegal	191-192
Somali Coast	179-180
Togo	268-269
Wallis & Futuna Isls.	90-91

French Revolution

Storming of the Bastille – CD83

French Revolution, 150th anniv. The surtax was for the defense of the colonies.

1939

Cameroun	B2-B6
Dahomey	B3-B7
Fr. Equatorial Africa	B4-B8, CB1
Fr. Guiana	B4-B8, CB1
Fr. Guinea	B3-B7
Fr. India	B7-B11
Fr. Polynesia	B6-B10, CB1
Fr. Sudan	B2-B6
Guadeloupe	B4-B8
Indo-China	B15-B19, CB1
Inini	B1-B5
Ivory Coast	B3-B7
Kwangchowan	B1-B5
Madagascar	B3-B7, CB1
Martinique	B3-B7
Mauritania	B4-B8
New Caledonia	B5-B9, CB1
Niger	B2-B6
Reunion	B5-B9, CB1
St. Pierre & Miquelon	B4-B8
Senegal	B4-B8, CB1
Somali Coast	B3-B7
Togo	B2-B6
Wallis & Futuna Isls.	B1-B5

Plane over Coastal Area CD85

All five denominations exist with colony name omitted.

1940

Dahomey	C1-C5
Fr. Guinea	C1-C5
Fr. Sudan	C1-C5
Ivory Coast	C1-C5
Mauritania	C1-C5
Niger	C1-C5
Senegal	C12-C16
Togo	C1-C5

Colonial Infantryman CD86

1941

Cameroun	B13B
Dahomey	B13
Fr. Equatorial Africa	B8B
Fr. Guiana	B10
Fr. India	B13
Fr. Polynesia	B12
Fr. Sudan	B12
Guadeloupe	B10
Indo-China	B19B
Inini	B7
Ivory Coast	B13
Kwangchowan	B7
Madagascar	B9
Martinique	B9
Mauritania	B14
New Caledonia	B11
Niger	B12
Reunion	B11
St. Pierre & Miquelon	B8B
Senegal	B14
Somali Coast	B9
Togo	B10B
Wallis & Futuna Isls.	B7

Cross of Lorraine & Four-motor Plane CD87

1941-5

Cameroun	C1-C7
Fr. Equatorial Africa	C17-C23
Fr. Guiana	C9-C10
Fr. India	C1-C6
Fr. Polynesia	C3-C9
Fr. West Africa	C1-C3
Guadeloupe	C1-C2
Madagascar	C37-C43
Martinique	C1-C2
New Caledonia	C7-C13
Reunion	C18-C24
St. Pierre & Miquelon	C1-C7
Somali Coast	C1-C7

Transport Plane CD88

Caravan and Plane CD89

1942

Dahomey	C6-C13
Fr. Guinea	C6-C13
Fr. Sudan	C6-C13
Ivory Coast	C6-C13
Mauritania	C6-C13
Niger	C6-C13
Senegal	C17-C25
Togo	C6-C13

Red Cross

Marianne CD90

The surtax was for the French Red Cross and national relief.

1944

Cameroun	B28
Fr. Equatorial Africa	B38
Fr. Guiana	B12
Fr. India	B14
Fr. Polynesia	B13
Fr. West Africa	B1
Guadeloupe	B12

Madagascar B15
Martinique B11
New Caledonia B13
Reunion B15
St. Pierre & Miquelon B13
Somali Coast B13
Wallis & Futuna Isls. B9

Eboue

CD91

Felix Eboue, first French colonial administrator to proclaim resistance to Germany after French surrender in World War II.

1945

Cameroun 296-297
Fr. Equatorial Africa 156-157
Fr. Guiana 171-172
Fr. India 210-211
Fr. Polynesia 150-151
Fr. West Africa 15-16
Guadeloupe 187-188
Madagascar 259-260
Martinique 196-197
New Caledonia 274-275
Reunion 238-239
St. Pierre & Miquelon 322-323
Somali Coast 238-239

Victory

Victory – CD92

European victory of the Allied Nations in World War II.

1946, May 8

Cameroun C8
Fr. Equatorial Africa C24
Fr. Guiana C11
Fr. India C7
Fr. Polynesia C10
Fr. West Africa C4
Guadeloupe C3
Indo-China C19
Madagascar C44
Martinique C3
New Caledonia C14
Reunion C25
St. Pierre & Miquelon C8
Somali Coast C8
Wallis & Futuna Isls. C1

Chad to Rhine

Leclerc's Departure from Chad – CD93

Battle at Cufra Oasis – CD94

Tanks in Action, Mareth – CD95

Normandy Invasion – CD96

Entering Paris – CD97

Liberation of Strasbourg – CD98

"Chad to the Rhine" march, 1942-44, by Gen. Jacques Leclerc's column, later French 2nd Armored Division.

1946, June 6

Cameroun C9-C14
Fr. Equatorial Africa C25-C30
Fr. Guiana C12-C17
Fr. India C8-C13
Fr. Polynesia C11-C16
Fr. West Africa C5-C10
Guadeloupe C4-C9
Indo-China C20-C25
Madagascar C45-C50
Martinique C4-C9
New Caledonia C15-C20
Reunion C26-C31
St. Pierre & Miquelon C9-C14
Somali Coast C9-C14
Wallis & Futuna Isls. C2-C7

UPU

French Colonials, Globe and Plane
CD99

Universal Postal Union, 75th anniv.

1949, July 4

Cameroun C29
Fr. Equatorial Africa C34
Fr. India C17
Fr. Polynesia C20
Fr. West Africa C15
Indo-China C26
Madagascar C55
New Caledonia C24
St. Pierre & Miquelon C18
Somali Coast C18
Togo C18
Wallis & Futuna Isls. C10

Tropical Medicine

Doctor
Treating
Infant
CD100

The surtax was for charitable work.

1950

Cameroun B29
Fr. Equatorial Africa B39
Fr. India B15
Fr. Polynesia B14
Fr. West Africa B3
Madagascar B17
New Caledonia B14
St. Pierre & Miquelon B14
Somali Coast B14
Togo B11

Military Medal

Medal, Early
Marine
and
Colonial Soldier
CD101

Centenary of the creation of the French Military Medal.

1952

Cameroun 332
Comoro Isls. 39
Fr. Equatorial Africa 186
Fr. India 233
Fr. Polynesia 179
Fr. West Africa 57
Madagascar 286
New Caledonia 295
St. Pierre & Miquelon 345
Somali Coast 267
Togo 327
Wallis & Futuna Isls. 149

Liberation

Allied Landing, Victory Sign and
Cross of Lorraine – CD102

Lberation of France, 10th anniv.

1954, June 6

Cameroun C32
Comoro Isls. C4
Fr. Equatorial Africa C38
Fr. India C18
Fr. Polynesia C22
Fr. West Africa C17
Madagascar C57
New Caledonia C25
St. Pierre & Miquelon C19
Somali Coast C19
Togo C19
Wallis & Futuna Isls. C11

FIDES

Plowmen
CD103

Efforts of FIDES, the Economic and Social Development Fund for Overseas Possessions (Fonds d' Investissement pour le Developpement Economique et Social).

Each stamp has a different design.

1956

Cameroun 326-329
Comoro Isls. 43
Fr. Polynesia 181
Fr. West Africa 65-72
Madagascar 292-295
New Caledonia 303
Somali Coast 268
Togo 331

Flower

CD104

Each stamp shows a different flower.

1958-9

Cameroun 333
Comoro Isls. 45
Fr. Equatorial Africa 200-201
Fr. Polynesia 192
Fr. So. & Antarctic Terr. 11
Fr. West Africa 79-83
Madagascar 301-302

New Caledonia 304-305
St. Pierre & Miquelon 357
Somali Coast 270
Togo 348-349
Wallis & Futuna Isls. 152

Human Rights

Sun, Dove and U.N. Emblem – CD105

10th anniversary of the signing of the Universal Declaration of Human Rights.

1958

Comoro Isls. 44
Fr. Equatorial Africa 202
Fr. Polynesia 191
Fr. West Africa 85
Madagascar 300
New Caledonia 306
St. Pierre & Miquelon 356
Somali Coast 274
Wallis & Futuna Isls. 153

C.C.T.A.

CD106

Commission for Technical Cooperation in Africa south of the Sahara, 10th anniv.

1960

Cameroun 335
Cent. Africa 3
Chad 66
Congo, P.R. 90
Dahomey 138
Gabon 150
Ivory Coast 180
Madagascar 317
Mali 9
Mauritania 117
Niger 104
Upper Volta 89

Air Afrique, 1961

Modern and Ancient Africa,
Map and Planes – CD107

Founding of Air Afrique (African Airlines).

1961-62

Cameroun C37
Cent. Africa C5
Chad C7
Congo, P.R. C5
Dahomey C17
Gabon C5
Ivory Coast C18
Mauritania C17
Niger C22
Senegal C31
Upper Volta C4

Anti-Malaria

CD108

World Health Organization drive to eradicate malaria.

1962, Apr. 7
Cameroun B36
Cent. Africa B1
Chad B1
Comoro Isls. B1
Congo, P.R. B3
Dahomey B15
Gabon B4
Ivory Coast B15
Madagascar B19
Mali B1
Mauritania B16
Niger B14
Senegal B16
Somali Coast B15
Upper Volta B1

Abidjan Games

CD109

Abidjan Games, Ivory Coast, Dec. 24-31, 1961. Each stamp shows a different sport.

1962
Chad 83-84
Cent. Africa 19-20
Congo, P.R. 103-104
Gabon 163-164, C6
Niger 109-111
Upper Volta 103-105

African and Malagasy Union

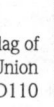

Flag of
Union
CD110

First anniversary of the Union.

1962, Sept. 8
Cameroun 373
Cent. Africa 21
Chad 85
Congo, P.R. 105
Dahomey 155
Gabon 165
Ivory Coast 198
Madagascar 332
Mauritania 170
Niger 112
Senegal 211
Upper Volta 106

Telstar

Telstar and Globe Showing Andover
and Pleumeur-Bodou – CD111

First television connection of the United States and Europe through the Telstar satellite, July 11-12, 1962.

1962-63
Andorra, French 154
Comoro Isls. C7
Fr. Polynesia C29
Fr. So. & Antarctic Terr. C5
New Caledonia C33
Somali Coast C31
St. Pierre & Miquelon C26
Wallis & Futuna Isls. C17

Freedom From Hunger

World Map
and Wheat
Emblem
CD112

U.N. Food and Agriculture Organization's "Freedom from Hunger" campaign.

1963, Mar. 21
Cameroun B37-B38
Cent. Africa B2

Chad B2
Congo, P.R. B4
Dahomey B16
Gabon B5
Ivory Coast B16
Madagascar B21
Mauritania B17
Niger B15
Senegal B17
Upper Volta B2

Red Cross Centenary

CD113

Centenary of the International Red Cross.

1963, Sept. 2
Comoro Isls. 55
Fr. Polynesia 205
New Caledonia 328
St. Pierre & Miquelon 367
Somali Coast 297
Wallis & Futuna Isls. 165

African Postal Union, 1963

UAMPT
Emblem,
Radio Masts,
Plane and
Mail
CD114

Establishment of the African and Malagasy Posts and Telecommunications Union.

1963, Sept. 8
Cameroun C47
Cent. Africa C10
Chad C9
Congo, P.R. C13
Dahomey C19
Gabon C13
Ivory Coast C25
Madagascar C75
Mauritania C22
Niger C27
Rwanda 36
Senegal C32
Upper Volta C9

Air Afrique, 1963

Symbols of Flight – CD115

First anniversary of Air Afrique and inauguration of DC-8 service.

1963, Nov. 19
Cameroun C48
Chad C10
Congo, P.R. C14
Gabon C18
Ivory Coast C26
Mauritania C26
Niger C35
Senegal C33

Europafrica

Europe and
Africa Linked
CD116

Signing of an economic agreement between the European Economic Community and the African and Malagasy Union, Yaounde, Cameroun, July 20, 1963.

1963-64
Cameroun 402
Chad C11
Cent. Africa C12
Congo, P.R. C16
Gabon C19
Ivory Coast C27
Niger C43
Upper Volta C11

Human Rights

Scales of
Justice and
Globe
CD117

15th anniversary of the Universal Declaration of Human Rights.

1963, Dec. 10
Comoro Isls. 58
Fr. Polynesia 206
New Caledonia 329
St. Pierre & Miquelon 368
Somali Coast 300
Wallis & Futuna Isls. 166

PHILATEC

Stamp Album, Champs Elysees Palace and Horses of Marly – CD118

Intl. Philatelic and Postal Techniques Exhibition, Paris, June 5-21, 1964.

1963-64
Comoro Isls. 60
France 1078
Fr. Polynesia 207
New Caledonia 341
St. Pierre & Miquelon 369
Somali Coast 301
Wallis & Futuna Isls. 167

Cooperation

CD119

Cooperation between France and the French-speaking countries of Africa and Madagascar.

1964
Cameroun 409-410
Cent. Africa 39
Chad 103
Congo, P.R. 121
Dahomey 193
France 1111
Gabon 175
Ivory Coast 221
Madagascar 360
Mauritania 181
Niger 143

Senegal 236
Togo 495

ITU

Telegraph,
Syncom Satellite
and
ITU Emblem
CD120

Intl. Telecommunication Union, Cent.

1965, May 17
Comoro Isls. C14
Fr. Polynesia C33
Fr. So. & Antarctic Terr. C8
New Caledonia C40
New Hebrides 124-125
St. Pierre & Miquelon C29
Somali Coast C36
Wallis & Futuna Isls. C20

French Satellite A-1

Diamant Rocket and Launching
Installation – CD121

Launching of France's first satellite, Nov. 26, 1965.

1965-66
Comoro Isls. C15-C16
France 1137-1138
Fr. Polynesia C40-C41
Fr. So. & Antarctic Terr. C9-C10
New Caledonia C44-C45
St. Pierre & Miquelon C30-C31
Somali Coast C39-C40
Wallis & Futuna Isls. C22-C23

French Satellite D-1

D-1 Satellite in Orbit – CD122

Launching of the D-1 satellite at Hammaguir, Algeria, Feb. 17, 1966.

1966
Comoro Isls. C17
France 1148
Fr. Polynesia C42
Fr. So. & Antarctic Terr. C11
New Caledonia C46
St. Pierre & Miquelon C32
Somali Coast C49
Wallis & Futuna Isls. C24

Air Afrique, 1966

Planes and Air Afrique Emblem – CD123

Introduction of DC-8F planes by Air Afrique.

1966
Cameroun C79
Cent. Africa C35
Chad C26
Congo, P.R. C42
Dahomey C42

Gabon...C47
Ivory Coast C32
Mauritania C57
Niger C63
Senegal C47
Togo C54
Upper Volta C31

African Postal Union, 1967

Telecommunications Symbols
and Map of Africa – CD124

Fifth anniversary of the establishment of
the African and Malagasy Union of Posts and
Telecommunications, UAMPT.

1967
Cameroun..C90
Cent. Africa C46
Chad C37
Congo, P.R. C57
Dahomey C61
Gabon...C58
Ivory Coast C34
Madagascar C85
Mauritania C65
Niger C75
Rwanda C1-C3
Senegal C60
Togo C81
Upper Volta C50

Monetary Union

Gold Token of
the Ashantis,
17-18th Centuries
CD125

West African Monetary Union, 5th anniv.

1967, Nov. 4
Dahomey 244
Ivory Coast....................................259
Mauritania 238
Niger 204
Senegal 294
Togo 623
Upper Volta 181

WHO Anniversary

Sun, Flowers and WHO Emblem
CD126

World Health Organization, 20th anniv.

1968, May 4
Afars & Issas 317
Comoro Isls. 73
Fr. Polynesia 241-242
Fr. So. & Antarctic Terr. 31
New Caledonia 367
St. Pierre & Miquelon 377
Wallis & Futuna Isls. 169

Human Rights Year

Human Rights
Flame
CD127

1968, Aug. 10
Afars & Issas 322-323
Comoro Isls. 76
Fr. Polynesia 243-244
Fr. So. & Antarctic Terr. 32
New Caledonia 369
St. Pierre & Miquelon 382
Wallis & Futuna Isls. 170

2nd PHILEXAFRIQUE

CD128

Opening of PHILEXAFRIQUE, Abidjan,
Feb. 14. Each stamp shows a local scene and
stamp.

1969, Feb. 14
Cameroun..C118
Cent. Africa C65
Chad C48
Congo, P.R. C77
Dahomey C94
Gabon..C82
Ivory Coast C38-C40
Madagascar C92
Mali C65
Mauritania C80
Niger C104
Senegal C68
Togo C104
Upper Volta C62

Concorde

Concorde
in Flight
CD129

First flight of the prototype Concorde supersonic plane at Toulouse, Mar. 1, 1969.

1969
Afars & Issas C56
Comoro Isls. C29
France C42
Fr. Polynesia C50
Fr. So. & Antarctic Terr. C18
New Caledonia C63
St. Pierre & Miquelon C40
Wallis & Futuna Isls. C30

Development Bank

Bank Emblem
CD130

African Development Bank, fifth anniv.

1969
Cameroun..499
Chad 217
Congo, P.R. 181-182
Ivory Coast 281
Mali 127-128
Mauritania 267
Niger 220
Senegal 317-318
Upper Volta 201

ILO

ILO Headquarters, Geneva,
and Emblem – CD131

Intl. Labor Organization, 50th anniv.
1969-70
Afars & Issas 337
Comoro Isls. 83
Fr. Polynesia 251-252
Fr. So. & Antarctic Terr. 35
New Caledonia 379
St. Pierre & Miquelon 396
Wallis & Futuna Isls. 172

ASECNA

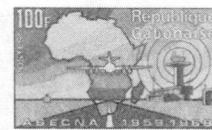

Map of Africa, Plane and Airport –
CD132

10th anniversary of the Agency for the
Security of Aerial Navigation in Africa and
Madagascar (ASECNA, Agence pour la
Securite de la Navigation Aerienne en Afrique
et a Madagascar).

1969-70
Cameroun..500
Cent. Africa 119
Chad 222
Congo, P.R. 197
Dahomey 269
Gabon..260
Ivory Coast 287
Mali 130
Niger 221
Senegal 321
Upper Volta 204

U.P.U. Headquarters

CD133

New Universal Postal Union headquarters,
Bern, Switzerland.

1970
Afars & Issas 342
Algeria 443
Cameroun................................503-504
Cent. Africa 125
Chad 225
Comoro Isls. 84
Congo, P.R. 216
Fr. Polynesia 261-262
Fr. So. & Antarctic Terr. 36
Gabon..258
Ivory Coast 295
Madagascar 444
Mali 134-135
Mauritania 283
New Caledonia 382
Niger 231-232
St. Pierre & Miquelon 397-398
Senegal 328-329
Tunisia 535
Wallis & Futuna Isls. 173

De Gaulle

CD134

First anniversay of the death of Charles de
Gaulle, (1890-1970), President of France.

1971-72
Afars & Issas 356-357
Comoro Isls. 104-105
France 1322-1325
Fr. Polynesia 270-271
Fr. So. & Antarctic Terr. 52-53
New Caledonia 393-394
Reunion 377, 380
St. Pierre & Miquelon 417-418
Wallis & Futuna Isls. 177-178

African Postal Union, 1971

UAMPT Building,
Brazzaville, Congo – CD135

10th anniversary of the establishment of
the African and Malagasy Posts and
Telecommunications Union, UAMPT.

Each stamp has a different native design.

1971, Nov. 13
Cameroun..C177
Cent. Africa C89
Chad C94
Congo, P.R. C136
Dahomey C146
Gabon..C120
Ivory Coast C47
Mauritania C113
Niger C164
Rwanda C8
Senegal C105
Togo C166
Upper Volta C97

West African Monetary Union

African Couple, City, Village and
Commemorative Coin – CD136

West African Monetary Union, 10th anniv.

1972, Nov. 2
Dahomey 300
Ivory Coast 331
Mauritania 299
Niger 258
Senegal 374
Togo 825
Upper Volta 280

African Postal Union, 1973

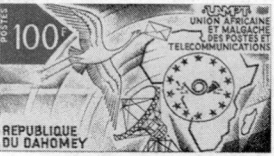

Telecommunications Symbols and
Map of Africa – CD137

11th anniversary of the African and
Malagasy Posts and Telecommunications
Union (UAMPT).

1973, Sept. 12
Cameroun..574
Cent. Africa 194
Chad 294
Congo, P.R. 289
Dahomey 311
Gabon..320
Ivory Coast 361
Madagascar 500
Mauritania 304
Niger 287
Rwanda 540
Senegal 393
Togo 849
Upper Volta 297

Philexafrique II — Essen

CD138

CD139

Designs: Indigenous fauna, local and German stamps.

Types CD138-CD139 printed horizontally and vertically se-tenant in sheets of 10 (2x5). Label between horizontal pairs alternately commemoratives Philexafrique II, Libreville, Gabon, June 1978, and 2nd International Stamp Fair, Essen, Germany, Nov. 1-5.

1978-1979
Benin	C285-C286
Central Africa	C200-C201
Chad	C238-C239
Congo Republic	C245-C246
Djibouti	C121-C122
Gabon	C215-C216
Ivory Coast	C64-C65
Mali	C356-C357
Mauritania	C185-C186
Niger	C291-C292
Rwanda	C12-C13
Senegal	C146-C147
Togo	C363-C364
Upper Volta	C253-C254

BRITISH COMMONWEALTH OF NATIONS

The listings follow established trade practices when these issues are offered as units by dealers. The Peace issue, for example, includes only one stamp from the Indian state of Hyderabad. The U.P.U. issue includes the Egypt set. Pairs are included for those varieties issues with bilingual designs se-tenant.

Silver Jubilee

Windsor Castle and King George V
CD301

Reign of King George V, 25th anniv.

1935
Antigua	77-80
Ascension	33-36
Bahamas	92-95
Barbados	186-189
Basutoland	11-14
Bechuanaland Protectorate	117-120
Bermuda	100-103
British Guiana	223-226
British Honduras	108-111
Cayman Islands	81-84
Ceylon	260-263
Cyprus	136-139
Dominica	90-93
Falkland Islands	77-80
Fiji	110-113
Gambia	125-128
Gibraltar	100-103
Gilbert & Ellice Islands	33-36
Gold Coast	108-111
Grenada	124-127
Hong Kong	147-150
Jamaica	109-112
Kenya, Uganda, Tanganyika	42-45
Leeward Islands	96-99
Malta	184-187

Mauritius	204-207
Montserrat	85-88
Newfoundland	226-229
Nigeria	34-37
Northern Rhodesia	18-21
Nyasaland Protectorate	47-50
St. Helena	111-114
St. Kitts-Nevis	72-75
St. Lucia	91-94
St. Vincent	134-137
Seychelles	118-121
Sierra Leone	166-169
Solomon Islands	60-63
Somaliland Protectorate	77-80
Straits Settlements	213-216
Swaziland	20-23
Trinidad & Tobago	43-46
Turks & Caicos Islands	71-74
Virgin Islands	69-72

The following have different designs but are included in the omnibus set:
Great Britain	226-229
Offices in Morocco	67-70, 226-229, 422-425, 508-510
Australia	152-154
Canada	211-216
Cook Islands	98-100
India	142-148
Nauru	31-34
New Guinea	46-47
New Zealand	199-201
Niue	67-69
Papua	114-117
Samoa	163-165
South Africa	68-71
Southern Rhodesia	33-36
South-West Africa	121-124

249 stamps

Coronation

Queen Elizabeth and King George VI
CD302

1937
Aden	13-15
Antigua	81-83
Ascension	37-39
Bahamas	97-99
Barbados	190-192
Basutoland	15-17
Bechuanaland Protectorate	121-123
Bermuda	115-117
British Guiana	227-229
British Honduras	112-114
Cayman Islands	97-99
Ceylon	275-277
Cyprus	140-142
Dominica	94-96
Falkland Islands	81-83
Fiji	114-116
Gambia	129-131
Gibraltar	104-106
Gilbert & Ellice Islands	37-39
Gold Coast	112-114
Grenada	128-130
Hong Kong	151-153
Jamaica	113-115
Kenya, Uganda, Tanganyika	60-62
Leeward Islands	100-102
Malta	188-190
Mauritius	208-210
Montserrat	89-91
Newfoundland	230-232
Nigeria	50-52
Northern Rhodesia	22-24
Nyasaland Protectorate	51-53
St. Helena	115-117
St. Kitts-Nevis	76-78
St. Lucia	107-109
St. Vincent	138-140
Seychelles	122-124
Sierra Leone	170-172
Solomon Islands	64-66
Somaliland Protectorate	81-83
Straits Settlements	235-237
Swaziland	24-26
Trinidad & Tobago	47-49
Turks & Caicos Islands	75-77
Virgin Islands	73-75

The following have different designs but are included in the omnibus set:
Great Britain	234
Offices in Morocco	82, 439, 514
Canada	237
Cook Islands	109-111
Nauru	35-38
Newfoundland	233-243

New Guinea	48-51
New Zealand	223-225
Niue	70-72
Papua	118-121
South Africa	74-78
Southern Rhodesia	38-41
South-West Africa	125-132

202 stamps

Peace

King George VI and
Parliament Buildings, London – CD303

Return to peace at the close of World War II.

1945-46
Aden	28-29
Antigua	96-97
Ascension	50-51
Bahamas	130-131
Barbados	207-208
Bermuda	131-132
British Guiana	242-243
British Honduras	127-128
Cayman Islands	112-113
Ceylon	293-294
Cyprus	156-157
Dominica	112-113
Falkland Islands	97-98
Falkland Islands Dep.	1L9-1L10
Fiji	137-138
Gambia	144-145
Gibraltar	119-120
Gilbert & Ellice Islands	52-53
Gold Coast	128-129
Grenada	143-144
Jamaica	136-137
Kenya, Uganda, Tanganyika	90-91
Leeward Islands	116-117
Malta	206-207
Mauritius	223-224
Montserrat	104-105
Nigeria	71-72
Northern Rhodesia	46-47
Nyasaland Protectorate	82-83
Pitcairn Island	9-10
St. Helena	128-129
St. Kitts-Nevis	91-92
St. Lucia	127-128
St. Vincent	152-153
Seychelles	149-150
Sierra Leone	186-187
Solomon Islands	80-81
Somaliland Protectorate	108-109
Trinidad & Tobago	62-63
Turks & Caicos Islands	90-91
Virgin Islands	88-89

The following have different designs but are included in the omnibus set:
Great Britain	264-265
Offices in Morocco	523-524
Aden	
Kathiri State of Seiyun	12-13
Qu'aiti State of Shihr and Mukalla	12-13
Australia	200-202
Basutoland	29-31
Bechuanaland Protectorate	137-139
Burma	66-69
Cook Islands	127-130
Hong Kong	174-175
India	195-198
Hyderabad	51
New Zealand	247-257
Niue	90-93
Pakistan-Bahawalpur	O16
Samoa	191-194
South Africa	100-102
Southern Rhodesia	67-70
South-West Africa	153-155
Swaziland	38-40
Zanzibar	222-223

164 stamps

Silver Wedding

King George VI and Queen Elizabeth
CD304   CD305

1948-49
Aden	30-31
Kathiri State of Seiyun	14-15
Qu'aiti State of Shihr and Mukalla	14-15
Antigua	98-99
Ascension	52-53
Bahamas	148-149
Barbados	210-211
Basutoland	39-40
Bechuanaland Protectorate	147-148
Bermuda	133-134
British Guiana	244-245
British Honduras	129-130
Cayman Islands	116-117
Cyprus	158-159
Dominica	114-115
Falkland Islands	99-100
Falkland Islands Dep.	1L11-1L12
Fiji	139-140
Gambia	146-147
Gibraltar	121-122
Gilbert & Ellice Islands	54-55
Gold Coast	142-143
Grenada	145-146
Hong Kong	178-179
Jamaica	138-139
Kenya, Uganda, Tanganyika	92-93
Leeward Islands	118-119
Malaya	
Johore	128-129
Kedah	55-56
Kelantan	44-45
Malacca	1-2
Negri Sembilan	36-37
Pahang	44-45
Penang	1-2
Perak	99-100
Perlis	1-2
Selangor	74-75
Trengganu	47-48
Malta	223-224
Mauritius	229-230
Montserrat	106-107
Nigeria	73-74
North Borneo	238-239
Northern Rhodesia	48-49
Nyasaland Protectorate	85-86
Pitcairn Island	11-12
St. Helena	130-131
St. Kitts-Nevis	93-94
St. Lucia	129-130
St. Vincent	154-155
Sarawak	174-175
Seychelles	151-152
Sierra Leone	188-189
Singapore	21-22
Solomon Islands	82-83
Somaliland Protectorate	110-111
Swaziland	48-49
Trinidad & Tobago	64-65
Turks & Caicos Islands	92-93
Virgin Islands	90-91
Zanzibar	224-225

The following have different designs but are included in the omnibus set:
Great Britain	267-268
Offices in Morocco	93-94, 525-526
Bahrain	62-63
Kuwait	82-83
Oman	25-26
South Africa	106
South-West Africa	159

138 stamps

U.P.U.

Mercury and Symbols of
Communications – CD306

Plane, Ship and Hemispheres CD307

Mercury Scattering Letters over Globe CD308

U.P.U. Monument, Bern CD309

Universal Postal Union, 75th anniversary.

1949

Aden	32-35
Kathiri State of Seiyun	16-19
Qu'aiti State of Shihr and Mukalla	16-19
Antigua	100-103
Ascension	57-60
Bahamas	150-153
Barbados	212-215
Basutoland	41-44
Bechuanaland Protectorate	149-152
Bermuda	138-141
British Guiana	246-249
British Honduras	137-140
Brunei	79-82
Cayman Islands	118-121
Cyprus	160-163
Dominica	116-119
Falkland Islands	103-106
Falkland Islands Dep.	1L14-1L17
Fiji	141-144
Gambia	148-151
Gibraltar	123-126
Gilbert & Ellice Islands	56-59
Gold Coast	144-147
Grenada	147-150
Hong Kong	180-183
Jamaica	142-145
Kenya, Uganda, Tanganyika	94-97
Leeward Islands	126-129
Malaya	
Johore	151-154
Kedah	57-60
Kelantan	46-49
Malacca	18-21
Negri Sembilan	59-62
Pahang	46-49
Penang	23-26
Perak	101-104
Perlis	3-6
Selangor	76-79
Trengganu	49-52
Malta	225-228
Mauritius	231-234
Montserrat	108-111
New Hebrides, British	62-65
New Hebrides, French	79-82
Nigeria	75-78
North Borneo	240-243
Northern Rhodesia	50-53
Nyasaland Protectorate	87-90
Pitcairn Islands	13-16
St. Helena	132-135
St. Kitts-Nevis	95-98
St. Lucia	131-134
St. Vincent	170-173
Sarawak	176-179
Seychelles	153-156
Sierra Leone	190-193
Singapore	23-26
Solomon Islands	84-87
Somaliland Protectorate	112-115
Southern Rhodesia	71-72
Swaziland	50-53
Tonga	87-90
Trinidad & Tobago	66-69
Turks & Caicos Islands	101-104
Virgin Islands	92-95
Zanzibar	226-229

The following have different designs but are included in the omnibus set:

Great Britain	276-279
Offices in Morocco	546-549
Australia	223
Bahrain	68-71
Burma	116-121
Ceylon	304-306
Egypt	281-283
India	223-226
Kuwait	89-92
Oman	31-34
Pakistan-Bahawalpur	26-29, O25-O28
South Africa	109-111
South-West Africa	160-162

319 stamps

University

Arms of University College CD310

Alice, Princess of Athlone CD311

1948 opening of University College of the West Indies at Jamaica.

1951

Antigua	104-105
Barbados	228-229
British Guiana	250-251
British Honduras	141-142
Dominica	120-121
Grenada	164-165
Jamaica	146-147
Leeward Islands	130-131
Montserrat	112-113
St. Kitts-Nevis	105-106
St. Lucia	149-150
St. Vincent	174-175
Trinidad & Tobago	70-71
Virgin Islands	96-97

28 stamps

Coronation

Queen Elizabeth II CD312

1953

Aden	47
Kathiri State of Seiyun	28
Qu'aiti State of Shihr and Mukalla	28
Antigua	106
Ascension	61
Bahamas	157
Barbados	234
Basutoland	45
Bechuanaland Protectorate	153
Bermuda	142
British Guiana	252
British Honduras	143
Cayman Islands	150
Cyprus	167
Dominica	141
Falkland Islands	121
Falkland Islands Dependencies	1L18
Fiji	145
Gambia	152
Gibraltar	131
Gilbert & Ellice Islands	60
Gold Coast	160
Grenada	170
Hong Kong	184
Jamaica	153
Kenya, Uganda, Tanganyika	101
Leeward Islands	132
Malaya	
Johore	155
Kedah	82
Kelantan	71
Malacca	27
Negri Sembilan	63
Pahang	71
Penang	27
Perak	126
Perlis	28
Selangor	101
Trengganu	74
Malta	241
Mauritius	250
Montserrat	127
New Hebrides, British	77
Nigeria	79
North Borneo	260
Northern Rhodesia	60

Nyasaland Protectorate	96
Pitcairn	19
St. Helena	139
St. Kitts-Nevis	119
St. Lucia	156
St. Vincent	185
Sarawak	196
Seychelles	172
Sierra Leone	194
Singapore	27
Solomon Islands	88
Somaliland Protectorate	127
Swaziland	54
Trinidad & Tobago	84
Tristan da Cunha	13
Turks & Caicos Islands	118
Virgin Islands	114

The following have different designs but are included in the omnibus set:

Great Britain	313-316
Offices in Morocco	579-582
Australia	259-261
Bahrain	92-95
Canada	330
Ceylon	317
Cook Islands	145-146
Kuwait	113-116
New Zealand	280-284
Niue	104-105
Oman	52-55
Samoa	214-215
South Africa	192
Southern Rhodesia	80
South-West Africa	244-248
Tokelau Islands	4

106 stamps

Royal Visit 1953

Separate designs for each country for the visit of Queen Elizabeth II and the Duke of Edinburgh.

1953

Aden	62
Australia	267-269
Bermuda	163
Ceylon	318
Fiji	146
Gibraltar	146
Jamaica	154
Kenya, Uganda, Tanganyika	102
Malta	242
New Zealand	286-287

13 stamps

West Indies Federation

Map of the Caribbean CD313

Federation of the West Indies, April 22, 1958.

1958

Antigua	122-124
Barbados	248-250
Dominica	161-163
Grenada	184-186
Jamaica	175-177
Montserrat	143-145
St. Kitts-Nevis	136-138
St. Lucia	170-172
St. Vincent	198-200
Trinidad & Tobago	86-88

30 stamps

Freedom from Hunger

Protein Food CD314

U.N. Food and Agricultural Organization's "Freedom from Hunger" campaign.

1963

Aden	65
Antigua	133
Ascension	89
Bahamas	180
Basutoland	83
Bechuanaland Protectorate	194
Bermuda	192
British Guiana	271
British Honduras	179
Brunei	100
Cayman Islands	168
Dominica	181
Falkland Islands	146
Fiji	198

Gambia	172
Gibraltar	161
Gilbert & Ellice Islands	76
Grenada	190
Hong Kong	218
Malta	291
Mauritius	270
Montserrat	150
New Hebrides, British	93
North Borneo	296
Pitcairn	35
St. Helena	173
St. Lucia	179
St. Vincent	201
Sarawak	212
Seychelles	213
Solomon Islands	109
Swaziland	108
Tonga	127
Tristan da Cunha	68
Turks & Caicos Islands	138
Virgin Islands	140
Zanzibar	280

37 stamps

Red Cross Centenary

Red Cross and Elizabeth II – CD315

1963

Antigua	134-135
Ascension	90-91
Bahamas	183-184
Basutoland	84-85
Bechuanaland Protectorate	195-196
Bermuda	193-194
British Guiana	272-273
British Honduras	180-181
Cayman Islands	169-170
Dominica	182-183
Falkland Islands	147-148
Fiji	203-204
Gambia	173-174
Gibraltar	162-163
Gilbert & Ellice Islands	77-78
Grenada	191-192
Hong Kong	219-220
Jamaica	203-204
Malta	292-293
Mauritius	271-272
Montserrat	151-152
New Hebrides, British	94-95
Pitcairn Islands	36-37
St. Helena	174-175
St. Kitts-Nevis	143-144
St. Lucia	180-181
St. Vincent	202-203
Seychelles	214-215
Solomon Islands	110-111
South Arabia	1-2
Swaziland	109-110
Tonga	134-135
Tristan da Cunha	69-70
Turks & Caicos Islands	139-140
Virgin Islands	141-142

70 stamps

Shakespeare

Shakespeare Memorial Theatre, Stratford-on-Avon – CD316

400th anniversary of the birth of William Shakespeare.

1964

Antigua	151
Bahamas	201
Bechuanaland Protectorate	197
Cayman Islands	171
Dominica	184
Falkland Islands	149
Gambia	192
Gibraltar	164
Montserrat	153
St. Lucia	196
Turks & Caicos Islands	141
Virgin Islands	143

12 stamps

ITU

ITU Emblem CD317

Intl. Telecommunication Union, cent.

1965
Antigua	153-154
Ascension	92-93
Bahamas	219-220
Barbados	265-266
Basutoland	101-102
Bechuanaland Protectorate	202-203
Bermuda	196-197
British Guiana	293-294
British Honduras	187-188
Brunei	116-117
Cayman Islands	172-173
Dominica	185-186
Falkland Islands	154-155
Fiji	211-212
Gibraltar	167-168
Gilbert & Ellice Islands	87-88
Grenada	205-206
Hong Kong	221-222
Mauritius	291-292
Montserrat	157-158
New Hebrides, British	108-109
Pitcairn Islands	52-53
St. Helena	180-181
St. Kitts-Nevis	163-164
St. Lucia	197-198
St. Vincent	224-225
Seychelles	218-219
Solomon Islands	126-127
Swaziland	115-116
Tristan da Cunha	85-86
Turks & Caicos Islands	142-143
Virgin Islands	159-160

64 stamps

Intl. Cooperation Year

ICY Emblem – CD318

1965
Antigua	155-156
Ascension	94-95
Bahamas	222-223
Basutoland	103-104
Bechuanaland Protectorate	204-205
Bermuda	199-200
British Guiana	295-296
British Honduras	189-190
Brunei	118-119
Cayman Islands	174-175
Dominica	187-188
Falkland Islands	156-157
Fiji	213-214
Gibraltar	169-170
Gilbert & Ellice Islands	104-105
Grenada	207-208
Hong Kong	223-224
Mauritius	293-294
Montserrat	176-177
New Hebrides, British	110-111
New Hebrides, French	126-127
Pitcairn Islands	54-55
St. Helena	182-183
St. Kitts-Nevis	165-166
St. Lucia	199-200
Seychelles	220-221
Solomon Islands	143-144
South Arabia	17-18
Swaziland	117-118
Tristan da Cunha	87-88
Turks & Caicos Islands	144-145
Virgin Islands	161-162

64 stamps

Churchill Memorial

Winston Churchill and St. Paul's, London, During Air Attack – CD319

1966
Antigua	157-160
Ascension	96-99
Bahamas	224-227
Barbados	281-284
Basutoland	105-108
Bechuanaland Protectorate	206-209
Bermuda	201-204
British Antarctic Territory	16-19
British Honduras	191-194
Brunei	120-123
Cayman Islands	176-179
Dominica	189-192
Falkland Islands	158-161
Fiji	215-218
Gibraltar	171-174
Gilbert & Ellice Islands	106-109
Grenada	209-212
Hong Kong	225-228
Mauritius	295-298
Montserrat	178-181
New Hebrides, British	112-115
New Hebrides, French	128-131
Pitcairn Islands	56-59
St. Helena	184-187
St. Kitts-Nevis	167-170
St. Lucia	201-204
St. Vincent	241-244
Seychelles	222-225
Solomon Islands	145-148
South Arabia	19-22
Swaziland	119-122
Tristan da Cunha	89-92
Turks & Caicos Islands	146-149
Virgin Islands	163-166

136 stamps

Royal Visit, 1966

Queen Elizabeth II and Prince Philip CD320

Caribbean visit, Feb. 4 - Mar. 6, 1966.

1966
Antigua	161-162
Bahamas	228-229
Barbados	285-286
British Guiana	299-300
Cayman Islands	180-181
Dominica	193-194
Grenada	213-214
Montserrat	182-183
St. Kitts-Nevis	171-172
St. Lucia	205-206
St. Vincent	245-246
Turks & Caicos Islands	150-151
Virgin Islands	167-168

26 stamps

World Cup Soccer

Soccer Player and Jules Rimet Cup CD321

World Cup Soccer Championship, Wembley, England, July 11-30.

1966
Antigua	163-164
Ascension	100-101
Bahamas	245-246
Bermuda	205-206
Brunei	124-125
Cayman Islands	182-183
Dominica	195-196
Fiji	219-220
Gibraltar	175-176
Gilbert & Ellice Islands	125-126
Grenada	230-231
New Hebrides, British	116-117
New Hebrides, French	132-133
Pitcairn Islands	60-61
St. Helena	188-189
St. Kitts-Nevis	173-174
St. Lucia	207-208
Seychelles	226-227
Solomon Islands	167-168
South Arabia	23-24
Tristan da Cunha	93-94

42 stamps

WHO Headquarters

World Health Organization Headquarters, Geneva – CD322

1966
Antigua	165-166
Ascension	102-103
Bahamas	247-248
Brunei	126-127
Cayman Islands	184-185
Dominica	197-198
Fiji	224-225
Gibraltar	180-181
Gilbert & Ellice Islands	127-128
Grenada	232-233
Hong Kong	229-230
Montserrat	184-185
New Hebrides, British	118-119
New Hebrides, French	134-135
Pitcairn Islands	62-63
St. Helena	190-191
St. Kitts-Nevis	177-178
St. Lucia	209-210
St. Vincent	247-248
Seychelles	228-229
Solomon Islands	169-170
South Arabia	25-26
Tristan da Cunha	99-100

46 stamps

UNESCO Anniversary

"Education" – CD323

"Science" (Wheat ears & flask enclosing globe). "Culture" (lyre & columns).
20th anniversary of the UNESCO.

1966-67
Antigua	183-185
Ascension	108-110
Bahamas	249-251
Barbados	287-289
Bermuda	207-209
Brunei	128-130
Cayman Islands	186-188
Dominica	199-201
Gibraltar	183-185
Gilbert & Ellice Islands	129-131
Grenada	234-236
Hong Kong	231-233
Mauritius	299-301
Montserrat	186-188
New Hebrides, British	120-122
New Hebrides, French	136-138
Pitcairn Islands	64-66
St. Helena	192-194
St. Kitts-Nevis	179-181
St. Lucia	211-213
St. Vincent	249-251
Seychelles	230-232
Solomon Islands	171-173
South Arabia	27-29
Swaziland	123-125
Tristan da Cunha	101-103
Turks & Caicos Islands	155-157
Virgin Islands	176-178

84 stamps

Silver Wedding, 1972

Queen Elizabeth II and Prince Philip CD324

Designs: borders differ for each country.

1972
Anguilla	161-162
Antigua	295-296
Ascension	164-165

Bahamas	344-345
Bermuda	296-297
British Antarctic Territory	43-44
British Honduras	306-307
British Indian Ocean Territory	48-49
Brunei	186-187
Cayman Islands	304-305
Dominica	352-353
Falkland Islands	223-224
Fiji	328-329
Gibraltar	292-293
Gilbert & Ellice Islands	206-207
Grenada	466-467
Hong Kong	271-272
Montserrat	286-287
New Hebrides, British	169-170
Pitcairn Islands	127-128
St. Helena	271-272
St. Kitts-Nevis	257-258
St. Lucia	328-329
St. Vincent	344-345
Seychelles	309-310
Solomon Islands	248-249
South Georgia	35-36
Tristan da Cunha	178-179
Turks & Caicos Islands	257-258
Virgin Islands	241-242

60 stamps

Princess Anne's Wedding

Princess Anne and Mark Phillips CD325

Wedding of Princess Anne and Mark Phillips, Nov. 14, 1973.

1973
Anguilla	179-180
Ascension	177-178
Belize	325-326
Bermuda	302-303
British Antarctic Territory	60-61
Cayman Islands	320-321
Falkland Islands	225-226
Gibraltar	305-306
Gilbert & Ellice Islands	216-217
Hong Kong	289-290
Montserrat	300-301
Pitcairn Island	135-136
St. Helena	277-278
St. Kitts-Nevis	274-275
St. Lucia	349-350
St. Vincent	358-359
St. Vincent Grenadines	1-2
Seychelles	311-312
Solomon Islands	259-260
South Georgia	37-38
Tristan da Cunha	189-190
Turks & Caicos Islands	286-287
Virgin Islands	260-261

44 stamps

Elizabeth II Coronation Anniv.

CD326   CD327

CD328

Designs: Royal and local beasts in heraldic form and simulated stonework. Portrait of Elizabeth II by Peter Grugeon.

25th anniversary of coronation of Queen Elizabeth II.

1978

Ascension	229
Barbados	474
Belize	397
British Antarctic Territory	71
Cayman Islands	404
Christmas Island	87
Falkland Islands	275
Fiji	384
Gambia	380
Gilbert Islands	312
Mauritius	464
New Hebrides, British	258
St. Helena	317
St. Kitts-Nevis	354
Samoa	472
Solomon Islands	368
South Georgia	51
Swaziland	302
Tristan da Cunha	238
Virgin Islands	337

20 sheets

Queen Mother Elizabeth's 80th Birthday

CD330

Designs: Photographs of Queen Mother Elizabeth. Falkland Islands issued in sheets of 50; others in sheets of 9.

1980

Ascension	261
Bermuda	401
Cayman Islands	443
Falkland Islands	305
Gambia	412
Gibraltar	393
Hong Kong	364
Pitcairn Islands	193
St. Helena	341
Samoa	532
Solomon Islands	426
Tristan da Cunha	277

12 stamps

Royal Wedding, 1981

Prince Charles
and Lady Diana
CD331

Wedding of Charles, Prince of Wales, and Lady Diana Spencer, St. Paul's Cathedral, London, July 29, 1981.

1981

Antigua	623-625
Ascension	294-296
Barbados	547-549
Barbuda	497-499
Bermuda	412-414
Brunei	268-270
Cayman Islands	471-473
Dominica	701-703
Falkland Islands	324-326
Falkland Islands Dep.	1L59-1L61
Fiji	442-444
Gambia	426-428
Ghana	759-761
Grenada	1051-1053
Grenada Grenadines	440-443
Hong Kong	373-375
Jamaica	500-503
Lesotho	335-337
Maldive Islands	906-908
Mauritius	520-522
Norfolk Island	280-282
Pitcairn Islands	206-208
St. Helena	353-355
St. Lucia	543-545
Samoa	558-560
Sierra Leone	509-517
Solomon Islands	450-452
Swaziland	382-384
Tristan da Cunha	294-296
Turks & Caicos Islands	486-488
Caicos Island	8-10
Uganda	314-316
Vanuatu	308-310
Virgin Islands	406-408

Princess Diana

CD332   CD333

Designs: Photographs and portrait of Princess Diana, wedding or honeymoon photographs, royal residences, arms of issuing country. Portrait photograph by Clive Friend. Souvenir sheet margins show family tree, various people related to the princess. 21st birthday of Princess Diana of Wales, July 1.

1982

Antigua	663-666
Ascension	313-316
Bahamas	510-513
Barbados	585-588
Barbuda	544-546
British Antarctic Territory	92-95
Cayman Islands	486-489
Dominica	773-776
Falkland Islands	348-351
Falkland Islands Dep.	1L72-1L75
Fiji	470-473
Gambia	447-450
Grenada	1101A-1105
Grenada Grenadines	485-491
Lesotho	372-375
Maldive Islands	952-955
Mauritius	548-551
Pitcairn Islands	213-216
St. Helena	372-375
St. Lucia	591-594
Sierra Leone	531-534
Solomon Islands	471-474
Swaziland	406-409
Tristan da Cunha	310-313
Turks and Caicos Islands	530A-534
Virgin Islands	430-433

250th anniv. of first edition of Lloyd's List (shipping news publication) & of Lloyd's marine insurance.

BAHAMAS 5c   CD335

Designs: First page of early edition of the list; historical ships, modern transportation or harbor scenes.

1984

Ascension	351-354
Bahamas	555-558
Barbados	627-630
Cayes of Belize	10-13
Cayman Islands	522-525
Falkland Islands	404-407
Fiji	509-512
Gambia	519-522
Mauritius	587-590
Nauru	280-283
St. Helena	412-415
Samoa	624-627
Seychelles	538-541
Solomon Islands	521-524
Vanuatu	368-371
Virgin Islands	466-469

Queen Mother 85th Birthday

CD336

Designs: Photographs tracing the life of the Queen Mother, Elizabeth. The high value in each set pictures the same photograph taken of the Queen Mother holding the infant Prince Henry.

1985

Ascension	372-376
Bahamas	580-584
Barbados	660-664
Bermuda	469-473
Falkland Islands	420-424
Falkland Islands Dep.	1L92-1L96
Fiji	531-535
Hong Kong	447-450
Jamaica	599-603
Mauritius	604-608
Norfolk Island	364-368
Pitcairn Islands	253-257
St. Helena	428-432
Samoa	649-653
Seychelles	567-571
Solomon Islands	543-547
Swaziland	476-480
Tristan da Cunha	372-376
Vanuatu	392-396
Zil Elwannyen Sesel	101-105

Queen Elizabeth II, 60th Birthday

CD337

1986, April 21

Ascension	389-393
Bahamas	592-596
Barbados	675-679
Bermuda	499-503
Cayman Islands	555-559
Falkland Islands	441-445
Fiji	544-548
Hong Kong	465-469
Jamaica	620-624
Kiribati	470-474
Mauritius	629-633
Papua New Guinea	640-644
Pitcairn Islands	270-274
St. Helena	451-455
Samoa	670-674
Seychelles	592-596
Solomon Islands	562-566
South Georgia	101-105
Swaziland	490-494
Tristan da Cunha	388-392
Vanuatu	414-418
Zambia	343-347
Zil Elwannyen Sesel	114-118

Royal Wedding

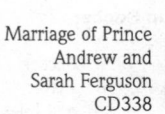

Marriage of Prince
Andrew and
Sarah Ferguson
CD338

1986, July 23

Ascension	399-400
Bahamas	602-603
Barbados	687-688
Cayman Islands	560-561
Jamaica	629-630
Pitcairn Islands	275-276
St. Helena	460-461
St. Kitts	181-182
Seychelles	602-603
Solomon Islands	567-568
Tristan da Cunha	397-398
Zambia	348-349
Zil Elwannyen Sesel	119-120

Queen Elizabeth II, 60th Birthday

Queen Elizabeth II
Inspecting Guard,
1946
CD339

Designs: Photographs tracing the life of Queen Elizabeth II.

1986

Anguilla	674-677
Antigua	925-928
Barbuda	783-786
Dominica	950-953
Gambia	611-614
Grenada	1371-1374
Grenada Grenadines	749-752
Lesotho	531-534
Maldive Islands	1172-1175
Sierra Leone	760-763
Uganda	495-498

Royal Wedding, 1986

CD340

Designs: Photographs of Prince Andrew and Sarah Ferguson during courtship, engagement and marriage.

1986

Antigua	939-942
Barbuda	809-812
Dominica	970-973
Gambia	635-638
Grenada	1385-1388
Grenada Grenadines	758-761
Lesotho	545-548
Maldive Islands	1181-1184
Sierra Leone	769-772
Uganda	510-513

Lloyds of London, 300th Anniv.

BAHAMAS   CD341

Designs: 17th century aspects of Lloyds, representations of each country's individual connections with Lloyds and publicized disasters insured by the organization.

1986

Ascension	454-457
Bahamas	655-658
Barbados	731-734
Bermuda	541-544
Falkland Islands	481-484
Liberia	1101-1104
Malawi	534-537
Nevis	571-574
St. Helena	501-504
St. Lucia	923-926
Seychelles	649-652
Solomon Islands	627-630
South Georgia	131-134
Trinidad & Tobago	484-487
Tristan da Cunha	439-442
Vanuatu	485-488
Zil Elwannyen Sesel	146-149

Moon Landing, 20th Anniv.

CD342

Designs: Equipment, crew photographs, spacecraft, official emblems and report profiles created for the Apollo Missions. Two stamps in each set are square in format rather than like the stamp shown; see individual country listings for more information.

1989

Ascension Is.	468-472
Bahamas	674-678
Belize	916-920
Kiribati	517-521
Liberia	1125-1129
Nevis	586-590
St. Kitts	248-252
Samoa	760-764
Seychelles	676-680
Solomon Islands	643-647
Vanuatu	507-511
Zil Elwannyen Sesel	154-158

Queen Mother, 90th Birthday

CD343   CD344

Designs: Portraits of Queen Elizabeth, the Queen Mother. See individual country listings for more information.

1990

Ascension Is.	491-492
Bahamas	698-699
Barbados	782-783
British Antarctic Territory	170-171
British Indian Ocean Territory	106-107
Cayman Islands	622-623
Falkland Islands	524-525
Kenya	527-528
Kiribati	555-556
Liberia	1145-1146
Pitcairn Islands	336-337
St. Helena	532-533
St. Lucia	969-970
Seychelles	710-711
Solomon Islands	671-672
South Georgia	143-144
Swaziland	565-566
Tristan da Cunha	480-481
Zil Elwannyen Sesel	171-172

Queen Elizabeth II, 65th Birthday, and Prince Philip, 70th Birthday

CD345   CD346

Designs: Portraits of Queen Elizabeth II and Prince Philip differ for each country. Printed in sheets of 10 + 5 labels (3 different) between. Stamps alternate, producing 5 different triptychs.

1991

Ascension Is.	505-506
Bahamas	730-731
Belize	969-970
Bermuda	617-618
Kiribati	571-572
Mauritius	733-734
Pitcairn Islands	348-349
St. Helena	554-555
St. Kitts	318-319
Samoa	790-791
Seychelles	723-724
Solomon Islands	688-689
South Georgia	149-150
Swaziland	586-587
Vanuatu	540-541
Zil Elwannyen Sesel	177-178

Royal Family Birthday, Anniversary

 CD347

Queen Elizabeth II, 65th birthday, Charles and Diana, 10th wedding anniversary: Various photographs of Queen Elizabeth II, Prince Philip, Prince Charles, Princess Diana and their sons William and Henry.

1991

Antigua	1446-1455
Barbuda	1229-1238
Dominica	1328-1337
Gambia	1080-1089
Grenada	2006-2015
Grenada Grenadines	1331-1340
Guyana	2440-2451
Lesotho	871-875
Maldive Islands	1533-1542
Nevis	666-675
St. Vincent	1485-1494
St. Vincent Grenadines	769-778
Sierra Leone	1387-1396
Turks & Caicos Islands	913-922
Uganda	918-927

Queen Elizabeth II's Accession to the Throne, 40th Anniv.

CD348

CD349

Various photographs of Queen Elizabeth II with local Scenes.

1992 - CD348

Antigua	1513-1518
Barbuda	1306-1309
Dominica	1414-1419
Gambia	1172-1177
Grenada	2047-2052
Grenada Grenadines	1368-1373
Lesotho	881-885
Maldive Islands	1637-1642
Nevis	702-707
St. Vincent	1582-1587
St. Vincent Grenadines	829-834
Sierra Leone	1482-1487
Turks and Caicos Islands	978-987
Uganda	990-995
Virgin Islands	742-746

1992 - CD349

Ascension Islands	531-535
Bahamas	744-748
Bermuda	623-627
British Indian Ocean Territory	119-123
Cayman Islands	648-652
Falkland Islands	549-553
Gibraltar	605-609
Hong Kong	619-623
Kenya	563-567
Kiribati	582-586
Pitcairn Islands	362-366
St. Helena	570-574
St. Kitts	332-336
Samoa	805-809
Seychelles	734-738
Soloman Islands	708-712
South Georgia	157-161
Tristan da Cunha	508-512
Vanuatu	555-559
Zambia	561-565
Zil Elwannyen Sesel	183-187

Royal Air Force, 75th Anniversary

CD350   FALKLAND ISLANDS

1993

Ascension	557-561
Bahamas	771-775
Barbados	842-846
Belize	1003-1008
Bermuda	648-651
British Indian Ocean Territory	136-140
Falkland Is.	573-577
Fiji	687-691
Montserrat	830-834
St. Kitts	351-355

Royal Air Force, 80th Anniv.

Design CD350 Re-inscribed

1998

Ascension	697-701
Bahamas	907-911
British Indian Ocean Terr	198-202
Cayman Islands	754-758
Fiji	814-818
Gibraltar	755-759
Samoa	957-961
Turks & Caicos Islands	1258-1265
Tuvalu	763-767
Virgin Islands	879-883

End of World War II, 50th Anniv.

 CD351

CD352

1995

Ascension	613-617
Bahamas	824-828
Barbados	891-895
Belize	1047-1050
British Indian Ocean Territory	163-167
Cayman Islands	704-708
Falkland Islands	634-638
Fiji	720-724
Kiribati	662-668
Liberia	1175-1179
Mauritius	803-805
St. Helena	646-654
St. Kitts	389-393
St. Lucia	1018-1022
Samoa	890-894
Solomon Islands	799-803
South Georgia & S. Sandwich Is.	198-200
Tristan da Cunha	562-566

UN, 50th Anniv.

CD353   BRITISH VIRGIN ISLANDS

1995

Bahamas	839-842
Barbados	901-904
Belize	1055-1058
Jamaica	847-851
Liberia	1187-1190
Mauritius	813-816
Pitcairn Islands	436-439
St. Kitts	398-401
St. Lucia	1023-1026
Samoa	900-903
Tristan da Cunha	568-571
Virgin Islands	807-810

Queen Elizabeth, 70th Birthday

CD354

1996

Ascension	632-635
British Antarctic Territory	240-243
British Indian Ocean Territory	176-180
Falkland Islands	653-657
Pitcairn Islands	446-449
St. Helena	672-676
Samoa	912-916
Tokelau	223-227
Tristan da Cunha	576-579
Virgin Islands	824-828

Diana, Princess of Wales (1961-97)

CD355   BAHAMAS   15c

1998

Ascension	696
Bahamas	901A-902
Barbados	950
Belize	1091
Bermuda	753
Botswana	659-663
British Antarctic Territory	258
British Indian Ocean Terr.	197
Cayman Islands	752A-753
Falkland Islands	694
Fiji	819-820
Gibraltar	754
Kiribati	719A-720
Namibia	909
Niue	706
Norfolk Island	644-645
Papua New Guinea	937
Pitcairn Islands	487
St. Helena	711
St. Kitts	437A-438
Samoa	955A-956
Seychelles	802
Solomon Islands	866-867
South Georgia & S. Sandwich Islands	220
Tokelau	253
Tonga	980
Niuafo'ou	201
Tristan da Cunha	618
Tuvalu	762
Vanuatu	719
Virgin Islands	878

Wedding of Prince Edward and Sophie Rhys-Jones

CD356

1999

Ascension	729-730
Cayman Islands	775-776
Falkland Islands	729-730
Pitcairn Islands	505-506
St. Helena	733-734
Samoa	971-972
Tristan da Cunha	636-637
Virgin Islands	908-909

1st Manned Moon Landing, 30th Anniv.

CD357

1999

Ascension	731-735
Bahamas	942-946
Barbados	967-971
Bermuda	778
Cayman Islands	777-781
Fiji	853-857
Jamaica	889-893
Kirbati	746-750
Nauru	465-469
St. Kitts	460-464
Samoa	973-977
Solomon Islands	875-879
Tuvalu	800-804
Virgin Islands	910-914

Queen Mother's Century

CD358

1999

Ascension	736-740
Bahamas	951-955
Cayman Islands	782-786
Falkland Islands	734-738
Fiji	858-862
Norfolk Island	688-692
St. Helena	740-744
Samoa	978-982
Solomon Islands	880-884
South Georgia & South Sandwich Islands	231-235
Tristan da Cunha	638-642
Tuvalu	805-809

British Commonwealth of Nations

Dominions, Colonies, Territories, Offices and Independent Members

Comprising stamps of the British Commonwealth and associated nations.

A strict observance of technicalities would bar some or all of the stamps listed under Burma, Ireland, Kuwait, Nepal, New Republic, Orange Free State, Samoa, South Africa, South-West Africa, Stellaland, Sudan, Swaziland, the two Transvaal Republics and others but these are included for the convenience of collectors.

1. Great Britain

Great Britain: Including England, Scotland, Wales and Northern Ireland.

2. The Dominions, Present and Past

AUSTRALIA

The Commonwealth of Australia was proclaimed on January 1, 1901. It consists of six former colonies as follows:

New South Wales	Victoria
Queensland	Tasmania
South Australia	Western Australia

Territories belonging to, or administered by Australia: Australian Antarctic Territory, Christmas Island, Cocos (Keeling) Islands, Nauru, New Guinea, Norfolk Island, Papua New Guinea.

CANADA

The Dominion of Canada was created by the British North America Act in 1867. The following provinces were former separate colonies and issued postage stamps:

British Columbia and Vancouver Island	Newfoundland
New Brunswick	Nova Scotia
	Prince Edward Island

FIJI

The colony of Fiji became an independent nation with dominion status on Oct. 10, 1970.

GHANA

This state came into existence Mar. 6, 1957, with dominion status. It consists of the former colony of the Gold Coast and the Trusteeship Territory of Togoland. Ghana became a republic July 1, 1960.

INDIA

The Republic of India was inaugurated on January 26, 1950. It succeeded the Dominion of India which was proclaimed August 15, 1947, when the former Empire of India was divided into Pakistan and the Union of India. The Republic is composed of about 40 predominantly Hindu states of three classes: governor's provinces, chief commissioner's provinces and princely states. India also has various territories, such as the Andaman and Nicobar Islands.

The old Empire of India was a federation of British India and the native states. The more important princely states were autonomous. Of the more than 700 Indian states, these 43 are familiar names to philatelists because of their postage stamps.

CONVENTION STATES

Chamba	Jhind
Faridkot	Nabha
Gwalior	Patiala

NATIVE FEUDATORY STATES

Alwar	Jammu
Bahawalpur	Jammu and Kashmir
Bamra	Jasdan
Barwani	Jhalawar
Bhopal	Jhind (1875-76)
Bhor	Kashmir
Bijawar	Kishangarh
Bundi	Las Bela
Bussahir	Morvi
Charkhari	Nandgaon
Cochin	Nowanuggur
Dhar	Orchha
Duttia	Poonch
Faridkot (1879-85)	Rajpeepla
Hyderabad	Sirmur
Idar	Soruth
Indore	Travancore
Jaipur	Wadhwan

NEW ZEALAND

Became a dominion on September 26, 1907. The following islands and territories are, or have been, administered by New Zealand:

Aitutaki	Ross Dependency
Cook Islands (Rarotonga)	Samoa (Western Samoa)
Niue	Tokelau Islands
Penrhyn	

PAKISTAN

The Republic of Pakistan was proclaimed March 23, 1956. It succeeded the Dominion which was proclaimed August 15, 1947. It is made up of all or part of several Moslem provinces and various districts of the former Empire of India, including Bahawalpur and Las Bela. Pakistan withdrew from the Commonwealth in 1972.

SOUTH AFRICA

Under the terms of the South African Act (1909) the self-governing colonies of Cape of Good Hope, Natal, Orange River Colony and Transvaal united on May 31, 1910, to form the Union of South Africa. It became an independent republic May 3, 1961.

Under the terms of the Treaty of Versailles, South-West Africa, formerly German South-West Africa, was mandated to the Union of South Africa.

SRI LANKA (CEYLON)

The Dominion of Ceylon was proclaimed February 4, 1948. The island had been a Crown Colony from 1802 until then. On May 22, 1972, Ceylon became the Republic of Sri Lanka.

3. Colonies, Past and Present; ControlledTerritory and Independent Members of the Commonwealth

Aden	Bechuanaland
Aitutaki	Bechuanaland Prot.
Antigua	Belize
Ascension	Bermuda
Bahamas	Botswana
Bahrain	British Antarctic Territory
Bangladesh	British Central Africa
Barbados	British Columbia and Vancouver Island
Barbuda	British East Africa
Basutoland	British Guiana
Batum	

British Honduras
British Indian Ocean Territory
British New Guinea
British Solomon Islands
British Somaliland
Brunei
Burma
Bushire
Cameroons
Cape of Good Hope
Cayman Islands
Christmas Island
Cocos (Keeling) Islands
Cook Islands
Crete,
  British Administration
Cyprus
Dominica
East Africa & Uganda
  Protectorates
Egypt
Falkland Islands
Fiji
Gambia
German East Africa
Gibraltar
Gilbert Islands
Gilbert & Ellice Islands
Gold Coast
Grenada
Griqualand West
Guernsey
Guyana
Heligoland
Hong Kong
Indian Native States
  (see India)
Ionian Islands
Jamaica
Jersey

Kenya
Kenya, Uganda & Tanzania
Kuwait
Labuan
Lagos
Leeward Islands
Lesotho
Madagascar
Malawi
Malaya
  Federated Malay States
  Johore
  Kedah
  Kelantan
  Malacca
  Negri Sembilan
  Pahang
  Penang
  Perak
  Perlis
  Selangor
  Singapore
  Sungei Ujong
  Trengganu
Malaysia
Maldive Islands
Malta
Man, Isle of
Mauritius
Mesopotamia
Montserrat
Muscat
Namibia
Natal
Nauru
Nevis
New Britain
New Brunswick
Newfoundland
New Guinea

New Hebrides
New Republic
New South Wales
Niger Coast Protectorate
Nigeria
Niue
Norfolk Island
North Borneo
Northern Nigeria
Northern Rhodesia
North West Pacific Islands
Nova Scotia
Nyasaland Protectorate
Oman
Orange River Colony
Palestine
Papua New Guinea
Penrhyn Island
Pitcairn Islands
Prince Edward Island
Queensland
Rhodesia
Rhodesia & Nyasaland
Ross Dependency
Sabah
St. Christopher
St. Helena
St. Kitts
St. Kitts-Nevis-Anguilla
St. Lucia
St. Vincent
Samoa
Sarawak
Seychelles
Sierra Leone
Solomon Islands
Somaliland Protectorate
South Arabia
South Australia
South Georgia

Southern Nigeria
Southern Rhodesia
South-West Africa
Stellaland
Straits Settlements
Sudan
Swaziland
Tanganyika
Tanzania
Tasmania
Tobago
Togo
Tokelau Islands
Tonga
Transvaal
Trinidad
Trinidad and Tobago
Tristan da Cunha
Trucial States
Turks and Caicos
Turks Islands
Tuvalu
Uganda
United Arab Emirates
Victoria
Virgin Islands
Western Australia
Zambia
Zanzibar
Zululand

**POST OFFICES IN
FOREIGN COUNTRIES**
Africa
  East Africa Forces
  Middle East Forces
Bangkok
China
Morocco
Turkish Empire

Colonies, Former Colonies, Offices, Territories Controlled by Parent States

Belgium
Belgian Congo
Ruanda-Urundi

Denmark
Danish West Indies
Faroe Islands
Greenland
Iceland

Finland
Aland Islands

France
COLONIES PAST AND PRESENT, CONTROLLED TERRITORIES
Afars & Issas, Territory of
Alaouites
Alexandretta
Algeria
Alsace & Lorraine
Anjouan
Annam & Tonkin
Benin
Cambodia (Khmer)
Cameroun
Castellorizo
Chad
Cilicia
Cochin China
Comoro Islands
Dahomey
Diego Suarez
Djibouti (Somali Coast)
Fezzan
French Congo
French Equatorial Africa
French Guiana
French Guinea
French India
French Morocco
French Polynesia (Oceania)
French Southern &
   Antarctic Territories
French Sudan
French West Africa
Gabon
Germany
Ghadames
Grand Comoro
Guadeloupe
Indo-China
Inini
Ivory Coast
Laos
Latakia
Lebanon
Madagascar
Martinique
Mauritania
Mayotte
Memel
Middle Congo
Moheli
New Caledonia
New Hebrides
Niger Territory
Nossi-Be
Obock
Reunion
Rouad, Ile
Ste.-Marie de Madagascar
St. Pierre & Miquelon
Senegal
Senegambia & Niger
Somali Coast
Syria
Tahiti
Togo
Tunisia
Ubangi-Shari
Upper Senegal & Niger
Upper Volta
Viet Nam
Wallis & Futuna Islands

POST OFFICES IN FOREIGN COUNTRIES
China
Crete
Egypt
Turkish Empire
Zanzibar

Germany
EARLY STATES
Baden
Bavaria
Bergedorf
Bremen
Brunswick
Hamburg
Hanover
Lubeck
Mecklenburg-Schwerin
Mecklenburg-Strelitz
Oldenburg
Prussia
Saxony
Schleswig-Holstein
Wurttemberg

FORMER COLONIES
Cameroun (Kamerun)
Caroline Islands
German East Africa
German New Guinea
German South-West Africa
Kiauchau
Mariana Islands
Marshall Islands
Samoa
Togo

Italy
EARLY STATES
Modena
Parma
Romagna
Roman States
Sardinia
Tuscany
Two Sicilies
   Naples
   Neapolitan Provinces
   Sicily

FORMER COLONIES, CONTROLLED TERRITORIES, OCCUPATION AREAS
Aegean Islands
   Calimno (Calino)
   Caso
   Cos (Coo)
   Karki (Carchi)
   Leros (Lero)
   Lipso
   Nisiros (Nisiro)
   Patmos (Patmo)
   Piscopi
   Rodi (Rhodes)
   Scarpanto
   Simi
   Stampalia
Castellorizo
Corfu
Cyrenaica
Eritrea
Ethiopia (Abyssinia)
Fiume
Ionian Islands
   Cephalonia
   Ithaca
   Paxos
Italian East Africa
Libya
Oltre Giuba
Saseno
Somalia (Italian Somaliland)
Tripolitania

POST OFFICES IN FOREIGN COUNTRIES
"ESTERO"*
Austria
China
   Peking
   Tientsin
Crete
Tripoli
Turkish Empire
   Constantinople
   Durazzo
   Janina
Jerusalem
Salonika
Scutari
Smyrna
Valona
*Stamps overprinted "ESTERO" were used in various parts of the world.

Netherlands
Aruba
Netherlands Antilles (Curacao)
Netherlands Indies
Netherlands New Guinea
Surinam (Dutch Guiana)

Portugal
COLONIES PAST AND PRESENT, CONTROLLED TERRITORIES
Angola
Angra
Azores
Cape Verde
Funchal
Horta
Inhambane
Kionga
Lourenco Marques
Macao
Madeira
Mozambique
Mozambique Co.
Nyassa
Ponta Delgada
Portuguese Africa
Portuguese Congo
Portuguese Guinea
Portuguese India
Quelimane
St. Thomas & Prince Islands
Tete
Timor
Zambezia

Russia
ALLIED TERRITORIES AND REPUBLICS, OCCUPATION AREAS
Armenia
Aunus (Olonets)
Azerbaijan
Batum
Estonia
Far Eastern Republic
Georgia
Karelia
Latvia
Lithuania
North Ingermanland
Ostland
Russian Turkestan
Siberia
South Russia
Tannu Tuva
Transcaucasian Fed. Republics
Ukraine
Wenden (Livonia)
Western Ukraine

Spain
COLONIES PAST AND PRESENT, CONTROLLED TERRITORIES
Aguera, La
Cape Juby
Cuba
Elobey, Annobon & Corisco
Fernando Po
Ifni
Mariana Islands
Philippines
Puerto Rico
Rio de Oro
Rio Muni
Spanish Guinea
Spanish Morocco
Spanish Sahara
Spanish West Africa

POST OFFICES IN FOREIGN COUNTRIES
Morocco
Tangier
Tetuan

UNITED STATES

yu-ˌnī-təd 'stāts

GOVT. — Republic
AREA — 3,615,211 sq. mi.
POP. — 248,709,873 (1990)
CAPITAL — Washington, DC

In addition to the 50 States and the District of Columbia, the Republic includes Guam, the Commonwealth of Puerto Rico, the Virgin Islands, American Samoa, Wake, Midway, and a number of small islands in the Pacific Ocean, all of which use stamps of the United States.

100 Cents = 1 Dollar

Catalogue values for unused stamps in this country are for Never Hinged items, beginning with Scott 772 in the regular postage section, Scott C19 in the air post section, Scott E17 in the special delivery section, Scott FA1 in the certified mail section, Scott O127 in officials section, Scott J88 in the postage due section, Scott RW1 in the hunting permit stamps section.

Watermarks

Wmk. 190—"USPS" in Single-lined Capitals

Wmk. 191—Double-lined "USPS" in Capitals

Watermark 191 has 9 letters for each horizontal row of 10 stamps. Watermark 190 has 8 to 9 letters for each horizontal row. Each watermark has 9 letters for each vertical row of 10 stamps. This results in a number of stamps in each pane showing only a small portion of 1 or more watermark letters. This is especially true of watermark 190.

Wmk. 190PI - PIPS, used in the Philippines
Wmk. 191PI - PIPS, used in the Philippines
Wmk. 191C - US-C, used for Cuba
Wmk. 191R - USIR

PROVISIONAL ISSUES BY POSTMASTERS

Values for Envelopes are for entires.

ALEXANDRIA, VA.

A1

Type I - 40 asterisks in circle.
Type II - 39 asterisks in circle.

Typeset 1846		Typeset	Imperf.
1X1	A1 5c black, buff, Type I		—
a.	5c black, buff, Type II		75,000.
1X2	A1 5c black, blue, Type I,		
	on cover		—

All known copies of Nos. 1X1-1X2 are cut to shape.

ANNAPOLIS, MD.

ENVELOPE

E1

1846

2XU1 E1 5c carmine red   225,000.

Handstamped impressions of the circular design with "2" in blue or red exist on envelopes and letter sheets. Values: blue $3,000, red $5,000.
A letter sheet exists with circular design and "5" handstamped in red. Values: blue $3,500, red $5,000.
A similar circular design in blue was used as a postmark.

BALTIMORE, MD.

Signature of Postmaster—A1

1845		Engr.	Imperf.
3X1	A1 5c black	5,000.	
3X2	A1 10c black, on cover	50,000.	
3X3	A1 5c black, bluish	65,000.	5,000.
3X4	A1 10c black, bluish		60,000.

Nos. 3X1-3X4 were printed from a plate of 12 (2x6) containing nine 5c and three 10c.

Envelopes

PAID 5

E1

The color given is that of the "PAID 5" and oval. "James M. Buchanan" is handstamped in black, blue or red. The paper is manila, buff, white, salmon or grayish.

1845			Handstamped
		Various Papers	
3XU1	E1	5c blue	7,000.
3XU2	E1	5c red	10,000.
3XU3	E1	10c blue	16,500.
3XU4	E1	10c red	20,000.

On the formerly listed "5+5" envelopes, the second "5" in oval is believed not to be part of the basic prepaid marking.

BOSCAWEN, N. H.

PAID 5 CENTS

A1

Typeset 1846(?)		Typeset	Imperf.
4X1	A1 5c dull blue, yellowish,		
	on cover		225,000.

BRATTLEBORO, VT.

Initials of Postmaster (FNP)—A1

Plate of 10 (5x2).

1846		Engr.	Imperf.
5X1	A1 5c black, buff		10,000.

LOCKPORT, N. Y.

A1

Handstamped, "5" in Black Ms

1846			
6X1	A1 5c red, buff, on cover		225,000.

MILLBURY, Mass.

George Washington—A1

Printed from a Woodcut

1846			Imperf.
7X1	A1 5c blue, bluish	130,000.	20,000.

NEW HAVEN, CONN.

Envelopes

E1

1845			Handstamped
		Signed in Blue, Black, Magenta or Red	
8XU1	E1 5c red (Bl or M)		80,000.
8XU2	E1 5c red, light bluish		
	(Bk)		110,000.
8XU3	E1 5c dull blue, buff (Bl)		110,000.
8XU4	E1 5c dull blue (Bl)		110,000.

Values of Nos. 8XU1-8XU4 are a guide to value. They are based on auction realizations and retail sales and take condition into consideration. All New Haven envelopes are of almost equal rarity. An entire of No. 8XU2 is the finest example known. The other envelopes are valued according to condition as much as rarity.
Reprints were made at various times between 1871 and 1932. They can be distinguished from the originals, primarily due to differences in paper.

NEW YORK, N. Y.

George Washington—A1

Plate of 40 (5x8). Nos. 9X1-9X3 and varieties unused are valued without gum. Examples with original gum are extremely scarce and will command higher prices.

1845-46		Engr.	Imperf.
		Bluish Wove Paper	
9X1	A1 5c blk, signed ACM,		
	connected ('46)	1,300.	500.
a.	Signed ACM, AC connected	1,600.	550.
b.	Signed A.C.M.	3,750.	700.
c.	Signed MMJr		9,000.
d.	Signed RHM	13,000.	3,250.
e.	Without signature	3,750.	750.

These stamps were usually initialed "ACM" in magenta ink, as a control, before being sold or passed through the mails.
A plate of 9 (3x3) was made from which proofs were printed in black on white and deep blue papers; also in blue, green, brown and red on white bond paper.

1847		Engr.	Imperf.
		Blue Wove Paper	
9X2	A1 5c blk, signed ACM,		
	connected	6,500.	3,500.
a.	Signed RHM		
d.	Without signature	11,000.	7,250.

On the listing example of No. 9X2a the "R" is illegible and does not match those of the other "RHM" signatures.

1847		Engr.	Imperf.
		Gray Wove Paper	
9X3	A1 5c blk, signed ACM,		
	connected	5,250.	2,100.
a.	Signed RHM		7,000.
b.	Without signature		7,000.

PROVIDENCE, R. I.

A1

A2

1846		Engr.	Imperf.
10X1	A1 5c gray black	375.	1,750.
10X2	A2 10c gray black	1,200.	15,000.
a.	Pair, #10X1-10X2	1,850.	

Plate of 12 (3x4) contains 11-5c and 1-10c.
Reprints were made in 1898. Each stamp bears one of the following letters on the back: B. O. G. E. R. T. D. U. R. B. I. N. Value of 5c, $50; 10c, $125; sheet, $725.
Reprint singles or sheets without back print sell for more.

ST. LOUIS, MO.

A1   A2   A3

Missouri Coat of Arms

Unused are valued without gum.

1845-46		Engr.	Imperf.
		Greenish Wove Paper	
11X1	A1 5c black	6,500.	4,250.
11X2	A2 10c black	6,500.	3,750.
11X3	A3 20c black		30,000.

Three varieties of 5c, 3 of 10c, 2 of 20c.

1846			
		Gray Lilac Paper	
11X4	A1 5c black	—	5,000.
11X5	A2 10c black	5,000.	2,500.
11X6	A3 20c black		22,500.

One variety of 5c, 3 of 10c, 2 of 20c.

1847			
		Pelure Paper	
11X7	A1 5c black bluish	—	6,500.
11X8	A2 10c blk, bluish	6,500.	
a.	Impression of 5c on back		—

Three varieties of 5c, 3 of 10c.

Values of Nos. 11X7-11X8 reflect the usual poor condition of these stamps, which were printed on fragile pelure paper. Attractive copies with minor defects sell for considerably more.

Used values are for pencanceled copies.

For Tuscumbia, Alabama, formerly listed as United States postmasters' provisional No. 12XU1, see the "3c 1861 Postmasters' Provisionals" section before the Confederate States of America Postmasters' Provisionals.

Please Note:

Stamps are valued in the grade of very fine unless otherwise indicated.

Values for early and valuable stamps are for examples with certificates of authenticity from acknowledged expert committees, or examples sold with the buyer having the right of certification. This applies to examples with original gum as well as examples without gum.

Beware of stamps offered "as is," as the gum on some unused stamps offered with "original gum" may be fraudulent, and stamps offered as unused without gum may in some cases be altered or faintly canceled used stamps.

GENERAL ISSUES
All Issues from 1847 to 1894 are Unwatermarked.

Benjamin Franklin A1

George Washington A2

1847, July 1		Engr.		Imperf.
1	A1	5c red brn, *bluish*	6,000.	600.
		No gum	2,600.	
a.		5c dark brown, *bluish*	6,500.	625.
		No gum	2,900.	
b.		5c orange brown, *bluish*	7,500.	850.
		No gum	3,150.	
c.		5c red orange, *bluish*	12,500.	6,000.
		No gum	7,000.	
d.		Double impression	—	
		Pen cancel		300.

The only known double impression shows part of the design doubled.

2	A2	10c black, *bluish*	27,500.	1,400.
		No gum	13,000.	
a.		Diagonal half used as 5c on cover		13,000.
b.		Vertical half used as 5c on cover		35,000.
c.		Horizontal half used as 5c on cover		—
		Pen cancel		750.

REPRODUCTIONS
Actually, official imitations made from new plates by order of the Post Office Department.

A3

A4

1875				Imperf.
Bluish Paper Without Gum				
3	A3	5c red brown		750.
4	A4	10c black		950.

Reproductions. The letters R. W. H. & E. at the bottom of each stamp are less distinct on the reproductions than on the originals.

5c. On the originals the left side of the white shirt frill touches the oval on a level with the top of the "F" of "Five." On the reproductions it touches the oval about on a level with the top of the figure "5." On the originals the bottom of the right leg of the "N" in "CENTS" is blunt. On the reproductions the "N" comes to a point at the bottom.

10c. On the reproductions, line of coat at left points to right tip of "X" and line of coat at right points to center of "S" of CENTS. On the originals, line of coat points to "T" of TEN and between "T" and "S" of CENTS. The bottom of the right leg of the "N" of "CENTS" shows the same difference as on the 5c originals and reproductions. On the reproductions the eyes have a sleepy look, the line of the mouth is straighter, and in the curl of hair near the left cheek is a strong black dot, while the originals have only a faint one.

Franklin — A5

ONE CENT
Type I. Has complete curved lines outside the labels with "U.S. Postage" and "One Cent." The scrolls below the lower label are turned under, forming little balls. The ornaments at top are substantially complete.

Values for type I are for stamps showing the marked characteristics plainly. Copies of type I showing the balls indistinctly sell for much lower prices.

Type Ib. Same as I but balls below the bottom label are not so clear. The plumelike scrolls at bottom are not complete.

A6

Type Ia. Same as I at bottom but top ornaments and outer line at top are partly cut away.

Type Ic. Same as Ia, but bottom right plume and ball ornament incomplete. Bottom left plume complete or nearly complete.

A7

Type II. The little balls of the bottom scrolls and the bottoms of the lower plume ornaments are missing. The side ornaments are substantially complete.

A8

Type III. The top and bottom curved lines outside the labels are broken in the middle. The side ornaments are complete.

Type IIIa. Similar to type III with the outer line broken at top or bottom but not both.

A9

Type IV. Similar to type II, but with the curved lines outside the labels recut at top or bottom or both.

Washington — A10

THREE CENTS
Type I. There is an outer frame line on all four sides.

Thomas Jefferson — A11

FIVE CENTS
Type I. There are projections on all four sides.

Washington — A12

TEN CENTS
Type I. The "shells" at the lower corners are practically complete. The outer line below the label is very nearly complete. The outer lines are broken above the middle of the top label and the "X" in each upper corner.

A13

Type II. The design is complete at the top. The outer line at the bottom is broken in the middle. The shells are partly cut away.

A14

Type III. The outer lines are broken above the top label and the "X" numerals. The outer line at the bottom and the shells are partly cut away, similar to Type II.

A15

Type IV. The outer lines have been recut at top or bottom or both.

Types I, II, III and IV have complete ornaments at the sides of the stamps and three pearls at each outer edge of the bottom panel.

Washington — A16

In Nos. 5-17, the 1c, 3c, and 12c have very small margins between the stamps. The 5c and 10c have moderate size margins. The values of these stamps take the margin size into consideration.

Values for No. 5A, 6b and 19b are for the less distinct positions. Best examples sell for more.

Values for No. 16 are for outer line recut at top. Other recuts sell for more.

1851-57				Imperf.
5	A5	1c blue, I	175,000.	45,000.

Values for No. 5 are for copies with margins touching or slightly cutting into the design. Value unused is for an example with no gum.

5A	A5	1c blue, Ib	15,000.	6,000.
		No gum	7,250.	
6	A6	1c blue, Ia ('57)	37,500.	10,000.
		No gum	20,000.	
b.		Type Ic	6,000.	1,400.
		No gum	2,750.	
7	A7	1c blue, II	1,200.	160.
		No gum	550.	
8	A8	1c blue, III	12,500.	2,750.
		No gum	6,000.	

Values for type III are for at least a 2mm break in each outer line. Examples of type III with wider breaks in outer lines command higher prices; those with smaller breaks sell for less.

8A	A8	1c blue, IIIa	4,250.	1,000.
		No gum	2,000.	

Stamps of type IIIa with bottom line broken command higher prices than those with top line broken. See note after No. 8 on width of break of outer lines.

9	A9	1c bl, IV ('52)	750.	125.
		No gum	325.	
a.		Printed on both sides, reverse inverted		
10	A10	3c org brown, I	3,000.	100.
		No gum	1,400.	
a.		Printed on both sides		12,000.
11	A10	3c dull red, I	240.	10.
		No gum	100.	
c.		Vertical half used as 1c on cover		5,000.
d.		Diagonal half used as 1c on cover		5,000.
e.		Double impression		5,000.
12	A11	5c red brown, I ('56)	19,000.	1,000.
		No gum	9,750.	
13	A12	10c grn, I ('55)	15,000.	800.
		No gum	7,250.	
14	A13	10c grn, II ('55)	4,000.	210.
		No gum	1,800.	
15	A14	10c grn, III ('55)	4,000.	210.
		No gum	1,800.	

16	A15	10c grn, IV ('55)	27,500.	1,600.
		No gum	14,000.	
17	A16	12c black	5,000.	325.
		No gum		2,250.
a.		Diagonal half used as 6c on cover		2,500.
b.		Vertical half used as 6c on cover		8,500.
c.		Printed on both sides		10,000.

Same Designs as 1851-56 Issues

Franklin—A20

ONE CENT
Type V. Similar to type III of 1851-57 but with side ornaments partly cut away.

Washington—A21

THREE CENTS
Type II. The outer frame line has been removed at top and bottom. The side frame lines were recut so as to be continuous from the top to the bottom of the plate. Stamps from the top or bottom rows show the ends of the side frame lines and may be mistaken for type IIa.

Type IIa. The side frame lines extend only to the top and bottom of the stamp design.

Jefferson — A22

FIVE CENTS
Type II. The projections at top and bottom are partly cut away.

Washington (Two typical examples) — A23

TEN CENTS
Type V. The side ornaments are slightly cut away. Usually only one pearl remains at each end of the lower label but some copies show two or three pearls at the right side.

At the bottom the outer line is complete and the shells nearly so. The outer lines at top are complete except over the right "X."

Washington A17

Franklin A18

Washington — A19

TWELVE CENTS
Plate I. Outer frame lines complete.
Plate III. Outer frame lines noticeably uneven or broken, sometimes partly missing.

Nos. 18-39 have small or very small margins. The values take into account the margin size.

1857-61				**Perf. 15½**
18	A5	1c blue, I ('61)	1,800.	600.
		No gum	825.	
19	A6	1c blue, Ia	22,500.	6,500.
		No gum	10,500.	
b.		Type Ic	2,750.	1,300.
		No gum	1,300.	
20	A7	1c blue, II	1,000.	250.
		No gum	450.	
21	A8	1c blue, III	12,500.	2,000.
		No gum	6,000.	
a.		Horiz. pair, imperf. btwn.		16,000.
22	A8	1c blue, IIIa	1,900.	475.
		No gum	925.	
b.		Horiz. pair, imperf. btwn.		5,000.

One pair of No. 22b has been reported. Beware of pairs with blind perforations.

23	A9	1c blue, IV	8,000.	700.
		No gum	3,800.	
24	A20	1c blue, V	175.	40.
		No gum	80.	
b.		Laid paper		—
25	A10	3c rose, I	2,500.	90.
		No gum	1,200.	
b.		Vert. pair, imperf. horiz.		10,000.
26	A21	3c dull red, II	75.	7.
		No gum	30.	
a.		3c dull red, IIa	225.	55.
		No gum	100.	
b.		Horiz. pair, imperf. vert., II	4,000.	—
c.		Vert. pair, imperf. horiz., II		10,000.
d.		Horiz. pair, imperf btwn., II		—
e.		Dbl. impression, II		2,500.
f.		Horiz. strip of 3, imperf. vert., IIa, on cover		8,250.
27	A11	5c brick red, I ('58)	25,000.	1,400.
		No gum	12,000.	
28	A11	5c red brn, I	4,500.	750.
		No gum	2,150.	
b.		5c bright red brown	4,750.	950.
		No gum	2,300.	
28A	A11	5c Indian red, I ('58)	30,000.	3,000.
		No gum	16,500.	
29	A11	5c brn, I ('59)	2,250.	350.
		No gum	1,025.	
30	A22	5c org brn, II ('61)	1,150.	1,100.
		No gum	525.	
30A	A22	5c brn, II ('60)	1,900.	275.
		No gum	875.	
b.		Printed on both sides	4,400.	4,650.
31	A12	10c green, I	16,500.	850.
		No gum	7,750.	
32	A13	10c green, II	5,000.	275.
		No gum	2,400.	
33	A14	10c green, III	5,000.	275.
		No gum	2,400.	
34	A15	10c green, IV	32,500.	2,250.
		No gum	17,500.	
35	A23	10c grn, V ('59)	275.	65.
		No gum	120.	
36	A16	12c black, plate I	1,400.	250.
		No gum	650.	
a.		Diagonal half used as 6c on cover (I)		17,500.
b.		12c black, plate III ('59)	750.	180.
		No gum	340.	
c.		Horizontal pair, imperf. between (I)		12,500.
37	A17	24c gray lil ('60)	1,600.	350.
a.		24c gray	1,600.	350.
		No gum	725.	
38	A18	30c orange ('60)	1,800.	450.
		No gum	825.	
39	A19	90c blue ('60)	2,750.	6,500.
		No gum	1,275.	
		Pen cancel		2,000.

See Die and Plate proofs in the Scott United States Specialized Catalogue for imperfs. of the 12c, 24c, 30c, 90c.

Genuine cancellations on the 90c are rare. Used examples must be accompanied by certificates of authenticty issued by recognized expertizing committees.

REPRINTS OF 1857-60 ISSUE
White Paper
Without Gum

1875				**Perf. 12**
40	A5	1c bright blue	625.	
41	A10	3c scarlet	3,000.	
42	A22	5c orange brown	1,200.	
43	A12	10c blue green	2,750.	
44	A16	12c greenish blk	3,250.	
45	A17	24c black violet	3,250.	
46	A18	30c yellow orange	3,250.	
47	A19	90c deep blue	4,500.	

Nos. 41-46 are valued in the grade of fine.
Nos. 40-47 exist imperf., value, set $25,000.

Essays-Trial Color Proofs

The paper of former Nos. 55-62 (Nos. 63E11e, 65-E15h, 67-E9e, 69-E6e, 72-E7h, Essay section, Nos. 70eTC, 71bTC, Trial Color Proof section, Scott U.S. Specialized) is thin and semitransparent.

That of the postage issues is thicker and more opaque, except Nos. 62B, 70c and 70d.

Franklin — A24

1c: There is a dash under the tip of the ornament at right of the numeral in upper left corner.
There is no dash on the essay.

Washington — A25

3c: Ornaments at corners are large and end in a small ball.
The ornaments are smaller and there is no ball on the essay.

Jefferson — A26

5c: Leaflets appear at each corner. These do not appear on the essay.

Washington — A27

A27a

A27

10c: On A27 a heavy curved line appears below the stars and an outer line above them which does not appear on A27a.

Washington — A28

12c: Ovals and scrolls appear at each corners.
These do not appear on the essay.

Washington　　　　Franklin
A29　　　　　　　A30

Washington — A31

90c: Two pairs of parallel lines form an angle above the ribbon with "U. S. Postage". Between these lines is a row of dashes, and there is a point of color to the apex of the lower pair.
These do not appear on the essay.

1861　　　　　　　　　　**Perf. 12**

62B	A27a 10c dark green	6,750.	950.
	No gum	3,250.	

1861-62　　　　　　　**Perf. 12**

63	A24 1c blue	325.00	32.50
	No gum	140.00	
	1c ultramarine	750.00	275.00
	No gum	350.00	
a.	1c dark blue	550.00	90.00
	No gum	250.00	
c.	Laid paper	—	—
d.	Vert. pair, imperf. horiz.	—	—
e.	Printed on both sides		2,500.
64	A25 3c pink	7,500.	750.00
	No gum	3,750.	
a.	3c pigeon blood pink	17,500.	3,500.
	No gum	9,000.	
b.	3c rose pink	550.00	140.00
	No gum	250.00	
65	A25 3c rose	130.00	2.50
	No gum	55.00	
b.	Laid paper	—	
d.	Vert. pair, imperf. horiz.	3,500.	750.00
e.	Printed on both sides	3,250.	2,750.
f.	Double impression		6,000.

The 3c lake can be found under No. 66 in the Trial Color Proofs section of the Scott U.S. Specialized Catalogue.
The imperf 3c lake under No. 66P in the same section.
The imperf 3c rose can be found in the Die and Plate Proofs section of the Specialized.

67	A26 5c buff	21,000.	800.00
a.	5c brown yellow	21,000.	850.00
	No gum	10,000.	
b.	5c olive yellow		1,050.

Values for Nos. 67, 67a, 67b reflect the normal small margins.

68	A27 10c yellow green	850.00	50.00
	No gum	400.00	
a.	10c dark green	900.00	62.50
	No gum	425.00	
b.	Vert. pair, imperf. horiz.		3,500.
69	A28 12c black	1,250.	100.00
	No gum	550.00	
70	A29 24c red lilac ('62)	2,000.	175.00
	No gum	900.00	
a.	24c brown lilac	1,600.	130.00
	No gum	725.00	
b.	24c steel blue	8,000.	650.00
	No gum	3,750.	
c.	24c violet, thin paper	9,500.	1,250.
	No gum	5,000.	
d.	24c pale gray violet, thin paper	3,250.	1,250.
	No gum	1,500.	
71	A30 30c orange	1,750.	160.00
	No gum	800.00	
a.	Printed on both sides		—

Values for No. 71 are for copies with small margins, especially at sides. Large margined examples sell for much more.

72	A31 90c blue	2,750.	425.00
	No gum	1,250.	
a.	90c pale blue	2,500.	425.00
	No gum	1,200.	
b.	90c dark blue	3,000.	550.00
	No gum	1,350.	

Nos. 70c, 70d are on a thinner, harder and more transparent paper than Nos. 70, 70a, 70b, or the later Nos. 78, 78a, 78b and 78c.

Please Note:

**Stamps are valued in the grade of very fine unless otherwise indicated.
Values for early and valuable stamps are for examples with certificates of authenticity from acknowledged expert committees, or examples sold with the buyer having the right of certification.
This applies to examples with original gum as well as examples without gum.
Beware of stamps offered "as is," as the gum on some unused stamps offered with "original gum" may be fraudulent, and stamps offered as unused without gum may in some cases be altered or faintly canceled used stamps.**

Designs as 1861 Issue

Andrew　　　　　Abraham
Jackson　　　　　Lincoln
A32　　　　　　　A33

1861-66　　　　　　　**Perf. 12**

73	A32 2c black ('63)	350.00	50.00
	No gum	140.00	
a.	Diag. half used as 1c as part of 3c rate on cover		1,150.
b.	Diagonal half used alone as 1c on cover		3,000.
c.	Horiz. half used alone as 1c on cover		3,500.
d.	Vert. half used as part of 3c rate on cover		1,250.
e.	Vert. half used alone as 1c on cover		—
f.	Printed on both sides		5,000.
g	Laid paper		—

The 3c scarlet can be found under No. 74 in the Scott U.S. Specialized Catalogue Trial Color Proofs section.

75	A26 5c red brown ('62)	4,500.	450.00
	No gum	2,100.	
76	A26 5c brown ('63)	1,300.	120.00
	No gum	575.00	
a.	5c black brown	1,350.	160.00
	No gum	600.00	
b.	Laid paper		—
77	A33 15c black ('66)	1,750.	160.00
	No gum	775.00	
78	A29 24c lilac ('63)	1,200.	110.00
a.	24c grayish lilac	1,200.	110.00
b.	24c gray	1,200.	110.00
	No gum	525.00	
c.	24c blackish violet	30,000.	2,500.
	No gum	20,000.	
d.	Printed on both sides		3,500.

Values for Nos. 75, 76, 76a reflect the normal small margins.

Grill

Same as 1861-66 Issues
Embossed with grills of various sizes

Grill with Points Up

Grills A and C were made by a roller covered with ridges shaped like an inverted V. Pressing the ridges into the stamp paper forced the paper into the pyramidal pits between the ridges, causing irregular breaks in the paper.
Grill B was made by a roller with raised bosses.

A. Grill covering the entire stamp

1867　　　　　　　　　**Perf. 12**

79	A25 3c rose	5,000.	1,100.
	No gum	2,400.	
b.	Printed on both sides		—
80	A26 5c brown	—	130,000.
a.	5c dark brown		130,000.
81	A30 30c orange		60,000.

Nos. 79, 79b, are valued for fine-very fine centering but with minor perforation faults.
An essay which is often mistaken for No. 79 (#79-E15) shows the points of the grill as small squares faintly impressed in the paper, but not cutting through it.
On No. 79 the grill breaks through the paper. Copies free from defects are rare.
Eight copies of Nos. 80 and 80a (four unused, four used), and eight copies of No. 81 (one in a museum and not available to collectors) are known. All are more or less faulty and/or off-center.
Values are for off-center examples with small perforation faults.
The imperf. of the 3c rose can be found in the Scott U.S. Specialized Catalogue, Die and Plate Proofs section.

B. Grill about 18x15mm (22 by 18 points)

82	A25 3c rose		175,000.

The four known copies of No. 82 are fine.

C. Grill about 13x16mm (16 to 17 by 18 to 21 points)

83	A25 3c rose	5,000.	950.
	No gum	2,400.	

The grilled area on each of four C grills in the sheet may total about 18x15mm when a

---

normal C grill adjoins a fainter grill extending to the right or left edge of the stamp.
This is caused by a partial erasure on the grill roller when it was changed to produce C grills instead of the all-over A grill.
The imperf. can be found in the Scott U.S. Specialized Catalogue Die and Plate Proofs section.

Grill with Points Down

The grills were produced by rollers with the surface covered by pyramidal bosses. On the Z grill the tips of the pyramids are very short horizontal ridges. On the D, E and F grills the ridges are vertical.

D. Grill about 12x14mm (15 by 17 to 18 points)

84	A32 2c black	15,000.	3,000.
	No gum	7,500.	

No. 84 is valued in the grade of fine.

85	A25 3c rose	6,000.	950.
	No gum	2,850.	

Z. Grill about 11x14mm (13 to 14 by 17 to 18 points)

85A	A24 1c blue		935,000.
85B	A32 2c black	7,000.	1,100.
	No gum	3,500.	
85C	A25 3c rose	12,500.	3,250.
	No gum	6,000.	
85D	A27 10c green		90,000.
85E	A28 12c black	11,000.	1,500.
	No gum	5,250.	
85F	A33 15c black		220,000.

Two copies of No. 85A are known. One is contained in the New York Public Library collection. Value represents 1998 auction sale price of the single example available to collectors.
Six copies of No. 85D are known. One is in the New York Public Library collection. Value is for a well-centered example with small faults.
Two copies of No. 85F are known. Value represents 1998 auction sale price of the much finer example.

E. Grill about 11x13mm (14 by 15 to 17 points)

86	A24 1c blue	2,750.	450.
	No gum	1,300.	
a.	1c dull blue	2,750.	425.
	No gum	1,300.	
87	A32 2c black	1,400.	140.
	No gum	625.	
a.	Diagonal half used as 1c on cover		2,000.
b.	Vertical half used as 1c on cover		2,000.
88	A25 3c rose	800.	22.50
	No gum	375.	
a.	3c lake red	875.	25.00
	No gum	400.	
89	A27 10c green	5,000.	300.
	No gum	2,200.	
90	A28 12c black	4,500.	350.
	No gum	2,000.	
91	A33 15c black	8,750.	625.
	No gum	4,000.	

F. Grill about 9x13mm (11 to 12 by 15 to 17 points)

92	A24 1c blue	1,000.	200.
a.	1c pale blue	1,000.	200.
	No gum	450.	
93	A32 2c black	475.	47.50
	No gum	210.	
a.	Vertical half used as 1c as part of 3c rate on cover		1,250.
b.	Diagonal half used as 1c as part of 3c rate on cover		1,250.
c.	Horizontal half used alone as 1c on cover		2,500.
d.	Diagonal half used alone as 1c on cover		2,500.
94	A25 3c red	360.	7.50
	3c rose	360.	7.50
	No gum	160.	
c.	Vert. pair, imperf. horiz.	1,100.	
d.	Printed on both sides	2,250.	

The imperf. 3c can be found in the Scott U.S. Specialized Catalogue Die and Plate Proofs section.

95	A26 5c brown	3,000.	750.
	No gum	1,400.	
a.	5c black brown	3,250.	950.
	No gum	1,500.	

Values for Nos. 95, 95a reflect the normal small margins.

96	A27 10c yel green	2,500.	200.
a.	10c dark green	2,500.	200.
	No gum	1,125.	
97	A28 12c black	2,800.	225.
	No gum	1,250.	
98	A33 15c black	3,250.	300.
	No gum	1,400.	
99	A29 24c gray lilac	6,000.	850.
	No gum	2,750.	
100	A30 30c orange	5,500.	750.
	No gum	2,500.	

Values for No. 100 are for copies with small margins, especially at sides. Large-margined examples sell for much more.

101	A31 90c blue	10,000.	1,500.
	No gum	4,750.	

Some authorities believe that more than one size of grill probably existed on one of the grill rolls.

Re-issue of 1861-66 Issues
Without Grill
Hard White Paper
White Crackly Gum

1875   *Perf. 12*

102	A24	1c blue	750.	1,100.
		No gum	400.	
103	A32	2c black	3,250.	5,000.
		No gum	1,950.	
104	A25	3c brown red	3,500.	5,750.
		No gum	2,100.	
105	A26	5c brown	2,750.	2,900.
		No gum	1,650.	
106	A27	10c green	3,000.	12,500.
		No gum	1,800.	
107	A28	12c black	4,250.	6,000.
		No gum	2,500.	
108	A33	15c black	4,250.	9,000.
		No gum	2,500.	
109	A29	24c deep violet	5,000.	9,000.
		No gum	3,000.	
110	A30	30c brownish org	5,000.	12,500.
		No gum	3,000.	
111	A31	90c blue	6,250.	50,000.
		No gum	3,800.	

These stamps can be distinguished from the 1861-66 issues by the shades and the paper which is hard and very white instead of yellowish. The gum is white and crackly.

Franklin — A34

Post Horse and Rider — A35

Locomotive A36

Washington A37

Shield and Eagle — A38

S. S. Adriatic — A39

Landing of Columbus — A40

FIFTEEN CENTS
Type I. Picture unframed.

A40a

Type II. Picture framed.
Type III. Same as type I but without fringe of brown shading lines around central vignette.

Declaration of Independence A41

Shield, Eagle and Flags A42

Lincoln — A43

G. Grill measuring 9½x9mm
(12 by 11 to 11½ points)

1869   *Perf. 12*

112	A34	1c buff	750.00	160.00
		No gum	350.00	
	b.	Without grill	6,000.	
113	A35	2c brown	700.00	75.00
		No gum	325.00	
	c.	Half used as 1c on cover, diagonal, vert. or horiz.		3,000.
	d.	Printed on both sides		9,000.
114	A36	3c ultramarine	300.00	20.00
	a.	Without grill	135.00	
	b.	Vertical one third used as 1c on cover	1,100.	
	c.	Vertical two thirds used as 2c on cover		4,000.
	e.	Printed on both sides		—
115	A37	6c ultramarine	2,750.	210.00
		No gum	1,250.	
	b.	Vertical half used as 3c on cover		—
116	A38	10c yellow	2,000.	140.
		No gum	925.	
117	A39	12c green	2,250.	150.
		No gum	1,000.	
118	A40	15c brn & bl, I	7,500.	650.
		No gum	3,600.	
	a.	Without grill	10,000.	
119	A40a	15c brn & bl, II	3,250.	250.
		No gum	1,500.	
	b.	Center inverted	275,000.	18,000.
	c.	Center dbl., one invtd.		35,000.
120	A41	24c green & vio	7,000.	750.
		No gum	3,400.	
	a.	Without grill	9,500.	
	b.	Center inverted	275,000.	19,000.
121	A42	30c ultra & car	7,000.	550.
		No gum	3,400.	
	a.	Without grill	11,000.	
	b.	Flags inverted	210,000.	65,000.
122	A43	90c car & black	9,250.	2,400.
		No gum	4,500.	
	a.	Without grill	16,000.	

Values of varieties of Nos. 112-122 without grill are for copies with original gum. Most copies of Nos. 119b, 120b are faulty. Values are for fine centered copies with only minimal faults.

Re-issues of the 1869 Issue
Without Grill
Hard White Paper
White Crackly Gum

1875   *Perf. 12*

123	A34	1c buff	500.	325.
		No gum	275.	
124	A35	2c brown	700.	475.
		No gum	375.	
125	A36	3c blue	5,250.	15,000.
		No gum	3,000.	

Used value for No. 125 is for an attractive copy with minimal faults.

126	A37	6c blue	1,600.	1,700.
		No gum	875.	
127	A38	10c yellow	2,100.	1,750.
		No gum	1,150.	
128	A39	12c green	2,750.	2,750.
		No gum	1,550.	
129	A40	15c brn & bl, III	2,000.	1,000.
		No gum	1,100.	
	a.	Imperf. horiz., single	4,000.	7,000.
		No gum	3,000.	

Type III is same as type I but without fringe of brown shading lines around central vignette.

130	A41	24c green & violet	2,250.	1,400.
		No gum	1,200.	
131	A42	30c ultra & car	3,000.	2,500.
		No gum	1,650.	
132	A43	90c car & blk	5,000.	5,500.
		No gum	2,750.	

1880-81

Soft Porous Paper

133	A34	1c buff	325.	200.
		No gum	150.	
	a.	1c brown orange ('81)	240.	175.

No. 133 was issued with gum, No. 133a without gum.

Printed by the National Bank Note Company

Franklin — A44

A44

A45

Jackson — A45

Washington — A46

A46

Lincoln — A47

A47

Edwin M. Stanton — A48

A48

Jefferson — A49

A49

Henry Clay — A50

A44

A50

Daniel Webster — A51

A51

Gen. Winfield Scott A52

Alexander Hamilton A53

Commodore O. H. Perry — A54

Two varieties of grill are known on this issue.

H. Grill about 10x12mm
(11 to 13 by 14 to 16 points)
On all values, 1c to 90c
I. Grill about 8½x10mm
(10 to 11 by 10 to 13 points)
On 1, 2, 3, 6, 7, 10 and 15c

On the 1870-71 stamps the grill impressions are usually faint or incomplete. This is especially true of the H grill, which often shows only a few points.

Values for 1c-7c are for stamps showing well-defined grills.

White Wove Paper

1870-71				Perf. 12
134	A44	1c ultramarine	2,000.	140.00
		No gum	900.00	
135	A45	2c red brown	1,200.	70.00
		No gum	550.00	
a.		Diagonal half used as 1c on cover	—	
b.		Vertical half used as 1c on cover	—	
136	A46	3c green	725.00	20.00
		No gum	325.00	

The imperf. 3c can be found in the Scott U.S. Specialized Catalogue Die and Plate Proofs section.

137	A47	6c carmine	4,250.	525.
		No gum	1,900.	
138	A48	7c ver ('71)	3,000.	425.
		No gum	1,350.	
139	A49	10c brown	4,750.	650.
		No gum	2,150.	
140	A50	12c dull violet	22,500.	3,000.
		No gum	11,000.	
141	A51	15c orange	5,750.	1,200.
		No gum	2,700.	
142	A52	24c purple	—	6,250.

No. 142 is valued in the grade of fine.

143	A53	30c black	14,000.	2,400.
		No gum	6,400.	
144	A54	90c carmine	13,500.	1,600.
		No gum	6,500.	

Without Grill
White Wove Paper

1870-71				Perf. 12
145	A44	1c ultramarine	475.00	15.00
		No gum	210.00	
146	A45	2c red brown	325.00	9.00
		No gum	140.00	
a.		Diagonal half used as 1c on cover		650.00
b.		Vertical half used as 1c on cover		750.00
c.		Horiz. half used as 1c on cover		750.00
d.		Double impression	—	
147	A46	3c green	300.00	1.50
		No gum	130.00	
a.		Printed on both sides		1,750.
b.		Double impression		1,250.

The imperf. 3c can be found in the Scott U.S. Specialized Catalogue Die and Plate Proofs section.

148	A47	6c carmine	675.00	25.00
		No gum	300.00	
a.		Vert. half used as 3c on cover		—
b.		Double impression		1,500.
149	A48	7c vermilion ('71)	850.00	90.00
		No gum	375.00	
150	A49	10c brown	750.00	20.00
		No gum	325.00	
151	A50	12c dull violet	1,750.	160.00
		No gum	800.00	
152	A51	15c bright orange	1,900.	160.00
		No gum	850.00	
a.		Double impression		1,650.
153	A52	24c purple	1,500.	140.00
		No gum	675.00	
154	A53	30c black	5,000.	190.00
		No gum	2,250.	
155	A54	90c carmine	4,000.	300.00
		No gum	1,850.	

Printed by the Continental Bank Note Co.

Designs of the 1870-71 Issue with secret marks on the values from 1c to 15c as described and illustrated below.

Franklin — A44a

1c. In pearl at left of numeral "1" is a small crescent.

Jackson — A45a

2c. Under the scroll at the left of "U. S." there is a small diagonal line. This mark seldom shows clearly. The stamp, No. 157, can be distinguished by its color.

Washington — A46a

3c. The under part of the upper tail of the left ribbon is heavily shaded.

Lincoln — A47a

6c. The first four vertical lines of the shading in the lower part of the left ribbon have been strengthened.

Stanton — A48a

7c. Two small semi-circles are drawn around the ends of the lines that outline the ball in the lower right hand corner.

Jefferson — A49a

10c. There is a small semi-circle in the scroll at the right end of the upper label.

Clay — A50a

12c. The balls of the figure "2" are crescent shaped.

Webster — A51a

15c. In the lower part of the triangle in the upper left corner two lines have been made heavier forming a "V."

This mark can be found on some of the Continental and American (1879) printings, but not all stamps show it.

Secret marks were added to the dies of the 24c, 30c and 90c but new plates can be distinguished only by the shades and paper.

White Wove Paper, thin to thick
Without Grill*

1873				Perf. 12
156	A44a	1c ultramarine	225.00	3.75
		No gum	95.00	
e.		With grill	2,000.	
f.		Imperf., pair	—	550.00
157	A45a	2c brown	375.00	17.50
		No gum	170.00	
c.		With grill	1,850.	750.00
d.		Double impression		

e.		Vertical half used as 1c on cover	—	
158	A46a	3c green	130.00	.60
		No gum	50.00	
e.		With grill	500.00	
h.		Horiz. pair, imperf. vert.	—	
i.		Horiz. pair, imperf. btwn.	1,300.	
j.		Double impression	2,500.	
k.		Printed on both sides		

The imperf 3c, with and without grill, can be found in the Scott U.S. Specialized Catalogue Die and Plate Proofs section.

159	A47a	6c dull pink	425.00	17.50
		No gum	190.00	
b.		With grill	1,800.	
160	A48a	7c orange ver	1,100.	80.00
		No gum	500.00	
b.		With grill	3,250.	
161	A49a	10c brown	700.00	18.00
		No gum	325.00	
c.		With grill	3,500.	
d.		Horiz. pair, imperf. btwn.		2,500.
162	A50a	12c black violet	1,800.	95.00
		No gum	800.00	
a.		With grill	5,250.	
163	A51a	15c yellow orange	2,100.	110.00
		No gum	950.00	
a.		With grill	5,250.	
164	A52	24c purple	—	—
165	A53	30c gray black	2,500.	100.00
		No gum	1,150.	
c.		With grill	22,500.	
166	A54	90c rose carmine	2,750.	250.00
		No gum	1,250.	

The Philatelic Foundation has certified as genuine a 24c on vertically ribbed paper, and that is the unique stamp listed as No. 164. Specialists believe that only Continental used ribbed paper. It is not known for sure whether or not Continental also printed the 24c value on regular paper; if it did, specialists currently are not able to distinguish these from No. 153.
* All values except 24c, 90c exist with experimental (J) grill, about 7x9 ½mm.

Special Printing of the 1873 Issue
Hard, White Wove Paper
Without Gum

1875				Perf. 12
167	A44a	1c ultramarine	11,500.	
168	A45a	2c dark brown	5,250.	
169	A46a	3c blue green	12,500.	
170	A47a	6c dull rose	12,500.	
171	A48a	7c redsh ver	3,000.	
172	A49a	10c pale brown	12,500.	
173	A50a	12c dark violet	4,250.	
174	A51a	15c bright orange	12,500.	
175	A52	24c dull purple	2,900.	5,000.
176	A53	30c greenish black	10,000.	
177	A54	90c violet car	12,500.	

Although perforated, these stamps were usually cut apart with scissors. As a result, the perforations are often much mutilated and the design is frequently damaged.

These can be distinguished from the 1873 issue by the shades, also by the paper, which is very white instead of yellowish.

These and the subsequent issues listed under this heading were special printings of stamps then in current use which, together with the reprints and reissues, were made for sale to collectors.

They were available for postage except for the Officials and demonetized issues.

Zachary Taylor — A55

Yellowish Wove Paper

1875, June 21				Perf. 12
178	A45a	2c vermilion	400.00	10.00
		No gum	175.00	
b.		Half used as 1c on cover		—
c.		With grill		750.00

The imperf 2c can be found in the Scott U.S. Specialized Catalogue Die and Plate Proofs section.

179	A55	5c blue	550.00	20.00
		No gum	250.00	
c.		With grill		1,000.

Almost all of the stamps of the Continental Bank Note Co. printing including the Department stamps and some of the Newspaper stamps may be found upon a paper that shows more or less of the characteristics of a ribbed paper.

Special Printing of the 1875 Issue
Hard, White Wove Paper
Without Gum

1875				
180	A45a	2c carmine ver	30,000.	
181	A55	5c bright blue	75,000.	

Printed by the American Bank Note Company
Same as 1870-75 Issues
Soft Porous Paper
Varying from Thin to Thick

1879				Perf. 12
182	A44a	1c dark ultra	300.00	3.50
		No gum	120.00	
183	A45a	2c vermilion	130.00	3.00
		No gum	55.00	
a.		Double impression		
184	A46a	3c green	100.00	.60
		No gum	37.50	
b.		Double impression		

The imperf 3c can be found in the Scott U.S. Specialized Catalogue Die and Plate Proofs section.

185	A55	5c blue	500.00	12.00
		No gum	225.00	
186	A47a	6c pink	950.00	20.00
		No gum	425.00	
187	A49	10c brn (without secret mark)	2,500.	25.00
		No gum	1,100.	
188	A49a	10c brown (with secret mark)	1,750.	25.00
		No gum	800.00	
189	A51a	15c red orange	350.00	22.50
		No gum	150.00	
190	A53	30c full black	1,100.	55.00
		No gum	500.00	
191	A54	90c carmine	2,250.	275.00
		No gum	1,050.	

The ABN Co. used many Continental plates to print the postage, Departmental and Newspaper stamps. Therefore, stamps bearing the Continental imprint were not always its product.

The ABN Co. also used the National 90c plate and possibly the 30c plate.

Early printings of No. 188 were from Continental plates 302 and 303 which contained the normal secret mark of 1873. After those plates were re-entered by the ABN Co. in 1880, pairs or multiple pieces contained combinations of normal, hairline or missing marks. The pairs or other multiples usually found contain at least one hairline mark which tended to disappear as the plate wore.

ABN Co. plates 377 and 378 were made in 1881 from the National transfer roll of 1870. No. 187 from those plates has no secret mark.

Perf 12 Trial Color Proofs on gummed stamp paper exist, as does a 15c without the blue "SAMPLE" overprint.

The imperf. 90c can be found in the Scott U.S. Specialized Catalogue Die and Plate Proofs section.

Special Printing of the 1879 Issue
Soft Porous Paper
Without Gum

1880				Perf. 12
192	A44a	1c dark ultra	25,000.	
193	A45a	2c black brown	10,000.	
194	A46a	3c blue green	40,000.	
195	A47a	6c dull rose	20,000.	
196	A48a	7c scar vermilion	3,500.	
197	A49a	10c deep brown	17,000.	
198	A50a	12c black purple	5,000.	
199	A51a	15c orange	17,000.	
200	A52	24c dark violet	5,000.	
201	A53	30c grnsh black	12,500.	
202	A54	90c dull carmine	15,000.	
203	A45a	2c scar vermilion	40,000.	
204	A55	5c deep blue	45,000.	

No. 197 was printed from Continental plate 302 (or 303) after plate was re-entered, therefore stamp may show normal, hairline or missing secret mark.

James A.
Garfield — A56

1882, Apr. 10   *Perf. 12*
205 A56 5c yellow brown   275.00   9.00
    No gum   100.00

Special Printing
Soft Porous Paper
Without Gum

1882
205C A56 5c gray brown   35,000.

Designs of 1873 Re-engraved

Franklin — A44b

1c. The vertical lines in the upper part of the stamp have been so deepened that the background often appears to be solid.
Lines of shading have been added to the upper arabesques.

Washington — A46b

3c. The shading at the sides of the central oval appears only about one-half the previous width.
A short horizontal dash has been cut about 1mm below the "TS" of "CENTS."

Lincoln — A47b

6c. On the original stamps four vertical lines can be counted from the edge of the panel to the outside of the stamp.
On the re-engraved stamps there are but three lines in the same place.

Jefferson — A49b

10c. On the original stamps there are five vertical lines between the left side of the oval and the edge of the shield. There are only four lines on the re-engraved stamps.
In the lower part of the latter, also, the horizontal lines of the background have been strengthened.

1881-82   *Perf. 12*
206 A44b 1c gray blue   80.00   .90
    No gum   27.50
207 A46b 3c blue green   80.00   .55
    No gum   27.50
   c.   Double impression
208 A47b 6c rose ('82)   550.00   80.00
    No gum   200.00
   a.   6c deep brown red   475.00   110.00
    No gum   190.00
209 A49b 10c brown ('82)   160.00   6.00
    No gum   60.00
   b.   10c black brown   1,000.   150.00
    No gum   400.00
   c.   Double impression
    Nos. 206-209 (4)   870.00   87.45

Specimen stamps (usually overprinted "Sample") without overprint exist in a brown shade that differs from No. 209. The unoverprinted brown specimen is cheaper than No. 209. Expertization is recommended.

Washington
A57

Jackson
A58

1883, Oct. 1   *Perf. 12*
210 A57 2c red brown   50.00   .60
    No gum   20.00
211 A58 4c blue green   275.00   17.50
    No gum   100.00

Imperfs can be found in the Scott U.S. Specialized Catalogue Die and Plate Proofs section.

Special Printing
Soft Porous Paper

1883-85
211B A57 2c pale red brown   500.   —
    Never hinged   750.
    No gum   200.
   c.   Horiz. pair, imperf. btwn.   2,000.
211D A58 4c deep blue grn   27,500.

No. 211D is without gum.

Franklin — A59

1887   *Perf. 12*
212 A59 1c ultramarine   110.00   1.75
    No gum   40.00
213 A57 2c green   50.00   .40
    No gum   17.50
   b.   Printed on both sides
214 A46b 3c vermilion   80.00   60.00
    No gum   30.00
    Nos. 212-214 (3)   240.00   62.15

Imperf 1c, 2c can be found in the Scott U.S. Specialized Catalogue Die and Plate Proofs section.

1888   *Perf. 12*
215 A58 4c carmine   225.00   20.00
    No gum   85.00
216 A56 5c indigo   240.00   14.00
    No gum   90.00
217 A53 30c orange brown   450.00   110.00
    No gum   170.00
218 A54 90c purple   1,300.   250.00
    No gum   500.00
    Nos. 215-218 (4)   2,465.   394.00

Imperfs can be found in the Scott U.S. Specialized Catalogue Die and Plate Proofs section.

IMPORTANT INFORMATION REGARDING VALUES FOR NEVER-HINGED STAMPS

Collectors should be aware that the values given for never-hinged stamps from No. 219 on are for stamps in the grade of very fine, just as the value of all stamps in the catalogue are for very fine stamps unless indicated otherwise. The never-hinged premium as a percentage of value will be larger for stamps in extremely fine or superb grades, and the premium will be smaller for fine-very fine, fine or poor examples. This is particularly true of the issues of the late-19th and early-20th centuries. For example, in the grade of very fine, an unused stamp from this time period may be valued at $100 hinged and $180 never hinged. The never-hinged premium is thus 80%. But in a grade of extremely fine, this same stamp will not only sell for more hinged, but the never-hinged premium will increase, perhaps to 100%-300% or more over the higher extremely fine value.

In a grade of superb, a hinged copy will sell for much more than a very fine copy, and additionally the never-hinged premium will be much larger, perhaps as large as 300%-400% or more. On the other hand, the same stamp in a grade of fine or fine-very fine not only will sell for less than a very fine stamp in hinged condition, but additionally the never-hinged premium will be smaller than the never-hinged premium on a very fine stamp, perhaps as small as 15%-30%.

Please note that the above statements and percentages are NOT a formula for arriving at the values of stamps in hinged or never-hinged condition in the grades of fine, fine to very fine, extremely fine or superb. The percentages given apply only to the size of the premium for never-hinged condition that might be added to the stamp value for hinged condition.

The marketplace will determine what this value will be for grades other than very fine. Further, the percentages given are only generalized estimates. Some stamps or grades may have percentages for never-hinged condition that are higher or lower than the ranges given.

VALUES FOR NEVER-HINGED STAMPS PRIOR TO SCOTT 219

This catalogue does not value pre-1890 stamps in never-hinged condition.

Premiums for never-hinged condition in the classic era invariably are even larger than those premiums listed for the post-1890 issues.

Generally speaking, the earlier the stamp is listed in the catalogue, the larger will be the never-hinged premium. On some early classics, the premium will be several multiples of the unused, hinged values given in the catalogue.

Franklin
A60

Washington
A61

Jackson
A62

Lincoln
A63

Ulysses S.
Grant
A64

Garfield
A65

William T.
Sherman
A66

Daniel
Webster
A67

Henry Clay
A68

Jefferson
A69

Perry — A70

1890-93   *Perf. 12*
219 A60 1c dull blue   27.50   .50
    Never hinged   55.00
219D A61 2c lake   250.00   1.00
    Never hinged   500.00
220 A61 2c carmine   22.50   .45
    Never hinged   45.00
   a.   Cap on left "2"   100.00   2.50
    Never hinged   200.00
   c.   Cap on both "2's"   500.00   20.00
    Never hinged   1,000.
221 A62 3c purple   80.00   7.50
    Never hinged   160.00
222 A63 4c dark brown   90.00   2.75
    Never hinged   180.00
223 A64 5c chocolate   80.00   2.75
    Never hinged   160.00
224 A65 6c brown red   85.00   20.00
    Never hinged   170.00
225 A66 8c lilac ('93)   60.00   13.00
    Never hinged   120.00
226 A67 10c green   190.00   3.50
    Never hinged   380.00
227 A68 15c indigo   250.00   20.00
    Never hinged   500.00
228 A69 30c black   400.00   30.00
    Never hinged   800.00
229 A70 90c orange   600.00   125.00
    Never hinged   1,250.
    Nos. 219-229 (12)   2,135.   226.45

The "cap on right 2" variety is due to imperfect inking, not a plate defect.
Imperfs. can be found in the Scott U.S. Specialized Catalogue Die and Plate Proofs section.

Columbian Exposition Issue

Columbus in Sight of Land
A71

Landing of Columbus
A72

Flagship of Columbus
A73

Fleet of Columbus A74

Columbus Soliciting Aid from Isabella A75

Columbus Welcomed at Barcelona A76

Columbus Restored to Favor A77

Columbus Presenting Natives A78

Columbus Announcing his Discovery — A79

Columbus at La Rábida A80

Recall of Columbus A81

Isabella Pledging her Jewels A82

Columbus in Chains A83

Columbus Describing his Third Voyage A84

Isabella & Columbus A85

Columbus A86

1893 — Perf. 12

230	A71	1c deep blue	22.50	.40
		Never hinged	45.00	
231	A72	2c brown violet	21.00	.25
		Never hinged	42.50	
232	A73	3c green	60.00	15.00
		Never hinged	120.00	
233	A74	4c ultra	87.50	7.50
		Never hinged	175.00	
a.		4c blue (error)	19,000.	15,000.
		Never hinged	27,500.	
234	A75	5c chocolate	95.00	8.00
		Never hinged	190.00	
235	A76	6c purple	85.00	22.50
		Never hinged	170.00	
a.		6c red violet	85.00	22.50
		Never hinged	170.00	
236	A77	8c magenta	75.00	11.00
		Never hinged	150.00	
237	A78	10c black brown	140.00	8.00
		Never hinged	280.00	
238	A79	15c dark green	240.00	65.00
		Never hinged	480.00	
239	A80	30c orange brn	300.00	85.00
		Never hinged	650.00	
240	A81	50c slate blue	600.00	160.00
		Never hinged	1,300.	
241	A82	$1 salmon	1,300.	650.00
		Never hinged	3,100.	
		No gum	675.00	
242	A83	$2 brown red	1,400.	600.00
		Never hinged	3,500.	
		No gum	675.00	
243	A84	$3 yellow green	2,100.	1,100.
		Never hinged	5,250.	
		No gum	1,150.	
a.		$3 olive green	2,100.	1,100.
		Never hinged	5,250.	
		No gum	1,150.	
244	A85	$4 crimson lake	2,900.	1,350.
		Never hinged	7,000.	
		No gum	1,500.	
a.		$4 rose carmine	2,900.	1,350.
		Never hinged	7,000.	
		No gum	1,500.	
245	A86	$5 black	3,250.	1,700.
		Never hinged	8,250.	
		No gum	1,750.	

World's Columbian Expo., Chicago, May 1-Oct. 30, 1893.
Nos. 230-245 are known imperf, but were not regularly issued.
See Scott U. S. Specialized Catalogue Die and Plate Proofs for the 2c.

Never-Hinged Stamps
See note after No. 218 regarding premiums for never-hinged stamps.

Bureau Issues
Starting in 1894, the Bureau of Engraving and Printing at Washington produced most U.S. postage stamps.
Until 1965 Bureau-printed stamps were engraved except Nos. 525-536, which are offset.
The combination of lithography and engraving (see #1253) was first used in 1964, and photogravure (see #1426) in 1971.

Franklin A87

Washington A88

Jackson A89

Lincoln A90

Grant A91

Garfield A92

Sherman A93

Webster A94

Clay A95

Jefferson A96

Perry A97

James Madison A98

John Marshall — A99

TWO CENTS

Triangle A (Type I)   Triangle B (Type II)

Type I. The horizontal lines of the ground work run across the triangle and are of the same thickness within it as without.

Type II. The horizontal lines cross the triangle but are thinner within it than without.

Triangle C (Types III and IV)

Type III. The horizontal lines do not cross the double frame lines of the triangle.
The lines within the triangle are thin, as in type II. Otherwise, design as type II.

Type IV

Type IV. Same triangle C as type III.
But other design differences include: (1) re-cutting and lengthening of hairline, (2) shaded toga button, (3) strengthening of lines on sleeve, (4) additional dots on ear, (5) "T" of "TWO" straight at right, (6) background lines extend into white oval opposite "U" of "UNITED." Many other differences exist.

ONE DOLLAR

Type I

Type I. The circles enclosing "$1" are broken where they meet the curved line below "One Dollar." The 15 left vert. rows of impressions from plate 76 are Type I, the balance Type II.

Type II

Type II. The circles are complete.

1894 — Unwmk. — Perf. 12

246	A87	1c ultramarine	32.50	4.50
		Never hinged	60.00	
247	A87	1c blue	67.50	2.25
		Never hinged	125.00	
248	A88	2c pink, Type I	27.50	3.25
		Never hinged	55.00	
249	A88	2c car lake, I	145.00	3.00
		Never hinged	290.00	
250	A88	2c car, I	30.00	1.20
		Never hinged	60.00	
a.		2c rose, I	30.00	2.25
		Never hinged	60.00	
b.		2c scarlet, I ('95)	30.00	.45
		Never hinged	60.00	
c.		Vert. pair, imperf. horiz.	4,500.	
d.		Horiz. pair, imperf. btwn.	2,000.	
251	A88	2c car, II	275.00	6.00
		Never hinged	550.00	
a.		2c scarlet, II	275.00	4.00
		Never hinged	550.00	
252	A88	2c car, III	120.00	6.00
		Never hinged	240.00	
a.		2c scarlet, III	120.00	6.00
		Never hinged	240.00	
b.		Horiz. pair, imperf. vert.	1,500.	
c.		Horiz. pair, imperf. btwn.	1,750.	
253	A89	3c purple	110.00	9.00
		Never hinged	220.00	
254	A90	4c dark brown	150.00	4.25
		Never hinged	300.00	
255	A91	5c chocolate	110.00	6.00
		Never hinged	220.00	
c.		Vert. pair, imperf. horiz.	2,500.	
256	A92	6c dull brown	175.00	22.50
		Never hinged	350.00	
a.		Vert. pair, imperf. horiz.	1,600.	
257	A93	8c vio brn ('95)	140.00	16.00
		Never hinged	280.00	
258	A94	10c dark green	275.00	11.00
		Never hinged	550.00	
259	A95	15c dark blue	300.00	55.00
		Never hinged	600.00	
260	A96	50c orange	550.00	120.00
		Never hinged	1,000.	
261	A97	$1 black, I	1,000.	350.00
		Never hinged	2,100.	
		No gum	350.	
261A	A97	$1 black, II	2,300.	700.00
		Never hinged	4,800.	
		No gum	750.	
262	A98	$2 bright blue	3,100.	1,100.
		Never hinged	6,750.	
		No gum	1,200.	
263	A99	$5 dark green	5,000.	2,250.
		Never hinged	11,000.	
		No gum	2,600.	

For imperfs. and the 2c pink, vert. pair, imperf. horiz., see Scott U. S. Specialized Catalogue Die and Plate Proofs.

Same as 1894 Issue
1895 — Wmk. 191 — Perf. 12

264	A87	1c blue	6.50	.30
		Never hinged	13.00	
265	A88	2c car, I	30.00	1.50
		Never hinged	60.00	
266	A88	2c car, II	30.00	3.25
		Never hinged	60.00	
267	A88	2c car, III	5.50	.25
		Never hinged	11.00	
a.		2c pink, III ('97	6.00	.60
		Never hinged	12.00	
b.		2c vermilion, III ('99)	27.50	
c.		2c rose car, III ('99)	—	

The three left vertical rows from plate 170 are type II, the balance being type III.

268	A89	3c purple	37.50	1.25
		Never hinged	75.00	
269	A90	4c dark brown	40.00	1.75
		Never hinged	80.00	
270	A91	5c chocolate	37.50	2.10
		Never hinged	75.00	
271	A92	6c dull brown	95.00	4.75
		Never hinged	190.00	
a.		Wmkd. USIR	9,000.	5,000.

272	A93	8c violet brown	65.00	1.40
		Never hinged	130.00	
a.		Wmkd. USIR	3,250.	600.00
273	A94	10c dark green	95.00	1.60
		Never hinged	190.00	
274	A95	15c dark blue	225.00	10.00
		Never hinged	450.00	
275	A96	50c orange	300.00	22.50
		Never hinged	600.00	
a.		50c red orange	325.00	27.50
		Never hinged	650.00	
276	A97	$1 blk, I	650.00	80.00
		Never hinged	1,350.	
		No gum	190.00	
276A	A97	$1 blk, II	1,300.	175.00
		Never hinged	2,700.	
		No gum	425.00	
277	A98	$2 bright blue	1,100.	350.00
		Never hinged	2,300.	
		No gum	400.00	
a.		$2 dark blue	1,100.	350.00
		Never hinged	2,300.	
		No gum	400.00	
278	A99	$5 dark green	2,400.	500.00
		Never hinged	5,000.	
		No gum	950.	

For imperfs. and the 1c horiz. pair, imperf. vert., see Scott U. S. Specialized Catalogue Die and Plate Proofs.
For "I.R." overprints see Nos. R155-R158.

TEN CENTS

Type I

Type I. Tips of foliate ornaments do not impinge on white curved line below "TEN CENTS."

Type II

Type II. Tips of ornaments break curved line below "E" of "TEN" and "T" of "CENTS."

1897-1903		**Wmk. 191**	*Perf. 12*	
279	A87	1c dp grn ('98)	9.00	.30
		Never hinged	18.00	
279B	A88	2c red, IV ('99)	9.00	.30
		Never hinged	18.00	
c.		2c rose car, IV ('99)	250.00	75.00
		Never hinged	500.00	
d.		2c org red, IV ('00)	10.00	.35
		Never hinged	20.00	
e.		Booklet pane of 6 ('00)	425.00	425.00
		Never hinged	750.00	
f.		2c carmine, IV	10.00	.30
		Never hinged	20.00	
g.		2c pink, IV	11.00	.45
		Never hinged	22.00	
h.		2c ver, IV ('99)	10.00	.30
		Never hinged	20.00	
i.		2c brn org, IV ('99)	100.00	6.00
		Never hinged	200.00	
280	A90	4c rose brn ('98)	30.00	1.00
		Never hinged	60.00	
a.		4c lilac brown	30.00	.90
		Never hinged	60.00	1.00
b.		4c orange brown	30.00	1.00
		Never hinged	60.00	
281	A91	5c dk bl ('98)	35.00	.85
		Never hinged	70.00	
282	A92	6c lake ('98)	45.00	2.75
		Never hinged	90.00	
a.		6c purple lake	60.00	3.75
		Never hinged	120.00	
282C	A94	10c brn, I ('98)	180.00	2.75
		Never hinged	360.00	
283	A94	10c org brn, II	110.00	2.25
		Never hinged	220.00	
284	A95	15c ol grn ('98)	150.00	8.25
		Never hinged	300.00	
		Nos. 279-284 (8)	568.00	18.45

For "I.R." overprints see Nos. R153-R154.

VALUES FOR VERY FINE STAMPS
Please note: Stamps are valued in the grade of very fine unless otherwise indicated.

Trans-Mississippi Exposition Issue

Marquette on the Mississippi
A100

Farming in the West
A101

Indian Hunting Buffalo
A102

Fremont on the Rocky Mountains
A103

Troops Guarding Wagon Train — A104

Hardships of Emigration
A105

Western Mining Prospector
A106

Western Cattle in Storm
A107

Mississippi River Bridge
A108

1898, June 17		**Wmk. 191**	*Perf. 12*	
285	A100	1c dk yel green	30.00	6.25
		Never hinged	60.00	
286	A101	2c copper red	27.50	1.60
		Never hinged	55.00	
287	A102	4c orange	150.00	24.00
		Never hinged	300.00	
288	A103	5c dull blue	140.00	21.00
		Never hinged	280.00	
289	A104	8c violet brown	180.00	42.50
		Never hinged	360.00	
a.		Vert. pair, imperf. horiz.	22,500.	
290	A105	10c gray violet	180.00	27.50
		Never hinged	360.00	
291	A106	50c sage green	650.00	190.00
		Never hinged	1,350.	
292	A107	$1 black	1,250.	550.00
		Never hinged	2,600.	
		No gum	600.	
293	A108	$2 orange brown	2,100.	1,000.
		Never hinged	4,500.	
		No gum	1,050.	
		Nos. 285-293 (9)	6,257.	1,862.

Trans-Mississippi Exposition, Omaha, Neb., June 1 to Nov. 1, 1898.
For "I.R." overprints see #R158A-R158B.

Never-Hinged Stamps
See note after No. 218 regarding premiums for never-hinged stamps.

Pan-American Exposition Issue

Fast Lake Navigation
A109

Farming in the West — *(see col 2)*

"Empire State" Express — A110

Electric Automobile
A111

Bridge at Niagara Falls — A112

Canal Locks at Sault Ste. Marie — A113

Fast Ocean Navigation
A114

1901, May 1		**Wmk. 191**	*Perf. 12*	
294	A109	1c green & black	18.00	3.00
		Never hinged	32.50	
a.		Center inverted	10,000.	8,500.
		Never hinged	15,000.	
295	A110	2c car & black	17.50	1.00
		Never hinged	31.00	
a.		Center inverted	42,500.	17,500.
296	A111	4c dp red brn & black	82.50	15.00
		Never hinged	150.00	
a.		Center inverted	22,500.	
297	A112	5c ultra & black	95.00	14.00
		Never hinged	175.00	
298	A113	8c brn vio & blk	120.00	50.00
		Never hinged	225.00	
299	A114	10c yel brn & blk	170.00	30.00
		Never hinged	325.00	
		Nos. 294-299 (6)	503.00	113.00
		Nos. 294-299, never hinged	938.50	

Buffalo, NY, May 1-Nov. 1, 1901.
No. 296a was a special printing.
Almost all unused copies of Nos. 295a and 296a have partial or disturbed gum. Values are for examples with full original gum that is slightly disturbed.

Franklin
A115

Washington
A116

Jackson
A117

Grant
A118

Lincoln
A119

Garfield
A120

Martha Washington
A121

Webster
A122

Benjamin Harrison
A123

Clay
A124

Jefferson
A125

David G. Farragut
A126

Madison
A127

Marshall
A128

1902-03		**Wmk. 191**	*Perf. 12*	
300	A115	1c blue grn ('03)	12.00	.20
		Never hinged	21.50	
b.		Booklet pane of 6	600.00	2,750.
		Never hinged	1,000.	

301	A116	2c carmine ('03)	16.00	.20
		Never hinged	29.00	
c.		Booklet pane of 6	500.00	2,250.
		Never hinged	850.00	
302	A117	3c brt violet ('03)	55.00	2.75
		Never hinged	100.00	
303	A118	4c brown ('03)	60.00	1.25
		Never hinged	110.00	
304	A119	5c blue ('03)	60.00	1.50
		Never hinged	110.00	
305	A120	6c claret ('03)	72.50	2.50
		Never hinged	130.00	
306	A121	8c violet black ('03)	45.00	2.00
		Never hinged	80.00	
307	A122	10c pale red brn ('03)	70.00	1.40
		Never hinged	125.00	
308	A123	13c purple black	50.00	7.50
		Never hinged	90.00	
309	A124	15c ol grn ('03)	170.00	4.75
		Never hinged	310.00	
310	A125	50c orange ('03)	475.00	22.50
		Never hinged	950.00	
311	A126	$1 black ('03)	775.00	55.00
		Never hinged	1,600.	
		No gum	180.00	
312	A127	$2 dk bl ('03)	1,250.	190.00
		Never hinged	2,600.	
		No gum	300.	
313	A128	$5 dk grn ('03)	3,000.	750.00
		Never hinged	6,500.	
		No gum	850.	
		Nos. 300-313 (14)	7,050.	1,041.

For listings of designs A127 and A128 with Perf. 10, see Nos. 479 and 480.

1906-08   *Imperf.*

314	A115	1c blue green	18.00	15.00
		Never hinged	33.00	
314A	A118	4c brown ('08)	40,000.	35,000.
315	A119	5c blue ('08)	250.00	600.00
		Never hinged	425.00	

No. 314A was issued imperforate but all copies were privately perforated with large oblong perforations at the sides (Schermack type III).

Beware of copies of No. 303 with trimmed perforations and fake private perfs added.

Used copies of Nos. 314 & 315 must have contemporaneous cancels.

Coil Stamps

Imperforate stamps are known fraudulently perforated to resemble coil stamps and part perforate varieties.

1908   *Perf. 12 Horizontally*

316	A115	1c bl grn, pair	115,000.	—
317	A119	5c blue, pair	14,000.	—
		Never hinged	22,500.	

Perf. 12 Vertically

318	A115	1c bl grn, pair	12,000.	—

Coil stamps for use in vending and affixing machines are perforated on two sides only, either horizontally or vertically.

They were first issued in 1908, using perf. 12. This was changed to 8½ in 1910, and to 10 in 1914.

Imperforate sheets of certain denominations were sold to the vending machine companies which applied a variety of private perforations and separations.

Several values of the 1902 and later issues are found on an apparently coarse ribbed paper caused by worn blankets on the printing press and are not true paper varieties.

All examples of Nos. 316-318 must be accompanied by certificates of authenticity issued by recognized expertizing committees.

Washington — A129

Type I   Type II

Type I. Leaf next to left "2" penetrates the border.
Type II. Strong line forming border left of leaf.

1903, Nov. 12   Wmk. 191   *Perf. 12*

319	A129	2c carmine, I	6.00	.20
		Never hinged	11.00	
a.		2c lake, I	—	—
b.		2c carmine rose, I	8.00	.35
		Never hinged	14.50	
c.		2c scarlet, I	6.00	.25
		Never hinged	11.00	
d.		Vert. pair, imperf. horiz.	6,000.	
e.		Vert. pair, imperf. btwn.	1,250.	
f.		2c lake, II	8.00	.25
		Never hinged	14.50	
g.		Booklet pane of 6, car, I	120.00	175.00
		Never hinged	200.00	
h.		As "g," II	290.00	
		Never hinged	475.00	
i.		2c carmine, II	27.50	50.00
		Never hinged	50.00	
j.		2c carmine rose, II	20.00	.75
		Never hinged	35.00	
k.		2c scarlet, II	18.00	.45
		Never hinged	32.50	
m.		As "g," lake, I	—	
n.		As "g," car rose, I	180.00	300.00
		Never hinged	300.00	
p.		As "g," scarlet, I	170.00	275.00
		Never hinged	275.00	
q.		As "g," lake, II	210.00	450.00
		Never hinged	350.00	

1906, Oct. 2   *Imperf.*

320	A129	2c carmine, I	18.00	12.00
		Never hinged	32.50	
a.		2c lake, II	50.00	40.00
		Never hinged	90.00	
b.		2c scarlet, I	18.00	12.50
		Never hinged	32.50	
c.		2c carmine rose, I	55.00	40.00
		Never hinged	100.00	
d.		2c carmine, II	—	

No. 320d was issued imperforate, but all copies were privately perforated with large oblong perforations at the sides (Schermack Type III).

Coil Stamps

1908   *Perf. 12 Horizontally*

321	A129	2c car, pair, I	125,000.	170,000.

Four or five authenticated unused pairs are known.

The used value is for a single on cover, of which two authenticated examples are known, both used from Indianapolis in 1908. Numerous counterfeits exist.

All examples of Nos. 321-322 must be accompanied by certificates of authenticity issued by recognized expertizing committees.

Perf. 12 Vertically

322	A129	2c car, pair, II	11,000.	—

Louisiana Purchase Exposition
St. Louis, Mo., Apr. 30 - Dec. 1, 1904

Robert R. Livingston A130

Thomas Jefferson A131

James Monroe A132

William McKinley A133

Map of Louisiana Purchase A134

1904, Apr. 30   Wmk. 191   *Perf. 12*

323	A130	1c green	30.00	4.00
		Never hinged	55.00	
324	A131	2c carmine	27.50	1.75
		Never hinged	50.00	
a.		Vert. pair, imperf. horiz.	10,000.	
325	A132	3c violet	90.00	30.00
		Never hinged	160.00	
326	A133	5c dark blue	95.00	20.00
		Never hinged	170.00	
327	A134	10c red brown	180.00	30.00
		Never hinged	340.00	
		Nos. 323-327 (5)	422.50	85.75
		Nos. 323-327, never hinged	775.00	

Jamestown Exposition Issue

Captain John Smith — A135

Founding of Jamestown A136

Pocahontas A137

1907   Wmk. 191   *Perf. 12*

328	A135	1c green	30.00	4.00
		Never hinged	55.00	
329	A136	2c carmine	35.00	3.50
		Never hinged	65.00	
330	A137	5c blue	135.00	27.50
		Never hinged	250.00	
		Nos. 328-330 (3)	200.00	35.00
		Nos. 328-330, never hinged	370.00	

Jamestown Expo., Hampton Roads, Va., Apr. 26 to Dec. 1.

Franklin A138   Washington A139

Washington — A140

There are several types of some of the 2c and 3c stamps of this and succeeding issues.

These types are described under the dates when they first appeared.

Illustrations of Types I-VII of the 2c (A140) and Types I-IV of the 3c (A140) are reproduced by permission of H. L. Lindquist.

TYPE I

Type I

THREE CENTS

Type I. Top line of the toga rope is weak and the rope shading lines are thin.
The fifth line from the left is missing.
The line between the lips is thin.
Used on both flat plate and rotary press printings.

1908-09   Wmk. 191   *Perf. 12*

331	A138	1c green	7.25	.20
		Never hinged	13.00	
a.		Booklet pane of 6	160.00	140.00
		Never hinged	250.00	
332	A139	2c carmine	6.75	.20
		Never hinged	12.00	
a.		Booklet pane of 6	135.00	125.00
		Never hinged	210.00	
333	A140	3c deep vio, I	35.00	2.50
		Never hinged	62.50	
334	A140	4c orange brown	42.50	1.00
		Never hinged	75.00	
335	A140	5c blue	52.50	2.00
		Never hinged	95.00	
336	A140	6c red orange	65.00	5.00
		Never hinged	115.00	
337	A140	8c olive green	50.00	2.50
		Never hinged	90.00	
338	A140	10c yellow ('09)	70.00	1.40
		Never hinged	125.00	
339	A140	13c bl grn ('09)	42.50	19.00
		Never hinged	75.00	
340	A140	15c pale ultra ('09)	70.00	5.50
		Never hinged	125.00	
341	A140	50c violet ('09)	350.00	20.00
		Never hinged	625.00	
342	A140	$1 vio brn ('09)	525.00	90.00
		Never hinged	950.00	
		Nos. 331-342 (12)	1,316.	149.30

For listings of China Clay papers see the Scott U.S. Specialized Catalogue.

For listing of other perforated stamps of designs A138, A139 and A140 see

#357-366	Bluish Paper	
#374-382, 405-407	Single line wmk.	Perf. 12
#424-430	Single line wmk.	Perf. 10
#461	Single line wmk.	Perf. 11
#462-469	Unwmkd.	Perf. 10
#498-507	Unwmkd.	Perf. 11
#519	Double line wmk.	Perf. 11
#525-530, 536	Offset printing	
#538-546	Rotary press printing	

Imperf

343	A138	1c green	5.00	4.50
		Never hinged	9.00	
344	A139	2c carmine	6.00	3.00
		Never hinged	11.00	
345	A140	3c dp violet, I	11.50	20.00
		Never hinged	21.00	
346	A140	4c org brn ('09)	19.00	22.50
		Never hinged	35.00	
347	A140	5c blue ('09)	36.00	35.00
		Never hinged	65.00	
		Nos. 343-347 (5)	77.50	85.00

For listings of other imperforate stamps of designs A138, A139 and A140, see #383-384, 408-409, 459 (single line wmk.), #481-485 (unwmkd.), #531-535 (offset printing).

Coil Stamps

1908-10   *Perf. 12 Horizontally*

348	A138	1c green	37.50	22.50
		Never hinged	67.50	
349	A139	2c carmine ('09)	80.00	12.50
		Never hinged	145.00	
350	A140	4c org brn ('10)	170.00	120.00
		Never hinged	310.00	
351	A140	5c blue ('09)	180.00	160.00
		Never hinged	325.00	
		Nos. 348-351 (4)	467.50	315.00

1909   *Perf. 12 Vertically*

352	A138	1c green	95.00	47.50
		Never hinged	170.00	
353	A139	2c carmine	95.00	12.50
		Never hinged	170.00	
354	A140	4c orange brown	220.00	85.00
		Never hinged	400.00	
355	A140	5c blue	230.00	120.00
		Never hinged	415.00	
356	A140	10c yellow	2,500.	1,250.
		Never hinged	4,500.	

Beware of stamps offered as No. 356 which may be examples of No. 338 with perforations trimmed at top and/or bottom.

Beware also of plentiful fakes in the marketplace of Nos. 348-355.

Authentication of all these coil stamps is advised.

For listings of other coil stamps of designs A138, A139 and A140, see #385-396, 410-413, 441-458 (single line wmk.), #486-496 (unwatermarked).

Bluish Paper

This was made with 35 percent rag stock instead of all wood pulp.

The grayish blue color goes through the paper showing clearly on the back as well as on the face.

1909   *Perf. 12*

357	A138	1c green	90.00	100.00
		Never hinged	160.00	
358	A139	2c carmine	85.00	100.00
		Never hinged	155.00	

359	A140	3c dp violet, I	2,000.	2,500.
		Never hinged	3,600.	
360	A140	4c org brn	24,000.	
		Never hinged	35,000.	
361	A140	5c blue	5,000.	12,500.
		Never hinged	8,750.	
362	A140	6c red orange	1,500.	5,000.
		Never hinged	2,700.	
363	A140	8c olive green	26,000.	
		Never hinged	37,500.	
364	A140	10c yellow	1,800.	4,500.
		Never hinged	3,250.	
365	A140	13c blue green	3,000.	2,500.
		Never hinged	5,400.	
366	A140	15c pale ultra	1,450.	9,000.
		Never hinged	2,600.	

Nos. 360, 363 not regularly issued.

Lincoln Centenary of Birth Issue

Lincoln — A141

1909, Feb. 12   Wmk. 191   *Perf. 12*

367	A141	2c carmine	5.50	1.75
		Never hinged	9.50	

Imperf

368	A141	2c carmine	21.00	20.00
		Never hinged	37.50	

1909   Bluish Paper   *Perf. 12*

369	A141	2c carmine	210.00	260.00
		Never hinged	380.00	

Alaska-Yukon-Pacific Exposition Issue

William H. Seward — A142

1909, June 1   Wmk. 191   *Perf. 12*

370	A142	2c carmine	8.75	2.00
		Never hinged	15.00	

1909   *Imperf.*

371	A142	2c carmine	24.00	22.50
		Never hinged	40.00	

Seattle, Wash., June 1 to Oct. 16.

Hudson-Fulton Celebration Issue

"Half Moon" and Steamship A143

1909, Sept. 25   Wmk. 191   *Perf. 12*

372	A143	2c carmine	12.50	4.50
		Never hinged	22.00	

Imperf

373	A143	2c carmine	27.50	25.00
		Never hinged	50.00	

Tercentenary of the discovery of the Hudson River and Centenary of Robert Fulton's steamship.

Designs of 1908-09 Issue

1910-11   Wmk. 190   *Perf. 12*

374	A138	1c green	6.75	.20
		Never hinged	12.00	
a.		Booklet pane of 6	175.00	125.00
		Never hinged	275.00	
375	A139	2c carmine	6.75	.20
		Never hinged	12.00	
a.		Booklet pane of 6	95.00	95.00
		Never hinged	160.00	
b.		2c lake	450.00	
		Never hinged	800.00	
c.		Double impression	500.00	
		Never hinged	1,000.	
376	A140	3c dp vio, I ('11)	20.00	1.50
		Never hinged	36.00	
377	A140	4c brown ('11)	32.50	.50
		Never hinged	57.50	
378	A140	5c blue ('11)	32.50	.50
		Never hinged	57.50	
379	A140	6c red org ('11)	37.50	.70
		Never hinged	67.50	
380	A140	8c ol grn ('11)	115.00	12.50
		Never hinged	210.00	
381	A140	10c yellow ('11)	105.00	3.75
		Never hinged	190.00	
382	A140	15c pale ultra ('11)	275.00	15.00
		Never hinged	500.00	
		Nos. 374-382 (9)	631.00	34.85

1910   *Imperf.*

383	A138	1c green	2.50	2.00
		Never hinged	4.25	
384	A139	2c carmine	4.00	2.50
		Never hinged	7.00	

Coil Stamps

1910   *Perf. 12 Horizontally*

385	A138	1c green	40.00	17.50
		Never hinged	72.50	
386	A139	2c carmine	70.00	22.50
		Never hinged	125.00	

1910-11   *Perf. 12 Vertically*

387	A138	1c green	160.00	55.00
		Never hinged	290.00	
388	A139	2c carmine	900.00	375.00
		Never hinged	1,600.	
389	A140	3c dp vio, I ('11)	57,500.	12,000.
		Never hinged	85,000.	

Stamps sold as Scott 388 frequently are privately perforated examples of No. 384, or examples of No. 375 with top and/or bottom perfs trimmed.
Stamps offered as No. 389 sometimes are examples of No. 376 with top and/or bottom perfs trimmed.
Expertization by competent authorities is recommended.

1910   *Perf. 8½ Horizontally*

390	A138	1c green	5.00	6.50
		Never hinged	9.00	
391	A139	2c carmine	40.00	14.00
		Never hinged	72.50	

1910-13   *Perf. 8½ Vertically*

392	A138	1c green	25.00	22.50
		Never hinged	45.00	
393	A139	2c carmine	47.50	8.50
		Never hinged	85.00	
394	A140	3c dp vio, I ('11)	57.50	52.50
		Never hinged	105.00	
395	A140	4c brown ('12)	57.50	47.50
		Never hinged	105.00	
396	A140	5c blue ('13)	57.50	47.50
		Never hinged	105.00	
		Nos. 392-396 (5)	245.00	178.50

Panama-Pacific Exposition Issue

Vasco Nunez de Balboa — A144

Pedro Miguel Locks, Panama Canal — A145

Golden Gate — A146

Discovery of San Francisco Bay — A147

1913   Wmk. 190   *Perf. 12*

397	A144	1c green	17.50	1.50
		Never hinged	35.00	
398	A145	2c carmine	21.00	.50
		Never hinged	37.50	
a.		2c carmine lake	1,000.	
		Never hinged	1,800.	
399	A146	5c blue	80.00	9.50
		Never hinged	140.00	
400	A147	10c orange yel	135.00	20.00
		Never hinged	240.00	
400A	A147	10c orange	225.00	16.00
		Never hinged	400.00	
		Nos. 397-400A (5)	478.50	47.50
		Nos. 397-400A, never hinged	852.50	

1914-15   *Perf. 10*

401	A144	1c green	25.00	5.50
		Never hinged	45.00	
402	A145	2c carmine ('15)	75.00	1.50
		Never hinged	135.00	
403	A146	5c blue ('15)	175.00	15.00
		Never hinged	310.00	
404	A147	10c orange ('15)	925.00	62.50
		Never hinged	1,650.	
		Nos. 401-404 (4)	1,200.	84.50
		Nos. 401-404, never hinged	2,140.	

San Francisco, Cal., Feb. 20 to Dec. 4.

Type I

TWO CENTS
Type I. One shading line in the first curve of the ribbon above the left "2". One in the second curve of the ribbon above the right "2."
Button of the toga has a faint outline.
Top line of the toga rope, from the button to the front of the throat, very faint.
Shading lines at face terminate in front of the ear with little or no joining, forming a lock of hair.
Used on both flat and rotary press printings.

1912-14   Wmk. 190   *Perf. 12*

405	A140	1c green	6.75	.20
		Never hinged	12.00	
a.		Vert. pair, imperf. horiz.	1,500.	—
b.		Booklet pane of 6	60.00	50.00
		Never hinged	100.00	
406	A140	2c carmine, I	6.75	.20
		Never hinged	12.00	
a.		Booklet pane of 6	60.00	60.00
		Never hinged	100.00	
b.		Double impression		
c.		2c lake, type II	500.00	—
407	A140	7c black ('14)	80.00	11.00
		Never hinged	145.00	
		Nos. 405-407 (3)	93.50	11.40

1912   *Imperf.*

408	A140	1c green	1.10	.55
		Never hinged	2.00	
409	A140	2c carmine, I	1.30	.60
		Never hinged	2.30	

Coil Stamps

1912   *Perf. 8½ Horizontally*

410	A140	1c green	6.00	4.00
		Never hinged	11.00	
411	A140	2c carmine, I	10.00	3.75
		Never hinged	18.00	

Perf. 8½ Vertically

412	A140	1c green	25.00	5.50
		Never hinged	45.00	
413	A140	2c carmine, I	50.00	1.10
		Never hinged	90.00	
		Nos. 410-413 (4)	91.00	14.35

Franklin — A148

1912-14   Wmk. 190   *Perf. 12*

414	A148	8c pale olive grn	45.00	1.25
		Never hinged	80.00	
415	A148	9c sal red ('14)	55.00	12.50
		Never hinged	100.00	
416	A148	10c orange yellow	45.00	.40
		Never hinged	80.00	
a.		10c brown yellow	850.00	—
			1,500.	
417	A148	12c claret brn ('14)	50.00	4.25
		Never hinged	90.00	
418	A148	15c gray	85.00	3.50
		Never hinged	155.00	
419	A148	20c ultra ('14)	200.00	15.00
		Never hinged	360.00	
420	A148	30c org red ('14)	125.00	15.00
		Never hinged	225.00	
421	A148	50c violet ('14)	425.00	17.50
		Never hinged	775.00	
		Nos. 414-421 (8)	1,030.	69.40

No. 421 almost always has an offset of the frame lines on the back under the gum.
No. 422 does not have this offset.

VALUES FOR VERY FINE STAMPS

Please note: Stamps are valued in the grade of Very Fine unless otherwise indicated.

1912, Feb. 12   Wmk. 191   Perf. 12

422	A148	50c violet	250.00	15.00
		Never hinged	450.00	
423	A148	$1 violet brown	525.00	60.00
		Never hinged	950.00	

Other stamps of type A148: #431-440 (single line wmk., perf. 10), #460 (double line wmk., perf. 10), #470-478 (unwmkd., perf. 10), #508-518 (unwmkd., perf. 11).

1914-15   Wmk. 190   Perf. 10

424	A140	1c green	2.50	.20
		Never hinged	4.50	
a.		Perf. 12x10	4,500.	4,000.
b.		Perf. 10x12		4,000.
c.		Vert. pair, imperf. horiz.	1,750.	1,500.
d.		Booklet pane of 6	5.25	3.25
		Never hinged	8.25	
e.		As "d," imperf.	1,600.	
f.		Vert. pair, imperf. btwn., straight edge at top	9,000.	

Most copies of No. 424b are precanceled Dayton, Ohio, to which the value applies.

All known examples of No. 424e are without gum.

425	A140	2c rose red, I	2.30	.20
		Never hinged	4.10	
c.		Perf. 10x12		
d.		Perf. 12x10	10,000.	4,500.
e.		Booklet pane of 6	17.50	15.00
		Never hinged	27.50	
426	A140	3c dp vio, I	15.00	1.25
		Never hinged	27.50	
427	A140	4c brown	35.00	.50
		Never hinged	62.50	
428	A140	5c blue	35.00	.50
		Never hinged	62.50	
a.		Perf. 12x10	7,000.	
429	A140	6c red orange	50.00	1.40
		Never hinged	90.00	
430	A140	7c black	90.00	4.00
		Never hinged	160.00	
431	A148	8c pale ol grn	36.00	1.50
		Never hinged	65.00	
432	A148	9c salmon red	50.00	7.50
		Never hinged	90.00	
433	A148	10c orange yellow	47.50	.40
		Never hinged	85.00	
434	A148	11c dk grn ('15)	25.00	7.50
		Never hinged	45.00	
435	A148	12c claret brown	27.50	4.00
		Never hinged	50.00	
a.		12c copper red	30.00	4.00
		Never hinged	55.00	
437	A148	15c gray	135.00	7.25
		Never hinged	250.00	
438	A148	20c ultra	220.00	4.00
		Never hinged	400.00	
439	A148	30c orange red	260.00	16.00
		Never hinged	475.00	
440	A148	50c violet ('15)	575.00	16.00
		Never hinged	1,050.	
		Nos. 424-440 (16)	1,605.	72.20

Coil Stamps

1914   Perf. 10 Horizontally

441	A140	1c green	1.00	1.00
		Never hinged	1.80	
442	A140	2c carmine, I	8.00	6.00
		Never hinged	18.00	

1914   Perf. 10 Vertically

443	A140	1c green	25.00	5.00
		Never hinged	45.00	
444	A140	2c carmine, I	40.00	1.50
		Never hinged	72.50	
a.		2c lake		1,250.
445	A140	3c violet, I	225.00	125.00
		Never hinged	400.00	
446	A140	4c brown	125.00	42.50
		Never hinged	225.00	
447	A140	5c blue	45.00	27.50
		Never hinged	80.00	
		Nos. 443-447 (5)	460.00	201.50

Type II

TWO CENTS

Type II. Shading lines in ribbons as on type I.

The toga button, rope, and shading lines are heavy.

The shading lines of the face at the lock of hair end in a strong vertical curved line.

Used on rotary press printings only.

Type III

TWO CENTS

Type III. Two lines of shading in the curves of the ribbons.

Other characteristics similar to type II.

Used on rotary press printings only.

Fraudulently altered copies of type III (Nos. 455, 488, 492 and 540) have had one line of shading scraped off to make them resemble type II (Nos. 454, 487, 491 and 539).

ROTARY PRESS STAMPS

The Rotary Press stamps are printed from plates that are curved to fit around a cylinder. This curvature produces stamps that are slightly larger, either horizontally or vertically, than those printed from flat plates.

Stamps from flat plates measure about 18½-19mm wide by 22mm high.

When the impressions are placed sideways on the curved plates the stamps are 19½-20mm wide; when they are placed vertically the stamps are 23mm high.

Coil Stamps

Rotary Press Printing

1915-16   Perf. 10 Horizontally

448	A140	1c green	6.00	3.25
		Never hinged	11.00	
449	A140	2c red, I	2,600.	600.00
		Never hinged	4,700.	
450	A140	2c car, III ('16)	10.00	3.00
		Never hinged	18.00	

1914-16   Perf. 10 Vertically

452	A140	1c green	10.00	2.00
		Never hinged	18.00	
453	A140	2c car rose, I	150.00	4.25
		Never hinged	270.00	
454	A140	2c red, II	82.50	10.00
		Never hinged	150.00	
455	A140	2c carmine, III	8.50	1.00
		Never hinged	15.00	
456	A140	3c vio, I ('16)	240.00	90.00
		Never hinged	430.00	
457	A140	4c brown ('16)	25.00	17.50
		Never hinged	45.00	
458	A140	5c blue ('16)	30.00	17.50
		Never hinged	55.00	
		Nos. 452-458 (7)	546.00	142.25

1914, June 30   Imperf.

459	A140	2c car, I	240.00	1,100.
		Never hinged	350.00	

No. 459 is a horizontal coil.

The used value is for a copy with an authenticated contemporaneous cancel.

Flat Plate Printings

1915, Feb. 8   Wmk. 191   Perf. 10

460	A148	$1 violet black	850.00	100.00
		Never hinged	1,500.	

1915, June 17   Wmk. 190   Perf. 11

461	A140	2c pale carmine red, I	150.00	275.00
		Never hinged	270.00	

Fraudulently perforated copies of No. 409 are offered as No. 461.

The used value is for a copy with a contemporaneous cancel.

Unwatermarked

From 1916 onward all postage stamps except Nos. 519 and 832b are on unwatermarked paper.

1916-17   Unwmk.   Perf. 10

462	A140	1c green	7.00	.35
		Never hinged	12.50	
a.		Booklet pane of 6	9.50	5.00
		Never hinged	15.00	
463	A140	2c carmine, I	4.50	.25
		Never hinged	8.00	
a.		Booklet pane of 6	95.00	65.00
		Never hinged	150.00	
464	A140	3c violet, I	75.00	14.00
		Never hinged	135.00	
465	A140	4c org brn	45.00	1.80
		Never hinged	80.00	
466	A140	5c blue	75.00	1.80
		Never hinged	135.00	
467	A140	5c car (error in plate of 2c, '17)	550.00	700.00
		Never hinged	1,000.	
468	A140	6c red orange	95.00	7.50
		Never hinged	170.00	
469	A140	7c black	130.00	12.50
		Never hinged	235.00	
470	A148	8c olive green	60.00	6.00
		Never hinged	110.00	
471	A148	9c salmon red	60.00	16.00
		Never hinged	110.00	
472	A148	10c orange yel	110.00	1.40
		Never hinged	200.00	
473	A148	11c dark green	40.00	17.50
		Never hinged	72.50	
474	A148	12c claret brown	55.00	5.50
		Never hinged	100.00	
475	A148	15c gray	200.00	12.50
		Never hinged	360.00	
476	A148	20c lt ultra	250.00	14.00
		Never hinged	450.00	
476A	A148	30c orange red	3,750.	—
		Never hinged	5,500.	
477	A148	50c lt violet ('17)	1,100.	65.00
		Never hinged	2,000.	
478	A148	$1 violet black	800.00	19.00
		Never hinged	1,450.	
		Nos. 462-466,468-476,477-478 (16)	3,171.	195.10

No. 476A is valued in the grade of fine.

Types of 1903 Issue

1917, Mar. 22   Perf. 10

479	A127	$2 dark blue	290.00	40.00
		Never hinged	525.00	
480	A128	$5 light green	240.00	40.00
		Never hinged	425.00	

Type Ia

TWO CENTS

Type Ia. Design characteristics similar to type I except that all lines of design are stronger.

The toga button, toga rope and rope shading lines are heavy.

The latter characteristics are those of type II, which, however, occur only on impressions from rotary plates.

Used only on flat plates 10208 and 10209.

Type II

THREE CENTS

Type II. The top line of the toga rope is strong and the rope shading lines are heavy and complete.

The line between the lips is heavy.

Used on both flat plate and rotary press printings.

1916-17   Imperf.

481	A140	1c green	1.00	.55
		Never hinged	1.80	
482	A140	2c carmine, I	1.40	1.25
		Never hinged	2.50	
482A	A140	2c dp rose, Ia		35,000.

No. 482A was issued imperforate but all copies were privately perforated with large oblong perforations at the sides (Schermack type III).

No. 500 exists with imperforate top sheet margin. Copies have been altered by trimming perforations. Some also have faked Schermack perfs.

483	A140	3c vio, I ('17)	13.00	7.50
		Never hinged	23.00	
484	A140	3c violet, II	10.00	5.00
		Never hinged	18.00	
485	A140	5c car (error in plate of 2c) ('17)	10,500.	
		Never hinged	15,000.	

Although #485 is valued as a single stamp, such examples are seldom seen in the marketplace.

#485 usually is seen as the center stamp in a block of 9 with 8 #482 (value with #485 never hinged, $17,000) or as two center stamps in a block of 12 (value with both #485 never hinged, $25,000).

Coil Stamps

Rotary Press Printing

1916-19   Perf. 10 Horizontally

486	A140	1c green ('18)	.90	.25
		Never hinged	1.50	
487	A140	2c car, II	13.50	3.00
		Never hinged	24.00	
488	A140	2c car, III ('19)	2.50	1.75
		Never hinged	4.50	
489	A140	3c violet, I ('17)	5.00	1.50
		Never hinged	9.00	
		Nos. 486-489 (4)	21.90	6.50

1916-22   Perf. 10 Vertically

490	A140	1c green	.55	.25
		Never hinged	1.00	
491	A140	2c car, II	2,200.	750.00
		Never hinged	3,750.	
492	A140	2c car, III	9.50	.25
		Never hinged	17.00	
493	A140	3c vio, I ('17)	16.00	3.00
		Never hinged	29.00	
494	A140	3c vio, II ('18)	10.00	1.00
		Never hinged	18.00	
495	A140	4c org brn ('17)	10.00	4.00
		Never hinged	18.00	
496	A140	5c blue ('19)	3.50	1.00
		Never hinged	6.25	
497	A148	10c org yel ('22)	20.00	10.50
		Never hinged	36.00	
		Nos. 490,492-497 (7)	69.55	20.00

See note above #448 regarding #487, 491.

Blind Perfs.

Listings of imperforate-between varieties are for examples which show no trace of "blind perfs.," traces of impressions from the perforating pins which do not cut into the paper.

Types of 1912-14 Issue

Flat Plate Printings

1917-19   Perf. 11

498	A140	1c green	.35	.25
		Never hinged	.60	
a.		Vert. pair, imperf. horiz.	600.00	
b.		Horiz. pair, imperf. btwn.	325.00	
		Never hinged	600.00	
c.		Vert. pair, imperf. btwn.	450.00	—
d.		Double impression	250.00	750.00
e.		Booklet pane of 6	2.50	1.00
		Never hinged	4.00	
f.		Booklet pane of 30	1,000.	
		Never hinged	1,600.	
499	A140	2c rose, I	.35	.25
		Never hinged	.60	
a.		Vert. pair, imperf. horiz.	175.00	
		Never hinged	300.00	
b.		Horiz. pair, imperf. vert.	300.00	225.00
		Never hinged	500.00	
c.		Vert. pair, imperf. btwn.	650.00	225.00
e.		Booklet pane of 6	4.00	1.25
		Never hinged	6.50	
f.		Booklet pane of 30	28,000.	
		Never hinged	36,000.	
g.		Double impression	175.00	—

No. 499b is valued in the grade of fine.

500	A140	2c dp rose, Ia	275.00	225.00
		Never hinged	500.00	
501	A140	3c lt violet, I	11.00	.25
		Never hinged	20.00	
b.		Booklet pane of 6	75.00	50.00
		Never hinged	120.00	
c.		Vert. pair, imperf. horiz.	750.00	
d.		Double impression	2,500.	2,500.
502	A140	3c dk violet, II	14.00	.40
		Never hinged	25.00	
b.		Booklet pane of 6	60.00	50.00
		Never hinged	100.00	
c.		Vert. pair, imperf. horiz.	450.00	
		Never hinged	800.00	
d.		Double impression	500.00	300.00
		Never hinged	850.00	
503	A140	4c brown	10.00	.25
		Never hinged	18.00	
b.		Double impression		—

504	A140	5c blue		9.00	.25
		Never hinged		16.00	
a.		Horiz. pair, imperf. btwn.		2,500.	—
b.		Double impression			900.00
505	A140	5c rose (error in plate of 2c)		350.00	500.00
		Never hinged		625.00	
506	A140	6c red orange		12.50	.25
		Never hinged		22.50	
507	A140	7c black		27.50	1.10
		Never hinged		50.00	
508	A148	8c olive bister		12.00	.50
		Never hinged		21.50	
b.		Vert. pair, imperf. btwn.			
509	A148	9c salmon red		14.00	1.75
		Never hinged		25.00	
510	A148	10c orange yellow		17.00	.20
a.		10c brown yellow		600.00	
		Never hinged		1,100.	
511	A148	11c lt green		9.00	2.50
		Never hinged		16.00	
512	A148	12c claret brown		9.00	.35
		Never hinged		16.00	
a.		12c brown carmine		9.50	.40
		Never hinged		17.00	
513	A148	13c apple grn ('19)		11.00	6.00
		Never hinged		20.00	
514	A148	15c gray		37.50	1.00
		Never hinged		67.50	
515	A148	20c light ultra		47.50	.25
		Never hinged		85.00	
b.		Vert. pair, imperf. btwn.		1,500.	
c.		Double impression		1,250.	

No. 515b is valued in the grade of fine. Beware of pairs with blind perforations inside the design of the top stamp that are offered as No. 515b.

516	A148	30c orange red		37.50	1.00
		Never hinged		67.50	
b.		Double impression		—	
517	A148	50c red violet		67.50	.50
		Never hinged		120.00	
b.		Vert. pair, imperf. btwn. & at bottom		—	6,000.
518	A148	$1 violet brown		52.50	1.50
		Never hinged		95.00	
b.		$1 deep brown		1,800.	1,050.
		Never hinged		3,000.	
		Nos. 498-504,506-518 (20)		674.20	243.55

No. 517b is valued in average condition and may be a unique used pair. The editors would like to see authenticated evidence of an unused pair.

No. 518b is valued in the grade of fine to very fine.

Type of 1908-09 Issue

1917, Oct. 10   Wmk. 191   Perf. 11

519	A139	2c carmine		450.00	1,100.
		Never hinged		750.00	

Fraudulently perforated copies of No. 344 are offered as No. 519.

The used value is for a stamp with an authenticated contemporaneous cancel.

Franklin — A149

1918, Aug. 19   Unwmk.   Perf. 11

523	A149	$2 org red & blk		600.00	230.00
		Never hinged		1,050.	
524	A149	$5 dp grn & blk		210.00	35.00
		Never hinged		375.00	

See No. 547 for $2 carmine & black.

Types of 1912-14 Issue

Type IV

TWO CENTS

Type IV. Top line of toga rope is broken. Shading lines in toga button are so arranged that the curving of the first and last form a "D (reversed) ID."

Line of color in left "2" is very thin and usually broken.

Used on offset printings only.

Type V

TWO CENTS

Type V. Top line of toga is complete.

Five vertical shading lines in toga button.

Line of color in left "2" is very thin and usually broken.

Shading dots on the nose and lip are as indicated on the diagram.

Used on offset printings only.

Type Va

TWO CENTS

Type Va. Characteristics same as type V, except in shading dots of nose. Third row from bottom has 4 dots instead of 6. Overall height of type Va is ½mm less than type V.

Used on offset printings only.

Type VI

TWO CENTS

Type VI. General characteristics same as type V, except that line of color in left "2" is very heavy.

Used on offset printings only.

Type VII

TWO CENTS

Type VII. Line of color in left "2" is invariably continuous, clearly defined, and heavier than in type V or Va, but not as heavy as in type VI. Additional vertical row of dots has been added to the upper lip.

Numerous additional dots have been added to hair on top of head.

Used on offset printings only.

Type III

THREE CENTS

Type III. The top line of the toga rope is strong but the fifth shading line is missing as in type I.

Center shading line of the toga button consists of two dashes with a central dot.

The "P" and "O" of "POSTAGE" are separated by a line of color.

The frame line at the bottom of the vignette is complete.

Used on offset printings only.

Type IV

THREE CENTS

Type IV. Shading lines of toga rope are complete.

Second and fourth shading lines in toga button are broken in the middle and the third line is continuous with a dot in the center.

"P" and "O" of "POSTAGE" are joined.

Frame line at bottom of vignette is broken.

Used on offset printings only.

1918-20   Offset Printing   Perf. 11

525	A140	1c gray green		2.50	.50
		Never hinged		4.50	
a.		1c dark green		3.25	.95
		Never hinged		5.75	
c.		Horiz. pair, imperf. btwn.		100.00	
d.		Double impression		40.00	30.00
		Never hinged		72.50	
526	A140	2c car, Type IV ('20)		27.50	3.50
		Never hinged		50.00	
527	A140	2c car, Type V ('20)		20.00	1.00
		Never hinged		36.00	
a.		Double impression		65.00	10.00
		Never hinged		120.00	
b.		Vert. pair, imperf. horiz.		600.00	
c.		Horiz. pair, imperf. vert.		1,000.	—
528	A140	2c car, Type Va ('20)		9.50	.25
		Never hinged		17.00	
c.		Double impression		27.50	
g.		Vert. pair, imperf. btwn.		3,500.	
528A	A140	2c car, Type VI ('20)		52.50	1.50
		Never hinged		95.00	
d.		Double impression		160.00	—
		Never hinged		290.00	
f.		Vert. pair, imperf. horiz.		—	
h.		Vert. pair, imperf. btwn.		1,000.	
528B	A140	2c car, Type VII ('20)		22.50	.35
		Never hinged		40.00	
e.		Double impression		70.00	
529	A140	3c vio, Type III		3.25	.25
		Never hinged		5.75	
a.		Double impression		40.00	—
b.		Printed on both sides		1,500.	
530	A140	3c pur, Type IV		1.60	.20
		Never hinged		2.80	
a.		Double impression		30.00	7.00
b.		Printed on both sides		350.00	
c.		Triple impression		750.00	
		Nos. 525-530 (8)		139.35	7.55

1918-20   Imperf.

531	A140	1c green ('19)		9.50	8.00
		Never hinged		17.00	
532	A140	2c car rose, Type IV ('20)		40.00	27.50
		Never hinged		72.50	
533	A140	2c car, Type V ('20)		120.00	80.00
		Never hinged		215.00	
534	A140	2c car, Type Va ('20)		11.00	6.50
		Never hinged		20.00	
534A	A140	2c car, Type VI ('20)		45.00	22.50
		Never hinged		80.00	
534B	A140	2c car, Type VII ('20)		2,100.	1,250.
		Never hinged		3,600.	
535	A140	3c vio, Type IV		9.00	5.00
		Never hinged		16.00	
a.		Double impression		100.00	
		Nos. 531-534A,535 (6)		234.50	149.50

1919, Aug. 15   Perf. 12½

536	A140	1c gray green		22.50	20.00
		Never hinged		40.00	
a.		Horiz. pair, imperf. vert.		900.00	

Victory Issue

"Victory" and Flags of the Allies — A150

Flat Plate Printing

1919, Mar. 3   Engr.   Perf. 11

537	A150	3c violet		9.00	3.25
		Never hinged		16.00	
a.		3c deep red violet		1,400.	2,000.
		Never hinged		2,250.	
b.		3c light reddish violet		9.00	3.00
		Never hinged		16.00	
c.		3c red violet		50.00	12.00
		Never hinged		90.00	

Victory of Allies in World War I.

No. 537a is valued in the grade of fine.

Rotary Press Printings

1919   Perf. 11x10

Size: 19½ to 20mm wide by 22 to 22¼mm high

538	A140	1c green		11.00	8.50
		Never hinged		20.00	
a.		Vert. pair, imperf. horiz.		50.00	100.00
		Never hinged		87.50	
539	A140	2c car rose, II		2,750.	4,750.
		Never hinged		4,000.	
540	A140	2c car rose, III		13.00	8.50
		Never hinged		23.50	
a.		Vert. pair, imperf. horiz.		50.00	100.00
		Never hinged		87.50	
b.		Horiz. pair, imperf. vert.		1,250.	
541	A140	3c vio, II		45.00	30.00
		Never hinged		80.00	

The part perforate varieties of Nos. 538a and 540a were issued in sheets and may be had in blocks; similar part perforate varieties, Nos. 490 and 492, are from coils and are found only in strips.

See note over No. 448 regarding No. 539.

No. 539 is valued in the grade of fine.

Size: 19x22½-22¾mm

1920, May 26   Perf. 10x11

542	A140	1c green		14.00	1.10
		Never hinged		25.00	

Size: 19x22½mm

1921   Perf. 10

543	A140	1c green		.50	.25
		Never hinged		.90	
a.		Horiz. pair, imperf. btwn.		1,750.	

Size: 19x22½mm

1922   Perf. 11

544	A140	1c green		15,000.	3,250.
		Never hinged		25,000.	

No. 544 is valued in the grade of fine.

Size: 19½-20x22mm

1921   Perf. 11

545	A140	1c green		190.00	175.00
		Never hinged		340.00	
546	A140	2c car rose, III		125.00	160.00
		Never hinged		225.00	

Flat Plate Printing

1920, Nov. 1   Perf. 11

547	A149	$2 carmine & black		180.00	40.00
		Never hinged		325.00	

Pilgrim Tercentenary Issue

"Mayflower"
A151

Landing of the
Pilgrims — A152

Signing of the
Compact — A153

1920, Dec. 21   *Perf. 11*
548 A151 1c green   4.50   2.25
    Never hinged   7.25
549 A152 2c carmine rose   6.50   1.60
    Never hinged   10.50
550 A153 5c deep blue   45.00   12.50
    Never hinged   72.50
    Nos. 548-550 (3)   56.00   16.35
    Nos. 548-550, never
    hinged   90.25

Tercentenary of the landing of the Pilgrims at Plymouth, Mass.

Nathan Hale
A154

Franklin
A155

Harding
A156

Washington
A157

Lincoln
A158

Martha
Washington
A159

Theodore
Roosevelt
A160

Garfield
A161

McKinley
A162

Grant
A163

Jefferson
A164

Monroe
A165

Rutherford B.
Hayes
A166

Grover
Cleveland
A167

American
Indian
A168

Statue of
Liberty
A169

Golden
Gate — A170

Niagara
Falls — A171

American
Buffalo
A172

Arlington
Amphitheater
A173

Lincoln
Memorial
A174

US Capitol
A175

Head of Freedom
Statue, Capitol
Dome — A176

1922-25   *Perf. 11*
551 A154 ½c olive brn
         ('25)   .20   .20
    Never hinged   .25
552 A155 1c dp green
         ('23)   1.50   .20
    Never hinged   2.50
 a. Booket pane of 6   6.00   2.00
    Never hinged   9.50
553 A156 1½c yel brn ('25) 2.60   .20
    Never hinged   4.25
554 A157 2c carmine
         ('23)   1.40   .20
    Never hinged   2.25
 a. Horiz. pair, imperf. vert. 300.00
 b. Vert. pair, imperf. horiz. 4,000.
 c. Booklet pane of 6   6.75   2.00
    Never hinged   10.50
555 A158 3c violet ('23)   18.00   1.00
    Never hinged   29.00
556 A159 4c yel brn ('23)   19.00   .25
    Never hinged   30.00
 a. Vert. pair, imperf. horiz. 10,500.
557 A160 5c dark blue   19.00   .20
    Never hinged   30.00
 a. Imperf., pair   1,500.
    Never hinged   2,350.
 b. Horiz. pair, imperf. vert.
558 A161 6c red orange   35.00   .85
    Never hinged   57.50
559 A162 7c black ('23)   9.25   .55
    Never hinged   15.00
560 A163 8c olive grn
         ('23)   50.00   .60
    Never hinged   80.00
561 A164 9c rose ('23)   14.00   1.10
    Never hinged   22.50
562 A165 10c orange ('23)   18.00   .20
    Never hinged   29.00
 a. Vert. pair, imperf. horiz. 1,500.
    Never hinged   2,350.
 b. Imperf., pair   1,500.
563 A166 11c light blue   1.40   .40
    Never hinged   2.20
 d. Imperf., pair   17,500.
564 A167 12c brn vio ('23) 6.00   .20
    Never hinged   9.50
 a. Horiz. pair, imperf. vert. 1,750.
565 A168 14c blue ('23)   4.00   .75
    Never hinged   6.50
566 A169 15c gray   23.00   .20
    Never hinged   37.50

567 A170 20c car rose
         ('23)   22.00   .20
    Never hinged   35.00
 a. Horiz. pair, imperf. vert. 1,500.
    Never hinged   2,400.
568 A171 25c yellow
         green   18.00   .45
    Never hinged   29.00
 b. Vert. pair, imperf. horiz. 2,000.
569 A172 30c olive brn
         ('23)   32.50   .35
    Never hinged   52.50
570 A173 50c lilac   55.00   .20
    Never hinged   87.50
571 A174 $1 vio black
         ('23)   45.00   .45
    Never hinged   72.50
572 A175 $2 dp bl ('23)   90.00   9.00
    Never hinged   145.00
573 A176 $5 car & bl
         ('23)   150.00 15.00
    Never hinged   240.00
 a. $5 car lake & dark bl 200.00 16.00
    Never hinged   325.00
    Nos. 551-573 (23)   634.85 32.75
    Nos. 551-573, never
    hinged   1,020.

No. 556a is unique. No. 568b is valued in the grade of fine.
For listings of other perforated stamps of designs A154 to A176 see

#578-579   Perf. 11x10
#581-591   Perf. 10
#594-595   Perf. 11
#632-642, 653, 692- Perf. 11x10½
696
#697-701   Perf. 10½x11

This series includes Nos. 622-623 (perf. 11).

1923-25   *Imperf.*
575 A155 1c green   7.25   5.00
    Never hinged   11.50
576 A156 1½c yel brn ('25) 1.50   1.50
    Never hinged   2.40
577 A157 2c carmine   1.60   1.25
    Never hinged   2.60
    Nos. 575-577 (3)   10.35   7.75
    Nos. 555-577, never hinged 16.50

The 1½c A156 rotary press imperforate is listed as No. 631.

Rotary Press Printings
                            Perf. 11x10
578 A155 1c green   100.00 160.00
    Never hinged   160.00
579 A157 2c carmine   90.00   140.00
    Never hinged   145.00

Nos. 578-579 were made from coil waste of Nos. 597, 599 and measure approximately 19¾x22¼mm.

1923-26   *Perf. 10*
581 A155 1c green   11.00   .65
    Never hinged   17.50
582 A156 1½c brown ('25)   5.50   .60
    Never hinged   8.75
583 A157 2c car ('24)   3.00   .25
    Never hinged   4.75
 a. Booklet pane of 6   90.00   50.00
    Never hinged   135.00
584 A158 3c violet ('25)   32.50   2.25
    Never hinged   52.50
585 A159 4c yel brn ('25)   19.00   .45
    Never hinged   30.00
586 A160 5c blue ('25)   19.00   .25
    Never hinged   30.00
 a. Horiz. pair, imperf. btwn.   8,500.
587 A161 6c red org ('25)   9.25   .35
    Never hinged   15.00
588 A162 7c black ('26)   13.50   5.50
    Never hinged   21.50
589 A163 8c ol grn ('26)   30.00   3.50
    Never hinged   47.50
590 A164 9c rose ('26)   6.00   2.25
    Never hinged   9.50
591 A165 10c orange ('25)   72.50   .25
    Never hinged   115.00
    Nos. 581-591 (11)   221.25 16.30
    Nos. 581-591, never
    hinged   352.00

                            Perf. 11
594 A155 1c green   19,000. 6,500.
595 A157 2c carmine   300.   325.
    Never hinged   475.

Nos. 594-595 were made from coil waste of Nos. 597 and 599, and measure approximately 19¾x22¼mm.
No. 594 unused is valued without gum; both unused and used are valued with perforations just touching frameline on one side.

                            Perf. 11
596 A155 1c green   85,000.
    Precanceled   65,000.

No. 596 was made from rotary press sheet waste and measures approximately 19¼x22½mm. A majority of the copies carry

the Bureau precancel "Kansas City, Mo." No. 596 is valued in the grade of fine.

ROTARY PRESS DOUBLE PAPER
The web of paper used on rotary presses must be continuous, therefore any break in the paper must be lapped and pasted, causing the "double paper" varieties. These are no longer listed since they may occur on any rotary press stamp.

Type I

Type II

Type I   Type II

Type I. No heavy hair lines at top center of head. Outline of left acanthus scroll generally faint at top and toward base at left side.
Type II. The heavy hair lines at top center of head; two being outstanding in the white area. Outline of left acanthus scroll very strong and clearly defined at top (under left edge of lettered panel) and at lower curve (above and to left of numeral oval). Type II is found only on Nos. 599A and 634A.

Coil Stamps
Rotary Press Printing
1923-29   *Perf. 10 Vertically*
597 A155 1c green   .30   .20
    Never hinged   .50
598 A156 1½c brown ('25)   1.00   .20
    Never hinged   1.60
599 A157 2c car, I ('23)   .40   .20
    Never hinged   .65
599A A157 2c car, II ('29) 125.00 11.00
    Never hinged   200.00
600 A158 3c violet ('24)   7.25   .20
    Never hinged   11.50
601 A159 4c yellow brown   4.50   .35
    Never hinged   7.25
602 A160 5c dk bl ('24)   1.75   .20
    Never hinged   2.80
603 A165 10c orange ('24)   4.00   .20
    Never hinged   6.50

          Perf. 10 Horizontally
604 A155 1c green ('24)   .35   .20
    Never hinged   .55
605 A156 1½c yel brn ('25) .35   .20
    Never hinged   .55
606 A157 2c carmine   .35   .20
    Never hinged   .55
    Nos. 597-599,600-606 (10) 20.25 2.15
    Nos. 597-599, 600-606,
    never hinged   32.45

Harding Memorial Issue

Warren G.
Harding — A177

Flat Plate Printing
(19¼x22¼mm)
1923, Sept. 1   *Perf. 11*
610 A177 2c black   .65   .20
    Never hinged   1.05
 a. Horiz. pair, imperf. vert. 2,000.

1923, Nov. 15 — Imperf.
611 A177 2c black — 6.25 / 4.00
Never hinged — 10.00

Rotary Press Printing
(19¼x22½mm)
1923, Sept. 12 — Perf. 10
612 A177 2c black — 17.50 / 1.75
Never hinged — 28.00

1923 — Perf. 11
613 A177 2c black — 35,000.

Tribute to President Warren G. Harding, who died August 2, 1923.
Nos. 610a, 613 valued in the grade of fine.

Huguenot-Walloon Tercentenary Issue

"New Netherland" A178

Landing at Fort Orange A179

Monument to Jan Ribault at Duvall County, Fla. — A180

Flat Plate Printings
1924, May 1 — Perf. 11
614 A178 1c dark green — 2.75 / 3.25
Never hinged — 4.25
615 A179 2c carmine rose — 5.50 / 2.25
Never hinged — 8.75
616 A180 5c dark blue — 22.50 / 13.00
Never hinged — 35.00
Nos. 614-616 (3) — 30.75 / 18.50
Nos. 614-616, never hinged — 48.00

Tercentenary of the settling of the Walloons and in honor of the Huguenots.

Lexington-Concord Issue

Washington at Cambridge A181

"Birth of Liberty," by Henry Sandham A182

The Minute Man, by Daniel Chester French A183

1925, Apr. 4 — Perf. 11
617 A181 1c deep green — 2.50 / 2.50
Never hinged — 4.00
618 A182 2c carmine rose — 5.00 / 4.00
Never hinged — 8.00
619 A183 5c dark blue — 20.00 / 13.00
Never hinged — 32.50
Nos. 617-619 (3) — 27.50 / 19.50
Nos. 617-619, never hinged — 44.50

150th anniv. of the Battle of Lexington-Concord.

Norse-American Issue
 A184   A185

1925, May 18 — Perf. 11
620 A184 2c "Restaurationen" — 4.00 / 3.00
Never hinged — 6.50
621 A185 5c Viking Ship — 16.00 / 10.50
Never hinged — 26.00

100th anniv. of the arrival in NY on Oct. 9, 1825, of the sloop "Restaurationen" with the first group of immigrants from Norway to the US.

Benjamin Harrison A186

Woodrow Wilson A187

1925-26 — Perf. 11
622 A186 13c green ('26) — 13.50 / .45
Never hinged — 21.00
623 A187 17c black — 15.00 / .25
Never hinged — 24.00

Sesquicentennial Exposition Issue

Liberty Bell A188

1926, May 10 — Perf. 11
627 A188 2c carmine rose — 3.25 / .50
Never hinged — 4.50

150th anniv. of the Declaration of Independence, Philadelphia, June 1-Dec. 1.

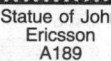
Statue of John Ericsson A189

Alexander Hamilton's Battery A190

Ericsson Memorial Issue
1926, May 29 — Perf. 11
628 A189 5c gray lilac — 6.50 / 3.25
Never hinged — 9.50

John Ericsson, builder of the "Monitor."

Battle of White Plains Issue
1926, Oct. 18 — Perf. 11
629 A190 2c carmine rose — 2.25 / 1.70
Never hinged — 3.25
a. Vertical pair, imperf. btwn. — —

Battle of White Plains, NY, 150th anniv.

International Philatelic Exhibition
Souvenir Sheet

A190a

1926, Oct. 18 — Perf. 11
630 A190a 2c carmine rose, sheet of 25 — 375.00 / 450.00
Never hinged — 550.00

Intl. Phil. Exhib. in NYC, Oct. 16-23. Size: 158-160¼x136-146½mm.
Condition Valued:
Centering: Overall centering will average very fine, but individual stamps may be better or worse.
Perforations: No folds along rows of perforations.
Gum: There may be some light gum bends but no gum creases.
Hinging: There may be hinge marks in the selvage and on up to two or three stamps, but no heavy hingling or hinge remnants (except in the ungummed portion of the wide selvage).
Margins: Top panes should have about ½ inch bottom margin and 1 inch top margin. Bottom panes should have about ½ inch top margin and just under ¾ inch bottom margin. Both will have one wide side (usually 1½ inches plus) and one narrow (½ inch) side margin. The wide margin corner will have a small diagonal notch on top panes.

Types of 1922-26
Rotary Press Printings
1926, Aug. 27 — Imperf.
631 A156 1½c yellow brown — 1.90 / 1.70
Never hinged — 2.75

1926-34 — Perf. 11x10½
632 A155 1c green ('27) — .20 / .20
Never hinged — .20
a. Booklet pane of 6 — 5.50 / 2.25
Never hinged — 7.00
b. Vert. pair, imperf. btwn. — 3,500. / 125.00
Never hinged — 5,500.
c. Horiz. pair, imperf. btwn. — 7,500.

No. 632c is valued in the grade of fine.

633 A156 1½c yel brn ('27) — 1.90 / .20
Never hinged — 2.60
634 A157 2c car, I — .20 / .20
Never hinged — .20
b. 2c carmine lake — —
c. Horiz. pair, imperf. btwn. — 7,000.
d. Booklet pane of 6 — 1.75 / 1.10
Never hinged — 2.50

No. 634c is valued in the grade of fine.

634A A157 2c car, II ('28) — 350.00 / 13.50
Never hinged — 500.00
635 A158 3c violet ('27) — .40 / .20
Never hinged — .55
a. 3c bright violet ('34) — .20 / .20
Never hinged — .30
636 A159 4c yel brn ('27) — 2.10 / .20
Never hinged — 3.00
637 A160 5c dk bl ('27) — 2.10 / .20
Never hinged — 3.00
638 A161 6c red org ('27) — 2.10 / .20
Never hinged — 3.00
639 A162 7c black ('27) — 2.10 / .20
Never hinged — 3.00
a. Vert. pair, imperf. btwn. — 300.00 / 100.00
Never hinged — 425.00
640 A163 8c ol grn ('27) — 2.10 / .20
Never hinged — 3.00
641 A164 9c rose ('27) — 2.10 / .20
Never hinged — 3.00
642 A165 10c org ('27) — 3.50 / .20
Never hinged — 5.00
Nos. 632-634,635-642 (11) — 18.80 / 2.20
Nos. 632-634, 635-642 never hinged — 26.45

The 1½c, 2c, 4c, 5c, 6c, 8c imperf. (dry print) are printer's waste.
For ½c, 11c-50c see Nos. 653, 692-701.

Vermont Sesquicentennial Issue

Green Mountain Boy — A191

Flat Plate Printing
1927, Aug. 3 — Perf. 11
643 A191 2c carmine rose — 1.40 / .80
Never hinged — 2.00

Battle of Bennington, Vt., and independence of the State of Vermont, 150th anniv.

"The Surrender of General Burgoyne at Saratoga," by John Trumbull A192

Washington at Prayer — A193

Burgoyne Campaign Issue
1927, Aug. 3 — Perf. 11
644 A192 2c carmine rose — 3.75 / 2.10
Never hinged — 5.50

Battles of Bennington, Oriskany, Fort Stanwix and Saratoga.

Valley Forge Issue
1928, May 26 — Perf. 11
645 A193 2c carmine rose — 1.05 / .40
Never hinged — 1.45
a. 2c lake — —
Never hinged — —

150th anniv. of Washington's encampment at Valley Forge, Pa.

Battle of Monmouth Issue

No. 634 Overprinted

Rotary Press Printing
1928, Oct. 20 — Perf. 11x10½
646 A157 2c carmine — 1.10 / 1.10
Never hinged — 1.50
a. "Pitcher" only — 750.00

The normal space between a vertical pair of the overprints is 18mm, but pairs are known with the space measuring 28mm.
150th anniv. of the Battle of Monmouth, NJ, as a memorial to "Molly Pitcher" (Mary Ludwig Hays), the heroine of the battle.
No. 646a is valued in the grade of fine.

Hawaii Sesquicentennial Issue

Nos. 634 and 637 Overprinted

Rotary Press Printing
1928, Aug. 13 — Perf. 11x10½
647 A157 2c carmine — 5.00 / 4.50
Never hinged — 7.00
648 A160 5c dark blue — 14.50 / 13.50
Never hinged — 20.00

150th anniv. of the discovery of the Hawaiian Islands by Captain Cook.
These stamps were on sale at post offices in the Hawaiian Islands and at the Postal Agency in Washington, DC.
They were not on sale at post offices in the Continental US, though they were valid for postage there.
Normally the overprints were placed 18mm apart vertically, but pairs exist with a space of 28mm between the overprints.

Aeronautics Conference Issue

Wright Airplane A194

Globe and Airplane A195

Flat Plate Printing

1928, Dec. 12   *Perf. 11*

649	A194	2c carmine rose	1.25	.80
		Never hinged	1.75	
650	A195	5c blue	5.25	3.25
		Never hinged	7.25	

Intl. Civil Aeronautics Conf. at Washington, DC, Dec. 12-14, 1928, and of the 25th anniv. of the 1st airplane flight by the Wright brothers, Dec. 17, 1903.

George Rogers Clark Issue

Surrender of Fort Sackville A196

1929, Feb. 25   *Perf. 11*

651	A196	2c carmine & black	.65	.50
		Never hinged	.90	

150th anniv. of the surrender of Fort Sackville, the present site of Vincennes, Ind., to George Rogers Clark.

Type of 1925
Rotary Press Printing

1929, May 25   *Perf. 11x10½*

653	A154	½c olive brown	.20	.20
		Never hinged	.20	

Edison's First Lamp A197   Maj. Gen. John Sullivan A198

Electric Light Jubilee Issue

1929   Flat Plate Printing   *Perf. 11*

654	A197	2c carmine rose	.70	.70
		Never hinged	1.00	

Rotary Press Printing
Perf. 11x10½

655	A197	2c carmine rose	.65	.20
		Never hinged	.90	

Coil Stamp (Rotary Press)
Perf. 10 Vertically

656	A197	2c carmine rose	14.00	1.75
		Never hinged	21.00	
		Nos. 654-656 (3)	15.35	2.65

50th anniv. of invention of the incandescent lamp by Thomas Alva Edison, Oct. 21, 1879. Issued: #654, June 5; #655-656, June 11.

Sullivan Expedition Issue
Flat Plate Printing

1929, June 17   *Perf. 11*

657	A198	2c carmine rose	.70	.60
		Never hinged	1.00	
a.		2c lake	400.00	—
		Never hinged	600.00	

150th anniv. of the Sullivan Expedition in NY State during the Revolutionary War.

Nos. 632-634, 635-642 Overprinted

Kans.

Rotary Press Printing

1929   *Perf. 11x10½*

658	A155	1c green	2.50	2.00
		Never hinged	3.75	
a.		Vert. pair, one without ovpt.	325.00	
659	A156	1½c brown	4.00	2.90
		Never hinged	6.00	
a.		Vert. pair, one without ovpt.	350.00	

660	A157	2c carmine	4.50	1.10
		Never hinged	6.75	
661	A158	3c violet	22.50	15.00
		Never hinged	34.00	
a.		Vert. pair, one without ovpt.	450.00	
		Never hinged	675.00	
662	A159	4c yellow brown	22.50	9.00
		Never hinged	34.00	
a.		Vert. pair, one without ovpt.	425.00	
663	A160	5c deep blue	14.00	9.75
		Never hinged	21.00	
664	A161	6c red orange	32.50	18.00
		Never hinged	50.00	
665	A162	7c black	30.00	27.50
		Never hinged	45.00	
a.		Vert. pair, one without ovpt.	—	
666	A163	8c olive green	110.00	75.00
		Never hinged	165.00	
667	A164	9c light rose	16.00	11.25
		Never hinged	24.00	
668	A165	10c orange yel	25.00	12.00
		Never hinged	37.50	
		Nos. 658-668 (11)	283.50	183.50
		Nos. 658-668, never hinged	427.00	

The existence of No. 665a has been questioned by specialists. The editors would like to see authenticated evidence of such a pair. See note following No. 679.

Nebr.

Overprinted

669	A155	1c green	4.00	2.25
		Never hinged	6.00	
a.		Vert. pair, one without ovpt.	—	
b.		No period after "Nebr." (19338, 19339 UR 26, 36)	50.00	
670	A156	1½c brown	3.75	2.50
		Never hinged	5.50	
671	A157	2c carmine	3.75	1.30
		Never hinged	5.50	
672	A158	3c violet	15.00	12.00
		Never hinged	22.50	
a.		Vert. pair, one without ovpt.	425.00	
673	A159	4c yellow brown	22.50	15.00
		Never hinged	34.00	
674	A160	5c deep blue	20.00	15.00
		Never hinged	30.00	
675	A161	6c red orange	47.50	24.00
		Never hinged	72.50	
676	A162	7c black	27.50	18.00
		Never hinged	41.00	
677	A163	8c olive green	37.50	25.00
		Never hinged	57.50	
678	A164	9c light rose	42.50	27.50
		Never hinged	65.00	
a.		Vert. pair, one without ovpt.	650.00	
679	A165	10c orange yel	135.00	22.50
		Never hinged	200.00	
		Nos. 669-679 (11)	359.00	165.05
		Nos. 669-679, never hinged	539.50	

Nos. 658-660, 669-673, 677 and 678 are known with the overprints on vertical pairs spaced 32mm apart instead of the normal 22mm.

The existence of No. 669a has been questioned by specialists. The editors would like to see authenticated evidence of such a pair.

Important: Nos. 658-679 with original gum have either one horizontal gum breaker ridge per stamp or portions of two at the extreme top and bottom of the stamps, 21mm apart.

Multiple complete gum breaker ridges indicate a fake overprint. Absence of the gum breaker ridges indicates either regumming or regumming and a fake overprint.

Gen. Anthony Wayne Memorial A199   Lock No. 5, Monongahela River A200

Battle of Fallen Timbers Issue
Flat Plate Printing

1929, Sept. 14   *Perf. 11*

680	A199	2c carmine rose	.80	.80
		Never hinged	1.10	

General Anthony Wayne memorial and 135th anniv. of the Battle of Fallen Timbers, Ohio.

Ohio River Canalization Issue

1929, Oct. 19   *Perf. 11*

681	A200	2c carmine rose	.70	.65
		Never hinged	.95	

Completion of the Ohio River Canalization Project between Cairo, Ill. and Pittsburgh.

Massachusetts Bay Colony Issue

Mass. Bay Colony Seal — A201

1930, Apr. 8   *Perf. 11*

682	A201	2c carmine rose	.60	.50
		Never hinged	.85	

300th anniv. Massachusetts Bay Colony.

Carolina-Charleston Issue

Gov. Joseph West & Chief Shadoo, a Kiowa — A202

1930, Apr. 10   *Perf. 11*

683	A202	2c carmine rose	1.20	1.20
		Never hinged	1.65	

260th anniv. of the Province of Carolina founding, and the 250th anniv. of the City of Charleston, SC.

Warren G. Harding A203   William H. Taft A204

Type of 1922-26 Issue
Rotary Press Printing

1930   *Perf. 11x10½*

684	A203	1½c brown	.35	.20
		Never hinged	.50	
685	A204	4c brown	.90	.20
		Never hinged	1.25	

Coil Stamps
Perf. 10 Vert.

686	A203	1½c brown	1.80	.20
		Never hinged	2.50	
687	A204	4c brown	3.25	.45
		Never hinged	4.50	

Braddock's Field Issue

Statue of Col. George Washington — A205

Flat Plate Printing

1930, July 9   *Perf. 11*

688	A205	2c carmine rose	1.00	.85
		Never hinged	1.40	

175th anniv. of the Battle of Braddock's Field, otherwise the Battle of Monongahela.

General von Steuben A206   General Casimir Pulaski A207

Von Steuben Issue

1930, Sept. 17   *Perf. 11*

689	A206	2c carmine rose	.55	.55
		Never hinged	.75	
a.		Imperf., pair	2,750.	
		Never hinged	3,500.	

Gen. Baron Friedrich Wilhelm von Steuben (1730-1794), German soldier who served with distinction in American Revolution.

Pulaski Issue

1931, Jan. 16   *Perf. 11*

690	A207	2c carmine rose	.30	.20
		Never hinged	.40	

150th anniv. (in 1929) of the death of Gen. Count Casimir Pulaski (1748-1779), Polish patriot and hero of American Revolution.

Types of 1922-26
Rotary Press Printing

1931   *Perf. 11x10½*

692	A166	11c light blue	2.60	.20
		Never hinged	3.70	
693	A167	12c brown violet	5.50	.20
		Never hinged	7.75	
694	A186	13c yellow green	2.00	.20
		Never hinged	2.80	
695	A168	14c dark blue	3.75	.25
		Never hinged	5.25	
696	A169	15c gray	8.00	.20
		Never hinged	11.25	

Perf. 10½x11

697	A187	17c black	4.50	.20
		Never hinged	6.25	
698	A170	20c carmine rose	8.25	.20
		Never hinged	11.50	
699	A171	25c blue green	8.50	.20
		Never hinged	12.00	
700	A172	30c brown	16.00	.20
		Never hinged	22.50	
701	A173	50c lilac	37.50	.20
		Never hinged	52.50	
		Nos. 692-701 (10)	96.60	2.05
		Nos. 692-701, never hinged	135.50	

"The Greatest Mother" — A208

Count de Rochambeau, Washington, Count de Grasse — A209

Red Cross Issue
Flat Plate Printing

1931, May 21   *Perf. 11*

702	A208	2c black & red	.25	.20
		Never hinged	.30	
a.		Red cross omitted	40,000.	

50th anniv. of the American Red Cross Society founding.

Yorktown Issue

1931, Oct. 19   *Perf. 11*

703	A209	2c car rose & blk	.40	.25
		Never hinged	.50	
a.		2c lake & black	4.50	.75
		Never hinged	6.25	
b.		2c dark lake & black	450.00	
		Never hinged	700.00	
c.		Horiz. pair, imperf. vert.	5,000.	
		Never hinged	6,250.	

Surrender of Yorktown, sesquicentennial.

Washington Bicentennial Issue
Various Portraits of George Washington

A210   A211

A212

A213

A214

A215

A216

A217

A216

A217

A218

A219

A220

A221

Rotary Press Printings
1932, Jan. 1 — *Perf. 11x10½*

704	A210	½c olive brown	.20	.20
		Never hinged	.20	
705	A211	1c green	.20	.20
		Never hinged	.20	
706	A212	1½c brown	.40	.20
		Never hinged	.55	
707	A213	2c carmine rose	.20	.20
		Never hinged	.20	
708	A214	3c deep violet	.55	.20
		Never hinged	.80	
709	A215	4c light brown	.25	.20
		Never hinged	.35	
710	A216	5c blue	1.60	.20
		Never hinged	2.25	
711	A217	6c red orange	3.25	.20
		Never hinged	4.50	
712	A218	7c black	.25	.20
		Never hinged	.35	
713	A219	8c olive bister	2.75	.50
		Never hinged	3.75	
714	A220	9c pale red	2.40	.20
		Never hinged	3.25	
715	A221	10c orange yellow	10.00	.20
		Never hinged	14.00	
	Nos. 704-715 (12)		22.05	2.70
	Nos. 704-715, never hinged		30.25	

200th anniv. of the birth of Washington.

Skier — A222

Boy and Girl Planting Tree — A223

Olympic Winter Games Issue
Flat Plate Printing
1932, Jan. 25 — *Perf. 11*

716	A222	2c carmine rose	.40	.20
		Never hinged	.50	

Olympic Winter Games, Lake Placid, NY, Feb. 4-13.

Arbor Day Issue
Rotary Press Printing
1932, Apr. 22 — *Perf. 11x10½*

717	A223	2c carmine rose	.20	.20
		Never hinged	.20	

60th anniv. of the 1st observance of Arbor Day in Nebr., April, 1872.

Birth centenary of Julius Sterling Morton, who conceived the plan and the name "Arbor Day," while a member of the Nebr. State Board of Agriculture.

10th Olympic Games Issue

Runner at Starting Mark A224

Myron's Discobolus A225

1932, June 15 — *Perf. 11x10½*

718	A224	3c violet	1.40	.20
		Never hinged	1.75	
719	A225	5c blue	2.20	.20
		Never hinged	2.75	

Los Angeles, Cal., July 30-Aug. 14.

Washington — A226

1932, June 16 — *Perf. 11x10½*

720	A226	3c deep violet	.20	.20
		Never hinged	.20	
b.		Booklet pane of 6	37.50	7.50
		Never hinged	50.00	
c.		Vert. pair, imperf. btwn.	1,250.	1,250.
		Never hinged	1,650.	

Coil Stamps
Rotary Press Printing
1932, June 24 — *Perf. 10 Vertically*

721	A226	3c deep violet	2.75	.20
		Never hinged	3.50	

1932, Oct. 12 — *Perf. 10 Horizontally*

722	A226	3c deep violet	1.50	.35
		Never hinged	2.00	

Garfield Type of 1922-26 Issue
1932, Aug. 18 — *Perf. 10 Vertically*

723	A161	6c deep orange	11.00	.30
		Never hinged	15.00	

William Penn A227

Daniel Webster A228

William Penn Issue
Flat Plate Printing
1932, Oct. 24 — *Perf. 11*

724	A227	3c violet	.30	.20
		Never hinged	.40	
a.		Vert. pair, imperf. horiz.	—	

250th anniv. of the arrival in America of William Penn (1644-1718), English Quaker and founder of Pennsylvania.

Daniel Webster Issue
1932, Oct. 24 — *Perf. 11*

725	A228	3c violet	.30	.25
		Never hinged	.40	

Daniel Webster (1782-1852), statesman.

Georgia Bicentennial Issue

Gen. James Edward Oglethorpe — A229

1933, Feb. 12 — *Perf. 11*

726	A229	3c violet	.30	.20
		Never hinged	.40	

200th anniv. of the Colony of Georgia founding and James Edward Oglethorpe, who landed from England, Feb. 12th, 1733, and personally supervised the establishing of the colony.

Peace of 1783 Issue

Washington's Headquarters, Newburgh, NY — A230

Rotary Press Printing
1933, Apr. 19 — *Perf. 10½x11*

727	A230	3c violet	.20	.20
		Never hinged	.20	

150th anniv. of the Proclamation of Peace between the U.S. and Great Britain at the end of the Revolutionary War. See No. 752.

Century of Progress Issue

Restoration of Fort Dearborn A231

Federal Building at Chicago, 1933 A232

1933, May 25 — *Perf. 10½x11*

728	A231	1c yellow green	.20	.20
		Never hinged	.20	
729	A232	3c violet	.20	.20
		Never hinged	.20	

"Century of Progress" Intl. Phil. Exhib., Chicago, 1933 and 100th anniv. of the incorporation of Chicago as a city.

American Philatelic Society Issue
Souvenir Sheets
Without Gum
Flat Plate Printing
1933, Aug. 25 — *Imperf.*

730		Sheet of 25	27.50	27.50
a.	A231	1c deep yellow green	.75	.45
731		Sheet of 25	25.00	25.00
a.	A232	3c deep violet	.65	.45

Sheet measures 134x120mm. See Nos. 766-767.

National Recovery Act Issue

Group of Workers — A233

Rotary Press Printing
1933, Aug. 15 — *Perf. 10½x11*

732	A233	3c violet	.20	.20
		Never hinged	.20	

Issued to direct attention to and arouse support of the Nation for the NRA.

Byrd Antarctic Issue

World Map on van der Grinten's Projection — A234

Flat Plate Printing
1933, Oct. 9 — *Perf. 11*

733	A234	3c dark blue	.50	.50
		Never hinged	.60	

Second Antarctic expedition of Rear Admiral Richard E. Byrd.
In addition to the 3 cents postage, letters sent by the ships of the expedition to be canceled in Little America were subject to a service charge of 50 cents each. See Nos. 735, 753.

Kosciuszko Issue

Statue of Gen. Tadeusz Kosciuszko — A235

1933, Oct. 13 — *Perf. 11*

734	A235	5c blue	.55	.25
		Never hinged	.65	
a.		Horiz. pair, imperf. vert.	2,250.	
		Never hinged	2,800.	

Gen. Tadeusz Kosciuszko (1746-1807), Polish soldier and statesman who served in American Revolution. 150th anniv. of grant of American citizenship.

National Stamp Exhibition Issue
Souvenir Sheet
Without Gum
1934, Feb. 10 — *Imperf.*

735		Sheet of 6	12.50	10.00
a.	A234	3c dark blue	2.00	1.65

Sheet measures 87x93mm. See #768.

Maryland Tercentenary Issue

"The Ark" and "The Dove" — A236

1934, Mar. 23 — *Perf. 11*

736	A236	3c carmine rose	.20	.20
		Never hinged	.20	

300th anniv. of the founding of Maryland.

Mothers of America Issue

Adaptation of Whistler's Portrait of his Mother A237

Rotary Press Printing
1934, May 2 — *Perf. 11x10½*

737	A237	3c deep violet	.20	.20
		Never hinged	.20	

Flat Plate Printing
Perf. 11

738	A237	3c deep violet	.20	.20
		Never hinged	.20	

Mother's Day. See No. 754.

Wisconsin Tercentenary Issue

Nicolet's Landing A238

1934, July 7 — *Perf. 11*

739	A238	3c deep violet	.20	.20
		Never hinged	.20	
a.		Vert. pair, imperf. horiz.	350.00	
		Never hinged	600.00	
b.		Horiz. pair, imperf. vert.	525.00	
		Never hinged	900.00	

Tercentenary of the arrival of French explorer Jean Nicolet at Green Bay, Wis. See No. 755.

National Parks Issue

El Capitan, Yosemite (California) A239

Old Faithful, Yellowstone (Wyoming) A243

Grand Canyon (Arizona) A240

Mt. Rainier and Mirror Lake (Washington) — A241

Mesa Verde (Colorado) A242

Crater Lake (Oregon) A244

Great Head, Acadia Park (Maine) A245

Great White Throne, Zion Park (Utah) A246

Great Smoky Mts. (North Carolina) A248

Mt. Rockwell (Mt. Sinopah) and Two Medicine Lake, Glacier Natl. Park (Montana) A247

1934		Flat Plate Printing	Perf. 11	
740	A239	1c green	.20	.20
		Never hinged	.20	
a.		Vert. pair, imperf. horiz., with gum	1,000.	
		Never hinged	1,700.	
741	A240	2c red	.20	.20
		Never hinged	.20	
a.		Vert. pair, imperf. horiz., with gum	475.00	
		Never hinged	800.00	
b.		Horiz. pair, imperf. vert., with gum	600.00	
		Never hinged	1,000.	
742	A241	3c deep violet	.20	.20
		Never hinged	.20	
a.		Vert. pair, imperf. horiz., with gum	700.00	
		Never hinged	1,200.	
743	A242	4c brown	.35	.40
		Never hinged	.45	
a.		Vert. pair, imperf. horiz., with gum	1,000.	
		Never hinged	1,700.	
744	A243	5c blue	.70	.65
		Never hinged	.95	
a.		Horiz. pair, imperf. vert., with gum	600.00	
		Never hinged	1,000.	
745	A244	6c dark blue	1.10	.85
		Never hinged	1.50	
746	A245	7c black	.60	.75
		Never hinged	.85	
a.		Horiz. pair, imperf. vert., with gum	725.00	
		Never hinged	1,250.	
747	A246	8c sage green	1.60	1.50
		Never hinged	2.20	
748	A247	9c red orange	1.50	.65
		Never hinged	2.10	

749	A248	10c gray black	3.00	1.25
		Never hinged	4.25	
		Nos. 740-749 (10)	9.45	6.65
		Nos. 740-749, never hinged	12.75	

National Parks Year. See Nos. 750-751, 756-765, 769-770, 797.

American Philatelic Society Issue
Souvenir Sheet

1934, Aug. 28			Imperf.	
750		Sheet of 6	30.00	27.50
		Never hinged	37.50	
a.		A241 3c deep violet	3.50	3.25
		Never hinged	4.50	

Sheet measures approximately 98x93mm. See #770.

Trans-Mississippi Philatelic Exposition Issue
Souvenir Sheet

1934, Oct. 10			Imperf.	
751		Sheet of 6	12.50	12.50
		Never hinged	16.00	
a.		A239 1c green	1.40	1.60
		Never hinged	1.85	

Sheet measures approximately 92x99mm. See #769.

Special Printing (Nos. 752-771)

"Issued for a limited time in full sheets as printed, and in blocks thereof, to meet the requirements of collectors and others who may be interested" - From Postal Bulletin, No. 16614.

Issuance of the following 20 stamps in complete sheets resulted from the protest of collectors and others at the practice of presenting, to certain government officials, complete sheets of unsevered panes, imperforate (except Nos. 752 and 753) and generally ungummed.

Without Gum

Note: In 1940 the P.O. Department offered to and did gum full sheets of Nos. 754 to 771 sent in by owners.

Type of Peace Issue
Issued in sheets of 400
Rotary Press Printing

1935, Mar. 15			Perf. 10½x11	
752	A230	3c violet	.20	.20

Type of Byrd Issue
Issued in sheets of 200
Flat Plate Printing
Perf. 11

753	A234	3c dark blue	.50	.45

No. 753 is similar to No. 733. Positive identification is by pairs or blocks showing a guide line between stamps. These lines are found only on No. 753.

Type of Mothers of America Issue
Issued in sheets of 200
Imperf

754	A237	3c deep violet	.60	.60

Type of Wisconsin Issue
Issued in sheets of 200
Imperf

755	A238	3c deep violet	.60	.60

Types of National Parks Issue
Issued in sheets of 200
Imperf

756	A239	1c green	.20	.20
757	A240	2c red	.25	.25
758	A241	3c deep violet	.50	.45
759	A242	4c brown	.95	.95
760	A243	5c blue	1.50	1.30
761	A244	6c dark blue	2.40	2.10
762	A245	7c black	1.50	1.40
763	A246	8c sage green	1.60	1.50
764	A247	9c red orange	1.90	1.65
765	A248	10c gray black	3.75	3.25
		Nos. 756-765 (10)	14.55	13.05

Souvenir Sheets
Type of Century of Progress Issue
Issued in sheets of 9 panes of 25 stamps each

Note: Single items from these sheets are identical with other varieties, 766 & 730, 766a & 730a, 767 & 731, 767a & 731a, 768 & 735, 768a & 735a, 769 & 756, 770 & 758.

Positive identification is by blocks or pairs showing wide gutters between stamps. These wide gutters occur only on Nos. 766-770 and measure, horiz., 13mm on Nos. 766-767; 16mm on No. 768, and 23mm on Nos. 769-770.

Imperf

766		Pane of 25	25.00	25.00
a.	A231	1c yellow green	.70	.40
767		Pane of 25	23.50	23.50
a.	A232	3c violet	.60	.40

National Exhibition Issue
Type of Byrd Issue
Issued in sheets of 25 panes of 6 stamps each
Imperf

768		Pane of 6	20.00	15.00
a.	A234	3c dark blue	2.80	2.40

Types of National Parks Issue
Issued in sheets of 20 panes of 6 stamps each
Imperf

769		Pane of 6	12.50	11.00
a.	A239	1c green	1.85	1.80
770		Pane of 6	30.00	24.00
a.	A241	3c deep violet	3.25	3.10

Type of Air Post Special Delivery
Issued in sheets of 200
Imperf

771	APSD1	16c dark blue	2.40	2.25

> Catalogue values for unused stamps in this section, from this point to the end of the section, are for Never Hinged items.

VALUES FOR HINGED STAMPS AFTER NO. 771
This catalogue does not value unused stamps after No. 771 in hinged condition. Hinged unused stamps from No. 772 to the present are worth considerably less than the values given for unused stamps, which are for never-hinged examples.

Connecticut Tercentenary Issue

Charter Oak A249

Rotary Press Printing

1935, Apr. 26			Perf. 11x10½	
772	A249	3c violet	.20	.20

300th anniv. of the settlement of Conn. See No. 778a.

California-Pacific Exposition Issue

View of San Diego Exposition A250

1935, May 29			Perf. 11x10½	
773	A250	3c purple	.20	.20

California-Pacific Expo., San Diego. See No. 778b.

Boulder Dam Issue

Boulder Dam — A251

Flat Plate Printing

1935, Sept. 30			Perf. 11	
774	A251	3c purple	.20	.20

Dedication of Boulder Dam.

Michigan Centenary Issue

Michigan State Seal A252

Rotary Press Printing

1935, Nov. 1			Perf. 11x10½	
775	A252	3c purple	.20	.20

Advance celebration of Michigan statehood centenary. Michigan was admitted to Union Jan. 26, 1837. See No. 778c.

Texas Centennial Issue

Sam Houston, Stephen F. Austin and the Alamo A253

1936, Mar. 2			Perf. 11x10½	
776	A253	3c purple	.20	.20

Centennial of Texas independence. See No. 778d.

Rhode Island Tercentenary Issue

Statue of Roger Williams — A254

1936, May 4			Perf. 10½x11	
777	A254	3c purple	.20	.20

Settlement of Rhode Island, 1636.

Third International Philatelic Exhibition Issue
Souvenir Sheet

A254a

Flat Plate Printing

1936, May 9			Imperf.	
778	A254a	Sheet of 4	1.75	1.75
a.		A249 3c violet	.40	.30
b.		A250 3c violet	.40	.30
c.		A252 3c violet	.40	.30
d.		A253 3c violet	.40	.30

Sheet measures 98x66mm.

Arkansas Centennial Issue

Arkansas Post, Old and New State Houses A255

Rotary Press Printing

1936, June 15			Perf. 11x10½	
782	A255	3c purple	.20	.20

Centennial of Arkansas statehood.

Map of Oregon Territory A256

Susan B. Anthony — A257

Oregon Territory Issue

1936, July 14   **Perf. 11x10½**
783 A256 3c purple   .20   .20

Centenary of Oregon Territory opening.

Susan B. Anthony Issue

1936, Aug. 26   **Perf. 11x10½**
784 A257 3c dark violet   .20   .20

Susan Brownell Anthony (1820-1906), woman suffrage advocate, honored on 16th anniv. of ratification of 19th Amendment granting American women the right to vote.

Army Issue

George Washington, Nathanael Greene and Mount Vernon — A258

Andrew Jackson, Winfield Scott and the Hermitage A259

Generals Sherman, Grant and Sheridan A260

Generals Robert E. Lee, "Stonewall" Jackson and Stratford Hall — A261

US Military Academy, West Point A262

1936-37   **Perf. 11x10½**
785 A258 1c green   .20   .20
786 A259 2c carmine ('37)   .20   .20
787 A260 3c purple ('37)   .20   .20
788 A261 4c gray ('37)   .30   .20
789 A262 5c ultra ('37)   .60   .20
    Nos. 785-789 (5)   1.50 1.00

Issued in honor of the United States Army.

Navy Issue

John Paul Jones and John Barry A263

Stephen Decatur and Thomas MacDonough — A264

Admirals David G. Farragut and David D. Porter A265

Admirals William T. Sampson, George Dewey and Winfield S. Schley A266

Seal of US Naval Academy and Naval Cadets A267

1936-37   **Perf. 11x10½**
790 A263 1c green   .20   .20
791 A264 2c carmine ('37)   .20   .20
792 A265 3c purple ('37)   .20   .20
793 A266 4c gray ('37)   .30   .20
794 A267 5c ultra ('37)   .60   .20
    Nos. 790-794 (5)   1.50 1.00

Issued in honor of the United States Navy.

Northwest Ordinance Sesquicentennial Issue

Manasseh Cutler, Rufus Putnam and Map of Northwest Territory A268

1937, July 13   **Perf. 11x10½**
795 A268 3c red violet   .20   .20

150th anniv. of the adoption of the Ordinance of 1787 and the creation of the Northwest Territory.

Virginia Dare Issue

Virginia Dare and Parents — A269

Flat Plate Printing

1937, Aug. 18   **Perf. 11**
796 A269 5c gray blue   .20   .20

350th anniv. of the birth of Virginia Dare and the settlement at Roanoke Island. Virginia was the first child born in America of English parents (Aug. 18, 1587).

Society of Philatelic Americans Souvenir Sheet

A269a

1937, Aug. 26   **Imperf.**
797 A269a 10c blue green   .60   .40

Sheet measures 67x78mm.

Constitution Sesquicentennial Issue

Signing of the Constitution A270

Rotary Press Printing

1937, Sept. 17   **Perf. 11x10½**
798 A270 3c bright red violet   .20   .20

Sesquicentennial of the Signing of the Constitution, Sept. 17, 1787.

Territorial Issues
Hawaii

Statue of Kamehameha I, Honolulu — A271

1937, Oct. 18   **Perf. 10½x11**
799 A271 3c violet   .20   .20

Alaska

Landscape with Mt. McKinley A272

1937, Nov. 12   **Perf. 11x10½**
800 A272 3c violet   .20   .20

Puerto Rico

La Fortaleza, San Juan A273

1937, Nov. 25   **Perf. 11x10½**
801 A273 3c bright violet   .20   .20

Virgin Islands

Charlotte Amalie A274

1937, Dec. 15   **Perf. 11x10½**
802 A274 3c light violet   .20   .20

Presidential Issue

Benjamin Franklin A275

George Washington A276

Martha Washington A277

John Adams A278

Thomas Jefferson A279

James Madison A280

White House A281

James Monroe A282

John Q. Adams A283

Andrew Jackson A284

Martin Van Buren A285

William H. Harrison A286

John Tyler — A287

James K. Polk — A288

Zachary Taylor A289

Millard Fillmore A290

Franklin Pierce A291

James Buchanan A292

Abraham Lincoln A293

Andrew Johnson A294

Ulysses S. Grant A295

Rutherford B. Hayes A296

James A. Garfield
A297

Chester A. Arthur
A298

Grover Cleveland
A299

Benjamin Harrison
A300

William McKinley
A301

Theodore Roosevelt
A302

William Howard Taft
A303

Woodrow Wilson
A304

Warren G. Harding
A305

Calvin Coolidge
A306

1938-54			Perf. 11x10½	
803	A275	½c deep orange	.20	.20
804	A276	1c green	.20	.20
b.		Booklet pane of 6	2.00	.35
805	A277	1½c bister brown	.20	.20
b.		Horiz. pair, imperf. btwn.	160.00	30.00
806	A278	2c rose carmine	.20	.20
b.		Booklet pane of 6	4.75	.85
807	A279	3c deep violet	.20	.20
a.		Booklet pane of 6	8.50	1.25
b.		Horiz. pair, imperf. btwn.	1,500.	—
c.		Imperf., pair	2,500.	
808	A280	4c red violet	.75	.20
809	A281	4½c dark gray	.20	.20
810	A282	5c bright blue	.20	.20
811	A283	6c red orange	.20	.20
812	A284	7c sepia	.25	.20
813	A285	8c olive green	.30	.20
814	A286	9c rose pink	.30	.20
815	A287	10c brown red	.25	.20
816	A288	11c ultra	.65	.20
817	A289	12c bright violet	.90	.20
818	A290	13c blue green	1.25	.20
819	A291	14c blue	.90	.20
820	A292	15c blue gray	.40	.20
821	A293	16c black	.90	.25
822	A294	17c rose red	.85	.20
823	A295	18c brown car	1.75	.20
824	A296	19c bright violet	1.25	.35
825	A297	20c brt blue grn	.70	.20
826	A298	21c dull blue	1.25	.20
827	A299	22c vermilion	1.00	.40
828	A300	24c gray black	3.50	.20
829	A301	25c deep red lil	.60	.20
830	A302	30c deep ultra	3.50	.20
831	A303	50c lt red violet	5.50	.20

Flat Plate Printing
Perf. 11

832	A304	$1 pur & black	7.00	.20
a.		Vert. pair, imperf. horiz.	1,600.	
b.		Wmkd. USIR ('51)	225.00	65.00
c.		$1 red violet & black ('54)	6.00	.20
d.		As "c," vert. pair, imperf. horiz.	1,500.	
e.		Vert. pair, imperf. btwn.	2,750.	
f.		As "c," vert. pair, imperf. btwn.	8,500.	

833	A305	$2 yel grn & blk	20.00	3.75
834	A306	$5 car & black	95.00	3.00
a.		$5 red brown & black	3,250.	7,000.
		Hinged	2,500.	
		Nos. 803-834 (32)	150.35	13.15

No. 805b used is always Bureau precanceled St. Louis Mo., and is generally with gum. Value is for gummed pair.

No. 832c is printed on thick white paper with smooth, colorless gum.

No. 834 can be chemically altered to resemble No. 834a. No. 834a should be purchased only with competent expert certification.

See Nos. 839-851.

Constitution Ratification Issue

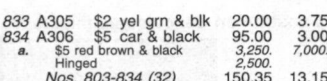

Old Court House, Williamsburg, Va. — A307

Rotary Press Printing
1938, June 21   Perf. 11x10½

835	A307	3c deep violet	.25	.20

150th anniv. of the ratification of the U.S. Constitution.

Landing of the Swedes and Finns — A308

Statue Symbolizing Colonization of the West — A309

Swedish-Finnish Tercentenary Issue
Flat Plate Printing
1938, June 27   Perf. 11

836	A308	3c red violet	.20	.20

Tercentenary of the Swedish and Finnish settlement at Wilmington, Del.

Northwest Territory Issue
Rotary Press Printing
1938, July 15   Perf. 11x10½

837	A309	3c bright violet	.20	.20

Sesquicentennial of the settlement of the Northwest Territory.

Iowa Territory Centennial Issue

Old Capitol, Iowa City A310

1938, Aug. 24   Perf. 11x10½

838	A310	3c violet	.20	.20

Centenary of Iowa Territory.

Presidential Types of 1938
Coil Stamps
Rotary Press Printing
1939   Perf. 10 Vertically

839	A276	1c green	.30	.20
840	A277	1½c bister brown	.30	.20
841	A278	2c rose carmine	.40	.20
842	A279	3c deep violet	.50	.20
843	A280	4c red violet	7.50	.40
844	A281	4½c dark gray	.70	.40
845	A282	5c bright blue	5.00	.35
846	A283	6c red orange	1.10	.20
847	A287	10c brown red	11.00	.50

Perf. 10 Horizontally

848	A276	1c green	.85	.20
849	A277	1½c bister brown	1.25	.30
850	A278	2c rose carmine	2.50	.40
851	A279	3c deep violet	2.25	.35
		Nos. 839-851 (13)	33.65	3.90

"Tower of the Sun"
A311

Trylon and Perisphere
A312

Golden Gate International Exposition Issue
Rotary Press Printing
1939, Feb. 18   Perf. 10½x11

852	A311	3c bright purple	.20	.20

Golden Gate Intl. Expo., San Francisco.

New York World's Fair Issue
1939, Apr. 1   Perf. 10½x11

853	A312	3c deep purple	.20	.20

Washington Inauguration Issue

George Washington Taking Oath of Office — A313

Flat Plate Printing
1939, Apr. 30   Perf. 11

854	A313	3c bright red violet	.40	.20

Sesquicentennial of George Washington's inauguration as 1st president.

Baseball Centennial Issue

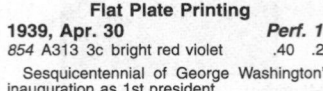

Sand-lot Baseball Game
A314

Rotary Press Printing
1939, June 12   Perf. 11x10½

855	A314	3c violet	1.75	.20

Centennial of baseball.

Panama Canal Issue

Theodore Roosevelt, Gen. George W. Goethals and Gaillard Cut — A315

Flat Plate Printing
1939, Aug. 15   Perf. 11

856	A315	3c deep red violet	.25	.20

25th anniv. of the Panama Canal opening.

Printing Tercentenary Issue

Stephen Daye Press — A316

Rotary Press Printing
1939, Sept. 25   Perf. 10½x11

857	A316	3c violet	.20	.20

300th anniv. of printing in Colonial America.

50th Anniversary of Statehood Issue

Map of North and South Dakota, Montana and Washington
A317

1939, Nov. 2   Perf. 11x10½

858	A317	3c rose violet	.20	.20

50th anniv. of admission to Statehood of North Dakota, South Dakota, Montana and Washington.

Famous Americans Issues
Authors

Washington Irving — A318

James Fenimore Cooper — A319

Ralph Waldo Emerson
A320

Louisa May Alcott
A321

Samuel L. Clemens (Mark Twain) — A322

1940   Perf. 10½x11

859	A318	1c bright blue green	.20	.20
860	A319	2c rose carmine	.20	.20
861	A320	3c bright red violet	.20	.20
862	A321	5c ultra	.30	.20
863	A322	10c dark brown	1.65	1.20
		Nos. 859-863 (5)	2.55	2.00

Poets

Henry W. Longfellow
A323

John Greenleaf Whittier
A324

James Russell Lowell
A325

Walt Whitman
A326

James Whitcomb Riley — A327

1940   *Perf. 10½x11*

864	A323	1c bright blue green	.20	.20
865	A324	2c rose carmine	.20	.20
866	A325	3c bright red violet	.20	.20
867	A326	5c ultra	.35	.20
868	A327	10c dark brown	1.75	1.25
	Nos. 864-868 (5)		2.70	2.05

Educators

Horace Mann A328   Mark Hopkins A329

Charles W. Eliot — A330   Frances E. Willard — A331

Booker T. Washington — A332

1940   *Perf. 10½x11*

869	A328	1c bright blue green	.20	.20
870	A329	2c rose carmine	.20	.20
871	A330	3c bright red violet	.20	.20
872	A331	5c ultra	.40	.20
873	A332	10c dark brown	1.25	1.10
	Nos. 869-873 (5)		2.25	1.90

Scientists

John James Audubon A333   Dr. Crawford W. Long A334

Luther Burbank A335   Dr. Walter Reed A336

Jane Addams — A337

1940   *Perf. 10½x11*

874	A333	1c bright blue green	.20	.20
875	A334	2c rose carmine	.20	.20
876	A335	3c bright red violet	.20	.20
877	A336	5c ultra	.25	.20
878	A337	10c dark brown	1.10	.85
	Nos. 874-878 (5)		1.95	1.65

Composers

Stephen Collins Foster — A338   John Philip Sousa — A339

Victor Herbert A340   Edward MacDowell A341

Ethelbert Nevin — A342

1940   *Perf. 10½x11*

879	A338	1c bright blue green	.20	.20
880	A339	2c rose carmine	.20	.20
881	A340	3c bright red violet	.20	.20
882	A341	5c ultra	.40	.20
883	A342	10c dark brown	3.75	1.20
	Nos. 879-883 (5)		4.75	2.00

Artists

Gilbert Charles Stuart A343   James A. McNeill Whistler A344

Augustus Saint-Gaudens A345   Daniel Chester French A346

Frederic Remington — A347

1940   *Perf. 10½x11*

884	A343	1c bright blue green	.20	.20
885	A344	2c rose carmine	.20	.20
886	A345	3c bright red violet	.20	.20
887	A346	5c ultra	.50	.20
888	A347	10c dark brown	1.75	1.25
	Nos. 884-888 (5)		2.85	2.05

Inventors

Eli Whitney — A348   Samuel F. B. Morse — A349

Cyrus Hall McCormick A350   Elias Howe A351

Alexander Graham Bell — A352

1940   *Perf. 10½x11*

889	A348	1c brt blue green	.20	.20
890	A349	2c rose carmine	.20	.20
891	A350	3c bright red violet	.25	.20
892	A351	5c ultra	1.10	.30
893	A352	10c dark brown	11.00	2.00
	Nos. 889-893 (5)		12.75	2.90
	Nos. 859-893 (35)		29.80	14.55

Pony Express Issue

Pony Express Rider A353

1940, Apr. 3   *Perf. 11x10½*

894	A353	3c henna brown	.25	.20

80th anniv. of the Pony Express.

Pan American Union Issue

The Three Graces from Botticelli's "Spring" — A354

1940, Apr. 14   *Perf. 10½x11*

895	A354	3c light violet	.20	.20

Pan American Union founding, 50th anniv.

Idaho Statehood Issue

Idaho Capitol, Boise A355

1940, July 3   *Perf. 11x10½*

896	A355	3c bright violet	.20	.20

Idaho statehood, 50th anniv.

Wyoming Statehood Issue

Wyoming State Seal — A356

1940, July 10   *Perf. 10½x11*

897	A356	3c brown violet	.20	.20

Wyoming statehood, 50th anniv.

Coronado Expedition Issue

"Coronado and His Captains," painted by Gerald Cassidy A357

1940, Sept. 7   *Perf. 11x10½*

898	A357	3c violet	.20	.20

400th anniv. of the Coronado Expedition.

National Defense Issue

Statue of Liberty — A358

90-millimeter Anti-aircraft Gun — A359

Torch of Enlightenment — A360

1940, Oct. 16   *Perf. 11x10½*

899	A358	1c bright blue green	.20	.20
a.		Vert. pair, imperf. btwn.	650.00	—
b.		Horiz. pair, imperf. btwn.	35.00	—
900	A359	2c rose carmine	.20	.20
a.		Horiz. pair, imperf. btwn.	40.00	—
901	A360	3c bright violet	.20	.20
a.		Horiz. pair, imperf. btwn.	27.50	—
	Nos. 899-901 (3)		.60	.60

Thirteenth Amendment Issue

"Emancipation," Statue of Lincoln and Slave, by Thomas Ball — A361

1940, Oct. 20   *Perf. 10½x11*

902	A361	3c deep violet	.20	.20

75th anniv. of the 13th Amendment to the Constitution.

Vermont Statehood Issue

Vermont Capitol, Montpelier A362

1941, Mar. 4   *Perf. 11x10½*

903	A362	3c light violet	.20	.20

Vermont statehood, 150th anniv.

Kentucky Statehood Issue

Daniel Boone and Three Frontiersmen, from mural by Gilbert White — A363

1942, June 1   *Perf. 11x10½*

904	A363	3c violet	.20	.20

Kentucky statehood, 150th anniv.

American Eagle — A364

Lincoln, Sun Yat-sen & Map A365

Win the War Issue

1942, July 4   **Perf. 11x10½**
905 A364 3c violet   .20   .20
   b.   3c purple

Chinese Resistance Issue

1942, July 7   **Perf. 11x10½**
906 A365 5c bright blue   .85   .20
   Five years' resistance of the Chinese people to Japanese aggression.

Allegory of Victory — A366

Allied Nations Issue

1943, Jan. 14   **Perf. 11x10½**
907 A366 2c rose carmine   .20   .20

Four Freedoms Issue

A367

1943, Feb. 12   **Perf. 11x10½**
908 A367 1c Liberty Holding Torch of Freedom & Enlightenment   .20 .20

Overrun Countries Issue

Flag of Poland A368

Frames Engraved, Centers Offset Letterpress
Rotary Press Printing
1943-44   **Unwmk.**   **Perf. 12**
909 A368 5c Poland   .20   .20
910 A368 5c Czechoslovakia   .20   .20
   a.   Double impression of "Czecho-slovakia"   —
911 A368 5c Norway   .20   .20
   a.   Double impression of "Norway"   —
912 A368 5c Luxembourg   .20   .20
   a.   Double impression of "Luxem-bourg"   —
913 A368 5c Netherlands   .20   .20
914 A368 5c Belgium   .20   .20
   a.   Double impression of "Belgium"   —
915 A368 5c France   .20   .20
916 A368 5c Greece   .35   .25
917 A368 5c Yugoslavia   .25   .20
   a.   Reverse printing of flag colors (red and blue over black)   —
918 A368 5c Albania   .20   .20
   a.   Double impression of "Albania"   —
919 A368 5c Austria   .20   .20
   a.   Double impression of "Austria"   —
920 A368 5c Denmark   .20   .20
921 A368 5c Korea ('44)   .20   .20
   a.   Double impression of "Korea"   —
     Nos. 909-921 (13)   2.80 2.65

Transcontinental Railroad Issue

"Golden Spike Ceremony" Painting by John McQuarrie A369

Engraved; Rotary Press Printing
1944, May 10   **Perf. 11x10½**
922 A369 3c violet   .20   .20
   75th anniv. of the completion of the first transcontinental railroad.

Steamship Issue

"Savannah" A370

1944, May 22   **Perf. 11x10½**
923 A370 3c violet   .20   .20
   125th anniv. of the first steamship to cross the Atlantic Ocean.

Telegraph Issue

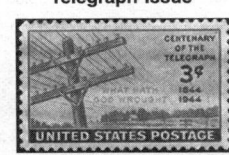

Telegraph Wires & the First Transmitted Words "What Hath God Wrought" A371

1944, May 24   **Perf. 11x10½**
924 A371 3c bright red violet   .20   .20
   100th anniv. of the 1st message transmitted by telegraph.

Philippines Issue

View of Corregidor A372

1944, Sept. 27   **Perf. 11x10½**
925 A372 3c deep violet   .20   .20
   Final resistance of the US and Philippine defenders on Corregidor.

Motion Pictures, 50th Anniv.

Motion Picture Showing for the Armed Forces in South Pacific A373

1944, Oct. 31   **Perf. 11x10½**
926 A373 3c deep violet   .20   .20

Florida Statehood Centenary

Old Florida Seal, St. Augustine Gates and State Capitol A374

1945, Mar. 3   **Perf. 11x10½**
927 A374 3c bright red violet   .20   .20

United Nations Conference Issue

A375

1945, Apr. 25   **Perf. 11x10½**
928 A375 5c ultramarine   .20   .20
   United Nations conference, San Francisco.

Iwo Jima (Marines) Issue

Marines Raising the Flag on Mt. Suribachi, Iwo Jima — A376

1945, July 11   **Perf. 10½x11**
929 A376 3c yellow green   .20   .20
   Achievements of the US Marines in WWII.

Franklin D. Roosevelt Issue

Roosevelt and Hyde Park Home A377

Roosevelt and "Little White House," Warm Springs, Georgia A378

Roosevelt and White House A379

Roosevelt, Globe and Four Freedoms A380

1945-46   **Perf. 11x10½**
930 A377 1c blue green   .20   .20
931 A378 2c carmine rose   .20   .20
932 A379 3c purple   .20   .20
933 A380 5c bright blue ('46)   .20   .20
     Nos. 930-933 (4)   .80   .80
   Franklin Delano Roosevelt (1882-1945).

Army Issue

US Troops Passing Arch of Triumph, Paris A381

1945, Sept. 28   **Perf. 11x10½**
934 A381 3c olive   .20   .20
   Achievements of the US Army in WWII.

Navy Issue

US Sailors A382

1945, Oct. 27   **Perf. 11x10½**
935 A382 3c blue   .20   .20
   Achievements of the US Navy in WWII.

Coast Guard Issue

Coast Guard Landing Craft and Supply Ship A383

1945, Nov. 10   **Perf. 11x10½**
936 A383 3c bright blue green   .20   .20
   Achievements of the US Coast Guard in WWII.

Alfred E. Smith — A384

US and Texas State Flags A385

Alfred E. Smith Issue

1945, Nov. 26   **Perf. 11x10½**
937 A384 3c purple   .20   .20
   Smith (1873-1944), governor of NY.

Texas Statehood Centenary

1945, Dec. 29   **Perf. 11x10½**
938 A385 3c dark blue   .20   .20

Liberty Ship Unloading Cargo A386

Honorable Discharge Emblem — A387

Merchant Marine Issue

1946, Feb. 26   **Perf. 11x10½**
939 A386 3c blue green   .20   .20
   Achievements of the US Merchant Marine in WWII.

Veterans of World War II Issue

1946, May 9   **Perf. 11x10½**
940 A387 3c dark violet   .20   .20
   Issued to honor all veterans of WWII.

Tennessee Statehood, 150th Anniv.

Andrew Jackson, John Sevier & Tennessee Capitol A388

1946, June 1   **Perf. 11x10½**
941 A388 3c dark violet   .20   .20

Iowa Statehood Centenary

Iowa State Flag & Map A389

1946, Aug. 3   **Perf. 11x10½**
942 A389 3c deep blue   .20   .20

Smithsonian Institution Issue

Smithsonian Institution — A390

1946, Aug. 10   *Perf. 11x10½*
943 A390 3c violet brown   .20   .20
Centenary of the establishment of the Smithsonian Institution, Washington, DC.

Kearny Expedition Issue

"Capture of Santa Fe" by Kenneth M. Chapman A391

1946, Oct. 16   *Perf. 11x10½*
944 A391 3c brown violet   .20   .20
Centenary of the entry of General Stephen Watts Kearny into Santa Fe.

Thomas Alva Edison Issue

Thomas A. Edison, Birth Centenary — A392

1947, Feb. 11   *Perf. 10½x11*
945 A392 3c bright red violet   .20   .20

Joseph Pulitzer Birth Centenary

Joseph Pulitzer & Statue of Liberty A393

1947, Apr. 10   *Perf. 11x10½*
946 A393 3c purple   .20   .20

U.S. Postage Stamp Centenary

Washington & Franklin; Early and Modern Mail-carrying Vehicles — A394

1947, May 17   *Perf. 11x10½*
947 A394 3c deep blue   .20   .20

Centenary International Philatelic Exhibition (CIPEX)

A395

Flat Plate Printing
1947, May 19   *Imperf.*
948 A395 Souvenir sheet of 2   .55   .45
   a.   A1 5c blue   .20   .20
   b.   A2 10c brown orange   .25   .25
Sheet size varies: 96-98x66-68mm

Doctors Issue

"The Doctor," by Sir Luke Fildes A396

Rotary Press Printing
1947, June 9   *Perf. 11x10½*
949 A396 3c brown violet   .20   .20
Issued to honor the physicians of America.

Utah Settlement Centenary

Pioneers Entering the Valley of Great Salt Lake A397

1947, July 24   *Perf. 11x10½*
950 A397 3c dark violet   .20   .20

US Frigate Constitution Issue

Naval Architect's Drawing of Frigate Constitution A398

1947, Oct. 21   *Perf. 11x10½*
951 A398 3c blue green   .20   .20
150th anniv. of the launching of the US Frigate Constitution ("Old Ironsides").

Everglades National Park Issue

Great White Heron and Map of Florida — A399

1947, Dec. 5   *Perf. 10½x11*
952 A399 3c bright green   .20   .20
Dedication of Everglades Natl. Park, Florida, Dec. 6, 1947.

Dr. George Washington Carver Issue

Dr. George Washington Carver — A400

1948, Jan. 5   *Perf. 10½x11*
953 A400 3c bright red violet   .20   .20
5th anniv. of the death of Dr. George Washington Carver, scientist.

California Gold Centennial Issue

Sutter's Mill, Coloma, California A401

1948, Jan. 24   *Perf. 11x10½*
954 A401 3c dark violet   .20   .20
Discovery of gold in California, centenary.

Mississippi Territory, 150th Anniv.

Map, Seal and Gov. Winthrop Sargent A402

1948, Apr. 7   *Perf. 11x10½*
955 A402 3c brown violet   .20   .20

Four Chaplains Issue

Four Chaplains and Sinking S.S. Dorchester A403

1948, May 28   *Perf. 11x10½*
956 A403 3c gray black   .20   .20
George L. Fox, Clark V. Poling, John P. Washington and Alexander D. Goode, the four chaplains who sacrificed their lives in the sinking of the S.S. Dorchester, Feb. 3, 1943.

Wisconsin Statehood Centenary

Map on Scroll & State Capitol A404

1948, May 29   *Perf. 11x10½*
957 A404 3c dark violet   .20   .20

Swedish Pioneer Issue

Swedish Pioneer with Covered Wagon Moving Westward - A405

1948, June 4   *Perf. 11x10½*
958 A405 5c deep blue   .20   .20
Centenary of the coming of the Swedish pioneers to the Middle West.

Progress of Women Issue

Elizabeth Stanton, Carrie C. Catt & Lucretia Mott A406

1948, July 19   *Perf. 11x10½*
959 A406 3c dark violet   .20   .20
Century of progress of American women.

William Allen White Issue

William Allen White, Editor and Author — A407

1948, July 31   *Perf. 10½x11*
960 A407 3c bright red violet   .20   .20

U.S.-Canada Friendship Centenary

Niagara Railway Suspension Bridge A408

1948, Aug. 2   *Perf. 11x10½*
961 A408 3c blue   .20   .20

Francis Scott Key Issue

Key and American Flags of 1814 and 1948 A409

1948, Aug. 9   *Perf. 11x10½*
962 A409 3c rose pink   .20   .20
Key (1779-1843), Maryland lawyer and author of "The Star-Spangled Banner" (1813).

Salute to Youth Issue

Girl and Boy Carrying Books A410

1948, Aug. 11   *Perf. 11x10½*
963 A410 3c deep blue   .20   .20
Youth of America and "Youth Month," Sept. 1948.

Oregon Territory Issue

John McLoughlin, Jason Lee & Wagon on Oregon Trail — A411

1948, Aug. 14   *Perf. 11x10½*
964 A411 3c brown red   .20   .20
Centenary of the establishment of Ore. Terr.

Harlan Fiske Stone Issue

Chief Justice Harlan Fiske Stone — A412

1948, Aug. 25   *Perf. 10½x11*
965 A412 3c bright red violet   .20   .20

Palomar Mountain Observatory Issue

Observatory, Palomar Mt., Cal. — A413

1948, Aug. 30   *Perf. 10½x11*
966 A413 3c blue   .20   .20
   a.   Vert. pair, imperf btwn.   550.00

Clara Barton, 1821-1912

Founder of the American Red Cross (1882) A414

1948, Sept. 7   *Perf. 11x10½*
967 A414 3c rose pink   .20   .20

Poultry Industry Issue

Light Brahma Rooster A415

1948, Sept. 9   *Perf. 11x10½*
968 A415 3c sepia   .20 .20
  Centenary of the establishment of the American poultry industry.

Gold Star Mothers Issue

Star and Palm Frond — A416

1948, Sept. 21   *Perf. 10½x11*
969 A416 3c orange yellow   .20 .20
  Honoring mothers of deceased members of the U.S. armed forces.

Fort Kearny Issue

Fort Kearny and Pioneer Group A417

1948, Sept. 22   *Perf. 11x10½*
970 A417 3c violet   .20 .20
  Establishment of Fort Kearny, Nebr., cent.

Volunteer Firemen Issue

Peter Stuyvesant; Early and Modern Fire Engines A418

1948, Oct. 4   *Perf. 11x10½*
971 A418 3c bright rose carmine   .20 .20
  300th anniv. of the organization of the 1st volunteer firemen in America by Peter Stuyvesant (1592-1672), Dutch colonial gov. of New Netherland.

Indian Centennial Issue

Map of Indian Territory & Seals of Five Tribes A419

1948, Oct. 15   *Perf. 11x10½*
972 A419 3c dark brown   .20 .20
  Cent. of the arrival in Indian Territory, later Okla., of the Five Civilized Indian Tribes.

Rough Riders Issue

Statue of Capt. William O. (Bucky) O'Neill A420

1948, Oct. 27   *Perf. 11x10½*
973 A420 3c violet brown   .20 .20
  50th anniv. of the organization of the Rough Riders of the Spanish-American War.

Low and Girl Scout Emblem A421

Will Rogers — A422

Juliette Low Issue
1948, Oct. 29   *Perf. 11x10½*
974 A421 3c blue green   .20 .20
  Juliette Gordon Low (1860-1927), organizer of the Girl Scouts of America.

Will Rogers Issue
1948, Nov. 4   *Perf. 10½x11*
975 A422 3c bright red violet   .20 .20
  Will Rogers, 1879-1935, humorist and political commentator.

Fort Bliss and Rocket — A423

Moina Michael and Poppy Plant A424

Fort Bliss Centennial Issue
1948, Nov. 5   *Perf. 10½x11*
976 A423 3c henna brown   .20 .20
  Centenary of Fort Bliss, Texas.

Moina Michael Issue
1948, Nov. 9   *Perf. 11x10½*
977 A424 3c rose pink   .20 .20
  Michael (1870-1944), educator who originated (1918) Flanders Field Poppy Day idea as memorial to war dead.

Gettysburg Address Issue

Lincoln and Quotation from Gettysburg Address A425

1948, Nov. 19   *Perf. 11x10½*
978 A425 3c bright blue   .20 .20
  85th anniv. of Abraham Lincoln's address at Gettysburg, Pa.

Torch and American Turners' Emblem A426

Joel Chandler Harris A427

American Turners Issue
1948, Nov. 20   *Perf. 10½x11*
979 A426 3c carmine   .20 .20
  Centenary of the formation of the American Turners Society.

Joel Chandler Harris Issue
1948, Dec. 9   *Perf. 10½x11*
980 A427 3c bright red violet   .20 .20
  Harris (1848-1908), editor and author.

Minnesota Territory Issue

Pioneer and Red River Oxcart A428

1949, Mar. 3   *Perf. 11x10½*
981 A428 3c blue green   .20 .20
  Cent. of the establishment of Minn. Terr.

Washington and Lee University Issue

George Washington, Robert E. Lee and University Building — A429

1949, Apr. 12   *Perf. 11x10½*
982 A429 3c ultramarine   .20 .20
  200th anniv. of the founding of Washington and Lee Univ.

Puerto Rico Election Issue

Puerto Rican Farmer Holding Cogwheel and Ballot Box A430

1949, Apr. 27   *Perf. 11x10½*
983 A430 3c green   .20 .20
  1st gubernatorial election in the Territory of P.R., Nov. 2, 1948.

Annapolis Tercentenary Issue

Stoddert's 1718 Map of Regions about Annapolis, Redrawn A431

1949, May 23   *Perf. 11x10½*
984 A431 3c aquamarine   .20 .20
  Founding of Annapolis, Md., 300th anniv

Union Soldier and GAR Veteran of 1949 A432

Edgar Allan Poe — A433

GAR Issue
1949, Aug. 29   *Perf. 11x10½*
985 A432 3c bright rose carmine   .20 .20
  Final encampment of the Grand Army of the Republic, Indianapolis, Aug. 28 to Sept. 1.

Edgar Allan Poe Issue
1949, Oct. 7   *Perf. 10½x11*
986 A433 3c bright red violet   .20 .20
  Poe (1809-1849), writer and poet.

Coin, Symbolizing Fields of Banking Service — A434

Samuel Gompers — A435

Bankers Issue
1950, Jan. 3   *Perf. 11x10½*
987 A434 3c yellow green   .20 .20
  75th anniv. of the formation of the American Bankers Assoc.

Samuel Gompers Issue
1950, Jan. 27   *Perf. 10½x11*
988 A435 3c bright red violet   .20 .20
  Gompers (1850-1924), labor leader.

National Capital Sesquicentennial Issue

Statue of Freedom on Capitol Dome — A436

Executive Mansion A437

Supreme Court Building A438

United States Capitol A439

1950   *Perf. 10½x11, 11x10½*
989 A436 3c bright blue   .20 .20
990 A437 3c deep green   .20 .20
991 A438 3c light violet   .20 .20
992 A439 3c bright red violet   .20 .20
  Nos. 989-992 (4)   .80 .80
  150th anniv. of the establishment of the National Capital, Washington, DC.
  Issued: Apr. 20; June 12; Aug. 2; Nov. 22.

Railroad Engineers Issue

"Casey" Jones and Locomotives of
1900 and 1950 — A440

1950, Apr. 29   *Perf. 11x10½*
993 A440 3c violet brown   .20   .20

Kansas City, Missouri, Issue

Kansas City Skyline, 1950 and
Westport Landing, 1850
A441

1950, June 3   *Perf. 11x10½*
994 A441 3c violet   .20   .20
Incorporation of Kansas City, Mo., cent.

Boy Scouts Issue

Three
Boys,
Statue of
Liberty and
Scout
Badge
A442

1950, June 30   *Perf. 11x10½*
995 A442 3c sepia   .20   .20
Honoring the BSA on the occasion of the
2nd Natl. Jamboree, held at Valley Forge, Pa.

Indiana Territory Issue

Gov. William Henry Harrison & First
Indiana Capitol, Vincennes
A443

1950, July 4   *Perf. 11x10½*
996 A443 3c bright blue   .20   .20
150th anniv. establishment of Ind. Terr.

California Statehood Centenary

Gold Miner,
Pioneers
and S.S.
Oregon
A444

1950, Sept. 9   *Perf. 11x10½*
997 A444 3c yellow orange   .20   .20

United Confederate Veterans Final Reunion Issue

Confederate
Soldier &
United
Confederate
Veteran
A445

1951, May 30   *Perf. 11x10½*
998 A445 3c gray   .20   .20
Final reunion of the United Confederate Veterans, Norfolk, Va, May 30, 1951.

Nevada Settlement Centennial

Carson
Valley,
c. 1851
A446

1951, July 14   *Perf. 11x10½*
999 A446 3c light olive green   .20   .20

Landing of Cadillac Issue

Detroit
Skyline and
Cadillac
Landing
A447

1951, July 24   *Perf. 11x10½*
1000 A447 3c blue   .20   .20
250th anniv. of the landing of Antoine de la
Mothe Cadillac at Detroit.

Colorado Statehood Issue

Colorado
Capitol and
Mount of
the Holy
Cross
A448

1951, Aug. 1   *Perf. 11x10½*
1001 A448 3c blue violet   .20   .20
Colorado statehood, 75th anniv. Design
includes columbine and statue, "The Bronco
Buster," by A. Phimister Proctor.

American Chemical Society Issue

A.C.S.
Emblem
and
Symbols of
Chemistry
A449

1951, Sept. 4   *Perf. 11x10½*
1002 A449 3c violet brown   .20   .20
American Chemical Soc., 75th anniv.

Battle of Brooklyn Issue

Gen.
George
Washington
Evacuating
Army
A450

1951, Dec. 10   *Perf. 11x10½*
1003 A450 3c violet   .20   .20
175th anniv. of the Battle of Brooklyn.
Design includes Fulton Ferry House.

Betsy Ross Issue

Betsy Ross Showing Flag to Gen.
George Washington, Robert Morris &
George Ross — A451

1952, Jan. 2   *Perf. 11x10½*
1004 A451 3c carmine rose   .20   .20
200th anniv. of the birth of Betsy Ross,
maker of the 1st American flag.

4-H Club Issue

Farm, Club
Emblem,
Boy and
Girl
A452

1952, Jan. 15   *Perf. 11x10½*
1005 A452 3c blue green   .20   .20

B. & O. Railroad Issue

Charter and Three Stages of Rail
Transportation — A453

1952, Feb. 28   *Perf. 11x10½*
1006 A453 3c bright blue   .20   .20
125th anniv. of the granting of a charter to
the Baltimore and Ohio Railroad Company by
the Maryland Legislature.

A. A. A., 50th Anniv.

School Girls and Safety Patrolman,
Automobiles of 1902 and
1952 — A454

1952, Mar. 4   *Perf. 11x10½*
1007 A454 3c deep blue   .20   .20

Torch of Liberty and
Globe — A455

Spillway,
Grand
Coulee
Dam
A456

NATO Issue

1952, Apr. 4   *Perf. 11x10½*
1008 A455 3c deep violet   .20   .20
3rd anniv. of the signing of the North Atlantic
Treaty.

Grand Coulee Dam Issue

1952, May 15   *Perf. 11x10½*
1009 A456 3c blue green   .20   .20
50 years of federal cooperation in developing the resources of rivers and streams in the
West.

Lafayette Issue

Marquis de Lafayette, Flags, Cannon
and Landing Party
A457

1952, June 13   *Perf. 11x10½*
1010 A457 3c bright blue   .20   .20
Arrival of Lafayette in America, 175th anniv.

Mt. Rushmore Memorial Issue

Sculptured Heads on
Mt.
Rushmore — A458

1952, Aug. 11   *Perf. 10½x11*
1011 A458 3c blue green   .20   .20
25th anniv. of the dedication of the Mt.
Rushmore Natl. Memorial.

Engineering Centennial Issue

George Washington Bridge & Covered
Bridge of 1850s — A459

1952, Sept. 6   *Perf. 11x10½*
1012 A459 3c violet blue   .20   .20
Centenary of the founding of the American
Soc. of Civil Engineers.

Service Women Issue

Women of
the Marine
Corps,
Army, Navy
and Air
Force
A460

1952, Sept. 11   *Perf. 11x10½*
1013 A460 3c deep blue   .20   .20
Honoring the women in the US Armed
Services.

Gutenberg Bible Issue

Gutenberg
Showing
Proof to the
Elector of
Mainz
A461

1952, Sept. 30   *Perf. 11x10½*
1014 A461 3c violet   .20   .20
500th anniv. of the printing of the 1st book,
the Holy Bible, from movable type, by Johann
Gutenberg.

Newspaper Boys Issue

Newspaper
Boy, Torch
and Group
of Homes
A462

1952, Oct. 4   *Perf. 11x10½*
1015 A462 3c violet   .20   .20

Red Cross Issue

Globe, Sun
and Cross
A463

1952, Nov. 21   *Perf. 11x10½*
                         Cross Typo.
1016 A463 3c deep blue & car   .20   .20

National Guard Issue

National Guardsman and Amphibious Landing A464

1953, Feb. 23   *Perf. 11x10½*
1017 A464 3c bright blue   .20   .20

Ohio Statehood Sesquicentennial

Map and Ohio State Seal — A465

1953, Mar. 2   *Perf. 11x10½*
1018 A465 3c chocolate   .20   .20

Washington Territory Issue

Medallion, Pioneers and Washington Scene A466

1953, Mar. 2   *Perf. 11x10½*
1019 A466 3c green   .20   .20
Centenary of the organization of Washington Territory.

Louisiana Purchase, 150th Anniv.

Monroe, Livingston and Barbé-Marbois — A467

1953, Apr. 30   *Perf. 11x10½*
1020 A467 3c violet brown   .20   .20

Opening of Japan Centennial Issue

Commodore Perry and 1st Anchorage off Tokyo Bay — A468

1953, July 14   *Perf. 11x10½*
1021 A468 5c green   .20   .20
Cent. of Commodore Matthew Calbraith Perry's negotiations with Japan, which opened her doors to foreign trade.

American Bar Association, 75th Anniv.

Section of Frieze, Supreme Court Room A469

1953, Aug. 24   *Perf. 11x10½*
1022 A469 3c rose violet   .20   .20

Sagamore Hill Issue

Home of Theodore Roosevelt A470

1953, Sept. 14   *Perf. 11x10½*
1023 A470 3c yellow green   .20   .20
Opening of Sagamore Hill, Theodore Roosevelt's home, as a national shrine.

Future Farmers Issue

Agricultural Scene and Future Farmer A471

1953, Oct. 13   *Perf. 11x10½*
1024 A471 3c deep blue   .20   .20
25th anniv. of the organization of Future Farmers of America.

Trucking Industry Issue

Truck, Farm and Distant City A472

1953, Oct. 27   *Perf. 11x10½*
1025 A472 3c violet   .20   .20
Trucking Industry in the US, 50th anniv.

General Patton Issue

Gen. George S. Patton, Jr., and Tank in Action A473

1953, Nov. 11   *Perf. 11x10½*
1026 A473 3c blue violet   .20   .20
Honoring Patton and the armored forces of the US army.

New York City, 300th Anniv.

Dutch Ship in New Amsterdam Harbor A474

1953, Nov. 20   *Perf. 11x10½*
1027 A474 3c bright red violet   .20   .20

Gadsden Purchase Issue

Map and Pioneer Group A475

1953, Dec. 30   *Perf. 11x10½*
1028 A475 3c copper brown   .20   .20
Centenary of James Gadsden's purchase of territory from Mexico, to adjust US-Mexico boundary.

Columbia University, 200th Anniv.

Low Memorial Library A476

1954, Jan. 4   *Perf. 11x10½*
1029 A476 3c blue   .20   .20

Wet and Dry Printings

In 1953 the Bureau of Engraving and Printing began experiments in printing on "dry" paper (moisture content 5-10 per cent). In previous "wet" printings the paper had a moisture content of 13-35 per cent.

The new process required a thicker, stiffer paper, special types of inks and greater pressure to force the paper into the recessed plates. The "dry" printings show whiter paper, a higher sheen on the surface, feel thicker and stiffer, and the designs stand out more clearly than on the "wet" printings.

Nos. 832c and 1041 (flat plate) were the first "dry" printings to be issued of flat-plate, regular-issue stamps. No. 1063 was the first rotary-press stamp to be produced entirely by "dry" printing.

All postage stamps have been printed by the "dry" process since the late 1950's.

See the Scott Specialized Catalogue of United States Stamps for listings of the wet and dry printings and for No. 1033 on Silkote paper.

Liberty Issue

Franklin A477

Washington A478

Palace of the Governors, Santa Fe — A478a

Mount Vernon — A479

Thomas Jefferson A480

Bunker Hill Monument, Mass. Flag, 1776 A481

Statue of Liberty A482

Abraham Lincoln A483

The Hermitage A484

James Monroe A485

Theodore Roosevelt A486

Woodrow Wilson A487

Statue of Liberty A488

Statue of Liberty A489

John J. Pershing A489a

The Alamo A490

Independence Hall — A491

Statue of Liberty A491a

Benjamin Harrison A492

John Jay A493

Paul Revere A495

Monticello A494

John Marshall A497

Patrick Henry A499

Robert E. Lee A496

Susan B. Anthony A498

Alexander Hamilton A500

Perf. 11x10½, 10½x11
1954-68   Rotary Press Printing
1030 A477   ½c red org
                    ('55)   .20   .20
1031 A478   1c dark grn   .20   .20
1031A A478a 1¼c turq ('60)   .20   .20

1032	A479	1½c brn car ('56)	.20	.20
1033	A480	2c car rose	.20	.20
1034	A481	2½c gray bl ('59)	.20	.20
1035	A482	3c deep vio	.20	.20
a.		Booklet pane of 6	4.00	.90
b.		Tagged ('66)	.25	.25
c.		Imperf., pair	2,000.	
d.		Horiz. pair, imperf btwn.	—	
g.		As "a," vert. imperf btwn.	5,000.	

No. 1057a measures about 19½x22mm; No. 1035c, about 18¾x22½mm.

1036	A483	4c red violet	.20	.20
a.		Booklet pane of 6 ('58)	2.75	.80
b.		Tagged ('63)	.60	.40
d.		As "a," imperf. horiz.	—	
1037	A484	4½c bl grn ('59)	.20	.20
1038	A485	5c deep blue	.20	.20
1039	A486	6c car ('55)	.25	.20
b.		Imperf., pair	11,000.	
1040	A487	7c rose car ('56)	.20	.20
a.		7c dark rose carmine	.20	.20

Flat Plate Printing
Perf. 11
Size: 22.7mm high

1041	A488	8c dk vio blue & car	.25	.20
a.		Double impression of carmine	650.00	

Rotary Press Printing
Size: 22.9mm high

1041B	A488	8c dk vio blue & car	.40	.20

Giori Press Printing
Redrawn Design

1042	A489	8c dk vio bl & car rose ('58)	.20	.20

Rotary Press Printing
Perf. 11x10½, 10½x11

1042A	A489a	8c brown ('61)	.20	.20
1043	A490	9c rose lil ('56)	.30	.20
a.		9c dark rose lilac	.30	
1044	A491	10c rose lake ('56)	.30	.20
b.		10c dark rose lake	.25	.20
d.		Tagged ('66)	2.00	1.00

Giori Press Printing
Perf. 11

1044A	A491a	11c car & dk vio blue ('61)	.30	.20
c.		Tagged ('67)	2.00	1.60

Rotary Press Printing
Perf. 11x10½, 10½x11

1045	A492	12c red ('59)	.35	.20
a.		Tagged ('68)	.35	.20
1046	A493	15c rose lake ('58)	.60	.20
a.		Tagged ('66)	1.10	.35
1047	A494	20c ultra ('56)	.40	.20
a.		20c deep bright ultra	.40	.20
1048	A495	25c green ('58)	1.10	.20
1049	A496	30c black ('55)	.70	.20
b.		30c intense black	.70	
1050	A497	40c brn red ('55)	1.50	.20
1051	A498	50c brt pur ('55)	1.50	.20
1052	A499	$1 purple ('55)	4.50	.20

Flat Plate Printing
Perf. 11

1053	A500	$5 black ('56)	70.00	6.75
	Nos. 1030-1053 (28)		85.05	12.15

Luminescence

During 1963 quantities of certain issues (Nos. C64a, 1213b, 1213c and 1229a) were overprinted with phosphorescent coating, "tagged," for use in testing automated facing and canceling machines. Listings for tagged varieties of stamps previously issued without tagging start with Nos. 1035b and C59a.

The entire printings of Nos. 1238, 1278, 1280-1281, 1283B, 1286-1288, 1298-1305, 1323-1340, 1342-1362, 1364, and C69-C75 and all following listings, unless otherwise noted, were tagged.

Stamps tagged with zinc orthosilicate glow yellow green. Airmail stamps with calcium silicate overprint glow orange red. Both tagging overprints are activated only by shortwave ultraviolet light.

Coil Stamps
Perf. 10 Vert., Horiz. (1¼c, 4½c)
1954-73

1054	A478	1c dark grn	.20	.20
b.		Imperf., pair	2,500.	—

1054A	A478a	1¼c turq ('60)	.20	.20
1055	A480	2c rose car	.20	.20
a.		Tagged ('68)	.20	.20
b.		Imperf., pair (Bureau precanceled)	550.00	
c.		As "a," imperf. pair	575.00	
1056	A481	2½c gray blue ('59)	.25	.25
1057	A482	3c dp violet	.20	.20
a.		Imperf., pair	1,750.	
b.		Tagged ('66)	1.00	.50

No. 1057a measures about 19½x22mm; No. 1035c, about 18¾x22½mm.

1058	A483	4c red vio ('58)	.20	.20
a.		Imperf., pair	120.00	120.00
1059	A484	4½c blue grn ('59)	1.50	1.20
1059A	A495	25c grn ('65)	.50	.30
b.		Tagged ('73)	.65	.20
c.		Imperf., pair	55.00	
	Nos. 1054-1059A (8)		3.25	2.75

Value for No. 1059Ac is for fine centering.

Nebraska Territory Issue

Mitchell Pass, Scotts Bluff & "The Sower," by Lee Lawrie A507

1954, May 7   *Perf. 11x10½*
1060 A507 3c violet   .20 .20
Establishment of the Nebraska Terr., cent.

Kansas Territory Issue

Wheat Field and Pioneer Wagon Train A508

1954, May 31   *Perf. 11x10½*
1061 A508 3c brown orange   .20 .20
Establishment of the Kansas Terr., cent.

George Eastman Issue

George Eastman (1854-1932), Inventor & Philanthropist — A509

1954, July 12   *Perf. 10½x11*
1062 A509 3c violet brown   .20 .20

Lewis and Clark Expedition Sesquicentennial

Landing of Lewis and Clark A510

1954, July 28   *Perf. 11x10½*
1063 A510 3c violet brown   .20 .20

Pennsylvania Academy of the Fine Arts

Charles Willson Peale in his Museum, Self-portrait — A511

1955, Jan. 15   *Perf. 10½x11*
1064 A511 3c violet brown   .20 .20
150th anniv. of the founding of the Pa. Acad. of the Fine Arts, Philadelphia.

Land Grant Colleges Issue

Open Book and Symbols of Subjects Taught A512

1955, Feb. 12   *Perf. 11x10½*
1065 A512 3c green   .20 .20
Cent. of the founding of Mich. State College and Penn. State Univ., 1st of the land-grant institutions.

Rotary International, 50th Anniv.

Torch, Globe and Rotary Emblem A513

1955, Feb. 23   *Perf. 11x10½*
1066 A513 8c deep blue   .20 .20

Armed Forces Reserve Issue

Marine, Coast Guard, Army, Navy, & Air Force Personnel A514

1955, May 21   *Perf. 11x10½*
1067 A514 3c purple   .20 .20

New Hampshire Issue

Great Stone Face — A515

1955, June 21   *Perf. 10½x11*
1068 A515 3c green   .20 .20
Honor NH on the occasion of the sesquicentennial of the discovery of the "Old Man of the Mountains."

Soo Locks Opening, Centenary

Map of Great Lakes and Two Steamers A516

1955, June 28   *Perf. 11x10½*
1069 A516 3c blue   .20 .20

Atoms for Peace Policy

Atomic Energy Encircling the Hemispheres — A517

1955, July 28   *Perf. 11x10½*
1070 A517 3c deep blue   .20 .20

Fort Ticonderoga Bicentenary

Map of the Fort, Ethan Allen and Artillery A518

1955, Sept. 18   *Perf. 11x10½*
1071 A518 3c light brown   .20 .20

Andrew W. Mellon Issue

Andrew W. Mellon — A519

1955, Dec. 20   *Perf. 10½x11*
1072 A519 3c rose carmine   .20 .20
Mellon, U.S. Sec. of the Treasury (1921-32), financier and art collector.

Benjamin Franklin Issue

"Franklin Taking Electricity from the Sky," by Benjamin West — A520

1956, Jan. 17   *Perf. 10½x11*
1073 A520 3c bright carmine   .20 .20
250th anniv. of the birth of Franklin.

Booker T. Washington Issue

Log Cabin A521

1956, Apr. 5   *Perf. 11x10½*
1074 A521 3c deep blue   .20 .20
Washington (1856-1915), black educator.

5th International Philatelic Exhibition Issue

A522

Flat Plate Printing

1956, Apr. 28   *Imperf.*

1075	A522	Souvenir sheet of 2	2.00	2.00
a.		A482 3c deep violet	.80	.80
b.		A488 8c dk vio bl & carmine	1.00	1.00

No. 1075 measures 108x73mm; Nos. 1075a and 1075b measure 24x28mm.

New York Coliseum & Columbus Monument A523

Rotary Press Printing
1956, Apr. 30   *Perf. 11x10½*
1076 A523 3c deep violet   .20 .20
FIPEX, New York City, Apr. 28-May 6.

Wildlife Conservation Issue

Wild Turkey
A524

Pronghorn Antelope
A525

King Salmon
A526

1956   *Perf. 11x10½*
1077 A524 3c rose lake   .20 .20
1078 A525 3c brown   .20 .20
1079 A526 3c blue green   .20 .20
   Nos. 1077-1079 (3)   .60 .60

Emphasizing the importance of Wildlife conservation in America.
Issued: May 5, June 22, Nov. 9.
See Nos. 1098, 1392.

Pure Food and Drug Laws, 50th Anniv.

Harvey W. Wiley — A527

1956, June 27   *Perf. 10½x11*
1080 A527 3c dark blue green   .20 .20

Wheatland Issue

President Buchanan's Home, "Wheatland," Lancaster, PA — A528

1956, Aug. 5   *Perf. 11x10½*
1081 A528 3c black brown   .20 .20

Labor Day Issue

Mosaic, AFL-CIO Headquarters
A529

1956, Sept. 3   *Perf. 10½x11*
1082 A529 3c deep blue   .20 .20

Nassau Hall Issue

Nassau Hall, Princeton, NJ — A530

1956, Sept. 22   *Perf. 11x10½*
1083 A530 3c black, *orange*   .20 .20

200th anniv. of Nassau Hall, Princeton University.

Devils Tower Issue

Devils Tower — A531

1956, Sept. 24   *Perf. 10½x11*
1084 A531 3c violet   .20 .20

50th anniv. of the Federal law providing for protection of American natural antiquities.
Devils Tower Natl. Monument, Wyoming, is an outstanding example.

Children's Issue

Children of the World
A532

1956, Dec. 15   *Perf. 11x10½*
1085 A532 3c dark blue   .20 .20

Promoting friendship among the world's children.

Alexander Hamilton Issue

Alexander Hamilton (1757-1804) and Federal Hall
A533

1957, Jan. 11   *Perf. 11x10½*
1086 A533 3c rose red   .20 .20

Polio Issue

Allegory — A534

1957, Jan. 15   *Perf. 10½x11*
1087 A534 3c red lilac   .20 .20

Honoring "those who helped fight polio," and 20th anniv. of the Natl. Foundation for Infantile Paralysis and the March of Dimes.

Coast and Geodetic Survey Issue

Flag of Coast and Geodetic Survey and Ships at Sea
A535

1957, Feb. 11   *Perf. 11x10½*
1088 A535 3c dark blue   .20 .20

150th anniv. of the establishment of the Coast and Geodetic Survey.

Architects Issue

Corinthian Capital and Mushroom Type Head & Shaft
A536

1957, Feb. 23   *Perf. 11x10½*
1089 A536 3c red lilac   .20 .20

Centenary of the American Institute of Architects.

Steel Industry Centenary

American Eagle and Pouring Ladle — A537

1957, May 22   *Perf. 10½x11*
1090 A537 3c bright ultra   .20 .20

International Naval Review Issue

Aircraft Carrier and Jamestown Festival Emblem
A538

1957, June 10   *Perf. 11x10½*
1091 A538 3c blue green   .20 .20

Intl. Naval Review and Jamestown Festival.

Oklahoma Statehood, 50th Anniv.

Map of Oklahoma, Arrow and Atom Diagram
A539

1957, June 14   *Perf. 11x10½*
1092 A539 3c dark blue   .20 .20

School Teachers Issue

Teacher and Pupils
A540

1957, July 1   *Perf. 11x10½*
1093 A540 3c rose lake   .20 .20

Honoring the school teachers of America.

Flag Issue

"Old Glory" (48 Stars)
A541

Giori Press Printing

1957, July 4   *Perf. 11*
1094 A541 4c dk blue & dp car   .20 .20

Shipbuilding Issue

"Virginia of Sagadahock" and Seal of Maine — A542

Rotary Press Printing

1957, Aug. 15   *Perf. 10½x11*
1095 A542 3c deep violet   .20 .20

350th anniv. of shipbuilding in America.

Champion of Liberty Issue

Ramon Magsaysay, (1907-1957), Philippines President — A543

Giori Press Printing

1957, Aug. 31   *Perf. 11*
1096 A543 8c car, ultra & ocher   .20 .20

For other Champion of Liberty issues, see Nos. 1110-1111, 1117-1118, 1125-1126, 1136-1137, 1147-1148, 1159-1160, 1165-1166, 1168-1169, 1174-1175.

Marquis de Lafayette
A544

Whooping Cranes
A545

Lafayette Bicentenary Issue
Rotary Press Printing

1957, Sept. 6   *Perf. 10½x11*
1097 A544 3c rose lake   .20 .20

Bicentenary of the birth of Lafayette.

Wildlife Conservation Issue
Giori Press Printing

1957, Nov. 22   *Perf. 11*
1098 A545 3c blue, ocher & grn   .20 .20

Emphasizing the importance of Wildlife Conservation in America.

Bible, Hat and Quill Pen — A546

"Bountiful Earth" — A547

Religious Freedom Issue
Rotary Press Printing

1957, Dec. 27   *Perf. 10½x11*
1099 A546 3c black   .20 .20

Flushing Remonstrance, 300th anniv.

Gardening-Horticulture Issue

1958, Mar. 15
1100 A547 3c green   .20 .20

Garden clubs of America and cent. of the birth of Liberty Hyde Bailey, horticulturist.

Brussels Fair Issue

US Pavilion at Brussels
A551

Rotary Press Printing

1958, Apr. 17   *Perf. 11x10½*
1104 A551 3c deep claret   .20 .20

Opening of the Universal and Intl. Exhib., Brussels, Apr. 17.

James Monroe Issue

James Monroe, by Gilbert Stuart — A552

1958, Apr. 28   *Perf. 11x10½*
1105 A552 3c purple   .20   .20
Monroe (1758-1831), 5th pres. of the US.

Minnesota Statehood Centenary

Minnesota Lakes and Pines A553

Rotary Press Printing
1958, May 11
1106 A553 3c green   .20   .20

Geophysical Year (IGY, 1957-58)

Solar Disc and Hands from Michelangelo's "Creation of Adam" — A554

Giori Press Printing
1958, May 31   *Perf. 11*
1107 A554 3c black & red orange   .20   .20

Gunston Hall Issue

Gunston Hall, Virginia A555

Rotary Press Printing
1958, June 12   *Perf. 11x10½*
1108 A555 3c light green   .20   .20
Bicent. of Gunston Hall and honoring George Mason, author of the Constitution of Va. and the Va. Bill of Rights.

Mackinac Bridge — A556   Simon Bolivar — A557

Mackinac Bridge Issue
1958, June 25   *Perf. 10½x11*
1109 A556 3c bright greenish bl   .20   .20
Dedication of Mackinac Bridge, Mich.

Champion of Liberty Issue
Rotary Press Printing
1958, July 24   *Perf. 10½x11*
1110 A557 4c olive bister   .20   .20
Giori Press Printing
Perf. 11
1111 A557 8c car, ultra & ocher   .20   .20
Simon Bolivar, So. American freedom fighter.

Atlantic Cable Centennial Issue

Neptune, Globe and Mermaid A558

Rotary Press Printing
1958, Aug. 15   *Perf. 11x10½*
1112 A558 4c reddish purple   .20   .20
Centenary of the Atlantic Cable, linking the Eastern and Western hemispheres.

Lincoln Sesquicentennial Issue

Lincoln, by George Healy A559   Lincoln, by Gutzon Borglum A560

Abraham Lincoln and Stephen A. Douglas Debating A561

Lincoln, by Daniel Chester French A562

1958-59   *Perf. 10½x11, 11x10½*
1113 A559 1c green ('59)   .20   .20
1114 A560 3c purple ('59)   .20   .20
1115 A561 4c sepia   .20   .20
1116 A562 4c dark blue ('59)   .20   .20
    Nos. 1113-1116 (4)   .80   .80
No. 1114 also for the founding of Cooper Union cent., NYC. No. 1115 also for the Lincoln-Douglas debates, cent.
Issue dates: Nos. 1113, 1114, 1116, Feb. 12, Feb. 27 and May 30. No. 1115, Aug. 27.

Lajos Kossuth, (1802-1892) A563   Early Press and Hand Holding Quill A564

Champion of Liberty Issue
Rotary Press Printing
1958, Sept. 19   *Perf. 10½x11*
1117 A563 4c green   .20   .20
Giori Press Printing
Perf. 11
1118 A563 8c car, ultra & ocher   .20   .20
Kossuth, Hungarian freedom fighter.

Freedom of Press Issue
Rotary Press Printing
1958, Sept. 22   *Perf. 10½x11*
1119 A564 4c black   .20   .20
Honoring journalism and freedom of the press in connection with the 50th anniv. of the 1st School of Journalism at the Univ. of Mo.

Overland Mail Centenary

Mail Coach and Map of Southwest US — A565

1958, Oct. 10   *Perf. 11x10½*
1120 A565 4c crimson rose   .20   .20

Noah Webster A566   Forest Scene A567

Noah Webster Issue
1958, Oct. 16   *Perf. 10½x11*
1121 A566 4c dark carmine rose   .20   .20
Webster (1758-1843), lexicographer.

Forest Conservation Issue
Giori Press Printing
1958, Oct. 27   *Perf. 11*
1122 A567 4c green, yel & brown   .20   .20
Publicizing forest conservation and the protection of natural resources and honoring Theodore Roosevelt, a leading forest conservationist, on the cent. of his birth.

Fort Duquesne Issue

Occupation of Fort Duquesne A568

Rotary Press Printing
1958, Nov. 25   *Perf. 11x10½*
1123 A568 4c blue   .20   .20
Bicentennial of Fort Duquesne (Fort Pitt).

Oregon Statehood Centenary

Covered Wagon and Mt. Hood A569

1959, Feb. 14   *Perf. 11x10½*
1124 A569 4c blue green   .20   .20

José de San Martin — A570   NATO Emblem — A571

Champion of Liberty Issue
Rotary Press Printing
1959, Feb. 25   *Perf. 10½x11*
1125 A570 4c blue   .20   .20
  a.   Horiz. pair, imperf. btwn.   1,500.
Giori Press Printing
Perf. 11
1126 A570 8c car, ultra & ocher   .20   .20
San Martin, South American soldier and statesman.

NATO Issue
Rotary Press Printing
1959, Apr. 1   *Perf. 10½x11*
1127 A571 4c blue   .20   .20
North Atlantic Treaty Organ., 10th anniv.

Arctic Explorations Issue

North Pole, Dog Sled and "Nautilus" A572

1959, Apr. 6   *Perf. 11x10½*
1128 A572 4c brt greenish blue   .20   .20
Conquest of the Arctic by land by Rear Admiral Robert Edwin Peary in 1909 and by sea by the submarine "Nautilus" in 1958.

World Peace Through World Trade Issue

Globe and Laurel A573

1959, Apr. 20   *Perf. 11x10½*
1129 A573 8c rose lake   .20   .20
Issued in conjunction with the 17th Cong. of the Intl. Chamber of Commerce, Washington, DC, Apr. 19-25.

Silver Centennial Issue

Henry Comstock at Mount Davidson Site A574

1959, June 8   *Perf. 11x10½*
1130 A574 4c black   .20   .20
Cent. of the discovery of silver at the Comstock Lode, Nev.

St. Lawrence Seaway Issue

Great Lakes, Maple Leaf and Eagle Emblems A575

Giori Press Printing
1959, June 26   *Perf. 11*
1131 A575 4c red & dark blue   .20   .20
Opening of the St. Lawrence Seaway, June 26, 1959. See Canada No. 387.

49-Star Flag Issue

US Flag, 1959 A576

1959, July 4   *Perf. 11*
1132 A576 4c ocher, dk blue & dp car   .20   .20

Soil Conservation Issue

Modern Farm A577

1959, Aug. 26
1133 A577 4c bl, grn & ocher   .20   .20
Tribute to farmers and ranchers who use soil and water conservation measures.

Petroleum Industry Issue

Oil Derrick — A578

Rotary Press Printing
1959, Aug. 27   **Perf. 10½x11**
1134 A578 4c brown   .20   .20
Cent. of the completion of the nation's 1st oil well at Titusville, Pa.

Dental Health Issue

Children
A579

1959, Sept. 14   **Perf. 11x10½**
1135 A579 4c green   .20   .20
Publicizing dental health and cent. of the American Dental Assoc.

Ernst Reuter
A580

Dr. Ephraim
McDowell
A581

Champion of Liberty Issue
Rotary Press Printing
1959, Sept. 29   **Perf. 10½x11**
1136 A580 4c gray   .20   .20
Giori Press Printing
Perf. 11
1137 A580 8c car, ultra & ocher   .20   .20
   a.   Ocher omitted   3,750.
   b.   Ultramarine omitted   3,750.
   c.   Ocher & ultramarine omitted   4,000.
   d.   All colors omitted   2,500.
Ernst Reuter, mayor of Berlin 1948-53.

Dr. Ephraim McDowell Issue
Rotary Press Printing
1959, Dec. 3   **Perf. 10½x11**
1138 A581 4c rose lake   .20   .20
   a.   Vert. pair, imperf. btwn.   450.00
   b.   Vert. pair, imperf. horiz.   350.00
Honoring McDowell on the 150th anniv. of the 1st successful ovarian operation performed in the US.

American Credo Issue

Quotation from Washington's Farewell Address, 1796 — A582

Benjamin
Franklin
Quotation
A583

Thomas
Jefferson
Quotation
A584

Francis
Scott Key
Quotation
A585

Abraham
Lincoln
Quotation
A586

Patrick
Henry
Quotation
A587

Giori Press Printing
1960-61   **Perf. 11**
1139 A582 4c dk vio blue & car   .20   .20
1140 A583 4c olive bister & grn   .20   .20
1141 A584 4c gray & vermilion   .20   .20
1142 A585 4c car & dark blue   .20   .20
1143 A586 4c magenta & green   .20   .20
1144 A587 4c green & brown   .20   .20
   Nos. 1139-1144 (6)   1.20   1.20
Re-emphasizing the ideals upon which America was founded and honoring those great Americans who wrote or uttered the credos.
Issued: 1/20; 3/31; 5/8; 9/14; 11/19; 1/11/61.

Boy Scout Jubilee Issue

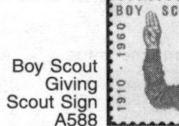

Boy Scout
Giving
Scout Sign
A588

Giori Press Printing
1960, Feb. 8   **Perf. 11**
1145 A588 4c red, dk bl & dk bis   .20   .20
Boy Scouts of America, 50th anniv.

Olympic Rings
and Snowflake
A589

Thomas G.
Masaryk
A590

Olympic Winter Games Issue
Rotary Press Printing
1960, Feb. 18   **Perf. 10½x11**
1146 A589 4c dull blue   .20   .20
Opening of the 8th Olympic Winter Games, Squaw Valley, Feb. 18-29.

Champion of Liberty Issue
Rotary Press Printing
1960, Mar. 7   **Perf. 10½x11**
1147 A590 4c blue   .20   .20
   a.   Vert. pair, imperf. btwn.   3,250.
Giori Press Printing
Perf. 11
1148 A590 8c car, ultra & ocher   .20   .20
   a.   Horiz. pair, imperf. btwn.   —
Masaryk, founder and pres. of Czechoslovakia (1918-35), 110th birth anniv.

World Refugee Year Issue

Refugee
Family
Walking
Toward
New Life
A591

Rotary Press Printing
1960, Apr. 7   **Perf. 11x10½**
1149 A591 4c gray black   .20   .20
WRY, July 1, 1959-June 30, 1960.

Water Conservation Issue

Water, from
Watershed
to
Consumer
A592

Giori Press Printing
1960, Apr. 18   **Perf. 11**
1150 A592 4c dk blue,
        brn org
        & green   .20   .20
   a.   Brown orange omitted   4,000.
Stressing the importance of water conservation, and 7th Watershed Cong., Washington, DC.

SEATO Issue

SEATO
Emblem — A593

Rotary Press Printing
1960, May 31   **Perf. 10½x11**
1151 A593 4c blue   .20   .20
   a.   Vert. pair, imperf. btwn.   160.00
South-East Asia Treaty Org. and the SEATO Conf., Washington, DC, May 31-June 3.

American Woman Issue

Mother and
Daughter
A594

1960, June 2   **Perf. 11x10½**
1152 A594 4c deep violet   .20   .20
A tribute to American women and their accomplishments in civic affairs, education, arts and industry.

50-Star Flag Issue

US Flag,
1960 — A595

Giori Press Printing
1960, July 4   **Perf. 11**
1153 A595 4c dark blue & red   .20   .20

Pony Express Centennial Issue

Pony
Express
Rider
A596

Rotary Press Printing
1960, July 19   **Perf. 11x10½**
1154 A596 4c sepia   .20   .20

Man in
Wheelchair
Operating Drill
Press — A597

5th World
Forestry
Congress
Seal — A598

Employ the Handicapped Issue
1960, Aug. 28   **Perf. 10½x11**
1155 A597 4c dark blue   .20   .20
Promoting employment of the physically handicapped and publicizing the 8th World Cong. of the Intl. Soc. for the Welfare of Cripples, NYC.

World Forestry Congress Issue
1960, Aug. 29   .20   .20
1156 A598 4c green   .20   .20
5th World Forestry Cong., Seattle, Wash., Aug. 29-Sept. 10.

A599

A600

Mexican Independence Issue
Giori Press Printing
1960, Sept. 16   **Perf. 11**
1157 A599 4c Independence Bell   .20   .20
150th anniv. of Mexican independence. See Mexico No. 910.

US-Japan Treaty Issue
1960, Sept. 28   **Perf. 11**
Washington Monument and Cherry Blossoms
1158 A600 4c blue & pink   .20   .20
Cent. of the US-Japan Treaty of Amity and Commerce.

Ignacy Jan
Paderewski
A601

Robert A. Taft
A602

Champion of Liberty Issue
Rotary Press Printing
1960, Oct. 8   **Perf. 10½x11**
1159 A601 4c blue   .20   .20
Giori Press Printing
Perf. 11
1160 A601 8c car, ultra & ocher   .20   .20
Paderewski (1866-1941), Polish statesman and musician.

Senator Taft Memorial Issue
Rotary Press Printing
1960, Oct. 10   **Perf. 10½x11**
1161 A602 4c dull violet   .20   .20
Senator Taft (1889-1953), of Ohio.

Wheels of Freedom Issue

Globe and Steering Wheel with Tractor, Car and Truck — A603

1960, Oct. 15   *Perf. 11x10½*
1162 A603 4c dark blue   .20 .20

Honoring the automotive industry and in connection with the National Automobile Show, Detroit, Oct. 15-23.

Boys' Clubs of America Issue

Profile of a Boy — A604

Giori Press Printing
1960, Oct. 18   *Perf. 11*
1163 A604 4c ind, sl & rose red   .20 .20

Boys' Clubs of America movement, cent.

Automated Post Office Issue

Architect's Sketch of New Post Office, Providence, RI — A605

1960, Oct. 20   *Perf. 11*
1164 A605 4c dk blue & carmine .20 .20

Opening of the 1st automated PO in the US.

Baron Gustaf Emil Mannerheim A606

Camp Fire Girls Emblem A607

Champion of Liberty Issue
Rotary Press Printing
1960, Oct. 26   *Perf. 10½x11*
1165 A606 4c blue   .20 .20
Giori Press Printing
Perf. 11
1166 A606 8c car, ultra & ocher .20 .20

Mannerheim (1867-1951), marshal and pres. of Finland.

Camp Fire Girls Issue
Giori Press Printing
1960, Nov. 1   *Perf. 11*
1167 A607 4c dk blue & brt red .20 .20

50th anniv. of the Camp Fire Girls' movement and with their Golden Jubilee Convention celebration.

Giuseppe Garibaldi (1807-1882) A608

Walter F. George (1878-1957) A609

Champion of Liberty Issue
Rotary Press Printing
1960, Nov. 2   *Perf. 10½x11*
1168 A608 4c green   .20 .20
Giori Press Printing
Perf. 11
1169 A608 8c car, ultra & ocher .20 .20

Garibaldi, Italian patriot and freedom fighter.

Senator George Memorial Issue
Rotary Press Printing
1960, Nov. 5   *Perf. 10½x11*
1170 A609 4c dull violet   .20 .20

Senator Walter F. George of Georgia.

Andrew Carnegie A610

John Foster Dulles A611

Andrew Carnegie Issue
1960, Nov. 25
1171 A610 4c deep claret   .20 .20

Carnegie (1835-1919), industrialist and philanthropist.

John Foster Dulles Memorial Issue
1960, Dec. 6   *Perf. 10½x11*
1172 A611 4c dull violet   .20 .20

Dulles (1888-1959), Sec. of State (1953-59).

Echo I—Communications for Peace Issue

Radio Waves Connecting Echo I and Earth A612

1960, Dec. 15   *Perf. 11x10½*
1173 A612 4c deep violet   .20 .20

World's 1st communications satellite, Echo I, placed in orbit by NASA, Aug. 12, 1960.

Champion of Liberty Issue

Mahatma Gandhi — A613

Rotary Press Printing
1961, Jan. 26   *Perf. 10½x11*
1174 A613 4c red orange   .20 .20
Giori Press Printing
Perf. 11
1175 A613 8c car, ultra & ocher .20 .20

Mohandas K. Gandhi, leader in India's struggle for independence.

Range Conservation Issue

The Trail Boss and Modern Range A614

Giori Press Printing
1961, Feb. 2   *Perf. 11*
1176 A614 4c bl, sl & brn org   .20 .20

Importance of range conservation and meeting of the American Soc. of Range Management, Washington, DC. "The Trail Boss" from a drawing by Charles M. Russell is the Society's emblem.

Horace Greeley Issue

Horace Greeley (1811-1872), Publisher and Editor — A615

Rotary Press Printing
1961, Feb. 3   *Perf. 10½x11*
1177 A615 4c dull violet   .20 .20

Civil War Centennial Issue

Sea Coast Gun of 1861 A616

Rifleman at Shiloh, 1862 A617

Blue and Gray at Gettysburg, 1863 A618

Battle of the Wilderness, 1864 A619

Appomattox, 1865 — A620

1961-65   *Perf. 11x10½*
1178 A616 4c light green   .20 .20
1179 A617 4c blk, *peach blossom*   .20 .20
Giori Press Printing
Perf. 11
1180 A618 5c gray & blue   .20 .20
1181 A619 5c dark red & black   .20 .20
1182 A620 5c Prus bl & blk   .25 .20
   a.   Horiz. pair, imperf. vert.   4,500.
   Nos. 1178-1182 (5)   1.05 1.00

Cent. of the firing on Fort Sumter, No. 1178; cent. of the Battle of Shiloh, No. 1179; cent. of the Battle of Gettysburg, No. 1180; cent. of the Battle of the Wilderness, No. 1181; cent. of the surrender of Gen. Robert E. Lee to Lt. Gen. Ulysses S. Grant at Appomattox Court House, No. 1182.
Issued: #1178-1182, 4/12; 4/7/62; 7/1/63; 5/5/64; 4/9/65.

Kansas Statehood Centenary

Sunflower, Pioneer Couple and Stockade A621

Giori Press Printing
1961, May 10   *Perf. 11*
1183 A621 4c brn, dk red & grn, *yellow*   .20 .20

Senator George W. Norris Issue

Norris and Norris Dam, Tenn. A622

Rotary Press Printing
1961, July 11   *Perf. 11x10½*
1184 A622 4c blue green   .20 .20

Norris (1861-1944) of Nebraska.

Naval Aviation, 50th Anniv.

Navy's First Plane (Curtiss A-1 of 1911) and Naval Air Wings A623

1961, Aug. 20
1185 A623 4c blue   .20 .20

Workmen's Compensation Issue

Scales of Justice, Factory, Worker and Family — A624

1961, Sept. 4   *Perf. 10½x11*
1186 A624 4c ultra, *grayish*   .20 .20

50th anniv. of the 1st successful Workmen's Compensation Law, enacted by the Wis. legislature.

Frederic Remington Issue

Remington's "Smoke Signal" — A625

Giori Press Printing
1961, Oct. 4   *Perf. 11*
1187 A625 4c multicolored   .20 .20

Frederic Remington (1861-1909), artist of the West. The design is from an oil painting, Amon Carter Museum of Western Art, Fort Worth, Texas.

Sun Yat-sen A626

Basketball A627

Republic of China, 50th Anniv.
Rotary Press Printing
1961, Oct. 10   *Perf. 10½x11*
1188 A626 4c blue   .20 .20

Naismith-Basketball Issue
1961, Nov. 6   *Perf. 10½x11*
1189 A627 4c brown   .20 .20

Honoring basketball and James Naismith (1861-1939), who invented the game in 1891.

Nursing Issue

Student Nurse Lighting Candle — A628

Giori Press Printing
1961, Dec. 28   *Perf. 11*
1190 A628 4c bl, grn, org & blk   .20   .20

New Mexico Statehood, 50th Anniv.

Shiprock A629

1962, Jan. 6   *Perf. 11*
1191 A629 4c lt bl, mar & bis   .20   .20

Arizona Statehood, 50th Anniv.

Giant Saguaro Cactus — A630

1962 Feb. 14   *Perf. 11*
1192 A630 4c car, vio bl & grn   .20   .20

Project Mercury Issue

"Friendship 7" Capsule and Globe A631

1962, Feb. 20   *Perf. 11*
1193 A631 4c dark blue & yellow   .20   .20

First orbital flight of a US astronaut, Lt. Col. John H. Glenn, Jr., Feb. 20, 1962. Imperfs. are printers waste.

Malaria Eradication Issue

Great Seal of US and WHO Symbol A632

1962, Mar. 30   *Perf. 11*
1194 A632 4c blue & bister   .20   .20

WHO drive to eradicate malaria.

Charles Evans Hughes A633

Space Needle and Monorail A634

Charles Evans Hughes Issue
Rotary Press Printing
1962, Apr. 11   *Perf. 10½x11*
1195 A633 4c black, *buff*   .20   .20

Hughes (1862-1948), Gov. of NY, Chief Justice of the US.

Seattle World's Fair Issue
Giori Press Printing
1962, Apr. 25   *Perf. 11*
1196 A634 4c red & dark blue   .20   .20

"Century 21" Intl. Expo., Seattle, Wash., Apr. 21-Oct. 21.

Louisiana Statehood Sesquicentennial

Riverboat on the Mississippi A635

1962, Apr. 30   *Perf. 11*
1197 A635 4c bl, dk sl grn & red   .20   .20

Homestead Act Centenary

Sod Hut and Settlers A636

Rotary Press Printing
1962, May 20   *Perf. 11x10½*
1198 A636 4c slate   .20   .20

Girl Scout of America, 50th Anniv.

Senior Girl Scout & Flag A637

1962, July 24   *Perf. 11x10½*
1199 A637 4c rose red   .20   .20

Senator Brien McMahon Issue

Brien McMahon & Atomic Diagram A638

1962, July 28   *Perf. 11x10½*
1200 A638 4c violet   .20   .20

Honoring Sen. McMahon, Conn., for his role in opening the way to peaceful uses of atomic energy.

Apprenticeship Issue

Machinist Handing Micrometer to Apprentice A639

1962, Aug. 31   *Perf. 11x10½*
1201 A639 4c black, *yellow bister* .20   .20

Natl. Apprenticeship Program and 25th anniv. of the Natl. Apprenticeship Act.

Sam Rayburn Issue

Sam Rayburn and Capitol — A640

Giori Press Printing
1962, Sept. 16   *Perf. 11*
1202 A640 4c dk bl & red brn   .20   .20

Sam Rayburn (1882-1961), Speaker of the House of Representatives.

Dag Hammarskjold Issue

UN Headquarters & Dag Hammarskjold — A641

Giori Press Printing
1962, Oct. 23   *Perf. 11*
1203 A641 4c black, brn & yel   .20   .20

Hammarskjold, UN Sec. Gen., 1953-61.

Hammarskjold Special Printing
1962, Nov. 16
1204 A641 4c blk, brn & yel (inverted)   .20   .20

No. 1204 was issued following discovery of No. 1203 with yellow background inverted.

Wreath and Candles — A642

Map of US and Lamp A643

Christmas Issue
Giori Press Printing
1962, Nov. 1   *Perf. 11*
1205 A642 4c green & red   .20   .20

Higher Education Issue
1962, Nov. 14   *Perf. 11*
1206 A643 4c blue green & black   .20   .20

Higher education's role in American cultural and industrial development in connection with the centenary celebrations of the signing of the law creating land-grant colleges and universities.

Winslow Homer Issue

"Breezing Up" — A644

1962, Dec. 15   *Perf. 11*
1207 A644 4c multicolored   .20   .20
   a.   Horiz. pair, imperf. btwn. &
        at right   6,750.

Winslow Homer (1836-1910), painter (showing his oil which hangs in the Natl. Gallery, Washington, DC).

Flag Issue

Flag over White House — A645

1963-66   *Perf. 11*
1208 A645 5c blue & red   .20   .20
   a.   Tagged ('66)   .20   .20
   b.   Horiz. pair, imperf. btwn. 1,500.

Issued: #1208, Jan. 9; #1208a, Aug. 25. Beware of pairs with faint blind perforations between offered as No. 1208b.

Regular Issue

Andrew Jackson A646

George Washington A650

Rotary Press Printing
1962-66   *Perf. 11x10½*
1209 A646 1c green ('63)   .20   .20
   a.   Tagged ('66)   .20   .20
1213 A650 5c dark blue gray   .20   .20
   a.   Booklet pane 5 + label   3.00 1.75
   b.   Tagged ('63)   .50   .20
   c.   As "a," tagged ('63)   2.00 1.50
   d.   Horiz. pair, imperf. btwn. 2,000.

See Luminescence note after No. 1053. Three different messages are found on the label in No. 1213a, and two messages on that of No. 1213c.
No. 1213d resulted from a paper foldover after perforating and before cutting into panes.
Unused catalogue numbers were left vacant for additional denominations.

Coil Stamps
Rotary Press
1962-66   *Perf. 10 Vert.*
1225 A646 1c green ('63)   .20   .20
   a.   Tagged ('66)   .20   .20
1229 A650 5c dk blue gray   1.25   .20
   a.   Tagged ('63)   1.40   .20
   b.   Imperf., pair   450.00

Carolina Charter Issue

First Page of Carolina Charter A662

Giori Press Printing
1963, Apr. 6   *Perf. 11*
1230 A662 5c dk car & brown   .20   .20

Carolina Charter, 1663, granting to 8 Englishmen lands, extending coast-to-coast roughly along the present border of Va. to the north and Fla. to the south. Original charter on display at Raleigh.

Food for Peace-Freedom from Hunger

Wheat — A663

1963, June 4   *Perf. 11*
1231 A663 5c green, buff & red   .20   .20

American "Food for Peace" program and FAO "Freedom from Hunger" campaign.

West Virginia Statehood Centenary

Map of West Virginia & State Capitol A664

1963, June 20
1232 A664 5c green, red & blk .20 .20

Emancipation Proclamation Issue

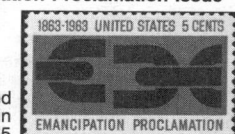

Severed Chain A665

1963, Aug. 16 *Perf. 11*
1233 A665 5c dk bl, blk & red .20 .20
Cent. of Lincoln's Emancipation Proclamation, freeing about 3,000,000 slaves in 10 southern states.

Alliance for Progress Issue

Alliance Emblem A666

1963, Aug. 17
1234 A666 5c ultra & green .20 .20
2nd anniv. of the Alliance for Progress, which aims to stimulate economic growth & raise living standards in Latin America.

Cordell Hull Issue

Cordell Hull (1871-1955), Sec. of State (1933-44) — A667

Rotary Press Printing
1963, Oct. 5 *Perf. 10½x11*
1235 A667 5c blue green .20 .20

Eleanor Roosevelt Issue

Mrs. Franklin D. Roosevelt (1884-1962) — A668

1963, Oct. 11 *Perf. 11x10½*
1236 A668 5c bright purple .20 .20

Science Issue

"The Universe" A669

Giori Press Printing
1963, Oct. 14 *Perf. 11*
1237 A669 5c Prus blue & black .20 .20
Honoring the sciences and cent. of the Natl. Academy of Science.

Free City Mail Delivery Centenary

Letter Carrier, 1863 — A670

1963, Oct. 26 **Tagged** *Perf. 11*
1238 A670 5c gray, dk bl & red .20 .20

International Red Cross Centenary

A671

Design features Cuban Refugees on S.S. Morning Light & Red Cross Flag

1963, Oct. 29 *Perf. 11*
1239 A671 5c bluish black & red .20 .20

Christmas Issue

Natl. Christmas Tree & White House — A672

1963, Nov. 1 *Perf. 11*
1240 A672 5c dk blue, bluish
   black & red .20 .20
   a. Tagged .65 .40
See Luminescence note after No. 1053.

Columbia Jays
A673

Sam Houston
A674

John J. Audubon Issue

1963, Dec. 7 *Perf. 11*
1241 A673 5c dark blue & multi .20 .20
John James Audubon (1785-1851), ornithologist and artist. The birds pictured are actually Collie's magpie jays.

Sam Houston Issue
Rotary Press Printing
1964, Jan. 10 *Perf. 10½x11*
1242 A674 5c black .20 .20
Sam Houston (1793-1863), soldier, pres. of Texas, US senator.

Charles M. Russell Issue

"Jerked Down" A675

Giori Press Printing
1964, Mar. 19 *Perf. 11*
1243 A675 5c ind, red brn & ol .20 .20
Russell (1864-1926), painter. The design is from a painting, Thomas Gilcrease Inst. of American History and Art, Tulsa, Okla.

New York World's Fair (1964-65)

Mall with Unisphere & "Rocket Thrower," by Donald De Lue A676

Rotary Press Printing
1964, Apr. 22 *Perf. 11x10½*
1244 A676 5c blue green .20 .20

John Muir Issue

John Muir (1838-1914), naturalist and conservationist and Redwood Forest — A677

Giori Press Printing
1964, Apr. 29 *Perf. 11*
1245 A677 5c brn, grn, yel grn & ol .20 .20

Kennedy Memorial Issue

Pres. John F. Kennedy (1917-63) and Eternal Flame A678

Rotary Press Printing
1964, May 29 *Perf. 11x10½*
1246 A678 5c blue gray .20 .20

New Jersey Tercentenary Issue

Philip Carteret Landing at Elizabethtown & Map of New Jersey — A679

1964, June 15 *Perf. 10½x11*
1247 A679 5c bright ultra .20 .20
300th anniv. of English colonization of NJ. The design is from a mural by Howard Pyle in the Essex County Courthouse, Newark.

Nevada Statehood Centenary

Virginia City and Map of Nevada A680

Giori Press Printing
1964, July 22 *Perf. 11*
1248 A680 5c red, yellow & blue .20 .20

Flag
A681

William Shakespeare
A682

Register and Vote Issue
Giori Press Printing
1964, Aug. 1 *Perf. 11*
1249 A681 5c dark blue & red .20 .20
Campaign to draw more voters to the polls.

Shakespeare Issue
Rotary Press Printing
1964, Aug. 14 *Perf. 10½x11*
1250 A682 5c black brown, tan .20 .20
400th anniv. of the birth of Shakespeare (1564-1616).

Doctors Mayo Issue

Drs. William and Charles Mayo — A683

1964, Sept. 11 *Perf. 10½x11*
1251 A683 5c green .20 .20
William (1861-1939) and his brother, Charles (1865-1939), surgeons who founded the Mayo Foundation for Medical Education and Research in affiliation with the Univ. of Minn. at Rochester. From a sculpture by James Earle Fraser.

American Music Issue

Lute, Horn, Laurel, Oak and Music Score A684

Giori Press Printing
1964, Oct. 15 *Perf. 11*
Gray Paper with Blue Threads
1252 A684 5c red, black & blue .20 .20
   a. Blue omitted 1,000.
50th anniv. of the founding of ASCAP (American Soc. of Composers, Authors and Publishers).
Beware of copies offered as No. 1252a which have traces of blue.

Homemakers Issue

Farm Scene Sampler A685

Lithographed, Engraved (Giori)
1964, Oct. 26 *Perf. 11*
1253 A685 5c multicolored .20 .20
Honoring American women as homemakers and 50th anniv. of the passage of the Smith-Lever Act. By providing economic experts under an extension service of the US Dept. of Agriculture, this legislation helped to improve homelife.

Christmas Issue

Holly
A686

Mistletoe
A687

Poinsettia
A688

Sprig of Conifer
A689

Giori Press Printing

1964, Nov. 9   *Perf. 11*
1254 A686 5c green, car & black   .25   .20
   a.   Tagged   .60   .50
   b.   Printed on gummed side
1255 A687 5c car, green & black   .25   .20
   a.   Tagged   .60   .50
1256 A688 5c car, green & black   .25   .20
   a.   Tagged   .60   .50
1257 A689 5c black, green & car   .25   .20
   a.   Tagged   .60   .50
   b.   Block of 4, #1254-1257   1.10   1.00
   c.   Block of 4, #1254a-1257a   2.50   2.25

Tagged stamps issued Nov. 10.
No. 1254b resulted from a paper foldover before printing and perforating.

Verrazano-Narrows Bridge Issue

Verrazano-Narrows Bridge and Map of NY Bay — A690

Rotary Press Printing

1964, Nov. 21   *Perf. 10½x11*
1258 A690 5c blue green   .20   .20

Opening of the Verrazano-Narrows Bridge connecting Staten Island and Brooklyn, NY.

Fine Arts Issue

Abstract Design by Stuart Davis A691

Giori Press Printing

1964, Dec. 2   *Perf. 11*
1259 A691 5c ultra, blk & dull red   .20   .20

Amateur Radio Issue

Radio Waves and Dial — A692

Rotary Press Printing

1964, Dec. 15   *Perf. 10½x11*
1260 A692 5c red lilac   .20   .20

Honoring radio amateurs on the 50th anniv. of the American Radio Relay League.

Battle of New Orleans Issue

General Andrew Jackson and Sesquicentennial Medal — A693

Giori Press Printing

1965, Jan. 8   *Perf. 11*
1261 A693 5c dp car, vio bl & gray   .20   .20

Battle of New Orleans, Chalmette Plantation, Jan. 8-18, 1815, which established 150 years of peace and friendship between the US and Great Britain.

Discus Thrower A694

Microscope and Stethoscope A695

Physical Fitness-Sokol Issue

1965, Feb. 15   *Perf. 11*
1262 A694 5c maroon & black   .20   .20

Importance of physical fitness and cent. of the founding of the Sokol (athletic) org. in America.

Crusade Against Cancer Issue

1965, Apr. 1   *Perf. 11*
1263 A695 5c blk, pur & red org   .20   .20

"Crusade Against Cancer" and stressing the importance of early diagnosis.

Churchill Memorial Issue

Winston Churchill — A696

Rotary Press Printing

1965, May 13   *Perf. 10½x11*
1264 A696 5c black   .20   .20

Sir Winston Spencer Churchill (1874-1965), British statesman and WWII leader.

Magna Carta Issue

Procession of Barons and King John's Crown A697

Giori Press Printing

1965, June 15   *Perf. 11*
1265 A697 5c blk, yel ocher & red lilac   .20   .20

750th anniv. of the Magna Carta, the basis of English and American common law.

International Cooperation Year Issue

ICY Emblem A698

1965, June 26   *Perf. 11*
1266 A698 5c dull blue & black   .20   .20

ICY, 1965, and 20th anniv. of the UN.

A699   A700

Salvation Army Issue

1965, July 2   *Perf. 11*
1267 A699 5c red, blk & dark bl   .20   .20

Cent. of the founding of the Salvation Army in London by William Booth.

Dante Alighieri Issue
Rotary Press Printing

1965, July 17   *Perf. 10½x11*
1268 A700 5c maroon, *tan*   .20   .20

Dante Alighieri (1265-1321), Italian poet. Design after a 16th cent. painting.

Herbert Hoover Issue

Pres. Herbert Clark Hoover (1874-1964) — A701

1965, Aug. 10   *Perf. 10½x11*
1269 A701 5c rose red   .20   .20

Robert Fulton Issue

Robert Fulton & Clermont A702

Giori Press Printing

1965, Aug. 19   *Perf. 11*
1270 A702 5c black & blue   .20   .20

Fulton (1765-1815), inventor of the 1st commercial steamship.

Settlement of Florida Issue

Spanish Explorer, Royal Flag of Spain and Ships — A703

Giori Press Printing

1965, Aug. 28   *Perf. 11*
1271 A703 5c red, yel & blk   .20   .20
   a.   Yellow omitted   350.00

400th anniv. of the settlement of Fla., and the 1st permanent European settlement in the continental US, St. Augustine, Fla.
See Spain #1312.

Traffic Safety Issue

Traffic Signal A704

1965, Sept. 3   *Perf. 11*
1272 A704 5c emer, blk & red   .20   .20

Traffic safety and the prevention of traffic accidents.

John Copley Issue

Elizabeth Clarke Copley — A705

1965, Sept. 17   1273 A705 5c blk, brn & olive   .20   .20

John Singleton Copley (1738-1815), painter. The portrait of the artist's daughter is from the oil painting "The Copley Family," which hangs in the Natl. Gallery of Art, Washington, DC.

International Telecommunication Union Centenary

Gall Projection World Map & Radio Sine Wave A706

1965, Oct. 6   *Perf. 11*
1274 A706 11c black, car & bis   .35   .20

Adlai E. Stevenson A707   Angel with Trumpet A708

Adlai E. Stevenson Issue

1965, Oct. 23   *Litho., Engr. (Giori)*
1275 A707 5c pale blue, blk, car & vio blue   .20   .20

Stevenson (1900-65), gov. of Ill., US ambassador to the UN.

Christmas Issue

Design features 1840 Weather Vane.

Giori Press Printing

1965, Nov. 2   *Perf. 11*
1276 A708 5c car, dk ol grn & bis   .20   .20
   a.   Tagged   .75   .25

Prominent Americans Issue

Thomas Jefferson A710   Albert Gallatin A711

Frank Lloyd Wright & Guggenheim Museum A712   Francis Parkman A713

Lincoln — A714

Washington — A715

Washington (Redrawn)
A715a

Franklin D.
Roosevelt
A716

Albert
Einstein
A717

Andrew
Jackson
A718

Henry Ford,
1909 Model T
A718a

John F.
Kennedy
A719

Oliver
Wendell
Holmes
A720

George
Catlett
Marshall
A721

Frederick
Douglass
A722

John Dewey
A723

Thomas
Paine
A724

Lucy Stone
A725

Eugene
O'Neill
A726

John Bassett
Moore — A727

Perf. 11x10½, 10½x11
1965-78   Rotary Press Printing

1278	A710	1c green, tagged	.20	.20
a.		Booklet pane of 8	1.00	
b.		Bklt. pane of 4 + 2 labels	.80	.30
c.		Untagged (Bureau precanceled)		.20
1279	A711	1¼c lt green	.20	.20
1280	A712	2c dk blue gray, tagged	.20	.20
a.		Booklet pane of 5 + label	1.25	.60
b.		Untagged (Bureau precanceled)		.20
c.		Booklet pane of 6	1.00	.50
1281	A713	3c vio, tagged	.20	.20
a.		Untagged (Bureau precanceled)		.20
1282	A714	4c black	.20	.20
a.		Tagged	.20	.20
1283	A715	5c blue	.20	.20
a.		Tagged	.20	.20
1283B	A715a	5c blue, tagged	.20	.20
d.		Untagged (Bureau precanceled)		.20
1284	A716	6c gray brown	.20	.20
a.		Tagged	.20	.20
b.		Booklet pane of 8	1.50	.75
c.		Booklet pane of 5 + label	1.50	.75
d.		Horiz. pair, imperf. btwn.		
1285	A717	8c violet	.20	.20
a.		Tagged	.20	.20
1286	A718	10c lilac, tagged	.20	.20
b.		Untagged (Bureau precanceled)		.20
1286A	A718a	12c black, tagged	.25	.20
a.		Untagged (Bureau precanceled)		.25
1287	A719	13c brn, tagged	.30	.20
a.		Untagged (Bureau precanceled)		.35
1288	A720	15c mag, tagged	.30	.20
a.		Untagged (Bureau precanceled)		.30
d.		Type II	.55	.20

Type II: necktie does not touch coat at bottom.

Perf. 10

1288B	A720	15c mag, from bklt. pane	.35	.20
c.		Booklet pane of 8	2.80	1.75
e.		As "c," vert. imperf. btwn.		

Perf. 11x10½, 10½x11

1289	A721	20c deep olive	.40	.20
a.		Tagged	.40	.20
1290	A722	25c rose lake	.55	.20
a.		Tagged	.45	.20
b.		25c magenta	25.00	—
1291	A723	30c red lilac	.65	.20
a.		Tagged	.50	.20
1292	A724	40c blue black	.85	.20
a.		Tagged	.65	.20
1293	A725	50c rose magenta	1.00	.20
a.		Tagged	.80	.20
1294	A726	$1 dull purple	2.25	.20
a.		Tagged	1.65	.20
1295	A727	$5 gray black	9.50	2.25
a.		Tagged	8.00	2.00
		Nos. 1278-1295 (21)	18.40	6.25

On No. 1283B the highlights and shadows have been softened.

No. 1288B issued in booklets only. All stamps have one or two straight edges.

Issued (without tagging)—1965: 4c, 11/19.
1966: 5c, 2/22; 6c, 1/29; 8c, 3/14; $5, 12/3.
1967: 1¼c, 1/30; 20c, 10/24; 25c, 2/14; $1, 10/16.
1968: 30c, 10/21; 40c, 1/29; 50c, 8/13.
Dates for tagged: 1965: 4c, 12/1.
1966: 2c, 6/8; 5c, 2/23; 6c, 12/29; 8c, 7/6.
1967: 3c, 9/16; #1283B, 11/17; #1284b, 12/28; 10c, 3/15; 13c, 5/29.
1968: 1c, #1284c, 1/12; #1280a, 1/8; 12c, 7/30; 15c, 3/8.
1973: 20c, 25c, 30c, 40c, 50c, $1, $5, 4/3.
1978: No. 1288B, 6/14.

Franklin D.
Roosevelt — A727a

Coil Stamps
Rotary Press Printing
1966-81   Tagged   Perf. 10 Horiz.

1297	A713	3c violet	.20	.20
a.		Imperf., pair	30.00	
b.		Untagged (Bureau precanceled)		.20
c.		As "b," imperf. pair		6.00
1298	A716	6c gray brn	.20	.20
a.		Imperf., pair	2,000.	

Perf. 10 Vertically

1299	A710	1c green	.20	.20
a.		Untagged (Bureau precanceled)		.20
b.		Imperf., pair	30.00	—
1303	A714	4c black	.20	.20
a.		Untagged (Bureau precanceled)		.20
b.		Imperf., pair	750.00	
1304	A715	5c blue	.20	.20
a.		Untagged (Bureau precanceled)		.20
b.		Imperf., pair	175.00	
e.		As "a," imperf. pair		400.00

No. 1304b is valued in the grade of fine.

1304C	A715a	5c blue	.20	.20
d.		Imperf., pair	800.	
1305	A727a	6c gray brn	.20	.20
a.		Imperf., pair	75.00	
b.		Untagged (Bureau precanceled)		.20
1305E	A720	15c magenta	.25	.20
f.		Untagged (Bureau precanceled)		.30
g.		Imperf., pair	30.00	
h.		Pair, imperf. between	200.00	
i.		Type II		.35
j.		Imperf., pair, type II	90.00	
1305C	A726	$1 dull pur	2.00	.40
d.		Imperf., pair	2,250.	
		Nos. 1297-1305C (9)	3.65	2.00

Issued: 1c, 1/12/68; 3c, 11/4/75; 4c, 5/28/66; #1304, 9/8/66; 6c, #1298, 12/28/67; #1305, 2/28/68;
$1, 1/12/73; 15c, 6/14/78.
See Nos. 1393-1395, 1397-1402 for more Prominent Americans.

Migratory Bird Treaty Issue

Migratory Birds over Canada-U.S.
Border — A728

Giori Press Printing
1966, Mar. 16   Perf. 11

1306	A728	5c blk, crim & dk blue	.20	.20

50th anniv. of the Migratory Bird Treaty between the U.S. and Canada.

Humane Treatment of Animals Issue

Mongrel
A729

Lithographed, Engraved (Giori)
1966, Apr. 9   Perf. 11

1307	A729	5c org brown & black	.20	.20

Humane treatment of all animals and cent. of the ASPCA.

Indiana Statehood Sesquicentennial

Sesquicentennial
Seal — A730

Giori Press Printing
1966, Apr. 16

1308	A730	5c yel, ocher & vio bl	.20	.20

Design features Sesquicentennial Seal; Map of Indiana with 19 Stars & Old Capitol at Corydon

American Circus Issue

Clown — A731

1966, May 2   Perf. 11

1309	A731	5c multicolored	.20	.20

Honoring the American circus on the cent. of the birth of John Ringling.

6th Intl. Phil. Exhib. Issues

Stamped
Cover
A732

A733

Lithographed, Engraved (Giori)
1966, May   Perf. 11

1310	A732	5c multicolored	.20	.20

Souvenir Sheet
Imperf

1311	A733	5c multicolored	.20	.20

SIPEX, Washington, DC, May 21-30.
No. 1311 measures 108x74mm.
Issue dates: #1310, 21st; #1311, 23rd.

"Freedom"
Checking
"Tyranny"
A734

Polish Eagle
and Cross
A735

Bill of Rights, 175th Anniv.
Giori Press Printing
1966, July 1   Perf. 11

1312	A734	5c car, dk & lt blue	.20	.20

Polish Millennium Issue
Rotary Press Printing
1966, July 30   Perf. 10½x11

1313	A735	5c red	.20	.20

1000th anniv. of the adoption of Christianity in Poland.

Tagging Extended
During 1966 experimental use of tagged stamps was extended to the Cincinnati Postal Region covering offices in Indiana, Kentucky and Ohio. To supply these offices about 12 percent of the following nine issues (Nos. 1314-1322) were tagged.

National Park Service Issue

National
Park
Service
Emblem
A736

Lithographed, Engraved (Giori)
1966, Aug. 25   Perf. 11

1314	A736	5c yel, black & green	.20	.20
a.		Tagged	.30	.25

50th anniv. of the Natl. Park Service of the Interior Dept. The design "Parkscape U.S.A." identifies Natl. Park Service facilities. No. 1314a was issued Aug. 26.

Marine Corps Reserve Issue

A737

Lithographed, Engraved (Giori)

1966, Aug. 29		Perf. 11
1315 A737 5c blk, bis, red & ultra	.20	.20
a. Tagged	.30	.20
b. Blk & bis (engr.) omitted	16,000.	

50th anniv. of the founding of the U.S. Marine Corps Reserve. Design includes Combat Marine, 1966; Frogman; WW II Flier; WW I "Devil Dog" & Marine, 1775.

General Federation of Women's Clubs

Women of 1890 and 1966
A738

Giori Press Printing

1966, Sept. 12		Perf. 11
1316 A738 5c black, pink & blue	.20	.20
a. Tagged	.30	.20

75 years of service by the Gen. Fed. of Women's Clubs. No. 1316a was issued 9/13.

American Folklore Issue

Johnny Appleseed — A739

1966, Sept. 24		Perf. 11
1317 A739 5c green, red & black	.20	.20
a. Tagged	.30	.20

Johnny Appleseed, (John Chapman, 1774-1845), who wandered over 100,000 square miles planting apple trees, and who gave away and sold seedlings to Midwest pioneers. No. 1317a issued Sept. 26.

Beautification of America Issue

Jefferson Memorial
A740

1966, Oct. 5		Perf. 11
1318 A740 5c emer, pink & blk	.20	.20
a. Tagged	.30	.20

Pres. Johnson's "Plant for a more beautiful America" campaign. Design features Jefferson Memorial, Tidal Basin & Cherry Blossoms.

Central U.S. Map With Great River Road — A741

Statue of Liberty & "Old Glory" — A742

Great River Road Issue
Lithographed, Engraved (Giori)

1966, Oct. 21		Perf. 11
1319 A741 5c ver, yel, bl & grn	.20	.20
a. Tagged	.30	.20

5,600-mile Great River Road connecting New Orleans with Kenora, Ontario, following the Mississippi most of the way. No. 1319a issued Oct. 22.

Savings Bond-Servicemen Issue

1966, Oct. 26		
1320 A742 5c red, dk & lt bl, blk	.20	.20
a. Tagged	.30	.20
b. Red, dark bl & blk omitted	4,250.	
c. Dark blue (engr.) omitted	8,500.	

25th anniv. of US Savings Bonds, and to honor American servicemen. No. 1320a issued Oct. 27.

Christmas Issue

Madonna and Child — A743

Lithographed, Engraved (Giori)

1966, Nov. 1		Perf. 11
1321 A743 5c multicolored	.20	.20
a. Tagged	.30	.20

The design is from "Madonna and Child with Angels," by the Flemish artist Hans Memling (c. 1430-1494), National Gallery of Art, Washington, DC. No. 1321a was issued Nov. 2. See No. 1336.

Mary Cassatt Issue

"The Boating Party"
A744

Giori Press Printing

1966, Nov. 17		Perf. 11
1322 A744 5c multicolored	.20	.20
a. Tagged	.30	.25

Cassatt (1844-1926), painter. The original painting is in the Natl. Gallery of Art, Washington, DC.

National Grange Issue

Grange Poster, 1870 — A745

1967, Apr. 17	Tagged	Perf. 11
1323 A745 5c multicolored		.20 .20

Cent. of the founding of the National Grange, American farmers' organization.

Phosphor Tagging

From No. 1323 onward, all postage issues are tagged, unless otherwise noted.

Tagging Omitted

Inadvertent omissions of tagging occurred on Nos. 1238, 1278, 1281, 1298 and 1305. In addition most tagged issues from 1967 on exist with tagging unintentionally omitted.

Canada Centenary Issue

Canadian Landscape
A746

Giori Press Printing

1967, May 25		Perf. 11
1324 A746 5c multicolored	.20	.20

Cent. of Canada's emergence as a nation.

Erie Canal Issue

Stern of Early Canal Boat
A747

Lithographed, Engraved (Giori)

1967, July 4		Perf. 11
1325 A747 5c multicolored	.20	.20

150th anniv. of the Erie Canal groundbreaking ceremony. The canal links Lake Erie and NYC.

"Peace"—Lions Issue

Peace Dove
A748

Giori Press Printing
1967, July 5 　　　　　Perf. 11
Gray Paper with Blue Threads

1326 A748 5c blue, red & black	.20	.20

Publicizing the Search for Peace. This was the theme of an essay contest for young men and women sponsored by Lions Intl. on its 50th anniv.

Henry David Thoreau Issue

Henry David Thoreau (1817-1862), Writer — A749

1967, July 12		
1327 A749 5c red, black & green	.20	.20

Nebraska Statehood Centenary

Hereford Steer and Corn
A750

Lithographed, Engraved (Giori)

1967, July 29		Perf. 11
1328 A750 5c dk red brn, lem & yel	.20	.20

Voice of America Issue

Radio Transmission Tower and Waves — A751

1967, Aug. 1	Giori Press Printing	
1329 A751 5c red, bl, blk & car	.20	.20

25th anniv. of the radio branch of the US Information Agency (USIA).

American Folklore Issue

Davy Crockett & Scrub Pines
A752

Lithographed, Engraved (Giori)

1967, Aug. 17		Perf. 11
1330 A752 5c grn, blk & yel	.20	.20
a. Vert. pair, imperf. btwn.	6,000.	
b. Green (engr.) omitted	—	
c. Blk & grn (engr.) omitted	—	

Crockett (1786-1836), frontiersman and congressman, died in defense of the Alamo.

A foldover on a pane of No. 1330 resulted in one example each of Nos. 1330b-1330c. Part of the colors appear on the back of the selvage and one freak stamp.

An engraved black-and-green-only impression appears on the gummed side of one almost-complete "stamp."

Space Accomplishments Issue

Space-Walking Astronaut — A753

Gemini 4 Capsule and Earth A754

Lithographed, Engraved (Giori)

1967, Sept. 29		Perf. 11
1331 A753 5c multicolored	.50	.20
1332 A754 5c multicolored	.50	.20
b. Pair, #1331-1332	1.10	1.25

US accomplishments in space.

View of Model City — A755

Finnish Coat of Arms — A756

Urban Planning Issue
Lithographed, Engraved (Giori)

1967, Oct. 2		
1333 A755 5c dk & lt blue, black	.20	.20

Importance of Urban Planning and the Intl. Conf. of the American Inst. of Planners, Washington, DC, Oct. 1-6.

Finnish Independence, 50th Anniv.
Engraved (Giori)

1967, Oct. 6		Perf. 11
1334 A756 5c blue	.20	.20

Thomas Eakins Issue

"The Biglin Brothers Racing" (Sculling on Schuylkill River, Philadelphia) — A757

1967, Nov. 2	Photo.	Perf. 12
1335 A757 5c gold & multi	.20	.20

Eakins (1844-1916), painter and sculptor. The painting is in the Natl. Gallery of Art, Washington, DC.

Christmas Issue

Madonna and Child,
by Hans
Memling — A758

Lithographed, Engraved (Giori)
1967, Nov. 6   *Perf. 11*
1336 A758 5c multicolored   .20   .20
See note after No. 1321.

Magnolia
A759

Flag and White
House — A760

Mississippi Statehood, 150th Anniv.
Giori Press Printing
1967, Dec. 11   *Perf. 11*
1337 A759 5c brt grnsh bl, grn &
red brn   .20   .20

Flag Issue
Giori Press Printing
1968-71   *Perf. 11*
Size: 19x22mm
1338 A760 6c dk bl, red &
grn   .20   .20
k.   Vert. pair, imperf. btwn.   550.00
s.   Red omitted   —
Vert. pairs have been offered as imperf.
horiz. Some have had the gum washed off to
make it difficult or impossible to detect blind
perfs.

Coil Stamp
Multicolor Huck Press
Perf. 10 Vert.
Size: 18¼x21mm
1338A A760 6c dk blue, red &
green ('69)   .20   .20
b.   Imperf., pair   500.00

Multicolor Huck Press
Perf. 11x10½
Size: 18¼x21mm
1338D A760 6c dk blue, red &
green ('70)   .20   .20
e.   Horiz. pair, imperf. btwn.   175.00
1338F A760 8c multi ('71)   .20   .20
i.   Vert. pair, imperf.   45.00
j.   Horiz. pair, imperf. btwn.   55.00
p.   Slate green omitted   400.00
t.   Horiz. pair, imperf. vert.   —
Issued: #1338, 1/2468; #1338A, 5/30/69;
#1338D, 8/7/70; 8c, 5/10/71.

Coil Stamp
1971, May 10   *Perf. 10 Vert.*
Size: 18¼x21mm
1338G A760 8c multi ('71)   .20   .20
h.   Imperf., pair   55.00

Farm House &
Fields of
Ripening Grain
A761

Map of North &
South America
A762

Illinois Statehood, 150th Anniv.
Lithographed, Engraved (Giori)
1968, Feb. 12   *Perf. 11*
1339 A761 6c multicolored   .20   .20

HemisFair '68 Issue
1968, Mar. 30   *Perf. 11*
1340 A762 6c blue, rose red &
white   .20   .20
a.   White omitted   1,300.
HemisFair '68 exhib. at San Antonio, Tex.,
4/6-10/6, for the 250th anniv. of San Antonio.

Airlift Issue

Eagle
Holding
Pennant
A763

Lithographed, Engraved (Giori)
1968, Apr. 4   Untagged   *Perf. 11*
1341 A763 $1 sep, dk blue,
ocher & brn red   2.25   1.25

Issued to pay for airlift of parcels from and to
US ports to servicemen overseas and in
Alaska, Hawaii and P.R. Valid for all regular
postage.
On Apr. 26, 1969, the POD ruled that
henceforth No. 1341 "may be used toward
paying the postage or fees for special services
on airmail articles."

Support Our Youth Issue

Girls &
Boys
A764

Lithographed, Engraved (Giori)
1968, May 1   *Perf. 11*
1342 A764 6c ultra & orange red   .20   .20

Support Our Youth program, and honoring
the Benevolent and Protective Order of Elks,
which extended its youth service program in
observance of its centennial year.

Policeman and
Small
Boy — A765

Eagle Weather
Vane — A766

Law and Order Issue
Giori Press Printing
1968, May 17   *Perf. 11*
1343 A765 6c chlky bl, blk & red   .20   .20
The police as protector and friend and
respect for law and order.

Register and Vote Issue
Lithographed, Engraved (Giori)
1968, June 27   *Perf. 11*
1344 A766 6c blk, yel & org   .20   .20
Campaign to draw more voters to the polls.
The weather vane is from an old house in the
Russian Hill section of San Francisco.

Historic Flag Series

Ft.
Moultrie,
1776
A767

Ft.
McHenry,
1795-1818
A768

Washington's Cruisers, 1775 — A769

Bennington,
1777
A770

Rhode
Island,
1775
A771

First Stars
and
Stripes,
1777
A772

Bunker Hill,
1775
A773

Grand
Union,
1776
A774

Philadelphia Light Horse,
1775 — A775

First Navy
Jack, 1775
A776

Engraved (Giori) (#1345-1348, 1350):
Engr. & Litho. (#1349, 1351-1354).
1968, July 4   *Perf. 11*
1345 A767 6c dark blue   .40   .25
1346 A768 6c dk blue & red   .30   .25
1347 A769 6c dk blue & ol green   .25   .25
1348 A770 6c dk blue & red   .25   .25
1349 A771 6c dk blue, yel & red   .25   .25
1350 A772 6c dk blue & red   .25   .25
1351 A773 6c dk bl, ol grn & red   .25   .25
1352 A774 6c dk blue & red   .25   .25
1353 A775 6c dk blue, yel & red   .25   .25
1354 A776 6c dk blue, red & yel   .25   .25
a.   Strip of 10, Nos. 1345-1354   2.75   2.75

Flags carried by American colonists and by
citizens of the new United States. The flag
sequence on the upper panes is as listed. On
the lower panes the sequence is reversed with
the Navy Jack in the 1st row and the Fort
Moultrie flag in the 10th.

Walt Disney Issue

Disney and Children
of the World — A777

1968, Sept. 11   Photo.   *Perf. 12*
1355 A777 6c multicolored   .20   .20
a.   Ocher (Walt Disney, 6c,
etc.) omitted   600.   —
b.   Vert. pair, imperf. horiz.   700.
c.   Imperf., pair   675.
d.   Black omitted   1,500.
e.   Horiz. pair, imperf. btwn.   4,750.
f.   Blue omitted   1,750.
Disney (1901-1966), cartoonist, film producer, creator of Mickey Mouse.

Father Marquette Issue

Father Marquette and Louis Jolliet
Exploring the Mississippi
A778

Giori Press Printing
1968, Sept. 20   *Perf. 11*
1356 A778 6c black, apple green
& org brn   .20   .20
Father Jacques Marquette (1637-1675).
French Jesuit missionary, who with Louis Jolliet explored the Mississippi and its tributaries.

American Folklore Issue
Daniel Boone (1734-1820)

Pennsylvania Rifle, Powder Horn,
Tomahawk Pipe & Knife — A779

Lithographed, Engraved (Giori)
1968, Sept. 26   *Perf. 11*
1357 A779 6c yel, dp yel, mar &
blk   .20   .20
Daniel Boone, frontiersman and trapper.

Arkansas River Navigation Issue

Ship's Wheel, Power Transmission
Tower & Barge — A780

1968, Oct. 1   *Perf. 11*
1358 A780 6c brt bl, dk bl & blk   .20   .20
Opening of the Arkansas River to commercial navigation.

Leif Erikson Issue

Leif Erikson, by
Stirling
Calder — A781

1968, Oct. 9   Litho., Engr.   Perf. 11
1359 A781 6c lt gray brn & blk
    brn   .20 .20

Erikson, 11th cent. Norse explorer, was the 1st European to set foot on the American continent, at a place he called Vinland. The statue by an American sculptor is in Reykjavik, Iceland.

The light gray brown ink carries the tagging element.

Cherokee Strip Issue

Homesteaders Racing to Cherokee Strip — A782

Rotary Press Printing
1968, Oct. 15   Perf. 11x10½
1360 A782 6c brown   .20 .20

75th anniv. of the opening of the Cherokee Strip to settlers, Sept. 16, 1893.

John Trumbull Issue

Detail from "The Battle of Bunker's Hill" — A783

Lithographed, Engraved
1968, Oct. 18   Perf. 11
1361 A783 6c multicolored   .20 .20
  b.   Blk (engr.) omitted   11,000.

Trumbull (1756-1843), painter. The stamp shows Lt. Thomas Grosvenor and his attendant, Peter Salem. The painting is at Yale Univ., New Haven, CT.

Waterfowl Conservation Issue

Wood Ducks A784

Lithographed, Engraved (Giori)
1968, Oct. 24   Perf. 11
1362 A784 6c black & multi   .20 .20
  a.   Vert. pair, imperf. btwn.   550.
  b.   Red & dark blue omitted   900.
  c.   Red omitted   —

Gabriel, from van Eyck's Annunciation A785

Chief Joseph, by Cyrenius Hall A786

Christmas Issue
Engraved (Multicolor Huck)
1968, Nov. 1   Tagged   Perf. 11
1363 A785 6c multicolored   .20 .20
  a.   Untagged   .20 .20
  b.   Imperf. pair, tagged 225.00
  c.   Light yellow omitted 65.00
  d.   Imperf. pair, untagged 300.00

"The Annunciation" by the 15th cent. Flemish artist Jan van Eyck is in the Natl. Gallery of Art, Washington, DC. No. 1363a was issued Nov. 2.

Luminescence
No. 1364 and all following postage stamps are tagged, unless otherwise noted.

American Indian Issue
Lithographed, Engraved (Giori)
1968, Nov. 4   Perf. 11
1364 A786 6c black & multi   .20 .20

Honoring American Indians and the opening of the Natl. Portrait Gallery, Oct. 5, 1968. Chief Joseph (Indian name Thunder Traveling over the Mountains) a leader of the Nez Percé tribe, was born c. 1840 in eastern Oregon and died at the Colesville Reservation in Washington in 1904.

Beautification of America Issue

Capitol, Azaleas and Tulips A787

Washington Monument, Potomac River and Daffodils — A788

Poppies and Lupines along Highway A789

Blooming Crabapples along Street A790

Lithographed, Engraved (Giori)
1969, Jan. 16   Perf. 11
1365 A787 6c multicolored   .30 .20
1366 A788 6c multicolored   .30 .20
1367 A789 6c multicolored   .30 .20
1368 A790 6c multicolored   .30 .20
  a.   Block of 4, #1365-1368 1.25 1.75

Natural Beauty Campaign for more beautiful cities, parks, highways and streets.

Eagle from Great Seal of US — A791

July Fourth, by Grandma Moses — A792

American Legion, 50th Anniv.
Lithographed, Engraved (Giori)
1969, Mar. 15   Perf. 11
1369 A791 6c red, blue & black .20 .20

American Folklore Issue
Grandma Moses
Lithographed, Engraved (Giori)
1969, May 1   Perf. 11
1370 A792 6c multicolored   .20 .20
  a.   Horiz. pair, imperf. btwn. 225.00
  b.   Black and Prus blue omitted 850.00

Grandma Moses (Anna Mary Robertson Moses, 1860-1961), primitive painter of American life.

Beware of pairs with blind perfs. being offered as No. 1370a. No. 1370b often comes with mottled or disturbed gum. Such stamps sell for about two-thirds as much as copies with perfect gum.

Apollo 8 Issue

Moon Surface and Earth — A793

Giori Press Printing
1969, May 5   Perf. 11
1371 A793 6c blk, bl & ocher .20 .20

Apollo 8 mission, which put the 1st men into orbit around the moon, Dec. 21-27, 1968. Imperfs. exist from printer's waste.

William Christopher Handy Issue

W. C. Handy (1873-1958), Jazz Musician and Composer — A794

Lithographed, Engraved (Giori)
1969, May 17   Perf. 11
1372 A794 6c multicolored   .20 .20

California Settlement, 200th Anniv.

Carmel Mission Belfry — A795

1969, July 16   Perf. 11
1373 A795 6c multicolored   .20 .20

John Wesley Powell Issue

Powell Exploring Colorado River A796

1969, Aug. 1   Perf. 11
1374 A796 6c multicolored   .20 .20

Powell (1834-1902), geologist and explorer of the Green and Colorado Rivers, 1869-1875.

Alabama Statehood, 150th Anniv.

Camellia & Yellow-shafted Flicker — A797

1969, Aug. 2   Perf. 11
1375 A797 6c multicolored   .20 .20

Botanical Congress Issue

Douglas Fir (Northwest) A798

Botanical Congress Issue

Lady's-slipper (Northeast) — A799

Ocotillo (Southwest) A800

Franklinia (Southeast) A801

Lithographed, Engraved (Giori)
1969, Aug. 23   Perf. 11
1376 A798 6c multicolored   .40 .20
1377 A799 6c multicolored   .40 .20
1378 A800 6c multicolored   .40 .20
1379 A801 6c multicolored   .40 .20
  a.   Block of 4, #1376-1379 1.75 2.25

11th Intl. Botanical Cong., Seattle, Wash., Aug. 24-Sept. 2.

Dartmouth College Case Issue

Daniel Webster & Dartmouth Hall — A802

Rotary Press Printing
1969, Sept. 22   Perf. 10½x11
1380 A802 6c green   .20 .20

Sesquicentennial of the Dartmouth College case, argued by Daniel Webster before the Supreme Court, which reasserted the sanctity of contracts.

Professional Baseball Centenary

Batter A803

Lithographed, Engraved (Giori)
1969, Sept. 24   Perf. 11
1381 A803 6c yel, red, blk &
    grn   .65 .20
  a.   Black (1869-1969, United
      States, 6c, Professional
      Baseball) omitted   1,100.

Intercollegiate Football Centenary

Football Player & Coach A804

1969, Sept. 26   Perf. 11
1382 A804 6c red & green   .20 .20

Dwight D. Eisenhower Issue

Dwight D.
Eisenhower
A805

Giori Press Printing

1969, Oct. 14		Perf. 11
1383 A805 6c blue, black & red	.20	.20

Gen. Eisenhower, 34th Pres. (1890-1969).

Christmas Issue

Winter
Sunday in
Norway,
Maine
A806

Engraved (Multicolor Huck)

1969, Nov. 3		Perf. 11x10½
1384 A806 6c dk green & multi	.20	.20
Precanceled		.50
b. Imperf., pair		1,000.
c. Light green omitted		22.50
d. Lt grn, red & yel omitted		1,000.
e. Yellow omitted		2,250.
g. Red & yellow omitted		—

The precancel value applies to the experimental precancel printed in four cities with the names between lines 4½mm apart: in black or green "ATLANTA, GA" and in green only "BALTIMORE, MD," "MEMPHIS, TN" and "NEW HAVEN, CT."

They were sold freely to the public and could be used on any class of mail at all post offices during the experimental program and thereafter.

Most examples of No. 1384c show orange where the offset green was.

Value is for this variety. Copies without orange sell for a premium.

Cured
Child — A807

"Old
Models" — A808

Hope for Crippled Issue
Lithographed, Engraved (Giori)

1969, Nov. 20		Perf. 11
1385 A807 6c multicolored	.20	.20

Issued to encourage the rehabilitation of crippled children and adults, and to honor the Natl. Soc. for Crippled Children and Adults (Easter Seal Soc.) on its 50th anniv.

William M. Harnett Issue

1969, Dec. 3		Perf. 11
1386 A808 6c multicolored	.20	.20

Harnett (1848-1892), painter. The painting is in the Museum of Fine Arts, Boston.

Natural History Issue

American Bald Eagle — A809

African Elephant Herd — A810

Tlingit Chief in Haida Ceremonial Canoe — A811

Brontosaurus, Stegosaurus & Allosaurus — A812

Lithographed, Engraved (Giori)

1970, May 6		Perf. 11
1387 A809 6c multicolored	.20	.20
1388 A810 6c multicolored	.20	.20
1389 A811 6c multicolored	.20	.20
1390 A812 6c multicolored	.20	.20
a. Block of 4, #1387-1390	.55	.60

1969-1970 celebration of the cent. of the American Museum of Natural History in NYC.
The design of No. 1390 is a detail from a mural by Rudolph Zallinger in Yale's Peabody Museum.

Maine Statehood Issue

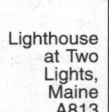

Lighthouse
at Two
Lights,
Maine
A813

Lithographed, Engraved (Giori)

1970, July 9		Perf. 11
1391 A813 6c black & multi	.20	.20

Sesquicentennial of Maine statehood. The painting by Edward Hopper (1882-1967) hangs in the Metropolitan Museum of Art, NYC.

Wildlife Conservation Issue

American
Buffalo
A814

Rotary Press Printing

1970, July 20		Perf. 10½x11
1392 A814 6c black, light brown	.20	.20

Regular Issue
Dwight David Eisenhower

A815

A815a

Dot between
"R" and "U"

No dot
between "R"
and "U"

Benjamin
Franklin
A816

USPS
Emblem
A817

Fiorello H.
LaGuardia
A817a

Ernest Taylor
Pyle
A818

Dr. Elizabeth
Blackwell
A818a

Amadeo P.
Giannini
A818b

Rotary (6c, 7c, 14c, 16c, 18c, 21c, #1395);
Giori (#1394); Photo. (#1396);

Perf. 11x10½, 10½x11; 11 (#1394)

1970-74

1393	A815	6c dark blue gray	.20	.20
a.		Booklet pane of 8	1.50	.65
b.		Booklet pane of 5 + label	1.50	.65
c.		Untagged (Bureau precanceled)		.20
1393D	A816	7c brt blue ('72)	.20	.20
e.		Untagged (Bureau precanceled)		.20
1394	A815a	8c blk, red & bl gray ('71)	.20	.20
b.		Red omitted		—
c.		Red and blue omitted		—
1395	A815	8c dp claret ('71)	.20	.20
a.		Booklet pane of 8	1.80	1.25
b.		Booklet pane of 6	1.25	.90
c.		Booklet pane of 4 + 2 labels ('72)	1.65	.80
d.		Bklt. pane of 7 + label ('72)	1.90	1.00
e.		Vert. pair, imperf. btwn.	600.00	
1396	A817	8c multi ('71)	.20	.20
1397	A817a	14c gray brn ('72)	.25	.20
a.		Untagged (Bureau precanceled)		.25
1398	A818	16c brown ('71)	.30	.20
a.		Untagged (Bureau precanceled)		.35
1399	A818a	18c violet ('74)	.35	.20
1400	A818b	21c green ('73)	.40	.20
		Nos. 1393-1400 (9)	2.30	1.80

No. 1395 was issued in booklets only. All stamps have one or two straight edges.

No. 1395e resulted from a paper foldover after perforating and before cutting into panes. At least 4 pairs are recorded from 3 panes (one No. 1395a and two No. 1395d) with different foldover patterns.

Issued: 6c, 8/6/70; 7c, 10/20/72; #1394-1395, 5/10/71; #1396, 7/1/71; 14c, 4/24/72; 16c, 5/7/71; 18c, 1/23/74; 21c, 6/27/73.

Coil Stamps
Rotary Press

1970-71			Perf. 10 Vert.
1401 A815 6c dark blue gray		.20	.20
a. Untagged (Bureau precanceled)			.20
b. Imperf., pair		2,000.	
1402 A815 8c deep claret		.20	.20
a. Imperf., pair		45.00	
b. Untagged (Bureau precanceled)			.20
c. Pair, imperf. btwn.		6,250.	

Issue dates: 6c, Aug. 6; 8c, May 10, 1971.

Edgar Lee Masters Issue

A819

Lithographed, Engraved (Giori)

1970, Aug. 22		Perf. 11
1405 A819 6c black & olive bister	.20	.20

Edgar Lee Masters (1869-1950), Poet

Woman Suffrage Issue

Suffragettes, 1920 & Woman Voter, 1970 — A820

Giori Press Printing

1970, Aug. 26		Perf. 11
1406 A820 6c blue	.20	.20

50th anniv. of the 19th Amendment, which gave women the vote.

South Carolina Issue

Symbols of
South
Carolina
A821

Lithographed, Engraved (Giori)

1970, Sept. 12		Perf. 11
1407 A821 6c bister, black & red	.20	.20

300th anniv. of the founding of Charles Town (Charleston), the 1st permanent settlement of SC.

Against a background of pine wood the line drawings of the design represent the economic and historic development of SC:

The spire of St. Phillip's Church, Capitol, state flag, a ship, 17th cent. man and woman, a Fort Sumter cannon, barrels, cotton, tobacco and yellow jessamine.

Stone Mountain Memorial Issue

A822

Giori Press Printing

1970, Sept. 19		Perf. 11
1408 A822 6c gray	.20	.20

Dedication of the Stone Mountain Confederate Memorial, featuring Robert E. Lee, Jefferson Davis & "Stonewall" Jackson, GA, May 9, 1970.

Fort Snelling Issue

Fort
Snelling,
Keelboat &
Tepees
A823

Lithographed, Engraved (Giori)

1970, Oct. 17		Perf. 11
1409 A823 6c yellow & multi	.20	.20

150th anniv. of Fort Snelling, MN, which was an important outpost for the opening of the Northwest.

Anti-Pollution Issue

Globe and Wheat
A824

Globe and City
A825

Globe and Bluegill
A826

Globe and Seagull
A827

1970, Oct. 28   Photo.   Perf. 11x10½

1410	A824	6c multicolored	.25	.20
1411	A825	6c multicolored	.25	.20
1412	A826	6c multicolored	.25	.20
1413	A827	6c multicolored	.25	.20
a.		Block of 4, #1410-1413	1.10	1.25

Christmas Issue

Nativity — A828

Tin and Cast-iron Locomotive
A829

Toy Horse on Wheels
A830

Mechanical Tricycle
A831

Doll Carriage
A832

1970, Nov. 5   Photo.   Perf. 10½x11

1414	A828	6c multicolored	.20	.20
a.		Precanceled	.20	.20
b.		Black omitted	550.00	
c.		As "a," blue omitted	1,500.	

Perf. 11x10½

1415	A829	6c multicolored	.30	.20
a.		Precanceled	.75	.20
b.		Black omitted	2,500.	
1416	A830	6c multicolored	.30	.20
a.		Precanceled	.75	.20
b.		Black omitted	2,500.	
c.		Imperf., pair (#1416, 1418)	4,000.	
1417	A831	6c multicolored	.30	.20
a.		Precanceled	.75	.20
b.		Black omitted	2,500.	

1418	A832	6c multicolored	.30	.20
a.		Precanceled	.75	.20
b.		Block of 4, #1415-1418	1.25	1.50
c.		As "b," precanceled	3.25	3.25
d.		Black omitted	2,500.	
e.		As "b," black omitted	10,000.	
		Nos. 1414-1418 (5)	1.40	1.00

No. 1414, Nativity, by Lorenzo Lotto (1480-1556). Nos. 1415-1418 are antique Christmas toys.

The precanceled stamps, Nos. 1414a-1418a, were furnished to 68 cities. The plates include two straight (No. 1414a) or two wavy (Nos. 1415a-1418a) black lines that make up the precancellation.

Unused values are for copies with gum and used values are for copies with an additional cancellation or without gum.

United Nations, 25th Anniv.

"UN" & UN Emblem
A833

Lithographed, Engraved (Giori)
1970, Nov. 20   Perf. 11

1419	A833	6c black, ver & ultra	.20	.20

Landing of the Pilgrims Issue

Mayflower & Pilgrims — A834

Lithographed, Engraved (Giori)
1970, Nov. 21   Perf. 11

1420	A834	6c blk, org, yel, brn, mag & bl	.20	.20
a.		Orange & yellow omitted	900.00	

Mayflower landing, 350th anniv.

Disabled Veterans & Servicemen Issue

A835   A836

Lithographed, Engraved (Giori)
1970, Nov. 24   Perf. 11
Engr.

1421	A835	6c multicolored	.20	.20
1422	A836	6c dk bl, blk & red	.20	.20
a.		Pair, #1421-1422	.30	.30

50th anniv. of the Disabled Veterans of America Organization (No. 1421).

Honoring the contribution of servicemen, particularly those who were prisoners of war or missing in action (No. 1422).

Ewe and Lamb
A837

Douglas MacArthur
A838

American Wool Industry Issue
Lithographed, Engraved (Giori)
1971, Jan. 19   Perf. 11

1423	A837	6c multicolored	.20	.20
b.		Teal blue ("United States") omitted	—	

450th anniv. of the introduction of sheep to the No. American continent and the beginning of the American wool industry.

No. 1423b was caused by the misregistration of the intaglio printing.

Gen. Douglas MacArthur Issue
Giori Press Printing
1971, Jan. 26

1424	A838	6c blk, red & dk bl	.20	.20
a.		Red omitted	—	

MacArthur (1880-1964), Chief of Staff, Supreme Commander for the Allied Powers in the Pacific Area during WW II and Supreme Commander in Japan after the war.

Blood Donor Issue

Giving Blood Saves Lives
A839

1971, Mar. 12   Perf. 11

1425	A839	6c lt blue, scar & ind	.20	.20

Salute to blood donors and spur to participation in the blood donor program.

Missouri Sesquicentennial Issue

"Independence and the Opening of the West" — A840

1971, May 8   Photo.   Perf. 11x10½

1426	A840	8c multicolored	.20	.20

Detail, by Thomas Hart Benton. The stamp design shows a Pawnee facing a hunter-trapper and a group of settlers.

Wildlife Conservation Issue

Trout
A841

Alligator — A842

Polar Bear, Cubs
A843

California Condor — A844

Lithographed, Engraved (Giori)
1971, June 12   Perf. 11

1427	A841	8c multicolored	.20	.20
a.		Red omitted	1,250.	
1428	A842	8c multicolored	.20	.20
1429	A843	8c multicolored	.20	.20
1430	A844	8c multicolored	.20	.20
a.		Block of 4, #1427-1430	.80	.90
b.		As "a," lt grn & dk grn omitted from #1427-1428	4,500.	
c.		As "a," red omitted from #1427, 1429-1430	7,500.	

Antarctic Treaty Issue

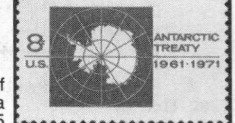

Map of Antarctica
A845

Giori Press Printing
1971, June 23

1431	A845	8c red & dark blue	.20	.20
b.		Both colors omitted	—	

10th anniv. of the Antarctic Treaty pledging peaceful uses of and scientific cooperation in Antarctica.

No. 1431b was caused by an extraneous piece of paper blocking the impression. It should be collected se-tenant with a normal stamp and/or a partially printed stamp.

American Revolution Bicentennial

Bicentennial Commission Emblem — A846

Lithographed, Engraved (Giori)
1971, July 4   Perf. 11

1432	A846	8c red, blue, gray & black	.20	.20
a.		Gray & black omitted	500.00	
b.		Gray ("U.S. Postage 8c") omitted	900.00	

John Sloan Issue

The Wake of the Ferry
A847

1971, Aug. 2   Perf. 11

1433	A847	8c multicolored	.20	.20
b.		Red engr. ("John Sloan" and "8") omitted	—	

Sloan (1871-1951), painter.

Space Achievement Decade Issue

Earth, Sun, Landing Craft on Moon
A848

Lunar Rover
A849

Lithographed, Engraved (Giori)
1971, Aug. 2   Perf. 11

1434	A848	8c blk, bl, yel & red	.20	.20
1435	A849	8c blk, bl, yel & red	.20	.20
b.		Pair, #1434-1435	.40	.45
d.		As "b," bl & red (litho.) omitted	1,500.	

Apollo 15 moon exploration mission July 26-Aug. 7.

Emily Elizabeth Dickinson
A850

Sentry Box, Morro Castle, San Juan
A851

Emily Dickinson Issue

Lithographed, Engraved (Giori)
1971, Aug. 28 *Perf. 11*
1436 A850 8c multi, *greenish* .20 .20
a. Black & olive (engr.) omitted 800.
b. Pale rose omitted 7,500.
c. Red omitted —

Dickinson (1830-1886), poet.

San Juan, PR, 450th Anniv.
1971, Sept. 12
1437 A851 8c multicolored .20 .20

VALUES FOR HINGED STAMPS AFTER NO. 771
This catalogue does not value unused stamps after No. 771 in hinged condition. Hinged unused stamps from No. 772 to the present are worth considerably less than the values given for unused stamps, which are for never-hinged examples.

Young Woman Drug Addict — A852

Hands Reaching for CARE — A853

Prevent Drug Abuse Issue
1971, Oct. 4 Photo. *Perf. 10½x11*
1438 A852 8c bl, dp bl & blk .20 .20
Drug Abuse Prevention Week, Oct. 3-9.

CARE Issue
1971, Oct. 27
1439 A853 8c multicolored .20 .20
a. Black omitted 4,750.
25th anniv. of CARE, a US-Canadian Cooperative for American Relief Everywhere.

Historic Preservation Issue

Decatur House, Washington, DC — A854

Whaling Ship Charles W. Morgan, Mystic, Conn. — A855

Cable Car, San Francisco — A856

San Xavier del Bac Mission, Tucson, Ariz. — A857

Lithographed, Engraved (Giori)
1971, Oct. 29 Buff Paper *Perf. 11*
1440 A854 8c blk brn & ocher .20 .20
1441 A855 8c blk brn & ocher .20 .20
1442 A856 8c blk brn & ocher .20 .20
1443 A857 8c blk brn & ocher .20 .20
a. Block of 4, #1440-1443 .75 .85
b. As "a," black brown omitted 2,250.
c. As "a," ocher omitted —

Christmas Issue

Adoration of the Shepherds, by Giorgione
A858

Partridge in a Pear Tree, by Jamie Wyeth
A859

1971, Nov. 10 Photo. *Perf. 10½x11*
1444 A858 8c gold & multi .20 .20
a. Gold omitted 550.00
1445 A859 8c multicolored .20 .20

Sidney Lanier (1842-1881)
A860

Peace Corps Poster, by David Battle
A861

Sidney Lanier Issue
Giori Press Printing
1972, Feb. 3 *Perf. 11*
1446 A860 8c blk, brn & lt bl .20 .20
Lanier, poet, musician, lawyer, educator.

Peace Corps Issue
1972, Feb. 11 Photo. *Perf. 10½x11*
1447 A861 8c dk bl, lt bl & red .20 .20

National Parks Centennial Issue

Hulk of Ship A862

Cape Hatteras Lighthouse A863

Laughing Gulls on Driftwood A864

Laughing Gulls and Dune A865

Wolf Trap Farm, Vienna, Va. — A866

Old Faithful, Yellowstone — A867

Mt. McKinley, Alaska A868

Lithographed, Engraved (Giori)
1972 *Perf. 11*
1448 A862 2c black & multi .20 .20
1449 A863 2c black & multi .20 .20
1450 A864 2c black & multi .20 .20
1451 A865 2c black & multi .20 .20
a. Block of 4, #1448-1451 .25 .25
b. As "a," black (litho.) omitted 2,250.
1452 A866 6c black & multi .20 .20
1453 A867 8c blk, blue, brn & multi .20 .20
1454 A868 15c black & multi .30 .30

Cent. of Yellowstone Natl. Park, the 1st Natl. Park, and of the Natl. Park System. The four 2c stamps were issued for Cape Hatteras, NC, Natl. Seashore.
Issued: 2c, 4/5; 6c, 6/26; 8c, 3/1; 15c, 7/28.
See No. C84.

Family Planning Issue

Family — A869

1972, Mar. 18
1455 A869 8c black & multi .20 .20
a. Yellow omitted 1,250.
b. Dark brown & olive omitted —
c. Dark brown omitted 9,500

American Bicentennial
Colonial American Craftsmen

Glassmaker A870

Silversmith A871

Wigmaker A872

Hatter A873

1972, July 4 Engr. *Perf. 11x10½*
Dull Yellow Paper
1456 A870 8c deep brown .20 .20
1457 A871 8c deep brown .20 .20
1458 A872 8c deep brown .20 .20
1459 A873 8c deep brown .20 .20
a. Block of 4, #1456-1459 .65 .75

Olympic Games Issue

Bicycling and Olympic Rings A874

Bobsledding A875

Running A876

1972, Aug. 17 Photo. *Perf. 11x10½*
1460 A874 6c multicolored .20 .20
1461 A875 8c multicolored .20 .20
1462 A876 15c multicolored .30 .20
a. Nos. 1460-1462 (3) .70 .60

11th Winter Olympic Games, Sapporo, Japan, Feb. 3-13, and 20th Summer Olympic Games, Munich, Germany, Aug. 26-Sept. 11. See No. C85.

Parent Teacher Association, 75th Anniv.

Blackboard A877

1972, Sept. 15 Photo. *Perf. 11x10½*
1463 A877 8c yellow & black .20 .20

Wildlife Conservation Issue

Fur Seals — A878

Cardinal — A879

Brown Pelican — A880

Bighorn Sheep — A881

Lithographed, Engraved
1972, Sept. 20   *Perf. 11*

1464	A878 8c multicolored		.20	.20
1465	A879 8c multicolored		.20	.20
1466	A880 8c multicolored		.20	.20
1467	A881 8c multicolored		.20	.20
a.	Block of 4, #1464-1467		.65	.75
b.	As "a," brown omitted	4,000.		
c.	As "a," green & blue omitted	4,500.		
d.	As "a," red & brown omitted	3,000.		

Mail Order Issue

Rural Post Office Store A882

1972, Sept. 27 Photo. *Perf. 11x10½*

1468	A882 8c multicolored		.20	.20

Cent. of mail order business, originated by Aaron Montgomery Ward, Chicago.

Osteopathic Medicine Issue

Man's Quest for Health — A883

1972, Oct. 9 Photo. *Perf. 10½x11*

1469	A883 8c yel, org & dk brn		.20	.20

75th anniv. of the American Osteopathic Assoc., founded by Dr. Andrew T. Still.

American Folklore Issue

Tom Sawyer, by Norman Rockwell — A884

Lithographed, Engraved (Giori)
1972, Oct. 13   *Perf. 11*

1470	A884 8c black & multi		.20	.20
a.	Horiz. pair, imperf. btwn.	4,500.		
b.	Red & black (engr.) omitted	1,900.		
c.	Yellow & tan (litho.) omitted	2,400.		

Tom Sawyer, hero of "The Adventures of Tom Sawyer," by Mark Twain.

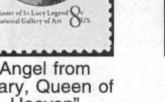

Angel from "Mary, Queen of Heaven" A885

Santa Claus A886

1972, Nov. 9 Photo. *Perf. 10½x11*

1471	A885 8c multicolored		.20	.20
a.	Pink omitted	150.00		
b.	Black omitted	4,000.		
1472	A886 8c multicolored		.20	.20

Design of No. 1471 shows detail from a painting by the Master of the St. Lucy Legend.

Pharmacy Issue

Mortar & Pestle, Bowl of Hygeia, 19th Century Medicine Bottles A887

Lithographed, Engraved (Giori)
1972, Nov. 10   *Perf. 11*

1473	A887 8c black & multi		.20	.20
a.	Blue & orange omitted	825.00		
b.	Blue omitted	2,250.		
c.	Orange omitted	2,250.		

Honoring American druggists, and 120th anniv. of the American Pharmaceutical Assoc.

Stamp Collecting Issue

U.S. No. 1 Under Magnifying Glass A888

1972, Nov. 17   *Perf. 11*

1474	A888 8c dark blue green, black & brown		.20	.20
a.	Black (litho.) omitted	600.00		

Love Issue

"Love," by Robert Indiana A889

1973, Jan. 26 Photo. *Perf. 11x10½*

1475	A889 8c red, emer & vio bl		.20	.20

American Bicentennial
Communications in Colonial Times

Printer and Patriots Examining Pamphlet A890

Posting a Broadside A891

Postrider A892

Drummer A893

1973 Giori Press Printing *Perf. 11*

1476	A890 8c ultra, grnsh blk & red		.20	.20
1477	A891 8c black, ver & ultra		.20	.20

Lithographed, Engraved (Giori)

1478	A892 8c multicolored		.20	.20
a.	Red omitted	—		
1479	A893 8c multicolored		.20	.20
	Nos. 1476-1479 (4)		.80	.80

Issued: No. 1476, Feb. 16; No. 1477, Apr. 13; No. 1478, June 22; No. 1479, Sept. 28.

Boston Tea Party

British Merchantman — A894

British Three-master — A895

Boats and Ship's Hull A896

Boat and Dock A897

Lithographed, Engraved (Giori)
1973, July 4   *Perf. 11*

1480	A894 8c black & multi		.20	.20
1481	A895 8c black & multi		.20	.20
1482	A896 8c black & multi		.20	.20
1483	A897 8c black & multi		.20	.20
a.	Block of 4, #1480-1483		.65	.75
b.	As "a," black (engr.) omitted	1,500.		
c.	As "a," black (litho.) omitted	1,400.		

American Arts Issue

Gershwin, Sportin' Life, Porgy & Bess A898

Robinson Jeffers, Man & Children of Carmel with Burro A899

Henry Ossawa Tanner, Palette & Rainbow A900

Willa Cather, Pioneer Family & Covered Wagon A901

1973 Photo. *Perf. 11*

1484	A898 8c dp grn & multi		.20	.20
a.	Vert. pair, imperf. horiz.	240.00		
1485	A899 8c Prus bl & multi		.20	.20
a.	Vert. pair, imperf. horiz.	250.00		
1486	A900 8c yel brn & multi		.20	.20
a.	Vert. pair, imperf. horiz.	275.00		
1487	A901 8c dp brn & multi		.20	.20
a.	Vert. pair, imperf. horiz.	275.00		
	Nos. 1484-1487 (4)		.80	.80

Honoring: No. 1484, George Gershwin (1898-1937), composer. No. 1485, Robinson Jeffers (1887-1962), poet. No. 1486, Henry Ossawa Tanner (1859-1937), black painter (portrait by Thomas Eakins). No. 1487, Willa Sibert Cather (1873-1947), novelist.

Issued: No. 1484, Feb. 28; No. 1485, Aug. 13; No. 1486, Sept. 10; No. 1487, Sept. 20.

Copernicus Issue

Nicolaus Copernicus (1473-1543), Polish Astronomer — A902

Lithographed, Engraved (Giori)
1973, Apr. 23   *Perf. 11*

1488	A902 8c black & orange		.20	.20
a.	Orange omitted	1,000.		
b.	Black (engraved) omitted	900.00		

The orange color can be chemically removed.

Postal Service Employees' Issue

Stamp Counter A903

Mail Collection A904

Letter Facing on Conveyor Belt — A905

Parcel Post Sorting — A906

UNITED STATES

43

Mail Canceling
A907

Manual Letter
Routing
A908

Electronic Letter
Routing — A909

Loading Mail on
Truck — A910

Mailman
A911

Rural Mail
Delivery
A912

1973, Apr. 30   Photo.   Perf. 10½x11

1489	A903	8c multicolored	.20	.20
1490	A904	8c multicolored	.20	.20
1491	A905	8c multicolored	.20	.20
1492	A906	8c multicolored	.20	.20
1493	A907	8c multicolored	.20	.20
1494	A908	8c multicolored	.20	.20
1495	A909	8c multicolored	.20	.20
1496	A910	8c multicolored	.20	.20
1497	A911	8c multicolored	.20	.20
1498	A912	8c multicolored	.20	.20
a.	Strip of 10, Nos. 1489-1498		1.75	1.75

A tribute to USPS employees. Emerald inscription on back, printed beneath gum in water-soluble ink, includes the USPS emblem, "People Serving You" and a statement, differing for each of the 10 stamps, about some aspect of postal service.

Each stamp in top or bottom row has a tab with blue inscription enumerating various jobs in postal service.

Harry S Truman Issue

Harry S Truman,
33rd President
(1884-1972)
A913

Giori Press Printing
1973, May 8   Perf. 11

1499	A913	8c car rose, blk & bl	.20	.20

Electronics Progress Issue

Marconi's
Spark Coil
and Gap
A914

Transistors
and Printed
Circuit
Board
A915

Microphone, Speaker, Vacuum Tube,
TV Camera Tube — A916

Lithographed, Engraved (Giori)
1973, July 10   Perf. 11

1500	A914	6c lilac & multi	.20	.20
1501	A915	8c tan & multi	.20	.20
a.	Black (inscriptions & "U.S. 8c") omitted		450.00	
b.	Tan (background) & lilac omitted		1,250.	
1502	A916	15c gray green & multi	.30	20
a.	Black (inscriptions & "U.S. 15c") omitted		1,350.	
	Nos. 1500-1502 (3)		.70	.60

No. 1501b hinged is ½ unhinged value.
See No. C86.

Lyndon B. Johnson Issue

Lyndon B.
Johnson (1908-
1973), 36th
President — A917

1973, Aug. 27   Photo.   Perf. 11

1503	A917	8c black & multi	.20	.20
a.	Horiz. pair, imperf. vert.		350.00	

Rural America Issue

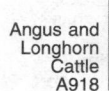

Angus and
Longhorn
Cattle
A918

Chautauqua Tent and Buggies — A919

Wheat
Fields and
Train
A920

Lithographed, Engraved (Giori)
1973-74   Perf. 11

1504	A918	8c multicolored	.20	.20
a.	Green & red brown omitted		950.00	
b.	Vert. pair, imperf. between		—	
1505	A919	10c multicolored	.20	.20
a.	Black (litho.) omitted		2,000.	
1506	A920	10c multicolored	.20	.20
a.	Black & blue (engr.) omitted		750.00	
	Nos. 1504-1506 (3)		.60	.60

Cent. of introduction of Aberdeen Angus cattle to US (No. 1504); of Chautauqua Institution (No. 1505); of introduction of hard winter wheat into Kansas by Mennonite immigrants (No. 1506).

Issue dates: No. 1504, Oct. 5, 1973; No. 1505, Aug. 6, 1974; No. 1506, Aug. 16, 1974.

Christmas Issue

Small Cowper
Madonna, by
Raphael
A921

Christmas Tree
in Needlepoint
A922

1973, Nov. 7   Photo.   Perf. 10½x11

1507	A921	8c tan & multi	.20	.20
1508	A922	8c green & multi	.20	.20
a.	Vert. pair, imperf. btwn.		300.00	

50-Star & 13-
Star Flags
A923

Jefferson
Memorial &
Signature
A924

Mail Transport
A925

Liberty Bell
A926

Multicolor Huck Press
1973-74   Tagged   Perf. 11x10½

1509	A923	10c red & blue	.20	.20
a.	Horiz. pair, imperf. btwn.		50.	
b.	Blue omitted		175.	
c.	Vert. pair, imperf.		950.	
d.	Horiz. pair, imperf. vert.		1,000.	

Rotary Press Printing

1510	A924	10c blue	.20	.20
a.	Untagged (Bureau pre-canceled)			.20
b.	Booklet pane of 5 + label		1.65	.55
c.	Booklet pane of 8		1.65	.70
d.	Booklet pane of 6 ('74)		5.25	1.00
e.	Vert. pair, imperf. horiz.		525.00	
f.	Vert. pair, imperf. btwn.		—	
1511	A925	10c multi, photo	.20	.20
a.	Yellow omitted		65.00	

The yellow can be chemically removed.

Coil Stamps
Perf. 10 Vert.
Rotary Press Printing

1518	A926	6.3c brick red	.20	.20
a.	Untagged (Bureau pre-canceled)			.20
b.	Imperf., pair		210.00	
c.	As "a," imperf. pair		100.00	

Multicolor Huck Press

1519	A923	10c red & blue	.20	.20
a.	Imperf., pair		37.50	

Rotary Press Printing

1520	A924	10c blue	.25	.20
a.	Untagged (Bureau pre-canceled)			.25
b.	Imperf., pair		40.00	

Issued: #1509, 1519, 12/8/73; #1510, 1520, 12/14/73; #1511, 1/4/74; #1518, 10/1/74.

Veterans of Foreign Wars Issue

V.F.W.
Emblem
A928

Giori Press Printing
1974, Mar. 11   Perf. 11

1525	A928	10c red & dark blue	.20	.20
b.	Blue omitted		—	

75th anniv. of Veterans of Spanish American and other Foreign Wars.

Robert Frost Issue

Robert Frost (1874-
1963), Poet — A929

Rotary Press Printing
1974, Mar. 26   Perf. 10½x11

1526	A929	10c black	.20	.20

EXPO '74 Issue

"Cosmic
Jumper"
A930

1974, Apr. 18   Photo.   Perf. 11

1527	A930	10c multicolored	.20	.20

EXPO '74, Spokane, Wash., May 4-Nov. 4. Theme, "Preserve the Environment."

Horse Racing Issue

Horses
Rounding
Turn
A931

1974, May 4   Photo.   Perf. 11x10½

1528	A931	10c yellow & multi	.20	.20
a.	Bl ("Horse Racing") omitted		900.00	
b.	Red ("U.S. postage 10 cents") omitted		—	

Beware of stamps offered as No. 1528b that have traces of red.

Skylab Issue

Skylab
A932

Lithographed, Engraved (Giori)
1974, May 14   Perf. 11

1529	A932	10c multicolored	.20	.20
a.	Vert. pair, imperf. btwn.		—	

1st anniv. of the launching of Skylab and to honor all who participated in the Skylab projects.

Centenary of UPU Issue

Michelangelo,
from School of
Athens — A933

Five Feminine
Virtues — A934

Old Time Letter
Rack — A935

Mlle. La
Vergne — A936

Lady Writing
Letter — A937

Inkwell and
Quill — A938

Mrs. John
Douglas — A939

Don Antonio
Noreiga — A940

1974, June 6   Photo.   Perf. 11

1530	A933	10c by Raphael	.20	.20
1531	A934	10c by Hokusai	.20	.20
1532	A935	10c by Peto	.20	.20
1533	A936	10c by Liotard	.20	.20
1534	A937	10c by Terborch	.20	.20
1535	A938	10c by Chardin	.20	.20
1536	A939	10c by Gains-borough	.20	.20
1537	A940	10c by Goya	.20	.20
a.		Block or strip, #1530-1537	1.75	1.60
b.		As "a" (block), imperf. vert.	7,500.	

Mineral Heritage Issue

Petrified
Wood
A941

Tourmaline — A942

Amethyst
A943

Rhodochrosite — A944

Lithographed, Engraved (Giori)
1974, June 13   Perf. 11

1538	A941	10c lt blue & multi	.20	.20
a.		Light blue & yellow omitted	—	
1539	A942	10c lt blue & multi	.20	.20
a.		Light blue omitted	—	
b.		Black & purple omitted	—	
1540	A943	10c lt blue & multi	.20	.20
a.		Light blue & yellow omitted	—	
1541	A944	10c lt blue & multi	.20	.20
a.		Block or strip, #1538-1541	.80	.90
b.		As "a," lt bl & yel omitted	1,900.	
c.		Light blue omitted	—	
d.		Black & red omitted	—	

Kentucky Settlement Issue

Fort Harrod — A945

Lithographed, Engraved (Giori)
1974, June 15   Perf. 11

1542	A945	10c green & multi	.20	.20
a.		Dull black (litho.) omitted	750.00	
b.		Grn (engr. & litho.), blk (engr. & litho.), bl omitted	3,000.	
c.		Green (engr.) omitted	—	
d.		Grn (engr.), blk (litho.) omitted	—	

American Bicentennial
First Continental Congress

Carpenters'
Hall
A946

A947

A948

Independence Hall — A949

Giori Press Printing
1974, July 4   Perf. 11

1543	A946	10c dark blue & red	.20	.20
1544	A947	10c gray, dk bl & red	.20	.20
1545	A948	10c gray, dk bl & red	.20	.20
1546	A949	10c red & dark blue	.20	.20
a.		Block of 4, #1543-1546	.80	.90

Energy Conservation Issue

A950

Lithographed, Engraved (Giori)
1974, Sept. 23   Perf. 11

1547	A950	10c multicolored	.20	.20
a.		Blue & orange omitted	850.00	
b.		Orange & green omitted	600.00	
c.		Green omitted	825.	

Design features molecules and drops of gasoline & oil to publicize the importance of conserving all forms of energy.

American Folklore Issue

Legend of
Sleepy
Hollow
A951

Lithographed, Engraved (Giori)
1974, Oct. 10   Perf. 11

1548	A951	10c dk bl, blk, org & yel	.20	.20

Legend of Sleepy Hollow, by Washington Irving.
Design features Headless Horseman pursuing Ichabod Crane.

Retarded Children Issue

Retarded
Child — A952

Giori Press Printing
1974, Oct. 12   Perf. 11

1549	A952	10c brn red & dk brn	.20	.20

Natl. Assoc. of Retarded Citizens.

Christmas Issue

Angel, from Perussis
Altarpiece,
1480 — A953

"The Road-Winter," by Currier &
Ives — A954

Dove
Weather
Vane
A955

1974   Photo.   Perf. 10½x11

1550	A953	10c multicolored	.20	.20

Perf. 11x10½

1551	A954	10c multicolored	.20	.20
a.		Buff omitted	35.00	

No. 1551a is difficult to identify. Competent expertization is necessary.

Die Cut, Paper Backing Rouletted
Self-adhesive
Inscribed "Precanceled"
Untagged

1552	A955	10c multicolored	.20	.20

Unused value of No. 1552 is for copy on rouletted paper backing as issued. Used value is for copy on piece, with or without postmark.
Most copies are becoming discolored, probably from the adhesive. Unused and used values are for discolored copies.
Die cutting includes crossed slashes through dove, applied to prevent removal and re-use of stamp. The stamp will separate into layers if soaked.

Issued: #1550-1551, 10/23; #1552, 11/15.

American Arts Issue

Benjamin West — A956

Paul Laurence Dunbar — A957

D. W. Griffith & Projector A958

1975   Photo.   Perf. 10½x11
1553 A956 10c multicolored   .20   .20
        Perf. 11
1554 A957 10c multicolored   .20   .20
    a.   Imperf., pair   1,300.
        Litho., Engr. (Giori)
1555 A958 10c multicolored   .20   .20
    a.   Brown (engr.) omitted   625.
    Nos. 1553-1555 (3)   .60   .60

Honoring: West (1738-1820), painter (#1553). Dunbar (1872-1906), poet (#1554). David Lewelyn Wark Griffith (1875-1948), motion picture producer (#1555).
    Issued: #1553, 2/10; #1554, 5/1; #1555, 5/27.

Space Issue

Pioneer 10 Passing Jupiter A959

Mariner 10, Venus & Mercury A960

Lithographed, Engraved (Giori)
1975   Perf. 11
1556 A959 10c lt yel, dk yel, red, blue, & 2 dk blues   .20   .20
    a.   Red & dk yel omitted   1,400.
    b.   Dk blues (engr.) omitted   950.
    d.   Dark yellow omitted   —
    Imperfs. exist from printer's waste.
1557 A960 10c blk, red, ultra & bis   .20   .20
    a.   Red omitted   450.00
    b.   Ultra & bister omitted   2,000.

U.S. unmanned accomplishments in space. Pioneer 10 passed within 81,000 miles of Jupiter, Dec. 3, 1973. Mariner 10 explored Venus and Mercury in 1974, and Mercury again in Mar. 1975.
    Issue dates: #1556, Feb. 28; #1557, Apr. 4.

Collective Bargaining Issue

"Labor and Management" — A961

1975, Mar. 13   Photo.   Perf. 11
1558 A961 10c multicolored   .20   .20
    Collective Bargaining Law, enacted 1935 with Wagner Act. Imperfs. are printers waste.

American Bicentennial
Contributors to the Cause

Sybil Ludington A962

Salem Poor A963

Haym Salomon A964

Peter Francisco A965

1975, Mar. 25   Photo.   Perf. 11x10½
1559 A962 8c multicolored   .20   .20
    a.   Back inscription omitted   225.00
1560 A963 10c multicolored   .20   .20
    a.   Back inscription omitted   225.00
1561 A964 10c multicolored   .20   .20
    a.   Back inscription omitted   225.00
    b.   Red omitted   250.00
1562 A965 18c multicolored   .35   .20
    Nos. 1559-1562 (4)   .95   .80

Ludington, age 16, rallied militia Apr. 26, 1777.
Poor, black freeman, fought in Battle of Bunker Hill.
Salomon, Jewish immigrant, raised money to finance Revolutionary War.
Francisco, Portuguese-French immigrant, joined Continental Army at 15.
An emerald inscription on back, printed beneath gum in water-soluble ink, gives a thumbnail sketch of the portrayed contributor.

Lexington-Concord Battle, 200th Anniv.

"Birth of Liberty," by Henry Sandham A966

1975, Apr. 19   Photo.   Perf. 11
1563 A966 10c multicolored   .20   .20
    a.   Vert. pair, imperf. horiz.   425.00

Battle of Bunker Hill, 200th Anniv.

Battle of Bunker Hill, by John Trumbull — A967

1975, June 17   Perf. 11
1564 A967 10c multicolored   .20   .20

Military Uniforms

Soldier with Flintlock Musket, Uniform Button — A968

Sailor with Grappling Hook, First Navy Jack, 1775 — A969

Marine with Musket, Full-rigged Ship — A970

Militiaman with Musket, Powder Horn — A971

1975, July 4   Perf. 11
1565 A968 10c multicolored   .20   .20
1566 A969 10c multicolored   .20   .20
1567 A970 10c multicolored   .20   .20
1568 A971 10c multicolored   .20   .20
    a.   Block of 4, #1565-1568   .85   .90

Bicentenary of US Military Services.

Apollo Soyuz Space Issue

Apollo & Soyuz After Docking, Earth — A972

Spacecraft Before Docking, Earth & Project Emblem — A973

1975, July 15   Photo.   Perf. 11
1569 A972 10c multicolored   .20   .20
1570 A973 10c multicolored   .20   .20
    a.   Pair, #1569-1570   .45   .40
    c.   As "a," vert. pair, imperf. horiz.   1,750.
    d.   As "a," yellow omitted

Apollo Soyuz space test project (Russo-American cooperation); launching, July 15; link-up, July 17.
Nos. 1569-1570 totally imperf are from printer's waste.
See Russia Nos. 4339-4340.

International Women's Year Issue

Worldwide Equality for Women A974

1975, Aug. 26   Photo.   Perf. 11x10½
1571 A974 10c bl, org & dk bl   .20   .20

Postal Service Bicentennial Issue

Stagecoach and Trailer Truck A975

Old and New Locomotives — A976

Early Mail Plane and Jet — A977

Satellite for Transmission of Mailgrams — A978

1975, Sept. 3   Photo.   Perf. 11x10½
1572 A975 10c multicolored   .20   .20
1573 A976 10c multicolored   .20   .20
1574 A977 10c multicolored   .20   .20
1575 A978 10c multicolored   .20   .20
    a.   Block of 4, #1572-1575   .85   .90
    b.   As "a," red ("10c") omitted   9,500.

World Peace Through Law Issue

Law Book, Olive Branch and Globe A979

Giori Press Printing
1975, Sept. 29   Perf. 11
1576 A979 10c green, Prus blue & rose brown   .20   .20
    b.   Horiz. pair, imperf. vert.

A prelude to 7th World Conf. of the World Peace Through Law Center at Washington, DC, Oct. 12-17.

Banking and Commerce Issue

Engine Turning, Indian Head Penny & Morgan Silver Dollar A980

Seated Liberty Quarter, $20 Gold (Double Eagle), Engine Turning A981

Lithographed, Engraved (Giori)
1975, Oct. 6   Perf. 11
1577 A980 10c multicolored   .25   .20
1578 A981 10c multicolored   .25   .20
    a.   Pair, #1577-1578   .50   .40
    b.   As "a," brown & blue (litho.) omitted   2,000.
    c.   As "a," brown, blue & yellow (litho.) omitted   2,500.

Banking and commerce in the US and for the Centennial Convention of the American Bankers Association.

Christmas Issue

Madonna, by
Domenico
Ghirlandaio
A982

Christmas Card,
by Louis Prang,
1878
A983

1975, Oct. 14   Photo.   Perf. 11

1579	A982	(10c) multicolored	.20	.20
	a.	Imperf., pair	90.00	

Perf. 11.2

1580	A983	(10c) multicolored	.20	.20
	a.	Imperf., pair	90.00	
	c.	Perf. 10.9	.25	.20

Perf. 10.5x11.3

1580B	A983	(10c) multicolored	.65	.20

Americana Issue

Inkwell and
Quill
A984

Speaker's
Stand
A985

Early Ballot
Box
A987

Books,
Bookmark,
Eyeglasses
A988

Dome of
Capitol
A994

Contemplation
of Justice
A995

Early
American
Printing
Press
A996

Torch
A997

Liberty Bell
A998

Eagle and
Shield
A999

Fort McHenry
Flag
A1001

Head, Statue
of Liberty
A1002

Old North
Church,
Boston
A1003

Fort Nisqually
A1004

Sandy Hook
Lighthouse,
NJ — A1005

Morris
Township
School No. 2,
Devils Lake,
ND — A1006

Iron "Betty"
Lamp, 17th-
18th Cent.
A1007

Rush Lamp
and Candle
Holder
A1008

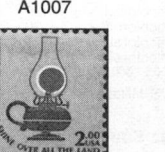

Kerosene
Table Lamp
A1009

Railroad
Conductor's
Lantern,
c. 1850
A1010

1975-81   Engr.   Perf. 11x10½

1581	A984	1c dk bl, *grnsh*	.20	.20
	a.	Untagged (Bureau pre-canceled)		.20
1582	A985	2c red brown, *grnsh*	.20	.20
	a.	Untagged (Bureau pre-canceled)		.20
	b.	Cream paper ('81)	.20	.20
1584	A987	3c olive, *grnsh*	.20	.20
	a.	Untagged (Bureau pre-canceled)		.20
1585	A988	4c rose mag, *cr*	.20	.20
	a.	Untagged (Bureau pre-canceled)		1.25

Size: 17½x20½mm

1590	A994	9c slate green	.45	.20

From bklt. pane #1623a.

Perf. 10x9¾

1590A	A994	9c slate green	22.50	15.00

From bklt. pane #1623Bc.

Size: 18½x22½mm

Perf. 11x10½

1591	A994	9c sl grn, *gray*	.20	.20
	a.	Untagged (Bureau pre-canceled)		.20
1592	A995	10c violet, *gray*	.20	.20
	a.	Untagged (Bureau pre-canceled)		.25
1593	A996	11c orange, *gray*	.20	.20
1594	A997	12c brown red, *beige*	.25	.20
1595	A998	13c brown	.30	.20
	a.	Booklet pane of 6	2.25	.75
	b.	Booklet pane of 7 + label	2.25	.75
	c.	Booklet pane of 8	2.25	1.00
	d.	Bklt. pane of 5 + label ('76)	1.75	.75
	e.	Vert. pair, imperf btwn.	800.00	

No. 1595e resulted from a paper foldover
after perforating and before cutting into panes.
Beware of printer's waste consisting of complete panes with perfs around all outside
edges.

Photo.

Perf. 11

1596	A999	13c multicolored	.25	.20
	a.	Imperf., pair	50.00	—
	b.	Yellow omitted	160.00	

Engr.

1597	A1001	15c gray, dk blue & red	.30	.20
	a.	Vert. pair, imperf.	20.00	
	b.	Gray omitted	600.00	
	c.	Vert. strip of 3, imperf. btwn. & at top or bottom	—	

Perf. 11x10½

1598	A1001	15c gray, dk blue & red	.40	.20
	a.	Booklet pane of 8	4.25	.80
1599	A1002	16c blue	.35	.20
1603	A1003	24c red, *blue*	.50	.20
1604	A1004	28c brown, *blue*	.55	.20
1605	A1005	29c blue, *blue*	.60	.20
1606	A1006	30c green, *blue*	.55	.20

Engr. & Litho.

Perf. 11

1608	A1007	50c tan, black & org	.85	.20
	a.	Black omitted	300.00	
	b.	Vert. pair, imperf. horiz.	1,750.	

Beware of copies offered as No. 1608b that
have blind perfs.

1610	A1008	$1 tan, brn, org & yel	2.00	.20
	a.	Brn (engraved) omitted	250.	
	b.	Tan, org & yel omitted	350.	
	c.	Brown inverted	13,000.	
1611	A1009	$2 tan, dk grn, org & yel	3.75	.75
1612	A1010	$5 tan, red brn, yel & org	8.25	1.75
		Nos. 1581-1612 (23)	43.25	21.50

Nos. 1590, 1590a, 1595, 1598 issued in
booklets only. All stamps have one or two
straight edges.

Years of issue: #1591, 1595-1596, 11c, 24c,
1975. #1590, 1c-4c, 10c, 1977. #1597-1598,
16c, 28c, 29c, $2, 1978. 30c-$1, $5, 1979.
12c, 1981.

Guitar
A1011

Saxhorns
A1012

Drum
A1013

Piano
A1014

Coil Stamps

Engr.

Perf. 10 Vertically

1613	A1011	3.1c brown, *yel*	.20	.20
	a.	Untagged (Bureau pre-canceled)		.50
	b.	Imperf., pair	1,400.	
1614	A1012	7.7c brown, *brt yel*	.20	.20
	a.	Untagged (Bureau pre-canceled)		.35
	b.	As "a," imperf., pair	1,600.	
1615	A1013	7.9c carmine, *yel*	.20	.20
	a.	Untagged (Bureau pre-canceled)		.20
	b.	Imperf., pair	600.00	
1615C	A1014	8.4c dk blue, *yel*	.20	.20
	d.	Untagged (Bureau pre-canceled)		.30
	e.	As "d," pair, imperf. btwn.	60.00	
	f.	As "d," imperf., pair	17.50	
1616	A994	9c sl green, *gray*	.20	.20
	a.	Imperf., pair	160.00	
	b.	Untagged (Bureau pre-canceled)		.35
	c.	As "b," imperf., pair	700.00	
1617	A995	10c violet, *gray*	.20	.20
	a.	Untagged (Bureau pre-canceled)		.25
	b.	Imperf., pair	60.00	
1618	A998	13c brown	.25	.20
	a.	Untagged (Bureau pre-canceled)		.45
	b.	Imperf., pair	25.00	
	g.	Vert. pair, imperf btwn.		
	h.	As "a," imperf., pair	—	
1618C	A1001	15c gray, dk blue & red	.40	.20
	d.	Imperf., pair	25.00	
	e.	Pair, imperf. between	150.00	
	f.	Gray omitted	40.00	

1619	A1002	16c blue	.35	.20
	a.	Huck press printing	.50	.20
		Nos. 1613-1619 (9)	2.20	1.80

The 15c was printed on two different
presses. Huck press printings have white
background without bluish tinge, are a fraction
of a millimeter smaller and have block instead
of overall tagging. Cottrell press printings show
a joint line.

Years of issue: 9c, 13c, 1975. 7.7c, 7.9c,
1976. 10c, 1977. 8.4c, 15c, 16c, 1978. 3.1c,
1979.

See Nos. 1811, 1813, 1816.

13-Star Flag,
Independence
Hall — A1015

Flag over
Capitol — A1016

Multicolor Huck Press

1975-81   Perf. 11x10¾

1622	A1015	13c dk bl & red	.25	.20
	a.	Horiz. pair, imperf. btwn.	50.00	
	b.	Vert. pair, imperf.	1,100.	
	e.	Horiz. pair, imperf. vert.	—	

No. 1622 has large block tagging and nearly
vertical multiple gum ridges.

Combination Press

Perf. 11¼

1622C	A1015	13c dark blue & red ('81)	1.00	.25
	d.	Vertical pair, imperf	150.00	

No. 1622C has small block tagging and flat
gum.

Booklet Stamps

Perf. 11x10½ on 2 or 3 Sides

1623	A1016	13c blue & red ('77)	.25	.20
	a.	Bklt. pane, #1590, 7 #1623)	2.25	1.10
	d.	Pair pair, #1590 & 1623	.70	.70

Perf. 10x9¾ on 2 or 3 Sides

1623B	A1016	13c blue & red	.80	.80
	c.	Booklet pane, #1590A, 7 #1623B	29.00	—
	e.	Pair, #1590A & #1623B	24.00	22.50

Coil Stamp

Perf. 10 Vertically

1625	A1015	13c dk bl & red	.25	.20
	a.	Imperf, pair	25.00	

American Bicentennial — Spirit of '76

Drummer Boy
A1019

Old Drummer
A1020

Fifer — A1021

Designed after painting "The Spirit of '76,"
by Archibald M. Willard.

1976, Jan. 1   Photo.   Perf. 11

1629	A1019	13c multicolored	.25	.20
	a.	Imperf., vert. pair		
1630	A1020	13c multicolored	.25	.20
1631	A1021	13c multicolored	.25	.20
	a.	Strip of 3, #1629-1631	.75	.65
	b.	As "a," imperf.	1,050.	
	c.	Imperf., vert. pair #1631	800.	

A1076

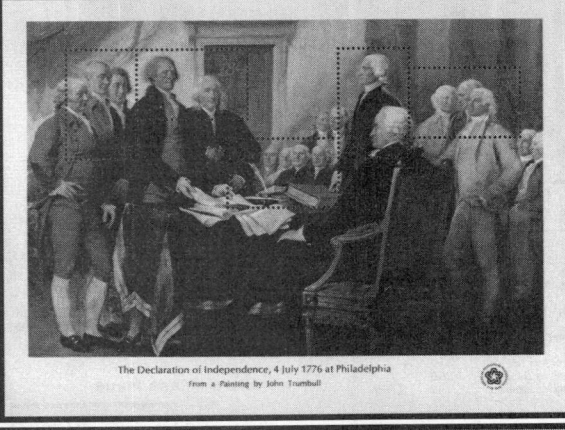

The Surrender of Lord Cornwallis at Yorktown
From a Painting by John Trumbull

A1077

The Declaration of Independence, 4 July 1776 at Philadelphia
From a Painting by John Trumbull

Washington Crossing the Delaware
From a Painting by Emanuel Leutze / Eastman Johnson

A1078

Washington Reviewing His Ragged Army at Valley Forge
From a Painting by William T. Trego

A1079

Interphil Issue

"Interphil
76"
A1022

Lithographed, Engraved (Giori)
1976, Jan. 17   **Perf. 11**
1632 A1022 13c dk blue & red
(engr.), ultra &
red (litho.)   .20   .20
  a. Dark blue & red (engr.) omitted   —

Interphil 76 Intl. Phil. Exhib., Philadelphia,
Pa., May 29-June 6.
No. 1632a is a top row stamp with all
engraved colors (wording) omitted due to a
color shift.

State Flags
A1023

1976, Feb. 23   **Photo.**   **Perf. 11**
1633	A1023	13c Delaware	.25 .20
1634	A1024	13c Pennsylvania	.25 .20
1635	A1025	13c New Jersey	.25 .20
1636	A1026	13c Georgia	.25 .20
1637	A1027	13c Connecticut	.25 .20
1638	A1028	13c Massachusetts	.25 .20
1639	A1029	13c Maryland	.25 .20
1640	A1030	13c South Carolina	.25 .20
1641	A1031	13c New Hamp-	
		shire	.25 .20
1642	A1032	13c Virginia	.25 .20
1643	A1033	13c New York	.25 .20
1644	A1034	13c North Carolina	.25 .20
1645	A1035	13c Rhode Island	.25 .20
1646	A1036	13c Vermont	.25 .20
1647	A1037	13c Kentucky	.25 .20
1648	A1038	13c Tennessee	.25 .20
1649	A1039	13c Ohio	.25 .20
1650	A1040	13c Louisiana	.25 .20
1651	A1041	13c Indiana	.25 .20
1652	A1042	13c Mississippi	.25 .20
1653	A1043	13c Illinois	.25 .20
1654	A1044	13c Alabama	.25 .20
1655	A1045	13c Maine	.25 .20
1656	A1046	13c Missouri	.25 .20
1657	A1047	13c Arkansas	.25 .20
1658	A1048	13c Michigan	.25 .20
1659	A1049	13c Florida	.25 .20
1660	A1050	13c Texas	.25 .20
1661	A1051	13c Iowa	.25 .20
1662	A1052	13c Wisconsin	.25 .20
1663	A1053	13c California	.25 .20
1664	A1054	13c Minnesota	.25 .20
1665	A1055	13c Oregon	.25 .20
1666	A1056	13c Kansas	.25 .20
1667	A1057	13c West Virginia	.25 .20
1668	A1058	13c Nevada	.25 .20
1669	A1059	13c Nebraska	.25 .20
1670	A1060	13c Colorado	.25 .20
1671	A1061	13c North Dakota	.25 .20
1672	A1062	13c South Dakota	.25 .20
1673	A1063	13c Montana	.25 .20
1674	A1064	13c Washington	.25 .20
1675	A1065	13c Idaho	.25 .20
1676	A1066	13c Wyoming	.25 .20
1677	A1067	13c Utah	.25 .20
1678	A1068	13c Oklahoma	.25 .20
1679	A1069	13c New Mexico	.25 .20
1680	A1070	13c Arizona	.25 .20
1681	A1071	13c Alaska	.25 .20
1682	A1072	13c Hawaii	.25 .20
a.		Pane of 50	15.00 —

Telephone Centenary Issue

Bell's
Telephone
Patent
Application
A1073

Engraved (Giori)
1976, Mar. 10   **Perf. 11**
1683 A1073 13c blk, pur &
red, *tan*   .25   .20
  a. Black & purple omitted   500.00

1st telephone call by Alexander Graham
Bell, Mar. 10, 1876.
No. 1683a comes from a partially printed
pane. The errors have only tiny traces of red
present so are best collected as a horiz. strip
of 5 with 2 or 3 error stamps.

Commercial Aviation Issue

A1074

1976, Mar. 19   **Photo.**   **Perf. 11**
1684 A1074 13c blue & multi   .25   .20

50th anniv. of 1st contract airmail flights:
Dearborn, MI to Cleveland, OH, 2/15/26; and
Pasco, WA to Elko, NV, 4/6/26. Design features Ford-Pullman Monoplane & Laird Swallow Biplane.

Chemistry Issue

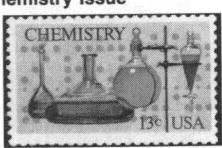

A1075

1976, Apr. 6   **Photo.**   **Perf. 11**
1685 A1075 13c multicolored   .25   .20

Cent. of the American Chemical Society.
Design features Various Flasks, Separatory
Funnel, Computer Tape, honoring American
chemists.

Designs, from Left to Right:
No. 1686, Surrender of Cornwallis at York-
town, by John Trumbull:
a, Two British officers. b, Gen. Benjamin Lin-
coln. c, George Washington. d, John Trumbull,
Col. Cobb, von Steuben, Lafayette, Thomas
Nelson, Alexander Hamilton, John Laurens,
Walter Stewart, all vert.
No. 1687, Declaration of Independence, by
John Trumbull:
a, John Adams, Roger Sherman, Robert R.
Livingston. b, Jefferson, Franklin. c, Thomas
Nelson, Jr., Francis Lewis, John Witherspoon,
Samuel Huntington. d, John Hancock, Charles
Thomson. e, George Read, John Dickinson,
Edward Rutledge

1687a, d, vert., b, c, e, horiz.
No. 1688, Washington Crossing the Delaware, by Emanuel Leutze/Eastman Johnson:
a, Boatsman. b, Washington. c, Flag bearer. d,
Men in boat. e, Men on shore
1688a, d, horiz., b, c, e, vert.
No. 1689, Washington Reviewing Army at
Valley Forge, by William T. Trego:
a, Two officers. b, Washington. c, Officer,
black horse. d, Officer, white horse. e, Three
soldiers.
1689a, c, e, horiz., b, d, vert.

1976, May 29   **Litho.**   **Perf. 11**
1686	A1076	Sheet of 5	3.25	—
a.-e.		13c multi, any single	.45	.40
f.		USA 13c omitted on "b,"		
		"c" & "d," imperf., tag-		
		ging omitted	—	2,250.
g.		USA 13c omitted on "a"		
		& "e"	450.	
h.		Imperf., tagging omitted	—	2,250.
i.		USA 13c omitted on "b,"		
		"c" & "d"	450.	
j.		USA 13c double on "b"	—	
k.		USA 13c omitted on "c"		
		& "d"	750.	
l.		USA 13c omitted on "e"	500.	
m.		USA 13c omitted, im-		
		perf., tagging omitted	—	
n.		As "g," imperf., tagging		
		omitted	—	
1687	A1077	Sheet of 5	4.25	—
a.-e.		18c multi, any single	.55	.55
f.		Design & marginal in-		
		scriptions omitted	3,000.	
g.		USA 18c omitted on "a"		
		& "c"	750.	
h.		USA 18c omitted on "b,"		
		"d" & "e"	450.	
i.		USA 18c omitted on "d"	500.	500.
j.		Black omitted in design	2,000.	
k.		USA 18c omitted, im-		
		perf., tagging omitted	3,000.	
m.		USA 18c omitted on "b"		
		& "e"	500.	
n.		USA 18c omitted on "b"		
		& "d"	—	
p.		Imperf., tagged	—	
q.		USA 18c omitted on "c"	—	
1688	A1078	Sheet of 5	5.25	—
a.-e.		24c multi, any single	.70	.70
f.		USA 24c omitted, im-		
		perf., tagging omitted	3,500.	
g.		USA 24c omitted on "d"		
		& "e"	450.	450.
h.		Design & marginal in-		
		scriptions omitted	3,500.	
i.		USA 24c omitted on "a,"		
		"b" & "c"	500.	
j.		Imperf., tagging omitted	3,000.	
k.		USA 24c of "d" & "e" in-		
		verted	—	
l.		As "i," imperf., tagging		
		omitted	3,500.	

American Bicentennial Issue

Declaration of Independence, by John Trumbull

A1081   A1082   A1083   A1084

1689	A1079	Sheet of 5	6.25	—
a.-e.		31c multi, any single	.85	.85
f.		USA 31c omitted, imperf.	2,750.	
g.		USA 31c omitted on "a" & "c"	400.	
h.		USA 31c omitted on "b," "d" & "e"	450.	
i.		USA 31c omitted on "e"	450.	
j.		Black omitted in design	2,000.	
k.		Imperf., tagging omitted		2,250.
l.		USA 31c omitted on "b" & "d"	—	
m.		USA 31c omitted on "a," "c" & "e"	—	
n.		As "m," imperf., tagging omitted	—	
p.		As "h," imperf., tagging omitted		2,500.
q.		As "g," imperf., tagging omitted	2,500.	
r.		USA 31c omitted on "d" & "e"	2,750.	
s.		As "f," tagging omitted	2,250.	
t.		"USA/31c" omitted on "d"	—	
		Nos. 1688-1689 (4)	19.00	

Nos. 1688-1689 exist with inverted perfs.
Size of sheets: 203x152mm; stamps: 25x39½mm, 39½x25mm.
Issued in connection with Interphil 76 Intl. Phil. Exhib., Philadelphia, Pa, May 29-June 6.

Benjamin Franklin Issue

Franklin & Map of North America, 1776
A1080

Lithographed, Engraved (Giori)
1976, June 1   *Perf. 11*

1690	A1080	13c ultra & multi	.25	.20
a.		Light blue omitted	250.00	

American Bicentennial; Franklin (1706-1790), deputy postmaster general for the colonies (1753-1774) and statesman.
See Canada No. 691.

1976, July 4   Photo.   *Perf. 11*

1691	A1081	13c multicolored	.30	.20
1692	A1082	13c multicolored	.30	.20
1693	A1083	13c multicolored	.30	.20
1694	A1084	13c multicolored	.30	.20
a.		Strip of 4, #1691-1694	1.20	1.10

Olympic Games Issue

Diving — A1085   Skiing — A1086   Running — A1087   Skating — A1088

1976, July 16   Photo.   *Perf. 11*

1695	A1085	13c multicolored	.25	.20
1696	A1086	13c multicolored	.25	.20
1697	A1087	13c multicolored	.25	.20

1698	A1088	13c multicolored	.25	.20
a.		Block of 4, #1695-1698	1.10	1.10
b.		As "a," imperf.	700.00	

12th Winter Olympic Games, Innsbruck, Austria, Feb. 4-15, and 21st Summer Olympic Games, Montreal, Canada, July 17-Aug. 1.

Clara Maass Issue

Clara Maass, Newark German Hospital Pin — A1089

1976, Aug. 18   Photo.   *Perf. 11*

1699	A1089	13c multicolored	.25	.20
a.		Horiz. pair, imperf. vert.	450.00	

Clara Maass (1876-1901), volunteer in fight against yellow fever, birth centenary.

Adolph S. Ochs Issue

Adolph S. Ochs, Publisher of the NY Times, 1896-1935
A1090

Giori Press Printing
1976, Sept. 18   *Perf. 11*

1700	A1090	13c black & gray	.25	.20

Christmas Issue

Nativity, by John Singleton Copley A1091

Winter Pastime, by Nathaniel Currier A1092

1976, Oct. 27   Photo.   *Perf. 11*

1701	A1091	13c multicolored	.25	.20
a.		Imperf., pair	100.00	
1702	A1092	13c multicolored	.25	.20
a.		Imperf., pair	100.00	
1703	A1092	13c multicolored	.25	.20
a.		Imperf., pair	110.00	
b.		Vert. pair, imperf. btwn.	—	
d.		Red omitted	—	
e.		Yellow omitted	—	
		Nos. 1701-1703 (3)	.75	.60

No. 1702 has overall tagging. Lettering at base is black and usually ½mm below design. As a rule, no "snowflaking" in sky or pond. Pane of 50 has margins on 4 sides with slogans.
No. 1703 has block tagging the size of printed area. Lettering at base is gray black and usually ¾mm below design. "Snowflaking" generally in sky and pond. Pane has margin only at right or left, and no slogans.
Copies are known with various amounts of red or yellow missing. Nos. 1703d and 1703e

have the color totally omitted. Expertization is recommended.

American Bicentennial Issue
Washington at Princeton

Washington, Nassau Hall, Hessians, 13-Star Flag — A1093

1977, Jan. 3   Photo.   *Perf. 11*

1704	A1093	13c by Charles Willson Peale	.25	.20
a.		Horiz. pair, imperf. vert.	550.00	

Washington's victory at Princeton over Lord Cornwallis, bicentennial.

Sound Recording Issue

Tin Foil Phonograph — A1094

Lithographed, Engraved (Giori)
1977, Mar. 23   *Perf. 11*

1705	A1094	13c black & multi	.25	.20

Centenary of invention of the phonograph by Thomas Alva Edison, and development of sophisticated recording industry.

American Folk Art Series
Pueblo Pottery

Zia — A1095

San Ildefonso A1096

Hopi — A1097

Acoma — A1098

1977, Apr. 13   Photo.   *Perf. 11*

1706	A1095	13c multicolored	.25	.20
1707	A1096	13c multicolored	.25	.20
1708	A1097	13c multicolored	.25	.20
1709	A1098	13c multicolored	.25	.20
a.		Block or strip of 4	1.00	1.00
b.		As "a," imperf. vert.	2,500.	

Pueblo art, 1880-1920, from museums in NM, AZ and CO.

Lindbergh Flight Issue

Spirit of St. Louis
A1099

1977, May 20   Photo.   *Perf. 11*

1710	A1099	13c multicolored	.25	.20
a.		Imperf., pair	1,050.	

Charles A. Lindbergh's solo transatlantic flight from NY to Paris, 50th anniv.

Colorado Statehood Issue

Columbine & Rocky Mountains — A1100

1977, May 21   Photo.   *Perf. 11*

1711	A1100	13c multicolored	.25	.20
a.		Horiz. pair, imperf. btwn.	600.00	
b.		Horiz. pair, imperf. vert.	900.00	

Colorado became a state in 1876.

Butterfly Issue

Swallowtail A1101

Checkerspot — A1102

Dogface A1103

Orange Tip A1104

1977, June 6   Photo.   *Perf. 11*

1712	A1101	13c tan & multi	.25	.20
1713	A1102	13c tan & multi	.25	.20
1714	A1103	13c tan & multi	.25	.20
1715	A1104	13c tan & multi	.25	.20
a.		Block of 4, #1712-1715	1.00	1.00
b.		As "a," imperf. horiz.	15,000.	

American Bicentennial Issues
Lafayette

Marquis de
Lafayette
A1105

1977, June 13   **Engr.**   *Perf. 11*
1716 A1105 13c bl, blk & red   .25   .20
  a.   Red omitted

200th anniv. of Lafayette's landing on the coast of SC, north of Charleston.

Skilled Hands for Independence

Seamstress
A1106

Blacksmith
A1107

Wheelwright — A1108

Leatherworker — A1109

1977, July 4   **Photo.**   *Perf. 11*
1717 A1106 13c multicolored   .25   .20
1718 A1107 13c multicolored   .25   .20
1719 A1108 13c multicolored   .25   .20
1720 A1109 13c multicolored   .25   .20
  a.   Block of 4, #1717-1720   1.00   1.00

Peace Bridge Issue

Peace
Bridge &
Dove
A1110

1977, Aug. 4   **Engr.**   *Perf. 11x10½*
1721 A1110 13c blue   .25   .20

50th anniv. of the Peace Bridge, connecting Buffalo, NY with Fort Erie, Ontario.

American Bicentennial Issue
Battle of Oriskany

Herkimer
at
Oriskany,
by Yohn
A1111

1977, Aug. 6   **Photo.**   *Perf. 11*
1722 A1111 13c multicolored   .25   .20

200th anniv. of Battle of Oriskany, American Militia led by Brig. Gen. Nicholas Herkimer (1728-1777).

Energy Issue
Energy Conservation
A1112

Energy Development
A1113

1977, Oct. 20   **Photo.**   *Perf. 11*
1723 A1112 13c multicolored   .25   .20
1724 A1113 13c multicolored   .25   .20
  a.   Pair, #1723-1724   .50   .50

Conservation and development of nation's energy resources.

Alta California Issue

Farm
Houses
A1114

Litho. & Engraved (Giori)
1977, Sept. 9   *Perf. 11*
1725 A1114 13c black & multi   .25   .20

El Pueblo de San José de Guadalupe, 1st civil settlement in Alta California, 200th anniv.

American Bicentennial Issue
Articles of Confederation

Members of
Continental
Congress
in
Conference
A1115

Engraved (Giori)
1977, Sept. 30   *Perf. 11*
1726 A1115 13c red & brn,
     cream   .25   .20
  b.   Red omitted   600.00
  c.   Red & brown omitted   400.00

200th anniv. of drafting the Articles of Confederation, York Town, Pa.
No. 1726b also has most of the brown color omitted. No. 1726c must be collected as a transition multiple, certainly with No. 1726b and preferably also with No. 1726.

Talking Picture, 50th Anniv. Issue

Movie Projector and
Phonograph — A1116

Litho. & Engraved (Giori)
1977, Oct. 6   *Perf. 11*
1727 A1116 13c multicolored   .25   .20

American Bicentennial Issue
Surrender at Saratoga

Surrender
of
Burgoyne,
by John
Trumbull
A1117

1977, Oct. 7   **Photo.**   *Perf. 11*
1728 A1117 13c multicolored   .25   .20

200th anniv. of Gen. John Burgoyne's surrender at Saratoga.

Christmas Issue

Washington at
Valley Forge
A1118

Rural Mailbox
A1119

1977, Oct. 21   **Photo.**   *Perf. 11*
1729 A1118 13c multicolored   .25   .20
  a.   Imperf., pair   75.00
1730 A1119 13c multicolored   .25   .20
  a.   Imperf., pair   300.00

Carl Sandburg Issue

Carl Sandburg, by
William A. Smith,
1952 — A1120

Engraved (Giori)
1978, Jan. 6   *Perf. 11*
1731 A1120 13c black & brown   .25   .20
  a.   Brown omitted

Sandburg (1878-1967), poet, biographer and collector of American folk songs.

Captain Cook Issue

Capt. Cook, by
Nathaniel Dance,
1776 — A1121

"Resolution" and "Discovery," by John
Webber — A1122

Giori Press Printing

1978, Jan. 20   *Perf. 11*
1732 A1121 13c dark blue   .25   .20
1733 A1122 13c green   .25   .20
  a.   Vert. pair, imperf. horiz.
  b.   Pair, #1732-1733   .50   .50
  c.   As "b," imperf. between   4,500.

Capt. James Cook, 200th anniv. of his arrival in Hawaii, at Waimea, Kauai, Jan. 20, 1778, and of his anchorage in Cook Inlet, near Anchorage, Alaska, June 1, 1778. Nos. 1732-1733 issued in panes of 50, containing 25 each of Nos. 1732-1733 including 5 No. 1732a. Design of No. 1733 is after etching "A View of Karakekooa in Owyhee."

Indian
Head
Penny,
1877
A1123

Eagle
A1124

Roses — A1126

Engraved (Giori)
1978, Jan. 11   *Perf. 11*
1734 A1123 13c brown & blue
     green, *bister*   .25   .20
  a.   Horiz. pair, imperf. vert.   300.00

1978, May 22   **Photo.**   *Perf. 11*
1735 A1124 (15c) orange   .25   .20
  a.   Imperf., pair   90.00
  b.   Vert. pair, imperf. horiz.   700.00

     Engr.   *Perf. 11x10½*
1736 A1124 (15c) orange   .25   .20
  a.   Booklet pane of 8   2.25   .90

See No. 1743

1978, July 11   **Engr.**   *Perf. 10*
1737 A1126 15c multicolored   .25   .20
  a.   Booklet pane of 8   2.25   .90
  b.   As "a," imperf.

Nos. 1736, 1737 issued in booklets only. All stamps have 1 or 2 straight edges.

Robertson
Windmill,
Williamsburg
A1127

Old
Windmill,
Portsmouth
A1128

Cape Cod
Windmill,
Eastham
A1129

Dutch Mill,
Batavia
A1130

Southwestern
Windmill — A1131

1980, Feb. 7   **Engr.**   *Perf. 11*
     Booklet Stamps
1738 A1127 15c sepia, *yellow*   .30   .20
1739 A1128 15c sepia, *yellow*   .30   .20
1740 A1129 15c sepia, *yellow*   .30   .20
1741 A1130 15c sepia, *yellow*   .30   .20
1742 A1131 15c sepia, *yellow*   .30   .20
  a.   Bklt. pane, 2 ea #1738-1742   3.50   3.00
  b.   Strip of 5, #1738-1742   1.50   1.40

Coil Stamp

1978, May 22   **Engr.**   *Perf. 10 Vert.*
1743 A1124 (15c) orange   .25   .20
  a.   Imperf., pair   90.00

No. 1743a is valued in the grade of fine.

Black Heritage Series

Harriet Tubman
(1820-1913), Cart
Carrying
Slaves — A1133

1978, Feb. 1   Photo.   Perf. 10½x11
1744 A1133 13c multicolored   .25   .20
   Tubman, born a slave, helped more than
300 slaves escape to freedom.

American Folk Art Series
American Quilts, Basket Design

A1134

A1135

A1136

A1137

1978, Mar. 8   Photo.   Perf. 11
1745 A1134 13c multicolored   .25   .20
1746 A1135 13c multicolored   .25   .20
1747 A1136 13c multicolored   .25   .20
1748 A1137 13c multicolored   .25   .20
  a.   Block of 4, #1745-1748   1.00   1.00

American Dance Issue

Ballet
A1138

Theater
A1139

Folk
Dance
A1140

Modern
Dance
A1141

1978, Apr. 26   Photo.   Perf. 11
1749 A1138 13c multicolored   .25   .20
1750 A1139 13c multicolored   .25   .20
1751 A1140 13c multicolored   .25   .20
1752 A1141 13c multicolored   .25   .20
  a.   Block of 4, #1749-1752   1.00   1.00

American Bicentennial Issue
French Alliance

Louis XVI and
Franklin,
Porcelain
Sculpture by C.
G. Sauvage
A1142

Giori Press Printing
1978, May 4   Perf. 11
1753 A1142 13c bl, blk & red   .25   .20
   Bicent. of French Alliance, signed in Paris,
Feb. 6, 1778, and ratified by Continental
Cong., May 4.

Early Cancer Detection Issue

Dr. George
Papanicolaou (1883-
1962)
A1143

1978, May 18   Engr.   Perf. 10½x11
1754 A1143 13c brown   .25   .20
   Papanicolaou, developer of Pap Test, early
cancer detection in women.

Performing Arts Series

Jimmie Rodgers
and Locomotive
A1144

George M.
Cohan, "Yankee
Doodle Dandy"
and Stars
A1145

1978   Photo.   Perf. 11
1755 A1144 13c multicolored   .25   .20
1756 A1145 15c multicolored   .30   .20
   Rodgers (1897-1933), the "Singing Brake-
man, Father of Country Music," and Cohan
(1878-1942), actor and playwright.
   Issue dates: #1755, May 24; #1756, July 3.

CAPEX Issue

Wildlife from Canadian-US
Border — A1146

Litho. & Engr. (Giori)
1978, June 10   Perf. 11
1757 A1146   Block of 8   2.00   2.00
  a. 13c Cardinal   .25   .20
  b. 13c Mallard   .25   .20
  c. 13c Canada goose   .25   .20
  d. 13c Blue jay   .25   .20
  e. 13c Moose   .25   .20
  f. 13c Chipmunk   .25   .20
  g. 13c Red fox   .25   .20
  h. 13c Raccoon   .25   .20
  i. Yellow, green, red, brown,
    blue, black (litho.) omitted   7,000.
  j. Strip of 4 (a-d), imperf. vert.   —
  k. Strip of 4 (e-h), imperf. vert.   —
   CAPEX, Canadian Intl. Phil. Exhib., Toronto,
Ont., June 9-18.

Photography Issue

Photographic
Equipment
A1147

1978, June 26   Photo.   Perf. 11
1758 A1147 15c multicolored   .30   .20

Viking Missions to Mars Issue

Viking 1
Lander
Scooping
Up Soil on
Mars
A1148

1978, July 20   Litho. & Engr.
1759 A1148 15c multicolored   .30   .20
   2nd anniv. of landing of Viking 1 on Mars.

American Owls Issue
Great Gray Owl   Saw-whet Owl
A1149   A1150

Barred Owl   Great Horned
A1151   Owl
                     A1152

Litho. & Engr.
1978, Aug. 26   Perf. 11
1760 A1149 15c multicolored   .30   .20
1761 A1150 15c multicolored   .30   .20
1762 A1151 15c multicolored   .30   .20
1763 A1152 15c multicolored   .30   .20
  a.   Block of 4, #1760-1763   1.25   1.25

American Trees Issue

Giant
Sequoia
A1153

White Pine
A1154

White Oak
A1155

Gray Birch
A1156

1978, Oct. 9   Photo.   Perf. 11
1764 A1153 15c multicolored   .30   .20
1765 A1154 15c multicolored   .30   .20
1766 A1155 15c multicolored   .30   .20
1767 A1156 15c multicolored   .30   .20
  a.   Block of 4, #1764-1767   1.25   1.25
  b.   As "a," imperf. horiz.   15,000.

Christmas Issue

Madonna and Child with Cherubim, by Andrea della Robbia A1157

Child on Hobby-horse and Christmas Trees A1158

1978, Oct. 18   Photo.   Perf. 11
1768 A1157 15c blue & multi   .30   .20
   a. Imperf., pair   90.00
1769 A1158 15c red & multi   .30   .20
   a. Imperf., pair   100.00
   b. Vert. pair, imperf. horiz.   2,000.
Value for #1768a is for an uncreased pair.

Robert F. Kennedy Issue

Robert F. Kennedy (1925-68), US Attorney General A1159

1979, Jan. 12   Engr.   Perf. 11
1770 A1159 15c blue   .35   .20

Black Heritage Series

Dr. Martin Luther King, Jr. (1929-68), and Civil Rights Marchers — A1160

1979, Jan. 13   Photo.   Perf. 11
1771 A1160 15c multicolored   .30   .20
   a. Imperf., pair   —
   Civil rights leader.

Year of the Child Issue

Children A1161

1979, Feb. 15   Engr.   Perf. 11
1772 A1161 15c orange red   .30   .20
International Year of the Child.

John Steinbeck A1162

Albert Einstein A1163

John Steinbeck Issue

1979, Feb. 27   Engr.   Perf. 10½x11
1773 A1162 15c dark blue   .30   .20
John Ernst Steinbeck (1902-68), novelist.

Albert Einstein Issue

1979, Mar. 4   Engr.   Perf. 10½x11
1774 A1163 15c chocolate   .35   .20
Einstein (1879-1955), theoretical physicist.

American Folk Art Series
Pennsylvania Toleware

Coffeepot A1164

Tea Caddy — A1165

Sugar Bowl — A1166

Coffeepot A1167

1979, Apr. 19   Photo.   Perf. 11
1775 A1164 15c multicolored   .30   .20
1776 A1165 15c multicolored   .30   .20
1777 A1166 15c multicolored   .30   .20
1778 A1167 15c multicolored   .30   .20
   a. Block of 4, #1775-1778   1.25   1.25
   b. As "a," imperf. horiz.   4,250.

American Architecture Series

Virginia Rotunda, by Thomas Jefferson A1168

Baltimore Cathedral, by Benjamin Latrobe A1169

Boston State House, by Charles Bulfinch A1170

Philadelphia Exchange, by William Strickland A1171

1979, June 4   Engr.   Perf. 11
1779 A1168 15c blk & brick red   .30   .20
1780 A1169 15c blk & brick red   .30   .20
1781 A1170 15c blk & brick red   .30   .20
1782 A1171 15c blk & brick red   .30   .20
   a. Block of 4, #1779-1782   1.25   1.25

Endangered Flora Issue

Persistent Trillium A1172

Hawaiian Wild Broadbean A1173

Contra Costa Wallflower A1174

Antioch Dunes Evening Primrose A1175

1979, June 7   Photo.   Perf. 11
1783 A1172 15c multicolored   .30   .20
1784 A1173 15c multicolored   .30   .20
1785 A1174 15c multicolored   .30   .20
1786 A1175 15c multicolored   .30   .20
   a. Block of 4, #1783-1786   1.25   1.25
   b. As "a," imperf.   600.00

Seeing Eye Dogs Issue

German Shepherd Leading Man — A1176

1979, June 15
1787 A1176 15c multicolored   .30   .20
   a. Imperf., pair   425.00

Special Olympics Issue

Child Holding Winner's Medal — A1177

1979, Aug. 9   Perf. 11
1788 A1177 15c multicolored   .30   .20
Special Olympics for special children, Brockport, NY, Aug. 8-13.

John Paul Jones Issue

John Paul Jones, by Charles Willson Peale — A1178

1979, Sept. 23   Photo.   Perf. 11x12
1789 A1178 15c multi   .30   .20
   c. Vert. pair, imperf. horiz.   175.
   Perf. 11
1789A A1178 15c multi   .55   .20
   d. Vert. pair, imperf. horiz.   150.
   Perf. 12
1789B A1178 15c multi   2,500.   1,000.
John Paul Jones (1747-1792), Naval Commander, American Revolution.
Imperfs, perf or imperf gutter pairs and blocks exist from printer's waste.

Olympic Games Issue

Javelin — A1179

Running A1180

Swimming A1181

Rowing A1182

Equestrian A1183

1979   Photo.   Perf. 11
1790 A1179 10c multicolored   .20   .20
1791 A1180 15c multicolored   .30   .20
1792 A1181 15c multicolored   .30   .20
1793 A1182 15c multicolored   .30   .20
1794 A1183 15c multicolored   .30   .20
   a. Block of 4, #1791-1794   1.25   1.25
   b. As "a," imperf.   1,500.
22nd Summer Olympic Games, Moscow, July 19-Aug. 3, 1980.
Issue dates: 10c, Sept. 5; 15c, Sept. 28.

Winter Olympic Games Issue

Speed Skating A1184

Downhill Skiing A1185

Ski Jump A1186

Ice Hockey
A1187

1980, Feb. 1   Photo.   Perf. 11¼x10½
1795 A1184 15c multicolored   .35   .20
1796 A1185 15c multicolored   .35   .20
1797 A1186 15c multicolored   .35   .20
1798 A1187 15c multicolored   .35   .20
  b.   Block of 4, #1795-1798   1.50   1.40
Perf. 11
1795A A1184 15c multicolored   1.05   .60
1796A A1185 15c multicolored   1.05   .60
1797A A1186 15c multicolored   1.05   .60
1798A A1187 15c multicolored   1.05   .60
  c.   Block of 4, #1795A-1798A   4.25   3.50

13th Winter Olympic Games, Lake Placid, NY, Feb. 12-24.

Christmas Issue

Virgin and Child, by Gerard David
A1188

Santa Claus, Christmas Tree Ornament
A1189

1979, Oct. 18   Photo.   Perf. 11
1799 A1188 15c multicolored   .30   .20
  a.   Imperf., pair   90.
  b.   Vert. pair, imperf. horiz.   700.
  c.   Vert. pair, imperf. btwn.   2,250.
1800 A1189 15c multicolored   .30   .20
  a.   Green & yellow omitted   625.
  b.   Grn, yel & tan omitted   700.

Nos. 1800a, 1800b always have the remaining colors misaligned.
No. 1800b is valued in the grade of fine.

Performing Arts Issue

Will Rogers (1879-1935), Actor and Humorist — A1190

1979, Nov. 4   Photo.   Perf. 11
1801 A1190 15c multicolored   .30   .20
  a.   Imperf., pair   225.00

Viet Nam Veterans Issue

Ribbon for Viet Nam Service Medal
A1191

1979, Nov. 11   Photo.   Perf. 11
1802 A1191 15c multicolored   .30   .20
A tribute to veterans of the Viet Nam War.

Performing Arts Series

W.C. Fields (1880-1946), actor and comedian — A1192

1980, Jan. 29   Photo.   Perf. 11
1803 A1192 15c multicolored   .30   .20
  a.   Imperf., pair

Black Heritage Series

Benjamin Banneker (1731-1806), Astronomer and Mathematician, Transverse — A1193

1980, Feb. 15   Photo.   Perf. 11
1804 A1193 15c multicolored   .35   .20
  a.   Horiz. pair, imperf. vert.   800.00

Imperf. printer's waste has been fraudulently perforated to simulate No. 1804a. Legitimate examples of No. 1804a do not have colors misregistered.

Letter Writing

Letters Preserve Memories
A1194

P.S. Write Soon
A1195

Letters Lift Spirits
A1196

Letters Shape Opinions
A1197

1980, Feb. 25
1805 A1194 15c multicolored   .30   .20
1806 A1195 15c purple & multi   .30   .20
1807 A1196 15c multicolored   .30   .20
1808 A1195 15c green & multi   .30   .20
1809 A1195 15c multicolored   .30   .20
1810 A1195 15c red & multi   .30   .20
  a.   Vert. strip of 6 #1805-1810   1.85   2.00
  Nos. 1805-1810 (6)   1.80   1.20

Natl. Letter Writing Week, Feb. 24-Mar. 1.

Americana Type

Weaver Violins — A1199

Coil Stamps

1980-81   Engr.   Perf. 10 Vert.
1811 A984 1c dk blue, *grnsh*   .20   .20
  a.   Imperf., pair   175.00
1813 A1199 3.5c purple, *yel*   .20   .20
  a.   Untagged (Bureau precanceled, lines only)   .20
  b.   Imperf., pair   225.00
1816 A997 12c brown red, *beige ('81)*   .25   .20
  a.   Untagged (Bureau precanceled)   .25
  b.   Imperf., pair   200.00
  c.   As "a," brownish red, *reddish beige*   .25

A1207

1981, Mar. 15   Photo.   Perf. 11x10½
1818 A1207 (18c) violet   .35   .20

Engr.   Perf. 10
Booklet Stamp
1819 A1207 (18c) violet   .40   .20
  a.   Booklet pane of 8   3.75   1.75
Coil Stamp
Perf. 10 Vert.
1820 A1207 (18c) violet   .40   .20
  a.   Imperf., pair   100.00
  Nos. 1818-1820 (3)   1.15   .60

Frances Perkins

Frances Perkins (1882-1965), Sec. of Labor, 1933-45 (1st Woman Cabinet Member) — A1208

1980, Apr. 10   Perf. 10½x11
1821 A1208 15c Prus blue   .30   .20

Dolley Madison

Dolley Madison (1768-1849), First Lady, 1809-1817 — A1209

1980, May 20   Perf. 11
1822 A1209 15c red bwn & sepia   .30   .20

Emily Bissell

Emily Bissell (1861-1948), Social Worker; Introduced Christmas seals in US — A1210

1980, May 31
1823 A1210 15c black & red   .35   .20
  a.   Vert. pair, imperf. horiz.   400.00

Helen Keller

Helen Keller and Anne Sullivan — A1211

1980, June 27   Litho. & Engr.   Perf. 11
1824 A1211 15c multicolored   .30   .20
Keller (1880-1968), blind and deaf writer and lecturer taught by Sullivan (1867-1936).

Veterans Administration Emblem
A1212

Gen. Bernardo de Galvez
A1213

Veterans Administration

1980, July 21   Photo.
1825 A1212 15c car & vio bl   .30   .20
  a.   Horiz. pair, imperf. vert.   450.00

General Bernardo de Galvez

1980, July 23   Engr.   Perf. 11
1826 A1213 15c multicolored   .30   .20
  a.   Red, brn & bl (engr.) omitted   800.
  b.   Red, brn, bl (engr.), bl & yel (litho.) omitted   1,400.

Galvez (1746-1786), helped defeat British in Battle of Mobile, 1780.

Coral Reefs

Brain Coral, Beaugregory Fish
A1214

Elkhorn Coral, Porkfish
A1215

Chalice Coral, Moorish Idol Fish
A1216

Finger Coral, Sabertooth Blenny Fish
A1217

1980, Aug. 26   Photo.   Perf. 11
1827 A1214 15c multicolored   .30   .20
1828 A1215 15c multicolored   .30   .20
1829 A1216 15c multicolored   .30   .20
1830 A1217 15c multicolored   .30   .20
  a.   Block of 4, #1827-1830   1.25   1.10
  b.   As "a," imperf.   1,000.
  c.   As "a," vert. imperf. btwn.   —
  d.   As "a," imperf. vert.   3,000.

American Bald Eagle
A1218

Edith Wharton
A1219

Organized Labor

1980, Sept. 1   Photo.   Perf. 11
1831 A1218 15c multicolored   .30   .20
  a.   Imperf., pair   375.00

Edith Wharton

1980, Sept. 5   Engr.   Perf. 10½x11
1832 A1219 15c purple   .30   .20
Edith Wharton (1862-1937), writer.

American Education

"Homage to the Square: Glow," by Josef Albers — A1220

1980, Sept. 12   Photo.   Perf. 11
1833 A1220 15c multicolored   .30   .20
  a.   Horiz. pair, imperf. btwn.   240.00

American Folk Art Series
Pacific Northwest Indian Masks

Heiltsuk, Bella
Bella
Tribe — A1221

Chilkat Tlingit
Tribe — A1222

Tlingit
Tribe — A1223

Bella Coola
Tribe — A1224

1980, Sept. 25

1834	A1221 15c multicolored	.30	.20
1835	A1222 15c multicolored	.30	.20
1836	A1223 15c multicolored	.30	.20
1837	A1224 15c multicolored	.30	.20
a.	Block of 4, #1834-1837	1.25	1.25

American Architecture Series

Smithsonian
Institution,
by James
Renwick
A1225

Trinity
Church,
Boston, by
Henry
Hobson
Richardson
A1226

Pennsylvania Academy of Fine Arts,
by Frank Furness — A1227

Lyndhurst,
Tarrytown,
NY, by
Alexander
Jackson
Davis
A1228

1980, Oct. 9   Engr.   Perf. 11

1838	A1225 15c black & brick red	.30	.20
1839	A1226 15c black & brick red	.30	.20
1840	A1227 15c black & brick red	.30	.20
1841	A1228 15c black & brick red	.30	.20
a.	Block of 4, #1838-1841	1.25	1.25
b.	As "a," red omitted on Nos. 1838, 1839	400.00	

No. 1841b was caused by a misregistration
of the perforations.

Christmas

Madonna and
Child
A1229

Wreath, Toys on
Windowsill
A1230

1980, Oct. 31   Photo.   Perf. 11

1842	A1229 15c multicolored	.30	.20
a.	Imperf., pair	70.00	
1843	A1230 15c multicolored	.30	.20
a.	Imperf., pair	70.00	
b.	Buff omitted	25.00	
c.	Vert. pair, imperf. horiz.		
d.	Horiz. pair, imperf. between	4,000.	

No. 1843b is difficult to identify and should
have a competent certificate.

Great Americans

Dorothea Dix
A1231

Igor Stravinsky
A1232

Henry Clay
A1233

Carl Schurz
A1234

Pearl Buck
A1235

Walter Lippmann
A1236

Abraham Baldwin
A1237

Henry Knox
A1238

Sylvanus Thayer
A1239

Richard Russell
A1240

Alden Partridge
A1241

Crazy Horse
A1242

Sinclair Lewis
A1243

Rachel Carson
A1244

George Mason
A1245

Sequoyah
A1246

Ralph Bunche
A1247

Thomas H. Gallaudet
A1248

Harry S Truman
A1249

John J. Audubon
A1250

Frank C. Laubach
A1251

Charles R Drew MD
A1252

Robert Millikan
A1253

Grenville Clark
A1254

Lillian M. Gilbreth
A1255

Chester W. Nimitz
A1256

**Perf. 11x10½, 11 (1, 6-11, 14, #1862,
22, 30, 39, 40, 50c)**

1980-85   Engr.

1844	A1231 1c black	.20	.20
a.	Imperf. pair	300.	
b.	Vert. pair, imperf. btwn. and at bottom	3,000.	
e.	Vert. pair, imperf. horiz.		
1845	A1232 2c brown black	.20	.20
1846	A1233 3c olive green	.20	.20
1847	A1234 4c violet	.20	.20
1848	A1235 5c henna brown	.20	.20
1849	A1236 6c orange ver	.20	.20
a.	Vert. pair, imperf. btwn. and at bottom	2,000.	
1850	A1237 7c brt carmine	.20	.20
1851	A1238 8c olive black	.20	.20
1852	A1239 9c dark green	.20	.20
1853	A1240 10c Prus blue	.25	.20
b.	Vert. pair, imperf. btwn. & at bottom	900.	
c.	Horiz. pair, imperf. btwn.	2,250.	

Completely imperforate tagged or untagged
stamps are from printer's waste.

1854	A1241 11c dark blue	.25	.20
1855	A1242 13c lt maroon	.25	.20

1856	A1243 14c slate green	.30	.20
b.	Vert. pair, imperf. horiz.	125.	
c.	Horiz. pair, imperf. btwn.	9.00	
d.	Vert. pair, imperf. btwn.	1,900.	
e.	All color omitted	—	

No. 1856e comes from a partially printed
pane and should be collected as a vertical
strip of 10, one stamp normal, one stamp transitional and 8 stamps with color omitted.

1857	A1244 17c green	.35	.20
1858	A1245 18c dark blue	.35	.20
1859	A1246 19c brown	.40	.20
1860	A1247 20c claret	.40	.20
1861	A1248 20c green	.45	.20
1862	A1249 20c black	.40	.20
1863	A1250 22c dk chalky bl	.55	.20
d.	Vert. pair, imperf. horiz.	2,500.	
e.	Vert. pair, imperf. btwn.	—	
f.	Horiz. pair, imperf. btwn.	2,500.	
1864	A1251 30c olive gray	.55	.20
1865	A1252 35c gray	.70	.20
1866	A1253 37c blue	.75	.20
1867	A1254 39c rose lilac	.80	.20
a.	Vert. pair, imperf. horiz.	600.	
b.	Vert. pair, imperf. btwn.	2,000.	
1868	A1255 40c dark green	.80	.20
1869	A1256 50c brown	.95	.20
f.	All color omitted	—	
	Nos. 1844-1869 (26)	10.30	5.20

No. 1869f must be collected se-tenant with
a normal stamp.

Years of issue: 19c, 1980. 17c, 18c, 35c,
1981. No. 1860, 2c, 13c, 37c, 1982. No. 1861,
1c, 3c-5c, 1983. No. 1862, 10c, 30c, 40c,
1984. 6c-9c, 11c, 14c, 22c, 39c, 50c, 1985.

Everett Dirksen
A1261

Whitney Moore Young
A1262

Everett Dirksen

1981, Jan. 4   Perf. 11

1874	A1261 15c gray	.30	.20
a.	All color omitted		

Everett Dirksen (1896-1969), Senate Minor-
ity Leader, 1960-69.

No. 1874a comes from a partially printed
pane and may be collected as either a vertical
strip of 3 or 5 (1 or 3 stamps normal, one
stamp transitional and one stamp with color
omitted) or as a pair with one partially printed
stamp.

Black Heritage Series

1981, Jan. 30   Photo.   Perf. 11

1875	A1262 15c multicolored	.35	.20

Whitney Moore Young (1921-71), civil rights
leader.

Flowers

Rose USA 18c
A1263

Camellia USA 18c
A1264

Dahlia USA 18c
A1265

A1266

1981, Apr. 23   *Perf. 11*
1876	A1263	18c multicolored	.35	.20
1877	A1264	18c multicolored	.35	.20
1878	A1265	18c multicolored	.35	.20
1879	A1266	18c multicolored	.35	.20
a.		Block of 4, #1876-1879	1.40	1.25

A1267   A1268

A1269   A1270

A1271   A1272

A1273   A1274

A1275   A1276

1981, May 14   Engr.   *Perf. 11*
Booklet Stamps
1880	A1267	18c Bighorn	.55	.20
1881	A1268	18c Puma	.55	.20
1882	A1269	18c Harbor seal	.55	.20
1883	A1270	18c American Buffa-lo	.55	.20
1884	A1271	18c Brown bear	.55	.20
1885	A1272	18c Polar bear	.55	.20
1886	A1273	18c Elk (wapiti)	.55	.20
1887	A1274	18c Moose	.55	.20
1888	A1275	18c White-tailed deer	.55	.20
1889	A1276	18c Pronghorn	.55	.20
a.		Bklt. pane of 10, #1880-1889	8.50	7.00
		Nos. 1880-1889 (10)	5.50	2.00

See No. 1949.

A1277   A1278

A1279   A1280

Multicolor Huck Press
1981, Apr. 24   *Perf. 11*
1890	A1277	18c multicolored	.35	.20
a.		Imperf., pair	125.00	
b.		Vert. pair, imperf. horiz.	850.00	

Coil Stamp
Perf. 10 Vert.
1891	A1278	18c multicolored	.35	.20
a.		Imperf., pair	30.00	
b.		Pair, imperf. btwn.	—	

Beware of pairs offered as imperf. between that have faint blind perfs.

Vertical pairs and blocks exist from printer's waste.

Booklet Stamps
Perf. 11
1892	A1279	6c multicolored	.50	.20
1893	A1280	18c multicolored	.30	.20
a.		Bklt. pane, 2 #1892, 6 #1893	3.00	2.25
b.		As "a," vert. imperf. btwn.	75.00	
c.		Pair, #1892, 1893	.90	1.00

Bureau Precanceled Coils
Starting with No. 1895b, Bureau precanceled coil stamps are valued unused as well as used. The coils issued with dull gum may be difficult to distinguish. When used normally these stamps do not receive any postal markings so that used stamps with an additional postal cancellation of any kind are worth considerably less than the values shown here.

A1281

1981, Dec. 17   *Perf. 11*
1894	A1281	20c blk, dk blue & red	.40	.20
a.		Vert. pair, imperf.	35.00	
b.		Vert. pair, imperf. horiz.	550.00	
c.		Dark blue omitted	85.00	
d.		Black omitted	325.00	

Coil Stamp
Perf. 10 Vertical
1895	A1281	20c blk, dk blue & red	.40	.20
b.		Untagged (Bureau precanceled)	.50	.50
d.		Imperf., pair	10.00	
e.		Pair, imperf. btwn.	1,250.	
f.		Black omitted	50.00	
g.		Dark blue omitted	1,500.	

Booklet Stamp
Perf. 11x10½
1896	A1281	20c blk, dk blue & red	.40	.20
a.		Booklet pane of 6	2.50	2.00
b.		Booklet pane of 10	4.25	3.25

Transportation Coils

A1283

A1284

A1284A   A1285

A1286   A1287

A1288   A1289

A1290   A1291

A1292

A1294

A1293

A1295

1981-84   Engr.   *Perf. 10 Vert.*
1897	A1283	1c violet	.20	.20
b.		Imperf., pair	675.00	
1897A	A1284	2c black	.20	.20
e.		Imperf., pair	55.00	

For similar designs to the 1c and 2c, see Nos. 2225-2226.

1898	A1284A	3c dk green	.20	.20
1898A	A1285	4c redsh brn	.20	.20
b.		Untagged (Bureau precanceled)	.20	
c.		As "b," imperf., pair	750.00	
d.		No. 1898A, imperf., pair	900.00	—
1899	A1286	5c gray green	.20	.20
a.		Imperf., pair	2,750.	
1900	A1287	5.2c carmine	.20	.20
a.		Untagged (Bureau precanceled)	.20	
1901	A1288	5.9c blue	.25	
a.		Untagged (Bureau precanceled, lines only)	.20	.20
b.		As "a," imperf., pair	200.00	
1902	A1289	7.4c brown	.20	.20
a.		Untagged (Bureau precanceled)	.20	
1903	A1290	9.3c car rose	.30	.20
a.		Untagged (Bureau precanceled, lines only)	.20	
b.		As "a," imperf., pair	125.00	
1904	A1291	10.9c purple	.30	.20
a.		Untagged (Bureau precanceled, lines only)	.30	.25
b.		As "a," imperf., pair	150.00	
1905	A1292	11c red	.30	.20
a.		Untagged	.25	.20
1906	A1293	17c ultra	.35	.20
a.		Untagged (Bureau precanceled, Presorted First Class)	.35	.35
b.		Imperf., pair	165.00	
c.		As "a," imperf., pair	650.00	
1907	A1294	18c dk brn	.35	.35
a.		Imperf., pair	150.00	
1908	A1295	20c vermilion	.35	.20
a.		Imperf., pair	110.00	
		Nos. 1897-1908 (14)	3.60	2.80

Years of issue: 9.3c, 17c-20c, 1981. 2c, 4c, 5.9c, 10.9c, 1982. 1c, 3c, 5c, 5.2c, 1983. 7.4, 11c, 1984.
See Nos. 2123-2136, 2225-2231, 2252-2266, 2451-2468.

A1296

Perf. 10 Vert. on 1 or 2 Sides
1983, Aug. 12   Photo.
1909	A1296	$9.35 multi	21.00	15.00
a.		Booklet pane of 3	65.00	—

A1297

A1298

American Red Cross Centennial
1981, May 1   *Perf. 10½x11*
1910	A1297	18c multicolored	.35	.20

Savings & Loan Sesquicentennial
1981, May 8   *Perf. 11*
1911	A1298	18c multicolored	.35	.20

Space Achievement

A1299

A1300

A1303

A1304

A1301

A1302

A1305

A1306

1981, May 21   *Perf. 11*
1912	A1299	18c multicolored	.40	.20
1913	A1300	18c multicolored	.40	.20
1914	A1301	18c multicolored	.40	.20
1915	A1302	18c multicolored	.40	.20
1916	A1303	18c multicolored	.40	.20
1917	A1304	18c multicolored	.40	.20
1918	A1305	18c multicolored	.40	.20
1919	A1306	18c multicolored	.40	.20
a.		Block of 8, #1912-1919	3.25	3.00
b.		As "a," imperf.	8,000.	

Professional Management

Joseph Wharton A1307

1981, June 18
1920 A1307 18c blue & black .35 .20

Preservation of Wildlife Habitats

A1308 A1309

A1310 A1311

1981, June 26
1921 A1308 18c multicolored .35 .20
1922 A1309 18c multicolored .35 .20
1923 A1310 18c multicolored .35 .20
1924 A1311 18c multicolored .35 .20
a. Block of 4, #1921-1924 1.50 1.25

International Year of the Disabled

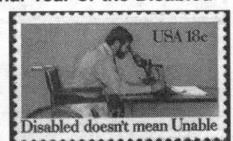

Man Looking through Microscope A1312

1981, June 29   Photo.   Perf. 11
1925 A1312 18c multicolored .35 .20
a. Vert. pair, imperf. horiz. 2,750.

Edna St. Vincent Millay, 1892-1950

A1313

Litho. & Engr.
1981, July 10   Perf. 11
1926 A1313 18c multicolored .35 .20
a. Black (engr.) inscriptions) omitted 300.00 —

Alcoholism

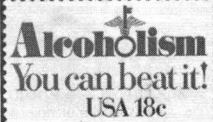

A1314

1981, Aug. 19   Engr.   Perf. 11
1927 A1314 18c blue & black .40 .20
a. Imperf., pair 400.
b. Vert. pair, imperf. horiz. 2,500.

American Architecture Series

New York University Library by Sanford White A1315

Biltmore House by Richard Morris Hunt A1316

Palace of the Arts by Bernard Maybeck A1317

National Farmer's Bank by Louis Sullivan A1318

1981, Aug. 28   Engr.   Perf. 11
1928 A1315 18c black & red .40 .20
1929 A1316 18c black & red .40 .20
1930 A1317 18c black & red .40 .20
1931 A1318 18c black & red .40 .20
a. Block of 4, #1928-1931 1.65 1.50

Athletes

Mildred Didrikson Zaharias A1319

Robert Tyre Jones A1320

1981, Sept. 22   Engr.   Perf. 10½x11
1932 A1319 18c purple .40 .20
1933 A1320 18c green .40 .20

Frederic Remington, 1861-1909

Coming Through the Rye A1321

1981, Oct. 9   Perf. 11
1934 A1321 18c gray, grn & brn .35 .20
a. Vert. pair, imperf. btwn. 275.00
b. Brown omitted 450.00

James Hoban, 1762?-1831

Irish-American Architect of White House — A1322

1981, Oct. 13   Photo.   Perf. 11
1935 A1322 18c multicolored .35 .20
1936 A1322 20c multicolored .35 .20
See Ireland No. 504.

American Bicentennial

Battle of Yorktown A1323

Battle of Virginia Capes A1324

Litho. & Engr.
1981, Oct. 16   Perf. 11
1937 A1323 18c multicolored .35 .20
1938 A1324 18c multicolored .35 .20
a. Pair, #1937-1938 .90 .75
b. As "a," black (engr., inscriptions) omitted 400.00

Christmas

Madonna and Child, Botticelli — A1325

Felt Bear on Sled A1326

1981, Oct. 28   Photo.   Perf. 11
1939 A1325 (20c) multicolored .40 .20
a. Imperf., pair 125.
b. Vert. pair, imperf. horiz. 1,650.
1940 A1326 (20c) multicolored .40 .20
a. Imperf., pair 275.
b. Vert. pair, imperf. horiz. 2,500.

John Hanson, 1721-1783

First President of Continental Congress — A1327

John Hanson President Continental Congress USA 20c

1981, Nov. 5   Photo.   Perf. 11
1941 A1327 20c multicolored .40 .20

Desert Plants

Barrel Cactus — A1328

Saguaro — A1331

Agave — A1329

Beavertail Cactus — A1330

1981, Dec. 11   Litho. & Engr.
1942 A1328 20c multicolored .35 .20
1943 A1329 20c multicolored .35 .20
1944 A1330 20c multicolored .35 .20
1945 A1331 20c multicolored .35 .20
a. Block of 4, #1942-1945 1.50 1.25
b. As "a," deep brown omitted 6,500.
c. No. 1945 imperf., vert. pair 5,250.

A1332   A1333

1981, Oct. 11   Photo.   Perf. 11x10½
1946 A1332 (20c) brown .40 .20
b. All color omitted

No. 1946b comes from a partially printed pane with most stamps normal. It must be collected as a vertical pair or strip with normal or partially printed stamps attached.

Coil Stamp
Perf. 10 Vert.
1947 A1332 (20c) brown .60 .20
a. Imperf., pair 1,500.

Booklet Stamp
Perf. 11
1948 A1333 (20c) brown .40 .20
a. Booklet pane of 10 4.50 3.00

A1334

1982, Jan. 8   Engr.   Perf. 11
1949 A1334 20c dk blue (from bklt. pane) .55 .20
a. Booklet pane of 10 5.50 2.50
b. As "a," vert. imperf. btwn. 110.00
c. Type II .55 .20
d. As "c," booklet pane of 10 11.00 —

No. 1949 is 18¾mm wide and has overall tagging. No. 1949c is 18½mm wide and has block tagging.
See No. 1880.

Franklin Delano Roosevelt

A1335

1982, Jan. 30   Engr.   Perf. 11
1950	A1335	20c blue	.40	.20

A1336

1982, Feb. 1   Photo.   Perf. 11¼
1951	A1336	20c multicolored	.40	.20
b.		Imperf., pair	275.00	
c.		Blue omitted	225.00	
d.		Yellow omitted	1,000.	
e.		Purple omitted	—	

No. 1951c is valued in the grade of fine.

Perf. 11¼x10½
1951A	A1336	20c multicolored	.75	.25

A1337   A1338

George Washington

1982, Feb. 22   Photo.   Perf. 11
1952	A1337	20c multicolored	.40	.20

State Birds & Flowers

Perf. 10½x11¼

1982, Apr. 14   Photo.
1953	A1338	20c Alabama	.50	.25
1954	A1339	20c Alaska	.50	.25
1955	A1340	20c Arizona	.50	.25
1956	A1341	20c Arkansas	.50	.25
1957	A1342	20c California	.50	.25
1958	A1343	20c Colorado	.50	.25
1959	A1344	20c Connecticut	.50	.25
1960	A1345	20c Delaware	.50	.25
1961	A1346	20c Florida	.50	.25
1962	A1347	20c Georgia	.50	.25
1963	A1348	20c Hawaii	.50	.25
1964	A1349	20c Idaho	.50	.25
1965	A1350	20c Illinois	.50	.25
1966	A1351	20c Indiana	.50	.25
1967	A1352	20c Iowa	.50	.25
1968	A1353	20c Kansas	.50	.25
1969	A1354	20c Kentucky	.50	.25
1970	A1355	20c Louisiana	.50	.25
1971	A1356	20c Maine	.50	.25
1972	A1357	20c Maryland	.50	.25
1973	A1358	20c Massachusetts	.50	.25
1974	A1359	20c Michigan	.50	.25
1975	A1360	20c Minnesota	.50	.25
1976	A1361	20c Mississippi	.50	.25
1977	A1362	20c Missouri	.50	.25
1978	A1363	20c Montana	.50	.25
1979	A1364	20c Nebraska	.50	.25
1980	A1365	20c Nevada	.50	.25
1981	A1366	20c New Hampshire	.50	.25
b.		Black (engr.) omitted	5,000.	
1982	A1367	20c New Jersey	.50	.25
1983	A1368	20c New Mexico	.50	.25
1984	A1369	20c New York	.50	.25
1985	A1370	20c North Carolina	.50	.25
1986	A1371	20c North Dakota	.50	.25
1987	A1372	20c Ohio	.50	.25
1988	A1373	20c Oklahoma	.50	.25
1989	A1374	20c Oregon	.50	.25
1990	A1375	20c Pennsylvania	.50	.25
1991	A1376	20c Rhode Island	.50	.25
b.		Black (engr.) omitted	5,000.	
1992	A1377	20c South Carolina	.50	.25
1993	A1378	20c South Dakota	.50	.25
1994	A1379	20c Tennessee	.50	.25
1995	A1380	20c Texas	.50	.25
1996	A1381	20c Utah	.50	.25
1997	A1382	20c Vermont	.50	.25
1998	A1383	20c Virginia	.50	.25
1999	A1384	20c Washington	.50	.25
2000	A1385	20c West Virginia	.50	.25
2001	A1386	20c Wisconsin	.50	.25
2002	A1387	20c Wyoming	.50	.25
b.		Pane of 50, #1953-2002	25.00	
d.		Pane of 50, imperf.	27,500.	

Perf. 11¼x11
1953A	A1338	20c Alabama	.55	.30
1954A	A1339	20c Alaska	.55	.30
1955A	A1340	20c Arizona	.55	.30
1956A	A1341	20c Arkansas	.55	.30
1957A	A1342	20c California	.55	.30
1958A	A1343	20c Colorado	.55	.30
1959A	A1344	20c Connecticut	.55	.30
1960A	A1345	20c Delaware	.55	.30
1961A	A1346	20c Florida	.55	.30
1962A	A1347	20c Georgia	.55	.30
1963A	A1348	20c Hawaii	.55	.30
1964A	A1349	20c Idaho	.55	.30
1965A	A1350	20c Illinois	.55	.30
1966A	A1351	20c Indiana	.55	.30
1967A	A1352	20c Iowa	.55	.30
1968A	A1353	20c Kansas	.55	.30
1969A	A1354	20c Kentucky	.55	.30
1970A	A1355	20c Louisiana	.55	.30
1971A	A1356	20c Maine	.55	.30
1972A	A1357	20c Maryland	.55	.30
1973A	A1358	20c Massachusetts	.55	.30
1974A	A1359	20c Michigan	.55	.30
1975A	A1360	20c Minnesota	.55	.30
1976A	A1360	20c Mississippi	.55	.30
1977A	A1361	20c Missouri	.55	.30
1978A	A1362	20c Montana	.55	.30
1979A	A1363	20c Nebraska	.55	.30
1980A	A1364	20c Nevada	.55	.30
1981A	A1364	20c New Hampshire	.55	.30
1982A	A1365	20c New Jersey	.55	.30
1983A	A1366	20c New Mexico	.55	.30
1984A	A1369	20c New York	.55	.30
1985A	A1370	20c North Carolina	.55	.30
1986A	A1371	20c North Dakota	.55	.30
1987A	A1372	20c Ohio	.55	.30
1988A	A1373	20c Oklahoma	.55	.30
1989A	A1374	20c Oregon	.55	.30
1990A	A1375	20c Pennsylvania	.55	.30
1991A	A1376	20c Rhode Island	.55	.30
1992A	A1377	20c South Carolina	.55	.30
1993A	A1378	20c South Dakota	.55	.30
1994A	A1379	20c Tennessee	.55	.30
1995A	A1380	20c Texas	.55	.30
1996A	A1381	20c Utah	.55	.30
1997A	A1382	20c Vermont	.55	.30
1998A	A1383	20c Virginia	.55	.30
1999A	A1384	20c Washington	.55	.30
2000A	A1385	20c West Virginia	.55	.30
2001A	A1386	20c Wisconsin	.55	.30
2002A	A1387	20c Wyoming	.55	.30
c.		Pane of 50, Nos. 1953A-2002A	27.50	—

US-Netherlands

200th Anniv. of Diplomatic Recognition by the Netherlands — A1388

1982, Apr. 20   Photo.   Perf. 11
2003	A1388	20c ver, brt blue & gray black	.40	.20
a.		Imperf., pair	325.00	

See Netherlands Nos. 640-641.

Library of Congress

A1389

1982, Apr. 21   Engr.   Perf. 11
2004	A1389	20c red & black	.40	.20
a.		All color missing	—	

No. 2004a must be collected se-tenant with transitional and normal stamps.

Consumer Education

A1390

Coil Stamp

1982, Apr. 27   Engr.   Perf. 10 Vert.
2005	A1390	20c sky blue	.55	.20
a.		Imperf., pair	100.00	

Knoxville World's Fair

A1391

A1392

A1393

A1394

1982, Apr. 29   Photo.   Perf. 11
2006	A1391	20c multicolored	.40	.20
2007	A1392	20c multicolored	.40	.20
2008	A1393	20c multicolored	.40	.20
2009	A1394	20c multicolored	.40	.20
a.		Block of 4, #2006-2009	1.65	1.50

American Author, 1832-1899

Frontispiece from "Ragged Dick" — A1395

1982, Apr. 30   Engr.   Perf. 11
2010	A1395	20c red & black, *tan*	.40	.20
a.		Red & Black omitted		

The Philatelic Foundation has issued a certificate for a pane of 50 with red and black colors omitted. Recognition of this error is by the paper and by a tiny residue of red ink from the tagging roller. The engraved plates did not strike the paper.

Aging Together

A1396

1982, May 21   Perf. 11
2011	A1396	20c brown	.40	.20

A1397   A1398

Performing Arts Series

Actors John, Ethel & Lionel Barrymore.

1982, June 8   Photo.   Perf. 11
2012	A1397	20c multicolored	.40	.20

Dr. Mary E. Walker, 1832-1919

1982, June 10   Photo.   Perf. 11
2013	A1398	20c multicolored	.40	.20

International Peace Garden

A1399

1982, June 30   Photo.   Perf. 11
2014	A1399	20c multicolored	.40	.20
a.		Blk & grn (engr.) omitted	260.00	

A1400   A1401

America's Libraries

1982, July 13   Engr.   Perf. 11
2015	A1400	20c red & black	.40	.20
a.		Vert. pair, imperf. horiz.	300.00	

Black Heritage Series

1982, Aug. 2   Photo.   Perf. 10½x11
2016	A1401	20c multicolored	1.10	.20

Jackie Robinson (1919-72), baseball player.

Touro Synagogue

A1402

Photogravure, Engraved

1982, Aug. 22   Perf. 11
2017	A1402	20c multicolored	.40	.20
a.		Imperf., pair	2,500.	

Wolf Trap Farm Park

A1403

1982, Sept. 1   Photo.   Perf. 11
2018	A1403	20c multicolored	.40	.20

American Architecture Series

Fallingwater, Mill Run, Pa., by Frank Lloyd Wright — A1404

Illinois Institute of Technology by Ludwig Mies van der Rohe A1405

Gropius House, Lincoln, Mass., by Walter Gropius A1406

Dulles Airport, by Eero Saarinen A1407

1982, Sept. 30   Engr.   Perf. 11
2019 A1404 20c black & brown   .45   .20
  b.   Red omitted
2020 A1405 20c black & brown   .45   .20
  a.   Red omitted
2021 A1406 20c black & brown   .45   .20
2022 A1407 20c black & brown   .45   .20
  a.   Block of 4, #2019-2022   2.00 1.60

St. Francis of Assisi, 1182-1226

A1408

1982, Oct. 7   Photo.   Perf. 11
2023 A1408 20c multicolored   .40   .20

Ponce de Leon, 1527-1591

A1409

1982, Oct. 12   Photo.   Perf. 11
2024 A1409 20c multicolored   .40   .20
  a.   Imperf., pair   500.00
  b.   Vert. pair, Imperf. btwn. and at top   —

Christmas

A1410

A1411

A1412

A1413

A1414

A1415

1982, Nov. 3   Photo.   Perf. 11
2025 A1410 13c multicolored   .25   .20
  a.   Imperf., pair   650.00

1982, Oct. 28
2026 A1411 20c multicolored   .40   .20
  a.   Imperf., pair   150.00
  b.   Horiz. pair, imperf. vert.   —
  c.   Vert. pair, imperf. horiz.   —
2027 A1412 20c multicolored   .50   .20
2028 A1413 20c multicolored   .50   .20
2029 A1414 20c multicolored   .50   .20
2030 A1415 20c multicolored   .50   .20
  a.   Block of 4, #2027-2030   2.25 1.50
  b.   As "a," imperf.   2,750.
  c.   As "a," imperf. horiz.
  Nos. 2025-2030 (6)   2.65 1.20

Science & Industry

A1416

Litho. & Engr.
1983, Jan. 19   Perf. 11
2031 A1416 20c multicolored   .40   .20
  a.   Black (engr.) omitted   1,400.

Balloons

A1417   A1420

A1418

A1419

1983, Mar. 31   Photo.   Perf. 11
2032 A1417 20c multicolored   .40   .20
2033 A1418 20c multicolored   .40   .20
2034 A1419 20c multicolored   .40   .20
2035 A1420 20c multicolored   .40   .20
  a.   Block of 4, #2032-2035   1.65 1.50
  b.   As "a," imperf.   4,250.
  c.   As "a," right stamp perf., otherwise imperf.   4,500.

US-Sweden

A1421

1983, Mar. 24   Engr.   Perf. 11
2036 A1421 20c multicolored   .40   .20
  See Sweden No. 1453.

Civilian Conservation Corps

A1422

1983, Apr. 5   Photo.   Perf. 11
2037 A1422 20c multicolored   .40   .20
  a.   Imperf., pair   2,750.
  b.   Vert. pair, imperf. horiz.

Joseph Priestley, 1733-1804

A1423

1983, Apr. 13   Photo.   Perf. 11
2038 A1423 20c multicolored   .40   .20

Voluntarism

A1424

1983, Apr. 20   Engr.   Perf. 11
2039 A1424 20c red & black   .40   .20
  a.   Imperf., pair   800.00

US-Germany

Concord, 1683 A1425

1983, Apr. 29   Perf. 11
2040 A1425 20c brown   .40   .20
  See Germany No. 1397.

Brooklyn Bridge

A1426

1983, May 17   Engr.   Perf. 11
2041 A1426 20c blue   .40   .20

T.V.A.

A1427

Photo. & Engr.
1983, May 18   Perf. 11
2042 A1427 20c multicolored   .40   .20

Physical Fitness

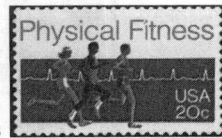

A1428

1983, May 14   Photo.   Perf. 11
2043 A1428 20c multicolored   .40   .20

Black Heritage Series

A1429

1983, June 9   Photo.
2044 A1429 20c multicolored   .40   .20
  a.   Imperf., pair   475.00
Scott Joplin (1868-1917), ragtime composer.

Medal of Honor

A1430

Litho. & Engr.
1983, June 7   Perf. 11
2045 A1430 20c multicolored   .40   .20
  a.   Red omitted   250.00

A1431   A1432

George Herman Ruth, 1895-1948
1983, July 6   Engr.   Perf. 10½x11
2046 A1431 20c blue   1.25   .20

Nathaniel Hawthorne, 1804-1864
1983, July 8   Photo.   Perf. 11
2047 A1432 20c multicolored   .45   .20

1984 Summer Olympics

Discus
A1433

High Jump
A1434

Archery
A1435

Boxing
A1436

1983, July 28   Photo.   *Perf. 11*
2048 A1433 13c multicolored   .35   .20
2049 A1434 13c multicolored   .35   .20
2050 A1435 13c multicolored   .35   .20
2051 A1436 13c multicolored   .35   .20
   a.   Block of 4, #2048-2051   1.50   1.25

Signing of Treaty of Paris

John Adams, Franklin, John Jay, David Hartley
A1437

1983, Sept. 2   Photo.   *Perf. 11*
2052 A1437 20c multicolored   .40   .20

Civil Service

A1438

1983, Sept. 9   Photo. & Engr.
2053 A1438 20c buff, blue & red   .40   .20

Metropolitan Opera

A1439

1983, Sept. 14   Litho. & Engr.
2054 A1439 20c yel & mar   .40   .20

American Inventors

A1440

A1441

A1442

A1443

1983, Sept. 21   Litho. & Engr
2055 A1440 20c multicolored   .45   .20
2056 A1441 20c multicolored   .45   .20
2057 A1442 20c multicolored   .45   .20
2058 A1443 20c multicolored   .45   .20
   a.   Block of 4, #2055-2058   1.80   1.25
   b.   As "a," black omitted   350.00

Streetcars

A1444

A1445

A1446

A1447

1983, Oct. 8   Photo. & Engr.
2059 A1444 20c multicolored   .45   .20
2060 A1445 20c multicolored   .45   .20
2061 A1446 20c multicolored   .45   .20
2062 A1447 20c multicolored   .45   .20
   a.   Block of 4, #2059-2062   1.80   1.40
   b.   As "a," black omitted   425.00
   c.   As "a," black omitted on #2059, 2061   —

Christmas

A1448

A1449

1983, Oct. 28   Photo.   *Perf. 11*
2063 A1448 20c multicolored   .40   .20
2064 A1449 20c multicolored   .40   .20
   a.   Imperf., pair   175.00

Martin Luther
A1450

Caribou and Alaska Pipeline — A1451

Martin Luther, 1483-1546
1983, Nov. 11   Photo.   *Perf. 11*
2065 A1450 20c multicolored   .40   .20

25th Anniv. of Alaska Statehood
1984, Jan. 3   Photo.   *Perf. 11*
2066 A1451 20c multicolored   .40   .20

Winter Olympic Games

Ice Dancing
A1452

Downhill Skiing
A1453

Cross-country Skiing
A1454

Hockey
A1455

1984, Jan. 6   *Perf. 10½x11*
2067 A1452 20c multicolored   .50   .20
2068 A1453 20c multicolored   .50   .20
2069 A1454 20c multicolored   .50   .20
2070 A1455 20c multicolored   .50   .20
   a.   Block of 4, #2067-2070   2.10   1.50
14th Winter Olympic Games, Sarajevo, Yugoslavia, Feb. 8-19.

A1456

A1457

Federal Deposit Insurance Corp., 50th Anniv.
1984, Jan. 12   *Perf. 11*
2071 A1456 20c multicolored   .40   .20

Love
1984, Jan. 31   Photo. & Engr.
2072 A1457 20c multicolored   .40   .20
   a.   Horiz. pair, imperf. vert.   175.00

Carter G. Woodson (1875-1950), Writer — A1458

Black Heritage Series
1984, Feb. 1   Photo.
2073 A1458 20c multicolored   .40   .20
   a.   Horiz. pair, imperf. vert.   1,600.

A1459

Dollar Sign, Coin — A1460

Soil and Water Conservation
1984, Feb. 6
2074 A1459 20c multicolored   .40   .20

50th Anniv. of Credit Union Act
1984, Feb. 10   Photo.   *Perf. 11*
2075 A1460 20c multicolored   .40   .20

Orchids

A1461

A1462

A1463

A1464

1984, Mar. 5
2076 A1461 20c Wild pink   .50   .20
2077 A1462 20c Yellow lady's-slipper   .50   .20
2078 A1463 20c Spreading pogonia   .50   .20
2079 A1464 20c Pacific calypso   .50   .20
   a.   Block of 4, #2076-2079   2.00   1.50

25th Anniv. of Hawaii Statehood

Eastern Polynesian Canoe, Golden Plover, Mauna Loa Volcano
A1465

1984, Mar. 12	**Photo.**		*Perf. 11*	
2080	A1465	20c multicolored	.40	.20

National Archives

Abraham Lincoln, George Washington — A1466

1984, Apr. 16	**Photo.**		*Perf. 11*	
2081	A1466	20c multicolored	.40	.20

1984 Los Angeles Olympics

Diving A1467   Long Jump A1468

Wrestling A1469   Kayak A1470

1984, May 4			*Perf. 11*	
2082	A1467	20c multicolored	.55	.20
2083	A1468	20c multicolored	.55	.20
2084	A1469	20c multicolored	.55	.20
2085	A1470	20c multicolored	.55	.20
a.		Block of 4, #2082-2085	2.40	1.90
b.		As "a," imperf. btwn. vert.	—	

New Orleans World Exposition

River Wildlife A1471

1984, May 11			*Perf. 11*	
2086	A1471	20c multicolored	.40	.20

Health Research

Lab Equipment A1472

1984, May 17			*Perf. 11*	
2087	A1472	20c multicolored	.40	.20

A1473   A1474

Performing Arts
Actor Douglas Fairbanks (1883-1939)

1984, May 23	**Photo. & Engr.**			
2088	A1473	20c multicolored	.40	.20
b.		Horiz. pair, imperf. btwn.		

Jim Thorpe, 1888-1953

1984, May 24	**Engr.**		*Perf. 11*	
2089	A1474	20c dark brown	.40	.20

Performing Arts

Tenor John McCormack (1884-1945) A1475

1984, June 6	**Photo.**		*Perf. 11*	
2090	A1475	20c multicolored	.40	.20

See Ireland No. 594.

25th Anniv. of St. Lawrence Seaway

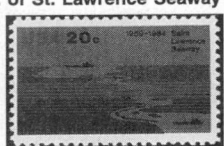

Aerial View of Seaway, Freighters A1476

1984, June 26	**Photo.**		*Perf. 11*	
2091	A1476	20c multicolored	.40	.20

50th Anniv. of Waterfowl Preservation Act

"Mallards Dropping In," by Jay N. Darling A1477

1984, July 2	**Engr.**		*Perf. 11*	
2092	A1477	20c blue	.50	.20
a.		Horiz. pair, imperf. vert.	400.00	

See No. RW1.

A1478   Author — A1479

Roanoke Voyages

1984, July 13	**Photo.**		*Perf. 11*	
2093	A1478	20c multicolored	.40	.20

Herman Melville (1819-1891)

1984, Aug. 1	**Engr.**		*Perf. 11*	
2094	A1479	20c sage green	.40	.20

Horace Moses (1862-1947)

Junior Achievement Founder — A1480

1984, Aug. 6	**Engr.**			
2095	A1480	20c org & dk brn	.45	.20

Smokey Bear — A1481   Clemente, Puerto Rican Flag — A1482

1984, Aug. 13	**Litho. & Engr.**			
2096	A1481	20c multicolored	.40	.20
a.		Horiz. pair, imperf. btwn.	300.	
b.		Vert. pair, imperf. btwn.	250.	
c.		Block of 4, imperf. btwn. vert. and horiz.	5,500.	
d.		Horiz. pair, imperf. vert.	1,750.	

Roberto Clemente (1934-1972)

1984, Aug. 17	**Photo.**		*Perf. 11*	
2097	A1482	20c multicolored	1.60	.20
a.		Horiz. pair, imperf. vert.	2,000.	

Dogs

Beagle, Boston Terrier A1483

Chesapeake Bay Retriever, Cocker Spaniel — A1484

Alaskan Malamute, Collie A1485

Black & Tan Coonhound, American Foxhound — A1486

1984, Sept. 7	**Photo.**		*Perf. 11*	
2098	A1483	20c multicolored	.45	.20
2099	A1484	20c multicolored	.45	.20
2100	A1485	20c multicolored	.45	.20
2101	A1486	20c multicolored	.45	.20
a.		Block of 4, #2098-2101	1.90	1.75

Crime Prevention

McGruff, The Crime Dog — A1487

1984, Sept. 26	**Photo.**		*Perf. 11*	
2102	A1487	20c multicolored	.40	.20

Hispanic Americans

A1488

1984, Oct. 31	**Photo.**		*Perf. 11*	
2103	A1488	20c multicolored	.40	.20
a.		Vert. pair, imperf. horiz.	2,250.	

A1489   A1490

Family Unity

1984, Oct. 1	**Photo. & Engr.**			
2104	A1489	20c multicolored	.40	.20
a.		Horiz. pair, imperf. vert.	550.00	
c.		Vert. pair, imperf. btwn. and at bottom		
d.		Horiz. pair, imperf. between	—	

Eleanor Roosevelt

1984, Oct. 11	**Engr.**		*Perf. 11*	
2105	A1490	20c deep blue	.40	.20

Nation of Readers

Lincoln, Son Tad — A1491

1984, Oct. 16	**Engr.**		*Perf. 11*	
2106	A1491	20c brown & mar	.40	.20

Christmas

Madonna and Child by Fra Filippo Lippi — A1492   Santa Claus — A1493

1984, Oct. 30	**Photo.**		*Perf. 11*	
2107	A1492	20c multicolored	.40	.20
2108	A1493	20c multicolored	.40	.20
a.		Horiz. pair, imperf. vert.	950.00	

No. 2108a is valued in the grade of fine.

Vietnam Veterans Memorial

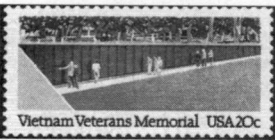

Memorial Wall — A1494

1984, Nov. 10   **Engr.**   *Perf. 11*
2109 A1494 20c multicolored   .40   .20

Performing Arts

Composer Jerome Kern (1885-1945) A1495

1985, Jan. 23   **Photo.**   *Perf. 11*
2110 A1495 22c multicolored   .40   .20

A1496   A1497

1985, Feb. 1   **Photo.**   *Perf. 11*
2111 A1496 (22c) green   .55   .20
  a. Vert. pair, imperf.   35.
  b. Vert. pair, imperf. horiz.   1,350.

Coil Stamp
Perf. 10 Vert.
2112 A1496 (22c) green   .60   .20
  a. Imperf., pair   47.50

Booklet Stamp
Perf. 11
2113 A1497 (22c) green   .80   .20
  a. Booklet pane of 10   8.50   3.00
  b. As "a," imperf. btwn. horiz.   —

A1498

Flag over Capitol Dome A1499

1985, Mar. 29   **Engr.**   *Perf. 11*
2114 A1498 22c bl, red & blk   .40   .20

Coil Stamp
Perf. 10 Vert.
2115 A1498 22c bl, red & blk   .40   .20
  c. Inscribed "T" at bottom ('87)   .50   .40
  d. Black field of stars   —
  e. Imperf., pair   15.00

Booklet Stamp
Perf. 10 Horiz. on 1 or 2 Sides
2116 A1499 22c bl, red & blk   .50   .20
  a. Booklet pane of 5   2.50   1.25

Seashells

Frilled Dogwinkle A1500   Reticulated Helmet A1501

 New England Neptune A1502   Calico Scallop A1503

 Lightning Whelk — A1504

1985, Apr. 4   **Engr.**   *Perf. 10*
Booklet Stamps
2117 A1500 22c black & brn   .40   .20
2118 A1501 22c multicolored   .40   .20
2119 A1502 22c black & brn   .40   .20
2120 A1503 22c black & violet   .40   .20
2121 A1504 22c multicolored   .40   .20
  a. Bklt. pane, 2 ea #2117-2121   4.00   2.50
  b. As "a," violet omitted   800.00
  c. As "a," vert. imperf. btwn.   600.00
  d. As "a," imperf.   —
  e. Strip of 5, #2117-2121   2.00

Eagle and Half Moon — A1505

Type I. Washed out, dull appearance most evident in the black of the body of the eagle, and the red in the background between the eagle's shoulder and the moon. "$10.75" appears splotchy or grainy (P# 11111).
Type II. Brighter, more intense colors most evident in the black on the eagle's body, and red in the background. "$10.75" appears smoother, brighter, and less grainy (P# 22222).

Perf. 10 Vert. on 1 or 2 Sides
1985, Apr. 29   **Photo.**   **Untagged**
2122 A1505 $10.75 multi, type I   19.00   7.50
  a. Booklet pane of 3   60.00   —
  b. Type II   21.00   —
  c. As "b," booklet pane of 3   65.00   —

Issued in booklets only.

Transportation Coils

 School Bus 1920s A1506   Buckboard 1880s A1507

 Star Route Truck A1508   Tricycle 1880s A1509

 Tractor 1920s A1510   Ambulance 1860s A1511

 Tow Truck 1920s A1512   Oil Wagon 1890s A1513

 Stutz Bearcat 1933 A1514   Stanley Steamer 1909 A1515

 Pushcart 1880s A1516   Iceboat 1880s A1517

 Dog Sled 1920s A1518   Bread Wagon 1880s A1519

1985-87   **Engr.**   *Perf. 10 Vert.*
2123 A1506 3.4c dk bluish green   .20   .20
  a. Untagged (Bureau precanceled)   .20   .20
2124 A1507 4.9c brn blk   .20   .20
  a. Untagged (Bureau precanceled)   .20   .20
2125 A1508 5.5c dp mag   .20   .20
  a. Untagged (Bureau precanceled)   .20   .20
2126 A1509 6c red brn   .20   .20
  a. Untagged (Bureau precanceled)   .20   .20
  b. As "a," imperf., pair   200.00
2127 A1510 7.1c lake   .20   .20
  a. Untagged (Bureau precanceled)   .20   .20
2128 A1511 8.3c green   .20   .20
  a. Untagged (Bureau precanceled)   .20   .20

For similar stamp see No. 2231.

2129 A1512 8.5c dk Prus green   .20   .20
  a. Untagged (Bureau precanceled)   .20   .20
2130 A1513 10.1c slate blue   .25   .20
  a. Untagged (Bureau precanceled)   .25   .25
  b. As "a," imperf., pair (red precancel)   15.00
    As "b," black precancel   100.00
2131 A1514 11c dk green   .25   .20
2132 A1515 12c dk bl, I   .25   .20
  a. Untagged (Bureau precanceled)   .25   .25
  b. Type II, untagged (Bureau precanceled)   .40   .30

Type II has "Stanley Steamer 1909" ½mm shorter (17 ½mm) than No. 2132 (18mm).

2133 A1516 12.5c ol grn   .25   .20
  a. Untagged (Bureau precanceled)   .25   .25
  b. As "a," imperf., pair   55.00
2134 A1517 14c sky bl, I   .30   .20
  a. Imperf., pair   100.00
  b. Type II   .30   .20

Type II design is ¼mm narrower (17¼mm) than No. 2134 (17½mm) and has block tagging. No. 2134 has overall tagging.

2135 A1518 17c sky blue   .30   .20
  a. Imperf., pair   500.00
2136 A1519 25c org brn   .45   .20
  a. Imperf., pair   10.00
  b. Pair, imperf. between   750.00
  Nos. 2123-2136 (14)   3.45   2.80

Years of issue: 3.4c, 4.9c, 6c, 8.3c, 10.1c-14c, 1985. 5.5c, 17c, 25c, 1986. 7.1c, 8.5c, 1987.
See Nos. 1897-1908, 2225-2231, 2252-2266, 2451-2468.

Black Heritage Series

Mary McLeod Bethune (1875-1955), Educator — A1520

1985, Mar. 5   **Photo.**   *Perf. 11*
2137 A1520 22c multicolored   .40   .20

American Folk Art Series
Duck Decoys

 Broadbill A1521

 Mallard A1522

 Canvasback A1523

 Redhead A1524

1985, Mar. 22   **Photo.**   *Perf. 11*
2138 A1521 22c multicolored   .65   .20
2139 A1522 22c multicolored   .65   .20
2140 A1523 22c multicolored   .65   .20
2141 A1524 22c multicolored   .65   .20
  a. Block of 4, #2138-2141   4.00   2.25

Winter Special Olympics

Ice Skater, Emblem, Skier A1525

1985, Mar. 25   **Photo.**   *Perf. 11*
2142 A1525 22c multicolored   .40   .20
  a. Vert. pair, imperf. horiz.   600.00

Love

A1526

1985, Apr. 17   **Photo.**
2143 A1526 22c multicolored   .40   .20
  a. Imperf., pair   1,500.

Rural Electrification Administration

Electrified Farm A1527

1985, May 11   **Photo. & Engr.**
2144 A1527 22c multicolored   .45   .20
  a. Vert. pair, imperf. btwn.

AMERIPEX '86

US No. 134 — A1528

1985, May 25   **Litho. & Engr.**
2145 A1528 22c multicolored   .40   .20
   a.   Red, black & blue omitted   200.
   b.   Red & black omitted   1,250.
   c.   Red omitted   —
   d.   Black omitted   —

US First Lady

Abigail Adams
(1744-1818)
A1529

1985, June 14   **Litho.**   *Perf. 11*
2146 A1529 22c multicolored   .40   .20
   a.   Imperf., pair   275.00

Architect, Sculptor

Frederic Auguste Bartholdi (1834-1904), Statue of Liberty — A1530

1985, July 18   **Litho. & Engr.**
2147 A1530 22c multicolored   .40   .20
   a.   Black (engr.) omitted   —

Examples exist with most, but not all, of the engraved black omitted. Expertization of No. 2147a is recommended.

George Washington, Washington Monument A1532

Envelopes A1533

COIL STAMPS

1985   **Photo.**   *Perf. 10 Vert.*
2149 A1532 18c multicolored   .35   .20
   a.   Untagged (Bureau precan-celed)   .35   .35
   b.   Imperf., pair   950.00
   c.   As "a," imperf., pair   800.00
2150 A1533 21.1c multicolored   .40   .20
   a.   Untagged (Bureau precan-celed)   .40   .40

Issue dates: 18c, Nov. 6; 21.1c, Oct. 22. Precancellations on Nos. 2149a ("PRESORTED FIRST CLASS"), 2150a ("ZIP+4") do not have lines.

Korean War Veterans

American Troops in Korea A1535

1985, July 26   **Engr.**   *Perf. 11*
2152 A1535 22c gray grn & rose red   .40   .20

Social Security Act, 50th Anniv.

Men, Women, Children, Corinthian Columns A1536

1985, Aug. 14   **Photo.**   *Perf. 11*
2153 A1536 22c dp bl & lt bl   .40   .20

World War I Veterans

The Battle of Marne, France, by Harvey Dunn A1537

1985, Aug. 26   **Engr.**   *Perf. 11*
2154 A1537 22c gray grn & rose red   .40   .20
   a.   Red omitted   —

Horses

Quarter Horse A1538

Morgan A1539

Saddlebred A1540

Appaloosa A1541

1985, Sept. 25   **Photo.**   *Perf. 11*
2155 A1538 22c multicolored   1.00   .20
2156 A1539 22c multicolored   1.00   .20
2157 A1540 22c multicolored   1.00   .20
2158 A1541 22c multicolored   1.00   .20
   a.   Block of 4, #2155-2158   6.00   4.50

Public Education in America

Quill Pen, Apple, Spectacles, Penmanship Quiz — A1542

1985, Oct. 1   **Photo.**   *Perf. 11*
2159 A1542 22c multicolored   .45   .20

International Youth Year

YMCA Youth Camping, Cent. A1543

Boy Scouts, 75th Anniv. A1544

Big Brothers/Big Sisters Fed., 40th Anniv. — A1545

Camp Fire, Inc., 75th Anniv. A1546

1985, Oct. 7   **Photo.**   *Perf. 11*
2160 A1543 22c multicolored   .65   .20
2161 A1544 22c multicolored   .65   .20
2162 A1545 22c multicolored   .65   .20
2163 A1546 22c multicolored   .65   .20
   a.   Block of 4, #2160-2163   3.00   2.25

Help End Hunger

Youths and the Elderly Suffering from Malnutrition A1547

1985, Oct. 15   **Photo.**
2164 A1547 22c multicolored   .45   .20

Christmas

Genoa Madonna, Enameled Terra-Cotta by Luca Della Robbia (1400-1482) A1548

Poinsettia Plants A1549

1985, Oct. 30   **Photo.**
2165 A1548 22c multicolored   .40   .20
   a.   Imperf., pair   100.00
2166 A1549 22c multicolored   .40   .20
   a.   Imperf., pair   130.00

Arkansas Statehood, 150th Anniv.

Old State House, Little Rock A1550

1986, Jan. 3   **Photo.**   *Perf. 11*
2167 A1550 22c multicolored   .40   .20
   a.   Vert. pair, imperf. horiz.   —

Great Americans

A1551

A1552

A1553   A1554

 A1555   A1556
 A1557   A1558
A1559   A1560
 A1561   A1562
A1563   A1564
 A1565   A1566
 A1567   A1568
 A1569   A1570
 A1571   A1572
 A1573   A1574
 A1575   A1576

A1577

A1578

Perf. 11, 11½x11 (#2185), 11.1x11 (#2179)

			Engr.	
1986-94				
2168	A1551	1c brnsh ver	.20	.20
2169	A1552	2c bright blue	.20	.20
a.		Untagged	.20	.20
2170	A1553	3c bright blue	.20	.20
a.		Untagged	.20	.20
2171	A1554	4c blue violet	.20	.20
a.		4c grayish violet, untagged	.20	.20
b.		4c deep grayish blue, un-tagged	.20	.20
2172	A1555	5c dk ol grn	.20	.20
2173	A1556	5c carmine	.20	.20
a.		Untagged	.20	.20
2175	A1557	10c lake	.20	.20
e.		10c carmine	.25	.20
2176	A1558	14c crimson	.25	.20
2177	A1559	15c claret	.30	.20
d.		All color omitted	—	
2178	A1560	17c dull bl grn	.35	.20
2179	A1561	20c red brown	.40	.20
a.		20c orange brown	.40	.20
2180	A1562	21c blue vio	.40	.20
2181	A1563	23c purple	.45	.20
2182	A1564	25c blue	.45	.20
a.		Booklet pane of 10 ('88)	4.50	3.75
d.		Horiz. pair, imperf btwn.	—	
2183	A1565	28c myrtle grn	.50	.20
2184	A1566	29c blue	.55	.20
2185	A1567	29c indigo	.50	.20
2186	A1568	35c black	.65	.20
2187	A1569	40c dark blue	.70	.20
2188	A1570	45c bright blue	.85	.20
a.		45c blue	1.65	—
2189	A1571	52c purple	1.10	.20
2190	A1572	56c scarlet	1.10	.20
2191	A1573	65c dark blue	1.20	.20
2192	A1574	75c dp magenta	1.30	.20
2193	A1575	$1 dk Prus grn	2.50	.50
2194	A1576	$1 intense deep blue	1.75	.50
b.		$1 deep blue	1.75	.50
d.		$1 dark blue	1.75	.50
e.		$1 blue	1.75	.60
2195	A1577	$2 brt violet	3.50	.50
2196	A1578	$5 copper red	8.00	1.00
		Nos. 2168-2196 (28)	28.20	7.30

Booklet Stamp
Perf. 10 on 2 or 3 sides

2197	A1564	25c blue	.45	.20
a.		Booklet pane of 6	3.00	2.25

No. 2177d must be collected se-tenant with a partially printed stamp or longer horizontal strip.

The intense deep blue of No. 2194 is much deeper than the deep blue and dark blue of the other $1 varieties.

Issued: #2182, 1/11/86; #2172, 2/27/86; $2, 3/19/86; 17c, 6/18/86; 1c, 6/30/86; 4c, 7/14/86; 56c, 9/3/86; 3c, 9/15/86; #2193, 9/23/86; 14c, 2/12/87; 2c, 2/28/87; 10c, 8/15/87; $5, 8/25/87; #2183a, 2197, 5/3/88; 15c, 6/6/88; 45c, 6/17/88; 21c, 10/21/88; 23c, 11/4/88; 65c, 11/5/88; # 2197, 1988; #2194, 6/7/89; 28c, 9/14/89; #2173, 2/18/90; 40c, 9/6/90; #2188a, 2194b, 1990; 35c, 4/3/91; 52c, 6/3/91; 75c, 2/16/92; #2184, 3/9/92; #2194d, 1992; #2185, 4/13/93; #2171b, 2194e, 1993; 20c, 10/24/94; #2170a, 1994.

Stamp Collecting

Handstamped Cover, No. 213, Philatelic Memorabilia — A1581

Boy Examining Stamp Collection A1582

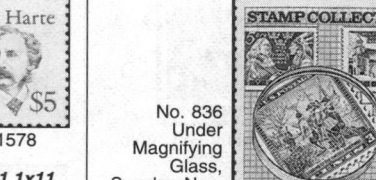
No. 836 Under Magnifying Glass, Sweden Nos. 268, 271 — A1583

1986 Presidents Miniature Sheet A1584

Perf. 10 Vert. on 1 or 2 Sides

1986, Jan. 23			**Litho. & Engr.**	
Booklet Stamps				
2198	A1581	22c multicolored	.45	.20
2199	A1582	22c multicolored	.45	.20
2200	A1583	22c multicolored	.45	.20
2201	A1584	22c multicolored	.45	.20
a.		Bklt. pane of 4, #2198-2201	2.00	1.75
b.		As "a," black omitted on #2198, 2201	65.00	
c.		As "a," blue (litho.) omitted on #2198-2200	2,500.	
d.		As "a," buff (litho.) omitted	2,500.	—

See Sweden Nos. 1585-1588.

A1585

A1586

Love

1986, Jan. 30		**Photo.**	**Perf. 11**	
2202	A1585	22c Puppy	.40	.20

Black Heritage Series

1986, Feb. 4		**Photo.**	**Perf. 11**	
2203	A1586	22c multicolored	.40	.20

Sojourner Truth (c. 1797-1883), abolitionist.

Republic of Texas, 150th Anniv.

Texas State Flag and Silver Spur — A1587

1986, Mar. 2			**Photo.**	
2204	A1587	22c dk bl, dk red & grysh blk	.40	.20
a.		Horiz. pair, imperf. vert.	1,100.	
b.		Dark red omitted	2,750.	
c.		Dark blue omitted	7,500.	

Fish

Muskellunge — A1588

Atlantic Cod A1589

Largemouth Bass — A1590

Bluefin Tuna A1591

Catfish A1592

Perf. 10 Horiz. on 1 or 2 Sides

1986, Mar. 21			**Photo.**	
Booklet Stamps				
2205	A1588	22c multicolored	.50	.20
2206	A1589	22c multicolored	.50	.20
2207	A1590	22c multicolored	.50	.20
2208	A1591	22c multicolored	.50	.20
2209	A1592	22c multicolored	.50	.20
a.		Bklt. pane of 5, #2205-2209	4.50	2.75
b.		As "a," red omitted		

Public Hospitals

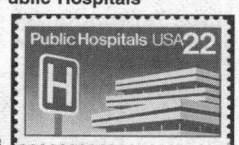
A1593

1986, Apr. 11		**Photo.**	**Perf. 11**	
2210	A1593	22c multicolored	.40	.20
a.		Vert. pair, imperf. horiz.	325.	
b.		Horiz. pair, imperf. vert.	1,350.	

Performing Arts

Edward Kennedy "Duke" Ellington (1899-1974), Jazz Composer — A1594

1986, Apr. 29		**Photo.**	**Perf. 11**	
2211	A1594	22c multicolored	.40	.20
a.		Vert. pair, imperf. horiz.	1,000.	—

Miniature Sheets

35 Presidents — A1599a

No. 2216: a, Washington. b, John Adams. c, Jefferson. d, Madison. e, Monroe. f, John Quincy Adams. g, Jackson. h, Van Buren. i, Harrison.

No. 2217; a, Tyler. b, Polk. c, Taylor. d, Fillmore. e, Pierce. f, Buchanan. g, Lincoln. h, Andrew Johnson. i, Grant.

No. 2218: a, Hayes. b, Garfield. c, Arthur. d, Cleveland. e, Harrison. f, McKinley. g, Theodore Roosevelt. h, Taft. i, Wilson.

No. 2219: a, Harding. b, Coolidge. c, Hoover. d, Franklin Delano Roosevelt. e, White House. f, Truman. g, Eisenhower. h, Kennedy. i, Lyndon B. Johnson.

1986, May 22			**Litho. & Engr.**	
2216	A1599a	Sheet of 9	4.25	—
a.-i.		22c any single	.45	.25
j.		Blue omitted	3,500.	
k.		Black inscription omitted	2,000.	
l.		Imperf.	10,500.	
2217	A1599b	Sheet of 9	4.25	—
a.-i.		22c any single	.45	—
j.		Black inscription omitted	3,750.	
2218	A1599c	Sheet of 9	4.25	—
a.-i.		22c any single	.45	.25
j.		Brown omitted		
k.		Black inscription omitted	2,900.	
2219	A1599d	Sheet of 9	4.25	—
a.-i.		22c any single	.45	.25
j.		Blackish blue (engr.) inscription omitted on a.-b., d.-e., g.-h.	—	
l.		Blackish blue (engr.) omitted	—	
		Nos. 2216-2219 (4)	17.00	

Issued at AMERIPEX '86 Intl. Phil. Exhib., Chicago, IL, May 22-June 1.

Arctic Explorers

Elisha Kent Kane A1600

Adolphus W. Greely A1601

Vilhjalmur Stefansson A1602

Robert E. Peary and Matthew Alexander Henson A1603

1986, May 28		**Photo.**	**Perf. 11**	
2220	A1600	22c multicolored	.65	.20
2221	A1601	22c multicolored	.65	.20
2222	A1602	22c multicolored	.65	.20

2223	A1603	22c multicolored	.65 .20
a.		Block of 4, #2220-2223	2.75 2.25
b.		As "a," blk (engr.) omitted	8,500.
c.		As "a," #2220 & 2221 black (engr.) omitted	—

Statue of Liberty, Cent. — A1604

1986, July 4   Engr.   Perf. 11

2224	A1604	22c scar & dk bl	.40 .20
a.		Scarlet omitted	—

See France No. 2014.

Transportation Coils
Types of 1982-85 and

A1604a   A1604b

1986-87   Engr.   Perf. 10 Vert.

2225	A1604a	1c violet	.20 .20
b.		Untagged	.20 .20
c.		Imperf., pair	2,000.
2226	A1604b	2c black ('87)	.20 .20
a.		Untagged	.20 .20
2228	A1285	4c reddish brown	.20 .20
b.		Imperf., pair	300.00
2231	A1511	8.3c grn (Bureau precancel)	.20 .20
		Nos. 2225-2231 (4)	.80 .80

Issued: 1c, 11/26; 2c, 3/6. Earliest known usage of 4c, 8/15/86; 8.3c, 8/29.
On No. 2228 "Stagecoach 1890s" is 17¾mm long, on No. 1898A 19¾mm long. On No. 2231 "Ambulance 1860s" is 18mm long, on No. 2128 18½mm long.
No. 2226 inscribed "2 USA;" No. 1897A inscribed "USA 2c."

America Folk Art Series
Navajo Art

A1605   A1606

A1607   A1608

Blankets in the Museum of the American Indian and Lowe Art Museum.

Litho. & Engr.

1986, Sept. 4   Perf. 11

2235	A1605	22c multicolored	.50 .20
2236	A1606	22c multicolored	.50 .20
2237	A1607	22c multicolored	.50 .20
2238	A1608	22c multicolored	.50 .20
a.		Block of 4, #2235-2238	2.50 2.00
b.		As "a," blk (engr.) omitted	350.00

Literary Arts

T. S. Eliot (1888-1965), Poet — A1609

1986, Sept. 26   Engr.   Perf. 11

2239	A1609	22c copper red	.40 .20

American Folk Art Series
Woodcarved Figurines

Highlander Figure   Ship Figurehead
A1610   A1611

Nautical Figure   Cigar Store Figure
A1612   A1613

1986, Oct. 1   Photo.   Perf. 11

2240	A1610	22c multicolored	.40 .20
2241	A1611	22c multicolored	.40 .20
2242	A1612	22c multicolored	.40 .20
2243	A1613	22c multicolored	.40 .20
a.		Block of 4, #2240-2243	1.75 1.75
b.		As "a," imperf. vert.	1,500.

Christmas

Madonna, by Perugino (c. 1450-1523)   Village Scene
A1614   A1615

1986, Oct. 24   Perf. 11

2244	A1614	22c multicolored	.40 .20
a.		Imperf., pair	800.00
2245	A1615	22c multicolored	.40 .20

Michigan Statehood Sesquicent.

White Pine — A1616

1987, Jan. 26   Photo.   Perf. 11

2246	A1616	22c multicolored	.40 .20

Pan American Games, Indianapolis, August 7-25

Runner in Full Stride A1617

1987, Jan. 29   Perf. 11

2247	A1617	22c multicolored	.40 .20
a.		Silver omitted	1,500.

No. 2247a is valued in the grade of fine.

A1618   A1619

Love

1987, Jan. 30   Photo.   Perf. 11½x11

2248	A1618	22c multicolored	.40 .20

Black Heritage Series

1987, Feb. 20   Photo.   Perf. 11

2249	A1619	22c multicolored	.40 .20

Jean Baptiste Pointe du Sable (c. 1750-1818), pioneer trader, founder of Chicago

A1620   A1621

Performing Arts Series
Photo. & Engr.

1987, Feb. 27   Perf. 11

2250	A1620	22c multicolored	.40 .20
a.		Black (engr.) omitted	5,000.

Enrico Caruso (1873-1921), Opera Tenor.

Girl Scouts, 75th Anniv.
Litho. & Engr.

1987, Mar. 12   Perf. 11

2251	A1621	22c 14 Achievement Badges	.40 .20
a.		All litho. colors omitted	2,500
b.		Red & black (engr.) omitted	2,000.

All known examples of No. 2251a have been expertized, and certificate must accompany purchase.
The unique pane of No. 2251b has been expertized, and a certificate exists for the pane of 50.

Transportation Coils

A1622   A1623

A1624   A1625

A1626   A1627

A1628   A1629

A1630   A1631

A1632   A1633

A1634   A1635

A1636

1987-88   Engr.   Perf. 10 Vert.

2252	A1622	3c claret	.20 .20
a.		Untagged	.20 .20
2253	A1623	5c black	.20 .20
2254	A1624	5.3c blk (Bureau precancel in scarlet)	.20 .20
2255	A1625	7.6c brn (Bureau precancel in scarlet)	.20 .20
2256	A1626	8.4c dp clar (Bureau precancel in red)	.20 .20
a.		Imperf., pair	700.00
2257	A1627	10c blue	.20 .20
e.		Imperf., pair	—
2258	A1628	13c blk (Bureau precancel in red)	.25 .25
2259	A1629	13.2c slate grn (Bureau precancel in red)	.25 .25
a.		Imperf., pair	100.00
2260	A1630	15c violet	.25 .20
c.		Imperf., pair	800.00
2261	A1631	16.7c rose (Bureau precancel in black)	.30 .30
a.		Imperf., pair	225.00

All known copies of No. 2261a are miscut top to bottom.

2262	A1632	17.5c dark violet	.30 .20
a.		Untagged (Bureau precancel)	.35 .30
b.		Imperf., pair	1,750.
2263	A1633	20c blue vio	.35 .20
a.		Imperf., pair	75.00
2264	A1634	20.5c rose (Bureau precancel in black)	.40 .40
2265	A1635	21c olive grn (Bureau precancel in red)	.40 .40
a.		Imperf., pair	65.00
2266	A1636	24.1c deep ultra (Bureau precancel)	.45 .45
		Nos. 2252-2266 (15)	4.15 3.85

The 5.3c, 7.6c, 8.4c, 13c, 13.2c, 16.7c, 20.5c, 21c and 24.1c are only available precanceled and are untagged.

Years of issue: 5c, 10c, 17.5c, 1987; others, 1988.
See Nos. 1897-1908, 2123-2136, 2225-2231, 2451-2468.

Special Occasions

Congratulations! 22 USA
A1637

Get Well! 22 USA
A1638

Thank You! 22 USA
A1639

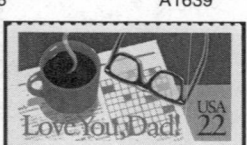
Love You, Dad! 22 USA
A1640

Best Wishes! 22 USA
A1641

Happy Birthday! USA 22
A1642

Love You, Mother! USA 22
A1643

Keep In Touch! 22 USA
A1644

Perf. 10 on 1, 2, or 3 sides

1987, Apr. 20   Photo.

Booklet Stamps

2267	A1637	22c multicolored	.60	.20
2268	A1638	22c multicolored	.75	.20
2269	A1639	22c multicolored	.75	.20
2270	A1640	22c multicolored	.75	.20
2271	A1641	22c multicolored	.75	.20
2272	A1642	22c multicolored	.60	.20
2273	A1643	22c multicolored	1.00	.20
2274	A1644	22c multicolored	.75	.20
a.		Bklt. pane of 8, #2268-2271, 2273-2274, 2 each #2267, 2272	8.00	5.00
		Nos. 2267-2274 (8)	5.95	1.60

United Way Centenary

United Way 1887-1987 Uniting Communities USA 22
Six Profiles
A1645

Litho. & Engr.

1987, Apr. 28   *Perf. 11*

2275	A1645	22c multicolored	.40	.20

22 USA
A1646

E Earth Domestic USA
A1647

USA 25
A1648

25 USA Yosemite
A1649

25 USA
Pheasant
A1649a

25 USA
Grosbeak
A1649b

25 USA
Owl
A1649c

25 USA
Honeybee
A1649d

Photo., Engr. (No. 2280), Litho. & Engr. (No. 2281)

1987-88   *Perf. 11*

2276	A1646	22c multi	.40	.20
a.		Booklet pane of 20	8.50	—
b.		As "a," vert. pair, imperf. btwn.	—	
2277	A1647	(25c) multi ('88)	.45	.20
2278	A1648	25c multi ('88)	.40	.20
		Nos. 2276-2278 (3)	1.25	.60

Coil Stamps

Perf. 10 Vertical

2279	A1647	(25c) multi ('88)	.45	.20
a.		Imperf., pair	90.00	—
2280	A1649	25c Green trees ('88)	.45	.20
c.		Imperf., pair	15.00	
e.		Black trees	100.00	—
f.		Pair, imperf. btwn.	800.00	
2281	A1649d	25c multi ('88)	.45	.20
a.		Imperf., pair	50.00	
b.		Black (engr.) omitted	60.00	
c.		Black (litho.) omitted	450.00	
d.		Pair, imperf. between	1,000.	
e.		Yellow (litho.) omitted	1,250.	
		Nos. 2279-2281 (3)	1.35	.60

Beware of copies with traces of the litho. black that are offered as No. 2281c. Vertical pairs or blocks of No. 2281 and imperfs. with the engr. black missing are from printer's waste.

No. 2280c is on prephosphored paper (mottled tagging). Imperfs are also known with large block tagging, value, unused pair, $35.

Booklet Stamps

Perf. 10 on 2 or 3 Sides, 11 on 2 or 3 sides (#2283)

2282	A1647	(25c) multi ('88)	.50	.20
a.		Booklet pane of 10	6.50	3.50

Vert. pairs, imperf between, are printer's waste. Other "varieties" probably exist.

2283	A1649a	25c multi ('88)	.50	.20
a.		Booklet pane of 10	6.00	3.50
b.		25c multi, red removed from sky	6.25	—
c.		As "b," booklet pane of 10	67.50	
d.		As "a," horiz. imperf. between	2,250.	

Imperfs. are printer's waste.

2284	A1649b	25c multi ('88)	.50	.20
2285	A1649c	25c multi ('88)	.50	.20
b.		Bklt. pane of 10, 5 each Nos. 2284-2285	5.00	3.50
		Pair, Nos. 2284-2285	1.10	.25
2285A	A1648	25c multi ('88)	.50	.20
c.		Booklet pane of 6	3.00	2.00
		Nos. 2282-2285A (5)	2.50	1.00

Issued: #2276, 5/9; #2277, 2279, 2282, 3/22; #2278, 5/6; #2280, 5/20; #2281, 9/2; #2283, 4/29; #2284-2285, 5/28; #2285A, 7/5.

22 USA Barn Swallow

North American Wildlife — A1650

1987, June 13   Photo.   *Perf. 11*

2286	A1650	22c Barn swallow	.85	.20
2287	A1651	22c Monarch butterfly	.85	.20
2288	A1652	22c Bighorn sheep	.85	.20
2289	A1653	22c Broad-tailed hummingbird	.85	.20
2290	A1654	22c Cottontail	.85	.20
2291	A1655	22c Osprey	.85	.20
2292	A1656	22c Mountain lion	.85	.20
2293	A1657	22c Luna moth	.85	.20
2294	A1658	22c Mule deer	.85	.20
2295	A1659	22c Gray squirrel	.85	.20
2296	A1660	22c Armadillo	.85	.20
2297	A1661	22c Eastern chipmunk	.85	.20
2298	A1662	22c Moose	.85	.20
2299	A1663	22c Black bear	.85	.20
2300	A1664	22c Tiger swallowtail	.85	.20
2301	A1665	22c Bobwhite	.85	.20
2302	A1666	22c Ringtail	.85	.20
2303	A1667	22c Red-winged blackbird	.85	.20
2304	A1668	22c American lobster	.85	.20
2305	A1669	22c Black-tailed jack rabbit	.85	.20
2306	A1670	22c Scarlet tanager	.85	.20
2307	A1671	22c Woodchuck	.85	.20
2308	A1672	22c Roseate spoonbill	.85	.20
2309	A1673	22c Bald eagle	.85	.20
2310	A1674	22c Alaskan brown bear	.85	.20
2311	A1675	22c Iiwi	.85	.20
2312	A1676	22c Badger	.85	.20
2313	A1677	22c Pronghorn	.85	.20
2314	A1678	22c River otter	.85	.20
2315	A1679	22c Ladybug	.85	.20
2316	A1680	22c Beaver	.85	.20
2317	A1681	22c White-tailed deer	.85	.20
2318	A1682	22c Blue jay	.85	.20
2319	A1683	22c Pika	.85	.20
2320	A1684	22c American Buffalo	.85	.20
2321	A1685	22c Snowy egret	.85	.20
2322	A1686	22c Gray wolf	.85	.20
2323	A1687	22c Mountain goat	.85	.20
2324	A1688	22c Deer mouse	.85	.20
2325	A1689	22c Black-tailed prairie dog	.85	.20
2326	A1690	22c Box turtle	.85	.20
2327	A1691	22c Wolverine	.85	.20
2328	A1692	22c American elk	.85	.20
2329	A1693	22c California sea lion	.85	.20
2330	A1694	22c Mockingbird	.85	.20
2331	A1695	22c Raccoon	.85	.20
2332	A1696	22c Bobcat	.85	.20
2333	A1697	22c Black-footed ferret	.85	.20
2334	A1698	22c Canada goose	.85	.20
2335	A1699	22c Red fox	.85	.20
a.		Pane of 50, #2286-2335	47.50	
b.		2286b-2335b, any single, red omitted	—	

Ratification of the Constitution

Dec 7, 1787 USA
Delaware 22
A1700

Dec 12, 1787 USA
Pennsylvania 22
A1701

Dec 18, 1787 USA
New Jersey 22
A1702

January 2, 1788
Georgia 22 USA
A1703

January 9, 1788
Connecticut 22 USA
A1704

Feb 6, 1788
Massachusetts 22 USA
A1705

April 28, 1788 USA
Maryland 22
A1706

May 23, 1788
South Carolina 25 USA
A1707

June 21, 1788 25 USA
New Hampshire
A1708

June 25, 1788 USA
Virginia 25
A1709

July 26, 1788 USA
New York 25
A1710

November 21, 1789
North Carolina 25 USA
A1711

May 29, 1790 25 USA
Rhode Island
A1712

Litho. & Engr., Photo. (#2337, 2343-2344, 2347)

1987-90   *Perf. 11*

2336	A1700	22c multi	.60	.20
2337	A1701	22c multi	.60	.20
2338	A1702	22c multi	.60	.20
a.		Black (engr.) omitted	5,500.	
2339	A1703	22c multi ('88)	.60	.20
2340	A1704	22c multi ('88)	.60	.20
2341	A1705	22c dk blue & dk red ('88)	.60	.20
2342	A1706	22c multi ('88)	.60	.20
2343	A1707	22c multi ('88)	.60	.20
a.		Strip of 3, vert. imperf. btwn.	—	
b.		Red omitted	—	
2344	A1708	25c multi ('88)	.60	.20
2345	A1709	25c multi ('88)	.60	.20
2346	A1710	25c multi ('88)	.60	.20
2347	A1711	25c multi ('89)	.60	.20
2348	A1712	25c multi ('90)	.60	.20
		Nos. 2336-2348 (13)	7.80	2.60

Issued: #2336, 7/4; #2337, 8/26; #2238, 9/11; #2339, 1/6; #2340, 1/9; #2341, 2/6; 32342, 2/15; #2343, 5/23; #2344, 6/21; #2345, 6/25; #2346, 7/26; # 2347, 8/22; #2348, 5/29.

US-Morocco Diplomatic Relations Bicentennial

Friendship with Morocco 1787-1987
USA 22
Arabesque, Dar Batha Palace, Fez — A1713

Litho. & Engr.

1987, July 18   *Perf. 11*

2349	A1713	22c scar & blk	.40	.20
a.		Black (engr.) omitted	275.00	

See Morocco No. 642.

Literary Arts

William Cuthbert Faulkner (1897-1962), Novelist — A1714

1987, Aug. 3   Engr.   Perf. 11
2350 A1714 22c bright green   .40   .20
    Imperfs. are from printer's waste.

American Folk Art Series
Lacemaking

A1715

A1716

A1717

A1718

Litho. & Engr.
1987, Aug. 14   Perf. 11
2351 A1715 22c ultra & white   .45   .20
2352 A1716 22c ultra & white   .45   .20
2353 A1717 22c ultra & white   .45   .20
2354 A1718 22c ultra & white   .45   .20
    a.   Block of 4, #2351-2354   1.90   1.90
    b.   As "a," white omitted   950.00

Drafting of the Constitution Bicentennial

A1719

A1720

A1721

A1722

A1723

Perf. 10 Horiz. on 1 or 2 Sides
1987, Aug. 28   Photo.
Booklet Stamps
2355 A1719 22c multicolored   .55   .20
    a.   Grayish grn (background) omitted   —
2356 A1720 22c multicolored   .55   .20
    a.   Grayish grn (background) omitted   —
2357 A1721 22c multicolored   .55   .20
    a.   Grayish grn (background) omitted   —
2358 A1722 22c multicolored   .55   .20
    a.   Grayish grn (background) omitted   —
2359 A1723 22c multicolored   .55   .20
    a.   Bklt. pane of 5, #2355-2359   2.75   2.25
    b.   Grayish grn (background) omitted   —

A1724

A1725

Signing of the Constitution
Litho. & Engr.
1987, Sept. 17   Perf. 11
2360 A1724 22c multicolored   .45   .20

Certified Public Accounting
1987, Sept. 21   Litho. & Engr.
2361 A1725 22c multicolored   1.90   .20
    a.   Black (engr.) omitted   725.00

Locomotives

Stourbridge Lion, 1829 — A1726

Best Friend of Charleston, 1830 — A1727

John Bull, 1831 A1728

Brother Jonathan, 1832 — A1729

Gowan & Marx, 1839 A1730

Perf. 10 Horiz. on 1 or 2 Sides
1987, Oct. 1
Booklet Stamps
2362 A1726 22c multicolored   .55   .20
2363 A1727 22c multicolored   .55   .20
2364 A1728 22c multicolored   .55   .20
2365 A1729 22c multicolored   .55   .20
    a.   Red omitted   —
2366 A1730 22c multicolored   .55   .20
    a.   Bklt. pane of 5, #2362-2366   2.75   2.50
    b.   As No. 2366, black (engr.) omitted (single)   —
    c.   As No. 2366, blue omitted (single)   —

Christmas

Moroni Madonna A1731

Christmas Ornaments A1732

1987, Oct. 23   Photo.   Perf. 11
2367 A1731 22c multicolored   .40   .20
2368 A1732 22c multicolored   .40   .20

1988 Winter Olympics, Calgary

Skiing — A1733

1988, Jan. 10   Photo.   Perf. 11
2369 A1733 22c multicolored   .40   .20

Australia Bicentennial

Caricature of Australian Koala & American Bald Eagle — A1734

1988, Jan. 10   Photo.   Perf. 11
2370 A1734 22c multicolored   .40   .20
    See Australia No. 1052.

Black Heritage Series

James Weldon Johnson, Author, Lyricist — A1735

1988, Feb. 2   Photo.   Perf. 11
2371 A1735 22c multicolored   .40   .20

Siamese, Exotic Shorthair A1736

Abyssinian, Himalayan A1737

Maine Coon, Burmese A1738

American Shorthair, Persian A1739

1988, Feb. 5   Perf. 11
2372 A1736 22c multicolored   .45   .20
2373 A1737 22c multicolored   .45   .20
2374 A1738 22c multicolored   .45   .20
2375 A1739 22c multicolored   .45   .20
    a.   Block of 4, #2372-2375   1.90   1.90

American Sports Issues

A1740

A1741

1988, Mar. 9   Litho. & Engr.
2376 A1740 22c multicolored   .40   .20
    Knute Kenneth Rockne (1888-1931), Notre Dame football coach.

1988, June 13   Photo.   Perf. 11
2377 A1741 25c multicolored   .45   .20
    Francis Ouimet (1893-1967), 1st amateur golfer to win the US Open Championship.

Love Issue

Rose — A1742

A1743

1988   Photo.   Perf. 11
2378 A1742 25c multicolored   .45   .20
    a.   Imperf., pair   3,000.
2379 A1743 45c multicolored   .65   .20
    Issue dates: 25c, July 4; 45c, Aug. 8.

1988 Summer Olympics, Seoul

Gymnastic Rings A1744

1988, Aug. 19   Photo.   Perf. 11
2380 A1744 25c multicolored   .45   .20

Classic Automobiles

1928 Locomobile — A1745

1929 Pierce-Arrow A1746

1931 Cord A1747

1932 Packard A1748

1935 Duesenberg — A1749

Perf. 10 Horiz. on 1 or 2 Sides
1988, Aug. 25 Litho. & Engr.
Booklet Stamps

2381	A1745	25c multicolored	.50	.20
2382	A1746	25c multicolored	.50	.20
2383	A1747	25c multicolored	.50	.20
2384	A1748	25c multicolored	.50	.20
2385	A1749	25c multicolored	.50	.20
a.	Bklt. pane of 5, #2381-2385	5.00	2.25
Nos. 2381-2385 (5)		2.50	1.00

Antarctic Explorers

Nathaniel Palmer (1799-1877) — A1750

Lt. Charles Wilkes (1798-1877) — A1751

Richard E. Byrd (1888-1957) — A1752

Lincoln Ellsworth (1880-1951) — A1753

1988, Sept. 14 Photo. ***Perf. 11***

2386	A1750	25c multicolored	.65	.20
2387	A1751	25c multicolored	.65	.20
2388	A1752	25c multicolored	.65	.20
2389	A1753	25c multicolored	.65	.20
a.	Block of 4, #2386-2389	2.75	2.00
b.	Black (engr.) omitted	1,500.	
c.	As "a," imperf. horiz.	3,000.	

Folk Art Series
Carousel Animals

Deer — A1754   Horse — A1755

Camel — A1756   Goat — A1757

1988, Oct. 1 Litho. & Engr. *Perf. 11*

2390	A1754	25c multicolored	.65	.20
2391	A1755	25c multicolored	.65	.20
2392	A1756	25c multicolored	.65	.20
2393	A1757	25c multicolored	.65	.20
a.	Block of 4, #2390-2393	3.00	2.00

Express Mail Rate

Eagle in Flight — A1758

1988, Oct. 4 Litho. & Engr. *Perf. 11*
2394 A1758 $8.75 multi 13.50 8.00

Special Occasions

Happy Birthday — A1759

Best Wishes — A1760

Thinking of You — A1761

Love You — A1762

Perf. 11 on 2 or 3 sides
1988, Oct. 22 Photo.
Booklet Stamps

2395	A1759	25c multicolored	.50	.20
2396	A1760	25c multicolored	.50	.20
a.	Bklt. pane of 6, 3 #2395 + 3 #2396 with gutter btwn.	3.50	3.25
2397	A1761	25c multicolored	.50	.20
2398	A1762	25c multicolored	.50	.20
a.	Bklt. pane of 6, 3 #2397 + 3 #2398 with gutter btwn.	3.50	3.25
b.	As "a," imperf. horiz.		
Nos. 2395-2398 (4)		2.00	.80

Madonna and Child, by Botticelli A1763   One-horse Open Sleigh & Village Scene A1764

Litho. & Engr., Photo. (No. 2400)
1988, Oct. 20 ***Perf. 11½***

2399	A1763	25c multicolored	.45	.20
a.	Gold omitted	30.00	
2400	A1764	25c multicolored	.45	.20

Montana Statehood Centennial

C.M. Russell and Friends, by Charles M. Russell (1865-1926) — A1765

Litho. & Engr.
1989, Jan. 15 ***Perf. 11***
2401 A1765 25c multicolored .45 .20

Imperfs without gum exist from printer's waste.

Black Heritage Series

Asa Philip Randolph (1889-1979), Labor & Civil Rights Leader — A1766

1989, Feb. 3 Photo. ***Perf. 11***
2402 A1766 25c multicolored .45 .20

North Dakota Statehood Centennial

A1767

1989, Feb. 21 ***Perf. 11***
2403 A1767 25c multicolored .45 .20

Washington Statehood Centennial

A1768

1989, Feb. 22 ***Perf. 11***
2404 A1768 25c multicolored .45 .20

Steamboats

Experiment, 1788-1790 — A1769

Phoenix, 1809 — A1770

New Orleans, 1812 — A1771

Washington, 1816 — A1772

Walk in the Water, 1818 — A1773

Perf. 10 Horiz. on 1 or 2 sides
1989, Mar. 3 Litho. & Engr.
Booklet Stamps

2405	A1769	25c multicolored	.45	.20
2406	A1770	25c multicolored	.45	.20
2407	A1771	25c multicolored	.45	.20
2408	A1772	25c multicolored	.45	.20
2409	A1773	25c multicolored	.45	.20
a.	Bklt. pane of 5, #2405-2409	2.25	1.75

A1774   A1775

World Stamp Expo '89
Nov. 17-Dec. 3, Washington, DC
Litho. & Engr.
1989, Mar. 16 ***Perf. 11***
2410 A1774 25c No. 122 .45 .20

Performing Arts
Arturo Toscanini (1867-1975), Italian Conductor
1989, Mar. 25 Photo. ***Perf. 11***
2411 A1775 25c multicolored .45 .20

Constitution Bicentennial

House of Representatives A1776   Senate A1777

Executive
Branch
A1778

Supreme Court
A1779

1989-90   Litho. & Engr.   Perf. 11
2412 A1776 25c multicolored   .50   .20
2413 A1777 25c multicolored   .50   .20
2414 A1778 25c multicolored   .50   .20
2415 A1779 25c multicolored   .50   .20
Nos. 2412-2415 (4)   2.00   .80
Issue dates: #2412, Apr. 4; #2413, Apr. 6; #2414, Apr. 16; #2415, Feb. 2, 1990.

South Dakota State Centenary

State Flower, Pioneer Woman & Sod
House on Grasslands
A1780

1989, May 3   Photo.   Perf. 11
2416 A1780 25c multicolored   .45   .20

American Sports

Henry Louis "Lou"
Gehrig (1903-1941),
Baseball Player for
the New York
Yankees — A1781

1989, June 10   Photo.   Perf. 11
2417 A1781 25c multicolored   .50   .20

Literary Arts

Ernest Hemingway
(1899-1961), Nobel
Prize-winner for
Literature,
1954 — A1782

1989, July 17   Photo.   Perf. 11
2418 A1782 25c multicolored   .45   .20
a.   Vert. pair, imperf. horiz.   —

Moon Landing, 20th Anniv.

Raising the
Flag on Lunar
Surface, July
20, 1969
A1783

Litho. & Engr.
1989, July 20   Perf. 11x11½
2419 A1783 $2.40 multicolored   4.00   2.00
a.   Black (engr.) omitted   2,500.
b.   Imperf., pair   750.00
c.   Black (litho.) omitted   3,250.

Natl. Assoc. of Letter Carriers, Cent.

Letter
Carriers
A1784

1989, Aug. 30   Photo.   Perf. 11
2420 A1784 25c multicolored   .45   .20

Constitution Bicentennial

Bill of
Rights — A1785

Litho. & Engr.
1989, Sept. 25   Perf. 11
2421 A1785 25c multicolored   .45   .20
a.   Black (engr.) omitted   325.00

Prehistoric Animals

Tyrannosaurus
Rex — A1786

Pteranodon
A1787

Stegosaurus
A1788

Brontosaurus
A1789

1989, Oct. 1   Litho. & Engr.   Perf. 11
2422 A1786 25c multicolored   .65   .20
2423 A1787 25c multicolored   .65   .20
2424 A1788 25c multicolored   .65   .20
2425 A1789 25c multicolored   .65   .20
a.   Block of 4, #2422-2425   3.00   2.00
b.   As "a," blk (engr.) omitted   750.00
The correct name for "Brontosaurus" is "Apatosaurus."
No. 2425b is valued in the grade of fine.

Pre-Columbian America Issue

Southwest Carved
Figure, A. D. 1150-
1350 — A1790

Emblem of the Postal Union of the Americas and Spain (UPAE) and Southwestern Wood-carved Ritual Figure, Mogollon Culture, Mimbres Period, a Forerunner of the Hopi Indian Kachina Doll, A.D. 1150-1350.

1989, Oct. 12   Photo.   Perf. 11
2426 A1790 25c multicolored   .45   .20
Discovery of America, 500th anniv. (in 1992). See No. C121.

Christmas

Madonna and
Child, by
Caracci
A1791

Sleigh Full of
Presents
A1792

Litho. & Engr.
1989, Oct. 19   Perf. 11½
2427 A1791 25c multicolored   .45   .20
a.   Booklet pane of 10   4.75   3.50
b.   Red (litho.) omitted   850.00
c.   As "a," imperf.   —

Photo.
Perf. 11
2428 A1792 25c multicolored   .45   .20
a.   Vert. pair, imperf. horiz.   2,000.

Booklet Stamp
Perf. 11½ on 2 or 3 sides
2429 A1792 25c multicolored   .45   .20
a.   Booklet pane of 10   4.75   3.50
b.   As "a," imperf. horiz.   —
c.   Vert. pair, imperf. horiz.   —
d.   As "a," red omitted   —
e.   Imperf., pair   —

Marked differences exist between Nos. 2428 and 2429: The runners on the sleigh in No. 2429 are twice as thick as those in No. 2428; in No. 2429 the package at upper left in the sleigh has a red bow, whereas the same package in No. 2428 has a red and black bow; and the ribbon on the upper right package in No. 2429 is green, whereas the same ribbon in No. 2428 is black.

Eagle and
Shield — A1793

1989, Nov. 10   Photo.   Die Cut
Self-Adhesive
2431 A1793 25c multicolored   .50   .20
a.   Booklet pane of 18   11.00
b.   Vert. pair, no die cutting between   850.00
c.   Pair, no die cutting   —
Issued unfolded in panes of 18; peelable paper backing is booklet cover. Sold for $5.
Also available in strips of 18 with stamps spaced for use in affixing machines to service first day covers. Sold for $5.
Sold in 15 test cities and through the philatelic agency only.

Souvenir Sheet

World Stamp Expo, Washington, DC,
Nov. 17-Dec. 3 — A1794

Litho. & Engr.   Litho. & Engr.
1989, Nov. 17   Imperf.
2433 A1794   Sheet of 4   14.00   9.00
a.   90c like No. 122   2.00   1.75
b.   90c like No. 132TC (blue frame, brown center)   2.00   1.75
c.   90c like No. 132TC (green frame, blue center)   2.00   1.75
d.   90c like No. 132TC (scarlet frame, blue center)   2.00   1.75

Traditional Mail Delivery

Stagecoach, c.
1850 — A1795

Paddlewheel
Steamer
A1796

Biplane — A1797

Depot-hack Type
Automobile
A1798

Litho. & Engr.
1989, Nov. 19   Perf. 11
2434 A1795 25c multicolored   .45   .20
2435 A1796 25c multicolored   .45   .20
2436 A1797 25c multicolored   .45   .20
2437 A1798 25c multicolored   .45   .20
a.   Block of 4, #2434-2437   2.00   2.00
b.   As "a," dark blue (engr.) omitted   700.00
No. 2437b is valued in the grade of fine. Very fine blocks exist and sell for somewhat more.

1989, Nov. 28   Imperf.
2438   Sheet of 4   4.00   1.75
a.   A1795 25c multicolored   .65   .25
b.   A1796 25c multicolored   .65   .25
c.   A1797 25c multicolored   .65   .25
d.   A1798 25c multicolored   .65   .25
e.   Dark blue & gray (engr.) omitted   5,500.
20th Universal Postal Union Congress.

VALUES FOR HINGED STAMPS AFTER NO. 771
This catalogue does not value unused stamps after No. 771 in hinged condition. Hinged unused stamps from No. 772 to the present are worth considerably less than the values given for unused stamps, which are for never-hinged examples.

Idaho State Centenary

Mountain Bluebird,
Sawtooth
Mountains — A1799

1990, Jan. 6   Photo.   Perf. 11
2439 A1799 25c multicolored   .45   .20

Love Issue

A1800

1990, Jan. 18   Photo.   Perf. 12½x13
2440 A1800 25c brt bl, dk pink
     & emer grn   .45 .20
  a. Imperf., pair   800.00

Booklet Stamp
Perf. 11½ on 2 or 3 sides
2441 A1800 25c ultra, brt pink
     & dk grn   .45 .20
  a. Booklet pane of 10 4.75 3.50
  b. As "a," bright pink omitted 1,900.
  c. As "b," single stamp 180.

No. 2441c may be obtained from booklet panes containing both normal and color-omitted stamps.

Black Heritage Series

Ida B. Wells (1862-1931), Journalist — A1801

1990, Feb. 1   Photo.   Perf. 11
2442 A1801 25c multicolored .45 .20

Beach Umbrella — A1802

1990, Feb. 3   Photo.   Perf. 11
Booklet Stamp
2443 A1802 15c multicolored .30 .20
  a. Booklet pane of 10 3.00 2.00
  b. As "a," blue omitted 1,750.
  c. As No. 2443, blue omitted 170.

Wyoming State Centenary

High Mountain Meadows, by Conrad Schwiering
A1803

Litho. & Engr.
1990, Feb. 23   **Perf. 11**
2444 A1803 25c multicolored .45 .20
  a. Black (engr.) omitted 2,250.

Classic Films

The Wizard of Oz — A1804

Gone With the Wind — A1805

Beau Geste — A1806

Stagecoach A1807

1990, Mar. 23   Photo.   Perf. 11
2445 A1804 25c multicolored 1.00 .20
2446 A1805 25c multicolored 1.00 .20
2447 A1806 25c multicolored 1.00 .20
2448 A1807 25c multicolored 1.00 .20
  a. Block of 4, #2445-2448 4.50 3.50

Literary Arts Series

Marianne Craig Moore (1887-1972), Poet — A1808

1990, Apr. 18   Photo.   Perf. 11
2449 A1808 25c multicolored .45 .20
  a. All colors omitted   —

No. 2449a must be collected se-tenant with a partially printed stamp or in a larger horizontal strip.

TRANSPORTATION ISSUE

 A1810   A1811

 A1811a   A1812

 A1816   A1822

 A1823   A1825

A1827

Engr., Photo. (#2452B, 2452D, 2454, 2458)
1990-95 Coil Stamps   Perf. 9.8 Vert.
Untagged: #2452B, 2452D, 2453, 2454, & 10c
2451 A1810 4c claret   .20 .20
  a. Imperf., pair   700.00
  b. Untagged   .20 .20
2452 A1811 5c carmine .20 .20
  a. Untagged   .20 .20
  c. Imperf., pair   900.00
2452B A1811 5c carmine .20 .20
2452D A1811a 5c carmine .20 .20
  e. Imperf., pair   —

2453 A1812 5c brn (Bureau precancel in gray) .20 .20
  a. Imperf., pair   350.00
  b. Gray omitted   —
2454 A1812 5c red (Bureau precancel in gray) .20 .20
2457 A1816 10c grn (Bureau precancel in gray) .20 .20
  a. Imperf., pair   350.00
2458 A1816 10c grn (Bureau precancel in black) .20 .20
2463 A1822 20c green   .40 .20
  a. Imperf., pair   150.00
2464 A1823 23c dark blue .45 .20
  a. Imperf., pair   175.00
2466 A1825 32c blue   .60 .20
  a. Imperf., pair   —
  b. 32c bright blue 6.00 4.50
2468 A1827 $1 bl & scar 1.75 .50
  a. Imperf., pair   2,500. —
   Nos. 2451-2468 (12) 4.80 2.70

Issued: $1, 4/20; #2452, 8/31; 4c, 1/25/91; #2453, 2457, 5/25/91; #2454, 10/22/91; 23c, 4/12/91; #2452B, 12/8/92; #2458, 5/25/94; #2452D, 3/20/95; 32c, 6/2/95; #2463, 6/9/95.
This is an expanding set. Numbers will change if necessary.
Some pairs of No. 2468 appear to be imperf but have some blind perfs on the gum. Beware of copies with the gum removed.

Lighthouses

Admiralty Head, WA — A1829

Cape Hatteras, NC — A1830

West Quoddy Head, ME — A1831

American Shoals, FL — A1832

Sandy Hook, NJ — A1833

Perf. 10 Vert. on 1 or 2 Sides
1990, Apr. 26   Litho. & Engr.
Booklet Stamps
2470 A1829 25c multicolored 1.00 .20
2471 A1830 25c multicolored 1.00 .20
2472 A1831 25c multicolored 1.00 .20
2473 A1832 25c multicolored 1.00 .20
2474 A1833 25c multicolored 1.00 .20
  a. Bklt. pane, #2470-2474 5.50 2.00
  b. As "a," white (USA 25) omitted 80.00

Flag

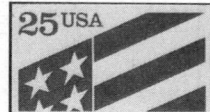

A1834

1990, May 18   Photo.   Die Cut
Self-adhesive
2475 A1834 25c dk red & dk bl .50 .25
  a. Pane of 12   6.00

Sold only in panes of 12; peelable plastic backing inscribed in light ultramarine. Available for a test period of six months at 22 First National Bank automatic teller machines in Seattle.

Flora and Fauna Series

American Kestrel
A1840   A1841

Eastern Bluebird A1842   Fawn A1843

Cardinal A1844   Pumpkinseed Sunfish A1845

Bobcat A1846

Perf. 11, 11.2 (#2477)
1990-95   **Litho.**
2476 A1840 1c multicolored .20 .20
2477 A1841 1c multicolored .20 .20
2478 A1842 3c multicolored .20 .20
  a. Vert. pair, imperf horiz. —
  b. Double impression of all colors except yellow —

Photo.
Perf. 11½x11
2479 A1843 19c multicolored .35 .20
  b. Red omitted   850.00

On No. 2479b other colors are shifted.
2480 A1844 30c multicolored .50 .20

Litho. & Engr.
Perf. 11
2481 A1845 45c multicolored .80 .20
  a. Black (engr.) omitted 525.00
2482 A1846 $2 multicolored 3.00 1.25
  a. Black (engr.) omitted 300.00
   Nos. 2476-2482 (7) 5.25 2.45

Issued: $2, 6/1/90; 19c, 3/11/91; 3c, 30c, #2476, 6/22/91; 45c, 12/2/92; #2477, 5/10/95.
See Nos. 3031, 3044. Compare design A1842 with A2336.

Blue Jay — A1847   Wood Duck — A1848

African Violets A1849   Peach A1850

Pear
A1851

Red Squirrel
A1852

Rose — A1853

Pine
Cone — A1854

Booklet Stamps

1991-95   **Perf. 10.9x9.8**

2483	A1847 20c multicolored	.50	.20
a.	Booklet pane of 10	5.25	2.25
b.	As "a," imperf	—	

See No. 3053.

Perf. 10 on 2 or 3 Sides

2484	A1848 29c blk & multi	.50	.20
a.	Booklet pane of 10	5.50	3.75
b.	Vert. pair, imperf. between		

Perf. 11 on 2 or 3 Sides

2485	A1848 29c red & multi	.50	.20
a.	Booklet pane of 10	5.50	4.00
b.	Vert. pair, imperf btwn.		
c.	Imperf, pair		

Perf. 10x11 on 2 or 3 Sides

2486	A1849 29c multicolored	.50	.20
a.	Booklet pane of 10	5.50	4.00
2487	A1850 32c multicolored	.60	.20
2488	A1851 32c multicolored	.60	.20
a.	Bkt. pane, 5 #2488b	6.00	4.25
b.	Pair, #2487-2488	1.25	.30

Issued: #2484-2485, 4/12/91; #2486, 10/8/93; 20c, 6/15/95; 32c 7/8/95.

Booklet Stamps

1993-95   **Photo.**

Self-Adhesive *Serpentine Die Cut*

2489	A1852 29c multicolored	.50	.20
a.	Booklet pane of 18	10.00	
b.	As "a," die cutting omitted		
2490	A1853 29c red, green & black	.50	.20
a.	Booklet pane of 18	10.00	
2491	A1854 29c multicolored	.50	.20
a.	Booklet pane of 18	11.00	
b.	Horiz. pair, no die cutting between	—	
c.	Coil with plate #B1	—	4.00

Serpentine Die Cut 11¼x11¾ on 2, 3 or 4 sides

2492	A1853 32c pk, grn & blk ('95)	.60	.20
a.	Booklet pane of 20+label	12.00	
b.	Bklt. pane of 15+label ('96)	8.75	
c.	Horiz. pair, no die cutting between	—	
d.	As "a," 2 stamps and parts of 7 others printed on backing liner	—	
e.	Booklet pane of 14	21.00	
f.	Booklet pane of 16	21.00	
g.	Coil with plate #S111	—	3.25
h.	Vert. pair, no die cutting between	—	

Serpentine Die Cut 8.8 on 2, 3 or 4 sides

2493	A1850 32c multi ('95)	.60	.20
2494	A1851 32c multi ('95)	.60	.20
a.	Booklet pane, 10 each #2493-2494+label	12.50	
b.	Pair, #2493-2494	1.20	

Coil Stamps

Serpentine Die Cut 8.8 Vert.

2495	A1850 32c multi ('95)	.60	.20
2495A	A1851 32c multi ('95)	.60	.20
b.	Pair, #2495-2495A	1.25	

Except for #2491c and 2492g with plate numbers, coil stamps of these issues are indistinguishable from booklet stamps once they are removed from the backing paper.
Issued: #2489, 6/25; #2490, 8/19; #2491, 11/5.
See Nos. 3048-3049, 3053-3054.

Scott values for used self-adhesive stamps are for examples either on piece or off piece.

Olympians

Jesse Owens, 1936
A1855

Ray Ewry, 1900-08
A1856

Hazel Wightman, 1924
A1857

Eddie Eagan, 1920, 1932
A1858

Helene Madison, 1932
A1859

1990, July 6   **Photo.**   **Perf. 11**

2496	A1855 25c multicolored	.60	.20
2497	A1856 25c multicolored	.60	.20
2498	A1857 25c multicolored	.60	.20
2499	A1858 25c multicolored	.60	.20
2500	A1859 25c multicolored	.60	.20
a.	Strip of 5, 2496-2500	3.25	2.50
b.	As "a," blue omitted		

Indian Headdresses

Assiniboin
A1860

Cheyenne
A1861

Comanche
A1862

Flathead
A1863

Shoshone
A1864

Perf. 11 on 2 or 3 sides

1990, Aug. 17   **Litho. & Engr.**

Booklet Stamps

2501	A1860 25c multicolored	.55	.20
2502	A1861 25c multicolored	.55	.20
2503	A1862 25c multicolored	.55	.20
2504	A1863 25c multicolored	.55	.20
2505	A1864 25c multicolored	.55	.20
a.	Bklt. pane, 2 ea #2501-2505	5.50	3.50
b.	As "a," blk (engr.) omitted	3,250.	
c.	Strip of 5, #2501-2505	2.75	1.00
d.	As "a," horiz. imperf. btwn.	—	

Micronesia, Marshall Islands

Canoe & Federated States of Micronesia Flag
A1865

Stick Chart, Canoe & Republic of the Marshall Islands Flag
A1866

1990, Sept. 28   **Perf. 11**

2506	A1865 25c multicolored	.45	.20
2507	A1866 25c multicolored	.45	.20
a.	Pair, #2506-2507	.90	.60
b.	As "a," blk (engr.) omitted	3,000.	

See Micronesia Nos. 124-126 and Marshall Islands No. 381.

Sea Creatures

Killer Whales
A1867

Northern Sea Lions
A1868

Sea Otter
A1869

Common Dolphin
A1870

1990, Oct. 3   **Litho. & Engr.**   **Perf. 11**

2508	A1867 25c multicolored	.45	.20
2509	A1868 25c multicolored	.45	.20
2510	A1869 25c multicolored	.45	.20
2511	A1870 25c multicolored	.45	.20
a.	Block of 4, #2508-2511	1.90	1.75
b.	As "a," blk (engr.) omitted	750.00	

See Russia Nos. 5933-5936.

Pre-Columbian America Issue

Grand Canyon
A1871

1990, Oct. 12   **Photo.**   **Perf. 11**

2512	A1871 25c multicolored	.45	.20

Dwight David Eisenhower

A1872

1990, Oct. 13   **Photo.**   **Perf. 11**

2513	A1872 25c multicolored	.60	.20
a.	Imperf., pair	2,250.	

Christmas

Madonna and Child by Antonello da Messina
A1873

Christmas Tree
A1874

Litho. & Engr.

1990, Oct. 18   **Perf. 11½**

2514	A1873 25c multicolored	.45	.20
a.	Booklet pane of 10	5.00	3.25

Photo.

Perf. 11

2515	A1874 25c multicolored	.45	.20
a.	Vert. pair, imperf horiz.	1,100.	

Perf. 11½x11 on 2 or 3 Sides

2516	A1874 25c multicolored	.45	.20
a.	Booklet pane of 10	5.00	3.25
	Nos. 2514-2516 (3)	1.35	.60

Marked differences exist between Nos. 2515 and 2516. The background red on No. 2515 is even while that on No. 2516 is splotchy. The bands across the tree and "GREETINGS" are blue green on No. 2515 and yellow green on No. 2516.

A1875

A1876

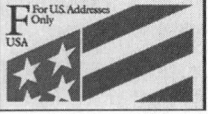

A1877

1991, Jan. 22   **Photo.**   **Perf. 13**

2517	A1875 (29c) yel, blk, red & yel grn	.50	.20
a.	Imperf., pair	750.00	
b.	Horiz. pair, imperf. vert.	1,250.	

Do not confuse No. 2517a with No. 2518a. See note after No. 2518.

Coil Stamp

Perf. 10 Vert.

2518	A1875 (29c) yel, blk, dull red & dk yel grn	.50	.20
a.	Imperf., pair	42.50	

"For U.S. addresses only" is 17½mm long on No. 2517, 16½mm long on No. 2518. Design of No. 2517 measures 21½x17½mm, No. 2518, 21x18mm.

Booklet Stamps
Perf. 11 on 2 or 3 Sides

2519 A1875 (29c) yel, blk, dull red & dk grn .50 .20
  a. Booklet pane of 10 6.50 4.50
2520 A1875 (29c) pale yel, blk, red & brt grn .50 .20
  a. Booklet pane of 10 18.00 4.50
  As "a," imperf horiz.

No. 2519 has bullseye perforations that measure approximately 11.2. No. 2520 has less pronounced black lines in the leaf, which is a much brighter green than on No. 2519.

Litho.
Perf. 11
2521 A1876 (4c) bister & car .20 .20
  a. Vert. pair, imperf. horiz. 110.00
  b. Imperf., pair 75.00

Photo.
Imperf., Die Cut
Self-Adhesive
2522 A1877 (29c) blk, dk blue & red .50 .25
  a. Pane of 12 7.00

No. 2522 sold only in panes of 12; peelable plastic backing inscribed in light ultramarine. Available during a test period at 22 First National Bank automatic teller machines in Seattle.

Flag Over Mt. Rushmore A1878

Flower A1879

1991, Mar. 29 Engr. Perf. 10 Vert.
Coil Stamps
2523 A1878 29c bl, red & cl .50 .20
  b. Imperf., pair 25.00
  c. Blue, red & brown 5.00 —

Photo.
2523A A1878 29c bl, red & brn .50 .20

On No. 2523A, USA and 29 are not outlined in white and appear farther from edge of design.
Issued: #2523, Mar. 29; #2523A, July 4.

1991-92 Photo. Perf. 11
2524 A1879 29c dull yel, blk, red & pale yel grn .50 .20
Perf. 13x12¾
2524A A1879 29c dull yel, blk, red & yel grn .75 .20

Coil Stamps
Roulette 10 Vert.
2525 A1879 29c pale yel, blk, red & yel grn .50 .20
Perf. 10 Vert.
2526 A1879 29c pale yel, blk, red & yel grn .50 .20

Perf. 11 on 2 or 3 Sides
Booklet Stamp
2527 A1879 29c pale yel, blk, red & brt grn .50 .20
  a. Booklet pane of 10 5.50 3.50
  b. As "a," imperf. vert. 1,500.
  c. Horiz. pair, imperf. vert. 300.
  d. As "a," imperf horiz. 2,750.

Flower on Nos. 2524-2524A has grainy appearance, inscriptions look rougher.
Issue dates: #2524, 2524A, 2527, Apr. 5; #2525, Aug. 16; #2526, Mar. 3, 1992.

Flag, Olympic Rings — A1880

Perf. 11 on 2 or 3 Sides
1991, Apr. 21 Photo.
Booklet Stamp
2528 A1880 29c multicolored .50 .20
  a. Booklet pane of 10 5.25 3.50
  b. As "a," horiz. imperf btwn., perfed at top and bottom —

  c. Vert. pair, imperf btwn, perfed at top and bottom —
  d. Vert. pair, imperf btwn —
  e. Vert. strip of 3, top or bottom pair imperf between —
  Vert. pair, imperf horiz. 2,000.

No. 2528c comes from the misperfed booklet pane of No. 2528b. No. 2528d resulted from paper foldovers after normal perforating and before cutting into panes. Two No. 2528d are known.
No. 2528e is valued in the grade of fine.

Fishing Boat A1881   Balloon A1882

1991-94 Photo. Perf. 9.8 Vert.
Coil Stamps
2529 A1881 19c multicolored .35 .20
  a. Type II ('93) .35 .20
  b. As "a," untagged ('93) 1.00 .40
2529C A1881 19c multicolored .50 .20

Design of Type II stamps is created by a finer dot pattern. The vertical sides of "1" are smooth on Type II and jagged on Type I stamps.
No. 2529C has one loop of rope tying boat to piling, numerals and USA are taller and thinner.
Issued: #2529, 8/8/91; #2529C, 6/25/94.

Perf. 10 on 2 or 3 Sides
1991, May 17 Photo.
Booklet Stamp
2530 A1882 19c multicolored .35 .20
  a. Booklet pane of 10 3.50 2.75

Flags on Parade A1883   Liberty Torch A1884

1991, May 30 Photo. Perf. 11
2531 A1883 29c multicolored .50 .20

1991, June 25 Photo. Die Cut
Booklet Pane
Self-Adhesive
2531A A1884 29c blk, gold & grn .55 .25
  b. Booklet pane of 18 10.50
  c. Pair, imperf

Switzerland, 700th Anniv.

A1887

1991, Feb. 22 Photo. Perf. 11
2532 A1887 50c multicolored 1.00 .25
  a. Vert. pair, imperf horiz. 2,250.

Imperfs exist from printers' waste.
See Switzerland No. 888.

A1888   A1889

Vermont Statehood Bicentennial
1991, Mar. 1 Perf. 11
2533 A1888 29c multicolored .55 .20

Savings Bonds, 50th Anniv.
1991, Apr. 30 Photo. Perf. 11
2534 A1889 29c multicolored .50 .20

Love

A1890   A1891

1991, May 9 Photo. Perf. 12½x13
2535 A1890 29c multicolored .50 .20
  b. Imperf., pair

Perf. 11
2535A A1890 29c multicolored .75 .20

Perf. 11 on 2 or 3 Sides
Booklet Stamp
2536 A1890 29c multicolored .50 .20
  a. Booklet pane of 10 5.25 3.50

"29" is closer to edge of design on No. 2536 than on No. 2535.

Perf. 11
2537 A1891 52c multicolored .90 .20

Literary Arts Series

William Saroyan A1892

1991, May 22 Photo. Perf. 11
2538 A1892 29c multicolored .50 .20
See Russia No. 6002.

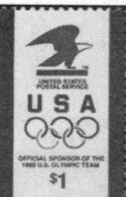
Eagle, Olympic Rings — A1893

1991, Sept. 29 Photo. Perf. 11
2539 A1893 $1 gold & multi 1.75 .50
  a. Black omitted

A1894

A1895

A1896

1991 Litho. & Engr. Perf. 11
Untagged (#2541-2542)
2540 A1894 $2.90 Priority 5.00 2.50
  a. Vert. pair, imperf horiz. —
2541 A1895 $9.95 Domestic express 15.00 7.50
  a. Imperf., pair
2542 A1896 $14 Intl. express 22.50 10.00
  a. Red (engr. inscriptions) omitted 1,500.
Nos. 2540-2542 (3) 42.50 20.00

Both Nos. 2540 and 2541 exist imperf and with color missing from printer's waste.
Issued: $2.90, 7/7; $9.95, 6/16; $14, 8/31.

Priority Mail Rate

Futuristic Space Shuttle A1897

Space Shuttle Challenger A1898

Litho. & Engr.
1993, June 3 Perf. 11x10½
2543 A1897 $2.90 multicolored 5.00 2.25

Litho. & Engr.
1995, June 22 Perf. 11.2
2544 A1898 $3 dated "1995" 5.25 2.25
  b. Dated "1996" 5.25 2.25
  c. Horiz. pair, imperf between
  d. As "b," imperf., pair 2,250.

Express Mail Rate

Space Shuttle Endeavour A1898a

Litho. & Engr.
1995, Aug. 4 Perf. 11
2544A A1898a $10.75 multi 17.50 7.50

Fishing Flies

Royal Wulff A1899

Jock Scott A1900

Apte Tarpon Fly A1901

Lefty's
Deceiver
A1902

Muddler
Minnow
A1903

Perf. 11 Horiz. on 1 or 2 Sides
1991, May 31   Photo.
Booklet Stamps

2545	A1899 29c multicolored	1.00	.20
a.	Black omitted	—	
2546	A1900 29c multicolored	1.00	.20
a.	Black omitted	—	
2547	A1901 29c multicolored	1.00	.20
a.	Black omitted	—	
2548	A1902 29c multicolored	1.00	.20
2549	A1903 29c multicolored	1.00	.20
a.	Bklt. pane of 5, #2545-2549	5.50	2.50

Horiz. pairs, imperf. vert., exist from printers' waste.

A1904   A1905

Performing Arts
Cole Porter (1891-1964), Composer
1991, June 8   Photo.   Perf. 11

2550	A1904 29c multicolored	.50	.20
a.	Vert. pair, imperf. horiz.	650.00	

Operations Desert Shield & Desert Storm
1991, July 2   Photo.   Perf. 11

2551	A1905 29c Southwest Asia service medal	.50	.20
a.	Vert. pair, imperf horiz.	1,500.	

No. 2551 is 21mm wide.

Perf. 11 Vert. on 1 or 2 Sides
Booklet Stamp

2552	A1905 29c multicolored	.50	.20
a.	Booklet pane of 5	2.75	2.25

No. 2552 is 20½mm wide. Inscriptions are shorter than on No. 2551.

Summer Olympics

Pole Vault
A1907

Discus
A1908

Women's
Sprints
A1909

Javelin
A1910

Women's
Hurdles
A1911

1991, July 12   Photo.   Perf. 11

2553	A1907 29c multicolored	.50	.20
2554	A1908 29c multicolored	.50	.20
2555	A1909 29c multicolored	.50	.20
2556	A1910 29c multicolored	.50	.20
2557	A1911 29c multicolored	.50	.20
a.	Strip of 5, #2553-2557	2.75	2.25

Numismatics

1858 Flying Eagle Cent, 1907 Standing Liberty Double Eagle, Series 1875 $1 Note, Series 1902 $10 National Currency Note — A1912

Litho. & Engr.
1991, Aug. 13   Perf. 11

2558	A1912 29c multicolored	.50	.20

World War II

A1913

Designs and events of 1941: a, Military vehicles (Burma Road, 717-mile lifeline to China). b, Recruits (America's 1st peacetime draft). c, Shipments for allies (US supports allies with Lend-Lease Act). d, Roosevelt, Churchill (Atlantic Charter sets war aims of allies). e, Tank (America becomes the "arsenal of democracy"). f, Sinking of Destroyer Reuben James, Oct. 31. g, Gas mask, helmet (Civil defense mobilizes Americans at home). h, Liberty Ship, sea gull (1st Liberty ship delivered Dec. 30). i, Sinking ships (Japanese bomb Pearl Harbor, Dec. 7). j, Congress in session (US declares war on Japan, Dec. 8). Central label is the size of 15 stamps and shows world map, extent of Axis control.

Illustration reduced.

Litho. & Engr.
1991, Sept. 3   Perf. 11

2559	A1913 Block of 10	5.25	4.50
a.-j.	29c any single	.50	.30
k.	Black (engr.) omitted	10,000.	

No. 2559 has selvage at left and right and either top or bottom.

Basketball, 100th Anniversary

Basketball, Hoop,
Players'
Arms — A1914

1991, Aug. 28   Photo.   Perf. 11

2560	A1914 29c multicolored	.55	.20

District of Columbia Bicentennial

Capitol Building from Pennsylvania
Avenue, Circa 1903 — A1915

Litho. & Engr.
1991, Sept. 7   Perf. 11

2561	A1915 29c multicolored	.50	.20
a.	Black (engr.) omitted	125.00	

Comedians

Stan Laurel
and Oliver
Hardy
A1916

Edgar
Bergen and
Charlie
McCarthy
A1917

Jack Benny
A1918

Fanny Brice
A1919

Bud Abbott
and Lou
Costello
A1920

Perf. 11 on 2 or 3 Sides
1991, Aug. 29   Litho. & Engr.
Booklet Stamps

2562	A1916 29c multicolored	.50	.20
2563	A1917 29c multicolored	.50	.20
2564	A1918 29c multicolored	.50	.20
2565	A1919 29c multicolored	.50	.20
2566	A1920 29c multicolored	.50	.20
a.	Bklt. pane, 2 ea #2562-2566	5.50	3.50
b.	As "a," scarlet & bright violet (engr.) omitted	700.00	—
c.	Strip of 5, #2562-2566	2.50	—

Black Heritage Series

Jan E. Matzeliger
(1852-1889),
Inventor — A1921

1991, Sept. 15   Photo.   Perf. 11

2567	A1921 29c multicolored	.50	.20
a.	Horiz. pair, imperf. vert.	1,500.	
b.	Vert. pair, imperf. horiz.	1,500.	
c.	Imperf, pair	1,250.	

Space Exploration

Mercury,
Mariner 10
A1922

Venus,
Mariner 2
A1923

Earth,
Landsat
A1924

Moon,
Lunar
Orbiter
A1925

Mars,
Viking
Orbiter
A1926

Jupiter,
Pioneer 11
A1927

Saturn,
Voyager 2
A1928

Uranus,
Voyager 2
A1929

Neptune,
Voyager 2
A1930

Pluto
A1931

Perf. 11 on 2 or 3 Sides
1991, Oct. 1   Photo.
Booklet Stamps

2568	A1922 29c multicolored	.85	.20
2569	A1923 29c multicolored	.85	.20
2570	A1924 29c multicolored	.85	.20
2571	A1925 29c multicolored	.85	.20
2572	A1926 29c multicolored	.85	.20
2573	A1927 29c multicolored	.85	.20
2574	A1928 29c multicolored	.85	.20
2575	A1929 29c multicolored	.85	.20
2576	A1930 29c multicolored	.85	.20
2577	A1931 29c multicolored	.85	.20
a.	Bklt. pane of 10, #2568-2577	9.00	3.50

Christmas

Madonna and Child by Antoniazzo Romano A1933

Santa Claus in Chimney A1934

Santa Checking List — A1935

Santa with Present — A1936

Santa at Fireplace — A1937

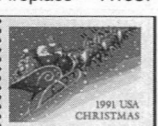

Santa and Sleigh — A1938

Litho. & Engr.

1991, Oct. 17   *Perf. 11*
2578 A1933 (29c) multicolored   .50   .20
   a.   Booklet pane of 10   5.75   3.25
   b.   As "a," single, red & black
      (engr.) omitted   3,500.

Photo.
2579 A1934 (29c) multicolored   .50   .20
   a.   Horiz. pair, imperf. vert.   325.00
   b.   Vert. pair, imperf. horiz.   525.00

Booklet Stamps

Size: 25x18½mm

Perf. 11 on 2 or 3 Sides
2580 A1934 (29c) Type I   1.75   .20
2581 A1934 (29c) Type II   1.75   .20
   a.   Pair, #2580, 2581   3.50   .25
   b.   Bklt. pane, 2 each #2580,
      2581   7.50   1.25
2582 A1935 (29c) multicolored   .50   .20
   a.   Booklet pane of 4   2.00   1.25
2583 A1936 (29c) multicolored   .50   .20
   a.   Booklet pane of 4   2.00   1.25
2584 A1937 (29c) multicolored   .50   .20
   a.   Booklet pane of 4   2.00   1.25
2585 A1938 (29c) multicolored   .50   .20
   a.   Booklet pane of 4   2.00   1.25
    Nos. 2578-2585 (8)   6.50   1.60

The extreme left brick in top row of chimney is missing from Type II, No. 2581.

A1939

A1942

A1944

James K. Polk (1795-1849)

1995, Nov. 2   Engr.   *Perf. 11.2*
2587 A1939 32c red brown   .60   .20

Surrender of Gen. John Burgoyne

1994, May 5   Engr.   *Perf. 11.5*
2590 A1942 $1 blue   1.90   .50

Washington and Jackson

1994, Aug. 19   Engr.   *Perf. 11.5*
2592 A1944 $5 slate green   8.00   2.50

Pledge of Allegiance A1946

Eagle and Shield A1947

A1950

Statue of Liberty — A1951

Perf. 10 on 2 or 3 sides

1992-93   **Photo.**

Booklet Stamps
2593 A1946 29c blk & multi   .50   .20
   a.   Booklet pane of 10   5.25   4.25

Perf. 11x10 on 2 or 3 Sides
2593B A1946 29c black & multi   1.00   .50
   c.   Bklt. pane of 10   10.00   6.00
2594 A1946 29c red & multi   .50   .20
   a.   Booklet pane of 10   5.25   4.25
   b.   Imperf., pair   900.00

Denomination is red on #2594 and black on #2593.
   Issued: #2593, 2593B, Sept. 8; #2594, 1993.

Litho. & Engr.1992-94 Litho. & Engr. *Die Cut*

Self-Adhesive
2595 A1947 29c brown & multi   .50   .25
   a.   Bklt. pane of 17 + label   13.00
   b.   Pair, no die cutting   225.00
   c.   Brown (engr.) omitted   475.00
   d.   As "a," no die cutting   1,800.

Photo.
2596 A1947 29c green & multi   .50   .25
   a.   Bklt. pane of 17 + label   12.00
2597 A1947 29c red & multi   .50   .25
   a.   Bklt. pane of 17 + label   10.00
2598 A1950 29c red, cream &
      blue   .50   .20
   a.   Booklet pane of 18   10.00
   b.   Coil with plate #111   —   3.50
2599 A1951 29c multicolored   .50   .20
   a.   Booklet pane of 18   10.00
   b.   Coil with plate #D111   —   3.75

Plate No. and inscription reads down on No. 2595a and up on Nos. 2596a-2597a. Design is sharper and more finely detailed on Nos. 2595, 2597.
Except for #2598b and 2599b with plate numbers, coil stamps of these issues are indistinguishable from booklet stamps once they are removed from the backing paper.
Issued unfolded in panes of 17 + label; peelable paper backing is booklet cover. Sold for $5.
Issue dates: No. 2598, Feb. 4, 1994; No. 2599, June 24, 1994; others, Sept. 25, 1992.
See Nos. 3122, 3122E.

A1956

A1957

A1959

A1960

Flag Over White House — A1961

1991-93   Photo.   *Perf. 10 Vert.*

Coil Stamps
2602 A1956 (10c) multi   .20   .20
   a.   Imperf., pair   —
2603 A1957 (10c) orange yel
      & multi   .20   .20
   a.   Imperf., pair   30.00
   b.   Tagged   2.00   1.50
2604 A1957 (10c) gold &
      multi   .20   .20
2605 A1959 23c multi (Bu-
      reau pre-
      cancel in
      blue)   .40   .40
2606 A1960 23c multi (Bu-
      reau Pre-
      canceled)   .40   .40
2607 A1960 23c multi (Bu-
      reau pre-
      canceled)   .40   .40
   c.   Imperf., pair   100.00
2608 A1960 23c vio blue,
      red & blk
      (Bureau
      Precan-
      celed)   .40   .40
   a.   Imperf., pair   .40   .40

"First Class" is 9½mm long on No. 2606, 9mm long on No. 2607, and 8½mm long on No. 2608.

Engr.
2609 A1961 29c blue & red   .50   .20
   a.   Imperf., pair   20.00
   b.   Pair, imperf between   100.00
    Nos. 2602-2609 (8)   2.70   2.40

Issued: #2602, 12/13/91; #2603-2604, 5/29/93; #2605, 9/27/91; #2606, 7/21/92; #2607, 10/9/92; #2608, 5/14/93; 29c, 4/23/92.
See Nos. 2907, 3270-3271.

Winter Olympics

Hockey A1963

Figure Skating A1964

Speed Skating A1965

Skiing A1966

Bobsledding A1967

1992, Jan. 11   Photo.   *Perf. 11*
2611 A1963 29c multicolored   .50   .20
2612 A1964 29c multicolored   .50   .20
2613 A1965 29c multicolored   .50   .20

2614 A1966 29c multicolored   .50   .20
2615 A1967 29c multicolored   .50   .20
   a.   Strip of 5, #2611-2615   2.75   2.25

A1968

A1969

World Columbian Stamp Expo

1992, Jan. 24   Litho. & Engr.
2616 A1968 29c Detail from #129   .50   .20

Black Heritage Series
Litho. & Engr.

1992, Jan. 31   *Perf. 11*
2617 A1969 29c multicolored   .50   .20

W.E.B. Du Bois (1868-1963), writer and civil rights leader.

Love

A1970

1992, Feb. 6   Photo.   *Perf. 11*
2618 A1970 29c multicolored   .50   .20
   a.   Horiz. pair, imperf vert.   800.00
   b.   As "a," green omitted

Olympic Baseball

A1971

1992, Apr. 3   Photo.   *Perf. 11*
2619 A1971 29c multicolored   .50   .20

Voyages of Columbus

Seeking Queen Isabella's Support A1972

Crossing the Atlantic A1973

Approaching Land — A1974

Coming Ashore A1975

Litho. & Engr.

1992, Apr. 24			Perf. 11	
2620	A1972	29c multicolored	.50	.20
2621	A1973	29c multicolored	.50	.20
2622	A1974	29c multicolored	.50	.20
2623	A1975	29c multicolored	.50	.20
a.		Block of 4, #2620-2623	2.00	1.90

See Italy Nos. 1877-1880.

Voyages of Columbus
Souvenir Sheets

A1976

A1977

A1978

A1979

A1980

A1981

Illustrations reduced.

Margins on Nos. 2624-2628 are lithographed. Nos. 2624a-2628c, 2629 are similar in design to Nos. 230-245 but are dated 1492-1992.

Litho. & Engr.

1992, May 22			Perf. 10½	
2624	A1976	Sheet of 3	1.75	—
a.	A71	1c deep blue	.20	.20
b.	A74	4c ultramarine	.20	.20
c.	A82	$1 salmon	1.65	1.00
2625	A1977	Sheet of 3	6.75	—
a.	A72	2c brown violet	.20	.20
b.	A73	3c green	.20	.20
c.	A85	$4 crimson lake	6.50	4.00
2626	A1978	Sheet of 3	1.40	—
a.	A75	5c chocolate	.20	.20
b.	A80	30c orange brown	.50	.30
c.	A81	50c slate blue	.80	.50
2627	A1979	Sheet of 3	5.25	—
a.	A76	6c purple	.20	.20
b.	A77	8c magenta	.20	.20
c.	A84	$3 yellow green	4.75	3.00
2628	A1980	Sheet of 3	3.75	—
a.	A78	10c black brown	.20	.20
b.	A79	15c dark green	.25	.20
c.	A83	$2 brown red	3.25	2.00
2629	A1981	Sheet of 1	8.50	—
a.	A86	$5 black, single stamp	8.00	5.00
		Nos. 2624-2629 (6)	27.40	

See Italy Nos. 1883-1888, Portugal Nos. 1918-1923 and Spain Nos. 2677-2682.

Imperforate examples are known of all the Columbus souvenir sheets, but these are not listed in this catalogue. Their appearance several years after the issue date, in substantial quantities of all six sheets at the same time and, evidently, from a single source, with many small faults such as wrinkles and light creases that are not normally seen on these sheets, raises serious concerns about the legitimacy of these imperforate sheets as issued errors.

These circumstances have led the Scott editors to adopt the position that these imperforate sheets are indeed almost certainly printer's waste rather than issued errors. While it is possible that actual imperforate errors of one or more of the sheets may exist that were legitimately sold by the USPS, it is not possible to separate these (should they exist) from the many more numerous examples that apparently are printer's waste.

New York Stock Exchange Bicentennial

A1982

Litho. & Engr.

1992, May 17			Perf. 11	
2630	A1982	29c grn, red & blk	.50	.20
a.		Black omitted		

Space Accomplishments

Cosmonaut, US Space Shuttle A1983

Astronaut, Russian Space Station A1984

Sputnik, Vostok, Apollo Command & Lunar Modules A1985

Soyuz, Mercury and Gemini Spacecraft A1986

1992, May 29		Photo.	Perf. 11	
2631	A1983	29c multicolored	.50	.20
2632	A1984	29c multicolored	.50	.20
2633	A1985	29c multicolored	.50	.20
2634	A1986	29c multicolored	.50	.20
a.		Block of 4, 2631-2634	2.00	1.75

See Russia Nos. 6080-6083.

Alaska Highway, 50th Anniversary

A1987

Litho. & Engr.

1992, May 30			Perf. 11	
2635	A1987	29c multicolored	.50	.20
a.		Black (engr.) omitted	500.00	

Most known examples of No. 2635a have poor to fine centering. It is valued in the grade of fine. Very fine examples sell for much more.

Kentucky Statehood Bicentennial

A1988

1992, June 1		Photo.	Perf. 11	
2636	A1988	29c multicolored	.50	.20
a.		Dark blue omitted	—	
b.		Dark blue and red omitted	—	
c.		All colors omitted	—	

Nos. 2636a-2636c must be collected se-tenant with normal stamps.

Summer Olympics

Soccer A1989

Gymnastics A1990

Volleyball A1991

Boxing A1992

Swimming A1993

1992, June 11		Photo.	Perf. 11	
2637	A1989	29c multicolored	.50	.20
2638	A1990	29c multicolored	.50	.20
2639	A1991	29c multicolored	.50	.20
2640	A1992	29c multicolored	.50	.20
2641	A1993	29c multicolored	.50	.20
a.		Strip of 5, #2637-2641	2.50	2.25

Hummingbirds

Ruby-throated A1994

Broad-billed A1995

Costa's A1996

Rufous A1997

Calliope — A1998

Perf. 11 Vert. on 1 or 2 sides

1992, June 15			Photo.	
		Booklet Stamps		
2642	A1994	29c multicolored	.50	.20
2643	A1995	29c multicolored	.50	.20
2644	A1996	29c multicolored	.50	.20
2645	A1997	29c multicolored	.50	.20
2646	A1998	29c multicolored	.50	.20
a.		Bklt. pane of 5, #2642-2646	2.75	2.25

Wildflowers

A1999

1992, July 24		Litho.	Perf. 11	
2647	A1999	29c Indian paint-brush	.50	.20
2648	A2000	29c Fragrant water lily	.50	.20
2649	A2001	29c Meadow beauty	.50	.20

2650	A2002	29c	Jack-in-the-pulpit	.50 .20
2651	A2003	29c	California poppy	.50 .20
2652	A2004	29c	Large-flowered trillium	.50 .20
2653	A2005	29c	Tickseed	.50 .20
2654	A2006	29c	Shooting star	.50 .20
2655	A2007	29c	Stream violet	.50 .20
2656	A2008	29c	Bluets	.50 .20
2657	A2009	29c	Herb Robert	.50 .20
2658	A2010	29c	Marsh marigold	.50 .20
2659	A2011	29c	Sweet white violet	.50 .20
2660	A2012	29c	Claret cup cactus	.50 .20
2661	A2013	29c	White mountain avens	.50 .20
2662	A2014	29c	Sessile bellwort	.50 .20
2663	A2015	29c	Blue flag	.50 .20
2664	A2016	29c	Harlequin lupine	.50 .20
2665	A2017	29c	Twinflower	.50 .20
2666	A2018	29c	Common sunflower	.50 .20
2667	A2019	29c	Sego lily	.50 .20
2668	A2020	29c	Virginia bluebells	.50 .20
2669	A2021	29c	Ohi'a lehua	.50 .20
2670	A2022	29c	Rosebud orchid	.50 .20
2671	A2023	29c	Showy evening primrose	.50 .20
2672	A2024	29c	Fringed gentian	.50 .20
2673	A2025	29c	Yellow lady's slipper	.50 .20
2674	A2026	29c	Passionflower	.50 .20
2675	A2027	29c	Bunchberry	.50 .20
2676	A2028	29c	Pasqueflower	.50 .20
2677	A2029	29c	Round-lobed hepatica	.50 .20
2678	A2030	29c	Wild columbine	.50 .20
2679	A2031	29c	Fireweed	.50 .20
2680	A2032	29c	Indian pond lily	.50 .20
2681	A2033	29c	Turk's cap lily	.50 .20
2682	A2034	29c	Dutchman's breeches	.50 .20
2683	A2035	29c	Trumpet honeysuckle	.50 .20
2684	A2036	29c	Jacob's ladder	.50 .20
2685	A2037	29c	Plains prickly pear	.50 .20
2686	A2038	29c	Moss campion	.50 .20
2687	A2039	29c	Bearberry	.50 .20
2688	A2040	29c	Mexican hat	.50 .20
2689	A2041	29c	Harebell	.50 .20
2690	A2042	29c	Desert five spot	.50 .20
2691	A2043	29c	Smooth Solomon's seal	.50 .20
2692	A2044	29c	Red maids	.50 .20
2693	A2045	29c	Yellow skunk cabbage	.50 .20
2694	A2046	29c	Rue anemone	.50 .20
2695	A2047	29c	Standing cypress	.50 .20
2696	A2048	29c	Wild flax	.50 .20
a.			Pane of 50, #2647-2696	25.00 —

World War II

A2049

Designs and events of 1942:
a, B-25's take off to raid Tokyo, Apr. 18. b, Ration coupons (food and other commodities rationed). c, Divebomber and deck crewman (U.S. wins Battle of the Coral Sea, May). d, Prisoners of war (Corregidor falls to Japanese, May 6). e, Dutch Harbor buildings on fire (Japan invades Aleutian Islands, June). f, Headphones, coded message (Allies decipher secret enemy codes). g, Yorktown lost, U.S. wins at Midway. h, Woman with drill (millions of women join war effort). i, Marines land on Guadalcanal, Aug. 7. j, Tank in desert (Allies land in North Africa, Nov.).
Central label is the size of 15 stamps and shows world map, extent of axis control.
Illustration reduced.

Litho. & Engr.

1992, Aug. 17				**Perf. 11**
2697	A2049		Block of 10	5.25 4.50
a.-j.		29c	any single	.50 .30
k.			Red (litho.) omitted	8,000.

No. 2697 has selvage at left and right and either top or bottom.

A2050   A2051

Literary Arts Series
Dorothy Parker

1992, Aug. 22		**Photo.**		**Perf. 11**
2698	A2050	29c	multicolored	.50 .20

Dr. Theodore von Karman

1992, Aug. 31		**Photo.**		**Perf. 11**
2699	A2051	29c	multicolored	.50 .20

Von Karman (1881-1963), rocket scientist.

Minerals

Azurite — A2052

Copper — A2053

Variscite A2054

Wulfenite A2055

Litho. & Engr.

1992, Sept. 17				**Perf. 11**
2700	A2052	29c	multicolored	.50 .20
2701	A2053	29c	multicolored	.50 .20
2702	A2054	29c	multicolored	.50 .20
2703	A2055	29c	multicolored	.50 .20
a.			Block or strip, #2700-2703	2.00 1.75
b.			As "a," silver (litho.) omitted	8,500.
c.			As "a," red (litho.) omitted	—
d.			As "a," silver omitted on two stamps	—

Juan Rodriguez Cabrillo

Cabrillo, Ship, Map of San Diego Bay Area — A2056

Litho. & Engr.

1992, Sept. 28				**Perf. 11**
2704	A2056	29c	multicolored	.50 .20
a.			Black (engr.) omitted	3,000.

Wild Animals

Giraffe A2057

Giant Panda A2058

Flamingo A2059

King Penguins A2060

White Bengal Tiger A2061

Perf. 11 Horiz. on 1 or 2 sides

1992, Oct. 1				**Photo.**
Booklet Stamps				
2705	A2057	29c	multicolored	.50 .20
2706	A2058	29c	multicolored	.50 .20
2707	A2059	29c	multicolored	.50 .20
2708	A2060	29c	multicolored	.50 .20
2709	A2061	29c	multicolored	.50 .20
a.			Booklet pane, #2705-2709	2.50 2.00
b.			As "a," imperforate	3,000.

Christmas

Madonna and Child, by Giovanni Bellini — A2062

A2063

A2064

A2065

A2066

1992		**Litho. & Engr.**		**Perf. 11.2**
2710	A2062	29c	multicolored	.50 .20
a.			Booklet pane of 10	5.25 3.50
Litho.				
				Perf. 11½x11
2711	A2063	29c	multicolored	.50 .20
2712	A2064	29c	multicolored	.50 .20
2713	A2065	29c	multicolored	.50 .20
2714	A2066	29c	multicolored	.50 .20
a.			Block of 4, #2711-2714	2.00 1.10

Booklet Stamps
Photo.
Perf. 11 on 2 or 3 Sides

2715	A2063	29c	multicolored	.85 .20
2716	A2064	29c	multicolored	.85 .20
2717	A2065	29c	multicolored	.85 .20
2718	A2066	29c	multicolored	.85 .20
a.			Bklt. pane of 4, #2715-2718	3.50 1.25
b.			As "a," imperf horiz.	—
c.			As "a," imperf	—

Self-Adhesive
Die Cut

2719	A2064	29c	multicolored	.60 .20
a.			Booklet pane of 18	11.00

"Greetings" is 27mm long on Nos. 2711-2714, 25mm long on Nos. 2715-2718 and 21½mm long on No. 2719. Nos. 2715-2719 differ in color from Nos. 2711-2714.
Issued: #2710-2718, 10/22; #2719, 10/28.

Chinese New Year

Year of the Rooster A2067

Litho. & Engr.

1992, Dec. 30				**Perf. 11**
2720	A2067	29c	multicolored	.50 .20

American Music Series

Elvis Presley A2068

Oklahoma! A2069

Hank Williams A2070

Elvis Presley A2071

Bill Haley A2072

Clyde
McPhatter
A2073

Ritchie
Valens
A2074

Otis
Redding
A2075

Buddy
Holly
A2076

Dinah
Washington
A2077

1993, Jan. 8   Photo.   Perf. 11
2721 A2068 29c multicolored   .50 .20
  a.   Imperf, pair   —

1993, Mar. 30   Photo.   Perf. 10
2722 A2069 29c multicolored   .50 .20

1993, June 9
2723 A2070 29c multicolored   .50 .20
Perf. 11.2x11.5
2723A A2070 29c multicolored   22.50 9.00

1993, June 16
2724 A2071 29c multicolored   .60 .20
2725 A2072 29c multicolored   .60 .20
2726 A2073 29c multicolored   .60 .20
2727 A2074 29c multicolored   .60 .20
2728 A2075 29c multicolored   .60 .20
2729 A2076 29c multicolored   .60 .20
2730 A2077 29c multicolored   .60 .20
  a.   Vert. strip, #2724-2730   4.25 —
Booklet Stamps
Perf. 11 Horiz.
2731 A2071 29c multicolored   .50 .20
2732 A2072 29c multicolored   .50 .20
2733 A2073 29c multicolored   .50 .20
2734 A2074 29c multicolored   .50 .20
2735 A2075 29c multicolored   .50 .20
2736 A2076 29c multicolored   .50 .20
2737 A2077 29c multicolored   .50 .20
  a.   Booklet pane, 2 #2731, 1 each
          #2732-2737   4.25 2.25
  b.   Booklet pane of 4, #2731,
          2735-2737 + tab   2.25 1.50

See Nos. 2769, 2771, 2775 and designs
A2112-A2117.

Space Fantasy

A2086   A2087

A2088   A2089

A2090

Perf. 11 Vert. on 1 or 2 Sides
1993, Jan. 25   Photo.
Booklet Stamps
2741 A2086 29c multicolored   .50 .20
2742 A2087 29c multicolored   .50 .20
2743 A2088 29c multicolored   .50 .20
2744 A2089 29c multicolored   .50 .20
2745 A2090 29c multicolored   .50 .20
  a.   Bklt. pane of 5, #2741-2745   2.50 2.25

Black Heritage Series

Percy Lavon Julian
(1899-1975),
Chemist — A2091

Litho. & Engr.
1993, Jan. 29   Perf. 11
2746 A2091 29c multicolored   .50 .20

Oregon Trail

          A2092

Litho. & Engr.
1993, Feb. 12   Perf. 11
2747 A2092 29c multicolored   .50 .20

World University Games

A2093

1993, Feb. 25   Photo.   Perf. 11
2748 A2093 29c multicolored   .50 .20

Grace Kelly (1929-1982)

Actress, Princess of
Monaco — A2094

1993, Mar. 24   Engr.   Perf. 11
2749 A2094 29c blue   .50 .20

See Monaco No. 1851.

Circus

Clown — A2095

Ringmaster
A2096

Trapeze
Artist — A2097

Elephant
A2098

Illustrations reduced.

1993, Apr. 6   Litho.   Perf. 11
2750 A2095 29c multicolored   .55 .20
2751 A2096 29c multicolored   .55 .20
2752 A2097 29c multicolored   .55 .20
2753 A2098 29c multicolored   .55 .20
  a.   Block of 4, #2750-2753   2.25 1.75

Cherokee Strip Land Run, Centennial

A2099

Litho. & Engr.
1993, Apr. 17   Perf. 11
2754 A2099 29c multicolored   .50 .20

Dean Acheson (1893-1971)

Secretary of
State — A2100

1993, Apr. 21   Engr.   Perf. 11
2755 A2100 29c greenish gray   .50 .20

Sporting Horses

Steeplechase — A2101

Thoroughbred Racing — A2102

Harness
Racing
A2103

Polo
A2104

Litho. & Engr.
1993, May 1   Perf. 11x11½
2756 A2101 29c multicolored   .50 .20
2757 A2102 29c multicolored   .50 .20
2758 A2103 29c multicolored   .50 .20
2759 A2104 29c multicolored   .50 .20
  a.   Block of 4, #2756-2759   2.00 1.75
  b.   As "a," black (engr.) omitted   1,250.

Garden Flowers

Hyacinth   Daffodil
A2105   A2106

Tulip — A2107   Iris — A2108

Lilac — A2109

Litho. & Engr.

1993, May 15			Perf. 11 Vert.
2760	A2105	29c multicolored	.50 .20
2761	A2106	29c multicolored	.50 .20
2762	A2107	29c multicolored	.50 .20
2763	A2108	29c multicolored	.50 .20
2764	A2109	29c multicolored	.50 .20
a.		Booklet pane, #2760-2764	2.50 2.00
b.		As "a," blk (engr.) omitted	250.00
c.		As "a," imperf	2,500.

World War II

A2110

Designs and events of 1943:
a, Destroyers (Allied forces battle German U-boats). b, Military medics treat the wounded. c, Amphibious landing craft on beach (Sicily attacked by Allied forces, July). d, B-24s hit Ploesti refineries, August. e, V-mail delivers letters from home. f, PT boat (Italy invaded by Allies, Sept.). g, Nos. WS7, WS8, savings bonds (Bonds and stamps help war effort). h, "Willie and Joe" keep spirits high. i, Banner in window (Gold Stars mark World War II losses). j, Marines assault Tarawa, Nov.
Central label is the size of 15 stamps and shows world map with extent of Axis control and Allied operations.
Illustration reduced.

Litho. & Engr.

1993, May 31			Perf. 11
2765	A2110	Block of 10 + label	5.25 4.50
a.-j.		29c any single	.50 .30

No. 2765 has salvage at left and right and either top or bottom.

Joe Louis (1914-1981)

A2111

Litho. & Engr.

1993, June 22			Perf. 11
2766	A2111	29c multicolored	.50 .20

American Music Series
Oklahoma! Type and

Show Boat
A2112

Porgy & Bess
A2113

My Fair Lady
A2114

Perf. 11 Horiz. on 1 or 2 Sides

1993, July 14			Photo.
Booklet Stamps			
2767	A2112	29c multicolored	.50 .20
2768	A2113	29c multicolored	.50 .20
2769	A2069	29c multicolored	.50 .20
2770	A2114	29c multicolored	.50 .20
a.		Booklet pane, #2767-2770	2.50 2.00

No. 2769 has smaller design size, brighter colors and shorter inscription than No. 2722, as well as a frameline around the design and other subtle design differences.

Hank Williams Type and

Patsy Cline
A2115

The Carter Family
A2116

Bob Wills
A2117

1993, Sept. 25		Photo.	Perf. 10
2771	A2070	29c multicolored	.55 .20
2772	A2115	29c multicolored	.55 .20
2773	A2116	29c multicolored	.55 .20
2774	A2117	29c multicolored	.55 .20
a.		Block or horiz. strip of 4, #2771-2774	2.20 1.75

Booklet Stamps
Perf. 11 Horiz.
With Black Frameline

2775	A2070	29c multicolored	.50 .20
2776	A2116	29c multicolored	.50 .20
2777	A2115	29c multicolored	.50 .20
2778	A2117	29c multicolored	.50 .20
a.		Booklet pane, #2775-2778	2.50 2.00
b.		As "a," imperf	—

Inscription at left measures 27mm on No. 2771, 27 ½mm on No. 2723 and 22mm on No. 2775. No. 2723 shows only two tuning keys on guitar, while No. 2771 shows those two and parts of two others.

National Postal Museum

Independence Hall, Benjamin Franklin, Printing Press, Colonial Post Rider — A2118

Pony Express Rider, Civil War Soldier, Concord Stagecoach A2119

JN-4H Biplane, Charles Lindbergh, Railway Mail Car, 1931 Model A Ford Mail Truck
A2120

California Gold Rush Miner's Letter, Nos. 39, 295, C3a, C13, Barcode & Circular Date Stamp
A2121

Litho. & Engr.

1993, July 30			Perf. 11
2779	A2118	29c multicolored	.50 .20
2780	A2119	29c multicolored	.50 .20
2781	A2120	29c multicolored	.50 .20
2782	A2121	29c multicolored	.50 .20
a.		Block or strip of 4, #2779-2782	2.00 1.75
b.		As "a," engr. maroon (USA/29) & black ("My Dear...") omitted	—
c.		As "a," imperf	3,500.

American Sign Language

A2122

A2123

1993, Sept. 20		Photo.	Perf. 11½
2783	A2122	29c multicolored	.50 .20
2784	A2123	29c multicolored	.50 .20
a.		Pair, #2783-2784	1.00 .65

Classic Books

A2124

A2125

A2126

A2127

Designs: No. 2785, Rebecca of Sunnybrook Farm, by Kate Douglas Wiggin. No. 2786, Little House on the Prairie, by Laura Ingalls Wilder. No. 2787, The Adventures of Huckleberry Finn, by Mark Twain. No. 2788, Little Women, by Louisa May Alcott.

Litho. & Engr.

1993, Oct. 23			Perf. 11
2785	A2124	29c multicolored	.50 .20
2786	A2125	29c multicolored	.50 .20
2787	A2126	29c multicolored	.50 .20
2788	A2127	29c multicolored	.50 .20
a.		Block or horiz. strip of 4, #2785-2788	2.00 1.75
b.		As "a," imperf	3,000.

Christmas

Madonna and Child in a Landscape, by Giovanni Battista Cima — A2128

Jack-in-the-Box
A2129

Red-Nosed Reindeer
A2130

Snowman
A2131

Toy Soldier Blowing Horn
A2132

Litho. & Engr.

1993, Oct. 21			Perf. 11
2789	A2128	29c multicolored	.50 .20

Booklet Stamp
Size: 18x25mm
Perf. 11½x11 on 2 or 3 Sides

2790	A2128	29c multicolored	.50 .20
a.		Booklet pane of 4	2.25 1.75
b.		Imperf pair	—
c.		As "a," imperf	—

No. 2790 has darker colors and smaller inscriptions than No. 2789.

1993		Photo.	Perf. 11½
2791	A2129	29c multicolored	.50 .20
2792	A2130	29c multicolored	.50 .20
2793	A2131	29c multicolored	.50 .20
2794	A2132	29c multicolored	.50 .20
a.		Block or strip, #2791-2794	2.00 1.75

Booklet Stamps
Size: 18x21mm
Perf. 11x10 on 2 or 3 Sides

2795	A2132	29c multicolored	.85	.20
2796	A2131	29c multicolored	.85	.20
2797	A2130	29c multicolored	.85	.20
2798	A2129	29c multicolored	.85	.20
a.		Booklet pane, 3 each #2795-2796, 2 each #2797-2798	8.50	4.00
b.		Booklet pane, 3 each #2797-2798, 2 each #2795-2796	8.50	4.00
c.		Block of 4, #2795-2798	3.40	1.75

Self-Adhesive
Size: 19½x26½mm
Die Cut

2799	A2131	29c multicolored	.50	.20
a.		Coil with plate #V1111111		3.50
2800	A2132	29c multicolored	.50	.20
2801	A2129	29c multicolored	.50	.20
2802	A2130	29c multicolored	.50	.20
a.		Bklt. pane, 3 ea #2799-2802	7.00	
b.		Block of 4, #2799-2802	2.00	

Size: 17x20mm

2803	A2131	29c multicolored	.50	.20
a.		Booklet pane of 18	10.00	

Except for #2799a with plate number, coil stamps are indistinguishable from booklet stamps once they are removed from the backing paper.

Snowman on Nos. 2793, 2799 has three buttons and seven snowflakes beneath nose (placement differs on both stamps). No. 2796 has two buttons and five snowflakes beneath nose. No. 2803 has two orange buttons and four snowflakes beneath nose.

Issued: #2791-2798, 10/21; #2799-2803, 10/28.

Mariana Islands

A2133

Litho. & Engr.
1993, Nov. 4   **Perf. 11**

2804	A2133	29c multicolored	.50	.20

Columbus' Landing in Puerto Rico, 500th Anniv.

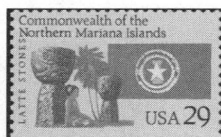

A2134

1993, Nov. 19   **Photo.**   **Perf. 11.2**

2805	A2134	29c multicolored	.50	.20

AIDS Awareness

A2135

1993, Dec. 1   **Photo.**   **Perf. 11.2**

2806	A2135	29c black & red	.50	.20
a.		Perf. 11 vert. on 1 or 2 sides, from bklt. pane	.50	.20
b.		As "a," booklet pane of 5	2.50	2.00

Winter Olympics

Slalom
A2136

Luge
A2137

Ice Dancing
A2138

Cross-Country Skiing
A2139

Ice Hockey — A2140

1994, Jan. 6   **Litho.**   **Perf. 11.2**

2807	A2136	29c multicolored	.50	.20
2808	A2137	29c multicolored	.50	.20
2809	A2138	29c multicolored	.50	.20
2810	A2139	29c multicolored	.50	.20
2811	A2140	29c multicolored	.50	.20
a.		Strip of 5, #2807-2811	2.50	2.25

Edward R. Murrow, Journalist (1908-65)

A2141

1994, Jan. 21   **Engr.**   **Perf. 11.2**

2812	A2141	29c brown	.50	.20

Love

A2142   A2143

A2144

Litho. & Engr. 1994 Litho. & Engr. Die Cut
Self-Adhesive (No. 2813)

2813	A2142	29c multicolored	.50	.20
a.		Booklet pane of 18	11.00	—
b.		Coil with plate #B1		3.50

Photo.
Perf. 10.9x11.1 on 2 or 3 Sides

2814	A2143	29c multicolored	.50	.20
a.		Booklet pane of 10	5.50	3.50
b.		As "a," imperf	—	
e.		Horiz. pair, imperf btwn.	—	

Litho. & Engr.
Perf. 11.1

2814C	A2143	29c multicolored	.50	.20

Photo. & Engr.
Perf. 11.2

2815	A2144	52c multicolored	1.00	.20

Size of No. 2814C is 20x28mm. No. 2814 is 18x24½mm.

Except for #2813b with plate number, coil stamps are indistinguishable from booklet stamps once they are removed from the backing paper.

Issued: No. 2813, Jan. 27; Nos. 2814-2815, Feb. 14; No. 2814C, June 11.

No. 2814 was issued in booklets only.

Black Heritage Series

Dr. Allison Davis (1902-83), Social Anthropologist, Educator — A2145

1994, Feb. 1   **Engr.**   **Perf. 11.2**

2816	A2145	29c red brn & brn	.50	.20

Chinese New Year

Year of the Dog
A2146

1994, Feb. 5   **Photo.**   **Perf. 11.2**

2817	A2146	29c multicolored	.55	.20

Buffalo Soldiers

A2147

Perf. 11.5x11.2
1994, Apr. 22   **Litho. & Engr.**

2818	A2147	29c multicolored	.50	.20
a.		Double impression (second impression light) of red brown (engr. inscriptions)	—	

Silent Screen Stars

Rudolph Valentino (1895-1926)
A2148

Clara Bow (1905-65)
A2149

Charlie Chaplin (1889-1977)
A2150

Lon Chaney (1883-1930)
A2151

John Gilbert (1895-1936)
A2152

Zasu Pitts (1898-1963)
A2153

Harold Lloyd (1894-1971)
A2154

Keystone Cops
A2155

Theda Bara (1885-1955)
A2156

Buster Keaton (1895-1966)
A2157

Litho. & Engr.
1994, Apr. 27   **Perf. 11.2**
Red, Blk & Brt Vio

2819	A2148	29c	.50	.20
2820	A2149	29c	.50	.20
2821	A2150	29c	.50	.20
2822	A2151	29c	.50	.20
2823	A2152	29c	.50	.20
2824	A2153	29c	.50	.20
2825	A2154	29c	.50	.20
2826	A2155	29c	.50	.20
2827	A2156	29c	.50	.20
2828	A2157	29c	.50	.20
a.		Block of 10, #2819-2828	5.00	4.00
b.		As "a," black (litho.) omitted		
c.		As "a," black, red & brt vio (litho.) omitted	—	

Garden Flowers

Lily — A2158   Zinnia — A2159

Gladiola
A2160

Marigold
A2161

Rose — A2162

Perf. 10.9 Vert.
1994, Apr. 28   **Litho. & Engr.**
Booklet Stamps

2829	A2158	29c multicolored	.50	.20
2830	A2159	29c multicolored	.50	.20
2831	A2160	29c multicolored	.50	.20
2832	A2161	29c multicolored	.50	.20

2833	A2162	29c multicolored	.50	.20
a.		Bklt. pane, #2829-2833	2.50	—
b.		As "a," imperf	2,250.	
c.		As "a," blk (engr.) omitted	300.00	

1994 World Cup Soccer Championships

A2163

A2164

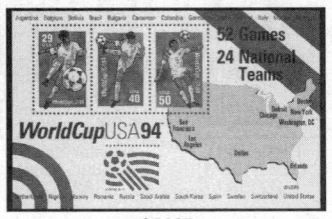

A2165

Design: 40c, Soccer player, diff.

1994, May 26   Photo.   Perf. 11.1

2834	A2163	29c multicolored	.50	.20
2835	A2163	40c multicolored	.80	.20
2836	A2164	50c multicolored	1.00	.20
		Nos. 2834-2836 (3)	2.30	.60

Souvenir Sheet of 3

2837	A2165	#a.-c.	2.50	2.00

Nos. 2834-2836 are printed on phosphor-coated paper, while Nos. 2837a (29c), 2837b (40c), 2837c (50c) are block tagged. No. 2837c has a portion of the yellow map in the LR corner.

World War II

A2166

Designs and events of 1944:
a, Allied forces retake New Guinea. b, P-51s escort B-17s on bombing raids. c, Troops running from landing craft (Allies in Normandy, D-Day, June 6). d, Airborne units spearhead attacks. e, Officer at periscope (Submarines shorten war in Pacific). f, Parade (Allies free Rome, June 4; Paris, Aug. 25). g, Soldier firing flamethrower (US troops clear Saipan bunkers). h, Red Ball Express speeds vital supplies. i, Battleship firing main battery (Battle for Leyte Gulf, Oct. 23-26). j, Soldiers in snow (Bastogne and Battle of the Bulge, Dec.).

Central label is size of 15 stamps and shows world map with extent of Axis control and Allied operations.

Illustration reduced.

Litho. & Engr.
1994, June 6   Perf. 10.9

2838	A2166	Block of 10 + label	6.00	4.50
a.-j.		29c any single	.60	.30

No. 2838 has stamp selvage at left and right and either top or bottom.

Norman Rockwell

A2167

A2168

Perf. 10.9x11.1
1994, July 1   Litho. & Engr.

2839	A2167	29c multicolored	.50	.20

Souvenir Sheet
Litho.

2840	A2168	Sheet of 4	4.00	2.75
a.		50c Freedom from Want	1.00	.65
b.		50c Freedom from Fear	1.00	.65
c.		50c Freedom of Speech	1.00	.65
d.		50c Freedom of Worship	1.00	.65

Moon Landing, 25th Anniv.

A2169

A2170

1994, July 20 Litho. Perf. 11.2x11.1
Miniature Sheet

2841	A2169	Sheet of 12	7.50	—
a.		29c Single stamp	.60	.60

Litho. & Engr.
Perf. 10.7x11.1

2842	A2170	$9.95 multicolored	17.50	7.50

Locomotives

Hudson's General
A2171

McQueen's Jupiter
A2172

Eddy's No. 242
A2173

Ely's No. 10
A2174

Buchanan's No. 999
A2175

Perf. 11 Horiz.
1994, July 28   Photo.
Booklet Stamps

2843	A2171	29c multicolored	.50	.20
2844	A2172	29c multicolored	.50	.20
2845	A2173	29c multicolored	.50	.20
2846	A2174	29c multicolored	.50	.20
2847	A2175	29c multicolored	.50	.20
a.		Booklet pane, #2843-2847	2.50	2.00
b.		As "a," imperf	—	

George Meany, Labor Leader (1894-1980)

A2176

1994, Aug. 16 Engr.   Perf. 11.1x11

2848	A2176	29c blue	.50	.20

American Music Series

Al Jolson (1886-1950) — A2177

Bing Crosby (1904-77) A2178

Ethel Waters (1896-1977) — A2179

Nat "King" Cole (1919-65) A2180

Ethel Merman (1908-84) A2181

Bessie Smith (1894-1937) — A2182

Muddy Waters (1915-83) A2183

Billie Holiday (1915-59) A2184

Robert Johnson (1911-38) A2185

Jimmy Rushing (1902-72) A2186

"Ma" Rainey (1886-1939) — A2187

Mildred Bailey (1907-51) A2188

Howlin' Wolf (1910-76) A2189

1994   Photo.   Perf. 10.1x10.2

2849	A2177	29c multicolored	.60	.20
2850	A2178	29c multicolored	.60	.20
2851	A2179	29c multicolored	.60	.20
2852	A2180	29c multicolored	.60	.20
2853	A2181	29c multicolored	.60	.20
a.		Vert. strip of 5, #2849-2853	3.00	2.00

Perf. 11x10.8
Litho.

2854	A2182	29c multicolored	.60	.20
2855	A2183	29c multicolored	.60	.20
2856	A2184	29c multicolored	.60	.20
2857	A2185	29c multicolored	.60	.20
2858	A2186	29c multicolored	.50	.20
2859	A2187	29c multicolored	.60	.20
2860	A2188	29c multicolored	.60	.20
2861	A2189	29c multicolored	.60	.20
a.		Block of 9, #2854-2861 +1 additional stamp	5.50	4.50

Issued: Nos. 2849-2853, 9/1/94; Nos. 2854-2861, 9/17/94.

Literary Arts Series

James Thurber
(1894-1961)
A2190

Litho. & Engr.
1994, Sept. 10   **Perf. 11**
2862 A2190 29c multicolored   .50   .20

Wonders Of The Sea

Diver,
Motorboat
A2191

Diver, Ship
A2192

Diver,
Ship's
Wheel
A2193

Diver, Coral
A2194

1994, Oct. 3   **Litho.**   **Perf. 11x10.9**
2863	A2191	29c multicolored	.50	.20
2864	A2192	29c multicolored	.50	.20
2865	A2193	29c multicolored	.50	.20
2866	A2194	29c multicolored	.50	.20
a.		Block of 4, #2863-2866	2.00	1.50
b.		As "a," imperf	1,750.	

Cranes

Black-Necked
A2195

Whooping
A2196

Litho. & Engr.
1994, Oct. 9   **Perf. 10.8x11**
2867	A2195	29c multicolored	.50	.20
2868	A2196	29c multicolored	.50	.20
a.		Pair, #2867-2868	1.00	.65
b.		Blk & mag (engr.) omitted	2,000.	
c.		As "a," dble. impression of engr. blk (Birds' names, "USA") & mag ("29")	5,000.	

---

  d. As "a," dble. impression of engr. blk ("USA") & mag ("29") —

See People's Republic of China Nos. 2528-2529.

Legends Of The West
Miniature Pane

A2197

g. Bill Pickett
(1870-1932)
(Revised)

Designs: a, Home on the Range. b, Buffalo Bill Cody (1846-1917). c, Jim Bridger (1804-81). d, Annie Oakley (1860-1926). e, Native American Culture. f, Chief Joseph (c. 1840-1904). h, Bat Masterson (1853-1921). i, John C. Fremont (1813-90). j, Wyatt Earp (1848-1929). k, Nellie Cashman (c. 1849-1925). l, Charles Goodnight (1826-1929). m, Geronimo (1823-1909). n, Kit Carson (1809-68). o, Wild Bill Hickok (1837-76). p, Western Wildlife. q, Jim Beckwourth (c. 1798-1866). r, Bill Tilghman (1854-1924). s, Sacagawea (c. 1787-1812). t, Overland Mail.

1994, Oct. 18   **Photo.**   **Perf. 10.1x10**
2869	A2197	Pane of 20	12.00	—
a.-t.		29c any single	.60	.20
u.		As No. 2869, a.-e. imperf, f.-j. part perf.	—	

Legends Of The West (Recalled)
Miniature Pane

g. Bill Pickett
(Recalled)

Nos. 2870b-2870d, 2870f-2870o, 2870q-2870s have a frameline around the vignette that is half the width of the frameline on similar stamps in No. 2869. Other design differences may exist.

1994   **Photo.**   **Perf. 10.1x10**
2870 A2197 29c Pane of 20   190.00

150,000 panes were made available through a drawing. Panes were delivered in an envelope. Value is for pane without envelope.

Christmas

Madonna and
Child, by
Elisabetta
Sirani
A2200

Stocking
A2201

Santa Claus
A2202

Cardinal in
Snow
A2203

Litho. & Engr.
1994, Oct. 20   **Perf. 11¼**
2871 A2200 29c multicolored   .50   .20
Booklet Stamp
Perf. 9¾x11
2871A	A2200	29c multicolored	.60	.20
b.		Booklet pane of 10	6.25	3.50
c.		As "b," imperf.	—	

Perf. 11¼
Litho.
2872	A2201	29c multicolored	.50	.20
a.		Booklet pane of 20	10.50	3.00
b.		Imperf., pair	—	
c.		As "a," imperf. horiz.	—	
d.		Quadruple impression of black, triple impression of blue, double impressions of red and yellow, green normal	—	

Booklet Stamps
Photo.
Die Cut
Self-Adhesive
2873	A2202	29c multicolored	.50	.20
a.		Booklet pane of 12	6.25	
b.		Coil with plate #V1111	—	3.50
2874	A2203	29c multicolored	.50	.20
a.		Booklet pane of 18	9.50	

Except for #2873b with plate number, coil stamps are indistinguishable from booklet stamps once they are removed from the backing paper.

Bureau Of Engraving & Printing
Souvenir Sheet

A2204

Litho. & Engr.
1994, Nov. 3   **Perf. 11**
2875	A2204	Sheet of 4	15.00	—
a.		$2 Single stamp	3.00	1.25

Chinese New Year

Year of the
Boar
A2205

Perf. 11.2x11.1
1994, Dec. 30   **Photo.**
2876 A2205 29c multicolored   .55   .20

A2206

A2207

A2208   A2208a

A2209   A2210

1994, Dec. 13   **Litho.**   **Perf. 11x10.8**
Untagged
2877	A2206	(3c) tan, bright blue & red	.20	.20
a.		Imperf, pair	200.00	
b.		Double impression of red	—	

Perf. 10.8x10.9
2878 A2206 (3c) tan, dark blue & red   .20   .20

Inscriptions on #2877 are in a thin typeface. Those on #2878 are in heavy, bold type.

Photo.
Perf. 11.2x11.1
Tagged
2879	A2207	(20c) black "G," yel & multi	.40	.20
a.		Imperf, pair		

Perf. 11x10.9
2880 A2207 (20c) red "G," yellow & multi   .50   .20

Perf. 11.2x11.1
2881	A2208	(32c) black "G" & multi	.75	.20
a.		Booklet pane of 10	6.00	3.75

Perf. 11x10.9
2882	A2208	(32c) red "G" & multi	.60	.20

Distance on #2882 from bottom of red G to top of flag immediately above is 13¾mm. Illustration A2208a shows #2885 superimposed over #2882.

Booklet Stamps
Perf. 10x9.9 on 2 or 3 Sides
2883	A2208	(32c) black "G" & multi	.60	.20
a.		Booklet pane of 10	6.25	3.75

Perf. 10.9 on 2 or 3 Sides
2884	A2208	(32c) blue "G" & multi	.60	.20
a.		Booklet pane of 10	6.00	3.75
b.		As "a," imperf	—	

Perf. 11x10.9 on 2 or 3 Sides
2885	A2208a	(32c) red "G" & multi	.65	.20
a.		Booklet pane of 10	6.50	3.75
b.		Pair, imperf vert.	—	
c.		Pair, imperf between	—	

Distance on #2885 from bottom of red G to top of flag immediately above is 13½mm. See note below #2882.
No. 2885c resulted from a paper foldover after perforating and before cutting into panes.

A2208b   A2208c

Die Cut
Self-Adhesive
2886	A2208b	(32c) gray, blue, lt bl, red & blk	.60	.20
a.		Booklet pane of 18	11.00	
b.		Coil with plate #V11111	—	3.25

No. 2886 is printed on pre-phosphored paper and has only a small number of blue shading dots in the white stripes immediately below the flag's blue field.
Except for #2886b with plate number, coil stamps are indistinguishable from booklet

stamps once they are removed from the backing paper.

2887	A2208c	(32c) blk, bl & red	.60	.20
a.		Booklet pane of 18	11.00	

No. 2887 has noticeable blue shading in the white stripes immediately below the blue field and has overall tagging.

COIL STAMPS

1994-95   Perf. 9.8 Vert.

2888	A2209	(25c) black "G"	.50	.20
2889	A2208	(32c) black "G"	.60	.20
a.		Imperf., pair	300.00	
2890	A2208	(32c) blue "G"	.60	.20
2891	A2208	(32c) red "G"	.60	.20

Rouletted 9.8 Vert.

2892	A2208	(32c) red "G"	.60	.20

Perf. 9.8 Vert.

2893	A2210	(5c) grn & multi	.20	.20

Nos. 2888-2892 issued 12/13/94. No. 2893 was only available through the Philatelic Fulfillment Center after its announcement 1/12/95.

Eagle and Shield Type of 1993 and:

Flag Over Porch A2212

Butte A2217

Mountain A2218

Auto A2220

Auto Tail Fin — A2223

Juke Box — A2225

Flag Over Field — A2230

1995-97   Photo.   Perf. 10.4

2897	A2212	32c multi	.60	.20
a.		Imperf., vert. pair	80.00	

COIL STAMPS
Self-Adhesive
(#2902B, 2904A-2904B, 2906-2907, 2910, 2912A-2912B, 2915-2915D, 2919-2921)
Photo.
Perf. 9.8 Vert.

2902	A2217	(5c) yel, red & bl	.20	.20
a.		Imperf., pair	750.00	

Serpentine Die Cut 11.5 Vert.

2902B	A2217	(5c) yel, red & bl	.20	.20

Perf. 9.8 Vert.

2903	A2218	(5c) purple & multi	.20	.20

Letters of inscription "USA NONPROFIT ORG." outlined in purple on #2903.

2904	A2218	(5c) bl & multi	.20	.20
c.		Imperf., pair	500.00	

Letters of inscription have no outline on #2904.

Serpentine Die Cut 11.2 Vert.

2904A	A2218	(5c) purple & multi	.20	.20

Serpentine Die Cut 9.8 Vert.

2904B	A2218	(5c) purple & multi	.20	.20

Letters of inscription outlined in purple on #2904B, not outlined on No. 2904A.

Perf. Perf. 9.8 Vert.

2905	A2220	(10c) blk, red brn & brn	.20	.20

Serpentine Die Cut 11.5 Vert.

2906	A2220	(10c) blk, brn & red brn	.20	.20
2907	A1957	(10c) gold & multi	.20	.20

Perf. 9.8 Vert.

2908	A2223	(15c) dk org yel & multi	.30	.30

No. 2908 has dark, bold colors, heavy shading lines and heavily shaded chrome.

2909	A2223	(15c) buff & multi	.30	.30

No. 2909 has shinier chrome, more subdued colors and finer details than No. 2908.

Serpentine Die Cut 11.5 Vert.

2910	A2223	(15c) buff & multi	.30	.30

Perf. 9.8 Vert.

2911	A2225	(25c) dk red, dk yel grn & multi	.50	.50
a.		Imperf., pair	—	

No. 2911 has dark, saturated colors and dark blue lines in the music selection board.

2912	A2225	(25c) brt org red, brt yel grn & multi	.50	.50

No. 2912 has bright colors, less shading and light blue lines in the music selection board.

Serpentine Die Cut 11.5 Vert.

2912A	A2225	(25c) brt org red, brt yel grn & multi	.50	.50

Serpentine Die Cut 9.8 Vert.

2912B	A2225	(25c) dk red, dk yel grn & multi	.50	.50

See No. 3132.

Perf. 9.8 Vert.

2913	A2212	32c bl, tan, brn, red & lt bl	.60	.20
a.		Imperf., pair	60.00	

No. 2913 has pronounced light blue shading in the flag and red "1995" at left bottom. See No. 3133.

2914	A2212	32c bl, yel brn, red & gray	.60	.20

No. 2914 has pale gray shading in the flag and blue "1995" at left bottom.

Serpentine Die Cut 8.7 Vert.

2915	A2212	32c multi	.60	.30

Serpentine Die Cut 9.8 Vert.

2915A	A2212	32c dk bl, tan, brn, red & lt bl	.60	.20
h.		Imperf., pair		
i.		Tan omitted	2,000.	
j.		Double die cutting, one through center of stamp	30.00	—

On the unique No. 2915Ai, all other colors except brown are severely shifted.

Serpentine Die Cut 11.5 Vert.

2915B	A2212	32c As #2915A	.60	.20

Serpentine Die Cut 10.9 Vert.

2915C	A2212	32c As #2915A	.60	.20

Serpentine Die Cut 9.8 Vert.

2915D	A2212	32c dk bl, tan, brn, red & lt bl	.60	.20

Die cutting on No. 2915A shows either 10 serpentine "peaks" on each side, 11 peaks on the left side and 10 peaks on the right side, or 10 peaks on the left side and 11 peaks on the right side. The last configuration is considered by specialists to be an error, and it is rare.

Stamps on multiples of No. 2915A touch, and are on a peelable backing the same size as the stamps, while those of No. 2915D are separated on the peelable backing, which is larger than the stamps.

No. 2915D has red "1997" at left bottom; No. 2915A has red "1996" at left bottom.

Sky on No. 3133 shows color gradation at lower right not on No. 2915D, and it has blue "1996" at left bottom.

Booklet Stamps
Perf. 10.8x9.8 on 2 or 3 Adjacent Sides

2916	A2212	32c bl, tan, brn, red & lt bl	.60	.20
a.		Booklet pane of 10	6.00	
b.		As "a," imperf	—	

Die Cut

2919	A2230	32c multi	.60	.20
a.		Booklet pane of 18	11.00	
b.		Vert. pair, no die cutting btwn.	—	

Serpentine Die Cut 8.7 on 2, 3 or 4 Adjacent Sides

2920	A2212	32c Large blue "1995" date	.60	.20
a.		Booklet pane of 20+label	12.00	
b.		Small blue "1995" date	3.00	.20
c.		As "b," booklet pane of 20+label	110.00	
f.		As #2920, pane of 15+label	9.00	
g.		As "a," partial pane of 10, 3 stamps and parts of 7 stamps printed on backing liner		
h.		As #2920, bklt. pane of 15	35.00	
i.		As No. 2920, imperf pair		

Serpentine Die Cut 11.3 on 3 sides

2920D	A2212	32c Dated blue "1996"	.70	.25
e.		Booklet pane of 10	7.50	

#2920D is dated "1996." Date on #2920 is nearly twice as large as date on #2920b. #2920f comes in various configurations.

No. 2920h is a pane of 16 with one stamp removed. The missing stamp is the lower right stamp in the pane. No. 2920h cannot be made from No. 2920f, a pane of 15 + label. The label is located in the second or third row of the pane and is die cut. If the label is removed, an impression of the die cutting appears on the backing paper.

Serpentine Die Cut 9.8 on 2 or 3 Adjacent Sides

2921	A2212	32c dk bl, tan, brn, red & lt bl, red "1996" date	.75	.20
a.		Booklet pane of 10, red "1996" date	7.50	
b.		As #2921, red "1997" date	.75	.20
c.		As "a," red "1997" date	7.50	
d.		Booklet pane of 5 + label, red "1997" date	3.75	
e.		As "a," imperf	300.00	

Issued: #2902, 2905, 3/10/95; #2908-2909, 2911-2912, 2919, 3/17/95; #2915, 2920, 4/18/95; #2897, 2913-2914, 2916, 5/19/95; #2920d, 1/20/96; #2904B, 2912B, 2915D, 2921d, 1/24/97; #2903-2904, 3/16/96; #2915A, 5/21/97; #2907, 2921, 5/21/96; #2902B, 2904A, 2906, 2910, 2912A, 2915B, 6/15/96; #2915C, 5/21/96.

See Nos. 3132-3133.

Scott values for used self-adhesive stamps are for examples either on piece or off piece.

Great Americans Issue

A2248

A2249

A2250

A2251

A2253

A2255

A2256

A2257

A2258

Perf. 11.2, Serpentine Die Cut 11.7x11.5 (#2941-2942)

1995-99   Engr.

Self-Adhesive (#2941-2942)

2933	A2248	32c brown	.60	.20
2934	A2249	32c green	.60	.20
2935	A2250	32c lake	.60	.20
2936	A2251	32c blue	.60	.20
2938	A2253	46c carmine	.90	.20
2940	A2255	55c green	1.10	.20
		Imperf., pair		
2941	A2256	55c black	1.10	.20
2942	A2257	77c blue	1.50	.20
2943	A2258	78c bright violet	1.60	.20
a.		78c dull violet	1.60	
b.		78c pale violet	1.75	.30
		Nos. 2933-2943 (9)	8.60	1.80

Issued: #2933, 9/13; 46c, 10/20; 55c, 7/11; 78c, 8/18; #2934, 5/26/96; #2935, 4/3/98; #2936, 7/16/98; #2942, 11/9/98; #2941, 7/17/99.

Love

Cherub from Sistine Madonna, by Raphael

     A2263   A2264

Litho. & Engr.

1995, Feb. 1   Perf. 11.2

2948	A2263	(32c) multicolored	.60	.20

Self-Adhesive
Die Cut

2949	A2264	(32c) multicolored	.60	.20
a.		Booklet pane of 20 + label	12.00	
b.		As No. 2949, red (engr.) omitted	450.00	
c.		As "a," red (engr.) omitted	9,000.	

Florida Statehood, 150th Anniv.

A2265

1995, Mar. 3   Litho.   Perf. 11.1

2950	A2265	32c multicolored	.60	.20

Earth Day

Earth Clean-Up A2266

Solar Energy A2267

Tree Planting A2268

Beach Clean-Up A2269

1995, Apr. 20 Litho. *Perf. 11.1x11*

2951	A2266	32c multicolored	.60 .20
2952	A2267	32c multicolored	.60 .20
2953	A2268	32c multicolored	.60 .20
2954	A2269	32c multicolored	.60 .20
a.		Block of 4, #2951-2954	2.40 1.75

Richard M. Nixon

Richard M. Nixon,
37th President
(1913-94) — A2270

Litho. & Engr.

1995, Apr. 26   *Perf. 11.2*

2955	A2270	32c multicolored	.60 .20
a.		Red (engr.) omitted	1,400.

No. 2955 is known with red (engr. "Richard Nixon") inverted, and with red (engr.) omitted but only half of Nixon portrait present, both from printer's waste.

No. 2955a shows a complete Nixon portrait.

Black Heritage Series

Bessie Coleman,
Aviator — A2271

1995, Apr. 27   Engr.   *Perf. 11.2*

2956	A2271	32c red & black	.60 .20

Love

A2272   A2273

A2274

Cherubs from Sistine Madonna, by Raphael

Litho. & Engr.

1995, May 12   *Perf. 11.2*

2957	A2272	32c multicolored	.60 .20
2958	A2273	55c multicolored	1.10 .20

BOOKLET STAMPS

Perf. 9.8x10.8

2959	A2272	32c multicolored	.60 .20
a.		Booklet pane of 10	6.00 3.25
b.		As "a," imperf	—

Self-Adhesive

Die Cut

2960	A2274	55c multicolored	1.10 .20
a.		Booklet pane of 20 + label	22.50

Recreational Sports

Volleyball
A2275

Softball
A2276

Bowling
A2277

Tennis
A2278

Golf
A2279

1995, May 20 Litho. *Perf. 11.2*

2961	A2275	32c multicolored	.60 .20
2962	A2276	32c multicolored	.60 .20
2963	A2277	32c multicolored	.60 .20
2964	A2278	32c multicolored	.60 .20
2965	A2279	32c multicolored	.60 .20
a.		Vert. strip of 5, #2961-2965	3.00 2.00
b.		As "a," imperf	2,500.
c.		As "a," yellow omitted	2,500.
d.		As "a," yel, bl & mag omitted	2,500.

Prisoners of War & Missing in Action

A2280

1995, May 29   *Perf. 11.2*

2966	A2280	32c multicolored	.60 .20

Legends of Hollywood

Marilyn Monroe
(1926-62) — A2281

1995, June 1   Photo.   *Perf. 11.1*

2967	A2281	32c multicolored	.60 .20
a.		Imperf., pair	600.00

Texas Statehood

A2282

1995, June 16   Litho.   *Perf. 11.2*

2968	A2282	32c multicolored	.60 .20

Great Lakes Lighthouses

Split Rock, Lake
Superior
A2283

St. Joseph, Lake
Michigan
A2284

Spectacle Reef,
Lake
Huron — A2285

Marblehead,
Lake
Erie — A2286

Thirty Mile Point,
Lake
Ontario — A2287

Perf. 11.2 Vert.

1995, June 17   **Photo.**

Booklet Stamps

2969	A2283	32c multicolored	.60 .20
2970	A2284	32c multicolored	.60 .20
2971	A2285	32c multicolored	.60 .20
2972	A2286	32c multicolored	.60 .20
2973	A2287	32c multicolored	.60 .20
a.		Booklet pane, #2969-2973	3.00 2.75

U.N., 50th Anniv.

A2288

1995, June 26   Engr.   *Perf. 11.2*

2974	A2288	32c blue	.60 .20

Civil War

A2289

Designs: a, Monitor and Virginia. b, Robert E. Lee. c, Clara Barton. d, Ulysses S. Grant. e, Battle of Shiloh. f, Jefferson Davis. g, David Farragut. h, Frederick Douglass. i, Raphael Semmes. j, Abraham Lincoln. k, Harriet Tubman. l, Stand Watie. m, Joseph E. Johnston. n, Winfield Hancock. o, Mary Chesnut. p, Battle of Chancellorsville. q, William T. Sherman.

r, Phoebe Pember. s, "Stonewall" Jackson. t, Battle of Gettysburg.

1995, June 29   Photo.   *Perf. 10.1*

2975	A2289	Pane of 20	12.00 —
a.-t.		32c any single	.60 .20
u.		As "No. 2975," a.-e. imperf, f.-j. part perf	—
v.		As "No. 2975," k.-t. imperf, f.-j. part perf	—
w.		As "No. 2975," imperf	1,500.
x.		Block of 9 (f.-h., k.-m., p.-r.), k.-l., p.-q. imperf vert.	—

American Folk Art Series
Carousel Horses

A2290   A2291

A2292   A2293

1995, July 21   Litho.   *Perf. 11*

2976	A2290	32c multicolored	.60 .20
2977	A2291	32c multicolored	.60 .20
2978	A2292	32c multicolored	.60 .20
2979	A2293	32c multicolored	.60 .20
a.		Block of 4, #2976-2979	2.40 1.75

Woman Suffrage

A2294

Litho. & Engr.

1995, Aug. 26   *Perf. 11.1x11*

2980	A2294	32c multicolored	.60 .20
a.		Black (engr.) omitted	425.00
b.		Imperf, pair	1,500.

No. 2980a is valued in the grade of fine. Very fine examples sell for much more.

World War II

A2295

Designs and events of 1945:

a, Marines raise flag on Iwo Jima. b, Fierce fighting frees Manila by March 3, 1945. c, Soldiers advancing (Okinawa, the last big battle). d, Destroyed bridge (U.S. and Soviets link up at Elbe River). e, Allies liberate Holocaust survivors. f, Germany surrenders at Reims. g, Refugees (by 1945, World War II has uprooted millions). h, Truman announces Japan's surrender. i, Sailor kissing nurse (news of victory hits home). j, Hometowns honor their returning veterans.

Central label is size of 15 stamps and shows world map with extent of Axis control and Allied operations.

Illustration reduced.

Litho. & Engr.
1995, Sept. 2   *Perf. 11.1*
2981 A2295   Block of 10 + la-
                  bel   6.00 4.50
  a.-j.   32c any single   .60   .30
  No. 2981 has selvage at left and right and
either top or bottom.

American Music Series

Louis Armstrong A2296

Coleman Hawkins A2297

James P. Johnson A2298

Jelly Roll Morton A2299

Charlie Parker A2300

Eubie Blake A2301

Charles Mingus A2302

Thelonious Monk A2303

John Coltrane A2304

Erroll Garner A2305

1995   **Litho.**   *Perf. 11.1x11*
2982 A2296 32c white "32c"   .60   .20
2983 A2297 32c multicolored   .80   .20
2984 A2296 32c black "32c"   .80   .20
2985 A2298 32c multicolored   .80   .20
2986 A2299 32c multicolored   .80   .20
2987 A2300 32c multicolored   .80   .20
2988 A2301 32c multicolored   .80   .20
2989 A2302 32c multicolored   .80   .20
2990 A2303 32c multicolored   .80   .20
2991 A2304 32c multicolored   .80   .20
2992 A2305 32c multicolored   .80   .20
  a.   Vert. block of 10, #2983-
               2992, top selvage   8.00   —
  b.   Pane of 20, dark blue (in-
               scriptions) omitted
  Issued: No. 2982, 9/1/95; others, 9/16/95.

Garden Flowers

A2306

A2307

A2308

A2309

A2310

                          Perf. 10.9 Vert.
1995, Sept. 19   **Litho. & Engr.**
                      Booklet Stamps
2993 A2306 32c Aster   .60   .20
2994 A2307 32c Chrysanthemum   .60   .20
2995 A2308 32c Dahlia   .60   .20
2996 A2309 32c Hydrangea   .60   .20
2997 A2310 32c Rudbeckia   .60   .20
  a.   Booklet pane, #2993-2997   3.00 2.25

Eddie Rickenbacker Issue

A2311

1995, Sept. 25   **Photo.**   *Perf. 11¼*
2998 A2311 60c Small "1995"   1.25   .25
  a.   Large "1995"   1.25   .25
  Eddie Rickenbacker (1890-1973), Aviator.
Date on No. 2998 is 1mm long, on No.
2998a 1½mm long.
  Issued: #2998a, 2000.

Republic of Palau

A2312

1995, Sept. 29   **Litho.**   *Perf. 11.1*
2999 A2312 32c multicolored   .60   .20

Comic Strips

A2313

  Designs: a, The Yellow Kid. b, Katzenjam-
mer Kids. c, Little Nemo in Slumberland. d,
Bringing Up Father. e, Krazy Kat. f, Rube
Goldberg's Inventions. g, Toonerville Folks. h,
Gasoline Alley. i, Barney Google. j, Little
Orphan Annie. k, Popeye. l, Blondie. m, Dick
Tracy. n, Alley Oop. o, Nancy. p, Flash
Gordon. q, Li'l Abner. r, Terry and the Pirates.
s, Prince Valiant. t, Brenda Starr, Reporter.

1995, Oct. 1   **Photo.**   *Perf. 10.1*
3000 A2313 Pane of 20   12.00   —
  a.-t.   32c any single   .60   .20
  u.   As No. 3000, a.-h. imperf.,
               i.-l. part perf   —
  v.   As No. 3000, m.-t. imperf.,
               i.-l. part perf   —
  w.   As No. 3000, a.-l. imperf.,
               m.-t. imperf vert.   —
  Inscriptions on back of each stamp describe
the comic strip.

U.S. Naval Academy, 150th Anniv.

A2314

1995, Oct. 10   **Litho.**   *Perf. 10.9*
3001 A2314 32c multicolored   .60   .20

Literary Arts Series

Tennessee Williams (1911-83) A2315

1995, Oct. 13   **Litho.**   *Perf. 11.1*
3002 A2315 32c multicolored   .60   .20

Christmas

Madonna and Child — A2316

Santa Claus Entering Chimney A2317

Child Holding Jumping Jack A2318

Child Holding Tree — A2319

Santa Claus Working on Sled — A2320

Midnight Angel A2321

Children Sledding A2322

1995   **Litho. & Engr.**   *Perf. 11.2*
3003 A2316 32c multicolored   .60   .20
  c.   Black (engr. denomina-
               tion) omitted   250.00
              Booklet Stamp
              Perf. 9.8x10.9
3003A A2316 32c multicolored   .65   .20
  b.   Booklet pane of 10   6.50 4.00
              Lithographed
3004 A2317 32c multicolored   .60   .20
3005 A2318 32c multicolored   .60   .20
3006 A2319 32c multicolored   .60   .20
3007 A2320 32c multicolored   .60   .20
  a.   Block or strip of 4, #3004-
               3007   2.40 1.25
  b.   Bklt. pane, 3 ea #3004-
               3005, 2 ea #3006-3007   6.00 4.00
  c.   Bklt. pane, 2 ea #3004-
               3005, 3 ea #3006-3007   6.00 4.00
  d.   As "a," imperf.   700.00
      Self-Adhesive Stamps
          Photogravure
        Serpentine Die Cut
3008 A2320 32c multicolored   .60   .20
3009 A2318 32c multicolored   .60   .20
3010 A2317 32c multicolored   .60   .20
3011 A2319 32c multicolored   .60   .20
  a.   Booklet pane of 20, 5
               each #3008-3011 + la-
               bel   12.00
          Lithographed
3012 A2321 32c multicolored   .60   .20
  a.   Bklt. pane of 20 + label   12.00
  c.   Bklt. pane of 15 + label   9.00
  d.   Booklet pane of 15
  No. 3003, Madonna and Child, by Giotto di
Bondone.
  Colors of No. 3012c are deeper than those
on #3012a.
  No. 3012d is a pane of 16 with one stamp
removed. The missing stamp is from the second row, either from the top or bottom, of the
pane. No. 3012d cannot be made from No.
3012c, a pane of 15 + label. The label is die
cut. If the label is removed, an impression of
the die cutting appears on the backing paper.
          Photogravure
            Die Cut
3013 A2322 32c multicolored   .60   .20
  a.   Booklet pane of 18   11.00
      Self-Adhesive Coil Stamps
        Serpentine Die Cut Vert.
3014 A2320 32c multicolored   .60   .30
3015 A2318 32c multicolored   .60   .30
3016 A2317 32c multicolored   .60   .30
3017 A2319 32c multicolored   .60   .30
  a.   Strip of 4, #3014-3017   2.40
          Lithographed
3018 A2321 32c multicolored   .60   .30
  #3014-3018 were only available through the
Philatelic Fullfillment Center in Kansas City.
  Issued: #3003-3003A, 3012-3013, 3018,
10/19; #3004-3011, 3014-3017, 9/30.

Antique Automobiles

1893 Duryea
A2323

1894 Haynes
A2324

1898 Columbia
A2325

1899 Winton
A2326

1901 White
A2327

1995, Nov. 3 Photo. Perf. 10.1x11.1

3019	A2323	32c multicolored	.60	.20
3020	A2324	32c multicolored	.60	.20
3021	A2325	32c multicolored	.60	.20
3022	A2326	32c multicolored	.60	.20
3023	A2327	32c multicolored	.60	.20
a.		Vert. or horiz. strip of 5, #3019-3023	3.00	2.00

Vert. or horiz. strips are all in different order.

Utah Statehood Centenary

Delicate Arch, Arches Natl. Park — A2328

1996, Jan. 4 Litho. Perf. 11.1

3024	A2328	32c multicolored	.60	.20

Garden Flowers

A2329   A2330

A2331   A2332

A2333

Perf. 10.9 Vert.
1996, Jan. 19 Litho. & Engr.
Booklet Stamps

3025	A2329	32c Crocus	.60	.20
3026	A2330	32c Winter Aconite	.60	.20
3027	A2331	32c Pansy	.60	.20
3028	A2332	32c Snowdrop	.60	.20
3029	A2333	32c Anemone	.60	.20
a.		Booklet pane, #3025-3029	3.00	2.50
b.		As "a," imperf	—	

Love

Cherub from Sistine Madonna — A2334

Serpentine Die Cut 11¼x11¾
1996, Jan. 20
Self-Adhesive
Booklet Stamp

3030	A2334	32c by Raphael	.60	.20
a.		Booklet pane of 20 + label	12.00	
b.		Booklet pane of 15 + label	9.00	
c.		Red omitted	750.00	

Flora and Fauna Series
Kestrel Type of 1995 and

Red-headed Woodpecker
A2335

Eastern Bluebird
A2336

Red Fox
A2339

Ring-necked Pheasant
A2350

Coral Pink Rose — A2351

Serpentine Die Cut 10¾
1996-2000 Litho.
Self-Adhesive

3031	A1841	1c multicolored	.20	.20

Serpentine Die Cut 11¼

3031A	A1841	1c multicolored	.20	.20

No. 3031A has blue inscription and year.

Perf. 11

3032	A2335	2c multicolored	.20	.20
3033	A2336	3c multicolored	.20	.20

Serpentine Die Cut 11½x11¼
Self-Adhesive

3036	A2339	$1 multicolored	2.00	.50

COIL STAMPS
Perf. 9¾ Vert.

3044	A1841	1c small date	.20	.20
a.		Large date	.20	.20
3045	A2335	2c multicolored	.20	.20

Date on #3044 is 1mm long, on #3044a 1.5mm.
Issued: #3032, 2/2/96; #3033, 4/3/96; #3044, 1/20/96; #3036, 8/14/98; #3045, 6/22/99; #3031, 11/19/99; #3031A, 10/00.

Blue Jay & Rose Types of 1993-95
Serpentine Die Cut 10½x10¾ on 3 Sides
1996-2000 Photo.
Self-Adhesive
Booklet Stamps

3048	A1847	20c multicolored	.40	.20
a.		Booklet pane of 10	4.00	
b.		Booklet pane of 4	1.60	
c.		Booklet pane of 6	2.40	

Nos. 3048b-3048c are from the vending machine booklet No. BK237 that has a glue strip at the top edge of the top pane, the peelable strip removed and the rouletting line 2mm lower than on No. 3048a, when the panes are compared with the bottoms aligned.

Serpentine Die Cut 11¼x11¾

3049	A1853	32c yel, org, grn & blk	.60	.20
a.		Booklet pane of 20 + label	12.00	
b.		Booklet pane of 4	2.75	
c.		Booklet pane of 5 + label	3.00	
d.		Booklet pane of 6	3.60	

Serpentine Die Cut 11¼ on 3 Sides

3050	A2350	20c multicolored	.40	.20
a.		Bklt. pane of 10, all stamps upright	4.00	

Serpentine Die Cut 10½x11 on 3 Sides

3051	A2350	20c multicolored	.60	.20
a.		Serpentine die cut 10½ on 3 sides	1.30	.20
b.		Booklet pane of 5, 4 #3051, 1 #3051a turned sideways at top	3.75	
c.		Booklet pane of 5, 4 #3051, 1 #3051a turned sideways at bottom	3.75	

Serpentine Die Cut 11½x11¼ on 2, 3 or 4 Sides

3052	A2351	33c multicolored	.65	.20
a.		Booklet pane of 4	2.60	
b.		Booklet pane of 5 + label	3.25	
c.		Booklet pane of 6	3.90	
d.		Booklet pane of 20 + label	13.00	
i.		Imperf, pair	—	

Serpentine Die Cut 10¾x10½ on 2 or 3 sides

3052E	A2351	33c multicolored	.65	.20
f.		Booklet pane of 20	13.00	
g.		As "f," all 12 stamps on one side with black ("33 USA," etc.) omitted	—	
h.		Horiz. pair, imperf between	—	

COIL STAMPS
Serpentine Die Cut 11½ Vert.

3053	A1847	20c multicolored	.40	.20

Serpentine Die Cut 9¾ Vert.
Litho.
Self-Adhesive

3054	A1853	32c yel, org, blk & grn	.60	.20
a.		Imperf, pair	90.00	
b.		Blk, yel & grn omitted	—	
c.		Blk, yel & grn omitted. imperf pair	—	
d.		Black omitted	—	
e.		Black omitted, imperf pair	—	

Nos. 3054b and 3054d also are miscut and with shifted die cuttings.

3055	A2350	20c multicolored	.40	.20
a.		Imperf, pair	—	

Issued: #3048, 3053, 8/2/96; #3049, 10/24/96; #3054, 8/1/97; #3050, 3055, 7/31/98; #3051, 7/99; #3052, 8/13/99; #3052E, 4/7/00.

Black Heritage Series

Ernest E. Just (1883-1941), Marine Biologist — A2358

1996, Feb. 1 Litho. Perf. 11.1

3058	A2358	32c gray & black	.60	.20
a.		All colors omitted	—	

No. 3058a must be collected se-tenant with "normal" misperfed stamps.

Smithsonian Institution, 150th Anniv.

A2359

1996, Feb. 7 Perf. 11.1

3059	A2359	32c multicolored	.60	.20

Chinese New Year

Year of the Rat — A2360

1996, Feb. 8 Photo. Perf. 11.1

3060	A2360	32c multicolored	.60	.20
a.		Imperf, pair	—	

Pioneers of Communication

Eadweard Muybridge
A2361

Ottmar Mergenthaler — A2362

Frederic E. Ives
A2363

William Dickson
A2364

1996, Feb. 22 Litho. Perf. 11.1x11

3061	A2361	32c multicolored	.60	.20
3062	A2362	32c multicolored	.60	.20
3063	A2363	32c multicolored	.60	.20
3064	A2364	32c multicolored	.60	.20
a.		Block or strip, #3061-3064	2.40	1.75

Muybridge (1830-1904), Photographer; Mergenthaler (1854-99), Inventor of Linotype; Ives (1856-1937), Developer of Halftone Process; Dickson (1860-1935), Co-developer of Kinetoscope.

Fulbright Scholarships, 50th Anniv.

A2365

Litho. & Engr.
1996, Feb. 28   *Perf. 11.1*
3065 A2365 32c multicolored   .60 .20

Jacqueline Cochran

A2366

Litho. & Engr.
1996, Mar. 9   *Perf. 11.1*
3066 A2366 50c multicolored   1.00 .20
   a.   Black (eng.) omitted   60.00
           Cochran (1910-80), Pilot.

Marathon

A2367

1996, Apr. 11   Litho.   Perf. 11.1
3067 A2367 32c multicolored   .60 .20

1996 Summer Olympic Games

A2368

Designs: a, Decathlon (javelin). b, Canoeing. c, Women's running. d, Women's diving.
e, Cycling. f, Freestyle wrestling. g, Women's
gymnastics. h, Women's sailboarding. i, Shot
put. j, Women's soccer. k, Beach volleyball. l,
Rowing. m, Sprints. n, Women's swimming. o,
Women's softball. p, Hurdles. q, Gymnastics. r,
Gymnastics (pommel horse). s, Equestrian. t,
Basketball.

1996, May 2   Photo.   Perf. 10.1
3068 A2368 Pane of 20   12.00   —
a.-t.   32c any single   .60   .20
u.   As No. 3068, imperf   1,500.
v.   As No. 3068, back inscrip-
          tions omitted on a, f, k,
          p, incorrect back inscrip-
          tions on others   —

   Inscription on back of each stamp describes
the sport shown.

Georgia O'Keeffe (1887-1986)

A2369

Perf. 11.6x11.4
1996, May 23   **Photo.**
3069 A2369 32c multicolored   .65 .20
   a.   Imperf, pair   200.00

Tennessee Statehood Bicentennial

A2370

1996, May 31   Photo.   Perf. 11.1
3070 A2370 32c multicolored   .60 .20
Booklet Stamp
Self-Adhesive
Serpentine Die Cut 9.9x10.8
3071 A2370 32c multicolored   .60 .30
   a.   Booklet pane of 20   12.00
   b.   Horiz. pair, no die cutting
           btwn.   —
   c.   Imperf., pair   —
   d.   Horiz. pair, imperf vert.   —

American Indian Dances

A2371   A2372

A2373   A2374

A2375

1996, June 7   Litho.   Perf. 11.1
3072 A2371 32c Fancy   .60 .20
3073 A2372 32c Butterfly   .60 .20
3074 A2373 32c Traditional   .60 .20
3075 A2374 32c Raven   .60 .20
3076 A2375 32c Hoop   .60 .20
   a.   Strip of 5, #3072-3076   3.00 1.75

Prehistoric Animals

A2376

A2377

A2378

   (Saber-tooth cat)

A2379

1996, June 8   Litho.   Perf. 11.1x11
3077 A2376 32c Eohippus   .60 .20
3078 A2377 32c Woolly Mam-
             moth   .60 .20
3079 A2378 32c Mastodon   .60 .20
3080 A2379 32c Saber-tooth Cat   .60 .20
   a.   Block or strip, #3077-3080 2.40 1.50

A2380   A2381

Breast Cancer Awareness
1996, June 15   Litho.   Perf. 11.1
3081 A2380 32c multicolored   .60 .20

Legends of Hollywood
James Dean (1931-55)
1996, June 24   Photo.   Perf. 11.1
3082 A2381 32c multicolored   .60 .20
   a.   Imperf. pair   350.00
   b.   As "a," red (USA 32c) omit-
           ted   —
   c.   As "a," tan ("James Dean")
           omitted   —
   d.   As "a," red & tan omitted   —

   Nos. 3082c-3082d come from the same
error pane. The top row is No. 3082d, rows 2-4
are No. 3082c.

Folk Heroes

A2382   A2383

Prehistoric Animals (right column)

A2384   A2385

1996, July 11   Litho.   Perf. 11.1x11
3083 A2382 32c multicolored   .60 .20
3084 A2383 32c multicolored   .60 .20
3085 A2384 32c multicolored   .60 .20
3086 A2385 32c multicolored   .60 .20
   a.   Block or strip, #3083-3086 2.40 1.50

Myron's   Young Corn, by
Discobolus   Grant Wood
A2386   A2387

Centennial Olympic Games
1996, July 19   Engr.   Perf. 11.1
3087 A2386 32c brown   .65 .20
   Sheet margin of the pane of 20 is
lithographed.

Iowa Statehood, 150th Anniversary
1996, Aug. 1   Litho.   Perf. 11.1
3088 A2387 32c multicolored   .60 .20
Booklet Stamp
Self-Adhesive
Serpentine Die Cut 11.6x11.4
3089 A2387 32c multicolored   .60 .30
   a.   Booklet pane of 20   12.00

Rural Free Delivery, Cent.

A2388

Litho. & Engr.
1996, Aug. 7   *Perf. 11.2x11*
3090 A2388 32c multicolored   .60 .20

Riverboats

Robt. E.
Lee
A2389

Sylvan Dell
A2390

Far West
A2391

Rebecca Everingham — A2392

Bailey
Gatzert
A2393

Self-Adhesive
Serpentine Die Cut 11x11.1
1996, Aug. 22   **Photo.**

3091	A2389	32c multicolored	.60	.20
3092	A2390	32c multicolored	.60	.20
3093	A2391	32c multicolored	.60	.20
3094	A2392	32c multicolored	.60	.20
3095	A2393	32c multicolored	.60	.20
a.		Vert. strip of 5, #3091-3095	3.00	
b.		As "a," with special die cutting	75.00	50.00

The serpentine die cutting runs through the peelable backing to which Nos. 3091-3095 are affixed. No. 3095a exists with stamps in different sequences.

On the long side of each stamp in No. 3095b, the die cutting is missing 3 "perforations" between the stamps, one near each end and one in the middle. This allows a complete strip to be removed from the backing paper for use on a first day cover.

American Music Series
Big Band Leaders

Count
Basie
A2394

Tommy &
Jimmy
Dorsey
A2395

Glenn
Miller
A2396

Benny
Goodman
A2397

Songwriters

Harold
Arlen
A2398

Johnny
Mercer
A2399

Dorothy
Fields
A2400

Hoagy
Carmichael
A2401

1996, Sept. 11 Litho. *Perf. 11.1x11*

3096	A2394	32c multicolored	.60	.20
3097	A2395	32c multicolored	.60	.20
3098	A2396	32c multicolored	.60	.20
3099	A2397	32c multicolored	.60	.20
a.		Block or strip, #3096-3099	2.40	1.50
3100	A2398	32c multicolored	.60	.20
3101	A2399	32c multicolored	.60	.20
3102	A2400	32c multicolored	.60	.20
3103	A2401	32c multicolored	.60	.20
a.		Block or strip, #3100-3103	2.40	1.50

Literary Arts Series

F. Scott Fitzgerald (1896-1940) — A2402

1996, Sept. 27 Photo. *Perf. 11.1*
3104	A2402	23c multicolored	.45	.20

Endangered Species

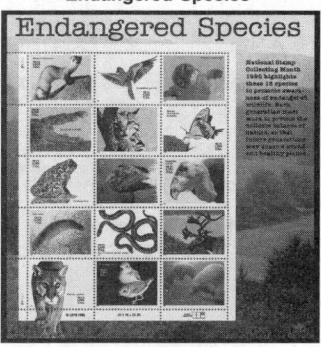

A2403

a, Black-footed ferret. b, Thick-billed parrot. c, Hawaiian monk seal. d, American crocodile. e, Ocelot. f, Schaus swallowtail butterfly. g, Wyoming toad. h, Brown pelican. i, California condor. j, Gila trout. k, San Francisco garter snake. l, Woodland caribou. m, Florida panther. n, Piping plover. o, Florida manatee.

1996, Oct. 2 Litho. *Perf. 11.1x11*
3105	A2403	Pane of 15	9.00	
a.-o.		32c any single	.60	.20

See Mexico No. 1995.

Computer Technology

A2404

Perf. 10.9x11.1
1996, Oct. 8   Litho. & Engr.
3106	A2404	32c multicolored	.60	.20

Christmas

Madonna and Child from Adoration of the Shepherds, by Paolo de Matteis — A2405

Family at
Fireplace
A2406

Decorating
Tree
A2407

Dreaming of
Santa Claus
A2408

Holiday
Shopping
A2409

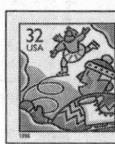

Skaters — A2410

1996 Litho. & Engr. *Perf. 11.1x11.2*
3107	A2405	32c multicolored	.60	.20

Litho.
Perf. 11.3
3108	A2406	32c multicolored	.60	.20
3109	A2407	32c multicolored	.60	.20
3110	A2408	32c multicolored	.60	.20
3111	A2409	32c multicolored	.60	.20
a.		Block or strip, #3108-3111	2.40	1.50
b.		Strip of 4, #3110-3111, 3108-3109, with #3109 imperf, #3108 imperf at right	—	

Self-Adhesive Booklet Stamps
Litho. & Engr.
Serpentine Die Cut 10 on 2, 3 or 4 Sides
3112	A2405	32c multicolored	.60	.20
a.		Booklet pane of 20 + label	12.00	
b.		No die cutting, pair	75.00	
c.		As "a," no die cutting	—	

Litho.
Serpentine Die Cut 11.8x11.5 on 2, 3 or 4 Sides
3113	A2406	32c multicolored	.60	.20
3114	A2407	32c multicolored	.60	.20
3115	A2408	32c multicolored	.60	.20
3116	A2409	32c multicolored	.60	.20
a.		Bklt. pane, 5 ea #3113-3116	12.00	
b.		As "a," no die cutting	—	

Photo.
Die Cut
3117	A2410	32c multicolored	.60	.20
a.		Booklet pane of 18	11.00	

Issued: #3108-3111, 3113-3117, 10/8; #3107, 3112, 11/1.

Hanukkah

A2411

Serpentine Die Cut 11.1
1996, Oct. 22   Photo.
Self-Adhesive
3118	A2411	32c multicolored	.60	.20

See Nos. 3352, 3547. See Israel No. 1289.

Cycling
Souvenir Sheet

A2412

1996, Nov. 1 Photo. *Perf. 11x11.1*
3119	A2412	Sheet of 2	2.00	2.00
a.		50c orange & multi	1.00	1.00
b.		50c blue green & multi	1.00	1.00

Chinese New Year

Year of the
Ox
A2413

1997, Jan. 5 Photo. *Perf. 11.2*
3120	A2413	32c multicolored	.60	.20

Black Heritage Series

Brig. Gen. Benjamin O. Davis, Sr. (1880-1970)
A2414

Self-Adhesive
Serpentine Die Cut 11.4
1997, Jan. 28   Litho.
3121	A2414	32c multicolored	.60	.20

Statue of Liberty Type of 1994
Serpentine Die Cut 11 on 2, 3 or 4 Sides
1997, Feb. 1   Photo.
Self-Adhesive
3122	A1951	32c red, lt bl, dk bl & yel	.60	.20
a.		Booklet pane of 20 + label	12.00	
b.		Booklet pane of 4	2.50	
c.		Booklet pane of 5 + label	3.20	
d.		Booklet pane of 6	3.60	
h.		As "a," no die cutting	—	

Serpentine Die Cut 11.5x11.8 on 2, 3 or 4 Sides
1997   Photo.
Self-Adhesive
3122E	A1951	32c red, lt bl, dk bl & yel	1.10	.20
f.		Booklet pane of 20 + label	35.00	
g.		Booklet pane of 6	7.00	

Love

A2415

Swans — A2416

Serpentine Die Cut 11.8x11.6 on 2, 3 or 4 Sides

1997, Feb. 4 Litho.
Self-Adhesive
3123 A2415 32c multicolored .60 .20
  a. Booklet pane of 20 + label 12.00
  b. No die cutting, pair 250.00
  c. As "a," no die cutting
  d. As "a," black omitted

Serpentine Die Cut 11.6x11.8 on 2, 3 or 4 Sides

3124 A2416 55c multicolored 1.00 .20
  a. Booklet pane of 20 + label 21.00

Helping Children Learn

A2417

Serpentine Die Cut 11.6x11.7
1997, Feb. 18 Photo.
Self-Adhesive
3125 A2417 32c multicolored .60 .20

Merian Botanical Prints

Citron, Moth, Larvae, Pupa, Beetle A2418

Flowering Pineapple, Cockroaches A2419

No. 3128 (r), No. 3129 (l), No. 3128a below

Serpentine Die Cut 10.9x10.2 on 2, 3 or 4 Sides
1997, Mar. 3 Photo.
Self-Adhesive
3126 A2418 32c multicolored .60 .20
3127 A2419 32c multicolored .60 .20
  a. Booklet pane of 20, 10 ea
    #3126-3127 + label 12.00
  b. Pair, #3126-3127 1.20
  c. Vert. pair, imperf between

Size: 18.5x24mm
Serpentine Die Cut 11.2x10.8 on 2 or 3 Sides
3128 A2418 32c multicolored .60 .20
  a. See footnote .60 .20
  b. Booklet pane of 5, 2 ea
    #3128-3129, 1 #3128a 3.00
3129 A2419 32c multicolored .60 .20
  a. See footnote .60 .20
  b. Booklet pane of 5, 2 ea
    #3128-3129, 1 #3129a 3.00
  c. Pair, #3128-3129 1.20

Nos. 3128a-3129a are placed sideways on the pane and are serpentine die cut 11.2 on

top and bottom, 10.8 on left side. The right side is 11.2 broken by a large perf where the stamp meets the vertical perforations of the two stamps above it. See illustration above.

Pacific 97

Sailing Ship — A2420

Stagecoach — A2421

1997, Mar. 13 Engr. **Perf. 11.2**
3130 A2420 32c blue .60 .20
3131 A2421 32c red .60 .20
  a. Pair, #3130-3131 1.25 .30

Juke Box and Flag Over Porch Types of 1995
COIL STAMPS
1997, Mar. 14 Photo. **Imperf.**
Self-Adhesive
3132 A2225 (25c) brt org red, brt yel grn & mul-ti .50 .50

Tagged
Serpentine Die Cut 9.9 Vert.
3133 A2212 32c dk bl, tan, brn, red & lt bl .60 .20

Nos. 3132-3133 were issued without backing paper. No. 3132 has simulated perforations ending in black bars at the top and bottom edges of the stamp.
Sky on No. 3133 shows color gradation at lower right that is not on Nos. 2915A or 2915D, and it has blue "1996" at left bottom.

Literary Arts

Thornton Wilder (1897-1975) — A2422

1997, Apr. 17 Litho. **Perf. 11.1**
3134 A2422 32c multicolored .60 .20

Raoul Wallenberg (1912-47)

Wallenberg and Jewish Refugees A2423

1997, Apr. 24 Litho. **Perf. 11.1**
3135 A2423 32c multicolored .60 .20

Dinosaurs

A2424

Designs: a, Ceratosaurus. b, Camptosaurus. c, Camarasaurus. d, Brachiosaurus. e, Goniopholis. f, Stegosaurus. g,

Allosaurus. h, Opisthias. i, Edmontonia. j, Einiosaurus. k, Daspletosaurus. l, Palaeosaniwa. m, Corythosaurus. n, Ornithominus. o, Parasaurolophus.
Illustration reduced.

1997, May 1 Litho. **Perf. 11x11.1**
3136 A2424 Sheet of 15 9.00 —
  a.-o. 32c any single .60 .20
  p. As #3136, bottom seven stamps imperf —
  q. As #3136, top eight stamp imperf —
  r. As #3136, all colors and tagging omitted —

Bugs Bunny

A2425

Serpentine Die Cut 11
1997, May 22 Photo.
3137 Pane of 10 6.00
  a. A2425 32c single .60 .20
  b. Booklet pane of 9 5.40
  c. Booklet pane of 1 .60

Die cutting on #3137b does not extend through the backing paper.

3138 Pane of 10 125.00
  a. A2425 32c single 2.00
  b. Booklet pane of 9 —
  c. Booklet pane of 1, imperf —

Die cutting on #3138b extends through the backing paper. Used examples of #3138a are identical to those of #3137a.
An untagged promotional piece similar to No. 3137c exists on the same backing paper as the booklet pane, with the same design image, but without Bugs' signature and the single stamp. Replacing the stamp is an enlarged "32 / USA" in the same style as used on the stamp.

Pacific 97

Franklin A2426

Washington A2427

1997 Litho. & Engr. **Perf. 10.5x10.4**
3139 Pane of 12 12.00 —
  a. A2426 50c single 1.00 .50
3140 Pane of 12 14.50 —
  a. A2427 60c single 1.20 .60

Selvage on Nos. 3139-3140 is lithographed.
Issued: No. 3139, 5/29; No. 3140, 5/30.

Marshall Plan, 50th Anniv.

Gen. George C. Marshall, Map of Europe — A2428

1997, June 4 **Perf. 11.1**
3141 A2428 32c multicolored .60 .20

Classic American Aircraft

A2429

Designs: a, Mustang. b, Model B. c, Cub. d, Vega. e, Alpha. f, B-10. g, Corsair. h, Stratojet. i, GeeBee. j, Staggerwing. k, Flying Fortress. l, Stearman. m, Constellation. n, Lightning. o, Peashooter. p, Tri-Motor. q, DC-3. r, 314 Clipper. s, Jenny. t, Wildcat.
Illustration reduced.

1997, July 19 Photo. **Perf. 10.1**
3142 A2429 Pane of 20 12.00 —
  a.-t. 32c any single .60 .20

Inscriptions on back of each stamp describe the airplane.

Football Coaches

Bear Bryant A2430

Pop Warner A2431

Vince Lombardi A2432

George Halas A2433

1997 Litho. **Perf. 11.2**
3143 A2430 32c multicolored .60 .20
3144 A2431 32c multicolored .60 .20
3145 A2432 32c multicolored .60 .20
3146 A2433 32c multicolored .60 —
  a. Block or strip, #3143-3146 2.40 —

With Red Bar Above Coach's Name
Perf. 11
3147 A2432 32c multicolored .60 .30
3148 A2430 32c multicolored .60 .30
3149 A2431 32c multicolored .60 .30
3150 A2433 32c multicolored .60 .30

Issued: #3143-3146, 7/25; #3147, 8/5; #3148, 8/7; #3149, 8/8; #3150, 8/16.

American Dolls

A2434

Designs: a, "Alabama Baby," and doll by Martha Chase. b, "Columbian Doll." c, Johnny Gruelle's "Raggedy Ann." d, Doll by Martha Chase. e, "American Child." f, "Baby Coos." g, Plains Indian. h, Doll by Izannah Walker. i, "Babyland Rag." j, "Scootles." k, Doll by Ludwig Greiner. l, "Betsy McCall." m, Percy Crosby's "Skippy." n, "Maggie Mix-up." o, Dolls by Albert Schoenhut.
Illustration reduced.

1997, July 28   Perf. 10.9x11.1
3151 A2434   Pane of 15   9.00 —
a.-o.   32c any single   .60   .20

A2435   A2436

Legends Of Hollywood
Humphrey Bogart (1899-1957)
1997, July 31   Photo.   Perf. 11.1
3152 A2435 32c multicolored   .60   .20
Perforations in corner of each stamp are star-shaped.

"The Stars and Stripes Forever!"
1997, Aug. 21   Perf. 11.1
3153 A2436 32c multicolored   .60   .20

American Music Series
Opera Singers

Lily Pons
A2437

Richard Tucker
A2438

Lawrence Tibbett
A2439

Rosa Ponselle
A2440

Classical Composers & Conductors

Leopold Stokowski
A2441

Arthur Fiedler
A2442

George Szell
A2443

Eugene Ormandy
A2444

Samuel Barber
A2445

Ferde Grofé
A2446

Charles Ives
A2447

Louis Moreau Gottschalk
A2448

1997   Litho.   Perf. 11
3154 A2437 32c multicolored   .65   .20
3155 A2438 32c multicolored   .65   .20
3156 A2439 32c multicolored   .65   .20
3157 A2440 32c multicolored   .65   .20
a.   Block or strip, #3154-3157 2.60 —
3158 A2441 32c multicolored   .65   .20
3159 A2442 32c multicolored   .65   .20
3160 A2443 32c multicolored   .65   .20
3161 A2444 32c multicolored   .65   .20
3162 A2445 32c multicolored   .65   .20
3163 A2446 32c multicolored   .65   .20
3164 A2447 32c multicolored   .65   .20
3165 A2448 32c multicolored   .65   .20
a.   Block of 8, #3158-3165   5.25 —
Issued: #3154-3157, 9/10; #3158-3165, 9/12.

Padre Félix Varela (1788-1853)

A2449

1997, Sept. 15   Litho.   Perf. 11.2
3166 A2449 32c purple   .60   .20

Department of the Air Force, 50th Anniv.

Thunderbirds Aerial Demonstration Squadron — A2450

Perf. 11.2x11.1
1997, Sept. 18   Litho.
3167 A2450 32c multicolored   .60   .20

Beginning with #3167, a hidden 3-D design can be seen on some stamps when they are viewed with a special viewer sold by the post office.

Classic Movie Monsters

A2451

A2452

A2453

A2454

quad='c'>
A2455

Designs: No. 3168, Lon Chaney as The Phantom of the Opera. No. 3169, Bela Lugosi as Dracula. No. 3170, Boris Karloff as Frankenstein's Monster. No. 3171, Boris Karloff as The Mummy. No. 3172, Lon Chaney, Jr. as The Wolf Man.

1997, Sept. 30   Photo.   Perf. 10.2
3168 A2451 32c multicolored   .60   .20
3169 A2452 32c multicolored   .60   .20
3170 A2453 32c multicolored   .60   .20
3171 A2454 32c multicolored   .60   .20
3172 A2455 32c multicolored   .60   .20
a.   Strip of 5, #3168-3172   3.00 —

First Supersonic Flight, 50th Anniv.

A2456

Serpentine Die Cut 11.4
1997, Oct. 14   Litho.
Self-Adhesive
3173 A2456 32c multicolored   .60   .20

Women In Military Service

A2457

1997, Oct. 18   Litho.   Perf. 11.1
3174 A2457 32c multicolored   .60   .20

Kwanzaa

A2458

Serpentine Die Cut 11
1997, Oct. 22   Photo.
Self-Adhesive
3175 A2458 32c multicolored   .60   .20
See Nos. 3368, 3548.

Christmas

Madonna and Child — A2459   Holly — A2460

Serpentine Die Cut 9.9 on 2, 3 or 4 Sides
1997   Litho.
Booklet Stamps
Self-Adhesive
3176 A2459 32c multicolored   .60   .20
a.   Booklet pane of 20 + label 12.00
Serpentine Die Cut 11.2x11.8 on 2, 3 or 4 Sides
3177 A2460 32c multicolored   .60   .20
a.   Booklet pane of 20 + label 12.00
b.   Booklet pane of 4   2.50
c.   Booklet pane of 5 + label 3.00
d.   Booklet pane of 6   3.75
Madonna and Child, by Sano di Pietro.
Issued: No. 3176, 10/27; No. 3177, 10/30.

Mars Pathfinder
Souvenir Sheet

Mars Rover Sojourner — A2461

Illustration reduced.

1997, Dec. 10 Photo. *Perf. 11x11.1*
3178 A2461 multicolored   6.00   3.00
  a. $3 single stamp   5.50   2.75

The perforations at the bottom of the stamp include the letters "USA." Vertical rouletting extends from the vertical perforations of the stamp to the bottom of the souvenir sheet.

Chinese New Year

Year of the Tiger — A2462

1998, Jan. 5 Photo. *Perf. 11.2*
3179 A2462 32c multicolored   .60   .20

A2463   A2464

Alpine Skiing
1998, Jan. 22 Litho. *Perf. 11.2*
3180 A2463 32c multicolored   .60   .20

Black Heritage Series
Serpentine Die Cut 11.6x11.3
1998, Jan. 28
Self-Adhesive
3181 A2464 32c sepia & black   .60   .20
  Madam C.J. Walker (1867-1919), entrepreneur.

Celebrate the Century

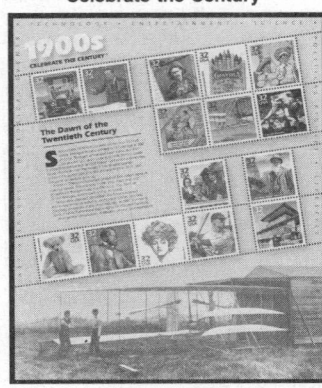

1900s — A2465

No. 3182: a, Model T Ford. b, Theodore Roosevelt. c, Motion picture "The Great Train Robbery," 1903. d, Crayola Crayons introduced, 1903. e, St. Louis World's Fair, 1904. f, Design used on Hunt's Remedy stamp (#RS56), Pure Food & Drug Act, 1906. g, Wright Brothers first flight, Kitty Hawk, 1903. h, Boxing match shown in painting "Stag at Sharkey's," by George Bellows of the Ash Can School. i, Immigrants arrive. j, John Muir, preservationist. k, "Teddy" Bear created. l, W.E.B. Du Bois, social activist. m, Gibson Girl. n, First baseball World Series, 1903. o, Robie

House, Chicago, designed by Frank Lloyd Wright.

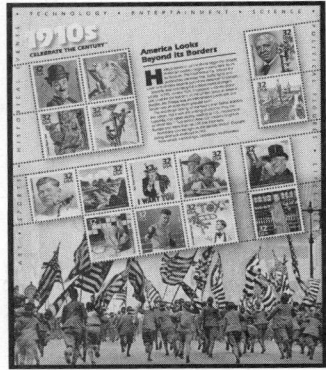

1910s — A2466

No. 3183: a, Charlie Chaplin as the Little Tramp. b, Federal Reserve System created, 1913. c, George Washington Carver. d, Avant-garde art introduced at Armory Show, 1913. e, First transcontinental telephone line, 1914. f, Panama Canal opens, 1914. g, Jim Thorpe wins decathlon at Stockholm Olympics, 1912. h, Grand Canyon National Park, 1919. i, U.S. enters World War I. j, Boy Scouts started in 1910, Girl Scouts formed in 1912. k, Woodrow Wilson. l, First crossword puzzle published, 1913. m, Jack Dempsey wins heavyweight title, 1919. n, Construction toys. o, Child labor reform.

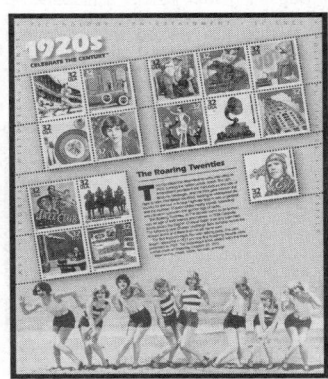

1920s — A2467

No. 3184: a, Babe Ruth. b, The Gatsby style. c, Prohibition enforced. d, Electric toy trains. e, 19th Amendment (woman voting). f, Emily Post's Etiquette. g, Margaret Mead, anthropologist. h, Flappers do the Charleston. i, Radio entertains America. j, Art Deco style (Chrysler Building). k, Jazz flourishes. l, Four Horsemen of Notre Dame. m, Lindbergh flies the Atlantic. n, American realism (The Automat, by Edward Hopper). o, Stock Market crash, 1929.

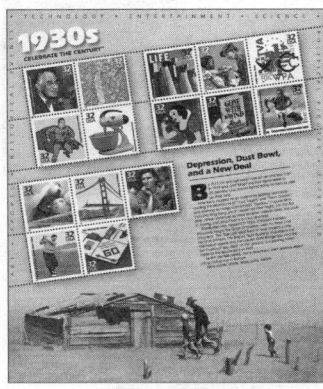

1930s — A2468

No. 3185: a, Franklin D. Roosevelt. b, The Empire State Building. c, 1st Issue of Life Magazine, 1936. d, Eleanor Roosevelt. e, FDR's New Deal. f, Superman arrives, 1938. g, Household conveniences. h, "Snow White and the Seven Dwarfs," 1937. i, "Gone with the Wind," 1936. j, Jesse Owens. k, Streamline design. l, Golden Gate Bridge. m, America

survives the Depression. n, Bobby Jones wins Grand Slam, 1938. o, The Monopoly Game.

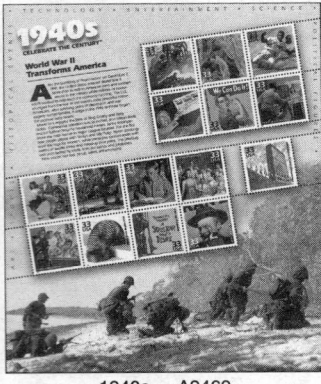

1940s — A2469

No. 3186: a, World War II. b, Antibiotics save lives. c, Jackie Robinson. d, Harry S Truman. e, Women support war effort. f, TV entertains America. g, Jitterbug sweeps nation. h, Jackson Pollock, Abstract Expressionism. i, GI Bill, 1944. j, Big Band Sound. k, Intl. style of architecture (UN Headquarters). l, Postwar baby boom. m, Slinky, 1945. n, "A Streetcar Named Desire," 1947. o, Orson Welles' "Citizen Kane."

1950s — A2470

No. 3187: a, Polio vaccine developed. b, Teen fashions. c, The "Shot Heard 'Round the World." d, US launches satellites. e, Korean War. f, Desegregating public schools. g, Tail fins, chrome. h, Dr. Seuss' "The Cat in the Hat." i, Drive-in movies. j, World Series rivals. k, Rocky Marciano, undefeated. l, "I Love Lucy." m, Rock 'n Roll. n, Stock car racing. o, Movies go 3-D.

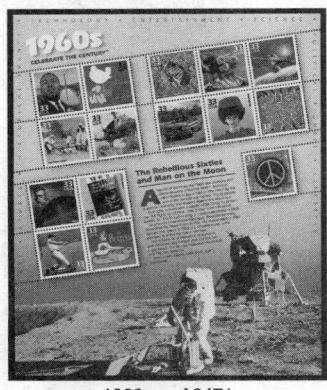

1960s — A2471

No. 3188: a, Martin Luther King, Jr., "I Have a Dream." b, Woodstock. c, Man walks on the moon. d, Green Bay Packers. e, Star Trek. f, The Peace Corps. g, Viet Nam War. h, Ford Mustang. i, Barbie Doll. j, Integrated circuit. k, Lasers. l, Super Bowl I. m, Peace symbol. n, Roger Maris, 61 in '61. o, The Beatles "Yellow Submarine."

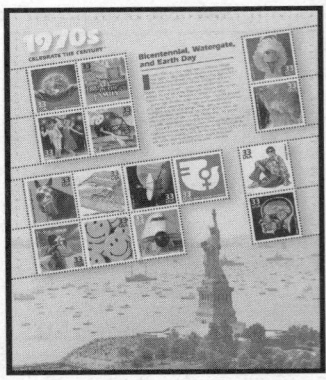

1970s — A2472

No. 3189: a, Earth Day celebrated. b, "All in the Family" television series. c, "Sesame Street" television series character, Big Bird. d, Disco music. e, Pittsburgh Steelers win four Super Bowls. f, US Celebrates 200th birthday. g, Secretariat wins Triple Crown. h, VCRs transform entertainment. i, Pioneer 10. j, Women's rights movement. k, 1970s fashions. l, "Monday Night Football." m, Smiley face buttons. n, Jumbo jets. o, Medical imaging.

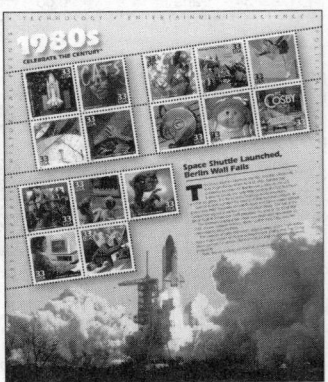

1980s — A2473

No. 3190: a, Space shuttle program. b, "Cats" Broadway show. c, San Francisco 49ers. d, Hostages in Iran come home. e, Figure skating. f, Cable TV. g, Vietnam Veterans Memorial. h, Compact discs. i, Cabbage Patch Kids. j, "The Cosby Show" television series. k, Fall of the Berlin Wall. l, Video games. m, "E. T. The Extra-Terrestrial" movie. n, Personal computers. o, Hip-hop culture.

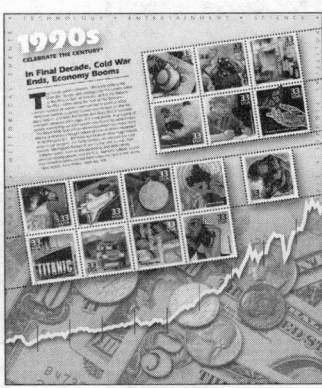

1990s — A2474

No. 3191: a, New baseball records. b, Gulf War. c, "Seinfeld" television series. d, Extreme sports. e, Improving education. f, Computer art and graphics. g, Recovering species. h, Return to space. i, Special Olympics. j, Virtual reality. k, Movie "Jurassic Park." l, Movie "Titanic." m, Sport utility vehicles. n, World Wide Web. o, Cellular phones.

Litho.; Litho. & Engr. (#3182m, 3183f, 3184m, 3185b, 3186k, 3187a, 3188c, 3189h)

1998-2000   Perf. 11½

3182	A2465	Pane of 15	9.00	—
a.-o.		32c any single	.60	.30
p.		Engr. red (No. 3182m, Gibson girl) omitted, in pane of 15		
3183	A2466	Pane of 15	9.00	—
a.-o.		32c any single	.60	.30
p.		Nos. 3183g, 3183 l-3183o imperf. in pane of 15		
3184	A2467	Pane of 15	9.00	—
a.-o.		32c any single	.60	.30
3185	A2468	Pane of 15	9.00	—
a.-o.		32c any single	.60	.30
3186	A2469	Pane of 15	9.75	—
a.-o.		33c any single	.65	.30
3187	A2470	Pane of 15	9.75	—
a.-o.		33c any single	.65	.30
3188	A2471	Pane of 15	9.75	—
a.-o.		33c any single	.65	.30
3189	A2472	Pane of 15	9.75	—
a.-o.		33c any single	.65	.30
3190	A2473	Pane of 15	9.75	—
a.-o.		33c any single	.65	.30
3191	A2474	Pane of 15	9.75	—
a.-o.		33c any single	.65	.30
		Nos. 3182-3191 (10)	94.50	

Issued: #3182-3183, 2/3; #3184, 5/28; #3185, 9/10; #3186, 2/18/99; #3187, 5/26/99; #3188, 9/17/99; #3189, 11/18/99; #3190, 1/12/00; #3191, 5/2/00.

"Remember The Maine"

A2475

Litho. & Engr.
1998, Feb. 15   **Perf. 11.2x11**

3192	A2475	32c red & black	.60	.20

Flowering Trees

Southern Magnolia
A2476

Blue Paloverde
A2477

Yellow Poplar — A2478

Prairie Crab Apple — A2479

Pacific Dogwood
A2480

Die Cut Perf 11.3
1998, Mar. 19   **Litho.**
Self-Adhesive

3193	A2476	32c multicolored	.60	.20
3194	A2477	32c multicolored	.60	.20
3195	A2478	32c multicolored	.60	.20
3196	A2479	32c multicolored	.60	.20
3197	A2480	32c multicolored	.60	.20
a.		Strip of 5, #3193-3197	3.00	

Alexander Calder, Sculptor

Black Cascade, 13 Verticals, 1959 — A2481

Untitled, 1965 — A2482

Rearing Stallion, 1928 — A2483

Portrait of a Young Man, c. 1945 — A2484

Un Effet du Japonais, 1945 — A2485

1998, Mar. 25   **Photo.**   **Perf. 10.2**

3198	A2481	32c multicolored	.60	.20
3199	A2482	32c multicolored	.60	.20
3200	A2483	32c multicolored	.60	.20
3201	A2484	32c multicolored	.60	.20
3202	A2485	32c multicolored	.60	.20
a.		Strip of 5, #3198-3202	3.00	—

Cinco De Mayo

A2486

Serpentine Die Cut 11.7x10.9
1998, Apr. 16   **Photo.**
Self-Adhesive

3203	A2486	32c multicolored	.60	.20

See No. 3309. See Mexico No. 2066.

A2487

A2488

Sylvester & Tweety
Serpentine Die Cut 11.1
1998, Apr. 27
Self-Adhesive

3204		Pane of 10	6.00	
a.	A2487	32c single	.60	.20
b.		Booklet pane of 9 #3204a	5.40	
c.		Booklet pane of 1 #3204a	.60	

Die cutting on #3204b does not extend through the backing paper.

3205		Pane of 10	10.00	
a.	A2487	32c single	.60	—
b.		Booklet pane of 9 #3205a	—	
c.		Booklet pane of 1, imperf.	—	

Die cutting on #3205a extends through the backing paper. Used examples of No. 3205a are identical to those of No. 3204a.

Wisconsin Statehood
Serpentine Die Cut 10.8x10.9
1998, May 29   **Photo.**
Self-Adhesive

3206	A2488	32c multicolored	.60	.30

See note after No. 3167.

Wetlands
A2489

Diner
A2490

COIL STAMPS
1998   **Photo.**   **Perf. 10 Vert.**
Self-Adhesive (#3207A, 3208A)

3207	A2489	(5c) multicolored	.20	.20

Serpentine Die Cut 9.7 Vert.

3207A	A2489	(5c) multicolored	.20	.20

Perf. 10 Vert.

3208	A2490	(25c) multicolored	.50	.50

Serpentine Die Cut 9.7 Vert.

3208A	A2490	(25c) multicolored	.50	.50

Issued: #3207-3208, 6/5; #3208A, 9/30; #3207A, 12/14.

1898 Trans-Mississippi Stamps, Centenary

A2491

Litho. & Engr.
1998, June 18   **Perf. 12x12.4**

3209	A2491	Pane of 9	7.75	5.00
a.	A100	1c green & black	.20	.20
b.	A108	2c red brown & black	.20	.20
c.	A102	4c orange & black	.20	.20
d.	A103	5c blue & black	.20	.20
e.	A104	8c dark lilac & black	.20	.20
f.	A105	10c purple & black	.20	.20
g.	A106	50c green & black	1.00	.60
h.	A107	$1 red & black	2.00	1.25
i.	A101	$2 red brown & black	4.00	2.50

Vignettes on Nos. 3209b and 3209i are reversed in comparison to the original issue.

3210	A107	$1 Pane of 9		
		#3209h	18.00	—

Berlin Airlift, 50th Anniv.

A2492

1998, June 26   **Photo.**   **Perf. 11.2**

3211	A2492	32c multicolored	.60	.20

American Music Series
Folk Singers

Huddie "Leadbelly" Ledbetter
A2493

Woody Guthrie
A2494

Sonny Terry
A2495

Josh White
A2496

Gospel Singers

Mahalia Jackson
A2497

Roberta Martin
A2498

Clara Ward
A2499

Sister Rosetta Tharpe
A2500

1998, June 26   *Perf. 10.1x10.2*
3212	A2493	32c multicolored	.60	.20
3213	A2494	32c multicolored	.60	.20
3214	A2495	32c multicolored	.60	.20
3215	A2496	32c multicolored	.60	.20
a.		Block or strip, #3212-3215	2.40	—

Perf. 10.1x10.3
1998, July 15   Photo.
3216	A2497	32c multicolored	.60	.20
3217	A2498	32c multicolored	.60	.20
3218	A2499	32c multicolored	.60	.20
3219	A2500	32c multicolored	.60	.20
a.		Block or strip, #3216-3219	2.40	—

Spanish Settlement of the Southwest

La Mision de San Miguel de San Gabriel, Española, NM — A2501

1998, July 11   Litho.   *Perf. 11.2*
3220	A2501	32c multicolored	.60	.20

Literary Arts Series

Stephen Vincent Benét — A2502

1998, July 22   Litho.   *Perf. 11.2*
3221	A2502	32c multicolored	.60	.20

Tropical Birds

Antillean Euphonia — A2503

Green-throated Carib — A2504

Crested Honeycreeper — A2505

Cardinal Honeyeater
A2506

1998, July 29   Litho.   *Perf. 11.2*
3222	A2503	32c multicolored	.60	.20
3223	A2504	32c multicolored	.60	.20
3224	A2505	32c multicolored	.60	.20
3225	A2506	32c multicolored	.60	.20
a.		Block or strip of 4, #3222-3225	2.40	—

A2507   A2508

Legends of Hollywood
1998, Aug. 3   Photo.   *Perf. 11.1*
3226	A2507	32c multicolored	.60	.20

Alfred Hitchcock (1899-1980). Perforations in corner of each stamp are star-shaped. Hitchcock's profile in the UL corner of each stamp is laser cut.

Organ & Tissue Donation
Serpentine Die Cut 11.7
1998, Aug. 5   Photo.
Self-Adhesive
3227	A2508	32c multicolored	.60	.20

Modern Bicycle

A2509

COIL STAMPS
Serpentine Die Cut 9.8 Vert.
1998, Aug. 14   Photo.   Untagged
Self-Adhesive
3228	A2509	(10c) multicolored, small "1998" year date	.20	.20
a.		Large date	.20	.20

Date on 3228a is approximately 1½mm; on 3228 approximately 1mm.

Perf. 9.9 Vert.
3229	A2509	(10c) multicolored	.20	.20

Bright Eyes

Dog
A2510

Fish
A2511

Cat
A2512

Parakeet
A2513

Hamster
A2514

Serpentine Die Cut 9.9
1998, Aug. 20   Photo.
Self-Adhesive
3230	A2510	32c multicolored	.60	.20
3231	A2511	32c multicolored	.60	.20
3232	A2512	32c multicolored	.60	.20
3233	A2513	32c multicolored	.60	.20
3234	A2514	32c multicolored	.60	.20
a.		Strip of 5, #3230-3234	3.00	

See note after No. 3167.

Klondike Gold Rush, Centennial

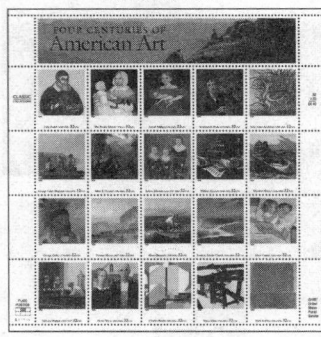

A2515

1998, Aug. 21   Litho.   *Perf. 11.1*
3235	A2515	32c multicolored	.60	.20

American Art

A2516

Paintings: a, "Portrait of Richard Mather," by John Foster. b, "Mrs. Elizabeth Freake and Baby Mary," by The Freake Limner. c, "Girl in Red Dress with Cat and Dog," by Ammi Phillips. d, "Rubens Peale with a Geranium," by Rembrandt Peale. e, "Long-billed Curlew, Numenius Longrostris," by John James Audubon. f, "Boatmen on the Missouri," by George Caleb Bingham. g, "Kindred Sprits," by Asher B. Durand. h, "The Westwood Children," by Joshua Johnson. i, "Music and Literature," by William Harnett. j, "The Fog Warning," by Winslow Homer. k, "The White Cloud, Head Chief of the Iowas," by George Catlin. l, "Cliffs of Green River," by Thomas Moran. m, "The Last of the Buffalo," by Albert Bierstadt. n, "Niagara," by Frederic Edwin Church. o, "Breakfast in Bed," by Mary Cassatt. p, "Nighthawks," by Edward Hopper. q, "American Gothic," by Grant Wood. r, "Two Against the White," by Charles Sheeler. s, "Mahoning," by Franz Kline. t, "No. 12," by Mark Rothko.

1998, Aug. 27   Photo.   *Perf. 10.2*
3236	A2516	Pane of 20	12.00	—
a.-t.		32c any single	.60	.20

Inscriptions on the back of each stamp describe the painting and the artist.

American Ballet

A2517

Perf. 10.9x11.1
1998, Sept. 16   Litho.
3237	A2517	32c multicolored	.60	.20

Space Discovery

A2518   A2519

A2520   A2521

A2522

1998, Oct. 1   Photo.   *Perf. 11.1*
3238	A2518	32c multicolored	.60	.20
3239	A2519	32c multicolored	.60	.20
3240	A2520	32c multicolored	.60	.20
3241	A2521	32c multicolored	.60	.20
3242	A2522	32c multicolored	.60	.20
a.		Strip of 5, #3238-3242	3.00	

See note after No. 3167.

Giving and Sharing

A2523

Serpentine Die Cut 11.1
1998, Oct. 7   Photo.
Self-Adhesive
3243	A2523	32c multicolored	.60	.20

Christmas

Madonna and Child — A2524

Wreaths

Evergreen
A2525

Victorian
A2526

Chili Pepper
A2527

Tropical
A2528

1998, Oct. 15 Litho.
Booklet Stamps
Serpentine Die Cut 10.1x9.9 on 2, 3 or 4 Sides

3244	A2524	32c multicolored	.60	.20
a.		Booklet pane of 20 + label	12.00	

Serpentine Die Cut 11.3x11.6 on 2 or 3 Sides

3245	A2525	32c multicolored	.75	.20
3246	A2526	32c multicolored	.75	.20
3247	A2527	32c multicolored	.75	.20
3248	A2528	32c multicolored	.75	.20
a.		Bklt. pane of 4, #3245-3248	4.00	
b.		Bklt. pane of 5, #3245-3246, 3248, 2 #3247 + label	5.00	
c.		Booklet pane of 6, #3247-3248, 2 each #3245-3246	6.00	

Size: 23x30mm
Serpentine Die Cut 11.4x11.6 on 2, 3 or 4 Sides

3249	A2525	32c multicolored	.60	.20
3250	A2526	32c multicolored	.60	.20
3251	A2527	32c multicolored	.60	.20
3252	A2528	32c multicolored	.60	.20
a.		Block or strip, #3249-3252	2.40	
b.		Bklt. pane, 5 #3252a + label	12.00	
c.		As "a," red ("Greetings 32 USA" and "1998") omitted on #3249, 3252)	—	

Madonna and Child, Florence, 15th Cent.

Weather Vane — A2529

Uncle Sam — A2530

Uncle Sam's Hat — A2531

Space Shuttle Landing — A2532

Piggyback Space Shuttle — A2533

1998 Litho. *Perf. 11.2*
Self-Adhesive (#3259, 3261-3263, 3265-3269)

3257	A2529	(1c) multi	.20	.20
a.		Black omitted	—	
3258	A2529	(1c) multi	.20	.20

No. 3257 is 18mm high, has thin letters, white USA, and black 1998. No. 3258 is 17mm high, has thick letters, pale blue USA and blue 1998.

Photo.
Serpentine Die Cut 10.8

3259	A2530	22c multi	.45	.20
a.		Die cut 10.8x10.5	1.00	.25

See No. 3353.

Perf. 11.2

3260	A2531	(33c)	.65	.20

Litho.
Serpentine Die Cut 11.5

3261	A2532	$3.20 multi	6.00	3.00
3262	A2533	$11.75 multi	22.50	11.50

COIL STAMPS
Photo.
Serpentine Die Cut 9.9 Vert.

3263	A2530	22c multi	.45	.20
a.		Imperf., pair	—	

See No. 3353.

Perf. 9.8 Vert.

3264	A2531	(33c)	.65	.20

Serpentine Die Cut 9.9 Vert.

3265	A2531	(33c) multi	.65	.20
a.		Imperf., pair	—	
b.		Red omitted	—	
c.		Black omitted	—	
d.		Black omitted, imperf., pair	—	

Unused examples of No. 3265 are on backing paper the same size as the stamps. On No. 3265b, the blue and gray colors are shifted down and to the right.

Serpentine Die Cut 9.9 Vert.

3266	A2531	(33c) multi	.65	.20

Unused examples of No. 3266 are on backing paper larger than the stamps. Corners of stamps are rounded, and the stamps are spaced approximately 2mm apart.

BOOKLET STAMPS
Serpentine Die Cut 9.9 on 2 or 3 Sides

3267	A2531	(33c) multi	.65	.20
a.		Booklet pane of 10	6.50	

Serpentine Die Cut on 2, 3 or 4 Sides
11¼ (#3268, 3268a), 11 (#3268b, 3268c)

3268	A2531	(33c) multi	.65	.20
a.		Booklet pane of 10	6.50	
b.		Serpentine die cut 11	.65	.20
c.		As "b," bklt. pane of 20 + label	13.00	

Die Cut 8 on 2, 3 or 4 Sides

3269	A2531	(33c) multi	.65	.20
a.		Booklet pane of 18	12.00	

Issued: No. 3262, 11/19; others, 11/9.

A2534

COIL STAMPS
1998, Dec. 14 Photo. *Perf. 9.8 Vert.*

3270	A2534	(10c) Small date	.20	.20
a.		Large date	.20	.20

Serpentine Die Cut 9.9 Vert.
Self-Adhesive

3271	A2534	(10c) Small date	.20	.20
b.		Large date	.20	.20

Dates on Nos. 3270a and 3271b are approximately 1¾mm; on Nos. 3270-3271 approximately 1¼mm.
Compare to Nos. 2602-2604, 2907.

Chinese New Year

Year of the Rabbit — A2535

1999, Jan. 5 Photo. *Perf. 11.2*

3272	A2535	33c multicolored	.65	.20

Black Heritage Series

Malcolm X — A2536

Serpentine Die Cut 11.4
1999, Jan. 20 Litho.
Self-Adhesive

3273	A2536	33c multicolored	.65	.20

Malcolm X (1925-65), Civil Rights Activist.

Love

A2537

A2538

1999, Jan. 28 Photo. *Die Cut*
Booklet Stamp
Self-Adhesive

3274	A2537	33c multicolored	.65	.20
a.		Booklet pane of 20	13.00	
b.		Imperf., pair	—	
3275	A2538	55c multicolored	1.10	.20

Hospice Care

A2539

Serpentine Die Cut 11.4
1998, Feb. 9 Litho.

3276	A2539	33c multicolored	.65	.20

Flag & City — A2540

1999 Photo. *Perf. 11.2*
Self-Adhesive (#3278-3279, 3281-3282)

3277	A2540	33c multicolored	.65	.20

No. 3277 has red date.

Serpentine Die Cut 11.1 on 2, 3 or 4 Sides

3278	A2540	33c multicolored	.65	.20
a.		Booklet pane of 4	2.60	
b.		Booklet pane of 5 + label	3.25	
c.		Booklet pane of 6	3.90	
d.		Booklet pane of 10	6.50	
e.		Booklet pane of 20 + label	13.00	
h.		As "e," imperf	—	

No. 3278 has black date.

BOOKLET STAMPS
Serpentine Die Cut 11½x11¾ on 2, 3 or 4 Sides

3278F	A2540	33c multicolored	.65	.20
g.		Booklet pane of 20 + label	13.00	

No. 3278f has black date.

Serpentine Die Cut 9.8 on 2 or 3 Sides

3279	A2540	33c multicolored	.65	.20
a.		Booklet pane of 10	6.50	

No. 3279 has red date.

COIL STAMPS
Perf. 9.9 Vert.

3280	A2540	33c multicolored, small "1999" year date	.65	.20
a.		Large date	.65	.20
b.		As "a," imperf pair		

Date on 3280a is approximately 1¾mm; on No. 3280 approximately 1¼mm.

Serpentine Die Cut 9.8 Vert.

3281	A2540	33c large "1999" year date	.65	.20
a.		Imperf., pair	25.00	
b.		Light blue & yellow omitted	600.00	
c.		Small date	.65	.20

Corners are square on #3281. Unused examples are on backing paper the same size as the stamps.
Date on No. 3281 is approximately 1¾mm; on No. 3281c approximately 1¼mm.

3282	A2540	33c multicolored	.65	.20

Corners are rounded on #3282. Unused examples are on backing paper larger than the stamps, and stamps are spaced approximately 2mm apart.

Flag & Chalkboard — A2541

Booklet Stamp
Serpentine Die Cut 7.9 on 2, 3 or 4 Sides
1999, Mar. 13 Photo.
Self-Adhesive

3283	A2541	33c multicolored	.65	.20
a.		Booklet pane of 18	12.00	

Irish Immigration

A2542

1999, Feb. 26 Litho. *Perf. 11.2*

3286	A2542	33c multicolored	.65	.20

See Ireland No. 1168.

Performing Arts Series

A2543

1999, Mar. 2   Litho.   Perf. 11.2
3287 A2543 33c multicolored   .65   .20
    Alfred Lunt (1892-1977), Lynn Fontanne
(1887-1983), Actors.

Arctic Animals

A2544

A2545

A2546

A2547

A2548

1999, Mar. 12   Litho.   Perf. 11
3288 A2544 33c Arctic Hare   .65   .20
3289 A2545 33c Arctic Fox   .65   .20
3290 A2546 33c Snowy Owl   .65   .20
3291 A2547 33c Polar Bear   .65   .20
3292 A2548 33c Gray Wolf   .65   .20
    a.   Strip of 5, #3288-3292   3.25   —

Sonoran Desert

A2549

Designs: a, Cactus wren, brittlebush, teddy
bear cholla. b, Desert tortoise. c, White-
winged dove, prickly pear. d, Gambel quail. e,
Saguaro cactus. f, Desert mule deer. g, Desert
cottontail, hedgehog cactus. h, Gila monster.
i, Western diamondback rattlesnake, cactus
mouse. j, Gila woodpecker.

Serpentine Die Cut Perf 11.2
1999, Apr. 6   Litho.
        Self-Adhesive
3293 A2549 Pane of 10   6.50
    a.-j.   33c any single   .65   .20

Berries

Blueberries
A2550

Raspberries
A2551

Strawberries
A2552

Blackberries
A2553

**Serpentine Die Cut 11½x11¾ on 2, 3
or 4 Sides**
1999, Apr. 10   Photo.
        Booklet Stamps
        Self-Adhesive
3294 A2550 33c multicolored   .65   .20
    a.   Dated "2000"   .65   .20
3295 A2551 33c multicolored   .65   .20
    a.   Dated "2000"   .65   .20
3296 A2552 33c multicolored   .65   .20
    a.   Dated "2000"   .65   .20
3297 A2553 33c multicolored   .65   .20
    a.   Dated "2000"   .65   .20
    b.   Booklet pane, 5 each
              #3294-3297 + label   13.00
    c.   Block of 4, #3294-3297 2.60
    d.   Booklet pane, 5 #3297e + la-
              bel   13.00
    e.   Block of 4, #3294a-3297a 2.60

Nos. 3297b and 3297d are double-sided
booklet panes with 12 stamps on one side and
8 stamps plus label on the other side.

**Serpentine Die Cut 9½x10 on 2 or 3
Sides**
3298 A2550 33c multicolored   .65   .20
3299 A2552 33c multicolored   .65   .20
3300 A2551 33c multicolored   .65   .20
3301 A2553 33c multicolored   .65   .20
    a.   Bklt. pane of 4, #3298-3301 2.60
    b.   Bklt. pane of 5, #3298-3299,
              3301, 2 #3300 + label 3.25
    c.   Booklet pane of 6, #3300-
              3301, 2 #3298-3299   4.00
    d.   Block of 4, #3298-3301 2.60

COIL STAMPS
Serpentine Die Cut 8.5 Vert.
3302 A2550 33c multicolored   .65   .20
3303 A2551 33c multicolored   .65   .20
3304 A2553 33c multicolored   .65   .20
3305 A2552 33c multicolored   .65   .20
    a.   Strip of 4, #3302-3305 2.60

    Issued: #3294a-3297a, 3/15/00.

A2554

A2555

Daffy Duck
Serpentine Die Cut 11.1
1999, Apr. 16   Photo.
        Self-Adhesive
3306   Pane of 10   6.50
    a.   A2554 33c single   .65   .20
    b.   Booklet pane, 9 #3306a 5.85
    c.   Booklet pane, 1 #3306a .65

Die cutting on #3306b does not extend
through the backing paper.

3307   Pane of 10   6.50
    a.   A2554 33c single   .65
    b.   Booklet pane, 9 #3307a —
    c.   Booklet pane, 1 #3307a imperf. —

Die cutting on #3307a extends through the
backing paper. Used examples of No. 3307a
are identical to those of No. 3306a.
Nos. 3306b-3306c and 3307b-3307c are
separated by a vertical line of
microperforations.

Literary Arts
Ayn Rand (1905-82)
1999, Apr. 22   Litho.   Perf. 11.2
3308 A2555 33c multicolored   .65   .20

Cinco De Mayo Type of 1998
Serpentine Die Cut 11.6x11.3
1999, Apr. 27   Litho.
        Self-Adhesive
3309 A2486 33c multicolored   .65   .20

Tropical Flowers

Bird of
Paradise
A2556

Royal
Poinciana
A2557

Gloriosa
Lily
A2558

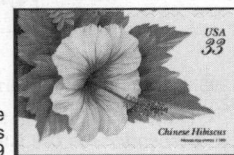

Chinese
Hibiscus
A2559

BOOKLET STAMPS
**Serpentine Die Cut 10.9 on 2 or 3
Sides**
1999, May 1   Photo.
        Self-Adhesive
3310 A2556 33c multicolored   .65   .20
3311 A2557 33c multicolored   .65   .20
3312 A2558 33c multicolored   .65   .20
3313 A2559 33c multicolored   .65   .20
    a.   Block of 4, #3310-3313 2.60
    b.   Booklet pane, 5 #3313a 13.00

No. 3313b is a double-sided booklet pane.

A2560

A2561

John (1699-1777) & William (1739-1823) Bartram, Botanists
Franklinia Alatamaha, by William
Bartram.

Serpentine Die Cut 11½
1999, May 18   Litho.
        Self-Adhesive
3314 A2560 33c multicolored   .65   .20

Prostate Cancer Awareness
Serpentine Die Cut 11
1999, May 28   Photo.
        Self-Adhesive
3315 A2561 33c multicolored   .65   .20

California Gold Rush, 150th Anniv.

A2562

1999, June 18   Litho.   Perf. 11¼
3316 A2562 33c multicolored   .65   .20

Aquarium Fish
Reef Fish

A2563

A2564

A2565

A2566

#3317, Yellow fish, red fish, cleaner shrimp.
#3318, Fish, thermometer. #3319, Red fish,
blue & yellow fish. #3320, Fish, heater/airator.

Serpentine Die Cut 11½
1999, June 24   Litho.
        Self-Adhesive
3317 A2563 33c multicolored   .65   .20
3318 A2564 33c multicolored   .65   .20
3319 A2565 33c multicolored   .65   .20
3320 A2566 33c multicolored   .65   .20
    b.   Strip of 4, #3317-3320 2.60

UNITED STATES

93

Extreme Sports

A2567   A2568

A2569   A2570

Serpentine Die Cut 11
1999, June 25   **Photo.**
Self-Adhesive

3321	A2567	33c	Skateboarding	.65	.20
3322	A2568	33c	BMX Biking	.65	.20
3323	A2569	33c	Snowboarding	.65	.20
3324	A2570	33c	Inline Skating	.65	.20
a.			Block or strip of 4, #3321-3324	2.60	

American Glass

Free-Blown   Mold-Blown
Glass — A2571   Glass — A2572

Pressed   Art
Glass — A2573   Glass — A2574

1999, June 29   **Litho.**   **Perf. 11**

3325	A2571	33c	multicolored	.65	.20
3326	A2572	33c	multicolored	.65	.20
3327	A2573	33c	multicolored	.65	.20
3328	A2574	33c	multicolored	.65	.20
a.			Strip or block of 4, #3325-3328	2.60	—

A2575   A2576

Legends of Hollywood
James Cagney (1899-1986)
1999, July 22   **Photo.**   **Perf. 11**

3329	A2575	33c	multicolored	.65	.20

Perforations in corner of each stamp are star-shaped.

Gen. William "Billy" L. Mitchell (1879-1936), Aviation Pioneer
Serpentine Die Cut 9¾x10
1999, July 30   **Photo.**
Self-Adhesive

3330	A2576	55c	multicolored	1.10	.20

Honoring Those Who Served

A2577

Serpentine Die Cut 11
1999, Aug. 16   **Photo.**
Self-Adhesive

3331	A2577	33c	black, blue & red	.65	.20

Universal Postal Union

A2578

1999, Aug. 25   **Litho.**   **Perf. 11**

3332	A2578	45c	multicolored	.90	.20

Famous Trains

Daylight
A2579

Congressional — A2580

20th
Century
Limited
A2581

Hiawatha
A2582

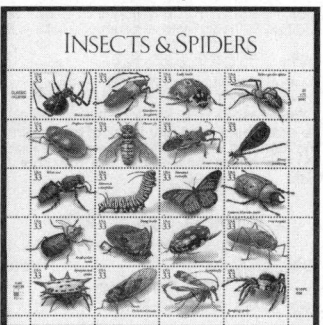

Super
Chief
A2583

1999, Aug. 26   **Litho.**   **Perf. 11**

3333	A2579	33c	multicolored	.65	.20
3334	A2580	33c	multicolored	.65	.20
3335	A2581	33c	multicolored	.65	.20
3336	A2582	33c	multicolored	.65	.20
3337	A2583	33c	multicolored	.65	.20
a.			Strip of 5, #3333-3337	3.25	—

Stamps in No. 3337a are arranged in four different orders.

Frederick Law Olmsted (1822-1903), Landscape Architect

A2584

1999, Sept. 12   **Litho.**   **Perf. 11**

3338	A2584	33c	multicolored	.65	.20

American Music Series
Hollywood Composers

Max Steiner (1888-1971) — A2585

Dimitri Tiomkin (1894-1975) — A2586

Bernard
Herrmann
(1911-75)
A2587

Franz
Waxman
(1906-67)
A2588

Alfred
Newman
(1907-70)
A2589

Erich Wolfgang Korngold (1897-1957) — A2590

1999, Sept. 16   **Litho.**   **Perf. 11**

3339	A2585	33c	multicolored	.65	.20
3340	A2586	33c	multicolored	.65	.20
3341	A2587	33c	multicolored	.65	.20
3342	A2588	33c	multicolored	.65	.20
3343	A2589	33c	multicolored	.65	.20
3344	A2590	33c	multicolored	.65	.20
a.			Block of 6, #3339-3344	3.90	—

Broadway Songwriters

Ira (1896-1983) & George (1898-1937)
Gershwin — A2591

Alan Jay
Lerner
(1918-86)
& Frederick
Loewe
(1901-88)
A2592

Lorenz Hart (1895-1943) — A2593

Richard Rodgers (1902-79) & Oscar
Hammerstein II (1895-1960) — A2594

Meredith
Willson
(1902-84)
A2595

Frank
Loesser
(1910-69)
A2596

1999, Sept. 21   **Litho.**   **Perf. 11**

3345	A2591	33c	multicolored	.65	.20
3346	A2592	33c	multicolored	.65	.20
3347	A2593	33c	multicolored	.65	.20
3348	A2594	33c	multicolored	.65	.20
3349	A2595	33c	multicolored	.65	.20
3350	A2596	33c	multicolored	.65	.20
a.			Block of 6, #3345-3350	3.90	—

Insects & Spiders

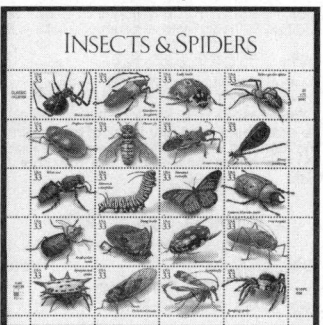

A2597

a, Black widow. b, Elderberry longhorn. c, Lady beetle. d, Yellow garden spider. e, Dogbane beetle. f, Flower fly. g, Assassin bug. h, Ebony jewelwing. i, Velvet ant. j, Monarch caterpillar. k, Monarch butterfly. l, Eastern

Hercules beetle. m, Bombardier beetle. n, Dung beetle. o, Spotted water beetle. p, True katydid. q, Spinybacked spider. r, Periodical cicada. s, Scorpionfly. t, Jumping spider.

1999, Oct. 1   Litho.   *Perf. 11*
3351 A2597 Pane of 20   13.00 —
a.-t.   33c any single   .65 .20

Hanukkah Type of 1996
Serpentine Die Cut 11
1999, Oct. 8   Photo.
Self-adhesive
3352 A2411 33c multicolored   .65 .20

Uncle Sam Type of 1998
COIL STAMP
1999, Oct. 8   Photo.   *Perf. 9¾ Vert.*
3353 A2530 22c multicolored   .45 .20

NATO, 50th Anniv.

A2598

1999, Oct. 13   Litho.   *Perf. 11¼*
3354 A2598 33c multicolored   .65 .20

Christmas

Madonna and Child, by Bartolomeo Vivarini A2599

Deer A2600

Serpentine Die Cut 11¼ on 2 or 3 sides
1999, Oct. 20   Litho.
Booklet Stamp
Self-Adhesive
3355 A2599 33c multicolored   .65 .20
a.   Booklet pane of 20   13.00

Serpentine Die Cut 11¼
3356 A2600 33c gold & red   .65 .20
3357 A2600 33c gold & blue   .65 .20
3358 A2600 33c gold & purple   .65 .20
3359 A2600 33c gold & green   .65 .20
a.   Block or strip, #3356-3359   2.60

Booklet Stamps
Serpentine Die Cut 11¼ on 2, 3 or 4 sides
3360 A2600 33c gold & red   .65 .20
3361 A2600 33c gold & blue   .65 .20
3362 A2600 33c gold & purple   .65 .20
3363 A2600 33c gold & green   .65 .20
a.   Booklet pane of 20, 5 each #3360-3363   13.00

Size: 21x19mm
Serpentine Die Cut 11½x11¼ on 2 or 3 sides
3364 A2600 33c gold & red   .65 .20
3365 A2600 33c gold & blue   .65 .20
3366 A2600 33c gold & purple   .65 .20
3367 A2600 33c gold & green   .65 .20
a.   Bkt. pane of 4, #3364-3367   2.60
b.   Bkt. pane, #3364, 3366, 3367, 2 #3365 + label   3.25
c.   Booklet pane of 6, #3365, 3367, 2 ea #3364, 3366   4.00

The frame on Nos. 3356-3359 is narrow and the space between it and the hoof is a hairline. The frame on Nos. 3360-3363 is much thicker, and the space between it and the hoof is wider.

Kwanzaa Type of 1997
Serpentine Die Cut 11
1999, Oct. 29   Photo.
Self-Adhesive
3368 A2458 33c multicolored   .65 .20

Year 2000

Baby New Year — A2601

Serpentine Die Cut 11¼
1999, Dec. 27   Litho.
Self-Adhesive
3369 A2601 33c multicolored   .65 .20

Chinese New Year

Year of the Dragon — A2602

2000, Jan. 6   Litho.   *Perf. 11¼*
3370 A2602 33c multicolored   .65 .20

Black Heritage

Patricia Roberts Harris — A2603

Serpentine Die Cut 11½x11¼
2000, Jan. 27   Litho.
Self-Adhesive
3371 A2603 33c indigo   .65 .20
Patricia Roberts Harris (1924-85), First Black Woman Cabinet Secretary.

Submarines

S Class A2604

Los Angeles Class A2605

Ohio Class A2606

USS Holland A2607

Gato Class — A2608

Illustration A2608 is reduced.

2000, Mar. 27   Litho.   *Perf. 11*
3372 A2605 33c multi   .65 .20

Booklet Stamps
3373 A2604 22c multi   .45 .20
3374 A2605 33c multi, no microprint   .65 .30
3375 A2606 55c multi   1.10 .50
3376 A2607 60c multi   1.25 .55
3377 A2608 $3.20 multi   6.50 3.00
a.   Booklet pane, #3373-3377   10.00

No. 3372 with microprinted "USPS" at base of sail. No. 3374 has no microprinting.
No. 3377a was issued with two types of text in the selvage.

Pacific Coast Rain Forest

A2609

Designs: a, Harlequin duck. b, Dwarf oregongrape, snail-eating ground beetle. c, American dipper, horiz. d, Cutthroat trout, horiz. e, Roosevelt elk. f, Winter wren. g, Pacific giant salamander, Rough-skinned newt. h, Western tiger swallowtail, horiz. i, Douglas squirrel, foliose lichen. j, Foliose lichen, banana slug.

Serpentine Die Cut 11¼x11½, 11½ (horiz. stamps)
2000, Mar. 29   Litho.
Self-Adhesive
3378 A2609 Pane of 10   6.50
a.-j.   33c any single   .65 .20

Louise Nevelson (1899-1988), Sculptor

Silent Music I — A2610

Royal Tide I — A2611

Black Chord — A2612

Nightsphere-Light — A2613

Dawn's Wedding Chapel I — A2614

2000, Apr. 6   Litho.   *Perf. 11x11¼*
3379 A2610 33c multicolored   .65 .20
3380 A2611 33c multicolored   .65 .20
3381 A2612 33c multicolored   .65 .20
3382 A2613 33c multicolored   .65 .20
3383 A2614 33c multicolored   .65 .20
a.   Strip of 5, #3379-3383   3.25 —

Hubble Space Telescope Images

Eagle Nebula — A2615   Ring Nebula — A2616

Lagoon Nebula — A2617   Egg Nebula — A2618

Galaxy NGC 1316 — A2619

2000, Apr. 10   Photo.   *Perf. 11*
3384 A2615 33c multicolored   .65 .20
3385 A2616 33c multicolored   .65 .20
3386 A2617 33c multicolored   .65 .20
3387 A2618 33c multicolored   .65 .20
3388 A2619 33c multicolored   .65 .20
a.   Strip of 5, #3384-3388   3.25 —
b.   As "a," imperf   1,200.

American Samoa

Samoan Double Canoe A2620

2000, Apr. 17   Litho.   *Perf. 11*
3389 A2620 33c multicolored   .65 .20

Library of Congress

A2621

2000, Apr. 24   Litho.   Perf. 11
3390 A2621 33c multicolored   .65   .20
Design features interior dome & arched windows in Main Reading Room, Thomas Jefferson Building.

Road Runner & Wile E. Coyote

A2622

Serpentine Die Cut 11
2000, Apr. 26   Litho.
Self-Adhesive
3391   Pane of 10   6.50
  a.   A2622 33c single   .65   .20
  b.   Booklet pane of 9 #3391a   5.85
  c.   Booklet pane of 1 #3391a   .65
  d.   All die cutting omitted, pane of
        10   8,500.
Die cutting on #3391 does not extend through the backing paper.
3392   Pane of 10   6.50
  a.   A2622 33c single   .65
  b.   Booklet pane of 9 #3392a   —
  c.   Booklet pane of 1, imperf.   —
Die cutting on #3392b extends through the backing paper. Used examples of No. 3392a are identical to those of No. 3391a.

Distinguished Soldiers

A2623

A2624

A2625

A2626

Designs: No. 3393, Maj. Gen. John L. Hines. No. 3394, Gen. Omar N. Bradley. No. 3395, Sgt. Alvin C. York. No. 3396, Second Lt. Audie L. Murphy.

2000, May 3   Litho.   Perf. 11
3393 A2623 33c multicolored   .65   .20
3394 A2624 33c multicolored   .65   .20
3395 A2625 33c multicolored   .65   .20
3396 A2626 33c multicolored   .65   .20
  a.   Block or strip, #3393-3396   2.60   —

Summer Sports

Runners
A2627

2000, May 5   Litho.   Perf. 11
3397 A2627 33c multicolored   .65   .20

Adoption

Stick Figures
A2628

Serpentine Die Cut 11½
2000, May 10   Litho.
Self-Adhesive
3398 A2628 33c multicolored   .65   .20

Youth Team Sports

A2629

A2630

A2631

A2632

2000, May 27   Litho.   Perf. 11
3399 A2629 33c Basketball   .65   .20
3400 A2630 33c Football   .65   .20
3401 A2631 33c Soccer   .65   .20
3402 A2632 33c Baseball   .65   .20
  a.   Block or strip, #3399-3402   2.60   —

The Stars and Stripes

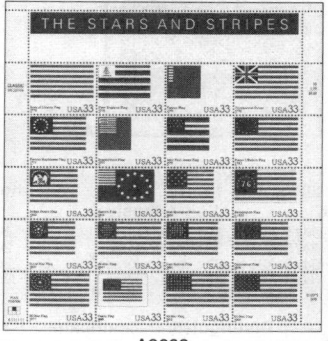

A2633

Designs: a, Sons of Liberty Flag, 1775. b, New England Flag, 1775. c, Forster Flag, 1775. d, Continental Colors, 1776. e, Francis Hopkinson Flag, 1777. f, Brandywine Flag, 1777. g, John Paul Jones Flag, 1779. h, Pierre L'Enfant Flag, 1783. i, Indian Peace Flag, 1803. j, Easton Flag, 1814. k, Star-Spangled Banner, 1814. l, Bennington Flag, c. 1820. m, Great Star Flag, 1837. n, 29-Star Flag, 1847. o, Fort Sumter Flag, 1861. p, Centennial Flag, 1876. q, 38-Star Flag, 1877. r, Peace Flag, 1891. s, 48-Star Flag, 1912. t, 50-Star Flag, 1960.

2000, June 14   Litho.   Perf. 10½x11
3403 A2633   Pane of 20   13.00
  a.-t.   33c any single   .65   .30
Inscriptions on the back of each stamp describe the flag.

Berries

Blueberries
A2634

Strawberries
A2635

Blackberries
A2636

Raspberries
A2637

Serpentine Die Cut 8½ Horiz.
2000, June 16   Photo.
Self-Adhesive
Coil Stamps
3404 A2634 33c multicolored   .65   .20
3405 A2635 33c multicolored   .65   .20
3406 A2636 33c multicolored   .65   .20
3407 A2637 33c multicolored   .65   .20
  a.   Strip of 4, #3404-3407   2.60
The adhesive on Nos. 3404-3407 is strong and can remove the ink from stamps in the roll.

Legends of Baseball

A2638

Designs: a, Jackie Robinson. b, Eddie Collins. c, Christy Mathewson. d, Ty Cobb. e, George Sisler. f, Rogers Hornsby. g, Mickey Cochrane. h, Babe Ruth. i, Walter Johnson. j, Roberto Clemente. k, Lefty Grove. l, Tris Speaker. m, Cy Young. n, Jimmie Foxx. o, Pie

Traynor. p, Satchel Paige. q, Honus Wagner. r, Josh Gibson. s, Dizzy Dean. t, Lou Gehrig.

Serpentine Die Cut 11¼
2000, July 6   Litho.
Self-Adhesive
3408 A2638   Pane of 20   13.00
  a.-t.   33c any single   .65   .20

Space
Souvenir Sheets

A2639

A2640

A2641

A2642

A2643

No. 3409, Probing the Vastness of Space:
a, Hubble Space Telescope. b, Radio inter-
ferometer very large array, New Mexico. c,
Optical and infrared telescopes, Keck Obser-
vatory, Hawaii. d, Optical telescopes, Cerro
Tololo Observatory, Chile. e, Optical tele-
scope, Mount Wilson Observatory, California.
f, Radio telescope, Arecibo Observatory,
Puerto Rico.
No. 3410, Exploring the Solar System:
a, Sun and corona. b, Cross-section of sun.
c, Sun and earth. d, Sun and solar flare. e,
Sun and clouds.
No. 3411, Escaping the Gravity of Earth:
a, Space Shuttle and Space Station. b,
Astronauts working in space.
No. 3412, Space Achievement &
Exploration.
No. 3413, Landing on the Moon
Illustrations reduced.

2000   Photo.   Perf. 10½x11

3409	A2639	Sheet of 6	7.50	—
a.-f.		60c any single	1.25	.60

Perf. 10¾

3410	A2640	Sheet of 5 + label	10.00	—
a.-e.		$1 any single	2.00	1.00
f.		As #3410, imperf		

Photogravure with Hologram Affixed
Perf. 10½, 10¾ (#3412)

3411	A2641	Sheet of 2	12.50	—
a.-b.		$3.20 any single	6.25	3.00
c.		Hologram omitted on right stamp		
3412	A2642	multi	22.50	11.50
a.		$11.75 Single stamp	20.00	10.00
b.		Hologram omitted		
c.		Hologram omitted on No. 3412 in uncut sheet of 5 panes		
3413	A2643	multi	22.50	11.50
a.		$11.75 Single stamp	20.00	10.00
b.		Double hologram		
c.		Double hologram on No. 3413 in uncut sheet of 5 panes		
d.		Hologram omitted on No. 3413 in uncut sheet of 5 panes		
		Nos. 3409-3413 (5)	75.00	

Issued: No. 3409, 7/10; No. 3410, 7/11; No.
3411, 7/9; No. 3412, 7/7; No. 3413, 7/8.
Warning: Soaking in water may affect
holographic images.

Stampin' the Future Children's Stamp Design Contest Winners

by Zachary Canter A2644

by Sarah Lipsey A2645

by Morgan Hill A2646

by Ashley Young A2647

Serpentine Die Cut 11¼
2000, July 13   Litho.
Self-Adhesive

3414	A2644	33c multicolored	.65	.20
3415	A2645	33c multicolored	.65	.20
3416	A2646	33c multicolored	.65	.20
3417	A2647	33c multicolored	.65	.20
a.		Horiz. strip of 4, #3414-3417	2.60	

Distinguished Americans

Gen. Joseph W. Stilwell A2650

Sen. Claude Pepper A2656

Sen. Hattie Caraway (1878-1950) — A2661

Perf. 11, Serpentine Die Cut 11 (#3431)
2000   Litho. & Engr.

3420	A2650	10c red & black	.20	.20
3426	A2656	33c red & black	.65	.20
3431	A2661	76c red & black	1.50	.20

This is an ongoing set. Numbers may
change. Issued: 10c, 8/24; 33c, 9/7, 75c,
2/21/01.

California Statehood, 150th Anniv.

Big Sur and Iceplant — A2668

Serpentine Die Cut 11
2000, Sept. 8   Photo.
Self-Adhesive

3438	A2668	33c multicolored	.65	.20

Deep Sea Creatures

Fanfin Anglerfish A2669

Sea Cucumber A2670

Fangtooth A2671

Amphipod A2672

Medusa A2673

2000, Oct. 2   Photo.   Perf. 10x10¼

3439	A2669	33c multicolored	.65	.20
3440	A2670	33c multicolored	.65	.20
3441	A2671	33c multicolored	.65	.20
3442	A2672	33c multicolored	.65	.20
3443	A2673	33c multicolored	.65	.20
a.		Vert. strip of 5, #3439-3443	3.25	—

Literary Arts

Thomas Wolfe (1900-38), Novelist — A2674

2000, Oct. 3   Litho.   Perf. 11

3444	A2674	33c multicolored	.65	.20

White House, 200th Anniv.

A2675

Serpentine Die Cut 11¼
2000, Oct. 18   Litho.
Self-Adhesive

3445	A2675	33c multicolored	.65	.20

Legends of Hollywood

A2676

2000, Oct. 24   Photo.   Perf. 11

3446	A2676	33c multicolored	.65	.20

Edward G. Robinson (1893-1973). Perforations in corner of each stamp are star-shaped.

New York Public Library Lion — A2677

Serpentine Die Cut 11½ Vert.
2000, Nov. 9   Photo.
Self-Adhesive
Coil Stamp

3447	A2677	(10c) multicolored	.20	.20

Flag Over Farm — A2678

2000, Dec. 15   Litho.   Perf. 11¼

3448	A2678	(34c) multicolored	.65	.20

Self-Adhesive
Serpentine Die Cut 11¼

3449	A2678	(34c) multicolored	.65	.20

Booklet Stamp
Self-Adhesive
Photo.
Serpentine Die Cut 8 on 2, 3 or 4 sides

3450	A2678	(34c) multicolored	.65	.20
a.		Booklet pane of 18	12.00	

A2679

Statue of Liberty — A2680

PHOTOGRAVURE
Serpentine Die Cut 11 on 2, 3 or 4 sides
2000, Dec. 15   Photo.
Self-Adhesive (#3451, 3453)
Booklet Stamp

3451	A2679	(34c) multicolored	.65	.20
a.		Booklet pane of 20	13.00	
b.		Booklet pane of 4	2.60	
c.		Booklet pane of 6	3.90	
d.		As "a," imperf	—	

Coil Stamps
Perf. 9¾ Vert.

3452	A2680	(34c) multicolored	.65	.20

Serpentine Die Cut 10 Vert.

3453	A2680	(34c) multicolored	.65	.20
a.		Imperf, pair	—	

A2681 A2682 A2683 A2684
Flowers

Serpentine Die Cut 10¼x10¾ on 2 or 3 sides
2000, Dec. 15   Photo.
Booklet Stamps
Self-Adhesive

3454	A2681	(34c) pur & multi	.65	.20
3455	A2682	(34c) tan & multi	.65	.20
3456	A2683	(34c) green & multi	.65	.20
3457	A2684	(34c) red & multi	.65	.20
a.		Block of 4, #3454-3457	2.60	
b.		Booklet pane of 4, #3454-3457	2.60	
c.		Booklet pane of 6, #3456, 3457, 2 each #3454-3455	3.90	
d.		Booklet pane of 6, #3454, 3455, 2 each #3456-3457	3.90	
e.		Booklet pane of 20, 5 each #3454-3457 + label	13.00	

Serpentine Die Cut 11½x11¾ on 2 or 3 sides

2000, Dec. 15   **Photo**

3458	A2681	(34c) pur & multi	.65	.20
3459	A2682	(34c) tan & multi	.65	.20
3460	A2683	(34c) grn & multi	.65	.20
3461	A2684	(34c) red & multi	.65	.20
a.	Block of 4, #3458-3461		2.60	
b.	Booklet pane of 20, 2 each #3461a, 3 each #3457a		13.00	
c.	Booklet pane of 20, 2 each #3457a, 3 each #3461a		13.00	

Coil Stamps
Serpentine Die Cut 8½ Vert.

3462	A2683	(34c) green & multi	.65	.20
3463	A2684	(34c) red & multi	.65	.20
3464	A2682	(34c) tan & multi	.65	.20
3465	A2681	(34c) pur & multi	.65	.20
a.	Strip of 4, #3462-3465		2.60	

Lettering on No. 3462 has black outline not found on No. 3456. Zeroes of "2000" are rounder on Nos. 3454-3457 than on Nos. 3462-3465.

Statue of Liberty
A2685

George Washington
A2686

American Buffalo
A2687

Flag Over Farm
A2688

Statue of Liberty — A2689

A2690

A2691

A2692

Flowers
A2693

Apple
A2694

Orange
A2695

Eagle
A2696

Capitol Dome — A2697

Washington Monument
A2698

Serpentine Die Cut 9¾ Vert.

2001   **Photo.**
Coil Stamp
Self-Adhesive

3466	A2685	34c multicolored	.65	.20

Litho.   Perf. 11¼
Self-Adhesive (#3468A, 3471A)

3467	A2687	21c multicolored	.40	.20

Serpentine Die Cut 11
Self-Adhesive (#3468, 3470-3471)

3468	A2687	21c multicolored	.40	.20

Serpentine Die Cut 11¼x11¾

3468A	A2686	23c green	.45	.20

Litho.
Perf. 11¼

3469	A2688	34c multicolored	.65	.20

Serpentine Die Cut 11¼

3470	A2688	34c multicolored	.65	.20

Photo.
Serpentine Die Cut 10¾

3471	A2696	55c multicolored	1.10	.20
3471A	A2696	57c multicolored	1.10	.20

Serpentine Die Cut 11¼x11½

3472	A2697	$3.50 multicolored	7.00	3.50
3473	A2698	$12.25 multicolored	22.50	10.00

COIL STAMPS
Self-Adhesive (#3475, 3477-3481)
Photo.
Serpentine Die Cut 8½ Vert.

3475	A2687	21c multicolored	.40	.20
3475A	A2686	23c green	.45	.20

Perf. 9¾ Vert.

3476	A2685	34c multicolored	.65	.20

Serpentine Die Cut 9¾ Vert.

3477	A2685	34c multicolored	.65	.20

No. 3477 has right angle corners and backing paper as high as the stamp. No. 3466 has rounded corners and is on backing paper larger than the stamp.

Serpentine Die Cut 8½ Vert.

3478	A2690	34c green & multi	.65	.20
3479	A2691	34c red & multi	.65	.20
3480	A2692	34c tan & multi	.65	.20
3481	A2693	34c purple & multi	.65	.20
a.	Strip of 4, #3478-3481		2.60	

BOOKLET STAMPS
Litho.
Self-Adhesive (#3482-3485, 3487-3492)
Serpentine Die Cut 11¼ on 3 Sides

3482	A2686	20c dark carmine	.40	.20
a.	Booklet pane of 10		4.00	
b.	Booklet pane of 4		1.60	
c.	Booklet pane of 6		2.40	

Serpentine Die Cut 10½x11¼ on 3 Sides

3483	A2686	20c dark carmine	.40	.20
a.	Booklet pane of 4, 2 #3482 at L, 2 #3483 at R		5.00	
b.	Booklet pane of 6, 3 #3482 at L, 3 #3483 at R		8.00	
c.	Booklet pane of 10, 5 #3482 at L, 5 #3483 at R		10.00	
d.	Booklet pane of 4, 2 #3483 at L, 2 #3482 at R		5.00	
e.	Booklet pane of 6, 3 #3483 at L, 3 #3482 at R		8.00	
f.	Booklet pane of 10, 5 #3483 at L, 5 #3482 at R		10.00	
g.	Pair, #3482 at L, #3483 at R		2.00	
h.	Pair, #3483 at L, #3482 at R		2.00	

Nos. 3483a and 3483b have No. 3482 at L and No. 3483 at R.

Serpentine Die Cut 11¼ on 3 Sides

3484	A2687	21c multicolored	.40	.20
b.	Booklet pane of 4		1.60	
c.	Booklet pane of 6		2.40	
d.	Booklet pane of 10		4.00	

Serpentine Die Cut 10½x11¼

3484A	A2687	21c multicolored	1.00	.30
e.	Booklet pane of 4, 2 #3484 at L, 2 #3484A at R		5.00	
f.	Booklet pane of 6, 3 #3484 at L, 3 #3484A at R		8.00	
g.	Booklet pane of 10, 5 #3484 at L, 5 #3484A at R		10.00	
h.	Booklet pane of 4, 2 #3484A at L, 2 #3484 at R		5.00	
i.	Booklet pane of 6, 3 #3484A at L, 3 #3484 at R		8.00	
j.	Booklet pane of 10, 5 #3484A at L, 5 #3484 at R		10.00	
k.	Pair, #3484 at L, #3484A at R		2.00	
l.	Pair, #3484A at L, #3484 at R		2.00	

Photo.
Serpentine Die Cut 11 on 2, 3 or 4 Sides

3485	A2689	34c multicolored	.65	.20
a.	Booklet pane of 10		6.50	
b.	Booklet pane of 20		13.00	
c.	Booklet pane of 4		2.60	
d.	Booklet pane of 6		3.90	

Photo.
Serpentine Die Cut 10¼x10¾ on 2 or 3 Sides

3487	A2693	34c purple & multi	.65	.20
3488	A2692	34c tan & multi	.65	.20
3489	A2690	34c green & multi	.65	.20
3490	A2691	34c red & multi	.65	.20
a.	Block of 4, #3487-3490		2.60	
b.	Booklet pane of 4, #3487-3490		2.60	
c.	Booklet pane of 6, #3489-3490, 2 each #3487-3488		3.90	
d.	Booklet pane of 6, #3487-3488, 2 each #3489-3490		3.90	
e.	Booklet pane of 20, 5 each #3490a + label		13.00	

Litho.
Serpentine Die Cut 11¼ on 2, 3 or 4 Sides

3491	A2694	34c multicolored	.65	.20
3492	A2695	34c multicolored	.65	.20
a.	Pair, #3491-3492		1.30	
b.	Booklet pane, 10 each #3491-3492		13.00	
c.	As "a," black ("34 USA") omitted		—	

Serpentine Die Cut 11½x10¾ on 2 or 3 Sides Tagged
Self-Adhesive
Booklet Stamps

3493	A2694	34c multicolored	.65	.20
3494	A2695	34c multicolored	.65	.20
a.	Pair, #3493-3494		1.30	
b.	Booklet pane, 2 each #3493-3494		2.60	
c.	Booklet pane, 3 each #3493-3494, #3493 at UL		3.90	
d.	Booklet pane, 3 each #3493-3494, #3494 at UL		3.90	

Photo.
Serpentine Die Cut 8 on 2, 3 or 4 sides

3495	A2688	34c multicolored	.65	.20
a.	Booklet pane of 18		12.00	

Issued: No. 3466, 1/7/01; Nos. 3472-3473, 1/29/01; Nos. 3468, 3471, 3475, 3482, 3483, 2/22; Nos. 3469, 3476-3481, 3485, 3487-3490, 2/7; Nos. 3470, 3491-3492, 3/6; 3493-3494, May; Nos. 3467, 3468A, 3471A, 3475A, 3484, 3484A, 9/20; 3495, 12/17.

Issued: $3.50, $12.25, 1/29.

Love

Rose, Apr. 20, 1763 Love Letter by John Adams
A2699

Rose, Apr. 20, 1763 Love Letter by John Adams
A2700

Rose, Aug. 11, 1763 Love Letter by John Adams — A2701

Serpentine Die Cut 11¾ on 2, 3 or 4 Sides

2001   **Litho.**
Self-Adhesive
Booklet Stamp

3496	A2699	(34c) multicolored	.65	.20
a.	Booklet pane of 20		13.00	
b.	Vert. pair, imperf horiz.		—	

Serpentine Die Cut 11¼

3497	A2700	34c multicolored	.65	.20
a.	Booklet pane of 20		13.00	

Size: 18x21mm
Serpentine Die Cut 11½x10¾ om 2 or 3 Sides

3498	A2700	34c multicolored	.65	.20
a.	Booklet pane of 4		2.60	
b.	Booklet pane of 6		3.90	

Issued: Nos. 3497-3498, 2/14.

3499	A2701	55c multicolored	1.10	.20

Issued: No. 3496, 1/19; 55c, 2/14. See No. 3551.

Chinese New Year

Year of the Snake
A2702

2001, Jan. 20   **Litho.**   **Perf. 11¼**

3500	A2702	34c multicolored	.65	.20

Black Heritage

Roy Wilkins (1901-81), Civil Rights Leader — A2703

Serpentine Die Cut 11½x11¼

2001, Jan. 24   **Litho.**
Self-Adhesive

3501	A2703	34c blue	.65	.20

American Illustrators

A2704

Designs: a, Marine Corps poster "First in the Fight, Always Faithful," by James Montgomery Flagg. b, "Interlude (The Lute Players)," by Maxfield Parrish. c, Advertisement for Arrow Collars and Shirts, by J. C. Leyendecker. d, Advertisement for Carrier Corp. Refrigeration, by Robert Fawcett. e, Advertisement for Luxite Hosiery, by Coles Phillips. f, Illustration for correspondence school lesson, by Al Parker. g, "Br'er Rabbit," by A. B. Frost. h, "An Attack on a Galleon," by Howard Pyle. i, Kewpie and Kewpie Doodle Dog, by Rose O'Neill. j, Illustration for cover of True Magazine, by Dean Cornwell. k, "Galahad's Departure," by Edwin Austin Abbey. l, "The First Lesson," by Jessie Willcox Smith. m, Illustration for cover of McCall's Magazine, by Neysa McMein. n, "Back Home For Keeps," by Jon Whitcomb. o, "Something for Supper," by Harvey Dunn. p, "A Dash for the Timber," by Frederic Remington. q, Illustration for "Moby Dick," by Rockwell Kent. r, "Captain Bill Bones," by N. C. Wyeth. s, Illustration for cover of The Saturday Evening Post, by Norman Rockwell. t, "The Girl He Left Behind," by John Held, Jr.

Serpentine Die Cut 11¼
2001, Feb. 1   **Photo.**
3502 A2704 Pane of 20   13.00
   a.-t.   34c any single   .65   .30

Diabetes Awareness

A2705

Serpentine Die Cut 11¼x11½
2001, Mar. 16   **Litho.**
Self-Adhesive
3503 A2705 34c multicolored   .65   .20

Nobel Prize Centenary

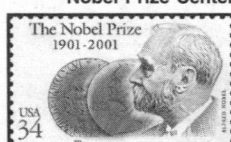

Alfred Nobel and Obverse of Medals A2706

Litho. & Engr.
2001, Mar. 22   **Perf. 11**
3504 A2706 34c multicolored   .65   .20
              See Sweden No. 2415.

Pan-American Exposition Invert Stamps, Cent.

A2707

Reproductions (dated 2001) of: a, #294a. b, #295a. c, #296a. d, Commemorative "cinderella" stamp depicting a buffalo.

Perf. 12 (#3505d), 12½x12 (others)
Litho. (#3505d), Engr. (others)
2001, Mar. 29
3505 A2707 Pane of 7,
              #3505a-3505c, 4
              #3505d   6.75   —
   a.   A109 1c green & black   .20   .20
   b.   A110 2c carmine & black   .20   .20
   c.   A111 4c deep red brown &
              black   .20   .20
   d.   80c red & blue   1.60   .35

Great Plains Prairie

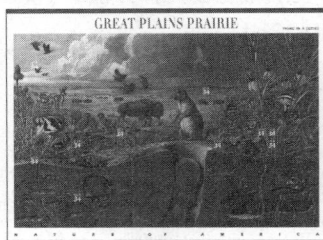

A2708

Wildlife and flowers: a, Pronghorns, Canada geese. b, Burrowing owls, American buffalos. c, American buffalo, Black-tailed prairie dogs, wild alfalfa, horiz. d, Black-tailed prairie dog, American buffalos,. e, Painted lady butterfly, American buffalo, prairie coneflowers, prairie wild roses, horiz. f, Western meadowlark, camel cricket, prairie coneflowers, prairie wild roses. g, Badger, harvester ants. h, Eastern short-horned lizard, plains pocket gopher. i, Plains spadefoot, dung beetle, prairie wild roses, horiz. j, Two-striped grasshopper, Ord's kangaroo rat.

Serpentine Die Cut 10
2001, Apr. 19   **Litho.**
Self-Adhesive
3506 A2708 Pane of 10   7.00
   a.-j.   34c Any single   .65   .20

Peanuts Comic Strip

Snoopy A2709

Serpentine Die Cut 11¼x11½
2001, May 17   **Litho.**
Self-Adhesive
3507 A2709 34c multicolored   .65   .20

Honoring Veterans

A2710

Serpentine Die Cut 11¼x11½
2001, May 23   **Litho.**
Self-Adhesive
3508 A2710 34c multicolored   .65   .20

Frida Kahlo (1907-54), Painter

Self-portrait A2711

2001, June 21   **Litho.**   **Perf. 11¼**
3509 A2711 34c multicolored   .65   .20

Legendary Playing Fields

Ebbets Field A2712

Tiger Stadium A2713

Crosley Field A2714

Yankee Stadium A2715

Polo Grounds A2716

Forbes Field A2717

Fenway Park A2718

Comiskey Park A2719

Shibe Park

Shibe Park A2720

Wrigley Field A2721

Serpentine Die Cut 11¼x11½
2001, June 27   **Photo.**
Self-Adhesive
3510 A2712 34c multicolored   .65   .20
3511 A2713 34c multicolored   .65   .20
3512 A2714 34c multicolored   .65   .20
3513 A2715 34c multicolored   .65   .20
3514 A2716 34c multicolored   .65   .20
3515 A2717 34c multicolored   .65   .20
3516 A2718 34c multicolored   .65   .20
3517 A2719 34c multicolored   .65   .20
3518 A2720 34c multicolored   .65   .20
3519 A2721 34c multicolored   .65   .20
   a.   Block of 10, #3510-3519   6.50

Atlas Statue, New York City

A2722

Serpentine Die Cut 8½ Vert.
2001, June 29   **Photo.**
Self-Adhesive
Coil Stamp
3520 A2722 (10c) multicolored   .20   .20

Leonard Bernstein (1918-90), Conductor

A2723

2001, July 10   **Litho.**   **Perf. 11¼**
3521 A2723 34c multicolored   .65   .20

Woody Wagon

A2724

Serpentine Die Cut 11½ Vert.
2001, Aug. 3   **Photo.**
Self-Adhesive
Coil Stamp
3522 A2724 (15c) multicolored   .30   .20

Legends of Hollywood

Lucille Ball (1911-89) — A2725

Serpentine Die Cut 11
2001, Aug. 6   Litho.
Self-Adhesive

3523	A2725	34c multicolored	.65 .20
a.		As No. 3523, die cutting omitted	—

American Treasures Series
Amish Quilts

Diamond in the Square, c. 1920 — A2726

Lone Star, c. 1920 — A2727

Sunshine and Shadow, c. 1910 — A2728

Double Ninepatch Variation A2729

Serpentine Die Cut 11¼x11½
2001, Aug. 9   Litho.
Self-Adhesive

3524	A2726	34c multicolored	.65 .20
3525	A2727	34c multicolored	.65 .20
3526	A2728	34c multicolored	.65 .20
3527	A2729	34c multicolored	.65 .20
a.		Block or strip of 4, #3524-3527	2.60

Carnivorous Plants

Venus Flytrap A2730   Yellow Trumpet A2731

Cobra Lily — A2732   English Sundew — A2733

Serpentine Die Cut 11½
2001, Aug. 23   Photo.
Self-Adhesive

3528	A2730	34c multicolored	.65 .20
3529	A2731	34c multicolored	.65 .20
3530	A2732	34c multicolored	.65 .20
3531	A2733	34c multicolored	.65 .20
a.		Block or strip of 4, #3528-3531	2.60

Eid

"Eid Mubarak" — A2734

Serpentine Die Cut 11¼
2001, Sept. 1   Photo.
Self-Adhesive

3532	A2734	34c multicolored	.65 .20

Enrico Fermi (1901-54), Physicist

A2735

2001, Sept. 29   Litho.   Perf. 11
Self-Adhesive

3533	A2735	34c multicolored	.65 .20

That's All Folks!

Porky Pig at Mailbox — A2736

Serpentine Die Cut 11
2001, Oct. 1   Photo.
Self-Adhesive

3534		Pane of 10	6.50
a.		A2736 34c single	.65 .20
b.		Booklet pane of 9 #3534a	5.85
c.		Booklet pane of 1 #3534a	.65

Die cutting on No. 3534b does not extend through the backing paper.

3535		Pane of 10	6.50
a.		A2736 34c single	.65
b.		Booklet pane of 9 #3535a	—
c.		Booklet pane of 1, imperf.	—

Die cutting on No. 3535a extends through backing paper. Used examples of No. 3535a are identical to those of No. 3534a.

Nos. 3534b-3534c and 3535b-3535c are separated by a vertical line of microperforations.

Christmas

Virgin and Child, by Lorenzo Costa — A2737

A2738	A2739
A2740	A2741

19th Century Chromolithographs of Santa Claus

Serpentine Die Cut 11½ on 2, 3 or 4 Sides
2001, Oct. 10   Photo.
Self-Adhesive
Booklet Stamps (#3536, 3541-3544)

3536	A2737	34c multicolored	.65 .20
a.		Booklet pane of 20	13.00

Serpentine Die Cut 10¾x11
Black Inscriptions

3537	A2738	34c multi, large date	.65 .20
a.		Small date (from booklet pane)	.65 .20
3538	A2739	34c multi, large date	.65 .20
a.		Small date (from booklet pane)	.65 .20
3539	A2740	34c multi, large date	.65 .20
a.		Small date (from booklet pane)	.65 .20
3540	A2741	34c multi, large date	.65 .20
a.		Small date (from booklet pane)	.65 .20
b.		Block of 4, #3537-3540	2.60
c.		Block of 4, small date, #3537a-3540a	2.60
d.		Booklet pane, 5 #3540c + label	13.00

Designs of Nos. 3537a-3540a are slightly taller than Nos. 3537-3540.

Serpentine Die Cut 11 on 2 or 3 Sides
Size: 21x18½mm
Green and Red Inscriptions

3541	A2738	34c multicolored	.65 .20
3542	A2739	34c multicolored	.65 .20
3543	A2740	34c multicolored	.65 .20
3544	A2741	34c multicolored	.65 .20
a.		Block of 4, #3541-3544	2.60
b.		Booklet pane of 4, #3541-3544	2.60
c.		Booklet pane of 6, #3543-3544, 2 #3541-3542	3.90
d.		Booklet pane of 6, #3541-3542, 2 #3543-3544	3.90
		Nos. 3536-3544 (9)	5.85 1.80

James Madison (1751-1836)

Madison and His Home, Montpelier — A2742

Litho. & Engr.
2001, Oct. 18   Perf. 11x11¼

3545	A2742	34c green & black	.65 .20

Thanksgiving

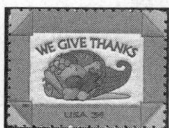

Cornucopia A2743

Serpentine Die Cut 11¼
2001, Oct. 19   Litho.
Self-Adhesive

3546	A2743	34c multicolored	.65 .20

Hanukkah Type of 1996
Serpentine Die Cut 11
2001, Oct. 21   Photo.
Self-Adhesive

3547	A2411	34c multicolored	.65 .20

Kwanzaa Type of 1997
Serpentine Die Cut 11
2001, Oct. 21   Photo.
Self-Adhesive

3548	A2458	34c multicolored	.65 .20

United We Stand

A2744

Serpentine Die Cut 11¼ on 2, 3, or 4 Sides
2001, Oct. 24   Litho.
Self-Adhesive
Booklet Stamp

3549	A2744	34c multicolored	.65 .20
a.		Booklet pane of 20	13.00

United We Stand Type of 2001
Serpentine Die Cut 9 ¾ Vert.
2001, Oct. 24   Photo.
Self-Adhesive
Coil Stamp

3550	A2744	34c multicolored	.65 .20
3550A	A2744	34c multicolored	.65 .20

No. 3550 has right angle corners and backing paper as high as the stamp. No. 3550A has rounded corners, the backing paper larger than the stamp, and the stamps are spaced approximately 2mm apart.

Love Letters Type of 2001
Serpentine Die Cut 11¼
2001, Nov. 19   Litho.
Self-Adhesive

3551	A2701	57c multicolored	1.10 .20

Winter Olympics

Ski Jumping A2745

Snowboarding — A2746

Ice Hockey A2747

Figure
Skating
A2748

Serpentine Die Cut 11½x10¾

2002, Jan. 8   Photo.

Self-Adhesive

3552	A2745	34c multicolored	.65	.20
3553	A2746	34c multicolored	.65	.20
3554	A2747	34c multicolored	.65	.20
3555	A2748	34c multicolored	.65	.20
a.		Block or strip of 4, #3552-3555	2.60	

Mentoring a Child

Child and
Adult
A2749

Serpentine Die Cut 11x10¾

2002, Jan. 10   Photo.

Self-Adhesive

3556	A2749	34c multicolored	.65	.20

Subject Index of Regular & Air Post Issues

UNITED STATES

SEMI-POSTAL STAMP

Breast Cancer Awareness

SP1

Serpentine Die Cut 11

1998, July 29   **Photo.**

Self-Adhesive

B1	SP1	(32c+8c) multicolored	.80	.25

The 8c surtax was for cancer research. Copies of #B1 sold after the Jan. 10, 1999 1st class postage rate change were 33c stamps with 7c surtax; after Jan. 7, 2001, 34c stamps with 6c surtax.

AIR POST STAMPS

For prepayment of postage on all mailable matter sent by airmail.

Curtiss Jenny — AP1

Engraved (Flat Plate Printing)

			1918	**Unwmk.**	**Perf. 11**
C1	AP1	6c orange		70.00	30.00
		Never hinged		110.00	

C2	AP1	16c green	90.00	35.00
		Never hinged	145.00	
C3	AP1	24c car rose & bl	90.00	35.00
		Never hinged	145.00	
a.		Center inverted	170,000.	
		Never hinged	200,000.	
		Nos. C1-C3 (3)	250.00	100.00
		Nos. C1-C3, never hinged	400.00	

Wooden Propeller and Radiator AP2

Emblem of Air Service AP3

De Havilland Biplane — AP4

1923

C4	AP2	8c dark green	25.00	14.00
		Never hinged	40.00	
C5	AP3	16c dark blue	90.00	30.00
		Never hinged	145.00	
C6	AP4	24c carmine	100.00	30.00
		Never hinged	160.00	
		Nos. C4-C6 (3)	215.00	74.00
		Nos. C4-C6, never hinged	345.00	

Map of US and Two Mail Planes — AP5

1926-27

C7	AP5	10c dark blue	2.80	.35
		Never hinged	4.50	
C8	AP5	15c olive brown	3.25	2.50
		Never hinged	5.25	
C9	AP5	20c yellow green ('27)	8.50	2.00
		Never hinged	13.50	
		Nos. C7-C9 (3)	14.55	4.85
		Nos. C7-C9, never hinged	23.25	

Lindbergh's Airplane "Spirit of St. Louis" — AP6

1927, June 18

C10	AP6	10c dark blue	7.75	2.50
		Never hinged	12.50	
a.		Booklet pane of 3	75.00	65.00
		Never hinged	110.00	

Singles from No. C10a are imperf. at sides or imperf. at sides and bottom.

Nos. C1-C10 were available for ordinary postage.

Beacon on Rocky Mountains AP7

1928, July 25   **Perf. 11**

C11	AP7	5c carmine & blue	5.25	.75
		Never hinged	8.50	
a.		Vertical pair, imperf. btwn.	5,500.	

Winged Globe — AP8

1930, Feb. 10   **Perf. 11**

Size: 46½x19mm

C12	AP8	5c violet	11.00	.50
		Never hinged	17.50	
a.		Horiz. pair, imperf. btwn.	4,500.	

See Nos. C16-C17, C19.

Graf Zeppelin Issue

Zeppelin over Atlantic Ocean — AP9

Zeppelin between Continents — AP10

Zeppelin Passing Globe — AP11

1930, Apr. 19   **Perf. 11**

C13	AP9	65c green	250.00	160.00
		Never hinged	360.00	
C14	AP10	$1.30 brown	475.00	375.00
		Never hinged	700.00	
C15	AP11	$2.60 blue	750.00	575.00
		Never hinged	1,100.	
		Nos. C13-C15 (3)	1,475.	1,110.
		Nos. C13-C15, never hinged	2,160.	

Issued for use on mail carried on first Europe-Pan-America round-trip flight of Graf Zeppelin, May, 1930.

Type of 1930 Issue

Rotary Press Printing

1931-32   **Perf. 10½x11**

Size: 47½x19mm

C16	AP8	5c violet	5.50	.60
		Never hinged	8.75	
C17	AP8	8c olive bister ('32)	2.40	.40
		Never hinged	3.75	

Century of Progress Issue

Airship "Graf Zeppelin" — AP12

Flat Plate Printing

1933, Oct. 2   **Perf. 11**

C18	AP12	50c green	75.00	70.00
		Never hinged	110.00	

Flight of the "Graf Zeppelin" in Oct. 1933, to Miami, Akron and Chicago, and from the last city to Europe.

> **Catalogue values for unused stamps in this section, from this point to the end of the section, are for Never Hinged items.**

Type of 1930 Issue

Rotary Press Printing

1934, June 30   **Perf. 10½x11**

C19	AP8	6c dull orange	3.50	.25

Transpacific Issues

The "China Clipper" over the Pacific AP13

Flat Plate Printing

1935, Nov. 22   **Perf. 11**

C20	AP13	25c blue	1.40	1.00

Issued to pay postage on mail carried on the Transpacific air post service inaugurated Nov. 22, 1935.

The "China Clipper" over the Pacific AP14

1937, Feb. 15   **Perf. 11**

C21	AP14	20c green	11.00	1.75
C22	AP14	50c carmine	10.00	5.00

Eagle Holding Shield, Olive Branch and Arrows AP15

1938, May 14   **Perf. 11**

C23	AP15	6c dk blue & carmine	.50	.20
a.		Vert. pair, imperf. horiz.	350.00	
b.		Horiz. pair, imperf. vert.	12,500.	

Transatlantic Issue

Winged Globe — AP16

1939, May 16   **Perf. 11**

C24	AP16	30c dull blue	10.50	1.50

Twin-Motored Transport Plane — AP17

Rotary Press Printing

1941-44   **Perf. 11x10½**

C25	AP17	6c carmine	.20	.20
a.		Booklet pane of 3 ('43)	5.00	1.50
b.		Horiz. pair, imperf. between	2,250.	
C26	AP17	8c olive grn ('44)	.20	.20
C27	AP17	10c violet	1.25	.20
C28	AP17	15c brown carmine	2.75	.35
C29	AP17	20c bright green	2.25	.30
C30	AP17	30c blue	2.50	.35
C31	AP17	50c orange	11.00	3.00
		Nos. C25-C31 (7)	20.15	4.60

Singles from No. C25a are imperf. at sides or imperf. at sides and bottom.

DC-4 Skymaster AP18

1946, Sept. 25   **Perf. 11x10½**

C32	AP18	5c carmine	.20	.20

DC-4 Skymaster — AP19

1947, Mar. 26   **Perf. 10½x11**

C33	AP19	5c carmine	.20	.20

See Nos. C37, C39, C41.

Pan American Union Building, Washington, DC — AP20

Statue of Liberty & New York Skyline AP21

Plane over San Francisco-Oakland Bay Bridge — AP22

1947   **Perf. 11x10½**
C34 AP20 10c black   .25 .20
C35 AP21 15c brt blue green   .35 .20
   a. Horiz. pair, imperf. between   2,250.
C36 AP22 25c blue   .85 .20
   Nos. C34-C36 (3)   1.45 .60

No. C35a is valued in the grade of fine.

Coil Stamp
1948, Jan. 15   **Perf. 10 Horiz.**
C37 AP19 5c carmine   1.00 .80

New York City Issue

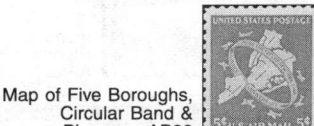

Map of Five Boroughs, Circular Band & Planes — AP23

1948, July 31   **Perf. 11x10½**
C38 AP23 5c bright carmine   .20 .20

50th anniv. of the consolidation of the 5 boroughs of NYC.

Type of 1947
1949, Jan. 18   **Perf. 10½x11**
C39 AP19 6c carmine   .20 .20
   a. Booklet pane of 6   10.00 5.00

Alexandria Bicentennial Issue

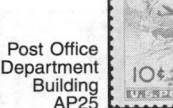

Home of John Carlyle, Alexandria Seal & Gadsby's Tavern AP24

Rotary Press Printing
1949, May 11   **Perf. 11x10½**
C40 AP24 6c carmine   .20 .20

Founding of Alexandria, Va, 200th anniv.

Type of 1947
Coil Stamp
1949, Aug. 25   **Perf. 10 Horiz.**
C41 AP19 6c carmine   3.25 .20

Universal Postal Union Issue

Post Office Department Building AP25

Globe & Doves Carrying Messages AP26

Boeing Stratocruiser & Globe — AP27

1949   **Unwmk.**   **Perf. 11x10½**
C42 AP25 10c violet   .20 .20
C43 AP26 15c ultramarine   .30 .25
C44 AP27 25c rose carmine   .50 .40
   Nos. C42-C44 (3)   1.00 .85

75th anniv. of the UPU.

Wright Brothers Issue

Wilbur & Orville Wright and their Plane AP28

1949, Dec. 17   **Perf. 11x10½**
C45 AP28 6c magenta   .20 .20

46th anniv. of the Wright Brothers' 1st flight, Dec. 17, 1903.

Diamond Head, Honolulu, Hawaii AP29

1952, Mar. 26   **Perf. 11x10½**
C46 AP29 80c brt red violet   5.00 1.25

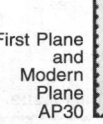

First Plane and Modern Plane AP30

Powered Flight Issue
1953, May 29   **Perf. 11x10½**
C47 AP30 6c carmine   .20 .20

50th anniversary of powered flight.

Eagle in Flight — AP31

For Domestic Post Cards
1954, Sept. 3   **Perf. 11x10½**
C48 AP31 4c bright blue   .20 .20

See No. C50.

Air Force Issue

B-52 Stratofortress and F-104 Starfighters — AP32

Rotary Press Printing
1957, Aug. 1   **Perf. 11x10½**
C49 AP32 6c blue   .20 .20

50th anniv. of US Air Force.

Flying Eagle Type of 1954
For Domestic Post Cards
1958, July 31   **Perf. 11x10½**
C50 AP31 5c rose red   .20 .20

Silhouette of Jet Airliner — AP33

1958, July 31   **Perf. 10½x11**
C51 AP33 7c blue   .20 .20
   a. Booklet pane of 6   13.00 7.00
   b. Vert. pair, imperf btwn. (from bklt. pane)   —

Coil Stamp
Perf. 10 Horizontally
C52 AP33 7c blue   2.25 .20

No. C51b resulted from a paper foldover after perforating and before cutting into panes. Two pairs are known.
See Nos. C60-C61.

Alaska Statehood Issue

Big Dipper, North Star & Map of Alaska AP34

Rotary Press Printing
1959, Jan. 3   **Perf. 11x10½**
C53 AP34 7c dark blue   .20 .20

Alaska's admission to statehood.

Balloon Jupiter Issue

Balloon & Crowd — AP35

Giori Press Printing
1959, Aug. 17   **Perf. 11**
C54 AP35 7c dark blue & red   .20 .20

Cent. of the carrying of mail by the balloon Jupiter from Lafayette to Crawfordsville, Ind.

Hawaii Statehood Issue

Alii Warrior, Map of Hawaii & Star of Statehood AP36

Rotary Press Printing
1959, Aug. 21   **Perf. 11x10½**
C55 AP36 7c rose red   .20 .20

Hawaii's admission to statehood.

Pan American Games Issue

Runner Holding Torch — AP37

Giori Press Printing
1959, Aug. 27   **Perf. 11**
C56 AP37 10c vio bl & brt red   .25 .25

3rd Pan American Games, Chicago, Aug. 27-Sept. 7.

Liberty Bell AP38

Statue of Liberty AP39

Abraham Lincoln AP40

Giori Press Printing
1959-66   **Perf. 11**
C57 AP38 10c blk & grn ('60)   1.25 .70
C58 AP39 15c black & orange   .35 .20
C59 AP40 25c blk & mar ('60)   .50 .20
   a. Tagged ('66)   .60 .30
   Nos. C57-C59 (3)   2.10 1.10

Luminescence
See note following No. 1053. "Tagged" varieties of untagged airmail stamps start with No. C59a and end with No. C67a.
Airmail stamps starting with No. C69 are tagged unless otherwise noted.

Type of 1958
Rotary Press Printing
1960, Aug. 12   **Perf. 10½x11**
C60 AP33 7c carmine   .20 .20
   a. Booklet pane of 6   16.00 8.00
   b. Vert. pair, imperf btwn. (from bklt. pane)   5,500.

No. C60b resulted from a paper foldover after perforating and before cutting into panes. Two pairs are known.

Type of 1958
Coil Stamp
1960, Oct. 22   **Perf. 10 Horiz.**
C61 AP33 7c carmine   4.25 .25

Type of 1959-60 and

Statue of Liberty AP41

Giori Press Printing
1961-67   **Perf. 11**
C62 AP38 13c black & red   .40 .20
   a. Tagged ('67)   .75 .50
C63 AP41 15c black & orange   .30 .20
   a. Tagged ('67)   .35 .20
   b. As "a," horiz. pair, imperf. vert.   15,000.

No. C63 has a gutter between the two parts of the design; No. C58 has none.

Jet Airliner Over Capitol — AP42

Rotary Press Printing
1962, Dec. 5   **Perf. 10½x11**
C64 AP42 8c carmine   .20 .20
   a. Tagged ('63)   .20 .20
   b. Booklet pane 5 + label   7.00 2.00
   c. As "b," tagged ('64)   2.00 .75

Three different messages are found on the label in No. C64b, and one on No. C64c.

Coil Stamp
Perf. 10 Horizontally
C65 AP42 8c carmine   .40 .20
   a. Tagged ('65)   .35 .20

The 1st luminescent tagged US issue was No. C64a issued Aug. 1, 1963, at Dayton, OH. Initial experiments there used tagged stamps and an automated facer-canceler to extract airmail as an aid to dispatch.

Montgomery Blair Issue

Montgomery Blair — AP43

Giori Press Printing
1963, May 3   Unwmk.   Perf. 11
C66 AP43 15c car, dp cl & bl   .60   .55

Blair (1813-1883), Postmaster Gen. (1861-64), who called the 1st Intl. Postal Conf., Paris, 1863, forerunner of the UPU.

Bald Eagle — AP44

For Domestic Post Cards
Rotary Press Printing
1963, July 12   Perf. 11x10½
C67 AP44 6c red   .20   .20
  a. Tagged ('67)   4.00   3.00

Amelia Earhart Issue

Amelia Earhart & Lockheed Electra — AP45

Giori Press Printing
1963, July 24   Perf. 11
C68 AP45 8c carmine & maroon   .20   .20
Earhart (1898-1937), 1st woman to fly across the Atlantic.

Dr. Robert H. Goddard Issue

Robert H. Goddard, Atlas Rocket & Launching Tower, Cape Kennedy AP46

1964, Oct. 5   Unwmk.   Tagged
C69 AP46 8c blue, red & bister   .40   .20
Goddard (1882-1945), physicist and pioneer rocket researcher.

Tlingit Totem, Southern Alaska AP47

"Columbia Jays," by Audubon AP48

Alaska Purchase Issue
Giori Press Printing
1967, Mar. 30   Perf. 11
C70 AP47 8c brown   .25   .20
Cent. of the Alaska Purchase.

The Tlingit totem is from the Alaska State Museum, Juneau.

1967, Apr. 26   Perf. 11
C71 AP48 20c multicolored   .80   .20
See note after No. 1241.

50-Star Runway — AP49

Rotary Press Printing
1968, Jan. 5   Unwmk.   Perf. 11x10½
C72 AP49 10c carmine   .20   .20
  b. Booklet pane of 8   2.00   .75
  c. Booklet pane of 5 + label 3.75   .75
  d. Vert. pair, imperf btwn. (from
     bklt. pane)   8,000.

Coil Stamp
Perf. 10 Vertically
C73 AP49 10c carmine   .30   .20
  a. Imperf., pair   600.00

No. C72d resulted from a paper foldover after perforating and before cutting into panes. Only one pair is known.

The $1 Air Lift stamp is listed as No. 1341.

Air Mail Service Issue

Curtiss Jenny AP50

Lithographed, Engraved (Giori)
1968, May 15   Perf. 11
C74 AP50 10c blue, black & red   .25   .20
50th anniv. of regularly scheduled US air mail service.

USA and Jet — AP51

1968, Nov. 22   Perf. 11
C75 AP51 20c red, blue & black   .35   .20
See No. C81.

Moon Landing Issue

First Man on the Moon — AP52

Litho. & Engr. (Giori)
1969, Sept. 9   Perf. 11
C76 AP52 10c multicolored   .25   .20
  a. Rose red (litho.) omitted 500.00   —

Man's 1st landing on the moon, July 20, 1969.
U.S. astronauts Neil A. Armstrong and Col. Edwin E. Aldrin, Jr., with Lieut. Col. Michael Collins piloting Apollo 11.
On No. C76a, the litho. rose red is missing from the entire vignette—the dots on top of the yellow areas as well as the flag shoulder patch.

Type of 1968 and:

Silhouette of Delta Wing Plane — AP53

Silhouette of Jet Airliner AP54

Winged Airmail Envelope AP55

Statue of Liberty AP56

Design: 21c, "USA" and jet (as #C75).

Rotary Press Printing
1971-73   Perf. 10½x11
C77 AP53 9c red   .20   .20
Perf. 11x10½
C78 AP54 11c carmine   .20   .20
  a. Booklet pane of 4 + 2 labels 1.25   .75
  b. Untagged (Bureau precanceled)   .30
C79 AP55 13c carmine ('73)   .25   .20
  a. Booklet pane of 5 + label ('73) 1.50   .75
  b. Untagged (Bureau precanceled)   .30

Giori Press Printing
Perf. 11
C80 AP56 17c bluish black, red &
    dark green   .35   .20

Litho. & Engr. (Giori)
Perf. 11
C81 AP51 21c red, blue & black   .40   .20
  b. Black (engr.) omitted
    Nos. C77-C81 (5)   1.40   1.00

Issued: 9c, 5/15; 11c, 5/7; 17c, 7/13; 21c, 5/21/71; 13c, 11/16/73.
The 9c was for use on domestic post cards. No. C78b is precanceled "WASHINGTON D.C." (or "DC") and No. C79b "WASHINGTON DC" for the use of Congressmen and the public.

Coil Stamps
Rotary Press Printing
1971-73   Perf. 10 Vertically
C82 AP54 11c carmine   .25   .20
  a. Imperf., pair   300.00
C83 AP55 13c carmine ('73)   .30   .20
  a. Imperf., pair   75.00

Issue dates: 11c, May 7; 13c, Dec. 27.

National Parks Centennial Issue

Kii Statue & Temple, City of Refuge, Hawaii — AP57

Litho. & Engr. (Giori)
1972, May 3   Perf. 11
C84 AP57 11c orange & multi   .20   .20
  a. Blue & green (litho) omitted 800.00

Cent. of the Natl. Parks system. No. C84 shows view of the City of Refuge Natl. Historical Park at Honaunau.

Olympic Games Issue

Skiing & Olympic Rings AP58

Photogravure (Andreotti)
1972, Aug. 17   Perf. 11x10½
C85 AP58 11c multicolored   .20   .20
11th Winter Olympic Games, Sapporo, Japan, Feb. 3-13, and 20th Summer Olympic Games, Munich, Germany, Aug. 26-Sept. 11.

Electronics Progress Issue

De Forest Audions AP59

Litho. & Engr. (Giori)
1973, July 10   Perf. 11
C86 AP59 11c multicolored   .20   .20
  a. Vermilion & olive (litho.) omit-
    ted   1,400.
  c. Olive omitted

Statue of Liberty AP60

Mt. Rushmore National Memorial AP61

1974   Giori Press Printing   Perf. 11
C87 AP60 18c car, black & ultra   .35   .25
C88 AP61 26c ultra, black & car   .50   .20
Issue dates: 18c, Jan. 11; 26c, Jan. 2.

Plane & Globes AP62

Plane, Globes & Flag AP63

Giori Press Printing
1976, Jan. 2   Perf. 11
C89 AP62 25c ultra, red & black   .50   .20
C90 AP63 31c ultra, red & black   .60   .20

Wright Brothers Issue

Orville and Wilbur Wright, Flyer A AP64

Wright Brothers, Flyer A and Shed AP65

Litho. & Engr.
1978, Sept. 23   Perf. 11
C91 AP64 31c ultra & multi   .65   .30
C92 AP65 31c ultra & multi   .65   .30
  a. Vert. pair, #C91-C92   1.30   1.10
  b. As "a," ultra & blk (engr.)
    omitted   800.00
  c. As "a," black (engr.) omitted   —
  d. As "a," blk, yel, mag, bl & brn
    (litho.) omitted   2,250.

75th anniv. of 1st powered flight, Kill Devil Hill, NC, Dec. 17, 1903.

Octave Chanute Issue

Chanute & Biplane Hangglider AP66

Biplane Hanggliders & Chanute AP67

Litho. & Engr.

1979, Mar. 29   *Perf. 11*
C93 AP66 21c ultra & multi .70 .30
C94 AP67 21c ultra & multi .70 .30
  a. Vert. pair, #C93-C94 1.40 1.10
  b. As "a," ultramarine & black
    (engr.) omitted 4,500.
Octave Chanute (1832-1910), civil engineer and aviation pioneer.

Wiley Post Issue

Wiley Post & "Winnie Mae" AP68   NR-105 W, Post in Pressurized Suit, Portrait AP69

Litho. & Engr.

1979, Nov. 20   *Perf. 11*
C95 AP68 25c ultra & multi 1.10 .35
C96 AP69 25c ultra & multi 1.10 .35
  a. Vert. pair, #C95-C96 2.25 1.25
Post (1899-1935), 1st man to fly around the world alone and high-altitude flying pioneer.

Olympic Games Issue

High Jump AP70

1979, Nov. 1   Photo.   *Perf. 11*
C97 AP70 31c multicolored .70 .30
22nd Olympic Games, Moscow, July 19-Aug. 3, 1980.

Philip Mazzei (1730-1816), Italian-born Political Writer — AP71

1980, Oct. 13   Photo.   *Perf. 11*
C98 AP71 40c multicolored .80 .20
  b. Imperf., pair 2,750.
    Perf. 10½x11¼
C98A AP71 40c multicolored 6.50 1.50
  c. Horiz. pair, imperf. vert.
Issued: #C98, 10/13; #C98A, 1982.

Blanche Stuart Scott (1886-1970) — AP72

Glenn Curtiss (1878-1930) — AP73

1980, Dec. 30
C99 AP72 28c multicolored .60 .20
  a. Imperf., pair 3,500.
C100 AP73 35c multicolored .65 .20
Scott, 1st woman pilot, and Curtiss, aviation pioneer and aircraft designer.

1984 Olympic Games

AP81

1983, June 17   *Perf. 11*
C101 AP81 28c Gymnast 1.00 .30
C102 AP81 28c Hurdler 1.00 .30
C103 AP81 28c Basketball 1.00 .30
C104 AP81 28c Soccer 1.00 .30
  a. Block of 4, #C101-C104 4.50 2.00
  b. As "a," imperf. vert.
  Nos. C101-C104 are vertical.

1983, Apr. 8
C105 AP81 40c Shot put .90 .40
C106 AP81 40c Gymnast .90 .40
C107 AP81 40c Swimmer .90 .40
C108 AP81 40c Weightlifting .90 .40
  b. Block of 4, #C105-C108 4.25 2.50
  d. As "b," imperf. 1,250.

1983, Nov. 4
C109 AP81 35c Women's fencing .90 .50
C110 AP81 35c Cycling .90 .50
C111 AP81 35c Women's volley- ball .90 .50
C112 AP81 35c Pole vaulting .90 .50
  a. Block of 4, #C109-C112 4.00 3.00

Alfred V. Verville AP86

Lawrence & Elmer Sperry AP87

1985, Feb. 13   Photo.
C113 AP86 33c multicolored .65 .20
  a. Imperf., pair 850.00
C114 AP87 39c multicolored .80 .25
  a. Imperf., pair 1,400.
Alfred V. Verville (1890-1970), aircraft designer, Lawrence Sperry (1892-1931), designer and pilot, and Elmer Sperry (1860-1930), inventor.

Transpacific Airmail AP88

1985, Feb. 15   Photo.
C115 AP88 44c multicolored .85 .25
  a. Imperf., pair 900.00

Fr. Junipero Serra (1713-84)
California Missionary

Outline Map of Southern California, Portrait, San Gabriel Mission AP89

1985, Aug. 22   Photo.   *Perf. 11*
C116 AP89 44c multicolored 1.00 .30
  a. Imperf., pair 1,500.

Settling of New Sweden, 350th Anniv. AP90

17th Cent. European settler negotiating with 2 American Indians, map of New Sweden, the Swedish ships *Kalmar Nyckel* and *Fogel Grip*, based on an 18th cent. illustration from a Swedish book about the Colonies.

1988, Mar. 29   Litho. & Engr.
C117 AP90 44c multicolored 1.00 .25
See Finland No. 768 and Sweden No. 1672.

Samuel Pierpont Langley (1834-1906)
Astronomer, Aviation Pioneer and Inventor

Langley and Unmanned Aerodrome No. 5 AP91

Litho. & Engr.

1988, May 14   *Perf. 11*
C118 AP91 45c multicolored .90 .20

Igor Sikorsky (1889-1972)
Aeronautic Engineer

Sikorsky and VS300 Helicopter, 1939 AP92

1988, June 23   Photo.   *Perf. 11*
C119 AP92 36c multicolored .70 .20

French Revolution, Bicent.

Liberty, Equality and Fraternity — AP93

Litho. & Engr.

1989, July 14   *Perf. 11½x11*
C120 AP93 45c multicolored .95 .20
See France Nos. 2143-2145a.

Pre-Columbian America Issue

UPAE Emblem & *Key Marco Cat* — AP94

Design features Southeastern Figure, *Key Marco Cat*, Calusa Culture, Pre-Columbian Mississippian Period, A.D. 700-1450

1989, Oct. 12   Photo.   *Perf. 11*
C121 AP94 45c multicolored .90 .20
Discovery of America, 500th anniv. (in 1992).

Futuristic Mail Delivery

Spacecraft AP95

Air-suspended Hover Car — AP96

Moon Rover — AP97

Space Shuttle — AP98

1989, Nov. 27   *Perf. 11*
C122 AP95 45c multicolored 1.00 .40
C123 AP96 45c multicolored 1.00 .40
C124 AP97 45c multicolored 1.00 .40
C125 AP98 45c multicolored 1.00 .40
  a. Block of 4, Nos. C122-C125 4.25 3.00
  b. As "a," lt bl (engr.) omitted 800.00

Litho. & Engr.

1989, Nov. 24   *Imperf.*
C126 Sheet of 4 4.75 3.75
  a. AP95 45c multicolored 1.00 .50
  b. AP96 45c multicolored 1.00 .50
  c. AP97 45c multicolored 1.00 .50
  d. AP98 45c multicolored 1.00 .50
World Stamp Expo '89, 20th UPU Congress. See Russia No. 5837.

Pre-Columbian America Issue

Tropical Coast AP99

1990, Oct. 12   Photo.   *Perf. 11*
C127 AP99 45c multicolored .90 .20

Harriet Quimby, Bleriot Aircraft AP100

1991, Apr. 27   Photo.   *Perf. 11*
C128 AP100 50c multicolored 1.00 .25
  a. Vert. pair, imperf. horiz. 2,000.
  b. Perf. 11.2 ('93) 1.10 .25

William T. Piper, Piper Cub AP101

1991, May 17
C129 AP101 40c multicolored .80 .20
See No. C132.

Antarctic Treaty, 30th Anniv. AP102

1991, June 21   Photo.   *Perf. 11*
C130 AP102 50c multicolored 1.00 .25

UNITED STATES

112

Pre-Columbian America Issue

First Americans Crossed Over From Asia
AP103

1991, Oct. 12   Photo.   *Perf. 11*
C131 AP103 50c multicolored   1.00   .25

Piper Type of 1991

1993   Photo.   *Perf. 11¼*
C132 AP101 40c multicolored   1.20   .20

Piper's hair touches top edge of design. Bullseye perf.

"All LC (Letters and Cards) mail receives First-Class Mail service in the United States, is dispatched by the fastest transportation available, and travels by airmail or priority service in the destination country. All LC mail should be marked 'AIRMAIL' or 'PAR AVION.'" (U.S. Postal Service, Pub. 51).

No. C133 listed below was issued to meet the LC rate to Canada and Mexico and is inscribed with the silhouette of a jet plane next to the denomination indicating the need for airmail service. This is unlike No. 2998, which met the LC rate to other countries, but contained no indication that it was intended for that use.

Future issues that meet a specific international airmail rate and contain the airplane silhouette will be treated by Scott as Air Post stamps. Stamps similar to No. 2998 will be listed in the Postage section.

Niagara Falls

AP104

1999, May 12   Photo.   *Perf. 11*
Self-Adhesive
C133 AP104 48c multicolored   .95   .20

Rio Grande

AP105

Serpentine Die Cut 11
1999, July 30   Photo.
Self-Adhesive
C134 AP105 40c multicolored   .80   .60

Grand Canyon

AP106

Serpentine Die Cut 11¼x11½
2000, Jan. 20   Litho.
Self-Adhesive
C135 AP106 60c multicolored   1.25   .25
   a.   Imperf, pair   —

Nine-Mile Prairie, Nebraska

AP107

Serpentine Die Cut 11¼x11½
2001, Mar. 6   Litho.
Self-Adhesive
C136 AP107 70c multicolored   1.40   .30

AIR POST STAMP

Mt. Mc Kinley

AP108

Serpentine Die Cut 11
2001, Apr. 17   Photo.
Self-Adhesive
C137 AP108 80c multicolored   1.60   .35

Acadia National Park

AP109

Serpentine Die Cut 11¼x11½
2001, May 30   Litho.
Self-Adhesive
C138 AP109 60c multicolored   1.25   .25

AIR POST SPECIAL DELIVERY STAMPS

To provide for the payment of both the postage and the special delivery fee in one stamp.

Great Seal of United States APSD1

Flat Plate Printing
1934   Unwmk.   *Perf. 11*
CE1 APSD1 16c dark blue   .60   .65
   Never hinged   .80

For imperforate variety see No. 771.

1936
CE2 APSD1 16c red & blue   .40   .25
   Never hinged   .50
   a.   Horiz. pair, imperf. vert.   4,000.

SPECIAL DELIVERY STAMPS

When affixed to any letter or article of mailable matter, secure immediate delivery, between 7 A. M. and midnight, at any post office.

Messenger Running SD1

Flat Plate Printing
1885   Unwmk.   *Perf. 12*
E1 SD1 10c blue   350.00   45.00
   Never hinged   700.00

Messenger Running SD2

1888
E2 SD2 10c blue   325.00   17.50
   Never hinged   650.00

1893
E3 SD2 10c orange   200.00   22.50
   Never hinged   400.00

Messenger Running SD3

Line under "Ten Cents"

1894
E4 SD3 10c blue   750.00   30.00
   Never hinged   1,500.

1895   *Wmk. 191*
E5 SD3 10c blue   160.00   3.50
   Never hinged   300.00
   b.   Printed on both sides   —

Messenger on Bicycle SD4

1902
E6 SD4 10c ultramarine   110.00   3.25
   Never hinged   200.00
   a.   10c blue   110.00   3.25
   Never hinged   200.00

Helmet of Mercury and Olive Branch — SD5

1908
E7 SD5 10c green   60.00   40.00
   Never hinged   110.00

1911   Wmk. 190   *Perf. 12*
E8 SD4 10c ultramarine   100.00   5.25
   Never hinged   185.00
   b.   10c violet blue   100.00   5.25
   Never hinged   185.00

1914   *Perf. 10*
E9 SD4 10c ultramarine   180.00   6.50
   Never hinged   340.00
   a.   10c blue   210.00   6.50
   Never hinged   390.00

1916   Unwmk.   *Perf. 10*
E10 SD4 10c pale ultra   275.00   27.50
   Never hinged   500.00
   a.   10c blue   310.00   27.50
   Never hinged   575.00

1917   *Perf. 11*
E11 SD4 10c ultramarine   20.00   .50
   Never hinged   37.50
   b.   10c gray violet   20.00   .50
   Never hinged   37.50
   c.   10c blue   50.00   2.50
   Never hinged   92.50

Postman and Motorcycle SD6

Post Office Truck SD7

1922-25
E12 SD6 10c gray violet   35.00   .50
   Never hinged   62.50
   a.   10c deep ultramarine   40.00   .60
   Never hinged   72.50
E13 SD6 15c deep orange ('25)   24.00   1.00
   Never hinged   45.00
E14 SD7 20c black ('25)   1.90   1.00
   Nos. E12-E14 (3)   60.90   2.50

No. E12 measures 36x21½mm

No. E15 measures 36½x21¾mm
No. E13 measures 36½x21½mm
No. E16 measures 36¾x22¼mm
No. E14 measures 35½x21½mm
No. E19 measures 36¼x22mm

Rotary Press Printing
1927-31   *Perf. 11x10½*
E15 SD6 10c gray violet   .60   .20
   Never hinged   .90
   a.   10c red lilac   .60   .20
   Never hinged   .90
   b.   10c gray lilac   .60   .20
   Never hinged   .90
   c.   Horiz. pair, imperf. btwn.   300.00
E16 SD6 15c orange ('31)   .70   .20
   Never hinged   1.05

> **Catalogue values for unused stamps in this section, from this point to the end of the section, are for Never Hinged items.**

1944-51
E17 SD6 13c blue   .60   .20
E18 SD6 17c orange yellow   2.75   1.75
E19 SD7 20c black ('51)   1.25   .20
   Nos. E17-E19 (3)   4.60   2.15

Special Delivery Letter, Hand to Hand SD8

1954-57   *Perf. 11x10½*
E20 SD8 20c deep blue   .40   .20
E21 SD8 30c lake ('57)   .50   .20

Arrows SD9

Giori Press Printing
1969-71   *Perf. 11*
E22 SD9 45c car & vio blue   1.25   .25
E23 SD9 60c vio blue & car ('71)   1.25   .20
   Issue dates: 45c, Nov. 21; 60c, May 10.

REGISTRATION STAMP

Issued for the prepayment of registry fees; not usable for postage.

Eagle — RS1

       Wmk. 190
1911, Dec. 1   Engr.   *Perf. 12*
F1 RS1 10c ultramarine   75.00   7.50
   Never hinged   130.00

CERTIFIED MAIL STAMP

For use on first-class mail for which no indemnity value is claimed, but for which proof of mailing and proof of delivery are available at less cost than registered mail.

> **Catalogue values for unused stamps in this section are for Never Hinged items.**

Letter
Carrier — CM1

Rotary Press Printing
1955, June 6 Unwmk. *Perf. 10½x11*
FA1 CM1 15c red .45 .30

POSTAGE DUE STAMPS

For affixing, by a postal clerk to any piece of mailable matter, to denote the amount to be collected from the addressee because of insufficient pre-payment of postage.

Unused Values for Nos. J1-J14 are for stamps with full original gum.

D1   D2

Printed by the American Bank Note Company

1879 Unwmk. Engraved Perf. 12

J1	D1	1c brown	65.00	8.50
J2	D1	2c brown	400.00	7.50
J3	D1	3c brown	62.50	4.50
J4	D1	5c brown	625.00	45.00
J5	D1	10c brown	675.00	25.00
a.		Imperf., pair	2,000.	
J6	D1	30c brown	350.00	50.00
J7	D1	50c brown	500.00	60.00
		Nos. J1-J7 (7)	2,677.	200.50

Special Printing

1879

J8	D1	1c deep brown	*12,500.*	
J9	D1	2c deep brown	*8,500.*	
J10	D1	3c deep brown	*12,500.*	
J11	D1	5c deep brown	*8,500.*	
J12	D1	10c deep brown	*4,000.*	
J13	D1	30c deep brown	*4,000.*	
J14	D1	50c deep brown	*4,000.*	

1884

J15	D1	1c red brown	55.00	4.50
J16	D1	2c red brown	67.50	4.50
J17	D1	3c red brown	1,000.	175.00
J18	D1	5c red brown	500.00	25.00
J19	D1	10c red brown	475.00	17.50
J20	D1	30c red brown	165.00	50.00
J21	D1	50c red brown	1,650.	175.00
		Nos. J15-J21 (7)	4,262.	451.50

1891

J22	D1	1c bright claret	26.00	1.00
J23	D1	2c bright claret	32.50	1.00
J24	D1	3c bright claret	62.50	8.00
J25	D1	5c bright claret	77.50	8.00
J26	D1	10c bright claret	125.00	17.50
J27	D1	30c bright claret	500.00	150.00
J28	D1	50c bright claret	525.00	150.00
		Nos. J22-J28 (7)	1,348.	335.50

See Die and Plate Proofs in the Scott U.S. Specialized for imperfs. on stamp paper.

Printed by the Bureau of Engraving and Printing

1894

J29	D2	1c vermilion	1,750.	500.
		Never hinged	3,100.	
J30	D2	2c vermilion	700.00	175.
		Never hinged	1,250.	

1894

J31	D2	1c deep claret	47.50	6.00
		Never hinged	85.00	
b.		Vert. pair, imperf. horiz.		
J32	D2	2c deep claret	40.00	4.00
		Never hinged	72.50	
J33	D2	3c deep claret	160.00	30.00
		Never hinged	290.00	
J34	D2	5c deep claret	240.00	35.00
		Never hinged	425.00	
J35	D2	10c deep claret	240.00	25.00
		Never hinged	425.00	

J36	D2	30c deep claret	400.00	90.00
		Never hinged	725.00	
a.		30c carmine	450.00	125.00
		Never hinged	800.00	
b.		30c pale rose	325.00	85.00
		Never hinged	575.00	
J37	D2	50c deep claret	1,350.	350.00
		Never hinged	2,400.	
a.		50c pale rose	1,200.	300.00
		Never hinged	2,150.	
		Nos. J31-J37 (7)	2,827.	540.00

Shades are numerous in the 1894 and later issues.

See Die and Plate Proofs in the Scott U.S. Specialized for 1c imperf. on stamp paper.

1895 Wmk. 191

J38	D2	1c deep claret	8.50	.75
		Never hinged	15.00	
J39	D2	2c deep claret	8.50	.70
		Never hinged	15.00	
J40	D2	3c deep claret	57.50	1.75
		Never hinged	100.00	
J41	D2	5c deep claret	65.00	1.75
		Never hinged	115.00	
J42	D2	10c deep claret	67.50	3.50
		Never hinged	120.00	
J43	D2	30c deep claret	550.00	50.00
		Never hinged	1,000.	
J44	D2	50c deep claret	350.00	37.50
		Never hinged	625.00	
		Nos. J38-J44 (7)	1,107.	95.95

1910-12 Wmk. 190

J45	D2	1c deep claret	32.50	3.00
		Never hinged	57.50	
a.		1c rose carmine	30.00	3.00
		Never hinged	55.00	
J46	D2	2c deep claret	32.50	1.00
		Never hinged	57.50	
a.		2c rose carmine	30.00	1.00
		Never hinged	55.00	
J47	D2	3c deep claret	600.00	30.00
		Never hinged	1,100.	
J48	D2	5c deep claret	95.00	6.50
		Never hinged	170.00	
a.		5c rose carmine	90.00	6.50
		Never hinged	160.00	
J49	D2	10c deep claret	115.00	12.50
		Never hinged	210.00	
a.		10c rose carmine	110.00	12.50
		Never hinged	200.00	
J50	D2	50c deep claret ('12)	1,000.	120.00
		Never hinged	2,000.	
		Nos. J45-J50 (6)	1,995.	173.00

1914 Perf. 10

J52	D2	1c carmine lake	60.00	11.00
		Never hinged	110.00	
a.		1c dull rose	70.00	11.00
		Never hinged	125.00	
J53	D2	2c carmine lake	47.50	.40
		Never hinged	85.00	
a.		2c dull rose	52.50	.50
		Never hinged	95.00	
b.		2c vermilion	52.50	.50
		Never hinged	95.00	
J54	D2	3c carmine lake	875.00	37.50
		Never hinged	1,600.	
a.		3c dull rose	875.00	37.50
		Never hinged	1,600.	
J55	D2	5c carmine lake	37.50	2.50
		Never hinged	67.50	
a.		5c dull rose	37.50	2.50
		Never hinged	67.50	
J56	D2	10c carmine lake	57.50	2.00
		Never hinged	105.00	
a.		10c dull rose	70.00	3.00
		Never hinged	125.00	
J57	D2	30c carmine lake	240.00	17.50
		Never hinged	425.00	
J58	D2	50c carmine lake	12,500.	900.00
		Never hinged	22,500.	
		Nos. J52-J58 (7)	14,717.	970.90

1916 Unwmk. Perf. 10

J59	D2	1c rose	3,000.	325.00
		Never hinged	5,500.	
J60	D2	2c rose	160.00	25.00
		Never hinged	290.00	

1917 Perf. 11

J61	D2	1c carmine rose	2.75	.25
		Never hinged	4.75	
a.		1c rose red	2.75	.25
		Never hinged	4.75	
b.		1c deep claret	2.75	.25
		Never hinged	4.75	
J62	D2	2c carmine rose	2.50	.25
		Never hinged	4.40	
a.		2c rose red	2.50	.25
		Never hinged	4.40	
b.		2c deep claret	2.50	.25
		Never hinged	4.40	
J63	D2	3c carmine rose	11.00	.25
		Never hinged	19.00	
a.		3c rose red	11.00	.25
		Never hinged	19.00	
b.		3c deep claret	11.00	.35
		Never hinged	19.00	
J64	D2	5c carmine	11.00	.25
		Never hinged	19.00	
a.		5c rose red	11.00	.25
		Never hinged	19.00	
b.		5c deep claret	11.00	.25
		Never hinged	19.00	
J65	D2	10c carmine rose	17.00	.30
		Never hinged	30.00	
a.		10c rose red	17.00	.25
		Never hinged	30.00	
b.		10c deep claret	17.00	.25
		Never hinged	30.00	
J66	D2	30c carmine rose	87.50	.75
		Never hinged	155.00	
a.		30c deep claret	87.50	.75
		Never hinged	155.00	

J67	D2	50c carmine rose	110.00	.30
		Never hinged	195.00	
a.		50c rose red	110.00	.30
		Never hinged	195.00	
b.		50c deep claret	110.00	.30
		Never hinged	195.00	
		Nos. J61-J67 (7)	241.75	2.35

1925

J68	D2	½c dull red	1.00	.25
		Never hinged	1.60	

D3   D4

1930 Perf. 11

J69	D3	½c carmine	4.50	1.40
		Never hinged	7.25	
J70	D3	1c carmine	3.00	.25
		Never hinged	4.75	
J71	D3	2c carmine	4.00	.25
		Never hinged	6.50	
J72	D3	3c carmine	21.00	1.75
		Never hinged	35.00	
J73	D3	5c carmine	19.00	2.50
		Never hinged	30.00	
J74	D3	10c carmine	40.00	1.00
		Never hinged	65.00	
J75	D3	30c carmine	110.00	2.00
		Never hinged	175.00	
J76	D3	50c carmine	150.00	.75
		Never hinged	250.00	
J77	D4	$1 carmine	30.00	.25
		Never hinged	47.50	
a.		$1 scarlet	25.00	.25
		Never hinged	40.00	
J78	D4	$5 carmine	37.50	.25
		Never hinged	60.00	
a.		$5 scarlet	32.50	.25
		Never hinged	52.50	
		Nos. J69-J78 (10)	419.00	10.40

Rotary Press Printing
1931-56 Perf. 11x10½

J79	D3	½c dull carmine	.90	.20
		Never hinged	1.30	
J80	D3	1c dull carmine	.20	.20
		Never hinged	.30	
J81	D3	2c dull carmine	.20	.20
		Never hinged	.30	
J82	D3	3c dull carmine	.25	.20
		Never hinged	.40	
J83	D3	5c dull carmine	.40	.20
		Never hinged	.60	
J84	D3	10c dull carmine	1.10	.20
		Never hinged	1.60	
J85	D3	30c dull carmine	7.50	.25
		Never hinged	10.00	
J86	D3	50c dull carmine	10.00	.25
		Never hinged	15.00	

Perf. 10½x11

J87	D4	$1 scarlet ('56)	32.50	.25
		Never hinged	47.50	
		Nos. J79-J87 (9)	53.05	1.95

J79a	D3	½c scarlet	.90	.20
		Never hinged	1.30	
J80a	D3	1c scarlet	.20	.20
		Never hinged	.30	
J81a	D3	2c scarlet	.20	.20
		Never hinged	.30	
J82a	D3	3c scarlet	.25	.20
		Never hinged	.40	
J83a	D3	5c scarlet	.40	.20
		Never hinged	.60	
J84a	D3	10c scarlet	1.10	.20
		Never hinged	1.60	
J85a	D3	30c scarlet	7.50	.25
		Never hinged	10.00	
J86a	D3	50c scarlet	10.00	.25
		Never hinged	15.00	
		Nos. J79a-J86a (8)	20.55	1.70

> **Catalogue values for unused stamps in this section, from this point to the end of the section, are for Never Hinged items.**

D5

Denominations added by rubber plates in an operation similar to precanceling.

Rotary Press Printing
Perf. 11x10½
1959, June 19 Unwmk.
Denomination in Black

J88	D5	½c carmine rose	1.50	1.10
J89	D5	1c carmine rose	.20	.20
a.		"1 CENT" omitted	300.00	
b.		Pair, one without "1 CENT"	525.00	

J90	D5	2c carmine rose	.20	.20
J91	D5	3c carmine rose	.20	.20
a.		Pair, one without "3 CENTS"	750.00	
J92	D5	4c carmine rose	.20	.20
J93	D5	5c carmine rose	.20	.20
a.		Pair, one without "5 CENTS"	1,250.	
J94	D5	6c carmine rose	.20	.20
a.		Pair, one without "6 CENTS"	850.00	
J95	D5	7c carmine rose	.20	.20
J96	D5	8c carmine rose	.20	.20
a.		Pair, one without "8 CENTS"	850.00	
J97	D5	10c carmine rose	.75	.20
J98	D5	30c carmine rose	.75	.20
J99	D5	50c carmine rose	1.10	.20

Straight Numeral Outlined in Black

J100	D5	$1 carmine rose	2.00	.20
J101	D5	$5 carmine rose	9.00	.20
		Nos. J88-J101 (14)	16.15	3.70

All single copies with value omitted are catalogued as No. J89a.

1978-85 Denomination in Black

J102	D5	11c carmine rose	.25	.20
J103	D5	13c carmine rose	.25	.20
J104	D5	17c carmine rose ('85)	.40	.35
		Nos. J102-J104 (3)	.90	.75
		Nos. J88-J104 (17)	17.05	4.45

Issue dates: Jan. 2, 1978, June 10, 1985.

UNITED STATES OFFICES IN CHINA

Issued for sale by the postal agency at Shanghai, at their surcharged value in local currency. Valid to the amount of their original values for the prepayment of postage on mail dispatched from the US postal agency at Shanghai to addresses in the US.

Nos. 498-499, 502-504, 506-510, 512, 514-518 Surcharged

1919 Unwmk. Perf. 11

K1	A140	2c on 1c green	25.00	27.50
		Never hinged	45.00	
K2	A140	4c on 2c rose, I	25.00	27.50
		Never hinged	45.00	
K3	A140	6c on 3c vio, II	52.50	65.00
		Never hinged	95.00	
K4	A140	8c on 4c brown	57.50	65.00
		Never hinged	105.00	
K5	A140	10c on 5c blue	65.00	65.00
		Never hinged	115.00	
K6	A140	12c on 6c red org	82.50	95.00
		Never hinged	150.00	
K7	A140	14c on 7c black	87.50	110.00
		Never hinged	160.00	
K8	A148	16c on 8c ol bis	65.00	70.00
		Never hinged	115.00	
a.		16c on 8c olive green	60.00	60.00
		Never hinged	110.00	
K9	A148	18c on 9c sal red	65.00	75.00
		Never hinged	115.00	
K10	A148	20c on 10c org yel	60.00	60.00
		Never hinged	110.00	
K11	A148	24c on 12c brn car	70.00	70.00
		Never hinged	125.00	
a.		24c on 12c claret brown	92.50	110.00
		Never hinged	165.00	
K12	A148	30c on 15c gray	87.50	125.00
		Never hinged	160.00	
K13	A148	40c on 20c dp ultra	140.00	190.00
		Never hinged	250.00	
K14	A148	60c on 30c org red	120.00	160.00
		Never hinged	220.00	
K15	A148	$1 on 50c lt vio	575.00	600.00
		Never hinged	1,050.	
K16	A148	$2 on $1 vio brown	450.00	500.00
		Never hinged	800.00	
a.		Double surcharge	5,000.	6,000.
		Never hinged	8,000.	
		Nos. K1-K16 (16)	2,027.	2,305.

Nos. 498 and 528B Surcharged

1922, July 3

K17	A140	2c on 1c green	110.00	110.00
		Never hinged	200.00	
K18	A140	4c on 2c car, VII	100.00	95.00
		Never hinged	180.00	

OFFICIAL STAMPS

The franking privilege having been abolished, as of July 1, 1873, these stamps were provided for each of the departments of Government for the pre-payment of postage on official matter.

These stamps were supplanted on May 1, 1879, by penalty envelopes and on July 5, 1884, were declared obsolete.

Designs, except Post Office, resemble those illustrated but are not identical. Each bears the name of Department. Portraits are as follows: 1c, Franklin; 2c, Jackson; 3c, Washington; 6c, Lincoln; 7c, Stanton; 10c, Jefferson; 12c, Clay; 15c, Webster; 24c, Scott; 30c, Hamilton; 90c, Perry.

Grade, condition and original gum are very important in valuing #O1-O120 unused.

Printed by the Continental Bank Note Co.
Thin Hard Paper

O1

1873   Unwmk.   Engr.   Perf. 12
AGRICULTURE

O1	O1	1c yellow	170.00	150.00
O2	O1	2c yellow	135.00	60.00
O3	O1	3c yellow	120.00	12.00
O4	O1	6c yellow	135.00	50.00
O5	O1	10c yellow	270.00	175.00
O6	O1	12c yellow	360.00	225.00
O7	O1	15c yellow	300.00	200.00
O8	O1	24c yellow	300.00	180.00
O9	O1	30c yellow	390.00	235.00
		Nos. O1-O9 (9)	2,180.	1,287.

Special printings overprinted "SPECIMEN" follow No. O120.

EXECUTIVE

O10	O1	1c carmine	650.00	400.00
O11	O1	2c carmine	425.00	200.00
O12	O1	3c carmine	475.00	160.00
a.		3c violet rose	475.00	160.00
O13	O1	6c carmine	725.00	475.00
O14	O1	10c carmine	700.00	550.00
		Nos. O10-O14 (5)	2,975.	1,785.

Special printings overprinted "SPECIMEN" follow No. O120.

INTERIOR

O15	O1	1c vermilion	37.50	8.00
O16	O1	2c vermilion	32.50	9.00
O17	O1	3c vermilion	50.00	5.00
O18	O1	6c vermilion	37.50	5.00
O19	O1	10c vermilion	37.50	15.00
O20	O1	12c vermilion	52.50	7.75
O21	O1	15c vermilion	90.00	17.00
O22	O1	24c vermilion	65.00	14.00
a.		Double impression		—
O23	O1	30c vermilion	90.00	14.00
O24	O1	90c vermilion	200.00	37.50
		Nos. O15-O24 (10)	692.50	132.25

Special printings overprinted "SPECIMEN" follow No. O120.

JUSTICE

O25	O1	1c purple	120.00	85.00
O26	O1	2c purple	210.00	85.00
O27	O1	3c purple	210.00	20.00
O28	O1	6c purple	190.00	30.00
O29	O1	10c purple	225.00	70.00
O30	O1	12c purple	170.00	45.00
O31	O1	15c purple	325.00	150.00
O32	O1	24c purple	875.00	325.00
O33	O1	30c purple	700.00	250.00
O34	O1	90c purple	1,050.	500.00
		Nos. O25-O34 (10)	4,575.	1,560.

Special printings overprinted "SPECIMEN" follow No. O120.

NAVY

O35	O1	1c ultramarine	80.00	40.00
a.		1c dull blue	90.00	40.00
O36	O1	2c ultramarine	65.00	17.00
a.		2c dull blue	75.00	15.00

O37	O1	3c ultramarine	62.50	9.00
a.		3c dull blue	72.50	11.00
O38	O1	6c ultramarine	62.50	14.00
a.		6c dull blue	72.50	14.50
O39	O1	7c ultramarine	425.00	175.00
a.		7c dull blue	450.00	175.00
O40	O1	10c ultramarine	85.00	30.00
a.		10c dull blue	90.00	30.00
O41	O1	12c ultramarine	100.00	30.00
O42	O1	15c ultramarine	180.00	57.50
O43	O1	24c ultramarine	200.00	65.00
a.		24c dull blue	200.00	—
O44	O1	30c ultramarine	150.00	35.00
O45	O1	90c ultramarine	725.00	225.00
a.		Double impression		3,750.
		Nos. O35-O45 (11)	2,135.	697.50

Special printings overprinted "SPECIMEN" follow No. O120.

O6

POST OFFICE

O47	O6	1c black	14.00	7.50
O48	O6	2c black	17.50	7.00
a.		Double impression	325.00	300.00
O49	O6	3c black	5.50	1.00
a.		Printed on both sides		3,000.
O50	O6	6c black	17.50	6.00
a.		Diagonal half used as 3c on cover		3,000.
O51	O6	10c black	75.00	40.00
O52	O6	12c black	37.50	8.25
O53	O6	15c black	50.00	14.00
O54	O6	24c black	65.00	17.00
O55	O6	30c black	65.00	17.00
O56	O6	90c black	95.00	14.00
		Nos. O47-O56 (10)	442.00	131.75

Stamps of the POD are often on paper with a gray surface. This is due to insufficient wiping of the plates during printing.

Special printings overprinted "SPECIMEN" follow No. O120.

Seward — O8

STATE

O57	O1	1c dark green	120.00	55.00
O58	O1	2c dark green	225.00	75.00
O59	O1	3c bright green	90.00	17.00
O60	O1	6c bright green	85.00	22.00
O61	O1	7c dark green	170.00	50.00
O62	O1	10c dark green	130.00	35.00
O63	O1	12c dark green	210.00	90.00
O64	O1	15c dark green	220.00	65.00
O65	O1	24c dark green	450.00	180.00
O66	O1	30c dark green	425.00	140.00
O67	O1	90c dark green	800.00	275.00
O68	O8	$2 green & black	900.00	750.00
O69	O8	$5 green & black	6,000.	3,500.
O70	O8	$10 green & black	4,000.	2,500.
O71	O8	$20 green & black	3,250.	1,800.

Nos. O68-O71 with pen cancels sell for approximately 25-40% of the values shown.

Special printings overprinted "SPECIMEN" follow No. O120.

TREASURY

O72	O1	1c brown	40.00	5.00
O73	O1	2c brown	50.00	5.00
O74	O1	3c brown	35.00	1.25
a.		Double impression		—
O75	O1	6c brown	45.00	2.50
O76	O1	7c brown	95.00	25.00
O77	O1	10c brown	95.00	7.75
O78	O1	12c brown	95.00	6.00
O79	O1	15c brown	90.00	7.75
O80	O1	24c brown	450.00	70.00
O81	O1	30c brown	150.00	9.00
O82	O1	90c brown	100.00	10.00
		Nos. O72-O82 (11)	1,305.	149.25

Special printings overprinted "SPECIMEN" follow No. O120.

WAR

O83	O1	1c rose	145.00	8.50
O84	O1	2c rose	130.00	9.50
O85	O1	3c rose	135.00	2.75
O86	O1	6c rose	450.00	6.00
O87	O1	7c rose	130.00	72.50

O88	O1	10c rose	45.00	15.00
O89	O1	12c rose	170.00	10.00
O90	O1	15c rose	40.00	10.00
O91	O1	24c rose	40.00	6.75
O92	O1	30c rose	42.50	6.75
O93	O1	90c rose	95.00	40.00
		Nos. O83-O93 (11)	1,422.	188.75

Special printings overprinted "SPECIMEN" follow No. O120.

Printed by the American Bank Note Co.
1879   Soft Porous Paper
AGRICULTURE

O94	O1	1c yel, no gum	3,250.	
O95	O1	3c yellow	300.00	65.00

INTERIOR

O96	O1	1c vermilion	250.00	220.00
O97	O1	2c vermilion	4.25	1.25
O98	O1	3c vermilion	3.75	1.00
O99	O1	6c vermilion	5.50	5.50
O100	O1	10c vermilion	70.00	60.00
O101	O1	12c vermilion	130.00	90.00
O102	O1	15c vermilion	325.00	225.00
O103	O1	24c vermilion	3,250.	

JUSTICE

O106	O1	3c bluish purple	100.00	65.00
O107	O1	6c bluish purple	225.00	175.00

POST OFFICE

O108	O6	3c black	16.00	5.00

TREASURY

O109	O1	3c brown	47.50	6.75
O110	O1	6c brown	90.00	35.00
O111	O1	10c brown	160.00	50.00
O112	O1	30c brown	1,300.	275.00
O113	O1	90c brown	2,100.	275.00
		Nos. O109-O113 (5)	4,247.	641.75

WAR

O114	O1	1c rose red	3.75	2.75
O115	O1	2c rose red	5.25	3.25
O116	O1	3c rose red	5.25	1.20
a.		Imperf., pair	900.00	
b.		Double impression	750.00	
O117	O1	6c rose red	4.75	1.00
O118	O1	10c rose red	40.00	37.50
O119	O1	12c rose red	32.50	10.00
O120	O1	30c rose red	85.00	67.50
		Nos. O114-O120 (7)	176.50	123.20

SPECIAL PRINTINGS

Special printings of Official stamps were made in 1875 at the time the other Reprints, Re-issues and Special Printings were printed. They are ungummed. Although perforated, these stamps were sometimes (but not always) cut apart with scissors. As a result the perforations may be mutilated and the design damaged.

All values exist imperforate.

Printed by the Continental Bank Note Co.

Overprinted in Block Letters

1875   Perf. 12
Thin, hard white paper
Type D
AGRICULTURE
Carmine Overprint

O1S	D	1c yellow	14.00	
a.		"Sepcimen" error	700.00	
b.		Small dotted "i" in "Specimen"	425.00	
c.		Horiz. ribbed paper	20.00	
O2S	D	2c yellow	27.50	
a.		"Sepcimen" error	750.00	
O3S	D	3c yellow	75.00	
a.		"Sepcimen" error	3,000.	
O4S	D	6c yellow	130.00	
a.		"Sepcimen" error	5,500.	
O5S	D	10c yellow	130.00	
a.		"Sepcimen" error	3,250.	
O6S	D	12c yellow	125.00	
a.		"Sepcimen" error	3,750.	
O7S	D	15c yellow	125.00	
a.		"Sepcimen" error	3,250.	
O8S	D	24c yellow	125.00	
a.		"Sepcimen" error	3,250.	
O9S	D	30c yellow	125.00	
a.		"Sepcimen" error	3,250.	
		Nos. O1S-O9S (9)	876.50	

EXECUTIVE
Blue Overprint

O10S	D	1c carmine	14.00	
a.		Small dotted "i" in "Specimen"	325.00	
b.		Ribbed paper	20.00	

O11S	D	2c carmine	27.50	
O12S	D	3c carmine	27.50	
O13S	D	6c carmine	27.50	
O14S	D	10c carmine	27.50	
		Nos. O10S-O14S (5)	124.00	

INTERIOR
Blue Overprint

O15S	D	1c vermilion	27.50	
O16S	D	2c vermilion	35.00	
a.		"Sepcimen" error	3,750.	
O17S	D	3c vermilion	475.00	
O18S	D	6c vermilion	450.00	
O19S	D	10c vermilion	450.00	
O20S	D	12c vermilion	475.00	
O21S	D	15c vermilion	475.00	
O22S	D	24c vermilion	475.00	
O23S	D	30c vermilion	475.00	
O24S	D	90c vermilion	475.00	
		Nos. O15S-O24S (10)	3,812.	

JUSTICE
Blue Overprint

O25S	D	1c purple	15.00	
a.		"Sepcimen" error	675.00	
b.		Small dotted "i" in "Specimen"	275.00	
c.		Horiz. ribbed paper	20.00	
O26S	D	2c purple	30.00	
a.		"Sepcimen" error	1,100.	
O27S	D	3c purple	250.00	
a.		"Sepcimen" error	3,750.	
O28S	D	6c purple	250.00	
O29S	D	10c purple	250.00	
O30S	D	12c purple	250.00	
a.		"Sepcimen" error	4,000.	
O31S	D	15c purple	275.00	
a.		"Sepcimen" error	4,000.	
O32S	D	24c purple	300.00	
a.		"Sepcimen" error	4,000.	
O33S	D	30c purple	300.00	
a.		"Sepcimen" error	4,000.	
O34S	D	90c purple	325.00	
		Nos. O25S-O34S (10)	2,245.	

NAVY
Carmine Overprint

O35S	D	1c ultramarine	17.50	
a.		"Sepcimen" error	550.00	
O36S	D	2c ultramarine	35.00	
a.		"Sepcimen" error	675.00	
O37S	D	3c ultramarine	300.00	
O38S	D	6c ultramarine	350.00	
O39S	D	7c ultramarine	150.00	
a.		"Sepcimen" error	3,000.	
O40S	D	10c ultramarine	350.00	
a.		"Sepcimen" error	4,250.	
O41S	D	12c ultramarine	300.00	
a.		"Sepcimen" error	4,000.	
O42S	D	15c ultramarine	300.00	
a.		"Sepcimen" error	7,500.	
O43S	D	24c ultramarine	300.00	
a.		"Sepcimen" error	4,000.	
O44S	D	30c ultramarine	300.00	
a.		"Sepcimen" error	4,500.	
O45S	D	90c ultramarine	300.00	
		Nos. O35S-O45S (11)	2,702.	

POST OFFICE
Carmine Overprint

O47S	D	1c black	25.00	
a.		"Sepcimen" error	650.00	
b.		Inverted overprint	1,000.	
O48S	D	2c black	65.00	
a.		"Sepcimen" error	1,750.	
O49S	D	3c black	450.00	
O50S	D	6c black	425.00	
O51S	D	10c black	275.00	
a.		"Sepcimen" error	4,250.	
O52S	D	12c black	400.00	
O53S	D	15c black	475.00	
a.		"Sepcimen" error	4,250.	
O54S	D	24c black	425.00	
a.		"Sepcimen" error	4,250.	
O55S	D	30c black	425.00	
O56S	D	90c black	425.00	
a.		"Sepcimen" error	8,000.	
		Nos. O47S-O56S (10)	3,390.	

STATE
Carmine Overprint

O57S	D	1c bluish green	15.00	
a.		"Sepcimen" error	400.00	
b.		Small dotted "i" in "Specimen"	400.00	
c.		Horiz. ribbed paper	20.00	
d.		Double overprint		
O58S	D	2c bluish green	30.00	
a.		"Sepcimen" error	550.00	
O59S	D	3c bluish green	45.00	
a.		"Sepcimen" error	2,000.	
O60S	D	6c bluish green	95.00	
a.		"Sepcimen" error	2,250.	
O61S	D	7c bluish green	47.50	
a.		"Sepcimen" error	1,750.	
O62S	D	10c bluish green	180.00	
a.		"Sepcimen" error	7,500.	
O63S	D	12c bluish green	190.00	
a.		"Sepcimen" error	3,500.	
O64S	D	15c bluish green	180.00	
a.		"Sepcimen" error	3,500.	
O65S	D	24c bluish green	180.00	
O66S	D	30c bluish green	180.00	
a.		"Sepcimen" error	3,750.	
O67S	D	90c bluish green	180.00	
a.		"Sepcimen" error	3,750.	
O68S	D	$2 green & black	7,500.	
O69S	D	$5 green & black	13,500.	
O70S	D	$10 green & black	19,000.	
O71S	D	$20 green & black	22,500.	
		Nos. O57S-O67S (11)	1,322.	

TREASURY
Blue Overprint

O72S	D	1c dark brown	27.50
O73S	D	2c dark brown	130.00
O74S	D	3c dark brown	475.00
O75S	D	6c dark brown	425.00
O76S	D	7c dark brown	275.00
O77S	D	10c dark brown	450.00
O78S	D	12c dark brown	475.00
O79S	D	15c dark brown	475.00
O80S	D	24c dark brown	375.00
O81S	D	30c dark brown	500.00
O82S	D	90c dark brown	500.00
Nos. O72S-O82S (11)			4,107.

WAR
Blue Overprint

O83S	D	1c deep rose	17.50
a.		"Sepcimen" error	550.00
O84S	D	2c deep rose	35.00
a.		"Sepcimen" error	1,000.
O85S	D	3c deep rose	350.00
a.		"Sepcimen" error	4,000.
O86S	D	6c deep rose	350.00
a.		"Sepcimen" error	4,250.
O87S	D	7c deep rose	72.50
a.		"Sepcimen" error	1,900.
O88S	D	10c deep rose	325.00
a.		"Sepcimen" error	4,250.
O89S	D	12c deep rose	375.00
a.		"Sepcimen" error	4,250.
O90S	D	15c deep rose	375.00
a.		"Sepcimen" error	4,250.
O91S	D	24c deep rose	375.00
a.		"Sepcimen" error	4,250.
O92S	D	30c deep rose	375.00
a.		"Sepcimen" error	4,250.
O93S	D	90c deep rose	375.00
a.		"Sepcimen" error	4,750.
Nos. O83S-O93S (11)			3,025.

SOFT POROUS PAPER
1881
EXECUTIVE
Blue Overprint

O10xS	D	1c violet rose	45.00

NAVY
Carmine Overprint

O35xS	D	1c gray blue	50.00
a.		Double overprint	850.00

STATE

O57xS	D	1c yellow green	200.00

OFFICIAL POSTAL SAVINGS MAIL

These stamps were used to prepay postage on official correspondence of the Postal Savings Division of the POD. Discontinued Sept. 23, 1914.

O11

1911 **Wmk. 191**

O121	O11	2c black	15.00	1.50
		Never hinged	25.00	
O122	O11	50c dark green	145.00	40.00
		Never hinged	240.00	
O123	O11	$1 ultra	135.00	11.00
		Never hinged	225.00	

Wmk. 190

O124	O11	1c dark violet	8.00	1.50
		Never hinged	13.50	
O125	O11	2c black	47.50	5.50
		Never hinged	80.00	
O126	O11	10c carmine	18.00	1.60
		Never hinged	30.00	
Nos. O121-O126 (6)			368.50	61.10

> **Catalogue values for unused stamps in this section, from this point to the end of the section, are for Never Hinged items.**

> **Catalogue values for used stamps are for regularly used copies, not copies removed from first day covers.**

> **From No. O127 onward, all official stamps are tagged unless noted.**

OFFICIAL MAIL

O12

O13

Type O13 has frame line completely around blue design.

1983-85 **Unwmk.** **Perf. 11**

O127	O12	1c red, bl & blk	.20	.20
O128	O12	4c red, bl & blk	.20	.25
O129	O12	13c red, bl & blk	.45	.75
O129A	O12	14c red, bl & blk		
		('85)	.45	.50
O130	O12	17c red, bl & blk	.60	.40
O132	O12	$1 red, bl & blk	2.00	1.00
O133	O12	$5 red, bl & blk	9.00	9.00
Nos. O127-O133 (7)			12.90	12.10

Coil Stamps
Perf. 10 Vert.

O135	O12	20c red, bl & blk	1.75	2.00
a.		Imperf., pair	2,000.	
O136	O12	22c red, bl & blk		
		('85)	.80	2.00

#O129A does not have a "c" after the "14."

Inscribed: Postal Card Rate D
1985, Feb. 4 **Perf. 11**

O138	O12	(14c) red, bl & blk	5.25	5.00

Coil Stamps

Inscribed: No. O139, Domestic Letter Rate D. No. O140, Domestic Mail E.

1985-88 **Perf. 10 Vert.**

O138A	O13	15c red, bl & blk	.45	.50
O138B	O13	20c red, bl & blk	.45	.30
O139	O12	(22c) red, bl & blk	5.25	3.00
O140	O13	(25c) red, bl & blk	.75	2.00
O141	O13	25c red, bl & blk	.65	.50
a.		Imperf., pair	1,750.	
Nos. O138A-O141 (5)			7.55	6.30

No. O139 is inscribed "D." No. O140 is inscribed "E."

Issue dates: 1985; E, Mar. 22, 1988; 15c, June 11; 20c, May 19; 25c, June 11.
See Nos. O143, O145-O151, O153-O156.

1989, July 5 **Litho.** **Perf. 11**

O143	O13	1c red, blue & black	.20	.20

O14

1991, Jan. 22 **Litho.** **Perf. 10 Vert.**
Coil Stamp

O144	O14	(29c) red, blue & blk	.75	.50

See No. O152.

Official Type of 1985
1991, May 24 **Litho.** **Perf. 10 Vert.**
Coil Stamp

O145	O13	29c red, blue & blk	.65	.30

1991-93 **Perf. 11**

O146	O13	4c red, bl & blk	.20	.30
O146A	O13	10c red, bl & blk	.25	.30
O147	O13	19c red, bl & blk	.40	.50
O148	O13	23c red, bl & blk	.45	.30
a.		Imperf., pair	200.00	
O151	O13	$1 red, bl & blk	2.00	.75

Nos. O146A, O151 have a line of microscopic printing below eagle.
Nos. O147 and O148 have blue background made up of crosshatched lines, thicker lettering and thinner numerals.
Issued: No. O146, 4/6; Nos. O147-O148, 5/24; 10c, 10/19/93; No. O151, 9/1993.

1994, Dec. 13 **Litho.** **Perf. 9.8 Vert.**
COIL STAMP

Inscribed: For U.S. addresses only G.

O152	O14	(32c) red, blue & blk	.65	—

Type of 1985
1995, May 9 **Litho.** **Perf. 9¾ Vert.**
COIL STAMP

O153	O13	32c red, blue & black	.65	.30

1995, May 9 **Perf. 11.2**

O154	O13	1c red, blue & blk, untagged	.20	.20
O155	O13	20c red, blue & black	.45	.30
O156	O13	23c red, blue & black	.50	.30

1999, Oct. 8 **Litho.** **Perf. 9¾ Vert.**
COIL STAMP

O157	O13	33c red, blue & black	.65	—

Nos. O153-O157 have a line of microscopic text below eagle.

Type of 1985
COIL STAMP
2001, Feb. 27 **Litho.** **Perf. 9¾ Vert.**

O158	O13	34c red, blue & black	.65	.30

NEWSPAPER STAMPS

For the prepayment of postage on bulk shipments of newspapers and periodicals. From 1875 on, the stamps were affixed to pages of receipt books, sometimes canceled and retained by the post office. Discontinued on July 1, 1898.

Virtually all used stamps of Nos. PR1-PR4 are canceled by blue brush strokes. All are rare. Most used stamps of Nos. PR9-PR32, PR57-PR79 and PR81-PR89 are pen canceled (or uncanceled).

Handstamp cancellations on any of these issues are rare and sell for much more than catalogue values which are for pen-canceled examples.

Used values for Nos. PR102-PR125 are for stamps with handstamp cancellations.

Washington — N1

Franklin — N2

Lincoln — N3

Printed by the National Bank Note Co.
Thin Hard Paper, No Gum
1865 **Unwmk.** **Typo.** **Perf. 12**
Size: 51x95mm
Colored Border

PR1	N1	5c dark blue	400.00	—
a.		5c light blue	425.00	
PR2	N2	10c blue green	150.00	—
a.		10c green	150.00	
b.		Pelure paper	175.00	
PR3	N3	25c orange red	200.00	—
a.		25c carmine red	230.00	
b.		Pelure paper	200.00	

White Border
Yellowish Paper

PR4	N1	5c light blue	90.00	—
a.		5c dark blue	90.00	
b.		Pelure paper	90.00	
Nos. PR1-PR4 (4)			840.00	

Reprints of 1865 Issue
Printed by the National Bank Note Co.
Hard White Paper, Without Gum
1875

PR5	N1	5c dull blue	115.00	
a.		Printed on both sides		
PR6	N2	10c dk bluish grn	120.00	
a.		Printed on both sides	2,150.	
PR7	N3	25c dark carmine	140.00	
Nos. PR5-PR7 (3)			375.00	

The 5c has white border, 10c and 25c have colored borders.

Printed by the American Bank Note Co.
1880 **Soft Porous Paper**
White Border

PR8	N1	5c dark blue	275.00

Statue of Freedom — N4

"Justice" — N5

Ceres — N6

"Victory" — N7

Clio — N8

Minerva — N9

Vesta — N10

"Peace" — N11

"Commerce" N12

Hebe N13

Indian Maiden — N14

Printed by the Continental Bank Note Co.
Engraved Thin Hard Paper

1875 Size: 24x35mm

PR9	N4	2c black	45.00	22.50
PR10	N4	3c black	50.00	25.00
PR11	N4	4c black	50.00	22.50
PR12	N4	6c black	65.00	25.00
PR13	N4	8c black	75.00	35.00
PR14	N4	9c black	160.00	80.00
PR15	N4	10c black	85.00	30.00
PR16	N5	12c rose	200.00	75.00
PR17	N5	24c rose	240.00	90.00
PR18	N5	36c rose	290.00	100.00
PR19	N5	48c rose	475.00	160.00
PR20	N5	60c rose	275.00	90.00
PR21	N5	72c rose	575.00	210.00
PR22	N5	84c rose	850.00	300.00
PR23	N5	96c rose	500.00	200.00
PR24	N6	$1.92 dark brn	625.00	275.00
PR25	N7	$3 vermilion	900.00	290.00
PR26	N8	$6 ultra	1,500.	425.00
PR27	N9	$9 yellow	1,900.	475.00
PR28	N10	$12 blue grn	2,250.	600.00
PR29	N11	$24 dk gray vio	2,250.	600.00
PR30	N12	$36 brn rose	2,500.	750.00
PR31	N13	$48 red brn	3,000.	900.00
PR32	N14	$60 violet	3,500.	900.00

Special Printing of the 1875 Issue Printed by the Continental Bank Note Co.
Hard White Paper, Without Gum

PR33	N4	2c gray black	350.
a.		Horizontally ribbed paper	350.
PR34	N4	3c gray black	375.
a.		Horizontally ribbed paper	425.
PR35	N4	4c gray black	450.
a.		Horizontally ribbed paper	500.
PR36	N4	6c gray black	500.
PR37	N4	8c gray black	550.
PR38	N4	9c gray black	675.
PR39	N4	10c gray black	850.
a.		Horizontally ribbed paper	
PR40	N5	12c pale rose	1,000.
PR41	N5	24c pale rose	1,450.
PR42	N5	36c pale rose	1,900.
PR43	N5	48c pale rose	2,250.
PR44	N5	60c pale rose	2,500.
PR45	N5	72c pale rose	3,000.
PR46	N5	84c pale rose	3,500.
PR47	N5	96c pale rose	5,250.
PR48	N6	$1.92 dk brown	11,500.
PR49	N7	$3 vermilion	21,500.
PR50	N8	$6 ultra	27,500.
PR51	N9	$9 yellow	42,500.
PR52	N10	$12 blue green	37,500.
PR53	N11	$24 dk gray vio	—
PR54	N12	$36 brown rose	—
PR55	N13	$48 red brown	—
PR56	N14	$60 violet	—

Nos. PR33 to PR56 exist imperf. but were not regularly issued. (See the Scott U.S. Specialized Catalogue.)

The existence of No. PR39a has been questioned by specialists. The editors would like to see evidence of its existence.

Printed by the American Bank Note Co.

1879 Soft Porous Paper

PR57	N4	2c black	20.00	5.50
PR58	N4	3c black	24.00	7.00
PR59	N4	4c black	22.50	7.00
PR60	N4	6c black	45.00	15.00
PR61	N4	8c black	45.00	15.00
PR62	N4	10c black	45.00	15.00
PR63	N5	12c red	235.00	60.00
PR64	N5	24c red	235.00	60.00
PR65	N5	36c red	500.00	175.00
PR66	N5	48c red	450.00	130.00
PR67	N5	60c red	375.00	110.00
a.		Imperf., pair	2,500.	
PR68	N5	72c red	725.00	210.00
PR69	N5	84c red	650.00	160.00
PR70	N5	96c red	425.00	110.00
PR71	N6	$1.92 pale brn	325.00	105.00
PR72	N7	$3 red ver	325.00	105.00
PR73	N8	$6 blue	600.00	160.00
PR74	N9	$9 orange	400.00	110.00
PR75	N10	$12 yellow grn	550.00	150.00
PR76	N11	$24 dk violet	650.00	180.00
PR77	N12	$36 Indian red	750.00	200.00
PR78	N13	$48 yel brn	850.00	275.00
PR79	N14	$60 purple	825.00	275.00
Nos. PR57-PR79 (14)			3,796.	1,079.

See the Scott U.S. Specialized Catalogue Die and Plate Proof section for other imperforates.

Special Printing of the 1879 Issue Printed by the American Bank Note Co.

1881

PR80	N4	2c intense black	550.00

1885

PR81	N4	1c black	30.00	7.50
PR82	N5	12c carmine	85.00	17.50
PR83	N5	24c carmine	80.00	20.00
PR84	N5	36c carmine	110.00	30.00
PR85	N5	48c carmine	160.00	45.00
PR86	N5	60c carmine	210.00	65.00
PR87	N5	72c carmine	210.00	70.00
PR88	N5	84c carmine	425.00	160.00
PR89	N5	96c carmine	350.00	120.00
Nos. PR81-PR89 (9)			1,660.	535.00

See the Scott U.S. Specialized Catalogue Die and Plate Proof section for imperforates.

Printed by the Bureau of Engraving and Printing

1894 Soft Wove Paper

PR90	N4	1c intense black	200.	—
PR91	N4	2c intense black	200.	
PR92	N4	4c intense black	225.	
PR93	N4	6c intense black	3,000.	
PR94	N4	10c intense black	600.	
PR95	N5	12c pink	1,350.	—
PR96	N5	24c pink	1,350.	
PR97	N5	36c pink	13,500.	
PR98	N5	60c pink	13,500.	
PR99	N5	96c pink	15,000.	
PR100	N7	$3 scarlet	18,000.	
PR101	N8	$6 pale blue	50,000.	—

Statue of Freedom N15

"Justice" N16

"Victory" N17

Clio N18

Vesta — N19

"Peace" N20

"Commerce" N21

Indian Maiden N22

1895 Unwmk.

Sizes: 1c-50c, 21x34mm, $2-$100, 24x35mm

PR102	N15	1c black	85.00	12.50
		Never hinged	150.00	
PR103	N15	2c black	85.00	12.50
		Never hinged	150.00	
PR104	N15	5c black	120.00	20.00
		Never hinged	210.00	
PR105	N15	10c black	240.00	52.50
		Never hinged	425.00	
PR106	N16	25c carmine	340.00	55.00
		Never hinged	600.00	
PR107	N16	50c carmine	750.00	150.00
		Never hinged	1,300.	
PR108	N17	$2 scarlet	875.00	110.00
		Never hinged	1,525.	
PR109	N18	$5 ultra	1,100.	225.00
		Never hinged	1,900.	
PR110	N19	$10 green	1,250.	250.00
		Never hinged	2,200.	
PR111	N20	$20 slate	1,650.	450.00
		Never hinged	2,850.	
PR112	N21	$50 dull rose	1,750.	450.00
		Never hinged	3,000.	
PR113	N22	$100 purple	2,000.	525.00
		Never hinged	3,500.	
Nos. PR102-PR113 (12)			12,145.	2,312.

1895-97 Wmk. 191

PR114	N15	1c black ('96)	6.00	5.00
		Never hinged	10.50	
PR115	N15	2c black	6.50	5.00
		Never hinged	11.25	
PR116	N15	5c black ('96)	10.00	7.50
		Never hinged	17.50	
PR117	N15	10c black	6.50	5.00
		Never hinged	11.25	
PR118	N16	25c carmine	12.50	12.50
		Never hinged	22.00	
PR119	N16	50c carmine	15.00	15.00
		Never hinged	26.50	
PR120	N17	$2 scar ('97)	20.00	22.50
		Never hinged	35.00	
PR121	N18	$5 dk bl ('96)	35.00	35.00
		Never hinged	62.50	
a.		$5 light blue	175.00	70.00
		Never hinged	300.00	
PR122	N19	$10 grn ('96)	35.00	35.00
		Never hinged	62.50	
PR123	N20	$20 slate ('96)	37.50	37.50
		Never hinged	65.00	
PR124	N21	$50 dl rose ('97)	50.00	42.50
		Never hinged	87.50	

PR125	N22	$100 pur ('96)	55.00	47.50
		Never hinged	95.00	
Nos. PR114-PR125 (12)			289.00	270.00
Nos. PR114-PR125, never hinged			506.50	

In 1899 the Government sold 26,989 sets of these stamps, but, as the stock of the high values was not sufficient to make up the required number, the $5, $10, $20, $50 and $100 were reprinted. These are virtually indistinguishable from earlier printings.

For overprints see Nos. R159-R160.

PARCEL POST STAMPS

Issued for the prepayment of postage on parcel post packages only.

Post Office Clerk — PP1

City Carrier PP2

Railway Postal Clerk — PP3

Rural Carrier PP4

Mail Train — PP5

Steamship and Mail Tender PP6

Automobile Service PP7

Airplane Carrying Mail — PP8

Manufacturing — PP9

Dairying
PP10

Harvesting
PP11

Fruit
Growing
PP12

1913 Engr. Wmk. 190 Perf. 12

Q1	PP1	1c carmine rose	5.25	1.50
		Never hinged	9.75	
Q2	PP2	2c carmine rose	6.75	1.25
		Never hinged	12.50	
Q3	PP3	3c carmine	13.50	5.75
		Never hinged	25.00	
Q4	PP4	4c carmine rose	37.50	3.00
		Never hinged	70.00	
Q5	PP5	5c carmine rose	32.50	2.25
		Never hinged	60.00	
Q6	PP6	10c carmine rose	52.50	3.00
		Never hinged	97.50	
Q7	PP7	15c carmine rose	67.50	12.00
		Never hinged	125.00	
Q8	PP8	20c carmine rose	140.00	25.00
		Never hinged	260.00	
Q9	PP9	25c carmine rose	67.50	6.75
		Never hinged	125.00	
Q10	PP10	50c carmine rose	280.00	40.00
		Never hinged	525.00	
Q11	PP11	75c carmine rose	95.00	35.00
		Never hinged	175.00	
Q12	PP12	$1 carmine rose	350.00	35.00
		Never hinged	650.00	
	Nos. Q1-Q12 (12)		1,148.	170.50
	Nos. Q1-Q12, never hinged		2,135.	

PARCEL POST POSTAGE DUE STAMPS

For affixing by a postal clerk, to any parcel post package, to denote the amount to be collected from the addressee because of insufficient prepayment of postage.

PPD1

1913 Engr. Wmk. 190 Perf. 12

JQ1	PPD1	1c dark green	11.00	4.50
		Never hinged	20.00	
JQ2	PPD1	2c dark green	85.00	17.50
		Never hinged	155.00	
JQ3	PPD1	5c dark green	15.00	5.50
		Never hinged	27.50	
JQ4	PPD1	10c dark green	175.00	45.00
		Never hinged	325.00	
JQ5	PPD1	25c dark green	105.00	5.00
		Never hinged	190.00	
	Nos. JQ1-JQ5 (5)		391.00	77.50
	Nos. JQ1-JQ5, never hinged		717.50	

SPECIAL HANDLING STAMPS

For use on fourth-class mail to secure the same expeditious handling accorded to first-class mail matter.

PP13

1925-29 Unwmk. Engr. Perf. 11

QE1	PP13	10c yel grn ('28)	1.60	1.00
		Never hinged	2.50	
QE2	PP13	15c yel grn ('28)	1.75	.90
		Never hinged	2.75	
QE3	PP13	20c yel grn ('28)	2.75	1.50
		Never hinged	4.40	
QE4	PP13	25c yel grn ('29)	22.50	7.50
		Never hinged	36.00	
a.		25c deep green ('25)	32.50	5.50
		Never hinged	52.50	
	Nos. QE1-QE4 (4)		28.60	10.90
	Nos. QE1-QE4, never hinged		45.65	

COMPUTER VENDED POSTAGE

CVP1

CVP2

1989, Aug. 23 Tagged Guillotined Self-Adhesive
Washington, DC, Machine 82
Date Other Than 1st Day

CVP1	CVP1	25c 1st Class	6.00	—
a.		1st day dated, serial #12501-15500	4.50	—
b.		1st day dated, serial #00001-12500	4.50	—
c.		1st day dated, serial over #27500	—	—
CVP2	CVP1	$1 3rd Class	—	—
a.		1st day dated, serial #24501-27500	—	—
b.		1st day dated, serial over #27500	—	—
CVP3	CVP2	$1.69 Parcel Post	—	—
a.		1st day dated, serial #21501-24500	—	—
b.		1st day dated, serial over #27500	—	—
CVP4	CVP1	$2.40 Priority Mail	—	—
a.		1st day dated, serial #18501-21500	—	—
b.		Priority Mail ($2.74), with bar code (CVP2)	100.00	—
c.		1st day dated, serial over #27500	—	—
CVP5	CVP1	$8.75 Express Mail	—	—
a.		1st day dated, serial #15501-18500	—	—
b.		1st day dated, serial over #27500	—	—
	Nos. CVP1a-CVP5a (5)		82.50	—

Washington, DC, Machine 83
Date Other Than 1st Day

CVP6	CVP1	25c 1st Class	6.00	—
a.		1st day dated, serial #12501-15500	4.50	—
b.		1st day dated, serial #00001-12500	4.50	—
c.		1st day dated, serial over #27500	—	—
CVP7	CVP1	$1 3rd Class	—	—
a.		1st day dated, serial #24501-27500	—	—
b.		1st day dated, serial over #27500	—	—
CVP8	CVP2	$1.69 Parcel Post	—	—
a.		1st day dated, serial #21501-24500	—	—
b.		1st day dated, serial over #27500	—	—
CVP9	CVP1	$2.40 Priority Mail	—	—
a.		1st day dated, serial #18501-21500	—	—
b.		1st day dated, serial over #27500	—	—
c.		Priority Mail ($2.74), with bar code (CVP2)	100.00	—
CVP10	CVP1	$8.75 Express Mail	—	—
a.		1st day dated, serial #15501-18500	—	—
b.		1st day dated, serial over #27500	—	—
	Nos. CVP6a-CVP10a (5)		57.50	—

1989, Sept. 1
Kensington, MD, Machine 82
Date Other Than 1st Day

CVP11	CVP1	25c 1st Class	6.00	—
a.		1st day dated, serial #12501-15500	4.50	—
b.		1st day dated, serial #00001-12500	4.50	—
c.		1st day dated, serial over #27500	—	—
CVP12	CVP1	$1 3rd Class	—	—
a.		1st day dated, serial #24501-27500	—	—
b.		1st day dated, serial over #27500	—	—
CVP13	CVP2	$1.69 Parcel Post	—	—
a.		1st day dated, serial #21501-24500	—	—
b.		1st day dated, serial over #27500	—	—
CVP14	CVP1	$2.40 Priority Mail	—	—
a.		1st day dated, serial #18501-21500	—	—
b.		1st day dated, serial over #27500	—	—
c.		Priority Mail ($2.74), with bar code (CVP2)	100.00	—
CVP15	CVP1	$8.75 Express Mail	—	—
a.		1st day dated, serial #15501-18500	—	—
b.		1st day dated, serial over #27500	—	—
	Nos. CVP11a-CVP15a (5)		57.50	—
	Nos. CVP1b, CVP11b (2)		9.00	—

Kensington, MD, Machine 83
Date Other Than 1st Day

CVP16	CVP1	25c 1st Class	6.00	—
a.		1st day dated, serial #12501-15500	4.50	—
b.		1st day dated, serial #00001-12500	4.50	—
c.		1st day dated, serial over #27500	—	—
CVP17	CVP1	$1 3rd Class	—	—
a.		1st day dated, serial #24501-27500	—	—
b.		1st day dated, serial over #27500	—	—
CVP18	CVP2	$1.69 Parcel Post	—	—
a.		1st day dated, serial #21501-24500	—	—
b.		1st day dated, serial over #27500	—	—
CVP19	CVP1	$2.40 Priority Mail	—	—
a.		1st day dated, serial #18501-21500	—	—
b.		1st day dated, serial over #27500	—	—
c.		Priority Mail ($2.74), with bar code (CVP2)	100.00	—
CVP20	CVP1	$8.75 Express Mail	—	—
a.		1st day dated, serial #15501-18500	—	—
b.		1st day dated, serial over #27500	—	—
	Nos. CVP16a-CVP20a (5)		57.50	—
	Nos. CVP6b, CVP16b (2)		9.00	—

1989, Nov.
Washington, DC, Machine 11

CVP21	CVP1	25c 1st Class	150.00	
a.		1st Class, with bar code (CVP2)	—	

Stamps in CVP1 design, probably certified 1st class, with $1.10 denominations exist.

CVP22	CVP1	$1 3rd Class	500.00	
CVP23	CVP2	$1.69 Parcel Post	500.00	
CVP24	CVP1	$2.40 Priority Mail	500.00	
a.		Priority Mail ($2.74), with bar code (CVP2)	—	
CVP25	CVP1	$8.75 Express Mail	500.00	

Washington, DC, Machine 12

CVP26	CVP1	25c 1st Class	150.00	

A $1.10 certified 1st Class stamp, dated Nov. 20, exists on cover.

CVP27	CVP1	$1 3rd Class	—	

A $1.40 Third Class stamp of type CVP2, dated Dec. 1 is known on a Dec. 2 cover.

CVP28	CVP2	$1.69 Parcel Post	—	
CVP29	CVP1	$2.40 Priority Mail	—	
a.		Priority Mail ($2.74), with bar code (CVP2)	—	
CVP30	CVP1	$8.75 Express Mail	—	

An $8.50 Express Mail stamp, dated Dec. 2, exists on cover.

CVP3 — Type I

CVP3 — Type II

1992, Aug. 20 Engr. Perf. 10 Horiz.
Coil Stamp

CVP31	CVP3	29c red & blue, type I	.60	.25
c.		32c, type II ('94)	.90	.40

No. CVP31 was available in all denominations from 1c to $99.99.

The listing is for the first class rate. Other denominations, se-tenant combinations, or "errors" will not be listed.

Type II denomination has large sans-serif numerals preceded by an asterisk measuring 2mm across. No. CVP31 has small numerals with serifs preceded by an asterisk 1½mm across.

CVP4

1994, Feb. 19 Photo. Perf. 9.9 Vert.
Coil Stamp

CVP32	CVP4	29c dk red & dk bl	.60	.25

No. CVP32 was available in all denominations from 19c to $99.99.

The listing is for the first class rate at time of issue. Other denominations, se-tenant combinations, or "errors" will not be listed.

1996, Jan. 26 Photo. Perf. 9.9 Vert.

CVP33	CVP4	32c brt red & bl	.60	.25

Letters in "USA" on No. CVP33 are thicker than on No. CVP32. Numerous other design differences exist in the moire pattern and in the bunting.

For No. CVP33, the 32c value has been listed because it was the first class rate at time of issue.

CVP5

Illustration reduced.

1999 Tagged Die Cut
Self-Adhesive

CVP34	CVP5	33c black	—	—

No. CVP34 was available from 15 NCR Automated Postal Center machines located in central Florida. Machines could produce values as low as 1c as well as values higher than 33c. The backing paper is taller and wider than the stamp.

CVP6

Illustration reduced.

1999 Tagged Die Cut
Self-Adhesive

CVP35	CVP6	33c black & red orange	—	—
a.		With Priority Mail inscription instead of identification number at LL	—	—

No. CVP35 was available from 18 IBM machines located in central Florida. The backing paper is taller than the stamp. Machines could produce values as low as 1c as well as values higher than 33c.

CARRIERS' STAMPS

OFFICIAL ISSUES

Issued by the US Government to facilitate payment of fees for delivering and collecting letters.

Franklin
OC1

Eagle
OC2

1851 Unwmk. Engr. Imperf.

LO1	OC1	(1c) dull blue, rose	5,000.	5,500.
LO2	OC2	1c blue	25.00	50.00

1875

REPRINTS OF 1851 ISSUE
Without Gum

LO3	OC1 (1c) blue, *rose,* imperf.		50.00
LO4	OC1 (1c) blue, perf. 12	16,000.	
LO5	OC2 1c blue, imperf.	25.00	
LO6	OC2 1c blue, perf. 12	160.00	

Reprints of the Franklin Carrier are printed in dark blue, instead of the dull blue or deep blue of the originals.

The reprints of the Eagle carrier are on hard white paper, ungummed and sometimes perforated, and also on a coarse wove paper. Originals are on yellowish paper with brown gum.

SEMI-OFFICIAL ISSUES

Issued by officials or employees of the US Government for the purpose of securing or indicating payment of carriers' fees.

BALTIMORE, MD.

C1

1850-55		**Typo.**		***Imperf.***
1LB1	C1 1c red, *bluish*		180.	160.
1LB2	C1 1c blue, *bluish*		200.	150.
a.	Bluish laid paper		—	—
1LB3	C1 1c blue		160.	100.
a.	Laid paper		200.	150.
1LB4	C1 1c green		—	850.
1LB5	C1 1c red		2,250.	1,750.

Ten varieties.

C2   C3

1856		**Typo.**	
1LB6	C2 1c blue	130.	90.
1LB7	C2 1c red	130.	90.

Shades exist of Nos. 1LB6-1LB7.

1857			
1LB8	C3 1c black	65.	50.
a.	"SENT"	100.	75.
b.	Short rays	100.	75.
1LB9	C3 1c red	100.	90.
a.	"SENT"	140.	110.
b.	Short rays	140.	110.
c.	As "b," double impression	—	

Ten varieties of C3.

BOSTON, MASS.

C6   C7

1849-50		**Typeset**	
3LB1	C6 1c blue	375.	180.
a.	Wrong ornament at left, on cover (not tied)		550.
3LB2	C7 1c bl (shades), *slate*	190.	100.

CHARLESTON, S. C.

C8   C10

1849		**Typo.**	
4LB1	C8 2c black, *brn rose*	10,000.	
	Cut to shape	4,000.	3,000.
4LB2	C8 2c black, *yellow,* cut to shape		

No. 4LB1 unused is a unique uncanceled stamp on piece. The used cut-to-shape stamp is also unique. In addition two covers exist bearing No. 4LB1.

No. 4LB2 unused (uncanceled) off cover is unique; four known on cover.

See the Scott U.S. Specialized Catalogue.

1854		**Typeset**	
4LB3	C10 2c black		1,500.

C11

1849-50		**Typeset**	
4LB5	C11 2c black, *bluish,* pelure	750.	500.
a.	"Ceuts"	5,750.	
4LB7	C11 2c black, *yellow*	750.	1,000.
a.	"Ccnts," ms. tied on cover		14,500.

Several varieties of C11.

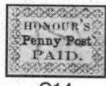

C13   C14   C15

1851-58		**Typeset**	
4LB8	C13 2c blk, *bluish*	350.	175.
a.	Period after "Paid"	500.	250.
b.	"Cens"	700.	900.
c.	"Conours" and "Bents"	—	
4LB9	C13 2c blk, *bluish,* pelure	850.	950.
4LB11	C14 (2c) blk, *bluish*	—	375.
4LB12	C14 (2c) blk, *bluish,* pelure		
4LB13	C15 (2c) blk, *bluish* ('58)	750.	400.
a.	Comma after "PAID"	1,100.	
b.	No period after "Post"	1,400.	

Several varieties of C13.

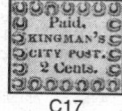

C16   C17

1851-58		**Typeset**	
4LB14	C16 2c black, *bluish*	1,400.	900.
4LB15	C17 2c black, *bluish*	800.	800.

Several varieties of each.

C18

1858		**Typeset**	
4LB16	C18 2c black, *bluish*	8,000.	

Several varieties.

Same as C19, but Inscribed "Beckmann's City Post"

1860		
4LB17	C19 2c black	

One copy exists, on cover.

C19   C20

1859		**Typeset**	
4LB18	C19 2c black, *bluish*	21,000.	
4LB19	C20 2c black, *bluish*	5,000.	—
4LB20	C20 2c black, *pink*	150.	—
4LB21	C20 2c black, *yellow*	150.	

CINCINNATI, OHIO

C20a

1854		**Litho.**	**Wove Paper**
9LB1	C20a 2c brown	3,000.	3,000.

CLEVELAND, OHIO

C20b   C20c

1854		**Wove Paper**	**Litho.**
10LB1	C20b blue	2,000.	2,000.
	Vertically Laid Paper		
10LB2	C20c 2c black, *bluish*	—	3,750.

LOUISVILLE, KY.

C21   C22

1857-58		**Litho.**	
5LB1	C21 (2c) bluish green	100.	
5LB2	C22 (2c) blue ('58)	200.	500.
5LB3	C22 (2c) black ('58)	4,500.	15,000.

NEW YORK, N.Y.

C23

1842		**Engr.**	
6LB1	C23 3c black, *grayish*		1,750.

Used copies are Carriers' stamps only when canceled with the regular government cancellation "U.S." in octagonal frame (see illustration), "U.S.CITY DESPATCH POST," or New York circular postmark.

When canceled "FREE" in frame they were used as local stamps. See No. 40L1 in the Scott Specialized Catalogue of United States Stamps.

C24

1842-45		**Engr.**
Unsurfaced Paper, Colored Through		
6LB2	C24 3c blk, *rosy buff*	2,500.
6LB3	C24 3c blk, *light blue*	500. 500.
6LB4	C24 3c black, *green*	11,500.

Some authorities consider No. 6LB2 to be an essay, and No. 6LB4 to be a color changeling.

Glazed Paper, Surface Colored			
6LB5	C24 3c blk, *bl grn* (shades)	175.	175.
a.	Double impression	1,500.	
b.	3c, black, *blue*	650.	250.
c.	As "b," dbl. impression		850.
d.	3c, black, *green*	1,000.	900.
e.	As "d," dbl. impression	—	
6LB6	C24 3c blk, *pink,* on cover front		14,500.

No. 6LB6 is unique.

No. 6LB5 Surcharged in Red — C25

1846		
6LB7	C25 2c on 3c, on cover	55,000.

The City Despatch 2c red is listed in the Scott U.S. Specialized Catalogue as a Local stamp.

C27

1849-50		**Typo.**	
6LB9	C27 1c black, *rose*	90.	90.
6LB10	C27 1c black, *yellow*	90.	90.
6LB11	C27 1c black, *buff*	90.	90.
a.	Pair, one stamp sideways	2,250.	

PHILADELPHIA, PA.

C28   C29

1849-50		**Typeset**	
7LB1	C28 1c blk, *rose* (with letters L.P.)	450.	
7LB2	C28 1c black, *rose* (with letter S)	3,000.	
7LB3	C28 1c blk, *rose* (with letter H)	275.	
7LB4	C28 1c blk, *rose* (with letters L.S.)	400.	500.
7LB5	C28 1c black, *rose* (with letters J.J.)		7,500.
7LB6	C29 1c black, *rose*	300.	250.
7LB7	C29 1c blk, *blue,* glazed	1,000.	
7LB8	C29 1c blk, *ver,* glazed	700.	
7LB9	C29 1c blk, *yel,* glazed	2,750.	2,250.

Several varieties of each.

Nos. 7LB1-7LB9 normally received no cancellation.

Two examples reported of No. 7LB5, one uncanceled on a cover front, the other uncanceled on full cover with U.S. 5c (No. 1).

Value here is for stamp on cover front; for full cover see the Scott U.S. Specialized Catalogue.

The 1c black on buff (unglazed), type C29, is believed to be a color changeling.

C30   C31

C32

1850-52   Litho.
7LB11	C30	1c gold, *black,* *glazed*	140.	110.
7LB12	C30	1c blue	350.	275.
7LB13	C30	1c black	750.	550.

25 varieties of C30.

Handstamped
7LB14	C31	1c blue, *buff*	3,000.	
7LB16	C31	1c black		5,000.

1856(?)
7LB18	C32	1c black	1,250.	2,000.

Labels in these designs are not believed to be Carrier stamps.

ST. LOUIS, MO.

C36   C37

Illustrations enlarged to show details of the two types (note upper corners especially).

1849   **White Wove Paper**   Litho.
           Two Types
8LB1	C36	2c black	7,000.	—
8LB2	C37	2c black	5,500.	—

C38

1857   Litho.
8LB3	C38	2c blue	22,500.

Carrier stamps Nos. 9LB1, 10LB1-10LB2 are listed following No. 4LB21.

STAMPED ENVELOPES & WRAPPERS

VALUES

Values are for cut squares in a grade of very fine.

Very fine cut squares will have the design well centered within moderately large margins. Precanceled cut squares must include the entire precancellation.

Values for unused entires are for those without printed or manuscript address. Values for letter sheets are for folded entires. Unfolded copies sell for more. A "full corner" includes back and side flaps and commands a premium.

Entire envelopes and wrappers are listed in the Scott U.S. Specialized Catalogue.

Wrappers are listed with envelopes of corresponding designs, and indicated by prefix letter "W" instead of "U."

Envelopes with the stamp printed by error in colorless embossing from an uninked die, are "albinos." They are

---

worth more than normal, inked impressions. Albinos of earlier issues, canceled while current, are scarce.

The papers of these issues vary greatly in texture, and in color from yellowish to bluish white and from amber to dark buff.

"+" Some authorities claim that Nos. U37, U48, U49, U110, U124, U125, U130, U133A, U137A, U137B, U137C, W138, U145, U162, U178A, U185, U220, U285, U286, U298, U299, UO3, UO32, UO38, UO45 and UO45A (each with "+" before number) were not regularly issued and are not known to have been used.

Washington
U1   U2

U1 — "THREE" in shor t label with curved ends; 13mm wide at top.
U2 — "THREE" in shor t label with straight ends; 15½mm wide at top.

U3   U4

U3 — "THREE" in shor t label with octagon ends.
U4 — "THREE" in wide label with str aight ends; 20mm wide at top.

U5   U6

U5 — "THREE" in medium wide label with curved ends; 14½mm wide at top.

U7   U8

U7 — "TEN" in shor t label; 15½mm wide at top.
U8 — "TEN" in wide label 20mm wide at top.

On Diagonally Laid Paper

1853-55
U1	U1	3c red	325.00	30.00
U2	U2	3c red, *buff*	95.00	15.00
U3	U2	3c red	1,100.	30.00
U4	U2	3c red, *buff*	310.00	25.00
U5	U2	3c red ('54)	6,000.	450.00
U6	U3	3c red, *buff* ('54)	1,500.	45.00
U7	U4	3c red	1,500.	90.00
U8	U4	3c red, *buff*	7,500.	110.00
U9	U5	3c red ('54)	35.00	3.50
U10	U5	3c red, *buff* ('54)	20.00	3.50
U11	U6	6c red	250.00	67.50
U12	U6	6c red, *buff*	150.00	65.00
U13	U6	6c green	300.00	110.00
U14	U6	6c green, *buff*	200.00	85.00
U15	U7	10c green ('55)	475.00	85.00
U16	U7	10c green, *buff* ('55)	125.00	55.00
a.		10c pale green, *buff*	110.00	50.00
U17	U8	10c green ('55)	325.00	125.00
a.		10c pale green	325.00	100.00
U18	U8	10c green, *buff* ('55)	400.00	75.00
a.		10c pale green, *buff*	350.00	75.00

Nos. U9, U10, U11, U12, U13, U14, U17 and U18 have been reprinted on white and buff papers, wove or vertically laid, and are not known entire. The originals are on diagonally laid paper. Value of 8 reprints on laid, $225. Reprints on wove sell for more.

Franklin, Period after "POSTAGE."
U9   U10

U10 — Bust touches inner fr ame-line at front and back.

 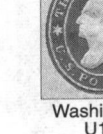

No period   Washington
after   U12
"POSTAGE"
U11

Envelopes are on diagonally laid paper. Wrappers on vert. or horiz. laid paper.

1860-61
W18B	U9	1c blue	4,500.	
U19	U9	1c blue, *buff*	37.50	15.00
W20	U9	1c blue, *buff* ('61)	70.00	50.00
W21	U9	1c bl, *man* ('61)	50.00	45.00
U21A	U9	1c blue, *org,* *entire*	2,250.	
W22	U9	1c blue, *org* ('61)	3,750.	
U23	U10	1c blue, *org*	650.00	350.00
U24	U11	1c blue, *buff*	300.00	125.00
W25	U11	1c bl, *man* ('61)	7,500.	2,000.
U26	U12	3c red	35.00	20.00
U27	U12	3c red, *buff*	26.00	13.00
U28	U12+9	3c + 1c red & blue	375.00	240.00
U29	U12+9	3c + 1c red & blue, *buff*	375.00	240.00
U30	U12	6c red	2,750.	1,250.
U31	U12	6c red, *buff*	3,500.	1,500.
U32	U12	10c green	1,500.	425.00
U33	U12	10c grn, *buff*	1,500.	250.00

Nos. U26, U27, U30 to U33 have been reprinted on the same vertically laid paper as the reprints of the 1853-55 issue and are not known entire. Value, Nos. U26-U27, $160; Nos. U30-U33, $100.

U13   U14

Washington
U15   U16

Envelopes are on diagonally laid paper. Nos. U36 and U45 come on vertically or horizontally laid paper.

1861
U34	U13	3c pink	26.00	5.75
U35	U13	3c pink, *buff*	24.00	5.25
U36	U13	3c pink, *bl (letter sheet)*	80.00	50.00
+U37	U13	3c pink, *org*	4,750.	
U38	U14	6c pink	110.00	80.00
U39	U14	6c pink, *buff*	70.00	62.50
U40	U15	10c yellow green	37.50	30.00
a.		10c blue green	35.00	27.50
U41	U15	10c yel green, *buff*	40.00	27.50
a.		10c blue green, *buff*	40.00	30.00
U42	U16	12c red & brown, *buff*	210.00	160.00
a.		12c lake & brown, *buff*	1,000.	
U43	U16	20c red & bl, *buff*	300.00	200.00
U44	U16	24c red & green, *buff*	240.00	200.00
a.		24c lake & green, *sal*	325.00	225.00
U45	U16	40c black & red, *buff*	375.00	350.00

Nos. U38 and U39 have been reprinted on the same papers as the reprints of the 1853-55 issue and are not known entire. Value of two reprints, $60.

Jackson   Jackson
U17   U18

"U.S. POSTAGE" above

U17 — The do wnstroke and tail of the "2" unite near the point.

U18 — The do wnstroke and tail of the "2" touch but do not merge.

Jackson — U19   Jackson — U20

"U.S. POST" above

U19 — Stamp measures 24-25mm in width.

U20 — Stamp measures 25½-26¼mm in width.

Envelopes are on diagonally laid paper. Wrappers on vert. or horiz. laid paper.

1863-64

U46	U17	2c black, *buff*	42.50	20.00
W47	U17	2c black, *dk man*	60.00	45.00
+U48	U18	2c black, *buff*	3,000.	
+U49	U18	2c black, *orange*	1,400.	
U50	U19	2c blk, *buff* ('64)	16.00	9.00
W51	U19	2c blk, *buff* ('64)	325.00	160.00
U52	U19	2c blk, *org* ('64)	14.00	9.00
W53	U19	2c black, *dk man* ('64)	45.00	35.00
U54	U20	2c blk, *buff* ('64)	15.00	9.00
W55	U20	2c blk, *buff* ('64)	90.00	57.50
U56	U20	2c blk, *org* ('64)	15.00	8.25
W57	U20	2c blk, *lt man* ('64)	19.00	11.50

Washington   Washington
U21   U22

1864-65

U58	U21	3c pink	8.00	1.60
U59	U21	3c pink, *buff*	6.50	1.25
U60	U21	3c brown ('65)	50.00	30.00
U61	U21	3c brn, *buff* ('65)	47.50	26.00
U62	U21	6c pink	77.50	29.00
U63	U21	6c pink, *buff*	40.00	27.50
U64	U21	6c purple ('65)	55.00	26.00
U65	U21	6c pur, *buff* ('65)	50.00	20.00
U66	U22	9c lem, *buff* ('65)	425.00	250.00
U67	U22	9c org, *buff* ('65)	125.00	90.00
a.		9c orange yellow, *buff*	125.00	90.00
U68	U22	12c brn, *buff* ('65)	325.00	250.00
U69	U22	12c red brn, *buff* ('65)	125.00	55.00
U70	U22	18c red, *buff* ('65)	95.00	95.00
U71	U22	24c bl, *buff* ('65)	100.00	95.00
U72	U22	30c grn, *buff* ('65)	125.00	75.00
a.		30c yellow green, *buff*	125.00	80.00
U73	U22	40c rose, *buff* ('65)	125.00	250.00

Reay Issue

The engravings in this issue are finely executed.

Franklin — U23   Jackson — U24

U23 — Bust points to the end of the "N" of "ONE."

U24 — Bust narrow at back. Small, thick figures of value.

Washington   Lincoln
U25   U26

U25 — Queue projects below bust.

U26 — Neck very long at the back.

Stanton — U27   Jefferson — U28

U27 — Bust pointed at the back, figures "7" are normal.

U28 — Queue forms straight line with the bust.

Clay — U29   Webster — U30

U29 — Ear partly concealed by hair, mouth large, chin prominent.

U30 — Has side whiskers.

Scott — U31   Hamilton — U32

U31 — Straggling locks of hair at top of head; ornaments around the inner oval end in squares.

U32 — Back of bust very narrow, chin almost straight; labels containing figures of value are exactly parallel.

Perry — U33

U33 — Front of bust very narrow and pointed; inner lines of shields project very slightly beyond the oval.

1870-71

U74	U23	1c blue	40.00	30.00
a.		1c ultramarine	65.00	35.00
U75	U23	1c blue, *amber*	32.50	27.50
a.		1c ultramarine, *amb*	60.00	30.00
U76	U23	1c blue, *org*	20.00	15.00
W77	U23	1c blue, *man*	42.50	35.00
U78	U24	2c brown	40.00	16.00
U79	U24	2c brown, *amb*	20.00	9.00
U80	U24	2c brown, *org*	12.00	6.50
W81	U24	2c brown, *man*	27.50	21.00
U82	U25	3c green	8.00	1.00
a.		3c brown (error), *entire*	12,000.	
U83	U25	3c green, *amb*	6.75	2.00
U84	U25	3c green, *cream*	10.00	4.25
U85	U26	6c dark red	25.00	16.00
a.		6c vermilion	25.00	16.00
U86	U26	6c dk red, *amb*	25.00	15.00
a.		6c vermilion, *amber*	25.00	15.00
U87	U26	6c dk red, *cr*	32.50	16.00
a.		6c vermilion, *cream*	32.50	16.00
U88	U27	7c ver, *amb* ('71)	50.00	190.00
U89	U28	10c olive black	850.00	750.00
U90	U28	10c ol blk, *amb*	850.00	900.00
U91	U28	10c brown	75.00	70.00
U92	U28	10c brn, *amb*	85.00	50.00
a.		10c dark brown, *amb*	85.00	50.00
U93	U29	12c plum	100.00	82.50
U94	U29	12c plum, *amb*	125.00	110.00
U95	U29	12c plum, *cr*	260.00	250.00
U96	U30	15c red orange	75.00	
a.		15c orange	75.00	
U97	U30	15c red org, *amb*	210.00	300.00
a.		15c orange, *amber*	210.00	
U98	U30	15c red org, *cr*	325.00	350.00
a.		15c orange, *cream*	325.00	
U99	U31	24c purple	140.00	140.00
U100	U31	24c pur, *amb*	200.00	325.00
U101	U31	24c pur, *cream*	260.00	500.00
U102	U32	30c black	80.00	110.00
U103	U32	30c blk, *amb*	250.00	500.00
U104	U32	30c blk, *cream*	225.00	500.00
U105	U33	90c carmine	150.00	350.00
U106	U33	90c car, *amb*	300.00	400.00
U107	U33	90c car, *cream*	250.00	2,500.

Plimpton Issue

The profiles in this issue are inferior to the fine engraving of the Reay issue.

U34   U35

U34 — Bust forms an angle at the back near the frame. Lettering poorly executed. Distinct circle in "O" of "POSTAGE."

U35 — Lower part of bust points to the end of the "E" in "ONE." Head inclined downward.

U36   U37

U36 — Bust narrow at back. Thin figures of value. The head of the "P" in "POSTAGE" is very narrow. The bust at front is broad and ends in sharp corners.

U37 — Bust broad. Figures of value in long ovals.

U38   U39

U38 — Similar to U37 but the figure "2" at the left touches the oval.

U39 — Similar to U37 but the "O" of "TWO" has the center netted instead of plain. The "G" of "POSTAGE" and the "C" of "CENTS" have diagonal crossline.

U40   U41

U40 — Bust broad; numerals in ovals short and thick.

U41 — Similar to U40 but the ovals containing the numerals are much heavier. A diagonal line runs from the upper part of the "U" to the white frame-line.

U42   U43

U42 — Similar to U40 but the middle stroke of "N" in "CENTS" is as thin as the vertical strokes.

U43 — Bottom of bust cut almost semi-circularly.

U44   U45

U44 — Thin lettering, long thin figures of value.

U45 — Thick lettering, well-formed figures of value, queue does not project below bust.

U46

U46 — Top of head egg-shaped; knot of queue well marked and projects triangularly.

Taylor — U47

Die 1   Die 2

Die 1: Figures of value with thick curved tops.

Die 2: Figures of value with long, thin tops.

U48   U49

U48 — Neck very short at the back.

U49 — Figures of value turned up at the ends.

U50   U51

U50 — Very large head.

U51 — Knot of queue stands out prominently.

U52   U53

U52 — Ear prominent, chin receding.

U53 — No side whiskers, forelock projects above head.

U54   U55

U54 — Hair does not project; ornaments around the inner oval end in points.

U55 — Back of bust rather broad, chin slopes considerably; labels containing figures of value are not exactly parallel.

U56

U56 — Front of bust sloping; inner lines of shields project considerably into the inner oval.

1874-86

U108	U34	1c dk blue	190.00	70.00
a.		1c light blue	190.00	70.00
U109	U34	1c dk blue, amb	160.00	75.00
+U110	U34	1c dk blue, cr	1,750.	
U111	U34	1c dk blue, org	25.00	17.50
a.		1c light blue, org	25.00	17.50
W112	U34	1c dk blue, man	60.00	40.00
U113	U35	1c light blue	1.75	1.00
a.		1c dark blue	8.50	7.50
U114	U35	1c lt bl, amb	4.25	4.00
a.		1c dark blue, amb	19.00	10.00
U115	U35	1c blue, cr	5.00	4.50
a.		1c dark blue, cr	19.00	8.50
U116	U35	1c lt bl, org	.80	.40
a.		1c dark blue, org	4.00	2.50
U117	U35	1c lt bl, bl ('80)	7.50	5.25
U118	U35	1c lt bl, fawn ('79)	7.50	5.25
U119	U35	1c lt bl, man ('86)	7.50	3.25
W120	U35	1c lt bl, man	1.60	1.10
a.		1c dark blue, man	8.50	8.00
U121	U35	1c lt blue, amb man ('86)	14.00	10.00
U122	U36	2c brown	110.00	40.00
U123	U36	2c brn, amb	60.00	40.00
+U124	U36	2c brn, cr	1,150.	
+U125	U36	2c brn, org	25,000.	
W126	U36	2c brn, man	140.00	70.00
W127	U36	2c ver, man	1,750.	250.00
U128	U37	2c brown	45.00	32.50
U129	U37	2c brn, amb	70.00	37.50
+U130	U37	2c brn, cr	50,000.	
W131	U37	2c brn, man	17.50	16.00
U132	U38	2c brown	70.00	27.50
U133	U38	2c brn, amb	300.00	65.00
+U133A	U38	2c brn, cr	75,000.	
U134	U39	2c brown	1,250.	140.00
U135	U39	2c brn, amb	475.00	125.00
U136	U39	2c brn, org	50.00	29.00
W137	U39	2c brn, man	65.00	35.00
+U137A	U39	2c vermilion	25,000.	
+U137B	U39	2c ver, amb	25,000.	
+U137C	U39	2c ver, org	25,000.	
+W138	U39	2c ver, man	32,500.	
U139	U40	2c brown ('75)	50.00	35.00
U140	U40	2c brn, amb ('75)	85.00	60.00
+U140A	U40	2c reddish brown, org ('75)	25,000.	
W141	U40	2c brn, man ('75)	35.00	26.00
U142	U40	2c ver ('75)	7.00	3.00
a.		2c pink	7.50	5.00
U143	U40	2c ver, amb ('75)	7.00	3.00
U144	U40	2c ver, cr ('75)	14.00	6.25
+U145	U40	2c ver, org ('75)	25,000.	
U146	U40	2c ver, bl ('80)	140.00	40.00
U147	U40	2c ver, fawn ('75)	6.75	4.50
W148	U40	2c ver, man ('75)	3.75	3.75
U149	U41	2c ver ('78)	55.00	30.00
a.		2c pink	55.00	30.00
U150	U41	2c ver, amb ('78)	30.00	17.50
U151	U41	2c ver, bl ('80)	13.00	9.25
a.		2c pink, blue	10.00	9.00

U152	U41	2c ver, fawn ('78)	11.00	4.75
U153	U42	2c ver ('76)	70.00	26.00
U154	U42	2c ver, amb ('76)	350.00	90.00
W155	U42	2c ver, man ('76)	22.50	9.50
U156	U43	2c ver ('81)	1,300.	150.00
U157	U43	2c ver, amb ('81)	57,500.	35,000.
W158	U43	2c ver, man ('81)	90.00	60.00
U159	U44	3c green	26.00	6.75
U160	U44	3c grn, amb	30.00	10.50
U161	U44	3c green, cr	37.50	15.00
+U162	U44	3c grn, blue	—	
U163	U45	3c green	1.40	.30
U164	U45	3c grn, amb	1.50	.70
U165	U45	3c green, cr	9.00	6.50
U166	U45	3c grn, blue	8.25	6.25
U167	U45	3c grn, fawn ('75)	5.00	3.50
U168	U46	3c grn ('81)	1,500.	75.00
U169	U46	3c grn, amb ('81)	260.00	110.00
U170	U46	3c grn, bl ('81)	12,500.	3,500.
U171	U46	3c grn, fawn ('81)	45,000.	3,250.
U172	U47	5c bl, die 1 ('75)	12.00	8.00
U173	U47	5c bl, die 1, amb ('75)	12.00	9.00
U174	U47	5c bl, die 1, cr ('75)	100.00	40.00
U175	U47	5c bl, die 1, bl ('75)	32.50	15.00
U176	U47	5c bl, die 1, fawn ('75)	125.00	57.50
U177	U47	5c bl, die 2 ('75)	9.00	6.75
U178	U47	5c bl, die 2, amb ('75)	9.00	7.50
+U178A	U47	5c bl, die 2, cr ('76)	16,000.	
U179	U47	5c bl, die 2, blue ('75)	22.50	9.00
U180	U47	5c bl, die 2, fawn ('75)	110.00	45.00
U181	U48	6c red	6.75	6.25
a.		6c vermilion	6.75	6.25
U182	U48	6c red, amb	11.50	6.25
a.		6c vermilion, amber	11.00	6.25
U183	U48	6c red, cr	40.00	13.00
a.		6c vermilion, cream	40.00	13.00
U184	U48	6c red, fawn	20.00	13.00
+U185	U49	7c vermilion	1,800.	
U186	U49	7c ver, amb	125.00	62.50
U187	U50	10c brown	37.50	20.00
U188	U50	10c brn, amb	70.00	32.50
U189	U51	10c choc ('75)	7.50	4.00
a.		10c bister brown	8.50	5.00
b.		10c yellow ocher	3,500.	
U190	U51	10c choc, amb ('75)	8.00	7.00
a.		10c bister brn, amb	8.50	7.50
b.		10c yel ocher, amb	3,500.	
U191	U51	10c brn, oriental buff ('86)	12.00	8.25
U192	U51	10c brn, bl ('86)	15.00	8.25
a.		10c gray black, bl	15.00	8.25
b.		10c red brown, blue	15.00	8.25
U193	U51	10c brn, man ('86)	16.00	10.00
a.		10c red brown, man	16.00	10.00
U194	U51	10c brn, amb man ('86)	19.00	8.50
a.		10c red brown, amber manila	21.00	9.00
U195	U52	12c plum	450.00	100.00
U196	U52	12c plum, amb	275.00	175.00
U197	U52	12c plum, cr	225.00	150.00
U198	U53	15c orange	47.50	37.50
U199	U53	15c org, amb	160.00	100.00
U200	U53	15c org, cr	600.00	350.00
U201	U54	24c purple	175.00	150.00
U202	U54	24c pur, amb	190.00	125.00
U203	U54	24c pur, cr	175.00	125.00
U204	U55	30c black	62.50	27.50
U205	U55	30c blk, amb	72.50	60.00
U206	U55	30c blk, cr	375.00	375.00
U207	U55	30c blk, oriental buff ('86)	100.00	82.50
U208	U55	30c blk, bl ('86)	110.00	82.50
U209	U55	30c blk, man ('86)	90.00	80.00
U210	U55	30c blk, amb man ('86)	175.00	85.00
U211	U56	90c car ('75)	110.00	85.00
U212	U56	90c car, amb ('75)	225.00	300.00
U213	U56	90c car, cr ('75)	1,250.	
U214	U56	90c car, oriental buff ('86)	200.00	275.00
U215	U56	90c car, bl ('86)	190.00	250.00
U216	U56	90c car, man ('86)	175.00	250.00
U217	U56	90c car, amb man ('86)	125.00	200.00

See Nos. U336-U347.

United States Centennial Issue

Single line under "POSTAGE" U57

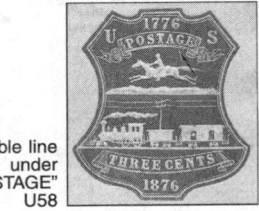

Double line under "POSTAGE" U58

1876

U218	U57	3c red	50.00	25.00
U219	U57	3c green	45.00	17.50
+U220	U58	3c red	40,000.	
U221	U58	3c green	52.50	21.00

Cent. of the US, and the World's Fair at Philadelphia. See No. U582.

Garfield   Washington
U59   U60

1882-86

U222	U59	5c brown	4.50	2.75
U223	U59	5c brown, amb	4.75	3.25
U224	U59	5c brn, oriental buff ('86)	125.00	72.50
U225	U59	5c brown, blue	70.00	35.00
U226	U59	5c brown, fawn	300.00	

1883, Oct.

U227	U60	2c red	3.75	2.25
a.		2c brown (error), entire	7,500.	
U228	U60	2c red, amber	4.75	2.75
U229	U60	2c red, blue	7.00	5.00
U230	U60	2c red, fawn	8.00	5.25

Wavy lines fine and clear — U61

Wavy lines thick and blurred — U62

Four Wavy Lines in Oval

1883, Nov.

U231	U61	2c red	3.75	2.25
U232	U61	2c red, amber	4.75	3.75
U233	U61	2c red, blue	8.00	7.25
U234	U61	2c red, fawn	5.75	4.75
W235	U61	2c red, manila	17.50	6.25

1884, June

U236	U62	2c red	10.00	4.00
U237	U62	2c red, amber	12.50	10.00
U238	U62	2c red, blue	21.00	10.00
U239	U62	2c red, fawn	15.00	10.00

See Nos. U260-W269.

3½ links over left "2" — U63

2 links below right "2" — U64

Round "O" in "TWO" — U65

U240	U63	2c red	85.00	42.50
U241	U63	2c red, amber	900.00	325.00
U242	U63	2c red, fawn		20,000.
U243	U64	2c red	100.00	57.50
U244	U64	2c red, amber	275.00	75.00
U245	U64	2c red, blue	450.00	200.00
U246	U64	2c red, fawn	400.00	140.00
U247	U65	2c red	2,750.	450.00
U248	U65	2c red, amber	4,250.	1,000.
U249	U65	2c red, fawn	1,100.	400.00

See Nos. U270-U276.

Jackson — U66

Die 1

Die 2

Die 1: Numeral at left is 2¾mm wide. Die 2: Numeral at left is 3¼mm wide.

1883-86

U250	U66	4c grn, die 1	3.75	3.50
U251	U66	4c grn, die 1, amb	4.75	3.50
U252	U66	4c grn, die 1, oriental buff ('86)	10.00	9.00
U253	U66	4c grn, die 1, bl ('86)	10.00	6.50
U254	U66	4c grn, die 1, man ('86)	12.50	7.50
U255	U66	4c grn, die 1, amb man ('86)	21.00	10.00
U256	U66	4c grn, die 2	8.00	5.00
U257	U66	4c grn, die 2, amb	14.00	7.00
U258	U66	4c grn, die 2, man ('86)	14.00	7.50
U259	U66	4c grn, die 2, amb man ('86)	14.00	7.50

1884, May

U260	U61	2c brown	14.00	5.75
U261	U61	2c brn, amber	14.00	6.50
U262	U61	2c brn, blue	16.00	10.00
U263	U61	2c brn, fawn	14.00	9.25
W264	U61	2c brn, manila	15.00	10.50

1884, June   Retouched Die

U265	U62	2c brown	16.00	6.25
U266	U62	2c brn, amber	67.50	40.00
U267	U62	2c brn, blue	17.50	6.25
U268	U62	2c brn, fawn	16.00	11.00
W269	U62	2c brn, manila	24.00	15.00

2 Links Below Right "2"

U270	U64	2c brown	100.00	40.00
U271	U64	2c brn, amber	400.00	95.00
U272	U64	2c brn, fawn	9,000.	2,500.

Round "O" in "Two"

U273	U65	2c brown	250.00	100.00
U274	U65	2c brn, amber	250.00	85.00
U275	U65	2c brn, blue		20,000.
U276	U65	2c brn, fawn	1,000.	700.00

Washington
U67   U68

U67 — Extremity of bust below the queue forms a point.

U68 — Extremity of bust is rounded.

Similar to U61
Two wavy lines in oval

1884-86

U277	U67	2c brown	.50	.20
a.		2c brown lake	22.50	21.00
U278	U67	2c brn, amber	.65	.50
a.		2c brown lake, amber	35.00	25.00
U279	U67	2c brn, oriental buff ('86)	4.00	2.10
U280	U67	2c brn, blue	2.50	2.10
U281	U67	2c brn, fawn	3.00	2.40
U282	U67	2c brn, man ('86)	11.00	4.00
W283	U67	2c brn, man	7.00	5.00
U284	U67	2c brn, amb man ('86)	7.00	5.75
+U285	U67	2c red	750.00	
+U286	U67	2c red, blue	325.00	
W287	U67	2c red, man	125.00	
U288	U68	2c brown	300.00	42.50
U289	U68	2c brn, amb	15.00	12.50
U290	U68	2c brn, blue	1,750.	250.00
U291	U68	2c brn, fawn	25.00	19.00
W292	U68	2c brn, man	20.00	17.50

Grant — US1

1886   **Letter Sheet**

U293	US1	2c green, entire	27.50	17.00

See the Scott U.S. Specialized Catalogue for perforation and inscription varieties..

Franklin   Washington
U69   U70

U70 — Bust points between 3rd and 4th notches of inner oval; "G" of "POSTAGE" has no bar.

U71   U72

U71 — Bust points between second and third notches of inner oval; "G" of "POSTAGE" has a bar; ear is indicated by one heavy line; one vertical line at corner of mouth.

U72 — Frame same as U71; upper part of head more rounded; ear indicated by two curved lines with two locks of hair in front; two vertical lines at corner of mouth.

Jackson — U73

Grant — U74   U75

U74 — There is a space between the beard and the collar of the coat. A button is on the collar.

U75 — The collar touches the beard and there is no button.

1887-94

U294	U69	1c blue	.55	.20
U295	U69	1c dk bl ('94)	7.50	2.50
U296	U69	1c bl, amb ('94)	3.50	1.25
U297	U69	1c dk bl, amb ('94)	47.50	22.50
+U298	U69	1c bl, oriental buff ('94)	12,500.	
+U299	U69	1c bl, bl ('94)	20,000.	
U300	U69	1c bl, man ('94)	.65	.35
W301	U69	1c bl, man ('94)	.45	.30
U302	U69	1c dk blue, man ('94)	27.50	10.00
W303	U69	1c dk blue, man ('94)	15.00	9.50
U304	U69	1c bl, amb man	7.50	4.25
U305	U70	2c green	16.00	9.00
U306	U70	2c grn, amb	32.50	14.00
U307	U70	2c grn, oriental buff	80.00	30.00
U308	U70	2c grn, blue	9,000.	1,250.
U309	U70	2c grn, man	17,500.	750.00
U310	U70	2c grn, amb man	1,800.	1,250.
U311	U71	2c green	.35	.20
U312	U71	2c grn, amb	.45	.20
a.		Double impression	—	
U313	U71	2c grn, oriental buff	.60	.25
U314	U71	2c grn, blue	.65	.30
U315	U71	2c grn, man	1.75	.50
W316	U71	2c grn, man	4.00	2.50
U317	U71	2c grn, amb man	2.75	1.90
U318	U72	2c green	140.00	12.50
U319	U72	2c grn, amb	175.00	25.00
U320	U72	2c grn, oriental buff	160.00	40.00
U321	U72	2c grn, blue	175.00	65.00
U322	U72	2c grn, man	250.00	65.00
U323	U72	2c grn, amb man	525.00	80.00
U324	U73	4c carmine	2.75	1.75
a.		4c lake	3.00	2.00
b.		4c scarlet ('94)	3.00	2.00
U325	U73	4c car, amb	3.25	2.25
a.		4c lake, amber	3.50	2.50
b.		4c scarlet, amber ('94)	3.50	3.25
U326	U73	4c car, oriental buff	6.00	3.00
a.		4c lake, oriental buff	7.00	3.50
U327	U73	4c car, blue	5.50	4.00
a.		4c lake, blue	5.50	4.00
U328	U73	4c car, man	7.00	5.50
a.		4c lake, manila	8.00	6.00
b.		4c pink, manila	12.50	4.50
U329	U73	4c car, amb man	5.25	2.75
a.		4c lake, amb manila	6.25	3.25
b.		4c pink, amb manila	12.50	3.75
U330	U74	5c blue	3.75	4.00
U331	U74	5c bl, amber	5.25	2.25
U332	U74	5c bl, oriental buff	5.25	3.75
U333	U74	5c bl, blue	10.00	5.50
U334	U75	5c blue ('94)	17.50	7.50
U335	U75	5c bl, amb ('94)	12.00	7.50
U336	U55	30c red brown	50.00	40.00
a.		30c yellow brown	55.00	45.00
b.		30c chocolate	62.50	47.50
U337	U55	30c red brn, amb	52.50	55.00
a.		30c yel brown, amber	50.00	55.00
b.		30c choc, amber	62.50	55.00
U338	U55	30c red brn, oriental buff	47.50	47.50
a.		30c yel brn, oriental buff	47.50	47.50
U339	U55	30c red brn, bl	47.50	47.50
a.		30c yellow brown, blue	47.50	47.50
U340	U55	30c red brn, manila	50.00	45.00
a.		30c brown, manila	47.50	40.00
U341	U55	30c red brown, amb man	55.00	30.00
a.		30c yel brn, amb man	55.00	30.00
U342	U56	90c purple	70.00	75.00
U343	U56	90c pur, amb	85.00	80.00
U344	U56	90c pur, oriental buff	85.00	85.00
U345	U56	90c pur, blue	85.00	90.00
U346	U56	90c pur, man	90.00	92.50
U347	U56	90c pur, amb manila	90.00	92.50

Columbian Exposition Issue

Columbus and Liberty — U76

1893

U348	U76	1c deep blue	2.25	1.10
U349	U76	2c violet	1.75	.50
a.		2c dark slate (error)	2,000.	
U350	U76	5c chocolate	8.50	7.50
a.		5c slate brown (error)	800.00	950.00
U351	U76	10c slate brown	35.00	30.00
		Nos. U348-U351 (4)	47.50	39.10

Franklin   Washington
U77   U78

U78 — Bust points to first notch of inner oval and is only slightly concave below.

U79   U80

U79 — Bust points to middle of second notch of inner oval and is quite hollow below. Queue has ribbon around it.

U80 — Same as U79 but hair flowing and no ribbon around queue.

Lincoln — U81

Pointed but not draped.

U82   U83

U82 — Bust broad and draped.

U83 — Head larger, inner oval has no notches.

Grant — U84

Similar to designs of 1887-95 but smaller

1899

U352	U77	1c green	.75	.20
U353	U77	1c grn, amb	5.25	1.50
U354	U77	1c grn, oriental buff	13.50	2.75
U355	U77	1c grn, bl	13.50	7.50
U356	U77	1c grn, man	2.25	.95
W357	U77	1c grn, man	2.50	1.10
U358	U78	2c carmine	3.00	1.75
U359	U78	2c car, amb	22.50	14.00
U360	U78	2c car, oriental buff	22.50	8.00
U361	U78	2c car, blue	62.50	27.50
U362	U79	2c carmine	.35	.20
a.		2c dark lake	30.00	30.00
U363	U79	2c car, amb	1.40	.20
U364	U79	2c car, oriental buff	1.20	.20
U365	U79	2c car, blue	1.50	.55
W366	U79	2c car, man	8.00	3.25
U367	U80	2c carmine	6.00	2.75
U368	U80	2c car, amber	9.00	6.75
U369	U80	2c car, oriental buff	25.00	12.50
U370	U80	2c car, blue	12.50	10.00

U371	U81	4c brown	19.00	11.00
U372	U81	4c brn, amb	19.00	12.50
U373	U81	4c brown	12,500.	1,100.
U374	U83	4c brown	14.00	8.00
U375	U83	4c brn, amb	50.00	17.50
W376	U83	4c brn, man	17.50	8.25
U377	U84	5c blue	12.50	9.50
U378	U84	5c blue, amb	16.00	10.00

Franklin   Washington
U85   U86

U86 — "D" of "UNITED" contains vertical line at right that parallels the left vertical line. One short and two long vertical lines at right of "CENTS."

Grant — U87

Lincoln — U88

1903

U379	U85	1c green	.70	.20
U380	U85	1c green, amb	13.50	2.00
U381	U85	1c grn, oriental buff	15.00	2.50
U382	U85	1c green, blue	20.00	2.50
U383	U85	1c grn, manila	4.00	.90
W384	U85	1c grn, manila	2.50	.40
U385	U86	2c carmine	.40	.20
U386	U86	2c car, amb	1.90	.20
U387	U86	2c car, oriental buff	1.75	.30
U388	U86	2c carmine, blue	1.30	.20
W389	U86	2c car, manila	17.50	9.50
U390	U87	4c chocolate	22.50	11.00
U391	U87	4c choc, amber	20.00	12.50
W392	U87	4c choc, manila	20.00	12.50
U393	U88	5c blue	20.00	12.50
U394	U88	5c blue, amber	20.00	12.50

U89

"D" of "UNITED" is well rounded at right. The three lines at the right of "CENTS" and at the left of "TWO" are usually all short; the lettering is heavier and the ends of the ribbons slightly changed.

1904   **Re-cut Die**

U395	U89	2c carmine	.50	.20
U396	U89	2c car, amber	8.00	1.00
U397	U89	2c car, oriental buff	5.50	1.10
U398	U89	2c carmine, blue	3.50	.90
W399	U89	2c car, manila	12.00	9.50

Franklin — U90   Die 1

Die 2

Die 3

Die 4

Die 1. Wide "D" in "UNITED."
Die 2. Narrow "D" in "UNITED."
Die 3. Wide "S-S" in "STATES" (1910).
Die 4. Sharp angle at back of bust, "N" and "E" of "ONE" are parallel (1912).

1907-16   Die 1

U400	U90 1c green	.30	.20
a.	Die 2	.80	.25
b.	Die 3	.80	.35
c.	Die 4	.75	.30
U401	U90 1c green, *amber*	1.60	.40
a.	Die 2	1.75	.70
b.	Die 3	2.00	.75
c.	Die 4	1.75	.65
U402	U90 1c grn, *oriental buff*	8.00	1.00
a.	Die 2	10.00	1.50
b.	Die 3	11.00	1.50
c.	Die 4	9.00	1.50
U403	U90 1c grn, *blue*	9.00	1.50
a.	Die 2	9.00	1.50
b.	Die 3	9.00	3.00
c.	Die 4	7.50	1.25
U404	U90 1c grn, *manila*	3.00	1.90
a.	Die 3	3.75	3.00
W405	U90 1c grn, *manila*	.80	.25
a.	Die 2	40.00	25.00
b.	Die 3	7.50	4.00
c.	Die 4	40.00	—

Die 1, Washington—U91

Die 2

Die 3

Die 4

Die 5

Die 6

Die 7

Die 8

Die 1. Oval "O" in "TWO" and "C" in "CENTS," front of bust broad.
Die 2. Similar to 1 but hair in two distinct locks at top of head.
Die 3. Round "O" in "TWO" and "C" in "CENTS," coarse lettering.
Die 4. Similar to 3 but lettering fine and clear, hair lines clearly embossed. Inner oval thin and clear.
Die 5. All "S's" wide (1910).
Die 6. Similar to 1 but front of bust narrow (1913).
Die 7. Similar to 6 but upper corner of front of bust cut away (1916).
Die 8. Similar to 7 but lower stroke of "S" in "CENTS" is a straight line. Hair as in Die 2 (1916).

Die I

U406	U91 2c brown red	.80	.20
a.	Die 2	35.00	6.25
b.	Die 3	.55	.20
U407	U91 2c brn red, *amb*	5.50	2.00
a.	Die 2	225.00	45.00
b.	Die 3	3.50	1.00
U408	U91 2c brown red, *oriental buff*	7.00	1.50
a.	Die 2	140.00	55.00
b.	Die 3	6.50	2.50
U409	U91 2c brn red, *blue*	4.50	1.75
a.	Die 2	175.00	100.00
b.	Die 3	4.50	1.50
W410	U91 2c brn red, *man*	40.00	32.50
U411	U91 2c carmine	.25	.20
a.	Die 2	.45	.20
b.	Die 3	.75	.35
c.	Die 4	.40	.20
d.	Die 5	.55	.30
e.	Die 6	.40	.20
f.	Die 7	30.00	25.00
g.	Die 8	32.50	25.00
h.	Die 1, with added impression of 1c grn (#U400), entire	325.00	
i.	Die 1, with added impression of 4c blk (#U416a), entire	300.00	
U412	U91 2c carmine, *amb*	.25	.20
a.	Die 2	.65	.25
b.	Die 3	1.30	.45
c.	Die 4	.40	.25
d.	Die 5	.60	.35
e.	Die 6	.55	.35
f.	Die 7	27.50	20.00
U413	U91 2c car, *oriental buff*	.45	.20
a.	Die 2	.65	.45
b.	Die 3	6.00	3.00
c.	Die 4	.40	.20
d.	Die 5	2.75	1.25
e.	Die 6	.55	.35
f.	Die 7	87.50	42.50
g.	Die 8	27.50	21.00
U414	U91 2c carmine, *blue*	.50	.20
a.	Die 2	.65	.35
b.	Die 3	.80	.60
c.	Die 4	.50	.25
d.	Die 5	.65	.30
e.	Die 6	.55	.30
f.	Die 7	30.00	19.00
g.	Die 8	30.00	19.00
W415	U91 2c car, *manila*	4.50	2.00
a.	Die 2	4.50	1.10
b.	Die 5	4.50	2.25
c.	Die 7	100.00	87.50

U90 4c Die 1

U90 4c Die 2

U416	U90 4c black, die 2	4.00	2.25
a.	Die 1	4.50	3.00
U417	U90 4c black, *amb*, die 2	5.50	2.50
a.	Die 1	5.50	2.50

Die 1-Tall "F" in "FIVE"

Die 2-Short "F" in "FIVE"

U418	U91 5c blue, die 2	6.50	2.25
a.	Die 1	6.50	2.25
b.	5c blue, *buff*, die 2 (error)	*2,500.*	
c.	5c blue, *blue*, die 2 (error)	*2,500.*	
d.	5c blue, *blue*, die 1 (error)	*2,500.*	
U419	U91 5c blue, *amber*, die 2	14.00	11.00
a.	Die 1	12.50	11.00

Franklin — U92

Die 1

Die 2

Die 3   Die 4   Die 5

(The 1c and 4c dies are the same except for figures of value.)
Die 1. UNITED nearer inner circle than outer circle.
Die 2. Large U; large NT closely spaced.
Die 3. Knob of hair at back of neck. Large NT widely spaced.
Die 4. UNITED nearer outer circle than inner circle.
Die 5. Narrow oval C, (also O and G).

1915-32   Die 1

U420	U92 1c green ('16)	.20	.20
a.	Die 2	125.00	55.00
b.	Die 3	.30	.20
c.	Die 4	.40	.40
d.	Die 5	.40	.35
U421	U92 1c grn, *amber* ('16)	.60	.30
a.	Die 2	425.00	175.00
b.	Die 3	1.10	.65
c.	Die 4	1.25	.85
d.	Die 5	1.00	.55
U422	U92 1c grn, *oriental buff* ('16)	2.00	.90
a.	Die 4	4.25	1.25
U423	U92 1c grn, *bl* ('16)	.45	.35
a.	Die 3	.75	.45
b.	Die 4	1.25	.65
c.	Die 5	.80	.35
U424	U92 1c grn, (unglazed), *manila* ('16)	6.50	4.00
W425	U92 1c grn, (unglazed), *manila* ('16)	.20	.20
a.	Die 3	160.00	125.00
U426	U92 1c grn, (glazed) *brown* ('20)	30.00	15.00
W427	U92 1c grn, (glazed) *brown* ('20)	65.00	
U428	U92 1c grn, (unglazed) *brown* ('20)	8.00	7.50

Washington — U93

Die 1

Die 2

Die 3

Die 4

Die 5

Die 6

Die 7

Die 8

Die 9

(The 1½c, 2c, 3c, 5c, and 6c are the same except for figures of value.)
Die 1. Letters broad. Numerals vertical. Large head (9¼mm) from tip of nose to back of neck. E closer to inner circle than N of cents.

Die 2. Similar to 1; but U far from left circle.
Die 3. Similar to 2; but all inner circles very thin (Rejected Die).
Die 4. Similar to 1; but C very close to left circle.
Die 5. Small head (8¾mm) from tip of nose to back of neck. T and S of CENTS close at bottom.
Die 6. Similar to 5; but T and S of CENTS far apart at bottom. Left numeral slopes to right.
Die 7. Large head. Both numerals slope to right. Clean cut lettering. All letters T have short top strokes.
Die 8. Similar to 7; but all letters T have long top strokes.
Die 9. Narrow oval C (also O and G).

Die 1

U429	U93	2c car, Dec. 20, 1915	.20	.20
a.		Die 2	12.50	6.00
b.		Die 3	40.00	25.00
c.		Die 4	27.50	15.00
d.		Die 5	.50	.35
e.		Die 6	.60	.20
f.		Die 7	.65	.25
g.		Die 8	.45	.20
h.		Die 9	.40	.20
i.		2c grn, error, die 1, entire	14,000.	
j.		2c car, die 1 with added impression of 1c grn (#U420), die 1	900.00	
k.		Die 1, with added impression of 4c blk (#U416a), entire	1,000.	
l.		Die 1, with added impression of 1c grn (#U400), die 1, entire	1,000.	
U430	U93	2c car, amber ('16)	.25	.20
a.		Die 2	14.00	7.50
b.		Die 4	45.00	20.00
c.		Die 5	1.10	.35
d.		Die 6	.95	.40
e.		Die 7	.70	.35
f.		Die 8	.65	.30
g.		Die 9	.60	.20
U431	U93	2c car, oriental buff ('16)	2.25	.65
a.		Die 2	150.00	40.00
b.		Die 4	70.00	60.00
c.		Die 5	2.75	1.75
d.		Die 6	3.00	2.00
e.		Die 7	2.75	1.75
U432	U93	2c carmine, blue ('16)	.25	.20
b.		Die 2	30.00	20.00
c.		Die 3	140.00	90.00
d.		Die 4	60.00	50.00
e.		Die 5	.80	.30
f.		Die 6	.85	.40
g.		Die 7	.75	.35
h.		Die 8	.60	.25
i.		Die 9	.90	.30
U432A	U93	2c car, manila, die 7, entire	35,000.	
W433	U93	2c car, manila ('16)	.25	.20
W434	U93	2c car, (glazed) brn ('20)	90.00	50.00
W435	U93	2c car, (unglazed) brn ('20)	95.00	50.00
U436	U93	3c dk vio ('17)	.55	.20
a.		3c purple, die 1 ('32)	.30	.20
b.		3c dark violet, die 5	1.65	.75
c.		3c dark violet, die 6	2.00	1.40
d.		3c dark violet, die 7	1.40	.95
e.		3c purple, die 7 ('32)	.65	.30
f.		3c purple, die 9 ('32)	.40	.20
g.		3c car (error), die 1	30.00	27.50
h.		3c car (error), die 5	32.50	30.00
i.		3c dk vio, die 1, with added impression of 1c grn (#U420), die 1, entire	800.00	
j.		3c dk vio, die 1, with added impression of 2c car (#U429), die 1, entire	900.00	950.00
U437	U93	3c dk vio, amb	3.25	1.25
a.		3c purple, die 1 ('32)	.35	.20
b.		3c dark vio, die 5	6.00	2.50
c.		3c dark vio, die 6	6.00	2.50
d.		3c dark vio, die 7	5.50	2.25
e.		3c purple, die 7 ('32)	.75	.20
f.		3c purple, die 9 ('32)	.50	.20
g.		3c car (error), die 5	450.00	275.00
h.		3c black (error), die 1	165.00	—
U438	U93	3c dk vio, oriental buff	22.50	1.50
a.		Die 5	22.50	1.00
b.		Die 6	32.50	1.65
c.		Die 7	32.50	3.50
U439	U93	3c dk violet, bl	6.50	2.00
a.		3c purple, die 1 ('32)	.30	.20
b.		3c dark violet, die 5	7.50	4.00
c.		3c dark violet, die 6	7.00	4.25
d.		3c dark violet, die 7	10.00	5.50
e.		3c purple, die 7 ('32)	.75	.25
f.		3c purple, die 9 ('32)	.50	.20
g.		3c car (error), die 5	325.00	300.00
U440	U92	4c black ('16)	1.50	.60
a.		4c black with added impression of 2c car (#U429), die 1, entire	400.00	
U441	U92	4c black, amb ('16)	3.00	.85
U442	U92	4c blk, bl ('21)	3.25	.85
U443	U93	5c blue ('16)	3.25	2.75
U444	U93	5c blue, amber ('16)	3.75	1.60
U445	U93	5c bl, blue ('21)	4.00	3.25

See Nos. U481-U485, U529-U531.

Listings of double or triple surcharges of 1920-25 are for specimens with the surcharges directly or partly upon the stamp.

Surcharged

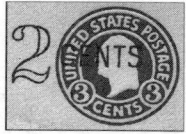

Type 1

1920-21

U446	U93	2c on 3c dk vio (U436, die 1)	12.00	10.00
a.		Die 5 (U436b)	12.00	10.00

Surcharged

Type 2

Rose Surcharge

U447	U93	2c on 3c dk vio (U436, die 1)	7.75	6.50
b.		Die 6 (U436c)	10.00	8.50

Black Surcharge

U447A	U93	2c on 2c car (U429, die 1)	—	
U447C	U93	2c on 2c car, amb (U430, die 1)	—	
U448	U93	2c on 3c dk vio (U436, die 1)	2.50	2.00
a.		Die 5 (U436b)	2.50	2.00
b.		Die 6 (U436c)	3.25	2.00
c.		Die 7 (U436d)	2.50	2.00
U449	U93	2c on 3c dk vio, amb (U437, die 1)	6.50	6.00
a.		Die 5 (U437b)	10.00	7.50
b.		Die 6 (U437c)	7.50	6.00
c.		Die 7 (U437d)	7.00	6.50
U450	U93	2c on 3c dk vio, oriental buff (U438, die 1)	17.50	14.00
a.		Die 5 (U438a)	17.50	14.00
b.		Die 6 (U438b)	17.50	14.00
c.		Die 7 (U438c)	100.00	90.00
U451	U93	2c on 3c dk vio, blue (U439, die 1)	12.50	10.00
b.		Die 5 (U439b)	12.50	10.00
c.		Die 6 (U439c)	12.50	10.00
d.		Die 7 (U439d)	25.00	20.00

Surcharged

Type 3

Bars 2mm apart

U451A	U90	2c on 1c grn (U400, die 1)	27,500.	
U452	U92	2c on 1c grn (U420, die 1)	3,000.	
a.		Die 3 (U420b)	3,000.	
b.		As No. U452, dbl. surch.	3,000.	
U453	U91	2c on 2c car (U411b, die 3)	4,250.	
a.		Die 1 (U411)	4,000.	
U453B	U91	2c on 2c car, bl (U414e, die 6)	2,750.	
U453C	U91	2c on 2c car, oriental buff (U413e, die 6)	1,900.	750.00
d.		Die 1 (U413)	2,000.	
U454	U93	2c on 2c car (U429e, die 6)	85.00	
a.		Die 1 (U429)	350.00	
b.		Die 5 (U429d)	500.00	
c.		Die 7 (U429f)	85.00	
U455	U93	2c on 2c car, amb (U430, die 1)	1,750.	
a.		Die 6 (U430d)	2,000.	
b.		Die 7 (U430e)	2,000.	

U456	U93	2c on 2c car, oriental buff (U431a, die 2)	275.00	
a.		Die 5 (U431c)	300.00	
b.		Die 7 (U431e)	350.00	
c.		As #U456, dbl. surch.	250.00	
U457	U93	2c on 2c car, bl (U432f, die 6)	300.00	
a.		Die 5 (U432e)	325.00	
b.		Die 7 (U432g)	750.00	
U458	U93	2c on 3c dk vio (U436, die 1)	.50	.35
a.		Die 5 (U436b)	.50	.40
b.		Die 6 (U436c)	.50	.35
c.		Die 7 (U436d)	.50	.35
d.		As #U458, dbl. surch.	14.00	7.50
e.		As #U458, trip. surch.	100.00	
f.		As #U458, dbl. surch., one in magenta	75.00	
g.		As #U458, dbl. surch., types 2 & 3	125.00	
h.		As "a," dbl. surch.	27.50	15.00
i.		As "a," triple surch.	100.00	
j.		As "a," dbl. surch., both magenta	65.00	
k.		As "b," dbl. surch.	16.00	8.00
l.		As "c," dbl. surch.	16.00	8.00
m.		As "c," triple surcharge	100.00	
U459	U93	2c on 3c dk vio, amb (U437c, die 6)	3.00	1.00
a.		Die 1 (U437)	4.00	1.00
b.		Die 5 (U437b)	4.00	1.00
c.		Die 7 (U437d)	3.00	1.00
d.		As #U459, dbl. surch.	24.00	
e.		As "a," dbl. surch.	24.00	
f.		As "b," dbl. surch.	24.00	
g.		As "b," dbl. surch., types 2 & 3	100.00	
h.		As "c," dbl. surch.	18.00	
U460	U93	2c on 3c dk vio, oriental buff (U438a, die 5)	2.75	1.00
a.		Die 1 (U438)	3.00	1.50
b.		Die 6 (U438b)	3.00	2.00
c.		As #U460, dbl. surch.	12.50	
d.		As "a," dbl. surch.	12.50	
e.		As "b," dbl. surch.	12.50	
f.		As "b," triple surcharge	150.00	
U461	U93	2c on 3c dk vio, bl (U439, die 1)	4.25	1.00
a.		Die 5 (U439b)	4.25	1.00
b.		Die 6 (U439c)	4.25	1.00
c.		Die 7 (U439d)	10.00	2.00
d.		As #U461, dbl. surch.	12.50	
e.		As "a," dbl. surch.	12.50	
f.		As "b," dbl. surch.	12.50	
g.		As "c," dbl. surch.	12.50	
U462	U87	2c on 4c choc (U390)	575.00	240.00
U463	U87	2c on 4c choc, amb (U391)	500.00	150.00
U463A	U90	2c on 4c blk (U416, die 2)	1,250.	375.00
U464	U93	2c on 5c bl (U443)	1,250.	

Surcharged

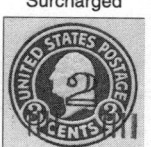

Type 4

Similar to Type 3, but bars 1½mm apart.

U465	U92	2c on 1c grn (U420, die 1)	1,400.	
a.		Die 3 (U420b)	1,500.	
U466	U91	2c on 2c car (U411e, die 6)	12,500.	
U466A	U93	2c on 2c car (U429, die 1)	750.00	
c.		Die 5 (U429d)	1,000.	
d.		Die 6 (U429e)	1,250.	
e.		Die 7 (U429f)	1,000.	
U466B	U93	2c on 2c car, amb (U430)	12,500.	
U467	U45	2c on 3c grn (U163)	350.00	
U468	U93	2c on 3c dk vio (U436, die 1)	.70	.45
a.		Die 5 (U436b)	.70	.50
b.		Die 6 (U436c)	.70	.50
c.		Die 7 (U436d)	.70	.50
d.		As #U468, dbl. surch.	15.00	
e.		As #U468, trip. surch.	15.00	
f.		As #U468, dbl. surch., types 2 & 4	85.00	
g.		As "a," double surcharge	15.00	
h.		As "b," double surcharge	15.00	
i.		As "c," double surcharge	15.00	
j.		As "c," triple surcharge	100.00	
k.		As "c," inverted surch.	75.00	
l.		2c on 3c car (error) (U436h)	650.00	

U469	U93	2c on 3c dk vio, amber (U437, die 1)	3.50	2.25
a.		Die 5 (U437b)	3.50	2.25
b.		Die 6 (U437c)	3.50	2.25
c.		Die 7 (U437d)	3.50	2.25
d.		As No. U469, dbl. surch.	20.00	
e.		As "a," double surcharge	20.00	
f.		As "a," double surcharge, types 2 & 4	70.00	
g.		As "b," double surcharge	20.00	
h.		As "c," double surcharge	20.00	
U470	U93	2c on 3c dk vio, oriental buff (U438, die 1)	4.50	2.50
a.		Die 5 (U438a)	4.50	2.50
b.		Die 6 (U438b)	4.50	2.50
c.		Die 7 (U438c)	35.00	32.50
d.		As No. U470, dbl. surch.	18.50	
e.		As No. U470, double surcharge, types 2 & 4	70.00	
f.		As "a," double surcharge	18.50	
g.		As "b," double surcharge	22.50	
U471	U93	2c on 3c dk vio, bl (U439, die 1)	4.50	1.75
a.		Die 5 (U439b)	4.50	1.75
b.		Die 6 (U439c)	4.50	1.75
c.		Die 7 (U439d)	10.00	6.00
d.		As No. U471, dbl. surch.	22.50	
e.		As No. U471, double surcharge, types 2 & 4	150.00	
f.		As "a," double surcharge	125.00	
g.		As "b," double surcharge	22.50	
U472	U87	2c on 4c choc (U390)	12.00	8.00
a.		Double surcharge	100.00	
U473	U87	2c on 4c choc, amb (U391)	16.00	10.00

Dbl. Surch., "1" and Type 4

U474	U93	2c on 1c on 3c dk vio (U436, die 1)	250.00	
a.		Die 5 (U436b)	325.00	
b.		Die 7 (U436d)	750.00	
U475	U93	2c on 1c on 3c dk vio, amb (U437, die 1)	275.00	

Surcharged

Type 5

U476	U93	2c on 3c dk vio, amb (U437, die 1)	275.00	
a.		Die 6 (U437c)	750.00	
b.		As #U476, double surch.	—	

Surcharged

Type 6

U477	U93	2c on 3c dk vio (U436, die 1)	125.00	
a.		Die 5 (U436b)	200.00	
b.		Die 6 (U436c)	200.00	
c.		Die 7 (U437d)	200.00	
U478	U93	2c on 3c dk vio, amb (U437, die 1)	250.00	

Handstamped Surcharge in Black or Violet—Type 7

U479	U93	2c on 3c dk vio (Bk) (U436b, die 5)	900.00	
a.		Die 1 (U436)	450.00	
b.		Die 7 (U436d)	400.00	

U480 U93 2c on 3c dk vio (V)
　(U436d, die 7)　5,000.
　a.　Double overprint　—

Expertization by competent authorities is recommended for Nos. U479-U480.

Type of 1916-32 Issue

1925-34

Die 1

U481	U93 1½c brown	.20	.20
a.	Die 8	.60	.25
b.	1½c purple (error) ('34)	90.00	
U482	U93 1½c brown, *amber*	.90	.40
a.	Die 8	1.40	.75
U483	U93 1½c brn, *bl*	1.50	.95
a.	Die 8	1.75	1.25
U484	U93 1½c brown, *manila*	6.00	3.00
W485	U93 1½c brown, *manila*	.80	.20
a.	With added impression of No. W433	120.00	—

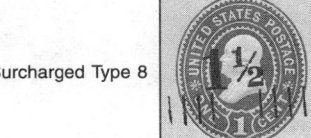

Surcharged Type 8

1925

U486	U71 1½c on 2c grn (U311)	700.00	
U487	U71 1½c on 2c grn, *amb* (U312)	850.00	
U488	U77 1½c on 1c grn (U352)	700.00	
U489	U77 1½c on 1c grn, *amb* (U353)	110.00	60.00
U490	U90 1½c on 1c grn, *die 1*	5.00	3.50
a.	Die 2 (U400a)	14.00	9.00
b.	Die 3 (U400b)	30.00	17.50
c.	Die 4 (U400c)	7.50	2.50
U491	U90 1½c on 1c grn, *amb* (U401c, die 4)	5.25	2.25
a.	Die 1 (U401)	9.00	2.50
b.	Die 2 (U401a)	90.00	65.00
c.	Die 3 (U401b)	42.50	30.00
U492	U90 1½c on 1c grn, *oriental buff* (U402a, die 2)	450.00	100.00
a.	Die 4 (U402c)	1,000.	100.00
U493	U90 1½c on 1c grn, *bl* (U403c, die 4)	100.00	55.00
a.	Die 2 (U403a)	90.00	55.00
U494	U90 1½c on 1c grn, *man* (U404, die 1)	350.00	80.00
a.	Die 3 (U404a)	1,000.	
U495	U92 1½c on 1c grn (U420, die 1)	.75	.25
a.	Die 2 (U420a)	70.00	52.50
b.	Die 3 (U420b)	1.60	.60
c.	Die 4 (U420c)	1.75	.75
d.	As No. U495, dbl. surch.	4.00	1.90
e.	As "b," double surcharge	7.00	3.00
f.	As "c," double surcharge	6.00	3.00
U496	U92 1½c on 1c grn, *amb* (U421, die 1)	17.50	12.50
a.	Die 3 (U421b)	600.00	
b.	Die 4 (U421c)	17.50	12.50
U497	U92 1½c on 1c grn, *oriental buff* (U422, die 1)	3.25	1.90
a.	Die 4 (U422b)	52.50	
U498	U92 1½c on 1c grn, *bl* (U423c, die 4)	1.25	.75
a.	Die 1 (U423)	2.25	1.50
b.	Die 3 (U423b)	1.75	1.50
U499	U92 1½c on 1c grn, *man* (U424)	12.50	6.00
U500	U92 1½c on 1c grn, *brn* (unglazed) (U428)	60.00	30.00
U501	U93 1½c on 1c grn, *brn* (glazed) (U426)	65.00	25.00
U502	U93 1½c on 2c car *die 1* (U429, die 1)	275.00	—
a.	Die 5 (U429d)	375.00	
b.	Die 7 (U429f)	375.00	
c.	Die 6 (U429e)	—	
d.	Die 8 (U429g)	—	
U503	U93 1½c on 2c car, *oriental buff* (U431c, die 5)	375.00	—
a.	Double surcharge		
b.	Dbl. surch., one inverted	700.00	

U504	U93 1½c on 2c car, *bl* (U432, die 1)	400.00	—
a.	Die 7 (U432g)	350.00	

On Envelopes of 1925

U505	U93 1½c on 1½c brn (U481, die 1)	450.00	
a.	Die 8 (U481a)	450.00	
U506	U93 1½c on 1½c brn, *bl* (U483a, die 8)	450.00	

The paper of No. U500 is not glazed and appears to be the same as that used for wrappers of 1920.

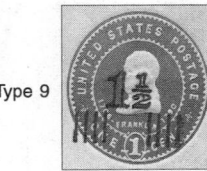

Surcharged Type 9

Black Surcharge

U507	U69 1½c on 1c bl (U294)	3,000.	
U508	U77 1½c on 1c grn, *amb* (U353)	67.50	
U508A	U85 1½c on 1c grn (U379)	4,250.	
U509	U85 1½c on 1c grn, *amb* (U380)	15.00	10.00
a.	Double surcharge	75.00	
U509B	U85 1½c on 1c grn, *oriental buff* (U381)	60.00	40.00
U510	U90 1½c on 1c grn, *die 1* (U400, die 1)	2.40	1.25
b.	Die 2 (U400a)	6.50	4.00
c.	Die 3 (U400b)	25.00	8.00
d.	Die 4 (U400c)	3.25	1.25
e.	As No. U510, double surcharge	8.00	
U511	U90 1½c on 1c grn, *amb* (U401, die 1)	225.00	72.50
U512	U90 1½c on 1c grn, *oriental buff* (U402, die 1)	7.00	4.00
a.	Die 4 (U402c)	17.50	14.00
U513	U90 1½c on 1c grn, *bl* (U403, die 1)	5.25	2.50
a.	Die 4 (U403c)	5.25	4.00
U514	U90 1½c on 1c grn, *man* (U404, die 1)	27.50	9.00
a.	Die 3 (U404a)	60.00	37.50
U515	U92 1½c on 1c grn (U420, die 1)	.35	.20
a.	Die 2 (U420a)	20.00	15.00
b.	Die 3 (U420b)	.35	.20
c.	Die 4 (U420c)	.35	.20
d.	As No. U515, dbl. surch.	6.00	
e.	As No. U515, inverted surch.	9.00	
f.	As No. U515, trip. surch.	9.00	
g.	As No. U515, dbl. surch., one invtd., entire	11.00	
h.	As "b," double surcharge	6.00	
i.	As "b," inverted surcharge	9.00	
j.	As "b," triple surcharge	11.00	
k.	As "c," double surcharge	6.00	
l.	As "c," inverted surcharge	9.00	
U516	U92 1½c on 1c grn, *amb* (U421c, die 4)	42.50	25.00
a.	Die 1 (U421)	47.50	30.00
U517	U92 1½c on 1c grn, *oriental buff* (U422, die 1)	4.25	1.25
a.	Die 4 (U422a)	5.50	1.50
U518	U92 1½c on 1c grn, *bl* (U423b, die 4)	4.50	1.25
a.	Die 1 (U423)	6.50	2.50
b.	Die 3 (U423a)	20.00	7.50
c.	As "a," double surcharge	9.00	
U519	U92 1½c on 1c grn, *man* (U424)	25.00	10.00
a.	Double surcharge	100.00	
U520	U93 1½c on 2c car (U429, die 1)	350.00	—
a.	Die 5 (U429d)	350.00	
b.	Die 6 (U429e)	350.00	
c.	Die 7 (U429f)	400.00	
U520D	U93 1½c on 2c car, *amber* (U430c, die 5), entire	—	

Magenta Surcharge

U521	U92 1½c on 1c grn (U420b, die 3)	4.50	3.50
a.	Double surcharge	50.00	

Sesquicentennial Exposition Issue

Liberty Bell — U94

Die 1. The center bar of "E" of "POSTAGE" is shorter than top bar.
Die 2. The center bar of "E" of "POSTAGE" is of same length as top bar.

1926

U522	U94 2c carmine, die 1	1.10	.50
a.	Die 2	7.00	3.75

See note below No. 627.

Washington Bicentennial Issue

Mount Vernon — U95

2 cent:
Die 1. "S" of "POSTAGE" normal.
Die 2. "S" of "POSTAGE" raised.

1932

U523	U95 1c olive green	1.00	.80
U524	U95 1½c chocolate	2.00	1.50
U525	U95 2c car, die 1	.40	.20
a.	Die 2	70.00	16.00
b.	Die 1, *blue, entire* (error)	27,500.	
U526	U95 3c violet	2.00	.35
U527	U95 4c black	18.00	16.00
U528	U95 5c dark blue	4.00	3.50
	Nos. U523-U528 (6)	27.40	22.35

Bicen. of the birth of Washington.

1932　　Die 7

U529	U93 6c orange	5.50	4.00
U530	U93 6c orange, *amber*	11.00	8.00
U531	U93 6c orange, *blue*	11.00	10.00

Franklin — U96

Die 1　　　　Die 2

Die 3

Die 1. Short (3½mm) and thick "1" in thick circle.
Die 2. Tall (4½mm) and thin "1" in thin circle; upper and lower bars of E in ONE long and 1mm from circle.
Die 3. As in Die 2, but E normal and 1½mm from circle.

1950

U532	U96 1c green, die 1	5.00	1.75
a.	Die 2	6.50	3.00
b.	Die 3	6.00	3.00
	Die 3, precanceled		.50

Washington — U97

Die 1　　　　Die 2

 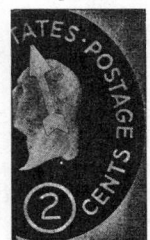

Die 3　　　　Die 4

Die 1. Thick "2" in circle; toe of "2" is an acute angle.
Die 2. Thin "2" in thin circle; toe of "2" is almost right angle; line through stand of "E" in POSTAGE goes considerably below tip of chin; "N" of UNITED is tall; "O" of TWO is high.
Die 3. Thin "2" in thin circle; toe of "2" is almost right angle; short UN in UNITED: thin crossbar in A of STATES.
Die 4. Tall UN in UNITED; thick crossbar in A of STATES; otherwise like Die 3.

U533	U97 2c carmine, die 3	.75	.25
a.	Die 1	.85	.30
b.	Die 2	1.50	.85
c.	Die 4	1.40	.60

Die 1　　　　Die 2

Die 3

Die 4　　　　Die 5

Die 1. Thick and tall (4½mm) "3" in thick circle; long top bars and short stems in T's of STATES.
Die 2. Thin and tall (4½mm) "3" in medium circle; short top bars and long stems in T's of STATES.
Die 3. Thin and short (4mm) "3" in thin circle; lettering wider than Dies 1 and 2; line from left stand of N to stand of E is distinctly below tip of chin.
Die 4. Figure and letters as in Die 3. Line hits tip of chin; short N in UNITED and thin crossbar in A of STATES.
Die 5. Figure, letter and chin line as in Die 4; but tall N in UNITED and thick crossbar in A of STATES.

U534	U97 3c dk violet, die 4	.40	.20
a.	Die 1	2.00	.70
b.	Die 2	.80	.50
c.	Die 3	.60	.25
d.	Die 5	.80	.45

Washington — U98

1952

U535	U98 1½c brown	5.00	3.50
	Precanceled		.50

Die 1

Die 2

Die 3

Die 1. Head high in oval (2mm below T of STATES). Circle near (1mm) bottom of colored oval.
Die 2. Head low in oval (3mm). Circle 1½mm from edge of oval. Right leg of A of POSTAGE shorter than left. Short leg on P.
Die 3. Head centered in oval (2½mm). Circle as in Die 2. Legs of A of POSTAGE about equal. Long leg on P.

1958

U536	U96	4c red violet, die 1	.80	.20
a.		Die 2	1.05	.20
b.		Die 3	1.05	.20

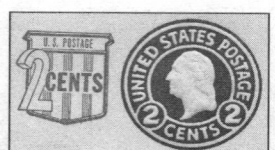

Nos. U429, U429f, U429h, U533, U533a-U533c Surcharged in Red - b

1958

U537	U93	2c + 2c car, die 1	3.25	1.50
a.		2c + 2c carmine, die 7	10.00	7.00
b.		2c + 2c carmine, die 9	5.00	5.00
U538	U97	2c + 2c car, die 1	.75	.20
a.		2c + 2c carmine, die 2	1.00	
b.		2c + 2c carmine, die 3	.80	.25
c.		2c + 2c carmine, die 4	.80	

Nos. U436a, U436e-U436f, U534a-U534d Surcharged in Green - a

U539	U93	3c +1c pur, die 1	15.00	11.00
a.		3c +1c purple, die 7	12.00	9.00
b.		3c +1c purple, die 9	30.00	15.00
U540	U97	3c +1c dk violet, die 3	.50	.20
a.		3c +1c dk vio, die 2, entire	2,500.	—
b.		3c +1c dark violet, die 4	.75	.20
c.		3c +1c dark violet, die 5	.75	.20

See No. U545.

Benjamin Franklin U99

George Washington U100

Die 1

Die 2

Dies of 1¼c

Die 1. The "4" is 3mm high. Upper leaf in left cluster 2mm from "U."
Die 2. The "4" is 3½mm high. Leaf clusters are larger. Upper leaf at left is 1mm from "U."

1960

U541	U99	1¼c turquoise, die 1	.75	.50
		Die 1, precanceled		.20
a.		Die 2, precanceled		1.50
U542	U100	2½c dull blue	.85	.50
		Precanceled		.25

Precanceled Cut Squares
Precanceled envelopes do not normally receive another cancellation. Since the lack of a cancellation makes it impossible to distinguish between cut squares from used and unused envelopes, they are valued here as used only.

Pony Express Centennial Issue

Pony Express Rider — U101

Envelope White Outside, Blue Inside
1960, July 19

U543	U101	4c brown	.60	.30

Abraham Lincoln — U102

Die 1

Die 2

Die 3

Die 1. Center bar of E of POSTAGE is above the middle. Center bar of E of STATES slants slightly upward. Nose sharper, more pointed. No offset ink specks inside envelope on back of die impression.
Die 2. Center bar of E in POSTAGE in middle. P of POSTAGE has short stem. Ink specks on back of die impression.
Die 3. Fl of FIVE closer than Die 1 or 2. Second T of STATES seems taller than ES. Ink specks on back of die impression.

1962, Nov. 19

U544	U102	5c dark blue, die 2	.85	.20
a.		Die 1	.85	.25
b.		Die 3	.90	.35
c.		Die 2 with albino impression of 4c (#U536)	60.00	
d.		Die 3 with albino impression of 4c (#U536)	80.00	
e.		Die 3 on complete impression of 4c (#U536)	—	

No. U536 Surcharged Type "a" in Green at Left of Stamp

Two types of surcharge "a":
Type I. "U.S. POSTAGE" 18½mm high. Serifs on cross of T both diagonal. Two lines of shading in C of CENT.
Type II. "U.S. POSTAGE" 17½mm high. Right serif on cross of T is vertical. Three shading lines in C.

1962, Nov.

U545	U96	4c +1c red vio, type I	1.40	.50
a.		Type II	1.10	.50

New York World's Fair (1964-65)

Globe with Satellite Orbit — U103

1964, Apr. 22

U546	U103	5c carmine rose	.60	.40

Liberty Bell — U104

Old Ironsides — U105

Eagle — U106

Head of Statue of Liberty — U107

1965-69   Tagged (6c)

U547	U104	1¼c brown		.20
U548	U104	1⁴⁄₁₀c brown ('68)		.20
U548A	U104	1⁴⁄₁₀c orange ('69)		.20
U549	U105	4c bright blue	.75	.20
U550	U106	5c bright purple	.75	.20
a.		Tagged ('67)	1.25	.20
U551	U107	6c lt green ('68)	.70	.20

Issue dates: 5c, Jan. 1; 1¼c, Jan. 6; 6c, Jan. 4; 1⁴⁄₁₀c, Mar. 26; 1⁴⁄₁₀c, June 16.
No. U550a has a luminescent panel 9x29mm at left of stamp. It glows yellow green under ultraviolet light.

Nos. U549-U550 Surcharged Types "b" and "a" in Red or Green at Left of Stamp

1968, Feb. 5

U552	U105	4c + 2c brt blue (R)	3.75	2.00
U553	U106	5c + 1c brt pur (G)	3.50	2.50
a.		Tagged	3.50	2.75

Tagging
Envelopes from No. U554 onward are tagged, with the tagging element in the ink unless otherwise noted.

Herman Melville Issue

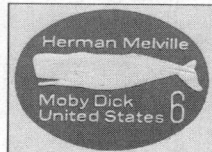

Moby Dick — U108

1970, Mar. 7

U554	U108	6c light blue	.50	.20

Herman Melville (1819-91), writer, and the whaling industry.

Youth Conference Issue

Youth Conference Emblem U109

1971, Feb. 24

U555	U109	6c light blue	.75	.20

White House Conference on Youth, Estes Park, Colo., Apr. 18-22.

Bell Type of 1965-69 and

Eagle — U110

1971   Untagged (1⁷⁄₁₀c)

U556	U104	1⁷⁄₁₀c deep lilac		.20
U557	U110	8c bright ultra	.40	.20

Issue dates: 1⁷⁄₁₀c, May 10; 8c, May 6.

Nos. U551 and U555 Surcharged in Green

1971, May 16

U561	U107	6c + (2c) light green	1.00	.30
U562	U109	6c + (2c) light blue	2.00	1.60

Bowling Issue

Bowling Ball and Pin — U111

1971, Aug. 21

U563	U111	8c rose red	.70	.20

Salute to bowling and 7th World Tournament of the Intl. Bowling Fed., Milwaukee, WI.

Aging Conference Issue

Conference Symbol — U112

1971, Nov. 5

U564	U112	8c light blue	.50	.20

White House Conference on Aging, Washington, DC, Nov. 28-Dec. 2, 1971.

International Transportation Exhibition Issue

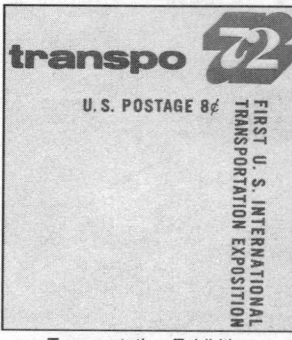

Transportation Exhibition Emblem — U113

Illustration ⅝ actual size.

1972, May 2

U565	U113	8c ultra & rose red	.50	.20

US Intl. Transportation Exhib., Dulles Intl. Airport, Washington, May 27-June 4.

No. U557 Surcharged Type "b" in Ultramarine at Left of Stamp

1973, Dec. 1

U566	U110	8c + 2c bright ultra	.40	.20

Liberty Bell — U114

1973, Dec. 5

U567	U114	10c emerald	.40	.20

"Volunteer Yourself" U115

1974, Aug. 23   **Untagged**
U568 U115   1⁸⁄₁₀c blue green   .20

US Tennis Centenary Issue

Tennis Racquet — U116

1974, Aug. 31
U569 U116   10c yel, brt bl & lt grn   .65   .20

Bicentennial Era Issue

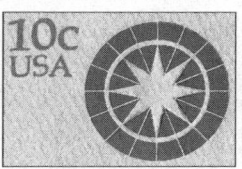

The Seafaring Tradition--Compass Rose — U118

The American Homemaker--Quilt Pattern — U119

The American Farmer--Sheaf of Wheat — U120

The American Doctor — U121

The American Craftsman--Tools, c. 1750 — U122

Designs (in brown on left side of envelope): 10c, Norwegian sloop Restaurationen. No. U572, Spinning wheel. No. U573, Plow. No. U574, Colonial era medical instruments and bottle. No. U575, Shaker rocking chair.

Light Brown Diagonally Laid Paper

1975-76
U571 U118   10c brown & blue   .30   .20
   a.   Brown ("10c/USA," etc.)
       omitted, entire   150.00
U572 U119   13c brn & bl grn   .35   .20
   a.   Brown ("13c/USA," etc.)
       omitted, entire   150.00
U573 U120   13c brn & brt grn   .35   .20
   a.   Brown ("13c/USA," etc.)
       omitted, entire   150.00

U574 U121   13c brown & orange   .35   .20
   a.   Brown ("13c/USA," etc.)
       omitted, entire
U575 U122   13c brown & car   .35   .20
   a.   Brown ("13c/USA," etc.)
       omitted, entire   150.00

Issued: 10c, 10/13; #U572, 2/2/76; #U573, 3/15/76; #574, 6/30/76; #U575, 8/6/76.

Liberty Tree, Boston, 1646 U123

1975, Nov. 8
U576 U123   13c orange brown   .30   .20

Precanceled Cut Squares
See note following No. U542.

Star and Pinweel U124

U125

U126

Eagle — U127

"Uncle Sam" — U128

1976-78   **Untagged (2c, 2.1c, 2.7c)**
U577 U124   2c red ('76)   .20
U578 U125   2.1c yel grn ('77)   .20
U579 U126   2.7c grn ('78)   .20
U580 U127   (15c) orange ('78)   .40   .20
U581 U128   15c red ('78)   .40   .20
Issued: 2c, 9/10; 2.1c 6/3; 2.7c, 7/5; A, 5/22; 15c, 6/3.

Bicentennial Issue

Centennial Envelope, 1876 — U129

1976, Oct. 15
U582 U129   13c emerald   .35   .20
See Nos. U218-U221.

Golf Issue

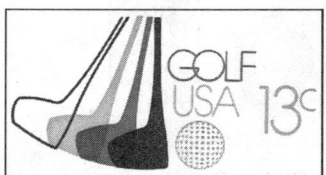

Golf Club in Motion and Golf Ball — U130

1977, Apr. 7
U583 U130   13c blk, bl & yel
       green   .65   .20
   a.   Black omitted, entire   650.00
   b.   Black & blue omitted, entire   550.00

Energy Issue

Energy Conservation U131

Energy Development U132

1977, Oct. 20
U584 U131   13c blk, red & yel   .40   .20
   a.   Red & yel omitted, entire   250.00
   b.   Yellow omitted, entire   175.00
   c.   Black omitted, entire   175.00
   d.   Black & red omitted, entire   425.00
U585 U132   13c blk, red & yel   .40   .20
Nos. U584-U585 have a luminescent panel at left of stamp.

Olive Branch and Star — U133

1978, July 28
U586 U133   15c on 16c blue   .35   .20
   a.   Surcharge omitted, entire   375.00
   b.   Surcharge on #U581, entire   —
   c.   As "a," with surcharge
       printed on envelope flap   175.00   —

Auto Racing Issue

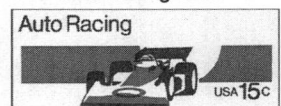

Indianapolis 500 Racing Car — U134

1978, Sept. 2
U587 U134   15c red, blue &
       black   .35   .20
   a.   Black omitted, entire   120.00
   b.   Black & blue omitted, entire   —
   c.   Red omitted, entire   120.00
   d.   Red & blue omitted, entire   —

No. U576 Surcharged at left of Stamp Like No. U586

1978, Nov. 28   **Embossed**
U588 U123   15c on 13c org brn   .35   .20

Precanceled Cut Squares
See note following No. U542.

U135

Weaver Violins — U136

U137

Eagle — U138

Star — U139

Eagle — U140

1979-82
    Untagged (3.1c, 3.5c, 5.9c)
U589 U135   3.1c ultramarine   .20
U590 U136   3.5c purple   .20
U591 U137   5.9c brown   .20
U592 U138   (18c) violet   .45   .20
U593 U139   18c dark blue   .45   .20
U594 U140   (20c) brown   .45   .20
Issued: 3.1c, 5/18; 3.5c, 6/23; 5.9c, 2/17/82; #U592, 3/15/81; #U593, 4/2/81; #U594, 10/11/81.

Veterinary Medicine Issue

Seal of Veterinarians U141

Design on left side of envelope shows 5 animals and a bird in brown and "Veterinary Medicine" in gray.

1979, July 24
U595 U141   15c brown & gray   .50   .20
   a.   Gray omitted, untagged, entire   750.00
   b.   Brown omitted, entire   1,050.
   c.   Gray & brown omitted, entire   —

Olympic Games Issue

U142

Design (multicolored on left side of envelope) shows two soccer players with ball.

1979, Dec. 10
U596 U142   15c red, grn & blk   .60   .20
   a.   Red & green omitted, untagged, entire   225.00
   b.   Blk omitted, untagged, entire   225.00
   c.   Blk & grn omitted, entire   225.00
   d.   Red omitted, untagged, entire   400.00

22nd Olympic Games, Moscow, 7/19-8/3/80.

Bicycling Issue

Highwheeler Bicycle — U143

Design (on left side of envelope) shows racing bicycle.

1980, May 16
U597 U143 15c bl & rose claret .40 .20
  a. Blue ("15c USA") omitted 100.00

America's Cup Yacht Races Issue

Racing Yacht — U144

1980, Sept. 15
U598 U144 15c light blue .40 .20

Italian Honeybee and Orange Blossoms U145

Bee & Petals Colorless Embossed
1980, Oct. 10
U599 U145 15c multicolored .35 .20
  a. Brown ("USA 15c") omitted, entire 125.00

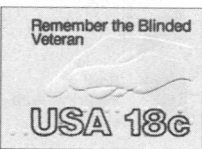

U146

Hand & Braille Colorless Embossed
1981, Oct. 11
U600 U146 18c blue & red .45 .20
  a. Blue omitted, untagged, entire —
  b. Red omitted, entire —

Capitol Dome U147

1981, Nov. 13
U601 U147 20c deep magenta .45 .20

U148

Illustration reduced.

1982, June 15
U602 U148 20c dk bl, blk & mag .45 .20
  a. Dark blue omitted, entire 150.00
  b. Dk bl & mag omitted, entire —

U149

1982, Aug. 6
U603 U149 20c purple & black .65 .20
  a. Black omitted, entire —
  b. Purple omitted, entire —

U150

1983, Mar. 21   Untagged
U604 U150 5.2c orange .20

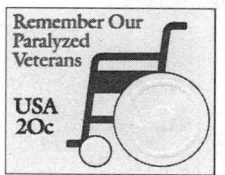

U151

1983, Aug. 3
U605 U151 20c red, bl & blk .45 .20
  a. Red omitted, entire —
  b. Blue omitted, entire —
  c. Red & black omitted, entire 140.00
  d. Blue & black omitted, entire 140.00
  e. Black omitted, entire 225.00

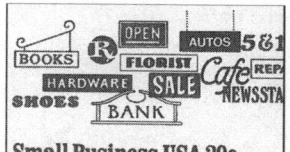

U152

Design shows storefronts at lower left. Stamp and design continue on back of envelope.

1984, May 7   Photo.
U606 U152 20c multicolored .50 .20

U153

1985, Feb. 1   Embossed
U607 U153 (22c) deep green .55 .20

American Buffalo U154

1985, Feb. 25   Embossed
U608 U154 22c violet brown .55 .20
  a. Untagged, precanceled with 3 blue lines .20

Frigate U.S.S. Constitution, "Old Ironsides" — U155

1985, May 3   Untagged
U609 U155 6c green blue .20

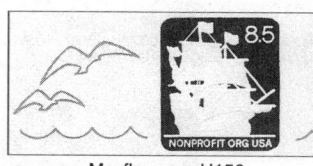

Mayflower — U156

Embossed
1986, Dec. 4   Untagged
Precanceled
U610 U156 8.5c black & gray .20

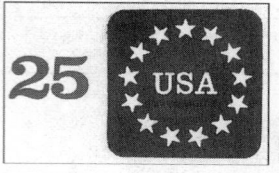

Stars U157

1988, Mar. 26   Embossed & Typo.
U611 U157 25c dk bl & dk red .60 .20
  a. Dk red ("25") omitted, entire 75.00

Sea Gulls, Frigate USS Constellation — U158

Embossed & Typo.
1988, Apr. 12   Untagged
Precanceled
U612 U158 8.4c blk & brt bl .20
  a. Black omitted, entire 600.00

Snowflake — U159

"Holiday Greetings!" inscribed at lower left.

1988, Sept. 8   Typo.
U613 U159 25c dark red & green .60 .25

Stars and "*Philatelic Mail*" Continuous in Dark Red Below Vignette — U160

1989, Mar. 10   Typo.
U614 U160 25c dk red & dp bl .50 .25

"USA" and Stars — U161

1989, July 10   Unwmk.
U615 U161 25c dk red & dp bl .50 .25
  a. Dark red omitted, entire

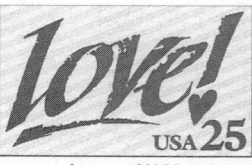

Love — U162

Litho. & Typo.
1989, Sept. 25   Unwmk.
U616 U162 25c dark red & blue .50 .25

Shuttle Docking at Space Station — U163

1989, Dec. 3   Typo.   Unwmk.
U617 U163 25c ultramarine .60 .30
  a. Ultramarine omitted, entire 600.00

A hologram, visible through the die cut window to the right of "USA 25," is affixed to the inside of the envelope. Available only in No. 9 size. No. 9 envelopes are 225mm by 100mm. See Nos. U625, U639.

Vince Lombardi Trophy, Football Players — U164

1990, Sept. 9   Litho.   Unwmk.
U618 U164 25c vermilion .60 .25

A hologram, visible through the die cut window to the right of "USA 25," is affixed to the inside of the envelope.

Star — U165

Has embossed bars above and below the design.

1991, Jan. 24   Embossed & Typo.
U619 U165 29c ultra & rose .60 .30
  a. Ultramarine omitted, entire 600.00
  b. Rose omitted, entire 400.00

Precanceled Cut Squares
See note following No. U542.

Birds — U166

Stamp and design continue on back of envelope.

1991, May 3   Typo.   Wmk.
Untagged
Precanceled
U620 U166 11.1c blue & red .20

Love — U167

1991, May 9   **Litho.**
U621 U167 29c lt bl, mar & brt rose   .60   .30
  a.   Bright rose omitted, entire   500.00

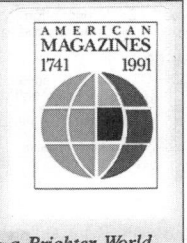

Magazine Industry, 250th Anniv. — U168

Photo. & Typo.
1991, Oct. 7   **Unwmk.**
U622 U168 29c multicolored   .60   .30
  The photogravure vignette, visible through the die cut window to the right of "USA 29," is affixed to the inside of the envelope. Available only in No. 10 size.

Star U169

Stamp and design continue on back of envelope.

1991, July 20   **Typo.**
U623 U169 29c ultra & rose   .60   .30
  a.   Ultra omitted, entire
  b.   Rose omitted, entire
  Lined with a blue design to provide security for enclosures. Available only in No. 9 size.

Country Geese U170

1991, Nov. 8   **Litho. & Typo.**   **Wmk.**
U624 U170 29c blue gray & yel   .60   .60

Space Shuttle Type of 1989
1992, Jan. 21   **Typo.**   **Unwmk.**
U625 U163 29c yellow green   .60   .25
  A hologram, visible through the die cut window to the right of "USA 29," is affixed to the inside of the envelope. Available only in No. 10 size.
  See No. U617a for envelopes with hologram only.

U171

Typo. & Litho.
1992, Apr. 10   **Unwmk.**   *Die Cut*
U626 U171 29c multicolored   .60   .30
  The lithographed vignette, visible through the die cut window to the right of "USA 29," is affixed to the inside of the envelope.

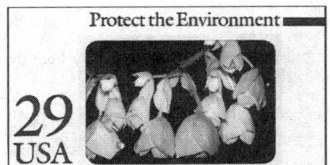

Hillebrandia — U172

Illustration reduced.

1992, Apr. 22
U627 U172 29c multicolored   .60   .30
  The lithographed vignette, visible through the die cut window to the right of "29 USA," is affixed to the inside of the envelope.

U173

Typo. & Embossed
1992, May 19   **Untagged**
Precanceled
U628 U173 19.8c red & blue   .40

Disabled Americans

U174

1992, July 22   **Typo.**   **Unwmk.**
U629 U174 29c red & blue   .60   .30

U175

Illustration reduced.

Typo. & Litho.
1993, Oct. 2   **Unwmk.**   *Die Cut*
U630 U175 29c multicolored   .60   .30
  The lithographed vignette, visible through the die cut window to the right of "USA 29," is affixed to the inside of the envelope.

U176

Typo. & Embossed
1994, Sept. 17   **Unwmk.**
U631 U176 29c brown & black   .60   .30
  a.   Blk ("29/USA") omitted, entire   400.00
  See No. U638.

Liberty Bell — U177

Typo. & Embossed
1995, Jan. 3   **Unwmk.**
U632 U177 32c greenish bl & bl   .65   .30
  a.   Greenish bl omitted, entire   525.00
  b.   Blue ("USA 32") omitted, entire   150.00

U178

  Design size: 49x38mm (#U633), 53x44mm (#U634).
  Stamp and design continue on back of envelope.

1995   **Typo.**   **Unwmk.**
U633 U178 (32c) blue & red   .65   .30
U634 U178 (32c) blue & red   .65   .30
  a.   Red and tagging omitted, entire   500.00
  b.   Blue omitted, entire   500.00
  Originally, Nos. U633-U634 were only available through the Philatelic Fulfillment Center after their announcement 1/12/95.

U179

  Design size: 58x25mm.
  Stamp and design continue on back of envelope.

1995, Mar. 10   **Typo.**   **Unwmk.**
Precanceled
U635 U179 (5c) grn & red brn   .20

Graphic Eagle — U180

1995, Mar. 10   **Typo.**   **Unwmk.**
Precanceled
U636 U180 (10c) dark car & bl   .20

Spiral Heart — U181

1995, May 12   **Typo.**   **Unwmk.**
U637 U181 32c red, *light blue*   .65   .30

Liberty Bell Type of 1995
1995, May 16   **Typo.**   **Unwmk.**
U638 U177 32c greenish bl & bl   .65   .30

Space Shuttle Type of 1989
Unwmk.
1995, Sept. 22   **Typo.**   *Die Cut*
U639 U163 32c carmine rose   .65   .35
  A hologram, visible through the die cut window to the right of "USA 32," is affixed to the inside of the envelope.

U182

Typo. & Litho.
1996, Apr. 20   **Unwmk.**   *Die Cut*
U640 U182 32c multicolored   .60   .30
  The lithographed vignette, visible through the die cut window to the right of "USA 32c," is affixed to the inside of the envelope.

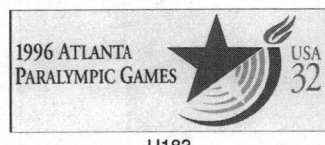

U183

1996, May 2
U641 U183 32c multicolored   .60   .30
  a.   Blue & red omitted, entire   500.00
  b.   Blue & gold omitted, entire   500.00
  c.   Red omitted, entire
  d.   Black & red omitted, entire   500.00

U184

Typo. & Embossed
1999, Jan. 11   **Unwmk.**
U642 U184 33c yel, bl & red   .65   .30
  a.   Tagging bar to right of design   .65   .30
  b.   Blue omitted, entire
  c.   Yellow omitted, entire
Typo.
U643 U184 33c blue & red   .65   .30

U185

1999, Jan. 28   **Litho.**
U644 U185 33c violet   .65   .30

Lincoln — U186

Typo. & Litho.
1999, June 5   **Unwmk.**
U645 U186 33c blue & black   .65   .30

Eagle
U187

Unwmk.
2001, Jan. 7   **Typo.**   **Tagged**
U646 U187 34c blue gray & gray   .65   .30
Many color shades known.

Lovebirds — U188

2001, Feb. 14   **Litho.**   **Unwmk.**
U647 U188 34c rose & dull violet   .65   .30

Community Colleges, Cent. — U189

2001, Feb. 20   **Typo.**   **Unwmk.**
U648 U189 34c dk bl & org brn   .65   .30

**AIR POST STAMPED ENVELOPES &
AIR LETTER SHEETS**

UC1   UC2

UC1 — Vertical rudder is not semi-circular but slopes down to the left. The tail of the plane projects into the G of POSTAGE.

UC2 — Vertical rudder is semi-circular. The tail of the plane touches but does not project into the G of POSTAGE.

6c — Same as UC2 except 3 types of numeral:
Die 2a—Numeral "6" 6½mm wide.
Die 2b—Numeral "6" 6mm wide.
Die 2c—Numeral "6" 5½mm wide.
Die 3—Vertical rudder leans forward. "S" closer to "O" than to "T" of POSTAGE. "E" of POSTAGE has short center bar.

1929-44   **Embossed**
UC1 UC1 5c blue   3.50   2.00
  a.   Orange & blue border,
         type b   325.00
UC2 UC2 5c blue   11.00   5.00
UC3 UC2 6c org, die 2a
        ('34)   1.45   .40
  a.   See footnote   4,000.

UC4 UC2 6c org, die 2b
        ('42)   2.75   2.00
UC5 UC2 6c org, die 2c
        ('44)   .75   .30
UC6 UC2 6c org, die 3 ('42)   1.00   .35
  a.   6c org, *blue* (error), entire 3,500. 2,400.
UC7 UC2 8c ol grn ('32)   13.00   3.50

No. UC3a is similiar in design to UC3, with added impression of 3c pur (#U436a). The entire is without border.

Surcharged in black on envelopes indicated by numbers in parentheses

1945
UC8 U93 6c on 2c (U429)   1.25   .65
  a.   6c on 1c grn, error, (U420)   1,750.
  b.   6c on 3c pur, error, (U436a)   2,000.
  c.   6c on 3c purple, error, amb
         (U437a)   3,000.
  d.   6c on 3c vio, error, (U526)   3,000.
UC9 U95 6c on 2c (U525)   75.00 40.00

Nos. UC8a-UC8d are known only entire.

Surcharged in
Black

Surcharged on 6c Orange Air Post Envelopes without borders

1946
UC10 UC2 5c on 6c, die 2a   2.75   1.50
  a.   Double surcharge   60.00
UC11 UC2 5c on 6c, die 2b   9.00   5.50
UC12 UC2 5c on 6c, die 2c   .75   .50
  a.   Double surcharge   60.00 60.00
UC13 UC2 5c on 6c, die 3   .80   .60
  a.   Double surcharge   60.00

The 6c borderless envelopes and the reval-ued envelopes were issued primarily for use to and from members of the armed forces.
The 5c rate came into effect Oct. 1, 1946.

DC-4
Skymaster
UC3

Die 1. The end of the wing at the right is a smooth curve. The juncture of the front end of the plane and the engine forms an acute angle. The first T of STATES and the E's of UNITED STATES lean to the left.
Die 2. The end of the wing at the right is a straight line. The juncture of the front end of the plane and the engine is wide open. The first T of STATES and the E's of UNITED STATES lean to the right.

1946   **Embossed**
UC14 UC3 5c carmine, die 1   .75   .20
UC15 UC3 5c carmine, die 2   .85   .25

See Nos. UC18, UC26.

DC-4
Skymaster — UC4

Letter Sheet for Foreign Postage
"Air Letter" on face, 2-line inscription on back.

1947, Apr. 29   **Typo.**
UC16 UC4 10c brt red, *pale
         bl*, entire   7.50   6.00
  a.   "Air Letter" on face, 4-line
         inscription on back ('51),
         entire   16.00 14.00
  b.   As "a," 10c chocolate,
         pale bl, entire   450.00

  c.   "Air Letter" and "Aero-
         gramme" on face, 4-line
         inscription on back ('53),
         entire   45.00 12.50
  d.   As "c," 3-line inscription
         on back ('55), entire   8.00   8.00

Washington & Franklin, Early and
Modern Mail-carrying Vehicles — UC5

Embossed, Rotary Press Printing
1947, May 21
UC17 UC5 5c car, (22¼mm high)   .40   .25
  a.   Flat plate (21¾mm high)   .50   .30

Cent. of the 1st postage stamps issued by the U.S. Government.

Type of 1946

Type I- 6's lean to right.
Type II- 6's upright.

1950, Sept. 22
UC18 UC3 6c carmine, type I   .35   .20
  a.   Type II   .75   .25

Several other types differ slightly from the two listed.

Nos. UC14, UC15, UC18 Surcharged
in Red

1951
UC19 UC3 6c on 5c car, die 1   .85   .50
UC20 UC3 6c on 5c car, die 2   .80   .50
  a.   6c on 6c car, error, entire   1,500.
  b.   6c on 5c, double surcharge 500.00   —

Nos. UC14, UC15 and UC17
Surcharged in Red at Left of Stamp

1952
UC21 UC3 6c on 5c, die 1   27.50 17.50
UC22 UC3 6c on 5c, die 2   3.50   2.50
  a.   Double surcharge   200.00
UC23 UC5 6c on 5c   1,250.

The 6c on 4c black (No. U440) is believed to be a favor printing.

Eagle in Flight — UC6

1956, May 2   **Embossed**
UC25 UC6 6c red   .75   .50

FIPEX, NYC, Apr. 28-May 6. Two types exist, differing mainly in the clouds at top.

Skymaster Type of 1946

1958, July 31
UC26 UC3 7c blue   .65   .50

Nos. UC3-UC5, UC18 and UC25
Surcharged in Green

1958
UC27 UC2 6c + 1c, die 2a   325.00 225.00
UC28 UC2 6c + 1c, die 2b   75.00 75.00
UC29 UC2 6c + 1c, die 2c   45.00 50.00
UC30 UC3 6c + 1c, type I   1.00   .50
  a.   Type II   1.00   .50
UC31 UC6 6c + 1c   1.00   .50

Jet
Airliner — UC7

Letter Sheet for Foreign Postage.

Two types:
Type I - Back inscription in 3 lines.
Type II - Back inscription in 2 lines.

1958-59   **Typo.**
UC32 UC7 10c bl & red, *bl*, II
         ('59), entire   6.00   5.00
  a.   Type I ('58), entire   10.00 5.00
  b.   Red omitted, II, entire   1,000.
  c.   Blue omitted, II, entire   1,000.
  d.   Red omitted, I, entire   1,000.

Silhouette of Jet Airliner -
UC8

1958, Nov. 21   **Embossed**
UC33 UC8 7c blue   .60   .25

1960, Aug. 18
UC34 UC8 7c carmine   .60   .25

Jet Plane and
Globe — UC9

Letter Sheet for Foreign Postage

1961, Nov. 16   **Typo.**
UC35 UC9 11c red & bl, *bl*,
         entire   2.75   1.50
  a.   Red omitted, entire   1,000.
  b.   Blue omitted, entire   1,000.

UC10   UC11

1962, Nov. 17   **Embossed**
UC36 UC10 8c red   .55   .20

1965, Jan. 7
UC37 UC11 8c red   .35   .20
  a.   Tagged ('67)   3.50   .30

No. UC37a has a luminescent panel ⅜x1 inches at left of stamp. It glows orange red under ultraviolet light.

Pres. John F.
Kennedy and
Jet Plane
UC12

Letter Sheets for Foreign Postage
1965-67   **Typo.**
UC38 UC12 11c red & dk bl,
          blue, entire   3.25   1.50
UC39 UC12 13c red & dk bl,
          blue, entire   3.00   1.50
  a.   Red omitted   900.00
  b.   Dark blue omitted   500.00

Issued: 11c, 5/29/65; 13c, 5/29/67.

UC13

1968, Jan. 8   **Tagged**   **Embossed**
UC40 UC13 10c red   .50   .20

No. UC37 Surcharged in Red

1968, Feb. 5
UC41 UC11 8c + 2c red   .65   .20

Tagging
Envelopes and Letter Sheets from No. UC42 onward are tagged unless otherwise noted.

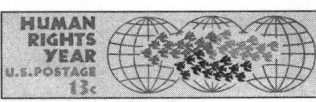

Globes and Flock of Birds — UC14

Letter Sheet for Foreign Postage
1968, Dec. 3   Photo.
UC42 UC14 13c gray, brn, org & blk, *blue,* entire   8.00 4.00
a.   Orange omitted, entire   —
b.   Brown omitted, entire   500.00
c.   Black omitted, entire   —

Intl. Human Rights Year, and 20th anniv. of the UN Declaration of Human Rights.

UC15

1971, May 6   Embossed
UC43 UC15 11c red & blue   .50   .20

Birds in Flight and "usa" — UC16

Letter Sheet for Foreign Postage
"postage 15c" in Gray
1971, May 28   Photo.
UC44 UC16 15c gray, red, white & blue, *blue,* entire   1.50 1.10
a.   "AEROGRAMME" added, entire   1.50 1.10

Folding instructions (2 steps) in capitals on No. UC44; (4 steps) in upper and lower case on No. UC44a. No. UC44a issued Dec. 13. See No. UC46.

No. UC40 Surcharged in Green

1971, June 28   Embossed
UC45 UC13 10c + (1c) red   1.50   .20

Letter Sheet for Foreign Postage
"usa" Type of 1971
Design: Three balloons and cloud at left in address section; no birds beside stamp.

"postage 15c" in Blue
1973, Feb. 10   Photo.
UC46 UC16 15c red, white & bl, *blue,* entire   .75   .40

Hot Air Ballooning World Championships, Albuquerque, NM, Feb. 10-17. Folding instructions as on No. UC44a, with "INTERNATIONAL HOT AIR BALLOONING" added to inscription.

Bird in Flight — UC17

1973, Dec. 1   Embossed
UC47 UC17 13c rose red   .30   .20

Beginning with No. UC48 all letter sheets are for Foreign Postage unless noted otherwise.

UC18

1974, Jan. 4   Photo.
UC48 UC18 18c red & blue, *blue,* entire   .90   .30
a.   Red omitted, entire   —

UC19

Design: "NATO" and NATO emblem in multicolor at left in address section.

1974, Apr. 4   Photo.
UC49 UC19 18c red & blue, *blue,* entire   .90   .40

25th anniv. of NATO.

UC20

1976, Jan. 16   Photo.
UC50 UC20 22c red & blue, *blue,* entire   .90   .40

UC21

1978, Nov. 3   Photo.
UC51 UC21 22c bl, *bl,* entire   .70   .25

UC22

Design (multicolored in bottom left corner) shows discus thrower.

1979, Dec. 5   Photo.
UC52 UC22 22c red, blk & grn, *bluish,* entire   1.50   .25

22nd Olympic Games, Moscow, July 19-Aug. 3, 1980.

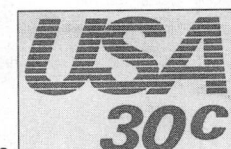

UC23

Design shows Statue of Liberty at lower left. Inscribed "Tour the United States," folding area shows tourist attractions.

1980-81   Photo.
UC53 UC23 30c bl, red & brn, *bl,* entire   .65   .30
a.   Red ("30c") omitted, entire   70.00
UC54 UC23 30c yel, magenta, bl & blk, *bl,* entire ('81)   .65   .30

Issued: Dec. 29, 1980; Sept. 21, 1981.

UC24

"Made in USA . . . world's best buys."

1982, Sept. 16   Photo.
UC55 UC24 30c multi, *bl,* entire   .65   .30

World Communications Year Issue

World Map Showing Locations of Satellite Tracking Stations — UC25

1983, Jan. 7   Photo.
UC56 UC25 30c multi, *bl,* entire   .65   .30

1984 Olympics

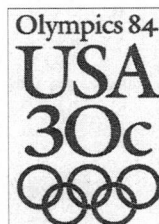

UC26

1983, Oct. 14   Photo.
UC57 UC26 30c multi, *bl,* entire   .65   .30

UC27

Design: Satellite over Earth at lower left, with Landsat photographs on folding area. Inscribed: Landsat views the Earth.

1985, Feb. 14   Photo.
UC58 UC27 36c multi, *bl,* entire   .70   .35

National Tourism Week

Urban Skyline UC28

1985, May 21   Photo.
UC59 UC28 36c multi, *bl,* entire   .70   .35
a.   Black omitted, entire   —

Mark Twain (1835-1910) and Halley's Comet

Comet Tail Viewed from Space - UC29

1985, Dec. 4   Photo.
UC60 UC29 36c multi, entire   .70   .35

UC30

1988, May 9   Litho.
UC61 UC30 39c multi, entire   .80   .40

Montgomery Blair and Pres. Lincoln — UC31

Design: Mail bags and text at lower left. Globe, locomotive, bust of Blair, UPU emblem and text contained on reverse folding area.

1989, Nov. 20   Litho.
UC62 UC31 39c multi, entire   .80   .40

UC32

1991, May 17   Litho.
UC63 UC32 45c gray, red & bl, *blue,* entire   .90   .45
a.   White paper, entire   .90   .45

Thaddeus Lowe (1832-1913), Balloonist — UC33

1995, Sept. 23   Litho.
UC64 UC33 50c multi, *blue,* entire   1.00   .50

Voyageurs
Natl. Park,
Minnesota
UC34

USA 60

1999, May 15   Litho.   Tagged
UC65 UC34 60c multi, *blue*, entire   1.25 .65

POSTAL CARDS
"R.F." CONTROL OVERPRINT
STAMPED ENVELOPES
are listed in the Scott Specialized
Catalogue of United States Stamps.
NEWSPAPER WRAPPERS
included in listings of Stamped Enve-
lopes with prefix "W" instead of "U"
LETTER SHEETS included with
Stamped Envelopes

OFFICIAL STAMPED ENVELOPES

Post Office Department

"2" 9mm
high — UO1

"3" 9mm
high — UO2

"6" 9½mm
high — UO3

1873
UO1	UO1	2c black, *lemon*	19.00	9.00
UO2	UO2	3c black, *lemon*	11.00	6.00
+UO3	UO2	3c black	22,500.	
UO4	UO3	6c black, *lemon*	21.00	15.00

"2" 9¼mm
high — UO4

"3" 9¼mm
high — UO5

"6" 10½mm
high — UO6

1874-79
UO5	UO4	2c black, *lemon*	8.00	4.00
UO6	UO4	2c black	100.00	32.50
UO7	UO5	3c black, *lemon*	3.00	.85
UO8	UO5	3c black	3,000.	2,250.
UO9	UO5	3c black, *amber*	80.00	35.00
UO10	UO5	3c black, *blue*	45,000.	
UO11	UO5	3c blue, *blue*	45,000.	
UO12	UO6	6c black, *lemon*	9.00	5.50
UO13	UO6	6c black	2,750.	1,500.

Postal Service

UO7

1877
UO14	UO7	black	6.00	3.75
UO15	UO7	black, *amber*	150.00	27.50
UO16	UO7	blue, *amber*	150.00	30.00
UO17	UO7	blue, *blue*	8.00	6.00
	Nos. UO14-UO17 (4)		314.00	67.25

War Department

Franklin
UO8

Jackson
UO9

UO8 — Bust points to the end of "N" of
"ONE."

UO9 — Bust narrow at the back.

Washington
UO10

Lincoln
UO11

UO10 — Queue projects below the bust.

UO11 — Neck very long at the back.

Jefferson
UO12

Clay
UO13

UO12 — Queue forms straight line with
bust.

UO13 — Ear partly concealed by hair,
mouth large, chin prominent.

Webster
UO14

Scott
UO15

UO14 — Has side whiskers.

Hamilton — UO16

Back of bust very narrow, chin almost
straight; the labels containing the letters "U S"
are exactly parallel.

1873
Reay Issue
UO18	UO8	1c dark red	550.00	300.00
UO19	UO9	2c dark red	1,800.	400.00
UO20	UO10	3c dark red	60.00	40.00
UO21	UO10	3c dark red, *amb*	40,000.	
UO22	UO10	3c dark red, *cr*	675.00	250.00
UO23	UO11	6c dark red	225.00	90.00
UO24	UO11	6c dark red, *cr*	8,250.	425.00
UO25	UO12	10c dark red	15,000.	1,500.
UO26	UO13	12c dark red	125.00	50.00
UO27	UO14	15c dark red	125.00	55.00
UO28	UO15	24c dark red	125.00	50.00
UO29	UO16	30c dark red	475.00	150.00

UO30	UO8	1c vermilion	160.00	
WO31	UO8	1c ver, *man*	14.00	12.50
+UO32	UO9	2c vermilion	450.00	
WO33	UO9	2c ver, *man*	210.00	
UO34	UO10	3c vermilion	85.00	40.00
UO35	UO10	3c ver, *amb*	95.00	
UO36	UO10	3c ver, *cr*	16.00	12.50
UO37	UO11	6c vermilion	85.00	
+UO38	UO11	6c ver, *cr*	500.00	

UO39	UO12	10c vermilion	275.00	
UO40	UO13	12c vermilion	140.00	
UO41	UO14	15c vermilion	210.00	
UO42	UO15	24c vermilion	375.00	
UO43	UO16	30c vermilion	475.00	

UO17

UO18

UO17--Bottom serif on "S" is thick and
short, bust at bottom below hair forms sharp
point.

UO18--Bottom serif on "S" is thick and short
front part of bust is rounded.

UO19

UO20

UO19--Bottom serif on "S" is short, queue
does not project below bust.

UO20--Neck very short at the back.

UO21

UO22

UO21--Knot of queue stands out
prominently.

UO22--Ear prominent, chin receding.

UO23

UO24

UO23--Has no side whiskers, forelock
projects above head.

UO24--Back of bust rather broad; chin
slopes considerably; the labels containing letters "U S" are not exactly parallel.

1875
Plimpton Issue
UO44	UO17	1c red	150.00	80.00
+UO45	UO17	1c red, *amb*	900.00	
+UO45A	UO17	1c red, *org*	37,500.	
WO46	UO17	1c red, *man*	4.00	2.75
UO47	UO18	2c red	100.00	—
UO48	UO18	2c red, *amb*	29.00	14.00
UO49	UO18	2c red, *org*	47.50	13.50
WO50	UO18	2c red, *man*	85.00	40.00
UO51	UO19	3c red	14.00	9.00
UO52	UO19	3c red, *amb*	16.00	9.00
UO53	UO19	3c red, *cr*	6.50	3.75
UO54	UO19	3c red, *bl*	3.50	2.75
UO55	UO19	3c red, *fawn*	4.50	2.75
UO56	UO20	6c red	47.50	30.00
UO57	UO20	6c red, *amb*	77.50	40.00
UO58	UO20	6c red, *cr*	200.00	85.00
UO59	UO21	10c red	200.00	80.00
UO60	UO21	10c red, *amb*	1,100.	
UO61	UO22	12c red	50.00	40.00
UO62	UO22	12c red, *amb*	675.00	
UO63	UO22	12c red, *cr*	550.00	
UO64	UO23	15c red	210.00	140.00
UO65	UO23	15c red, *amb*	925.00	
UO66	UO23	15c red, *cr*	725.00	
UO67	UO24	30c red	170.00	140.00
UO68	UO24	30c red, *amb*	950.00	
UO69	UO24	30c red, *cr*	950.00	

POSTAL SAVINGS STAMPED ENVELOPES

UO25

1911
UO70	UO25	1c green	67.50	20.00
UO71	UO25	1c grn, *oriental buff*	200.00	67.50
UO72	UO25	2c carmine	11.00	3.75
a.		2c car, *manila* (error)	1,750.	1,000.

Used Values
Catalogue values for regularly used
entires. Those with first day cancels
generally sell for much less.

OFFICIAL MAIL

UO26

1983, Jan. 12
UO73 UO26 20c blue, entire   1.25 30.00

UO27

1985, Feb. 26
UO74 UO27 22c blue, entire   .90 10.00

UO28

1987, Mar. 2   Typo.
UO75 UO28 22c blue, entire   1.00 20.00
Used exclusively to mail US Savings Bonds.

UO29

1988, Mar. 22   Typo.
UO76 UO29 (25c) blk & bl, en-
tire   1.10 20.00
Used exclusively to mail US Saving Bonds.

UO30

1988, Apr. 11   Embossed & Typo.
UO77 UO30 25c blk & bl, entire   .80 15.00
a.   Denomination & lettering as
        No. UO78

Official Mail 25 USA UO31

1988, Apr. 11   **Typo.**
UO78 UO31 25c blk & bl, entire   .90   25.00
  a. Denomination & lettering as
      No. UO77   —   —
Used exclusively to mail US Saving Bonds.

Used Values
The appearance in the marketplace of postally used examples of the entires used to mail passports (Nos. UO79-UO82, UO86-UO87) is so infrequent that it currently is not possible to establish accurate values.

1990, Mar. 17   **Typo.**
UO79 UO31 45c blk & bl, entire   1.25   —
UO80 UO31 65c blk & bl, entire   1.75   —
Used exclusively to mail US passports.

Official Mail 45 USA UO32

Type UO32: sharp impression, stars and "E Pluribus Unum" are clear and distinct. Official is 14½mm long, USA is 17mm long.

1990, Aug. 10   **Typo.**
UO81 UO32 45c blk & bl, entire   1.25   —
UO82 UO32 65c blk & bl, entire   1.60   —
Used exclusively to mail US passports.

Official Mail F USA For U.S. addresses only UO33

1991, Jan. 22   **Typo.**   **Wmk.**
UO83 UO33 (29c) blk & bl, en-
    tire   1.10   20.00
Used exclusively to mail US Saving Bonds.

Official Mail USA 29 UO34

1991, Apr. 6   **Typo. & Embossed**
UO84 UO34 29c blk & bl, entire   .75   2.00

Official Mail USA 29 UO35

1991, Apr. 17   **Typo.**   **Wmk.**
UO85 UO35 29c blk & bl, entire   .70   20.00
Used exclusively to mail US Saving Bonds.

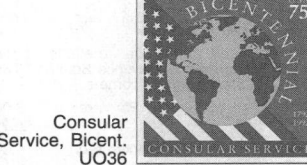

Consular Service, Bicent.
UO36

1992, July 10   **Litho.**   **Unwmk.**
UO86 UO36 52c bl & red, entire   1.60   —
UO87 UO36 75c bl & red, entire   3.00   —
Used exclusively to mail US passports.

Official Mail USA 32 UO37

Typo. & Embossed
1995-99   **Unwmk.**
UO88 UO37 32c bl & red, entire   .80   10.00
UO89 UO37 33c bl & red, entire   .70   10.00
UO90 UO37 34c blue & red, entire   .85   —
Issued: 32c, 5/9; 33c, 2/22/99; 34c, 2/27/01.

OFFICIAL WRAPPERS
Included in listings of Official Stamped Envelopes with prefix letters "WO" instead of "UO"

REVENUE STAMPS

Nos. R1-R102 were used to pay taxes on documents and proprietary articles including playing cards. Until Dec. 25, 1862, the law stated that a revenue stamp could be used only for payment of the tax upon the particular instrument or article specified on its face. After that date stamps, except the Proprietary, could be used indiscriminately.
Values quoted are for pen-canceled copies. Stamps with handstamped cancellations sell at higher prices. Stamps canceled with cuts, punches or holes sell for less. See the Scott U.S. Specialized Catalogue.

General Issue
First Issue. Head of Washington in Oval. Various Frames as Illustrated.

Nos. R1b to R42b, part perforate, occur perforated sometimes at sides only and sometimes at top and bottom only. The higher values, part perforate, are perforated at sides only. Imperforate and part perforate revenues often bring much more in pairs or blocks than as single copies.
The experimental silk paper is a variety of the old paper and has only a very few minute fragments of fiber.
Some of the stamps were in use eight years and were printed several times. Many color variations occurred, particularly when unstable pigments were used and the color was intended to be purple or violet, such as the 4c Proprietary, 30c and $2.50 stamps. Before 1868 dull colors predominate on these and the early red stamps. In later printings of the 4c Proprietary, 30c and $2.50 stamps, red predominates in the mixture, and on the dollar values the red is brighter. The early $1.90 stamp is dull purple, imperf. or perforated. In a later printing, perforated only, the purple is darker.

  R1
  R2

  R3

R4   R5

1862-71   Engr.   Perf. 12
Old Paper

R1c	R1	1c Express, red	1.25
a.		Imperf.	60.00
b.		Part perf.	40.00
d.		Silk paper	90.00
e.		Vertical pair, imperf. between, old paper	200.00
R2c	R1	1c Playing Cards, red	140.00
a.		Imperf.	1,200.
b.		Part perf.	1,250.
R3c	R1	1c Proprietary, red	.50
a.		Imperf.	775.00
b.		Part perf.	140.00
d.		Silk paper	27.50
R4c	R1	1c Telegraph, red	12.00
a.		Imperf.	400.00
R5c	R2	2c Bank Check, blue	.25
a.		Imperf.	1.00
b.		Part perf.	1.75
e.		Vert. pair, imperf btwn., old paper	400.00
R6c	R2	2c Bank Check, orange	.25
b.		Part perf.	55.00
d.		Silk paper	250.00
e.		Old paper, *green*	425.00
R7c	R2	2c Certificate, blue	25.00
a.		Imperf.	12.50
R8c	R2	2c Certificate, orange	27.50
R9c	R2	2c Express, blue	.40
a.		Imperf.	12.50
b.		Part perf.	20.00
R10c	R2	2c Express, orange	7.50
b.		Part perf.	750.00
d.		Silk paper	80.00
R11c	R2	2c Playing Cards, blue	4.00
b.		Part perf.	200.00
R12c	R2	2c Playing Cards, org	42.50
R13c	R2	2c Proprietary, blue	.40
a.		Imperf.	500.00
b.		Part perf.	150.00
d.		Silk paper	60.00
e.		Ultramarine	200.00
R14c	R2	2c Proprietary, orange	40.00
R15c	R2	2c U.S. Int. Rev., orange ('64)	.20
d.		Silk paper	.25
e.		Old paper, *green*	600.00
R16c	R3	3c For. Exch., green	3.50
b.		Part perf.	300.00
d.		Silk paper	60.00
R17c	R3	3c Playing Cards, green ('63)	130.00
a.		Imperf.	10,000.
R18c	R3	3c Proprietary, green	3.25
b.		Part perf.	350.00
d.		Silk paper	37.50
e.		Printed on both sides, old paper	1,800.
R19c	R3	3c Telegraph, green	2.75
a.		Imperf.	70.00
b.		Part perf.	25.00
R20c	R3	4c Inland Exch., brown ('63)	1.75
d.		Silk paper	62.50
R21c	R3	4c Playing Cards, slate ('63)	500.00
R22c	R3	4c Proprietary, purple	6.50
a.		Imperf.	250.00
d.		Silk paper	77.50

Many shade and color variations of Nos. R21-R22. See foreword, "Revenue Stamps."

R23c	R3	5c Agreement, red	.30
d.		Silk paper	1.50
R24c	R3	5c Certificate, red	.30
a.		Imperf.	2.50
b.		Part perf.	11.00
d.		Silk paper	.35
R25c	R3	5c Express, red	.30
a.		Imperf.	5.00
b.		Part perf.	6.00
R26c	R3	5c Foreign Exch., red	.30
b.		Part perf.	—
d.		Silk paper	300.00
R27c	R3	5c Inland Exch., red	.25
a.		Imperf.	5.00
b.		Part perf.	3.75
d.		Silk paper	17.50
R28c	R3	5c Playing Cards, red ('63)	20.00
R29c	R3	5c Proprietary, red ('64)	25.00
d.		Silk paper	120.00

R30c	R3	6c Inland Exch., org ('63)	1.75
d.		Silk paper	75.00
R31c	R3	6c Proprietary, org ('71)	*1,700.*

Nearly all copies of No. R31 are faulty or repaired and poorly centered.
The Catalogue value is for a fine centered copy with minor faults which do not detract from its appearance.

R32c	R3	10c Bill of Lading, blue	1.00
a.		Imperf.	50.00
b.		Part perf.	300.00
R33c	R3	10c Certificate, blue	.25
a.		Imperf.	150.00
b.		Part perf.	300.00
d.		Silk paper	5.00
R34c	R3	10c Contract, blue	.35
b.		Part perf.	200.00
d.		Silk paper	2.25
e.		Ultramarine, part perf.	425.00
f.		Ultramarine, old paper	1.00
R35c	R3	10c For. Exch., blue	7.00
d.		Silk paper	—
e.		ultra, old paper	9.75
R36c	R3	10c Inland Exch., blue	.20
a.		Imperf.	200.00
b.		Part perf.	4.00
d.		Silk paper	37.50
R37c	R3	10c Power of Attorney, blue	.50
b.		Part perf.	500.00
d.		Silk paper	25.00
R38c	R3	10c Proprietary, blue ('64)	17.50
R39c	R3	15c For. Exch., brown ('63)	15.00
R40c	R3	15c Inland Exch., brown	1.25
a.		Imperf.	30.00
b.		Part perf.	12.50
R41c	R3	20c For. Exch., red	32.50
a.		Imperf.	50.00
R42c	R3	20c Inland Exch., red	.35
a.		Imperf.	15.00
b.		Part perf.	17.50
R43c	R4	25c Bond, red	2.50
a.		Imperf.	180.00
b.		Part perf.	6.00
R44c	R4	25c Certificate, red	.25
a.		Imperf.	10.00
b.		Part perf.	6.00
d.		Silk paper	2.75
e.		Printed on both sides, old paper	4,500.
f.		Impression of No. R48 on back, old paper	—
R45c	R4	25c Entry of Goods, red	.75
a.		Imperf.	17.50
b.		Part perf.	70.00
d.		Silk paper	27.50
R46c	R4	25c Insurance, red	.25
a.		Imperf.	10.00
b.		Part perf.	10.00
d.		Silk paper	4.50
R47c	R4	25c Life Insurance, red	6.50
a.		Imperf.	35.00
b.		Part perf.	275.00
R48c	R4	25c Power of Attorney, red	.30
a.		Imperf.	6.00
b.		Part perf.	27.50
R49c	R4	25c Protest, red	6.75
a.		Imperf.	30.00
b.		Part perf.	350.00
R50c	R4	25c Warehouse Receipt, red	22.50
a.		Imperf.	45.00
b.		Part perf.	300.00
R51c	R4	30c For. Exch., lilac	52.50
a.		Imperf.	75.00
b.		Part perf.	1,050.
d.		Silk paper	—
R52c	R4	30c Inland Exch., lilac	3.50
a.		Imperf.	50.00
b.		Part perf.	65.00
d.		Silk paper	—

Many shade and color variations of Nos. R51-R52. See foreword, "Revenue Stamps."

R53c	R4	40c Inland Exch., brown	3.50
a.		Imperf.	650.00
b.		Part perf.	7.00
f.		Double impression	—
R54c	R5	50c Conveyance, blue	.20
a.		Imperf.	14.00
b.		Part perf.	1.60
d.		Silk paper	3.00
e.		Ultramarine, old paper	.25
f.		Ultramarine, silk paper	—
R55c	R5	50c Entry of Goods, blue	.40
b.		Part perf.	12.00
d.		Silk paper	42.50
R56c	R5	50c For. Exch., blue	5.00
a.		Imperf.	50.00
b.		Part perf.	60.00
R57c	R5	50c Lease, blue	8.50
a.		Imperf.	25.00
b.		Part perf.	70.00
R58c	R5	50c Life Insurance, blue	1.00
a.		Imperf.	30.00
b.		Part perf.	45.00
R59c	R5	50c Mortgage, blue	.50
a.		Imperf.	14.00
b.		Part perf.	2.50
R60c	R5	50c Original Process, blue	.60
a.		Imperf.	3.00
b.		Part perf.	600.00
d.		Silk paper	1.60
R61c	R5	50c Passage Ticket, blue	1.25
a.		Imperf.	80.00
b.		Part perf.	175.00
R62c	R5	50c Probate of Will, blue	19.00
a.		Imperf.	40.00
b.		Part perf.	70.00
R63c	R5	50c Surety Bond, blue	.30
a.		Imperf.	200.00
b.		Part perf.	2.50
e.		Ultramarine, old paper	.75

R6

R7

R8

R9

R10

R64c	R5	60c Inland Exch., org	6.00
a.		Imperf.	85.00
b.		Part perf.	47.50
d.		Silk paper	37.50
R65c	R5	70c For. Exch., green	8.00
a.		Imperf.	400.00
b.		Part perf.	100.00
d.		Silk paper	60.00

(Illustration sideways)
R11

Old Paper

R66c	R6	$1 Conveyance, red	17.50
a.		Imperf.	12.00
b.		Part perf.	425.00
d.		Silk paper	100.00
R67c	R6	$1 Entry of Goods, red	1.90
a.		Imperf.	35.00
d.		Silk paper	60.00
R68c	R6	$1 For. Exch., red	.60
a.		Imperf.	80.00
d.		Silk paper	55.00
R69c	R6	$1 Inland Exch., red	.45
a.		Imperf.	12.50
b.		Part perf.	325.00
d.		Silk paper	3.00
R70c	R6	$1 Lease, red	2.25
a.		Imperf.	40.00
R71c	R6	$1 Life Insurance, red	6.50
a.		Imperf.	180.00
R72c	R6	$1 Manifest, red	27.50
a.		Imperf.	42.50
R73c	R6	$1 Mortgage, red	175.00
a.		Imperf.	20.00
R74c	R6	$1 Passage Ticket, red	200.00
a.		Imperf.	275.00
R75c	R6	$1 Power of Attorney, red	2.10
a.		Imperf.	75.00
R76c	R6	$1 Probate of Will, red	35.00
a.		Imperf.	70.00
R77c	R7	$1.30 For. Exch., orange ('63)	60.00
a.		Imperf.	4,000.
R78c	R7	$1.50 Inland Exch., blue	3.25
a.		Imperf.	25.00
R79c	R7	$1.60 For. Exch., green ('63)	120.00
a.		Imperf.	900.00
R80c	R7	$1.90 For. Exch., pur ('63)	100.00
a.		Imperf.	5,500.
d.		Silk paper	—

Many shade and color variations of No. R80. See foreword, "Revenue Stamps."

R81c	R8	$2 Conveyance, red	2.75
a.		Imperf.	150.00
b.		Part perf.	1,500.
d.		Silk paper	25.00
R82c	R8	$2 Mortgage, red	3.00
a.		Imperf.	120.00
d.		Silk paper	55.00
R83c	R8	$2 Probate of Will, red ('63)	60.00
a.		Imperf.	4,500.
R84c	R8	$2.50 Inland Exch., pur ('63)	6.50
a.		Imperf.	5,000.
d.		Silk paper	25.00
R85c	R8	$3 Charter Party, green	5.00
a.		Imperf.	140.00
d.		Silk paper	95.00
e.		Printed on both sides	2,000.
g.		Impression of #RS208 on back	4,000.
R86c	R8	$3 Manifest, green	30.00
a.		Imperf.	140.00

R87c	R8	$3.50 Inland Exch., blue ('63)	60.00
a.		Imperf.	4,500.
e.		Printed on both sides	

Many shade and color variations of the $2.50. See foreword, "Revenue Stamps." The $3.50 has stars in upper corners.

R88c	R9	$5 Charter Party, red	6.00
a.		Imperf.	300.00
d.		Silk paper	75.00
R89c	R9	$5 Conveyance, red	6.00
a.		Imperf.	40.00
d.		Silk paper	75.00
R90c	R9	$5 Manifest, red	80.00
a.		Imperf.	120.00
R91c	R9	$5 Mortgage, red	17.00
a.		Imperf.	120.00
R92c	R9	$5 Probate of Will, red	17.50
a.		Imperf.	500.00
R93c	R9	$10 Charter Party, green	25.00
a.		Imperf.	650.00
R94c	R9	$10 Conveyance, green	70.00
a.		Imperf.	100.00
R95c	R9	$10 Mortgage, green	25.00
a.		Imperf.	450.00
R96c	R9	$10 Probate of Will, green	27.50
a.		Imperf.	1,250.
R97c	R10	$15 Mortgage, blue	150.00
a.		Imperf.	1,400.
e.		Ultramarine, old paper	200.00
R98c	R10	$20 Conveyance, org	70.00
a.		Imperf.	125.00
d.		Silk paper	125.00
R99c	R10	$20 Probate of Will, orange	1,250.
a.		Imperf.	1,500.
R100c	R10	$25 Mortgage, red ('63)	125.00
a.		Imperf.	1,000.
d.		Silk paper	200.00
e.		Horiz. pair, imperf. btwn., old paper	1,100.
R101c	R10	$50 U.S. Int. Rev., green ('63)	100.00
a.		Imperf.	200.00
R102c	R11	$200 U.S. Int. Rev., green & red ('64)	700.00
a.		Imperf.	1,500.

DOCUMENTARY STAMPS

Second Issue

After release of the First Issue revenue stamps, the Bureau of Internal Revenue received many reports of fraudulent cleaning and re-use. The Bureau ordered a Second Issue with new designs and colors, using a patented "chameleon" paper which is usually slightly violet or pinkish, with silk fibers.

R12

R12a

R13

R13a

R13b

Head of Washington in Black within Octagon. Various Frames and Numeral Arrangements.

1871   *Perf. 12*

R103	R12	1c blue & black	50.00
		Cut cancel	22.50
a.		Inverted center	1,500.
R104	R12	2c blue & black	1.10
		Cut cancel	.20
a.		Inverted center	6,000.
R105	R12a	3c blue & black	20.00
		Cut cancel	10.00
R106	R12a	4c blue & black	65.00
		Cut cancel	32.50
R107	R12a	5c blue & black	1.50
		Cut cancel	.50
a.		Inverted center	2,750.
R108	R12a	6c blue & black	110.00
		Cut cancel	55.00
R109	R12a	10c blue & black	1.00
		Cut cancel	.20
a.		Inverted center	2,000.
R110	R12a	15c blue & black	30.00
		Cut cancel	15.00
R111	R12a	20c blue & black	6.00
		Cut cancel	2.75
a.		Inverted center	8,000.

Nos. R109a, R111a are valued in the grade of fine.

Head of Washington in Black within Circle
Various Frames

R112	R13	25c blue & black	.60
		Cut cancel	.20
a.		Inverted center	10,000.
b.		Sewing machine perf.	95.00
c.		Perf. 8	275.00
R113	R13	30c blue & black	80.00
		Cut cancel	42.50
R114	R13	40c blue & black	50.00
		Cut cancel	25.00
R115	R13a	50c blue & black	.60
		Cut cancel	.20
a.		Sewing machine perf.	75.00
b.		Inverted center	850.00
		Punch cancellation	275.00
R116	R13a	60c blue & black	110.00
		Cut cancel	55.00
R117	R13a	70c blue & black	45.00
		Cut cancel	22.50
a.		Inverted center	3,500.
		Cut cancel	2,000.
R118	R13b	$1 blue & black	3.00
		Cut cancel	1.25
a.		Inverted center	5,000.
		Punch cancel	900.00
R119	R13b	$1.30 blue & black	350.00
		Cut cancel	175.00
R120	R13b	$1.50 blue & black	12.50
		Cut cancel	7.00
a.		Sewing machine perf.	450.00
R121	R13b	$1.60 blue & black	450.00
		Cut cancel	250.00
R122	R13b	$1.90 blue & black	250.00
		Cut cancel	140.00
R123	R13b	$2 blue & black	15.00
		Cut cancel	7.50
R124	R13b	$2.50 blue & black	30.00
		Cut cancel	16.00
R125	R13b	$3 blue & black	32.50
		Cut cancel	17.50
R126	R13b	$3.50 blue & black	200.00
		Cut cancel	100.00
R127	R13b	$5 blue & black	17.50
		Cut cancel	9.00
a.		Inverted center	3,000.
		Punch cancel	950.00
R128	R13b	$10 blue & black	130.00
		Cut cancel	70.00
R129	R13b	$20 blue & black	400.00
		Cut cancel	260.00
R130	R13b	$25 blue & black	400.00
		Cut cancel	260.00
R131	R13b	$50 blue & black	450.00
		Cut cancel	275.00
R132	R13b	$200 red, bl & blk	5,000.
		Cut cancel	2,800.
R133	R13b	$500 red org, grn & blk	13,000.

Fraudulently produced inverted centers exist, some excellently made.

Value for No. R133 is for a very fine appearing example with a light cut cancel or with minor flaws.

Third Issue

Violet "Chameleon" Paper with Silk Fibers. Various Frames and Numeral Arrangements.

1871-72   *Perf. 12*

R134	R12	1c claret & blk ('72)	35.00
		Cut cancel	19.00
R135	R12	2c orange & blk	.20
		Cut cancel	.20
a.		2c vermilion & black (error)	650.00
b.		Inverted center	375.00
c.		Imperf., pair	
R136	R12a	4c brown & blk ('72)	42.50
		Cut cancel	21.00
R137	R12a	5c orange & black	.25
		Cut cancel	.20
a.		Inverted center	3,500.

No. R137a is valued in the grade of fine.

R138	R12a	6c orange & blk ('72)	50.00
		Cut cancel	25.00
R139	R12a	15c brown & blk ('72)	10.00
		Cut cancel	4.75
a.		Inverted center	15,000.
R140	R13	30c orange & blk ('72)	15.00
		Cut cancel	7.50
a.		Inverted center	2,750.
		Cut cancel	1,750.
R141	R13	40c brown & blk ('72)	40.00
		Cut cancel	20.00
R142	R13	60c orange & blk ('72)	75.00
		Cut cancel	37.50

R143	R13	70c green & blk ('72)	55.00
		Cut cancel	27.50
R144	R13b	$1 green & blk ('72)	1.35
		Cut cancel	.55
a.		Inverted center	5,500.
R145	R13b	$2 ver & black ('72)	22.50
		Cut cancel	14.00
R146	R13b	$2.50 claret & blk ('72)	40.00
		Cut cancel	22.00
a.		Inverted center	20,000.
R147	R13b	$3 green & blk ('72)	40.00
		Cut cancel	21.00
R148	R13b	$5 ver & black ('72)	22.50
		Cut cancel	11.00
R149	R13b	$10 green & blk ('72)	85.00
		Cut cancel	45.00
R150	R13b	$20 org & blk ('72)	500.00
		Cut cancel	260.00
a.		$20 vermilion & black (error)	600.00

1874   *Perf. 12*

R151	R12	2c org & blk, *grn*	.20
		Cut cancel	.20
a.		Inverted center	400.00

Liberty — R14

1875-78   *Perf. 12*

R152a	R14	2c bl, *blue*, silk paper	.20
b.		Wmk. 191R ('78)	.20
c.		Wmk. 191R, rouletted	32.50
d.		Vert. pair, imperf. horiz.	500.00
e.		As "b," imperf., pair	250.00

The rouletted stamps probably were introduced in 1881.

Nos. 279, 267a, 267, 279Bg, 279B, 272-274 Overprinted in Red or Blue

I. R.   I.R.
a   b

1898   **Wmk. 191**   *Perf. 12*

R153	A87(a)	1c grn (R)	3.00	2.50
R154	A87(b)	1c grn (R)	.20	.20
a.		Overprint inverted	20.00	17.50
b.		Ovpt. on back instead of face, invtd.	—	
c.		Pair, one without ovpt.	—	
R155	A88(b)	2c pink, III	.20	.20
		(Bl)		
b.		2c carmine, III	.25	.20
c.		As #R155, ovpt. invtd.	4.50	2.75
d.		Vert. pair, one without ovpt.	750.00	
e.		Horiz. pair, one without ovpt.	—	
f.		As #R155, ovpt. on back instead of face, invtd.	—	
R155A	A88(b)	2c pink, IV	.20	.20
		(Bl)		
g.		2c carmine, IV	.20	.20
h.		As #R155A, ovpt. invtd.	2.50	1.75

Handstamped Type "b"

R156	A93	8c vio brn	4,500.
R157	A94	10c dark grn	3,750.
R158	A95	15c dark blue	4,750.

Nos. R156-R158 were emergency provisionals, privately prepared, not officially issued.

Privately Prepared Provisionals

No. 285 Overprinted   **I. R.**
in Red   **L. H. C.**

1898   **Wmk. 191**   *Perf. 12*

R158A	A100	1c dk yel grn	9,500.	10,000.

Same Overprinted "I.R./P.ID. & Son" in Red

R158B	A100	1c dk yel grn	—	22,500.

No. R158B is valued with small faults as each of the four recorded examples have faults.

Nos. R158A-R158B were overprinted with federal government permission by the Purvis Printing Co. upon order of Capt. L.H. Chapman of the Chapman Steamboat Line. Both the Chapman line and P.I. Daprix & Son operated freight-carrying steamboats on the Erie Canal. The Chapman Line touched at Syracuse, Utica, Little Falls and Fort Plain; the Daprix boat ran between Utica and Rome. 250 of each stamp were overprinted.

Dr. Kilmer & Co. provisional overprints are listed in the Scott Specialized Catalogue of United States Stamps under Private Die uMedicine Stamps, Nos. RS307-RS315.

Newspaper Stamp No. PR121 Surcharged Vertically in Red

1898   **Wmk. 191**   *Perf. 12*
Reading Down

R159	N18	$5 on $5 dk blue	400.00	160.00

Reading Up

R160	N18	$5 on $5 dk blue	110.00	70.00

Battleship — R163

Inscribed: "Series of 1898" and "Documentary."

There are 2 styles of rouletting for the 1898 proprietary and documentary stamps, an ordinary roulette 5½ and one where small rectangles of the paper are cut out, called hyphen hole perf. 7.

1898   **Wmk. 191R**   *Rouletted 5½*

R161	R15	½c orange	2.50	7.50
R162	R15	½c dark gray	.25	.20
a.		Vert. pair, imperf. horiz.	75.00	
R163	R15	1c pale blue	.20	.20
a.		Vert. pair, imperf. horiz.	7.50	
b.		Imperf., pair	400.00	
R164	R15	2c car rose	.25	.25
a.		Vert. pair, imperf. horiz.	65.00	
b.		Imperf., pair	200.00	
c.		Horiz. pair, imperf. vert.		
R165	R15	3c dark blue	2.00	.20
R166	R15	4c pale rose	1.25	.20
a.		Vert. pair, imperf. horiz.	125.00	
R167	R15	5c lilac	.20	.20
a.		Pair, imperf. horiz. or vert.	200.00	150.00
b.		Horiz. pair, imperf. btwn.		450.00
R168	R15	10c dark brown	1.50	.20
a.		Vert. pair, imperf. horiz.	35.00	30.00
b.		Horiz. pair, imperf. vert.		
R169	R15	25c pur brown	2.50	.20
R170	R15	40c blue lilac	125.00	1.00
		Cut cancellation		.30
R171	R15	50c slate violet	17.50	.20
a.		Imperf., pair	300.00	
R172	R15	80c bister	100.00	.25
		Cut cancellation		.20

No. R167b may not be genuine.

Hyphen Hole Perf. 7

R163p	1c	.25	.20
R164p	2c	.30	.20
R165p	3c	20.00	1.00
R166p	4c	7.50	1.50
R167p	5c	7.50	.20
R168p	10c	5.00	.20
R169p	25c	8.00	.25
R170p	40c	175.00	35.00
R171p	50c	35.00	.75
b.	Horiz. pair, imperf. btwn.		250.00
R172p	80c	200.00	45.00

Commerce — R16

1898   *Rouletted 5½*

R173	R16	$1 dark green	8.00	.20
a.		Vert. pair, imperf. horiz.		300.00
b.		Horiz. pair, imperf. vert.	17.50	.65
c.		Hyphen hole perf. 7		
R174	R16	$3 dark brown	22.50	.85
		Cut cancellation		.20
a.		Horiz. pair, imperf. vert.		450.00
b.		Hyphen hole perf. 7	35.00	2.25
		Cut cancellation	.20	.25
R175	R16	$5 orange red	30.00	1.40
		Cut cancellation		.20
R176	R16	$10 black	80.00	2.75
		Cut cancellation		.50
a.		Horiz. pair, imperf. vert.		
R177	R16	$30 red	275.00	120.00
		Cut cancellation		45.00
R178	R16	$50 gray brown	125.00	5.50
		Cut cancellation		2.00

See Nos. R182-R183.

INT. REV.
$5.
DOCUMENTARY.

John Marshall R17

Alexander Hamilton R18

James Madison R19

Inscribed "Series of 1898"

1899   **Without Gum**   *Imperf.*

R179	R17	$100 yel brn & black	130.00	30.00
		Cut cancellation		20.00
R180	R18	$500 car lake & black	1,100.	750.00
		Cut cancellation		225.00
R181	R19	$1000 grn & blk	900.00	300.00
		Cut cancellation		110.00

See #R224-R227, R246-R252, R282-R286.

Type of 1898

1900   **Hyphen-Hole Perf. 7**

R182	R16	$1 carmine	17.50	.50
		Cut cancellation		.20
R183	R16	$3 lake	130.00	45.00
		Cut cancellation		7.00

Warning: The ink on No. R183 will run in water.

Surcharged in Black

a

Surcharged type "a"

1900

R184	R16	$1 gray	12.50	.20
		Cut cancellation		.20
a.		Horiz. pair, imperf. vert.	—	
b.		Surcharge omitted	125.00	
		As "b," cut cancellation		80.00

R185	R16	$2 gray	12.50	.20
		Cut cancellation		.20
R186	R16	$3 gray	65.00	11.00
		Cut cancellation		3.00
R187	R16	$5 gray	42.50	6.50
		Cut cancellation		1.00
R188	R16	$10 gray	75.00	17.50
		Cut cancellation		3.00
R189	R16	$50 gray	900.00	425.00
		Cut cancellation		90.00

Surcharged type "b"

1902

R190	R16	$1 green	20.00	3.75
		Cut cancellation		.20
a.		Inverted surcharge		175.00
R191	R16	$2 green	17.50	1.30
		Cut cancellation		.25
a.		Surcharged as #R185	75.00	75.00
b.		Surch. as #R185, in vio	1,300.	—
c.		As "a," double surcharge	100.00	
d.		As "a," triple surcharge	—	
R192	R16	$5 green	140.00	25.00
		Cut cancellation		4.00
a.		Surcharge omitted	160.00	
b.		Pair, one without surch.	350.00	
R193	R16	$10 green	325.00	125.00
		Cut cancellation		45.00
R194	R16	$50 green	950.00	800.00
		Cut cancellation		225.00

Warning: If Nos. R190-R194 are soaked, the center part of the surcharged numeral may wash off. Before surcharging, a square of soluble varnish was applied to the middle of some stamps.

R20

Liberty — R21

Inscribed "Series of 1914"
Offset Printing

1914   **Wmk. 190**   *Perf. 10*

R195	R20	½c rose	7.50	3.50
R196	R20	1c rose	1.40	.20
R197	R20	2c rose	2.00	.20
R198	R20	3c rose	50.00	30.00
R199	R20	4c rose	14.00	2.00
R200	R20	5c rose	4.00	.20
R201	R20	10c rose	3.25	.20
R202	R20	25c rose	30.00	.55
R203	R20	40c rose	17.50	1.00
R204	R20	50c rose	6.00	.20
R205	R20	80c rose	95.00	10.00
Nos. R195-R205 (11)			230.65	48.05

Wmk. 191R

R206	R20	½c rose	1.50	.50
R207	R20	1c rose	.20	.20
R208	R20	2c rose	.20	.20
R209	R20	3c rose	1.40	.20
R210	R20	4c rose	3.50	.45
R211	R20	5c rose	1.75	.25
R212	R20	10c rose	.60	.20
R213	R20	25c rose	5.00	1.25
R214	R20	40c rose	75.00	12.50
		Cut cancellation		.45
R215	R20	50c rose	15.00	.20
R216	R20	80c rose	110.00	17.50
		Cut cancellation		1.00
Nos. R206-R216 (11)			214.15	33.50

Engr.

R217	R21	$1 green	35.00	.30
		Cut cancellation		.20
a.		$1 yellow green		.20
R218	R21	$2 carmine	50.00	.50
		Cut cancellation		.20
R219	R21	$3 purple	60.00	2.50
		Cut cancellation		.45
R220	R21	$5 blue	50.00	2.75
		Cut cancellation		.50
R221	R21	$10 orange	125.00	5.00
		Cut cancellation		.75
R222	R21	$30 vermilion	250.00	11.00
		Cut cancellation		2.00
R223	R21	$50 violet	1,300.	800.00
		Cut cancellation		350.00

See #R240-R245, R257-R259, R276-R281.

Portrait Types of 1899 Inscribed "Series of 1915" (#R224), or "Series of 1914"

1914-15   **Without Gum**   *Perf. 12*

R224	R19	$60 brn (Lincoln)	175.00	100.00
		Cut cancellation		45.00
R225	R17	$100 grn (Washington)	60.00	40.00
		Cut cancellation		15.00

R226	R18	$500 blue	—	600.00
		Cut cancellation		250.00
R227	R19	$1000 orange	—	500.00
		Cut cancellation		240.00

The stamps of types R17, R18 and R19 in this and subsequent issues are issued in vert. strips of 4 which are imperf. at the top, bottom and right side; therefore, single copies are always imperf. on 1 or 2 sides.

R22

Offset Printing
1917 Wmk. 191R   Perf. 11

R228	R22	1c carmine rose	.20	.20
R229	R22	2c carmine rose	.20	.20
R230	R22	3c carmine rose	1.25	.35
R231	R22	4c carmine rose	.50	.20
R232	R22	5c carmine rose	.20	.20
R233	R22	8c carmine rose	1.75	.30
R234	R22	10c carmine rose	.35	.20
R235	R22	20c carmine rose	.60	.20
R236	R22	25c carmine rose	1.10	.20
R237	R22	40c carmine rose	1.50	.40
R238	R22	50c carmine rose	2.00	.20
R239	R22	80c carmine rose	5.00	.20
		Nos. R228-R239 (12)	14.65	2.85

Type of 1914 without "Series 1914"
1917-33   Engr.

R240	R21	$1 yellow green	6.50	.20
a.		$1 green	6.50	.20
R241	R21	$2 rose	11.00	.20
R242	R21	$3 violet	35.00	.75
		Cut cancellation		.20
R243	R21	$4 yel brn ('33)	25.00	1.75
		Cut cancellation		.20
R244	R21	$5 dark blue	17.50	.25
		Cut cancellation		.20
R245	R21	$10 orange	30.00	.90
		Cut cancellation		.20

Portrait Types of 1899-1915 without "Series of" and Date
Portraits: $30, Grant. $100, Washington.

1917   Without Gum   Perf. 12

R246	R17	$30 dp org, grn numerals	45.00	10.00
		Cut cancellation		1.00
a.		Imperf., pair		750.00
b.		Numerals in blue	70.00	1.90
		As "b," cut cancellation		1.00
R247	R19	$60 brown	55.00	7.00
		Cut cancellation		.80
R248	R17	$100 green	32.50	1.00
		Cut cancellation		.35
R249	R18	$500 blue, red numerals	300.00	35.00
		Cut cancellation		11.00
a.		Numerals in orange	350.00	50.00
R250	R19	$1000 orange	140.00	12.50
		Cut cancellation		4.00
a.		Imperf., pair		900.00

See note after No. R227.

1928-29   Offset Printing   Perf. 10

R251	R22	1c carmine rose	2.00	1.50
R252	R22	2c carmine rose	.60	.20
R253	R22	4c carmine rose	5.50	3.75
R254	R22	5c carmine rose	1.25	.50
R255	R22	10c carmine rose	1.75	1.25
R256	R22	20c carmine rose	5.50	4.50
		Nos. R251-R256 (6)	16.60	11.70

Engr.

R257	R21	$1 green	100.00	30.00
		Cut cancellation		5.00
R258	R21	$2 rose	40.00	2.50
R259	R21	$10 orange	130.00	40.00
		Cut cancellation		25.00

1929   Offset Printing   Perf. 11x10

R260	R22	2c carmine rose	2.75	2.50
R261	R22	5c carmine rose	2.00	1.75
R262	R22	10c carmine rose	7.50	6.50
R263	R22	20c carmine rose	15.00	8.00

Used values for Nos. R264-R734 are for copies which are neither cut nor perforated with initials. Copies with cut cancellations or perforated initials are valued in the Scott U. S. Specialized Catalogue.

Types of 1917-33 Overprinted in Black   **SERIES 1940**

1940   Offset Printing   Perf. 11

R264	R22	1c rose pink	2.75	2.25
R265	R22	2c rose pink	2.75	1.75
R266	R22	3c rose pink	8.25	4.00
R267	R22	4c rose pink	3.50	.55
R268	R22	5c rose pink	3.75	.90
R269	R22	8c rose pink	16.00	12.50
R270	R22	10c rose pink	1.75	.45
R271	R22	20c rose pink	2.25	.60
R272	R22	25c rose pink	5.50	1.00
R273	R22	40c rose pink	5.50	.65
R274	R22	50c rose pink	6.00	.50
R275	R22	80c rose pink	11.00	.99
		Nos. R264-R275 (12)	69.00	26.05

Engr.

R276	R21	$1 green	40.00	.80
R277	R21	$2 rose	40.00	1.00
R278	R21	$3 violet	55.00	25.00
R279	R21	$4 yellow brown	95.00	30.00
R280	R21	$5 dark blue	55.00	11.00
R281	R21	$10 orange	140.00	27.50

Types of 1917 Handstamped in Green Like Nos. R264-R281
Perf. 12
Without Gum

R282	R17	$30 vermilion		600.
a.		With black 2-line handstamp in larger type		6,000.
R283	R19	$60 brown		800.
a.		As #R282a, cut cancel		—
R284	R17	$100 green		2,000.
R285	R18	$500 blue		1,400.
a.		As #R282a,	2,750.	2,500.
b.		Blue handstamp, double transfer		—
c.		Violet handstamp, double transfer		1,500.
R286	R19	$1000 orange		650.
a.		Double overprint (cut cancel)		—

Alexander Hamilton — R23

Levi Woodbury — R24   Thomas Corwin — R25

Portraits: 2c, Oliver Wolcott, Jr. 3c, Samuel Dexter. 4c, Albert Gallatin. 5c, George Washington Campbell. 8c, Alexander Dallas. 10c, William H. Crawford. 20c, Richard Rush. 25c, Samuel D. Ingham. 40c, Louis McLane. 50c, William J. Duane. 80c, Roger B. Taney. $2, Thomas Ewing. $3, Walter Forward. $4, John Canfield Spencer. $5, George M. Bibb. $10, Robert J. Walker. $20, William M. Meredith. $50, James Guthrie. $60, Howell Cobb. $100, P. F. Thomas. $500, John Adams Dix. $1,000, Salmon P. Chase.

Overprinted in Black Like Nos. R264-R281
1940   Perf. 11
Various Portraits

R288	R23	1c carmine	4.00	3.00
R289	R23	2c carmine	4.50	2.75
R290	R23	3c carmine	17.50	9.00
R291	R23	4c carmine	45.00	20.00
R292	R23	5c carmine	3.00	.60
R293	R23	8c carmine	65.00	45.00
R294	R23	10c carmine	2.50	.45
R295	R23	20c carmine	3.75	2.50
R296	R23	25c carmine	2.75	.50
R297	R23	40c carmine	45.00	20.00
R298	R23	50c carmine	4.50	.40
R299	R23	80c carmine	100.00	60.00
R300	R24	$1 carmine	40.00	.55
R301	R24	$2 carmine	47.50	.75
R302	R24	$3 carmine	135.00	75.00
R303	R24	$4 carmine	80.00	30.00
R304	R24	$5 carmine	47.50	2.00
R305	R24	$10 carmine	85.00	6.00
R305A	R24	$20 carmine	1,750.	750.00
b.		Imperf., pair		600.00

Various Frame Designs
Perf. 12
Without Gum

R306	R25	$30 carmine	130.00	45.00
R306A	R25	$50 carmine	—	2,750.
R307	R25	$60 carmine	260.00	60.00
a.		Vert. pair, imperf btwn.		1,450.
R308	R25	$100 carmine	190.00	65.00
R309	R25	$500 carmine	—	2,100.
R310	R25	$1000 carmine	—	425.00

The $30 to $1,000 denominations in this and following similar issues, and the $2,500, $5,000 and $10,000 stamps of 1952-58 have straight edges on one or two sides. They were issued without gum through No. R723.

Overprinted in Black "SERIES 1941"
1941   Size: 19x22mm   Perf. 11

R311	R23	1c carmine	3.00	2.25
R312	R23	2c carmine	3.00	.90
R313	R23	3c carmine	7.50	3.50
R314	R23	4c carmine	5.00	1.25
R315	R23	5c carmine	1.00	.20
R316	R23	8c carmine	14.00	7.50
R317	R23	10c carmine	1.25	.20
R318	R23	20c carmine	3.00	.45
R319	R23	25c carmine	1.75	.20
R320	R23	40c carmine	11.00	2.50
R321	R23	50c carmine	2.50	.20
R322	R23	80c carmine	55.00	10.00
		Nos. R311-R322 (12)	108.00	29.20

Size: 21½x36¼mm

R323	R24	$1 carmine	10.00	.25
R324	R24	$2 carmine	12.50	.35
R325	R24	$3 carmine	20.00	2.75
R326	R24	$4 carmine	35.00	17.50
R327	R24	$5 carmine	40.00	.60
R328	R24	$10 carmine	60.00	3.50
R329	R24	$20 carmine	550.00	190.00

Size: 28½x42mm
Perf. 12
Without Gum

R330	R25	$30 carmine	125.00	40.00
R331	R25	$50 carmine	375.00	325.00
R332	R25	$60 carmine	175.00	60.00
R333	R25	$100 carmine	75.00	25.00
R334	R25	$500 carmine	—	240.00
R335	R25	$1000 carmine	—	125.00

Overprinted in Black "SERIES 1942"
1942   Size: 19x22mm   Perf. 11

R336	R23	1c carmine	.50	.45
R337	R23	2c carmine	.45	.45
R338	R23	3c carmine	.70	.60
R339	R23	4c carmine	1.20	.90
R340	R23	5c carmine	.45	.20
R341	R23	8c carmine	5.50	4.25
R342	R23	10c carmine	1.20	.25
R343	R23	20c carmine	1.20	.45
R344	R23	25c carmine	2.10	.45
R345	R23	40c carmine	4.75	1.20
R346	R23	50c carmine	3.00	.20
R347	R23	80c carmine	17.50	10.00
		Nos. R336-R347 (12)	38.55	19.40

Size: 21½x36¼mm

R348	R24	$1 carmine	9.00	.25
R349	R24	$2 carmine	10.00	.25
R350	R24	$3 carmine	17.50	2.00
R351	R24	$4 carmine	25.00	3.75
R352	R24	$5 carmine	27.50	.90
R353	R24	$10 carmine	65.00	2.50
R354	R24	$20 carmine	120.00	35.00

Size: 28½x42mm
Perf. 12
Without Gum

R355	R25	$30 carmine	70.00	30.00
R356	R25	$50 carmine	1,250.	550.00
R357	R25	$60 carmine	1,500.	750.00
R358	R25	$100 carmine	160.00	120.00
R359	R25	$500 carmine	1,500.	225.00
R360	R25	$1000 carmine	—	100.00

Overprinted in Black "SERIES 1943"
1943   Size: 19x22mm   Perf. 11

R361	R23	1c carmine	.60	.50
R362	R23	2c carmine	.45	.35
R363	R23	3c carmine	2.50	2.50
R364	R23	4c carmine	1.00	1.00
R365	R23	5c carmine	.50	.30
R366	R23	8c carmine	4.25	3.00
R367	R23	10c carmine	.60	.25
R368	R23	20c carmine	1.90	.65
R369	R23	25c carmine	1.50	.25
R370	R23	40c carmine	5.00	2.25
R371	R23	50c carmine	1.25	.20
R372	R23	80c carmine	15.00	5.50
		Nos. R361-R372 (12)	34.55	16.75

Size: 21½x36¼mm

R373	R24	$1 carmine	6.00	.35
R374	R24	$2 carmine	11.00	.25
R375	R24	$3 carmine	20.00	2.25
R376	R24	$4 carmine	27.50	3.25
R377	R24	$5 carmine	35.00	.60
R378	R24	$10 carmine	55.00	4.00
R379	R24	$20 carmine	110.00	22.50

Size: 28½x42mm
Perf. 12
Without Gum

R380	R25	$30 carmine	55.00	18.00
R381	R25	$50 carmine	110.00	30.00
R382	R25	$60 carmine	260.00	75.00
R383	R25	$100 carmine	25.00	10.00
R384	R25	$500 carmine	—	200.00
R385	R25	$1000 carmine	—	160.00

Overprinted in Black "Series 1944"
1944   Size: 19x22mm   Perf. 11

R386	R23	1c carmine	.40	.35
R387	R23	2c carmine	.40	.35
R388	R23	3c carmine	.40	.35
R389	R23	4c carmine	.55	.50
R390	R23	5c carmine	.30	.20
R391	R23	8c carmine	1.75	1.25
R392	R23	10c carmine	.40	.20
R393	R23	20c carmine	.75	.20
R394	R23	25c carmine	1.40	.20
R395	R23	40c carmine	2.75	.60
R396	R23	50c carmine	3.00	.20
R397	R23	80c carmine	15.00	4.00
		Nos. R386-R397 (12)	27.10	8.40

Size: 21½x36¼mm

R398	R24	$1 carmine	7.50	.20
R399	R24	$2 carmine	10.00	.25
R400	R24	$3 carmine	16.00	2.00
R401	R24	$4 carmine	22.50	10.00
R402	R24	$5 carmine	25.00	.25
R403	R24	$10 carmine	50.00	1.40
R404	R24	$20 carmine	100.00	15.00

Size: 28½x42mm
Perf. 12
Without Gum

R405	R25	$30 carmine	75.00	25.00
R406	R25	$50 carmine	35.00	17.50
R407	R25	$60 carmine	200.00	60.00
R408	R25	$100 carmine	40.00	9.00
R409	R25	$500 carmine	—	2,500.
R410	R25	$1000 carmine	—	275.00

Overprinted in Black "Series 1945"
1945   Size: 19x22mm   Perf. 11

R411	R23	1c carmine	.20	.20
R412	R23	2c carmine	.25	.20
R413	R23	3c carmine	.50	.45
R414	R23	4c carmine	.30	.20
R415	R23	5c carmine	.25	.20
R416	R23	8c carmine	4.25	2.00
R417	R23	10c carmine	.80	.20
R418	R23	20c carmine	4.50	1.00
R419	R23	25c carmine	1.10	.30
R420	R23	40c carmine	4.75	1.00
R421	R23	50c carmine	2.75	.20
R422	R23	80c carmine	20.00	8.00
		Nos. R411-R422 (12)	39.65	14.05

Size: 21½x36¼mm

R423	R24	$1 carmine	8.50	.20
R424	R24	$2 carmine	9.00	.25
R425	R24	$3 carmine	17.50	2.25
R426	R24	$4 carmine	25.00	3.00
R427	R24	$5 carmine	25.00	.40
R428	R24	$10 carmine	50.00	1.40
R429	R24	$20 carmine	100.00	11.00

Size: 28½x42mm
Without Gum
Perf. 12

R430	R25	$30 carmine	125.00	35.00
R431	R25	$50 carmine	150.00	35.00
R432	R25	$60 carmine	250.00	55.00
R433	R25	$100 carmine	50.00	15.00
R434	R25	$500 carmine	300.00	175.00
R435	R25	$1000 carmine	200.00	90.00

Overprinted in Black "Series 1946"
1946   Wmk. 191R   Perf. 11
Size: 19x22mm

R436	R23	1c carmine	.20	.25
R437	R23	2c carmine	.35	.30
R438	R23	3c carmine	.35	.30
R439	R23	4c carmine	.60	.50
R440	R23	5c carmine	.30	.20
R441	R23	8c carmine	1.25	1.10
R442	R23	10c carmine	.70	.20
R443	R23	20c carmine	1.25	.40
R444	R23	25c carmine	4.00	.75
R445	R23	40c carmine	2.50	.75
R446	R23	50c carmine	3.00	.20
R447	R23	80c carmine	12.50	4.25
		Nos. R436-R447 (12)	27.00	8.65

Size: 21½x36¼mm

R448	R24	$1 carmine	9.00	.20
R449	R24	$2 carmine	12.50	.20
R450	R24	$3 carmine	19.00	5.00
R451	R24	$4 carmine	25.00	10.00
R452	R24	$5 carmine	25.00	.45
R453	R24	$10 carmine	50.00	1.50
R454	R24	$20 carmine	100.00	11.00

Size: 28½x42mm
Without Gum
Perf. 12

R455	R25	$30 carmine	45.00	12.00
R456	R25	$50 carmine	35.00	10.00
R457	R25	$60 carmine	70.00	17.50
R458	R25	$100 carmine	50.00	10.00
R459	R25	$500 carmine	—	105.00
R460	R25	$1000 carmine	—	100.00

Overprinted in Black "Series 1947"

1947   Wmk. 191R   Perf. 11
Size: 19x22mm

R461	R23	1c carmine	.65	.50
R462	R23	2c carmine	.55	.50
R463	R23	3c carmine	.55	.50
R464	R23	4c carmine	.70	.60
R465	R23	5c carmine	.35	.30
R466	R23	8c carmine	1.20	.70
R467	R23	10c carmine	1.10	.25
R468	R23	20c carmine	1.80	.50
R469	R23	25c carmine	2.40	.60
R470	R23	40c carmine	3.75	.90
R471	R23	50c carmine	3.00	.25
R472	R23	80c carmine	8.25	6.00
		Nos. R461-R472 (12)	24.30	11.60

Size: 21½x36¼mm

R473	R24	$1 carmine	6.00	.25
R474	R24	$2 carmine	9.50	.50
R475	R24	$3 carmine	12.00	5.00
R476	R24	$4 carmine	14.00	4.50
R477	R24	$5 carmine	21.00	.50
R478	R24	$10 carmine	50.50	2.00
R479	R24	$20 carmine	75.00	10.00

Size: 28½x42mm
Perf. 12
Without Gum

R480	R25	$30 carmine	100.00	20.00
R481	R25	$50 carmine	50.00	14.00
R482	R25	$60 carmine	120.00	40.00
R483	R25	$100 carmine	50.00	11.00
R484	R25	$500 carmine	—	150.00
R485	R25	$1000 carmine	—	80.00

Overprinted in Black "Series 1948"

1948   Wmk. 191R   Perf. 11
Size: 19x22mm

R486	R23	1c carmine	.25	.25
R487	R23	2c carmine	.35	.30
R488	R23	3c carmine	.45	.35
R489	R23	4c carmine	.40	.30
R490	R23	5c carmine	.35	.20
R491	R23	8c carmine	.75	.35
R492	R23	10c carmine	.60	.20
R493	R23	20c carmine	1.75	.30
R494	R23	25c carmine	1.50	.20
R495	R23	40c carmine	4.50	1.50
R496	R23	50c carmine	2.25	.20
R497	R23	80c carmine	7.50	4.50
		Nos. R486-R497 (12)	20.65	8.65

Size: 21½x36¼mm

R498	R24	$1 carmine	7.50	.20
R499	R24	$2 carmine	12.50	2.00
R500	R24	$3 carmine	17.50	2.50
R501	R24	$4 carmine	25.00	2.75
R502	R24	$5 carmine	21.00	.50
R503	R24	$10 carmine	50.00	1.00
a.		Pair, one dated "1946"	—	
R504	R24	$20 carmine	95.00	10.00

Size: 28½x42mm
Perf. 12
Without Gum

R505	R25	$30 carmine	65.00	22.50
R506	R25	$50 carmine	65.00	20.00
a.		Vert. pair, imperf. btwn.	—	
R507	R25	$60 carmine	125.00	35.00
a.		Vert. pair, imperf. btwn.	1,100	
R508	R25	$100 carmine	55.00	10.00
a.		Vert. pair, imperf. btwn.	850.00	
R509	R25	$500 carmine	250.00	125.00
R510	R25	$1000 carmine	175.00	75.00

Overprinted in Black "Series 1949"

1949   Wmk. 191R   Perf. 11
Size: 19x22mm

R511	R23	1c carmine	.25	.25
R512	R23	2c carmine	.55	.35
R513	R23	3c carmine	.40	.35
R514	R23	4c carmine	.60	.50
R515	R23	5c carmine	.35	.20
R516	R23	8c carmine	.70	.60
R517	R23	10c carmine	.40	.25
R518	R23	20c carmine	1.30	.60
R519	R23	25c carmine	1.80	.70
R520	R23	40c carmine	4.25	2.10
R521	R23	50c carmine	3.50	.30
R522	R23	80c carmine	10.00	4.75
		Nos. R511-R522 (12)	24.10	10.95

Size: 21½x36¼mm

R523	R24	$1 carmine	8.50	.40
R524	R24	$2 carmine	11.00	2.00
R525	R24	$3 carmine	17.50	6.00
R526	R24	$4 carmine	21.00	6.00
R527	R24	$5 carmine	21.00	2.25
R528	R24	$10 carmine	50.00	2.50
R529	R24	$20 carmine	95.00	9.00

Size: 28½x42mm
Perf. 12
Without Gum

R530	R25	$30 carmine	85.00	25.00
R531	R25	$50 carmine	100.00	40.00
R532	R25	$60 carmine	175.00	40.00
R533	R25	$100 carmine	50.00	15.00
R534	R25	$500 carmine	—	200.00
R535	R25	$1000 carmine	—	110.00

Overprinted in Black "Series 1950"

1950   Wmk. 191R   Perf. 11
Size: 19x22mm

R536	R23	1c carmine	.20	.20
R537	R23	2c carmine	.30	.25
R538	R23	3c carmine	.35	.30
R539	R23	4c carmine	.50	.40
R540	R23	5c carmine	.30	.20
R541	R23	8c carmine	1.25	.65
R542	R23	10c carmine	.60	.20
R543	R23	20c carmine	1.00	.35
R544	R23	25c carmine	1.50	.35
R545	R23	40c carmine	3.25	1.75
R546	R23	50c carmine	4.00	.20
R547	R23	80c carmine	9.00	4.00
		Nos. R536-R547 (12)	22.25	8.85

Size: 21½x36¼mm

R548	R24	$1 carmine	9.00	.25
R549	R24	$2 carmine	11.00	2.00
R550	R24	$3 carmine	12.50	4.00
R551	R24	$4 carmine	17.50	5.00
R552	R24	$5 carmine	21.00	.80
R553	R24	$10 carmine	47.50	8.50
R554	R24	$20 carmine	95.00	9.00

Size: 28½x42mm
Perf. 12
Without Gum

R555	R25	$30 carmine	70.00	40.00
R556	R25	$50 carmine	65.00	15.00
a.		Vert. pair, imperf. horiz.	—	
R557	R25	$60 carmine	150.00	55.00
R558	R25	$100 carmine	55.00	17.50
R559	R25	$500 carmine	—	100.00
R560	R25	$1000 carmine	—	75.00

Overprinted in Black "Series 1951"

1951   Wmk. 191R   Perf. 11
Size: 19x22mm

R561	R23	1c carmine	.20	.20
R562	R23	2c carmine	.30	.25
R563	R23	3c carmine	.25	.25
R564	R23	4c carmine	.30	.25
R565	R23	5c carmine	.30	.20
R566	R23	8c carmine	1.00	.35
R567	R23	10c carmine	.55	.20
R568	R23	20c carmine	1.25	.45
R569	R23	25c carmine	1.25	.40
R570	R23	40c carmine	3.00	1.25
R571	R23	50c carmine	2.50	.35
R572	R23	80c carmine	7.50	2.50
		Nos. R561-R572 (12)	18.40	6.65

Size: 21½x36¼mm

R573	R24	$1 carmine	9.00	.20
R574	R24	$2 carmine	11.00	.50
R575	R24	$3 carmine	16.00	3.50
R576	R24	$4 carmine	21.00	5.00
R577	R24	$5 carmine	17.50	.60
R578	R24	$10 carmine	42.50	2.25
R579	R24	$20 carmine	90.00	8.50

Size: 28½x42mm
Perf. 12
Without Gum

R580	R25	$30 carmine	70.00	10.00
a.		Imperf., pair	750.00	
R581	R25	$50 carmine	85.00	20.00
R582	R25	$60 carmine	140.00	45.00
R583	R25	$100 carmine	45.00	12.50
R584	R25	$500 carmine	250.00	100.00
R585	R25	$1000 carmine	—	95.00

Overprinted in Black "Series 1952"

Designs: 55c, $1.10, $1.65, $2.20, $2.75, $3.30, L. J. Gage; $2500, William Windom; $5000, C. J. Folger; $10,000, W. Q. Gresham.

1952   Wmk. 191R   Perf. 11
Size: 19x22mm

R586	R23	1c carmine	.20	.20
R587	R23	2c carmine	.35	.25
R588	R23	3c carmine	.30	.25
R589	R23	4c carmine	.30	.25
R590	R23	5c carmine	.25	.20
R591	R23	8c carmine	.65	.45
R592	R23	10c carmine	.40	.20
R593	R23	20c carmine	1.00	.35
R594	R23	25c carmine	1.50	.40
R595	R23	40c carmine	3.00	1.00
R596	R23	50c carmine	2.75	.20
R597	R23	55c carmine	20.00	10.00
R598	R23	80c carmine	12.50	3.00
		Nos. R586-R598 (13)	43.20	16.75

Size: 21½x36¼mm
Perf. 12

R599	R24	$1 carmine	5.00	1.50
R600	R24	$1.10 carmine	42.50	25.00
R601	R24	$1.65 carmine	140.00	45.00
R602	R24	$2 carmine	9.50	.65
R603	R24	$2.20 carmine	115.00	60.00
R604	R24	$2.75 carmine	130.00	60.00
R605	R24	$3 carmine	25.00	4.00
a.		Horiz. pair, imperf. btwn.	600.00	
R606	R24	$3.30 carmine	115.00	60.00
R607	R24	$4 carmine	22.50	4.00
R608	R24	$5 carmine	22.50	1.25
R609	R24	$10 carmine	45.00	1.25
R610	R24	$20 carmine	70.00	9.00

Size: 28½x42mm
Perf. 12
Without Gum

R611	R25	$30 carmine	47.50	18.00
R612	R25	$50 carmine	42.50	12.00
R613	R25	$60 carmine	300.00	50.00
R614	R25	$100 carmine	37.50	8.00
R615	R25	$500 carmine	—	100.00
R616	R25	$1000 carmine	—	30.00
R617	R25	$2500 carmine	—	165.00
R618	R25	$5000 carmine	—	3,000.
R619	R25	$10,000 carmine	—	1,250.

Overprinted in Black "Series 1953"

1953   Wmk. 191R   Perf. 11
Size: 19x22mm

R620	R23	1c carmine	.20	.20
R621	R23	2c carmine	.20	.20
R622	R23	3c carmine	.25	.25
R623	R23	4c carmine	.35	.25
R624	R23	5c carmine	.20	.20
a.		Vert. pair, imperf. horiz.	650.00	
R625	R23	8c carmine	.75	.35
R626	R23	10c carmine	.40	.20
R627	R23	20c carmine	.75	.40
R628	R23	25c carmine	1.00	.50
R629	R23	40c carmine	1.75	1.00
R630	R23	50c carmine	2.50	.20
R631	R23	55c carmine	3.50	2.00
a.		Horiz. pair, imperf. vert.	350.00	
R632	R23	80c carmine	6.00	2.00
		Nos. R620-R632 (13)	17.85	7.70

Size: 21½x36¼mm

R633	R24	$1 carmine	4.00	.25
R634	R24	$1.10 carmine	7.00	2.25
a.		Horiz. pair, imperf. vert.	500.00	
b.		Imperf., pair	550.00	
R635	R24	$1.65 carmine	8.00	4.00
R636	R24	$2 carmine	6.00	.65
R637	R24	$2.20 carmine	12.50	6.00
R638	R24	$2.75 carmine	17.50	7.00
R639	R24	$3 carmine	10.00	3.00
R640	R24	$3.30 carmine	26.00	8.00
R641	R24	$4 carmine	20.00	7.50
R642	R24	$5 carmine	20.00	1.00
R643	R24	$10 carmine	45.00	1.75
R644	R24	$20 carmine	85.00	18.00

Size: 28½x42mm
Perf. 12
Without Gum

R645	R25	$30 carmine	65.00	15.00
R646	R25	$50 carmine	120.00	30.00
R647	R25	$60 carmine	450.00	200.00
R648	R25	$100 carmine	37.50	12.00
R649	R25	$500 carmine	500.00	140.00
R650	R25	$1000 carmine	250.00	65.00
R651	R25	$2500 carmine	1,600.	900.00
R652	R25	$5000 carmine	—	3,500.
R653	R25	$10,000 carmine	—	2,500.

Types of 1940 without Overprint

1954   Wmk. 191R   Perf. 11
Size: 19x22mm

R654	R23	1c carmine	.20	.20
a.		Horiz. pair, imperf. vert.	—	
R655	R23	2c carmine	.20	.20
R656	R23	3c carmine	.20	.20
R657	R23	4c carmine	.20	.20
R658	R23	5c carmine	.20	.20
R659	R23	8c carmine	.25	.20
R660	R23	10c carmine	.25	.20
R661	R23	20c carmine	.50	.30
R662	R23	25c carmine	.60	.35
R663	R23	40c carmine	1.25	.60
R664	R23	50c carmine	1.65	.20
a.		Horiz. pair, imperf. vert	240.00	
R665	R23	55c carmine	1.50	1.25
R666	R23	80c carmine	2.25	1.75
		Nos. R654-R666 (13)	9.25	5.85

Size: 21½x36¼mm

R667	R24	$1 carmine	1.50	.30
R668	R24	$1.10 carmine	3.25	2.50
R669	R24	$1.65 carmine	95.00	65.00
R670	R24	$2 carmine	1.75	.35
R671	R24	$2.20 carmine	4.50	3.75
R672	R24	$2.75 carmine	100.00	60.00
R673	R24	$3 carmine	3.00	2.00
R674	R24	$3.30 carmine	6.50	4.00
R675	R24	$4 carmine	4.00	3.50
R676	R24	$5 carmine	6.00	.45
R677	R24	$10 carmine	12.50	1.25
R678	R24	$20 carmine	32.50	5.75

Overprinted in Black "Series 1954"

Perf. 12
Size: 28½x42mm
Without Gum

R679	R25	$30 carmine	50.00	14.00
R680	R25	$50 carmine	65.00	20.00
R681	R25	$60 carmine	100.00	22.50
R682	R25	$100 carmine	50.00	7.00
R683	R25	$500 carmine	—	75.00
R684	R25	$1000 carmine	300.00	60.00
R685	R25	$2500 carmine	—	210.00
R686	R25	$5000 carmine	—	850.00
R687	R25	$10,000 carmine	—	1,000.

Overprinted in Black "Series 1955"
Without Gum

1955   Wmk. 191R   Perf. 12
Size: 28½x42mm

R688	R25	$30 carmine	65.00	12.50
R689	R25	$50 carmine	65.00	15.00
R690	R25	$60 carmine	110.00	30.00
R691	R25	$100 carmine	55.00	8.00
R692	R25	$500 carmine	—	125.00
R693	R25	$1000 carmine	—	35.00
R694	R25	$2500 carmine	—	140.00
R695	R25	$5000 carmine	1,750.	1,250.
R696	R25	$10,000 carmine	—	1,000.

Overprinted in Black "Series 1956"
Without Gum

1956   Size: 28½x42mm

R697	R25	$30 carmine	85.00	15.00
R698	R25	$50 carmine	90.00	19.00
R699	R25	$60 carmine	110.00	40.00
R700	R25	$100 carmine	85.00	14.00
R701	R25	$500 carmine	—	85.00
R702	R25	$1000 carmine	550.00	65.00
R703	R25	$2500 carmine	—	400.00
R704	R25	$5000 carmine	—	1,600.
R705	R25	$10,000 carmine	—	500.00

Overprinted in Black "Series 1957"
Without Gum

1957   Size: 28½x42mm

R706	R25	$30 carmine	105.00	30.00
R707	R25	$50 carmine	85.00	27.50
R708	R25	$60 carmine	—	175.00
R709	R25	$100 carmine	75.00	15.00
R710	R25	$500 carmine	350.00	100.00
R711	R25	$1000 carmine	—	80.00
R712	R25	$2500 carmine	—	600.00
R713	R25	$5000 carmine	—	1,100.
R714	R25	$10,000 carmine	—	450.00

Overprinted in Black "Series 1958"
Without Gum

1958   Size: 28½x42mm

R715	R25	$30 carmine	80.00	20.00
R716	R25	$50 carmine	65.00	20.00
R717	R25	$60 carmine	110.00	30.00
R718	R25	$100 carmine	50.00	10.00
R719	R25	$500 carmine	250.00	75.00
R720	R25	$1000 carmine	—	67.50
R721	R25	$2500 carmine	—	750.00
R722	R25	$5000 carmine	—	1,750.
R723	R25	$10,000 carmine	—	900.00

Documentary Stamps and Type of 1940 Without Overprint
With Gum

1958   Size: 28½x42mm

R724	R25	$30 carmine	37.50	7.00
a.		Vert. pair, imperf. horiz.		
R725	R25	$50 carmine	42.50	7.00
a.		Vert. pair, imperf. horiz.		
R726	R25	$60 carmine	80.00	20.00
R727	R25	$100 carmine	19.00	4.75
R728	R25	$500 carmine	85.00	25.00
R729	R25	$1000 carmine	55.00	20.00
a.		Vert. pair, imperf. horiz.	750.00	
R730	R25	$2500 carmine	—	160.00
R731	R25	$5000 carmine	—	150.00
R732	R25	$10,000 carmine	—	125.00

Internal Revenue Building, Washington, DC — R26

Giori Press Printing

1962, July 1   Unwmk.   Perf. 11

R733	R26	10c vio bl & brt grn	.80	.35
		Never hinged	1.10	

Centenary of Internal Revenue Service.

"Established 1862" Removed

1963

R734	R26	10c vio bl & brt grn	2.50	.35
		Never hinged	3.50	

Documentary revenue stamps were no longer required after Dec. 31, 1967.

PROPRIETARY STAMPS

Stamps for use on proprietary articles were included in the first general issue of 1862-71. They are Nos. R3, R13-R14, R18, R22, R29, R31, R38.

Washington — RB1

Various Frames and Sizes
Violet or Green Paper with Silk Threads

1871-74   Engr.   *Perf. 12*

a. left column = Violet Paper (1871)
b. right column = Green Paper (1874)

RB1	RB1	1c grn & blk	5.00	10.00
c.		Imperf.	80.00	
d.		Inverted center	3,000.	
RB2	RB1	2c grn & blk	6.00	22.50
c.		Invtd. center, black	40,000.	
d.		Invtd. center, *violet*		8,500.

RB2d is valued with small faults.

RB3	RB1	3c grn & blk	17.50	50.00
c.		Sewing machine perf.	275.00	
d.		Inverted center	16,000.	

No. RB3d is valued with small faults as 6 of the 7 recorded examples have faults.

RB4	RB1	4c grn & blk	10.00	17.50
c.		Inverted center	19,000.	

No. RB4c is valued with small faults as all recorded examples have faults.

RB5	RB1	5c grn & blk	150.00	160.00
c.		Inverted center	130,000.	

No. RB5c is unique. Value represents price realized in 2000 auction sale.

RB6	RB1	6c grn & blk	35.00	110.00
RB7	RB1	10c green & blk ('73)	175.00	55.00
RB8	RB1	50c green & blk ('73)	500.00	900.00
RB9	RB1	$1 green & blk ('73)	1,100.	8,000.
RB10	RB1	$5 green & blk ('73)	7,000.	25,000.

No. RB10b is valued with small faults.

Washington — RB2

Various Frames and Sizes
Green Paper
Wmk. 191R, Unwmkd. (Silk Paper)

1875-81

b. left column = Perf.
c. right column = Rouletted 6

RB11	RB2	1c green	.40	80.00
a.		Silk paper	1.90	
d.		Vert. pair, imperf btwn.		250.00
RB12	RB2	2c brown	1.40	100.00
a.		Silk paper	2.50	
RB13	RB2	3c orange	3.00	100.00
a.		Silk paper	12.50	
d.		Horiz. pair, imperf. btwn.		—
RB14	RB2	4c red brown	5.50	
a.		Silk paper	6.75	
RB15	RB2	4c red	4.50	150.00
RB16	RB2	5c black	90.00	1,500.
a.		Silk paper	110.00	
RB17	RB2	6c violet blue	20.00	260.00
a.		Silk paper	25.00	
RB18	RB2	6c violet	30.00	
RB19	RB2	10c blue ('81)	300.00	

Many fraudulent roulettes exist.

The existence of No. RB18c has been questioned by specialists. The editors would like to see authenticated evidence proving its existence.

Battleship — RB3

Rouletted 5½

1898   Wmk. 191R   Engr.

RB20	RB3	⅛c yel grn	.20	.20
a.		Vert. pair, imperf. horiz.		
RB21	RB3	¼c brown	.20	.20
a.		¼c red brown	.20	
b.		¼c yellow brown	.20	
c.		¼c orange brown	.20	
d.		¼c bister	.20	
e.		Vert. pair, imperf. horiz.	—	
f.		Printed on both sides	—	
RB22	RB3	⅜c dp org	.20	.20
a.		Horiz. pair, imperf. vert.	10.00	
b.		Vert. pair, imperf. horiz.	—	

RB23	RB3	⅝c deep ultra	.20	.20
a.		Vert. pair, imperf. horiz.	75.00	—
b.		Horiz. pair, imperf. btwn.	300.00	
RB24	RB3	1c dark green	2.00	.20
a.		Vert. pair, imperf. horiz.	300.00	
RB25	RB3	1¼c violet	.20	.20
a.		1¼c brown violet	.20	
b.		Vert. pair, imperf. btwn.	—	
RB26	RB3	1⅞c dull blue	11.50	1.50
RB27	RB3	2c vio brown	1.00	.20
a.		Horiz. pair, imperf. vert.	50.00	
RB28	RB3	2½c lake	4.00	.20
a.		Vert. pair, imperf. horiz.	175.00	
RB29	RB3	3¾c olive gray	40.00	10.00
RB30	RB3	4c purple	12.50	1.00
RB31	RB3	5c brown org	12.50	1.00
a.		Vert. pair, imperf. horiz.		300.00
b.		Horiz. pair, imperf. vert.		400.00
		Nos. RB20-RB31 (12)	84.50	15.10

Hyphen Hole Perf. 7

RB20p		⅛c	.20	.20
RB21p		¼c	.20	.20
g.		¼c yellow brown	.20	.20
h.		¼c orange brown	.20	.20
RB22p		⅜c	.25	.25
RB23p		⅝c	.25	.25
RB24p		1c	20.00	12.50
RB25p		1¼c	.20	.20
c.		1¼c brown violet	.25	.20
RB26p		1⅞c	30.00	7.50
RB27p		2c	6.00	.75
RB28p		2½c	5.00	.25
RB29p		3¾c	70.00	20.00
RB30p		4c	60.00	17.50
RB31p		5c	65.00	20.00

See note before No. R161.

   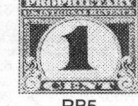

RB4   RB5

Offset Printing

1914   Wmk. 190   Perf. 10

RB32	RB4	⅛c black	.20	.20
RB33	RB4	¼c black	2.00	1.00
RB34	RB4	⅜c black	.20	.20
RB35	RB4	⅝c black	4.50	1.75
RB36	RB4	1¼c black	3.00	.80
RB37	RB4	1⅞c black	40.00	15.00
RB38	RB4	2½c black	9.00	2.50
RB39	RB4	3⅛c black	90.00	50.00
RB40	RB4	3¾c black	40.00	20.00
RB41	RB4	4c black	60.00	27.50
RB42	RB4	4⅜c black	1,100.	
RB43	RB4	5c black	120.00	70.00
		Nos. RB32-RB41,RB43 (11)	368.90	188.95

Wmk. 191R

RB44	RB4	⅛c black	.20	.20
RB45	RB4	¼c black	.20	.20
RB46	RB4	⅜c black	.60	.30
RB47	RB4	½c black	3.00	2.75
RB48	RB4	⅝c black	.20	.20
RB49	RB4	1c black	4.25	4.00
RB50	RB4	1¼c black	.35	.25
RB51	RB4	1½c black	3.00	2.25
RB52	RB4	1⅞c black	1.00	.60
RB53	RB4	2c black	5.00	4.00
RB54	RB4	2½c black	1.25	1.00
RB55	RB4	3c black	4.00	2.75
RB56	RB4	3⅛c black	5.00	3.00
RB57	RB4	3¾c black	11.00	7.50
RB58	RB4	4c black	.30	.20
RB59	RB4	4⅜c black	14.00	8.00
RB60	RB4	5c black	3.00	2.50
RB61	RB4	6c black	55.00	40.00
RB62	RB4	8c black	17.50	11.00
RB63	RB4	10c black	11.00	7.00
RB64	RB4	20c black	22.50	17.50
		Nos. RB44-RB64 (21)	162.35	115.20

1919   Perf. 11

RB65	RB5	1c dark blue	.20	.20
RB66	RB5	2c dark blue	.20	.20
RB67	RB5	3c dark blue	1.00	.60
RB68	RB5	4c dark blue	1.00	.50
RB69	RB5	5c dark blue	1.25	.60
RB70	RB5	8c dark blue	14.00	9.00
RB71	RB5	10c dark blue	5.00	2.00
RB72	RB5	20c dark blue	7.50	3.00
RB73	RB5	40c dark blue	45.00	10.00
		Nos. RB65-RB73 (9)	75.15	26.10

FUTURE DELIVERY STAMPS

Issued to facilitate the collection of a tax upon each sale, agreement of sale or agreement to sell any products or merchandise at any exchange or board of trade, or other similar place for future delivery.

Documentary Stamps Nos. R228-R250 Overprinted in Black or Red

FUTURE

DELIVERY

Offset Printing

1918-34   Wmk. 191R   Perf. 11
Overprint Horizontal
(Lines 8mm apart)

RC1	R22	2c car rose	4.50	.20
RC2	R22	3c car rose	30.00	22.50
		('34)		12.50
		Cut cancellation		
RC3	R22	4c car rose	7.50	.20
RC3A	R22	5c car rose	75.00	5.00
		('33)		
RC4	R22	10c car rose	12.50	.20
a.		Double overprint	—	5.00
b.		"FUTURE" omitted	—	200.00
		"DELIVERY FUTURE"		35.00
RC5	R22	20c car rose	17.50	.20
a.		Double overprint		20.00
RC6	R22	25c car rose	40.00	.40
		Cut cancellation		.20
RC7	R22	40c car rose	45.00	.75
		Cut cancellation		.20
RC8	R22	50c car rose	10.00	.20
a.		"DELIVERY" omitted		100.00
RC9	R22	80c car rose	85.00	10.00
		Cut cancellation		1.00
a.		Double overprint		35.00
b.		Cut cancellation		6.00
		Nos. RC1-RC9 (10)	327.00	39.65

Overprint Vertical, Reading Up
(Lines 2mm apart)
Engr.

RC10	R21	$1 green (R)	35.00	.25
		Cut cancellation		.20
a.		Overprint reading down		275.00
b.		Black overprint	—	
		Cut cancellation		125.00
RC11	R21	$2 rose	40.00	.25
		Cut cancellation		.20
RC12	R21	$3 violet (R)	90.00	2.50
		Cut cancellation		.20
a.		Overprint reading down		50.00
RC13	R21	$5 dk bl (R)	70.00	.35
		Cut cancellation		.20
RC14	R21	$10 orange	90.00	.75
		Cut cancellation		.20
a.		"DELIVERY FUTURE"		100.00
RC15	R21	$20 olive bis	170.00	4.00
		Cut cancellation		.50
		Nos. RC10-RC15 (6)	495.00	8.10

Perf. 12

Overprint Horizontal
(Lines 11½mm apart)
Without Gum

RC16	R17	$30 ver, green numerals	70.00	3.50
a.		Cut cancellation		1.25
		Numerals in blue	60.00	3.50
		Cut cancellation		1.50
b.		As "a," imperf.		100.00
RC17	R19	$50 olive grn	47.50	1.25
		Cut cancellation		.40
a.		$50 olive bister	47.50	1.00
		Cut cancellation		.40
RC18	R19	$60 brown	70.00	2.25
		Cut cancellation		.75
a.		Vert. pair, imperf. horiz.	400.00	
RC19	R17	$100 yel green	110.00	27.50
		('34)		
		Cut cancellation		7.00
RC20	R18	$500 blue, red numerals (R)	80.00	11.00
a.		Cut cancellation		4.50
		Numerals in orange		50.00
		Cut cancellation		11.00
RC21	R19	$1000 orange	95.00	5.50
		Cut cancellation		1.50
a.		Vert. pair, imperf. horiz.		1,000.
		Nos. RC16-RC21 (6)	472.50	51.00

See note after No. R227.

1923-24   Offset Printing   Perf. 11
Overprint Horiz.
(Lines 2mm apart)

RC22	R22	1c carmine rose	1.00	.20
RC23	R22	80c carmine rose	75.00	1.75
		Cut cancellation		.35

FUTURE

Documentary Stamps of 1917 Overprinted in Red or Black

DELIVERY

1925-34   Engr.

RC25	R21	$1 green (R)	35.00	.75
		Cut cancellation		.20
RC26	R21	$10 orange (Bk)	100.00	15.00
		('34)		
		Cut cancellation		10.00

Overprinted like Nos. RC1-RC9

1928-29   Offset Printing   Perf. 10

RC27	R22	10c carmine rose	1,500.	
RC28	R22	20c carmine rose	1,500.	

STOCK TRANSFER STAMPS

Issued to facilitate the collection of a tax on all sales or agreements to sell, or memoranda of sales or delivery of, or transfers of legal title to shares or certificates of stock.

Documentary Stamps Nos. R228-R259 Overprinted in Black or Red

STOCK

TRANSFER

Offset Printing

1918-29   Wmk. 191R   Perf. 11
Overprint Horiz. (Lines 8mm apart)

RD1	R22	1c car rose	.85	.20
a.		Double overprint	—	
RD2	R22	2c car rose	.20	.20
a.		Double overprint		5.00
		Cut cancellation		2.50
RD3	R22	4c car rose	.20	.20
a.		Double overprint		4.00
b.		"STOCK" omitted		2.00
d.		Overprint lines 10mm apart		10.00
RD4	R22	5c car rose	.25	.20
RD5	R22	10c car rose	.25	.20
a.		Double overprint		5.00
b.		"STOCK" omitted		2.50
RD6	R22	20c car rose	.50	.20
a.		Double overprint		6.00
b.		"STOCK" double		—
RD7	R22	25c car rose	1.50	.20
		Cut cancellation		.20
RD8	R22	40c car rose	1.25	.20
		('22)		
RD9	R22	50c car rose	.65	.20
a.		Double overprint		—
RD10	R22	80c car rose	3.00	.30
		Nos. RD1-RD10 (10)	8.65	2.10

Overprint Vertical, Reading Up
(Lines 2mm apart)
Engr.

RD11	R21	$1 green (R)	85.00	20.00
		Cut cancellation		3.00
a.		Ovpt. reading down	125.00	20.00
		Cut cancellation		7.50
RD12	R21	$1 green (Bk)	2.50	.25
a.		Pair, one without ovpt.	—	150.00
b.		Ovptd. on back instead of face, inverted		100.00
c.		Ovpt. reading down	—	6.00
d.		$1 yellow green	2.75	.20
RD13	R21	$2 rose	2.50	.20
a.		Ovpt. reading down		10.00
		Cut cancellation		1.50
b.		Vert. pair, imperf. horiz.	500.00	
RD14	R21	$3 violet (R)	17.50	4.25
RD15	R21	$4 yellow brn	9.00	.20
		Cut cancellation		.20
RD16	R21	$5 dk blue (R)	6.00	.20
		Cut cancellation		.20
a.		Ovpt. reading down	20.00	1.00
		Cut cancellation		.20
RD17	R21	$10 orange	16.00	.30
		Cut cancellation		.20
RD18	R21	$20 ol bis ('21)	75.00	20.00
		Nos. RD11-RD18 (8)	213.50	45.40

1918   Without Gum   Perf. 12
Overprint Horizontal (Lines 11½mm apart)

RD19	R17	$30 ver, green numerals	17.50	4.50
a.		Cut cancellation		1.00
		Numerals in blue		55.00
RD20	R19	$50 olive green, (Cleveland)	110.00	55.00
		Cut cancellation		20.00
RD21	R19	$60 brown	110.00	20.00
		Cut cancellation		9.00
RD22	R17	$100 green	22.50	5.50
		Cut cancellation		2.25
RD23	R18	$500 blue (R)	300.00	125.00
		Cut cancellation		65.00
a.		Numerals in orange		140.00
RD24	R19	$1000 orange	165.00	72.50
		Cut cancellation		25.00

See note after No. R227.

1928-32   Offset Printing   Perf. 10
Overprint Horiz. (Lines 8mm apart)

RD25	R22	2c carmine rose	2.50	.25
RD26	R22	4c carmine rose	2.50	.25
RD27	R22	10c carmine rose	2.00	.25
a.		Inverted overprint		1,000.
RD28	R22	20c carmine rose	3.00	.25
RD29	R22	50c carmine rose	3.50	.25

Overprint Vertical, Reading Up
(Lines 2mm apart)
Engr.

RD30	R21	$1 green	30.00	.20
a.		$1 yellow green		—
RD31	R21	$2 car rose	30.00	.20
a.		Pair, one without ovpt.	200.00	175.00

RD32	R21	$10 orange	32.50	.35
		Cut cancellation		.20
		Nos. RD25-RD32 (8)	106.00	2.00

STOCK

Overprinted Horiz. in Black

TRANSFER

1920-28 Offset Printing Perf. 11

RD33	R22	2c carmine rose	7.50	.70
RD34	R22	10c carmine rose	1.25	.30
b.		Inverted overprint	*1,500.*	
RD35	R22	20c carmine rose	1.00	.20
a.		Horiz. pair, one without overprint	175.00	
d.		Invtd. ovpt. (perf. initials)		—
RD36	R22	50c carmine rose	3.00	.20

Engr.

RD37	R21	$1 green	45.00	8.00
		Cut cancellation		.25
RD38	R21	$2 rose	40.00	8.00
		Cut cancellation		.25
		Nos. RD33-RD38 (6)	97.75	17.40

Shifted overprints on the 10c, 20c and 50c result in "TRANSFER STOCK," "TRANSFER" omitted, "STOCK" omitted, pairs, one without overprint and other varieties.

Perf. 10
Offset Printing

RD39	R22	2c carmine rose	6.50	.70
RD40	R22	10c carmine rose	1.50	.50
RD41	R22	20c carmine rose	2.50	.25
		Nos. RD39-RD41 (3)	10.50	1.25

Used values for Nos. RD42-RD372 are for copies which are neither cut nor perforated with initials. Copies with cut cancellations or perforated initials are valued in the Scott U.S. Specialized Catalogue.

SERIES 1940

Documentary Stamps of 1917-33 Overprinted in Black

STOCK
TRANSFER

1940 Perf. 11

RD42	R22	1c rose pink	3.00	.45
a.		"Series 1940" inverted		— 250.00

No. RD42a always comes with a natural straight edge at left.

RD43	R22	2c rose pink	3.00	.50
RD45	R22	4c rose pink	3.00	.20
RD46	R22	5c rose pink	3.50	.20
RD48	R22	10c rose pink	3.50	.20
RD49	R22	20c rose pink	7.50	.20
RD50	R22	25c rose pink	7.50	.60
RD51	R22	40c rose pink	5.00	.75
RD52	R22	50c rose pink	6.00	.25
RD53	R22	80c rose pink	95.00	50.00
		Nos. RD42-RD53 (10)	137.00	53.35

Engr.

RD54	R21	$1 green	27.50	.35
RD55	R21	$2 rose	27.50	.60
RD56	R21	$3 violet	160.00	10.00
RD57	R21	$4 yel brown	55.00	1.10
RD58	R21	$5 dark blue	55.00	1.10
RD59	R21	$10 orange	120.00	7.00
RD60	R21	$20 olive bister	260.00	75.00
		Nos. RD54-RD60 (7)	705.00	95.15

Stock Transfer Stamps of 1918 Handstamped in Blue "Series 1940"

1940 Without Gum Perf. 12

RD61	R17	$30 vermilion	*900.*	650.00
RD62	R19	$50 olive grn	*900.*	900.00
a.		Dbl. ovpt. (perf. initials canc.)		*500.*
RD63	R19	$60 brown	*2,250.*	2,100.
RD64	R17	$100 green	*750.*	575.
RD65	R18	$500 blue		*2,200.*
RD66	R19	$1000 orange		*2,400.*

Alexander Hamilton ST1

Levi Woodbury ST2

Thomas Corwin — ST3

Portraits (see R23-R25): 2c, Wolcott. 4c, Gallatin. 5c, Campbell. 10c, Crawford. 20c, Rush. 25c, Ingham. 40c, McLane. 50c, Duane. 80c, Taney. $2, Ewing. $3, Forward. $4, Spencer. $5, Bibb. $10, Walker. $20, Meredith. $50, Guthrie. $60, Cobb. $100, Thomas. $500, Dix. $1,000, Chase.

Overprinted in Black **SERIES 1940**

1940 Wmk. 191R Perf. 11
Various Portraits
Size: 19x22mm

RD67	ST1	1c brt green	11.00	3.00
RD68	ST1	2c brt green	7.00	1.60
RD70	ST1	4c brt green	12.50	4.25
RD71	ST1	5c brt green	7.50	1.60
a.		Without overprint (cut canc.)		*250.00*
RD73	ST1	10c brt green	11.00	2.00
RD74	ST1	20c brt green	12.50	2.25
RD75	ST1	25c brt green	35.00	9.00
RD76	ST1	40c brt green	65.00	32.50
RD77	ST1	50c brt green	11.00	2.00
RD78	ST1	80c brt green	85.00	55.00
		Nos. RD67-RD78 (10)	257.50	113.20

Size: 21½x36¼mm

RD79	ST2	$1 brt green	37.50	4.00
a.		Without overprint (perf. initials canc.)		*225.00*
RD80	ST2	$2 brt green	42.50	10.00
RD81	ST2	$3 brt green	65.00	12.50
RD82	ST2	$4 brt green	280.00	210.00
RD83	ST2	$5 brt green	60.00	14.00
RD84	ST2	$10 brt green	145.00	40.00
RD85	ST2	$20 brt green	750.00	80.00

Perf. 12
Without Gum
Size: 28½x42mm
Various Frame Designs

RD86	ST3	$30 brt green	—	150.00
RD87	ST3	$50 brt green	600.00	450.00
RD88	ST3	$60 brt green	—	1,000.
RD89	ST3	$100 brt green	—	300.00
RD90	ST3	$500 brt green	—	1,900.
RD91	ST3	$1000 brt green	—	1,900.

Overprinted in Black "Series 1941" **SERIES 1941**

1941 Size: 19x22mm Perf. 11

RD92	ST1	1c brt green	.65	.50
RD93	ST1	2c brt green	.45	.25
RD95	ST1	4c brt green	.45	.20
RD96	ST1	5c brt green	.35	.20
RD98	ST1	10c brt green	.75	.20
RD99	ST1	20c brt green	1.75	.25
RD100	ST1	25c brt green	1.75	.40
RD101	ST1	40c brt green	2.50	.75
RD102	ST1	50c brt green	3.75	.35
RD103	ST1	80c brt green	22.50	7.50
		Nos. RD92-RD103 (10)	34.90	10.60

Size: 21½x36¼mm

RD104	ST2	$1 brt green	15.00	.20
RD105	ST2	$2 brt green	16.00	.25
RD106	ST2	$3 brt green	24.00	1.50
RD107	ST2	$4 brt green	42.50	6.50
RD108	ST2	$5 brt green	42.50	6.00
RD109	ST2	$10 brt green	90.00	4.00
RD110	ST2	$20 brt green	250.00	65.00
		Nos. RD104-RD110 (7)	480.00	78.05

Perf. 12
Without Gum
Size: 28½x42mm

RD111	ST3	$30 brt green	225.00	225.00
RD112	ST3	$50 brt green	550.00	400.00
RD113	ST3	$60 brt green	1,000.	325.00
RD114	ST3	$100 brt green	—	150.00
RD115	ST3	$500 brt green	1,500.	1,500.
RD116	ST3	$1000 brt green	—	1,100.

Overprinted in Black "Series 1942"

1942 Size: 19x22mm Perf. 11

RD117	ST1	1c brt green	.50	.30
RD118	ST1	2c brt green	.40	.35
RD119	ST1	4c brt green	3.00	1.00
RD120	ST1	5c brt green	.40	.20
a.		Ovpt. invtd. (cut cancel)		*225.00*
RD121	ST1	10c brt green	1.75	.20
RD122	ST1	20c brt green	2.00	.20
RD123	ST1	25c brt green	2.00	.20
RD124	ST1	40c brt green	4.25	.35

RD125	ST1	50c brt green	5.25	.20
RD126	ST1	80c brt green	22.50	5.75
		Nos. RD117-RD126 (10)	42.05	8.75

Size: 21½x36¼mm

RD127	ST2	$1 brt green	14.00	.35
RD128	ST2	$2 brt green	20.00	.35
RD129	ST2	$3 brt green	27.50	1.00
RD130	ST2	$4 brt green	42.50	20.00
RD131	ST2	$5 brt green	37.50	.35
a.		Dbl. ovpt. (perf. initials cancel)		—
RD132	ST2	$10 brt green	70.00	8.00
RD133	ST2	$20 brt green	160.00	35.00
		Nos. RD127-RD133 (7)	371.50	65.05

Perf. 12
Without Gum
Size: 28½x42mm

RD134	ST3	$30 brt green	200.00	60.00
RD135	ST3	$50 brt green	350.00	125.00
RD136	ST3	$60 brt green	400.00	190.00
RD137	ST3	$100 brt green	*500.00*	80.00
RD138	ST3	$500 brt green	—	9,500.
RD139	ST3	$1000 brt green	—	550.00

Overprinted in Black "Series 1943"

1943 Size: 19x22mm Perf. 11

RD140	ST1	1c brt green	.40	.25
RD141	ST1	2c brt green	.50	.40
RD142	ST1	4c brt green	1.75	.20
RD143	ST1	5c brt green	.50	.20
RD144	ST1	10c brt green	1.00	.20
RD145	ST1	20c brt green	1.75	.20
RD146	ST1	25c brt green	3.75	.25
RD147	ST1	40c brt green	3.75	.25
RD148	ST1	50c brt green	3.75	.20
RD149	ST1	80c brt green	15.00	4.50
		Nos. RD140-RD149 (10)	32.15	6.65

Size: 21½x36¼mm

RD150	ST2	$1 brt green	15.00	.20
RD151	ST2	$2 brt green	17.50	.35
RD152	ST2	$3 brt green	21.00	1.00
RD153	ST2	$4 brt green	42.50	15.00
RD154	ST2	$5 brt green	60.00	.35
RD155	ST2	$10 brt green	85.00	4.50
RD156	ST2	$20 brt green	150.00	37.50
		Nos. RD150-RD156 (7)	391.00	58.90

Perf. 12
Without Gum
Size: 28½x42mm

RD157	ST3	$30 brt green	325.00	140.00
RD158	ST3	$50 brt green	650.00	140.00
RD159	ST3	$60 brt green	—	700.00
RD160	ST3	$100 brt green	110.00	60.00
RD161	ST3	$500 brt green	—	800.00
RD162	ST3	$1000 brt green	—	250.00

Overprinted in Black "Series 1944"

Portraits: $2,500, William Windom. $5,000, C. J. Folger. $10,000, Walter Q. Gresham.

1944 Wmk. 191R Perf. 11
Size: 19x22mm

RD163	ST1	1c brt green	.65	.60
RD164	ST1	2c brt green	.45	.20
RD165	ST1	4c brt green	.60	.25
RD166	ST1	5c brt green	.50	.20
RD167	ST1	10c brt green	.75	.20
RD168	ST1	20c brt green	1.25	.20
RD169	ST1	25c brt green	2.00	.30
RD170	ST1	40c brt green	8.00	5.00
RD171	ST1	50c brt green	4.50	.20
RD172	ST1	80c brt green	9.00	4.50
		Nos. RD163-RD172 (10)	27.70	11.65

Size: 21½x36¼mm

RD173	ST2	$1 brt green	10.00	.40
RD174	ST2	$2 brt green	37.50	.50
RD175	ST2	$3 brt green	35.00	1.25
RD176	ST2	$4 brt green	40.00	5.00
RD177	ST2	$5 brt green	37.50	.90
RD178	ST2	$10 brt green	75.00	4.50
RD179	ST2	$20 brt green	125.00	9.00
		Nos. RD173-RD179 (7)	360.00	21.65

Perf. 12
Without Gum
Size: 28½x42mm
Bright Green

RD180	ST3	$30	200.00	75.00
RD181	ST3	$50	140.00	60.00
RD182	ST3	$60	240.00	140.00
RD183	ST3	$100	200.00	60.00
RD184	ST3	$500	—	500.00
RD185	ST3	$1000	—	800.00
RD185A	ST3	$2500	—	—
RD185B	ST3	$5000	—	—
RD185C	ST3	$10,000		
		(cut cancel)		*1,500.*

Overprinted in Black "Series 1945"

1945 Wmk. 191R Perf. 11
Size: 19x22mm

RD186	ST1	1c brt green	.20	.20
RD187	ST1	2c brt green	.25	.20
RD188	ST1	4c brt green	.25	.20
RD189	ST1	5c brt green	.25	.20
RD190	ST1	10c brt green	.75	.35
RD191	ST1	20c brt green	1.25	.30

RD192	ST1	25c brt green	2.00	.35
RD193	ST1	40c brt green	3.00	.20
RD194	ST1	50c brt green	3.50	.25
RD195	ST1	80c brt green	7.50	3.00
		Nos. RD186-RD195 (10)	18.95	5.25

Size: 21½x36¼mm

RD196	ST2	$1 brt green	16.00	.25
RD197	ST2	$2 brt green	21.00	.45
RD198	ST2	$3 brt green	37.50	.80
RD199	ST2	$4 brt green	37.50	2.50
RD200	ST2	$5 brt green	24.00	.50
RD201	ST2	$10 brt green	55.00	6.50
RD202	ST2	$20 brt green	125.00	12.50

Perf. 12
Without Gum
Size: 28½x42mm
Bright green

RD203	ST3	$30	140.00	70.00
RD204	ST3	$50	65.00	25.00
RD205	ST3	$60	240.00	150.00
RD206	ST3	$100	85.00	40.00
RD207	ST3	$500	—	900.00
RD208	ST3	$1000	1,500.	900.00
RD208A	ST3	$2500		
		(cut cancel)		20,000.
RD208B	ST3	$5000	—	—
RD208C	ST3	$10,000		
		(cut cancel)		7,000.

Overprinted in Black "Series 1946"

1946 Wmk. 191R Perf. 11
Size: 19x22mm

RD209	ST1	1c brt green	.20	.20
a.		Pair, one dated "1945"	475.00	
RD210	ST1	2c brt green	.35	.20
RD211	ST1	4c brt green	.30	.20
RD212	ST1	5c brt green	.35	.20
RD213	ST1	10c brt green	.75	.20
RD214	ST1	20c brt green	1.50	.20
RD215	ST1	25c brt green	1.50	.25
RD216	ST1	40c brt green	3.50	.60
RD217	ST1	50c brt green	4.50	.20
RD218	ST1	80c brt green	11.00	6.00
		Nos. RD209-RD218 (10)	23.95	8.25

Size: 21½x36¼mm

RD219	ST2	$1 brt green	10.00	.50
RD220	ST2	$2 brt green	11.00	.50
RD221	ST2	$3 brt green	21.00	1.25
RD222	ST2	$4 brt green	21.00	6.25
RD223	ST2	$5 brt green	32.50	1.10
RD224	ST2	$10 brt green	60.00	2.60
RD225	ST2	$20 brt green	150.00	45.00
		Nos. RD219-RD225 (7)	305.50	57.20

Perf. 12
Without Gum
Size: 28½x42mm

RD226	ST3	$30 brt grn	115.00	42.50
RD227	ST3	$50 brt grn	90.00	47.50
RD228	ST3	$60 brt grn	210.00	100.00
RD229	ST3	$100 brt grn	125.00	55.00
RD230	ST3	$500 brt grn	—	180.00
RD231	ST3	$1000 brt grn	—	200.00
RD232	ST3	$2500 brt grn	—	—
		(cut cancel)		12,500.
RD233	ST3	$5000 brt grn	—	
		(cut cancel)		7,000.
RD234	ST3	$10,000 brt grn	—	
		(cut cancel)		2,000.

Overprinted in Black "Series 1947"

1947 Wmk. 191R Perf. 11
Size: 19x22mm

RD235	ST1	1c brt green	.65	.55
RD236	ST1	2c brt green	.60	.50
RD237	ST1	4c brt green	.50	.40
RD238	ST1	5c brt green	.45	.35
RD239	ST1	10c brt green	.60	.50
RD240	ST1	20c brt green	1.10	.50
RD241	ST1	25c brt green	1.75	.50
RD242	ST1	40c brt green	3.00	.75
RD243	ST1	50c brt green	4.00	.30
RD244	ST1	80c brt green	17.50	10.00
		Nos. RD235-RD244 (10)	30.15	14.35

Size: 21½x36¼mm

RD245	ST2	$1 brt green	10.00	.50
RD246	ST2	$2 brt green	16.00	.75
RD247	ST2	$3 brt green	25.00	1.50
RD248	ST2	$4 brt green	40.00	6.00
RD249	ST2	$5 brt green	35.00	1.50
RD250	ST2	$10 brt green	55.00	5.00
RD251	ST2	$20 brt green	100.00	30.00
		Nos. RD245-RD251 (7)	281.00	45.25

Perf. 12
Without Gum
Size: 28½x42mm

RD252	ST3	$30 brt grn	100.00	50.00
RD253	ST3	$50 brt grn	200.00	110.00
RD254	ST3	$60 brt grn	300.00	150.00
RD255	ST3	$100 brt grn	110.00	40.00
RD256	ST3	$500 brt grn	—	400.00
RD257	ST3	$1000 brt grn	—	100.00
RD258	ST3	$2500 brt grn	—	
		(cut cancel)		400.00
RD259	ST3	$5000 brt grn	—	
		(cut cancel)		300.00
RD260	ST3	$10,000 brt grn	—	
		(cut cancel)		55.00
a.		Horiz. pair, imperf. vert. (cut canc.)		—

Overprinted in Black "Series 1948"

1948		Wmk. 191R	Perf. 11

Size: 19x22mm

RD261 ST1	1c brt green	.25	.25
RD262 ST1	2c brt green	.25	.25
RD263 ST1	4c brt green	.30	.30
RD264 ST1	5c brt green	.25	.25
RD265 ST1	10c brt green	.30	.25
RD266 ST1	20c brt green	1.40	.35
RD267 ST1	25c brt green	1.40	.40
RD268 ST1	40c brt green	1.75	.75
RD269 ST1	50c brt green	4.25	.30
RD270 ST1	80c brt green	14.00	6.00
Nos. RD261-RD270 (10)		24.15	9.10

Size: 21½x36¼mm

RD271 ST2	$1 brt green	10.00	.40
RD272 ST2	$2 brt green	17.50	.60
RD273 ST2	$3 brt green	18.00	3.75
RD274 ST2	$4 brt green	21.00	11.00
RD275 ST2	$5 brt green	32.50	2.50
RD276 ST2	$10 brt green	55.00	4.50
RD277 ST2	$20 brt green	95.00	18.00
Nos. RD271-RD277 (7)		249.00	40.75

Perf. 12
Without Gum
Size: 28½x42mm

RD278 ST3	$30 brt grn	150.00	60.00
RD279 ST3	$50 brt grn	100.00	60.00
RD280 ST3	$60 brt grn	250.00	140.00
RD281 ST3	$100 brt grn	85.00	22.50
RD282 ST3	$500 brt grn	—	240.00
RD283 ST3	$1000 brt grn	—	120.00
RD284 ST3	$2500 brt grn	600.00	350.00
RD285 ST3	$5000 brt grn	—	275.00
RD286 ST3	$10,000 brt grn		
	(cut cancel)		55.00

Overprinted in Black "Series 1949"

1949		Wmk. 191R	Perf. 11

Size: 19x22mm

RD287 ST1	1c brt green	.50	.45
RD288 ST1	2c brt green	.50	.45
RD289 ST1	4c brt green	.60	.50
RD290 ST1	5c brt green	.60	.50
RD291 ST1	10c brt green	1.30	.60
RD292 ST1	20c brt green	2.10	.50
RD293 ST1	25c brt green	3.00	.85
RD294 ST1	40c brt green	5.50	1.50
RD295 ST1	50c brt green	5.00	.25
RD296 ST1	80c brt green	14.00	6.50
Nos. RD287-RD296 (10)		33.10	12.10

Size: 21½x36¼mm

RD297 ST2	$1 brt green	12.50	.75
RD298 ST2	$2 brt green	18.00	.90
RD299 ST2	$3 brt green	40.00	4.50
RD300 ST2	$4 brt green	37.50	7.50
RD301 ST2	$5 brt green	47.50	2.00
RD302 ST2	$10 brt green	65.00	4.00
RD303 ST2	$20 brt green	140.00	15.00
Nos. RD297-RD303 (7)		360.50	34.65

Perf. 12
Without Gum
Size: 28½x42mm

RD304 ST3	$30 brt grn	150.00	85.00
RD305 ST3	$50 brt grn	225.00	110.00
RD306 ST3	$60 brt grn	375.00	225.00
RD307 ST3	$100 brt grn	150.00	70.00
RD308 ST3	$500 brt grn	—	250.00
RD309 ST3	$1000 brt grn	—	100.00
RD310 ST3	$2500 brt grn	—	
	(cut cancel)		450.00
RD311 ST3	$5000 brt grn		
	(cut cancel)		400.00
RD312 ST3	$10,000 brt grn	—	400.00
a.	Pair, one without ovpt.		
	(cut cancel)		4,500.

No. RD312a is unique.

Overprinted in Black "Series 1950"

1950		Wmk. 191R	Perf. 11

Size: 19x22mm

RD313 ST1	1c brt green	.40	.35
RD314 ST1	2c brt green	.40	.30
RD315 ST1	4c brt green	.40	.35
RD316 ST1	5c brt green	.40	.20
RD317 ST1	10c brt green	2.00	.30
RD318 ST1	20c brt green	3.00	.50
RD319 ST1	25c brt green	4.25	.60
RD320 ST1	40c brt green	5.00	.90
RD321 ST1	50c brt green	8.25	.35
RD322 ST1	80c brt green	12.50	5.00
Nos. RD313-RD322 (10)		36.60	8.85

Size: 21½x36¼mm

RD323 ST2	$1 brt green	12.50	.40
RD324 ST2	$2 brt green	22.50	.75
RD325 ST2	$3 brt green	35.00	4.00
RD326 ST2	$4 brt green	42.50	9.00
RD327 ST2	$5 brt green	42.50	1.75
RD328 ST2	$10 brt green	125.00	5.00
RD329 ST2	$20 brt green	140.00	25.00
Nos. RD323-RD329 (7)		420.00	45.90

Perf. 12
Without Gum
Size: 28½x42mm

RD330 ST3	$30 brt grn	140.00	70.00
RD331 ST3	$50 brt grn	160.00	90.00
RD332 ST3	$60 brt grn	250.00	140.00

RD333 ST3	$100 brt grn	100.00	45.00
a.	Vert. pair, imperf btwn.		1,500.
RD334 ST3	$500 brt grn	—	250.00
RD335 ST3	$1000 brt grn	—	85.00
RD336 ST3	$2500 brt grn	—	1,100.
RD337 ST3	$5000 brt grn	—	725.00
RD338 ST3	$10,000 brt grn	—	800.00

Overprinted in Black "Series 1951"

1951		Wmk. 191R	Perf. 11

Size: 19x22mm

RD339 ST1	1c brt green	1.10	.35
RD340 ST1	2c brt green	1.10	.30
RD341 ST1	4c brt green	1.50	.50
RD342 ST1	5c brt green	1.10	.35
RD343 ST1	10c brt green	1.50	.30
RD344 ST1	20c brt green	3.75	.90
RD345 ST1	25c brt green	5.00	.90
RD346 ST1	40c brt green	15.00	9.00
RD347 ST1	50c brt green	10.00	.90
RD348 ST1	80c brt green	18.00	10.00
Nos. RD339-RD348 (10)		58.05	23.50

Size: 21½x36¼mm

RD349 ST2	$1 brt green	21.00	.80
RD350 ST2	$2 brt green	32.50	1.25
RD351 ST2	$3 brt green	42.50	10.00
RD352 ST2	$4 brt green	50.00	12.00
RD353 ST2	$5 brt green	60.00	2.50
RD354 ST2	$10 brt green	95.00	8.50
RD355 ST2	$20 brt green	160.00	17.50
Nos. RD349-RD355 (7)		461.00	52.55

Perf. 12
Without Gum
Size: 28½x42mm

RD356 ST3	$30 brt grn	160.00	75.00
RD357 ST3	$50 brt grn	150.00	65.00
RD358 ST3	$60 brt grn	—	1,400.
RD359 ST3	$100 brt grn	150.00	65.00
RD360 ST3	$500 brt grn	—	350.00
RD361 ST3	$1000 brt grn	—	85.00
RD362 ST3	$2500 brt grn	—	2,500.
RD363 ST3	$5000 brt grn	—	1,400.
RD364 ST3	$10,000 brt grn	1,500.	150.00

Overprinted in Black "Series 1952"

1952		Wmk. 191R	Perf. 11

Size: 19x22mm

RD365 ST1	1c brt green	35.00	17.50
RD366 ST1	10c brt green	35.00	17.50
RD367 ST1	20c brt green	400.00	—
RD368 ST1	25c brt green	500.00	—
RD369 ST1	40c brt green	100.00	40.00

Size: 21½x36¼mm

RD370 ST2	$4 brt green	1,250.	550.
RD371 ST2	$10 brt green	2,500.	—
RD372 ST2	$20 brt green	5,750.	—

Stock Transfer stamps were discontinued in 1952.

See the *Scott United States Specialized Catalogue* for other categories of Revenue stamps.

HUNTING PERMIT STAMPS

The receipts of the sales of these "Migratory Bird Hunting" stamps help to maintain waterfowl life in the United States.

Unused values are for stamps with never-hinged original gum.

Minor natural gum skips and bends are normal on Nos. RW1-RW20.

No gum stamps are without signature or other cancel.

Beginning with No. RW2, the used value is for stamps with manuscript signature.

Used Values

Used value for No. RW1 is for stamp with handstamp or manuscript cancel, though technically it was illegal to deface the stamp.

Beginning with No. RW2, the used value is for stamps with manuscript signature.

> **Catalogue values for unused stamps in this section are for Never Hinged items.**

Department of Agriculture
Various Designs Inscribed
"U. S. Department of Agriculture"

HP1

Engraved; Flat Plate Printing

1934		Unwmk.	Perf. 11

"Void after June 30, 1935"

RW1 HP1	$1 blue	750.00	125.00
	Hinged	350.00	
	No gum	160.00	
a.	Imperf., pair	—	
b.	Vert. pair, imperf. horiz.	—	

1935		**"Void after June 30, 1936"**	
RW2	$1 Canvasback Ducks Taking to Flight	675.00	140.00
	Hinged	375.00	
	No gum	190.00	

1936		**"Void after June 30, 1937"**	
RW3	$1 Canada Geese in Flight	325.00	75.00
	Hinged	175.00	
	No gum	110.00	

1937		**"Void after June 30, 1938"**	
RW4	$1 Scaup Ducks Taking to Flight	275.00	57.50
	Hinged	150.00	
	No gum	75.00	

1938		**"Void after June 30, 1939"**	
RW5	$1 Pintail Drake and Duck Alighting	400.00	57.50
	Hinged	190.00	
	No gum	75.00	

Department of the Interior
Various Designs Inscribed
"U. S. Department of the Interior"

Green-Winged Teal — HP2

1939		**"Void after June 30, 1940"**	
RW6 HP2	$1 chocolate	225.00	45.00
	Hinged	110.00	
	No gum	50.00	

1940		**"Void after June 30, 1941"**	
RW7	$1 Black Mallards	200.00	45.00
	Hinged	110.00	
	No gum	50.00	

1941		**"Void after June 30, 1942"**	
RW8	$1 Family of Ruddy Ducks	200.00	45.00
	Hinged	110.00	
	No gum	50.00	

1942		**"Void after June 30, 1943"**	
RW9	$1 Baldpates	225.00	45.00
	Hinged	110.00	
	No gum	50.00	

1943		**"Void after June 30, 1944"**	
RW10	$1 Wood Ducks	75.00	32.50
	Hinged	50.00	
	No gum	42.50	

1944		**"Void after June 30, 1945"**	
RW11	$1 White-fronted Geese	87.50	25.00
	Hinged	50.00	
	No gum	32.50	

1945		**"Void after June 30, 1946"**	
RW12	$1 Shoveller Ducks in Flight	60.00	25.00
	Hinged	35.00	
	No gum	27.50	

1946		**"Void after June 30, 1947"**	
RW13	$1 Redhead Ducks	45.00	16.00
	No gum	18.00	
a.	$1 bright rose pink	—	

1947		**"Void after June 30, 1948"**	
RW14	$1 Snow Geese	45.00	16.00
	No gum	18.00	

1948		**"Void after June 30, 1949"**	
RW15	$1 Bufflehead Ducks in Flight	50.00	15.00
	No gum	21.00	

Goldeneye Ducks — HP3

1949		**"Void after June 30, 1950"**	
RW16 HP3	$2 bright green	60.00	14.00
	No gum	22.50	

1950		**"Void after June 30, 1951"**	
RW17	$2 Trumpeter Swans in Flight	75.00	11.00
	No gum	22.50	

1951		**"Void after June 30, 1952"**	
RW18	$2 Gadwall Ducks	75.00	11.00
	No gum	22.50	

1952		**"Void after June 30, 1953"**	
RW19	$2 Harlequin Ducks	75.00	11.00
	No gum	22.50	

1953		**"Void after June 30, 1954"**	
RW20	$2 Blue-winged Teal	75.00	11.00
	No gum	22.50	

1954		**"Void after June 30, 1955"**	
RW21	$2 Ring-necked Ducks	75.00	10.50
	No gum	22.50	

1955		**"Void after June 30, 1956"**	
RW22	$2 Blue Geese	75.00	10.50
	No gum	22.50	
a.	Back inscription inverted	—	

1956		**"Void after June 30, 1957"**	
RW23	$2 American Merganser	75.00	10.50
	No gum	22.50	

1957		**"Void after June 30, 1958"**	
RW24	$2 American Eiders	75.00	10.50
	No gum	22.50	
a.	Back inscription inverted	—	

1958		**"Void after June 30, 1959"**	
RW25	$2 Canada Geese	75.00	10.50
	No gum	22.50	

Labrador Retriever Carrying Mallard Drake — HP4

1959		**Giori Press Printing "Void after June 30, 1960"**	
RW26 HP4	$3 blue, ocher & blk	100.00	11.00
	No gum	35.00	
a.	Back inscription inverted	—	

Redhead Ducks — HP5

1960		**"Void after June 30, 1961"**	
RW27 HP5	$3 red brn, dk bl & bister	85.00	10.50
	No gum	35.00	

1961	"Void after June 30, 1962"		
RW28	$3 Mallard Hen & Ducklings	85.00	10.50
	No gum	37.50	

Pintail Drakes — HP6

1962	"Void after June 30, 1963"		
RW29	HP6 $3 Coming in for Landing	95.00	10.50
	No gum	55.00	
a.	Back inscription omitted	—	

1963	"Void after June 30, 1964"		
RW30	$3 Pair of Brant landing	100.00	10.50
	No gum	55.00	

1964	"Void after June 30, 1965"		
RW31	$3 Hawaiian Nene Geese	95.00	10.50
	No gum	55.00	

1965	"Void after June 30, 1966"		
RW32	$3 3 Canvasback Drakes	95.00	10.50
	No gum	55.00	

Whistling Swans — HP7

1966	"Void after June 30, 1967"		
RW33	HP7 $3 ultra, sl grn & blk	95.00	10.50
	No gum	55.00	

1967	"Void after June 30, 1968"		
RW34	$3 Old Squaw Ducks	100.00	10.00
	No gum	55.00	

1968	"Void after June 30, 1969"		
RW35	$3 Hooded Mergansers	57.50	10.00
	No gum	25.00	

White-winged Scoters — HP8

1969	"Void after June 30, 1970"		
RW36	HP8 $3 gray, brn, indigo & brn red	60.00	7.00
	No gum	25.00	

1970	Litho. & Engr.		
	"Void after June 30, 1971"		
RW37	$3 Ross' Geese	65.00	7.00
	No gum	24.00	

1971	"Void after June 30, 1972"		
RW38	$3 3 Cinnamon Teal	40.00	7.75
	No gum	21.00	

1972	"Void after June 30, 1973"		
RW39	$5 Emperor Geese	25.00	7.00
	No gum	12.50	

1973	"Void after June 30, 1974"		
RW40	$5 Steller's Eiders	20.00	7.00
	No gum	11.50	

1974	"Void after June 30, 1975"		
RW41	$5 Wood Ducks	18.00	6.00
	No gum	9.50	

1975	"Void after June 30, 1976"		
RW42	$5 Weathered canvasback duck decoy & flying ducks	15.00	6.00
	No gum	8.00	

1976	Engr.		
	"Void after June 30, 1977"		
RW43	$5 Family of Canada Geese	15.00	6.00
	No gum	7.50	

1977	Engr. & Litho.		
	"Void after June 30, 1978"		
RW44	$5 Ross' Geese, pair	15.00	6.00
	No gum	7.50	

Hooded Merganser — HP9

1978	"Void after June 30, 1979"		
RW45	HP9 $5 multicolored	12.50	6.00
	No gum	7.00	

1979	"Void after June 30, 1980"		
RW46	$7.50 Green-winged teal	14.00	7.00
	No gum	8.50	

1980	"Void after June 30, 1981"		
RW47	$7.50 Mallards	14.00	7.00
	No gum	8.50	

1981	"Void after June 30, 1982"		
RW48	$7.50 Ruddy Ducks	14.00	7.00
	No gum	8.50	

1982	"Void after June 30, 1983"		
RW49	$7.50 Canvasbacks	15.00	7.00
	No gum	8.50	
a.	Orange & violet omitted		

1983	"Void after June 30, 1984"		
RW50	$7.50 Pintails	15.00	7.00
	No gum	8.50	

1984	"Void after June 30, 1985"		
RW51	$7.50 Widgeons	15.00	7.00
	No gum	8.50	

1985	"Void after June 30, 1986"		
RW52	$7.50 Cinnamon Teal	15.00	7.00
	No gum	8.50	

1986	"Void after June 30, 1987"		
RW53	$7.50 Fulvous Whistling Duck	15.00	7.00
	No gum	8.50	
a.	Black omitted	3,750.	

1987	Perf. 11½x11		
	"Void after June 30, 1988"		
RW54	$10 Redheads	17.50	9.50
	No gum	10.00	

1988	"Void after June 30, 1989"		
RW55	$10 Snow Goose	15.00	10.00
	No gum	11.00	

1989	"Void after June 30, 1990"		
RW56	$12.50 Lesser Scaups	19.00	10.00
	No gum	12.00	

1990	"Void after June 30, 1991"		
RW57	$12.50 Black Bellied Whistling Duck	19.00	10.00
	No gum	12.00	
a.	Back inscription omitted	425.00	

The back inscription is on top of the gum so beware of copies with gum removed. Used examples of No. RW57a cannot exist.

King Eiders — HP10

1991	"Void after June 30, 1992"		
RW58	HP10 $15 multicolored	22.50	11.00
	No gum	15.00	
a.	Black (engr.) omitted	8,500.	

1992	"Void after June 30, 1993"		
RW59	$15 Spectacled Eider	24.00	12.50
	No gum	15.00	

1993	"Void after June 30, 1994"		
RW60	$15 Canvasbacks	22.50	11.00
	No gum	15.00	
a.	Black (engr.) omitted	3,250.	

1994	"Void after June 30, 1995"		
RW61	$15 Red-breasted mergansers	24.00	11.00
	No gum	15.00	

1995	"Void after June 30, 1996"		
RW62	$15 Mallards	24.00	11.00
	No gum	15.00	

1996   "Void after June 30, 1997"
RW63 $15 Surf Scoters   22.50 11.00
      No gum   15.00

1997   "Void after June 30, 1998"
RW64 $15 Canada Goose   22.50 11.00
      No gum   15.00

Nos. RW65 and later issues were sold in panes of 30 (RW65 and RW66) or 20 (RW67 and later issues). The self-adhesives starting with No. RW65A were sold in panes of 1. The self-adhesives are valued unused as complete panes and used as single stamps.

1998   "Void after June 30, 1999"
RW65 $15 Barrow's
          Goldeneye   22.50 11.00
      No gum   15.00

Self-Adhesive
Serpentine Die Cut
RW65A $15 Barrow's
          Goldeneye   22.50 12.50

1999   "Void after June 30, 2000"
RW66 $15 Greater Scaup   22.50 11.00
      No gum   15.00

Self-Adhesive
Die Cut 10
RW66A $15 Greater Scaup   22.50 12.50

2000   Perf. 11¼
"Void after June 30, 2001"
RW67 $15 Mottled Duck   22.50 11.00
      No gum   15.00

Self-Adhesive
Die Cut 10
RW67A $15 Mottled Duck   22.50 11.00

2001   Perf. 11¼
"Void after June 30, 2002"
RW68 $15 Northern pintail 22.50 11.00
      No gum   15.00

Self-Adhesive
Die Cut 10
RW68A $15 Northern pintail 22.50 11.00

CONFEDERATE STATES

3c 1861 POSTMASTERS' PROVISIONALS

With the secession of South Carolina from the Union on Dec. 20, 1860, a new era began in U.S. history as well as its postal history. Other Southern states quickly followed South Carolina's lead, which in turn led to the formation of the provisional government of the Confederate States of America on Feb. 4, 1861.

President Jefferson Davis' cabinet was completed Mar. 6, 1861, with the acceptance of the position of Postmaster General by John H. Reagan of Texas. The provisional government had already passed regulations that required payment for postage in cash and that effectively carried over the U.S. 3c rate until the new Confederate Post Office Department took over control of the system.

Soon after entering on his duties, Reagan directed the postmasters in the Confederate States and in the newly seceded states to "continue the performance of their duties as such, and render all accounts and pay all moneys (sic) to the order of the Government of the U.S. as they have heretofore done, until the Government of the Confederate States shall be prepared to assume control of its postal affairs."

As coinage was becoming scarce, postal patrons began having problems buying individual stamps or paying for letters individually, especially as stamp stocks started to run short in certain areas. Even though the U.S. Post Office Department was technically in control of the postal system and southern postmasters were operating under Federal authority, the U.S.P.O. was hesitant in re-supplying seceded states with additional stamps and stamped envelopes.

The U.S. government had made the issuance of postmasters' provisionals illegal many years before, but the southern postmasters had to do what they felt was necessary to allow patrons to pay for postage and make the system work. Therefore, a few postmasters took it upon themselves to issue provisional stamps in the 3c rate then in effect.

Interestingly, these were stamps and envelopes that the U.S. government did not recognize as legal, but they did do postal duty unchallenged in the Confederate States. Yet the proceeds were to be remitted to the U.S. government in Washington! Six authenticated postmasters' provisionals in the 3c rate have been recorded.

On May 13, 1861, Postmaster General Reagan issued his proclamation "assuming control and direction of postal service within the limits of the Confederate States of America on and after the first day of June," with new postage rates and regulations.

The Federal government suspended operations in the Confederate States (except for western Virginia and the seceding state of Tennessee) by a proclamation issued by Postmaster General Montgomery Blair on May 27, 1861, effective from May 31, 1861, and June 10 for western and middle Tennessee.

As Tennessee did not join the Confederacy until July 2, 1861, the unissued 3c Nashville provisional was produced in a state that was in the process of seceding, while the other provisionals were used in the Confederacy before the June 1 assumption of control of postal service by the Confederate States of America.

Illustrations are reduced in size.
XU numbers are envelope entires.

HILLSBORO, N.C.

A1

Handstamped Adhesive
1AX1 A1 3c bluish blk, on cover

This is the same handstamp used for No. 39X1. 3c usage is determined from the May 27, 1861 circular date stamp.
No. 1AX1 is unique.
See Nos. 39X1, 39XU1.

JACKSON, MISS.

E1

Handstamped Envelope
2AXU1 E1 3c black   1,000.
See Nos. 43XU1-43XU4.

MADISON COURT HOUSE, FLA.

A1

"CNETS"

Typeset Adhesive
3AX1 A1 3c gold   —   10,000.
   a. "CNETS"   14,000.
      No. 3AX1a is unique.
See No. 137XU1.

NASHVILLE, TENN.

A1

Typeset Adhesive (5 varieties)
4AX1 A1 3c carmine   150.
No. 4AX1 was prepared by Postmaster McNish with the U.S. rate, but the stamp was never issued.
See Nos. 61X2-61XU2.

SELMA, ALA.

E1

Handstamped Envelope
5AXU1 E1 3c black   1,500.
See Nos. 77XU1-77XU3.

TUSCUMBIA, ALA.

E1

Handstamped Envelope
Impression at upper right
6AXU1 E1 3c dull red, buff 16,500.
See Nos. 84XU1-84XU3.

PROVISIONAL ISSUES

These stamps and envelopes were issued by individual postmasters generally between June 1, 1861, when the use of U.S. stamps stopped in the Confederacy, and Oct. 16, 1861, when the 1st Confederate Government stamps were issued.

They were occasionally issued at later periods, especially in Texas, when regular issues of Government stamps were unavailable.

Canceling stamps of the post offices were often used to produce envelopes, some of which were supplied in advance by private citizens.

These envelopes and other stationery therefore may be found in a wide variety of papers, colors, sizes & shapes, including patriotic and semi-official types.

It is often difficult to determine whether the impression made by the canceling stamp indicates provisional usage or merely postage paid at the time the letter was deposited in the post office. Occasionally the same mark was used for both purposes.

The *press-printed* provisional envelopes are in a different category. They were produced in quantity, using envelopes procured in advance by the postmaster, such as those of Charleston, Lynchburg, Memphis, etc.

The press-printed envelopes are listed and valued on all known papers.

The handstamped provisional envelopes are listed and valued according to type and variety of handstamp, but not according to paper. Many exist on such a variety of papers that they defy accurate, complete listing.

The value of a handstamped provisional envelope is determined *primarily* by the clarity of the markings and its overall condition and attractiveness, rather than type of paper.

All handstamped provisional envelopes, when used, should also show the postmark of the town of issue.

Most handstamps are impressed at top right, although they exist from some towns in other positions.

Illustrations in this section are reduced in size.
XU numbers are envelope entires.

ABERDEEN, MISS.

E1

Handstamped Envelopes
1XU1 E1 5c black   6,000.
1XU2 E1 10c (ms.) on 5c blk   —
No. 1XU2 is unique.

ABINGDON, VA.

E1

Handstamped Envelopes
2XU1 E1 2c black   11,000.
2XU2 E1 5c black   1,000.
2XU3 E1 10c black   2,200. 3,500.
No. 2XU3 unused and used are each unique.

ALBANY, GA.

E1

E2

Handstamped Envelopes

3XU1	E1	5c grnsh blue		700.
3XU2	E1	10c grnsh blue		2,000.
3XU3	E1	10c on 5c grnsh blue		3,500.
3XU5	E2	5c grnsh blue		—
3XU6	E2	10c grnsh blue		2,500.

Only one example recorded of No. 3XU3.

ANDERSON COURT HOUSE, S.C.

E1

Handstamped Envelopes

4XU1	E1	5c black	500.	2,250.
4XU2	E1	10c (ms.) black		3,000.

ATHENS, GA.

A1 - Type I

A1 - Type II

Typographed Adhesives

Two types of Type A1 exist.

5X1	A1	5c purple (shades)	900.	1,100.
a.		Vertical tete beche pair		7,500.
5X2	A1	5c red	—	4,250.

ATLANTA, GA.

E1

E2

E3

Handstamped Adhesives

6XU1	E1	5c red		3,500.
6XU2	E1	5c black	175.	600.
6XU3	E1	10c on 5c black		1,500.
6XU4	E2	2c black		3,000.
6XU5	E2	5c black		1,500.
6XU6	E2	10c black		850.
6XU7	E2	10c on 5c black		2,500.
6XU8	E3	5c black		3,500.
6XU9	E3	10c blk ("10" upright)		2,750.

AUGUSTA, GA.

E1

Handstamped Envelope

7XU1 E1 5c black

Provisional status questioned. Indistinguishable from a handstamp paid cover when used.

The only known example purported to be a postmaster Provisional has a general CSA issue used over the marking.

The editors intend to delist this item unless evidence of a certified unused envelope with the marking is furnished.

AUSTIN, MISS.

E1

Press-printed Envelope (typeset)

8XU1 E1 5c red, *amber* 75,000.

No. 8XU1 is unique.

AUSTIN, TEX.

E1a

Handstamped Adhesive

9X1 E1a 10c black —

Handstamped Envelope

9XU1 E1a 10c black 1,500.

AUTAUGAVILLE, ALA.

E1

E2

Handstamped Envelopes

10XU1	E1	5c black	10,000.
10XU2	E2	5c black	12,500.

No. 10XU2 is unique.

BALCONY FALLS, VA.

E1

Handstamped Envelope

122XU1 E1 5c black 1,500.

BARNWELL COURT HOUSE, S.C.

E1

Handstamped Envelope

123XU1 E1 5c black 1,500.

These are two separate handstamps.

BATON ROUGE, LA.

A1

A2

A3

A4

Ten varieties each of A1, A2 & A3

Typeset Adhesives

11X1	A1	2c green	5,250.	4,000.
a.		"McCcrmick"	14,000.	8,500.
11X2	A2	5c green & car	1,250.	1,100.
a.		"McCcrmick"		2,000.
11X3	A3	5c green & car	4,500.	2,250.
a.		"McCcrmick"		3,250.
11X4	A4	10c blue		6,000.

Only one example each is recorded of No. 11X1a unused, used and on cover.

BEAUMONT, TEX.

A1

A2

Several varieties of A1

Typeset Adhesives

12X1	A1	10c black, *yellow*, on cover		55,000.
12X2	A1	10c black, *pink*		12,500.
12X3	A2	10c blk, *yel*, on cover		90,000.

BLUFFTON, S.C.

E1

A1

Handstamped Envelope

124XU1 E1 5c black 2,500.

Only one example recorded of No. 124XU1.

BRIDGEVILLE, ALA.

Handstamped Adhesive

13X1 A1 5c black & red 20,000.

CAMDEN, S.C.

E1

E2

Handstamped Envelopes

125XU1	E1	5c black		3,500.
125XU2	E2	10c black		450.

No. 125XU2 unused was privately carried and is addressed but has no postal markings. No. 125XU2 is indistinguishable from a handstamp paid cover when used.

CANTON, MISS.

E1

Handstamped Envelopes

14XU1	E1	5c black	2,250.
14XU2	E1	10c (ms.) on 5c black	5,000.

CAROLINA CITY, N.C.

E1

Handstamped Envelope

118XU1 E1 5c black 3,500.

CARTERSVILLE, GA.

E1

Handstamped Envelope

126XU1 E1 (5c) red 1,250.

CHAPEL HILL, N.C.

E1

Handstamped Envelope

15XU1 E1 5c black 2,500.

CHARLESTON, S.C.

A1

E1

E2

Lithographed Adhesive

16X1	A1	5c blue	900.	750.

Press-printed Envelopes
(typographed from woodcut)

16XU1	E1	5c blue	1,100.	3,500.
16XU2	E1	5c blue, *amber*	1,100.	3,500.
16XU3	E1	5c blue, *org*	1,100.	3,500.
16XU4	E1	5c blue, *buff*	1,100.	3,500.
16XU5	E1	5c blue, *blue*	1,100.	3,500.
16XU6	E2	10c blue, *org*		77,500.

Handstamped Cut Square

16XU7	E2	10c black	3,000.

The No. 16XU6 entire is unique. There is also only one copy known of No. 16XU7. It is a cut-out, not an entire. It may not have been mailed from Charleston and may not have paid postage.

CHARLOTTESVILLE, VA.

E1   PAID

Handstamped Envelopes
Manuscript Initials

127XU1	E1	5c blue	—
127XU2	E1	10c blue	

CHATTANOOGA, TENN.

E1

Handstamped Envelopes

17XU2	E1	5c black	1,600.
17XU3	E1	5c on 2c black	3,250.

CHRISTIANSBURG, VA.

E1

Handstamped Envelopes
Impressed at top right

99XU1	E1	5c black, *blue*	2,000.
99XU2	E1	5c blue	1,400.
99XU3	E1	5c black, *orange*	2,000.
99XU4	E1	5c green, on US envelope #U27	4,500.
99XU5	E1	10c blue	3,500.

COLAPARCHEE, GA.

E1

Control

Handstamped Envelope

119XU1	E1	5c black	3,500.

COLUMBIA, S.C.

E1   E2

Handstamped Envelopes

18XU1	E1	5c blue	500.	900.
18XU2	E1	5c black	600.	900.
18XU3	E1	10c on 5c blue		3,500.
18XU4	E2	5c blue (seal on front)		2,500.
a.		Seal on back		1,000.
18XU5	E2	10c blue (seal on back)		2,750.

Three types of "PAID" for Nos. 18XU4-18XU5, one in circle.

Circular Seal similar to E2, 27mm diameter

18XU6	E2	5c blue (seal on back)	4,000.

E1   E1a

COLUMBIA, TENN.
Handstamped Envelope

113XU1	E1	5c red	3,500.

COLUMBUS, GA.

Handstamped Envelopes

19XU1	E1a	5c blue	700.
19XU2	E1a	10c red	2,250.

E1   E1a

COURTLAND, ALA.
Handstamped Envelopes from Woodcut

103XU1	E1	5c black	
103XU2	E1	5c red	10,000.

Provisional status of #103XU1 questioned.

DALTON, GA.

Handstamped Envelopes

20XU1	E1a	5c black	500.
a.		Denomination omitted (5c rate)	650.
20XU2	E1a	10c black	700.
20XU3	E1a	10c (ms.) on 5c black	1,500.

DANVILLE, VA.

A1   Design measures 60x37mm — E1

E2   E3

wBs

  E4

Typeset Adhesives

21X1	A1	5c red, wove paper	5,500.

One of the four recorded cut-to-shape examples is reported to be on laid paper.

Press-printed Envelopes
(typographed)

Design E1 measures 60x37mm. Two types: "SOUTHERN" in straight or curved line.

21XU1	E1	5c black	5,500.
21XU2	E1	5c black, *amber*	5,500.
21XU3	E1	5c blk, *dark buff*	5,250.

Unissued 10c envelopes (type E1, in red) are known. All recorded examples are envelopes on which added stamps paid the postage.

Handstamped Envelopes

21XU3A	E4	5c blk (ms "WBP")	1,000.
21XU4	E2	10c black	2,000.
21XU5	E2	10c blue	
21XU6	E3	10c black	2,750.
21XU7	E4	10c blk (ms "WBP")	

The existence of #21XU5 has been questioned.

DEMOPOLIS, ALA.

E1

Handstamped Envelopes
Ms Signature

22XU1	E1	5c black ("Jno. Y. Hall")	3,500.
22XU2	E1	5c black ("J. Y. Hall")	3,500.
22XU3	E1	5c (ms.) blk ("J. Y. Hall")	4,000.

EATONTON, GA.

E1

Handstamped Envelopes

23XU1	E1	5c black	3,000.
23XU2	E1	5c + 5c black	4,500.

Only one example is recorded of No. 23XU2.

EMORY, VA.

PAID

A1   E1

PAID

E2

Handstamped Adhesive
On sheet selvage of US 1857
1c stamps
Perf. 15 on Three Sides

24X1	A1	5c blue	15,000.

No. 24X1 exists with "5" above or below "PAID."

Handstamped Envelopes

24XU1	E1	5c blue	2,000.
24XU2	E2	10c blue	7,500.

Only one example recorded of No. 24XU2.

E1   E1a

FINCASTLE, VA.
Press-printed Envelope (typeset)

104XU1	E1	10c black	20,000.

No. 104XU1 is unique.

FORSYTH, GA.

Handstamped Envelope

120XU1	E1a	10c black	1,350.

E1   E1a

FRANKLIN, N.C.
Press-printed Envelope (typeset)

25XU1	E1	5c blue, *buff*	30,000.

No. 25XU1 is unique.

FRAZIERSVILLE, S.C.

Handstamped Envelope
Manuscript "5"

128XU1	E1a	5c black	2,250.

One example recorded of No. 128XU1.

FREDERICKSBURG, VA.

A1

Typeset Adhesives
Ten varieties
Thin Bluish Paper

26X1	A1	5c blue, *bluish*	250.	750.
26X2	A1	10c red (shades), *bluish*	900.	

GAINESVILLE, ALA.

E1   E2

Handstamped Envelopes

27XU1	E1	5c black	5,000.
27XU2	E2	10c black	6,000.

GALVESTON, TEX.

E1

E2

Handstamped Envelopes

98XU1	E1	5c black	500.	1,500.
98XU2	E1	10c black		2,000.
98XU3	E2	10c black	550.	2,400.
98XU4	E2	20c black		3,500.

GASTON, N.C.

E1

Handstamped Envelope

129XU1	E1	5c black	4,000.

One example recorded of No. 129XU1.

GEORGETOWN, S.C.

E1

Control

Handstamped Envelope

28XU1	E1	5c black	800.

GOLIAD, TEX.

A1

A2

Typeset Adhesives
Several varieties of A1 and A2

29X1	A1	5c black	7,000.
29X2	A1	5c black, gray	6,500.
29X3	A1	5c black, rose	7,000.
29X4	A1	10c black	— 7,000.
29X5	A1	10c black, rose	7,000.

Type A1 stamps bear ms. control: "Clarke P.M."

29X6	A2	5c black, gray	10,000.
a.		"Goilad"	12,000.
29X7	A2	10c black, gray	7,500.
a.		"Goilad"	8,000.
29X8	A2	5c blk, dk bl, on cover	7,000.
29X9	A2	10c black, dark blue	—

GONZALES, TEX.

A1

Lithographed Adhesives
on colored glazed paper

30X1	A1	(5c) gold, dark blue	15,000.
30X2	A1	(10c) gold, garnet, on cover, 1864	12,500.
30X3	A1	(10c) gold, black, on cover, 1865	—

No. 30X1 must bear double-circle town cancel as validating control.

The control was applied to the labels in the sheet before their sale as stamps.

When used, the stamps bear an additional Gonzales double-circle postmark.

GREENSBORO, ALA.

E1

E2

Handstamped Envelopes

31XU1	E1	5c black	1,500.
31XU2	E1	10c black	2,750.
31XU3	E2	10c black	4,250.

GREENSBORO, N.C.

E1

Handstamped Envelope

32XU1	E1	10c red	1,250.

GREENVILLE, ALA.

A1

A2

Typeset Adhesives
on pinkish surface-colored
glazed paper

33X1	A1	5c blue & red	22,500.
33X2	A2	10c red & blue	—

Nos. 33X1-33X2 exist used on cover.

GREENVILLE COURT HOUSE, S.C.

E1

Control

Handstamped Envelopes
Several types

34XU1	E1	5c black	2,000.
34XU2	E1	10c black	2,250.
34XU3	E1	20c (ms.) on 10c blk	3,000.

Envelopes must bear the black circle control on the back.

GREENWOOD DEPOT, VA.

A1

Handstamped "PAID" Adhesive
Ms Value & Signature
Laid Paper
Uncanceled

35X1	A1	10c black, gray blue, on cover	20,000.

Six examples are known of No. 35X1, all on covers.

On only one cover is the stamp tied.

GRIFFIN, GA.

E1

Handstamped Envelope

102XU1	E1	5c black	2,000.

A1

A1a

GROVE HILL, ALA.
Handstamped Adhesive
(from woodcut)

36X1	A1	5c black	—

Two examples are recorded:

One is on cover tied by the postmark.

The other is canceled by magenta pen on a cover front.

HALLETTSVILLE, TEX.

Handstamped Adhesive
Ruled Letter Paper

37X1	A1a	10c black, gray blue, on cover	15,000.

HAMBURGH, S.C.

E1

Handstamped Envelope

112XU1	E1	5c black	2,000.

HARRISBURGH (Harrisburg), TEX.

E1

Handstamped Envelope

130XU1	E1	5c black	—

No. 130XU1 is indistinguishable from a handstamp paid cover when used.

A1

A1a

HELENA, TEX.
Typeset Adhesives
Several varieties

38X1	A1	5c black, buff	7,500.	6,000.
38X2	A1	10c black, gray		5,000.

On 10c "Helena" is in upper and lower case italics.

Used examples are valued with small faults or repairs, as all recorded have faults.

HILLSBORO, N.C.

Handstamped Adhesive

39X1	A1a	5c black, on cover	15,000.

Manuscript Envelope

39XU1		10c "paid 10"	—

No. 39XU1 has undated town cancel as control on face.

See 3c 1861 Postmaster Provisional No. 1AX1.

E1

E1a

HOLLANDALE, TEX.
Handstamped Envelope

132XU1	E1	5c black	—

HOUSTON, TEX.

Handstamped Envelopes

40XU1	E1a	5c red	— 700.
40XU2	E1a	10c red	1,500.
40XU3	E1a	10c black	2,250.
40XU4	E1a	5c + 10c red	2,500.
40XU5	E1a	10c + 10c red	2,500.
40XU6	E1a	10c (ms.) on 5c red	3,000.

HUNTSVILLE, TEX.

E1

Control

Handstamped Envelope

92XU1	E1	5c black	5,000.

No. 92XU1 exists with "5" outside or within control circle.

A1

E1

INDEPENDENCE, TEX.
Handstamped Adhesives

41X1	A1	10c blk, buff, on cover	20,000.
41X2	A1	10c blk, dull rose, on cover	
41X3	A1	10c blk, buff	32,500.

No. 41X1 is unique.

All known examples of Nos. 41X1-41X3 are uncanceled on covers with black "INDEPENDANCE TEX." (sic) postmark.

The existence of No. 41X2 has been questioned by specialists.

The editors would like to see authenticated evidence of the existence of this item.

No. 41X3 small "10," Manuscript "Pd," on cover, cut to shape.

ISABELLA, GA.

Handstamped Envelope
Manuscript "5"

133XU1	E1	5c black	2,000.

I·U·KA
PAID 5cts
E1

E1a

IUKA, MISS.
Handstamped Envelope

42XU1	E1	5c black	1,600.

JACKSON, MISS.

Handstamped Envelopes

43XU1	E1a	5c black	500.
43XU2	E1a	10c black	2,000.
43XU3	E1a	10c on 5c black	2,750.
43XU4	E1a	10c on 5c blue	2,750.

The 5c also exists on a lettersheet. See 3c 1861 Postmaster Provisional No. 2AXU1.

E1

PAID
5
E1a

JACKSONVILLE, ALA.
Handstamped Envelope

110XU1	E1	5c black	— 3,000.

JACKSONVILLE, FLA.

Handstamped Envelope

134XU1	E1a	5c black	—

Undated double circle postmark control on reverse.

A1

E1

JETERSVILLE, VA.
Handstamped "5"; Ms "AHA."
Adhesive
Laid Paper

44X1	A1	5c black, vert. pair on cover, uncanceled	16,000.

JONESBORO, TENN.

Handstamped Envelopes

45XU1	E1	5c black	3,750.
45XU2	E1	5c dark blue	7,000.

KINGSTON, GA.

PAID
5
CENTS
E1

PAID
c **5** s
CENTS
E2

KINGSTON
PAID
5
CENTS
GA.
E4

KINGSTON PAID
Ga' 5
JUNE 13 1861 CENTS
E3

Envelopes
Typeset
(probably impressed by hand, possibly press printed)

46XU1	E1	5c black	2,000.
46XU2	E2	5c black	— 3,250.
a.		No "C" or "S" at sides of numeral	—
46XU3	E2	5c black, amber	2,750.
46XU4	E3	5c black	—

Handstamped

46XU5	E4	5c black	2,000.

Only one example of No. 46XU3 is recorded.

KNOXVILLE, TENN.

A1

Typographed Adhesives
(stereotype from woodcut)
Grayish White Laid Paper

47X1	A1	5c brick red	1,250.	900.
47X2	A1	5c carmine	1,750.	1,500.
47X3	A1	10c grn, on cover	57,750.	

The 5c has been reprinted in red, brown and chocolate on white and bluish wove and laid paper.

E1

KNOXVILLE
PAID
5
Ten.
E2

Press-printed Envelopes
(typographed)

47XU1	E1	5c blue	750.	1,750.
47XU2	E1	5c blue, orange	750.	2,000.
47XU3	E1	10c red		2,100.
47XU4	E1	10c red, orange		2,100.

Handstamped Envelopes

47XU5	E1	5c black	750.	1,500.
47XU6	E2	10c on 5c black		3,500.

Type E2 exists with "5" above or below "PAID."

Nos. 47XU3 and 47XU4 cut to shape.

LA GRANGE, TEX.

LA GRANGE
PAID
10
TEX
E1

Handstamped Envelopes

48XU1	E1	5c black	2,000.
48XU2	E1	10c black	2,500.

LAKE CITY, FLA.

PAID
10
E1

LAKE CITY
FLA.
Control

Handstamped Envelope

96XU1	E1	10c black	2,000.

Envelopes have black circle control mark, or printed name of E.R. Ives, postmaster, on face or back.

LAURENS COURT HOUSE, S.C.

PAID

5
E1

Handstamped Envelope

116XU1	E1	5c black	1,500.

LENOIR, N.C.

LENOIR
N **5** C
PAID
A1

LENOIR
PAID
5
N.C.
E1

Handstamped Adhesive
from Woodcut

Paper has ruled lines in orange

49X1	A1	5c blue	3,250.	2,750.

Handstamped Envelopes

49XU1	A1	5c black	3,500.
49XU2	A1	10c (5c + 5c) blue	25,000.
49XU3	E1	5c blue	4,500.
49XU4	E1	5c black	

The existence of No. 49XU4 has been questioned.

No. 49XU2 is unique.

LEXINGTON, MISS.

LEXINGTON
PAID
5
E.H. P.M.
MISS.
E1

Handstamped Envelopes

50XU1	E1	5c black	5,000.
50XU2	E1	10c black	5,000.

LEXINGTON, VA.

PAID
10
E1

Handstamped Envelopes

135XU1	E1	5c blue	500.
135XU2	E1	10c blue	750.

Nos. 135XU1-135XU2 by themselves are indistinguishable from a handstamp paid cover when used.

LIBERTY, VA.
(and SALEM, VA.)

PAID
A1 5cts.

5
A1a

Typeset Adhesive
Laid Paper

74X1	A1	5c blk, on cover, uncanceled	35,000.

Three known on covers:
Two on covers with Liberty, Va. postmark;
One on cover with Salem, Va. postmark.

LIMESTONE SPRINGS, S.C.

Handstamped Adhesive

121X1	A1	5c black, on cover	10,000.

Stamps are cut round, square or rectangular. Covers are not postmarked.

LIVINGSTON, ALA.

A1

Lithographed Adhesive

51X1	A1	5c blue	7,000.

LYNCHBURG, VA.

A1

5
PAID.
E1

Typographed Adhesives
(stereotype from woodcut)

52X1	A1	5c blue (shades)	1,500.	1,000.

Press-printed Envelopes
(typographed)

52XU1	E1	5c black		2,500.
52XU2	E1	5c black, amber	650.	2,500.
52XU3	E1	5c black, buff		2,500.
52XU4	E1	5c black, brown	900.	2,500.

MACON, GA.

POST OFFICE
FIVE
CENTS
MACON GA
A1

FIVE
CENTS
A2

FIVE
CENTS
A3

TWO CENTS
A4

MACON, GEO.
PAID
5
E1

Several varieties of each. Ten of A2.

Typeset Adhesives
Wove Paper

53X1	A1	5c blk, *lt blue green*		850.	600.
53X3	A2	5c black, *yellow*		2,500.	800.
53X4	A3	5c black, *yel (shades)*		2,750.	1,250.
a.	Vertical tete beche pair				
53X5	A4	2c black, *gray grn*			—

No. 53X4a is unique.

Laid Paper

53X6	A2	5c black, *yellow*	3,000.	3,500.
53X7	A3	5c black, *yellow*	6,000.	
53X8	A1	5c blk, *lt blue green*	1,750.	2,000.

Handstamped Envelope
Two types of "PAID" and "5"

53XU1	E1	5c black	250.	500.

E1

E1a

MADISON, GA.
Handstamped Envelope

136XU1	E1	5c red	500.

No. 136XU1 is indistinguishable from a handstamp paid cover when used.

MADISON COURT HOUSE, FLA.

Typeset Envelope

137XU1	E1a	5c black, *yellow*	23,000.	

No. 137XU1 is unique.
See 3c 1861 Postmaster Provisional No. 3AX1.

MARIETTA, GA.

E1

E2

Handstamped Envelopes
Two types of "PAID" and numerals

54XU1	E1	5c black		300.
54XU2	E1	10c on 5c black		1,750.
54XU3	E1	10c black		
54XU4	E2	5c black		2,000.

The existence of No. 54XU3 is questioned.

MARION, VA.

A1

Adhesives with Typeset frame
Handstamped Numeral in center
Wove Paper

55X1	A1	5c black		6,500.
55X2	A1	10c black	16,500.	10,000.

Bluish Laid Paper

55X3	A1	5c black	

The 2c, 3c, 15c and 20c are believed to be bogus items printed later using the original typeset frame.

MEMPHIS, TENN.

A1

A2

Typographed Adhesives
(stereotyped from woodcut)

56X1	A1	2c blue (shades)	90.	1,250.
56X2	A2	5c red (shades)	140.	175.
a.	Tete beche pair			1,500.
b.	Pair, one sideways		750.	
c.	Pelure paper		—	

Press-printed Envelopes
(typographed)

56XU1	A2	5c red	2,500.
56XU2	A2	5c red, *amber*	4,000.
56XU3	A2	5c red, *orange*	2,500.

MICANOPY, FLA.

E1

Handstamped Envelope

105XU1	E1	5c black	11,500.

No. 105X1 is unique.

MILLEDGEVILLE, GA.

E1

E2

E3

Handstamped Envelopes

57XU1	E1	5c black		250.
57XU2	E1	5c blue		800.
57XU3	E1	10c on 5c black		1,000.
57XU4	E2	10c black	225.	1,000.
57XU5	E3	10c black		700.

The existence of No. 57XU2 as a provisional has been questioned by specialists. The editors would like to see authenticated evidence of provisional use of this marking.

E1

E1a

MILTON, N.C.
Handstamped Envelope
Manuscript "5"

138XU1	E1	5c black	2,000.

Two examples of No. 138XU1 are recorded.

MOBILE, ALA.

Lithographed Adhesives

58X1	A1	2c black	2,000.	1,000.
58X2	A1	5c blue	275.	225.

MONTGOMERY, ALA.

E1

E2

E3

Handstamped Envelopes

59XU1	E1	5c red		1,000.
59XU2	E1	5c blue	400.	900.
59XU3	E1	10c red		800.
59XU4	E1	10c blue		1,500.
59XU5	E1	10c black		800.
59XU6	E1	10c on 5c red		2,750.

The 10c design is larger than the 5c.

59XU7	E2	2c red		2,500.
59XU7A	E2	2c blue		3,500.
59XU8	E2	5c black		2,250.
59XU9	E3	10c black		2,750.
59XU10	E3	10c red		1,500.

MT. LEBANON, LA.

A1

Woodcut Adhesive
(mirror image of design)

60X1	A1	5c red brn, on cover	385,000.

No. 60X1 is unique. Value represents sale price at 1999 auction.

NASHVILLE, TENN.

A2

E1

Typographed Adhesives
(stereotyped from woodcut)
Gray Blue Ribbed Paper

61X2	A2	5c car (shades)	850.	500.
a.	Vertical tete beche pair			3,000.
61X3	A2	5c brick red	850.	450.
61X4	A2	5c gray (shades)	850.	625.
61X5	A2	5c violet brown	750.	475.
a.	Vertical tete beche pair		3,500.	2,500.
61X6	A2	10c green	3,000.	3,000.

Handstamped Envelopes

61XU1	E1	5c blue		850.
61XU2	E1	5c + 10c blue		2,400.

See 3c Postmaster Provisional No. 4AX1.

NEW ORLEANS, LA.

A1

A2

J.L.RIDDELL.P.M

Pᴰ5ᶜᵀˢ
N O.P.O
E1

Stereotyped Adhesives
from Woodcut

62X1	A1	2c blue	150.	500.
a.	Printed on both sides			
62X2	A1	2c red (shades)	125.	1,000.
62X3	A2	5c brown, *white*	250.	150.
a.	5c ocher		650.	1,750.
b.	5c ocher			600.
62X4	A2	5c red brn, *bluish*	280.	175.
a.	Printed on both sides			2,750.
62X5	A2	5c yel brn, *off-white*	125.	225.
62X6	A2	5c red	—	7,500.
62X7	A2	5c red, *bluish*		10,000.

Handstamped Envelopes

62XU1	E1	5c black		4,500.
62XU2	E1	10c black		12,500.

"J L. RIDDELL, P.M." omitted

62XU3	E1	2c black	9,500.

A1

E1

NEW SMYRNA, FLA.
Handstamped Adhesive

63X1	A1	10c ("01") on 5c black	45,000.

No. 63X1 is unique.

NORFOLK, VA.

Handstamped Envelopes
Ms Initials on Front or Back

139XU1	E1	5c blue		1,250.
139XU2	E1	10c blue		1,750.

A1

E1

OAKWAY, S.C.
Handstamped Adhesive
(from woodcut)

115X1	A1	5c black, on cover	66,000.

Two used examples of No. 115X1 are recorded, both on cover.
Value represents 1997 auction realization for the cover on which the stamp is tied by manuscript "Paid."

PENSACOLA, FLA.

Handstamped Envelopes

106XU1	E1	5c black	3,750.
106XU2	E1	10c (ms.) on 5c black	4,250.

A1

A1a

PETERSBURG, VA.
Typeset Adhesive (10 varieties)

65X1	A1	5c red (shades)	1,750.	500.

PITTSYLVANIA COURT HOUSE, VA.

Typeset Adhesives

66X1	A1a	5c red, wove paper	6,000.	5,000.
66X2	A1a	5c red, laid paper		6,500.

PLAINS OF DURA, GA.

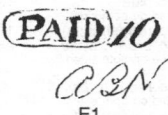

E1

Handstamped Envelopes
Ms. initials

140XU1	E1	5c black	—
140XU2	E1	10c black	—

A1

E1

PLEASANT SHADE, VA.
Typeset Adhesive
(5 varieties)

67X1	A1	5c blue	2,500.	20,000.

PLUM CREEK, TEX.

Manuscript Adhesive

141X1	E1	10c black, *blue*, on cover	—

The ruled lines and "10" are done by hand. Size and shape of the stamp varies.

PORT GIBSON, MISS.

PAID 5

E1

Handstamped Envelope
Ms Signature

142XU1	E1	5c black	—

A1

E1

PORT LAVACA, TEX.
Typeset Adhesive

107X1	A1	10c black, on cover	25,000.

No. 107X1 is unique.

RALEIGH, N.C.

Handstamped Envelopes

68XU1	E1	5c red	500.
68XU2	E1	5c blue	2,500.

A1

E1

RHEATOWN, TENN.
Typeset Adhesive
Three varieties

69X1	A1	5c red	2,000.	2,750.

RICHMOND, TEX.

Handstamped Envelopes
or Letter Sheets

70XU1	E1	5c red	1,500.
70XU2	E1	10c red	1,000.
70XU3	E1	10c on 5c red	5,000.
70XU4	E1	15c (ms.) on 10c red	5,000.

E1

E1a

RINGGOLD, GA.
Handstamped Envelope

71XU1	E1	5c blue black	3,000.

RUTHERFORDTON, N.C.

Handstamped Adhesive
"Paid 5cts" in ms.
Cut round

72X1	E1a	5c black, on cover (un-canceled)	25,000.

No. 72X1 is unique.

SALEM, N.C.

"Paid 5" in Ms.—E1

"Paid 5"
Handstamped—E2

Handstamped Envelopes

73XU1	E1	5c black	1,150.
73XU2	E1	10c black	1,500.
73XU3	E2	5c black	1,500.
73XU4	E2	10c on 5c black	2,800.

Reprints exist on various papers. They either lack the "Paid" and value or have them counterfeited.

Salem, Va.
See No. 74X1 under Liberty, Va.

SALISBURY, N.C.

E1

Press-printed Envelope
(Typeset)

Impressed at top left

75XU1	E1	5c black, *grnsh*	5,000.

One example known with part of envelope torn away, leaving part of design missing. Illustration E1 partly suppositional.

SAN ANTONIO, TEX.

E1

E2

Control

Handstamped Envelopes

76XU1	E1	10c black	275.	2,000.
76XU1A	E2	5c black		1,500.
76XU2	E1	10c black		2,500.

Black circle control mark is on front or back.

SAVANNAH, GA.

E1

Control

PAID 10

E2

Handstamped Envelopes

101XU1	E1	5c black	300.
101XU2	E2	5c black	600.
101XU3	E1	10c black	750.
101XU4	E2	10c black	750.
101XU5	E1	10c on 5c black	1,500.
101XU6	E2	20c on 5c black	2,000.

Envelope must bear octagonal control mark. One example is known of No. 101XU6.

E1

E1a

SELMA, ALA.
Handstamped Envelopes
Ms Signature

77XU1	E1	5c black	1,250.
77XU2	E1	10c black	2,500.
77XU3	E1	10c on 5c black	3,000.

See 3c Postmaster Provisional No. 5AXU1.

SPARTA, GA.

Handstamped Envelopes

93XU1	E1a	5c red	—1,000.
93XU2	E1a	10c red	2,500.

SPARTANBURG, S.C.

A1

A2

SAN ANTONIO / continued

E2

Handstamped Adhesives
on Ruled or Plain
Wove Paper

78X1	A1	5c black	3,500.
a.		"5" omitted	4,000.
78X2	A2	5c black, *bluish*	4,000.
78X3	A2	5c black, *brown*	4,000.

Most examples of Nos. 78X1-78X3 are cut round.
Cut square examples in sound condition are worth much more.

STATESVILLE, N.C.

E1

Handstamped Envelopes

79XU1	E1	5c black	250.	600.
79XU2	E1	10c on 5c black		2,250.

Fakes exist of No. 79XU1 unused.

SUMTER, S.C.

E1

Handstamped Envelopes

80XU1	E1	5c black	400.
80XU2	E1	10c black	400.
80XU3	E1	10c on 5c black	800.
80XU4	E1	2c (ms.) on 10c black	1,100.

Used examples of Nos. 80XU1-80XU2 are indistinguishable from handstamped "Paid" covers.

TALBOTTON, GA.

E1

Handstamped Envelopes

94XU1	E1	5c black	1,000.
94XU2	E1	10c black	1,000.
94XU3	E1	10c on 5c black	2,000.

PAID 10

E1

A1

TALLADEGA, ALA.
Handstamped Envelopes

143XU1	E1	5c black	—	—
143XU2	E1	10c black	—	—

TELLICO PLAINS, TENN.

Typeset Adhesives
Laid Paper

81X1	A1	5c red	1,250.
81X2	A1	10c red	2,500.

THOMASVILLE, GA.

E1

Control

E2

Handstamped Envelopes

82XU1	E1	5c black	500.
82XU2	E2	5c black	900.

On No. 82XU1, the control is on the reverse of the cover.

TULLAHOMA, TENN.

E1

Control

Handstamped Envelope

111XU1 E1 10c black 3,000.

E1

E1a

TUSCALOOSA, ALA.
Handstamped Envelopes

83XU1	E1	5c black	250.
83XU2	E1	10c black	250.

Used examples of Nos. 83XU1-83XU2 are indistinguishable from handstamped "Paid" covers.

TUSCUMBIA, ALA.

Handstamped Envelopes

84XU1	E1a	5c black	2,250.
84XU2	E1a	5c red	3,000.
84XU3	E1a	10c black	3,500.

See 3c 1861 Postmasters Provisional No. 6AXU1.

Union City, Tenn.

E1

The use of E1 to produce provisional envelopes is doubtful.

A1

A1a

UNIONTOWN, ALA.
Typeset Adhesives
in settings of 4 (2x2)
Laid Paper
(4 varieties of each value)

86X1	A1	2c dk bl, *gray bl* on cover	—
86X2	A1	2c dk blue, sheet of 4	57,500.
86X3	A1	5c grn, *gray bl*	3,000.	2,000.
86X4	A1	5c green	3,000.	2,000.
86X5	A1	10c red, *gray blue*	—

The only recorded examples of No. 86X2 are in a unique sheet of 4.
No. 86X5 used is an uncanceled stamp on a large piece with part of addressee's name in manuscript.
Another example also known on full cover.

UNIONVILLE, S.C.

Handstamped Adhesive
Wove Paper
with Blue Ruled Lines

87X1 A1a 5c black, *grayish* —

VALDOSTA, GA.

E1

Control

Handstamped Envelopes

100XU1	E1	10c black	2,000.
100XU2	E1	5c + 5c black

The black circle control must appear on front or back of envelope. There is one recorded cover each of Nos. 100XU1-100XU2.

VICTORIA, TEX.

A1

A2

Typeset Adhesives

88X1	A1	5c red brn, *grn*	9,000.
88X2	A1	10c red brn, *grn*	10,000.	5,500.

Pelure Paper

88X3 A2 10c red brn, *grn* 10,000. 10,000.

No. 88X3, "10" is in bold face type.

WALTERBOROUGH, S.C.

E1

Handstamped Envelopes

108XU1	E1	10c black, *buff*	4,000.
108XU2	E1	10c carmine	4,000.

WARRENTON, GA.

E1

Handstamped Envelopes

89XU1	E1	5c black	1,250.
89XU2	E1	10c (ms.) on 5c black	850.

Fakes of the Warrenton provisional marking based on the illustration shown are known on addressed but postally unused covers.

E1

E1a

WASHINGTON, GA.
Handstamped Envelope

117XU1 E1 10c black 2,000.

WEATHERFORD, TEX.

Handstamped Envelopes
Woodcut with "PAID"
inserted in type

109XU1	E1a	5c black	2,000.
109XU2	E1a	5c + 5c black	11,000.

One example is known of No. 109XU2.

WINNSBOROUGH, S.C.

E1

Control

Handstamped Envelopes

97XU1	E1	5c black	1,500.
97XU2	E1	10c black	3,500.

Envelopes must bear black circle control on front or back.

WYTHEVILLE, VA.

Control

E1

Handstamped Envelope

114XU1 E1 5c black 900.

For later additions, listed out of numerical sequence, see:

#74X1, Liberty, Va. (& Salem, Va.)
#92XU1, Huntsville, Tex.
#93XU1, Sparta, Ga.
#94XU1, Talbotton, Ga.
#96XU1, Lake City, Fla.
#97XU1, Winnsborough, S.C.
#98XU1, Galveston, Tex.
#99XU1, Christiansburg, Va.
#100XU1, Valdosta, Ga.
#101XU1, Savannah, Ga.
#102XU1, Griffin, Ga.
#103XU1, Courtland, Ala.
#104XU1, Fincastle, Va.
#105XU1, Micanopy, Fla.
#106XU1, Pensacola, Fla.
#107X1, Port Lavaca, Tex.
#108XU1, Walterborough, S.C.
#109XU1, Weatherford, Tex.
#110XU1, Jacksonville, Ala.
#111XU1, Tullahoma, Tenn.
#112XU1, Hamburgh, S.C.
#113XU1, Columbia, Tenn.
#114XU1, Wytheville, Va.
#115X1, Oakway, S.C.
#116XU1, Laurens Court House, S.C.
#117XU1, Washington, Ga.
#118XU1, Carolina City, N.C.
#119XU1, Colaparchee, Ga.
#120XU1, Forsyth, Ga.
#121XU1, Limestone Springs, S.C.
#122XU1, Balcony Falls, Va.
#123XU1, Barnwell Court House, S.C.
#124XU1, Bluffton, S.C.
#125XU1, Camden, S.C.
#126XU1, Cartersville, Ga.
#127XU1, Charlottesville, Va.
#128XU1, Fraziersville, S.C.
#129XU1, Gaston, N.C.
#130XU1, Harrisburgh, Tex.
#132XU1, Hollandale, Tex.
#133XU1, Isabella, Ala.
#134XU1, Jacksonville, Fla.
#135XU1, Lexington, Va.
#136XU1, Madison, Ga.
#137XU1, Madison Court House, Fla.
#138XU1, Milton, N.C.
#139XU1, Norfolk, Va.
#140XU1, Plains of Dura, Ga.
#141X1, Plum Creek, Tex.
#142XU1, Port Gibson, Miss.
#143XU1, Talladega, Ala.

GENERAL ISSUES

Jefferson Davis A1 — Thomas Jefferson A2

1861		Unwmk.	Litho.	Imperf.
1	A1	5c green	250.00	150.00
		No gum	175.00	
a.		5c light green	250.00	150.00
		No gum	175.00	
b.		5c dark green	300.00	175.00
		No gum	210.00	
c.		5c olive green	350.00	175.00
		No gum	240.00	
2	A2	10c blue	280.00	190.00
		No gum	200.00	
a.		10c light blue	280.00	190.00
		No gum	200.00	
b.		10c dark blue	550.00	240.00
		No gum	400.00	
c.		10c indigo	2,750.	2,250.
		No gum	2,000.	
d.		Printed on both sides	—	—
e.		10c greenish blue	650.00	300.00
		No gum	450.00	

The earliest printings of No. 2 were made by Hoyer & Ludwig, the later ones by J. T. Paterson & Co.
Stamps of the later printings usually have a small colored dash below the lowest point of the upper left spandrel.
See Nos. 4-5.

Andrew Jackson A3 — Jefferson Davis A4

1862				
3	A3	2c green	700.00	650.00
		No gum	500.00	
a.		2c bright yellow green	1,750.	—
		No gum	1,300.	
4	A1	5c blue	180.00	110.00
		No gum	125.00	
a.		5c dark blue	240.00	160.00
		No gum	170.00	
b.		5c light milky blue	270.00	200.00
		No gum	190.00	
5	A2	10c rose	1,400.	500.00
		No gum	1,000.	
a.		10c carmine	2,800.	1,750.
		No gum	2,000.	

Typo.

|6|A4|5c lt blue (London print)|10.00|27.50|
| | |No gum|7.00| |

7	A4	5c blue (local print)	13.00	20.00
		No gum	9.00	
a.		5c deep blue	16.00	35.00
		No gum	11.00	
b.		Printed on both sides	2,500.	950.00

No. 6 has fine, clear impression. No. 7 has coarser impression and the color is duller and often blurred.

Both 2c and 10c stamps, types A4 and A10, were privately printed in various colors.

Andrew Jackson — A5

1863   **Engr.**

8	A5	2c brown red	70.00	350.00
		No gum	52.50	
a.		2c pale red	90.00	450.00
		No gum	65.00	

Jefferson Davis
A6   A6a

Thick or Thin Paper

9	A6	10c blue	850.	525.
		No gum	600.	
a.		10c milky blue	850.	525.
		No gum	600.	
b.		10c gray blue	900.	625.
		No gum	650.	
10	A6a	10c blue (with frame line)	4,500.	1,400.
		No gum	3,400.	
a.		10c milky blue	4,500.	1,400.
		No gum	3,400.	
b.		10c greenish blue	5,000.	1,500.
		No gum	3,750.	
c.		10c dark blue	5,000.	1,500.
		No gum	3,750.	

Values of Nos. 10, 10a, 10b and 10c are for copies showing parts of lines on at least three sides. Stamps showing 4 complete lines sell for 300%-400% of the values given.

A7   A8

There are many slight differences between A7 and A8, the most noticeable being the additional line outside the ornaments at the corners of A8.

11	A7	10c blue	9.00	15.00
		No gum	6.50	
a.		10c milky blue	22.50	37.50
		No gum	16.00	
b.		10c dark blue	18.50	25.00
		No gum	13.00	
c.		10c greenish blue	17.50	17.50
		No gum	12.50	
d.		10c green	80.00	75.00
		No gum	55.00	
e.		Officially perforated 12½	300.00	275.00
12	A8	10c blue	11.00	17.50
		No gum	8.00	
a.		10c milky blue	25.00	35.00
		No gum	17.50	
b.		10c light blue	11.00	17.50
		No gum	8.00	
c.		10c greenish blue	20.00	45.00
		No gum	14.00	
d.		10c dark blue	11.00	20.00
		No gum	8.00	
e.		10c green	175.00	150.00
		No gum	130.00	
f.		Officially perforated 12½	325.00	300.00

The paper of Nos. 11 and 12 varies from thin hard to thick soft. The so-called laid paper is probably due to thick streaky gum.

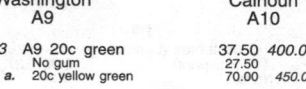

George Washington   John C. Calhoun
A9   A10

13	A9	20c green	37.50	400.00
		No gum	27.50	
a.		20c yellow green	70.00	450.00

	b.	20c dark green	65.00	500.00
		No gum	45.00	
	c.	Diag. half used as 10c on cover		2,000.
	d.	Horiz. half used as 10c on cover		3,500.

1862   **Typo.**

14	A10	1c orange	100.00	
		No gum	70.00	
a.		1c deep orange	125.00	
		No gum	90.00	

The 1c was never put in use.

CANAL ZONE

kə-ˈnal ˈzōn

LOCATION — A strip of land 10 miles wide, extending through the Republic of Panama, between the Atlantic and Pacific Oceans.

GOVT. — From 1904-79 a US Government Reservation; from 1979-99 under joint control of the Republic of Panama and the US.

AREA — 552.8 sq. mi.

POP. — 41,800 (est. 1976)

The Canal Zone, site of the Panama Canal, was leased in perpetuity to the US for a cash payment of $10,000,000 and a yearly rental. Treaties between the two countries provided for joint jurisdiction by the US and Panama, 1979-1999, with Panama handling postal service. At the end of 1999, the canal, in its entirety, reverted to Panama.

100 Centavos = 1 Peso
100 Centesimos = 1 Balboa
100 Cents = 1 Dollar

> **Catalogue values for unused stamps in this country are for Never Hinged items, beginning with Scott 118 in the regular postage section and Scott C6 in the air post section.**

Watermarks

Wmk. 190- "USPS" in Single-lined Capitals   Wmk. 191- Double-lined "USPS" in Capitals

Map of Panama — A1

Violet to Violet-blue Handstamp, "CANAL ZONE," on Panama Nos. 72-72c, 78 and 79

1904   **Unwmk.**   **Engr.**   *Perf. 12*

1	A1	2c rose, both "PANAMA" up or down	550.00	425.00
a.		"CANAL ZONE" inverted	950.00	850.00
b.		"CANAL ZONE" double	2,500.	2,000.
c.		"CANAL ZONE" double, both inverted	15,000.	
d.		"PANAMA" reading down and up	700.00	650.00
e.		As "d," "CANAL ZONE" inverted	6,500.	6,500.
f.		Vert. pair, "PANAMA" reading up on top 2c, down on other	2,100.	2,100.
2	A1	5c blue	225.00	175.00
a.		"CANAL ZONE" inverted	725.00	600.00
b.		"CANAL ZONE" double	2,250.	1,500.
c.		Pair, one without "CANAL ZONE"	5,000.	5,000.
d.		"CANAL ZONE" diagonal, running down to right	700.00	700.00
3	A1	10c yellow	375.00	250.00
a.		"CANAL ZONE" inverted	725.00	600.00
b.		"CANAL ZONE" double		15,000.

c.	Pair, one without "CANAL ZONE"		6,000.	5,000.
	Nos. 1-3 (3)		1,150.	850.00

On the 2c stamp "PANAMA" is normally about 13mm; on the 5c and 10c about 15mm. Varieties of "PANAMA" overprint exist on the 2c with inverted "V" for "A," accent on "A," inverted "N," etc.
Counterfeit "CANAL ZONE" overprints exist.

U.S. Nos. 300, 319, 304, 306 and 307 Overprinted in Black

1904   **Wmk. 191**

4	A115	1c blue green	32.50	22.50
5	A129	2c carmine	30.00	25.00
		2c scarlet	35.00	30.00
6	A119	5c blue	100.00	65.00
7	A121	8c violet black	175.00	85.00
8	A122	10c pale red brown	150.00	90.00
		Nos. 4-8 (5)	487.50	287.50

Beware of fake overprints.

A2   A3

CANAL   CANAL
ZONE   ZONE
Regular   Antique
Type   Type

Black Overprint on Stamps of Panama

1904-06   **Unwmk.**

9	A2	1c green	2.75	2.25
a.		"CANAL" in antique type	100.00	100.00
b.		"ZONE" in antique type	70.00	70.00
c.		Inverted overprint	5,000.	2,250.
d.		Double overprint	2,000.	1,500.
10	A2	2c rose	4.50	3.00
a.		Inverted overprint	225.00	275.00
b.		"L" of "CANAL" sideways	2,500.	2,500.

Overprinted "CANAL ZONE" in Black, "PANAMA" and Bar in Red on Panama Nos. 77-79
"PANAMA" 15mm long

11	A3	2c rose	7.50	5.00
a.		"ZONE" in antique type	200.00	200.00
b.		"PANAMA" inverted, bar at bottom	350.00	350.00
12	A3	5c blue	8.00	3.75
a.		"CANAL" in antique type	75.00	65.00
b.		"ZONE" in antique type	75.00	65.00
c.		"CANAL ZONE" double	600.00	600.00
d.		"PANAMA" ovpt. dbl.	1,050.	1,000.
e.		"PANAMA" inverted, bar at bottom		1,250.
13	A3	10c yellow	22.50	12.50
a.		"CANAL" in antique type	200.00	200.00
b.		"ZONE" in antique type	175.00	160.00
c.		"PANAMA" ovpt. dbl.	650.00	650.00
d.		"PANAMA" overprint in red brown	27.50	27.50
		Nos. 11-13 (3)	38.00	21.25

With Added Surcharge in Red on Panama No. 81

8 cts

14	A3	8c on 50c bis brn	32.50	22.50
a.		"ZONE" in antique type	1,100.	1,100.
b.		"CANAL ZONE" invtd.	425.00	400.00
c.		Rose brown overprint	40.00	40.00
d.		As "c," "CANAL" in antique type	2,250.	
e.		As "c," "ZONE" in antique type	2,250.	
f.		As "c," "8 cts" double	850.00	
g.		As "c," "8" omitted	4,250.	

Panama No. 74 Overprinted "CANAL ZONE" in Regular Type in Black and Surch. Like No. 14 in Red. Both "PANAMA" Reading Up. "PANAMA" 13mm long.

1905

15	A3	8c on 50c bis brn	2,600.	*4,500.*
a.		"PANAMA" reading down & up	6,500.	—

On No. 15 with original gum the gum is almost always disturbed.

Panama Nos. 19 and 21 Surcharged in Black:

a	PANAMA **CANAL ZONE 1 ct.** PANAMA
b	PANAMA **CANAL ZONE 1 ct.** PANAMA
c	PANAMA **CANAL ZONE 1 ct.** PANAMA
d	PANAMA **CANAL ZONE 2 cts.** PANAMA
e	PANAMA **CANAL ZONE 2 cts.** PANAMA
f	PANAMA **CANAL ZONE 2 cts.** PANAMA

There were 3 printings of each denomination differing mainly in the relative position of the various parts of the surcharges. Varieties occur with invtd. "V" for the 3rd "A" in "PANAMA," "CA" spaced, "ZO" spaced, "2c" spaced, accents in various positions, and with bars shifted so that 2 bars appear on top or bottom of the stamp (either with or without the corresponding bar on top or bottom) and sometimes with only 1 bar at top or bottom.

1906

16	A4	1c on 20c vio, type a	2.00	1.60
a.		Surcharge type b	2.00	1.60
b.		Surcharge type c	2.00	1.60
c.		As #16, double surcharge		2,000.
17	A4	2c on 1p lake, type d	2.75	2.75
a.		Surcharge type e	2.75	2.75
b.		Surcharge type f	20.00	20.00

Panama No. 74 Overprinted "CANAL ZONE" in Regular Type in Black and Surcharged in Red

8 cts.   **8 cts**
b   c

Both "PANAMA" reading up

1905-06

18	A3 (b)	8c on 50c bis brn	55.00	50.00
a.		"ZONE" in antique type	200.00	180.00
b.		"PANAMA" down & up	175.00	160.00
19	A3 (c)	8c on 50c bis brn ('06)	55.00	45.00
a.		"CANAL" in antique type	210.00	180.00
b.		"ZONE" in antique type	210.00	180.00
c.		"8 cts." double	1,100.	1,100.
d.		"PANAMA" down & up	110.00	110.00

On Nos. 18-19 with original gum the gum is usually disturbed.

Panama No. 81 Overprinted "CANAL ZONE" in Regular Type in Black and Surcharged in Red Type "c" plus Period.

"PANAMA" reading up and down

20	A3	8c on 50c bis brn	45.00	40.00
a.		"CANAL" in antique type	200.00	180.00
b.		"ZONE" in antique type	200.00	180.00
c.		"8 cts" omitted	750.00	750.00
d.		"8 cts" double	1,500.	

Numerous minor varieties of all these surcharges exist. Nos. 14, 18, 19 and 20 exist without CANAL ZONE overprint but were not regularly issued.

Vasco Nunez de Balboa A5

Francisco Hernandez de Cordoba A6

Justo Arosemena A7

Manuel J. Hurtado A8

Jose de Obaldia — A9

Stamps of Panama Ovptd. in Black

1906-07

Overprint Reading Up

21	A6	2c red & black	25.00	25.00
a.		"CANAL" only	4,000.	

Overprint Reading Down

22	A5	1c green & black	2.25	1.25
a.		Horiz. pair, imperf. btwn.	1,300.	1,300.
b.		Vert. pair, imperf. btwn.	1,750.	1,750.
c.		Vert. pair, imperf. horiz.	2,250.	1,750.
d.		Invtd. ovpt., reading up	550.00	550.00
e.		Double overprint	275.00	275.00
f.		Dbl. ovpt., one diagonal	1,350.	1,350.
g.		Inverted center and ovpt. reading up	4,000.	2,750.
23	A6	2c red & black	3.25	1.40
a.		Horiz. pair, imperf. btwn.	2,000.	1,750.
b.		Vertical pair, one without overprint	1,750.	1,750.
c.		Double overprint	500.00	500.00
d.		Dbl. ovpt., one diagonal	750.00	750.00
e.		Pair, Nos. 23, 23d	1,750.	
f.		2c carmine red & black	5.00	2.75
g.		As "f," inverted center and overprint reading up		5,000.
h.		As "d," one "ZONE CANAL"	4,000.	
i.		"CANAL" double	3,250.	
24	A7	5c ultra & black	6.50	2.25
c.		Double overprint	450.00	350.00
d.		"CANAL" only	3,500.	
e.		"ZONE CANAL"	4,500.	
25	A8	8c purple & black	22.50	8.00
a.		Horizontal pair, imperf. between and at left margin	2,000.	
26	A9	10c violet & black	20.00	8.00
a.		"CANAL" only, one reading up	3,750.	
b.		Overprint reading up	4,000.	
		Nos. 22-26 (5)	54.50	20.90

Nos. 22 to 25 occur with "CA" spaced.

Cordoba A11

Arosemena A12

Hurtado A13

Jose de Obaldia A14

Overprint Reading Down

1909

27	A11	2c ver & blk	12.50	6.50
a.		Horiz. pair, one without ovpt.	2,600.	
b.		Vert. pair, one without ovpt.	2,750.	
28	A12	5c dp bl & blk	45.00	12.50
29	A13	8c violet & black	37.50	14.00
30	A14	10c violet & black	40.00	15.00
a.		Horiz. pair, one without ovpt.	2,400.	
b.		Vert. pair, one without ovpt.	2,600.	
		Nos. 27-30 (4)	135.00	48.00

Nos. 27-30 occur with "CA" spaced. Do not confuse #27 with #39d or 53a. For designs A11-A14 with overprints reading up, see Nos. 32-35, 39-41, 47-48, 53-54, 56-57.

Vasco Nunez de Balboa — A15   Type I

Black Overprint, Reading Up

Type I Overprint: "C" with serifs both top and bottom. "L" "Z" and "E" with slanting serif.
Compare Type I overprint with Types II to V illustrated before Nos. 38, 46, 52 and 55. Illustrations of Types I to V are considerably enlarged and do not show actual spacing between lines of overprint.

1909-10

31	A15	1c dk green & blk	4.00	1.60
a.		Inverted center and overprint reading down		15,000.
c.		Bklt. pane of 6 handmade, perf. margins	575.00	
32	A11	2c vermilion & blk	4.50	1.60
a.		Vert. pair, imperf. horiz	1,000.	1,000.
c.		Bklt. pane of 6, handmade, perf. margins	750.00	
d.		Double overprint		—
33	A12	5c dp blue & blk	15.00	4.00
a.		Double overprint	375.00	375.00
34	A13	8c vio & blk ('10)	11.00	5.25
a.		Vert. pair, one without ovpt.	1,500.	
35	A14	10c violet & black	50.00	20.00
		Nos. 31-35 (5)	84.50	32.45

See Nos. 38, 46, 52, 55.

A16   A17

Black Surcharge

1911

36	A16	10c on 13c gray	6.00	2.25
a.		"10 cts." inverted	275.00	275.00
b.		"10 cts." omitted	275.00	

1914

37	A17	10c gray		55.00	12.50

Type II: "C" with serif at top only. "L" and "E" with vertical serifs. "O" tilts to left

Black Overprint, Reading Up

1912-16

38	A15	1c grn & blk ('13)	11.00	3.00
a.		Vert. pair, one without ovpt.	1,500.	1,500.
b.		Booklet pane of 6	625.00	
c.		As "b," handmade, perf. margins	1,000.	
39	A11	2c vermilion & blk	8.50	1.40
a.		Horiz. pair, right stamp without ovpt.	1,250.	
b.		Horiz. pair, left stamp without ovpt.	1,750.	
c.		Booklet pane of 6	500.00	
d.		Overprint reading down	175.00	
e.		As "d," inverted center	700.00	750.00
f.		As "e," booklet pane of 6 handmade, perf. margins	8,000.	
g.		As "c," handmade, perf. margins	1,000.	
h.		As #39, "CANAL" only		1,100.
40	A12	5c dp blue & blk	22.50	3.25
a.		With portrait of 2c		8,750.
41	A14	10c vio & blk ('16)	47.50	8.50
		Nos. 38-41 (4)	89.50	16.15

Map of Panama Canal — A18

Balboa Takes Possession of the Pacific Ocean — A19

Gatun Locks — A20

Culebra Cut — A21

Blue Overprint, Type II

1915

42	A18	1c dark green & black	8.50	6.50
43	A19	2c carmine & black	10.00	4.25
44	A20	5c blue & black	11.00	5.75
45	A21	10c orange & black	22.50	11.00
		Nos. 42-45 (4)	52.00	27.50

Type III: Similar to Type I but letters appear thinner, particularly the lower bar of "L," "Z" and "E." Impressions are often light, rough and irregular

Black Overprint, Reading Up

1915-20

46	A15	1c green & black	160.00	95.00
a.		Overprint reading down	375.00	
b.		Double overprint	300.00	
c.		"ZONE" double	4,250.	
d.		Dbl. ovpt., one "ZONE CANAL"	1,750.	
47	A11	2c orange ver & blk	3,250.	100.00
48	A12	5c dp blue & black	600.00	175.00
		Nos. 46-48 (3)	4,010.	370.00

S.S. "Panama" in Culebra Cut — A22

S.S. "Panama" in Culebra Cut — A23

S.S. "Cristobal" in Gatun Locks — A24

Blue Overprint, Type II

1917

49	A22	12c purple & black	17.50	5.50
50	A23	15c brt blue & black	55.00	25.00
51	A24	24c yel brown & black	45.00	15.00
		Nos. 49-51 (3)	117.50	45.50

Type IV: "C" thick at bottom, "E" with center bar same length as top and bottom bars

Black Overprint, Reading Up

1918-20

52	A15	1c green & black	32.50	11.00
a.		Overprint reading down	175.00	—
b.		Booklet pane of 6	650.00	
c.		Bklt. pane of 6, left vert. row of 3 without ovpt.	7,500.	
d.		Bklt. pane of 6, right vert. row of 3 with dbl. ovpt.	7,500.	
e.		Horiz. bklt. pair, left stamp without overprint	3,000.	
f.		Horiz. bklt. pair, right stamp with dbl. overprint	3,000.	
53	A11	2c vermilion & blk	115.00	7.00
a.		Overprint reading down	150.00	150.00
b.		Horizontal pair, right stamp without overprint	2,000.	
c.		Booklet pane of 6	1,000.	
d.		Bklt. pane of 6, left vert. row of 3 without ovpt.	8,000.	
e.		Horiz. bklt. pair, left stamp without overprint	3,000.	4,500.
54	A12	5c dp blue & black ('20)	175.00	35.00
		Nos. 52-54 (3)	322.50	53.00

Normal spacing between words of overprint on Nos. 52 and 53 is 9¼mm. On No. 54 and the booklet printings of Nos. 52 and 53, the normal spacing is 9mm. Minor spacing varieties are known.

No. 53e used is unique and is on cover.

Type V: Smaller block type 1¾mm high. "A" with flat top

Black Overprint, Reading Up

1920-21

55	A15	1c lt green & black	22.50	3.50
a.		Overprint reading down	250.00	225.00
b.		Horiz. pair, right stamp without ovpt.	1,750.	
c.		Horiz. pair, left stamp without ovpt.	1,000.	
d.		"ZONE" only	2,750.	
e.		Booklet pane of 6	1,750.	
f.		"CANAL" double	1,400.	
56	A11	2c orange ver & blk	8.50	2.25
a.		Double overprint	600.00	
b.		Double overprint, one reading down	650.00	
c.		Horiz. pair, right stamp without ovpt.	1,500.	
d.		Horiz. pair, left stamp without ovpt.	1,000.	
e.		Vert. pair, one without overprint	1,500.	
f.		"ZONE" double	1,000.	
g.		Booklet pane of 6	850.00	
h.		"CANAL" double	1,000.	
57	A12	5c dp blue & black	300.00	55.00
a.		Horiz. pair, right stamp without ovpt.	2,500.	
b.		Horiz. pair, left stamp without ovpt.	2,500.	
		Nos. 55-57 (3)	331.00	60.75

Drydock at Balboa — A25

Ship in Pedro Miguel Locks — A26

Black Overprint, Type V

1920

58	A25	50c orange & black	275.00	160.00
59	A26	1b dk violet & black	160.00	65.00

Jose Vallarino A27

The "Land Gate" A28

Bolivar's Tribute — A29

Municipal Building in 1821 and 1921 — A30

Statue of Balboa A31

Tomas Herrera A32

Jose de Fabrega — A33

Black or Red Overprint, Type V

1921
60	A27	1c green	3.75	1.40
a.		"CANAL" double	2,500.	
b.		Booklet pane of 6	900.00	
61	A28	2c carmine	3.00	1.50
a.		Overprint reading down	225.00	225.00
b.		Double overprint	900.00	
c.		Vert. pair, one without over-print	3,500.	
d.		"CANAL" double	1,900.	
f.		Booklet pane of 6	2,100.	
62	A29	5c blue (R)	11.00	4.50
a.		Overprint reading down (R)	60.00	
63	A30	10c violet	18.00	7.50
a.		Overprint reading down	90.00	
64	A31	15c light blue	47.50	17.50
65	A32	24c black brown	70.00	22.50
66	A33	50c black	150.00	100.00
		Nos. 60-66 (7)	303.25	154.90

Experts question the status of the 5c blue with a small type V overprint in red or black.

Black Overprint, Type III

1924
67	A27	1c green	500.	200.
a.		"ZONE CANAL" reading down	850.	
b.		"ZONE" reading down	1,900.	

Coat of Arms — A34

Black Overprint

1924
68	A34	1c dark green	11.00	4.50
69	A34	2c carmine	8.25	2.75

The 5c to 1b values were prepared but never issued. See listing in the Scott U.S. Specialized Catalogue.

US Nos. 551-554, 557, 562, 564-566, and 569-571 Overprinted in Red or Black

CANAL

Type A

ZONE

Letters "A" with Flat Tops
Flat Plate Printing

1924-25   *Perf. 11*
70	A154	½c olive brown (R)	1.25	.75
71	A155	1c deep green	1.40	.90
a.		Inverted overprint	500.00	500.00
b.		"ZONE" inverted	350.00	325.00
c.		"CANAL" only	1,750.	
d.		"ZONE CANAL"	500.00	
e.		Booklet pane of 6	90.00	
72	A156	1½c yellow brown	1.90	1.70
73	A157	2c carmine	7.50	1.70
a.		Booklet pane of 6	175.00	
74	A160	5c dark blue	19.00	8.50
75	A165	10c orange	45.00	25.00

76	A167	12c brown violet	35.00	32.50
a.		"ZONE" inverted	3,750.	3,000.
77	A168	14c dark blue	30.00	22.50
78	A169	15c gray	50.00	37.50
79	A172	30c olive brown	35.00	22.50
80	A173	50c lilac	77.50	45.00
81	A174	$1 violet brown	225.00	95.00
		Nos. 70-81 (12)	528.55	293.55

The space between the two lines of the overprint, on both type A and B, varies on some settings.

US Nos. 554, 555, 557, 562, 564-567, 569-571 and 623 Overprinted in Black or Red

CANAL

Type B

ZONE

Letters "A" with Sharp Pointed Tops
1925-26
84	A157	2c carmine	30.00	8.00
a.		"CANAL" ONLY	1,600.	
b.		"ZONE CANAL"	375.00	
c.		Horiz. pair, one without overprint	3,500.	
d.		Booklet pane of 6	175.00	
85	A158	3c violet	4.00	3.75
a.		"ZONE ZONE"	600.00	550.00
86	A160	5c dark blue	4.00	2.25
a.		"ZONE ZONE"	1,250.	
b.		"CANAL" inverted	950.00	
c.		Inverted overprint	500.00	
d.		Pair, one without overprint	3,250.	
e.		"ZONE CANAL"	325.00	
f.		"ZONE" only	2,000.	
g.		Pair, one without ovpt., other ovpt. invtd.	2,250.	
h.		"CANAL" only	2,250.	
87	A165	10c orange	35.00	12.00
a.		"ZONE ZONE"	3,000.	
88	A167	12c brown violet	22.50	14.00
a.		"ZONE ZONE"	5,250.	
89	A168	14c dark blue	20.00	16.00
90	A169	15c gray	7.00	4.50
a.		"ZONE ZONE"	5,500.	
91	A187	17c black (R)	4.00	3.00
a.		"ZONE" only	900.00	
b.		"CANAL" only	1,700.	
c.		"ZONE CANAL"	175.00	
92	A170	20c carmine rose	7.25	3.25
a.		"CANAL" inverted	3,850.	
b.		"ZONE" inverted	3,850.	
c.		"ZONE CANAL"	3,600.	
93	A172	30c olive brown	5.00	4.00
94	A173	50c lilac	225.00	165.00
95	A174	$1 violet brown	125.00	60.00
		Nos. 84-95 (12)	488.75	295.25

Overprint Type B on US Sesquicentennial Stamp No. 627

1926
96	A188	2c carmine rose	4.50	3.75

On this stamp there is a space of 5mm between the two words of the overprint.

Overprint Type B on US Nos. 583, 584 and 591

1927   *Perf. 10*
97	A157	2c carmine	65.00	11.00
a.		Pair, one without overprint	3,250.	
b.		Booklet pane of 6	600.00	
c.		"CANAL" only	2,000.	
d.		"ZONE" only	2,750.	
98	A158	3c violet	8.00	4.25
99	A165	10c orange	17.50	7.50
		Nos. 97-99 (3)	90.50	22.75

Overprint Type B on US Nos. 632, 634, 635, 637 and 642

1927-31   *Perf. 11x10½*
100	A155	1c green	2.25	1.40
a.		Pair, one without overprint	4,000.	
101	A157	2c carmine	2.50	1.00
a.		Booklet pane of 6	175.00	
102	A158	3c violet	4.25	2.75
a.		Booklet pane of 6, handmade, perf. margins	6,500.	
103	A160	5c dark blue	30.00	10.00
104	A165	10c orange	17.50	10.00
		Nos. 100-104 (5)	56.50	25.15

Wet and Dry Printings

Canal Zone stamps printed by both the "wet" and "dry" process are Nos. 105, 108-109, 111-114, 117, 138-140, C21-C24, C26, J25, J27. Starting with Nos. 147 and C27, the Bureau of Engraving and Printing used the "dry" method exclusively. See note following US Scott 1029.

Maj. Gen. William Crawford Gorgas A35

Maj. Gen. George Washington Goethals A36

Gaillard Cut — A37

Maj. Gen. Harry Foote Hodges A38

Lt. Col. David D. Gaillard A39

Maj. Gen. William L. Sibert — A40

Jackson Smith — A41

Rear Adm. Harry H. Rousseau A42

Col. Sydney B. Williamson A43

J.C.S. Blackburn — A44

1928-40   *Perf. 11*
105	A35	1c green	.20	.20
106	A36	2c carmine	.20	.20
a.		Booklet pane of 6	15.00	20.00
107	A37	5c blue ('29)	1.00	.40
108	A38	10c orange ('32)	.20	.20
109	A39	12c violet brown ('29)	.75	.60
110	A40	14c blue ('37)	.85	.85
111	A41	15c gray ('32)	.40	.35
112	A42	20c olive brown ('32)	.60	.20
113	A43	30c brown black ('40)	.80	.70
114	A44	50c lilac ('29)	1.50	.65
		Nos. 105-114 (10)	6.50	4.35

For surcharges & overprints see #J21-J24, O1-O8.

United States Nos. 720 and 695 Overprinted type B

1933   *Perf. 11x10½*
115	A226	3c deep violet	2.75	.25
b.		"CANAL" only	2,600.	
c.		Bkt. pane of 6, handmade, perf. margins	225.00	
116	A168	14c dark blue	4.50	3.50
a.		"ZONE CANAL"	1,500.	

Gen. George Washington Goethals — A45

1934, Aug. 15   *Perf. 11*
117	A45	3c deep violet	.20	.20
a.		Booklet pane of 6	45.00	32.50
b.		As "a," handmade, perf. margins	225.00	—

20th anniv. of the Panama Canal opening. See No. 153.

> Catalogue values for unused stamps in this section, from this point to the end of the section, are for Never Hinged items.

US Nos. 803 and 805 Overprinted in Black

1939   *Perf. 11x10½*
118	A275	½c deep orange	.20	.20
119	A277	1½c bister brown	.20	.20

Panama Canal Anniversary Issue

Balboa-Before — A46

Balboa-After — A47

Gaillard Cut-Before A48

Gaillard Cut-After A49

Bas Obispo-Before — A50

Bas Obispo-After A51

Gatun Locks-Before — A52

Gatun Locks-After A53

Canal Channel-Before A54

Canal Channel-After — A55

Gamboa-Before A56

Gamboa-After — A57

Pedro Miguel Locks-Before — A58

Pedro Miguel Locks-After A59

Gatun Spillway-Before A60

Gatun Spillway-After — A61

1939, Aug. 15   **Perf. 11**
120 A46 1c yellow green .65 .30
121 A47 2c rose carmine .65 .35
122 A48 3c purple .65 .20
123 A49 5c dark blue 1.60 1.25
124 A50 6c red orange 3.00 3.00
125 A51 7c black 3.25 3.00
126 A52 8c green 4.75 3.50
127 A53 10c ultramarine 3.50 3.00
128 A54 11c blue green 8.00 8.50
129 A55 12c brown carmine 7.50 8.00
130 A56 14c dark violet 7.50 8.00
131 A57 15c olive green 10.00 6.00
132 A58 18c rose pink 10.00 8.50
133 A59 20c brown 12.50 7.50
134 A60 25c orange 17.50 17.50
135 A61 50c violet brown 22.50 6.00
   Nos. 120-135 (16) 113.55 84.60

25th anniv. of the Panama Canal.

Maj. Gen. George W. Davis A62

Gov. Charles E. Magoon A63

Theodore Roosevelt A64

John F. Stevens A65

John F. Wallace — A66

1946-49   **Size: 19x22mm**   **Perf. 11**
136 A62 ½c bright red ('48) .40 .25
137 A63 1½c chocolate ('48) .40 .25
138 A64 2c rose carmine ('49) .20 .20
139 A65 5c deep blue .35 .20
140 A66 25c yellow green ('48) .85 .55
   Nos. 136-140 (5) 2.20 1.45

See #155, 162, 164. For overprint see #O9.

Map of Biological Area and Coati-Mundi A67

1948, Apr. 17   **Perf. 11**
141 A67 10c black 1.25 .80

Establishment of the Canal Zone Biological Area on Barro Colorado Is., 25th anniv.

"Forty-niners" Arriving at Chagres A68

Journey by "Bungo" to Las Cruces A69

Las Cruces Trail to Panama A70

Departure for San Francisco A71

1949, June 1   **Perf. 11**
142 A68 3c blue .50 .25
143 A69 6c violet .65 .30
144 A70 12c bright green 1.10 .90
145 A71 18c deep red lilac 2.00 1.50
   Nos. 142-145 (4) 4.25 2.95

Centenary of the California Gold Rush.

Workers in Culebra Cut — A72

Early Railroad Scene — A73

1951, Aug. 15
146 A72 10c carmine 2.25 1.50

Contribution of West Indian laborers in the construction of the Canal.

1955, Jan. 28   **Perf. 11**
147 A73 3c violet .60 .50

Cent. of the completion of the Panama Railroad and the 1st transcontinental railroad trip in Americas.

Gorgas Hospital and Ancon Hill — A74

1957, Nov. 17
148 A74 3c black, *blue green* .45 .35

75th anniv. of Gorgas Hospital. Printed on two shades of blue green paper.

S.S. Ancon A75

1958, Aug. 30   **Unwmk.**
149 A75 4c greenish blue .40 .30

Roosevelt Medal and Map — A76

1958, Nov. 15   **Perf. 11**
150 A76 4c brown .40 .30

Theodore Roosevelt (1858-1919).

Boy Scout Badge — A77

Administration Building — A78

1960, Feb. 8   **Perf. 11**
151 A77 4c dk blue, red & bister .50 .40

Boy Scouts of America, 50th anniv.

1960, Nov. 1   **Perf. 11**
152 A78 4c rose lilac .20 .20

Types of 1934, 1960 and 1946 Coil Stamps

1960-62   **Perf. 10 Vert.**
153 A45 3c deep violet .20 .20
   Perf. 10 Horizontally
154 A78 4c deep rose lilac .20 .20
   Perf. 10 Vertically
155 A65 5c deep blue .25 .20
   Nos. 153-155 (3) .65 .60

Issued: 3c, 4c, 1960; 5c, Feb. 10, 1962.

Girl Scout Badge and Camp at Gatun Lake A79

1962, Mar. 12   **Perf. 11**
156 A79 4c bl, dk grn & bister .40 .30

50th anniv. of Girl Scouts.

Thatcher Ferry Bridge and Map of Western Hemisphere A80

1962, Oct. 12
157 A80 4c black & silver .35 .25
   a. Silver (bridge) omitted 7,500.

Opening of the Thatcher Ferry Bridge, spanning the Panama Canal.

Goethals Memorial, Balboa A81

Fort San Lorenzo A82

1968-71   **Perf. 11**
158 A81 6c green & ultra .30 .30
159 A82 8c multicolored .35 .20

Issued: 6c, Mar. 15, 1968; 8c, July 14, 1971.

Portrait Type of 1928-48 Coil Stamps

1975, Feb. 14   **Perf. 10 Vert.**
160 A35 1c green .20 .20
161 A38 10c orange .70 .40
162 A66 25c yellow green 2.75 2.75
   Nos. 160-162 (3) 3.65 3.35

Dredge Cascadas A83

1976, Feb. 23   **Perf. 11**
163 A83 13c multicolored .35 .20
   a. Booklet pane of 4 3.00 —

Stevens Type of 1946

1977   **Perf. 11x10½**
    Size: 19x22½mm
164 A65 5c deep blue .60 .85
   a. Tagged 12.00 15.00

Towing Locomotive, Ship in Lock — A84

1978, Oct. 25   **Perf. 11**
165 A84 15c dp grn & bl grn .35 .20

AIR POST STAMPS

Nos. 105-106 Surcharged in Dark Blue

Type I- Flag of "5" pointing up **15**

Type II- Flag of "5" curved **15**

1929   **Engr.**   **Unwmk.**   **Perf. 11**
C1 A35 15c on 1c green, I 8.00 5.50
C2 A35 15c on 1c green, II 85.00 75.00
C3 A36 25c on 2c carmine 3.50 2.00
   Nos. C1-C3 (3) 96.50 82.50

Nos. 114 and 106 Surcharged

1929, Dec. 31

C4	A44	10c on 50c lilac	7.50	6.50
C5	A36	20c on 2c carmine	5.00	1.75
a.		Dropped "2" in surcharge	80.00	60.00

Catalogue values for unused stamps in this section, from this point to the end of the section, are for Never Hinged items.

Gaillard Cut — AP1

1931-49   Engr.

C6	AP1	4c red violet ('49)	.75	.70
C7	AP1	5c yellow green	.60	.45
C8	AP1	6c yellow brown ('46)	.75	.35
C9	AP1	10c orange	1.00	.35
C10	AP1	15c blue	1.25	.30
C11	AP1	20c red violet	2.00	.30
C12	AP1	30c rose lake ('41)	3.50	1.00
C13	AP1	40c yellow	3.50	1.10
C14	AP1	$1 black	8.50	1.90
		Nos. C6-C14 (9)	21.85	6.45

For overprints see Nos. CO1-CO14.

Panama Canal Anniversary Issue

Douglas Plane over Sosa Hill — AP2

Planes and Map of Central America AP3

Pan American Clipper and Scene near Fort Amador AP4

Pan American Clipper at Cristobal Harbor AP5

Pan American Clipper over Gaillard Cut — AP6

Pan American Clipper Landing AP7

1939, July 15

C15	AP2	5c greenish black	3.75	2.25
C16	AP3	10c dull violet	3.00	2.25
C17	AP4	15c light brown	4.25	1.25
C18	AP5	25c blue	13.00	8.00
C19	AP6	30c rose carmine	12.00	6.75
C20	AP7	$1 green	35.00	22.50
		Nos. C15-C20 (6)	71.00	43.00

10th anniv. of Air Mail service and the 25th anniv. of the opening of the Panama Canal.

Globe and Wing — AP8

1951, July 16   Unwmk.   Perf. 11

C21	AP8	4c red violet	.75	.35
C22	AP8	6c brown	.50	.25
C23	AP8	10c red orange	.90	.35
C24	AP8	21c blue	7.50	4.00
C25	AP8	31c cerise	7.50	3.75
a.		Horiz. pair, imperf. vert.	1,000.	
C26	AP8	80c gray black	4.50	1.50
		Nos. C21-C26 (6)	21.65	10.20

1958, Aug. 16

C27	AP8	5c yellow green	1.00	.60
C28	AP8	7c olive	1.00	.45
C29	AP8	15c brown violet	3.75	2.75
C30	AP8	25c orange yellow	10.00	2.75
C31	AP8	35c dark blue	6.25	2.75
		Nos. C27-C31 (5)	22.00	9.30
		Nos. C21-C31 (11)	43.65	19.50

See No. C34.

Emblem of US Army Caribbean School AP9

1961, Nov. 21   Perf. 11

C32	AP9	15c red & dk blue	1.25	.75

Malaria Eradication Emblem and Mosquito AP10

1962, Sept. 24   Unwmk.   Perf. 11

C33	AP10	7c yellow & black	.45	.40

WHO drive to eradicate malaria.

Type of 1951

1963, Jan. 7   Perf. 10½x11

C34	AP8	8c carmine	.40	.30

Alliance Emblem AP11

1963, Aug. 17   Unwmk.   Perf. 11

C35	AP11	15c gray, green & dk ultra	1.10	.85

2nd anniv. of the Alliance for Progress, which aims to stimulate economic growth and raise living standards in Latin America.

Jet over Cristobal AP12

Designs: 8c, Gatun Locks. 15c, Madden Dam. 20c, Gaillard Cut. 30c, Miraflores Locks. 80c, Balboa.

1964, Aug. 15   Perf. 11

C36	AP12	6c green & black	.45	.35
C37	AP12	8c rose red & black	.45	.35
C38	AP12	15c blue & black	1.00	.75
C39	AP12	20c rose lilac & blk	1.50	1.00
C40	AP12	30c redsh brn & blk	2.25	2.25
C41	AP12	80c ol bister & black	3.75	3.00
		Nos. C36-C41 (6)	9.40	7.70

50th anniv. of the Panama Canal.

Seal and Jet Plane AP13

1965, July 15   Unwmk.   Perf. 11

C42	AP13	6c green & black	.35	.30
C43	AP13	8c rose red & black	.30	.20
C44	AP13	15c blue & black	.50	.20
C45	AP13	20c lilac & black	.55	.20

C46	AP13	30c redsh brn & blk	.80	.30
C47	AP13	80c bister & black	2.00	.75
		Nos. C42-C47 (6)	4.50	2.05

1968-76

C48	AP13	10c dull orange & blk	.25	.20
a.		Booklet pane of 4 (70)	4.25	
C49	AP13	11c olive & blk	.25	.20
a.		Booklet pane of 4	3.50	
C50	AP13	13c emerald & black	.80	.25
a.		Booklet pane of 4	6.00	
C51	AP13	22c violet & black	.75	2.00
C52	AP13	25c pale yel green & blk	.60	.70
C53	AP13	35c salmon & black	.90	2.00
		Nos. C48-C53 (6)	3.55	5.35

Issued: 10c, 3/15/68; 11c, 9/24/71; 13c, 2/11/74; 22c, 35c, 5/10/76.

AIR POST OFFICIAL STAMPS

Officials and Air Post Officials were sold to the public only with a Balboa Heights, Canal Zone wavy line parcel post cancel while current. After being withdrawn from use, unused copies (except for Nos. CO8-CO12, O3 and O8) were sold at face value for three months beginning Jan. 2, 1952.

Used values are for the CTO copies, postally used copies being worth more.

Nos. C7, C9-C14 Overprinted in Black

Two Types of Overprint

1941-42   Unwmk.   Engr.   Perf. 11   "PANAMA CANAL" 19-20mm

CO1	AP1	5c yellow green	5.50	1.50
CO2	AP1	10c orange	8.50	2.00
CO3	AP1	15c blue	11.00	2.00
CO4	AP1	20c red violet	12.50	4.00
CO5	AP1	30c rose lake ('42)	17.50	5.00
CO6	AP1	40c yellow	17.50	7.50
CO7	AP1	$1 black	20.00	10.00
		Nos. CO1-CO7 (7)	92.50	32.00

Overprint varieties occur on Nos. CO1-CO7 and CO14. "O" over "N" of "PANAMA" (entire 3rd row). "O" broken at top (pos. 31). "O" over 2nd "A" of "PANAMA" (pos. 45). 1st "F" of "OFFICIAL" over 2nd "A" of "PANAMA" (pos. 50).

1941

"PANAMA CANAL" 17mm long

CO8	AP1	5c light green	—	160.00
CO9	AP1	10c orange	—	275.00
CO10	AP1	20c red violet	—	175.00
CO11	AP1	30c rose lake	—	65.00
CO12	AP1	40c yellow	—	180.00
		Nos. CO8-CO12 (5)		855.00

Same Overprint on No. C8

1947, Nov.

"PANAMA CANAL" 19-20mm long

CO14	AP1	6c yellow brown	12.50	5.00
a.		Inverted overprint		2,500.

POSTAGE DUE STAMPS

Postage Due Stamps of the US Nos. J45a, J46a and J49a Overprinted in Black

CANAL ZONE

Wmk. 190

1914, Mar.   Engr.   Perf. 12

J1	D2	1c rose carmine	85.00	15.00
J2	D2	2c rose carmine	250.00	45.00
J3	D2	10c rose carmine	850.00	40.00
		Nos. J1-J3 (3)	1,185.	100.00

Castle Gate (See footnote) — D1

Statue of Columbus D2

Pedro J. Sosa D3

Blue Overprint, Type II, on Postage Due Stamps of Panama

1915   Unwmk.

J4	D1	1c olive brown	12.50	5.00
J5	D2	2c olive brown	200.00	17.50
J6	D3	10c olive brown	50.00	10.00
		Nos. J4-J6 (3)	262.50	32.50

The 1c was intended to show a gate of San Lorenzo Castle, Chagres. By error the stamp actually shows the main gate of San Geronimo Castle, Portobelo.

Surcharged in Red   CANAL 2 ZONE

J7	D1	1c on 1c olive brn	105.00	15.00
J8	D2	2c on 2c olive brn	25.00	7.00
J9	D3	10c on 10c olive brn	22.50	5.00
		Nos. J7-J9 (3)	152.50	27.00

Columbus Statue — D4

Capitol, Panama City — D5

Carmine Surcharge

1919

J10	D4	2c on 2c olive brown	30.00	12.50
J11	D5	4c on 4c olive brown	35.00	15.00
a.		"ZONE" omitted	7,500.	
b.		"4" omitted	7,500.	

US Postage Due Stamps Nos. J61, J62b and J65b Overprinted in Black

CANAL

Type A

ZONE

Letters "A" with Flat Tops

1924   Perf. 11

J12	D2	1c carmine rose	110.00	27.50
J13	D2	2c deep claret	60.00	10.00
J14	D2	10c deep claret	250.00	50.00
		Nos. J12-J14 (3)	420.00	87.50

US Postage Stamps Nos. 552, 554 and 562 Overprinted Type A and additional Overprint in Red or Blue

POSTAGE DUE

1925

J15	A155	1c deep green	90.00	13.00
J16	A157	2c carmine (Bl)	22.50	7.00
J17	A165	10c orange	50.00	11.00
a.		"POSTAGE DUE" double	500.00	
b.		"E" of "POSTAGE" missing	450.00	
c.		As "a" and "b"	3,250.	
		Nos. J15-J17 (3)	162.50	31.00

"CANAL ZONE" Type B Overprinted on US Nos. J61, J62, J65, J65b Letters "A" with Sharp Pointed Tops

1925

J18	D2	1c carmine rose	8.00	3.00
a.		"ZONE ZONE"	1,250.	
J19	D2	2c carmine rose	15.00	4.00
a.		"ZONE ZONE"	1,500.	
J20	D2	10c carmine rose	150.00	20.00
a.		Pair, one without overprint	1,750.	
b.		10c rose red	250.00	150.00
c.		As "b," double overprint	450.00	
		Nos. J18-J20 (3)	173.00	27.00

No. 107 Surcharged in Black

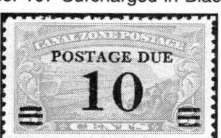

1929-30

J21	A37	1c on 5c blue	4.50	1.75
a.		"POSTAGE DUE" omitted	5,500.	
J22	A37	2c on 5c blue	7.50	2.50
J23	A37	5c on 5c blue	7.50	2.75
J24	A37	10c on 5c blue	7.50	2.75
		Nos. J21-J24 (4)	27.00	9.75

On No. J23 the horizontal bars in the lower corners of the surcharge are omitted.

Canal Zone Seal — D6

1932-41

J25	D6	1c claret	.20	.20
J26	D6	2c claret	.20	.20
J27	D6	5c claret	.35	.20
J28	D6	10c claret	1.40	1.50
J29	D6	15c claret ('41)	1.10	1.00
		Nos. J25-J29 (5)	3.25	3.10

The 1c and 5c are found in both "wet" and "dry" printings. (See note after US No. 1029.) The dry printings are in red violet.

OFFICIAL STAMPS

See note at beginning of Air Post Official Stamps.

Regular Issues of 1928-34
Overprinted in Black

OFFICIAL	
PANAMA	OFFICIAL
CANAL	PANAMA CANAL
Type 1	Type 2

Type 1 - "PANAMA" 10mm long.
Type 1A - "PANAMA" 9mm long.

1941		**Unwmk.**	**Engr.**	**Perf. 11**	
O1	A35	1c yel green (1)	2.25	.40
O2	A45	3c deep violet (1)	4.00	.75
O3	A37	5c blue (2)	1,000.	32.50
O4	A38	10c orange (1)	7.00	1.90
O5	A41	15c gray (1)	12.50	2.25
O6	A42	20c olive brown (1)	15.00	2.75
O7	A44	50c lilac (1)	37.50	5.50
O8	A44	50c rose lilac (1A)		525.00

Same Overprint on No. 139

1947

O9	A65	5c deep blue (1)	9.00	3.50

CUBA

ˈkyü-bə

LOCATION — The largest island of the West Indies; south of Florida.
GOVT. — socialist; under US military governor 1899-1902 and US provisional governor 1906-1909.
AREA — 44,206 sq. mi.
POP. — 9,710,000 (1981)
CAPITAL — Havana

Formerly a Spanish possession, Cuba's attempts to gain freedom led to US intervention in 1898. Under Treaty of Paris of that year, Spain relinquished the island to US trust. In 1902, a republic was established and Cuban Congress took over government from US military authorities.

100 Cents = 1 Dollar

Watermark

Wmk. 191- Double-lined "USPS" in Capitals

Values for Nos. 176-220 are for stamps in the grade of fine and in sound condition where such exist. Values for Nos. 221-J4 are for very fine examples.

King Alfonso XIII
A19   N2
**United States Administration
Puerto Principe Issue**
Issues of Cuba of 1898 & 1896
Surcharged

HABILITADO

**HABILITADO
1
cent.**
a

**HABILITADO
2
cents.**
c

**HABILITADO
3
cents.**
e

**HABILITADO
5
cents.**
g

**HABILITADO
5
cents.**
i

**HABILITADO
3
cents.**
k

**1
cents.**
b

**HABILITADO
2
cents.**
d

**HABILITADO
3
cents.**
f

**HABILITADO
5
cents.**
h

**HABILITADO
5
cents.**
j

**HABILITADO
3
cents.**
l

**HABILITADO
10
cents.**
m

Types a, c, d, e, f, g and h are 17½mm high, the others are 19½mm high.

Black Surcharge on #156-158, 160
1898-99
#176-189 are Orange Brown

176	A19 (a)	1c on 1m	50.	30.
177	A19 (b)	1c on 1m	45.	35.
a.		Broken figure "1"	75.	65.
b.		Inverted surcharge		200.
d.		As "a," inverted		250.
178	A19 (c)	2c on 2m	22.50	18.
a.		Inverted surcharge	250.	50.
179	A19 (d)	2c on 2m	40.	35.
a.		Inverted surcharge	350.	100.
179B	A19 (k)	3c on 1m	300.	175.
c.		Double surcharge	1,500.	750.
179D	A19 (l)	3c on 1m	1,500.	750.
e.		Double surcharge	—	
179F	A19 (e)	3c on 2m		1,500.

Value for No. 179F is for copies with minor faults.

179G	A19 (f)	3c on 2m	—	2,000.

Value for No. 179G is for copies with minor faults.

180	A19 (e)	3c on 3m	27.50	30.
a.		Inverted surcharge		110.
181	A19 (f)	3c on 3m	75.	75.
a.		Inverted surcharge		200.
182	A19 (g)	5c on 1m	700.	200.
a.		Inverted surcharge		500.
183	A19 (h)	5c on 1m	1,300.	500.
a.		Inverted surcharge		700.
184	A19 (g)	5c on 2m	750.	250.
185	A19 (h)	5c on 2m	1,500.	500.
186	A19 (g)	5c on 3m	650.	175.
a.		Inverted surcharge	1,200.	700.
187	A19 (h)	5c on 3m		400.
a.		Inverted surcharge		1,000.
188	A19 (g)	5c on 5m	80.	60.
a.		Inverted surcharge	400.	200.
b.		Double surcharge	—	—
189	A19 (h)	5c on 5m	350.	250.
a.		Inverted surcharge	—	400.
b.		Double surcharge	—	—

Values for Nos. 188, 189 are for the 1st printing.
The 2nd printing was surcharged using a shiny ink.

189C	A19 (i)	5c on 5m org brn		7,500.

Black Surcharge on No. P25

190	N2 (g)	5c on ½m bl grn	250.	75.
a.		Inverted surcharge	500.	150.
b.		Pair, one without surch.		500.

Value for No. 190b is for pair with unsurcharged copy at right. Exists with unsurcharged stamp at left.

191	N2 (h)	5c on ½m bl grn	300.	90.
a.		Inverted surcharge		200.
192	N2 (i)	5c on ½m bl grn	550.	200.
a.		Dbl. surch., one diagonal		11,500.
193	N2 (j)	5c on ½m bl grn	800.	300.

Red Surcharge on No. 161

196	A19	3c on 1c blk vio (k)	65.	35.
a.		Inverted surcharge		300.
197	A19 (l)	3c on 1c blk vio	125.	55.
a.		Inverted surcharge		300.
198	A19 (i)	3c on 1c blk vio	25.	30.
a.		Inverted surcharge		125.
b.		Vert. surch., reading up		3,500.
c.		Double surcharge	400.	600.
d.		Double invtd. surcharge	—	

No. 198b exists reading down.

199	A19 (j)	5c on 1c blk vio	55.	55.
a.		Inverted surcharge		250.
b.		Vertical surcharge		2,000.
c.		Double surcharge	1,000.	600.
200	A19 (m)	10c on 1c blk vio	20.	50.
a.		Broken figure "1"	40.	100.

Black Surcharge on Nos. P26-P30

201	N2 (k)	3c on 1m bl grn	350.	350.
a.		Inverted surcharge		450.
b.		"EENTS"	550.	450.
c.		As "b," inverted		850.
202	N2 (l)	3c on 1m bl grn	550.	400.
a.		Inverted surcharge		850.
203	N2 (k)	3c on 2m bl grn	850.	350.
a.		"EENTS"	1,250.	500.
b.		Inverted surcharge		850.
c.		As "a," inverted		850.
204	N2 (l)	3c on 2m bl grn	1,250.	600.
a.		Inverted surcharge		750.
205	N2 (k)	3c on 3m bl grn	900.	350.
a.		Inverted surcharge		500.
b.		"EENTS"	1,250.	450.
c.		As "b," inverted		700.
206	N2 (l)	3c on 3m bl grn	1,200.	550.
a.		Inverted surcharge		700.
211	N2 (i)	5c on 1m bl grn	—	1,800.
a.		"EENTS"		2,500.
212	N2 (j)	5c on 1m bl grn		2,250.
213	N2 (i)	5c on 2m bl grn	—	1,800.
a.		"EENTS"		1,900.
214	N2 (j)	5c on 2m bl grn		1,750.
215	N2 (i)	5c on 3m bl grn	—	550.
a.		"EENTS"		1,000.
216	N2 (j)	5c on 3m bl grn	—	1,000.
217	N2 (i)	5c on 4m bl grn	2,500.	900.
a.		"EENTS"	3,000.	1,500.
b.		Inverted surcharge		2,000.
c.		As "a," inverted		2,000.
218	N2 (j)	5c on 4m bl grn	—	1,250.
a.		Inverted surcharge		2,000.

219	N2 (i)	5c on 8m bl grn	2,500.	1,250.
a.		Inverted surcharge		1,500.
b.		"EENTS"	—	1,800.
c.		As "b," inverted		2,500.
220	N2 (j)	5c on 8m bl grn		2,000.
a.		Inverted surcharge		2,500.

CUBA

U.S. Nos. 279, 267, 267b, 279Bf, 279Bh, 268, 281, 282C and 283 Surcharged in Black

**1 c.
de PESO.**

1899		**Wmk. 191**		**Perf. 12**	
221	A87	1c on 1c yel grn	5.25	.35
222	A88	2c on 2c reddish car, III	10.00	.75
b.		2c on 2c vermilion, III	10.00	.75
222A	A88	2c on 2c reddish car, IV	5.75	.40
c.		2c on 2c vermilion, IV	5.75	.40
d.		As #222A, inverted surcharge	3,500.	3,500.
223	A88	2½c on 2c reddish car, III	5.00	.80
b.		2½c on 2c vermilion, III	5.00	.80
223A	A88	2½c on 2c reddish car, IV	3.50	.50
c.		2½c on 2c vermilion, IV	3.50	.50
224	A89	3c on 3c purple	12.50	1.75
a.		"CUB.A"	37.50	35.00
225	A91	5c on 5c blue	12.50	2.00
226	A94	10c on 10c brn, I	22.50	6.50
b.		"CUBA" omitted	4,000.	4,000.
226A	A94	10c on 10c brn, II	6,000.	
		Nos. 221-226 (8)	77.00	13.05

The 2½c was sold and used as a 2 centavo stamp.

Excellent counterfeits of this and the preceding issue exist, especially inverted and double surcharges.

Issues of the Republic under U.S. Military Rule

Statue of Columbus
A20

Royal Palms
A21

"Cuba"
A22

Ocean Liner
A23

Cane Field — A24

1899		**Engr.**		**Wmk. U S-C (191C)**	**Perf. 12**	
227	A20	1c yellow green	3.50	.20
228	A21	2c carmine	3.50	.20
a.		2c scarlet	3.50	.20
b.		Booklet pane of 6	2,000.	
229	A22	3c purple	3.50	.20
230	A23	5c blue	4.50	.20
231	A24	10c brown	11.00	.50
		Nos. 227-231 (5)	26.00	1.30

Unwatermarked stamps of designs A20-A24 were re-engraved and issued by the Cuban Republic. See Volume 2 for details of the re-engraving.

SPECIAL DELIVERY STAMPS

United States Administration

U.S. No. E5
Surcharged
in Red

1899   Wmk. 191   *Perf. 12*

E1	SD3	10c on 10c blue	130.00	100.00
a.		No period after "CUBA"	450.00	400.00

Issues of the Republic under U.S. Military Rule

Special Delivery Messenger SD2

Inscribed: "Immediata"

1899   Wmk. 191C   *Engr.*

E2	SD2	10c orange	50.00	15.00

POSTAGE DUE STAMPS

United States Administration
Postage Due Stamps of the US Nos.
J38, J39, J41 & J42
Surcharged in Black Like Nos. 221-226A

1899   Wmk. 191   *Perf. 12*

J1	D2	1c on 1c dp claret	45.00	5.25
J2	D2	2c on 2c dp claret	45.00	5.25
a.		Inverted surcharge		2,750.
J3		5c on 5c dp claret	45.00	5.25
J4	D2	10c on 10c deep cl	27.50	2.50
		Nos. J1-J4 (4)	162.50	18.25

DANISH WEST INDIES

'dā-nish 'west 'in-dēs

LOCATION — Group of islands in the West Indies, lying east of Puerto Rico
GOVT. — Danish colony
AREA — 132 sq. mi.
POP. — 27,086 (1911)
CAPITAL — Charlotte Amalie

The US bought these islands in 1917 and they became the US Virgin Islands, using US stamps and currency.

100 Cents = 1 Dollar
100 Bit = 1 Franc (1905)

Watermarks

Wmk. 111- Small Crown

Wmk. 112- Crown

Wmk. 113- Crown

Wmk. 114- Multiple Crosses

Coat of Arms — A1

Yellowish Paper
Yellow Wavy-line Burelage, UL to LR

1856   Wmk. 111   *Typo.*   *Imperf.*

1	A1	3c dk car, brn gum	150.	175.
a.		3c dark car, yellow gum	175.	190.
b.		3c carmine, white gum	4,000.	—

Reprint: 1981, carmine, back-printed across two stamps ("Reprint by Dansk Post og Telegrafmuseum 1978"), value, pair, $10.

White Paper
Yellow Wavy-line Burelage, UR to LL

1866

2	A1	3c rose	40.00	60.00

No. 2 reprints unwatermarked: 1930 carmine, value $100. 1942 rose carmine, back-printed across each row ("Nytryk 1942 G. A. Hagemann Danmark og Dansk Vestindiens Friemaerker Bind 2"), value $50.

1872   *Perf. 12½*

3	A1	3c rose	75.00	150.00

1873
Without Burelage

4	A1	4c dull blue	160.00	325.00
a.		Imperf., pair	750.00	
b.		Horiz. pair, imperf. vert.	525.00	

#4 reprints, unwatermarked, imperf.: 1930, ultramarine, value $100. 1942, blue back-printed like 1942 reprint of #2, value $50.

A2

Normal Frame

Inverted Frame

The arabesques in the corners have a main stem and a branch. When the frame is in normal position, in the upper left corner the branch leaves the main stem half way between two little leaflets. In the lower right corner the branch starts at the foot of the second leaflet. When the frame is inverted the corner designs are, of course, transposed.

White Wove Paper
Varying from Thin to Thick

1874-79   Wmk. 112   *Perf. 14x13½*

5	A2	1c green & brn red	13.00	21.00
a.		1c grn & rose lilac, thin paper	75.00	125.00
b.		1c grn & red vio, medium paper	40.00	65.00
c.		1c green & violet, thick paper	13.00	21.00
d.		Inverted frame	13.00	21.00
6	A2	3c blue & carmine	17.50	12.00
a.		3c lt bl & rose car, thin paper	65.00	50.00
b.		3c dp bl & dk car, medium paper	35.00	16.00

---

c.		3c greenish blue & lake, thick paper	17.50	12.00
d.		Imperf., pair	325.00	
e.		Inverted frame	17.50	12.00
7	A2	4c brn & dull blue	9.75	12.00
a.		4c brown & ultramarine	150.00	200.00
c.		Diagonal half used as 2c on cover		110.00
d.		As "b," inverted frame	750.00	1,250.
8	A2	5c grn & gray ('76)	17.50	13.50
a.		5c yel grn & dk gray, thin paper	45.00	30.00
b.		Inverted frame	17.50	13.50
9	A2	7c lilac & orange	21.00	77.50
a.		7c lilac & yellow	77.50	77.50
b.		Inverted frame	52.50	125.00
10	A2	10c blue & brn ('76)	19.00	21.00
a.		10c dk bl & blk brn, thin paper	70.00	45.00
b.		"cent.s"	30.00	30.00
c.		Inverted frame	21.00	25.00
11	A2	12c red lilac & yel green ('77)	35.00	110.00
a.		12c lilac & deep green	125.00	140.00
12	A2	14c lilac & green ('79)	450.00	850.00
a.		Inverted frame	1,500.	2,750.
13	A2	50c violet, thin paper ('79)	160.00	225.00
a.		50c gray vio, thick porous paper	210.00	325.00
		Nos. 5-13 (9)	742.75	1,342.

The central element in the fan-shaped scrollwork at the outside of the lower corner of Nos. 5a and 7b looks like an elongated diamond.

See Nos. 16-20. For surcharges see Nos. 14-15, 23-28, 40.

Nos. 9 & 13 Surcharged in Black

1887-95

14	A2	1c on 7c lilac & org	65.00	175.00
a.		1c on 7c lilac & yellow	65.00	175.00
b.		Double surcharge	175.00	350.00
c.		Inverted frame	85.00	300.00
15	A2	10c on 50c violet, thin paper ('95)	37.50	60.00

Type of 1874-79

1896-1901   *Perf. 13*

16	A2	1c grn & red vio ('98)	11.00	16.00
a.		Normal frame	225.00	325.00
17	A2	3c blue & lake ('98)	9.00	12.50
a.		Normal frame	200.00	325.00
18	A2	4c bis & dl bl ('01)	10.00	10.00
a.		Diagonal half used as 2c on cover		40.00
b.		Inverted frame	45.00	85.00
c.		As "b," diagonal half used as 2c on cover		250.00
19	A2	5c green & gray	27.50	29.00
a.		Normal frame	550.00	850.00
20	A2	10c blue & brn ('01)	60.00	110.00
a.		Inverted frame	750.00	1,300.
b.		"cent.s"	100.00	150.00
		Nos. 16-20 (5)	117.50	177.50

Arms — A5

1900

21	A5	1c light green	2.50	2.50
22	A5	5c light blue	14.00	17.50

See #29-30. For surcharges see #41-42.

Nos. 6, 17, 20 Surcharged

Surcharge "c" in Black

1902   *Perf. 14x13½*

23	A2	2c on 3c blue & car	300.00	350.00
a.		"2" in date with straight tail	325.00	375.00
b.		Normal frame	3,500.	

Perf. 13

24	A2	2c on 3c blue & lake	9.00	20.00
a.		"2" in date with straight tail	11.50	22.50
b.		Dated "1901"	375.00	400.00
c.		Normal frame	150.00	225.00
d.		Dark green surcharge	1,750.	
e.		As "d" & "a"		
f.		As "d" & "c"		
25	A2	8c on 10c blue & brn	20.00	32.50
a.		"2" with straight tail	22.50	35.00
b.		On No. 20b	20.00	37.50
c.		Inverted frame	200.00	325.00

Only one copy of No. 24f can exist.

Surcharge "d" in Black

1902

27	A2	2c on 3c blue & lake	11.00	30.00
a.		Normal frame	225.00	375.00
28	A2	8c on 10c blue & brn	11.00	11.00
a.		On No. 20b	17.50	20.00
b.		Inverted frame	175.00	350.00
		Nos. 23-28 (5)	351.00	443.50

1903   Wmk. 113

29	A5	2c carmine	6.00	10.00
30	A5	8c brown	22.50	42.50

King Christian IX — A8

St. Thomas Harbor — A9

1905   *Typo.*   *Perf. 13*

31	A8	5b green	3.50	3.00
32	A8	10b red	3.50	3.00
33	A8	20b green & blue	8.00	7.00
34	A8	25b ultramarine	8.00	8.00
35	A8	40b red & gray	8.00	7.00
36	A8	50b yellow & gray	9.00	9.00

Frame Typo., Center Engr.
Wmk. Two Crowns (113)
Perf. 12

37	A9	1fr green & blue	17.50	37.50
38	A9	2fr org red & brown	30.00	50.00
39	A9	5fr yellow & brown	75.00	210.00
		Nos. 31-39 (9)	162.50	334.50

Favor cancels exist on #37-39. Value 25% less.

Nos. 18, 22, 30 Surcharged in Black

1905   Wmk. 112   *Perf. 13*

40	A2	5b on 4c bis & dl bl	13.50	40.00
a.		Inverted frame	40.00	75.00
41	A5	5b on 5c light blue	12.50	32.50

Wmk. 113

42	A5	5b on 8c brown	12.50	32.50
		Nos. 40-42 (3)	38.50	105.00

Favor cancels exist on #40-42. Value 25% less.

Frederik VIII
A10

Christian X
A11

Frame Typo., Center Engr.

1907-08		Wmk. 113		Perf. 13
43	A10	5b green	1.75	1.25
44	A10	10b red	1.75	1.25
45	A10	15b violet & brown	3.50	3.50
46	A10	20b green & blue	30.00	22.50
47	A10	25b blue & dk blue	1.50	1.75
48	A10	30b claret & slate	42.50	42.50
49	A10	40b ver & gray	4.50	5.25
50	A10	50b yellow & brown	4.50	9.00
		Nos. 43-50 (8)	90.00	87.00

1915		Wmk. 114		Perf. 14x14½
51	A11	5b yellow green	3.50	3.00
52	A11	10b red	3.50	35.00
53	A11	15b lilac & red brown	3.50	40.00
54	A11	20b green & black	3.50	40.00
55	A11	25b blue & dark blue	3.50	10.00
56	A11	30b claret & black	3.50	50.00
57	A11	40b orange & black	3.50	50.00
58	A11	50b yellow & brown	3.50	50.00
		Nos. 51-58 (8)	28.00	278.00

Forged and favor cancellations exist.

POSTAGE DUE STAMPS

Royal Cipher,
"Christian 9 Rex"
D1

1902		Unwmk.	Litho.		Perf. 11½
J1	D1	1c dark blue		4.00	11.00
J2	D1	4c dark blue		9.00	17.50
J3	D1	6c dark blue		17.50	45.00
J4	D1	10c dark blue		15.00	45.00
		Nos. J1-J4 (4)		45.50	118.50

There are five types of each value. On the 4c they may be distinguished by differences in the figures "4"; on the other values the differences are minute.

Used values of Nos. J1-J4 are for canceled copies. Uncanceled examples without gum have probably been used. Value 60% of unused.

Counterfeits of Nos. J1-J4 exist.

D2

1905-13				Perf. 13
J5	D2	5b red & gray	4.00	6.25
J6	D2	20b red & gray	7.00	12.50
J7	D2	30b red & gray	6.00	12.50
J8	D2	50b red & gray	5.50	32.50
a.		Perf. 14x14½ ('13)	35.00	125.00
b.		Perf. 11½	400.00	
		Nos. J5-J8 (4)	22.50	63.75

All values of this issue are known imperforate, but were not regularly issued.

Used values of Nos. J5-J8 are for canceled copies. Uncanceled examples without gum have probably been used. Value 60% of unused.

Counterfeits of Nos. J5-J8 exist.

Danish West Indies stamps were replaced by those of the US in 1917, after the US bought the islands.

GUAM
'gwäm

LOCATION — One of the Mariana Islands in the Pacific Ocean, about 1450 miles east of the Philippines
GOVT. — United States Possession
AREA — 206 sq. mi.
POP. — 9,000 (est. 1899)
CAPITAL — Agaña

Formerly a Spanish possession, Guam was ceded to the United States in 1898 following the Spanish-American War. Stamps overprinted "Guam" were superseded by the regular postage stamps of the United States in 1901.

100 Cents = 1 Dollar

US Nos. 279, 279B, 279Bc, 268, 280a, 281, 282, 272, 282C, 283, 284, 275, 275a, 276 and 276A
Overprinted in Black (1c-50c) or Red ($1)

1899		Wmk. 191		Perf. 12
1	A87	1c deep green	20.00	25.00
2	A88	2c red, type IV	17.50	25.00
a.		2c rose carmine, type IV	22.50	30.00
3	A89	3c purple	125.00	175.00
4	A90	4c lilac brown	135.00	175.00
5	A91	5c blue	30.00	45.00
6	A92	6c lake	125.00	200.00
7	A93	8c violet brown	125.00	200.00
8	A94	10c brown, type I	45.00	55.00
9	A94	10c brown, type II	4,000.	
10	A95	15c olive green	150.00	175.00
11	A96	50c orange	350.00	425.00
a.		50c red orange	550.00	
12	A97	$1 black, type I	350.00	400.00
13	A97	$1 black, type II	4,500.	
		Nos. 1-8,10-12 (11)	1,472.	1,900.

SPECIAL DELIVERY STAMP

United States No. E5 Overprinted in Red

1899		Wmk. 191		Perf. 12
E1	SD3	10c blue	150.00	200.00

Guam Guard Mail stamps of 1930 are listed in the Scott Specialized United States Catalogue.

HAWAII
hə-'wä-yē

LOCATION — Group of 20 islands in the Pacific Ocean, about 2,000 miles southwest of San Francisco.
GOVT. — Former Kingdom and Republic
AREA — 6,435 sq. mi.
POP. — 150,000 (est. 1899)
CAPITAL — Honolulu

Until 1893 an independent kingdom, from 1893 to 1898 a republic, the Hawaiian Islands were annexed to the US in 1898. The Territory of Hawaii achieved statehood in 1959.

100 Cents = 1 Dollar

Values for Nos. 1-4 are for examples with minor damage that has been skillfully repaired.

A1

A2

A3

Pelure Paper

1851-52		Unwmk.	Typeset	Imperf.
1	A1	2c blue	660,000.	200,000.
2	A1	5c blue	45,000.	25,000.
3	A2	13c blue	22,500.	17,500.
4	A3	13c blue	40,000.	27,500.

Two varieties of each.
No. 1 unused is unique.

King Kamehameha III
A4   A5

Thick White Wove Paper

1853				Engr.
5	A4	5c blue	1,350.	1,050.
a.		Line through "Honolulu" (Pos. 2)	2,750.	2,500.
6	A5	13c dark red	600.	1,100.

See Nos. 8-11.

A6

1857				
7	A6	5c on 13c dark red	6,750.	9,000.

Thin White Wove Paper

1857				
8	A4	5c blue	650.	625.
a.		Line through "Honolulu" (Pos. 2)	1,250.	1,250.
b.		Double impression	3,500.	3,500.

Thin Bluish Wove Paper

1861				
9	A4	5c blue	350.	250.
a.		Line through "Honolulu" (Pos. 2)	750.	900.

Re-issues

Ordinary White Wove Paper

1868				
10	A4	5c blue		25.00
a.		Line through "Honolulu" (Pos. 2)		55.00
11	A5	13c dull rose		250.00

Reprints:

5c — Originals have two small dots near the left side of the square in the upper right corner. These dots are missing in the reprints.

13c — The bottom of the 3 of 13 in the upper left corner is flattened in the originals and rounded in the reprints. The "t" of "Cts" on the left side is as tall as the "C" in the reprints, but shorter in the originals.

On August 19, 1892, the remaining supply of reprints was overprinted in black "REPRINT." The reprints (both with and without overprint) were sold at face value. See Scott's U.S. Specialized Catalogue.

Unused values for the Numeral stamps, Nos. 12-26, are for examples without gum.

A7

A8

A9

1859-62				Typeset
12	A7	1c lt blue, bluish white	8,750.	7,250.
a.		"1 Ce" omitted		16,000.
b.		"nt" omitted		
13	A7	2c lt blue, bluish white	6,000.	3,500.
a.		2c dark blue, grayish white	6,500.	3,750.
b.		Comma after "Cents"		6,000.
c.		No period after "Leta"	—	
14	A7	2c blk, grnsh blue ('62)	6,500.	4,250.
a.		"2-Cents."		

1863				
15	A7	1c black, grayish	450.	1,000.
a.		Tete beche pair	3,500.	
b.		"NTER"		
c.		Period omitted after "Post-age"	700.	
16	A7	2c black, grayish	900.	675.
a.		"2" at top of rectangle	3,500.	3,500.
b.		Printed on both sides	—	20,000.
c.		"NTER"	3,000.	3,000.
d.		2c black, grayish white	950.	700.
e.		Period omitted after "Cents"	—	
f.		Overlapping impressions	—	
g.		"TAGE."	—	
17	A7	2c dk blue, bluish	7,500.	6,500.
a.		"ISL"	—	
18	A7	2c black, blue gray	3,000.	4,500.

1864-65				
19	A7	1c black	475.	1,000.
20	A7	2c black	700.	1,150.
21	A8	5c blue, blue ('65)	750.	550.
a.		Tete beche pair	10,000.	
b.		5c bluish black, grayish white	12,000.	
22	A9	5c blue, blue ('65)	525.	850.
a.		Tete beche pair	8,500.	
b.		5c blue, grayish white	—	
c.		Overlapping impressions	—	

1864				Laid Paper
23	A7	1c black	250.	2,000.
a.		HA instead of HAWAIIAN	3,500.	
b.		Tete beche pair	6,000.	
c.		Tete beche pair, #23, 23a	17,500.	
24	A7	2c black	275.	1,000.
a.		"NTER"	3,500.	
b.		"S" of "POSTAGE" omitted	1,000.	
c.		Tete beche pair	5,250.	

A10

1865				Wove Paper
25	A10	1c dark blue		275.
a.		Double impression	—	
b.		With invtd. impression of #21	10,500.	
26	A10	2c dark blue		275.

Nos. 12 to 26 were typeset and were printed in settings of ten, each stamp differing from the others.

King Kamehameha IV — A11

1861-63				Litho.

Horizontally Laid Paper

27	A11	2c pale rose	275.	250.
a.		2c carmine rose ('63)	2,000.	2,000.

Vertically Laid Paper

28	A11	2c pale rose	275.	150.
a.		2c carmine rose ('63)	300.	350.

1869		Engr.	Thin Wove Paper	
29	A11	2c red	45.00	—

No. 29 was a re-issue sold only at the Honolulu post office, at first without overprint and later with overprint "CANCELLED."
See #50-51 and note following #51.

Princess Victoria
Kamamalu — A12

King Kamehameha
IV — A13

King Kamehameha V
A14　　　　　A15

Mataio
Kekuanaoa — A16

1864-86　　　　　Engr.　　　　Perf. 12
Wove Paper

30	A12	1c purple ('86)		9.00	7.50
a.		1c mauve ('71)		40.00	20.00
b.		1c violet ('78)		17.50	10.00
31	A13	2c rose vermilion		15.00	9.00
a.		2c vermilion ('86)		35.00	12.50
b.		Half used as 1c on cover with #32			8,500.
32	A14	5c blue ('66)		175.00	30.00
33	A15	6c yel grn ('71)		25.00	9.00
a.		6c bluish green ('78)		25.00	9.00
34	A16	18c dull rose ('71)		85.00	35.00
		Nos. 30-34 (5)		309.00	90.50

No. 32 has traces of rectangular frame lines surrounding the design. Nos. 39 and 52C have no such frame lines.

For overprints see #53, 58-60, 65, 66C, 71.

King David　　　　Prince William
Kalakaua　　　　Pitt Leleiohoku
A17　　　　　　　A18

1875

35	A17	2c brown		7.50	3.00
36	A18	12c black		55.00	27.50

See Nos. 38, 43, 46. For overprints see Nos. 56, 62-63, 66, 69.

Princess　　　　King David
Likelike　　　　Kalakaua
A19　　　　　　A20

Queen
Kapiolani — A21

Statue of King　　　King William
Kamehameha　　　Lunalilo — A23
I — A22

Queen Emma
Kaleleonalani — A24

1882

37	A19	1c blue		6.00	10.00
38	A17	2c lilac rose		125.00	45.00
39	A14	5c ultramarine		15.00	3.25
a.		Vert. pair, imperf. horiz.		4,250.	4,250.
40	A20	10c black		35.00	20.00
41	A21	15c red brown		55.00	25.00
		Nos. 37-41 (5)		236.00	103.25

1883-86

42	A19	1c green		2.75	1.90
43	A17	2c rose ('86)		4.00	1.00
a.		2c dull red		62.50	21.00
44	A20	10c red brown ('84)		30.00	10.00
45	A20	10c vermilion		32.50	12.50
46	A18	12c red lilac		75.00	32.50
47	A22	25c dark violet		140.00	60.00
48	A23	50c red		160.00	85.00
49	A24	$1 rose red		240.00	140.00
		Maltese cross cancellation			100.00
		Nos. 42-49 (8)		684.25	342.90

Other fiscal cancellations exist on No. 49. For overprints see Nos. 54-55, 57, 61-61B, 64, 67-68, 70, 72-73.

Reproduction and Reprint
Yellowish Wove Paper

1886-89　　　　　　　　　　Imperf.

50	A11	2c orange vermilion	160.00	
51	A11	2c carmine ('89)	25.00	

In 1885 the Postmaster General wished to have on sale complete sets of Hawaii's stamps as far back as type A11, but was unable to find either the stone from which Nos. 27 and 28, or the plate from which No. 29 was printed. He therefore sent a copy of No. 29 to the American Bank Note Co., with an order to engrave a new plate and print 10,000 stamps, of which 5000 were overprinted "Specimen" in blue.

The original No. 29 was printed in sheet of 15 (5x3), but the plate of these "Official Imitations" was made up of 50 stamps (10x5). Later, in 1887, the original die for No. 29 was discovered, and after retouching, a new plate was made and 37,500 stamps were printed. These, like the originals, were printed in sheets of 15. They were delivered during 1889 and 1890. In 1892 all remaining unsold in the Post Office were overprinted "Reprint."

No. 29 is red in color, and printed on very thin white wove paper. No. 50 is orange vermilion in color, on medium, white to buff paper. In No. 50 the vertical line on the left side of the portrait touches the horizontal line over the label "Elua Keneta", while in the other two varieties, Nos. 29 and 51, it does not touch the horizontal line by half a millimeter. In No. 51 there are three parallel lines on the left side of the King's nose, while in No. 29 and No. 50 there are no such lines. No. 51 is carmine in color and printed on thick, yellowish to buff wove paper.

It is claimed that both Nos. 50 and 51 are available for postage, although not made to fill a postal requirement.

Queen
Liliuokalani — A25

1890-91　　　　　　　　　Perf. 12

52	A25	2c dull violet ('91)		4.50	1.50
a.		Vert. pair, imperf. horiz.		4,000.	
52C	A14	5c deep indigo		110.00	140.00

Stamps of 1864-91
Overprinted in Red

Three categories of double overprints:
　I. Both overprints heavy.
　II. One overprint heavy, one of moderate strength.
　III. One overprint heavy, one of light or weak strength.

1893

53	A12	1c purple		7.50	12.50
a.		"189" instead of "1893"		475.00	
b.		No period after "GOVT"		210.00	210.00
f.		Double overprint		550.00	
54	A19	1c blue		6.00	12.50
b.		No period after "GOVT"		140.00	140.00
d.		Double overprint (I)		1,250.	
f.		Double overprint (III)		400.00	
55	A19	1c green		1.50	3.00
d.		Double overprint (I)		625.00	450.00
f.		Double overprint (III)		200.00	
g.		Pair, one without ovpt.		10,000.	
56	A17	2c brown		10.00	20.00
b.		No period after "GOVT"		300.00	—
57	A25	2c dull violet		1.50	1.25
d.		"18 3" instead of "1893"		650.00	500.00
f.		Double overprint (III)		1,200.	650.00
g.		Double overprint (III)		160.00	
		Inverted overprint		4,000.	3,500.
58	A14	5c deep indigo		10.00	25.00
b.		No period after "GOVT"		225.00	250.00
f.		Double overprint (III)		1,250.	
59	A14	5c ultramarine		6.00	2.50
d.		Double overprint (I)		6,500.	
f.		Double overprint (III)		4,000.	4,000.
		Double overprint (III)			400.00
g.		Inverted overprint		1,500.	1,500.
60	A15	6c green		15.00	25.00
f.		Double overprint (III)		1,000.	
61	A20	10c black		9.00	15.00
d.		Double overprint (I)		750.00	
f.		Double overprint (III)		200.00	
61B	A20	10c red brown		14,000.	29,000.
62	A18	12c black		9.00	17.50
d.		Double overprint (I)		2,000.	
e.		Double overprint (II)		1,750.	
63	A18	12c red lilac		150.00	250.00
64	A22	25c dark violet		26.00	40.00
b.		No period after "GOVT"		325.00	325.00
f.		Double overprint (III)		1,000.	
		Nos. 53-61,62-64 (12)		251.50	424.25

Overprinted in Black

65	A13	2c vermilion		67.50	75.00
b.		No period after "GOVT"		250.00	250.00
66	A17	2c rose		1.25	2.25
b.		No period after "GOVT"		50.00	60.00
d.		Double overprint (I)		4,000.	
e.		Double overprint (II)		2,750.	
f.		Double overprint (III)		300.00	
66C	A15	6c green		14,000.	29,000.
67	A20	10c vermilion		15.00	30.00
f.		Double overprint (III)		1,250.	
68	A20	10c red brown		7.50	12.50
f.		Double overprint (III)		1,750.	
69	A18	12c red lilac		275.00	500.00
70	A21	15c red brown		20.00	30.00
e.		Double overprint (II)		2,000.	
71	A16	18c dull rose		25.00	35.00
b.		"18 3" instead of "1893"		475.00	475.00
b.		No period after "GOVT"		300.00	300.00
d.		Double overprint (I)		450.00	
f.		Double overprint (III)		225.00	
g.		Pair, one without ovpt.		2,500.	
72	A23	50c red		60.00	90.00
b.		No period after "GOVT"		400.00	400.00
f.		Double overprint (III)		1,000.	
73	A24	$1 rose red		110.00	175.00
b.		No period after "GOVT"		450.00	450.00
		Nos. 65-66,67-73 (9)		581.25	949.75

Coat of
Arms — A26

View of
Honolulu — A27

Statue of
Kamehameha
I — A28

Stars and
Palms — A29

S.S. Arawa — A30

Pres. Sanford
Ballard
Dole — A31

"CENTS"
Added — A32

1894

74	A26	1c yellow		2.00	1.25
75	A27	2c brown		2.25	.60
76	A28	5c rose lake		4.00	1.50
77	A29	10c yellow green		6.00	4.50
78	A30	12c blue		12.50	17.50
79	A31	25c deep blue		12.50	17.50
		Nos. 74-79 (6)		39.25	42.85

1899

80	A26	1c dark green		1.50	1.25
81	A27	2c rose		1.40	1.00
a.		2c salmon		1.50	1.25
b.		Vert. pair, imperf. horiz.		4,500.	
82	A32	5c blue		5.50	3.00
		Nos. 80-82 (3)		8.40	5.25

OFFICIAL STAMPS

Lorrin Andrews
Thurston — O1

1896　　　Unwmk.　　Engr.　　Perf. 12

O1	O1	2c green		40.00	17.50
O2	O1	5c black brown		40.00	17.50
O3	O1	6c deep ultra		40.00	17.50
O4	O1	10c bright rose		40.00	17.50
O5	O1	12c orange		40.00	17.50
O6	O1	25c gray violet		40.00	17.50
		Nos. O1-O6 (6)		240.00	105.00

Used values for #O1-O6 are for copies cto "FOREIGN OFFICE/HONOLULU H.I." in double circle without date.

The stamps of Hawaii were replaced by those of the United States.

PHILIPPINES

ˌfi-lə-ˈpēnz

LOCATION — Group of 7,100 islands and islets in the Malay Archipelago, north of Borneo, in the North Pacific Ocean
GOVT. — US Admin., 1898-1946
AREA — 115,748 sq. mi.
POP. — 16,971,100 (est. 1941)
CAPITAL — Quezon City

The islands were ceded to the US by Spain in 1898. On Nov. 15, 1935, they were given their independence, subject to a transition period which ended July 4, 1946. On that date the Commonwealth became the "Republic of the Philippines."

　　100 Cents = 1 Dollar (1899)
　　100 Centavos = 1 Peso (1906)

Watermarks

Wmk. 191PI-　　　Wmk. 190PI-
Double-lined PIPS　Single-lined PIPS

Wmk. 257- Curved
Wavy Lines

Issued under US Administration

Issues of the US
Overprinted in Black

On No. 260

1899-1901		**Unwmk.**	**Perf. 12**	
212	A96	50c orange	400.00	250.00

On Nos. 279, 279B, 279Bd, 279Be,
279Bf, 279Bc, 268, 281, 282C, 283,
284, 275 and 275a

Wmk. 191

213	A87	1c yellow green	3.00	.60
a.		Inverted overprint	13,500.	
214	A88	2c red, IV	1.25	.60
a.		2c orange red, IV ('01)	1.25	.60
b.		Bklt. pane of 6, red, IV ('00)	250.00	200.00
c.		2c reddish car, IV	1.90	.90
d.		2c rose car, IV	2.25	1.10
215	A89	3c purple	5.75	1.25
216	A91	5c blue	5.50	.90
a.		Inverted overprint	3,750.	
217	A94	10c brown, I	17.50	4.00
217A	A94	10c org brn, II	160.00	27.50
218	A95	15c olive green	32.50	8.00
219	A96	50c orange	125.00	37.50
a.		50c red orange	250.00	
		Nos. 213-219 (8)	350.50	80.35

No. 216a is valued in the grade of fine.

On Nos. 280b, 282 and 272

1901				
220	A90	4c orange brown	22.50	5.00
221	A92	6c lake	29.00	7.00
222	A93	8c violet brown	29.00	7.50
		Nos. 220-222 (3)	80.50	19.50

On Nos. 276, 276A, 277a and 278

Red Overprint

223	A97	$1 black, I	425.	275.
223A	A97	$1 black, II	2,250.	750.
224	A98	$2 dark blue	450.	350.
225	A99	$5 dark green	800.	900.

On Nos. 300-313 and shades

1903-04

Black Overprint

226	A115	1c blue green	4.00	.30
227	A116	2c carmine	7.50	1.10
228	A117	3c bright violet	67.50	12.50
229	A118	4c brown ('04)	75.00	22.50
a.		4c orange brown	75.00	20.00
230	A119	5c blue	11.00	1.00
231	A120	6c brnsh lake ('04)	80.00	22.50
232	A121	8c vio blk ('04)	45.00	15.00
233	A122	10c pale red brn ('04)	20.00	2.25
a.		10c red brown	25.00	3.00
b.		Pair, one without ovpt.		1,500.
234	A123	13c purple black	32.50	17.50
a.		13c brown violet	32.50	17.50
235	A124	15c olive green	60.00	15.00
236	A125	50c orange	125.00	35.00
		Nos. 226-236 (11)	527.50	144.65

Red Overprint

237	A126	$1 black	450.	275.
238	A127	$2 dk blue ('04)	750.	850.
239	A128	$5 dk green ('04)	950.	1,000.

On Nos. 319, 319c in Black

1904

240	A129	2c carmine	5.50	2.25
a.		Booklet pane of 6	1,100.	
b.		2c scarlet	6.25	2.75
c.		As "b," booklet pane of 6	—	

Jose Rizal
A40

Arms of
Manila
A41

Designs: 4c, McKinley. 6c, Magellan. 8c,
Miguel Lopez de Legaspi. 10c, Gen. Henry W.
Lawton. 12c, Lincoln. 16c, Adm. William T.
Sampson. 20c, Washington. 26c, Francisco
Carriedo. 30c, Franklin.

Each Inscribed "Philippine
Islands/United States of America"

1906, Sept. 8		**Engr.**	**Wmk. 191PI**	
241	A40	2c deep green	.25	.20
a.		2c yellow green ('10)	.40	.20
b.		Booklet pane of 6	475.00	
242	A40	4c carmine	.30	.20
a.		4c carmine lake ('10)	.60	.20
b.		Booklet pane of 6	650.00	
243	A40	6c violet	1.25	.20
244	A40	8c brown	2.50	.70
245	A40	10c blue	1.75	.20
a.		10c dark blue	1.75	
246	A40	12c brown lake	5.00	2.00
247	A40	16c violet black	3.75	.20
248	A40	20c orange brown	4.00	.30
249	A40	26c violet brown	6.00	2.25
250	A40	30c olive green	4.75	1.50
251	A41	1p orange	27.50	7.00
252	A41	2p black	35.00	1.25
253	A41	4p dark blue	100.00	15.00
254	A41	10p dark green	225.00	70.00
		Nos. 241-254 (14)	417.05	101.00

Change of Colors

1909-13			**Perf. 12**	
255	A40	12c red orange	8.50	2.50
256	A40	16c olive green	3.50	.75
257	A40	20c yellow	7.50	1.25
258	A40	26c blue green	1.75	.75
259	A40	30c ultramarine	10.00	3.25
260	A41	1p pale violet	30.00	5.00
260A	A41	2p vio brown ('13)	85.00	15.00
		Nos. 255-260A (7)	146.25	16.25

1911		**Wmk. 190PI**	**Perf. 12**	
261	A40	2c green	.65	.20
a.		Booklet pane of 6	550.00	
262	A40	4c carmine lake	2.50	.20
a.		4c carmine	—	
b.		Booklet pane of 6	600.00	
263	A40	6c deep violet	2.00	.20
264	A40	8c brown	8.50	.45
265	A40	10c blue	3.25	.20
266	A40	12c orange	2.50	.45
267	A40	16c olive green	2.50	.20
a.		16c pale olive green	2.50	
268	A40	20c yellow	2.00	.20
a.		20c orange	2.00	
269	A40	26c blue green	3.00	.20
270	A40	30c ultramarine	3.50	.40
271	A41	1p pale violet	22.50	.55
272	A41	2p violet brown	27.50	.75
273	A41	4p deep blue	625.00	80.00
274	A41	10p deep green	225.00	25.00
		Nos. 261-274 (14)	930.40	109.00

1914				
275	A40	30c gray	10.00	.40

1914-23			**Perf. 10**	
276	A40	2c green	1.75	.20
a.		Booklet pane of 6	450.00	
277	A40	4c carmine	1.75	.20
a.		Booklet pane of 6	450.00	
278	A40	6c light violet	37.50	9.00
a.		6c deep violet	42.50	6.00
279	A40	8c brown	40.00	10.00
280	A40	10c dark blue	25.00	.20
281	A40	16c olive green	75.00	4.50
282	A40	20c orange	22.50	.85
283	A40	30c gray	55.00	2.75
284	A41	1p pale violet	110.00	3.00
		Nos. 276-284 (9)	368.50	30.70

1918-26			**Perf. 11**	
285	A40	2c green	20.00	4.25
a.		Booklet pane of 6	750.00	
286	A40	4c carmine	25.00	2.50
a.		Booklet pane of 6	1,350.	
287	A40	6c deep violet	35.00	1.75
287A	A40	6c light brown	200.00	25.00
288	A40	10c dark blue	52.50	1.50
289	A40	16c olive green	90.00	6.75
289A	A40	20c orange	60.00	7.50
289C	A40	30c gray	55.00	12.50
289D	A41	1p pale violet	70.00	14.00
		Nos. 285-289D (9)	607.50	75.75

1917-25		**Unwmk.**	**Perf. 11**	
290	A40	2c yellow green	.20	.20
a.		2c dark green	.20	.20
b.		Vert. pair, imperf. horiz.	1,500.	
c.		Horiz. pair, imperf. btwn.	1,500.	—
d.		Vert. pair, imperf. btwn.	1,750.	
e.		Booklet pane of 6	27.50	
291	A40	4c carmine	.20	.20
a.		4c light rose	.20	.20
b.		Booklet pane of 6	17.50	
292	A40	6c deep violet	.30	.20
a.		6c lilac	.35	.20
b.		6c red violet	.35	
c.		Booklet pane of 6	550.00	
293	A40	8c yellow brown	.20	.20
a.		8c orange brown	.20	
294	A40	10c deep blue	.20	.20
295	A40	12c red orange	.30	.20
296	A40	16c light olive green	55.00	.25
a.		16c olive bister	55.00	.40
297	A40	20c orange yellow	.30	.20
298	A40	26c green	.45	.45
a.		26c blue green	.55	.25
299	A40	30c gray	.55	.20
300	A41	1p pale violet	27.50	1.00
a.		1p red lilac	27.50	1.00
b.		1p pale rose lilac	27.50	1.10

301	A41	2p violet brown	25.00	.75
302	A41	4p blue	22.50	.45
a.		4p dark blue	22.50	.45
		Nos. 290-302 (13)	132.70	4.50

1923-26

Design: 16c, Adm. George Dewey.

303	A40	16c olive bister	.90	.20
a.		16c olive green	1.25	.20
304	A41	10p deep green ('26)	45.00	5.00

See Nos. 326-353. For surcharges see Nos.
368-369, 450. For overprints see Nos. C1-
C28, C36-C46, C54-C57, O5-O14.

Legislative
Palace — A42

1926, Dec. 20		**Unwmk.**	**Perf. 12**	
319	A42	2c green & black	.40	.25
a.		Horiz. pair, imperf. btwn.	300.00	
b.		Vert. pair, imperf. between	550.00	
320	A42	4c car & black	.40	.35
a.		Horiz. pair, imperf. between	300.00	
b.		Vert. pair, imperf. between	575.00	
321	A42	16c ol grn & black	.75	.65
a.		Horiz. pair, imperf. btwn.	350.00	
b.		Vert. pair, imperf. between	625.00	
c.		Double impression of center	675.00	
322	A42	18c lt brn & black	.85	.50
a.		Double impression of center	700.00	
b.		Vert. pair, imperf. between	675.00	
323	A42	20c orange & black	1.25	.80
a.		20c orange & brown	600.00	
b.		Vert. pair, imperf. between	575.00	575.00
c.		As "a," imperf. pair	950.00	
d.		Vert. pair, imperf. between	675.00	
324	A42	24c gray & black	.85	.55
a.		Vert. pair, imperf. between	675.00	
325	A42	1p rose lilac & blk	45.00	30.00
a.		Vert. pair, imperf. between	675.00	
		Nos. 319-325 (7)	49.50	33.10

Opening of the Legislative Palace.
For overprints see Nos. O1-O4.

Coil Stamp
Rizal Type of 1906

1928			**Perf. 11 Vertically**	
326	A40	2c green	7.50	15.00

Types of 1906-23

1925-31		**Unwmk.**	**Imperf.**	
340	A40	2c yel grn ('31)	.20	.20
a.		green ('25)	.25	.20
341	A40	4c car rose ('31)	.20	.20
a.		carmine ('25)	.40	.20
342	A40	6c violet ('31)	1.00	1.00
a.		deep violet ('25)	8.00	4.00
343	A40	8c brown ('31)	.90	.90
a.		yellow brown ('25)	6.00	3.00
344	A40	10c blue ('31)	1.75	1.40
a.		deep blue ('25)	25.00	7.00
345	A40	12c dp org ('31)	2.50	2.10
a.		red orange ('25)	25.00	7.00
346	A40	16c olive green (Dewey) ('31)	2.00	1.50
a.		bister green ('25)	20.00	5.50
347	A40	20c org yel ('31)	2.00	1.50
a.		yellow ('25)	20.00	5.50
348	A40	26c green ('31)	2.00	1.50
a.		blue green ('25)	25.00	7.00
349	A40	30c light gray ('31)	2.25	1.75
a.		gray ('25)	25.00	7.00
350	A41	1p lt violet ('31)	4.00	4.00
a.		violet ('25)	90.00	35.00
351	A41	2p brn vio ('31)	10.00	10.00
a.		violet brown ('25)	200.00	75.00
352	A41	4p blue ('31)	35.00	30.00
a.		deep blue ('25)	1,000.	375.00
353	A41	10p deep green ('31)	100.00	100.00
a.		deep green ('25)	2,000.	750.00
		Nos. 340-353 (14)	163.80	156.05
		Nos. 340a-353a (14)	4,569.	1,281.

Mount Mayon,
Luzon — A43

Post Office,
Manila — A44

Pier No. 7, Manila Bay
A45

(See
footnote)
A46

Rice Planting
A47

Rice Terraces
A48

Baguio
Zigzag — A49

1932, May 3   **Perf. 11**

354	A43	2c yellow green	.40	.20
355	A44	4c rose carmine	.35	.20
356	A45	12c orange	.50	.50
357	A46	18c red orange	25.00	9.00
358	A47	20c yellow	.65	.55
359	A48	24c deep violet	1.00	.65
360	A49	32c olive brown	1.00	.70
		Nos. 354-360 (7)	28.90	11.85

The 18c vignette was intended to show Pag-
sanjan Falls in Laguna, central Luzon, and is
so labeled. Through error, the stamp pictures
Vernal Falls in Yosemite Natl. Park, CA.
For overprints see #C29-C35, C47-C51,
C63.

Nos. 302, 302a
Surcharged in Orange
or Red

1932

368	A41	1p on 4p blue (O)	2.00	.45
a.		1p on 4p dark blue (O)	2.75	1.25
369	A41	2p on 4p dark blue (R)	3.50	.75
a.		2p on 4p blue (R)	3.50	.75

Baseball — A50

Tennis — A51

Basketball — A52

1934, Apr. 14		**Typo.**	**Perf. 11½**	
380	A50	2c yellow brown	1.50	.80
381	A51	6c ultramarine	.25	.20
a.		Vert. pair, imperf. between	1,250.	
382	A52	16c violet brown	.50	.50
a.		Vert. pair, imperf. horiz.	1,250.	
		Nos. 380-382 (3)	2.25	1.50

Tenth Far Eastern Championship Games.

Jose Rizal
A53

Woman and Carabao
A54

La Filipina — A55

Pearl Fishing — A56

Fort Santiago — A57

Salt Spring — A58

Magellan's Landing, 1521
A59

"Juan de la Cruz"
A60

Rice Terraces — A61

"Blood Compact," 1565 — A62

Barasoain Church, Malolos
A63

Battle of Manila Bay, 1898 — A64

Montalban Gorge
A65

George Washington — A66

1935, Feb. 15   Engr.   *Perf. 11*

383	A53	2c rose	.20 .20
384	A54	4c yellow green	.20 .20
385	A55	6c dark brown	.20 .20
386	A56	8c violet	.20 .20

387	A57	10c rose carmine	.20 .20
388	A58	12c black	.25 .20
389	A59	16c dark blue	.25 .20
390	A60	20c light olive green	.25 .20
391	A61	26c indigo	.30 .25
392	A62	30c orange red	.30 .20
393	A63	1p red orange & black	1.75 1.25
394	A64	2p bister brn & black	4.50 1.25
395	A65	4p blue & black	5.00 3.00
396	A66	5p green & black	10.00 3.00
		Nos. 383-396 (14)	23.60 10.60

For overprints & surcharges see #411-424, 433-446, 449, 463-466, 468, 472-474, 478-484, 485-494, C52-C53, O15-O36, O38, O40-O43, N2-N9, N28, NO2-NO6.

Commonwealth Issues

The Temples of Human Progress — A67

1935, Nov. 15

397	A67	2c carmine rose	.20 .20
398	A67	6c deep violet	.20 .20
399	A67	16c blue	.20 .20
400	A67	36c yellow green	.35 .30
401	A67	50c brown	.55 .55
		Nos. 397-401 (5)	1.50 1.45

Inauguration of the Philippine Commonwealth, Nov. 15th, 1935.

Jose Rizal — A68

President Manuel L. Quezon — A69

1936, June 19   *Perf. 12*

402	A68	2c yellow brown	.20 .20
403	A68	6c slate blue	.20 .20
a.		Horiz. pair, imperf. vert.	1,350.
404	A68	36c red brown	.50 .45
		Nos. 402-404 (3)	.90 .85

75th anniv. of the birth of Jose Rizal.

1936, Nov. 15   *Perf. 11*

408	A69	2c orange brown	.20 .20
409	A69	6c yellow green	.20 .20
410	A69	12c ultramarine	.20 .20
		Nos. 408-410 (3)	.60 .60

1st anniv. of the Commonwealth.
For overprints see Nos. 467, 475.

Nos. 383-396 Overprinted in Black

a

b

1936-37   *Perf. 11*

411	A53 (a)	2c rose	.20 .20
a.		Booklet pane of 6	2.50 2.00
412	A54 (b)	4c yel grn ('37)	.50 4.00
413	A55 (a)	6c dark brown	.20 .20
414	A56 (b)	8c violet ('37)	.25 .20
415	A57 (b)	10c rose carmine	.20 .20
a.		"COMMONWEALT"	—
416	A58 (b)	12c black ('37)	.20 .20
417	A59 (b)	16c dark blue	.20 .20
418	A60 (a)	20c lt ol grn ('37)	.65 .40
419	A61 (b)	26c indigo ('37)	.45 .35
420	A62 (b)	30c orange red	.35 .20
421	A63 (b)	1p red org & black	.65 .20
422	A64 (b)	2p bister brn & black ('37)	5.00 2.75

423	A65 (b)	4p blue & blk ('37)	22.50 5.00
424	A66 (b)	5p grn & blk ('37)	3.00 1.50
		Nos. 411-424 (14)	34.35 15.60

Map of Philippines
A70

Arms of Manila
A71

1937, Feb. 3

425	A70	2c yellow green	.20 .20
426	A70	6c light brown	.20 .20
427	A70	12c sapphire	.20 .20
428	A70	20c deep orange	.25 .20
429	A70	36c deep violet	.50 .40
430	A70	50c carmine	.65 .35
		Nos. 425-430 (6)	2.00 1.55

33rd Eucharistic Congress.

1937, Aug. 27   *Perf. 11*

431	A71	10p gray	4.25 2.00
432	A71	20p henna brown	2.25 1.40

For overprints see Nos. 495-496. For surcharges see Nos. 451, C58.

Nos. 383-396 Overprinted in Black

COMMON-WEALTH   COMMONWEALTH
a   b

1938-40   *Perf. 11*

433	A53 (a)	2c rose ('39)	.20 .20
a.		Booklet pane of 6	3.50 2.50
b.		"WEALTH COMMON-"	4,000.
c.		Hyphen omitted	
434	A54 (b)	4c yel grn ('40)	1.25 30.00
435	A55 (a)	6c dk brn ('39)	.20 .20
a.		6c golden brown	.20 .20
436	A56 (b)	8c violet ('39)	.20 .20
a.		"COMMONWEALT" (LR 31)	90.00
437	A57 (b)	10c rose car ('39)	.20 .20
a.		"COMMONWEALT" (LR 31)	—
438	A58 (b)	12c black ('40)	.20 .20
439	A59 (b)	16c dark blue	.20 .20
440	A60 (a)	20c lt ol grn ('39)	.20 .20
441	A61 (b)	26c indigo ('40)	.20 .20
442	A62 (b)	30c org red ('39)	1.40 .70
443	A63 (b)	1p red org & blk	.40 .20
444	A64 (b)	2p bis brn & blk	2.75 .20
445	A65 (b)	4p bl & blk ('40)	150.00 150.00
446	A66 (b)	5p grn & blk ('40)	6.00 3.25
		Nos. 433-446 (14)	163.40
		Nos. 433,435-446 (13)	156.50

Overprint "b" measures 18½x1¾mm. No. 433b occurs in booklet pane, No. 433a, position 5; all copies are straight-edged, left and bottom.

Stamps of 1917-37 Surcharged in Red, Violet or Black

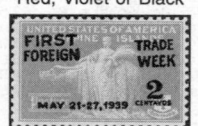
FIRST FOREIGN TRADE WEEK
MAY 21-27, 1939
2 CENTAVOS

FIRST FOREIGN TRADE WEEK
MAY 21-27, 1939
6 CENTAVOS 6

50 CENTAVOS 50
FIRST FOREIGN TRADE WEEK
MAY 21-27, 1939

1939, July 5

449	A54	2c on 4c yel green (R)	.20 .20
450	A40	6c on 26c blue grn (V)	.20 .20
a.		6c on 26c green	.65 .30
451	A71	50c on 20p henna brn (Bk)	1.00 1.00
		Nos. 449-451 (3)	1.40 1.40

Foreign Trade Week.

Triumphal Arch — A72

Malacanan Palace — A73

1939, Nov. 15   *Perf. 11*

452	A72	2c yellow green	.20 .20
453	A72	6c carmine	.20 .20
454	A72	12c bright blue	.20 .20
		Nos. 452-454 (3)	.60 .60

For overprints see Nos. 469, 476.

1939, Nov. 15

455	A73	2c green	.20 .20
456	A73	6c orange	.20 .20
457	A73	12c carmine	.20 .20
		Nos. 455-457 (3)	.60 .60

#452-457 for 4th anniv. of the Commonwealth.
For overprint see No. 470.

Quezon Taking Oath of Office
A74

Jose Rizal
A75

1940, Feb. 8

458	A74	2c dark orange	.20 .20
459	A74	6c dark green	.20 .20
460	A74	12c purple	.25 .20
		Nos. 458-460 (3)	.65 .60

4th anniversary of Commonwealth.
For overprints see Nos. 471, 477.

Rotary Press Printing
1941, Apr. 14   *Perf. 11x10½*
Size: 19x22½mm

461	A75	2c apple green	.20 .50

Flat Plate Printing
1941-43   *Perf. 11*
Size: 18¾x22mm

462	A75	2c apple green ('43)	.20 .20
a.		2c pale apple green	.20 .50
b.		Bklt. pane of 6 #462 ('43)	1.25 5.00
c.		Bklt. pane of 6 #462a	2.50 2.75

No. 462 was issued only in booklet panes and all copies have straight edges.
Further printings were made in 1942 and 1943 in different shades from the first supply of stamps sent to the islands.
For type A75 overprinted see Nos. 464, O37, O39, N1, NO1.

Philippine Stamps of 1935-41, Handstamped in Violet
VICTORY

1944   *Perf. 11, 11x10½*

463	A53	2c (#411)	325.00 160.00
a.		Booklet pane of 6	3,250.
463B	A53	2c (#433)	1,400. 1,350.
464	A75	2c (#461)	3.75 3.00
465	A54	4c (#384)	42.50 42.50
466	A55	6c (#385)	1,900. 1,650.
467	A69	6c (#409)	150.00 110.00
468	A58	12c (#413)	875.00 800.00
469	A72	6c (#453)	150.00 125.00
470	A73	6c (#456)	850.00 725.00
471	A74	6c (#459)	225.00 190.00
472	A56	8c (#436)	17.50 24.00
473	A57	10c (#415)	125.00 82.50
474	A57	10c (#437)	150.00 125.00
475	A69	12c (#410)	750.00 300.00
476	A72	12c (#454)	4,000. 2,250.
477	A74	12c (#460)	275.00 160.00
478	A59	16c (#389)	800.00
479	A59	16c (#417)	650.00 450.00
480	A59	16c (#439)	300.00 190.00
481	A60	20c (#440)	35.00 35.00
482	A62	30c (#420)	350.00 225.00
483	A62	30c (#442)	475.00 350.00
484	A63	1p (#443)	6,250. 4,500.

Nos. 463-484 are valued in the grade of fine to very fine.

Types of 1935-37 Overprinted

a

b

1945 — Perf. 11
485	A53 (a)	2c rose	.20 .20
486	A54 (b)	4c yellow green	.20 .20
487	A55 (a)	6c golden brown	.20 .20
488	A56 (b)	8c violet	.20 .20
489	A57 (b)	10c rose carmine	.20 .20
490	A58 (b)	12c black	.20 .20
491	A59 (b)	16c dark blue	.25 .20
492	A60 (a)	20c lt olive green	.30 .20
493	A62 (b)	30c orange red	.40 .35
494	A63 (b)	1p red org & black	1.10 .25

Nos. 431-432 Overprinted in Black
495	A71	10p gray	40.00 13.50
496	A71	20p henna brown	35.00 15.00
	Nos. 485-496 (12)	78.25 30.70

Jose Rizal — A76

1946, May 28 — Perf. 11x10½
497 A76 2c sepia — .20 .20

For overprints see No. 503 (Philippines, Vol. 5) and No. O44.

Succeeding issues, released by the Philippine Republic on and after July 4, 1946, are listed in Vol. 5.

AIR POST STAMPS

Madrid-Manila Flight Issue
Regular Issue of 1917-26 Overprinted in Red or Violet

1926, May 13 — Unwmk. — Perf. 11
C1	A40	2c green (R)	8.75 8.75
C2	A40	4c carmine	11.50 11.50
a.	Inverted overprint	2,500. —
C3	A40	6c lilac (R)	55.00 55.00
C4	A40	8c org brown	57.50 57.50
C5	A40	10c deep blue (R)	57.50 57.50
C6	A40	12c red orange	57.50 57.50
C7	A40	16c lt olive green (Sampson)	2,000. 1,600.
C8	A40	16c ol bister (Sampson) (R)	3,750. 3,000.
C9	A40	16c olive green (Dewey)	70.00 30.00
C10	A40	20c orange yellow	70.00 70.00
C11	A40	26c blue green	70.00 70.00
C12	A40	30c gray	70.00 70.00
C13	A41	2p vio brown (R)	550.00 300.00
C14	A41	4p dark blue (R)	750.00 500.00
C15	A41	10p deep green	1,350. 700.00

Same Overprint on No. 269 — Wmk. 190PI — Perf. 12
C16 A40 26c blue green — 3,000.

Same Overprint on No. 284 — Perf. 10
C17 A41 1p pale violet — 200.00 175.00

Flight of Spanish aviators Gallarza and Loriga from Madrid to Manila.

London-Orient Flight Issue
Regular Issue of 1917-25 Overprinted in Red

1928, Nov. 9 — Unwmk. — Perf. 11
C18	A40	2c green	.50 .30
C19	A40	4c carmine	.60 .50
C20	A40	6c violet	2.10 1.75
C21	A40	8c orange brown	2.25 1.90
C22	A40	10c deep blue	2.25 1.90
C23	A40	12c red orange	3.25 2.75
C24	A40	16c ol green (Dewey)	2.40 1.90
C25	A40	20c orange yellow	3.25 2.75
C26	A40	26c blue green	9.50 6.50
C27	A40	30c gray	9.50 6.50

Same Overprint on No. 271 — Wmk. 190PI — Perf. 12
C28 A41 1p pale violet — 50.00 25.00
Nos. C18-C28 (11) — 85.60 51.75

Flight from London to Manila.

Nos. 354-360 Overprinted

1932, Sept. 27 — Unwmk. — Perf. 11
C29	A43	2c yellow green	.40 .30
C30	A44	4c rose carmine	.40 .30
C31	A45	12c orange	.60 .50
C32	A46	18c red orange	3.50 3.25
C33	A47	20c yellow	1.75 1.50
C34	A48	24c deep violet	1.75 1.50
C35	A49	32c olive brown	1.75 1.50
	Nos. C29-C35 (7)	10.15 8.85

Visit of Capt. Wolfgang von Gronau on his round-the-world flight.

Regular Issue of 1917-25 Overprinted

1933, Apr. 11
C36	A40	2c green	.40 .35
C37	A40	4c carmine	.45 .35
C38	A40	6c deep violet	.80 .75
C39	A40	8c orange brown	2.50 1.50
C40	A40	10c dark blue	2.25 1.00
C41	A40	12c orange	2.00 1.00
C42	A40	16c ol green (Dewey)	2.00 1.00
C43	A40	20c yellow	2.00 1.00
C44	A40	26c orange	2.25 1.50
a.	26c blue green	3.00 1.75
C45	A40	30c gray	3.00 1.50
	Nos. C36-C45 (10)	17.65 10.20

Flight from Madrid to Manila of aviator Fernando Rein y Loring.

Stamp of 1917 Overprinted

1933, May 26 — Unwmk. — Perf. 11
C46 A40 2c green — .50 .40

Regular Issue of 1932 Overprinted

C47	A44	4c rose carmine	.20 .20
C48	A45	12c orange	.30 .20
C49	A47	20c yellow	.30 .20
C50	A48	24c deep violet	.40 .20
C51	A49	32c olive brown	.50 .35
	Nos. C46-C51 (6)	2.20 1.60

Nos. 387 & 392 Overprinted in Gold

1935, Dec. 2
C52 A57 10c rose carmine — .30 .20
C53 A62 30c orange red — .50 .35

China Clipper flight from Manila to San Francisco, Dec. 2-5, 1935.

Regular Issue of 1917-25 Surcharged in Various Colors

1936, Sept. 6 — Perf. 11
C54	A40	2c on 4c carmine (Bl)	.20 .20
C55	A40	6c on 12c red org (V)	.20 .20
C56	A40	16c on 26c bl grn (Bk)	.25 .20
a.	16c on 26c green (Bk)	1.25 .70
	Nos. C54-C56 (3)	.65 .60

Manila-Madrid flight by aviators Antonio Arnaiz and Juan Calvo.

Regular Issue of 1917-37 Surcharged in Black or Red

1939, Feb. 17
C57	A40	8c on 26c blue green	.75 .40
a.	8c on 26c green	1.60 .55
C58	A71	1p on 10p gray (R)	3.00 2.25

1st Air Mail Exhib., Feb. 17-19, 1939.

Moro Vinta and Clipper — AP1

1941, June 30
C59	AP1	8c carmine	1.00 .60
C60	AP1	20c ultramarine	1.25 .45
C61	AP1	60c blue green	1.75 1.00
C62	AP1	1p sepia	.70 .50
	Nos. C59-C62 (4)	4.70 2.55

For overprint see No. NO7. For surcharges see Nos. N10-N11, N35-N36.

No. C47 Handstamped in Violet — **VICTORY**

1944, Dec. 3 — Unwmk. — Perf. 11
C63 A44 4c rose carmine — 2,500. 2,500.

SPECIAL DELIVERY STAMPS

U.S. No. E5 Overprinted in Red

1901, Oct. 15 — Wmk. 191 — Perf. 12
E1 SD3 10c dark blue — 125.00 100.00

Special Delivery Messenger — SD2

1906 — Engr. — Wmk. 191PI
E2 SD2 20c ultramarine — 30.00 7.50
b. 20c pale ultramarine — 30.00 7.50

See Nos. E3-E6. For overprints see Nos. E7-E10, EO1.

Special Printing
Ovptd. in Red as #E1 on US #E6
1907
E2A SD4 10c ultramarine — 2,750.

1911 — Wmk. 190PI
E3 SD2 20c deep ultramarine — 20.00 1.75

1916 — Perf. 10
E4 SD2 20c deep ultra — 175.00 75.00

1919 — Unwmk. — Perf. 11
E5 SD2 20c ultramarine — .60 .20
a. 20c pale blue — .75 .20
b. 20c dull violet — .60 .20

Type of 1906 Issue

1925-31 — Imperf.
E6 SD2 20c dull violet ('31) — 20.00 50.00
a. 20c violet blue ('25) — 40.00 27.50

Type of 1919 Overprinted in Black

1939 — Perf. 11
E7 SD2 20c blue violet — .25 .20

Nos. E5b and E7, Handstamped in Violet

1944 — Perf. 11
E8 SD2 20c (On #E5b) — 800.00 550.00
E9 SD2 20c (On #E7) — 225.00 175.00

Type SD2 Overprinted "VICTORY" As No. 486

1945
E10 SD2 20c blue violet — .70 .55
a. "IC" close together — 3.25 2.75

SPECIAL DELIVERY OFFICIAL STAMP

Type of 1906 Issue Overprinted

1931   **Unwmk.**   *Perf. 11*

EO1	SD2 20c dull violet	.65	75.00
a.	No period after "B"	20.00	15.00
b.	Double overprint		

It is recommended that expert opinion be acquired for No. EO1 used.

POSTAGE DUE STAMPS

Postage Due Stamps of the U.S. Nos. J38-J44 Overprinted in Black

1899, Aug. 16   **Wmk. 191**   *Perf. 12*

J1	D2 1c deep claret	6.50	1.50
J2	D2 2c deep claret	6.50	1.25
J3	D2 5c deep claret	15.00	2.50
J4	D2 10c deep claret	19.00	5.50
J5	D2 50c deep claret	200.00	100.00

No. J1 was used to pay regular postage Sept. 5-19, 1902.

1901, Aug. 31

J6	D2 3c deep claret	17.50	7.00
J7	D2 30c deep claret	225.00	110.00
	Nos. J1-J7 (7)	489.50	227.75

Post Office Clerk — D3

Unwmk.

1928, Aug. 21   **Engr.**   *Perf. 11*

J8	D3 4c brown red	.20	.20
J9	D3 6c brown red	.20	.20
J10	D3 8c brown red	.20	.20
J11	D3 10c brown red	.20	.20
J12	D3 12c brown red	.20	.20
J13	D3 16c brown red	.20	.20
J14	D3 20c brown red	.20	.20
	Nos. J8-J14 (7)	1.40	1.40

For overprints see Nos. O16-O22, NJ1. For surcharge see No. J15.

No. J8 Surcharged in Blue

1937

J15	D3 3c on 4c brown red	.20	.20

Nos. J8-J14 Handstamped in Violet **VICTORY**

1944

J16	D3 4c brown red	140.00	—
J17	D3 6c brown red	90.00	—
J18	D3 8c brown red	95.00	—
J19	D3 10c brown red	90.00	—
J20	D3 12c brown red	90.00	—
J21	D3 16c brown red	95.00	—
J22	D3 20c brown red	95.00	—
	Nos. J16-J22 (7)	695.00	

OFFICIAL STAMPS

Official Handstamped Overprints

"Officers purchasing stamps for government business may, if they so desire, overprint them with the letters "O.B." either in writing with black ink or by rubber stamps but in such a manner as not to obliterate the stamp that postmasters will be unable to determine whether the stamps have been previously used." C. M. Cotterman, Director of Posts, Dec. 26, 1905.

Beginning Jan. 1, 1906, all branches of the Insular Government used postage stamps to prepay postage instead of franking them as before. Some officials used manuscript, some

utilized typewriting machines, some made press-printed overprints, but by far the larger number provided themselves with rubber stamps.

The majority of these read "O.B." but other forms were: "OFFICIAL BUSINESS" or "OFFICIAL MAIL" in 2 lines, with variations on many of these.

These "O.B." overprints are known on US 1899-1901 stamps; on 1903-06 stamps in red and blue; on 1906 stamps in red, blue, black, yellow and green.

"O.B." overprints were also made on the centavo and peso stamps of the Philippines, per order of May 25, 1907.

Beginning in 1926, the Bureau of Posts issued press-printed official stamps, but many government offices continued to handstamp ordinary postage stamps "O.B."

Regular Issue of 1926 Overprinted in Red

1926, Dec. 20   **Unwmk.**   *Perf. 12*

O1	A42 2c green & black	2.25	1.00
O2	A42 4c carmine & black	2.25	1.25
a.	Vertical pair, imperf. between	750.00	
O3	A42 18c lt brown & black	7.00	4.00
O4	A42 20c orange & black	6.75	1.75
	Nos. O1-O4 (4)	18.25	8.00

Opening of the Legislative Palace.

Regular Issue of 1917-26 Overprinted

1931   *Perf. 11*

O5	A40 2c green	.20	.20
a.	No period after "B"	15.00	5.00
b.	No period after "O"		
O6	A40 4c carmine	.20	.20
a.	No period after "B"	15.00	5.00
O7	A40 6c deep violet	.20	.20
O8	A40 8c yellow brn	.20	.20
O9	A40 10c deep blue	.30	.20
O10	A40 12c red orange	.25	.20
a.	No period after "B"	32.50	
O11	A40 16c lt ol green	.25	.20
	(Dewey)		
a.	16c olive bister	1.25	.20
O12	A40 20c orange yellow	.25	.20
a.	No period after "B"	22.50	15.00
O13	A40 26c green	.40	.30
a.	26c blue green	1.00	.65
O14	A40 30c gray	.30	.20
	Nos. O5-O14 (10)	2.55	2.15

Same Overprint on Nos. 383-392

1935

O15	A53 2c rose	.20	.20
a.	No period after "B"	15.00	5.00
O16	A54 4c yellow green	.20	.20
a.	No period after "B"	15.00	8.50
O17	A55 6c dark brown	.20	.20
a.	No period after "B"	20.00	17.50
O18	A56 8c violet	.20	.20
O19	A57 10c rose carmine	.20	.20
O20	A58 12c black	.20	.20
O21	A59 16c dark blue	.20	.20
O22	A60 20c lt olive green	.20	.20
O23	A61 26c indigo	.25	.20
O24	A62 30c orange red	.30	.20
	Nos. O15-O24 (10)	2.15	2.05

Same Overprint on Nos. 411 and 418

1937-38   *Perf. 11*

O25	A53 2c rose	.20	.20
a.	No period after "B"	4.25	2.25
b.	Period after "B" raised (UL 4)		
O26	A60 20c lt olive green ('38)	.65	.50

Nos. 383-392 Overprinted in Black:

a

b

1938-40

O27	A53(a) 2c rose	.20	.20
a.	Hyphen omitted	20.00	20.00
b.	No period after "B"	25.00	25.00
O28	A54(b) 4c yellow green	.20	.20
O29	A55(a) 6c dark brown	.20	.20
O30	A56(b) 8c violet	.20	.20
O31	A57(b) 10c rose carmine	.20	.20
a.	No period after "O"	30.00	30.00
O32	A58(b) 12c black	.20	.20
O33	A59(b) 16c dark blue	.20	.20
O34	A60(a) 20c lt ol grn ('40)	.25	.25
O35	A61(b) 26c indigo	.30	.30
O36	A62(b) 30c orange red	.25	.25
	Nos. O27-O36 (10)	2.20	2.20

No. 461 Overprinted in Black

Perf. 11x10½

1941, Apr. 14   **Unwmk.**

O37	A75 2c apple green	.20	.20

Official Stamps Handstamped in Violet **VICTORY**

1944   *Perf. 11, 11x10½*

O38	A53 2c #O27	250.00	150.00
O39	A75 2c #O37	6.50	3.00
O40	A54 4c #O16	42.50	30.00
O40A	A55 6c #O29	5,000.	—
O41	A57 10c #O31	150.00	
a.	No period after "O"		
O42	A60 20c #O22	6,000.	
O43	A60 20c #O26	1,550.	

No. 497 Overprinted Like No. O37 in Black

Perf. 11x10½

1946, June 19   **Unwmk.**

O44	A76 2c sepia	.20	.20

OCCUPATION STAMPS

Issued under Japanese Occupation

Nos. 461, 438 and 439 Overprinted with Bars in Black

1942-43   **Unwmk.**   *Perf. 11x10½, 11*

N1	A75 2c apple green	.20	.20
a.	Pair, one without overprint		
N2	A58 12c black ('43)	.20	.20
N3	A59 16c dark blue	5.00	3.75
	Nos. N1-N3 (3)	5.40	4.15

Nos. 435, 442, 443 and 423 Surcharged in Black

a

b

c

d

Perf. 11

N4	A55 5c on 6c golden brn	.20	.20
a.	Top bar shorter, thinner	.20	.20
b.	5c on 6c dark brown	.20	.20
c.	As "b" and "a"	.20	.20
N5	A62 16c on 30c orange red ('43)	.25	.25
N6	A63 50c on 1p red org & black ('43)	.60	.60
a.	Double surcharge		300.00
N7	A65 1p on 4p blue & black ('43)	125.00	200.00
	Nos. N4-N7 (4)	126.05	201.05

On Nos. N4 and N4b, the top bar measures 1½x22½mm. On Nos. N4a and N4c, the top bar measures 1x21mm and the "5" is smaller and thinner.

No. N7 used is valued with a postal cancellation. Used examples exist with first day cancellations and these are worth somewhat less.

No. 384 Surcharged in Black

1942, May 18

N8	A54 2c on 4c yellow green	6.00	6.00

Japan's capture of Bataan and Corregidor. The American-Filipino forces finally surrendered May 7, 1942.

No. 384 Surcharged in Black

1942, Dec. 8

N9	A54 5c on 4c yellow green	.50	.50

1st anniv. of the "Greater East Asia War."

Nos. C59 and C62 Surcharged in Black

1943, Jan. 23

N10	AP1 2(c) on 8c carmine	.25	.25
N11	AP1 5c on 1p sepia	.50	.50

Philippine Executive Commission, 1st anniv.

Nipa Hut OS1

Rice Planting OS2

Mt. Mayon and Mt. Fuji OS3

Moro Vinta OS4

Engr., Typo. (2, 6, 25c)

1943-44   **Wmk. 257**   *Perf. 13*

N12	OS1 1c deep orange	.20	.20
N13	OS2 2c bright green	.20	.20
N14	OS1 4c slate green	.20	.20
N15	OS3 5c orange brown	.20	.20
N16	OS2 6c red	.20	.20
N17	OS3 10c blue green	.20	.20

N18 OS4 12c steel blue 1.00 1.00
N19 OS4 16c dark brown .20 .20
N20 OS1 20c rose violet 1.25 1.25
N21 OS3 21c violet .20 .20
N22 OS2 25c pale brown .20 .20
N23 OS3 1p deep carmine .75 .75
N24 OS4 2p dull violet 5.50 5.50
N25 OS4 5p dark olive 14.00 9.00
Nos. N12-N25 (14) 24.30 19.30

For surcharges see Nos. NB5-NB7.

Map of Manila
Bay Showing
Bataan and
Corregidor
OS5

1943, May 7 Photo. Unwmk.
N26 OS5 2c carmine red .20 .20
N27 OS5 5c bright green .25 .25

Fall of Bataan and Corregidor, 1st anniv.

No. 440 Surcharged in
Black

1943, June 20 Engr. Perf. 11
N28 A60 12c on 20c lt olive green .20 .20
a. Double surcharge —

350th anniv. of the printing press in the Philippines. "Limbagan" is Tagalog for "printing press."

Rizal
Monument,
Filipina and
Philippine
Flag — OS6

1943, Oct. 14 · Photo. Perf. 12
N29 OS6 5c light blue .20 .20
a. Imperf. .20 .20
N30 OS6 12c orange .20 .20
a. Imperf. .20 .20
N31 OS6 17c rose pink .20 .20
a. Imperf. .20 .20
Nos. N29-N31 (3) .60 .60

"Independence of the Philippines." Japan granted "independence" Oct. 14, 1943, when the puppet republic was founded.
The imperforate stamps were issued without gum.

Jose Rizal
OS7

Rev. Jose
Burgos
OS8

Apolinario
Mabini — OS9

1944, Feb. 17 Litho. Perf. 12
N32 OS7 5c blue .20 .20
a. Imperf. .20 .20
N33 OS8 12c carmine .20 .20
a. Imperf. .20 .20
N34 OS9 17c deep orange .20 .20
a. Imperf. .20 .20
Nos. N32-N34 (3) .60 .60

Nos. C60 and C61 Surcharged in
Black

1944, May 7 Perf. 11
N35 AP1 5c on 20c ultra .50 .35
N36 AP1 12c on 60c blue green 1.25 .85

Fall of Bataan and Corregidor, 2nd anniv.

Jose P.
Laurel — OS10

Without Gum
1945, Jan. 12 Litho. Imperf.
N37 OS10 5c dull violet brown .20 .20
N38 OS10 7c blue green .20 .20
N39 OS10 20c chalky blue .20 .20
Nos. N37-N39 (3) .60 .60

1st anniv. of the puppet Philippine Republic (Oct. 14, 1944). "S" stands for "sentimos."

OCCUPATION SEMI-POSTAL STAMPS

Woman, Farming
and
Cannery — OSP1

Unwmk.
1942, Nov. 12 Litho. Perf. 12
NB1 OSP1 2c + 1c pale vio .20 .20
NB2 OSP1 5c + 1c brt green .25 .20
NB3 OSP1 16c + 2c orange 32.50 32.50
Nos. NB1-NB3 (3) 32.95 32.90

Campaign to produce and conserve food. The surtax aided the Red Cross.

Souvenir Sheet

OSP2

Without Gum
1943, Oct. 14 Imperf.
NB4 OSP2 Sheet of 3 50.00 10.00

"Independence of the Philippines."
No. NB4 contains Nos. N29a-N31a. Lower inscription from Rizal's "Last Farewell." Sold for 2.50p.

Nos. N18, N20 and
N21 Surcharged in
Black

1943, Dec. 8 Wmk. 257 Perf. 13
NB5 OS4 12c + 21c steel blue .20 .20
NB6 OS1 20c + 36c rose violet .20 .20
NB7 OS3 21c + 40c violet .20 .20
Nos. NB5-NB7 (3) .60 .60

The surtax was for the benefit of victims of a Luzon flood.

"Baha" is Tagalog for "flood."

Souvenir Sheet

OSP3

Without Gum
1944, Feb. 9 Litho. Imperf.
NB8 OSP3 Sheet of 3 5.00 3.00

No. NB8 contains Nos. N32a-N34a.
Sheet sold for 1p, surtax going to a fund for the care of heroes' monuments.

OCCUPATION POSTAGE DUE STAMP

No. J15 Ovptd. with Bar in Blue

1942, Oct. 14 Unwmk. Perf. 11
NJ1 D3 3c on 4c brown red 35.00 20.00

On copies of No. J15, two lines were drawn in India ink with a ruling pen across "United States of America" by employees of the Short Paid Section of the Manila Post Office.
This was to make a provisional 3c postage due stamp which was used from Sept. 1, 1942, (when the letter rate was raised from 2c to 5c) until Oct. 14 when No. NJ1 went on sale.

OCCUPATION OFFICIAL STAMPS

Nos. 461, 413, 435, 435a & 442
Overprinted or Surcharged in Black
with Bars and

1943-44 Unwmk. Perf. 11x10½, 11
NO1 A75 2c apple green .20 .20
a. Double overprint 500.00
NO2 A55 5c on 6c dk brown
(#413, '44) 45.00 45.00
NO3 A55 5c on 6c gldn brn
(No. 435a) .20 .20
a. Narrower spacing btwn.
bars .20 .20
b. 5c on 6c dark brown (#435) .20 .20
c. As "b," narrower spacing
between bars .20 .20
d. Double surcharge —
NO4 A62 16c on 30c org red .30 .30
a. Wider spacing btwn bars .30 .30
Nos. NO1-NO4 (4) 45.70 45.70

On Nos. NO3 and NO3b, the bar deleting "United States of America" is 9¾-10mm above the bar deleting "Common-." On Nos. NO3a and NO3c, the spacing is 8-8½mm.
On No. NO4 the center bar is 19mm long, 3½mm below the top bar and 6mm above the Japanese characters.
On No. NO4a, the center bar is 20½mm long, 9mm below the top bar and 1mm above the Japanese characters.
"K. P." (Kagamitang Pampamahalaan) is Tagalog for "Official Business."

Nos. 435 & 435a
Surcharged in Black

1944 Perf. 11
NO5 A55 5c on 6c golden brown .20 .20
a. 5c on 6c dark brown .20 .20

Nos. O34 & C62 Overprinted in Black

a

b

NO6 A60(a) 20c lt olive green .25 .25
NO7 AP1(b) 1p sepia .65 .65

PUERTO RICO

ˌpwer-tə-'rē-ˌkō

(Porto Rico)

LOCATION — Large island in the West Indies, east of Hispaniola
GOVT. — Former Spanish possession
AREA — 3,435 sq. mi.
POP. — 953,243 (1899)
CAPITAL — San Juan

The island was ceded to the US by the Treaty of 1898.
Spanish issues of 1855-73 used in both Puerto Rico and Cuba are listed as Cuba Nos. 1-4, 9-14, 18-21, 32-34, 35A-37, 39-41, 43-45, 47-49, 51-53, 55-57.
Spanish issues of 1873-1898 for Puerto Rico only are listed in Vol. 4 of this Catalogue.

100 Cents = 1 Dollar (1898)

Issued under US Administration
Ponce Issue

A11

1898 Unwmk. Imperf.
200 A11 5c violet, yellowish 7,000.

The only way No. 200 is known used is handstamped on envelopes.
Both unused stamps and used envelopes have a violet control mark.
Counterfeits exist of Nos. 200-201.

Coamo Issue

A12

1898 Unwmk. Imperf.
201 A12 5c black 650. 1,050.

There are ten varieties in the setting (see the Scott United States Specialized Catalogue).
The stamps bear the control mark "F. Santiago" in violet.

U.S. Nos. 279, 279Bf, 281, 272 &
282C Overprinted in Black at 36
degree angle

1899	Wmk. 191	Perf. 12	
210 A87	1c yellow green	5.00	1.40
a.	Ovpt. at 25 degree angle	7.50	2.25
211 A88	2c redsh car, IV	4.25	1.25
a.	Ovpt. at 25 degree angle	5.50	2.25
212 A91	5c blue	9.00	2.50
213 A93	8c violet brown	27.50	17.50
a.	Ovpt. at 25 degree angle	32.50	19.00
c.	"PORTO RIC"	125.00	110.00
214 A94	10c brown, I	17.50	6.00
	Nos. 210-214 (5)	63.25	28.65

Misspellings of the overprint, actually broken letters (PORTO RICU, PORTU RICO, FORTO RICO), are found on 1c, 2c, 8c and 10c.

U.S. Nos. 279 and
279B Overprinted
Diagonally in Black

1900			
215 A87	1c yellow green	6.50	1.40
216 A88	2c red, IV	4.75	2.00
b.	Inverted overprint		8,250.

POSTAGE DUE STAMPS

U.S. Nos. J38, J39, J42 Overprinted
like Nos. 210-214

1899	Wmk. 191	Perf. 12	
J1 D2	1c deep claret	22.50	5.50
a.	Overprint at 25 degree angle	22.50	7.50
J2 D2	2c deep claret	20.00	6.00
a.	Overprint at 25 degree angle	20.00	7.00
J3 D2	10c deep claret	160.00	60.00
a.	Overprint at 25 degree angle	175.00	85.00
	Nos. J1-J3 (3)	202.50	71.50

Stamps of Puerto Rico were replaced by those of the US.

RYUKYU ISLANDS

rē-'yü-ˌkyü 'ī-lənds

LOCATION — Chain of 63 islands between Japan and Formosa, separating the East China Sea from the Pacific Ocean
GOVT. — Semi-autonomous under United States administration
AREA — 848 sq. mi.
POP. — 945,465 (1970)
CAPITAL — Naha, Okinawa

The Ryukyus were part of Japan until American forces occupied them in 1945. The islands reverted to Japan May 15, 1972.

Before the general issue of 1948, a number of provisional stamps were used. These included a mimeographed-handstamped adhesive for Kume Island, and various current stamps of Japan handstamped with chops by the postmasters of Okinawa, Amami, Miyako and Yaeyama. Although authorized by American authorities, these provisionals were local in nature, so are omitted in the listings that follow. They are listed in the Scott United States Specialized Catalogue.

100 Sen = 1 Yen
100 Cents = 1 Dollar (1958)

Catalogue values for all unused stamps in this country are for Never Hinged items.

Watermark

Wmk. 257

Cycad — A1   Lily — A2

Sailing Ship — A3   Farmer — A4

Wmk. 257

1949, July 18	Typo.	Perf. 13	
Second Printing			
1 A1	5s magenta	1.50	1.50
2 A2	10s yellow green	6.00	5.50
3 A1	20s yellow green	2.50	2.50
4 A3	30s vermilion	1.50	1.50
5 A2	40s magenta	1.50	1.50
6 A3	50s ultramarine	3.00	3.25
7 A4	1y ultramarine	6.00	5.50
	Nos. 1-7 (7)	22.00	21.25

First Printing			
1a A1	5s magenta	2.50	3.50
2a A2	10s yellow green	1.40	2.00
3a A1	20s yellow green	1.40	2.00
4a A3	30s vermilion	2.50	3.25
5a A2	40s magenta	50.00	50.00
6a A3	50s ultramarine	2.50	3.50
7a A4	1y ultramarine	450.00	290.00
	Nos. 1a-7a (7)	510.30	354.25

First printing: thick yellow gum, dull colors, rough perforations, grayish paper.
Second printing: white gum, sharp colors, cleancut perforations, white paper.

Tile Rooftop and Shishi — A5

1y, Ryukyu girl. 2y, Shuri Castle. 3y, Guardian dragon. 4y, Two women. 5y, Sea shells.

	Perf. 13x13½		
1950, Jan. 21	Unwmk.	Photo.	
8 A5	50s dark carmine rose	.20	.20
a.	White paper	.50	.50
9 A5	1y deep blue	2.50	2.00
10 A5	2y rose violet	11.00	6.00
11 A5	3y carmine rose	25.00	11.00
12 A5	4y grnsh gray	15.00	11.00
13 A5	5y blue green	7.50	5.00
	Nos. 8-13 (6)	61.20	35.20

No. 8a is on whiter paper with colorless gum. Issued Sept. 6, 1958.
No. 8 is on toned paper with yellowish gum. For surcharges see Nos. 16-17.

Ryukyu University A6

1951, Feb. 12		Perf. 13½x13	
14 A6	3y red brown	55.00	20.00

Opening of Ryukyu University, Feb. 12.

Pine Tree — A7

1951, Feb. 19		Perf. 13	
15 A7	3y dark green	50.00	20.00

Reforestation Week, Feb. 18-24.

Nos. 8 and 10
Surcharged in Black

Three types of 10y surcharge:
I - Narrow-spaced rules, "10" normal spacing.
II - Wide-spaced rules, "10" normal spacing.
III - Rules and "10" both wide-spaced.

1952		Perf. 13x13½	
16 A5	10y on 50s, type II	9.00	9.00
a.	Type I	35.00	35.00
b.	Type III	40.00	40.00
17 A5	100y on 2y rose vio	1,900.	1,200.
	Hinged		1,500.

Surcharge forgeries are known of No. 17. Authentication by competent experts is recommended.

Dove, Bean Sprout and Map — A8

1952, Apr. 1		Perf. 13½x13	
18 A8	3y deep plum	120.00	35.00

Establishment of the Government of the Ryukyu Islands (GRI), Apr. 1, 1952.

Madanbashi Bridge — A9

1952-53

Designs: 2y, Main Hall, Shuri Castle. 3y, Shurei Gate. 6y, Stone Gate, Sogenji temple, Naha. 10y, Benzaiten-do temple. 30y, Sonohan Utaki (altar) at Shuri Castle. 50y, Tamaudum (royal mausoleum), Shuri. 100y, Stone Bridge, Hosho Pond.

19 A9	1y red	.20	.20
20 A9	2y green	.25	.25
21 A9	3y aqua	.30	.30
22 A9	6y blue	1.75	1.75
23 A9	10y crimson rose	2.50	.90
24 A9	30y olive green	11.00	6.50
a.	30y light olive green ('58)	30.00	
25 A9	50y rose violet	15.00	8.25
26 A9	100y claret	20.00	6.25
	Nos. 19-26 (8)	51.00	24.40

Issued: 1y, 2y, 3y, 11/20/52; others, 1/20/53.

Reception at Shuri Castle — A10

Perry and American Fleet A11

1953, May 26	Perf. 13½x13, 13x13½		
27 A10	3y deep magenta	12.50	6.50
28 A11	6y dull blue	1.25	1.25

Centenary of the arrival of Commodore Matthew Calbraith Perry at Naha, Okinawa.

Chofu Ota and Pencil-shaped Matrix — A12

1953, Oct. 1		Perf. 13½x13	
29 A12	4y yellow brown	10.00	5.00

3rd Newspaper Week.

Shigo Toma and Pen — A13

1954, Oct. 1			
30 A13	4y blue	13.00	7.50

4th Newspaper Week.

Ryukyu Pottery — A14   Noguni Shrine and Sweet Potato Plant — A15

15y, Lacquerware. 20y, Textile design.

1954-55	Photo.	Perf. 13	
31 A14	4y brown	1.00	.60
32 A14	15y vermilion	4.00	2.00
33 A14	20y yellow orange	2.25	2.00
	Nos. 31-33 (3)	7.25	4.60

Issue dates: June 25, 1954, June 20, 1955. For surcharges see Nos. C19, C21, C23.

1955, Nov. 26			
34 A15	4y blue	11.00	7.00

350th anniv. of the introduction of the sweet potato to the Ryukyu Islands.

Stylized Trees — A16

1956, Feb. 18		Unwmk.	
35 A16	4y bluish green	10.00	5.00

Arbor Week, Feb. 18-24.

Willow Dance — A17

1956, May 1 — Perf. 13

Design: 8y, Straw hat dance. 14y, Dancer in warrior costume with fan.

36	A17	5y rose lilac	.90	.60
37	A17	8y violet blue	2.00	1.65
38	A17	14y reddish brown	3.00	2.00
		Nos. 36-38 (3)	5.90	4.25

For surcharges see Nos. C20, C22.

Telephone — A18

1956, June 8

| 39 | A18 | 4y violet blue | 15.00 | 8.00 |

Establishment of dial telephone system.

Garland of Pine, Bamboo and Plum — A19

1956, Dec. 1 — Perf. 13½x13

| 40 | A19 | 2y multicolored | 2.00 | 2.00 |

New Year, 1957.

Map of Okinawa and Pencil Rocket — A20

1957, Oct. 1 — Photo. — Perf. 13½x13

| 41 | A20 | 4y deep violet blue | .75 | .75 |

7th annual Newspaper Week, Oct. 1-7.

Phoenix — A21

1957, Dec. 1 — Unwmk. — Perf. 13

| 42 | A21 | 2y multicolored | .25 | .25 |

New Year, 1958.

Ryukyu Stamps — A22

1958, July 1 — Perf. 13½

| 43 | A22 | 4y multicolored | .80 | .80 |

10th anniversary of first Ryukyu stamps.

Yen Symbol and Dollar Sign — A23

1958, Sept. 16 — Typo. — Perf. 11
Without Gum

44	A23	½c orange	.90	.90
a.		Imperf., pair	1,000.	
b.		Horiz. pair, imperf. btwn.	100.00	
c.		Vert. pair, imperf. btwn.	150.00	
d.		Vert. strip of 3, imperf. btwn.	500.00	
45	A23	1c yellow green	1.40	1.40
a.		Horiz. pair, imperf. btwn.	150.00	
b.		Vert. pair, imperf. btwn.	110.00	
c.		Vert. strip of 3, imperf. btwn.	450.00	
d.		Vert. strip of 4, imperf. btwn.	500.00	
e.		Block of 4, imperf. btwn. vert & horiz.	—	
46	A23	2c dark blue	2.25	2.25
a.		Horiz. pair, imperf. btwn.	150.00	
b.		Vert. pair, imperf. btwn.	1,500.	
c.		Horiz. strip of 3, imperf. btwn.	300.00	
d.		Horiz. strip of 4, imperf. btwn.	500.00	
47	A23	3c deep carmine	1.75	1.50
a.		Horiz. pair, imperf. btwn.	150.00	
b.		Vert. pair, imperf. btwn.	110.00	
c.		Vert. strip of 3, imperf. btwn.	300.00	
d.		Vert. strip of 4, imperf. btwn.	550.00	
e.		Block of 4, imperf. btwn. vert	—	
48	A23	4c bright green	2.25	2.25
a.		Horiz. pair, imperf. btwn.	500.00	
b.		Vert. pair, imperf. btwn.	150.00	
49	A23	5c orange	4.25	3.75
a.		Horiz. pair, imperf. btwn.	150.00	
b.		Vert. pair, imperf. btwn.	750.00	
50	A23	10c aqua	5.75	4.75
a.		Horiz. pair, imperf. btwn.	200.00	
b.		Vert. pair, imperf. btwn.	150.00	
c.		Vert. strip of 3, imperf. btwn.	500.00	
51	A23	25c brt vio blue	8.00	6.00
a.		Gummed paper ('61)	9.50	8.50
b.		Horiz. pair, imperf. btwn.	1,400.	
c.		Vert. pair, imperf. btwn.	—	
d.		Vert. strip of 3, imperf. btwn.	600.00	
52	A23	50c gray	17.50	10.00
a.		Gummed paper ('61)	10.50	10.00
b.		Horiz. pair, imperf. btwn.	1,200.	
53	A23	$1 rose lilac	12.50	5.50
a.		Horiz. pair, imperf. btwn.	400.00	
b.		Vert. pair, imperf. btwn.	1,750.	
		Nos. 44-53 (10)	56.55	38.30

Printed locally. Perforation, paper and shade varieties exist. See chart in the *Scott United States Specialized Catalogue*.

Nos. 51a, 52a are on off-white paper and perf 10.3.

Gate of Courtesy — A24

1958, Oct. 15 — Photo. — Perf. 13½

| 54 | A24 | 3c multicolored | 1.25 | 1.25 |

Restoration of Shureimon, Gate of Courtesy, on road leading to Shuri City. Counterfeits exist.

Lion Dance — A25

1958, Dec. 10 — Unwmk. — Perf. 13½

| 55 | A25 | 1½c multicolored | .25 | .25 |

New Year, 1959.

Trees and Mountains — A26

1959, Apr. 30 — Litho. — Perf. 13½x13

| 56 | A26 | 3c bl, yel grn, grn & red | .70 | .60 |

"Make the Ryukyus Green" movement.

Yonaguni Moth A27

1959, July 23 — Photo. — Perf. 13

| 57 | A27 | 3c multicolored | 1.10 | 1.00 |

Meeting of the Japanese Biological Education Society in Okinawa.

Hibiscus — A28

3c, Fish (Moorish idol). 8c, Sea shell (Phalium bandatum). 13c, Butterfly (Kallima inachus Eucerca), denomination at left, butterfly going up. 17c, Jellyfish (Dactylometra pacifera Goette).

Inscribed 琉球郵便

1959, Aug. 10 — Perf. 13x13½

58	A28	½c multicolored	.20	.20
59	A28	3c multicolored	.75	.40
60	A28	8c lt ultra, blk & ocher	10.00	5.50
61	A28	13c lt bl, gray & org	2.50	1.75
62	A28	17c vio bl, red & yel	20.00	9.00
		Nos. 58-62 (5)	33.45	16.85

Four-character inscription measures 10x2mm on ½c; 12x3mm on 3c, 8c; 8½x2mm on 13c, 17c. See Nos. 76-80.

Toy (Yakaji) — A29

1959, Dec. 1 — Litho.

| 63 | A29 | 1½c gold & multi | .55 | .45 |

New Year, 1960.

University Badge A30

1960, May 22 — Photo. — Perf. 13

| 64 | A30 | 3c multicolored | .95 | .75 |

Opening of Ryukyu University, 10th anniv.

Dancer — A31

Designs: Various Ryukyu Dances.

1960, Nov. 1 — Photo. — Perf. 13
Dark Gray Background

65	A31	1c yellow, red & vio	1.25	.80
66	A31	2½c crimson, bl & yel	3.00	1.00
67	A31	5c dk blue, yel & red	.65	.50
68	A31	10c dk blue, yel & car	.80	.65
		Nos. 65-68 (4)	5.70	2.95

See Nos. 81-87, 220.

Torch and Nago Bay A32

Runners at Starting Line A33

1960, Nov. 8

| 72 | A32 | 3c lt bl, grn & red | 5.50 | 3.00 |
| 73 | A33 | 8c orange & slate grn | .75 | .75 |

8th Kyushu Inter-Prefectural Athletic Meet, Nago, Northern Okinawa, Nov. 6-7.

Little Egret and Rising Sun A34

1960, Dec. 1 — Unwmk. — Perf. 13

| 74 | A34 | 3c reddish brown | 5.50 | 3.50 |

National census.

Okinawa Bull Fight — A35

1960, Dec. 10 — Perf. 13½

| 75 | A35 | 1½c bis, dk bl & red brn | 1.75 | 1.50 |

New Year, 1961.

Type of 1959 With Japanese
Inscription Redrawn:

1960-61　　Photo.　Perf. 13x13½
76　A28　½c multicolored ('61)　.45　.45
77　A28　3c multicolored ('61)　.90　.35
78　A28　8c lt ultra, blk &
　　　　　ocher　.90　.80
79　A28　13c blue, brn & red　1.10　.90
80　A28　17c violet bl, red & yel　15.00　6.00
　　Nos. 76-80 (5)　18.35　8.50

Size of Japanese inscription on Nos. 78-80 is 10½x11½mm. On No. 79 the denomination is at right, butterfly going down.
Issued: 8c-17c, July 1; 3c, Aug. 23; ½c, Oct.

Dancer Type of 1960 with "RYUKYUS"
Added in English

1961-64　　　　　　　Perf. 13
81　A31　1c multicolored　.20　.20
82　A31　2½c multicolored ('62)　.20　.20
83　A31　5c multicolored ('62)　.25　.25
84　A31　10c multicolored ('62)　.45　.40
84A　A31　20c multicolored ('64)　3.00　1.40
85　A31　25c multicolored ('62)　1.00　.90
86　A31　50c multicolored　2.50　1.40
87　A31　$1 multicolored　6.00　.25
　　Nos. 81-87 (8)　13.60　5.00

Issued: 50c, $1, Sept. 1; 1c, Dec. 5; 25c, Feb. 1; 2½c, 5c, 10c, June 20; 20c, Jan. 20.

Pine Tree — A36

1961, May 1　　Photo.　Perf. 13
88　A36　3c yellow green & red　1.50　1.25
"Make the Ryukyus Green" movement.

Naha, Steamer and Sailboat A37

1961, May 20
89　A37　3c aqua　2.10　1.50
40th anniversary of Naha.

White Silver Temple — A38

1961, Oct. 1　　Typo.　Perf. 11
90　A38　3c red brown　2.00　1.50
　a.　Horiz. pair, imperf. between　500.00
　b.　Vert. pair, imperf. between　600.00
Merger of townships Takamine, Kanegushiku and Miwa with Itoman.

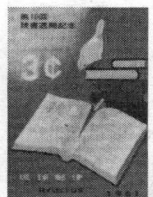

Books and Bird — A39

1961, Nov. 12　Litho.　Perf. 13
91　A39　3c multicolored　1.10　.90
Issued for Book Week.

Rising Sun and Eagles — A40

1961, Dec. 10　　Photo.　Perf. 13½
92　A40　1½c gold, ver & blk　2.00　2.00
New Year, 1962.

Symbolic Steps, Trees and Government Building — A41

1962, Apr. 1　Unwmk.　Perf. 13½
Design: 3c, Government Building.
93　A41　1½c multicolored　.60　.60
94　A41　3c brt grn, red & gray　.80　.80
10th anniv. of the Government of the Ryukyu Islands (GRI).

Anopheles Hyrcanus Sinensis — A42

8c, Malaria eradication emblem, Shurei gate.

1962, Apr. 7　　Perf. 13½x13
95　A42　3c multicolored　.60　.60
96　A42　8c multicolored　.90　.75
WHO drive to eradicate malaria.

Dolls and Toys — A43

1962, May 5　Litho.　Perf. 13½
97　A43　3c red, blk, bl & buff　1.10　1.00
Issued for Children's Day.

Linden or Sea Hibiscus — A44

1962, June 1　　　　Photo.
Flowers: 3c, Indian coral tree. 8c, Iju (Schima liukiuensis Nakai). 13c, Touch-me-not (garden balsam). 17c, Shell flower (Alpinia speciosa).
98　A44　½c multicolored　.20　.20
99　A44　3c multicolored　.35　.20
100　A44　8c multicolored　.40　.40
101　A44　13c multicolored　.60　.55
102　A44　17c multicolored　1.00　.80
　　Nos. 98-102 (5)　2.55　2.15
See #107, 114 for other flower stamps.
For surcharge see No. 190.

Earthenware A45

1962, July 5　　Perf. 13½x13
103　A45　3c multicolored　3.50　2.50
Issued for Philatelic Week.

Japanese Fencing (Kendo) A46

1962, July 25　　　Perf. 13
104　A46　3c multicolored　4.00　3.00
All-Japan Kendo Meeting, Okinawa, July 25.

Rabbit Playing near Water, Bingata Cloth Design — A47

1962, Dec. 10　　Perf. 13x13½
105　A47　1½c gold & multi　1.00　.80
New Year, 1963.

Young Man and Woman, Stone Relief — A48

1963, Jan. 15　　Photo.　Perf. 13½
106　A48　3c gold, black & blue　.90　.80
Issued for Adult Day.

Gooseneck Cactus — A49

1963, Apr. 5　　Perf. 13x13½
107　A49　1½c dk bl, grn, yel & pink　.20　.20

Trees and Wooded Hills — A50

1963, Mar. 25　　Perf. 13½x13
108　A50　3c ultra, grn & red brn　1.00　.80
"Make the Ryukyus Green" movement.

Map of Okinawa — A51

1963, Apr. 30　Unwmk.　Perf. 13½
109　A51　3c multicolored　1.25　1.00
Opening of the Round Road on Okinawa.

Hawks over Islands — A52

1963, May 10　　　　Photo.
110　A52　3c multicolored　1.10　.95
Issued for Bird Day, May 10.

Shioya Bridge — A53

1963, June 5
111　A53　3c multicolored　1.10　.95
Opening of Shioya Bridge over Shioya Bay.

Tsuikin-wan Lacquerware Bowl — A54

1963, July 1　Unwmk.　Perf. 13½
112　A54　3c multicolored　3.00　2.50
Issued for Philatelic Week.

Map of Far East and JCI Emblem A55

1963, Sept. 16　Photo.　Perf. 13½
113　A55　3c multicolored　.70　.70
Meeting of the Intl. Junior Chamber of Commerce (JCI), Naha, Okinawa, Sept. 16-19.

Mamaomoto — A56

1963, Oct. 15　　Perf. 13x13½
114　A56　15c multicolored　2.00　.80

Site of Nakagusuku Castle — A57

1963, Nov. 1　　Perf. 13½x13
115　A57　3c multicolored　.70　.60
Protection of national cultural treasures.

Flame — A58

1963, Dec. 10　　Perf. 13½
116　A58　3c red, dk bl & yel　.70　.60
15th anniversary of the Universal Declaration of Human Rights.

Dragon — A59

1963, Dec. 10   **Photo.**
117 A59 1½c Bingata Pattern   .60 .50
New Year, 1964.

Carnation — A60

1964, May 10   **Perf. 13½**
118 A60 3c blue, yel, blk & car   .40 .35
Issued for Mother's Day.

Pineapples and
Sugar Cane — A61

1964, June 1
119 A61 3c multicolored   .40 .35
Agricultural census.

Minsah Obi (Sash
Woven of
Kapok) — A62

1964, July 1   Unwmk.   Perf. 13½
120 A62 3c dp bl, rose pink &
            ocher   .55 .50
a.   3c dp bl, dp car & ocher   .70 .65
Issued for Philatelic Week.

Girl Scout and
Emblem
A63

1964, Aug. 31   **Photo.**
121 A63 3c multicolored   .40 .35
10th anniversary of Ryukyuan Girl Scouts.

Shuri Relay
Station — A64

Parabolic
Antenna and
Map — A65

1964, Sept. 1   Unwmk.   Perf. 13½
Black Overprint
122 A64 3c deep green   .65 .65
a.   Figure "1" inverted   27.50 27.50
123 A65 8c ultra   1.25 1.25
Opening of the Ryukyu Islands-Japan
microwave system carrying telephone & telegraph messages between the Ryukyus and
Japan.
Nos. 122-123 not issued without overprint.

Gate of Courtesy,
Olympic Torch and
Emblem — A66

1964, Sept. 7   Photo.   Perf. 13½x13
124 A66 3c ultra, yellow & red   .20 .20
Relaying of the Olympic torch on Okinawa
en route to Tokyo.

"Naihanchi,"
Karate
Stance — A67

"Makiwara,"
Strengthening
Hands and
Feet — A68

"Kumite,"
Simulated
Combat — A69

1964-65   Photo.   Perf. 13½
125 A67 3c dull claret, yel & blk   .50 .45
126 A68 3c yellow & multi ('65)   .40 .40
127 A69 3c gray, red & blk ('65)   .40 .40
    Nos. 125-127 (3)   1.30 1.25
Karate, Ryukyuan self-defense sport.
Issued: #125, 10/5; #126, 2/5; #127, 6/5.

Miyara
Dunchí — A70

1964, Nov. 1   **Perf. 13½**
128 A70 3c multicolored   .25 .25
Protection of national cultural treasures.
Miyara Dunchi was built as a residence by
Miyara-pechin Toen in 1819.

Snake and Iris
(Bingata) — A71

1964, Dec. 10   **Photo.**
129 A71 1½c multicolored   .30 .25
New Year, 1965.

Boy
Scouts — A72

1965, Feb. 6   **Perf. 13½**
130 A72 3c lt blue & multi   .45 .40
10th anniversary of Ryukyuan Boy Scouts.

Main
Stadium,
Onoyama
A73

1965, July 1   **Perf. 13x13½**
131 A73 3c multicolored   .25 .25
Inauguration of the main stadium of the
Onoyama athletic facilities.

Samisen of
King
Shoko — A74

1965, July 1   Photo.   Perf. 13½
132 A74 3c buff & multi   .45 .40
Issued for Philatelic Week.

Kin Power
Plant — A75

1965, July 1
133 A75 3c green & multi   .25 .25
Completion of Kin power plant.

ICY Emblem,
Ryukyu Map — A76

1965, Aug. 24   Photo.   Perf. 13½
134 A76 3c multicolored   .20 .20
UN, 20th anniv.; Intl. Cooperation Year,
1964-65.

Naha City
Hall — A77

1965, Sept. 18   Unwmk.   Perf. 13½
135 A77 3c blue & multi   .20 .20
Completion of Naha City Hall.

Chinese Box
Turtle — A78

Turtles: No. 137, Hawksbill turtle (denomination at top, country name at bottom). No.
138, Asian terrapin (denomination and country
name on top).

1965-66   Photo.   Perf. 13½
136 A78 3c gldn brn & multi   .30 .30
137 A78 3c black, yel & brn   .30 .30
138 A78 3c gray & multi   .30 .30
    Nos. 136-138 (3)   .90 .90
Issue dates: No. 136, Oct. 20, 1965. No.
137, Jan. 20, 1966. No. 138, Apr. 20, 1966.

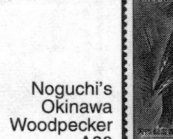

Horse
(Bingata) — A79

1965, Dec. 10   Photo.   Perf. 13½
139 A79 1½c multicolored   .20 .20
a.   Gold omitted   1,200. —
New Year, 1966.
There are 92 unused and 2 used examples
of No. 139a known.

Noguchi's
Okinawa
Woodpecker
A80

Sika Deer — A81

1966   Photo.   Perf. 13½
140 A80 3c shown   .20 .20
141 A81 3c shown   .25 .25
142 A81 3c Dugong   .25 .25
    Nos. 140-142 (3)   .70 .70
Nature conservation.
Issued: #140, 2/15; #141, 3/15; #142, 4/20.

Ryukyu Bungalow
Swallow — A82

1966, May 10   Photo.   Perf. 13½
143 A82 3c sky blue, blk & brn   .20 .20
4th Bird Week, May 10-16.

Lilies and
Ruins
A83

1966, June 23   **Perf. 13x13½**
144 A83 3c multicolored   .20 .20
Memorial Day, commemorating the end of
the Battle of Okinawa, June 23, 1945.

University
of the
Ryukyus
A84

1966, July 1
145 A84 3c multicolored   .20 .20
    Transfer of the University of the Ryukyus
from US authority to the Ryukyu Government.

Lacquerware, 18th
Century — A85

1966, Aug. 1   **Perf. 13½**
146 A85 3c gray & multi   .20 .20
    Issued for Philatelic Week.

Tile-Roofed House
and UNESCO
Emblem — A86

1966, Sept. 20   Photo.   Perf. 13½
147 A86 3c multicolored   .20 .20
    UNESCO, 20th anniv.

Government
Museum and
Dragon
Statue — A87

1966, Oct. 6
148 A87 3c multicolored   .20 .20
    Completion of the GRI (Government of the
Ryukyu Islands) Museum, Shuri.

Tomb of Nakasone-Tuimya Genga,
Ruler of Miyako — A88

1966, Nov. 1   Photo.   Perf. 13½
149 A88 3c multicolored   .20 .20
    Protection of national cultural treasures.

Ram in Iris Wreath
(Bingata) — A89

1966, Dec. 10   Photo.   Perf. 13½
150 A89 1½c dk blue & multi   .20 .20
    New Year, 1967.

Clown
Fish — A90

1966-67
    #152, Young boxfish (white numeral at lower
left). #153, Forceps fish (pale buff numeral at
lower right). #154, Spotted triggerfish (orange
numeral). #155, Saddleback butterflyfish (carmine numeral, lower left).

151 A90 3c org red & multi   .20 .20
152 A90 3c org yel & multi ('67) .20 .20
153 A90 3c multi ('67)   .30 .25
154 A90 3c multi ('67)   .30 .25
155 A90 3c multi ('67)   .30 .25
    Nos. 151-155 (5)   1.30 1.15
    Issue dates: #151, Dec. 20. #152, Jan. 10.
#153, Apr. 10. #154, May 25. #155, June 10.

Tsuboya Urn — A91

1967, Apr. 20
156 A91 3c yellow & multi   .20 .20
    Issued for Philatelic Week.

Episcopal
Miter — A92

1967-68   Photo.   Perf. 13½
    Seashells: No. 158, Venus comb murex. No.
159, Chiragra spider. No. 160, Green turban.
No. 161, Euprotomus bulla.

157 A92 3c lt green & multi   .20 .20
158 A92 3c grnsh bl & multi   .20 .20
159 A92 3c emerald & multi   .25 .20
160 A92 3c lt blue & multi   .30 .25
161 A92 3c brt blue & multi   .60 .50
    Nos. 157-161 (5)   1.55 1.35
    Issued: #157, 7/20; #158, 8/30; #159,
1/18/68; #160, 2/20/68; #161, 6/5/68.

Red-tiled
Roofs and
ITY Emblem
A93

1967, Sept. 11   Photo.   Perf. 13½
162 A93 3c multicolored   .20 .20
    International Tourist Year.

Mobile TB
Clinic — A94

1967, Oct. 13   Photo.   Perf. 13½
163 A94 3c lilac & multi   .20 .20
    Anti-Tuberculosis Society, 15th anniv.

Hojo Bridge,
Enkaku
Temple,
1498 — A95

1967, Nov. 1
164 A95 3c blue grn & multi   .20 .20
    Protection of national cultural treasures.

Monkey
(Bingata) — A96

1967, Dec. 11   Photo.   Perf. 13½
165 A96 1½c silver & multi   .25 .20
    New Year 1968.

TV Tower and
Map — A97

1967, Dec. 22
166 A97 3c multicolored   .25 .25
    Opening of Miyako and Yaeyama television
stations.

Dr. Kijin Nakachi
and Helper — A98

1968, Mar. 15   Photo.   Perf. 13½
167 A98 3c multicolored   .25 .25
    120th anniv. of the first vaccination in the
Ryukyu Islands, performed by Dr. Kijin
Nakachi.

Pill Box (Inro) — A99

1968, Apr. 18
168 A99 3c gray & multi   .45 .45
    Philatelic Week.

Young Man,
Library, Book
and Map of
Ryukyu
Islands
A100

1968, May 13
169 A100 3c multicolored   .30 .25
    10th International Library Week.

Mailmen's
Uniforms
and Stamp
of 1948
A101

1968, July 1   Photo.   Perf. 13x13½
170 A101 3c multicolored   .30 .25
    1st Ryukyuan postage stamps, 20th anniv.

Main Gate,
Enkaku
Temple
A102

Photo. & Engr.

1968, July 15   **Perf. 13½**
171 A102 3c multicolored   .30 .25
    Restoration of the main gate of the Enkaku
Temple, built 1492-1495, and destroyed during
WWII.

Old Man's
Dance — A103

1968, Sept. 15   Photo.   Perf. 13½
172 A103 3c gold & multi   .30 .25
    Issued for Old People's Day.

Mictyris
Longicarpus
A104

    Crabs: #174, Uca dubia stimpson. #175,
Baptozius vinosus. #176, Cardisoma carnifex.
#177, Ocypode ceratophthalma pallas.

1968-69   Photo.   Perf. 13½
173 A104 3c blue, ocher & blk   .30 .25
174 A104 3c bl grn & multi   .35 .30
175 A104 3c lt green & multi   .35 .30
176 A104 3c lt ultra & multi   .45 .40
177 A104 3c lt ultra & multi   .45 .40
    Nos. 173-177 (5)   1.90 1.65
    Issued: #173, 10/10; #174, 2/5/69; #175,
3/5/69; #176, 5/15/69; #177, 6/2/69.

Saraswati
Pavilion
A105

1968, Nov. 1   Photo.   Perf. 13½
178 A105 3c multicolored   .30 .25
    Restoration of the Saraswati Pavilion (in
front of Enkaku Temple), destroyed during
WWII.

Tennis Player — A106

1968, Nov. 3   Photo.   Perf. 13½
179 A106 3c green & multi   .40 .35
35th All-Japan East-West Men's Soft-ball Tennis Tournament, Naha City, Nov. 23-24.

Cock and Iris (Bingata) — A107

1968, Dec. 10
180 A107 1½c orange & multi   .25 .20
New Year, 1969.

Boxer — A108

1969, Jan. 3
181 A108 3c gray & multi   .40 .30
20th All-Japan Amateur Boxing Championships, University of the Ryukyus, Jan. 3-5.

Ink Slab Screen — A109

1969, Apr. 17   Photo.   Perf. 13½
182 A109 3c salmon, indigo & red   .40 .35
Philatelic Week.

Box Antennas and Map of Radio Link — A110

1969, July 1   Photo.   Perf. 13½
183 A110 3c multicolored   .25 .20
Opening of the UHF (radio) circuit system between Okinawa and the outlying Miyako-Yaeyama Islands.

Gate of Courtesy and Emblems — A111

1969, Aug. 1   Photo.   Perf. 13½
184 A111 3c Prus bl, gold & ver   .25 .20
22nd All-Japan Formative Education Study Conference, Naha, Aug. 1-3.

Tug of War Festival A112

Hari Boat Race A113

Izaiho Ceremony, Kudaka Island A114

Mortardrum Dance — A115

Sea God Dance A116

1969-70   Photo.   Perf. 13
185 A112 3c multicolored   .30 .25
186 A113 3c multicolored   .35 .30
187 A114 3c multicolored   .35 .30
188 A115 3c multicolored ('70)   .50 .45
189 A116 3c multicolored ('70)   .50 .45
  Nos. 185-189 (5)   2.00 1.75
Folklore. Issued: #185, 8/1; #186, 9/5; #187, 10/3; #188, 1/20; #189, 2/27.

No. 99 Surcharged

1969, Oct. 15   Photo.   Perf. 13½
190 A44   ½c on 3c multi   .90 .90

Nakamura-ke Farm House, Built 1713-51 A117

1969, Nov. 1   Photo.   Perf. 13½
191 A117 3c multicolored   .20 .20
Protection of national cultural treasures.

Statue of Kyuzo Toyama, Maps of Hawaiian and Ryukyu Islands A118

1969, Dec. 5   Photo.   Perf. 13½
192 A118 3c lt ultra & multi   .40 .40
  a. Without overprint   2,500.
  b. Wide-spaced bars   725.00
Ryukyu-Hawaii emigration led by Kyuzo Toyama, 70th anniversary.
The overprint - "1969" at lower left and bars across "1970" at upper right - was applied before No. 192 was issued.

Dog and Flowers (Bingata) — A119

1969, Dec. 10
193 A119 1½c pink & multi   .20 .20
New Year, 1970.

Sake Flask Made from Coconut A120

1970, Apr. 15   Photo.   Perf. 13½
194 A120 3c multicolored   .25 .25
Philatelic Week.

Classic Opera Issue

"The Bell" (Shushin Kaneiri) A121

Child and Kidnapper (Chu-nusudu) A122

Robe of Feathers (Mekarushi) A123

Vengeance of Two Young Sons (Nidotichiuchi) A124

The Virgin and the Dragon (Kokonomaki) A125

1970   Photo.   Perf. 13½
195 A121 3c dull bl & multi   .40 .40
196 A122 3c lt blue & multi   .40 .40
197 A123 3c bluish grn & multi   .40 .40
198 A124 3c dull bl grn & multi   .40 .40
199 A125 3c multicolored   .40 .40
  Nos. 195-199 (5)   2.00 2.00
  195a-199a, 5 sheets of 4   22.50 25.00
Issue dates: #195, Apr. 28; #196, May 29; #197, June 30; #198, July 30; #199, Aug. 25.

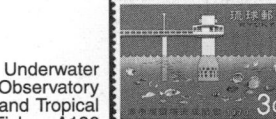

Underwater Observatory and Tropical Fish — A126

1970, May 22
200 A126 3c blue grn & multi   .30 .25
Completion of the underwater observatory at Busena-Misaki, Nago.

Noboru Jahana (1865-1908), Politician — A127

Portraits: No. 202, Saion Gushichan Bunjaku (1682-1761), statesman. No. 203, Choho Giwan (1823-1876), regent and poet.

1970-71   Engr.   Perf. 13½
201 A127 3c rose claret   .50 .45
202 A127 3c dull blue green   .75 .65
203 A127 3c black   .50 .45
  Nos. 201-203 (3)   1.75 1.55
Issued: #201, 9/25; #202, 12/22; #203, 1/22/71.

Map of Okinawa and People — A128

1970, Oct. 1   Photo.
204 A128 3c red & multi   .25 .25
Oct. 1, 1970 census.

Great Cycad of Une — A129

1970, Nov. 2   Photo.   Perf. 13½
205 A129 3c gold & multi   .25 .25
Protection of national treasures.

Japanese Flag, Diet and Map of Ryukyus A130

1970, Nov. 15   Photo.   Perf. 13½
206 A130 3c ultra & multi   .80 .75
Citizens' participation in national administration according to Japanese law of 4/24/70.

Wild Boar and Cherry Blossoms (Bingata) — A131

1970, Dec. 10
207 A131 1½c multicolored   .20 .20
New Year, 1971.

Low Hand Loom (Jibata) A132

Farmer Wearing Palm Bark Raincoat and Kuba Leaf Hat — A133

Fisherman's
Wooden Box
and Scoop
A134

#209, Woman running a filature (reel). #211,
Woman hulling rice with cylindrical "Shiri-
iushi."

1971   **Photo.**   **Perf. 13½**

208 A132 3c lt blue & multi	.30	.25
209 A132 3c pale grn & multi	.30	.25
210 A133 3c lt blue & multi	.35	.30
211 A132 3c yellow & multi	.40	.35
212 A134 3c gray & multi	.35	.30
Nos. 208-212 (5)	1.70	1.45

Issue dates: #208, Feb. 16; #209, Mar. 16;
#210, Apr. 30; #211, May 20; #212, June 15.

Water Carrier
(Taku) — A135

1971, Apr. 15   **Photo.**   **Perf. 13½**
213 A135 3c blue grn & multi   .35 .30
Philatelic Week.

Old and
New
Naha,
and City
Emblem
A136

1971, May 20   **Perf. 13**
214 A136 3c ultra & multi   .25 .20
50th anniversary of Naha as a municipality.

Caesalpinia
Pulcherrima — A137

Design: 2c, Madder (Sandanka).

1971   **Photo.**   **Perf. 13**
215 A137 2c gray & multi   .20 .20
216 A137 3c gray & multi   .20 .20
Issue dates: 2c, Sept. 30; 3c, May 10.

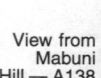

View from
Mabuni
Hill — A138

Mt. Arashi
from Haneji
Sea — A139

Yabuchi Island
from Yakena
Port — A140

1971-72
217 A138 3c green & multi   .20 .20
218 A139 3c blue & multi   .20 .20
219 A140 4c multi ('72)   .25 .20
Nos. 217-219 (3)   .65 .60
Government parks. Issued: #217, July 30;
#218, Aug. 30, 1971; #219, Jan. 20, 1972.

Dancer — A141

1971, Nov. 1   **Photo.**   **Perf. 13**
220 A141 4c Prus blue & multi   .20 .20

Deva King, Torinji
Temple — A142

1971, Dec. 1
221 A142 4c dp blue & multi   .20 .20
Protection of national cultural treasures.

Rat and
Chrysanthemums
A143

1971, Dec. 10
222 A143 2c brown org & multi   .20 .20
New Year 1972.

Student
Nurse — A144

1971, Dec. 24
223 A144 4c lilac & multi   .20 .20
Nurses' training, 25th anniversary.

Birds on
Seashore
A145

Sun over Islands
A147

Coral
Reef — A146

1972   **Photo.**   **Perf. 13**
224 A145 5c brt blue & multi   .40 .35
225 A146 5c gray & multi   .40 .35
226 A147 5c ocher & multi   .40 .35
Nos. 224-226 (3)   1.20 1.05
Issued: #224, 4/14; #225, 3/30; #226, 3/21.

Dove, US and
Japanese
Flags — A148

1972, Apr. 17   **Photo.**   **Perf. 13**
227 A148 5c brt blue & multi   .60 .60
Ratification of the Reversion Agreement
with US under which the Ryukyu Islands were
returned to Japan.

Antique Sake Pot
(Yushibin) — A149

1972, Apr. 20
228 A149 5c ultra & multi   .50 .50
Philatelic Week.
Ryukyu stamps were replaced by those of
Japan after May 15, 1972.

AIR POST STAMPS

Dove and Map of
Ryukyus — AP1

Perf. 13x13½

			Photo.
1950, Feb. 15		**Unwmk.**	
C1 AP1 8y bright blue	125.00	60.00
C2 AP1 12y green	35.00	30.00
C3 AP1 16y rose carmine	15.00	15.00
Nos. C1-C3 (3)	175.00	105.00

Heavenly
Maiden
AP2

1951-54
C4 AP2 13y blue	2.50	1.50
C5 AP2 18y green	3.50	2.25
C6 AP2 30y cerise	6.00	1.75
C7 AP2 40y red violet	7.00	5.50
C8 AP2 50y yellow orange	9.00	6.50
Nos. C4-C8 (5)	28.00	17.50

Issue dates: Oct. 1, 1951, Aug. 16, 1954.

Heavenly
Maiden
Playing
Flute — AP3

1957, Aug. 1   **Engr.**   **Perf. 13½**
C9 AP3 15y blue green	9.00	3.50
C10 AP3 20y rose carmine	15.00	5.50
C11 AP3 35y yellow green	15.00	6.50
a. 35y light yellow green ('58)	150.00	
C12 AP3 45y reddish brown	16.00	8.00
C13 AP3 60y gray	18.00	10.00
Nos. C9-C13 (5)	73.00	33.50

Same
Surcharged in
Brown Red or
Light
Ultramarine

1959, Dec. 20
C14 AP3 9c on 15y (BrR)	2.50	1.50
a. Inverted surcharge	950.00	

C15 AP3 14c on 20y (LU)	3.00	3.00
C16 AP3 19c on 35y (BrR)	8.00	5.00
C17 AP3 27c on 45y (LU)	17.50	6.00
C18 AP3 35c on 60y (BrR)	15.00	9.00
Nos. C14-C18 (5)	46.00	24.50

Nos. 31-33, 36 and 38
Surcharged in Black,
Brown, Red, Blue or
Green

1960, Aug. 3   **Photo.**   **Perf. 13**
C19 A14 9c on 4y	3.50	1.00
a. Surch. invtd. and trans-posed	15,000.	15,000.
b. Invtd. surch. (legend only)	12,000.	
c. Surcharge transposed	1,500.	
d. Legend of surcharge only	4,000.	
e. Vert. pair, one without surch.	—	
C20 A17 14c on 5y (Br)	4.00	2.25
C21 A14 19c on 15y (R)	2.50	2.00
C22 A17 27c on 14y (Bl)	9.00	2.75
C23 A14 35c on 20y (G)	6.00	4.50
Nos. C19-C23 (5)	25.00	12.50

Nos. C19c and C19d are from a single
sheet of 100 with surcharge shifted downward.
Ten examples of No. C19c exist with "9c" also
in bottom selvage. No. C19d is from the top
row of the sheet.
No. C19e is unique, pos. 100, caused by
paper foldover.

Wind
God — AP4

9c, Heavenly Maiden (as on AP2). 14c,
Heavenly Maiden (as on AP3). 27c, Wind God
at right. 35c, Heavenly Maiden over treetops.

1961, Sept. 21   **Photo.**   **Perf. 13½**
C24 AP4 9c multicolored	.30	.20
C25 AP4 14c multicolored	.70	.60
C26 AP4 19c multicolored	.70	.70
C27 AP4 27c multicolored	3.00	.60
C28 AP4 35c multicolored	1.50	1.25
Nos. C24-C28 (5)	6.20	3.35

Jet over Gate
of Courtesy
AP5

Jet Plane
AP6

1963, Aug. 28   **Perf. 13x13½**
C29 AP5 5½c multicolored   .25 .25
C30 AP6 7c multicolored   .25 .25

SPECIAL DELIVERY STAMP

Sea Horse and Map of
Ryukyus — SD1

Perf. 13x13½
1950, Feb. 15   **Unwmk.**   **Photo.**
E1 SD1 5y bright blue   30.00 16.00

UNITED NATIONS, OFFICES IN NEW YORK

yu-ˌnī-təd ˈnā-shənz

United Nations stamps are used on
UN official mail sent from UN Headquarters in New York City, the UN European Office in Geneva, Switzerland, or
from the Donaupark Vienna International Center or Atomic Energy Agency

in Vienna, Austria to points throughout the world. They may be used on private correspondence sent through the UN post offices and are valid only at the individual UN post offices.

The UN stamps issued for use in Geneva and Vienna are listed in separate sections. They are denominated in centimes and francs, and are valid only in Geneva or Vienna. The UN stamps issued for use in New York, denominated in cents and dollars, are valid only in New York.

Letters bearing Nos. 170-174 provide an exception as they were carried by the Canadian postal system.

See Switzerland Nos. 7O1-7O39 in Volume 6 of the Scott *Standard Postage Stamp Catalogue* for stamps issued by the Swiss Government for official use of the UN European Office in Geneva.

> Catalogue values for all unused stamps in this section are for Never Hinged items.

> Stamps are inscribed in English, French, or Spanish or are multilingual.

Watermark

Wmk. 309- Wavy Lines

Peoples of the World — A1

UN Headquarters Building — A2

"Peace, Justice, Security" — A3

UN Flag — A4

UN Children's Fund — A5

World Unity — A6

Perf. 13x12½, 12½x13, 12½x13½ (2c, 5c)

		1951	Unwmk.	Engr. & Photo.	
1	A1	1c magenta		.20	.20
2	A2	1½c blue green		.20	.20
3	A3	2c purple		.20	.20
4	A4	3c magenta & blue		.20	.20
5	A5	5c blue		.20	.20
6	A1	10c chocolate		.25	.25
7	A4	15c violet & blue		.25	.25
8	A6	20c dark brown		.35	.20
9	A4	25c ol gray & blue		.40	.20
10	A2	50c indigo		2.25	1.50
11	A3	$1 red		1.50	.65
		Nos. 1-11 (11)		6.00	3.95

See Offices in Geneva Nos. 4, 14.

Veteran's War Memorial Building, San Francisco A7

1952, Oct. 24   Engr.   Perf. 12

12	A7	5c blue	.20	.20

7th anniv. of the signing of the UN charter.

Globe and Encircled Flame A8

1952, Dec. 10   Perf. 13½x14

13	A8	3c deep green	.20	.20
14	A8	5c blue	.20	.20

Fourth anniv. of the adoption of the Universal Declaration of Human Rights.

Refugee Family — A9

1953, Apr. 24   Perf. 12½x13

15	A9	3c dk red brn & rose brn	.20	.20
16	A9	5c indigo & blue	.25	.25

"Protection for Refugees."

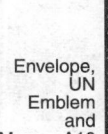

Envelope, UN Emblem and Map — A10

1953, June 12   Unwmk.   Perf. 13

17	A10	3c black brown	.20	.20
18	A10	5c dark blue	.50	.45

Issued to honor the UPU.

Gearwheels and UN Emblem — A11

1953, Oct. 24   Perf. 13x12½

19	A11	3c dark gray	.20	.20
20	A11	5c dark green	.30	.30

UN activities in the field of technical assistance.

Hands Reaching Toward Flame — A12

Ear of Wheat — A13

1953, Dec. 10   Perf. 12½x13

21	A12	3c bright blue	.20	.20
22	A12	5c rose red	1.00	.50

Human Rights Day.

1954, Feb. 11

23	A13	3c dark green & yellow	.40	.20
24	A13	8c indigo & yellow	.85	.50

Issued to honor the FAO.

UN Emblem and Anvil — A14

1954, May 10   Perf. 12½x13

25	A14	3c brown	.20	.20
26	A14	8c magenta	1.25	.75

Honoring the ILO.

UN European Office, Geneva A15

1954, Oct. 25   Perf. 14

27	A15	3c dark blue violet	1.90	1.10
28	A15	8c red	.25	.25

UN Day.

Mother and Child — A16

1954, Dec. 10   Perf. 14

29	A16	3c red orange	6.75	2.00
30	A16	8c olive green	.25	.25

Human Rights Day.

Symbol of Flight A17

1955, Feb. 9   Perf. 13½x14

31	A17	3c blue	1.75	.65
32	A17	8c rose carmine	.75	.75

International Civil Aviation Organization.

UNESCO Emblem A18

1955, May 11   Perf. 13½x14

33	A18	3c lilac rose	.20	.20
34	A18	8c light blue	.20	.20

Honoring the UN Educational, Scientific and Cultural Organization.

UN Charter A19

1955, Oct. 24   Perf. 13½x14

35	A19	3c deep plum	.90	.50
36	A19	4c dull green	.35	.20
37	A19	8c bluish black	.20	.20
		Nos. 35-37 (3)	1.45	.90

Souvenir Sheet
Imperf
Wmk. 309

38		Sheet of 3	110.00	32.50
		Hinged	80.00	
a.	A19	3c deep plum	10.00	1.50
b.	A19	4c dull green	10.00	1.50
c.	A19	8c bluish black	10.00	1.50

10th anniv. of the UN.
Two printings were made of No. 38. The first may be distinguished by the broken line of background shading on the 8c. It leaves a small white spot below the left leg of the "n" of "Unies." For the 2nd printing, the broken line was retouched, eliminating the white spot.

Hand Holding Torch — A20

1955, Dec. 9   Unwmk.   Perf. 14x13½

39	A20	3c ultra	.20	.20
40	A20	8c green	.20	.20

Human Rights Day, Dec. 10.

Symbols of Telecommunication — A21

1956, Feb. 17   Perf. 14

41	A21	3c turquoise blue	.20	.20
42	A21	8c deep carmine	.30	.30

Honoring the ITU.

Globe & Caduceus — A22

1956, Apr. 6   Perf. 14

43	A22	3c bright greenish blue	.20	.20
44	A22	8c golden brown	.20	.20

Honoring the World Health Organization.

General Assembly A23

1956, Oct. 24　　　　*Perf. 14*
45　A23　3c dark blue　　　　.20　.20
46　A23　8c gray olive　　　　.20　.20

UN Day, Oct. 24.

Flame and
Globe
A24

1956, Dec. 10　　　　*Perf. 14*
47　A24　3c plum　　　　.20　.20
48　A24　8c dark blue　　　　.20　.20

Human Rights Day.

Weather
Balloon — A25

1957, Jan. 28　　　　*Perf. 14*
49　A25　3c violet blue　　　　.20　.20
50　A25　8c dark carmine rose　　　　.20　.20

Honoring the World Meteorological
Organization.

Badge of UN
Emergency
Force — A26

1957, Apr. 8　　　　*Perf. 14x12½*
51　A26　3c light blue　　　　.20　.20
52　A26　8c rose carmine　　　　.20　.20

UN Emergency Force.

Re-engraved
1957, Apr.-May
53　A26　3c blue　　　　.20　.20
54　A26　8c rose carmine　　　　.35　.20

On Nos. 53-54 the background within and
around the circles is shaded lightly, giving a
halo effect. The letters are more distinct with a
line around each letter.

UN Emblem and
Globe — A27

1957, Oct. 24　　Engr.　　*Perf. 12½x13*
55　A27　3c orange brown　　　　.20　.20
56　A27　8c dark blue green　　　　.20　.20

Honoring the Security Council.

Flaming Torch — A28

1957, Dec. 10　　　　*Perf. 14*
57　A28　3c red brown　　　　.20　.20
58　A28　8c black　　　　.20　.20

Human Rights Day.

Atom & UN
Emblem — A29

1958, Feb. 10　　　　*Perf. 12*
59　A29　3c olive　　　　.20　.20
60　A29　8c blue　　　　.20　.20

Honoring the International Atomic Energy
Agency.

Central Hall,
Westminster — A30

1958, Apr. 14　　　　*Perf. 12*
61　A30　3c violet blue　　　　.20　.20
62　A30　8c rose claret　　　　.20　.20

Central Hall, Westminster, London, was the
site of the first session of the UN General
Assembly 1946.

UN Seal
A31

Gearwheels
A32

1958　　　　*Perf. 13½x14*
63　A31　4c red orange　　　　.20　.20
　　　　Perf. 13x14
64　A31　8c bright blue　　　　.20　.20

Issue dates: 4c, Oct. 24; 8c, June 2.

1958, Oct. 24　　Engr.　　*Perf. 12*
65　A32　4c dark blue green　　　　.20　.20
66　A32　8c vermilion　　　　.20　.20

Honoring the Economic and Social Council.

Hands
Upholding
Globe — A33

1958, Dec. 10　　　　**Unwmk.**
67　A33　4c yellow green　　　　.20　.20
68　A33　8c red brown　　　　.20　.20

Human Rights Day and the 10th anniv. of
the signing of the Universal Declaration of
Human Rights.

New York
City
Building,
Flushing
Meadows
A34

1959, Mar. 30　　　　*Perf. 12*
69　A34　4c light lilac rose　　　　.20　.20
70　A34　8c aqua　　　　.20　.20

Site of many General Assembly meetings,
1946-50.

UN Emblems and
Symbols of
Agriculture,
Industry and
Trade — A35

Figure Adapted
from Rodin's
"Age of
Bronze" — A36

1959, May 18　　　　*Perf. 12*
71　A35　4c blue　　　　.20　.20
72　A35　8c red orange　　　　.20　.20

Honoring the UN Economic Commission for
Europe.

1959, Oct. 23　　Engr.　　*Perf. 12*
73　A36　4c bright red　　　　.20　.20
74　A36　8c dark olive green　　　　.20　.20

Honor the Trusteeship Council.

World Refugee
Year
Emblem — A37

1959, Dec. 10　　　　**Unwmk.**
75　A37　4c olive & red　　　　.20　.20
76　A37　8c ol & brt greenish bl　　　　.20　.20

World Refugee Year, 7/1/59-6/30/60.

Chaillot Palace,
Paris — A38

1960, Feb. 29　　　　*Perf. 14*
77　A38　4c rose lilac & blue　　　　.20　.20
78　A38　8c dull green & brown　　　　.20　.20

Chaillot Palace in Paris was the site of General
Assembly meetings in 1948 and 1951.

Map of Far
East and
Steel Beam
A39

1960, Apr. 11　　Photo.　　*Perf. 13x13½*
79　A39　4c dp cl, bl grn & dl yel　　　　.20　.20
80　A39　8c ol green, blue & rose　　　　.20　.20

Honoring the Economic Commission for
Asia and the Far East (ECAFE).

Tree, FAO and UN
Emblems — A40

1960, Aug. 29　　　　*Perf. 13½*
81　A40　4c green, dk blue & org　　　.20　.20
　a.　　Imperf., pair
82　A40　8c yel green, black & org　　.20　.20

5th World Forestry Congress, Seattle,
Wash., Aug. 29-Sept. 10.

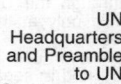

UN
Headquarters
and Preamble
to UN
Charter — A41

1960, Oct. 24　　Engr.　　*Perf. 11*
83　A41　4c blue　　　　.20　.20
84　A41　8c gray　　　　.20　.20

Souvenir Sheet
Imperf
85　　Sheet of 2　　　.50　.50
　a.　A41 4c blue　　　.25　.25
　b.　A41 8c gray　　　.25　.25

15th anniv. of the UN.

Block and
Tackle — A42

Scales of
Justice — A43

1960, Dec. 9　Photo.　　*Perf. 13½x13*
86　A42　4c multicolored　　　　.20　.20
87　A42　8c multicolored　　　　.20　.20
　a.　　Imperf., pair　　　　—

Honoring the International Bank for Reconstruction
and Development.
No. 86 exists imperf.

1961, Feb. 13　　　　**Unwmk.**
88　A43　4c yel, org brn & blk　　　　.20　.20
89　A43　8c yellow, green & black　　　.20　.20

Honoring the International Court of Justice.
The design was taken from Raphael's
"Stanze."
Nos. 88-89 exist imperf.

Seal of International Monetary
Fund — A44

1961, Apr. 17　　　　*Perf. 13x13½*
90　A44　4c bright bluish green　　　.20　.20
91　A44　7c fawn & yellow　　　　.20　.20

Honoring the International Monetary Fund.
No. 90 exists imperf.

Abstract
Group of
Flags — A45

1961, June 5　　　　*Perf. 11½*
92　A45　30c multicolored　　　　.40　.20

See Offices in Geneva No. 10.

Cogwheel and Map
of Latin
America — A46

1961, Sept. 18　　　　*Perf. 13½*
93　A46　4c blue, red & citron　　　　.20　.20
94　A46　11c green, lilac & org ver　　.25　.20

Honoring the Economic Commission for
Latin America.

Africa House, Addis Ababa, and Map — A47

1961, Oct. 24   Photo.   Perf. 11½
95 A47 4c ultra, org, yel & brown   .20 .20
96 A47 11c emer, org, yel & brn   .25 .20

Honoring the Economic Commission for Africa.

Mother Bird Feeding Young and UNICEF Seal — A48

1961, Dec. 4   Unwmk.   Perf. 11½
97 A48 3c brown, gold, org & yel   .20 .20
98 A48 4c brn, gold, bl & emer   .20 .20
99 A48 13c dp grn, gold, pur & pink   .20 .20
       Nos. 97-99 (3)   .60 .60

15th anniv. of the UN Children's Fund.

Family and Symbolic Buildings A49

1962, Feb. 28   Photo.   Perf. 14½x14
Central design multicolored
100 A49 4c bright blue   .20 .20
  a.   Black omitted   200.00
  b.   Yellow omitted   —
  c.   Brown omitted   —
101 A49 7c orange brown   .20 .20
  a.   Red omitted   —
  b.   Black omitted   —

UN program for housing and urban development.

"The World Against Malaria" — A50

1962, Mar. 30   Perf. 14x14½
Word frame in gray
102 A50 4c org, yel, green & black   .20 .20
103 A50 11c green, yel, brn & ind   .25 .20

Honoring the WHO and to call attention to the international campaign to eradicate malaria from the world.

"Peace" — A51

UN Flag — A52

Hands Combining "UN" and Globe — A53

UN Emblem over Globe — A54

Photogravure; Engraved (5c)
1962, May 25   Perf. 14x14½
104 A51 1c ver, blue, black & gray .20 .20
105 A52 3c lt green, Prus blue, yel & gray   .20 .20
Perf. 12
Size: 36½x23½mm
106 A53 5c dark carmine rose   .20 .20
Perf. 12½
107 A54 11c dk & lt blue & gold   .25 .20
       Nos. 104-107 (4)   .85 .80

See #167 and UN Offices in Geneva #2, 6. Compare A51 with A76.

Flag at Half-mast and UN Headquarters A55

World Map Showing Congo A56

1962, Sept. 17   Unwmk.   Perf. 11½
108 A55 5c black, lt blue & blue   .20 .20
109 A55 15c black, gray ol & blue   .20 .20

1st anniv. of the death of Dag Hammarskjold, Secretary General of the UN 1953-61, in memory of those who died in the service of the UN.

1962, Oct. 24
110 A56 4c olive, org, black & yel   .20 .20
111 A56 11c bl grn, org, blk & yel   .20 .20

UN Operation in the Congo.

Globe in Universe and Palm Frond — A57

1962, Dec. 3   Engr.   Perf. 14x13½
112 A57 4c violet blue   .20 .20
113 A57 11c rose claret   .25 .20

Honoring the Committee on Peaceful Uses of Outer Space.

Development Decade Emblem — A58

Perf. 11½
1963, Feb. 4   Unwmk.   Photo.
114 A58 5c pale grn, mar, dk blue & Prus blue   .20 .20
115 A58 11c yel, mar, dk blue & Prus blue   .20 .20

UN Development Decade and the UN Conference on the Application of Science and Technology for the Benefit of the Less Developed Areas, Geneva, Feb. 4-20.

Stalks of Wheat — A59

1963, Mar. 22   Perf. 11½
116 A59 5c ver, green & yellow   .20 .20
117 A59 11c ver, dp claret & yel   .25 .20

"Freedom from Hunger" campaign of the FAO.

Bridge over Map of New Guinea — A60

1963, Oct. 1   Unwmk.   Perf. 11½
118 A60 25c blue, green & gray   .45 .30

1st anniv. of the UN Temporary Executive Authority (UNTEA) in West New Guinea (West Irian).

General Assembly Building, New York — A61

1963, Nov. 4   Photo.   Perf. 13
119 A61 5c violet blue & multi   .20 .20
120 A61 11c green & multi   .20 .20

Since Oct. 1955 all sessions of the General Assembly have been held in the General Assembly Hall, UN Headquarters, N.Y.

Flame — A62

1963, Dec. 10   Perf. 13
121 A62 5c green, gold, red & yel   .20 .20
122 A62 11c car, gold, blue & yel   .20 .20

15th anniv. of the signing of the Universal Declaration of Human Rights.

Ships at Sea and IMCO Emblem A63

1964, Jan. 13   Perf. 11½
123 A63 5c blue, ol, ocher & yel   .20 .20
124 A63 11c bl, dk grn, emer & yel   .20 .20

Honoring the Intergovernmental Maritime Consultative Organization.

Map of the World — A64

UN Emblem — A65

Three Men United Before Globe — A66

Stylized Globe and Weather Vane — A67

1964   Unwmk.   Photo.   Perf. 14
125 A64 2c lt bl, dk blue, org & yel green   .20 .20
  a.   Perf. 13x13½ (71)   .20 .20
Perf. 11½
126 A65 7c dk bl, org brn & blk   .20 .20
127 A66 10c bl grn, ol grn & blk   .20 .20
128 A67 50c multicolored   .75 .45
       Nos. 125-128 (4)   1.35 1.05

Issued: 2c, 7c, 10c, May 29; 50c, Mar. 6. See UN Offices in Geneva Nos. 3, 12.

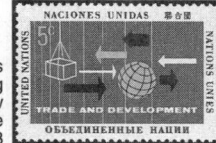

Arrows Showing Global Flow of Trade A68

1964, June 15   Perf. 13
129 A68 5c black, red & yellow   .20 .20
130 A68 11c black, olive & yellow   .20 .20

UN Conference on Trade and Development, Geneva, Mar. 23-June 15.

Poppy Capsule and Hands A69

1964, Sept. 21   Engr.   Perf. 12
131 A69 5c rose red & black   .20 .20
132 A69 11c emerald & black   .20 .20

International efforts and achievements in the control of narcotics.

Padlocked Atomic Blast — A70

Photogravure and Engraved
1964, Oct. 23   Perf. 11x11½
133 A70 5c dark red & dk brown   .20 .20

Signing of the nuclear test ban treaty pledging an end to nuclear explosions in the atmosphere, outer space and under water.

"Education for Progress" A71

1964, Dec. 7   Photo.   Perf. 12½
134 A71 4c multicolored   .20 .20
135 A71 5c multicolored   .20 .20
136 A71 11c multicolored   .20 .20
       Nos. 134-136 (3)   .60 .60

UNESCO world campaign for universal literacy and for free compulsory primary education.

Progress Chart, Key & Globe — A72

Perf. 13½x13
1965, Jan. 25   Unwmk.
137 A72   5c multicolored   .20 .20
138 A72   11c multicolored   .20 .20
   a.   Black omitted (UN emblem on key)   —

Special Fund Program, which aims to speed economic growth and social advancement in low-income countries.

Leaves & View of Cyprus — A73

1965, Mar. 4   Photo.   Perf. 11½
139 A73   5c org, olive & black   .20 .20
140 A73   11c yel grn, blue grn & blk   .20 .20

UN Peace-keeping Force on Cyprus.

"From Semaphore to Satellite" A74

1965, May 17   Unwmk.   Perf. 11½
141 A74   5c multicolored   .20 .20
142 A74   11c multicolored   .20 .20

Cent. of the ITU.

ICY Emblem — A75

1965, June 26   Engr.   Perf. 14x13½
143 A75   5c dark blue   .20 .20
144 A75   15c lilac rose   .20 .20

Souvenir Sheet
145 A75   Sheet of 2, #143-144   .35 .30

UN 25th anniv. and Intl. Cooperation Year.

"Peace" — A76   Opening Words, UN Charter — A77

UN Headquarters, Emblem — A78   UN Emblem — A79

UN Emblem A80

1965-66   Photo.   Perf. 13½
146 A76   1c ver, bl, blk & gray   .20 .20
   Perf. 14
147 A77   15c ol bis, dull yel, blk & dp claret   .25 .20

Perf. 12
148 A78   20c dk bl, bl, red & yel   .30 .70
   a.   Yellow omitted   —
Lithographed and Embossed
   Perf. 14
149 A79   25c lt bl & dk blue   .35 .20
   Photo.
   Perf. 11½
150 A80 $1 aqua & sapphire   1.75 1.50
   Nos. 146-150 (5)   2.85 2.30

Issued: 1c, 25c, 9/20; 15c, 20c, 10/25; $1, 3/25/66.
See UN Offices in Geneva Nos. 5, 9, 11.

Fields & People — A81

1965, Nov. 29   Photo.   Perf. 12
151 A81   4c multicolored   .20 .20
152 A81   5c multicolored   .20 .20
153 A81   11c multicolored   .20 .20
   Nos. 151-153 (3)   .60 .60

Emphasize the importance of the world's population growth and its problems and to call attention to population trends and developments.

Globe & Flags of UN Members — A82

1966, Jan. 31   Photo.   Perf. 11½
154 A82   5c multicolored   .20 .20
155 A82   15c multicolored   .20 .20

World Federation of UN Associations.

WHO Headquarters, Geneva — A83

1966, May 26   Photo.   Perf. 12½x12
Granite Paper
156 A83   5c multicolored   .20 .20
157 A83   11c multicolored   .20 .20

WHO Headquarters, Geneva.

Coffee — A84

1966, Sept. 19   Perf. 13½x13
158 A84   5c multicolored   .20 .20
159 A84   11c multicolored   .20 .20

International Coffee Agreement of 1962.

UN Observer — A85

1966, Oct. 24   Photo.   Perf. 11½
Granite Paper
160 A85   15c multicolored   .25 .20

Peace Keeping UN Observers.

Children of Various Races — A86

1966, Nov. 28   Litho.   Perf. 13x13½

Designs: 5c, Children riding locomotive and tender. 11c, Children in open railroad car playing medical team.

161 A86   4c pink & multi   .20 .20
162 A86   5c pale green & multi   .20 .20
   a.   Yellow omitted   —
163 A86   11c ultra & multi   .20 .20
   a.   Imperf., pair   —
   b.   Dark blue omitted   —
   Nos. 161-163 (3)   .60 .60

20th anniv. of UNICEF.

Hand Rolling up Sleeve & Chart Showing Progress A87

1967, Jan. 23   Photo.   Perf. 12½
164 A87   5c multicolored   .20 .20
165 A87   11c multicolored   .20 .20

UN Development Program.

Type of 1962 and

UN Headquarters, New York & World Map — A88

1967   Photo.   Perf. 11½
166 A88   1½c ultra, blk, org & ocher   .20 .20
   Size: 33x23mm
167 A53   5c red brn, brn & org yel   .20 .20
   Issue dates: 1½c, Mar. 17; 5c, Jan. 23.
   See UN Offices in Geneva No. 1.

Fireworks — A89

1967, Mar. 17   Perf. 14x14½
168 A89   5c dark blue & multi   .20 .20
169 A89   11c brown lake & multi   .20 .20

Honoring all nations which gained independence since 1945.

"Peace" — A90

UN Pavilion, EXPO '67 — A91

Litho. & Engr.; Litho. (8c)
1967, Apr. 28   Perf. 11
170 A90   4c shown   .20 .20
171 A90   5c Justice   .20 .20
172 A91   8c shown   .20 .20
173 A90   10c Fraternity   .20 .20
174 A90   15c Truth   .20 .20
   Nos. 170-174 (5)   1.00 1.00

Montreal World's Fair, EXPO '67, Apr. 28-Oct. 27. Under special agreement with the Canadian Government Nos. 170-174 were valid for postage only on mail posted at the UN pavilion during the fair. The denominations are expressed in Canadian currency.

Luggage Tags and UN Emblem A92

1967, June 19   Litho.   Perf. 14
Unwmk.
175 A92   5c multicolored   .20 .20
176 A92   15c multicolored   .25 .20

International Tourist Year, 1967.

Quotation from Isaiah 2:4 — A93

1967, Oct. 24   Photo.
177 A93   6c multicolored   .20 .20
178 A93   13c multicolored   .20 .20

UN General Assembly's resolutions on general and complete disarmament and for suspension of nuclear and thermonuclear tests.

Art at UN Issue
Miniature Sheet

Memorial Window — A94

"The Kiss of Peace" — A95

Sizes: a, 41x46mm. b, 24x46mm. c, 41x33½mm. d, 36x33½mm. e, 29x33½mm. f, 41½x47mm.

1967, Nov. 17   Litho.   Rouletted 9
179 A94   Sheet of 6, a.-f.   .40 .30
   Perf. 12½x13½
180 A95   6c multicolored   .20 .20

No. 179 contains six 6c stamps, each rouletted on 3 sides, imperf. on fourth side. On Nos. 179a-179c, "United Nations. 6c" appears at top; on Nos. 179d-179f, at bottom. No. 179f includes name "Marc Chagall."

Globe and Major UN Organs A96

1968, Jan. 16   Photo.   Perf. 11½
181 A96 6c multicolored   .20 .20
182 A96 13c multicolored   .20 .20
Honoring the UN Secretariat.

Statue by Henrik
Starcke — A97

Art at UN Issue
1968, Mar. 1   Photo.   Perf. 11½
183 A97 6c blue & multi   .20 .20
184 A97 75c rose lake & multi   1.10 .85
The 6c is part of the "Art at UN" series. The 75c belongs to the definitive series. The 6c exists imperforate.
The Starcke statue represents mankind's search for freedom and happiness.
See UN Offices in Geneva No. 13.

Factories and
Chart — A98

1968, Apr. 18   Litho.   Perf. 12
185 A98 6c multicolored   .20 .20
186 A98 13c multicolored   .20 .20
UN Industrial Development Organization.

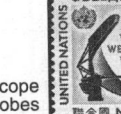

UN Headquarters
A99

1968, May 31   Litho.   Perf. 13½
187 A99 6c multicolored   .20 .20

Radarscope
and Globes
A100

1968, Sept. 19   Photo.   Perf. 13x13½
188 A100 6c green & multi   .20 .20
189 A100 20c lilac & multi   .30 .20
World Weather Watch, a new weather system directed by the World Meterological Organization.

Human Rights
Flame — A101   Books and UN
                    Emblem — A102

Photogravure; Foil Embossed
1968, Nov. 22   Perf. 12½
190 A101 6c brt bl, dp ultra & gold .20 .20
191 A101 13c rose red, dk red &
            gold   .20 .20
International Human Rights Year.

1969, Feb. 10   Litho.   Perf. 13½
192 A102 6c yel green & multi   .20 .20
193 A102 13c bluish lilac & multi   .25 .20
UN Institute for Training and Research (UNITAR).

UN
Building,
Santiago,
Chile
A103

1969, Mar. 14   Litho.   Perf. 14
194 A103 6c lt blue, vio bl & lt grn .20 .20
195 A103 15c pink, cr & red brown   .25 .20
The UN Building in Santiago, Chile is the seat of the UN Economic Commission for Latin America and of the Latin American Institute for Economic and Social Planning.

"UN" and UN   UN Emblem and
Emblem — A104   Scales of
                   Justice — A105

1969, Mar. 14   Photo.   Perf. 13½
196 A104 13c brt blue, black & gold .20 .20
See UN Offices in Geneva No. 7.

1969, Apr. 21   Photo.   Perf. 11½
Granite Paper
197 A105 6c brt grn, ultra & gold   .20 .20
198 A105 13c crim, lilac & gold   .20 .20
20th anniv. session of the UN Intl. Law Commission.

Allegory of
Labor,
Emblems
of UN and
ILO
A106

1969, June 5   Photo.   Perf. 13
199 A106 6c bl, dp bl, yel & gold   .20 .20
200 A106 20c org ver, mag, yel &
            gold   .25 .20
"Labor and Development" and the 50th anniv. of the ILO.

Art at UN Issue

Ostrich, Tunisian
Mosaic, 3rd
Century — A107

Design: 13c, Pheasant.

1969, Nov. 21   Photo.   Perf. 14
201 A107 6c blue & multi   .20 .20
202 A107 13c red & multi   .20 .20

Art at UN Issue

Peace Bell, Gift
of Japanese — A108

1970, Mar. 13   Photo.   Perf. 13½x13
203 A108 6c vio blue & multi   .20 .20
204 A108 25c claret & multi   .35 .25

Mekong River,
Power Lines
and Map of
Delta — A109

1970, Mar. 13   Perf. 14
205 A109 6c dk blue & multi   .20 .20
206 A109 13c dp plum & multi   .20 .20
Lower Mekong Basin, Viet Nam, Development project under UN auspices.

"Fight Cancer"
A110

1970, May 22   Litho.   Perf. 14
207 A110 6c blue & black   .20 .20
208 A110 13c olive & black   .20 .20
Fight against cancer in connection with the 10th Intl. Cancer Congress of the International Union Against Cancer, Houston, Texas, May 22-29.

UN Emblem
and Olive
Branch
A111

UN Emblem — A112

1970, June 26   Photo.   Perf. 11½
209 A111 6c red, gold, dk & lt bl   .20 .20
210 A111 13c dk bl, gold, grn & red .20 .20
Perf. 12½
211 A112 25c dk bl, gold & lt bl   .35 .25
    Nos. 209-211 (3)   .75 .65
Souvenir Sheet
Imperf
212   Sheet of 3   .60 .60
  a. A111 6c multicolored   .20 .20
  b. A111 13c multicolored   .20 .20
  c. A112 25c multicolored   .30 .20
25th anniv. of the UN.

Scales, Olive   Sea Bed, Fish,
Branch,   Underwater
Progress   Research
Symbol   A114
A113

1970, Nov. 20   Photo.   Perf. 13½
213 A113 6c gold & multi   .20 .20
214 A113 13c silver & multi   .20 .20
publicizing "Peace, Justice and Progress" in connection with the 25th anniv. of the UN.

Photogravure and Engraved
1971, Jan. 25   Perf. 13
215 A114 6c blue & multi   .20 .20
Peaceful uses of the sea bed. See Offices in Geneva No. 15.

Refugees,
Sculpture by
Kaare K.
Nygaard
A115

1971, Mar. 12   Litho.   Perf. 13x12½
216 A115 6c brown, ocher & black .20 .20
217 A115 13c ultra, grnsh bl & blk .20 .20
International support for refugees. See Offices in Geneva No. 16.

Wheat and
Globe — A116

1971, Apr. 13   Photo.   Perf. 14
218 A116 13c brn red, gold & grn   .20 .20
Publicizing the UN World Food Program. See Offices in Geneva No. 17.

UPU
Headquarters,
Bern — A117

1971, May 28   Photo.   Perf. 11½
219 A117 20c brown org & multi   .35 .25
Opening of new UPU Headquarters, Bern. See Offices in Geneva No. 18.

"Eliminate Racial
Discrimination"
A118

A119

1971, Sept. 21   Photo.   Perf. 13½
220 A118 8c yel green & multi   .20 .20
221 A119 13c blue & multi   .20 .20
International Year Against Racial Discrimination. See Offices in Geneva Nos. 19-20.

UN Headquarters, New York — A120

UN
Emblem
and
Symbolic
Flags
A121

1971, Oct. 22   Perf. 13½; 13 (60c)
222 A120 8c vio blue & multi   .20 .20
223 A121 60c ultra & multi   .75 .50

Maia by Pablo Picasso — A122

1971, Nov. 19   Photo.   *Perf. 11½*
224 A122   8c olive & multi   .20   .20
225 A122   21c ultra & multi   .30   .20
UN Intl. School. See Off. in Geneva No. 21.

Letter Changing Hands A123

1972, Jan. 5   Litho.   *Perf. 14*
226 A123   95c blue & multi   1.25   1.00

"No More Nuclear Weapons" A124

1972, Feb. 14   Photo.   *Perf. 13½x14*
227 A124   8c dull rose, blk, bl & gray   .20   .20
To promote non-proliferation of nuclear weapons. See Offices in Geneva No. 23.

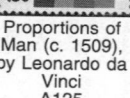

Proportions of Man (c. 1509), by Leonardo da Vinci A125

"Human Environment" A126

Lithographed and Engraved
1972, Apr. 7   *Perf. 13x13½*
228 A125   15c black & multi   .25   .20
World Health Day, Apr. 7. See Offices in Geneva No. 24.

Lithographed and Embossed
1972, June 5   *Perf. 12½x14*
229 A126   8c multicolored   .20   .20
230 A126   15c multicolored   .25   .20
UN Conference on Human Environment, Stockholm, June 5-16, 1972. See Offices in Geneva Nos. 25-26.

"Europe" and UN Emblem — A127

The Five Continents, by José Maria Sert — A128

1972, Sept. 11   Litho.   *Perf. 13x13½*
231 A127   21c yel brown & multi   .35   .20
Economic Commission for Europe, 25th anniv.
See Offices in Geneva No. 27.

Art at UN Issue
1972, Nov. 17   Photo.   *Perf. 12x12½*
232 A128   8c gold, brn & gldn brn   .20   .20
233 A128   15c gold, brn & blue grn   .30   .20
See Offices in Geneva Nos. 28-29.

Olive Branch and Broken Sword A129

1973, Mar. 9   Litho.   *Perf. 13½x13*
234 A129   8c blue & multi   .20   .20
235 A129   15c lilac rose & multi   .35   .20
Disarmament Decade, 1970-79. Nos. 234-235 exist imperf. See Offices in Geneva Nos. 30-31.

Poppy Capsule and Skull — A130

1973, Apr. 13   Photo.   *Perf. 13½*
236 A130   8c multicolored   .20   .20
237 A130   15c multicolored   .35   .25
Fight against drug abuse. See Offices in Geneva No. 32.

Honeycomb A131

1973, May 25   Photo.   *Perf. 14*
238 A131   8c olive bister & multi   .20   .20
239 A131   21c gray blue & multi   .35   .25
5th anniv. of the UN Volunteer Program. See UN Offices in Geneva No. 33.

Map of Africa with Namibia A132

1973, Oct. 1   Photo.   *Perf. 13½*
240 A132   8c emerald & multi   .20   .20
241 A132   15c brt rose & multi   .35   .25
To publicize Namibia (South-West Africa), for which the UN General Assembly ended the mandate of South Africa and established the UN Council for Namibia to administer the territory until independence. See Offices in Geneva No. 34.

UN Emblem, Human Rights Flame A133

1973, Nov. 16   Photo.   *Perf. 13½*
242 A133   8c dp carmine & multi   .20   .20
243 A133   15c blue & multi   .35   .25
25th anniv. of the adoption and proclamation of the Universal Declaration of Human Rights. See Offices in Geneva Nos. 35-36.

ILO Headquarters, Geneva A134

1974, Jan. 11   Photo.   *Perf. 14*
244 A134   10c ultra & multi   .20   .20
245 A134   21c blue green & multi   .35   .25
New Headquarters of Intl. Labor Organization. See Offices in Geneva Nos. 37-38.

Post Horn Encircling Globe A135

1974, Mar. 22   Photo.   *Perf. 14*
246 A135   10c multicolored   .25   .20
UPU, cent. See Off. in Geneva #39-40.

Art at UN Issue

Peace Mural, by Candido Portinari A136

1974, May 6   Photo.   *Perf. 14*
247 A136   10c gold & multi   .20   .20
248 A136   18c ultra & multi   .40   .30
See Offices in Geneva Nos. 41-42.

Dove & UN Emblem A137

UN Headquarters A138

Globe, UN Emblem, Flags A139

1974, June 10   Photo.   *Perf. 14*
249 A137   2c dk bl & lt blue   .20   .20
250 A138   10c multicolored   .20   .20
251 A139   18c multicolored   .30   .20
    Nos. 249-251 (3)   .70   .60

Children of the World — A140

Law of the Sea — A141

1974, Oct. 18   Photo.   *Perf. 14*
252 A140   10c lt blue & multi   .20   .20
253 A140   18c lilac & multi   .40   .25
World Population Year. See Offices in Geneva Nos. 43-44.

1974, Nov. 22   Photo.   *Perf. 14*
254 A141   10c green & multi   .20   .20
255 A141   26c multicolored   .40   .25
UN General Assembly declared the sea bed common heritage of mankind, exempt from arms race. See Offices in Geneva No. 45.

Satellite and Globe — A142

1975, Mar. 14   Litho.   *Perf. 13*
256 A142   10c multicolored   .20   .20
257 A142   26c multicolored   .40   .30
Peaceful uses of outer space (meteorology, industry, fishing, communications). See Offices in Geneva Nos. 46-47.

Equality Between Men and Women — A143

1975, May 9   Litho.   *Perf. 15*
258 A143   10c multicolored   .20   .20
259 A143   18c multicolored   .40   .25
International Women's Year 1975. See Offices in Geneva Nos. 48-49.

UN Flag and "XXX" — A144

1975, June 26   Litho.   *Perf. 13*
260 A144   10c multicolored   .20   .20
261 A144   26c purple & multi   .50   .35
Souvenir Sheet
Imperf
262   Sheet of 2   .65   .50
   a.   A144 10c olive bister & multi   .20   .20
   b.   A144 26c purple & multi   .40   .25
30th anniv. of the UN. See Offices in Geneva Nos. 50-52.

Hand Reaching up over Map of Africa & Namibia — A145

1975, Sept. 22   Photo.   *Perf. 13½*
263 A145   10c multicolored   .20   .20
264 A145   18c multicolored   .35   .20
"Namibia—United Nations direct responsibility." See note after No. 241. See Offices in Geneva Nos. 53-54.

Wild Rose Growing from Barbed Wire — A146

1975, Nov. 21   Engr.   *Perf. 12½*
265 A146   13c ultramarine   .25   .20
266 A146   26c rose carmine   .50   .45
UN Peace-keeping Operations. See Offices in Geneva Nos. 55-56.

Symbolic Flags
Forming
Dove — A147

UN
Emblem — A149

People of
All Races
A148

UN Flag
A150

Dove and
Rainbow
A151

Perf. 13x13½, 13½x13, 14 (9c)
1976   **Litho.; Photo. (9c)**
267 A147 3c multicolored   .20 .20
268 A148 4c multicolored   .20 .20
269 A149 9c multicolored   .20 .20
270 A150 30c blue, emer & black .40 .35
271 A151 50c multicolored   .70 .65
    Nos. 267-271 (5)   1.70 1.60
  Issue dates: 9c, Nov. 19; others, Jan. 9.
  See Offices in Vienna No. 8.

Interlocking
Bands — A152

1976, Mar. 12   Photo.   Perf. 14
272 A152 13c blue, green & black .20 .20
273 A152 26c green & multi   .35 .30
  World Federation of UN Association. See
Offices in Geneva No. 57.

Cargo, Globe
and
Graph — A153

Houses Around
Globe — A154

1976, Apr. 23   Photo.   Perf. 11½
274 A153 13c multicolored   .20 .20
275 A153 31c multicolored   .40 .30
  UN Conference on Trade and Development
(UNCTAD), Nairobi, Kenya, May 1976. See
Offices in Geneva No. 58.

1976, May 28   Photo.   Perf. 14
276 A154 13c multicolored   .20 .20
277 A154 25c green & multi   .40 .30
  Habitat, UN Conference on Human Settlements, Vancouver, Canada, May 31-June 11.
See Offices in Geneva Nos. 59-60.

Magnifying
Glass, Sheet
of Stamps, UN Emblem
A155

1976, Oct. 8   Photo.   Perf. 11½
278 A155 13c blue & multi   .20 .20
279 A155 31c green & multi   1.25 1.25
  UN Postal Administration, 25th anniv.
Sheets of 20. See Offices in Geneva #61-62.

Grain — A156

1976, Nov. 19   Litho.   Perf. 14½
280 A156 13c multicolored   .25 .20
  World Food Council. See Off. in Geneva #63.

WIPO Headquarters, Geneva — A157

1977, Mar. 11   Photo.   Perf. 14
281 A157 13c citron & multi   .20 .20
282 A157 31c brt green & multi   .45 .30
  World Intellectual Property Organization.
See Geneva No. 64.

Drops of Water
Falling into
Funnel — A158

1977, Apr. 22   Photo.   Perf. 13½x13
283 A158 13c yellow & multi   .20 .20
284 A158 25c salmon & multi   .45 .30
  UN Water Conf., Mar del Plata, Argentina,
Mar. 14-25. See Offices in Geneva #65-66.

Burning Fuse
Severed
A159

1977, May 27   Photo.   Perf. 14
285 A159 13c purple & multi   .20 .20
286 A159 31c dk blue & multi   .45 .30
  UN Security Council. See Geneva #67-68.

"Combat
Racism"
A160

1977, Sept. 19   Litho.   Perf. 13½x13
287 A160 13c black & yellow   .20 .20
288 A160 25c black & vermilion   .40 .30
  Fight against racial discrimination. See
Geneva Nos. 69-70.

Atom, Grain, Fruit
and Factory — A161

1977, Nov. 18   Photo.
289 A161 13c yellow bister & multi .20 .20
290 A161 18c dull green & multi .35 .25
  Peaceful uses of atomic energy. See
Geneva Nos. 71-72.

Opening
Words of UN
Charter
A162

"Live Together
in Peace"
A163

People of the
World — A164

1978, Jan. 27   Litho.   Perf. 14½
291 A162 1c gold, brown & red   .20 .20
292 A163 25c multicolored   .35 .30
293 A164 $1 multicolored   1.10 1.10
    Nos. 291-293 (3)   1.65 1.60
  See Offices in Geneva No. 73.

Smallpox
Virus — A165

1978, Mar. 31   Photo.   Perf. 12x11½
294 A165 13c rose & black   .20 .20
295 A165 31c blue & black   .45 .40
  Global eradication of smallpox. See Offices
in Geneva Nos. 74-75.

Open Handcuff
A166

Multicolored
Bands and
Clouds
A167

1978, May 5   Photo.   Perf. 12
296 A166 13c multicolored   .20 .20
297 A166 18c multicolored   .30 .20
  Liberation, justice and cooperation for
Namibia. See Offices in Geneva No. 76.

1978, June 12   Photo.   Perf. 14
298 A167 13c multicolored   .20 .20
299 A167 25c multicolored   .40 .30
  Intl. Civil Aviation Organization for "Safety in
the Air." See Offices in Geneva #77-78.

General
Assembly
A168

1978, Sept. 15   Photo.   Perf. 13½
300 A168 13c multicolored   .20 .20
301 A168 18c multicolored   .35 .25
  See Offices in Geneva Nos. 79-80.

Hemispheres
as Cogwheels
A169

1978, Nov. 17   Photo.   Perf. 14
302 A169 13c multicolored   .20 .20
303 A169 31c multicolored   .50 .40
  Technical Cooperation Among Developing
Countries Conf., Buenos Aires, Argentina,
Sept. 1978. See Offices in Geneva No. 81.

Hand Holding
Olive
Branch — A170

Tree of Various
Races — A171

Globe, Dove
with Olive
Branch — A172

Birds and
Globe — A173

1979, Jan. 19   Photo.   Perf. 14
304 A170 5c multicolored   .20 .20
305 A171 14c multicolored   .20 .20
306 A172 15c multicolored   .30 .25
307 A173 20c multicolored   .30 .25
    Nos. 304-307 (4)   1.00 .90

UNDRO
Against Fire
and
Water — A174

1979, Mar. 9   Photo.   Perf. 14
308 A174 15c multicolored   .25 .20
309 A174 20c multicolored   .35 .30
  Office of the UN Disaster Relief Coordinator. See Offices in Geneva Nos. 82-83.

Child and ICY
Emblem
A175

1979, May 4   Photo.   Perf. 14
310 A175 15c multicolored   .20 .20
311 A175 31c multicolored   .35 .30
  International Year of the Child. See Offices
in Geneva Nos. 84-85.

Map of Namibia, Olive Branch — A176

Scales and Sword of Justice — A177

1979, Oct. 5　　Litho.　　Perf. 13½

312	A176	15c multicolored	.20	.20
313	A176	31c multicolored	.40	.35

For a free and independent Namibia. See Offices in Geneva No. 86.

1979, Nov. 9　　Litho.　　Perf. 13x13½

314	A177	15c multicolored	.20	.20
315	A177	20c multicolored	.40	.35

Intl. Court of Justice, The Hague, Netherlands. See Offices in Geneva Nos. 87-88.

Graph of Economic Trends — A178

Key — A179

1980, Jan. 11　　　　Perf. 15x14½

316	A178	15c multicolored	.20	.20
317	A179	31c multicolored	.50	.35

New International Economic Order. See Offices in Geneva No. 89; Vienna No. 7.

Women's Year Emblems A180

1980, Mar. 7　　Litho.　　Perf. 14½x15

318	A180	15c multicolored	.20	.20
319	A180	20c multicolored	.30	.25

UN Decade for Women. See Offices in Geneva Nos. 90-91; Vienna Nos. 9-10.

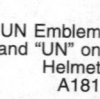
UN Emblem and "UN" on Helmet A181

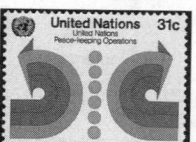
Arrows and UN Emblem A182

1980, May 16　　Litho.　　Perf. 14x13

320	A181	15c black & brt blue	.25	.20
321	A182	31c multicolored	.45	.40

UN Peace-keeping Operations. See Offices in Geneva No. 92; Vienna No. 11.

"35" and Flags — A183

Globe and Laurel — A184

1980, June 26　　Litho.　　Perf. 13

322	A183	15c multicolored	.20	.20
323	A184	31c multicolored	.40	.30

Souvenir Sheet
Imperf

324		Sheet of 2	.70	.60
a.		A183 15c multicolored	.20	
b.		A184 31c multicolored	.40	

35th anniv. of the UN. See Offices in Geneva Nos. 93-95; Vienna Nos. 12-14.

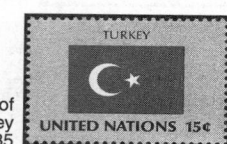
Flag of Turkey A185

1980, Sept. 26　　Litho.　　Perf. 12
Granite Paper

325	A185	15c shown	.20	.20
326	A185	15c Luxembourg	.20	.20
327	A185	15c Fiji	.20	.20
328	A185	15c Viet Nam	.20	.20
a.		Se-tenant block of 4	.80	—
329	A185	15c Guinea	.20	.20
330	A185	15c Surinam	.20	.20
331	A185	15c Bangladesh	.20	.20
332	A185	15c Mali	.20	.20
a.		Se-tenant block of 4	.80	—
333	A185	15c Yugoslavia	.20	.20
334	A185	15c France	.20	.20
335	A185	15c Venezuela	.20	.20
336	A185	15c El Salvador	.20	.20
a.		Se-tenant block of 4	.80	—
337	A185	15c Madagascar	.20	.20
338	A185	15c Cameroon	.20	.20
339	A185	15c Rwanda	.20	.20
340	A185	15c Hungary	.20	.20
a.		Se-tenant block of 4	.80	—
		Nos. 325-340 (16)	3.20	3.20

Issued in 4 sheets of 16. Each sheet contains 4 blocks of 4 (Nos. 325-328, 329-332, 333-336, 337-340). A se-tenant block of 4 designs centers each sheet.
See #350-365, 374-389, 399-414, 425-440, 450-465, 477-492, 499-514, 528-543, 554-569, 690-697; 719-726, 744-751, 795-802.

Symbolic Flowers A186

Symbols of Progress A187

1980, Nov. 21　　Litho.　　Perf. 13½x13

341	A186	15c multicolored	.30	.25
342	A187	20c multicolored	.40	.35

Economic and Social Council (ECOSOC). See Offices in Geneva Nos. 96-97; Vienna Nos. 15-16.

Inalienable Rights of the Palestinian People A188

1981, Jan. 30　　　　Photo.

343	A188	15c multicolored	.25	.20

See Offices in Geneva #98; Vienna #17.

Interlocking Puzzle Pieces — A189

Stylized Person — A190

1981, Mar. 6　　　　Photo.

344	A189	20c multicolored	.30	.20
345	A190	35c multicolored	.55	.40

Intl. Year of the Disabled. See Offices in Geneva Nos. 99-100; Vienna Nos. 18-19.

Divislava and Sebastocrator Kaloyan, Bulgarian Mural, 1259, Boyana Church, Sofia — A191

1981, Apr. 15　　Photo.　　Perf. 11½
Granite Paper

346	A191	20c multicolored	.30	.25
347	A191	31c multicolored	.45	.35

See Offices in Geneva #101; Vienna #20.

Solar Energy A192

Conference Emblem — A193

1981, May 29　　Litho.　　Perf. 13

348	A192	20c multicolored	.30	.25
349	A193	40c multicolored	.55	.50

Conference on New and Renewable Sources of Energy, Nairobi, Aug. 10-21. See Offices in Geneva No. 102; Vienna No. 21.

Flag Type of 1980
1981, Sept. 25　　　　Litho.
Granite Paper

350	A185	20c Djibouti	.25	.20
351	A185	20c Sri Lanka	.25	.20
352	A185	20c Bolivia	.25	.20
353	A185	20c Equatorial Guinea	.25	.20
a.		Se-tenant block of 4	1.40	—
354	A185	20c Malta	.25	.20
355	A185	20c Czechoslovakia	.25	.20
356	A185	20c Thailand	.25	.20
357	A185	20c Trinidad & Tobago	.25	.20
a.		Se-tenant block of 4	1.40	—
358	A185	20c Ukrainian SSR	.25	.20
359	A185	20c Kuwait	.25	.20
360	A185	20c Sudan	.25	.20
361	A185	20c Egypt	.25	.20
a.		Se-tenant block of 4	1.40	—
362	A185	20c US	.25	.20
363	A185	20c Singapore	.25	.20
364	A185	20c Panama	.25	.20
365	A185	20c Costa Rica	.25	.20
a.		Se-tenant block of 4	1.40	—
		Nos. 350-365 (16)	4.00	3.20

See note after No. 340.

Seedling and Tree Cross Section A194

"10" and Symbols of Progress A195

1981, Nov. 13　　　　Litho.

366	A194	18c multicolored	.35	.25
367	A195	28c multicolored	.65	.50

UN Volunteers Program, 10th anniv. See Offices in Geneva #103-104; Vienna #22-23.

Respect for Human Rights — A196

Independence of Colonial Countries and People — A197

Second Disarmament Decade — A198

1982, Jan. 22　　　　Perf. 11½x12

368	A196	17c multicolored	.30	.20
369	A197	28c multicolored	.50	.35
370	A198	40c multicolored	.80	.60
		Nos. 368-370 (3)	1.60	1.15

10th Anniv. of UN Environment Program

A199　　　　A200

1982, Mar. 19　　Litho.　　Perf. 13½x13

371	A199	20c multicolored	.25	.25
372	A200	40c multicolored	.75	.65

See Offices in Geneva #107-108; Vienna #25-26.

UN Emblem and Olive Branch in Outer Space A201

Perf. 13 x 13½
1982, June 11　　　　Litho.

373	A201	20c multicolored	.45	.35

Exploration and Peaceful Uses of Outer Space. See Offices in Geneva Nos. 109-110; Vienna No. 27.

Flag Type of 1980
1982, Sept. 24　　Litho.　　Perf. 12
Granite Paper

374	A185	20c Austria	.25	.20
375	A185	20c Malaysia	.25	.20
376	A185	20c Seychelles	.25	.20
377	A185	20c Ireland	.25	.20
a.		Se-tenant block of 4	1.40	—
378	A185	20c Mozambique	.25	.20
379	A185	20c Albania	.25	.20
380	A185	20c Dominica	.25	.20
381	A185	20c Solomon Islands	.25	.20
a.		Se-tenant block of 4	1.40	—
382	A185	20c Philippines	.25	.20
383	A185	20c Swaziland	.25	.20
384	A185	20c Nicaragua	.25	.20
385	A185	20c Burma	.25	.20
a.		Se-tenant block of 4	1.40	

386	A185	20c	Cape Verde	.25	.20
387	A185	20c	Guyana	.25	.20
388	A185	20c	Belgium	.25	.20
389	A185	20c	Nigeria	.25	.20
a.			Se-tenant block of 4	1.40	—
			Nos. 374-389 (16)	4.00	3.20

See note after No. 340.

Conservation and Protection of Nature — A202

1982, Nov. 19   Photo.   Perf. 14
390	A202	20c	Leaf	.35	.30
391	A202	28c	Butterfly	.50	.45

See Off. in Geneva #111-112; Vienna #28-29.

A203

World Communications Year — A204

1983, Jan. 28   Litho.   Perf. 13
392	A203	20c	multicolored	.25	.25
393	A204	40c	multicolored	.70	.65

See Offices in Geneva #113; Vienna #30.

Safety at Sea
A205   A206

1983, Mar. 18   Litho.   Perf. 14½
394	A205	20c	multicolored	.30	.30
395	A206	37c	multicolored	.60	.50

See Off. in Geneva #114-115; Vienna #31-32.

World Food Program
A207

1983, Apr. 22   Engr.   Perf. 13½
396	A207	20c	rose lake	.35	.30

See Offices in Geneva #116; Vienna #33-34.

Trade and Development
A208   A209

1983, June 6   Litho.   Perf. 14
397	A208	20c	multicolored	.30	.25
398	A209	28c	multicolored	.65	.60

See Off. in Geneva #117-118; Vienna #35-36.

Flag Type of 1980
1983, Sept. 23   Photo.   Perf. 12
Granite Paper
399	A185	20c	Great Britain	.25	.20
400	A185	20c	Barbados	.25	.20
401	A185	20c	Nepal	.25	.20
402	A185	20c	Israel	.25	.20
a.			Se-tenant block of 4	1.60	—
403	A185	20c	Malawi	.25	.20
404	A185	20c	Byelorussian SSR	.25	.20
405	A185	20c	Jamaica	.25	.20
406	A185	20c	Kenya	.25	.20
a.			Se-tenant block of 4	1.60	—
407	A185	20c	People's Republic of China	.25	.20
408	A185	20c	Peru	.25	.20
409	A185	20c	Bulgaria	.25	.20
410	A185	20c	Canada	.25	.20
a.			Se-tenant block of 4	1.60	—
411	A185	20c	Somalia	.25	.20
412	A185	20c	Senegal	.25	.20
413	A185	20c	Brazil	.25	.20
414	A185	20c	Sweden	.25	.20
a.			Se-tenant block of 4	1.60	—
			Nos. 399-414 (16)	4.00	3.20

See note after No. 340.

A210

35th Anniv. of the Universal Declaration of Human Rights — A211

Photogravure and Engraved
1983, Dec. 9   Perf. 13½
415	A210	20c	Window Right	.30	.25
416	A211	40c	Peace Treaty with Nature	.70	.65

See Off. in Geneva #119-120, Vienna #37-38.

Intl. Population Conference
A212

1984, Feb. 3   Litho.   Perf. 14
417	A212	20c	multicolored	.30	.25
418	A212	40c	multicolored	.60	.55

See Offices in Geneva #121; Vienna #39.

Tractor Plowing
A213

Rice Paddy
A214

1984, Mar. 15   Litho.   Perf. 14½
419	A213	20c	multicolored	.30	.30
420	A214	40c	multicolored	.60	.60

World Food Day, Oct. 16. See Offices in Geneva Nos. 122-123; Vienna Nos. 40-41.

Grand Canyon
A215

Ancient City of Polonnaruwa, Sri Lanka
A216

1984, Apr. 18   Litho.   Perf. 14
421	A215	20c	multicolored	.25	.20
422	A216	50c	multicolored	.70	.70

World Heritage (protection of world cultural and natural sites). See #601-602; Offices in Geneva #124-125, 211-212; Vienna #42-43, 125-126.

A217   A218

1984, May 29   Photo.   Perf. 11½
423	A217	20c	multicolored	.40	.35
424	A218	50c	multicolored	1.00	.85

Future for Refugees. See Offices in Geneva Nos. 126-127; Vienna Nos. 44-45.

Flag Type of 1980
1984, Sept. 21   Photo.   Perf. 12
Granite Paper
425	A185	20c	Burundi	.55	.40
426	A185	20c	Pakistan	.55	.40
427	A185	20c	Benin	.55	.40
428	A185	20c	Italy	.55	.40
a.			Se-tenant block of 4	2.75	—
429	A185	20c	Tanzania	.55	.40
430	A185	20c	United Arab Emirates	.55	.40
431	A185	20c	Ecuador	.55	.40
432	A185	20c	Bahamas	.55	.40
a.			Se-tenant block of 4	2.75	—
433	A185	20c	Poland	.55	.40
434	A185	20c	Papua New Guinea	.55	.40
435	A185	20c	Uruguay	.55	.40
436	A185	20c	Chile	.55	.40
a.			Se-tenant block of 4	2.75	—
437	A185	20c	Paraguay	.55	.40
438	A185	20c	Bhutan	.55	.40
439	A185	20c	Central African Republic	.55	.40
440	A185	20c	Australia	.55	.40
a.			Se-tenant block of 4	2.75	—
			Nos. 425-440 (16)	8.80	6.40

See note after No. 340.

Intl. Youth Year — A219   ILO Turin Center — A220

1984, Nov. 15   Litho.   Perf. 13½
441	A219	20c	multicolored	.50	.35
442	A219	35c	multicolored	1.50	1.10

See Offices in Geneva #128; Vienna #46-47.

1985, Feb. 1   Engr.
443	A220	23c	Turin Center emblem	.60	.45

See Off. in Geneva #129-130; Vienna #48.

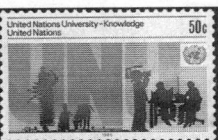

UN University
A221

1985, Mar. 15   Photo.   Perf. 13½
444	A221	50c	multicolored	1.25	1.00

See Off. in Geneva #131-132; Vienna #49.

Peoples of the World — A222

Painting UN Emblem
A223

1985, May 10   Litho.   Perf. 14
445	A222	22c	multicolored	.35	.30
446	A223	$3	multicolored	4.00	1.00

See Offices in Geneva #133-134; Vienna #50-51.

The Corner
A224

Alvaro Raking Hay
A225

Oil paintings (details) by American artist Andrew Wyeth.

1985, June 26   Photo.   Perf. 12x11½
447	A224	22c	multicolored	.50	.35
448	A225	45c	multicolored	1.25	.85

Souvenir Sheet
Imperf
449			Sheet of 2	1.60	1.25
a.	A224	22c	multicolored	.50	—
b.	A225	45c	multicolored	1.00	—

40th anniv. of the UN. No. 449 has multicolored margin with inscription and UN emblem. Size: 75x83mm. See Offices in Geneva Nos. 135-137; Vienna Nos. 52-54.

Flag Type of 1980
1985, Sept. 20   Photo.   Perf. 12
Granite Paper
450	A185	22c	Grenada	.55	.50
451	A185	22c	Federal Republic of Germany	.55	.50
452	A185	22c	Saudi Arabia	.55	.50
453	A185	22c	Mexico	.55	.50
a.			Se-tenant block of 4	3.25	—
454	A185	22c	Uganda	.55	.50
455	A185	22c	St. Thomas & Prince	.55	.50
456	A185	22c	USSR	.55	.50
457	A185	22c	India	.55	.50
a.			Se-tenant block of 4	3.25	—
458	A185	22c	Liberia	.55	.50
459	A185	22c	Mauritius	.55	.50
460	A185	22c	Chad	.55	.50
461	A185	22c	Dominican Republic	.55	.50
a.			Se-tenant block of 4	3.25	—
462	A185	22c	Sultanate of Oman	.55	.50
463	A185	22c	Ghana	.55	.50
464	A185	22c	Sierra Leone	.55	.50
465	A185	22c	Finland	.55	.50
a.			Se-tenant block of 4	3.25	—
			Nos. 450-465 (16)	8.80	8.00

See note after No. 340.

A226   A227

Photogravure and Engraved
1985, Nov. 22   **Perf. 13½**
466 A226 22c Asian child   .35   .30
467 A226 33c Breastfeeding   .65   .60

UNICEF Child Survival Campaign. See Offices in Geneva #138-139; Vienna #55-56.

1986, Jan. 31   Photo.   Perf. 11½
468 A227 22c Abstract Painting by Wosene Kos-rof   .50   .45

Africa in Crisis, campaign against hunger. See Offices in Geneva #140; Vienna #57.

Water Resources A228

1986, Mar. 14   Photo.   Perf. 13½
469 A228 22c Dam   1.00   .90
470 A228 22c Irrigation 1.00   .90
471 A228 22c Hygiene   1.00   .90
472 A228 22c Well   1.00   .90
a.   Block of 4, #469-472   4.00 4.00

UN Development program. No. 472a has continuous design. See Offices in Geneva #141-144; Vienna #58-61.

Human Rights Stamp of 1954 — A229

Stamp collecting: 44c, Engraver.

1986, May 22   Engr.   Perf. 12½
473 A229 22c dk violet & brt blue .30 .25
474 A229 44c brown & emer green   .80 .70

See Offices in Geneva #146-147; Vienna #62-63.

Birds Nest in Tree — A230

Peace in Seven Languages A231

Photo. & Embossed
1986, June 20   **Perf. 13½**
475 A230 22c multicolored   .50   .40
476 A231 33c multicolored 1.50 1.25

Intl. Peace Year. See Offices in Geneva Nos. 148-149; Vienna Nos. 64-65.

Flag Type of 1980
1986, Sept. 19   Photo.   Perf. 12
Granite Paper
477 A185 22c New Zealand   .60 .45
478 A185 22c Lao PDR   .60 .45
479 A185 22c Burkina Faso   .60 .45
480 A185 22c Gambia   .60 .45
a.   Se-tenant block of 4 3.25 —
481 A185 22c Maldives   .60 .45
482 A185 22c Ethiopia   .60 .45
483 A185 22c Jordan   .60 .45
484 A185 22c Zambia   .60 .45
a.   Se-tenant block of 4 3.25

485 A185 22c Iceland   .60 .45
486 A185 22c Antigua & Barbu-da .60 .45
487 A185 22c Angola   .60 .45
488 A185 22c Botswana   .60 .45
a.   Se-tenant block of 4 3.25 —
489 A185 22c Romania   .60 .45
490 A185 22c Togo   .60 .45
491 A185 22c Mauritania   .60 .45
492 A185 22c Colombia   .60 .45
a.   Se-tenant block of 4 3.25 —
Nos. 477-492 (16)   9.60 7.20
See note after No. 340.

Souvenir Sheet

World Federation of UN Associations, 40th Anniv. — A232

22c, Mother Earth, by Edna Hibel, US. 33c, Watercolor by Salvador Dali (b. 1904), Spain. 39c, New Dawn, by Dong Kingman, US. 44c, Watercolor by Chaim Gross, US.

1986, Nov. 14   Litho.   Perf. 13x13½
493 A232   Sheet of 4   4.75 2.50
a.   22c multicolored   .60   —
b.   33c multicolored   .75   —
c.   39c multicolored   1.10   —
d.   44c multicolored   1.25   —
See Offices in Geneva #150; Vienna #66.

Trygve Halvdan Lie (1896-1968), 1st Secretary-General A233

Photogravure and Engraved
1987, Jan. 30   **Perf. 13½**
494 A233 22c multicolored   .90 .75
See Offices in Geneva #151; Vienna #67.

Intl. Year of Shelter for the Homeless A234

Perf. 13½x12½
1987, Mar. 13   **Litho.**
495 A234 22c Surveying, blueprint .40 .25
496 A234 44c Cutting lumber 1.25 1.00
See Offices in Geneva #154-155; Vienna #68-69.

Fight Drug Abuse A235

1987, June 12   Litho.   Perf. 14½x15
497 A235 22c Construction   .65 .50
498 A235 33c Education   1.25 1.00
See Offices in Geneva #156-157; Vienna #70-71.

Flag Type of 1980
1987, Sept. 18   Photo.   Perf. 12
Granite Paper
499 A185 22c Comoros   .60 .50
500 A185 22c Yemen PDR   .60 .50
501 A185 22c Mongolia   .60 .50
502 A185 22c Vanuatu   .60 .50
a.   Se-tenant block of 4 3.25 —
503 A185 22c Japan   .60 .50
504 A185 22c Gabon   .60 .50
505 A185 22c Zimbabwe   .60 .50
506 A185 22c Iraq   .60 .50
a.   Se-tenant block of 4 3.25

507 A185 22c Argentina   .60 .50
508 A185 22c Congo   .60 .50
509 A185 22c Niger   .60 .50
510 A185 22c St. Lucia   .60 .50
a.   Se-tenant block of 4 3.25 —
511 A185 22c Bahrain   .60 .50
512 A185 22c Haiti   .60 .50
513 A185 22c Afghanistan   .60 .50
514 A185 22c Greece   .60 .50
a.   Se-tenant block of 4 3.25 —
Nos. 499-514 (16)   9.60 8.00
See note after No. 340.

UN Day — A236

Multinational people in various occupations.

1987, Oct. 23   Litho.   Perf. 14½x15
515 A236 22c multicolored   .40 .35
516 A236 39c multicolored   .70 .65
See Offices in Geneva #158-159; Vienna #74-75.

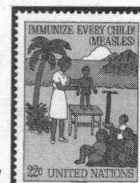

Immunize Every Child — A237

1987, Nov. 20   Litho.   Perf. 15x14½
517 A237 22c Measles   1.25 .60
518 A237 44c Tetanus   2.50 1.75
See Offices in Geneva #160-161; Vienna #76-77.

Intl. Fund for Agricultural Development (IFAD) — A238

1988, Jan. 29   Litho.   Perf. 13½
519 A238 22c Fishing   .50 .40
520 A238 33c Farming   1.00 .85
See Offices in Geneva #162-163; Vienna #78-79.

A239

1988, Jan. 29   Photo.   Perf. 13½x14
521 A239 3c multicolored ('88) .20 .20

Survival of the Forests A240

1988, Mar. 18   Litho.   Perf. 14x15
522 A240 25c multicolored 1.00 1.00
523 A240 44c multicolored 1.75 1.75
a.   Pair, #522-523   3.25 3.25

#523a has continuous design. See Off. in Geneva #165-166; Vienna #80-81.

Intl. Volunteer Day — A241

1988, May 6   Perf. 13x14, 14x13
524 A241 25c Education, vert.   .45 .40
525 A241 50c Vocational training 1.10 1.00
See Offices in Geneva #167-168; Vienna #82-83.

Health in Sports — A242

Perf. 13½x13, 13x13½
1988, June 17   **Litho.**
526 A242 25c Cycling, vert.   .50 .45
527 A242 38c Marathon   1.25 1.10
See Offices in Geneva #169-170; Vienna #84-85.

Flag Type of 1980
1988, Sept. 16   Photo.   Perf. 12
Granite Paper
528 A185 25c Spain   .60 .45
529 A185 25c St. Vincent & Grenadines .60 .45
530 A185 25c Ivory Coast   .60 .45
531 A185 25c Lebanon   .60 .45
a.   Se-tenant block of 4 3.25 —
532 A185 25c Yemen (Arab Republic) .60 .45
533 A185 25c Cuba   .60 .45
534 A185 25c Denmark   .60 .45
535 A185 25c Libya   .60 .45
a.   Se-tenant block of 4 3.25 —
536 A185 25c Qatar   .60 .45
537 A185 25c Zaire   .60 .45
538 A185 25c Norway   .60 .45
539 A185 25c German Democratic Republic .60 .45
a.   Se-tenant block of 4 3.25 —
540 A185 25c Iran   .60 .45
541 A185 25c Tunisia   .60 .45
542 A185 25c Samoa   .60 .45
543 A185 25c Belize   .60 .45
a.   Se-tenant block of 4 3.25 —
Nos. 528-543 (16)   9.60 7.20
See note after No. 340.

A243   A244

1988, Dec. 9   Photo. & Engr.
544 A243 25c multicolored   .55 .40
Souvenir Sheet
545 A243 $1 multicolored   1.25 1.25

Universal Declaration of Human Rights, 40th anniv.
See Offices in Geneva #171-172; Vienna #86-87.

1989, Jan. 27   Litho.   Perf. 13x14
546 A244 25c Energy and nature .75 .45
547 A244 45c Agriculture   1.50 1.00

World Bank. See Offices in Geneva Nos. 173-174; Vienna Nos. 88-89.

UN Peace-Keeping Force, 1988 Nobel Peace Prize Winner — A245

1989, Mar. 17   Litho.   Perf. 14x13½
548 A245 25c multicolored   .50   .40
See Offices in Geneva #175, Vienna #90.

Aerial Photograph of New York Headquarters — A246

1989, Mar. 17   Perf. 14½x14
549 A246 45c multicolored   .70   .60

World Weather Watch, 25th Anniv. (in 1988) — A247

Satellite photographs: 25c, Storm system off the East Coast, US. 36c, Typhoon Abby in the North-West Pacific.

1989, Apr. 21   Litho.   Perf. 13x14
550 A247 25c multicolored   .75   .50
551 A247 36c multicolored   1.50   1.25
See Offices in Geneva #176-177; Vienna #91-92.

A248   A249

Photo. & Engr., Photo.
1989, Aug. 23   Perf. 14
552 A248 25c multicolored   2.75   .50
553 A249 90c multicolored   2.25   1.75
Offices in Vienna, 10th anniv. See Offices in Geneva Nos. 178-179; Vienna Nos. 93-94.

Flag Type of 1980
1989, Sept. 22   Photo.   Perf. 12
Granite Paper
554 A185 25c Indonesia   .65   .55
555 A185 25c Lesotho   .65   .55
556 A185 25c Guatemala   .65   .55
557 A185 25c Netherlands   .65   .55
 a.   Se-tenant block of 4   3.75   —
558 A185 25c South Africa   .65   .55
559 A185 25c Portugal   .65   .55
560 A185 25c Morocco   .65   .55
561 A185 25c Syrian Arab Re-
         public   .65   .55
 a.   Se-tenant block of 4   3.75   —
562 A185 25c Honduras   .65   .55
563 A185 25c Kampuchea   .65   .55
564 A185 25c Guinea-Bissau   .65   .55
565 A185 25c Cyprus   .65   .55
 a.   Se-tenant block of 4   3.75   —
566 A185 25c Algeria   .65   .55
567 A185 25c Brunei   .65   .55
568 A185 25c St. Kitts and Nev-
         is   .65   .55
569 A185 25c United Nations   .65   .55
 a.   Se-tenant block of 4   3.75   —
      Nos. 554-569 (16)   10.40   8.80
See note after No. 340.

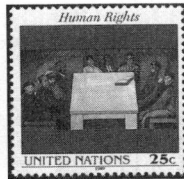

Declaration of Human Rights, 40th Anniv. (in 1988) — A250

Paintings: 25c, *The Table of Universal Brotherhood*, by Jose Clemente Orozco. 45c, *Study for Composition II*, by Vassily Kandinsky.

1989, Nov. 17   Litho.   Perf. 13½
570 A250 25c multicolored   .40   .30
571 A250 45c multicolored   .90   .80
Printed in sheets of 12+12 se-tenant labels containing Articles 1 (25c) or 2 (45c) inscribed in English, French or German.
See Nos. 582-583, 599-600, 616-617, 627-628; Offices in Geneva Nos. 180-181, 193-194, 209-210, 224-225, 234-235; Vienna Nos. 95-96, 108-109, 123-124, 139-140, 150-151.

Intl. Trade Center A251

1990, Feb. 2   Litho.   Perf. 14½x15
572 A251 25c multicolored   1.60   1.25
See Offices in Geneva #182; Vienna #97.

Fight AIDS Worldwide A252

Perf. 13½x12½
1990, Mar. 16   Litho.
573 A252 25c shown   .50   .40
574 A252 40c Shadow over
         crowd   1.50   1.25
See Offices in Geneva #184-185; Vienna #99-100.

Medicinal Plants — A253

1990, May 4   Photo.   Perf. 11½
Granite Paper
575 A253 25c *Catharanthus
         roseus*   .75   .65
576 A253 90c *Panax quinquefoli-
         um*   2.00   1.50
See Off. in Geneva #186-187; Vienna #101-102.

United Nations, 45th Anniv. A254

1990, June 26   Litho.   Perf. 14½x13
577 A254 25c shown   .80   .70
578 A254 45c "45," emblem   2.75   2.50
Souvenir Sheet
579 Sheet of 2, #577-578   7.75   6.00
See Off. in Geneva #188-189; Vienna #103-104.

Crime Prevention — A255

1990, Sept. 13   Photo.   Perf. 14
580 A255 25c Crimes of youth   1.10   .70
581 A255 36c Organized crime   2.50   1.25
See Off. in Geneva #191-192; Vienna #106-107.

Human Rights Type of 1989
Artwork: 25c, Fragment from the sarcophagus of Plotinus, c. 270 A.D. 45c, Combined Chambers of the High Court of Appeal by Charles Paul Renouard.

1990, Nov. 16   Litho.   Perf. 13½
582 A250 25c black, gray & tan   .45   .35
583 A250 45c black & brown   .90   .75
See Off. in Geneva #193-194; Vienna #108-109.
Printed in sheets of 12+12 se-tenant labels containing Articles 7 (25c) or 8 (45c) inscribed in English, French or German.

Economic Commission for Europe A256

1991, Mar. 15   Litho.   Perf. 14
584 A256 30c Two storks   1.10   .90
585 A256 30c Woodpecker, ibex   1.10   .90
586 A256 30c Capercaille, plover   1.10   .90
587 A256 30c Falcon, marmot   1.10   .90
 a.   Block of 4, #584-587   4.50   3.75

Namibian Independence A257

1991, May 10   Litho.   Perf. 14
588 A257 30c Dunes, Namib De-
         sert   1.00   .65
589 A257 50c Savanna   2.00   1.50
See Off. in Geneva #199-200; Vienna #114-115.

A258

The Golden Rule by Norman Rockwell — A259

1991, Sept. 11   Litho.   Perf. 13½
590 A258 30c multicolored   .90   .55
Photo.
Perf. 12x11½
591 A259 50c multicolored   1.50   1.00

UN Headquarters, New York — A260

1991, May 10   Engr.   Perf. 13½
592 A260 $2 dark blue   3.00   2.50

Rights of the Child — A261

1991, June 14   Litho.   Perf. 14½
593 A261 30c Children, globe   1.25   1.00
594 A261 70c Houses, rainbow   3.25   2.25
See Off. in Geneva #203-204; Vienna #117-118.

Banning of Chemical Weapons A262

90c, Hand holding back chemical drums.

1991, Sept. 11   Litho.   Perf. 13½
595 A262 30c multicolored   1.75   1.40
596 A262 90c multicolored   5.50   4.00
See Off. in Geneva #205-206; Vienna #119-120.

UN Postal Administration, 40th Anniv. — A263

1991, Oct. 24   Litho.   Perf. 14x15
597 A263 30c No. 1   1.10   .90
598 A263 40c No. 3   1.90   1.25
See Off. in Geneva #207-208; Vienna #121-122.

Human Rights Type of 1989
Artwork: 30c, The Last of England, by Ford Madox Brown. 50c, The Emigration to the East, by Tito Salas.

1991, Nov. 20   Litho.   Perf. 13½
599 A250 30c multicolored   .60   .45
600 A250 50c multicolored   1.25   1.00
Printed in sheets of 12+12 se-tenant labels containing Articles 13 (30c) or 14 (50c) inscribed in English, French or German.
See Off. in Geneva #209-210; Vienna #123-124.

World Heritage Type of 1984
Designs: 30c, Uluru Natl. Park, Australia. 50c, The Great Wall of China.

1992, Jan. 24   Litho.   Perf. 13
Size: 35x28mm
601 A215 30c multicolored   .70   .60
602 A215 50c multicolored   1.25   1.00
See Off. in Geneva #211-212; Vienna #125-126.

Clean Oceans — A264

1992, Mar. 13   Litho.   Perf. 14
603 A264 29c Ocean surface   .55   .55
604 A264 29c Ocean bottom   .55   .55
  a.   Pair, #603-604   1.10 1.10
Printed in sheets of 12 containing 6 #604a.
See Off. in Geneva #214-215; Vienna #127-128.

Earth Summit — A265

#605, Globe at LR. #606, Globe at LL. #607, Globe at UR. #608, Globe at UL.

1992, May 22   Photo.   Perf. 11½
605 A265 29c multicolored   1.50 1.25
606 A265 29c multicolored   1.50 1.25
607 A265 29c multicolored   1.50 1.25
608 A265 29c multicolored   1.50 1.25
  a.   Block of 4, #605-608   6.00 5.00
See Off. in Geneva #216-219, Vienna #129-132.

Mission to Planet Earth — A266

#609, Satellites over city, sailboats, fishing boat. #610, Satellite over coast, passenger liner, dolphins, whale, volcano.

1992, Sept. 4   Photo.   Rouletted 8
Granite Paper
609 A266 29c multicolored   3.25 3.00
610 A266 29c multicolored   3.25 3.00
  a.   Pair, #609-610   6.50 6.00
See Off. in Geneva #220-221, Vienna #133-134.

Science and Technology for Development — A267

Design: 50c, Animal, man drinking.

1992, Oct. 2   Litho.   Perf. 14
611 A267 29c multicolored   .50   .45
612 A267 50c multicolored   .85   .70
See Off. in Geneva #222-223, Vienna #135-136.

UN University Building, Tokyo A268

UN Headquarters A269

40c, UN University Building, Tokyo, diff.

Perf. 14, 13½x13 (29c)
1992, Oct. 2
613 A268 4c multicolored   .20   .20
614 A269 29c multicolored   .70   .55
615 A268 40c multicolored   .90   .75
  Nos. 613-615 (3)   1.80 1.50

Human Rights Type of 1989
Artwork: 29c, Lady Writing a Letter With her Maid, by Vermeer. 50c, The Meeting, by Ester Almqvist.

1992, Nov. 20   Litho.   Perf. 13½
616 A250 29c multicolored   .90   .75
617 A250 50c multicolored   1.10 1.00
Printed in sheets of 12+12 se-tenant labels containing Articles 19 (29c) and 20 (50c) inscribed in English, French or German.
See Off. in Geneva #224-225; Vienna #139-140.

Aging With Dignity — A270

29c, Elderly couple, family. 52c, Old man, physician, woman holding fruit basket.

1993, Feb. 5   Litho.   Perf. 13
618 A270 29c multicolored   1.00 .75
619 A270 52c multicolored   1.75 1.40
See Off. in Geneva #226-227; Vienna #141-142.

Endangered Species A271

Designs: No. 620, Hairy-nosed wombat. No. 621, Whooping crane. No. 622, Giant clam. No. 623, Giant sable antelope.

1993, Mar. 3   Litho.   Perf. 13x12½
620 A271 29c multicolored   .55   .50
621 A271 29c multicolored   .55   .50
622 A271 29c multicolored   .55   .50
623 A271 29c multicolored   .55   .50
  a.   Block of 4, #620-623   2.25 2.25
See #639-642, 657-660, 674-677, 700-703, 730-733, 757-760, 773-776, 789-792; Offices in Geneva #228-231, 246-249, 264-267, 280-283, 298-301, 318-321, 336-339, 367-370; Vienna #143-146, 162-165, 180-183, 196-199, 214-217, 235-238, 253-256, 284-287.

Healthy Environment A272

Designs: 29c, Personal. 50c, Family.

1993, May 7   Litho.   Perf. 15x14½
624 A272 29c Man   .70   .50
625 A272 50c Family   1.10 .85
WHO, 45th anniv.
See Off. in Geneva #232-233; Vienna #147-148.

A273

1993, May 7   Litho.   Perf. 15x14
626 A273 5c multicolored   .20   .20

Human Rights Type of 1989
Artwork: 29c, Shocking Corn, by Thomas Hart Benton. 35c, The Library, by Jacob Lawrence.

1993, June 11   Litho.   Perf. 13½
627 A250 29c multicolored   .90   .65
628 A250 35c multicolored   1.25 1.00
Printed in sheets of 12 + 12 se-tenant labels containing Articles 25 (29c) and 26 (35c) inscribed in English, French or German.
See Off. in Geneva #234-235; Vienna #150-151.

Intl. Peace Day — A274

Denomination at: No. 629, UL. No. 630, UR. No. 631, LL. No. 632, LR.

Rouletted 12½
1993, Sept. 21   Litho. & Engr.
629 A274 29c blue & multi   2.00 1.50
630 A274 29c blue & multi   2.00 1.50
631 A274 29c blue & multi   2.00 1.50
632 A274 29c blue & multi   2.00 1.50
  a.   Block of 4, #629-632   9.00 7.00
See Off. in Geneva #236-239; Vienna #152-155.

Environment-Climate — A275

Designs: No. 633, Chameleon. No. 634, Palm trees, top of funnel cloud. No. 635, Bottom of funnel cloud, deer, antelope. No. 636, Bird of paradise.

1993, Oct. 29   Litho.   Perf. 14½
633 A275 29c multicolored   .85   .75
634 A275 29c multicolored   .85   .75
635 A275 29c multicolored   .85   .75
636 A275 29c multicolored   .85   .75
  a.   Strip of 4, #633-636   3.50 3.25
See Off. in Geneva #240-243; Vienna #156-159.

Intl. Year of the Family — A276

Designs: 29c, Mother holding child, two children, woman. 45c, People tending crops.

1994, Feb. 4   Litho.   Perf. 13.1
637 A276 29c green & multi   1.25 1.00
638 A276 45c blue & multi   2.00 1.50
See Off. in Geneva #244-245; Vienna #160-161.

Endangered Species Type of 1993
Designs: No. 639, Chimpanzee. No. 640, St. Lucia Amazon. No. 641, American crocodile. No. 642, Dama gazelle.

1994, Mar. 18   Litho.   Perf. 12.7
639 A271 29c multicolored   .60   .50
640 A271 29c multicolored   .60   .50
641 A271 29c multicolored   .60   .50
642 A271 29c multicolored   .60   .50
  a.   Block of 4, #639-642   2.50 2.25
See Off. in Geneva #246-249; Vienna #162-165.

Protection for Refugees — A277

1994, Apr. 29   Litho.   Perf. 14.3x14.8
643 A277 50c multicolored   1.25 1.00
See Offices in Geneva #250; Vienna #166.

Dove of Peace — A278

Sleeping Child, by Stanislaw Wyspianski A279

Mourning Owl, by Vanessa Isitt A280

1994, Apr. 29   Litho.   Perf. 12.9
644 A278 10c multicolored   .20   .20
645 A279 19c multicolored   .65   .40

Engr.
Perf. 13.1
646 A280 $1 red brown   2.50 2.00

Intl. Decade for Natural Disaster Reduction A281

Earth viewed from space, outline map of: No. 647, North America. No. 648, Eurasia. No. 649, South America. No. 650, Australia and South Asia.

1994, May 27   Litho.   Perf. 13.9x14.2
647 A281 29c multicolored   1.75 1.25
648 A281 29c multicolored   1.75 1.25
649 A281 29c multicolored   1.75 1.25
650 A281 29c multicolored   1.75 1.25
  a.   Block of 4, #647-650   8.00 3.00
See Off. in Geneva #251-254; Vienna #170-173.

Population and Development — A282

Designs: 29c, Children playing. 52c, Family with house, car, other possessions.

1994, Sept. 1   Litho.   Perf. 13.2x13.6
651 A282 29c multicolored   .75   .60
652 A282 52c multicolored   1.25 1.00
See Off. in Geneva #258-259; Vienna #174-175.

UNCTAD, 30th Anniv. A283

1994, Oct. 28
653	A283	29c multicolored	.55	.50
654	A283	50c multi, diff.	.95	.70

See Off. in Geneva #260-261; Vienna #176-177.

UN, 50th Anniv. — A284

1995, Jan. 1   Litho. & Engr.   Perf. 13.4
655	A284	32c multicolored	1.25	.90

See Offices in Geneva #262; Vienna #178.

Social Summit, Copenhagen A285

Photo. & Engr.
1995, Feb. 3   Perf. 13.6x13.9
656	A285	50c multicolored	1.10	1.00

See Offices in Geneva #263; Vienna #179.

Endangered Species Type of 1993
Designs: No. 657, Giant armadillo. No. 658, American bald eagle. No. 659, Fijian/Tongan banded iguana. No. 660, Giant panda.

1995, Mar. 24   Litho.   Perf. 13x12½
657	A271	32c multicolored	.65	.55
658	A271	32c multicolored	.65	.55
659	A271	32c multicolored	.65	.55
660	A271	32c multicolored	.65	.55
a.		Block of 4, 657-660	2.75	2.25

See Off. in Geneva #264-267; Vienna #180-183.

Intl. Youth Year, 10th Anniv. — A286

32c, Seated child. 55c, Children cycling.

1995, May 26   Litho.   Perf. 14.4x14.7
661	A286	32c multicolored	1.00	.45
662	A286	55c multicolored	1.75	.85

See Off. in Geneva #268-269; Vienna #184-185.

UN, 50th Anniv. — A287

Designs: 32c, Hand with pen signing UN Charter, flags. 50c, Veterans' War Memorial, Opera House, San Francisco.

Perf. 13.3x13.6
1995, June 26   Engr.
663	A287	32c black	.65	.45
664	A287	50c maroon	1.00	.70

Souvenir Sheet
Litho. & Engr.
Imperf
665		Sheet of 2, #663-664	2.25	2.00
a.	A287	32c black	.90	.75
b.	A287	50c maroon	1.25	1.10

See Off. in Geneva #270-271; Vienna #186-187.

4th World Conference on Women, Beijing A288

Designs: 32c, Mother and child. 40c, Seated woman, cranes flying above.

1995, Sept. 5   Photo.   Perf. 12
666	A288	32c multicolored	.80	.40
		Size: 28x50mm		
667	A288	40c multicolored	1.10	.90

See Off. in Geneva #273-274; Vienna #189-190.

UN Headquarters — A289

1995, Sept. 5   Litho.   Perf. 15
668	A289	20c multicolored	.35	.20

Miniature Sheet

United Nations, 50th Anniv. — A290

Designs: #669a-669 l, Various people in continuous design (2 blocks of six stamps with gutter between).

1995, Oct. 24   Litho.   Perf. 14
669		Sheet of 12	15.00	12.50
a.-l.		A290 32c any single	1.25	.80
670		Souvenir booklet	20.00	
a.		A290 32c Bklt. pane, vert. strip of 3 from UL of sheet	5.00	5.00
b.		A290 32c Bklt. pane, vert. strip of 3 from UR of sheet	5.00	5.00
c.		A290 32c Bklt. pane, vert. strip of 3 from LL of sheet	5.00	5.00
d.		A290 32c Bklt. pane, vert. strip of 3 from LR of sheet	5.00	5.00

See Off. in Geneva #275-276; Vienna #191-192.

WFUNA, 50th Anniv. — A291

1996, Feb. 2   Litho.   Perf. 13x13½
671	A291	32c multicolored	.50	.35

See Offices in Geneva #277; Vienna #193.

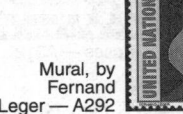

Mural, by Fernand Leger — A292

1996, Feb. 2   Litho.   Perf. 14½x15
672	A292	32c multicolored	.50	.35
673	A292	60c multi, diff.	1.00	.75

Endangered Species Type of 1993
#674, Masdevallia veitchiana. #675, Saguaro cactus. #676, West Australian pitcher plant. #677, Encephalartos horridus.

1996, Mar. 14   Litho.   Perf. 12½
674	A271	32c multicolored	.75	.65
675	A271	32c multicolored	.75	.65
676	A271	32c multicolored	.75	.65
677	A271	32c multicolored	.75	.65
a.		Block of 4, #674-677	3.25	3.00

See Off. in Geneva #280-283; Vienna #196-199.

City Summit (Habitat II) — A293

Designs: No. 678, Deer. No. 679, Man, child, dog sitting on hill, overlooking town. No. 680, People walking in park, city skyline. No. 681, Tropical park, Polynesian woman, boy. No. 682, Polynesian village, orchids, bird.

1996, June 3   Litho.   Perf. 14x13½
678	A293	32c multicolored	.85	.60
679	A293	32c multicolored	.85	.60
680	A293	32c multicolored	.85	.60
681	A293	32c multicolored	.85	.60
682	A293	32c multicolored	.85	.60
a.		Strip of 5, #678-682	4.25	3.50

See Off. in Geneva #284-288; Vienna #200-204.

Sport and the Environment A294

1996 Summer Olympic Games, Atlanta, GA: 32c, Men's basketball. 50c, Women's volleyball, horiz.

Perf. 14x14½, 14½x14
1996, July 19   Litho.
683	A294	32c multicolored	1.00	.75
684	A294	50c multicolored	2.00	1.50

Souvenir Sheet
685	A294	Sheet of 2, #683-684	2.50	1.60

See Off. in Geneva #289-291; Vienna #205-207.

Plea for Peace — A295

Designs: 32c, Doves. 60c, Stylized dove.

1996, Sept. 17   Litho.   Perf. 14½x15
686	A295	32c multicolored	.65	.45
687	A295	60c multicolored	1.25	.90

See Off. in Geneva #292-293; Vienna #208-209.

UNICEF, 50th Anniv. — A296

Fairy Tales: 32c, Yeh-Shen, China. 60c, The Ugly Duckling, by Hans Christian Andersen.

1996, Nov. 20   Litho.   Perf. 14½x15
688	A296	32c multicolored	.65	.50
689	A296	60c multicolored	1.50	1.25

Panes of 8 + label.
See Off. in Geneva #294-295; Vienna #210-211.

Flag Type of 1980
1997, Feb. 12   Photo.   Perf. 12
Granite Paper
690	A185	32c Tadjikistan	.65	.50
691	A185	32c Georgia	.65	.50
692	A185	32c Armenia	.65	.50
693	A185	32c Namibia	.65	.50
a.		Block of 4, #690-693	4.00	3.00
694	A185	32c Liechtenstein	.65	.50
695	A185	32c Republic of Korea	.65	.50
696	A185	32c Kazakhstan	.65	.50
697	A185	32c Latvia	.65	.50
a.		Block of 4, #694-697	4.00	3.00

See note after No. 340.

Cherry Blossoms, UN Headquarters A297

Peace Rose — A298

1997, Feb. 12   Litho.   Perf. 14½
698	A297	8c multicolored	.40	.35
699	A298	55c multicolored	2.00	1.75

Endangered Species Type of 1993
Designs: No. 700, African elephant. No. 701, Major Mitchell's cockatoo. No. 702, Black-footed ferret. No. 703, Cougar.

1997, Mar. 13   Litho.   Perf. 12½
700	A271	32c multicolored	.65	.50
701	A271	32c multicolored	.65	.50
702	A271	32c multicolored	.65	.50
703	A271	32c multicolored	.65	.50
a.		Block of 4, #700-703	2.75	2.00

See Off. in Geneva #298-301; Vienna #214-217.

Earth Summit, 5th Anniv. A299

Designs: No. 704, Sailboat. No. 705, Three sailboats. No. 706, Two people watching sailboat, sun. No. 707, Person, sailboat. $1, Combined design similar to #704-707.

1997, May 30   Photo.   Perf. 11.5
Granite Paper
704	A299	32c multicolored	1.10	.80
705	A299	32c multicolored	1.10	.80
706	A299	32c multicolored	1.10	.80
707	A299	32c multicolored	1.10	.80
a.		Block of 4, #704-707	4.50	3.50

Souvenir Sheet
708	A299	$1 multicolored	4.00	4.00
a.		Ovptd. in sheet margin	20.00	20.00

No. 708 contains one 60x43mm stamp. Overprint in sheet margin of No. 708a reads "PACIFIC 97 / World Philatelic Exhibition / San Francisco, California / 29 May - 8 June 1997."
See Off. in Geneva #302-306; Vienna #218-222.

Transportation A300

Ships: No. 709, Clipper ship. No. 710, Paddle steamer. No. 711, Ocean liner. No. 712, Hovercraft. No. 713, Hydrofoil.

1997, Aug. 29   Litho.   Perf. 14x14½

709	A300	32c multicolored	.65	.30
710	A300	32c multicolored	.65	.30
711	A300	32c multicolored	.65	.30
712	A300	32c multicolored	.65	.30
713	A300	32c multicolored	.65	.30
a.		Strip of 5, #709-713	3.25	1.50

No. 713a has continuous design.
See Off. in Geneva #307-311; Vienna #223-227.

Philately — A301

1997, Oct. 14   Litho.   Perf. 13½x14

714	A301	32c No. 473	2.50	2.25
715	A301	50c No. 474	4.00	3.50

See Off. in Geneva #312-313; Vienna #228-229.

World Heritage Convention, 25th Anniv. — A302

Terracotta warriors of Xian: 32c, Single warrior. 60c, Massed warriors.

No. 718: a, like #716. b, like #717. c, like Geneva #314. d, like Geneva #315. e, like Vienna #230. f, like Vienna #231.

1997, Nov. 19   Litho.   Perf. 13½

716	A302	32c multicolored	1.10	.75
717	A302	60c multicolored	2.10	1.75
718		Souvenir bklt.	8.50	
a.-f.		A302 8c any single	.30	.30
g.		Booklet pane of 4 #718a	1.25	1.25
h.		Booklet pane of 4 #718b	1.25	1.25
i.		Booklet pane of 4 #718c	1.25	1.25
j.		Booklet pane of 4 #718d	1.25	1.25
k.		Booklet pane of 4 #718e	1.25	1.25
l.		Booklet pane of 4 #718f	1.25	1.25

See Off. in Geneva #314-316; Vienna #230-232.

Flag Type of 1980

1998, Feb. 13   Photo.   Perf. 12
Granite Paper

719	A185	32c Micronesia	.75	.50
720	A185	32c Slovakia	.75	.50
721	A185	32c Democratic People's Republic of Korea	.75	.50
722	A185	32c Azerbaijan	.75	.50
a.		Block of 4, #719-722	3.50	—
723	A185	32c Uzbekistan	.75	.50
724	A185	32c Monaco	.75	.50
725	A185	32c Czech Republic	.75	.50
726	A185	32c Estonia	.75	.50
a.		Block of 4, #723-726	3.50	—

See note after No. 340.

A303

A304

A305

1998, Feb. 13   Litho.   Perf. 14½x15

727	A303	1c multicolored	.20	.20
728	A304	2c multicolored	.20	.20

Perf. 15x14½

729	A305	21c multicolored	.45	.20

Endangered Species Type of 1993

#730, Lesser galago. #731, Hawaiian goose. #732, Golden birdwing. #733, Sun bear.

1998, Mar. 13   Litho.   Perf. 12½

730	A271	32c multicolored	.65	.30
731	A271	32c multicolored	.65	.30
732	A271	32c multicolored	.65	.30
733	A271	32c multicolored	.65	.30
a.		Block of 4, #730-733	2.75	1.40

See Off. in Geneva #318-321; Vienna #235-238.

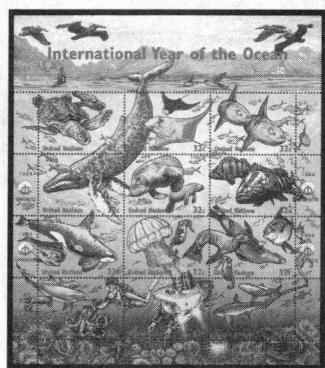

Intl. Year of the Ocean — A306

1998, May 20   Litho.   Perf. 13x13½

734	A306	Sheet of 12	8.00	6.50
a.-l.		32c any single	.65	.50

See Offices in Geneva #322; Vienna #239.

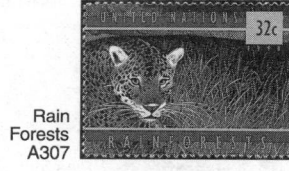

Rain Forests A307

1998, June 19   Litho.   Perf. 13x13½

735	A307	32c Jaguar	.75	.65

Souvenir Sheet

736	A307	$2 like #735	4.00	3.00

See Off. in Geneva #323-324; Vienna #240-241.

U.N. Peacekeeping Forces, 50th Anniv. — A308

Designs: 33c, Commander with binoculars. 40c, Two soldiers on vehicle.

1998, Sept. 15   Photo.   Perf. 12

737	A308	33c multicolored	.85	.60
738	A308	40c multicolored	1.25	.90

See Off. in Geneva #325-326; Vienna #242-243.

Universal Declaration of Human Rights, 50th Anniv. — A309

Stylized people: 32c, Carrying flag. 55c, Carrying pens.

Litho. & Photo.   Perf. 13

739	A309	32c multicolored	.75	.65
740	A309	55c multicolored	1.25	1.25

See Off. in Geneva #327-328; Vienna #244-245.

Schönnbrun Palace, Vienna — A310

Designs: 33c, #743f, The Gloriette. 60c, #743b, Wall painting on fabric (detail), by Johann Wenzl Bergl, vert. No. 743a, Blue porcelain vase, vert. No. 743c, Porcelain stove, vert. No. 743d, Palace. No. 743e, Great Palm House (conservatory).

1998, Dec. 4   Litho.   Perf. 14

741	A310	33c multicolored	.75	.50
742	A310	60c multicolored	1.50	.90
743		Souvenir bklt.	6.00	
a.-c.		A310 11c any single	.40	.40
d.-f.		A310 15c any single	.50	.50
g.		Booklet pane, 4 #743d	2.00	
h.		Booklet pane, 3 #743a	1.20	
i.		Booklet pane, 3 #743b	1.20	
j.		Booklet pane, 3 #743c	1.20	
k.		Booklet pane, 4 #743e	2.00	
l.		Booklet pane, 4 #743f	2.00	

See Off. in Geneva #329-331; Vienna #246-248.

Flag Type of 1980

1999, Feb. 5   Photo.   Perf. 12

744	A185	33c Lithuania	.70	.50
745	A185	33c San Marino	.70	.50
746	A185	33c Turkmenistan	.70	.50
747	A185	33c Marshall Islands	.70	.50
a.		Block of 4, #744-747	3.00	—
748	A185	33c Moldova	.70	.50
749	A185	33c Kyrgyzstan	.70	.50
750	A185	33c Bosnia & Herzegovina	.70	.50
751	A185	33c Eritrea	.70	.50
a.		Block of 4, #748-751	3.00	—

See note after No. 340.

Flags and Globe — A311

Roses — A312

1999, Feb. 5   Litho.   Perf. 14x13½

752	A311	33c multicolored	.65	.30

Photo.
Granite Paper
Perf. 11½x12

753	A312	$5 multicolored	8.50	2.00

World Heritage Sites, Australia A313

33c, #756f, Willandra Lakes region. 60c, #756b, Wet tropics of Queensland. No. 756a, Tasmanian wilderness. No. 756c, Great Barrier Reef. No. 756d, Uluru-Kata Tjuta Natl. Park. No. 756e, Kakadu Natl. Park.

1999, Mar. 19   Litho.   Perf. 13

754	A313	33c multicolored	.85	.75
755	A313	60c multicolored	1.75	1.50
756		Souvenir booklet	5.00	
a.-c.		A313 5c any single	.20	.20
d.-f.		A313 15c any single	.30	.30
g.		Booklet pane of 4, #756a	.40	
h.		Booklet pane of 4, #756d	1.25	
i.		Booklet pane of 4, #756b	.40	
j.		Booklet pane of 4, #756e	1.25	
k.		Booklet pane of 4, #756c	.40	
l.		Booklet pane of 4, #756f	1.25	

See Off. in Geneva Nos. 333-335; Vienna Nos. 250-252.

Endangered Specied Type of 1993

#757, Tiger. #758, Secretary bird. #759, Green tree python. #760, Long-tailed chinchilla.

1999, Apr. 22   Litho.   Perf. 12½

757	A271	33c multicolored	.65	.20
758	A271	33c multicolored	.65	.20
759	A271	33c multicolored	.65	.20
760	A271	33c multicolored	.65	.20
a.		Block of 4, #757-760	2.60	

See Off. in Geneva Nos. 336-339; Vienna Nos. 253-256.

UNISPACE III, Vienna — A314

#761, Probe on planet's surface. #762, Planetary rover. #763, Composite of #761-762.

1999, July 7   Photo.   Rouletted 8

761	A314	33c multicolored	.95	.60
762	A314	33c multicolored	.95	.60
a.		Pair, #761-762	1.95	1.50

Souvenir Sheet
Perf. 14½

763	A314	$2 multicolored	4.25	2.00
a.		Ovptd. in sheet margin	10.00	5.00

No. 763a was issued 7/7/00 and is overprinted in violet blue "WORLD STAMP EXPO 2000 / ANAHEIM, CALIFORNIA / U.S.A./ 7-16 JULY 2000."
See Off. in Geneva #340-342; Vienna #257-259.

UPU, 125th Anniv. — A315

Various people, 19th century methods of mail transportation, denomination at: No. 764, UL. No. 765, UR. No. 766, LL. No. 767, LR.

1999, Aug. 23   Photo.   Perf. 11¾

764	A315	33c multicolored	.65	.30
765	A315	33c multicolored	.65	.30
766	A315	33c multicolored	.65	.30
767	A315	33c multicolored	.65	.30
a.		Block of 4, #764-767	2.60	

See Off. in Geneva #343-346; Vienna #260-263.

In Memoriam A316

UN Headquarters. Size of $1 stamp: 34x63mm.

1999, Sept. 21   Litho.   Perf. 14½x14

768	A316	33c multicolored	2.00	1.75

Souvenir Sheet
Perf. 14

769	A316	$1 multicolored	2.00	1.00

See Off. in Geneva #347-348, Vienna #264-265.

Education, Keystone to the 21st Century — A317

Perf. 13½x13¾
1999, Nov. 18			Litho.	
770	A317	33c Two readers	.65	.30
771	A317	60c Heart	1.25	.60

See Off. in Geneva #349-350, Vienna #266-267.

International Year of Thanksgiving A318

2000, Jan. 1		Litho.	Perf. 13¼x13½	
772	A318	33c multicolored	.90	.75

On No. 772 portions of the design were applied by a thermographic process producing a shiny, raised effect. See Off. in Geneva #351, Vienna #268.

Endangered Species Type of 1993

Designs: No. 773, Brown bear. No. 774, Black-bellied bustard. No. 775, Chinese crocodile lizard. No. 776, Pygmy chimpanzee.

2000, Apr. 6		Litho.	Perf. 12¾x12½	
773	A271	33c multicolored	.65	.30
774	A271	33c multicolored	.65	.30
775	A271	33c multicolored	.65	.30
776	A271	33c multicolored	.65	.30
a.		Block of 4, #773-776	2.60	2.00

See Off. in Geneva #352-355; Vienna #269-272.

Our World 2000 A319

Winning artwork in Millennium painting competition: 33c, Crawling Toward the Millennium, by Sam Yeates, US. 60c, Crossing, by Masakazu Takahata, Japan, vert.

Perf. 13x13½, 13½x13
2000, May 30			Litho.	
777	A319	33c multicolored	.65	.30
778	A319	60c multicolored	1.25	.60

See Off. in Geneva #356-357, Vienna #273-274.

UN, 55th Anniv. — A320

Designs: 33c, Workmen removing decorative discs in General Assembly Hall, 1956. 55c, UN Building in 1951.

2000, July 7		Litho.	Perf. 13¼x13	
779	A320	33c multicolored	.65	.30
780	A320	55c multicolored	1.10	.55

Souvenir Sheet
781	A320	Sheet of 2, #779-780	2.25	2.00

See Off. in Geneva #358-360, Vienna #275-277.

International Flag of Peace — A321

2000, Sept. 15		Litho.	Perf. 14½x14	
782	A321	33c multicolored	.65	.30

The UN in the 21st Century — A322

No. 783: a, Farmers, animals in rice paddy. b, Vehicle chassis being lifted. c, People voting. d, Baby receiving inoculation. e, Woman, man at pump. f, Mason, construction workers.

2000, Sept. 15			Litho.	Perf. 14	
783	A322	Sheet of 6		4.00	3.00
a.-f.		33c any single		.65	.30

See Off. in Geneva #361; Vienna #278.

World Heritage Sites, Spain — A323

Designs: 33c, #786a, Alhambra, Generalife and Albayzin, Granada. 60c, #786d, Amphitheater of Mérida. #786b, Walled Town of Cuenca. #786c, Aqueduct of Segovia. #786e, Toledo. #786f, Güell Park, Barcelona.

2000, Oct. 6		Litho.	Perf. 14¾x14½	
784	A323	33c multicolored	.65	.30
785	A323	60c multicolored	1.25	.60

Souvenir Booklet
786		Booklet	5.00	
a.-c.		A323 5c any single	.20	.20
d.-f.		A323 15c any single	.30	.30
g.		Booklet pane of 4, #786a	.40	—
h.		Booklet pane of 4, #786d	1.25	—
i.		Booklet pane of 4, #786b	.40	—
j.		Booklet pane of 4, #786e	1.25	—
k.		Booklet pane of 4, #786c	.40	—
l.		Booklet pane of 4, #786f	1.25	—

See Offices in Geneva Nos. 362-364, Vienna Nos. 279-281.

Respect for Refugees A324

2000, Nov. 9		Litho.	Perf. 13¼x12¾	
787	A324	33c multicolored	.65	.30

Souvenir Sheet
788	A324	$1 multicolored	2.00	1.00

See Offices in Geneva Nos. 365-366, Vienna Nos. 282-283.

Endangered Species Type of 1993

Designs: No. 789, Common spotted cuscus. No. 790, Resplendent quetzal. No. 791, Gila monster. No. 792, Guereza.

2001, Feb. 1		Litho.	Perf. 12¾x12½	
789	A271	34c multicolored	.65	.30
790	A271	34c multicolored	.65	.30
791	A271	34c multicolored	.65	.30
792	A271	34c multicolored	.65	.30
a.		Block of 4, #789-792	2.60	—

See Offices in Geneva Nos. 367-370; Vienna Nos. 284-287.

Intl. Volunteers Year — A325

Paintings by: 34c, Jose Zaragoza, Brazil. 80c, John Terry, Australia.

2001, Mar. 29		Litho.	Perf. 13¼	
793	A325	34c multicolored	.65	.30
794	A325	80c multicolored	1.60	.80

See Offices in Geneva Nos. 371-372; Vienna Nos. 288-289.

Flag Type of 1980
2001, May 25		Photo.	Perf. 12	
		Granite Paper		
795	A185	34c Slovenia	.65	.30
796	A185	34c Palau	.65	.30
797	A185	34c Tonga	.65	.30
798	A185	34c Croatia	.65	.30
a.		Block of 4, #795-798	2.60	—
799	A185	34c Former Yugoslav Republic of Macedonia	.65	.30
800	A185	34c Kiribati	.65	.30
801	A185	34c Andorra	.65	.30
802	A185	34c Nauru	.65	.30
a.		Block of 4, #799-802	2.60	—
		Nos. 795-802 (8)	5.20	2.40

Sunflower A326

Rose — A327

2001, May 25		Litho.	Perf. 13¼x13¾	
803	A326	7c multicolored	.20	.20
804	A327	34c multicolored	.65	.30

World Heritage Sites, Japan — A328

Designs: 34c, #807a, Kyoto. 70c, #807d, Shirakawa-Go and Gokayama. #807b, Nara. #807c, Himeji-Jo. #807e, Itsukushima Shinto Shrine. #807f, Nikko.

2001, Aug. 1		Litho.	Perf. 12¾x13¼	
805	A328	34c multicolored	.65	.30
806	A328	70c multicolored	1.40	.70

Souvenir Booklet
807		Booklet	6.00	
a.-c.		A328 5c any single	.20	.20
d.-f.		A328 20c any single	.40	.40
g.		Booklet pane of 4, #807a	1.60	—
h.		Booklet pane of 4, #807d	.40	—
i.		Booklet pane of 4, #807b	1.60	—
j.		Booklet pane of 4, #807e	.40	—
k.		Booklet pane of 4, #807c	1.60	—
l.		Booklet pane of 4, #807f	.40	—

See Offices in Geneva Nos. 373-375, Vienna Nos. 290-292.

Dag Hammarskjöld (1905-61), UN Secretary General — A329

2001, Sept. 18		Engr.	Perf. 11x11¼	
808	A329	80c blue	1.60	.80

See Offices in Geneva No. 376, Vienna No. 293.

A330

UN Postal Administration, 50th Anniv. — A331

2001, Oct. 18		Litho.	Perf. 13½	
809	A330	34c Stamps, streamers	.65	.30
810	A330	80c Stamps, gifts	1.60	.80

Souvenir Sheet
811	A331	Sheet of 2 #811a	4.00	2.00
a.		$1 blue & light blue, 38mm diameter	2.00	1.00

See Offices in Geneva Nos. 377-379, Vienna Nos. 294-296.

Climate Change — A332

Designs: No. 812, Canada geese, greenhouses, butterfly, thistle. No. 813, Canada geese, iceberg, penguins, tomato plant. No. 814, Palm tree, solar collector. No. 815, Hand planting ginkgo cutting.

2001, Nov. 16   Litho.   Perf. 13¼
812	A332 34c multicolored	.65	.30
813	A332 34c multicolored	.65	.30
814	A332 34c multicolored	.65	.30
815	A332 34c multicolored	.65	.30
a.	Horiz. strip, #812-815	2.60	—

See Offices in Geneva Nos. 380-383, Vienna Nos. 297-300.

Awarding of Nobel Peace Prize to Secretary General Kofi Annan and UN — A333

2001, Dec. 10   Litho.   Perf. 13¼
816	A333 34c multicolored	.65	.30

See Offices in Geneva Nos. 384, Vienna Nos. 301.

AIR POST

Plane and Gull — AP1

Swallows and UN Emblem AP2

Unwmk.
1951, Dec. 14   Engr.   Perf. 14
C1	AP1 6c henna brown	.20	.20
C2	AP1 10c bright blue green	.20	.20
C3	AP2 15c deep ultra	.20	.25
a.	15c Prussian blue	100.00	
C4	AP2 25c gray black	.70	.35
	Nos. C1-C4 (4)	1.30	1.00

The 6c, 15c and 25c exist imperforate.

Airplane Wing and Globe — AP3

1957, May 27   Perf. 12½x14
C5	AP3 4c maroon	.20	.20

1959, Feb. 9   Perf. 12½x13½
C6	AP3 5c rose red	.20	.20

UN Flag and Plane AP4

1959, Feb. 9   Perf. 13½x14
C7	AP4 7c ultramarine	.20	.20

Outer Space — AP5

UN Emblem — AP6

"Flight Across Globe" — AP8

Bird of Laurel Leaves — AP7

Jet Plane and Envelope AP9

1963-64   Photo.   Perf. 11½
C8	AP5 6c blk, blue & yel grn	.20	.20
C9	AP6 8c yel, ol green & red	.20	.20

Perf. 12½x12
C10	AP7 13c ultra, aqua, gray & car	.20	.20

Perf. 11½x12, 12x11½
C11	AP8 15c violet, buff, gray & pale grn ('64)	.25	.20
a.	Gray omitted		
C12	AP9 25c yel, org, gray, blue & red ('64)	.50	.30
	Nos. C8-C12 (5)	1.35	1.10

Dates of issue: 6c, 8c, 13c, June 17, 1963; 15c, 25c, May 1. See Offices in Geneva No. 8.

Jet Plane and UN Emblem AP10

1968, Apr. 18   Litho.   Perf. 13
C13	AP10 20c multicolored	.30	.25

Wings, Envelopes and UN Emblem AP11

1969, Apr. 21   Litho.
C14	AP11 10c org ver, org, yel & black	.20	.20

UN Emblem and Stylized Wing — AP12

Birds in Flight — AP13

Clouds AP14

"UN" and Plane — AP15

Lithograved and Engraved
1972, May 1   Perf. 13x13½
C15	AP12 9c lt blue, dark red & vio blue	.20	.20

Photo.   Perf. 14x13½
C16	AP13 11c blue & multi	.20	.20

Perf. 13½x14
C17	AP14 17c yel, red & org	.25	.20

Perf. 13
C18	AP15 21c silver & multi	.25	.25
	Nos. C15-C18 (4)	.90	.85

Globe and Jet — AP16

Pathways Radiating from UN Emblem AP17

Bird in Flight, UN Headquarters AP18

Perf. 13, 12½x13 (18c)
1974, Sept. 16   Litho.
C19	AP16 13c multicolored	.20	.20
C20	AP17 18c multicolored	.25	.20
C21	AP18 26c blue & multi	.35	.30
	Nos. C19-C21 (3)	.80	.70

Winged Airmail Letter — AP19

Symbolic Globe and Plane — AP20

1977, June 27   Photo.   Perf. 14
C22	AP19 25c grnsh blue & multi	.35	.25
C23	AP20 31c magenta	.40	.30

U.N. OFFICES IN GENEVA, SWITZERLAND

For use only on mail posted at the Palais des Nations (UN European Office), Geneva. Inscribed in French unless otherwise stated.

100 Centimes = 1 Franc

Catalogue values for all unused stamps in this country are for Never Hinged items.

Stamps are inscribed in English, French or Spanish or are multilingual.

For use only on mail posted at the Palais des Nations (UN European Office), Geneva. Inscribed in French unless otherwise stated.

100 Centimes = 1 Franc

Types of UN Issues 1961-69 and

UN European Office, Geneva — G1

Designs: 5c, UN Headquarters, New York, and world map. 10c, UN flag. 20c, Three men united before globe. 50c, Opening words of UN Charter. 60c, UN emblem over globe. 70c, "UN" and UN emblem.
75c, "Flight Across Globe." 80c, UN Headquarters and emblem. 90c, Abstract group of flags. 1fr, UN Emblem. 2fr, Stylized globe and weather vane. 3fr, Statue by Henrik Starcke. 10fr, "Peace, Justice, Security."

Photogravure; Lithographed & Embossed (1fr); Engraved (10fr)

1969-70   **Unwmk.**
Perf. 13 (5c, 70c, 90c); Perf. 12½x12
(10c); Perf. 11½ (20c-60c, 3fr);
Perf. 11½x12 (75c); Perf. 13½x14
(80c); Perf. 14 (1fr);
Perf. 12x11½ (2fr); Perf. 12 (10fr)

1	A88	5c purple & multi	.20	.20
a.		Green omitted		—
2	A52	10c salmon & multi	.20	.20
3	A66	20c black & multi	.20	.20
4	G1	30c dk blue & multi	.20	.20
5	A77	50c ultra & multi	.20	.20
6	A54	60c dk brown, sal & gold	.20	.20
7	A104	70c red, black & gold	.20	.20
8	AP8	75c car rose & multi	.25	.25
9	A78	80c blue grn, red & yel	.25	.25
10	A45	90c blue & multi	.25	.25
11	A79	1fr lt & dk green	.30	.30
12	A67	2fr blue & multi	.60	.60
13	A97	3fr olive & multi	.95	.95
14	A3	10fr deep blue	2.75	2.75
		Nos. 1-14 (14)	6.75	6.75

The 20c, 80c and 90c are inscribed in French. The 75c and 10fr carry French inscription at top, English at bottom.
Issued: 60c, 10fr, 4/17/70; 70c, 80c, 90c, 2fr, 9/22/70; others, 10/4/69.

Sea Bed Type
Photogravure and Engraved
1971, Jan. 25   *Perf. 13*

15	A114	30c green & multi	.20	.20

Refugee Type
1971, Mar. 12   **Litho.**   *Perf. 13x12½*

16	A115	50c dp car, dp org & black	.20	.20

Food Program Type
1971, Apr. 13   **Photo.**   *Perf. 14*

17	A116	50c dk purple, gold & grn	.20	.20

UPU Headquarters Type
1971, May 28   **Photo.**   *Perf. 11½*

18	A117	75c green & multi	.30	.30

Eliminate Discrimination Types
1971, Sept. 21   **Photo.**   *Perf. 13½*

19	A118	30c blue & multi	.20	.20
20	A119	50c multicolored	.25	.25

Picasso Type
1971, Nov. 19   **Photo.**   *Perf. 11½*

21	A122	1.10fr carmine & multi	.75	.65

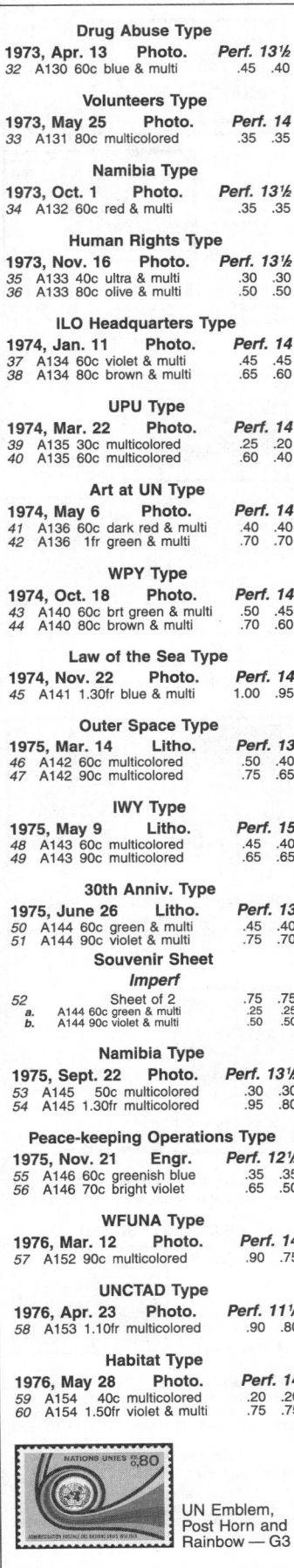

Palais des Nations, Geneva — G2

1972, Jan. 5   **Photo.**   *Perf. 11½*

22	G2	40c olive & multi	.20	.20

Nuclear Weapons Type
1972, Feb. 14   **Photo.**   *Perf. 13½x14*

23	A124	40c yel green, blk, rose & gray	.25	.25

World Health Day Type
Lithographed and Engraved
1972, Apr. 7   *Perf. 13x13½*

24	A125	80c black & multi	.40	.40

Environment Type
Lithographed and Embossed
1972, June 5   *Perf. 12½x14*

25	A126	40c multicolored	.20	.20
26	A126	80c multicolored	.40	.40

ECE Type
1972, Sept. 11   **Litho.**   *Perf. 13x13½*

27	A127	1.10fr red & multi	1.00	.90

Art at UN Type
1972, Nov. 17   **Photo.**   *Perf. 12x12½*

28	A128	40c gold, brown & red	.30	.30
29	A128	80c gold, brown & olive	.60	.60

Disarmament Type
1973, Mar. 9   **Litho.**   *Perf. 13½x13*

30	A129	60c violet & multi	.40	.35
31	A129	1.10fr olive & multi	.85	.75

Nos. 30-31 exist imperf.

Drug Abuse Type
1973, Apr. 13   **Photo.**   *Perf. 13½*

32	A130	60c blue & multi	.45	.40

Volunteers Type
1973, May 25   **Photo.**   *Perf. 14*

33	A131	80c multicolored	.35	.35

Namibia Type
1973, Oct. 1   **Photo.**   *Perf. 13½*

34	A132	60c red & multi	.35	.35

Human Rights Type
1973, Nov. 16   **Photo.**   *Perf. 13½*

35	A133	40c ultra & multi	.30	.30
36	A133	60c olive & multi	.50	.50

ILO Headquarters Type
1974, Jan. 11   **Photo.**   *Perf. 14*

37	A134	60c violet & multi	.45	.45
38	A134	80c brown & multi	.65	.60

UPU Type
1974, Mar. 22   **Photo.**   *Perf. 14*

39	A135	30c multicolored	.25	.20
40	A135	60c multicolored	.60	.40

Art at UN Type
1974, May 6   **Photo.**   *Perf. 14*

41	A136	60c dark red & multi	.40	.40
42	A136	1fr green & multi	.70	.70

WPY Type
1974, Oct. 18   **Photo.**   *Perf. 14*

43	A140	60c brt green & multi	.50	.45
44	A140	80c brown & multi	.70	.60

Law of the Sea Type
1974, Nov. 22   **Photo.**   *Perf. 14*

45	A141	1.30fr blue & multi	1.00	.95

Outer Space Type
1975, Mar. 14   **Litho.**   *Perf. 13*

46	A142	60c multicolored	.50	.40
47	A142	90c multicolored	.75	.65

IWY Type
1975, May 9   **Litho.**   *Perf. 15*

48	A143	60c multicolored	.45	.40
49	A143	90c multicolored	.65	.65

30th Anniv. Type
1975, June 26   **Litho.**   *Perf. 13*

50	A144	60c green & multi	.45	.40
51	A144	90c violet & multi	.75	.70

Souvenir Sheet
Imperf

52		Sheet of 2	.75	.75
a.		A144 60c green & multi	.25	.25
b.		A144 90c violet & multi	.50	.50

Namibia Type
1975, Sept. 22   **Photo.**   *Perf. 13½*

53	A145	50c multicolored	.30	.30
54	A145	1.30fr multicolored	.95	.80

Peace-keeping Operations Type
1975, Nov. 21   **Engr.**   *Perf. 12½*

55	A146	60c greenish blue	.35	.35
56	A146	70c bright violet	.65	.50

WFUNA Type
1976, Mar. 12   **Photo.**   *Perf. 14*

57	A152	90c multicolored	.90	.75

UNCTAD Type
1976, Apr. 23   **Photo.**   *Perf. 11½*

58	A153	1.10fr multicolored	.90	.80

Habitat Type
1976, May 28   **Photo.**   *Perf. 14*

59	A154	40c multicolored	.20	.20
60	A154	1.50fr violet & multi	.75	.75

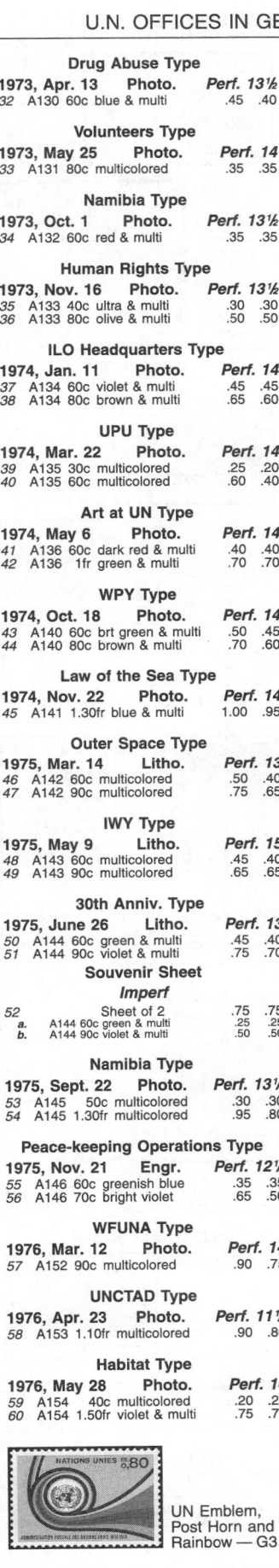

UN Emblem, Post Horn and Rainbow — G3

1976, Oct. 8   **Photo.**   *Perf. 11½*

61	G3	80c tan & multi	.50	.50
62	G3	1.10fr lt green & multi	1.60	1.60

Sheets of 20.

Food Council Type
1976, Nov. 19   **Litho.**   *Perf. 14½*

63	A156	70c multicolored	.50	.45

WIPO Type
1977, Mar. 11   **Photo.**   *Perf. 14*

64	A157	80c red & multi	.65	.60

Drop of Water and Globe — G4

1977, Apr. 22   **Photo.**   *Perf. 13½x13*

65	G4	80c ultra & multi	.55	.50
66	G4	1.10fr dark car & multi	.85	.75

UN Water Conference, Mar del Plata, Argentina, Mar. 14-25.

Hands Protecting UN Emblem — G5

1977, May 24   **Photo.**   *Perf. 14*

67	G5	80c blue & multi	.55	.50
68	G5	1.10fr emerald & multi	.85	.75

UN Security Council.

Colors of Five Races Spun into One Firm Rope — G6

1977, Sept. 19   **Litho.**   *Perf. 13*

69	G6	40c multicolored	.25	.25
70	G6	1.10fr multicolored	.65	.65

Fight against racial discrimination.

Atomic Energy Turning Partly into Olive Branch — G7

1977, Nov. 18   **Photo.**

71	G7	80c dark car & multi	.60	.60
72	G7	1.10fr Prus blue & multi	.80	.80

Peaceful uses of atomic energy.

"Tree" of Doves — G8

1978, Jan. 27   **Litho.**   *Perf. 14½*

73	G8	35c multicolored	.20	.20

Globes with Smallpox Distribution G9

1978, Mar. 31   **Photo.**   *Perf. 12x11½*

74	G9	80c yellow & multi	.60	.50
75	G9	1.10fr lt green & multi	.90	.75

Global eradication of smallpox.

Namibia Type
1978, May 5   **Photo.**   *Perf. 12*

76	A166	80c multicolored	.85	.75

Jets and Flight Patterns — G10

1978, June 12   **Photo.**   *Perf. 14*

77	G10	70c multicolored	.40	.30
78	G10	80c multicolored	.70	.60

International Civil Aviation Organization for "Safety in the Air."

General Assembly, Flags and Globe G11

1978, Sept. 15   **Photo.**   *Perf. 13½*

79	G11	70c multicolored	.50	.45
80	G11	1.10fr multicolored	.90	.75

Technical Cooperation Type
1978, Nov. 17   **Photo.**   *Perf. 14*

81	A169	80c multicolored	.70	.60

Seismograph Recording Earthquake G12

1979, Mar. 9   **Photo.**   *Perf. 14*

82	G12	80c multicolored	.50	.40
83	G12	1.50fr multicolored	.80	.75

Office of the UN Disaster Relief Coordinator (UNDRO).

Children and Rainbow G13

1979, May 4   **Photo.**   *Perf. 14*

84	G13	80c multicolored	.35	.35
85	G13	1.10fr multicolored	.65	.65

International Year of the Child.

Namibia Type
1979, Oct. 5   **Litho.**   *Perf. 13½*

86	A176	1.10fr multicolored	.50	.50

International Court of Justice, Scales — G14

1979, Nov. 9   **Litho.**   *Perf. 13x13½*

87	G14	80c multicolored	.40	.40
88	G14	1.10fr multicolored	.60	.60

International Court of Justice, The Hague, Netherlands.

Economic Order Type
1980, Jan. 11   *Perf. 15x14½*

89	A179	80c multicolored	.85	.75

Women's Year Emblem G15

1980, Mar. 7   Litho.   Perf. 14½x15
90 G15 40c multicolored   .30 .30
91 G15 70c multicolored   .75 .65
UN Decade for Women.

Peace-keeping Operations Type
1980, May 16   Litho.   Perf. 14x13
92 A181 1.10fr blue & green   .85 .75

35th Anniv. Type and

Dove and "35" — G16

1980, June 26   Litho.   Perf. 13
93 G16 40c multicolored   .35 .30
94 A183 70c multicolored   .65 .60

Souvenir Sheet
Imperf
95   Sheet of 2   .70 .60
a.   G16 40c multicolored   .25 —
b.   A183 70c multicolored   .45 —
35th anniv. of the UN.

ECOSOC Type and

Family Climbing Line Graph — G17

1980, Nov. 21   Litho.   Perf. 13½x13
96 G17 40c multicolored   .30 .30
97 G17 70c multicolored   .60 .50

Palestinian Rights Type
1981, Jan. 30   Photo.
98 A188 80c multicolored   .55 .50

Disabled Type of UN, Vienna
1981, Mar. 6   Photo.
99 A190 40c multicolored   .25 .25
100 V4 1.50fr multicolored   1.00 1.00

Art Type
1981, Apr. 15   Photo.   Perf. 11½
101 A191 80c multicolored   .85 .75

Energy Type
1981, May 29   Litho.   Perf. 13
102 A192 1.10fr multicolored   .70 .60

Volunteers Program Type and Symbols of Science, Agriculture and Industry — G18

1981, Nov. 13   Litho.   Perf. 13½x13
103 A194 40c multicolored   .50 .40
104 G18 70c multicolored   1.00 .90

Fight Against Apartheid G19   Flower of Flags G20

1982, Jan. 22   Photo.   Perf. 11½x12
105 G19 30c multicolored   .25 .20
106 G20 1fr multicolored   .80 .70

Human Environment — G21

1982, Mar. 19   Litho.   Perf. 13½x13
107 G21 40c multicolored   .35 .25
108 A199 1.20fr multicolored   1.25 1.00

Outer Space Type and

Satellite Applications of Space Technology G22

1982, June 11   Litho.   Perf. 13x13½
109 A201 80c multicolored   .70 .60
110 G22 1fr multicolored   .90 .90

Conservation and Protection of Nature
1982, Nov. 19   Photo.   Perf. 14
111 A202 40c Bird   .50 .40
112 A202 1.50fr Reptile   1.20 1.00

World Communications Year Type
1983, Jan. 28   Litho.   Perf. 13
113 A204 1.20fr multicolored   1.25 1.00

Safety at Sea Type and

Life Preserver and Radar — G23

1983, Mar. 18   Litho.   Perf. 14½
114 A205 40c multicolored   .40 .40
115 G23 80c multicolored   .80 .80

World Food Program Type
1983, Apr. 22   Engr.   Perf. 13½
116 A207 1.50fr blue   1.25 1.00

Type of UN and

G24

1983, June 6   Litho.   Perf. 14
117 A208 80c multicolored   .55 .55
118 G24 1.10fr multicolored   .95 .90

35th Anniv. of the Universal Declaration of Human Rights G25   G26

Perf. 13½
1983, Dec. 9   Photo.   Engr.
119 G25 40c Homo Humus Humanitas .45 .45
120 G26 1.20fr Right to Create   .95 .90

Intl. Population Conference Type
1984, Feb. 3   Litho.   Perf. 14
121 A212 1.20fr multicolored   1.00 .90

Fishing G27

Women Farm Workers, Africa G28

1984, Mar. 15   Litho.   Perf. 14½
122 G27 50c multicolored   .35 .30
123 G28 80c multicolored   .65 .55
World Food Day.

Valletta, Malta — G29

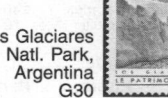

Los Glaciares Natl. Park, Argentina G30

1984, Apr. 18   Litho.   Perf. 14
124 G29 50c multicolored   .55 .50
125 G30 70c multicolored   .75 .70
World Heritage. See Nos. 211-212.

G31   G32

1984, May 29   Photo.   Perf. 11½
126 G31 35c multicolored   .35 .30
127 G32 1.50fr multicolored   1.25 1.00
Refugees.

International Youth Year — G33

1984, Nov. 15   Litho.   Perf. 13½
128 G33 1.20fr multicolored   1.40 1.25

ILO Type of UN and

Turin Center — G34

1985, Feb. 1   Engr.
129 A220 80c Turin Center emblem .70 .60
130 G34 1.20fr U Thant Pavilion 1.10 1.00

UN University Type
1985, Mar. 15   Photo.   Perf. 13½
131 A221 50c Farmer, discussion group .65 .60
132 A221 80c As above   1.00 .90

Postman G35

Doves — G36

1985, May 10   Litho.   Perf. 14
133 G35 20c multicolored   .25 .20
134 G36 1.20fr multicolored   1.60 1.25

40th Anniv. Type
1985, June 26   Photo.   Perf. 12x11½
135 A224 50c multicolored   .60 .50
136 A225 70c multicolored   .90 .75

Souvenir Sheet
Imperf
137   Sheet of 2   2.25 1.50
a.   A224 50c multicolored   .75 —
b.   A225 70c multicolored   1.00 —

UNICEF Child Survival Campaign
Photo. & Engr.
1985, Nov. 22   Perf. 13½
138 A226 50c Three girls   .40 .30
139 A226 1.20fr Infant drinking 1.00 1.00

Africa in Crisis Type
Abstract painting by Alemayehou Gabremedhin.
1986, Jan. 31   Photo.   Perf. 11½
140 A227 1.40fr Mother, hungry children 1.40 1.00

UN Development Program Type
1986, Mar. 14   Photo.   Perf. 13½
141 A228 35c Erosion control   1.60 1.50
142 A228 35c Logging   1.60 1.50
143 A228 35c Lumber transport   1.60 1.50
144 A228 35c Nursery   1.60 1.50
a.   Block of 4, #141-144   6.50 6.00
No. 144a has a continuous design.

Doves and Sun — G37

1986, Mar. 14   Litho.   Perf. 15x14½
145 G37 5c multicolored   .20 .20

UN Stamp Collecting Type
Designs: 50c, UN Human Rights stamp. 80c, UN stamps.
1986, May 22   Engr.   Perf. 12½
146 A229 50c dk green & hn brn   1.00 .75
147 A229 80c dk green & yel org 1.50 1.25

Flags and Globe as Dove — G38

Peace in French — G39

Photo. & Embossed
1986, June 20   Perf. 13½
148 G38 45c multicolored   .75 .60
149 G39 1.40fr multicolored   1.60 1.50
Intl. Peace Year.

WFUNA Anniv. Type
Souvenir Sheet

Designs: 35c, Abstract by Benigno Gomez, Honduras. 45c, Abstract by Alexander Calder (1898-1976), US. 50c, Abstract by Joan Miro (b. 1893), Spain. 70c, Sextet with Dove, by Ole Hamann, Denmark.

1986, Nov. 14   Litho.   Perf. 13x13½
150	Sheet of 4	4.00	3.25
a.	A232 35c multicolored	.55	—
b.	A232 45c multicolored	.75	—
c.	A232 50c multicolored	.95	—
d.	A232 70c multicolored	1.25	—

Trygve Lie Type
Photo. & Engr.

1987, Jan. 30   Perf. 13½
151	A233 1.40fr multicolored	1.25	1.00

Sheaf of Colored Bands, by Georges Mathieu — G40

Armillary Sphere, Palais des Nations — G41

Photo., Photo. & Engr. (No. 153)
Perf. 11½x12, 13½ (No. 153)

1987, Jan. 30
152	G40 90c multicolored	.75	.60
153	G41 1.40fr multicolored	1.40	1.25

Perf. 13½x12½
154	A234 50c Construction	.50	.45
155	A234 90c Finishing interior	1.00	.90

(Litho.)

Fight Drug Abuse Type

1987, June 12   Litho.   Perf. 14½
156	A235 80c Mother and child	.55	.55
157	A235 1.20fr Workers in rice paddy	.90	.80

UN Day Type

Designs: Multinational people in various occupations.

1987, Oct. 23   Litho.   Perf. 14½x15
158	A236 35c multicolored	.40	.35
159	A236 50c multicolored	.65	.65

Immunize Every Child Type

1987, Nov. 20   Litho.   Perf. 15x14½
160	A237 90c Whooping cough	1.50	1.25
161	A237 1.70fr Tuberculosis	2.75	2.25

IFAD Type

1988, Jan. 29   Litho.   Perf. 13½
162	A238 35c Flocks	.40	.35
163	A238 1.40fr Fruit	1.40	1.25

G42

1988, Jan. 29   Photo.   Perf. 14
164	G42 50c multicolored	.90	.70

Survival of the Forests Type

1988, Mar. 18   Litho.   Perf. 14x15
165	A240 50c Pine forest	1.50	1.25
166	A240 1.10fr as 50c	4.00	3.50
a.	Pair, #165-166	5.50	5.00

No. 166a has a continuous design.

Intl. Volunteer Day Type
Perf. 13x14, 14x13

1988, May 6   Litho.
167	A241 80c Agriculture, vert.	.80	.60
168	A241 90c Veterinary medicine	1.00	.90

Health in Sports Type
Perf. 13½x13, 13x13½

1988, June 17   Litho.
169	A242 50c Soccer, vert.	.40	.35
170	A242 1.40fr Swimming	1.40	1.25

Human Rights Declaration Anniv. Type
Photo. & Engr.

1988, Dec. 9   Perf. 12
171	A243 90c multicolored	.75	.60

Souvenir Sheet
172	A243 2fr multicolored	3.00	2.50

World Bank Type

1989, Jan. 27   Litho.   Perf. 13x14
173	A244 80c Telecommunications	1.00	.90
174	A244 1.40fr Industry	2.25	2.00

Peace-Keeping Force Type

1989, Mar. 17   Litho.   Perf. 14x13½
175	A245 90c multicolored	1.00	1.00

World Weather Watch Anniv. Type

Satellite photographs: 90c, Europe under the influence of Arctic air. 1.10fr, Surface temperatures of sea, ice and land surrounding the Kattegat between Denmark and Sweden.

1989, Apr. 21   Litho.   Perf. 13x14
176	A247 90c multicolored	1.25	1.00
177	A247 1.10fr multicolored	2.00	1.75

G43   G44

Photo. & Engr., Photo.

1989, Aug. 23   Perf. 14
178	G43 50c multicolored	1.10	1.00
179	G44 2fr multicolored	3.50	3.00

Offices in Vienna, 10th anniv.

Human Rights Type of 1989

Paintings and sculpture: 35c, *Young Mother Sewing*, by Mary Cassatt. 80c, *The Unknown Slave*, sculpture by Albert Mangones.

1989, Nov. 17   Litho.   Perf. 13½
180	A250 35c multicolored	.35	.30
181	A250 80c multicolored	1.00	.90

Printed in sheets of 12+12 se-tenant labels containing Articles 3 (35c) or 4 (80c) inscribed in French, German or English.

Intl. Trade Center Type

1990, Feb. 2   Litho.   Perf. 14½x15
182	A251 1.50fr multicolored	2.50	2.00

G45

1990, Feb. 2   Photo.   Perf. 14x13½
183	G45 5fr multicolored	4.00	3.25

G46

Fight AIDS Worldwide - G46a

Perf. 13½x12½

1990, Mar. 16   Litho.
184	G46 50c multicolored	1.10	1.00
185	G46a 80c multicolored	1.75	1.25

Medicinal Plants Type
Granite Paper

1990, May 4   Photo.   Perf. 11½
186	A253 90c *Plumeria rubra*	1.10	1.00
187	A253 1.40fr *Cinchona officinalis*	2.25	1.75

UN 45th Anniv. Type

"45," emblem and: 90c, Symbols of clean environment, transportation and industry. 1.10fr, Dove in silhouette.

1990, June 26   Litho.   Perf. 14½x13
188	A254 90c multicolored	1.25	1.00
189	A254 1.10fr multicolored	2.25	1.75

Souvenir Sheet
190	A254 Sheet of 2, #188-189	6.50	5.00

Crime Prevention Type

1990, Sept. 13   Photo.   Perf. 14
191	A255 50c Official corruption	1.50	1.25
192	A255 2fr Environmental crime	3.50	3.00

Human Rights Type of 1989

Paintings: 35c, The Prison Courtyard by Vincent Van Gogh. 90c, Katho's Son Redeems the Evil Doer From Execution by Albrecht Durer.

1990, Nov. 16   Litho.   Perf. 13½
193	A250 35c multicolored	.50	.40
194	A250 90c black & brown	1.40	1.25

Printed in sheets of 12+12 se-tenant labels containing Articles 9 (35c) or 10 (90c) inscribed in French, German or English.

Economic Commission for Europe Type

1991, Mar. 15   Litho.   Perf. 14
195	A256 90c Owl, gull	1.40	1.10
196	A256 90c Bittern, otter	1.40	1.10
197	A256 90c Swan, lizard	1.40	1.10
198	A256 90c Great crested grebe	1.40	1.10
a.	Block of 4, #195-198	6.00	5.00

Namibian Independence Type

1991, May 10   Litho.   Perf. 14
199	A257 70c Mountains	1.50	1.25
200	A257 90c Baobab tree	2.50	2.00

Ballots Filling Ballot Box — G47

UN Emblem — G48

1991, May 10   Litho.   Perf. 15x14½
201	G47 80c multicolored	1.60	1.25
202	G48 1.50fr multicolored	3.00	2.50

G49

Rights of the Child G50

1991, June 14   Litho.   Perf. 14½
203	G49 80c Hands holding infant	1.50	1.25
204	G50 1.10fr Children, flowers	2.25	2.00

Perf. 13½x12½

G51

Banning of Chemical Weapons G52

1991, Sept. 11   Litho.   Perf. 13½
205	G51 80c multicolored	1.75	1.50
206	G52 1.40fr multicolored	3.25	2.75

UN Postal Administration, 40th Anniv. Type

1991, Oct. 24   Litho.   Perf. 14x15
207	A263 50c UN NY #7	1.25	1.00
208	A263 1.60fr UN NY #10	2.75	2.25

Human Rights Type of 1989

Artwork: 50c, Early Morning in Ro...1925, by Paul Klee. 90c, The Marriage of Giovanni Arnolfini and Fiovanna Cenami, by Jan Van Eyck.

1991, Nov. 20   Litho.   Perf. 13½
209	A250 50c multicolored	.90	.80
210	A250 90c multicolored	1.50	1.25

Printed in sheets of 12+12 se-tenant labels containing Articles 15 (50c) and 16 (90c) inscribed in French, German or English.

World Heritage Type of 1984

Designs: 50c, Sagarmatha Natl. Park, Nepal. 1.10fr, Stonehenge, United Kingdom.

1992, Jan. 24   Perf. 13
Size: 35x28mm
211	G29 50c multicolored	1.25	1.00
212	G29 1.10fr multicolored	2.50	2.25

G53

1992, Jan. 24   Perf. 15x14½
213	G53 3fr multicolored	3.75	3.25

Clean Oceans Type

1992, Mar. 13   Litho.   Perf. 14
214	A264 80c Ocean surface, diff.	.90	.90
215	A264 80c Ocean bottom, diff.	.90	.90
a.	Pair, #214-215	1.80	1.60

Printed in sheets of 12 containing 6 #215a.

Earth Summit Type

Designs: No. 216, Rainbow. No. 217, Faces shaped as clouds. No. 218, Two sailboats. No. 219, Woman with parasol, sailboat, flowers.

1992, May 22   Photo.   Perf. 11½
216	A265 75c multicolored	1.15	1.00
217	A265 75c multicolored	1.15	1.00
218	A265 75c multicolored	1.15	1.00
219	A265 75c multicolored	1.15	1.00
a.	Block of 4, #216-219	5.50	4.50

Mission to Planet Earth Type

Designs: No. 220, Space station. No. 221, Probes near Jupiter.

1992, Sept. 4   Photo.   Rouletted 8
Granite Paper
220	A266 1.10fr multicolored	2.50	2.00
221	A266 1.10fr multicolored	2.50	2.00
a.	Pair, #220-221	5.00	4.00

Science and Technology Type

Designs: 90c, Doctor, nurse. 1.60fr, Graduate seated before computer.

1992, Oct. 2   Litho.   Perf. 14
222	A267 90c multicolored	1.50	1.25
223	A267 1.60fr multicolored	3.50	2.75

Human Rights Type of 1989

Artwork: 50c, The Oath of the Tennis Court, by Jacques Louis David. 90c, Rocking Chair I, by Henry Moore.

		1992, Nov. 20	**Litho.**	**Perf. 13½**	
224	A250	50c multicolored		1.00	.90
225	A250	90c multicolored		1.75	1.50

Printed in sheets of 12+12 se-tenant labels containing Articles 21 (50c) and 22 (90c) inscribed in French, German or English.

Aging With Dignity Type

Designs: 50c, Older man coaching soccer. 1.50fr, Older man working at computer terminal.

		1993, Feb. 5	**Litho.**	**Perf. 13**	
226	A270	50c multicolored		.75	.65
227	A270	1.50fr multicolored		2.40	2.25

Endangered Species Type

Designs: No. 228, Pongidae (gorilla). No. 229, Falco peregrinus (peregrine falcon). No. 230, Trichechus inunguis (Amazonian manatee). No. 231, Panthera uncia (snow leopard).

		1993, Mar. 3	**Litho.**	**Perf. 13x12½**	
228	A271	80c multicolored		1.10	.90
229	A271	80c multicolored		1.10	.90
230	A271	80c multicolored		1.10	.90
231	A271	80c multicolored		1.10	.90
a.		Block of 4, #228-231		4.50	4.00

Healthy Environment Type

		1993, May 7	**Litho.**	**Perf. 15x14½**	
232	A272	60c Neighborhood		1.10	1.00
233	A272	1fr Urban skyscrapers		2.25	2.00

Human Rights Type of 1989

Artwork: 50c, Three Musicians, by Pablo Picasso. 90c, Voice of Space, by Rene Magritte.

		1993, June 11	**Litho.**	**Perf. 13½**	
234	A250	50c multicolored		.90	.90
235	A250	90c multicolored		2.00	1.75

Printed in sheets of 12 + 12 se-tenant labels containing Article 27 (50c) and 28 (90c) inscribed in French, German or English.

Intl. Peace Day Type

Denomination at: No. 236, UL. No. 237, UR. No. 238, LL. No. 239, LR.

		Rouletted 12½			
		1993, Sept. 21	**Litho. & Engr.**		
236	A274	60c purple & multi		2.20	1.75
237	A274	60c purple & multi		2.20	1.75
238	A274	60c purple & multi		2.20	1.75
239	A274	60c purple & multi		2.20	1.75
a.		Block of 4, #236-239		9.00	7.50

Environment-Climate Type

Designs: No. 240, Polar bears. No. 241, Whale sounding. No. 242, Elephant seal. No. 243, Penguins.

		1993, Oct. 29	**Litho.**	**Perf. 14½**	
240	A275	1.10fr multicolored		1.50	1.25
241	A275	1.10fr multicolored		1.50	1.25
242	A275	1.10fr multicolored		1.50	1.25
243	A275	1.10fr multicolored		1.50	1.25
a.		Strip of 4, #240-243		6.00	5.00

Intl. Year of the Family Type of 1993

Designs: 80c, Parents teaching child to walk. 1fr, Two women and child picking plants.

		1994, Feb. 4	**Litho.**	**Perf. 13.1**	
244	A276	80c rose violet & multi		1.25	1.00
245	A276	1fr brown & multi		1.75	1.50

Endangered Species Type of 1993

Designs: No. 246, Mexican prairie dog. No. 247, Jabiru. No. 248, Blue whale. No. 249, Golden lion tamarin.

		1994, Mar. 18	**Litho.**	**Perf. 12.7**	
246	A271	80c multicolored		1.10	1.00
247	A271	80c multicolored		1.10	1.00
248	A271	80c multicolored		1.10	1.00
249	A271	80c multicolored		1.10	1.00
a.		Block of 4, #246-249		4.50	4.25

Protection for Refugees Type of 1994

Design: 1.20fr, Hand lifting figure over chasm.

		1994, Apr. 29	**Litho.**	**Perf. 14.3x14.8**	
250	A277	1.20fr multicolored		2.75	2.50

Intl. Decade for Natural Disaster Reduction Type of 1994

Earth seen from space, outline map of: No. 251, North America. No. 252, Eurasia. No. 253, South America. No. 254, Australia and South Pacific region.

		1994, May 27	**Litho.**	**Perf. 13.9x14.2**	
251	A281	60c multicolored		2.00	1.50
252	A281	60c multicolored		2.00	1.50
253	A281	60c multicolored		2.00	1.50
254	A281	60c multicolored		2.00	1.50
a.		Block of 4, #251-254		8.50	7.00

Palais des Nations, Geneva G54

Creation of the World, by Oili Maki — G55

		1994, Sept. 1	**Litho.**	**Perf. 14.3x14.6**	
255	G54	60c multicolored		.75	.65
256	G55	80c multicolored		1.00	.90
257	G54	1.80fr multi, diff.		2.50	2.25

Population and Development Type of 1994

Designs: 60c, People shopping at open-air market. 80c, People on vacation crossing bridge.

		1994, Sept. 1	**Litho.**	**Perf. 13.2x13.6**	
258	A282	60c multicolored		1.25	1.00
259	A282	80c multicolored		1.75	1.50

UNCTAD Type of 1994

		1994, Oct. 28			
260	A283	80c multi, diff.		1.25	1.00
261	A283	1fr multi, diff.		1.75	1.50
a.		Grayish green omitted		—	

UN 50th Anniv. Type of 1995

		1995, Jan. 1	**Litho. & Engr.**		
			Perf. 13.4		
262	A284	80c multicolored		1.40	1.25

Social Summit Type of 1995

		1995, Feb. 3	**Photo. & Engr.**		
			Perf. 13.6x13.9		
263	A285	1fr multi, diff.		1.50	1.25

Endangered Species Type of 1993

Designs: No. 264, Crowned lemur, Lemur coronatus. No. 265, Giant Scops owl, Otus gurneyi. No. 266, Zetek's frog, Atelopus varius zeteki. No. 267, Wood bison, Bison bison athabascae.

		1995, Mar. 24	**Litho.**	**Perf. 13x12½**	
264	A271	80c multicolored		1.40	1.25
265	A271	80c multicolored		1.40	1.25
266	A271	80c multicolored		1.40	1.25
267	A271	80c multicolored		1.40	1.25
a.		Block of 4, 264-267		5.75	5.00

Intl. Youth Year Type of 1995

Designs: 80c, Farmer on tractor, fields at harvest time. 1fr, Couple standing by fields at night.

		1995, May 26	**Litho.**	**Perf. 14.4x14.7**	
268	A286	80c multicolored		1.75	1.50
269	A286	1fr multicolored		2.75	2.00

UN, 50th Anniv. Type of 1995

Designs: 60c, Like No. 663. 1.80fr, Like No. 664.

		Perf. 13.3x13.6			
		1995, June 26		**Engr.**	
270	A287	60c maroon		1.00	.80
271	A287	1.80fr green		3.25	2.50
		Souvenir Sheet			
		Litho. & Engr.			
		Imperf			
272		Sheet of 2, #270-271		4.25	4.25
a.		A287 60c maroon		1.00	1.00
b.		A287 1.80fr green		3.25	3.25

Conference on Women Type of 1995

Designs: 60c, Black woman, cranes flying above. 1fr, Women, dove.

		1995, Sept. 5	**Photo.**	**Perf. 12**	
273	A288	60c multicolored		1.50	1.00
		Size: 28x50mm			
274	A288	1fr multicolored		2.50	1.75

UN People, 50th Anniv. Type of 1995

		1995, Oct. 24	**Litho.**	**Perf. 14**	
275		Sheet of 12		17.50	12.50
a.-l.		A290 30c any single		1.40	1.25
276		Souvenir booklet		20.00	
a.		A290 30c Booklet pane of 3, vert. strip of 3 from UL of sheet		4.75	4.75
b.		A290 30c Booklet pane of 3, vert. strip of 3 from UR of sheet		4.75	4.75
c.		A290 30c Booklet pane of 3, vert. strip of 3 from LL of sheet		4.75	4.75
d.		A290 30c Booklet pane of 3, vert. strip of 3 from LR of sheet		4.75	4.75

WFUNA, 50th Anniv. Type of 1996

		1996, Feb. 2	**Litho.**	**Perf. 13x13½**	
277	A291	80c multicolored		1.50	1.00

The Galloping Horse Treading on a Flying Swallow, Chinese Bronzework, Eastern Han Dynasty (25-220 A.D.) — G56

Palais des Nations, Geneva G57

		1996, Feb. 2	**Litho.**	**Perf. 14½x15**	
278	G56	40c multicolored		.65	.60
279	G57	70c multicolored		1.10	.90

Endangered Species Type of 1993

Designs: No. 280, Paphiopedilum delenatii. No. 281, Pachypodium baronii. No. 282, Sternbergia lutea. No. 283, Darlingtonia californica.

		1996, Mar. 14	**Litho.**	**Perf. 12½**	
280	A271	80c multicolored		1.10	.90
281	A271	80c multicolored		1.10	.90
282	A271	80c multicolored		1.10	.90
283	A271	80c multicolored		1.10	.90
a.		Block of 4, #280-283		4.50	4.25

City Summit Type of 1996

Designs: No. 284, Asian family. No. 285, Oriental garden. No. 286, Fruit, vegetable vendor, mosque. No. 287, Boys playing ball. No. 288, Couple reading newspaper.

		1996, June 3	**Litho.**	**Perf. 14x13½**	
284	A293	70c multicolored		1.00	.75
285	A293	70c multicolored		1.00	.75
286	A293	70c multicolored		1.00	.75
287	A293	70c multicolored		1.00	.75
288	A293	70c multicolored		1.00	.75
a.		Strip of 5, #284-288		5.00	4.75

Sport and the Environment Type of 1996

Designs: 70c, Cycling, vert. 1.10fr, Sprinters.

			Perf. 14x14½, 14½x14		
		1996, July 19		**Litho.**	
289	A294	70c multicolored		1.40	1.25
290	A294	1.10fr multicolored		2.00	1.50
		Souvenir Sheet			
291	A294	Sheet of 2, #289-290		3.00	2.85

Plea for Peace Type of 1996

Designs: 90c, Tree filled with birds, vert. 1.10fr, Bouquet of flowers in rocket tail vase, vert.

		1996, Sept. 17	**Litho.**	**Perf. 15x14½**	
292	A295	90c multicolored		1.75	1.25
293	A295	1.10fr multicolored		2.50	1.50

UNICEF Type of 1996

Fairy Tales: 70c, The Sun and the Moon, South America. 1.80fr, Ananse, Africa.

		1996, Nov. 20	**Litho.**	**Perf. 14½x15**	
294	A296	70c multicolored		1.00	.75
295	A296	1.80fr multicolored		2.50	2.00

Panes of 8 + label.

UN Flag — G58

Palais des Nations Under Construction, by Massimo Campigli G59

		1997, Feb. 12	**Litho.**	**Perf. 14½**	
296	G58	10c multicolored		.20	.20
297	G59	1.10fr multicolored		1.50	1.25

Endangered Species Type of 1993

Designs: No. 298, Ursus maritimus (polar bear). No. 299, Goura cristata (blue-crowned pigeon). No. 300, Amblyrhynchus cristatus (marine iguana). No. 703, Lama guanicoe (guanaco).

		1997, Mar. 13	**Litho.**	**Perf. 12½**	
298	A271	80c multicolored		1.10	.90
299	A271	80c multicolored		1.10	.90
300	A271	80c multicolored		1.10	.90
301	A271	80c multicolored		1.10	.90
a.		Block of 4, #298-301		4.50	4.00

Earth Summit Anniv. Type of 1997

Designs: No. 302, Person flying over mountain. No. 303, Mountain, person's face. No. 304, Person standing on mountain, sailboats. No. 305, Person, mountain, trees. 1.10fr, Combined design similar to Nos. 302-305.

		1997, May 30	**Photo.**	**Perf. 11.5**	
			Granite Paper		
302	A299	45c multicolored		1.50	1.25
303	A299	45c multicolored		1.50	1.25
304	A299	45c multicolored		1.50	1.25
305	A299	45c multicolored		1.50	1.25
a.		Block of 4, #302-305		7.00	5.50
		Souvenir Sheet			
306	A299	1.10fr multicolored		3.50	3.00

Transportation Type of 1997

Air transportation: No. 307, Zeppelin, Fokker tri-motor. No. 308, Boeing 314 Clipper, Lockheed Constellation. No. 309, DeHavilland Comet. No. 310, Boeing 747, Illyushin jet. No. 311, Concorde.

		1997, Aug. 29	**Litho.**	**Perf. 14x14½**	
307	A300	70c multicolored		1.10	.90
308	A300	70c multicolored		1.10	.90
309	A300	70c multicolored		1.10	.90
310	A300	70c multicolored		1.10	.90
311	A300	70c multicolored		1.10	.90
a.		Strip of 5, #307-311		5.50	5.00

No. 311a has continuous design.

Philately Type of 1997

Designs: 70c, No. 146. 1.10fr, No. 147.

		1997, Oct. 14	**Litho.**	**Perf. 13½x14**	
312	A301	70c multicolored		2.00	1.50
313	A301	1.10fr multicolored		2.75	2.50

World Heritage Convention Type of 1997

Terracotta warriors of Xian: 45c, Single warrior. 70c, Massed warriors. No. 316a, like #716. No. 316b, like #717. No. 316c, like Geneva #314. No. 316d, like Geneva #315. No. 316e, like Vienna #230. No. 316f, like Vienna #231.

		1997, Nov. 19	**Litho.**	**Perf. 13½**	
314	A302	45c multicolored		1.50	1.25
315	A302	70c multicolored		2.50	2.25
316		Souvenir booklet		8.50	
a.-f.		A302 10c any single		.35	.35
g.		Booklet pane of 4 #316a		1.40	1.40
h.		Booklet pane of 4 #316b		1.40	1.40
i.		Booklet pane of 4 #316c		1.40	1.40
j.		Booklet pane of 4 #316d		1.40	1.40
k.		Booklet pane of 4 #316e		1.40	1.40
l.		Booklet pane of 4 #316f		1.40	1.40

Palais des
Nations,
Geneva
G60

1998, Feb. 13   Litho.   Perf. 14½x15
317 G60 2fr multicolored   2.75 1.40

Endangered Species Type of 1993

Designs: No. 318, Macaca thibetana (short-tailed Tibetan macaque). No. 319, Phoenicopterus ruber (Caribbean flamingo). No. 320, Ornithoptera alexandrae (Queen Alexandra's birdwing). No. 321, Dama mesopotamica (Persian fallow deer).

1998, Mar. 13   Litho.   Perf. 12½
318 A271 80c multicolored   1.10 .55
319 A271 80c multicolored   1.10 .55
320 A271 80c multicolored   1.10 .55
321 A271 80c multicolored   1.10 .55
  a.   Block of 4, #318-321   4.50 2.25

Intl. Year of the Ocean — G61

1998, May 20   Litho.   Perf. 13x13½
322   G61 Sheet of 12   12.00 10.00
  a.-l. 45c any single   .80   .65

Rain Forests Type
1998, June 19   Perf. 13x13½
323 A307 70c Orangutans   1.00 .50
Souvenir Sheet
324 A307 3fr like #323   6.00 5.00

Peacekeeping Type

Designs: 70c, Soldier with two children. 90c, Two soldiers, children.

1998, Sept. 15   Photo.   Perf. 12
325 A308 70c multicolored   1.25 1.00
326 A308 90c multicolored   1.75 1.50

Declaration of Human Rights Type

Designs: 90c, Stylized birds. 1.80fr, Stylized birds flying from hand.

Litho. & Photo.
1998, Oct. 27   Perf. 13
327 A309 90c multicolored   1.40 1.25
328 A309 1.80fr multicolored   2.75 2.50

Schönnbrun Palace Type

Designs: 70c, #331b, Great Palm House. 1.10fr, #331d, Blue porcelain vase, vert. No. 331a, Palace. No. 331c, The Gloriette (archway). No. 331e, Wall painting on fabric (detail), by Johann Wenzl Bergl, vert. No. 331f, Porcelain stove, vert.

1998, Dec. 4   Litho.   Perf. 14
329   A310 70c multicolored   1.00 .90
330   A310 1.10fr multicolored   1.50 1.25
331   Souvenir
             booklet   7.00
  a.-c.   A310 10c any single   .20   .20
  d.-f.   A310 30c any single   .50   .50
  g.   Booklet pane, 4 #331a   .75   .60
  h.   Booklet pane, 3 #331d   1.50 1.30
  i.   Booklet pane, 3 #331e   1.50 1.30
  j.   Booklet pane, 3 #331f   1.50 1.30
  k.   Booklet pane, 4 #331b   .75   .60
  l.   Booklet pane, 4 #331c   .75   .60

Palais Wilson,
Geneva
G62

1999, Feb. 5   Photo.   Perf. 11½
Granite Paper
332 G62 1.70fr brown red   3.00 2.50

World Heritage, Australia Type

90c, #335e, Kakadu Natl. Park. 1.10fr, #335c, Great Barrier Reef. #335a, Tasmanian Wilderness. #335b, Wet tropics of Queensland. #335d, Uluru-Kata Tjuta Natl. Park. #335f, Willandra Lakes region.

1999, Mar. 19   Litho.   Perf. 13
333 A313 90c multicolored   1.40 1.25
334 A313 1.10fr multicolored   1.50 1.25
335   Souvenir booklet   6.50
  a.-c.   A313 10c any single   .20   .20
  d.-f.   A313 20c any single   .40   .40
  g.   Booklet pane of 4, #335a .55   .40
  h.   Booklet pane of 4, #335d 1.60 1.40
  i.   Booklet pane of 4, #335b .55   .40
  j.   Booklet pane of 4, #335e 1.60 1.40
  k.   Booklet pane of 4, #335c .55   .40
  l.   Booklet pane of 4, #335f 1.60 1.40

Endangered Specied Type of 1993

Designs: No. 336, Equus hemionus (Asiatic wild ass). No. 337, Anodorhynchus hyacinthinus (hyacinth macaw). No. 338, Epicrates subflavus (Jamaican boa). No. 339, Dendrolagus bennettianus (Bennetts' tree kangaroo).

1999, Apr. 22   Litho.   Perf. 12½
336 A271 90c multicolored   1.40 1.25
337 A271 90c multicolored   1.40 1.25
338 A271 90c multicolored   1.40 1.25
339 A271 90c multicolored   1.40 1.25
  a.   Block of 4, #336-339   5.75 5.50

UNISPACE III Type

No. 340, Farm, satellite dish. No. 341, City, satellite in orbit. No. 342, Composite of #340-341.

1999, July 7   Photo.   Rouletted 8
340 A314 45c multicolored   .60   .50
341 A314 45c multicolored   .60   .50
  a.   Pair, #340-341   2.00 1.75

Souvenir Sheet
Perf. 14½
342 A314 2fr multicolored   4.50 3.50
  a.   Ovptd. in sheet margin   9.50 6.00

No. 342a is overprinted in violet blue "PHILEXFRANCE 99 / LE MONDIAL DU TIMBRE / PARIS / 2 AU 11 JUILLET 1999."

UPU Type

Various designs, early 20th century methods of mail transportation, denomination at: No. 343, UL. No. 344, UR. No. 345, LL. No. 346, LR.

1999, Aug. 23   Photo.   Perf. 11¾
343 A315 70c multicolored   1.00 .75
344 A315 70c multicolored   1.00 .75
345 A315 70c multicolored   1.00 .75
346 A315 70c multicolored   1.00 .75
  a.   Block of 4, #343-346   4.00 3.50

In Memoriam Type

Armillary sphere, Palais de Nations. Size of 2fr stamp: 34x63mm.

1999, Sept. 21   Litho.   Perf. 14½x14
347 A316 1.10fr multicolored   1.60 1.25

Souvenir Sheet
Perf. 14
348 A316 2fr multicolored   3.00 2.50

Education Type
Perf. 13½x13¾
1999, Nov. 18   Litho.
349 A317 90c Rainbow over
             globe   1.40 1.10
350 A317 1.80fr Fish, tree,
             globe, book   2.50 2.25

Intl. Year Of Thanksgiving Type
2000, Jan 1   Litho.   Perf. 13¼x13½
351 A318 90c multicolored   1.40 1.25

On No. 351 portions of the design were applied by a thermographic process producing a shiny, raised effect.

Endangered Species Type of 1993

#352, Hippopotamus amphibius (hippopotamus). #353, Coscoroba coscoroba (Coscoroba swan). #354, Varanus prasinus (emerald monitor). #355, Enhydra lutris (sea otter).

2000, Apr. 6   Litho.   Perf. 12¾x12½
352 A271 90c multicolored   1.25 1.00
353 A271 90c multicolored   1.25 1.00
354 A271 90c multicolored   1.25 1.00
355 A271 90c multicolored   1.25 1.00
  a.   Block of 4, #352-355   5.00 4.50

Our World 2000 Type

Winning artwork in Millennium painting competition: 90c, The Embrace, by Rita Adaimy, Lebanon. 1.10fr, Living Single, by Richard Kimanthi, Kenya, vert.

Perf. 13x13½, 13½x13
2000, May 30   Litho.
356 A319 90c multicolored   1.25 1.00
357 A319 1.10fr multicolored   1.50 1.25

55th Anniversary Type

Designs: 90c, Trygve Lie, Harry S Truman, workers at cornerstone dedication ceremony, 1949. 1.40fr, Window cleaner on Secretariat Building, General Assembly Hall under construction, 1951.

2000, July 7   Litho.   Perf. 13¼x13
358 A320 90c multicolored   1.25 .60
359 A320 1.40fr multicolored   2.00 1.00

Souvenir Sheet
360 A320   Sheet of 2,
              #358-359   3.25 1.60

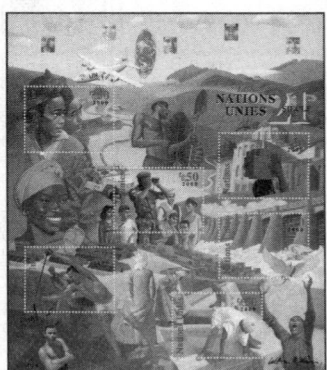

The UN in the 21st Century — G63

No. 361: a, Two people, terraced rice paddy. b, Man carrying bricks on head. c, UN Peacekeeper with binoculars. d, Dam, doves. e, Men with shovels. f, People working on irrigation system.

2000, Sept. 15   Litho.   Perf. 14
361   G63 Sheet of 6   4.00 3.00
  a.-f. 50c any single   .65   .30

World Heritage, Spain Type

1fr, #364b, Walled Town of Cuenca. 1.20fr, #364e, Toledo. #364a, Alhambra, Generalife and Albayzin, Granada. #364c, Aqueduct of Segovia. #364d, Amphitheater of Mérida. #364f, Güell Park, Barcelona.

2000, Oct. 6   Litho.   Perf. 14¾x14½
362   A323 1fr multicolored   1.40 .70
363   A323 1.20fr multicolored   1.60 .80

Souvenir Booklet
364   Booklet   5.50
  a.-c.   A323 10c any single   .20   .20
  d.-f.   A323 20c any single   .30   .30
  g.   Booklet pane of 4, #364a .55   .50
  h.   Booklet pane of 4, #364d 1.25 1.10
  i.   Booklet pane of 4, #364b .55   .50
  j.   Booklet pane of 4, #364e 1.25 1.10
  k.   Booklet pane of 4, #364c .55   .50
  l.   Booklet pane of 4, #364f 1.25 1.10

Respect for Refugees Type

Refugee with cane, four other refugees.

2000, Nov. 9   Litho.   Perf. 13¼x12¾
365 A324 80c multicolored   1.10 .55

Souvenir Sheet
366 A324 1.80fr multicolored   2.40 1.25

Endangered Species Type of 1993

Designs: No. 367, Felis lynx canadensis (North American lynx). No. 368, Pavo muticus (green peafowl). No. 369, Geochelone elephantopus (Galapagos giant tortoise). No. 370, Lepilemur spp. (sportive lemur).

2001, Feb. 1   Litho.   Perf. 12¾x12½
367 A271 90c multicolored   1.25 .60
368 A271 90c multicolored   1.25 .60
369 A271 90c multicolored   1.25 .60
370 A271 90c multicolored   1.25 .60
  a.   Block of 4, #367-370   5.00 —

Intl.
Volunteers
Year — G64

Paintings by: 90c, Ernest Pignon-Ernest, France. 1.30fr, Paul Siché, France.

2001, Mar. 29   Litho.   Perf. 13¼
371 G64 90c multicolored   1.10 .55
372 G64 1.10fr multicolored   1.60 .80

World Heritage, Japan Type

Designs: 1.10fr, #375b, Nara. 1.30fr, #375e, Itsukushima Shinto Shrine. #375a, Kyoto. #375c, Himeji-Jo. #375d, Shirakawa-Go and Gokayama. #375f, Nikko.

2001, Aug. 1   Litho.   Perf. 12¾x13¼
373 A328 1.10fr multicolored   1.40 .70
374 A328 1.30fr multicolored   1.60 .80

Souvenir Booklet
375   Booklet   6.00
  a.-c.   A328 10c any single   .20   .20
  d.-f.   A328 30c any single   .35   .35
  g.   Booklet pane of 4, #375a .50   —
  h.   Booklet pane of 4, #375d 1.50 —
  i.   Booklet pane of 4, #375b .50   —
  j.   Booklet pane of 4, #375e 1.50 —
  k.   Booklet pane of 4, #375c .50   —
  l.   Booklet pane of 4, #375f 1.50

Dag Hammarskjöld Type
2001, Sept. 18   Engr.   Perf. 11x11¼
376 A329 2fr carmine lake   2.50 1.25

UN Postal Administration, 50th Anniv. Types
2001, Oct. 18   Litho.   Perf. 13½
377 A330 90c Stamps, globe   1.10 .55
378 A330 1.30fr Stamps, horns   1.60 .80

Souvenir Sheet
379 A331   Sheet of 2   4.00 2.00
  a.   1.30fr red & light blue, 38mm diameter   1.75 .85
  b.   1.80fr red & light blue, 38mm diameter   2.25 1.10

Climate Change Type

Designs: No. 380, Lizard, flowers, shoreline. No. 381, Windmills, construction workers. No. 382, Non-polluting factory. No. 383, Solar oven, city, village, picnickers.

2001, Nov. 16   Litho.   Perf. 13¼
380 A332 90c multicolored   1.10 .55
381 A332 90c multicolored   1.10 .55
382 A332 90c multicolored   1.10 .55
383 A332 90c multicolored   1.10 .55
  a.   Horiz. strip, #380-383   4.50

Nobel Peace Prize Type
2001, Dec. 10   Litho.   Perf. 13¼
384 A333 90c multicolored   1.10 .55

U.N. OFFICES IN VIENNA, AUSTRIA

For use only on mail posted at the Vienna International Center for the UN and the International Atomic Energy Agency.

100 Groschen = 1 Schilling
100 Cents = 1 Euro (2002)

Catalogue values for all unused stamps in this country are for Never Hinged items.

Stamps are inscribed in English, French or Spanish or are multilingual.

For use only on mail posted at the Vienna International Center for the UN and the International Atomic Energy Agency.

100 Groschen = 1 Schilling

Type of Geneva 1978, UN Types of 1961-72 and

Donaupark, Vienna — V1

Aerial View — V2

Perf. 11½
1979, Aug. 24   Photo.   Unwmk.
Granite Paper

1	G8	50g multicolored	.20	.20
2	A52	1s multicolored	.20	.20
3	V1	4s multicolored	.20	.20
4	AP13	5s multicolored	.25	.25
5	V2	6s multicolored	.35	.30
6	A45	10s multicolored	.50	.45
		Nos. 1-6 (6)	1.70	1.60

No. 6 has no frame.

Economic Order Type
1980, Jan. 11   Litho.   *Perf. 15x14½*
7	A178	4s multicolored	.70	.50

Dove Type
1980, Jan. 11   Litho.   *Perf. 13x13½*
8	A147	2.50s multicolored	.25	.20

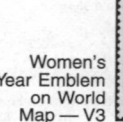

Women's Year Emblem on World Map — V3

1980, Mar. 7   Litho.   *Perf. 14½x15*
9	V3	4s lt green & dk green	.40	.35
10	V3	6s bister brown	.65	.65

UN Decade for Women.

Peace-keeping Operations Type
1980, May 16   Litho.   *Perf. 14x13*
11	A182	6s multicolored	.40	.35

35th Anniv. Types of Geneva and UN
1980, June 26   Litho.   *Perf. 13*
12	G16	4s multicolored	.40	.35
13	A184	6s multicolored	.70	.65

Souvenir Sheet
Imperf
14		Sheet of 2	.55	.55
a.		G16 4s multicolored	.20	—
b.		A184 6s multicolored	.35	—

35th anniv. of the UN.

ECOSOC Types of UN and Geneva
1980, Nov. 21   Litho.   *Perf. 13½x13*
15	A187	4s multicolored	.30	.20
16	G17	6s multicolored	.60	.20

Palestinian Rights Type
1981, Jan. 30   Photo.
17	A188	4s multicolored	.45	.45

Disabled Type of UN and

Interlocking Stitches — V4

1981, Mar. 6   Photo.
18	A189	4s multicolored	.40	.35
19	V4	6s multicolored	.60	.50

Art Type
1981, Apr. 15   Photo.   *Perf. 11½*
20	A191	6s multicolored	.75	.65

Energy Type
1981, May 29   Litho.   *Perf. 13*
21	A193	7.50s multicolored	.70	.60

Volunteers Program Types of UN and Geneva
1981, Nov. 13   Litho.   *Perf. 13½x13*
22	A195	5s multicolored	.50	.45
23	G18	7s multicolored	1.00	.90

"For a Better World" — V5

1982, Jan. 22   Photo.   *Perf. 11½x12*
24	V5	3s multicolored	.35	.30

Human Environment Types of UN and Geneva
1982, Mar. 19   Litho.   *Perf. 13½x13*
25	A200	5s multicolored	.40	.40
26	G21	7s multicolored	.80	.70

Outer Space Type of Geneva
1982, June 11   Litho.   *Perf. 13x13½*
27	G22	5s multicolored	.60	.60

Conservation and Protection of Nature Type
1982, Nov. 19   Photo.   *Perf. 14*
28	A202	5s Fish	.50	.40
29	A202	7s Animal	.70	.60

World Communications Year Type
1983, Jan. 28   Litho.   *Perf. 13*
30	A203	4s multicolored	.40	.40

Safety at Sea Types of Geneva and UN
1983, Mar. 18   Litho.   *Perf. 14½*
31	G23	4s multicolored	.40	.30
32	A206	6s multicolored	.65	.55

World Food Program Type
1983, Apr. 22   Engr.   *Perf. 13½*
33	A207	5s green	.50	.40
34	A207	7s brown	.70	.65

Trade and Development Types of Geneva and UN
1983, June 6   Litho.   *Perf. 14*
35	G24	4s multicolored	.30	.25
36	A209	8.50s multicolored	.75	.65

35th Anniv. of the Universal Declaration of Human Rights
V6   V7

Photogravure and Engraved
Perf. 13½
1983, Dec. 9
37	V6	5s The Second Skin	.50	.40
38	V7	7s Right to Think	.75	.70

Intl. Population Conference Type
1984, Feb. 3   Litho.   *Perf. 14*
39	A212	7s multicolored	.65	.60

Field Irrigation V8

Pest Control V9

1984, Mar. 15   Litho.   *Perf. 14½*
40	V8	4.50s multicolored	.45	.40
41	V9	6s multicolored	.70	.60

World Food Day.

Serengeti Park, Tanzania V10

Ancient City of Shiban, People's Democratic Rep. of Yemen — V11

1984, Apr. 18   Litho.   *Perf. 14*
42	V10	3.50s multicolored	.25	.25
43	V11	15s multicolored	1.40	1.25

World Heritage. See Nos. 125-126.

V12   V13

1984, May 29   Photo.   *Perf. 11½*
44	V12	4.50s multicolored	.55	.45
45	V13	8.50s multicolored	1.40	1.25

Refugees.

International Youth Year — V14

1984, Nov. 15   Litho.   *Perf. 13½*
46	V14	3.50s multicolored	.50	.40
47	V14	6.50s multicolored	.75	.65

ILO Type of Geneva
1985, Feb. 1   Engr.   *Perf. 13½*
48	G34	7.50s U Thant Pavilion	.85	.75

UN University Type
1985, Mar. 15   Photo.   *Perf. 13½*
49	A221	8.50s Rural scene, scientist	.85	.80

Ship of Peace   Sharing
V15   Umbrella
                       V16

1985, May 10   Litho.   *Perf. 14*
50	V15	4.50s multicolored	.35	.30
51	V16	15s multicolored	2.25	2.00

40th Anniv. Type
1985, June 26   Photo.   *Perf. 12x11½*
52	A224	6.50s multicolored	1.00	.90
53	A225	8.50s multicolored	1.50	1.25

Souvenir Sheet
Imperf
54		Sheet of 2	2.75	2.50
a.		A224 6.50s multicolored	.70	.60
b.		A225 8.50s multicolored	.90	.75

UNICEF Child Survival Campaign
Photogravure and Engraved
1985, Nov. 22   *Perf. 13½*
55	A226	4s Spoonfeeding children	.75	.65
56	A226	6s Mother hugging infant	1.40	1.25

Africa in Crisis Type
Abstract painting by Tesfaye Tessema.

1986, Jan. 31   Photo.   *Perf. 11½*
57	A227	8s multicolored	.80	.70

UN Development Program Type
1986, Mar. 14   Photo.   *Perf. 13½*
58	A228	4.50s Developing crop strains	1.50	1.25
59	A228	4.50s Animal husbandry	1.50	1.25
60	A228	4.50s Technical instruction	1.50	1.25
61	A228	4.50s Nutrition education	1.50	1.25
a.		Block of 4, #58-61	6.25	5.50

No. 61a has a continuous design.

UN Stamp Collecting Type
Designs: 3.50s, UN stamps. 6.50s, Engraver.

1986, May 22   Engr.   *Perf. 12½*
62	A229	3.50s dk ultra & dk brown	.50	.35
63	A229	6.50s int blue & brt rose	1.10	1.00

Olive Branch, Rainbow, Earth — V17

Photogravure and Embossed
1986, June 20   *Perf. 13½*
64	V17	5s shown	.90	.80
65	V17	6s Doves, UN emblem	1.10	1.00

Intl. Peace Year.

WFUNA Anniv. Type
Souvenir Sheet
Designs: 4c, White Stallion, by Elisabeth von Janota-Bzowski, Germany. 5s, Surrealistic landscape by Ernst Fuchs, Austria. 6s, Geometric abstract by Victor Vasarely (b. 1908), France. 7s, Mythological abstract by Wolfgang Hutter (b. 1928), Austria.

1986, Nov. 14   Litho.   *Perf. 13x13½*
66		Sheet of 4	4.00	3.75
a.	A232	4s multicolored	.75	.60
b.	A232	5s multicolored	.85	.70
c.	A232	6s multicolored	1.00	.80
d.	A232	7s multicolored	1.25	1.00

Trygve Lie Type
Photogravure and Engraved
1987, Jan. 30   *Perf. 13½*
67	A233	8s multicolored	.80	.75

Shelter for the Homeless Type
Perf. 13½x12½
1987, Mar. 13   Litho.
68	A234	4s Family, homes	.65	.60
69	A234	9.50s Entering home	1.25	1.10

Fight Drug Abuse Type
1987, June 12   Litho.   *Perf. 14½x15*
70	A235	5s Soccer players	.60	.50
71	A235	8s Family	1.00	.85

Donaupark,
Vienna
V18

Peace
Embracing
the
Earth — V19

1987, June 12   *Perf. 14½x15*
72   V18   2s multicolored   .35   .25
73   V19   17s multicolored   1.90   1.50

UN Day Type
1987, Oct. 23   Litho.   *Perf. 14½x15*
74   A236   5s multicolored   .85   .65
75   A236   10s multicolored   1.00   1.00

Immunize Every Child Type
1987, Nov. 20   *Perf. 15x14½*
76   A237   4s Polio   .75   .65
77   A237   9.50s Diphtheria   2.00   1.75

IFAD Type
1988, Jan. 29   Litho.   *Perf. 13½*
78   A238   4s Grains   .50   .40
79   A238   6s Vegetables   1.00   .90

Survival of the Forests Type
Deciduous forest in fall.
1988, Mar. 18   Litho.   *Perf. 14x15*
80   A240   4s multicolored   2.25   2.00
81   A240   6s multicolored   3.25   3.00
   a.   Pair, #80-81   5.50   5.50
No. 81a has a continuous design.

Intl. Volunteer Day Type
Perf. 13x14, 14x13
1988, May 6   **Litho.**
82   A241   6s Medical care,
       vert.   .85   .70
83   A241   7.50s Construction   1.25   1.10

Health in Sports Type
Perf. 13½x13, 13x13½
1988, June 17   **Litho.**
84   A242   6s Skiing, vert.   .85   .75
85   A242   8s Tennis   1.25   1.10

Human Rights Declaration Anniv. Type
Photo. & Engr.
1988, Dec. 9   *Perf. 12*
86   A243   5s multicolored   .50   .40
Souvenir Sheet
87   A243   11s multicolored   1.25   .50

World Bank Type
1989, Jan. 27   Litho.   *Perf. 13x14*
88   A244   5.50s Transportation   1.25   1.10
89   A244   8s Health care, edu-
       cation   1.90   1.75

Peace-Keeping Force Type
1989, Mar. 17   Litho.   *Perf. 14x13½*
90   A245   6s multicolored   .90   .80

World Weather Watch Anniv. Type
Designs: 4s, Helical cloud formation over Italy, the eastern Alps and parts of Yugoslavia. 9.50s, Rainfall in Tokyo, Japan.
1989, Apr. 21   Litho.   *Perf. 13x14*
91   A247   4s multicolored   1.00   .90
92   A247   9.50s multicolored   2.25   2.25

V20

V21

Photo. & Engr., Photo.
1989, Aug. 23   *Perf. 14*
93   V20   5s multicolored   4.50   3.75
94   V21   7.50s multicolored   1.00   .90
Offices in Vienna, 10th anniv.

Human Rights Type
Paintings: 4s, *The Prisoners*, by Kathe Kollwitz. 6s, *Justice*, by Raphael.
1989, Nov. 17   Litho.   *Perf. 13½*
95   A250   4s multicolored   .65   .60
96   A250   6s multicolored   .90   .90
Printed in sheets of 12+12 se-tenant labels containing Articles 5 (4s) or 6 (6s) inscribed in German, English or French.

Intl. Trade Center Type
1990, Feb. 2   Litho.   *Perf. 14½x15*
97   A251   12s multicolored   1.40   1.25

Painting by
Kurt
Regschek
V22

1990, Feb. 2   Litho.   *Perf. 13x13½*
98   V22   1.50s multicolored   .30   .20

Fight
AIDS
Worldwide
V23

Perf. 13½x12½
1990, Mar. 16   **Litho.**
99   V23   5s "AIDS"   1.00   .90
100   V23   11s Stylized figures, ink
       blot   2.25   2.00

Medicinal Plants Type
1990, May 4   **Photo.**   *Perf. 11½*
Granite Paper
101   A253   4.50s *Bixa orellana*   1.00   .90
102   A253   9.50s *Momordica
       charantia*   2.25   2.00

UN 45th Anniv. Type
"45" and emblem.
1990, June 26   Litho.   *Perf. 14½x13*
103   A254   7s multicolored   1.25   1.10
104   A254   9s multi, diff.   2.25   2.00
Souvenir Sheet
105   A254   Sheet of 2, #103-
       104   5.50   4.75

Crime Prevention Type
1990, Sept. 13   Photo.   *Perf. 14*
106   A255   6s Domestic violence   1.25   1.10
107   A255   7s Crime against cul-
       tural heritage   2.50   2.25

Human Rights Type of 1989
Paintings: 4.50s, Before the Judge by Sandor Bihari. 7s, Young Man Greeted by a Woman Writing a Poem by Suzuki Harunobu.
1990, Nov. 16   Litho.   *Perf. 13½*
108   A250   4.50s multicolored   .40   .30
109   A250   7s multicolored   1.25   1.10
Printed in sheets of 12+12 se-tenant labels containing Articles 11 (4.50s) or 12 (7s) inscribed in German, English or French.

Economic Commission for Europe Type
1991, Mar. 15   Litho.   *Perf. 14*
110   A256   5s Weasel, hoopoe   1.25   1.00
111   A256   5s Warbler, swans   1.25   1.00
112   A256   5s Badgers, squirrel   1.25   1.00
113   A256   5s Fish   1.25   1.00
   a.   Block of 4, #110-113   5.50   4.75

Namibian Independence Type
1991, May 10   Litho.   *Perf. 14*
114   A257   6s Mountain, clouds   1.00   .90
115   A257   9.50s Dune, Namib
       Desert   2.50   2.25

V24

1991, May 10   Litho.   *Perf. 15x14½*
116   V24   20s multicolored   3.50   2.75

V25

Rights of
the
Child — V26

1991, June 14   Litho.   *Perf. 14½*
117   V25   7s Stick drawings   1.50   1.25
118   V26   9s Child, clock, fruit   2.00   1.75

V27

Banning of
Chemical
Weapons
V28

1991, Sept. 11   Litho.   *Perf. 13½*
119   V27   5s multicolored   1.25   1.10
120   V28   10s multicolored   2.75   2.25

UN Postal Administration, 40th Anniv. Type
1991, Oct. 24   Litho.   *Perf. 14x15*
121   A263   5s UN NY No. 8   .85   .75
122   A263   8s UN NY No. 5   2.00   1.90

Human Rights Type of 1989
Artwork: 4.50s, Pre-columbian Mexican pottery, c. 600 A.D. 7s, Windows, 1912, by Robert Delaunay.
1991, Nov. 20   Litho.   *Perf. 13½*
123   A250   4.50s black & brown   .75   .75
124   A250   7s multicolored   1.25   1.25
Printed in sheets of 12+12 se-tenant labels containing Articles 17 (4.50s) and 18 (7s) inscribed in German, English or French.

World Heritage Type of 1984
Designs: 5s, Iguacu Natl. Park, Brazil. 9s, Abu Simbel, Egypt.
1992, Jan. 24   Litho.   *Perf. 13*
Size: 35x28mm
125   V10   5s multicolored   1.25   1.10
126   V10   9s multicolored   2.25   2.00

Clean Oceans Type
1992, Mar. 13   Litho.   *Perf. 14*
127   A264   7s Ocean surface, diff.   1.10   1.00
128   A264   7s Ocean bottom, diff.   1.10   1.00
   a.   Pair, #127-128   2.25   2.00
Printed in sheets of 12 containing 6 #128a.

Earth Summit Type
1992, May 22   Photo.   *Perf. 11½*
129   A265   5.50s Man in space   1.30   1.00
130   A265   5.50s Sun   1.30   1.00
131   A265   5.50s Man fishing   1.30   1.00
132   A265   5.50s Sailboat   1.30   1.00
   a.   Block of 4, #129-132   6.50   4.25

Mission to Planet Earth Type
Designs: No. 133, Satellite, person's mouth. No. 134, Satellite, person's ear.

1992, Sept. 4   Photo.   *Rouletted 8*
Granite Paper
133   A266   10s multicolored   2.90   2.50
134   A266   10s multicolored   2.90   2.50
   a.   Pair, #133-134   6.00   5.00

Science and Technology Type
Designs: 5.50s, Woman emerging from computer screen. 7s, Green thumb growing flowers.
1992, Oct. 2   Litho.   *Perf. 14*
135   A267   5.50s multicolored   .80   .75
136   A267   7s multicolored   1.50   1.50

V29   Intl. Center,
Vienna — V30

1992, Oct. 2   Litho.   *Perf. 13x13½*
137   V29   5.50s multicolored   1.00   .90
Perf. 13½x13
138   V30   7s multicolored   1.50   1.50

Human Rights Type of 1989
Artwork: 6s, Les Constructeurs, by Fernand Leger. 10s, Sunday Afternoon on the Island of La Grande Jatte, by Georges Seurat.
1992, Nov. 20   Litho.   *Perf. 13½*
139   A250   6s multicolored   1.00   .85
140   A250   10s multicolored   1.75   1.50
Printed in sheets of 12+12 se-tenant labels containing Articles 23 (6s) and 24 (10s) inscribed in German, English or French.

Aging With Dignity Type
Designs: 5.50s, Elderly couple, family working in garden. 7s, Older woman teaching.
1993, Feb. 5   Litho.   *Perf. 13*
141   A270   5.50s multicolored   1.00   1.00
142   A270   7s multicolored   1.60   1.50

Endangered Species Type
Designs: No. 143, Equus grevyi (Grevy's zebra). No. 144, Spheniscus humboldti (Humboldt's penguins). No. 145, Varanus griseus (desert monitor). No. 146, Canis lupus (gray wolf).
1993, Mar. 3   Litho.   *Perf. 13x12½*
143   A271   7s multicolored   1.25   1.00
144   A271   7s multicolored   1.25   1.00
145   A271   7s multicolored   1.25   1.00
146   A271   7s multicolored   1.25   1.00
   a.   Block of 4, #143-146   5.00   4.00

Healthy Environment Type
1993, May 7   Litho.   *Perf. 15x14½*
147   A272   6s Wave in ocean   1.40   1.25
148   A272   10s Globe   2.25   2.00

V31

1993, May 7   Photo.   *Perf. 11½*
Granite Paper
149   V31   13s multicolored   3.00   2.50

Human Rights Type of 1989
Artwork: 5s, Lower Austrian Peasants' Wedding, by Ferdinand G. Waldmuller. 6s, Outback, by Sally Morgan.
1993, June 11   Litho.   *Perf. 13½*
150   A250   5s multicolored   1.25   1.10
151   A250   6s multicolored   1.25   1.25
Printed in sheets of 12 + 12 se-tenant labels containing Article 29 (5s) and 30 (6s) inscribed in German, English or French.

Intl. Peace Day Type
Denomination at: No. 152, UL. No. 153, UR. No. 154, LL. No. 155, LR.

Rouletted 12½

1993, Sept. 21   Litho. & Engr.

152	A274	5.50s green & multi	2.00	1.75
153	A274	5.50s green & multi	2.00	1.75
154	A274	5.50s green & multi	2.00	1.75
155	A274	5.50s green & multi	2.00	1.75
a.		Block of 4, #152-155	8.50	7.00

Environment-Climate Type

Designs: No. 156, Monkeys. No. 157, Bluebird, industrial pollution, volcano. No. 158, Volcano, nuclear power plant, tree stumps. No. 159, Cactus, tree stumps, owl.

1993, Oct. 29   Litho.   Perf. 14½

156	A275	7s multicolored	1.50	1.25
157	A275	7s multicolored	1.50	1.25
158	A275	7s multicolored	1.50	1.25
159	A275	7s multicolored	1.50	1.25
a.		Strip of 4, #156-159	6.00	5.00

Intl. Year of the Family Type of 1993

Designs: 5.50s, Adults, children holding hands. 8s, Two adults, child planting crops.

1994, Feb. 4   Litho.   Perf. 13.1

160	A276	5.50s blue green & multi	1.25	1.25
161	A276	8s red & multi	2.00	1.75

Endangered Species Type of 1993

Designs: No. 162, Ocelot. No. 163, White-breasted silver-eye. No. 164, Mediterranean monk seal. No. 165, Asian elephant.

1994, Mar. 18   Litho.   Perf. 12.7

162	A271	7s multicolored	1.40	1.25
163	A271	7s multicolored	1.40	1.25
164	A271	7s multicolored	1.40	1.25
165	A271	7s multicolored	1.40	1.25
a.		Block of 4, #162-165	5.75	5.00

Protection for Refugees Type of 1994

Design: 12s, Protective hands surround group of refugees.

1994, Apr. 29   Litho.   Perf. 14.3x14.8

166	A277	12s multicolored	1.50	1.25

V32

V33

V34

1994, Apr. 29   Litho.   Perf. 12.9

167	V32	50g multicolored	.20	.20
168	V33	4s multicolored	.70	.60
169	V34	30s multicolored	5.00	4.00
		Nos. 167-169 (3)	5.90	4.80

Intl. Decade for Natural Disaster Reduction Type of 1994

Earth seen from space, outline map of: No. 170, North America. No. 171, Eurasia. No. 172, South America. No. 173, Australia and South Asia.

1994, May 27   Litho.   Perf. 13.9x14.2

170	A281	6s multicolored	1.90	1.50
171	A281	6s multicolored	1.90	1.50
172	A281	6s multicolored	1.90	1.50
173	A281	6s multicolored	1.90	1.50
a.		Block of 4, #170-173	8.00	7.00

Population and Development Type of 1994

Designs: 5.50s, Women teaching, running machine tool, coming home to family. 7s, Family on tropical island.

1994, Sept. 1   Litho.   Perf. 13.2x13.6

174	A282	5.50s multicolored	1.25	1.10
175	A282	7s multicolored	1.50	1.25

UNCTAD Type of 1994

1994, Oct. 28

176	A283	6s multi, diff.	1.50	1.25
177	A283	7s multi, diff.	1.75	1.50

UN 50th Anniv. Type of 1995

Litho. & Engr.

1995, Jan. 1   Perf. 13.4

178	A284	7s multicolored	1.60	1.25

Social Summit Type of 1995

Photo. & Engr.

1995, Feb. 3   Perf. 13.6x13.9

179	A285	14s multi, diff.	2.50	2.25

Endangered Species Type of 1993

Designs: No. 180, Black rhinoceros, Diceros bicornis. No. 181, Golden conure, Aratinga guarouba. No. 182, Douc langur, Pygathrix nemaeus. No. 183, Arabian oryx, Oryx leucoryx.

1995, Mar. 24   Litho.   Perf. 13x12½

180	A271	7s multicolored	1.25	1.25
181	A271	7s multicolored	1.25	1.25
182	A271	7s multicolored	1.25	1.25
183	A271	7s multicolored	1.25	1.25
a.		Block of 4, 180-183	5.00	5.00

Intl. Youth Year Type of 1995

Designs: 6s, Village in winter. 7s, Teepees.

1995, May 26   Litho.   Perf. 14.4x14.7

184	A286	6s multicolored	1.50	1.25
185	A286	7s multicolored	1.75	1.50

UN, 50th Anniv. Type of 1995

Designs: 7s, Like No. 663. 10s, Like No. 664.

Perf. 13.3x13.6

1995, June 26   Engr.

186	A287	7s green	1.40	1.25
187	A287	10s black	2.00	1.75

Souvenir Sheet

Litho. & Engr.

Imperf

188		Sheet of 2, #186-187	4.50	4.50
a.		A287 7s green	1.75	1.75
b.		A287 10s black	2.50	2.50

Conference on Women Type of 1995

Designs: 5.50s, Women amid tropical plants. 6s, Woman reading, swans on lake.

1995, Sept. 5   Photo.   Perf. 12

189	A288	5.50s multicolored	1.25	1.00

Size: 28x50mm

190	A288	6s multicolored	2.25	1.75

UN People, 50th Anniv. Type of 1995

1995, Oct. 24   Litho.   Perf. 14

191		Sheet of 12	19.00	19.00
a.-l.		A290 3s any single	1.50	1.25
192		Souvenir booklet	21.00	
a.		A290 3s Booklet pane of 3, vert. strip of 3 from UL of sheet	5.00	5.00
b.		A290 3s Booklet pane of 3, vert. strip of 3 from UR of sheet	5.00	5.00
c.		A290 3s Booklet pane of 3, vert. strip of 3 from LL of sheet	5.00	5.00
d.		A290 3s Booklet pane of 3, vert. strip of 3 from LR of sheet	5.00	5.00

WFUNA, 50th Anniv. Type of 1996

Design: 7s, Harlequin holding dove.

1996, Feb. 2   Litho.   Perf. 13x13½

193	A291	7s multicolored	1.35	.65

UN Flag — V35

Abstract, by Karl Korab — V36

1996, Feb. 2   Litho.   Perf. 15x14½

194	V35	1s multicolored	.20	.20
195	V36	10s multicolored	2.00	1.75

Endangered Species Type of 1993

Designs: No. 196, Cypripedium calceolus. No. 197, Aztekium ritteri. No. 198, Euphorbia cremersii. No. 199, Dracula bella.

1996, Mar. 14   Litho.   Perf. 12½

196	A271	7s multicolored	1.30	1.00
197	A271	7s multicolored	1.30	1.00
198	A271	7s multicolored	1.30	1.00
199	A271	7s multicolored	1.30	1.00
a.		Block of 4, #196-199	5.25	4.25

City Summit Type of 1996

Designs: No. 200, Arab family selling fruits, vegetables. No. 201, Woman beside stream, camels. No. 202, Woman carrying bundle on head, city skyline. No. 203, Woman threshing grain, yoke of oxen in field. No. 204, Native village, elephant.

1996, June 3   Litho.   Perf. 14x13½

200	A293	6s multicolored	1.40	1.10
201	A293	6s multicolored	1.40	1.10
202	A293	6s multicolored	1.40	1.10
203	A293	6s multicolored	1.40	1.10
204	A293	6s multicolored	1.40	1.10
a.		Strip of 5, #200-204	7.00	6.25

Sport and the Environment Type of 1996

Designs: 6s, Men's parallel bars (gymnastics), vert. 7s, Hurdles.

Perf. 14x14½, 14½x14

1996, July 19   Litho.

205	A294	6s multicolored	1.25	1.10
206	A294	7s multicolored	1.75	1.50

Souvenir Sheet

207	A294	Sheet of 2, #205-206	3.25	2.75

Plea for Peace Type of 1996

7s, Dove & butterflies. 10s, Stylized dove, diff.

1996, Sept. 17   Litho.   Perf. 14½x15

208	A295	7s multicolored	1.25	1.10
209	A295	10s multicolored	1.90	1.50

UNICEF Type of 1996

Fairy Tales: 5.50s, Hansel and Gretel, by the Brothers Grimm. 8s, How Maui Stole Fire from the Gods, South Pacific.

1996, Nov. 20   Litho.   Perf. 14½x15

210	A296	5.50s multicolored	1.00	.80
211	A296	8s multicolored	1.50	1.25

Panes of 8 + label.

V37

Phoenixes Flying Down (Detail), by Sagenji Yoshida — V38

1997, Feb. 12   Litho.   Perf. 14½

212	V37	5s multicolored	.85	.75
213	V38	6s multicolored	1.00	.90

Endangered Species Type of 1993

No. 214, Macaca sylvanus (Barbary macaque). No. 215, Anthropoides paradisea (blue crane). No. 216, Equus przewalskii (Przewalski horse). No. 217, Myrmecophaga tridactyla (giant anteater).

1997, Mar. 13   Litho.   Perf. 12½

214	A271	7s multicolored	1.50	1.25
215	A271	7s multicolored	1.50	1.25
216	A271	7s multicolored	1.50	1.25
217	A271	7s multicolored	1.50	1.25
a.		Block of 4, #214-217	6.00	5.25

Earth Summit Anniv. Type of 1997

Designs: No. 218, Person running. No. 219, Hills, stream, trees. No. 220, Tree with orange leaves. No. 221, Tree with pink leaves. 11s, Combined design similar to Nos. 218-221.

1997, May 30   Photo.   Perf. 11.5

Granite Paper

218	A299	3.50s multicolored	1.50	1.25
219	A299	3.50s multicolored	1.50	1.25
220	A299	3.50s multicolored	1.50	1.25
221	A299	3.50s multicolored	1.50	1.25
a.		Block of 4, #218-221	6.00	5.25

Souvenir Sheet

222	A299	11s multicolored	2.75	2.75

Transportation Type of 1997

Ground transportation: No. 223, 1829 Rocket, 1901 Darraque. No. 224, Steam engine from Vladikawska Railway, trolley. No. 225, Double-decker bus. No. 226, 1950s diesel locomotive, semi-trailer. No. 227, High-speed train, electric car.

1997, Aug. 29   Litho.   Perf. 14x14½

223	A300	7s multicolored	2.25	2.00
224	A300	7s multicolored	2.25	2.00
225	A300	7s multicolored	2.25	2.00
226	A300	7s multicolored	2.25	2.00
227	A300	7s multicolored	2.25	2.00
a.		Strip of 5, #223-227	12.00	10.00

No. 227a has continuous design.

Philately Type of 1997

Designs: 6.50s, No. 62. 7s, No. 63.

1997, Oct. 14   Litho.   Perf. 13½x14

228	A301	6.50s multicolored	1.25	1.10
229	A301	7s multicolored	1.75	1.50

World Heritage Convention Type of 1997

Terracotta warriors of Xian: 3s, Single warrior. 6s, Massed warriors. No. 232a, like #716. No. 232b, like #717. No. 232c, like Geneva #314. No. 232d, like Geneva #315. No. 232e, like Vienna #230. No. 232f, like Vienna #231.

1997, Nov. 19   Litho.   Perf. 13½

230	A302	3s multicolored	1.25	1.00
231	A302	6s multicolored	2.50	2.00
232		Souvenir booklet	8.00	
a.-f.		A302 1s any single	.35	.30
g.		Booklet pane of 4 #232a	1.25	1.20
h.		Booklet pane of 4 #232b	1.25	1.20
i.		Booklet pane of 4 #232c	1.25	1.20
j.		Booklet pane of 4 #232d	1.25	1.20
k.		Booklet pane of 4 #232e	1.25	1.20
l.		Booklet pane of 4 #232f	1.25	1.20

Japanese Peace Bell, Vienna — V39

Vienna Subway, Vienna Intl. Center — V40

1998, Feb. 13   Litho.   Perf. 15x14½

233	V39	6.50s multicolored	1.00	.90
234	V40	9s multicolored	1.50	1.25

Endangered Species Type of 1993

Designs: No. 235, Chelonia mydas (green turtle). No. 236, Speotyto cunicularia (burrowing owl). No. 237, Trogonoptera brookiana (Rajah Brooke's birdwing). No. 238, Ailurus fulgens (lesser panda).

1998, Mar. 13   Litho.   Perf. 12½

235	A271	7s multicolored	1.50	1.25
236	A271	7s multicolored	1.50	1.25
237	A271	7s multicolored	1.50	1.25
238	A271	7s multicolored	1.50	1.25
a.		Block of 4, #235-238	6.00	5.00

Intl. Year of the Ocean — V41

1998, May 20   Litho.   Perf. 13x13½

239	V41	Sheet of 12	12.00	9.00
a.-l.		3.50s any single	1.00	.75

Rain Forests Type

1998, June 19   Perf. 13x13½

240	A307	6.50s Ocelot	1.00	.90

Souvenir Sheet

241	A307	22s like #240	3.50	3.00

Peacekeeping Type

Designs: 4s, Soldier passing out relief supplies. 7.50s, UN supervised voting.

1998, Sept. 15   Photo.   Perf. 12

242	A308	4s multicolored	.70	.60
243	A308	7.50s multicolored	1.25	1.10

Declaration of Human Rights Type

Designs: 4.50s, Stylized person. 7s, Gears.

Litho. & Photo.

1998, Oct. 27   Perf. 13

244	A309	4.50s multicolored	.80	.70
245	A309	7s multicolored	1.25	1.10

Schönnbrun Palace Type

Designs: 3.50s, #248d, Palace. 7s, #248c, Porcelain stove, vert. No. 248a, Blue porcelain vase, vert. No. 248b, Wall painting on fabric (detail), by Johann Wenzl Bergl, vert. No. 248e, Great Palm House (conservatory). No. 248f, The Gloriette (archway).

1998, Dec. 4   Litho.   Perf. 14

246	A310	3.50s multicolored	.60	.50
247	A310	7s multicolored	1.10	1.00
248		Souvenir booklet	6.50	
a.-c.		A310 1s any single	.25	.25
d.-f.		A310 2s any single	.35	.35
g.		Booklet pane, 4 #248d	1.40	1.25
h.		Booklet pane, 3 #248a	.75	.65
i.		Booklet pane, 3 #248b	.75	.65
j.		Booklet pane, 3 #248c	.75	.65
k.		Booklet pane, 3 #248e	1.40	1.25
l.		Booklet pane, 4 #248f	1.40	1.25

Volcanic
Landscape — V42

1999, Feb. 5   Litho.   Perf. 13x13½

249	V42	8s multicolored	2.00	1.75

World Heritage, Australia Type

Designs: 4.50s, #252d, Uluru-Kata Tjuta Natl. Park. 6.50s, #252a, Tasmanian Wilderness. No. 252b, Wet tropics of Queensland. No. 252c, Great Barrier Reef. No. 252e, Kakadu Natl. Park. No. 252f, Willandra Lakes region.

1999, Mar. 19   Litho.   Perf. 13

250	A313	4.50s multicolored	.75	.65
251	A313	6.50s multicolored	1.10	1.00
252		Souvenir booklet	6.75	
a.-c.		A313 1s any single	.20	.20
d.-f.		A313 2s any single	.35	.35
g.		Booklet pane, 4, #252a	.80	
h.		Booklet pane, 4, #252d	1.40	
i.		Booklet pane, 4, #252b	.80	
j.		Booklet pane, 4, #252e	1.40	
k.		Booklet pane, 4, #252c	.80	
l.		Booklet pane, 4, #252f	1.40	

Endangered Specied Type of 1993

No. 253, Pongo pygmaeus (oran-utan). No. 254, Pelecanus crispus (Dalmatian pelican). No. 255, Eunectes notaeus (yellow anaconda). No. 256, Caracal.

1999, Apr. 22   Litho.   Perf. 12½

253	A271	7s multicolored	1.10	1.00
254	A271	7s multicolored	1.10	1.00
255	A271	7s multicolored	1.10	1.00
256	A271	7s multicolored	1.10	1.00
a.		Block of 4, #253-256	4.50	4.25

UNISPACE III Type

#257, Satellite over ships. #258, Satellite up close. #259, Composite of #257-258.

1999, July 7   Photo.   Rouletted 8

257	A314	3.50s multicolored	.75	.65
258	A314	3.50s multicolored	.75	.65
a.		Pair, #257-258	2.00	1.50

Souvenir Sheet
Perf. 14½

259	A314	13s multicolored	4.50	3.50

UPU Type

Various people, late 20th century methods of mail transportation, denomination at: No. 260, UL. No. 261, UR. No. 262, LL. No. 263, LR.

1999, Aug. 23   Photo.   Perf. 11¾

260	A315	6.50s multicolored	1.10	1.00
261	A315	6.50s multicolored	1.10	1.00
262	A315	6.50s multicolored	1.10	1.00
263	A315	6.50s multicolored	1.10	1.00
a.		Block of 4, #260-263	4.50	4.25

In Memoriam Type

Donaupark. Size of 14s stamp: 34x63mm.

1999, Sept. 21   Litho.   Perf. 14½x14

264	A316	6.50s multicolored	1.10	1.00

Souvenir Sheet
Perf. 14

265	A316	14s multicolored	2.40	2.00

Education Type
Perf. 13½x13¾

1999, Nov. 18   Litho.

266	A317	7s Boy, girl, book	1.25	1.10
267	A317	13s Group reading	2.25	2.00

Intl. Year of Thanksgiving Type

2000, Jan. 1   Litho.   Perf. 13¼x13½

268	A318	7s multicolored	1.25	1.10

On No. 268 portions of the design were applied by a thermographic process producing a shiny, raised effect.

Endangered Species Type of 1993

Designs: No. 269, Panthera pardus (leopard). No. 270, Platalea leucorodia (white spoonbill). No. 271, Hippocamelus bisulcus (huemal). No. 272, Orcinus orca (killer whale).

2000, Apr. 6   Litho.   Perf. 12¾x12½

269	A271	7s multicolored	1.10	1.00
270	A271	7s multicolored	1.10	1.00
271	A271	7s multicolored	1.10	1.00
272	A271	7s multicolored	1.10	1.00
a.		Block of 4, #269-272	4.50	4.25

Our World 2000 Type

Winning artwork in Millennium painting competition: 7s, Tomorrow's Dream, by Voltaire Perez, Philippines. 8s, Remembrance, by Dimitris Nalbandis, Greece, vert.

Perf. 13x13½, 13½x13

2000, May 30   Litho.

273	A319	7s multicolored	1.10	1.00
274	A319	8s multicolored	1.25	1.10

55th Anniversary Type

Designs: 7s, Secretariat Building, unfinished dome of General Assembly Hall, 1951. 9s, Trygve Lie and Headquarters Advisory Committee at topping-out ceremony, 1949.

2000, July 7   Litho.   Perf. 13¼x13

275	A320	7s multicolored	1.10	1.00
276	A320	9s multicolored	1.50	1.25

Souvenir Sheet

277	A320	Sheet of 2, #275-276	2.60	1.40

The UN in the 21st Century — V43

No. 278: a, Farm machinery. b, UN Peacekeepers and children. c, Oriental farm workers. d, Peacekeepers searching for mines. e, Medical research. f, Handicapped child.

2000, Sept. 15   Litho.   Perf. 14

278	V43	Sheet of 6	3.25	2.25
a.-f.		3.50s any single	.50	.30

World Heritage, Spain Type

4.50s, #281c, Aqueduct of Segovia. 6.50s, #281f, Güell Park, Barcelona. #281a, Alhambra, Generalife and Albayzin, Granada. #281b, Walled Town of Cuenca. #281d, Amphitheater of Mérida. #281e, Toledo.

2000, Oct. 6   Litho.   Perf. 14¾x14½

279	A323	4.50s multicolored	.70	.35
280	A323	6.50s multicolored	.95	.50

Souvenir Booklet

281		Booklet	5.50	
a.-c.		A323 1s any single	.20	.20
d.-f.		A323 2s any single	.30	.30
g.		Booklet pane of 4, #281a	.55	.50
h.		Booklet pane of 4, #281d	1.25	1.10
i.		Booklet pane of 4, #281b	.55	.50
j.		Booklet pane of 4, #281e	1.25	1.10
k.		Booklet pane of 4, #281c	.55	.50
l.		Booklet pane of 4, #281f	1.25	1.10

Respect for Refugees Type

Refugee with hat, three other refugees.

2000, Nov. 9   Litho.   Perf. 13¼x12¾

282	A324	7s multicolored	1.10	.55

Souvenir Sheet

283	A324	25s multicolored	3.75	1.90

Endangered Species Type of 1993

Designs: No. 284, Tremarctos ornatus (spectacled bear). No. 285, Anas laysanensis (Laysan duck). No. 286, Proteles cristatus (aardwolf). No. 287, Trachypithecus cristatus (silvered leaf monkey).

2001, Feb. 1   Litho.   Perf. 12¾x12½

284	A271	7s multicolored	1.00	.50
285	A271	7s multicolored	1.00	.50
286	A271	7s multicolored	1.00	.50
287	A271	7s multicolored	1.00	.50
a.		Block of 4, #284-287	4.00	

Intl. Volunteers Year — V44

Paintings by: 10s, Nguyen Thanh Chuong, Viet Nam. 12s, Ikko Tanaka, Japan.

2001, Mar. 29   Litho.   Perf. 13¼

288	V44	10s multicolored	1.40	.70
289	V44	12s multicolored	1.75	.85

World Heritage, Japan Type

Designs: 7s, #290c, Himeji-Jo. 15s, #291f, Nikko. #292a, Kyoto. #292b, Nara. #292d, Shirakawa-Go and Gokayama. #292e, Itsukushima Shinto Shrine.

2001, Aug. 1   Litho.   Perf. 12¾x13¼

290	A328	7s multicolored	1.00	.50
291	A328	15s multicolored	2.10	1.00

Souvenir Booklet

292		Booklet	5.00	
a.-c.		A328 1s any single	.20	.20
d.-f.		A328 2s any single	.25	.25
g.		Booklet pane of 4, #292a	.55	
h.		Booklet pane of 4, #292d	1.10	
i.		Booklet pane of 4, #292b	.55	
j.		Booklet pane of 4, #292e	1.10	
k.		Booklet pane of 4, #292c	.55	
l.		Booklet pane of 4, #292f	1.10	

Dag Hammarskjöld Type

2001, Sept. 18   Engr.   Perf. 11x11¼

293	A329	7s green	1.00	.50

UN Postal Administration, 50th Anniv. Types

2001, Oct. 18   Litho.   Perf. 13½

294	A330	7s Stamps, balloons	1.00	.50
295	A330	8s Stamps, cake	1.10	.55

Souvenir Sheet

296	A331	Sheet of 2	4.00	2.00
a.		7s green & light blue, 38mm diameter	1.00	.50
b.		21s green & light blue, 38mm diameter	3.00	1.50

Climate Change Type

Designs: No. 297, Solar panels, automobile at pump. No. 298, Blimp, bicyclists, horse and rider. No. 299, Balloon, sailboat, lighthouse, train. No. 300, Bird, train, traffic signs.

2001, Nov. 16   Litho.   Perf. 13¼

297	A332	7s multicolored	1.00	.50
298	A332	7s multicolored	1.00	.50
299	A332	7s multicolored	1.00	.50
300	A332	7s multicolored	1.00	.50
a.		Horiz. strip, #297-300	4.00	

Nobel Peace Prize Type

2001, Dec. 10   Litho.   Perf. 13¼

301	A333	7s multicolored	1.00	.50

U.N., KOSOVO

These stamps were issued by the United Nations Interim Administration Mission in Kosovo and the Post & Telecommunications of Kosovo. Service was local for the first two months, with international use to start in mid-May.

100 pfennigs = 1 mark

> **Catalogue values for all unused stamps in this country are for Never Hinged items.**

Peace in
Kosovo — A1

Designs: 20pf, Mosaic depicting Orpheus, c. 5th-6th cent., Podujeve. 30pf, Dardinian idol, Museum of Kosovo. 50pf, Silver coin of Damastion from 4th cent. B.C. 1m, Statue of Mother Teresa, Prizren. 2m, Map of Kosovo.

Perf. 13½x13, 13½x13¼ (30pf)

2000, Mar. 14   Litho.   Unwmk.

1	A1	20pf multicolored	.20	.20
2	A1	30pf multicolored	.30	.30
3	A1	50pf multicolored	.50	.50
4	A1	1m multicolored	1.00	1.00
5	A1	2m multicolored	2.00	2.00
		Nos. 1-5 (5)	4.00	4.00

U.N., WEST NEW GUINEA
Temporary Executive Authority

LOCATION — Western half of New Guinea, southwest Pacific Ocean
GOVT. — Province of Indonesia
AREA — In 1958, the size was 151,789 sq. mi.
POP. — estimated at 730,000 in 1958
CAPITAL — Hollandia

The former Netherlands New Guinea became a territory under the administration of the United Nations Temporary Executive Authority on Oct. 1, 1962. The territory came under Indonesian administration on May 1, 1963. For stamps issued by Indonesia see West Irian in Vol. 6.

100 Cents = 1 Gulden

> **Catalogue values for all unused stamps in this country are for Never Hinged items.**

Netherlands New Guinea Stamps of 1950-60 Overprinted

Perf. 12½x12, 12½x13½

1962-63	Photo.		Unwmk.
1	A4	1c vermilion & yel	.20	.20
2a	A1	2c deep orange	.35	.25
3	A4	5c choc & yel	.40	.25
4a	A5	7c org red, bl & brn vio	.35	.35
5	A4	10c aqua & red brn	.40	.40
6	A5	12c grn, bl & brn vio	.40	.40
7	A4	15c dp yel & red brn	.65	.55
8	A5	17c brn vio & bl	.75	.75
9	A4	20c lt bl grn & red brn	.75	.75
10	A6	25c red	.65	.55
11	A6	30c deep blue	1.25	1.00
12	A6	40c deep orange	1.25	1.00
13	A6	45c dark olive	2.75	2.25
14	A6	55c slate blue	1.40	1.10
15a	A6	80c dl gray vio	11.00	10.00
16	A6	85c dk vio brn	6.50	5.25
17	A6	1g plum	4.25	3.50

Engr.

18a	A3	2g reddish brn	12.50	11.00
19	A3	5g green	6.25	5.25
		Nos. 1-19 (19)	52.05	44.80

The overprint exists in four types:
1) Size 17½mm. Applied locally and sold in 1962 in West New Guinea. Top of "N" is slightly lower than the "U," and the base of the "T" is straight, or nearly so.
2) Size 17½mm. Applied in the Netherlands and sold in 1963 by the UN in New York. Top of the "N" is slightly higher than the "U," and the base of the "T" is concave.
3) Size 14mm. Exists on eight values.
4) Size 19mm. Exists on 1c and 10c.
Types 3 and 4 were applied in West New Guinea and it is doubtful whether they were regularly issued.
Note: Nos. 2a, 4a, 15a and 18a are from the second printing. Nos. 1, 3, 5-14, 16-17 and 19 are from the first printing.
See the *U. S. Specialized Catalogue* for complete listings and values of the UNTEA overprints.

collecting accessories

MINT SHEET BINDERS & PAGES

Keep those mint sheets intact in a handsome, 3-ring binder. Just like the cover album, the Mint Sheet album features the "D" ring mechanism on the right hand side of binder so you don't have to worry about damaging your stamps when turning the pages. Mint Sheet binder available in four colors.

ITEM		RETAIL
MBRD	Mint Sheet Binder - Red	$9.95
MBBL	Mint Sheet Binder - Blue	$9.95
MBGY	Mint Sheet Binder - Gray	$9.95
MBBK	Mint Sheet Binder - Black	$9.95
MS1	Mint Sheet Pages (25 per pack)	$5.95

STOCK PAGE BINDER AND SLIPCASE

Keep all your stock pages neat and tidy with binder and accompanying slipcase. Available in two colors.

ITEM	COLOR	RETAIL
SSBSRD	Red	$19.95
SSBSBL	Blue	$19.95

COVER BINDERS & PAGES

Padded, durable, 3-ring binder will hold up to 100 covers. Features the "D" ring mechanism on the right hand side of album so you don't have to worry about creasing or wrinkling covers when opening or closing binder.
Cover pages sold separately.

ITEM		RETAIL
CBRD	Cover Binder - Red	$7.95
CBBL	Cover Binder - Blue	$7.95
CBGY	Cover Binder - Gray	$7.95
CBBK	Cover Binder - Black	$7.95
T2	Cover Pages Black (25 per pack)	$4.95
T2C	Cover Pages Clear (25 per pack)	$4.95

scott**mounts**

ABU DHABI

ȧ-bü-'thä-bē

LOCATION — Arabia, on Persian Gulf
GOVT. — Sheikdom under British
  protection
POP. — 25,000 (estimated)
CAPITAL — Abu Dhabi

Abu Dhabi is one of six Persian Gulf
sheikdoms to join the United Arab Emirates, which proclaimed its independence Dec. 2, 1971. See United Arab
Emirates.

100 Naye Paise = 1 Rupee
1000 Fils = 1 Dinar (1966)

**Catalogue values for all unused
stamps in this country are for
Never Hinged items.**

Sheik Shakbut bin
Sultan — A1

Palace — A2

Designs: 40np, 50np, 75np, Gazelle. 5r, 10r,
Oil rig and camels.

Perf. 14½

			Unwmk.	
1	A1	5np brt yellow green	1.25	1.50
2	A1	15np brown	1.75	.95
3	A1	20np brt ultra	1.90	.75
4	A1	30np red orange	2.75	1.10
5	A1	40np brt violet	2.75	.55
6	A1	50np brown olive	3.25	1.50
7	A1	75np gray	3.25	2.50

Engr.   Perf. 13x13½

8	A2	1r light green	3.50	.95
9	A2	2r black	6.50	2.50
10	A2	5r carmine rose	13.50	7.00
11	A2	10r dark blue	20.00	10.50
		Nos. 1-11 (11)	60.40	29.80

For surcharges see Nos. 15-25.

Falcon Perched on
Wrist — A3

40np, Falcon facing left. 2r, Falcon facing
right.

1965, Mar. 30   Photo.   Perf. 14½

12	A3	20np chlky blue & brn	7.75	1.75
13	A3	40np ultra & brown	10.00	2.75
14	A3	2r brt blue grn & gray brn	17.00	13.00
		Nos. 12-14 (3)	34.75	17.50

Nos. 1-11 Surcharged

a   b

c

1966, Oct. 1   Photo.   Perf. 14½

15	A1 (a)	5f on 5np	6.75	4.75
16	A1 (a)	15f on 15np	6.75	4.50
17	A1 (a)	20f on 20np	8.00	6.00
18	A1 (a)	30f on 30np	7.50	11.00
19	A1 (b)	40f on 40np	11.00	.75
20	A1 (b)	50f on 50np	17.00	17.00
21	A1 (b)	75f on 75np	17.00	16.00

Engr.   Perf. 13x13½

22	A2 (c)	100f on 1r	13.50	3.00
23	A2 (c)	200f on 2r	15.00	10.50
24	A2 (c)	500f on 5r	25.00	32.50
25	A2 (c)	1d on 10r	32.50	57.50
		Nos. 15-25 (11)	160.00	163.50

Overprint on No. 25 has "1 Dinar" on 1 line
and 3 bars through old denomination.

Sheik Zaid bin Sultan al Nahayan
A4   A6

Dorcas Gazelle — A5

Designs: 5f, 15f, 20f, 35f, Crossed flags of
Abu Dhabi. 200f, Falcon. 500f, 1d, Palace.

Engr.; Flags Litho.   1967, Apr. 1   Perf. 13x13½

26	A4	5f dull grn & red	.20	.20
27	A4	15f dk brown & red	.30	.20
28	A4	20f dk blue & red	.30	.20
29	A4	35f purple & red	.60	.20

Engr.

30	A4	40f green	.75	.20
31	A4	50f brown	1.00	.30
32	A4	60f blue	1.25	.30
33	A4	100f car rose	2.25	.40

Litho.

34	A5	125f green & brn ol	2.75	1.25
35	A5	200f sky blue & brn	4.50	2.75
36	A5	500f org & brt pur	11.00	5.00
37	A5	1d green & vio bl	25.00	9.00
		Nos. 26-37 (12)	49.90	20.00

In 1969, the 15f was surcharged "25" in
Arabic in black with a numbering machine.

1967, Aug. 6   Photo.   Perf. 14½x14

38	A6	40f Prussian green	1.00	.75
39	A6	50f brown	1.25	.60
40	A6	60f blue	2.25	.75
41	A6	100f carmine rose	5.50	1.40
		Nos. 38-41 (4)	10.00	3.50

Human
Rights
Flame
and
Sheik
Zaid
A6a

Perf. 14½x14   1968, Apr. 1   Photo.   Unwmk.
Emblem in Red and Green

42	A6a	35f peacock bl & gold	1.25	.50
43	A6a	60f dk blue & gold	2.00	.75
44	A6a	150f dk brown & gold	4.75	1.75
		Nos. 42-44 (3)	8.00	3.00

International Human Rights Year.

Sheik
Zaid
and
Coat
of
Arms
A7

Perf. 14x14½   1968, Aug. 6   Photo.   Unwmk.

45	A7	5f multicolored	.45	.20
46	A7	10f multicolored	.70	.20
47	A7	100f multicolored	4.25	1.00
48	A7	125f multicolored	6.00	1.60
		Nos. 45-48 (4)	11.40	3.00

Accession of Sheik Zaid, 2nd anniversary.

Abu Dhabi Airport — A8

5f, Buildings under construction and earth-
moving equipment. 35f, New bridge and falcon. Each stamp shows different portrait of
Sheik Zaid.

Perf. 12, 12½x13 (10f)   1969, Mar. 28   Litho.
Size: 5f, 35f, 59x34mm

49	A8	5f multicolored	1.50	.25
50	A8	10f multicolored	3.00	.60
51	A8	35f multicolored	9.25	5.00
		Nos. 49-51 (3)	13.75	5.85

Issued to publicize progress made in Abu
Dhabi during preceding 2 years.

Sheik
Zaid and
Abu
Dhabi
Petroleum
Co. — A9

Designs: 60f, Abu Dhabi Marine Areas drilling platform and helicopter. 125f, Zakum Field
separator at night. 200f, Tank farm.

1969, Aug. 6   Litho.   Perf. 14x13½

52	A9	35f olive grn & multi	1.00	.25
53	A9	60f yel brown & multi	1.75	.65
54	A9	125f multicolored	4.00	1.10
55	A9	200f red brown & multi	7.25	4.00
		Nos. 52-55 (4)	14.00	6.00

Accession of Sheik Zaid, 3rd anniversary.

Sheik Zaid — A10

Sheik
Zaid
and
Stallion
A11

5f, 25f, 60f, 90f, Oval frame around portrait.
150f, Gazelle and Sheik. 500f, Fort Jahili and
Sheik. 1d, Grand Mosque and Sheik.

1970-71   Litho.   Perf. 14

56	A10	5f lt green & multi	.25	.20
57	A10	10f bister & multi	.35	.20
58	A10	25f lilac & multi	.65	.20
59	A10	35f violet & multi	.85	.30
60	A10	50f sepia & multi	1.25	.40
61	A10	60f violet & multi	1.40	.45
62	A10	70f rose red & multi	2.00	.65
63	A10	90f car rose & multi	3.00	.70
64	A11	125f multi ('71)	5.00	.90
65	A11	150f multi ('71)	6.00	2.00
66	A11	500f multi ('71)	17.50	5.00
67	A11	1d multi ('71)	30.00	9.00
		Nos. 56-67 (12)	68.25	20.00

For surcharge see No. 80.

Sheik Zaid and Mt. Fuji — A12

1970, Aug.   Litho.   Perf. 13½x13

68	A12	25f multicolored	2.00	1.00
69	A12	35f multicolored	3.50	1.25
70	A12	60f multicolored	6.50	1.75
		Nos. 68-70 (3)	12.00	4.00

Issued to publicize EXPO '70 International
Exhibition, Osaka, Japan, Mar. 15-Sept. 13.

Abu
Dhabi
Airport
A13

Designs: 60f, Airport entrance. 150f, Aerial
view of Abu Dhabi Town, vert.

Perf. 14x13½, 13½x14   1970, Sept. 22   Litho.

71	A13	25f multicolored	1.50	.50
72	A13	60f multicolored	4.00	1.25
73	A13	150f multicolored	9.00	3.00
		Nos. 71-73 (3)	14.50	4.75

Accession of Sheik Zaid, 4th anniversary.

Gamal Abdel Nasser — A14

1971, May 3   Litho.   Perf. 14

74	A14	25f deep rose & blk	3.50	2.00
75	A14	35f rose violet & blk	5.50	3.00

In memory of Gamal Abdel Nasser (1918-
1970), President of UAR.

Scout
Cars
A15

Designs: 60f, Patrol boat. 125f, Armored car
in desert. 150f, Meteor jet fighters.

1971, Aug. 6   Litho.   Perf. 13

76	A15	35f multicolored	2.50	.80
77	A15	60f multicolored	3.50	1.10
78	A15	125f multicolored	7.25	1.60
79	A15	150f multicolored	9.25	2.50
		Nos. 76-79 (4)	22.50	6.00

Accession of Sheik Zaid, 5th anniversary.

5 فلوس

No. 60 Surcharged
in Green

5 Fils

1971, Dec. 8   *Perf. 14*
80   A10   5f on 50f multi   70.00 47.50

Dome of the Rock,
Jerusalem — A16

Different views of Dome of the Rock.

1972, June 3   *Perf. 13*
81   A16   35f lt violet & multi   8.50   2.00
82   A16   60f lt violet & multi   12.50   4.50
83   A16 125f lilac & multi   24.00   5.50
     Nos. 81-83 (3)   45.00 10.00

Nos. 80-83 were issued after Abu Dhabi joined the United Arab Emirates Dec. 2, 1971. Stamps of UAE replaced those of Abu Dhabi. UAE Nos. 1-12 were used only in Abu Dhabi except the 10f and 25f which were issued later in Dubai and Sharjah.

ADEN

ˈä-dən

LOCATION — Southern Arabia
GOVT. — British colony and
    protectorate
AREA — 112,075 sq. mi.
POP. — 220,000 (est. 1964)
CAPITAL — Aden

Aden used India stamps before 1937. In January, 1963, the colony of Aden (the port) and the sheikdoms and emirates of the Western Aden Protectorate formed the Federation of South Arabia. This did not include the Eastern Aden Protectorate with Kathiri and Qu'aiti States. Stamps of Aden, except those of Kathiri and Qu'aiti States, were replaced Apr. 1, 1965, by those of the Federation of South Arabia. See South Arabia and People's Democratic Republic of Yemen, Vol. 6.

12 Pies = 1 Anna
16 Annas = 1 Rupee
100 Cents = 1 Shilling (1951)

Catalogue values for unused stamps in this country are for Never Hinged items.

Dhow — A1

1937, Apr. 1   Engr.   Wmk. 4
                Perf. 13x11½
1   A1   ½a lt green   3.25   1.25
2   A1   9p dark green   3.25   1.50
3   A1   1a black brown   3.25   .65
4   A1   2a red   3.25   1.75
5   A1   2½a blue   3.25   .75
6   A1   3a carmine rose   8.00   5.75
7   A1   3½a gray blue   6.75   1.75
8   A1   8a rose lilac   18.00   5.00
9   A1   1r brown   26.00   5.50
10 A1   2r orange yellow   42.50 14.50

11 A1   5r rose violet   80.00 57.50
12 A1 10r olive green   200.00 240.00
     Nos. 1-12 (12)   397.50 335.90
     Set, hinged   250.00

Common Design Types
pictured following the introduction.

Coronation Issue
Common Design Type

1937, May 12   *Perf. 13½x14*
13   CD302   1a black brown   .80   .75
14   CD302   2½a blue   .95   1.35
15   CD302   3½a gray blue   1.25   2.40
     Nos. 13-15 (3)   3.00   4.50

Aidrus
Mosque — A2

Designs: ¾a, 5r, Camel Corpsman. 1a, 2r, Aden Harbor. 1½a, 1r, Adenese dhow. 2½a, 8a, Mukalla. 3a, 14a, 10r, Capture of Aden, 1839.

1939-48   Engr.   Wmk. 4   Perf. 12½
16   A2   ½a green   .45   .45
17   A2   ¾a red brown ('46) 1.00   1.00
18   A2   1a brt lt blue   .20   .25
19   A2   1½a red   .50   .55
20   A2   2a dark brown ('46) .20   .25
21   A2   2½a brt ultra   .35   .30
22   A2   3a rose car & dk brn .55   .25
23   A2   8a orange   .50   .40
23A A2   14a lt bl & brn blk
              ('45)   2.00   1.00
24   A2   1r bright green   2.00   1.40
25   A2   2r dp mag & bl blk
              ('44)   4.25   1.90
26   A2   5r dp ol & lake brn
              ('44)   10.50   7.25
27   A2   10r brt vio & brt sep 27.50 11.00
     Nos. 16-27 (13)   50.00 26.00

For shades, see the *Scott Classic Specialized Catalogue*.

Peace Issue
Common Design Type
Perf. 13½x14

1946, Oct. 15   Engr.   Wmk. 4
28   CD303   1½a carmine   .20   .85
29   CD303   2½a deep blue   .30   .30

Return to peace at end of World War II.

Silver Wedding Issue
Common Design Types

1949, Jan. 17   Photo.   Perf. 14x14½
30   CD304   1½a scarlet   .40   .75
    Engraved; Name Typographed
               Perf. 11½x11
31   CD305   10r purple   25.00 27.50

25th anniv. of the marriage of King George VI and Queen Elizabeth.

UPU Issue
Common Design Types
Surcharged with New Values
in Annas and Rupees
Engr.; Name typo. on Nos. 33-34
1949, Oct. 10   Perf. 13½, 11x11½
32   CD306   2½a on 20c dp ultra .60   1.25
33   CD307   3a on 30c dp car   1.40   1.25
34   CD308   8a on 50c org   1.25   1.25
35   CD309   1r on 1sh blue   1.75   2.25
     Nos. 32-35 (4)   5.00   6.00

75th anniv. of the formation of the UPU.

Nos. 18 and 20-27 Surcharged with
New Values in Black or Carmine
1951, Oct. 1   Wmk. 4   Perf. 12½
36   A2   5c on 1a   .20   .35
37   A2   10c on 2a   .20   .40
38   A2   15c on 2½a   .20   1.10
 a.   Double surcharge   650.00
39   A2   20c on 3a   .25   .35
40   A2   30c on 8a (C)   .25   .60
41   A2   50c on 8a   .25   .30
42   A2   70c on 14a   1.50   1.40
43   A2   1sh on 1r   .40   .25
44   A2   2sh on 2r   6.75   2.50
45   A2   5sh on 5r   14.00   7.75
46   A2 10sh on 10r   21.00 10.00
     Nos. 36-46 (11)   45.00 25.00

Surcharge on No. 40 includes 2 bars.

Coronation Issue
Common Design Type

1953, June 2   Engr.   Perf. 13½x13
47   CD312   15c dark grn & black   .45   .35

Minaret — A10   Camel
                  Transport — A11

15c, Crater. 25c, Mosque. 35c, Dhow. 50c, Map. 70c, Salt works. 1sh, Dhow building. 1sh, 25c, Colony Badge. 2sh, Aden Protectorate levy. 5sh, Crater Pass. 10sh, Tribesman. 20sh, Aden in 1572.

Perf. 12, 12x13½ ('56)
1953-59   Engr.   Wmk. 4
        Size: 29x23, 23x29mm
48   A10   5c grn, perf
              12x13½
              ('56)   .20   .20
 a.   Perf. 12 ('55)   .20   .20
 b.   5c bluish grn, perf 12x13½
              ('56)   .50 2.50
49   A11 10c orange   .20   .20
 a.   10c vermilion ('55)   .20   .35
50   A11 15c blue green   .90   .50
 a.   15c grayish grn ('59)   4.25 5.00
51   A11 25c carmine   .60   .35
 a.   25c deep rose red ('56) 2.25 1.00
52   A10 35c ultra, perf 12 1.75 1.75
 a.   35c dp bl, perf 12x13½ ('58) 3.00 2.00
 b.   35c vio bl, perf 12x13½ ('59) 7.50 2.50
53   A10 50c blue, perf 12   .20   .20
 a.   As "b," perf 12x13½ ('56) .55 .20
 b.   50c deep bl, perf 12 ('55) 1.00 1.50
54   A10 70c gray, perf 12   .20   .20
 a.   As "b," perf 12x13½ ('56) .60 .20
 b.   70c grayish blk, perf 12 ('54) 1.00 .35
55   A11   1sh pur & sepia   .20   .20
55A A11   1sh vio & black
              ('55)   1.10   .20
56   A10 1sh25c blk & lt blue
              ('56)   1.65   .50
57   A10   2sh car rose &
              sep   .90   .40
57A A10   2sh car & black
              ('56)   4.25   .40
58   A10   5sh blue & sepia   .90   .40
58A A10   5sh dk blue & blk
              ('56)   3.75   .50
59   A10 10sh olive & sepia 1.25 6.75
60   A10 10sh ol gray & blk
              ('54)   9.50 1.10

        Size: 36½x27mm
        Perf. 13½x13
61   A11 20sh rose vio & dk
              brn   4.75 8.50
61A A11 20sh lt vio & blk
              ('57)   30.00 12.00
     Nos. 48-61A (18)   62.30 34.35

No. 60 has heavier shading on tribesman's lower garment than No. 59.
See #66-75. For overprints see #63-64.

Type of 1953
Inscribed: "Royal Visit 1954"
1954, Apr. 27   *Perf. 12*
62   A11   1sh purple & sepia   .40   .40

Nos. 50 & 56 Overprinted in Red

No. 63

No. 64

1959, Jan. 26   Perf. 12, 12x13½
63   A11   15c dark blue green   .30   .30
64   A10   1sh25c blk & light blue .80 .80

Introduction of a revised constitution.

Freedom from Hunger Issue
Common Design Type
Perf. 14x14½
1963, June 4   Photo.   Wmk. 314
65   CD314   1sh25c green   1.50 1.00

Types of 1953-57
Perf. 12x13½, 12 (#67-69, 73)
1964-65   Engr.   Wmk. 314
66   A10   5c green ('65)   .50 3.00
67   A11   10c orange   .25   .75
68   A11   15c Prus green   .30 2.75
69   A11   25c carmine   .50   .35
70   A10   35c dk blue   2.50 2.50
71   A10   50c dull blue   1.00   .25
72   A10   70c gray   1.25 1.50
73   A11   1sh vio & black   8.00 2.00
74   A10 1sh25c blk & lt blue   8.00 1.90
75   A10   2sh car & blk ('65)   5.00 20.00
     Nos. 66-75 (10)   27.30 35.00

KATHIRI STATE OF SEIYUN

LOCATION — In Eastern Aden
    Protectorate
GOVT. — Sultanate
CAPITAL — Seiyun

The stamps of the Kathiri State of Seiyun were valid for use throughout Aden. Used copies generally bear Aden GPO or Aden Camp cancels. Examples with cancels from offices in the Eastern Protectorate command a premium.

Sultan Ja'far   Seiyun — A2
bin Mansur al
Kathiri — A1

Minaret at
Tarim — A3

Designs: 2½a, Mosque at Seiyun. 3a, Palace at Tarim. 8a, Mosque at Seiyun, horiz. 1r, South Gate, Tarim. 2r, Kathiri House. 5r, Mosque at Tarim.

1942   Engr.   Wmk. 4   Perf. 13⅜x14
1   A1   ½a dark green   .20   .45
2   A1   ¾a copper brown   .30   .60
3   A1   1a deep blue   .40   .45
        Perf. 13x11½, 11½x13
4   A2   1½a carmine   .40   .50
5   A3   2a sepia brown   .30   .75
6   A2   2½a deep blue   .70 1.00
7   A2   3a dk car rose & dull
              brn   1.25 1.75
8   A2   8a orange red   .55   .90
9   A3   1r green   .90 1.50
10 A2   2r rose vio & dk blue 6.50 9.50
11 A3   5r gray green & fawn 17.50 12.50
     Nos. 1-11 (11)   30.00 29.90

For surcharges see Nos. 20-27.

Nos. 4, 6 Ovptd. in Black or Red:

a

b

Perf. 13x11½, 11½x13
1946, Oct. 15   **Wmk. 4**
12 A2 (a) 1½a dark car rose   .20 .50
13 A3 (b) 2½a deep blue (R)   .25 .25
a. Inverted overprint   425.00
b. Double overprint   —

Victory of the Allied Nations in WWII.
All examples of No. 13b have the 2nd overprint almost directly over the 1st.

Silver Wedding Issue
Common Design Types
1949, Jan. 17   Photo.   Perf. 14x14½
14 CD304 1½a scarlet   .35 2.00
Engraved; Name Typo.
Perf. 11½x11
15 CD305 5r green   13.50 10.00
25th anniv. of the marriage of King George VI and Queen Elizabeth.

UPU Issue
Common Design Types
Surcharged with New Values in Annas and Rupees
Engr.; Name Typo. on Nos. 17-18
1949, Oct. 10   Perf. 13½, 11x11½
16 CD306 2½a on 20c dp ultra   .25 .50
17 CD307 3a on 30c dp car   1.00 .65
18 CD308 8a on 50c orange   .55 .75
19 CD309 1r on 1sh blue   1.00 1.10
       Nos. 16-19 (4)   2.80 3.00
75th anniv. of the formation of the UPU.

Nos. 3 and 5-11 Surcharged with New Values in Carmine or Black
Perf. 14, 13x11½, 11½x13
1951, Oct. 1   Engr.   Wmk. 4
20 A1 5c on 1a (C)   .20 .20
21 A3 10c on 2a   .30 .20
22 A3 15c on 2½a   .50 .50
23 A2 20c on 3a   .25 .60
24 A2 50c on 8a   .30 .25
25 A3 1sh on 1r   1.90 .75
26 A2 2sh on 2r   3.50 15.00
27 A3 5sh on 5r   14.50 27.50
       Nos. 20-27 (8)   21.45 45.00

Coronation Issue
Common Design Type
1953, June 2   Perf. 13½x13
28 CD312 15c dk green & blk   .30 .50

Sultan Hussein A10

Qarn Adh Dhabi A11

15c, Seiyun scene, horiz. 25c, Minaret at Tarim. 35c, Mosque at Seiyun. 50c, Palace at Tarim, horiz. 1sh, Mosque at Seiyun, horiz. 2sh, South Gate, Tarim. 5sh, Kathiri house, horiz. 10sh, Mosque entrance, Tarim.

1954, Jan. 15   Engr.   Perf. 12½
29 A10 5c dark brown   .20 .20
30 A10 10c deep blue   .20 .20
Perf. 13x11½, 11½x13
31 A11 15c dk blue green   .20 .20
32 A11 25c dk car rose   .20 .20
33 A11 35c deep blue   .20 .20
34 A11 50c dk car rose & dk brn .20 .20
35 A11 1sh deep orange   .20 .20
36 A11 2sh gray green   3.25 1.25
37 A11 5sh vio & dk blue   5.25 3.50
38 A11 10sh vio & yel brn   5.25 5.25
       Nos. 29-38 (10)   15.15 11.40

Perf. 11½x13, 13x11½
1964, July 1   Wmk. 314
Designs: 1sh25c, Seiyun, horiz. 1sh50c, View of Gheil Omer, horiz.
39 A11 70c black   1.50 1.00
40 A11 1sh25c bright green   1.50 4.50
41 A11 1sh50c purple   1.50 4.50
       Nos. 39-41 (3)   4.50 10.00

QUAITI STATE OF SHIHR AND MUKALLA

LOCATION — In Eastern Aden Protectorate
GOVT. — Sultanate
CAPITAL — Mukalla

The stamps of the Quaiti State of Shihr and Mukalla were valid for use throughout Aden. Used copies generally bear Aden GPO or Aden Camp cancels. Examples with cancels from offices in the Eastern Protectorate command a premium.

Sultan Sir Saleh bin Ghalib al Qu'aiti — A1

Mukalla Harbor — A2

Buildings at Shibam — A3

2a, Gateway of Shihr. 3a, Outpost of Mukalla. 8a, View of 'Einat. 1r, Governor's Castle, Du'an. 3r, Mosque in Hureidha. 5r, Meshhed.

1942   Engr.   Wmk. 4   Perf. 13¾x14
1   A1 ½a blue green   .50 .40
2   A1 ¾a copper brown   .50 .30
3   A1 1a deep blue   .60 .55
Perf. 13x11½, 11½x13
4   A2 1½a deep carmine   .80 .40
5   A2 2a black brown   1.10 .90
6   A3 2½a deep blue   .40 .30
7   A2 3a dk car rose & dl brn .75 .55
8   A3 8a orange red   .50 .40
9   A3 1r green   2.40 1.75
10 A3 2r rose vio & dk blue 9.75 7.50
11 A3 5r gray green & fawn 13.50 10.00
       Nos. 1-11 (11)   30.80 23.05
For surcharges see Nos. 20-27.

Nos. 4, 6 Ovptd. in Black or Carmine like Kathiri Nos. 12-13
1946, Oct. 15   Perf. 11½x13, 13x11½
12 A2 (b) 1½a dk car rose   .20 .50
13 A3 (a) 2½a deep blue (C)   .25 .20
Victory of the Allied Nations in WWII.

Silver Wedding Issue
Common Design Types
1949, Jan. 17   Photo.   Perf. 14x14½
14 CD304 1½a scarlet   .45 2.25
Engraved; Name Typo.
Perf. 11½x11
15 CD305 5r green   14.00 10.50
25th anniv. of the marriage of King George VI and Queen Elizabeth.

UPU Issue
Common Design Types
Surcharged with New Values in Annas and Rupees
Engr.; Name Typo. on Nos. 17 and 18
1949, Oct. 10   Perf. 13½, 11x11½
16 CD306 2½a on 20c dp ultra .20 .20
17 CD307 3a on 30c dp car   1.00 .50
18 CD308 8a on 50c org   .80 .80
19 CD309 1r on 1sh blue   2.25 2.25
a. Surcharge omitted   1,250.
       Nos. 16-19 (4)   4.25 3.75

Nos. 3 and 5-11 Surcharged with New Values in Carmine or Black
Perf. 14, 13x11½, 11½x13
1951, Oct. 1   Engr.   Wmk. 4
20 A1 5c on 1a (C)   .20 .20
21 A2 10c on 2a   .20 .20
22 A3 15c on 2½a   .20 .20
23 A2 20c on 3a   .30 .20
24 A2 50c on 8a   .20 .40
25 A2 1sh on 1r   .75 .30
26 A3 2sh on 2r   6.00 8.75
27 A3 5sh on 5r   9.00 13.50
       Nos. 20-27 (8)   16.85 23.75

Coronation Issue
Common Design Type
1953, June 2   Engr.   Perf. 13½x13
28 CD312 15c dk blue & black .60 .60

Qu'aiti State in Hadhramaut

Metal Work — A10

Fisheries A11

Designs: 10c, Mat making. 15c, Weaving. 25c, Pottery. 35c, Building. 50c, Date cultivation. 90c, Agriculture. 1sh25c, 10sh, Lime burning. 2sh, Dhow building. 5sh, Agriculture.

Perf. 11½x13, 13½x14
1955, Sept. 1   Engr.   Wmk. 4
29 A10 5c greenish blue   .25 .20
30 A10 10c black   .40 .20
31 A10 15c dk green   .40 .20
32 A10 25c carmine   .35 .20
33 A10 35c ultra   .50 .20
34 A10 50c red orange   .35 .20
35 A10 90c brown   .40 .20
36 A11 1sh purple & blk   .45 .20
37 A11 1sh25c red org & blk .45 .45
38 A11 2sh dk blue & blk   3.50 .80
39 A11 5sh green & blk   4.25 2.50
40 A11 10sh car & black   4.75 5.50
       Nos. 29-40 (12)   16.00 10.85

Types of 1955 with Portrait of Sultan Awadh Bin Saleh El-Qu'aiti
Design: 70c, Agriculture. Others as before.

1963, Oct. 20   Wmk. 314
41 A10 5c greenish blue   .20 .50
42 A10 10c black   .20 .50
43 A10 15c dark green   .20 .50
44 A10 25c carmine   .20 .30
45 A10 35c ultra   .30 .65
46 A10 50c red orange   .40 .35
47 A10 70c brown   .65 .35
48 A11 1sh purple & blk   .85 .20
49 A11 1sh25c red org & blk 1.00 2.00
50 A11 2sh dk blue & blk   2.50 .90
51 A11 5sh green & blk   10.00 14.50
52 A11 10sh car & black   12.50 14.50
       Nos. 41-52 (12)   29.00 35.25

AFARS AND ISSAS
French Territory of the

ä-färz and ē-'säz

LOCATION — East Africa
GOVT. — French Overseas Territory
AREA — 8,880 sq. mi.
POP. — 150,000 (est. 1974)
CAPITAL — Djibouti (Jibuti)

The French overseas territory of Somali Coast was renamed the French Territory of the Afars and Issas in 1967.

It became the Djibouti Republic (which see) on June 27, 1977.

100 Centimes = 1 Franc

Catalogue values for all unused stamps in this country are for Never Hinged items.

Imperforates
Most stamps of Afars and Issas exist imperforate in issued and trial colors, and also in small presentation sheets in issued colors.

Grayheaded Kingfisher — A48

1967   Engr.   Unwmk.   Perf. 13
310 A48 10fr Halcyon leucocephala   2.00 1.25
311 A48 15fr Haematopus os-tralegus 2.50 1.75
312 A48 50fr Tringa nebularia   7.50 4.25
313 A48 55fr Coracias abys-sinicus 10.00 5.50
314 A48 60fr Xerus rutilus, vert.   13.00 9.50
       Nos. 310-314 (5)   35.00 22.25
       Nos. 310-314,C50 (6)   51.00 29.75
Issued: 10fr, 55fr, Aug. 21; 15fr, 50fr, 60fr, Sept. 25. See No. C50.

Soccer A49

1967, Dec. 18   Engr.   Perf. 13
315 A49 25fr shown   1.90 1.25
316 A49 30fr Basketball   2.40 1.75

Common Design Types
Pictured in section at front of book.

WHO Anniversary Issue
Common Design Type
1968, May 4   Engr.   Perf. 13
317 CD126 15fr multicolored   1.25 1.10
20th anniv. of WHO.

Damerdjog Fortress A50

Administration Buildings: 25fr, Ali Adde. 30fr, Dorra. 40fr, Assamo.

1968, May 17   Engr.   Perf. 13
318 A50 20fr slate, brn & emer   .90 .55
319 A50 25fr brt grn, bl & brn 1.00 .60
320 A50 30fr brn ol, brn org & sl 1.10 .80
321 A50 40fr brn ol, sl & brt grn 2.00 1.60
       Nos. 318-321 (4)   5.00 3.55

Human Rights Year Issue
Common Design Type
1968, Aug. 10   Engr.   Perf. 13
322 CD127 10fr purple, ver & org 1.00 .65
323 CD127 70fr green, pur & org 1.75 1.10
International Human Rights Year.

Radio-television Station, Djibouti — A52

High Commission Palace, Djibouti — A53

Designs: 2fr, Justice Building. 5fr, Chamber of Deputies. 8fr, Great Mosque. 15fr, Monument of Free French Forces, vert. 40fr, Djibouti Post Office. 70fr, Residence of Gov. Léonce Lagarde at Obock. No. 332, Djibouti Harbormaster's Building. No. 333, Control tower, Djibouti Airport.

1968-70		**Engr.**	**Perf. 13**
324	A52	1fr multicolored	.25 .20
325	A52	2fr multicolored	.25 .20
326	A52	5fr multicolored	.35 .20
327	A52	8fr multicolored	.40 .20
328	A52	15fr multicolored	3.00 2.00
329	A52	40fr multicolored	2.00 1.00
330	A53	60fr multicolored	2.25 1.50
331	A53	70fr multicolored	3.00 1.50
332	A53	85fr multicolored	4.00 2.00
333	A52	85fr multicolored	4.50 2.50
		Nos. 324-333 (10)	20.00 11.30

Issue years: 1968 - 60fr; 1969 - 1fr-15fr; 70fr, 85fr; 1970 - 40fr, 85fr.

Locust A54

Designs: 50fr, Pest control by helicopter. 55fr, Pest control by plane.

1969, Oct. 6		**Engr.**	**Perf. 13**
334	A54	15fr brn, grn & slate	3.00 1.50
335	A54	50fr dk grn, bl & ol brn	1.60 1.10
336	A54	55fr red brn, bl & brn	2.40 1.50
		Nos. 334-336 (3)	7.00 4.10

Campaign against locusts.

ILO Issue
Common Design Type

1969, Nov. 24		**Engr.**	**Perf. 13**
337	CD131	30fr org, gray & lil	1.40 .90

Afar Dagger in Ornamental Scabbard A56

1970, Apr. 3		**Engr.**	**Perf. 13**
338	A56	10fr multicolored	.50 .35
339	A56	15fr multicolored	.60 .35
340	A56	20fr multicolored	.80 .55
341	A56	25fr multicolored	1.10 .55
		Nos. 338-341 (4)	3.00 1.80

See No. 364.

UPU Headquarters Issue
Common Design Type

1970, May 20		**Engr.**	**Perf. 13**
342	CD133	25fr brn, brt grn & choc	1.10 .70

Trapshooting — A57

Motorboats A58

Designs: 50fr, Steeplechase. 55fr, Sailboat, vert. 60fr, Equestrians.

1970		**Engr.**	**Perf. 13**
343	A57	30fr dp brn, yel grn & brt bl	1.40 .85
344	A58	48fr blue & multi	2.10 1.10
345	A58	50fr cop red, bl & pur	2.50 1.25
346	A58	55fr red brn, bl & ol	2.25 1.25
347	A58	60fr ol, blk & red brn	3.25 1.75
		Nos. 343-347 (5)	11.50 6.20

Issued: 30fr, 6/5; 48fr, 10/9; 50fr, 60fr, 11/6.

Automatic Ferry, Tadjourah A59

1970, Nov. 25			
348	A59	48fr blue, brn & grn	2.25 1.40

Volcanic Geode A60

Diabase and Chrysolite A61

10fr, Doleritic basalt. 15fr, Olivine basalt.

1971		**Photo.**	**Perf. 13**
349	A61	10fr black & multi	1.75 .75
350	A61	15fr black & multi	2.50 .75
351	A60	25fr black, crim & brn	5.00 2.25
352	A61	40fr black & multi	7.50 3.50
		Nos. 349-352 (4)	16.75 7.25

Issued: 10fr, 11/22; 15fr, 10/8; 25fr, 4/26; 40fr, 1/25.

A62   A63

1971, July 1		**Photo.**	**Perf. 12x12½**
353	A62	4fr Manta birostris	1.25 .50
354	A62	5fr Coryphaena hippurus	1.25 .50
355	A62	9fr Pristis pectinatus	2.50 1.50
		Nos. 353-355 (3)	5.00 2.50

See No. C60.

De Gaulle Issue
Common Design Type

Designs: 60fr, Gen. Charles de Gaulle, 1940. 85fr, Pres. de Gaulle, 1970.

1971, Nov. 9		**Engr.**	**Perf. 13**
356	CD134	60fr dk vio bl & blk	2.50 1.50
357	CD134	85fr dk vio bl & blk	3.00 1.50

1972, Mar. 8		**Photo.**	**Perf. 12½x13**

Shells: 4fr, Strawberry Top. 9fr, Cypraea pantherina. 20fr, Bull-mouth helmet. 50fr, Ethiopian volute.

358	A63	4fr olive & multi	1.25 .40
359	A63	9fr dk blue & multi	1.50 .60
360	A63	20fr dp green & multi	3.75 1.00
361	A63	50fr dp claret & multi	7.50 1.50
		Nos. 358-361 (4)	14.00 3.50

Shepherd — A64

Design: 10fr, Dromedary breeding.

1973, Apr. 11		**Photo.**	**Perf. 13**
362	A64	9fr blue & multi	1.00 .30
363	A64	10fr blue & multi	1.00 .30

Afar Dagger — A65

1974, Jan. 29		**Engr.**	**Perf. 13**
364	A65	30fr slate grn & dk brn	1.10 .65

For surcharge see No. 379.

Flamingos, Lake Abbe — A66

Flamingos and different views of Lake Abbe.

1974, Feb. 22		**Photo.**	**Perf. 13**
370	A66	5fr multicolored	1.25 .25
371	A66	15fr multicolored	.60 .50
372	A66	50fr multicolored	1.90 1.25
		Nos. 370-372 (3)	3.75 2.00

Soccer Ball — A67

1974, May 24		**Engr.**	**Perf. 13**
373	A67	25fr black & emerald	1.25 .80

World Cup Soccer Championship, Munich, June 13-July 7.

Letters Around UPU Emblem — A68

Oleo Chrysophylla A69

1974, Oct. 9		**Engr.**	**Perf. 13**
374	A68	20fr multicolored	1.00 .50
375	A68	100fr multicolored	2.50 2.00

Centenary of Universal Postal Union.

1974, Nov. 22			**Photo.**
376	A69	10fr not shown	.75 .40
377	A69	15fr *Ficus species*	1.00 .60
378	A69	20fr *Solanum adoense*	2.25 1.00
		Nos. 376-378 (3)	4.00 2.00

Day Primary Forest.

No. 364 Surcharged with New Value and Two Bars in Red

1975, Jan. 1		**Engr.**	**Perf. 13**
379	A65	40fr on 30fr multi	1.50 .90

Treasury — A70

Design: 25fr, Government buildings.

1975, Jan. 7		**Engr.**	**Perf. 13**
380	A70	8fr blue, gray & red	.55 .35
381	A70	25fr red, blue & indigo	1.25 .75

Darioconus Textile — A71

Sea Shells: No. 383, Murex palmarosa. 10fr, Conus sumatrensis. 15fr, Cypraea pulchra. No. 386, 45fr, Murex scolopax. No. 387, Cypraea exhusta. 40fr, Ranella spinosa. 55fr, Cypraea erythraensis. 60fr, Conus taeniatus.

1975-76		**Engr.**	**Perf. 13**
382	A71	5fr blue grn & brn	1.25 .60
383	A71	5fr blue & multi ('76)	1.50 .60
384	A71	10fr lilac, blk & brn	1.25 .60
385	A71	15fr blue, ind & brn	2.25 1.000
386	A71	20fr purple & lt brn	3.00 2.00
387	A71	20fr brt grn & multi ('76)	1.50 .60
388	A71	40fr green & brown	7.00 2.50
389	A71	45fr green, bl & bister	6.00 2.00
390	A71	55fr turq & multi ('76)	4.00 2.25
391	A71	60fr buff & sepia ('76)	7.00 3.00
		Nos. 382-391 (10)	34.75 15.15

Hypolimnas Misippus A72

Butterflies: 40fr, Papilio nireus. 50fr, Acraea anemosa. 65fr, Holocerina smilax menieri. 70fr, Papilio demodocus. No. 397, Papilio dardanus. No. 398, Balachowsky gonimbrasca. 150fr, Vanessa cardui.

1975-76	**Photo.**	**Perf. 13**	
392 A72	25fr emerald & multi	1.90	1.00
393 A72	40fr yellow & multi	2.00	1.00
394 A72	50fr ultra & multi		
	('76)	3.00	1.50
395 A72	65fr ol & multi ('76)	3.25	1.50
396 A72	70fr violet & multi	4.25	2.00
397 A72	100fr blue & multi	5.50	2.00
398 A72	100fr Prus bl & multi		
	('76)	5.50	2.00
399 A72	150fr grn & multi ('76)	7.00	2.00
	Nos. 392-399 (8)	32.40	13.00

A73

Perf. 13x12½, 12½x13

1975-76			**Photo.**
400 A73	10fr Hyaena hyaena	.55	.35
401 A73	15fr Cercopithecus aethiops	1.10	.50
402 A73	15fr Equus asinus somalicus	1.00	.50
403 A73	30fr Dorcatragus megalotis	1.60	.90
404 A73	50fr Ichneumia albicauda	2.25	1.00
405 A73	60fr Hystrix galasta	2.75	1.25
406 A73	70fr Ictonyx striatus	4.00	1.75
407 A73	200fr Orycteropus afar	6.75	3.75
	Nos. 400-407 (8)	20.00	10.00

Nos. 401-402, 405 are vert.
Issued: 50fr, 60fr, 70fr, 2/21; No. 401, 200fr, 10/24; 10fr, No. 402, 30fr, 2/4/76.

A74

A75

1975-76	**Photo.**	**Perf. 12½x13**	
413 A74	20fr Vidua macroura	1.25	.80
414 A74	25fr Psittacula krameri	1.25	.40
415 A74	50fr Cinnyris venustus	2.50	1.50
416 A74	60fr Ardea goliath	4.00	1.75
417 A74	100fr Scopus umbretta	5.50	2.50
418 A74	100fr Oena capensis	4.00	1.75
419 A74	300fr Platalea alba	10.00	4.00
	Nos. 413-419 (7)	28.50	12.70

Issued: 300fr, 6/15/76; 25fr, No. 418, 10/13/76; others 11/21 and 12/19/75.

1975, Dec. 19	**Engr.**	**Perf. 13**	
421 A75	20fr Palms	1.00	.40

Satellite and Alexander Graham Bell — A76

1976, Mar. 10	**Engr.**	**Perf. 13**	
422 A76	200fr dp bl, org & sl grn	4.50	2.25

Centenary of the first telephone call by Alexander Graham Bell, Mar. 10, 1876.

Basketball A77

1976, July 7	**Litho.**	**Perf. 12½**	
423 A77	10fr shown	.45	.20
424 A77	15fr Bicycling	.60	.30
425 A77	40fr Soccer	1.10	.50
426 A77	60fr Running	1.40	.80
	Nos. 423-426 (4)	3.55	1.80

21st Olympic Games, Montreal, Canada, July 17-Aug. 1.

Pterois Radiata — A78

1976, Aug. 10	**Photo.**	**Perf. 13x13½**	
428 A78	45fr blue & multi	3.50	1.00

Psammophis Elegans — A79

Design: 70fr, Naja nigricollis, vert.

Perf. 13x13½, 13½x13

1976, Sept. 27			**Photo.**
430 A79	70fr ocher & multi	2.75	1.50
431 A79	80fr emerald & multi	3.25	1.75

Motorcyclist A80

1977, Jan. 27	**Litho.**	**Perf. 12x12½**	
432 A80	200fr multicolored	5.50	2.75

Moto-Cross motorcycle race.

Conus Betulinus — A81

Sea Shells: 5fr, Cyprea tigris. 70fr, Conus striatus. 85fr, Cyprea mauritiana.

1977	**Engr.**	**Perf. 13**	
433 A81	5fr multicolored	.90	.50
434 A81	30fr multicolored	1.40	.60
435 A81	70fr multicolored	4.75	1.75
436 A81	85fr multicolored	5.00	2.00
	Nos. 433-436 (4)	12.05	4.85

Gaterin Gaterinus A82

1977, Apr. 15	**Photo.**	**Perf. 13x12½**	
437 A82	15fr shown	1.10	.40
438 A82	65fr Barracudas	3.25	1.10

AIR POST STAMPS

AP16

AP17

Unwmk.

1967, Aug. 21	**Engr.**	**Perf. 13**	
C50 AP16	200fr Aquila rapax belisarius	16.00	7.50

1968	**Engr.**	**Perf. 13**	
C51 AP17	48fr Parachutists	2.75	1.50
C52 AP17	85fr Water skier & skin diver	3.75	2.50

Issue dates: 48fr, Jan. 5; 85fr, Mar. 15.

Aerial Map of the Territory — AP18

1968, Nov. 15	**Engr.**	**Perf. 13**	
C53 AP18	500fr bl, dk brn & ocher	26.00	8.00

Buildings Type of Regular Issue

100fr, Cathedral. 200fr, Sayed Hassan Mosque.

1969	**Engr.**	**Perf. 13**	
C54 A53	100fr multi, vert.	2.25	1.50
C55 A53	200fr multi, vert.	5.25	3.00

Issue dates: 100fr, Apr. 4; 200fr, May 8.

Concorde Issue
Common Design Type

1969, Apr. 17			
C56 CD129	100fr org red & ol	18.00	10.00

Arta Ionospheric Station — AP19

Japanese Sword Guard, Fish Design — AP20

1970, May 8	**Engr.**	**Perf. 13**	
C57 AP19	70fr multicolored	3.00	2.00

Gold embossed

1970, Oct. 26		**Perf. 12½**	

200fr, Japanese sword guard, horse design.

C58 AP20	100fr multicolored	7.50	5.00
C59 AP20	200fr multicolored	9.50	5.50

EXPO '70 International Exposition, Osaka, Japan, Mar. 15-Sept. 13.

Scarus vetula — AP21

1971, July 1	**Photo.**	**Perf. 12½**	
C60 AP21	30fr black & multi	4.00	2.50

Djibouti Harbor — AP22

1972, Feb. 3			
C61 AP22	100fr blue & multi	4.00	2.25

New Djibouti harbor.

AP23

AP24

1972   Photo.   Perf. 12½x13

C62	AP23	30fr Pterocles		
		lichtensteini	2.50	1.40
C63	AP23	49fr Uppupa epops	4.50	2.50
C64	AP23	66fr Capella media	5.75	3.25
C65	AP23	500fr Francolinus		
		ochropectus	24.00	9.00
		Nos. C62-C65 (4)	36.75	16.15

Issue dates: #C65, Nov. 3; others Apr. 21.

1972, June 8   Engr.   Perf. 13

Olympic Rings and: 5fr, Running. 10fr, Basketball. 55fr, Swimming, horiz. 60fr, Olympic torch and Greek frieze, horiz.

C66	AP24	5fr multicolored	.45	.25
C67	AP24	10fr multicolored	.55	.40
C68	AP24	55fr multicolored	1.75	1.10
C69	AP24	60fr multicolored	2.25	1.25
		Nos. C66-C69 (4)	5.00	3.00

20th Olympic Games, Munich, 8/26-9/11.

Louis Pasteur — AP25

100fr, Albert Calmette and C. Guérin.

1972, Oct. 5   Engr.   Perf. 13

C70	AP25	20fr multicolored	1.50	.50
C71	AP25	100fr multicolored	4.00	2.50

Pasteur, Calmette, Guerin, chemists and bacteriologists, benefactors of mankind.

Map and Views of Territory — AP26

200fr, Woman and Mosque of Djibouti, vert.

1973, Jan. 15   Photo.   Perf. 13

C72	AP26	30fr brown & multi	4.50	3.50
C73	AP26	200fr multicolored	8.50	6.00

Visit of Pres. Georges Pompidou of France, Jan. 15-17.

AP27

1973, Feb. 26   Photo.   Perf. 13x12½

C74	AP27	30fr Oryx beisa	2.00	1.00
C75	AP27	50fr Madogua saltiana	2.75	1.50
C76	AP27	66fr Felis caracal	3.75	2.00
		Nos. C74-C76 (3)	8.50	4.50

See Nos. C94-C96.

Celts — AP28

Various pre-historic flint tools. 40fr, 60fr, horiz.

1973   Perf. 13

C77	AP28	20fr yel grn, blk &		
		brn	2.25	1.50
C78	AP28	40fr yellow & multi	2.75	2.00
C79	AP28	49fr lilac & multi	5.00	3.00
C80	AP28	60fr blue & multi	3.75	2.50
		Nos. C77-C80 (4)	13.75	9.00

Issued: 20fr, 49fr, 3/16; 40fr, 60fr, 9/7.

AP29

1973, Mar. 16

C81	AP29	40fr Octopus		
		macropus	3.00	1.00
C82	AP29	60fr Halicore dugong	5.00	2.50

AP30

AP31

Copernicus: 8fr, Nicolaus Copernicus, Polish astronomer. 9fr, William C. Roentgen, physicist, X-ray discoverer. No. C85, Edward Jenner, physician, discoverer of vaccination. No. C86, Marie Curie, discoverer of radium and polonium. 49fr, Robert Koch, physician

and bacteriologist. 50fr, Clement Ader (1841-1925), French aviation pioneer. 55fr, Guglielmo Marconi, Italian electrical engineer, inventor. 85fr, Moliere, French playwright. 100fr, Henri Farman (1874-1937), French aviation pioneer. 150fr, Andre-Marie Ampere (1775-1836), French physicist. 250fr, Michelangelo Buonarroti (1475-1564), Italian sculptor, painter and architect.

1973-75   Engr.   Perf. 13

C83	AP30	8fr multicolored	1.00	.30
C84	AP30	9fr multicolored	1.00	.40
C85	AP30	10fr multicolored	1.25	.50
C86	AP30	10fr multicolored	.75	.40
C87	AP30	49fr multicolored	3.25	1.60
C88	AP30	50fr multicolored	2.50	1.25
C89	AP30	55fr multicolored	2.25	1.00
C90	AP30	85fr multicolored	4.00	1.75
C91	AP30	100fr multicolored	4.00	2.00
C92	AP30	150fr multicolored	4.00	2.00
C93	AP30	250fr multicolored	7.50	3.50
		Nos. C83-C93 (11)	31.50	14.70

Issued: 8fr, 85fr, 5/9/73; 9fr, #C85, 49fr, 10/12/73; 100fr, 1/29/74; 55fr, 3/22/74; #C86, 8/23/74; 150fr, 7/24/75; 250fr, 6/26/75; 50fr, 9/25/75.

Perf. 12½x13, 13x12½

1973, Dec. 12   Photo.

C94	AP31	20fr Papio anubis	1.50	.60
C95	AP31	50fr Genetta tigrina,		
		horiz.	3.00	.90
C96	AP31	66fr Lapus habes-		
		sinicus	4.25	1.50
		Nos. C94-C96 (3)	8.75	3.00

Spearfishing — AP32

1974, Apr. 14   Engr.   Perf. 13

C97	AP32	200fr multicolored	7.50	4.50

No. C97 was prepared for release in Nov. 1972, for the 3rd Underwater Spearfishing Contest in the Red Sea. Dates were obliterated with a rectangle and the stamp was not issued without this obliteration.

Rock Carvings, Balho — AP33

1974, Apr. 26

C98	AP33	200fr carmine & slate	7.00	5.00

Lake Assal — AP34

Designs (Lake Assal): 50fr, Rock formations on shore. 85fr, Crystallized wood.

1974, Oct. 25   Photo.   Perf. 13

C99	AP34	49fr multicolored	1.50	.75
C100	AP34	50fr multicolored	2.00	1.00
C101	AP34	85fr multicolored	4.00	2.25
		Nos. C99-C101 (3)	7.50	4.00

Columba
Guinea — AP35

1975, May 23   Photo.   Perf. 13

C102	AP35	500fr multicolored	18.00	6.50

Djibouti Airport — AP36

1977, Mar. 1   Litho.   Perf. 12

C103	AP36	500fr multicolored	11.00	7.50

Opening of new Djibouti Airport.

Thomas A. Edison and
Phonograph — AP37

Design: 75fr, Alexander Volta, electric train, lines and light bulb.

1977, May 5   Engr.   Perf. 13

C104	AP37	55fr multicolored	3.25	1.50
C105	AP37	75fr multicolored	4.75	2.50

Famous inventors: Thomas Alva Edison and Alexander Volta (1745-1827).

POSTAGE DUE STAMPS

Nomad's Milk
Jug — D3

Perf. 14x13

1969, Dec. 15   Engr.   Unwmk.

J49	D3	1fr red brn, red lil & sl	.20	.20
J50	D3	2fr red brn, emer & sl	.20	.20
J51	D3	5fr red brn, bl & slate	.30	.30
J52	D3	10fr red brn, brn & slate	.80	.80
		Nos. J49-J52 (4)	1.50	1.50

AFGHANISTAN

af-'ga-nə-,stan

LOCATION — Central Asia, bounded by Iran, Turkmenistan, Uzbekistan, Tajikistan, Pakistan, and China
GOVT. — Republic
AREA — 251,773 sq. mi.
POP. — 23,500,000 (1995 est.)
CAPITAL — Kabul

Afghanistan changed from a constitutional monarchy to a republic in July 1973.

12 Shahi = 6 Sanar = 3 Abasi =
2 Krans = 1 Rupee Kabuli
60 Paisas = 1 Rupee (1921)
100 Pouls = 1 Rupee Afghani (1927)

Catalogue values for unused stamps in this country are for Never Hinged items, beginning with Scott 364 in the regular postage section, Scott B1 in the semipostal section, Scott C7 in the airpost section, Scott O8 in officials section, and Scott RA6 in the postal tax section.

1871-78   A7   A8
Sanar.   Abasi.   6 Shahi.

1871-78   1871   1872
1 Rupee.   ½ Rupee.

1874   1876(A8)   1876 (A7)
1 Rupee.

Rupee.
1872   1874   1876 (A8)
1877-78

From 1871 to 1892 and 1898 the Moslem year date appears on the stamp. Numerals as follows:

۱	۲	۳	۴	۵
1	2	3	4	5
۶	۷	۸	۹	۰
6	7	8	9	0

Until 1891 cancellation consisted of cutting or tearing a piece from the stamps. Such copies should not be considered as damaged.

Values are for cut square examples of good color. Cut to shape or faded copies sell for much less, particularly Nos. 2-10.

Nos. 2-108 are on laid paper of varying thickness except where wove is noted.

Until 1907 all stamps were issued ungummed.

The tiger's head on types A2 to A11 symbolizes the name of the contemporary amir, Sher (Tiger) Ali.

Kingdom of Kabul

Tiger's Head
A2

(Both circles dotted)

1871   Unwmk.   Litho.   *Imperf.*
Dated "1288"

2	A2	1sh black	90.00	22.50
3	A2	1sa black	75.00	32.50
4	A2	1ab black	40.00	35.00
		Nos. 2-4 (3)	205.00	90.00

Thirty varieties of the shahi, 10 of the sanar and 5 of the abasi.
Similar designs without the tiger's head in the center are revenues.

A3

(Outer circle dotted)
Dated "1288"

5	A3	1sh black	175.00	35.00
6	A3	1sa black	75.00	27.50
7	A3	1ab black	37.50	22.50
		Nos. 5-7 (3)	287.50	85.00

Five varieties of each.

A4

1872
Toned Wove Paper
Dated "1289"

| 8 | A4 | 6sh violet | 850. | 750. |
| 9 | A4 | 1rup violet | 1,300. | 1,100. |

Two varieties of each. Date varies in location. Printed in sheets of 4 (2x2) containing two of each denomination.
Most used copies are smeared with a greasy ink cancel.

A4a

1873
White Laid Paper
Dated "1290"

10	A4a	1sh black	10.00	4.50
a.		Corner ornament missing	450.00	375.00
b.		Corner ornament retouched	60.00	25.00

15 varieties. Nos. 10a, 10b are the sixth stamp on the sheet.

A5

1873

| 11 | A5 | 1sh black | | 2.25 | 2.00 |
| 11A | A5 | 1sh violet | | 500.00 | |

Sixty varieties of each.

1874

Dated "1291"

12	A5	1ab black	40.00	25.00
13	A5	½rup black	20.00	17.50
14	A5	1rup black	22.50	20.00
		Nos. 12-14 (3)	82.50	62.50

Five varieties of each.
Nos. 12-14 were printed on the same sheet. Se-tenant varieties exist.

A6   A7

1875

Dated "1292"

15	A6	1sa black	300.00	250.00
a.		Wide outer circle	600.00	
16	A6	1ab black	350.00	300.00
17	A6	1sa brown violet	22.50	22.50
a.		Wide outer circle	110.00	
18	A6	1ab brown violet	40.00	25.00

Ten varieties of the sanar, five of the abasi.
Nos. 15-16 and 17-18 were printed in the same sheets. Se-tenant pairs exist.

1876

Dated "1293"

19	A7	1sh black	300.00	150.00
20	A7	1sa black	375.00	200.00
21	A7	1ab black	600.00	325.00
22	A7	½rup black	375.00	200.00
23	A7	1rup black	550.00	200.00
24	A7	1sh violet	375.00	200.00
25	A7	1sa violet	350.00	200.00
26	A7	1ab violet	425.00	200.00
27	A7	½rup violet	90.00	55.00
28	A7	1rup violet	90.00	75.00

12 varieties of the shahi and 3 each of the other values.

A8

1876

Dated "1293"

29	A8	1sh gray	5.00	4.00
30	A8	1sa gray	7.50	4.00
31	A8	1ab gray	15.00	7.50
32	A8	½rup gray	17.50	10.00
33	A8	1rup gray	22.50	10.00
34	A8	1sh olive blk	125.00	
35	A8	1sa olive blk	175.00	
36	A8	1ab olive blk	350.00	
37	A8	½rup olive blk	250.00	
38	A8	1rup olive blk	275.00	
39	A8	1sh green	22.50	3.75
40	A8	1sa green	35.00	15.00
41	A8	1ab green	50.00	37.50
42	A8	½rup green	100.00	40.00
43	A8	1rup green	100.00	80.00
44	A8	1sh ocher	22.50	7.50
45	A8	1sa ocher	35.00	15.00
46	A8	1ab ocher	60.00	27.50
47	A8	½rup ocher	75.00	60.00
48	A8	1rup ocher	125.00	110.00
49	A8	1sh violet	22.50	5.50
50	A8	1sa violet	22.50	7.50

51	A8	1ab violet	35.00	10.00
52	A8	½rup violet	60.00	22.50
53	A8	1rup violet	75.00	35.00

24 varieties of the shahi, 4 of which show denomination written:

12 varieties of the sanar, 6 of the abasi and 3 each of the ½ rupee and rupee.

A9

1877

Dated "1294"

54	A9	1sh gray	3.50	2.25
55	A9	1sa gray	6.00	3.00
56	A9	1ab gray	9.00	6.00
57	A9	½rup gray	12.00	12.00
58	A9	1rup gray	12.00	12.00
59	A9	1sh black	10.00	
60	A9	1sa black	17.50	
61	A9	1ab black	42.50	
62	A9	½rup black	45.00	
63	A9	1rup black	45.00	
64	A9	1sh green	4.50	3.50
a.		Wove paper	12.00	
65	A9	1sa green	7.50	3.50
a.		Wove paper	16.00	12.00
66	A9	1ab green	10.00	10.00
a.		Wove paper	27.50	
67	A9	½rup green	14.00	14.00
a.		Wove paper	30.00	30.00
68	A9	1rup green	14.00	14.00
a.		Wove paper	30.00	30.00
69	A9	1sh ocher	3.50	2.00
70	A9	1sa ocher	10.00	3.50
71	A9	1ab ocher	17.50	16.00
72	A9	½rup ocher	30.00	30.00
73	A9	1rup ocher	30.00	30.00
74	A9	1sh violet	3.75	2.00
75	A9	1sa violet	7.50	2.75
76	A9	1ab violet	11.00	7.50
77	A9	½rup violet	17.50	14.00
78	A9	1rup violet	17.50	14.00

25 varieties of the shahi, 8 of the sanar, 3 of the abasi and 2 each of the ½ rupee and rupee.

A10   A11

1878

Dated "1295"

79	A10	1sh gray	1.50	1.50
80	A10	1sa gray	1.75	1.75
81	A10	1ab gray	3.75	3.75
82	A10	½rup gray	10.00	7.50
83	A10	1rup gray	10.00	7.50
84	A10	1sh black	3.00	
85	A10	1sa black	3.00	
86	A10	1ab black	10.00	
87	A10	½rup black	20.00	
88	A10	1rup black	20.00	
89	A10	1sh green	21.00	20.00
90	A10	1sa green	3.00	3.00
91	A10	1ab green	11.00	10.00
92	A10	½rup green	21.00	17.50
93	A10	1rup green	21.00	17.50
94	A10	1sh ocher	10.00	3.00
95	A10	1sa ocher	3.00	2.25
96	A10	1ab ocher	11.00	10.00
97	A10	½rup ocher	21.00	21.00
98	A10	1rup ocher	16.00	16.00
99	A10	1sh violet	1.75	1.75
100	A10	1sa violet	1.75	1.75
101	A10	1ab violet	5.50	5.50
102	A10	½rup violet	21.00	17.50
103	A10	1rup violet	21.00	17.50
104	A11	1sh gray	2.00	1.75
105	A11	1sh black	90.00	
106	A11	1sh green	1.75	1.75
107	A11	1sh ocher	1.40	1.40
108	A11	1sh violet	2.00	1.75

40 varieties of the shahi, 30 of the sanar, 6 of the abasi and 2 each of the ½ rupee and 1 rupee.

The 1876, 1877 and 1878 issues were printed in separate colors for each main post office on the Peshawar-Kabul-Khulm (Tashkurghan) postal route. Some specialists consider the black printings to be proofs or trial colors.

There are many shades of these colors.

1ab, Type I (26mm) — A12 | 1ab, Type II (28mm) — A13

A14 | A15

Dated "1298", numerals scattered through design

Handstamped, in watercolor

1881-90
Thin White Laid Batonne Paper

109	A12	1ab violet	1.75	1.10
109A	A13	1ab violet	3.50	3.50
110	A12	1ab black brn	3.50	1.75
111	A12	1ab rose	2.00	2.00
b.		Se-tenant with No. 111A	16.00	
111A	A13	1ab rose	2.50	2.00
112	A14	2ab violet	1.75	1.50
113	A14	2ab black brn	5.00	4.00
114	A14	2ab rose	3.00	3.00
115	A15	1rup violet	2.50	1.50
116	A15	1rup black brn	6.50	6.50
117	A15	1rup rose	3.00	3.00

Thin White Wove Batonne Paper

118	A12	1ab violet	6.50	4.00
119	A12	1ab vermilion	4.25	
120	A12	1ab rose		
121	A14	2ab violet		
122	A14	2ab vermilion	5.00	
122A	A14	2ab black brn		
123	A15	1rup violet	8.25	
124	A15	1rup vermilion	6.50	
125	A15	1rup black brn	8.25	

Thin White Laid Batonne Paper

126	A12	1ab brown org	2.50	2.50
126A	A13	1ab brn org (II)	3.50	3.50
127	A12	1ab carmine lake	2.50	2.50
a.		Laid paper		
128	A14	2ab brown org	2.50	2.50
129	A14	2ab carmine lake	3.00	3.00
130	A15	1rup brown org	10.00	10.00
131	A15	1rup car lake	4.25	4.25

Yellowish Laid Batonne Paper

132	A12	1ab purple		3.50
133	A12	1ab red	6.50	3.50

1884
Colored Wove Paper

133A	A13	1ab purple, yel (II)	17.50	17.50
134	A12	1ab purple, grn	20.00	
135	A12	1ab purple, blue	32.50	21.00
136	A12	1ab red, grn	37.50	
137	A12	1ab red, yel	1.75	
139	A12	1ab red, rose	6.00	
140	A14	2ab red, yel	6.00	
142	A14	2ab red, rose	5.50	
143	A15	1rup red, yel	6.50	6.50
145	A15	1rup red, rose	7.00	7.00

Thin Colored Ribbed Paper

146	A14	2ab red, yellow	3.00	
147	A15	1rup red, yellow	8.25	
148	A12	1ab lake, lilac	4.00	
149	A14	2ab lake, lilac	5.00	
150	A15	1rup lake, lilac	4.00	
151	A12	1ab lake, green	2.00	
152	A14	2ab lake, green	4.00	
153	A15	1rup lake, green	4.00	

1886-88
Colored Wove Paper

155	A12	1ab black, magenta	27.50	
156	A12	1ab claret brn, org	20.00	
156A	A12	1ab red, org	2.00	
156B	A14	2ab red, org	4.75	
156C	A15	1rup red, org	3.50	

Laid Batonné Paper

157	A12	1ab black, lavender	2.75	
158	A12	1ab cl brn, grn	6.50	
159	A12	1ab black, pink	17.50	
160	A14	2ab black, pink	35.00	
161	A15	1rup black, pink	20.00	

Laid Paper

162	A12	1ab black, pink	6.50	
163	A14	2ab black, pink	6.50	
164	A15	1rup black, pink	6.50	
165	A12	1ab brown, yel	6.50	
166	A14	2ab brown, yel	6.50	
167	A15	1rup brown, yel	6.50	

168	A12	1ab blue, grn	6.50	
169	A14	2ab blue, grn	6.50	
170	A15	1rup blue, grn	6.50	

1891
Colored Wove Paper

175	A12	1ab green, rose	22.50	
176	A15	1rup pur, grn batonne	22.50	

Nos. 109-176 fall into three categories:
1. Those regularly issued and in normal postal use from 1881 on, handstamped on thin white laid or wove paper in strip sheets containing 12 or more impressions of the same denomination arranged in two irregular rows, with the impressions often touching or overlappng.
2. The 1884 postal issues provisionally printed on smooth or ribbed colored wove paper as needed to supplement low stocks of the normal white paper stamps.
3. The "special" printings made in a range of colors on several types of laid or wove colored papers, most of which were never used for normal printings. These were produced periodically from 1886 to 1891 to meet philatelic demands. Although nominally valid for postage, most of the special printings were exported directly to fill dealers' orders. Many were ever postally used. Many of the sheets contained all three denominations with impressions separated by ruled lines. Sometimes different colors were used, so se-tenant multiples of denomination or color exist. Many combinations of stamp and paper colors exist besides those listed.
Various shades of each color exist.
Type A12 is known dated "1297."
Counterfeits, lithographed or typographed, are plentiful.

Kingdom of Afghanistan

A16

A17 | A18

1891   Pelure Paper   Litho.
Dated "1309"

177	A16	1ab slate blue	.85	.85
a.		Tete beche pair	14.00	
178	A17	2ab slate blue	6.00	5.00
179	A18	1rup slate blue	12.50	10.00
		Nos. 177-179 (3)	19.35	15.85

Revenue stamps of similar design exist in various colors.
Nos. 177-179 were printed in panes on the same sheet, so se-tenant gutter pairs exist. Examples in black or red are proofs.

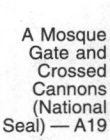

A Mosque Gate and Crossed Cannons (National Seal) — A19

Dated "1310" in Upper Right Corner

1892
Flimsy Wove Paper

180	A19	1ab black, green	2.00	1.60
181	A19	1ab black, orange	2.50	2.50
182	A19	1ab black, yellow	2.00	1.60
183	A19	1ab black, pink	2.50	1.60
184	A19	1ab black, lil rose	2.50	2.50
185	A19	1ab black, blue	4.25	3.50
186	A19	1ab black, salmon	2.50	2.00
187	A19	1ab black, magenta	2.50	2.50
188	A19	1ab black, violet	2.50	2.50
188A	A19	1ab black, scarlet	2.50	1.75

Many shades exist.

A20

A21

Undated

1894
Flimsy Wove Paper

189	A20	2ab black, green	6.50	6.50
190	A21	1rup black, green	10.00	10.00

24 varieties of the 2 abasi and 12 varieties of the rupee.
Nos. 189-190 and F3 were printed se-tenant in the same sheet. Pairs exist.

A21a

Dated "1316"

1898
Flimsy Wove Paper

191	A21a	2ab black, pink	2.50	
192	A21a	2ab black, magenta	2.50	
193	A21a	2ab black, yellow	1.10	
193A	A21a	2ab black, salmon	3.00	
194	A21a	2ab black, green	1.40	
195	A21a	2ab black, purple	1.75	
195A	A21a	2ab black, blue	17.50	
		Nos. 191-195A (7)	29.75	

Nos. 191-195A were not regularly issued. Genuinely used copies are scarce. No. 195A was found in remainder stocks and probably was never released.

A22 | A23

A24

1907   Engr.   Imperf.
Medium Wove Paper

196	A22	1ab blue green	10.00	2.50
a.		1ab emerald	17.00	5.00
b.		Double impression	125.00	
197	A22	1ab brt blue	15.00	10.00
198	A23	2ab deep blue	5.00	5.00
199	A24	1rup blue green	9.00	10.00
a.		1rup blue green	10.00	12.50

Zigzag Roulette 10

200	A22	1ab blue green	55.00	
201	A23	2ab blue	90.00	
201A	A24	1rup blue green	110.00	

1908   Perf. 12

202	A22	1ab green	14.00	20.00
203	A23	2ab deep blue	5.00	5.00
a.		Horiz. pair, imperf between	175.00	
204	A24	1rup blue green	17.50	17.50
		Nos. 202-204 (3)	36.50	42.50

Twelve varieties of the 1 abasi, 6 of the 2 abasi, 4 of the 1 rupee.
Nos. 196-204 were issued in small sheets containing 3 or 4 panes. Gutter pairs, normal and tête bêche, exist.

A25 | A26

A27

1909-19   Typo.   Perf. 12

205	A25	1ab ultra	3.00	1.00
a.		Imperf., pair	20.00	
206	A25	1ab red ('16)	.60	.60
a.		Imperf.	22.50	
207	A25	1ab rose ('18)	.80	.70
208	A26	2ab green	.50	.25
a.		Imperf., pair	20.00	
b.		Horiz. pair, imperf. btwn.		
208C	A26	2ab yellow ('16)	2.00	2.00
209	A26	2ab bis ('18-'19)	.90	1.25
210	A27	1rup lilac brn	4.00	4.00
a.		1rup red brown	4.00	4.00
211	A27	1rup ol bis ('16)	6.00	6.00
		Nos. 205-211 (8)	17.80	15.80

A28

1913

212	A28	2pa drab brown	1.25	1.25
a.		2pa red brown	1.25	1.25

No. 212 is inscribed "Tiket waraq dak" (Postal card stamps). It was usable only on postcards and not accepted for postage on letters.
Nos. 196-212 sometimes show letters of a papermaker's watermark, "Howard & Jones, London."

Royal Star — A29

1920, Aug. 24   Perf. 12
Size: 39x47mm

214	A29	10pa rose	30.00	20.00
215	A29	20pa red brown	50.00	40.00
216	A29	30pa green	100.00	100.00
		Nos. 214-216 (3)	180.00	160.00

Issued in sheets of two.

1921, Mar.
Size: 22½x28¼mm

217	A29	10pa rose	1.00	1.00
a.		Perf. 11 ('27)	12.00	10.00
218	A29	20pa red brown	2.00	2.00
219	A29	30pa yel green	3.00	2.50
a.		Tete beche pair	20.00	20.00
b.		30pa green	3.00	2.75
c.		As "b," Tete beche pair	20.00	20.00
		Nos. 217-219 (3)	6.00	5.50

Two types of the 10pa, three of the 20pa.

Crest of King Amanullah
A30 | A32

1924, Feb. 26   **Perf. 12**
220 A30 10pa chocolate   27.50 27.50
  a. Tete beche pair   90.00 70.00
6th Independence Day.
Printed in sheets of four consisting of two
tete beche pairs, and in sheets of two. Two
types exist.

Some authorities believe that Nos.
Q15-Q16 were issued as regular postage stamps.

1925, Feb. 26   **Perf. 12**
Size: 29x37mm
222 A32 10pa light brown   35.00 30.00
7th Independence Day.
Printed in sheets of 8 (two panes of 4).

1926, Feb. 28
Wove Paper
Size: 26x33mm
224 A32 10pa dark blue   5.00   5.00
  a. Imperf., pair   25.00
  b. Horiz. pair, imperf. btwn.   50.00
  c. Vert. pair, imperf. btwn.   50.00
  d. Laid paper   10.00 10.00
7th anniv. of Independence. Printed in
sheets of 4, and in sheets of 8 (two panes of
4). Tete beche gutter pairs exist.

Tughra and Crest of
Amanullah — A33

1927, Feb.
225 A33 10pa magenta   10.00   9.00
  a. Vertical pair, imperf. between 47.50   70
Dotted Background
226 A33 10pa magenta   12.00 10.00
  a. Horiz. pair, imperf. between   50.00
The surface of No. 226 is covered by a net
of fine dots.
8th anniv. of Independence. Printed in
sheets of 8 (two panes of 4). Tete beche gutter pairs exist.

National
Seal — A34   A35

A35a

A36

1927, Oct.   **Imperf.**
227 A34 15p pink   1.00   1.00
228 A35 30p Prus green   2.00   .90
229 A36 60p light blue   3.00   2.50
  a. Tete beche pair   7.50
    Nos. 227-229 (3)   6.00   4.40

1927-30   **Perf. 11, 12**
230 A34 15p pink   1.00   1.00
231 A34 15p ultra ('29)   1.00   1.00
232 A35 30p Prus green   2.00   1.00
233 A35a 30p dp green ('30)   1.00   .90

---

234 A36 60p bright blue   2.00   1.00
  a. Tete beche pair   9.00   9.00
235 A36 60p black ('29)   2.50   1.75
    Nos. 230-235 (6)   9.50   6.65
Nos. 230, 232 and 234 are usually imperforate on one or two sides.
No. 233 has been redrawn. A narrow border of pearls has been added and "30," in
European and Arabic numerals, inserted in the
upper spandrels.

Tughra and Crest of Amanullah — A37

1928, Feb. 27
236 A37 15p pink   4.00   4.00
  a. Tete beche pair   9.00   7.50
  b. Horiz. pair, imperf. vert.   17.50 15.00
  c. As "a," imperf. vert., block of 4 25.00
9th anniv. of Independence. This stamp is
always imperforate on one or two sides.
A 15p blue of somewhat similar design was
prepared for the 10th anniv., but was not
issued due to Amanullah's dethronement.
Value, $15.

A38

A39

A40   A41

A42

1928-30   **Perf. 11, 12**
237 A38 2p dull blue   2.50   1.60
  a. Vertical pair, imperf. between 17.50
238 A38 2p lt rose ('30)   .25   .25
239 A39 10p gray green   1.00   .20
  a. Tete beche pair   12.00   5.00
  b. Vert. pair, imperf. horiz.   10.00 10.00
  c. Vertical pair, imperf. between
240   10p choc ('30)   1.25   1.00
  a. 10p brown purple ('29)   8.00   4.00
241 A40 25p car rose   1.00   .25
242 A40 25p Prus green ('29)   1.50   1.00
243 A41 40p ultra   1.25   .35
  a. Tete beche pair   13.00 15.00
244 A41 40p rose ('29)   1.50   1.25
  a. Tete beche pair   12.50
  b. Vert. pair, imperf. horiz.   10.00
245 A42 50p red   .60   .50
246 A42 50p dk blue ('29)   1.75   1.25
    Nos. 237-246 (10)   12.60   7.65
The sheets of these stamps are often imperforate at the outer margins.
Nos. 237-238 are newspaper stamps.

This handstamp was used for ten
months by the Revolutionary Gov't in
Kabul as a control mark on outgoing
mail. It occasionally fell on the stamps
but there is no evidence that it was officially used as an overprint. Unused
copies were privately made.

Independence
Monument
A46

Wmk. Large Seal in the Sheet
1931, Aug.   **Litho.**   **Perf. 12**
Laid Paper
Without Gum
262 A46 20p red   1.00   .60
13th Independence Day.

National
Assembly
Chamber
A47

A48

A50

National
Assembly
Building
A49

National
Assembly
Chamber
A51

National
Assembly
Building
A52

1932   Unwmk.   Typo.   Perf. 12
Wove Paper
263 A47 40p olive   1.00   .40
264 A48 60p violet   .65   .50
265 A49 80p dark red   1.00   .80
266 A50 1af black   10.00   4.25
267 A51 2af ultra   3.50   2.75
268 A52 3af gray green   4.25   3.50
    Nos. 263-268 (6)   20.40 12.20
Formation of the Natl. Council. Imperforate
or perforated examples on ungummed chalky
paper are proofs.
See Nos. 304-305.

Mosque at
Balkh — A53

Kabul
Fortress
A54

Parliament
House, Darul
Funun — A55

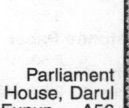

Parliament
House, Darul
Funun — A56

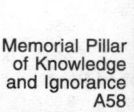

Arch of Qalai
Bist — A57

Memorial Pillar
of Knowledge
and Ignorance
A58

Independence
Monument — A59

Minaret at
Herat — A60

Arch of
Paghman
A61

Ruins at
Balkh — A62

Minarets of
Heret — A63

Great Buddha at
Bamian — A64

1932   Typo.   Perf. 12

269	A53	10p brown	.50	.20
270	A54	15p dk brown	.60	.20
271	A55	20p red	.30	.20
272	A56	25p dk green	.75	.20
273	A57	30p red	.40	.30
274	A58	40p orange	.65	.35
275	A59	50p blue	.80	.35
a.		Tete beche pair	5.50	
276	A60	60p blue	1.50	.50
277	A61	80p violet	1.75	1.00
278	A62	1af dark blue	2.75	.60
279	A63	2af dk red violet	3.75	2.00
280	A64	3af claret	4.25	2.50
		Nos. 269-280 (12)	18.00	8.40

Counterfeits of types A53-A65 exist.
See Nos. 290-295, 298-299, 302-303.

Entwined 2's — A65

Two types:
Type I - Numerals shaded. Size about
21x29mm.
Type II - Numerals unshaded. Size about
21¾x30mm.

1931-38   Perf. 12, 11x12

281	A65	2p red brn (I)	.25	.20
282	A65	2p olive blk (I) ('34)	.35	.20
283	A65	2p grnsh gray (I) ('34)	.35	.20
283A	A65	2p black (II) ('36)	.35	.20
284	A65	2p salmon (II) ('38)	.25	.20
284A	A65	2p rose (I) ('38)	.25	.20
b.		Imperf., pair	3.00	

Imperf

285	A65	2p black (II) ('37)	.75	.20
286	A65	2p salmon (II) ('38)	.25	.20
		Nos. 281-286 (8)	2.70	1.60

The newspaper rate was 2 pouls.

A66   A67

1932, Aug.   Perf. 12

287 A66 1af Independence Monument   2.75 1.50
14th Independence Day.

1932, Oct.   Typo.

1929 Liberation Monument, Kabul.

288 A67 80p red brown   .85 .50

Arch of Paghman — A68

1933, Aug.
289 A68 50p light ultra   1.25 1.25
15th Independence Day.

Types of 1932 and

Royal
Palace,
Kabul
A69

Darrah- Shikari
Pass, Hindu
Kush — A70

1934-38   Typo.   Perf. 12

290	A53	10p deep violet	.20	.20
291	A54	15p turq green	.20	.20
292	A55	20p magenta	.25	.20
293	A56	25p deep rose	.30	.20
294	A57	30p orange	.40	.20
295	A58	40p blue black	.75	.30
296	A69	45p dark blue	1.50	1.00
297	A69	45p red ('38)	.50	.20
298	A59	50p orange	.30	.20
299	A60	60p purple	.85	.20
300	A70	75p red	1.00	.35
301	A70	75p dk blue ('38)	.60	.40
302	A61	80p brown vio	1.00	.50
303	A62	1af red violet	1.60	1.00
304	A51	2af gray black	3.00	2.00
305	A52	3af ultra	5.00	3.00
		Nos. 290-305 (16)	17.45	10.15

Nos. 290, 292, 300, 304, 305 exist imperf.

Independence Monument — A71

1934, Aug.   Litho.
Without Gum

306 A71 50p pale green   2.50 1.25
a.   Tete beche pair   10.00 3.50

16th year of Independence. Each sheet of
40 (4x10) included 4 tete beche pairs as lower
half of sheet was inverted.

Independence
Monument — A74

Fireworks
Display
A75

1935, Aug. 15
Laid Paper
309 A74 50p dark blue   1.25 1.25
17th year of Independence.

1936, Aug. 15   Perf. 12
Wove Paper
310 A75 50p red violet   1.25 1.00
18th year of Independence.

Independence Monument and Nadir
Shah — A76

1937
311 A76 50p vio & bis brn   1.00 .60
a.   Imperf., pair   2.25
19th year of Independence.

Mohammed Nadir Shah
A77   A78

1938   Perf. 11x12
Without Gum
315 A77 50p brt blue & sepia   5.00 2.50
a.   Imperf. in pair   20.00
20th year of Independence.

1939   Perf. 11, 12x11
317 A78 50p deep salmon   1.75 1.00
21st year of Independence.

National
Arms
A79

Parliament House, Darul Funun — A80

Royal
Palace,
Kabul
A81

Independence
Monument — A82

Independence Monument and Nadir
Shah — A83

Mohammed Zahir Shah — A84

Mohammed
Zahir Shah
A85

Perf. 11, 11x12, 12x11, 12

1939-61   Typo.

318	A79	2p intense blk	.20	.20
318A	A79	2p brt pink ('61)	1.50	.50
319	A80	10p brt purple	.20	.20
320	A80	15p brt green	.20	.20
321	A80	20p red lilac	.20	.20
322	A81	25p rose red	1.00	.25
322A	A81	25p green ('41)	.50	.20
323	A81	30p orange	.20	.20
324	A81	40p dk gray	.20	.20
325	A82	45p brt carmine	.20	.20
326	A82	50p dp orange	.30	.20
327	A82	60p violet	.60	.20
328	A83	75p ultra	3.00	.75
328A	A83	75p red vio ('41)	.75	.30
328C	A83	75p brt red ('44)	3.00	3.00
328D	A83	75p chnt brn ('49)	4.00	3.00
329	A83	80p chocolate	.50	.50
a.		80p dull red violet (error)		
330	A84	1af brt red violet	1.50	.75
330A	A85	1af brt red vio ('44)	3.00	1.50
331	A85	2af copper red	1.75	.50
a.		2af deep rose red	2.50	1.40
332	A84	3af deep blue	3.75	1.60
		Nos. 318-332 (21)	26.55	14.65

Many shades exist in this issue.
On No. 332 the King faces slightly left.
No. 318A issued with and without gum.
See #795A-795B. For similar design see
#907A.

Mohammed Nadir
Shah — A86

1940, Aug. 23   Perf. 11
333 A86 50p gray green   .75 .60
22nd year of Independence.

 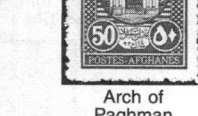

Independence   Arch of
Monument   Paghman
A87   A88

1941, Aug. 23   Perf. 12
334 A87 15p gray green   8.00 2.75
335 A88 50p red brown   1.25 .85
23rd year of Independence.

Sugar
Factory,
Baghlan
A89

1942, Apr.   **Perf. 12**
336 A89 1.25af blue (shades)   2.00 1.00
  a.   1.25af ultra   2.00 1.00

In 1949, a 1.50af brown, type A89, was sold
for 3af by the Philatelic Office, Kabul. It was
not valid for postage. Value $3.50.

Independence
Monument — A90

Mohammed
Nadir Shah
and Arch of
Paghman
A91

1942, Aug. 23   **Perf. 12**
337 A90 35p bright green   2.75 2.00
338 A91 125p chalky blue   1.40 1.10

24th year of Independence.

Independence Monument and Nadir
Shah — A92

Mohammed Nadir
Shah — A93

Perf. 11x12, 12x11
1943, Aug. 25   Typo.   Unwmk.
339 A92 35p carmine   18.00 6.00
340 A93 1.25af dark blue   3.00 1.75

25th year of Independence.

Tomb of Gohar
Shad, Herat — A94

Ruins of
Qalai
Bist — A95

1944, May 1   **Perf. 12, 11x12**
341 A94 35p orange   .50 .30
342 A95 70p violet   1.00 .60
  a.   70p rose lilac   3.50 .75

A96

A97

1944, Aug.   **Perf. 12**
343 A96 35p crimson   .80 .60
344 A97 1.25af ultra   1.40 1.10

26th year of Independence.

A98

A99

1945, July
345 A98 35p deep red lilac   .75 .65
346 A99 1.25af blue   1.75 1.50

27th year of Independence.

Mohammed Zahir Shah — A100

Independence   Mohammed Nadir
Monument   Shah
A101   A102

1946, July
347 A100 15p emerald   .45 .35
348 A101 20p dp red lilac   .70 .55
349 A102 125p blue   1.75 1.75
  Nos. 347-349 (3)   2.90 2.65

28th year of Independence.

Zahir Shah
and Ruins of
Qalai
Bist — A103

A104

A105

1947, Aug.
350 A103 15p yellow green   .30 .20
351 A104 35p plum   .40 .20
352 A105 125p deep blue   1.40 1.40
  Nos. 350-352 (3)   2.10 1.80

29th year of Independence.

Begging
Child
A106

A107

1948, May Unwmk. Typo. Perf. 12
353 A106 35p yel green   3.00 2.00
354 A107 125p gray blue   3.00 2.25

Children's Day, May 29, 1948, and valid only
on that day. Proceeds were used for Child
Welfare.

A108   A109

A110

1948, Aug.
355 A108 15p green   .20 .20
356 A109 20p magenta   .40 .20
357 A110 125p dark blue   .75 .70
  Nos. 355-357 (3)   1.35 1.10

30th year of Independence.

United Nations Emblem — A111

1948, Oct. 24
358 A111 125p dk violet blue   7.00 7.00

UN, 3rd anniv. Valid one day only. Sheets of
9.

Maiwand Victory
Column,
Kandahar — A112

Zahir Shah
and Ruins
of Qalai
Bist
A113

Independence Monument and Nadir
Shah — A114

1949, Aug.   Typo.   Perf. 12
359 A112 25p green   .25 .20
360 A113 35p magenta   .35 .25
361 A114 1.25af blue   .90 .75
  Nos. 359-361 (3)   1.50 1.20

31st year of Independence.

> **Catalogue values for unused
> stamps in this section, from this
> point to the end of the section, are
> for Never Hinged items.**

Nadir
Shah — A117

1950, Aug.
364 A117 35p red brown   .30 .30
365 A117 125p blue   .65 .65

32nd year of Independence.

Medical
School
and
Nadir Shah
A119

1950, Dec. 22   Typo.   Perf. 12
Size: 38x25mm
367 A119 35p emerald   .60 .60

Size: 46x30mm

368	A119	1.25af deep blue	1.90 1.90
a.		1.25af black (error)	6.00

19th anniv. of the founding of Afghanistan's Faculty of Medicine. On sale and valid for use on Dec. 22-28, 1950.

Minaret, Herat
A120

Zahir Shah
A121

Mosque of Khodja Abu Parsar, Balkh — A122

A123

A124

20p, Buddha at Bamian. 40p, Ruined arch. 45p, Maiwand Victory onument. 50p, View of Kandahar. 60p, Ancient tower. 70p, Afghanistan flag. 80p, 1af, Profile of Zahir Shah in uniform.

Photogravure, Engraved, Engraved and Lithographed
Perf. 12, 12½, 13x12½, 13½
1951, Mar. 21   Unwmk.
Imprint: "Waterlow & Sons Limited, London"

369	A120	10p yellow & brn	.20 .20
370	A120	15p blue & brn	.25 .20
371	A120	20p black	7.50 2.75
372	A121	25p green	.30 .20
373	A122	30p cerise	.35 .20
374	A121	35p violet	.40 .20
375	A120	40p chestnut brn	.40 .20
376	A120	45p deep blue	.40 .20
377	A122	50p olive black	1.25 .35
378	A120	60p black	1.50 .50
379	A122	70p dk grn, blk, red & grn	.50 .20
380	A123	75p cerise	.75 .35
381	A123	80p carmine & blk	1.00 .35
382	A123	1af dp grn & vio	.75 .35
383	A124	1.25af rose lil & blk	5.00 .35
384	A124	2af ultra	1.10 .35
385	A124	3af ultra & blk	2.50 .90
		Nos. 369-385 (17)	24.15 7.70

Nos. 372, 374 and 381 to 385 are engraved, No. 379 is engraved and lithographed.
Imperfs. exist of the photogravure stamps.
See Nos. 445-451, 453, 552A-552D. For surcharges see Nos. B1-B2.

Arch of Paghman
A125

Nadir Shah and Independence Monument — A126

Overprint in Violet

Perf. 13½x13, 13
1951, Aug. 25   Engr.

386	A125	35p dk green & blk	1.00 .50
387	A126	1.25af deep blue	2.00 1.00

Overprint reads "Sol 33 Istiqlal" or "33rd Year of Independence." Overprint measures about 11mm wide.
See Nos. 398-399B, 441-442.

Proposed Flag of Pashtunistan — A127

Design: 125p, Flag and Pashtunistan warrior.

1951, Sept. 2   Litho.   Perf. 11½

388	A127	35p dull chocolate	.80 .65
389	A127	125p blue	2.00 1.75

Issued to publicize "Free Pashtunistan" Day.

Imperforates
From 1951 to 1958, quantities of nearly all locally-printed stamps were left imperforate and sold by the government at double face. From 1959 until March, 1964, many of the imperforates were sold for more than face value.

Avicenna — A128

1951, Nov. 4   Typo.   Perf. 11½

390	A128	35p deep claret	.50 .35
391	A128	125p blue	1.40 1.10

20th anniv. of the founding of the natl. Graduate School of Medicine.

A129

Dove and UN Symbols
A130

1951, Oct. 24

392	A129	35p magenta	1.40 1.00
393	A130	125p blue	3.50 2.75

7th anniv. of the UN.

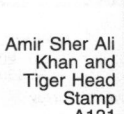

Amir Sher Ali Khan and Tiger Head Stamp
A131

Nos. 395, 397, Zahir Shah and stamp.

1951, Dec. 23   Litho.

394	A131	35p chocolate	.35 .35
395	A131	35p rose lilac	.35 .35
396	A131	125p ultra	.65 .60
a.		Cliche of 35p in plate of 125p	80.00 80.00
397	A131	125p aqua	.65 .60
		Nos. 394-397 (4)	2.00 1.90

76th anniv. of the UPU.

Stamps of 1951 Without Overprint
Perf. 13½x13, 13
1952, Aug. 24   Engr.

398	A125	35p dk green & blk	1.25 1.25
399	A126	1.25af deep blue	1.25 1.25

For overprints see #399A-399B, 441-442.

Same Overprinted in Violet

399A	A125	35p dk grn & blk	.60 .40
399B	A126	1.25af deep blue	1.60 1.00

#398-399B issued for 34th Independence Day.

Globe — A132

Perf. 11½
1952, Oct. 25   Unwmk.   Litho.

400	A132	35p rose	.55 .45
401	A132	125p aqua	1.10 1.00

Issued to honor the United Nations.

Symbol of Medicine
A134

Tribal Warrior, Natl. Flag — A135

1952, Nov.   Perf. 11½

403	A134	35p chocolate	.40 .35
404	A134	125p violet blue	1.10 1.10

21st anniv. of the natl. Graduate School of Medicine.
No. 404 is inscribed in French with white letters on a colored background.

1952, Sept. 1   Perf. 11

405	A135	35p red	.30 .30
406	A135	125p dark blue	.60 .60

No. 406 is inscribed in French "Pashtunistan Day, 1952."

Flags of Afghanistan & Pashtunistan
A139

Badge of Pashtunistan
A140

Perf. 10½x11, 11
1953, Sept. 1   Unwmk.

411	A139	35p vermilion	.20 .20
412	A140	125p blue	.60 .45

Issued to publicize "Free Pashtunistan" Day.

Nadir Shah and Flag Bearer
A141

A142

1953, Aug. 24   Perf. 11

413	A141	35p green	.20 .20
414	A142	125p violet	.75 .60

35th anniv. of Independence.

United Nations Emblem — A143

1953, Oct. 24

415	A143	35p lilac	.60 .60
416	A143	125p violet blue	1.50 1.25

United Nations Day, 1953.

A144

Nadir Shah — A145

1953, Nov. 29

417	A144	35p orange	.65 .65
418	A145	125p chalky blue	1.50 1.50

22nd anniv. of the founding of the natl. Graduate School of Medicine.

Redrawn

35p. Original- Right character in second line of Persian inscription: ۳

Redrawn- Persian character: ۲

125p: Original- Inscribed "XXIII," "MADECINE" and "ANNIVERAIRE" Redrawn- Inscribed "XXII," "MEDECINE" and "ANNIVERSAIRE"

1953
419 A144 35p deep orange   3.50
420 A145 125p chalky blue   4.25

Nadir Shah and Symbols of Independence — A146

1954, Aug.   Typo.   Perf. 11
421 A146 35p carmine rose   .35   .30
422 A146 125p violet blue   1.00   .80
    36th year of Independence.

Raising Flag of Pashtunistan A147

1954, Sept.   Perf. 11½
423 A147 35p chocolate   .35   .30
424 A147 125p blue   1.00   .80
    Issued to publicize "Free Pashtunistan" Day.

UN Flag and Map — A148

1954, Oct. 24   Perf. 11
425 A148 35p carmine rose   .65   .65
426 A148 125p dk violet blue 2.00 2.00
    9th anniv. of the United Nations.

UN Symbols A149

Design: 125p, UN emblem & flags.

1955, June 26   Litho.   Perf. 11
    Size: 26½x36mm
427 A149 35p dark green   .45   .40
    Size: 28½x36mm
428 A149 125p aqua   1.10   .90
    10th anniv. of the UN charter.

Nadir Shah (center) and Brothers A150

1929 Civil War Scene and Zahir Shah — A151

Tribal Elders' Council and Pashtun Flag — A152

1955, Aug.   Unwmk.   Perf. 11
429 A150 35p brt pink   .30   .30
430 A150 35p violet blue   .30   .30
431 A151 125p rose lilac   .90   .75
432 A151 125p light violet   .90   .75
    Nos. 429-432 (4)   2.40 2.10
    37th anniv. of Independence.

1955, Sept. 5
433 A152 35p orange brown   .20   .20
434 A152 125p yellow green   .90   .65
    Issued for "Free Pashtunistan" Day.

UN Flag — A153   A154

1955, Oct. 24   Unwmk.   Perf. 11
435 A153 35p orange brown   .75   .60
436 A153 125p brt ultra   1.40 1.10
    10th anniv. of the United Nations.

1956, Aug.   Litho.
437 A154 35p lt green   .25   .20
438 A154 140p lt violet blue .90   .75
    38th year of Independence.

Jesh'n Exhibition Hall A155

1956, Aug. 25
439 A155 50p chocolate   .25   .20
440 A155 50p lt violet blue   .25   .20
    International Exposition at Kabul.
    Of the 50p face value, only 35p paid postage. The remaining 15p went to the Exposition.

Nos. 398-399 Handstamped in Violet

a

b

1957, Aug.   Engr.   Perf. 13½x13, 13
441 A125 (a) 35p dk green & blk .40   .20
442 A126 (b) 1.25af deep blue   .60   .50
    Arabic overprint measures 19mm.
    39th year of independence.

Pashtunistan Flag — A156

1957, Sept. 1   Litho.   Perf. 11
443 A156 50p pale lilac rose   .60   .40
444 A156 155p light violet   .90   .75
    Issued for "Free Pashtunistan" Day. French inscription on No. 444. 15p of each stamp went to the Pashtunistan Fund.

Types of 1951 and

Game of Buzkashi A157

Perf. 12, 12½, 12½x13, 13, 13x12, 13x12½, 13½x14
Photo., Engr., Engr.& Litho.
1957, Nov. 23   Unwmk.
Imprint: "Waterlow & Sons Limited, London"
445 A122 30p brown   .20   .20
446 A122 40p rose red   .20   .20
447 A122 50p yellow   .35   .20
448 A120 60p ultra   .40   .20
449 A123 75p brt violet   .50   .20
450 A123 80p violet & brn   .50   .20
451 A123 1af carmine & ultra 1.00 .20
452 A157 140p olive & dp claret 2.00 .50
453 A124 3af orange & blk   2.50 .50
    Nos. 445-453 (9)   7.65 2.40
    No. 452 lacks imprint.

Nadir Shah and Flag-bearer A158

1958, Aug. 25   Perf. 13½x14
454 A158 35p dp yellow green .20   .20
455 A158 140p brown   .55   .35
    40th year of Independence.

Exposition Buildings A159

1958, Aug. 23   Litho.   Perf. 11
456 A159 35p brt blue green   .20   .20
457 A159 140p vermilion   .50   .40
    International Exposition at Kabul.

Pres. Celal Bayar of Turkey — A160

Flags of UN and Afghanistan A161

1958, Sept. 13   Unwmk.
458 A160 50p lt blue   .20   .20
459 A160 100p brown   .35   .30
    Visit of President Celal Bayar of Turkey.

1958, Oct. 24   Photo.   Perf. 14x13½
Flags in Original Colors
460 A161 50p dark gray   .60   .60
461 A161 100p green   1.10   .90
    United Nations Day, Oct. 24.

Atomic Energy Encircling the Hemispheres — A162

1958, Oct. 20   Perf. 13½x14
462 A162 50p blue   .60   .35
463 A162 100p dp red lilac   .90   .55
    Issued to promote Atoms for Peace.

UNESCO Building, Paris A163

1958, Nov. 3
464 A163 50p dp yellow grn   .50   .40
465 A163 100p brown olive   .75   .60
    UNESCO Headquarters in Paris opening, Nov. 3.

Globe and Torch A164

Perf. 13½x14
1958, Dec. 10   Unwmk.
466 A164 50p lilac rose   .35   .35
467 A164 100p maroon   .65   .65
    10th anniv. of the signing of the Universal Declaration of Human Rights.

Nadir Shah and Flags A165

1959, Aug.   Litho.   Perf. 11 Rough
468 A165 35p light vermilion .20   .20
469 A165 165p light violet   .65   .40
    41st year of Independence.

Uprooted Oak Emblem — A166

1960, Apr. 7   Perf. 11
470 A166 50p deep orange   .20   .20
471 A166 165p blue   .35   .30
    World Refugee Year, 7/1/59-6/30/60.
    Two imperf. souvenir sheets exist. Both contain a 50p and a 165p, type A166, with marginal inscriptions and WRY emblem in maroon. On one sheet the stamps are in the colors of Nos. 470-471 (size 108x81mm). On the other, the 50p is blue and the 165p is deep orange (size 107x80mm). Value $4 each.
    For surcharges see Nos. B35-B36.

Buzkashi
A167

1960, May 4   *Perf. 11, Imperf.*
472 A167 25p rose red   .25   .20
473 A167 50p bluish green   .50   .35
   a. Cliche of 25p in plate of 50p   20.00 20.00
      See Nos. 549-550A.

Independence
Monument
A168

1960, Aug.   *Perf. 11, 12*
474 A168 50p light blue   .20   .20
475 A168 175p bright pink   .40   .40
     42nd Independence Day.

Globe and
Flags
A169

1960, Oct. 24   *Litho.*   *Perf. 11, 12*
476 A169 50p rose lilac   .25   .20
477 A169 175p ultra   .75   .65
       UN Day.
An imperf. souvenir sheet contains one each of Nos. 476-477 with marginal inscriptions ("La Journée des Nations Unies 1960" in French and Persian) and UN emblem in light blue. Size: 127x85½mm. Value $4.
   This sheet was surcharged "+20ps" in 1962. Value $8.50.

Teacher
Pointing to
Globe
A170

1960, Oct. 23   *Perf. 11*
478 A170 50p brt pink   .20   .20
479 A170 100p brt green   .70   .45
    Issued to publicize Teacher's Day.

Mohammed Zahir Shah — A171

1960, Oct. 15
480 A171 50p red brown   .30   .20
481 A171 150p dk car rose   .90   .30
   Honoring the King on his 46th birthday.

Buzkashi
A172

1960, Nov. 9   *Perf. 11*
482 A172 175p lt red brown   1.00   .40
      See Nos. 551-552.

No. 482 Overprinted "1960" and
Olympic Rings in Bright Green.

1960, Dec. 24
483 A172 175p red brown   2.00 1.75
   a. Souv. sheet of 1, imperf.   8.50
   17th Olympic Games, Rome, 8/25-9/11.

Mir Wais — A173

1961, Jan. 5   *Unwmk.*   *Perf. 10½*
484 A173 50p brt rose lilac   .20   .20
485 A173 175p ultra   .60   .40
   a. Souv. sheet of #484-485, imperf.   2.00 2.00
   Mir Wais (1665-1708), national leader.

No Postal Need
existed for the 1p-15p denominations issued with sets of 1961-63 (between Nos. 486 and 649, B37 and B65).
   The lowest denomination actually used for non-philatelic postage in that period was 25p (except for the 2p newspaper rate for which separate stamps were provided).

Horse,
Sheep and
Camel
A174

#487, 175p, Rock partridge. 10p, 100p, Afghan hound. 15p, 150p, Grain & grasshopper, vert.

1961, Mar. 29   *Photo.*   *Perf. 13½x14*
486 A174 2p maroon & buff
487 A174 2p ultra & org
488 A174 5p brown & yel
489 A174 10p black & salmon
490 A174 15p blue grn & yel
491 A174 25p black & pink
492 A174 50p black & citron
493 A174 100p black & pink
494 A174 150p green & yel
495 A174 175p ultra & pink
     Nos. 486-495 (10)   2.00
Two souvenir sheets, perf. and imperf., contain 2 stamps, 1 each of #492-493. Value $2 each.

Afghan
Fencing
A175

Designs: No. 497, 5p, 25p, 50p, Wrestlers. 10p, 100p, Man with Indian clubs. 15p, 150p, Afghan fencing. 175p, Children skating.

1961, July 6   *Perf. 13½x14*
496 A175 2p green & rose lil
497 A175 2p brown & citron
498 A175 5p gray & rose
499 A175 10p blue & bister
500 A175 15p sl bl & dl lil

---

501 A175 25p black & dl bl
502 A175 50p sl grn & bis brn
503 A175 100p brown & bl grn
504 A175 150p brown & org yel
505 A175 175p black & blue
     Nos. 496-505 (10)   3.00
   Issued for Children's Day.
A souvenir sheet exists, perf. and imperf., containing one each of Nos. 502-503. Value $4.50 each.
For surcharges see Nos. B37-B41.

Bande Amir
Lakes
A176

1961, Aug. 7   *Photo.*   *Perf. 13½x14*
506 A176 3af brt blue   .35   .30
507 A176 10af rose claret   1.10 1.00

Nadir
Shah — A177

Girl Scout — A178

1961, Aug. 23   *Perf. 14x13½*
508 A177 50p rose red & blk   .50   .40
509 A177 175p brt grn & org brn   1.00   .80
     43rd Independence Day.
Two souvenir sheets, perf. and imperf., contain one each of Nos. 508-509. Value, each $2.50.

      Perf. 14x13½
1961, July 23   *Unwmk.*
510 A178 50p dp car & dk gray   .40   .20
511 A178 175p dp grn & rose brn   .90   .40
     Issued for Women's Day.
Two souvenir sheets exist, perf. and imperf., containing one each of Nos. 510-511. Value $3 each.

Exhibition
Hall, Kabul
A179

1961, Aug. 23   *Perf. 13½x14*
512 A179 50p yel brn & yel grn   .20   .20
513 A179 175p blue & brn   .40   .30
    International Exhibition at Kabul.

Pathan with
Pashtunistan
Flag — A180

1961, Aug. 31   *Photo.*   *Perf. 14x13½*
514 A180 50p blk, lil & red   .20   .20
515 A180 175p brn, grnsh bl & red   .35   .30
    Issued for "Free Pashtunistan Day."

Souvenir sheets exist perf. and imperf. containing one each of Nos. 514-515. Value $2 each.

Assembly
Building
A181

1961, Sept. 10   *Perf. 12*
516 A181 50p dk gray & brt grn   .20   .20
517 A181 175p ultra & brn   .45   .30
   Anniv. of the founding of the Natl. Assembly.
Souvenir sheets exist, perf. and imperf., containing one each of Nos. 516-517. Value $1 each.

Exterminating Anopheles
Mosquito — A182

1961, Oct. 5   *Perf. 13½x14*
518 A182 50p blk & brn lil   .50   .30
519 A182 175p maroon & brt grn   1.10   .50
   Anti-Malaria campaign. Souvenir sheets exist, perf. and imperf., containing one each of Nos. 518-519. Value $4 each.

Zahir
Shah — A183

1961, Oct. 15   *Perf. 13½*
520 A183 50p lilac & blue   .20   .20
521 A183 175p emerald & red brn   .40   .35
   Issued to honor King Mohammed Zahir Shah on his 47th birthday.
   See Nos. 609-612.

Pomegranates — A184

Fruit: No. 523, 5p, 25p, 50p, Grapes. 10p, 150p, Apples. 15p, 175p, Pomegranates. 100p, Melons.

1961, Oct. 16   *Perf. 13½x14*
     Fruit in Natural Colors
522 A184 2p black
523 A184 2p green
524 A184 5p lilac rose
525 A184 10p lilac
526 A184 15p dk blue
527 A184 25p dull red
528 A184 50p purple
529 A184 100p brt blue
530 A184 150p brown
531 A184 175p olive gray
     Nos. 522-531 (10)   1.75
   For Afghan Red Crescent Society.
Souvenir sheets exist, perf. and imperf., containing one each of Nos. 528-529. Value $1.50 each.
   For surcharges see Nos. B42-B46.

UN Headquarters, NY — A185

1961, Oct. 24   Perf. 13½x14
Vertical Borders in Emerald, Red and Black
532 A185   1p rose lilac
533 A185   2p slate
534 A185   3p brown
535 A185   4p ultra
536 A185   50p rose red
537 A185   75p gray
538 A185   175p brt green
          Nos. 532-538 (7)   1.50

16th anniv. of the UN. Souvenir sheets exist, perf. and imperf., containing one each of Nos. 536-538. Value $2 each.

Children Giving Flowers to Teacher — A186

People Raising UNESCO Symbol — A187

#540, 5p, 25p, 50p, Tulips. 10p, 100p, Narcissus. 15p, 150p, Children giving flowers to teacher. 175p, Teacher with children in front of school.

1961, Oct. 26   Photo.   Perf. 12
539 A186   2p multicolored
540 A186   2p multicolored
541 A186   5p multicolored
542 A186   10p multicolored
543 A186   15p multicolored
544 A186   25p multicolored
545 A186   50p multicolored
546 A186   100p multicolored
547 A186   150p multicolored
548 A186   175p multicolored
          Nos. 539-548 (10)   1.75

Issued for Teacher's Day.
Souvenir sheets exist, perf. and imperf. containing one each of Nos. 545-546. Value, 2 sheets, $4.
For surcharges see Nos. B47-B51.

Buzkashi Types of 1960
1961-72   Litho.   Perf. 10½, 11
549 A167   25p violet   .20   .20
 b.   25p brt vio, typo. ('72)   .20   .20
549A A167   25p citron ('63)   .20   .20
550 A167   50p blue   .30   .20
550A A167   50p yel org ('69)   .20   .20
551 A172   100p citron   .45   .20
551A A172   150p orange ('64)   .30   .20
552 A172   2af lt green   1.10   .45
          Nos. 549-552 (7)   2.75   1.65

Zahir Shah Types of 1951
Photo., Engr., Engr. & Litho.
1962   Perf. 13x12, 13
Imprint: "Thomas De La Rue & Co. Ltd."
552A A123   75p brt purple   1.10   .25
552B A123   1af car & ultra   1.40   .35
552C A124   2af blue   1.75   .75
552D A124   3af orange & blk   4.00   1.10
          Nos. 552A-552D (4)   8.25   2.45

1962, July 2   Photo.   Perf. 14x13½
553 A187   2p rose lil & brn
554 A187   2p ol bis & brn
555 A187   5p dp org & dk grn
556 A187   10p gray & mag
557 A187   15p blue & brn
558 A187   25p org yel & pur
559 A187   50p lt grn & pur

560 A187   75p brt cit & brn
561 A187   100p dp org & brn
          Nos. 553-561 (9)   1.60

15th anniv. of UNESCO. Souvenir sheets exist, perf. and imperf. One contains Nos. 558-559; the other contains Nos. 560-561. Value, $3 each.
For surcharges see Nos. B52-B60.

Ahmad Shah — A188

Afghan Hound — A189

1962, Feb. 24   Photo.   Perf. 13½
562 A188   50p red brn & gray   .20   .20
563 A188   75p green & salmon   .25   .20
564 A188   100p claret & bister   .40   .30
          Nos. 562-564 (3)   .85   .70

Ahmad Shah (1724-73), founded the Afghan kingdom in 1747 and ruled until 1773.

1962, Apr. 21   Perf. 14x13½
Designs: 5p, 75p, Afghan cock. 10p, 100p, Kondjid plant. 15p, 125p, Astrakhan skins.
565 A189   2p rose & brn
566 A189   2p lt green & brn
567 A189   5p dp rose & claret
568 A189   10p lt grn & sl grn
569 A189   15p blue grn & blk
570 A189   25p blue & brn
571 A189   50p gray & brn
572 A189   75p rose lil & lil
573 A189   100p gray & dl grn
574 A189   125p rose brn & blk
          Nos. 565-574 (10)   2.00

Agriculture Day. Perf. and imperf. souvenir sheets exist. Set of 4 sheets, value $4.

Athletes with Flag and Nadir Shah — A190

Woman in National Costume — A191

1962, Aug. 23   Perf. 12
575 A190   25p multicolored   .20   .20
576 A190   50p multicolored   .20   .20
577 A190   150p multicolored   .25   .20
          Nos. 575-577 (3)   .65   .60

44th Independence Day.

1962, Aug. 30   Perf. 11½x12
578 A191   25p lilac & brn   .20   .20
579 A191   50p green & brn   .25   .20
          Nos. 578-579,C15-C16 (4)   1.90   1.85

Issued for Women's Day. A souvenir sheet exists containing one each of #578-579, C15-C16. Value $3.

Man and Woman with Flag — A192

Malaria Eradication Emblem and Swamp — A193

1962, Aug. 31   Photo.
580 A192   25p black, pale bl & red   .20   .20
581 A192   50p black, grn & red   .20   .20
582 A192   150p black, pink & red   .45   .20
          Nos. 580-582 (3)   .85   .60

Issued for "Free Pashtunistan Day."

1962, Sept. 5   Perf. 14x13½
583 A193   2p dk grn & ol gray
584 A193   2p dk green & sal
585 A193   5p red brn & ol
586 A193   10p red brn & brt grn
587 A193   15p red brn & gray
588 A193   25p brt bl & bluish grn
589 A193   50p brt bl & rose lil
590 A193   75p black & blue
591 A193   100p black & brt pink
592 A193   150p black & bis brn
593 A193   175p black & orange
          Nos. 583-593 (11)   2.50

WHO drive to eradicate malaria. Perf. and imperf. souvenir sheets exist. Set of 4 sheets, value $6.50.
For surcharges see Nos. B61-B71.

National Assembly Building — A194

Perf. 10½, 11 (100p)
1962, Sept. 10   Unwmk.   Litho.
594 A194   25p lt green   .35   .25
595 A194   50p blue   .55   .35
596 A194   75p rose   .75   .55
597 A194   100p violet   1.10   .90
598 A194   125p ultra   1.25   1.10
          Nos. 594-598 (5)   4.00   3.15

Establishment of the National Assembly.

Horse Racing — A195

Designs: 2p, Pole vaulting. 3p, Wrestling. 4p, Weight lifting. 5p, Soccer.

1962, Sept. 22   Photo.   Perf. 12
Black Inscriptions
599 A195   1p lt ol & red brn
600 A195   2p lt grn & red brn
601 A195   3p yellow & dk pur
602 A195   4p pale bl & grn
603 A195   5p bluish grn & dk brn
          Nos. 99-603, C17-C22 (11)   2.50

4th Asian Games, Djakarta, Indonesia. Two souvenir sheets exist. A perforated one contains a 125p blue, dark blue and brown stamp in horse racing design. An imperf. one contains a 2af buff, purple and black stamp in soccer design. Value, $3.50 each.

Runners A196

1p, 2p, Diver, vert. 4p, Peaches. 5p, Iris, vert.

Perf. 11½x12, 12x11½
1962, Oct. 2   Unwmk.
604 A196   1p rose lil & brn
605 A196   2p blue & brn
606 A196   3p brt blue & lil
607 A196   4p ol gray & multi
608 A196   5p gray & multi
          Nos. 604-608, C23-C25 (8)   2.00

Issued for Children's Day.

King Type of 1961, Dated "1962"
1962, Oct. 15   Perf. 13½
Various Frames
609 A183   25p lilac rose & brn   .20   .20
610 A183   50p orange brn & grn   .20   .20
611 A183   75p blue & lake   .20   .20
612 A183   100p green & red brn   .30   .20
          Nos. 609-612 (4)   .90   .80

Issued to honor King Mohammed Zahir Shah on his 48th birthday.

Grapes A197

1962, Oct. 16   Perf. 12
613 A197   1p shown
614 A197   2p Grapes
615 A197   3p Pears
616 A197   4p Wistaria
617 A197   5p Blossoms
          Nos. 613-617, C26-C28 (8)   1.00

For the Afghan Red Crescent Society.

UN Headquarters, NY and Flags of UN and Afghanistan — A198

1962, Oct. 24   Unwmk.
618 A198   1p multicolored
619 A198   2p multicolored
620 A198   3p multicolored
621 A198   4p multicolored
622 A198   5p multicolored
          Nos. 618-622, C29-C31 (8)   2.00

UN Day. Souvenir sheets exist. One contains a single 4af ultramarine stamp, perforated; the other, a 4af ocher stamp, imperf. Value, 2 sheets, $5.

Boy Scout — A199

Pole Vault — A200

1962, Oct. 18   Photo.   Perf. 12
623 A199   1p yel, dk grn & sal
624 A199   2p dl yel, slate & sal
625 A199   3p rose, blk & sal
626 A199   4p multicolored
          Nos. 623-626, C32-C35 (8)   2.25

Issued to honor the Boy Scouts.

1962, Oct. 25   Unwmk.   *Perf. 12*

3p, High jump. 4p, 5p, Different blossoms.

627 A200 1p lilac & dk grn
628 A200 2p yellow grn & brn
629 A200 3p bister & vio
630 A200 4p sal pink, grn & ultra
631 A200 5p yellow, grn & bl
Nos. 627-631, C36-C37 (7)   1.25

Issued for Teacher's Day.

Rockets
A201

1962, Nov. 29

632 A201 50p pale lil & dk bl   .45
633 A201 100p lt blue & red brn   .85

UN World Meteorological Day. A souvenir sheet contains one 5af pink and green stamp. Value $6.

Ansari Mausoleum, Herat — A202

Perf. 13½
1963, Jan. 3   Unwmk.   Photo.

634 A202 50p purple & green   .20 .20
635 A202 75p gray & magenta   .20 .20
636 A202 100p orange brn & brn   .30 .30
Nos. 634-636 (3)   .70 .70

Khwaja Abdullah Ansari, Sufi, religious leader and poet, on the 900th anniv. of his death.

Sheep
A203

Silkworm, Cocoons, Moth and Mulberry Branch
A204

1963, Mar. 1   *Perf. 12*

637 A203 1p grnsh blue & blk
638 A203 2p yellow grn & blk
639 A203 3p lilac rose & blk
640 A204 4p gray, grn & brn
641 A204 5p red lil, grn & brn
Nos. 637-641, C42-C44 (8) 2.25

Issued for the Day of Agriculture.

Rice — A205

Designs: 3p, Corn. 300p, Wheat emblem.

1963, Mar. 27   Unwmk.   *Perf. 14*

642 A205 2p gray, claret & grn   .20 .20
643 A205 3p green, yel & ocher   .20 .20
644 A205 300p dk blue & yel   .30 .30
Nos. 642-644 (3)   .70 .70

FAO "Freedom from Hunger" campaign.

Meteorological Measuring Instrument — A206

Designs: 3p, 10p, Weather station. 4p, 5p, Rockets in space.

1963, May 23   Photo.   *Perf. 13½x14*

645 A206 1p dp magenta & brn
646 A206 2p brt blue & brn
647 A206 3p red & brown
648 A206 4p orange & lilac
649 A206 5p green & dl vio

Imperf

650 A206 10p red brn & grn
Nos. 645-650, C46-C50 (11)   7.50

3rd UN World Meteorological Day, Mar. 23.

Independence Monument
A207

1963, Aug. 23   Litho.   *Perf. 10½*

651 A207 25p lt green   .20 .20
652 A207 50p orange   .20 .20
653 A207 150p rose carmine   .35 .20
Nos. 651-653 (3)   .75 .60

45th Independence Day.

Pathans in Forest
A208

1963, Aug. 31   Unwmk.   *Perf. 10½*

654 A208 25p pale violet   .20 .20
655 A208 50p sky blue   .20 .20
655A A208 150p dull red brn   .45 .35
Nos. 654-655A (3)   .85 .75

Issued for "Free Pashtunistan Day."

4th Asian Games, Djakarta
A208a

2p, 250p, 300p, Wrestling. 3p, 10p, Tennis. 4p, 500p, Javelin. 5p, 9af, Shot put.

1963, Sept. 3   Litho.   *Perf. 12*

656 A208a 2p rose vio & brn
656A A208a 3p olive grn & brn
656B A208a 4p blue & brn
656C A208a 5p yel grn & brn
656D A208a 10p lt bl grn & brn
656E A208a 300p yellow & vio
656F A208a 500p lt yel bis & brn
656G A208a 9af pale grn & vio
Nos. 656-656G (8)   1.75

Souvenir Sheets

656H A208a 250p lilac & vio   1.50
656I A208a 300p blue & blk   1.50
Nos. 656-656F are airmail. Nos. 656-656I exist imperf.

National Assembly Building — A209

1963, Sept. 10   *Perf. 11*

657 A209 25p gray   .20 .20
658 A209 50p dull red   .20 .20
659 A209 75p brown   .20 .20
660 A209 100p olive   .30 .20
661 A209 125p lilac   .40 .20
Nos. 657-661 (5)   1.30 1.00

Issued to honor the National Assembly.

Balkh Gate
A210

1963, Oct. 8

662 A210 3af choc (screened margins)   .40 .30
a.   White margins   1.50 .50

In the original printing a halftone screen extended across the plate, covering the space between the stamps. A retouch removed the screen between the stamps (No. 662a).

Intl. Red Cross, Cent.
A210a

4p, 5p, 200p, 3af, Nurse holding patient, vert. 10p, 4af, 6af, Crown Prince Ahmed Shah.

1963, Oct. 9   *Perf. 13½*

662B A210a 2p olive, blk & red
662C A210a 3p blue, blk & red
662D A210a 4p lt grn, blk & red
662E A210a 5p lt vio, blk & red
662F A210a 10p gray grn, red & blk
662G A210a 100p dull bl grn, red & blk
662H A210a 200p lt brn, blk & blk
662I A210a 4af brt bl grn, red & blk
m.   Souvenir sheet of 1   1.25
662J A210a 6af lt brn, red & blk
Nos. 662B-662J (9)   1.25

Souvenir Sheet

662K A210a 3af dl blue, blk & red   1.25

Nos. 662G-662K are airmail. Nos. 662B-662K exist imperf.

Zahir Shah — A211

Kemal Ataturk — A212

1963, Oct. 15   *Perf. 10½*

663 A211 25p green   .20 .20
663A A211 50p gray   .20 .20
663B A211 75p carmine rose   .20 .20
663C A211 100p dull redsh brn   .30 .20
Nos. 663-663C (4)   .90 .80

King Mohammed Zahir Shah, 49th birthday.

1963, Oct. 10   *Perf. 10½*

664 A212 1af blue   .20 .20
665 A212 3af rose lilac   .40 .35

25th anniv. of the death of Kemal Ataturk, president of Turkey.

Protection of Nubian Monuments
A213

Designs: 5af, 7.50af, 10af, Ruins, vert.

Perf. 12, Imperf. (150p, 250p, 10af)
1963, Nov. 16   Photo.

666 A213 100p lil rose & blk
666A A213 150p rose lil & blk
666B A213 200p brown & blk
666C A213 250p ultra & blk
666D A213 500p green & blk
666E A213 5af greenish blue & gray bl
666F A213 7.50af red brn & gray
666G A213 10af ver & gray bl
Nos. 666-666G (8)   2.50

#666E-666G are airmail. #666D exists imperf.

Women's Day — A213a

Boy and Girl Scouts — A213c

A213b

1964, Jan. 5   *Perf. 14x13½*

667 A213a 2p multicolored
667A A213a 3p multicolored
667B A213a 4p multicolored
667C A213a 5p multicolored
667D A213a 10p multicolored
Nos. 667-667D (5)   1.00

Exist imperf.

1964, Jan. 5   *Perf. 13½x14, 14x13½*

#668F-668G, 668K-668M, Girl with flag.

668	A213b	2p multi	
668A	A213b	3p multi	
668B	A213b	4p multi	
668C	A213b	5p multi	
668D	A213b	10p multi	
668E	A213c	2af multi	
668F	A213c	2af multi	
668G	A213c	2.50af multi	
668H	A213c	3af multi	
668I	A213c	4af multi	
668J	A213c	5af multi	
668K	A213c	12af multi	
	Nos. 668-666K (12)	3.00	

Souvenir Sheets

668L	A213c	6af multi	.75
668M	A213c	6af multi	.75
668N	A213c	6af multi	1.25
668O	A213c	10af multi	1.25

Nos. 668E-668O are airmail. Nos 668-668K, 668N-668O exist imperf.

Children — A213d

1964, Jan. 22   *Perf. 12*

669	A213d	2p Playing ball	
669A	A213d	3p like #669	
669B	A213d	4p Swinging, jumping rope, vert.	
669C	A213d	5p Skiing, vert.	
669D	A213d	10p like #669	
669E	A213d	200p like #669C	
669F	A213d	300p like #669B	
	Nos. 669-666F (7)	2.00	

Nos. 669E-669F are airmail. All exist imperf.

Red Crescent Society — A213e

Designs: 100p, 200p, Pierre and Marie Curie, physicists. 2.50af, 7.50af Nurse examining child. 3.50af, 5af, Nurse and patients.

Perf. 14, Imperf. (#670A, 670C-670D)
1964, Feb. 8

670	A213e	100p multi	
670A	A213e	100p multi	
670B	A213e	200p multi	
670C	A213e	2.50af multi	
670D	A213e	3.50af multi	
670E	A213e	5af multi	
670F	A213e	7.50af multi	
	Nos. 670-670F (7)	3.00	

Nos. 670B-670D are airmail.

Teachers' Day — A213f

Flowers: 2p, 3p, 3af, 4af, Tulips. 4p, 5p, 3.50af, 6af, Flax. 10p, 1.50af, 2af, Iris.

Perf. 12, Imperf. (1.50af, 2af)
1964, Mar. 3

671	A213f	2p multicolored	
671A	A213f	3p multicolored	
671B	A213f	4p multicolored	
671C	A213f	5p multicolored	
671D	A213f	10p multicolored	
671E	A213f	1.50af multicolored	
671F	A213f	2af multicolored	
671G	A213f	3af multicolored	
671H	A213f	3.50af multicolored	
	Nos. 671-671H (9)	2.00	

Souvenir Sheets

671I	A213f	4af multi	1.50
671J	A213f	6af multi, imperf	4.00

#671E-671J are airmail. #671-671D exist imperf.

A213g

UN Day: 5p, 10p, 2af, 3af, 4af, Doctor and nurse, vert.

1964, Mar. 9   *Perf. 14*

672	A213g	2p multicolored	
672A	A213g	3p multicolored	
672B	A213g	4p multicolored	
672C	A213g	5p multicolored	
672D	A213g	10p multicolored	
672E	A213g	100p multicolored	
672F	A213g	2af multicolored	
672G	A213g	3af multicolored	
	Nos. 672-672G (8)	3.00 2.75	

Souvenir Sheets

672H	A213g	4af multi, imperf.	10.00
672I	A213g	5af multi	3.00

Nos. 672E-672G are airmail. Nos. 672-672G exist imperf.
For surcharges see Nos. B71A-B71J.

UNICEF A213h

Design: 5af, 7.50af, 10af, Children eating.

Perf. 14x13½, Imperf. (150p, 250p, 10af)
1964, Mar. 15

673	A213h	100p multicolored	
673A	A213h	150p multicolored	
673B	A213h	200p multicolored	
673C	A213h	250p multicolored	
673D	A213h	5af multicolored	
673E	A213h	7.50af multicolored	
673F	A213h	10af multicolored	
	Nos. 673-673F (7)	10.00	

Nos. 673D-673F are airmail.

Eradication of Malaria — A213i

4p, 5p, 5af, 10af Spraying mosquitoes.

1964, Mar. 15   *Perf. 13½*

674	A213i	2p lt red brn & yel grn	
674A	A213i	3p olive grn & buff	
674B	A213i	4p dk vio & bl grn	
674C	A213i	5p brn & grn	
674D	A213i	2af Prus bl & ver	
h.	Souvenir sheet of 1	.35	
674E	A213i	5af dk grn & lt red brn, imperf.	
i.	Souv. sheet of 1, imperf.	2.00	
674F	A213i	10af red brn & grnsh bl	
	Nos. 674-674F (7)	1.50	

674G A213i 10p on 4p Prus bl & rose   .60

No. 674G not issued without surcharge. Nos. 674-674C, 674G exist imperf. Nos. 674D-674F are airmail. Exists imperf.

"Tiger's Head" of 1878 — A214

1964, Mar. 22   Photo.   *Perf. 12*

675	A214	1.25af gold, grn & blk	.25	.20
676	A214	5af gold, rose car & blk	.55	.35

Issued to honor philately.

Unisphere and Flags A215

1964, May 3   *Perf. 13½x14*

677 A215 6af crimson, gray & grn   .30   .20

New York World's Fair, 1964-65.

Hand Holding Torch — A216

1964, May 12   Photo.   *Perf. 14x13½*

678 A216 3.75af multicolored   .20   .20

1st UN Seminar on Human Rights in Kabul, May 1964. The denomination in Persian at right erroneously reads "3.25" but the stamp was sold and used as 3.75af.

Kandahar Airport A217

1964, Apr.   Litho.   *Perf. 10½, 11*

679	A217	7.75af dk red brown	.40	.20
680	A217	9.25af lt green	.50	.20
681	A217	10.50af lt green	.50	.30
682	A217	13.75af carmine rose	.70	.40
	Nos. 679-682 (4)	2.10	1.10

Inauguration of Kandahar Airport.

Snow Leopard A218

50p, Ibex, vert. 75p, Head of argali. 5af, Yak.

1964, June 25   Photo.   *Perf. 12*

683	A218	25p yellow & blue	.20	.20
684	A218	50p dl red & grn	.20	.20
685	A218	75p Prus bl & lil	.20	.20
686	A218	5af brt grn & dk brn	.30	.30
	Nos. 683-686 (4)	.90	.90

View of Herat A219

Flag and Map of Afghanistan A220

Tourist publicity: 75p, Tomb of Queen Gowhar Shad, vert.

1964, July 12   *Perf. 13½x14, 14x13½*

687	A219	25p sepia & bl	.20	.20
688	A219	75p dp blue & buff	.20	.20
689	A220	3af red, blk & grn	.30	.20
	Nos. 687-689 (3)	.70	.60

Wrestling A221

25p, Hurdling, vert. 1af, Diving, vert. 5af, Soccer.

1964, July 26   *Perf. 12*

690	A221	25p ol bis, blk & car	.20	.20
691	A221	1af bl grn, blk & car	.20	.20
692	A221	3.75af yel grn, blk & car	.20	.20
693	A221	5af brn, blk & car	.30	.30
a.	Souv. sheet of #690-693, imperf.	.90	.90
	Nos. 690-693 (4)	.90	.90

18th Olympic Games, Tokyo, Oct. 10-25, 1964. No. 693a sold for 15af. The additional 5af went to the Afghanistan Olympic Committee.

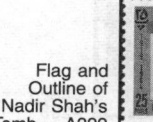

Flag and Outline of Nadir Shah's Tomb — A222

1964, Aug. 24   Photo.

695	A222	25p multicolored	.20	.20
696	A222	75p multicolored	.20	.20

Independence Day. The stamps were printed with an erroneous inscription in upper left corner: "33rd year of independence." This was locally obliterated with a typographed gold bar.

Pashtunistan Flag — A223

Zahir Shah — A225

1964, Sept. 1   Unwmk.

697 A223 100p gold, blk, red, bl & grn   .20   .20

Issued for "Free Pashtunistan Day."

1964, Oct. 17   **Perf. 14x13½**
699	A225	1.25af gold & yel grn	.20 .20
700	A225	3.75af gold & rose	.20 .20
701	A225	50af gold & gray	2.00 1.75
		Nos. 699-701 (3)	2.40 2.15

King Mohammed Zahir Shah, 50th birthday.

Coat of Arms of Afghanistan and UN Emblem A226

1964, Oct. 24   **Perf. 13½x14**
702	A226	5af gold, blk & dl bl	.20 .20

Issued for United Nations Day.

Emblem of Afghanistan Women's Association A227

1964, Nov. 9   **Photo.**   **Unwmk.**
703	A227	25p pink, dk bl & emer	.50 .25
704	A227	75p aqua, dk bl & emer	.75 .35
705	A227	1af sil, dk bl & emer	1.00 1.00
		Nos. 703-705 (3)	2.25 1.10

Issued for Women's Day.

Poet Mowlana Nooruddin Abdul Rahman Jami (1414-1492) A228

Perf. 11 Rough

1964, Nov. 23   **Litho.**
706	A228	1.50af blk, emer & yel	.85 .85

Woodpecker A229

Birds: 3.75af, Black-throated jay, vert. 5af, Impeyan pheasant, vert.

Perf. 13½x14, 14x13½

1965, Apr. 20   **Photo.**   **Unwmk.**
707	A229	1.25af multi	1.00 .50
708	A229	3.75af multi	1.75 .75
709	A229	5af multi	2.50 1.00
		Nos. 707-709 (3)	5.25 2.25

ITU Emblem, Old and New Communication Equipment — A230

1965, May 17   **Perf. 13½x14**
710	A230	5af lt bl, blk & red	.35 .35

Cent. of the ITU.

"Red City," Bamian — A231

Designs: 3.75af, Ruins of ancient Bamian city. 5af, Bande Amir, mountain lakes.

1965, May 30   **Perf. 13x13½**
711	A231	1.25af pink & multi	.20 .20
712	A231	3.75af lt blue & multi	.20 .20
713	A231	5af yellow & multi	.30 .30
		Nos. 711-713 (3)	.70 .70

Issued for tourist publicity.

ICY Emblem A232

1965, June 25   **Perf. 13½x13**
714	A232	5af multicolored	.25 .25

International Cooperation Year, 1965.

ARIANA Air Lines Emblem and DC-3 A233

5af, DC-6 at right. 10af, DC-3 on top.

Perf. 13½x14

1965, July 15   **Photo.**   **Unwmk.**
715	A233	1.25af brt bl, gray & blk	.20 .20
716	A233	5af red lil, blk & bl	.30 .30
717	A233	10af bis, blk, bl gray & grn	.75 .75
a.		Souv. sheet, #715-717, imperf	1.00 1.00
		Nos. 715-717 (3)	1.25 1.25

10th anniv. of Afghan Air Lines, ARIANA.

Nadir Shah — A234

1965, Aug. 23   **Perf. 14x13½**
718	A234	1af dl grn, blk & red brn	.25 .20

For the 47th Independence Day.

Flag of Pashtunistan — A235

Perf. 13½x14

1965, Aug. 31   **Photo.**   **Unwmk.**
719	A235	1af multicolored	.25 .20

Issued for "Free Pashtunistan Day."

Zahir Shah Signing Constitution — A236

1965, Sept. 11   **Perf. 13x13½**
720	A236	1.50af brt grn & blk	.25 .25

Promulgation of the new Constitution.

Zahir Shah and Oak Leaves — A237

1965, Oct. 14   **Perf. 14x13½**
721	A237	1.25af blk, ultra & salmon	.20 .20
722	A237	6af blk, lt bl & rose lil	.40 .35

King Mohammed Zahir Shah, 51st birthday.

Flags of UN and Afghanistan A238

1965, Oct. 24   **Perf. 13½x14**
723	A238	5af multicolored	.20 .20

Issued for United Nations Day.

Dappled Ground Gecko A239

Designs: 4af, Caucasian agamid (lizard). 8af, Horsfield's tortoise.

Perf. 13½x14

1966, May 10   **Photo.**   **Unwmk.**
724	A239	3af tan & multi	.75 .35
725	A239	4af brt grn & multi	.85 .40
726	A239	8af violet & multi	1.50 .75
		Nos. 724-726 (3)	3.10 1.50

Soccer Player and Globe — A240

1966, July 31   **Litho.**   **Perf. 14x13½**
727	A240	2af rose red & blk	.65 .20
728	A240	6af violet bl & blk	1.10 .25
729	A240	12af bister brn & blk	2.25 .55
		Nos. 727-729 (3)	4.00 1.00

World Cup Soccer Championship, Wembley, England, July 11-30.

Cotton Flower and Boll — A241

5af, Silkworm. 7af, Farmer plowing with oxen.

1966, July 31   **Perf. 13½x14**
730	A241	1af multicolored	.50 .20
731	A241	5af multicolored	1.00 .30
732	A241	7af multicolored	1.40 .40
		Nos. 730-732 (3)	2.90 .90

Issued for the Day of Agriculture.

Independence Monument — A242

1966, Aug. 23   **Photo.**   **Perf. 13½x14**
733	A242	1af multicolored	.25 .25
734	A242	3af multicolored	.75 .25

Issued to commemorate Independence Day.

Flag of Pashtunistan — A243

Perf. 11 Rough

1966, Aug. 31   **Litho.**
735	A243	1af bright blue	.50 .20

"Free Pashtunistan Day."

Bagh-i-Bala Park Casino A244

Tourist publicity: 2af, Map of Afghanistan. 8af, Tomb of Abd-er-Rahman. The casino on 4af is the former summer palace of Abd-er-Rahman near Kabul.

1966, Oct. 3   **Photo.**   **Perf. 13½x14**
736	A244	2af red & multi	.20 .20
737	A244	4af multicolored	.40 .30
738	A244	8af multicolored	.65 .60
a.		Souvenir sheet of 3, #736-738, imperf.	3.50 3.50
		Nos. 736-738 (3)	1.25 1.10

Zahir Shah — A245

UNESCO Emblem — A246

1966, Oct. 14   Perf. 14x13½
739 A245 1af dk slate grn   .20 .20
740 A245 5af red brown   .50 .25
 King Mohammed Zahir Shah, 52nd birthday. See Nos. 760-761.

1967, Mar. 6   Litho.   Perf. 12
741 A246 2af multicolored   .60 .20
742 A246 5af multicolored   .75 .20
743 A246 12af multicolored   1.50 .30
 Nos. 741-743 (3)   2.85 .70
 20th anniv. of UNESCO.

Zahir Shah and UN Emblem A247

1967   Photo.
744 A247 5af multicolored   .40 .20
745 A247 10af multicolored   .75 .30
 UN Intl. Org. for Refugees, 20th anniv.

New Power Station A248

 5af, Carpet, vert. 8af, Cement factory.

1967, Jan. 7   Photo.   Perf. 13½x14
746 A248 2af red lil & ol grn   .20 .20
747 A248 5af multicolored   .20 .20
748 A248 8af blk, dk bl & tan   .40 .25
 Nos. 746-748 (3)   .80 .65
 Issued to publicize industrial development.

International Tourist Year Emblem A249

 Designs: 6af, International Tourist Year emblem and map of Afghanistan.

1967, May 11   Photo.   Perf. 12
749 A249 2af yel, blk & lt bl   .20 .20
750 A249 6af bis brn, blk & lt bl   .40 .20
 a. Souv. sheet, #749-750, imperf   1.00 1.00
 Intl. Tourist Year, 1967. No. 750a sold for 10af.

Power Dam, Dorunta A250

Macaque — A251

 6af, Sirobi Dam, vert. 8af, Reservoir at Jalalabad.

1967, July 2   Photo.   Perf. 12
751 A250 1af dk green & lil   .20 .20
752 A250 6af red brn & grnsh bl   .35 .35
753 A250 8af plum & dk bl   .50 .50
 Nos. 751-753 (3)   1.05 1.05
 Progress in agriculture through electricity.

1967, July 28   Photo.   Perf. 12
 Designs: 6af, Striped hyena, horiz. 12af, Persian gazelles, horiz.
754 A251 2af dull yel & indigo   .25 .20
755 A251 6af lt green & sepia   .70 .35
756 A251 12af lt bl & red brn   1.50 .75
 Nos. 754-756 (3)   2.45 1.30

Pashtun Dancers A252

1967, Sept. 1   Photo.   Perf. 12
757 A252 2af magenta & violet   .50 .20
 Issued for "Free Pashtunistan Day."

Retreat of British at Maiwand A253

Fireworks and UN Emblem — A254

1967, Aug. 24
758 A253 1af dk brn & org ver   .25 .20
759 A253 2af dk brn & brt pink   .50 .20
 Issued to commemorate Independence Day.

 King Type of 1966
1967, Oct. 15   Photo.   Perf. 14x13½
760 A245 2af brown red   .20 .20
761 A245 8af dark blue   .50 .25
 Issued to honor King Mohammed Zahir Shah on his 53rd birthday.

1967, Oct. 24   Litho.   Perf. 12
762 A254 10af violet bl & multi   .65 .35
 Issued for United Nations Day.

Greco-Roman Wrestlers A255

Said Jamalluddin Afghan — A256

 Design: 6af, Free style wrestlers.
1967, Nov. 20   Photo.
763 A255 4af ol grn & rose lil   .50 .20
764 A255 6af dp carmine & brn   .80 .20
 a. Souv. sheet, #763-764, imperf   5.00 5.00
 1968 Olympic Games.

1967, Nov. 27
765 A256 1af magenta   .20 .20
766 A256 5af brown   .35 .20
 Said Jamalluddin Afghan, politician (1839-97).

Bronze Vase, 11th-12th Centuries — A257

WHO Emblem A258

 Design: 7af, Bronze vase, Ghasnavide era, 11th-12th centuries.

1967, Dec. 23   Photo.   Perf. 12
767 A257 3af lt green & brn   .20 .20
768 A257 7af yel & slate grn   .40 .30
 a. Souv. sheet, #767-768, imperf   2.50 2.50

1968, Apr. 7   Photo.   Perf. 12
769 A258 2af citron & brt bl   .20 .20
770 A258 7af rose & brt bl   .30 .20
 20th anniv. of the WHO.

Karakul A259

1968, May 20   Photo.   Perf. 12
771 A259 1af yellow & blk   .25 .20
772 A259 6af lt blue & blk   .70 .20
773 A259 12af ultra & dk brn   1.25 .40
 Nos. 771-773 (3)   2.20 .80
 Issued for the Day of Agriculture.

Map of Afghanistan A260

Victory Tower, Ghazni — A261

 Design: 16af, Mausoleum, Ghazni.
1968, June 3   Perf. 13½x14, 12
774 A260 2af red, blk, lt bl & grn   .20 .20
775 A261 3af yel, dk brn & lt bl   .20 .20
776 A261 16af pink & multi   .95 .50
 Nos. 774-776 (3)   1.35 .90
 Issued for tourist publicity.

Cinereous Vulture — A262

 6af, Eagle owl. 7af, Greater flamingoes.

1968, July 3   Perf. 12
777 A262 1af sky blue & multi   .75 .20
778 A262 6af yellow & multi   1.50 .20
779 A262 7af multicolored   1.75 .30
 Nos. 777-779 (3)   4.00 .70

Game of "Pegsticking" A263

 2af, Olympic flame & rings, vert. 12af, Buzkashi.

1968, July 20   Photo.   Perf. 12
780 A263 2af multicolored   .20 .20
781 A263 8af orange & multi   .65 .30
782 A263 12af multicolored   1.00 .45
 Nos. 780-782 (3)   1.85 .95
 19th Olympic Games, Mexico City, 10/12-27.

Flower-decked Armored Car — A264

1968, Aug. 23
783 A264 6af multicolored   .40 .20
 Issued to commemorate Independence Day.

Flag of Pashtunistan A265

1968 Aug. 31   Photo.   Perf. 12
784 A265 3af multicolored   .25 .20
 Issued for "Free Pashtunistan Day."

Zahir Shah — A266   Human Rights Flame — A267

1968, Oct. 14   Photo.   Perf. 12
785 A266 2af ultra   .20 .20
786 A266 8af brown   .45 .30
 King Mohammed Zahir Shah, 54th birthday.

1968, Oct. 24
787 A267 1af multicolored   .20 .20
788 A267 2af violet, bis & blk   .20 .20
789 A267 6af vio blk, bis & vio   .40 .20
 Nos. 787-789 (3)   .80 .60

 Souvenir Sheet
 Imperf
790 A267 10af plum, bis & red org   1.50 1.50
 International Human Rights Year.

Maolana Djalalodine Balkhi — A268   Kushan Mural — A269

1968, Nov. 26   Photo.   Perf. 12
791 A268 4af dk green & mag   .25 .20
 Balkhi (1207-73), historian.

1969, Jan. 2   *Perf. 12*
Design: 3af, Jug shaped like female torso.
792 A269 1af dk grn, mar & yel   .25 .20
793 A269 3af violet, gray & mar   .75 .20
  a.   Souv. sheet, #792-793, imperf   1.50 1.50
Archaeological finds at Bagram, 1st cent. B.C. to 2nd cent. A.D.

ILO Emblem A270

1969, Mar. 23   *Photo.*   *Perf. 12*
794 A270 5af lt yel, lemon & blk   .30 .20
795 A270 8af lt bl, grnsh bl & blk   .50 .30
50th anniv. of the ILO.

Arms Type of 1939
1969, May (?)   *Typo.*
795A A79 100p dark green   .20 .20
795B A79 150p deep brown   .25 .20
Nos. 795A-795B were normally used as newspaper stamps.

Badakhshan Scene A271

Tourist Publicity: 2af, Map of Afghanistan. 7af, Three men on mules ascending the Pamir Mountains.

1969, July 6   *Photo.*   *Perf. 13½x14*
796 A271 2af ocher & multi   .20 .20
797 A271 4af multicolored   .30 .20
798 A271 7af multicolored   .75 .20
  a.   Souv. sheet, #796-798, imperf   1.75 1.75
    Nos. 796-798 (3)   1.25 .60
No. 798a sold for 15af.

Bust, from Hadda Treasure, 3rd-5th Centuries — A272

Zahir Shah and Queen Humeira — A273

Designs: 5af, Vase and jug. 10af, Statue of crowned woman. 5af and 10af from Bagram treasure, 1st-2nd centuries.

1969, Aug. 3   *Photo.*   *Perf. 14x13½*
799 A272 1af olive grn & gold   .20 .20
800 A272 5af purple & gold   .20 .20
801 A272 10af dp blue & gold   .40 .30
    Nos. 799-801 (3)   .80 .70

1969, Aug. 23   *Perf. 12*
802 A273 5af gold, dk bl & red brn   .35 .20
803 A273 10af gold, dp lil & bl grn   .65 .35
Issued to commemorate Independence Day.

Map of Pashtunistan and Rising Sun — A274

1969, Aug. 31   *Typo.*   *Perf. 10½*
804 A274 2af lt blue & red   .20 .20
Issued for "Free Pashtunistan Day."

Zahir Shah — A275

1969, Oct. 14   *Photo.*   *Perf. 12*
Portrait in Natural Colors
805 A275 2af dk brown & gold   .20 .20
806 A275 6af brown & gold   .45 .20
King Mohammed Zahir Shah, 55th birthday.

UN Emblem and Flag of Afghanistan — A276

1969, Oct. 24   *Litho.*   *Perf. 13½*
807 A276 5af blue & multi   .25 .20
Issued for United Nations Day.

ITU Emblem — A277

Wild Boar — A278

1969, Nov. 12
808 A277 6af ultra & multi   .30 .20
809 A277 12af rose & multi   .60 .35
Issued for World Telecommunications Day.

1969, Dec. 7   *Photo.*   *Perf. 12*
1af, Long-tailed porcupine. 8af, Red deer.
810 A278 1af yellow & multi   .25 .20
811 A278 3af blue & multi   .75 .50
812 A278 8af pink & multi   2.00 1.00
    Nos. 810-812 (3)   3.00 1.70

Man's First Footprints on Moon, and Earth — A279

1969, Dec. 28   *Perf. 13½x14*
813 A279 1af yel grn & multi   .20 .20
814 A279 3af yellow & multi   .25 .20
815 A279 6af blue & multi   .40 .20
816 A279 10af rose & multi   .65 .30
    Nos. 813-816 (4)   1.50 .90
Moon landing. See note after Algeria #427.

Anti-cancer Symbol — A280

Mirza Abdul Quader Bedel — A281

1970, Apr. 7   *Photo.*   *Perf. 14*
817 A280 2af dk grn & rose car   .20 .20
818 A280 6af dk bl & rose claret   .40 .20
Issued to publicize the fight against cancer.

1970, May 6   *Perf. 14x13½*
819 A281 5af multicolored   .25 .20
Mirza Abdul Quader Bedel (1643-1720), poet.

Education Year Emblem A282

Mother and Child A283

1970, June 7   *Photo.*   *Perf. 12*
820 A282 1af black   .20 .20
821 A282 6af deep rose   .35 .20
822 A282 12af green   .75 .35
    Nos. 820-822 (3)   1.30 .75
International Education Year 1970.

1970, June 15   *Perf. 13½*
823 A283 6af yellow & multi   .25 .20
Issued for Mother's Day.

UN Emblem, Scales of Justice, Spacecraft A284

1970, June 26
824 A284 4af yel, dk bl & dp bl   .20 .20
825 A284 6af pink, dk bl & brt bl   .35 .20
25th anniversary of United Nations.

Mosque of the Amir of the two Swords, Kabul A285

2af, Map of Afghanistan. 7af, Arch of Paghman.

1970, July 6   *Perf. 12*
Size: 30½x30½mm
826 A285 2af lt bl, blk & citron   .20 .20
Size: 36x26mm
827 A285 3af pink & multi   .20 .20
828 A285 7af yellow & multi   .40 .20
    Nos. 826-828 (3)   .80 .60
Issued for tourist publicity.

Zahir Shah Reviewing Troops — A286

1970, Aug. 23   *Photo.*   *Perf. 13½*
829 A286 8af multicolored   .60 .25
Issued to commemorate Independence Day.

Pathans — A287

1970, Aug. 31   *Typo.*   *Perf. 10½*
830 A287 2af ultra & red   .20 .20
Issued for "Free Pashtunistan Day."

Quail — A288

4af, Golden eagle. 6af, Ringnecked pheasant.

1970, Sept.   *Photo.*   *Perf. 12*
831 A288 2af multicolored   .50 .25
832 A288 4af multicolored   1.00 .50
833 A288 6af multicolored   1.50 .75
    Nos. 831-833 (3)   3.00 1.50

Zahir Shah — A289

Red Crescents
A290

1970, Oct. 14   Photo.   Perf. 14x13½
834 A289 3af green & vio .20 .20
835 A289 7af dk bl & vio brn .60 .25

King Mohammed Zahir Shah, 56th birthday.

1970, Oct. 16   Typo.   Perf. 10½
836 A290 2af black, gold & red .20 .20

Issued for the Red Crescent Society.

UN Emblem and Charter
A291

1970, Oct. 24   Photo.   Perf. 14
837 A291 1af gold & multi .20 .20
838 A291 5af gold & multi .20 .20

United Nations Day.

Tiger Heads of 1871 — A292

1970, Nov. 10   Perf. 12
839 A292 1af sal, lt grnsh bl & blk .25 .20
840 A292 4af lt ultra, yel & blk .50 .20
841 A292 12af lilac, lt bl & blk .85 .35
Nos. 839-841 (3) 1.60 .75

Cent. of the 1st Afghan postage stamps. The postal service was established in 1870, but the 1st stamps were issued in May, 1871.

Globe and Waves
A293

1971, May 17   Photo.   Perf. 13½
842 A293 12af green, blk & bl .60 .35

3rd World Telecommunications Day.

Callimorpha Principalis
A294

Designs: 3af, Epizygaenella species. 5af, Parnassius autocrator.

1971, May 30   Perf. 13½x14
843 A294 1af vermilion & multi 1.00 .50
844 A294 3af yellow & multi 2.25 1.00
845 A294 5af ultra & multi 3.00 1.50
Nos. 843-845 (3) 6.25 3.00

"UNESCO" and Half of Ancient Kushan Statue — A295

1971, June 26   Photo.   Perf. 13½
846 A295 6af ocher & vio .40 .20
847 A295 10af lt blue & mar .65 .30

UNESCO-sponsored Intl. Kushani Seminar.

Tughra and Independence Monument — A296

1971, Aug. 23
848 A296 7af rose red & multi .40 .20
849 A296 9af red orange & multi .65 .30

Independence Day.

Pashtunistan Square, Kabul — A297

1971, Aug. 31   Typo.   Perf. 10½
850 A297 5af deep rose lilac .25 .20

"Free Pashtunistan Day."

Zahir Shah — A298

A299

1971, Oct. 14   Photo.   Perf. 12½x12
851 A298 9af lt green & multi .40 .30
852 A298 17af yellow & multi .75 .55

King Mohammed Zahir Shah, 57th birthday.

1971, Oct. 16   Perf. 14x13½
Design: Map of Afghanistan, red crescent, various activities.
853 A299 8af lt bl, red, grn & blk .45 .25

For Afghan Red Crescent Society.

Equality Year Emblem
A300

1971, Oct. 24   Perf. 12
854 A300 24af brt blue 1.25 .70

International Year Against Racial Discrimination and United Nations Day.

"Your Heart is your Health" — A301

Tulip — A302

1972, Apr. 7   Photo.   Perf. 14
855 A301 9af pale yellow & multi .75 .30
856 A301 12af gray & multi 1.50 .35

World Health Day.

1972, June 5   Photo.   Perf. 14
Designs: 10af, Rock partridge, horiz. 12af, Lynx, horiz. 18af, Allium stipitatum (flower).
857 A302 7af green & multi .50 .25
858 A302 10af blue & multi .75 .35
859 A302 12af lt green & multi 1.00 .35
860 A302 18af blue grn & multi 1.25 .60
Nos. 857-860 (4) 3.50 1.55

Buddhist Shrine, Hadda
A302a

Designs: 7af, Greco-Bactrian animal seal, 250 B.C. 9af, Greco-Oriental temple, Ai-Khanoum, 3rd-2nd centuries B.C.

1972, July 16   Photo.   Perf. 12
861 A302a 3af brown & dl bl .50 .20
862 A302a 7af rose claret & dl grn .80 .20
863 A302a 9af green & lilac 1.10 .30
Nos. 861-863 (3) 2.40 .70

Tourist publicity.

King and Queen Reviewing Parade — A303

1972, Aug. 23   Photo.   Perf. 13½
864 A303 25af gold & multi 4.00 1.00

Independence Day.
Used as a provisional in 1978 with king and queen portion removed.

Wrestling
A304

10af, 19af, 21af, Wrestling, different hold.

1972, Aug. 26
865 A304 4af ol bis & multi .25 .20
866 A304 8af lt blue & multi .50 .25
867 A304 10af yel grn & multi .60 .30
868 A304 19af multicolored 1.25 .40
869 A304 21af lilac & multi 1.40 .45
a. Souv. sheet, #865-869, imperf 3.00 3.00
Nos. 865-869 (5) 4.00 1.60

20th Olympic Games, Munich, Aug. 26-Sept. 11. No. 869a sold for 60af.

Pathan and View of Tribal Territory — A305

Zahir Shah — A306

1972, Aug. 31   Perf. 12½x12
870 A305 5af ultra & multi .25 .20

Pashtunistan day.

1972, Oct. 14   Photo.   Perf. 14x13½
871 A306 7af gold, blk & Prus bl 1.50 .30
872 A306 14af gold, blk & lt brn 2.50 .50

58th birthday of King Mohammed Zahir Shah.

City Destroyed by Earthquake, Refugees — A307

1972, Oct. 16   Perf. 13½
873 A307 7af lt bl, red & blk .40 .20

For Afghan Red Crescent Society.

UN Emblem A308

1972, Oct. 24
874 A308 12af lt ultra & blk .65 .35

UN Economic Commission for Asia and the Far East (ECAFE), 25th anniv.

Ceramics
A309

Designs: 9af, Leather coat, vert. 12af, Metal ware, vert. 16af, Inlaid artifacts.

1972, Dec. 10   Photo.   Perf. 12
875 A309 7af gold & multi   .40 .20
876 A309 9af gold & multi   .55 .30
877 A309 12af gold & multi   .70 .35
878 A309 16af gold & multi   1.00 .50
  a. Souv. sheet, #875-878, imperf 2.25 2.25
  Nos. 875-878 (4)   2.65 1.35

Handicraft industries. No. 878a sold for 45af.

WMO and National Emblems — A310

1973, Apr. 3   Photo.   Perf. 14
879 A310 7af lt lil & dk grn   .40 .20
880 A310 14af lt bl & dp claret   .85 .45

Cent. of intl. meteorological cooperation.

Abu Rayhan al-Biruni — A311

1973, June 16   Photo.   Perf. 13½
881 A311 10af multicolored   .55 .30

Millennium of birth (973-1048), philosopher and mathematician.

Family — A312

1973, June 30   Photo.   Perf. 13½
882 A312 9af orange & red lil   .50 .30

Intl. Family Planning Fed., 21st anniv.

Republic

Impeyan Pheasant A313

Birds: 9af, Great crested grebe. 12af, Himalayan snow cock.

1973, July 29   Photo.   Perf. 12x12½
883 A313 8af yellow & multi   1.25 .25
884 A313 9af blue & multi   1.75 .30
885 A313 12af multicolored   2.00 .35
  Nos. 883-885 (3)   5.00 .90

Stylized Buzkashi Horseman A314

1973, Aug.   Perf. 13½
886 A314 8af black   .30 .25

Tourist publicity.

Fireworks A315

1973, Aug. 23   Photo.   Perf. 12
887 A315 12af multicolored   .45 .35

55th Independence Day.

Lake Abassine, Pashtunistan Flag — A316

1973, Aug. 31   Perf. 14x13½
888 A316 9af multicolored   .50 .30

Pashtunistan Day.

Red Crescent A317

1973, Oct. 16   Perf. 13½
889 A317 10af red, blk & gold   .60 .30

Red Crescent Society.

Kemal Ataturk A318

1973, Oct. 28   Litho.   Perf. 10½
890 A318 1af blue   .20 .20
891 A318 7af reddish brown   .40 .20

50th anniversary of the Turkish Republic.

Human Rights Flame, Arms of Afghanistan A319

1973, Dec. 10   Photo.   Perf. 12
892 A319 12af sil, blk & lt bl   .45 .35

25th anniversary of the Universal Declaration of Human Rights.

Asiatic Black Bears A320

1974, Mar. 26   Litho.   Perf. 12
893 A320 5af shown   .35 .20
894 A320 7af Afghan hound   .50 .20
895 A320 10af Persian goat   .70 .30
896 A320 12af Leopard   .90 .35
  a. Souv. sheet, #893-896, imperf 5.00 5.00
  Nos. 893-896 (4)   2.45 1.05

Worker and Farmer A321

1974, May 1   Photo.   Perf. 13½x12½
897 A321 9af rose red & multi   .40 .25

International Labor Day, May 1.

Independence Monument and Arch — A322

1974, May 27   Photo.   Perf. 12
898 A322 4af blue & multi   .20 .20
899 A322 11af gold & multi   .35 .30

56th Independence Day.

Arms of Afghanistan and Symbol of Cooperation — A323

Pres. Mohammad Daoud Khan — A324

5af, Flag of Republic of Afghanistan. 15af, Soldiers, coat of arms of the Republic.

1974, July 25   Perf. 13½x12½, 14
Sizes: 4af, 15af, 36x22mm; 5af, 7af, 36x26, 26x36mm

900 A323 4af multicolored   .20 .20
901 A323 5af multicolored   .25 .20
902 A324 7af green, brn & blk   .30 .20
  a. Souv. sheet, #901-902, imperf .70 .70
903 A323 15af multicolored   .65 .40
  a. Souv. sheet, #900, 903, imperf 1.00 1.00
  Nos. 900-903 (4)   1.40 1.00

1st anniv. of the Republic of Afghanistan.

Lesser Spotted Eagle A325

Birds: 6af, White-fronted goose, ruddy shelduck and gray-lag goose. 11af, European coots and European crane.

1974, Aug. 6   Photo.   Perf. 13½x13
904 A325 1af car rose & multi   .25 .20
905 A325 6af blue & multi   .75 .20
906 A325 11af yellow & multi   1.50 .40
  a. Strip of 3, #904-906   2.50 .80

Flags of Pashtunistan and Afghanistan — A326

1974, Aug. 31   Photo.   Perf. 14
907 A326 5af multicolored   .25 .20

Pashtunistan Day.

Natl. Arms A326a

1974, Aug.   Typo.   Rough Perf. 11
907A A326a 100p green

Coat of Arms A327

1974, Oct. 9
908 A327 7af gold, grn & blk   .25 .20

Centenary of Universal Postal Union.

"un" and UN Emblem A328

1974, Oct. 24   Photo.   Perf. 14
909 A328 5af lt ultra & dk bl   .25 .20

United Nations Day.

Minaret of Jam — A329

Buddha,
Hadda — A330

14af, Lady riding griffin, 2nd century,
Bagram.

1975, May 5   Photo.   *Perf. 13½*
910	A329	7af multicolored	.25	.20
911	A330	14af multicolored	.60	.30
912	A330	15af multicolored	.65	.30
a.		Souv. sheet, #910-912, imperf.	3.50	3.50
		Nos. 910-912 (3)	1.50	.80

South Asia Tourism Year 1975.

New Flag
of
Afghanistan
A331

1975, May 27   Photo.   *Perf. 12*
913	A331	16af multicolored	.75	.35

57th Independence Day.

Celebrating Crowd — A332

1975, July 17   Photo.   *Perf. 13½*
914	A332	9af blue & multi	.45	.20
915	A332	12af carmine & multi	.55	.30

Second anniversary of the Republic.

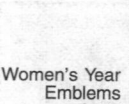

Women's Year
Emblems
A333

1975, Aug. 24   Photo.   *Perf. 12*
916	A333	9af car, lt bl & blk	.30	.20

International Women's Year 1975.

Pashtunistan
Flag, Sun Rising
Over Mountains
A334

Mohammed Akbar
Khan
A335

1975, Aug. 31   *Perf. 13½*
917	A334	10af multicolored	.30	.25

Pashtunistan Day.

1976, Feb. 4   Photo.   *Perf. 14*
918	A335	15af lt brown & multi	.45	.35

Mohammed Akbar Khan (1816-1846), warrior son of Amir Dost Mohammed Khan.

A336

Pres. Mohammad
Daoud
Khan — A337

1974-78   Photo.   *Perf. 14*
919	A336	10af multi	.55	.20
920	A336	16af multi ('78)	2.00	.75
921	A336	19af multi	.75	.40
922	A336	21af multi	1.10	.45
923	A336	22af multi ('78)	3.00	1.60
924	A336	30af multi ('78)	4.00	2.25
925	A337	50af multi ('75)	2.25	1.10
926	A337	100af multi ('75)	4.50	2.00
		Nos. 919-926 (8)	18.15	8.75

Arms of Republic, Independence
Monument — A338

1976, June 1   Photo.   *Perf. 14*
927	A338	22af blue & multi	.65	.45

58th Independence Day.

Flag
Raising — A339

1976, July 17   Photo.   *Perf. 14*
928	A339	30af multicolored	.90	.75

Republic Day.

Mountain Peaks
and Flag of
Pashtunistan
A340

1976, Aug. 31   Photo.   *Perf. 14*
929	A340	16af multicolored	.50	.40

Pashtunistan Day.

Coat of
Arms
A340a

1976, Sept.   Litho.   *Perf. 11 Rough*
930	A340a	25p salmon	.25	.20
931	A340a	50p lt green	.25	.20
932	A340a	1af ultra	.25	.20
		Nos. 930-932 (3)	.75	.60

Flag and
Views on
Open Book
A341

1977, May 27   Photo.   *Perf. 14*
937	A341	20af green & multi	.60	.50

59th Independence Day.

Pres. Daoud and National
Assembly — A342

President
Taking
Oath of
Office
A343

Designs: 10af, Inaugural address. 18af, Promulgation of Constitution.

1977, June 22
938	A342	7af multicolored	.65	.45
939	A343	8af multicolored	.70	.60
940	A343	10af multicolored	.90	.75
941	A342	18af multicolored	1.60	1.25
a.		Souvenir sheet of 4	3.00	3.00
		Nos. 938-941 (4)	3.85	3.05

Election of 1st Pres. and promulgation of
Constitution. No. 941a contains 4 imperf.
stamps similar to Nos. 938-941.

Jamalluddin
Medal
A344

1977, July 6   Photo.   *Perf. 14*
942	A344	12af blue, blk & gold	.35	.30

Sajo Jamalluddin Afghani, reformer, 80th
death anniversary.

Afghanistan Flag
over
Crowd — A345

1977, July 17
943	A345	22af multicolored	.65	.55

Dancers, Fountain, Pashtunistan
Flag — A346

1977, Aug. 31
944	A346	30af multicolored	.90	.75

Pashtunistan Day.

Arms and
Carrier
Pigeon
A346a

1977, Oct. 30   Litho.   *Perf. 11*
944A	A346a	1af black & blue	.20	.20

Members of Parliament Congratulating
Pres. Daoud — A347

1978, Feb. 5   Litho.   *Perf. 14*
945	A347	20af multicolored	1.75	

Election of first president, first anniversary.

Map of Afghanistan, UPU
Emblem — A348

1978, Apr. 1   Photo.   *Perf. 14*
946	A348	10af green, blk & gold	.30	.25

Afghanistan's UPU membership, 50th anniv.

Wall
Telephone
and
Satellite
Station
A349

1978, Apr. 12
947	A349	8af multicolored	.25	.20

Afghanistan's ITU membership, 50th anniv.

Democratic Republic

Arrows
Pointing to
Crescent,
Cross and
Lion — A350

1978, July 6   Litho.   *Perf. 11 Rough*
948	A350	3af black	1.00	.50

50th anniv. of Afghani Red Crescent Soc.

Khalq Party Emblem — A350a

1978, Aug. **Litho.** **Perf. 11**
948A A350a 1af rose red & gold 1.25 .50
948B A350a 4af rose red & gold 1.75 .75

Qalai Bist Arch A351

1978, Aug. 19 **Perf. 14**
949 A351 16af Bamian Buddha 1.00 .40
949A A351 22af shown 1.25 .55
949B A351 30af Hazara Women 1.75 .90
Nos. 949-949B (3) 4.00 1.85

Men with Pashtunistan Flag — A352

Coat of Arms and Emblems A353

1978, Aug. 31 **Perf. 11 Rough**
950 A352 7af ultra & red .20 .20
Pashtunistan Day.

1978, Sept. 8 **Perf. 11**
951 A353 20af rose red .60 .50
World Literacy Day.

A354

Perf. 11½ Rough
1978, Oct. 25 **Litho.**
952 A354 18af light green .55 .45
Hero of Afghanistan.

Khalq Party Flag A355

1978, Oct. 19 **Photo.** **Perf. 11½**
953 A355 8af black, red & gold .25 .20
954 A355 9af black, red & gold .30 .20
"The mail serving the people."

Nour Mohammad Taraki — A356

1979, Jan. 1 **Litho.** **Perf. 12**
955 A356 12af multicolored .35 .20
Nour Mohammad Taraki, founder of People's Democratic Party of Afghanistan, installation as president.

Woman Breaking Chain — A357

1979, Mar. 8 **Litho.** **Perf. 11**
956 A357 14af red & ultra 1.50 .50
Women's Day. Inscribed "POSSTES."

Map of Afghanistan, Census Emblem — A358

1979, Mar. 25 **Litho.** **Perf. 12**
957 A358 3af multicolored .75 .50
First comprehensive population census.

Farmers A359

1979, Mar. 21
958 A359 1af multicolored .50 .25
Agricultural advances.

Pres. Taraki Reading First Issue of Khalq — A360

1979, Apr. 11 **Perf. 12½x12**
959 A360 2af multicolored .25 .20
Khalq, newspaper of People's Democratic Republic of Afghanistan.

Pres. Noor Mohammad Taraki A361

Plaza with Tank Monument and Fountain — A362

House where Revolution Started — A363

Designs: 50p, Taraki, tank. 12af, House where 1st Khalq Party Congress was held.

Perf. 12, 12½x12 (A362)
1979, Apr. 27 **Litho.**
959A A363 50p multicolored .20 .20
960 A361 4af multicolored .20 .20
961 A362 5af multicolored .25 .20
962 A363 6af multicolored .30 .25
963 A363 12af multicolored .50 .45
Nos. 959A-963 (5) 1.45 1.30
1st anniversary of revolution.

Carpenter and Blacksmith A364

1979, May 1 **Perf. 12**
964 A364 10af multicolored .30 .25
Int'l Labor Day.

Children, Flag and Map of Afghanistan — A366

1979, June 1 **Litho.** **Perf. 12½x12**
966 A366 16af multicolored 1.50 .75
International Year of the Child.

Doves Circling Asia in Globe A366a

1979 **Litho.** **Perf. 11x10½**
966A A366a 2af red & blue 1.00 .20

Armed Afghans, Kabul Memorial and Arch — A367

Pashtunistan Citizens, Flag — A368

1979, Aug. 19 **Litho.** **Perf. 12**
967 A367 30af multicolored 1.25 .75
60th independence day.

1979, Aug. 31
968 A368 9af multicolored .30 .20
Pashtunistan Day.

UPU Day A369

1979, Oct. 9 **Litho.** **Perf. 12**
969 A369 15af multicolored .45 .40

Tombstone — A369a

1979, Oct. 25 **Litho.** **Perf. 12½x12**
969A A369a 22af multicolored 2.00 1.00

International Women's Day — A370

1980, Mar. 8 **Litho.** **Perf. 12**
970 A370 8af multicolored 1.25 .40

Farmers' Day — A371

1980, Mar. 21 **Litho.** **Perf. 11½x12**
971 A371 2af multicolored 1.40 .45

Non-smoker and Smoker
A372

1980, Apr. 7　　　　　*Perf. 11½*
972 A372 5af multicolored　　　1.25 .40
Anti-smoking campaign; World Health Day.

Lenin, 110th Birth Anniversary
A373

1980, Apr. 22　　*Perf. 12x12½*
973 A373 12af multicolored　　1.75 .50

People and Fist on Map of Afghanistan — A374

1980, Apr. 27 Litho. Perf. 12½x12
974 A374 1af multicolored　　　.50 .20
Saur Revolution, 2nd anniversary.

International Workers' Solidarity Day — A375

1980, May 1
975 A375 9af multicolored　　　.35 .20

Wrestling, Moscow '80 Emblem A376

1980, July 19 Perf. 12½x12½, 12½x12
976 A376　3af Soccer, vert.　.55　.20
977 A376　6af shown　　　.60　.20
978 A376　9af Buzkashi　　.65　.25
979 A376　10af Pegsticking　.75　.25
　Nos. 976-979 (4)　　　2.55　.90
22nd Summer Olympic Games, Moscow, July 19-Aug. 3.

61st Anniversary of Independence — A377

1980, Aug. 19 Litho. Perf. 12½x12
980 A377 3af multicolored　　　.45 .20

Pashtunistan Day — A378

1980, Aug. 30
981 A378 25af multicolored　　　.75 .35

Intl. UPU Day A379

1980, Oct. 9 Litho. Perf. 12½x12
982 A379 20af multicolored　　　.60 .25

The resistance group headed by Amin Wardak released some stamps in 1980. Some of these are inscribed "WARDAK AFGHANISTAN," others "Solidarite Internationale Avec la Resistance Afghane." The status of these labels is questionable.

International Women's Day — A381

1981, Mar. 9 Litho. Perf. 12½x12
984 A381 15af multicolored　　　.90 .30

Farmers' Day — A382

1981, Mar. 20 Litho. Perf. 12½x12
985 A382 1af multicolored　　　.75 .25

Bighorn Mountain Sheep (Protected Species) A383

1981, Apr. 4　　　*Perf. 12x12½*
986 A383 12af multicolored　　.90 .40

Saur Revolution, 3rd Anniversary A384

Intl. Workers' Solidarity Day — A385

1981, Apr. 27　　　　*Perf. 11*
987 A384 50p brown　　　　.45 .20

1981, May 1　　　*Perf. 12½x12*
988 A385 10af multicolored　　.75 .25

13th World Telecommunications Day — A387

1981, May 17 Litho. Perf. 12½x12
990 A387 9af multicolored　　　.40 .20

Intl. Children's Day — A388

1981, June 1　　*Perf. 12x12½*
991 A388 15af multicolored　　.75 .30

People's Independence Monument
62nd Anniv. of Independence — A389

1981, Aug. 19
992 A389 4af multicolored　　　.75 .30

Pashtunistan Day — A390

1981, Aug. 31 Litho. Perf. 12
992A A390 2af multicolored　　　.45 .20

Intl. Tourism Day — A391

1981, Sept. 27　　*Perf. 12½x12½*
993 A391 5af multicolored　　　.45 .20

World Food Day — A392

1981, Oct. 16
995 A392 7af multicolored　　　.50 .20

Asia-Africa Solidarity Meeting — A393

1981, Nov. 18 Litho. Perf. 11
996 A393 8af blue　　　　　.55 .20

Struggle Against Apartheid — A394

1300th Anniv. of Bulgaria A395

1981, Dec. 1　　　*Perf. 12½x12*
997 A394 4af multicolored　　　.35 .20

1981, Dec. 9　　　*Perf. 12x12½*
998 A395 20af multicolored　　1.00 .35

Buzkashi Game A395a

1980　　　Photo.　　*Perf. 14*
998A A395a 50af multicolored　1.50 .75
998B A395a 100af multicolored　3.00 1.50

Intl. Women's Day A396

1982, Mar. 8   Litho.   Perf. 12
999 A396 6af multicolored   .40 .20

Farmers' Day — A397

1982, Mar. 21
1000 A397 4af multicolored   .40 .20

Judas Trees — A398   Saur Revolution, 4th Anniv. — A399

Designs: Various local plants.

1982, Apr. 9   Litho.   Perf. 12
1001 A398 3af shown   .20 .20
1002 A398 4af Rose of Sharon   .45 .20
1003 A398 16af Rhubarb plant   .75 .25
    Nos. 1001-1003 (3)   1.40 .65

1982, Apr. 27
1004 A399 1af multicolored   .85 .30

George Dimitrov (1882-1947), First Prime Minister of Bulgaria — A400

Intl. Workers' Solidarity Day A401

1982, Apr. 30
1005 A400 30af multicolored   1.40 .50

1982, May 1
1006 A401 10af multicolored   .60 .25

Storks — A402

1982, May 31
1007 A402 6af shown   1.00 .35
1008 A402 11af Nightingales   1.25 .45

Hedgehogs A403

1982, July 6   Litho.   Perf. 12
1009 A403 3af shown   .40 .20
1010 A403 14af Cobra   1.00 .35
    See Nos. 1020-1022.

63rd Anniv. of Independence — A404

1982, Aug. 19
1011 A404 20af multicolored   .85 .30

Pashtunistan Day — A405

1982, Aug. 31
1012 A405 32af multicolored   1.40 .50

World Tourism Day A406

1982, Sept. 27   Litho.   Perf. 12
1013 A406 9af multicolored   .65 .25

UPU Day A407

1982, Oct. 9
1014 A407 4af multicolored   .50 .20

World Food Day A408

1982, Oct. 16
1015 A408 9af multicolored   .75 .25

37th Anniv. of UN — A409

1982, Oct. 24
1016 A409 15af multicolored   .60 .25

ITU Plenipotentiaries Conference, Nairobi, Sept. — A410

1982, Oct. 26
1017 A410 8af multicolored   .40 .20

TB Bacillus Centenary A411   Human Rights Declaration, 34th Anniv. A412

1982, Nov. 24   Litho.   Perf. 12
1018 A411 7af multicolored   .35 .20

1982, Dec. 10
1019 A412 5af multicolored   .35 .20

Animal Type of 1982
1982, Dec. 16
1020 A403 2af Lions   .20 .20
1021 A403 7af Donkeys   .45 .20
1022 A403 12af Marmots, vert.   .75 .25
    Nos. 1020-1022 (3)   1.40 .65

Intl. Women's Day — A413   Mir Alicher Nawai Research Decade — A414

1983, Mar. 8
1023 A413 3af multicolored   .30 .20

1983, Mar. 19
1024 A414 22af multicolored   .70 .25

Farmers' Day A415

1983, Mar. 21   Litho.   Perf. 12
1025 A415 10af multicolored   .40 .20

5th Anniv. of Saur Revolution A416

1983, Apr. 27   Litho.   Perf. 12
1026 A416 15af multicolored   .60 .25

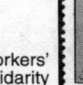

Intl. Workers' Solidarity Day — A417

1983, May 1
1027 A417 2af multicolored   .45 .20

World Communications Year — A418

1983, May 17
1028 A418 4af Modes of communication   .25 .20
1029 A418 11af Building   .50 .25

Intl. Children's Day — A419

1983, June 1   Litho.   Perf. 12
1030 A419 25af multicolored   .60 .25

2nd Anniv. of National Front — A420

1983, June 15
1031 A420 1af multicolored   .20 .20

Local Butterflies A421

Various butterflies. 9af, 13af vert.

1983, July 6
1032 A421 9af multicolored   .40 .30
1033 A421 13af multicolored   1.00 .55
1034 A421 21af multicolored   1.25 .65
    Nos. 1032-1034 (3)   2.65 1.50

Struggle Against Apartheid — A422

1983, Aug. 1   Litho.   Perf. 12
1035 A422 10af multicolored   .30 .20

64th Anniv of Independence — A423

1983, Aug. 19
1036 A423 6af multicolored .25 .20

Parliament House A423a

1983, Sept. Litho. **Perf. 12**
1036A A423a 50af shown 2.00 .65
1036B A423a 100af Afghan Woman, Camel 4.00 1.25

A424

World Tourism Day — A425

1983, Sept. 27 Litho. **Perf. 12**
1037 A424 5af shown .25 .20
1038 A424 7af shown .35 .20
1039 A424 12af Golden statues .40 .20
1040 A425 16af Stone carving .50 .20
Nos. 1037-1040 (4) 1.50 .80

World Communications Year — A426

1983, Oct. 9 Litho. **Perf. 12**
1041 A426 14af Dish antenna, dove .50 .20
1042 A426 15af Building, flag .50 .20

World Food Day — A427

1983, Oct. 16 Litho. **Perf. 12**
1043 A427 14af multicolored .60 .25

Sports A428

1983, Nov. 1 Litho. **Perf. 12**
1044 A428 1af Soccer .20 .20
1045 A428 18af Boxing .70 .25
1046 A428 21af Wrestling .80 .25
Nos. 1044-1046 (3) 1.70 .70

Pashtunistan Day — A428a

1983,Nov. Litho. **Perf. 12**
1046A A428a 3af Pathans Waving Flag .25 .20

Handicrafts A429

1983, Nov. 22
1047 A429 2af Jewelry .20 .20
1048 A429 8af Stone ashtrays, dishes .30 .20
1049 A429 19af Furniture .55 .20
1050 A429 30af Leather goods 1.25 .40
Nos. 1047-1050 (4) 2.30 1.00

UN Declaration of Human Rights, 35th Anniv. A430

1983, Dec. 10 Litho. **Perf. 12**
1051 A430 20af multicolored .75 .25

Kabul Polytechnical Institute, 20th Anniv. — A431

1983, Dec. 28 **Perf. 12½x12**
1052 A431 30af multicolored 1.00 .35

1984 Winter Olympics A432

1984, Jan. **Perf. 12**
1053 A432 5af Figure skating .25 .20
1054 A432 9af Skiing .30 .20
1055 A432 11af Speed skating .40 .20
1056 A432 15af Hockey .50 .20
1057 A432 18af Biathlon .55 .20
1058 A432 20af Ski jumping .60 .25
1059 A432 22af Bobsledding .70 .25
Nos. 1053-1059 (7) 3.30 1.50

Intl. Women's Day — A433

1984, Mar. 8
1060 A433 4af multicolored .40 .25

Farmers' Day A434

Various agricultural scenes.

1984, Mar. 21 Litho. **Perf. 12**
1061 A434 2af multicolored .20 .20
1062 A434 4af multicolored .20 .20
1063 A434 7af multicolored .20 .20
1064 A434 9af multicolored .20 .20
1065 A434 15af multicolored .30 .20
1066 A434 18af multicolored .35 .20
1067 A434 20af multicolored .40 .20
Nos. 1061-1067 (7) 1.85 1.40

World Aviation Day A435

1984, Apr. 12
1068 A435 5af Luna 1 .25 .20
1069 A435 8af Luna 2 .35 .20
1070 A435 11af Luna 3 .45 .20
1071 A435 17af Apollo 11 .55 .20
1072 A435 22af Soyuz 6 .70 .25
1073 A435 28af Soyuz 7 .70 .25
1074 A435 34af Soyuz 6, 7, 8 1.00 .35
Nos. 1068-1074 (7) 4.00 1.65

Souvenir Sheet
Perf. 12x12½
1075 A435 25af S. Koroliov 1.00 .70

No. 1075 contains one 30x41mm stamp.

Saur Revolution, 6th Anniv. A436

1984, Apr. 27 **Perf. 12**
1076 A436 3af multicolored .25 .20

65th Anniv. of Independence — A437

1984, Aug. 19 Litho. **Perf. 12**
1077 A437 6af multicolored .30 .20

Pashto's and Balutchi's Day A438

1984, Aug. 31
1078 A438 3af Symbolic sun, tribal terr. .20 .20

Wildlife A439

Perf. 12½x12, 12x12½
1984, May 5 Litho.
1079 A439 1af Cape hunting dog, vert. .20 .20
1080 A439 2af Argali sheep, vert. .20 .20
1081 A439 6af Przewalski's horse .40 .20
1082 A439 8af Wild boar, vert. .55 .20
1083 A439 17af Snow leopard 1.00 .30
1084 A439 19af Tiger 1.25 .40
1085 A439 22af Indian elephant, vert. 1.40 .45
Nos. 1079-1085 (7) 5.00 1.95

19th UPU Congress, Hamburg A440

1984, June 18 **Perf. 12x12½**
1086 A440 25af German post-man, 17th cent. .90 .30
1087 A440 35af Postrider, 16th cent. 1.40 .45
1088 A440 40af Carrier pigeon, letter 1.60 .55
Nos. 1086-1088 (3) 3.90 1.30

Souvenir Sheet
1089 A440 50af Hamburg No. 3 in black 2.50 1.50

No. 1089 contains one 30x40mm stamp.

Natl. Aviation, 40th Anniv. A441

Soviet civil aircraft.

1984, June 29
1090 A441 1af Antonov AN-2 .20 .20
1091 A441 4af Ilyushin IL-12 .25 .20
1092 A441 9af Tupolev TU-104 .55 .25
1093 A441 10af Ilyushin IL-18 .60 .25
1094 A441 13af Tupolev TU-134 .80 .25
1095 A441 17af Ilyushin IL-62 1.00 .30
1096 A441 21af Ilyushin IL-28 1.25 .40
Nos. 1090-1096 (7) 4.65 1.85

Ettore Bugatti (1881-1947), Type 43, Italy — A442

Classic automobiles and their designers: 5af, Henry Ford, 1903 Model A, US. 8af, Rene Panhard (1841-1908), 1899 Landau, France. 11af, Gottlieb Daimler (1834-1900), 1935 Daimler-Benz, Germany. 12af, Carl Benz (1844-1929), 1893 Victoris, Germany. 15af, Armand Peugeot (1848-1915), 1892 Vis-a-Vis, France. 22af, Louis Chevrolet (1879-1941), 1925 Sedan, US.

1984, June 30
1097 A442 2af multicolored .20 .20
1098 A442 5af multicolored .20 .20
1099 A442 8af multicolored .45 .20
1100 A442 11af multicolored .55 .20
1101 A442 12af multicolored .65 .25
1102 A442 15af multicolored .75 .25
1103 A442 22af multicolored 1.10 .35
Nos. 1097-1103 (7) 3.90 1.65

Qalai Bist Arch
A443

World Tourism Day: 2af, Ornamental buck-led harness. 5af, Victory Monument and Memorial Arch, Kabul. 9af, Standing sculpture of Afghani ruler and attendants. 15af, Buffalo riders in snow. 19af, Camel driver, tent, camel in caparison. 21af, Horsemen playing buzkashi.

1984, Sept. 27
1104	A443	1af multicolored	.20	.20
1105	A443	2af multicolored	.20	.20
1106	A443	5af multicolored	.20	.20
1107	A443	9af multicolored	.20	.20
1108	A443	15af multicolored	.40	.20
1109	A443	19af multicolored	.65	.25
1110	A443	21af multicolored	.65	.25
		Nos. 1104-1110 (7)	2.50	1.50

UN World Food Day — A444

Fruit-bearing trees.

1984, Oct. 16
1111	A444	2af multicolored	.20	.20
1112	A444	4af multicolored	.20	.20
1113	A444	6af multicolored	.25	.20
1114	A444	9af multicolored	.30	.20
1115	A444	13af multicolored	.40	.20
1116	A444	15af multicolored	.45	.20
1117	A444	26af multicolored	.70	.25
		Nos. 1111-1117 (7)	2.50	1.45

People's Democratic Party, 20th Anniv. A445

1985, Jan. 1
1118	A445	25af multicolored	1.00	.35

Farmer's Day
A446

1985, Mar. 2
1119	A446	1af Oxen	.20	.20
1120	A446	3af Mare, foal	.20	.20
1121	A446	7af Brown horse	.20	.20
1122	A446	8af White horse, vert.	.35	.20
1123	A446	15af Sheep, sheep-skins	.40	.20
1124	A446	16af Shepherd, cattle, sheep	.60	.25
1125	A446	25af Family, camels	.85	.30
		Nos. 1119-1125 (7)	2.80	1.55

Geologist's Day — A447

1985, Apr. 5
1126	A447	4af multicolored	.25	.20

Lenin Leading Red Army, 1917 — A448

Lenin and: 10af, Soviet Workers' Party deputies, Smolny. 15af, Revolutionaries, 1917, Leningrad. 50af, Portrait.

1985, Apr. 21   *Perf. 12x12½*
1127	A448	10af multicolored	.55	.20
1128	A448	15af multicolored	.70	.25
1129	A448	25af multicolored	1.25	.40
		Nos. 1127-1129 (3)	2.50	.85

Souvenir Sheet
1130	A448	50af multicolored	1.50	1.25

Saur Revolution, 7th Anniv. — A449

1985, Apr. 27
1131	A449	21af multicolored	.85	.30

Berlin-Treptow Soviet War Memorial, Red Army at Siege of Berlin, 1945 — A450

9af, Victorious Motherland monument, fireworks over Kremlin. 10af, Caecilienhof, site of Potsdam Treaty signing, Great Britain, USSR & US flags.

1985, May 9   *Perf. 12½x12*
1132	A450	6af multicolored	.40	.20
1133	A450	9af multicolored	.55	.20
1134	A450	10af multicolored	.65	.25
		Nos. 1132-1134 (3)	1.60	.65

End of World War II, defeat of Nazi Germany, 40th anniv.

INTELSAT, 20th Anniv.
A451

Designs: 6af, INTELSAT satellite orbiting Earth. 9af, INTELSAT III. 10af, Rocket launch, Baikanur Space Center, vert.

Perf. 12x12½, 12½x12
1985, Apr. 6   Litho.
1135	A451	6af multicolored	.40	.20
1136	A451	9af multicolored	.45	.20
1137	A451	10af multicolored	.60	.20
		Nos. 1135-1137 (3)	1.45	.60

12th World Youth Festival, Moscow — A452

1985, May 5
1138	A452	7af Olympic stadium, Moscow	.20	.20
1139	A452	12af Festival emblem	.45	.20
1140	A452	13af Kremlin	.45	.20
1141	A452	18af Folk doll, emblem	.65	.25
		Nos. 1138-1141 (4)	1.75	.85

Intl. Child Survival Campaign
A453

1985, June 1
1142	A453	1af Weighing child	.20	.20
1143	A453	2af Immunization	.20	.20
1144	A453	4af Breastfeeding	.25	.20
1145	A453	5af Mother, child	.25	.20
		Nos. 1142-1145 (4)	.90	.80

Flowers
A454

1985, July 5
1146	A454	2af Oenothera affinis	.20	.20
1147	A454	4af Erythrina cristagalli	.25	.20
1148	A454	8af Tillandsia aeranthos	.40	.20
1149	A454	13af Vinca major	.70	.25
1150	A454	18af Mirabilis jalapa	1.00	.35
1151	A454	25af Cypella herbertii	1.40	.45
1152	A454	30af Clytostoma callistegioides	1.75	.60
		Nos. 1146-1152 (7)	5.70	2.25

Souvenir Sheet
Perf. 12½x11½
1153	A454	75af Sesbania punicea, horiz.	4.00	3.00

ARGENTINA '85.

Independence, 66th Anniv. — A455

1985, Aug. 19   *Perf. 12x12½*
1154	A455	33af Mosque	1.40	.45

Pashto's and Balutchi's Day
A456

1985, Aug. 30
1155	A456	25af multicolored	1.00	.35

UN Decade for Women
A457

1985, Sept. 22
1156	A457	10af Emblems	.45	.20

World Tourism Day, 10th Anniv. A457a

1985, Sept. 27   Litho.   *Perf. 12*
1156A	A457a	1af Guldara Stupa	.20	.20
1156B	A457a	2af Mirwais Tomb, vert.	.20	.20
1156C	A457a	10af Statue of Bamyan, vert.	.30	.20
1156D	A457a	13af No Gumbad Mosque, vert.	.45	.20
1156E	A457a	14af Pule Kheshti Mosque	.45	.20
1156F	A457a	15af Bost Citadel	.50	.20
1156G	A457a	20af Ghazni Minaret, vert.	.75	.25
		Nos. 1156A-1156G (7)	2.85	1.45

Sports
A457b

Perf. 12x12½, 12½x12
1985, Oct. 3   Litho.
1156H	A457b	1af Boxing	.20	.20
1156I	A457b	2af Volleyball	.20	.20
1156J	A457b	3af Soccer, vert.	.20	.20
1156K	A457b	12af Buzkashi	.45	.20
1156L	A457b	14af Weight lifting	.50	.20
1156M	A457b	18af Wrestling	.60	.25
1156N	A457b	25af Peg sticking	1.10	.35
		Nos. 1156H-1156N (7)	3.25	1.60

World Food Day
A457c

1985, Oct. 16
1156O	A457c	25af multicolored	.85	.30

UN 40th Anniv. — A458   Birds — A459

1985, Oct. 24   *Perf. 12½x12*
1157	A458	22af multicolored	.85	.30

1985, Oct. 25   *Perf. 12½x12, 12x12½*
1158	A459	2af Jay	.20	.20
1159	A459	4af Plover, hummingbird	.60	.25
1160	A459	8af Pheasant	.60	.25
1161	A459	13af Hoopoe	.95	.30
1162	A459	18af Falcon	1.25	.40
1163	A459	25af Partridge	1.60	.50
1164	A459	30af Pelicans, horiz.	2.10	.70
		Nos. 1158-1164 (7)	7.30	2.55

Souvenir Sheet
Perf. 12x12½
1165 A459 75af Parakeets　　　6.00 5.00

Mushrooms
A460

1985, June 10　Litho.　Perf. 12½x12
1165A	A460	3af	Tricholomopsis rutilans	.20 .20
1166	A460	4af	Boletus miniatoporus	.25 .20
1167	A460	7af	Amanita rubescens	.45 .20
1168	A460	11af	Boletus scaber	.65 .25
1169	A460	12af	Coprinus atramentarius	.75 .25
1170	A460	18af	Hypholoma	1.10 .35
1171	A460	20af	Boletus aurantiacus	1.25 .40
		Nos. 1165A-1171 (7)		4.65 1.85

World Wildlife Fund — A461

1985, Nov. 25
1172	A461	2af	Leopard, cubs	.40 .20
1173	A461	9af	Adult's head	1.40 .45
1174	A461	11af	Adult	2.25 .75
1175	A461	15af	Cub	3.50 1.10
		Nos. 1172-1175 (4)		7.55 2.50

Motorcycle, Cent. — A462

Designs: Different makes and landmarks.

1985, Dec. 16
1176	A462	2af	multicolored	.20 .20
1177	A462	4af	multicolored	.20 .20
1178	A462	8af	multicolored	.25 .20
1179	A462	13af	multicolored	.65 .25
1180	A462	18af	multicolored	.80 .25
1181	A462	25af	multicolored	1.10 .35
1182	A462	30af	multicolored	1.25 .40
		Nos. 1176-1182 (7)		4.45 1.85

Souvenir Sheet
Perf. 11½x12½
1183 A462 75af multicolored　　3.50 2.50

People's Democratic Party, 21st
Anniv. — A463

1986, Jan. 1　　　Perf. 12½x12
1184 A463 2af multicolored　　　.30 .20

27th Soviet Communist Party
Congress — A464

1986, Mar. 31
1185 A464 25af Lenin　　　　　.75 .25

First Man in Space, 25th
Anniv. — A465

Designs: 3af, Spacecraft. 7af, Soviet space achievement medal, vert. 9af, Rocket lift-off, vert. 11af, Yuri Gagarin, military decorations, vert. 13af, Gagarin, cosmonaut. 15af, Gagarin, politician. 17af, Gagarin wearing flight suit, vert.

Perf. 12½x12, 12x12½
1986, Apr. 12　　　　　　Litho.
1186	A465	3af	multicolored	.20 .20
1187	A465	7af	multicolored	.25 .20
1188	A465	9af	multicolored	.40 .20
1189	A465	11af	multicolored	.45 .20
1190	A465	13af	multicolored	.50 .20
1191	A465	15af	multicolored	.55 .20
1192	A465	17af	multicolored	.65 .25
		Nos. 1186-1192 (7)		4.50 4.50

Loya Jirgah (Grand Assembly) of the
People's Democratic Republic, 1st
Anniv.
A465a

1986, Apr. 23　Litho.　Perf. 12x12½
1192A A465a 3af multicolored　　.25 .20

Intl. Day of Labor
Solidarity — A465b

1986, May 1　　　　Perf. 12½x12
1192B A465b 5af multicolored　　.25 .20

Intl. Red
Crescent
Day
A465c

1986, May 8　　　　　Perf. 12x12½
1192C A465c 7af multicolored　　.40 .20

Intl.
Children's
Day
A466

1986, June 1　　　　　　Perf. 12
1193	A466	1af	Mother, children, vert.	.20 .20
1194	A466	3af	Mother, child, vert.	.20 .20
1195	A466	9af	Children, map	.30 .20
		Nos. 1193-1195 (3)		.70 .60

World
Youth Day
A466a

1986, July 31　　　　　Perf. 12x12½
1195A A466a 15af multicolored　　.60 .25

Pashtos'
and
Baluchis'
Day
A467

1986, Aug. 31　　　　　Perf. 12x12½
1196 A467 4af multicolored　　　.25 .20

Intl. Peace
Year — A468

1986, Sept. 30　Photo.　Perf. 12½x12
1197 A468 12af black & Prus blue　.50 .20

A469

1986 World Cup Soccer
Championships, Mexico — A470

Various soccer plays.

1986, Apr. 15　　Litho.　　Perf. 12
1198	A469	3af	multi, vert.	.20 .20
1199	A469	4af	multicolored	.20 .20
1200	A469	7af	multicolored	.25 .20
1201	A469	11af	multi, vert.	.40 .20
1202	A469	12af	multicolored	.45 .20
1203	A469	18af	multi, vert.	.70 .25
1204	A469	20af	multi, vert.	.80 .25
		Nos. 1198-1204 (7)		4.50 4.50

Souvenir Sheet
Perf. 12½x12
1205 A470 75af multicolored　　4.00 3.00

A471

A472

1986, Apr. 21　　　　Perf. 12½x12
1206 A471 16af Lenin　　　　　.60 .40

1986, Apr. 27　Litho.　Perf. 12½x12
1207 A472 8af multicolored　　　.30 .20

Saur revolution, 8th anniv.

Natl.
Independence,
67th
Anniv. — A473

1986, Aug. 19　Litho.　Perf. 12½x12
1208 A473 10af multicolored　　.45 .20

Literacy
Day
A474

1986, Sept. 18　　　　Perf. 12x12½
1209 A474 2af multicolored　　　.25 .20

Dogs — A475

Lizards — A476

1986, May 19　Litho.　Perf. 12x12½
1210	A475	5af	St. Bernard	.25 .20
1211	A475	7af	Collie	.30 .20
1212	A475	8af	Pointer	.35 .20
1213	A475	9af	Golden retriever	.40 .20
1214	A475	11af	German shepherd	.50 .20
1215	A475	15af	Bulldog	.65 .25
1216	A475	20af	Afghan hound	.85 .30
		Nos. 1210-1216 (7)		4.50 4.50

1986, July 7　　Perf. 12x12½, 12½x12
1217	A476	3af	Cobra	.20 .20
1218	A476	4af	shown	.25 .20
1219	A476	5af	Praying mantis	.25 .20
1220	A476	8af	Beetle	.30 .20
1221	A476	9af	Tarantula	.35 .20
1222	A476	10af	Python	.35 .20
1223	A476	11af	Scorpions	.40 .20
		Nos. 1217-1223 (7)		3.00 3.00

Nos. 1217, 1219, 1221-1223 horiz.

STOCKHOLMIA '86 — A477

Ships.

1986, Aug. 28   Perf. 12½x12
1224 A477 4af multicolored   .25   .20
1225 A477 5af multicolored   .30   .20
1226 A477 6af multicolored   .40   .20
1227 A477 7af multicolored   .45   .20
1228 A477 8af multicolored   .55   .20
1229 A477 9af multicolored   .55   .20
1230 A477 11af multicolored   .65   .25
     Nos. 1224-1230 (7)   3.00 3.00

Souvenir Sheet
1231 A477 50af Galley   2.50 2.00

A479   A480

1986, Sept. 14   Perf. 12
1232 A479 3af lt blue, blk & olive
            gray   .35   .20
Reunion of Afghan tribes under the
Supreme Girgah.

1986, Oct. 25   Perf. 12½x12
1233 A480 3af black & brt ver   .35   .20
     Natl. youth solidarity.

Locomotives — A481

1986, June 21   Perf. 12½x12
1234 A481 4af multicolored   .25   .20
1235 A481 5af multicolored   .25   .20
1236 A481 6af multicolored   .35   .20
1237 A481 7af multicolored   .40   .20
1238 A481 8af multicolored   .50   .20
1239 A481 9af multicolored   .60   .20
1240 A481 11af multicolored   .65   .25
     Nos. 1234-1240 (7)   3.00 3.00

Fish
A482

Various fish.

1986, May 25
1241 A482 5af multicolored   .25   .20
1242 A482 7af multicolored   .30   .20
1243 A482 8af multicolored   .40   .20
1244 A482 9af multicolored   .45   .20
1245 A482 11af multicolored   .55   .20
1246 A482 15af multicolored   .70   .25
1247 A482 20af multicolored   .90   .30
     Nos. 1241-1247 (7)   4.50 4.50

Saur
Revolution,
9th Anniv.
A483

1987, Apr. 27   Perf. 12
1248 A483 3af multicolored   .25   .20

Natl. Reconciliation — A484

1987, May 27   Perf. 12x12½
1249 A484 3af multicolored   .25   .20

A485   A486

UN Child Survival
Campaign — A487

1987, June 1   Perf. 12
1250 A485 1af multicolored   .20   .20
1251 A486 5af multicolored   .20   .20
1252 A487 9af multicolored   .25   .20
     Nos. 1250-1252 (3)   .65   .60

Conference
of
Clergymen
and Ulema,
1st Anniv.
A488

1987, June 30
1253 A488 5af multicolored   .30   .20

Butterflies — A489   A490

1987, July 3
1254 A489 7af multicolored   .30   .20
1255 A489 9af multi, diff.   .40   .20
1256 A489 10af multi, diff.   .45   .20
1257 A489 12af multi, diff.   .50   .25
1258 A489 15af multi, diff.   .55   .25
1259 A489 22af multi, diff.   .80   .40
1260 A489 25af multi, diff.   1.00   .50
     Nos. 1254-1260 (7)   6.00 6.00

     10af, 15af and 22af horiz.

1987, Aug. 11
1261 A490 1af multicolored   .20   .25
1st election of local representatives for State
Power and Administration.

Natl. Independence, 68th
Anniv. — A490a

1987, Aug. 19
1261A A490a 3af multicolored   .20   .20

1st Artificial
Satellite (Sputnik),
30th
Anniv. — A491

1987, Oct. 4   Litho.   Perf. 12½x12
1262 A491 10af Sputnik   .35   .20
1263 A491 15af Rocket launch   .50   .20
1264 A491 25af Soyuz   .65   .25
     Nos. 1262-1264 (3)   3.00 3.00

World Post
Day
A492

1987, Oct. 9   Perf. 12x12½
1265 A492 22af multicolored   .75   .50

Intl. Communications and Transport
Day — A493

1987, Oct. 24   Perf. 12½x12
1266 A493 42af multicolored   2.00 1.00

October   Mice — A495
Revolution in
Russia, 70th
Anniv. — A494

1987, Nov. 7
1267 A494 25af Lenin   .90   .50

1987, Dec. 6   Perf. 12½x12, 12x12½
     Various mice. Nos. 1269-1272 horiz.

1268 A495 2af multicolored   .20   .20
1269 A495 4af multi, diff.   .25   .20
1270 A495 8af multi, diff.   .30   .20
1271 A495 16af multi, diff.   .55   .20
1272 A495 20af multi, diff.   .70   .25
     Nos. 1268-1272 (5)   3.00 3.00

Medicinal   Pashto's and
Plants — A496   Baluchis'
                   Day — A497

1987, Nov. 11   Litho.   Perf. 12
1273 A496 3af Castor bean   .20   .20
1274 A496 6af Licorice   .25   .20
1275 A496 9af Chamomile   .40   .20
1276 A496 14af Datura   .65   .25
1277 A496 18af Dandelion   .75   .30
     Nos. 1273-1277 (5)   2.25 1.15

1987, Aug. 30
1278 A497 4af multicolored   .25   .20

Dinosaurs
A498

Pashtos' and
Baluchis'
Day — A499

Perf. 12½x12, 12x12½
1988, June 6   Litho.
1279 A498 3af Mesosaurus   .20   .20
1280 A498 5af Styracosaurus   .25   .20
1281 A498 10af Uinatherium   .45   .20
1282 A498 15af Protoceratops   .70   .25
1283 A498 20af Stegosaurus   .90   .30
1284 A498 25af Ceratosaurus   1.10   .35
1285 A498 30af Dinornis max-
            imus   1.50   .60
     Nos. 1279-1285 (7)   5.10 2.10

     Nos. 1280-1283 horiz.

1988, Aug. 30   Perf. 12½x12
1286 A499 23af multicolored   .75   .50

Afghan-Soviet   Valentina
Joint Space   Tereshkova, 1st
Flight — A500   Woman in Space,
                   25th
                   Anniv. — A501

1988, Aug. 30
1287 A500 32af multicolored   .75   .40

1988, Oct. 16   Perf. 12x12½, 12½x12
1288 A501 10af Portrait, rocket,
            horiz.   .45   .25
1289 A501 15af Lift-off, dove   .65   .30
1290 A501 25af Spacecraft,
            Earth, horiz.   .90   .45
     Nos. 1288-1290 (3)   2.00 1.00

Traditional
Crafts — A502

Precious and
Semiprecious
Gems — A503

Perf. 12x12½, 12½x12

1988, Nov. 9   **Litho.**
1291	A502	2af Pitcher, bowls	.20	.20
1292	A502	4af Vases	.20	.20
1293	A502	5af Dress	.20	.20
1294	A502	9af Mats, napkins	.25	.20
1295	A502	15af Pocketbooks	.40	.20
1296	A502	23af Jewelry	.65	.25
1297	A502	50af Furniture	1.25	.50
		Nos. 1291-1297 (7)	3.15	1.75

Nos. 1291-1292, 1294-1297 horiz.

1988, Dec. 5   **Perf. 12½x12**
1298	A503	13af Emeralds	.65	.25
1299	A503	37af Lapiz lazuli	1.50	.60
1300	A503	40af Rubies	1.75	.75
		Nos. 1298-1300 (3)	3.90	1.60

1988 Winter
Olympics,
Calgary — A504

1988, Dec. 25
1301	A504	2af Women's figure skating	.20	.20
1301A	A504	5af Skiing	.20	.20
1301B	A504	9af Bobsledding	.30	.20
1301C	A504	22af Biathlon	.80	.35
1301D	A504	37af Speed skating	1.50	.65

Size: 80x60mm
1302	A504	75af Ice hockey	2.50	2.50
		Nos. 1301-1302 (6)	5.50	4.10

A510

A511

A512

A513

A513a

Flowers — A514

Various flowering plants.

Perf. 12x12½, 12½x12

1988, Jan. 27   **Litho.**
1303	A510	3af multicolored	.20	.20
1304	A511	5af multicolored	.25	.20
1305	A511	7af multi, vert.	.35	.20
1306	A512	9af multicolored	.40	.20
1307	A513	12af multicolored	.50	.25
1308	A513a	15af multicolored	.60	.25
1309	A514	24af multicolored	1.00	.50
		Nos. 1303-1309 (7)	3.30	1.75

Traditional
Musical
Instruments
A515

String and percussion instruments.

1988, Jan. 15   **Litho.**   **Perf. 12**
1310	A515	1af shown	.20	.20
1311	A515	3af drums	.20	.20
1312	A515	5af multi, diff.	.20	.20
1313	A515	15af multi, diff.	.50	.20
1314	A515	18af multi, diff.	.55	.25
1315	A515	25af multi, diff.	.85	.35
1316	A515	33af multi, diff.	1.10	.45
		Nos. 1310-1316 (7)	3.60	1.85

Admission of
Afghanistan to the
ITU and UPU, 60th
Anniv. — A516

1988, Apr. 13   **Litho.**   **Perf. 12**
1317	A516	20af multicolored	.60	.30

Saur
Revolution,
10th Anniv.
A517

1988, Apr. 23
1318 A517 10af multicolored   .45   .25

Fruit
A518

1988, July 18   **Litho.**   **Perf. 12**
1319	A518	2af Baskets, compote	.20	.20
1320	A518	4af Four baskets	.20	.20
1321	A518	7af Basket	.25	.20
1322	A518	8af Grapes, vert.	.30	.20
1323	A518	16af Market	.50	.25
1324	A518	22af Market, diff.	.75	.30
1325	A518	25af Vendor, vert.	.90	.40
		Nos. 1319-1325 (7)	3.10	1.70

Jawaharlal Nehru
(1889-1964), 1st
Prime Minister of
Independent
India — A519

1988, Nov. 14
1326 A519 40af multicolored   1.50   .75

Natl. Independence, 69th
Anniv. — A520

1988, Aug. 1
1327 A520 24af multicolored   .80   .40

Intl. Red Cross and
Red Crescent
Organizations,
125th
Anniv. — A521

1988, Sept. 26
1328 A521 10af multicolored   .50   .25

Natl. Reconciliation Institute, 2nd
Anniv. — A522

1989, Jan. 4
1329 A522 4af multicolored   .20   .20

Chess
A523

Boards, early matches and hand-made
chessmen.

1989, Feb. 2   **Litho.**   **Perf. 12x12½**
1330	A523	2af Bishop	.20	.20
1331	A523	3af Queen	.25	.20
1332	A523	4af King (bust)	.30	.20
1333	A523	7af King, diff.	.35	.20
1334	A523	16af Knight	.55	.20
1335	A523	24af Pawn	.85	.30
1336	A523	45af Bishop, diff.	1.50	.50
		Nos. 1330-1336 (7)	4.00	1.80

Paintings by
Picasso — A524

Fauna — A525

Designs: 4af, *The Old Jew.* 6af, *The Two
Mountebanks.* 8af, *Portrait of Ambrouse Vol-
lar.* 22af, *Woman of Majorca.* 35af, *Acrobat on
the Ball.* 75af, *Usine a Horta de Ebro.*

1989, Feb. 13   **Litho.**   **Perf. 12½x12**
1341	A524	4af multicolored	.20	.20
1342	A524	6af multicolored	.25	.20
1343	A524	8af multicolored	.40	.20
1344	A524	22af multicolored	.90	.30
1345	A524	35af multicolored	1.25	.40

Size: 71x90mm
Imperf
1346	A524	75af multicolored	3.00	2.50
		Nos. 1341-1346 (6)	6.00	3.80

1989, Feb. 20   **Litho.**   **Perf. 12½x12**
1347	A525	3af *Allactaga euphratica*	.20	.20
1348	A525	4af *Equus hemionus*	.25	.20
1349	A525	14af *Felis lynx*	.70	.30
1350	A525	35af *Gypaetus barbatus*	1.75	1.25
1351	A525	44af *Capra falconeri*	1.75	1.00

Size: 71x91mm
Imperf
1352	A525	100af *Naja oxiana*	4.50	3.00
		Nos. 1347-1352 (6)	9.15	5.95

Intl. Women's
Day — A526

1989, Mar. 8   **Perf. 12½x12**
1353 A526 8af multicolored   .25   .20

Restoration and Development of
San'a, Yemen — A527

1988, Dec. 27   **Litho.**   **Perf. 12**
1354 A527 32af multicolored   1.00   .50

Agriculture
Day
A528

1989, Mar. 21
1355 A528 1af Cattle .20 .20
1356 A528 2af Old and new plows .20 .20
1357 A528 3af Field workers .20 .20
Nos. 1355-1357 (3) .60 .60

World Meteorology Day — A529

1989, Mar. 23
1358 A529 27af shown .95 .50
1359 A529 32af Emblems 1.10 .60
1360 A529 40af Weather station,
balloon, vert. 1.40 .75
Nos. 1358-1360 (3) 3.45 1.85

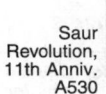

Saur
Revolution,
11th Anniv.
A530

1989, Apr. 27
1361 A530 20af multicolored .75 .25

Classic Automobiles — A531

1989, Dec. 30   Litho.   Perf. 12½x12
1362 A531 5af 1910 Duchs,
Germany .20 .20
1363 A531 10af 1911 Ford, US .35 .20
1364 A531 20af 1911 Renault,
France .60 .30
1365 A531 25af 1911, Russo-
Balte, Russia .85 .35
1366 A531 30af 1926 Fiat, Italy 1.00 .40

Asia-Pacific Telecommunity, 10th
Anniv. — A532

1989, Aug. 3   Perf. 12
1367 A532 3af shown .20 .20
1368 A532 27af Emblem, satellite
dish .80 .50

Teacher's
Day
A533

1989, May 30   Litho.   Perf. 12
1369 A533 42af multicolored 1.25 .60

French Revolution,
Bicent. — A534

1989, July   Litho.   Perf. 12
1370 A534 25af multicolored .90 .50

Natl. Independence, 70th
Anniv. — A535

1989, Aug. 18   Litho.   Perf. 12
1371 A535 25af multicolored .90 .50

A536   Birds — A537

1989, Aug. 30
1372 A536 3af multicolored .20 .20
Pashtos' and Baluchis' Day.

1989, Dec. 5   Litho.   Perf. 12
1373 A537 3af Platalea
leucorodia .20 .20
1374 A537 5af Porphyrio
porhyrio .25 .20
1375 A537 10af Botaurus stellaris, horiz. .45 .20
1376 A537 15af Pelecanus
onocrotalus .65 .35
1377 A537 20af Netta rufina .85 .40
1378 A537 25af Cygnus olor 1.10 .50
1379 A537 30af Phalacrocorax
carbo, horiz. 1.25 .60
Nos. 1373-1379 (7) 4.75

Tourism — A538

1989, Dec.
1380 A538 1af Mosque .20 .20
1381 A538 2af Minaret .20 .20
1382 A538 3af Buzkashi, horiz. .20 .20
1383 A538 4af Jet over Hendo
Kush, horiz. .20 .20
Nos. 1380-1383 (4) .80

Mavlavi Allahdad Balkhi, President of
Post of the Afghanistan Postal Administration, has declared that "the stamps
which have been printed after year
1989 are false stamps."
The status of the issues of 1996 to
date will be reviewed once more information is available.

Mushrooms
A539

1996, July 20   Litho.   Perf. 12½x13
Designs: 100af, Suillus luteus. 300af, Russula virescens. 400af, Clitocybe inversa.
500af, Volvariella bombycina. 600af,
Macrolepiota procera. 800af, Cystoderma
cinnabarinum.
4000af, Lycoperdon umbrinum.

A539   Set of 6
Souvenir Sheet
A539 4000af multicolored
Souv. sheet contains one 32x40mm stamp.

Bears
A540

Designs: 500af, Ursus americanus, vert.
600af, Ursus maritimus. 800af, Helarctos
malayanus. 900af, Ursus arctos horribilis.
1000af, Ursus arctos pyreneicus, vert.
4000af, Ursus arctos syriacus, vert.

Perf. 12½x13, 13x12½
1996, Aug. 15   Litho.
A540   Set of 5
Souvenir Sheet
Perf. 13
A540 4000af multicolored
Souv. sheet contains one 32x40mm stamp.

1998 World Cup
Soccer
Championships,
France — A541

Various soccer players.

1996, Sept. 18   Litho.   Perf. 13
Background Color
A541 500af green
A541 600af purple
A541 700af brown
Size: 28x42mm
A541 800af yellow
A541 900af blue
A541 1000af vermilion
Souvenir Sheet
Perf. 12½
A541 4000d multicolored
Souv. sheet contains one 32x40mm stamp.

Silkworms
A542

Designs: 300af, Arctia caja. 400af, Sphinx
ligustri. 500af, Zerynthia polyxema. 600af,
Papilio machaon. 700af, Cerura vinula. 800af,
Celerio euphorbiae.
3000af, Abraxes grossulariata.

1996, Oct. 7   Perf. 12½
A542   Set of 6
Souvenir Sheet
Perf. 13
A542 3000af multicolored
Souv. sheet contains one 40x32mm stamp.

Domestic
Cats — A543

Designs: 200af, American shorthair. 500af,
Japanese bobtail. 600af, British shorthair.
800af, Devon rex. 1000af, Colorpoint
shorthair. 1200af, Somali.
4000af, Sphinx.

1996   Litho.   Perf. 12½
A543   Set of 6
Souvenir Sheet
A543 4000af multicolored
Souv. sheet contains one 40x32mm stamp.

Horses
A544

200af, Eohippus. 300af, Miohippus. 400af,
Merychippus. 500af, Pliohippus. 600af,
Equus.

1996   Litho.1996, Nov. 5   Perf. 12½
A544   Set of 5
Souvenir Sheet
Perf. 13
A544 3000af Trotter, sulky
Souvenir sheet contains one 40x32mm
stamp. Inscription on 200af reads "Echippus."

Tulips — A545

Designs: 300af, Jewel of Spring. 400af, Mrs.
John Scheepers. 500af, Absalon. 600af,
Queen of Sheba. 800af, Marlette. 1000af,
Mary Housley,
3000af, Fosteriana Purissima.

1997   Litho.   Perf. 12½
A545   Set of 6
Souvenir Sheet
A545 3000af multicolored
Souv. sheet contains one 32x40mm stamp.

Llamas
and
Camels
A546

Designs: 400af, Lama vicugna, vert. 600af,
Lama guanicoe. 800af, Camelus dromedarius.
1000af, Lama guanicoe pacos, vert. 1200af,

Lama guanicoe glama. 1500af, Camelus ferus bactrianus. 4000af, Camelus dromedarius, vert.

1997
A546   Set of 6
Souvenir Sheet
A546   4000af multicolored
Souv. sheet contains one 32x40mm stamp.

Islamic Revolution, 4th Anniv. — A547

800af, shown. 1500af, Farmer plowing beside stream.

1996   Litho.   Perf. 13
A547   Set of 6

Independence, 77th Anniv. — A548

In Honor of Prophet Mohammed A549

A548, 700af. A549, 1500af.

1996
A548-A549   Set of 2

Domestic Cats A550

Designs: 30af, Norwegian forest. 50af, Ragdoll. 100af, Longhair Scottish fold. 200af, Oriental longhair. 300af, Manx. 500af, Sphinx. 1200af, Manx, diff.

1997   Perf. 12½
A550   Set of 6
Souvenir Sheet
Perf. 13
A550   1200af multicolored
Souv. sheet contains one 40x32mm stamp.

Wildflowers A551

Designs: 50af, Nymphaea odorata. 100af, Nymphaea lotus. 200af, Aponogeton distachyus. 500af, Nymphaea capensis. 800af, Numphaea rubra. 1000af, Pontederia cordata. 3000af, Nymphaea daubenyana, horiz.

1997   Litho.   Perf. 12½
A551   Set of 6
Souvenir Sheet
A551   3000af multicolored
Souv. sheet contains one 40x32mm stamp.

Early Sailing Ships — A552

Designs: 400af, Hanseatic cog. 600af, Northern Europe dromond. 800af, Venetian cargo ship. 1000af, Northern Europe merchant ship. 1200af, Ladia Russian war ship. 1500af, Genoa merchant ship. 4000af, Egyptian merchant ship.

1997   Litho.   Perf. 12½
A552   Set of 3 pairs
Souvenir Sheet
A552   4000af multicolored
400af-600af, 800af-1000af, 1200af-1500af issued in setenant pairs.

1998 World Cup Soccer Championships, France — A553

French flag, various soccer plays.

1997   Litho.   Perf. 12½
A553   Set of 6
Souvenir Sheet
A553   4000af multicolored
Souv. sheet contains one 32x40mm stamp.

Mushrooms A554

Designs: 400af, Gomphidius glutinosus. 600af, Collybia fusipes. 800af, Stropharia aeruginosa. 1000af, Craterellus cornucopioides. 1200af, Guepinia helvelloides. 1500af, Ixocomus elegans. 4000af, Cantharellus cibarius.

1998   Litho.   Perf. 12½
A554   Set of 6
Souvenir Sheet
Perf. 13
A554   4000af multicolored
Souv. sheet contains one 40x32mm stamp.

Butterflies, Moths A556

Designs: 400af, Fabriciana adippe, vert. 600af, Nymphalis antiopa. 800af, Polygonia c-album. 1000af, Nymphalis polychloros. 1200af, Pararge aegeria. 1500af, Melitaea phoebe, vert. 4000af, Aglais urticae.

1998, July 3   Litho.   Perf. 12½
A556   Set of 6
Souvenir Sheet
Perf. 13
A556   4000af multicolored
Souv. sheet contains one 40x32mm stamp.

A sheet of 9 stamps memorializing Princess Diana also has been sold in the philatelic market.

Ovis Vignei A557

World Wildlife Fund: 800af, Male. 1000af, Female nursing young. 1200af, Two males walking. 10,000af, Two males butting heads.

1998   Litho.   Perf. 12½
A557   Strip of 4

Wildlife — A558

400af lilac, Panthera tigris, vert. 400af orange, Cepreolus capreolus, vert. 600af blue, Lutra lutra, vert. 600af brown, Cervus elaphus, vert. 800af blue green, Dama dama, vert. 800af red, Acinonyx jubatus, vert. 1000af violet, Panthera leo. 1000af green, Sus scrofa. 1200af brown, Martes foina. 1200af blue, Martes martes. 1500af black, Vulpes vulpes. 1500af green blue, Capra ibex.

1998   Litho.   Perf. 12½
A558   Set of 12

Dogs A559

400af, Bloodhound, vert.. 600af, St. Bernard, vert. 800af, Rottweiler, vert. 1000af, Borzoi, vert. 1200af, Basset hound. 1500af, Chow chow.

1998, Mar. 25   Litho.   Perf. 12¾
A559   Set of 6
Souvenir Sheet
Perf. 13
A559   4000af Vizsla, vert.
Souv. sheet contains one 32x40mm stamp.

Trains A560

400af, Large Bloomer, Great Britain. 600af, Mogul 2-6-0, US. 800af, Saddle Tank 0-4-0, US. 1000af, A4-4498, Great Britain. 1200af, 020201, Germany. 1500af, 3801, Australia. 4000af, Royal Hudson 2860, Canada.

1998, May   Litho.   Perf. 12¾
A560   Set of 6   .05

Souvenir Sheet
Perf. 12½
A560   4000af multi
Souv. sheet contains one 36x28mm stamp.

Prehistoric Animals A561

400af, Mammuthu primigenius. 600af, Megaloceros. 800af, Ursus spelaeus. 1000af, Synthetoceras. 1200af, Coelodonta. 1500af, Hipparion. 4000af, Smilodon.

1998, May   Litho.   Perf. 12¾
A561   Set of 6
Souvenir Sheet
Perf. 12½
A561   4000af multi
Souv. sheet contains one 32x40mm stamp.

SEMI-POSTAL STAMPS

Catalogue values for unused stamps in this section are for Never Hinged items.

No. 373 Surcharged in Violet

1952, July 12   Unwmk.   Perf. 12½
B1   A122   40p + 30p cerise   10.00   1.50
B2   A122   125p + 30p cerise   12.50   2.00
1000th anniv. of the birth of Avicenna.

Children at Play — SP1

1955, July 3   Typo.   Perf. 11
B3   SP1   35p + 15p dk green   .50   .35
B4   SP1   125p + 25p purple   1.00   .85
The surtax was for child welfare.

Amir Sher Ali Khan, Tiger Head Stamp and Zahir Shah — SP2

Children at Play — SP3

1955, July 2   Litho.
B5   SP2   35p + 15p carmine   .40   .30
B6   SP2   125p + 25p pale vio bl   .85   .55
   85th anniv. of the Afghan post.

1956, June 20   Typo.
B7   SP3   35p + 15p brt vio bl   .75   .25
B8   SP3   140p + 15p dk org brn   1.25   .75
   Issued for Children's Day. The surtax was for child welfare. No. B8 inscribed in French.

Pashtunistan Monument, Kabul — SP4

1956, Sept. 1   Litho.
B9   SP4   35p + 15p dp violet   .20   .20
B10   SP4   140p + 15p brown   .60   .60
   "Free Pashtunistan" Day. The surtax aided the "Free Pashtunistan" movement.
   No. B9 measures 30½x19½mm; No. B10, 29x19mm. On sale and valid for use only on Sept. 1-2.

Globe and Sun — SP5

Children on Seesaw SP6

1956, Oct. 24   Perf. 11
B11   SP5   35p + 15p ultra   .65   .60
B12   SP5   140p + 15p red brown   1.25   1.00
   Afghanistan's UN admission, 10th anniv.

1957, June 20   Unwmk.
B13   SP6   35p + 15p brt rose   .75   .25
B14   SP6   140p + 15p ultra   1.50   .90
   Children's Day. Surtax for child welfare.

UN Headquarters and Emblems SP7

1957, Oct. 24   Perf. 11 Rough
B15   SP7   35p + 15p red brown   .35   .20
B16   SP7   140p + 15p lt ultra   .65   .55
   United Nations Day.

Swimming Pool and Children SP8

1958, June 22   Perf. 11
B17   SP8   35p + 15p rose   .25   .20
B18   SP8   140p + 15p dl red brn   .75   .60
   Children's Day. Surtax for child welfare.

Pashtunistan Flag — SP9

1958, Aug. 31
B19   SP9   35p + 15p lt blue   .20   .20
B20   SP9   140p + 15p red brown   .60   .60
   Issued for "Free Pashtunistan Day."

Children Playing Tug of War — SP10

1959, June 23   Litho.   Perf. 11
B21   SP10   35p + 15p brown vio   .50   .20
B22   SP10   165p + 15p brt pink   1.00   .60
   Children's Day. Surtax for child welfare.

Pathans in Tribal Dance SP11

Perf. 11 Rough
1959, Sept.   Unwmk.
B23   SP11   35p + 15p green   .50   .20
B24   SP11   165p + 15p orange   1.00   .60
   Issued for "Free Pashtunistan Day."

Afghan Cavalryman with UN Flag — SP12

1959, Oct. 24   Perf. 11 Rough
B25   SP12   35p + 15p orange   .20   .20
B26   SP12   165p + 15p lt bl grn   .45   .40
   Issued for United Nations Day.

Children SP13

1960, Oct. 23   Litho.
B27   SP13   75p + 25p lt ultra   .75   .20
B28   SP13   175p + 25p lt green   1.50   .35
   Children's Day. Surtax for child welfare.

Man with Spray Gun SP14

1960, Sept. 6   Perf. 11 Rough
B29   SP14   50p + 50p orange   .80   1.00
B30   SP14   175p + 50p red brown   2.25   2.25
   11th anniversary of the WHO malaria control program in Afghanistan.

SP15

1960, Sept. 1   Unwmk.
B31   SP15   35p + 50p rose   .25   .20
B32   SP15   175p + 50p dk blue   .55   .45
   Issued for "Free Pashtunistan Day."

Ambulance — SP16

1960, Oct. 16   Perf. 11
    Crescent in Red
B33   SP16   50p + 50p violet   .40   .30
B34   SP16   175p + 50p blue   .90   .75
   Issued for the Red Crescent Society.

Nos. 470-471 Surcharged in Blue or Orange
1960, Dec. 31   Litho.   Perf. 11
B35   A166   50p + 25p dp org (Bl)   1.50   1.50
B36   A166   165p + 25p blue (O)   1.50   1.50
   The souvenir sheets described after No. 471 were surcharged in carmine "+25 Ps" on each stamp. Value $5 each.
   See general note after No. 485.

Nos. 496-500 Surcharged

1961   Unwmk.   Photo.   Perf. 13½x14
B37   A175   2p + 25p green & rose lil
B38   A175   2p + 25p brown & cit
B39   A175   5p + 25p gray & rose
B40   A175   10p + 25p blue & bis
B41   A175   15p + 25p sl bl & dl lil
     Nos. B37-B41 (5)   1.50
   UNICEF. The same surcharge was applied to an imperf. souvenir sheet like that noted after No. 505. Value $4.50.

Nos. 522-526 Surcharged "+25PS" and Crescent in Red
1961, Oct. 16   Perf. 13½x14
B42   A184   2p + 25p black
B43   A184   2p + 25p green
B44   A184   5p + 25p lilac rose
B45   A184   10p + 25p lilac
B46   A184   15p + 25p dk blue
     Nos. B42-B46 (5)   2.00
   Issued for the Red Crescent Society.

Nos. 539-543 Surcharged in Red: "UNESCO + 25PS"
1962   Perf. 12
B47   A186   2p + 25p multi
B48   A186   2p + 25p multi
B49   A186   5p + 25p multi
B50   A186   10p + 25p multi
B51   A186   15p + 25p multi
     Nos. B47-B51 (5)   1.50
   UNESCO. The same surcharge was applied to the souvenir sheets mentioned after No. 548. Value, 2 sheets, $3.50.

Nos. 553-561 Surcharged: "Dag Hammarskjöld +20PS"
1962, Sept. 17   Perf. 14x13½
B52   A187   2p + 20p
B53   A187   2p + 20p
B54   A187   5p + 20p
B55   A187   10p + 20p
B56   A187   15p + 20p
B57   A187   25p + 20p
B58   A187   50p + 20p

B59   A187   75p + 20p
B60   A187   100p + 20p
     Nos. B52-B60 (5)   2.00
   In memory of Dag Hammarskjold, Sec. Gen. of the UN, 1953-61. Perf. and imperf. souvenir sheets exist. Value, 2 sheets, $3.

Nos. 583-593 Surcharged "+15PS"
1963, Mar. 15   Perf. 14x13½
B61   A193   2p + 15p
B62   A193   2p + 15p
B63   A193   5p + 15p
B64   A193   10p + 15p
B65   A193   15p + 15p
B66   A193   25p + 15p
B67   A193   50p + 15p
B68   A193   75p + 15p
B69   A193   100p + 15p
B70   A193   150p + 15p
B71   A193   175p + 15p
     Nos. B61-B71 (11)   7.50
   WHO drive to eradicate malaria.
   Postally used copies of Nos. B37-B71 are uncommon and command a considerable premium over the values for unused copies.

Nos. 672-672G, 672I Surcharged in Various Positions

1964, Mar. 9
B71A   A213g   2p + 50p
B71B   A213g   3p + 50p
B71C   A213g   4p + 50p
B71D   A213g   5p + 50p
B71E   A213g   10p + 50p
B71F   A213g   100p + 50p
B71G   A213g   2af + 50p
B71H   A213g   3af + 50p
     Souvenir Sheet
B71J   A213g   5af + 50p
   Nos. B71E-B71G are airmail semi-postals.

Blood Transfusion Kit — SP17

1964, Oct. 18   Litho.   Perf. 10½
B72   SP17   1af + 50p black & rose   .50   .20
   Issued for the Red Crescent Society and Red Crescent Week, Oct. 18-24.

First Aid Station SP18

1965, Oct.   Photo.   Perf. 13½x14
B73   SP18   1.50af + 50p multi   1.00   .50
   Issued for the Red Crescent Society.

Children Playing SP19

1966, Nov. 28   Photo.   Perf. 13½x14

B74 SP19 1af + 1af yel grn & cl	.35	.20
B75 SP19 3af + 2af yel & brn	.75	.20
B76 SP19 7af + 3af rose lil & grn	1.25	.40
Nos. B74-B76 (3)	2.35	.80

Children's Day.

Nadir Shah Presenting Society Charter SP20

1967   Photo.   Perf. 13x14

B77 SP20 2af + 1af red & dk grn	.25	.20
B78 SP20 5af + 1af lil rose & brn	.50	.25

Issued for the Red Crescent Society.

Vaccination SP21

Red Crescent — SP22

1967, June 6   Photo.   Perf. 12

B79 SP21 2af + 1af yellow & blk	.75	.20
B80 SP21 5af + 2af pink & brn	1.00	.25

The surtax was for anti-tuberculosis work.

1967, Oct. 18   Photo.   Perf. 12
Crescent in Red

B81 SP22 3af + 1af gray ol & blk	.50	.20
B82 SP22 5af + 1af dl bl & blk	.75	.20

Issued for the Red Crescent Society.

Queen Humeira SP23   Red Crescent SP24

1968, June 14   Photo.   Perf. 12

B83 SP23 2af + 2af red brown	.25	.20
B84 SP23 7af + 2af dull green	.75	.50

Issued for Mother's Day.

1968, Oct. 16   Photo.   Perf. 12

B85 SP24 4af + 1af yel, blk & red	.45	.25

Issued for the Red Crescent Society.

Red Cross, Crescent, Lion and Sun Emblems — SP25   Mother and Child — SP26

1969, May 5   Litho.   Perf. 14x13½

B86 SP25 3af + 1af multicolored	.75	.20
B87 SP25 5af + 1af multicolored	1.25	.30

League of Red Cross Societies, 50th anniv.

1969, June 14   Photo.   Perf. 12

B88 SP26 1af + 1af yel org & brn	.25	.20
B89 SP26 4af + 1af rose lil & pur	.40	.25
a. Souvenir sheet of 2	1.00	1.00

Mother's Day. No. B89a contains 2 imperf. stamps similar to Nos. B88-B89. Sold for 10af.

Red Crescent — SP27

1969, Oct. 16   Photo.   Perf. 12

B90 SP27 6af + 1af multi	.75	.30

Issued for the Red Crescent Society.

UN and FAO Emblems, Farmer — SP28

1973, May 24   Photo.   Perf. 13½

B91 SP28 14af + 7af grnsh bl & lil	1.10	.75

World Food Program, 10th anniversary.

Dome of the Rock, Jerusalem SP29

1977, Sept. 11   Photo.   Perf. 14

B92 SP29 12af + 3af multi	1.50	.35

Surtax for Palestinian families and soldiers.

15 Cent. (lunar) of Islamic Pilgrimage (Hegira) — SP30

1981, Jan. 17   Litho.   Perf. 12½x12

B93 SP30 13af + 2af multi	1.50	1.00

Red Crescent Aid Programs SP31

1981, May 8   Perf. 12x12½

B94 SP31 1af + 4af multi	.50	.60

Intl. Year of the Disabled SP32

1981, Oct. 12   Perf. 12x12½

B95 SP32 6af + 1af multi	.35	.25

AIR POST STAMPS

Plane over Kabul AP1

Perf. 12, 12x11, 11

1939, Oct. 1   Typo.   Unwmk.

C1 AP1 5af orange	3.75	2.25
a. Imperf., pair ('47)	22.50	22.50
b. Horiz. pair, imperf. vert.	20.00	
C2 AP1 10af blue	3.75	1.75
a. 10af lt bl	5.00	5.00
b. Imperf., pair ('47)	22.50	
c. Horiz. pair, imperf. vert.	20.00	
C3 AP1 20af emerald	7.50	5.00
a. Imperf., pair ('47)	22.50	
b. Horiz. pair, imperf. vert.	22.50	
c. Vert. pair, imperf. horiz.	22.50	
Nos. C1-C3 (3)	15.00	9.00

These stamps come with clean-cut or rough perforations. Counterfeits exist.

1948, June 14   Perf. 12x11½

C4 AP1 5af emerald	15.00	15.00
C5 AP1 10af red orange	15.00	15.00
C6 AP1 20af blue	15.00	15.00
Nos. C4-C6 (3)	45.00	45.00

Imperforates exist.

> **Catalogue values for unused stamps in this section, from this point to the end of the section, are for Never Hinged items.**

Plane over Palace Grounds, Kabul AP2

1951-54   Engr.   Perf. 13½
Imprint: "Waterlow & Sons, Limited, London"

C7 AP2 5af henna brn	2.50	.55
C8 AP2 5af dp grn ('54)	3.50	.50
C9 AP2 10af gray	4.00	1.40
C10 AP2 20af dark blue	6.50	2.25

1957

C11 AP2 5af ultra	.90	.35
C12 AP2 10af dark vio	1.75	.75
Nos. C7-C12 (6)	19.15	5.80

See No. C38.

Ariana Plane over Hindu Kush AP3

1960-63   Litho.   Unwmk.

C13 AP3 75p light vio	.30	.30
C14 AP3 125p blue	.40	.40

Perf. 10½, 11

C14A AP3 5af citron ('63)	1.10	1.10
Nos. C13-C14A (3)	1.80	1.80

Perf. 11, Imperf.

Girl Scout — AP4

1962, Aug. 30   Photo.   Perf. 11½x12

C15 AP4 100p ocher & brn	.60	.60
C16 AP4 175p brt yel grn & brn	.85	.85

Women's Day. See #578-579 and note on souvenir sheet.

Sports Type of Regular Issue, 1962

25p, 50p, Horse racing. 75p, 100p, Wrestling. 150p, Weight lifting. 175p, Soccer.

1962, Sept. 25   Unwmk.   Perf. 12
Black Inscriptions

C17 A195 25p rose & red brn		
C18 A195 50p gray & red brn		
C19 A195 75p pale vio & dk grn		
C20 A195 100p gray ol & dk pur		
C21 A195 150p rose lil & grn		
C22 A195 175p sal & brn		
Nos. C17-C22 (6)	2.25	

Children's Day Type of Regular Issue
Perf. 11½x12, 12x11½

1962, Oct. 14   Unwmk.

C23 A196 75p Runners	
C24 A196 150p Peaches	
C25 A196 200p Iris, vert.	

A souvenir sheet contains one each of Nos. C23-C25. Value $2.50.

Red Crescent Type of Regular Issue

1962, Oct. 16   Perf. 12
Fruit and Flowers in Natural Colors; Carmine Crescent

C26 A197 25p Grapes	
C27 A197 50p Pears	
C28 A197 100p Wistaria	

Two souvenir sheets exist. One contains a 150p gray brown stamp in blossom design, the other a 200p gray stamp in wistaria design, imperf. Value, each $5.

UN Type of Regular Issue

1962, Oct. 24   Photo.
Flags in Original Colors, Black Inscriptions

C29 A198 75p blue	
C30 A198 100p lt brn	
C31 A198 125p brt grn	

Boy Scout Type of Regular Issue

1962, Oct. 25   Unwmk.   Perf. 12

C32 A199 25p gray, blk, dl grn & sal	
C33 A199 50p grn, brn & sal	
C34 A199 75p bl grn, red brn & sal	
C35 A199 100p bl, slate & sal	

Teacher's Day Type of Regular Issue

1962, Oct. 25   Photo.

C36 A200 100p Pole vault	
C37 A200 150p High jump	

A souvenir sheet contains one 250p pink and slate green stamp in design of 150p. Value $2.50.

Type of 1951-54

1962   Engr.   Perf. 13½
Imprint: "Thomas De La Rue & Co. Ltd."

C38 AP2 5af ultra	6.00	1.00

Agriculture Types of Regular Issue
Unwmk.

1963, Mar. 1   Photo.   Perf. 12

C42 A204 100p dk car, grn & brn	
C43 A203 200p ocher & blk	
C44 A204 200p ultra, grn & brn	

Hands Holding Wheat Emblem AP5

1963, Mar. 27   Photo.   Perf. 14

C45 AP5 500p lil, lt brn & brn	1.75	.60

FAO "Freedom from Hunger" campaign. Two souvenir sheets exist. One contains a 1000p blue green, light brown and brown, type AP5, imperf. The other contains a 200p brown and green and 300p ultramarine, yellow and ocher in rice and corn designs, type A205. Values $6 and $2.50.

Meteorological Day Type of Regular Issue

Designs: 100p, 500p, Meteorological measuring instrument. 200p, 400p, Weather station. 300p, Rockets in space.

1963, May 23   *Imperf.*

C46 A206 100p brn & bl

Perf. 13½x14

C47	A206	200p brt grn & lil	
C48	A206	300p dk bl & rose	
C49	A206	400p bl & dl red brn	
C50	A206	500p car rose & gray grn	

Nos. C47 and C50 printed se-tenant. Two souvenir sheets exist. One contains a 125p red and brown stamp in rocket design. The other contains a 100p blue and dull red brown in "rockets in space" design. Values $5 and $7.50.

Kabul International Airport — AP8

Perf. 12x11½

1964, Apr.		**Unwmk.**		**Photo.**
C57	AP8	10af red lil & grn	.55	.20
C58	AP8	20af dk grn & red lil	.80	.40
a.		Perf. 12 ('68)	5.00	3.00
C59	AP8	50af dk bl & grnsh bl	2.25	1.00
a.		Perf. 12 ('68)	8.00	5.00
		Nos. C57-C59 (3)	3.60	1.60

Inauguration of Kabul Airport Terminal. Nos. C58a-C59a are 36mm wide. Nos. C58-C59 are 35½mm wide.

Zahir Shah and Kabul Airport — AP9

100af, Zahir Shah and Ariana Plane.

1971	**Photo.**		**Perf. 12½x13½**	
C60	AP9	50af multi	10.00	8.00
C61	AP9	100af blk, red & grn	5.00	3.00

Remainders of No C60 were used, starting in 1978, with king's portrait removed.

REGISTRATION STAMPS

R1

Dated "1309"

1891	**Unwmk.**	**Litho.**	*Imperf.*
	Pelure Paper		
F1	R1	1r slate blue	2.00
a.		Tete beche pair	12.50

Genuinely used copies of No. F1 are rare. Counterfeit cancellations exist.

R2

Dated "1311"

1893		**Thin Wove Paper**	
F2	R2	1r black, *green*	1.60

Genuinely used copies of No. F2 are rare. Counterfeit cancellations exist.

R3

Undated

1894				
F3	R3	2ab black, *green*	7.50	8.00

12 varieties. See note below Nos. 189-190.

R4

Undated

1898-1900				
F4	R4	2ab black, *deep rose*	3.50	3.50
F5	R4	2ab black, *lilac rose*	4.00	4.00
F6	R4	2ab black, *magenta*	5.00	4.00
F7	R4	2ab black, *salmon*	3.00	3.50
F8	R4	2ab black, *orange*	3.50	3.50
F9	R4	2ab black, *yellow*	3.50	3.50
F10	R4	2ab black, *green*	3.50	3.50
		Nos. F4-F10 (7)	26.00	25.50

Many shades of paper. Nos. F4-F10 come in two sizes, measured between outer frame lines: 52x36mm, 1st printing; 46x33mm, 2nd printing. The outer frame line (not pictured) is 3-6mm from inner frame line. Used on P.O. receipts.

OFFICIAL STAMPS

(Used only on interior mail.)

Coat of Arms O1

1909	**Unwmk.**	**Typo.**	*Perf. 12*	
	Wove Paper			
O1	O1	red	1.00	1.00
a.		Carmine ('19?)	2.25	6.00

Later printings of No. O1 in scarlet, vermilion, claret, etc., on various types of paper, were issued until 1927.

Coat of Arms — O2

1939-68?	**Typo.**		*Perf. 11, 12*	
O3	O2	15p emerald	.50	.50
O4	O2	30p ocher ('40)	.65	.65
O5	O2	45p dark carmine	.55	.55
O6	O2	50p brt car ('68)	.30	.30
a.		50p carmine rose ('55)	.50	.50
O7	O2	1af brt red violet	1.00	1.00
		Nos. O3-O7 (5)	3.00	3.00

Size of 50p, 24x31mm, others 22½x28mm.

> **Catalogue values for unused stamps in this section, from this point to the end of the section, are for Never Hinged items.**

1964-65		**Litho.**	*Perf. 11*	
O8	O2	50p rose	.75	.75
a.		50p salmon ('65)	1.50	1.50

Stamps of this type are revenues.

PARCEL POST STAMPS

Coat of Arms — PP1

PP2

PP3

PP4

1909	**Unwmk.**	**Typo.**	*Perf. 12*	
Q1	PP1	3sh bister	1.00	2.00
a.		Imperf., pair	1.00	
Q2	PP2	1kr olive gray	1.60	3.00
a.		Imperf., pair		
Q3	PP3	1r orange	3.00	3.00
Q4	PP3	1r olive green	18.00	4.00
Q5	PP4	2r red	3.50	3.50
		Nos. Q1-Q5 (5)	27.10	15.50

1916-18				
Q6	PP1	3sh green	1.60	3.00
Q7	PP2	1kr pale red	2.50	1.25
a.		1kr rose red ('18)	3.25	3.25
Q8	PP3	1r brown org	1.25	1.25
a.		1r deep brown ('18)	10.00	2.50
Q9	PP4	2r blue	4.50	5.00
		Nos. Q6-Q9 (4)	9.85	10.50

Nos. Q1-Q9 sometimes show letters of the papermaker's watermark "HOWARD & JONES LONDON."

Ungummed copies are remainders. They sell for one-third the price of mint examples.

Old Habibia College, Near Kabul — PP5

1921				
	Wove Paper			
Q10	PP5	10pa chocolate	3.00	3.00
a.		Tete beche pair	15.00	15.00
Q11	PP5	15pa light brn	6.00	5.00
a.		Tete beche pair	20.00	
Q12	PP5	30pa red violet	9.00	7.00
a.		Tete beche pair	30.00	
b.		Laid paper	15.00	10.00
Q13	PP5	1r brt blue	10.00	9.00
a.		Tete beche pair	50.00	
		Nos. Q10-Q13 (4)	28.00	24.00

Stamps of this issue are usually perforated on one or two sides only.

The laid paper of No. Q12b has a papermaker's watermark in the sheet.

PP6

1924-26		**Wove Paper**		
Q15	PP6	5kr ultra ('26)	35.00	35.00
Q16	PP6	5r lilac	15.00	15.00

A 15r rose exists, but is not known to have been placed in use.

PP7

PP8

1928-29		*Perf. 11, 11xImperf.*		
Q17	PP7	2r yellow orange	10.00	3.00
Q18	PP7	2r green ('29)	3.00	3.00
Q19	PP8	3r deep green	7.50	4.00
Q20	PP8	3r brown ('29)	5.00	5.00
		Nos. Q17-Q20 (4)	25.50	15.00

POSTAL TAX STAMPS

Aliabad
Hospital
near
Kabul
PT1

Pierre
and
Marie
Curie
PT2

Perf. 12x11½, 12

1938, Dec. 22   Typo.   Unwmk.
RA1 PT1 10p peacock grn   2.50 4.00
RA2 PT2 15p dull blue   2.50 4.00

Obligatory on all mail Dec. 22-28, 1938. The
money was used for the Aliabad Hospital. See
note with CD80.

PT3

Begging
Child — PT4

1949, May 28   Typo.   Perf. 12
RA3 PT3 35p red orange   2.50 1.60
RA4 PT4 125p ultra   2.75 1.60

United Nations Children's Day, May 28.
Obligatory on all foreign mail on that date.
Proceeds were used for child welfare.

Paghman
Arch and
UN
Emblem
PT5

1949, Oct. 24
RA5 PT5 125p dk blue green   10.00 6.00

4th anniv. of the UN. Valid one day only.
Issued in sheets of 9 (3x3).

| Catalogue values for unused |
| stamps in this section, from this |
| point to the end of the section, are |
| for Never Hinged items. |

Zahir Shah and Map of
Afghanistan — PT6

1950, Mar. 30   Typo.
RA6 PT6 125p blue green   2.00 1.25

Return of Zahir Shah from a trip to Europe
for his health. Valid for two weeks. The tax was
used for public health purposes.

Hazara
Youth — PT7

1950, May 28   Typo.   Perf. 11½
RA7 PT7 125p dk blue green   2.00 1.50

Tax for Child Welfare. Obligatory and valid
only on May 28, 1950, on foreign mail.

Ruins of Qalai Bist and Globe — PT8

1950, Oct. 24
RA8 PT8 1.25af ultramarine   7.50 4.00

5th anniv. of the UN. Proceeds went to
Afghanistan's UN Projects Committee.

Zahir
Shah and
Medical
Center
PT9

1950, Dec. 22   Typo.   Perf. 11½
Size: 38x25mm
RA9 PT9 35p carmine   1.00 1.00
RA10 PT9 1.25af black   4.50 2.25

The tax was for the national Graduate
School of Medicine.

Koochi Girl
with Lamb
PT10

Kohistani Boy and Sheep — PT11

1951, May 28
RA11 PT10 35p emerald   .75 .65
RA12 PT11 1.25af ultramarine   .75 .65

The tax was for Child Welfare.

Distributing Gifts
to
Children — PT12

Qandahari
Boys
Dancing the
"Attan"
PT13

1952, May 28   Litho.
RA13 PT12 35p chocolate   .25 .25
RA14 PT13 125p violet   .75 .75

The tax was for Child Welfare.

Soldier Receiving
First Aid — PT14

1952, Oct.
RA15 PT14 10p light green   .50 .35

Stretcher-bearers and
Wounded — PT15

Soldier Assisting Wounded — PT16

1953, Oct.
RA16 PT15 10p yel grn & org red   .50 .40
RA17 PT16 10p vio brn & org red   .50 .40

Prince
Mohammed
Nadir — PT17

Map and
Young
Musicians
PT18

1953, May 28
RA18 PT17 35p orange yellow   .20 .20
RA19 PT17 125p chalky blue   .55 .55

No. RA19 is inscribed in French "Children's
Day." The tax was for child welfare.

1954, May 28   Unwmk.   Perf. 11
RA20 PT18 35p purple   .30 .20
RA21 PT18 125p ultra   1.10 1.10

No. RA21 is inscribed in French. The tax
was for child welfare.

PT19

Red Crescent
PT20

1954, Oct. 17   Perf. 11½
RA22 PT19 20p blue & red   .25 .20

1955, Oct. 18   Perf. 11
RA23 PT20 20p dull grn & car   .50 .25

Zahir Shah and
Red Crescent
PT21

1956, Oct. 18
RA24 PT21 20p lt grn & rose car .25 .20

Red Crescent Headquarters,
Kabul — PT22

1957, Oct. 17
RA25 PT22 20p lt ultra & car   .75 .50

Map and Crescent PT23

1958, Oct.   **Unwmk.**   *Perf. 11*
RA26 PT23 25p yel grn & red   .30 .30

PT24

1959, Oct. 17   **Litho.**   *Perf. 11*
RA27 PT24 25p lt violet & red   .20 .20

The tax on Nos. RA15-RA17, RA22-RA27 was for the Red Crescent Society. Use of these stamps was required for one week.

AGUERA, LA

LOCATION — An administrative district in southern Rio de Oro on the northwest coast of Africa.
GOVT. — Spanish possession
AREA — Because of indefinite political boundaries, figures for area and population are not available.

100 Centimos = 1 Peseta

Type of 1920 Issue of Rio de Oro Overprinted

LA AGÜERA

1920, June   **Unwmk.**   *Perf. 13*
1	A8	1c blue green	1.75	1.75
2	A8	2c olive brown	1.75	1.75
3	A8	5c deep green	1.75	1.75
4	A8	10c light red	1.75	1.75
5	A8	15c yellow	1.75	1.75
6	A8	20c lilac	1.75	1.75
7	A8	25c deep blue	1.75	1.75
8	A8	30c dark brown	1.75	1.75
9	A8	40c pink	1.75	1.75
10	A8	50c bright blue	5.50	5.50
11	A8	1p red brown	10.00	10.00
12	A8	4p dark violet	30.00	30.00
13	A8	10p orange	60.00	60.00
		Nos. 1-13 (13)	121.25	121.25
		Set, never hinged	180.00	

Very fine examples of Nos. 1-13 will be somewhat off center. Well centered examples are uncommon and will sell for more.

King Alfonso XIII — A2

1922, June   **Typo.**
14	A2	1c turquoise blue	.75	.75
15	A2	2c dark green	.75	.75
16	A2	5c blue green	.75	.75
17	A2	10c red	.75	.75
18	A2	15c red brown	.75	.75
19	A2	20c yellow	.75	.75
20	A2	25c deep blue	.75	.75
21	A2	30c dark brown	.75	.75
22	A2	40c rose red	1.00	1.00
23	A2	50c red violet	3.50	3.25
24	A2	1p rose	7.00	6.50
25	A2	4p violet	17.50	17.00
26	A2	10p orange	26.00	26.00
		Nos. 14-26 (13)	61.00	59.75
		Set, never hinged	92.50	

For later issues see Spanish Sahara.

AITUTAKI

ïit-ə-'täk-ē

LOCATION — One of the larger Cook Islands, in the South Pacific Ocean northeast of New Zealand
GOVT. — A dependency of New Zealand
AREA — 7 sq. mi.
POP. — 2,335 (1981)

The Cook Islands were attached to New Zealand in 1901. Stamps of Cook Islands were used in 1892-1903 and 1932-72.
Aitutaki acquired its own postal service in August 1972, though remaining part of Cook Islands.

12 Pence = 1 Shilling
100 Cents = 1 Dollar (1972)

Catalogue values for unused stamps in this country are for Never Hinged items, beginning with Scott 37.

Watermark

Wmk. 61- Single-lined NZ and Star Close Together

Stamps of New Zealand Surcharged in Red or Blue:

a   b

1903   **Engr.**   **Wmk. 61**   *Perf. 14*
1	A18(a)	½p green (R)	4.25	6.00
2	A35(b)	1p rose car (Bl)	4.50	6.25

c

d   e

AITUTAKI.

f Tal Tiringl.

Perf. 11
3	A22(c)	2½p blue (R)	9.75	15.00
4	A23(d)	3p yel brn (Bl)	16.00	14.00
5	A26(e)	6p red (Bl)	30.00	27.50
6	A29(f)	1sh scarlet (Bl)	55.00	80.00
a.		1sh orange red (Bl)	60.00	87.50

1911   **Typo.**   *Perf. 14x15*
7	A41(a)	½p yellow grn (R)	1.00	3.00

Engr.
Perf. 14
9	A22(c)	2½p deep blue (R)	7.50	16.00

AITUTAKI.

Ono Pene. g   Tal Tiringl. h

1913-16   **Typo.**
10	A42(b)	1p rose (Bl)	2.75	9.00

Engr.
12	A41(g)	6p car rose (Bl) ('16)	42.50	87.50
13	A41(h)	1sh ver (Bl) ('14)	50.00	125.00

1916-17   *Perf. 14x13½, 14x14½*
17	A45(g)	6p car rose (Bl)	10.00	24.00
18	A45(h)	1sh ver (Bl) ('17)	32.50	80.00
		Nos. 1-18 (13)	265.75	493.25

New Zealand Stamps of 1909-19 Overprinted in Red or Dark Blue

1917-20   **Typo.**   *Perf. 14x15*
19	A43	½p yellow grn ('20)	.95	5.50
20	A42	1p car (Bl) ('20)	3.00	19.50
21	A47	1½p gray black	3.50	27.50
22	A47	1½p brown org ('19)	.80	6.50
23	A43	3p choc (Bl) ('19)	3.25	14.00

Perf. 14x13½, 14x14½
Engr.
24	A44	2½p dull blue ('18)	1.60	14.00
25	A45	3p vio brn (Bl) ('18)	1.75	17.50
26	A45	6p car rose (Bl)	4.50	19.00
27	A45	1sh vermilion (Bl)	11.50	26.00
		Nos. 19-27 (9)	30.85	149.50

Landing of Capt. Cook A15

Avarua Waterfront A16

Capt. James Cook — A17

Palm — A18

Houses at Arorangi — A19

Avarua Harbor — A20

1920   **Engr.**   **Unwmk.**   *Perf. 14*
28	A15	½p green & black	3.25	22.50
29	A16	1p car & black	3.25	16.00
30	A17	1½p brown & blk	5.50	11.00
31	A18	3p dp blue & blk	2.25	14.00
32	A19	6p sl & red brn	6.25	15.00
33	A20	1sh claret & blk	9.00	24.00
		Nos. 28-33 (6)	29.50	102.50

Inverted centers, double frames, etc. are from printers waste.

Rarotongan Chief (Te Po) — A21

1924-27   **Wmk. 61**   *Perf. 14*
34	A15	½p green & blk ('27)	2.00	9.00
35	A16	1p carmine & blk	5.75	6.00
36	A21	2½p blue & blk ('27)	7.50	47.50
		Nos. 34-36 (3)	15.25	62.50

Catalogue values for unused stamps in this section, from this point to the end of the section, are for Never Hinged items.

Cook Islands Nos. 199-200, 202, 205-206, 210, 212-213, 215-217 Overprinted

1972 Photo. Unwmk.   *Perf. 14x13½*
37	A34	½c gold & multi	.50	.70
38	A34	1c gold & multi	1.25	1.25
39	A34	2½c gold & multi	3.75	6.25
40	A34	4c gold & multi	1.25	.75
41	A34	5c gold & multi	4.25	6.50
42	A34	10c gold & multi	4.25	5.00
43	A34	20c gold & multi	2.10	.90
44	A34	25c gold & multi	1.25	.90
45	A34	50c gold & multi	4.75	2.50
46	A35	$1 gold & multi	7.00	5.00
47	A35	$2 gold & multi	.85	.65
		Nos. 37-47 (11)	31.20	30.40

Overprint horizontal on Nos. 46-47. On $2, overprint is in capitals of different font; size: 21x3mm.
Issued: Nos. 37-46, Aug. 9; No. 47, Nov. 24.

Same Overprint Horizontal in Silver On Cook Islands Nos. 330-332
1972, Oct. 27   *Perf. 13½*
48	A53	5c gold & multi	.20	.20
49	A53	5c gold & multi	.25	.25
50	A53	10c gold & multi	.40	.40
		Nos. 48-50 (3)	.85	.85

Fluorescence
Starting in 1972, stamps carry a "fluorescent security underprinting" in a multiple pattern of New Zealand's coat of arms with "Aitutaki" above, "Cook Islands" below and two stars at each side.

Silver Wedding Type of Cook Islands
1972, Nov. 20   **Photo.**   *Perf. 13½*
Size: 29x40mm
51	A54	5c silver & multi	3.25	2.50

Size: 66x40mm
52	A54	15c silver & multi	1.50	1.10

25th anniversary of the marriage of Queen Elizabeth II and Prince Philip. Nos. 51-52 printed in sheets of 5 stamps and one label.

Flower Issue of Cook Islands Overprinted

1972, Dec. 11   **Photo.**   *Perf. 14x13½*
53	A34	½c on #199	.20	.20
54	A34	1c on #200	.20	.20
55	A34	2½c on #202	.20	.20

56	A34	4c on #205	.25	.20
57	A34	5c on #206	.25	.20
58	A34	10c on #210	.40	.25
59	A34	20c on #212	1.00	.50
60	A34	25c on #213	.50	.60
61	A34	50c on #215	.75	.90
62	A35	$1 on #216	1.25	2.00
		Nos. 53-62 (10)	5.00	5.25

See Nos. 73-76.

The Passion of Christ, by Mathias Grunewald — A22

Paintings: No. 63b, St. Veronica, by Rogier van der Weyden. No. 63c, Crucifixion, by Raphael. No. 63d, Resurrection, by della Francesca. No. 64a, Last Supper, by Master of Amiens. No. 64b, Condemnation of Christ, by Hans Holbein, the Elder. No. 64c, Crucifixion, by Rubens. No. 64d, Resurrection, by El Greco. No. 65a, Passion of Christ, by El Greco. No. 65b, St. Veronica, by Jakob Cornelisz. No. 65c, Crucifixion, by Rubens. No. 65d, Resurrection, by Dierik Bouts.

Perf. 13½

1973, Apr. 6   Photo.   Unwmk.

63		Block of 4	.30	.30
a.-d.	A22	1c any single	.20	.20
64		Block of 4	.80	.80
a.-d.	A22	5c any single	.20	.20
65		Block of 4	1.90	1.90
a.-d.	A22	10c any single	.45	.45
		Nos. 63-65 (3)	3.00	3.00

Easter. Printed in blocks of 4 in sheets of 40. Design descriptions in top and bottom margins.

Coin Type of Cook Islands

Queen Elizabeth II Coins: 1c, Taro leaf. 2c, Pineapples. 5c, Hibiscus. 10c, Oranges. 20c, Fairy terns. 50c, Bonito. $1, Tangaroa, Polynesian god of creation, vert.

1973, May 14   Perf. 13x13½

Size: 37x24mm

66	A55	1c dp car & multi	.20	.20
67	A55	2c blue & multi	.20	.20
68	A55	5c green & multi	.20	.20

Size: 46x30mm

69	A55	10c vio blue & multi	.20	.20
70	A55	20c green & multi	.30	.25
71	A55	50c dp car & multi	.60	.50

Size: 32x54½mm

72	A55	$1 blue, blk & sil	1.00	.75
		Nos. 66-72 (7)	2.70	2.30

Cook Islands coinage commemorating silver wedding anniv. of Queen Elizabeth II.

Printed in sheets of 20 stamps and label showing Westminster Abbey.

Cook Islands Nos. 208, 210, 212 and 215 Overprinted Like Nos. 53-62 and: "TENTH ANNIVERSARY/ CESSATION/ OF/ NUCLEAR TESTING/ TREATY"

1973, July   Photo.   Perf. 14x13½

73	A34	8c gold & multi	.20	.20
74	A34	10c gold & multi	.20	.20
75	A34	20c gold & multi	.50	.50
76	A34	50c gold & multi	1.10	1.10
		Nos. 73-76 (4)	2.00	2.00

Nuclear Test Ban Treaty, 10th anniv., protest against French nuclear testing on Mururoa Atoll.

Princess Anne, Hibiscus A23

Design: 30c, Mark Phillips and hibiscus.

1973, Nov. 14   Photo.   Perf. 13½x14

77	A23	25c gold & multi	.30	.30
78	A23	30c gold & multi	.40	.40
a.		Souvenir sheet of 2, #77-78	.80	.80

Wedding of Princess Anne and Capt. Mark Phillips.

Virgin and Child, by Il Perugino — A24

Paintings of the Virgin and Child by various masters - #79: a, Van Dyck. b, Bartolommeo Montagna. c, Carlo Crivelli. d, Il Perugino. #80: a, Cima da Conegliano. b, Memling. c, Verones. d, Verones. #81: a, Raphael. b, Lorenzo Lotto. c, Del Colle. d, Memling.

1973, Dec.   Photo.   Perf. 13

79	A24	1c Block of 4, #a.-d.	.25	.25
80	A24	5c Block of 4, #a.-d.	.75	.75
81	A24	10c Block of 4, #a.-d.	2.00	2.00
		Nos. 79-81 (3)	3.00	3.00

Christmas. Printed in blocks of 4 in sheets of 48. Design descriptions in margins.

Murex Ramosus A25

Terebra Maculata — A26

Pacific Shells: 1c, Nautilus macromphalus. 2c, Harpa major. 3c, Phalium strigatum. 4c, Cypraea talpa. 5c, Mitra stictica. 8c, Charonia tritonis. 10c, Murex triremis. 20c, Oliva sericea. 25c, Tritonalia rubeta. 60c, Strombus latissimus. $1, Biplex perca. $5, Cypraea hesitata.

1974-75   Photo.   Perf. 13

82	A25	½c silver & multi	.50	.50
83	A25	1c silver & multi	.50	.40
84	A25	2c silver & multi	.50	.40
85	A25	3c silver & multi	.50	.40
86	A25	4c silver & multi	.50	.40
87	A25	5c silver & multi	.50	.40
88	A25	8c silver & multi	1.10	.50
89	A25	10c silver & multi	1.10	.50
90	A25	20c silver & multi	1.50	1.00
91	A25	25c silver & multi	1.75	1.00
92	A25	60c silver & multi	6.00	1.75
93	A25	$1 silver & multi	4.75	3.00

Perf. 14

94	A26	$2 silver & multi	7.50	4.25
95	A26	$5 silver & multi	27.50	15.50
		Nos. 82-95 (14)	54.20	30.00

Issued: #82-93, 1/31/74; $2, 1/20/75; $5, 2/28/75.

For overprints see Nos. O1-O16.

1974, Apr. 11   Photo.   Perf. 13

Size: 38x22mm

96	A27	1c shown	.20	.20
97	A27	1c "Bounty" at sea	.20	.20
a.		Pair, #96-97	.20	.20
98	A27	5c Bligh and "Bounty" off Aitutaki	.45	.45
99	A27	5c Chart of Aitutaki, 1856	.45	.45
a.		Pair, #98-99	.90	.90
100	A27	8c James Cook and "Resolution"	.95	.95
101	A27	8c Maps of Aitutaki and Pacific Ocean	.95	.95
a.		Pair, #100-101	1.90	1.90
		Nos. 96-101,C1-C6 (12)	8.70	8.70

Capt. William Bligh (1754-1817), European discoverer of Aitutaki, Apr. 11, 1789.

Aitutaki Nos. 1 & 2 Map and UPU Emblem A28

Design: 50c, Aitutaki Nos. 4 and 28, map of Aitutaki and UPU emblem.

1974, July 15   Photo.   Perf. 13½

102	A28	25c blue & multi	.55	.55
103	A28	50c blue & multi	1.10	1.10
a.		Souvenir sheet of 2, #102-103	2.00	2.00

UPU, cent. Printed in sheets of 5 plus label showing UPU emblem.

A29

Designs: Paintings of the Virgin and Child.

1974, Oct. 11   Photo.   Perf. 13½

104	A29	1c Van der Goes	.20	.20
105	A29	5c Giovanni Bellini	.20	.20
106	A29	8c Gerard David	.20	.20
107	A29	10c Antonello da Messina	.20	.20
108	A29	25c Joos van Cleve	.50	.50
109	A29	30c Maitre de St. Catherine	.55	.55
a.		Souvenir sheet of 6, #104-109	2.00	2.00
		Nos. 104-109 (6)	1.85	1.85

Christmas. #104-109 printed in sheets of 15 stamps and corner label. See #B1-B6.

A30

1974, Nov. 29   Photo.   Perf. 14

Designs: Churchill portraits.

110	A30	10c Dublin, Age 5	.20	.20
111	A30	25c As young man	.25	.20
112	A30	30c Inspecting troops, WWII	.35	.20
113	A30	50c Painting	.70	.40
114	A30	$1 Giving V sign	1.40	.80
a.		Souvenir sheet of 5, #110-114 + label, perf. 13½	4.25	3.75
		Nos. 110-114 (5)	2.90	1.80

Sir Winston Churchill (1874-1965). Nos. 110-114 printed in sheets of 5 stamps and corner label.

Emblem US & USSR Flags A31

50c, Icarus and Apollo Soyuz spacecraft.

1975, July 24   Photo.   Perf. 13x14½

115	A31	25c multicolored	.35	.35
116	A31	50c multicolored	.90	.90
a.		Souvenir sheet of 2	1.75	1.75

Apollo Soyuz space test project (Russo-American cooperation), launching July 15; link-up July 17. Nos. 115 and 116 each printed in sheets of 5 stamps and one label showing area of Apollo splash-downs. No. 116a contains one each of Nos. 115-116 with gold and black border and inscription.

Madonna and Child, by Pietro Lorenzetti — A32

Paintings: 7c, Adoration of the Kings, by Rogier van der Weyden. 15c, Madonna and Child, by Bartolommeo Montagna. 20c, Adoration of the Shepherds.

1975, Nov. 24   Photo.   Perf. 14x13½

117	A32	Strip of 3	.30	.30
a.		6c St. Francis	.20	.20
b.		6c Madonna and Child	.20	.20
c.		6c St. John the Evangelist	.20	.20
118	A32	Strip of 3	.30	.30
a.		7c One King	.20	.20
b.		7c Madonna and Child	.20	.20
c.		7c Two Kings	.20	.20
119	A32	Strip of 3	.75	.75
a.		15c St. Joseph	.25	.25
b.		15c Madonna and Child	.25	.25
c.		15c St. John the Baptist	.25	.25
120	A32	Strip of 3	1.25	1.25
a.		20c One Shepherd	.40	.40
b.		20c Madonna and Child	.40	.40
c.		20c Two Shepherds	.40	.40
d.		Souv. sheet of 12, #117-120, perf. 13½	3.50	3.50
		Nos. 117-120 (4)	2.60	2.60

Christmas. Nos. 117-120 printed in sheets of 30 (10 strips of 3).
For surcharges see Nos. B7-B10.

Descent from the Cross, detail — A33

Designs (Painting, Flemish School, 16th Century): 30c, Virgin Mary, disciple and body of Jesus. 35c, Mary Magdalene and disciple.

1976, Apr. 5   Photo.   Perf. 13½

121	A33	15c gold & multi	.20	.20
122	A33	30c gold & multi	.30	.30
123	A33	35c gold & multi	.70	.70
a.		Souvenir sheet of 3	1.60	1.60
		Nos. 121-123 (3)	1.20	1.20

Easter. No. 123a contains 3 stamps similar to Nos. 121-123, perf. 13, in continuous design without gold frames and white margins.

Declaration of Independence — A34

William Bligh and "Bounty" A27

Paintings by John Trumbull: 35c, Surrender of Cornwallis at Yorktown. 50c, Washington's Farewell Address. a, "1976 BICENTENARY." b, "UNITED STATES." c, "INDEPENDENCE 1776."

1976, June 1   Photo.   Perf. 13½

124	A34	Strip of 3	1.50	1.50
a.-c.		30c any single	.50	.50
125	A34	Strip of 3	2.00	2.00
a.-c.		35c any single	.65	.65
126	A34	Strip of 3	2.75	2.75
a.-c.		50c any single	.90	.90
d.		Souvenir sheet of 9 (3x3)	6.25	6.25
		Nos. 124-126 (3)	6.25	6.25

American Bicentennial. Nos. 124-126 printed in sheets of 5 strips of 3 and 3-part corner label showing portrait of John Trumbull, commemorative inscription and portraits of Washington (30c), John Adams (35c) and Jefferson (50c). No. 126d contains 3 strips similar to Nos. 124-126.

Bicycling
A35

Montreal Olympic Games Emblem and: 35c, Sailing. 60c, Field hockey. 70c, Running.

1976, July 15   Photo.   Perf. 13x14

127	A35	15c multicolored	.25	.20
128	A35	35c multicolored	.55	.45
129	A35	60c multicolored	.90	.75
130	A35	70c multicolored	1.10	.85
a.		Souvenir sheet of 4	3.00	2.25
		Nos. 127-130 (4)	2.80	2.25

21st Olympic Games, Montreal, Canada, July 17-Aug. 1. Nos. 127-130 printed in sheets of 5 stamps and label showing coat of Arms and Montreal Olympic Games emblem. No. 130a contains 4 stamps similar to Nos. 127-130 with gold margin around each stamp.

Nos. 127-130a Overprinted Diagonally: "ROYAL VISIT JULY 1976"

1976, July 30

131	A35	15c multicolored	.20	.20
132	A35	35c multicolored	.55	.55
133	A35	60c multicolored	.75	.75
134	A35	70c multicolored	1.00	1.00
a.		Souvenir sheet of 4	3.00	3.00
		Nos. 131-134 (4)	2.50	2.50

Visit of Queen Elizabeth II to Montreal and official opening of the Games. Each stamp of No. 134a has diagonal overprint. Sheet margin has additional overprint: "ROYAL VISIT OF H.M. QUEEN ELIZABETH II/OFFICIALLY OPENED 17 JULY 1976."

Annunciation — A36

Designs: Nos. 137-138, Angel appearing to the shepherds. Nos. 139-140, Nativity. Nos. 141-142, Three Kings.

1976, Oct. 18   Perf. 13½x13

135	6c	dk green & gold	.20	.20
136	6c	dk green & gold	.20	.20
a.	A36	Pair, #135-136		
137	7c	dk brown & gold	.20	.20
138	7c	dk brown & gold	.20	.20
a.	A36	Pair, #137-138	.25	.25
139	15c	dk blue & gold	.20	.20
140	15c	dk blue & gold	.20	.20
a.	A36	Pair, #139-140	.30	.30
141	20c	purple & gold	.25	.25
142	20c	purple & gold	.25	.25
a.	A36	Pair, #141-142	.50	.50
b.		Souvenir sheet of 8	1.90	1.90
		Nos. 135-142 (8)	1.70	1.70

Christmas. No. 142a contains 8 stamps similar to Nos. 135-142 with white margin around each pair of stamps.

A. G. Bell and 1876 Telephone — A38

Design: 70c, Satellite and radar.

1977, Mar. 3   Photo.   Perf. 13½x13

143	A38	25c rose & multi	.25	.25
144	A38	70c violet & multi	.85	.85
a.		Souvenir sheet of 2	1.65	1.65

Centenary of first telephone call by Alexander Graham Bell, Mar. 10, 1876. No. 144a contains a 25c in colors of 70c and 70c in colors of 25c.

Calvary (detail), by Rubens A39

Paintings by Rubens: 20c, Lamentation. 35c, Descent from the Cross.

1977, Mar. 31   Photo.   Perf. 13½x14

145	A39	15c gold & multi	.55	.55
146	A39	20c gold & multi	.70	.70
147	A39	35c gold & multi	1.00	1.00
a.		Souv. sheet of #145-147, perf. 13	2.75	2.75
		Nos. 145-147 (3)	2.25	2.25

Easter, and 400th birth anniv. of Peter Paul Rubens (1577-1640), Flemish painter.

Capt. Bligh, "Bounty" and George III — A40

Designs: 35c, Rev. John Williams, George IV, First Christian Church. 50c, British flag, map of Aitutaki, Queen Victoria. $1, Elizabeth II and family on balcony after coronation.

1977, Apr. 21   Perf. 13½

148	A40	25c gold & multi	.20	.20
149	A40	35c gold & multi	.30	.30
150	A40	50c gold & multi	.50	.50
151	A40	$1 gold & multi	3.00	3.00
a.		Souvenir sheet of 4, #148-151	2.75	2.75
		Nos. 148-151 (4)	4.00	4.00

Reign of Queen Elizabeth II, 25th anniv. For overprint & surcharge see #O11, O15.

Annunciation — A41

Designs: No. 154, Virgin, Child and ox. No. 155, Joseph and donkey (Nativity). No. 156, Three Kings. No. 157, Virgin and Child. No. 158, Joseph. No. 159, Virgin, Child and donkey (Flight into Egypt).

1977, Oct. 14   Photo.   Perf. 13½x14

152	6c	multicolored	.20	.20
153	6c	multicolored	.20	.20
a.	A41	Pair, #152-153	.25	.25
154	7c	multicolored	.20	.20
155	7c	multicolored	.20	.20
a.	A41	Pair, #154-155	.25	.25
156	15c	multicolored	.20	.20
157	15c	multicolored	.20	.20
a.	A41	Pair, #156-157	.40	.40
158	20c	multicolored	.25	.25
159	20c	multicolored	.25	.25
a.	A41	Pair, #158-159	.50	.50
b.		Souvenir sheet of 8, #152-159	1.60	1.60
		Nos. 152-159 (8)	1.70	1.70

Christmas.

For surcharges see Nos. B19-B26a.

Hawaiian Wood Figurine — A43

Designs: 50c, Talbot hunting dog, figurehead of "Resolution", horiz. $1, Temple figure.

1978, Jan. 19   Litho.   Perf. 13½

160	A43	35c multicolored	.55	.55
161	A43	50c multicolored	.75	.75
162	A43	$1 multicolored	1.40	1.40
a.		Souvenir sheet of 3, #160-162	3.00	3.00
		Nos. 160-162 (3)	2.70	2.70

Bicentenary of Capt. Cook's arrival in Hawaii. Nos. 160-162 issued in sheets of 6.

Jesus Carrying Cross, by Simone di Martini A44

Paintings: 20c, Avignon Pietà, 15th Century. 35c, Christ at Emmaus, by Rembrandt.

1978, Mar. 17   Photo.   Perf. 13½x14

163	A44	15c gold & multi	.20	.20
164	A44	20c gold & multi	.30	.30
165	A44	35c gold & multi	.50	.50
a.		Souvenir sheet of 3	1.25	1.25
		Nos. 163-165 (3)	1.00	1.00

Easter. No. 165a contains one each of Nos. 163-165, perf. 13½, and label showing Louvre, Paris. See Nos. B27-B29.

Elizabeth II — A45

Virgin and Child, by Dürer — A46

Souvenir Sheets

1978, June 15   Photo.   Perf. 13½x13

166		Sheet of 6	2.75	2.75
a.	A45	$1 Yale of Beaufort	.25	.25
b.	A45	$1 shown	.25	.25
c.	A45	$1 Ancestral statue	.25	.25
d.		Souvenir sheet of 6	1.50	1.50

25th anniv. of coronation of Queen Elizabeth II. No. 166 contains 2 each of Nos. 166a-166c, silver marginal inscription and coats of arms. No. 166d contains 2 strips of Nos. 166a-166c separated by horizontal slate green gutter showing Royal family on balcony, silver marginal inscription.

1978, Dec. 4   Photo.   Perf. 14½x13

Designs: Various paintings of the Virgin and Child by Albrecht Dürer.

167	A46	15c multicolored	.30	.25
168	A46	17c multicolored	.35	.30
169	A46	30c multicolored	.70	.50
170	A46	35c multicolored	.90	.75
		Nos. 167-170 (4)	2.25	1.80

Christmas; 450th death anniv. of Albrecht Dürer (1471-1528), German painter. Nos. 167-170 issued in sheets of 5 stamps and corner label. See No. B30.

Capt. Cook, by Nathaniel Dance — A47

Boy Holding Hibiscus, IYC Emblem — A48

Design: 75c, "Resolution" and "Adventure," by William Hodges.

1979, July 20   Photo.   Perf. 14x13½

171	A47	50c multicolored	1.25	1.25
172	A47	75c multicolored	1.75	1.75
a.		Souvenir sheet of 2, #171-172	2.50	2.50

Capt. James Cook (1728-1779), explorer, death bicentenary.

1979, Oct. 1   Photo.   Perf. 14x13½

IYC Emblem and: 35c, Boy playing guitar. 65c, Boys in outrigger canoe.

173	A48	30c multicolored	.20	.20
174	A48	35c multicolored	.30	.30
175	A48	65c multicolored	.55	.55
		Nos. 173-175 (3)	1.05	1.05

See No. B31.

Aitutaki No. 102, Hill, Penny Black A49

Designs: Nos. 176, 178-179, 181, paintings of letter writers, Flemish School, 17th century.

1979, Nov. 14   Photo.   Perf. 13

176	A49	50c Gabriel Metsu	.45	.45
177	A49	50c shown	.45	.45
178	A49	50c Jan Vermeer	.45	.45
a.		Strip of 3, #176-178	1.35	1.35
179	A49	65c Gerard Terborch	.55	.55
180	A49	65c No. 103 (like No. 177)	.55	.55
181	A49	65c Jan Vermeer	.55	.55
a.		Strip of 3, #179-181	1.65	1.65
		Nos. 176-181 (6)	3.00	3.00

Souvenir Sheet

182		Sheet of 6	2.50	2.50
a.	A49	30c like No. 176	.40	.40
b.	A49	30c like No. 177	.40	.40
c.	A49	30c like No. 178	.40	.40
d.	A49	30c like No. 179	.40	.40
e.	A49	30c like No. 180	.40	.40
f.	A49	30c like No. 181	.40	.40

Sir Rowland Hill (1795-1879), originator of penny postage. Nos. 176-178 and 179-181 printed in sheets of 9.

Descent from the Cross, Detail — A50

Albert Einstein — A51

Easter: 30c, 35c, Descent from the Cross, by Quentin Metsys (details).

1980, Apr. 3   Photo.   Perf. 13x13½
183	A50	20c multicolored	.40 .40
184	A50	30c multicolored	.50 .50
185	A50	35c multicolored	.60 .60
		Nos. 183-185 (3)	1.50 1.50

See No. B32.

1980, July 21   Photo.   Perf. 14
186	A51	12c shown	.55 .55
187	A51	12c Formula, atom structure	.55 .55
a.		Pair, #186-187	1.10 1.10
188	A51	15c Portrait, diff.	.65 .65
189	A51	15c Atomic blast	.65 .65
a.		Pair, #188-189	1.30 1.30
190	A51	20c Portrait, diff.	.90 .90
191	A51	20c Atomic blast, trees	.90 .90
a.		Pair, #190-191	1.80 1.80
b.		Souv. sheet of 6, #186-191, perf. 13	4.25 4.25
		Nos. 186-191 (6)	4.20 4.20

Albert Einstein (1879-1955), theoretical physicist.

A52   A53

1980, Sept. 26   Photo.   Perf. 14
192	A52	6c Ancestral Figure, Aitutaki	.20 .20
193	A52	6c God image staff, Rarotonga	.20 .20
194	A52	6c Trade adze, Mangaia	.20 .20
195	A52	6c Tangaroa carving, Rarotonga	.20 .20
a.		Block of 4, #192-195	.35 .35
196	A52	12c Wooden image, Aitutaki	.20 .20
197	A52	12c Hand club, Rarotonga	.20 .20
198	A52	12c Carved mace, Mangaia	.20 .20
199	A52	12c Fisherman's god, Rarotonga	.20 .20
a.		Block of 4, #196-199	.70 .70
200	A52	15c Ti'i image, Aitutaki	.20 .20
201	A52	15c Fisherman's god, diff.	.20 .20
202	A52	15c Carved mace, Cook Islands	.20 .20
203	A52	15c Tangaroa, diff.	.20 .20
a.		Block of 4, #200-203	.90 .90
204	A52	20c Chief's headdress, Aitutaki	.30 .30
205	A52	20c Carved mace, diff.	.30 .30
206	A52	20c God image staff, diff.	.30 .30
207	A52	20c like #195	.30 .30
a.		Block of 4, #2-4-207	1.20 1.20
b.		Souvenir sheet of 16, #192-207	3.50

Third South Pacific Arts Festival, Port Moresby, Papua New Guinea.

1980, Nov. 21   Photo.   Perf. 13x13½

Virgin and Child, Sculptures.
208	A53	15c 13th cent.	.20 .20
209	A53	20c 14th cent.	.20 .20
210	A53	25c 15th cent.	.25 .25
211	A53	35c 15th cent., diff.	.35 .35
		Nos. 208-211 (4)	1.00 1.00

Christmas. See No. B33.

Mourning Virgin, by Pedro Roldan — A54

Sturnus Vulgaris — A55

Easter (Roldan Sculptures): 40c, Christ. 50c, Mourning St. John.

1981, Mar. 31   Photo.   Perf. 14
212	A54	30c green & gold	.35 .35
213	A54	45c brt purple & gold	.45 .45
214	A54	50c dk blue & gold	.60 .60
		Nos. 212-214 (3)	1.40 1.40

See No. B34.

1981-82   Perf. 14x13½, 13½x14
215	A55	1c shown	.25 .20
216	A55	1c Poephila gouldiae	.25 .20
a.		Pair, #215-216	.50 .20
217	A55	2c Petroica multicolor	.35 .20
218	A55	2c Pachycephala pectoralis	.35 .20
a.		Pair, #217-218	.70 .20
219	A55	3c Falco peregrinus	.40 .20
220	A55	3c Rhipidura rufifrous	.40 .20
a.		Pair, #219-220	.80 .20
221	A55	4c Tyto alba	.45 .20
222	A55	4c Padda oryzivora	.45 .20
a.		Pair, #221-222	.90 .30
223	A55	5c Artamus leucorhynchus	.50 .20
224	A55	5c Vini peruviana	.50 .20
a.		Pair, #223-224	1.00 .35
225	A55	6c Columba livia	.60 .20
226	A55	6c Porphyrio porphyria	.60 .20
a.		Pair, #225-226	1.20 .40
227	A55	10c Geopelia striata	.80 .35
228	A55	10c Lonchura castaneothorax	.80 .35
a.		Pair, #227-228	1.60 .70
229	A55	12c Acridotheres tristis	.80 .40
230	A55	12c Egretta sacra	.80 .40
a.		Pair, #229-230	1.60 .80
231	A55	15c Diomeda melanophris	.90 .45
232	A55	15c Numenius phaeopus	.90 .45
a.		Pair, #231-232	1.80 .90
233	A55	20c Gygis alba	1.00 .65
234	A55	20c Pluvialis dominica	1.00 .65
a.		Pair, #233-234	2.00 1.30
235	A55	25c Sula leucogaster	1.10 .80
236	A55	25c Anas superciliosa	1.10 .80
a.		Pair, #235-236	2.20 1.60
237	A55	30c Anas acuta	1.90 .90
238	A55	30c Fregata minor	1.90 .90
a.		Pair, #237-238	3.80 1.80
239	A55	35c Stercorarius pomarinus	2.00 1.10
240	A55	35c Conopoderas caffra	2.00 1.10
a.		Pair, #239-240	4.00 2.20
241	A55	40c Lalage maculosa	2.25 1.10
242	A55	40c Gallirallus philippensis	2.25 1.10
a.		Pair, #241-242	4.50 2.20
243	A55	50c Vini stepheni	2.50 1.50
244	A55	50c Diomedea epomophora	2.50 1.50
a.		Pair, #243-244	5.00 3.00
245	A55	70c Ptilinopus victor	5.00 2.00
246	A55	70c Erythrura cyaneovirens	5.00 2.00
e.		Pair, #245-246	10.00 4.00

Photo.   Perf. 13½
Size: 35x47mm
246A	A55	$1 Myiagra azureocapilla	5.50 3.50
246B	A55	$2 Myiagra vanikorensis	9.00 7.00
246C	A55	$4 Amandava amandava	15.00 12.00
246D	A55	$5 Halcyon recurvirostris	16.00 15.00
		Nos. 215-246D (36)	87.10 58.40

Issued: #215-230, 4/6; #231-238, 5/8; #239-246, 1/14/82; #246A-246B, 2/15/82.
Nos. 231-246 horiz.
For surcharges and overprint see Nos. 293-306, 452-454, O40-O41.

Prince Charles and Lady Diana — A56

Perf. 13x13½, 13½x13

1981, June 10   Photo.
247	A56	60c Charles, vert.	.55 .55
248	A56	80c Lady Diana, vert.	.70 .70
249	A56	$1.40 Shown	1.00 1.00
		Nos. 247-249 (3)	2.25 2.25

Royal Wedding. Issued in sheets of 4.
For overprints and surcharges see Nos. 265-267, 307, 309, 355, 405-407, B35-B37.

1982 World Cup Soccer — A57

Designs: Various soccer players.

1981, Nov. 30   Photo.   Perf. 14
250	A57	12c Pair, #250a-250b	.85 .85
251	A57	15c Pair, #251a-251b	1.00 1.00
252	A57	20c Pair, #252a-252b	1.40 1.40
253	A57	25c Pair, #253a-253b	1.75 1.75
		Nos. 250-253 (4)	5.00 5.00

See No. B38.

Christmas A58

Rembrandt Etchings: 15c, Holy Family, 1632, vert. 30c, Virgin with Child, 1634, vert. 40c, Adoration of the Shepherds, 1654. 50c, Holy Family with Cat, 1644.

1981, Dec. 10   Perf. 14
254	A58	15c gold & dk brown	.40 .40
255	A58	30c gold & dk brown	.65 .65
256	A58	40c gold & dk brown	.85 .85
257	A58	50c gold & dk brown	1.10 1.10
		Nos. 254-257 (4)	3.00 3.00

Souvenir Sheets
258	A58	80c + 5c like #254	.90 .90
259	A58	80c + 5c like #255	.90 .90
260	A58	80c + 5c like #256	.90 .90
261	A58	80c + 5c like #257	.90 .90

Nos. 258-261 have multicolored margins showing entire etching. Surtax on Nos. 258-261 was for local charities.

21st Birthday of Princess Diana — A59

1982, June 24   Photo.   Perf. 14
262	A59	70c shown	.75 1.60
263	A59	$1 Wedding portrait	1.90 1.00
264	A59	$2 Diana, diff.	3.50 2.25
a.		Souvenir sheet of 3, #262-264	6.00 5.00
		Nos. 262-264 (3)	6.15 4.85

See #268-270a. For surcharges see #308, 310.

Nos. 247-249 Overprinted: "21 June 1982 PRINCE WILLIAM OF WALES" or "COMMEMORATING THE ROYAL BIRTH"

1982, July 13   Perf. 13x13½, 13½x13
265	A56	60c multicolored	1.00 1.00
266	A56	80c multicolored	1.50 1.50
267	A56	$1.40 multicolored	2.50 2.50
		Nos. 265-267 (3)	5.00 5.00

Nos. 262-264a Inscribed: "ROYAL BIRTH 21 JUNE 1982 PRINCE WILLIAM OF WALES"

1982, Aug. 5   Perf. 14
268	A59	70c multicolored	1.10 1.10
269	A59	$1 multicolored	1.50 1.50
270	A59	$2 multicolored	3.00 3.00
a.		Souvenir sheet of 3	6.00 6.00
		Nos. 268-270 (3)	5.60 5.60

Christmas — A60

Madonna and Child Sculptures, 12th-15th Cent.

1982, Dec. 10   Photo.   Perf. 13
271	A60	18c multicolored	.55 .55
272	A60	36c multicolored	.70 .70
273	A60	48c multicolored	.90 .90
274	A60	60c multicolored	1.10 1.10
		Nos. 271-274 (4)	3.25 3.25

Souvenir Sheet
275		Sheet of 4	4.00 4.00
a.	A60	18c + 2c like 18c	.45 .45
b.	A60	36c + 2c like 36c	.80 .80
c.	A60	48c + 2c like 48c	1.10 1.10
d.	A60	60c + 2c like 60c	1.25 1.25

Surtax was for children's charities.

Commonwealth Day — A61

1983, Mar. 14   Photo.   Perf. 13x13½
276	A61	48c Bananas	1.25 1.25
277	A61	48c Ti'i statuette	1.25 1.25
278	A61	48c Boys canoeing	1.25 1.25
279	A61	48c Capt. Bligh, Bounty	1.25 1.25
a.		Block of 4, #276-279	5.00 5.00

Scouting Year A62

1983, Apr. 18   Photo.   Perf. 14
280	A62	36c Campfire	.50 .50
281	A62	48c Salute	.60 .60
282	A62	60c Hiking	.65 .65
		Nos. 280-282 (3)	1.75 1.75

Souvenir Sheet
Perf. 13½
283		Sheet of 3	3.00 3.00
a.	A62	36c + 3c like #280	.75 .75
b.	A62	48c + 3c like #281	.90 .90
c.	A62	60c + 3c like #282	1.25 1.25

Surtax was for benefit of Scouting.

Nos. 280-283 Overprinted: "15th WORLD SCOUT JAMBOREE"

1983, July 11   Photo.   Perf. 14
284	A62	36c multicolored	.90 .90
285	A62	48c multicolored	1.10 1.10
286	A62	60c multicolored	1.25 1.25
		Nos. 284-286 (3)	3.25 3.25

Souvenir Sheet
287		Sheet of 3	3.00 3.00
a.	A62	36c + 3c like #284	.75 .75
b.	A62	48c + 3c like #285	.90 .90
c.	A62	60c + 3c like #286	1.25 1.25

A63

A64

Manned Flight Bicentenary: Modern sport balloons.

1983, July 22	Photo.		Perf. 14x13	
288	A63	18c multicolored	.60	.60
289	A63	36c multicolored	.80	.80
290	A63	48c multicolored	1.00	1.00
291	A63	60c multicolored	1.10	1.10
		Nos. 288-291 (4)	3.50	3.50

Souvenir Sheet

292	A63	$2.50 multicolored	3.00	3.00

Nos. 233-246, 246D, 248-249, 263-264 Surcharged

1983, Sept. 22				
293	A55	18c on 20c, #233	2.25	.35
294	A55	18c on 20c, #234	2.25	.35
a.		Pair, #293-294	4.50	.70
295	A55	36c on 25c, #235	3.00	.70
296	A55	36c on 25c, #236	3.00	.70
a.		Pair, #295-296	6.00	1.40
297	A55	36c on 30c, #237	3.00	.70
298	A55	36c on 30c, #238	3.00	.70
a.		Pair, #297-298	6.00	1.40
299	A55	36c on 35c, #239	3.00	.70
300	A55	36c on 35c, #240	3.00	.70
a.		Pair, #299-300	6.00	1.40
301	A55	48c on 40c, #241	3.50	.95
302	A55	48c on 40c, #242	3.50	.95
a.		Pair, #301-302	7.00	1.90
303	A55	48c on 50c, #243	3.50	.95
304	A55	48c on 50c, #244	3.50	.95
a.		Pair, #303-304	7.00	1.90
305	A55	72c on 70c, #245	6.25	1.50
306	A55	72c on 70c, #246	6.25	1.50
a.		Pair, #305-306	12.50	3.00
307	A56	96c on 80c, #248	2.75	1.90
308	A59	96c on $1, #263	2.75	1.90
309	A56	$1.20 on $1.40, #249	2.50	2.50
310	A59	$1.20 on $2, #264	2.75	2.50

Size: 35x47mm

311	A55	$5.60 on $5, #246D	18.00	11.00
		Nos. 293-311 (19)	77.50	31.50

Nos. 307-308, 310-311 vert.

1983, Sept. 29	Photo.		Perf. 14	
312	A64	48c shown	.65	.65
313	A64	60c Global coverage	.85	.85
314	A64	96c Communications satellite	1.50	1.50
a.		Souvenir sheet of 3, #312-314	3.00	3.00
		Nos. 312-314 (3)	3.00	3.00

World Communications Year.

Christmas
A65

Raphael Paintings.

1983, Nov. 21	Photo.		Perf. 13½x14	
315	A65	36c Madonna of the Chair	.75	.75
316	A65	48c Alba Madonna	.95	.95
317	A65	60c Connestabile Madonna	1.25	1.25
		Nos. 315-317 (3)	2.95	2.95

Souvenir Sheet

318		Sheet of 3	2.75	2.75
a.	A65	36c + 3c like #315	.70	.70
b.	A65	48c + 3c like #316	.85	.85
c.	A65	60c + 3c like #317	1.00	1.00

1983, Dec. 15			Imperf.	
		Size: 46x46mm		
319	A65	85c + 5c like #315	1.25	1.25
320	A65	85c + 5c like #316	1.25	1.25
321	A65	85c + 5c like #317	1.25	1.25
		Nos. 319-321 (3)	3.75	3.75

Surtax was for children's charities.

Local Birds — A66

1984	Photo.		Perf. 14	
322	A66	2c as No. 216	.25	.25
323	A66	3c as No. 215	.25	.25
324	A66	5c as No. 217	.25	.25
325	A66	10c as No. 218	.25	.25
326	A66	12c as No. 220	.35	.35
327	A66	18c as No. 219	.45	.45
328	A66	24c as No. 221	.65	.65
329	A66	30c as No. 222	.75	.75
330	A66	36c as No. 223	.90	.90
331	A66	48c as No. 224	1.25	1.25
332	A66	50c as No. 225	.90	.90
333	A66	60c as No. 226	1.25	1.25
334	A66	72c as No. 227	1.50	1.50
335	A66	96c as No. 228	2.00	2.00
336	A66	$1.20 as No. 229	2.25	2.25
337	A66	$2.10 as No. 230	4.00	4.00
338	A66	$3 as No. 246A	5.75	5.75
339	A66	$4.20 as No. 246B	7.00	7.00
340	A66	$5.60 as No. 246C	7.50	7.50
341	A66	$9.60 as No. 246D	12.50	12.50
		Nos. 322-341 (20)	50.00	50.00

For overprints and surcharges see Nos. O17-O39.

1984 Summer Olympics — A67

1984, July 24	Photo.		Perf. 13x13½	
342	A67	36c Javelin	.35	.35
343	A67	48c Shot put	.45	.45
344	A67	60c Hurdles	.55	.55
345	A67	$2 Handball	1.75	1.75
		Nos. 342-345 (4)	3.10	3.10

Souvenir Sheet

346		Sheet of 4	3.50	3.50
a.	A67	36c + 5c like #342	.40	.40
b.	A67	48c + 5c like #343	.50	.50
c.	A67	60c + 5c like #344	.60	.60
d.	A67	$2 + 5c like #345	1.75	1.75

Surtax was for benefit of local sports.

Nos. 342-345 Overprinted in Gold on Black with Winners' Names, Event, Nationality

1984, Aug. 21	Photo.		Perf. 13x13½	
347	A67	36c multicolored	.40	.40
348	A67	48c multicolored	.55	.55
349	A67	60c multicolored	.65	.65
350	A67	$2 multicolored	1.90	1.90
		Nos. 347-350 (4)	3.50	3.50

Ausipex '84 — A68

1984, Sept. 14	Photo.		Perf. 14	
351	A68	60c William Bligh, map	3.25	3.25
352	A68	96c Bounty, map	3.25	3.25
353	A68	$1.40 Stamps, map	3.25	3.25
		Nos. 351-353 (3)	9.75	9.75

Souvenir Sheet

354		Sheet of 3	6.25	6.25
a.	A68	60c + 5c like #351	1.40	1.40
b.	A68	96c + 5c like #352	1.90	1.90
c.	A68	$1.40 + 5c like #353	2.50	2.50

For overprint see No. 399.

No. 247 Surcharged with Black Bar and New Value in Gold and: "15.9.84 Birth/Prince Henry"

1984, Oct. 10	Photo.		Perf. 13x13½	
355	A56	$3 multicolored	4.00	4.00

Issued in sheets of 4.

A69

A70

1984, Nov. 16	Photo.		Perf. 13	
356	A69	36c Annunciation	.40	.40
357	A69	48c Nativity	.50	.50
358	A69	60c Epiphany	.60	.60
359	A69	96c Flight into Egypt	1.00	1.00
		Nos. 356-359 (4)	2.50	2.50

Souvenir Sheets
Size: 45x53mm
Imperf

360	A69	90c + 7c like #356	.90	.90
361	A69	90c + 7c like #357	.90	.90
362	A69	90c + 7c like #358	.90	.90
363	A69	90c + 7c like #359	.90	.90

Christmas.

1984, Dec. 10	Photo.		Perf. 13½x14	
364	A70	48c Diana, Henry	2.00	2.00
365	A70	60c William, Henry	2.00	2.00
366	A70	$2.10 Family	3.50	3.50
		Nos. 364-366 (3)	7.50	7.50

Souvenir Sheet

367		Sheet of 3	7.00	7.00
a.	A70	96c + 7c like #364	2.25	2.25
b.	A70	96c + 7c like #365	2.25	2.25
c.	A70	96c + 7c like #366	2.25	2.25

Christmas, Birth of Prince Henry, Sept. 15. Surtax was for benefit of local children's charities.

Audubon Birth Bicentenary A71

Illustrations of bird species by John J. Audubon.

1985, Mar. 22	Litho.		Perf. 13	
368	A71	55c Gray kingbird	.80	.80
369	A71	65c Bohemian waxwing	.95	.95
370	A71	75c Summer tanager	1.25	1.25
371	A71	95c Cardinal	1.50	1.50
372	A71	$1.15 White-winged crossbill	1.75	1.75
		Nos. 368-372 (5)	6.25	6.25

Queen Mother, 85th Birthday A72

Photographs: 55c, Lady Elizabeth Bowes-Lyon, age 7. 65c, Engaged to the Duke of York, 75c, Duchess of York with daughter, Elizabeth. $1.30, Holding the infant Prince Charles. $3, Portrait taken on 63rd birthday.

1985-86			Perf. 13½x13	
373	A72	55c multicolored	.50	.50
374	A72	65c multicolored	.60	.60
375	A72	75c multicolored	.65	.65
376	A72	$1.30 multicolored	1.25	1.25
a.		Souvenir sheet of 4, #373-376	3.25	3.25
		Nos. 373-376 (4)	3.00	3.00

Souvenir Sheet

377	A72	$3 multicolored	2.25	2.25

Nos. 373-376 printed in sheets of 4. Issued: #376a, 8/4/86; others, 6/14/85.

Intl. Youth Year A73

Designs: 75c, The Calmady Children, by Thomas Lawrence (1769-1830). 90c, Madame Charpentier's Children, by Renoir (1841-1919). $1.40, Young Girls at Piano, by Renoir.

1985, Sept. 16	Photo.		Perf. 13	
378	A73	75c multicolored	1.40	1.40
379	A73	90c multicolored	1.65	1.65
380	A73	$1.40 multicolored	2.75	2.75
		Nos. 378-380 (3)	5.80	5.80

Souvenir Sheet

381		Sheet of 3	3.75	3.75
a.	A73	75c + 10c like #378	.90	.90
b.	A73	90c + 10c like #379	1.10	1.10
c.	A73	$1.40 + 10c like #380	1.75	1.75

Surcharged for children's activities.

Adoration of the Magi, by Giotto di Bondone (1276-1337) — A74

1985, Nov. 15	Photo.		Perf. 13½x13	
382	A74	95c multicolored	1.10	1.10
383	A74	95c multicolored	1.10	1.10
a.		Pair, #382-383	2.20	2.20
384	A74	$1.15 multicolored	1.40	1.40
385	A74	$1.15 multicolored	1.40	1.40
a.		Pair, #384-385	2.80	2.80
		Nos. 382-385 (4)	5.00	5.00

Souvenir Sheet
Imperf

386	A74	$6.40 multicolored	7.50	7.50

Christmas, return of Halley's Comet, 1985-86.

Halley's Comet A75

Designs: 90c, Halley's Comet, A.D. 684, wood engraving, Nuremberg Chronicles. $1.25, Sighting of 1066, Bayeux Tapestry, detail, c. 1092, France. $1.75, The Comet Inflicting Untold Disasters, 1456, Lucerne Chronicles, by Diebolt Schilling. $4.20, Melancolia I, engraving by Durer.

1986, Feb. 25	Photo.		Perf. 13½x13	
387	A75	90c multicolored	1.00	1.00
388	A75	$1.25 multicolored	1.40	1.40
389	A75	$1.75 multicolored	2.00	2.00
		Nos. 387-389 (3)	4.40	4.40

Souvenir Sheets

390		Sheet of 3 + label	3.00	3.00
a.	A75	95c, like #387	1.00	1.00
b.	A75	95c, like #388	1.00	1.00
c.	A75	95c, like #389	1.00	1.00

Imperf

391	A75	$4.20 multicolored	4.75	4.75

Elizabeth II, 60th
Birthday — A76

1986, Apr. 21   Perf. 14
392 A76 95c Coronation por-
          trait   1.10 1.10
Souvenir Sheet
Perf. 13½
393 A76 $4.20 Portrait, diff.   5.00 5.00

No. 392 printed in sheets of 5 with label
picturing U.K. flag and Queen's flag for New
Zealand.

Statue of
Liberty,
Cent.
A77

1986, June 27   Photo.   Perf. 14
394 A77 $1 Liberty head   1.10 1.10
395 A77 $2.75 Statue   3.00 3.00
Souvenir Sheet
Perf. 13½
396   Sheet of 2   2.75 2.75
a.   A77 $1.25 like $1   1.25 1.25
b.   A77 $1.25 like $2.75   1.25 1.25

For surcharges see Nos B44, B49.

Wedding of
Prince Andrew
and Sarah
Ferguson — A78

1986, July 23   Perf. 14
397 A78 $2 multicolored   2.25 2.25
Souvenir Sheet
Perf. 13½
398 A78 $5 multicolored   5.75 5.75

No. 397 printed in sheets of 5 plus label
picturing Westminster Abbey.
For surcharge see No. B48.

No. 354 Ovptd. with Gold Circle over
AUSIPEX Emblem, Black and Gold
STAMPEX '86 Emblem

1986, Aug. 4   Photo.   Perf. 14
399   Sheet of 3   6.00 6.00
a.   A68 60c + 5c like #351   1.25 1.25
b.   A68 96c + 5c like #352   2.00 2.00
c.   A68 $1.40 + 5c like #353   2.75 2.75

STAMPEX '86, Adelaide, Aug. 4-10.

Christmas
A79

Paintings by Albrecht Durer: 75c, No. 404a,
St. Anne with Virgin and Child. $1.35, No.
404b, Virgin and Child. $1.95, No. 404c, Ado-
ration of the Magi. $2.75, No. 404d, Rosary
Festivity.

1986, Nov. 21   Litho.   Perf. 13½
400 A79 75c multicolored   .80   .80
401 A79 $1.35 multicolored   1.50 1.50
402 A79 $1.95 multicolored   2.00 2.00
403 A79 $2.75 multicolored   3.00 3.00
     Nos. 400-403 (4)   7.30 7.30
Souvenir Sheet
404   Sheet of 4   7.00 7.00
a.-d. A79 $1.65 any single   1.75 1.75

For surcharges see Nos. B39-B44, B46-
B47, B50-B54.

Nos. 247-249 Surcharged in Gold and
Black

1987, Nov. 20   Photo.   Perf. 13x12½
405 A56 $2.50 on 60c No. 247   3.00 3.00
406 A56 $2.50 on 80c No. 248   3.00 3.00
407 A56 $2.50 on $1.40 No. 249   3.00 3.00
     Nos. 405-407 (3)   9.00 9.00

Issued in sheets of 4 with margin inscriptions overprinted with gold bar and "40th Anniversary of the Royal Wedding / 1947-1987" in
black; "OVERPRINTED BY NEW ZEALAND
GOVERNMENT PRINTER, / WELLINGTON,
NOVEMBER 1987" at left.

A80

The Virgin with Garland, by
Rubens — A81

Painting details.

1987, Dec. 10   Photo.   Perf. 13x13½
408 A80 70c UL   .90   .90
409 A80 85c UR   1.10 1.10
410 A80 $1.50 LL   2.00 2.00
411 A80 $1.85 LR   2.50 2.50
     Nos. 408-411 (4)   6.50 6.50
Souvenir Sheets
412   Sheet of 4   6.00 6.00
a.   A80 95c like No. 408   1.50 1.50
b.   A80 95c like No. 409   1.50 1.50
c.   A80 95c like No. 410   1.50 1.50
d.   A80 95c like No. 411   1.50 1.50
Perf. 13
413 A81 $6 multicolored   7.75 7.75
Christmas.

1988 Summer Olympics, Seoul — A82

Flags of Korea, Aitutaki, ancient and modern events, and Seoul Games emblem or $50
silver coin issued to commemorate the participation of Aitutaki athletes in the Olympics for
the 1st time: 70c, No. 418a, Obverse of silver
coin, chariot race, running. 85c, Emblem, running, soccer. 95c, Emblem, boxing, handball.
$1.40, No. 418b, Reverse of coin, spearmen,
women's tennis.

1988, Aug. 22   Photo.   Perf. 14½x15
414 A82 70c multicolored   .95   .95
415 A82 85c multicolored   1.10 1.10
416 A82 95c multicolored   1.25 1.25
417 A82 $1.40 multicolored   1.90 1.90
     Nos. 414-417 (4)   5.20 5.20
Souvenir Sheet
418   Sheet of 2   5.50 5.50
a.-b. A82 $2 any single   2.75 2.75

Nos. 414-417 Ovptd. with Names of
1988 Olympic Gold Medalists
a. "FLORENCE GRIFFTH JOYNER /
UNITED STATES / 100 M AND 200 M"
b. "GELINDO BORDIN / ITALY /
MARATHON"
c. "HITOSHI SAITO / JAPAN / JUDO"
d. "STEFFI GRAF / WEST GERMANY /
WOMEN'S TENNIS"

1988, Oct. 10   Litho.   Perf. 14½x15
419 A82 (a) 70c on No. 414   .95   .95
420 A82 (b) 85c on No. 415   1.10 1.10
421 A82 (c) 95c on No. 416   1.25 1.25
422 A82 (d) $1.40 on No. 417   1.90 1.90
     Nos. 419-422 (4)   5.20 5.20

Griffith is spelled incorrectly on No. 419.

Christmas
A83

Paintings by Rembrandt: 55c, Adoration of
the Shepherds (detail), National Gallery,
London. 70c, Holy Family, Alte Pinakothek,
Munich. 85c, Presentation in the Temple, Kun-
sthalle, Hamburg. 95c, The Holy Family, Louvre, Paris. $1.15, Presentation in the Temple,
diff., Mauritshuis, The Hague. $4.50, Adora-
tion of the Shepherds (entire painting).

1988, Nov. 2   Photo.   Perf. 13½
423 A83 55c multicolored   .70   .70
424 A83 70c multicolored   .90   .90
425 A83 85c multicolored   1.10 1.10
426 A83 95c multicolored   1.25 1.25
427 A83 $1.15 multicolored   1.50 1.50
     Nos. 423-427 (5)   5.45 5.45
Souvenir Sheet
Perf. 14
428 A83 $4.50 multicolored   5.75 5.75

No. 428 contains one 52x34mm stamp.

A84

Mutiny on the Bounty, 200th
Anniv. — A85

1989, July 3   Photo.   Perf. 13½
429 A84 55c Ship, Capt.
          Bligh   1.25 1.25
430 A84 65c Breadfruit   1.40 1.40
431 A84 75c Bligh, chart   1.60 1.60
432 A84 95c Bounty off
          Aitutaki   2.00 2.00
433 A84 $1.65 Christian, Bligh   3.75 3.75
     Nos. 429-433 (5)   10.00 10.00
Souvenir Sheet
434 A85 $4.20 Castaways   9.00 9.00

Discovery of Aitutaki by William Bligh, bicent.

1st Moon Landing, 20th Anniv. — A86

Apollo 11 mission emblem, American flag,
eagle, "The Eagle has landed" and: 75c,
Astronaut standing on the lunar surface.
$1.15, Conducting an experiment in front of
the lunar module. $1.80, Carrying equipment.
$6.40, Raising the flag.

1989, July 28   Photo.   Perf. 13½x13
435 A86 75c multicolored   .90   .90
436 A86 $1.15 multicolored   1.40 1.40
437 A86 $1.80 multicolored   2.25 2.25
     Nos. 435-437 (3)   4.55 4.55
Souvenir Sheet
Perf. 13½
438 A86 $6.40 multicolored   7.50 7.50

No. 438 contains one 42x31mm stamp.

Christmas — A87

Details from Virgin in Glory, by Titian: 70c,
Virgin. 85c, Christ child. 95c, Angel. $1.25,
Cherubs. $6, Entire painting.

1989, Nov. 20   Photo.   Perf. 13½x13
439 A87 70c multicolored   .90   .90
440 A87 85c multicolored   1.10 1.10
441 A87 95c multicolored   1.25 1.25
442 A87 $1.25 multicolored   1.60 1.60
     Nos. 439-442 (4)   4.85 4.85
Souvenir Sheet
Perf. 13½
443 A87 $6 multicolored   7.75 7.75

No. 443 contains one 45x60mm stamp.

World Environmental Protection — A88

Designs: a, Human comet, World Philatelic
Programs emblem. b, Comet tail and "Protect
The Endangered Earth!" $3, Human comet,
emblem and inscription.
Illustration reduced.

1990, Feb. 16   Photo.   Perf. 13½x13
444 A88   Pair   4.50 4.50
a.-b. $1.75 any single   2.25 2.25
Souvenir Sheet
445 A88 $3 multicolored   4.00 4.00

No. 376a Ovptd. "Ninetieth / Birthday"
in Black on Gold

Designs: 55c, Lady Elizabeth Bowes-Lyon,
1907. 65c, Lady Elizabeth engaged to Duke of
York. 75c, As Duchess of York with daughter
Elizabeth. $1.30, As Queen Mother with
grandson.

1990, July 16   Litho.   Perf. 13½x13
446   Sheet of 4   4.00 4.00
a.   A72 55c multicolored   .65   .65
b.   A72 65c multicolored   .75   .75
c.   A72 75c multicolored   .90   .90
d.   A72 $1.30 multicolored   1.50 1.50

Christmas — A89

Paintings: 70c, Madonna of the Basket by Correggio. 85c, Virgin and Child by Morando. 95c, Adoration of the Child by Tiepolo. $1.75, Mystic Marriage of St. Catherine by Memling. $6, Donne Triptych by Memling.

1990, Nov. 28   Litho.   Perf. 14
447	A89	70c multicolored	.85	.85
448	A89	85c multicolored	1.00	1.00
449	A89	95c multicolored	1.10	1.10
450	A89	$1.75 multicolored	2.25	2.25

Nos. 447-450 (4)   5.20 5.20

Souvenir Sheet
451	A89	$6 multicolored	7.50	7.50

Nos. 246A-246B Overprinted

1990, Dec. 5   Photo.   Perf. 13½
452	A55	$1 multicolored	1.90	1.90
453	A55	$2 multicolored	3.75	3.75

Birdpex '90, 20 Intl. Ornithological Congress, New Zealand.

No. 246D Overprinted
"COMMEMORATING 65TH BIRTHDAY OF H.M. QUEEN ELIZABETH II"

1991, Apr. 22   Photo.   Perf. 13
454	A55	$5 multicolored	6.25	6.25

Christmas — A90

Paintings: 80c, The Holy Family, by Mengs. 90c, Virgin and Child, by Fra Filippo Lippi. $1.05, Virgin and Child, by Durer. $1.75, Adoration of the Shepherds, by De La Tour. $6, The Holy Family, by Michelangelo.

1991, Nov. 13   Litho.   Perf. 14
455	A90	80c multicolored	.90	.90
456	A90	90c multicolored	1.10	1.10
457	A90	$1.05 multicolored	1.25	1.25
458	A90	$1.75 multicolored	2.00	2.00

Nos. 455-458 (4)   5.25 5.25

Souvenir Sheet
459	A90	$6 multicolored	7.00	7.00

1992 Summer Olympics, Barcelona — A91

1992, July 29   Litho.   Perf. 14
460	A91	95c Hurdles	1.00	1.00
461	A91	$1.25 Weight lifting	1.40	1.40
462	A91	$1.50 Judo	1.75	1.75
463	A91	$1.95 Soccer	2.25	2.25

Nos. 460-463 (4)   6.40 6.40

6th Festival of Pacific Arts, Rarotonga — A92

Canoes: 30c, Vaka Motu. 50c, Hamatafua. 95c, Alia Kalia Ndrua. $1.75, Hokule'a Hawaiian. $1.95, Tuamotu Pahi.

1992, Oct. 16   Litho.   Perf. 14x15
464	A92	30c multicolored	.35	.35
465	A92	50c multicolored	.55	.55
466	A92	95c multicolored	1.10	1.10
467	A92	$1.75 multicolored	2.00	2.00
468	A92	$1.95 multicolored	2.25	2.25

Nos. 464-468 (5)   6.25 6.25

For overprints see #524-528.

Overprinted "ROYAL VISIT"

1992, Oct. 16
469	A92	30c on #464	.35	.35
470	A92	50c on #465	.55	.55
471	A92	95c on #466	1.10	1.10
472	A92	$1.75 on #467	2.00	2.00
473	A92	$1.95 on #468	2.25	2.25

Nos. 469-473 (5)   6.25 6.25

Christmas A93

Designs: Different details from Virgin's Nativity, by Guido Reni.

1992, Nov. 19   Litho.   Perf. 13½
474	A93	80c multicolored	.90	.90
475	A93	90c multicolored	1.10	1.10
476	A93	$1.05 multicolored	1.25	1.25
477	A93	$1.75 multicolored	1.90	1.90

Nos. 474-477 (4)   5.15 5.15

Souvenir Sheet
478	A93	$6 like #476	6.50	6.50

No. 478 contains one 39x50mm stamp.

Discovery of America, 500th Anniv. — A94

Designs: $1.25, Columbus being blessed as he departs from Spain. $1.75, Map of Columbus' four voyages. $1.95, Columbus landing in New World.

1992, Dec. 11   Perf. 14x15
479	A94	$1.25 multicolored	1.40	1.40
480	A94	$1.75 multicolored	1.90	1.90
481	A94	$1.95 multicolored	2.25	2.25

Nos. 479-481 (3)   5.55 5.55

Coronation of Queen Elizabeth II, 40th Anniv. — A95

Designs: a, Victoria, Edward VII. b, George V, George VI. c, Elizabeth II.

1993, June 4   Litho.   Perf. 14
482	A95	$1.75 Strip of 3, #a.-c.	6.00	6.00

Christmas — A96

Religious sculpture: 80c, Madonna and Child, by Nino Pisano. 90c, Virgin on Rosebush, by Luca Della Robbia. $1.15, Virgin with Child and St. John, by Juan Francisco Rustici. $1.95, Virgin with Child, by Michelangelo. $3, Madonna and Child, by Jacopo Della Quercia.

1993, Oct. 29   Litho.   Perf. 14
483	A96	80c multicolored	.90	.90
484	A96	90c multicolored	1.00	1.00
485	A96	$1.15 multicolored	1.25	1.25
486	A96	$1.95 multicolored	2.25	2.25

Size: 32x47mm
Perf. 13½
487	A96	$3 multicolored	3.50	3.50

Nos. 483-487 (5)   8.90 8.90

1994 Winter Olympics, Lillehammer — A97

Designs: a, Ice hockey. b, Ski jumping. c, Cross-country skiing.

1994, Feb. 11   Litho.   Perf. 14
488	A97	$1.15 Strip of 3, #a.-c.	4.00	4.00

Flowers — A98

Hibiscus A98a

1994-97   Litho.   Perf. 13½
489	A98	5c Prostrate morning glory	.20	.20
490	A98	10c White frangipani	.20	.20
491	A98	15c Red hibiscus	.20	.20
492	A98	20c Yellow allamanda	.20	.20
493	A98	25c Royal poinciana	.25	.25
494	A98	30c White gardenia	.35	.35
495	A98	50c Pink frangipani	.55	.55
496	A98	80c Morning glory	.90	.90
497	A98	85c Yellow mallow	.95	.95
498	A98	90c Red coral tree	1.00	1.00
499	A98	$1 Cup of gold	1.10	1.10
500	A98	$2 Red cordia	2.25	2.25
501	A98a	$3 multicolored	3.75	3.75
502	A98a	$5 multicolored	6.25	6.25
503	A98a	$8 multicolored	10.00	10.00

Nos. 489-503 (15)   28.15 28.15

Issued: 5c-90c, 2/17; $1, $2, 4/29; $3, $5, 11/18; $8, 11/21/97. This is an expanding set. Numbers may change.

First Manned Moon Landing, 25th Anniv. A99

#506, Astronauts Collins, Armstrong, Aldrin. #507, Splash down in South Pacific.

1994, July 20   Litho.   Perf. 14
506	A99	$2 multicolored	2.25	2.25
507	A99	$2 multicolored	2.25	2.25

Christmas — A100

Paintings: No. 508a, The Madonna of the Basket, by Corregio. b, Virgin & Child with Saints, by Hans Memling. c, The Virgin & Child with Flowers, by Dolci. d, Virgin & Child with Angels, by Bergognone.
No. 509a, The Adoration of the Kings, by Dosso. b, The Virgin & Child, by Bellini. c, The Virgin & Child, by Schiavone. d, Adoration of the Kings, by Dolci.

1994, Nov. 30   Litho.   Perf. 14
508	A100	85c Block of 4, #a.-d.	3.75	3.75
509	A100	90c Block of 4, #a.-d.	4.00	4.00

End of World War II, 50th Anniv. — A101

Designs: a, Battle of Britain, 1940. b, Battle of Midway, June 1942.

1995, Sept. 4   Litho.   Perf. 13½x13
510	A101	$4 Pair, #a.-b.	10.50	10.50

No. 510 issued in sheets of 4 stamps.

Queen Mother, 95th Birthday A102

1995, Sept. 14   Litho.   Perf. 13x13½
511 A102 $4 multicolored   5.25 5.25

UN, 50th Anniv. — A103

1995, Oct. 18   Litho.   Perf. 13½
512 A103 $4.25 multicolored   5.50 5.50

Year of the Sea Turtle A104

1995, Dec. 1   Litho.   Perf. 14x13½
513 A104 95c Green   1.25 1.25
514 A104 $1.15 Leatherback   1.50 1.50
515 A104 $1.50 Olive Ridley   2.00 2.00
516 A104 $1.75 Loggerhead   2.25 2.25
   Nos. 513-516 (4)   7.00 7.00

Queen Elizabeth II, 70th Birthday A105

1996, June 24   Litho.   Perf. 14
517 A105 $4.50 multicolored   6.00 6.00
No. 517 was issued in sheets of 4.

Modern Olympic Games, Cent. A106

Designs: No. 518, Pierre de Coubertin, Olympic torch, parading athletes, 1896. No. 519, Modern sprinters, US flag, Atlanta, 1996.

1996, July 11   Litho.   Perf. 14
518 A106 $2 multicolored   2.75 2.75
519 A106 $2 multicolored   2.75 2.75
  a.   Pair, #518-519   5.50 5.50

Queen Elizabeth II and Prince Philip, 50th Wedding Anniv. A107

$2.50, Queen Elizabeth II, Prince Philip, Queen Mother, and King George VI. $6, like #520, close-up.

1997, Nov. 20   Litho.   Perf. 14
520 A107 $2.50 multicolored   3.25 3.25
   Souvenir Sheet
521 A107 $6 multicolored   7.75 7.75
No. 520 was issued in sheets of 4.

Diana, Princess of Wales (1961-97) — A108

1998, Apr. 15   Litho.   Perf. 14
522 A108 $1 multicolored   1.25 1.25
   Souvenir Sheet
523 A108 $4 like #522   4.75 4.75
No. 522 was issued in sheets of 5 + label. No. 523 is a continuous design. For surcharge see No. B55.

Nos. 464-468 Overprinted "KIA ORANA / THIRD MILLENNIUM"

1999, Dec. 31   Litho.   Perf. 14x15
524 A92 30c on #464   .30 .30
525 A92 50c on #465   .50 .50
526 A92 95c on #466   .95 .95
527 A92 $1.75 on #467   1.75 1.75
528 A92 $1.95 on #468   1.90 1.90
   Nos. 524-528 (5)   5.40 5.40

Queen Mother, 100th Birthday — A109

No. 529: a, Wearing crown, blue-toned photograph. b, Wearing crown, color photograph. c, Wearing hat. d, With King George VI. Illustration reduced.

2000, Oct. 20   Litho.   Perf. 14
529 A109 $3 Sheet of 4, #a-d   9.50 9.50
   Souvenir Sheet
530 A109 $7.50 With flowers   6.00 6.00

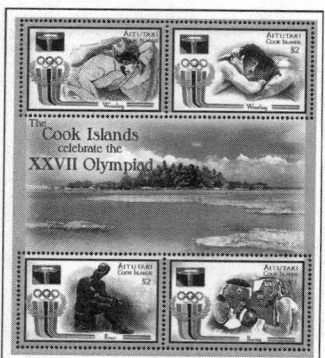

2000 Summer Olympics, Sydney — A110

No. 531: a, Ancient wrestling. b, Wrestling. c, Ancient boxer. d, Boxing. Illustration reduced.

2000, Dec. 14   Litho.   Perf. 14
531 A110 $2 Sheet of 4, #a-d   7.25 7.25
   Souvenir Sheet
532 A110 $2.75 Torch relay   2.50 2.50

SEMI-POSTAL STAMPS

Christmas Type of 1974

Designs: 1c+1c, like #104. 5c+1c, like #105. 8c+1c, like #106. 10c+1c, like #107. 25c+1c, like #108. 30c+1c, like #109.

1974, Dec. 2   Photo.   Perf. 13½
B1 A29 1c + 1c multicolored   .20 .20
B2 A29 5c + 1c multicolored   .20 .20
B3 A29 8c + 1c multicolored   .20 .20
B4 A29 10c + 1c multicolored   .20 .20
B5 A29 25c + 1c multicolored   .30 .30
B6 A29 30c + 1c multicolored   .30 .30
   Nos. B1-B6 (6)   1.40 1.40
Surtax was for child welfare.

Nos. 117-120 Surcharged in Silver

1975, Dec. 19   Photo.   Perf. 14x13½
B7 A32 Strip of 3   .30 .30
  a.-c.   6c+1c any single   .20 .20
B8 A32 Strip of 3   .35 .35
  a.-c.   7c+1c any single   .20 .20
B9 A32 Strip of 3   .90 .90
  a.-c.   15c+1c any single   .30 .30
B10 A32 Strip of 3   1.25 1.25
  a.-c.   20c+1c any single   .40 .40
   Nos. B7-B10 (4)   2.80 2.80

Christmas. The surtax was for children's activities during holiday season.

Nos. 135-142a Surcharged in Silver

1976, Nov. 19   Photo.   Perf. 13½x13
B11 A36 6c + 1c multicolored   .20 .20
B12 A37 6c + 1c multicolored   .20 .20
  a.   Pair, #B11-B12   .20 .20
B13 A36 7c + 1c multicolored   .20 .20
B14 A37 7c + 1c multicolored   .20 .20
  a.   Pair, #B13-B14   .25 .25
B15 A36 15c + 1c multicolored   .20 .20
B16 A37 15c + 1c multicolored   .20 .20
  a.   Pair, #B15-B16   .45 .45
B17 A36 20c + 1c multicolored   .30 .30
B18 A37 20c + 1c multicolored   .30 .30
  a.   Pair, #B17-B18   .60 .60
  b.   Souvenir sheet of 8   1.60 1.60

Surtax was for child welfare. Stamps of No. B18a each surcharged 2c.

Nos. 152-159a Surcharged in Black

1977, Nov. 15   Perf. 13½x14
B19 A41 6c + 1c multicolored   .20 .20
B20 A42 6c + 1c multicolored   .20 .20
  a.   Pair, #B19-B20   .20 .20
B21 A41 7c + 1c multicolored   .20 .20
B22 A42 7c + 1c multicolored   .20 .20
  a.   Pair, #B21-B22   .25 .25
B23 A41 15c + 1c multicolored   .20 .20
B24 A42 15c + 1c multicolored   .20 .20
  a.   Pair, #B23-B24   .45 .45
B25 A41 20c + 1c multicolored   .30 .30
B26 A42 20c + 1c multicolored   .30 .30
  a.   Pair, #B25-B26   .60 .60
  b.   Souvenir sheet of 8   1.60 1.60
   Nos. B19-B26 (8)   1.80 1.80

Surtax was for child welfare. Stamps of No. B26a each surcharged 2c.

Easter Type of 1978
Souvenir Sheets

Paintings: No. B27, like No. 163. No. B28, like No. 164. No. B29, like No. 165.

1978, Mar. 17   Photo.   Perf. 14
B27 A44 50c + 5c multicolored   .70 .70
B28 A44 50c + 5c multicolored   .70 .70
B29 A44 50c + 5c multicolored   .70 .70
Nos. B27-B29 contain one stamp 33x25mm.

Christmas Type of 1978
Souvenir Sheet

1978, Dec. 4   Photo.   Perf. 14½x13
B30 Sheet of 4   2.25 2.25
  a.   A46 15c + 2c like #167   .30 .30
  b.   A46 17c + 2c like #168   .35 .35
  c.   A46 30c + 2c like #169   .55 .55
  d.   A46 35c + 2c like #170   .60 .60

Year of the Child Type
Souvenir Sheet

1979, Oct. 1   Photo.   Perf. 14x13½
B31 Sheet of 3   1.40 1.40
  a.   A48 30c + 3c like #173   .30 .30
  b.   A48 35c + 3c like #174   .35 .35
  c.   A48 65c + 3c like #175   .60 .60

Easter Type of 1980
Souvenir Sheet

#B32 shows entire painting in continuous design. #B32a-B32c similar to #183-185. Size of #B32a-B32c: 25x50mm.

1980, Apr. 3   Photo.   Perf. 13x13½
B32 Sheet of 3   1.40 1.40
  a.   A50 20c + 2c multicolored   .35 .35
  b.   A50 30c + 2c multicolored   .45 .45
  c.   A50 35c + 2c multicolored   .55 .55

Christmas Type of 1980
Souvenir Sheet

1980, Nov. 21   Photo.   Perf. 13x13½
B33 Sheet of 4   1.40 1.40
  a.   A53 15c + 2c like #208   .20 .20
  b.   A53 20c + 2c like #209   .30 .30
  c.   A53 25c + 2c like #210   .35 .35
  d.   A53 35c + 2c like #211   .45 .45

Easter Type of 1981
Souvenir Sheet

1981, Mar. 31   Photo.   Perf. 13½
B34 Sheet of 3   1.65 1.65
  a.   A54 30c + 2c like #212   .35 .35
  b.   A54 40c + 2c like #213   .50 .50
  c.   A54 50c + 2c like #214   .65 .65

Nos. 247-249 Surcharged

1981, Nov. 23   Photo.   Perf. 13x13½
B35 A56 60 + 5c multi   .90 .90
B36 A56 80 + 5c multi   1.10 1.10
B37 A56 $1.40 + 5c multi   2.00 2.00
   Nos. B35-B37 (3)   4.00 4.00

Intl. Year of the Disabled. Surtax was for the handicapped.

Soccer Type of 1981
Souvenir Sheet

1981, Nov. 30   Perf. 14
B38 A57 Sheet of 8, multi   2.50 2.50
No. B38 contains stamps with 2c surtax similar to Nos. 250-253. Surtax was for local sports.

Nos. 400-404 Surcharged "NOVEMBER/21-24 1986/FIRST VISIT TO SOUTH/PACIFIC" and 10c in Silver

1986, Nov. 25   Litho.   Perf. 13½
B39 A79 75c + 10c multi   1.25 1.25
B40 A79 $1.35 + 10c multi   2.00 2.00
B41 A79 $1.95 + 10c multi   3.00 3.00
B42 A79 $2.75 + 10c multi   4.00 4.00
   Nos. B39-B42 (4)   10.25 10.25
   Souvenir Sheet
B43 Sheet of 4   13.00 13.00
  a.-d.   A79 $1.65 +10c on #404a-404d   3.25 3.25

State visit of Pope John Paul II. For surcharges see Nos. B51-B54.

Nos. 394-395, 397 and 400-403 Surcharged "HURRICANE RELIEF/ + 50c" in Silver or Black

1987, Apr. 29   Litho.   Perf. 13½, 14
B44 A79 75c + 50c #400   2.00 2.00
B45 A77 $1 + 50c #394   2.50 2.50
   (B)
B46 A79 $1.35 + 50c #401   3.00 3.00
B47 A79 $1.95 + 50c #402   3.25 3.25
B48 A78 $2 + 50c #397   3.25 3.25
B49 A77 $2.75 + 50c #395   4.25 4.25
   (B)
B50 A79 $2.75 + 50c #403   4.25 4.25
   Nos. B44-B50 (7)   22.50 22.50

Nos. B39-B42 Surcharged "HURRICANE RELIEF / +50c" in Silver

1987, Apr. 29   Litho.   Perf. 13½
B51 A79 75c + 50c No. B39   2.00 2.00
B52 A79 $1.35 + 50c No. B40   2.50 2.50
B53 A79 $1.95 + 50c No. B41   3.00 3.00
B54 A79 $2.75 + 50c No. B42   3.50 3.50
   Nos. B51-B54 (4)   11.00 11.00

Souvenir Sheet
No. 523 Surcharged "CHILDREN'S/CHARITIES" in Silver

1998, Nov. 19   Litho.   Perf. 14
B55 A108 $4 + $1 multicolored   6.25 6.25

AIR POST STAMPS

Capt. Bligh Type of 1974

1974, Sept. 9		**Litho.**		**Perf. 13**	
		Size: 46x26mm			
C1	A27	10c Bligh and "Bounty"		.75	.75
C2	A27	10c "Bounty" at sea		.75	.75
a.		Pair, #C1-C2		1.50	1.50
C3	A27	25c Bligh and "Bounty"		.90	.90
C4	A27	25c Chart, 1856		.90	.90
a.		Pair, #C3-C4		1.80	1.80
C5	A27	30c Cook and "Resolution"		1.10	1.10
C6	A27	30c Maps		1.10	1.10
a.		Pair, #C5-C6		2.20	2.20
		Nos. C1-C6 (6)		5.50	5.50

See note after No. 101.

OFFICIAL STAMPS

Nos. 83-90, 92-95, 150-151
Overprinted or Surcharged in Black,
Silver or Gold

1978-79		**Photo.**		**Perf. 13x13½**	
O1	A25	1c multi		.20	.20
O2	A25	2c multi		.20	.20
O3	A25	3c multi		.20	.20
O4	A25	4c multi (G)		.20	.20
O5	A25	5c multi		.20	.20
O6	A25	8c multi		.20	.20
O7	A25	10c multi		.20	.20
O8	A25	15c on 60c multi		.20	.20
O9	A25	18c on 60c multi		.25	.25
O10	A40	20c multi (G)		.30	.25
O11	A40	50c multi		.75	.70
O12	A25	60c multi		.90	.80
O13	A25	$1 multi		1.40	1.25
O14	A26	$2 multi		3.00	2.25
O15	A40	$4 on $1 multi (S)		6.00	4.50
O16	A26	$5 multi		7.25	5.00
		Nos. O1-O16 (16)		21.45	16.60

Overprint on 4c, 20c, $1 diagonal.
Issued: #O14-O16, 2/20/79; others, 11/3/78.

Stamps of 1983-84 Ovptd. or
Surcharged in Green

or Gold (#O29-O32)

1985, Aug. 9			**Perf. 14, 13x13½**		
O17	A66	2c No. 322		.20	.20
O18	A66	2c No. 324		.20	.20
O19	A66	10c No. 325		.20	.20
O20	A66	12c No. 326		.20	.20
O21	A66	18c No. 327		.20	.20
O22	A66	20c on 24c No. 328		.20	.20
O23	A66	30c No. 329		.35	.35
O24	A66	40c on 36c No. 330		.45	.45
O25	A66	50c No. 332		.55	.55
O26	A66	55c on 48c No. 331		.65	.65
O27	A66	60c No. 333		.70	.70
O28	A66	65c on 72c No. 334		.75	.75
O29	A61	75c on 48c No. 276		.85	.85
O30	A61	75c on 48c No. 277		.85	.85
O31	A61	75c on 48c No. 278		.85	.85
O32	A61	75c on 48c No. 279		.85	.85
a.		Block of 4, Nos. O29-O32		3.50	3.50
O33	A66	80c on 96c No. 335		.90	.90
		Nos. O17-O33 (17)		8.95	8.95

Nos. 336-341, 246C-246D Overprinted
or Surcharged Like Nos. O17-O28,
O33 in Metallic Green or Blue

1986, Oct. 1				**Perf. 14**	
O34	A66	$3 multi		3.00	3.00
O35	A66	$4.20 multi		4.25	4.25
O36	A66	$5.60 multi		5.75	5.75
O37	A66	$9.60 multi		10.00	10.00
1988-91				**Perf. 14**	
O38	A66	$1.20 multi		1.50	1.50
O39	A66	$2.10 multi		2.50	2.50
				Perf. 13½	
O40	A55	$14 on $4 (B)		17.50	17.50
O41	A55	$18 on $5 (B)		22.50	22.50
		Nos. O34-O41 (8)		67.00	67.00

Issue dates: July 2, 1991; others, June 15.

AJMAN

äj-'man

LOCATION — Oman Peninsula, Arabia, on Persian Gulf
GOVT. — Sheikdom under British Protection
AREA — 100 sq. mi.
POP. — 4,400
CAPITAL — Ajman

Ajman is one of six Persian Gulf sheikdoms to join the United Arab Emirates, which proclaimed its independence Dec. 2, 1971. See United Arab Emirates.

100 Naye Paise = 1 Rupee

Catalogue values for all unused stamps in this country are for Never Hinged items.

Sheik Rashid bin Humaid al Naimi &
Arab Stallion — A1

Designs: 2np, 50np, Regal angelfish. 3np, 70np, Camel. 4np, 1r, Angelfish. 5np, 1.50r, Green turtle. 10np, 2r, Jewelfish. 15np, 3r, White storks. 20np, 5r, White-eyed gulls. 30np, 10r, Lanner falcon. 40np as 1np.

1964		**Photo. & Litho.**			
		Unwmk.		**Perf. 14**	
		Size: 35x22mm			
1	A1	1np gold & multi		.20	.20
2	A1	2np gold & multi		.20	.20
3	A1	3np gold & multi		.20	.20
4	A1	4np gold & multi		.20	.20
5	A1	5np gold & multi		.20	.20
6	A1	10np gold & multi		.20	.20
7	A1	15np gold & multi		.20	.20
8	A1	20np gold & multi		.20	.20
9	A1	30np gold & multi		.20	.20
		Size: 42x27mm			
10	A1	40np gold & multi		.20	.20
11	A1	50np gold & multi		.25	.20
12	A1	70np gold & multi		.25	.20
13	A1	1r gold & multi		.40	.20
14	A1	1.50r gold & multi		.50	.20
15	A1	2r gold & multi		.85	.20
		Size: 53x33½mm			
16	A1	3r gold & multi		1.00	.20
17	A1	5r gold & multi		1.50	.40
18	A1	10r gold & multi		3.25	.75
		Nos. 1-18 (18)		10.00	4.35

Issued: #1-9, 6/20; #10-15, 9/7; #16-18, 11/4.

Pres. and Mrs.
John F.
Kennedy with
Caroline — A2

Pres. Kennedy: 10np, As a boy in football uniform. 15np, Diving. 50np, As navy lieutenant, receiving Navy and Marine Corps Medal from Capt. Frederic L. Conklin. 1r, Sailing with Jacqueline Kennedy. 2r, With Eleanor Roosevelt. 5r, With Lyndon B. Johnson and Hubert H. Humphrey. 10r, Portrait.

1964, Dec. 15		**Photo.**	**Perf. 13½x14**		
19	A2	10np grn & red lil		.20	.20
20	A2	15np Prus bl & vio		.20	.20
21	A2	50np org brn & dk bl		.20	.20
22	A2	1r brn & Prus grn		.45	.20
23	A2	2r red lil & dp ol		.70	.20
24	A2	3r grn & red brn		1.25	.50
25	A2	5r vio & brn		2.00	1.00
26	A2	10r dk bl & red brn		5.00	2.25
		Nos. 19-26 (8)		10.00	4.75

John F. Kennedy (1917-63). A souvenir sheet contains one each of Nos. 23-26.

Runners at
Start — A3

10np, 1.50r, Boxing. 25np, 2r, Judo. 50np, 5r, Gymnast on vaulting horse. 1r, 3r, Sailing yacht.

1965, Jan. 12		**Photo.**	**Perf. 13½x14**		
27	A3	5np red brn, brt pink & Prus grn		.20	.20
28	A3	10np dk ol grn, bl gray & red brn		.20	.20
29	A3	15np dk vio, grn & sep		.20	.20
30	A3	25np bl sal pink & blk		.20	.20
31	A3	50np mar, bl & ind		.20	.20
32	A3	1r dk grn, lil & ultra		.40	.25
33	A3	1.50r lil, grn & brn		.60	.40
34	A3	2r red org, bis & dk bl		1.00	.70
35	A3	3r dk brn, grnsh bl & lil		1.50	.95
36	A3	5r grn, yel & red brn		2.00	1.60
		Nos. 27-36 (10)		6.50	4.90

18th Olympic Games, Tokyo, Oct. 10-25, 1964. A souvenir sheet contains four stamps similar to Nos. 33-36 in changed colors.

Stanley Gibbons Catalogue, 1865,
U.S. No. 1X2 — A4

Designs: 10np, Austria, Scarlet Mercury 1856. 15np, British Guiana 1c, 1856. 25np, Canada 12p, 1851. 50np, Hawaii 2c, 1851. 1r, Mauritius 2p, 1847. 3r, Switzerland, Geneva 10c, 1843. 5r, Tuscany 31, 1860. 5np, 15np, 50np and 3r show first edition of Stanley Gibbons Catalogue; 10np, 25np, 1r and 5r show 1965 Elizabethan Catalogue.

1965, May 6		**Unwmk.**	**Perf. 13**		
37	A4	5np multi		.20	.20
38	A4	10np multi		.20	.20
39	A4	15np multi		.20	.20
40	A4	25np multi		.20	.20
41	A4	50np multi		.20	.20
42	A4	1r multi		.45	.20
43	A4	3r multi		.75	.20
a.		Souv. sheet of 4, #38-39, 42-43		2.50	
44	A4	5r multi		1.25	.30
a.		Souv. sheet of 4, #37, 40-41, 44		2.50	
		Nos. 37-44 (8)		3.45	1.70

Gibbons Catalogue Cent. Exhib., London, Feb. 17-20. Nos. 43a and 44a for 125th anniv. of 1st postage stamp. Sheets exist imperf.

Stamps of Ajman were replaced in 1972 by those of United Arab Emirates.

AIR POST STAMPS

Type of Regular Issue, 1964

Designs: 15np, Arab stallion. 25np, Regal angelfish. 35np, Camel. 50np, Angelfish. 75np, Green turtle. 1r, Jewelfish. 2r, White storks. 3r, White-eyed gulls. 5r, Lanner falcon.

1965		**Photo. & Litho.**			
		Unwmk.		**Perf. 14**	
		Size: 42x25½mm			
C1	A1	15np silver & multi		.20	.20
C2	A1	25np silver & multi		.20	.20
C3	A1	35np silver & multi		.25	.20
C4	A1	50np silver & multi		.30	.20
C5	A1	75np silver & multi		.55	.20
C6	A1	1r silver & multi		.40	.20
		Size: 53x33½mm			
C7	A1	2r silver & multi		.75	.20
C8	A1	3r silver & multi		2.00	.20
C9	A1	5r silver & multi		3.25	.30
		Nos. C1-C9 (9)		7.90	1.90

Issued: #C1-C6, Nov. 15; C7-C9, Dec. 18.

AIR POST OFFICIAL STAMPS

Type of Regular Issue, 1964

Designs: 75np, Jewelfish. 2r, White storks. 3r, White-eyed gulls. 5r, Lanner falcon.

1965, Dec. 18		**Photo. & Litho.**			
		Unwmk.		**Perf. 14**	
		Size: 42x25½mm			
CO1	A1	75np gold & multi		.35	.20
		Size: 53x33½mm			
CO2	A1	2r gold & multi		1.00	.20
CO3	A1	3r gold & multi		1.50	.20
CO4	A1	5r gold & multi		3.00	.35
		Nos. CO1-CO4 (4)		5.85	.95

OFFICIAL STAMPS

Type of Regular Issue, 1964

25np, Arab stallion. 40np, Regal angelfish. 50np, Camel. 75np, Angelfish. 1r, Green turtle.

1965, Dec. 1		**Photo. & Litho.**			
		Unwmk.		**Perf. 14**	
		Size: 42x25½mm			
O1	A1	25np gold & multi		.20	.20
O2	A1	40np gold & multi		.20	.20
O3	A1	50np gold & multi		.25	.20
O4	A1	75np gold & multi		.30	.20
O5	A1	1r gold & multi		.55	.20
		Nos. O1-O5 (5)		1.50	1.00

ALAOUITES

'al-au-ˌwītz

LOCATION — A division of Syria, in Western Asia
GOVT. — Under French Mandate
AREA — 2,500 sq. mi.
POP. — 278,000 (approx. 1930)
CAPITAL — Latakia

This territory became an independent state in 1924, although still administered under the French Mandate. In 1930 it was renamed Latakia and Syrian stamps overprinted "Lattaquie" superseded the stamps of Alaouites. For these and subsequent issues see Latakia and Syria.

100 Centimes = 1 Piaster

Issued under French Mandate
Stamps of France Surcharged:

Nos. 1-6, 16-18   Nos. 7-15, 19-21

1925		**Unwmk.**	**Perf. 14x13½**
1	A16	10c on 2c vio brn	1.00 1.00
2	A22	25c on 5c orange	.75 .75
3	A20	75c on 15c gray grn	1.40 1.40
4	A22	1p on 20c red brn	.80 .80
5	A22	1.25p on 25c blue	1.10 1.10
6	A22	1.50p on 30c red	3.75 3.75
7	A22	2p on 35c violet	1.00 1.00
8	A18	2p on 40c red & pale bl	1.75 1.75
9	A18	2p on 45c grn & bl	3.75 3.75
10	A18	3p on 60c vio & ultra	2.50 2.50
11	A20	3p on 60c lt vio	2.50 2.50
b.		Double surcharge	67.50 67.50
12	A20	4p on 85c vermilion	.80 .80
13	A18	5p on 1fr cl & ol grn	2.50 2.50
14	A18	10p on 2fr org & pale bl	3.75 3.75
15	A18	25p on 5fr bl & buff	4.50 4.50
		Nos. 1-15 (15)	33.10 33.10

For overprints see Nos. C1-C4.

Same Surcharges on Pasteur Stamps of France

16	A23	50c on 10c green	.90 .90
17	A23	75c on 15c green	.90 .90
18	A23	1.50p on 30c red	.90 .90
19	A23	2p on 45c red	1.25 1.25
20	A23	2.50p on 50c blue	1.25 1.25
21	A23	4p on 75c blue	1.75 1.75
		Nos. 16-21 (6)	6.95 6.95

Inverted Surcharges

1a	A16	10c on 2c vio brn	10.00
2a	A22	25c on 5c orange	10.00
3a	A20	75c on 15c gray grn	10.00
4a	A22	1p on 20c red brn	10.00
5a	A22	1.25p on 25c blue	10.00
6a	A22	1.50p on 30c red	14.00
7a	A22	2p on 35c violet	14.00
8a	A18	2p on 40c red & pale bl	14.00
9a	A18	2p on 45c grn & bl	14.00
10a	A18	3p on 60c vio & ultra	10.00
11a	A20	3p on 60c lt vio	10.00
12a	A20	4p on 85c vermilion	10.00
13a	A18	5p on 1fr cl & ol grn	10.00
14a	A18	10p on 2fr org & pale bl	10.00
15a	A18	25p on 5fr bl & buff	10.00
16a	A23	50c on 10c green	7.50
17a	A23	75c on 15c green	7.50
18a	A23	1.50p on 30c red	7.50
19a	A23	2p on 45c red	7.50
20a	A23	2.50p on 50c blue	7.50
21a	A23	4p on 75c blue	7.50

Stamps of Syria, 1925, Overprinted in Red, Black or Blue:

On A3, A5

On A4

1925, Mar. 1			**Perf. 12½, 13½**
25	A3	10c dk violet (R)	.35 .35
a.		Double overprint	14.00 14.00
b.		Inverted overprint	10.00
c.		Black overprint	12.00 12.00
26	A4	25c olive black (R)	.50 .50
a.		Inverted overprint	10.00
b.		Blue overprint	18.00 18.00
27	A4	50c yellow green	.45 .45
a.		Inverted overprint	10.00
b.		Blue overprint	18.00 18.00
c.		Red overprint	17.50 17.50
28	A4	75c brown orange	.45 .45
a.		Inverted overprint	10.00
b.		Double overprint	25.00
29	A5	1p magenta	.65 .65
a.		Inverted overprint	10.00
30	A4	1.25p deep green	.50 .50
a.		Red overprint	15.00 15.00
31	A4	1.50p rose red (Bl)	.50 .50
a.		Inverted overprint	17.50 17.50
b.		Black overprint	10.00
32	A4	2p dk brown (R)	.45 .45
a.		Blue overprint	—
b.		Inverted overprint	10.00

33	A4	2.50p pck blue (R)	.80 .80
a.		Black overprint	—
34	A4	3p orange brown	.45 .45
a.		Inverted overprint	10.00
b.		Blue overprint	22.50 22.50
35	A4	5p violet	.60 .60
a.		Red overprint	22.50 22.50
36	A4	10p violet brown	1.00 1.00
37	A4	25p ultra (R)	2.00 2.00
		Nos. 25-37 (13)	8.70 8.70

For overprints see Nos. C5-C19.

Stamps of Syria, 1925, Surcharged in Black or Red:

Nos. 38-42

Nos. 43-45

1926			
38	A4	3.50p on 75c brn org	.75 .60
a.		Surcharged on face and back	5.00 4.50
39	A4	4p on 25c ol blk (R)	1.00 1.00
40	A4	6p on 2.50p pck bl (R)	.80 .60
41	A4	12p on 1.25p dp grn	.70 .60
a.		Inverted surcharge	10.00 10.00
42	A4	20p on 1.25p dp grn	1.25 1.10
43	A4	4.50p on 75c brn org	2.50 1.25
a.		Inverted surcharge	25.00
44	A4	7.50p on 2.50p pck bl	2.00 1.25
45	A4	15p on 25p ultra	3.50 2.00
		Nos. 38-45 (8)	12.50 8.00

For overprint see No. C21.

Syria #199 Ovptd. like #25 in Red

1928			
46	A3	5c on 10c dk violet	.30 .30
a.		Double surcharge	13.00

Syria Nos. 178 and 174 Surcharged like Nos. 43-45 in Red

47	A4	2p on 1.25p dp green	6.00 3.50
48	A4	4p on 25c olive black	3.25 2.50

For overprint see No. C20.

49	A4	4p on 25c olive black	35.00 30.00
a.		Double impression	—
		Nos. 46-49 (4)	44.55 36.30

AIR POST STAMPS

Nos. 8, 10, 13 & 14 with Additional Overprint in Black

1925, Jan. 1		**Unwmk.**	**Perf. 14x13½**
C1	A18	2p on 40c	3.50 3.50
a.		Overprint reversed	60.00
C2	A18	3p on 60c	5.25 5.25
a.		Overprint reversed	60.00 60.00
C3	A18	5p on 1fr	3.50 3.50
C4	A18	10p on 2fr	3.50 3.50
		Nos. C1-C4 (4)	15.75 15.75

Nos. 32, 34, 35 & 36 With Additional Overprint in Green

1925, Mar. 1			**Perf. 13½**
C5	A4	2p dark brown	1.00 1.00
C6	A4	3p orange brown	1.00 1.00
C7	A4	5p violet	1.00 1.00
C8	A4	10p violet brown	1.00 1.00
		Nos. C5-C8 (4)	4.00 4.00

Nos. 32, 34, 35 & 36 With Additional Overprint in Red

1926, May 1			
C9	A4	2p dark brown	1.75 1.90
C10	A4	3p orange brown	1.75 1.90
C11	A4	5p violet	1.75 1.90
C12	A4	10p violet brown	1.75 1.90
		Nos. C9-C12 (4)	7.00 7.60

No. C9 has the original overprint in black. Double or inverted overprints, original or plane, are known on most of Nos. C9-C12. Value, $8-$10.

The red plane overprint was also applied to Nos. C5-C8. These are believed to have been essays, and were not regularly issued.

Nos. 27, 29, and 37 With Additional Overprint of Airplane in Red or Black

1929, June-July			
C17	A4	50c yel grn (R)	.75 .75
a.		Plane overprint double	15.00
b.		Plane ovpt. on face and back	11.00
c.		Pair with plane overprint tete beche	35.00
C18	A5	1p magenta (Bk)	2.75 2.75
C19	A4	25p ultra (R)	15.00 10.00
a.		Plane overprint inverted	60.00 60.00
		Nos. C17-C19 (3)	18.50 13.50

Nos. 47 and 45 With Additional Overprint of Airplane in Red

1929-30			
C20	A4	2p on 1.25p ('30)	1.25 1.40
a.		Surcharge inverted	4.00
b.		Double surcharge	3.50
C21	A4	15p on 25p (Bk + R)	19.00 14.00
a.		Plane overprint inverted	35.00 35.00

POSTAGE DUE STAMPS

Postage Due Stamps of France, 1893-1920, Surcharged Like No. 1 (Nos. J1-J2) or No. 7 (Nos. J3-J5)

1925		**Unwmk.**	**Perf. 14x13½**
J1	D2	50c on 10c choc	1.90 1.90
J2	D2	1p on 20c ol grn	1.90 1.90
J3	D2	2p on 30c red	1.90 1.90
J4	D2	3p on 50c vio brn	1.90 1.90
J5	D2	5p on 1fr red brn, straw	1.90 1.90
		Nos. J1-J5 (5)	9.50 9.50

Postage Due Stamps of Syria, 1925, Overprinted Like No. 26 (Type D5) or No. 25 (Type D6) in Black, Blue or Red

1925			**Perf. 13½**
J6	D5	50c brown, *yel*	.60 .60
J7	D6	1p vio, *rose* (Bl)	.60 .60
a.		Black overprint	9.00 9.00
b.		Double overprint (Bk + Bl)	14.00 14.00
J8	D5	2p blk, *blue*	1.00 1.00
J9	D5	3p blk, *red org*	1.40 1.40
J10	D5	5p blk, *bl grn* (R)	2.40 2.40
		Nos. J6-J10 (5)	6.00 6.00

The stamps of Alaouites were superseded in 1930 by those of Latakia.

ALBANIA

al-'bā-nē-ə

LOCATION — Southeastern Europe
GOVT. — Republic
AREA — 11,101 sq. mi.
POP. — 3,364,571 (1999 est.)
CAPITAL — Tirana

After the outbreak of World War I, the country fell into a state of anarchy when the Prince and all members of the International Commission left Albania. Subsequently General Ferrero in command of Italian troops declared Albania an independent country. A constitution was adopted and a republican form of government was instituted which continued until 1928 when, by constitutional amendment, Albania was declared to be a monarchy. The President of the republic, Ahmed Zogu, became king of the new state. Many unlisted varieties or surcharges and lithographed labels are said to have done postal duty in Albania and Epirus during this unsettled period.

In March 1939, Italy invaded Albania. King Zog fled but did not abdicate. The King of Italy acquired the crown.

Germany occupied Albania from September, 1943, until late 1944 when it became an independent state. The People's Republic began in January, 1946.

40 Paras = 1 Piaster = 1 Grossion
100 Centimes = 1 Franc (1917)
100 Qintar = 1 Franc
100 Qintar (Qindarka) = 1 Lek (1947)

Catalogue values for unused stamps in this country are for Never Hinged items, beginning with Scott 458 in the regular postage section, Scott B34 in the semipostal section, and Scott C67 in the airpost section.

Watermarks

Wmk. 125—Lozenges   Wmk. 220—Double Headed Eagle

Stamps of Turkey Handstamped

Handstamped on Issue of 1908
Perf. 12, 13½ and Compound

1913, June			**Unwmk.**
1	A19	2½pi violet brown	450.00 300.00

With Additional Overprint in Carmine

2	A19	10pa blue green	425.00 350.00

The eagle handstamp was applied to other Turkish stamps of 1908: 25pi green and 50 pi red brown. The 5pa ocher, Albania No. 4, was surcharged "2 paras." These three stamps were retained by officials. Values, $2,500, $5,750, $450.

Handstamped on Issue of 1909

4	A21	5pa ocher	250.00 240.00
5	A21	10pa blue green	200.00 110.00
6	A21	20pa car rose	175.00 110.00
7	A21	1pi ultra	150.00 110.00
8	A21	2pi blue black	190.00 175.00
10	A21	5pi dark violet	675.00 500.00
11	A21	10pi dull red	2,250. 2,000.

For surcharge see No. 19.

With Additional Overprint in Blue or Carmine

14	A21	20pa car rose (Bl)	450.00	450.00
15	A21	1pi brt blue (C)	900.00	800.00

Handstamped on Newspaper Stamp of 1911

17	A21	2pa olive green	250.00	240.00

Handstamped on Postage Due Stamp of 1908

18	A19	1pi black, dp rose	1,600.	1,250.

No. 18 was used for regular postage.

No. 6 Surcharged With New Value

19	A21	10pa on 20pa car rose	650.00	550.00

The overprint on #1-19 was handstamped and is found inverted, double, etc.

Nos. 6, 7 and 8 exist with the handstamp in red, blue or violet, but these varieties are not known to have been regularly issued.

Excellent counterfeits exist of Nos. 1 to 19.

A1

1913, July — Imperf.
Handstamped on White Laid Paper Without Eagle and Value

20	A1	(1pi) black	210.00	210.00
		Cut to shape	110.00	110.00
a.		Sewing machine perf.	275.00	275.00

Counterfeits exist.

1913, Aug.
Value Typewritten in Violet With Eagle

21	A1	10pa violet	6.25	5.00
22	A1	20pa red & black	8.00	6.75
23	A1	1gr black	8.00	8.00
24	A1	2gr blue & violet	12.50	10.00
25	A1	5gr violet & blue	15.00	14.00
26	A1	10gr blue	21.00	20.00
		Nos. 21-26 (6)	70.75	63.75

Nos. 21-26 exist with the eagle inverted or omitted and with numerous errors in the figures of value and the spelling of the word "grosh."

A2

Skanderbeg (George Castriota) — A3

1913, Nov. — Perf. 11½
Handstamped on White Laid Paper Eagle and Value in Black

27	A2	10pa green	2.50	2.00
b.		Eagle and value in green	650.00	650.00
c.		10pa red (error)	20.00	20.00
d.		10pa violet (error)	20.00	20.00
29	A2	20pa red	4.00	3.50
b.		20pa green (error)	20.00	20.00
30	A2	30pa violet	4.00	3.50
a.		30pa ultramarine (error)	20.00	20.00
b.		30pa red (error)	20.00	20.00
31	A2	1gr ultramarine	4.75	5.00
a.		1gr green (error)	20.00	20.00
b.		1gr black (error)	20.00	20.00
c.		1gr violet (error)	20.00	20.00
33	A2	2gr black	7.50	7.00
a.		2gr violet (error)	25.00	25.00
b.		2gr blue (error)	25.00	25.00
		Nos. 27-33 (5)	22.75	21.00

The stamps of this issue are known with eagle or value inverted or omitted.

1st anniv. of Albanian independence.

Counterfeits exist.

1913, Dec. — Typo. — Perf. 14

35	A3	2q orange brn & buff	1.60	.80
36	A3	5q green & blue grn	1.60	.80
37	A3	10q rose red	1.60	.80
38	A3	25q dark blue	1.60	.80
39	A3	50q violet & red	4.25	2.00
40	A3	1fr deep brown	9.00	4.50
		Nos. 35-40 (6)	19.65	9.70

For overprints and surcharges see Nos. 41-52, 105, J1-J9.

Nos. 35-40 Handstamped in Black or Violet

1914, Mar. 7

41	A3	2q orange brn & buff	22.50	17.50
42	A3	5q grn & bl grn (V)	22.50	17.50
43	A3	10q rose red	22.50	17.50
44	A3	25q dark blue (V)	22.50	17.50
45	A3	50q violet & red	22.50	17.50
46	A3	1fr deep brown	22.50	17.50
		Nos. 41-46 (6)	135.00	105.00

Issued to celebrate the arrival of Prince Wilhelm zu Wied on Mar. 7, 1914.

Nos. 35-40 Surcharged in Black:

a

b

1914, Apr. 2

47	A3 (a)	5pa on 2q	1.10	1.10
48	A3 (a)	10pa on 5q	1.10	1.10
49	A3 (a)	20pa on 10q	1.75	1.50
50	A3 (b)	1gr on 25q	1.75	1.50
51	A3 (b)	2gr on 50q	1.75	1.50
52	A3 (b)	5gr on 1fr	10.00	8.50
		Nos. 47-52 (6)	17.45	15.20

For overprints see Nos. 105, J6-J9.

Inverted Surcharge

47a	A3 (a)	5pa on 2q	7.50	7.50
48a	A3 (a)	10pa on 5q	7.00	7.00
49a	A3 (a)	20pa on 10q	8.00	8.00
50a	A3 (b)	1gr on 25q	8.00	8.00
51a	A3 (b)	2gr on 50q	9.00	9.00
52b	A3 (b)	5gr on 1fr	32.50	32.50
		Nos. 47a-52b (6)	72.00	72.00

Korce (Korytsa) Issues

A4

1914 — Handstamped — Imperf.

52A	A4	10pa violet & red	90.00	90.00
c.		10pa black & red	90.00	90.00
53	A4	25pa violet & red	90.00	90.00
a.		25pa black & red	150.00	150.00

Nos. 52A-53a originally were handstamped directly on the cover, so the paper varies. Later they were also produced in sheets; these are rarely found. Nos. 52A-53a were issued by Albanian military authorities.

Counterfeits exist of Nos. 52A and 53.

A5

A6

1917 — Typo. & Litho. — Perf. 11½

54	A5	1c dk brown & grn	12.00	10.00
55	A5	2c red & green	12.00	10.00
56	A5	3c gray grn & grn	9.00	6.50
57	A5	5c green & black	12.00	10.00
58	A5	10c rose red & black	7.00	4.25
59	A5	25c blue & black	7.00	4.25
60	A5	50c violet & black	12.00	9.00
61	A5	1fr brown & black	14.00	9.00
		Nos. 54-61 (8)	85.00	63.00

1917-18

62	A6	1c dk brown & grn	2.75	2.75
63	A6	2c red brown & grn	2.75	2.75
a.		"CTM" for "CTS"	30.00	25.00
64	A6	3c black & green	2.75	2.75
a.		"CTM" for "CTS"	35.00	30.00
65	A6	5c green & black	4.25	4.25
66	A6	10c dull red & black	4.25	4.25
67	A6	50c violet & black	11.50	9.00
68	A6	1fr red brn & black	15.00	12.00
		Nos. 62-68 (7)	43.25	37.00

Counterfeits abound of Nos. 54-68, 80-81.

QARKU

I

KORÇËS

25 CTS

No. 65 Surcharged in Red

1918

80	A6	25c on 5c green & blk	55.00	45.00

A7

1918

81	A7	25c blue & black	35.00	30.00

General Issue

A8

A9

Handstamped in Rose or Blue — XVI MCMXIX

1919 — Perf. 12½

84	A8	(2)q on 2h brown	12.50	12.50
85	A8	5q on 16h green	12.50	12.50
86	A8	10q on 8h rose (Bl)	12.50	12.50
87	A8	25q on 64h blue	12.50	12.50
88	A9	25q on 64h blue	275.00	275.00
89	A8	50q on 32h violet	12.50	12.50
90	A8	1fr on 1.28k org, bl	12.50	12.50
		Nos. 84-90 (7)	350.00	350.00

See Nos. J10-J13. Compare with types A10-A14. For overprints see Nos 91-104.

Handstamped in Rose or Blue

1919, Jan. 16

91	A8	(2)q on 2h brown	8.50	8.50
92	A8	5q on 16h green	8.50	8.50
93	A8	10q on 8h rose (Bl)	8.50	8.50
94	A8	25q on 64h blue	35.00	35.00
95	A9	25q on 64h blue	35.00	35.00
96	A8	50q on 32h violet	8.50	8.50
97	A8	1fr on 1.28k org, bl	8.50	8.50
		Nos. 91-97 (7)	112.50	112.50

Handstamped in Violet

1919

98	A8	(2)q on 2h brown	7.50	7.50
99	A8	5q on 16h green	7.50	7.50
100	A8	10q on 8h rose	7.50	7.50
101	A8	25q on 64h blue	10.00	10.00
102	A9	25q on 64h blue	75.00	65.00
103	A8	50q on 32h violet	7.50	7.50
104	A8	1fr on 1.28k org, bl	7.50	7.50
		Nos. 98-104 (7)	122.50	112.50

No. 50 Overprinted in Violet — SHKODER • 1919

1919 — Perf. 14

105	A3	1gr on 25q blue	5.00	7.50

A10

A11

1919, June 5 — Perf. 11½, 12½

106	A10	10q on 2h brown	3.50	4.00
107	A11	15q on 8h rose	3.50	4.00
108	A11	20q on 16h green	3.50	4.00
109	A10	25q on 64h blue	3.50	4.00
110	A11	50q on 32h violet	3.50	4.00
111	A11	1fr on 96h orange	3.50	4.00
112	A10	2fr on 1.60k vio, buff	14.00	17.50
		Nos. 106-112 (7)	35.00	41.50

Nos. 106-108, 110 exist with inverted surcharge.

A12

A13

Black or Violet Surcharge

1919

113	A12	10q on 8h car	3.50	4.00
114	A12	15q on 8h car (V)	3.50	4.00
115	A13	20q on 16h green	3.50	4.00
116	A13	25q on 35h violet	3.50	4.00
117	A13	50q on 64h blue	9.25	11.00
118	A13	1fr on 96h orange	4.75	5.50
119	A12	2fr on 1.60k vio, buff	7.00	8.00
		Nos. 113-119 (7)	35.00	40.50

A14

A15

Overprinted in Blue or Black Without New Value

1920 — Perf. 12½

120	A14	1q gray (Bl)	22.50	22.50
121	A14	10q rose (Bk)	1.75	2.75
a.		Double overprint	24.00	27.50
122	A14	20q brown (Bl)	11.00	11.00
123	A14	25q blue (Bk)	110.00	110.00
124	A14	50q brown vio (Bk)	14.00	16.00
		Nos. 120-124 (5)	159.25	162.25

Counterfeit overprints exist of Nos. 120-128.

Surcharged with New Value

125	A14	2q on 10q rose (R)	4.25	4.25
126	A14	5q on 10q rose (G)	4.25	4.25
127	A14	25q on 10q rose (Bl)	4.25	4.25
128	A14	50q on 10q rose (Br)	4.25	4.25
		Nos. 125-128 (4)	17.00	17.00

Stamps of type A14 (Portrait of the Prince zu Wied) were not placed in use without overprint or surcharge.

Post Horn Overprinted in Black

1920 — Perf. 14x13

129	A15	2q orange	3.75	3.25
130	A15	5q deep green	6.25	6.00
131	A15	10q red	11.00	11.00
132	A15	25q light blue	20.00	11.00

133	A15	50q gray green	4.25	4.00
134	A15	1fr claret	4.25	4.00
		Nos. 129-134 (6)	49.50	39.25

Type A15 was never placed in use without post horn or "Besa" overprint.

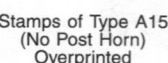

Stamps of Type A15 (No Post Horn) Overprinted

1921

135	A15	2q orange	3.00	3.00
136	A15	5q deep green	3.00	3.00
137	A15	10q red	6.00	6.00
138	A15	25q light blue	11.00	11.00
139	A15	50q gray green	6.00	6.00
140	A15	1fr claret	6.00	6.00
		Nos. 135-140 (6)	35.00	35.00

For surcharge & overprints see #154, 156-157.

Stamps of these types, and with "TAKSE" overprint, were unauthorized and never placed in use. They are common.

Gjirokaster
A18

Korcha
A19

Designs: 5q, Kanina. 10q, Berati. 25q, Bridge at Vezirit. 50q, Rozafat. 2fr, Dursit.

1923 Typo. Perf. 12½, 11½

147	A18	2q orange	.60	.60
148	A18	5q yellow green	.50	.50
149	A18	10q carmine	.50	.50
150	A18	25q dark blue	.50	.50
151	A18	50q dark green	.50	.50
152	A19	1fr dark violet	.65	.65
153	A19	2fr olive green	1.75	1.75
		Nos. 147-153 (7)	5.00	5.00

For overprints & surcharges see #158-185, B1-B8.

No. 135 Surcharged

1922

154	A15	1q on 2q orange	3.00	3.00

Perf. 14x13

Stamps of Type A15 (No Post Horn) Overprinted

1922

156	A15	5q deep green	3.00	2.50
157	A15	10q red	3.00	2.50

Nos. 147-151 Overprinted (top line in Black; diamond in Violet)

1924, Jan. Perf. 12½

158	A18	2q red orange	4.00	3.75
159	A18	5q yellow green	4.00	3.75
160	A18	10q carmine	4.00	3.75
161	A18	25q dark blue	4.00	3.75
162	A18	50q dark green	4.00	3.75
		Nos. 158-162 (5)	20.00	18.75

The words "Mbledhje Kushtetuese" are in taller letters on the 25q than on the other values. Opening of the Constituent Assembly. Counterfeits of Nos. 158 and 161 abound.

No. 147 Surcharged

1924

163	A18	1q on 2q red orange	2.25	2.25

Nos. 163, 147-152 Overprinted

1924

164	A18	1g on 2q orange	1.75	2.50
165	A18	2g orange	1.75	2.50
166	A18	5g yellow green	1.75	2.50
167	A18	10g carmine	1.75	2.50
168	A18	25g dark blue	1.75	2.50
169	A18	50g dark green	1.75	2.50
170	A19	1fr dark violet	1.75	2.50
		Nos. 164-170 (7)	12.25	17.50

Issued to celebrate the return of the Government to the Capital after a revolution.

Nos. 163, 147-152 Overprinted

1925

171	A18	1g on 2q orange	1.75	2.50
172	A18	2g orange	1.75	2.50
173	A18	5g yellow green	1.75	2.50
174	A18	10g carmine	1.75	2.50
175	A18	25g dark blue	1.75	2.50
176	A18	50g dark green	1.75	2.50
177	A19	1fr dark violet	1.75	2.50
		Nos. 171-177 (7)	12.25	17.50

Proclamation of the Republic, Jan. 21, 1925. The date "1921" instead of "1925" occurs once in each sheet of 50.
Counterfeits exist.

Nos. 163, 147-153 Overprinted

1925

178	A18	1g on 2q orange	.55	.75
a.		Inverted overprint	7.00	7.00
179	A18	2g orange	.55	.75
180	A18	5g yellow green	.55	.75
a.		Inverted overprint	7.00	7.00
181	A18	10g carmine	.55	.75
182	A18	25g dark blue	.55	.75

183	A18	50g dark green	.55	.75
184	A19	1fr dark violet	.65	.90
185	A19	2fr olive green	.65	.90
		Nos. 178-185 (8)	4.60	6.30

Counterfeits exist.

President Ahmed Zogu
A25   A26

1925 Perf. 13½, 13½x13

186	A25	1q orange	.20	.20
187	A25	2q red brown	.20	.20
188	A25	5q green	.20	.20
189	A25	10q rose red	.20	.20
190	A25	15q gray brown	1.50	1.50
191	A25	25q dark blue	.20	.20
192	A25	50q blue green	.55	.55
193	A26	1fr red & ultra	.95	.95
194	A26	2fr green & orange	1.25	1.25
195	A26	3fr brown & violet	2.00	2.00
196	A26	5fr violet & black	5.00	5.00
		Nos. 186-196 (11)	12.25	12.25

No. 193 in ultramarine and brown, and No. 194 in green and brown were not regularly issued. Value, both $15.
For overprints & surcharges see #197-209, 238-248.

Nos. 186-196 Overprinted in Various Colors

1927

197	A25	1q orange (V)	.60	.40
198	A25	2q red brn (G)	.25	.20
199	A25	5q green (R)	1.25	.20
200	A25	10q rose red (Bl)	.25	.20
201	A25	15q gray brn (G)	5.00	7.50
202	A25	25q dk blue (R)	.60	.20
203	A25	50q blue grn (Bl)	.60	.20
204	A26	1fr red & ultra (Bk)	.90	.30
205	A26	2fr green & org (Bk)	.90	.30
206	A26	3fr brown & vio (Bk)	1.40	.30
207	A26	5fr violet & blk (Bk)	2.10	1.25
		Nos. 197-207 (11)	13.85	11.50

No. 200 exists perf. 11.
For surcharges see Nos. 208-209, 238-240.

Nos. 200, 202 Surcharged in Black or Red

1928

208	A25	1q on 10q rose red	.40	.30
a.		Inverted surcharge	3.75	3.75
209	A25	5q on 25q dk blue (R)	.40	.30
a.		Inverted surcharge	3.75	3.75

A27   King Zog I — A28

1928 Perf. 14x13½
Black Overprint

210	A27	1q orange brown	2.25	2.25
211	A27	2q slate	2.25	2.25
212	A27	5q blue green	2.25	2.25
213	A27	10q rose red	2.25	2.25
214	A27	15q bister	12.00	12.00
215	A27	25q deep blue	1.75	1.75
216	A27	50q lilac rose	2.25	2.25

Red Overprint
Perf. 13½x14

217	A28	1fr blue & slate	2.50	2.50
		Nos. 210-217 (8)	27.50	27.50

Compare with types A29-A32.

A29   A30

1928 Perf. 14x13½
Black or Red Overprint

218	A29	1q orange brown	8.25	8.25
219	A29	2q slate (R)	8.25	8.25
220	A29	5q blue green	7.00	7.00
221	A29	10q rose red	4.50	4.50
222	A29	15q bister	4.75	4.75
223	A29	25q deep blue (R)	4.75	4.75
224	A29	50q lilac rose	5.25	5.25

Perf. 13½x14

225	A30	1fr blue & slate (R)	7.75	7.75
226	A30	2fr green & slate (R)	9.50	9.50
		Nos. 218-226 (9)	60.00	60.00

Proclamation of Ahmed Zogu as King of Albania.

A31   A32

1928 Perf. 14x13½
Black Overprint

227	A31	1q orange brown	.35	.35
228	A31	2q slate	.35	.25
229	A31	5q blue green	3.00	.25
230	A31	10q rose red	.35	.25
231	A31	15q bister	6.75	8.00
232	A31	25q deep blue	.35	.25
233	A31	50q lilac rose	.60	.25

Perf. 13½x14
Black Overprint

234	A32	1fr blue & slate	1.25	1.10
235	A32	2fr green & slate	1.25	1.25
236	A32	3fr dk red & ol bis	2.10	1.75
237	A32	5fr dull vio & gray	2.75	4.50
		Nos. 227-237 (11)	19.10	18.30

The overprint reads "Kingdom of Albania."

Mbr. Shqiptare

Nos. 203, 202, 200 Surcharged in Black

1929 Perf. 13½x13, 11½

238	A25	1q on 50q blue green	.35	.35
239	A25	5q on 25q dark blue	.35	.35
240	A25	15q on 10q rose red	.55	.50
		Nos. 238-240 (3)	1.25	1.20

RROFT·MBRETI

Nos. 186-189, 191-194 Overprinted in Black or Red

8·X·1929.

1929 Perf. 11½, 13½

241	A25	1q orange	4.00	4.00
242	A25	2q red brown	4.00	4.00
243	A25	5q green	4.00	4.00
244	A25	10q rose red	4.00	4.00

245	A25	25q dark blue	4.00	4.00
246	A25	50q blue green (R)	4.75	4.75
247	A26	1fr red & ultra	7.00	7.00
248	A26	2fr green & orange	8.75	8.75
		Nos. 241-248 (8)	40.50	40.50

34th birthday of King Zog. The overprint reads "Long live the King."

Lake Butrinto — A33

King Zog I — A34

Zog Bridge — A35

Ruin at Zog Manor — A36

Perf. 14, 14½
1930, Sept. 1   Photo.   Wmk. 220

250	A33	1q slate	.20	.20
251	A33	2q orange red	.20	.20
252	A34	5q yellow green	.20	.20
253	A34	10q carmine	.20	.20
254	A34	15q dark brown	.20	.20
255	A34	25q dark ultra	.20	.20
256	A33	50q slate green	.30	.30
257	A35	1fr violet	.75	.75
258	A35	2fr indigo	.85	.85
259	A36	3fr gray green	1.90	1.90
260	A36	5fr orange brown	3.25	3.25
		Nos. 250-259 (11)		

2nd anniversary of accession of King Zog I.
For overprints see Nos. 261-270, 299-309, J39. For surcharges see Nos. 354-360.

Nos. 250-259 Overprinted in Black

1934, Dec. 24

261	A33	1q slate	8.50	8.50
262	A33	2q orange red	8.50	8.50
263	A34	5q yellow green	8.50	8.50
264	A34	10q carmine	8.50	8.50
265	A34	15q dark brown	8.50	8.50
266	A34	25q dark ultra	8.50	8.50
267	A33	50q slate green	8.50	8.50
268	A35	1fr violet	8.50	8.50
269	A35	2fr indigo	9.00	9.00
270	A36	3fr gray green	12.50	12.50
		Nos. 261-270 (10)	89.50	89.50

Tenth anniversary of the Constitution.

Allegory of Death of Skanderbeg A37

Albanian Eagle in Turkish Shackles A38

5q, 25q, 40q, 2fr, Eagle with wings spread.

1937   Unwmk.   Perf. 14

271	A37	1q brown violet	.20	.20
272	A38	2q brown	.30	.30
273	A38	5q lt green	.35	.35
274	A37	10q olive brown	.40	.40
275	A38	15q rose red	.55	.55
276	A38	25q blue	1.00	1.00
277	A37	50q deep green	1.40	1.40
278	A37	1fr violet	2.25	2.25
279	A38	2fr orange brown	5.75	5.75
		Nos. 271-279 (9)	12.20	12.20

Souvenir Sheet

280		Sheet of 3	15.00	13.00
a.	A37	20q red violet	3.00	3.00
b.	A38	30q olive brown	3.00	3.00
c.	A38	40q red	3.00	3.00

25th anniv. of independence from Turkey, proclaimed Nov. 26, 1912.

Queen Geraldine and King Zog — A40

1938   Perf. 14

281	A40	1q slate violet	.20	.20
282	A40	2q red brown	.20	.20
283	A40	5q green	.20	.20
284	A40	10q olive brown	.35	.35
285	A40	15q rose red	.60	.60
286	A40	25q blue	.85	.85
287	A40	50q Prus green	2.50	2.50
288	A40	1fr purple	5.25	5.25
		Nos. 281-288 (8)	10.15	10.15

Souvenir Sheet

289		Sheet of 4	18.00	18.00
a.	A40	20q dark red violet	1.75	1.75
b.	A40	30q brown olive	1.75	1.75

Wedding of King Zog and Countess Geraldine Apponyi, Apr. 27, 1938.
No. 289 contains 2 each of Nos. 289a, 289b.

Queen Geraldine — A42

National Emblems — A43

Designs: 10q, 25q, 30q, 1fr, King Zog.

1938

290	A42	1q dp red violet	.20	.20
291	A43	2q red orange	.20	.20
292	A42	5q deep green	.20	.20
293	A42	10q red brown	.20	.20
294	A42	15q deep rose	.55	.55
295	A42	25q deep blue	.70	.70
296	A43	50q gray black	1.75	1.75
297	A42	1fr slate green	6.00	6.00
		Nos. 290-297 (8)	9.80	9.80

Souvenir Sheet

298		Sheet of 3	18.00	18.00
b.	A43	20q Prussian green	2.00	2.00
c.	A42	30q deep violet	2.00	2.00

10th anniv. of royal rule. They were on sale for 3 days (Aug. 30-31, Sept. 1) only, during which their use was required on all mail.
No. 298 contains Nos. 294, 298b, 298c.

Issued under Italian Dominion

Nos. 250-260 Overprinted in Black

1939   Wmk. 220   Perf. 14

299	A33	1q slate	.20	.20
300	A33	2q orange red	.20	.20
301	A34	5q yellow green	.20	.20
302	A34	10q carmine	.40	.40
303	A34	15q dark brown	.40	.40
304	A34	25q dark ultra	.60	.60
305	A33	50q slate green	.90	.90
306	A35	1fr violet	1.60	1.60
307	A35	2fr indigo	2.50	2.50
308	A36	3fr gray green	5.00	5.00
309	A36	5fr orange brown	7.00	7.00
		Nos. 299-309 (11)	19.00	19.00

Resolution adopted by the Natl. Assembly, Apr. 12, 1939, offering the Albanian Crown to Italy.

A46

A47

Native Costumes — A48

King Victor Emmanuel III
A49   A50

Native Costume — A51

Monastery A52

Designs: 2fr, Bridge at Vezirit. 3fr, Ancient Columns. 5fr, Amphitheater.

1939   Unwmk.   Photo.   Perf. 14

310	A46	1q blue gray	.20	.20
311	A47	2q olive green	.20	.20
312	A48	3q golden brown	.20	.20
313	A49	5q green	.20	.20
314	A50	10q brown	.20	.20
315	A50	15q crimson	.25	.20
316	A50	25q sapphire	.40	.25
317	A50	30q brt violet	.55	.35
318	A51	50q dull purple	.70	.35
319	A49	65q red brown	1.00	1.00
320	A52	1fr myrtle green	1.25	1.10
321	A52	2fr brown lake	3.00	3.00
322	A52	3fr brown black	5.75	5.75
323	A52	5fr gray violet	12.00	12.00
		Nos. 310-323 (14)	25.90	25.00

For overprints and surcharges see Nos. 331-353.

King Victor Emmanuel III — A56

1942   Photo.

324	A56	5q green	.20	.20
325	A56	10q brown	.25	.25
326	A56	15q rose red	.35	.35
327	A56	25q blue	.85	.85
328	A56	65q red brown	1.25	1.25
329	A56	1fr myrtle green	2.40	2.40
330	A56	2fr gray violet	5.25	5.25
		Nos. 324-330 (7)	10.55	10.55

Conquest of Albania by Italy, 3rd anniv.

No. 311 Surcharged in Black

331	A47	1q on 2q olive green	1.00	1.00

Issued under German Administration

Stamps of 1939 Overprinted in Carmine or Brown

1943

332	A47	2q olive green	1.10	2.25
333	A48	3q golden brown	1.10	2.25
334	A49	5q green	1.10	2.25
335	A50	10q brown	1.10	2.25
336	A50	15q crimson (Br)	1.10	2.25

337	A50	25q sapphire	1.10	2.25
338	A50	30q brt violet	1.10	2.25
339	A49	65q red brown	1.25	4.50
340	A52	1fr myrtle green	7.75	13.50
341	A52	2fr brown lake	10.50	45.00
342	A52	3fr brown black	45.00	125.00

Surcharged with New Values

343	A48	1q on 3q gldn brn	1.10	2.25
344	A49	50q on 65q red brn	1.25	4.50
		Nos. 332-344 (13)	74.55	210.50

Proclamation of Albanian independence. The overprint "14 Shtator 1943" on Nos. 324 to 328 is private and fraudulent.

Independent State

Nos. 312 to 317 and 319 to 321 Surcharged with New Value and Bars in Black or Carmine, and:

1945

345	A48	30q on 3q gldn brn	3.00	3.00
346	A49	40q on 5q green	3.00	3.00
347	A50	50q on 10q brown	3.00	3.00
348	A50	60q on 15q crimson	3.00	3.00
349	A50	80q on 65q saph (C)	3.00	3.00
350	A50	1fr on 30q brt violet	3.00	3.00
351	A49	2fr on 65q red brn	3.00	3.00
352	A52	3fr on 1fr myr green	3.00	3.00
353	A52	5fr on 2fr brown lake	3.00	3.00
		Nos. 345-353 (9)	27.00	27.00

"DEMOKRATIKE" is not abbreviated on Nos. 352 and 353.

Nos. 250, 251, 256 and 258 Surcharged in Black or Carmine, and

1945   Wmk. 220

354	A33	30q on 1q slate	1.10	1.10
355	A33	60q on 1q slate	1.25	1.25
356	A33	80q on 1q slate	1.50	1.50
357	A33	1fr on 1q slate	2.10	2.10
358	A33	2fr on 2q org red	3.00	3.00
359	A33	3fr on 50q sl grn	7.25	7.25
360	A35	5fr on 2fr indigo	9.25	9.25
		Nos. 354-360 (7)	25.45	25.45

Albanian Natl. Army of Liberation, 2nd anniv. The surcharge on No. 360 is condensed to fit the size of the stamp.

Country House, Labinot — A57

40q, 60q, Bridge at Berat. 1fr, 3fr, Permet.

Perf. 11½
1945, Nov. 28   Unwmk.   Typo.

361	A57	20q bluish green	.20	.20
362	A57	30q deep orange	.40	.40
363	A57	40q brown	.40	.40
364	A57	60q red violet	.60	.60
365	A57	1fr rose red	1.40	1.40
366	A57	3fr dark blue	6.00	6.00
		Nos. 361-366 (6)	9.00	9.00

Counterfeits: lithographed; genuine: typographed.
For overprints and surcharges see Nos. 367-378, 418-423, B28-B33.

Nos. 361 to 366 Overprinted in Black

1946

367	A57	20q bluish green	.60	.60
368	A57	30q deep orange	.60	.60
369	A57	40q brown	.95	.95
370	A57	60q red violet	1.60	1.60
371	A57	1fr rose red	4.75	4.75
372	A57	3fr dark blue	7.50	7.50
		Nos. 367-372 (6)	16.00	16.00

Convocation of the Constitutional Assembly, Jan. 10, 1946.

People's Republic

#361-366
Overprinted in
Black

1946   Perf. 11
373	A57	20q bluish green	.30	.40
374	A57	30q deep orange	.45	.55
375	A57	40q brown	.75	1.10
376	A57	60q red violet	1.50	2.00
377	A57	1fr rose red	4.50	5.50
378	A57	3fr dark blue	7.50	8.00
	Nos. 373-378 (6)		15.00	17.55

Proclamation of the Albanian People's
Republic.
Some values exist perf 11½.
For surcharges see Nos. 418-423.

Globe, Dove
and Olive
Branch — A60

Perf. 11½, Imperf.
1946, Mar. 8   Typo.
Denomination in Black
379	A60	20q lilac & dull red	.20	.30
380	A60	40q dp lilac & dull red	.35	.50
381	A60	50q violet & dull red	.50	.75
382	A60	1fr lt blue & red	.80	1.00
383	A60	2fr dk blue & red	1.60	2.00
	Nos. 379-383 (5)		3.45	4.55

International Women's Congress.
Counterfeits exist.

Athletes
with Shot
and Indian
Club
A61

Perf. 11½
1946, Oct. 6   Litho.   Unwmk.
384	A61	1q grnsh black	5.25	5.25
385	A61	2q green	5.25	5.25
386	A61	5q brown	5.25	5.25
387	A61	10q crimson	5.25	5.25
388	A61	20q ultra	5.25	5.25
389	A61	40q rose violet	5.25	5.25
390	A61	1fr deep orange	8.50	8.50
	Nos. 384-390 (7)		40.00	40.00

Balkan Games, Tirana, Oct. 6-13.

Qemal
Stafa — A62

1947, May 5   Perf. 12½x11½
391	A62	20q brn & yel brn	4.00	4.50
392	A62	28q dk blue & blue	4.00	4.50
393	A62	40q brn blk & gray brn	4.00	4.50
a.	Souvenir sheet, #391-393		8.00	8.00
	Nos. 391-393 (3)		12.00	13.50

5th anniv. of the death of Qemal Stafa.

Young
Railway
Laborers
A64

1947, May 16   Perf. 11½
395	A64	1q brn blk & gray brn	1.75	.60
396	A64	4q dk green & green	1.75	.60
397	A64	10q blk brn & bis brn	1.75	.60
398	A64	15q dk red & red	2.00	.60
399	A64	20q indigo & bl gray	2.75	.90
400	A64	28q dk blue & blue	4.25	.90
401	A64	40q brn vio & rose vio	11.00	4.25

Perf. 13x12½
402	A64	68q dk brn & org brn	17.50	7.75
	Nos. 395-402 (8)		42.75	16.20

Issued to publicize the construction of the
Durres Elbasan Railway by Albanian youths.
The 4q, 20q, 28q and 40q exist perf
13x12½.

Citizens Led
by Hasim
Zeneli — A65

Enver Hoxha
and Vasil
Shanto — A66

Vojo
Kushi — A68

Inauguration
of Vithkuq
Brigade
A67

1947, July 10   Litho.
403	A65	16q brn org & red brn	3.25	3.25
404	A66	20q org brn & dk brn	3.25	3.25
405	A67	28q blue & dk blue	3.50	3.50
406	A68	40q lilac & dk brn	5.00	5.00
	Nos. 403-406 (4)		15.00	15.00

4th anniv. of the formation of Albania's
army, July 10, 1943.

Conference
Building Ruins,
Peza — A69

Disabled
Soldiers — A70

1947, Sept. 16
407	A69	2 l red violet	2.25	2.00
408	A69	2.50 l deep blue	2.25	2.00

Peza Conf., Sept. 16, 1942, 5th anniv.

1947, Nov. 17   Perf. 12½x11½
408A	A70	1 l red	6.00	6.00

Disabled War Veterans Cong., 11/14-20/47.

A71

A73

2 l, Banquet. 2.50 l, Peasants rejoicing.

Perf. 11½x12½, 12½x11½
1947, Nov. 17   Unwmk.
409	A71	1.50 l dull violet	2.50	2.50
410	A71	2 l brown	2.50	2.50
411	A71	2.50 l blue	2.50	2.50
412	A73	3 l rose red	2.50	2.50
	Nos. 409-412 (4)		10.00	10.00

Agrarian reform law of 11/17/46, 1st anniv.

Burning
Farm
Buildings
A74

Designs: 2.50 l, Trench scene. 5 l, Firing
line. 8 l, Winter advance. 12 l, Infantry column.

1947, Nov. 29   Perf. 11½x12½
413	A74	1.50 l red	1.75	1.50
414	A74	2.50 l rose brown	2.50	2.00
415	A74	5 l blue	3.00	2.50
416	A74	8 l purple	5.00	4.00
417	A74	12 l brown	7.50	6.00
	Nos. 413-417 (5)		19.75	16.00

3rd anniv. of Albania's liberation.

Nos. 373 to 378 Surcharged with New
Value and Bars in Black

1948, Feb. 22   Perf. 11
418	A57	50q on 30q dp org	.35	.25
419	A57	1 l on 20q bluish grn	.70	.60
420	A57	2.50 l on 60q red vio	1.40	1.00
421	A57	3 l on 1fr rose red	1.75	1.25
422	A57	5 l on 3fr dk bl	3.25	2.25
423	A57	12 l on 40q brown	6.50	4.75
	Nos. 418-423 (6)		13.95	10.00

The two bars consist of four type squares
each set close together.
Some values exist perf 11½.

Map, Train and
Construction
Workers
A75

1948, June 1   Litho.   Perf. 11½
424	A75	50q dk car rose	1.10	.55
425	A75	1 l lt green & blk	1.25	.55
426	A75	1.50 l deep rose	1.25	.55
427	A75	2.50 l org brn & dk brn	1.25	.55
428	A75	5 l dull blue	1.50	1.10
429	A75	8 l sal & dk brn	3.50	2.00
430	A75	12 l red vio & dk vio	4.75	2.25
431	A75	20 l olive gray	9.00	5.00
	Nos. 424-431 (8)		23.60	12.55

Issued to publicize the construction of the
Durres-Tirana Railway.

Marching
Soldiers
A76

Design: 8 l, Battle scene.

1948, July 10
432	A76	2.50 l yellow brown	1.25	1.25
433	A76	5 l dark blue	1.75	1.75
434	A76	8 l violet gray	3.25	3.25
	Nos. 432-434 (3)		6.25	6.25

5th anniv. of the formation of Albania's army.

Bricklayer, Flag,
Globe and
"Industry" — A77

Map and
Soldier — A78

1949, May 1   Photo.   Perf. 12½x12
435	A77	2.50 l olive brown	.30	.30
436	A77	5 l blue	.70	.70
437	A77	8 l violet brown	1.10	1.10
	Nos. 435-437 (3)		2.10	2.10

Issued to publicize Labor Day, May 1, 1949.

1949, July 10   Unwmk.
438	A78	2.50 l brown	.50	.50
439	A78	5 l light ultra	.75	.75
440	A78	8 l brown orange	1.50	1.50
	Nos. 438-440 (3)		2.75	2.75

6th anniv. of the formation of Albania's army.

Enver Hoxha
A79

Albanian
Citizen and
Spasski
Tower,
Kremlin
A80

1949, Oct. 16   Engr.   Perf. 12½
441	A79	50q purple	.20	.20
442	A79	1 l dull green	.20	.20
443	A79	1.50 l car lake	.20	.20
444	A79	2.50 l brown	.30	.20
445	A79	5 l violet blue	.65	.20
446	A79	8 l sepia	1.10	.90
447	A79	12 l rose lilac	2.50	1.50
448	A79	20 l gray blue	5.00	2.50
	Nos. 441-448 (8)		10.15	5.90

1949, Sept. 10   Photo.   Perf. 12½x12
449	A80	2.50 l orange brown	.50	.50
450	A80	5 l deep ultra	1.00	1.00

Albanian-Soviet friendship.

Albanian Soldier
and Flag — A81

Battle
Scene — A82

1949, Nov. 29   Unwmk.   Perf. 12
451	A81	2.50 l brown	.25	.25
452	A82	3 l dark red	.50	.50
453	A81	5 l violet	.60	.60
454	A82	8 l black	1.75	1.75
	Nos. 451-454 (4)		3.10	3.10

Fifth anniversary of Albania's liberation.

Joseph V. Stalin — A83

Symbols of UPU and Postal Transport A84

1949, Dec. 21
455	A83	2.50 l dark brown	.45	.50
456	A83	5 l violet blue	1.25	1.25
457	A83	8 l rose brown	2.00	2.25
		Nos. 455-457 (3)	3.70	4.00

70th anniv. of the birth of Joseph V. Stalin.

Canceled to Order
Beginning in 1950, Albania sold some issues in sheets canceled to order. Values in second column when much less than unused are for "CTO" copies. Postally used stamps are valued at slightly less than, or the same as, unused.

Catalogue values for unused stamps in this section, from this point to the end of the section, are for Never Hinged items.

1950, July 1   Photo.   Perf. 12x12½
458	A84	5 l blue	1.60	1.25
459	A84	8 l rose brown	2.25	1.75
460	A84	12 l sepia	2.75	2.25
		Nos. 458-460 (3)	6.60	5.25

75th anniv. (in 1949) of the UPU.

Sami Frasheri — A85

Arms and Albanian Flags — A86

Authors: 2.50 l, Andon Zako. 3 l, Naim Frasheri. 5 l, Kostandin Kristoforidhi.

1950, Nov. 5   Perf. 14
461	A85	2 l dark green	.70	.35
462	A85	2.50 l red brown	.90	.40
463	A85	3 l brown carmine	1.40	.60
464	A85	5 l deep blue	2.00	.75
		Nos. 461-464 (4)	5.00	2.10

"Jubilee of the Writers of the Renaissance."

1951, Jan. 11   Engr.   Perf. 14x13½
465	A86	2.50 l brown carmine	1.10	.25
466	A86	5 l deep blue	2.00	.50
467	A86	8 l sepia	3.00	1.00
		Nos. 465-467 (3)	6.10	1.75

5th anniv. of the formation of the Albanian People's Republic.

Skanderbeg — A87

Enver Hoxha and Congress of Permet — A88

1951, Mar. 1
468	A87	2.50 l brown	.75	.25
469	A87	5 l violet	1.50	.50
470	A87	8 l olive bister	2.50	1.00
		Nos. 468-470 (3)	4.75	1.75

483rd anniv. of the death of George Castriota (Skanderbeg).

1951, May 24   Photo.   Perf. 12
471	A88	2.50 l dark brown	.45	.20
472	A88	3 l rose brown	.70	.30
473	A88	5 l violet blue	1.10	.50
474	A88	8 l rose lilac	1.90	.80
		Nos. 471-474 (4)	4.15	1.80

Congress of Permet, 7th anniversary.

Child and Globe — A89

Weighing Baby — A90

1951, July 16
475	A89	2 l green	1.00	.75
476	A90	2.50 l brown	1.50	.90
477	A90	3 l red	2.00	1.10
478	A89	5 l blue	3.00	1.25
		Nos. 475-478 (4)	7.50	4.00

Intl. Children's Day, June 1, 1951.

Enver Hoxha and Birthplace of Albanian Communist Party — A91

1951, Nov. 8   Photo.   Perf. 14
479	A91	2.50 l olive brown	.30	.20
480	A91	3 l rose brown	.45	.35
481	A91	5 l dark slate blue	.70	.60
482	A91	8 l black	1.00	.85
		Nos. 479-482 (4)	2.45	2.00

Albanian Communist Party, 10th anniv.

Battle Scene A92

Designs: 5 l, Schoolgirl, "Agriculture and Industry." 8 l, Four portraits.

1951, Nov. 28   Perf. 12x12½
483	A92	2.50 l brown	.40	.20
484	A92	5 l blue	.65	.40
485	A92	8 l brown carmine	1.40	.75
		Nos. 483-485 (3)	2.45	1.35

Albanian Communist Youth Org., 10th anniv.

Albanian Heroes (Haxhija, Lezhe, Giyebegej, Mezi and Dedej) — A93

#486-489 each show 5 "Heroes of the People"; #490 shows 2 (Stafa and Shanto).

1950, Dec. 25   Unwmk.   Perf. 14
486	A93	2 l dark green	.60	.20
487	A93	2.50 l purple	.80	.20
488	A93	3 l scarlet	1.25	.25
489	A93	3 l brt blue	1.75	.35
490	A93	8 l olive brown	4.50	1.00
		Nos. 486-490 (5)	8.90	2.00

6th anniv. of Albania's liberation.

Tobacco Factory, Shkoder A94

Composite, Lenin Hydroelectric Plant — A95

Designs: 1 l, Canal. 2.50 l, Textile factory. 3 l, "8 November" Cannery. 5 l, Motion Picture Studio, Tirana. 8 l, Stalin Textile Mill, Tirana. 20 l, Central Hydroelectric Dam.

1953, Aug. 1   Perf. 12x12½, 12½x12
491	A94	50q red brown	.20	.20
492	A94	1 l dull green	.30	.20
493	A94	2.50 l brown	.50	.20
494	A94	3 l rose brown	.65	.20
495	A94	5 l blue	1.25	.20
496	A94	8 l brown olive	1.75	.20
497	A95	12 l deep plum	2.10	.30
498	A94	20 l slate blue	3.25	.50
		Nos. 491-498 (8)	10.00	2.00

Liberation Scene — A96

1954, Nov. 29   Perf. 12x12½
499	A96	50q brown violet	.20	.20
500	A96	1 l olive green	.25	.20
501	A96	2.50 l yellow brown	.65	.20
502	A96	3 l carmine rose	.80	.20
503	A96	5 l gray blue	1.10	.20
504	A96	8 l rose brown	2.00	.55
		Nos. 499-504 (6)	5.00	1.55

10th anniversary of Albania's liberation.

School — A97

Pandeli Sotiri, Petro Nini Luarasi, Nuci Naci — A98

1956, Feb. 23   Unwmk.
505	A97	2 l rose violet	.35	.20
506	A98	2.50 l lt green	.50	.20
507	A98	5 l ultra	1.10	.35
508	A97	10 l brt grnsh blue	2.25	.65
		Nos. 505-508 (4)	4.20	1.40

Opening of the 1st Albanian school, 70th anniv.

Flags — A99

Designs: 5 l, Labor Party headquarters, Tirana. 8 l, Marx and Lenin.

1957, June 1   Engr.   Perf. 11½x11
509	A99	2.50 l brown	.45	.20
510	A99	5 l lt violet blue	.90	.20
511	A99	8 l rose lilac	2.00	1.00
		Nos. 509-511 (3)	3.35	1.40

Albania's Labor Party, 15th anniv.

Congress Emblem A100

1957, Oct. 4   Unwmk.   Perf. 11½
512	A100	2.50 l gray brown	.50	.20
513	A100	3 l rose red	.70	.20
514	A100	5 l dark blue	.90	.20
515	A100	8 l green	1.60	.65
		Nos. 512-515 (4)	3.70	1.25

4th Intl. Trade Union Cong., Leipzig, 10/4-15.

Lenin and Cruiser "Aurora" A101

1957, Nov. 7   Litho.   Perf. 10½
516	A101	2.50 l violet brown	.45	.20
517	A101	5 l violet blue	.95	.20
518	A101	8 l gray	1.25	.30
		Nos. 516-518 (3)	2.65	.70

40th anniv. of the Russian Revolution.

Albanian Fighter Holding Flag A102

Naum Veqilharxhj A103

1957, Nov. 28   Perf. 10½
519	A102	1.50 l magenta	.40	.20
520	A102	2.50 l brown	.60	.20
521	A102	5 l blue	1.00	.35
522	A102	8 l green	2.00	.65
		Nos. 519-522 (4)	4.00	1.40

Proclamation of independence, 45th anniv.

1958, Feb. 1   Unwmk.
523	A103	2.50 l dark brown	.50	.20
524	A103	5 l violet blue	1.00	.20
525	A103	8 l rose lilac	2.00	.60
		Nos. 523-525 (3)	3.50	1.00

160th anniv. of the birth of Naum Veqilharxhj, patriot and writer.

Luigi Gurakuqi A104

Soldiers A105

1958, Apr. 15   Photo.   Perf. 10½
526	A104	1.50 l dark green	.30	.20
527	A104	2.50 l brown	.45	.25
528	A104	5 l blue	.75	.25
529	A104	8 l sepia	1.50	.50
		Nos. 526-529 (4)	3.00	1.20

Transfer of the ashes of Luigi Gurakuqi.

1958, July 10   Litho.

2.50 l, 11 l, Airman, sailor, soldier and tank.

530 A105 1.50 l blue green   .20   .20
531 A105 2.50 l dark red brown   .30   .20
532 A105   8 l rose red   1.00   .30
533 A105   11 l bright blue   1.50   .50
     Nos. 530-533 (4)   3.00   1.20

15th anniversary of Albanian army.

Cerciz Topulli   Buildings and
and Mihal   Tree
Grameno   A107
A106

1958, July 1

534 A106 2.50 l dk olive bister   .35   .20
535 A107   3 l green   .45   .20
536 A106   5 l blue   .75   .20
537 A107   8 l red brown   1.25   .40
     Nos. 534-537 (4)   2.80   1.00

50th anniversary, Battle of Mashkullore.

Ancient
Amphitheater
and Goddess
of Butrinto
A108

1959, Jan. 25   Litho.   Perf. 10½

538 A108 2.50 l redsh brown   .65   .20
539 A108 6.50 l lt blue green   1.60   .30
540 A108   11 l dark blue   2.50   .75
     Nos. 538-540 (3)   4.75   1.25

Cultural Monuments Week.

Frederic Joliot-Curie   Basketball
and World Peace   A110
Congress Emblem
A109

1959, July 1   Unwmk.

541 A109 1.50 l carmine rose   1.00   .20
542 A109 2.50 l rose violet   1.75   .30
543 A109   11 l blue   5.00   1.50
     Nos. 541-543 (3)   7.75   2.00

10th anniv. of the World Peace Movement.

1959, Nov. 20   Perf. 10½

Sports: 2.50 l, Soccer, 5 l, Runner. 11 l, Man
and woman runners with torch and flags.

544 A110 1.50 l bright violet   .40   .20
545 A110 2.50 l emerald   .55   .20
546 A110   5 l carmine rose   1.50   .25
547 A110   11 l ultra   4.00   1.75
     Nos. 544-547 (4)   6.45   2.40

1st Albanian Spartacist Games.

Fighter and
Flags — A111

Designs: 2.50 l, Miner with drill standing
guard. 3 l, Farm woman with sheaf of grain.
6.50 l, Man and woman in laboratory.

1959, Nov. 29

548 A111 1.50 l brt carmine   .50   .20
549 A111 2.50 l red brown   .70   .20
550 A111   3 l brt blue green   .90   .30
551 A111 6.50 l bright red   2.00   .50
   a.   Souvenir sheet   6.00   6.00
         Nos. 548-551 (4)   4.10   1.20

15th anniversary of Albania's liberation.
No. 551a contains one each of Nos. 548-
551, imperf. and all in bright carmine.
Inscribed ribbon frame of sheet and frame
lines for each stamp are blue green.

Mother and
Child, UN
Emblem
A112

1959, Dec. 5   Unwmk.

552 A112 5 l lt grnsh blue   3.00   1.00
   a.   Miniature sheet   4.00   4.00

10th anniv. (in 1958) of the signing of the
Universal Declaration of Human Rights.
No. 552a contains one imperf. stamp similar
to No. 552; ornamental border.

Woman with   Alexander
Olive Branch   Moissi
A113   A114

1960, Mar. 8   Litho.   Perf. 10½

553 A113 2.50 l chocolate   .45   .20
554 A113   11 l rose carmine   2.00   .50

50th anniv. of Intl. Women's Day, Mar. 8.

1960, Apr. 20

555 A114   3 l deep brown   .35   .20
556 A114   11 l Prus green   1.40   .30

80th anniversary of the birth of Alexander
Moissi (Moisiu) (1880-1935), German actor.

Lenin — A115   School
                    Building — A116

1960, Apr. 22

557 A115   4 l Prus blue   1.60   .20
558 A115   11 l lake   3.50   .40

90th anniversary of birth of Lenin.

1960, May 30   Litho.   Perf. 10½

559 A116   5 l green   1.25   .35
560 A116 6.50 l plum   1.25   .35

1st Albanian secondary school, 50th anniv.

Soldier on Guard   Liberation
Duty   Monument,
A117   Tirana, Family
                      and Policeman
                          A118

1960, May 12   Unwmk.   Perf. 10½

561 A117 1.50 l carmine rose   .30   .20
562 A117   11 l Prus blue   1.60   .40

15th anniversary of the Frontier Guards.

1960, May 14

563 A118 1.50 l green   .30   .20
564 A118 8.50 l brown   1.60   .40

15th anniversary of the People's Police.

Congress   Pashko
Site — A119   Vasa — A120

1960, Mar. 25

565 A119 2.50 l sepia   .25   .20
566 A119 7.50 l dull blue   1.00   .25

40th anniversary, Congress of Louchnia.

1960, May 5

Designs: 1.50 l, Jani Vreto. 6.50 l, Sami
Frasheri. 11 l, Page of statutes of association.

567 A120   1 l gray olive   .40   .20
568 A120   5 l brown   .50   .20
569 A120 6.50 l blue   1.10   .25
570 A120   11 l rose red   2.00   .35
     Nos. 567-570 (4)   4.00   1.00

80th anniv. (in 1959) of the Association of
Albanian Authors.

Albanian   TU-104 Plane, Clock
Fighter and   Tower, Tirana, and
Cannon   Kremlin, Moscow
A121   A122

1960, Aug. 2   Litho.   Perf. 10½

571 A121 1.50 l olive brown   .40   .20
572 A121 2.50 l maroon   .50   .30
573 A121   5 l dark blue   1.25   .40
     Nos. 571-573 (3)   2.15   .90

Battle of Viona (against Italian troops), 40th
anniv.

1960, Aug. 18

574 A122   1 l redsh brown   .40   .20
575 A122 7.50 l brt grnsh blue   1.50   .35
576 A122 11.50 l gray   2.75   .60
     Nos. 574-576 (3)   4.65   1.15

TU-104 flights, Moscow-Tirana, 2nd anniv.

Rising Sun and   Ali Kelmendi
Federation   A124
Emblem
A123

1960, Nov. 10   Unwmk.   Perf. 10½

577 A123 1.50 l ultra   .30   .20
578 A123 8.50 l red   1.10   .30

Intl. Youth Federation, 15th anniv.

1960, Dec. 5   Litho.   Perf. 10½

579 A124 1.50 l pale gray grn   .30   .20
580 A124   11 l dull rose lake   .70   .30

Ali Kelmendi, communist leader, 60th
birthday.

Flags of Russia   Marx and
and Albania   Lenin — A126
and Clasped
Hands — A125

1961, Jan. 10   Unwmk.   Perf. 10½

581 A125 2 l violet   .30   .20
582 A125 8 l dull red brown   .70   .30

15th anniv. of the Albanian-Soviet Friendship Society.

1961, Feb. 13   Litho.

583 A126 2 l rose red   .30   .20
584 A126 8 l violet blue   1.10   .30

Fourth Communist Party Congress.

Man from
Shkoder — A127

Otter — A128

Costumes: 1.50 l, Woman from Shkoder.
6.50 l, Man from Lume. 11 l, Woman from
Mirdite.

1961, Apr. 28   Perf. 10½

585 A127   1 l slate   .35   .20
586 A127 1.50 l dull claret   .60   .25
587 A127 6.50 l ultra   1.90   .45
588 A127   11 l red   3.25   1.05
     Nos. 585-588 (4)   6.10   2.15

1961, June 25   Unwmk.   Perf. 10½

Designs: 6.50 l, Badger. 11 l, Brown bear.

589 A128 2.50 l grayish blue   1.50   .25
590 A128 6.50 l blue green   2.75   .50
591 A128   11 l dark red brown   5.75   .85
     Nos. 589-591 (3)   10.00   1.60

Dalmatian   Cyclamen
Pelicans   A130
A129

1961, Sept. 30   Perf. 14

592 A129 1.50 l shown   2.00   .25
593 A129 7.50 l Gray herons   3.00   .60
594 A129   11 l Little egret   5.00   .75
     Nos. 592-594 (3)   10.00   1.60

1961, Oct. 27   Litho.

595 A130 1.50 l shown   1.00   .20
596 A130   8 l Forsythia   2.75   .50
597 A130   11 l Lily   3.75   .60
     Nos. 595-597 (3)   7.50   1.30

Milosh G.
Nikolla — A131

Flag with Marx
and
Lenin — A132

1961, Oct. 30   **Perf. 14**

598	A131	50q violet brown	.30	.20
599	A131	8.50 l Prus green	1.25	.30

50th anniv. of the birth of Milosh Gjergi
Nikolla, poet.

1961, Nov. 8

600	A132	2.50 l vermilion	.50	.20
601	A132	7.50 l dull red brown	1.00	.30

20th anniv. of the founding of Albania's
Communist Party.

Worker, Farm
Woman and
Emblem — A133

Yuri Gagarin and
Vostok 1 — A134

1961, Nov. 23   **Unwmk.**   **Perf. 14**

602	A133	2.50 l violet blue	.50	.20
603	A133	7.50 l rose claret	1.00	.30

20th anniv. of the Albanian Workers' Party.

1962, Feb. 15   **Unwmk.**   **Perf. 14**

604	A134	50q blue	.40	.20
605	A134	4 l red lilac	1.60	.20
606	A134	11 l dk slate grn	2.00	.60
		Nos. 604-606 (3)	4.00	1.00

1st manned space flight, made by Yuri A.
Gagarin, Soviet astronaut, Apr. 12, 1961.
Nos. 604-606 were overprinted with an over-
all yellow tint and with "POSTA AJRORE" (Air
Mail) in maroon in 1962. Value, set $50.

Petro Nini
Luarasi — A135

Malaria
Eradication
Emblem — A136

1962, Feb. 28   **Litho.**

607	A135	50q Prus blue	.25	.20
608	A135	8.50 l olive gray	1.50	.25

50th anniv. (in 1961) of the death of Petro
Nini Luarasi, Albanian patriot.

1962, Apr. 30   **Unwmk.**   **Perf. 14**

609	A136	1.50 l brt green	.20	.20
610	A136	2.50 l brown red	.20	.20
611	A136	10 l red lilac	.55	.25
612	A136	11 l blue	.90	.35
		Nos. 609-612 (4)	1.85	1.00

WHO drive to eradicate malaria.
Souvenir sheets, perf. and imperf., contain
one each of Nos. 609-612. Value $20 each.
Nos. 609-612 imperf., value, set $14.

Camomile
A137

Woman Diver
A138

Medicinal plants.

1962, May 10

613	A137	50q shown	.20	.20
614	A137	8 l Linden	.75	.25
615	A137	11.50 l Garden sage	1.75	.45
		Nos. 613-615 (3)	2.70	.90

Value, imperf. set $12.

1962, May 31   **Perf. 14**

2.50 l, Pole vault. 3 l, Mt. Fuji & torch, horiz.
9 l, Woman javelin thrower. 10 l, Shot putting.

616	A138	50q brt grnsh bl & blk	.20	.20
617	A138	2.50 l gldn brn & sepia	.20	.20
618	A138	3 l blue & gray	.40	.20
619	A138	9 l rose car & dk brn	1.10	.25
620	A138	10 l olive & blk	1.25	.30
		Nos. 616-620 (5)	3.15	1.15

1964 Olympic Games, Tokyo. Value, imperf.
set $25. A 15 l (like 3 l) exists in souv. sheet,
perf. and imperf.

Globe and
Orbits — A139

Dog Laika and
Sputnik
2 — A140

Designs: 1.50 l, Rocket to the sun. 20 l,
Lunik 3 photographing far side of the moon.

1962, June   **Unwmk.**   **Perf. 14**

621	A139	50q violet & org	.20	.20
622	A140	1 l blue grn & brn	.35	.20
623	A140	1.50 l yellow & ver	.50	.20
624	A139	20 l magenta & bl	3.50	.80
		Nos. 621-624 (4)	4.55	1.40

Russian space explorations.
#621-624 exist imperf in changed colors.
Two miniature sheets exist, containing one
14-lek picturing Sputnik 1. The perforated 14-
lek is yellow and brown; the imperf. red and
brown.

Soccer Game,
Map of South
America
A141

2.50 l, 15 l, Soccer game and globe as ball.

1962, July   **Litho.**

625	A141	1 l org & dk pur	.20	.20
626	A141	2.50 l emer & bluish grn	.25	.20
627	A141	6.50 l lt brn & pink	.90	.20
628	A141	15 l bluish grn & mar	1.50	.40
		Nos. 625-628 (4)	2.85	1.00

World Soccer Championships, Chile, 5/30-
6/17.
Exist imperforate in changed colors.
Two miniature sheets exist, each containing
a single 20-lek in design similar to A141. The
perf. sheet is brown and green; the imperf.,
brown and orange.

Map of Europe
and
Albania — A142

Woman of
Dardhe — A143

Designs: 1 l, 2.50 l, Map of Adriatic Sea and
Albania and Roman statue.

1962, Aug.

630	A142	50q multicolored	.40	.35
631	A142	1 l ultra & red	1.00	.80
632	A142	2.50 l blue & red	3.00	2.50
633	A142	11 l multicolored	6.00	5.00
		Nos. 630-633 (4)	10.40	8.65

Tourist propaganda. Imperforates in
changed colors exist.
Miniature sheets containing a 7 l and 8 l
stamp, perf. and imperf., exist.

1962, Sept.

Regional Costumes: 1 l, Man from Devoll.
2.50 l, Woman from Lunxheri. 14 l, Man from
Gjirokaster.

635	A143	50q car, bl & pur	.20	.20
636	A143	1 l red brn & ocher	.20	.20
637	A143	2.50 l vio, yel grn & blk	.65	.30
638	A143	14 l red brn & pale grn	2.25	.75
		Nos. 635-638 (4)	3.30	1.45

Value, imperf. set $18.

Chamois
A144

Ismail Qemali
A145

Animals: 1 l, Lynx, horiz. 1.50 l, Wild boar,
horiz. 15 l, 20 l, Roe deer.

1962, Oct. 24   **Unwmk.**   **Perf. 14**

639	A144	50q sl grn & dk pur	.65	.20
640	A144	1 l orange & blk	1.10	.20
641	A144	1.50 l red brn & blk	1.50	.20
642	A144	15 l yel ol & red brn	7.75	1.00
		Nos. 639-642 (4)	11.00	1.60

Miniature Sheet

643	A144	20 l yel ol & red brn	45.00	50.00

Imperfs. in changed colors, value #639-642
$25, #643 $25.

1962, Dec. 28   **Litho.**

Designs: 1 l, Albania eagle. 16 l, Eagle over
fortress formed by "RPSH."

644	A145	1 l red & red brn	.30	.20
645	A145	3 l org brn & blk	.55	.20
646	A145	16 l dk car rose & blk	3.50	.50
		Nos. 644-646 (3)	4.35	.90

50th anniv. of independence. Imperfs. in
changed colors, value $12.50.

Monument of
October
Revolution — A146

Henri Dunant,
Cross, Globe
and
Nurse — A147

1963, Jan. 5   **Unwmk.**   **Perf. 14**

647	A146	5 l shown	.50	.20
648	A146	10 l Lenin statue	1.25	.35

October Revolution (Russia, 1917), 45th
anniv.

1963, Jan 25   **Unwmk.**   **Perf. 14**

649	A147	1.50 l rose lake, red & blk	.25	.20
650	A147	2.50 l lt bl, red & blk	.30	.20
651	A147	6 l emerald, red & blk	.75	.25
652	A147	10 l dull yel, red & blk	1.40	.50
		Nos. 649-652 (4)	2.70	1.15

Cent. of the Geneva Conf., which led to the
establishment of the Intl. Red Cross in 1864.
Imperfs. in changed colors, value, set $20.

Stalin and
Battle of
Stalingrad
A148

Andrian G.
Nikolayev — A149

1963, Feb. 2

653	A148	8 l dk green & slate	2.75	.75

Battle of Stalingrad, 20th anniv. See #C67.

1963, Feb. 28   **Litho.**

Designs: 7.50 l, Vostoks 3 and 4 and globe,
horiz. 20 l, Pavel R. Popovich. 25 l, Nikolayev,
Popovich and globe with trajectories.

654	A149	2.50 l vio bl & sepia	.40	.20
655	A149	7.50 l lt blue & blk	.75	.20
656	A149	20 l violet & sepia	2.25	.50
		Nos. 654-656 (3)	3.40	1.10

Miniature Sheet

657	A149	25 l vio bl & sepia	12.00	12.00

1st group space flight of Vostoks 3 and 4,
Aug. 11-15, 1962. Imperfs. in changed colors,
value #654-656 $12, #657 $12.

"Albania"
Decorating Police
Officer — A150

Polyphylla
Fullo — A151

1963, Mar. 20   **Unwmk.**   **Perf. 14**

658	A150	2.50 l crim, mag & blk	.40	.20
659	A150	7.50 l org ver, dk red & blk	1.40	.25

20th anniversary of the security police.

1963, Mar. 20

Beetles: 1.50 l, Lucanus cervus. 8 l,
Procerus gigas. 10 l, Cicindela Albanica.

660	A151	50q ol grn & brn	.25	.20
661	A151	1.50 l blue & brn	.55	.20
662	A151	8 l dl rose & blk vio	2.75	1.10
663	A151	10 l brt citron & blk	3.00	1.25
		Nos. 660-663 (4)	6.55	2.75

1913 Stamp
and Postmark
A152

10 l, Stamps of 1913, 1937 and 1962.

1963, May 5
| 664 | A152 | 5 l | yel, buff, bl & blk | .70 | .25 |
| 665 | A152 | 10 l | car rose, grn & blk | 1.40 | .45 |

50th anniversary of Albanian stamps.

Boxer — A153   Crested Grebe — A154

Designs: 3 l, Basketball baskets. 5 l, Volleyball. 6 l, Bicyclists. 9 l, Gymnast. 15 l, Hands holding torch, and map of Japan.

1963, May 25   **Perf. 13½**
666	A153	2 l	yel, blk & red brn	.25	.20
667	A153	3 l	ocher, brn & bl	.35	.20
668	A153	5 l	gray bl, red brn & brn	.60	.20
669	A153	6 l	gray, dk gray & grn	.80	.25
670	A153	9 l	rose, red brn & bl	1.50	.30
		Nos. 666-670 (5)		3.50	1.15

Miniature Sheet
| 671 | A153 | 15 l | lt bl, car, blk & brn | 9.00 | 9.00 |

1964 Olympic Games in Tokyo. Value, imperfs. #666-670 $7.50, #671 $8.

1963, Apr. 20   **Litho.**   **Perf. 14**

Birds: 3 l, Golden eagle. 6.50 l, Gray partridges. 11 l, Capercaillie.
672	A154	50q	multicolored	.20	.20
673	A154	3 l	multicolored	1.10	.25
674	A154	6.50 l	multicolored	2.50	.55
675	A154	11 l	multicolored	4.00	.85
		Nos. 672-675 (4)		7.80	1.85

Soldier and Building A155

2.50 l, Soldier with pack, ship, plane. 5 l, Soldier in battle. 6 l, Soldier, bulldozer.

1963, July 10   **Unwmk.**   **Perf. 12**
676	A155	1.50 l	brick red, yel & blk	.30	.20
677	A155	2.50 l	bl, ocher & brn	.40	.20
678	A155	5 l	bluish grn, gray & blk	.90	.20
679	A155	6 l	red brn, buff & bl	1.25	.25
		Nos. 676-679 (4)		2.85	.85

Albanian army, 20th anniversary.

Maj. Yuri A. Gagarin A156

Designs: 5 l, Maj. Gherman Titov. 7 l, Maj. Andrian G. Nikolayev. 11 l, Lt. Col. Pavel R. Popovich. 14 l, Lt. Col. Valeri Bykovski. 20 l, Lt. Valentina Tereshkova.

1963, July 30
Portraits in Yellow and Black
680	A156	3 l	brt purple	.30	.20
681	A156	5 l	dull blue	.45	.20
682	A156	7 l	gray	.60	.20
683	A156	11 l	deep claret	1.10	.35
684	A156	14 l	blue green	1.60	.55
685	A156	20 l	ultra	2.25	1.00
		Nos. 680-685 (6)		6.30	2.50

Man's conquest of space. Value, imperf. set $18.

Volleyball A157

1963, Aug. 31   **Perf. 12x12½**
686	A157	2 l	shown	.20	.20
687	A157	3 l	Weight lifting	.35	.20
688	A157	5 l	Soccer	.65	.20
689	A157	7 l	Boxing	.80	.20
690	A157	8 l	Rowing	1.50	.30
		Nos. 686-690 (5)		3.50	1.15

European championships. Imperfs. in changed colors, value set $16.

Papilio Podalirius A158

1963, Sept. 29   **Litho.**
Various Butterflies and Moths in Natural Colors
691	A158	1 l	red	.20	.20
692	A158	2 l	blue	.75	.20
693	A158	4 l	dull lilac	1.25	.25
694	A158	5 l	pale green	2.25	.40
695	A158	8 l	bister	2.75	.55
696	A158	10 l	light blue	4.50	.70
		Nos. 691-696 (6)		11.70	2.30

Oil Refinery, Cerrik — A159   Flag and Shield — A160

2.50 l, Food processing plant, Tirana, horiz. 30 l, Fruit canning plant. 50 l, Tannery, horiz.

1963, Nov. 15   **Unwmk.**   **Perf. 14**
697	A159	2.50 l	rose red, pnksh	.20	.20
698	A159	20 l	slate grn, grnsh	.90	.20
699	A159	30 l	dull pur, grysh	1.90	.50
700	A159	50 l	ocher, yel	1.90	.75
		Nos. 697-700 (4)		4.90	1.65

Industrial development in Albania. For surcharges see #841-846.

1963, Nov. 24   **Perf. 12½x12**
| 701 | A160 | 2 l | grnsh bl, blk, ocher & red | .35 | .20 |
| 702 | A160 | 8 l | blue, blk, ocher & red | 1.00 | .50 |

1st Congress of Army Aid Assn.

Chinese, Caucasian and Negro Men — A161

1963, Dec. 10   **Perf. 12x11½**
703	A161	3 l	bister & blk	.50	.20
704	A161	5 l	bister & ultra	1.00	.20
705	A161	7 l	bister & vio	1.50	.30
		Nos. 703-705 (3)		3.00	.70

15th anniv. of the Universal Declaration of Human Rights.

Slalom Ascent — A162   Lenin — A163

Designs: 50q, Bobsled, horiz. 6.50 l, Ice hockey, horiz. 12.50 l, Women's figure skating. No. 709A, Ski jumper.

1963, Dec. 25   **Perf. 14**
706	A162	50q	grnsh bl & blk	.20	.20
707	A162	2.50 l	red, gray & blk	.30	.20
708	A162	6.50 l	yel, blk & gray	.75	.20
709	A162	12.50 l	red, blk & yel grn	1.75	.50
		Nos. 706-709 (4)		3.00	1.10

Miniature Sheet
| 709A | A162 | 12.50 l | multi | 10.00 | 7.50 |

9th Winter Olympic Games, Innsbruck, Jan. 29-Feb. 9, 1964. Imperfs. in changed colors, value #706-709 $25, #709A $30.

1964, Jan. 21   **Perf. 12½x12**
| 710 | A163 | 5 l | gray & bister | .40 | .20 |
| 711 | A163 | 10 l | gray & ocher | .75 | .20 |

40th anniversary, death of Lenin.

Hurdling — A164

Fish — A165

Designs: 3 l, Track, horiz. 6.50 l, Rifle shooting, horiz. 8 l, Basketball.

Perf. 12½x12, 12x12½
1964, Jan. 30   **Litho.**
712	A164	2.50 l	pale vio & ultra	.20	.20
713	A164	3 l	lt grn & red brn	.35	.20
714	A164	6.50 l	blue & claret	.60	.25
715	A164	8 l	lt blue & ocher	1.00	.35
		Nos. 712-715 (4)		2.15	1.00

1st Games of the New Emerging Forces, GANEFO, Jakarta, Indonesia, Nov. 10-22, 1963.

1964, Feb. 26   **Unwmk.**   **Perf. 14**
716	A165	50q	Sturgeon	.20	.20
717	A165	1 l	Gilthead	.20	.20
718	A165	1.50 l	Striped mullet	.40	.20
719	A165	2.50 l	Carp	.60	.20
720	A165	6.50 l	Mackerel	1.60	.40
721	A165	10 l	Lake Ohrid trout	3.00	.50
		Nos. 716-721 (6)		6.00	1.70

Wild Animals A166

1964, Mar. 28   **Perf. 12½x12**
722	A166	1 l	Red Squirrel	.30	.20
723	A166	1.50 l	Beech marten	.60	.20
724	A166	2 l	Red fox	.60	.20
725	A166	2.50 l	Hedgehog	.90	.20
726	A166	3 l	Hare	1.25	.20
727	A166	5 l	Jackal	1.50	.25
728	A166	7 l	Wildcat	2.40	.35
729	A166	8 l	Wolf	3.00	.50
		Nos. 722-729 (8)		10.55	2.10

Lighting Olympic Torch — A167

5 l, Torch, globes. 7 l, 15 l, Olympic flag, Mt. Fuji. 10 l, National Stadium, Tokyo.

1964, May 18   **Perf. 12x12½**
730	A167	3 l	lt yel grn, yel & buff	.25	.20
731	A167	5 l	red & vio blue	.35	.20
732	A167	7 l	lt bl, ultra & yel	.55	.20
733	A167	10 l	orange, bl & vio	.75	.25
		Nos. 730-733 (4)		1.90	.85

Miniature Sheet
| 734 | A167 | 15 l | lt bl, ultra & org | 11.00 | 11.00 |

18th Olympic Games, Tokyo, Oct. 10-25, 1964. No. 734 contains one 49x62mm stamp. Imperfs. in changed colors, value #730-733 $11, #734 $14.
See No. 745.

Partisans — A168

5 l, Arms of Albania. 8 l, Enver Hoxha.

Perf. 12½x12
1964, May 24   **Litho.**   **Unwmk.**
735	A168	2 l	orange, red & blk	.65	.20
736	A168	5 l	multicolored	1.50	.30
737	A168	8 l	red brn, blk & red	3.25	.85
		Nos. 735-737 (3)		5.40	1.35

20th anniv. of the Natl. Anti-Fascist Cong. of Liberation, Permet, May 24, 1944. The label attached to each stamp, without perforations between, carries a quotation from the 1944 Congress.

Albanian Flag and Revolutionists A169

Perf. 12½x12
1964, June 10   **Litho.**   **Unwmk.**
| 738 | A169 | 2.50 l | red & gray | .25 | .20 |
| 739 | A169 | 7.50 l | lilac rose & gray | .75 | .25 |

Albanian revolution of 1924, 40th anniv.

Full Moon — A170

1964, June 27   **Perf. 12x12½**

Designs: 5 l, New moon. 8 l, Half moon. 11 l, Waning moon. 15 l, Far side of moon.
740	A170	1 l	purple & yel	.25	.20
741	A170	5 l	violet & yel	.60	.20
742	A170	8 l	blue & yel	1.10	.30
743	A170	11 l	green & yel	1.75	.45
		Nos. 740-743 (4)		3.70	1.15

Miniature Sheet
Perf. 12 on 2 sides
| 744 | A170 | 15 l | ultra & yel | 12.50 | 12.50 |

No. 744 contains one stamp, size: 35x36mm, perforated at top and bottom. Imperfs. in changed colors, value #740-743 $12.50, #744 $12.50.

No. 733 with Added Inscription:
"Rimini 25-VI-64"

1964 *Perf. 12x12½*
745 A167 10 l orange, bl & vio 3.50 3.00
"Toward Tokyo 1964" Phil. Exhib. at Rimini, Italy, June 25-July 6.

Wren — A171

Birds: 1 l, Penduline titmouse. 2.50 l, Green woodpecker. 3 l, Tree creeper. 4 l, Nuthatch. 5 l, Great titmouse. 6 l, Goldfinch. 18 l, Oriole.

1964, July 31 *Perf. 12x12½*
746 A171 50q multi .20 .20
747 A171 1 l orange & multi .40 .20
748 A171 2.50 l multi .60 .20
749 A171 3 l blue & multi .80 .20
750 A171 4 l yellow & multi 1.00 .25
751 A171 5 l blue & multi 1.25 .25
752 A171 6 l lt vio & multi 1.40 .50
753 A171 18 l pink & multi 3.00 1.25
Nos. 746-753 (8) 8.65 3.05

Running and Gymnastics A172

Sport: 2 l, Weight lifting, judo. 3 l, Equestrian, bicycling. 4 l, Soccer, water polo. 5 l, Wrestling, boxing. 6 l, Pentathlon, hockey. 7 l, Swimming, sailing. 8 l, Basketball, volleyball. 9 l, Rowing, canoeing. 10 l, Fencing, pistol shooting. 20 l, Three winners.

Perf. 12x12½
1964, Sept. 25 Litho. Unwmk.
754 A172 1 l lt bl, rose & emer .20 .20
755 A172 2 l bis brn, bluish grn & vio .20 .20
756 A172 3 l vio, red org & ol bis .20 .20
757 A172 4 l grnsh bl, ol & ultra .20 .20
758 A172 5 l grnsh bl, car & pale lil .30 .20
759 A172 6 l dk bl, org & lt bl .35 .20
760 A172 7 l dk bl, lt ol & org .35 .20
761 A172 8 l emer, gray & yel .50 .20
762 A172 9 l bl, yel & lil rose .65 .30
763 A172 10 l brt grn, org brn & yel grn 1.60 .50
Nos. 754-763 (10) 4.55 2.40

Miniature Sheet
Perf. 12
764 A172 20 l violet & lemon 16.00 16.00
18th Olympic Games, Tokyo, Oct. 10-25. No. 764 contains one stamp, size: 41x68mm. Imperfs. in changed colors, value #754-763 $12.50, #764 $12.50.

Arms of People's Republic of China — A173

Mao Tse-tung and Flag A174

1964, Oct. 1 *Perf. 11½x12, 12x11½*
765 A173 7 l black, red & yellow 2.00 .40
766 A174 8 l black, red & yellow 3.00 .60
People's Republic of China, 15th anniv.

Karl Marx A175

Jeronim de Rada — A176

Designs: 5 l, St. Martin's Hall, London. 8 l, Friedrich Engels.

1964, Nov. 5 *Perf. 12x11½*
767 A175 2 l red, lt vio & blk .55 .20
768 A175 5 l gray blue 1.10 .25
769 A175 8 l ocher, blk & red 2.25 .55
Nos. 767-769 (3) 3.90 1.00
Centenary of First Socialist International.

1964, Nov. 15 *Perf. 12½x11½*
770 A176 7 l slate green 1.10 .35
771 A176 8 l dull violet 1.60 .55
Birth of Jeronim de Rada, poet, 150th anniv.

Arms of Albania — A177

Factories A178

Designs: 3 l, Combine harvester. 4 l, Woman chemist. 10 l, Hands holding Constitution, hammer and sickle.

Perf. 11½x12, 12x11½
1964, Nov. 29
772 A177 1 l multicolored .35 .20
773 A178 2 l red, yel & vio bl .45 .20
774 A178 3 l red, yel & brn .85 .20
775 A178 4 l red, yel & gray grn 1.00 .20
776 A177 10 l red, bl & blk 1.60 .45
Nos. 772-776 (5) 4.25 1.25
20th anniversary of liberation.

Planet Mercury — A179

Planets: 2 l, Venus and rocket. 3 l, Earth, moon and rocket. 4 l, Mars and rocket. 5 l, Jupiter. 6 l, Saturn. 7 l, Uranus. 8 l, Neptune. 9 l, Pluto. 15 l, Solar system and rocket.

1964, Dec. 15 *Perf. 12x12½*
777 A179 1 l yellow & pur .20 .20
778 A179 2 l multicolored .20 .20
779 A179 3 l multicolored .20 .20
780 A179 4 l multicolored .25 .20
781 A179 5 l yel, dk pur & brn .45 .20
782 A179 6 l lt grn, vio brn & yel .60 .20
783 A179 7 l yellow & grn .70 .20
784 A179 8 l yellow & vio .85 .25
785 A179 9 l lt grn, yel & blk 1.25 .35
Nos. 777-785 (9) 4.70 2.00

Miniature Sheet
Perf. 12 on 2 sides
786 A179 15 l car, bl, yel & grn 15.00 15.00
No. 786 contains one stamp, size: 62x51mm, perforated at top and bottom. Imperfs. in changed colors. Value #777-785, $15; #786, $17.50.

European Chestnut A180

Symbols of Industry A181

1965, Jan. 25 *Perf. 11½x12*
787 A180 1 l shown .20 .20
788 A180 2 l Medlars .25 .20
789 A180 3 l Persimmon .50 .20
790 A180 4 l Pomegranate .55 .20
791 A180 5 l Quince .80 .20
792 A180 10 l Orange 1.60 .35
Nos. 787-792 (6) 3.90 1.35

1965, Feb. 20
Designs: 5 l, Books, triangle and compass. 8 l, Beach, trees and hotel.
793 A181 2 l blk, car rose & pink 1.75 .50
794 A181 5 l yel, gray & blk 3.50 1.00
795 A181 8 l blk, vio bl & lt bl 5.75 1.60
Nos. 793-795 (3) 11.00 3.10
Professional trade associations, 20th anniv.

Water Buffalo A182

Various designs: Water buffalo.

1965, Mar. *Perf. 12x11½*
796 A182 1 l lt yel grn, yel & brn blk .30 .20
797 A182 2 l lt bl, dk gray & blk .85 .20
798 A182 3 l yellow, brn & grn 1.10 .20
799 A182 7 l brt grn, yel & brn blk 2.75 .35
800 A182 12 l pale lil, dk brn & ind 4.00 .65
Nos. 796-800 (5) 9.00 1.60

Mountain View, Valbona — A183

1.50 l, Seashore. 3 l, Glacier and peak. 4 l, Gorge. 5 l, Mountain peaks. 9 l, Lake and hills.

1965, Mar. Litho. *Perf. 12*
801 A183 1.50 l multi .60 .20
802 A183 2.50 l multi 1.40 .20
803 A183 3 l multi 1.40 .25
804 A183 4 l multi, vert. 1.75 .40
805 A183 5 l multi 2.10 .50
806 A183 9 l multi 6.00 .75
Nos. 801-806 (6) 13.25 2.30

Frontier Guard — A184

Small-bore Rifle Shooting, Prone — A185

1965, Apr. 25 Unwmk.
807 A184 2.50 l lt blue & multi .85 .20
808 A184 12.50 l lt ultra & multi 3.50 .90
20th anniversary of the Frontier Guards.

1965, May 10
Designs: 2 l, Rifle shooting, standing. 3 l, Target over map of Europe, showing Bucharest. 4 l, Pistol shooting. 15 l, Rifle shooting, kneeling.
809 A185 1 l lil, car rose, blk & brn .20 .20
810 A185 2 l bl, blk, brn & vio bl .35 .20
811 A185 3 l pink & car rose .45 .20
812 A185 4 l bis, blk & vio brn .60 .20
813 A185 15 l brt grn, brn & vio brn 2.25 .50
Nos. 809-813 (5) 3.85 1.30
European Shooting Championships, Bucharest.

ITU Emblem, Old and New Communications Equipment A186

Col. Pavel Belyayev — A187

1965, May 17 *Perf. 12½x12*
814 A186 2.50 l brt grn, blk & lil rose .50 .20
815 A186 12.50 l vio, blk & brt bl 3.25 .30
Centenary of the ITU.

1965, June 15 *Perf. 12*
Designs: 2 l, Voskhod II. 6.50 l, Lt. Col. Alexei Leonov. 20 l, Leonov floating in space.
816 A187 1.50 l lt blue & brn .20 .20
817 A187 2 l dk bl, lt vio & lt ultra .20 .20
818 A187 6.50 l lilac & brn .70 .20
819 A187 20 l chlky bl, yel & blk 1.90 .40
Nos. 816-819 (4) 3.00 1.00

Miniature Sheet
Perf. 12 on 2 sides
820 A187 20 l brt bl, org & blk 6.00 6.00
Space flight of Voskhod II and 1st man walking in space, Lt. Col. Alexei Leonov. No. 820 contains one stamp, size: 51x59½mm, perforated at top and bottom. Imperf., brt grn background, value $6.

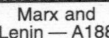

Marx and Lenin — A188

Mother and Child — A189

1965, June 21   *Perf. 12*
821	A188	2.50 l dk brn, red & yel	.85	.20
822	A188	7.50 l sl grn, red, org ver & buff	2.25	.25

6th Conf. of Postal Ministers of Communist Countries, Peking, June 21-July 15.

Perf. 12½x12, 12x12½

1965, June 29   *Litho.*   *Unwmk.*

2 l, Pioneers. 3 l, Boy and girl at play, horiz. 4 l, Child on beach. 15 l, Girl with book.

823	A189	1 l brt bl, rose lil & blk	.20	.20
824	A189	2 l salmon, vio & blk	.35	.20
825	A189	3 l green, org & vio	.50	.20
826	A189	4 l multicolored	.70	.20
827	A189	15 l lil rose, brn & ocher	2.25	.50
		Nos. 823-827 (5)	4.00	1.35

Issued for International Children's Day.

Statue of Magistrate A190

Flowers A191

Designs: 1 l, Amphora. 2 l, Illyrian armor. 3 l, Mosaic, horiz. 15 l, Torso, Apollo statue.

1965, July 20   *Perf. 12*
828	A190	1 l lt ol, org & brn	.20	.20
829	A190	2 l gray grn, grn & brn	.25	.20
830	A190	3 l tan, brn, car & lil	.50	.20
831	A190	4 l green, bis & brn	.70	.25
832	A190	15 l gray & pale claret	1.75	.65
		Nos. 828-832 (5)	3.40	1.50

1965, Aug. 11   *Perf. 12½x12*
833	A191	1 l Fuchsia	.20	.20
834	A191	2 l Cyclamen	.30	.20
835	A191	3 l Tiger lily	.50	.20
836	A191	3.50 l Iris	.60	.25
837	A191	4 l Dahlia	.70	.25
838	A191	4.50 l Hydrangea	.80	.25
839	A191	5 l Rose	1.00	.30
840	A191	7 l Tulips	1.90	.35
		Nos. 833-840 (8)	6.00	2.00

Nos. 698-700 Surcharged New Value and Two Bars

1965, Aug. 16   *Perf. 14*
841	A159	5q on 30 l	.20	.20
842	A159	15q on 30 l	.30	.20
843	A159	25q on 30 l	.45	.20
844	A159	80q on 50 l	.80	.20
845	A159	1.10 l on 20 l	1.50	.30
846	A159	2 l on 20 l	2.75	.60
		Nos. 841-846 (6)	6.00	1.70

White Stork — A192

"Homecoming," by Bukurosh Sejdini — A193

Migratory Birds: 20q, Cuckoo. 30q, Hoopoe. 40q, European bee-eater. 50q, European nightjar. 1.50 l, Quail.

1965, Aug. 31   *Perf. 12*
847	A192	10q yel, blk & gray	.20	.20
848	A192	20q brt pink, blk & dk bl	.35	.20
849	A192	30q violet, blk & bis	.65	.25
850	A192	40q emer, blk yel & org	1.40	.30
851	A192	50q ultra, brn & red brn	1.60	.35
852	A192	1.50 l bis, red brn & dp org	4.50	1.00
		Nos. 847-852 (6)	8.70	2.30

1965, Sept. 26   *Litho.*   *Perf. 12x12½*
853	A193	25q olive black	1.25	.20
854	A193	65q blue black	3.75	.55
855	A193	1.10 l black	5.00	1.25
		Nos. 853-855 (3)	10.00	2.00

Second war veterans' meeting.

Hunting — A194

Oleander — A195

1965, Oct. 6   *Litho.*   *Unwmk.*
856	A194	10q Capercaillie	.25	.20
857	A194	20q Deer	.40	.20
858	A194	30q Pheasant	.70	.20
859	A194	40q Mallards	1.10	.20
860	A194	50q Boar	1.25	.20
861	A194	1 l Rabbit	3.75	.55
		Nos. 856-861 (6)	7.45	1.60

1965, Oct. 26   *Perf. 12½x12*

Flowers: 20q, Forget-me-nots. 30q, Pink. 40q, White water lily. 50q, Bird's foot. 1 l, Corn poppy.

862	A195	10q brt bl, grn & car rose	.20	.20
863	A195	20q org red, bl, brn & grn	.40	.20
864	A195	30q vio, car rose & grn	.60	.20
865	A195	40q emerald, yel & blk	.80	.20
866	A195	50q org brn, yel & grn	1.00	.20
867	A195	1 l yel grn, blk & rose red	2.00	.70
		Nos. 862-867 (6)	5.00	1.70

Hotel Turizmi, Fier — A196

Freighter "Teuta" — A197

Buildings: 10q, Hotel, Peshkopi. 15q, Sanatorium, Tirana. 25q, Rest home, Pogradec.

65q, Partisan Sports Arena, Tirana. 80q, Rest home, Mali Dajt. 1.10 l, Culture House, Tirana. 1.60 l, Hotel Adriatik, Durres. 2 l, Migjeni Theater, Shkoder. 3 l, Alexander Moissi House of Culture, Durres.

1965, Oct.   *Perf. 12x12½*
868	A196	5q blue & blk	.20	.20
869	A196	10q ocher & blk	.20	.20
870	A196	15q dull grn & blk	.20	.20
871	A196	25q violet & blk	.20	.20
872	A196	65q lt brn & blk	.65	.20
873	A196	80q yel grn & blk	.90	.20
874	A196	1.10 l lilac & blk	1.25	.20
875	A196	1.60 l lt vio bl & blk	1.90	.40
876	A196	2 l dull rose & blk	2.50	.50
877	A196	3 l gray & blk	4.00	1.00
		Nos. 868-877 (10)	12.00	3.00

1965, Nov. 16

Ships: 20q, Raft. 30q, Sailing ship, 19th cent. 40q, Sailing ship, 18th cent. 50q, Freighter "Vlora." 1 l, Illyric galleys.

878	A197	10q brt grn & dk grn	.20	.20
879	A197	20q ol bis & dk grn	.20	.20
880	A197	30q lt & dp ultra	.35	.20
881	A197	40q vio & dp vio	.60	.20
882	A197	50q pink & dk red	.75	.20
883	A197	1 l bister & brn	1.50	.45
		Nos. 878-883 (6)	3.60	1.45

Brown Bear — A198

Basketball and Players — A199

Various Albanian bears. 50q, 55q, 60q, horiz.

1965, Dec. 7   *Perf. 11½x12*
884	A198	10q bister & dk brn	.30	.20
885	A198	20q pale brn & dk brn	.40	.20
886	A198	30q bis, dk brn & car	.65	.20
887	A198	35q pale brn & dk brn	.80	.20
888	A198	40q bister & dk brn	1.25	.20
889	A198	50q bister & dk brn	1.50	.20
890	A198	55q bister & dk brn	1.50	.30
891	A198	60q pale brn, dk brn & car	1.75	.50
		Nos. 884-891 (8)	8.15	2.00

1965, Dec. 15   *Litho.*   *Perf. 12½x12*

10q, Games' emblem (map of Albania and basket). 30q, 50q, Players with ball (diff. designs). 1.40 l, Basketball medal on ribbon.

892	A199	10q blue, yel & car	.20	.20
893	A199	20q rose lil, lt brn & blk	.35	.20
894	A199	30q bis, lt brn, red & blk	.45	.20
895	A199	50q lt grn, lt brn & blk	.95	.20
896	A199	1.40 l rose, blk, brn & yel	1.75	.50
		Nos. 892-896 (5)	3.70	1.30

7th Balkan Basketball Championships, Tirana, Dec. 15-19.

Arms of Republic and Smokestacks A200

Arms and: 10q, Book. 30q, Wheat. 60q, Book, hammer & sickle. 80q, Factories.

1966, Jan. 11   *Litho.*   *Perf. 11½x12*
Coat of Arms in Gold
897	A200	10q crimson & brn	.20	.20
898	A200	20q blue & vio bl	.20	.20
899	A200	30q org yel & brn	.35	.20
900	A200	60q yel grn & brt grn	.50	.20
901	A200	80q crimson & brn	1.10	.20
		Nos. 897-901 (5)	2.35	1.00

Albanian People's Republic, 20th anniv.

Cow A201

1966, Feb. 25   *Perf. 12½x12, 12x12½*
902	A201	10q shown	.20	.20
903	A201	20q Pig	.35	.20
904	A201	30q Ewe & lamb	.45	.20
905	A201	35q Ram	.65	.20
906	A201	40q Dog	.95	.20
907	A201	50q Cat, vert.	1.00	.20
908	A201	55q Horse, vert.	1.25	.25
909	A201	60q Ass, vert.	1.50	.30
		Nos. 902-909 (8)	6.35	1.75

Soccer Player and Map of Uruguay — A202

Andon Zako Cajupi — A203

5q, Globe in form of soccer ball. 15q, Player, map of Italy. 20q, Goalkeeper, map of France. 25q, Player, map of Brazil. 30q, Player, map of Switzerland. 35q, Player, map of Sweden. 40q, Player, map of Chile. 50q, Player, map of Great Britain. 70q, World Championship cup & ball.

1966, Mar. 20   *Litho.*   *Perf. 12*
910	A202	5q gray & dp org	.20	.20
911	A202	10q lt brn, bl & vio	.20	.20
912	A202	15q cit, dk bl & brt bl	.20	.20
913	A202	20q org, vio bl & brt bl	.25	.20
914	A202	25q salmon & sepia	.30	.20
915	A202	30q lt yel grn & brn	.30	.20
916	A202	35q lt ultra & emer	.35	.20
917	A202	40q pink & brown	.55	.20
918	A202	50q pale grn, mag & rose red	.55	.20
919	A202	70q gray, brn, yel & blk	.70	.30
		Nos. 910-919 (10)	3.60	2.10

World Cup Soccer Championship, Wembley, England, July 11-30.

1966, Mar. 27   *Unwmk.*
920	A203	40q bluish blk	.50	.20
921	A203	1.10 l dark green	1.50	.40

Andon Zako Cajupi, poet, birth centenary .

Painted Lady — A204

WHO Headquarters, Geneva, and Emblem — A205

Designs: 20q, Blue dragonfly. 30q, Cloudless sulphur butterfly. 35q, 40q, Splendid dragonfly. 50q, Machaon swallow-tail. 55q, Sulphur butterfly. 60q, Whitemarbled butterfly.

1966, Apr. 21   *Litho.*   *Perf. 11½x12*
922	A204	10q multicolored	.25	.20
923	A204	20q yellow & multi	.40	.20
924	A204	30q yellow & multi	.65	.20
925	A204	35q sky blue & multi	.80	.20
926	A204	40q multicolored	.85	.20
927	A204	50q rose & multi	1.10	.20
928	A204	55q multicolored	1.25	.20
929	A204	60q multicolored	2.00	.35
		Nos. 922-929 (8)	7.30	1.80

Perf. 12x12½, 12½x12
1966, May 3   **Litho.**

Designs (WHO Emblem and): 35q, Ambulance and stretcher bearers, vert. 60q, Albanian mother and nurse weighing infant, vert. 80q, X-ray machine and hospital.

930	A205	25q lt blue & blk	.30 .20
931	A205	35q salmon & ultra	.55 .20
932	A205	60q lt grn, bl & red	.90 .20
933	A205	80q yel, bl, grn & lt brn	1.25 .25

Nos. 930-933 (4)   3.00 .85

Inauguration of the WHO Headquarters, Geneva.

Bird's Foot Starfish A206

Designs: 25q, Starfish. 35q, Brittle star. 45q, But-thorn starfish. 50q, Starfish. 60q, Sea cucumber. 70q, Sea urchin.

1966, May 10   **Perf. 12x12½**

934	A206	15q multicolored	.25 .20
935	A206	25q multicolored	.45 .20
936	A206	35q multicolored	.65 .20
937	A206	45q multicolored	.90 .20
938	A206	50q multicolored	1.10 .20
939	A206	60q multicolored	1.25 .20
940	A206	70q multicolored	1.90 .35

Nos. 934-940 (7)   6.50 1.55

Luna 10 — A207

30q, 80q, Trajectory of Luna 10, earth & moon.

1966, June 10   **Perf. 12x12½**

941	A207	20q blue, yel & blk	.35 .20
942	A207	30q yel grn, blk & bl	.50 .20
943	A207	70q vio, yel & blk	.90 .20
944	A207	80q yel, vio, grn & blk	1.25 .50

Nos. 941-944 (4)   3.00 1.15

Launching of the 1st artificial moon satellite, Luna 10, Apr. 3, 1966.

Jules Rimet Cup and Soccer A208

Designs: Various scenes of soccer play.

1966, July 12   **Litho.**   **Perf. 12x12½**
Black Inscriptions

945	A208	10q ocher & lilac	.20 .20
946	A208	20q lt blue & cit	.20 .20
947	A208	30q brick red & Prus bl	.25 .20
948	A208	35q lt ultra & rose	.30 .20
949	A208	40q yel grn & lt red brn	.35 .20
950	A208	50q lt red brn & yel grn	.60 .20
951	A208	55q rose lil & yel grn	.65 .20
952	A208	60q dp rose & ocher	1.25 .25

Nos. 945-952 (8)   3.80 1.65

World Cup Soccer Championship, Wembley, England, July 11-30.

Water Level Map of Albania — A209

30q, Water measure & fields. 70q, Turbine & pylon. 80q, Hydrological decade emblem.

1966, July   **Perf. 12½x12**

953	A209	20q brick red, blk & org	.30 .20
954	A209	30q emer, blk & lt brn	.50 .20
955	A209	70q brt violet & blk	1.10 .25
956	A209	80q brt bl, org, yel & blk	1.25 .45

Nos. 953-956 (4)   3.15 1.10

Hydrological Decade (UNESCO), 1965-74.

Greek Turtle — A210

Designs: 15q, Grass snake. 25q, European pond turtle. 30q, Wall lizard. 35q, Wall gecko. 45q, Emerald lizard. 50q, Slowworm. 90q, Horned viper (or sand viper).

1966, Aug. 10   **Litho.**   **Perf. 12½x12**

957	A210	10q gray & multi	.20 .20
958	A210	15q yellow & multi	.20 .20
959	A210	25q ultra & multi	.30 .20
960	A210	30q multicolored	.45 .20
961	A210	35q multicolored	.60 .20
962	A210	45q multicolored	.70 .25
963	A210	50q orange & multi	.80 .30
964	A210	90q lilac & multi	1.75 .55

Nos. 957-964 (8)   5.00 2.10

Persian Cat A211

Cats: 10q, Siamese, vert. 15q, European tabby, vert. 25q, Black kitten. 60q, 65q, 80q, Various Persians.

Perf. 12x12½, 12½x12
1966, Sept. 20   **Litho.**

965	A211	10q multicolored	.20 .20
966	A211	15q blk, sepia & car	.25 .20
967	A211	25q blk, dk & lt brn	.35 .20
968	A211	45q blk, org & yel	.80 .20
969	A211	60q blk, brn & yel	1.40 .30
970	A211	65q multicolored	1.40 .40
971	A211	80q blk, gray & yel	1.60 .50

Nos. 965-971 (7)   6.00 2.00

Pjeter Budi, Writer — A212

1966, Oct. 5   **Perf. 12x12½**

972	A212	25q buff & slate grn	.25 .20
973	A212	1.75 l gray & dull claret	1.75 .45

UNESCO Emblem A213

Designs (UNESCO Emblem and): 15q, Open book, rose and school. 25q, Male folk dancers. 1.55 l, Jug, column and old building.

1966, Oct. 20   **Litho.**   **Perf. 12**

974	A213	5q lt gray & multi	.20 .20
975	A213	15q dp blue & multi	.30 .20
976	A213	25q gray & multi	.50 .20
977	A213	1.55 l multi	2.00 .50

Nos. 974-977 (4)   3.00 1.10

20th anniv. of UNESCO.

A214   A215

Designs: 15q, Hand holding book with pictures of Marx, Engels, Lenin and Stalin. 25q, Map of Albania, hammer and sickle, symbols of agriculture and industry. 65q, Symbolic grain and factories. 95q, Fists holding rifle, spade, axe, sickle and book.

1966, Nov. 1   **Litho.**   **Perf. 11½x12**

978	A214	15q vermilion & gold	.30 .20
979	A214	25q multicolored	.55 .20
980	A214	65q brn, brn org & gold	1.25 .20
981	A214	95q yellow & multi	1.90 .40

Nos. 978-981 (4)   4.00 1.00

Albanian Communist Party, 5th Cong.

1966, Nov. 8

Designs: 15q, Hammer and sickle, Party emblem in sunburst. 25q, Partisan and sunburst. 65q, Steel worker and blast furnace. 95q, Combine harvester, factories, and pylon.

982	A215	15q orange & multi	.30 .20
983	A215	25q red & multi	.40 .20
984	A215	65q multicolored	1.10 .40
985	A215	95q blue & multi	1.50 .40

Nos. 982-985 (4)   3.30 1.00

25th anniv. of the founding of the Albanian Workers Party.

Russian Wolfhound — A216

Dogs: 15q, Sheep dog. 25q, English setter. 45q, English springer spaniel. 60q, Bulldog. 65q, Saint Bernard. 80q, Dachshund.

1966   **Litho.**   **Perf. 12½x12**

986	A216	10q green & multi	.20 .20
987	A216	15q multicolored	.30 .20
988	A216	25q lilac & multi	.40 .20
989	A216	45q rose & multi	.75 .35
990	A216	60q brown & multi	1.00 .40
991	A216	65q ultra & multi	1.10 .45
992	A216	80q blue grn & multi	1.50 .50

Nos. 986-992 (7)   5.25 2.30

Ndre Mjeda A217   Proclamation A218

1966   **Perf. 12½x12**

993	A217	25q brt bl & dk brn	.50 .20
994	A217	1.75 l brt grn & dk brn	2.00 .65

Birth Centenary of the priest Ndre Mjeda.

1966   **Perf. 11½x12, 12x11½**

Designs: 10q, Banner, man and woman holding gun and axe, horiz. 1.85 l, man with axe and banner and partisan with gun.

995	A218	5q lt brn, red & blk	.20 .20
996	A218	10q red, blk, gray & bl	.20 .20
997	A218	1.85 l red, blk & salmon	1.50 .30

Nos. 995-997 (3)   1.90 .70

Albanian Communist Party, 25th anniv.

Golden Eagle — A219

Birds of Prey: 15q, European sea eagle. 25q, Griffon vulture. 40q, Common sparrowhawk. 50q, Osprey. 70q, Egyptian vulture. 90q, Kestrel.

1966, Dec. 20   **Litho.**   **Perf. 11½x12**

998	A219	10q gray & multi	.20 .20
999	A219	15q multicolored	.25 .20
1000	A219	25q citron & multi	.45 .20
1001	A219	40q multicolored	.80 .20
1002	A219	50q multicolored	1.00 .25
1003	A219	70q yellow & multi	1.40 .35
1004	A219	90q multicolored	1.90 .45

Nos. 998-1004 (7)   6.00 1.85

Hake A220

Fish: 15q, Red mullet. 25q, Opah. 40q, Atlantic wolf fish. 65q, Lumpfish. 80q, Swordfish. 1.15 l, Shorthorn sculpin.

1967, Jan.   **Photo.**   **Perf. 12x11½**
Fish in Natural Colors

1005	A220	10q blue	.20 .20
1006	A220	15q lt yellow grn	.25 .20
1007	A220	25q Prus blue	.35 .20
1008	A220	40q emerald	.85 .20
1009	A220	65q brt blue grn	.95 .25
1010	A220	80q blue	1.40 .35
1011	A220	1.15 l brt green	1.75 .60

Nos. 1005-1011 (7)   5.75 2.00

White Pelican A221

Designs: Various groups of pelicans.

1967, Feb. 22   **Litho.**   **Perf. 12**

1012	A221	10q pink & multi	.20 .20
1013	A221	15q pink & multi	.25 .20
1014	A221	25q pink & multi	.55 .20
1015	A221	50q pink & multi	1.00 .20
1016	A221	2 l pink & multi	3.75 .75

Nos. 1012-1016 (5)   5.75 1.55

Camellia A222

Flowers: 10q, Chrysanthemum. 15q, Hollyhock. 25q, Flowering Maple. 35q, Peony. 65q, Gladiolus. 80q, Freesia. 1.15 l, Carnation.

Unwmk.
1967, Apr. 12   Litho.   *Perf. 12*
Flowers in Natural Colors
1017	A222	5q pale brown	.20	.20
1018	A222	10q lt lilac	.20	.20
1019	A222	15q gray	.25	.20
1020	A222	25q ultra	.40	.20
1021	A222	35q lt blue	.70	.20
1022	A222	65q lt blue grn	1.00	.20
1023	A222	80q lt bluish gray	1.50	.25
1024	A222	1.15 l dull yellow	2.00	.40
		Nos. 1017-1024 (8)	6.25	1.85

Congress Emblem and Power Station — A223

1967, Apr. 24   Litho.   *Perf. 12*
1025	A223	25q multi	.25	.20
1026	A223	1.75 l multi	2.25	.45

Cong. of the Union of Professional Workers, Tirana, Apr. 24.

Rose — A224

1967, May 15   *Perf. 12x12½*
Various Roses in Natural Colors.
1027	A224	5q blue gray	.20	.20
1028	A224	10q brt blue	.20	.20
1029	A224	15q rose violet	.20	.20
1030	A224	25q lemon	.35	.20
1031	A224	35q brt grnsh blue	.45	.20
1032	A224	65q gray	.85	.20
1033	A224	80q brown	1.10	.25
1034	A224	1.65 l gray green	2.50	.45
		Nos. 1027-1034 (8)	5.85	1.90

Seashore, Bregdet Borsh — A225

Views: 15q, Buthrotum, vert. 25q, Shore, Fshati Piqeras. 45q, Shore, Bregdet. 50q, Shore, Bregdet Himare. 65q, Ship, Sarande (Santi Quaranta). 80q, Shore, Dhermi. 1 l, Sunset, Bregdet, vert.

Perf. 12x12½, 12½x12
1967, June 10
1035	A225	15q multicolored	.20	.20
1036	A225	20q multicolored	.25	.20
1037	A225	25q multicolored	.30	.20
1038	A225	45q multicolored	.80	.20
1039	A225	50q multicolored	.90	.20
1040	A225	65q multicolored	1.25	.20
1041	A225	80q multicolored	1.40	.25
1042	A225	1 l multicolored	1.90	.35
		Nos. 1035-1042 (8)	7.00	1.80

Fawn A226

Roe Deer: 20q, Stag, vert. 25q, Doe, vert. 30q, Young stag and doe. 35q, Doe and fawn.

40q, Young stag, vert. 65q, Stag and doe, vert. 70q, Running stag and does.

Perf. 12½x12, 12x12½
1967, July 20   Litho.
1043	A226	15q multicolored	.35	.20
1044	A226	20q multicolored	.35	.20
1045	A226	25q multicolored	.55	.20
1046	A226	30q multicolored	.65	.20
1047	A226	35q multicolored	.80	.20
1048	A226	40q multicolored	1.10	.20
1049	A226	65q multicolored	1.60	.30
1050	A226	70q multicolored	1.60	.50
		Nos. 1043-1050 (8)	7.00	2.00

Man and Woman from Madhe A227

Regional Costumes: 20q, Woman from Zadrimes. 25q, Dancer and drummer, Kukesit. 45q, Woman spinner, Dardhes. 50q, Farm couple, Myseqese. 65q, Dancer with tambourine, Tirana. 80q, Man and woman, Dropullit. 1 l, Piper, Laberise.

1967, Aug. 25   *Perf. 12*
1051	A227	15q tan & multi	.20	.20
1052	A227	20q lt yellow grn	.20	.20
1053	A227	25q multicolored	.20	.20
1054	A227	45q sky blue & multi	.35	.20
1055	A227	50q lemon & multi	.55	.25
1056	A227	65q pink & multi	.60	.35
1057	A227	80q multicolored	.80	.40
1058	A227	1 l gray & multi	1.10	.55
		Nos. 1051-1058 (8)	4.00	2.35

Fighters and Newspaper — A228

75q, Printing plant, newspapers, microphone. 2 l, People holding newspaper.

1967, Aug. 25   *Perf. 12½x12*
1059	A228	25q multicolored	.40	.20
1060	A228	75q pink & multi	.85	.25
1061	A228	2 l multicolored	2.25	.55
		Nos. 1059-1061 (3)	3.50	1.00

Issued for the Day of the Press.

Street Scene, by Kolë Idromeno — A229

Hakmarrja Battalion, by Sali Shijaku — A230

Designs: 20q, David, fresco by Onufri, 16th century, vert. 45q, Woman's head, ancient mosaic, vert. 50q, Men on horseback from 16th century icon, vert. 65q, Farm Women, by Zef Shoshi. 80q, Street Scene, by Vangjush Mio. 1 l, Bride, by Kolë Idromeno, vert.

Perf. 12, 12x12½, (A230)
1967, Oct. 25   Litho.
1062	A229	15q multicolored	.20	.20
1063	A229	20q multicolored	.25	.20
1064	A230	25q multicolored	.35	.20
1065	A229	45q multicolored	.75	.20
1066	A229	50q multicolored	.95	.20
1067	A230	65q multicolored	1.10	.20
1068	A230	80q multicolored	1.50	.25
1069	A230	1 l multicolored	2.40	.30
		Nos. 1062-1069 (8)	7.50	1.75

Lenin at Storming of Winter Palace — A231

Rabbit — A232

Designs: 15q, Lenin and Stalin, horiz. 50q, Lenin and Stalin addressing meeting. 1.10 l, Storming of the Winter Palace, horiz.

1967, Nov. 7   *Perf. 12*
1070	A231	15q red & multi	.25	.20
1071	A231	25q slate grn & blk	.55	.20
1072	A231	50q brn, blk & brn		
		vio	.85	.20
1073	A231	1.10 l lilac, gray & blk	2.75	.25
		Nos. 1070-1073 (4)	4.40	.85

50th anniv. of the Russian October Revolution.

1967, Nov. 25

Designs: Various hares and rabbits. The 15q, 25q, 35q, 40q and 1 l are horizontal.
1074	A232	15q orange & multi	.20	.20
1075	A232	20q brt yel & multi	.20	.20
1076	A232	25q lt brn & multi	.25	.20
1077	A232	35q multicolored	.35	.20
1078	A232	40q yellow & multi	.65	.20
1079	A232	50q pink & multi	.75	.20
1080	A232	65q multicolored	1.25	.30
1081	A232	1 l lilac & multi	2.00	.50
		Nos. 1074-1081 (8)	5.65	2.00

University, Torch and Book — A233

1967   Litho.   *Perf. 12*
1082	A233	25q multi	.25	.20
1083	A233	1.75 l multi	1.50	.35

10th anniv. of the founding of the State University, Tirana.

Coat of Arms and Soldiers A234

65q, Arms, Factory, grain, flag, gun, radio tower. 1.20 l, Arms, hand holding torch.

1967   *Perf. 12x11½*
1084	A234	15q multi	.20	.20
1085	A234	65q multi	.55	.20
1086	A234	1.20 l multi	1.00	.20
		Nos. 1084-1086 (3)	1.75	.60

25th anniversary of the Democratic Front.

Turkey A235

Designs: 20q, Duck. 25q, Hen. 45q, Rooster. 50q, Guinea fowl. 65q, Goose, horiz. 80q, Mallard, horiz. 1 l, Chicks, horiz.

Perf. 12x12½, 12½x12
1967, Nov. 25   Photo.
1087	A235	15q gold & multi	.25	.20
1088	A235	20q gold & multi	.25	.20
1089	A235	25q gold & multi	.30	.20
1090	A235	45q gold & multi	.50	.20
1091	A235	50q gold & multi	.75	.20
1092	A235	65q gold & multi	.95	.20
1093	A235	80q gold & multi	1.75	.30
1094	A235	1 l gold & multi	2.25	.40
		Nos. 1087-1094 (8)	7.00	1.90

Skanderbeg A236

Designs: 10q, Arms of Skanderbeg. 25q, Helmet and sword. 30q, Kruje Castle. 35q, Petreles Castle. 65q, Berati Castle. 80q, Skanderbeg addressing national chiefs. 90q, Battle of Albulenes.

1967, Dec. 10   Litho.   *Perf. 12x12½*
Medallion in Bister and Dark Brown
1095	A236	10q gold & violet	.20	.20
1096	A236	15q gold & rose car	.20	.20
1097	A236	25q gold & vio bl	.20	.20
1098	A236	30q gold & dk blue	.25	.20
1099	A236	35q gold & maroon	.35	.20
1100	A236	65q gold & green	.60	.20
1101	A236	80q gold & gray brn	.95	.25
1102	A236	90q gold & ultra	1.75	.30
		Nos. 1095-1102 (8)	4.50	1.75

500th anniv. of the death of Skanderbeg (George Castriota), national hero.

10th Winter Olympic Games, Grenoble, France, Feb. 6-18 — A237

Designs: 15q, 2 l, Winter Olympics emblem. 25q, Ice hockey. 30q, Women's figure skating. 50q, Slalom. 80q, Downhill skiing. 1 l, Ski jump.

1967-68
1103	A237	15q multicolored	.20	.20
1104	A237	25q multicolored	.20	.20
1105	A237	30q multicolored	.20	.20
1106	A237	50q multicolored	.30	.20
1107	A237	80q multicolored	.60	.20
1108	A237	1 l multicolored	1.25	.25
		Nos. 1103-1108 (6)	2.75	1.25

Miniature Sheet
Imperf
1109	A237	2 l red, gray & brt bl ('68)	6.00	6.00

Nos. 1103-1108 issued Dec. 29, 1967.

Skanderbeg Monument, Kruje — A238

Designs: 10q, Skanderbeg monument, Tirana. 15q, Skanderbeg portrait, Uffizi Galleries, Florence. 25q, engraved portrait of Gen. Tanush Topia. 35q, Portrait of Gen.

Gjergj Arianti, horiz. 65q, Portrait bust of Skanderbeg by O. Paskali. 80q, Title page of "The Life of Skanderbeg." 90q, Skanderbeg battling the Turks, painting by S. Rrota, horiz.

Perf. 12x12½, 12½x12

1968, Jan. 17   **Litho.**

1110	A238	10q multicolored	.20 .20
1111	A238	15q multicolored	.25 .20
1112	A238	25q blk, yel & lt bl	.35 .20
1113	A238	30q multicolored	.40 .20
1114	A238	35q lt vio, pink & blk	.65 .20
1115	A238	65q multicolored	1.00 .25
1116	A238	80q pink, blk & yel	1.25 .45
1117	A238	90q beige & multi	1.75 .60
		Nos. 1110-1117 (8)	5.85 2.30

500th anniv. of the death of Skanderbeg (George Castriota), national hero.

Carnation
A239

1968, Feb. 15   **Perf. 12**
Various Carnations in Natural Colors

1118	A239	15q green	.20 .20
1119	A239	20q dk brown	.20 .20
1120	A239	25q brt blue	.20 .20
1121	A239	50q gray olive	.75 .20
1122	A239	80q bluish gray	1.10 .20
1123	A239	1.10 l violet gray	1.50 .40
		Nos. 1118-1123 (6)	3.95 1.40

"Electrification"
A240

65q, Farm tractor, horiz. 1.10 l, Cow & herd.

1968, Mar. 5   **Litho.**   **Perf. 12**

1124	A240	25q multi	.25 .20
1125	A240	65q multi	.75 .20
1126	A240	1.10 l multi	1.00 .35
		Nos. 1124-1126 (3)	2.00 .80

Fifth Farm Cooperatives Congress.

Goat
A241

Various goats. 15q, 20q, 25q are vertical.

1968, Mar. 25   **Perf. 12x12½, 12½x12**

1127	A241	15q multi	.20 .20
1128	A241	20q multi	.20 .20
1129	A241	25q multi	.20 .20
1130	A241	30q multi	.30 .20
1131	A241	40q multi	.40 .20
1132	A241	50q multi	.45 .20
1133	A241	80q multi	.80 .20
1134	A241	1.40 l multi	2.00 .35
		Nos. 1127-1134 (8)	4.55 1.75

Zef N.
Jubani — A242

Physician and
Hospital — A243

1968, Mar. 30   **Perf. 12**

1135	A242	25q yellow & choc	.25 .20
1136	A242	1.75 l lt violet & blk	1.25 .50

Sesquicentennial of the birth of Zef N. Jubani, writer and scholar.

Perf. 12½x12, 12x12½

1968, Apr. 7   **Litho.**

Designs (World Health Organization Emblem and): 65q, Hospital and microscope, horiz. 1.10 l, Mother feeding child.

1137	A243	25q green & claret	.20 .20
1138	A243	65q black, yel & bl	.55 .25
1139	A243	1.10 l black & dp org	1.00 .35
		Nos. 1137-1139 (3)	1.75 .80

20th anniv. of WHO.

Scientist
A244

Women: 15q, Militia member. 60q, Farm worker. 1 l, Factory worker.

1968, Apr. 14   **Perf. 12**

1140	A244	15q ver & dk red	.35 .20
1141	A244	25q blue grn & grn	.50 .20
1142	A244	60q dull yel & brn	.80 .20
1143	A244	1 l lt vio & vio	2.00 .40
		Nos. 1140-1143 (4)	3.65 1.00

Albanian Women's Organization, 25th anniv.

Karl Marx
A245

Designs: 25q, Marx lecturing to students. 65q, "Das Kapital," "Communist Manifesto" and marching crowd. 95q, Full-face portrait.

1968, May 5   **Litho.**   **Perf. 12**

1144	A245	15q gray, dk bl & bis	.25 .20
1145	A245	25q brn vio, dk brn & dl yel	.50 .20
1146	A245	65q gray, blk, brn & car	1.25 .20
1147	A245	95q gray, ocher & blk	2.25 .50
		Nos. 1144-1147 (4)	4.25 1.10

Karl Marx, 150th birth anniversary.

Heliopsis
A246

Flowers: 20q, Red flax. 25q, Orchid. 30q, Gloxinia. 40q, Turk's-cap lily. 80q, Amaryllis. 1.40 l, Red magnolia.

1968, May 10   **Perf. 12x12½**

1148	A246	15q gold & multi	.20 .20
1149	A246	20q gold & multi	.20 .20
1150	A246	25q gold & multi	.30 .20
1151	A246	30q gold & multi	.35 .20
1152	A246	40q gold & multi	.35 .20
1153	A246	1 l gold & multi	1.00 .40
1154	A246	1.40 l gold & multi	1.60 .60
		Nos. 1148-1154 (7)	4.00 2.00

Proclamation of Prizren — A247

25q, Abdyl Frasheri. 40q, House in Prizren.

1968, June 10   **Litho.**   **Perf. 12**

1155	A247	25q emerald & blk	.20 .20
1156	A247	40q multicolored	.45 .20
1157	A247	85q yellow & multi	.85 .25
		Nos. 1155-1157 (3)	1.50 .65

League of Prizren against the Turks, 90th anniv.

Shepherd, by
A. Kushi — A248

Paintings from Tirana Art Gallery: 20q, View of Tirana, by V. Mio, horiz. 25q, Mountaineer, by G. Madhi. 40q, Refugees, by A. Buza. 80q, Guerrillas of Shahin Matrakut, by S. Xega. 1.50 l, Portrait of an Old Man, by S. Papadhimitri. 1.70 l, View of Scutari, by S. Rrota. 2.50 l, Woman in Scutari Costume, by Z. Colombi.

1968, June 20   **Perf. 12x12½**

1158	A248	15q gold & multi	.20 .20
1159	A248	20q gold & multi	.20 .20
1160	A248	25q gold & multi	.25 .20
1161	A248	40q gold & multi	.45 .20
1162	A248	80q gold & multi	.75 .20
1163	A248	1.50 l gold & multi	1.25 .25
1164	A248	1.70 l gold & multi	1.50 .50
		Nos. 1158-1164 (7)	4.60 1.75

Miniature Sheet
Perf. 12½xImperf.

1165	A248	2.50 l multi	2.00 2.00

No. 1165 contains one stamp, size: 50x71mm.

Soldier and Guns — A249

25q, Sailor, warships. 65q, Aviator, planes, vert. 95q, Militiamen, woman.

1968, July 10   **Litho.**   **Perf. 12**

1166	A249	15q multicolored	.30 .20
1167	A249	25q multicolored	.45 .20
1168	A249	65q multicolored	1.25 .20
1169	A249	95q multicolored	2.50 .20
		Nos. 1166-1169 (4)	4.50 .80

25th anniversary of the People's Army.

Squid
A250

Designs: 20q, Crayfish. 25q, Whelk. 50q, Crab. 70q, Spiny lobster. 80q, Shore crab. 90q, Norway lobster.

1968, Aug. 20

1170	A250	15q multicolored	.20 .20
1171	A250	20q multicolored	.20 .20
1172	A250	25q multicolored	.25 .20
1173	A250	50q multicolored	.45 .20
1174	A250	70q multicolored	.75 .25
1175	A250	80q multicolored	.90 .30
1176	A250	90q multicolored	1.25 .35
		Nos. 1170-1176 (7)	4.00 1.70

Women's Relay Race — A251

Sport: 20q, Running. 25q, Women's discus. 30q, Equestrian. 40q, High jump. 50q, Women's hurdling. 80q, Soccer. 1.40 l, Woman diver. 2 l, Olympic stadium.

1968, Sept. 23   **Photo.**   **Perf. 12**

1177	A251	15q multicolored	.20 .20
1178	A251	20q multicolored	.20 .20
1179	A251	25q multicolored	.20 .20
1180	A251	30q multicolored	.20 .20
1181	A251	40q multicolored	.25 .20
1182	A251	50q multicolored	.35 .20
1183	A251	80q multicolored	.60 .20
1184	A251	1.40 l multicolored	1.00 .35
		Nos. 1177-1184 (8)	3.00 1.75

Souvenir Sheet
Perf. 12½ Horizontally

1185	A251	2 l multicolored	2.25 2.00

19th Olympic Games, Mexico City, Oct. 12-27. No. 1185 contains one rectangular stamp, size: 64x54mm. Value of imperfs., #1177-1184 $7, #1185 $5.

Enver
Hoxha — A252

1968, Oct. 16   **Litho.**   **Perf. 12**

1186	A252	25q blue gray	.35 .20
1187	A252	35q rose brown	.50 .20
1188	A252	80q violet	.90 .35
1189	A252	1.10 l brown	1.10 .50
		Nos. 1186-1189 (4)	2.85 1.25

Souvenir Sheet
Imperf

1190	A252	1.50 l rose red, bl vio & gold	55.00 40.00

60th birthday of Enver Hoxha, First Secretary of the Central Committee of the Communist Party of Albania.

Book and
Pupils
A253

1968, Nov. 14   **Photo.**

1191	A253	15q mar & slate grn	.45 .20
1192	A253	85q gray olive & sepia	2.75 .20

60th anniv. of the Congress of Monastir, Nov. 14-22, 1908, which adopted a unified Albanian alphabet.

Waxwing — A254

Birds: 20q, Rose-colored starling. 25q, King-fishers. 50q, Long-tailed tits. 80q, Wallcreeper. 1.10 l, Bearded tit.

1968, Nov. 15   **Litho.**
Birds in Natural Colors

1193	A254	15q lt blue & blk	.20	.20
1194	A254	20q bister & blk	.30	.20
1195	A254	25q pink & blk	.30	.20
1196	A254	50q lt yel grn & blk	.60	.20
1197	A254	80q bis brn & blk	1.25	.30
1198	A254	1.10 l pale grn & blk	1.75	.50
		Nos. 1193-1198 (6)	4.40	1.60

Mao Tse-tung — A255

1968, Dec. 26   **Litho.**   **Perf. 12½x12**

1199	A255	25q gold, red & blk	.40	.20
1200	A255	1.75 l gold, red & blk	2.00	.30

75th birthday of Mao Tse-tung.

Adem Reka and Crane — A256

Portraits: 10q, Pjeter Lleshi and power lines. 15q, Mohammed Shehu and Myrteza Kepi. 25q, Shkurte Vata and women railroad work-ers. 65q, Agron Elezi, frontier guard. 80q, Ismet Bruçaj and mountain road. 1.30 l, Fuat Cela, blind revolutionary.

1969, Feb. 10   **Litho.**   **Perf. 12x12½**

1201	A256	5q multicolored	.20	.20
1202	A256	10q multicolored	.20	.20
1203	A256	15q multicolored	.20	.20
1204	A256	25q multicolored	.20	.20
1205	A256	65q multicolored	.40	.20
1206	A256	80q multicolored	.75	.20
1207	A256	1.30 l multicolored	1.25	.20
		Nos. 1201-1207 (7)	3.20	1.40

Contemporary heroine and heroes.

Meteorological Instruments — A257

Designs: 25q, Water gauge. 1.60 l, Radar, balloon and isobars.

1969, Feb. 25   **Perf. 12**

1208	A257	15q multicolored	.25	.20
1209	A257	25q ultra, org & blk	.45	.20
1210	A257	1.60 l rose vio, yel & blk	2.50	.60
		Nos. 1208-1210 (3)	3.20	1.00

20th anniv. of Albanian hydrometeorology.

Partisans, 1944, by F. Haxmiu — A258

Paintings: 5q, Student Revolutionists, by P. Mele, vert. 65q, Steel Mill, by C. Ceka. 80q, Reconstruction, by V. Kilica. 1.10 l, Harvest, by N. Jonuzi. 1.15 l, Terraced Landscape, by S. Kaceli. 2 l, Partisans' Meeting.

Perf. 12x12½, 12½x12
1969, Apr. 25   **Litho.**
Size: 31½x41½mm

1211	A258	5q buff & multi	.20	.20

Size: 51½x30½mm

1212	A258	25q buff & multi	.20	.20

Size: 40½x32mm

1213	A258	65q buff & multi	.30	.20

Size: 51½x30½mm

1214	A258	80q buff & multi	.65	.20
1215	A258	1.10 l buff & multi	.70	.20
1216	A258	1.15 l buff & multi	.95	.20
		Nos. 1211-1216 (6)	3.00	1.20

Miniature Sheet
Imperf
Size: 111x90mm

1217	A258	2 l ocher & multi	2.25	1.75

Leonardo da Vinci, Self-portrait A259

Designs (after Leonardo da Vinci): 35q, Lil-ies. 40q, Design for a flying machine, horiz. 1 l, Portrait of Beatrice. No. 1222, Portrait of a Noblewoman. No. 1223, Mona Lisa.

Perf. 12x12½, 12½x12
1969, May 2   **Litho.**

1218	A259	25q gold & sepia	.20	.20
1219	A259	35q gold & sepia	.40	.20
1220	A259	40q gold & sepia	.45	.20
1221	A259	1 l gold & multi	1.25	.20
1222	A259	2 l gold & sepia	2.25	.55
		Nos. 1218-1222 (5)	4.55	1.35

Miniature Sheet
Imperf

1223	A259	2 l gold & multi	3.25	2.25

Leonardo da Vinci (1452-1519), painter, sculptor, architect and engineer.

First Congress Meeting Place A260

Designs: 1 l, Albanian coat of arms. 2.25 l, Two partisans with guns and flag.

1969, May 24   **Perf. 12**

1224	A260	25q lt grn, blk & red	.35	.20
1225	A260	2.25 l multi	2.50	.85

Souvenir Sheet

1226	A260	1 l gold, bl, blk & red	25.00	20.00

25th anniversary of the First Anti-Fascist Congress of Permet, May 24, 1944.

Albanian Violet — A261

Designs: Violets and Pansies.

1969, June 30   **Litho.**   **Perf. 12x12½**

1227	A261	5q gold & multi	.20	.20
1228	A261	10q gold & multi	.20	.20
1229	A261	15q gold & multi	.30	.20
1230	A261	20q gold & multi	.35	.20
1231	A261	25q gold & multi	.35	.20
1232	A261	80q gold & multi	1.00	.30
1233	A261	1.95 l gold & multi	1.60	.65
		Nos. 1227-1233 (7)	4.00	2.00

Plum, Fruit and Blossoms A262

Designs: Blossoms and Fruits.

1969, Aug. 10   **Litho.**   **Perf. 12**

1234	A262	10q shown	.20	.20
1235	A262	15q Lemon	.20	.20
1236	A262	25q Pomegranate	.30	.20
1237	A262	50q Cherry	.60	.20
1238	A262	80q Peach	.95	.20
1239	A262	1.20 l Apple	1.75	.35
		Nos. 1234-1239 (6)	4.00	1.35

Basketball A263

Designs: 10q, 80q, 2.20 l, Various views of basketball game. 25q, Hand aiming ball at basket and map of Europe, horiz.

1969, Sept. 15   **Litho.**   **Perf. 12**

1240	A263	10q multi	.20	.20
1241	A263	15q buff & multi	.20	.20
1242	A263	25q blue & multi	.25	.20
1243	A263	80q multi	.65	.20
1244	A263	2.20 l multi	1.60	.50
		Nos. 1240-1244 (5)	2.90	1.30

16th European Basketball Championships, Naples, Italy, Sept. 27-Oct. 5.

Runner A264

Designs: 5q, Games' emblem. 10q, Woman gymnast. 20q, Pistol shooting. 25q, Swimmer at start. 80q, Bicyclist. 95q, Soccer.

1969, Sept. 30

1245	A264	5q multicolored	.20	.20
1246	A264	10q multicolored	.20	.20
1247	A264	15q multicolored	.20	.20
1248	A264	20q multicolored	.30	.20
1249	A264	25q multicolored	.40	.20
1250	A264	80q multicolored	.80	.20
1251	A264	95q multicolored	1.25	.20
		Nos. 1245-1251 (7)	3.35	1.40

Second National Spartakiad.

Electronic Technicians, Steel Ladle — A265

25q, Mao Tse-tung with microphones. 1.40 l, Children holding Mao's red book.

1969, Oct. 1   **Litho.**   **Perf. 12**

1252	A265	25q multi, vert.	.35	.20
1253	A265	85q multi	1.40	.40
1254	A265	1.40 l multi, vert.	2.25	.60
		Nos. 1252-1254 (3)	4.00	1.20

People's Republic of China, 20th anniv.

Enver Hoxha A266

Designs: 80q, Pages from Berat resolution. 1.45 l, Partisans with flag.

1969, Oct. 20   **Litho.**   **Perf. 12**

1255	A266	25q multicolored	.30	.20
1256	A266	80q gray & multi	.60	.20
1257	A266	1.45 l ocher & multi	1.90	.40
		Nos. 1255-1257 (3)	2.80	.80

25th anniv. of the 2nd reunion of the Natl. Antifascist Liberation Council, Berat.

Soldiers — A267

Designs: 30q, Oil refinery. 35q, Combine harvester. 45q, Hydroelectric station and dam. 55q, Militia woman, man and soldier. 1.10 l, Dancers and musicians.

1969, Nov. 29

1258	A267	25q multi	.25	.20
1259	A267	30q multi	.30	.20
1260	A267	35q multi	.40	.20
1261	A267	45q multi	.70	.20
1262	A267	55q multi	1.00	.25
1263	A267	1.10 l multi	1.75	.40
		Nos. 1258-1263 (6)	4.40	1.45

25th anniv. of the socialist republic.

Joseph V. Stalin, (1879-1953), Russian Political Leader — A268

1969, Dec. 21   Litho.   *Perf. 12*
1264	A268	15q lilac	.20	.20
1265	A268	25q slate blue	.20	.20
1266	A268	1 l brown	.75	.20
1267	A268	1.10 l violet blue	1.25	.20
		Nos. 1264-1267 (4)	2.40	.80

Head of Woman A269

Greco-Roman Mosaics: 25q, Geometrical floor design, horiz. 80q, Bird and tree, horiz. 1.10 l, Floor with birds and grapes, horiz. 1.20 l, Fragment with corn within oval design.

1969, Dec. 25   *Perf. 12½x12*
1268	A269	15q gold & multi	.20	.20
1269	A269	25q gold & multi	.20	.20
1270	A269	80q gold & multi	.45	.20
1271	A269	1.10 l gold & multi	.70	.20
1272	A269	1.20 l gold & multi	.95	.30
		Nos. 1268-1272 (5)	2.50	1.10

Cancellation of 1920 — A270

25q, Proclamation and congress site.

1970, Jan. 21   Litho.   *Perf. 12*
1273	A270	25q red, gray & blk	.20	.20
1274	A270	1.25 l dk grn, yel & blk	1.25	.20

Congress of Louchnia, 50th anniversary.

Worker, Student and Flag A271

1970, Feb. 11   *Perf. 12½x12*
1275	A271	25q red & multi	.25	.25
1276	A271	1.75 l red & multi	1.75	.50

Vocational organizations in Albania, 25th anniv.

Turk's-cap Lily — A272

Lilies: 5q, Cernum, vert. 15q, Madonna, vert. 25q, Royal, vert. 1.10 l, Tiger. 1.15 l, Albanian.

Perf. 11½x12, 12x11½
1970, Mar. 10   Litho.
1277	A272	5q multi	.20	.20
1278	A272	15q multi	.20	.20
1279	A272	25q multi	.35	.20
1280	A272	80q multi	.75	.20
1281	A272	1.10 l multi	1.10	.20
1282	A272	1.15 l multi	1.40	.25
		Nos. 1277-1282 (6)	4.00	1.25

Lenin A273

Designs (Lenin): 5q, Portrait, vert. 25q, As volunteer construction worker. 95q, Addressing crowd. 1.10 l, Saluting, vert.

1970, Apr. 22   Litho.   *Perf. 12*
1283	A273	5q multi	.20	.20
1284	A273	15q multi	.20	.20
1285	A273	25q multi	.20	.20
1286	A273	95q multi	.60	.20
1287	A273	1.10 l multi	1.10	.20
		Nos. 1283-1287 (5)	2.30	1.00

Centenary of birth of Lenin (1870-1924).

Frontier Guard A274

1970, Apr. 25
1288	A274	25q multi	.25	.20
1289	A274	1.25 l multi	2.50	.50

25th anniversary of Frontier Guards.

Soccer Players — A275

Designs: 5q, Jules Rimet Cup and globes. 10q, Aztec Stadium, Mexico City. 25q, Defending goal. 65q, 80q, No. 1296, Two soccer players in various plays. No. 1297, Mexican horseman and volcano Popocatepetl.

1970, May 15   Litho.   *Perf. 12½x12*
1290	A275	5q multicolored	.20	.20
1291	A275	10q multicolored	.20	.20
1292	A275	15q multicolored	.20	.20
1293	A275	25q lt green & multi	.20	.20
1294	A275	65q pink & multi	.30	.20
1295	A275	80q lt blue & multi	.55	.20
1296	A275	2 l yellow & multi	1.50	.30
		Nos. 1290-1296 (7)	3.15	1.45

Souvenir Sheet
Perf 12 x Imperf
1297	A275	2 l multicolored	2.25	1.75

World Soccer Championships for the Jules Rimet Cup, Mexico City, May 31-June 21, 1970. No. 1297 contains one large horizontal stamp. Nos. 1290-1297 exist imperf.

UPU Headquarters and Monument, Bern — A276

1970, May 30   Litho.   *Perf. 12½x12*
1298	A276	25q ultra, gray & blk	.20	.20
1299	A276	1.10 l org, buff & blk	.65	.20
1300	A276	1.15 l grn, gray & blk	.90	.25
		Nos. 1298-1300 (3)	1.75	.65

Inauguration of the new UPU Headquarters in Bern.

Bird and Grapes Mosaic A277

Mosaics, 5th-6th centuries, excavated near Pogradec: 10q, Waterfowl and grapes. 20q, Bird and tree stump. 25q, Bird and leaves. 65q, Fish. 2.25 l, Peacock, vert.

1970, July 10   *Perf. 12½x12, 12x12½*
1301	A277	5q multi	.20	.20
1302	A277	10q multi	.20	.20
1303	A277	20q multi	.20	.20
1304	A277	25q multi	.30	.20
1305	A277	65q multi	.55	.20
1306	A277	2.25 l multi	1.75	.35
		Nos. 1301-1306 (6)	3.20	1.35

Fruit Harvest and Dancers A278

Designs: 25q, Contour-plowed fields and conference table. 80q, Cattle and newspapers. 1.30 l, Wheat harvest.

1970, Aug. 28   Litho.   *Perf. 12x11½*
1307	A278	15q brt violet & blk	.20	.20
1308	A278	25q dp blue & blk	.20	.20
1309	A278	80q dp brown & blk	.60	.20
1310	A278	1.30 l org brn & blk	.90	.20
		Nos. 1307-1310 (4)	1.90	.80

25th anniv. of the agrarian reform law.

Attacking Partisans — A279

Designs: 25q, Partisans with horses and flag. 1.60 l, Partisans.

1970, Sept. 3   *Perf. 12*
1311	A279	15q org brn & blk	.20	.20
1312	A279	25q brn, yel & blk	.20	.20
1313	A279	1.60 l dp grn & blk	1.25	.30
		Nos. 1311-1313 (3)	1.65	.70

50th anniversary of liberation of Vlona.

Miners, by Nexhmedin Zajmi — A280

Paintings from the National Gallery, Tirana: 5q, Bringing in the Harvest, by Isuf Sulovari, vert. 15q, The Activists, by Dhimitraq Trebicka, vert. 65q, Instruction of Partisans, by Hasan Nallbani. 95q, Architectural Planning, by Vilson Kilica. No. 1319, Woman Machinist, by Zef Shoshi, vert. No. 1320, Partisan Destroying Tank, by Sali Shijaku, vert.

Perf. 12½x12, 12x12½
1970, Sept. 25   Litho.
1314	A280	5q multicolored	.20	.20
1315	A280	15q multicolored	.20	.20
1316	A280	25q multicolored	.20	.20
1317	A280	65q Architectural plan	.25	.20
1318	A280	95q multicolored	.40	.20
1319	A280	2 l multicolored	1.75	.30
		Nos. 1314-1319 (6)	3.00	1.30

Miniature Sheet
Imperf
1320	A280	2 l multicolored	2.00	1.25

Electrification Map of Albania — A281

Designs: 25q, Light bulb, hammer and sickle emblem, map of Albania and power graph. 80q, Linemen at work. 1.10 l, Use of electricity on the farm, in home and business.

1970, Oct. 25   Litho.   *Perf. 12*
1321	A281	15q multi	.20	.20
1322	A281	25q multi	.20	.20
1323	A281	80q multi	.70	.20
1324	A281	1.10 l multi	1.00	.20
		Nos. 1321-1324 (4)	2.10	.80

Albanian village electrification completion.

Friedrich Engels A282

Designs: 1.10 l, Engels as young man. 1.15 l, Engels addressing crowd.

1970, Nov. 28   Litho.   *Perf. 12x12½*
1325	A282	25q bister & dk bl	.20	.20
1326	A282	1.10 l bis & dp claret	.60	.20
1327	A282	1.15 l bis & dk ol grn	.70	.25
		Nos. 1325-1327 (3)	1.50	.65

150th anniv. of the birth of Friedrich Engels (1820-95), German socialist, collaborator with Karl Marx.

Ludwig van Beethoven A283

Designs: 5q, Birthplace, Bonn. 25q, 65q, 1.10 l, various portraits. 1.80 l, Scene from Fidelio, horiz.

1970, Dec. 16   Litho.   *Perf. 12*
1328	A283	5q dp plum & gold	.20	.20
1329	A283	15q brt rose lil & gold	.20	.20
1330	A283	25q green & gold	.20	.20
1331	A283	65q magenta & sil	.30	.20
1332	A283	1.10 l dk blue & gold	.60	.25
1333	A283	1.80 l black & sil	1.40	.45
		Nos. 1328-1333 (6)	2.90	1.50

Ludwig van Beethoven (1770-1827), composer.

Coat of Arms A284

Designs: 25q, Proclamation. 80q, Enver Hoxha reading proclamation. 1.30 l, Young people and proclamation.

1971, Jan. 11   Litho.   *Perf. 12*
1334	A284	15q lt bl, gold, blk & red	.20	.20
1335	A284	25q rose lil, blk, gold & gray	.20	.20
1336	A284	80q emerald, blk & gold	.55	.20
1337	A284	1.30 l yel org, blk & gold	.85	.25
		Nos. 1334-1337 (4)	1.80	.85

Declaration of the Republic, 25th anniv.

"Liberty"
A285

Black Men
A286

Designs: 50q, Women's brigade. 65q, Street battle, horiz. 1.10 l, Execution, horiz.

Perf. 12x11½, 11½x12

1971, Mar. 18   Litho.
1338	A285	25q dk bl & bl	.20	.20
1339	A285	50q slate green	.35	.20
1340	A285	65q dk brn & chest	.50	.20
1341	A285	1.10 l purple	.75	.20
		Nos. 1338-1341 (4)	1.80	.80

Centenary of the Paris Commune.

1971, Mar. 21   **Perf. 12x12½**

1.10 l, Men of 3 races. 1.15 l, Black protest.
1342	A286	25q blk & bis brn	.20	.20
1343	A286	1.10 l blk & rose car	.60	.20
1344	A286	1.15 l blk & ver	.70	.20
		Nos. 1342-1344 (3)	1.50	.60

Intl. year against racial discrimination.

Tulip — A287

Horseman, by Dürer — A288

Designs: Various tulips.

1971, Mar. 25
1345	A287	5q multi	.20	.20
1346	A287	10q yellow & multi	.20	.20
1347	A287	15q pink & multi	.20	.20
1348	A287	20q lt blue & multi	.20	.20
1349	A287	25q multi	.25	.20
1350	A287	80q multi	.50	.20
1351	A287	1 l multi	.75	.20
1352	A287	1.45 l citron & multi	1.10	.20
		Nos. 1345-1352 (8)	3.40	1.65

Perf. 11½x12, 12x11½

1971, May 15   Litho.

Art Works by Dürer: 15q, Three peasants. 25q, Dancing peasant couple. 45q, The bagpiper. 65q, View of Kalkrebut, horiz. 2.40 l, View of Trent, horiz. 2.50 l, Self-portrait.
1353	A288	10q blk & pale grn	.20	.20
1354	A288	15q black & pale lil	.20	.20
1355	A288	25q black & pale bl	.25	.20
1356	A288	45q blk & pale rose	.40	.20
1357	A288	65q black & multi	.60	.20
1358	A288	2.40 l black & multi	2.25	.35
		Nos. 1353-1358 (6)	3.90	1.35

Miniature Sheet
Imperf
1359	A288	2.50 l multi	3.00	1.75

Albrecht Dürer (1471-1528), German painter and engraver.

Satellite Orbiting Globe — A289

Designs: 1.20 l, Government Building, Tirana, and Red Star emblem. 2.20 l, like 60q, 2.50 l, Flag of People's Republic of China forming trajectory around globe.

1971, June 10   Litho.   **Perf. 12x12½**
1360	A289	60q purple & multi	.40	.20
1361	A289	1.20 l ver & multi	1.00	.25
1362	A289	2.20 l green & multi	1.60	.45

Imperf
1363	A289	2.50 l vio blk & multi	2.50	.90
		Nos. 1360-1363 (4)	5.50	1.80

Space developments of People's Republic of China.

Mao Tse-tung
A290

Designs: 1.05 l, House where Communist Party was founded, horiz. 1.20 l, Peking crowd with placards, horiz.

1971, July 1   **Perf. 12x12½, 12½x12**
1364	A290	25q silver & multi	.30	.20
1365	A290	1.05 l silver & multi	.95	.20
1366	A290	1.20 l silver & multi	1.25	.25
		Nos. 1364-1366 (3)	2.50	.65

50th anniv. of Chinese Communist Party.

Crested Titmouse — A291

1971, Aug. 15   Litho.   **Perf. 12½x12**
1367	A291	5q shown	.20	.20
1368	A291	10q European serin	.20	.20
1369	A291	15q Linnet	.20	.20
1370	A291	25q Firecrest	.45	.20
1371	A291	45q Rock thrush	.70	.20
1372	A291	60q Blue tit	1.00	.50
1373	A291	2.40 l Chaffinch	4.25	2.50
a.		Block of 7, #1367-1373 + label	10.00	5.00
		Nos. 1367-1373 (7)	7.00	4.00

Continuous design with bird's nest label at upper left.

Olympic Rings and Running — A292

Designs (Olympic Rings and): 10q, Hurdles. 15q, Canoeing. 25q, Gymnastics. 80q, Fencing. 1.05 l, Soccer. 2 l, Runner at finish line. 3.60 l, Diving, women's.

1971, Sept. 15
1374	A292	5q green & multi	.20	.20
1375	A292	10q multicolored	.20	.20
1376	A292	15q blue & multi	.20	.20
1377	A292	25q violet & multi	.20	.20
1378	A292	80q lilac & multi	.35	.20
1379	A292	1.05 l multicolored	.45	.20
1380	A292	3.60 l multicolored	2.50	.50
		Nos. 1374-1380 (7)	4.10	1.70

Souvenir Sheet
Imperf
1381	A292	2 l brt blue & multi	2.50	2.00

20th Olympic Games, Munich, Aug. 26-Sept. 10, 1972.

Workers with Flags
A293

Designs: 1.05 l, Party Headquarters, Tirana, and Red Star. 1.20 l, Rifle, star, flag and "VI."

1971, Nov. 1   **Perf. 12**
1382	A293	25q multi	.20	.20
1383	A293	1.05 l multi	.65	.20
1384	A293	1.20 l multi, vert.	.80	.25
		Nos. 1382-1384 (3)	1.65	.65

6th Congress of Workers' Party.

Factories and Workers
A294

Designs: 80q, "XXX" and flag, vert. 1.55 l, Enver Hoxha and flags.

1971, Nov. 8
1385	A294	15q gold, sil, lil & yel	.20	.20
1386	A294	80q gold, sil & red	.70	.20
1387	A294	1.55 l gold, sil, red & brn	1.40	.25
		Nos. 1385-1387 (3)	2.30	.65

30th anniversary of Workers' Party.

Construction Work, by M. Fushekati — A295

Contemporary Albanian Paintings: 5q, Young Man, by R. Kuci, vert. 25q, Partisan, by D. Jukniu, vert. 80q, Fliers, by S. Kristo. 1.20 l, Girl in Forest, by A. Sadikaj. 1.55 l, Warriors with Spears and Shields, by S. Kamberi. 2 l, Freedom Fighter, by I. Lulani.

Perf. 12x12½, 12½x12
1971, Nov. 20
1388	A295	5q gold & multi	.20	.20
1389	A295	15q gold & multi	.20	.20
1390	A295	25q gold & multi	.20	.20
1391	A295	80q gold & multi	.40	.20
1392	A295	1.20 l gold & multi	.90	.20
1393	A295	1.55 l gold & multi	1.10	.25
		Nos. 1388-1393 (6)	3.00	1.25

Miniature Sheet
Imperf
1394	A295	2 l gold & multi	2.25	1.75

Young Workers' Emblem — A296

1971, Nov. 23   **Perf. 12x12½**
1395	A296	15q lt blue & multi	.20	.20
1396	A296	1.35 l grnsh gray & multi	1.10	.25

Albanian Young Workers' Union, 30th anniv.

"Halili and Hajria" Ballet — A297

Scenes from "Halili and Hajria" Ballet: 10q, Brother and sister. 15q, Hajria before Sultan Suleiman. 50q, Hajria and husband. 80q, Execution of Halili. 1.40 l, Hajria killing her husband.

1971, Dec. 27   **Perf. 12½x12**
1397	A297	5q silver & multi	.20	.20
1398	A297	10q silver & multi	.20	.20
1399	A297	15q silver & multi	.20	.20
1400	A297	50q silver & multi	.45	.20
1401	A297	80q silver & multi	.70	.20
1402	A297	1.40 l silver & multi	1.10	.20
		Nos. 1397-1402 (6)	2.85	1.35

Albanian ballet Halili and Hajria after drama by Kol Jakova.

Biathlon and Olympic Rings — A298

Designs (Olympic Rings and): 10q, Sledding. 15q, Ice hockey. 20q, Bobsledding. 50q, Speed skating. 1 l, Slalom. 2 l, Ski jump. 2.50 l, Figure skating, pairs.

1972, Feb. 10
1403	A298	5q lt olive & multi	.20	.20
1404	A298	10q lt violet & multi	.20	.20
1405	A298	15q multicolored	.20	.20
1406	A298	20q pink & multi	.20	.20
1407	A298	50q lt blue & multi	.30	.20
1408	A298	1 l ocher & multi	.75	.20
1409	A298	2 l lilac & multi	1.50	.35
		Nos. 1403-1409 (7)	3.35	1.55

Souvenir Sheet
Imperf
1410	A298	2.50 l blue & multi	2.25	1.75

11th Winter Olympic Games, Sapporo, Japan, Feb. 3-13.

Wild Strawberries
A299

Wild Fruits and Nuts: 10q, Blackberries. 15q, Hazelnuts. 20q, Walnuts. 25q, Strawberry-tree fruit. 30q, Dogwood berries. 2.40 l, Rowan berries.

1972, Mar. 20   Litho.   **Perf. 12**
1411	A299	5q lt grn & multi	.20	.20
1412	A299	10q yellow & multi	.20	.20
1413	A299	15q lt vio & multi	.20	.20
1414	A299	20q pink & multi	.25	.20
1415	A299	25q multi	.25	.20
1416	A299	30q multi	.40	.20
1417	A299	2.40 l multi	2.50	.45
		Nos. 1411-1417 (7)	4.00	1.65

"Your Heart is your Health" A300

Worker and Student — A301

World Health Day: 1.20 l, Cardiac patient and electrocardiogram.

1972, Apr. 7   **Perf. 12x12½**
1418	A300	1.10 l multicolored	.75	.40
1419	A300	1.20 l rose & multi	3.00	1.25

1972, Apr. 24   Litho.   Perf. 11½x12½

7th Trade Union Cong., May 8: 2.05 l, Assembly Hall, dancers and emblem.
1420	A301	25q multi	.25	.20
1421	A301	2.05 l blue & multi	1.50	.40

Qemal Stafa A302

Designs: 15q, Memorial flame. 25q, Monument "Spirit of Defiance," vert.

1972, May 5   Perf. 12½x12, 12x12½
1422	A302	15q gray & multi	.20	.20
1423	A302	25q sal rose, blk & gray	.20	.20
1424	A302	1.90 l dull yel & blk	1.10	.30
		Nos. 1422-1424 (3)	1.50	.70

30th anniversary of the murder of Qemal Stafa and of Martyrs' Day.

Camellia A303

Designs: Various camellias.

1972, May 10   Perf. 12x12½
Flowers in Natural Colors
1425	A303	5q lt blue & blk	.20	.20
1426	A303	10q citron & blk	.20	.20
1427	A303	15q grnsh gray & blk	.20	.20
1428	A303	25q pale sal & blk	.25	.20
1429	A303	45q gray & blk	.35	.20
1430	A303	50q sal pink & blk	.80	.20
1431	A303	2.50 l bluish gray & blk	3.00	.80
		Nos. 1425-1431 (7)	5.00	2.00

High Jump — A304

Designs (Olympic and Motion Emblems and): 10q, Running. 15q, Shot put. 20q, Bicycling. 25q, Pole vault. 50q, Hurdles, women's. 75q, Hockey. 2 l, Swimming. 2.50 l, Diving, women's.

1972, June 30   Litho.   Perf. 12½x12
1432	A304	5q multicolored	.20	.20
1433	A304	10q lt brn & multi	.20	.20
1434	A304	15q lt lil & multi	.20	.20
1435	A304	20q multicolored	.20	.20
1436	A304	25q lt vio & multi	.20	.20
1437	A304	50q lt grn & multi	.40	.20
1438	A304	75q multicolored	.80	.20
1439	A304	2 l multicolored	1.50	.30
		Nos. 1432-1439 (8)	3.70	1.70

Miniature Sheet
Imperf
1440	A304	2.50 l multi	2.25	1.50

20th Olympic Games, Munich, Aug. 26-Sept. 11. Nos. 1432-1439 each issued in sheets of 8 stamps and one label (3x3) showing Olympic rings in gold.

Autobus A305

25q, Electric train. 80q, Ocean liner Tirana. 1.05 l, Automobile. 1.20 l, Trailer truck.

1972, July 25   Litho.   Perf. 12
1441	A305	15q org brn & multi	.20	.20
1442	A305	25q gray & multi	.20	.20
1443	A305	80q dp grn & multi	.40	.20
1444	A305	1.05 l multi	.55	.20
1445	A305	1.20 l multi	.65	.20
		Nos. 1441-1445 (5)	2.00	1.00

Arm Wrestling A306

Folk Games: 10q, Piggyback ball game. 15q, Women's jumping. 25q, Rope game (srum). 90q, Leapfrog. 2 l, Women throwing pitchers.

1972, Aug. 18
1446	A306	5q multi	.20	.20
1447	A306	10q lt bl & multi	.20	.20
1448	A306	15q rose & multi	.20	.20
1449	A306	25q lt bl & multi	.20	.20
1450	A306	90q ocher & multi	.65	.20
1451	A306	2 l lt grn & multi	1.25	.25
		Nos. 1446-1451 (6)	2.70	1.25

1st National Festival of People's Games.

Mastheads — A307

30th Press Day: 25q, Printing press. 1.90 l, Workers reading paper.

1972, Aug. 25
1452	A307	15q lt bl & blk	.20	.20
1453	A307	25q red, grn & blk	.20	.20
1454	A307	1.90 l lt vio & blk	1.25	.35
		Nos. 1452-1454 (3)	1.65	.75

Map of Peza Area, Memorial Tablet A308

1972, Sept. 16
1455	A308	15q shown	.20	.20
1456	A308	25q Guerrillas with flag	.30	.20
1457	A308	1.90 l Peza Conference memorial	1.75	.35
		Nos. 1455-1457 (3)	2.25	.75

30th anniversary, Conference of Peza.

Partisans, by Sotir Capo — A309

Paintings: 10q, Woman, by Ismail Lulani, vert. 15q, "Communists," by Lec Shkreli, vert. 20q, View of Nendorit, 1941, by Sali Shijaku, vert. 50q, Woman with Sheaf, by Zef Shoshi, vert. 1 l, Landscape with Children, by Dhimitraq Trebicka. 2 l, Women on Bicycles, by Vilson Kilica. 2.30 l, Folk Dance, by Abdurrahim Buza.

Perf. 12½x12, 12x12½
1972, Sept. 25   Litho.
1458	A309	5q gold & multi	.20	.20
1459	A309	10q gold & multi	.20	.20
1460	A309	15q gold & multi	.20	.20
1461	A309	20q gold & multi	.20	.20
1462	A309	50q gold & multi	.35	.20
1463	A309	1 l gold & multi	.70	.20
1464	A309	2 l gold & multi	1.50	.35
		Nos. 1458-1464 (7)	3.35	1.55

Miniature Sheet
Imperf
1465	A309	2.30 l gold & multi	2.00	1.50

No. 1465 contains one 41x68mm stamp.

Congress Emblem — A310

Design: 2.05 l, Young worker with banner.

1972, Oct. 23   Litho.   Perf. 12
1466	A310	25q silver, red & gold	.20	.20
1467	A310	2.05 l silver & multi	1.60	.45

Union of Working Youth, 6th Congress.

Hammer and Sickle A311

Ismail Qemali A312

Design: 1.20 l, Lenin as orator.

1972, Nov. 7   Litho.   Perf. 11½x12
1468	A311	1.10 l multi	.55	.20
1469	A311	1.20 l multi	.60	.25

Russian October Revolution, 55th anniv.

Perf. 12x11½, 11½x12
1972, Nov. 29

Designs: 15q, Albanian fighters, horiz. 65q, Rally, horiz. 1.25 l, Coat of arms.
1470	A312	15q red, brt bl & blk	.20	.20
1471	A312	25q yel, blk & red	.20	.20
1472	A312	65q red, sal & blk	.50	.20
1473	A312	1.25 l dl red & blk	.95	.25
		Nos. 1470-1473 (4)	1.85	.85

60th anniv. of independence.

Cock, Mosaic A313

Mosaics, 2nd-5th centuries, excavated near Buthrotum and Apollonia: 10q, Bird, vert. 15q, Partridges, vert. 25q, Warrior's legs. 45q, Nymph riding dolphin, vert. 50q, Fish, vert. 2.50 l, Warrior with helmet.

1972, Dec. 10   Perf. 12½x12, 12x12½
1474	A313	5q silver & multi	.20	.20
1475	A313	10q silver & multi	.20	.20
1476	A313	15q silver & multi	.20	.20
1477	A313	25q silver & multi	.40	.20
1478	A313	45q silver & multi	.40	.20
1479	A313	50q silver & multi	.60	.20
1480	A313	2.50 l silver & multi	3.00	.70
		Nos. 1474-1480 (7)	5.00	1.90

Nicolaus Copernicus A314

Designs: 10q, 25q, 80q, 1.20 l, Various portraits of Copernicus. 1.60 l, Heliocentric solar system.

1973, Feb. 19   Litho.   Perf. 12x12½
1481	A314	5q lil rose & multi	.20	.20
1482	A314	10q dull ol & multi	.20	.20
1483	A314	25q multicolored	.20	.20
1484	A314	80q lt violet & multi	.60	.20
1485	A314	1.20 l blue & multi	.85	.25
1486	A314	1.60 l gray & multi	1.25	.35
		Nos. 1481-1486 (6)	3.30	1.40

500th anniversary of the birth of Nicolaus Copernicus (1473-1543), Polish astronomer.

Flowering Cactus — A315

Designs: Various flowering cacti.

1973, Mar. 25   Litho.   Perf. 12
1487	A315	10q multicolored	.20	.20
1488	A315	15q multicolored	.20	.20
1489	A315	20q beige & multi	.20	.20
1490	A315	25q gray & multi	.25	.20
1491	A315	30q beige & multi	3.75	1.25
1492	A315	65q gray & multi	.55	.20
1493	A315	80q multicolored	.60	.20
1494	A315	2 l multicolored	1.25	.50
a.		Block of 8, #1487-1494	7.50	5.00
		Nos. 1487-1494 (8)	7.00	2.95

Guard and Factories
A316

1.80 l, Guard and guards with prisoner.

1973, Mar. 20　Litho.　Perf. 12½x12

1495	A316	25q ultra & blk	.30	.20
1496	A316	1.80 l dk red & multi	1.40	.40

30th anniv. of the State Security Branch.

Common Tern — A317

Sea Birds: 15q, White-winged black terns, vert. 25q, Black-headed gull, vert. 45q, Great black-headed gull. 80q, Slender-billed gull, vert. 2.40 l, Sandwich terns.

1973, Apr. 30　Perf. 12½x12, 12x12½

1497	A317	5q gold & multi	.20	.20
1498	A317	15q gold & multi	.20	.20
1499	A317	25q gold & multi	.30	.20
1500	A317	45q gold & multi	.35	.20
1501	A317	80q gold & multi	.80	.20
1502	A317	2.40 l gold & multi	2.50	.50
		Nos. 1497-1502 (6)	4.35	1.50

Letters, 1913 Cancellation and Post Horn — A318

Design: 1.80 l, Mailman, 1913 cancel.

1973, May, 5　Litho.　Perf. 12x11½

1503	A318	25q red & multi	.40	.20
1504	A318	1.80 l red & multi	2.50	.50

60th anniversary of Albanian stamps.

Farmer, Worker, Soldier
A319

Design: 25q, Woman and factory, vert.

1973, June 4　Perf. 12

1505	A319	25q carmine rose	.25	.20
1506	A319	1.80 l	1.50	.45

7th Congress of Albanian Women's Union.

Creation of General Staff, by G. Madhi — A320

Designs: 40q, "August 1949," sculpture by Sh. Haderi, vert. 60q, "Generation after Generation," sculpture by H. Dule, vert. 80q, "Defend Revolutionary Victories," by M. Fushekati.

1973, July 10　Litho.　Perf. 12½x12

1507	A320	25q gold & multi	5.50	5.50
1508	A320	40q gold & multi	5.50	5.50
1509	A320	60q gold & multi	5.50	5.50
1510	A320	80q gold & multi	5.50	5.50
		Nos. 1507-1510 (4)	22.00	22.00

30th anniversary of the People's Army.

"Electrification," by S. Hysa — A321

Albanian Paintings: 10q, Woman Textile Worker, by N. Nallbani. 15q, Gymnasts, by M. Fushekati. 50q, Aviator, by F. Stamo. 80q, Fascist Prisoner, by A. Lakuriqi. 1.20 l, Workers with Banner, by P. Mele. 1.30 l, Farm Woman, by Zef Shoshi. 2.05 l, Battle of Tenda, by F. Haxhiu. 10q, 50q, 80q, 1.20 l, 1.30 l, vertical.

Perf. 12½x12, 12x12½
1973, Aug. 10

1511	A321	5q gold & multi	.20	.20
1512	A321	10q gold & multi	.20	.20
1513	A321	15q gold & multi	.20	.20
1514	A321	50q gold & multi	.25	.20
1515	A321	80q gold & multi	.55	.20
1516	A321	1.20 l gold & multi	.90	.20
1517	A321	1.30 l gold & multi	.95	.20
		Nos. 1511-1517 (7)	3.25	1.40

Souvenir Sheet
Imperf

1518	A321	2.05 l multi	2.25	1.25

Mary Magdalene, by Caravaggio
A322

Paintings by Michelangelo da Caravaggio: 10q, The Lute Player, horiz. 15q, Self-portrait. 50q, Boy Carrying Fruit and Flowers. 80q, Still Life, horiz. 1.20 l, Narcissus. 1.30 l, Boy Peeling Apple. 2.05 l, Man with Feathered Hat.

Perf. 12x12½, 12½x12
1973, Sept. 28

1519	A322	5q gold & multi	.20	.20
1520	A322	10q gold & multi	.20	.20
1521	A322	15q gold, blk & gray	.20	.20
1522	A322	50q gold & multi	.25	.20
1523	A322	80q gold & multi	.60	.20
1524	A322	1.20 l gold & multi	.80	.25
1525	A322	1.30 l gold & multi	.90	.25
		Nos. 1519-1525 (7)	3.15	1.50

Souvenir Sheet
Imperf

1526	A322	2.05 l multi	3.75	2.00

Michelangelo da Caravaggio (Merisi; 1573?-1609), Italian painter. No. 1526 contains one stamp, size: 63x73mm.

Soccer — A323

Designs: 5q-1.25 l, Various soccer scenes. 2.05 l, Ball in goal and list of cities where championships were held.

1973, Oct. 30　Litho.　Perf. 12½x12

1527	A323	5q multi	.20	.20
1528	A323	10q multi	.20	.20
1529	A323	15q multi	.20	.20
1530	A323	20q multi	.20	.20
1531	A323	25q multi	.20	.20
1532	A323	90q multi	.65	.20
1533	A323	1.20 l multi	.95	.20
1534	A323	1.25 l multi	1.10	.20
		Nos. 1527-1534 (8)	3.70	1.60

Minature Sheet
Imperf

1535	A323	2.05 l multi	2.00	1.50

World Soccer Cup, Munich 1974.

Weight Lifter — A324

Designs: Various stages of weight lifting. 1.20 l, 1.60 l, horiz.

1973, Oct. 30　Litho.　Perf. 12

1536	A324	5q multi	.20	.20
1537	A324	10q multi	.20	.20
1538	A324	25q multi	.20	.20
1539	A324	90q multi	.55	.20
1540	A324	1.20 l multi	.45	.20
1541	A324	1.60 l multi	.95	.20
		Nos. 1536-1541 (6)	2.55	1.20

Weight Lifting Championships, Havana, Cuba.

Ballet — A325

Harvester Combine
A326

Designs: 5q, Cement factory, Kavaje. 10q, Ali Kelmendi truck factory and tank cars, horiz. 25q, "Communication." 35q, Skiers and hotel, horiz. 60q, Resort, horiz. 80q, Mountain lake. 1 l, Mao Tse-tung textile mill. 1.20 l, Steel workers. 2.40 l, Welder and pipe. 3 l, Skanderbeg Monument, Tirana. 5 l, Roman arches, Durres.

Perf. 12½x12, 12x12½

1973-74				Litho.
1543	A325	5q gold & multi	.20	.20
1544	A325	10q gold & multi	.20	.20
1545	A325	15q gold & multi	.20	.20
1545A	A326	20q gold & multi	.20	.20
1546	A326	25q gold & multi	.20	.20
1547	A326	35q gold & multi	.20	.20
1548	A326	60q gold & multi	.35	.20
1549	A326	80q gold & multi	.50	.20
1549A	A326	1 l gold & multi	.45	.20
1549B	A326	1.20 l gold & multi	.75	.20
1549C	A326	2.40 l gold & multi	1.50	.35
1550	A326	3 l gold & multi	1.75	.35
1551	A326	5 l gold & multi	2.75	.60
		Nos. 1543-1551 (13)	9.25	3.30

Issue dates: Nos. 1545-1546, 1549-1550, Dec. 5, 1973; others, 1974.

Mao Tse-tung — A327

80th birthday of Mao Tse-tung: 1.20 l, Mao Tse-tung addressing crowd.

1973, Dec. 26　Perf. 12

1552	A327	85q multicolored	.80	.20
1553	A327	1.20 l multicolored	1.25	.20

Old Man and Dog, by Gericault
A328

Paintings by Jean Louis André Theodore Gericault: 10q, Horse's Head. 15q, Male Model. 25q, Head of Black Man. 1.20 l, Self-portrait. 2.05 l, Raft of the Medusa, horiz. 2.20 l, Battle of the Giants.

Perf. 12x12½, 12½x12
1974, Jan. 18　　　　Litho.

1554	A328	10q gold & multi	.20	.20
1555	A328	15q gold & multi	.20	.20
1556	A328	20q gold & multi	.20	.20
1557	A328	25q gold & blk	.25	.20
1558	A328	1.20 l gold & multi	.90	.20
1559	A328	2.20 l gold & multi	1.75	.35
		Nos. 1554-1559 (6)	3.50	1.35

Souvenir Sheet
Imperf

1560	A328	2.05 l gold & multi	2.00	1.50

No. 1560 contains one 87x78mm stamp.

Lenin, by Pandi Mele — A329

Designs: 25q, Lenin with Sailors on Cruiser Aurora, by Dhimitraq Trebicka, horiz. 1.20 l, Lenin, by Vilson Kilica.

1974, Jan. 21　Perf. 12½x12, 12x12½

1561	A329	25q gold & multi	.20	.25
1562	A329	60q gold & multi	.60	.20
1563	A329	1.20 l gold & multi	1.75	.55
		Nos. 1561-1563 (3)	2.55	1.00

50th anniv. of the death of Lenin.

Swimming Duck, Mosaic — A330

Designs: Mosaics from the 5th-6th Centuries A.D., excavated near Buthrotium, Pogradec and Apollonia.

1974, Feb. 20　Litho.　Perf. 12½x12

1564	A330	5q shown	.20	.20
1565	A330	10q Bird, flower	.20	.20
1566	A330	15q Vase, grapes	.20	.20
1567	A330	25q Duck	.20	.20
1568	A330	40q Donkey, bird	.30	.20
1569	A330	2.50 l Sea horse	1.50	.35
		Nos. 1564-1569 (6)	2.60	1.35

Soccer — A331

Various scenes from soccer. 2.05 l, World Soccer Cup & names of participating countries.

1974, Apr. 25   Litho.   Perf. 12½x12
1570	A331	10q	gold & multi	.20	.20
1571	A331	15q	gold & multi	.20	.20
1572	A331	20q	gold & multi	.20	.20
1573	A331	25q	gold & multi	.20	.20
1574	A331	40q	gold & multi	.30	.20
1575	A331	80q	gold & multi	.55	.20
1576	A331	1 l	gold & multi	.85	.25
1577	A331	1.20 l	gold & multi	1.10	.35
		Nos. 1570-1577 (8)		3.60	1.80

Souvenir Sheet
Imperf
1578	A331	2.05 l	gold & multi	2.50	.90

World Cup Soccer Championship, Munich, June 13-July 7. No. 1578 contains one stamp (60x60mm) with simulated perforations. Nos. 1570-1577 exist imperf, No. 1578 with simulated perfs omitted.

Arms of Albania, Soldier — A332

Design: 1.80 l, Soldier and front page of 1944 Congress Book.

1974, May 24   Litho.   Perf. 12
1579	A332	25q	multicolored	.20	.20
1580	A332	1.80 l	multicolored	1.25	.25

30th anniversary of the First Anti-Fascist Liberation Congress of Permet.

Medicinal Plants A333

40q, 80q, 2.20 l, horiz.

1974, May 5   Perf. 12x12½
1581	A333	10q	Bittersweet	.20	.20
1582	A333	15q	Arbutus	.20	.20
1583	A333	20q	Lilies of the valley	.20	.20
1584	A333	25q	Autumn crocus	.20	.20
1585	A333	40q	Borage	.25	.20
1586	A333	80q	Soapwort	.85	.20
1587	A333	2.20 l	Gentian	1.90	.40
		Nos. 1581-1587 (7)		3.80	1.60

Revolutionaries with Albanian Flag — A334

1.80 l, Portraits of 5 revolutionaries, vert.

Perf. 12½x12, 12x12½
1974, June 10
1588	A334	25q	red, blk & lil	.30	.20
1589	A334	1.80 l	yel, red & blk	1.25	.40

50th anniversary Albanian Bourgeois Democratic Revolution.

European Redwing — A335

Designs: Songbirds; Nos. 1597-1600 vert.

Perf. 12½x12, 12x12½
1974, July 15   Litho.
1594	A335	10q	shown	.20	.20
1595	A335	15q	European robin	.20	.20
1596	A335	20q	Greenfinch	.20	.20
1597	A335	25q	Bullfinch	.20	.20
1598	A335	40q	Hawfinch	.35	.20
1599	A335	80q	Blackcap	.85	.20
1600	A335	2.20 l	Nightingale	1.90	.45
		Nos. 1594-1600 (7)		3.90	1.65

Globe — A336

Cent. of UPU: 1.20 l, UPU emblem. 2.05 l, Jet over globe.

1974, Aug. 25   Litho.   Perf. 12x12½
1601	A336	85q	grn & multi	.80	.20
1602	A336	1.20 l	vio & ol grn	1.25	.20

Miniature Sheet
Imperf
1603	A336	2.05 l	blue & multi	12.00	12.00

Widows, by Sali Shijaku — A337

Albanian Paintings: 15q, Drillers, by Danish Jukniu, vert. 20q, Workers with Blueprints, by Clirim Ceka. 25q, Call to Action, by Spiro Kristo, vert. 40q, Winter Battle, by Sabaudin Xhaferi. 80q, Comrades, by Clirim Ceka, vert. 1 l, Aiding the Partisans, by Guri Madhi. 1.20 l, Teacher with Pupils, by Kleo Nini Brezat. 2.05 l, Comrades in Arms, by Guri Madhi.

Perf. 12½x12, 12x12½
1974, Sept. 25
1604	A337	10q	silver & multi	.20	.20
1605	A337	15q	silver & multi	.20	.20
1606	A337	20q	silver & multi	.20	.20
1607	A337	25q	silver & multi	.20	.20
1608	A337	40q	silver & multi	.40	.20
1609	A337	80q	silver & multi	.75	.20
1610	A337	1 l	silver & multi	.95	.20
1611	A337	1.20 l	silver & multi	1.00	.20
		Nos. 1604-1611 (8)		3.90	1.60

Miniature Sheet
Imperf
1612	A337	2.05 l	silver & multi	2.00	1.50

Crowd on Tien An Men Square A338

Design: 1.20 l, Mao Tse-tung, vert.

1974, Oct. 1   Perf. 12
1613	A338	85q	gold & multi	.80	.20
1614	A338	1.20 l	gold & multi	1.25	.20

25th anniversary of the proclamation of the People's Republic of China.

Women's Volleyball A339

Spartakiad Medal and: 15q, Women hurdlers. 20q, Women gymnasts. 25q, Mass exercises in Stadium. 40q, Weight lifter. 80q, Wrestlers. 1 l, Military rifle drill. 1.20 l, Soccer.

1974, Oct. 9   Perf. 12x12½
1615	A339	10q	multi	.20	.20
1616	A339	15q	multi	.20	.20
1617	A339	20q	multi	.20	.20
1618	A339	25q	gray & multi	.20	.20
1619	A339	40q	multi	.25	.20
1620	A339	80q	multi	.50	.20
1621	A339	1 l	multi	.65	.20
1622	A339	1.20 l	tan & multi	1.00	.20
		Nos. 1615-1622 (8)		3.20	1.60

National Spartakiad, Oct. 9-17.

View of Berat — A340

Designs: 80q, Enver Hoxha addressing Congress, bas-relief, horiz. 1 l, Hoxha and leaders leaving Congress Hall.

Perf. 12x12½, 12½x12
1974, Oct. 20   Litho.
1623	A340	25q	rose car & blk	.30	.20
1624	A340	80q	yel, brn & blk	.70	.20
1625	A340	1 l	dp lilac & blk	1.10	.30
		Nos. 1623-1625 (3)		2.10	.70

30th anniversary of 2nd Congress of Berat.

Anniversary Emblem, Factory Guards — A341

35q, Chemical industry. 50q, Agriculture. 80q, Arts. 1 l, Atomic diagram & computer. 1.20 l, Youth education. 2.05 l, Crowd & History Book.

1974, Nov. 29   Litho.   Perf. 12½x12
1626	A341	25q	green & multi	.20	.20
1627	A341	35q	ultra & multi	.20	.20
1628	A341	50q	brown & multi	.20	.20
1629	A341	80q	multicolored	.40	.20
1630	A341	1 l	violet & multi	.50	.20
1631	A341	1.20 l	multicolored	1.00	.25
		Nos. 1626-1631 (6)		2.50	1.25

Miniature Sheet
Imperf
1632	A341	2.05 l	gold & multi	2.50	2.00

30th anniv. of liberation from Fascism.

Artemis, from Apolloni A342

1974, Dec. 25   Photo.   Perf. 12x12½
1633	A342	10q	shown	.20	.20
1634	A342	15q	Zeus statue	.20	.20
1635	A342	20q	Poseidon statue	.20	.20
1636	A342	25q	Illyrian helmet	.25	.20
1637	A342	40q	Amphora	.30	.20
1638	A342	80q	Agrippa	.60	.25
1639	A342	1 l	Demosthenes	.80	.30
1640	A342	1.20 l	Head of Bilia	1.50	.40
		Nos. 1633-1640 (8)		4.05	1.95

Miniature Sheet
Imperf
1641	A342	2.05 l	Artemis & amphora	2.50	1.50

Archaeological discoveries in Albania.

Workers and Factories A343

25q, Handshake, tools and book, vert.

1975, Feb. 11   Litho.   Perf. 12
1642	A343	25q	brown & multi	.30	.20
1643	A343	1.80 l	yellow & multi	1.50	.35

Albanian Trade Unions, 30th anniversary.

Chicory A344

1975, Feb. 15
1644	A344	5q	shown	.20	.20
1645	A344	10q	Houseleek	.20	.20
1646	A344	15q	Columbine	.20	.20
1647	A344	20q	Anemone	.20	.20
1648	A344	25q	Hibiscus	.20	.20
1649	A344	30q	Gentian	.20	.20
1650	A344	35q	Hollyhock	.50	.20
1651	A344	2.70 l	Iris	2.50	.40
		Nos. 1644-1651 (8)		4.20	1.80

Protected flowers.

Jesus, from Doni Madonna A345

Works by Michelangelo: 10q, Slave, sculpture. 15q, Head of Dawn, sculpture. 20q, Awakening Giant, sculpture. 25q, Cumaenian Sybil, Sistine Chapel. 30q, Lorenzo di Medici, sculpture. 1.20 l, David, sculpture. 2.05 l, Self-portrait. 3.90 l, Delphic Sybil, Sistine Chapel.

1975, Mar. 20   Litho.   Perf. 12x12½

1652	A345	5q gold & multi	.20	.20
1653	A345	10q gold & multi	.20	.20
1654	A345	15q gold & multi	.20	.20
1655	A345	20q gold & multi	.20	.20
1656	A345	25q gold & multi	.20	.20
1657	A345	30q gold & multi	.30	.20
1658	A345	1.20 l gold & multi	.50	.20
1659	A345	3.90 l gold & multi	2.00	.50
		Nos. 1652-1659 (8)	3.80	1.90

Miniature Sheet
Imperf

1660	A345	2.05 l gold & multi	2.50	1.75

Michelangelo Buonarroti (1475-1564), Italian sculptor, painter and architect.

Two-wheeled Cart — A346

Albanian Transportation of the Past: 5q, Horseback rider. 15q, Lake ferry. 20q, Coastal three-master. 25q, Phaeton. 3.35 l, Early automobile on bridge.

1975, Apr. 15   Litho.   Perf. 12½x12

1661	A346	5q bl grn & multi	.20	.20
1662	A346	10q ol & multi	.20	.20
1663	A346	15q lil & multi	.20	.20
1664	A346	20q multi	.20	.20
1665	A346	25q multi	.20	.20
1666	A346	3.35 l ocher & multi	2.00	.50
		Nos. 1661-1666 (6)	3.00	1.50

Guard at Frontier
Stone — A347

Guardsman and
Militia — A348

1975, Apr. 25   Perf. 12

1667	A347	25q multi	.30	.20
1668	A348	1.80 l multi	1.50	.35

30th anniversary of Frontier Guards.

Posting Illegal Poster — A349

Designs: 60q, Partisans in battle. 1.20 l, Partisan killing German soldier, and Albanian coat of arms.

1975, May 9   Perf. 12½x12

1669	A349	25q multi	.20	.20
1670	A349	60q multi	.50	.20
1671	A349	1.20 l red & multi	1.00	.25
		Nos. 1669-1671 (3)	1.70	.65

30th anniversary of victory over Fascism.

European Widgeons — A350

Waterfowl: 10q, Red-crested pochards. 15q, White-fronted goose. 20q, Northern pintails. 25q, Red-breasted merganser. 30q, Eider ducks. 35q, Whooper swan. 2.70 l, Shovelers.

1975, June 15   Litho.   Perf. 12

1672	A350	5q brt blue & multi	.20	.20
1673	A350	10q yel grn & multi	.20	.20
1674	A350	15q brt rose lil & multi	.20	.20
1675	A350	20q bl grn & multi	.20	.20
1676	A350	25q multicolored	.20	.20
1677	A350	30q multicolored	.25	.20
1678	A350	35q orange & multi	.40	.20
1679	A350	2.70 l multi	3.00	.75
		Nos. 1672-1679 (8)	4.65	2.15

Shyqyri
Kanapari, by
Musa
Qarri — A351

Albanian Paintings: 10q, Woman Saving Children in Sea, by Agim Faja. 15q, "November 28, 1912" (revolution), by Petrit Ceno, horiz. 20q, "Workers Unite," by Sali Shijaku. 25q, The Partisan Shota Galica, by Ismail Lulani. 30q, Victorious Resistance Fighters, 1943, by Nestor Jonuzi. 80q, Partisan Couple in Front of Red Flag, by Vilson Halimi. 2.05 l, Dancing Procession, by Abdurahim Buza. 2.25 l, Republic Day Celebration, by Fatmir Haxhiu, horiz.

Perf. 12x12½, 12½x12

1975, July 15   Litho.

1680	A351	5q gold & multi	.20	.20
1681	A351	10q gold & multi	.20	.20
1682	A351	15q gold & multi	.20	.20
1683	A351	20q gold & multi	.20	.20
1684	A351	25q gold & multi	.20	.20
1685	A351	30q gold & multi	.20	.20
1686	A351	80q gold & multi	.40	.20
1687	A351	2.25 l gold & multi	1.40	.40
		Nos. 1680-1687 (8)	3.00	1.80

Miniature Sheet
Imperf

1688	A351	2.05 l gold & multi	2.10	1.50

Nos. 1680-1687 issued in sheets of 8 stamps and gold center label showing palette and easel.

Farmer
Holding
Reform
Law — A352

Design: 2 l, Produce and farm machinery.

1975, Aug. 28   Perf. 12

1689	A352	15q multicolored	.25	.20
1690	A352	2 l multicolored	1.25	.50

Agrarian reform, 30th anniversary.

Alcyonium
Palmatum
A353

Corals: 10q, Paramuricea chamaeleon. 20q, Coralium rubrum. 25q, Eunicella covalini. 3.70 l, Cladocora cespitosa.

1975, Sept. 25   Litho.   Perf. 12

1691	A353	5q blue, ol & blk	.20	.20
1692	A353	10q blue & multi	.20	.20
1693	A353	20q blue & multi	.20	.20
1694	A353	25q blue & blk	.20	.20
1695	A353	3.70 l blue & blk	2.50	.60
		Nos. 1691-1695 (5)	3.30	1.40

Bicycling
A354

Designs (Montreal Olympic Games Emblem and): 10q, Canoeing. 15q, Fieldball. 20q, Basketball. 25q, Water polo. 30q, Hockey. 1.20 l, Pole vault. 2.05 l, Fencing. 2.15 l, Montreal Olympic Games emblem and various sports.

1975, Oct. 20   Litho.   Perf. 12½

1696	A354	5q multi	.20	.20
1697	A354	10q multi	.20	.20
1698	A354	15q multi	.20	.20
1699	A354	20q multi	.25	.20
1700	A354	25q multi	.25	.20
1701	A354	30q multi	.25	.20
1702	A354	1.20 l multi	.75	.25
1703	A354	2.05 l multi	1.50	.40
		Nos. 1696-1703 (8)	3.60	1.85

Miniature Sheet
Imperf

1704	A354	2.15 l org & multi	3.00	2.00

21st Olympic Games, Montreal, July 18-Aug. 8, 1976. Nos. 1696-1703 exist imperf.

Power Lines
Leading to
Village
A355

Designs: 25q, Transformers and insulators. 80q, Dam and power station. 85q, Television set, power lines, grain and cogwheel.

1975, Oct. 25   Perf. 12x12½

1705	A355	15q ultra & yel	.20	.20
1706	A355	25q brt vio & pink	.20	.20
1707	A355	80q lt grn & gray	.40	.20
1708	A355	85q ocher & brn	1.00	.40
		Nos. 1705-1708 (4)	1.80	1.00

General electrification, 5th anniversary.

Child, Rabbit and Teddy Bear Planting
Tree — A356

Fairy Tales: 10q, Mother fox. 15q, Ducks in school. 20q, Little pigs building house. 25q, Animals watching television. 30q, Rabbit and bear at work. 35q, Working and playing ants. 2.70 l, Wolf in sheep's clothes.

1975, Dec. 25   Litho.   Perf. 12½x12

1709	A356	5q black & multi	.20	.20
1710	A356	10q black & multi	.20	.20
1711	A356	15q black & multi	.20	.20
1712	A356	20q black & multi	.20	.20
1713	A356	25q black & multi	.20	.20
1714	A356	30q black & multi	.25	.20
1715	A356	35q black & multi	.25	.20
1716	A356	2.70 l black & multi	3.00	.60
		Nos. 1709-1716 (8)	4.50	2.00

Arms,
People,
Factories
A357

Design: 1.90 l, Arms, government building, celebrating crowd.

1976, Jan. 11   Litho.   Perf. 12

1717	A357	25q gold & multi	.25	.20
1718	A357	1.90 l gold & multi	1.25	.35

30th anniversary of proclamation of Albanian People's Republic.

Ice Hockey,
Olympic
Games'
Emblem
A358

Designs: 10q, Speed skating. 15q, Biathlon. 50q, Ski jump. 1.20 l, Slalom. 2.15 l, Figure skating, pairs. 2.30 l, One-man bobsled.

1976, Feb. 4

1719	A358	5q silver & multi	.20	.20
1720	A358	10q silver & multi	.20	.20
1721	A358	15q silver & multi	.20	.20
1722	A358	50q silver & multi	.25	.20
1723	A358	1.20 l silver & multi	.65	.20
1724	A358	2.30 l silver & multi	1.50	.35
		Nos. 1719-1724 (6)	3.00	1.35

Miniature Sheet
Perf. 12 on 2 sides x Imperf.

1725	A358	2.15 l silver & multi	2.10	1.75

12th Winter Olympic Games, Innsbruck, Austria, Feb. 4-15.

Meadow
Saffron
A359

Medicinal Plants: 10q, Deadly night-shade. 15q, Yellow gentian. 20q, Horse chestnut. 70q, Shield fern. 80q, Marshmallow. 2.30 l, Thorn apple.

1976, Apr. 10   Litho.   Perf. 12x12½

1726	A359	5q	black & multi	.20	.20
1727	A359	10q	black & multi	.20	.20
1728	A359	15q	black & multi	.20	.20
1729	A359	20q	black & multi	.20	.20
1730	A359	70q	black & multi	.30	.20
1731	A359	80q	black & multi	.60	.20
1732	A359	2.30 l	black & multi	1.60	.35
		Nos. 1726-1732 (7)		3.30	1.55

Bowl and Spoon — A360

15q, Flask, vert. 20q, Carved handles, vert. 25q, Pistol and dagger. 80q, Wall hanging, vert. 1.20 l, Earrings and belt buckle. 1.40 l, Jugs, vert.

1976   Litho.   Perf. 12½x12, 12x12½

1733	A360	10q	lilac & multi	.20	.20
1734	A360	15q	gray & multi	.20	.20
1735	A360	20q	multi	.20	.20
1736	A360	25q	car & multi	.20	.20
1737	A360	80q	yellow & multi	.50	.20
1738	A360	1.20 l	multi	.75	.25
1739	A360	1.40 l	tan & multi	1.10	.35
		Nos. 1733-1739 (7)		3.15	1.60

Natl. Ethnographic Conf., Tirana, June 28. For surcharge see No. 1873.

Founding of Cooperatives, by Zef Shoshi — A361

Paintings: 10q, Going to Work, by Agim Zajmi, vert. 25q, Crowd Listening to Loudspeaker, by Vilson Kilica. 40q, Woman Welder, by Sabaudin Xhaferi, vert. 50q, Factory, by Isuf Sulovari, vert. 1.20 l, 1942 Revolt, by Lec Shkreli, vert. 1.60 l, Coming Home from Work, by Agron Dine. 2.05 l, Honoring a Young Pioneer, by Andon Lakuriqi.

Perf. 12½x12, 12x12½

1976, Aug. 8   Litho.

1740	A361	5q	gold & multi	.20	.20
1741	A361	10q	gold & multi	.20	.20
1742	A361	25q	gold & multi	.20	.20
1743	A361	40q	gold & multi	.25	.20
1744	A361	50q	gold & multi	.25	.20
1745	A361	1.20 l	gold & multi	1.00	.50
1746	A361	1.60 l	gold & multi	1.50	.75
		Nos. 1740-1746 (7)		3.60	2.25

Miniature Sheet
Perf. 12 on 2 sides x Imperf.

1747	A361	2.05 l	gold & multi	2.50	2.00

Red Flag, Agricultural Symbols — A362

Enver Hoxha, Partisans and Albanian Flag — A363

Design: 1.20 l, Red flag and raised pickax.

1976, Nov. 1

1748	A362	25q	multi	.20	.20
1749	A362	1.20 l	multi	.80	.20

7th Workers Party Congress.

1976, Oct. 28   Perf. 12x12½

1.90 l, Demonstrators with Albanian flag.

1750	A363	25q	multi	.20	.20
1751	A363	1.90 l	multi	1.00	.30

Anti-Fascist demonstrations, 35th anniv.

Attacking Partisans, Meeting House A364

Designs (Red Flag and): 25q, Partisans, pickax and gun. 80q, Workers, soldiers, pickax and gun. 1.20 l, Agriculture and industry. 1.70 l, Dancers, symbols of science and art.

1976, Nov. 8   Litho.   Perf. 12x12½

1752	A364	15q	gold & multi	.20	.20
1753	A364	25q	gold & multi	.20	.20
1754	A364	80q	gold & multi	.30	.20
1755	A364	1.20 l	gold & multi	.50	.20
1756	A364	1.70 l	gold & multi	1.00	.20
		Nos. 1752-1756 (5)		2.20	1.00

35th anniv. of 1st Workers Party Cong.

Young Workers and Track A365

1.25 l, Young soldiers and Albanian flag.

1976, Nov. 23   Perf. 12

1757	A365	80q	yellow & multi	.55	.20
1758	A365	1.25 l	carmine & multi	.75	.20

Union of Young Communists, 35th anniv.

"Cuca e Maleve" Ballet A366

Scenes from ballet "Mountain Girl."

1976, Dec. 14   Perf. 12

1759	A366	10q	gold & multi	.20	.20
1760	A366	15q	gold & multi	.20	.20
1761	A366	20q	gold & multi	.20	.20
1762	A366	25q	gold & multi	.20	.20
1763	A366	80q	gold & multi	.55	.20
1764	A366	1.20 l	gold & multi	.75	.20
1765	A366	1.40 l	gold & multi	.90	.25
		Nos. 1759-1765 (7)		3.00	1.45

Miniature Sheet
Perf. 12 on 2 sides x Imperf.

1766	A366	2.05 l	gold & multi	1.75	.45

Bashtoves Castle A367

Albanian Castles: 15q, Gjirokastres. 20q, Ali Pash Tepelenes. 25q, Petreles. 80q, Beratit. 1.20 l, Durresit. 1.40 l, Krujes.

1976, Dec. 30   Litho.   Perf. 12

1767	A367	10q	black & dull bl	.20	.20
1768	A367	15q	black & grn	.20	.20
1769	A367	20q	black & gray	.20	.20
1770	A367	25q	black & brn	.20	.20
1771	A367	80q	black & rose	.40	.20
1772	A367	1.20 l	black & vio	.45	.20
1773	A367	1.40 l	black & brn red	.90	.20
		Nos. 1767-1773 (7)		2.55	1.40

Skanderbeg's Shield and Spear — A368

Skanderbeg's Weapons: 80q, Helmet, sword and scabbard. 1 l, Halberd, quiver with arrows, crossbow and spear.

1977, Jan. 28   Litho.   Perf. 12

1774	A368	15q	silver & multi	.50	.20
1775	A368	80q	silver & multi	2.25	.20
1776	A368	1 l	silver & multi	3.25	.25
		Nos. 1774-1776 (3)		6.00	.65

Skanderbeg (1403-1468), national hero.

Ilia Oiqi, Messenger in Storm — A369

Modern Heroes: 10q, Ilia Dashi, sailor in battle. 25q, Fran Ndue Ivanaj, fisherman in storm. 80q, Zeliha Allmetaj, woman rescuing child. 1 l, Ylli Zaimi, rescuing goats from flood. 1.90 l, Isuf Plloci, fighting forest fire.

1977, Feb. 28   Litho.   Perf. 12x12½

1777	A369	5q	brown & multi	.20	.20
1778	A369	10q	ultra & multi	.20	.20
1779	A369	25q	blue & multi	.20	.20
1780	A369	80q	ocher & multi	.50	.20
1781	A369	1 l	brown & multi	.80	.20
1782	A369	1.90 l	brown & multi	1.40	.20
		Nos. 1777-1782 (6)		3.30	1.20

Polyvinylchloride Plant, Vlore — A370

6th Five-year plan: 25q, Naphtha fractioning plant, Ballsh. 65q, Hydroelectric station and dam, Fjerzes. 1 l, Metallurgical plant and blast furnace, Elbasan.

1977, Mar. 29   Litho.   Perf. 12½x12

1783	A370	15q	silver & multi	.20	.20
1784	A370	25q	silver & multi	.30	.20
1785	A370	65q	silver & multi	.65	.20
1786	A370	1 l	silver & multi	1.10	.20
		Nos. 1783-1786 (4)		2.25	.80

Qerime Halil Galica — A371

Victory Monument, Tirana — A372

Design: 1.25 l, Qerime Halil Galica "Shota" and father Azem Galica.

1977, Apr. 20   Litho.   Perf. 12

1787	A371	80q	dark red	.65	.20
1788	A371	1.25 l	gray blue	1.10	.20

"Shota" Galica, communist fighter.

1977, May 5   Litho.   Perf. 12

Red Star and: 80q, Clenched fist, Albanian flag. 1.20 l, Bust of Qemal Stafa, poppies.

1789	A372	25q	multi	.30	.20
1790	A372	80q	multi	.90	.20
1791	A372	1.20 l	multi	1.50	.20
		Nos. 1789-1791 (3)		2.70	.60

35th anniversary of Martyrs' Day.

Physician Visiting Farm, Mobile Clinic — A373

10q, Cowherd, cattle ranch. 20q, Militia woman helping with harvest, rifle, combine. 80q, Modern village, highway, power lines. 2.95 l, Tractor, greenhouses.

1977, June 18

1792	A373	5q	multi	.20	.20
1793	A373	10q	multi	.20	.20
1794	A373	20q	multi	.20	.20
1795	A373	80q	multi	.40	.20
1796	A373	2.95 l	multi	2.50	.40
		Nos. 1792-1796 (5)		3.50	1.20

"Socialist transformation of the villages."

Armed Workers, Flag and Factory — A374

1.80 l, Workers with proclamation and flags.

1977, June 20

1797	A374	25q	multi	.20	.20
1798	A374	1.80 l	multi	1.25	.20

9th Labor Unions Congress.

Kerchief Dance — A375

Designs: Various folk dances.

1977, Aug. 20   Litho.   Perf. 12

1799	A375	5q	multi	.20	.20
1800	A375	10q	multi	.20	.20
1801	A375	15q	multi	.20	.20
1802	A375	25q	multi	.20	.20
1803	A375	80q	multi	.30	.20
1804	A375	1.20 l	multi	.60	.20
1805	A375	1.55 l	multi	.75	.25
		Nos. 1799-1805 (7)		2.45	1.45

Miniature Sheet
Perf. 12 on 2 sides x Imperf.

1806	A375	2.05 l	multi	1.25	.40

See Nos. 1836-1840, 1884-1888.

Attack
A376

Designs: 25q, Enver Hoxha addressing Army. 80q, Volunteers and riflemen. 1 l, Volunteers, hydrofoil patrolboat and MiG planes. 1.90 l, Volunteers and Albanian flag.

1977, July 10   Litho.   *Perf. 12*
1807	A376	15q gold & multi	.20	.20
1808	A376	25q gold & multi	.20	.20
1809	A376	80q gold & multi	.45	.20
1810	A376	1 l gold & multi	.70	.20
1811	A376	1.90 l gold & multi	1.25	.20
		Nos. 1807-1811 (5)	2.80	1.00

"One People-One Army."

Armed Workers, Article 3 of Constitution
A377

Design: 1.20 l, Symbols of farming and fertilizer industry, Article 25 of Constitution.

1977, Oct.
1812	A377	25q red, gold & blk	.25	.20
1813	A377	1.20 l red, gold & blk	.95	.20

New Constitution.

Picnic — A378

Film Frames: 15q, Telephone lineman in winter. 25q, Two men and a woman. 80q, Workers. 1.20 l, Boys playing in street. 1.60 l, Harvest.

1977, Oct. 25   Litho.   *Perf. 12½x12*
1814	A378	10q blue green	.20	.20
1815	A378	15q multi	.20	.20
1816	A378	25q black	.20	.20
1817	A378	80q multi	.55	.20
1818	A378	1.20 l deep claret	.95	.20
1819	A378	1.60 l multi	1.25	.20
		Nos. 1814-1819 (6)	3.35	1.20

Albanian films.

Farm Workers in Field, by V. Mio
A379

Paintings by V. Mio: 10q, Landscape in Snow. 15q, Grazing Sheep under Walnut Tree in Spring. 25q, Street in Korce. 80q, Horseback Riders on Mountain Pass. 1 l, Boats on Shore. 1.75 l, Tractors Plowing Fields. 2.05 l, Self-portrait.

1977, Dec. 25   Litho.   *Perf. 12½x12*
1820	A379	5q gold & multi	.20	.20
1821	A379	10q gold & multi	.20	.20
1822	A379	15q gold & multi	.20	.20
1823	A379	25q gold & multi	.20	.20
1824	A379	80q gold & multi	.40	.20
1825	A379	1 l gold & multi	.45	.20
1826	A379	1.75 l gold & multi	.80	.20
		Nos. 1820-1826 (7)	2.45	1.40

Miniature Sheet
Imperf.; Perf. 12 Horiz. between Vignette and Value Panel
1827	A379	2.05 l gold & multi	2.00	.35

Pan Flute — A380

Albanian Flag, Monument and People — A381

Folk Musical Instruments: 25q, Single-string goat's-head fiddle. 80q, Woodwind. 1.20 l, Drum. 1.70 l, Bagpipe. Background shows various woven folk patterns.

1978, Jan. 20   *Perf. 12x12½*
1828	A380	15q multi	.20	.20
1829	A380	25q multi	.25	.20
1830	A380	80q multi	.70	.20
1831	A380	1.20 l multi	1.10	.20
1832	A380	1.70 l multi	1.50	.20
		Nos. 1828-1832 (5)	3.75	1.00

1978   *Perf. 12½x12, 12x12½*

25q, Ismail Qemali, fighters, horiz. 1.65 l, People dancing around Albanian flag, horiz.

1833	A381	15q multi	.20	.20
1834	A381	25q multi	.30	.20
1835	A381	1.65 l multi	1.50	.20
		Nos. 1833-1835 (3)	2.00	.60

65th anniversary of independence.

Folk Dancing Type of 1977

Designs: Various dances.

1978, Feb. 15   Litho.   *Perf. 12*
1836	A375	5q multi	.20	.20
1837	A375	25q multi	.20	.20
1838	A375	80q multi	.35	.20
1839	A375	1 l multi	.50	.20
1840	A375	2.30 l multi	1.00	.20
		Nos. 1836-1840 (5)	2.25	1.00

Nos. 1836-1840 have white background around dancers, Nos. 1799-1805 have pinkish shadows.

Tractor Drivers, by Dhimitraq Trebicka
A382

Working Class Paintings: 80q, Steeplejack, by Spiro Kristo. 85q, "A Point in the Discussion," by Skender Milori. 90q, Oil rig crew, by Anesti Cini, vert. 1.60 l, Metal workers, by Ramadan Karanxha. 2.20 l, Political discussion, by Sotiraq Sholla.

1978, Mar. 25   Litho.   *Perf. 12*
1841	A382	25q multi	.20	.20
1842	A382	80q multi	.35	.20
1843	A382	85q multi	.35	.20
1844	A382	90q multi	.40	.20
1845	A382	1.60 l multi	.80	.20
		Nos. 1841-1845 (5)	2.10	1.00

Miniature Sheet
Perf. 12 on 2 sides x Imperf.
1846	A382	2.20 l multi	1.75	.40

Woman with Rifle and Pickax
A383

1.95 l, Farm & Militia women, industrial plant.

1978, June 1   Litho.   *Perf. 12*
1847	A383	25q gold & red	.25	.20
1848	A383	1.95 l gold & red	1.40	.25

8th Congress of Women's Union.

Children and Flowers — A384

Designs: 10q, Children with rifle, ax, book and flags. 25q, Dancing children in folk costume. 1.80 l, Children in school.

1978, June 1   Litho.
1849	A384	5q multi	.20	.20
1850	A384	10q multi	.20	.20
1851	A384	25q multi	.25	.20
1852	A384	1.80 l multi	1.50	.20
		Nos. 1849-1852 (4)	2.15	.80

International Children's Day.

Spirit of Skanderbeg as Conqueror
A385

10q, Battle at Mostar Bridge. 80q, Marchers, Albanian flag. 1.20 l, Riflemen in winter battle. 1.65 l, Abdyl Frasheri (1839-92). 2.20 l, Rifles, scroll, pen, League building. 2.60 l, League headquarters, Prizren.

1978, June 10   Litho.   *Perf. 12*
1853	A385	10q multi	.20	.20
1854	A385	25q multi	.20	.20
1855	A385	80q multi	.25	.20
1856	A385	1.20 l multi	.50	.20
1857	A385	1.65 l multi	.85	.20
1858	A385	2.60 l multi	1.00	.30
		Nos. 1853-1858 (6)	3.00	1.30

Miniature Sheet
Perf. 12 on 2 sides x Imperf.
1859	A385	2.20 l multi	2.00	.35

Centenary of League of Prizren.

Guerrillas and Flag, 1943 — A386

Designs: 25q, Soldier, sailor, airman, militiaman, horiz. 1.90 l, Members of armed forces, civil guards, and Young Pioneers.

1978, July 10   *Perf. 11½x12½*
1860	A386	5q multi	.20	.20
1861	A386	25q multi	.45	.20
1862	A386	1.90 l multi	3.25	.20
		Nos. 1860-1862 (3)	3.90	.60

35th anniversary of People's Army.

Woman with Machine Carbine — A387

Kerchief Dance — A388

25q, Man with target rifle, horiz. 95q, Man shooting with telescopic sights, horiz. 2.40 l, Woman target shooting with pistol.

Children and Flowers — A384

1978, Sept. 20   Litho.
1863	A387	25q black & yel	.20	.20
1864	A387	80q orange & blk	.35	.20
1865	A387	95q red & blk	.50	.20
1866	A387	2.40 l carmine & blk	1.10	.30
		Nos. 1863-1866 (4)	2.15	.90

32nd National Rifle-shooting Championships, Sept. 20.

1978, Oct. 6   *Perf. 12*

15q, Musicians. 25q, Fiddler with single-stringed instrument. 80q, Dancers, men. 1.20 l, Saber dance. 1.90 l, Singers, women.

1867	A388	10q multi	.20	.20
1868	A388	15q multi	.20	.20
1869	A388	25q multi	.20	.20
1870	A388	80q multi	.30	.20
1871	A388	1.20 l multi	.60	.20
1872	A388	1.90 l multi	.95	.25
		Nos. 1867-1872 (6)	2.45	1.25

National Folklore Festival.
See Nos. 2082-2085, 2289-2290.

No. 1736 Surcharged with New Value, 2 Bars and "RICCIONE 78"

1978   Litho.   *Perf. 12½x12*
1873	A360	3.30 l on 25q multi	5.00	1.10

Riccione 78 Philatelic Exhibition.

Enver Hoxha
A389

1978, Oct. 16   Litho.   *Perf. 12x12½*
1874	A389	80q red & multi	.30	.20
1875	A389	1.20 l red & multi	.45	.20
1876	A389	2.40 l red & multi	.90	.25
		Nos. 1874-1876 (3)	1.65	.65

Miniature Sheet
Perf. 12½ on 2 sides x Imperf.
1877	A389	2.20 l red & multi	1.75	.40

70th birthday of Enver Hoxha, First Secretary of Central Committee of the Communist Party of Albania.

Woman and Wheat — A390

25q, Woman with egg crates. 80q, Shepherd, sheep. 2.60 l, Milkmaid, cows.

1978, Dec. 15   *Perf. 12x12½*
1878	A390	15q multicolored	.20	.20
1879	A390	25q multicolored	.40	.20
1880	A390	80q multicolored	.90	.20
1881	A390	2.60 l multicolored	2.50	.50
		Nos. 1878-1881 (4)	4.00	1.10

Dora d'Istria — A391   Tower House — A392

Design: 1.10 l, Full portrait of Dora d'Istria, author; birth sesquicentennial.

1979, Jan. 22   Litho.   *Perf. 12*
1882	A391	80q lt grn & blk	.70	.20
1883	A391	1.10 l vio brn & blk	.80	.20

Costume Type of 1977

Designs: Various folk dances.

1979, Feb. 25

1884	A375	15q multi	.20	.20
1885	A375	25q multi	.20	.20
1886	A375	80q multi	.35	.20
1887	A375	1.20 l multi	.50	.20
1888	A375	1.40 l multi	.75	.20
		Nos. 1884-1888 (5)	2.00	1.00

#1884-1888 have white background. Denomination in UL on #1885, in UR on #1802; LL on #1886, UL on #1803.

1979, Mar. 20

Traditional Houses: 15q, Stone gallery house, horiz. 80q, House with wooden galleries, horiz. 1.20 l, Galleried tower house. 1.40 l, 1.90 l, Tower houses, diff.

1889	A392	15q multi	.20	.20
1890	A392	25q multi	.20	.20
1891	A392	80q multi	.35	.20
1892	A392	1.20 l multi	.50	.20
1893	A392	1.40 l multi	.75	.20
		Nos. 1889-1893 (5)	2.00	1.00

Miniature Sheet

Perf. 12 on 2 sides x Imperf.

1894	A392	1.90 l multi	1.50	.40

See Nos. 2015-2018.

Soldier, Factories, Wheat A393

1.65 l, Soldiers, workers and coat of arms.

1979, May 14   Litho.   Perf. 12

1895	A393	25q multi	.45	.20
1896	A393	1.65 l multi	2.00	.20

Congress of Permet, 35th anniversary.

Albanian Flag A394

1979, June 4

1897	A394	25q multi	.50	.20
1898	A394	1.65 l multi	2.50	.20

5th Congress of Albanian Democratic Front.

Alexander Moissi, (1880-1935), Actor — A395

1979, Apr 2

1899	A396	80q multi	.80	.20
1900	A396	1.10 l multi, diff.	1.00	.20

Vasil Shanto, (1913-44) A396

Design: 25q, 90q, Qemal Stafa (1921-42).

1979, May 5

1901	A395	15q multi	.20	.20
1902	A395	25q multi	.20	.20
1903	A395	60q multi	.60	.20
1904	A395	90q multi	.80	.20
		Nos. 1901-1904 (4)	1.80	.80

Shanto and Stafa, anti-Fascist fighters. For similar design see A410.

Winter Campaign, by Arben Basha — A397

Paintings of Military Scenes by: 25q, Ismail Lulani. 80q, Myrteza Fushekati. 1.20 l, Muhamet Deliu. 1.40 l, Jorgji Gjikopulli. 1.90 l, Fatmir Haxhiu.

1979, July 15   Litho.   Perf. 12½x12

1905	A397	15q multi	.20	.20
1906	A397	25q multi	.20	.20
1907	A397	80q multi	.35	.20
1908	A397	1.20 l multi	.60	.20
1909	A397	1.40 l multi	.65	.20
		Nos. 1905-1909 (5)	2.00	1.00

Miniature Sheet

Perf. 12 on 2 sides x Imperf.

1910	A397	1.90 l multi	1.75	.40

Athletes Surrounding Flag — A398

Literary Society Headquarters A399

1979, Oct. 1   Litho.   Perf. 12

1911	A398	15q shown	.20	.20
1912	A398	25q Shooting	.20	.20
1913	A398	80q Dancing	.25	.20
1914	A398	1.20 l Soccer	.50	.20
1915	A398	1.40 l High jump	.65	.20
		Nos. 1911-1915 (5)	1.80	1.00

Liberation Spartakiad, 35th anniversary.

1979, Oct. 12

Albanian Literary Society Centenary: 25q, Seal and charter. 80q, Founder. 1.55 l, 1879 Headquarters. 1.90 l, Founders.

1916	A399	25q multi	.20	.20
1917	A399	80q multi	.40	.20
1918	A399	1.20 l multi	.60	.20
1919	A399	1.55 l multi	.80	.20
		Nos. 1916-1919 (4)	2.00	.80

Miniature Sheet

Perf. 12½ on 2 sides x Imperf.

1920	A399	1.90 l multi	2.00	.40

Congress Statute, Coat of Arms — A400

1979, Oct. 20   Photo.   Perf. 12x12½

1921	A400	50q multi	.50	.20
1922	A400	1.65 l multi	2.50	.25

2nd Congress of Berat, 35th anniversary.

Children Entering School, Books — A401

1979   Litho.   Perf. 12½x12

1923	A401	5q shown	.20	.20
1924	A401	10q Communications	.20	.20
1925	A401	15q Steel workers	.20	.20
1926	A401	20q Dancers, instruments	.20	.20
1927	A401	25q Newspapers, radio, television	.20	.20
1928	A401	60q Textile worker	.40	.20
1929	A401	80q Armed forces	.55	.20
1930	A401	1.20 l Industry	.80	.20
1931	A401	1.60 l Transportation	1.00	.20
1932	A401	2.40 l Agriculture	1.50	.35
1932A	A401	3 l Medicine	1.90	.50
		Nos. 1923-1932A (11)	7.15	2.75

Workers and Factory A402

Worker, Red Flag and: 80q, Hand holding sickle and rifle. 1.20 l, Red star and open book. 1.55 l, Open book and cogwheel.

1979, Nov. 29

1933	A402	25q multi	.20	.20
1934	A402	80q multi	.20	.20
1935	A402	1.20 l multi	.50	.20
1936	A402	1.55 l multi	.60	.20
		Nos. 1933-1936 (4)	1.50	.80

35th anniversary of independence.

Joseph Stalin — A403

Design: 1.10 l, Stalin on dais, horiz.

1979, Dec. 21   Litho.   Perf. 12

1937	A403	80q red & dk bl	.75	.20
1938	A403	1.10 l red & dk bl	1.00	.20

Joseph Stalin (1879-1953), birth centenary.

Fireplace and Pottery, Korcar A404

Home Furnishings: 80q, Cupboard bed, dagger, pistol, ammunition pouch, Shkodar. 1.20 l, Stool, pot, chair, Mirdit. 1.35 l, Chimney, dagger, jacket, Gjirokaster.

1980, Feb. 27   Litho.   Perf. 12

1939	A404	25q multi	.20	.20
1940	A404	80q multi	.35	.20
1941	A404	1.20 l multi	.55	.20
1942	A404	1.35 l multi	.60	.30
		Nos. 1939-1942 (4)	1.70	.90

See Nos. 1985-1988.

Pipe, Painted Flask A405

1980, Mar. 4

1943	A405	25q shown	.20	.20
1944	A405	80q Leather handbags	.35	.20
1945	A405	1.20 l Carved eagle, embroidered rug	.55	.20
1946	A405	1.35 l Lace	.60	.30
		Nos. 1943-1946 (4)	1.70	.90

Prof. Aleksander Xhuvanit Birth Centenary A406

1980, Mar. 14

1947	A406	80q multi	.55	.20
1948	A406	1 l multi	.70	.20

Revolutionaries on Horseback — A407

Insurrection at Kosove, 70th Anniversary: 1 l, Battle scene.

1980, Apr. 4

1949	A407	80q red & black	.60	.20
1950	A407	1 l red & black	.75	.20

Soldiers and Workers Laboring to Aid the Stricken Populations, by D. Jukinui and I. Lulani — A408

1980, Apr. 15   Litho.   Perf. 12½

1951	A408	80q lt blue & multi	.60	.20
1952	A408	1 l lt blue grn & multi	.75	.20

Lenin, 110th Birth Anniversary A409

1980, Apr. 22

1953	A409	80q multi	.90	.20
1954	A409	1 l multi	1.10	.20

Misto Mame and Ali Demi, War Martyrs A410

War Martyrs: 80q, Sadik Staveleci, Vojo Kusji, Hoxhi Martini. 1.20 l, Bule Naipi, Persefoni Kokedhima. 1.35 l, Ndoc Deda, Hydajet Lezha, Naim Gyylbegu, Ndoc Mazi, Ahmed Haxha.

1980, May 5
1955	A410	25q multi	.20	.20
1956	A410	80q multi	.40	.20
1957	A410	1.20 l multi	.55	.20
1958	A410	1.35 l multi	.70	.30
	Nos. 1955-1958 (4)		1.85	.90

See Nos. 2012A-2012D, 2025-2028, 2064-2067, 2122-2125, 2171-2174, 2207-2209.

Scene from "Mirela"
A411

1980, June 7
1959	A411	15q shown	.20	.20
1960	A411	25q The Scribbler	.20	.20
1961	A411	80q Circus Bears	.35	.20
1962	A411	2.40 l Waterdrops	1.00	.35
	Nos. 1959-1962 (4)		1.75	.95

Carrying Iron Castings in the Enver Hoxha Tractor Combine, by S. Shijaku and M. Fushekati — A412

Paintings (Gallery of Figurative Paintings, Tirana): 80q, The Welder, by Harilla Dhima. 1.20 l, Steel Erectors, by Petro Kokushta. 1.35 l, Pandeli Lena, 1.80 l Communists, by Vilson Kilica.

1980, July 22
1963	A412	25q multi	.20	.20
1964	A412	80q multi	.35	.20
1965	A412	1.20 l multi	.50	.20
1966	A412	1.35 l multi	.65	.25
	Nos. 1963-1966 (4)		1.70	.85

Souvenir Sheet
1967	A412	1.80 l multi	1.40	.40

Gate, Parchment Miniature, 11th Cent. — A413

Bas reliefs of the Middle Ages: 80q, Eagle, 13th cent. 1.20 l, Heraldic lion, 14th cent. 1.35 l, Pheasant, 14th cent.

1980, Sept. 27   Litho.   Perf. 12
1968	A413	25q gold & blk	.20	.20
1969	A413	80q gold & blk	.25	.20
1970	A413	1.20 l gold & blk	.45	.20
1971	A413	1.35 l gold & blk	.55	.25
	Nos. 1968-1971 (4)		1.45	.85

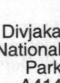

Divjaka National Park
A414

1980, Nov. 6   Photo.
1972	A414	80q shown	.50	.20
1973	A414	1.20 l Lura	.85	.25
1974	A414	1.60 l Thethi	1.10	.25
	Nos. 1972-1974 (3)		2.45	.70

Souvenir Sheet
Perf. 12½
1975	A414	1.80 l Llogara Park	2.00	.75

Citizens, Flag and Arms of Albania
A415

1981, Jan. 11   Litho.   Perf. 12
1976	A415	80q shown	.50	.20
1977	A415	1 l People's Party Headquarters, Tirana	.75	.25

35th anniversary of the Republic.

Child's Bed
A416

1981, Mar. 20   Litho.   Perf. 12
1978	A416	25q shown	.20	.20
1979	A416	80q Wooden bucket, brass bottle	.35	.20
1980	A416	1.20 l Shoes	.55	.25
1981	A416	1.35 l Jugs	.60	.35
	Nos. 1978-1981 (4)		1.70	1.00

A417

A419

1981, Apr. 20
1982	A417	80q Soldiers	.40	.20
1983	A417	1 l Sword combat	.60	.25

Souvenir Sheet
Perf. 12½ Vert.
1984	A417	1.80 l Soldier with pistol	1.25	.80

Battle of Shtimje centenary.

Home Furnishings Type of 1980
1981, Feb. 25   Litho.   Perf. 12
1985	A404	25q House interior, Labara	.20	.20
1986	A404	80q Labara, diff.	.35	.20
1987	A404	1.20 l Mat	.55	.25
1988	A404	1.35 l Dibres	.55	.35
	Nos. 1985-1988 (4)		1.65	1.00

1981, June   Perf. 12

Designs: Children's circus.
1989	A419	15q multi	.20	.20
1990	A419	25q multi	.20	.20
1991	A419	80q multi	.35	.20
1992	A419	2.40 l multi	1.00	.60
	Nos. 1989-1992 (4)		1.75	1.20

Soccer Players
A420

1982 World Cup Soccer Elimination Games: Various soccer players.

1981, Mar. 31   Litho.   Perf. 12
1993	A420	25q multi	.25	.25
1994	A420	80q multi	1.90	.40
1995	A420	1.20 l multi	2.75	.60
1996	A420	1.35 l multi	3.50	.80
	Nos. 1993-1996 (4)		8.40	2.00

Allies, by S. Hysa
A421

Paintings: 80q, Warriors, by A. Buza. 1.20 l, Rallying to the Flag, Dec. 1911, by A. Zajmi, vert. 1.35 l, My Flag is My Heart, by L. Cefa, vert. 1.80 l, Circling the Flag in a Common Cause, by N. Vasia.

1981, July 10   Perf. 12½x12
1997	A421	25q multi	.20	.20
1998	A421	80q multi	.35	.20
1999	A421	1.20 l multi	.50	.25
2000	A421	1.35 l multi	.55	.35
	Nos. 1997-2000 (4)		1.60	1.00

Souvenir Sheet
2001	A421	1.80 l multi	1.40	.85

#2001 contains one 55x55mm stamp.

Rifleman
A422

1981, Aug. 30   Perf. 12
2002	A422	25q shown	.20	.20
2003	A422	80q Weight lifting	.40	.20
2004	A422	1.20 l Volleyball	.55	.25
2005	A422	1.35 l Soccer	.65	.35
	Nos. 2002-2005 (4)		1.80	1.00

Albanian Workers' Party, 8th Congress
A423

1981, Nov. 1
2006	A423	80q Flag, star	.30	.20
2007	A423	1 l Flag, hammer & sickle	.40	.25

Albanian Workers' Party, 40th Anniv. — A424

Communist Youth Org., 40th Anniv. — A425

1981, Nov. 8
2008	A424	80q Symbols of industrialization	.35	.25
2009	A424	2.80 l Fist, emblem	1.25	.70

Souvenir Sheet
2010	A424	1.80 l Enver Hoxha, Memoirs	2.00	.85

1981, Nov. 23
2011	A425	80q Star, ax, map	.65	.20
2012	A425	1 l Flags, star	.85	.25

War Martyrs Type of 1980

25q, Perlat Rexhepi (1919-42) and Branko Kadia (1921-42). 80q, Xheladin Beqiri (1908-44) and Hajdar Dushi (1916-44). 1.20 l, Koci Bako (1905-41), Vasil Laci (1923-41) and Mujo Ulqinaku (1898-1939). 1.35 l, Mine Peza (1875-1942) and Zoja Cure (1920-44).

1981, May 5   Litho.   Perf. 12
2012A	A410	25q silver & multi	.20	.20
2012B	A410	80q gold & multi	.75	.40
2012C	A410	1.20 l silver & multi	1.25	.55
2012D	A410	1.35 l gold & multi	1.40	.60
	Nos. 2012A-2012D (4)		3.60	1.75

Fan S. Noli, Writer, Birth Centenary
A426

1982, Jan. 6   Litho.   Perf. 12
2013	A426	80q lt ol grn & gold	.40	.20
2014	A426	1.10 l lt red brn & gold	.60	.20

Traditional Houses Type of 1979
1982, Feb.   Perf. 12½x12
2015	A392	25q Bulqize	.30	.20
2016	A392	80q Lebush	.35	.20
2017	A392	1.20 l Bicaj	.55	.30
2018	A392	1.55 l Klos	.80	.40
	Nos. 2015-2018 (4)		2.00	1.10

TB Bacillus Centenary
A428

1982, Mar. 24   Perf. 12
2019	A428	80q Globe	1.00	.25
2020	A428	1.10 l Koch	1.40	.35

Albanian League House, Prizren, by K. Buza — A429

Kosova Landscapes: 25q, Castle at Prizrenit, by G. Madhi. 1.20 l, Mountain Gorge at Rogove, by K. Buza. 1.55 l, Street of the Hadhji at Zekes, by G. Madhi. 25q, 1.20 l, 1.55 l vert.

Perf. 12x12½, 12½x12
1982, Apr. 15   Litho.
2021	A429	25q multi	.20	.20
2022	A429	80q multi	.50	.20
2023	A429	1.20 l multi	.70	.20
2024	A429	1.55 l multi	1.00	.30
	Nos. 2021-2024 (4)		2.40	.90

War Martyr Type of 1980

Designs: 25q, Hibe Palikuqi, Liri Gero. 80q, Mihal Duri, Kajo Karafili. 1.20 l, Fato Dudumi, Margarita Tutulani, Shejnaze Juka. 1.55 l, Memo Meto, Gjok Doci.

1982, May   Perf. 12
2025	A410	25q multi	.20	.20
2026	A410	80q multi	.35	.20
2027	A410	1.20 l multi	.60	.30
2028	A410	1.55 l multi	.85	.45
	Nos. 2025-2028 (4)		2.00	1.15

Loading Freighter — A430

Children's Paintings.

1982, June 15			**Perf. 12½x12**		
2029	A430	15q	shown	.20	.20
2030	A430	80q	Forest	.55	.20
2031	A430	1.20 l	City	.90	.30
2032	A430	1.65 l	Park	1.25	.45
	Nos. 2029-2032 (4)			2.90	1.15

9th Congress of Trade Unions A431

1982, June 6		**Litho.**		**Perf. 12**	
2033	A431	80q	Workers, factories	.80	.20
2034	A431	1.10 l	Emblem, flag	1.10	.25

Alpine Village Festival, by Danish Jukniu A432

Industrial Development Paintings: 80q, Hydroelectric Station Builders, by Ali Miruku. 1.20 l, Steel Workers, by Clirim Ceka. 1.55 l, Oil drillers, by Pandeli Lena. 1.90 l, Trapping the Furnace, by Jorgji Gjikopulli.

1982, July				**Perf. 12½**	
2035	A432	25q	multi	.20	.20
2036	A432	80q	multi	.50	.20
2037	A432	1.20 l	multi	.75	.20
2038	A432	1.55 l	multi	1.00	.30
	Nos. 2035-2038 (4)			2.45	.90

Souvenir Sheet
Perf. 12

2039	A432	1.90 l	multi	1.75	.40

No. 2039 contains one 54x48mm stamp.

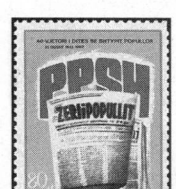

Communist Party Newspaper "Voice of the People," 40th Anniv. — A432a

1982, Aug. 25		**Litho.**		**Perf. 12**	
2039A	A432a	80q	Newspapers		
2039B	A432a	1.10 l	Paper, press		

40th Anniv. of Democratic Front A433

1982, Sept. 16				**Perf. 12**	
2040	A433	80q	Glory to the Heroes of Peza Monument	.80	.20
2041	A433	1.10 l	Marchers	1.10	.25

8th Youth Congress — A434

Handmade Shoulder Bags — A435

1982, Oct. 4					
2042	A434	80q	multi	.80	.20
2043	A434	1.10 l	multi	1.10	.25

1982, Nov.					
2044	A435	25q	Rug, horiz.	.20	.20
2045	A435	80q	shown	.40	.20
2046	A435	1.20 l	Wooden pots, bowls, horiz.	.60	.20
2047	A435	1.55 l	Jug	.80	.30
	Nos. 2044-2047 (4)			2.00	.90

70th Anniv. of Independence — A436

1982, Nov. 28					
2048	A436	20q	Ishamil Qemali	.20	.20
2049	A436	1.20 l	Partisans	.55	.20
2050	A436	2.40 l	Partisans, diff.	1.25	.40
	Nos. 2048-2050 (3)			2.00	.80

Souvenir Sheet

2051	A436	1.90 l	Independence Monument, Tirana	1.75	.40

Dhermi Beach A437

1982, Dec. 20					
2052	A437	25q	shown	.20	.20
2053	A437	80q	Sarande	.50	.20
2054	A437	1.20 l	Ksamil	.75	.25
2055	A437	1.55 l	Lukove	1.00	.35
	Nos. 2052-2055 (4)			2.45	1.00

Handkerchief Dancers — A438

Folkdancers.

1983, Feb. 20		**Litho.**		**Perf. 12**	
2056	A438	25q	shown	.20	.20
2057	A438	80q	With kerchief, drum	.40	.20
2058	A438	1.20 l	With guitar, flute, tambourine	.60	.25
2059	A438	1.55 l	Women	.80	.35
	Nos. 2056-2059 (4)			2.00	1.00

A439

A440

1983, Mar. 14		**Litho.**		**Perf. 12**	
2060	A439	80q	multi	1.10	.20
2061	A439	1.10 l	multi	1.50	.25

Karl Marx (1818-83).

1983, Apr. 20					
2062	A440	80q	Electricity generation	.40	.20
2063	A440	1.10 l	Gas & oil production	.55	.25

Energy development.

War Martyr Type of 1980

Designs: 25q, Asim Zeneli (1916-43), Nazmi Rushiti (1919-42). 80q, Shyqyri Ishmi (1922-42), Shyqyri Alimerko (1923-43), Myzafer Asqeriu (1918-42). 1.20 l, Qybra Sokoli (1924-44), Qeriba Derri (1905-44), Ylbere Bilibashi (1928-44). 1.55 l, Themo Vasi (1915-43), Abaz Shehu (1905-42).

1983, May 5		**Litho.**		**Perf. 12**	
2064	A410	25q	multi	.20	.20
2065	A410	80q	multi	.40	.20
2066	A410	1.20 l	multi	.60	.25
2067	A410	1.55 l	multi	.80	.35
	Nos. 2064-2067 (4)			2.00	1.00

Women's Union, 9th Congress A441

1983, June 1		**Litho.**		**Perf. 12x12½**	
2068	A441	80q	red & gold	.85	.20
2069	A441	1.10 l	blue & gold	1.10	.25

Bicycling A442

1983, June 20				**Perf. 12**	
2070	A442	25q	shown	.20	.20
2071	A442	80q	Chess	.40	.20
2072	A442	1.20 l	Gymnastics	.60	.25
2073	A442	1.55 l	Wrestling	.80	.35
	Nos. 2070-2073 (4)			2.00	1.00

40th Anniv. of People's Army — A443

1983, July 10					
2074	A443	20q	Armed services	.20	.20
2075	A443	1.20 l	Soldier, gun barrels	.85	.30
2076	A443	2.40 l	Factory guard, crowd	1.60	.50
	Nos. 2074-2076 (3)			2.65	1.00

Sunny Day, by Myrteza Fushekati — A444

Paintings: 80q, Messenger of the Grasp, by Niko Progi. 1.20 l, 29 November 1944, by Harilla Dhimo. 1.55 l, Fireworks, by Pandi Mele. 1.90 l, Partisan Assault, by Sali Shijaku and M. Fushekati.

1983, Aug. 28		**Litho.**		**Perf. 12½x12**	
2077	A444	25q	multi	.20	.20
2078	A444	80q	multi	.40	.20
2079	A444	1.20 l	multi	.60	.25
2080	A444	1.55 l	multi	.80	.35
	Nos. 2077-2080 (4)			2.00	1.00

Souvenir Sheet
Perf. 12

2081	A444	1.90 l	multi	4.00	.50

Folklore Festival Type of 1978

Gjirokaster Folklore Festival: folkdances.

1983, Oct. 6		**Litho.**		**Perf. 12**	
2082	A388	25q	Sword dance	.20	.20
2083	A388	80q	Kerchief dance	.50	.20
2084	A388	1.20 l	Shepherd flautists	.75	.20
2085	A388	1.55 l	Garland dance	1.00	.35
	Nos. 2082-2085 (4)			2.45	1.00

World Communications Year — A446

1983, Nov. 10					
2086	A446	60q	multi	.40	.20
2087	A446	1.20 l	multi	.85	.25

75th Birthday of Enver Hoxha A447

1983, Oct. 16		**Litho.**		**Perf. 12½**	
2088	A447	80q	multi	.40	.20
2089	A447	1.20 l	multi	.60	.25
2090	A447	1.80 l	multi	.90	.40
	Nos. 2088-2090 (3)			1.90	.85

Souvenir Sheet
Perf. 12

2091	A447	1.90 l	multi	1.40	.50

The Right to a Joint Triumph, by J. Keraj A448

Era of Skanderbeg in Figurative Art: 80q, The Heroic Center of the Battle of Krujes, by N. Bakalli. 1.20 l, The Rights of the Enemy after our Triumph, by N. Progri. 1.55 l, The

Discussion at Lezhes, by B. Ahmeti. 1.90 l, Victory over the Turks, by G. Madhi.

1983, Dec. 10   *Perf. 12½x12*
2092	A448	25q multi	.20	.20
2093	A448	80q multi	.65	.20
2094	A448	1.20 l multi	.90	.25
2095	A448	1.55 l multi	1.25	.35
	Nos. 2092-2095 (4)		3.00	1.00

Souvenir Sheet
Perf. 12
2096	A448	1.90 l multi	2.25	.50

Greco-Roman Ruins of Illyria — A449

1983, Dec. 28   *Perf. 12*
2097	A449	80q Amphitheater, Buthroxtum	.65	.20
2098	A449	1.20 l Colonnade, Apollonium	.95	.25
2099	A449	1.80 l Vaulted gallery, amphitheater at Epidamnus	1.40	.40
	Nos. 2097-2099 (3)		3.00	.85

Archeological Discoveries A450

Designs: Apollo, 3rd cent. 25q, Tombstone, Korce, 3rd cent. 80q, Apollo, diff. 1st cent. 1.10 l, Earthenware pot (child's head), Tren, 1st cent. 1.20 l, Man's head, Dyrrah, 2.20 l, Eros with Dolphin, statue Bronze Dyrrah, 3rd cent.

1984, Feb. 25   *Perf. 12x12½*
2100	A450	15q multi	.20	.20
2101	A450	25q multi	.20	.20
2102	A450	80q multi	.35	.20
2103	A450	1.10 l multi	.55	.20
2104	A450	1.20 l multi	.60	.25
2105	A450	2.20 l multi	1.10	.50
	Nos. 2100-2105 (6)		3.00	1.55

Clock Towers — A451

1984, Mar. 30   Litho.   *Perf. 12*
2106	A451	15q Gjirokaster	.20	.20
2107	A451	25q Kavaje	.20	.20
2108	A451	80q Elbasan	.35	.20
2109	A451	1.10 l Tirana	.55	.20
2110	A451	1.20 l Peqin	.60	.25
2111	A451	2.20 l Kruje	1.10	.50
	Nos. 2106-2111 (6)		3.00	1.55

40th Anniv. of Liberation A452

1984, Apr. 20   Litho.   *Perf. 12*
2112	A452	15q Student & microscope	.20	.20
2113	A452	25q Guerrilla with flag	.20	.20

2114	A452	80q Children with flag	.35	.20
2115	A452	1.10 l Soldier	.55	.20
2116	A452	1.20 l Workers with flag	.60	.25
2117	A452	2.20 l Militia at dam	1.10	.50
	Nos. 2112-2117 (6)		3.00	1.55

Children — A453

1984, May   Litho.   *Perf. 12*
2118	A453	15q Children reading	.20	.20
2119	A453	25q Young pioneers	.25	.20
2120	A453	60q Gardening	.60	.20
2121	A453	2.80 l Kite flying	2.75	.60
	Nos. 2118-2121 (4)		3.80	1.20

War Martyr Type of 1980

Designs: 15q, Manush Almani, Mustafa Matohiti, Kastriot Muco. 25q, Zaho Koka, Reshit Collaku, Maliq Muco. 1.20 l, Lefter Talo, Tom Kola, Fuat Babani. 2.20 l, Myslysm Shyri, Dervish Hexali, Skender Caci.

1984, May 5   Litho.   *Perf. 12*
2122	A410	15q multi	.20	.20
2123	A410	15q multi	.20	.20
2124	A410	1.20 l multi	.95	.30
2125	A410	2.20 l multi	1.75	.60
	Nos. 2122-2125 (4)		3.10	1.30

A454

1984, May 24   Litho.   *Perf. 12*
2126	A454	80q Enver Hoxha	.80	.20
2127	A454	1.10 l Resistance fighter	1.25	.30

40th anniv. of Permet Congress.

1984, June 12   Litho.   *Perf. 12*
2128	A455	15q Goalkeeper	.20	.20
2129	A455	25q Referee	.20	.20
2130	A455	1.20 l Map of Europe	.85	.45
2131	A455	2.20 l Field diagram	1.75	.90
	Nos. 2128-2131 (4)		3.00	1.75

European soccer championships.

Freedom Came, by Myrteza Fushekati — A456

Paintings, Tirana Gallery of Figurative Art: 25q, Morning, by Zamir Mati, vert. 80q, My Darling, by Agim Zajmi, vert. 2.60 l, For the Partisans, by Arben Basha. 1.90 l, Eagle, by Zamir Mati, vert.

1984, June 12   *Perf. 12½*
2132	A456	15q multi	.20	.20
2133	A456	25q multi	.25	.20
2134	A456	80q multi	.80	.25
2135	A456	2.60 l multi	2.75	.80
	Nos. 2132-2135 (4)		4.00	1.45

Souvenir Sheet
Perf. 12 Horiz.
2136	A456	1.90 l multi	3.00	.60

Flora — A457

1984, Aug. 20   Litho.   *Perf. 12*
2137	A457	15q Moraceae L.	.35	.20
2138	A457	25q Plantaginaceae	.65	.20
2139	A457	1.20 l Hypericaceae L.	2.75	.60
2140	A457	2.20 l Leontopodium alpinum	5.25	1.10
	Nos. 2137-2140 (4)		9.00	2.10

AUSIPEX '84, Melbourne, Sept. 21-30 — A458

Perf. 12 Horiz.
1984, Sept. 21   Litho.
2141	A458	1.90 l Sword dancers, emblem	1.50	.75

A459

A460

Forestry, logging, UNFAO emblem.

1984, Sept. 25   *Perf. 12*
2142	A459	15q Beech trees, transport	.20	.20
2143	A459	25q Pine forest, logging cable	.20	.20
2144	A459	1.20 l Firs, sawmill	.85	.45
2145	A459	2.20 l Forester clearing woods	1.75	.90
	Nos. 2142-2145 (4)		3.00	1.75

1984, Oct. 13   *Perf. 12½*
2146	A460	1.20 l View of Gjirokaster	2.00	.45

EURPHILA '84, Rome.

5th National Spartakiad A461

1984, Oct. 19   *Perf. 12*
2147	A461	15q Soccer	.20	.20
2148	A461	25q Women's track & field	.20	.20
2149	A461	80q Weight lifting	.60	.30
2150	A461	2.20 l Pistol shooting	1.75	.60
	Nos. 2147-2150 (4)		2.75	1.60

Souvenir Sheet
Perf. 12 Horiz.
2151	A461	1.90 l Opening ceremony, red flags	2.00	.75

November 29 Revolution, 40th Anniv. A462

1984, Nov. 29   *Perf. 12*
2152	A462	80q Industrial reconstruction	1.25	.30
2153	A462	1.10 l Natl. flag, partisans	1.60	.40

Souvenir Sheet
Perf. 12 Horiz.
2154	A462	1.90 l Gen. Enver Hoxha reading 1944 declaration	2.00	.75

Archaeological Discoveries from Illyria — A463

Designs: 15q, Iron Age water container. 80q, Terra-cotta woman's head, 6th-7th cent. B.C. 1.20 l, Aphrodite, bust, 3rd cent. B.C. 1.70 l, Nike, A.D. 1st-2nd cent. bronze statue.

1985, Feb. 25   *Perf. 12x12½*
2155	A463	15q multi	.20	.20
2156	A463	80q multi	.80	.40
2157	A463	1.20 l multi	1.10	.55
2158	A463	1.70 l multi	1.75	.85
	Nos. 2155-2158 (4)		3.85	2.00

Hysni Kapo (1915-1980), Natl. Labor Party Leader — A464

1985, Mar. 4   *Perf. 12*
2159	A464	90q red & blk	.85	.45
2160	A464	1.10 l chlky bl & blk	1.10	.55

OLYMPHILEX '85, Lausanne — A465

1985, Mar. 18
2161	A465	25q Women's track & field	.25	.20
2162	A465	60q Weight lifting	.60	.30
2163	A465	1.20 l Soccer	1.10	.55
2164	A465	1.50 l Women's pistol shooting	1.25	.65
		Nos. 2161-2164 (4)	3.20	1.70

Johann Sebastian Bach — A466

1985, Mar. 31
2165	A466	80q Portrait, manuscript	2.00	.40
2166	A466	1.20 l Eisenach, birthplace	3.00	.55

Gen. Enver Hoxha (1908-1985) A467

1985, Apr. 11   *Perf. 12½*
2167	A467	80q multicolored	.80	.40

Souvenir Sheet
Imperf
2168	A467	1.90 l multicolored	2.00	1.00

Natl. Frontier Guards, 40th Anniv. A468

1985, Apr. 25   *Perf. 12*
2169	A468	25q Guardsman, family	.35	.20
2170	A468	80q At frontier post	1.10	.40

War Martyrs Type of 1980

25q, Mitro Xhani (1916-44), Nimete Progonati (1929-44), Kozma Nushi (1909-44). 40q, Ajet Xhindoli (1922-43), Mustafa Kacaci (1903-44), Estref Caka Osaja (1919-44). 60q, Celo Sinani (1929-44), Lt. Ambro Andoni (1920-44), Meleq Gosnishti (1913-44). 1.20 l, Thodhori Mastora (1920-44), Fejzi Micoli (1919-45), Hysen Cino (1920-44).

1985, May 5
2171	A410	25q multi	.25	.20
2172	A410	40q multi	.40	.20
2173	A410	60q multi	.60	.30
2174	A410	1.20 l multi	1.25	.55
		Nos. 2171-2174 (4)	2.50	1.25

Victory over Fascism A469

25q, Rifle, red flag, inscribed May 9. 80q, Hand holding rifle, globe, broken swastika.

1985, May 9
2175	A469	25q multi	.65	.20
2176	A469	80q multi	2.00	.40

End of World War II, 40th anniv.

Primary School, by Thoma Malo A470

Paintings, Tirana Gallery of Figurative Art: 80q, The Heroes, by Hysen Devolli, vert. 90q, In Our Days, by Angjelin Dodmasej, vert. 1.20 l, Going Off to Sow, by Ksenofon Dilo. 1.90 l, Foundry Workers, by Mikel Gurashi.

1985, June 25   *Perf. 12½*
2177	A470	25q multi	.25	.20
2178	A470	80q multi	.80	.40
2179	A470	90q multi	.85	.45
2180	A470	1.20 l multi	1.10	.55
		Nos. 2177-2180 (4)	3.00	1.60

Souvenir Sheet
Perf. 12 Horiz.
2181	A470	1.90 l multi	2.00	1.00

Basketball Championships, Spain — A471

Fruits — A472

Various plays.

1985, July 20   Litho.   *Perf. 12*
2182	A471	25q dull bl & blk	.25	.20
2183	A471	80q dull grn & blk	.80	.40
2184	A471	1.20 l dl vio & blk	1.10	.60
2185	A471	1.60 l dl rose & blk	1.50	.80
		Nos. 2182-2185 (4)	3.65	2.00

1985, Aug. 20
2186	A472	25q Oranges	.25	.20
2187	A472	80q Plums	.80	.40
2188	A472	1.20 l Apples	1.10	.60
2189	A472	1.60 l Cherries	1.50	.80
		Nos. 2186-2189 (4)	3.65	2.00

Architecture A473

1985, Sept. 20
2190	A473	25q Kruja	.25	.20
2191	A473	80q Gjirokastra	.80	.40
2192	A473	1.20 l Berati	1.10	.60
2193	A473	1.60 l Shkodera	1.50	.80
		Nos. 2190-2193 (4)	3.65	2.00

Natl. Folk Theater Festival — A474

Various scenes from folk plays.

1985, Oct. 6
2194	A474	25q multi	.25	.20
2195	A474	80q multi	.80	.40
2196	A474	1.20 l multi	1.10	.60
2197	A474	1.60 l multi	1.50	.75

Size: 56x82mm
Imperf
2198	A474	1.90 l multi	3.50	1.90
		Nos. 2194-2198 (5)	7.15	3.85

Socialist People's Republic, 40th Anniv. — A475

1986, Jan. 11   Litho.   *Perf. 12½*
2199	A475	25q Natl. crest, vert.	.70	.20
2200	A475	80q Proclamation, 1946	2.25	.40

A476

Designs: 25q, Dam, River Drin, Melgun. 80q, Bust of Enver Hoxha, dam power house.

1986, Feb. 20   *Perf. 12*
2201	A476	25q multi	1.25	.20
2202	A476	80q multi	3.75	.40

Enver Hoxha hydro-electric power station, Koman.

A477

1986, Mar. 20   Litho.   *Perf. 12*

Flowers: 25q,   Gymnospermium shqipetarum.1.20 l, Leucojum valentinum.
2203	A477	25q multi	.35	.20
2204	A477	1.20 l multi	1.90	.60
a.		Pair, #2203-2204	2.25	1.00

No. 2204a sold only in booklets of 2; exists imperf.

A478

Famous Men — A479

Designs: 25q, Maxim Gorky, Russian author. 80q, Andre Marie Ampere, French physicist. 1.20 l, James Watt, English inventor of modern steam engine. 2.40 l, Franz Liszt, Hungarian composer.

1986, Apr. 20
2205		Strip of 4	4.40	2.20
a.	A478	25q dull red brown	.25	.20
b.	A478	80q dull violet	.75	.40
c.	A478	1.20 l blue green	1.10	.60
d.	A478	2.40 l dull lilac rose	2.25	.90

Size: 88x72mm
Imperf
2206	A479	1.90 l multi	1.75	.90

No. 2206 has central area picturing Gorky, Ampere, Watt and Liszt, perf. 12½.

War Martyrs Type of 1980

25q, Ramiz Aranitasi (1923-43), Inajete Dumi (1924-44) and Laze Nuro Ferraj (1897-1944). 80q, Dine Kalenja (1919-44), Kozma Naska (1921-44), Met Hasa (1929-44) and Fahri Ramadani (1920-44). 1.20 l, Hiqmet Buzi (1927-44), Bajram Tusha (1922-42), Mumin Selami (1923-42) and Hajrfdin Bylyshi (1923-42).

1986, May 5   *Perf. 12*
2207	A410	25q multi	.65	.20
2208	A410	80q multi	2.25	.40
2209	A410	1.20 l multi	3.00	.55
		Nos. 2207-2209 (3)	5.90	1.15

A480

1986 World Cup Soccer Championships, Mexico — A481

1986, May 31   Litho.   *Perf. 12*
2210	A480	25q Globe, world cup	.25	.20
2211	A480	1.20 l Player, soccer ball	1.25	.60

Size: 97x64mm
Imperf
2212	A481	1.90 l multi	1.75	.90
		Nos. 2210-2212 (3)	3.25	1.70

No. 2212 has central label, perf. 12½.

Transportation Workers' Day, 40th Anniv. — A482

1986, Aug. 10   Litho.   *Perf. 12*
2213	A482	1.20 l multi	3.00	.60

Prominent Albanians A483

Designs: 30q, Naim Frasheri (1846-1900), poet. 60q, Ndre Mjeda (1866-1937), poet. 90q, Petro Nini Luarasi (1865-1911), poet, journalist. 1 l, Andon Zako Cajupi (1866-1930), poet. 1.20 l, Millosh Gjergj Nikolla Migjeni (1911-1938), novelist. 2.60 l, Urani Rumbo (1884-1936), educator.

1986, Sept. 20		**Litho.**	**Perf. 12**	
2214	A483	30q multi	.30	.20
2215	A483	60q multi	.60	.30
2216	A483	90q multi	.90	.45
2217	A483	1 l multi	.95	.50
2218	A483	1.20 l multi	1.10	.60
2219	A483	2.60 l multi	2.50	1.25
		Nos. 2214-2219 (6)	6.35	3.30

Albanian Workers' Party, 9th Congress, Tirana A484

1986, Nov. 3	**Litho.**	**Perf. 12**	
2220	A484 30q multi	1.90	.25

A485   A486

Albanian Workers' Party, 45th Anniv.: 30q, Handstamp, signature of Hoxha. 1.20 l, Marx, Engels, Lenin and Stalin, party building.

1986, Nov. 8			
2221	A485 30q multi	.60	.20
2222	A485 1.20 l multi	2.25	.60

Statue of Mother Albania.

1986, Nov. 29			**Perf. 12x12½**	
2223	A486	10q peacock blue	.20	.20
2224	A486	20q henna brn	.20	.20
2225	A486	30q vermilion	.30	.20
2226	A486	50q dk olive bis	.50	.25
2227	A486	60q lt olive grn	.60	.30
2228	A486	80q rose	.80	.40
2229	A486	90q ultra	.90	.45
2230	A486	1.20 l green	1.10	.60
2231	A486	1.60 l red vio	1.50	.75
2232	A486	2.20 l myrtle grn	2.00	1.10
2233	A486	3 l brn org	2.75	1.40
2234	A486	6 l yel bister	5.50	2.25
		Nos. 2223-2234 (12)	16.35	8.10

For surcharges see Nos. 2435-2439.

Artifacts A487

Designs: 30q, Head of Aesoulapius, 5th cent. B.C. Byllis, marble. 80q, Aphrodite, 3rd cent. B.C., Fier, terracotta. 1 l, Pan, 3rd-2nd cent, B.C., Byllis, bronze. 1.20 l, Jupiter, A.D. 2nd cent., Tirana, limestone.

1987, Feb. 20				
2235	A487	30q multi	.30	.20
2236	A487	80q multi	.75	.40
2237	A487	1 l multi	.95	.45
2238	A487	1.20 l multi	1.10	.60
		Nos. 2235-2238 (4)	3.10	1.65

A488

A489

Gun, quill pen, book of the alphabet and: 30q, Monument, vert. 80q, School, Korca. 1.20 l, Students.

1987, Mar. 7		**Perf. 12**	
2239	A488 30q multi	.35	.20
2240	A488 80q multi	.85	.40
2241	A488 1.20 l multi	1.25	.60
	Nos. 2239-2241 (3)	2.45	1.20

First Albanian school, cent.

1987, Apr. 20

Famous Men: 30q, Victor Hugo, French author. 80q, Galileo Galilei, Italian mathematician, philosopher. 90q, Charles Darwin, British biologist. 1.30 l, Miguel Cervantes, Spanish novelist.

2242	A489	30q multi	.30	.20
2243	A489	80q multi	.75	.40
2244	A489	90q multi	.90	.45
2245	A489	1.30 l multi	1.25	.80
		Nos. 2242-2245 (4)	3.20	1.85

World Food Day — A490

10th Trade Unions Cong. — A491

1987, May 20				
2246	A490	30q Forsythia europaea	.30	.20
2247	A490	90q Moltkia doerfleri	.85	.45
2248	A490	2.10 l Wulfenia baldacii	2.00	1.00
		Nos. 2246-2248 (3)	3.15	1.65

1987, June 25			
2249	A491 1.20 l multi	2.25	.60

Sowing, by Bujar Asllani — A492

Paintings in the Eponymous Museum, Tirana: 30q, The Sustenance of Industry, by Myrteza Fushekati, vert. 80q, The Gifted Partisan, by Skender Kokobobo, vert. 1.20 l, At the Forging Block, by Clirim Ceka.

	Perf. 12x12½, 12½x12		
1987, July 20		**Litho.**	
2250	A492 30q multi	.30	.20
2251	A492 80q multi	.80	.40
2252	A492 1 l shown	1.00	.50
2253	A492 1.20 l multi	1.25	.60
	Nos. 2250-2253 (4)	3.35	1.70

A493

OLYMPHILEX '87, Rome, Aug. 29-Sept. 6 — A494

Illustration A494 reduced.

1987, Aug. 29		**Litho.**	**Perf. 12½**	
2254	A493	30q Hammer throw	.30	.20
2255	A493	90q Running	.90	.45
2256	A493	1.10 l Shot put	1.25	.60
		Size: 85x60mm		
2257	A494	1.90 l Runner, globe	2.00	1.00
		Nos. 2254-2257 (4)	4.45	2.25

Famous Men A495

Designs: 30q, Themistokli Germenji (1871-1917), author, politician. 80q, Bajram Curri (1862-1925), founder of the Albanian League. 90q, Aleks Stavre Drenova (1872-1947), poet. 1.30 l, Gjerasim D. Qiriazi (1861-1894), teacher, journalist.

1987, Sept. 30			**Perf. 12**	
2258	A495	30q multi	.30	.20
2259	A495	80q multi	.80	.40
2260	A495	90q multi	.90	.45
2261	A495	1.30 l multi	1.25	.65
		Nos. 2258-2261 (4)	3.25	1.70

Albanian Labor Party Congress, Tirana A496

1987, Oct. 22	**Litho.**	**Perf. 12**	
2262	A496 1.20 l multi	1.90	.60

Natl. Independence, 75th Anniv. — A497

Postal Administration, 75th Anniv. — A498

1987, Nov. 27			
2263	A497 1.20 l State flag	1.90	.60

1987, Dec. 5			
2264	A498 90q P.O. emblem	2.00	.45
2265	A498 1.20 l State seal	2.50	.60

Art & Literature — A499

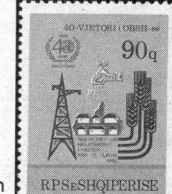

WHO, 40th Anniv. — A500

Portraits: 30q, Lord Byron (1788-1824), English Poet. 1.20 l, Eugene Delacroix (1798-1863), French painter.

1988, Mar. 10				
2266	A499	30q org brn & blk	1.00	.20
2267	A499	1.20 l pale vio & blk	4.00	.60

1988, Apr. 7				
2268	A500	90q multi	2.00	.45
2269	A500	1.20 l multi	2.50	.60

Flowers — A501

1988, May 20				
	Booklet Stamps			
2270	A501	30q Sideritis raeseri	.75	.20
2271	A501	90q Lunaria telekiana	2.25	.45
2272	A501	2.10 l Sanguisorba albanica	5.50	1.10
a.		Bklt. pane of 3, plus label	8.50	
		Nos. 2270-2272 (3)	8.50	1.75

10th Women's Federation Congress A502

1988, June 6
2273 A502 90q blk, red & dark
org   2.50 .45

European Soccer
Championships — A503

Various athletes.
1.90 l, Goalie designs of Nos. 2274-2276.

1988, June 10
2274 A503   30q multicolored   .30 .20
2275 A503   80q multicolored   .80 .40
2276 A503 1.20 l multicolored   1.25 .60

Size: 79x68mm
Imperf

2277 A503 1.90 l multicolored   1.90 .95
   Nos. 2274-2277 (4)   4.25 2.15

League of
Prizren, 110th
Anniv. — A504

People's Army,
45th
Anniv. — A505

1988, June 10   Litho.   Perf. 12
2278 A504   30q Hands
2279 A504 1.20q House

1988, July 10
2280 A505   60q shown
2281 A505   90q Soldier statue

Famous
Albanians
A506

Designs: 30q, Mihal Grameno (1871-1931),
author. 90q, Bajo Topulli (1868-1930), freedom fighter. 1 l, Murat Toptani (1868-1917),
poet. 1.20 l, Jul Variboba, poet.

1988, Aug. 15
2282 A506   30q multi
2283 A506   90q multi
2284 A506   1 l multi
2284A A506 1.20 l multi

Migjeni (1911-1938), Poet — A507

1988, Aug. 26   Litho.   Perf. 12
2285 A507 90q silver & brown   2.50 .50

Ballads
A508

1988, Sept. 5
2286 A508   30q Dede Skurra   1.00 .20
2287 A508   90q Omeri Iri   3.00 .50
2288 A508 1.20 l Gjergj Elez Alia   4.00 .65
   Nos. 2286-2288 (3)   8.00 1.35

Folklore Festival Type of 1978

1988, Oct. 6
2289 A388   30q Kerchief Dance 1.25 .20
2290 A388 1.20 l Dancers with
         raised arm   4.75 .65

Enver
Hoxha
Museum
A510

Perf. 12x12½, 12½x12
1988, Oct. 16   Litho.
2291 A510   90q Portrait, vert. 1.10 .35
2292 A510 1.20 l shown   1.40 .50

Hoxha (1908-85), Communist leader.

Monastir
Congress,
80th Anniv.
A511

1988, Nov. 14   Litho.   Perf. 12
2293 A511 60q Scroll
2294 A511 90q Book, building

Locomotives, Map Showing Rail
Network — A512

1989, Feb. 28   Litho.   Perf. 12½x12
2295 A512   30q 1947   .20 .20
2296 A512   90q 1949   .65 .35
2297 A512 1.20 l 1978   .85 .40
2298 A512 1.80 l 1985   1.25 .65
2299 A512 2.40 l 1988   1.60 .85
   Nos. 2295-2299 (5)   4.55 2.45

Archaeological Treasures — A513

30q, Illyrian grave. 90q, Warrior on
horseback.

1989, Mar. 10   Litho.   Perf. 12
2300 A513   30q blk & tan   .20 .20
2301 A513   90q blk & dl grn   .65 .35
2302 A513 2.10 l shown   1.50 .75
   Nos. 2300-2302 (3)   2.35 1.30

Folklore
A514

1989, Apr. 5   Litho.   Perf. 12x12½
2303 A514   30q multicolored   .20 .20
2304 A514   80q multi, diff.   .55 .30
2305 A514   1 l multi, diff.   .70 .35
2306 A514 1.20 l multi, diff.   .85 .45
   Nos. 2303-2306 (4)   2.30 1.30

Flowers — A515

Famous
People — A516

Designs: 30q, Aster albanicus. 90q, Orchis
x paparisti. 2.10 l, Orchis albanica.

1989, May 10   Perf. 12
2307 A515   30q multicolored   .20 .20
2308 A515   80q multicolored   .65 .35
2309 A515 2.10 l multicolored   1.50 .75
   Nos. 2307-2309 (3)   2.35 1.30

1989, June 3
Designs: 30q, Johann Strauss the Younger
(1825-1899), composer. 80q, Marie Curie
(1867-1834), chemist. 1 l, Federico Garcia
Lorca (1898-1936), poet. 1.20 l, Albert Einstein (1879-1955), physicist.

2310 A516   30q gold & blk brn   .20 .20
2311 A516   80q gold & blk brn   .60 .30
2312 A516   1 l gold & blk brn   .75 .35
2313 A516 1.20 l gold & blk brn   .85 .45
   Nos. 2310-2313 (4)   2.40 1.30

6th
Congress
of Albanian
Democratic
Front
A517

1989, June 26
2314 A517 1.20 l multicolored   1.50 .65

French Revolution, Bicent. — A518

90q, Storming of the Bastille. 1.20 l, Statue.

1989, July 7   Litho.   Perf. 12½
2315 A518   90q multicolored   .75 .40
2316 A518 1.20 l shown   1.00 .50

Illyrian Ship
A519

1989, July 25   Perf. 12
2317 A519   30q shown   .25 .20
2318 A519   80q Caravel   .60 .30
2319 A519   90q 3-masted
         schooner   .65 .35
2320 A519 1.30 l Modern cargo
         ship   1.00 .50
   Nos. 2317-2320 (4)   2.50 1.35

A520

A521

Famous Men: 30q, Pjeter Bogdani (1625-
1689), writer. 80q, Gavril Dara (1826-1889),
poet. 90q, Thimi Mitko (1820-1890), writer.
1.30 l, Kole Idromeno (1860-1939), painter.

1989, Aug. 30   Litho.   Perf. 12
2321 A520   30q multicolored   .30 .20
2322 A520   80q multicolored   .80 .40
2323 A520   90q multicolored   .90 .45
2324 A520 1.30 l multicolored   1.25 .65
   Nos. 2321-2324 (4)   3.25 1.70

1989, Sept. 29
2325 A521   90q shown   .70 .35
2326 A521 1.20 l Workers   .95 .50

First Communist International, 125th anniv.

Spartakiad
Games
A522

1989, Oct. 27   Perf. 12x12½
2327 A522   30q Gymasnastics   .20 .20
2328 A522   80q Soccer   .55 .30
2329 A522   1 l Cycling   .70 .35
2330 A522 1.20 l Running   .85 .45
   Nos. 2327-2330 (4)   2.30 1.30

Miniature Sheet

45th Anniv. of Liberation — A523

1989, Nov. 29   Perf. 12x12½
2331 A523 Sheet of 4   2.50 1.25
  a.   30q Revolutionary   .20 .20
  b.   80q "45"   .55 .30
  c.   1 l Coat of arms   .70 .35
  d.   1.20 l Workers   .85 .45

Rupicapra
Rupicapra
A524

1990, Mar. 15   *Perf. 12*
2332 A524 10q Two adults   .25 .20
2333 A524 30q Adult, kid   .50 .20
2334 A524 80q Adult   1.25 .60
2335 A524 90q Adult head   1.50 .75
  a.   Block of 4, #2332-2335   3.50 1.75

World Wildlife Fund.

Tribal Masks
A525

1990, Apr. 4   *Perf. 12x12½*
2336 A525 30q shown   .30 .20
2337 A525 90q multi, diff.   .95 .50
2338 A525 1.20 l multi, diff.   1.25 .65
2339 A525 1.80 l multi, diff.   1.90 .95
  Nos. 2336-2339 (4)   4.40 2.30

Mushrooms
A526

1990, Apr. 28   **Litho.**   *Perf. 12*
2340 A526 30q Amanita caesa-
                rea   .25 .20
2341 A526 90q Lepiota procera   .75 .40
2342 A526 1.20 l Boletus edulis   1.00 .50
2343 A526 1.80 l Clathrus cance-
                latus   1.50 .75
  Nos. 2340-2343 (4)   3.50 1.85

First
Postage
Stamp,
150th
Anniv.
A527

1990, May 6   *Perf. 12*
2344 A527 90q shown   1.00 .50
2345 A527 1.20 l Post rider   1.25 .60
2346 A527 1.80 l Carriage   1.75 .90
  a.   Bklt. pane of 3, #2344-2346 +
       label   4.25
  Nos. 2344-2346 (3)   4.00 2.00

World Cup
Soccer,
Italy
A528

1990, June   **Litho.**   *Perf. 12*
2347 A528 30q multicolored   .50 .25
2348 A528 90q multi, diff.   1.40 .75
2349 A528 1.20 l multi, diff.   2.00 1.00

Size: 80x63mm
Imperf
2350 A528 3.30 l multi, diff.   5.25 2.75
  Nos. 2347-2350 (4)   9.15 4.75

Vincent
Van Gogh,
Death
Cent.
A529

Self portraits and: 30q, Details from various paintings. 90q, Woman in field. 2.10 l, Asylum. 2.40 l, Self-portrait.

1990, July 27
2351 A529 30q multicolored   .50 .25
2352 A529 90q multicolored   1.40 .75
2353 A529 2.10 l multicolored   3.50 1.75

Size: 87x73mm
Imperf
2354 A529 2.40 l multicolored   1.90 .95
  Nos. 2351-2354 (4)   7.30 3.70

Albanian Folklore — A530

Scenes from medieval folktale of "Gjergj Elez Alia": 30q, Alia lying wounded. 90q, Alia being helped onto horse. 1.20 l, Alia fighting Bajloz. 1.80 l, Alia on horseback over severed head of Bajloz.

1990, Aug. 30   *Perf. 12½x12*
2355 A530 30q multicolored   .50 .25
2356 A530 90q multicolored   1.40 .70
2357 A530 1.20 l multicolored   2.00 .95
2358 A530 1.80 l multicolored   3.00 1.50
  Nos. 2355-2358 (4)   6.90 3.40

Founding of
Berat, 2400th
Anniv.
A531

Designs: 30q, Xhamia E Plumbit. 90q, Kisha E Shen Triadhes. 1.20 l, Ura E Beratit. 1.80 l, Onufri-Piktor Mesjetar. 2.40 l, Nikolla-Piktor Mesjetar.

1990, Sept. 20   *Perf. 12½*
2359   Block of 5 + 4 labels   4.25 2.10
  a.   A531 30q multi   .20 .20
  b.   A531 90q multi   .65 .30
  c.   A531 1.20 l multi   .70 .35
  d.   A531 1.80 l multi   1.25 .65
  e.   A531 2.40 l multi   1.40 .70

No. 2359 was sold in souvenir folders for 9.90 l.

Illyrian
Heroes — A532

1990, Oct. 20   *Perf. 12*
2360 A532 30q Pirroja   .50 .25
2361 A532 90q Teuta   1.40 .70
2362 A532 1.20 l Bato   2.00 .95
2363 A532 1.80 l Bardhyli   3.00 1.50
  Nos. 2360-2363 (4)   6.90 3.40

Intl.
Literacy
Year
A533

1990, Oct. 30
2364 A533 90q lt bl & multi   1.40 .70
2365 A533 1.20 l pink & multi   2.00 .95

Albanian
Horseman by
Eugene
Delacroix
A534

Designs: 1.20 l, Albanian Woman by Camille Corot. 1.80 l, Skanderbeg by unknown artist.

1990, Nov. 30   *Perf. 12x12½*
2366 A534 30q multicolored   .50 .25
2367 A534 1.20 l multicolored   1.90 .95
2368 A534 1.80 l multicolored   3.00 1.50
  Nos. 2366-2368 (3)   5.40 2.70

A535   A536

1991, Jan. 23   **Litho.**   *Perf. 12x12½*
2369 A535 90q shown   .65 .30
2370 A535 1.20 l Boletini stand-
                ing   .90 .45

Isa Boletini (1864-1916), freedom fighter.

1991, Jan. 30   **Litho.**   *Perf. 12*
Background Color
2371 A536 90q pale yellow
2372 A536 1.20 l pale gray

Arberi State, 800th anniv.

Pierre Auguste Renoir (1841-1919),
Painter — A537

Paintings: 30q, Girl Reading, 1876, vert. 90q, The Swing, 1876, vert. 1.20 l, Boating Party, 1868-1869. 1.80 l, Flowers and grapes, 1878. 3 l, Self-portrait.

1991, Feb. 25   *Perf. 12½x12*
2373 A537 30q multicolored   .20 .20
2374 A537 90q multicolored   .65 .30
2375 A537 1.20 l multicolored   .90 .45
2376 A537 1.80 l multicolored   1.25 .65

Size: 95x75mm
Imperf
2377 A537 3 l multicolored   4.75 2.50
  Nos. 2373-2377 (5)   7.75 4.10

Flowers — A538

1991, Mar. 30   *Perf. 12*
2378 A538 30q Cistus al-
                banicus   .50 .25
2379 A538 90q Trifolium pilczii   1.40 .75
2380 A538 1.80 l Lilium al-
                banicum   3.00 1.50
  Nos. 2378-2380 (3)   4.90 2.50

Legend of
Rozafa
A539

Various scenes from legend.

1991, Sept. 30   **Litho.**   *Perf. 12x12½*
2381 A539 30q multicolored   .50 .25
2382 A539 90q multicolored   1.40 .70
2383 A539 1.20 l multicolored   2.00 .95
2384 A539 1.80 l multicolored   3.00 1.50
  Nos. 2381-2384 (4)   6.90 3.40

For surcharges see #2586, 2604.

Wolfgang
Amadeus Mozart,
Death
Bicent. — A540

1991, Oct. 5   **Litho.**   *Perf. 12*
2385 A540 90q Conducting   .70 .35
2386 A540 1.20 l Portrait   .90 .45
2387 A540 1.80 l Playing piano   1.40 .70

Size: 89x70mm
Imperf
2388 A540 3 l Medal, score   4.00 4.00
  Nos. 2385-2388 (4)   7.00 5.50

Airplanes — A541

Designs: 30q, Glider, Otto Lilienthal, 1896. 80q, Avion III, Clement Ader, 1897. 90q, Flyer, Wright Brothers, 1903. 1.20 l, Concorde. 1.80 l, Tupolev 114. 2.40 l, Dornier 31 E.

1992, Jan. 27   **Litho.**   *Perf. 12½x12*
2389 A541 30q multicolored   .50 .25
2390 A541 80q multicolored   1.25 .65
2391 A541 90q multicolored   1.40 .70
2392 A541 1.20 l multicolored   2.00 .90
2393 A541 1.80 l multicolored   3.00 1.50
2394 A541 2.40 l multicolored   4.00 2.00
  Nos. 2389-2394 (6)   12.15 6.00

No. 2393 misidentifies a Tupolev 144.

Explorers — A542

1992, Jan. 10
2395	A542	30q Bering	.50	.25
2396	A542	90q Columbus	1.40	.70
2397	A542	1.80 l Magellan	3.00	1.50
		Nos. 2395-2397 (3)	4.90	2.45

1992 Winter Olympics, Albertville A543

1992, Feb. 15   Litho.   Perf. 12½
2398	A543	30q Ski jumping	.25	.20
2399	A543	90q Cross country skiing	.70	.35
2400	A543	1.20 l Pairs figure skating	.95	.50
2401	A543	1.80 l Luge	1.40	.70
		Nos. 2398-2401 (4)	3.30	1.75

For surcharge see No. 2598.

Participation of Albania in Conference on Security and Cooperation in Europe, Berlin (1991) — A544

1992, Mar. 31   Litho.   Perf. 12½x12
2402	A544	90q shown	.95	.95
2403	A544	1.20 l Flags, map	1.25	1.25
a.		Pair, #2402-2403	2.25	2.25

Dated 1991. Issued in sheets containing 2 #2403a, 3 each #2402-2403 + 2 labels.

Albanian Admission to CEPT — A545

1992, Apr. 25   Litho.   Perf. 12½
2404	A545	90q Envelopes, CEPT emblem	.80	.80
2405	A545	1.20 l blk, pur & red lil	1.10	1.10
a.		Pair, #2404-2405	2.00	2.00

Issued in sheets containing 2 #2405a, 3 each #2404-2405 and 2 labels.

Martyrs' Day — A546

1992, May 5   Perf. 12x12½
2406	A546	90q Freedom flame, vert.	1.00	1.00

Perf. 12½x12
2407	A546	4.10 l Flowers	4.50	4.50

European Soccer Championships, Sweden'92 — A547

Various stylized designs of soccer plays.

1992, June 10   Litho.   Perf. 12
2408	A547	30q green & lt grn	.20	.20
2409	A547	90q blue & pink	.25	.25
2410	A547	10.80 l henna & tan	3.00	3.00

Size: 90x70mm

Imperf
2411	A547	5 l tan, lt green & pink	1.40	1.40
		Nos. 2408-2411 (4)	4.85	4.85

1992 Summer Olympics, Barcelona A548

1992, June 14   Litho.   Perf. 12
2412	A548	30q Tennis	.35	.35
2413	A548	90q Baseball	1.00	1.00
2414	A548	1.80 l Table tennis	2.00	2.00

Size: 90x70mm

Imperf
2415	A548	5 l Torch bearer	1.50	1.50
		Nos. 2412-2415 (4)	4.85	4.85

United Europe A549

1992, July 10   Litho.   Perf. 12
2416	A549	1.20 l multicolored	.75	.40

Horses A550

1992, Aug. 10   Litho.   Perf. 12
2417	A550	30q Native	.20	.20
2418	A550	90q Nonius	.25	.25
2419	A550	1.20 l Arabian, vert.	.35	.35
2420	A550	10.60 l Haflinger, vert.	2.75	2.75
		Nos. 2417-2420 (4)	3.55	3.55

Discovery of America, 500th Anniv. A551

Map of North and South America and: 60q, Columbus, sailing ships. 3.20 l, Columbus meeting natives.

1992, Aug. 20
2421	A551	60q blk, bl & gray	.35	.35
2422	A551	3.20 l blk, brn & gray	1.50	1.50

Size: 90x70mm

Imperf
2423	A551	5 l Map, Columbus	50.00	

Mother Theresa, Infant — A552   A553

1992, Oct. 4   Litho.   Perf. 12x12½
2424	A552	40q fawn	.20	.20
2425	A552	60q brown	.20	.20
2426	A552	1 l violet	.20	.20
2427	A552	1.80 l gray	.25	.25
2428	A552	2 l red	.30	.30
2429	A552	2.40 l green	.35	.35
2430	A552	3.20 l blue	.50	.50
2431	A552	5.60 l rose violet	1.00	1.00
2432	A552	7.20 l olive	1.10	1.10
2433	A552	10 l org brn	1.50	1.50
		Nos. 2424-2433 (10)	5.60	5.60

See Nos. 2472-2476.

1993, Apr. 25   Litho.   Perf. 12
2434	A553	16 l multicolored	2.50	2.50

Visit of Pope John Paul II.

Nos. 2223-2226, 2229 Surcharged

1993, May 2   Litho.   Perf. 12x12½
2435	A486	3 l on 10q	.60	.60
2436	A486	6.50 l on 20q	1.25	1.25
2437	A486	13 l on 30q	2.50	2.50
2438	A486	20 l on 90q	4.00	4.00
2439	A486	30 l on 50q	5.75	5.75
		Nos. 2435-2439 (5)	14.10	14.10

Lef Nosi (1873-1945), Minister of Posts A554

1993, May 5   Litho.   Perf. 12
2440	A554	6.50 l olive brn & bister	.90	.90

First Albanian postage stamps, 80th anniv.

Europa A555

Contemporary paintings by: 3 l, A. Zajmi, vert. 7 l, E. Hila. 20 l, B. Ahmeti-Peizazh.

1993, May 28   Litho.   Perf. 12
2441	A555	3 l multicolored	.60	.60
2442	A555	7 l multicolored	1.40	1.40

Size: 116x122mm
2443	A555	20 l multicolored	4.25	4.25
		Nos. 2441-2443 (3)	6.25	6.25

1993 Mediterranean Games, France — A556

1993, June 20   Litho.   Perf. 12
2444	A556	3 l Running	.55	.55
2445	A556	16 l Kayaking	3.00	3.00
2446	A556	21 l Cycling	3.75	3.75

Size: 111x78mm

Imperf
2447	A556	20 l Mediterranean map	3.50	3.50
		Nos. 2444-2447 (4)	10.80	10.80

Frang Bardhi, Author, 350th Death Anniv. A557

1993, Aug. 20   Litho.   Perf. 12x12½
2448	A557	6.50 l shown	1.10	1.10

Size: 89x101mm

Imperf
2449	A557	20 l Writing at desk	3.50	3.50

A558

A559

1994, July 17   Litho.   Perf. 12
2450	A558	42 l shown	1.50	1.50
2451	A558	68 l Mascot, ball, US map	2.50	2.50

1994 World Cup Soccer Championships, US.

1994, Dec. 31   Litho.   Perf. 14

European Inventors, Discoveries: 50 l, Gjovalin Gjadri, engineer. 100 l, Karl von Ghega, Austrian engineer. 150 l, Sketch of road project.
2452	A559	50 l multicolored	1.50	1.50
2453	A559	100 l multicolored	3.50	3.50

Size: 50x70mm

Imperf
2454	A559	150 l multicolored	5.00	5.00
		Nos. 2452-2454 (3)	10.00	10.00

Europa (#2454).

Ali Pasa of Tepelene (Lion of Janina) (1744-1822) — A560

1995, Jan. 28   Perf. 14
2455	A560	60 l shown	2.50	2.50

Size: 70x50mm

Imperf
2456	A560	100 l Tepelene Palace	4.00	4.00

Intl. Olympic Committee,
Cent. — A561

1995, Feb. 2   *Imperf.*
2457 A561 80 l multicolored   3.25 3.25

Karl Benz (1844-1929), Automobile
Pioneer — A562

Designs: 5 l, Automobile company emblem,
Benz. 10 l, Modern Mercedes Benz automobile. 60 l, First four-wheel Benz 1886 motor
car. 125 l, Pre-war Mercedes touring car.

1995, Jan. 21 Litho.   Perf. 14
2458 A562 5 l multicolored   .20   .20
2459 A562 10 l multicolored   .30   .30
2460 A562 60 l multicolored   1.60 1.60
2461 A562 125 l multicolored   3.50 3.50
    Nos. 2458-2461 (4)   5.60 5.60

Liberation,
50th Anniv.
(in 1994)
A563

1995, Jan. 28 Litho.   Perf. 14
2462 A563 50 l black, gray & red   2.00 2.00

Dated 1994.

Miniature Sheet

Albania '93 — A564

Composers: a, 3 l, Wagner. b, 6.50 l, Grieg.
c, 11 l, Gounod. d, 20 l, Tchaikovsky.

1995, Jan. 26   *Perf. 12*
2463 A564 Sheet of 4, #a.-d.   2.00 2.00

Veskopoja
Academy, 250th
Anniv. — A565

Buildings of Veskopoja.

1995, Feb. 2
2464 A565 42 l multicolored   1.50 1.50
2465 A565 68 l multicolored   2.50 2.50
    a.   Pair, #2464-2465   4.00 4.00

Bleta
Apricula — A566

Peace &
Freedom — A567

1995, Aug. 20   Litho.   Perf. 12
2466 A566 5 l On flower   .20   .20
2467 A566 10 l Honeycomb, bee   .40   .40
2468 A566 25 l Emerging from
                  cell of honey-
                  comb   1.00 1.00
    Nos. 2466-2468 (3)   1.60 1.60

1995, Aug. 10   Perf. 13½x14
Stylized hands reaching for: 50 l, Olive
branch. 100 l, Peace dove.
150 l, Stylized person.

2469 A567 50 l multicolored   1.50 1.50
2470 A567 100 l multicolored   3.00 3.00
    Size: 80x60mm
    Imperf
2471 A567 150 l multicolored   6.00 6.00
    Nos. 2469-2471 (3)   10.50 10.50

Europa.
For surcharges, see Nos. B39-B40.

Mother Teresa Type of 1992

1994-95   Litho.   Perf. 12x12½
2472 A552 5 l violet   .25   .25
2473 A552 18 l orange   .85   .85
2474 A552 20 l rose lilac   .95   .95
2475 A552 25 l green   1.10 1.10
2476 A552 60 l olive   2.75 2.75
    Nos. 2472-2476 (5)   5.90 5.90

Issued: 20 l, 1994; 60 l, 1995; others, 7/94.

Arctic Explorers — A568

Designs: a, Fridtjof Nansen (1861-1930),
Norway. b, James Cook (1728-79), England.
c, Roald Amundsen (1872-1928), Norway. d,
Robert F. Scott (1872-1928), Great Britain.

1995, Sept. 14   Litho.   Perf. 13½x14
2477 A568 25 l Block of 4, #a.-d. 4.25 4.25

UN, 50th
Anniv.
A569

1995, Sept. 14   Litho.   Perf. 14x13½
2478 A569 2 l shown   .20   .20
2479 A569 100 l like #2478, flags
                  streaming to
                  right   4.25 4.25

Poets — A570

1995   *Perf. 13½x14*
2480 A570 25 l Pol Elyar   1.10 1.10
2481 A570 50 l Sergej Esnin   2.25 2.25
    a.   Pair, #2480-2481   3.50 3.50

Entry into
Council of
Europe
A571

Designs: 25 l, Doves flying from headquarters, Strasbourg. 85 l, Albanian eagle over
map of Europe.

1995   *Perf. 14x13½*
2482 A571 25 l multicolored   1.10 1.10
2483 A571 85 l multicolored   3.75 3.75

For surcharge see No. 2583

Jan Kukuzeli,
Composer
A572

Stylized figure: 18 l, Writing. 20 l, Holding
hand to head. 100 l, Holding up scroll of paper.

1995, Oct. 17   Perf. 13½x14
2484 A572 18 l multicolored   .85   .85
2485 A572 20 l multicolored   .95   .95
    Size: 74x74mm
2486 A572 100 l multicolored   4.50 4.50
    Nos. 2484-2486 (3)   6.30 6.30

World Tourism
Organization, 20th
Anniv. — A573

Stylized designs: 18 l, Church, saint holding
scroll. 20 l, City, older buildings. 42 l, City,
modern buildings.

1995, Oct. 17
2487 A573 18 l multicolored   1.00 1.00
2488 A573 20 l multicolored   1.10 1.10
2489 A573 42 l multicolored   2.50 2.50
    Nos. 2487-2489 (3)   4.60 4.60

Fables of
Jean de la
Fontaine
(1621-95)
A574

Designs: 2 l, Raptor, turtle, wolf, goose,
mouse, lion, rats. 3 l, Crow, goose, dog, foxes.
25 l, Insect, doves, frogs. 60 l, Drawings of Da
la Fontaine, animals, birds.

1995, Aug. 20   Litho.   Perf. 14x13½
2490 A574 2 l multicolored   .20   .20
2491 A574 3 l multicolored   .20   .20
2492 A574 25 l multicolored   .85   .85
    Imperf
    Size: 73x56mm
2493 A574 60 l multicolored   2.75 2.75
    Nos. 2490-2493 (4)   4.00 4.00

Folklore Festival,
Berat — A575

Motion Pictures,
Cent. — A576

Stylized designs: 5 l, Men's choir. 50 l, Costumed woman seated in chair.

1995, Oct. 17   Litho.   Perf. 13½x14
2494 A575 5 l multicolored   .20   .20
2495 A575 50 l multicolored   2.25 2.25

1995, Nov. 17
2496 A576 10 l Louis Lumiere   .45   .45
2497 A576 85 l Auguste Lumiere   3.75 3.75
    a.   Pair, #2496-2497   4.20 4.20

Elvis
Presley
(1935-77)
A577

1995, Nov. 20 Litho. Perf. 14x13½
2498 A577 3 l orange & multi .20 .20
2499 A577 60 l green & multi 2.50 2.50

A578

A579

1995, Nov. 25 Perf. 13½x14
2500 A578 10 l 1925 Bank notes .45 .45
2501 A578 25 l 1995 Bank notes 1.10 1.10

National Bank, 70th anniv.

1995, Nov. 27 Litho. Perf. 13½x14
2502 A579 5 l shown .20 .20
2503 A579 50 l Maiden planting
tree 2.25 2.25

Democracy, 5th anniv.

A580

Designs: 25 l, Soccer ball, British flag, map of Europe, stadium. 100 l, Soccer ball, player.

1996, June 4 Perf. 14
2504 A580 25 l multicolored 1.10 1.10
2505 A580 100 l multicolored 4.50 4.50

Euro '96, European Soccer Championships, Great Britain.

Mother Teresa — A581

1996, May 5 Perf. 13½x14
2506 A581 25 l blue & multi 1.00 1.00
2507 A581 100 l red & multi 3.25 3.25

Size: 52x74mm

Imperf
2508 A581 150 l Mother Teresa, diff. 6.00 6.00
Nos. 2506-2508 (3) 10.25 10.25

Europa. For overprints see Nos. 2551, 2582.

GSM Cellular Telephone Transmission A582

Designs: 10 l, Satellite transmitting signals. 60 l, Uses for cellular telephone, vert.

Perf. 13x13½, 13½x13
1996, Aug. 1 Litho.
2509 A582 10 l multicolored .45 .45
2510 A582 60 l multicolored 2.50 2.50

1996 Summer Olympic Games, Atlanta — A583

Stylized designs.

1996, Aug. 3 Litho. Perf. 13x14
2511 A583 5 l Runners .20 .20
2512 A583 25 l Throwers 1.00 1.00
2513 A583 60 l Jumpers 2.40 2.40

Size: 52x37mm

Imperf
2514 A583 100 l Emblem, US flag 4.00 4.00
Nos. 2511-2514 (4) 7.60 7.60

Gottfried Wilhelm Leibniz (1646-1716), Mathematician — A584

85 l, René Descartes (1596-1650), mathematician.

1996, Sept. 20 Litho. Perf. 14
2515 A584 10 l multicolored .40 .40
2516 A584 85 l multicolored 3.50 3.50

Paintings by Francisco Goya (1746-1828) A585

Designs: 10 l, The Naked Maja. 60 l, Dona Isabel Cobos de Porcel. 100 l, Self portrait.

1996, Sept. 25 Perf. 14x13½
2517 A585 10 l multicolored .40 .40
2518 A585 60 l multicolored 2.50 2.50

Souvenir Sheet
2519 A585 100 l multicolored 4.00 4.00

Religious Engravings — A586

Designs: a, 5 l, Book cover showing crucifixion, angels. b, 25 l, Medallion of crucifixion. c, 85 l, Book cover depicting life of Christ.

1996, Nov. 5 Perf. 13x13½
2520 A586 Block of 3, #a.-c. + label 4.75 4.75

UNICEF, 50th Anniv. — A587

1996, Nov. 11 Perf. 13½
Children's paintings: 5 l, Fairy princess. 10 l, Doll, sun. 25 l, Sea life. 50 l, House, people.

2521 A587 5 l multicolored .20 .20
2522 A587 10 l multicolored .45 .45
2523 A587 25 l multicolored 1.10 1.10
2524 A587 50 l multicolored 2.25 2.25
Nos. 2521-2524 (4) 4.00 4.00

Gjergj Fishta (1871-1940), Writer, Priest — A588

1996, Dec. 20 Perf. 13½x14
2525 A588 10 l shown .40 .40
2526 A588 60 l Battle scene, portrait 2.50 2.50

Omar Khayyam — A589

1997, Mar. 6 Perf. 14
2527 A589 20 l shown .70 .70
2528 A589 50 l Portrait, diff. 1.75 1.75

A590   A591

1997, Mar. 20 Perf. 14x14½
2529 A590 20 l Portrait .70 .70
2530 A590 60 l Printing press 2.15 2.15
a. Pair, #2529-2530 2.85 2.85

Johannes Gutenberg (1397?-1468).

1997, May 5 Litho. Perf. 13x14
The Azure Eye (Stories and Legends): 30 l, Dragon on rock looking at warrior, donkey. 100 l, Dragon drinking water from pond, warrior.

2531 A591 30 l multicolored .75 .75
2532 A591 100 l multicolored 3.00 3.00

Europa.

A592   A593

1997, Apr. 10 Perf. 14
2533 A592 10 l Pelicanus crispus .40 .40
2534 A592 80 l Pelicans, diff. 3.00 3.00
a. Pair, #2533-2534 3.40 3.40

No. 2534a is a continuous design.

1997, June 25 Litho. Perf. 14
2535 A593 10 l blk & dark brn .40 .40
2536 A593 25 l blk & blue blk 1.00 1.00

Souvenir Sheet
2537 A593 80 l gray brown 2.90 2.90

Faik Konica (1875-1942), writer and politician.
No. 2537 contains one 22x26mm stamp.

A594

1997 Mediterranean Games, Bari: 20 l, Man running. 30 l, Woman running, 3-man canoe. 100 l, Man breaking finish line, silhouettes of man and woman.

1997, June 13
2538 A594 20 l Man running .75 .75
2539 A594 30 l Woman running, canoe 1.10 1.10

Size: 52x74mm

Imperf
2540 A594 100 l multicolored 3.60 3.60

Skanderbeg — A595

1997, Aug. 25 Litho. Perf. 13
2541 A595 5 l red brn & red .20 .20
2542 A595 10 l dp ol & ol .40 .40
2543 A595 20 l dp grn & grn .80 .80
2544 A595 25 l dp mag & red lil 1.00 1.00
2545 A595 30 l dk vio & vio 1.25 1.25
2546 A595 50 l black 2.00 2.00
2547 A595 60 l brn & lt brn 2.40 2.40
2548 A595 80 l dk brown & brn 3.25 3.25
2549 A595 100 l dk red brown & red brn 4.00 4.00
2550 A595 110 l dark blue 4.25 4.25
Nos. 2541-2550 (10) 19.55 19.55

No. 2507 Ovptd. in Silver "HOMAZH / 1910-1997"

1997 Perf. 13½x14
2551 A581 100 l red & multi 6.50 6.50

Religious Manuscripts — A596

Albanian Codex: a, 10 l, 11th cent. b, 25 l, 6th cent. c, 60 l, 6th cent., diff.

1997, Nov. 15　Litho.　Perf. 13x14
2552　A596　Block of 3, #a.-c. +
　　　　　　label　　　　　3.50　3.50
　　　　　　See No. 2575.

Post and Telecommunications
Administration, 85th Anniv. — A597

1997, Dec. 4　　　　　Perf. 13½
2553　A597　10 l　multi　　　.40　.40
2554　A597　30 l　multi, diff.　1.10　1.10

A598

1998, Mar. 25　Litho.　Perf. 14
2555　A598　30 l　red brn & multi　.75　.75
2556　A598　100 l　tan & multi　2.75　2.75
　a.　Pair, #2555-2556　　3.50　3.50

Nikete Dardani, musician.

A599

1998, Apr. 15

Legends of Pogradecit: a, 30 l, Old man
seated at table. b, 50 l, Three Graces. c, 60 l,
Two women, fountain. d, 80 l, Iceman.

2557　A599　Block of 4, #a.-d.　5.50　5.50

A600

1998, May 5　Litho.　Perf. 13x14
2558　A600　60 l　shown　　1.50　1.50
2559　A600　100 l　multi, diff.　2.50　2.50

Size: 50x72mm
Imperf
2560　A600　150 l　multi, diff.　3.75　3.75

Europa (folk festivals).

A601

1998, June 10　Litho.　Perf. 13½x13
Albanian League of Prizren, 120th anniv.: a,
30 l, Abdyl Frasheri. b, 50 l, Sulejman Vokshi.
c, 60 l, Iljaz Pashe Dibra. d, 80 l, Ymer
Prizreni.

2561　A601　Block of 4, #a.-d.　5.50　5.50

1998 World Cup
Soccer
Championships,
France — A602

Perf. 13½

1998, June 10

Stylized soccer players.

2562　A602　60 l　multicolored　1.50　1.50
2563　A602　100 l　multicolored　2.50　2.50

Size: 50x73mm
Imperf
2564　A602　120 l　Mascot　　3.00　3.00

European Youth Greco-Roman
Wrestling Championships,
Albania — A603

1998, July 5　　　　　Perf. 13½
2565　A603　30 l　shown　　.75　.75
2566　A603　60 l　Wrestlers, diff.　1.50　1.50
　a.　Pair, #2565-2566　　2.25　2.25

Eqerem Cabej
(1908-1980),
Albanian
Etymologist — A604

1998, Aug. 7　　　　　Perf. 14
2567　A604　60 l　yel brn & multi　1.50　1.50
2568　A604　80 l　brn red & multi　2.00　2.00
　a.　Pair, #2567-2568　　3.50　3.50

Paul
Gauguin
(1848-1903)
A605

Paintings (details): 60 l, The Vision after the
Sermon. 80 l, Ea Haere la Oe.
120 l, Stylized design to resemble self-
portrait.

1998, Sept. 10　　　　Perf. 13½
2569　A605　60 l　multicolored　1.50　1.50
2570　A605　80 l　multicolored　2.00　2.00
　a.　Pair, #2569-2570　　3.50　3.50

Size: 50x73mm
Imperf
2571　A605　120 l　multicolored　3.00　3.00

Epitaph of Gllavenica, 14th Cent.
Depiction of Christ — A606

Designs: 30 l, Entire cloth showing artwork.
80 l, Closer view.
100 l, Upper portion of cloth, vert.

1998, Oct. 5　　　　　Perf. 14½x14
2572　A606　30 l　multicolored　.75　.75
2573　A606　80 l　multicolored　2.00　2.00

Souvenir Sheet
Perf. 13
2574　A606　100 l　multicolored　2.50　2.50
No. 2574 contains one 25x29mm stamp.

Religious Manuscripts Type of 1997

Illustrations from Purple Codex, Gold
Codex: a, 30 l, Manuscript, columns on sides,
arched top. b, 50 l, Manuscript cover with
embossed pictures of icons. c, 80 l, Manuscript picturing cathedral, birds.

1998, Oct. 15　　　　Perf. 13x14
2575　A596　Block of 3, #a.-c. +
　　　　　　label　　　　　4.00　4.00

Mikel Koliqi (1902-
97), First Albanian
Cardinal — A607

1998, Nov. 28　　　　Perf. 14
2576　A607　30 l　shown　　.75　.75
2577　A607　100 l　Portrait, facing　2.50　2.50
　a.　Pair, #2576-2577　　3.25　3.25

Mother Teresa
(1910-97) — A608

Diana, Princess
of Wales (1961-
97) — A609

Perf. 14x13½, 13½x14
1998, Sept. 5　　　　Photo.
2578　A608　60 l　With child,
　　　　　　horiz.　　1.50　1.50
2579　A608　100 l　shown　　2.50　2.50
　　　　See Italy Nos. 2254-2255.

1998, Aug. 31　Litho.　Perf. 13½
2580　A609　60 l　shown　　1.50　1.50
2581　A609　100 l　With Mother
　　　　　　Teresa　　2.50　2.50

No. 2508 Ovptd. in Blue

1998, Oct. 23　Litho.　Imperf.
2582　A581　150 l　multicolored　6.25　6.25

No. 2482 Surcharged

1999, Apr. 20　Litho.　Perf. 14x13½
2583　A571　150 l　on 25 l　multi　2.25　2.25

Famous Americans — A610

a, Washington. b, Lincoln. c. Martin Luther
King, Jr.

1999, Mar. 15　　　　Perf. 14
2584　A610　150 l　Block of 3, #a.-
　　　　　　c. + label　6.25　6.25

Monacus Albiventris — A611

Seals: a, 110 l, One looking left, one looking
right. b, 150 l, Both looking right. c, 110 l,
Mirror image of #2585b. d, 150 l, Mirror image
of #2585a.

1999, Apr. 10
2585　A611　Sheet of 4, #a.-d.　7.50　7.50

No. 2382 Surcharged

1999, Apr. 24   Litho.   Perf. 12x12¼
2586 A539 150 l on 90 l multi   4.00 4.00
IBRA '99, Nuremburg.

A612

1999, Apr. 25   Litho.   Perf. 13½x13¾
2587 A612   10 l blue & multi   .25   .25
2588 A612 100 l green & multi   2.50 2.50
Souvenir Sheet
Perf. 13
2589 A612 250 l green & multi   6.75 6.75
NATO, 50th anniv. No. 2589 contains one 30x50mm stamp.

A613

1999, Apr. 30   Litho.   Perf. 13x13¾
Cartoon mouse: a, 80 l, Writing. b, 110 l, Holding chin. c, 150 l, Wearing bow tie. d, 60 l, Pointing.
2590 A613   Strip of 4, #a.-d.   10.50 10.50
Animated films.

Europa
A614

1999, May 1   Litho.   Perf. 13¾x13
2591 A614   90 l Thethi Park   2.40 2.40
2592 A614 310 l Lura Park   8.25 8.25
Imperf
Size: 80x60mm
2592A A614 350 l Kombetare
                   Park   9.50 9.50
      Nos. 2591-2592A (3)   20.15 20.15

Illyrian
Coins
A615

Designs: a, 200 l, Kings of Illyria - Monumiou c. 300-280 BC cow suckling calf, square containing double stellate pattern, and Epidamos-Dyrrachium c. 623 BC, square with double stellate. b, 20 l, Damastion c. 395-380 BC siver drachm portable ingot, Byllis c. 238-168 BC AE13 serpent entwined around cornucopia, Skodra after 168 BC, AE17 war galley, and other war galley coin. c, 10l, Epirote Republic before 238 BC silver tetrabol with jugate busts of Zeus and Dione on obverse and thunderbolt within oak wreath reverse.
310 l, Kings of Illyria - Genthos c. 197-168 BC head wearing kausia.

1999, June 1   Litho.   Perf. 13¾x13¼
2593 A615   Strip of 3, #a.-c.   6.25 6.25
Souvenir Sheet
Perf. 13
2594 A615 310 l multicolored   8.50 8.50

Charlie
Chaplin — A616

Designs: 30 l, Holding cigarette. 50 l, Tipping hat. 250 l, Dancing.

1999, June 20   Litho.   Perf. 14x14¼
2595 A616   30 l multicolored   .75   .75
2596 A616   50 l multicolored   1.25 1.25
2597 A616 250 l multicolored   6.75 6.75
  a. Booklet pane, 2 each #2595-
      2597, perf. 14¼ vert.   17.50
      Complete booklet   17.50
      Nos. 2595-2597 (3)   8.75 8.75
In No. 2597a, the 30 l stamps are at the ends of the pane and the 250 l stamps are in the middle.

No. 2398 Surcharged

1999, July 2   Litho.   Perf. 12½
2598 A543 150 l on 30q multi   4.25 4.25
PhilexFrance 99.

Holocaust — A617

1999, July 6   Litho.   Perf. 14x14¼
2599 A617   30 l brown & multi   .80   .80
2600 A617 150 l gray & multi   4.00 4.00

First Manned
Moon Landing,
30th
Anniv. — A618

No. 2601: a, 30 l, Astronaut, earth. b, 150 l, Lunar Module. c, 300 l, Astronaut, flag. 280 l, Lift-off.

1999, July 25   Litho.   Perf. 13¼x14
2601 A618   Strip of 3, #a.-c   13.00 13.00
Souvenir Sheet
Perf. 13
2602 A618 280 l multicolored   7.25 7.25
No. 2602 contains one 25x29mm stamp.

UPU, 125th
Anniv. — A619

1999, Aug. 1   Litho.   Perf. 14x14¼
Background colors: a, 20 l, aquamarine and brown. b, 60 l, bister and dark blue.
2603 A619   Pair, #a.-b.   2.10 2.10

No. 2383 Surcharged in Brown,
Symbol in Red and Green

1999   Method & Perf. as Before
2604 A539 150 l on 1.20 l multi   3.25 3.25
China 1999 World Philatelic Exhibition.

A620   A621

Background colors: a, 10 l, Yellow. b, 20 l, Orange. c, 200 l, Green.

1999, Sept. 2   Litho.   Perf. 14x14¼
2605 A620   Strip of 3, #a.-c.   4.75 4.75
First Natl. Track & Field Championships, 70th anniv.

1999, Oct. 30   Perf. 14
2606 A621   30 l Madonna and
                   Child   .60   .60
2607 A621 300 l shown   6.00 6.00
  a. Souv. sheet, 2 ea #2606-
      2607   14.00 14.00
Art by Onufri of Elbasan.

Famous Albanians — A622

Designs: a, 10 l, Bilal Golemi (1899-1955), veterinarian. b, 20 l, Azem Galica (1889-1924), freedom fighter. c, 50 l, Viktor Eftimiu (1889-1972), writer. d, 300 l, Lasgush Poradeci (1900-87), poet.

1999, Nov. 28   Litho.   Perf. 14¼x14
2608 A622   Block of 4, #a.-d.   7.75 7.75

Carnival
Masks — A623

1999, Dec. 1   Perf. 13¾
2609 A623   30 l shown   .60   .60
2610 A623 300 l Turkey head   6.00 6.00

Millennium
A624

2000, Mar. 27   Litho.   Perf. 13½x14
2611 A624   40 l red & multi   .90   .90
2612 A624   90 l blue & multi   2.00 2.00

Native
Costumes — A625

a, 5 l, Librazhdi. b, 10 l, Malesia e Madhe woman. c, 15 l, Malesia e Madhe man. d, 20 l, Tropoje. e, 30 l, Dumrea. f, 35 l, Tirana man. g, 40 l, Tirana woman. h, 45 l, Arbereshe. i, 50 l, Gjirokaster. j, 55 l, Lunxheri. k, 70 l, Cameria. l, 90 l, Laberia.
Illustration reduced.

2000, Mar. 28   Perf. 13x13¾
2613   Booklet pane of 12   13.00 13.00
  a.-l. A625 any single   1.10 1.10
         Booklet, #2613   13.00

Gustave Mayer (1850-1900), Student of Albanian Culture — A626

Colors: a, 50 l, olive green. b, 130 l, carmine lake.
Illustration reduced.

2000, Mar. 30   **Perf. 13½x14**
2614 A626   Pair, #a-b   3.75 3.75

Cartoon Duck — A627

Duck with: a, 250 l, Top hat. b, 10 l, Ten-gallon hat. c, 30 l, Cap. d, 90 l, Bow.

2000, Apr. 6   **Litho.**   **Perf. 13x13¾**
2615 A627   Strip of 4, #a-d   8.25 8.25

Grand Prix Race Cars — A628

Various cars.

2000, Apr. 10   **Litho.**   **Perf. 14¼x14**
2616   Bklt. pane of 10 + 2 labels   9.25 9.25
a.-j.   A628 30 l any single   .90 .90
    Booklet, #2616   9.25

Holy Year 2000 A629

Designs: 15 l, Church with bell tower. 40 l, Church with conical roof. 90 l, Ruins. 250 l, Aerial view of ruins.

2000, Apr. 22   **Litho.**   **Perf. 13¾x14**
2617-2619 A629   Set of 3   3.25 3.25
Souvenir Sheet
Perf. 13¾
2620 A629 250 l multi   5.50 5.50
No. 2620 contains one 38x38mm stamp.

Europa, 2000
Common Design Type
2000, May 9   **Perf. 13x13¾**
2621 CD17 130 l multi   2.75 2.75
Souvenir Sheet
Perf. 13
2622 CD17 300 l Detail of #2621   6.50 6.50
No. 2622 contains one 25x29mm stamp.

Miniature Sheet

Wild Animals — A630

No. 2623: a, 10 l, Canis lupus. b, 40 l, Ursus arctos. c, 90 l, Sus scrofa. d, 220 l, Vulpes vulpes.
Illustration reduced.

2000, May 17   **Perf. 14¼x13¾**
2623 A630   Sheet of 4, #a-d   7.75 7.75

Gustav Mahler (1860-1911), Composer A631

2000, May 30   **Perf. 13½x14**
2624 A631 130 l multi   2.75 2.75
WIPA 2000 Stamp Exhibition, Vienna.

European Soccer Championships — A632

10 l, Goalie. 120 l, Player heading ball. 260 l, Player kicking ball.

2000, June 1   **Perf. 13¾x13¼**
2625-2626 A632   Set of 2   2.75 2.75
Imperf
Size: 81x60mm
2627 A632 260 l multi   5.50 5.50

Paintings by Pablo Picasso — A633

Various unnamed paintings or self-portraits: 30 l, Brown panel. 40 l, Green panel. 130 l, Self-portrait, with Espana 2000 philatelic exhibition emblem, vert. 250 l, Blue panel.

2000   **Litho.**   **Perf. 13¾**
2628-2631 A633   Set of 4   9.50 9.50
Souvenir Sheet
Perf. 13
2632 A633 400 l Self-portrait   8.50 8.50
No. 2632 contains one 25x29mm stamp. Issued: 130 l, 10/6; others 6/7.

2000 Summer Olympics, Sydney — A634

No. 2633: a, 10 l, Basketball. b, 40 l, Soccer. c, 90 l, Runner. d, 250 l, Cycling.

2000, July 1   **Perf. 14x14¼**
2633 A634   Block of 4, #a-d   8.25 8.25

First Zeppelin Flight, Cent. — A635

No. 2634: a, 15 l, LZ-1 over Friedrichshafen. b, 30 l, Airship over Paris. c, 300 l, R34 over New York.
Illustration reduced.

2000, July 2   **Perf. 13¾x13**
2634 A635   Sheet of 3, #a-c   7.50 7.50
Souvenir Sheet
Perf. 13
2635 A635 300 l Ferdinand von Zeppelin   6.50 6.50
No. 2634 contains three 40x28mm stamps.

Flowers — A636

No. 2636: a, 50 l, Gentiana lutea. b, 70 l, Gentiana cruciata.
Illustration reduced.

2000, Oct. 10   **Perf. 13¼x14**
2636 A636   Pair, #a-b   2.60 2.60

Famous Albanians — A637

a, 30 l, Naim Frasheri, writer (1845-1900). b, 50 l, Bajram Curri, politician (1862-1925).
Illustration reduced.

2000, Nov. 28   **Perf. 14¼x13¾**
2637 A637   Pair, #a-b   1.75 1.75

UN High Commissioner on Refugees, 50th Anniv. — A638

50 l, Mother & child. 90 l, Mother & child, diff.

2000, Dec. 14   **Perf. 13¾x14¼**
2638-2639 A638   Set of 2   3.00 3.00

Famous Albanians — A639

No. 2640: a, Ahmed Myftar Dede. b, Sali Njazi Dede.
Illustration reduced.

2001, Feb. 22   **Litho.**   **Perf. 14¼x14**
2640 A639 90 l Horiz. pair, #a-b   3.00 3.00

Native Costumes — A640

No. 2641: a, Man from Tropoje. b, Woman from Lume. c, Woman from Mirdite. d, Man from Lume. e, Woman from Zadrime. f, Woman from Shpati. g, Man from Kruje. h, Woman from Macukulli. i, Woman from Dardhe. j, Man from Lushnje. k, Woman from Dropulli. l, Woman from Shmili.

2001, Mar. 15   **Perf. 13x13¾**
2641 A640 20 l Sheet of 12, #a-l   4.00 4.00
    Booklet, #2641   4.00

Flowers — A641

No. 2642: a, 10 l, Magnolia grandiflora. b, 20 l, Rosa virginiana. c, 90 l, Dianthus barbatus. d, 140 l, Syringa vulgaris.

2001, Mar. 30   *Perf. 14x14¼*
2642 A641   Block of 4, #a-d   5.50 5.50

Cartoon Dog — A642

Denominations: a, 50 l. b, 90 l. c, 140 l, d, 20 l. Illustration reduced.

2001, Apr. 6   *Perf. 13x13¾*
2643 A642   Strip of 4, #a-d   5.00 5.00

Opera Composers — A643

Designs: No. 2644, 90 l, Vincenzo Bellini (1801-35). No. 2645, 90 l, Giuseppe Verdi (1813-1901).
300 l, Bellini and Verdi.

2001, Apr. 20   *Perf. 13¾x13*
2644-2645 A643   Set of 2   3.00 3.00
Souvenir Sheet
Perf. 13¾
2646 A643   300 l multi   5.00 5.00

Europa
A644

Designs: 40 l, Waterfall, cliffs. 110 l, Waterfall, boulders. 200 l, Water, shoreline. 350 l, Ripples in water, vert.

2001, Apr. 29   *Perf. 13¾x14*
2647-2649 A644   Set of 3   6.75 6.75
Souvenir Sheet
Perf. 12¾x13
2650 A644   350 l multi   6.75 6.75
No. 2650 contains one 25x29mm stamp.

Domestic Animals — A645

No. 2651: a, 10 l, Horse. b, 15 l, Donkey. c, 80 l, Cat. d, 90 l, Dog.
300 l, Cat.

2001, May 17   *Perf. 14¼x14*
2651 A645   Sheet of 4, #a-d   3.25 3.25
Souvenir Sheet
Perf. 12¾x13
2652 A645   300 l shown   5.00 5.00
No. 2651 contains four 42x26mm stamps.

2001 Mediterranean Games, Tunis, Tunisia — A646

No. 2653: a, 10 l, Swimmer. b, 90 l, Runners. c, 140 l, Cyclists.
260 l, Discus thrower.

2001, June 1   *Perf. 14¼x14*
2653 A646   Vert. strip of 3, #a-c   4.00 4.00
Souvenir Sheet
Perf. 13x12¾
2654 A646   260 l multi   4.50 4.50
No. 2654 contains one 29x25mm stamp.

History of Aviation — A647

No. 2655: a, Clement Ader's flight of Eole, Oct. 9, 1890. b, Louis Blériot's flight of Blériot IX over English Channel, July 25, 1909. c, Charles Lindbergh's solo transatlantic flight of Spirit of St. Louis, May, 1927. d, Flight over Tirana, May 30, 1925. e, Antonov AN-10, 1956. f, First Concorde flight, Feb. 9, 1969. g, First Boeing 747 flight, Jan. 22, 1970. h, First flight of Space Shuttle Columbia, Apr. 12, 1981.

2001, June 20   *Perf. 13¾x13*
2655 A647   40 l Sheet of 8, #a-h   5.50 5.50

Bridges — A648

No. 2656: a, 10 l, Tabakeve. b, 20 l, Kamares. c, 40 l, Golikut. d, 90 l, Mesit.
250 l, Tabakeve.

2001, July 20   *Perf. 13¾x13¼*
2656 A648   Sheet of 4, #a-d   2.75 2.75
Souvenir Sheet
Perf. 12¾x13
2657 A648   250 l shown   4.00 4.00
No. 2656 contains four 38x30mm stamps.

Coats of Arms — A649

Arms of: 20 l, Dimitri of Arber. 45 l, Balsha. 50 l, Muzaka. 90 l, George Castrioti (Skanderbeg).

2001, Sept. 12   *Perf. 12¾x13*
2658 A649   20 l multi   .35 .35
  a.   Booklet pane of 4   1.40
2659 A649   45 l multi   .80 .80
  a.   Booklet pane of 4   3.25
2660 A649   50 l multi   .85 .85
  a.   Booklet pane of 4   3.50
2661 A649   90 l multi   1.60 1.60
  a.   Booklet pane of 4   6.50
    Booklet, #2658a-2661a   15.00
    Nos. 2658-2661 (4)   3.60 3.60

Year of Dialogue Among Civilizations
A650

Colors of denomination: 45 l, Green. 50 l, Black. 120 l, White.

2001, Oct. 6   *Perf. 13½x14*
2662-2664 A650   Set of 3   3.50 3.50

Nobel Prizes, Cent.
A651

Laureates: 10 l, Doctors Without Borders, Peace, 1999. 20 l, Wilhelm C. Roentgen, Physics, 1901. 90 l, Ferid Murad, Physiology or Medicine, 1988. 200 l, Mother Teresa, Peace, 1979.

2001, Dec. 1   *Perf. 13¾x13¼*
2665-2668 A651   Set of 4   5.25 5.25

SEMI-POSTAL STAMPS

Nos. 148-151 Surcharged in Red and Black

1924, Nov. 1
B1 A18   5q + 5q yel grn   5.00 6.50
B2 A18   10q + 5q carmine   5.00 6.50
B3 A18   25q + 5q dark blue   5.00 6.50
B4 A18   50q + 5q dark grn   5.00 6.50
    Nos. B1-B4 (4)   20.00 26.00

Nos. B1 to B4 with Additional Surcharge in Red and Black

1924
B5 A18   5q + 5q + 5q yel grn   5.00 6.50
B6 A18   10q + 5q + 5q car   5.00 6.50
B7 A18   25q + 5q + 5q dk bl   5.00 6.50
B8 A18   50q + 5q + 5q dk grn   5.00 6.50
    Nos. B5-B8 (4)   20.00 26.00

Issued under Italian Dominion

Nurse and Child — SP1

Unwmk.
**1943, Apr. 1   Photo.   *Perf. 14*
B9 SP1   5q + 5q dark grn   .25 .25
B10 SP1   10q + 10q olive brn   .25 .25
B11 SP1   15q + 10q rose red   .35 .35
B12 SP1   25q + 15q saphire   .50 .50
B13 SP1   30q + 20q violet   .60 .60
B14 SP1   50q + 25q dk org   .75 .75
B15 SP1   65q + 30q grnsh blk   1.10 1.10
B16 SP1   1fr + 40q chestnut   2.50 2.50
    Nos. B9-B16 (8)   6.30 6.30
The surtax was for the control of tuberculosis.
For surcharges see Nos. B24-B27.

Issued under German Administration

War Victims
SP2

1944, Sept. 22
B17 SP2   5g + 5(q) dp grn   2.10 2.75
B18 SP2   10g + 5(q) dp brn   2.10 2.75
B19 SP2   15g + 5(q) car lake   2.10 2.75
B20 SP2   25g + 10(q) dp blue   2.10 2.75
B21 SP2   1fr + 50q dk olive   2.10 2.75
B22 SP2   2fr + 1(fr) purple   2.10 2.75
B23 SP2   3fr + 1.50(fr) dk org   2.10 2.75
    Nos. B17-B23 (7)   14.70 19.25
Surtax for victims of World War II.

Independent State

Nos. B9 to B12 Surcharged in Carmine

**1945, May 4   Unwmk.   *Perf. 14*
B24 SP1   30q +15q on 5q+5q   1.75 1.75
B25 SP1   50q +25q on
    10q+10q   1.75 1.75
B26 SP1   1fr +50q on
    15q+10q   5.00 5.00
B27 SP1   2fr +1fr on 25q+15q   8.75 8.75
    Nos. B24-B27 (4)   17.25 17.25
The surtax was for the Albanian Red Cross.

People's Republic

Nos. 361 to 366 Overprinted in Red (cross) and Surcharged in Black

1946, July 16   **Perf. 11**
B28	A57	20q + 10q bluish grn	6.50	6.50
B29	A57	30q + 15q dp org	6.50	6.50
B30	A57	40q + 20q brown	6.50	6.50
B31	A57	60q + 30q red vio	6.50	6.50
B32	A57	1fr + 50q rose red	6.50	6.50
B33	A57	3fr + 1.50fr dk bl	6.50	6.50
		Nos. B28-B33 (6)	39.00	39.00

To honor and benefit the Congress of the Albanian Red Cross.
Counterfeits: lithographed; genuine: typographed.

> Catalogue values for unused stamps in this section, from this point to the end of the section, are for Never Hinged items.

SP3   SP4

First Aid and Red Cross: 25q+5q, Nurse carrying child on stretcher. 65q+25q, Symbolic blood transfusion. 80q+40q, Mother and child.

1967, Dec. 1   Litho.   Perf. 11½x12
B34	SP3	15 + 5q blk, red & brn	.90	.45
B35	SP3	25 + 5q multi	1.00	.60
B36	SP3	65 + 25q multi	3.00	.65
B37	SP3	80 + 40q multi	5.00	1.50
		Nos. B34-B37 (4)	9.90	3.20

6th congress of the Albanian Red Cross.

1996, Aug. 5   Litho.   Perf. 13½x13
B38	SP4	50 l +10 l multi	2.50	2.50

Albanian Red Cross, 75th anniv.

Nos. 2469-2470 Surcharged

2001, Mar. 12
B39	A567	80 l +10 l on 50 l multi	3.00	3.00
B40	A567	130 l +20 l on 100 l multi	4.50	4.50

AIR POST STAMPS

Airplane Crossing Mountains AP1

Wmk. 125

1925, May 30   Typo.   Perf. 14
C1	AP1	5q green	.50	.50
C2	AP1	10q rose red	.50	.50
C3	AP1	25q deep blue	.50	.50
C4	AP1	50q dark green	1.00	1.00
C5	AP1	1fr dk vio & blk	1.90	1.90

C6	AP1	2fr ol grn & vio	3.00	3.00
C7	AP1	3fr brn org & dk grn	5.25	5.25
		Nos. C1-C7 (7)	12.65	12.65

Nos. C1-C7 exist imperf.
For overprint see Nos. C8-C28.

Nos. C1-C7 Overprinted

1927, Jan. 18
C8	AP1	5q green	3.00	3.00
a.		Dbl. overprint, one invtd.	35.00	
C9	AP1	10q rose red	3.00	3.00
a.		Inverted overprint	30.00	
b.		Dbl. overprint, one invtd.	35.00	
C10	AP1	25q deep blue	1.60	1.60
C11	AP1	50q dark grn	1.60	1.60
a.		Inverted overprint	30.00	
C12	AP1	1fr dk vio & blk	1.60	1.60
a.		Inverted overprint	30.00	
b.		Double overprint	30.00	
C13	AP1	2fr ol grn & vio	1.60	1.60
C14	AP1	3fr brn org & dk grn	2.75	2.75
		Nos. C8-C14 (7)	15.15	15.15

Nos. C1-C7 Overprinted

1928, Apr. 21
C15	AP1	5q green	1.40	1.50
a.		Inverted overprint	22.50	
C16	AP1	10q rose red	1.40	1.50
C17	AP1	25q deep blue	1.40	1.50
C18	AP1	50q dark green	3.00	2.50
C19	AP1	1fr dk vio & blk	15.00	19.00
C20	AP1	2fr ol grn & vio	15.00	19.00
C21	AP1	3fr brn org & dk grn	15.00	19.00
		Nos. C15-C21 (7)	52.20	64.00

First flight across the Adriatic, Valona to Brindisi, Apr. 21, 1928.
The variety "SHQYRTARE" occurs once in the sheet for each value. Value 3 times normal.

Nos. C1-C7 Overprinted in Red Brown

1929, Dec. 1
C22	AP1	5q green	2.75	2.75
C23	AP1	10q rose red	2.75	2.75
C24	AP1	25q deep blue	5.75	5.75
C25	AP1	50q dk grn	17.00	17.00
C26	AP1	1fr dk vio & blk	80.00	80.00
C27	AP1	2fr ol grn	97.50	97.50
C28	AP1	3fr brn org & dk grn	190.00	190.00
		Nos. C22-C28 (7)	395.75	395.75

Excellent counterfeits exist.

King Zog and Airplane over Tirana AP2

AP3

1930, Oct. 8   Photo.   Unwmk.
C29	AP2	5q yellow green	.35	.30
C30	AP2	15q rose red	.45	.40
C31	AP2	20q slate blue	.60	.55
C32	AP2	50q olive green	.85	.75
C33	AP3	1fr dark blue	1.75	1.60
C34	AP3	2fr olive brown	5.50	5.25
C35	AP3	3fr purple	7.50	7.00
		Nos. C29-C35 (7)	17.00	15.85

For overprints and surcharges see Nos. C36-C45.

Nos. C29-C35 Overprinted

1931, July 6
C36	AP2	5q yellow grn	2.10	2.10
a.		Double overprint	65.00	
C37	AP2	15q rose red	2.10	2.10
C38	AP2	20q slate blue	2.10	2.10
C39	AP2	50q olive grn	2.10	2.10
C40	AP3	1fr dark blue	12.50	12.50
C41	AP3	2fr olive brn	12.50	12.50
C42	AP3	3fr purple	12.50	12.50
a.		Inverted overprint	175.00	
		Nos. C36-C42 (7)	45.90	45.90

1st air post flight from Tirana to Rome.
Only a very small part of this issue was sold to the public. Most of the stamps were given to the Aviation Company to help provide funds for conducting the service.

Issued under Italian Dominion

Nos. C29-C30 Overprinted in Black

1939, Apr. 19   Unwmk.   Perf. 14
C43	AP2	5q yel green	1.25	1.10
C44	AP2	15q rose red	1.25	1.10

No. C32 With Additional Surcharge
C45	AP2	20q on 50q ol grn	2.00	2.00
a.		Inverted overprint		
		Nos. C43-C45 (3)	4.50	4.20

See note after No. 309.

King Victor Emmanuel III and Plane over Mountains AP4

1939, Aug. 4   Photo.
C46	AP4	20q brown	13.00	4.00

Shepherds AP5

Map of Albania Showing Air Routes — AP6

Designs: 20q, Victor Emmanuel III and harbor view. 50q, Woman and river valley. 1fr, Bridge at Vezirit. 2fr, Ruins. 3fr, Women waving to plane.

1940, Mar. 20   Unwmk.
C47	AP5	5q green	.25	.25
C48	AP6	15q rose red	.25	.25
C49	AP5	20q deep blue	.25	.25
C50	AP6	50q brown	.75	.75
C51	AP5	1fr myrtle green	1.25	1.25
C52	AP6	2fr brown black	4.25	4.25
C53	AP6	3fr rose violet	10.00	10.00
		Nos. C47-C53 (7)	17.00	17.00

People's Republic

Vuno-Himare AP12

Albanian Towns: 1 l, 10 l, Rozafat-Shkoder. 2 l, 20 l, Keshtjelle-Butrinto.

1950, Dec. 15   Engr.   Perf. 12½x12
C54	AP12	50q gray black	.25	.25
C55	AP12	1 l red brown	.25	.25
C56	AP12	2 l ultra	.50	.50
C57	AP12	5 l deep green	1.00	1.00
C58	AP12	10 l deep blue	2.25	2.25
C59	AP12	20 l purple	5.75	5.75
		Nos. C54-C59 (6)	10.00	10.00

Nos. C56-C58 Surcharged with New Value and Bars in Red or Black

1952-53
C60	AP12	50q on 2 l (R)	40.00	40.00
C61	AP12	50q on 5 l	10.00	5.00
C62	AP12	2.50 l on 5 l (R)	60.00	60.00
C63	AP12	2.50 l on 10 l	10.00	5.00
		Nos. C60-C63 (4)	120.00	110.00

Issued: #C60, C62, 12/26/52; #C61, C63, 3/14/53.

> Catalogue values for unused stamps in this section, from this point to the end of the section, are for Never Hinged items.

Banner with Lenin, Map of Stalingrad and Tanks — AP13

1963, Feb. 2   Litho.   Perf. 14
C67	AP13	7 l grn & dp car	3.00	.60

20th anniversary, Battle of Stalingrad.

Sputnik and Sun AP14

Designs: 3 l, Lunik 4. 5 l, Lunik 3 photographing far side of the Moon. 8 l, Venus space probe. 12 l, Mars 1.

1963, Oct. 31   Unwmk.   Perf. 12
C68	AP14	2 l org, yel & blk	.25	.30
C69	AP14	3 l multi	.50	.30
C70	AP14	5 l rose lil, yel & blk	.90	.45
C71	AP14	8 l multi	1.25	.85
C72	AP14	12 l blue & org	2.25	2.50
		Nos. C68-72 (5)	5.15	4.40

Russian interplanetary explorations.

Nos. C68 and C71 Overprinted: "Riccione 23-8-1964"

1964, Aug. 23
C73	AP14	2 l org, yel & blk	5.50	5.50
C74	AP14	8 l multicolored	9.50	9.50

Intl. Space Exhib. in Riccione, Italy.

Plane over Berat AP15

1975, Nov. 25   Litho.   Perf. 12
C75	AP15	20q multi	.20	.20
C76	AP15	40q Gjirokaster	.20	.20
C77	AP15	60q Sarande	.20	.20
C78	AP15	90q Durres	.50	.20
C79	AP15	1.20 l Kruje	.80	.20
C80	AP15	2.40 l Boga	1.60	.35
C81	AP15	4.05 l Tirana	2.50	.65
		Nos. C75-C81 (7)	6.00	2.00

SPECIAL DELIVERY STAMPS

Issued under Italian Dominion

King Victor
Emmanuel
III — SD1

1940   Unwmk.   Photo.   Perf. 14
E1	SD1	25q bright violet	1.40	.60
E2	SD1	50q red orange	2.40	2.00

Issued under German Administration

No. E1
Overprinted
in Carmine

1943
E3	SD1	25q bright violet	15.00	17.50

Proclamation of Albanian independence.

POSTAGE DUE STAMPS

Nos. 35-39
Handstamped in
Various Colors

1914, Feb. 23   Unwmk.   Perf. 14
J1	A3	2q org brn & buff (Bl)	6.00	1.60
J2	A3	5q green (R)	6.00	2.50
J3	A3	10q rose red (Bl)	8.00	1.60
J4	A3	25q dark blue (R)	10.00	1.60
J5	A3	50q vio & red (Bk)	14.00	5.00
		Nos. J1-J5 (5)	44.00	12.30

The two parts of the overprint are hand-stamped separately. Stamps exist with one or both handstamps inverted, double, omitted or in wrong color.

Nos. 48-51
Overprinted in Black

1914, Apr. 16
J6	A3	(a) 10pa on 5q green	2.75	2.25
J7	A3	(a) 20pa on 10q rose red	2.75	2.25
J8	A3	(b) 1gr on 25q blue	2.75	2.25
J9	A3	(b) 2gr on 50q vio & red	2.75	2.25
		Nos. J6-J9 (4)	11.00	9.00

Same Design as Regular Issue of 1919, Overprinted

1919, Feb. 10   Perf. 11½, 12½
J10	A8	(4)q on 4h rose	5.00	4.50
J11	A8	(10)q on 10k red, grn	5.00	4.50
J12	A8	20q on 2k org, gray	5.00	4.50
J13	A8	50q on 5k brn, yel	5.00	4.50
		Nos. J10-J13 (4)	20.00	18.00

Fortress at
Scutari — D3

D5

Post Horn Overprinted in Black

1920, Apr. 1   Perf. 14x13
J14	D3	4q olive green	.40	.40
J15	D3	10q rose red	.85	.85
J16	D3	20q bister brn	.85	.85
J17	D3	50q black	2.00	2.00
		Nos. J14-J17 (4)	4.10	4.10

1922   Perf. 12½, 11½

Background of Red Wavy Lines
J23	D5	4q black, red	1.00	1.00
J24	D5	10q black, red	1.00	1.00
J25	D5	20q black, red	1.00	1.00
J26	D5	50q black, red	1.00	1.00
		Nos. J23-J26 (4)	4.00	4.00

Same Overprinted in White

1925
J27	D5	4q black, red	1.00	1.00
J28	D5	10q black, red	1.00	1.00
J29	D5	20q black, red	1.00	1.00
J30	D5	50q black, red	1.00	1.00
		Nos. J27-J30 (4)	4.00	4.00

The 10q with overprint in gold was a trial printing. It was not put in use.

D7

Coat of Arms — D8

Overprinted "QINDAR" in Red

1926, Dec. 24   Perf. 13½x13
J31	D7	10q dark blue	.25	.20
J32	D7	20q green	.50	.40
J33	D7	30q red brown	.80	.60
J34	D7	50q dark brown	1.25	1.00
		Nos. J31-J34 (4)	2.80	2.20

Wmk. Double Headed Eagle (220)
1930, Sept. 1   Photo.   Perf. 14, 14½
J35	D8	10q dark blue	7.50	7.50
J36	D8	20q rose red	2.50	2.50
J37	D8	30q violet	2.50	2.50
J38	D8	50q dark green	2.50	2.50
		Nos. J35-J38 (4)	15.00	15.00

Nos. J36-J38 exist with overprint "14 Shtator 1943" (see Nos. 332-344) which is private and fraudulent on these stamps.

No. 253 Overprinted **Taksë**

1936   Perf. 14
J39	A34	10q carmine	3.50	4.75
a.		Hyphens on each side of "Taksë" ('39)	20.00	20.00

Issued under Italian Dominion

Coat of Arms — D9

1940   Unwmk.   Photo.   Perf. 14
J40	D9	4q red orange	16.00	16.00
J41	D9	10q bright violet	16.00	16.00
J42	D9	20q brown	16.00	16.00
J43	D9	30q dark blue	16.00	16.00
J44	D9	50q carmine rose	16.00	16.00
		Nos. J40-J44 (5)	80.00	80.00

ALEXANDRETTA

ˌa-lig-ˌzan-ˈdre-tə

LOCATION — A political territory in northern Syria, bordering on Turkey
GOVT. — French mandate
AREA — 10,000 sq. mi. (approx.)
POP. — 270,000 (approx.)

Included in the Syrian territory mandated to France under the Versailles Treaty, the name was changed to Hatay in 1938. The following year France returned the territory to Turkey in exchange for certain concessions. See Hatay.

100 Centimes = 1 Piaster

Stamps of Syria, 1930-36, Overprinted or Surcharged in Black or Red:

a

b

c

d

e

1938   Unwmk.   Perf. 12x12½
1	A6(a)	10c vio brn	.60	.60
2	A6(a)	20c brn org	.60	.60
		Perf. 13½		
3	A9(b)	50c vio (R)	.75	.75
4	A10(b)	1p bis brn	.85	.85
5	A9(b)	2p dk vio (R)	1.25	1.25
6	A13(b)	3p yel grn (R)	2.00	2.00
7	A10(b)	4p yel org	2.50	2.50
8	A16(b)	6p grnsh blk (R)	2.25	2.25
9	A18(b)	25p vio brn	7.25	7.25
10	A15(c)	75c org red	1.10	1.10
11	A10(d)	2.50p on 4p yel org	1.50	1.50
12	AP2(e)	12.50p on 15p org red	3.25	3.25
		Nos. 1-12 (12)	23.90	23.90
		Set, never hinged	35.00	

Issue dates: #1-9, Apr. 14, #10-12, Sept. 2.

Nos. 4, 7, 10-12 Overprinted in Black

1938, Nov. 10
13	A15	75c	30.00	32.50
14	A10	1p	17.50	19.00
15	A10	2.50p on 4p	11.00	12.50
16	A10	4p	15.00	15.00
17	AP2	12.50p on 15p	30.00	32.50
		Nos. 13-17 (5)	103.50	111.50
		Set, never hinged	140.00	

Death of Kemal Ataturk, pres. of Turkey.

AIR POST STAMPS

Air Post Stamps of Syria, 1937, Overprinted Type "b" in Red or Black

1938, Apr. 14   Unwmk.   Perf. 13
C1	AP14	½p dark vio (R)	.75	.85
C2	AP15	1p black (R)	.75	.50
C3	AP14	2p blue grn (R)	1.60	1.75
C4	AP15	3p deep ultra	1.75	2.00
C5	AP14	5p rose lake	4.00	4.75
C6	AP15	10p red brown	4.50	5.25
C7	AP14	15p lake brown	5.25	6.00
C8	AP15	25p dk blue (R)	7.25	8.00
		Nos. C1-C8 (8)	25.85	29.10
C		Set, never hinged	37.50	

POSTAGE DUE STAMPS

Postage Due Stamps of Syria, 1925-31, Ovptd. Type "b" in Black or Red

1938, Apr. 14   Unwmk.   Perf. 13½
J1	D5	50c brown, yel	1.40	2.00
J2	D6	1p violet, rose	2.10	2.25
J3	D5	2p blk, blue (R)	2.75	2.75
J4	D5	3p blk, red org	4.50	5.00
J5	D5	5p blk, bl grn (R)	6.75	7.00
J6	D7	8p blk, gray bl (R)	7.50	8.50
		Nos. J1-J6 (6)	25.00	27.50
J		Set, never hinged	32.50	

On No. J2, the overprint is vertical, reading up, other denominations, horizontal.
Stamps of Alexandretta were discontinued in 1938 and replaced by those of Hatay.

ALGERIA

al-'jir-ē-ə

LOCATION — North Africa
GOVT. — Republic
AREA — 919,595 sq. mi.
POP. — 29,300,000 (1998 est.)
CAPITAL — Algiers

The former French colony of Algeria became an integral part of France on Sept. 1, 1958, when French stamps replaced Algerian stamps. Algeria became an independent country July 3, 1962.

100 Centimes = 1 Franc
100 Centimes = 1 Dinar (1964)

Catalogue values for unused stamps in this country are for Never Hinged items, beginning with Scott 109 in the regular postage section, Scott B27 in the semipostal section, Scott C1 in the airpost section, Scott CB1 in the airpost semi-postal section, and Scott J25 in the postage due section.

Stamps of France Overprinted in Red, Blue or Black:

a

b

c

d

1924-26		Unwmk.	Perf. 14x13½	
1	A16(a)	1c dk gray (R)	.20	.20
2	A16(a)	2c violet brn	.20	.20
3	A16(a)	3c orange	.20	.20
4	A16(a)	4c yel brn (Bl)	.20	.20
5	A22(a)	5c orange (Bl)	.20	.20
6	A16(a)	5c green ('25)	.40	.30
7	A23(a)	10c green	.30	.20
b.		Booklet pane of 10	6.00	
8	A22(a)	10c green ('25)	.50	.20
9	A20(a)	15c slate grn	.20	.20
10	A22(a)	15c green ('25)	.60	.20
11	A22(a)	15c red brn (Bl) ('26)	.20	.20
12	A22(a)	20c red brn (Bl)	.25	.20
13	A23(a)	25c blue (R)	.20	.20
a.		Booklet pane of 10	45.00	
14	A23(a)	30c red (Bl)	.90	.20
15	A22(a)	30c cerise ('25)	.70	.50
a.		"ALGÉRIE" double	140.00	
16	A22(a)	30c lt bl (R) ('25)	.30	.20
a.		Booklet pane of 10	35.00	
17	A22(a)	35c violet	.30	.20
18	A18(a)	40c red & pale bl	.30	.20
19	A22(a)	40c ol brn (R) ('25)	.75	.50
20	A18(b)	45c grn & bl (R)	.40	.30
a.		Double overprint	175.00	
21	A23(a)	45c red (Bl) ('25)	.60	.20
22	A23(a)	50c blue (R)	.40	.20
23	A20(a)	60c lt violet	.65	.35
a.		Inverted overprint		1,750.
24	A20(a)	65c rose (Bl)	.35	.20
25	A23(a)	75c blue (R)	.60	.30
a.		Double overprint	150.00	

26	A20(a)	80c ver ('26)	.90	.40
27	A20(a)	85c ver (Bl)	.60	.20
28	A18(b)	1fr cl & ol grn	1.00	.30
29	A22(a)	1.05fr ver ('26)	1.00	.40
30	A18(c)	2fr org & pale bl	1.00	.55
31	A18(b)	3fr vio & bl ('26)	3.00	.80
32	A18(d)	5fr bl & buff (R)	8.00	4.75
		Nos. 1-32 (32)	25.40	13.45

No. 15 was issued precanceled only. Values for precanceled stamps in first column are for those which have not been through the post and have original gum. Values in second column are for postally used, gumless stamps.
For surcharges see Nos. 75, P1.

Street in Kasbah, Algiers A1

Mosque of Sidi Abd-er-Rahman A2

La Pêcherie Mosque — A3

Marabout of Sidi Yacoub A4

1926-39		Typo.	Perf. 14x13½	
33	A1	1c olive	.20	.20
34	A1	2c red brown	.20	.20
35	A1	3c orange	.20	.20
36	A1	5c blue green	.20	.20
37	A1	10c brt violet	.20	.20
a.		Booklet pane of 10	25.00	
38	A2	15c orange brn	.20	.20
39	A2	20c green	.20	.20
40	A2	20c deep rose	.20	.20
41	A2	25c blue grn	.20	.20
42	A2	25c blue ('27)	.35	.20
43	A2	25c vio bl ('39)	.20	.20
44	A2	30c blue	.25	.20
45	A2	30c bl grn ('27)	.65	.40
46	A2	35c dp violet	1.00	.65
47	A2	40c olive green	.25	.20
a.		Booklet pane of 10	30.00	
48	A3	45c violet brn	.35	.20
49	A3	50c blue	.25	.20
a.		Booklet pane of 10	35.00	
50	A3	50c dk red ('30)	.20	.20
a.		Booklet pane of 10	40.00	
51	A3	60c yellow grn	.25	.20
52	A3	65c blk brn ('27)	1.60	1.10
53	A3	65c ultra ('38)	.25	.20
a.		Booklet pane of 10	25.00	
54	A3	75c carmine	.50	.35
55	A3	75c blue ('29)	2.00	.25
56	A3	80c orange red	.50	.25
57	A3	90c red ('27)	4.50	2.00
58	A4	1fr gray grn & red brn	.50	.25
59	A3	1.05fr lt brown	.50	.35
60	A3	1.10fr mag ('27)	4.50	1.25
61	A4	1.25fr dk bl & ultra	.80	.60
62	A4	1.50fr dk bl & ultra ('27)	2.40	.25
63	A4	2fr Prus bl & blk brn	1.90	.25
64	A4	3fr violet & org	3.50	.80
65	A4	5fr red & violet	6.00	2.25
66	A4	10fr ol brn & rose ('27)	37.50	22.50
67	A4	20fr vio & grn ('27)	4.50	3.50
		Nos. 33-67 (35)	77.00	40.60

Type A4, 50c blue and rose red, inscribed "CENTENAIRE-ALGERIE" is France No. 255. See design A24. For stamps and types surcharged see Nos. 68-74, 131, 136, 187, B1-B13, J27, P2.

Stamps of 1926 Surcharged with New Values

1927				
68	A2	10c on 35c dp violet	.20	.20
69	A2	25c on 30c blue	.20	.20
70	A2	30c on 25c blue grn	.20	.20
71	A3	65c on 60c yel grn	.75	.50
72	A3	90c on 80c org red	.20	.20
73	A3	1.10fr on 1.05fr lt brn	.30	.20

74	A4	1.50fr on 1.25fr dk bl & ultra	1.25	.75
		Nos. 68-74 (7)	3.40	2.25

Bars cancel the old value on #68, 69, 73, 74.

No. 4 Surcharged

1927				
75	A16	5c on 4c yellow brown	.50	.25

Bay of Algiers A5

1930, May 4		Engr.	Perf. 11, 12½	
78	A5	10fr red brown	9.50	7.50
a.		Imperf., pair	27.50	

Cent. of Algeria and for Intl. Phil. Exhib. of North Africa, May, 1930.
One copy of No. 78 was sold with each 10fr admission.

Travel across the Sahara A6

Arch of Triumph, Lambese A7

Admiralty Building, Algiers A8

Kings' Tombs near Touggourt A9

El-Kebir Mosque, Algiers A10

Oued River at Colomb-Bechar A11

Sidi Bon Medine Cemetery at Tlemcen A13

View of Ghardaia A12

No. 4 Surcharged

ALGÉRIE 5c

1936-41		Engr.	Perf. 13	
79	A6	1c ultra	.20	.20
80	A11	2c dk violet	.20	.20
81	A7	3c dk blue grn	.20	.20
82	A12	5c red violet	.20	.20
83	A8	10c emerald	.20	.20
84	A9	15c red	.20	.20
85	A13	20c dk blue grn	.20	.20
86	A10	25c rose vio	.30	.20
87	A12	30c yellow grn	.30	.20
88	A9	40c brown vio	.20	.20
89	A13	45c deep ultra	.65	.40
90	A8	50c red	.20	.20
91	A6	65c red brn	3.25	2.10
92	A6	65c rose car ('37)	.35	.20
93	A6	70c red brn ('39)	.20	.20
94	A11	75c slate bl	.20	.20
95	A7	90c henna brn	1.00	.55
96	A10	1fr brown	.20	.20
97	A8	1.25fr lt violet	.35	.20
98	A8	1.25fr car rose ('39)	.30	.20
99	A11	1.50fr turq blue	1.25	.20
99A	A11	1.50fr rose ('40)	.35	.20
100	A12	1.75fr henna brn	.20	.20
101	A7	2fr dk brown	.20	.20
102	A6	2.25fr yellow grn	9.50	6.50
103	A12	2.50fr dk ultra ('41)	.30	.25
104	A13	3fr magenta	.25	.20
105	A10	3.50fr pck blue	2.10	1.75
106	A8	5fr slate blue	.30	.20
107	A11	10fr henna brn	.30	.20
108	A9	20fr turq blue	.70	.40
		Nos. 79-108 (31)	24.55	16.75

See Nos. 124-125, 162.
Nos. 82 and 100 with surcharge "E. F. M. 30frs" (Emergency Field Message) were used in 1943 to pay cable tolls for US and Canadian servicemen.
For other surcharges see Nos. 122, B27.

Catalogue values for unused stamps in this section, from this point to the end of the section, are for Never Hinged items.

Algerian Pavilion — A14

1937			Perf. 13	
109	A14	40c brt green	.30	.35
110	A14	50c rose carmine	.20	.20
111	A14	1.50fr blue	.50	.25
112	A14	1.75fr brown black	.60	.50
		Nos. 109-112 (4)	1.60	1.30

Paris International Exposition.

Constantine in 1837 — A15

1937				
113	A15	65c deep rose	.30	.20
114	A15	1fr rose	2.50	.50
115	A15	1.75fr blue green	.40	.20
116	A15	2.15fr red violet	.20	.20
		Nos. 113-116 (4)	3.40	1.10

Taking of Constantine by the French, cent.

Ruins of a Roman Villa — A16

1938				
117	A16	30c green	.50	.30
118	A16	65c ultra	.20	.20
119	A16	75c rose violet	.55	.40
120	A16	3fr carmine rose	1.40	1.40
121	A16	5fr yellow brown	2.25	2.25
		Nos. 117-121 (5)	4.90	4.55

Centenary of Philippeville.

No. 90 Surcharged in Black

1938

122	A8	25c on 50c red	.20	.20
a.		Double surcharge	35.00	30.00
b.		Inverted surcharge	20.00	18.00

Types of 1936

1939
Numerals of Value on Colorless Background

124	A7	90c henna brown	.20	.20
125	A10	2.25fr blue green	.20	.20

For surcharge see No. B38.

American Export Liner Unloading Cargo
A17

1939

126	A17	20c green	.65	.65
127	A17	40c red violet	.65	.50
128	A17	90c brown black	.35	.20
129	A17	1.25fr rose	2.25	.80
130	A17	2.25fr ultra	.65	.60
		Nos. 126-130 (5)	4.55	2.75

New York World's Fair.

Type of 1926, Surcharged in Black

Two types of surcharge:
I — Bars 6mm
II — Bars 7mm

1939-40   **Perf. 14x13½**

131	A1	1fr on 90c crimson (I)	.20	.20
a.		Booklet pane of 10	35.00	
b.		Double surcharge (I)	35.00	
c.		Inverted surcharge (I)	22.50	
d.		Pair, one without surch. (I)	800.00	
e.		Type II ('40)	1.75	.20
f.		Inverted surcharge (II)	27.50	
g.		Pair, one without surch. (II)	800.00	

View of Algiers — A18

1941   **Typo.**

132	A18	30c ultra	.20	.20
133	A18	70c sepia	.20	.20
134	A18	1fr carmine rose	.20	.20
		Nos. 132-134 (3)	.60	.60

See No. 163.

Marshal Pétain
A19   A20

1941   **Engr.**   **Perf. 13**

135	A19	1fr dark blue		.30	.20

For stamp and type surcharged see #B36-B37.

No. 53 Surcharged in Black with New Value and Bars

1941   **Perf. 14x13½**

.136	A1	50c on 65c ultra	.30	.20
a.		Booklet pane of 10		
b.		Inverted surcharge	21.00	
c.		Pair, one without surch.	52.50	

1942   **Perf. 14x13**

137	A20	1.50fr orange red	.20	.20

Four other denominations of type A20 exist (4, 5, 10, 20fr), but were not placed in use.

Constantine
A21

Oran
A22

Arms of Algiers — A23

Engraver's Name at Lower Left

1942-43   **Photo.**   **Perf. 12**

138	A21	40c dark vio ('43)	.20	.20
139	A21	60c rose ('43)	.20	.20
140	A21	1.20fr yel grn ('43)	.20	.20
141	A23	1.50fr car rose	.20	.20
142	A22	2fr sapphire	.20	.20
143	A21	2.40fr rose ('43)	.20	.20
144	A23	3fr sapphire	.20	.20
145	A21	4fr blue ('43)	.20	.20
146	A22	5fr yel grn ('43)	.20	.20
		Nos. 138-146 (9)	1.80	1.80

For type surcharged see No. 166.

Imperforates
Nearly all of Algeria Nos. 138-285, B39-B96, C1-C12 and CB1-CB3 exist imperforate. See note after France No. 395.

Without Engraver's Name

1942-45   **Typo.**   **Perf. 14x13½**

147	A23	10c dull brn vio ('45)	.20	.20
148	A22	30c dp bl grn ('45)	.20	.20
149	A21	40c dull brn vio ('45)	.20	.20
150	A22	60c rose ('45)	.20	.20
151	A21	70c deep bl ('45)	.20	.20
152	A23	80c dk bl grn ('43)	.25	.25
153	A21	1.20fr dp bl grn ('45)	.20	.20
154	A23	1.50fr brt rose ('43)	.20	.20
155	A22	2fr dp blue ('45)	.20	.20
156	A21	2.40fr rose ('45)	.30	.25
157	A23	3fr dp blue ('45)	.20	.20
158	A22	4.50fr brown vio	.20	.20
		Nos. 147-158 (12)	2.55	2.50

For surcharge see No. 190.

La Pêcherie Mosque — A24

1942   **Typo.**

159	A24	50c dull red	.20	.20
a.		Booklet pane of 10	2.75	

1942   **Photo.**   **Perf. 12**

160	A24	40c gray green	.20	.20
161	A24	50c red	.20	.20

Types of 1936-41, Without "RF"

1942   **Engr.**   **Perf. 13**

162	A11	1.50fr rose		.30	.20

          Typo.   **Perf. 14x13½**

163	A18	30c ultra		.20	.20

"One Aim Alone - Victory"
A25   A26

1943   **Litho.**   **Perf. 12**

164	A25	1.50fr deep rose	.20	.20
165	A26	1.50fr dark blue	.20	.20

Type of 1942-3 Surcharged with New Value in Black

1943   **Photo.**

166	A22	2fr on 5fr red orange	.20	.20
a.		Surcharge omitted	140.00	

Summer Palace, Algiers
A27

1944, Dec. 1   **Litho.**

167	A27	15fr slate	.80	.80
168	A27	20fr lt blue grn	.60	.40
169	A27	50fr dk carmine	.60	.50
170	A27	100fr deep blue	1.50	1.25
171	A27	200fr dull bis brn	2.50	1.40
		Nos. 167-171 (5)	6.00	4.35

Marianne
A28

Gallic Cock
A29

1944-45

172	A28	10c gray	.20	.20
173	A28	30c red violet	.20	.20
174	A29	40c rose car ('45)	.20	.20
175	A28	50c red	.20	.20
176	A28	80c emerald	.20	.20
177	A29	1fr green ('45)	.20	.20
178	A28	1.20fr rose lilac	.20	.20
179	A28	1.50fr dark blue	.20	.20
a.		Double impression	20.00	
180	A29	2fr red	.20	.20
a.		Double impression	22.50	
181	A29	2fr dk brown ('45)	.20	.20
182	A28	2.40fr rose red	.20	.20
183	A29	3fr purple	.20	.20
184	A29	4fr ultra ('45)	.20	.20
185	A28	4.50fr olive blk	.30	.25
186	A29	10fr grnsh blk ('45)	.50	.35
		Nos. 172-186 (15)	3.40	3.20

No. 38 Surcharged in Black

1944   **Perf. 14x13½**

187	A2	30c on 15c orange brn	.20	.20
a.		Inverted surcharge	10.00	4.00

This stamp exists precanceled only. See note below No. 32.

No. 154 Surcharged "RF" and New Value

1945

190	A23	50c on 1.50fr brt rose	.20	.20
a.		Inverted surcharge	15.00	

Stamps of France, 1944, Overprinted Type "a" of 1924 in Black

1945-46

191	A99	80c yellow grn	.20	.20
192	A99	1fr grnsh blue	.20	.20
193	A99	1.20fr violet	.20	.20
194	A99	2fr violet brown	.25	.20
195	A99	2.40fr carmine rose	.25	.20
196	A99	3fr orange	.25	.20
		Nos. 191-196 (6)	1.35	1.20

Same Overprint on Stamps of France, 1945-47, in Black, Red or Carmine

1945-47

197	A145	40c lilac rose	.20	.20
198	A145	50c violet bl (R)	.20	.20
199	A146	60c brt ultra (R)	.25	.20
200	A146	1fr rose red ('47)	.20	.20
201	A146	1.50fr rose lilac ('47)	.20	.20
202	A147	2fr myr grn (R) ('46)	.20	.20
203	A147	3fr deep rose	.20	.20
204	A147	4.50fr ultra (C) ('47)	.55	.20
205	A147	5fr lt green ('46)	.20	.20
206	A147	10fr ultra	.50	.25
		Nos. 197-206 (10)	2.70	2.05

Same Overprint on France No. 383 and New Value Surcharged in Black

1946

207	A99	2fr on 1.50fr henna brn	.20	.20
a.		Without "2F"	110.00	

Same Overprint on France Nos. 562 and 564, in Carmine or Blue

1947

208	A153	10c dp ultra & blk (C)	.25	.25
209	A155	50c brown, yel & red (Bl)	.30	.30

Constantine
A30

Algiers
A31

Arms of Oran — A32

          Perf. 14x13½

1947-49   **Unwmk.**   **Typo.**

210	A30	10c dk grn & brt red	.20	.20
211	A31	50c black & orange	.20	.20
212	A32	1fr ultra & yellow	.20	.20
213	A30	1.30fr blk & grnsh bl	.55	.35
214	A31	1.50fr pur & org yel	.20	.20
215	A32	2fr blk & brt grn	.20	.20
216	A30	2.50fr blk & brt red	.35	.30
217	A31	3fr vio brn & grn	.20	.20
218	A32	3.50fr lt grn & rose lil	.20	.20
219	A30	4fr dk brn & brt grn	.20	.20
220	A31	4.50fr ultra & scar	.20	.20
221	A31	5fr blk & grnsh bl	.25	.20
222	A32	6fr brown & scarlet	.25	.20
223	A32	8fr choc & ultra ('48)	.20	.20
224	A32	10fr car & choc ('48)	.35	.20
225	A31	15fr black & red ('49)	.35	.20
		Nos. 210-225 (16)	4.05	3.45

See Nos. 274-280, 285.

Peoples of the World
A33

1949, Oct. 24   **Engr.**   **Perf. 13**

226	A33	5fr green	1.00	.80
227	A33	15fr scarlet	1.25	.80
228	A33	25fr ultra	2.75	2.50
		Nos. 226-228 (3)	5.00	4.10

75th anniv. of the UPU.

Grapes
A34

Apollo of Cherchell
A35

25fr, Dates. 40fr, Oranges and lemons.

1950, Feb. 25
229 A34 20fr multicolored 1.25 .35
230 A34 25fr multicolored 1.40 .40
231 A34 40fr multicolored 2.75 .80
Nos. 229-231 (3) 5.40 1.55

1952 Unwmk. Perf. 13
Designs: 12fr, 18fr, Isis statue, Cherchell. 15fr, 20fr, Child with eagle.
240 A35 10fr gray black .25 .20
241 A35 12fr orange brn .35 .20
242 A35 15fr deep blue .25 .20
243 A35 18fr rose red .35 .25
244 A35 20fr deep green .35 .20
245 A35 30fr deep blue .65 .35
Nos. 240-245 (6) 2.20 1.40

War Memorial, Algiers — A38

Fossilized Nautilus — A39

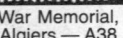

Phonolite Dike A40

1952, Apr. 11
246 A38 12fr dark green .50 .35
Issued to honor the French Africa Army.

1952, Aug. 11
247 A39 15fr brt crimson .85 .50
248 A40 30fr deep ultra .90 .65
19th Intl. Geological Cong., Algiers, 9/8-15.

French and Algerian Soldiers and Camel — A41

1952, Nov. 30
249 A41 12fr chestnut brown .75 .50
50th anniv. of the establishment of the Sahara Companies.

Eugène Millon A42

François C. Maillot — A43

Oranges — A44

Portrait: 50fr, Alphonse Laveran.

Unwmk.
1954, Jan. 4 Engr. Perf. 13
250 A42 25fr dk grn & choc 1.10 .20
251 A43 40fr org brn & brn car 1.75 .60
252 A42 50fr ultra & indigo 1.75 .20
Nos. 250-252 (3) 4.60 1.00
Military Health Service.

1954, May 8
253 A44 15fr indigo & blue .70 .40
3rd Intl. Cong. on Agronomy, Algiers, 1954.

Type of France, 1954 Overprinted type "a" in Black

Unwmk.
1954, June 6 Engr. Perf. 13
254 A240 15fr rose carmine .55 .45
Liberation of France, 10th anniversary.

Darguinah Hydroelectric Works A45

Patio of Bardo Museum A46

1954, June 19
255 A45 15fr lilac rose .65 .45
Opening of Darguinah hydroelectric works.

1954 Typo. Perf. 14x13½
257 A46 12fr red brn & brn org .60 .25
258 A46 15fr dk blue & blue .60 .25
See Nos. 267-271.

Type of France, 1954, Overprinted type "a" in Carmine
1954 Engr. Perf. 13
260 A247 12fr dark green .50 .45
150th anniv. of the 1st Legion of Honor awards at Camp de Boulogne.

St. Augustine — A47

1954, Nov. 11
261 A47 15fr chocolate .75 .65
1600th anniv. of the birth of St. Augustine.

Aesculapius Statue and El Kattar Hospital, Algiers A48

1955, Apr. 3 Unwmk. Perf. 13
262 A48 15fr red .50 .35
Issued to publicize the 30th French Congress of Medicine, Algiers, April 3-6, 1955.

Chenua Mountain and View of Tipasa A49

1955, May 31
263 A49 50fr brown carmine .50 .20
2000th anniv. of the founding of Tipasa.

Type of France, 1955 Overprinted type "a" in Red
1955, June 13
264 A251 30fr deep ultra .60 .45
Rotary Intl., 50th anniv.

Marianne — A50

Great Kabylia Mountains A51

1955, Oct. 3 Typo. Perf. 14x13½
265 A50 15fr carmine .50 .25
See No. 284.

1955, Dec. 17 Engr. Perf. 13
266 A51 100fr indigo & ultra 2.00 .20

Bardo Type of 1954, "Postes" and "Algerie" in White
Perf. 14x13½
1955-57 Unwmk. Typo.
267 A46 10fr dk brn & lt brn .25 .20
268 A46 12fr red brn & brn org ('56) .20 .20
269 A46 18fr crimson & ver ('57) .45 .20
270 A46 20fr grn & yel grn ('57) .35 .25
271 A46 25fr purple & brt purple .50 .20
Nos. 267-271 (5) 1.75 1.05

Marshal Franchet d'Esperey A52

1956, May 25 Engr. Perf. 13
272 A52 15fr sapphire & indigo .70 .60
Birth cent. of Marshal Franchet d'Esperey.

Marshal Jacques Leclerc A53

1956, Nov. 29
273 A53 15fr red brown & sepia .50 .50
Death of Marshal Leclerc.
For design surcharged see No. B90.

Type of 1947-49 and

Arms of Bône — A54

Arms: 2fr, Tizi-Quzou. 3fr, Mostaganem. 5fr, Tlemcen. 10fr, Setif. 12fr, Orleansville.

1956-58 Typo. Perf. 14x13½
274 A54 1fr green & ver .25 .20
275 A54 2fr ver & ultra ('58) .45 .25
276 A54 3fr ultra & emer ('58) .45 .25
277 A54 5fr ultra & yellow .25 .20
278 A31 6fr red & grn ('57) .45 .30
279 A54 10fr dp cl & emer ('58) .50 .30
280 A54 12fr ultra & red ('58) .50 .30
Nos. 274-280 (7) 2.85 1.80
Nos. 275 and 279 are inscribed "Republique Francaise." See No. 285.

View of Oran — A55

1956-58 Engr. Perf. 13
281 A55 30fr dull purple .45 .20
282 A55 35fr car rose ('58) .75 .45

Electric Train Crossing Bridge A56

1957, Mar. 25
283 A56 40fr dk blue grn & emer .60 .20

Marianne Type of 1955 Inscribed "Algerie" Vertically
1957, Dec. 2 Typo. Perf. 14x13½
284 A50 20fr ultra .40 .20

Arms Type of 1947-49 Inscribed "Republique Francaise"
1958, July
285 A31 6fr red & green 10.00 10.00

Independent State
France Nos. 939, 968, 945-946 and 1013 Overprinted "EA" and Bars, Handstamped or Typographed, in Black or Red

1962, July 2
286 A336 10c brt green .25 .20
a. Typographed overprint .30 .20
287 A349 25c lake & gray .20 .20
a. Handstamped overprint .25 .20
288 A339 45c brt vio & ol gray 3.50 3.00
a. Handstamped overprint 15.00 10.00
289 A339 50c sl grn & lt claret 5.00 5.00
a. Handstamped overprint 15.00 12.00
290 A372 1fr dk bl, sl & bis 2.75 1.00
a. Handstamped overprint 3.50 1.50
Nos. 286-290 (5) 11.70 7.40

Post offices were authorized to overprint their stock of these 5 French stamps. The size of the letters was specified as 3x6mm each, but various sizes were used. The post offices had permission to make their own rubber stamps. Typography, pen or pencil were also used. Many types exist. Colors of hand-stamped overprints include black, red, blue, violet. "EA" stands for Etat Algérien.

Mosque, Tlemcen — A57

Roman Gates of Lodi, Médéa A58

5c, Kerrata Gorge. 10c, Dam at Foum el Gherza. 95c, Oil field, Hassi Messaoud.

1962, Nov. 1 Engr. Perf. 13
291 A57 5c Prus grn, grn & choc .20 .20
292 A58 10c ol blk & dk bl .20 .20
293 A57 25c sl grn, brn & ver .40 .20
294 A57 95c dk bl, blk & bis 1.50 .55
295 A58 1fr green & blk 1.50 1.10
Nos. 291-295 (5) 3.80 2.25

The designs of Nos. 291-295 are similar to French issues of 1959-61 with "Republique Algerienne" replacing "Republique Francaise."

Flag, Rifle, Olive Branch — A59

Design: Nos. 300-303, Broken chain and rifle added to design A59.

1963, Jan. 6   Litho.   Perf. 12½
Flag in Green and Red

296	A59	5c bister brown	.25	.20
297	A59	10c blue	.25	.20
298	A59	25c vermilion	1.50	.20
299	A59	95c violet	1.25	.45
300	A59	1fr green	1.00	.20
301	A59	2fr brown	2.50	.45
302	A59	5fr lilac	4.00	1.25
303	A59	10fr gray	14.00	7.00
	Nos. 296-303 (8)		24.75	9.95

Nos. 296-299 for the successful revolution and Nos. 300-303 the return of peace.

Men of Various Races, Wheat Emblem and Globe A60

1963, Mar. 21   Engr.   Perf. 13
304 A60 25c maroon, dl grn & yel   .30 .25
FAO "Freedom from Hunger" campaign.

Map of Algeria and Emblems — A61

Physicians from 13th Century Manuscript — A62

1963, July 5   Unwmk.   Perf. 13
305 A61 25c bl, dk brn, grn & red   .40 .25
1st anniv. of Algeria's independence.

1963, July 29   Engr.
306 A62 25c brn red, grn & bis   1.00 .35
2nd Congress of the Union of Arab physicians.

Orange and Blossom — A63

Scales and Scroll A64

1963   Perf. 14x13

307	A63	8c gray grn & org	.65	.65
308	A63	20c slate & org red	.75	.75
309	A63	40c grnsh bl & org	1.00	1.00
310	A63	55c ol grn & org red	2.00	2.00
	Nos. 307-310 (4)		4.40	4.40

Nos. 307-310 issued precanceled only. See note below No. 32.

1963, Oct. 13   Unwmk.   Perf. 13
311 A64 25c blk, grn & rose red   .40 .25
Issued to honor the new constitution.

Guerrillas — A65   Centenary Emblem — A66

1963, Nov. 1
312 A65 25c dk brn, yel grn & car   .55 .25
9th anniversary of Algerian revolution.

1963, Dec. 8   Photo.   Perf. 12
313 A66 25c lt vio bl, yel & dk red   .55 .30
Centenary of International Red Cross.

UNESCO Emblem, Scales and Globe — A67

Workers — A68

1963, Dec. 16   Unwmk.   Perf. 12
314 A67 25c lt blue & blk   .55 .25
15th anniv. of the Universal Declaration of Human Rights.

1964, May 1   Engr.   Perf. 13
315 A68 50c dull red, red org & bl   .90 .50
Issued for the Labor Festival.

Map of Africa and Flags A69

1964, May 25   Unwmk.   Perf. 13
316 A69 45c blue, orange & car   .55 .30
Africa Day on the 1st anniv. of the Addis Ababa charter on African unity.

Ramses II Battling the Hittites (from Abu Simbel) — A70

Design: 30c, Two statues of Ramses II.

1964, June 28   Engr.   Perf. 13
317 A70 20c choc, red & vio bl   .55 .30
318 A70 30c brn, red & grnsh bl   .65 .40
UNESCO world campaign to save historic monuments in Nubia.

A71

A72

5c, 25c, 85c, Tractors. 10c, 30c, 65c, Men working with lathe. 12c, 15c, 45c, Electronics center & atom symbol. 20c, 50c, 95c, Draftsman & bricklayer.

1964-65   Typo.   Perf. 14x13½

319	A71	5c red lilac	.20	.20
320	A71	10c brown	.20	.20
321	A71	12c emerald ('65)	.40	.20
322	A71	15c dk blue ('65)	.25	.20
323	A71	20c yellow	.40	.20
324	A71	25c red	.50	.20
325	A71	30c purple ('65)	.40	.20
326	A71	45c rose car	.50	.20
327	A71	50c ultra	.60	.20
328	A71	65c orange	.80	.20
329	A71	85c green	1.40	.25
330	A71	95c car rose	1.75	.30
	Nos. 319-330 (12)		7.40	2.55

For surcharges see Nos. 389, 424.

1964, Aug. 30   Engr.   Perf. 13
331 A72 85c Communications tower   1.50 .75
Inauguration of the Hertzian cable telephone line Algiers-Annaba.

Industrial & Agricultural Symbols — A73

1964, Sept. 26   Typo.   Perf. 13½x14
332 A73 25c lt ultra, yel & red   .60 .45
1st Intl. Fair at Algiers, Sept. 26-Oct. 11.

Gas Flames and Pipes — A74

1964, Sept. 27
333 A74 30c violet, blue & yel   .45 .35
Arzew natural gas liquification plant opening.

Planting Trees — A75   Children and UNICEF Emblem — A76

1964, Nov. 29   Unwmk.
334 A75 25c slate grn, yel & car   .30 .20
National reforestation campaign.

1964, Dec. 13   Perf. 13½x14
335 A76 15c pink, vio bl & lt grn   .25 .20
Issued for Children's Day.

Decorated Camel Saddle — A77

1965, May 29   Typo.   Perf. 13½x14
336 A77 20c blk, red, emer & brn   .25 .20
Handicrafts of Sahara.

ICY Emblem A78

1965, Aug. 29   Engr.   Perf. 13
337 A78 30c blk, mar & bl grn   .45 .30
338 A78 60c blk, brt bl & bl grn   .85 .40
International Cooperation Year, 1965.

ITU Emblem A79

1965, Sept. 19
339 A79 60c purple, emer & buff   .45 .30
340 A79 95c dk brn, mar & buff   .65 .35
Cent. of the ITU.

Musicians A80

Miniatures by Mohammed Racim: 60c, Two female musicians. 5d, Algerian princess and antelope.

1965, Dec. 27   Photo.   Perf. 11½

341	A80	30c multicolored	1.10	.45
342	A80	60c multicolored	1.50	.85
343	A80	5d multicolored	9.00	5.25
	Nos. 341-343 (3)		11.60	6.55

Bulls, Painted in 6000 B.C. — A81

Wall Paintings from Tassili-N-Ajjer, c. 6000
B.C.: No. 345, Shepherd, vert. 2d, Fleeing
ostriches. 3d, Two girls, vert.

1966, Jan. 29   Photo.   Perf. 11½
344 A81 1d brn, bis & red brn   3.00 1.75
345 A81 1d gray, blk, ocher &
          dk brn   3.00 1.75
346 A81 2d brn, ocher & red
          brn   6.50 3.00
347 A81 3d buff, blk, ocher &
          brn red   7.50 4.00
    Nos. 344-347 (4)   20.00 10.50
       See Nos. 365-368.

Pottery — A82

Handicrafts from Great Kabylia: 50c, Weaving, woman at loom, horiz. 70c, Jewelry.

1966, Feb. 26   Engr.   Perf. 13
348 A82 40c Prus bl, brn red & blk   .30 .25
349 A82 50c dk red, ol & ocher   .40 .30
350 A82 70c vio bl, blk & red   .65 .40
    Nos. 348-350 (3)   1.35 .95

Weather Balloon, Compass Rose and
Anemometer — A83

1966, Mar. 23   Engr.   Unwmk.
351 A83 1d claret, brt bl & grn   .85 .40
       World Meteorological Day.

Book, Grain,
Cogwheel and
UNESCO
Emblem — A84

Design: 60c, Grain, cogwheel, book and
UNESCO emblem.

1966, May 2   Typo.   Perf. 13x14
352 A84 30c yellow bis & blk   .25 .20
353 A84 60c dk red, gray & blk   .40 .25
       Literacy as basis for development.

WHO Headquarters, Geneva — A85

1966, May 30   Engr.   Perf. 13
354 A85 30c multicolored   .35 .30
355 A85 60c multicolored   .70 .40
Inauguration of the WHO Headquarters,
Geneva.

Algerian Scout
Emblem — A86

Arab Jamboree
Emblem — A87

1966, July 23   Photo.   Perf. 12x12½
356 A86 30c multicolored   .65 .50
357 A87 1d multicolored   1.75 1.25
No. 356 commemorates the 30th anniv. of
the Algerian Mohammedan Boy Scouts. No.
357, the 7th Arab Boy Scout Jamboree, held
at Good Daim, Libya, Aug. 12.

Map of Palestine
and Victims
A88

Abd-el-Kader
A89

1966, Sept. 26   Typo.   Perf. 10½
358 A88 30c red & black   .80 .40
       Deir Yassin Massacre, Apr. 9, 1948.

1966, Nov. 2   Photo.   Perf. 11½
359 A89 30c multicolored   .40 .20
360 A89 95c multicolored   1.10 .35
Transfer from Damascus to Algiers of the
ashes of Abd-el-Kader (1807?-1883), Emir of
Mascara. See Nos. 382-387.

UNESCO
Emblem — A90

1966, Nov. 19   Typo.   Perf. 10½
361 A90 1d multicolored   1.00 .35
       20th anniv. of UNESCO.

Horseman
A91

Miniatures by Mohammed Racim: 1.50d,
Woman at her toilette. 2d, The pirate Barba-
rossa in front of the Admiralty.

1966, Dec. 17   Photo.   Perf. 11½
Granite Paper
362 A91 1d multicolored   3.25 1.00
363 A91 1.50d multicolored   4.25 1.50
364 A91 2d multicolored   7.00 2.00
    Nos. 362-364 (3)   14.50 5.00

Wall Paintings Type of 1966
Wall Paintings from Tassili-N-Ajjer, c. 6000
B.C.: 1d, Cow. No. 366, Antelope. No. 367,
Archers. 3d, Warrior, vert.

1967, Jan. 28   Photo.   Perf. 11½
365 A81 1d brn, bis & dl vio   2.75 1.50
366 A81 2d brn, ocher & red
          brn   4.00 2.25
367 A81 2d brn, yel & red brn   4.50 2.75
368 A81 3d blk, gray, yel & red
          brn   6.25 3.50
    Nos. 365-368 (4)   17.50 10.00

Bardo
Museum
A92

La Kalaa
Minaret — A93

Design: 1.30d, Ruins at Sedrata.

1967, Feb. 27   Photo.   Perf. 13
369 A92 35c multicolored   .20 .20
370 A93 95c multicolored   .45 .30
371 A92 1.30d multicolored   .75 .40
    Nos. 369-371 (3)   1.40 .90

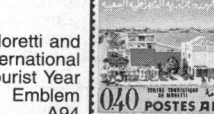

Moretti and
International
Tourist Year
Emblem
A94

Design: 70c, Tuareg riding camel, Tassili,
and Tourist Year Emblem, vert.

1967, Apr. 29   Litho.   Perf. 14
372 A94 40c multi   .50 .25
373 A94 70c multi   1.00 .35
       International Tourist Year, 1967.

Spiny-tailed
Agamid
A95

Designs: 20c, Ostrich, vert. 40c, Slender-
horned gazelle, vert. 70c, Fennec.

1967, June 24   Photo.   Perf. 11½
374 A95 5c bister & blk   .60 .50
375 A95 20c ocher, blk & pink   1.25 .80
376 A95 40c ol bis, blk & red brn   2.00 1.00
377 A95 70c gray, blk & dp org   3.50 2.00
    Nos. 374-377 (4)   7.35 4.30

Dancers — A96

Typographed and Engraved
1967, July 4   Perf. 10½
378 A96 50c gray vio, yel & blk   .45 .35
       National Youth Festival.

Map of the Mediterranean and Sport
Scenes — A97

1967, Sept. 2   Typo.   Perf. 10½
379 A97 30c black, red & blue   .25 .20
Issued to publicize the 5th Mediterranean
Games, Tunis, Sept. 8-17.

Skiers — A98

Olympic
Emblem
and Sports
A99

1967, Oct. 21   Engr.   Perf. 13
380 A98 30c brt blue & ultra   .35 .20
381 A99 95c brn org, pur & brt
          grn   .80 .55
Issued to publicize the 10th Winter Olympic
Games, Grenoble, Feb. 6-18, 1968.

Abd-el-Kader Type of 1966
Lithographed, Photogravure
1967-71   Perf. 13½, 11½
382 A89 5c dull pur ('68)   .20 .20
383 A89 10c green   .85 .35
383A A89 10c sl grn (litho., '69)   .20 .20
383B A89 25c orange ('71)   .20 .20
384 A89 30c black ('68)   .50 .20
385 A89 30c lt violet ('68)   .75 .30
386 A89 50c rose claret   .65 .20
387 A89 70c violet blue   .85 .25
     Nos. 382-387 (8)   4.20 1.90

No. 383, 50c and 70c, issued Nov. 13, 1967,
are on granite paper, photo. The 5c, No.383A,
25c and 30c are litho., perf. 13½; others, perf.
11½.
The three 1967 stamps (No. 383, 50c, 70c)
have numerals thin, narrow and close
together; the Arabic inscription at lower right is
2mm high. The 5 litho. stamps are redrawn,
with numerals thicker and spaced more widely;
Arabic at lower right 3mm high.

Boy Scouts
Holding
Jamboree
Emblem
A100

1967, Dec. 23   Engr.   Perf. 13
388 A100 1d multicolored   1.00 .80
12th Boy Scout World Jamboree, Farragut
State Park, Idaho, Aug. 1-9.

No. 324 Surcharged
1967   Typo.   Perf. 14x13½
389 A71 30c on 25c red   .50 .20

Mandolin — A101

1968, Feb. 17 Photo. Perf. 12½x13
390 A101 30c shown   .35 .25
391 A101 40c Lute   .40 .25
392 A101 1.30d Rebec   1.40 .65
   Nos. 390-392 (3)   2.15 1.15

Nememcha Rug — A102

Algerian Rugs: 70c, Guergour. 95c, Djebel-Amour. 1.30d, Kalaa.

1968, Apr. 13 Photo. Perf. 11½
393 A102 30c multi   .75 .75
394 A102 70c multi   1.50 1.50
395 A102 95c multi   2.00 2.00
396 A102 1.30d multi   2.50 2.50
   Nos. 393-396 (4)   6.75 6.75

Human Rights Flame A103

1968, May 18 Typo. Perf. 10½
397 A103 40c blue, red & yel   .40 .30
International Human Rights Year, 1968.

WHO Emblem A104

1968, May 18
398 A104 70c blk, lt bl & yel   .55 .30
20th anniv. of the WHO.

Welder — A105

Athletes, Olympic Flame and Rings — A106

1968, June 15 Engr. Perf. 13
399 A105 30c gray, brn & ultra .25 .20
Algerian emigration to Europe.

1968, July 4 Photo.
50c, Soccer player. 1d, Mexican pyramid, emblem, Olympic flame, rings & athletes, horiz.
400 A106 30c green, red & yel   .35 .30
401 A106 50c rose car & multi   .60 .30
402 A106 1d dk grn, org, brn & red 1.10 .65
   Nos. 400-402 (3)   2.05 1.25
19th Olympic Games, Mexico City, 10/12-27.

Scouts and Emblem — A107

Barbary Sheep — A108

1968, July 4 Perf. 13
403 A107 30c multicolored   .50 .20
8th Arab Boy Scout Jamboree, Algiers, 1968.

1968, Oct. 19 Photo. Perf. 11½
404 A108 40c shown   .50 .25
405 A108 1d Red deer 1.25 .60

Hunting Scenes, Djemila A109

"Industry" A110

Design: 95c, Neptune's chariot, Timgad, horiz. Both designs are from Roman mosaics.

Perf. 12½x13, 13x12½
1968, Nov. 23 Photo.
406 A109 40c gray & multi   .35 .25
407 A109 95c gray & multi   .85 .50

1968, Dec. 14 Perf. 11½
Designs: No. 409, Miner with drill. 95c, "Energy" (circle and rays).
408 A110 30c dp orange & sil   .25 .20
409 A110 30c brown & multi   .25 .20
410 A110 95c silver, red & blk .75 .35
   Nos. 408-410 (3)   1.25 .75
Issued to publicize industrial development.

Opuntia Ficus Indica — A111

Flowers: 40c, Carnations. 70c, Roses. 95c, Bird-of-paradise flower.

1969, Jan. Photo. Perf. 11½
Flowers in Natural Colors
411 A111 25c pink & blk   .55 .25
412 A111 40c yellow & blk   .65 .35
413 A111 70c gray & blk   1.25 .45
414 A111 95c brt blue & blk 2.00 .80
   Nos. 411-414 (4)   4.45 1.85
See Nos. 496-499.

Irrigation Dam at Djorf Torba-Oued Guir — A112

Design: 1.50d, Truck on Highway No. 51 and camel caravan.

1969, Feb. 22 Photo. Perf. 11½
415 A112 30c multi   .25 .20
416 A112 1.50d multi 1.25 .65
Public works in the Sahara.

Mail Coach A113

1969, Mar. 22 Photo. Perf. 11½
417 A113 1d multicolored 1.10 .60
Issued for Stamp Day, 1969.

Capitol, Timgad — A114

1d, Septimius Temple, Djemila, horiz.

1969, Apr. 5 Photo. Perf. 13x12½
418 A114 30c gray & multi .35 .20
419 A114 1d gray & multi   .85 .35
Second Timgad Festival, Apr. 4-8.

ILO Emblem A115

Arabian Saddle — A116

1969, May 24 Photo. Perf. 11½
420 A115 95c dp car, yel & blk 1.00 .40
50th anniv. of the ILO.

1969, June 28 Photo. Perf. 12x12½
Algerian Handicrafts: 30c, Bookcase. 60c, Decorated copper plate.
Granite Paper
421 A116 30c multicolored   .30 .20
422 A116 60c multicolored   .55 .25
423 A116 1d multicolored   1.00 .45
   Nos. 421-423 (3)   1.85 .90

No. 321 Surcharged

1969 Typo. Perf. 14x13½
424 A71 20c on 12c emerald .25 .20

Pan-African Culture Festival Emblem — A117

African Development Bank Emblem — A118

1969, July 19 Photo. Perf. 12½
425 A117 30c multicolored .35 .20
1st Pan-African Culture Festival, Algiers, 7/21-8/1.

1969, Aug. 23 Typo. Perf. 10½
426 A118 30c dull blue, yel & blk .35 .20
5th anniv. of the African Development Bank.

Astronauts and Landing Module on Moon — A119

Perf. 12½x11½
1969, Aug. 23 Photo.
427 A119 50c gold & multi .60 .35
Man's 1st landing on the moon, July 20, 1969. US astronauts Neil A. Armstrong and Col. Edwin E. Aldrin, Jr., with Lieut. Col. Michael Collins piloting Apollo 11.

Algerian Women, by Dinet — A120

1.50d, The Watchmen, by Etienne Dinet.

1969, Nov. 29 Photo. Perf. 14½
428 A120 1d multi   1.75 .90
429 A120 1.50d multi   2.75 1.40

Mother and Child — A121

1969, Dec. 27 Photo. Perf. 11½
430 A121 30c multicolored .35 .25
Issued to promote mother and child protection.

Agricultural Growth Chart, Tractor and Dam A122

30c, Transportation and development. 50c, Abstract symbols of industrialization.

1970, Jan. 31   Photo.   *Perf. 12½*
Size: 37x23mm
431 A122 25c dk brn, yel & org   .20 .20

Litho.   *Perf. 14*
Size: 49x23mm
432 A122 30c blue & multi   .25 .20

Photo.   *Perf. 12½*
Size: 37x23mm
433 A122 50c rose lilac & blk   .30 .20
    Nos. 431-433 (3)   .75 .60
Four-Year Development Plan.

Old and New Mail Delivery — A123

Spiny Lobster — A124

1970, Feb. 28   Photo.   *Perf. 11½*
Granite Paper
434 A123 30c multicolored   .30 .20
    Issued for Stamp Day.

1970, Mar. 28
Designs: 40c, Mollusks. 75c, Retepora cellulosa. 1d, Red coral.
435 A124 30c ocher & multi   .35 .20
436 A124 40c multicolored   .50 .25
437 A124 75c ultra & multi   .90 .35
438 A124 1d lt blue & multi   1.25 .50
    Nos. 435-438 (4)   3.00 1.30

Oranges, EXPO '70 Emblem A125

Designs (EXPO '70 Emblem and): 60c, Algerian pavilion. 70c, Grapes.

1970, Apr. 25   Photo.   *Perf. 12½x12*
439 A125 30c lt blue, grn & org   .50 .20
440 A125 60c multicolored   .65 .20
441 A125 70c multicolored   1.00 .35
    Nos. 439-441 (3)   2.15 .75
EXPO '70 International Exhibition, Osaka, Japan, Mar. 15-Sept. 13, 1970.

Olives, Oil Bottle — A126

Saber — A127

1970, May 16   Photo.   *Perf. 12½x12*
442 A126 1d yellow & multi   1.00 .65
    Olive Year, 1969-1970.

Common Design Types pictured following the introduction.

UPU Headquarters Issue
Common Design Type
1970, May 30   *Perf. 13*
Size: 36x26mm
443 CD133 75c multicolored   .50 .40

1970, June 27   Photo.   *Perf. 12½*
Designs: 40c, Guns, 18th century, horiz. 1d, Pistol, 18th century, horiz.
444 A127 40c yellow & multi   .65 .25
445 A127 75c red & multi   .80 .40
446 A127 1d multicolored   1.25 .50
    Nos. 444-446 (3)   2.70 1.15

Map of Arab Countries and Arab League Flag A128

Typographed and Engraved
1970, July 25   *Perf. 10½*
447 A128 30c grn, ocher & lt bl   .30 .20
    25th anniversary of the Arab League.

Lenin — A129

1970, Aug. 29   Litho.   *Perf. 11½x12*
448 A129 30c brown & buff   .25 .20
    Lenin (1870-1924), Russian communist leader.

Exhibition Hall and Algiers Fair Emblem — A130

1970, Sept. 11   Engr.   *Perf. 14x13½*
449 A130 60c lt olive green   .40 .30
    New Exhibition Hall for Algiers Intl. Fair.

Education Year Emblem, Blackboard, Atom Symbol — A131

Koran Page — A132

1970, Oct. 24   Photo.   *Perf. 14*
450 A131 30c pink, blk, gold & lt bl   .25 .20
451 A132 3d multicolored   2.50 1.50
    Issued for International Education Year.

Great Mosque, Tlemcen A133

Design: 40c, Ketchaoua Mosque, Algiers, vert. 1d, Mosque, Sidi-Okba, vert.

1970-71   Litho.   *Perf. 14*
456 A133 30c multicolored   .20 .20
457 A133 40c sepia & lemon ('71)   .25 .20
458 A133 1d multicolored   .65 .30
    Nos. 456-458 (3)   1.10 .70

Symbols of the Arts A134

1970, Dec. 26   Photo.   *Perf. 13x12½*
459 A134 1d grn, lt grn & org   .80 .45

Main Post Office, Algiers A135

1971, Jan. 23   *Perf. 11½*
460 A135 30c multicolored   .30 .20
    Stamp Day, 1971.

Hurdling A136

40c, Vaulting, vert. 75c, Basketball, vert.

1971, Mar. 7   Photo.   *Perf. 11½*
461 A136 20c lt blue & slate   .25 .20
462 A136 40c lt ol grn & slate   .35 .35
463 A136 75c salmon pink & slate   .65 .50
    Nos. 461-463 (3)   1.25 1.05
Mediterranean Games, Izmir, Turkey, Oct. 1971.

Symbolic Head — A137

1971, Mar. 27   *Perf. 12½*
464 A137 60c car rose, blk & sil   .30 .20
    Intl. year against racial discrimination.

Emblem and Technicians A138

1971, Apr. 24   Photo.   *Perf. 12½x12*
465 A138 70c cl, org & bluish blk   .40 .30
    Founding of the Institute of Technology.

Woman from Aurès — A139

Regional Costumes: 70c, Man from Oran. 80c, Man from Algiers. 90c, Woman from Amour Mountains.

1971, Oct. 16   *Perf. 11½*
466 A139 50c gold & multi   1.50 .65
467 A139 70c gold & multi   1.75 1.00
468 A139 80c gold & multi   2.25 1.10
469 A139 90c gold & multi   2.50 1.25
    Nos. 466-469 (4)   8.00 4.00
    See Nos. 485-488, 534-537.

UNICEF Emblem, Birds and Plants — A140

1971, Dec. 6   *Perf. 11½*
470 A140 60c multicolored   .55 .30
    25th anniv. of UNICEF.

Lion of St. Mark A141

1.15d, Bridge of Sighs, Venice, vert.

1972, Jan. 24   Litho.   *Perf. 12*
471 A141 80c multi   .60 .35
472 A141 1.15d multi   .90 .50
    UNESCO campaign to save Venice.

Javelin — A142

Book and Book Year Emblem — A143

Designs: 25c, Bicycling, horiz. 60c, Wrestling. 1d, Gymnast on rings.

1972, Mar. 25   Photo.   Perf. 11½
473 A142 25c maroon & multi   .30   .20
474 A142 40c ocher & multi   .35   .25
475 A142 60c ultra & multi   .40   .40
476 A142 1d rose & multi   1.00   .50
    Nos. 473-476 (4)   2.05   1.35

20th Olympic Games, Munich, 8/26-9/11.

1972, Apr. 15
477 A143 1.15d bister, brn & red   .65   .50

International Book Year 1972.

Mailmen A144   Flowers A145

1972, Apr. 22
478 A144 40c gray & multi   .25   .20

Stamp Day 1972.

1972, May 27
479 A145 50c Jasmine   .65   .30
480 A145 60c Violets   .75   .35
481 A145 1.15d Tuberose   1.50   .55
    Nos. 479-481 (3)   2.90   1.20

Olympic Stadium, Chéraga A146

1972, June 10
482 A146 50c gray, choc & grn   .60   .30

New Day, Algerian Flag — A147

1972, July 5
483 A147 1d green & multi   .65   .40

10th anniversary of independence.

Festival Emblem — A148   Mailing a Letter — A149

1972, July 5   Litho.   Perf. 10½
484 A148 40c grn, dk brn & org   .25   .20

1st Arab Youth Festival, Algiers, July 5-11.

Costume Type of 1971

Regional Costumes: 50c, Woman from Hoggar. 60c, Kabyle woman. 70c, Man from Mzab. 90c, Woman from Tlemcen.

1972, Nov. 18   Photo.   Perf. 11½
485 A139 50c gold & multi   .80   .70
486 A139 60c gold & multi   1.10   .90
487 A139 70c gold & multi   1.25   1.10
488 A139 90c gold & multi   1.75   1.25
    Nos. 485-488 (4)   4.90   3.95

1973, Jan. 20   Photo.   Perf. 11
489 A149 40c orange & multi   .40   .20

Stamp Day.

Ho Chi Minh, Map of Viet Nam — A150

1973, Feb. 17   Photo.   Perf. 11½
490 A150 40c multicolored   .75   .50

To honor the people of Viet Nam.

Embroidery from Annaba A151

Designs: 60c, Tree of Life pattern from Algiers. 80c, Constantine embroidery.

1973, Feb. 24
491 A151 40c gray & multi   .75   .40
492 A151 60c blue and multi   1.00   .60
493 A151 80c dk red, gold & blk   1.50   .80
    Nos. 491-493 (3)   3.25   1.80

Stylized Globe and Wheat — A152

1973, Mar. 26   Photo.   Perf. 11½
494 A152 1.15d brt rose lil, org & grn   .75   .40

World Food Program, 10th anniversary.

Soldier and Flag A153

1973, Apr. 23   Photo.   Perf. 14x13½
495 A153 40c multicolored   .25   .20

Honoring the National Service.

Flower Type of 1969

30c, Opuntia ficus indica. 40c, Roses. 1d, Carnations. 1.15d, Bird-of-paradise flower.

1973, May 21   Photo.   Perf. 11½
Flowers in Natural Colors
496 A111 30c pink & blk   .40   .20
497 A111 40c gray & blk   .50   .20
498 A111 1d yellow & multi   .90   .40
499 A111 1.15d multi   1.25   .50
    Nos. 496-499 (4)   3.05   1.30

For overprints and surcharges see #518-519, 531.

OAU Emblem — A154

1973, May 28   Photo.   Perf. 12½x13
500 A154 40c multicolored   .40   .20

Org. for African Unity, 10th anniv.

Desert and Fruitful Land, Farmer and Family A155

1973, June 18   Perf. 11½
501 A155 40c gold & multi   .50   .40

Agricultural revolution.

Map of Africa, Scout Emblem — A156

1973, July 16   Litho.   Perf. 10½
502 A156 80c purple   1.00   .50

24th Boy Scout World Conference (1st in Africa), Nairobi, Kenya, July 16-21.

Algerian PTT Emblem A157

1973, Aug. 6   Perf. 14
503 A157 40c blue & orange   .25   .20

Adoption of new emblem for Post, Telegraph and Telephone System.

Conference Emblem — A158

Perf. 13½x12½
1973, Sept. 5   Photo.
504 A158 40c dp rose & multi   .20   .20
505 A158 80c blue grn & multi   .50   .25

4th Summit Conference of Non-aligned Nations, Algiers, Sept. 5-9.

Port of Skikda A159

1973, Sept. 29   Photo.   Perf. 11½
506 A159 80c ocher, blk & ultra   .50   .25

New port of Skikda.

Young Workers — A160

1973, Oct. 22   Photo.   Perf. 13
507 A160 40c multicolored   .25   .20

Voluntary work service.

Arms of Algiers A161

1973, Dec. 22   Photo.   Perf. 13
508 A161 2d gold & multi   1.60   1.10

Millennium of Algiers.

Infant — A162

1974, Jan. 7   Litho.   Perf. 10½x11
509 A162 80c orange & multi   .60   .35

Fight against tuberculosis.

Man and Woman, Industry and Transportation — A163

1974, Feb. 18   Photo.   Perf. 11½
510 A163 80c multicolored   .50 .20
Four-year plan.

A164

1974, Feb. 25   Photo.   Perf. 11½
511 A164 1.50d multi   1.10 .65
Millennium of the birth of abu-al-Rayhan al-Biruni (973-1048), philosopher and mathematician.

Map and Colors of Algeria, Tunisia, Morocco A165

1974, Mar. 4   Photo.   Perf. 13
512 A165 40c gold & multi   .30 .20
Maghreb Committee for Coordination of Posts and Telecommunications.

Hand Holding Rifle — A166   Mother and Children — A167

1974, Mar. 25   Perf. 11½
513 A166 80c red & black   .30 .20
Solidarity with the struggle of the people of South Africa.

1974, Apr. 8   Perf. 13½
514 A167 85c multicolored   .35 .25
Honoring Algerian mothers.

Village A168

Designs: 80c, Harvest. 90c, Tractor and sun. Designs after children's drawings.

1974, June 15
Size: 45x26mm
515 A168 70c multicolored   .40 .20
Size: 48x33mm
516 A168 80c multicolored   .50 .30
517 A168 90c multicolored   .60 .40
Nos. 515-517 (3)   1.50 .90

Nos. 498-499 Overprinted "FLORALIES/1974"

1974, June 22   Photo.   Perf. 11½
518 A111 1d multi   .65 .35
519 A111 1.15d multi   .70 .40
1974 Flower Show.

Stamp Vending Machine — A169

1974, Oct. 7   Photo.   Perf. 13
520 A169 80c multicolored   .40 .20
Stamp Day 1974.

UPU Emblem and Globe A170

1974, Oct. 14   Perf. 14
521 A170 80c multicolored   .50 .30
Centenary of Universal Postal Union.

"Revolution" — A171

Soldiers and Mountains A172

Raising New Flag — A173

Design: 1d, Algerian struggle for independence (people, sun and fields).

1974, Nov. 4   Photo.   Perf. 14
522 A171 40c multicolored   .30 .20
523 A172 70c multicolored   .40 .20
524 A173 95c multicolored   .50 .25
525 A171 1d multicolored   .60 .30
Nos. 522-525 (4)   1.80 .95
20th anniv. of the start of the revolution.

"Horizon 1980" — A174

Ewer and Basin — A175

1974, Nov. 23   Photo.   Perf. 13
526 A174 95c ocher, dk red & blk   .55 .25
10-year development plan, 1971-1980.

1974, Dec. 21   Perf. 11½
527 A175 50c shown   .25 .20
528 A175 60c Coffee pot   .30 .20
529 A175 95c Sugar bowl   .45 .30
530 A175 1d Bath tub   .50 .35
Nos. 527-530 (4)   1.50 1.05
17th century Algerian copperware.

No. 497 Surcharged with New Value and Heavy Bar

1975, Jan. 4
531 A111 50c on 40c multi   .50 .40

Mediterranean Games' Emblem — A176

1975, Jan. 27   Perf. 13½
532 A176 50c purple, yel & grn   .30 .20
533 A176 1d orange, bl & mar   .60 .25
Mediterranean Games, Algiers, 1975.

Costume Type of 1971

Regional Costumes: No. 534, Woman from Hoggar. No. 535, Woman from Algiers. No. 536, Woman from Oran. No. 537, Man from Tlemcen.

1975, Feb. 22   Photo.   Perf. 11½
534 A139 1d gold & multi   .90 .80
535 A139 1d gold & multi   .90 .80
536 A139 1d gold & multi   .90 .80
537 A139 1d gold & multi   .90 .80
Nos. 534-537 (4)   3.60 3.20

Map of Arab Countries, ALO Emblem A177

1975, Mar. 10   Litho.   Perf. 10½x11
538 A177 50c red brown   .25 .20
Arab Labor Organization, 10th anniversary.

Blood Transfusion A178

1975, Mar. 15   Perf. 14
539 A178 50c car rose & multi   .30 .20
Blood donation and transfusions.

Post Office, Al-Kantara A179   Policeman and Map of Algeria A180

1975, May 10   Photo.   Perf. 11½
Granite Paper
540 A179 50c multicolored   .25 .20
Stamp Day 1975.

1975, June 1   Photo.   Perf. 13
541 A180 50c multicolored   .75 .40
Natl. Security and 10th Natl. Police Day.

Ground Receiving Station A181

Designs: 1d, Map of Algeria with locations of radar sites, transmission mast and satellite. 1.20d, Main and subsidiary stations.

1975, June 28   Photo.   Perf. 13
542 A181 50c blue & multi   .30 .20
543 A181 1d blue & multi   .55 .20
544 A181 1.20d blue & multi   .60 .25
Nos. 542-544 (3)   1.45 .65
National satellite telecommunications network.

Revolutionary with Flag — A182

1975, Aug. 20   Photo.   Perf. 11½
545 A182 1d multicolored   .50 .20
August 20th Revolutionary Movement (Skikda), 20th anniversary.

Swimming and Games' Emblem A183

Perf. 13x13½, 13½x13
1975, Aug. 23   Photo.
546 A183 25c shown   .20 .20
547 A183 50c Judo, map   .25 .20
548 A183 70c Soccer, vert.   .50 .20
549 A183 1d Running, vert.   .55 .25
550 A183 1.20d Handball, vert.   .70 .40
Nos. 546-550 (5)   2.20 1.25
a. Souv. sheet; #546-550, perf 13   4.50 4.50
7th Mediterranean Games, Algiers, 8/23-9/46.
No. 550a sold for 4.50d. Exists imperf., same value.

Setif, Guelma, Kherrata — A184

1975   Litho.   *Perf. 13½x14*
551	A184	5c orange & blk	.20 .20
552	A184	10c emerald & brn	.20 .20
553	A184	25c dl blue & blk	.20 .20
554	A184	30c lemon & blk	.20 .20
555	A184	50c brt grn & blk	.25 .20
556	A184	70c fawn & blk	.35 .20
557	A184	1d vermilion & blk	.50 .25

Nos. 551-557 (7)   1.90 1.45

30th anniv. of victory in World War II.
Issued: 50c, 1d, Nov. 3; others, Dec. 17.
For surcharge see No. 611.

Map of
Maghreb
and APU
Emblem
A185

1975, Nov. 20   Photo.   *Perf. 11½*
558 A185 1d multicolored   .55 .30

10th Cong. of Arab Postal Union, Algiers.

Mosaic, Bey
Constantine's
Palace
A186

Dey-Alger Palace — A187

Famous buildings: 2d, Prayer niche,
Medersa Sidi-Boumediene, Tlemcen.

1975, Dec. 22
559	A186	1d lt blue & multi	.60 .25
560	A186	2d buff & multi	1.10 .60
561	A187	2.50d buff & blk	1.60 .90

Nos. 559-561 (3)   3.30 1.75

Al-Azhar
University
A188

Perf. 11½x12½

1975, Dec. 29   Litho.
562 A188 2d multicolored   1.10 .60

Millennium of Al-Azhar University.

Red-billed
Firefinch — A189

Birds: 1.40d, Black-headed bush shrike,
horiz. 2d, Blue tit. 2.50d, Blackbellied sand-
grouse, horiz.

1976, Jan. 24   Photo.   *Perf. 11½*
563	A189	50c multi	.35 .20
564	A189	1.40d multi	.85 .55
565	A189	2d multi	1.10 .65
566	A189	2.50d multi	1.50 .90

Nos. 563-566 (4)   3.80 2.30

See Nos. 595-598.

Telephones 1876   Map of Africa
and 1976 — A190   with Angola and
               its Flag — A191

1976, Feb. 23   Photo.   *Perf. 13½x13*
567 A190 1.40d rose, dk & lt bl   .65 .40

Centenary of first telephone call by Alexander Graham Bell, Mar. 10, 1876.

1976, Feb. 23   *Perf. 11½*
568 A191 50c brown & multi   .25 .20

Algeria's solidarity with the People's Republic of Angola.

A192

A193

Sahraoui flag and child, map of former
Spanish Sahara.

1976, Mar. 15   Photo.   *Perf. 11½*
569 A192 50c multicolored   .25 .20

Algeria's solidarity with Sahraoui Arab Democratic Republic, former Spanish Sahara.

1976, Mar. 22
570 A193 1.40d Mailman   .60 .30

Stamp Day 1976.

Microscope,
Slide with
TB Bacilli,
Patients
A194

1976, Apr. 26   *Perf. 13x13½*
571 A194 50c multicolored   .40 .20

Fight against tuberculosis.

"Setif, Guelma,
Kherrata" — A195

1976, May 24   Photo.   *Perf. 13½x13*
572 A195 50c blue & yellow   .35 .20
a.	Booklet pane of 6	4.75
b.	Booklet pane of 10	4.00

No. 572 was issued in booklets only.

Ram's Head over   People Holding
Landscape   Torch, Map of
A196   Algeria
               A197

1976, June 17   Photo.   *Perf. 11½*
573 A196 50c multicolored   .40 .20

Livestock breeding.

1976, June 29   Photo.   *Perf. 14x13½*
574 A197 50c multicolored   .25 .20

National Charter.

Palestine Map and
Flag — A198

Map of
Africa — A199

1976, July 12   *Perf. 11½*
          Granite Paper
575 A198 50c multicolored   2.00 1.00

Solidarity with the Palestinians.

1976, Oct. 3   Litho.   *Perf. 10½x11*
576 A199 2d dk blue & multi   1.00 .50

2nd Pan-African Commercial Fair, Algiers.

Blind
Brushmaker
A200

The
Blind,
by
Dinet
A201

1976, Oct. 23   Photo.   *Perf. 14½*
577	A200	1.20d blue & multi	.65 .35
578	A201	1.40d gold & multi	1.50 .75

Rehabilitation of the blind.

"Constitution 1976" — A202

1976, Nov. 19   Photo.   *Perf. 11½*
579 A202 2d multicolored   1.00 .55

New Constitution.

Soldiers Planting
Seedlings
A203

1976, Nov. 25   Litho.   *Perf. 12*
580 A203 1.40d multicolored   .75 .35

Green barrier against the Sahara.

Ornamental Border and
Inscription — A204

1976, Dec. 18   Photo.   *Perf. 11½*
          Granite Paper
581 A204 2d multicolored   1.25 .75

Re-election of Pres. Houari Boumediene.
See No. 627.

Map with Charge   People and
Zones and Dials   Buildings
A205   A206

1977, Jan. 22   *Perf. 13*
582 A205 40c silver & multi   .30 .20

Inauguration of automatic national and international telephone service.

1977, Jan. 29   Photo.   *Perf. 11½*
583 A206 60c on 50c multi   .35 .20

2nd General Population and Buildings Census. No. 583 was not issued without the typographed red brown surcharge, date, and bars.

Sahara
Museum,
Uargla
A207

1977, Feb. 12   Litho.   *Perf. 14*
584 A207 60c multicolored   .35 .20

El-Kantara
Gorge — A208

Perf. 12½x13½
1977, Feb. 19   Photo.
585 A208 20c green & yellow   .20 .20
a.   Bkt. pane, 3 #585, 4 #586 + label 8.00
b.   Bkt. pane, 5 #585, 2 #587 + label 6.50
586 A208 60c brt lilac & yel   .20 .20
587 A208 1d brown & yellow   .40 .20
Nos. 585-587 (3)   .80 .60

National Assembly — A209

1977, Feb. 27   *Perf. 11½*
588 A209 2d multicolored   1.00 .60

People and   Soldier and
Flag — A210   Flag — A211

Perf. 13½, 11½ (3d)
1977, Mar. 12   Photo.
589 A210 2d multicolored   1.25 .40
590 A211 3d multicolored   1.75 .65
Solidarity with the peoples of Zimbabwe
(Rhodesia), 2d; Namibia, 3d.

Winter, Roman
Mosaic
A212

The Seasons from Roman Villa, 2nd century
A.D.: 1.40d, Fall. 2d, Summer. 3d, Spring.

1977, Apr. 21   Photo.   *Perf. 11½*
Granite Paper
591 A212 1.20d multi   .95 .50
592 A212 1.40d multi   1.25 .55
593 A212 2d multi   1.65 .95
594 A212 3d multi   2.50 1.60
a.   Souv. sheet, #591-594   10.00 10.00
Nos. 591-594 (4)   6.35 3.60
No. 594a sold for 8d and exists imperf.

Bird Type of 1976
Birds: 60c, Tristram's warbler. 1.40d,
Moussier's redstart, horiz. 2d, Temminck's
horned lark, horiz. 3d, Eurasian hoopoe.

1977, May 21   Photo.   *Perf. 11½*
595 A189 60c multi   .75 .25
596 A189 1.40d multi   1.25 .40
597 A189 2d multi   1.75 .65
598 A189 3d multi   2.50 1.10
Nos. 595-598 (4)   6.25 2.40

Horseman — A213

Design: 5d, Attacking horsemen, horiz.

1977, June 25   Photo.   *Perf. 11½*
599 A213 2d multicolored   1.75 .75
600 A213 5d multicolored   3.50 2.00

Flag Colors, Games
Emblem — A214

Wall
Painting,
Games
Emblem
A215

1977, Sept. 24   Photo.   *Perf. 11½*
601 A214 60c multi   .35 .25
602 A215 1.40d multi   .80 .45
3rd African Games, Algiers 1978.

Village
and
Tractor
A216

1977, Nov. 12   *Perf. 14x13*
603 A216 1.40d multi   .90 .65
Socialist agricultural village.

Almohades Dirham, 12th
Century — A217

Ancient Coins: 1.40d, Almohades coin, 12th
century. 2d, Almoravides dinar, 11th century.

1977, Dec. 17   Photo.   *Perf. 11½*
604 A217 60c ultra, sil & blk   .50 .35
605 A217 1.40d grn, gold & brn   1.10 .50
606 A217 2d red brn, gold &
   brn   1.50 .90
Nos. 604-606 (3)   3.10 1.75

Flowering
Trees — A218

1978, Feb. 11   Photo.   *Perf. 11½*
607 A218 60c Cherry   .35 .25
608 A218 1.20d Peach   .85 .50
609 A218 1.30d Almond   .85 .50
610 A218 1.40d Apple   .90 .55
Nos. 607-610 (4)   2.95 1.80

No. 555 Surcharged with New Value
and Bar
1978, Feb. 11   Litho.   *Perf. 13½x14*
611 A184 60c on 50c   .50 .20

Children
with Traffic
Signs and
Car — A219

1978, Apr. 29   Photo.   *Perf. 11½*
612 A219 60c multicolored   .30 .20
Road safety and protection of children.

Sports and
Games
Emblems
A220

Designs (Games Emblem and): 60c, Rower,
vert. 1.20d, Flag colors. 1.30d, Fireworks, vert.
1.40d, Map of Africa and dancers, vert.

1978, July 13   Photo.   *Perf. 11½*
613 A220 40c mul   .20 .20
614 A220 60c multi   .30 .20
615 A220 1.20d multi   .60 .30
616 A220 1.30d multi   .60 .35
617 A220 1.40d multi   .65 .35
Nos. 613-617 (5)   2.35 1.40
3rd African Games, Algiers, July 13-28.

TB Patient Returning to
Family — A221

1978, Oct. 5   Photo.   *Perf. 13½x14*
618 A221 60c multicolored   .35 .20
Anti-tuberculosis campaign.

Holy
Kaaba — A222

1978, Oct. 28   Photo.   *Perf. 11½*
619 A222 60c multicolored   .30 .20
Pilgrimage to Mecca.

National
Servicemen
Building
Road — A223

1978, Nov. 4
620 A223 60c multicolored   .30 .20
African Unity Road from El Goleah to In
Salah, inauguration.

Fibula   Pres. Boumediene
A224   A225

Jewelry: 1.35d, Pendant. 1.40d, Ankle ring.

1978, Dec. 21   Photo.   *Perf. 12x11½*
621 A224 1.20d multi   .65 .30
622 A224 1.35d multi   .70 .30
623 A224 1.40d multi   1.10 1.10
Nos. 621-623 (3)   2.45 1.70

1979, Jan. 7   Photo.   *Perf. 12x11½*
624 A225 60c green, red & brown   .30 .20
Houari Boumediene, pres. of Algeria 1965-
1978.

Torch and
Books
A226

1979, Jan. 27   Photo.   *Perf. 11½*
625 A226 60c multicolored   .30 .20
Natl. Front of Liberation Party Cong.

Pres. Boumediene — A227

1979, Feb. 4   Photo.   *Perf. 11½*
626 A227 1.40d multi   .65 .30
40 days after death of Pres. Houari
Boumediène.

Ornamental Type of 1976
Proclamation of new President.

1979, Feb. 10
627 A204 2d multicolored   1.00 .35
Election of Pres. Chadli Bendjedid.

A229

A230

1979, Apr. 18   Photo.   Perf. 11½
628 A229 60c multicolored   .30 .20
Sheik Abdul-Hamid Ben Badis (1889-1940).

1979, May 19   Photo.   Perf. 13½x14
Designs: 1.20d, Telephone dial, map of Africa. 1.40d, Symbolic Morse key and waves.
629 A230 1.20d multi   .55 .20
630 A230 1.40d multi   .60 .25
Telecom '79 Exhib., Geneva, Sept. 20-26.

Harvest, IYC Emblem A231

1.40d, Dancers and IYC emblem, vert.

Perf. 11½x11, 11x11½
1979, June 21
631 A231 60c multi   .40 .20
632 A231 1.40d multi   .60 .45
International Year of the Child.

A232

1979, Oct. 20   Photo.   Perf. 11½
633 A232 1.40d Nuthatch   .90 .40

1979, Nov. 1   Photo.   Perf. 12½
Designs: 1.40d, Flag, soldiers and workers. 3d, Revolutionaries and emblem.
634 A233 1.40d multi   .90 .25
Size: 37x48mm
Perf. 11½
635 A233 3d multi   2.25 .65
November 1 revolution, 25th anniversary.

A233

Hegira, 1500 Anniv. A234

1979, Dec. 2   Photo.   Perf. 11½
636 A234 3d multicolored   1.25 .65

Camels, Lion, Men and Slave — A235

Dionysian Procession (Setif Mosaic): 1.35d, Elephants, tigers and women. Men in tiger-drawn cart. No. 639a has continuous design.

1980, Feb. 16   Photo.   Perf. 11½
Granite Paper
637 A235 1.20d multi   .55 .20
638 A235 1.35d multi   .60 .35
639 A235 1.40d multi   .65 .55
a.   Strip of 3, #637-639   1.80 1.25

Science Day — A236

1980, Apr. 19   Photo.   Perf. 12
640 A236 60c multicolored   .30 .20

Dam and Workers A237

1980, June 17   Photo.   Perf. 11½
641 A237 60c multicolored   .30 .20
Extraordinary Congress of the National Liberation Front Party.

Olympic Sports, Moscow '80 Emblem A238

1980, June 28
642 A238 50c Flame, rings, vert.   .25 .20
643 A238 1.40d shown   .65 .35
22nd Summer Olympic Games, Moscow, July 19-Aug. 3.

20th Anniversary of OPEC — A239

Perf. 11x10½, 10½x11
1980, Sept. 15   Engr.
644 A239   60c Men holding OPEC
                emblem, vert.   .30 .20
645 A239 1.40d shown   .65 .35

Aures Valley A240

1980, Sept. 25   Litho.   Perf. 13½x14
646 A240 50c shown   .25 .20
647 A240   1d El Oued Oasis   .40 .20
648 A240 1.40d Tassili Rocks   .60 .25
649 A240   2d View of Algiers   .90 .40
Nos. 646-649 (4)   2.15 1.05
World Tourism Conf., Manila, Sept. 27.

Avicenna (980-1037), Philosopher and Physician A241

1980, Oct. 25   Photo.   Perf. 12
650 A241 2d multicolored   1.50 .75

Ruins of El Asnam A242

1980, Nov. 13   Photo.   Perf. 12
651 A242 3d multicolored   1.25 .45
Earthquake relief.

Crown A243

1980, Dec. 20   Photo.   Perf. 12
Granite Paper
652 A243 60c Necklace, vert.   .30 .20
653 A243 1.40d Earrings, bracelet,
                vert.   .60 .30
654 A243   2d shown   .80 .45
Nos. 652-654 (3)   1.70 .95
See Nos. 705-707.

1980-1984 Five-Year Plan — A244

1981, Jan. 29   Litho.   Perf. 14
655 A244 60c multicolored   .25 .20

Basket Weaving — A245

1981, Feb. 19   Photo.   Perf. 12½
Granite Paper
656 A245 40c shown   .20 .20
657 A245 60c Rug weaving   .30 .20
658 A245 1d Coppersmith   .40 .20
659 A245 1.40d Jeweler   .60 .30
Nos. 656-659 (4)   1.50 .90

Cedar Tree A246

Arbor Day: 1.40d, Cypress tree, vert.

1981, Mar. 19   Photo.   Perf. 12
Granite Paper
660 A246 60c multi   .30 .20
661 A246 1.40d multi   .60 .30

Mohamed Bachir el Ibrahimi (1869-1965) A247

Children Going to School A248

1981, Apr. 16
Granite Paper
662 A247 60c multicolored   .25 .20
663 A248 60c multicolored   .25 .20
Science Day.

12th International Hydatidological Congress, Algiers — A249

1981, Apr. 23   Perf. 14x13½
664 A249 2d multicolored   .80 .30

13th World Telecommunications Day — A250

1981, May 14   Photo.   *Perf. 14x13½*
665 A250 1.40d multi   .60 .20

Disabled People and Hand Offering Flower — A251

Perf. 12½x13, 13x12½
1981, June 20   Litho.
666 A251 1.20d Symbolic globe, vert.   .55 .20
667 A251 1.40d shown   .60 .20

Intl. Year of the Disabled.

Papilio Machaon A252

1981, Aug. 20   Photo.   *Perf. 11½*
Granite Paper
668 A252 60c shown   .25 .20
669 A252 1.20d Rhodocera rhamni   .55 .20
670 A252 1.40d Charaxes jasius   .60 .25
671 A252 2d Papilio podalirius   .80 .40
      Nos. 668-671 (4)   2.20 1.05

Monk Seal — A253

1981, Sept. 17   *Perf. 14x13½*
672 A253 60c shown   .25 .20
673 A253 1.40d Macaque   .60 .35

World Food Day — A254

Cave Drawings of Tassili — A255

1981, Oct. 16   Photo.   *Perf. 14x14½*
674 A254 2d multicolored   .65 .35

1981, Nov. 21   *Perf. 11½*
Various cave drawings. 1.60d, 2d horiz.
675 A255 60c multi   .30 .20
676 A255 1d multi   .50 .20
677 A255 1.60d multi   .75 .35
678 A255 2d multi   .90 .40
      Nos. 675-678 (4)   2.45 1.15

Galley, 17-18th Cent. A256

1981, Dec. 17   Photo.   *Perf. 11½*
679 A256 60c shown   .40 .20
680 A256 1.60d Ship, diff.   .90 .35

1982 World Cup Soccer A257

Designs: Various soccer players.

Perf. 13x12½x 12½x13
1982, Feb. 25   Litho.
681 A257 80c multi, vert.   .35 .20
682 A257 2.80d multi   1.10 .50

TB Bacillus Centenary A258

1982, Mar. 20   Photo.   *Perf. 14½x14*
683 A258 80c multi   .35 .20

Painted Stand A259

1982, Apr. 24   Photo.   *Perf. 11½*
Granite Paper
684 A259 80c Mirror, vert.   .30 .20
685 A259 2d shown   .75 .40
      Size: 48x33mm
686 A259 2.40d Chest   .90 .55
      Nos. 684-686 (3)   1.95 1.15

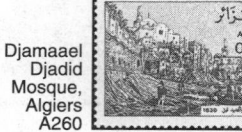

Djamaael Djadid Mosque, Algiers A260

1982, May 15   Litho.   *Perf. 14*
687 A260 80c shown   .30 .20
688 A260 2.40d Sidi Boumediene Mosque, Tlemcen   .80 .50
689 A260 3d Garden of Dey, Algiers   1.00 .55
      Nos. 687-689 (3)   2.10 1.25

See Nos. 731-734, 745-747, 774, 778-783.

A261   A262

Designs: Medicinal plants.

1982, May 27   Photo.   *Perf. 11½*
Granite Paper
690 A261 50c Callitris articulata   .25 .20
691 A261 80c Artemisia herba-alba   .30 .20
692 A261 1d Ricinus communis   .60 .20
693 A261 2.40d Thymus fontanesii   1.10 .45
      Nos. 690-693 (4)   2.25 1.05

1982, July 5
Granite Paper
694 A262 50c Riflemen   .20 .20
695 A262 80c Soldiers, horiz.   .35 .20
696 A262 2d Symbols, citizens, horiz.   .80 .45
      Nos. 694-696 (3)   1.35 .85

Souvenir Sheet
697 A262 5d Emblem   2.25 2.25

Independence, 20th anniv.
No. 697 contains one 32x39mm stamp.

Soummam Congress A263

1982, Aug. 20   Litho.
698 A263 80c Congress building   .35 .20

Scouting Year — A264

1982, Oct. 21   Photo.
Granite Paper
699 A264 2.80d multi   1.00 .45

Palestinian Child — A265

1982, Nov. 25   Litho.   *Perf. 10½*
700 A265 1.60d multi   3.00 .75

Perf. 15x14, 14x15
1982, Dec. 23   Photo.
Protected birds. 50c, 2d horiz.
701 A266 50c Geronticus eremita   .40 .20
702 A266 80c shown   .65 .20
703 A266 2d Aguila rapax   1.25 .40

Chlamydotis Undulata — A266

704 A266 2.40d Gypaetus barbatus   1.75 .45
      Nos. 701-704 (4)   4.05 1.25

Jewelry Type of 1980

1983, Feb. 10   *Perf. 11½*
Granite Paper
705 A243 50c Picture frame   .20 .20
706 A243 1d Flaska   .35 .25
707 A243 2d Brooch, horiz.   .65 .45
      Nos. 705-707 (3)   1.20 .90

A267

A268

1983, Mar. 17   Photo.
Granite Paper
708 A267 80c Abies numidica, vert.   .25 .20
709 A267 2.80d Acacia raddiana   .75 .60

Intl. Arbor Day.

Perf. 12x12½, 12½x12
1983, Apr. 21   Photo.
Various minerals. 1.20d, 2.40d horiz.

Granite Paper
710 A268 70c multi   .30 .20
711 A268 80c multi   .35 .20
712 A268 1.20d multi   .50 .30
713 A268 2.40d multi   1.00 .60
      Nos. 710-713 (4)   2.15 1.30

30th Anniv. of Intl. Customs Cooperation Council A269

1983, May 14   Photo.   *Perf. 11½*
Granite Paper
714 A269 80c multi   .35 .20

Emir Abdelkader Death Centenary — A270

1983, May 22   Photo.   *Perf. 12*
Granite Paper
715 A270 4d multi   1.60 .75

A271   A272

Local mushrooms.

1983, July 21   *Perf. 14x15*
716 A271 50c Amanita muscaria   .25 .20
717 A271 80c Amanita phalloides   .50 .25

718	A271	1.40d Pleurotus eryngii	1.00	.50
719	A271	2.80d Tefezia leonis	2.25	1.00
		Nos. 716-719 (4)	4.00	1.95

1983, Sept. 1   Photo.   Perf. 11½

| 720 | A272 | 80c multi | .35 | .20 |

ibn-Khaldun, historian, philosopher.

World Communications Year — A273

Perf. 11½x12½

1983, Sept. 22   Litho.

| 721 | A273 | 80c Post Office, Algiers | .35 | .20 |
| 722 | A273 | 2.40d Telephone, circuit box | 1.00 | .40 |

Goat and Tassili Mountains A274

1983, Oct. 20   Litho.   Perf. 12½x13

723	A274	50c shown	.20	.20
724	A274	80c Tuaregs in native costume	.30	.20
725	A274	2.40d Animals, rock painting	1.00	.40
726	A274	2.80d Rock formation	1.00	.60
		Nos. 723-726 (4)	2.50	1.40

Sloughi Dog — A275

Perf. 14x14½, 14½x14

1983, Nov. 24   Photo.

| 727 | A275 | 80c shown | .60 | .40 |
| 728 | A275 | 2.40d Sloughi, horiz. | 1.50 | .75 |

Natl. Liberation Party, 5th Congress — A276

1983, Dec. 19   Photo.   Perf. 11½

| 729 | A276 | 80c Symbols of development | .35 | .25 |

Souvenir Sheet

| 730 | A276 | 5d Emblem | 3.00 | 2.50 |

No. 730 contains one 32x38mm stamp.

View Type of 1982

1984, Jan. 26   Litho.   Perf. 14

731	A260	10c View of Oran, 1830	.20	.20
732	A260	1d Sidi Abderahman and Taalibi Mosques	.40	.20
733	A260	2d Bejaia, 1830	.80	.35
734	A260	4d Constantine, 1830	2.00	.60
		Nos. 731-734 (4)	3.40	1.35

See Nos. 745-747, 781, 783.

Pottery A278

Perf. 11½x12, 12x11½

1984, Feb. 23   Photo.

Granite Paper

735	A278	80c Jug, vert.	.35	.20
736	A278	1d Platter	.50	.25
737	A278	2d Oil lamp, vert.	1.00	.45
738	A278	2.40d Pitcher	1.50	.60
		Nos. 735-738 (4)	3.35	1.50

Fountains of Old Algiers — A279   1984 Summer Olympics — A280

Various fountains.

1984, Mar. 22   Photo.   Perf. 11½

Granite Paper

739	A279	50c multi	.20	.20
740	A279	80c multi	.35	.20
741	A279	2.40d multi	1.00	.60
		Nos. 739-741 (3)	1.55	1.00

1984, May 19   Photo.   Perf. 11½

Granite Paper

| 742 | A280 | 1d multi | .45 | .30 |

Brown Stallion A281

1984, June 14   Photo.   Perf. 11½

Granite Paper

| 743 | A281 | 80c shown | .35 | .20 |
| 744 | A281 | 2.40d White mare | 1.00 | .60 |

View Type of 1982

1984   Litho.   Perf. 14

745	A260	5c Mustapha Pacha	.20	.20
746	A260	20c Bab Azzoun	.20	.20
746A	A260	30c Algiers	.20	.20
746B	A260	40c Kolea	.20	.20
746C	A260	80c Algiers	.20	.20
747	A260	70c Mostaganem	.35	.20
		Nos. 745-747 (6)	1.35	1.20

Issued: #745, 746, 747, 7/19; #746A-746C, 10/20.

Lute A282

Native musical instruments.

1984, Sept. 22   Litho.   Perf. 15x14

748	A282	80c shown	.20	.20
749	A282	1d Drum	.25	.20
750	A282	2.40d Fiddle	.60	.35
751	A282	2.80d Bagpipe	.70	.40
		Nos. 748-751 (4)	1.75	1.15

30th Anniv. of Algerian Revolution — A284

1984, Nov. 3   Photo.   Perf. 11½x12

| 757 | A284 | 80c Partisans | .20 | .20 |

Souvenir Sheet

| 758 | A284 | 5d Algerian flags, vert. | 2.00 | 1.00 |

M'Zab Valley A285

1984, Dec. 15   Perf. 15x14, 14x15

| 759 | A285 | 80c Map of valley | .20 | .20 |
| 760 | A285 | 2.40d Town of M'Zab, vert. | .50 | .30 |

18th and 19th Century Metalware — A286

1985, Jan. 26   Photo.   Perf. 11½

761	A286	80c Coffee pot	.20	.20
762	A286	2d Bowl, horiz.	.50	.25
763	A286	2.40d Covered bowl	.65	.30
		Nos. 761-763 (3)	1.35	.75

Fish A287

1985, Feb. 23   Photo.   Perf. 15x14

764	A287	50c Thunnus thynnus	.20	.20
765	A287	80c Sparus aurata	.20	.20
766	A287	2.40d Epinephelus guaza	.60	.30
767	A287	2.80d Mustelus mustelus	.65	.35
		Nos. 764-767 (4)	1.65	1.05

National Games A288

1985, Mar. 28   Perf. 11½x12

Granite Paper

| 768 | A288 | 80c Doves, emblem | .20 | .20 |

Environmental Conservation — A289

1985, Apr. 25   Perf. 13½

| 769 | A289 | 80c Stylized trees | .20 | .20 |
| 770 | A289 | 1.40d Stylized waves | .35 | .20 |

View Type of 1982 and

The Casbah A290   View of Constantine A290a

Street Scene in Algiers — A290b

Designs: 2.50d, Djamaael Djadid Mosque, Algiers. 2.90d, like #746. 5d, like #746A. 1.50d, like #746B. 4.20d, like #764.

Perf. 13½x12½, 13 (#774, 4.20d),
Perf. 13½x14 (#775)
Perf. 14½x14 (2d)

Photo., Litho. (2d, 6,20d, 7.50d, #775)

1985-94

771	A290	20c dk blue & buff	.20	.20
772	A290	80c sage grn & buff	.20	.20
773	A290a	1d dk olive grn	.50	.25
a.		Bklt. pane of 5 + label	2.50	
774	A290	1.50d dull red	.55	.30
775	A290b	1.50d red brn & brn	.25	.20
a.		Booklet pane of 6	1.50	
776	A290b	2d dk bl & lt bl	.20	.20
a.		Booklet pane of 5 + label	.95	
777	A290	2.40d chestnut & buff	.60	.30
a.		Bklt. pane of 5 (20c, 3 80c, 2.40d) + label	1.40	
778	A260	2.50d bluish green	1.00	.50
779	A260	2.90d slate	1.15	.60
780	A260	4.20d gray green	1.60	.85
781	A260	5d dp bis & blk	2.00	1.00

Perf. 14

782	A260	6.20d like #731	1.00	.50
783	A260	7.50d like #745	1.25	.65
		Nos. 771-783 (13)	10.50	5.75

Nos. 771-772, 777 issued only in booklet panes.

Issued: 20c, 80c, 2.40d, 6/1/85; 1d, 1/26/89; 2.50d, 2.90d, 5d, 2/23/89; #774, 4.20d, 3/21/91; #775, 5/20/92; 6.20d, 7.50d, 4/22/92; 2d, 10/21/93; #776a, 10/21/94.

See No. 1010.

UN, 40th Anniv. — A291

Natl. Youth Festival — A292

1985, June 26   Photo.   Perf. 14

| 784 | A291 | 1d Dove, emblem, 40 | .25 | .20 |

1985, July 5   Litho.   Perf. 13½

| 785 | A292 | 80c multicolored | .25 | .20 |

Intl. Youth Year
A293

1985, July 5
786 A293 80c Silhouette, globe,
          emblem, vert.   .25 .20
787 A293 1.40d Doves, globe .45 .20

World Map, OPEC — A294

1985, Sept. 14 Photo. *Perf. 12½x13*
788 A294 80c multicolored   .25 .20
Organization of Petroleum Exporting Countries, 25th anniv.

Family Planning — A295

1985, Oct. 3   Litho.   *Perf. 14*
789 A295 80c Mother and sons   .20 .20
790 A295 1.40d Weighing infant .35 .20
791 A295 1.70d Breast-feeding   .45 .20
        Nos. 789-791 (3)   1.00 .60

El-Meniaa Township — A296

1985, Oct. 24   Engr.   *Perf. 13*
792 A296 80c Chetaibi Bay,
          horiz.   .20 .20
793 A296 2d shown   .50 .25
794 A296 2.40d Bou Noura Town,
          horiz.   .65 .30
        Nos. 792-794 (3)   1.35 .75

The Palm Grove, by N. Dinet — A297

1985, Nov. 21 Photo. *Perf. 11½x12*
            Granite Paper
795 A297 2d multi   .50 .25
796 A297 3d multi, diff.   .85 .40

Tapestries A298

Various designs.

1985, Dec. 19
            Granite Paper
797 A298 80c multi   .20 .20
798 A298 1.40d multi   .40 .20
799 A298 2.40d multi   .60 .30
800 A298 2.80d multi   .75 .40
        Nos. 797-800 (4)   1.95 1.10

Wildcats A299

1986, Jan. 23   *Perf. 12x11½, 11½x12*
            Granite Paper
801 A299 80c Felis margarita .50 .20
802 A299 1d Felis caracal   .70 .20
803 A299 2d Felis sylvestris 1.40 .80
804 A299 2.40d Felis serval, vert. 1.90 .95
        Nos. 801-804 (4)   4.50 2.15

UN Child Survival Campaign — A300 | Algerian General Worker's Union, 30th Anniv. — A301

1986, Feb. 13   Litho.   *Perf. 13½*
805 A300 80c Oral vaccine   .25 .20
806 A300 1.40d Mother, child, sun .60 .25
807 A300 1.70d Three children 1.00 .35
        Nos. 805-807 (3)   1.85 .80

1986, Feb. 24   *Perf. 12½*
            Granite Paper
808 A301 2d multi   .50 .25

National Charter — A302 | Natl. Day of the Disabled — A303

1986, Mar. 6   Photo.   *Perf. 11½*
            Granite Paper
809 A302 4d multi   1.00 .45

1986, Mar. 15   *Perf. 12½x13*
810 A303 80c multi   .20 .20

A304 | A305

1986, Apr. 17 Litho. *Perf. 14x15*
811 A304 80c multi   .20 .20
Anti-Tuberculosis campaign.

1986, Apr. 24   *Perf. 14*
812 A305 2d Soccer ball, sombrero .50 .25
813 A305 2.40d Soccer players .65 .30
1986 World Cup Soccer Championships, Mexico.

Inner Courtyards — A306

Blood Donation Campaign A307

1986, May 15   Photo.   *Perf. 11½*
            Granite Paper
814 A306 80c multi   .20 .20
815 A306 2.40d multi, diff. .65 .30
816 A306 3d multi, diff.   .80 .40
        Nos. 814-816 (3)   1.65 .90

1986, June 26   Litho.   *Perf. 13½*
817 A307 80c multi   .25 .20

Southern District Radio Communication Inauguration A308

1986, July   *Perf. 13*
818 A308 60c multi   .20 .20

Mosque Gateways A309

1986, Sept. 27 Photo. *Perf. 12x11½*
            Granite Paper
819 A309 2d Door   .50 .25
820 A309 2.40d Ornamental arch .65 .30

Intl. Peace Year A310

1986, Oct. 16   *Perf. 13½x14½*   **Photo.**
821 A310 2.40d multi   .65 .30

Folk Dancing A311

1986, Nov. 22 Litho. *Perf. 14x13½*
822 A311 80c Woman, scarf   .25 .20
823 A311 2.40d Woman, diff. .65 .30
824 A311 2.80d Man, sword   .70 .40
        Nos. 822-824 (3)   1.60 .90

Flowers — A312

1986, Dec. 18   Photo.   *Perf. 14*
825 A312 80c Narcissus tazetta .25 .20
826 A312 1.40d Iris unguicularis .40 .20
827 A312 2.40d Capparis spinosa .65 .30
828 A312 2.80d Gladiolus
          segetum   .70 .40
        Nos. 825-828 (4)   2.00 1.10
        See Nos. 936-938.

Abstract Paintings by Mohammed Issia Khem — A313

1987, Jan. 29   *Perf. 11½x12, 12x11½*   **Litho.**
829 A313 2d Man and woman,
          vert.   .65 .35
830 A313 5d Man and books   1.60 .80

Jewelry from Aures A314

1987, Feb. 27   Photo.   *Perf. 12*
            Granite Paper
831 A314 1d Earrings   .35 .20
832 A314 1.80d Bracelets   .60 .30
833 A314 2.90d Nose rings   1.00 .50
834 A314 3.30d Necklace   1.10 .55
        Nos. 831-834 (4)   3.05 1.55
        Nos. 831-833 vert.

Petroglyphs, Atlas — A315

1987, Mar. 26   Litho.   *Perf. 12x11½*
Granite Paper
835 A315   1d Man and woman   .35   .20
836 A315   2.90d Goat   1.00   .50
837 A315   3.30d Horse, bull   1.10   .60
   Nos. 835-837 (3)   2.45   1.30

Syringe as an
Umbrella — A316

1987, Apr. 7   *Perf. 11½*
Granite Paper
838 A316   1d multi   .35   .20
   Child Immunization Campaign, World
Health Day.

Volunteers
A317

Third General
Census — A318

1987, Apr. 23   *Perf. 10½*
839 A317   1d multi   .35   .20

1987, May 21   *Perf. 13½*
840 A318   1d multi   .35   .20

Algerian Postage, 25th Anniv. — A319

War Orphans' Fund label (1fr + 9fr) of 1962.

1987, July 5   Photo.   *Perf. 11½x12*
Granite Paper
841 A319   1.80d multi   .60   .30

A320

A321

1987, July 5
Granite Paper
842 A320   1d multi   .35   .20
Souvenir Sheet
843 A321   5d multi   1.75   1.60
   Natl. independence, 25th anniv.

Amateur
Theater
Festival,
Mostaganem
A322

1987, July 20   *Perf. 12x11½*
Granite Paper
844 A322   1d Actors on stage   .35   .20
845 A322   1.80d Theater   .60   .30
   a.   Pair, #844-845   1.00   .50

   No. 845a has continuous design.

Mediterranean Games,
Latakia — A323

1987, Aug. 6   *Perf. 13x12½, 12½x13*
846 A323   1d Discus   .35   .20
847 A323   2.90d Tennis, vert.   1.00   .50
848 A323   3.30d Team handball   1.50   .55
   Nos. 846-848 (3)   2.85   1.25

Birds — A324

1987   Litho.   *Perf. 13½*
849 A324   1d Phoenicopterus
   ruber roseus   .50   .25
850 A324   1.80d Porphyrio
   porphyrio   .90   .50
851 A324   2.50d Elanus caeruleus   1.25   .65
852 A324   2.90d Milvus milvus   1.50   .75
   Nos. 849-852 (4)   4.15   2.15

Agriculture
A325

Perf. 10½x11, 11x10½
1987, Nov. 26   Litho.
853 A325   1d Planting   .35   .20
854 A325   1d Reservoir   .35   .20
855 A325   1d Harvesting crop,
   vert.   .35   .20
856 A325   1d Produce, vert.   .35   .20
   Nos. 853-856 (4)   1.40   .80

African Telecommunications
Day — A326

1987, Dec. 7   *Perf. 10½*
857 A326   1d multi   .35   .20

Transportation — A327

1987, Dec. 18   Litho.   *Perf. 10½x11*
858 A327   2.90d shown   1.00   .50
859 A327   3.30d Diesel train   1.10   .55

Algerian
Universities
A328

Various campuses.

1987, Dec. 26   *Perf. 10½x11, 11x10½*
860 A328   1d shown   .35   .20
861 A328   2.50d multi, diff.   1.00   .40
862 A328   2.90d multi, diff.   1.50   .50
863 A328   3.30d multi, diff., vert.   1.75   .55
   Nos. 860-863 (4)   4.60   1.65

Intl. Rural Development Fund, 10th
Anniv. — A329

1988, Jan. 27   *Perf. 10½x11*
864 A329   1d multi   .50   .25

Autonomy of
State-owned
Utilities — A330

1988, Feb. 27   Litho.   *Perf. 11x10½*
865 A330   1d multi   .50   .25

Intl. Women's
Day — A331

Arab Scouts, 75th
Anniv. — A332

1988, Mar. 10   Litho.   *Perf. 11x10½*
866 A331   1d multi   .50   .25

1988, Apr. 7   Litho.   *Perf. 10½*
867 A332   2d multi   .95   .50

1988 Summer
Olympics,
Seoul — A333

Hot
Springs — A334

1988, July 23   Litho.   *Perf. 10½*
868 A333   2.90d multi   1.40   .70

1988, July 16
869 A334   1d shown   .50   .25
870 A334   2.90d Caverns, horiz.   1.40   .70
871 A334   3.30d Gazebo, foun-
   tain, horiz.   1.60   .80
   Nos. 869-871 (3)   3.50   1.75

World
Wildlife
Fund
A335

Barbary apes, *Macaca sylvanus.*

1988, Sept. 17   Litho.   *Perf. 10½*
872 A335   50c Adult   .25   .20
873 A335   90c Family   .45   .25
874 A335   1d Close-up, vert.   .50   .25
875 A335   1.80d Seated on
   branch, vert.   .90   .45
   Nos. 872-875 (4)   2.10   1.15

Intl. Literacy
Day — A336

WHO, 40th
Anniv. — A337

1988, Sept. 10   Photo.   *Perf. 10½*
876 A336 2.90d multi   1.40 .70

1988, Oct. 15
877 A337 2.90d multi   1.40 .70

Fight
Apartheid
A338

1988, Nov. 19   Litho.   *Perf. 10½x11*
878 A338 2.50d multi   1.25 .60

Natl. Front
Congress — A339

1988, Nov. 29   *Perf. 11x10½*
879 A339 1d multi   .50 .25

Agriculture
A340

1988, Dec. 24   *Perf. 10½*
880 A340 1d Irrigation   .50 .25
881 A340 1d Orchard, fields, live-
              stock   .50 .25

Natl.   Airports — A343
Goals — A342

1989, Mar. 9   Litho.   *Perf. 11½*
Granite Paper
886 A342 1d shown   .50 .25
887 A342 1d Ancient fort   .50 .25
888 A342 1d Telecommunications   .50 .25
889 A342 1d Modern buildings   .50 .25
       Nos. 886-889 (4)   2.00 1.00
            Nos. 887-889 horiz.

1989, Mar. 23   *Perf. 10½x11, 11x10½*
890 A343 2.90d Oran Es Senia,
              horiz.   1.25 .70
891 A343 3.30d Tebessa, horiz.   1.50 .80
892 A343 5d shown   2.25 1.25
       Nos. 890-892 (3)   5.00 2.75

Development of the South — A344

1989, Apr. 24   Litho.   *Perf. 13½*
893 A344 1d Irrigation   .45 .25
894 A344 1.80d Building   .90 .45
895 A344 2.50d Fossil fuel ex-
              traction, vert.   1.25 .60
       Nos. 893-895 (3)   2.60 1.30

Eradicate
Locusts
A345

1989, May 25   *Perf. 10½*
896 A345 1d multi   .50 .25

National
Service — A346

1989, May 11   Litho.   *Perf. 13½*
897 A346 2d multicolored   .80 .40

1st Moon
Landing,
20th Anniv.
A347

4d, Astronaut, lunar module, Moon's
surface.

1989, July 23   Litho.   *Perf. 13½*
898 A347 2.90d shown   1.00 .55
899 A347 4d multi, vert.   1.40 .75

Interparliamentary Union,
Cent. — A348

1989, Sept. 4   *Perf. 10½*
900 A348 2.90d gold, brt rose lil
              & blk   1.10 .55

Produce
A349

1989, Sept. 23   Litho.   *Perf. 11½*
Granite Paper
901   Strip of 3   4.00 2.00
  a. A349 2d multi, diff.   .75 .40
  b. A349 3d multi, diff.   1.10 .55
  c. A349 5d shown   2.00 1.00

Fish — A350

1989, Oct. 27   Litho.   *Perf. 13½*
902 A350 1d *Sarda sarda*   .30 .20
903 A350 1.80d *Zeus faber*   .50 .35
904 A350 2.90d *Pagellus
              bogaraveo*   .90 .55
905 A350 3.30d *Xiphias gladius*   1.00 .65
       Nos. 902-905 (4)   2.70 1.75

Algerian
Revolution, 35th
Anniv. — A351

1989, Nov. 4   Litho.   *Perf. 13½*
906 A351 1d multicolored   .40 .20

African
Development
Bank, 25th
Anniv. — A352

1989, Nov. 18   *Perf. 10½*
907 A352 1d multicolored   .40 .20

Mushrooms
A353

1989, Dec. 16   *Perf. 13½*
908 A353 1d *Boletus satanas*   .30 .20
909 A353 1.80d *Psalliota
              xanthoderma*   .60 .35
910 A353 2.90d *Lepiota procera*   1.00 .55
911 A353 3.30d *Lactarius delici-
              osus*   1.10 .65
       Nos. 908-911 (4)   3.00 1.75

A354   A355

1990, Jan. 18   Litho.   *Perf. 10½*
912 A354 1d multicolored   .40 .20

Pan-African Postal Union, 10th anniv.

1990, Feb. 22   Litho.   *Perf. 14*
913 A355 1d Energy conserva-
              tion   .25 .20

A356   A357

1990, Mar. 2   Photo.   *Perf. 11½*
914 A356 3d multicolored   .65 .30

African Soccer Championships.

1990, May 17   Litho.   *Perf. 13½*
917 A357 2.90d shown   .75 .40
918 A357 5d Trophy   1.25 .65

World Cup Soccer Championships, Italy.

Rural Electrification — A358

1990, June 21
919 A358 2d multicolored   .50 .25

Youth
A359

Youth Holding
Rainbow — A360

1990, July 6   *Perf. 13½*
920 A359 2d multicolored   .50 .25
921 A360 3d multicolored   .75 .35

Maghreb Arab
Union — A361

1990   *Perf. 14x13½*
922 A361 1d multicolored   .40 .20

Vocations
A362

1990, Apr. 26   Litho.   *Perf. 12½*
923 A362 2d Craftsmen   .75 .40
924 A362 2.90d Auto mechanics   1.10 .60
925 A362 3.30d Deep sea fishing   1.25 .65
       Nos. 923-925 (3)   3.10 1.65

Organization of Petroleum Exporting
Countries (OPEC), 30th
Anniv. — A363

1990 *Perf. 13½*
926 A363 2d multicolored .75 .40

Savings
Promotion
A364

1990, Oct. 31 *Litho.* *Perf. 14*
927 A364 1d multicolored .20 .20

Namibian Independence — A365

1990, Nov. 8
928 A365 3d multicolored .60 .50

A366

A367

Farm animals.

1990, Nov. 29 *Perf. 13½*
929 A366 1d Duck .35 .20
930 A366 2d Rabbit, horiz. .65 .40
931 A366 2.90d Turkey .90 .55
932 A366 3.30d Rooster, horiz. 1.10 .65
Nos. 929-932 (4) 3.00 1.80

1990, Dec. 11
933 A367 1d multicolored .25 .20
Anti-French Riots, 30th anniv.

A368

A369

1990, Dec. 20 *Perf. 14*
934 A368 1d multicolored .25 .20
Fight against respiratory diseases.

1991, Feb. 24 *Litho.* *Perf. 13½*
935 A369 1d multicolored .25 .20
Constitution, 2nd anniv.

Flower Type of 1986
1991, May 23 *Litho.* *Perf. 13½*
Size: 26x36mm
936 A312 2d Jasminum fruticans .60 .30
937 A312 4d Dianthus crinitus 1.10 .65
938 A312 5d Cyclamen africanum 1.50 .85
Nos. 936-938 (3) 3.20 1.80

Children's
Drawings
A370

1991, June 3 *Litho.* *Perf. 13½*
939 A370 3d shown 1.00 .50
940 A370 4d Children playing 1.25 .65

Maghreb Arab
Union
Summit — A371

1991, June 10
941 A371 1d multicolored .30 .20

Geneva Convention on Refugees, 40th
Anniv. — A372

1991, July 28 *Litho.* *Perf. 14½x13½*
942 A372 3d multicolored 1.00 .50

Postal
Service
A373

1991, Oct. 12 *Perf. 14*
943 A373 1.50d shown .55 .25
944 A373 4.20d Expo emblem, vert. 1.50 .75
Telecom '91, 6th World Forum and Exposition on Telecommunications, Geneva, Switzerland (No. 944).

Butterflies
A374

1991, Nov. 21 *Litho.* *Perf. 11½*
Granite Paper
945 A374 2d Zerynthia rumina .30 .20
946 A374 4d Melitaea didyma .65 .30
947 A374 6d Vanessa atalanta 1.00 .50
948 A374 7d Nymphalis polychloros 1.10 .55
Nos. 945-948 (4) 3.05 1.55

A375

A376

1991, Dec. 21 *Perf. 12*
Granite Paper
949 A375 3d Necklace .40 .25
950 A375 4d Jewelry of Southern Tuaregs .60 .30
951 A375 5d Brooch .70 .40
952 A375 7d Rings, horiz. 1.00 .55
Nos. 949-952 (4) 2.70 1.50

1992, Mar. 8 *Litho.* *Perf. 14*
953 A376 1.50d Algerian Women .20 .20

Gazelles
A377

Designs: 1.50d, Gazella dorcas. 6.20d, Gazella cuvieri. 8.60d, Gazella dama.

1992, May 13 *Perf. 14½x13*
954 A377 1.50d multicolored .25 .20
955 A377 6.20d multicolored .95 .50
956 A377 8.60d multicolored 1.25 .65
Nos. 954-956 (3) 2.45 1.35

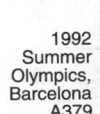

1992
Summer
Olympics,
Barcelona
A379

1992, June 24 *Litho.* *Perf. 14*
958 A379 6.20d Runners 1.00 .55

A381

A382

1992, July 7 *Litho.* *Perf. 14*
960 A381 5d multicolored .90 .45
Independence, 30th anniv.

1992, Sept. 23 *Litho.* *Perf. 14*
Designs: Medicinal plants.
961 A382 1.50d Ajuga iva .20 .20
962 A382 5.10d Rhamnus alaternus .60 .35
963 A382 6.20d Silybum marianum .70 .40
964 A382 8.60d Lavandula stoechas 1.00 .55
Nos. 961-964 (4) 2.50 1.50

Post Office
Modernization
A383

1992, Oct. 10 *Litho.* *Perf. 14*
965 A383 1.50d multicolored .20 .20

Marine
Life — A384

Designs: 1.50d, Hippocampus hippocampus. 2.70d, Caretta caretta. 6.20d, Muraena helena. 7.50d, Palinurus elephas.

1992, Dec. 23
966 A384 1.50d multicolored .20 .20
967 A384 2.70d multicolored .35 .20
968 A384 6.20d multicolored .85 .40
969 A384 7.50d multicolored 1.00 .50
Nos. 966-969 (4) 2.40 1.30

Pres. Mohammad Boudiaf (1919-92) — A385

1992, Nov. 3 *Litho.* *Perf. 11½*
Granite Paper
970 A385 2d green & multi .30 .20
971 A385 8.60d blue & multi 1.10 .55

Coins
A386

1992, Dec. 16   Litho.   Perf. 11½
Granite Paper
972 A386 1.50d Numidia, 2nd   .20   .20
         cent. BC
973 A386   2d Dinar, 14th cent.   .30   .20
974 A386   5.10d Dinar, 11th cent.   .65   .35
975 A386   6.20d Abdelkader, 19th   .85   .40
         cent.
       Nos. 972-975 (4)   2.00 1.15

Door Knockers — A387

Flowering Trees — A388

1993, Feb. 17   Litho.   Perf. 14
976 A387   2d Algiers   .30   .20
977 A387   5.60d Constantine   .75   .40
978 A387   8.60d Tlemcen   1.10   .60
       Nos. 976-978 (3)   2.15 1.20

1993, Mar. 17   Perf. 12x11½, 11½x12
Granite Paper
979 A388   4.50d Neflier (medlar),   .50   .30
         horiz.
980 A388   8.60d Cognassier   1.00   .60
         (quince)
981 A388   11d Abricotier (apri-   1.25   .75
         cot)
       Nos. 979-981 (3)   2.75 1.65

Natl. Coast Guard Service, 20th Anniv. A389

1993, Apr. 3   Litho.   Perf. 14
982 A389   2d multicolored   .30   .20

Traditional Grain Processing A390

1993, May 19   Litho.   Perf. 14
983 A390   2d Container   .25   .20
984 A390   5.60d Millstone   .75   .40
985 A390   8.60d Press   1.00   .55
       Nos. 983-985 (3)   2.00 1.15

Royal Mausoleums — A391

1993, June 16   Litho.   Perf. 14
986 A391   8.60d Mauretania   1.10   .60
987 A391   12d El Khroub   1.60   .80

Ports A392

1993, Oct. 20   Litho.   Perf. 14x13½
988 A392   2d Annaba   .20   .20
989 A392   8.60d Arzew   1.00   .55

Varanus Griseus A393

Design: 2d, Chamaeleo vulgaris, vert.

Perf. 13½x14, 14x13½
1993, Nov. 20
990 A393   2d multicolored   .25   .20
991 A393   8.60d multicolored   1.10   .55

Tourism A394

1993, Dec. 18   Litho.   Perf. 14x13½
992 A394   2d Tipaza   .20   .20
993 A394   8.60d Kerzaz   .80   .40

A395

Chahid Day — A396

1994, Jan. 2   Perf. 13½x14
994 A395   2d multicolored   .20   .20
SONATRACH (Natl. Society for Research, Transformation, and Commercialization of Hydrocarbons), 30th anniv.

1994, Feb. 18   Litho.   Perf. 13½x14
995 A396   2d multicolored   .20   .20

1994 World Cup Soccer Championships, US — A397

1994, Mar. 16   Perf. 14x13½
996 A397   8.60d multicolored   .80   .40

A398

A399

Orchids: 5.60d, Orchis simia lam. 8.60d, Ophrys lutea cavan. 11d, Ophrys apifera huds.

1994, Apr. 20   Litho.   Perf. 11½
Granite Paper
997 A398   5.60d multicolored   .55   .30
998 A398   8.60d multicolored   .85   .40
999 A398   11d multicolored   1.10   .55
       Nos. 997-999 (3)   2.50 1.25

1994, May 21   Litho.   Perf. 13x14
Ancient petroglyphs.
1000 A399   3d Inscriptions   .35   .20
1001 A399   10d Man on horse   1.25   .60

A400

A401

1994, June 25
1002 A400   12d multicolored   1.25   .65
Intl. Olympic Committee, cent.

1994, July 13
1003 A401   3d multicolored   .35   .20
World Population Day.

Views of Algiers Type of 1992
Design: 3d, like #775.

1994, July 13   Litho.   Perf. 14
1010 A290b   3d dk blue & lt blue   .35   .20
This is an expanding set. Number may change.

Jewelry from Saharan Atlas Region A402

Perf. 13½x14, 14x13½
1994, Oct. 18   Litho.
1019 A402   3d Fibules, vert.   .20   .20
1020 A402   5d Belt   .25   .20
1021 A402   12d Bracelets   .55   .30
       Nos. 1019-1021 (3)   1.00   .70

A403

A404

1994, Nov. 3   Litho.   Perf. 13½x14
1022 A403   3d multicolored   .40   .20
Algerian Revolution, 40th anniv.

1994, Nov. 16   Litho.   Perf. 13½x14
1023 A404   3d Ladybugs   .20   .20
1024 A404   12d Beetles   .55   .30

Fight Against AIDS A405

1994, Dec. 1   Litho.   Perf. 14x13½
1025 A405   3d multicolored   .38   .20

Folk Dances — A406

Minerals — A407

1994, Dec. 17   Litho.   Perf. 13½x14
1026 A406   3d Algeroise   .20   .20
1027 A406   10d Constantinoise   .50   .25
1028 A406   12d Alaoui   .55   .30
       Nos. 1026-1028 (3)   1.25   .75
See Nos. 1170-1172.

1994, Sept. 21
1029 A407   3d Gres lite-erode   .20   .20
1030 A407   5d Cipolin   .25   .20
1031 A407   10d Marne a turitella   .50   .25
       Nos. 1029-1031 (3)   .95   .65

World Tourism Organization, 20th Anniv. — A408

1995, Jan. 28   Litho.   Perf. 14x13½
1032 A408   3d multicolored   .35   .20

Honey Bees — A409

Flowers — A410

1995, Feb. 22 Perf. 13½x14, 14x13½
1033 A409 3d shown .35 .20
1034 A409 13d On flower, horiz. 1.50 .75

1995, Mar. 29 Photo. Perf. 11½
Granite Paper
1035 A410 3d Dahlias .25 .20
1036 A410 10d Zinnias 1.00 .55
1037 A410 13d Lilacs 1.25 .75
Nos. 1035-1037 (3) 2.50 1.50

Decorative Stonework — A411

Various patterns.

1995, Apr. 19 Perf. 14
1039 A411 3d brown .35 .20
1040 A411 4d green .45 .25
1041 A411 5d deep claret .55 .30
Nos. 1039-1041 (3) 1.35 .75

This is an expanding set. Numbers may change.

End of World War II, 50th Anniv. A413

1995, May 3 Perf. 14x13½
1048 A413 3d multicolored .35 .20

Souvenir Sheet

VE Day, 50th Anniv. — A414

Illustration reduced.

1995, May 10 Litho. Perf. 13½x14
1049 A414 13d multicolored 1.50 .85

Volleyball, Cent. — A415

Environmental Protection — A416

1995, June 14
1050 A415 3d multicolored .40 .20

1995, June 5
1051 A416 3d Air, water pollution .35 .20
1052 A416 13d Air pollution 1.50 .85

General Electrification A417

1995, July 5 Litho. Perf. 13½x14
1053 A417 3d multicolored .45 .20

UN, 50th Anniv. A418

1995, Oct. 24 Perf. 14x13½
1054 A418 13d multicolored 2.00 1.00

Pottery — A419

10d, Pot, Lakhdaria. 20d, Pitcher, Aokas. 21d, Jar, Larbaa Nath Iraten. 30d, Vase, Ouadhia.

1995, Nov. 14 Litho. Perf. 14
1055 A419 10d dark brown 1.50 .75
1056 A419 20d dull maroon 3.00 1.50
1057 A419 21d golden brown 3.25 1.60
1058 A419 30d dark rose brown 4.50 2.25
Nos. 1055-1058 (4) 12.25 6.10

Aquatic Birds A420

1995, Dec. 20 Litho. Perf. 14x13½
1059 A420 3d Tadorna tadorna .40 .20
1060 A420 5d Gallinago gallinago .70 .35

1996 Summer Olympics, Atlanta A421

1996, Jan. 24 Litho. Perf. 14x13½
1061 A421 20d multicolored 2.50 1.25

Touareg Leather Crafts A422

Perf. 14x13½, 13½x14
1996, Feb. 14 Litho.
1062 A422 5d shown .60 .40
1063 A422 16d Saddle bag, vert. 2.25 1.00

Pasteur Institute of Algeria — A423

1996, Mar. 20 Litho. Perf. 13½x14
1064 A423 5d multicolored .75 .40

Youm El Ilm — A424

Designs: 16d, Dove, stylus, vert. 23d, Open book showing pencil, stylus, compass, satellite in earth orbit, vert.

Perf. 14x13½, 13½x14
1996, Apr. 16 Litho.
1065 A424 5d multicolored .50 .40
1066 A424 16d multicolored 2.00 1.00
1067 A424 23d multicolored 3.00 1.50
Nos. 1065-1067 (3) 5.50 2.90

Minerals A425

Mineral, region: 10d, Iron, Djebel-Ouenza. 20d, Gold, Tirek-Amesmessa.

1996, May 6 Litho. Perf. 14x13½
1068 A425 10d multicolored .75 .25
1069 A425 20d multicolored 2.00 .60

Butterflies A426

Designs: 5d, Pandoriana pandora. 10d, Coenonympha pamphilus. 20d, Cynthia cardui. 23d, Melanargia galathea.

1996, June 12 Litho. Perf. 11½
Granite Paper
1070 A426 5d multicolored .30 .20
1071 A426 10d multicolored .75 .20
1072 A426 20d multicolored 1.50 .35
1073 A426 23d multicolored 2.00 .40
Nos. 1070-1073 (4) 4.55 1.15

Civil Protection A427

5d, Giving medical aid, ambulance. 23d, Prevention of natural disasters, vert.

Perf. 14x13½, 13½x14
1996, Oct. 9 Litho.
1074 A427 5d multicolored .40 .20
1075 A427 23d multicolored 1.25 .40

World Day Against Use of Illegal Drugs A428

1996, June 26 Litho. Perf. 14x13½
1076 A428 5d multicolored .40 .20

UNICEF, 50th Anniv. — A429

Stylized designs: 5d, Two children, wreath, pencils, flowers. 10d, Five children, pencil, key, flower, flag, hypodermic.

1996, Nov. 20 Litho. Perf. 13½x14
1077 A429 5d multicolored .30 .20
1078 A429 10d multicolored .50 .20

4th General Census A430

1997, Feb. 12 Litho. Perf. 14x13½
1079 A430 5d multicolored .20 .20

Protest at Ouargla, 35th Anniv. — A431

1997, Feb. 27 Perf. 13½x14
1080 A431 5d multicolored .20 .20

Interior Courts of Algerian Dwellings A432

1996, Dec. 18 Litho. Perf. 13½x14
Designs: 5d, Palace of Hassan Pasha. 10d, Khedaouj El-Amia, Algiers. 20d, Palace of Light. 30d, Abdellatif Villa.
1081 A432 5d multicolored .20 .20
1082 A432 10d multicolored .35 .20
1083 A432 20d multicolored .70 .35
1084 A432 30d multicolored 1.10 .55
Nos. 1081-1084 (4) 2.35 1.30

Paintings by Ismail Samson (1934-88) A433

20d, Woman with Pigeons. 30d, Interrogation.

1996, Dec. 25   **Perf. 14**
1085 A433 20d multicolored   1.00 .35
1086 A433 30d multicolored   1.50 .55

Victory Day, 35th Anniv. A434

1997, Mar. 19   **Perf. 14x13½**
1087 A434 5d multicolored   .20 .20

Flowers — A435

Designs: 5d, Ficaria verna. 16d, Lonicera arborea. 23d, Papaver rhoeas.

1997, Apr. 23 **Litho.** **Perf. 13½x14**
1088 A435 5d multicolored   .20 .20
1089 A435 16d multicolored   .55 .30
1090 A435 23d multicolored   .80 .40
    Nos. 1088-1090 (3)   1.55 .90

World Day to Stop Smoking — A436

Legislative Elections — A437

1997, May 31 **Litho.** **Perf. 13½x14**
1091 A436 5d multicolored   .20 .20

1997, June 4
1092 A437 5d multicolored   .20 .20

Scorpions A438

Designs: 5d, Buthus occitanus tunetanus. 10d, Androctonus australis hector.

1997, June 18   **Perf. 14x13½**
1093 A438 5d multicolored   .20 .20
1094 A438 10d multicolored   .35 .20

Natl. Independence, 35th Anniv. — A439

Designs: 5d, Crowd celebrating, flags. 10d, Doves, broken chain, "35," flag.

1997, July 5 **Litho.** **Perf. 14x13½**
1095 A439 5d multicolored   .20 .20
   Souvenir Sheet
   Perf. 14
1096 A439 10d multicolored   .35 .20
No. 1096 contains one 30x40mm stamp.

Wood Carvings — A440

Designs: 5d, Inscription, Nedroma Mosque. 23d, Door, Ketchaoua Mosque.

1997, Jan. 15 **Litho.** **Perf. 13½x14**
1097 A440 5d multicolored   .20 .20
1098 A440 23d multicolored   .80 .40

Moufdi Zakaria (1908-77), poet. — A441

1997, Aug. 17 **Litho.** **Perf. 13½x14**
1099 A441 5d multicolored   .20 .20

Textile Patterns A442

1997, Sept. 17 **Litho.** **Perf. 14**
1100 A442 3d Dokkali   .20 .20
1101 A442 5d Tellis   .20 .20
1102 A442 10d Bou-Taleb   .35 .20
1103 A442 20d Ddil   .70 .35
    Nos. 1100-1103 (4)   1.45 .95

Natl. Police Force, 25th Anniv. A443

1997, Oct. 6   **Perf. 14x13½**
1104 A443 5d multicolored   .20 .20

Express Mail Service A444

1997, Oct. 9
1105 A444 5d multicolored   .20 .20

Local Elections — A445

1997, Oct. 23   **Perf. 13½x14**
1106 A445 5d multicolored   .20 .20

Lighthouses A446

  Perf. 14x13½, 13½x14
1997, Nov. 5   **Litho.**
1107 A446 5d Tenes   .20 .20
1108 A446 10d Cape Caxine, vert.   .35 .20

New Airpost Service, 1st Anniv. A447

1997, Nov. 17   **Perf. 14x13½**
1109 A447 5d multicolored   .20 .20

Shells A448

Designs: 5d, Chlamys varia. 10d, Bolinus brandaris. 20d, Hinia reticulata, vert.

  Perf. 14x13½, 13½x14
1997, Dec. 17   **Litho.**
1110 A448 5d multicolored   .20 .20
1111 A448 10d multicolored   .35 .20
1112 A448 20d multicolored   .70 .35
    Nos. 1110-1112 (3)   1.25 .75

A449

A450

1997, Dec. 25   **Perf. 13½x14**
1113 A449 5d multicolored   .20 .20
  Election of the Natl. Council.

1997, Dec. 30 **Litho.** **Perf. 13½x14**
Completion of Government Reforms: a, Natl. flag, people, book, ballot box. b, People, open book, torch. c, Ballot box. d, Flag, rising sun, flower. e, Ballots, building, flag.

1114 A450 5d Strip of 5, #a.-e.   .85 .45

Bombing of Sakiet Sidi Youcef, 40th Anniv. A451

1998, Feb. 8 **Litho.** **Perf. 14x13½**
1115 A451 5d multicolored   .20 .20

National Archives A452

1998, Feb. 16
1116 A452 5d multicolored   .20 .20

Intl. Women's Day A453

1998, Mar. 8 **Litho.** **Perf. 14x13½**
1117 A453 5d multicolored   .20 .20

Expo '98, Lisbon A454

1998, Jan. 21 **Litho.** **Perf. 14x13½**
1118 A454 5d shown   .25 .20
   Size: 80x75mm
   Imperf
1119 A454 24d Mosaic   1.25 .60

1998 World Cup Soccer Championships, Paris — A455

1998, Apr. 15 **Litho.** **Perf. 13½x14**
1120 A455 24d multi   1.25 .60

Algiers
Casbah
A456

Designs: 5d, Aerial view, vert. 10d, Buildings, vert. 24d, Aerial view, diff.

1998, Apr. 22   Perf. 13½x14, 14x13½
1121 A456 5d multi .25 .20
1122 A456 10d multi .50 .20
1123 A456 24d multi 1.25 .60
    Nos. 1121-1123 (3) 2.00 1.00

Zaatcha Resistance — A457

1998, May 20   Perf. 13¼x13
1124 A457 5d multi .25 .20

Tourism
A458

5d, Mountains, farm, desert, vert. 10d, Youths, modes of transportation. 24d, Taghit.

Perf. 13½x14, 14x13½
1998, June 4   Litho.
1125 A458 5d multi .25 .20
1126 A458 10d multi .50 .25
1127 A458 24d multi 1.25 .60
    Nos. 1125-1127 (3) 2.00 1.05

Arab Post
Day
A459

1998, Aug. 3   Litho.   Perf. 14x13½
1128 A459 5d multi .25 .20

Interpol,
75th Anniv.
A460

1998, Sept. 7   Litho.   Perf. 14x13½
1129 A460 5d multi .25 .20

Creation of Provisional Government,
40th Anniv. — A461

1998, Sept. 19   Perf. 13¼x13
1130 A461 5d multi .25 .20

Natl.
Diplomacy
Day
A462

1998, Oct. 8   Perf. 14
1131 A462 5d multi .25 .20

Algerian
Olympic
Committee,
35th Anniv.
A463

1998, Oct. 18   Perf. 14x13½
1132 A463 5d multi .25 .20

Birds
A464

Designs: 5d, Pandion haliaetus. 10d, Larus audouinii. 24d, Phalacrocorax aristotelis, vert. 30d, Phalacrocorax carbo, vert.

Perf. 14x13½, 13½x14
1998, Nov. 11
1133 A464 5d multi .25 .20
1134 A464 10d multi .50 .25
1135 A464 24d multi 1.25 .60
1136 A464 30d multi 1.50 .75
    Nos. 1133-1136 (4) 3.50 1.80

See Nos. 1204-1207.

Universal
Declaration
of Human
Rights, 50th
Anniv.
A465

1998, Dec. 10   Litho.   Perf. 14x13½
1137 A465 5d Profiles, emblem .25 .20
1138 A465 24d shown 1.25 .60

Spinning
and
Weaving
Tools
A466

Designs: 5d, Comb, vert. 10d, Cards. 20d, Spindle, vert. 24d, Loom, vert.

1999, Jan. 20   Perf. 13½x14, 14x13½
1139 A466 5d multi .25 .20
1140 A466 10d multi .50 .25
1141 A466 20d multi 1.00 .50
1142 A466 24d multi 1.25 .60
    Nos. 1139-1142 (4) 3.00 1.55

Natl. Chahid
Day — A467

1999, Feb. 18   Perf. 13x13¼
1143 A467 5d multi .25 .20

Flowering
Trees
A468

1999, Mar. 17   Perf. 14x13½, 13½x14
1144 A468 5d Pear .25 .20
1145 A468 10d Plum .50 .25
1146 A468 24d Orange, vert. 1.25 .60
    Nos. 1144-1146 (3) 2.00 1.05

Presidential
Elections
A469

1999, Apr. 15   Perf. 13x13¼
1147 A469 5d multi .25 .20

Handicrafts
A470

Designs: 5d, Tlemcen mosaic, 14th cent., vert. 10d, Mosaic, Al Qal'a of Beni Hammad, 11th cent, vert. 20d, Cradle. 24d, Table.

1999, Apr. 18   Perf. 13¼x14, 14x13¼
1148 A470 5d multi .25 .20
1149 A470 10d multi .50 .25
1150 A470 20d multi 1.00 .50
1151 A470 24d multi 1.25 .60
    Nos. 1148-1151 (4) 3.00 1.55

7th African Games,
Johannesburg — A471

Stylized athletes and: 5d, Map of Africa, vert. 10d, South African flag.

1999, May 12   Perf. 13¼x14, 14x13¼
1152 A471 5d multi .25 .20
1153 A471 10d multi .50 .25

A472

A473

1999, June 6   Perf. 13¼x14
Rocks.
1154 A472 5d Gneiss .25 .20
1155 A472 20d Granite 1.00 .50
1156 A472 24d Schist 1.25 .60
    Nos. 1154-1156 (3) 2.50 1.30

1999, July 12   Perf. 13x13¼
1157 A473 5d multi .25 .20

Organization of African Unity, 35th summit.

A474

A475

1999, July 12   Perf. 13¼x14
1158 A474 5d multi .25 .20

Organization of African Unity Convention on Refugees.

1999, July 22   Perf. 13x13¼
1159 A475 5d Police Day .25 .20

Intl. Year of
Culture and
Peace (in
2000)
A476

1999, Sept. 14   Litho.   Perf. 14
1160 A476 5d multi .25 .20

Fish
A477

Designs: 5d, Dentex dentex. 10d, Mullus surmuletus. 20d, Dentex gibbosus. 24d, Diplodus sargus.

1999, Sept. 15   **Perf. 14x13¼**
1161	A477	5d multi	.25 .20
1162	A477	10d multi	.50 .25
1163	A477	20d multi	1.00 .50
1164	A477	24d multi	1.25 .60
		Nos. 1161-1164 (4)	3.00 1.55

Civil Peace
Referendum
A478

1999, Sept. 16   **Perf. 13¼x14**
1165 A478 5d multi   .25 .20

UPU, 125th
Anniv.
A479

1999, Oct. 9   **Perf. 14x13¼**
1166 A479 5d multi   .25 .20

World Post
Day
A480

1999, Oct. 9   **Litho.**   **Perf. 14x13½**
1167 A480 5d multi   .25 .20

Intl. Rural
Women's
Day
A481

1999, Oct. 14   **Litho.**   **Perf. 14x13¼**
1168 A481 5d multi   .25 .20

Algerian Revolution, 45th
Anniv. — A482

Soldiers and : a, Helicopters, burning flag. b, Burning flag
Illustration reduced.

1999, Nov. 1   **Perf. 13x13¼**
1169 A482 5d Pair, #a.-b.   .50 .25

Folk Dances Type of 1994
1999, Dec. 15   **Perf. 13¼x14**
1170	A406	5d Chaoui	.25 .20
1171	A406	10d Targuie	.50 .25
1172	A406	24d Mzab	1.25 .60
		Nos. 1170-1172 (3)	2.00 1.05

Millennium — A483

No. 1173: a, Doves, UN emblem. b, Sun, plant, trees. c, Umbrella over wheat and corn plants. d, Microscope and flasks. e, Crane, ship, truck. f, Train, Concorde, satellite dish, satellite, Moon. g, Windmills. h, Globe, ballot box. i, Apollo 15 astronauts on Moon. j, Film, inkwell, musical instrument and notes.
No. 1174: a, Dove with olive branch. b, Hand, flora, fauna. c, Satellites, computer, map of Africa and Europe. d, Heart, staff of Aesculapius, Red Cross, Red Crescent. e, Stylized globe and arrows. f, Animals, film, violin, painting, book. g, Flame, sun, water. h, Hand holding plant. i, symbols of democracy. j, Satellite, planets, space shuttle, astronaut.

Sawtooth Die Cut 6¼ Vert.
2000, Jan. 19
Self-Adhesive
Booklet Stamps
1173		Bklt. pane of 10+2 labels	2.50
a.-j.		A483 5d any single	.25 .20
1174		Bklt. pane of 10+2 labels	2.50
a.-j.		A483 5d any single	.25 .20

Expo 2000,
Hanover
A485

2000, Feb. 16   **Litho.**   **Perf. 14x13¼**
1179 A485 5d multi   .25 .20

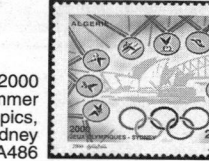

2000
Summer
Olympics,
Sydney
A486

2000, Mar. 22
1180 A486 24d multi   1.25 .60

Telethon
2000 — A487

2000, Apr. 8   **Perf. 13¼x14**
1181 A487 5d multi   .25 .20

Civil Concord
A488

Designs: 5d, Dove, handshake, crowd, vert. 10d, Handshake, hands releasing dove. 20d, Handshake, doves, flowers. 24d, Doves, flowers, handshake, vert.

Perf. 11½x11¾, 11¾x11½
2000, Apr. 15
1182-1185 A488   Set of 4   3.00 1.50

National Library — A489

2000, Apr. 16   **Perf. 13½x13**
1186 A489 5d multi   .25 .20

Blood
Donation — A490

2000, May 2   **Perf. 13¼x14**
1187 A490 5d multi   .25 .20

Tuareg
Handicrafts
A491

Background colors: 5d, Rose. 10d, Buff, vert.

2000, May 17   **Perf. 14**
1188-1189 A491   Set of 2   .75 .40

Famous Men — A492

#1190, Mohammed Dib (b. 1920), writer. #1191, Mustapha Kateb (1920-89), actor. #1192, Ali Maachi (1927-58), musician. #1193, Mohamed Racim (1896-1975), artist.

2000, June 8   **Perf. 13¼x13**
1190-1193 A492 10d Set of 4   2.00 1.00

Insects — A493

#1194, 5d, Hanneton. #1195, 5d, Anthrene. 10d, Vrillete du pain. 24d, Carabe.

2000, Sept. 20   **Perf. 13¼x14**
1194-1197 A493   Set of 4   2.25 1.10

Roman Cinerary
Urns Found at
Tipasa — A494

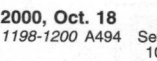

2000, Oct. 18   **Litho.**   **Perf. 14**
1198-1200 A494 Set of 3, 5d,
     10d, 24d   1.90 1.90

Orchids — A495

Designs: 5d, Limodorum abortivum. 10d, Orchis papilionacea. 24d, Orchis provincialis.

2000, Dec. 13   **Litho.**   **Perf. 14**
1201-1203 A495   Set of 3   1.00 1.00

Bird Type of 1998
Designs: No. 1204, 5d, Anser anser. No. 1205, 5d, Recurvirosta avosetta, vert. 10d, Botaurus stellaris, vert. 24d, Numenius arquata.

2001, Jan. 24
1204-1207 A464   Set of 4   1.10 1.10

Handicrafts — A496

Designs: 5d, Skampla, vert. 10d, Etagere. 24d, Mirror, vert.

2001, Feb. 21
1208-1210 A496   Set of 3   1.00 1.00

National
Parks
A497

Designs: 5d, Belezma, vert. 10d, Gouraya. 20d, Théniet el Had. 24d, El Kala, vert.

2001, Mar. 21   **Perf. 13¼x14, 14x13¼**
1211-1214 A497   Set of 4   1.50 1.50

1st Intl. Colloquium on St. Augustine
of Hippo — A498

Designs: 5d, Statue of St. Augustine (25x37mm). 24d, Mosaic.

Perf. 13¼x14, 13¼x13 (24d)
2001, Mar. 31
1215-1216 A498   Set of 2   .75 .75

Silver Coins — A499

Designs: 5d, 1830 Ryal boudjou. 10d, 1826 Double boudjou. 24d, 1771 Ryal drahem.

2001, Apr. 25   Litho.   Perf. 13½x13
1217-1219 A499   Set of 3   1.00 1.00

Natl. Scouting Day — A500

2001, May 27   Litho.   Perf. 14
1220 A500 5d multi   .20 .20

Palestinian Intifada — A501

2001, June 2
1221 A501 5d multi   .20 .20

Children's Games A502

Designs: No. 1222, 5d, Jacks. No. 1223, 5d, Hopscotch. No. 1224, 5d, Top spinning. No. 1225, 5d, Marbles.

2001, June 2
1222-1225 A502   Set of 4   .50 .50

Natl. Asthma Day — A503

2001, June 9
1226 A503 5d multi   .20 .20

14th Mediterranean Games, Tunis, Tunisia — A504

Designs: No. 1227, 5d, Map, "50." No. 1228, 5d, Runners, emblem.

2001, July 25   Litho.   Perf. 14
1227-1228 A504   Set of 2   .30 .30

15th World Festival of Youth and Students — A505

2001, Aug. 8
1229 A505 5d multi   .20 .20

Natl. Mujahedeen Day — A506

2001, Aug. 20   Perf. 13¼x14
1230 A506 5d multi   .20 .20

SEMI-POSTAL STAMPS

Regular Issue of 1926 Surcharged in Black or Red

1927		**Unwmk.**	**Perf. 14x13½**	
B1	A1	5c +5c bl grn	.50	.50
B2	A1	10c +10c lilac	.50	.50
B3	A2	15c +15c org brn	.50	.50
B4	A2	20c +20c car rose	.50	.50
B5	A2	25c +25c bl grn	.50	.50
B6	A2	30c +30c lt bl	.50	.50
B7	A2	35c +35c dp vio	.55	.55
B8	A2	40c +40c ol grn	.60	.60
B9	A3	50c +50c dp bl (R)	.60	.60
a.		Double surcharge	200.00	200.00
B10	A3	80c +80c red org	.60	.60
B11	A4	1fr +1fr gray grn & red brn	.65	.65
B12	A4	2fr +2fr Prus bl & blk brn	15.00	15.00
B13	A4	5fr +5fr red & vio	21.00	21.00
		Nos. B1-B13 (13)	42.00	42.00

The surtax was for the benefit of wounded soldiers. Government officials speculated in this issue.

Railroad Terminal, Oran SP1

Ruins at Djemila SP2   Mosque of Sidi Abd-er-Rahman SP3

Designs: 10c+10c, Rummel Gorge, Constantine. 15c+15c, Admiralty Buildings, Algiers. 25c+25c, View of Algiers. 30c+30c, Trajan's Arch, Timgad. 40c+40c, Temple of the North, Djemila. 75c+75c Mansourah Minaret, Tlemcen. 1f+1f, View of Ghardaia. 1.50f+1.50f, View of Tolga. 2f+2f, Tuareg warriors. 3f+3f, Kasbah, Algiers.

1930		**Engr.**	**Perf. 12½**	
B14	SP1	5c +5c orange	5.00	5.00
B15	SP1	10c +10c ol grn	5.00	5.00
B16	SP1	15c +15c dk brn	5.00	5.00

B17	SP1	25c +25c black	5.00	5.00
B18	SP1	30c +30c dk red	5.00	5.00
B19	SP1	40c +40c ap grn	5.00	5.00
B20	SP2	50c +50c ultra	5.00	5.00
B21	SP2	75c +75c red pur	5.00	5.00
B22	SP2	1fr +1fr org red	5.00	5.00
B23	SP2	1.50fr +1.50fr deep ultra	5.00	5.00
B24	SP2	2fr +2fr dk car	5.00	5.00
B25	SP2	3fr +3fr dk grn	5.00	5.00
B26	SP3	5fr +5fr grn & car	12.00	12.00
a.		Center inverted	450.00	
		Nos. B14-B26 (13)	72.00	72.00

Centenary of the French occupation of Algeria. The surtax on the stamps was given to the funds for the celebration.
Nos. B14-B26 exist imperf. Value, set in pairs, $350.

> **Catalogue values for unused stamps in this section, from this point to the end of the section, are for Never Hinged items.**

No. 102 Surcharged in Red

1938   Perf. 13
B27 A6 65c +35c on 2.25fr yel grn   .50 .40

20th anniversary of Armistice.

René Caillié, Charles Lavigerie and Henri Duveyrier SP14

1939			**Engr.**	
B28	SP14	30c +20c dk bl grn	1.00	.60
B29	SP14	90c +60c car rose	1.25	.65
B30	SP14	2.25fr +75c ultra	6.75	6.25
B31	SP14	5fr +5fr brn blk	14.00	14.00
		Nos. B28-B31 (4)	23.00	21.50

Pioneers of the Sahara.

French and Algerian Soldiers SP15

1940		**Photo.**	**Perf. 12**	
B32	SP15	1fr +1fr bl & car	.50	.40
B33	SP15	1fr +2fr brn rose & blk	.50	.40
B34	SP15	1fr +4fr dp grn & red	.70	.60
B35	SP15	1fr +9fr brn & car	1.00	1.00
		Nos. B32-B35 (4)	2.70	2.40

The surtax was used to assist the families of mobilized men.

Type of Regular Issue, 1941 Surcharged in Carmine

1941   Engr.   Perf. 13
B36 A19 1fr +4fr black   .20 .20

No. 135 Surcharged in Carmine

B37 A19 1fr +4fr dark blue   .20 .20

The surtax was for National Relief.

No. 124 Surcharged in Black "+60c"
1942
B38 A7 90c +60c henna brn   .20 .20
a.   Double surcharge   55.00

The surtax was used for National Relief. The stamp could also be used as 1.50 francs for postage.

Mother and Child — SP16

1943, Dec. 1		**Litho.**	**Perf. 12**	
B39	SP16	50c +4.50fr brt pink	.50	.25
B40	SP16	1.50fr +8.50fr lt grn	.50	.25
B41	SP16	3fr +12fr dp bl	.50	.25
B42	SP16	5fr +15fr vio brn	.50	.25
		Nos. B39-B42 (4)	2.00	1.00

The surtax was for the benefit of soldiers and prisoners of war.

Planes over Fields SP17

Unwmk.
1945, July 2   Engr.   Perf. 13
B43 SP17 1.50fr +3.50fr lt ultra, red org & blk   .25 .25

The surtax was for the benefit of Algerian airmen and their families.

France No. B192 Overprinted Type "a" of 1924 in Black
1945
B44 SP146 4fr +6fr dk vio brn   .35 .20

The surtax was for war victims of the P.T.T.

Overprinted in Blue on Type of France, 1945
1945, Oct. 15
B45 SP150 2fr +3fr dk brn   .40 .40
For Stamp Day.

Overprinted in Blue on Type of France, 1946
1946, June 29
B46 SP160 3fr +2fr red   .45 .45
For Stamp Day.

Children Playing by Stream SP18

Girl — SP19   Athlete — SP20

Repatriated Prisoner and Bay of Algiers SP21

1946, Oct. 2   Engr.   Perf. 13
B47 SP18 3fr +17fr dark grn   .65 .65
B48 SP19 4fr +21fr red   .65 .65
B49 SP20 8fr +27fr rose lilac   2.75 2.75
B50 SP21 10fr +35fr dark blue   .70 .70
Nos. B47-B50 (4)   4.75 4.75

Type of France, 1947, Overprinted type "a" of 1924 in Carmine
1947, Mar. 15
B51 SP172 4.50fr +5.50fr dp ultra   .40 .40
For Stamp Day.

Same on Type of France, 1947, Surcharged Like No. B36 in Carmine
1947, Nov. 13
B52 A173 5fr +10fr dk Prus grn   .55 .40

Type of France, 1948, Overprinted in Dark Green—f

1948, Mar. 6
B53 SP176 6fr +4fr dk grn   .55 .45
For Stamp Day.

Type of France, 1948, Overprinted type "a" of 1924 in Blue and New Value
1948, May
B54 A176 6fr +4fr red   .55 .35

Battleship Richelieu and the Admiralty, Algiers SP22

Aircraft Carrier Arromanches — SP23

Unwmk.
1949, Jan. 15   Engr.   Perf. 13
B55 SP22 10fr +15fr dp blue   4.50 4.50
B56 SP23 18fr +22fr red   4.50 4.50
The surtax was for naval charities.

Type of France, 1949, Overprinted in Blue—g

1949, Mar. 26
B57 SP180 15fr +5fr lilac rose   1.25 1.10
For Stamp Day, Mar. 26-27.

Type of France, 1950, Overprinted type "f" in Green
1950, Mar. 11
B58 SP183 12fr +3fr blk brn   1.25 1.10
For Stamp Day, Mar. 11-12.

Foreign Legionary — SP24

1950, Apr. 30
B59 SP24 15fr +5fr dk grn   1.10 1.10

Charles de Foucauld and Gen. J. F. H. Laperrine SP25

1950, Aug. 21   Unwmk.   Perf. 13
B60 SP25 25fr +5fr brn ol & brn blk   3.00 3.00
50th anniversary of the presence of the French in the Sahara.

Emir Abd-el-Kader and Marshal T. R. Bugeaud — SP26

1950, Aug. 21
B61 SP26 40fr +10fr dk brn & blk brn   3.00 3.00
Unveiling of a monument to Emir Abd-el-Kader at Cacheron.

Col. Colonna d'Ornano and Fine Arts Museum, Algiers SP27

1951, Jan. 11
B62 SP27 15fr +5fr blk brn, vio brn & red brn   .65 .65
Death of Col. Colonna d'Ornano, 10th anniv.

Type of France, 1951, Overprinted type "a" of 1924 in Black
1951, Mar. 10
B63 SP186 12fr +3fr brown   .85 .85
For Stamp Day.

Type of France, 1952, Overprinted type "g" in Dark Blue
1952, Mar. 8   Unwmk.   Perf. 13
B64 SP190 12fr +3fr dk bl   1.25 1.25
For Stamp Day.

French Military Medal — SP28

1952, July 5   Unwmk.   Perf. 13
B65 SP28 15fr +5fr grn, yel & brn 1.75 1.25
Centenary of the creation of the French Military Medal.

Type of France 1952, Surcharged type "g" and Surtax in Black
1952, Sept. 15
B66 A222 30fr +5fr dp ultra   1.40 1.25
10th anniv. of the defense of Bir-Hakeim.

View of El Oued SP29

Design: 12fr+3fr, View of Bou-Noura.
1952, Nov. 15   Engr.
B67 SP29 8fr +2fr ultra & red   1.25 1.10
B68 SP29 12fr +3fr red   2.25 1.90
The surtax was for the Red Cross.

Type of France, 1953, Overprinted type "a" of 1924 in Black
1953, Mar. 14   Engr.
B69 SP193 12fr +3fr purple   1.00 .90
For Stamp Day. Surtax for Red Cross.

Victory of Cythera — SP30

Unwmk.
1953, Dec. 18   Engr.   Perf. 13
B70 SP30 15fr +5fr blk brn & brn   .65 .60
The surtax was for army welfare work.

Type of France, 1954, Overprinted type "a" of 1924 in Black
1954, Mar. 20   Unwmk.   Perf. 13
B71 SP196 12fr +3fr scarlet   .75 .65
For Stamp Day.

Soldiers and Flags SP31   Foreign Legionary SP32

1954, Mar. 27
B72 SP31 15fr +5fr dk brn   .65 .50
The surtax was for old soldiers.

1954, Apr. 30
B73 SP32 15fr +5fr dk grn   1.25 1.00
The surtax was for the welfare fund of the Foreign Legion.

Nurses and Verdun Hospital, Algiers SP33

15fr+5fr, J. H. Dunant & ruins at Djemila.
1954, Oct. 30
B74 SP33 12fr +3fr indigo & red   2.00 1.75
B75 SP33 15fr +5fr pur & red   2.50 2.00
The surtax was for the Red Cross.

Earthquake Victims and Ruins — SP34

First Aid — SP35

Design: #B80-B81, Removing wounded.
1954, Dec. 5
B76 SP34 12fr +4fr dk vio brn   1.00 1.00
B77 SP34 15fr +5fr dp bl   1.00 1.00
B78 SP35 18fr +6fr lil rose   1.75 1.75
B79 SP35 20fr +7fr violet   1.75 1.75
B80 SP35 25fr +8fr rose brn   2.00 2.00
B81 SP35 30fr +10fr brt bl grn   2.00 2.00
Nos. B76-B81 (6)   9.50 9.50
The surtax was for victims of the Orleansville earthquake disaster of September 1954.

Type of France, 1955, Overprinted type "a" of 1924 in Black
1955, Mar. 19
B82 SP199 12fr +3fr dp ultra   1.00 1.00
For Stamp Day, Mar. 19-20.

Women and Children
SP36

Cancer Victim
SP37

1955, Nov. 5
B83 SP36 15fr +5fr blue & indigo .60 .60
The tax was for war victims.

1956, Mar. 3 **Unwmk.** *Perf. 13*
B84 SP37 15fr +5fr dk brn .75 .50
The surtax was for the Algerian Cancer Society. The male figure in the design is Rodin's "Age of Bronze."

Type of France, 1956, Overprinted type "a" of 1924 in Black
1956, Mar.
B85 SP202 12fr +3fr red .90 .60
For Stamp Day, Mar. 17-18.

Foreign Legion Rest Home
SP38

1956, Apr. 29
B86 SP38 15fr +5fr dk bl grn .90 .90
Honoring the French Foreign Legion.

Type of France, 1957, Overprinted type "f" in Black
1957, Mar. 16 **Engr.** *Perf. 13*
B87 SP204 12fr +3fr dull purple .70 .70
For Stamp Day and to honor the Maritime Postal Service.

Fennec
SP39

Design: 15fr+5fr, Stork flying over roofs.
1957, Apr. 6
B88 SP39 12fr +3fr red brn & red 3.75 3.75
B89 SP39 15fr +5fr sepia & red 3.75 3.75
The surtax was for the Red Cross.

Type of Regular Issue, 1956 Surcharged in Dark Blue

1957, June 18
B90 A53 15fr +5fr scar & rose red .95 .95
17th anniv. of General de Gaulle's appeal for a Free France.

The Giaour, by Delacroix — SP40

On the Banks of the Oued, by Fromentin
SP41

Design: 35fr+10fr, Dancer, by Chasseriau.

Unwmk.
1957, Nov. 30 **Engr.** *Perf. 13*
B91 SP40 15fr +5fr dk car 3.75 3.75
B92 SP41 20fr +5fr grn 3.75 3.75
B93 SP40 35fr +10fr dk bl 3.75 3.75
Nos. B91-B93 (3) 11.25 11.25
Surtax for army welfare organizations.

Type of France Overprinted type "f" in Blue
1958, Mar. 15 **Unwmk.** *Perf. 13*
B94 SP206 15fr +5fr org brn .75 .75
For Stamp Day.

Bird-of-Paradise Flower — SP42

Arms & Marshal's Baton — SP43

1958, June 14 **Engr.** *Perf. 13*
B95 SP42 20fr +5fr grn, org & vio 2.25 2.25
The surtax was for Child Welfare.

1958, July 20
B96 SP43 20fr +5fr ultra, car & grn 1.00 1.00
Marshal de Lattre Foundation.

Independent State

Clasped Hands, Wheat, Olive Branch — SP44

Burning Books — SP45

1963, May 27 **Unwmk.** *Perf. 13*
B97 SP44 50c +20c sl grn, brt grn & car .80 .60
Surtax for the Natl. Solidarity Fund.

1965, June 7 **Engr.** *Perf. 13*
B98 SP45 20c +5c ol grn, red & blk .50 .40
Burning of the Library of Algiers, 6/7/62.

Soldiers and Woman Comforting Wounded Soldier — SP46

1966, Aug. 20 **Photo.** *Perf. 11½*
B99 SP46 30c +10c multi 1.25 .70
B100 SP46 95c +10c multi 1.75 1.10
Day of the Moudjahid (Moslem volunteers).

Red Crescent, Boy and Girl — SP47

1967, May 27 **Litho.** *Perf. 14*
B101 SP47 30c +10c brt grn, brn & car .45 .35
Algerian Red Crescent Society.

Flood Victims — SP48

Design: 95c+25c, Rescuing flood victims.
1969, Nov. 15 **Typo.** *Perf. 10½*
B102 SP48 30c +10c multi .45 .35
Litho.
B103 SP48 95c +25c multi 1.00 .65

Red Crescent Flag SP49

1971, May 17 **Engr.** *Perf. 10½*
B104 SP49 30c +10c slate grn & car .35 .30
Algerian Red Crescent Society.

Intl. Children's Day — SP50

1989, June 1 **Litho.** *Perf. 10½x11*
B105 SP50 1d +30c multi .65 .50
Surtax for child welfare.

Solidarity with Palestinians
SP51

1990, Dec. 9 **Litho.** *Perf. 10½x11*
B106 SP51 1d +30c multi .50 .30

Natl. Solidarity with Education
SP52

1995, Sept. 20 **Litho.** *Perf. 13x14*
B107 SP52 3d +50c multi .50 .25

Red Crescent Society
SP53

1998, May 2 **Litho.** *Perf. 13x13¼*
B108 SP53 5d +1d multi .30 .20

World Children's Day
SP54

1998, June 1 *Perf. 14x13½, 13½x14*
B109 SP54 5d +1d shown .30 .20
B110 SP54 5d +1d Flower, child, adult, vert. .30 .20

AIR POST STAMPS

Catalogue values for unused stamps in this section are for Never Hinged items.

Plane over Algiers Harbor AP1

Two types of 20fr:
Type I - Monogram "F" without serifs. "POSTE" indented 3mm.
Type II - Monogram "F" with serifs. "POSTE" indented 4½mm.

Unwmk.
1946, June 20 **Engr.** *Perf. 13*
C1 AP1 5fr red .25 .20
C2 AP1 10fr deep blue .25 .20
C3 AP1 15fr deep green .45 .20
C4 AP1 20fr brown (II) .25 .20
C4A AP1 20fr brown (I) 100.00 65.00

C5　AP1　25fr violet　.55　.20
C6　AP1　40fr gray black　.75　.20
　Nos. C1-C4,C5-CC6 (6)　2.50　1.20
For surcharges see Nos. C7, CB1-CB2.

No. C1
Surcharged
in Black

1947, Jan. 18
C7　AP1　(4.50fr) on 5fr red　.25　.20

Storks over
Mosque — AP2

Plane over
Village
AP3

1949-53
C8　AP2　50fr green　2.00　.25
C9　AP3　100fr brown　1.75　.25
C10　AP2　200fr bright red　4.00　3.00
C11　AP3　500fr ultra ('53)　14.00　10.00
　Nos. C8-C11 (4)　21.75　13.50

Beni Bahdel
Dam — AP4

1957, July 1　Unwmk.　Perf. 13
C12　AP4　200fr dark red　3.25　.75

Caravelle over Ghardaia — AP5

Designs: 2d, Caravelle over El Oued. 5d,
Caravelle over Tipasa.

1967-68　Engr.　Perf. 13
C13　AP5　1d lil, org brn & emer　1.00　.50
C14　AP5　2d brt bl, org brn & em-
　er　2.50　1.25
C15　AP5　5d brt bl, grn & org brn
　('68)　6.00　2.75
　Nos. C13-C15 (3)　9.50　4.50

Plane over Casbah, Algiers — AP6

Designs: 3d, Plane over Oran. 4d, Plane
over Rhumel Gorge.

1971-72　Photo.　Perf. 12½
C16　AP6　2d grysh blk & multi　1.60　.80
C17　AP6　3d violet & blk　2.50　1.40
C18　AP6　4d blk & multi　3.25　1.75
　Nos. C16-C18 (3)　7.35　3.95

Issued: 2d, 6/12/71; 3d, 4d, 2/28/72.

Storks and
Plane — AP7

1979, Mar. 24　Photo.　Perf. 11½
C19　AP7　10d multi　4.00　1.60

Plane Approaching Coastal
City — AP8

1991, Apr. 26　Litho.　Perf. 13½
C20　AP8　10d shown　3.00　1.50
C21　AP8　20d Plane over city　6.00　3.00

Plane Over
Djidjelli
Corniche — AP9

1993, Sept. 25　Engr.　Perf. 13½x14
C22　AP9　50d blue, grn & brn　6.25　3.25

AIR POST SEMI-POSTAL STAMPS

**Catalogue values for unused
stamps in this section are for
Never Hinged items.**

No. C2 Surcharged in Carmine

1947, June 18　Perf. 13
CB1　AP1　10fr +10fr deep blue　.75　.60
7th anniv. of Gen. Charles de Gaulle's
speech in London, June 18, 1940.

No. C1
Surcharged
in Blue

1948, June 18
CB2　AP1　5fr +10fr red　.70　.60
8th anniv. of Gen. Charles de Gaulle's
speech in London, June 18, 1940.

Monument, Clock
Tower and
Plane — SPAP1

1949, Nov. 10　Engr.　Unwmk.
CB3　SPAP1　15fr +20fr dk brn　3.50　3.50
25th anniv. of Algeria's 1st postage stamps.

POSTAGE DUE STAMPS

D1　　　　D2

1926-27　Typo.　Perf. 14x13½
J1　D1　5c light blue　.20　.20
J2　D1　10c dk brn　.20　.20
J3　D1　20c olive grn　.20　.20
J4　D1　25c car rose　.35　.35
J5　D1　30c rose red　.20　.20
J6　D1　45c blue grn　.50　.50
J7　D1　50c brn vio　.20　.20
J8　D1　60c green ('27)　1.25　.30
J9　D1　1fr red brn, straw　.20　.20
J10　D1　2fr lil rose ('27)　.20　.20
J11　D1　3fr deep blue ('27)　.20　.20
　Nos. J1-J11 (11)　3.70　2.75

See Nos. J25-J26, J28-J32. For surcharges,
see Nos. J18-J20.

1926-27
J12　D2　1c olive grn　.20　.20
J13　D2　10c violet　.40　.20
J14　D2　30c bister　.25　.20
J15　D2　60c dull red　.20　.20
J16　D2　1fr brt vio ('27)　11.00　1.75
J17　D2　2fr lt bl ('27)　7.50　.65
　Nos. J12-J17 (6)　19.55　3.20

See note below France No. J51.
For surcharges, see Nos. J21-J24.

Stamps of 1926 Surcharged

1927
J18　D1　60c on 20c olive grn　.90　.25
J19　D1　2fr on 45c blue grn　1.10　.65
J20　D1　3fr on 25c car rose　.75　.25
　Nos. J18-J20 (3)　2.75　1.15

Recouvrement Stamps
of 1926 Surcharged

1927-32
J21　D2　10c on 30c bis ('32)　2.25　1.50
J22　D2　1fr on 1c olive grn　.65　.60
J23　D2　1fr on 60c dl red ('32)　11.00　.25
J24　D2　2fr on 10c violet　6.25　6.25
　Nos. J21-J24 (4)　20.15　8.60

**Catalogue values for unused
stamps in this section, from this
point to the end of the section, are
for Never Hinged items.**

Type of 1926, Without "R F"

1942　Typo.　Perf. 14x13½
J25　D1　30c dark red　.20　.20
J26　D1　2fr magenta　.20　.20

Type of 1926
Surcharged in Red

1944　Perf. 14x13½
J27　A2　50c on 20c yel grn　.20　.20
　a.　Inverted surcharge　3.50
　b.　Double surcharge　9.50
No. J27 was issued precanceled only. See
note after No. 32.

Type of 1926

1944　Litho.　Perf. 12
J28　D1　1.50fr brt rose lilac　.30　.20
J29　D1　2fr greenish blue　.30　.20
J30　D1　5fr rose carmine　.30　.20
　Nos. J28-J30 (3)　.90　.60

Type of 1926

1947　Typo.　Perf. 14x13½
J32　D1　5fr green　.60　.45

France Nos. J80-J81 Overprinted Type
"a" of 1925 in Carmine or Black

1947
J33　D5　10c sepia (C)　.20　.20
J34　D5　30c bright red violet　.20　.20

D3

Perf. 14x13
1947-55　Unwmk.　Engr.
J35　D3　20c red　.20　.20
J36　D3　60c ultra　.25　.20
J37　D3　1fr dk org brn　.20　.20
J38　D3　1.50fr dull green　.40　.40
J39　D3　2fr red　.20　.20
J40　D3　3fr violet　.20　.20
J41　D3　5fr ultra ('49)　.25　.25
J42　D3　6fr black　.25　.20
J43　D3　10fr lil rose　.35　.20
J44　D3　15fr ol grn ('55)　.45　.45
J45　D3　20fr brt grn　.25　.20
J46　D3　30fr red org ('55)　.65　.40
J47　D3　50fr indigo ('51)　1.25　.95
J48　D3　100fr brt bl ('53)　5.50　3.50
　Nos. J35-J48 (14)　10.40　7.50

Independent State

France Nos. J93-J97 Overprinted "EA"
in Black like Nos. 286-290

1962, July 2　Typo.　Perf. 14x13½
Handstamped Overprint
J49　D6　5c bright pink　2.25　1.60
J50　D6　10c red orange　2.25　1.40
J51　D6　20c olive bister　2.25　1.40
J52　D6　50c dark green　3.00　2.75
J53　D6　1fr deep green　4.25　4.00
　Nos. J49-J53 (5)　14.00　11.15

Typographed Overprint
J49a　D6　5c bright pink　6.00　6.00
J50a　D6　10c red orange　6.00　6.00
J51a　D6　20c olive bister　5.50　5.50
J52a　D6　50c dark green　14.00　14.00
J53a　D6　1fr deep green　25.00　25.00
　Nos. J49a-J53a (5)　56.50　56.50

See note after No. 290.

Scales — D4　　Grain — D5

1963, June 25　Perf. 14x13½
J54　D4　5c car rose & blk　.20　.20
J55　D4　10c olive & car　.20　.20
J56　D4　20c ultra & blk　.20　.20
J57　D4　50c bister brn & grn　.50　.30
J58　D4　1fr lilac & org　.90　.50
　Nos. J54-J58 (5)　2.00　1.40

#J58 Surcharged with New Value & 3
Bars

1968, Mar. 28　Typo.　Perf. 14x13½
J59　D4　60c on 1fr lilac & org　.40　.30

1972-93　Litho.　Perf. 13½x14
J60　D5　10c bister　.20　.20
J61　D5　20c deep brown　.20　.20
J62　D5　40c orange　.20　.20
J63　D5　50c dk vio blue　.20　.20
J64　D5　80c dk olive gray　.40　.20
J65　D5　1d green　.45　.25
J66　D5　2d blue　.95　.40

J67	D5	3d violet	.45	.20
J68	D5	4d lilac rose	.60	.30
		Nos. J60-J68 (9)	3.65	2.15

Issued: 3d, 4d, 1/21/93; others, 10/21/72.

NEWSPAPER STAMPS

Nos. 1 and 33
Surcharged in Red

1924-26   **Unwmk.**   **Perf. 14x13½**

P1	A16	½c on 1c dk gray	.20	.20
a.		Triple surcharge	87.50	
P2	A1	½c on 1c olive ('26)	.20	.20

ALLENSTEIN
'a-lən-,shtin

LOCATION — In East Prussia
AREA — 4,457 sq. mi.
POP. — 540,000 (estimated 1920)
CAPITAL — Allenstein

Allenstein, a district of East Prussia, held a plebiscite in 1920 under the Versailles Treaty, voting to join Germany rather than Poland. Later that year, Allenstein became part of the German Republic.

100 Pfennig = 1 Mark

Stamps of Germany, 1906-20, Overprinted

Perf. 14, 14½, 14x14½, 14½x14
1920   **Wmk. 125**

1	A16	5pf green	.20	.30
2	A16	10pf carmine	.20	.30
3	A22	15pf dk vio	.20	.30
4	A22	15pf vio brn	4.50	5.50
5	A16	20pf bl vio	.20	.30
6	A16	30pf org & blk, buff	.25	.30
7	A16	40pf lake & blk	.20	.30
8	A16	50pf pur & blk, buff	.20	.30
9	A16	75pf grn & blk	.20	.30
10	A17	1m car rose	.55	.55
a.		Double overprint	—	—
11	A17	1.25m green	.50	.50
a.		Double overprint	—	—
12	A17	1.50m yel brn	.50	.70
13	A21	2.50m lilac rose	1.00	6.25
14	A19	3m blk vio	1.10	1.10
a.		Double overprint	55.00	275.00
		Never hinged	82.50	
b.		Inverted overprint	—	—
		Nos. 1-14 (14)	9.80	17.00
		Set, never hinged	18.00	

The 5pf brown (Germany #118), 10pf orange (#119), 20pf green (#121), 30pf blue (#123) and 40pf (#124) exist with this overprint but were not regularly issued. Value, each: $75 hinged, $115 never hinged.

Overprinted

15	A16	5pf green	.20	.30
16	A16	10pf carmine	.20	.30
17	A22	15pf dark vio	.20	.35
18	A22	15pf vio brn	18.00	24.00
19	A16	20pf blue vio	.20	.35
20	A16	30pf org & blk, buff	.30	.30
21	A16	40pf lake & blk	.30	.30
22	A16	50pf pur & blk, buff	.20	.30
23	A16	75pf grn & blk	.20	.45
24	A17	1m car rose	.55	.55
a.		Inverted overprint	425.00	550.00
		Never hinged	550.00	

25	A17	1.25m green	.50	.55
26	A17	1.50m yel brn	.50	.55
27	A21	2.50m lilac rose	1.10	2.75
28	A19	3m blk vio	.85	.85
a.		Inverted overprint	275.00	700.00
		Never hinged	500.00	
b.		Double overprint	150.00	425.00
		Never hinged	425.00	
		Nos. 15-28 (14)	23.30	31.90
		Set, never hinged	47.50	

The 40pf carmine rose (Germany No. 124) exists with this oval overprint, but it is doubtful whether it was regularly issued. Value $85 hinged, $175 never hinged.

ANDORRA, SPANISH ADMIN.

an-'dor-ə

LOCATION — On the southern slope of the Pyrenees Mountains between France and Spain.
GOVT. — Co-principality
AREA — 179 sq. mi.
POP. — 72,766 (July 1, 1996)
CAPITAL — Andorra la Vella

Andorra is subject to the joint control of France and the Spanish Bishop of Urgel and pays annual tribute to each. The country has no monetary unit of its own, the peseta and franc both being in general use.

100 Centimos = 1 Peseta
100 Centimes = 1 Franc
100 Cents = 1 Euro (2002)

Catalogue values for unused stamps in the Spanish Administration for this country are for Never Hinged items, beginning with Scott 50 in the regular postage section and Scott C2 in the airpost section; for the French Administration of this country, Never Hinged items begin at Scott 78 for regular postage, Scott B1 for the semi-postal section, Scott C1 for the airpost section, and Scott J21 for the postage due section.

A majority of the Spanish Andorra stamps issued to about 1950 are poorly centered. The very fine examples that are valued will be somewhat off center. Very poorly centered examples (perfs cutting design) sell for less. Well centered stamps are scarce and sell for approximately twice the values shown (#1-24, E1-E3), or 50% more (#25-49, E4-E5).

Stamps of Spain, 1922-26, Overprinted in Red or Black

Perf. 13½x12½, 12½x11½, 14
1928   **Unwmk.**

1	A49	2c olive green	.35	.30

Control Numbers on Back

2	A49	5c car rose (Bk)	.45	.35
3	A49	10c green	.45	.35
4	A49	15c slate blue	2.00	2.00
5	A49	20c violet	2.25	2.00
6	A49	25c rose red (Bk)	2.00	2.00
7	A49	30c black brown	10.00	8.25
8	A49	40c deep blue	10.00	5.75
9	A49	50c orange (Bk)	10.00	7.50
10	A49a	1p blue blk	12.00	12.50
11	A49a	4p lake (Bk)	80.00	90.00
12	A49a	10p brown (Bk)	140.00	140.00
		Nos. 1-12 (12)	269.50	271.00
		Set, never hinged	375.00	

Counterfeit overprints exist.
#1-12 perf 14 are worth much more. See the *Scott Classic Specialized Catalogue.*

 La Vall — A1

 St. Juan de Caselles — A2

 St. Julia de Loria — A3

 St. Coloma — A4

 General Council — A5

1929, Nov. 25   **Engr.**   **Perf. 14**

13	A1	2c olive green	1.00	.50

Control Numbers on Back

14	A2	5c carmine lake	2.25	1.25
15	A3	10c yellow green	2.25	2.50
16	A4	15c slate green	2.25	2.50
17	A3	20c violet	2.25	2.50
18	A4	25c carmine rose	5.50	5.50
19	A1	30c olive brown	100.00	100.00
20	A4	40c dark blue	4.50	2.75
21	A3	50c deep orange	4.50	3.50
22	A5	1p slate	11.00	11.00
23	A5	4p deep rose	65.00	65.00
24	A5	10p bister brown	75.00	85.00
		Nos. 13-24 (12)	275.50	282.00
		Set, never hinged	350.00	

Nos. 13-24 exist imperforate. Value, $700.

1931-38
Perf. 11½

13a	A1	2c	4.00	1.25

Control Numbers on Back

14a	A2	5c	7.00	5.25
15a	A3	10c	7.00	3.00
16a	A4	15c	20.00	16.00
17a	A3	20c	9.00	7.00
18a	A4	25c	6.50	4.00
19a	A1	30c ('33)	100.00	55.00
20a	A4	40c ('35)	10.00	8.00
22a	A5	1p ('38)	25.00	16.00
b.		Control number omitted	1,400.	
		Nos. 13a-22a (9)	188.50	115.50
		Set, never hinged	250.00	

Without Control Numbers
1936-43   **Perf. 11½x11**

25	A1	2c red brown ('37)	2.00	1.00
26	A2	5c dark brown	2.00	1.00
27	A3	10c deep green	9.00	4.00
a.		10c yellow green	72.50	60.00
		Never hinged	92.50	
28	A4	15c blue green ('37)	4.00	3.50
a.		15c yellow green	5.75	3.75
29	A3	20c violet	6.00	3.50
30	A4	25c deep rose ('37)	2.00	3.00
31	A1	30c carmine	3.00	2.75
31A	A2	40c dark blue	600.00	
		Never hinged	750.00	
32	A1	45c rose red ('37)	3.00	1.75
33	A3	50c deep orange	7.00	4.00
34	A1	60c deep blue ('37)	5.00	3.50
34A	A5	1p slate	1,500.	
		Never hinged	2,000.	
35	A5	4p deep rose ('43)	35.00	35.00
36	A5	10p bister brn ('43)	35.00	45.00
		Nos. 25-31,32-34,35-36 (12)	113.00	108.00
		Set, never hinged	160.00	

Exist imperforate. Value, $175.

Edelweiss — A6   Provost — A7

 Coat of Arms — A8

 Plaza of Ordino — A9

 Chapel of Meritxell — A10

 Map — A11

1948-53   **Unwmk.**   **Photo.**   **Perf. 12½**

37	A6	2c dark ol grn ('51)	.40	.70
38	A6	5c deep org ('53)	.40	.70
39	A6	10c deep blue ('53)	.45	.70

Engr.   **Perf. 9½x10**

40	A7	20c brown vio	6.25	2.75
41	A7	25c org, perf. 12½ ('53)	4.50	2.10
42	A8	30c dk slate grn	8.00	3.25
43	A9	50c deep green	9.50	4.75
44	A10	75c dark blue	14.00	4.75
45	A9	90c dp car rose	6.25	3.75
46	A10	1p brt orange ver	9.50	4.75
47	A8	1.35p dk blue vio	6.25	5.75

Perf. 10

48	A11	4p ultra ('53)	9.50	9.50
49	A11	10p dk vio brn ('51)	20.00	9.50
		Nos. 37-49 (13)	95.00	52.95
		Set, never hinged	125.00	

Catalogue values for unused stamps in this section, from this point to the end of the section, are for Never Hinged items.

 Bridge of St. Anthony — A12

 Madonna of Meritxell, 8th Century — A13

Designs: 70c, Aynos pasture. 1p, View of Canillo. 2p, St. Coloma. 2.50p, Arms of Andorra. 3p, Old Andorra, horiz. 5p, View of Ordino, horiz.

1963-64   **Unwmk.**   **Engr.**   **Perf. 13**

50	A12	25c dk gray & sepia	.20	.20
51	A12	70c dk sl grn & brn blk	.20	.20
52	A12	1p slate & dull pur	.25	.20
53	A12	2p violet & dull pur	.25	.20
54	A12	2.50p rose claret	.70	.55
55	A12	3p blk & grnsh gray	1.25	.55
56	A12	5p dk brn & choc	1.75	1.00
57	A13	6p sepia & car	2.75	1.00
		Nos. 50-57 (8)	7.35	3.90

Issued: 25c-2p, 7/20/63; 2.50p-6p, 2/29/64.

 Narcissus — A14

 Encamp Valley — A15

1966, June 10   **Engr.**   **Perf. 13**

58	A14	50c shown	.20	.20
59	A14	1p Pinks	.20	.20
60	A14	5p Jonquils	.95	.50
61	A14	10p Hellebore	2.10	.60
		Nos. 58-61 (4)	3.45	1.50

312

ANDORRA, SPANISH ADMIN.

Common Design Types pictured following the introduction.

Europa Issue 1972
Common Design Type

1972, May 2   Photo.   Perf. 13
Size: 25½x38mm

62	CD15	8p multicolored	100.00	62.50

1972, July 4   Photo.   Perf. 13
Tourist publicity: 1.50p, Massana (village). 2p, Skiing on De La Casa Pass. 5p, Pessons Lake, horiz.

63	A15	1p multicolored	.20	.20
64	A15	1.50p multicolored	.60	.50
65	A15	2p multicolored	1.50	.50
66	A15	1.90p multicolored	1.90	.80
		Nos. 63-66 (4)	4.20	2.00

Butterfly
Stroke
A16

Design: 2p, Volleyball, vert.

1972, Oct.   Photo.   Perf. 13

67	A16	2p lt blue & multi	.20	.20
68	A16	5p multicolored	.25	.20

20th Olympic Games, Munich, 8/26-9/11.

St. Anthony
Singers
A17

1972, Dec. 5   Photo.   Perf. 13

69	A17	1p shown	.20	.20
70	A17	1.50p Les Caramelles (boys' choir)	.20	.20
71	A17	2p Nativity scene	.20	.20
72	A17	5p Man holding giant cigar, vert	.45	.20
73	A17	8p Hermit of Meritxell, vert	.60	.30
74	A17	15p Marratxa dancers	1.40	.45
		Nos. 69-74 (6)	3.05	1.55

Andorran customs. No. 71 is for Christmas.

Europa Issue 1973
Common Design Type and

Symbol of
Unity
A18

1973, Apr. 30   Photo.   Perf. 13

75	A18	2p ultra, red & blk	.20	.20

Size: 37x25mm

76	CD16	8p tan, red & blk	.75	.40

Nativity — A19   Virgin of
Ordino — A20

Christmas: 5p, Adoration of the Kings. Designs are from altar panels of Meritxell Parish Church.

1973, Dec. 14   Photo.   Perf. 13

77	A19	2p multicolored	.20	.20
78	A19	5p multicolored	.55	.35

1974, Apr. 29   Photo.   Perf. 13
Europa: 8p, Les Banyes Cross.

79	A20	2p multicolored	1.00	.35
80	A20	8p slate & brt blue	3.00	.95

Cupboard — A21   Crowns of Virgin
and Child of
Roser — A22

1974, July 30   Photo.   Perf. 13

81	A21	10p multicolored	1.40	.45
82	A22	25p dark red & multi	3.50	1.40

UPU
Monument,
Bern
A23

1974, Oct. 9   Photo.   Perf. 13

83	A23	15p multicolored	1.10	.50

Centenary of Universal Postal Union.

Nativity
A24

Christmas: 5p, Adoration of the Kings.

1974, Dec. 4   Photo.   Perf. 13

84	A24	2p multicolored	.45	.20
85	A24	5p multicolored	1.50	.40

Mail Delivery,
Andorra, 19th
Century — A25   12th Century
Painting, Ordino
Church — A26

1975, Apr. 4   Photo.   Perf. 13

86	A25	3p multicolored	.25	.20

Espana 75 Intl. Philatelic Exhibition, Madrid, 4/4-13.

1975, Apr. 28   Photo.   Perf. 13
Design: 12p, Christ in Glory, 12th century Romanesque painting, Ordino church.

87	A26	3p multicolored	1.00	.30
88	A26	12p multicolored	2.50	.75

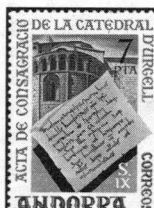

Urgel Cathedral
and
Document — A27

1975, Oct. 4   Photo.   Perf. 13

89	A27	7p multicolored	.75	.45

Millennium of consecration of Urgel Cathedral, and Literary Festival 1975.

Nativity,
Ordino
A28

Christmas: 7p, Adoration of the Kings, Ordino.

1975, Dec. 3   Photo.   Perf. 13

90	A28	3p multicolored	.20	.20
91	A28	7p multicolored	.35	.25

Caldron and
CEPT
Emblem — A29   Slalom and
Montreal
Olympic
Emblem — A30

Europa: 12p, Chest and CEPT emblem.

1976, May 3   Photo.   Perf. 13

92	A29	3p bister & multi	.20	.20
93	A29	12p yel & multi, horioz.	.50	.20

1976, July 9   Photo.   Perf. 13
Design: 15p, One-man canoe and Montreal Olympic emblem, horiz.

94	A30	7p multicolored	.20	.20
95	A30	15p multicolored	.35	.25

21st Olympic Games, Montreal, Canada, July 17-Aug. 1.

Nativity
A31

Christmas: 25p, Adoration of the Kings. Wall paintings in La Massana Church.

1976, Dec. 7   Photo.   Perf. 13

96	A31	3p multicolored	.20	.20
97	A31	25p multicolored	.35	.25

View of Ansalonge — A32

Europa: 12p, Xuclar, valley, mountains.

1977, May 2   Litho.   Perf. 13

98	A32	3p multicolored	.20	.20
99	A32	12p multicolored	.40	.25

Cross of
Terme — A33   Map of Post
Offices — A34

Christmas: 12p, Church of St. Miguel d'Engolasters.

1977, Dec. 2   Photo.   Perf. 13x12½

100	A33	5p multicolored	.25	.25
101	A33	12p multicolored	.60	.45

Souvenir Sheet

Designs: 10p, Mail delivery. 20p, Post Office, 1928. 25p, Andorran coat of arms.

1978, Mar. 31   Photo.   Perf. 13x13½

102		Sheet of 4	.75	.75
a.	A34	5p multicolored	.20	.20
b.	A34	10p multicolored	.20	.20
c.	A34	20p multicolored	.20	.20
d.	A34	25p multicolored	.20	.20

Spanish postal service in Andorra, 50th anniv.

La
Vall — A35

Europa: 12p, St. Juan de Caselles.

1978, May 2   Perf. 13

103	A35	5p multicolored	.20	.20
104	A35	12p multicolored	.25	.20

Crown,
Bishop's
Mitre and
Staff
A36

1978, Sept. 24   Photo.   Perf. 13

105	A36	5p brown, car & yel	.30	.20

700th anniversary of the signing of treaty establishing Co-Principality of Andorra.

Holy Family — A37

Christmas: 25p, Adoration of the Kings. Both designs after frescoes in the Church of St. Mary d'Encamp.

1978, Dec. 5   Photo.   Perf. 13

106	A37	5p multicolored	.20	.20
107	A37	25p multicolored	.30	.20

Young
Woman — A38

1979, Feb. 14   Photo.   Perf. 13

Designs: 5p, Young man. 12p, Bridegroom and bride riding mule.

108	A38	3p multicolored	.20	.20
109	A38	5p multicolored	.20	.20
110	A38	12p multicolored	.20	.20
		Nos. 108-110 (3)	.60	.60

Old Mail Truck A39

Europa: 12p, Stampless covers of 1846 & 1854.

1979, Apr. 30   Engr.   Perf. 13

111	A39	5p yel grn & dk blue	.20	.20
112	A39	12p dk red & violet	.25	.20

Children Holding Hands A40

1979, Oct. 18   Photo.   Perf. 13

113	A40	19p multicolored	.30	.20

International Year of the Child.

St. Coloma's Church — A41

Christmas: 25p, Agnus Dei roundel, St. Coloma's Church.

1979, Nov. 28   Photo.   Perf. 13½

114	A41	8p multicolored	.20	.20
115	A41	25p multicolored	.30	.25

Bishop Pere d'Arg A42

Bishops of Urgel: 5p, Josep Caixal. 13p, Joan Benlloch.

1979, Dec. 27   Engr.

116	A42	1p dk blue & brown	.20	.20
117	A42	5p rose lake & purple	.20	.20
118	A42	13p brown & dk green	.20	.20
		Nos. 116-118 (3)	.60	.60

See Nos. 132-133, 159, 175, C4.

Antoni Fiter, Magistrate — A43

Europa: 19p, Francesc Cairat, magistrate.

1980, Apr. 28   Photo.   Perf. 13x13½

119	A43	8p bister, blk & brn	.20	.20
120	A43	19p lt green & blk	.25	.20

Boxing, Moscow '80 Emblem A44

1980, July 23   Photo.   Perf. 13½x13

121	A44	5p Downhill skiing	.20	.20
122	A44	8p shown	.20	.20
123	A44	50p Target shooting	.60	.45
		Nos. 121-123 (3)	1.00	.85

12th Winter Olympic Games, Lake Placid, NY, Feb. 12-24 (5p); 22nd Summer Olympic Games, Moscow, July 19-Aug. 3.

Nativity A45

1980, Dec. 12   Litho.   Perf. 13

124	A45	10p Nativity, vert.	.20	.20
125	A45	22p shown	.30	.20

Christmas 1980.

Children Dancing at Santa Anna Feast A46

Europa: 30p, Going to church on Aplec de la Verge de Canolich Day.

1981, May 7   Photo.   Perf. 13

126	A46	12p multicolored	.20	.20
127	A46	30p multicolored	.35	.25

50th Anniv. of Police Force A47

1981, July 2   Photo.   Perf. 13½x13

128	A47	30p multicolored	.35	.20

Intl. Year of the Disabled A48

1981, Oct. 8   Photo.   Perf. 13½

129	A48	50p multicolored	.55	.25

Christmas 1981 A49

Designs: Encamp Church retable.

1981, Dec. 3   Photo.   Perf. 13½

130	A49	12p Nativity	.20	.20
131	A49	30p Adoration	.35	.20

Bishops of Urgel Type of 1979

1981, Dec. 12   Engr.   Perf. 13½

132	A42	7p Salvador Casanas	.20	.20
133	A42	20p Josep de Boltas	.25	.20

Natl. Arms — A51

1982, Feb. 17   Photo.   Perf. 13x13½

134	A51	1p bright pink	.20	.20
135	A51	3p bister brown	.20	.20
136	A51	7p red orange	.20	.20
137	A51	12p lake	.20	.20
138	A51	15p ultra	.20	.20
139	A51	20p blue green	.25	.20
140	A51	30p crimson rose	.30	.20

Perf. 13½x12½

1982, Sept. 30   Engr.

Size: 25½x30½mm

141	A51	50p dark green	.70	.20
142	A51	100p dark blue	1.40	.45
		Nos. 134-142 (9)	3.65	2.05

For type A51 without "PTA" see #192-198.

Europa 1982 A52

1982, May 12   Photo.   Perf. 13

143	A52	14p New Reforms, 1866, vert.	.20	.20
144	A52	33p Reform of Institutions, 1981	.40	.25

1982 World Cup — A53

Designs: Various soccer players.

1982, June 13   Photo.   Perf. 13x13½

145	A53	14p multicolored	.40	.40
146	A53	33p multicolored	.85	.85
a.		Pair, #145-146 + label	1.25	1.25

A54   A55

Anniversaries: 9p, Permanent Spanish and French delegations, cent. 14p, 50th anniv. of Andorran stamps. 23p, St. Francis of Assisi (1182-1226). 33p, Anyos Pro-Vicarial District membership centenary (Relacio sobre la Vall de Andorra titlepage).

1982, Sept. 7   Engr.   Perf. 13

147	A54	9p dk blue & brown	.20	.20
148	A54	14p black & green	.45	.20
149	A54	23p dk blue & brown	.25	.20
150	A54	33p black & olive grn	.50	.40
		Nos. 147-150 (4)	1.40	1.00

Perf. 13x13½, 13½x13

1982, Dec. 9   Photo.

Christmas: 14p, Madonna and Child, Andorra la Vieille Church, vert. 33p, El Tio de Nadal (children in traditional costumes striking hollow tree).

151	A55	14p multicolored	.20	.20
152	A55	33p multicolored	.40	.25

Europa 1983 A56

1983, June 7   Photo.   Perf. 13

153	A56	16p La Cortinada Church, architect, 12th cent.	.20	.20
154	A56	38p Water mill, 16th cent.	.50	.35

Local Mushrooms — A57

1983, July 20   Photo.   Perf. 13x12½

155	A57	16p Lactarius sanguifluus	.95	.40

See Nos. 165, 169, 172.

Universal Suffrage, 50th Anniv. A58

Photogravure and Engraved

1983, Sept. 6   Perf. 13

156	A58	10p multicolored	.20	.20

Visit of Monsignor Jacinto Verdaguer Bishop and Co-Prince A59

1983, Sept. 6

157	A59	50p multicolored	.70	.40

Christmas 1983 — A60

Saint Cerni de Nagol, Romanesque fresco, Church of San Cerni de Nagol.

1983, Nov. 24   Photo.   Perf. 13½

158	A60	16p multicolored	.25	.20

Bishops of Urgel Type of 1979

1983, Dec. 7   Engr.   Perf. 13

159	A42	26p Joan J. Laguarda Fenollera	.30	.20

1984 Winter Olympics A62

1984, Feb. 17   Litho.   Perf. 13½x14

160	A62	16p Ski jumping	.30	.20

ESPANA '84 — A63

1984, Apr. 27   Photo.   Perf. 13
161 A63 26p Emblems   .30 .20

Europa (1959-84) A64

1984, May 5   Engr.
162 A64 16p brown   .20 .20
163 A64 38p blue   .50 .30

1984 Summer Olympics A65

1984, Aug. 9   Litho.   Perf. 13½x14
164 A65 40p Running   .50 .30

Mushroom Type of 1983

1984, Sept. 27   Photo.   Perf. 13x12½
165 A57 11p Morchella esculenta   8.50 1.25

Christmas 1984 A66

1984, Dec. 6   Photo.   Perf. 13½
166 A66 17p Nativity carving   .25 .20

Europa 1985 A67

18p, Mossen Enric Arfany, composer, natl. hymn score. 45p, Musician Playing Viol, Romanesque fresco detail, La Cortinada Church, vert.

1985, May 3   Engr.   Perf. 13½
167 A67 18p dk vio, grn & chocolate   .20 .20
168 A67 45p green & chocolate   .65 .20

Mushroom Type of 1983
Perf. 13½x12½
1985, Sept. 19   Photo.
169 A57 30p Gyromitra esculenta   .45 .20

Pal Village — A68

1985, Nov. 7   Engr.   Perf. 13½
170 A68 17p brt ultra & dk blue   .25 .20

Christmas 1985 A69

Fresco: Angels Playing Trumpet and Psaltery, St. Bartholomew Chapel.

1985, Dec. 11   Photo.   Perf. 13½x13
171 A69 17p multicolored   .25 .20

Mushroom Type of 1983
Perf. 13½x12½
1986, Apr. 10   Photo.
172 A57 30p Marasmius oreades   .45 .20

Europa 1986 — A70

1986, May 5   Engr.   Perf. 13
173 A70 17p Water   .20 .20
174 A70 45p Soil and air   .60 .20

Bishops of Urgel Type of 1979
1986, Sept. 11   Engr.   Perf. 13½
175 A42 35p Justi Guitart   .45 .20

A72   A73

Santa Roma de Les Bons Church bell.

1986, Dec. 11   Litho.   Perf. 14
176 A72 19p multicolored   .25 .20
                  Christmas.

1987, Mar. 27   Photo.   Perf. 14
Contemporary Natl. Coat of Arms.
177 A73 48p multicolored   .60 .35
Visit of the co-princes: the Bishop of Urgel and president of France, September 26, 1986.

Europa 1987 A74

Modern architecture: 19p, Meritxell Sanctuary interior. 48p, Sanctuary exterior, vert.

1987, May 15   Engr.   Perf. 14x13½
178 A74 19p dark blue & brown   .20 .20
179 A74 48p dark blue & brown   .60 .20

Souvenir Sheet

1992 Summer Olympics, Barcelona A75

20p, House of the Valleys. 50p, Bell tower, Chapel of the Archangel Michael, and torchbearer.

1987, July 20   Photo.   Perf. 14
180   Sheet of 2   3.50 3.50
  a. A75 20p multicolored   1.00 1.00
  b. A75 50p multicolored   2.40 2.40

Local Mushrooms — A76

1987, Sept. 11   Perf. 13½x12½
181 A76 100p Boletus edulis   1.25 .50

Christmas A77

Design: Detail from a Catalan manuscript, De Nativitat, by R. Llull.

1987, Nov. 18   Litho.   Perf. 14
182 A77 20p multicolored   .25 .20

Lance and Arrowhead (Bronze Age) A78

1988, Mar. 25   Photo.   Perf. 14
183 A78 50p multicolored   .65 .25

Europa 1988 — A79   Pyrenean Mastiff — A80

Transport and communications: 20p, Les Bons, a medieval road. 45p, Trader and pack mules, early 20th cent.

1988, May 5   Engr.   Perf. 14x13½
184 A79 20p dark bl & dark red   .20 .20
185 A79 45p dark bl & dark red   .50 .20

1988, July 26   Litho.   Perf. 14x13½
186 A80 20p multicolored   .25 .20

Bishop of Urgel and Seigneur of Caboet Confirming Co-Principality, 700th Anniv. — A81

1988, Oct. 24   Litho.   Perf. 14x13½
187 A81 20p gold, blk & int blue   .25 .20

Christmas 1988 A82

1988, Nov. 30   Litho.   Perf. 14x13½
188 A82 20p multicolored   .25 .20

Arms Type of 1982 Without "PTA"
1988, Dec. 2   Photo.   Perf. 13x13½
192 A51 20p brt blue green   .25 .20
          Size: 25x30½mm
          Perf. 13½x12½
194 A51 50p grnsh black   .65 .25
196 A51 100p dark blue   1.25 .45
198 A51 500p dark brown   6.50 2.10
  Nos. 192-198 (4)   8.65 3.00
This is an expanding set. Numbers will change if necessary.

Europa 1989 A83

Perf. 14x13½, 13½x14
1989, May 8   Litho. & Engr.
200 A83 20p Leapfrog, vert.   .25 .20
201 A83 45p Tug of war   .50 .20

Santa Roma Church, Les Bons A84

Litho. & Engr.
1989, June 20   Perf. 13½x14
202 A84 50p blk, dp bl & grn bl   .55 .20

Anniv. Emblem — A85   Christmas — A86

1989, Oct. 26   Litho.   Perf. 14x13½
203 A85 20p multicolored   .25 .20
Intl. Red Cross and Red Crescent societies, 125th annivs.; Year for the Protection of Human Life.

1989, Dec. 1
204 A86 20p *The Immaculate Conception*   .25 .20

Europa 1990 A87

Post offices.

Perf. 13½x14, 14x13½
1990, May 17   Photo.
205 A87 20p shown   .25 .20
206 A87 50p Post office, vert.   .60 .25

Gomphidius Rutilus — A88

1990, June 21   Litho.   Perf. 13x13½
207 A88 45p multicolored   .60 .30

Plandolit House — A89

Christmas — A90

Litho. & Engr.
1990, Oct. 17   **Perf. 13x12½**
208 A89 20p brown & org yel   .30   .20

1990, Nov. 26   Litho.   Perf. 14x13½
209 A90 25p lake, brn & bister   .35   .20

4th Games of the Small European States A91

1991, Apr. 29   Photo.   Perf. 13½x14
210 A91 25p Discus   .35   .20
211 A91 45p High jump, runner   .65   .30

Europa — A92

Perf. 14x13½, 13½x14
1991, May 10   **Litho.**
212 A92 25p Olympus-1 satellite   .40   .20
213 A92 55p Olympus-1, horiz.   .80   .40

A93   Christmas — A94

1991, Sept. 20   Litho.   Perf. 13x12½
214 A93 45p Macrolepiota procera   .60   .30

1991, Nov. 29   Photo.   Perf. 14x13½
215 A94 25p multicolored   .35   .20

Woman Carrying Water Pails A95

1992, Feb. 14   Photo.   Perf. 13½x14
216 A95 25p multicolored   .35   .20

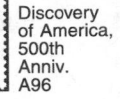

Discovery of America, 500th Anniv. A96

Perf. 14x13½, 13½x14
1992, May 8   **Photo.**
217 A96 27p Santa Maria, vert.   .45   .20
218 A96 45p King Ferdinand   .70   .30

Europa.

1992 Summer Olympics, Barcelona A97

1992, July 22   Photo.   Perf. 13½x14
219 A97 27p Kayak   .55   .25

Nativity Scene, by Fra Angelico — A98

1992, Nov. 18   Photo.   Perf. 14
220 A98 27p multicolored   .45   .20

Natl. Automobile Museum A99

Litho. & Engr.
1992, Sept. 10   **Perf. 13½x14**
221 A99 27p 1894 Benz   .45   .25

Cantharellus Cibarius — A100

1993, Mar. 25   Photo.   Perf. 13½x14
222 A100 28p multicolored   .55   .25

Contemporary Paintings — A101

Europa: 28p, Upstream, by John Alan Morrison. 45p, Rhythm, by Angel Calvente, vert.

Perf. 13½x14, 14x13½
1993, May 20   **Litho.**
223 A101 28p multicolored   .55   .25
224 A101 45p multicolored   1.00   .45

Art and Literature Society, 25th Anniv. — A102

1993, Sept. 23   Litho.   Perf. 14
225 A102 28p multicolored   .60   .25

Christmas — A103

Litho. & Engr.
1993, Nov. 25   **Perf. 14x13½**
226 A103 28p multi   .60   .25

Souvenir Sheet

Constitution, 1st Anniv. — A104

1994, Mar. 14   Photo.   Perf. 14
227 A104 29p multicolored   .65   .65

Sir Alexander Fleming (1881-1955), Co-discoverer of Penicillin — A105

1994, May 6   Photo.   Perf. 13½x14
228 A105 29p Portrait   .65   .65
229 A105 55p AIDS virus   1.25 1.25

Europa.

Hygrophorus Gliocyclus — A106

1994, Sept. 27   Photo.   Perf. 14
230 A106 29p multicolored   .65   .65

Christmas — A107

1994, Nov. 29   Photo.   Perf. 14x13½
231 A107 29p multicolored   .65   .65

Nature Conservation in Europe — A108

1995, Mar. 23   **Perf. 14**
232 A108 30p Farm in valley   .70   .70
233 A108 60p Stone fence, valley 1.40 1.40

Europa A109

1995, May 8   Photo.   Perf. 14
234 A109 60p multicolored   1.40 1.40

Christmas — A110

1995, Nov. 8   Photo.   Perf. 14
235 A110 30p Flight to Egypt   .70   .70

Entrance Into Council of Europe A111

1995, Nov. 10
236 A111 30p multicolored   .70   .70

Mushrooms — A112

1996, Apr. 30   Photo.   Perf. 14
237 A112 30p Ramaria aurea   .70   .70
238 A112 60p Tuber mela-nosporum   1.40 1.40

Isabelle Sandy (1884-1975), Writer — A113

1996, May 7
239 A113 60p brown & violet   1.50 1.50

Europa.

Intl. Museum Day A114

Design: Antique coal-heated iron.

1996, Sept. 12   Photo.   Perf. 14
240 A114 60p multicolored   .80   .80

Christmas A115

The Annunciation, by Andrew Martin, 1753,
St. Eulalia d'Encamp Church.

1996, Nov. 26　　Photo.　　Perf. 14
241 A115 30p multicolored　　　　.40　.40

Museums
of Andorra
A116

Early bicycles designed by: 32p, Karl Drais,
1818. 65p, Pierre Michaux, 1861.

1997, Apr. 28　　Photo.　　Perf. 14
242 A116 32p multicolored　　　　.40　.40
243 A116 65p multicolored　　　　.75　.75
　　　　See Nos. 248-249.

A117　　　　　UNESCO — A118

Europa (Stories and Legends): Hikers
watching family of bears crossing over river on
fallen tree.

1997, May 6　　Photo.　　Perf. 14
244 A117 65p multicolored　　　　.75　.75

1997, Sept. 30　　Photo.　　Perf. 14
245 A118 32p multicolored　　　　.40　.40

Christmas — A119

1997, Nov. 25　　Photo.　　Perf. 14
246 A119 32p multicolored　　　　.40　.40

1998
Winter
Olympic
Games,
Nagano
A120

1998, Feb. 23　　Photo.　　Perf. 14
247 A120 35p Slalom skier　　　　.40　.40

Museums of Andorra Type of 1997

Early bicycles: 35p, Kangaroo, 1878. 70p,
Hirondelle, 1889.

1998, Apr. 24　　Photo.　　Perf. 13½x14
248 A116 35p multicolored　　　　.40　.40
249 A116 70p multicolored　　　　.75　.75

Harlequins,
Canillas
Carnival
A121

1998, May 22　　Photo.　　Perf. 14
250 A121 70p multicolored　　　　.80　.80
　　　　Europa.

Manual Digest,
250th
Anniv. — A122

1998, Sept. 30　　Photo.　　Perf. 14
251 A122 35p multicolored　　　　.45　.45

Inauguration of the Postal Museum of
Andorra — A123

1998, Nov. 19　　Photo.　　Perf. 14
252 A123 70p multicolored　　　　.85　.85

Christmas
A124

1998, Nov. 26
253 A124 35p multicolored　　　　.45　.45

Museums
of Andorra
A125

Early bicycles designed by: 35p, Salvo,
1878, vert. 70p, Rudge, 1883.

1999, Jan. 29　　Photo.　　Perf. 14
254 A125 35p multicolored　　　　.45　.45
255 A125 70p multicolored　　　　.85　.85

Council of
Europe,
50th Anniv.
A126

1999, Apr. 29　　Photo.　　Perf. 14
256 A126 35p multicolored　　　　.40　.40

Incles
Valley
A127

1999, May 6
257 A127 70p multicolored　　　　.75　.75
　　　　Europa.

Transporting Mail on
Horseback — A128

1999, Feb. 18　　Photo.　　Perf. 14
258 A128 35p black & sepia　　　　.45　.45

Restoration
of Casa
Rull,
Sispony,
La
Massana
A129

1999, Sept. 22　　Photo.　　Perf. 13½x14
259 A129 35p multicolored　　　　.40　.40

Christmas — A130　　St. Coloma's
　　　　　　　　　　Church — A131

1999, Nov. 10　　Engr.　　Perf. 14x13½
260 A130 35p orange brn & brn　　.40　.40

1999, Nov. 12　　　　　　　Photo.
261 A131 35p multicolored　　　　.40　.40
　　　　European heritage.

Europa, 2000
Common Design Type
2000, May 11　　Photo.　　Perf. 13¾
262 CD17 70p multi　　　　.75　.75

Angonella
Lakes
A132

2000, June 29　　Photo.　　Perf. 13¾x14
263 A132 35p multi　　　　.40　.40

Casa
Lacruz
A133

2000, July 20　　Photo.　　Perf. 13¾x14
264 A133 35p multi　　　　.40　.40

China, Areny-
Plandolit
Museum — A134

2000, July 27　　　　　Perf. 14x13¾
265 A134 70p multi　　　　.80　.80

2000 Summer
Olympics,
Sydney — A135

2000, Sept. 29　　Photo.　　Perf. 14x13½
266 A135 70p multi　　　　.75　.75

European
Convention
on Human
Rights,
50th Anniv.
A136

2000, Nov. 3　　　　　Perf. 13½x14
267 A136 70p multi　　　　.75　.75

Natl. Archives,
25th
Anniv. — A137

2000, Nov. 14　　　　　Perf. 14x13½
268 A137 35p multi　　　　.35　.35

Christmas — A138

2000, Nov. 22
269 A138 35p multi　　　　.35　.35

Rec de
Solà — A139

2001, Mar. 30　　Photo.　　Perf. 14x13¾
270 A139 40p multi　　　　.40　.40

Europa
A140

2001, May 16　　　　　Perf. 13¾x14
271 A140 75p multi　　　　.80　.80

Casa Palau, Sant Julià de Lòria — A141

2001, June 20 Photo. Perf. 14x13¾

272 A141 75p multi .80 .80

Chapel of the Virgin of Meritxell, 25th Anniv. of Rebuilding — A142

2001, Sept. 7 Photo. Perf. 14x13¾

273 A142 40p multi .45 .45

Natl. Auditorium, 10th Anniv. A143

2001, Sept. 20 Perf. 13¾x14

274 A143 75p multi .85 .85

Christmas A144

2001, Nov. 20 Photo. Perf. 13¾x14

275 A144 40p multi .45 .45

AIR POST STAMPS

AP1

Unwmk.

1951, June 27 Engr. Perf. 11

C1 AP1 1p dark violet brown 19.00 4.25

> Catalogue values for unused stamps in this section, from this point to the end of the section, are for Never Hinged items.

AP2 AP3

Litho. & Engr.

1983, Oct. 20 Perf. 13

C2 AP2 20p brown & bis brn .25 .20

Jaime Sansa Nequi, Episcopal Church official.

1984, Oct. 25 Photo. Perf. 13

C3 AP3 20p multicolored .30 .20

Pyrenees Art Center.

Bishops of Urgel Type of 1979

1985, June 13 Engr. Perf. 13½

C4 A42 20p Ramon Iglesias .30 .20

SPECIAL DELIVERY STAMPS

Special Delivery Stamp of Spain, 1905 Overprinted

1928 Unwmk. Perf. 14

Without Control Number on Back

E1 SD1 20c red 62.50 65.00
    Never hinged 85.00

With Control Number on Back

E2 SD1 20c pale red 40.00 45.00
    Never hinged 52.50

Eagle over Mountain Pass — SD2

1929 Perf. 14

With Control Number on Back

E3 SD2 20c scarlet 18.00 18.00
    Never hinged 24.00

Perf 11½ examples are numbered A000.000 and are specimens. Value, $300.

1937 Perf. 11½x11

Without Control Number on Back

E4 SD2 20c red 6.75 6.50
    Never hinged 7.50

Arms and Squirrel — SD3

1949 Unwmk. Engr. Perf. 10x9½

E5 SD3 25c red 4.00 4.00

ANDORRA, FRENCH ADMIN.

Stamps and Types of France, 1900-1929, Overprinted

Perf. 14x13½

1931, June 16 Unwmk.

1	A16	1c gray	.45	.60
a.		Double overprint	1,000.	1,000.
2	A16	2c red brown	.45	.70
3	A16	3c orange	.45	.70
4	A16	5c green	1.25	1.25
5	A16	10c lilac	2.25	1.75
6	A22	15c red brown	3.00	3.00
7	A22	20c red brown	4.25	4.00
8	A22	25c yellow brn	5.75	4.00
9	A22	30c green	4.75	4.00
10	A22	40c ultra	5.75	6.75
11	A20	45c lt violet	9.50	7.25
12	A20	50c vermilion	7.00	6.00
13	A20	65c gray green	14.00	12.75
14	A22	75c rose lilac	16.00	14.75
15	A22	90c red	20.00	17.50
16	A20	1fr dull blue	21.00	20.00
17	A22	1.50fr light blue	24.00	25.00

Overprinted

18	A18	2fr org & pale bl	15.00	17.50
19	A18	3fr brt vio & rose	57.50	62.50
20	A18	5fr dk bl & buff	72.50	100.00
21	A18	10fr grn & red	175.00	210.00
22	A18	20fr mag & grn	225.00	275.00
		Nos. 1-22 (22)	684.85	795.00

See No. P1 for ½c on 1c gray.
Nos. 9, 15 and 17 were not issued in France without overprint.

Chapel of Meritxell A50

Bridge of St. Anthony A51

St. Miguel d'Engolasters A52 Gorge of St. Julia A53

Old Andorra A54

1932-43 Engr. Perf. 13

23	A50	1c gray blk	.25	.25
24	A50	2c violet	.40	.40
25	A50	3c brown	.30	.30
26	A50	5c blue green	.40	.40
27	A51	10c dull lilac	.65	.60
28	A50	15c deep red	1.00	1.00
29	A51	20c lt rose	6.25	4.50
30	A52	25c brown	2.25	2.25
31	A51	25c brn car ('37)	4.50	6.50
32	A51	30c emerald	1.75	1.50
33	A51	40c ultra	5.00	4.25
34	A51	40c brn blk ('39)	.65	.60
35	A51	45c lt red	6.00	5.00
36	A51	45c bl grn ('39)	3.00	2.50
37	A52	50c lilac rose	6.50	5.00
38	A51	50c lt vio ('39)	3.00	2.50
38A	A51	50c grn ('40)	1.40	1.40
39	A51	55c lt vio ('38)	9.50	6.00
40	A51	60c yel brn ('38)	.60	.50
41	A52	65c yel grn	35.00	35.00
42	A51	65c blue ('38)	6.50	5.50
43	A52	70c red ('39)	1.25	1.00
44	A52	75c violet	3.25	2.50
45	A51	75c ultra ('39)	2.50	2.25
46	A51	80c green ('38)	13.00	9.50
46A	A53	80c bl grn ('40)	.25	.30
47	A53	90c deep rose	3.25	2.25
48	A53	90c dk grn ('39)	3.25	2.25
49	A53	1fr blue grn	9.50	6.00
50	A53	1fr scarlet ('38)	15.00	15.00
51	A53	1fr dp ultra ('39)	.25	.25
51A	A53	1.20fr brt vio ('42)	.25	.25
52	A50	1.25fr rose car ('33)	35.00	25.00
52A	A50	1.25fr rose ('38)	3.00	1.40
52B	A53	1.30fr sepia ('40)	.25	.25
53	A54	1.50fr ultra	8.25	7.50
53A	A53	1.50fr crim ('40)	.25	.25
54	A53	1.75fr violet ('33)	80.00	80.00
55	A53	1.75fr dk bl ('38)	30.00	22.50
56	A53	2fr red violet	3.75	3.50
56A	A50	2fr rose red ('40)	1.00	.65
56B	A50	2fr dk bl grn ('42)	.25	.20
57	A50	2.15fr dk vio ('38)	40.00	27.50
58	A50	2.25fr ultra ('39)	4.00	3.00
58A	A50	2.40fr red ('42)	.25	.20
59	A50	2.50fr gray blk ('39)	4.00	3.00
59A	A50	2.50fr dp ultra ('40)	1.40	1.25
60	A53	3fr orange brn	3.75	3.50
60A	A50	3fr red brn ('40)	.30	.25
60B	A50	4fr sl bl ('42)	.30	.25
60C	A50	4.50fr dp vio ('42)	.75	.75
61	A54	5fr brown	.40	.35
62	A54	10fr violet	.45	.40
62B	A54	15fr dp ultra ('42)	.50	.40
63	A54	20fr rose lake	.50	.40
63A	A51	50fr turq bl ('43)	1.00	.65
		Nos. 23-63A (56)	365.00	310.50

A 20c ultra exists. Value $12,500.

No. 37 Surcharged with Bars and New Value in Black

1935, Sept. 25

64	A52	20c on 50c lil rose	11.00	10.00
a.		Double surcharge	1,900.	

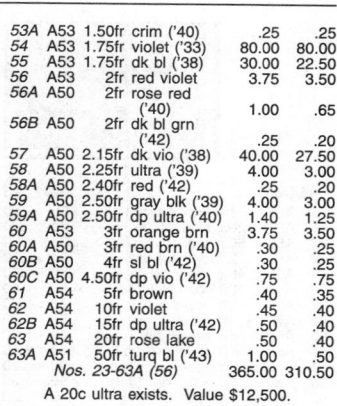

Coat of Arms
A55 A56

1936-42 Perf. 14x13

65	A55	1c black ('37)	.20	.20
66	A55	2c blue	.20	.20
67	A55	3c brown	.20	.20
68	A55	5c rose lilac	.20	.20
69	A55	10c ultra ('37)	.20	.20
70	A55	15c red violet	.50	.50
71	A55	20c emerald ('37)	.20	.20
72	A55	30c cop red ('38)	.30	.30
72A	A55	30c blk brn ('42)	.20	.20
73	A55	35c Prus grn ('38)	30.00	30.00
74	A55	40c cop red ('42)	.20	.20
75	A55	50c Prus grn ('42)	.20	.20
76	A55	60c turq bl ('42)	.20	.20
77	A55	70c vio ('42)	.20	.20
		Nos. 65-77 (14)	33.00	33.00

> Catalogue values for unused stamps in this section, from this point to the end of the section, are for Never Hinged items.

1944

78	A56	10c violet	.20	.20
79	A56	30c deep magenta	.20	.20
80	A56	40c dull blue	.20	.20
81	A56	50c orange red	.20	.20
82	A56	60c black	.20	.20
83	A56	70c brt red violet	.20	.20
84	A56	80c blue green	.20	.20
		Nos. 78-84 (7)	1.40	1.40

See No. 114.

St. Jean de Caselles A57

La Maison des Vallees A58

Old Andorra A59

Provost
A60

1944-47　　　　　　　　　**Perf. 13**
85	A57	1fr brown violet	.35	.20
86	A57	1.20fr blue	.20	.20
87	A57	1.50fr red	.35	.20
88	A57	2fr dk blue grn	.20	.20
89	A58	2.40fr rose red	.30	.20
90	A58	2.50fr rose red ('46)	4.50	1.40
91	A58	3fr sepia	.20	.20
92	A58	4fr ultra	.35	.20
93	A59	4.50fr brown blk	.40	.20
94	A58	4.50fr dk bl grn ('47)	7.00	3.50
95	A59	5fr ultra	.30	.20
96	A59	5fr Prus grn ('46)	.55	.30
97	A59	6fr rose car ('45)	.40	.20
98	A59	10fr Prus green	.20	.20
99	A59	10fr ultra ('46)	.30	.20
100	A60	15fr rose lilac	.65	.25
101	A60	20fr deep blue	.75	.45
102	A60	25fr lt rose red ('46)	4.50	2.25
103	A60	40fr dk green ('46)	4.50	3.00
104	A60	50fr sepia	2.00	1.10
		Nos. 85-104 (20)	28.00	14.65

1948-49
105	A58	4fr lt blue grn	1.00	.80
106	A59	6fr violet brn	.50	.40
107	A59	8fr indigo	1.50	1.25
108	A59	12fr bright red	1.00	.90
109	A59	12fr blue grn ('49)	1.10	.90
110	A59	15fr crimson ('49)	.60	.50
111	A59	18fr deep blue	3.75	2.00
112	A60	20fr dark violet	3.00	2.25
113	A60	25fr ultra ('49)	2.00	1.50
		Nos. 105-113 (9)	14.45	10.50

1949-51　　　　　　　　**Perf. 14x13, 13**
114	A56	1fr deep blue	1.25	.75
115	A57	3fr red ('51)	6.00	5.00
116	A57	4fr sepia	3.00	2.50
117	A58	5fr emerald	3.50	3.00
118	A58	5fr purple ('51)	6.00	5.00
119	A58	6fr blue grn ('51)	5.00	4.50
120	A58	8fr brown	1.50	1.00
121	A59	15fr blk brn ('51)	6.50	5.00
122	A59	18fr rose red ('51)	17.50	12.00
123	A60	30fr ultra ('51)	30.00	12.00
		Nos. 114-123 (10)	80.25	50.75

Les Escaldres
Spa — A61

St. Coloma
Belfry
A62

Designs: 15fr-25fr, Gothic cross. 30fr-75fr, Village of Les Bons.

1955-58　**Unwmk.**　**Engr.**　**Perf. 13**
124	A61	1fr dk gray bl	.20	.20
125	A61	2fr dp green	.20	.20
126	A61	3fr red	.25	.20
127	A61	5fr chocolate	.25	.20
128	A62	6fr dk bl grn	.50	.40
129	A62	8fr rose brown	.50	.45
130	A62	10fr brt violet	.80	.55
131	A62	12fr indigo	.90	.60
132	A61	15fr red	1.25	.85
133	A61	18fr blue grn	1.25	.85
134	A61	20fr dp purple	1.90	1.50
135	A61	25fr sepia	2.25	1.50
136	A62	30fr deep blue	26.00	16.00
137	A62	35fr Prus bl ('57)	10.00	6.75
138	A62	40fr dk green	27.50	18.00
139	A62	50fr cerise	3.50	2.25
140	A62	65fr purple ('58)	9.50	5.75
141	A62	70fr chestnut ('57)	6.50	5.75
142	A62	75fr violet blue	45.00	32.50
		Nos. 124-142 (19)	138.25	94.50

Issued: 35fr, 70fr, 8/19; 65fr, 2/10; others, 2/15.

Coat of Arms — A63

Gothic
Cross,
Meritxell
A64

65c, 85c, 1fr, Engolasters Lake.

1961, June 19　**Typo.**　**Perf. 14x13**
143	A63	5c brt green & blk	.20	.20
144	A63	10c red, pink & blk	.20	.20
145	A63	15c blue & black	.20	.20
146	A63	20c yellow & brown	.20	.20

　　　　　　　　Engr.　　　**Perf. 13**
147	A64	25c violet, bl & grn	.25	.25
148	A64	30c mar, ol grn & brn	.30	.30
149	A64	45c indigo, bl & grn	13.00	6.50
150	A64	50c pur, lt brn & ol grn	1.00	1.00
151	A64	65c bl, ol & brn	17.50	14.00
152	A64	85c rose lil, vio bl & brn	17.50	14.00
153	A64	1fr grnsh bl, ind & brn	1.00	1.00
		Nos. 143-153 (11)	51.35	37.85

See Nos. 161-166A.

Imperforates

Most stamps of Andorra, French Administration, from 1961 onward exist imperforate in issued and trial colors, and also in small presentation sheets in issued colors.

Telstar and Globe Showing Andover
and Pleumeur-Bodou — A65

1962, Sept. 29　　　　　　**Engr.**
154	A65	50c ultra & purple	.90	.90

1st television connection of the US and Europe through the Telstar satellite, 7/11-12.

"La
Sardane"
A66

Charlemagne Crossing Andorra — A67

1fr, Louis le Debonnaire giving founding charter.

1963, June 22　**Unwmk.**　**Perf. 13**
155	A66	20c lil rose, cl & ol grn	2.75	2.75
156	A67	50c sl grn & dk car rose	4.50	4.50
157	A67	1fr red brn, ultra & dk grn	7.00	7.00
		Nos. 155-157 (3)	14.25	14.25

Old Andorra Church and Champs-
Elysées Palace — A68

1964, Jan. 20　　　　　　　**Engr.**
158	A68	25c blk, grn & vio brn	.90	.75

"PHILATEC," Intl. Philatelic and Postal Techniques Exhib., Paris, June 5-21, 1964.

Bishop of Urgel and Seigneur of
Caboet Confirming Co-Principality,
1288 — A69

Design: 60c, Napoleon re-establishing Co-principality, 1806.

1964, Apr. 25　**Engr.**　　**Perf. 13**
159	A69	60c dk brn, red brn & sl grn	9.00	9.00
160	A69	1fr brt bl, org brn & blk	9.00	9.00

Arms Type of 1961

1964, May 16　**Typo.**　**Perf. 14x13**
161	A63	1c dk blue & gray	.25	.20
162	A63	2c black & orange	.25	.20
163	A63	12c purple, emer & yel	.50	.40
164	A63	18c black, lil & pink	.50	.40
		Nos. 161-164 (4)	1.50	1.20

Scenic Type of 1961

Designs: 40c, 45c, Gothic Cross, Meritxell. 60c, 90c, Pond of Engolasters.

1965-71　　**Engr.**　　**Perf. 13**
165	A64	40c dk brn, org brn & sl grn	.50	.50
165A	A64	45c vio bl, ol bis & slate	.90	.75
166	A64	60c org brn & dk brn	.60	.60
166A	A64	90c ultra, bl grn & bister	.50	.50
		Nos. 165-166A (4)	2.50	2.35

Issued: 40c, 60c, Apr. 24, 1965. 45c, June 13, 1970. 90c, Aug. 28, 1971.

Syncom Satellite
over Pleumeur-
Bodou
Station — A70

1965, May 17　　　　　　**Unwmk.**
167	A70	60c dp car, lil & bl	3.25	3.00

Cent. of the ITU.

Andorra House,
Paris — A71

1965, June 5
168	A71	25c dk bl, org brn & ol gray	.80	.65

Ski
Lift — A72

Design: 25c, Chair lift, vert.

1966, Apr. 2　**Engr.**　　**Perf. 13**
169	A72	25c brt bl, grn & dk brn	.80	.70
170	A72	40c mag, brt ultra & sep	1.10	1.00

Winter sports in Andorra.

FR-1 Satellite — A73

1966, May 7　　　　　　**Perf. 13**
171	A73	60c brt bl, grn & dk grn	1.25	1.10

Issued to commemorate the launching of the scientific satellite FR-1, Dec. 6, 1965.

Common Design Types
pictured following the introduction.

Europa Issue, 1966
Common Design Type

1966, Sept. 24　　　　**Perf. 13**
Size: 21½x35½mm
172	CD9	60c brown		2.50	2.00

Folk Dancers,
Sculpture by
Josep
Viladomat — A74

Telephone
Encircling the
Globe — A75

1967, Apr. 29　**Engr.**　**Perf. 13**
173	A74	30c ol grn, dp grn & slate	.55	.30

Cent. (in 1966) of the New Reform, which reaffirmed and strengthened political freedom in Andorra.

Europa Issue, 1967
Common Design Type

1967, Apr. 29
Size: 22x36mm
174	CD10	30c bluish blk & lt bl	4.50	2.50
175	CD10	60c dk red & brt pink	6.50	3.50

1967, Apr. 29
176	A75	60c dk car, vio & blk	.90	.60

Automatic telephone service.

Injured
Father at
Home
A76

1967, Sept. 23　**Engr.**　**Perf. 13**
177	A76	2.30fr ocher, dk red brn & brn red	6.00	4.50

Introduction of Social Security System.

Jesus in Garden of
Gethsemane — A77

Designs (from 16th century frescoes in La
Maison des Vallees): 30c, The Kiss of Judas.
60c, The Descent from the Cross (Pieta).

1967, Sept. 23
178 A77 25c black & red brn .40 .35
179 A77 30c purple & red lilac .40 .35
180 A77 60c indigo & Prus blue 1.00 .70
Nos. 178-180 (3) 1.80 1.40

See Nos. 185-187.

Downhill
Skier — A78

1968, Jan. 27 Engr. Perf. 13
181 A78 40c org, ver & red lil .65 .55
10th Winter Olympic Games, Grenoble,
France, Feb. 6-18.

Europa Issue, 1968
Common Design Type
1968, Apr. 27 Engr. Perf. 13
Size: 36x22mm
182 CD11 30c gray & brt bl 6.50 3.50
183 CD11 60c brown & lilac 8.50 4.75

High Jump
A79

1968, Oct. 12 Engr. Perf. 13
184 A79 40c brt blue & brn .90 .70
19th Olympic Games, Mexico City, Oct. 12-27.

Fresco Type of 1967
Designs (from 16th century frescoes in La
Maison des Vallees): 25c, The Scourging of
Christ. 30c, Christ Carrying the Cross. 60c,
The Crucifixion. (All horiz.)

1968, Oct. 12
185 A77 25c dk grn & gray grn .35 .35
186 A77 30c dk brown & lilac .40 .40
187 A77 60c dk car & vio brn 1.25 1.25
Nos. 185-187 (3) 2.00 2.00

Europa Issue, 1969
Common Design Type
1969, Apr. 26 Engr. Perf. 13
188 CD12 40c rose car, gray & dl bl 7.50 4.00
189 CD12 70c indigo, dl red & ol 11.50 6.00
10th anniv. of the Conf. of European Postal
and Telecommunications Administrations.

Kayak on Isere   Drops of Water
River   & Diamond
A80   A80a

1969, Aug. 2 Engr. Perf. 13
190 A80 70c dk sl grn, ultra & ind 1.75 1.75
Intl. Canoe & Kayak Championships, Bourg-
Saint-Maurice, Savoy, July 31-Aug. 6.

1969, Sept. 27 Engr. Perf. 13
191 A80a 70c blk, dp ultra & grnsh bl 3.50 2.00
European Water Charter.

St. John,
the Woman
and the
Dragon
A81

The Revelation (From the Altar of St. John,
Caselles): 40c, St. John Hearing Voice from
Heaven on Patmos. 70c, St. John and the
Seven Candlesticks.

1969, Oct. 18
192 A81 30c brn, dp pur & brn red .40 .40
193 A81 40c gray, dk brn & brn ol .80 .80
194 A81 70c dk red, maroon & brt rose lilac 1.25 1.25
Nos. 192-194 (3) 2.45 2.45

See Nos. 199-201, 207-209, 214-216.

Field Ball — A82   Shot Put — A83

1970, Feb. 21 Engr. Perf. 13
195 A82 80c multi 1.60 1.10
Issued to publicize the 7th International
Field Ball Games, France, Feb. 26-Mar. 8.

Europa Issue, 1970
Common Design Type
1970, May 2 Engr. Perf. 13
Size: 36x22mm
196 CD13 40c orange 6.00 3.25
197 CD13 80c violet blue 11.50 6.00

1970, Sept. 11 Engr. Perf. 13
198 A83 80c bl & dk brn 1.75 1.25
1st European Junior Athletic Championships, Colombes, France, Sept. 11-13.

Altar Type of 1969
The Revelation (from the Altar of St. John,
Caselles): 30c, St. John recording angel's
message. 40c, Angel erecting column symbolizing faithful in heaven. 80c, St. John's trial in
kettle of boiling oil.

1970, Oct. 24
199 A81 30c dp car, dk brn & brt pur .60 .55
200 A81 40c violet & slate grn 1.00 .85
201 A81 80c ol, dk bl & car rose 1.75 1.50
Nos. 199-201 (3) 3.35 2.90

Ice Skating
A84

1971, Feb. 20 Engr. Perf. 13
202 A84 80c dk red, red lil & pur 1.75 1.50
World Figure Skating Championships,
Lyons, France, Feb. 23-28.

Capercaillie — A85

Nature protection: No. 204, Brown bear.

1971, Apr. 24 Photo. Perf. 13
203 A85 80c multicolored 2.00 1.50
Engr.
204 A85 80c blue, grn & brn 3.00 2.00

Europa Issue, 1971
Common Design Type
1971, May 8 Engr. Perf. 13
Size: 35½x22mm
205 CD14 50c rose red 6.50 3.50
206 CD14 80c lt blue green 11.50 6.00

Altar Type of 1969
The Revelation (from the Altar of St. John,
Caselles): 30c, St. John preaching, Rev. 1:3.
50c, "The Sign of the Beast . . ." Rev. 16:1-2.
90c, The Woman, Rev. 17:1.

1971, Sept. 18
207 A81 30c dl grn, ol & brt grn .65 .55
208 A81 50c rose car, org & ol brn .75 .55
209 A81 90c blk, dk pur & bl 1.50 1.25
Nos. 207-209 (3) 2.90 2.35

Europa Issue 1972
Common Design Type
1972, Apr. 29 Photo. Perf. 13
Size: 21½x37mm
210 CD15 50c brt mag & multi 6.50 3.50
211 CD15 90c multicolored 12.00 6.50

Golden
Eagle
A86

1972, May 27 Engr.
212 A86 60c dk grn, olive & plum 3.25 2.00
Nature protection.

Shooting
A87

1972, July 8
213 A87 1fr dk purple 2.00 1.50
20th Olympic Games, Munich, 8/26-9/11.

Altar Type of 1969
The Revelation (from the Altar of St. John,
Caselles): 30c, St. John, bishop and servant.
50c, Resurrection of Lazarus. 90c, Angel with
lance and nails.

1972, Sept. 16 Engr. Perf. 13
214 A81 30c dk ol, gray & red lil .65 .55
215 A81 50c vio blue & slate .75 .75
216 A81 90c dk Prus bl & sl grn 1.50 1.40
Nos. 214-216 (3) 2.90 2.70

De Gaulle as
Coprince of
Andorra — A88

90c, De Gaulle in front of Maison des
Vallées.

1972, Oct. 23 Engr. Perf. 13
217 A88 50c violet blue 1.00 .90
218 A88 90c dk carmine 1.50 1.40
a. Pair, #217-218 + label 2.75 2.75
Visit of Charles de Gaulle to Andorra, 5th
anniv.
See Nos. 399-400.

Europa Issue 1973
Common Design Type
1973, Apr. 28 Photo. Perf. 13
Size: 36x22mm
219 CD16 50c violet & multi 6.00 3.25
220 CD16 90c dk red & multi 10.00 6.00

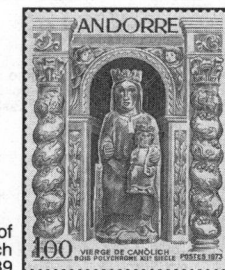

Virgin of
Canolich
A89

1973, June 16 Engr. Perf. 13
221 A89 1fr ol, Prus bl & vio 1.40 1.10

Lily — A90   Blue
                    Titmouse — A91

45c, Iris. 50c, Columbine. 65c, Tobacco.
No. 226, Pinks. No. 227, Narcissuses.

1973-74 Photo. Perf. 13
222 A90 30c car rose & multi .30 .30
223 A90 45c yel grn & multi .20 .20
224 A90 50c buff & multi 1.00 1.00
225 A90 65c gray & multi .30 .30
226 A90 80c ultra & multi .75 .75
227 A90 90c grnsh bl & multi .65 .65
Nos. 222-227 (6) 3.20 3.20

See Nos. 238-240.

1973-74 Photo. Perf. 13
Nature protection: 60c, Citril finch and mistletoe. 80c, Eurasian bullfinch. 1fr, Lesser
spotted woodpecker.
228 A91 60c buff & multi 3.00 1.50
229 A91 80c gray & multi 2.25 1.25
230 A91 90c gray & multi 1.75 1.00
231 A91 1fr yel grn & multi 1.75 1.25
Nos. 228-231 (4) 8.75 5.00

Europa Issue 1974

Virgin of Pal — A92

90c, Virgin of Santa Coloma. Statues are polychrome 12th cent. carvings by rural artists.

1974, Apr. 27   Engr.   Perf. 13
232 A92 50c multicolored   9.50 5.00
233 A92 90c multicolored   13.00 7.00

Arms of Andorra and Cahors Bridge — A93

1974, Aug. 24   Engr.   Perf. 13
234 A93 1fr blue, vio & org   .90 .60

First anniv. of meeting of the co-princes of Andorra: Pres. Georges Pompidou of France and Msgr. Juan Marti Alanis, Bishop of Urgel.

Mail Box, Chutes and Globe — A94

1974, Oct. 5   Engr.   Perf. 13
235 A94 1.20fr multi   1.00 .90

Centenary of Universal Postal Union.

Coronation of St. Marti, 16th Century — A95

Europa: 80c, Crucifixion, 16th cent., vert.

Perf. 11½x13, 13x11½
1975, Apr. 26   Photo.
236 A95 80c gold & multi   4.25 2.75
237 A95 1.20fr gold & multi   5.75 3.50

Flower Type of 1973

Designs: 60c, Gentian. 80c, Anemone. 1.20fr, Autumn crocus.

1975, May 10   Photo.   Perf. 13
238 A90 60c olive & multi   .25 .25
239 A90 80c brt rose & multi   .80 .50
240 A90 1.20fr green & multi   .50 .45
Nos. 238-240 (3)   1.55 1.20

Abstract Design — A96

1975, June 7   Engr.   Perf. 13
241 A96 2fr bl, magenta & emer   1.40 1.25
ARPHILA 75 International Philatelic Exhibition, Paris, June 6-16.

A97   A98

1975, Aug. 23   Engr.   Perf. 13
242 A97 80c violet bl & blk   .65 .60

Georges Pompidou (1911-74), pres. of France and co-prince of Andorra (1969-74).

1975, Nov. 8   Engr.   Perf. 13
243 A98 1.20fr Costume, IWY Emblem   .90 .65

International Women's Year.

Skier and Snowflake A99

1976, Jan. 31   Engr.   Perf. 13
244 A99 1.20fr multicolored   .90 .65

12th Winter Olympic Games, Innsbruck, Austria, Feb. 4-15.

Telephone and Satellite — A100

1976, Mar. 20   Engr.   Perf. 13
245 A100 1fr multicolored   .70 .60

Centenary of first telephone call by Alexander Graham Bell, Mar. 10, 1976.

Catalan Forge A101

Europa: 1.20fr, Lacemaker.

1976, May 8   Engr.   Perf. 13
246 A101 80c multi   1.75 1.00
247 A101 1.20fr multi   2.75 1.50

Thomas Jefferson A102   Trapshooting A103

1976, July 3   Engr.   Perf. 13
248 A102 1.20fr multi   .90 .70

American Bicentennial.

1976, July 17   Engr.   Perf. 13
249 A103 2fr multi   1.40 .90

21st Olympic Games, Montreal, Canada, July 17-Aug. 1.

Meritxell Sanctuary and Old Chapel — A104

1976, Sept. 4   Engr.   Perf. 13
250 A104 1fr multi   .70 .60

Dedication of rebuilt Meritxell Church, Sept. 8, 1976.

Apollo — A105   Ermine — A106

Design: 1.40fr, Morio butterfly.

1976, Oct. 16   Photo.   Perf. 13
251 A105 80c black & multi   1.60 1.00
252 A105 1.40fr salmon & multi   2.00 1.75

Nature protection.

1977, Apr. 2   Photo.   Perf. 13
253 A106 1fr vio bl, gray & blk   1.40 1.25

Nature protection.

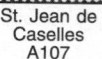

St. Jean de Caselles A107   Manual Digest, 1748, Arms of Andorra A108

Europa: 1.40fr, Sant Vicens Castle.

1977, Apr. 30   Engr.   Perf. 13
254 A107 1fr multi   3.00 1.50
255 A107 1.40fr multi   4.00 2.25

1977, June 11   Engr.   Perf. 13
256 A108 80c grn, bl & brn   .65 .55

Establishment of Institute of Andorran Studies.

St. Romanus of Caesarea A109

1977, July 23   Engr.   Perf. 12½x13
257 A109 2fr multi   1.10 .90

Design from altarpiece in Church of St. Roma de les Bons.

General Council Chamber A110

Guillem d'Arény Plandolit — A111

1977, Sept. 24   Engr.   Perf. 13
258 A110 1.10fr multi   1.50 .90
259 A111 2fr car & dk brn   1.25 .80

Andorran heritage. Guillem d'Arény Plandolit started Andorran reform movement in 1866.

Squirrel — A112

1978, Mar. 18   Engr.   Perf. 13
260 A112 1fr multi   .80 .50

Flag and Valira River Bridge — A113

1978, Apr. 8
261 A113 80c multi   .40 .30

Signing of the treaty establishing the Co-Principality of Andorra, 700th anniv.

Pal Church A114

Europa: 1.40fr, Charlemagne's Castle, Charlemagne on horseback, vert.

1978, Apr. 29   Engr.   Perf. 13
262 A114   1fr multi   2.50 1.25
263 A114   1.40fr multi   3.50 2.25

Virgin of
Sispony
A115

1978, May 20   Engr.   Perf. 12x13
264 A115   2fr multi   1.10 .90

Visura
Tribunal
A116

1978, June 24   Engr.   Perf. 13
265 A116   1.20fr multi   .65 .40

Preamble of 1278 Treaty — A117

1978, Sept. 2   Engr.   Perf. 13x12½
266 A117   1.70fr multi   .65 .40
700th anniversary of the signing of treaty establishing Co-Principality of Andorra.

Pyrenean
Chamois
A118

White Partridges
A119

1979, Mar. 26   Engr.   Perf. 13
267 A118   1fr multi   .40 .35

1979, Apr. 9   Photo.   Perf. 13
268 A119   1.20fr multi   .75 .60
Nature protection. See Nos. 288-289.

French Mailman,
1900 — A120

Europa: 1.70fr, 1st French p.o. in Andorra.

1979, Apr. 28   Engr.   Perf. 13
269 A120   1.20fr multi   1.10 .90
270 A120   1.70fr multi   1.60 1.10

Falcon,
Pre-Roman
Painting
A121

1979, June 2   Engr.   Perf. 12½x13
271 A121   2fr multi   .90 .65

Child with Lambs,
Church, IYC
Emblem. — A122

1979, July 7   Photo.   Perf. 13
272 A122   1.70fr multi   .70 .50
International Year of the Child.

Bas-relief,
Trobada
Monument.
A123

1979, Sept. 29   Engr.   Perf. 13
273 A123   2fr multi   .90 .65
Co-Principality of Andorra, 700th anniv

Judo Hold
A124

Farm House,
Cortinada
A125

1979, Nov. 24   Engr.   Perf. 13
274 A124   1.30fr multi   .65 .45
World Judo Championships, Paris, Dec. 1979.

1980, Jan. 26   Engr.   Perf. 13
275 A125   1.10fr multi   .35 .25

Cross-Country Skiing — A126

1980, Feb. 9
276 A126   1.80fr ultra & lil rose   1.10 .70
13th Winter Olympic Games, Lake Placid, NY, Feb. 12-24.

A128   A129

1980, Aug. 30   Engr.   Perf. 13
278 A128   1.20fr multi   .40 .25
World Bicycling championships.

1980, Apr. 26   Engr.   Perf. 13
Europa: 1.30fr, Charlemagne (742-814). 1.80fr, Napoleon I (1769-1821).
279 A129   1.30fr multi   .40 .30
280 A129   1.80fr gray grn & brn   .60 .40

Pyrenees
Lily — A130

1980   Photo.
281 A130   1.10fr Dog-toothed violet   .40 .25
282 A130   1.30fr shown   .45 .30
Nature protection. Issue dates: 1.10fr, June 21; 1.30fr, May 17.

De La Vall
House,
400th
Anniversary
of
Restoration
A131

1980, Sept. 6   Engr.
283 A131   1.40fr multi   .40 .30

Angel, Church of St. Cerni de Nagol,
Pre-Romanesque Fresco — A132

1980, Oct. 27   Perf. 13x12½
284 A132   2fr multi   .75 .60

Bordes de
Mereig
Mountain
Village
A133

1981, Mar. 21   Engr.   Perf. 13
285 A133   1.40fr bl gray & dk brn   .45 .35

Europa Issue 1981

Ball de
l'Ossa,
Winter
Game
A134

1981, May 16   Engr.
286 A134   1.40fr shown   .55 .40
287 A134   2fr El Contrapas dance   .55 .55

Bird Type of 1979
1981, June 20   Photo.
288 A119   1.20fr Phylloscopus bonelli   .50 .35
289 A119   1.40fr Tichodroma muraria   .55 .40

World Fencing Championship,
Clermont-Ferrand, July 2-13 — A135

1981, July 4   Engr.
290 A135   2fr bl & blk   .60 .45

St. Martin,
12th Cent.
Tapestry
A136

1981, Sept. 5   Engr.   Perf. 12x13
291 A136   3fr multi   1.00 .75

Intl. Drinking
Water Decade
A137

Intl. Year of the
Disabled
A138

1981, Oct. 17   Perf. 13
292 A137   1.60fr multi   .45 .30

1981, Nov. 7
293 A138   2.30fr multi   .70 .55

Europa
1982
A139

1982, May 8   Engr.   Perf. 13
294 A139   1.60fr Creation of Andorran govt., 1982   .50 .35
295 A139   2.30fr Land Council, 1419   .75 .50

1982 World Cup — A140

Various soccer players.

1982, June 12   Engr.   Perf. 13
296   1.60fr red & dk brn   .45 .35
297   2.60fr red & dk brn   .60 .50
a. A140 Pair, #296-297 + label   1.25 .85

Souvenir Sheet

No. 52 — A141

1982, Aug. 21   **Engr.**
298 A141 5fr blk & rose car   1.25 1.25
1st Andorran Stamp Exhib., 8/21-9/19.

Horse, Roman Wall Painting — A142

1982, Sept. 4   **Photo.**   *Perf. 13x12½*
299 A142 3fr multi   1.00 .80

Wild Cat — A143

1982, Oct. 9   **Engr.**   *Perf. 13*
300 A143 1.80fr shown   1.10 .75
301 A143 2.60fr Pine trees   .75 .55

TB Bacillus Centenary A144

St. Thomas Aquinas (1225-74) A145

1982, Nov. 13
302 A144 2.10fr Koch, lungs   .55 .45

1982, Dec. 4
303 A145 2fr multi   .55 .45

Manned Flight Bicentenary A146

1983, Feb. 26   **Engr.**
304 A146 2fr multi   .55 .45

Nature Protection A147

1983, Apr. 16   **Engr.**   *Perf. 13*
305 A147 1fr Birch trees   .35 .25
306 A147 1.50fr Trout   .50 .35
See Nos. 325-326.

Europa 1983 A148

Catalane Gold Works.

1983, May 7   **Engr.**   *Perf. 13*
307 A148 1.80fr Exterior   .70 .50
308 A148 2.60fr Interior   .90 .60

30th Anniv. of Customs Cooperation Council — A149

1983, May 14
309 A149 3fr Letter of King Louis XIII   1.10 .75

First Arms of Valleys of Andorra A150

1983, Sept. 3   **Engr.**   *Perf. 13*
310 A150   5c olive grn & red   .20 .20
311 A150 10c grn & olive grn   .20 .20
312 A150 20c brt pur & red   .20 .20
313 A150 30c brn vio & red   .25 .20
314 A150 40c dk bl & ultra   .25 .20
315 A150 50c gray & red   .20 .20
316 A150   1fr deep magenta   .20 .20
317 A150   2fr org red & red brn   .60 .40
318 A150   5fr dk brn & red   1.75 1.40
    Nos. 310-318 (9)   3.85 3.20
See Nos. 329-335, 380-385, 464-465.

Painting, Cortinada Church A151

1983, Sept. 24   *Perf. 12x13*
319 A151 4fr multi   1.25 .75

Plandolit House — A152

1983, Oct. 15   **Photo.**   *Perf. 13*
320 A152 1.60fr dp ultra & brn   .45 .30

1984 Winter Olympics A153

1984, Feb. 18   **Engr.**
321 A153 2.80fr multicolored   .75 .50

Pyrenees Region Work Community (Labor Org.) A154

1984, Apr. 28   **Engr.**   *Perf. 13*
322 A154 3fr brt blue & sepia   .85 .60

Europa (1959-84) A155

1984, May 5   **Engr.**
323 A155   2fr brt grn   .90 .60
324 A155 2.80fr rose car   1.10 .75

Nature Protection Type of 1983

1984, July 7   **Engr.**   *Perf. 13*
325 A147 1.70fr Chestnut tree   .50 .30
326 A147 2.10fr Walnut tree   .70 .50

Pyrenees Art Center A155a

1984, Sept. 7   **Engr.**
327 A155a 3fr multi   .90 .65

Romanesque Fresco, Church of St. Cerni de Nagol — A156

1984, Nov. 17   *Perf. 12x13*
328 A156 5fr multi   1.60 1.25

First Arms Type of 1983

1984-87   **Engr.**   *Perf. 13*
329 A150 1.90fr emerald   .90 .60
330 A150 2.20fr red orange   .50 .35
   a.   Bklt. pane, 2 #329, 6 #330   5.50
331 A150   3fr bl grn & red brn   1.00 .65
332 A150   4fr brt org & brn   1.50 .90
333 A150   10fr brn org & blk   2.25 1.50
334 A150   15fr grn & dk grn   3.75 2.25
335 A150   20fr brt bl & red brn   4.75 3.00
    Nos. 329-335 (7)   14.65 9.25
Nos. 329-330 issued in booklets only.
Issued: 3fr, 20fr, 12/1/84; 10fr, 2/9/85; 4fr, 15fr, 4/19/86; 1.90fr, 2.20fr, 3/28/87.

Saint Julia Valley A157

1985, Apr. 13   **Engr.**
336 A157 2fr multi   .80 .55

Europa 1985 — A158   Intl. Youth Year — A159

1985, May 4   **Engr.**
337 A158 2.10fr Le Val D'Andorre   1.25 .85
338 A158   3fr Instruments   1.75 1.10

1985, June 8   **Engr.**
339 A159 3fr multi   .90 .60

Wildlife Conservation — A160

1985, Aug. 3   **Photo.**
340 A160 1.80fr Anas platyrhynchos .65 .40
341 A160 2.20fr Carduelis carduelis .85 .60

Two Saints, Medieval Fresco in St. Cerni de Nagol Church A161

1985, Sept. 14   **Engr.**   *Perf. 12½x13*
342 A161 5fr multi   1.50 1.10

Postal Museum Inauguration A162

1986, Mar. 22   **Engr.**   *Perf. 13*
343 A162 2.20fr like No. 269   .80 .40

Europa 1986 A163

1986, May 3   **Engr.**   *Perf. 13*
344 A163 2.20fr Ansalonga   1.25 .75
345 A163 3.20fr Isard   2.00 1.25

1986 World Cup Soccer Championships, Mexico — A164

1986, June 14
346 A164 3fr multi   .90 .50

Angonella Lake A165

1986, June 28
347 A165 2.20fr multi   .65 .40

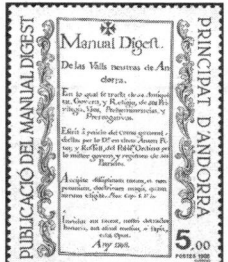

Manual Digest Frontispiece, 1748 — A166

1986, Sept. 6   Engr.
348 A166 5fr chnt brn, gray ol & blk   1.60 .80

Intl. Peace Year A167

1986, Sept. 29
349 A167 1.90fr bl gray & grnsh bl   .65 .40

A168

1986, Oct. 18   Engr.   Perf. 13½x13
350 A168 1.90fr St. Vicenc D'Enclar .75 .40

Contemporary Natl. Coat of Arms — A169

1987, Mar. 27   Litho.   Perf. 12½x13
351 A169 2.20fr multi   1.50 .80

Visit of the French co-prince.

Europa 1987 A170

1987, May 2   Engr.   Perf. 13
352 A170 2.20fr Meritxell Sanctuary   1.00 .65
353 A170 3.40fr Pleta D'Ordino   1.50 .90

Ransol Village — A171

1987, June 13   Photo.
354 A171 1.90fr multicolored   1.00 .50

Nature A172

1987, July 4
355 A172 1.90fr Cavall rogenc   1.10 .60
356 A172 2.20fr Graellsia isabellae   1.40 .70

Aryalsu, Romanesque Painting, La Cortinada Church — A173

Litho. & Engr.
1987, Sept. 5   Perf. 12½x13
357 A173 5fr multi   2.00 1.00

Hiker Looking at Map A174

1987, Sept. 19   Engr.   Perf. 13
358 A174 2fr olive, grn & dark brn vio   .80 .45

Medieval Iron Key, La Cortinada A175

1987, Oct. 17   Litho.
359 A175 3fr multi   1.10 .60

Andorran Coat of Arms — A176

Booklet Stamp
1988, Feb. 6   Engr.   Perf. 13
360 A176 2.20fr red   .80 .40
  a. Bkt. pane of 5   4.00
      Complete bklt., 2 #360a   8.00

See Nos. 388-389B.

Shoemaker's Last from Roc de l'Oral — A177

1988, Feb. 13   Photo.
361 A177 3fr multi   1.25 .60

Rugby A178

1988, Mar. 19   Engr.   Perf. 13½x13
362 A178 2.20fr emer grn, Prus grn & brn   .95 .50

Europa 1988 A179   Hot Springs, Escaldes A180

Transport and communication: 2.20fr, Broadcast tower. 3.60fr, Computer graphics.

1988, May 2   Engr.   Perf. 13
363 A179 2.20fr multicolored   1.25 .75
364 A179 3.60fr multicolored   1.75 1.25

1988, May 14   Engr.
365 A180 2.20fr Prus blue, org brn & emer   .85 .50

Tor D'Ansalonga Farmhouse, Ansalonga Pass — A181

1988, June 13   Engr.
366 A181 2fr multi   .75 .40

Sheepdog — A182

1988, July 2   Photo.
367 A182   2fr shown   .90 .50
368 A182 2.20fr Hare   1.10 .60

Roman Fresco, 8th Cent., St. Steven's Church, Andorre-La-Vieille — A183

1988, Sept. 3   Engr.   Perf. 13x12½
369 A183 5fr multicolored   1.75 .90

French Revolution, Bicent. — A184

1989, Jan. 1   Litho.   Perf. 13
370 A184 2.20fr red & vio bl   .85 .50

Poble de Pal Village A185

1989, Mar. 4   Engr.   Perf. 13
371 A185 2.20fr indigo & lilac   .80 .45

Europa 1989 A186

Children's games.

1989, June 9   Engr.   Perf. 13
372 A186 2.20fr Human tower   1.00 .50
373 A186 3.60fr The handkerchief   1.25 .75

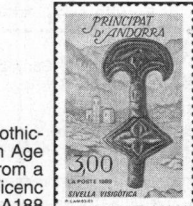

Red Cross A187

1989, May 6
374 A187 3.60fr multi   1.25 .65

Visigothic-Merovingian Age Cincture from a Column, St. Vicenc D'Anclar — A188

1989, June 3   Photo.
375 A188 3fr multi   1.00 .50

Wildlife A189

1989, Sept. 18   Engr.   Perf. 13
376 A189 2.20fr Wild boar   .90   .50
377 A189 3.60fr Newt   1.40   .75

Scene of Salome from the Retable of
St. Michael of Mosquera,
Encamp — A190

1989, Oct. 16   Perf. 13x13½
378 A190 5fr multi   1.50   .80

La
Margineda
Bridge
A191

1990, Feb. 26   Engr.   Perf. 13
379 A191 2.30fr multi   .80   .45

Tourism.

Arms Types of 1983 and 1988
1990-93   Engr.   Perf. 13
380 A150 2.10fr green   .80   .30
381 A150 2.20fr green   1.50   .60
382 A150 2.30fr vermilion   .85   .30
383 A150 2.40fr green   .90   .40
384 A150 2.50fr vermilion   1.75   .70
385 A150 2.80fr vermilion   1.00   .40
      Nos. 380-385 (6)   6.80 2.70

Booklet Stamps
Perf. 13
386 A176 2.30fr red   .85   .30
  a. Booklet pane of 5   4.25
387 A176 2.50fr red   1.75   .65
  a. Booklet pane of 5   8.50
388 A176 2.80fr red   1.00   .40
  c. Booklet pane of 5   5.00
      Nos. 386-388 (3)   3.60 1.35

Issued: 2.20fr, #384, 10/28/91; #387,
10/21/91; 2.40fr, 2.80fr, 8/9/93; 2.10fr, 2.30fr,
1990.

Llorts
Mines
A193

1990, Apr. 21   Engr.   Perf. 12½x13
390 A193 3.20fr multicolored   1.25   .60

Europa
A194

Designs: 2.30fr, Early post office. 3.20fr,
Modern post office.

1990, May 5   Perf. 13
391 A194 2.30fr blk & scar   .95   .50
392 A194 3.20fr scar & vio   1.40   .80

Otter
A195

1990, May 25   Perf. 12x13
393 A195 2.30fr Roses, vert.   .95   .50
394 A195 3.20fr shown   1.40   .75

Censer of
St. Roma
of Les
Bons
A196

1990, June 25   Perf. 12½x13
395 A196 3fr multicolored   1.10   .60

Tobacco
Drying
Sheds, Les
Bons
A197

1990, Sept. 15   Engr.   Perf. 12½x13
396 A197 2.30fr multi   .85   .50

St. Coloma
(Detail)
A198

1990, Oct. 8   Perf. 12½x13
397 A198 5fr multi   2.00 1.00

Coin from
Church of
St. Eulalia
d'Encamp
A199

1990, Oct. 27   Litho.   Perf. 13
398 A199 3.20fr multi   1.10   .60

De Gaulle Type of 1972 Dated 1990
1990, Oct. 23   Engr.   Perf. 13
399 A88 2.30fr vio bl   1.00   .55
400 A88 3.20fr dk car   1.40   .75
  a. Pair, #399-400 + label   2.40 2.00

Birth centenary of De Gaulle.

4th Games of the
Small European
States — A200

1991, Apr. 8   Photo.   Perf. 13
401 A200 2.50fr multicolored   .90   .50

Chapel of
St. Roma
Dels Vilars
A201

1991, Mar. 9   Engr.   Perf. 13
402 A201 2.50fr multicolored   .90   .50

Europa — A202

1991, Apr. 27   Perf. 13x12½, 12½x13
403 A202 2.50fr TV satellite   1.10   .60
404 A202 3.50fr Telescope, horiz. 1.25   .75

Bottles from
Tombs of
St. Vincenc
d'Enclar
A203

1991, May 11   Photo.   Perf. 13
405 A203 3.20fr multicolored   1.25   .60

Farm
Animals
A204

1991, June 22   Engr.   Perf. 13
406 A204 2.50fr Sheep   .90   .50
407 A204 3.50fr Cow   1.25   .65

Petanque World
Championships — A205

1991, Sept. 14   Engr.   Perf. 13
408 A205 2.50fr multicolored   .90   .40

Wolfgang
Amadeus
Mozart,
Death
Bicent.
A206

1991, Oct. 5
409 A206 3.40fr multicolored   1.40   .75

Virgin and
Child of St.
Julia and
St. Germa
A207

1991, Nov. 16   Engr.   Perf. 12½x13
410 A207 5fr multicolored   2.00 1.00

1992 Winter
Olympics,
Albertville — A208

1992, Feb. 10   Litho.   Perf. 13
411 A208 2.50fr Slalom skiing   .95   .50
412 A208 3.40fr Figure skating   1.25 1.10
  a. Pair, #411-412 + label   2.25 1.10

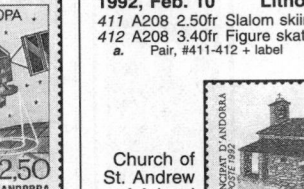

Church of
St. Andrew
of Arinsal
A209

1992, Mar. 21   Engr.   Perf. 12x13
413 A209 2.50fr black & tan   1.10   .60

Discovery
of America,
500th
Anniv.
A210

1992, Apr. 25   Perf. 13
414 A210 2.50fr Columbus' fleet   1.00   .60
415 A210 3.40fr Landing in New
                 World   1.50 1.00
      Europa.

1992 Summer   European
Olympics,   Globeflower
Barcelona   A212
A211

1992, June 8   Litho.   Perf. 13
416 A211 2.50fr Kayaking   1.00   .60
417 A211 3.40fr Shooting   1.40   .90
  a. Pair, #416-417 + label   2.40   .90

1992, July 6

Design: 3.40fr, Vulture, horiz.

418 A212 2.50fr multicolored   1.00   .60
419 A212 3.40fr multicolored   1.40   .90

Martyrdom
of St.
Eulalia
A213

1992, Sept. 14   Photo.   Perf. 13
420 A213 4fr multicolored   1.50   .80

Sculpture
by Mauro
Staccioli
A214

1992, Oct. 5   Engr.   Perf. 12½x13
421 A214 5fr multicolored   2.00 1.00

Ordino Arcalis '91.

Tempest in a Tea Cup, by Dennis Oppenheim — A215

1992, Nov. 14   Engr.   Perf. 13x12½
422 A215 5fr multicolored   2.00 1.00

Skiing in Andorra — A216

Ski resorts: No. 423: a, 2.50fr, Soldeu El Tarter. b, 3.40fr, Arinsal.
No. 424: a, 2.50fr, Pas de la Casa-Grau Roig. b, 2.50fr, Ordino Arcalis. c, 3.40fr, Pal.

1993, Mar. 13   Litho.   Perf. 13
423 A216 Pair, #a.-b. + label   2.25 1.10
424 A216 Strip of 3, #a.-c.   3.25 1.75

Sculptures — A217

Europa: 2.50fr, "Estructures Autogeneradores," by Jorge du Bon, vert. 3.40fr, Sculpture, "Fisicromia per Andorra," by Carlos Cruz-Diez.

1993, May 15   Engr.   Perf. 12½x13
425 A217 2.50fr multicolored   .75 .50
Litho.
Perf. 14x13½
426 A217 3.40fr multicolored   1.25 .75

Butterflies A218

1993, June 28   Litho.   Perf. 13
427 A218 2.50fr Polymmatus icarus   .95 .50
428 A218 4.20fr Nymphalidae   1.50 .80

Tour de France Bicycle Race — A219

1993, July 20   Litho.   Perf. 13
429 A219 2.50fr multicolored   .90 .50

Andorra School, 10th Anniv. A220

1993, Sept. 20   Litho.   Perf. 13
430 A220 2.80fr multicolored   1.00 .60

Un Lloc Paga, by Michael Warren A221

1993, Oct. 18   Engr.   Perf. 12½x13
431 A221 5fr blue & black   1.75 1.00

Sculpture, by Erik Dietman A222

1993, Nov. 8   Engr.   Perf. 12½x13
432 A222 5fr multicolored   1.75 1.00

1994 Winter Olympics, Lillehammer A223

1994, Feb. 21   Litho.   Perf. 13
433 A223 3.70fr multicolored   1.25 .75

1st Anniversary of the Constitution — A224

Designs: 2.80fr, Monument, by Emili Armengol. 3.70fr, Stone tablet with inscription.

1994, Mar. 15   Litho.   Perf. 13
434 A224 2.80fr multicolored   1.00 .60
435 A224 3.70fr multicolored   1.40 .90
  a. Pair, #434-435 + label   2.40 2.00

European Discoveries A225

Europa: 2.80fr, Discovery of AIDS virus. 3.70fr, Radio diffusion.

1994, May 9   Litho.   Perf. 13
436 A225 2.80fr multicolored   1.00 .60
437 A225 3.70fr multicolored   1.25 .75

1994 World Cup Soccer Championships, US — A226

1994, June 20
438 A226 3.70fr multicolored   1.50 .90

Tourist Sports — A227

#439, Mountain climbing. #440, Fishing. #441, Horseback riding. #442, Mountain biking.

1994, July 11
439 A227 2.80fr multicolored   1.10 .60
440 A227 2.80fr multicolored   1.10 .60
  a. Pair, #439-440 + label   2.25 2.00
441 A227 2.80fr multicolored   1.10 .60
442 A227 2.80fr multicolored   1.10 .60
  a. Pair, #441-442 + label   2.25 2.00
      Nos. 439-442 (4)   4.40 2.40

Butterflies A228

1994, Sept. 5   Litho.   Perf. 13
443 A228 2.80fr Iphiclides podalirus   1.10 .60
444 A228 4.40fr Aglais urticae   1.75 1.00

A229   A230

1994, Oct. 22   Litho.   Perf. 13
445 A229 2.80fr multicolored   1.25 .75
Meeting of the Co-Princes, 1st anniv.

1995, Feb. 27   Litho.   Perf. 13
446 A230 2.80fr multicolored   1.25 .75
European Nature Conservation Year

1995 World Cup Rugby Championships — A231

1995, Apr. 24   Litho.   Perf. 13
447 A231 2.80fr multicolored   1.25 .75

Peace & Freedom A232

Europa: 2.80fr, Dove with olive branch. 3.70fr, Flock of doves.

1995, May 2
448 A232 2.80fr multicolored   1.00 .60
449 A232 3.70fr multicolored   1.25 .80

Caritas in Andorra, 15th Anniv. A233

1995, May 15   Litho.   Perf. 13
450 A233 2.80fr multicolored   1.25 1.00

Caldea Health Spa — A234

1995, June 26   Litho.   Perf. 13
451 A234 2.80fr multicolored   1.25 1.00

Ordino Natl. Auditorium A235

1995, July 10   Litho. & Engr.
452 A235 3.70fr black & buff   1.60 1.25

Virgin of Meritxell — A236

1995, Sept. 11   Litho.   Perf. 14
453 A236 4.40fr multicolored   1.90 1.50

Protection of Nature A237

Butterflies: 2.80fr, Papallona llimonera, vert. 3.70fr, Papallona melanargia galathea.

1995, Sept. 25   Litho.   Perf. 13
454 A237 2.80fr multicolored   1.25 1.00
455 A237 3.70fr multicolored   1.60 1.25

UN, 50th Anniv. — A238

1995, Oct. 21   Litho.   Perf. 13
456 A238 2.80fr Flag, emblem   1.25 1.00
457 A238 3.70fr Emblem, "50," flag   1.60 1.25
  a. Pair, #456-457 + label   3.00 3.00

326 ANDORRA, FRENCH ADMIN.

Andorra's Entrance into Council of Europe
A239

1995, Nov. 4
458 A239 2.80fr multicolored   1.25 1.00

World Skiing Championships, Ordino Arcalis — A240

1996, Jan. 29   Litho.   Perf. 13
459 A240 2.80fr multicolored   1.25 1.25

Basketball in Andorra — A241

1996, Jan. 29   Litho.   Perf. 13
460 A241 3.70fr multicolored   1.60 1.60

Our Lady of Meritxell Special School, 25th Anniv. A242

1996, Feb. 17   Litho.   Perf. 13
461 A242 2.80fr multicolored   1.25 1.25

Songbirds A243

1996, Mar. 25
462 A243 3fr Pit riog   1.25 1.25
463 A243 3.80fr Mallarenga carbonera 1.60 1.60

First Arms Type of 1983

1996, Apr. 17   Engr.   Perf. 13
464 A150 2.70fr green   1.25 1.25
465 A150 3fr red   1.40 1.40

Cross of St. James d'Engordany A244

1996, Apr. 20   Litho.
466 A244 3fr multicolored   1.40 1.40

Censer of St. Eulalia d'Encamp A245

1996, Apr. 20
467 A245 3.80fr multicolored   1.75 1.75

Europa — A246   Chess — A247

1996, May 6
468 A246 3fr Ermessenda de Castellbo   1.25 .75

1996, June 8   Litho.   Perf. 13
469 A247 4.50fr multicolored   2.00 2.00

1996 Summer Olympic Games, Atlanta A248

1996, June 29   Litho.   Perf. 13
470 A248 3fr multicolored   1.25 1.25

Arms of the Community of Canillo — A249

Serpentine Die Cut 7 Vert.
1996, June 10   Litho.
Self-Adhesive
471 A249 (3fr) multicolored   1.75 1.75

Natl. Children's Choir, 5th Anniv. A250

1996, Sept. 14   Litho.   Perf. 13
472 A250 3fr multicolored   1.40 1.40

Livestock Fair A251

1996, Oct. 26   Engr.   Perf. 12x13
473 A251 3fr multicolored   1.25 1.25

Churches A252

#474, St. Romá de Les Bons. #475, St. Coloma.

1996, Nov. 16   Litho.   Perf. 13
474 A252 6.70fr multicolored   2.75 2.75
475 A252 6.70fr multicolored   2.75 2.75

A253   A254

1997, Jan. 7   Litho.   Perf. 13
476 A253 3fr multicolored   1.25 1.25
Pres. Francois Mitterrand (1916-96).

Sawtooth Die Cut 7 Vert. x Straight Die Cut
1997, Feb. 24   Litho.
Self-Adhesive
477 A254 (3fr) Arms of Encamp   1.25 1.25
a. Booklet pane of 10   12.50

By its nature, No. 477a is a complete book-let. The peelable paper backing serves as a booklet cover.

A255   A256

1997, Mar. 22   Perf. 13
478 A255 3fr Volleyball   1.25 1.25

1997, May 12   Litho.   Perf. 13
479 A256 3fr "The White Lady"   1.00 .50
Europa (Stories and Legends).

Oreneta Cuablanca A257

1997, May 31   Litho.   Perf. 13
480 A257 3.80fr multicolored   1.60 1.60

Paintings of Mills A258

1997, Sept. 15   Litho.   Perf. 13
481 A258 3fr Cal Pal, vert.   1.10 1.10
482 A258 4.50fr Mas d'en Sole   1.75 1.75

Religious Artifacts A259

Designs: 3fr, Monstrance of St. Iscle and St. Victoria. 15.50fr, Altar piece of St. Pierre d'Alxirivall.

1997, Oct. 27
483 A259   3fr multicolored   1.10 1.10
484 A259 15.50fr multicolored   5.75 5.75
a. Pair, #483-484 + label   7.00 7.00

Legends — A260

Designs: No. 485, Legend of Meritxell. No. 486, The cross of seven arms. 3.80fr, The fountain of Esmelicat.

1997, Nov. 22   Litho.   Perf. 13
485 A260   3fr multicolored   1.10 1.10
486 A260   3fr multicolored   1.10 1.10
487 A260 3.80fr multicolored   1.40 1.40
a. Strip of 3, #485-487   3.75 3.75

Monaco Intl. Philatelic Exhibition — A261

1997, Nov. 28   Litho.   Perf. 13
488 A261 3fr Chapel of St. Mi-guel d'Engolasters   1.10 1.10

Happy Anniversary A262   1998 Winter Olympic Games, Nagano A263

1998, Jan. 3   Litho.   Perf. 13
489 A262 3fr Juggling candles   1.10 1.10

1998, Feb. 14
490 A263 4.40fr multicolored   1.75 1.75

Arms of Ordino — A264

Serpentine Die Cut Vert.
1998, Mar. 7   Litho.
Booklet Stamp
Self-Adhesive
491 A491 (3fr) multicolored   1.10 1.10
a. Booklet pane of 10   11.00
Complete booklet, #491a   11.00

See Nos. 504, 518, 531.

Mesa de Vila Church — A265

1998, Mar. 28   Perf. 13
492 A265 4.50fr multicolored   1.75 1.75

Rotary Club
of Andorra,
20th Anniv.
A265a

1998, Apr. 11
493 A265a 3fr multicolored   1.10 1.10

Finch
A266

1998   **Litho.**   **Perf. 13**
494 A266 3.80fr multicolored   1.40 1.40

1998 World Cup
Soccer
Championships,
France — A267

1998, June 6   **Litho.**   **Perf. 13**
495 A267 3fr multicolored   1.10 1.10

For overprint see No. 499.

Music
Festival
A268

1998, June 20   **Litho.**   **Perf. 13**
496 A268 3fr multicolored   1.00 .60

Europa.

Expo '98,
Lisbon
A269

1998, July 6
497 A269 5fr multicolored   1.75 1.75

Chalice, House of
the Valleys — A270

1998, Sept. 19   **Litho.**   **Perf. 13**
498 A270 4.50fr multicolored   1.60 1.60

No. 495 Ovptd. "FINAL /
FRANCA/BRASIL / 3-0"
1998, Nov. 16
499 A267 3fr multicolored   1.10 1.10

Early Maps
of Andorra
A271

1998, Nov. 16
500 A271   3fr 1717, vert.   1.10 1.10
501 A271 15.50fr 1777   5.75 5.75

Inauguration of the Postal
Museum — A272

1998, Nov. 19   **Litho.**   **Perf. 13**
502 A272 3fr multicolored   1.10 1.10

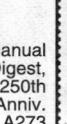

Manual
Digest,
250th
Anniv.
A273

1998, Dec. 7
503 A273 3.80fr multicolored   1.40 1.40

Arms Type of 1998
Serpentine Die Cut Vert.
1999, Jan. 18
Booklet Stamp
Self-Adhesive
504 A264 (3fr) La Massana   1.10 1.10
   a.   Booklet pane of 10   11.00

No. 504a is a complete booklet.

Recycling
A274

1999, Mar. 13   **Litho.**   **Perf. 13**
505 A274 5fr multicolored   1.75 1.75

Sorteny Valley — A275

Illustration reduced.

1999, Apr. 10
506 A275 3fr multicolored   1.00 .60

Europa.

Council of
Europe,
50th Anniv.
A276

1999, May 5   **Litho.**   **Perf. 13**
507 A276 3.80fr multicolored   1.40 1.40

First Stage
Coach — A277

1999, May 15
508 A277 2.70fr multi   1.00 1.00

1999 European National Soccer
Championships — A278

1999, June 10   **Photo.**   **Perf. 13**
509 A278 4.50fr multicolored   1.75 1.75

PhilexFrance 99 — A279

1999, July 2   **Litho.**   **Perf. 13x13¼**
510 A279 3fr multicolored   1.10 1.10

Historic
View of
Pal — A280

Perf. 13x13¼, 13¼x13
1999, July 10   **Litho.**
511 A280 3fr shown   1.10 1.10
512 A280 3fr Different view, vert.   1.10 1.10

International Federation of
Photographic Art, 50th Anniv. — A281

1999, July 24   **Litho.**   **Perf. 13**
513 A281 4.40fr multicolored   1.60 1.60

Casa Rull,
Sispony
A282

1999, Sept. 6   **Litho.**   **Perf. 13x13¼**
514 A282 15.50fr multi   5.50 5.50

Chest With Six Locks — A283

1999, Oct. 9   **Litho.**   **Perf. 13x13¼**
515 A283 6.70fr multicolored   2.40 2.40

Christmas
A284

1999, Nov. 27   **Litho.**   **Perf. 13**
516 A284 3fr multi   1.00 1.00

Year 2000
A285

2000, Jan. 5   **Litho.**   **Perf. 13x13¼**
517 A285 3fr multi   .95 .95

Arms Type of 1998
Serpentine Die Cut 6½ Vert.
2000, Feb. 26
Booklet Stamp
Self-Adhesive
518 A264 (3fr) Andorra-la-Vielle   .95 .95
   a.   Booklet pane of 10   9.50

No. 518a is a complete booklet.

Snowboarding
A286

2000, Mar. 17   **Litho.**   **Perf. 13**
519 A286 4.50fr multi   1.40 1.40

Montserrat
Caballé
Chant
Competition
A287

2000, Apr. 3   **Perf. 13x13¼**
520 A287 3.80fr multi   1.10 1.10

Campanula
Cochleariifolia
A288

2000, Apr. 17   **Litho.**   **Perf. 13**
521 A288 2.70fr multi   .75 .75

Europa, 2000
Common Design Type
2000, May 9   **Perf. 13½x13**
522 CD17 3fr multi   .80 .80

Festivals
A289

No. 523: a, Canòlic. b, Meritxell.

2000, May 27   Litho.   Perf. 13
523   Pair + central label   1.75 1.75
a.-b.   A289 3fr Any single   .85   .85

Pardal
Comú — A290

2000, July 7   Litho.   Perf. 13
524 A290 4.40fr multi   1.25 1.25

A291   A292

2000, Sept. 11   Litho.   Perf. 13
525 A291 5fr multi   1.40 1.40

2000 Summer Olympics, Sydney.

2000, Sept. 28
526 A292 3fr multi   .85   .85

World Tourism Day.

Expo 2000,
Hanover
A293

2000, Oct. 6   Litho.   Perf. 13
527 A293 3fr multi   .80   .80

Arms Type of 1998
Serpentine Die Cut 6½ Vert.
2001, Feb. 19   Litho.
Booklet Stamp
Self-Adhesive
531 A264 (3fr) Sant Julià de
Lòria   .75   .75
a.   Booklet, 10 #531   7.50

Canillo Aliga
Mountain
Station — A297

2001, Feb. 10   Litho.   Perf. 13
532 A297 4.50fr multi   1.25 1.25

Casa
Cristo
Museum
A298

2001, Feb. 17   Perf. 13¼x13
533 A298 6.70fr multi   1.90 1.90

Andorran Heritage — A299

No. 534: a, Legend of Engolasters Lake. b,
Foundation of Andorra.

2001, Mar. 23   Perf. 13
534 A299 3fr Pair, #a-b, with central label   1.60 1.60

Intl. Book   Europa — A301
Day — A300

2001, Apr. 23   Litho.   Perf. 13
535 A300 3.80fr multi   1.00 1.00

2001, Apr. 28
536 A301 3fr multi   .80   .80

A302

2001, May 12
537 A302   3fr Raspberries,
vert.   .80   .80
538 A302 4.40fr shown   1.10 1.10

European
Language
Year
A303

2001, June 16   Litho.   Perf. 13
539 A303 3.80fr multi   1.00 1.00

Escaldes-Engordany Jazz
Festival — A304

2001, July 7
540 A304 3fr multi   .85   .85

General
Council's
Kitchen
A305

2001, Aug. 10
541 A305 5fr multi   1.40 1.40

Chapel of the Virgin of Meritxell, 25th
Anniv. of Rebuilding — A306

2001, Sept. 7   Litho.   Perf. 13
542 A306 3fr multi   .85   .85

Hotel
Pla — A307

2001, Oct. 12
543 A307 15.50fr multi   4.25 4.25

─────────────────

SEMI-POSTAL STAMP

┌─────────────────────────────────┐
│ Catalogue values for unused   │
│ stamps in this section are for   │
│ Never Hinged items.   │
└─────────────────────────────────┘

Virgin of St.
Coloma — SP1

Unwmk.
1964, July 25   Engr.   Perf. 13
B1 SP1 25c + 10c multi   20.00 20.00

The surtax was for the Red Cross.

─────────────────

AIR POST STAMPS

┌─────────────────────────────────┐
│ Catalogue values for unused   │
│ stamps in this section are for   │
│ Never Hinged items.   │
└─────────────────────────────────┘

Chamois
AP1

Unwmk.
1950, Feb. 20   Engr.   Perf. 13
C1 AP1 100fr indigo   65.00 45.00

East Branch of
Valira River — AP2

1955-57
C2 AP2 100fr dark green   8.50   6.50
C3 AP2 200fr cerise   17.50 14.00
C4 AP2 500fr dp bl ('57)   90.00 65.00
    Nos. C2-C4 (3)   116.00 85.50

D'Inclès
Valley
AP3

1961-64   Unwmk.   Perf. 13
C5 AP3 2fr red, ol gray & cl   1.00   .65
C6 AP3 3fr bl, mar & slate grn   1.25 1.25
C7 AP3 5fr rose lil & red org   2.00 1.75
C8 AP3 10fr bl grn & slate grn   3.75 3.50
    Nos. C5-C8 (4)   8.00 7.15

Issued: 10fr, 4/25/64; others, 6/19/61.

POSTAGE DUE STAMPS

Postage Due Stamps of France, 1893-
1931, Overprinted

On Stamps of 1893-1926
1931-33   Unwmk.   Perf. 14x13½
J1 D2 5c blue   1.00 1.00
J2 D2 10c brown   1.00 1.00
J3 D2 30c rose red   .40   .40
J4 D2 50c violet brn   1.00 1.00
J5 D2 60c green   10.00 10.00
J6 D2 1fr red brn,
straw   .50   .50
J7 D2 2fr brt violet   6.00 6.00
J8 D2 3fr magenta   1.10 1.10
    Nos. J1-J8 (8)   21.00 21.00
On Stamps of 1927-31
J9 D4 1c olive grn   1.25 1.25
J10 D4 10c rose   2.75 2.75
J11 D4 60c red   16.00 16.00
J12 D4 1fr Prus grn
('32)   65.00 65.00
J13 D4 1.20fr on 2fr bl   50.00 50.00
J14 D4 2fr ol brn ('33)   140.00 140.00
J15 D4 5fr on 1fr vio   65.00 65.00
    Nos. J9-J15 (7)   340.00 340.00

D5   D6

1935-41   Typo.
J16 D5 1c gray green   2.25 1.25
J17 D6 5c light blue ('37)   3.75   *4.50*
J18 D6 10c brown ('41)   3.00   *4.50*
J19 D6 2fr violet ('41)   6.00 3.25
J20 D6 5fr red orange ('41)   11.00 3.25
    Nos. J16-J20 (5)   26.00 16.75

┌─────────────────────────────────┐
│ Catalogue values for unused   │
│ stamps in this section, from this │
│ point to the end of the section, are │
│ for Never Hinged items.   │
└─────────────────────────────────┘

Wheat Sheaves — D7

1943-46			Perf. 14x13½	
J21	D7	10c sepia	1.00	1.00
J22	D7	30c brt red vio	1.50	1.50
J23	D7	50c blue grn	1.75	1.75
J24	D7	1fr brt ultra	.80	.80
J25	D7	1.50fr rose red	5.75	5.75
J26	D7	2fr turq blue	1.50	1.50
J27	D7	3fr brown org	2.75	2.75
J28	D7	4fr dp vio ('45)	4.50	4.50
J29	D7	5fr brt pink	4.50	4.50
J30	D7	10fr red org ('45)	5.75	5.75
J31	D7	20fr olive brn ('46)	6.00	6.00
		Nos. J21-J31 (11)	35.80	35.80

Inscribed: "Timbre Taxe"

1946-53				
J32	D7	10c sepia ('46)	1.10	1.10
J33	D7	1fr ultra	.75	.75
J34	D7	2fr turq blue	1.00	1.00
J35	D7	3fr orange brn	2.00	2.00
J36	D7	4fr violet	2.75	2.75
J37	D7	5fr brt pink	1.75	1.75
J38	D7	10fr red orange	2.75	2.75
J39	D7	20fr olive brn	6.25	6.25
J40	D7	50fr dk green ('50)	16.50	16.50
J41	D7	100fr dp green ('53)	87.50	87.50
		Nos. J32-J41 (10)	122.35	122.35

Inscribed: "Timbre Taxe"

1961, June 19			Perf. 14x13½	
J42	D7	5c rose pink	3.00	3.00
J43	D7	10c red orange	6.00	6.00
J44	D7	20c olive	9.00	9.00
J45	D7	50c dark slate green	15.00	15.00
		Nos. J42-J45 (4)	33.00	33.00

D8

D9

1964-71		Typo.	Perf. 14x13½	
J46	D8	5c Centaury ('65)	.20	.20
J47	D8	10c Gentian ('65)	.20	.20
J48	D8	15c Corn poppy	.20	.20
J49	D8	20c Violets ('71)	.20	.20
J50	D8	30c Forget-me-not	.20	.20
J51	D8	40c Columbine ('71)	.20	.20
J52	D8	50c Clover ('65)	.30	.30
		Nos. J46-J52 (7)	1.50	1.50

1985, Oct. 21		Engr.	Perf. 13	
J53	D9	10c Holly	.20	.20
J54	D9	20c Blueberries	.20	.20
J55	D9	30c Raspberries	.20	.20
J56	D9	40c Bilberries	.20	.20
J57	D9	50c Blackberries	.20	.20
J58	D9	1fr Broom	.35	.30
J59	D9	2fr Rosehips	.65	.35
J60	D9	3fr Nightshade	1.00	.60
J61	D9	4fr Nabiu	1.40	.75
J62	D9	5fr Strawberries	1.75	1.00
		Nos. J53-J62 (10)	6.15	4.00

NEWSPAPER STAMP

France No. P7
Overprinted

1931		Unwmk.	Perf. 14x13½	
P1	A16	½c on 1c gray		.75	.75

ANGOLA

aŋ-'gō-lə

LOCATION — S.W. Africa between Zaire and Namibia.
GOVT. — Republic
AREA — 481,351 sq. mi.
POP. — 11,177,537 (1999 est.)
CAPITAL — Luanda

Angola was a Portuguese overseas territory until it became independent November 11, 1975, as the People's Republic of Angola.

1000 Reis = 1 Milreis
100 Centavos = 1 Escudo (1913, 1954)
100 Centavos = 1 Angolar (1932)
10 Lweys = 1 Kwanza (1977)

Catalogue values for unused stamps in this country are for Never Hinged items, beginning with Scott 328 in the regular postage section, Scott C26 in the airpost section, Scott J31 in the postage due section, and Scott RA7 in the postal tax section.

Watermark

Wmk. 232—Maltese Cross

Portuguese
Crown — A1

1870-77		Typo.	Perf. 12½, 13½	
1	A1	5r black	2.00	1.00
a.		Perf. 13½	8.00	3.00
2	A1	10r yellow	20.00	9.00
3	A1	20r bister	2.00	1.10
a.		Perf. 13½	275.00	200.00
4	A1	25r red	8.00	4.25
c.		25r rose, perf. 14	225.00	125.00
d.		Perf. 13½	18.00	11.00
5	A1	40r blue ('77)	150.00	100.00
6	A1	50r green	40.00	10.00
a.		Perf. 13½	200.00	85.00
7	A1	100r lilac	3.00	1.75
a.		Perf. 12½	7.00	3.00
8	A1	200r orange ('77)	2.75	1.75
a.		Perf. 12½	4.00	2.10
9	A1	300r choc ('77)	3.00	1.75
a.		Perf. 12½	13.00	6.50

1881-85				
10	A1	10r green ('83)	4.00	1.50
a.		Perf. 12½	20.00	2.25
11	A1	20r carmine rose ('85)	9.00	5.00
12	A1	25r violet ('85)	4.00	2.00
a.		Perf. 13½	6.00	2.75
13	A1	40r buff ('82)	5.00	2.00
a.		Perf. 13½	6.00	2.00
15	A1	50r blue	12.00	1.75
a.		Perf. 13½	20.00	1.75
		Nos. 10-15 (5)	34.00	12.25

Two types of numerals are found on #2, 11, 13, 15.

The cliche of 40r in plate of 20r error, was discovered before the stamps were issued. All copies were defaced by a blue pencil mark. Value, $750.00.

In perf. 12½, Nos. 1-4, 4a and 6, as well as 7a, were printed in 1870 on thicker paper and 1875 on normal paper. Stamps of the earlier printing sell for 2 to 5 times more than those of the 1875 printing.

Some reprints of the 1870-85 issues are on a smooth white chalky paper, ungummed and perf. 13½.

Other reprints of these issues are on thin ivory paper with shiny white gum and clear-cut perf. 13½.

King Luiz — A2

King Carlos — A3

1886		Embossed	Perf. 12½	
16	A2	5r black	3.50	2.50
a.		Perf. 13½	11.50	8.50
17	A2	10r green	3.50	2.50
a.		Perf. 13½	13.00	7.25
18	A2	20r rose	10.00	6.25
a.		Perf. 13½	12.50	6.50
19	A2	25r red violet	7.50	1.50
20	A2	40r chocolate	8.00	5.00
21	A2	50r blue	10.50	2.00
22	A2	100r yellow brn	14.00	6.00
23	A2	200r gray violet	18.00	10.00
24	A2	300r orange	20.00	12.00
		Nos. 16-24 (9)	95.00	47.75

For surcharges see #61-69, 172-174, 208-210.
Reprints of 5r, 20r & 100r have cleancut perf. 13½.

1893-94		Typo.	Perf. 11½, 12½, 13½	
25	A3	5r yellow	1.00	.85
26	A3	10r redsh violet	2.00	.90
27	A3	15r chocolate	2.75	1.25
28	A3	20r lavender	2.75	1.25
29	A3	25r green	1.25	1.00
a.		Perf. 12½	4.00	2.00
30	A3	50r light blue	3.25	1.25
a.		Perf. 13½	5.00	2.75
31	A3	75r carmine	6.00	3.50
a.		Perf. 11½	8.00	6.25
32	A3	80r lt green	7.50	3.50
33	A3	100r brown, buff	6.75	3.50
a.		Perf. 11½	50.00	32.50
34	A3	150r car, rose	12.00	10.00
35	A3	200r dk blue, lt bl	14.00	11.00
36	A3	300r dk blue, sal	15.00	11.00
		Nos. 25-36 (12)	74.25	49.00

For surcharges see Nos. 70-81, 175-179, 213-216, 234.

No. P1 Surcharged in Blue

1894, Aug.				
37	N1	25r on 2½r brown	80.00	22.50

King Carlos — A5

1898-1903			Perf. 11½	
Name and Value in Black except 500r				
38	A5	2½r gray	.20	.20
39	A5	5r orange	.20	.20
40	A5	10r yellow grn	.20	.20
41	A5	15r violet brn	1.50	.70
42	A5	15r gray grn ('03)	.65	.50
43	A5	20r gray violet	.25	.20
44	A5	25r sea green	1.00	.40
45	A5	25r car ('03)	.50	.20
46	A5	50r blue	1.60	.35
47	A5	50r brown ('03)	3.00	2.00
48	A5	65r dull blue ('03)	12.00	7.00
49	A5	75r rose	4.50	1.60
50	A5	75r red violet ('03)	1.25	.90
51	A5	80r violet	4.50	2.00
52	A5	100r dk blue, blue	.90	.65
53	A5	115r org brn, pink ('03)	9.00	6.50
54	A5	130r brn, straw ('03)	9.00	6.50
55	A5	150r brn, straw	8.00	5.00
56	A5	200r red vio, pink	2.25	1.00
57	A5	300r dk blue, rose	3.25	3.25
58	A5	400r dull bl, straw ('03)	5.00	3.50
59	A5	500r blk & red, bl ('01)	3.50	3.00
60	A5	700r vio, yelsh ('01)	14.00	10.00
		Nos. 38-60 (23)	86.25	55.85

For surcharges & overprints see #83-102, 113-117, 159-171, 181-183, 217-218, 221-225.

Stamps of 1886-94 Surcharged in Black or Red

Two types of surcharge:
I - 3mm between numeral and REIS.
II - 4½mm spacing.

1902			Perf. 12½	
61	A2	65r on 40r choc	4.50	3.50
62	A2	65r on 300r org, I	4.50	3.50
a.		Type II	32.50	25.00
63	A2	115r on 10r green	4.00	3.25
a.		Inverted surcharge	30.00	20.00
b.		Perf. 13½	18.00	17.00
64	A2	115r on 200r gray vio	4.00	2.75
65	A2	130r on 50r blue	6.50	4.75
66	A2	130r on 100r brown	5.00	3.00
67	A2	400r on 20r rose	60.00	30.00
a.		Perf. 13½	60.00	45.00
68	A2	400r on 25r violet	9.00	6.00
69	A2	400r on 5r black (R)	8.00	6.25
a.		Double surcharge	30.00	20.00
		Nos. 61-69 (9)	105.50	63.00

For surcharges see Nos. 172-174, 208-210.

			Perf. 11½, 12½, 13½	
70	A3	65r on 5r yel, I	4.00	2.75
a.		Type II	10.00	10.00
71	A3	65r on 10r red vio, I	3.25	2.25
a.		Type II	13.00	5.25
b.		Perf. 11½, type I	8.75	5.25
c.		Perf. 11½, type II	3.50	2.50
72	A3	65r on 20r lav	5.00	3.00
a.		Type II	6.50	6.00
73		65r on 25r green	4.00	2.50
a.		Perf. 11½	9.25	7.25
74	A3	115r on 80r lt grn	6.00	4.00
75	A3	115r on 100r brn, buff	6.00	3.50
76	A3	115r on 150r car, rose	8.50	5.25
a.		Perf. 13½	10.00	6.00
77	A3	130r on 15r choc	3.50	2.00
78	A3	130r on 75r carmine	3.50	2.25
a.		Perf. 13½	14.00	11.50
79	A3	130r on 300r dk bl, sal	9.00	6.50
80	A3	400r on 50r lt bl	3.00	2.75
81	A3	400r on 200r bl, bl	3.00	3.25
a.		Perf. 13½	21.00	8.75
82	N1	400r on 2½r brn	1.75	1.10
a.		Type II	2.50	2.25
		Nos. 70-82 (13)	60.50	41.10

For surcharges see #175-180, 211-216, 234-235.
Reprints of Nos. 65, 67, 68 and 69 have clean-cut perforation 13½.

Stamps of 1898 Overprinted—a

1902			Perf. 11½	
83	A5	15r brown	1.25	.60
84	A5	25r sea green	1.00	.35
85	A5	50r blue	1.75	.85
86	A5	75r rose	3.00	2.00
		Nos. 83-86 (4)	7.00	3.80

For surcharge see No. 116.

No. 48 Surcharged in Black

1905				
87	A5	50r on 65r dull blue	3.00	1.25

For surcharge see No. 183.

Stamps of 1898-1903 Overprinted—b in Carmine or Green

1911				
88	A5	2½r gray	.20	.20
89	A5	5r orange yel	.20	.20
90	A5	10r light green	.25	.20
91	A5	15r gray green	.25	.20

92	A5	20r gray violet	.25	.20
93	A5	25r carmine (G)	.25	.20
94	A5	50r brown	1.50	.90
95	A5	75r lilac	2.50	2.50
96	A5	100r dk blue, *bl*	2.50	2.50
97	A5	115r org brn, *pink*	1.00	.60
98	A5	130r brown, *straw*	1.00	.60
99	A5	200r red lil, *pnksh*	1.00	.60
100	A5	400r dull bl, *straw*	1.50	.65
101	A5	500r blk & red, *bl*	1.25	.65
102	A5	700r violet, *yelsh*	1.75	.70
		Nos. 88-102 (15)	15.40	10.90

Inverted and double overprints of Nos. 88-102 were made intentionally.

For surcharges see #217-218, 221-222, 224.

King Manuel II — A6   Ceres — A7

Overprinted in Carmine or Green

1912   **Perf. 11½x12**

103	A6	2½r violet	.25	.50
104	A6	5r black	.25	.50
105	A6	10r gray green	.35	.30
106	A6	20r carmine (G)	.35	.30
107	A6	25r violet brown	.35	.30
108	A6	50r dk blue	.60	.50
109	A6	75r bister brown	.65	1.00
110	A6	100r brown, *lt green*	1.60	.70
111	A6	200r dk green, *salmon*	1.10	.70
112	A6	300r black, *azure*	1.10	.70
		Nos. 103-112 (10)	6.60	5.50

For surcharges see Nos. 219-220, 226-227.

No. 91 Surcharged with New Values as

1912, June   **Perf. 11½**

113	A5	2½r on 15r gray green	2.25	2.25
114	A5	5r on 15r gray green	1.75	1.50
115	A5	10r on 15r gray green	1.75	1.50
		Nos. 113-115 (3)	5.75	5.25

Inverted and double surcharges of Nos. 113-115 were made intentionally.

Nos. 86 and 50 Surcharged "25" in Black and Overprinted in Violet—c

1912

116	A5	25r on 75r rose	70.00	50.00
117	A5	25r on 75r red violet	2.75	1.50
a.		"REUPBLICA"	22.50	20.00
b.		"25" omitted	27.50	25.00
c.		"REPUBLICA" omitted	32.50	27.50

1914-26   Typo.   Perf. 12x11½, 15x14
Name and Value in Black

118	A7	¼c olive brown	.20	.20
a.		Inscriptions inverted	8.00	
119	A7	½c black	.20	.20
120	A7	1c blue green	.20	.20
121	A7	1c yel grn ('22)	.20	.20
122	A7	1½c lilac brown	.20	.20
123	A7	2c carmine	.20	.20
124	A7	2c gray ('25)	.30	1.00
125	A7	2½c lt violet	.20	.20
126	A7	3c orange ('21)	.20	.60
127	A7	4c dull rose ('21)	.20	.20
128	A7	4½c gray ('21)	.20	.80
130	A7	5c blue	.20	.20
131	A7	6c lilac ('21)	.20	.20
132	A7	7c ultra ('21)	.20	.20
133	A7	7½c yellow brn	.20	.20
134	A7	8c slate	.20	.20
135	A7	10c orange brn	.20	.20
136	A7	12c olive brn ('21)	.35	.25
137	A7	12c dp green ('25)	.20	.20
138	A7	15c plum	.75	.20
139	A7	15c brn rose ('21)	.20	.20
140	A7	20c yel green	.25	.20
141	A7	24c ultra ('25)	1.25	.75
142	A7	25c choc ('25)	1.25	.75
143	A7	30c brown, *green*	2.00	2.00
144	A7	30c gray grn ('21)	.75	.20
145	A7	40c brown, *pink*	3.50	2.00

146	A7	40c turq blue ('21)	.75	.20
147	A7	50c orange, *sal*	6.00	4.25
148	A7	50c lt violet ('25)	1.50	.20
149	A7	60c dk blue ('22)	1.25	.20
150	A7	60c dp rose ('26)	25.00	50.00
151	A7	80c pink ('22)	1.25	.20
152	A7	1e green, *blue*	3.50	2.25
153	A7	1e rose ('22)	2.25	.25
154	A7	1e dp blue ('25)	4.00	3.00
155	A7	2e dk violet ('22)	1.25	.50
156	A7	5e buff ('25)	15.00	2.25
157	A7	10e pink ('25)	30.00	10.00
158	A7	20e pale turq ('25)	55.00	35.00
		Nos. 118-158 (40)	160.75	120.20

Two kinds of paper, chalky-surfaced paper and ordinary, were used for Nos. 118-120, 122-123, 125, 130, 133-135, 138 and 140. Those on coated paper sell unused for 10 to 40 times the values listed; used for about 5 to 20 times.

All but #143, 145, 147 come perf 12x11½.
All but #124, 137, 141-142, 146, 148, 151, 153-154, 156-158 come perf 15x14.
For surcharges see Nos. 228-229, 236-239.

Stamps of 1898-1903 Overprinted type "c" in Red or Green
On Stamps of 1898-1903

1914   **Perf. 11½, 12**

159	A5	10r yel green (R)	3.25	2.75
160	A5	15r gray green (R)	3.25	2.75
161	A5	20r gray violet (G)	.80	1.00
163	A5	75r red violet (G)	.80	1.00
164	A5	100r blue, *blue* (R)	1.25	1.25
165	A5	115r org brn, *pink* (R)	80.00	
167	A5	200r red vio, *pnksh* (R)	.90	.50
169	A5	400r dl bl, *straw* (R)	40.00	30.00
170	A5	500r blk & red, *bl* (R)	5.00	3.00
171	A5	700r vio, *yelsh* (G)	15.00	12.00

Inverted and double overprints were made intentionally. No. 165 was not regularly issued. Red overprints on the 20r, 75r, 200r were not regularly issued. The 130r was not regularly issued without surcharge (No. 225).

On Nos. 63-65, 74-76, 78-79, 82
Perf. 11½, 12½, 13½

172	A2	115r on 10r (R)	20.00	10.00
a.		Perf. 13½	30.00	
173	A2	115r on 200r (R)	20.00	10.00
174	A2	130r on 50r (R)	35.00	20.00
175	A3	115r on 80r (R)	100.00	75.00
176	A3	115r on 100r (R)	250.00	150.00
177	A3	115r on 150r (G)	165.00	125.00
178	A3	130r on 75r (G)	1.75	1.60
179	A3	130r on 300r (R)	4.00	3.25
a.		Perf. 12½	7.00	4.50
180	N1	400r on 2½r (R)	.40	.40
a.		Perf. 11½	1.60	1.25
		Nos. 172-180 (9)	596.15	395.25

Overprinted

On Stamps of 1902
Perf. 11½, 12

181	A5	50r blue (R)	.90	.60
182	A5	75r rose (G)	2.75	2.00

On No. 87

183	A5	50r on 65r dull blue (R)	2.50	2.50
		Nos. 181-183 (3)	6.15	5.10

Inverted and double surcharges of Nos. 181-183 were made intentionally.

Common Design Types pictured following the introduction.

Vasco da Gama Issue of Various Portuguese Colonies
Common Design Types Surcharged

On Stamps of Macao

1913   **Perf. 12½ to 16**

184	CD20	¼c on ½a	4.00	4.00
185	CD21	½c on 1a	3.00	3.00
186	CD22	1c on 2a	3.00	3.00
187	CD23	2½c on 4a	2.00	2.00
188	CD24	5c on 8a	2.00	2.00
189	CD25	7½c on 12a	5.50	5.50

190	CD26	10c on 16a	4.00	4.00
191	CD27	15c on 24a	4.00	4.00
		Nos. 184-191 (8)	27.50	27.50

On Stamps of Portuguese Africa
Perf. 14 to 15

192	CD20	¼c on 2½r	.75	.75
193	CD21	½c on 5r	.75	.75
194	CD22	1c on 10r	.75	.75
195	CD23	2½c on 25r	.75	.75
196	CD24	5c on 50r	.75	.75
197	CD25	7½c on 75r	2.50	2.50
198	CD26	10c on 100r	1.25	1.25
199	CD27	15c on 150r	1.75	1.75
		Nos. 192-199 (8)	9.25	9.25

On Stamps of Timor

200	CD20	¼c on ½a	2.00	2.00
201	CD21	½c on 1a	2.00	2.00
202	CD22	1c on 2a	2.00	2.00
203	CD23	2½c on 4a	2.00	2.00
204	CD24	5c on 8a	2.00	2.00
205	CD25	7½c on 12a	3.00	3.00
206	CD26	10c on 16a	2.00	2.00
207	CD27	15c on 24a	2.00	2.00
		Nos. 200-207 (8)	17.00	17.00
		Nos. 184-207 (24)	53.75	53.75

Provisional Issue of 1902 Overprinted in Carmine

1915   **Perf. 11½, 12½, 13½**

208	A2	115r on 10r green	1.00	2.00
209	A2	115r on 200r gray vio	.90	2.00
210	A2	130r on 100r brown	.70	2.00
211	A3	115r on 80r lt green	1.10	2.00
212	A3	115r on 100r brn, *buff*	.90	2.00
a.		Perf. 11½	17.00	17.00
213	A3	115r on 150r car, *rose*	1.75	2.00
214	A3	130r on 15r choc	.65	2.00
a.		Perf. 12½	7.00	7.00
215	A3	130r on 75r carmine	1.50	1.75
216	A3	130r on 300r dk bl, *sal*	1.10	1.75
		Nos. 208-216 (9)	9.60	17.50

Stamps of 1911-14 Surcharged in Black:

d   e

On Stamps of 1911

1919   **Perf. 11½**

217	A5 (d)	½c on 75r red lilac	1.50	2.00
218	A5 (d)	2½c on 100r blue, *grysh*		

On Stamps of 1912
Perf. 11½x12

219	A6 (e)	½c on 75r bis brn	.65	.60
220	A6 (e)	2½c on 100r brn, *lt grn*	.75	.40

On Stamps of 1914

221	A5 (d)	½c on 75r red lil	.65	.40
222	A5 (d)	2½c on 100r bl, *grysh*	.70	.60
		Nos. 217-222 (5)	4.25	4.00

Inverted and double surcharges were made for sale to collectors.

Nos. 163, 98 and Type of 1914 Surcharged with New Values and Bars in Black

1921

223	A5 (c)	00.5c on 75r	350.00	350.00
224	A5 (b)	4c on 130r (#98)	.70	.70
225	A5 (c)	4c on 130r brn, *straw*	2.75	2.50

Nos. 109 and 108 Surcharged with New Values and Bars in Black

226	A6	00.5c on 75c	.85	.85
227	A6	1c on 50r	.75	.65

Nos. 133 and 138 Surcharged with New Values and Bars in Black

228	A7	00.5c on 7½c	.70	.60
229	A7	04c on 15c	1.10	1.10
		Nos. 224-229 (6)	6.85	6.40
		Nos. 223-229 (7)	356.85	356.40

The 04c surcharge exists on the 15c brown rose, perf 12x11½, No. 139. Vale, 30 cents.

Nos. 81-82 Surcharged

República / 40 C.

1925   **Perf. 12½**

234	A3	40c on 400r on 200r bl, *bl*	.80	.65
a.		Perf. 13½	3.25	2.25
235	N1	40c on 400c on 2½r brn	.60	.60
a.		Perf. 13½	.60	.60

Nos. 150-151, 154-155 Surcharged

70 C.

1931   **Perf. 11½**

236	A7	50c on 60c deep rose	1.50	.80
237	A7	70c on 80c pink	3.00	1.00
238	A7	70c on 1e deep blue	4.00	1.10
239	A7	1.40e on 2e dark violet	5.00	1.10
		Nos. 236-239 (4)	13.50	4.00

Ceres — A14

1932-46   **Typo.**   **Wmk. 232**
    Perf. 12x11½

243	A14	1c bister brn	.20	.20
244	A14	5c dk brown	.20	.20
245	A14	10c dp violet	.20	.20
246	A14	15c black	.20	.20
247	A14	20c gray	.25	.20
248	A14	30c myrtle grn	.25	.20
249	A14	35c yel grn ('46)	4.50	2.00
250	A14	40c dp orange	.25	.20
251	A14	45c lt blue	.85	.65
252	A14	50c lt brown	.20	.20
253	A14	60c olive grn	.30	.20
254	A14	70c orange brn	.65	.20
255	A14	80c emerald	.25	.20
256	A14	85c rose	2.00	2.00
257	A14	1a claret	.65	.20
258	A14	1.40a dk blue	4.50	1.10
258A	A14	1.75a dk blue ('46)	6.00	1.10
259	A14	2a dull vio	2.25	.35
260	A14	5a pale yel grn	3.00	.50
261	A14	10a olive bis	10.00	.90
262	A14	20a orange	17.50	2.00
		Nos. 243-262 (21)	54.20	13.00

For surcharges see Nos. 263-267, 271-273, 294A-300, J31-J36.

Surcharged with New Value and Bars
5½mm between bars and new value.

1934

263	A14	10c on 45c lt bl	1.25	.70
264	A14	20c on 85c rose	1.10	.70
265	A14	30c on 1.40a dk bl	1.10	.70
266	A14	70c on 2a dl vio	2.00	1.10
267	A14	80c on 5a pale yel grn	3.50	1.00
		Nos. 263-267 (5)	8.95	4.20

See Nos. 294A-300.

CORREIOS

Nos. J26, J30 Surcharged in Black

= 5 CENTAVOS

1935   **Unwmk.**   **Perf. 11½**

268	D2	5c on 6c lt brown	.90	.60
269	D2	30c on 50c gray	.90	.60
270	D2	40c on 50c gray	.90	.60
		Nos. 268-270 (3)	2.70	1.80

No. 255 Surcharged in Black

0,15 Cent.

1938   **Wmk. 232**   **Perf. 12x11½**

271	A14	5c on 80c emerald	.40	1.00
272	A14	10c on 80c emerald	.50	1.75
273	A14	15c on 80c emerald	.65	2.50
		Nos. 271-273 (3)	1.55	5.25

Vasco da Gama Issue
Common Design Types
Engr.; Name & Value Typo. in Black
Perf. 13½x13

1938, July 26   Unwmk.

274	CD34	1c gray green	.20	.20
275	CD34	5c orange brn	.20	.20
276	CD34	10c dk carmine	.20	.20
277	CD34	15c dk violet brn	.20	.20
278	CD34	20c slate	.20	.20
279	CD35	30c rose violet	.25	.20
280	CD35	35c brt green	.35	.20
281	CD35	40c brown	.25	.20
282	CD35	50c brt red vio	.25	.20
283	CD36	60c gray black	.35	.20
284	CD36	70c brown vio	.30	.30
285	CD36	80c orange	.30	.30
286	CD36	1a red	.30	.20
287	CD37	1.75a blue	.85	.30
288	CD37	2a brown car	1.50	.30
289	CD37	5a olive grn	3.00	.30
290	CD38	10a blue vio	6.50	.60
291	CD38	20a red brown	15.00	1.10
		Nos. 274-291 (18)	30.20	5.20

For surcharges see Nos. 301-304.

Marble Column and Portuguese Arms with Cross — A20

1938, July 29   *Perf. 12½*

292	A20	80c blue green	1.00	1.00
293	A20	1.75a deep blue	5.00	1.00
294	A20	20a dk red brown	14.00	11.00
		Nos. 292-294 (3)	20.00	13.00

Visit of the President of Portugal to this colony in 1938.

Stamps of 1932 Surcharged with New Value and Bars

8mm between bars and new value.

1941-45   Wmk. 232   *Perf. 12x11½*

294A	A14	5c on 80c emer ('45)	.25	.20
295	A14	10c on 45c lt blue	.65	.55
296	A14	15c on 45c lt blue	1.00	.70
297	A14	20c on 85c rose	.65	.55
298	A14	35c on 85c rose	.65	.55
299	A14	50c on 1.40a dk blue	.65	.55
300	A14	60c on 1a claret	8.00	4.00
		Nos. 294A-300 (7)	11.85	7.10

Nos. 285 to 287 Surcharged with New Values and Bars in Black or Red

1945   Unwmk.   *Perf. 13½x13*

301	CD36	5c on 80c org	.30	.20
302	CD36	10c on 1a red	.60	.20
303	CD37	50c on 1.75a bl (R)	.40	.20
304	CD37	50c on 1.75a bl	.60	.20
		Nos. 301-304 (4)	1.90	.80

Sao Miguel Fort, Luanda — A21

John IV — A22

Designs: 10c, Our Lady of Nazareth Church, Luanda. 50c, Salvador Correia de Sa e Bene vides. 1a, Surrender of Luanda. 1.75a, Diogo Cao. 2a, Manuel Cerveira Pereira. 5a, Stone Cliffs, Yelala. 10a, Paulo Dias de Novais. 20a, Massangano Fort.

Perf. 14½

1948, May   Unwmk.   Litho.

305	A21	5c dk violet	.20	.20
306	A21	10c dk brown	.25	.20
307	A22	30c blue grn	.20	.20
308	A22	50c vio brown	.20	.20
309	A21	1a carmine	.35	.20
310	A21	1.75a slate blue	.65	.20
311	A22	2a green	.65	.20
312	A21	5a gray black	1.25	.35
313	A22	10a rose lilac	2.50	.35

314	A21	20a gray blue	6.00	1.10
a.		Sheet of 10, #305-314	40.00	40.00
		Nos. 305-314 (10)	12.25	3.20

300th anniv. of the restoration of Angola to Portugal. No. 314a sold for 42.50a.

Lady of Fatima Issue
Common Design Type

1948, Dec.

315	CD40	50c carmine	.65	.50
316	CD40	3a ultra	2.00	1.00
317	CD40	6a red orange	7.00	2.50
318	CD40	9a dp claret	17.00	3.00
		Nos. 315-318 (4)	26.65	7.00

Our Lady of the Rosary at Fatima, Portugal.

Chiumbe River — A24

Black Rocks — A25

Designs: 50c, View of Luanda. 2.50a, Sa da Bandeira. 3.50a, Mocamedes. 15a, Cubal River. 50a, Duke of Bragança Falls.

1949   Unwmk.   *Perf. 13½*

319	A24	20c dk slate blue	.20	.20
320	A25	40c black brown	.20	.20
321	A24	50c rose brown	.20	.20
322	A24	2.50a blue violet	1.10	.25
323	A24	3.50a slate gray	1.10	.25
323A	A24	15a dk green	8.25	1.50
324	A24	50a dp green	22.50	3.75
		Nos. 319-324 (7)	33.55	6.35

Sailing Vessel — A26

UPU Symbols — A27

1949, Aug.   *Perf. 14*

325	A26	1a chocolate	2.00	.35
326	A26	4a dk Prus green	5.00	.85

Centenary of founding of Mocamedes.

1949, Oct.

327	A27	4a dk grn & lt grn	2.50	1.50

75th anniv. of the UPU.

Catalogue values for unused stamps in this section, from this point to the end of the section, are for Never Hinged items.

Stamp of 1870 — A28

1950, Apr. 2   *Perf. 11½x12*

328	A28	50c yellow green	.80	.25
329	A28	1a fawn	.80	.25
330	A28	4a black	3.25	.70
a.		Sheet of 3, #328-330	7.50	7.50
		Nos. 328-330 (3)	4.85	1.20

Angola's first philatelic exhibition, marking the 80th anniversary of Angola's first stamps. No. 330a contains Nos. 328, 329 (inverted), 330, perf. 11½ and sold for 6.50a. All copies carry an oval exhibition cancellation in the margin but the stamps were valid for postage.

Holy Year Issue
Common Design Types

1950, May   *Perf. 13x13½*

331	CD41	1a dull rose vio	.35	.20
332	CD42	4a black	3.00	.35

Dark Chanting Goshawk — A31

European Bee Eater — A32

10c, Racquet-tailed roller. 15c, Bateleur eagle. 50c, Giant kingfisher. 1a, Yellow-fronted barbet. 1.50a, Openbill (stork). 2a, Southern ground hornbill. 2.50a, African skimmer. 3a, Shikra. 3.50a, Denham's bustard. 4a, African golden oriole. 4.50a, Long-tailed shrike. 5a, Red-shouldered glossy starling. 6a, Sharp-tailed glossy starling. 7a, Red-shouldered widow bird. 10a, Half-colored kingfisher. 12.50a, White-crowned shrike. 15a, White-winged babbling starling. 20a, Yellow-billed hornbill. 25a, Amethyst starling. 30a, Orange-breasted shrike. 40a, Secretary bird. 50a, Rosy-faced lovebird.

Photogravure and Lithographed
1951   Unwmk.   *Perf. 11½*
Birds in Natural Colors

333	A31	5c lt blue	.20	.50
334	A32	10c aqua	.20	.20
335	A32	15c salmon pink	.25	1.00
336	A32	20c pale yellow	.50	.25
337	A31	50c gray blue	.30	.20
338	A31	1a lilac	.30	.20
339	A31	1.50a gray buff	.40	.20
340	A31	2a cream	.40	.20
341	A32	2.50a gray	.40	.20
342	A32	3a lemon yel	.40	.20
343	A31	3.50a lt gray	.40	.20
344	A31	4a rose buff	1.25	.20
345	A32	4.50a rose lilac	1.25	3.00
346	A31	5a green	6.25	.20
347	A31	6a blue	6.25	.55
348	A31	7a orange	6.25	.75
349	A31	10a lilac rose	25.00	1.10
350	A32	12.50a slate gray	8.50	1.75
351	A31	15a pale olive	8.50	1.75
352	A31	20a pale bis brn	25.00	4.50
353	A31	25a lilac rose	20.00	2.50
354	A32	30a pale salmon	20.00	3.00
355	A31	40a yellow	40.00	3.75
356	A31	50a turquoise	75.00	14.00
		Nos. 333-356 (24)	247.00	40.40

Holy Year Extension Issue
Common Design Type

1951, Oct.   Litho.   *Perf. 14*

357	CD43	4a orange + label	1.25	.50

Sheets contain alternate vertical rows of stamps and labels bearing quotations from Pope Pius XII or the Patriarch Cardinal of Lisbon. Stamp without label attached sells for less.

Medical Congress Issue
Common Design Type

Design: Medical examination

1952, June   *Perf. 13½*

358	CD44	1a vio blue & brn blk	.40	.20

Head of Christ — A35

1952, Oct.   Unwmk.   *Perf. 13*

359	A35	10c dk blue & buff	.20	.20
360	A35	50c dk ol grn & ol gray	.20	.20
361	A35	2a rose vio & cream	1.25	.20
		Nos. 359-361 (3)	1.65	.60

Exhibition of Sacred Missionary Art, Lisbon, 1951.

Leopard — A36

Sable Antelope — A37

Animals: 20c, Elephant. 30c, Eland. 40c, African crocodile. 50c, Impala. 1a, Mountain zebra. 1.50a, Sitatunga. 2a, Black rhinoceros. 2.30a, Gemsbok. 2.50a, Lion. 3a, Buffalo. 3.50a, Springbok. 4a, Brindled gnu. 5a, Harte-beest. 7a, Wart hog. 10a, Defassa waterbuck. 12.50a, Hippopotamus. 15a, Greater kudu. 20a, Giraffe.

1953, Aug. 15   *Perf. 12½*

362	A36	5c multicolored	.20	.20
363	A37	10c multicolored	.20	.20
364	A37	20c multicolored	.20	.20
365	A37	30c multicolored	.20	.20
366	A36	40c multicolored	.20	.20
367	A37	50c multicolored	.20	.20
368	A37	1a multicolored	.20	.20
369	A37	1.50a multicolored	.20	.20
370	A36	2a multicolored	.20	.20
371	A37	2.30a multicolored	.25	.20
372	A37	2.50a multicolored	.30	.20
373	A36	3a multicolored	.30	.20
374	A37	3.50a multicolored	.20	.20
375	A37	4a multicolored	3.00	.25
376	A37	5a multicolored	.35	.20
377	A37	7a multicolored	.75	.25
378	A31	10a multicolored	1.25	.20
379	A37	12.50a multicolored	4.00	2.50
380	A37	15a multicolored	4.00	2.00
381	A37	20a multicolored	5.00	.35
		Nos. 362-381 (20)	21.20	8.35

Stamp of Portugal and Arms of Colonies — A38

1953, Nov.   Photo.   *Perf. 13*
Stamp and Arms Multicolored

382	A38	50c gray & dark gray	.55	.35

Cent. of Portugal's 1st postage stamps.

Map and Plane — A39

Typographed and Lithographed
1954, May 27   *Perf. 13½*

383	A39	35c multicolored	.20	.20
384	A39	4.50e multicolored	.70	.30

Visit of Pres. Francisco H C. Lopes.

Sao Paulo Issue
Common Design Type

1954   Litho.

385	CD46	1e bister & gray	.32	.20

Map of Angola — A41

Artur de Paiva — A42

1955, Aug.   Unwmk.   *Perf. 13½*

386	A41	5c multicolored	.20	.20
387	A41	20c multicolored	.20	.20
388	A41	50c multicolored	.20	.20
389	A41	1e multicolored	.20	.20
390	A41	2.30e multicolored	.30	.20
391	A41	4e multicolored	.50	.20

392	A41	10e multicolored	.50	.20
393	A41	20e multicolored	1.00	.20
		Nos. 386-393 (8)	3.10	1.60

For overprints see Nos. 593, 598, 604.

1956, Oct. 9   **Perf. 13½x12½**

| 394 | A42 | 1e blk, dk bl & ocher | .20 | .20 |

Cent. of the birth of Col. Artur de Paiva.

Man of Malange — A43   Jose M. Antunes — A44

Various Costumes in Multicolor; Inscriptions in Black Brown

1957, Jan. 1   **Photo.**   **Perf. 11½**
Granite Paper

395	A43	5c gray	.20	.20
396	A43	10c orange yel	.20	.20
397	A43	15c lt blue grn	.20	.20
398	A43	20c pale rose vio	.20	.20
399	A43	30c brt rose	.20	.20
400	A43	40c blue gray	.20	.20
401	A43	50c pale olive	.20	.20
402	A43	80c lt violet	.20	.20
403	A43	1.50e buff	1.00	.20
404	A43	2.50e lt yel grn	1.00	.20
405	A43	4e salmon	.50	.20
406	A43	10e salmon pink	1.00	.25
		Nos. 395-406 (12)	5.10	2.45

1957, Apr.   **Perf. 13½**

| 407 | A44 | 1e aqua & brown | .65 | .20 |

Birth cent. of Father Jose Maria Antunes.

Fair Emblem, Globe and Arms — A45

1958, July   **Litho.**   **Perf. 12x11½**

| 408 | A45 | 1.50e multicolored | .25 | .20 |

World's Fair, Brussels, Apr. 17-Oct. 19.

Tropical Medicine Congress Issue
Common Design Type

Design: Securidaca longipedunculata.

1958, Dec. 15   **Perf. 13½**

| 409 | CD47 | 2.50e multicolored | 1.10 | .70 |

Medicine Man — A47

Welwitschia Mirabilis A48

Designs: 1.50e, Early government doctor. 2.50e, Modern medical team.

1958, Dec. 18   **Perf. 11½x12**

410	A47	1e blue blk & brown	.20	.20
411	A47	1.50e gray, blk & brown	.50	.40
412	A47	2.50e multicolored	.75	.40
		Nos. 410-412 (3)	1.45	.80

75th anniversary of the Maria Pia Hospital, Luanda.

1959, Oct. 1   **Litho.**   **Perf. 14½**
Various Views of Plant and Various Frames

413	A48	1.50e lt brn, grn & blk	.55	.45
414	A48	2.50e multicolored	.85	.50
415	A48	5e multicolored	1.10	.75
416	A48	10e multicolored	2.75	1.00
		Nos. 413-416 (4)	5.25	2.70

Centenary of discovery of Welwitschia mirabilis, desert plant.

Map of West Africa, c. 1540, by Jorge Reinel — A49

1960, June 25   **Perf. 13½**

| 417 | A49 | 2.50e multicolored | .20 | .20 |

500th anniv. of the death of Prince Henry the Navigator.

Distributing Medicines A50

Girl of Angola — A51

1960, Oct.   **Litho.**   **Perf. 14½**

| 418 | A50 | 2.50e multicolored | .30 | .20 |

10th anniv. of the Commission for Technical Co-operation in Africa South of the Sahara (C.C.T.A.).

1961, Nov. 30   **Unwmk.**   **Perf. 13**

Various portraits.

419	A51	10c multicolored	.20	.20
420	A51	15c multicolored	.20	.20
421	A51	30c multicolored	.20	.20
422	A51	40c multicolored	.20	.20
423	A51	60c multicolored	.20	.20
424	A51	1.50e multicolored	.20	.20
425	A51	2e multicolored	.60	.20
426	A51	2.50e multicolored	.85	.20
427	A51	3e multicolored	2.00	.30
428	A51	4e multicolored	1.25	.20
429	A51	5e multicolored	1.00	.20
430	A51	7.50e multicolored	1.25	.50
431	A51	10e multicolored	1.00	.25
432	A51	15e multicolored	1.00	.40
432A	A51	25e multicolored	2.00	.65
432B	A51	50e multicolored	4.00	1.00
		Nos. 419-432B (16)	16.15	5.00

Sports Issue
Common Design Type

Sports: 50c, Flying. 1e, Rowing. 1.50e, Water polo. 2.50e, Hammer throwing. 4.50e, High jump. 15e, Weight lifting.

1962, Jan. 18   **Perf. 13½**
Multicolored Design

433	CD48	50c lt blue	.40	.20
434	CD48	1e olive bister	1.00	.20
435	CD48	1.50e salmon	.50	.20
436	CD48	2.50e lt green	.50	.20
437	CD48	4.50e pale blue	.50	.25
438	CD48	15e yellow	1.75	.65
		Nos. 433-438 (6)	4.65	1.70

For overprint see No. 608.

Anti-Malaria Issue
Common Design Type

Design: Anopheles funestus.

1962, April   **Litho.**   **Perf. 13½**

| 439 | CD49 | 2.50e multicolored | .85 | .50 |

Gen. Norton de Matos — A54

Locusts — A56

1962, Aug. 8   **Unwmk.**   **Perf. 14½**

| 440 | A54 | 2.50e multicolored | .40 | .20 |

50th anniv. of the founding of Nova Lisboa.

1963, June 2   **Litho.**   **Perf. 14**

| 447 | A56 | 2.50e multicolored | .55 | .25 |

15th anniv. of the Intl. Anti-Locust Organ.

Arms of Luanda A57

Vila de Santo Antonio do Zaire — A58

Coats of Arms (Provinces and Cities): 10c, Massangano. 15c, Sanza-Pombo. 25c, Ambriz. 30c, Muxima. 40c, Ambrizete. 50c, Carmona. 60c, Catete. 70c, Quibaxe. No. 458, Maquelo do Zombo. 1e, Salazar. 1.20e, Bembe. No. 461, Malanje. No. 462, Caxito. 1.80e, Dondo. 2e, Henrique de Carvalho. No. 465, Moçamedes. No. 466, Damba. 3e, Novo Redondo. 3.50e, S. Salvador do Congo. 4e, Cuimba. 5e, Luso. 6.50e, Negage. 7e, Quitexe. 7.50e, S. Filipe de Benguela. 8e, Mucaba. 9e, 31 de Janeiro. 10e, Lobito. 11e, Nova Caipemba. 12.50e, Gabela. 14e, Songo. 15e Sá da Bandeira. 17e, Quimbele. 17.50e, Silva Porto. 20e, Nova Lisboa. 22.50e, Cabinda. 25e, Noqui. 30e, Serpa Pinto. 35e, Santa Cruz. 50e, General Freire.

1963   **Perf. 13½**
Arms in Original Colors; Red and Violet Blue Inscriptions

448	A57	5c tan	.20	.20
449	A57	10c lt blue	.20	.20
450	A58	15c salmon	.20	.20
451	A58	20c olive	.20	.20
452	A57	25c lt blue	.20	.20
453	A57	30c buff	.20	.20
454	A58	40c gray	.20	.20
455	A57	50c lt green	.20	.20
456	A58	60c brt yellow	.20	.20
457	A58	70c dull rose	.20	.20
458	A58	1e pale lilac	.30	.20
459	A58	1e dull yellow	.20	.20
460	A57	1.20e rose	.20	.20
461	A57	1.50e pale salmon	.60	.20
462	A58	1.50e lt green	.40	.20
463	A58	1.80e yel olive	.25	.20
464	A57	2e lt yel green	.30	.20
465	A57	2.50e lt gray	1.50	.20
466	A58	2.50e dull blue	1.25	.20
467	A57	3e yel olive	.45	.20
468	A57	3.50e gray	.50	.20
469	A58	4e citron	.35	.20
470	A57	5e citron	.40	.25
471	A58	6.50e tan	.40	.25
472	A58	7e rose lilac	1.25	2.00
473	A57	7.50e pale lilac	1.25	2.00
474	A58	8e lt aqua	.45	.30
475	A58	9e yellow	1.25	1.50
476	A58	10e dp salmon	.70	.35
477	A58	11e dull yel grn	2.00	1.50
478	A57	12.50e pale blue	.90	.45
479	A58	14e lt gray	2.00	1.00
480	A57	15e lt blue	1.00	.45
481	A58	17e pale blue	3.00	2.00
482	A57	17.50e dull yellow	1.50	1.00

483	A57	20e lt aqua	1.50	.70
484	A57	22.50e gray	1.50	1.00
485	A57	25e citron	1.50	.70
486	A57	30e yellow	2.00	1.25
487	A58	35e grysh blue	2.00	1.50
488	A58	50e dp yellow	3.00	1.25
		Nos. 448-488 (41)	35.10	22.10

Pres. Américo Rodrigues Thomaz — A59

1963, Sept. 16   **Litho.**

| 489 | A59 | 2.50e multicolored | .40 | .20 |

Visit of the President of Portugal.

Airline Anniversary Issue
Common Design Type

1963, Oct. 5   **Unwmk.**   **Perf. 14½**

| 490 | CD50 | 1e lt blue & multi | .50 | .20 |

Cathedral of Sá da Bandeira — A61

Malange Cathedral A62

Churches: 20c, Landana. 30c, Luanda Cathedral. 40c, Gabela. 50c, St. Martin's Chapel, Baia dos Tigres. 1.50e, St. Peter, Chibia. 2e, Church of Our Lady, Benguela. 2.50e, Church of Jesus, Luanda. 3e, Camabatela. 3.50e, Mission, Cabinda. 4e, Vila Folgares. 4.50e, Church of Our Lady, Lobito. 5e, Church of Cabinda. 7.50e, Cacuso Church, Malange. 10e, Lubango Mission. 12.50e, Huila Mission. 15e, Church of Our Lady, Luanda Island.

1963, Nov. 1   **Litho.**
Multicolored Design and Inscription

491	A61	10c gray blue	.20	.20
492	A61	20c pink	.20	.20
493	A61	30c lt blue	.20	.20
494	A61	40c tan	.20	.20
495	A61	50c lt green	.20	.20
496	A62	1e buff	.20	.20
497	A61	1.50e lt vio blue	.20	.20
498	A62	2e pale rose	.20	.20
499	A62	2.50e gray	.20	.20
500	A62	3e buff	.20	.20
501	A61	3.50e olive	.25	.20
502	A62	4e buff	.25	.20
503	A62	4.50e pale blue	.40	.25
504	A61	5e tan	.50	.25
505	A62	7.50e gray	.70	.30
506	A61	10e dull yellow	.80	.35
507	A62	12.50e bister	1.00	.70
508	A62	15e pale gray vio	2.00	.60
		Nos. 491-508 (18)	7.90	4.85

National Overseas Bank Issue
Common Design Type

Design: Antonio Teixeira de Sousa.

1964, May 16   **Perf. 13½**

| 509 | CD51 | 2.50e multicolored | .40 | .25 |

Commerce Building and Arms of Chamber of Commerce A64

1964, Nov.   **Litho.**   **Perf. 12**

| 510 | A64 | 1e multicolored | .20 | .20 |

Luanda Chamber of Commerce centenary.

ITU Issue
Common Design Type
1965, May 17   Unwmk.   Perf. 14½
511 CD52 2.50e gray & multi   .70 .25

Plane over Luanda
Airport — A65

Harquebusier,
1539 — A66

1965, Dec. 3   Litho.   Perf. 13
512 A65 2.50e multicolored   .25 .20
25th anniv. of DTA, Direccao dos Transportes Aereos.

1966, Feb. 25   Litho.   Perf. 14½
50c, Harquebusier, 1539. 1e, Harquebusier, 1640. 1.50e, Infantry officer, 1777. 2e, Standard bearer, infantry, 1777. 2.50e, Infantry soldier, 1777. 3e, Cavalry officer, 1783. 4e, Cavalry soldier, 1783. 4.50e, Infantry officer, 1807. 5e, Infantry soldier, 1807. 6e, Cavalry officer, 1807. 8e, Cavalry soldier, 1807. 9e, Infantry soldier, 1873.

513	A66	50c multicolored	.20	.20
514	A66	1e multicolored	.20	.20
515	A66	1.50e multicolored	.20	.20
516	A66	2e multicolored	.20	.20
517	A66	2.50e multicolored	.20	.20
518	A66	3e multicolored	.20	.20
519	A66	4e multicolored	.35	.25
520	A66	4.50e multicolored	.35	.25
521	A66	5e multicolored	.50	.20
522	A66	6e multicolored	.65	.45
523	A66	8e multicolored	1.00	.75
524	A66	9e multicolored	1.25	.90
		Nos. 513-524 (12)	5.30	4.00

National Revolution Issue
Common Design Type
Design: St. Paul's Hospital and Commercial and Industrial School.

1966, May 28   Litho.   Perf. 12
525 CD53 1e multicolored   .20 .20

Emblem of Holy
Ghost Society — A68

1966   Litho.   Perf. 13
526 A68 1e blue & multi   .20 .20
Centenary of the Holy Ghost Society.

Navy Club Issue
Common Design Type
Designs: 1e, Mendes Barata and cruiser Dom Carlos I. 2.50e, Capt. Augusto de Castilho and corvette Mindelo.

1967, Jan. 31   Litho.   Perf. 13
527 CD54 1e multicolored   .40 .20
528 CD54 2.50e multicolored   .65 .20

Fatima
Basilica — A70

Angola Map,
Manuel Cerveira
Pereira — A71

1967, May 13   Litho.   Perf. 12½x13
529 A70 50c multicolored   .20 .20
50th anniv. of the apparition of the Virgin Mary to 3 shepherd children at Fatima.

1967, Aug. 15   Litho.   Perf. 12½x13
530 A71 50c multicolored   .20 .20
350th anniv. of the founding of Benguela.

Administration Building,
Carmona — A72

1967   Litho.   Perf. 12
531 A72 1e multicolored   .20 .20
50th anniv. of the founding of Carmona.

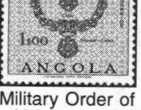

Military Order of
Valor — A73

Our Lady of
Hope — A74

50c, Ribbon of the Three Orders. 1.50e, Military Order of Avis. 2e, Military Order of Christ. 2.50e, Military Order of St. John of Espada. 3e, Order of the Empire. 4e, Order of Prince Henry. 5e, Order of Benemerencia. 10e, Order of Public Instruction. 20e, Order for Industrial & Agricultural Merit.

1967, Oct. 31   Perf. 14
532	A73	50c lt gray & multi	.20	.20
533	A73	1e lt green & multi	.20	.20
534	A73	1.50e yellow & multi	.20	.20
535	A73	2e multicolored	.20	.20
536	A73	2.50e multicolored	.20	.20
537	A73	3e lt olive & multi	.20	.20
538	A73	4e gray & multi	.20	.20
539	A73	5e multicolored	.40	.20
540	A73	10e lilac & multi	.55	.20
541	A73	20e lt blue & multi	1.25	.45
		Nos. 532-541 (10)	3.60	2.25

1968, Apr. 22   Litho.   Perf. 14
1e, Belmonte Castle, horiz. 1.50e, St. Jerome's Convent. 2.50e, Cabral's Armada.

542	A74	50c yellow & multi	.20	.20
543	A74	1e gray & multi	.25	.20
544	A74	1.50e lt blue & multi	.40	.20
545	A74	2.50e buff & multi	.60	.20
		Nos. 542-545 (4)	1.45	.80

500th anniv. of the birth of Pedro Alvares Cabral, navigator who took possession of Brazil for Portugal.

Francisco Inocencio
de Souza
Coutinho — A75

1969, Jan. 7   Litho.   Perf. 14
546 A75 2e multicolored   .25 .20
Founding of Novo Redondo, 200th anniv.

Admiral Coutinho Issue
Common Design Type
Design: Adm. Gago Coutinho and his first ship.

1969, Feb. 17   Litho.   Perf. 14
547 CD55 2.50e multicolored   .30 .20

Compass Rose
A77

Portal of St.
Jeronimo's
Monastery
A79

1969, Aug. 29   Litho.   Perf. 14
548 A77 1e multicolored   .20 .20
500th anniv. of the birth of Vasco da Gama (1469-1524), navigator.

Administration Reform Issue
Common Design Type
1969, Sept. 25   Litho.   Perf. 14
549 CD56 1.50e multicolored   .20 .20

1969, Dec. 1   Litho.   Perf. 14
550 A79 3e multicolored   .20 .20
500th anniv. of the birth of King Manuel I.

Angolasaurus Bocagei — A80

Fossils and Minerals: 1e, Ferrometeorite. 1.50e, Dioptase crystals. 2e, Gondwanidium. 2.50e, Diamonds. 3e, Estromatolite. 3.50e, Procarcharodon megalodon. 4e, Microceratodus angolensis. 4.50e, Moscovite. 5e, Barite. 6e, Nostoceras. 10e, Rotula orbiculus angolensis.

1970, Oct. 31   Litho.   Perf. 13
551	A80	50c tan & multi	.20	.20
552	A80	1e multicolored	.25	.20
553	A80	1.50e multicolored	.30	.20
554	A80	2e multicolored	.35	.20
555	A80	2.50e lt gray & multi	.40	.20
556	A80	3e multicolored	.50	.20
557	A80	3.50e blue & multi	.60	.20
558	A80	4e lt gray & multi	.70	.20
559	A80	4.50e gray & multi	.80	.20
560	A80	5e gray & multi	.90	.25
561	A80	6e pink & multi	1.00	.30
562	A80	10e lt blue & multi	2.00	.50
		Nos. 551-562 (12)	8.00	2.85

Marshal Carmona Issue
Common Design Type
1970, Nov. 15   Perf. 14
563 CD57 2.50e multicolored   .25 .20

Arms of
Malanje, Cotton
Boll and
Field — A82

1970, Nov. 20   Perf. 13
564 A82 2.50e multicolored   .25 .20
Centenary of the municipality of Malanje.

Mail Ships
and Angola
No. 1
A83

4.50e, Steam locomotive and Angola No. 4.

1970, Dec. 1   Perf. 13½
565 A83 1.50e multicolored   .40 .25
566 A83 4.50e multicolored   .75 .40
Cent. of stamps of Angola. See No. C36. For overprint see No. 616B.

Map of Africa,
Diagram of
Seismic
Tests — A84

Galleon on Congo
River — A85

1971, Aug. 22   Litho.   Perf. 13
567 A84 2.50e multicolored   .20 .20
5th Regional Conference of Soil and Foundation Engineers, Luanda, Aug. 22-Sept. 5.

1972, May 25   Litho.   Perf. 13
568 A85 1e emerald & multi   .20 .20
4th centenary of the publication of The Lusiads by Luiz Camoens.

Olympic Games Issue
Common Design Type
1972, June 20   Perf. 14x13½
569 CD59 50c multicolored   .20 .20

Lisbon-Rio de Janeiro Flight Issue
Common Design Type
1972, Sept. 20   Litho.   Perf. 13½
570 CD60 1e multicolored   .20 .20

WMO Centenary Issue
Common Design Type
1973, Dec. 15   Litho.   Perf. 13
571 CD61 1e dk gray & multi   .20 .20

Radar
Station
A89

1974, June 25   Litho.   Perf. 13
572 A89 2e multicolored   .25 .20
Establishment of satellite communications network via Intelsat among Portugal, Angola and Mozambique.
For overprint see No. 616A

Harpa
Doris — A90

Designs: Sea shells.

1974, Oct. 25   Litho.   Perf. 12x12½
573	A90	25c shown	.20	.20
574	A90	30c Murex me-lanamathos	.20	.20
575	A90	50c Venus foliaceo lamellosa	.20	.20
576	A90	70c Lathyrus filosus	.20	.20
577	A90	1e Cymbium cisium	.20	.20
578	A90	1.50e Cassis tesselata	.20	.20
579	A90	2e Cypraea stercoraria	.20	.20
580	A90	2.50e Conus prome-theus	.20	.20
581	A90	3e Strombus latus	.20	.20
582	A90	3.50e Tympanotonus fuscatus	.20	.20
583	A90	4e Cardium cos-tatum	.25	.20
584	A90	5e Natica fulminea	.25	.20
585	A90	6e Lyropecten nodosus	.35	.20
586	A90	7e Tonna galea	.75	.25
587	A90	10e Donax rugosus	.90	.30
588	A90	25e Cymatium trigonum	1.50	.40

589	A90	30e	Olivancilaria acuminata	2.50	.75
590	A90	35e	Semifusus morio	2.50	.75
591	A90	40e	Clavatula lineata	3.00	1.00
592	A90	50e	Solarium granulatum	4.00	1.50
		Nos. 573-592 (20)		18.00	7.55

For overprints see Nos. 605-607, 617-630.

No. 386 Overprinted in Blue: "1974 / FILATELIA / JUVENIL"

1974, Dec. 21   Litho.   Perf. 13½
593 A41 5c multicolored   .20 .20

Youth philately.

Republic

Star and Hand Holding Rifle — A91

1975, Nov. 11   Litho.   Perf. 13x13½
594 A91 1.50e red & multi   .20 .20

Independence in 1975.

Diquiche Mask — A92

Design: 3e, Bui ou Congolo mask.

1976, Feb. 6   Perf. 13½
595 A92 50c lt blue & multi   .20 .20
596 A92 3e multicolored   .20 .20

Workers — A93

President Agostinho Neto — A94

1976, May 1   Litho.   Perf. 12
597 A93 1e red & multi   .20 .20

International Workers' Day.

No. 392 Overprinted Bar and: "DIA DO SELO / 15 Junho 1976 / REP. POPULAR / DE"

1976, June 15   Litho.   Perf. 13½
598 A41 10e multicolored   .40 .25

Stamp Day.

1976, Nov. 11   Litho.   Perf. 13
599 A94 50c yel & dk brown   .20 .20
600 A94 2e lt gray & plum   .20 .20
601 A94 3e gray & indigo   .20 .20
602 A94 5e buff & brown   .20 .20
603 A94 10e tan & sepia   .40 .20
  a. Souv. sheet of 1, imperf.   2.00 1.25
     Nos. 599-603 (5)   1.20 1.00

First anniversary of independence.

Nos. 393, 588-589, 592 Overprinted with Bar over Republica Portuguesa and: "REPUBLICA POPULAR DE"

1977, Feb. 9   Perf. 13½, 12x12½
604 A41 20e multicolored   1.75 .25
605 A90 25e multicolored   2.25 .35
606 A90 30e multicolored   2.75 .50
607 A90 50e multicolored   4.50 .75
     Nos. 604-607 (4)   11.25 1.85

Overprint in 3 lines on No. 604, in 2 lines on others.

No. 438 Overprinted with Bar over Republica Portuguesa and: "S. Silvestre / 1976 / Rep. Popular / de"

1976, Dec. 31   Perf. 13½
608 CD48 15e multicolored   3.50 .20

Child and WHO Emblem — A95

Map of Africa, Flag of Angola — A96

1977   Litho.   Perf. 10½
609 A95 2.50k blk & lt blue   .20 .20

Campaign for vaccination against poliomyelitis.

1977   Photo.
610 A96 6k blk, red & blue   .20 .20

First Congress of Popular Movement for the Liberation of Angola.

Anti-Apartheid Emblem — A97

1979, June 20   Litho.   Perf. 13½
611 A97 1k multicolored   .20 .20

Anti-Apartheid Year.

Human Rights Emblem — A98

Child Flowers, Globe, IYC Emblem — A99

1979, June 15   Litho.   Perf. 13½
612 A98 2.50k multicolored   .20 .20

Declaration of Human Rights, 30th anniv. (in 1975).

1980, May 1   Litho.   Perf. 14x14½
613 A99 3.50k multicolored   .20 .20

International Year of the Child (1979).

Running, Moscow '80 Emblem — A100

5th Anniv. of Independence A101

1980, Dec. 15   Litho.   Perf. 13½
614 A100 9k shown   .30 .20
615 A100 12k Swimming, horiz.   .40 .20

22nd Summer Olympic Games, Moscow, July 19-Aug. 3.

1980, Nov. 11
616 A101 5.50k multicolored   .20 .20

Nos. 572, 566 Overprinted with Bar and: "REPUBLICA POPULAR / DE"

1980-81   Litho.   Perf. 13½x13
616A A89   2e multi (bar only)   .50
616B A83   4.50e multicolored   1.00

Issued: 2e, 5/17/81; 4.50e, 6/15/80. See No. C37.

Nos. 577-580, 582-591 Overprinted with Black Bar over "Republica Portuguesa"

1981, June 15   Litho.   Perf. 12x12½
617 A90   1e multicolored
618 A90   1.50e multicolored
619 A90   2e multicolored
620 A90   2.50e multicolored
621 A90   3.50e multicolored
622 A90   4e multicolored
623 A90   5e multicolored
624 A90   6e multicolored
625 A90   7e multicolored
626 A90   10e multicolored
627 A90   25e multicolored
628 A90   30e multicolored
629 A90   35e multicolored
630 A90   40e multicolored
     Nos. 617-630 (14)   15.00 8.00

Man Walking with Canes, Tchibinda Ilunga Statue — A102

1981, Sept. 5   Litho.   Perf. 13½
631 A102 9k multicolored   .30 .20

Turipex '81 tourism exhibition.

M.P.L.A. Workers' Party Congress A103

1980, Dec. 23   Litho.   Perf. 14
632 A103   50 l Millet   .20 .20
633 A103   5k Coffee   .20 .20
634 A103   7.50k Sunflowers   .30 .20
635 A103   13.50k Cotton   .40 .20
636 A103   14k Oil   .45 .25
637 A103   16k Diamonds   .45 .25
     Nos. 632-637 (6)   2.00 1.30

People's Power — A104

Natl. Heroes' Day — A105

1980, Nov. 11
638 A104 40k lt blue & blk   1.25 .40

1980, Sept. 17   Perf. 14x13½
639 A105 4.50k Former Pres. Neto   .20 .20
640 A105 50k Neto, diff.   1.50 .65

Soweto Uprising, 5th Anniv. A106

1981
641 A106 4.50k multicolored   .20 .20

2nd Central African Games — A107

1981, Sept. 3   Litho.   Perf. 13½
642 A107 50 l Bicycling, tennis   .20 .20
643 A107 5k Judo, boxing   .20 .20
644 A107 6k Basketball, volleyball   .25 .20
645 A107 10k Handball, soccer   .35 .25
     Nos. 642-645 (4)   1.00 .85

Souvenir Sheet
Imperf
646 A107 15k multicolored   2.00

Charaxes Kahldeni A108

1982, Feb. 26   Litho.   Perf. 13½
647 A108 50 l shown   .20 .20
648 A108 1k Abantis zambesiaca   .20 .20
649 A108 5k Catacroptera cloanthe   .20 .20
650 A108 9k Myrina ficedula, vert.   .40 .20
651 A108 10k Colotis danae   .40 .20
652 A108 15k Acraea acrita   .55 .25
653 A108 100k Precis hierta   2.75 1.25
  a.   Souvenir sheet   3.00 2.00
     Nos. 647-653 (7)   4.70 2.50

No. 653a contains Nos. 647-653, imperf., and sold for 30k (stamps probably not valid individually).

5th Anniv. of UN Membership — A109

5.50k, The Silence of the Night, by Musseque Catambor. 7.50k, Cotton picking, Catete.

1982, Sept. 22   Litho.
654 A109 5.50k multicolored   .20 .20
655 A109 7.50k multicolored   .25 .20

20th Anniv.
of
Engineering
Laboratory
A110

1982, Dec. 21   Litho.   Perf. 14
656 A110   9k Lab   .25 .20
657 A110   13k Worker, vert.   .40 .20
658 A110 100k Equipment, vert.   3.25 1.25
     Nos. 656-658 (3)   3.90 1.65

Local Flowers — A111

1983, Feb. 18   Perf. 13½
659 A111   5k Dichrostachys
                glomerata   .20 .20
660 A111 12k Amblygonocarpus
                obtusangulus   .40 .20
661 A111 50k Albizzia versicolor   2.00 .60
     Nos. 659-661 (3)   2.60 1.00

Women's Org.,
First Congress
A112

1983   Litho.   Perf. 13½
662 A112 20k multicolored   .80 .80

Africa
Day — A113

1983, June 30   Perf. 13
663 A113 6.5k multi   .25 .25

World Communications Year — A114

1983, June 30   Litho.   Perf. 13½
664 A114 6.5k M'pungi   .25 .25
665 A114   12k Mondu   .40 .40

BRASILIANA '83 Stamp Exhibition,
Rio de Janeiro, July 29-Aug. 7 — A115

Crop-eating insects.

1983, July 29   Litho.   Perf. 13
666 A115 4.5k Antestiopsis lineat-
                icollis   .20 .20
667 A115 6.5k Stephanoderes
                hampei ferr.   .25 .25
668 A115   10k Zonocerus varie-
                gatus   .40 .40
     Nos. 666-668 (3)   .85 .85

25th Anniv. of Economic Commission
for Africa — A116

1983, Aug. 2
669 A116 10k Map, emblem   .40 .40

185th
Anniv. of
Post Office
A117

1983, Dec. 7   Litho.   Perf. 13½
670 A117   50 l Mail collection,
                vert.   .20 .20
671 A117 3.5k Unloading mail
                plane   .20 .20
672 A117   5k Sorting mail   .20 .20
673 A117   15k Mailing letter,
                vert.   .60 .60
674 A117   30k Post office box
                delivery   1.25 1.25
  a.   Min. sheet of 3, #671-672, 674 4.00 4.00
     Nos. 670-674 (5)   2.45 2.45
     No. 674a sold for 100k.

Local
Butterflies
A118

1984, Jan. 20   Litho.   Perf. 13½
675 A118   50 l Parasa karschi   .20 .20
676 A118   1k Diaphone
                angolensis   .20 .20
677 A118 3.5k Choeropasis
                jucunda   .20 .20
678 A118 6.5k Hespagarista
                rendalli   .40 .25
679 A118   15k Euchromia
                guineensis   .75 .60
680 A118 17.5k Mazuca roseistri-
                ga   1.00 .70
681 A118   20k Utetheisa callima   1.50 .85
     Nos. 675-681 (7)   4.25 3.00

A119

A120

1984, Apr. 11   Litho.   Perf. 13½
682 A119 30k multicolored   1.25 1.25
     First Natl. Worker's Union Congress, Apr.
11-16 .

1984, Oct. 24   Litho.   Perf. 13½
     Local birds.
683 A120 10.50k Bucorvos
                leadbeateri   .45 .35
684 A120   14k Gypohicax
                angolensis   .55 .50
685 A120   16k Ardea goliath   .75 .50
686 A120 19.50k Pelicanus
                onocrotalus   1.00 .75
687 A120   22k Platelea alba   1.25 .90
688 A120   26k Balearica
                pavonnia   2.00 1.00
     Nos. 683-688 (6)   6.00 4.00

Local
Animals
A121

1984, Nov. 12
689 A121   1k Tragelephus strep-
                sicerus   .20 .20
690 A121   4k Antidorcos mar-
                supialis
                angolerusis   .20 .20
691 A121   5k Pan troglodytes   .20 .20
692 A121   10k Sycerus caffer   .40 .40
693 A121   15k Hippotragus niger
                variani   .60 .60
694 A121   20k Orycteropus afer   .80 .80
695 A121   25k Crocuta crocuta   1.00 1.00
     Nos. 689-695 (7)   3.40 3.40

Angolese
Monuments
A122

1985, Feb. 21   Litho.   Perf. 13½
696 A122   5k San Pedro da
                Barra   .25 .25
697 A122 12.5k Nova Oeiras   .55 .55
698 A122   18k M'Banza Kongo   .80 .80
699 A122   26k Massangano   1.10 1.10
700 A122   39k Escravatura Mu-
                seum   1.60 1.60
     Nos. 696-700 (5)   4.30 4.30

United
Workers'
Party, 25th
Anniv.
A123

1985, May   Litho.   Perf. 12
701 A123 77k XXV, red flags   1.50 1.50
     Printed in sheets of 5.

A124

A125

1985, May
702 A124   1k Flags   .20 .20
703 A124   11k Oil drilling plat-
                form, Cabinda   .25 .25
704 A124   57k Conference   1.10 1.10
  a.   Strip of 3, #702-704   1.40 1.40
     Southern African Development Council, 5th
anniv.

Lithographed and Typographed
1985, July 5   Perf. 11
     Medicinal plants.
705 A125   1k Lonchocarpus
                sericeus   .20 .20
706 A125   4k Gossypium   .20 .20
707 A125   11k Cassia oc-
                cidentalis   .25 .25
708 A125 25.50k Gloriosa super-
                ba   .50 .50
709 A125   55k Cochlos-
                permum
                angolensis   1.10 1.10
     Nos. 705-709 (5)   2.25 2.25
     ARGENTINA '85 exhibition.

5th Natl.
Heroes Day
A126

     Natl. flag and: 10.50k, Portrait of Agostinho
Neto, party leader. 36.50k, Neto working.

1985   Litho.   Perf. 13½
710 A126 10.50k multicolored   .20 .20
711 A126 36.50k multicolored   .70 .70

Ministerial Conference of Non-Aligned
Countries, Luanda — A127

1985, Sept. 4   Photo.   Perf. 11
712 A127 35k multicolored   1.50 1.50

UN, 40th
Anniv.
A128

1985, Oct. 29   Litho.   Perf. 11
713 A128 12.50k multicolored   .55 .55

Industry and Natural
Resources — A129

1985, Nov. 11
714	A129	50 l Cement Factory	.20	.20
715	A129	5k Logging	.25	.25
716	A129	7k Quartz	.30	.30
717	A129	10k Iron mine	.45	.45
a.		Souvenir sheet of 4, #714-717, imperf.	2.00	2.00

Nos. 714-717 (4)   1.20 1.20

Natl. independence, 10th anniv.

2nd Natl. Workers' Party Congress (MPLA) — A130

1985, Nov. 28   *Perf. 13½*
718 A130 20k multicolored   .85 .85

Demostenes de Almeida Clington Races, 30th Anniv. — A131

Various runners.

1985, Dec. 13
719	A131	50 l multicolored	.20	.20
720	A131	5k multicolored	.25	.25
721	A131	6.50k multicolored	.30	.30
722	A131	10k multicolored	.40	.40

Nos. 719-722 (4)   1.15 1.15

1986 World Cup Soccer Championships, Mexico — A132

Map, soccer field and various plays.

1986, May 6   Litho.   *Perf. 11½x11*
723	A132	50 l multi	.20	.20
724	A132	3.50k multi	.20	.20
725	A132	5k multi	.25	.25
726	A132	7k multi	.30	.30
727	A132	10k multi	.45	.45
728	A132	18k multi	.85	.85

Nos. 723-728 (6)   2.25 2.25

Struggle Against Portugal, 25th Anniv. A133

1986, May 6   *Perf. 11x11½*
729 A133 15k multicolored   .65 .65

First Man in Space, 25th Anniv. A134

1986, Aug. 21   Litho.   *Perf. 11x11½*
730	A134	50 l Skylab, US	.20	.20
731	A134	1k Spacecraft	.20	.20
732	A134	5k A. Leonov space-walking	.25	.25
733	A134	10k Lunokhod on Moon	.40	.40

734	A134	13k Apollo-Soyuz link-up	.60	.60

Nos. 730-734 (5)   1.65 1.65

Admission of Angola to UN, 10th Anniv. A135

1986, Dec. 1   Litho.   *Perf. 11x11½*
735 A135 22k multi   .90 .90

Liberation Movement, 30th Anniv. — A136

Angolese at work, fighting and: No. 736a, "1956." No. 736b, Congress emblem, "1980." No. 736c, Labor Party emblem, "1985."

1986, Dec. 3   *Perf. 11½x11*
736	A136	Strip of 3	.65	.65
a.-c.		5k any single	.20	.20

Agostinho Neto University, 10th Anniv. A137

1986, Dec. 30   Litho.   *Perf. 11x11½*
737	A137	50 l Mathematics	.20	.20
738	A137	1k Law	.20	.20
739	A137	10k Medicine	.45	.45

Nos. 737-739 (3)   .85 .85

Tribal Hairstyles — A138

1987, Apr. 15   Litho.   *Perf. 11½x11*
740	A138	1k Ouioca	.20	.20
741	A138	1.50k Luanda	.20	.20
742	A138	5k Humbe	.20	.20
743	A138	7k Muila	.20	.20
744	A138	20k Muila, diff.	.45	.45
745	A138	30k Dilolo	.75	.75

Nos. 740-745 (6)   2.00 2.00

Landscapes A139

Lenin — A140

Perf. 11½x12, 12x11½
1987, July 7   Litho.
746	A139	50 l Pambala Shore	.20	.20
747	A139	1.50k Dala Waterfalls	.20	.20
748	A139	3.50k Black Stones	.20	.20
749	A139	5k Cuango River	.20	.20
750	A139	10k Launda coast	.25	.25
751	A139	20k Hills of Leba	.50	.50

Nos. 746-751 (6)   1.55 1.55

Nos. 746-747, 749 and 751 horiz.

1987, Nov. 25   *Perf. 12x12½*
752 A140 15k multi   .60 .60

October Revolution, Russia, 70th anniv.

2nd Congress of the Organization of Angolan Women (OMA) — A141

1988, May 30   Litho.   *Perf. 13x13½*
753	A141	2k shown	.20	.20
754	A141	10k Soldier, nurse, technician, student	.35	.35

Victory Carnival, 10th Anniv. A142

Various carnival scenes.

1988, June 15   Litho.   *Perf. 13½x13*
755	A142	5k shown	.20	.20
756	A142	10k multi, diff.	.35	.35

Augusto N'Gangula (1956-1968), Youth Pioneer Killed by Portuguese Colonial Army — A143

Agostinho Neto Pioneers' Organization (OPA), 25th Anniv. — A144

1989, Oct. 2   Litho.   *Perf. 12x11½*
757	A143	12k multicolored	.40	.40
758	A144	15k multicolored	.50	.50

Pioneer Day.

10th Natl. Soccer Championships, Benguela, May 1 — A145

1989, Oct. 16
759	A145	5k shown	.20	.20
760	A145	5k Luanda, 3 years	.20	.20
761	A145	5k Luanda, 5 years	.20	.20

Nos. 759-761 (3)   .60 .60

Intl. Fund for Agricultural Development, 10th Anniv. — A146

1990, Feb. 15   Litho.   *Perf. 11½x12*
762 A146 10k multicolored   .70 .70

Ingombotas' Houses — A147

Architecture: 2k, Alta Train Station. 5k, National Museum of Anthropology. 15k, Ana Joaquina Palace. 23k, Iron Palace. 36k, Meteorological observatory, vert. 50k, People's Palace.

1990, Feb. 20   *Perf. 12x11½, 11½x12*
763	A147	1k shown	.20	.20
764	A147	2k multicolored	.20	.20
765	A147	5k multicolored	.35	.35
766	A147	15k multicolored	1.00	1.00
767	A147	23k multicolored	1.50	1.50
768	A147	36k multicolored	2.25	2.25
769	A147	50k multicolored	3.25	3.25

Nos. 763-769 (7)   8.75 8.75

Luanda and Benguela Railways A148

Various maps and locomotives.

1990, Mar. 1   *Perf. 12x11½*
770	A148	5k shown	.35	.35
771	A148	12k Garrat T (left)	.80	.80
772	A148	12k Garrat T (right)	.80	.80
a.		Pair, #771-772	1.60	1.60
773	A148	14k Mikado	.95	.95

Nos. 770-773 (4)   2.90 2.90

Souvenir Sheet
774 A148 25k Diesel electric   2.35 2.35

No. 772a has a continuous design.

Southern Africa Development Coordinating Conf. (SADCC), 10th Anniv. — A149

1990, Apr. 1   Litho.   *Perf. 14*
775	A149	5k shown	7.00	4.00
776	A149	9k Floating oil rig	10.00	6.00

Pan-African Postal Union (PAPU), 10th Anniv. A150

1990, Apr. 6
777	A150	4k shown	.75	.75
778	A150	10k Simulated stamp, map	1.50	1.50

Paintings by Raul Indipwo
A151

1990, Apr. 24
779	A151	6k	*Tres Gracas*	.40 .40
780	A151	9k	*Muxima*, vert.	.65 .65

Stamp World London 90.

Hippotragus Niger Variani, Adult Male and Female — A152

1990, May 9   **Perf. 14x13½**
781	A152	5k	Adult male	.35 .35
782	A152	5k	shown	.35 .35
783	A152	5k	Adult female	.35 .35
784	A152	5k	Female, calf	.35 .35
			Nos. 781-784 (4)	1.40 1.40

World Wildlife Fund. Various combinations available in blocks or strips of four.

Rosa de Porcelana
A153

1990, June 2   **Litho.**   **Perf. 14**
785	A153	5k	shown	.35 .35
786	A153	8k	Cravo burro	.55 .55
787	A153	10k	Alamandra	.70 .70
			Nos. 785-787 (3)	1.60 1.60

Souvenir Sheet
788	A153	40k	Hibiscus	2.70 2.70

Belgica '90.

Miniature Sheet

Intl. Literacy Year — A154

Various animals and forest scenes.

1990, July 26   **Litho.**   **Perf. 14**
789	A154		Sheet of 30	6.00 6.00
a.-ad.			1k any single	.50 .50
790	A154	5k	Zebra	.35 .35
791	A154	5k	Butterfly	.35 .35
792	A154	5k	Horse	.35 .35
a.			Block of 3, #790-792 + label	1.10 1.10

People's Assembly, 10th Anniv.
A155

1990, Nov. 11   **Perf. 14**
793	A155	10k	multicolored	.70 .70

3rd Natl. Labor Congress
A156

1990   **Litho.**   **Perf. 13½**
794	A156	14k	multicolored	1.40 1.40

War of Independence, 30th Anniv. — A157

Uniforms.

1991, Feb. 28   **Litho.**   **Perf. 14**
795	A157	6k	Machete, 1961	.40 .40
a.			Perf. 13½ vert.	.40 .40
796	A157	6k	Rifle, 1962-63	.40 .40
a.			Perf. 13½ vert.	.40 .40
797	A157	6k	Rifle, 1968	.40 .40
a.			Perf. 13½ vert.	.40 .40
798	A157	6k	Automatic rifle, 1972	.40 .40
a.			Perf. 13½ vert.	.40 .40
b.			Bklt. pane of 4, #795a-798a	1.70
			Nos. 795-798 (4)	1.60 1.60

Musical Instruments
A158

Designs: a, Marimba. b, Mucupela. c, Ngoma la Txina. d, Kissange.

1991, Apr. 5   **Litho.**   **Perf. 14**
799	A158	6k	Block or strip of 4, #799a-799d	1.75 1.75

Tourism
A159

Designs: 3k, Iona National Park. 7k, Kalandula Waterfalls. 35k, Lobito Bay. 60k, Weltwitschia Mirabilis plant.

1991, June 25   **Litho.**   **Perf. 14**
800	A159	3k	multi	.20 .20
801	A159	7k	multi	.25 .25
802	A159	35k	multi	1.10 1.10
803	A159	60k	multi	2.00 2.00
			Nos. 800-803 (4)	3.55 3.55

Dogs
A160

1991, July 5   **Litho.**   **Perf. 14**
804	A160	5k	Kabir of dembos	.20 .20
805	A160	7k	Ombua	.25 .25
806	A160	11k	Kabir massongo	.40 .40
807	A160	12k	Kawa tchowe	.40 .40
			Nos. 804-807 (4)	1.25 1.25

1992 Summer Olympics, Barcelona
A161

1991, July 26   **Perf. 13**
808	A161	4k	Judo	.20 .20
809	A161	6k	Sailing	.20 .20
810	A161	10k	Running	.35 .35
811	A161	100k	Swimming	3.50 3.50
			Nos. 808-811 (4)	4.25 4.25

Navigation Aids
A162

1991, Nov. 8   **Litho.**   **Perf. 12**
812	A162	5k	Quadrant	.20 .20
813	A162	15k	Astrolabe	.50 .50
814	A162	20k	Cross-staff	.70 .70
815	A162	50k	Portolano	1.75 1.75
			Nos. 812-815 (4)	3.15 3.15

Iberex '91.

Rays
A163

1992, Mar. 30   **Litho.**   **Perf. 14**
816	A163	40k	Myliobatis aquila	.20 .20
817	A163	50k	Aetobatus narinari	.20 .20
818	A163	66k	Manta birostris	.25 .25
819	A163	80k	Raja miraletus	.35 .35
			Nos. 816-819 (4)	1.00 1.00

Souvenir Sheet
Perf. 13½
820	A163	25k	Manta birostris, diff.	.20 .20

A164

Quioca masks.

1992, Apr. 30   **Litho.**   **Perf. 13½**
821	A164	60k	Kalelwa	.20 .20
822	A164	100k	Mukixe Wa Kino	.40 .40
823	A164	150k	Cikunza	.50 .50

824	A164	250k	Mukixi Wa Mbwesu	.90 .90
			Nos. 821-824 (4)	2.00 2.00

See #854-857, 868-871, 883-886, 895-898.

1992, May 8   **Perf. 14**
Medicinal Plants: 200k, Ptaeroxylon obliquum. 300k, Spondias mombin. 500k, Parinari curatellifolia. 600k, Cochlospermum angolense.
825	A165	200k	brown & pale yel	.75 .75
826	A165	300k	brown & pale yel	1.10 1.10
827	A165	500k	brown & pale yel	1.90 1.90
828	A165	600k	brown & pale yel	2.25 2.25
a.			Block or strip of 4, #825-828	6.00 6.00

Evangelization of Angola, 500th Anniv. — A166

1992, May 10   **Perf. 13½**
829	A166	150k	King, missionaries	.55 .55
830	A166	420k	Ruins of M'banza Congo	1.50 1.50
831	A166	470k	Maxima Church	1.75 1.75
832	A166	500k	Faces of people	1.90 1.90
			Nos. 829-832 (4)	5.70 5.70

Traditional Houses — A167

Perf. 14, 13½ Vert. (#832A)
1992, May 22
832A	A167	150k	Dimbas	4.00 4.00
b.			Bklt. pane of 4, #832A, 833a-835a	10.00
833	A167	330k	Cokwe	1.25 1.25
a.			Perf. 13½ vert.	1.25 1.25
834	A167	360k	Mbali	1.40 1.40
a.			Perf. 13½ vert.	1.40 1.40
835	A167	420k	Ambwelas	1.60 1.60
a.			Perf. 13½ vert.	1.60 1.60
836	A167	500k	Upper Zambezi	1.90 1.90
			Nos. 832A-836 (5)	10.15 10.15

Expo '92, Seville.

Agapornis Roseicollis
A168

1992, June 2   **Perf. 12x11½**
837	A168	150k	Two birds on branch	.55 .55
838	A168	200k	Birds feeding	.75 .75
839	A168	250k	Hand holding bird	.90 .90
840	A168	300k	Bird on perch	1.10 1.10
a.			Strip of 4, #837-840	3.35 3.35

Expo '92, Seville.

Souvenir Sheet

Visit of Pope John Paul II to Angola — A169

Abstract paintings: a, 340k, The Crucifixion. b, 370k, The Resurrection.

A165

1992, June 4   Litho.   Perf. 13½
841 A169 Sheet of 2, #a.-b. + 2
          labels   1.75 1.75

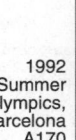

1992
Summer
Olympics,
Barcelona
A170

1992, July 30   Perf. 14
842 A170 120k Hurdles   .30   .30
843 A170 180k Cycling   .50   .50
844 A170 240k Roller hockey   .65   .65
845 A170 360k Basketball   1.00 1.00
     Nos. 842-845 (4)   2.45 2.45

Native
Fishing — A171

1992, Aug. 5   Perf. 11½x12
846 A171 65k Building traps   .20   .20
847 A171 90k Using nets   .25   .25
848 A171 100k Laying traps   .30   .30
849 A171 120k Fisherman in
              boats   .35   .35
     Nos. 846-849 (4)   1.10 1.10

Souvenir Sheet

Discovery of America, 500th
Anniv. — A172

1992, Sept. 18   Litho.   Perf. 12
850 A172 500k multicolored   1.75 1.75

Genoa '92.

First Free
Elections in
Angola — A173

Designs: 120k, People voting. 150k, Map,
ballot box, peace doves. 200k, People, dove,
hand dropping ballot into ballot box.

1992, Oct. 27   Litho.   Perf. 11½x12
851 A173 120k multicolored   .30   .30
852 A173 150k multicolored   .40   .40
853 A173 200k multicolored   .55   .55
     Nos. 851-853 (3)   1.25 1.25

Quioca Mask Type of 1992

1992, Nov. 6   Perf. 13½
854 A164 72k Cihongo   .30   .30
855 A164 80k Mbwasu   .35   .35
856 A164 120k Cinhanga   .45   .45
857 A164 210k Kalewa   .80   .80
     Nos. 854-857 (4)   1.90 1.90

Inauguration of Express Mail
Service — A174

1992, Dec. 14   Litho.   Perf. 12x11½
858 A174 450k Truck   1.10 1.10
859 A174 550k Airplane   1.25 1.25

Meteorological
Instruments
A175

1993, Mar. 23   Litho.   Perf. 11½x12
860 A175 250k Weather balloon .65   .65
861 A175 470k Actinometer   1.10 1.10
862 A175 500k Rain gauge   1.25 1.25
     Nos. 860-862 (3)   3.00 3.00

Seashells
A176

1993, Apr. 6   Perf. 12x11½
863 A176 210k Trochita
              trochiformis   .50   .50
864 A176 330k Strombus latus .75   .75
865 A176 400k Aporrhais pes-
              gallinae   .95   .95
866 A176 500k Fusos aff. al-
              binus   1.25 1.25
     Nos. 863-866 (4)   3.45 3.45
Souvenir Sheet
867 A176 1000k Pusionella nifat 2.25 2.25

Quioca Art Type of 1992

1993, June 7   Litho.   Perf. 12
868 A164 72k Men with vehicles .20 .20
869 A164 210k Cavalier   .45   .45
870 A164 420k Airplane   .90   .90
871 A164 600k Men carrying
              stretcher   1.25 1.25
     Nos. 868-871 (4)   2.80 2.80

Flowering
Plants — A177

1993, June 28   Perf. 11½x12
872 A177 360k Sansevieria cylin-
              drica   .75   .75
873 A177 400k Euphorbia tirucalli .90 .90
874 A177 500k Opuntia ficus-in-
              dica   1.10 1.10
875 A177 600k Dracaena aubry-
              ana   1.25 1.25
     Nos. 872-875 (4)   4.00 4.00

Souvenir Sheet

Africa Day — A178

1993, May 31   Perf. 12
876 A178 1500k Leopard   3.15 3.15

Tribal
Pipes — A179

1993, Aug. 16   Litho.   Perf. 11½x12
877 A179 72k Vimbundi   .20   .20
878 A179 200k Vimbundi, diff. .45   .45
879 A179 420k Mutopa   .90   .90
880 A179 600k Pexi   1.25 1.25
     Nos. 877-880 (4)   2.80 2.80

Souvenir Sheet

Union of Portuguese Speaking
Capitals — A180

1993, July 30   Perf. 12x11½
881 A180 1500k multicolored   3.25 3.25

Turtles — A181

Designs: a, 180k, Chelonia mydas (b). b,
450k, Eretmochelys imbricata. c, 550k,
Dermochelys coriacea. d, 630k, Caretta
caretta.

1993, July 9   Litho.   Perf. 12½x12
882 A181 Block of 4, #a.-d. 3.50 3.50

Quioca Art Type of 1992

1993, Sept. 1   Litho.   Perf. 12
883 A164 300k Leopard   .65   .65
884 A164 600k Malhado   1.25 1.25
885 A164 800k Birds   1.60 1.60
886 A164 1000k Chickens   2.00 2.00
     Nos. 883-886 (4)   5.50 5.50

Mushrooms
A182

1993, Dec. 5   Litho.   Perf. 12
887 A182 300k Tricholoma ge-
              orgii   .55   .55
  a.   Perf. 11½ vert.   .55   .55
888 A182 500k Amanita phal-
              loides   .95   .95
  a.   Perf. 11½ vert.   .95   .95
889 A182 600k Amanita
              vaginata   1.10 1.10
  a.   Perf. 11½ vert.   1.10 1.10
890 A182 1000k Macrolepiota
              procera   1.90 1.90
  a.   Perf. 11½ vert.   1.90 1.90
  b.   Booklet pane of 4, #887a-890a 4.50
     Nos. 887-890 (4)   4.50 4.50

A183

1994, Jan. 10   Litho.   Perf. 12
Natl. Culture Day: 500k, Cinganji, wood
carving of dancer. 1000k, Ohunya yo soma,
staff with woman's face. 1200k, Ongende,
sculpture of man on donkey. 2200k, Upi, corn
pestle.

891 A183 500k multicolored   .45   .45
892 A183 1000k multicolored   .90   .90
893 A183 1200k multicolored 1.10 1.10
894 A183 2200k multicolored 2.00 2.00
     Nos. 891-894 (4)   4.45 4.45

Hong Kong '94.

Quioca Art Type of 1992

1994, Feb. 21   Litho.   Perf. 12
895 A164 500k Bird on flower .30   .30
896 A164 2000k Plant with roots 1.25 1.25
897 A164 2500k Feto   1.60 1.60
898 A164 3000k Plant   2.00 2.00
     Nos. 895-898 (4)   5.15 5.15

Social
Responsibilities of
AIDS — A184

500k, Mass of people. 1000k, Witchdoctor
receiving AIDS through needle, people being
educated. 3000k, Stylized man, woman.

1994, May 5   Litho.   Perf. 12
899 A184 500k multicolored   .35   .35
900 A184 1000k multicolored   .65   .65
901 A184 3000k multicolored 2.00 2.00
     Nos. 899-901 (3)   3.00 3.00

1994 World Cup Soccer
Championships, US — A185

1994, June 17   Perf. 14
902 A185 500k Large arrows,
              small ball   .30   .30
903 A185 700k Small arrows,
              large ball   .45   .45
904 A185 2200k Ball in goal 1.50 1.50
905 A185 2500k Ball, foot   1.60 1.60
     Nos. 902-905 (4)   3.85 3.85

Dinosaurs
A186

1994, Aug. 16		**Litho.**	**Perf. 12**	
906	A186	1000k Brachiosaurus	.20	.20
907	A186	3000k Spinosaurus	.55	.55
908	A186	5000k Ouranosaurus	.90	.90
909	A186	10,000k Lesothosaurus	1.90	1.90
		Nos. 906-909 (4)	3.55	3.55

Souvenir Sheet

910	A186	19,000k Lesothosaurus, map of Africa	3.50	3.50

PHILAKOREA '94, SINGPEX '94. No. 910 contains one 44x34mm stamp.

Tourism
A187

1994, Sept. 27		**Litho.**	**Perf. 12x11½**	
911	A187	2000k Birds	.20	.20
912	A187	4000k Wild animals	.35	.35
913	A187	8000k Native women	.75	.75
914	A187	10,000k Native men	.90	.90
		Nos. 911-914 (4)	2.20	2.20

Post Boxes — A188

Designs: 5000k, Letters, bundled mail wall box. 7500k, Wall box for letters. 10,000k, Pillar box. 21,000k, Multi-function units.

1994, Oct. 7			**Perf. 14½**	
915	A188	5000k multicolored	.45	.45
916	A188	7500k multicolored	.75	.75
917	A188	10,000k multicolored	.90	.90
918	A188	21,000k multicolored	1.90	1.90
		Nos. 915-918 (4)	4.00	4.00

Cotton Pests — A189

Insects: 5000k, Heliothis armigera. 6000k, Bemisia tabasi. 10,000k, Dysdercus. 27,000k, Spodoptera exigua.

1994, Nov. 11		**Litho.**	**Perf. 14**	
919	A189	5000k multicolored	.45	.45
920	A189	6000k multicolored	.55	.55
921	A189	10,000k multicolored	.95	.95
922	A189	27,000k multicolored	2.50	2.50
		Nos. 919-922 (4)	4.45	4.45

Intl. Olympic Committee, Cent. A190

1994, Dec. 15				
923	A190	27,000k multicolored	2.75	2.75

Tribal Culture A191

Designs: 10,000k. Rubbing sticks to start fire. 15,000k, Extracting sap from tree. 20,000k, Smoking tribal pipe. 25,000k, Shooting bow & arrow. 28,000k, Mothers, children. 30,000k, Cave art.

1995, Jan. 6		**Litho.**	**Perf. 14**	
924	A191	10,000k multicolored	.40	.40
925	A191	15,000k multicolored	.65	.65
926	A191	20,000k multicolored	.85	.85
927	A191	25,000k multicolored	1.00	1.00
928	A191	28,000k multicolored	1.10	1.10
929	A191	30,000k multicolored	1.25	1.25
		Nos. 924-929 (6)	5.25	5.25

Traditional Ceramics A192

Designs: No. 930, Pitcher with bust of a woman as stopper. No. 931, Cone-shaped vase. No. 932, Bird-shaped vase. No. 933, Pitcher with bust of a man as stopper.

1995, Jan. 2		**Litho.**	**Perf. 14½**	
930	A192	(2) 2nd class natl.		
931	A192	(1) 1st class natl.		
932	A192	(2) 2nd class intl.		
933	A192	(1) 1st class intl.		
		Nos. 930-933 (4)	3.25	

Rotary Intl., 90th Anniv. A193

1995, Feb. 23		**Litho.**	**Perf. 14**	
934		Strip of 3	2.25	2.25
a.-c.	A193	27,000k any single	.75	.75
935		Strip of 3	2.25	2.25
a.-c.	A193	27,000k any single	.75	.75

Souvenir Sheet

936	A193	81,000k multicolored	4.00	4.00
a.		English inscription	4.00	4.00

a, Immunizing boy against polio. b, Medical examination. c, Immunizing girl against polio. No. 936, Dove over map.

No. 934 has Portuguese inscriptions. No. 935 has English inscriptions. Both were issued in sheets of 9 stamps.
No. 936 contains Portuguese inscription in sheet margin.

Rotary Intl., 90th Anniv. — A194

Illustration reduced.

Litho. & Embossed

1995, Feb. 23			**Perf. 11½x12**	
937	A194	81,000k gold		

World Telecommunications Day — A195

Designs: No. 938, 1957 Sputnik 1. No. 939, Shuttle, Intelsat satellite.

1995		**Litho.**	**Perf. 14**	
938	A195	27,000k multicolored	1.50	1.50
939	A195	27,000k multicolored	1.50	1.50
a.		Souvenir sheet, #938-939	3.00	3.00

Independence, 20th Anniv. — A196

1995, Nov. 11		**Litho.**	**Perf. 14**	
940	A196	2900k multicolored	1.50	1.50

4th World Conference on Women, Beijing — A197

Designs: 375k, Women working in fields. 1106k, Woman teaching, girls with book. 1265k, Woman in industry, career woman. 2900k, Woman in native headdress, vert. 1500k, Native mother, children, vert.

1996, Jan. 29		**Litho.**	**Perf. 14**	
941	A197	375k multicolored	.20	.20
942	A197	1106k multicolored	.35	.35
943	A197	1265k multicolored	.45	.45
944	A197	2900k multicolored	1.00	1.00
		Nos. 941-944 (4)	2.00	2.00

Souvenir Sheet

945	A197	1500k multicolored	.50	.50

UN Assistance Programs — A198

Designs: 200k, Boy, highlift moving supplies. 1265k, Supply ship arriving. No. 948, Two high lifts. No. 949, Tractor-trailer traveling past vultures, native girl. No. 950, Man, ship.

1996		**Litho.**	**Perf. 14**	
946	A198	200k multicolored	.20	.20
947	A198	1265k multicolored	.50	.50
948	A198	2583k multicolored	1.00	1.00
949	A198	2583k multicolored	1.00	1.00
		Nos. 946-949 (4)	2.70	2.70

Souvenir Sheet

950	A198	1265k multicolored	.50	.50

Flora and Fauna A199

1500k, Verdant hawkmoth. 4400k, Water lily. 5100k, Panther toad. 6000k, African wild dog.
1500k: a, Western honey buzzard. b, Bateleuer. c, Common kestrel.
4400k; d, Red-crested turaco. e, Giraffe. f, Elephant.
5100k: g, Hippopotamus. h, Cattle egret. i, Lion.
6000k: j, Helmeted turtle. k, African pygmy goose. l, Egyptian plover.
12,000k, Spotted hyena.

1996, Apr. 20		**Litho.**	**Perf. 14**	
951-954	A199	Set of 4	1.00	1.00
955	A199	Sheet of 12, #a.-l.	4.00	4.00

Souvenir Sheet

956	A199	12,000k multicolored	.80	.80

Sheets of 12

Birds — A200

Fowl: No. 957a, California quail. b, Greater prairie chicken. c, Painted quail. d, Golden pheasant. e, Roulroul partridge. f, Ceylon sourfowl. g, Himalayan snowcock. h, Temminicks tragopan. i, Lady Amherst's pheasant. j, Great curassow. k, Red-legged partridge. l, Impeyan pheasant.
Hummingbirds: No. 958a, Anna's. b, Blue-throated. c, Broad-tailed. d, Costa's. e, White-eared. f, Calliope. g, Violet-crowned. h, Rufous. i, Crimson topaz. j, Broad-billed. k, Frilled coquette. l, Ruby-throated.
No. 959, Ring-necked pheasant. No. 960, Racquet-tail hummingbird.

1996, Apr. 20				
957-958	A200	5500k #a.-l., ea	4.25	4.25

Souvenir Sheets

959-960	A200	12,000k each	.80	.80

Lubrapex '96 A201

Wild animals: a, 180k, Lions attacking zebra. b, 450k, Zebras, lions, diff. c, 180k, Zebras grazing, lions stalking. d, 450k, Panthera leo. e, 550k, Cheetah. f, 630k, Cheetah running. g, 550k, Cheetah chasing antilope. h, 630k, Cheetah attacking antelope. i, 180k, Antilope (gnu) being attacked by wild dogs. j, 450k, Antelope, wild dogs. k, 180k, Pack of wild dogs. l, 450k, Licaon pictus. m, 550k, Panthera pardus. n, 630k, Oryx. o, 550k, Oryx, diff. p, 630k, Leopard attacking oryx.

1996, Apr. 27				
961	A201	Sheet of 16, #a.-p.	6.00	6.00

Sheets of 6

Ships A202

Designs: No. 962a, Styrbjorn, Sweden, 1789. b, Constellation, US, 1797. c, Taureau, France, 1865. d, Bomb Ketch, France, 1682. e, Sardegna, Italy, 1881. f, HMS Glasgow, England, 1867.
No. 963a, Essex, US, 1812. b, HMS Inflexible, England, 1881. c, HMS Minotaur, England, 1863. d, Napoleon, France, 1854. e, Sophia Amalia, Denmark, 1650. f, Massena, France, 1887.
No. 964, HMS Tremendous, England, 1806, vert. No. 965, Royal Prince, England, 1666.

1996, May 4				
962-963	A202	6000k #a.-f., ea	2.50	2.50

Souvenir Sheets

964-965	A202	12,000k each	.80	.80

UN, 50th Anniv. (in 1995) A203

Designs: No. 966, Boys pumping water. No. 967, Man, woman with girl.
8000k, Unloading supplies from ship.

1996, Apr. 27		**Litho.**	**Perf. 14**	
966	A203	3500k multicolored	1.00	1.00

967 A203 3500k multicolored 1.00 1.00
Souvenir Sheet
968 A203 8000k multicolored 1.00 1.00

Sonangol, 20th Anniv. A204

MPLA (Liberation Movement), 40th Anniv. — A208

Face in traditional mask, costume, native birds, and: No. 969, Oil derricks. No. 970, Oil storage tanks, ship. 2500k, Refinery equipment. 5000k, Cargo shipment, jet.

1996, May 12
969 A204 1000k multicolored .20 .20
970 A204 1000k multicolored .20 .20
971 A204 2500k multicolored .25 .25
972 A204 5000k multicolored .55 .55
    Nos. 969-972 (4) 1.20 1.20

Brapex '96 — A205

#973, Slaves in hold. #974, Slaves fleeing ship as it's overturned. #975, Slave boats approaching ship. #976, Slaves talking with captain.
50,000k, like #975.

1996, Oct. 19   Litho.   Perf. 14
973 A205 20,000k multicolored 1.25 1.25
974 A205 20,000k multicolored 1.25 1.25
975 A205 30,000k multicolored 1.90 1.90
976 A205 30,000k multicolored 1.90 1.90
    Nos. 973-976 (4) 6.30 6.30
Souvenir Sheet
977 A205 50,000k multicolored 3.25 3.25

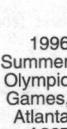

Churches — A206

5,000k, Mission, Huila. #979, Church of the Nazarene. #980, Church of Our Lady of Pó Pulo. 25,000k, St. Adrião Church.

1996, Dec. 6   Litho.   Perf. 14
978 A206 5,000k multicolored .30 .30
979 A206 10,000k multicolored .65 .65
980 A206 10,000k multicolored .65 .65
981 A206 25,000k multicolored 1.60 1.60
    Nos. 978-981 (4) 3.20 3.20

1996 Summer Olympic Games, Atlanta A207

1996, Dec. 9
982 A207 5,000k Handball, vert. .30 .30
983 A207 10,000k Swimming .65 .65
984 A207 25,000k Track & field, vert. 1.60 1.60
985 A207 35,000k Shooting 2.25 2.25
    Nos. 982-985 (4) 4.80 4.80
Souvenir Sheet
986 A207 65,000k Basketball 4.00 4.00

From this point the value of Angolan currency is in question.

1996, Dec. 10   Litho.   Perf. 14
987 A208 30,000k Dolphins, map 1.75 1.75

Trains A209

Trains A209a

No. 988: a, AVE, Spain. b, Bullet Train, Japan. c, GM F7 Warbonnet, US. d, Deltic, Great Britain. e, Eurostar, France/Great Britain. f, ETR 450, Italy.
No. 989: a, Class E1300, Morocco. b, ICE, Germany. c, X2000, Sweden. d, TGV Duplex, France.
No. 989E: f, Steam engine. g, Garrat. h, General Electric.
No. 990, Canadian Pacific 4-4-0, Canada. No. 991, Via Rail Canadian, Canada.

1997, May 29   Litho.   Perf. 14
Sheets of 6, 4 or 3
988 A209 100,000k #a.-f. 6.00 6.00
989 A209 140,000k #a.-d. 6.00 6.00
989E A209a 250,000k Sheet of 3, #f.-h. 5.75 5.75
Souvenir Sheets
Perf. 13½
990-991 A209 110,000k each 4.00 4.00
    Nos. 990-991 contain one 38x50 or 50x38mm stamp, respectively. PACIFIC 97.

Horses A210

No. 992: a, Thoroughbred. b, Palomino, appaloosa. c, Arabians. d, Arabian colt. e, Thoroughbred colt. f, Mustang. g, Mustang, diff. h, Furioso.
No. 993: a, Thoroughbred. b, Arabian, palomino. c, Arabian, chincoteague. d, Pintos. e, Przewalski's horse. f, Thoroughbred colt. g, Arabians. h, New forest pony.
No. 994: a, Selle Francais. b, Fjord. c, Percheron. d, Italian heavy draft. e, Shagya Arab. f, Avelignese. g, Czechoslovakian warmblood. h, New forest pony.
    215,000k, Thoroughbreds. 220,000k, Thoroughbreds, diff.

1997, July 5   Litho.   Perf. 14
Sheets of 8
992 A210 100,000k #a.-h. 4.00 4.00
993 A210 120,000k #a.-h. 5.00 5.00
994 A210 140,000k #a.-h. 5.50 5.50
Souvenir Sheets
995 A210 215,000k multicolored 4.00 4.00
996 A210 220,000k multicolored 4.00 4.00
    PACIFIC 97.

1998 World Cup Soccer Championships, France — A211

Winners holding World Cup trophy: No. 997: a, Uruguay, 1930. b, Germany, 1954. c, Brazil, 1970. d, Argentina, 1986. e, Brazil, 1994.
Winning team pictures: No. 998a, Germany, 1954. b, Uruguay, 1958. c, Italy, 1938. d, Brazil, 1962. e, Brazil, 1970. f, Uruguay, 1930.
220,000k, Angolan team members standing. 250,000k, 1997 Angolan team picture.

1997, July 5   Litho.   Perf. 14
Sheets of 5 or 6
997 A211 100,000k #a.-e. + label 5.00 5.00
998 A211 100,000k #a.-f. 6.00 6.00
Souvenir Sheets
999 A211 220,000k multicolored 3.50 3.50
1000 A211 250,000k multicolored 4.00 4.00

ENSA (Security System), 20th Anniv. — A212

"Star" emblem, and stylized protection of "egg:" #1001, Industry. #1002, Recreation. #1003, Homes, shelters. #1004, Accident prevention.
350,000k, Emblem.

1998   Litho.   Perf. 13½
1001-1004 A212 240,000k Set of 4 7.50 7.50
Souvenir Sheet
Perf. 13½x13
1005 A212 350,000k multicolored 2.75 2.75
    No. 1005 contains one 60x40mm stamp.

GURN (Natl. Unity & Reconciliation Government), 1st Anniv. — A213

Emblem, portion of country map and: 100,000k, a, Sea, swordfish, ships, oil derrick. b, Sea, ships, swordfish. c, Sea, swordfish, ships, mining car on railroad track. d, Sea, power lines.
200,000k: e, Train on track, antelope. f, Mining cars on track, tractor pulling cart. g, Railroad track across rivers, tractor plowing. h, Power lines. i, UR corner of map, crystals. j, Train on track. k, Elephant, tree. l, Trunk of tree, bottom edge of map.

1998
1006 A213 Sheet of 12, #a.-l. 15.00 15.00

Souvenir Sheet

Education in Angola — A214

Illustration reduced.

1998
1007 A214 400,000k multicolored 3.25 3.25

Diana, Princess of Wales (1961-97) — A215

Various portraits, color of sheet margin: No. 1008, pale green. No. 1009, pale yellow. 400,000k, Wearing protective clothing.

1998, May 21   Litho.   Perf. 14
Sheets of 6
1008-1009 A215 100,000k #a.-f., each 4.75 4.75
Souvenir Sheet
1010 A215 400,000k multicolored 3.25 3.25
    See No. 1028.

Expo '98, Lisbon A216

Marine life: No. 1011, 100,000k, Anemones. No. 1012, 100,000k, Sea urchin. No. 1013, 100,000k, Sea horses. No. 1014, 100,000k, Coral (Caravela). No. 1015, 240,000k, Sea slug. No. 1016, 240,000k, Worms (Tunicados).

1998, May 21   Perf. 13½
1011-1016 A216 Set of 6 7.00 7.00

Butterflies — A217

No. 1017: a, Metamorpha stelene. b, Papilio glaucus. c, Danaus plexippus. d, Catonephele numili. e, Plebejus argus. f, Hypolimnas bolina.
No. 1018: a, Terinos terpander. b, Bematistes aganice. c, Hebomoia glaucippe. d, Colias eurytheme. e, Pereute leucodrosime. f, Lycaenia dispar.
No. 1019, horiz.: a, Dynastor napolean. b, Zeuxidia amethystus. c, Battus philenor. d, Phoebis philea. e, Danaus chrysippus. f, Glaucopsyche alexis.
No. 1020, Euphaedra neophron. No. 1021, Thecla betulae, horiz. No. 1022, Uraneis ucubis, armillaria staminea.

1998, May 21   Perf. 14
Sheets of 6
1017-1019 A217 120,000k #a.-f., each 6.00 6.00
Souvenir Sheets
1020-1022 A217 250,000k each 4.00 4.00

Cats and Dogs A218

Cats: No. 1023a, British tortoiseshell. b, Chinchilla. c, Russian blue. d, Black Persian (longhair). e, British red tabby. f, Birman.
Dogs: No. 1024a, West Highland terrier. b, Irish setter. c, Dachshund. d, St. John water dog. e, Shetland sheep dog. f, Dalmatian.
No. 1025, Turkish van (swimming cat). No. 1026, Labrador retriever.

1998, May 21 Litho. Perf. 14x13½
Sheets of 6
1023-1024 A218 140,000k #a.-f.,
  each 6.75 6.75
Souvenir Sheets
1025-1026 A218 500,000k each 4.00 4.00

Wild Animals A219

100,000k: a, Panthera leo. b, Hippopotamus amphibius. c, Loxodonta africana. d, Giraffa camelopardalis.
220,000k: e, Syncerus caffer-caffer. f, Gorilla gorilla. g, Ceratotherim simum. h, Oryx gazella.

1998, July 24 Litho. Perf. 14
1027 A219 Sheet of 8, #a.-h. 10.00 10.00

Diana, Princes of Wales Type of 1998

Pictures showing Diana's campaign to ban land mines: a, With girl. b, With two boys. c, Wearing protective clothing.

1998, Aug. 31 Litho. Perf. 14
1028 A215 150,000k Strip of 3, #a.-c. 4.75 4.75

No. 1028 was issued in sheets of 6 stamps.

Intl. Year of the Ocean — A220

Marine life: No. 1029a, Pagurites. b, Callinectes marginatus. c, Thais forbesi. d, Ostrea tulipa. e, Balanus amohitrite. f, Uca tangeri.
No. 1030: a, Littorina angulifera. b, Semifusus morio. c, Thais coronata. d, Cerithium atratum (red branch). e, Ostrea tulipa. f, Cerithium atratum (green branch).
No. 1031, Goniopsis, horiz. No. 1032, Unidentified shell.

1998, Sept. 4
Sheets of 6
1029 A220 100,000k #a.-f. 3.00 3.00
1030 A220 170,000k #a.-f. 5.00 5.00
Souvenir Sheets
1031-1032 A220 300,000k each 4.00 4.00

Souvenir Sheet

Battle Against Polio in Angola — A221

Illustration reduced.

1998, Aug. 28 Litho. Perf. 13½
1033 A221 500,000k multicolored 2.50 2.50

Traditional Boats A222

Designs: No. 1034, 250,000k, Boat, Bimba. No. 1035, 250,000k, Canoe with sail, Ndongo. 500,000k, Constructing boat, Ndongo.

1998, Sept. 4 Perf. 14
1034-1036 A222 Set of 3 5.00 5.00

Titanic A223

Views of Titanic: a, Under tow. b, Stern. c, Starboard side at night. d, At dock.

1998, Sept. 4
1037 A223 350,000k Sheet of 4, #a.-d. 7.00 7.00

#1037c is 76x30mm, #1037d is 38x61mm.

Angolan Food A224

Various vegetables, fruits: #1038, 100,000k, 4 fruits. #1039, 100,000k, Squash sliced in half. #1040, 120,000k, Ears of corn. #1041, 120,000k, Green beans. #1042, 140,000k, Fruit with red seeds sliced in half. #1043, 140,000k, Sliced bananas.

1998
1038-1043 A224 Set of 6 5.50 5.50

Portugal '98.

Airplanes A225

No. 1044, IL-62 M. No. 1045, B737 100.
No. 1046: a, Ultralight. b, Gyroplane. c, Business jet. d, onvertible plane (e). e, Chuterplane (a, b, d). f, Twin rotors (e). g, Skycrane. h, Aerospatiale Concorde (i). i, Flying boat.
No. 1047: a, Pedal power (b). b, Sail plane (a, e). c, Aerobatic (f). d, Hang gliding (g). e, Balloon (h). f, Glidercraft (e, i). g, Model airplane. h, Air racing (i). i, Solar cells.
No. 1048, Boeing 777. No. 1049, Columbia Space Shuttle, vert. No. 1049A, Boeing 737-200. No. 1049B, Boeing 747-300.

1998-99 Litho. Perf. 14
1044 A225 200,000k multicolored 1.50 1.50
1045 A225 200,000k multicolored 1.50 1.50
Sheets of 9
1046 A225 150,000k #a.-i. 4.50 4.50
1047 A225 250,000k #a.-i. 6.00 6.00
Souvenir Sheets
1048-1049B A225 1,000,000k ea 5.00 5.00
Nos. 1048-1049B each contain one 85x28mm stamp.
Issued: Nos. 1049A-1049B, 3/25/99; others 12/24/98.

Dinosaurs A226

Designs, vert: No. 1050, Parasaurolophus. No. 1051, Maiasaura. No. 1052, Iguanodon. No. 1053, Elaphosaurus.
No. 1054, vert: a, Brontosaurus. b, Plateosaurus. c, Brachiosaurus. d, Anatosaurus. e, Tyrannosaurus. f, Carnotaurus. g, Corythosaurus. h, Stegosaurus. i, Iguanodon, diff.
No. 1055: a, Hadrosaurus. b, Ouranosaurus. c, Hypsilophodon. d, Brachiosaurus. e, Shunosaurus. f, Amargasaurus. g, Tuojiangosaurus. h, Monoclonius. i, Struthiosaurus.

No. 1056, Triceratops, vert. No. 1057, Tyrannosaurus, vert.

1998, Dec. 28
1050-1053 A226 120,000k Set of 4 6.00 6.00
Sheets of 9
1054-1055 A226 120,000k #a.-i., each 7.50 7.50
Souvenir Sheets
1056-1057 A226 550,000k each 2.00 2.00

World Wildlife Fund — A227

Lesser flamingo: a, Facing left. b, Body facing forward. c, Head and neck. d, With wings spread.

1999 Litho. Perf. 14
Strip of 4
1058 A227 300,000k #a.-d. 3.25 3.25
No. 1058 was issued in sheets of 16 stamps.

Fauna A228

Designs: No. 1059, Equis caballus przewalski. No. 1060, Sphenisciformes, vert. No. 1061, Haliaeetus leucocephalus, vert. No. 1062, Anodorhynchus hyacinthinus.
No. 1063: a, Vulpes velox hebes. b, Odocoileus. c, Pongo pygmaeus. d, Leontopitecus rosalia. e, Panthera tigris. f, Tragelaphus eurycerus.
No. 1064: a, Tremarctos ornatus. b, Aphelocoma. c, Otus insularis. d, Balaeniceps rex. e, Lepidochelys kempii. f, Lutra canadensis.
No. 1065, Ailuropoda melanoleuca, vert. No. 1066, Ursus arctos horribilis.

1999
1059-1062 A228 300,000k Set of 4 9.25 9.25
Sheets of 6
1063-1064 A228 300,000k #a.-f., each 6.00 6.00
Souvenir Sheets
1065-1066 A228 1,000,000k each 4.00 4.00

These Flora and Fauna stamps, formerly Nos. 1067-1078, were not authorized by Angola postal authorities.

Other items inscribed "Angola" that were not authorized but which have appeared on the market include sheets with the themes of Disney and History of Animation, Millennium, Animals, Trains, Flora, Muhammad Ali & Lennox Lewis, Bruce Lee, Albert Einstein / Moon Landing, Elvis Presley and other entertainers, Great Personalities, John Kennedy and Marilyn Monroe, Martin Luther King, Jr., Payne Stewart, Colin Montgomerie, Babe Ruth, Cardinal John O'Connor, Pope John Paul II / Mother Teresa and Queen Elizabeth II / Winston Churchill.

World Telecommunications Day — A230

1999, May 17 Litho. Perf. 14
1079 A230 500,000k multi .50 .50

Souvenir Sheet

Waterfalls A231

a, Andulo. b, Chiumbo. c, Ruacaná. d, Coemba.

1999, June 5 Sheet of 4
1080 A231 500,000k #a.-d. 2.00 2.00

A232

African Men's Basketball Championships - No. 1081: a, Poster. b, Basketball, hoop, tan background. c, Basketball, hoop, green background. d, Welwitschia plant holding basketball.
2,500,000k, Similar to No. 1081c.

1999, July 29 Perf. 13½
Sheet of 4
1081 A232 1,500,000k #a.-d. 3.00 3.00
Souvenir Sheet
Perf. 13x13½
1082 A232 2,500,000k multi 2.00 2.00
No. 1082 contains one 40x30mm stamp.

A233

1999, Aug. 17 Perf. 14
1083 A233 1,000,000k multi .80 .80
Southern African Development Community. Issued in sheets of 4.

A234

A235

Tribal kings - No. 782: a, Ekuikui II. b, Mvemba Nzinga. c, Mwata Yamvu Naweji II. d, Njinga Mbande.
1,000,000k, Mandume Ndemufayo.

1999, Sept. 17　　　**Sheet of 4**
1084 A234 500,000k #a.-d.　　　2.00 2.00
Souvenir Sheet
1085 A234 1,000,000k multi　　　1.00 1.00

1999, Sept. 17　　　**Litho.**
Queen Mother (b. 1900) - No. 1086: a, With King George VI. b, Wearing brooch. c, Wearing tiara. d, Wearing hat.
500,000k, Wearing academic gown.
Sheet of 4
1086 A235 200,000k #a.-d.　　　6.00 6.00
Souvenir Sheet
Perf. 13¾
1087 A235 500,000k multi　　　3.75 3.75
No. 1087 contains one 38x51mm stamp.

Ships
A236

No. 1088: a, Egyptian bark, 1300 B.C. b, Flemish carrack, 1480. c, Beagle, 1830. d, North Star, 1852. e, Fram, 1892. f, Unyon Maru, 1909. g, Juan Sebastian de Elcano, 1927. h, Tovarishch, 1933.
No. 1089: a, Bucentauro, 1728. b, Clermont, 1807. c, Savannah, 1819. d, Dromedary, 1844. e, Iberia, 1881. f, S.S. Gluckauf, 1886. g, City of Paris, 1888. h, Mauretania, 1906.
No. 1090: a, Gloire, 1859. b, L'Ocean, 1868. c, Dandalo, 1876, stern of HMS Dreadnought, 1906. d, Bow of Dreadnought. e, Bismarck, 1939, stern of USS Cleveland, 1946. f, Bow of Cleveland. g, USS Boston, 1942, stern of USS Long Beach, 1959. h, Bow of Long Beach.
No. 1091, Chinese junk. No. 1092, Madre de Deus, 1609. No. 1093, Catamaran, 1861. No. 1094, Natchez, 1870.

1999, Sept. 23　　　**Litho.**　　　**Perf. 14**
Sheets of 8
1088-1090 A236 950,000k #a.-h.,
　　　　　　each 6.00 6.00
Souvenir Sheets
1091-1094 A236 5,000,000k each 3.00 3.00

Mushrooms
A237

#1095, Amanita caesarea. #1096, Psalliota xanthoderma. #1097, Hygrocybe conica. #1098, Boletus chrysenteron. #1099, Coprinus comatus. #1100, Boletus luteus.
#1101: a, Morchella crassipes. b, Boletus rufescens. c, Amanita phalloides. d, Collybia iocephala. e, Tricholoma aurantium. f, Cortinarius violaceus. g, Mycena polygramma. h, Psalliota augusta.
#1102: a, Amanita muscaria. b, Boletus aereus. c, Coprinus comatus. d, Amanita rubescens. e, Cortinarius collinitus. f, Boletus satanas. g, Lepiota procera. h, Clitocybe geotropa.
#1103: a, Russula nigricans. b, Boletus granulatus. c, Mycena strobilinoides. d, Amanita caesarea. e, Amanita muscaria. f, Boletus, crocipodius. g, Russula virescens. h, Lactarius deliciosus.
#1104, Psalliota haemorrhoidaria.
#1105, Mycena lilacifolia.

1999, Sept. 23　　　**Litho.**　　　**Perf. 14**
1095 A237 1,250,000k multi　　.95 .95
1096 A237 1,250,000k multi　　.95 .95
1097 A237 1,250,000k multi　　.95 .95
1098 A237 1,250,000k multi　　.95 .95
1099 A237 1,250,000k multi　　.95 .95
1100 A237 1,250,000k multi　　.95 .95
　　Nos. 1095-1100 (6)　　5.70 5.70
Sheets of 8
1101 A237 1,000,000k #a-h　　6.50 6.50
1102 A237 1,000,000k #a-h　　6.50 6.50
1103 A237 1,000,000k #a-h　　6.50 6.50
Souvenir Sheets
1104 A237 5,000,000k multi　　3.00 3.00
1105 A237 5,000,000k multi　　3.00 3.00

A238

First Manned Moon Landing, 30th Anniv. A239

No. 1107: a, Astronaut spacewalking. b, Mariner 8. c, Viking 10. d, GINGA satellite. e, Soyuz 19. f, Voyager.
No. 1108, vert.: a, Space telescope. b, Space shuttle Atlantis. c, Uhuru satellite. d, Mir space station. e, Gemini 7. f, Venera 7.
No. 1109: a, Mercury, Venus. b, Jupiter. c, Neptune, Pluto. d, Earth, Mars. e, Saturn. f, Uranus.
No. 1110: a, Explorer 17. b, Intelsat 4A. c, GOES-D Satellite. d, Intelsat 2. e, Navstar. f, S.M.S.
No. 1111, Lunar rover, vert. No. 1112, Apollo 17 astronaut on moon, vert. No. 1113, Neil Armstrong, vert. No. 1114, Space shuttle Columbia. No. 1115, SBS-4, vert.

Perf. 13¾ (A238), 14 (A239)
1999, Nov. 15　　　**Litho.**
Sheets of 6, #a.-f.
1107-1108 A238 3,500,000k　　7.25 7.25
1109-1110 A239 3,500,000k　　7.25 7.25
Souvenir Sheets
1111-1112 A238　6,000,000k ea　1.60 1.60
1113-1115 A239 12,000,000k ea　3.25 3.25

Hokusai Paintings — A240

No. 1116: a, Night attack. b, Usigafuchi No Kudan. c, Drawing of man and bowl. d, Wildlife. e, Pheasant. f, People on bridge.
No. 1117: a, Tree and shoreline. b, Kabuki theater. c, Hen. d, Cooper. e, Trip to Enoshima. f, Sumida River landscape.
No. 1118, Yama-uba and Kintori, vert. No. 1119, Woman, vert.

1999, Dec. 13　　**Litho.**　　**Perf. 13¾**
Sheets of 6, #a.-f.
1116-1117 A240　3,500,000k ea　4.50 4.50
Souvenir Sheets
1118-1119 A240 12,000,000k ea　4.00 4.00
On Dec. 13, the date of issue of these stamps, Angola devalued its currency, with approximately 1,000,000k being the equivalent of 1k after the devaluation.

Souvenir Sheets

PhilexFrance 99 — A241

No. 1120, 4-8-4 Linder Compound express. No. 1121, Hovertrain prototype.
Illustration reduced.

2000, Mar. 13　　**Litho.**　　**Perf. 13¾**
1120-1121 A241 12k Set of 2　　8.00 8.00

A242

Wildlife — A243

1.50k, Zebra. 2k, Fruit bat. 3k, California condor. 5.50k, Lion.
No. 1126, horiz.: a, Equus zebra. b, Ploceus xanthops. c, Lycaon protus. d, Acinonyx jubatus. e, Oryx gazella. f, Nursing Otocyon megalotis. g, Giraffa camelopardalis. h, Canis adustus. i, Perodicticus potto. j, Panthera leo. k, Coracius caudata. l, Pair of Otocyon megalotis.
No. 1127, horiz.: a, Struthio camelus. b, Felis lybica. c, Aepyceros melampus. d, Cercopithecus aethiops. e, Diceros bicornis. f, Papio sp. g, Felis caracal. h, Sagittarius serpentarius. i, Phacochoerus aethiopicus. j, Arctocephalus pusillus. k, Alcedo cristata. l, Hippopotamus amphibius.
No. 1128: a, Deer. b, Turkey. c, Beaver. d, Frog. e, Manatee. f, Trout.
No. 1129: a, Macaque. b, Toucan. c, Bothriopsis bilineata. d, Hyla leucopyliata. e, Tamarin. f, Eagle.
No. 1130, vert.: a, Mountain gorilla. b, Rhinoceros. c, Water buffalo. d, Chameleon. e, Cobra. f, Meerkats.
No. 1131, vert.: a, Kangaroo. b, Koala. c, Kingfishers. d, Frog on tree root. e, Three fish. f, Turtle.
No. 1132, Sloth. No. 1133, Lemur, vert. No. 1134, Cheetah, vert. No. 1135, Orangutan, vert. No. 1136, Cercopithecus aethiops, diff. No. 1137, Loxodonta africana.
Illustration A243 reduced.

2000, Apr. 7　　　**Perf. 14**
1122-1125 A242　Set of 4　　2.50 2.50
Sheets of 12
1126 A243 1.50k #a-l　　3.75 3.75
1127 A243　2k #a-l　　5.00 5.00
Sheets of 6, #a-f
1128-1131 A242 3.50k Set of 4 17.00 17.00
Souvenir Sheets
1132-1135 A242 12k Set of 4 10.00 10.00
1136-1137 A243 12k Set of 4 10.00 10.00

Birds of Prey
A244

1.50k, Harpy eagle. 2k, Unidentified bird. 3k, Vulture, vert. 5.50k, King vulture, vert.
No. 1142: a, Acolpiler gentilis. b, Surnis ulula. c, Falco peregrinus. d, Otus asio. e, Haliaetus vocifer. f, Herpetothers cachinnans.
No. 1143: a, Falco sperterius. b, Pulsetrix perspicillata. c, Elemus leucurus. d, Ninox novaseelandiae. e, Polemactus bellicosus. f, Polyborus plancus.
No. 1144: a, Verreaux's eagle. b, Aguia gigante. c, Aguia peixe.
No. 1145, vert.: a, Aguia despeida. b, Aguia dourada. c, Aguia devoradora de macacos.
No. 1146, King vulture, diff. No. 1147, Falcon, vert. No. 1148, Sagittarius serpentarius. No. 1149, Aquila chrysectos.

2000, Apr. 10
1138-1141 A244　Set of 4　　2.75 2.75
Sheets of 6, #a-f
1142-1143 A244 3.50k Set of 2　8.50 8.50

Sheets of 3, #a-c
1144-1145 A244 6.50k Set of 2　8.00 8.00
Souvenir Sheets
1146-1147 A244 12k Set of 2　5.00 5.00
1148-1149 A244 15k Set of 2　6.50 6.50

Millennium — A245

Highlights of the 16th Century: a, Paintings by Lai-Ji. b, The Last Judgment, by Luca Signorelli. c, Garden of Earthly Delights by Hieronymus Bosch. d, The Prince, written by Niccolò Machiavelli. e, Utopia, written by Sir Thomas More. f, Martin Luther. g, Charles I of Spain becomes Holy Roman Emperor Charles V. h, The School of Athens, by Raphael. i, Juan Sebastián de Elcano circumnavigates globe. j, Henry VIII of England. k, Spanish conquest of Aztecs and Incas. l, Placentia Cathedral. m, Potatoes introduced to Europe. n, Heliocentric theory of Copernicus. o, Portuguese reach Japan. p, Death of Albrecht Dürer (60x40mm). q, Bartolomé de Las Casas promotes rights for Indians.
Illustration reduced.

2000, Oct. 2　　**Litho.**　　**Perf. 12¾x12½**
1150 A245 2.50k Sheet of 17,
　　　#a-q, + label　6.00 6.00

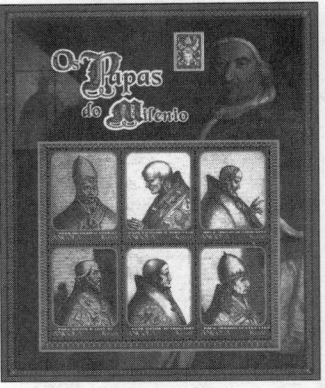

War Damage in Angola
A246

#1151, 3k, B.N.A. Building, Kuito. #1152, 3k, Kunje St., Kuito. #1153, 4k, Post office. #1154, 4k, Police headquarters. #1155, 5k, Apartment house. #1156, 5k, Independence Square. #1157, 6k, Child waving from upper floor of apartment house. #1158, 6k, Building, man carrying pack.

2000, Sept. 29　　**Litho.**　　**Perf. 14**
1151-1158 A246　Set of 8　　4.25 4.25

Popes — A247

#1159: a, Nicholas II, 1059-61. b, Paschal II, 1099-1118. c, Sergius IV, 1009-1012. d, Victor II, 1055-57. e, Victor III, 1086-87. f, Urban III, 1185-87.

#1160: a, Innocent II, 1130-43. b, John XIII, 965-72. c, Agapetus II, 946-55. d, John XV, 985-96. e, John XVIII, 1003-09. f, Lucius II, 1144-45.

#1161: a, Celestine II, 1143-44. b, Clement II, 1046-47. c, Clement III, 1187-91. d, Gelasius II, 1118-19. e, Benedict VII, 974-83. f, Gregory V, 996-99.

#1162, Leo IX, 1049-54. #1163, Gregory VII, 1073-85. #1164, Leo XIII, 1878-1903. Illustration reduced.

2000, Oct. 2   **Perf. 12x12¼**
Sheets of 6, #a-f
1159-1161 A247 Set of 3   6.25 6.25
Souvenir Sheets
1162-1164 A247 Set of 3   4.25 4.25

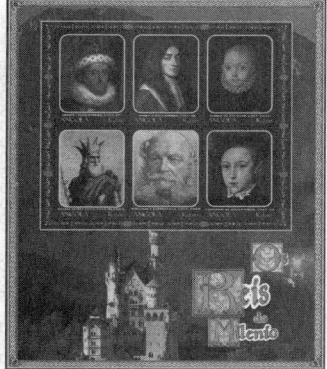

Monarchs — A248

#1165: a, Henry II, King of Germany and Holy Roman Emperor, 1002-24. b, Marina Mniszek, wife of false Russian czar Dmitri, 1605-06. c, Ivan IV of Russia, 1533-84. d, Ivan III of Russia, 1462-1505.

#1166: a, Charles II of Great Britain, 1660-85. b, Lady Jane Grey of England, 1533. c, Leopold III of Belgium, 1934-51. d, Louis XV of France, 1715-74.

#1167: a, James I of Great Britain, 1603-25. b, James II of Great Britain, 1685-88. c, James IV of Scotland, 1567-1625. d, Brian Boru of Ireland, 1002-14. e, Wilhelm I, King of Prussia and German Emperor, 1861-88. f, Edward VI of England, 1547-53.

#1168, Feodor I of Russia, 1584-98. #1169, False Russian czar Dmitri, 1605-06. #1170, William IV of Great Britain, 1830-37. Illustration reduced.

2000, Oct. 2
Sheets of 4, #a-d
1165-1166 A248 Set of 2   2.75 2.75
Sheet of 6
1167   A248 #a-f   2.10 2.10
Souvenir Sheets
1168-1170 A248 Set of 3   4.25 4.25

Children's Drawings A249

Various designs. Denominations: 3k, 4k, 5k.

2000, Nov. 7   **Perf. 14**
1171-1173 A249 Set of 3   1.40 1.40

Post Office Buildings A250

Designs: No. 1174, 5k , Former Secretary of Communications Building, Luanda. No. 1175, 5k, Mbanza Congo Post Office. No. 1176, 5k, Namibe Post Office. No. 1177, 8k, Facade of Luanda Post Office. No. 1178, 8k, Luanda Post Office, diff. No. 1179, 8k, Lobito Post Office.

2000, Sept. 29   **Litho.**   **Perf. 14**
1174-1179 A250 Set of 6   6.00 6.00

National Radio and Television, 25th Anniv. — A251

No. 1180, 9.50k: a, Woman at computer in newsroom. b, Reporter with tape recorder reporting on tank battle. c, Rescuing victims from airplane crash.

No. 1181, 9.50k: a, People and equipment in newsroom. b, Cameraman filming tank battle. c, Refugees.

No. 1182, 20k, Reporter with tape recorder. No. 1183, 20k, Cameraman, vert.

Perf. 13¼x13½, 13½x13¼
2000, Dec. 7
Sheets of 3, #a-c
1180-1181 A251 Set of 2   8.50 8.50
Souvenir Sheets
1182-1183 A251 Set of 2   6.00 6.00

Souvenir Sheet

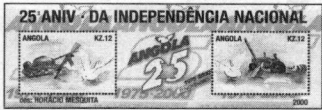

Independence, 25th Anniv. — A252

No. 1184: a, Tank, rifle, dove. b, Dove, hoe, tractor.

2001, Feb. 13   **Litho.**   **Perf. 14¼x14**
1184 A252 12k Sheet of 2, #a-b   2.60 2.60

Africa Day A253

Designs: No. 1185, 10k, Shown. No. 1186, 10k, Xylophone.

30k, Map, musical instruments, native with mask, elephant, satellite dishes and computer.

2001, May 25   **Perf. 13x13¼**
1185-1186 A253 Set of 2   2.00 2.00
Souvenir Sheet
1187 A253 30k multi   3.00 3.00

Flowers A254

Butterfly and: 8k, Nicolaia speciosa. 9k, Allamanda cathartica. No. 1190, 10k, Welwitschia mirabilis. No. 1191, 10k, Tagetes patula. 30k, Welwitschia mirabilis.

2001, June 9
1188-1191 A254 Set of 4   3.75 3.75
Souvenir Sheet
1192 A254 30k multi   3.00 3.00
Belgica 2001 Intl. Stamp Exhibition, Brussels (#1192).

Souvenir Sheet

Total Solar Eclipse, June 21 — A255

2001, June 21
1193 A255 30k multi   3.25 3.25

SEMI-POSTAL STAMPS

Angolan Red Cross — SP1

1991, Sept. 19   **Litho.**   **Perf. 14**
B1 SP1 20k +5k Mother and child 1.00 1.00
B2 SP1 40k +5k Zebra and foal   2.50 2.50

AIR POST STAMPS

Common Design Type
1938, July 26   **Engr.**   **Perf. 13½x13**
Name and Value in Black
C1 CD39 10c red orange   .20 .20
C2 CD39 20c purple   .25 .20
C3 CD39 50c orange   .20 .20
C4 CD39 1a ultra   .40 .20
C5 CD39 2a lilac brn   .85 .20
C6 CD39 3a dk green   2.25 .25
C7 CD39 5a red brown   3.25 .35
C8 CD39 9a rose carmine   4.25 1.10
C9 CD39 10a magenta   5.50 1.10
   Nos. C1-C9 (9)   17.15 3.80

No. C7 exists with overprint "Exposicao Internacional de Nova York, 1939-1940" and Trylon and Perisphere.

AP2

Planes Circling Globe — AP3

1947, Aug.   **Litho.**   **Perf. 10½**
C10 AP2 1a red brown   6.25 1.60
C11 AP2 2a yellow grn   6.25 1.60
C12 AP2 3a orange   8.00 1.60
C13 AP2 3.50a orange   10.00 4.00
C14 AP2 5a olive grn   90.00 15.00
C15 AP2 6a rose   90.00 17.50
C16 AP2 9a red   275.00 200.00
C17 AP2 10a green   175.00 60.00
C18 AP2 20a blue   175.00 60.00
C19 AP2 50a black   400.00 200.00
C20 AP2 100a yellow   750.00 600.00
   Nos. C10-C20 (11)   1,985. 1,161.

1949, May 1   **Photo.**   **Perf. 11½**
C21 AP3 1a henna brown   .20 .20
C22 AP3 2a red brown   .40 .20
C23 AP3 3a plum   .65 .20
C24 AP3 6a dull green   2.00 .40
C25 AP3 9a violet brown   3.00 1.00
   Nos. C21-C25 (5)   6.25 2.00

Catalogue values for unused stamps in this section, from this point to the end of the section, are for Never Hinged items.

Cambambe Dam AP4

Designs: 1.50e, Oil refinery, vert. 3e, Salazar Dam. 4e, Capt. Teófilo Duarte Dam. 4.50e, Craveiro Lopes Dam. 5e, Cuango Dam. 6e, Quanza River Bridge. 7e, Capt. Teófilo Duarte Bridge. 8.50e, Oliveira Salazar Bridge. 12.50e, Capt. Silva Carvalho Bridge.

Perf. 11½x12, 12x11½
1965, July 12   **Litho.**
C26 AP4 1.50e multicolored 1.00 .20
C27 AP4 2.50e multicolored .60 .20
C28 AP4 3e multicolored 1.00 .20
C29 AP4 4e multicolored .40 .20
C30 AP4 4.50e multicolored .40 .20
C31 AP4 5e multicolored .65 .20
C32 AP4 6e multicolored .65 .20
C33 AP4 7e multicolored 1.00 .20
C34 AP4 8.50e multicolored 1.25 .55
C35 AP4 12.50e multicolored 1.50 .65
   Nos. C26-C35 (10)   8.45 2.80

Stamp Centenary Type
Design: 2.50e, Boeing 707 jet & Angola #2.

1970, Dec. 1   **Litho.**   **Perf. 13½**
C36 A83 2.50e multicolored   .45 .20
   a.   Souv. sheet of 3, #565-566, C36 2.50 2.50
No. C36a sold for 15e.

No. C36 Overprinted with Bar and:
"REPUBLICA POPULAR / DE"
1980, June 15   **Litho.**   **Perf. 13½**
C37 A83 2.50e multicolored   .20

POSTAGE DUE STAMPS

D1   D2

1904 Unwmk. Typo. Perf. 11½x12
J1 D1 5r yellow grn   .25 .20
J2 D1 10r slate   .25 .20
J3 D1 20r yellow brn   .35 .30
J4 D1 30r orange   .60 .60
J5 D1 50r gray brown   .60 .60
J6 D1 60r red brown   4.00 2.50
J7 D1 100r lilac   1.75 1.60
J8 D1 130r dull blue   1.75 1.60
J9 D1 200r carmine   4.00 3.00
J10 D1 500r gray violet   4.00 3.00
   Nos. J1-J10 (10)   17.55 13.60

Postage Due Stamps of 1904 Overprinted in Carmine or Green

REPUBLICA

1911
J11 D1 5r yellow grn   .20 .20
J12 D1 10r slate   .20 .20
J13 D1 20r yellow brn   .20 .20
J14 D1 30r orange   .30 .30
J15 D1 50r gray brown   .30 .30
J16 D1 60r red brown   .60 .60
J17 D1 100r lilac   .60 .60
J18 D1 130r dull blue   .60 .60
J19 D1 200r carmine (G)   .60 .60
J20 D1 500r gray violet   .70 .70
   Nos. J11-J20 (10)   4.30 4.30

1921 ***Perf. 11½***

J21	D2	½c yellow green	.20	.20
J22	D2	1c slate	.20	.20
J23	D2	2c orange brown	.20	.20
J24	D2	3c orange	.20	.20
J25	D2	5c gray brown	.20	.20
J26	D2	6c lt brown	.20	.20
J27	D2	10c red violet	.20	.20
J28	D2	13c dull blue	.20	.20
J29	D2	20c carmine	.20	.20
J30	D2	50c gray	.20	.20
		Nos. J21-J30 (10)	2.00	2.00

For surcharges see Nos. 268-270.

Catalogue values for unused stamps in this section, from this point to the end of the section, are for Never Hinged items.

Stamps of 1932 Surcharged in Black

1948 **Wmk. 232** ***Perf. 12x11½***

J31	A14	10c on 20c gray	.20	.20
J32	A14	20c on 30c myrtle grn	.40	.20
J33	A14	30c on 50c lt brown	.60	.45
J34	A14	40c on 1a claret	.75	.45
J35	A14	50c on 2a dull vio	1.25	.45
J36	A14	1a on 5a pale yel grn	3.00	1.00
		Nos. J31-J36 (6)	6.20	2.75

Common Design Type

Photogravure and Typographed

1952 **Unwmk.** ***Perf. 14***

Numeral in Red, Frame Multicolored

J37	CD45	10c red brown	.20	.20
J38	CD45	30c olive green	.20	.20
J39	CD45	50c chocolate	.20	.20
J40	CD45	1a dk vio blue	.20	.20
J41	CD45	2a red brown	.20	.20
J42	CD45	5a black brown	.35	.35
		Nos. J37-J42 (6)	1.35	1.35

NEWSPAPER STAMP

N1

1893 **Typo.** ***Perf. 11½, 12½, 13½***

P1	N1	2½r brown	1.00	.70

No. P1 was also used for ordinary postage. For surcharges see Nos. 37, 82, 180, 235.

POSTAL TAX STAMPS

Pombal Issue

Common Design Types

1925, May 8 **Unwmk.** ***Perf. 12½***

RA1	CD28	15c lilac & black	.35	.25
RA2	CD29	15c lilac & black	.35	.25
RA3	CD30	15c lilac & black	.35	.25
		Nos. RA1-RA3 (3)	1.05	.75

"Charity" PT1

Coat of Arms PT2

1929 **Litho.** ***Perf. 11***

Without Gum

RA4	PT1	50c dark blue	2.00	.70

1939 **Without Gum** ***Perf. 10½***

RA5	PT2	50c turq green	1.00	.20
RA6	PT2	1a red	6.00	1.50

A 1.50a, type PT2, was issued for fiscal use.

Catalogue values for unused stamps in this section, from this point to the end of the section, are for Never Hinged items.

Old Man — PT3

Mother and Child — PT4

Designs: 1e, Boy. 1.50e, Girl.

Imprint: "Foto-Lito-E.G.A.-Luanda"

1955 **Unwmk.** ***Perf. 13***

Heads in dark brown

RA7	PT3	50c dk ocher	.20	.20
RA8	PT3	1e orange ver	.75	.40
RA9	PT3	1.50e brt yel grn	.50	.25
		Nos. RA7-RA9 (3)	1.45	.85

A 2.50e, type PT3 showing an old woman, was issued for revenue use.

See Nos. RA16, RA19-RA21, RA25-RA27.

No. RA7 Surcharged with New Values and two Bars in Red or Black

1957-58

Head in dark brown

RA11	PT3	10c on 50c dk ocher (R)	.25	.25
RA12	PT3	10c on 50c dk ocher ('58)	.20	.20
RA13	PT3	30c on 50c dk ocher	.25	.25
		Nos. RA11-RA13 (3)	.70	.70

1959 **Litho.** ***Perf. 13***

Design: 30c, Boy and girl.

RA14	PT4	10c orange & blk	.20	.20
RA15	PT4	30c slate & blk	.20	.20

Type of 1955 Redrawn

Design: 1e, Boy.

1961, Nov. ***Perf. 13***

RA16	PT3	1e salmon pink & dk brn	.20	.20

Denomination in italics.

Yellow, White and Black Men — PT5

1962, July 1 **Typo.** ***Perf. 10½***

Without Gum

RA17	PT5	50c multicolored	.65	.65
RA18	PT5	1e multicolored	.35	.35

Issued for the Provincial Settlement Committee (Junta Provincial do Povoamento). The tax was used to promote Portuguese settlement in Angola, and to raise educational and living standards of recent immigrants.

Denominations higher than 1e were used for revenue purposes.

Head Type of 1955

Without Imprint

Designs: 50c, Old man. 1e, Boy. 1.50e, Girl.

1964-65 **Litho.** ***Perf. 11½***

Heads in dark brown

RA19	PT3	50c orange	.20	.20
RA20	PT3	1e dull red org ('65)	.20	.20
RA21	PT3	1.50e yel grn ('65)	.25	.25
		Nos. RA19-RA21 (3)	.65	.65

No. RA20 is second redrawing of 1e, with bolder lettering and denomination in gothic. Space between "Assistencia" and denomination on RA19-RA21 is ½mm; on 1955 issue space is 2mm.

Map of Angola, Industrial and Farm Workers — PT6

1965, Sept. 1 **Litho.** ***Perf. 13***

RA22	PT6	50c multicolored	.35	.20
RA23	PT6	1e multicolored	.35	.25

The 2e was used for revenue purposes.

Head Type of 1955

Imprint: "I.N.A." or "INA" (1e)

Designs: 50c, Old man. 1e, Boy. 1.50e, Girl.

1966

Heads in dark brown

RA25	PT3	50c dull orange	.20	.20
RA26	PT3	1e dull brick red	.20	.20
RA27	PT3	1.50e lt yel grn	.35	.20
		Nos. RA25-RA27 (3)	.75	.60

Woman Planting Tree — PT7

1972 **Litho.** ***Perf. 13***

RA28	PT7	50c shown	.20	.20
RA29	PT7	1e Workers	.20	.20
RA30	PT7	2e Produce	.20	.20
		Nos. RA28-RA30 (3)	.60	.60

POSTAL TAX DUE STAMPS

Pombal Issue

Common Design Types

1925, May 8 **Unwmk.** ***Perf. 12½***

RAJ1	CD28	30c lilac & black	.50	*1.25*
RAJ2	CD29	30c lilac & black	.50	*1.25*
RAJ3	GD30	30c lilac & black	.50	*1.25*
		Nos. RAJ1-RAJ3 (3)	1.50	*3.75*

See note after Portugal No. RAJ4.

ANGRA

'aŋ-grə

LOCATION — An administrative district of the Azores, consisting of the islands of Terceira, Sao Jorge and Graciosa.
GOVT. — A district of Portugal
AREA — 275 sq. mi.
POP. — 70,000 (approx.)
CAPITAL — Angra do Heroismo

1000 Reis = 1 Milreis

King Carlos
A1 A2

1892-93 **Typo.** ***Perf. 12½***

1	A1	5r yellow	3.00	1.25
a.		Perf. 11½	8.50	4.75
b.		Perf. 13½	2.75	1.25
2	A1	10r redsh violet	3.00	1.25
a.		Perf. 13½	3.75	2.00
3	A1	15r chocolate	3.50	2.00
a.		Perf. 13½	3.75	2.00
4	A1	20r lavender	5.00	2.00
a.		Perf. 13½	5.00	2.00
5	A1	25r green	4.50	.50
a.		Perf. 13½	7.00	2.50
b.		Perf. 11½	4.25	1.00
7	A1	50r blue	7.75	3.00
a.		Perf. 13½	10.00	4.50
8	A1	75r carmine	9.00	3.50
9	A1	80r yellow green	10.00	7.00
10	A1	100r brown, *yel*, perf. 13½ ('93)	35.00	10.00
a.		Perf. 12½	140.00	95.00
11	A1	150r car, *rose* ('93)	50.00	25.00
a.		Perf. 13½	55.00	40.00
12	A1	200r dk blue, *bl* ('93)	50.00	25.00
a.		Perf. 13½	55.00	40.00
13	A1	300r dk blue, *sal* ('93)	50.00	25.00
a.		Perf. 13½	55.00	40.00
		Nos. 1-13 (12)	230.75	105.50

Reprints of 50r, 150r, 200r and 300r, made in 1900, are perf. 11½ and ungummed. Value, each $7.50. Reprints of all values, made in 1905, have shiny white gum and clean-cut perf. 13½.

1897-1905 ***Perf. 11½***

Name and Value in Black except Nos. 26 and 35

14	A2	2½r gray	.65	.35
15	A2	5r orange	.65	.35
a.		Diagonal half used as 2½r on cover		*26.00*
16	A2	10r yellow grn	.70	.40
17	A2	15r brown	8.25	4.00
18	A2	15r gray grn ('99)	.90	.45
19	A2	20r gray violet	1.50	.90
20	A2	25r sea green	2.75	.90
21	A2	25r car rose ('99)	.70	.40
22	A2	50r dark blue	5.00	1.75
23	A2	50r ultra ('05)	12.50	9.00
24	A2	65r slate bl ('98)	1.00	.40
25	A2	75r rose	3.00	1.00
26	A2	75r gray brn & car, *straw* ('05)	12.50	*9.00*
27	A2	80r violet	1.50	1.00
28	A2	100r dk blue, *bl*	2.50	1.25
29	A2	115r org brn, *pink* ('98)	2.50	1.40
30	A2	130r gray brn, *straw* ('98)	2.50	1.40
31	A2	150r lt brn, *straw*	2.50	1.40
32	A2	180r sl, *pnksh* ('98)	3.00	2.00
33	A2	200r red vio, *pnksh*	5.00	2.75
34	A2	300r blue, *rose*	7.50	4.00
35	A2	500r blk & red, *bl*	16.00	10.00
a.		Perf. 12½	21.00	12.50
		Nos. 14-35 (22)	93.10	54.10

Azores stamps were used in Angra from 1906 to 1931, when they were superseded by those of Portugal.

ANGUILLA

aŋ-gwi-lə

LOCATION — In the West Indies southeast of Puerto Rico
GOVT. — British territory
AREA — 60 sq. mi.
POP. — 10,663 (est. 1997)
CAPITAL — The Valley

Anguilla separated unilaterally from the Associated State of St. Kitts-Nevis-Anguilla in 1967, formalized in 1980 following direct United Kingdom intervention some years before. A British Commissioner exercises executive authority.

100 Cents = 1 Eastern Caribbean Dollar

Catalogue values for all unused stamps in this country are for Never Hinged items.

St. Kitts-Nevis Nos. 145-160 Overprinted

Independent
Anguilla
On Type A14

Independent
Anguilla
On Type A15

1967, Sept. 4		**Photo.**	**Perf. 14**	
1	A14	½c blue & dk brn	25.00	22.50
2	A15	1c multicolored	25.00	7.00
3	A14	2c multicolored	25.00	2.00
4	A14	3c multicolored	25.00	5.00
5	A15	4c multicolored	25.00	6.00
6	A15	5c multicolored	100.00	20.00
7	A15	6c multicolored	50.00	10.00
8	A15	10c multicolored	25.00	7.50
9	A14	15c multicolored	55.00	12.00
10	A15	20c multicolored	85.00	20.00
11	A14	25c multicolored	70.00	22.50
12	A15	50c multicolored	2,000.	500.00
13	A14	60c multicolored	2,500.	900.00
14	A14	$1 multicolored	1,600.	425.00
15	A15	$2.50 multicolored	1,600.	325.00
16	A14	$5 multicolored	1,300.	325.00
		Nos. 1-16 (16)	11,985.	2,609.

Counterfeit overprints exist.

Mahogany Tree, The Quarter — A1

Designs: 2c, Sombrero Lighthouse. 3c, St. Mary's Church. 4c, Valley Police Station. 5c, Old Plantation House, Mt. Fortune. 6c, Valley Post Office. 10c, Methodist Church, West End. 15c, Wall-Blake Airport. 20c, Plane over Sandy Ground. 25c, Island Harbor. 40c, Map of Anguilla. 60c, Hermit crab and starfish. $1, Hibiscus. $2.50, Coconut harvest. $5, Spiny lobster.

1967-68		**Litho.**	**Perf. 12½x13**	
17	A1	1c orange & multi	.20	.35
18	A1	2c gray green & blk	.20	.35
19	A1	3c emerald & blk	.20	.20
20	A1	4c brt blue & blk	.20	.20
21	A1	5c lt blue & multi	.20	.20
22	A1	6c ver & black	.20	.20
23	A1	10c multicolored	.20	.20
24	A1	15c multicolored	.50	.20
25	A1	20c multicolored	.70	.55
26	A1	25c multicolored	.50	.20
27	A1	40c blue & multi	.70	.25
28	A1	60c yellow & multi	2.50	2.25
29	A1	$1 lt green & multi	1.50	2.40
30	A1	$2.50 multicolored	1.75	2.75
31	A1	$5 multicolored	2.75	3.50
		Nos. 17-31 (15)	12.30	13.80

Issued: 1c, 5c, 10c, 20c, 25c, 40c, 11/27/67; 3c, 4c, 15c, 60c, $1, $5, 2/10/68; 2c, 6c, $2.50, 3/21/68.
For overprints see Nos. 53-67, 78-82.

Sailboats A2

Designs: 15c, Boat building. 25c, Schooner Warspite. 40c, Yacht Atlantic Star.

1968, May 11			**Perf. 14**	
32	A2	10c rose & multi	.40	.20
33	A2	15c olive & multi	.45	.20
34	A2	25c lilac rose & multi	.65	.30
35	A2	40c dull blue & multi	.75	.50
		Nos. 32-35 (4)	2.25	1.20

Purple-throated Carib — A3

Girl Guide Badge — A4

Anguillan Birds: 15c, Bananaquit. 25c, Black-necked stilt, horiz. 40c, Royal tern, horiz.

1968, July 8				
36	A3	10c dull yel & multi	.90	.20
37	A3	15c yel green & multi	1.10	.30
38	A3	25c multicolored	1.40	.30
39	A3	40c multicolored	1.60	.40
		Nos. 36-39 (4)	5.00	1.20

1968, Oct. 14		**Perf. 13x13½, 13½x13**		

10c, Girl Guide badge, horiz. 25c, Badge and Headquarters, horiz. 40c, Merit Badges.

40	A4	10c lt green & multi	.20	.20
41	A4	15c lt blue & multi	.20	.20
42	A4	25c multicolored	.30	.20
43	A4	40c multicolored	.40	.20
		Nos. 40-43 (4)	1.10	.80

Anguillan Girl Guides, 35th anniversary.

Three Kings A5

Christmas: 10c, Three Kings seeing Star, vert. 15c, Holy Family, vert. 40c, Shepherds seeing Star. 50c, Holy Family and donkey.

1968, Nov. 18				
44	A5	1c lilac rose & black	.20	.20
45	A5	10c blue & black	.20	.20
46	A5	15c brown & black	.20	.20
47	A5	40c brt ultra & black	.20	.20
48	A5	50c green & black	.20	.20
		Nos. 44-48 (5)	1.00	1.00

Bagging Salt — A6

Salt Industry: 15c, Packing salt. 40c, Salt pond. 50c, Loading salt.

1969, Jan. 4			**Perf. 13**	
49	A6	10c red & multi	.30	.20
50	A6	15c lt blue & multi	.35	.20
51	A6	40c emerald & multi	.40	.20
52	A6	50c purple & multi	.45	.20
		Nos. 49-52 (4)	1.50	.80

Nos. 17-31 Overprinted:
"INDEPENDENCE/JANUARY, 1969"

1969, Jan. 9			**Perf. 12½x13**	
53	A1	1c orange & multi	.20	.20
54	A1	2c gray green & blk	.20	.20
55	A1	3c emerald & blk	.20	.20
56	A1	4c brt blue & blk	.20	.20
57	A1	5c lt blue & multi	.20	.20
58	A1	6c vermilion & blk	.20	.20
59	A1	10c multicolored	.20	.20
60	A1	15c multicolored	.20	.20
61	A1	20c multicolored	.25	.25
62	A1	25c multicolored	.35	.35
63	A1	40c blue & multi	.45	.50
64	A1	60c yellow & multi	.60	.70
65	A1	$1 lt green & multi	1.00	1.25
66	A1	$2.50 multicolored	2.50	3.00
67	A1	$5 multicolored	5.50	6.25
		Nos. 53-67 (15)	12.25	13.90

Crucifixion, School of Quentin Massys A7

Easter: 40c, The Last Supper, ascribed to Roberti.

1969, Mar. 31		**Litho.**	**Perf. 13½**	
68	A7	25c multicolored	.30	.20
69	A7	40c multicolored	.50	.20

Amaryllis A8

1969, June 10			**Perf. 14**	
70	A8	10c shown	.25	.20
71	A8	15c Bougainvillea	.30	.20
72	A8	40c Hibiscus	.60	.50
73	A8	50c Cattleya orchid	1.60	1.00
		Nos. 70-73 (4)	2.75	2.00

Turban and Star Shells A9

Sea Shells: 15c, Spiny oysters. 40c, Scotch, royal and smooth bonnets. 50c, Triton trumpet.

1969, Sept. 22				
74	A9	10c multicolored	.30	.20
75	A9	15c multicolored	.45	.25
76	A9	40c multicolored	.85	.30
77	A9	50c multicolored	1.10	.35
		Nos. 74-77 (4)	2.70	1.10

Nos. 17, 25-28 Overprinted "CHRISTMAS 1969" and Various Christmas Designs

1969, Oct. 27		**Perf. 12½x13**		
78	A1	1c orange & multi	.20	.20
79	A1	20c multicolored	.20	.20
80	A1	25c multicolored	.25	.20
81	A1	40c blue & multi	.50	.25
82	A1	60c yellow & multi	1.10	.30
		Nos. 78-82 (5)	2.25	1.15

Red Goatfish A10

Designs: 15c, Blue-striped grunts. 40c, Mutton grouper. 50c, Banded butterfly-fish.

1969, Dec. 1			**Perf. 14**	
83	A10	10c multicolored	.25	.20
84	A10	15c multicolored	.35	.20
85	A10	40c multicolored	1.00	.40
86	A10	50c multicolored	1.25	.60
		Nos. 83-86 (4)	2.85	1.40

Morning Glory — A11

1970, Feb. 23				
87	A11	10c shown	.40	.20
88	A11	15c Blue petrea	.60	.20
89	A11	40c Hibiscus	.90	.25
90	A11	50c Flamboyant	1.10	.35
		Nos. 87-90 (4)	3.00	1.00

The Way to Calvary, by Tiepolo — A12

Easter: 20c, Crucifixion, by Masaccio, vert. 40c, Descent from the Cross, by Rosso Fiorentino, vert. 60c, Jesus Carrying the Cross, by Murillo.

1970, Mar. 26			**Perf. 13½**	
91	A12	10c multicolored	.20	.20
92	A12	15c multicolored	.25	.20
93	A12	40c multicolored	.40	.25
94	A12	60c multicolored	.60	.35
		Nos. 91-94 (4)	1.45	1.00

Anguilla Map, Scout Badge A13

Designs: 15c, Cub Scouts practicing first aid. 40c, Monkey bridge. 50c, Scout Headquarters, The Valley, and Lord Baden-Powell.

1970, Aug. 10			**Perf. 13**	
95	A13	10c multicolored	.25	.20
96	A13	15c multicolored	.35	.25
97	A13	40c multicolored	.45	.40
98	A13	50c multicolored	.70	.40
		Nos. 95-98 (4)	1.75	1.25

Anguilla Boy Scouts, 40th anniversary.

Boat Building A14

Designs: 2c, Road construction. 3c, Blowing Point dock. 4c, Radio announcer. 5c, Cottage Hospital extension. 6c, Valley secondary school. 10c, Hotel extension. 15c, Sandy Ground. 20c, Supermarket and movie house. 25c, Bananas and mangoes. 40c, Wall-Blake airport. 60c, Sandy Ground jetty. $1, Administration building. $2.50, Cow and calf. $5, Sandy Hill Bay.

1970, Nov. 23		**Litho.**	**Perf. 14**	
99	A14	1c multicolored	.35	.20
100	A14	2c multicolored	.35	.20
101	A14	3c multicolored	.35	.20
102	A14	4c multicolored	.50	.20
103	A14	5c multicolored	.35	.20
104	A14	6c multicolored	.35	.20
105	A14	10c multicolored	.35	.20
106	A14	15c multicolored	.35	.25
107	A14	20c multicolored	.70	.30
108	A14	25c multicolored	.40	.35
109	A14	40c multicolored	.60	.55
110	A14	60c multicolored	3.00	.90
111	A14	$1 multicolored	.80	1.50
112	A14	$2.50 multicolored	1.50	3.50
113	A14	$5 multicolored	1.90	7.25
		Nos. 99-113 (15)	11.85	16.00

Adoration of the Shepherds, by Guido Reni — A15

Christmas: 20c, Virgin and Child, by Benozzo Gozzoli. 25c, Nativity, by Botticelli. 40c, Santa Margherita Madonna, by Mazzola. 50c, Adoration of the Kings, by Tiepolo.

1970, Dec. 11			**Perf. 13½**	
114	A15	1c multicolored	.20	.20
115	A15	20c multicolored	.25	.20
116	A15	25c multicolored	.30	.25
117	A15	40c multicolored	.50	.35
118	A15	50c multicolored	.55	.45
		Nos. 114-118 (5)	1.80	1.45

Angels Weeping over the Dead Christ, by Guercino — A16

Easter: 10c, Ecce Homo, by Correggio, vert. 15c, Christ Appearing to St. Peter, by Carracci, vert. 50c, The Supper at Emmaus, by Caravaggio.

1971, Mar. 29
119	A16	10c pink & multi	.20	.20
120	A16	15c lt blue & multi	.25	.20
121	A16	40c yel green & multi	.45	.20
122	A16	50c violet & multi	.55	.20
		Nos. 119-122 (4)	1.45	.80

Hypolimnas Misippus — A17

Butterflies: 15c, Junonia lavinia. 40c, Agraulis vanillae. 50c, Danaus plexippus.

1971, June 21 Perf. 14x14½
123	A17	10c multicolored	1.75	.90
124	A17	15c multicolored	1.75	1.00
125	A17	40c multicolored	2.25	1.60
126	A17	50c multicolored	2.25	1.90
		Nos. 123-126 (4)	8.00	5.40

Magnanime and Aimable in Battle — A18

Ships: 15c, HMS Duke and Agamemnon against Glorieux. 25c, HMS Formidable and Namur against Ville de Paris. 40c, HMS Canada. 50c, HMS St. Albans and wreck of Hector.

1971, Aug. 30 Litho. Perf. 14
127	A18	10c multicolored	.35	.35
128	A18	15c multicolored	.60	.65
129	A18	25c multicolored	1.25	1.40
130	A18	40c multicolored	2.00	2.25
131	A18	50c multicolored	2.75	3.00
a.		Strip of 5, #127-131	7.25	7.25

West Indies sea battles.

Ansidei Madonna, by Raphael — A19

Christmas: 25c, Mystic Nativity, by Botticelli. 40c, Virgin and Child, School of Seville, inscribed Murillo. 50c, Madonna of the Iris, ascribed to Dürer.

1971, Nov. 29 Perf. 14x13½
132	A19	20c green & multi	.25	.30
133	A19	25c blue & multi	.25	.30
134	A19	40c lilac rose & multi	.35	.40
135	A19	50c violet & multi	.40	.50
		Nos. 132-135 (4)	1.25	1.50

Map of Anguilla and St. Maarten, by Jefferys, 1775 — A20

Jesus Buffeted, Stained-glass Window — A21

Maps of Anguilla by: 15c, Samuel Fahlberg, 1814. 40c, Thomas Jefferys, 1775, horiz. 50c, Capt. E. Barnett, 1847, horiz.

1972, Jan. 24 Perf. 14x13½, 13½x14
136	A20	10c lt blue & multi	.20	.20
137	A20	15c lt green & multi	.35	.25
138	A20	40c lt green & multi	.75	.50
139	A20	50c lt ultra & multi	1.00	.50
		Nos. 136-139 (4)	2.30	1.45

1972, Mar. 14 Perf. 14x13½
Easter (19th cent. Stained-glass Windows, Bray Church): 15c, Jesus Carrying the Cross. 25c, Crucifixion. 40c, Descent from the Cross. 50c, Burial.
140	A21	10c multicolored	.30	.30
141	A21	15c multicolored	.40	.40
142	A21	25c multicolored	.40	.40
143	A21	40c multicolored	.45	.45
144	A21	50c multicolored	.55	.55
a.		Strip of 5, #140-144	2.50	2.50

Spear Fishing — A22

Sandy Ground — A23

1972-75 Perf. 13½
145	A22	1c shown	.20	.20
146	A23	2c Loblolly tree, vert.	.20	.20
147	A22	3c shown	.20	.20
148	A23	4c Ferry, Blowing Point, vert.	1.00	.20
149	A23	5c Agriculture	.20	.50
150	A23	6c St. Mary's Church, vert.	.20	.20
151	A23	10c St. Gerard's Church	.20	.20
152	A22	15c Cottage Hospital	.30	.30
153	A23	20c Public Library	.35	.35
154	A23	25c Sunset, Blowing Point	.50	1.50
155	A22	40c Boat building	3.00	1.50
156	A22	60c Hibiscus	3.75	3.00
157	A23	$1 Man-o-war bird	7.75	7.00
158	A23	$2.50 Frangipani	5.50	8.00
159	A23	$5 Brown pelican	13.50	12.00
160	A22	$10 Green-back turtle	13.50	16.00
		Nos. 145-160 (16)	51.55	51.35

Issued: $10, 5/20/75; others 10/30/72.
For overprints see Nos. 229-246.

Common Design Types pictured following the introduction.

Silver Wedding Issue, 1972
Common Design Type
Design: Queen Elizabeth II, Prince Philip, schooner and dolphin.

1972, Nov. 20 Photo. Perf. 14x14½
161	CD324	25c olive & multi	1.00	.75
162	CD324	40c maroon & multi	1.00	.75

Flight into Egypt — A24

1972, Dec. 4 Litho. Perf. 13½
163	A24	1c shown	.20	.20
164	A24	20c Star of Bethlehem	.20	.20
165	A24	25c Nativity	.20	.20
166	A24	40c Three Kings	.20	.25
167	A24	50c Adoration of the Kings	.25	.30
a.		Vert. strip of 4, #164-167	1.00	1.00
		Nos. 163-167 (5)	1.05	1.15

Christmas.

Betrayal of Jesus — A25

1973, Mar. 26
168	A25	1c shown	.20	.20
169	A25	10c Man of Sorrow	.20	.20
170	A25	20c Jesus Carrying Cross	.20	.25
171	A25	25c Crucifixion	.25	.25
172	A25	40c Descent from Cross	.25	.25
173	A25	50c Resurrection	.25	.35
a.		Souvenir sheet of 6	1.25	1.50
b.		Vert. strip of 5, #169-173	1.00	1.00
		Nos. 168-173 (6)	1.35	1.50

Easter. #173a contains 6 stamps similar to #168-173 with bottom panel in lilac rose.

Santa Maria A26

1973, Sept. 10
174	A26	1c shown	.20	.20
175	A26	20c Old West Indies map	1.25	1.25
176	A26	40c Map of voyages	1.50	1.50
177	A26	70c Sighting land	1.75	1.75
178	A26	$1.20 Columbus landing	2.40	2.40
a.		Souvenir sheet of 5, #174-178	7.00	7.75
b.		Horiz. strip of 4, #175-178	7.00	7.00
		Nos. 174-178 (5)	7.10	7.10

Discovery of West Indies by Columbus.

Princess Anne's Wedding Issue
Common Design Type

1973, Nov. 14 Wmk. 314 Perf. 13½
179	CD325	60c blue grn & multi	.20	.20
180	CD325	$1.20 lilac & multi	.40	.30

Wedding of Princess Anne and Capt. Mark Phillips, Nov. 14, 1973.

Adoration of the Shepherds, by Guido Reni — A27

Paintings: 10c, Virgin and Child, by Filippino Lippi. 20c, Nativity, by Meester Van de Brunswijkse Diptiek. 25c, Madonna of the Meadow, by Bellini. 40c, Virgin and Child, by Cima. 50c, Adoration of the Kings, by Geertgen Tot Sint Jans.

1973, Dec. 2 Unwmk.
181	A27	1c multicolored	.20	.20
182	A27	10c multicolored	.20	.20
183	A27	20c multicolored	.20	.20
184	A27	25c multicolored	.20	.20
185	A27	40c multicolored	.20	.20
186	A27	50c multicolored	.20	.20
a.		Souvenir sheet of 6, #181-186	1.25	1.25
b.		Horiz. strip of 6, #182-186	1.00	1.00
		Nos. 181-186 (6)	1.20	1.20

Christmas.

Crucifixion, by Raphael — A28

Easter (Details from Crucifixion by Raphael): 15c, Virgin Mary and St. John. 20c, The Two Marys. 25c, Left Angel. 40c, Right Angel. $1, Christ on the Cross.

1974, Mar. 30
187	A28	1c lilac & multi	.20	.20
188	A28	15c gray & multi	.20	.20
189	A28	20c salmon & multi	.20	.20
190	A28	25c yel green & multi	.20	.20
191	A28	40c orange & multi	.20	.20
192	A28	$1 lt blue & multi	.25	.25
a.		Souvenir sheet of 6, #187-192	1.50	1.75
b.		Vert. strip of 6, #188-192	1.00	1.00
		Nos. 187-192 (6)	1.25	1.25

Churchill Making Victory Sign — A29

20c, Roosevelt, Churchill, US, British flags. 25c, Churchill broadcasting during the war. 40c, Blenheim Palace. 60c, Churchill Statue & Parliament. $1.20, Chartwell.

1974, June 24
193	A29	1c multicolored	.20	.20
194	A29	20c multicolored	.25	.25
195	A29	25c multicolored	.35	.35
196	A29	40c multicolored	.40	.40
197	A29	60c multicolored	.40	.40
198	A29	$1.20 multicolored	.50	.50
a.		Souvenir sheet of 6, #193-198	2.25	2.50
b.		Horiz. strip of 5, #194-198	2.25	2.25
		Nos. 193-198 (6)	2.10	2.10

Sir Winston Spencer Churchill (1874-1965).

UPU Emblem, Map of Anguilla — A30

1974, Aug. 27

199	A30	1c black & ultra	.20	.20
200	A30	20c black & orange	.20	.20
201	A30	25c black & yellow	.20	.20
202	A30	40c black & brt lilac	.25	.25
203	A30	60c black & lt green	.35	.35
204	A30	$1.20 black & blue	.55	.55
a.		Souvenir sheet of 6	1.75	2.00
b.		Horiz. strip of 5, #200-204	1.50	1.50
		Nos. 199-204 (6)	1.75	1.75

UPU, centenary. No. 204a contains one each of Nos. 199-204 with second row (40c, 60c, $1.20) perf. 15 at bottom.

Fishermen Seeing Star — A31

Christmas: 20c, Nativity. 25c, King offering gift. 40c, Star over map of Anguilla. 60c, Family looking at star. $1.20, Two angels with star and "Peace."

1974, Dec. 16   Litho.   Perf. 14½

205	A31	1c brt blue & multi	.20	.20
206	A31	20c dull grn & multi	.20	.20
207	A31	25c gray & multi	.20	.20
208	A31	40c car & multi	.20	.20
209	A31	60c dp blue & multi	.20	.20
210	A31	$1.20 ultra & multi	.25	.25
a.		Souvenir sheet of 6, #205-210	1.50	1.75
b.		Horiz. strip of 5, #206-210	1.25	1.25
		Nos. 205-210 (6)	1.25	1.25

Virgin Mary, St. John, Mary Magdalene A32

Paintings from Isenheim Altar, by Matthias Grunewald: 10c, Crucifixion. 15c, John the Baptist. 20c, St. Sebastian and Angels. $1, Burial of Christ, horiz. $1.50, St. Anthony, the Hermit.

1975, Mar. 25   Perf. 13½

211	A32	1c multicolored	.20	.20
212	A32	10c multicolored	.20	.20
213	A32	15c multicolored	.20	.20
214	A32	20c multicolored	.20	.20
215	A32	$1 multicolored	.25	.35
216	A32	$1.50 multicolored	.30	.45
a.		Souvenir sheet of 6	1.75	2.00
b.		Horiz. strip of 5, #212-216	1.25	1.25
		Nos. 211-216 (6)	1.35	1.60

Easter. No. 216a contains 6 stamps similar to Nos. 211-216 with simulated perforations.

Statue of Liberty, N.Y. Skyline — A33

10c, Capitol, Washington, DC. 15c, Congress voting independence. 20c, Washington, map & his battles. $1, Boston Tea Party. $1.50, Bicentennial emblem, historic US flags.

1975, Nov. 10

217	A33	1c multicolored	.20	.20
218	A33	10c multicolored	.20	.20
219	A33	15c multicolored	.30	.20
220	A33	20c multicolored	.35	.20
221	A33	$1 multicolored	.50	.45
222	A33	$1.50 multicolored	.55	.70
a.		Souvenir sheet of 6	1.75	2.50
b.		Horiz. strip of 5, #218-222	2.00	2.00
		Nos. 217-222 (6)	2.10	1.95

American Bicentennial. No. 222a contains one each of Nos. 217-222 with second row (20c, $1, $1.50) perf. 15 at bottom.

Virgin and Child with St. John, by Raphael — A34

Paintings, Virgin and Child by: 10c, Cima. 15c, Dolci. 20c, Durer. $1, Bellini. $1.50, Botticelli.

1975, Dec. 8   Perf. 14x13½

223	A34	1c ultra & multi	.20	.20
224	A34	10c Prus blue & multi	.20	.20
225	A34	15c plum & multi	.20	.20
226	A34	20c car rose & multi	.20	.20
227	A34	$1 brt grn & multi	.35	.25
228	A34	$1.50 blue grn & multi	.45	.40
a.		Souvenir sheet of 6, #223-228	2.75	2.75
b.		Horiz. strip of 5, #224-228	1.50	1.50
		Nos. 223-228 (6)	1.60	1.45

Christmas.

Nos. 145-146, 148, 150-160
Overprinted "NEW CONSTITUTION 1976"

1976   Litho.   Perf. 13½

229	A22	1c #145	.25	.35
230	A22	2c on 1c #145	.25	.35
231	A23	2c #146	4.25	1.60
232	A22	3c on 40c #155	.65	.60
233	A23	4c #148	.85	.90
234	A22	5c on 40c #155	.25	.45
235	A23	6c #150	.25	.45
236	A23	10c on 20c #153	.25	.45
237	A23	10c #151	4.25	3.75
238	A22	15c #152	.25	.80
239	A22	20c #153	.25	.45
240	A23	25c #154	.25	.45
241	A22	40c #155	.85	.65
242	A22	60c #156	.60	.65
243	A23	$1 #157	5.25	2.00
244	A23	$2.50 #158	2.00	2.00
245	A23	$5 #159	6.50	6.00
246	A22	$10 #160	2.50	5.50
		Nos. 229-246 (18)	29.70	27.40

Flowering Trees — A35

1976, Feb. 16   Perf. 13½x14

247	A35	1c Almond	.20	.20
248	A35	10c Clusia rosea	.30	.30
249	A35	15c Calabash	.30	.30
250	A35	20c Cordia	.30	.30
251	A35	$1 Papaya	.40	.40
252	A35	$1.50 Flamboyant	.50	.50
a.		Souvenir sheet of 6, #247-252	2.25	2.25
b.		Horiz. strip of 5, #248-252	2.00	2.00
		Nos. 247-252 (6)	2.00	2.00

The Three Marys — A36

Designs: 10c, Crucifixion. 15c, Two soldiers. 20c, Annunciation. $1, Altar tapestry, 1470, Monastery of Rheinau, Switzerland, horiz. $1.50, "Noli me Tangere" (Jesus and Mary Magdalene). Designs of vertical stamps show details from tapestry shown on $1 stamp.

1976, Apr. 5   Perf. 14x13½, 13½x14

253	A36	1c multicolored	.20	.20
254	A36	10c multicolored	.20	.20
255	A36	15c multicolored	.20	.20
256	A36	20c multicolored	.20	.20
257	A36	$1 multicolored	.65	.65

258	A36	$1.50 multicolored	.80	.80
a.		Souvenir sheet of 6	2.50	2.75
b.		Horiz. strip of 5, #254-258	2.25	2.25
		Nos. 253-258 (6)	2.25	2.25

Easter. No. 258a contains 6 stamps similar to Nos. 253-258 with simulated perforations.

Le Desius and La Vaillante Approaching Anguilla — A37

Sailing Ships: 3c, Sailboat leaving Anguilla for Antigua to get help. 15c, HMS Lapwing in battle with frigate Le Desius and brig La Vaillante. 25c, La Vaillante aground off St. Maarten. $1, Lapwing. $1.50, Le Desius burning.

1976, Nov. 8   Litho.   Perf. 13½x14

259	A37	1c multicolored	.20	.20
260	A37	3c multicolored	.75	.25
261	A37	15c multicolored	1.00	.30
262	A37	25c multicolored	1.25	.50
263	A37	$1 multicolored	2.50	2.25
264	A37	$1.50 multicolored	3.25	3.00
a.		Souvenir sheet of 6, #259-264	8.50	8.50
b.		Strip of 5, #260-264	8.50	8.50
		Nos. 259-264 (6)	8.95	6.50

Bicentenary of Battle of Anguilla between French and British ships.

Christmas Carnival — A38

Children's Paintings: 3c, 3 children dreaming of Christmas gifts. 15c, Caroling. 25c, Candlelight procession. $1, Going to Church on Christmas Eve. $1.50, Airport, coming home for Christmas.

1976, Nov. 22

265	A38	1c multicolored	.20	.20
266	A38	3c multicolored	.20	.20
267	A38	15c multicolored	.20	.20
268	A38	25c multicolored	.20	.20
269	A38	$1 multicolored	.65	.65
270	A38	$1.50 multicolored	.85	.75
a.		Souvenir sheet of 6, #265-270	2.50	2.75
b.		Strip of 5, #266-270	2.00	1.75
		Nos. 265-270 (6)	2.30	2.20

Christmas. For overprints and surcharges see Nos. 305-310a.

Prince Charles and HMS Minerva, 1973 — A39

Designs: 40c, Prince Philip landing at Road Bay, 1964. $1.20, Homage to Queen at Coronation. $2.50, Coronation regalia and map of Anguilla.

1977, Feb. 9

271	A39	25c multicolored	.20	.20
272	A39	40c multicolored	.20	.20
273	A39	$1.20 multicolored	.40	.35
274	A39	$2.50 multicolored	.75	.70
a.		Souvenir sheet of 4, #271-274	1.50	2.00
		Nos. 271-274 (4)	1.55	1.45

25th anniv. of reign of Queen Elizabeth II. For overprints see Nos. 297-300.

Yellow-crowned Night Heron — A40

Designs: 2c, Great barracuda. 3c, Queen conch. 4c, Spanish bayonet (Yucca). 5c, Trunkfish. 6c, Cable and telegraph building. 10c, American sparrow hawk. 15c, Ground orchids. 20c, Parlorfish. 22c, Lobster fishing boat. 35c, Boat race. 50c Sea bean (flowers). $1, Sandy Island with palms. $2.50, Manchineel (fruit). $5, Ground lizard. $10, Red-billed tropic bird.

1977-78   Litho.   Perf. 13½x14

275	A40	1c multicolored	.30	.75
276	A40	2c multicolored	.30	1.25
277	A40	3c multicolored	1.10	1.90
278	A40	4c multicolored	.35	.30
279	A40	5c multicolored	1.40	.30
280	A40	6c multicolored	.30	.35
281	A40	10c multicolored	3.75	2.25
282	A40	15c multicolored	2.50	1.90
283	A40	20c multicolored	1.90	.80
284	A40	22c multicolored	.40	.65
285	A40	35c multicolored	1.25	.75
286	A40	50c multicolored	.85	.50
287	A40	$1 multicolored	.60	.50
288	A40	$2.50 multicolored	1.00	1.00
289	A40	$5 multicolored	1.75	1.75
290	A40	$10 multicolored	8.25	4.75
		Nos. 275-290 (16)	26.00	19.70

Issued: #275-280, 290, 4/18/77; others 2/20/78.

For overprints and surcharges see Nos. 319-324, 337-342, 387-390, 402-404, 407-415, 417-423.

Crucifixion, by Quentin Massys — A41

Easter (Paintings): 3c, Betrayal of Christ, by Ugolino. 22c, Way to Calvary, by Ugolino. 30c, The Deposition, by Ugolino. $1, Resurrection, by Ugolino. $1.50, Crucifixion, by Andrea del Castagno.

1977, Apr. 25

291	A41	1c multicolored	.20	.20
292	A41	3c multicolored	.20	.25
293	A41	22c multicolored	.25	.25
294	A41	30c multicolored	.30	.30
295	A41	$1 multicolored	.75	.75
296	A41	$1.50 multicolored	1.10	1.10
a.		Souvenir sheet of 6, #291-296	2.75	2.75
b.		Strip of 5, #292-296	2.75	2.75
		Nos. 291-296 (6)	2.80	2.80

Nos. 271-274, 274a Overprinted:
"ROYAL VISIT/TO WEST INDIES"

1977, Oct. 26   Litho.   Perf. 13½x14

297	A39	25c multicolored	.20	.20
298	A39	40c multicolored	.20	.20
299	A39	$1.20 multicolored	.50	.60
300	A39	$2.50 multicolored	1.00	1.25
a.		Souvenir sheet of 4	1.75	2.00
		Nos. 297-300 (4)	1.90	2.25

Visit of Queen Elizabeth II to West Indies.

Suzanne Fourment in Velvet Hat, by Rubens — A42

Rubens Paintings: 40c, Helena Fourment with her Children. $1.20, Rubens with his wife. $2.50, Marchesa Brigida Spinola-Doria.

1977, Nov. 1   *Perf. 14x13½*

301	A42	25c black & multi	.20	.20
302	A42	40c black & multi	.20	.20
303	A42	$1.20 multicolored	.75	.75
304	A42	$2.50 black & multi	1.50	1.50
a.		Souvenir sheet of 4, #301-304	3.00	3.00
		Nos. 301-304 (4)	2.65	2.65

Peter Paul Rubens, 400th birth anniv. Nos. 301-304 printed in sheets of 5 stamps and blue label with Rubens' portrait.

Nos. 265-270b Overprinted 1977 and Surcharged

1977, Nov. 7   *Perf. 13½x14*

305	A38	1c multicolored	.20	.20
306	A38	5c on 3c multi	.20	.20
307	A38	12c on 15c multi	.20	.20
308	A38	18c on 25c multi	.20	.20
309	A38	$1 multicolored	.65	.65
310	A38	$2.50 on $1.50 multi	1.75	1.75
a.		Souvenir sheet of 6, #305-310	3.75	3.75
b.		Strip of 5, #306-310	3.00	3.00
		Nos. 305-310 (6)	3.20	3.20

Christmas. Stamps and souvenir sheets have "1976" and old denomination obliterated with variously shaped rectangles.

Nos. 301-304a Ovptd. in Gold: "EASTER 1978"

1978, Mar. 6   *Perf. 14x13½*

311	A42	25c black & multi	.20	.20
312	A42	40c black & multi	.25	.25
313	A42	$1.20 black & multi	.65	.65
314	A42	$2.50 black & multi	1.40	1.40
a.		Souvenir sheet of 4, #311-314	2.50	2.50
		Nos. 311-314 (4)	2.50	2.50

Buckingham Palace — A43

Designs: 50c, Coronation procession. $1.50, Royal family on balcony. $2.50, Royal coat of arms.

1978, Apr. 6   *Perf. 14*

315	A43	22c multicolored	.20	.20
316	A43	50c multicolored	.20	.20
317	A43	$1.50 multicolored	.35	.45
318	A43	$2.50 multicolored	.50	.70
a.		Souvenir sheet of 4, #315-318	2.00	2.00
		Nos. 315-318 (4)	1.25	1.55

25th anniv. of coronation of Queen Elizabeth II.
#315-318 each exist in a booklet pane of 2.

Nos. 284-285 and 288 Ovptd. and Surcharged: "VALLEY / SECONDARY / SCHOOL / 1953-1978"

1978, Aug. 14   Litho.   *Perf. 13½x14*

319	A40	22c multicolored	.20	.20
320	A40	35c multicolored	.25	.20
321	A40	$1.50 on $2.50 multi	1.25	1.25
		Nos. 319-321 (3)	1.70	1.65

Valley Secondary School, 25th anniv. Surcharge on No. 321 includes heavy bar over old denomination.

Nos. 286-287, 289 Ovptd. and Surcharged: "ROAD / METHODIST / CHURCH / 1878-1978"

1978, Aug. 14

322	A40	50c multicolored	.40	.40
323	A40	$1 multicolored	.75	.75
324	A40	$1.20 on $5 multi	1.00	1.00
		Nos. 322-324 (3)	2.15	2.15

Road Methodist Church, centenary. Surcharge on No. 324 includes heavy bar over old denomination.

Mother and Child — A44

Christmas: 12c, Christmas masquerade. 18c, Christmas dinner. 22c, Serenade. $1, Star over manger. $2.50, Family going to church.

1978, Dec. 11   Litho.   *Perf. 13½*

325	A44	5c multicolored	.20	.20
326	A44	12c multicolored	.20	.20
327	A44	18c multicolored	.20	.20
328	A44	22c multicolored	.20	.20
329	A44	$1 multicolored	.50	.50
330	A44	$2.50 multicolored	1.00	1.00
a.		Souvenir sheet of 6, #325-330	2.75	2.75
		Nos. 325-330 (6)	2.30	2.30

Type A44 in Changed Colors with IYC Emblem and Inscription.

1979, Jan. 15   Litho.   *Perf. 13½*

331	A44	5c multicolored	.20	.20
332	A44	12c multicolored	.20	.20
333	A44	18c multicolored	.20	.20
334	A44	22c multicolored	.20	.20
335	A44	$1 multicolored	.50	.50
336	A44	$2.50 multicolored	1.00	1.00
a.		Souvenir sheet of 6, #331-336	3.50	3.50
		Nos. 331-336 (6)	2.30	2.30

Intl. Year of the Child. For overprint see #416.

1979, Feb. 8   Litho.   *Perf. 13½x14*

337	A40	12c on 2c multi	.45	.45
338	A40	14c on 4c multi	.50	.50
339	A40	18c on 4c multi	.75	.75
340	A40	25c on 6c multi	1.00	.90
341	A40	38c on 10c multi	2.25	1.75
342	A40	40c on 1c multi	2.25	2.00
		Nos. 337-342 (6)	7.20	6.35

Valley Methodist Church A45

Church Interiors: 12c, St. Mary's Anglican Church, The Valley. 18c, St. Gerard's Roman Catholic Church, The Valley. 22c, Road Methodist Church. $1.50, St. Augustine's Anglican Church, East End. $2.50, West End Methodist Church.

1979, Mar. 30   Litho.   *Perf. 14*

343	A45	5c multicolored	.20	.20
344	A45	12c multicolored	.20	.20
345	A45	18c multicolored	.20	.20
346	A45	22c multicolored	.20	.20
347	A45	$1.50 multicolored	.90	.90
348	A45	$2.50 multicolored	1.25	1.25
a.		Souvenir sheet of 6	2.75	2.75
b.		Strip of 6, #343-348	2.50	2.50

Easter. No. 348a contains Nos. 343-348 in 2 horizontal rows of 3.

US No. C3a A46

No. 350, Cape of Good Hope #1. No. 351, Penny Black. No. 352, Germany #C36. No. 353, US #245. No. 354, Great Britain #93.

1979, Apr. 23   Litho.   *Perf. 14*

349	A46	1c multicolored	.20	.20
350	A46	1c multicolored	.20	.20
351	A46	22c multicolored	.20	.20
352	A46	35c multicolored	.20	.20
353	A46	$1.50 multicolored	.75	.75
354	A46	$2.50 multicolored	1.10	1.10
a.		Souvenir sheet of 6, #349-353	2.50	2.50
		Nos. 349-354 (6)	2.65	2.65

Sir Rowland Hill (1795-1879), originator of penny postage.

Wright's Flyer A — A47

History of Aviation: 12c, Louis Bleriot landing at Dover, 1909. 18c, Vickers Vimy, 1919. 22c, Spirit of St. Louis, 1927. $1.50, LZ127 Graf Zeppelin, 1928. $2.50, Concorde, 1979.

1979, May 21   Litho.   *Perf. 14*

355	A47	5c multicolored	.20	.20
356	A47	12c multicolored	.20	.20
357	A47	18c multicolored	.25	.25
358	A47	22c multicolored	.25	.25
359	A47	$1.50 multicolored	.90	.90
360	A47	$2.50 multicolored	1.90	1.90
a.		Souvenir sheet of 6, #355-360	4.00	3.75
		Nos. 355-360 (6)	3.70	3.60

Map of Anguilla, Map and View of Sombrero Island A48

Map of Anguilla, Map and View of: 12c, Anguillita Island. 18c, Sandy Island. 25c, Prickly Pear Cays. $1, Dog Island. $2.50, Scrub Island.

1979   Litho.   *Perf. 14*

361	A48	5c multicolored	.20	.20
362	A48	12c multicolored	.20	.20
363	A48	18c multicolored	.20	.20
364	A48	25c multicolored	.20	.20
365	A48	$1 multicolored	.40	.40
366	A48	$2.50 multicolored	1.00	1.00
a.		Souvenir sheet of 6, #361-366	3.50	3.50
		Nos. 361-366 (6)	2.20	2.20

Anguilla's Outer Islands.

Red Poinsettia — A49

1979, Oct. 22   Litho.   *Perf. 14½*

367	A49	22c shown	.20	.20
368	A49	35c Kalanchoe	.20	.20
369	A49	$1.50 Cream poinsettia	.85	.75
370	A49	$2.50 White poinsettia	1.50	1.25
a.		Souvenir sheet of 4, #367-370	3.00	3.00
		Nos. 367-370 (4)	2.75	2.40

Christmas.

Booths and Frames A50

50c, Earls Court Exhibition Hall. $1.50, Penny Black, Great Britain #2. $2.50, Exhibition emblem.

1979, Dec. 10   Litho.   *Perf. 13*

371	A50	35c multicolored	.20	.20
372	A50	50c multicolored	.20	.20
373	A50	$1.50 multicolored	.75	.75
374	A50	$2.50 multicolored	1.00	1.00
b.		Souvenir sheet of 4, #371-374	3.25	3.25
		Nos. 371-374 (4)	2.15	2.15

            Perf. 14½

371a	A50	35c	.20	.20
372a	A50	50c	.20	.20
373a	A50	$1.50	.75	.75
374a	A50	$2.50	1.00	1.00
c.		Souvenir sheet of 4, #371-374	3.25	3.25
		Nos. 371a-374a (4)	2.15	2.15

London 1980 Intl. Stamp Exhibition, May 6-14, 1980.

Lake Placid and Olympic Rings — A51

Olympic Rings and: 18c, Ice Hockey. 35c, Figure skating. 50c, Bobsledding. $1, Ski jump. $2.50, Luge.

1980, Jan.   Litho.   *Perf. 13½, 14½*

375	A51	5c multicolored	.20	.20
376	A51	18c multicolored	.20	.20
377	A51	35c multicolored	.20	.20
378	A51	50c multicolored	.20	.20
379	A51	$1 multicolored	.35	.35
380	A51	$2.50 multicolored	.60	.60
a.		Souvenir sheet of 6, #375-380	2.25	2.25
		Nos. 375-380 (6)	1.75	1.75

13th Winter Olympic Games, Lake Placid, NY, Feb. 12-24.

Salt Field A52

1980, Apr. 14   Litho.   *Perf. 14*

381	A52	5c shown	.20	.20
382	A52	12c Tallying salt	.20	.20
383	A52	18c Unloading salt flats	.20	.20
384	A52	22c Storage pile	.20	.20
385	A52	$1 Bagging and grinding	.40	.40
386	A52	$2.50 Loading onto boats	.90	.90
a.		Souvenir sheet of 6, #381-386	2.00	2.00
		Nos. 381-386 (6)	2.10	2.10

Salt industry.

Nos. 281, 288 Overprinted: "50th Anniversary / Scouting 1980"

1980, Apr. 16   *Perf. 13½x14*

387	A40	10c multicolored	1.10	.40
388	A40	22c multicolored	2.00	1.75

Nos. 283, 289 Overprinted: "75th Anniversary / Rotary 1980" and Rotary Emblem

1980, Apr. 16   *Perf. 13½x14*

389	A40	20c multicolored	.90	.40
390	A40	$5 multicolored	2.75	2.50

Rotary International, 75th anniversary.

Big Ben, Great Britain #643, London 1980 Emblem — A53

Designs: $1.50, Canada #756. $2.50, Statue of Liberty, US #1632.

1980, May

391	A53	50c multicolored	.75	.75
392	A53	$1.50 multicolored	1.00	1.00
393	A53	$2.50 multicolored	1.50	1.50
a.		Souvenir sheet of 3, #391-393	3.50	3.50
		Nos. 391-393 (3)	3.25	3.25

London 1980 International Stamp Exhibition, May 6-14.

Queen Mother
Elizabeth, 80th
Birthday — A54

1980, Aug. 4   Litho.   Perf. 14
394 A54 35c multicolored   .50   .20
395 A54 50c multicolored   .75   .30
396 A54 $1.50 multicolored   1.25   .90
397 A54 $3 multicolored   3.00 1.75
 a. Souvenir sheet of 4, #394-397 6.00 6.00
     Nos. 394-397 (4)   5.50 3.15

Pelicans — A55

1980, Nov. 10   Litho.   Perf. 14
398 A55 5c shown   .50   .20
399 A55 22c Great gray her-
           ons   1.25   .25
400 A55 $1.50 Swallows   2.25 1.50
401 A55 $3 Hummingbirds   3.00 2.00
 a. Souvenir sheet of 4, #398-401 11.00 9.00
     Nos. 398-401 (4)   7.00 3.95

Christmas. For overprints see #405-406.

Nos. 275, 278, 280-290, 334, 400-401
Overprinted: "SEPARATION 1980"
Perf. 13½x14, 14 (A55)
1980, Dec. 18   Litho.
402 A40 1c #275   .20   .20
403 A40 2c on 4c #278   .20   .20
404 A40 5c on 15c #282   .20   .20
405 A55 5c on $1.50 #400   .20   .20
406 A55 5c on $3 #401   .20   .20
407 A40 10c #281   .20   .20
408 A40 12c on $1 #287   .25   .20
409 A40 14c on $2.50 #288   .25   .20
410 A40 15c #282   .30   .20
411 A40 18c on $5 #289   .30   .20
412 A40 20c #283   .30   .20
413 A40 22c #284   .30   .20
414 A40 25c on 15c #282   .35   .20
415 A40 35c #285   .35   .25
416 A44 38c on 22c #334   .35   .30
417 A40 40c on 1c #275   .30   .35
418 A40 50c #286   .40   .40
419 A40 $1 #287   .55   .65
420 A40 $2.50 #288   1.10 2.00
421 A40 $5 #289   2.50 4.00
422 A40 $10 #290   5.75 8.00
423 A40 $10 on 6c #280   5.75 8.00
     Nos. 402-423 (22)   20.30 26.55

Petition for Separation, 1825 — A56

1980, Dec. 18   Perf. 14
424 A56 18c shown   .20   .20
425 A56 22c Referendum ballot,
           1967   .20   .20
426 A56 35c Airport blockade,
           1967   .25   .25
427 A56 50c Anguilla flag   .30   .30
428 A56 $1 Separation celebra-
           tion, 1980   .50   .50
 a. Souvenir sheet of 5, #424-428 1.50 1.60
     Nos. 424-428 (5)   1.45 1.45

Separation from St. Kitts-Nevis.

Nelson's
Dockyard,
by R.
Granger
Barrett
A57

Ship Paintings: 35c, Agamemnon, Van-
guard, Elephant, Captain and Victory, by
Nicholas Pocock. 50c, Victory, by Monamy
Swaine. $3, Battle of Trafalgar, by Clarkson
Stanfield. $5, Lord Nelson, by L.F. Abbott and
Nelson's arms.

1981, Mar. 2   Litho.   Perf. 14
429 A57 22c multicolored   1.25   .75
430 A57 35c multicolored   1.50 1.00
431 A57 50c multicolored   2.00 1.25
432 A57 $3 multicolored   2.50 1.75
     Nos. 429-432 (4)   7.25 4.75
Souvenir Sheet
433 A57 $5 multicolored   4.50 4.50

Lord Horatio Nelson (1758-1805), 175th
death anniversary (1980).

Minnie
Mouse
A58

Easter: Various Disney characters in Easter
outfits.

1981, Mar. 30   Litho.   Perf. 13½
434 A58 1c multicolored   .20   .20
435 A58 2c multicolored   .20   .20
436 A58 3c multicolored   .20   .20
437 A58 5c multicolored   .20   .20
438 A58 7c multicolored   .20   .20
439 A58 9c multicolored   .20   .20
440 A58 10c multicolored   .20   .20
441 A58 $2 multicolored   1.50 1.50
442 A58 $3 multicolored   2.00 2.00
     Nos. 434-442 (9)   4.90 4.90
Souvenir Sheet
443 A58 $5 multicolored   5.50 5.50

Prince
Charles,
Lady
Diana, St.
Paul's
Cathedral
A59

1981, June 15   Litho.   Perf. 14
444 A59 50c shown   .20   .25
 a. Souvenir sheet of 2   .30   .30
 b. Wmk. 380   .30   .30
 c. Booklet pane of 4 #444b   1.25 1.25
445 A59 $2.50 Althorp   .45   .60
 a. Souvenir sheet of 2   1.60 1.60
446 A59 $3 Windsor Castle   .55   .75
 a. Souvenir sheet of 2   2.00 2.00
 b. Wmk. 380   2.00 2.00
 c. Booklet pane of 4 #446b   8.00 8.00
     Nos. 444-446 (3)   1.20 1.60
Souvenir Sheet
447 A59 $5 Buckingham Pal-
           ace   2.00 2.00

Royal Wedding. Nos. 444a-446a contain
stamps in different colors.

Boys
Climbing
Tree
A60

1981   Litho.   Perf. 14
448 A60 5c shown   .20   .20
449 A60 10c Boys sailing boats .25   .25
450 A60 15c Children playing in-
           struments   .35   .35
451 A60 $3 Children with ani-
           mals   2.50 2.50
     Nos. 448-451 (4)   3.30 3.30

Souvenir Sheet
452 A60 $4 Boys playing soc-
           cer, vert.   5.00 5.00

UNICEF, 35th anniv.
Issued: 5c-15c, July 31; $3-$4, Sept. 30.

"The Children were Nestled all Snug in
their Beds" — A61

Christmas: Scenes from Walt Disney's The
Night Before Christmas.

1981, Nov. 2   Litho.   Perf. 13½
453 A61 1c multicolored   .20   .20
454 A61 2c multicolored   .20   .20
455 A61 3c multicolored   .20   .20
456 A61 5c multicolored   .20   .20
457 A61 7c multicolored   .20   .20
458 A61 10c multicolored   .20   .20
459 A61 12c multicolored   .20   .20
460 A61 $2 multicolored   3.00 1.75
461 A61 $3 multicolored   3.00 2.25
     Nos. 453-461 (9)   7.40 5.40
Souvenir Sheet
462 A61 $5 multicolored   6.00 6.00

Red Grouper — A62

1982, Jan. 1   Litho.   Perf. 14
463 A62 1c shown   .20   .60
464 A62 5c Ferries, Blowing
           Point   .30   .60
465 A62 10c Racing boats   .20   .60
466 A62 15c Majorettes   .20   .60
467 A62 20c Launching boat,
           Sandy Hill   .40   .60
468 A62 25c Coral   1.25   .60
469 A62 30c Little Bay cliffs   .30   .75
470 A62 35c Fountain Cave   1.25   .80
471 A62 40c Sandy Isld.   .30   .75
472 A62 45c Landing, Som-
           brero   .50   .80
473 A62 50c on 45c, #472   .50   .35
474 A62 60c Seine fishing   3.00 2.25
475 A62 75c Boat race,
           Sandy Ground   .85 1.75
476 A62 $1 Bagging lob-
           ster, Island
           Harbor   2.25 1.75
477 A62 $5 Pelicans   14.00 10.00
478 A62 $7.50 Hibiscus   11.00 11.00
479 A62 $10 Queen trigger-
           fish   14.00 12.00
     Nos. 463-479 (17)   50.50 45.80

For overprints & surcharges see #507-510,
546A-546D, 578-582, 606-608, 640-647.

Easter — A63   Princess Diana,
                          21st
                      Birthday — A64

Designs: Butterflies on flowers.

1982, Apr. 5
480 A63 10c Zebra, anthurium   .50   .20
481 A63 35c Caribbean buckeye 1.25   .35
482 A63 75c Monarch, allamanda 1.50   .75
483 A63 $3 Red rim, orchid   2.25 2.25
     Nos. 480-483 (4)   5.50 3.55
Souvenir Sheet
484 A63 $5 Flambeau, amaryllis 4.25 4.25

1982, May 17
Designs: Portraits, 1961-1981.
485 A64 10c 1961   .20   .20
486 A64 30c 1968   .20   .20
487 A64 40c 1970   .25   .25
488 A64 60c 1974   .40   .40
489 A64 $2 1981   1.40 1.40
490 A64 $3 1981   2.00 2.00
 a. Souvenir sheet of 6, #485-490 4.50 4.50
     Nos. 485-490 (6)   4.45 4.45
Souvenir Sheet
491 A64 $5 1981   5.00 5.00

For overprints see Nos. 639A-639G.

1982 World Cup — A65

Various Disney characters playing soccer.

1982, Aug. 3   Litho.   Perf. 11
492 A65 1c multicolored   .20   .20
493 A65 3c multicolored   .20   .20
494 A65 4c multicolored   .20   .20
495 A65 5c multicolored   .20   .20
496 A65 7c multicolored   .20   .20
497 A65 9c multicolored   .20   .20
498 A65 10c multicolored   .20   .20
499 A65 $2.50 multicolored   2.50 2.25
500 A65 $3 multicolored   2.50 2.25
     Nos. 492-500 (9)   6.40 5.90
Souvenir Sheet
Perf. 14
501 A65 $5 multicolored   7.00 7.00

Scouting
Year
A66

1982, July 5
502 A66 10c Pitching tent   .60   .50
503 A66 35c Marching band   1.00   .75
504 A66 75c Sailing   1.50 1.25
505 A66 $3 Flag bearers   4.00 3.00
     Nos. 502-505 (4)   7.10 5.50
Souvenir Sheet
506 A66 $5 Camping   6.00 6.00

Nos. 465, 474-475, 477 Overprinted:
"COMMONWEALTH / GAMES 1982"
1982, Oct. 18   Litho.   Perf. 14
507 A62 10c multicolored   .20   .20
508 A62 60c multicolored   .55   .55
509 A62 75c multicolored   .75   .75
510 A62 $5 multicolored   4.00 4.00
     Nos. 507-510 (4)   5.50 5.50

12th Commonwealth Games, Brisbane,
Australia, Sept. 30-Oct. 9.

Christmas — A67

Scenes from Walt Disney's Winnie the
Pooh.

1982, Nov. 29
511 A67 1c multicolored   .20   .20
512 A67 2c multicolored   .20   .20
513 A67 3c multicolored   .20   .20
514 A67 5c multicolored   .25   .20
515 A67 7c multicolored   .25   .20
516 A67 10c multicolored   .25   .20
517 A67 12c multicolored   .35   .25

518	A67	20c multicolored	.60	.50
519	A67	$5 multicolored	6.00	5.00
		Nos. 511-519 (9)	8.30	6.95

Souvenir Sheet

| 520 | A67 | $5 multicolored | 7.50 | 7.50 |

Commonwealth Day (Mar. 14) — A68

1983, Feb. 28   Litho.   Perf. 14

521	A68	10c Carnival proces-		
		sion	.20	.20
522	A68	35c Flags	.50	.50
523	A68	75c Economic cooper-		
		ation	1.00	1.00
524	A68	$2.50 Salt pond	4.00	4.00
		Nos. 521-524 (4)	5.70	5.70

Souvenir Sheet

| 525 | A68 | $5 Map showing | | |
| | | Commonwealth | 4.50 | 4.00 |

Easter — A69

Ten Commandments.

1983, Mar. 31   Litho.   Perf. 14

526	A69	1c multicolored	.20	.20
527	A69	2c multicolored	.20	.20
528	A69	3c multicolored	.20	.20
529	A69	10c multicolored	.25	.20
530	A69	35c multicolored	.55	.30
531	A69	60c multicolored	1.00	.50
532	A69	75c multicolored	1.10	.55
533	A69	$2 multicolored	2.75	2.00
534	A69	$2.50 multicolored	3.00	2.00
535	A69	$5 multicolored	4.75	3.00
		Nos. 526-535 (10)	14.00	9.15

Souvenir Sheet

| 536 | A69 | $5 Moses Taking | | |
| | | Tablets | 4.00 | 4.00 |

Local Turtles and World Wildlife Fund
Emblem — A70

1983, Aug. 10   Litho.   Perf. 13½

537	A70	10c Leatherback	2.00	1.00
538	A70	35c Hawksbill	4.00	2.00
539	A70	75c Green	5.50	2.75
540	A70	$1 Loggerhead	6.50	3.25
		Nos. 537-540 (4)	18.00	9.00

Souvenir Sheet

| 541 | A70 | $5 Leatherback, diff. | 11.00 | 5.50 |

1983, Aug. 10   Litho.   Perf. 12

537a	A70	10c Leatherback	2.00	1.00
538a	A70	35c Hawksbill	7.00	3.50
539a	A70	75c Green	9.00	4.50
540a	A70	$1 Loggerhead	11.00	5.50
		Nos. 537a-540a (4)	29.00	14.50

Manned Flight
Bicentenary
A71

1983, Aug. 22   Perf. 14

542	A71	10c Montgolfiere,		
		1783	.35	.25
543	A71	60c Blanchard & Jef-		
		fries, 1785	1.00	.60
544	A71	$1 Giffard's airship,		
		1852	1.50	1.00
545	A71	$2.50 Lilienthal's glider,		
		1890	2.25	1.75
		Nos. 542-545 (4)	5.10	3.60

Souvenir Sheet

| 546 | A71 | $5 Wright Brothers' | | |
| | | plane, 1909 | 4.00 | 4.00 |

Nos. 465, 471, 476-477 Overprinted:
150TH ANNIVERSARY / ABOLITION
OF SLAVERY ACT

1983, Oct. 24   Litho.   Perf. 14

546A	A62	10c Racing boats	.20	.20
546B	A62	40c Sandy Isld	.40	.35
546C	A62	$1 Bagging lobster,		
		Island Harbor	1.00	.90
546D	A62	$5 Pelicans	4.75	4.50
		Nos. 546A-546D (4)	6.35	5.95

Jiminy
Cricket
A72

Designs: Various Disney productions.

1983, Nov. 14   Perf. 13½

547	A72	1c shown	.20	.20
548	A72	2c Jiminy Cricket, ket-		
		tle	.20	.20
549	A72	3c Jiminy Cricket, toys	.20	.20
550	A72	4c Mickey and Morty	.20	.20
551	A72	5c Scrooge McDuck	.20	.20
552	A72	6c Minnie and Goofy	.20	.20
553	A72	10c Goofy and Elf	.20	.20
554	A72	$2 Scrooge McDuck,		
		diff.	3.00	2.25
555	A72	$3 Disney characters	3.50	2.50
		Nos. 547-555 (9)	7.90	6.15

Souvenir Sheet

| 556 | A72 | $5 Scrooge McDuck | 7.50 | 7.50 |

Boys' Brigade Centenary — A73

1983, Sept. 12   Litho.   Perf. 14

557	A73	10c Anguilla company,		
		banner	.25	.25
558	A73	$5 Marching with drum-		
		mer	4.25	4.25
a.		Souvenir sheet of 2, #557-558	4.00	4.00

1984 Olympics, Los Angeles — A74

Mickey Mouse Competing in Decathlon.

1984, Feb. 20   Litho.   Perf. 14

559	A74	1c 100-meter run	.20	.20
560	A74	2c Long jump	.20	.20
561	A74	3c Shot put	.20	.20
562	A74	4c High jump	.20	.20
563	A74	5c 400-meter run	.20	.20
564	A74	6c Hurdles	.20	.20
565	A74	10c Discus	.20	.20

566	A74	$1 Pole vault	2.50	2.50
567	A74	$4 Javelin	4.50	4.50
		Nos. 559-567 (9)	8.40	8.40

Souvenir Sheet

| 568 | A74 | $5 1500-meter run | 8.00 | 8.00 |

1984, Apr. 24   Perf. 12½x12

559a	A74	1c	.20	.20
560a	A74	2c	.20	.20
561a	A74	3c	.20	.20
562a	A74	4c	.20	.20
563a	A74	5c	.20	.20
564a	A74	6c	.20	.20
565a	A74	10c	.20	.20
566a	A74	$1	3.00	3.00
567a	A74	$4	5.50	5.50
		Nos. 559a-567a (9)	9.90	9.90

Souvenir Sheet

| 568a | A74 | $5 With Olympic rings | | |
| | | emblem | 8.00 | 8.00 |

Nos. 559a-567a inscribed with Olympic
rings emblem. Printed in sheets of 5 plus
label.

Easter
A75

Ceiling and Wall Frescoes, La Stanze della
Segnatura, by Raphael (details).

1984, Apr. 19   Perf. 13½x14

569	A75	10c Justice	.20	.20
570	A75	25c Poetry	.30	.30
571	A75	35c Philosophy	.40	.40
572	A75	40c Theology	.40	.40
573	A75	$1 Abraham & Paul	1.10	1.10
574	A75	$2 Moses & Matthew	2.25	2.25
575	A75	$3 John & David	3.00	3.00
576	A75	$4 Peter & Adam	3.50	3.50
		Nos. 569-576 (8)	11.15	11.15

Souvenir Sheet

| 577 | A75 | $5 Astronomy | 4.50 | 4.50 |

Nos. 463, 469, 477-479 Surcharged

1984   Litho.   Perf. 14

578	A62	25c on $7.50 #478	.45	.45
579	A62	35c on 30c #469	.50	.50
580	A62	60c on 1c #463	.55	.55
581	A62	$2.50 on $5 #477	2.25	2.25
582	A62	$2.50 on $10 #479	1.75	1.75
		Nos. 578-582 (5)	5.50	5.50

Issue dates: 25c, May 17, others, Apr. 24.

Ausipex '84 — A76

Australian stamps.

1984, July 16   Litho.   Perf. 13½

583	A76	10c No. 2	.40	.40
584	A76	75c No. 18	1.25	1.25
585	A76	$1 No. 130	1.75	1.75
586	A76	$2.50 No. 178	2.25	2.25
		Nos. 583-586 (4)	5.65	5.65

Souvenir Sheet

| 587 | A76 | $5 Nos. 378, 379 | 5.50 | 5.50 |

Slavery Abolition
Sesquicentennial — A77

Abolitionists and Vignettes: 10c, Thomas
Fowell Buxton, planting sugar cane. 25c, Abraham Lincoln, cotton field. 35c, Henri Christophe, armed slave revolt. 60c, Thomas Clark-
son, addressing Anti-Slavery Society. 75c,
William Wilberforce, Slave auction. $1,
Olaudah Equiano, slave raid on Benin coast.
$2.50, General Gordon, slave convoy in
Sudan. $5, Granville Sharp, restraining ship
captain from boarding slave.

1984, Aug. 1   Perf. 12

588	A77	10c multicolored	.20	.20
589	A77	25c multicolored	.35	.35
590	A77	35c multicolored	.50	.50
591	A77	60c multicolored	.65	.65
592	A77	75c multicolored	.90	.90
593	A77	$1 multicolored	1.00	1.00
594	A77	$2.50 multicolored	2.00	2.00
595	A77	$4 multicolored	4.00	4.00
a.		Miniature sheet of 8, #588-595	9.50	9.50
		Nos. 588-595 (8)	9.60	9.60

For overprints see Nos. 688-695a.

Christmas — A78

Various Disney characters and celebrations.

Perf. 14, 12½x12 ($2)

1984, Nov. 12   Litho.

596	A78	1c multicolored	.20	.20
597	A78	2c multicolored	.20	.20
598	A78	3c multicolored	.20	.20
599	A78	4c multicolored	.20	.20
600	A78	5c multicolored	.20	.20
601	A78	10c multicolored	.20	.20
602	A78	$1 multicolored	2.75	2.50
603	A78	$2 multicolored	3.50	3.25
604	A78	$4 multicolored	5.50	5.00
		Nos. 596-604 (9)	12.95	11.95

Souvenir Sheet

| 605 | A78 | $5 multicolored | 7.50 | 7.50 |

Nos. 464-465, 477 Overprinted or
Surcharged: "U.P.U. CONGRESS /
HAMBURG 1984"

1984, Aug. 13   Litho.

606	A62	5c #464	.30	.20
607	A62	20c on 10c #465	.45	.30
608	A62	$5 #477	6.00	4.50
		Nos. 606-608 (3)	6.75	4.50

Intl. Civil
Aviation
Org., 40th
Anniv.
A79

1984, Dec. 3   Litho.   Perf. 14

609	A79	60c Icarus, by Hans		
		Erni	.75	.75
610	A79	75c Sun Princess, by		
		Sadiou Diouf	1.00	1.00
611	A79	$2.50 Anniv. emblem,		
		vert.	2.50	2.50
		Nos. 609-611 (3)	4.25	4.25

Souvenir Sheet

| 612 | A79 | $5 Map of the Carib- | | |
| | | bean | 4.50 | 4.50 |

Audubon Birth   Queen Mother
Bicent. — A80   85th
                        Birthday — A81

Illustrations by artist and naturalist J. J.
Audubon (1785-1851).

1985, Apr. 30 **Litho.** *Perf. 14*
613 A80 10c Hirundo rustica .60 .50
614 A80 60c Mycteria americana 1.10 1.00
615 A80 75c Sterna dougallii 1.10 1.00
616 A80 $5 Pandion haliaetus 4.25 3.75
Nos. 613-616 (4) 7.05 6.25

Souvenir Sheets
617 A80 $4 Vireo solitarus, horiz. 3.75 3.75
618 A80 $4 Piranga ludoviciana, horiz. 3.75 3.75

1985, July 2
Photographs: 10c, Visiting the children's ward at King's College Hospital. $2, Inspecting Royal Marine Volunteer Cadets at Deal. $3, Outside Clarence House in London. $5, In an open carriage at Ascot.
619 A81 10c multicolored .20 .20
620 A81 $2 multicolored 1.25 1.25
621 A81 $3 multicolored 1.90 1.90
Nos. 619-621 (3) 3.35 3.35

Souvenir Sheet
622 A81 $5 multicolored 3.25 3.25
Nos. 619-621 printed in sheetlets of 5.

Birds
A82

1985-86 **Litho.** *Perf. 13½x14*
623 A82 5c Brown pelican 1.60 1.00
624 A82 10c Turtle dove 1.60 1.00
625 A82 15c Man-o-war 1.60 1.00
626 A82 20c Antillean crested hummingbird 1.60 1.00
627 A82 25c White-tailed tropicbird 1.60 1.25
628 A82 30c Caribbean elaenia 1.60 1.25
629 A82 35c Black-whiskered vireo 6.25 5.00
629A A82 35c Lesser Antillean bullfinch ('86) 1.60 1.25
630 A82 40c Yellow-crowned night heron 1.60 1.25
631 A82 45c Pearly-eyed thrasher 1.60 1.25
632 A82 50c Laughing bird 1.60 1.25
633 A82 65c Brown booby 1.60 1.25
634 A82 80c Gray kingbird 2.10 2.75
635 A82 $1 Audubon's shearwater 2.10 2.75
636 A82 $1.35 Roseate tern 1.60 2.75
637 A82 $2.50 Bananaquit 4.75 6.00
638 A82 $5 Belted kingfisher 4.00 7.00
639 A82 $10 Green heron 6.75 9.00
Nos. 623-639 (18) 45.15 48.00

Issued: 25c, 65c, $1.35, $5, 7/22; 45c, 50c, 80c, $1, $10, 9/30; 5c-20c, 30c, #629, 40c, $2.50, 11/11; #629A, 3/10.
For overprints & surcharges see #678-682, 713-716, 723-739, 750-753, 764-767.

Nos. 485-491 Overprinted "PRINCE HENRY / BIRTH 15.9.84."

1985, Oct. 31 **Litho.** *Perf. 14*
639A A64 10c multicolored .20 .20
639B A64 30c multicolored .20 .20
639C A64 40c multicolored .30 .30
639D A64 60c multicolored .45 .45
639E A64 $2 multicolored 1.50 1.50
639F A64 $3 multicolored 4.25 4.25
h. Souv. sheet of 6, #639A-639F 4.80 4.80
Nos. 639A-639F (6) 6.90 6.90

Souvenir Sheet
639G A64 $5 multicolored 3.50 3.50

Nos. 464, 469 and 477 Ovptd. with Anniversary Emblem and "GIRL GUIDES 75th ANNIVERSARY / 1910-1985"

1985, Oct. 14 **Litho.** *Perf. 14*
640 A62 5c multicolored .20 .20
641 A62 30c multicolored .40 .30
642 A62 75c multicolored .55 .50
643 A62 $5 multicolored 6.00 5.00
Nos. 640-643 (4) 7.15 6.00

Nos. 465 and 469 Overprinted or Surcharged with Organization Emblem and "80th ANNIVERSARY ROTARY 1985."

1985, Nov. 18
644 A62 10c multicolored .20 .20
645 A62 35c on 30c multi .30 .30

Nos. 476, 469 Surcharged or Ovptd. with Emblem, Text and "INTERNATIONAL YOUTH YEAR"

1985, Nov. 18
646 A62 $1 multicolored 1.00 1.00
647 A62 $5 on 30c multi 4.50 4.50

Brothers Grimm — A83

Christmas: Disney characters in Hansel and Gretel.

1985, Nov. 11 **Litho.** *Perf. 14*
648 A83 5c multicolored .20 .20
649 A83 50c multicolored .75 .70
650 A83 90c multicolored 1.25 1.10
651 A83 $4 multicolored 3.50 3.25
Nos. 648-651 (4) 5.70 5.25

Souvenir Sheet
652 A83 $5 multicolored 6.25 6.25

Mark Twain (1835-1910), Author — A84

Disney characters in Huckleberry Finn.

1985, Nov. 11
653 A84 10c multicolored .30 .30
654 A84 60c multicolored 1.10 1.10
654A A84 $1 multicolored 1.75 1.75
655 A84 $3 multicolored 3.50 3.50
Nos. 653-655 (4) 6.65 6.65

Souvenir Sheet
656 A84 $5 multicolored 6.75 6.75
Christmas. No. 654A printed in sheets of 8.

Statue of Liberty Centennial A85

1985, Nov. 25
657 A85 10c Danmark, Denmark .55 .65
658 A85 20c Eagle, USA .75 .90
659 A85 60c Amerigo Vespucci, Italy 1.40 1.50
660 A85 75c Sir Winston Churchill, G.B. 1.40 1.50
661 A85 $2 Nippon Maru, Japan 2.00 2.25
662 A85 $2.50 Gorch, Germany 2.25 2.50
Nos. 657-662 (6) 8.35 9.30

Souvenir Sheet
663 A85 $5 Statue of Liberty, vert. 7.25 6.00

Easter — A86

Stained glass windows.

1986, Mar. 27 **Litho.** *Perf. 14*
664 A86 10c multicolored .25 .25
665 A86 25c multicolored .45 .45
666 A86 45c multicolored .80 .80
667 A86 $4 multicolored 4.00 4.00
Nos. 664-667 (4) 5.50 5.50

Souvenir Sheet
668 A86 $5 multi, horiz. 6.25 6.25

Halley's Comet A87

A88

Designs: 5c, Johannes Hevelius (1611-1687), Mayan temple observatory. 10c, US Viking probe landing on Mars, 1976. 60c, Theatri Cosmicum (detail), 1668. $4, Sighting, 1835. $5, Comet over Anguilla.

1986, Mar. 24
669 A87 5c multicolored .25 .25
670 A87 10c multicolored .30 .30
671 A87 60c multicolored 1.00 1.00
672 A87 $4 multicolored 4.00 4.00
Nos. 669-672 (4) 5.55 5.55

Souvenir Sheet
673 A88 $5 multicolored 5.25 5.25

Queen Elizabeth II, 60th Birthday
Common Design Type

1986, Apr. 21
674 CD339 20c Inspecting guards, 1946 .20 .20
675 CD339 $2 Garter Ceremony, 1985 1.75 1.75
676 CD339 $3 Trooping the color 2.50 2.50
Nos. 674-676 (3) 4.45 4.45

Souvenir Sheet
677 CD339 $5 Christening, 1926 4.50 4.50

Nos. 623, 631, 635, 637 and 639 Ovptd. "AMERIPEX 1986"

1986, May 22 *Perf. 13½x14*
678 A82 5c multicolored .45 .45
679 A82 45c multicolored .75 .75
680 A82 $1 multicolored 1.40 1.40
681 A82 $2.50 multicolored 2.50 2.50
682 A82 $10 multicolored 6.50 6.50
Nos. 678-682 (5) 11.60 11.60

Wedding of Prince Andrew and Sarah Ferguson — A89

1986, July 23 **Litho.** *Perf. 14, 12*
683 A89 10c Couple .20 .25
684 A89 35c Andrew .25 .30
685 A89 $2 Sarah 1.50 1.75
686 A89 $3 Couple, diff. 2.25 2.75
Nos. 683-686 (4) 4.20 5.05

Souvenir Sheet
687 A89 $6 Westminster Abbey 7.00 7.00

Nos. 588-595 Ovptd. "INTERNATIONAL / YEAR OF / PEACE"

1986, Sept. 29 **Litho.** *Perf. 12*
688 A77 10c multicolored .30 .30
689 A77 25c multicolored .50 .50
690 A77 35c multicolored .60 .60
691 A77 60c multicolored .90 .90
692 A77 75c multicolored 1.10 1.10
693 A77 $1 multicolored 1.25 1.25
694 A77 $2.50 multicolored 2.25 2.25
695 A77 $5 multicolored 3.50 3.50
a. Miniature sheet, #688-695 12.50 12.50
Nos. 688-695 (8) 10.40 10.40

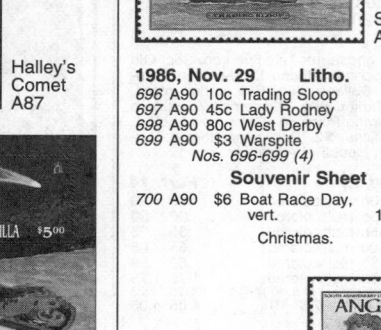

Ships
A90

1986, Nov. 29 **Litho.** *Perf. 14*
696 A90 10c Trading Sloop .75 .75
697 A90 45c Lady Rodney 1.25 1.25
698 A90 80c West Derby 1.75 1.75
699 A90 $3 Warspite 3.50 3.50
Nos. 696-699 (4) 7.25 7.25

Souvenir Sheet
700 A90 $6 Boat Race Day, vert. 10.00 10.00

Christmas.

Discovery of America, 500th Anniv. (in 1992) — A91

Dragon Tree — A92

5c, Christopher Columbus, astrolabe. 10c, Aboard ship. 35c, Santa Maria. 80c, Ferdinand, Isabella. $4, Indians. No. 707, Caribbean manatee.
Illustration A92 reduced.

1986, Dec. 22
701 A91 5c multi .30 .35
702 A91 10c multi .50 .55
703 A91 35c multi 1.25 1.40
704 A91 80c multi, horiz. 1.50 1.75
705 A91 $4 multi 3.25 3.50
Nos. 701-705 (5) 6.80 7.55

Souvenir Sheets
706 A92 $5 shown 6.50 6.50
707 A92 $5 multi, horiz. 6.50 6.50

Butterflies
A93

1987, Apr. 14　Litho.　Perf. 14
708	A93	10c Monarch	.75	.75
709	A93	80c White peacock	2.25	2.25
710	A93	$1 Zebra	2.50	2.50
711	A93	$2 Caribbean buckeye	4.00	4.00
		Nos. 708-711 (4)	9.50	9.50

Souvenir Sheet
|712|A93|$6 Flambeau|9.00|9.00|

Easter.

Nos. 629A, 631, 634 and 639 Ovptd. with CAPEX '87 Emblem in Red

1987, May 25　Litho.　Perf. 13½x14
713	A82	35c on No. 629A	.75	.80
714	A82	45c on No. 631	.85	.90
715	A82	80c on No. 634	1.25	1.40
716	A82	$10 on No. 639	7.00	7.50
		Nos. 713-716 (4)	9.85	10.60

Separation from St. Kitts and Nevis, 20th Anniv. — A94

10c, Old goose iron, electric iron. 35c, Old East End School, Albena Lake-Hodge Comprehensive College. 45c, Old market place, People's Market. 80c, Old ferries & modern ferry at Blowing Point. $1, Old & new cable & wireless offices. $2, Public meeting at Burrowes Park, House of Assembly.

1987, May 25　Perf. 14
717	A94	10c multicolored	.20	.20
718	A94	35c multicolored	.30	.30
719	A94	45c multicolored	.35	.35
720	A94	80c multicolored	.65	.65
721	A94	$1 multicolored	.80	.80
722	A94	$2 multicolored	1.75	1.75
a.		Souvenir sheet of 6, #717-722	5.25	5.25
		Nos. 717-722 (6)	4.05	4.05

Nos. 623, 625-628, 629A-639 Ovptd. "20 YEARS OF PROGRESS / 1967-1987" in Red or Surcharged in Red & Black

1987, Sept. 4　Litho.　Perf. 13½x14
723	A82	5c No. 623	.75	.80
724	A82	10c on 15c No. 625	.75	.80
725	A82	15c No. 625	1.00	1.10
726	A82	20c No. 626	1.00	1.10
727	A82	25c No. 627	1.00	1.10
728	A82	30c No. 628	1.00	1.10
729	A82	35c No. 629A	1.00	1.10
730	A82	40c No. 630	1.00	1.10
731	A82	45c No. 631	1.00	1.10
732	A82	50c No. 632	1.00	1.10
733	A82	65c No. 633	1.40	1.50
734	A82	80c No. 634	1.50	1.60
735	A82	$1 No. 635	1.60	1.75
736	A82	$1.35 No. 636	2.00	2.25
737	A82	$2.50 No. 637	2.25	2.50
738	A82	$5 No. 638	3.50	3.75
739	A82	$10 No. 639	6.00	6.50
		Nos. 723-739 (17)	27.75	30.25

Cricket World Cup — A95

Various action scenes.

1987, Oct. 5　Perf. 14
740	A95	10c multicolored	.65	.60
741	A95	35c multicolored	1.10	1.00
742	A95	45c multicolored	1.25	1.10
743	A95	$2.50 multicolored	3.00	2.75
		Nos. 740-743 (4)	6.00	5.45

Souvenir Sheet
|744|A95|$6 multicolored|8.00|8.50|

Sea Shells, Crabs A96

1987, Nov. 2
745	A96	10c West Indian top shell	.50	.50
746	A96	35c Ghost crab	.80	.80
747	A96	50c Spiny Caribbean vase	1.50	1.50
748	A96	$2 Great land crab	2.50	2.50
		Nos. 745-748 (4)	5.30	5.30

Souvenir Sheet
|749|A96|$6 Queen conch|7.00|7.50|

Christmas.

Nos. 629A, 635-636 and 639 Ovptd. "40TH WEDDING ANNIVERSARY / H.M. QUEEN ELIZABETH II / H.R.H. THE DUKE OF EDINBURGH" in Scarlet

1987, Dec. 14　Litho.　Perf. 13½x14
750	A82	35c multicolored	.30	.30
751	A82	$1 multicolored	.70	.75
752	A82	$1.35 multicolored	1.00	1.00
753	A82	$10 multicolored	7.00	7.50
		Nos. 750-753 (4)	9.00	9.55

Easter (Lilies) — A97

1988, Mar. 28　Litho.　Perf. 14
754	A97	30c Crinum erubescens	.30	.30
755	A97	45c Hymenocallis caribaea	.40	.40
756	A97	$1 Crinum macowanii	.90	.90
757	A97	$2.50 Hemerocallis fulva	2.25	2.25
		Nos. 754-757 (4)	3.85	3.85

Souvenir Sheet
|758|A97|$6 Lilium longiflorum|5.00|5.50|

1988 Summer Olympics, Seoul — A98

1988, July 25　Litho.　Perf. 14
759	A98	35c 4x100-Meter relay	.30	.25
760	A98	45c Windsurfing	.45	.40
761	A98	80c Tennis	1.10	1.00
762	A98	80c Basketball	2.00	1.75
		Nos. 759-762 (4)	3.85	3.40

Souvenir Sheet
|763|A98|$6 Women's 200 meters|5.00|6.00|

Nos. 629A, 634-635 and 637 Ovptd. "H.R.H. PRINCESS / ALEXANDRA'S / VISIT NOVEMBER 1988"

1988, Dec. 14　Litho.　Perf. 13½x14
764	A82	35c multicolored	.75	.60
765	A82	80c multicolored	1.25	1.40
766	A82	$1 multicolored	1.50	1.60
767	A82	$2.50 multicolored	2.50	2.75
		Nos. 764-767 (4)	6.00	6.35

Marine Life — A99

1988, Dec. 5　Litho.　Perf. 14
768	A99	35c Common sea fan	.35	.35
769	A99	80c Coral crab	.75	.75
770	A99	$1 Grooved brain coral	1.00	1.00
771	A99	$1.60 Old wife	1.75	1.75
		Nos. 768-771 (4)	3.85	3.85

Souvenir Sheet
|772|A99|$6 West Indies spiny lobster|5.00|5.00|

Christmas.

Lizards — A100

1989, Feb. 20　Litho.　Perf. 13½x14
773	A100	45c Wood slave	.50	.35
774	A100	80c Slippery back	.75	.70
775	A100	$2.50 Iguana	2.25	2.75
		Nos. 773-775 (3)	3.50	3.80

Souvenir Sheet
|776|A100|$6 Tree lizard|4.75|5.00|

Easter — A101

Paintings: 35c, Christ Crowned with Thorns, by Hieronymous Bosch (c. 1450-1516). 80c, Christ Bearing the Cross, by David. $1, The Deposition, by David. $1.60, Pieta, by Rogier van der Weyden (1400-1464). $6, Crucified Christ with the Virgin Mary and Saints, by Raphael.

1989, Mar. 23　Litho.　Perf. 14x13½
777	A101	35c multicolored	.30	.35
778	A101	80c multicolored	.60	.70
779	A101	$1 multicolored	.75	.75
780	A101	$1.60 multicolored	1.25	1.75
		Nos. 777-780 (4)	2.90	3.55

Souvenir Sheet
|781|A101|$6 multicolored|4.75|5.50|

University of the West Indies, 40th Anniv. — A102

1989, Apr. 24　Litho.　Perf. 14x13½
|782|A102|$5 Coat of arms|4.00|4.50|

Nos. 634-636 and 638 Ovptd. "20th / ANNIVERSARY / MOON / LANDING"

1989, July 3　Litho.　Perf. 13½X14
783	A82	80c multicolored	.60	.60
784	A82	$1 multicolored	.75	.75
785	A82	$1.35 multicolored	1.00	1.00
786	A82	$5 multicolored	3.75	3.75
		Nos. 783-786 (4)	6.10	6.10

Christmas — A103

Well-known and historic houses.

1989, Dec. 4　Litho.　Perf. 13½x14
787	A103	5c Lone Star, 1930	.20	.20
788	A103	35c Whitehouse, 1906	.30	.30
789	A103	45c Hodges House	.35	.35
790	A103	80c Warden's Place	.60	.60
		Nos. 787-790 (4)	1.45	1.45

Souvenir Sheet
|791|A103|$6 Wallblake House, 1787|4.50|4.50|

Fish A104

1990, Apr. 2　Litho.　Perf. 13½x14
792	A104	5c Blear eye	.20	.20
793	A104	10c Redman	.20	.20
794	A104	15c Speckletail	.20	.20
795	A104	25c Grunt	.20	.20
796	A104	30c Amber jack	.20	.20
797	A104	35c Red hind	.25	.25
798	A104	40c Goatfish	.30	.30
799	A104	45c Old wife	.35	.35
800	A104	50c Butter fish	.40	.40
801	A104	65c Shell fish	.50	.50
802	A104	80c Yellowtail snapper	.60	.60
803	A104	$1 Katy	.75	.75
804	A104	$1.35 Mutton grouper	1.00	1.00
805	A104	$2.50 Doctor fish	1.90	1.90
806	A104	$5 Angelfish	3.75	3.75
807	A104	$10 Barracuda	7.50	7.50
		Nos. 792-807 (16)	18.30	18.30

Nos. 792-793, 797 exist inscribed 1992. For overprints and surcharge see #821-824, 849. For booklet see #890.

Easter — A105

1990, Apr. 2　Perf. 14x13½
811	A105	35c Last Supper	.25	.25
812	A105	45c Trial	.35	.35
813	A105	$1.35 Calvary	1.00	1.00
814	A105	$2.50 Empty tomb	1.90	1.90
		Nos. 811-814 (4)	3.50	3.50

Souvenir Sheet
|815|A105|$6 The Resurrection|4.50|4.50|

See Nos. 834-838.

Cape of Good Hope #7 A106

Stamps of Great Britain and exhibition emblem: 25c, #1, vert. 50c, #2, vert. $2.50, #93. $6, #1-2.

1990, Apr. 30　Perf. 14
816	A106	25c multicolored	.20	.20
817	A106	50c multicolored	.35	.35
818	A106	$1.50 shown	1.10	1.10
819	A106	$2.50 multicolored	1.90	1.90
		Nos. 816-819 (4)	3.55	3.55

Souvenir Sheet
|820|A106|$6 multicolored|4.50|4.50|

Stamp World London '90, Penny Black 150th anniv.

Nos. 803-806 Overprinted:
a. EXPO '90
b. 1990 INTERNATIONAL / LITERACY YEAR
c. WORLD CUP FOOTBALL / CHAMPIONSHIPS 1990
d. 90TH BIRTHDAY / H.M. THE QUEEN MOTHER

1990, Sept. 24   Litho.   Perf. 13½x14
821	A104(a)	$1 Katy	.75	.75
822	A104(b)	$1.35 Mutton grouper	1.00	1.00
823	A104(c)	$2.50 Doctor fish	1.90	1.90
824	A104(d)	$3.50 Angelfish	3.75	3.75
		Nos. 821-824 (4)	7.40	7.40

Christmas — A107

Birds.

1990, Dec. 3   Perf. 14
825	A107	10c Laughing gull	.20	.20
826	A107	35c Brown booby	.35	.35
827	A107	$1.50 Bridled tern	1.40	1.40
828	A107	$3.50 Brown pelican	3.50	3.50
		Nos. 825-828 (4)	5.45	5.45

Souvenir Sheet
829	A107	$6 Least tern	7.00	7.00

Flags A108

1991, Nov. 5   Litho.   Perf. 13½x14
830	A108	50c Mermaid	.40	.40
831	A108	80c New Anguilla official	.60	.60
832	A108	$1 Three dolphins	.75	.75
833	A108	$5 Governor's official	3.75	3.75
		Nos. 830-833 (4)	5.50	5.50

Nos. 811-815 Inscribed or Overprinted "1991"

1991, Apr. 30   Litho.   Perf. 14x13½
834	A105	35c like #811	.25	.25
835	A105	45c like #812	.35	.35
836	A105	$1.35 like #813	1.00	1.00
837	A105	$2.50 like #814	1.90	1.90
		Nos. 834-837 (4)	3.50	3.50

Souvenir Sheet
838	A105	$6 like #815	7.75	7.75

Easter. "1990" obliterated by black bar in souvenir sheet margin.

Christmas — A109

Perf. 14x13½, 13½x14
1991, Dec.   Litho.
839	A109	5c Angel, vert.	.20	.20
840	A109	35c Santa, vert.	.25	.25
841	A109	80c shown	.60	.60
842	A109	$1 Palm trees, poinsettias	.75	.75
		Nos. 839-842 (4)	1.80	1.80

Souvenir Sheet
843	A109	$5 Homes, holly	3.75	3.75

Easter A110

Designs: 35c, Church, angels holding palms, vert. 45c Church, angels singing, vert. 80c, Village. $1, People going to church, vert. $5, People at beach, sailboats.

1992   Litho.   Perf. 14
844	A110	35c multicolored	.30	.30
845	A110	45c multicolored	.40	.40
846	A110	80c multicolored	.70	.70
847	A110	$1 multicolored	.85	.85
848	A110	$5 multicolored	4.25	4.25
		Nos. 844-848 (5)	6.50	6.50

No. 796 Surcharged

1992, June 10   Litho.   Perf. 13½x14
849	A104	$1.60 on 30c #796	1.40	1.40

No. 849 inscribed "1992."

Independence, 25th Anniv. — A111

1992, Aug. 10   Litho.   Perf. 14
850	A111	80c Official seal, flag	.60	.60
851	A111	$1 Official seal	.70	.70
852	A111	$1.60 Flags, airport	1.25	1.25
853	A111	$2 First seal	1.40	1.40
		Nos. 850-853 (4)	3.95	3.95

Souvenir Sheet
854	A111	$10 #1, 8-11, 15-16	8.50	8.50

No. 854 contains one 85x85mm stamp. For booklet see No. 970.

Sailboat Racing — A112

Designs: 20c, On course. 35c, Stylized boat poster. 45c, Start of race. No. 858, Blue Bird, 1971, vert. No. 859, Construction plans for Blue Bird, vert. $1, Stylized boat poster, diff. $6, Like Nos. 855 & 857.

Perf. 13½x14, 14x13½
1992, Oct. 12   Litho.
855	A112	20c multicolored	.20	.20
856	A112	35c multicolored	.25	.25
857	A112	45c multicolored	.35	.35
858	A112	80c multicolored	.55	.55
859	A112	80c multicolored	.55	.55
a.		Pair, #858-859	1.10	1.10
860	A112	$1 multicolored	.70	.70
		Nos. 855-860 (6)	2.60	2.60

Souvenir Sheet
861	A112	$6 multicolored	4.55	4.55

No. 861 contains one 96x31mm stamp.

Discovery of America, 500th Anniv. A113

1992, Dec. 15   Litho.   Perf. 14
862	A113	80c Landfall	.70	.70
863	A113	$1 Columbus, vert.	.85	.85
864	A113	$2 Fleet	1.75	1.75
865	A113	$3 Pinta	2.50	2.50
		Nos. 862-865 (4)	5.80	5.80

Souvenir Sheet
866	A113	$6 Map of voyage, vert.	5.00	5.00

Christmas A114

Various Christmas trees and: 20c, Mucka Jumbie on stilts. 70c, Masquerading house to house. $1.05, Christmas baking, old oven style. $2.40, $5, Collecting presents.

1992, Dec. 7
867	A114	20c multicolored	.20	.20
868	A114	70c multicolored	.60	.60
869	A114	$1.05 multicolored	.90	.90
870	A114	$2.40 multicolored	2.00	2.00
		Nos. 867-870 (4)	3.70	3.70

Souvenir Sheet
871	A114	$5 Sheet of 1 + 3 labels	4.25	4.25

Labels on No. 871 are similar to Nos. 867-869, but without denomination.

Easter — A115

Children's drawings: 20c, Kite flying. 45c, Cliff top village service. 80c, Morning devotion on Sombrero. $1.50, Hilltop church service. $5, Good Friday kites.

1993, Mar. 29   Litho.   Perf. 14
872	A115	20c multicolored	.20	.20
873	A115	45c multicolored	.40	.40
874	A115	80c multicolored	.65	.65
875	A115	$1.50 multicolored	1.25	1.25
		Nos. 872-875 (4)	2.50	2.50

Souvenir Sheet
876	A115	$5 multicolored	4.25	4.25

No. 876 contains one 42x56mm stamp.

Native Industries A116

1993, June 23   Litho.   Perf. 14
877	A116	20c Salt	.20	.20
878	A116	80c Tobacco	.65	.65
879	A116	$1 Cotton	.80	.80
880	A116	$2 Sugar cane	1.60	1.60
		Nos. 877-880 (4)	3.25	3.25

Souvenir Sheet
881	A116	$6 Fishing	4.75	4.75

Coronation of Queen Elizabeth II, 40th Anniv. — A117

Designs: 80c, Lord Great Chamberlain presents the spurs of chivalry. $1, The benediction. $2 Queen Elizabeth II, coronation photograph. $3, St. Edward's Crown. $6, Queen, Prince Philip in Gold State Coach.

1993, Aug. 16   Litho.   Perf. 14
882	A117	80c multicolored	.65	.65
883	A117	$1 multicolored	.80	.80
884	A117	$2 multicolored	1.75	1.75
885	A117	$3 multicolored	2.50	2.50
		Nos. 882-885 (4)	5.70	5.70

Souvenir Sheet
886	A117	$6 multicolored	4.75	4.75

Anguilla Carnival — A118

1993, Aug. 23   Litho.   Perf. 14
887	A118	20c Pan musician	.20	.20
888	A118	45c Pirates	.35	.35
889	A118	80c Stars	.65	.65
890	A118	$1 Playing mas	.80	.80
		Booklet, 5 ea #796, 890	5.00	
891	A118	$2 Masqueraders	1.75	1.75
892	A118	$3 Commandos	2.50	2.50
		Nos. 887-892 (6)	6.25	6.25

Souvenir Sheet
893	A118	$5 Carnival fantasy	4.00	4.00

Christmas A119

Mail Delivery — A120

Traditional Christmas customs: 20c, Mucka Jumbies. 35c, Serenaders. 45c, Baking. $3, Five-fingers Christmas tree. $4, Mucka Jumbies and serenaders.

1993, Dec. 7   Litho.   Perf. 14x13½
894	A119	20c multicolored	.20	.20
895	A119	35c multicolored	.30	.30
896	A119	45c multicolored	.40	.40
897	A119	$3 multicolored	2.50	2.50
		Nos. 894-897 (4)	3.40	3.40

Souvenir Sheet
Perf. 14
898	A119	$4 multicolored	3.50	3.50

No. 898 contains one 54x42mm stamp.

1993, Feb. 11   Litho.   Perf. 14

Designs: 20c, Traveling Branch mail van, Sandy Ground, horiz. 45c, Mail boat, Betsy R, The Forest. 80c, Old post office, horiz. $1, Mail by jeep, Island Harbor. $4, New post office, 1993, horiz.

899	A120	20c multicolored	.20 .20
900	A120	45c multicolored	.40 .40
901	A120	80c multicolored	.70 .70
902	A120	$1 multicolored	.85 .85
903	A120	$4 multicolored	3.50 3.50
		Nos. 899-903 (5)	5.65 5.65

Royal Visits — A121

1994, Feb. 18

904	A121	45c Princess Alexandra	.35 .35
905	A121	50c Princess Alice	.45 .45
906	A121	80c Prince Philip	.70 .70
907	A121	$1 Prince Charles	.85 .85
908	A121	$2 Queen Elizabeth II	1.75 1.75
a.		Souvenir sheet of 4, #904-908	4.00 4.00
		Nos. 904-908 (5)	4.10 4.10

Easter — A122

1994, Apr. 6   Litho.   Perf. 14x15

Stained glass windows: 20c, Crucifixion. 45c, Empty tomb. 80c, Resurrection. $3, Risen Christ with disciples.

909	A122	20c multicolored	.20 .20
910	A122	45c multicolored	.40 .40
911	A122	80c multicolored	.75 .75
912	A122	$3 multicolored	2.75 2.75
		Nos. 909-912 (4)	4.10 4.10

Christmas — A123

Designs: 20c, Adoration of the shepherds. 30c, Magi, shepherds. 35c, The Annunciation. 45c, Nativity Scene. $2.40, Flight into Egypt.

1994, Nov. 22   Litho.   Perf. 14

913	A123	20c multicolored	.20 .20
914	A123	30c multicolored	.30 .30
915	A123	35c multicolored	.35 .35
916	A123	45c multicolored	.45 .45
917	A123	$2.40 multicolored	2.50 2.50
		Nos. 913-917 (5)	3.80 3.80

1994 World Cup Soccer Championships, US — A124

Soccer player and: 20c, Pontiac Silverdome, Detroit. 70c, Foxboro Stadium, Boston. $1.80, RFK Memorial Stadium, Washington. $2.40, Soldier Field, Chicago. $6, Two players.

1994, Oct. 3   Litho.   Perf. 13½x14

918	A124	20c multicolored	.20 .20
919	A124	70c multicolored	.65 .65
920	A124	$1.80 multicolored	1.60 1.60
921	A124	$2.40 multicolored	1.90 1.90
		Nos. 918-921 (4)	4.35 4.35

Souvenir Sheet

922	A124	$6 multicolored	5.50 5.50

Easter A125

Turtle dove: 45c, One on tree branch. 50c, One on nest, one on branch. $5, Mother with young.

1995, Apr. 10   Litho.   Perf. 14

923	A125	20c multicolored	.20 .20
924	A125	45c multicolored	.40 .40
925	A125	50c multicolored	.45 .45
926	A125	$5 multicolored	4.75 4.75
		Nos. 923-926 (4)	5.80 5.80

UN, 50th Anniv. A126

Secretaries general and: 20c, Trygve Lie (1946-53), general assembly. 80c, UN flag, UN headquarters with "50" (no portrait). $1, Dag Hammarskjold (1953-61), charter, U Thant (1961-71). $5, UN complex, New York, vert. (no portrait).

Perf. 13½x14, 14x13½

1995, June 26   Litho.

927	A126	20c multicolored	.20 .20
928	A126	80c multicolored	.75 .75
929	A126	$1 multicolored	.95 .95
930	A126	$5 multicolored	4.75 4.75
		Nos. 927-930 (4)	6.65 6.65

Caribbean Development Bank, 25th Anniv. — A127

Designs: 45c, Emblem, map of Anguilla. $5, Local headquarters along waterfront.

1995, Aug. 15   Litho.   Perf. 13½x14

931	A127	45c multicolored	.45 .45
932	A127	$5 multicolored	5.00 5.00
a.		Pair, #931-932	5.45 5.45

Whales — A128

Perf. 13½x14, 14x13½

1995, Nov. 24   Litho.

933	A128	20c Blue whale	.20 .20
934	A128	45c Right whale, vert.	.40 .40
935	A128	$1 Sperm whale	.90 .90
936	A128	$5 Humpback whale	4.25 4.25
		Nos. 933-936 (4)	5.75 5.75

Christmas A129

1995, Dec. 12   Perf. 14½

937	A129	10c Palm tree	.20 .20
938	A129	25c Fish net floats	.20 .20
939	A129	45c Sea shells	.40 .40
940	A129	$5 Fish	4.25 4.25
		Nos. 937-940 (4)	5.05 5.05

Corals A130

1996, June 21   Litho.   Perf. 14x14½

941	A130	20c Deep water gorgonia	.20 .20
942	A130	80c Common sea fan	.70 .70
943	A130	$5 Venus sea fern	4.25 4.25
		Nos. 941-943 (3)	5.15 5.15

A131   A132

1996 Summer Olympic Games, Atlanta: 20c, Running. 80c, Javelin, wheelchair basketball. $1, High jump. $3.50, Olympic torch, Greek, US flags.

1996, Dec. 12   Litho.   Perf. 14

944	A131	20c multicolored	.20 .20
945	A131	80c multicolored	.65 .65
946	A131	$1 multicolored	.80 .80
947	A131	$3.50 multicolored	2.75 2.75
		Nos. 944-947 (4)	4.40 4.40

1996, Dec. 12

Battle for Anguilla, bicent.: 60c, Sandy Hill Fort, HMS Lapwing. 75c, French troops destroy church, horiz. $1.50, HMS Lapwing defeats Valiant, Decius, horiz. $4, French troops land, Rendezvous Bay.

948	A132	60c multicolored	.50 .50
949	A132	75c multicolored	.60 .60
950	A132	$1.50 multicolored	1.25 1.25
951	A132	$4 multicolored	3.25 3.25
		Nos. 948-951 (4)	5.60 5.60

Fruits and Nuts A133

1997, Apr. 30   Litho.   Perf. 14

952	A133	10c Gooseberry	.20 .20
953	A133	20c West Indian cherry	.20 .20
954	A133	40c Tamarind	.25 .30
955	A133	50c Pomme-surette	.30 .40
956	A133	60c Sea almond	.40 .50
957	A133	75c Sea grape	.55 .65
958	A133	80c Banana	.55 .65
959	A133	$1 Genip	.70 .80
960	A133	$1.10 Coco plum	.80 .85
961	A133	$1.25 Pope	.90 .95
962	A133	$1.50 Papaya	1.00 1.10
963	A133	$2 Sugar apple	1.40 1.40
964	A133	$3 Soursop	2.00 2.25
965	A133	$4 Pomegrante	2.75 3.00
966	A133	$5 Cashew	3.25 3.50
967	A133	$10 Mango	6.75 7.00
		Nos. 952-967 (16)	22.00 23.75

Iguanas — A134

World Wildlife Fund: a, 20c, Baby iguanas emerging from eggs, juvenile iguana. b, 50c, Adult on rock. c, 75c, Two iguanas on tree limbs. d, $3, Adult up close, adult on tree branch.

1997, Oct. 13   Litho.   Perf. 13½x14

968	A134	Strip of 4, #a.-d.	4.00 4.00

Diana, Princess of Wales (1961-67) A135

Designs: a, 15c, In red & white. b, $1, In yellow. c, $1.90, Wearing tiara. d, $2.25, Wearing blouse with Red Cross emblem.

1998, Apr. 14   Litho.   Perf. 14

969	A135	Strip of 4, #a.-d.	4.00 4.00

No. 969 was issued in sheets of 16 stamps.

Fountain Cavern Carvings A136

30c, Rainbow Deity (Juluca). $1.25, Lizard. $2.25, Solar Chieftan. $2.75, Creator.

1997, Nov. 17   Litho.   Perf. 14x14½

970	A136	30c multicolored	.25 .25
		Booklet, 5 ea #851, 970	4.75
971	A136	$1.25 multicolored	1.10 1.10
972	A136	$2.25 multicolored	1.90 1.90
973	A136	$2.75 multicolored	2.25 2.25
		Nos. 970-973 (4)	5.50 5.50

1998 Intl. Arts Festival A137

Paintings: 15c, "Treasure Island." 30c, "Posing in the Light." $1, "Pescadores de Anguilla." $1.50, "Fresh Catch." $1.90, "The Bell Tower of St. Mary's."

1998, Aug. 24   Litho.   Perf. 14

974	A137	15c multi	.20 .20
975	A137	30c multi, vert.	.25 .25
976	A137	$1 multi, vert.	.80 .80
		Booklet, 5 ea #975-976	5.25
977	A137	$1.50 multi	1.25 1.25
978	A137	$1.90 multi, vert.	1.50 1.50
		Nos. 974-978 (5)	4.00 4.00

Christmas A138

Paintings of "Hidden beauty of Anguilla:" 15c, Woman cooking over open fire, girl seated on steps." $1, Person looking over fruits and vegetables. $1.50, Underwater scene. $3, Cacti growing along shore.

1998

979	A138	15c multicolored	.20	.20
980	A138	$1 multicolored	.80	.80
981	A138	$1.50 multicolored	1.25	1.25
982	A138	$3 multicolored	2.40	2.40
		Nos. 979-982 (4)	4.65	4.65

Royal Air Force, 80th Anniv. A139

Designs: 30c, Sopwith Camel, Bristol F2B. $1, Supermarine Spitfire II, Hawker Hurricane Mk1. $1.50, Avro Lancaster. $1.90, Harrier GR7, Panavia Tornado F3.

1998   **Litho.**   **Perf. 13½**
Granite Paper (No. 983)

983	A139	30c multicolored	.25	.25
984	A139	$1 multicolored	.80	.80
985	A139	$1.50 multicolored	1.25	1.25
986	A139	$1.90 multicolored	1.50	1.50
		Nos. 983-986 (4)	3.80	3.80

University of the West Indies, 50th Anniv. — A140

Designs: $1.50, Anguilla campus. $1.90, Anguilla campus, torchbearer, University arms.

1998   **Litho.**   **Perf. 13¼**
Granite Paper (#988)

987-988	A140	Set of 2	2.60	2.60

First Manned Moon Landing, 30th Anniv. — A141

Designs: 30c, Lift-off of Apollo 11, Command and Service Modules in lunar orbit. $1, Buzz Aldrin on Moon, footprint. $1.50, Lunar Module leaving Moon. $1.90, Splashdown.

1999, May 6   **Litho.**   **Perf. 13¾**

989	A141	30c multi	.25	.25
990	A141	$1 multi	.75	.75
991	A141	$1.50 multi	1.10	1.10
992	A141	$1.90 multi	1.40	1.40
		Nos. 989-992 (4)	3.50	3.50

Heroes of Anguilla's Revolution A142

Designs: 30c, Albena Lake Hodge (1920-85). $1, Collins O. Hodge (1926-78). $1.50, Edwin W. Rey (1906-80). $1.90, Walter G. Hodge (1920-89).

1999, July 5   **Perf. 14½x14¼**

993	A142	30c multi	.25	.25
994	A142	$1 multi	.75	.75
995	A142	$1.50 multi	1.10	1.10
996	A142	$1.90 multi	1.40	1.40
		Nos. 993-996 (4)	3.50	3.50

Modern Architecture A143

Designs: No. 997, 30c, Library and resource center. No. 998, 65c, Parliamentary building and court house. No. 999, $1, Caribbean Commercial Bank. No. 999A, $1.50, Police headquarters. No. 1000, $1.90, Post office.

1999   **Litho.**   **Perf. 14x14½**

997-1000	A143	Set of 5	4.00	4.00

Christmas and Millennium Celebrations — A144

Designs: 30c, Fireworks display and barbecue. $1, Globe, musicians. $1.50, Family dinner. $1.90, Decorated tree.

1999   **Litho.**   **Perf. 13¼**

1001	A144	30c multi	.25	.25
1002	A144	$1 multi	.75	.75
1003	A144	$1.50 multi	1.10	1.10
1004	A144	$1.90 multi	1.40	1.40
		Nos. 1001-1004 (4)	3.50	3.50

Beaches — A145

1005, 15c, Shoal Bay. 1006, 30c, Maundys Bay. 1007, $1, Rendezvous Bay. 1008, $1.50, Meads Bay. 1009, $1.90, Little Bay. 1010, $2, Sandy Ground.

1999   **Perf. 12**

1010a	A145	Sheet of 6, #1005-1010	5.00	5.00
b.		As "a," with show emblem in margin	5.00	5.00

The Stamp Show 2000, London (No. 1010b). Issued: No. 1010b, 5/22/00.

Easter A146

Toys: 25c, Banjo. 30c, Top. $1.50, Slingshot. $1.90, Roller. $2.50, Killy ban.
No. 1016: a, 75c, Rag doll. b, $1, Kite. c, $1.25, Cricket ball. d, $4, Pond boat.

2000   **Perf. 13¼**

1011	A146	25c multi	.20	.20
1012	A146	30c multi	.25	.25
1013	A146	$1.50 multi	1.10	1.10
1014	A146	$1.90 multi	1.40	1.40
1015	A146	$2.50 multi	1.90	1.90
		Nos. 1011-1015 (5)	4.85	4.85

Souvenir Sheet

1016	A146	Sheet of 4, #a-d	5.25	5.25

100th Test Match at Lord's Ground — A147

$2, Lanville Harrigan. $4, Cardigan Connor.

2000, May 5   **Litho.**   **Perf. 13¾x13¼**

1017-1018	A147	Set of 2	4.50	4.50

Souvenir Sheet

Design: $6, Lord's Ground, horiz.

1018A	A147	$6 multi	4.50	4.50

Prince William, 18th Birthday — A148

Prince William and: 30c, Queen Elizabeth II, Princes Philip and Charles. $1, Princess Diana, Princes Harry and Charles. $1.90, Princes Harry and Charles. $2.25, Princes Charles and Harry, in winter wear.

2000, July 20   **Perf. 13¼**

1019-1022	A148	Set of 4	4.00	4.00

Souvenir Sheet

1023	A148	$8 Prince William, vert.	6.00	6.00

Queen Mother, 100th Birthday — A149

Queen Mother and: 30c, Prince William. $1.50, Anguilla shoreline. $1.90, Clarence House. $5, Castle of Mey.

2000, Aug. 4

1024-1027	A149	Set of 4	6.50	6.50

Intl. Arts Festival A150

Artwork: 15c, Anguilla Montage, by Werne Caster. 30c, Serenity, by Damien Carty. 65c, Inter-island Cargo, by Paula Walden. $1.50, Rainbow City Where Spirits Find Form, by Fiona Percy. $1.90, Sailing Silver Seas, by Valerie Carpenter.
$7, Historic Anguilla, by Melsadis Fleming.

2000, Sept. 21   **Perf. 14¼x14½**

1028-1032	A150	Set of 5	3.50	3.50

Souvenir Sheet
Perf. 14¼

1033	A150	$7 multi	5.25	5.25

No. 1033 contains one 43x28mm stamp.

Christmas A151

Flower and Garden Show flower arrangements by: 15c, Rowena Carty. 25c, Yvonda Hodge. 30c, Carty, diff. $1, Simon Rogers. $1.50, Lady Josephine Gumbs. $1.90, Carty, diff.

2000, Nov. 22   **Perf. 13¼**

1034-1039	A151	Set of 6	3.75	3.75

Natl. Bank of Anguilla, 15th Anniv. — A152

Designs: 30c, Soccer team in annual primary school tournament. $1, Sponsored sailboat, De Chan, vert. $1.50, Bank's crest, vert. $1.90, New bank building.

2000, Nov. 27

1040-1043	A152	Set of 4	3.50	3.50

Ebenezer Methodist Church, 170th Anniv. — A153

Church in: 30c, Sepia tones. $1.90, Full color.

2000, Dec. 4

1044-1045	A153	Set of 2	1.60	1.60

UN Women's Human Rights Campaign — A154

Designs: 25c, Soroptimist Day Care Center. 30c, Britannia Idalla Gumbs, vert. $2.25, Woman, vert.

2001   **Litho.**   **Perf. 13¼**

1046-1048	A154	Set of 3	2.10	2.10

American Revolution, 225th Anniv. — A155

Designs: 30c, John Paul Jones, USS Ranger. $1, George Washington, Battle of Yorktown. $1.50, Thomas Jefferson, Submission of Declaration of Independence. $1.90, John Adams, Adams and Benjamin Franklin signing peace treaty.

2001, July 4   **Litho.**   **Perf. 13¼**

1049-1052	A155	Set of 4	3.75	3.75

Designs: 30c, White-cheeked pintail. $1, Black-faced grassquits, vert. $1.50, Brown noddy. $2, Black-necked stilts, vert. $3, Snowy plovers.
No. 1058: a, 25c, Snowy egret. b, 65c, Red-billed tropicbird. $1.35, Greater yellowlegs. $2.25, Sooty tern.

2001, Aug. 7
| 1053-1057 | A156 | Set of 5 | 6.00 | 6.00 |

Souvenir Sheet
| 1058 | A156 | Sheet of 4, #a-d | 3.50 | 3.50 |

Year of Dialogue Among Civilizations — A157

2001, Oct. 9   Perf. 13¼x13
| 1059 | A157 | $1.90 multi | 1.50 | 1.50 |

Christmas — A158

Musical instruments: 15c, Triangle. 25c, Maracas. 30c, Guiro, vert. $1.50, Marimba. $1.90, Tambu, vert. $2.50, Bath pan, vert.
No. 1066, vert.: a, 75c, Banjo. b, $1, Quatro. c, $1.25, Ukulele. d, $3, Cello.

2001, Nov. 5   Litho.   Perf. 13¼
| 1060-1065 | A158 | Set of 6 | 5.00 | 5.00 |

Souvenir Sheet
| 1066 | A158 | Sheet of 4, #a-d | 4.50 | 4.50 |

ANJOUAN

'an-jü-wän

LOCATION — One of the Comoro Islands in the Mozambique Channel between Madagascar and Mozambique.
GOVT. — French colony.
AREA — 89 sq. mi.
POP. — 20,000 (approx. 1912)
CAPITAL — Mossamondu
    See Comoro Islands.

100 Centimes = 1 Franc

Navigation and Commerce — A1

1892-1907   Typo.   Perf. 14x13½
Name of Colony in Blue or Carmine
1	A1	1c black, *blue*	1.00	1.00
2	A1	2c brown, *buff*	1.25	1.25
3	A1	4c claret, *lav*	2.10	1.75
4	A1	5c green, *grnsh*	4.50	3.25
5	A1	10c blk, *lavender*	5.00	3.50
6	A1	10c red ('00)	17.50	15.00
7	A1	15c bl, quadrille paper	6.50	4.50
8	A1	15c gray, *lt gray* ('00)	10.00	7.50
9	A1	20c red, *green*	6.00	5.00
10	A1	25c black, *rose*	7.00	5.50
11	A1	25c blue ('00)	10.00	8.00

12	A1	30c brn, *bister*	15.00	10.00
13	A1	35c blk, *yel* ('06)	7.25	5.00
14	A1	40c red, *straw*	25.00	17.00
15	A1	45c blk, *gray grn* ('07)	90.00	75.00
16	A1	50c car, *rose*	26.00	18.00
17	A1	50c brn, *azure* ('00)	15.00	12.00
18	A1	75c vio, *orange*	24.00	18.00
19	A1	1fr brnz grn, *straw*	55.00	45.00
		Nos. 1-19 (19)	328.10	256.25

Perf. 13½x14 stamps are counterfeits.

Issues of 1892-1907 Surcharged in Black or Carmine

1912
20	A1	5c on 2c brn, *buff*	.50	.50
21	A1	5c on 4c claret, *lav* (C)	.80	.80
22	A1	5c on 15c blue (C)	.80	.80
23	A1	5c on 20c red, *green*	.80	.80
24	A1	5c on 25c blk, *rose* (C)	.80	.80
25	A1	5c on 30c brn, *bis* (C)	.80	.80
26	A1	10c on 40c red, *straw*	1.00	1.00
27	A1	10c on 45c blk, *gray grn* (C)	1.25	1.25
28	A1	10c on 50c car, *rose*	2.50	2.50
29	A1	10c on 75c vio, *org*	1.50	1.50
30	A1	10c on 1fr brnz grn, *straw*	1.75	1.75
		Nos. 20-30 (11)	12.50	12.50

Nos. 21-23, 30 exist in pairs, one without surcharge. Value, $550 each.
Two spacings between the surcharged numerals are found on Nos. 20-30.
Nos. 20-30 were available for use in Madagascar and the Comoro archipelago.

The stamps of Anjouan were superseded by those of Madagascar, and in 1950 by those of Comoro Islands.

ANNAM AND TONKIN

a-'nam and 'tän-'kin

LOCATION — In French Indo-China bordering on the China Sea on the east and Siam on the west.
GOVT. — French Protectorate
AREA — 97,503 sq. mi.
POP. — 14,124,000 (approx. 1890)
CAPITAL — Annam: Hue; Tonkin: Hanoi

For administrative purposes, the Protectorates of Annam, Tonkin, Cambodia, Laos and the Colony of Cochin-China were grouped together and were known as French Indo-China.

100 Centimes = 1 Franc

Catalogue values for unused stamps are for examples without gum as most stamps were issued in that condition.

Stamps of French Colonies, 1881-86
Handstamped Surcharged in Black:

Perf. 14x13½
1888, Jan. 21   Unwmk.
1	A9	1c on 2c brn, *buff*	20.00	18.00
a.		Inverted surcharge	90.00	90.00
b.		Sideways surcharge	90.00	90.00
2	A9	1c on 4c claret, *lav*	16.00	12.50
a.		Inverted surcharge	90.00	90.00
b.		Double surcharge	110.00	110.00
c.		Sideways surcharge	90.00	90.00
3	A9	5c on 10c blk, *lav*	16.00	13.50
a.		Inverted surcharge	90.00	90.00

| b. | | Double surcharge | 110.00 | 110.00 |

Hyphen between "A" and "T"
7	A9	1c on 2c brn, *buff*	200.00	175.00
a.		Inverted surcharge	400.00	
8	A9	1c on 4c claret, *lav*	325.00	325.00
9	A9	5c on 10c blk, *lav*	150.00	140.00

A 5c on 2c was prepared but not issued. Value $6,000.
In these surcharges there are different types of numerals and letters.
There are numerous other errors in the placing of the surcharges, including double one inverted, double both inverted, double one sideways, pair #1, 7, and pair one without surcharge. Such varieties command substantial premiums.
These stamps were superseded in 1892 by those of Indo-China.

ANTIGUA

an-'tēg-,wə

LOCATION — In the West Indies, southeast of Puerto Rico
GOVT. — Independent state
AREA — 171 sq. mi.
POP. — 64,246 (est. 1999)
CAPITAL — St. John's

Antigua was one of the presidencies of the former Leeward Islands colony until becoming a Crown Colony in 1956. It became an Associated State of the United Kingdom in 1967 and an independent nation on November 1, 1981, taking the name of Antigua and Barbuda.
Antigua stamps were discontinued in 1890 and resumed in 1903. In the interim, stamps of Leeward Islands were used. Between 1903-1956, stamps of Antigua and Leeward Islands were used concurrently.

12 Pence = 1 Shilling
20 Shillings = 1 Pound
100 Cents = 1 Dollar (1951)

Catalogue values for unused stamps in this country are for Never Hinged items, beginning with Scott 96.

Watermark

Wmk. 5- Star

Values for unused stamps are for examples with original gum as defined in the catalogue introduction. Any exceptions will be noted. Very fine examples of Nos. 1-8, 11, 18-20 will have perforations touching at least one frameline due to the narrow spacing of the stamps on the plates. Stamps with perfs clear of the framelines on all four sides are extremely scarce and will command higher prices.

Queen Victoria
A1   A2

Rough Perf. 14-16
1862   Engr.   Unwmk.
1	A1	6p blue green	900.	575.
a.		Perf. 11-13	5,000.	
b.		Perf. 11-13x14-16	2,750.	
c.		Perf. 11-13 compound with 14-16	3,000.	

There is a question whether Nos. 1a-1c ever did postal duty.
Values for No. 1 are for stamps with perfs. cutting into the design. Values for No. 1b are for copies without gum.

1863-67   Wmk. 5
2	A1	1p lilac rose	110.00	32.50
a.		Vert. pair, imperf. btwn.	15,000.	
3	A1	1p vermilion ('67)	300.00	25.00
a.		Horiz. pair, imperf. btwn.	16,000.	
4	A1	6p green	375.00	27.50
a.		6p yellow green	3,500.	70.00
b.		Pair, imperf. between		

1872   Wmk. 1   Perf. 12½
5	A1	1p lake	100.00	22.50
6	A1	1p vermilion	140.00	22.50
7	A1	6p blue green	525.00	9.00
		Nos. 5-7 (3)	765.00	54.00

1873-79   Perf. 14
| 8 | A1 | 1p lake | 100.00 | 11.00 |
| a. | | Half used as ½p on cover | 2,750. | |

Typo.
| 9 | A2 | 2½p red brown ('79) | 600.00 | 160.00 |
| 10 | A2 | 4p blue ('79) | 275.00 | 16.00 |

Engr.
| 11 | A1 | 6p blue green ('76) | 300.00 | 13.00 |

1882-86   Typo.   Wmk. 2
12	A2	½p green	2.50	10.00
13	A2	2½p red brown	125.00	55.00
14	A2	2½p ultra ('86)	7.00	12.00
15	A2	4p blue	275.00	16.00
16	A2	4p brown org ('86)	2.00	3.00
17	A2	1sh violet ('86)	160.00	125.00

Engr.
| 18 | A1 | 1p carmine ('84) | 1.50 | 2.75 |
| 19 | A1 | 6p deep green | 60.00 | 150.00 |

No. 18 was used for a time in St. Christopher and is identified by the "A12" cancellation.

1884   Perf. 12
| 20 | A1 | 1p rose red | 50.00 | 15.00 |

Seal of the Colony — A3

King Edward VII — A4

1903   Typo.   Perf. 14
21	A3	½p blue grn & blk	3.25	5.00
a.		Bluish paper ('09)	100.00	100.00
22	A3	1p car & black	5.00	.90
a.		Bluish paper ('09)	90.00	90.00
23	A3	2p org brn & vio	6.00	22.50
24	A3	2½p ultra & black	7.50	13.50
25	A3	3p ocher & gray green	9.00	19.00
26	A3	6p black & red vio	26.00	45.00
27	A3	1sh violet & ultra	40.00	45.00
28	A3	2sh pur & gray green	65.00	82.50
29	A3	2sh6p red vio & blk	20.00	45.00
30	A4	5sh pur & gray green	70.00	90.00
		Nos. 21-30 (10)	251.75	368.40

The 2½p, 1sh and 5sh exist on both ordinary and chalky paper.

1908-15   Wmk. 3
31	A3	½p green	2.10	3.50
32	A3	1p carmine	4.50	1.75
a.		1p scarlet ('15)	5.00	2.75
33	A3	2p org brn & dull vio ('12)	3.75	24.00
34	A3	2½p ultra	9.00	14.00
35	A3	3p ocher & grn ('12)	6.00	18.00
36	A3	6p blk & red vio ('11)	7.00	35.00
37	A3	1sh vio & ultra	14.00	62.50
38	A3	2sh vio & green ('12)	57.50	77.50
		Nos. 31-38 (8)	103.85	236.25

Nos. 33, 35-38 are on chalky paper.
For overprints see Nos. MR1-MR3.

George V — A6   St. John's Harbor — A7

1913
41 A6 5sh violet & green   70.00 *110.00*

1921-29   **Wmk. 4**
42 A7 ½p green   1.60 .30
43 A7 1p rose red   1.40 .30
44 A7 1p dp violet ('23)   2.40 1.40
45 A7 1½p orange ('22)   2.25 6.50
46 A7 1½p rose red ('26)   3.50 1.75
47 A7 1½p fawn ('29)   2.25 .55
48 A7 2p gray   1.75 .75
49 A7 2½p ultra   3.25 5.00
50 A7 2½p orange ('23)   1.75 16.00

Chalky Paper
51 A7 3p violet, *yel* ('25)   3.75 8.00
52 A7 6p vio & red vio   2.75 6.25
53 A7 1sh black, *emer* ('29)   5.75 7.50
54 A7 2sh vio & ultra, *blue* ('27)   9.50 50.00
55 A7 2sh6p blk & red, *blue* ('27)   17.50 24.00
56 A7 3sh grn & vio ('22)   24.00 75.00
57 A7 4sh blk & red ('22)   45.00 57.50
Nos. 42-57 (16)   128.40 260.80

Wmk. 3
Chalky Paper
58 A7 3p violet, *yel*   3.50 10.50
59 A7 4p black & red, *yel* ('22)   1.60 5.00
60 A7 1sh black, *emerald*   3.50 7.00
61 A7 2sh vio & ultra, *bl*   11.00 17.50
62 A7 2sh6p blk & red, *bl*   12.50 42.50
63 A7 5sh grn & red, *yel* ('22)   8.25 40.00
64 A7 £1 vio & black, *red* ('22)   200.00 275.00
Nos. 58-64 (7)   240.35 397.50

Old Dockyard, English Harbour — A8

Govt. House, St. John's — A9

Nelson's "Victory," 1805 — A10

Sir Thomas Warner's Ship, 1632 — A11

1932, Jan. 27   Engr.   Perf. 12½
67 A8 ½p green   1.75 5.25
68 A8 1p scarlet   2.40 4.25
69 A8 1½p lt brown   3.00 4.00
70 A9 2p gray   3.50 14.00
71 A9 2½p ultra   3.50 8.00
72 A9 3p orange   4.50 11.50
73 A10 6p violet   12.50 11.50
74 A10 1sh olive green   17.00 24.00
75 A10 2sh6p claret   37.50 45.00

76 A11 5sh red brn & black   95.00 110.00
Nos. 67-76 (10)   180.65 237.50
Tercentenary of the colony.

Common Design Types pictured following the introduction.

Silver Jubilee Issue
Common Design Type
1935, May 6   Perf. 13½x14
77 CD301 1p car & blue   1.90 2.25
78 CD301 1½p gray blk & ultra   2.50 1.00
79 CD301 2½p blue & brn   5.75 3.00
80 CD301 1sh brt vio & ind   9.50 12.50
Nos. 77-80 (4)   19.65 18.75
Set, never hinged   27.50

Coronation Issue
Common Design Type
1937, May 12   Perf. 11x11½
81 CD302 1p carmine   .30 .75
82 CD302 1½p brown   .40 .85
83 CD302 2½p deep ultra   1.00 1.50
Nos. 81-83 (3)   1.70 3.10
Set, never hinged   2.25

English Harbour — A14   Nelson's Dockyard — A15

Fort James — A16   St. John's Harbor — A17

1938-48   Engr.   Perf. 12½
84 A14 ½p green   .20 .90
85 A15 1p red   1.90 1.75
86 A15 1½p brown violet   1.25 1.25
87 A14 2p dark gray   .30 .50
88 A15 2½p deep ultra   .40 .75
89 A16 3p pale orange   .35 .80
90 A17 6p purple   .75 .80
91 A17 1sh brown & blk   1.90 1.00
92 A16 2sh6p deep claret   15.00 7.50
93 A17 5sh grayish ol grn   10.00 6.50
94 A15 10sh red vio ('48)   11.00 22.50
95 A16 £1 Prus blue ('48)   17.00 30.00
Nos. 84-95 (12)   60.05 74.25
Set, never hinged   80.00

See Nos. 107-113, 115-116, 118-121, 136-142, 144-145.
For overprint see Nos. 125-126.

Catalogue values for unused stamps in this section, from this point to the end of the section, are for Never Hinged items.

Peace Issue
Common Design Type
1946, Nov. 1   Wmk. 4   Perf. 13½x14
96 CD303 1½p brown   .25 .25
97 CD303 3p deep orange   .25 .30

Silver Wedding Issue
Common Design Types
1949, Jan. 3   Photo.   Perf. 14x14½
98 CD304 2½p bright ultra   .40 1.00
Engraved; Name Typographed
Perf. 11½x11
99 CD305 5sh dk brown olive   7.50 8.00

UPU Issue
Common Design Types
Perf. 13½, 11x11½
1949, Oct. 10   Wmk. 4
Engr.; Name Typo. on 3p and 6p
100 CD306 2½p deep ultra   .40 .50
101 CD307 3p orange   1.40 1.60
102 CD308 6p purple   1.10 1.10
103 CD309 1sh red brown   1.25 1.25
Nos. 100-103 (4)   4.15 4.45

University Issue
Common Design Types
1951, Feb. 16   Engr.   Perf. 14x14½
104 CD310 3c chocolate & blk   .40 .45
105 CD311 12c purple & blk   .60 .70

Coronation Issue
Common Design Type
1953, June 2   Engr.   Perf. 13½x13
106 CD312 2c dk green & blk   .50 .75

Types of 1938 with Portrait of Queen Elizabeth II

Martello Tower — A24

Perf. 13x13½, 13½x13
1953-56   Wmk. 4
107 A16 ½c dk red brn ('56)   .25 .25
108 A14 1c gray   .25 .50
109 A15 2c deep green   .25 .20
110 A15 3c yellow & blk   .35 .20
111 A14 4c rose red (shades)   .95 .20
112 A15 5c dull vio & blk   1.90 .30
113 A15 6c orange   1.50 .20
114 A24 8c deep blue   1.75 .20
115 A17 12c violet   1.75 .20
116 A17 24c chocolate & blk   1.90 .20
117 A24 48c dp bl & rose lil   5.25 2.00
118 A16 60c claret   5.75 .55
119 A17 $1.20 olive green   1.75 .50
120 A15 $2.40 magenta   7.50 8.50
121 A16 $4.80 greenish blue   11.50 16.00
Nos. 107-121 (15)   42.60 30.00

See #143. For overprint see #125-126.

West Indies Federation
Common Design Type
1958, Apr. 22   Engr.   Perf. 11½x11
122 CD313 3c green   .90 .25
123 CD313 6c blue   1.25 2.00
124 CD313 12c carmine rose   1.40 .50
Nos. 122-124 (3)   3.55 2.75

Nos. 110 and 115 Overprinted in Red or Black: "Commemoration Antigua Constitution 1960"
Perf. 13x13½, 13½x13
1960, Jan. 1   Wmk. 4
125 A15 3c yellow & black   .20 .20
126 A17 12c violet (Blk)   .20 .20
Constitutional reforms effective Jan. 1, 1960.

Lord Nelson and Nelson's Dockyard A26

Perf. 11½x11
1961, Nov. 14   Wmk. 314
127 A26 20c brown & lilac   .90 .90
128 A26 30c dk blue & green   1.10 1.10
Completion of the restoration of Lord Nelson's headquarters, English Harbour.

Stamp of 1862 and Royal Mail Steam Packet in English Harbour A27

1962, Aug. 1   Engr.   Perf. 13
129 A27 3c dull green & pur   .50 .20
130 A27 10c dull green & ultra   .60 .20
131 A27 12c dull green & blk   .65 .20
132 A27 50c dull grn & brn org   1.25 1.10
Nos. 129-132 (4)   3.00 1.70
Centenary of first Antigua postage stamp.

Freedom from Hunger Issue
Common Design Type
1963, June 4   Photo.   Perf. 14x14½
133 CD314 12c green   .30 .30

Red Cross Centenary Issue
Common Design Type
1963, Sept. 2   Litho.   Perf. 13
134 CD315 3c black & red   .20 .25
135 CD315 12c ultra & red   .80 1.25

Types of 1938-53 with Portrait of Queen Elizabeth II
Perf. 13x13½, 13½x13
1963-65   Engr.
136 A16 ½c brown ('65)   1.40 .30
137 A14 1c gray ('65)   .90 .30
138 A15 2c deep green   .55 .20
139 A15 3c orange yel & blk   .40 .20
140 A14 4c brown red   .25 .35
141 A15 5c dull vio & black   .20 .35
142 A16 6c orange   .55 .40
143 A24 8c deep blue   .25 .45
144 A17 12c violet   .30 .50
145 A17 24c choc & black   3.50 .75
Nos. 136-145 (10)   8.30 3.80
For surcharge see No. 152.

Shakespeare Issue
Common Design Type
1964, Apr. 23   Photo.   Perf. 14x14½
151 CD316 12c red brown   .35 .20

No. 144 Surcharged with New Value and Bars
1965, Apr. 1   Engr.   Perf. 13½x13
152 A17 15c on 12c violet   .25 .25

ITU Issue
Common Design Type
1965, May 17   Litho.   Perf. 11x11½
153 CD317 2c blue & ver   .20 .20
154 CD317 50c orange & vio bl   1.40 1.10

Intl. Cooperation Year Issue
Common Design Type
1965, Oct. 25   Perf. 14½
155 CD318 4c blue grn & claret   .20 .20
156 CD318 15c lt vio & green   .40 .25

Churchill Memorial Issue
Common Design Type
1966, Jan. 24   Photo.   Perf. 14
Design in Black, Gold and Carmine Rose
157 CD319 ½c bright blue   .20 1.25
158 CD319 4c green   .25 .20
159 CD319 25c brown   .75 .30
160 CD319 35c violet   .85 .40
Nos. 157-160 (4)   2.05 2.15

Royal Visit Issue
Common Design Type
1966, Feb. 4   Litho.   Perf. 11x12
Portraits in Black
161 CD320 6c violet blue   1.25 .90
162 CD320 15c dark car rose   2.00 1.10

World Cup Soccer Issue
Common Design Type
1966, July 1   Wmk. 314   Perf. 14
163 CD321 6c multicolored   .20 .25
164 CD321 35c multicolored   .65 .25

WHO Headquarters Issue
Common Design Type
1966, Sept. 20   Perf. 14
165 CD322 2c multicolored   .20 .20
166 CD322 15c multicolored   .70 .35

Nelson's Dockyard A35

Designs: 1c, Old post office, St. John's. 2c, Health Center. 3c, Teachers' Training College.

4c, Martello Tower, Barbuda. 5c, Ruins of officers quarters, Shirley Heights. 6c, Government House, Barbuda. 10c, Princess Margaret School. 15c, Air terminal. 25c, General post office. 35c, Clarence House. 50c, Government House. 75c, Administration building. $1, Court House, St. John's. $2.50, Magistrates' Court. $5, St. John's Cathedral.

1966, Nov. 1   Engr.   Perf. 11½x11

167	A35	½c green & blue	.20	.20
168	A35	1c purple & rose	.20	.25
169	A35	2c slate & org	.20	.25
170	A35	3c rose red & blk	.20	.25
171	A35	4c dull vio & brn	.20	.20
172	A35	5c vio bl & olive	.20	.20
a.		Booklet pane of 4 ('68)	.40	
173	A35	6c dp org & pur	.20	.20
174	A35	10c brt grn & rose red	.20	.20
a.		Booklet pane of 4 ('68)	1.00	
175	A35	15c brn & blue	1.00	.20
a.		Booklet pane of 4 ('68)	1.25	
176	A35	25c slate & brn	.50	.20
177	A35	35c dp rose & sep	1.00	.60
178	A35	50c green & black	.90	1.50
179	A35	75c Prus bl & vio blue	1.25	1.75
180	A35	$1 dp rose & olive	4.50	2.00
181	A35	$2.50 black & rose	3.75	5.50
182	A35	$5 ol grn & dl vio	5.50	6.50
		Nos. 167-182 (16)	20.00	20.00

For surcharge see No. 231.

1969   Perf. 13½

167a	A35	½c	.20	.40
168a	A35	1c	.20	.50
169a	A35	2c	.20	.20
170a	A35	3c	.20	.20
171a	A35	4c	.20	.20
172b	A35	5c	.20	.20
173a	A35	6c	.20	.50
174b	A35	10c	.20	.20
175b	A35	15c	.30	.30
176a	A35	25c	.50	.20
177a	A35	35c	.60	.75
178a	A35	50c	.95	2.00
180a	A35	$1	2.00	3.00
181a	A35	$2.50	5.50	6.00
182a	A35	$5	19.00	24.00
		Nos. 167a-182a (15)	30.45	38.75

The ½c, 3c, 6c are on ordinary paper. The 15c through $5 on glazed paper. The others exist on both papers.

UNESCO Anniversary Issue
Common Design Type

1966, Dec. 1   Litho.   Perf. 14

183	CD323	4c "Education"	.20	.20
184	CD323	25c "Science"	.40	.20
185	CD323	$1 "Culture"	1.40	2.00
		Nos. 183-185 (3)	2.00	2.40

Independent State

Flag of Antigua, Spiny Lobster, Maps of Antigua and Barbuda
A37

Designs: 15c, 35c, Flag of Antigua. 25c, Flag and Premier's Office Building.

1967, Feb. 27   Photo.   Perf. 14

186	A37	4c multicolored	.20	.20
187	A37	15c multicolored	.20	.20
188	A37	25c multicolored	.20	.20
189	A37	35c multicolored	.20	.20
		Nos. 186-189 (4)	.80	.80

Antigua's independence, Feb. 27, 1967.

Gilbert Memorial Church, Antigua — A38

25c, Nathaniel Gilbert's House. 35c, Map of the Caribbean and Central America.

1967, May 18   Photo.   Perf. 14x13½

190	A38	4c brt red & black	.20	.20
191	A38	25c emerald & black	.20	.20
192	A38	35c ultra & black	.20	.20
		Nos. 190-192 (3)	.60	.60

Attainment of autonomy by the Methodist Church in the Caribbean and the Americas,

and the opening of headquarters near St. John's, Antigua, May 1967.

Antiguan and British Royal Arms — A39

1967, July 21   Perf. 14½x14

193	A39	15c dark green & multi	.20	.20
194	A39	35c deep blue & multi	.20	.20

Granting of a new coat of arms to the State of Antigua; 300th anniv. of the Treaty of Breda.

Sailing Ship, 17th Century
A40

Design: 6c, 35c, Map of Barbuda from Jan Blaeu's Atlas, 1665.

1967, Dec. 14   Engr.   Perf. 11½x11

195	A40	4c dark blue	.20	.20
196	A40	6c deep plum	.20	.75
197	A40	25c green	.30	.20
198	A40	35c black	.40	.30
		Nos. 195-198 (4)	1.10	1.45

Resettlement of Barbuda, 300th anniv.

Dow Hill Antenna — A41

Designs: 15c, Antenna and rocket blasting off. 25c, Nose cone orbiting moon. 50c, Re-entry of space capsule.

1968, Mar. 29   Photo.   Perf. 14½x14

199	A41	4c dk blue, org & black	.20	.20
200	A41	15c dk blue, org & black	.20	.20
201	A41	25c dk blue, org & black	.20	.20
202	A41	50c dk blue, org & black	.20	.20
		Nos. 199-202 (4)	.80	.80

Dedication of the Dow Hill tracking station in Antigua for the NASA Apollo project.

Beach and Sailfish
A42

Designs: ½c, 50c, Limbo dancer, flames and dancing girls. 15c, Three girls on a beach and water skier. 35c, Woman scuba diver, corals and fish.

1968, July 1   Photo.   Perf. 14

203	A42	½c red & multi	.20	.20
204	A42	15c sky blue & multi	.20	.20
205	A42	25c blue & multi	.30	.20
206	A42	35c brt blue & multi	.30	.20
207	A42	50c multicolored	.50	.90
		Nos. 203-207 (5)	1.50	1.70

Issued for tourist publicity.

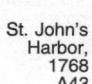

St. John's Harbor, 1768
A43

St. John's Harbor: 15c, 1829. 25c, Map of deep-sea harbor, 1968. 35c, Dock, 1968. 2c, Like $1.

Engr. & Litho.; Engr. ($1)

1968, Oct. 31   Perf. 13

208	A43	2c dp car & lt blue	.20	.30
209	A43	15c sepia & yel grn	.35	.20
210	A43	25c dk blue & yel	.40	.20
211	A43	35c dp green & sal	.50	.20
212	A43	$1 black	.90	1.25
		Nos. 208-212 (5)	2.35	2.15

Opening of St. John's deep-sea harbor.

Mace and Parliament A44

Mace and: 15c, Mace bearer. 25c, House of Representatives, interior. 50c, Antigua coat of arms and great seal.

1969, Feb. 3   Photo.   Perf. 12½

213	A44	4c crimson & multi	.20	.20
214	A44	15c crimson & multi	.20	.20
215	A44	25c crimson & multi	.25	.20
216	A44	50c crimson & multi	.35	1.00
		Nos. 213-216 (4)	1.00	1.60

300th anniversary of Antigua Parliament.

CARIFTA Cargo — A45

4c, 15c, Ship, plane and trucks, horiz.

Perf. 13½x13, 13x13½

1969, Apr. 14   Litho.

217	A45	4c blk & brt lilac rose	.20	.20
218	A45	15c blk & brt grnsh blue	.20	.20
219	A45	25c bister & black	.20	.20
220	A45	35c tan & black	.20	.25
		Nos. 217-220 (4)	.80	.85

1st anniv. of CARIFTA (Caribbean Free Trade Area).

Map of Redonda Island A46

25c, View of Redonda from the sea & seagulls.

1969, Aug. 1   Photo.   Perf. 13x13½

221	A46	15c ultra & multi	.25	.20
222	A46	25c multicolored	.25	.20
223	A46	50c salmon & multi	.50	.50
		Nos. 221-223 (3)	1.00	.90

Centenary of Redonda phosphate industry.

Adoration of the Kings, by Gugliemo Marcillat A47

Christmas: 10c, 50c, Holy Family, by anonymous German artist, 15th century.

1969, Oct. 15   Litho.   Perf. 13x14

224	A47	6c bister brn & multi	.20	.20
225	A47	10c fawn & multi	.20	.20
226	A47	35c gray olive & multi	.20	.20
227	A47	50c gray blue & multi	.30	.20
		Nos. 224-227 (4)	.90	.80

Arms of Antigua — A48

Coil Stamps

1970, Jan. 30   Photo.   Perf. 14½x14

228	A48	5c bright blue	.20	.20
a.		Wmk. 373 ('77)	7.00	
229	A48	10c bright green	.20	.20
a.		Wmk. 373, invtd. ('77)		.80
230	A48	25c deep magenta	.45	.20
a.		Wmk. 373 ('77)	12.50	
		Nos. 228-230 (3)	.85	.60

No. 176 Surcharged

1970, Jan. 2   Engr.   Perf. 11½x11

231	A35	20c on 25c slate & brown	.25	.20

Sikorsky S-38 A49

Aircraft: 20c, Dornier DO-X. 35c, Hawker Siddeley 748. 50c, Douglas C-124C Globemaster II. 75c, Vickers VC 10.

1970, Feb. 16   Litho.   Perf. 14½

232	A49	5c brt green & multi	.40	.20
233	A49	20c ultra & multi	1.00	.20
234	A49	35c blue grn & multi	1.25	.20
235	A49	50c blue & multi	1.40	1.00
236	A49	75c vio blue & multi	1.50	1.75
		Nos. 232-236 (5)	5.55	3.35

40th anniversary of air service.

Dickens and Scene from "Pickwick Papers" A50

Charles Dickens (1812-1870), English novelist and Scene from: 5c, "Nicholas Nickleby." 35c, "Oliver Twist." $1, "David Copperfield."

1970, May 19   Litho.   Perf. 14

237	A50	5c olive & sepia	.20	.20
238	A50	20c aqua & sepia	.25	.20
239	A50	35c violet & sepia	.30	.20
240	A50	$1 scarlet & sepia	.75	.50
		Nos. 237-240 (4)	1.50	1.10

Carib Indian and War Canoe A51

Ships: 1c, Columbus and "Nina." 2c, Sir Thomas Warner's arms and sailing ship. 3c, Viscount Hood and "Barfleur." 4c, Sir George Rodney and "Formidable." 5c, Capt. Horatio Nelson and "Boreas." 6c, King William IV and "Pegasus." 10c, Blackbeard (Edward Teach) and pirate ketch. 15c, Capt. Cuthbert Collingwood and "Pelican." 20c, Admiral Nelson and "Victoria." 25c, Paddle steamer "Solent" and Steam Packet Company emblem. 35c, King George V and corvette "Canada." 50c, Cruiser "Renown" and royal badge. 75c, S.S. "Federal Maple" and maple leaf. $1, Racing yacht "Sol-Quest" and Gallant 53 class emblem. $2.50,

Missile destroyer "London" and her emblem. $5, Tug "Pathfinder" and arms of Antigua.

Wmk. 314 Sideways
1970, Aug. 19   Litho.   Perf. 14

241	A51	½c ocher & multi	.20	.55
242	A51	1c Prus bl & multi	.25	.65
243	A51	2c yel grn & multi	.30	1.25
244	A51	3c ol bis & multi	.30	1.00
245	A51	4c bl gray & multi	.30	1.25
246	A51	5c fawn & multi	.40	.35
247	A51	6c rose lil & multi	.55	1.40
248	A51	10c brn org & multi	.60	.20
249	A51	15c ultra & multi	3.00	.30
250	A51	20c ol grn & multi	1.00	.30
251	A51	25c olive & multi	1.00	.30
252	A51	35c dull red brn & multi	1.40	.65
253	A51	50c lt brn & multi	3.75	2.75
254	A51	75c beige & multi	5.50	4.50
255	A51	$1 Prus green & multi	5.50	1.60
256	A51	$2.50 gray & multi	5.50	6.00
257	A51	$5 yel & multi	5.50	6.25
		Nos. 241-257 (17)	35.05	29.80

1972-74   Wmk. 314 Upright

241a	A51	½c	.20	.25
242a	A51	1c	.20	.50
244a	A51	3c	.20	.40
245a	A51	4c	.20	1.00
246a	A51	5c	.20	1.50
247a	A51	6c	.20	1.50
248a	A51	10c	1.60	.50
249a	A51	15c	.20	.20
254a	A51	75c	3.25	2.00
255a	A51	$1	3.50	1.60
256a	A51	$2.50	6.00	7.50
257a	A51	$5	6.75	10.50
		Nos. 241a-257a (12)	22.50	26.15

For surcharge see No. 368.

1975, Jan. 21   Wmk. 373

257b	A51	$5 yellow & multi	5.00	11.00

Nativity, by Albrecht Dürer — A52

Christmas: 10c, 50c, Adoration of the Magi, by Albrecht Dürer.

Engr. & Litho.
1970, Oct. 28   Perf. 13½x14

258	A52	3c brt grnsh blue & blk	.20	.20
259	A52	10c pink & plum	.20	.20
260	A52	35c brick red & black	.25	.20
261	A52	50c lilac & violet	.35	.25
		Nos. 258-261 (4)	1.00	.85

1970, Dec. 1   Litho.   Perf. 14x13½

Military Uniforms: ½c, Drummer Boy, 4th King's Own Regiment, 1759. 20c, Grenadier Company Officer, 60th Regiment, The Royal American, 1809. 35c, Light Company Officer, 93rd Regiment, The Sutherland Highlanders, 1826-1834. 75c, Private, 3rd West India Regiment, 1851.

Private, 4th West India Regiment, 1804 — A53

262	A53	½c lake & multi	.20	.20
263	A53	10c brn org & multi	.40	.20
264	A53	20c Prus grn & multi	1.00	.20
265	A53	35c dl pur & multi	1.25	.20
266	A53	75c dk ol grn & multi	3.00	2.00
a.		Souv. sheet #262-266 + label	8.00	9.00
		Nos. 262-266 (5)	5.85	2.80

See #274-278, 283-287, 307-311, 329-333.

Market Woman Voting — A54

Voting by: 20c, Businessman. 35c, Mother (and child). 50c, Workman.

1971, Feb. 1   Photo.   Perf. 14½x14

267	A54	5c brown	.20	.20
268	A54	20c olive black	.20	.20
269	A54	35c rose magenta	.20	.20
270	A54	50c violet blue	.20	.20
		Nos. 267-270 (4)	.80	.80

Adult suffrage, 20th anniversary.

Last Supper, from The Small Passion, by Dürer — A55

Woodcuts by Albrecht Dürer: 35c, Crucifixion from Eichstaff Missal. 75c, Resurrection from The Great Passion.

1971, Apr. 7   Litho.   Perf. 14x13½

271	A55	5c gray, red & black	.20	.20
272	A55	35c gray, violet & black	.20	.20
273	A55	75c gray, gold & black	.20	.20
		Nos. 271-273 (3)	.60	.60

Easter.

Military Uniform Type of 1970

Military Uniforms: ½c, Private, Suffolk Regiment, 1704. 10c, Grenadier, South Staffordshire, 1751. 20c, Fusilier, Royal Northumberland, 1778. 35c, Private, Northamptonshire. 1793, 75c, Private, East Yorkshire, 1805.

1971, July 12   Litho.   Wmk. 314

274	A53	½c gray grn & multi	.20	.20
275	A53	10c bluish blk & multi	.40	.25
276	A53	20c dk pur & multi	.80	.30
277	A53	35c dk ol & multi	1.40	.35
278	A53	75c brown & multi	2.75	3.25
a.		Souv. sheet, #274-278 + label	6.75	7.50
		Nos. 274-278 (5)	5.55	4.35

Virgin and Child, by Veronese — A56

Christmas: 5c, 50c, Adoration of the Shepherds, by Bonifazio Veronese.

1971, Oct. 4   Perf. 14x13½

279	A56	3c multicolored	.20	.20
280	A56	20c multicolored	.20	.20
281	A56	35c multicolored	.25	.20
282	A56	50c multicolored	.45	.30
		Nos. 279-282 (4)	1.10	.90

Uniform Type of 1970

Military Uniforms: ½c, Officer, King's Own Borderers Regiment, 1815. 10c, Sergeant, Buckinghamshire Regiment, 1837. 20c, Private, South Hampshire Regiment, 1853. 35c, Officer, Royal Artillery, 1854. 75c, Private, Worcestershire Regiment, 1870.

1972, July 1

283	A53	½c ol brn & multi	.20	.20
284	A53	10c dp grn & multi	.35	.20
285	A53	20c brt vio & multi	.70	.25
286	A53	35c mar & multi	1.25	.35

287	A53	75c dk vio bl & multi	2.50	3.00
a.		Souvenir sheet of 5, #283-287 + label	7.50	8.50
		Nos. 283-287 (5)	5.00	4.00

Reticulated Helmet Cowrie — A57

Sea Shells: 5c, Measled cowrie. 35c, West Indian fighting conch. 50c, Hawkwing conch.

1972, Aug. 1   Perf. 14½x14

288	A57	3c multicolored	.20	.20
289	A57	5c ver & multi	.35	.20
290	A57	35c lt vio & multi	1.25	.25
291	A57	50c rose red & multi	2.00	2.50
		Nos. 288-291 (4)	3.80	3.15

St. John's Cathedral, 1745-1843 — A58

Christmas: 50c, Interior of St. John's. 75c, St. John's rebuilt.

1972, Nov. 6   Litho.   Perf. 14

292	A58	35c org brn & multi	.20	.20
293	A58	50c vio & multi	.30	.30
294	A58	75c multicolored	.50	.50
a.		Souv. sheet, #292-294, perf 15	1.00	1.25
		Nos. 292-294 (3)	1.00	1.00

Silver Wedding Issue, 1972
Common Design Type

1972, Nov. 20   Photo.   Perf. 14x14½

295	CD324	20c ultra & multi	.20	.20
296	CD324	35c steel blue & multi	.20	.20

Map of Antigua, Batsman Driving Ball — A60

Designs: 35c, Batsman and wicketkeeper. $1, Emblem of Rising Sun Cricket Club.

1972, Dec. 15   Perf. 13½x14

297	A60	5c multicolored	.25	.25
298	A60	35c multicolored	1.10	.50
299	A60	$1 multicolored	2.75	3.25
a.		Souvenir sheet of 3, #297-299	5.50	6.50
		Nos. 297-299 (3)	4.10	4.00

Rising Sun Cricket Club, St. John's, 50th anniv.

Map of Antigua and Yacht — A61

1972, Dec. 29   Perf. 14½

300	A61	35c shown	.20	.20
301	A61	50c Racing yachts	.20	.20
302	A61	75c St. John's G.P.O.	.30	.25
303	A61	$1 Statue of Liberty	.30	.25
a.		Souvenir sheet of 2, #301, 303	1.50	1.50
		Nos. 300-303 (4)	1.00	.90

Opening of Antigua and Barbuda Information Office in New York City.

Window with Episcopal Coat of Arms — A62

Stained glass windows from Cathedral of St. John: 35c, Crucifixion. 75c, Arm of Rt. Rev. D.G. Davis, 1st bishop of Antigua.

1973, Apr. 16   Litho.   Perf. 13½

304	A62	5c yellow & multi	.20	.20
305	A62	35c brt lilac & multi	.20	.20
306	A62	75c blue & multi	.30	.20
		Nos. 304-306 (3)	.70	.60

Easter.

Uniform Type of 1970

Military Uniforms: ½c, Private, Col. Zacharia Tiffin's Regiment, 1701. 10c, Private, 63rd Regiment, 1759. 20c, Officer, 35th Sussex Regiment, 1828. 35c, Private, 2nd West India Wales Regiment, 1853. 75c, Sergeant, Princess of Wales Regiment, Hertfordshire, 1858.

Perf. 14x13½

1973, July 1   Wmk. 314

307	A53	½c dp ultra & multi	.20	.20
308	A53	10c rose lilac & multi	.20	.20
309	A53	20c gray & multi	.40	.25
310	A53	35c multicolored	.60	.25
311	A53	75c multicolored	1.60	1.10
a.		Souv. sheet #307-311 + label	3.50	3.00
		Nos. 307-311 (5)	3.00	2.00

Butterfly Costumes — A63

Designs: 20c, Carnival revelers. 35c, Costumed group. 75c, Carnival Queen.

Perf. 13½x14

1973, July 30   Unwmk.

312	A63	5c multicolored	.20	.20
313	A63	20c multicolored	.20	.20
314	A63	35c multicolored	.20	.20
315	A63	75c multicolored	.20	.20
a.		Souvenir sheet of 4, #312-315	1.10	1.25
		Nos. 312-315 (4)	.85	.80

Carnival, July 29-Aug. 7.

Virgin of the Porridge, by David — A64

Christmas: 5c, Adoration of the Kings, by Stomer. 20c, Virgin of the Grand Duke, by Raphael. 35c, Nativity with God the Father and Holy Ghost, by Tiepolo. $1, Madonna and Child, by Murillo.

1973, Oct. 15   Photo.   Perf. 14½

316	A64	3c brt blue & multi	.20	.20
317	A64	5c emerald & multi	.20	.20
318	A64	20c gold & multi	.20	.20
319	A64	35c violet & multi	.25	.20
320	A64	$1 red & multi	.40	.40
a.		Souvenir sheet of 5, #316-320	1.75	2.00
		Nos. 316-320 (5)	1.25	1.20

Princess Anne and Mark
Phillips — A65

Design: $2, different border.

1973, Nov. 14   Litho.   Perf. 13½
321	A65	35c dull ultra & multi	.20	.20
322	A65	$2 yel grn & multi	.25	.25
a.		Souvenir sheet of 2, #321-322	.75	.75

Wedding of Princess Anne and Capt. Mark
Phillips.
Nos. 321-322 were issued in sheets of 5
plus label.

Nos. 321-322 and 322a Overprinted
Vertically: "HONEYMOON / VISIT /
DECEMBER 16th / 1973"

1973, Dec. 15   Litho.   Perf. 13½
323	A65	35c multicolored	.20	.20
324	A65	$2 multicolored	.50	.50
a.		Souvenir sheet of 2, #323-324	.75	.75

Visit of Princess Anne and Mark Phillips to
Antigua, Dec. 16. Same overprint in sheet
margins of Nos. 323-324 and 324a.
Overprint lithographed. Also exists
typographed.

Arms of
Antigua
and U.W.I.
A66

Designs: 20c, Dancers. 35c, Antigua campus. 75c, Chancellor Sir Hugh Wooding.

1974, Feb. 18   Wmk. 314
325	A66	5c multicolored	.20	.20
326	A66	20c multicolored	.20	.20
327	A66	35c multicolored	.20	.20
328	A66	75c multicolored	.20	.20
		Nos. 325-328 (4)	.80	.80

University of the West Indies, 24th anniv.

Uniform Type of 1970

Military Uniforms: ½c, Officer, 59th Foot,
1797. 10c, Gunner, Royal Artillery, 1800. 20c,
Private, 1st West India Regiment, 1830. 35c,
Officer, Gordon Highlanders, 1843. 75c, Private, Royal Welsh Fusiliers, 1846.

1974, May 1   Perf. 14x13½
329	A53	½c dull grn & multi	.20	.20
330	A53	10c ocher & multi	.40	.20
331	A53	20c multicolored	.65	.20
332	A53	35c gray bl & multi	.80	.20
333	A53	75c dk gray & multi	1.25	1.50
a.		Souvenir sheet of 5, #329-333	3.00	2.50
		Nos. 329-333 (5)	3.30	2.30

English Mailman and Coach,
Helicopter — A67

UPU, Cent.: 1c, English bellman, 1846; Orinoco mailboat, 1851; telecommunications satellite. 2c, English mailtrain guard, 1852; Swiss
post passenger bus, 1906; Italian hydrofoil. 5c,
Swiss messenger, 16th century; Wells Fargo
coach, 1800; Concorde. 20c, German position, 1820; Japanese mailmen, 19th century;
carrier pigeon. 35c, Contemporary Antiguan
mailman; radar station; aquaplane. $1, Medie-
val French courier; American train, 1884; British Airways jet.

1974, July 15   Litho.   Perf. 14½
334	A67	½c multicolored	.20	.20
335	A67	1c multicolored	.20	.20
336	A67	2c multicolored	.20	.20
337	A67	5c multicolored	.20	.20
338	A67	20c multicolored	.30	.20
339	A67	35c multicolored	.65	.25

340	A67	$1 multicolored	1.75	1.50
a.		Souvenir sheet of 7, #334-340 + label, perf. 13	4.50	3.50
		Nos. 334-340 (7)	3.50	2.75

For surcharges see Nos. 365-367.

Traditional
Steel Band
A68

Carnival 1974 (Steel Bands): 5c, Traditional
players, vert. 35c, Modern steel band. 75c,
Modern players, vert.

1974, Aug. 1   Wmk. 314   Perf. 14
341	A68	5c rose red, dk red & blk	.20	.20
342	A68	20c ocher, brn & blk	.20	.20
343	A68	35c yel grn, grn & blk	.20	.20
344	A68	75c dl bl, dk bl & blk	.20	.50
a.		Souvenir sheet of 4, #341-344	.75	.75
		Nos. 341-344 (4)	.80	1.10

Soccer — A69

Designs: Games' emblem and soccer.

1974, Sept. 23   Unwmk.   Perf. 14½
345	A69	5c multicolored	.20	.20
346	A69	35c multicolored	.20	.20
347	A69	75c multicolored	.25	.25
348	A69	$1 multicolored	.35	.35
a.		Souvenir sheet of 4	1.25	1.25
		Nos. 345-348 (4)	1.00	1.00

World Cup Soccer Championship, Munich,
June 13-July 7. Nos. 345-348 issued in sheets
of 5 plus label showing Soccer Cup. No. 348a
contains one each of Nos. 345-348, perf. 13½,
and 2 labels.
For overprints and surcharges see Nos.
361-364.

Winston Churchill (1874-1965) at
Harrow — A70

Designs: 35c, St. Paul's during bombing and
Churchill portrait. 75c, Churchill's coat of arms
and catafalque. $1, Churchill during Boer war,
warrant for arrest and map of his escape route.

1974, Oct. 20   Unwmk.   Perf. 14½
349	A70	5c multicolored	.20	.20
350	A70	35c multicolored	.20	.20
351	A70	75c multicolored	.25	.30
352	A70	$1 multicolored	.35	.50
a.		Souvenir sheet of 4, #349-352	1.25	1.75
		Nos. 349-352 (4)	1.00	1.20

Virgin and Child,
by Giovanni
Bellini — A71

Christmas: Paintings of the Virgin and Child.

1974, Nov. 18   Litho.   Perf. 14½
353	A71	½c shown	.20	.20
354	A71	1c Raphael	.20	.20
355	A71	2c Van der Weyden	.20	.20
356	A71	3c Giorgione	.20	.20
357	A71	5c Andrea Mantegna	.20	.20
358	A71	20c Alvise Vivarini	.20	.20

359	A71	35c Bartolommeo Montagna	.25	.20
360	A71	75c Lorenzo Costa	.35	.60
a.		Souv. sheet, #357-360, perf 13½	1.25	1.50
		Nos. 353-360 (8)	1.80	2.00

Nos. 346-348 Overprinted and No.
344 Surcharged and Overprinted:
"EARTHQUAKE / RELIEF"

1974, Oct. 16   Litho.   Perf. 14½, 14
361	A69	35c multicolored	.30	.20
362	A69	75c multicolored	.40	.25
363	A69	$1 multicolored	.55	.35
364	A68	$5 on 75c multi	1.75	1.75
		Nos. 361-364 (4)	3.00	2.55

Earthquake of Oct. 8, 1974.

Nos. 338-340 and 254a Surcharged
with New Value and Two Bars

1974-75   Wmk. 314   Perf. 14½
365	A67	50c on 20c	1.25	1.25
366	A67	$2.50 on 35c	2.75	3.75
367	A67	$5 on $1	5.75	5.25

Perf. 14
368	A51	$10 on 75c	4.25	5.75
		Nos. 365-368 (4)	14.00	16.00

Carib War
Canoe,
English
Harbour
A72

Designs (Nelson's Dockyard): 15c, Raising
ship, 1770. 35c, Lord Nelson and "Boreas."
50c, Yachts arriving for Sailing Week, 1974.
$1, "Anchorage" in Old Dockyard, 1970.

1975, Mar. 17   Unwmk.   Perf. 14½
369	A72	5c multicolored	.25	.20
370	A72	15c multicolored	.75	.20
371	A72	35c multicolored	1.25	.25
372	A72	50c multicolored	1.25	1.00
373	A72	$1 multicolored	1.75	1.75
		Nos. 369-373 (5)	5.25	3.40

Souvenir Sheet
Perf. 13½
373A	A72	Sheet of 5, #369-373	4.00	3.00

Stamps in No. 373A are 43x28mm.

Lady of
the Valley
Church
A73

Churches of Antigua: 20c, Gilbert Memorial.
35c, Grace Hill Moravian. 50c, St. Phillip's. $1,
Ebenezer Methodist.

1975, May 19   Litho.   Perf. 14½
374	A73	5c multicolored	.20	.20
375	A73	20c multicolored	.20	.20
376	A73	35c multicolored	.20	.20
377	A73	50c multicolored	.20	.20
378	A73	$1 multicolored	.20	.20
a.		Souvenir sheet of 3, #376-378, perf. 13½	1.00	1.50
		Nos. 374-378 (5)	1.00	1.00

Antigua, Senex's Atlas, 1721, and
Hevelius Sextant, 1640
A74

Maps of Antigua: 20c, Jeffery's Atlas, 1775,
and 18th century engraving of ship. 35c, Barbuda and Antigua, 1775 and 1975. $1, St.
John's and English Harbour, 1973.

1975, July 21   Wmk. 314
379	A74	5c multicolored	.30	.20
380	A74	20c multicolored	.60	.20
381	A74	35c multicolored	.75	.20
382	A74	$1 multicolored	1.50	1.75
a.		Souvenir sheet of 4, #379-382	3.75	2.75
		Nos. 379-382 (4)	3.15	2.35

Bugler
and
Sunset
A75

Nordjamb 75 Emblem and: 20c, Black and
white Scouts, tents and flags. 35c, Lord
Baden-Powell and tents. $2, Dahomey
dancers.

1975, Aug. 26   Litho.   Perf. 14
383	A75	15c multicolored	.25	.20
384	A75	20c multicolored	.35	.20
385	A75	35c multicolored	.50	.25
386	A75	$2 multicolored	2.50	2.00
a.		Souvenir sheet of 4, #383-386	4.00	4.25
		Nos. 383-386 (4)	3.60	2.65

Nordjamb 75, 14th Boy Scout Jamboree, Lillehammer, Norway, July 29-Aug. 7.

Eurema
Elathea
A76

Butterflies: 1c, Danaus plexippus. 2c,
Phoebis philea. 5c, Marpesia petreus thetys.
20c, Eurema proterpia. 35c, Papilio
polydamas. $2, Vanessa cardui.

1975, Oct. 30   Litho.   Perf. 14
387	A76	½c multicolored	.20	.20
388	A76	1c multicolored	.20	.20
389	A76	2c multicolored	.25	.20
390	A76	5c multicolored	.20	.20
391	A76	20c multicolored	1.00	.50
392	A76	35c multicolored	1.60	1.25
393	A76	$2 multicolored	4.75	6.00
a.		Miniature sheet of 4, #390-393	9.00	10.00
		Nos. 387-393 (7)	8.20	8.55

Virgin and Child,
by
Correggio — A77

Christmas: Virgin and Child paintings.

1975, Nov. 17   Unwmk.
394	A77	½c shown	.20	.20
395	A77	1c El Greco	.20	.20
396	A77	2c Durer	.20	.20
397	A77	3c Antonello	.20	.20
398	A77	5c Bellini	.20	.20
399	A77	10c Durer	.20	.20
400	A77	35c Bellini	.40	.20
401	A77	$2 Durer	.75	.60
a.		Souvenir sheet of 4, #398-401	2.25	2.25
		Nos. 394-401 (8)	2.35	2.00

West
Indies
Team
A78

Designs: 5c, Batsman I.V.A. Richards and
cup, vert. 35c, Bowler A.M.E. Roberts and
cup, vert.

1975, Dec. 15   Litho.   Perf. 14
402	A78	5c multicolored	1.10	.20
403	A78	35c multicolored	2.10	.50
404	A78	$2 multicolored	4.00	7.00
		Nos. 402-404 (3)	7.20	7.70

World Cricket Cup, victory of West Indies
team.

A number of unissued items, imperfs., part perfs., missing color varieties, etc., were made available when the Format International inventory was liquidated. Imperfs of some or all of the Antigua stamps are included: #405-422, 503-507, 515-517, 703-707, 745-749, 755-759, 808-816, 819-826, 905-909, 934-937.
See footnote after #962.

Antillean Crested Hummingbird — A79

Irrigation System, Diamond Estate — A80

Designs: 1c, Imperial parrot. 2c, Zenaida dove. 3c, Loggerhead kingbird. 4c, Red-necked pigeon. 5c, Rufous-throated solitaire. 6c, Orchid tree. 10c, Bougainvillea. 15c, Geiger tree. 20c, Flamboyant. 25c, Hibiscus. 35c, Flame of the Woods. 50c, Cannon at Fort James. 75c, Premier's Office. $1, Potworks Dam. $5, Government House. $10, Coolidge International Airport.

1976, Jan. 19		Litho.	Perf. 15	
405	A79	½c multicolored	.20	.35
406	A79	1c multicolored	.20	.35
407	A79	2c multicolored	.20	.35
408	A79	3c multicolored	.20	.40
409	A79	4c multicolored	.20	.40
410	A79	5c multicolored	.20	.20
411	A79	6c multicolored	.20	.40
412	A79	10c multicolored	.20	.20
413	A79	15c multicolored	.20	.20
414	A79	20c multicolored	.20	.20
415	A79	25c multicolored	.20	.20
416	A79	35c multicolored	.25	.25
417	A79	50c multicolored	.35	.35
418	A79	75c multicolored	.50	.60
419	A79	$1 multicolored	.70	.80
		Perf. 13½x14		
420	A80	$2.50 rose & multi	1.50	2.50
421	A80	$5 lilac & multi	3.25	4.50
422	A80	$10 multicolored	6.75	8.00
		Nos. 405-422 (18)	15.50	20.25

Nos. 405-422 exist inscribed "1978."
For overprints see Nos. 607-617.

Privates, Clark's Illinois Regiment — A81

1c, Riflemen, Pennsylvania Militia. 2c, Decorated American powder horn. 5c, Water bottle of Maryland troops. 35c, "Liberty Tree" and "Rattlesnake" flags. $1, American privateer Montgomery. $2.50, Congress Flag. $5, Continental Navy sloop Ranger.

1976, Mar. 17		Litho.	Perf. 14½	
423	A81	½c multicolored	.20	.20
424	A81	1c multicolored	.20	.20
425	A81	2c multicolored	.20	.20
426	A81	5c multicolored	.20	.20
427	A81	35c multicolored	.50	.20
428	A81	$1 multicolored	1.50	.25
429	A81	$5 multicolored	3.00	3.00
		Nos. 423-429 (7)	5.80	4.25
		Souvenir Sheet		
		Perf. 13		
430	A81	$2.50 multicolored	2.50	3.50
		American Bicentennial.		

High Jump, Olympic Rings A82

Olympic Rings and: 1c, Boxing. 2c, Pole vault. 15c, Swimming. 30c, Running. $1, Bicycling. $2, Shot put.

1976, July 12		Litho.	Perf. 14½	
431	A82	½c yellow & multi	.20	.20
432	A82	1c purple & multi	.20	.20
433	A82	2c emerald & multi	.20	.20
434	A82	15c brt blue & multi	.20	.20
435	A82	30c olive & multi	.30	.20
436	A82	$1 orange & multi	.50	.25
437	A82	$2 red & multi	.75	.75
a.		Souvenir sheet of 4	2.00	2.50
		Nos. 431-437 (7)	2.35	2.00

21st Olympic Games, Montreal, Canada, July 17-Aug. 1. No. 437a contains one each of Nos. 434-437, perf. 13½.

Water Skiing A83

Water Sports: 1c, Sailfish sailing. 2c, Snorkeling. 20c, Deep-sea fishing. 50c, Scuba diving. $2, Swimming.

1976, Aug. 26			Perf. 14	
438	A83	½c yel grn & multi	.20	.20
439	A83	1c sepia & multi	.20	.20
440	A83	2c gray & multi	.20	.20
441	A83	20c multicolored	.20	.20
442	A83	50c brt vio & multi	.35	.40
443	A83	$2 lt gray & multi	1.10	1.25
a.		Souvenir sheet of 3, #441-443	2.00	2.50
		Nos. 438-443 (6)	2.25	2.45

French Angelfish — A84

1976, Oct. 4		Litho.	Perf. 13½x14	
444	A84	15c shown	.55	.20
445	A84	30c Yellowfish grouper	.80	.25
446	A84	50c Yellowtail snappers	1.00	.45
447	A84	90c Shy hamlet	1.40	.75
		Nos. 444-447 (4)	3.75	1.65

The Annunciation A85

Christmas: 10c, Flight into Egypt. 15c, Three Kings. 50c, Shepherds and star. $1, Kings presenting gifts to Christ Child.

1976, Nov. 15		Litho.	Perf. 14	
448	A85	8c multicolored	.20	.20
449	A85	10c multicolored	.20	.20
450	A85	15c multicolored	.20	.20
451	A85	50c multicolored	.20	.20
452	A85	$1 multi	.20	.20
		Nos. 448-452 (5)	1.00	1.00

 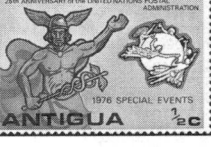

Mercury and UPU Emblem A86

Designs: 1c, Alfred Nobel, symbols of prize categories. 10c, Viking spacecraft. 50c, Vivi Richards (batsman) and Andy Roberts (bowler). $1, Alexander G. Bell, telephones, 1876 and 1976. $2, Schooner Freelance.

1976, Dec. 28		Litho.	Perf. 14	
453	A86	½c multicolored	.20	.20
454	A86	1c multicolored	.20	.20
455	A86	10c multicolored	.25	.20
456	A86	50c multicolored	2.50	1.25
457	A86	$1 multicolored	.75	1.25
458	A86	$2 multicolored	1.75	2.50
a.		Souvenir sheet of 4, #455-458	6.00	8.00
		Nos. 453-458 (6)	5.65	5.60

Special 1976 Events: UN Postal Admin., 25th anniv. (½c); Nobel Prize, 75th anniv. (1c); Viking Space Mission to Mars (10c); World Cricket Cup victory (50c); Telephone cent. ($1); Operation Sail, American Bicent. ($2).

Royal Family — A87

Designs: 30c, Elizabeth II and Prince Philip touring Antigua. 50c, Queen enthroned. 90c, Queen wearing crown. $2.50, Queen and Prince Charles. $5, Queen and Prince Philip.

1977, Feb. 7			Perf. 13½x14	
459	A87	10c multicolored	.20	.20
460	A87	30c multicolored	.20	.20
461	A87	50c multicolored	.20	.20
462	A87	90c multicolored	.20	.20
463	A87	$2.50 multicolored	.20	.40
		Nos. 459-463 (5)	1.00	1.20
		Souvenir Sheet		
464	A87	$5 multicolored	.80	1.00

Reign of Queen Elizabeth II, 25th anniv.
Nos. 459-463 were printed in sheets of 40. Sheets of 5 plus label, perf. 12, probably were not sold by the Antigua Post Office.
A booklet of self-adhesive stamps contains one pane of six rouletted and die cut 50c stamps in design of 90c, and one pane of one die cut 50c. Stamps have changed colors. Panes have marginal inscriptions.
For overprints see Nos. 477-482.

Scouts Camping A88

Boy Scout Emblem and: 1c, Scouts on hike. 2c, Rock climbing. 10c, Cutting logs. 30c, Map and compass reading. 50c, First aid. $2, Scouts on raft.

1977, May 23		Litho.	Perf. 14	
465	A88	½c multicolored	.20	.20
466	A88	1c multicolored	.20	.20
467	A88	2c multicolored	.20	.20
468	A88	10c multicolored	.20	.20
469	A88	30c multicolored	.25	.20
470	A88	50c multicolored	.45	.35
471	A88	$2 multicolored	1.50	1.75
a.		Souvenir sheet of 3, #469-471	2.75	2.75
		Nos. 465-471 (7)	3.00	3.10

Caribbean Boy Scout Jamboree, Jamaica.

Carnival Queen Holding Horseshoe — A89

30c, Carnival Queen in feather costume. 50c, Butterfly costume. 90c, Carnival Queen with ornaments. $1, Carnival King, Queen.

1977, July 18		Litho.	Perf. 14	
472	A89	10c multicolored	.20	.20
473	A89	30c multicolored	.20	.20
474	A89	50c multicolored	.25	.25
475	A89	90c multicolored	.50	.40
476	A89	$1 multicolored	.60	.55
a.		Souvenir sheet of 4, #473-476	1.75	2.25
		Nos. 472-476 (5)	1.75	1.60

21st Summer Carnival.

Nos. 459-464 Overprinted: "ROYAL VISIT / 28th OCTOBER 1977"
Perf. 13½x14, 12

1977, Oct. 17			Litho.	
477	A87	10c multicolored	.20	.20
478	A87	30c multicolored	.20	.20
479	A87	50c multicolored	.20	.20
480	A87	90c multicolored	.40	.40
481	A87	$2.50 multicolored	1.25	1.00
		Nos. 477-481 (5)	2.25	2.00
		Souvenir Sheet		
482	A87	$5 multicolored	3.00	3.25

Visit of Queen Elizabeth II, Oct. 28.

Virgin and Child, by Cosimo Tura — A90

Virgin and Child by: 1c, $2, Carlo Crivelli (different). 2c, 25c, Lorenzo Lotto (different). 8c, Jacopo da Pontormo. 10c, Tura.

1977, Nov. 15		Litho.	Perf. 14	
483	A90	½c multicolored	.20	.20
484	A90	1c multicolored	.20	.20
485	A90	2c multicolored	.20	.20
486	A90	8c multicolored	.20	.20
487	A90	10c multicolored	.20	.20
488	A90	25c multicolored	.20	.20
489	A90	$2 multicolored	1.00	.80
a.		Souvenir sheet of 4, #486-489	1.50	2.00
		Nos. 483-489 (7)	2.20	2.00

Christmas.

Pineapple A91

10th anniv. of Statehood: 15c, Flag of Antigua. 50c, Police band. 90c, Prime Minister V. C. Bird. $2, Coat of Arms.

1977, Dec. 28		Litho.	Perf. 13x13½	
490	A91	10c multicolored	.20	.20
491	A91	15c multicolored	.20	.20
492	A91	50c multicolored	.75	.40
493	A91	90c multicolored	.35	.40
494	A91	$2 multicolored	.50	.60
a.		Souv. sheet, #491-494, perf 14	2.00	1.75
		Nos. 490-494 (5)	2.00	1.80

Wright Glider III, 1902 A92

1c, Flyer I in air, 1903. 2c, Weight and derrick launch system and Wright engine, 1903. 10c, Orville Wright, vert. 50c, Flyer III, 1905. 90c, Wilbur Wright, vert. $2, Wright Model B, 1910. $2.50, Flyer I, 1903, on ground.

1978, Mar. 28			Perf. 14	
495	A92	½c multicolored	.20	.20
496	A92	1c multicolored	.20	.20
497	A92	2c multicolored	.20	.20
498	A92	25c multicolored	.20	.20
499	A92	50c multicolored	.25	.20

500	A92	90c multicolored	.50 .30
501	A92	$2 multicolored	1.10 .90
		Nos. 495-501 (7)	2.65 2.20

Souvenir Sheet

502	A92	$2.50 multicolored	2.00 3.00

1st powered flight by Wright brothers, 75th anniv.

Sunfish Regatta A93

Sailing Week 1978: 50c, Fishing and work boat race. 90c, Curtain Bluff race. $2, Powerboat rally. $2.50, Guadeloupe-Antigua race.

1978, Apr. 29   Litho.   Perf. 14½

503	A93	10c multicolored	.20 .20
504	A93	50c multicolored	.30 .20
505	A93	90c multicolored	.50 .35
506	A93	$2 multicolored	1.10 1.25
		Nos. 503-506 (4)	2.10 2.00

Souvenir Sheet

507	A93	$2.50 multicolored	2.00 2.25

Elizabeth II and Prince Philip — A94

Designs: 30c, Coronation. 50c, State coach. 90c, Elizabth II and Archbishop. $2.50, Elizabeth II. $5, Elizabeth II, Prince Philip, Prince Charles and Princess Anne as children.

1978, June 2   Litho.   Perf. 14, 12

508	A94	10c multicolored	.20 .20
509	A94	30c multicolored	.20 .20
510	A94	50c multicolored	.20 .20
511	A94	90c multicolored	.30 .30
512	A94	$2.50 multicolored	.60 .60
		Nos. 508-512 (5)	1.50 1.50

Souvenir Sheet

513	A94	$5 multicolored	2.00 2.00

25th anniv. of coronation of Queen Elizabeth II.
Nos. 508-512 were printed in sheets of 50 (2 panes of 25), perf. 14, and in sheets of 3 plus label, perf. 12, with frames in changed colors.

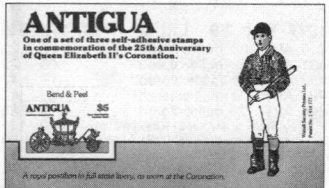

Glass Coach — A95

Royal Coaches: 50c, Irish state coach. $5, Coronation coach.

1978, June 2   Litho.   Imperf.
Self-adhesive

514		Souvenir booklet	2.50
a.	A95	Bklt. pane, 3 each 25c, 50c	1.00
b.	A95	Bklt. pane, 1 $5	1.50

25th anniversary of coronation of Queen Elizabeth II. No. 514 contains 2 booklet panes printed on peelable paper backing showing royal processions.

Soccer — A96

Purple Wreath — A97

Designs: Various soccer scenes. Stamps in souvenir sheet horizontal.

1978, Aug. 18   Litho.   Perf. 15

515	A96	10c multicolored	.20 .20
516	A96	15c multicolored	.20 .20
517	A96	$3 multicolored	2.00 1.75
		Nos. 515-517 (3)	2.40 2.15

Souvenir Sheet

518		Sheet of 4	3.00 2.50
a.	A96	25c multicolored	.20 .20
b.	A96	30c multicolored	.30 .30
c.	A96	50c multicolored	.50 .50
d.	A96	$2 multicolored	2.00 1.75

11th World Cup Soccer Championship, Argentina, June 1-25.

1978, Oct.   Litho.   Perf. 14

519	A97	25c shown	.20 .20
520	A97	50c Sunflowers	.30 .20
521	A97	90c Frangipani	.60 .35
522	A97	$2 Passionflower	1.50 1.25
		Nos. 519-522 (4)	2.60 2.00

Souvenir Sheet

523	A97	$2.50 Red hibiscus	2.00 2.25

St. Ildefonso Receiving Chasuble, by Rubens A98

Christmas: 25c, Flight of St. Barbara, by Rubens. $2, Holy Family, by Sebastiano del Piombo. $4, Annunciation, by Rubens.

1978, Oct. 30   Litho.   Perf. 14

524	A98	8c multicolored	.20 .20
525	A98	25c multicolored	.25 .20
526	A98	80c multicolored	.80 .65
		Nos. 524-526 (3)	1.25 1.05

Souvenir Sheet

527	A98	$4 multicolored	2.50 3.00

Antigua #2 — A99   Crucifixion, by Durer — A100

Designs: 50c, Great Britain Penny Black, 1840. $1, Woman posting letter in pillar box, and coach. $2, Mail train, ship, plane and Concorde. $2.50, Rowland Hill.

1979, Feb. 12   Litho.   Perf. 14

528	A99	25c multicolored	.20 .20
529	A99	50c multicolored	.20 .20
530	A99	$1 multicolored	.40 .25
531	A99	$2 multicolored	.85 .50
		Nos. 528-531 (4)	1.65 1.15

Souvenir Sheet

532	A99	$2.50 multicolored	1.25 1.40

Sir Rowland Hill (1795-1879), originator of penny postage.
Nos. 528-531 were printed in sheets of 50 (2 panes of 25), perf. 14, and in sheets of 5 plus label, perf. 12, with frames in changed colors.
For overprints, see Nos. 571A-571D.

1979, Mar. 15

Designs (after Dürer): 10c, Deposition. $2.50, Crucifixion. $4, Man of Sorrows.

533	A100	10c multicolored	.20 .20
534	A100	50c multicolored	.60 .25
535	A100	$4 multicolored	1.40 1.10
		Nos. 533-535 (3)	2.20 1.55

Souvenir Sheet

536	A100	$2.50 multicolored	1.25 1.25

Easter.

Child Playing with Sailboat — A101

IYC emblem, child's hand holding toy: 50c, Rocket. 90c, Automobile. $2, Train. $5, Plane.

1979, Apr. 9   Litho.   Perf. 14

537	A101	25c multicolored	.20 .20
538	A101	50c multicolored	.25 .20
539	A101	90c multicolored	.50 .35
540	A101	$2 multicolored	1.25 1.10
		Nos. 537-540 (4)	2.20 1.85

Souvenir Sheet

541	A101	$5 multicolored	2.50 2.50

International Year of the Child.

Yellowjacks — A102

Sport Fish: 50c, Bluefin tunas. 90c, Sailfish. $2.50, Barracuda. $3, Wahoos.

1979, May   Litho.   Perf. 14½

542	A102	30c multicolored	.40 .25
543	A102	50c multicolored	.50 .30
544	A102	90c multicolored	.75 .40
545	A102	$3 multicolored	2.25 1.50
		Nos. 542-545 (4)	3.90 2.45

Souvenir Sheet

546	A102	$2.50 multicolored	2.00 1.75

Capt. Cook and his Birthplace at Marton — A103   Holy Family — A104

Capt. James Cook (1728-1779) and: 50c, HMS Endeavour. 90c, Marine timekeeper. $2.50, HMS Resolution. $3, Landing at Botany Bay.

1979, July 2   Litho.   Perf. 14

547	A103	25c multicolored	.40 .30
548	A103	50c multicolored	.50 .40
549	A103	90c multicolored	.50 .55
550	A103	$3 multicolored	1.75 2.50
		Nos. 547-550 (4)	3.15 3.75

Souvenir Sheet

551	A103	$2.50 multicolored	2.50 2.00

1979, Oct. 1   Litho.   Perf. 14

Stained-glass Windows: 25c, Flight into Egypt. 50c, Shepherd and star. $3, Angel with trumpet. $4, Three Kings offering gifts.

552	A104	8c multicolored	.20 .20
553	A104	25c multicolored	.20 .20
554	A104	50c multicolored	.30 .30
555	A104	$4 multicolored	1.10 2.00
		Nos. 552-555 (4)	1.80 2.70

Souvenir Sheet
Perf. 12x12½

556	A104	$3 multicolored	1.50 2.00

Christmas.

Javelin, Olympic Rings — A105

1980, Feb. 7   Litho.   Perf. 14

557	A105	10c shown	.20 .20
558	A105	25c Running	.25 .25
559	A105	$1 Pole vault	.55 .55
560	A105	$2 Hurdles	.75 .75
		Nos. 557-560 (4)	1.75 1.75

Souvenir Sheet

561	A105	$3 Boxing, horiz.	1.00 1.25

22nd Summer Olympic Games, Moscow, July 19-Aug. 3.

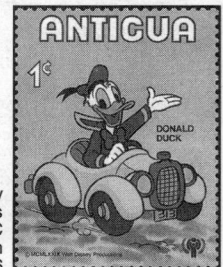

Disney Characters and IYC Emblem A106

Designs: Transportation scenes. ½c, 2c, 3c, 4c, 5c, $1, $2.50, horiz.

1980, Mar. 24   Litho.   Perf. 11

562	A106	½c Mickey, plane	.20 .20
563	A106	1c Donald, car	.20 .20
564	A106	2c Goofy driving taxi	.20 .20
565	A106	3c Mickey, Minnie in sidecar	.20 .20
566	A106	4c Huey, Dewey and Louie	.20 .20
567	A106	5c Grandma Duck	.20 .20
568	A106	10c Mickey in jeep	.20 .20
569	A106	$1 Chip and Dale sailing	1.00 1.25
570	A106	$4 Donald on train	3.50 4.50
		Nos. 562-570 (9)	5.90 7.15

Souvenir Sheet

571	A106	$2.50 Goofy in glider	5.00 4.00

Nos. 528-531 in Changed Colors
Overprinted "LONDON 1980"

1980, May 6   Litho.   Perf. 12

571A	A99	25c multicolored	.20 .20
571B	A99	50c multicolored	.25 .25
571C	A99	$1 multicolored	.45 .45
571D	A99	$2 multicolored	2.10 2.10
		Nos. 571A-571D (4)	3.00 3.00

London '80 Intl. Stamp Exhib., May 6-14.

Birth of Venus, by Botticelli — A106a

10c, David, by Donatello. 50c, Reclining Couple, sarcophagus, Cerveteri. 90c, The Garden of Earthly Delights, by Hieronymus Bosch. $1, Portinari Altarpiece, by Hugo van der Goes. $4, Eleanora of Toledo and her Son Giovanni de Medici, by Bronzino. $5, The Holy Family, by Rembrandt.

Perf. 13½x14, 14x13½
1980, June 23 Litho.
572 A106a 10c multi, vert. .20 .20
573 A106a 30c multi .25 .20
574 A106a 50c multi .35 .30
575 A106a 90c multi .45 .45
576 A106a $1 multi .50 .50
577 A106a $4 multi, vert. 2.75 3.00
Nos. 572-577 (6) 4.50 4.65
Souvenir Sheet
Perf. 14
578 A106a $5 multicolored 3.00 2.50

Anniversary Emblem, Intl.
Headquarters, Evanston, IL — A107

1980, July 21 Litho. **Perf. 14**
579 A107 30c shown .25 .25
580 A107 50c Antigua club banner .30 .35
581 A107 90c Map of Antigua .45 .60
582 A107 $3 Paul. P. Harris, emblem 2.00 2.75
Nos. 579-582 (4) 3.00 3.95
Souvenir Sheet
583 A107 $5 Emblems, Antigua flags 2.25 2.75

Rotary International, 75th anniv.

A108 A109

1980, Sept. 15
584 A108 10c multicolored .20 .20
585 A108 $2.50 multicolored 1.65 2.00
Souvenir Sheet
Perf. 12
586 A108 $3 multicolored 1.75 2.50

Queen Mother Elizabeth, 80th birthday.

1980, Nov. 3 Litho. **Perf. 14**
587 A109 10c Ringed Kingfisher .50 .25
588 A109 30c Plain pigeon .75 .40
589 A109 $1 Green-throated carib 1.00 1.00
590 A109 $2 Black-necked stilt 2.00 2.75
Nos. 587-590 (4) 4.25 4.40
Souvenir Sheet
591 A109 $2.50 Roseate tern 5.75 5.25

Sleeping Beauty and the Prince — A110

Christmas: Various scenes from Walt Disney's Sleeping Beauty. $4 vert.

1980, Dec. 23 **Perf. 11, 13½x14 ($4)**
592 A110 ½c multicolored .20 .20
593 A110 1c multicolored .20 .20
594 A110 2c multicolored .20 .20
595 A110 4c multicolored .20 .20
596 A110 8c multicolored .20 .20
597 A110 10c multicolored .20 .20
598 A110 25c multicolored .25 .25

599 A110 $2 multicolored 1.75 1.75
600 A110 $2.50 multicolored 2.25 2.25
Nos. 592-600 (9) 5.45 5.45
Souvenir Sheet
601 A110 $4 multicolored 5.25 4.50

Sugar-cane Railway Diesel Locomotive No. 15 — A111

1981, Jan. 12 **Perf. 14**
602 A111 25c shown .20 .20
603 A111 50c Narrow-gauge steam locomotive .35 .40
604 A111 90c Diesels #1, #10 .60 .65
605 A111 $3 Hauling sugar-cane 2.00 2.25
Nos. 602-605 (4) 3.15 3.50
Souvenir Sheet
606 A111 $2.50 Sugar factory, train yard 2.50 2.50

Nos. 411-412, 414-422 Overprinted: "INDEPENDENCE 1981"
1981, Mar. 31 Litho.
607 A79 6c multicolored .20 .20
608 A79 10c multicolored .20 .20
609 A79 20c multicolored .20 .20
610 A79 25c multicolored .20 .20
611 A79 35c multicolored .25 .25
612 A79 50c multicolored .45 .45
613 A79 75c multicolored .50 .50
614 A79 $1 multicolored .75 .75
615 A80 $2.50 multicolored 1.25 1.50
616 A80 $5 multicolored 2.25 2.75
617 A80 $10 multicolored 4.50 5.75
Nos. 607-617 (11) 10.75 12.75

Pipes of Pan, by Picasso — A112

Paintings by Pablo Picasso (1881-1973): 50c, Seated Harlequin. 90c, Paulo as Harlequin. $4, Mother and Child. $5, Three Musicians.

1981, May 5 Litho. **Perf. 14**
618 A112 10c multicolored .20 .20
619 A112 50c multicolored .35 .35
620 A112 90c multicolored .60 .60
621 A112 $4 multicolored 2.50 2.50
Nos. 618-621 (4) 3.65 3.65
Souvenir Sheet
Perf. 14x14½
622 A112 $5 multicolored 3.00 3.25

Royal Wedding Issue
Common Design Type
1981, June 16 Litho. **Perf. 14**
623 CD331 25c Couple .20 .20
624 CD331 50c Glamis Castle .20 .20
625 CD331 $4 Charles 1.40 1.40
Nos. 623-625 (3) 1.80 1.80
Souvenir Sheet
626 CD331 $5 Glass coach 2.00 2.00
627 CD331 Booklet 9.00
a. Pane of 6 (2x25c, 2x$1, 2x$2), Charles 3.00
b. Pane of 1, $5, Couple 2.00
No. 627 contains imperf., self-adhesive stamps.
Nos. 623-625 also printed in sheets of 5 plus label, perf. 12 in changed colors.
For surcharges see #792, 795, 802, 805.

Campfire Sing A113

1981, Oct. 28 Litho. **Perf. 15**
628 A113 10c Irene Joshua .20 .20
629 A113 50c shown .30 .25
630 A113 90c Sailing .65 .55
631 A113 $2.50 Milking cow 1.60 1.75
Nos. 628-631 (4) 2.75 2.75
Souvenir Sheet
632 A113 $5 Flag raising 5.00 4.00
Girl Guides, 50th anniv.

A114 A115

1981, Nov. 1 Litho. **Perf. 15**
633 A114 10c Arms .20 .20
634 A114 50c Flag .40 .20
635 A114 90c Prime Minister Bird .50 .45
636 A114 $2.50 St. John's Cathedral, horiz. 1.40 2.25
Nos. 633-636 (4) 2.50 3.10
Souvenir Sheet
637 A114 $5 Map 4.25 3.75
Independence .
No. 637 contains one 41x41mm stamp.

1981, Nov. 16
Christmas (Virgin and Child Paintings by): 8c, Holy Night, by Jacques Stella (1596-1657). 30c Julius Schnorr von Carolfeld (1794-1872). $1, Alonso Cano (1601-1667). $3, Lorenzo de Credi (1459-1537). $5, Holy Family, by Pieter von Avoni (1600-1652).
638 A115 8c multicolored .20 .20
639 A115 30c multicolored .55 .20
640 A115 $1 multicolored 1.10 .85
641 A115 $3 multicolored 1.90 3.50
Nos. 638-641 (4) 3.75 4.75
Souvenir Sheet
642 A115 $5 multicolored 3.75 5.00

Intl. Year of the Disabled A116

1981, Dec. 1 Litho. **Perf. 15**
643 A116 10c Swimming .20 .20
644 A116 50c Discus .25 .30
645 A116 90c Archery .45 .50
646 A116 $2 Baseball 1.10 1.40
Nos. 643-646 (4) 2.00 2.40
Souvenir Sheet
647 A116 $4 Basketball 4.50 2.50

1982 World Cup Soccer A117

Designs: Various soccer players.

1982, Apr. 15 Litho. **Perf. 14**
648 A117 10c multicolored .25 .20
649 A117 50c multicolored .50 .30
650 A117 90c multicolored .95 .65
651 A117 $4 multicolored 3.75 3.25
Nos. 648-651 (4) 5.45 4.40
Souvenir Sheet
652 A117 $5 multicolored 6.50 7.50
Also issued in sheetlets of 5 + label in changed colors, perf. 12.

A118 A119

1982, June 17 Litho. **Perf. 14½**
653 A118 10c A-300 Airbus .20 .20
654 A118 50c Hawker-Siddeley 748 .40 .40
655 A118 90c De Havilland Twin Otter DCH6 .65 .65
656 A118 $2.50 Britten-Norman Islander 1.75 1.75
Nos. 653-656 (4) 3.00 3.00
Souvenir Sheet
657 A118 $5 Jet, horiz. 3.50 4.00
Coolidge Intl. Airport opening.

1982, June 28 Litho. **Perf. 14½**
658 A119 10c Cordia, vert. .20 .20
659 A119 50c Golden spotted mongoose .35 .30
660 A119 90c Corallita, vert. .60 .60
661 A119 $3 Bulldog bats 2.00 3.00
Nos. 658-661 (4) 3.15 4.10
Souvenir Sheet
662 A119 $5 Caribbean monk seals 6.50 7.00
Charles Darwin's death centenary.

Princess Diana Issue
Common Design Type
1982, July 1 Litho. **Perf. 14½x14**
663 CD332 90c Greenwich Palace .90 .90
664 CD332 $1 Wedding 1.00 1.00
665 CD332 $4 Diana 4.00 4.00
Nos. 663-665 (3) 5.90 5.90
Souvenir Sheet
666 CD332 $5 Diana, diff. 5.00 4.75
For overprints and surcharges see Nos. 672-675, 797, 799, 803, 806.

Scouting Year A120

Designs: Independence Day celebration.

1982, July 15 **Perf. 14**
667 A120 10c Decorating buildings .20 .20
668 A120 50c Helping woman .45 .35
669 A120 90c Princess Margaret .75 .65
670 A120 $2.20 Cub Scout giving directions 1.60 2.40
Nos. 667-670 (4) 3.00 3.60
Souvenir Sheet
671 A120 $5 Baden-Powell 5.25 5.00

Nos. 663-666 Overprinted: "ROYAL BABY / 21.6.82"
1982, Aug. 30 Litho. **Perf. 14½x14**
672 CD332 90c multicolored .50 .50
673 CD332 $1 multicolored .60 .60
674 CD332 $4 multicolored 2.40 1.90
Nos. 672-674 (3) 3.50 3.00
Souvenir Sheet
675 CD332 $5 multicolored 3.25 3.25
For surcharges see Nos. 798, 800, 804, 807.

Roosevelt Driving by "The Little White House" A121

1982, Sept. 20 — Perf. 15

676	A121	10c shown	.20	.20
677	A121	25c Washington as blacksmith	.35	.20
678	A121	45c Churchill, Roosevelt, Stalin	.90	.35
679	A121	60c Washington crossing Delaware, vert.	.90	.35
680	A121	$1 Roosevelt on train, vert.	1.25	.90
681	A121	$3 Roosevelt, vert.	1.40	2.50
		Nos. 676-681 (6)	5.00	4.50

Souvenir Sheets

682	A121	$4 Washington, vert.	3.25	3.00
683	A121	$4 Eleanor and Franklin	3.25	3.00

George Washington's 250th birth anniv. and Franklin D. Roosevelt's birth centenary.

Christmas — A122

Raphael Paintings.

1982, Nov. — Litho. — Perf. 14

684	A122	10c Annunciation	.20	.20
685	A122	30c Adoration of the Magi	.20	.20
686	A122	$1 Presentation at the Temple	.55	.55
687	A122	$4 Coronation of the Virgin	2.40	2.40
		Nos. 684-687 (4)	3.35	3.35

Souvenir Sheet

688	A122	$5 Marriage of the Virgin	3.00	2.75

500th Birth Anniv. of Raphael — A123

1983, Jan. 28. — Litho. — Perf. 14½

689	A123	45c Galatea taking Reins of Dolphins, vert.	.25	.30
690	A123	50c Sea Nymphs carried by Tritons, vert.	.35	.40
691	A123	60c Winged Angel Steering Dolphins	.40	.45
692	A123	$4 Cupids Shooting Arrows	2.25	2.60
		Nos. 689-692 (4)	3.25	3.75

Souvenir Sheet

693	A123	$5 Galatea	3.00	3.25

A124

1983, Mar. 14 — Perf. 14

694	A124	25c Pineapple crop	.20	.20
695	A124	45c Carnival	.35	.40
696	A124	60c Tourists, sailboat	.45	.50
697	A124	$3 Control Tower	2.00	2.50
		Nos. 694-697 (4)	3.00	3.60

Commonwealth Day.

World Communications Year — A125

1983, Apr. 5 — Litho. — Perf. 14

698	A125	15c TV screen, camera	.35	.20
699	A125	50c Police radio, car	2.00	1.40
700	A125	60c Long distance phone call	2.00	1.40
701	A125	$3 Dish antenna, planets	4.00	4.50
		Nos. 698-701 (4)	8.35	7.50

Souvenir Sheet

702	A125	$5 Comsat satellite	3.50	4.00

Imperforates
See note following No. 404.

Bottlenose Dolphin A126

1983, May 9 — Litho. — Perf. 15

703	A126	15c shown	.75	.25
704	A126	50c Finback whale	1.60	1.25
705	A126	60c Bowhead whale	1.75	1.25
706	A126	$3 Spectacled porpoise	3.25	4.25
		Nos. 703-706 (4)	7.35	7.00

Souvenir Sheet

707	A126	$5 Unicorn whale	7.50	6.00

Cashew Nut A127

1983, July 11 — Perf. 14

708	A127	1c shown	.20	.45
709	A127	2c Passion fruit	.20	.45
710	A127	3c Mango	.20	.45
711	A127	5c Grapefruit	.20	.35
712	A127	10c Pawpaw	.35	.20
713	A127	15c Breadfruit	.40	.20
714	A127	20c Coconut	.40	.20
715	A127	25c Oleander	.45	.25
716	A127	30c Banana	.50	.30
717	A127	40c Pineapple	.60	.30
718	A127	45c Cordcia	.65	.40
719	A127	50c Cassia	.75	.45
720	A127	60c Poui	1.25	.75
721	A127	$1 Frangipani	1.90	1.25
722	A127	$2 Flamboyant	3.25	3.00
723	A127	$2.50 Lemon	3.75	4.00
724	A127	$5 Lignum vitae	6.00	8.00
725	A127	$10 Arms	9.25	11.50
		Nos. 708-725 (18)	30.30	32.50

1985 — Perf. 12½x12

708a	A127	1c	.20	.45
709a	A127	2c	.20	.45
710a	A127	3c	.20	.45
711a	A127	5c	.25	.35
712a	A127	10c	.30	.20
713a	A127	15c	.40	.20
714a	A127	20c	.50	.20
715a	A127	25c	.50	.20
716a	A127	30c	.60	.25
717a	A127	40c	.65	.25
718a	A127	45c	.70	.35
719a	A127	50c	1.00	.35
720a	A127	60c	1.25	.80
721a	A127	$1	1.90	1.10
722a	A127	$2	3.25	3.00
723a	A127	$2.50	3.75	4.00
724a	A127	$5	6.00	8.00
725a	A127	$10	9.25	11.50
		Nos. 708a-725a (18)	30.90	32.10

Issue dates: $2-$5, Dec; others Mar.

Manned Flight Bicentenary — A128

1983, Aug. 15 — Perf. 15

726	A128	30c Dornier DoX	.80	.30
727	A128	50c Supermarine S-6B	.95	.60
728	A128	60c Curtiss F9C, USS Akron	1.00	.65
729	A128	$4 Pro Juventute balloon	3.25	5.00
		Nos. 726-729 (4)	6.00	6.55

Souvenir Sheet

730	A128	$5 Graf Zeppelin	3.25	3.50

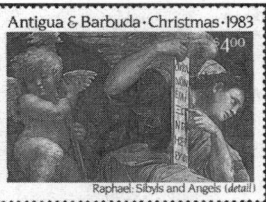

Christmas — A129

Raphael Paintings: 10c, 30c, $1, $4, Sybils and Angels details. $5, Vision of Ezekiel.

1983, Oct. 4 — Litho. — Perf. 14

731	A129	10c Angel flying with scroll	.30	.20
732	A129	30c Angel, diff.	.70	.30
733	A129	$1 Inscribing tablet	1.50	1.25
734	A129	$4 Angel showing tablet	3.25	4.50
		Nos. 731-734 (4)	5.75	6.25

Souvenir Sheet

735	A129	$5 multicolored	2.00	2.50

Methodist Church, Anniv. — A130

1984 Olympics, Los Angeles — A131

Designs: 15c, John Wesley founder of Methodism. 50c, Nathaniel Gilbert, Antiguan founder. 60c, St. John's Methodist Church Steeple. $3, Ebenezer Methodist Church.

1983, Nov. — Litho. — Perf. 14

736	A130	15c multicolored	.30	.20
737	A130	50c multicolored	.85	.45
738	A130	60c multicolored	.95	.60
739	A130	$3 multicolored	2.40	3.75
		Nos. 736-739 (4)	4.50	5.00

1984, Jan. — Litho. — Perf. 15

740	A131	25c Discus	.20	.20
741	A131	50c Gymnastics	.30	.20
742	A131	90c Hurdling	.60	.65
743	A131	$3 Bicycling	2.00	2.25
		Nos. 740-743 (4)	3.10	3.30

Souvenir Sheet

744	A131	$5 Volleyball, horiz.	3.25	4.00

Booker Vanguard A132

1984, June 4 — Litho. — Perf. 15

745	A132	45c shown	1.00	.45
746	A132	50c Canberra	1.25	.70
747	A132	60c Yachts	1.60	.85
748	A132	$4 Fairwind	3.00	6.00
		Nos. 745-748 (4)	6.85	8.00

Souvenir Sheet

749	A132	$5 Man-of-war, vert.	3.25	4.00

Local Flowers A133

US Presidents A134

1984, June 25 — Litho. — Perf. 15

755	A133	15c multicolored	.30	.20
756	A133	50c multicolored	.90	.60
757	A133	60c multicolored	1.00	.90
758	A133	$3 multicolored	2.75	5.50
		Nos. 755-758 (4)	4.95	7.20

Souvenir Sheet

759	A133	$5 multicolored	3.25	3.25

1984, July 18 — Litho. — Perf. 14

760	A134	10c Lincoln	.20	.20
761	A134	20c Truman	.20	.20
762	A134	30c Eisenhower	.25	.25
763	A134	40c Reagan	.45	.45
764	A134	90c Lincoln, diff.	.80	.80
765	A134	$1.10 Truman, diff.	1.10	1.10
766	A134	$1.50 Eisenhower, diff.	1.40	1.40
767	A134	$2 Reagan, diff.	1.50	1.50
		Nos. 760-767 (8)	5.90	5.90

Slavery Abolition Sesquicentennial — A135

1984, Aug. 1

768	A135	40c Moravian Mission	.70	.45
769	A135	50c Antigua Courthouse, 1823	.80	.60
770	A135	60c Sugar cane planting	.85	.70
771	A135	$3 Boiling House, Delaps' Estate	3.50	4.00
		Nos. 768-771 (4)	5.85	5.75

Souvenir Sheet

772	A135	$5 Willoughby Bay	6.00	6.00

Song Birds — A136

1984, Aug. 15 — Perf. 15

773	A136	40c Rufous-sided towhee	1.10	.70
774	A136	50c Parula warbler	1.25	.90
775	A136	60c House wren	1.40	1.25
776	A136	$2 Ruby-crowned kinglet	1.75	3.00
777	A136	$3 Yellow-shafted flicker	2.50	4.00
		Nos. 773-777 (5)	8.00	9.85

Souvenir Sheet

778	A136	$5 Yellow-breasted chat	3.75	5.00

 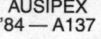

AUSIPEX '84 — A137

The Blue Dancers, by Degas — A137a

1984, Sept. 21 — Perf. 15

779	A137	$1 Grass skiing	1.50	1.50
780	A137	$5 Australian rules football	3.50	5.00

Souvenir Sheet

781	A137	$5 Boomerang	3.50	4.00

1984, Oct. — Litho. — Perf. 15

Paintings by Correggio: 25c, Virgin and Infant with Angels and Cherubs. 60c, The Four Saints. 90c, Saint Catherine. $3, The Campori Madonna. #790, St. John the Baptist.

Paintings by Degas: 50c, The Pink Dancers. 70c, Two Dancers. $4, Dancers at the Bar. #791, Folk Dancers.

782	A137a	15c multicolored	.30	.20
783	A137a	25c multicolored	.35	.20
784	A137a	50c multicolored	.75	.50
785	A137a	60c multicolored	.75	.40
786	A137a	70c multicolored	1.00	.70
787	A137a	90c multicolored	1.00	.75
788	A137a	$3 multicolored	2.00	3.50
789	A137a	$4 multicolored	2.25	3.75
		Nos. 782-789 (8)	8.40	10.00

Souvenir Sheets

790	A137a	$5 multicolored	3.00	3.00
791	A137a	$5 multi, horiz.	3.00	3.00

Nos. 623-626, 663-666, 672-675, 694-697 Surcharged in Black or Gold

1984, June   Perf. 14, 14½x14

792	CD331	$2 on 25c #623	2.75	2.75
793	CD334	$2 on 25c #694	2.10	1.10
794	CD334	$2 on 45c #695	2.10	1.10
795	CD331	$2 on 50c #624	2.75	2.75
796	CD334	$2 on 60c #696	2.10	1.10
797	CD332	$2 on 90c #663 (G)	2.25	2.00
798	CD332	$2 on 90c #672 (G)	2.25	2.00
799	CD332	$2 on $1 #664 (G)	2.25	2.00
800	CD332	$2 on $1 #673 (G)	2.25	2.00
801	CD334	$2 on $3 #697	2.10	1.10
802	CD331	$2 on $4 #625	2.75	2.75
803	CD332	$2 on $4 #665 (G)	2.25	2.00
804	CD332	$2 on $4 #674 (G)	2.25	2.00
		Nos. 792-804 (13)	30.15	24.65

Souvenir Sheets

805	CD331	$2 on $5 #626	3.50	3.50
806	CD332	$2 on $5 #666	3.50	3.50
807	CD332	$2 on $5 #675	3.50	3.50

Nos. 797-800, 803-804 exist with silver surcharge.

Christmas 1984 and 50th Anniv. of Donald Duck A138

Scenes from various Donald Duck comics.

1984, Nov.   Litho.   Perf. 11

808	A138	1c multicolored	.20	.20
809	A138	2c multicolored	.20	.20
810	A138	3c multicolored	.20	.20
811	A138	4c multicolored	.20	.20
812	A138	5c multicolored	.20	.20
813	A138	10c multicolored	.20	.20
814	A138	$1 multicolored	1.50	1.00
815	A138	$2 multicolored	2.25	2.25
816	A138	$5 multicolored	3.25	3.75
		Nos. 808-816 (9)	8.20	8.20

Souvenir Sheets
Perf. 14

817	A138	$5 multi, horiz.	4.50	5.50
818	A138	$5 Donald on beach	4.50	5.50

20th Century Leaders A139

1984, Nov. 19   Litho.   Perf. 15

819	A139	60c John F. Kennedy (1917-1963), vert.	1.00	1.25
820	A139	60c Winston Churchill (1874-1965), vert.	1.00	1.25
821	A139	60c Mahatma Gandhi (1869-1948), vert.	1.00	1.25
822	A139	60c Mao Tse-Tung (1883-1976), vert.	1.00	1.25
823	A139	$1 Kennedy in Berlin	1.25	1.50
824	A139	$1 Churchill in Paris	1.25	1.50
825	A139	$1 Gandhi in Great Britain	1.25	1.50
826	A139	$1 Mao in Peking	1.25	1.50
		Nos. 819-826 (8)	9.00	11.00

Souvenir Sheet

827	A139	$5 Flags of Great Britain, India, China, USA	7.00	4.50

Statue of Liberty Centennial A140

1985, Jan. 7

828	A140	25c Torch on display, 1885	.20	.20
829	A140	30c Restoration, 1984-1986, vert.	.20	.20
830	A140	50c Bartholdi supervising construction, 1876	.30	.30
831	A140	90c Statue on Liberty Island	.50	.50
832	A140	$1 Dedication Ceremony, 1886, vert.	.80	.80
833	A140	$3 Operation Sail, 1976, vert.	1.50	1.75
		Nos. 828-833 (6)	3.50	3.75

Souvenir Sheet

834	A140	$5 Port of New York	3.75	3.75

Traditional Scenes A141

1985, Jan. 21

835	A141	15c Ceramics, Arawak pot shard	.20	.20
836	A141	50c Tatooing, body design	.35	.40
837	A141	60c Harvesting Manioc, god Yocahu	.45	.50
838	A141	$3 Caribs in battle, war club	2.00	2.25
		Nos. 835-838 (4)	3.00	3.35

Souvenir Sheet

839	A141	$5 Tainos worshiping	3.25	3.50

Invention of the Motorcycle, Cent. — A142

1985, Mar. 7   Perf. 14

840	A142	10c Triumph 2HP Jap, 1903	.30	.20
841	A142	30c Indian Arrow, 1949	.50	.25
842	A142	60c BMW R100RS, 1976	.75	.60
843	A142	$4 Harley Davidson Model II, 1916	2.50	3.00
		Nos. 840-843 (4)	4.05	4.05

Souvenir Sheet

844	A142	$5 Laverda Jota, 1975	3.75	4.25

John J. Audubon, 200th Birth Anniv. A143

1985, Mar. 25   Perf. 14

845	A143	90c Horned grebe	.80	.70
846	A143	$1 Least petrel	.90	.75
847	A143	$1.50 Great blue heron	1.10	1.25
848	A143	$3 Double-crested cormorant	1.75	3.00
		Nos. 845-848 (4)	4.55	5.70

Souvenir Sheet

849	A143	$5 White-tailed tropic bird, vert.	3.50	2.75

See Nos.910-914.

Butterflies A144

1985, Apr. 16   Perf. 14

850	A144	25c Polygrapha cyanea	.40	.20
851	A144	60c Leodonta dysoni	1.00	.50
852	A144	90c Junea doraete	1.25	.60
853	A144	$4 Prepona xenagoras	2.75	3.50
		Nos. 850-853 (4)	5.40	4.80

Souvenir Sheet

854	A144	$5 Caerois gerdrudtus	4.25	5.00

Cessna 172 A145

1985, Apr. 30

855	A145	30c shown	.40	.20
856	A145	90c Fokker DVII	.90	.40
857	A145	$1.50 Spad VII	1.25	1.10
858	A145	$3 Boeing 747	1.75	2.50
		Nos. 855-858 (4)	4.30	4.20

Souvenir Sheet

859	A145	$5 Twin Otter, Coolidge Intl. Airport	3.25	4.00

40th anniv. of the ICAO. Nos. 855, 858-859 show the ICAO and UN emblems.

Maimonides (1135-1204), Judaic Philosopher and Physician — A146

1985, June 17   Litho.   Perf. 14

860	A146	$2 yellow green	1.35	1.25

Souvenir Sheet

861	A146	$5 deep brown	3.00	2.00

Intl. Youth Year A147

1985, July 1

862	A147	25c Agriculture	.20	.20
863	A147	50c Hotel management	.25	.30
864	A147	60c Environmental studies	.30	.50
865	A147	$3 Windsurfing	2.25	3.00
		Nos. 862-865 (4)	3.00	4.00

Souvenir Sheet

866	A147	$5 Youths, national flag	3.25	3.50

Queen Mother, 85th Birthday — A148

Designs: 90c, $1, Attending a church service. No. 867A, $1.50, Touring the London Gardens, children in a sandpit. $2.50, $3, Photograph (1979). $5, With Prince Edward at the wedding of Prince Charles and Lady Diana Spencer.

Perf. 14, 12x12½ (90c, $1, $3)

1985, July 15

866A	A148	90c multi ('86)	.65	.65
867	A148	$1 multi	.75	.75
867A	A148	$1 multi ('86)	.75	.75
868	A148	$1.50 multi	1.10	1.10
869	A148	$2.50 multi	1.75	1.75
869A	A148	$3 multi ('86)	2.00	2.00
		Nos. 866A-869A (6)	7.00	7.00

Souvenir Sheet

870	A148	$5 multicolored	3.25	3.25

Nos. 866A, 867A, 869A issued in sheets of 5 plus label on Jan. 13, 1986.

Marine Life — A149

Johann Sebastian Bach — A150

1985, Aug. 1   Perf. 14

871	A149	15c Fregata magnificens	.30	.20
872	A149	45c Diploria labyrinthiformis	.50	.25
873	A149	60c Oreaster reticulatus	.55	.45
874	A149	$3 Gymnothorax moringa	1.75	2.25
		Nos. 871-874 (4)	3.10	3.15

Souvenir Sheet

875	A149	$5 Acropora palmata	3.25	3.25

1985, Aug. 26   Litho.   Perf. 14

876	A150	25c Bass trombone	.30	.20
877	A150	50c English horn	.50	.30
878	A150	$1 Violino piccolo	.65	.35
879	A150	$3 Bass rackett	1.75	1.90
		Nos. 876-879 (4)	3.20	2.75

Souvenir Sheet

880	A150	$5 Portrait	3.25	3.50

Girl Guides, 75th Anniv. A151

Public service and growth-oriented activities.

1985, Sept. 10

881	A151	15c Public service	.40	.20
882	A151	45c Guides meeting	.50	.40
883	A151	60c Lord and Lady Baden-Powell	1.75	2.25
884	A151	$3 Nature study	1.75	2.25
		Nos. 881-884 (4)	3.40	3.35

Souvenir Sheet

885	A151	$5 Barn swallow	3.25	3.25

State Visit of Elizabeth II, Oct. 24 — A152

1985, Oct. 24   Litho.   Perf. 14½

886	A152	60c National flags	.55	.45
887	A152	$1 Elizabeth II, vert.	.75	.75
888	A152	$4 HMY Britannia	2.25	3.00
		Nos. 886-888 (3)	3.55	4.20

Souvenir Sheet

889	A152	$5 Map of Antigua	3.25	3.25

Mark Twain — A153

Disney characters in Roughing It.

1985, Nov. 4 *Perf. 14*
890 A153 25c Cowboys and Indians .30 .20
891 A153 50c Canoeing .50 .30
892 A153 $1.10 Pony Express .90 1.00
893 A153 $1.50 Buffalo hunt in
Missouri 1.10 1.50
894 A153 $2 Nevada silver
mine 1.75 2.25
Nos. 890-894 (5) 4.55 5.25

Souvenir Sheet
895 A153 $5 Stagecoach on
Kansas plains 4.50 4.50

Jacob and Wilhelm Grimm, Fabulists
and Philologists — A154

Disney characters in Spindle, Shuttle and
Needle.

1985, Nov. 11
896 A154 30c multicolored .40 .25
897 A154 60c multicolored .50 .40
898 A154 70c multicolored .60 .45
899 A154 $1 multicolored 1.25 1.10
900 A154 $3 multicolored 2.50 3.00
Nos. 896-900 (5) 5.25 5.20

Souvenir Sheet
900A A154 $5 multicolored 4.50 4.50

UN 40th Anniv. A155

Stamps of UN and portraits: 40c, No. 18 and
Benjamin Franklin. $1, No. 391 and George
Washington Carver, agricultural chemist. $3,
No. 299 and Charles Lindbergh. $5, Marc
Chagall, artist, vert.

1985, Nov. 18 *Perf. 13½x14*
901 A155 40c multicolored .40 .30
902 A155 $1 multicolored .75 .75
903 A155 $3 multicolored 1.75 2.25
Nos. 901-903 (3) 2.90 3.30

Souvenir Sheet
Perf. 14x13½
904 A155 $5 multicolored 3.25 2.50

Christmas — A156

Religious paintings: 10c, Madonna and
Child, by De Landi. 25c, Madonna and Child,
by Bonaventura Berlinghieri (d. 1244). 60c,
The Nativity, by Fra Angelico (1400-1455). $4,
Presentation in the Temple, by Giovanni di
Paolo Grazia (c.1403-1482). $5, The Nativity,
by Antoniazzo Romano.

1985, Dec. 30 *Perf. 15*
905 A156 10c multicolored .20 .20
906 A156 25c multicolored .40 .20
907 A156 60c multicolored .55 .45
908 A156 $4 multicolored 2.00 3.00
Nos. 905-908 (4) 3.15 3.85

Souvenir Sheet
909 A156 $5 multicolored 3.25 3.50

Audubon Type of 1985

Illustrations of North American ducks.

1986, Jan. 6 *Perf. 12½x12*
910 A143 60c Mallard .70 .50
911 A143 90c Dusky duck .80 .65
912 A143 $1.50 Common pintail 1.10 1.50
913 A143 $3 Widgeon 1.50 2.25
Nos. 910-913 (4) 4.10 4.90

Souvenir Sheet
Perf. 14
914 A143 $5 Common eider 3.25 2.50

1986 World Cup Soccer
Championships, Mexico — A157

1986, Mar. 17 *Litho.* *Perf. 14*
915 A157 30c shown .40 .20
916 A157 60c Heading the ball .60 .35
917 A157 $1 Referee .75 .60
918 A157 $4 Goal 2.25 3.00
Nos. 915-918 (4) 4.00 4.15

Souvenir Sheet
919 A157 $5 Action 3.25 2.75
Nos. 916-917 vert.
For overprints see Nos. 963-967.

A158

Halley's Comet — A159

Designs: 5c, Edmond Halley, Greenwich
Observatory. 10c, Me 163B Komet. German
WWII fighter plane. 60c, Montezuma sighting
comet, 1517. $4, Pocahontas saving Capt.
John Smith's life, 1607 sighting as sign for
Powhatan Indians to raid Jamestown. $5,
Comet over Antigua.

1986, Mar. 24
920 A158 5c multicolored .20 .20
921 A158 10c multicolored .20 .20
922 A158 60c multicolored .75 .35
923 A158 $4 multicolored 2.25 2.50
Nos. 920-923 (4) 3.40 3.25

Souvenir Sheet
924 A159 $5 multicolored 3.50 3.50
For overprints see Nos. 973-977.

Queen Elizabeth II, 60th Birthday
Common Design Type

1986, Apr. 21
925 CD339 60c Wedding, 1947 .60 .65
926 CD339 $1 Trooping the col-
or 1.00 1.10
927 CD339 $4 Visiting Scotland 2.75 3.00
Nos. 925-927 (3) 4.35 4.75

Souvenir Sheet
928 CD339 $5 Held by Queen
Mary, 1927 3.50 4.50

Boats — A160

1986, May 15
929 A160 30c Tugboat .25 .20
930 A160 60c Fishing boat .45 .35
931 A160 $1 Sailboat 2056 .75 .60
932 A160 $4 Lateen-rigged sail-
boat 2.50 3.00
Nos. 929-932 (4) 3.95 4.15

Souvenir Sheet
933 A160 $5 Boatbuilding 3.50 4.50

A number of unissued items,
imperfs., part perfs., missing color varieties, etc., were made available when
the Format International inventory was
liquidated. Imperfs of some or all of the
Antigua stamps in the following sets are
included: #405-422, 503-507, 515-517,
703-707, 745-749, 755-759, 808-816,
819-826, 905-909, 934-937.
See footnote after #962.

AMERIPEX '86 — A161

American trains.

1986, May 22 *Perf. 15*
934 A161 25c Hiawatha .50 .20
935 A161 50c Grand Canyon .60 .40
936 A161 $1 Powhattan Arrow .75 .90
937 A161 $3 Empire State 1.50 2.50
Nos. 934-937 (4) 3.35 4.00

Souvenir Sheet
938 A161 $5 Daylight 3.50 5.50

**Wedding of Prince Andrew and
Sarah Ferguson**
Common Design Type

1986, July 23 *Perf. 14*
939 CD340 45c Couple .35 .35
940 CD340 60c Prince Andrew .45 .45
941 CD340 $4 Princes Andrew,
Philip 2.75 3.50
Nos. 939-941 (3) 3.55 4.30

Souvenir Sheet
942 CD340 $5 Couple, diff. 3.25 3.50

Conch Shells — A162

1986, Aug. 6 *Litho.* *Perf. 15*
943 A162 15c Say fly-specked
cerith .25 .20
944 A162 45c Gmelin smooth
scotch bonnet .55 .35
945 A162 60c Linne West Indian
crown conch .65 .65
946 A162 $3 Murex ciboney 2.25 3.50
Nos. 943-946 (4) 3.70 4.70

Souvenir Sheet
947 A162 $5 Atlantic natica 3.50 3.75

Flowers A163

1986, Aug. 25 *Litho.* *Perf. 15*
948 A163 10c Water lily .20 .20
949 A163 15c Queen of the night .20 .20
950 A163 50c Cup of gold .50 .50
951 A163 60c Beach morning
glory .75 .75
952 A163 70c Golden trumpet .85 .85
953 A163 $1 Air plant .90 1.10
954 A163 $3 Purple wreath 1.75 2.50
955 A163 $4 Zephyr lily 2.00 3.25
Nos. 948-955 (8) 7.15 9.35

Souvenir Sheets
956 A163 $4 Dozakie 2.50 3.00
957 A163 $5 Four o'clock 3.25 3.75

Fungi — A164

1986, Sept. 15
958 A164 10c Hygrocybe oc-
cidentalis scarle-
tina .40 .20
959 A164 50c Trogia buccinalis .60 .35
960 A164 $1 Collybia subprui-
nosa .90 .75
961 A164 $4 Leucocoprinus
brebissonii 2.50 2.50
Nos. 958-961 (4) 4.40 3.80

Souvenir Sheet
962 A164 $5 Pyrrhoglossum
pyrrhum 3.50 3.50

An unissued $3 stamp and #961 inscribed
"4$" were made available when the Format
International inventory was liquidated

Nos. 915-919 Ovptd. "WINNERS
Argentina 3 W. Germany 2" in Gold in
2 or 3 lines

1986, Sept. 15 *Perf. 14*
963 A157 30c multicolored .20 .20
964 A157 60c multicolored .30 .45
965 A157 $1 multicolored .75 .75
966 A157 $4 multicolored 2.75 3.00
Nos. 963-966 (4) 4.00 4.40

Souvenir Sheet
967 A157 $5 multicolored 3.25 3.25

Automobile, Cent. — A165

Carl Benz and classic automobiles.

1986, Oct. 20
968 A165 10c 1933 Auburn
Speedster .20 .20
968A A165 15c 1986 Mercury
Sable .20 .20
969 A165 50c 1959 Cadillac .40 .25
970 A165 60c 1950 Studebaker .50 .35
970A A165 70c 1939 Lagonda V-
12 .60 .50
970B A165 $1 1930 Adler Stan-
dard .75 .60
970C A165 $3 1956 DKW 2.00 2.00
971 A165 $4 1936 Mercedes
500K 2.75 2.75
Nos. 968-971 (8) 7.40 6.85

Souvenir Sheets
972 A165 $5 1921 Mercedes
Knight 3.50 3.25
972A A165 $5 1896 Daimler 3.50 3.25

Nos. 920-924 Ovptd. with Halley's Comet Emblem in Black or Silver

1986, Oct. 22   Litho.   *Perf. 14*

973	A158	5c multicolored	.20	.20
974	A158	10c multicolored	.20	.20
975	A158	60c multicolored	.45	.30
976	A158	$4 multicolored	3.00	2.75
		Nos. 973-976 (4)	3.85	3.45

Souvenir Sheet

977	A159	$5 multicolored (S)	3.75	3.75

Christmas — A166

Disney characters as children.

1986, Nov. 4   *Perf. 11*

978	A166	25c Mickey	.30	.25
979	A166	3cc Mickey, Minnie	.35	.30
980	A166	40c Aunt Matilda, Goofy	.40	.35
981	A166	60c Goofy, Pluto	.50	.55
982	A166	70c Pluto, Donald, Daisy	.60	.65
983	A166	$1.50 Stringing popcorn	1.25	2.00
984	A166	$3 Grandma Duck, Minnie	2.25	2.75
985	A166	$4 Donald, Pete	2.75	3.25
		Nos. 978-985 (8)	8.40	10.10

Souvenir Sheets
Perf. 14

986	A166	$5 Playing with presents	3.50	3.50
987	A166	$5 Reindeer	3.50	3.50

Nos. 985 printed in sheets of 8.

Coat of Arms
A167

Natl. Flag
A168

1986, Nov. 25   Litho.   *Perf. 14x14½*

988	A167	10c bright blue	.20	.20
989	A168	25c orange	.25	.25

Marc Chagall (1887-1985), Artist A169

Designs: No. 990, The Profile, 1957. No. 991, Portrait of the Artist's Sister, 1910. No. 992, Bride with Fan, 1911. No. 993, David in Profile, 1914. No. 994, Fiancee with Bouquet, 1977. No. 995, Self-portrait with Brushes, 1909. No. 996, The Walk, 1973. No. 997, Candles, 1938. No. 998, Fall of Icarus, 1975. No. 999, Myth of Orpheus, 1977.

1987, Mar. 30   *Perf. 13½x14*

990	A169	10c multicolored	.20	.20
991	A169	30c multicolored	.25	.20
992	A169	40c multicolored	.30	.30
993	A169	60c multicolored	.35	.35
994	A169	90c multicolored	.60	.60
995	A169	$1 multicolored	.65	.65
996	A169	$3 multicolored	2.00	2.25
997	A169	$4 multicolored	2.75	3.00

Size: 110x95mm
Imperf

998	A169	$5 multicolored	3.25	3.25
999	A169	$5 multicolored	3.25	3.25
		Nos. 990-999 (10)	13.60	14.05

A170

America's Cup — A171

1987, Feb. 5   *Perf. 15*

1000	A170	30c Canada I, 1981	.25	.20
1001	A170	60c Gretel II, 1970	.30	.35
1002	A170	$1 Sceptre, 1958	.70	.75
1003	A170	$3 Vigilant, 1893	1.50	2.25
		Nos. 1000-1003 (4)	2.75	3.55

Souvenir Sheet

1004	A171	$5 Australia II, Liberty, 1983	2.75	3.50

Fish, World Wildlife Fund A172

Marine Birds A173

1987, Feb. 23   Litho.   *Perf. 14*

1005	A172	15c Bridled burrfish	.50	.20
1006	A173	30c Brown noddy	.90	.25
1007	A172	40c Nassau grouper	.65	.30
1008	A173	50c Laughing gull	1.25	.50
1009	A172	60c French angelfish	.90	.50
1010	A172	$1 Porkfish	.90	.60
1011	A173	$2 Royal tern	1.75	1.65
1012	A173	$3 Sooty tern	2.00	2.00
		Nos. 1005-1012 (8)	8.85	6.00

Souvenir Sheets

1013	A172	$5 Banded butterfly fish	5.00	5.00
1014	A173	$5 Brown booby	5.00	5.00

The 30c, 50c, $2, $3 and Nos. 1013-1014 do not picture the WWF emblem. For overprints see Nos. 1137-1139A.

Statue of Liberty, Cent. A174

Photographs by Peter B. Kaplan.

1987, Apr. 20   *Perf. 14*

1015	A174	15c Lee Iacocca	.20	.20
1016	A174	30c Statue at dusk	.25	.25
1017	A174	45c Crown, head	.45	.45
1018	A174	50c Iacocca, torch	.50	.50
1019	A174	60c Crown observatory	.50	.50
1020	A174	90c Interior restoration	.70	.70
1021	A174	$1 Head	.80	.80
1022	A174	$2 Statue at sunset	1.65	1.75
1023	A174	$3 Men on scaffold, flag	1.75	2.50
1024	A174	$5 Statue at night	3.00	4.00
		Nos. 1015-1024 (10)	9.80	11.65

Nos. 1015-1018, 1021-1022, 1024 vert.

A175

Transportation Innovations — A175a

1987, Apr. 19   *Perf. 15*

1025	A175	10c Spirit of Australia, 1978	.20	.20
1026	A175a	15c Siemens' Electric locomotive, 1879	.30	.20
1027	A175	30c USS Triton, 1960	.30	.20
1028	A175a	50c Trevithick, 1801	.35	.30
1029	A175	60c USS New Jersey, 1942	.40	.35
1030	A175a	70c Draisine bicycle, 1818	.40	.40
1031	A175	90c SS United States, 1952	.60	.60
1032	A175a	$1.50 Cierva C-4, 1923	.75	1.50
1033	A175a	$2 Curtiss NC-4, 1919	.90	1.60
1034	A175	$3 Queen Elizabeth II, 1969	1.50	1.75
		Nos. 1025-1034 (10)	5.70	7.10

Reptiles and Amphibians — A176

1987, June 15   *Perf. 14*

1035	A176	30c Eleutherodactylus martinicensis	.35	.20
1036	A176	60c Thecadactylus bapicauda	.50	.45
1037	A176	$1 Anolis bimaculatus leachi	.70	.60
1038	A176	$3 Geochelone carbonaria	1.75	2.25
		Nos. 1035-1038 (4)	3.30	3.50

Souvenir Sheet

1039	A176	$5 Ameiva griswoldi	3.25	3.25

Entertainers A177

1987, May 11

1040	A177	15c Grace Kelly	.30	.20
1041	A177	30c Marilyn Monroe	.60	.25
1042	A177	45c Orson Welles	.30	.20
1043	A177	50c Judy Garland	.30	.20
1044	A177	60c John Lennon	.75	.35
1045	A177	$1 Rock Hudson	.50	.35
1046	A177	$2 John Wayne	.75	.70
1047	A177	$3 Elvis Presley	2.00	1.25
		Nos. 1040-1047 (8)	5.50	3.50

No. 1047 Overprinted

1987, Sept. 9   Litho.   *Perf. 14*

1047A	A177	$3 multicolored	2.50	2.50

1988 Summer Olympics, Seoul A178

1987, Mar. 23

1048	A178	10c Basketball	.20	.20
1049	A178	60c Fencing	.50	.25
1050	A178	$1 Women's gymnastics	.70	.70
1051	A178	$3 Soccer	1.75	2.50
		Nos. 1048-1051 (4)	3.15	3.65

Souvenir Sheet

1052	A178	$5 Boxing glove	3.25	3.50

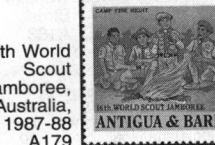

16th World Scout Jamboree, Australia, 1987-88 A179

1987, Nov. 2   Litho.   *Perf. 15*

1053	A179	10c Campfire, red kangaroo	.30	.20
1054	A179	60c Kayaking, blue-winged kookaburra	.75	.45
1055	A179	$1 Obstacle course, ring-tailed rock wallaby	.75	.50
1056	A179	$3 Field kitchen, koalas	1.25	2.25
		Nos. 1053-1056 (4)	3.05	3.40

Souvenir Sheet

1057	A179	$5 Flags	3.25	3.25

US Constitution Bicent. — A180

Designs: 15c, Virginia House of Burgesses exercising right of freedom of speech. 45c, Connecticut state seal. 60c, Delaware state seal. $4, Gouverneur Morris (1752-1816), principal writer of the Constitution, vert. $5, Roger Sherman (1721-1793), jurist and statesman, vert.

1987, Nov. 16   Litho.   *Perf. 14*

1058	A180	15c multicolored	.20	.20
1059	A180	45c multicolored	.25	.30
1060	A180	60c multicolored	.35	.40
1061	A180	$4 multicolored	2.25	2.75
		Nos. 1058-1061 (4)	3.05	3.65

Souvenir Sheet

1062	A180	$5 multicolored	3.25	3.25

A181

A182

Christmas (Paintings): 45c, Madonna and Child, by Bernardo Daddi (1290-1355). 60c, Joseph, detail from The Nativity, by Sano Di Pietro (1406-1481). $1, Mary, detail from Di Pietro's The Nativity. $4, Music-making Angel, by Melozzo Da Forli (1438-1494). $5, The Flight into Egypt, by Di Pietro.

1987, Dec. 1

1063	A181	45c multicolored	.30	.20
1064	A181	60c multicolored	.45	.30
1065	A181	$1 multicolored	.75	.70
1066	A181	$4 multicolored	2.25	3.00
		Nos. 1063-1066 (4)	3.75	4.20

Souvenir Sheet

1067	A181	$5 multicolored	3.25	3.25

1988, Feb. 8   Litho.   **Perf. 14**

1068	A182	25c Wedding portrait	.20	.20
1069	A182	60c Elizabeth II, c. 1970	.45	.50
1070	A182	$2 Christening of Charles, 1948	1.25	1.50
1071	A182	$3 Elizabeth II, c. 1980	1.75	2.00
		Nos. 1068-1071 (4)	3.65	4.20

Souvenir Sheet

1072	A182	$5 Royal family, c. 1951	3.25	3.25

40th wedding anniv. of Queen Elizabeth II and Prince Philip.

Tropical Birds
A183

1988, Mar. 1

1073	A183	10c Great blue heron, vert.	.25	.20
1074	A183	15c Ringed kingfisher	.25	.20
1075	A183	50c Bananaquit	.50	.40
1076	A183	60c Purple gallinule	.50	.45
1077	A183	70c Blue-hooded euphonia	.60	.55
1078	A183	$1 Caribbean parakeet, vert.	.75	.65
1079	A183	$3 Troupial	2.50	2.25
1080	A183	$4 Hummingbird	2.50	3.00
		Nos. 1073-1080 (8)	7.85	7.70

Souvenir Sheets

1081	A183	$5 Roseate flamingo, vert.	3.25	3.25
1082	A183	$5 Brown pelicans, vert.	3.25	3.25

Salvation Army — A184

1988, Mar. 7

1083	A184	25c Day-care, Antigua	.30	.25
1084	A184	30c Penicillin inoculation, Indonesia	.30	.25
1085	A184	40c Day-care Center, Bolivia	.40	.30
1086	A184	45c Rehabilitation, India	.40	.30
1087	A184	50c Training the blind, Kenya	.45	.50
1088	A184	60c Infant care, Ghana	.45	.50
1089	A184	$1 Job training, Zambia	.75	.90
1090	A184	$2 Food distribution, Sri Lanka	1.25	1.75
		Nos. 1083-1090 (8)	4.30	4.75

Souvenir Sheet

1091	A184	$5 General Eva Burrows	3.25	3.25

A185

Discovery of America, 500th Anniv. (in 1992) — A186

Anniv. emblem and: 10c, Fleet. 30c, View of fleet in harbor from Paino Indian village. 45c, Caravel anchored in harbor, Paino village. 60c, Columbus, 3 Indians in canoe. 90c, Indian, parrot, Columbus. $1, Columbus in longboat. $3, Spanish guard, fleet in harbor. $4, Ships under full sail. No. 1100, Stone cross given to Columbus by Queen Isabella. No. 1101, Gold exelente.

1988, Mar. 14   Litho.   **Perf. 14**

1092	A185	10c multicolored	.30	.20
1093	A185	30c multicolored	.30	.20
1094	A185	45c multicolored	.35	.25
1095	A185	60c multicolored	.35	.30
1096	A185	90c multicolored	.70	.50
1097	A185	$1 multicolored	.70	.70
1098	A185	$3 multicolored	1.25	1.25
1099	A185	$4 multicolored	1.50	2.00
		Nos. 1092-1099 (8)	5.45	5.40

Souvenir Sheets

1100	A186	$5 multicolored	3.25	3.25
1101	A186	$5 multicolored	3.25	3.25

Paintings by Titian
A187

Details: 30c, Bust of Christ. 40c, Scourging of Christ. 45c, Madonna in Glory with Saints. 50c, The Averoldi Polyptych. $1, Christ Crowned with Thorns. $2, Christ Mocked. $3, Christ and Simon of Cyrene. $4, Crucifixion with Virgin and Saints. No. 1110, Ecce Homo. No. 1111, Noli Me Tangere.

1988, Apr. 11   Litho.   **Perf. 13½x14**

1102	A187	30c shown	.35	.25
1103	A187	40c multicolored	.40	.30
1104	A187	45c multicolored	.40	.30
1105	A187	50c multicolored	.45	.45
1106	A187	$1 multicolored	.75	.75
1107	A187	$2 multicolored	1.25	1.40
1108	A187	$3 multicolored	2.00	2.25
1109	A187	$4 multicolored	2.25	2.50
		Nos. 1102-1109 (8)	7.85	8.20

Souvenir Sheets

1110	A187	$5 multicolored	3.25	3.75
1111	A187	$5 multicolored	3.25	3.75

Sailing Week
A188

1988, Apr. 18   **Perf. 15**

1112	A188	30c Canada I, 1980	.20	.20
1113	A188	60c Gretel II, Australia, 1970	.50	.55
1114	A188	$1 Sceptre, GB, 1958	.80	.85
1115	A188	$3 Vigilant, US, 1893	1.75	3.00
		Nos. 1112-1115 (4)	3.25	4.60

Souvenir Sheet

1116	A188	$5 Australia II, 1983	3.25	4.25

Walt Disney Animated Characters and Epcot Center, Walt Disney World — A189

1988, May 3   **Perf. 14x13½, 13½x14**

1116A	A189	1c like 25c	.20	.20
1116B	A189	2c like 30c	.20	.20
1116C	A189	3c like 40c	.20	.20
1116D	A189	4c like 60c	.20	.20
1116E	A189	5c like 70c	.20	.20
1116F	A189	10c like $1.50	.20	.20
1117	A189	25c The Living Seas	.20	.20
1118	A189	30c World of Motion	.25	.25
1119	A189	40c Spaceship Earth	.25	.25
1120	A189	60c Universe of Energy	.30	.30
1121	A189	70c Journey to Imagination	.40	.40
1122	A189	$1.50 The Land	1.25	1.25
1123	A189	$3 Communicore	2.25	2.25
1124	A189	$4 Horizons	2.50	2.50
		Nos. 1116A-1124 (14)	8.60	8.60

Souvenir Sheets

1125	A189	$5 Epcot Center	3.50	3.75
1126	A189	$5 The Contemporary Resort Hotel	3.50	3.75

30c, 40c, $1.50, $3 and No. 1126 are vert.

Flowering Trees
A190

A186

1988, May 16   **Perf. 14**

1127	A190	10c Jacaranda	.30	.20
1128	A190	30c Cordia	.35	.25
1129	A190	50c Orchid tree	.50	.50
1130	A190	90c Flamboyant	.60	.60
1131	A190	$1 African tulip tree	.75	.75
1132	A190	$2 Potato tree	1.50	1.75
1133	A190	$3 Crepe myrtle	2.00	2.25
1134	A190	$4 Pitch apple	2.50	3.00
		Nos. 1127-1134 (8)	8.50	9.30

Souvenir Sheets

1135	A190	$5 Cassia	3.25	3.50
1136	A190	$5 Chinaberry	3.25	3.50

Nos. 1135-1136 are continuous designs.

Nos. 1011-1012, 1014 and 1013 Ovptd. in Black for Philatelic Exhibitions

a

b

c

d

1988, May 9   Litho.   **Perf. 14**

1137	A173 (a)	$2 multicolored	1.25	1.50
1138	A173 (b)	$3 multicolored	2.00	2.25

Souvenir Sheets

1139	A173 (c)	$5 multicolored	3.25	3.25
1139A	A172 (d)	$5 multicolored	3.25	3.25

1988 Summer Olympics, Seoul
A192

1988, June 10

1140	A192	40c Gymnastic rings, vert.	.30	.30
1141	A192	60c Weight lifting, vert.	.45	.45
1142	A192	$1 Water polo	.70	.75
1143	A192	$3 Boxing	1.75	2.25
		Nos. 1140-1143 (4)	3.20	3.75

Souvenir Sheet

1144	A192	$5 Torch-bearer, vert.	3.25	3.75

Butterflies
A193

1988-90   Litho.   **Perf. 14**

1145	A193	1c Monarch	.20	.35
1146	A193	2c Jamaican clearwing	.35	.45
1147	A193	3c Yellow-barred ringlet	.35	.45
1148	A193	5c Cracker	.45	.45
1149	A193	10c Jamaican mestra	.55	.25
1150	A193	15c Mimic	.65	.25
1151	A193	20c Silver spot	.70	.25
1152	A193	25c Zebra	.70	.25
1153	A193	30c Fiery sulphur	.70	.25
1154	A193	40c Androgeus swallowtail	.75	.25
1155	A193	45c Giant brimstone	.75	.25
1156	A193	50c Orbed sulphur	.80	.45
1157	A193	60c Blue-backed skipper	.90	.50
1158	A193	$1 Common white skipper	1.40	.85
1159	A193	$2 Baracoa skipper	2.50	2.75
1160	A193	$2.50 Mangrove skipper	3.00	3.50
1161	A193	$5 Silver king	4.50	5.00
1161A	A193	$10 Pygmy skipper	6.25	7.50
1162	A193	$20 Parides lycimenes	12.50	13.50
		Nos. 1145-1162 (19)	38.00	37.50

Issued: $20, Feb. 19, 1990; others, Aug. 29.

John F. Kennedy
A194

1988, Nov. 22		**Litho.**	**Perf. 14**	
1162A	A194	1c like 30c	.20	.20
1162B	A194	2c like $4	.20	.20
1162C	A194	3c like $1	.20	.20
1162D	A194	4c like 60c	.20	.20
1163	A194	30c First family	.25	.20
1164	A194	60c Motorcade, Mexico	.45	.40
1165	A194	$1 Funeral procession	.70	.70
1166	A194	$4 Aboard PT109	2.25	2.50
		Nos. 1162A-1166 (8)	4.45	4.60

Souvenir Sheet

1167	A194	$5 Taking Oath of Office	3.25	3.75

Miniature Sheet

Christmas, Mickey Mouse 60th Anniv. — A195

Walt Disney characters - #1168: a, Morty and Ferdie. b, Goofy. c, Chip-n-Dale. d, Huey and Dewey. e, Minnie Mouse. f, Pluto. g, Mickey Mouse. h, Donald Duck and Louie.
No. 1169, Goofy driving Mickey and Minnie in a horse-drawn carriage. No. 1170, Characters on roller skates, caroling.

1988, Dec. 1		**Perf. 13½x14, 14x13½**		
1168	A195	Sheet of 8	6.00	6.00
a.-h.		$1 any single	.75	.75

Souvenir Sheets

1169	A195	$7 multicolored	5.00	5.00
1170	A195	$7 multi, horiz.	5.00	5.00

1988, Dec. 1		**Litho.**	**Perf. 14**	
1171	A195	10c like No. 1168e	.20	.20
1172	A195	25c like No. 1168f	.20	.20
1173	A195	30c like No. 1168g	.25	.25
1174	A195	70c like No. 1168h	.50	.50
		Nos. 1171-1174 (4)	1.15	1.15

Arawak Indian Whip Dance — A196

UPAE and discovery of America emblems and: a, Five adults. b, Eight adults. c, Seven adults. d, Three adults, three children.

1989, May 16		**Litho.**	**Perf. 14**	
1175		Strip of 4	4.50	4.50
a.-d.	A196	$1.50 any single	1.10	1.10

Souvenir Sheet

1176	A196	$6 Arawak chief	4.50	4.50

Discovery of America 500th anniv. (in 1992), pre-Columbian societies and customs.

Jet Flight, 50th Anniv. A197

Various jet aircraft.

1989, May 29		**Litho.**	**Perf. 14x13½**	
1177	A197	10c DeHavilland Comet 4	.20	.20
1178	A197	30c Messerschmitt Me262	.25	.20
1179	A197	40c Boeing 707	.25	.30
1180	A197	60c Canadair F-86 Sabre	.30	.25
1181	A197	$1 Lockheed F-104 Starfighter	.40	.35
1182	A197	$2 McDonnell Douglas DC-10	.80	1.00

1183	A197	$3 Boeing 747	1.00	1.10
1184	A197	$4 McDonnell F-4 Phantom	1.00	1.10
		Nos. 1177-1184 (8)	4.20	4.50

Souvenir Sheets

1185	A197	$7 Grumman F-14 Tomcat	4.75	5.00
1186	A197	$7 Concorde	4.75	5.00

Caribbean Cruise Ships A198

1989, June 20		**Litho.**	**Perf. 14**	
1187	A198	25c TSS Festivale	.20	.20
1188	A198	45c M.S. Southward	.30	.20
1189	A198	50c M.S. Sagafjord	.40	.20
1190	A198	60c MTS Daphne	.45	.30
1191	A198	75c M.V. Cunard Countess	.55	.45
1192	A198	90c M.S. Song of America	.70	.65
1193	A198	$3 M.S. Island Princess	2.00	2.25
1194	A198	$4 S.S. Galileo	2.00	2.25
		Nos. 1187-1194 (8)	6.60	6.50

Souvenir Sheets

1195	A198	$6 S.S. Norway	4.25	4.75
1196	A198	$6 S.S. Oceanic	4.25	4.75

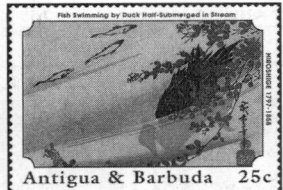

Paintings by Hiroshige — A199

Designs: 25c, Fish Swimming by Duck Half-submerged in Stream. 45c, Crane and Wave. 50c, Sparrows and Morning Glories. 60c, Crested Blackbird and Flowering Cherry. $1, Great Knot Sitting among Water Grass. $2, Goose on a Bank of Water. $3, Black Paradise Flycatcher and Blossoms. $4, Sleepy Owl Perched on a Pine Branch. No. 1205, Bullfinch Flying Near a Clematis Branch. No. 1206, Titmouse on a Cherry Branch.

1989, July 3		**Perf. 14x13½**		
1197	A199	25c multicolored	.45	.20
1198	A199	45c multicolored	.55	.35
1199	A199	50c multicolored	.60	.35
1200	A199	60c multicolored	.70	.45
1201	A199	$1 multicolored	.80	.60
1202	A199	$2 multicolored	1.75	1.75
1203	A199	$3 multicolored	2.00	2.00
1204	A199	$4 multicolored	2.00	2.00
		Nos. 1197-1204 (8)	8.85	7.70

Souvenir Sheets

1205	A199	$5 multicolored	3.25	3.25
1206	A199	$5 multicolored	3.25	3.25

Hirohito (1901-1989) and enthronement of Akihito as emperor of Japan.

PHILEXFRANCE '89 — A200

Walt Disney characters, French landmarks: 1c, Helicopter over the Seine. 2c, Arc de Triomphe. 3c, Painting Notre Dame Cathedral. 4c, Entrance to the Metro. 5c, Fashion show. 10c, Follies. No. 1213, Shopping stalls on the Seine. $6, Sidewalk cafe, Left Bank. No. 1215, Hot air balloon Ear Force One. No. 1216, Dining.

1989, July 7		**Perf. 14x13½**		
1207	A200	1c multicolored	.20	.20
1208	A200	2c multicolored	.20	.20
1209	A200	3c multicolored	.20	.20
1210	A200	4c multicolored	.20	.20
1211	A200	5c multicolored	.20	.20
1212	A200	10c multicolored	.20	.20

1213	A200	$5 multicolored	3.25	3.75
1214	A200	$6 multicolored	3.75	4.00
		Nos. 1207-1214 (8)	8.20	8.95

Souvenir Sheets

1215	A200	$5 multicolored	3.25	3.25
1216	A200	$5 multicolored	3.25	3.25

1990 World Cup Soccer Championships, Italy — A201

Natl. flag, various actions of a defending goalie.

1989, Aug. 21		**Perf. 14**		
1217	A201	15c multicolored	.45	.20
1218	A201	25c multicolored	.50	.20
1219	A201	$1 multicolored	1.00	.75
1220	A201	$4 multicolored	2.00	3.50
		Nos. 1217-1220 (4)	3.95	4.65

Souvenir Sheets

1221	A201	$5 2 players, horiz.	3.25	3.50
1222	A201	$5 3 players, horiz.	3.25	3.50

For overprints see Nos. 1344-1349.

Mushrooms — A202

1989, Oct. 12		**Litho.**	**Perf. 14**	
1223	A202	10c Lilac fairy helmet	.20	.20
1224	A202	25c Rough psathyrella, vert.	.25	.20
1225	A202	50c Golden tops	.60	.40
1226	A202	60c Blue cap, vert.	.60	.45
1227	A202	75c Brown cap, vert.	.75	.55
1228	A202	$1 Green gill, vert.	1.00	.75
1229	A202	$3 Red pinwheel	2.00	2.50
1230	A202	$4 Red chanterelle	2.00	2.50
		Nos. 1223-1230 (8)	7.40	7.55

Souvenir Sheets

1231	A202	$6 Slender stalk	4.25	4.00
1232	A202	$6 Paddy straw mushroom	4.25	4.00

Nos. 1224, 1226-1228, 1231 vert.

Wildlife A203

1989, Oct. 19		**Litho.**	**Perf. 14**	
1233	A203	25c Hutia	.30	.25
1234	A203	45c Caribbean monk seal	.75	.40
1235	A203	60c Mustache bat, vert.	.50	.45
1236	A203	$4 Manatee, vert.	1.50	2.25
		Nos. 1233-1236 (4)	3.05	3.35

Souvenir Sheet

1237	A203	$5 West Indies giant rice rat	3.25	3.75

American Philatelic Soc. Emblem, Stamps on Stamps and Walt Disney Characters Promoting Philately A204

Designs: 1c, Israel #150, printing press. 2c, Italy #1238, first day cancel. 3c, US #143L4,

Pony Express recruits. 4c, Denmark #566, early radio broadcast. 5c, German Democratic Republic #702, television. 10c, Great Britain #1, stamp collector. $4, Japan #1414, integrated circuits. $6, Germany #B667, boom box. No. 1246, US #1355, C3a, and Jenny biplane over Disneyland, horiz. No. 1247, US #940, 1421 and stamps for the wounded.

1989, Nov. 2		**Perf. 13½x14, 14x13½**		
1238	A204	1c multicolored	.20	.20
1239	A204	2c multicolored	.20	.20
1240	A204	3c multicolored	.20	.20
1241	A204	4c multicolored	.20	.20
1242	A204	5c multicolored	.20	.20
1243	A204	10c multicolored	.20	.20
1244	A204	$4 multicolored	3.00	3.25
1245	A204	$6 multicolored	4.00	4.25
		Nos. 1238-1245 (8)	8.20	8.70

Souvenir Sheets

1246	A204	$5 multicolored	3.50	3.75
1247	A204	$5 multicolored	3.50	3.75

Locomotives and Walt Disney Characters — A205

		Perf. 14x13½, 13½x14		
1989, Nov. 17				
1248	A205	25c John Bull, 1831	.50	.50
1249	A205	45c Atlantic, 1832	.60	.50
1250	A205	50c William Crook's, 1861	.60	.50
1251	A205	60c Minnetonka, 1869	.70	.65
1252	A205	$1 Thatcher Perkins, 1863	.75	.75
1253	A205	$2 Pioneer, 1848	1.50	2.00
1254	A205	$3 Peppersass, 1869	1.75	2.50
1255	A205	$4 Gimbels Flyer	2.00	2.50
		Nos. 1248-1255 (8)	8.40	9.90

Souvenir Sheets

1256	A205	$6 #6100 Class S-1 & 1835 Thomas Jefferson	4.25	4.50
1257	A205	$6 Jupiter & #119	4.25	4.50

New York World's Fair, 50th anniv., and World Stamp Expo '89, Washington, DC.

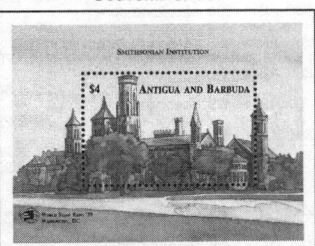

1st Moon Landing, 20th Anniv. A206

1989, Nov. 24		**Litho.**	**Perf. 14**	
1258	A206	10c Apollo 11 liftoff	.20	.20
1259	A206	45c Aldrin walking on Moon	.35	.20
1260	A206	$1 Eagle ascending from Moon	.70	.60
1261	A206	$4 Recovery after splashdown	2.75	3.25
		Nos. 1258-1261 (4)	4.00	4.25

Souvenir Sheet

1262	A206	$5 Armstrong	3.50	3.75

Nos. 1258-1259 and 1262, vert.

Souvenir Sheet

Smithsonian Institution, Washington, DC — A207

1989, Nov. 17		**Litho.**	**Perf. 14**	
1263	A207	$4 multicolored	3.00	3.00

World Stamp Expo '89.

Christmas — A208

Religious paintings: 10c, *The Small Cowper Madonna.* 25c, *Madonna of the Goldfinch.* 30c, *The Alba Madonna.* 50c, *Bologna Altarpiece* (attendant). 60c, *Bologna Altarpiece* (heralding angel). 70c, *Bologna Altarpiece* (archangel). $4, *Bologna Altarpiece* (saint holding ledger). No. 1271, *Madonna of Foligno.* No. 1272, *The Marriage of the Virgin.* No. 1273, *Bologna Altarpiece* (Madonna and Child).
Bologna Altarpiece by Giotto. Other paintings by Raphael.

1989, Dec. 11   Litho.   Perf. 14

1264	A208	10c multicolored	.20	.20
1265	A208	25c multicolored	.20	.20
1266	A208	30c multicolored	.20	.20
1267	A208	50c multicolored	.45	.35
1268	A208	60c multicolored	.50	.40
1269	A208	70c multicolored	.55	.45
1270	A208	$4 multicolored	2.75	3.00
1271	A208	$5 multicolored	3.50	4.00
		Nos. 1264-1271 (8)	8.35	8.80

Souvenir Sheets

1272	A208	$5 multicolored	3.50	4.00
1273	A208	$5 multicolored	3.50	4.00

America Issue — A210

Orchids — A211

UPAE, discovery of America 500th anniv. emblems and marine life: 10c, Star-eyed hermit crab. 20c, Spiny lobster. 25c, Magnificent banded fanworm. 45c, Cannonball jellyfish. 60c, Red-spiny sea star. $2, Peppermint shrimp. $3, Coral crab. $4, Branching fire coral. No. 1283, Common sea fan. No. 1284, Portuguese man-of-war.

1990, Mar. 26   Litho.   Perf. 14

1275	A210	10c multicolored	.20	.20
1276	A210	20c multicolored	.20	.20
1277	A210	25c multicolored	.25	.25
1278	A210	45c multicolored	.45	.45
1279	A210	60c multicolored	.70	.70
1280	A210	$2 multicolored	1.75	2.00
1281	A210	$3 multicolored	2.00	2.25
1282	A210	$4 multicolored	2.50	2.75
		Nos. 1275-1282 (8)	8.05	8.80

Souvenir Sheets

1283	A210	$5 multicolored	3.50	4.00
1284	A210	$5 multicolored	3.50	4.00

1990, Apr. 17   Perf. 14

1285	A211	15c *Vanilla mexicana*	.35	.25
1286	A211	45c *Epidendrum ibaguense*	.50	.25
1287	A211	50c *Epidendrum secundum*	.55	.30
1288	A211	60c *Maxillaria conferta*	.60	.35
1289	A211	$1 *Oncidium altissimum*	.90	.70
1290	A211	$2 *Spiranthes lanceolata*	1.25	1.50
1291	A211	$3 *Tonopsis utricularioides*	1.75	2.25
1292	A211	$5 *Epidendrum nocturnum*	3.50	3.75
		Nos. 1285-1292 (8)	9.40	9.35

Souvenir Sheets

1293	A211	$6 *Octomeria graminifolia*	4.00	4.50
1294	A211	$6 *Rodriguezia lanceolata*	4.00	4.50

EXPO '90, Osaka.

Fish A212

1990, May 21   Perf. 14

1295	A212	10c Flamefish	.35	.35
1296	A212	15c Coney	.40	.35
1297	A212	50c Squirrelfish	.60	.45
1298	A212	60c Sergeant major	.60	.45
1299	A212	$1 Yellowtail snapper	.85	.65
1300	A212	$2 Rock beauty	1.50	1.75
1301	A212	$3 Spanish hogfish	2.00	2.25
1302	A212	$4 Striped parrotfish	2.00	2.25
		Nos. 1295-1302 (8)	8.30	8.50

Souvenir sheets

1303	A212	$5 Blackbar soldierfish	3.50	4.00
1304	A212	$5 Foureye butterflyfish	3.50	4.00

Victoria and Elizabeth II — A213

1990, May 3   Litho.   Perf. 15x14

1305	A213	45c green	.60	.30
1306	A213	60c bright rose	.70	.50
1307	A213	$5 bright ultra	3.25	4.00
		Nos. 1305-1307 (3)	4.55	4.80

Souvenir Sheet

1308	A213	$6 black	4.25	4.75

Penny Black, 150th anniv.

Royal Mail Transport A214

Designs: 50c, Steam packet *Britannia,* 1840. 75c, Railway mail car, 1892. $4, *Centaurus* seaplane, 1938. $6, Subway, 1927.

1990, May 3   Perf. 13½

1309	A214	50c red & deep green	.55	.30
1310	A214	75c red & vio brn	.75	.70
1311	A214	$4 red & brt ultra	3.00	3.75
		Nos. 1309-1311 (3)	4.30	4.75

Souvenir Sheet

1312	A214	$6 red & black	4.25	4.75

Stamp World London '90.

Miniature Sheet

Space Achievements — A215

Designs: a, *Voyager 2* passing Saturn. b, *Pioneer 11* photographing Saturn. c, Manned maneuvering unit. d, *Columbia* space shuttle. e, Splashdown of Apollo 10 command module. f, *Skylab.* g, Ed White space walking, Gemini 4 mission. h, Apollo module, Apollo-Soyuz mission. i, Soyuz module, Apollo-Soyuz mission. j, *Mariner 1* passing Venus. k, Gemini 4 module. l, *Sputnik.* m, Hubble Space Telescope. n, X-15 rocket plane. o, Bell X-1 breaking sound barrier. p, Astronaut, Apollo 17 mission. r, American lunar rover. r, Lunar module, Apollo 14 mission. s, First men on the Moon, Apollo 11 mission. t, Lunokhod, Soviet lunar rover.

1990, June 11   Litho.   Perf. 14

1313	A215	Sheet of 20	6.75	6.75
a.-t.		45c any single	.30	.30

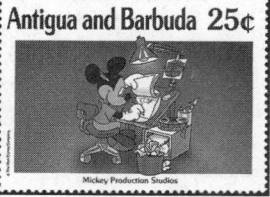

Mickey Production Studios — A216

Walt Disney characters in Hollywood: 45c, Minnie Mouse reading script. 50c, Director Mickey Mouse, take 1 of Minnie. 60c, Make-up artist Daisy Duck. $1, Clarabelle as Cleopatra. $2, Mickey, Goofy, Donald Duck. $3, Goofy destroying set. $4, Mickey, Donald editing film. No. 1323, Minnie, Daisy, Clarabelle in musical.

1990, Sept. 3   Litho.   Perf. 14x13½

1314	A216	25c shown	.25	.20
1315	A216	45c multicolored	.45	.20
1316	A216	50c multicolored	.55	.25
1317	A216	60c multicolored	.60	.30
1318	A216	$1 multicolored	.80	.60
1319	A216	$2 multicolored	1.50	1.75
1320	A216	$3 multicolored	2.00	2.25
1321	A216	$4 multicolored	2.00	2.25
		Nos. 1314-1321 (8)	8.15	7.80

Souvenir Sheets

1322	A216	$5 multicolored	3.50	3.50
1323	A216	$5 multicolored	3.50	3.50

A217   A218

1990, Aug. 27   Litho.   Perf. 14

1324	A217	15c multicolored	.20	.20
1325	A217	35c multi, diff.	.30	.20
1326	A217	75c multi, diff.	.55	.55
1327	A217	$3 multi, diff.	2.00	2.50
		Nos. 1324-1327 (4)	3.05	3.45

Souvenir Sheet

1328	A217	$6 multi, diff.	4.00	4.50

Queen Mother, 90th birthday.

1990, Oct. 1   Litho.   Perf. 14

1329	A218	50c 20-Kilometer Walk	.55	.30
1330	A218	75c Triple jump	.70	.65
1331	A218	$1 10,000 meter run	.90	.85
1332	A218	$5 Javelin	3.00	4.25
		Nos. 1329-1332 (4)	5.15	6.05

Souvenir Sheet

1333	A218	$6 Opening ceremony, Los Angeles, 1984	4.25	5.50

1992 Summer Olympics, Barcelona.

Intl. Literacy Year — A219

Walt Disney characters in scenes from books by Charles Dickens: 15c, Huey and Dewey, Christmas Stories. 45c, Donald Duck, Bleak House. 50c, Dewey, Bad Pete, Oliver Twist. 60c, Daisy Duck, Old Curiosity Shop. $1, Little Nell. $2, Scrooge McDuck, Pickwick Papers. $3, Mickey and Minnie Mouse, Dombey and Son. $5, Minnie, Our Mutual Friend. No. 1342, Mickey and friends, David Copperfield. No. 1343, Pinocchio, Oliver Twist.

1990, Oct. 15   Litho.   Perf. 14

1334	A219	15c multicolored	.20	.20
1335	A219	45c multicolored	.35	.35
1336	A219	50c multicolored	.40	.40
1337	A219	60c multicolored	.45	.45
1338	A219	$1 multicolored	.70	.70
1339	A219	$2 multicolored	1.25	1.75
1340	A219	$3 multicolored	1.75	2.25
1341	A219	$5 multicolored	2.50	3.00
		Nos. 1334-1341 (8)	7.60	9.10

Souvenir Sheets

1342	A219	$6 multicolored	4.25	4.50
1343	A219	$6 multicolored	4.25	4.50

Nos. 1217-1222 Overprinted

Winners West Germany 1 Argentina 0

1990, Nov. 11

1344	A201	15c multicolored	.40	.20
1345	A201	25c multicolored	.40	.20
1346	A201	$1 multicolored	1.00	1.00
1347	A201	$4 multicolored	2.50	3.25
		Nos. 1344-1347 (4)	4.30	4.65

Souvenir Sheets

1348	A201	$5 on #1221	3.50	3.75
1349	A201	$5 on #1222	3.50	3.75

Overprint on Nos. 1348-1349 is 32x13mm.

Birds A220

1990, Nov. 19

1350	A220	10c Pearly-eyed thrasher	.30	.30
1351	A220	25c Purple-throated carib	.35	.35
1352	A220	50c Common yellow-throat	.40	.40
1353	A220	60c American kestrel	.70	.70
1354	A220	$1 Yellow-bellied sapsucker	.75	.75
1355	A220	$3 Purple gallinule	1.75	2.00
1356	A220	$3 Yellow-crowned night heron	2.25	2.50
1357	A220	$4 Blue-hooded euphonia	2.25	2.50
		Nos. 1350-1357 (8)	8.75	9.50

Souvenir Sheets

1358	A220	$6 Brown pelican	4.25	4.75
1359	A220	$6 Frigate bird	4.25	4.75

Christmas — A221

Paintings: 25c, Madonna and Child with Saints by del Piombo. 30c, Virgin and Child with Angels by Grunewald, vert. 40c, Holy Family and a Shepherd by Titian. 60c, Virgin and Child by Fra Filippo Lippi, vert. $1, Jesus, St. John and Two Angels by Rubens. $2, Adoration of the Shepherds by Catena. $4, Adoration of the Magi by Giorgione. $5, Virgin and Child Adored by a Warrior by Catena. No. 1368, Allegory of the Blessings of Jacob by Rubens, vert. No. 1369, Adoration of the Magi by Fra Angelico, vert.

Perf. 14x13½, 13½x14

1990, Dec. 10   Litho.

1360	A221	25c multicolored	.25	.20
1361	A221	30c multicolored	.30	.20
1362	A221	40c multicolored	.40	.25
1363	A221	60c multicolored	.55	.35
1364	A221	$1 multicolored	.75	.60

1365	A221	$2 multicolored	1.60	1.75
1366	A221	$4 multicolored	2.75	3.00
1367	A221	$5 multicolored	2.75	3.00
		Nos. 1360-1367 (8)	9.35	9.35

Souvenir Sheets

1368	A221	$6 multicolored	4.25	4.50
1369	A221	$6 multicolored	4.25	4.50

Peter Paul Rubens (1577-1640),
Painter — A222

Entire paintings or different details from: 25c, Rape of the Daughters of Leucippus. 45c, $2, $4, Bacchanal. 50c, $1, $3, Rape of the Sabine Women. 60c, Battle of the Amazons. No. 1378, Rape of Hippodameia. No. 1379, Battle of the Amazons.

1991, Jan. 21　　Litho.　　Perf. 14

1370	A222	25c multicolored	.45	.30
1371	A222	45c multicolored	.65	.45
1372	A222	50c multicolored	.70	.50
1373	A222	60c multicolored	.75	.65
1374	A222	$1 multicolored	.90	.90
1375	A222	$2 multicolored	1.25	1.50
1376	A222	$3 multicolored	2.00	2.25
1377	A222	$4 multicolored	2.75	3.00
		Nos. 1370-1377 (8)	9.45	9.55

Souvenir Sheets

1378	A222	$6 multicolored	4.25	4.50
1379	A222	$6 multicolored	4.25	4.50

World War II Milestones A223

Designs: 10c, US troops enter Germany, Sept. 11, 1944. 15c, All axis forces surrender in North Africa, May 12, 1943. 25c, US troops invade Kwajalein, Jan. 31, 1944. 45c, Roosevelt and Churchill meet in Casablanca, Jan. 14, 1943. 50c, Marshal Badoglio signs agreement with allies, Sept. 1, 1943. $1, Mountbatten appointed Supreme Allied Commander, Southeast Asia Command, Aug. 25, 1943. $2, Major Greek tactical victory, Koritza, Nov. 22, 1940. $4, Britain and USSR sign mutual assistance pact, July 12, 1941. $5, Operation Torch, Nov. 8, 1942. No. 1389, Japanese attack on Pearl Harbor, Dec. 7, 1941. No. 1390, American bombing attack on Schweinfurt, Oct. 14, 1943.

1991, Mar. 11　　Litho.　　Perf. 14

1380	A223	10c multicolored	.25	.25
1381	A223	15c multicolored	.30	.20
1382	A223	25c multicolored	.35	.35
1383	A223	45c multicolored	.70	.50
1384	A223	50c multicolored	.60	.45
1385	A223	$1 multicolored	.75	.65
1386	A223	$2 multicolored	1.50	1.75
1387	A223	$4 multicolored	2.25	2.50
1388	A223	$5 multicolored	2.25	2.50
		Nos. 1380-1388 (9)	8.95	9.15

Souvenir Sheets

1389	A223	$6 multicolored	4.25	4.50
1390	A223	$6 multicolored	4.25	4.50

Cog Railways of the World A224

Designs: 25c, Prince Regent, Middleton Colliery, 1812. 30c, Snowdon Mountain Railway, Wales. 40c, 1st Railcar at Hell Gate, Manitou and Pike's Peak Railway. 60c, PNKA Rack Railway, Amberawa, Java. $1, Green Mountain Railway, Mt. Desert Island, Maine, 1883. $2, Cog locomotive, Pike's Peak, 1891. $4, Vitznau-Rigi Cog Railway, Lake Lucerne. $5, Leopoldina Railway, Brazil. No. 1399, Electric Cog Donkey Engines, Panama Canal. No. 1400, Gornergratbahn, 1st electric cog railway in Switzerland, vert.

1991, Mar. 18　　Litho.　　Perf. 14

1391	A224	25c multicolored	.20	.20
1392	A224	30c multicolored	.25	.25
1393	A224	40c multicolored	.30	.30
1394	A224	60c multicolored	.45	.45
1395	A224	$1 multicolored	1.00	.75
1396	A224	$2 multicolored	1.75	1.50
1397	A224	$4 multicolored	3.00	3.00
1398	A224	$5 multicolored	3.00	3.75
		Nos. 1391-1398 (8)	9.95	10.20

Souvenir Sheets

1399	A224	$6 multicolored	4.25	4.25
1400	A224	$6 multicolored	4.25	4.25

Butterflies A225

1991, Apr. 15　　Litho.　　Perf. 14

1401	A225	10c Zebra	.20	.20
1402	A225	35c Southern daggertail	.25	.25
1403	A225	50c Red anartia	.40	.40
1404	A225	75c Malachite	.55	.55
1405	A225	$1 Polydamas swallowtail	.70	.75
1406	A225	$2 Orion	1.25	1.50
1407	A225	$4 Mimic	2.75	3.00
1408	A225	$5 Cracker	3.25	3.75
		Nos. 1401-1408 (8)	9.35	10.40

Souvenir Sheets
Caterpillars

1409	A225	$6 Monarch, vert.	4.25	4.25
1410	A225	$6 Painted lady, vert.	4.25	4.25

Voyages of Discovery A226

Designs: 10c, Hanno, Phoenicia, c. 450 B.C. 15c, Pytheas, Greece, 325 B.C. 45c, Eric the Red, Viking, A.D. 985. 60c, Leif Erikson, Viking, A.D. 1000. $1, Scylax, Greece, A.D. 518. $2, Marco Polo, A.D. 1259. $4, Queen Hatsheput, Egypt, 1493 B.C. $5, St. Brendan, Ireland, 500 A.D. No. 1419, Columbus, bareheaded. No. 1420, Columbus, wearing hat.

1991, Apr. 22

1411	A226	10c multicolored	.20	.20
1412	A226	15c multicolored	.20	.20
1413	A226	45c multicolored	.35	.35
1414	A226	60c multicolored	.45	.45
1415	A226	$1 multicolored	.70	.75
1416	A226	$2 multicolored	1.25	1.50
1417	A226	$4 multicolored	2.50	3.00
1418	A226	$5 multicolored	3.00	3.75
		Nos. 1411-1418 (8)	8.65	10.20

Souvenir Sheets

1419	A226	$6 multicolored	4.00	4.00
1420	A226	$6 multicolored	4.00	4.00

Discovery of America, 500th anniv. (in 1992).

Paintings by Vincent Van Gogh A227

Designs: 5c, Portrait of Camille Roulin. 10c, Portrait of Armand Roulin. 15c, Young Peasant Woman with Straw Hat Sitting in the Wheat. 25c, Portrait of Adeline Ravoux. 30c, The Schoolboy (Camille Roulin). 40c, Portrait of Doctor Gachet. 50c, Portrait of a Man. 75c, Two Children. $2, Portrait of Postman Joseph Roulin. $3, The Seated Zouave. $4, L'arlesienne: Madame Ginoux with Books. No. 1432, Self Portrait, November/December 1888. No. 1433, Flowering Garden. No. 1434, Farmhouse in Provence. $6, The Bridge at Trinquetaille.

1991, May 13　　Perf. 13½

1421	A227	5c multicolored	.20	.20
1422	A227	10c multicolored	.20	.20
1423	A227	15c multicolored	.20	.20
1424	A227	25c multicolored	.20	.20
1425	A227	30c multicolored	.25	.25
1426	A227	40c multicolored	.30	.30
1427	A227	50c multicolored	.35	.35
1428	A227	75c multicolored	.55	.55
1429	A227	$2 multicolored	1.25	1.50
1430	A227	$3 multicolored	2.00	2.25
1431	A227	$4 multicolored	2.50	3.00
1432	A227	$5 multicolored	3.00	3.75
		Nos. 1421-1432 (12)	11.00	12.75

Size: 102x76mm
Imperf

1433	A227	$5 multicolored	3.50	3.50
1434	A227	$5 multicolored	3.50	3.50
1435	A227	$6 multicolored	4.25	4.25

Phila Nippon '91 — A228

Walt Disney characters demonstrating Japanese martial arts: 10c, Mickey as champion sumo wrestler, vert. 15c, Goofy using tonfa. 45c, Ninja Donald in full field dress. 60c, Mickey using weapon in kung fu, vert. $1, Goofy tries kendo, vert. $2, Mickey, Donald demonstrating special technique of aikido. $4, Mickey flips Donald with judo throw. $5, Mickey demonstrates yabusame (target shooting from running horse), vert. No. 1444, Mickey using karate. No. 1445, Mickey demonstrating tamashiwara (powerbreaking), vert.

Perf. 13½x14, 14x13½
1991, June 29　　Litho.

1436	A228	10c multicolored	.20	.20
1437	A228	15c multicolored	.20	.20
1438	A228	45c multicolored	.35	.35
1439	A220	60c multicolored	.45	.45
1440	A228	$1 multicolored	.70	.75
1441	A228	$2 multicolored	1.25	1.50
1442	A220	$4 multicolored	2.50	3.00
1443	A228	$5 multicolored	3.00	3.75
		Nos. 1436-1443 (8)	8.65	10.20

Souvenir Sheets

1444	A228	$6 multicolored	4.25	4.25
1445	A228	$6 multicolored	4.25	4.25

Royal Family Birthday, Anniversary
Common Design Type

1991, July 8　　Litho.　　Perf. 14

1446	CD347	10c multicolored	.20	.20
1447	CD347	15c multicolored	.20	.20
1448	CD347	20c multicolored	.20	.20
1449	CD347	40c multicolored	.30	.30
1450	CD347	$1 multicolored	.70	.75
1451	CD347	$2 multicolored	1.25	1.50
1452	CD347	$4 multicolored	2.50	3.00
1453	CD347	$5 multicolored	3.00	3.75
		Nos. 1446-1453 (8)	8.35	9.90

Souvenir Sheets

1454	CD347	$4 Elizabeth, Philip	2.75	2.75
1455	CD347	$4 Charles, Diana, sons	2.75	2.75

10c, 40c, $1, $5, No. 1455, Charles and Diana, 10th wedding anniversary. Others, Queen Elizabeth II, 65th birthday.

Walt Disney Characters Playing Golf — A229

Designs: 10c, Daisy Duck teeing off. 15c, Goofy using 3-Wood. 45c, Mickey using 3-Iron. 60c, Mickey missing ball using 6-Iron. $1, Donald trying 8-Iron to get out of pond. $2, Minnie using 9-Iron. $4, Donald digging hole with sand wedge. $5, Goofy trying new approach with putter. No. 1464, Grandma Duck using pitching wedge. No. 1465, Mickey

cheering Minnie as she uses her 5-Wood, horiz.

Perf. 13½x14, 14x13½
1991, Aug. 7　　Litho.

1456	A229	10c multicolored	.20	.20
1457	A229	15c multicolored	.20	.20
1458	A229	45c multicolored	.35	.35
1459	A229	60c multicolored	.45	.45
1460	A229	$1 multicolored	.70	.75
1461	A229	$2 multicolored	1.25	1.50
1462	A229	$4 multicolored	2.50	3.00
1463	A229	$5 multicolored	3.00	3.75
		Nos. 1456-1463 (8)	8.65	10.20

Souvenir Sheets

1464	A229	$6 multicolored	4.25	4.25
1465	A229	$6 multicolored	4.25	4.25

1992 Summer Olympics, Barcelona A230

Archie Comics, 50th anniv.: 10c, Moose receiving gold medal. 25c, Archie, Veronica, Mr. Lodge, polo match, horiz. 40c, Archie & Betty, fencing. 60c, Archie, women's volleyball. $1, Archie, tennis. $2, Archie, marathon race. $4, Archie, judging women's gymnastics, horiz. $5, Archie, Betty, Veronica, basketball. No. 1474, Archie, soccer. No. 1475, Archie, Betty, baseball, horiz.

Perf. 13½x14, 14x13½
1991, Aug. 19

1466	A230	10c multicolored	.20	.20
1467	A230	25c multicolored	.20	.20
1468	A230	40c multicolored	.30	.30
1469	A230	60c multicolored	.45	.45
1470	A230	$1 multicolored	.75	.75
1471	A230	$2 multicolored	1.50	1.50
1472	A230	$4 multicolored	3.00	3.00
1473	A230	$5 multicolored	3.75	3.75
		Nos. 1466-1473 (8)	10.15	10.15

Souvenir Sheets

1474	A230	$6 multicolored	4.50	4.50
1475	A230	$6 multicolored	4.50	4.50

Charles de Gaulle, Birth Cent. A231

Charles de Gaulle: 10c, and Pres. Kennedy, families, 1961. 15c, and Pres. Roosevelt, 1945, vert. 45c, and Chancellor Adenauer, 1962, vert. 60c, Liberation of Paris, 1944, vert. $1, Crossing the Rhine, 1945. $2, In Algiers, 1944. $4, and Pres. Eisenhower, 1960. $5, Returning from Germany, 1968, vert. No. 1484, and Churchill at Casablanca, 1943. No. 1485, and Citizens.

1991, Sept. 11　　Litho.　　Perf. 14

1476	A231	10c multicolored	.20	.20
1477	A231	15c multicolored	.20	.20
1478	A231	45c multicolored	.35	.35
1479	A231	60c multicolored	.45	.45
1480	A231	$1 multicolored	.70	.75
1481	A231	$2 multicolored	1.25	1.50
1482	A231	$4 multicolored	2.50	3.00
1483	A231	$5 multicolored	3.00	3.75
		Nos. 1476-1483 (8)	8.65	10.20

Souvenir Sheets

1484	A231	$6 multicolored	4.25	4.25
1485	A231	$6 multicolored	4.25	4.25

Independence, 10th Anniv. — A232

Designs: 10c, Island maps, government building. $6, Old P. O., St. Johns, #1 & #635.

1991, Oct. 28
1486 A232 10c multicolored   .20 .20

Souvenir Sheet
1487 A232 $6 multicolored 4.25 4.25
No. 1487 contains one 50x38mm stamp.

Miniature Sheet

Attack on Pearl Harbor, 50th Anniv. A233

Designs: No. 1488a, Bow of Nimitz class carrier, Ticonderoga class cruiser. b, Tourist boat to Arizona Memorial. c, USS Arizona Memorial. d, Aircraft salute to missing men. e, White tern. f, Japanese Kate torpedo bombers. g, Japanese Zero fighters. h, Battleship row in flames. i, USS Nevada breaking out. j, Zeros returning to carriers.

1991, Dec. 9   *Perf. 14½x15*
1488 A233 $1 Sheet of 10, #a.-j. 7.50 7.50
Inscription for No. 1488f incorrectly describes torpedo bombers as Zekes.

3rd Antigua Methodist Cub Scout Pack, 60th Anniv. A234

Designs: $2, Lord Robert Baden-Powell, scouts, vert. $3.50, Scouts around campfire. $5, Antigua & Barbuda flag, Jamboree emblem, vert.

1991, Dec. 9   *Perf. 14*
1489 A234 75c multicolored .60 .60
1490 A234 $2 multicolored 1.25 1.50
1491 A234 $3.50 multicolored 2.25 2.75
   Nos. 1489-1491 (3) 4.10 4.85

Souvenir Sheet
1492 A234 $5 multicolored 3.25 3.25
17th World Scout Jamboree, Korea.

Wolfgang Amadeus Mozart, Death Bicent. A235

Portrait of Mozart and: $1.50, Scene from opera, Don Giovanni. $4, St. Peter's Cathedral, Salzburg.

1991, Dec. 9
1493 A235 $1.50 multicolored 1.10 1.10
1494 A235 $4 multicolored 2.50 3.00

Anniversaries and Events — A236

Designs: $2, Otto Lilienthal's glider No. 5. $2.50, Locomotive cab, vert.

1991, Dec. 9   Litho. *Perf. 14*
1495 A236 $2 multicolored 1.25 1.50
1496 A236 $2.50 multicolored 1.60 1.90
First glider flight, cent. (No. 1495). Trans-Siberian Railway, cent. (No. 1496). Numbers have been reserved for additional values in this set.

Brandenburg Gate, Bicent. — A237

25c, Demonstrators in autos, German flag. $2, Statue. $3, Portions of decorative frieze.

1991, Dec. 9   Litho. *Perf. 14*
1499 A237 25c multicolored .20 .20
1500 A237 $2 multicolored 1.25 1.50
1501 A237 $3 multicolored 2.00 2.25
   Nos. 1499-1501 (3) 3.45 3.95

Souvenir Sheet
1502 A237 $4 multicolored 3.00 3.00

Christmas A238

Paintings by Fra Angelico: 10c, The Annunciation. 30c, Nativity. 40c, Adoration of the Magi. 60c, Presentation in the Temple. $1, Circumcision. $3, Flight into Egypt. $4, Massacre of the Innocents. $5, Christ Teaching in the Temple. Nos. 1511, Adoration of the Magi, diff. No. 1512, Adoration of the Magi (Cook Tondo).

1991, Dec. 12   *Perf. 12*
1503 A238 10c multicolored .20 .20
1504 A238 30c multicolored .25 .25
1505 A238 40c multicolored .30 .30
1506 A238 60c multicolored .45 .45
1507 A238 $1 multicolored .70 .75
1508 A238 $3 multicolored 2.00 2.25
1509 A238 $4 multicolored 2.50 3.00
1510 A238 $5 multicolored 3.00 3.75
   Nos. 1503-1510 (8) 9.40 10.95

Souvenir Sheets
1511 A238 $6 multicolored 4.25 4.25
1512 A238 $6 multicolored 4.25 4.25

Queen Elizabeth II's Accession to the Throne, 40th Anniv.
Common Design Type

Queen Elizabeth II and various island scenes.

1992, Feb. 6   Litho. *Perf. 14*
1513 CD348 10c multicolored .20 .20
1514 CD348 30c multicolored .20 .20
1515 CD348 $1 multicolored .70 .75
1516 CD348 $5 multicolored 3.00 3.75
   Nos. 1513-1516 (4) 4.10 4.90

Souvenir Sheets
1517 CD348 $6 Beach 4.25 4.25
1518 CD348 $6 Flora 4.25 4.25

Mushrooms A239

1992   Litho. *Perf. 14*
1519 A239 10c Amanita caesarea .20 .20
1520 A239 15c Collybia fusipes .20 .20
1521 A239 30c Boletus aereus .20 .20
1522 A239 40c Laccaria amethystina .30 .30
1523 A239 $1 Russula virescens .70 .75
1524 A239 $2 Tricholoma auratum 1.25 1.50

1525 A239 $4 Calocybe gambosa 2.50 3.00
1526 A239 $5 Panus tigrinus 3.00 3.75
   Nos. 1519-1526 (8) 8.35 9.90

Souvenir Sheet
1527 A239 $6 Auricularia auricula 4.25 4.25
1528 A239 $6 Clavariadelphus truncatus 4.25 4.25
Issued: 10c, 30c, $1, $5, #1528, May 18; others, Mar.

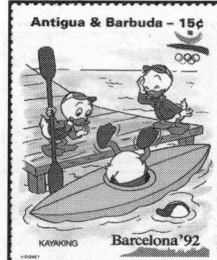

Disney Characters at Summer Olympics, Barcelona A240

Designs: 10c, Mickey presenting gold medal to mermaid for swimming. 15c, Dewey and Huey watching Louie in kayak. 30c, Uncle McScrooge, Donald yachting. 50c, Donald, horse trying water polo. $1, Big Pete weight lifting. $2, Donald, Goofy fencing. $4, Mickey, Donald playing volleyball. $5, Goofy vaulting over horse. No. 1537, Mickey playing basketball, horiz. No. 1538, Minnie Mouse on uneven parallel bars, horiz. No. 1539, Mickey, Goofy, and Donald judging Minnie's floor exercise, horiz. No. 1540, Mickey running after soccer ball.

1992, Mar. 16   *Perf. 13*
1529 A240 10c multicolored .20 .20
1530 A240 15c multicolored .20 .20
1531 A240 30c multicolored .20 .20
1532 A240 50c multicolored .40 .40
1533 A240 $1 multicolored .70 .75
1534 A240 $2 multicolored 1.25 1.50
1535 A240 $4 multicolored 2.50 3.00
1536 A240 $5 multicolored 3.00 3.75
   Nos. 1529-1536 (8) 8.45 10.00

Souvenir Sheets
1537-1540 A240 $6 each 4.25 4.25

Dinosaurs A241

1992, Apr. 6   *Perf. 14*
1541 A241 10c Pteranodon .20 .20
1542 A241 15c Brachiosaurus .20 .20
1543 A241 30c Tyrannosaurus rex .20 .20
1544 A241 50c Parasaurolophus .40 .40
1545 A241 $1 Deinonychus .70 .75
1546 A241 $2 Triceratops 1.25 1.50
1547 A241 $4 Protoceratops 2.50 3.00
1548 A241 $5 Stegosaurus 3.00 3.75
   Nos. 1541-1548 (8) 8.45 10.00

Souvenir Sheets
1549 A241 $6 Apatosaurus 4.25 4.25
1550 A241 $6 Allosaurus 4.25 4.25
Nos. 1541-1544 are vert.

Easter — A242

Paintings: 10c, Supper at Emmaus, by Caravaggio. 15c, The Vision of St. Peter, by Francisco de Zurbaran. 30c, $1, Christ Driving the Money Changers from the Temple, by Tiepolo (detail on $1). 40c, Martyrdom of St. Bartholomew (detail), by Jusepe de Ribera. $2, Crucifixion (detail), by Albrecht Altdorfer. $4, $5, The Deposition (diff. detail), by Fra Angelico. No. 1559, Crucifixion, by Albrecht Altdorfer, vert. No. 1560, The Last Supper, by Vicente Juan Masip.

1992   *Perf. 14x13½*
1551 A242 10c multicolored .20 .20
1552 A242 15c multicolored .20 .20
1553 A242 30c multicolored .20 .20
1554 A242 40c multicolored .30 .30
1555 A242 $1 multicolored .70 .75
1556 A242 $2 multicolored 1.25 1.50
1557 A242 $4 multicolored 2.50 3.00
1558 A242 $5 multicolored 3.00 3.75
   Nos. 1551-1558 (8) 8.35 9.90

Souvenir Sheet
Perf. 13½x14
1559 A242 $6 multicolored 4.25 4.25
1560 A242 $6 multicolored 4.25 4.25

Spanish Art — A243

Designs: 10c, The Miracle at the Well, by Alonso Cano. 15c, The Poet Luis de Gongora y Argote, by Velazquez. 30c, The Painter Francisco Goya, by Vincente Lopez Portana. 40c, Maria de Las Nieves Michaela Fourdiniere, by Luis Paret y Alcazar. $1, Charles III Eating before His Court, by Paret y Alcazar, horiz. $2, A Rain Shower in Granada, by Antonio Munoz Degrain, horiz. $4, Sarah Bernhardt, by Santiago Rusinol y Subias. $5, The Hermitage Garden, by Joaquin Mir Trinxet. No. 1569, Olympus: Battle with the Giants, by Francisco Bayeu y Subias. No. 1570, The Ascent of Monsieur Boucle's Montgolfier Balloon in the Gardens of Aranjuez, by Antonio Carnicero.

1992, May 11
1561 A243 10c multicolored .20 .20
1562 A243 15c multicolored .20 .20
1563 A243 30c multicolored .20 .20
1564 A243 40c multicolored .30 .30
1565 A243 $1 multicolored .70 .70
1566 A243 $2 multicolored 1.25 1.50
1567 A243 $4 multicolored 2.50 3.00
1568 A243 $5 multicolored 3.00 3.75

Size: 120x95mm
Imperf
1569 A243 $6 multicolored 3.75 4.50
1570 A243 $6 multicolored 3.75 4.50
   Nos. 1561-1570 (10) 15.85 18.90
Granada '92.

Discovery of America, 500th Anniv. A244

Designs: 15c, San Salvador Island. 30c, Martin Alonzo Pinzon, captain of Pinta. 40c, Columbus, signature, coat of arms. $1, Pinta. $2, Nina. $4, Santa Maria. No. 1577, Sea monster. No. 1578, Map, sailing ship.

1992, May 25   Litho. *Perf. 14*
1571 A244 15c multicolored .20 .20
1572 A244 30c multicolored .20 .20
1573 A244 40c multicolored .30 .30
1574 A244 $1 multicolored .70 .75
1575 A244 $2 multicolored 1.25 1.50
1576 A244 $4 multicolored 2.50 3.00
   Nos. 1571-1576 (6) 5.15 5.95

Souvenir Sheets
1577 A244 $6 multicolored 4.25 4.25
1578 A244 $6 multicolored 4.25 4.25
World Columbian Stamp Expo '92, Chicago.

Hummel Figurines — A245

Wanderers: 15c, No. 1587a, Boy sitting on rock pointing to flower in cap. 30c, No. 1587b, Girl sitting on fence. 40c, No. 1587c, Boy holding binoculars. 50c, No. 1587d, Boy holding umbrella. $1, No. 1588a, Two boys looking up at direction marker. $2, No. 1588b, Boy carrying basket on back, walking with stick. $4, No. 1588c, Two girls, goat. $5, No. 1588d, Boy carrying walking stick.

1993, Jan. 6   Litho.   Perf. 14

1579	A245	15c multicolored	.20	.20
1580	A245	30c multicolored	.20	.20
1581	A245	40c multicolored	.30	.30
1582	A245	50c multicolored	.40	.40
1583	A245	$1 multicolored	.70	.75
1584	A245	$2 multicolored	1.25	1.50
1585	A245	$4 multicolored	2.50	3.00
1586	A245	$5 multicolored	3.00	3.75
		Nos. 1579-1586 (8)	8.55	10.10

Souvenir Sheets of 4

1587	A245	$1.50 #a.-d.	4.25	4.25
1588	A245	$1.50 #a.-d.	4.25	4.25

Hummingbirds and Flowers — A246

Designs: 10c, Antillean crested, wild plantain. 25c, Green mango, parrot's plantain. 45c, Purple-throated carib, lobster claws. 60c, Antillean mango, coral plant. $1, Vervain, cardinal's guard. $2, Rufous breasted hermit, heliconia. $4, Blue-headed, red ginger. $5, Green-throated carib, ornamental banana. No. 1597, Bee, jungle flame. No. 1598, Western streamertails, bignonia.

1992, Aug. 10   Litho.   Perf. 14

1589	A246	10c multicolored	.20	.20
1590	A246	25c multicolored	.20	.20
1591	A246	45c multicolored	.35	.35
1592	A246	60c multicolored	.45	.45
1593	A246	$1 multicolored	.70	.75
1594	A246	$2 multicolored	1.25	1.50
1595	A246	$4 multicolored	2.50	3.00
1596	A246	$5 multicolored	3.00	3.75
		Nos. 1589-1596 (8)	8.65	10.20

Souvenir Sheets

1597	A246	$6 multicolored	6.75	6.75
1598	A246	$6 multicolored	6.75	6.75

Genoa '92.

Discovery of America, 500th Anniv. — A247

1992   Litho.   Perf. 14½

1599	A247	$1 Coming ashore	.75	.75
1600	A247	$2 Natives, ships	1.25	1.50

Organization of East Caribbean States.

Souvenir Sheet

Madison Square Garden, NYC — A248

1992   Litho.   Perf. 14

1601	A248	$6 multicolored	5.00	5.00

Postage Stamp Mega-Event, Jacob Javits Center, New York City.

Elvis Presley (1935-1977) A249

Various pictures of Elvis Presley.

1992   Perf. 13½x14

1602	A249	$1 Sheet of 9, #a.-i.	7.00	7.00

Inventors and Pioneers A250

Designs: 10c, Ts'ai Lun, paper. 25c, Igor I. Sikorsky, 4-engine airplane. 30c, Alexander Graham Bell, telephone. 40c, Johannes Gutenberg, printing press. 60c, James Watt, steam engine. $1, Anton van Leeuwenhoek, microscope. $4, Louis Braille, Braille printing. $5, Galileo, telescope. No. 1607, Phonograph. No. 1608, Steamboat.

1992, Oct. 19   Litho.   Perf. 14

1603	A250	10c multicolored	.20	.20
1604	A250	25c multicolored	.20	.20
1605	A250	30c multicolored	.25	.25
1605A	A250	40c multicolored	.40	.40
1605B	A250	60c multicolored	.45	.45
1605C	A250	$1 multicolored	.75	.75
1605D	A250	$4 multicolored	3.00	3.00
1606	A250	$5 multicolored	3.75	3.75
		Nos. 1603-1606 (8)	9.00	9.00

Souvenir Sheet

1607	A250	$6 multicolored	4.00	4.00
1608	A250	$6 multicolored	4.00	4.00

Christmas A251

Details from Paintings: 10c, Virgin and Child with Angels, by School of Piero Della Francesca. 25c, Madonna Degli Alberelli, by Giovanni Bellini. 30c, Madonna and Child with St. Anthony Abbot and St. Sigismund, by Neroccio di Landi. 40c, Madonna and the Grand Duke, by Raphael. 60c, The Nativity, by George de la Tour. $1, Holy Family, by Jacob Jordaens. $4, Madonna and Child Enthroned, by Margaritone. $5, Madonna and Child on a Curved Throne, by Byzantine artist. No. 1617, Madonna and Child, by Domenico Ghirlandaio (both names misspelled). No. 1618, The Holy Family, by Pontormo.

1992   Perf. 13½x14

1609	A251	10c multicolored	.20	.20
1610	A251	25c multicolored	.20	.20
1611	A251	30c multicolored	.25	.25
1612	A251	40c multicolored	.30	.30
1613	A251	60c multicolored	.45	.45
1614	A251	$1 multicolored	.75	.75
1615	A251	$4 multicolored	3.00	3.00
1616	A251	$5 multicolored	3.75	3.75
		Nos. 1609-1616 (8)	8.90	8.90

Souvenir Sheet

1617	A251	$6 multicolored	4.50	4.50
1618	A251	$6 multicolored	4.50	4.50

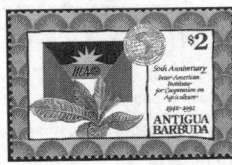

A252

A253

Anniversaries and Events: 10c, Cosomonauts. 40c, Graf Zeppelin, Goodyear blimp. 45c, Right Rev. Daniel C. Davis, St. John's Cathedral. 75c, Konrad Adenauer. $1, Bus Mosbacher, Weatherly. $1.50, Rain forest. No. 1625, Felis tigris. No. 1626, Flag, emblems, plant. No. 1627, Women acting on stage. $2.25, Women carrying baskets of food on their heads. $3, Lions Club emblem, club member. No. 1630, West German, NATO flags. No. 1631, China's Long March Booster Rocket. No. 1632, Dr. Hugo Eckener. No. 1633, The Hindenburg. No. 1634, Brandenburg Gate, German flag. No. 1635, Monarch butterfly. No. 1636, Hermes Shuttle, Columbus Space Station.

1992   Litho.   Perf. 14

1619	A252	10c multicolored	.20	.20
1620	A252	40c multicolored	.30	.30
1621	A253	45c multicolored	.35	.35
1622	A252	75c multicolored	.60	.60
1623	A252	$1 multicolored	.75	.75
1624	A252	$1.50 multicolored	1.10	1.10
1625	A252	$2 multicolored	1.50	1.50
1626	A253	$2 multicolored	1.50	1.50
1627	A253	$2 multicolored	1.50	1.50
1628	A252	$2.25 multicolored	1.75	1.75
1629	A252	$3 multicolored	2.25	2.25
1630	A252	$4 multicolored	3.00	3.00
1631	A252	$4 multicolored	3.00	3.00
1632	A252	$6 multicolored	4.50	4.50
		Nos. 1619-1632 (14)	22.30	22.30

Souvenir Sheets

1633-1636	A252	$6 each	4.50	4.50

Intl. Space Year (#1619, 1631, 1636). Count Zeppelin, 75th anniv. of death (#1620, 1632-1633). Diocese of Northeast Caribbean and Aruba District, 150th anniv. (#1621). Konrad Adenauer, 25th anniv. of death (#1622, 1630, 1634). 1962 winner of America's Cup (#1623). Earth Summit, Rio (#1624-1625, 1635). Inter-American Institute for Cooperation on Agriculture, 50th anniv. (#1626). Cultural Development, 40th anniv. (#1627). WHO Intl. Conf. on Nutrition, Rome (#1628). Lions Club, 75th anniv. (#1629).

Issued: #1619, 1621-1623, 1626-1631, 1634, 1636, Nov.; #1624-1625, 1635, Dec. 14.

Euro Disney, Paris — A254

Disney characters: 10c, Golf course. 25c, Davy Crockett Campground. 30c, Cheyenne Hotel. 40c, Santa Fe Hotel. $1, New York Hotel. $2, In car, map showing location. $4, Pirates of the Caribbean. $5, Adventureland. No. 1645, Mickey Mouse on map with star, vert. No. 1646, Roof turret at entrance, Mickey Mouse in uniform. No. 1646A, Mickey Mouse, colored spots on poster, vert. No. 1646B, Mickey on poster, vert., diff.

1992-93   Litho.   Perf. 14x13½

1637	A254	10c multicolored	.20	.20
1638	A254	25c multicolored	.20	.20
1639	A254	30c multicolored	.25	.25
1640	A254	40c multicolored	.30	.30
1641	A254	$1 multicolored	.75	.75
1642	A254	$2 multicolored	1.50	1.50
1643	A254	$4 multicolored	3.00	3.00
1644	A254	$5 multicolored	3.75	3.75
		Nos. 1637-1644 (8)	9.95	9.95

Souvenir Sheets

Perf. 13½x14

1645-1646B	A254	$6 each	4.50	4.50

Issued: #1638-1639, 1642-1643, 1646-1646B, 2/22/93; others, 12/1992.

Miniature Sheets

Louvre Museum, Bicent. A255

Details or entire paintings, by Peter Paul Rubens: No. 1647a, Destiny of Marie de' Medici. b, Birth of Marie de'Medici. c, Marie's Education. d, Destiny of Marie de'Medici, diff. e, Henry IV Receives the Portrait. f, The Meeting at Lyons. g, The Marriage. h, The Birth of Louis XIII.

No. 1648a, The Capture of Juliers. b, The Exchange of Princesses. c, The Happiness of the Regency. d, The Majority of Louis XIII. e, The Flight from Blois. f, The Treaty of Angouleme. g, The Peace of Angers. h, The Queen's Reconciliation with Her Son.

$6, Helene Fourment Au Carosse.

1993, Mar. 22   Litho.   Perf. 12

Sheets of 8 + Label

1647	A255	$1 #a.-h.	6.00	6.00
1648	A255	$1 #a.-h.	6.00	6.00

Souvenir Sheet

Perf. 14½

1649	A255	$6 multicolored	4.50	4.50

No. 1649 contains one 55x88mm stamp.

Flowers — A256

1993, Mar. 15   Litho.   Perf. 14

1650	A256	15c Cardinal's guard	.20	.20
1651	A256	25c Giant granadilla	.20	.20
1652	A256	30c Spider flower	.25	.25
1653	A256	40c Gold vine	.30	.30
1654	A256	$1 Frangipani	.75	.75
1655	A256	$2 Bougainvillea	1.50	1.50
1656	A256	$4 Yellow oleander	3.00	3.00
1657	A256	$5 Spicy jatropha	3.75	3.75
		Nos. 1650-1657 (8)	9.95	9.95

Souvenir Sheets

1658	A256	$6 Bird lime tree	4.50	4.50
1659	A256	$6 Fairy lily	4.50	4.50

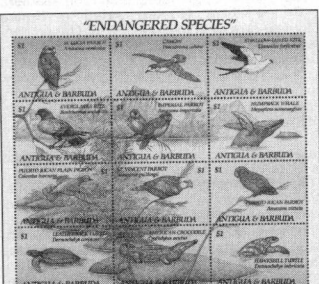

Endangered Species — A257

Designs: No. 1660a, St. Lucia parrot. b, Cahow. c, Swallow-tailed kite. d, Everglades kite. e, Imperial parrot. f, Humpback whale. g, Puerto Rican plain pigeon. h, St. Vincent parrot. i, Puerto Rican parrot. j, Leatherback turtle. k, American crocodile. l, Hawksbill turtle. No. 1662, West Indian manatee.

1993, Apr. 5
1660 A257 $1 Sheet of 12, #a.-l. 9.00 9.00

Souvenir Sheets
1661 A257 $6 like #1660f 4.50 4.50
1662 A257 $6 multicolored 4.50 4.50

Philatelic Publishing
Personalities — A258

Portrait, stamp: No. 1663, J. Walter Scott (1842-1919), US "#C3a," Antigua #1. No. 1664, Theodore Champion, France #8, Antigua #1. No. 1665, E. Stanley Gibbons (1856-1913), cover of his first price list and catalogue, Antigua #1. No. 1666, Hugo Michel (1866-1944), Bavaria #1, Antigua #1. No. 1667, Alberto (1877-1944) and Giulio (1902-1987) Bolaffi, Sardinia #1, Great Britain #3. No. 1668, Richard Borek (1874-1947), Brunswick #24, Bavaria #1.
Front pages, Mekeel's Weekly Stamp News: No. 1669a, Jan. 7, 1890. b, Feb. 12, 1993.

1993, June 14
1663 A258 $1.50 multicolored 1.10 1.10
1664 A258 $1.50 multicolored 1.10 1.10
1665 A258 $1.50 multicolored 1.10 1.10
1666 A258 $1.50 multicolored 1.10 1.10
1667 A258 $1.50 multicolored 1.10 1.10
1668 A258 $1.50 multicolored 1.10 1.10
  Nos. 1663-1668 (6) 6.60 6.60

Souvenir Sheet of 2
1669 A258 $3 #a.-b. 4.50 4.50

Mekeel's Weekly Stamp News, cent. (in 1891; #1669).

Miniature Sheets

Coronation of Queen Elizabeth II, 40th Anniv. A259

Coronation: 1670a, 30c, Official photograph. b, 40c, Crown of Queen Elizabeth, the Queen Mother. c, $2, Dignitaries attending ceremony. d, $4, Queen, Prince Edward.
$6, Portrait, by Denis Fildes.
First decade, 1953-1963: No. 1671a, Wedding photograph of Princess Margaret and Antony Armstrong-Jones. b, Queen opening Parliament, Prince Philip. c, Queen holding infant. d, Royal family. e, Queen Elizabeth II, formal portrait. f, Queen, Charles de Gaulle. g, Queen, Pope John XXIII. h, Queen inspecting troops.
Second decade, 1963-1973: No. 1672a, Investiture of Charles as Prince of Wales. b, Queen opening Parliament, Prince Philip, diff. c, Queen holding infant, diff. d, Queen, Prince Philip, children. e, Wearing blue robe, diadem. f, Prince Philip, Queen seated. g, Prince Charles, Queen at microphone. h, Queen conversing, model airplane.
Third decade, 1973-1983: No. 1673a, Wedding photograph of Prince Charles and Princess Diana. b, Queen opening Parliament, Prince Philip, diff. c, Princess Diana with infant. d, Princess Anne with infant. e, Portrait of Queen. f, Queen waving, diff. g, Queen, Pope John Paul II. h, Wedding portrait of Mark Phillips and Princess Anne.
Fourth decade, 1983-1993: No. 1674a, Wedding photograph of Sarah Ferguson and Prince Andrew. b, Queen opening Parliament, Prince Philip, diff. c, Princess Diana holding infant. diff. d, Sarah Ferguson, infant. e, Queen wearing blue dress. f, Queen waving from carriage, Prince Philip. g, Queen wearing military uniform. h, Queen Mother.

1993, June 2 Litho. Perf. 13½x14
1670 A259 Sheet, 2 each
  #a.-d. 10.00 10.00

Sheets of 8
1671 A259 $1 #a.-h. + label 6.00 6.00
1672 A259 $1 #a.-h. + label 6.00 6.00
1673 A259 $1 #a.-h. + label 6.00 6.00
1674 A259 $1 #a.-h. + label 6.00 6.00

Souvenir Sheet
Perf. 14
1675 A259 $6 multicolored 4.50 4.50
No. 1675 contains one 28x42mm stamp.

Wedding of Japan's Crown Prince Naruhito and Masako Owada A260

Cameo photos of couple and: 40c, Crown Prince. $3, Princess.
$6, Princess wearing white coat, vert.

1993, Aug. 16 Litho. Perf. 14
1676 A260 40c multicolored .30 .30
1677 A260 $3 multicolored 2.25 2.25

Souvenir Sheet
1678 A260 $6 multicolored 4.50 4.50

Picasso (1881-1973) — A261

Paintings: 30c, Cat and Bird, 1939. 40c, Fish on a Newspaper, 1957. $5, Dying Bull, 1934. $6, Woman with a Dog, 1953.

1993, Aug. 16 Litho. Perf. 14
1679 A261 30c multicolored .25 .25
1680 A261 40c multicolored .30 .30
1681 A261 $5 multicolored 4.00 4.00
  Nos. 1679-1681 (3) 4.55 4.55

Souvenir Sheet
1682 A261 $6 multicolored 4.50 4.50

Copernicus (1473-1543) A262

Designs: 40c, Astronomical devices. $4, Photograph of supernova. $5, Copernicus.

1993, Aug. 16
1683 A262 40c multicolored .30 .30
1684 A262 $4 multicolored 3.25 3.25

Souvenir Sheet
1685 A262 $5 multicolored 3.75 3.75

Willy Brandt (1913-1992), German Chancellor — A263

Designs: 30c, Helmut Schmidt, George Leber, Brandt. $4, Brandt, newspaper headlines. $6, Brandt at Warsaw Ghetto Memorial, 1970.

1993, Aug. 16
1686 A263 30c multicolored .25 .25
1687 A263 $4 multicolored 3.25 3.25

Souvenir Sheet
1688 A263 $6 multicolored 4.50 4.50

Polska '93 A264

Paintings: $1, Study of a Woman Combing Her Hair, by Wladyslaw Slewinski, 1897. $3, Artist's Wife with Cat, by Konrad Kryzanowski, 1912. $6, General Confusion, by S. I. Witkiewicz, 1930, vert.

1993, Aug. 16
1689 A264 $1 multicolored .80 .80
1690 A264 $3 multicolored 2.50 2.50

Souvenir Sheet
1691 A264 $6 multicolored 4.50 4.50

Inauguration of Pres. William J. Clinton — A265

Designs: $5, Pres. Clinton driving car. $6, Pres. Clinton, inauguration ceremony, vert.

1993, Aug. 16
1692 A265 $5 multicolored 4.00 4.00

Souvenir Sheet
1693 A265 $6 multicolored 4.50 4.50
No. 1693 contains one 43x57mm stamp.

1994 Winter Olympics, Lillehammer, Norway — A266

15c, Irina Rodnina, Alexei Ulanov, gold medalists, pairs figure skating, 1972. $5, Alberto Tomba, gold medal, giant slalom, 1988, 1992. $6, Yvonne van Gennip, Andrea Ehrig, gold, bronze medalists, speedskating, 1988.

1993, Aug. 16
1694 A266 15c multicolored .20 .20
1695 A266 $5 multicolored 4.00 4.00

Souvenir Sheet
1696 A266 $6 multicolored 4.50 4.50

1994 World Cup Soccer Championships, US — A267

English soccer players: No. 1697, Gordon Banks. No. 1698, 1709, Bobby Moore. No. 1699, Peter Shilton. No. 1700, Nobby Stiles. No. 1701, Bryan Robson. No. 1702, Geoff Hurst. No. 1703, Gary Lineker. No. 1704, Bobby Charlton. No. 1705, Martin Peters. No. 1706, John Barnes. No. 1707, David Platt. No. 1708, Paul Gascoigne. No. 1710, Player holding 1990 Fair Play Winners Trophy.

1993, July 30 Litho. Perf. 14
1697-1708 A267 $2 Set of 12 18.00 18.00

Souvenir Sheets
1709 A267 $6 multicolored 4.50 4.50
1710 A267 $6 multicolored 4.50 4.50
Nos. 1697-1708 issued in sheets of five plus label identifying player.

Aviation Anniversaries — A268

Designs: 30c, Dr. Hugo Eckener, Dr. Wm. Beckers, zeppelin over Lake George, NY. No. 1712, Chicago Century of Progress Exhibition seen from zeppelin. No. 1713, George Washington, Blanchard's balloon, vert. No. 1714, Gloster E.28/39, first British jet plane. $4, Pres. Wilson watching take-off of first scheduled air mail plane. No. 1716, Hindenburg over Ebbets Field, Brooklyn, NY, 1937. No. 1717, Gloster Meteor in combat. No. 1718, Eckener, vert. No. 1719, Alexander Hamilton, Pres. Washington, John Jay, gondola of Blanchard's balloon. No. 1720, PBY-5.

1993, Oct. 11
1711 A268 30c multicolored .20 .20
1712 A268 40c multicolored .30 .30
1713 A268 40c multicolored .30 .30
1714 A268 40c multicolored .30 .30
1715 A268 $4 multicolored 3.00 3.00
1716 A268 $5 multicolored 3.75 3.75
1717 A268 $5 multicolored 3.75 3.75
  Nos. 1711-1717 (7) 11.60 11.60

Souvenir Sheets
1718 A268 $6 multicolored 4.50 4.50
1719 A268 $6 multicolored 4.50 4.50
1720 A268 $6 multicolored 4.50 4.50
Dr. Hugo Eckener, 125th anniv. of birth (#1711-1712, 1716, 1718). First US balloon flight, bicent. (#1713, 1715, 1719). Royal Air Force, 75th anniv. (#1714, 1717, 1720).
No. 1720 contains one 57x43mm stamp.

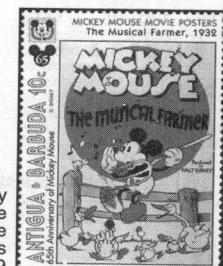

Mickey Mouse Movie Posters A269

Nos. 1721-1729: 10c, The Musical Farmer, 1932. 15c, Little Whirlwind, 1941. 30c, Pluto's Dream House, 1940. 40c, Gulliver Mickey, 1934. 50c, Alpine Climbers, 1936. $1, Mr. Mouse Takes a Trip, 1940. $2, The Nifty Nineties, 1941. $4, Mickey Down Under, 1948. $5, The Pointer, 1939.
#1730, The Simple Things, 1953. #1731, The Prince and the Pauper, 1990.

1993, Oct. 25 Litho. Perf. 13½x14
1721-1729 A269 Set of 9 12.00 12.00

Souvenir Sheets
1730-1731 A269 $6 each 4.50 4.50

St. John's Lodge #492, 150th Anniv. A270

Designs: 10c, W.K. Heath, Grand Inspector 1961-82, vert. 30c, Present Masonic Hall. 40c, 1st Masonic Hall. 60c, J.L.E. Jeffery, Grand Inspector 1953-61, vert.

1993, Aug. 16 Litho. Perf. 14
1732-1735 A270 Set of 4 1.10 1.10

First Ford Engine and Benz's First 4-Wheel Car, Cent. A271

30c, Lincoln Continental. 40c, 1914 Mercedes racing car. $4, 1966 Ford GT40. $5, 1954

ANTIGUA
375

Mercedes Benz gull wing coupe, street version. No. 1740, Mustang emblem. No. 1741, US #1286A, Germany #471.

1993, Oct. 11 Litho. Perf. 14
1736-1739 A271 Set of 4   7.00 7.00
Souvenir Sheets
1740-1741 A271 $6 each   4.50 4.50

Christmas — A272

Nos. 1742-1750, Disney characters in The Nutcracker: 10c, 15c, 20c, 30c, 40c, 50c, 60c, $3, $6. 1751, Minnie and Mickey. No. 1752, Mickey, vert.

1993, Nov. 8 Perf. 14x13½, 13½x14
1742-1750 A272 Set of 9   8.50 8.50
Souvenir Sheets
1751-1752 A272 $6 each   4.50 4.50

Fine Art — A273

Paintings by Rembrandt: No. 1753, 15c, Hannah and Samuel. 30c, Isaac & Rebecca (The Jewish Bride). 40c, Jacob Wrestling with the Angel. $5, Moses with the Tablets of the Law.
Paintings by Matisse: No. 1754, 15c, Guitarist. 60c, Interior with a Goldfish Bowl. $1, Portrait of Mlle. Yvonne Landsberg. $4, The Toboggan, Plate XX from Jazz. No. 1761, The Blinding of Samson by the Philistines, by Rembrandt. No. 1762, The Three Sisters, by Matisse.

1993, Nov. 22 Perf. 13½x14
1753-1760 A273 Set of 8   9.00 9.00
Souvenir Sheets
1761-1762 A273 $6 each   4.50 4.50

A274

Hong Kong '94 A275

Stamps, fishing boats at Shau Kei Wan: No. 1763, Hong Kong #370, bow of boat. No. 1764, Stern of boat, #1300.
Museum of Qin figures, Shaanxi Province, Tomb of Qin First Emperor: No. 1765a, Inside museum. b, Cavalryman, horse. c, Warriors in battle formation. d, Painted bronze horses, chariot. e, Pekingese dog (not antiquity). f, Chin warrior figures, horses.

1994, Feb. 18 Litho. Perf. 14
1763 A274 40c multicolored   .30 .30
1764 A274 40c multicolored   .30 .30
   a. Pair, #1763-1764   .60 .60
Miniature Sheet
1765 A275 40c Sheet of 6, #a.-f.   1.75 1.75
Nos. 1763-1764 issued in sheets of 5 pairs. No. 1764a is a continuous design.
New Year 1994 (Year of the Dog) (#1765e).

Hong Kong '94 — A276

Disney characters: 10c, Mickey's "Pleasure Junk." 15c, Mandarin Minnie. 30c, Donald, Daisy journey by house boat. 50c, Mickey, Birdman of Mongkok. $1, Pluto encounters a good-luck dog. $2, Minnie, Daisy celebrate Bun Festival. $4, Goofy, the noodle maker. $5, Goofy pulls Mickey in a rickshaw.
No. 1774, Mickey celebrating New Year with Dragon Dance, horiz. No. 1775, View of Hong Kong Harbor, horiz.

1994, Feb. 18 Litho. Perf. 13½x14
1766-1773 A276 Set of 8   10.00 10.00
Souvenir Sheets
Perf. 14x13½
1774-1775 A276 $5 each   3.75 3.75

Miniature Sheets of 8

Sierra Club, Cent. — A277

No. 1776: a, Bactrian camel, emblem UR. b, Bactrian camel, emblem UL. c, African elephant, emblem UL. d, African elephant, emblem UR. e, Leopard, blue background. f, Leopard, emblem UR. g, Leopard, emblem UL. h, Club emblem.
No. 1777: a, Sumatran rhinoceros, lying on ground. b, Sumatran rhinoceros, looking straight ahead. c, Ring-tailed lemur standing. d, Ring-tailed lemur sitting on branch. e, Red-fronted brown lemur on branch. f, Red-fronted brown lemur, diff.
No. 1778, Sumatran rhinoceros, horiz. No. 1779, Ring-tailed lemur, horiz. No. 1780, Bactrian camel, horiz. No. 1781, African elephant, horiz.

1994, Mar. 1 Litho. Perf. 14
1776 A277 $1.50 #a.-h.   9.00 9.00
1777 A277 $1.50 #a.-g, #1776h   9.00 9.00
Souvenir Sheets
1778-1781 A277 $1.50 each   1.10 1.10

Miniature Sheets

New Year 1994 (Year of the Dog) — A278

Small breeds of dogs: No. 1782a, West highland white terrier. b, Beagle. c, Scottish terrier. d, Pekingese. e, Dachshund. f, Yorkshire terrier. g, Pomeranian. h, Poodle. i, Shetland sheepdog. j, Pug. k, Shih tzu. l, Chihuahua.
Large breeds of dogs: No. 1783a, Mastiff. b, Border collie. c, Samoyed. d, Airedale terrier. e, English setter. f, Rough collie. g, Newfoundland. h, Weimaraner. i, English springer spaniel. j, Dalmatian. k, Boxer. l, Old English sheepdog.
No. 1784, Welsh corgi. No. 1785, Labrador retriever.

1994, Apr. 5 Perf. 14
1782 A278 50c Sheet of 12, #a.-l.   4.50 4.50
1783 A278 75c Sheet of 12, #a.-l.   6.75 6.75
Souvenir Sheets
1784-1785 A278 $6 each   4.50 4.50

Orchids — A279   Butterflies — A280

Designs: 10c, Spiranthes lanceolata. 20c, Ionopsis utricularioides. 30c, Tetramicra canaliculata. 50c, Oncidium picturatum. $1, Epidendrum difforme. $2, Epidendrum ciliare. $4, Epidendrum ibaguense. $5, Epidendrum nocturnum.
No. 1794, Encyclia cochleata. No. 1795, Rodriguezia lanceolata.

1994, Apr. 11 Perf. 14
1786-1793 A279 Set of 8   10.00 10.00
Souvenir Sheets
1794-1795 A279 $6 each   4.50 4.50

1994, June 27 Perf. 14
Designs: 10c, Monarch. 15c, Florida white. 30c, Little sulphur. 40c, Troglodyte. $1, Common long-tail skipper. $2, Caribbean buckeye. $4, Polydamas swallowtail. $5, Zebra. #1804, Cloudless sulphur. #1805, Hanno blue.
1796-1803 A280 Set of 8   10.00 10.00
Souvenir Sheets
1804-1805 A280 $6 each   4.50 4.50

Miniature Sheet of 9

Marine Life — A281

Designs: No. 1806a, Bottlenose dolphin. b, Killer whale (a). c, Spinner dolphin (b). d, Ocean sunfish (a). e, Caribbean reef shark, short fin pilot whale (d, f). f, Butterfly fish. g, Moray eel. h, Trigger fish. i, Red lobster (h).
#1807, Blue marlin, horiz. #1808, Sea horse.

1994, July 21 Litho. Perf. 14
1806 A281 50c a.-i.   3.50 3.50
Souvenir Sheets
1807-1808 A281 $6 each   4.50 4.50

Intl. Year of the Family A282

1994, Aug. 4
1809 A282 90c multicolored   .70 .70

D-Day, 50th Anniv. A283

Designs: 40c, Short Sunderland attacks U-boat. $2, Lockheed P-38 Lightning attacks train. $3, B-26 Marauders of 9th Air Force. $6, Hawker Typhoon Fighter Bombers.

1994, Aug. 4
1810-1812 A283 Set of 3   4.25 4.25
Souvenir Sheet
1813 A283 $6 multicolored   4.50 4.50

A284

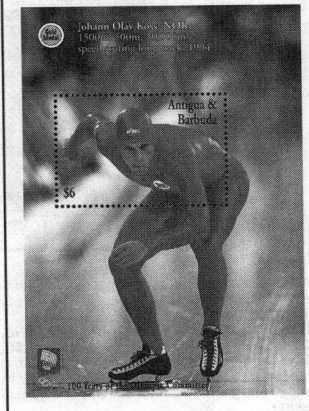

Intl. Olympic Committee, Cent. — A285

Designs: 50c, Edwin Moses, US, hurdles, 1984. $1.50, Steffi Graf, Germany, tennis, 1988. $6, Johann Olav Koss, Norway, speed skating, 1994.

1994, Aug. 4
1814 A284 50c multicolored   .40 .40
1815 A284 $1.50 multicolored   1.10 1.10
Souvenir Sheet
1816 A285 $6 multicolored   4.50 4.50

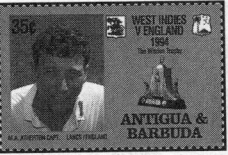

English Touring Cricket, Cent. A286

35c, M.A. Atherton, England, Wisden Trophy. 75c, I.V.A. Richards, Leeward Islands, vert. $1.20, R.B. Richardson, Leeward Islands, Wisden Trophy. $3, First English team, 1895.

1994, Aug. 4
1817-1819 A286 Set of 3   1.75 1.75
Souvenir Sheet
1820 A286 $3 multicolored   2.25 2.25

Miniature Sheets of 6

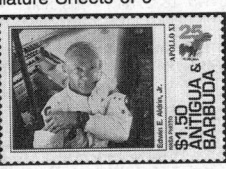

First Manned Moon Landing, 25th Anniv. A287

No. 1821: a, Edwin E. Aldrin, Jr. b, First footprint on Moon. c, Neil A. Armstrong. d, Aldrin descending to lunar surface. e, Aldrin deploys ALSET. f, Aldrin, US flag, Tranquility Base.
No. 1822: a, Scientific research, Tranquility Base. b, Plaque on Moon. c, Eagle ascending to docking. d, Command module in lunar orbit. e, US No. C76 made from die carried to Moon. f, Pres. Nixon, Apollo 11 crew.
$6, Armstrong, Aldrin, Postmaster General Blount.

1994, Aug. 4
1821-1822 A287 $1.50 #a.-f.   6.75 6.75
Souvenir Sheet
1823 A287 $6 multicolored   4.50 4.50

A288

PHILAKOREA
'94 — A289

40c, Entrance bridge, Songgwangsa Temple. 90c, Song-op Folk Village, Cheju. $3, Panoramic view, Port Sogwip'o.
Ceramics, Koryŏ & Choson Dynasties: No. 1827a, Long-necked bottle. b, Jar. c, Jar, diff. d, Ewer in form of bamboo shoot. e, Jar, diff. f, Pear-shaped bottle. g, Porcelain jar with dragon design. h, Porcelain jar with bonsai design.
$4, Ox, ox herder, vert.

1994, Aug. 4   Perf. 14, 13½ (#1827)
1824-1826 A288 Set of 3   3.50 3.50
Miniature Sheet of 8
1827 A289 75c #a.-h.   6.00 6.00
Souvenir Sheet
1828 A288 $4 multicolored   3.00 3.00

Miniature Sheets of 8

Stars of Country & Western Music — A290

No. 1829: a, Patsy Cline. b, Tanya Tucker. c, Dolly Parton. d, Anne Murray. e, Tammy Wynette. f, Loretta Lynn. g, Reba McEntire. h, Skeeter Davis.
No. 1830a, Travis Tritt. b, Dwight Yoakam. c, Billy Ray Cyrus. d, Alan Jackson. e, Garth Brooks. f, Vince Gill. g, Clint Black. h, Eddie Rabbit.
No. 1831: a, Hank Snow. b, Gene Autry. c, Jimmie Rogers. d, Ernest Tubb. e, Eddy Arnold. f, Willie Nelson. g, Johnny Cash. h, George Jones.
No. 1832, Kitty Wells, horiz. No. 1833, Hank Williams, Sr. No. 1834, Hank Williams, Jr.

1994, Aug. 18   Litho.   Perf. 14
1829-1831 A290 75c #a.-h., each   4.50 4.50
Souvenir Sheets
1832-1834 A290 $6 each   4.50 4.50

1994 World Cup Soccer Championships, US — A291

Designs: 15c, Hugo Sanchez, Mexico. 35c, Juergen Klinsman, Germany. 65c, Antigua player. $1.20, Cobi Jones, US. $4, Roberto Baggio, Italy. $5, Bwalya Kalusha, Zambia.
No. 1841, FIFA World Cup Trophy, vert. No. 1842, Maldive Islands player, vert.

1994, Sept. 19
1835-1840 A291 Set of 6   8.50 8.50
Souvenir Sheets
1841-1842 A291 $6 each   4.50 4.50

Order of the Caribbean Community — A292

First award recipients: 65c, Sir Shridath Ramphal, statesman, Guyana. 90c, William Demas, economist, Trinidad & Tobago. $1.20, Derek Walcott, writer, St. Lucia.

1994, Sept. 26
1843-1845 A292 Set of 3   2.00 2.00

Herman E. Sieger (1902-54) A293

Germany #C35, Graf Zeppelin, Sieger.

1994   Litho.   Perf. 14
1846 A293 $1.50 multicolored   1.25 1.25

Birds A294

Designs: 10c, Magnificent frigate birds. 15c, Bridled quail dove. 30c, Magnificent frigate bird hatchling. 40c, Purple-throated carib, vert. No. 1851, $1, Antigua broad-wing hawk, vert. No. 1852, $1, Magnificent frigate bird, vert. $3, Magnificent frigate bird, white head. $4, Yellow warbler.
No. 1855, West Indian Whistling duck. No. 1856, Magnificent frigate bird, diff., vert.

1994, Dec. 12   Litho.   Perf. 14
1847-1854 A294 Set of 8   7.50 7.50
Souvenir Sheets
1855-1856 A294 $6 each   4.50 4.50
World Wildlife Fund (#1847, 1849, 1852-1853).

Christmas A295

Paintings of Madonnas: 15c, The Virgin and Child by the Fireside, by Robert Campin. 35c, The Reading Madonna, by Giorgione. 40c, Madonna and Child, by Giovanni Bellini. 45c, The Litta Madonna, by da Vinci. 65c, The Virgin and Child Under the Apple Tree, by Lucas Cranach the Elder. 75c, Madonna and Child, by Master of the Female Half-Lengths. $1.20, An Allegory of the Church, by Alessandro Allori. $5, Madonna and Child Wreathed with Flowers, by Jacob Jordaens.
No. 1865, The Virgin Enthroned with Child, by Bohemian Master. No. 1866, Madonna and Child with (painting's) Commissioners, by Palma Vecchio.

1994, Dec. 12   Perf. 13½x14
1857-1864 A295 Set of 8   6.75 6.75
Souvenir Sheets
1865-1866 A295 $6 each   4.50 4.50

Birds — A296

Designs: 15c, Magnificent frigate bird. 25c, Blue-hooded euphonia. 35c, Meadowlark. 40c, Red-billed tropic bird. 45c, Greater flamingo. 60c, Yellow-faced grassquit. 65c, Yellow-billed cuckoo. 70c, Purple-throated carib. 75c, Bananaquit. 90c, Painted bunting. $1.20, Red-legged honeycreeper. $2, Jacana. $5, Greater antillean bullfinch. $10, Caribbean elaenia. $20, Trembler.

1995, Feb. 6   Perf. 14½x14
1867 A296 15c multicolored   .20   .20
1868 A296 25c multicolored   .20   .20
1869 A296 35c multicolored   .20   .20
1870 A296 40c multicolored   .20   .20
1871 A296 45c multicolored   .30   .30
1872 A296 60c multicolored   .35   .35
1873 A296 65c multicolored   .45   .45
1874 A296 70c multicolored   .45   .45
1875 A296 75c multicolored   .50   .50
1876 A296 90c multicolored   .60   .60
1877 A296 $1.20 multicolored .75   .75
1878 A296 $2 multicolored   1.25 1.25
1879 A296 $5 multicolored   3.00 3.00
1880 A296 $10 multicolored   6.25 6.25
1881 A296 $20 multicolored 13.00 13.00
Nos. 1867-1881 (15)   27.70 27.70

Prehistoric Animals A297

Designs, vert.: 15c, Pachycephalosaurus. 20c, Afrovenator. 65c, Centrosaurus. 90c, Pentaceratops. $1.20, Tarbosaurus. $5, Styracosaur.
No. 1888a, Kronosaur. b, Ichthyosaur. c, Plesiosaur. d, Archelon. e, Two tyrannosaurs. f, One tyrannosaur. g, One parasaurolophus. h, Two parasaurolophuses. i, Oviraptor. j, Protoceratops with eggs. k, Pteranodon, protoceratops. l, Protoceratops.
#1889, Carnotaurus. #1890, Corythosaurus.

1995, May 15   Litho.   Perf. 14
1882-1887 A297 Set of 6   6.25 6.25
Miniature Sheet of 12
1888 A297 75c #a.-l.   6.75 6.75
Souvenir Sheets
1889-1890 A297 $6 each   4.50 4.50

1996 Summer Olympics, Atlanta A298

Gold medalists: 15c, Al Oerter, US, discus. 20c, Greg Louganis, US, diving. 65c, Naim Suleymanoglu, Turkey, weight lifting. 90c, Louise Ritter, US, high jump. $1.20, Nadia Comaneci, Romania, gymnastics. $5, Olga Bardarenko, USSR, 10,000-meter run.
No. 1897, Lutz Hessilch, Germany, 1000-meter sprint cycling, vert. No. 1898, US team, eight-oared shell, 800-, 1500-meters.

1995, June 6   Litho.   Perf. 14
1891-1896 A298 Set of 6   6.00 6.00
Souvenir Sheets
1897-1898 A298 $6 each   4.50 4.50

Miniature Sheets of 6 or 8

End of World War II, 50th Anniv. A299

No. 1899: a, Chiang Kai-Shek. b, Gen. MacArthur. c, Gen. Chennault. d, Brigadier Orde C. Wingate. e, Gen. Stillwell. f, Field Marshall William Slim.
No. 1900: a, Map of Germany showing battle plan. b, Tanks, infantry advance. c, Red Army at gates of Berlin. d, German defenses smashed. e, Airstrikes on Berlin. f, German soldiers give up. g, Berlin falls to Russians. h, Germany surrenders.
$3, Plane, ship, Adm. Chester Nimitz. $6, Gen. Konev at command post outside Berlin, vert.

1995, July 20
1899 A299 $1.20 #a.-f. + label   5.50 5.50
1900 A299 $1.20 #a.-h. + label   7.25 7.25
Souvenir Sheets
1901 A299 $3 multicolored   2.25 2.25
1902 A299 $6 multicolored   4.50 4.50

UN, 50th Anniv. — A300   FAO, 50th Anniv. — A301

No. 1903: a, 75c, Earl of Halifax, signatures. b, 90c, Virginia Gildersleeve. c, $1.20, Harold Stassen.
$6, Franklin D. Roosevelt.

1995, July 20   Litho.   Perf. 14
1903 A300 Strip of 3, #a.-c.   2.25 2.25
Souvenir Sheet
1904 A300 $6 multicolored   4.50 4.50
No. 1903 is a continuous design.

1995, July 20
Street market scene: No. 1905a, 75c, Two women, bananas. b, 90c, Women, crates, produce. c, $1.20, Women talking, one with box of food on head.
$6, Tractor.
1905 A301 Strip of 3, #a.-c.   2.25 2.25
Souvenir Sheet
1906 A301 $6 multicolored   4.50 4.50
No. 1905 is a continuous design.

Rotary Intl., 90th Anniv. — A302

1995, July 20
1907 A302 $5 shown   3.75 3.75
Souvenir Sheet
1908 A302 $6 Natl. flag, Rotary emblem   4.50 4.50

Queen Mother, 95th Birthday A303

#1909: a, Drawing. b, White & dark pink hat. c, Formal portrait. d, Blue green hat, dress. #1910, Light blue dress, pearls.

1995, July 20   Perf. 13½x14
1909 A303 $1.50 Strip or block of 4, #a.-d.   4.50 4.50
Souvenir Sheet
1910 A303 $6 multicolored   4.50 4.50
No. 1909 was issued in sheets of 2 each.

Miniature Sheet of 12

Ducks — A304

No. 1911: a, Ring-necked duck. b, Ruddy duck. c, Green-winged teal (d). d, Wood duck. e, Hooded merganser (f). f, Lesser scaup (g). g, West Indian tree duck (h, k, l). h, Fulvous whistling duck (l). i, Bahama pintail. j, Shoveler (i). k, Masked duck (l). l, American widgeon. $6, Blue-winged teal.

1995, Aug. 31   Litho.   Perf. 14
1911 A304 75c #a.-l.   6.75 6.75
Souvenir Sheet
1912 A304 $6 multicolored   4.50 4.50

Bees
A305

Designs: 90c, Mining bee. $1.20, Solitary bee. $1.65, Leaf-cutter. $1.75, Honey bee. $6, Solitary mining bee.

1995, Sept. 7
1913-1916 A305   Set of 4   4.25 4.25
Souvenir Sheet
1917 A305 $6 multicolored   4.50 4.50

Miniature Sheet of 12

Domestic
Cats
A306

Designs: a, Somali. b, Persian. c, Devon rex. d, Turkish angora. e, Himalayan. f, Maine coon. g, Nonpedigree. h, American wirehair. i, British shorthair. j, American curl. k, Black nonpedigree. l, Birman. $6, Siberian, vert.

1995, Sept. 7
1918 A306 45c #a.-l.   4.00 4.00
Souvenir Sheet
1919 A306 $6 multicolored   4.50 4.50

Miniature Sheet

Tourism
A307

Stylized paintings depicting: a, Caring. b, Marketing. c, Working. d, Enjoying life.

1995, July 31   Litho.   Perf. 14
1920 A307 $2 Sheet of 4, #a.-d. 6.00 6.00
Date of issue is in question. First day cover of Aug. 10, 1995, has been seen.

Greenbay
Moravian Church,
150th
Anniv. — A308

20c, 1st structure, wood & stone. 60c, 1st stone, concrete building, 3/67. 75c, $2, Present structure. 90c, John A. Buckley, 1st minister of African descent. $1.20, John Ephraim Knight, longest serving minister. $6, Front of present structure.

1995, Sept. 4
1921-1926 A308   Set of 6   4.25 4.25
Souvenir Sheet
1927 A308 $6 multicolored   4.50 4.50

Miniature Sheet of 12

Flowers — A309

No. 1928: a, Narcissus. b, Camellia. c, Iris. d, Tulip. e, Poppy. f, Peony. g, Magnolia. h, Oriental lily. i, Rose. j, Pansy. k, Hydrangea. l, Azaleas.
$6, Bird of paradise, calla lily.

1995, Sept. 7
1928 A309 75c #a.-l.   6.75 6.75
Souvenir Sheet
1929 A309 $6 multicolored   4.50 4.50

1995 Boy Scout Jamboree,
Holland — A310

Tents - #1930: a, Explorer. b, Camper. c, Wall.
#1931: a, Trail tarp. b, Miner's. c, Voyager.
#1932, Scout with camping equipment, vert.
#1933, Scout making camp fire.

1995, Oct. 5   Strip of 3
1930-1931 A310 $1.20 #a.-c., ea 2.75 2.75
Souvenir Sheets
1932-1933 A310 $6 each   4.50 4.50
For overprints see Nos. 1963-1966.

Trains
A311

Designs: 35c, Gabon. 65c, Canadian. 75c, US. 90c, British high-speed. $1.20, French high-speed. No. 1939, American high-speed (Amtrak).
No. 1940: a, Australian diesel. b, Italian high-speed. c, Thai diesel. d, US steam. e, South African steam. f, Natal steam. g, US war train. h, British steam. i, British steam, diff.
No. 1941, Australian diesel, vert. No. 1942, Asian steam, vert.

1995, Oct. 23   Litho.   Perf. 14
1934-1939 A311   Set of 6   7.50 7.50
Miniature Sheet of 9
1940 A311 $1.20 #a.-i.   8.25 8.25
Souvenir Sheets
1941-1942 A311 $6 each   4.50 4.50

Birds — A312

No. 1943: a, Purple-thoated carib. b, Antillean crested hummingbird. c, Bananaquit (d). d, Mangrove cuckoo. e, Troupial. f, Green-throated carib (e, g). g, Yellow warbler (h). h, Blue-hooded Euphonia. i, Scally-breasted thrasher. j, Burrowing owl (i). k, Caribbean crackle (k). l, Adelaide's warbler.
$6, Purple gallinule.

1995
Miniature Sheet of 12
1943 A312 75c #a.-l.   6.75 6.75
Souvenir Sheet
1944 A312 $6 multicolored   4.50 4.50

Miniature Sheets of 9

Nobel Prize Fund Established,
Cent. — A313

Recipients: No. 1945a, S.Y. Agnon, literature, 1966. b, Kipling, literature, 1907. c, Aleksandr Solzhenitsyn, literature, 1970. d, Jack Steinberger, physics, 1988. e, Andrei Sakharov, peace, 1975. f, Otto Stern, physics, 1943. g, Steinbeck, literature, 1962. h, Nadine Gordimer, literature, 1991. i, Faulkner, literature, 1949.
No. 1946: a, Hammarskjold, peace, 1961. b, Georg Wittig, chemistry, 1979. c, Wilhelm Ostwald, chemistry, 1909. d, Koch, physiology or medicine, 1945. e, Karl Ziegler, chemistry, 1963. f, Fleming, physiology or medicine, 1945. g, Hermann Staudinger, chemistry, 1953. h, Manfred Eigen, chemistry, 1967. i, Arno Penzias, physics, 1978.
No. 1947, Elie Wiesel, peace, 1986, vert. No. 1948, Dalai Lama, peace, 1989, vert.

1995, Nov. 8
1945-1946 A313 $1 #a.-i. + label,
each   6.75 6.75
Souvenir Sheets
1947-1948 A313 $6 each   4.50 4.50

Christmas
A314

Details or entire paintings: 15c, Rest on the Flight into Egypt, by Veronese. 35c, Madonna with The Child, by Van Dyck. 65c, Sacred Conversation Piece, by Veronese. 75c, Vision of Saint Anthony, by Van Dyck. 90c, The Virgin and the Infant, by Van Eyck. No. 1954, The Immaculate Conception, by Tiepolo.
$5, Christ Appearing to His Mother, by Van Der Weyden. No. 1956, Infant Jesus and the Young St. John, by Murillo.

1995, Dec. 18   Litho.   Perf. 13½x14
1949-1954 A314   Set of 6   6.75 6.75
Souvenir Sheets
1955 A314 $5 multicolored   3.75 3.75
1956 A314 $6 multicolored   4.50 4.50

Miniature Sheet

Elvis Presley
(1935-77)
A315

Nos. 1957-1958, Various portraits depicting Presley's life.

1995, Dec. 8   Perf. 14
1957 A315 $1 Sheet of 9, #a.-i. 6.75 6.75
Souvenir Sheet
1958 A315 $6 multicolored   4.50 4.50

John Lennon
(1940-80),
Entertainer — A316

45c, 50c, 65c, 75c, Various portraits of Lennon.

1995, Dec. 8
1959-1962 A316   Set of 4   1.75 1.75
1962A A316 $6 like 75c   4.50 4.50
Nos. 1959-1962 were each issued in miniature sheets of 16.
No. 1962A has a continuous design.

Nos. 1930-1933 Ovptd.

1995, Dec. 14   Strips of 3
1963-1964 A310 $1.20 #a.-c., ea 2.75 2.75
Souvenir Sheets
1965-1966 A310 $6 each   4.50 4.50
Size and location of overprint varies.

Mushrooms
A317

#1967: a, Hygrophoropsis aurantiaca. b, Hygrophorus bakerensis. c, Hygrophorus conicus. d, Hygrophorus miniatus.
#1968: a, Suillus brevipes. b, Suillus luteus. c, Suillus granulatus. d, Suillus caerulescens. No. 1969, Conocybe filaris. No. 1970, Hygrocybe flavescens.

1996, Apr. 22   Litho.   Perf. 14
Strip of 4
1967-1968 A317 75c #a.-d., ea   2.25 2.25
Souvenir Sheets
1969-1970 A317 $6 each   4.50 4.50
#1967-1968 were each issued in sheets of 12 stamps.

Sailing Ships
A318

Designs: 15c, Resolution. 25c, Mayflower. 45c, Santa Maria. No. 1970D, 75c, Aemilia, Holland, 1630. No. 1970E, 75c, Sovereign of the Seas, England, 1637. 90c, HMS Victory, England, 1765.

Battleships: No. 1971: a, Aemila, Holland, 1630. b, Sovereign of the Seas, England, 1637. c, Royal Louis, France, 1692. d, HMS Royal George, England, 1715. e, Le Protecteur, France, 1761. f, HMS Victory, England, 1765.

Ships of exploration: No. 1972: a, Santa Maria. b, Victoria. c, Golden Hinde. d, Mayflower. e, Griffin. f, Resolution.

No. 1973, Grande Hermine. No. 1974, USS Constitution, 1797.

1996, Apr. 25
1970A-1970F	A318	Set of 6	2.50 2.50

Sheets of 6
1971	A318	$1.20 #a.-f.	5.50 5.50
1972	A318	$1.50 #a.-f.	6.75 6.75

Souvenir Sheets
1973-1974	A318	$6 each	4.50 4.50

1996 Summer Olympics, Atlanta
A319

Designs: 65c, Florence Griffith Joyner, women's track, vert. 75c, Olympic Stadium, Seoul, 1988. 90c, Allison Jolly, yachting. $1.20, 2000m Tandem cycling.

Medalists: No. 1979a, Wolfgang Nordwig, pole vault. b, Shirley Strong, women's 100m hurdles. c, Sergei Bubka, pole vault. d, Filbert Bayi, 3000m steeplechase. e, Victor Saneyev, triple jump. f, Silke Renk, women's javelin. g, Daley Thompson, decathlon. h, Bob Richards, pole vault. i, Parry O'Brien, shot put.

Diving medalists: No. 1980a, Ingrid Kramer, women's platform. b, Kelly McCormick, women's springboard. c, Gary Tobian, men's springboard. d, Greg Louganis, men's diving. e, Michelle Mitchell, women's platform. f, Zhou Jihong, women's platform. g, Wendy Wyland, women's platform. h, Xu Yanmei, women's platform. i, Fu Mingxia, women's platform.

$5, Bill Toomey, decathlon. $6, Mark Lenzi, men's springboard.

1996, May 6
1975-1978	A319	Set of 4	2.50 2.50

Sheets of 9
1979-1980	A319	90c #a.-i., each	6.25 6.25

Souvenir Sheets
1981	A319	$5 multicolored	3.75 3.75
1982	A319	$6 multicolored	4.50 4.50

Sea Birds
A320

No. 1983: a, Black skimmer. b, Black-capped petrel. c, Sooty tern. d, Royal tern.

No. 1984 a, Pomarina jaegger. b, White-tailed tropicbird. c, Northern gannet. d, Laughing gull.

$5, Great frigatebird. $6, Brown pelican.

1996, May 13
Vertical Strip of 4
1983-1984	A320	75c #a.-d., ea	2.25 2.25

Souvenir Sheets
1985	A320	$5 multicolored	3.75 3.75
1986	A320	$6 multicolored	4.50 4.50

Nos. 1983-1984 were each issued in sheets of 12 stamps with each strip in sheet having a different order.

Disney Characters In Scenes from Jules Verne's Science Fiction Novels — A321

Designs: 1c, Around the World in Eighty Days. 2c, Journey to the Center of the Earth. 5c, Michel Strogoff. 10c, From the Earth to the Moon. 15c, Five Weeks in a Balloon. 20c, Around the World in Eighty Days, diff. $1, The Mysterious Island. $2, From the Earth to the Moon, diff. $3, Captain Grant's Children. $5, Twenty Thousand Leagues Under the Sea.

No. 1997, Twenty Thousand Leagues Under the Sea, diff. No. 1998, Journey to the Center of the Earth, diff.

1996, June 6　Litho.　Perf. 14x13½
1987-1996	A321	Set of 10	8.75 8.75

Souvenir Sheets
1997-1998	A321	$6 each	4.50 4.50

Bruce Lee (1940-73), Martial Arts Expert — A322

Various portraits.

1996, June 13　　Perf. 14
1999	A322	75c Sheet of 9, #a.-i.	5.25 5.25

Souvenir Sheet
2000	A322	$5 multicolored	3.75 3.75

China '96 (#1999).

Queen Elizabeth II, 70th Birthday — A323

Designs: a, In blue dress, pearls. b, Carrying bouquet of flowers. c, In uniform. $6, Painting as younger woman.

1996, July 17　　Perf. 13½x14
2001	A323	$2 Strip of 3, #a.-c.	4.50 4.50

Souvenir Sheet
2002	A323	$6 multicolored	4.50 4.50

No. 2001 was issued in sheets of 9 stamps.

Traditional Cavalry
A324

a, Ancient Egyptian. b, 13th cent. English. c, 16th cent. Spanish. d, 18th cent. Chinese. $6, 19th cent. French.

1996, July 24　Litho.　Perf. 14
2003	A324	60c Block of 4, #a.-d.	1.75 1.75

Souvenir Sheet
2004	A324	$6 multicolored	4.50 4.50

No. 2003 was issued in sheets of 16 stamps.

A325

A326

UNICEF, 50th Anniv.: 75c, Girl. 90c, Children. $1.20, Woman holding baby. $6, Girl, diff.

1996, July 30
2005-2007	A325	Set of 3	2.00 2.00

Souvenir Sheet
2008	A325	$6 multicolored	4.50 4.50

1996, July 30

Site, flower: 75c, Tomb of Zachariah, verbascum sinuatum. 90c, Pool of Siloam, hyacinthus orientalis. $1.20, Hurva Synagogue, ranunculus asiaticus. $6, Model of Herod's Temple.
2009-2011	A326	Set of 3	2.25 2.25

Souvenir Sheet
2012	A326	$6 multicolored	4.50 4.50

Jerusalem, 3000th anniv.

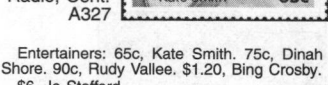

Radio, Cent.
A327

Entertainers: 65c, Kate Smith. 75c, Dinah Shore. 90c, Rudy Vallee. $1.20, Bing Crosby. $6, Jo Stafford.

1996, July 30
2013-2016	A327	Set of 4	2.75 2.75

Souvenir Sheet
2017	A327	$6 multicolored	4.50 4.50

Christmas
A328

Details or entire paintings, by Filippo Lippi: 60c, Madonna Enthroned. 90c, Adoration of the Child and Saints. $1, Annunciation. $1.20, Birth of the Virgin. $1.60, Adoration of the Child. $1.75, Madonna and Child.

No. 2024, Madonna and Child, diff. No. 2025, Circumcision.

1996, Nov. 25　　Perf. 13½x14
2018-2023	A328	Set of 6	5.25 5.25

Souvenir Sheets
2024-2025	A328	$6 each	4.50 4.50

Disney Pals — A329

1c, Goofy, Wilbur. 2c, Donald, Goofy. 5c, Donald, Panchito, Jose Carioca. 10c, Mickey, Goofy. 15c, Dale, Chip. 20c, Pluto, Mickey. $1, Daisy, Minnie at ice cream shop. $2, Daisy, Minnie. $3, Gus Goose, Donald.

No. 2035, Donald, vert. No. 2036, Goofy.

1997, Feb. 17　Litho.　Perf. 14x13½
2026-2034	A329	Set of 9	5.00 5.00

Souvenir Sheets
Perf. 13½x14, 14x13½
2035-2036	A329	$6 each	4.50 4.50

Salute to Broadway
A330

Stars, show: No. 2037: a, Robert Preston, The Music Man. b, Michael Crawford, Phantom of the Opera. c, Zero Mostel, Fiddler on the Roof. d, Patti Lupone, Evita. e, Raul Julia, Threepenny Opera. f, Mary Martin, South Pacific. g, Carol Channing, Hello Dolly. h, Yul Brynner, The King and I. i, Julie Andrews, My Fair Lady.

$6, Mickey Rooney, Sugar Babies.

1997　　Perf. 14
2037	A330	$1 Sheet of 9, #a.-i.	6.80 6.80

Souvenir Sheet
2038	A330	$6 multicolored	4.50 4.50

Butterflies — A331

Designs: 90c, Charaxes porthos. $1.20, Aethiopana honorius. $1.60, Charaxes hadrianus. $1.75, Precis westermanni.

No. 2043: a, Charaxes protoclea. b, Byblia ilithyia. c, Black-headed tchagra (bird). d, Charaxes nobilis. e, Pseudacraea boisduvali. f, Charaxes smaragdalis. g, Charaxes lasti. h, Pseudacraea poggei. i, Graphium colonna.

No. 2044a, Carmine bee-eater (bird). b, Pseudacraea eurytus. c, Hypolimnas monteironis. d, Charaxes anticlea. e, Graphium leonidas. f, Graphium illyris. g, Nepheronia argia. h, Graphium policenes. i, Papilio dardanus.

No. 2045, Euxanthe tiberius, horiz. No. 2046, Charaxes lactitinctus, horiz. No. 2047, Euphaedra neophron.

1997, Mar. 10
2039-2042	A331	Set of 4	4.00 4.00

Sheets of 9
2043-2044	A331	$1.10 #a.-i., ea	7.50 7.50

Souvenir Sheets
2045-2047	A331	$6 each	4.50 4.50

UNESCO, 50th Anniv. — A332

World Heritage Sites: 60c, Convent of the Companions of Jesus, Morelia, Mexico. 90c, Fortress, San Lorenzo, Panama, vert. $1, Canaima Natl. Park, Venezuela, vert. $1.20, Huascarán Natl. Park, Peru, vert. $1.60, Church of San Francisco, Guatemala, vert. $1.75, Santo Domingo, Dominican Republic, vert.

No. 2054, vert: a-c, Guanajuato, Mexico. d, Jesuit missions of the Chiquitos, Bolivia. e, Huascarán Natl. Park, Peru. f, Jesuit missions, La Santisima, Paraguay. g, Cartagena, Colombia. h, Old Havana fortification, Cuba.

No. 2055: a, Tikal Natl. Park, Guatemala. b, Rio Platano Reserve, Honduras. c, Ruins of Copán, Honduras. d, Church of El Carmen, Antigua, Guatemala. e, Teotihuacán, Mexico.

No. 2056, Teotihuacán, Mexico, diff. No. 2057, Tikal Natl. Park, Guatemala, diff.

1997, Apr. 10	Litho.	Perf. 14
2048-2053 A332	Set of 6	5.25 5.25

Sheets of 8 or 5

| 2054 A332 | $1.10 #a.-h. + label | 6.75 6.75 |
| 2055 A332 | $1.65 #a.-e. + label | 6.25 6.25 |

Souvenir Sheets

| 2056-2057 A332 | $6 each | 4.50 4.50 |

Fauna — A333

No. 2058: a, Red bishop. b, Yellow baboon. c, Superb starling. d, Ratel. e, Hunting dog. f, Serval.

No. 2059: a, Okapi. b, Giant forest squirrel. c, Masked weaver. d, Common genet. e, Yellow-billed stork. f, Red-headed agama.

No. 2060, Malachite kingfisher. No. 2061, Gray crowned crane. No. 2062, Bat-eared fox.

1997, Apr. 24

Sheets of 6

| 2058 A333 | $1.20 #a.-f. | 5.50 5.50 |
| 2059 A333 | $1.65 #a.-f. | 7.50 7.50 |

Souvenir Sheets

| 2060-2062 A333 | $6 each | 4.50 4.50 |

Charlie Chaplin (1889-1977), Comedian, Actor A334

Various portraits.

1997, Feb. 24	Litho.	Perf. 14
2063 A334	$1 Sheet of 9, #a.-i.	6.75 6.75

Souvenir Sheet

| 2064 A334 | $6 multicolored | 4.50 4.50 |

Paul P. Harris (1868-1947), Founder of Rotary, Intl. — A335

Designs: $1.75, Service above self, James Grant, Ivory Coast, 1994, portrait of Harris. $6, Group study exchange, New Zealand.

1997, June 12	Litho.	Perf. 14
2065 A335	$1.75 multicolored	1.25 1.25

Souvenir Sheet

| 2066 A335 | $6 multicolored | 4.50 4.50 |

Heinrich von Stephan (1831-97) A336

Portrait of Von Stephan and: No. 2067: a, Kaiser Wilhelm I. b, UPU emblem. c, Pigeon Post.
$6, Von Stephan, Basel messenger, 1400's.

1997, June 12

| 2067 A336 | $1.75 Sheet of 3, #a.-c. | 4.00 4.00 |

Souvenir Sheet

| 2068 A336 | $6 multicolored | 4.50 4.50 |

PACIFIC 97.

Queen Elizabeth II, Prince Philip, 50th Wedding Anniv. A337

No. 2069: a, Queen. b, Royal arms. c, Queen, Prince in royal attire. d, Queen, King riding in open carriage. e, Balmoral Castle. f, Prince Philip.
$6, Early portrait of Queen, King in royal attire.

1997, June 12

| 2069 A337 | $1 Sheet of 6, #a.-f. | 4.50 4.50 |

Souvenir Sheet

| 2070 A337 | $6 multicolored | 4.50 4.50 |

Grimm's Fairy Tales A338

Scenes from "Cinderella:" No. 2071: a, Mother, stepsisters. b, Cinderella, fairy godmother. c, Cinderella, Prince Charming.
$6, Prince trying shoe on Cinderella.

1997, June 13	Perf. 13½x14
2071 A338	$1.75 Sheet of 3, #a.-c.	4.00 4.00

Souvenir Sheet

| 2072 A338 | $6 multicolored | 4.50 4.50 |

Chernobyl Disaster, 10th Anniv. A339

Designs: $1.65, UNESCO. $2, Chabad's Children of Chernobyl.

1997, June 12

| 2073 A339 | $1.65 multicolored | 1.25 1.25 |
| 2074 A339 | $2 multicolored | 1.50 1.50 |

Mushrooms — A340

Designs: 45c, Marasmius rotula. 65c, Cantharellus cibarius. 70c, Lepiota cristata. 90c, Auricularia mesenterica. $1, Pholiota alnicola. $1.65, Leccinum aurantiacum.

No. 2081: a, Entoloma serrulatum. b, Panaeolus sphinctrinus. c, Volvariella bombycina. d, Conocybe percincta. e, Pluteus cervinus. f, Russula foetens.

No. 2082, Panellus serotinus. No. 2083, Amanita cothurnata.

1997, Aug. 12	Litho.	Perf. 14
2075-2080 A340	Set of 6	4.00 4.00

Sheets of 6

| 2081 A340 | $1.75 #a.-f. | 8.00 8.00 |

Souvenir Sheets

| 2082-2083 A340 | $6 each | 4.50 4.50 |

Orchids — A341

Designs: 45c, Odontoglossum cervantesii. 65c, Medford star. 75c, Motes resplendent. 90c, Debutante. $1, Apple blossom. $2, Dendrobium.

No. 2090: a, Angel lace. b, Precious stones. c, Orange theope butterfly. d, Promenaea xanthina. e, Lycaste macrobulbon. f, Amesiella philippinensis. g, Machu Picchu. h, Zuma urchin.

No. 2091: a, Sophia Martin. b, Dogface butterfly. c, Mini purple. d, Showgirl. e, Mem. Dorothy Bertsch. f, Black II. g, Leeanum. h, Paphiopedilum macranthum.

No. 2092, Seine. No. 2093, Paphiopedilum gratrixianum.

1997, Aug. 19	Litho.	Perf. 14
2084-2089 A341	Set of 6	4.25 4.25

Sheets of 8

| 2090-2091 A341 | $1.65 #a.-h., each | 5.00 5.00 |

Souvenir Sheets

| 2092-2093 A341 | $6 each | 4.50 4.50 |

1998 World Cup Soccer Championships, France — A342

Designs: 60c, Maradona, Argentina, 1986. 75c, Fritzwalter, W. Germany, 1954. 90c, Zoff, Italy, 1982. $1.20, Moore, England, 1966. $1.65, Alberto, Brazil, 1970. $1.75, Matthäus, W. Germany.

No. 2100, vert: a, Ademir, Brazil, 1950. b, Eusebio, Portugal, 1966. c, Fontaine, France, 1958. d, Schillaci, Italy, 1990. e, Leonidas, Brazil, 1938. f, Stabile, Argentina, 1930. g, Nejedly, Czechoslovakia, 1934. h, Muller, W. Germany, 1970.

No. 2101, Players, W. Germany, 1990. No. 2102, Bebeto, Brazil, vert.

1997, Oct. 6	Litho.	Perf. 14
2094-2099 A342	Set of 6	6.00 6.00

Sheet of 8 + Label

| 2100 A342 | $1 #a.-h. | 6.00 6.00 |

Souvenir Sheets

| 2101-2102 A342 | $6 each | 4.50 4.50 |

Domestic Animals A343

Dogs: No. 2103: a, Dachshund. b, Staffordshire terrier. c, Sharpei. d, Beagle. e, Norfolk terrier. f, Golden retriever.

Cats: No. 2104: a, Scottish fold. b, Japanese bobtail. c, Tabby manx. d, Bicolor American shorthair. e, Sorrel abyssinian. f, Himalayan blue point.

No. 2105, Siberian husky, vert. No. 2106, Red tabby American shorthair kitten, vert.

1997, Oct. 27	Litho.	Perf. 14
2103-2104 A343	$1.65 #a.-f., ea	7.50 7.50

Souvenir Sheets

| 2105-2106 A343 | $6 each | 4.50 4.50 |

Early Trains A344

No. 2107: a, Original Trevithick drawing, 1804. b, "Puffing Billy," William Hedley, 1860. c, Crampton locomotive, Northern Railway, France, 1858. d, Twenty-five ton locomotive, Lawrence Machine Shop, 1860's. e, First locomotive, "Mississippi," built in England. f, "Coppernob," locomotive by Edward Bury, Furness Railway.

No. 2108: a, "Jenny Lind," by David Joy for E.B. Wilson. b, "Atlantic" type locomotive, by Schenectady Locomotive Works, 1899. c, British built tank engine, Japan, by Kisons of Leeds, 1881. d, Express freight locomotive, 4-8-2 type, Pennsylvania Railroad. e, Four-cylinder locomotive, by Karl Golsdorf, Austria. f, "E" series 0-10-0 locomotive, produced by Lugansk Works, Russia, 1930.

No. 2109, "Patente" George Stephenson, 1843. No. 2110, Brunel's Trestle, Lynher River.

1997, Nov. 10

Sheets of 6

| 2107-2108 A344 | $1.65 #a.-f., ea | 7.50 7.50 |

Souvenir Sheets

| 2109-2110 A344 | $6 each | 4.50 4.50 |

Christmas A345

Entire paintings or details: 15c, The Angel Leaving Tobias and His Family, by Rembrandt. 25c, The Resurrection, by Martin Knoller. 60c, Astronomy, by Raphael. 75c, Music-making Angel, by Melozzo da Forli. 90c, Amor, by Parmigianino. $1.20, Madonna and Child with

Saints John the Baptist, Anthony, Stephen and Jerome, by Rosso Fiorentino.
No. 2117, The Portinari Altarpiece, by Hugo Van Der Goes. No. 2118, The Wedding of Tobiolo, by Gianantonio and Francesco Guardi.

1997, Dec. 2   **Litho.**   **Perf. 14**
2111-2116 A345   Set of 6   5.25 5.25
Souvenir Sheets
2117-2118 A345 $6 each   4.50 4.50

Diana, Princess of Wales (1961-97) — A346

Various portraits, color of sheet margin: No. 2119, Pale green. No. 2120, Pale pink. No. 2121, With her sons (in margin). No. 2122, With Pope John Paul II (in margin).

1998, Jan. 19   **Litho.**   **Perf. 14**
Sheets of 6
2119-2120 A346 $1.65 #a.-f., ea   7.50 7.50
Souvenir Sheets
2121-2122 A346 $6 each   4.50 4.50

Fish
A347

Designs: 75c, Yellow damselfish. 90c, Barred hamlet. $1, Jewelfish. $1.20, Bluehead wrasse. $1.50, Queen angelfish. $1.75, Queen triggerfish.
No. 2129: a, Jack-knife fish. b, Cuban hogfish. c, Sergeant major. d, Neon goby. e, Jawfish. f, Flamefish.
No. 2130: a, Rock beauty. b, Yellowtail snapper. c, Creole wrasse. d, Slender filefish. e, Squirrel fish. f, Fairy basslet.
No. 2131, Black-capped gramma. No. 2132, Porkfish.

1998, Feb. 19
2123-2128 A347   Set of 6   5.50 5.50
Sheets of 6
2129-2130 A347 $1.65 #a.-f., ea   7.50 7.50
Souvenir Sheets
2131-2132 A347 $6 each   4.50 4.50

Cedar Hall Moravian Church, 175th Anniv. A348

Designs: 20c, First church, manse, 1822-40. 45c, Cedar Hall School, 1840. 75c, Hugh A. King, former minister. 90c, Present structure. $1.20, Water tank, 1822. $2, Former manse demolished, 1978.
$6, Present structure, diff.

1998, Mar. 16   **Litho.**   **Perf. 14**
2133-2138 A348   Set of 6   4.25 4.25
Souvenir Sheet
2139 A348 $6 multicolored   4.50 4.50
No. 2139 contains one 50x37mm stamp.

Lighthouses — A349

Lighthouse, location: 45c, Trinity, Europa Point, Gibraltar, vert. 65c, Tierra Del Fuego, Argentina. 75c, Point Loma, California, US.

90c, Groenpoint, South Africa, vert. $1, Youghal, County Cork, Ireland, vert. $1.20, Launceston, Tasmania, Australia, vert. $1.65, Point Abino, Ontario, Canada. $1.75, Great Inagua, Bahamas.
$6, Capa Hatteras, North Carolina, US.

1998, Apr. 20
2140-2147 A349   Set of 8   6.50 6.50
Souvenir Sheet
2148 A349 $6 multi, vert.   4.50 4.50

Winnie the Pooh
A350

No. 2149: a, Pooh, Tigger in January. b, Pooh, Piglet in February. c, Piglet in March. d, Tigger, Pooh, Piglet in April. e, Kanga, Roo in May. f, Pooh, Owl in June.
No. 2150: a, Pooh, Eeyore, Tigger, Piglet in July. b, Pooh, Piglet in August. c, Christopher Robin in September. d, Eeyore in October. e, Pooh, Rabbit in November. f, Pooh, Piglet in December.
No. 2151, Pooh, Rabbit holding blanket, Spring. No. 2152, Pooh holding hand to mouth, Summer. No. 2153, Pooh holding rake, Fall. No. 2154, Eeyore, Pooh, Winter.

1998, May 11   **Litho.**   **Perf. 13½x14**
Sheets of 6
2149-2150 A360 $1 #a.-f., each   4.50 4.50
Souvenir Sheet
2151-2154 A350 $6 each   4.50 4.50

Thomas Oliver Robinson Memorial High School, Cent. A351

Designs: 20c, $6, Nellie Robinson (1880-1972), founder, vert. 45c, School picture, 1985. 65c, Former building, 1930-49. 75c, Students with present headmistress, Natalie Hurst. 90c, Ina Loving (1908-96), educator, vert. $1.20, Present building, 1950.

1998, July 23   **Litho.**   **Perf. 14**
2155-2160 A351   Set of 6   3.25 3.25
Souvenir Sheet
2161 A351 $6 multicolored   4.50 4.50
No. 2161 is a continuous design.

Intl. Year of the Ocean A352

Marine life, "20,000 Leagues Under the Sea:" No. 2162: a, Spotted eagle ray. b, Manta ray. c, Hawksbill turtle. d, Jellyfish. e, Queen angelfish. f, Octopus. g, Emperor angelfish. h, Regal angelfish. i, Porkfish. j, Raccoon butterfly fish. k, Atlantic barracuda. l, Sea horse. m, Nautilus. n, Trumpet fish. o, White tip shark. p, Spanish galleon. q, Black tip shark. r, Longnosed butterfly fish. s, Green moray eel. t, Captain Nemo. u, Treasure chest. v, Hammerhead shark. w, Divers. x, Lion fish. y, Clown fish.
Wildlife and birds: No. 2163: a, Maroon tailed conure. b, Cocoi heron. c, Common tern. d, Rainbow lorikeet. e, Saddleback butterfly fish. f, Goatfish, cat shark. g, Blue shark, stingray. h, Majestic snapper. i, Nassau grouper. j, Black-cap gramma, blue tang. k, Stingrays. l, Stingrays, giant starfish.
#2164, Fiddler ray. #2165, Humpback whale.

1998, Aug. 17
2162 A352 40c Sheet of 25, #a.-
       y.   7.50 7.50

2163 A352 75c Sheet of 12, #a.-l. 6.75 6.75
Souvenir Sheets
2164-2165 A352 $6 each   4.50 4.50

Ships
A353

No. 2166: a, Savannah. b, Viking ship. c, Greek warship.
No. 2167: a, Clipper. b, Dhow. c, Fishing cat.
No. 2168, Dory, vert. No. 2169, Baltimore clipper. No. 2170, English warship, 13th cent.

1998, Aug. 18   **Perf. 14x14½**
Sheets of 3
2166-2167 A353 $1.75 #a.-c., ea   4.00 4.00
Souvenir Sheets
Perf. 14
2168-2170 A353 $6 each   4.50 4.50

CARICOM, 25th Anniv. — A354

1998, Aug. 20   **Litho.**   **Perf. 13½**
2171 A354 $1 multicolored   .75 .75

Antique Automobiles — A355

No. 2172: a, 1911 Torpedo. b, 1913 Mercedes 22. c, 1920 Rover. d, 1956 Mercedes Benz. e, 1934 Packard V12. f, 1924 Opel.
Fords: No. 2173: a, 1896. b, 1903 Model A. c, 1928 Model T. d, 1922 Model T. e, 1929 Blackhawk. f, 1934 Sedan. #2174, 1908. #2175, 1929.

1998, Sept. 1   **Perf. 14**
Sheets of 6
2172-2173 A355 $1.65 #a.-f., ea   7.50 7.50
Souvenir Sheets
2174-2175 A355 $6 each   4.50 4.50
Nos. 2174-2175 each contain one 60x40mm stamp.

Aircraft A356

No. 2176: a, NASA Space Shuttle. b, Saab Grippen. c, Eurofighter EF2000. d, Sukhoi SU 27. e, Northrop B-2. f, Lockheed F-117 Nighthawk.
No. 2177: a, Lockheed-Boeing General Dynamics Yf-22. b, Dassault-Breguet Rafale BO 1. c, MiG 29. d, Dassault-Breguet Mirage 2000D. e, Rockwell B-1B Lancer. f, McDonnell-Douglas C-17A.
No. 2178, Sukhoi SU 35. No. 2179, F18 Hornet.

1998, Sept. 21
Sheets of 6
2176-2177 A356 $1.65 #a.-f., ea   7.50 7.50
Souvenir Sheets
2178-2179 A356 $6 each   4.50 4.50

Famous People of the 20th Cent. — A357

Inventors and their inventions: No. 2180: a, Rudolf Diesel (1858-1913). b, Internal combustion, diesel engines. c, Zeppelin war balloon, Intrepid. d, Ferdinand von Zeppelin (1838-1917). e, Wilhelm Conrad Röntgen (1845-1923). f, X-ray machine. g, Saturn rocket. h, Wernher von Braun (1912-77).
No. 2181: a, Carl Benz (1844-1929). b, Internal combustion engine, automobile. c, Atomic bomb. d, Albert Einstein. e, Leopold Godowsky, Jr. (1901-83) and Leopold Damrosch Mannes (1899-1964). f, Kodachrome film. g, First turbo jet airplane. h, Hans Pabst von Ohain (1911-98).
No. 2182, Hans Geiger (1882-1945), inventor of the Geiger counter. No. 2183, William Shockley (1910-89), developer of transistors.

1998, Nov. 10   **Litho.**   **Perf. 14**
Sheets of 8
2180-2181 A357 $1 #a.-h., each   6.00 6.00
Souvenir Sheets
2182-2183 A357 $6 each   4.50 4.50
Nos. 2180b-2180c, 2180f-2180g, 2181b-2181c, 2181f-2181g are 53x38mm.

Diana, Princess of Wales (1961-97) A358

1998, Nov. 18
2184 A358 $1.20 multicolored   .90 .90
No. 2184 was issued in sheets of 6.

Gandhi — A359

Portraits: 90c, Up close, later years. $1, Seated with hands clasped. $1.20, Up close, early years. $1.65, Primary school, Rajkot, age 7. $6, With stick, walking with boy (in margin).

1998, Nov. 18
2185-2188 A359   Set of 4   2.75 2.75
Souvenir Sheet
2189 A359 $6 multicolored   4.50 4.50

Picasso — A360

Paintings: $1.20, Figures on the Seashore, 1931, horiz. $1.65, Three Figures Under a Tree, 1907. $1.75, Two Women Running on the Beach, 1922, horiz.
$6, Bullfight, 1900, horiz.

1998, Nov. 18
2190-2192 A360 Set of 3   3.50 3.50
Souvenir Sheet
2193 A360 $6 multicolored   4.50 4.50

1998 World Scouting Jamboree, Chile A361

90c, Handshake. $1, Scouts hiking. $1.20, Sign. $6, Lord Baden-Powell.

1998, Oct. 8   Litho.   *Perf. 14*
2194-2196 A361 Set of 3   2.50 2.50
Souvenir Sheet
2197 A361 $6 multicolored   4.50 4.50

Organization of American States, 50th Anniv. A362

1998, Nov. 18   *Perf. 13½*
2198 A362 $1 multicolored   .75 .75

Enzo Ferrari (1898-1988), Automobile Manufacturer — A363

No. 2199: a, Top view of Dino 246 GT-GTS. b, Front view of Dino 246 GT-GTS. c, 1977 365 GT4 BB. $6, Dino 246 GT-GTS.

1998, Nov. 18   *Perf. 14*
2199 A363 $1.75 Sheet of 3, #a.-c.   4.00 4.00
Souvenir Sheet
2200 A363 $6 multicolored   4.50 4.50
No. 2200 contains one 92x35mm stamp.

Royal Air Force, 80th Anniv. A364

No. 2201: a, McDonnell Douglas Phantom FGR1. b, Sepecat Jaguar GR1A. c, Panavia Tornado F3. d, McDonnell Douglas Phantom FGR2.
No. 2202, Eurofighter 2000, Hurricane. No. 2203, Hawk, biplane.

1998, Nov. 18
2201 A364 $1.75 Sheet of 4, #a.-d.   4.00 4.00
Souvenir Sheets
2202-2203 A364 $6 each   4.50 4.50

Sea Birds A365

Designs: 15c, Brown pelican. 25c, Dunlin. 45c, Atlantic puffin. 90c, Pied cormorant.

No. 2208: a, King eider. b, Inca tern. c, Dovekie. d, Ross's bull. e, Brown noddy. f, Marbled murrelet. g, Northern gannet. h, Razorbill. i, Long-tailed jaeger. j, Black guillemot. k, Whimbrel. l, Oystercatcher.
No. 2209, Rhynchops niger. No. 2210, Diomedea exulans.

1998, Nov. 24
2204-2207 A365 Set of 4   1.25 1.25
2208 A365 75c Sheet of 12, #a.-l. 6.75 6.75
Souvenir Sheets
2209-2210 A365 $6 each   4.50 4.50

Christmas A366

Dogs with Christmas decorations: 15c, Border collie. 25c, Dalmatian. 65c, Weimaraner. 75c, Scottish terrier. 90c, Long-haired dachshund. $1.20, Golden retriever. $2, Pekingese.
No. 2218, Dalmatian, diff. No. 2219, Jack Russell terrier.

1998, Dec. 10
2211-2217 A366 Set of 7   4.50 4.50
Souvenir Sheet
2218-2219 A366 $6 each   4.50 4.50

Disney Characters in Water Sports A367

Water skiing - No. 2220: a, Goofy, maroon skis. b, Mickey. c, Goofy, Mickey. d, Donald. e, Goofy, blue skis. f, Minnie.
Surfing - No. 2221: a, Goofy running with board. b, Mickey. c, Donald holding board. d, Donald, riding board. e, Minnie. f, Goofy in water.
Sailing & sailboarding - No. 2221G: h, Mickey wearing cap. i, Mickey, Goofy, counterbalancing boat. j, Goofy sailboarding. k, Mickey, seagull overhead. l, Goofy puffing at sail. m, Mickey sailboarding.
No. 2222, Mickey. No. 2223, Minnie. No. 2224, Goofy. No. 2225, Donald.

1999, Jan. 11   Litho.   *Perf. 13½x14*
Sheets of 6
2220-2221 A367 $1 #a.-f., each   4.50 4.50
2221G A367 $1 #h.-m.   4.50 4.50
Souvenir Sheets
2222-2225 A367 $6 each   4.50 4.50
Mickey Mouse, 70th anniv.

Hell's Gate Steel Orchestra, 50th Anniv. A368

Designs: 20c, Nelson's Dockyard, 1996. 60c, Holiday Inn, Rochester, New York, 1992. 75c, Early years, 1950. 90c, World's Fair, 1964, Eustace Henry (AKA Manning). $1.20, Alston Henry playing double tenor.
No. 2231, like #2229, vert. No. 2232, The early years, vert.

1999, Feb. 1   Litho.   *Perf. 14*
2226-2230 A368 Set of 5   2.75 2.75
Souvenir Sheets
2231-2232 A368 $4 each   3.00 3.00

Flowers A369

Designs, vert: 60c, Tulip. 75c, Fuschia. $1.20, Calla lily. $1.65, Sweet pea.
No. 2237: a, Morning glory. b, Geranium. c, Blue hibiscus. d, Marigolds. e, Sunflower. f, Impatiens. g, Petunia. h, Pansy. i, Saucer magnolia.
No. 2238: a, Primrose. b, Bleeding heart. c, Pink dogwood. d, Peony. e, Rose. f, Hellebores. g, Lily. h, Violet. i, Cherry blossoms.
No. 2239, Lily, vert. no. 2240, Zinnias, vert.

1999, Apr. 19   Litho.   *Perf. 14*
2233-2236 A369 Set of 4   3.25 3.25
Sheets of 9
2237 A369 90c #a.-i.   6.00 6.00
2238 A369 $1 #a.-i.   6.75 6.75
Souvenir Sheets
2239-2240 A369 $6 each   4.50 4.50

Elle Macpherson, Model — A370

Various portraits.

1999, Apr. 26   *Perf. 13½*
2241 A370 $1.20 Sheet of 8, #a.-h.   7.25 7.25
Australia '99 World Stamp Expo.

John Glenn's Space Flight — A371

John Glenn, 1962 - No. 2242: a, Climbing into Mercury Capsule. b, Formal portrait. c, Having helmet adjusted. d, Entering pressure chamber.
No. 2243: a, Luna 2. b, Mariner 2. c, Giotto space probe. d, Rosat. e, Intl. Ultraviolet Explorer. f, Ulysses Space Probe.
No. 2244: a, Mariner 10. b, Luna 9. c, Advanced X-ray Astrophysics Facility. d, Magellan Spacecraft. e, Pioneer-Venus 2. f, Infra-red Astronomy Satellite.
No. 2245, Salyut 1, horiz. No. 2246, MIR, horiz.

1999, May 6   Litho.   *Perf. 14*
2242 A371 $1.75 Sheet of 4, #a.-d.   5.25 5.25

Space Exploration A372

Sheets of 6
2243-2244 A372 $1.65 #a.-f., ea   7.50 7.50
Souvenir Sheets
2245-2246 A372 $6 each   4.50 4.50
Nos. 2245-2246 are incorrectly inscribed.

Prehistoric Animals A373

Designs: 65c, Brachiosaurus. 75c, Oviraptor, vert. $1, Homotherium. $1.20, Macrauchenia, vert.
No. 2251: a, Leptictidium. b, Ictitherium. c, Plesictis. d, Hemicyon. e, Diacodexis. f, Stylinodon. g, Kanuites. h, Chriacus. i, Argyrolagus.
No. 2252: a, Struthiomimus. b, Corythosaurus. c, Dsungaripterus. d, Compognathus. e, Prosaurolophus. f, Montanoceratops. g, Stegosaurus. h, Deinonychus. i, Ouranosaurus.
No. 2253, Pteranodon. No. 2254, Eurhinodelphus.

1999, May 26
2247-2250 A373 Set of 4   3.50 3.50
Sheets of 9
2251-2252 A373 $1.65 #a.-i., each   11.50 11.50
Souvenir Sheets
2253-2254 A373 $6 each   4.50 4.50
Illustrations on Nos. 2247-2248 are switched.

IBRA'99, World Stamp Exhibition, Nuremberg — A374

Exhibition emblem, Leipzig-Dresden Railway and: No. 2255, $1, Caroline Islands #19. No. 2257, $1.65, Caroline Islands #4.
Emblem, Gölsdorf 4-4-0 and: No. 2256, $1.20, Caroline Islands #16. No. 2258, $1.90, Caroline Islands #8, #10.
$6, Registered label on cover. Illustration reduced.

1999, June 24   Litho.   *Perf. 14*
2255-2258 A374 Set of 4   4.50 4.50
Souvenir Sheet
2259 A374 $6 multicolored   5.00 5.00

Paintings by Hokusai (1760-1849) — A375

Details or entire paintings: No. 2260: a, Asakusa Honganji. b, Dawn at Isawa in Kai Province. c, Samurai with Bow and Arrow (bows level). d, Samurai with Bow and Arrow (bows at different angles). e, Kajikazawa in Kai Province. f, A Great Wave.
No. 2261: a, People on the Balcony of the Sazaido. b, Nakahara in Sagami Province. c, Defensive Positions (2 men). d, Defensive Positions (3 men). e, Mount Fuji in Clear Weather. f, Nihonbashi in Edo.
No. 2262, Cotenyama At Shinagawa on Tokaido Highway, vert. No. 2263, A Netsuke Workshop, vert.

1999, June 24
Sheets of 6
2260-2261 A375 $1.65 #a.-f., ea   7.50 7.50
Souvenir Sheets
2262-2263 A375 $6 each   4.50 4.50

Johann Wolfgang von Goethe (1749-1832), Poet — A376

No. 2264: a, Three archangels in "Faust." b, Portraits of Goethe and Friedrich von Schiller (1759-1805). c, Faust reclining in landscape with spirits.
$6, Profile portrait of Goethe.

1999, June 24   Litho.   Perf. 14
2264 A376 $1.75 Sheet of 3, #a.-
            c.   4.00 4.00
Souvenir Sheet
2265 A376 $6 multicolored   4.50 4.50

Souvenir Sheets

Philexfrance '99, World Philatelic Exhibition — A377

Locomotives: #2266, Crampton 1855-69. #2267, 232-U1 4-Cylinder Compound 4-6-4, 1949.
Illustration reduced.

1999, June 24   Perf. 13¾
2266 A377 $6 multicolored   4.50 4.50
2267 A377 $6 multicolored   4.50 4.50

A378

Wedding of Prince Edward and Sophie Rhys-Jones - No. 2268: a, Sophie. b, Sophie, Edward. c, Edward.
$6, Horse and carriage, couple.

1999, June 24   Perf. 13½
2268 A378 $3 Sheet of 3, #a.-c.   6.75 6.75
Souvenir Sheet
2269 A378 $6 multicolored   4.50 4.50

A379

1999, May 25   Litho.   Perf. 14½x14
Various white kittens: 35c, 45c, 60c, 75c, 90c, $1.
No. 2276: a, One holding paw on another. b, Black & white. c, White kitten, black kitten. d, One with yarn. e, Two in basket. f, One looking up.
No. 2277: a, One playing with red yarn. b, Two long-haired. c, Yellow tabby. d, One with mouse. e, Yellow tabby on pillow. f, Black & gray tabby.
No. 2278, Tabby cat carrying kitten. No. 2279, Yellow kitten in tree.

2270-2275 A379 Set of 6   3.00 3.00

Sheets of 6
2276-2277 A379 $1.65 #a.-f., ea   7.50 7.50
Souvenir Sheets
2278-2279 A379 $6 each   4.50 4.50
Australia '99, World Stamp Expo (#2276-2279).

A380

UN Rights of the Child Convention, 10th Anniv. - No. 2280: a, Three children. b, Adult hand taking child's hand, silhouette of mother holding infant. c, UN Building, member flags, dove.
$6, Dove.

1999, June 22   Perf. 14
2280 A380 $3 Sheet of 3, #a.-c.   6.75 6.75
Souvenir Sheet
2281 A380 $6 multicolored   4.50 4.50

A381

1999, June 24   Litho.   Perf. 13x11
Boats and ships: 25c, Missa Ferdie. 45c, Sailboats. 60c, Jolly Roger Pirate Ship. 90c, $4, Freewinds. $1.20, Monarch of the Seas.

2282-2286 A381 Set of 5   2.60 2.60
2286a   Souvenir sheet,
           #2282-2286   2.60 2.60
Souvenir Sheet
       Perf. 13¾
2287 A381 $4 multicolored   3.00 3.00
No. 2287 contains one 51x38mm stamp.

A382

Butterflies: 65c, Fiery jewel. 75c, Hewitson's blue hairstreak. $1.20, Scarce bamboo page, horiz. $1.65, Paris peacock, horiz.
No. 2292, horiz.: a, California dog face. b, Small copper. c, Zebra swallowtail. d, White M hairstreak. e, Old world swallowtail. f, Buckeye. g, Apollo. h, Sonoran blue. i, Purple emperor.
No. 2293, Monarch. No. 2294, Cairns birdwing, horiz.

1999, Aug. 16   Perf. 14
2288-2291 A382 Set of 4   3.25 3.25
2292 A382 $1 Sheet of 9, #a.-i.   6.75 6.75
Souvenir Sheets
2293-2294 A382 $6 each   4.50 4.50

Christmas A383

15c, Madonna and child in a Wreath of Flowers by Peter Paul Rubens. 25c, Shroud of Christ Held by Two Angels, by Albrecht Dürer. 45c, Madonna and Child Enthroned Between Two Saints, by Raphael. 60c, Holy Family with the Lamb, by Raphael. $2, The Transfiguration, by Raphael. $4, Three Putti Holding a Coat of Arms, by Dürer.
$6, The Coronation of the Holy St. Catherine, by Rubens.

1999, Nov. 22   Litho.   Perf. 13¾
2295-2300 A383 Set of 6   5.50 5.50
Souvenir Sheet
2301 A383 $6 multicolored   4.50 4.50

Famous Elderly People A384

Designs: a, Katharine Hepburn. b, Martha Graham. c, Eubie Blake. d, Agatha Christie. e, Eudora Welty. f, Helen Hayes. g, Vladimir Horowitz. h, Katharine Graham. i, Pablo Casals. j, Pete Seeger. k, Andres Segovia. l, Frank Lloyd Wright.

2000, Jan. 18   Litho.   Perf. 14
2302 A384 90c Sheet of 12, #a-l   8.00 8.00

Charlie Chaplin A385

Designs: a, "Modern Times," street scene. b, "The Gold Rush," with other actor. c, Unidentified film. d, "Modern Times," on gears. e, "The Gold Rush," arms akimbo. f, "The Gold Rush," with cane.

2000, Jan. 18   Perf. 13¾
2303 A385 $1.65 Sheet of 6, #a-f   7.25 7.25

Sir Cliff Richard, Rock Musician A386

2000, Jan. 18   Perf. 13¼
2304 A386 $1.65 multi   1.25 1.25
Issued in sheets of 6.

Birds A387

Designs: 75c, Streamertail. 90c, Yellow-bellied sapsucker. $1.20, Rufous-tailed jacamar. $2, Spectacled owl.
No. 2309: a, Ground dove. b, Wood stork. c, Saffron finch. d, Green-backed heron. e, Lovely cotinga. f, St. Vincent parrot. g, Cuban grassquit. h, Red-winged blackbird.
No. 2310: a, Scarlet macaw. b, Yellow-fronted amazon. c, Queen-of-Bavaria. d, Nanday conure. e, Jamaican tody. f, Smooth-billed ani. g, Puerto Rican woodpecker. h, Ruby-throated hummingbird.
No. 2311, Vermilion flycatcher. No. 2312, Red-capped manakin, vert.

2000, Apr. 17   Litho.   Perf. 14
2305-2308 A387 Set of 4   3.75 3.75
Sheets of 8, #a-h
       Perf. 13¾x14
2309-2310 A387 $1.20 Set of
                2   14.00 14.00
Souvenir Sheets
       Perf. 13¾
2311-2312 A387 $6 Set of 2   9.00 9.00
The Stamp Show 2000, London (Nos. 2309-2312). Size of stamps: Nos. 2309-2310, 48x31mm; No. 2311, 50x38mm; No. 2312, 38x50mm.

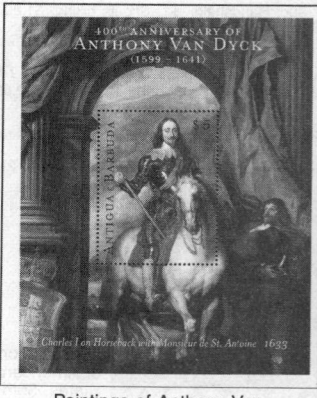

Paintings of Anthony Van Dyck — A388

No. 2313: a, Arthur Goodwin. b, Sir Thomas Wharton. c, Mary Villers (as Venus), Daughter of the Duke of Buckingham. d, Christina Bruce, Countess of Devonshire. e, James Hamilton, 3rd Marquis and 1st Duke of Hamilton. f, Henry Danvers, Earl of Danby.
No. 2314: a, Charles I in Robes of State. b, Henrietta Maria. c, Queen Henrietta Maria with Her Dwarf Sir Jeffrey Hudson. d, Charles I in Armor. e, Henrietta Maria in Profile, facing right. f, Queen Henrietta Maria.
No. 2315: a, Marie de Raet, Wife of Philippe le Roy. b, Jacomo de Cachiopin. c, Princess Henrietta of Lorraine Attended by a Page. d, Portrait of a Man. e, Portrait of a Woman. f, Philippe le Roy, Seigneur de Ravels.
No. 2316, Charles I on Horseback with Monsieur de St. Antoine. No. 2317, Le Roi a La Chasse (Charles I hunting). No. 2318, Charles I in Three Positions. No. 2319, Charles I and Queen Henrietta. No. 2320, Portrait of Two Young English Gentlemen, Sons of the Duke of Lenox. No. 2321, George, Lord Digby, and William, Lord Russell.
Illustration reduced.

2000, May 15   Perf. 13¾
Sheets of 6, #a-f
2313-2315 A388 $1.20 Set of
                3   15.00 15.00
Souvenir Sheets
2316-2319 A388 $5 Set of 4   15.00 15.00
2320-2321 A388 $6 Set of 2   9.00 9.00

Butterflies — A389

No. 2322: a, Orange theope. b, Sloane's urania. c, Gold-drop helicopis. d, Papilio velovis. e, Graphium androcles. f, Cramer's mesene.
No. 2323, horiz.: a, Euploea miniszeki. b, Doris. c, Evenus coronata. d, Anchisiades

swallowtail. e, White-spotted tadpole. f, Morpho patroclus.
No. 2324, horiz.: a, Mesosemia loruhama. b, Bia actorion. c, Ghost brimstone. d, Blue tharops. e, Catasticta manco. f, White-tailed page.
No. 2325, Reakirt's blue. No. 2326, Graphium encelades, horiz. No. 2327, Graphium milon, horiz.
Illustration reduced.

2000, May 29		Perf. 14
Sheets of 6, #a-f		
2322-2324 A389 $1.65 Set of 3		22.50 22.50
Souvenir Sheets		
2325-2327 A389 $6 Set of 3		13.00 13.00

Prince William, 18th Birthday — A390

Prince William - No. 2328: a, With checked shirt, waving. b, In jacket and white shirt. c, With arms clasped. d, In striped shirt, waving.
$6, With Prince Harry, Princess Diana and unidentified man.
Illustration reduced.

2000, June 21		Perf. 14
2328 A390 $1.65 Sheet of 4, #a-d		5.00 5.00
Souvenir Sheet		
Perf. 13¾		
2329 A390 $6 multi		4.50 4.50

100th Test Cricket Match at Lord's Ground — A391

90c, Richie Richardson. $5, Viv Richard. $6, Lord's Ground, horiz.

2000, June 26		Perf. 14
2330-2331 A391 Set of 2		4.50 4.50
Souvenir Sheet		
2332 A391 $6 multi		4.50 4.50

Souvenir Sheet

2000 Summer Olympics, Sydney — A392

Designs: a, Cyclist. b, Diver. c, Italian flag, Flaminio Stadium, Rome. d, Ancient Greek javelin thrower.

Illustration reduced.

2000, June 26		
2333 A392 $2 Sheet of 4, #a-d		6.00 6.00

First Zeppelin Flight, Cent. — A393

No. 2334: a, LZ-1. b, LZ-2. c, LZ-3. $6, LZ-7.
Illustration reduced.

2000, June 26		Perf. 13½
2334 A393 $3 Sheet of 3, #a-c		6.75 6.75
Souvenir Sheet		
Perf. 14¼		
2335 A393 $6 multi		4.50 4.50

No. 2334 contains three 45x27mm stamps.

Cats — A394

No. 2336: a, Long-haired blue & white. b, Snow shoe. c, Persian. d, Chocolate lynx point. e, Brown & white sphynx. f, White tortoiseshell.
$6, Lavender tortie.
Illustration reduced.

2000, May 29	Litho.	Perf. 14
2336 A394 $1.65 Sheet of 6, #a-f		7.50 7.50
Souvenir Sheet		
2337 A394 $6 multi		4.50 4.50

Souvenir Sheet

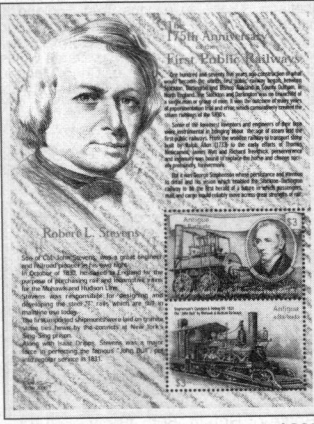

Public Railways, 175th Anniv. — A395

Designs: a, Locomotion No. 1, George Stephenson. b, John Bull.
Illustration reduced.

2000, June 26		
2338 A395 $3 Sheet of 2, #a-b		4.50 4.50

The Stamp Show 2000, London.

Souvenir Sheet

Johann Sebastian Bach (1685-1750) — A396

Illustration reduced.

2000, June 26		
2339 A396 $6 multi		4.50 4.50

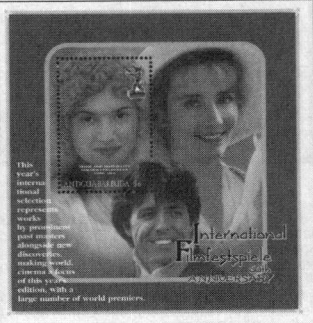

Berlin Film Festival, 50th Anniv. — A397

No. 2340: a, Une Femme Est Une Femme. b, Carmen Jones. c, Die Ratten. d, Die Vier im Jeep. e, Lilies of the Field. f, Invitation to the Dance.
$6, Sense and Sensibility.
Illustration reduced.

2000, June 26		
2340 A397 $1.65 Sheet of 6, #a-f		7.50 7.50
Souvenir Sheet		
2341 A397 $6 multi		4.50 4.50

Flowers — A398

Designs: 45c, Epidendrum pseudepidndrum. 65c, Odontoglossum cervantesii. 75c, Cattleya dowiana. 90c, Beloperone guttata. $1, Colliandra haematocephala. $1.20, Brassavola nodosa.
No. 2348, $1.65: a, Masdevallia coccinea. b, Paphinia cristata. c, Vanilla planifolia. d, Cattleya forbesii. e, Lycaste skinneri. f, Cattleya percivaliana.
No. 2349, $1.65: a, Anthurium andreanum. b, Doxantha unguiscati. c, Hibiscus rosa-sinensis. d, Canna indica. e, Heliconius umilis. f, Strelitzia reginae.
No. 2350, $1.65: a, Pseudocalymna alliaceum. b, Datura candida. c, Ipomoea tuberosa. d, Allamanda cathartica. e, Aspasia epidendroides. f, Maxillaria cucullata.
No. 2351, Strelitzia reginae. No. 2352, Cattleya leopoldii. No. 2353, Rossioglossum grande.

2000, May 29	Litho.	Perf. 14
2342-2347 A398 Set of 6		3.75 3.75
Sheets of 6, #a-f		
2348-2350 A398 Set of 3		22.50 22.50
Souvenir Sheets		
2351-2353 A398 $6 Set of 3		13.50 13.50

Dogs — A399

Designs: 90c, Boxer. $1, Wire-haired pointer (inscribed Alaskan malamute). $2, Alaskan malamute (inscribed Wire-haired pointer). $4, Saluki.
No. 2358: a, Bearded collie. b, Cardigan Welsh corgi. c, Saluki. d, Basset hound. e, Standard poodle. f, Boston terrier.
No. 2359, Cavalier King Charles Spaniel.

2000, May 29		
2354-2357 A399 Set of 4		6.00 6.00
2358 A399 $1.65 Sheet of 6, #a-f		7.25 7.25
Souvenir Sheet		
2359 A399 $6 multi		4.50 4.50

Space Achievements — A400

No. 2360, $1.65: a, Sputnik 1. b, Explorer 1. c, Mars Express. d, Luna 1. e, Ranger 7. f, Mariner 4.
No. 2361, $1.65: a, Mariner 10. b, Soho. c, Mariner 2. d, Giotto. e, Exosat. f, Pioneer.
No. 2362, Hubble Space Telescope. No. 2363, Vostok 1.
Illustration reduced.

2000, June 26		
Sheets of 6, #a-f		
2360-2361 A400 Set of 2		15.00 15.00
Souvenir Sheets		
2362-2363 A400 $6 Set of 2		9.00 9.00

World Stamp Expo 2000, Anaheim.

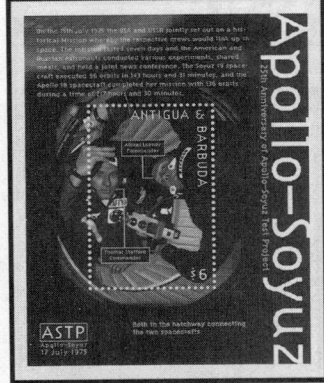

Apollo-Soyuz Mission, 25th Anniv. — A401

No. 2364: a, Alexei Leonov. b, Soyuz 19. c, Valeri Kubasov.
$6, Leonov and Thomas Stafford.
Illustration reduced.

2000, June 26		
2364 A401 $3 Sheet of 3, #a-c		6.75 6.75
Souvenir Sheet		
2365 A401 $6 multi		4.50 4.50

Souvenir Sheet

Albert Einstein (1879-1955) — A402

Illustration reduced.

| **2000, June 26** | | **Perf. 14¼** |
| 2366 A402 | $6 multi | 4.50 4.50 |

Girls'
Brigade
A403

Designs: 20c, Outreach program to Sunshine Home for Girls. 60c, Ullida Rawlins Gill, Intl. vice-president, vert. 75c, Officers and girls. 90c, Raising the flag, vert. $1.20, Members with 8th Antigua Company flag. $5, Emblem, vert.

2000, July 13		**Perf. 14**
2367-2371 A403	Set of 5	2.75 2.75
Souvenir Sheet		
2372 A403	$5 multi	3.75 3.75

A404

Queen Mother, 100th Birthday — A405

No. 2373: a, As child. b, In 1940. c, With Princess Anne, 1951. d, In Canada, 1989. $6, Inspecting the troops. $20, In gardens. Illustration reduced.

Litho., Margin Embossed

| **2000, Aug. 4** | | **Perf. 14** |
| 2373 A404 | $2 Sheet of 4, #a-d, + label | 6.00 6.00 |

Souvenir Sheet
Perf. 13¾

| 2374 A404 | $6 multi | 4.50 4.50 |

Without Gum
Litho. & Embossed
Die Cut 8¾x9

| 2375 A405 | $20 gold & multi | |

No. 2374 contains one 38x51mm stamp.

Popes — A406

No. 2376: a, Alexander VI, 1492-1503, hands clasped. b, Benedict XIII, 1724-30. c, Boniface IX, 1389-1404. d, Alexander VI, no hands. e, Clement VIII, 1592-1605. f, Clement VI, 1342-52.

No. 2377: a, John Paul II, 1978-present. b, Benedict XV, 1914-22. c, John XXIII, 1958-63. d, Pius XI, 1922-39. e, Pius XII, 1939-58. f, Paul VI, 1963-78.

No. 2378, Pius II, 1458-1464. No. 2379, Pius VII, 1800-23.
Illustration reduced.

2000, Aug. 21 Litho. Perf. 13¾		
Sheets of 6, #a-f		
2376-2377 A406	$1.65 Set of 2	15.00 15.00
Souvenir Sheets		
2378-2379 A406	$6 Set of 2	9.00 9.00

Monarchs — A407

No. 2380: a, Donaldbane of Scotland, 1093-97. b, Duncan I of Scotland, 1034-40. c, Duncan II of Scotland, 1094. d, Macbeth of Scotland, 1040-57. e, Malcolm III of Scotland, 1057-93. f, Edgar of Scotland, 1097-1107.

No. 2381: a, Charles I of Great Britain, 1625-49. b, Charles II of Great Britain, 1660-85. c, George III of Great Britain, 1760-1820. d, James II of Great Britain, 1685-89. e, James II of Scotland, 1437-60. f, James III of Scotland, 1460-88.

No. 2382, Robert I of Scotland, 1306-29. No. 2383, Anne of Great Britain, 1702-14.
Illustration reduced.

2000, Aug. 21		
Sheets of 6, #a-f		
2380-2381 A407	$1.65 Set of 2	15.00 15.00
Souvenir Sheets		
2382-2383 A407	$6 Set of 2	9.00 9.00

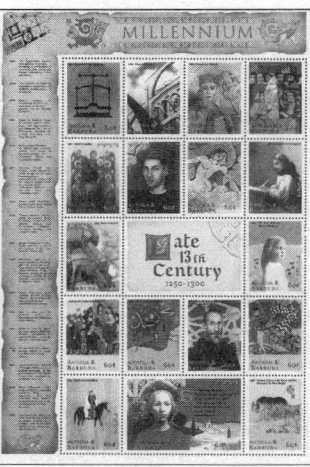

Millennium (#2385) — A408

No. 2384 - Chinese paintings: a, Admonitions of the Instructress to the Court Ladies, attributed to Ku K'ai-chih. b, Ink drawing on silk, 3rd cent. B.C. c, Ink and color drawing on silk, 2nd cent. B.C. d, Scholars of the Northern Qi Collating Texts (detail), attributed to Yang Zihua. e, Sprinting Outing (detail), attributed to Zhan Ziqian. f, Portrait of the Emperors (detail), attributed to Yen Liben. g, Sailing Boats and a Riverside Mansion, attributed to Li Sixun. h, Two Horses and a Groom (detail), by Han Kan. i, King's Portrait (detail), attributed to Wu Daozi. j, Margaret, Queen of Scotland. k, Jewish exodus from England. l, Mount Kuanglu, by Jiang Hao. m, Pheasant and Small Birds by a Jujube Shrub, by Huang Jucai. n, Deer Among Red Maples, by anonymous painter. o, Distant Mountain Forest (hills in foreground). p, Literary Gathering, by Han Huang (60x40mm). q, Sketches of Birds and Insects (detail), by Huang Quan.

Perf. 12¾x12½

| **2000, Aug. 21** | | **Litho.** |
| 2384 A408 | 25c Sheet of 17, #a-q, + label | 3.25 3.25 |

Highlights of 1250-1300: a, Expansion of the Inquisition. b, Chartres Cathedral. c, Sculptures in Naumburg Cathedral. d, 1st English Parliament. e, The Madonna in Majesty (Maestà), by Cimabue. f, Marco Polo. g Divine wind. h, Death of St. Thomas Aquinas. i, Arezzo Cathedral. j, Margaret, Queen of Scotland. k, Jewish exodus from England. l, Fall of Acre to Muslims. m, Moses de León writes much of The Zohar. n, German Civil War. o, Death of Kublai Khan. p, Dante writes La Vita Nuova (60x40mm). q, Chao Meng-fu paints Autumn Colors on the Quiao and Hua Mountains.

| **2000, Aug. 21** | | |
| 2385 A408 | 60c Sheet of 17, #a-q + label | 7.50 7.50 |

Battle of Britain, 60th Anniv. — A409

No. 2386, $1.20: a, Bristol Blenheim. b, Winston Churchill. c, Bristol Blenheim and barrage balloon. d, Heinkel. e, Spitfire. f, German rescue vessel. g, Messerschmitt 109. h, RAF air and sea rescue launch.

No. 2387, $1.20: a, German lookout. b, Children being evacuated. c, Youngsters evacuated from hospitals. d, Hurricane. e, Rescue workers. f, British political cartoon. g, King George VI and Queen Elizabeth inspect wreckage. h, Barrage balloon over Tower Bridge.

No. 2388, $6, Spitfires. No. 2389, $6, Junkers 87B.

2000, Oct. 16 Litho. Perf. 14		
Sheets of 8, #a-h		
2386-2387 A409	Set of 2	14.50 14.50
Souvenir Sheets		
2388-2389 A409	Set of 2	9.00 9.00

Rainforest
Fauna — A410

Designs: 75c, Agouti. 90c, Capybara. $1.20, Basilisk lizard. $2, Heliconid butterfly.

No. 2394, $1.65: a, Green violet-ear hummingbird. b, Harpy eagle. c, Three-toed sloth. d, White uakari monkey. e, Anteater. f, Coati.

No. 2395, $1.75: a, Red-eyed tree frog. b, Black spider monkey. c, Emerald toucanet. d, Kinkajou. e, Spectacled bear. f, Tapir.

No. 2396, $6, Keel-billed toucan, horiz. No. 2397, $6, Scarlet macaw, horiz.

2000, Sept. 25 Litho. Perf. 14		
2390-2393 A410	Set of 4	3.75 3.75
Sheets of 6, #a-f		
2394-2395 A410	Set of 2	15.00 15.00
Souvenir Sheets		
2396-2397 A410	Set of 2	9.00 9.00

Submarines — A411

Designs: 65c, Sea Cliff. 75c, Beaver Mark IV. 90c, Reef Ranger. $1, Cubmarine. $1.20, Alvin. $3, Argus.

No. 2404, $2: a, Revenge. b, Walrus. c, Los Angeles. d, Daphne. e, USS Ohio. f, USS Skipjack.

No. 2405, $6, Trieste. No. 2406, $6, German Type 209.

2000, Oct. 2		
2398-2403 A411	Set of 6	5.50 5.50
2404 A411	$2 Sheet of 6, #a-f	9.00 9.00
Souvenir Sheets		
2405-2406 A411	Set of 2	9.00 9.00

Paintings from the Prado — A412

No. 2407, $1.65: a, Three men. b, Man's head. c, Three women. d, Man on white horse. e, Man on brown horse. f, Man leading horse. a-c from Family Portrait, by Adriaen Thomasz Key. d-f from The Devotion of Rudolf I, by Peter Paul Rubens and Jan Wildens.

No. 2408, $1.65: a, Seated man. b, Man with sash. c, Group of men. d, Laureated figure. e, Men working at anvil. f, Two workers. a-c from The Defense of Cadiz Against the English by Francisco de Zurbaran. d-f from Vulcan's Forge, by Diego Velázquez

No. 2409, $1.65: a, Mandolin player. b, Woman with fan. c, Two men. d, Bald man. e, Two Magi. f, Jesus, Mary and Joseph. a-c from The Concert, by Vicente Palmaroli y Gonzalez. d-f from The Adoration of the Magi, by Juan Bautista Maino

No. 2410, $6, The Seller of Fans, by José del Castillo. No. 2411, $6, Portrati of a Family in a Garden, by Jan van Kessel, the Younger. No. 2412, $6, The Deliverance of St. Peter, by José de Ribera, horiz.
Illustration reduced.

2000, Oct. 6 — Perf. 12x12¼, 12¼x12
Sheets of 6, #a-f
2407-2409 A412 Set of 3   22.50 22.50
Souvenir Sheets
2410-2412 A412 Set of 3   13.50 13.50

España 2000 Intl. Philatelic Exhibition.

Christmas — A413

Designs (background): 25c, #2417a, Angels, full body (blue). 45c, #2417b, Angel's heads (orange). 90c, #2417c, Angel's heads (blue). $5, #2417d, Angels, full body (yellow).

2000, Dec. 4 — Perf. 14
2413-2416 A413 Set of 4   5.00 5.00
2417 A413 $1.75 Sheet of 4, #a-d   5.25 5.25
Souvenir Sheet
2418 A413 $6 Jesus   4.50 4.50

Rijksmuseum, Amsterdam, Bicent. (in 2000) — A414

No. 2419, $1: a, Dr. Ephraim Bueno, by Rembrandt. b, Woman Writing a Letter, by Frans van Mieris, the Elder. c, Mary Magdalene, by Jan van Scorel. d, Portrait of a Woman (inscribed Anna Coddle), by Maarten van Heemskerck. e, Cleopatra's Banquet, by Gerard Lairesse. f, Titus van Rijn in Friar's Habit, by Rembrandt.

No. 2420, $1.20: a, Saskia van Uylenburgh, by Rembrandt. b, In the Month of July, by Paul Joseph Constantin Gabriel. c, Maria Trip, by Rembrandt. d, Still Life with Flowers, by Jan van Huysum. e, Hesje van Cleyburgh, by Rembrandt. f, Girl in a White Kimono, by George Hendrik Breitner.

No. 2421, $1.65: a, Man and woman at spinning wheel, by Pieter Pietersz. b, Self-portrait, by Rembrandt. c, Jeremiah Lamenting the Destruction of Jerusalem, by Rembrandt. d, The Jewish Bride, by Rembrandt. e, Tobit and Anna with a Kid, by Rembrandt. f, The Prophetess Anna, by Rembrandt.

No. 2422, $6, Doubting Thomas, by Hendrick ter Brugghen. No. 2423, $6, Still Life with Cheeses, by Floris van Dijck. No. 2424, $6, Isaac Blessing Jacob, by Govert Flinck.

2001, Jan. 15 — Litho. — Perf. 13¾
Sheets of 6, #a-f
2419-2421 A414 Set of 3   17.50 17.50
Souvenir Sheets
2422-2424 A414 Set of 3   13.50 13.50

Pokémon — A415

No. 2425: a, Starmie. b, Misty. c, Brock. d, Geodude. e, Krabby. f, Ash.

2001, Feb. 13
2425 A415 $1.75 Sheet of 6, #a-f   8.00 8.00
Souvenir Sheet
2426 A415 $6 Charizard   4.50 4.50

Mushrooms A416

Designs: 25c, Blue-toothed entoloma. 90c, Common morel. $1, Red cage fungus. $1.75, Fawn shield-cap.

No. 2431, $1.65: a, Lilac bonnet. b, Silky volvar. c, Poplar field cap. d, St. George's mushroom. e, Red-stemmed tough shank. f, Fly agaric.

No. 2432, $1.65: a, Copper trumpet. b, Meadow mushroom. c, Green-gilled parasol. d, Panther. e, Death cap. f, King bolete.

No. 2433, $6, Yellow parasol. No. 2434, Mutagen milk cap.

2001, Mar. 26 — Perf. 13¾x13¼
2427-2430 A416 Set of 4   3.00 3.00
Sheets of 6, #a-f
2431-2432 A416 Set of 2   15.00 15.00
Souvenir Sheets
2433-2434 A416 Set of 2   9.00 9.00

Hong Kong 2001 Stamp Exhibition (2431-2434).

Population and Housing Census — A417

Map of Antigua with various graphs. Denominations: 15c, 25c, 65c, 90c.

2001, Apr. 2 — Perf. 13¾
2435-2438 A417 Set of 4   1.50 1.50
Souvenir Sheet
2439 A417 $6 Map, emblem   4.50 4.50

Phila Nippon '01, Japan — A418

Designs: 45c Two women facing right, from Yuna (Bath-house Women). 60c, Woman facing left, from Yuna. 65c, Two women, from Yuna. 75c, Man with stringed instrument at top, from Hikone Screen. $1, Woman with stringed instrument at bottom, from Hikone Screen. $1.20, Two people, from Hikone Screen.

No. 2446 - Namban Screen, by Naizen Kano: a, Ship's stern. b, Ship's bow. c, Man with closed umbrella. d, Man with open umbrella.

No. 2447 - Merry Making Under the Cherry Blossoms, by Naganobu Kano: a, Steps. b, Tree. c, Four people near building. d, Four people, mountains. e, Three people. f, One person.

No. 2448, $6, Visiting a Shrine on a Rainy Night, by Harunobu Suzuki. No. 2449, $6, Harunobu Suzuki, by Kokan Shiba. No. 2450, $6, Daruma, by Tsujo Kano.

2001, May 28 — Litho. — Perf. 14¼x14
2440-2445 A418 Set of 6   3.50 3.50
2446 A418 $1.65 Sheet of 4, #a-d   5.00 5.00
2447 A418 $1.65 Sheet of 6, #a-f   7.50 7.50
Souvenir Sheets
Perf. 13¾
2448-2450 A418 Set of 3   13.50 13.50

Nos. 2448-2450 each contain one 38x51mm stamp.

Orchids A419

Designs: 45c, Hintleya burtii. 75c, Neomoovea irrovata. 90c, Comparettia speciosa. $1, Cypripedium crapeanum.

No. 2455, $1.20, vert.: a, Trichoceuos muralis. b, Dracula rampira. c, Psychopsis papilio. d, Lycaste clenningiana. e, Telipogon nevuosus. f, Masclecallia ayahbacana.

No. 2456, $1.65, vert.: a, Rhyncholaelia glanca. b, Oncidium barbatum. c, Phaius tankervillege. d, Ghies brechtiana. e, Angraecum leonis. f, Cychnoches loddigesti.

No. 2457, $1.65, vert.: a, Cattleya dowiana. b, Dendrobium cruentum. c, Bulbophyllum lobbi. d, Chysis laevis. e, Ancistrochilus rothschildicanus. f, Angraecum sororium.

No. 2458, $6, Trichopilia fragrans, vert. No. 2459, $6, Symphalossum sanguinem, vert.

2001, June 11 — Perf. 14
2451-2454 A419 Set of 4   2.40 2.40
Sheets of 6, #a-f
2455-2457 A419 Set of 3   20.00 20.00
Souvenir Sheets
2458-2459 A419 Set of 2   9.00 9.00

Souvenir Sheets

I Love Lucy — A420

Designs: No. 2460, $6, Fred and Ricky. No. 2461, $6, Lucy and Ethel. No. 2462, $6, Lucy and fireplace. No. 2463, $6, Lucy and open door.

2001, Mar. 5 — Litho. — Perf. 13¾
2460-2463 A420 Set of 4   18.00 18.00

See Nos. 2522-2525.

Marine Life and Birds A421

Designs: 25c, Yellowtail damselfish. 45c, Indigo hamlet. 65c, Great white shark. No. 2467, 90c, Bottlenose dolphin. No. 2468, 90c, Palette surgeonfish. $1, Octopus.

No. 2470, $1.20: a, Common dolphin. b, Franklin's gull. c, Rock beauty. d, Bicolor angelfish. e, Beaugregory. f, Banded butterflyfish.

No. 2471, $1.20: a, Common tern. b, Flying fish. c, Queen angelfish. d, Blue-striped grunt. e, Porkfish. f, Blue tang.

No. 2472, $1.65: a, Dugong. b, White-tailed tropicbird. c, Bull shark and Spanish grunt. d, Manta ray. e, Green turtle. f, Spanish grunt.

No. 2473, $1.65: a, Red-footed booby. b, Bottlenose dolphin. c, Hawksbill turtle. d, Monk seal. e, Bull shark and coral. f, Lemon shark.

No. 2474, $5, Sailfish. No. 2475, $5, Beaugregory and brown pelican, vert. No. 2476, $6, Hawksbill turtle. No. 2477, $6, Queen triggerfish.

2001, June 11 — Perf. 14
2464-2469 A421 Set of 6   3.25 3.25
Sheets of 6, #a-f
2470-2473 A421 Set of 4   26.00 26.00
Souvenir Sheets
2474-2477 A421 Set of 4   16.00 16.00

Ship Freewinds — A422

Designs: 30c, Maiden voyage anniversary in Antigua. 45c, In St. Barthelemy. 75c, In Caribbean at sunset. 90c, In Bonaire. $1.50, In Bequia.

No. 2483, $4, With lights on during eclipse. No. 2484, $4, In Curacao.

2001, June 15
2478-2482 A422 Set of 5   3.00 3.00
Souvenir Sheets
2483-2484 A422 Set of 2   6.00 6.00

Toulouse-Lautrec Paintings — A423

No. 2485: a, Monsieur Georges-Henri Manuel Standing. b, Monsieur Louis Pascal. c, Roman Coolus. d, Monsieur Fourcade. $5, Dancing at the Moulin de la Galette.

2001, July 3			Perf. 13¾	
2485	A423	$2 Sheet of 4, #a-d	6.00	6.00
		Souvenir Sheet		
2486	A423	$5 multi	3.75	3.75

Giuseppe Verdi (1813-1901), Opera Composer — A424

No. 2487: a, Verdi in hat. b, Character and score from Don Carlos. c, Conductor and score for Aida. d, Musicians and score for Rigoletto.

2001, July 3			Perf. 14	
2487	A424	$2 Sheet of 4, #a-d	6.00	6.00
		Souvenir Sheet		
2488	A424	$5 Verdi, score	3.75	3.75

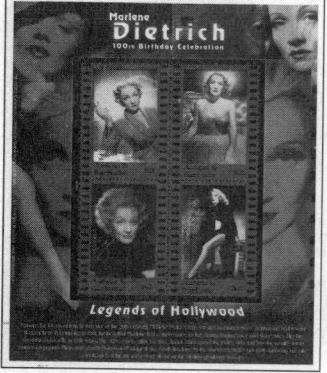

Marlene Dietrich — A425

No. 2489: a, With cigarette. b, On sofa. c, Color photograph. d, With piano.

2001, July 3			Perf. 13¾	
2489	A425	$2 Sheet of 4, #a-d	6.00	6.00

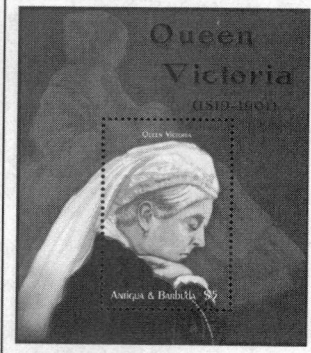

Queen Victoria (1819-1901) — A426

No. 2490: a, Blue dress. b, Red hat. c, Crown. d, Crown and blue sash.

2001, July 3			Perf. 14	
2490	A426	$2 Sheet of 4, #a-d	6.00	6.00
		Souvenir Sheet		
2491	A426	$5 As old woman	3.75	3.75

Queen Elizabeth II, 75th Birthday — A427

No. 2492: a, At birth, 1926. b, In 1938. c, In 1939. d, At coronation, 1953. e, In 1956. f, In 1985.

2001, July 3				
2492	A427	$1 Sheet of 6, #a-f	4.50	4.50
		Souvenir Sheet		
2493	A427	$6 In 1940	4.50	4.50

Photomosaic of Queen Elizabeth II — A428

2001, July 3		Litho.	Perf. 14	
2494	A428	$1 multi	.75	.75

Queen Elizabeth II, 75th birthday. Issued in sheets of 8.

Monet Paintings — A429

No. 2495, horiz.: a, Water Lilies. b, Rose Portals, Giverny. c, The Water Lily Pond, Harmony in Green. d, The Artist's Garden, Irises. $5, Jerusalem Artichokes.

2001, July 3			Perf. 13¾	
2495	A429	$2 Sheet of 4, #a-d	6.00	6.00
		Souvenir Sheet		
2496	A429	$5 multi	3.75	3.75

Endangered Animals — A430

Designs: 25c, Collared peccary. 30c, Baird's tapir. 45c, Agouti. 75c, Bananaquit. 90c, Six-banded armadillo. $1, Roseate spoonbill.

No. 2503: a, Mouse opossum. b, Magnificent black frigatebird. c, Northern jacana. d, Painted bunting. e, Haitian solenodon. f, St. Lucia iguana.

No. 2504: a, West Indian iguana. b, Scarlet macaw. c, Cotton-topped tamarin. d, Kinkajou. No. 2505, $6, Ocelot, vert. No. 2506, $6, King vulture, vert.

2001, Sept. 10			Perf. 14	
2497-2502	A430	Set of 6	2.75	2.75
2503	A430	$1.80 Sheet of 6, #a-f	8.25	8.25
2504	A430	$2.50 Sheet of 4, #a-d	7.50	7.50
		Souvenir Sheets		
2505-2506	A430	Set of 2	9.00	9.00

Rudolph Valentino (1895-1926), Actor — A431

No. 2507, $1: a, Blood and Sand. b, Eyes of Youth. c, All Night. d, Last known photo of Valentino. e, Camille. f, Cobra.

No. 2508, $1: a, The Son of the Sheik. b, The Young Rajah. c, The Eagle. d, The Sheik. e, A Sainted Devil. f, Monsieur Beaucaire.

No. 2509, $6, The Four Horsemen of the Apocalypse. No. 2510, $6, Valentino with Natasha Rambova.

2001, Oct. 2			Perf. 13¾	
		Sheets of 6, #a-f		
2507-2508	A431	Set of 2	9.00	9.00
		Souvenir Sheets		
2509-2510	A431	Set of 2	9.00	9.00

Scenes From Shirley Temple Movies — A432

No. 2511, $1.65 - Scenes from Baby, Take a Bow, with Temple: a, In polka-dot dress. b, With man on steps. c, With man holding gun. d, With woman.

No. 2512, $1.80, horiz. - Scenes from The Little Princess, with Temple: a, With man. b, Washing floor. c, With woman and child. d, With old woman.

No. 2513, $1.50 - Scenes from The Little Princess, with Temple: a, With woman. b, In pink dress. c, Holding doll. d, On throne. e, With man. f, With birthday cake.

No. 2514, $1.65, horiz. - Scenes from Baby, Take a Bow, with Temple: a, With woman and

five children. b, With arms around man. c, Being tucked in bed. d, With man. e, Standing with man and woman. f, Looking in cradle.

No. 2515, $6, In polka-dot dress, from Baby, Take a Bow. No. 2516, With soldiers, from The Little Princess.

2001, Oct. 2			Sheets of 4, #a-d	
2511-2512	A432		10.50	10.50
		Sheets of 6, #a-f		
2513-2514	A432	Set of 2	14.00	14.00
		Souvenir Sheets		
2515-2516	A432	Set of 2	9.00	9.00

Nobel Prizes, Cent. — A433

No. 2517, $1.50 - Chemistry laureates: a, Melvin Calvin, 1961. b, Linus C. Pauling, 1954. c, Vincent du Vigneaud, 1955. d, Richard Synge, 1952. e, Archer Martin, 1952. f, Alfred Werner, 1913.

No. 2518, $1.50 - Chemistry laureates: a, Robert F. Curl, Jr., 1996. b, Alan J. Heeger, 2000. c, Michael Smith, 1993. d, Sidney Altman, 1989. e, Elias James Corey, 1990. f, William Francis Giauque, 1949.

No. 2519, $6, Ernest Rutherford, Chemistry, 1908. No. 2520, $6, International Red Cross, Peace, 1944. No. 2521, $6, Ernst Otto Fischer, Chemistry, 1973.

2001, Nov. 29			Perf. 14	
		Sheets of 6, #a-f		
2517-2518	A433	Set of 2	13.50	13.50
		Souvenir Sheets		
2519-2521	A433	Set of 3	13.50	13.50

I Love Lucy Type of 2001

Designs: No. 2522, $6, Fred at desk. No. 2523, $6, Lucy and Fred. No. 2524, $6, Lucy, closed door. No. 2525, $6, Fred and Ricky at desk, horiz.

2001			Perf. 13¾	
2522-2525	A420	Set of 4	18.00	18.00

WAR TAX STAMPS

No. 31 and Type A3 Overprinted in Black or Red

1916-18		Wmk. 3	Perf. 14	
MR1	A3	½p green	.75	1.50
MR2	A3	½p green (R) ('17)	1.00	1.75
MR3	A3	1½p orange ('18)	.75	1.00
		Nos. MR1-MR3 (3)	2.50	4.25

ARGENTINA

ˌär-jən-ˈtē-nə

LOCATION — In South America
GOVT. — Republic
AREA — 1,084,120 sq. mi.
POP. — 36,737,664 (est. 1999)
CAPITAL — Buenos Aires

100 Centavos = 1 Peso (1858, 1992)
100 Centavos = 1 Austral (1985)

Catalogue values for unused stamps in this country are for Never Hinged items, beginning with Scott 587 in the regular postage section, Scott B12 in the semipostal section, Scott C59 in the airpost section, Scott CB1 in the airpost semi-postal section and Scott O79 in the officials section.

Watermarks

Wmk. 84- Italic RA

Wmk. 85- Small Sun, 4½mm

Wmk. 86- Large Sun, 6mm

Wmk. 87- Honeycomb

Wmk. 88- Multiple Suns

Wmk. 89- Large Sun

In this watermark the face of the sun is 7mm in diameter, the rays are heavier than in the large sun watermark of 1896-1911 and the watermarks are placed close together, so that parts of several frequently appear on one stamp. This paper was intended to be used for fiscal stamps and is usually referred to as "fiscal sun paper."

Wmk. 90- RA in Sun

In 1928 watermark 90 was slightly modified, making the diameter of the Sun 9mm instead of 10mm. Several types of this watermark exist.

Wmk. 205- AP in Oval

The letters "AP" are the initials of "AHORRO POSTAL." This paper was formerly used exclusively for Postal Savings stamps.

Wmk. 287- Double Circle and Letters in Sheet

Wmk. 288- RA in Sun with Straight Rays

Wmk. 365- Argentine Arms, "Casa de Moneda de la Nacion" & "RA" Multiple

Values for Unused

Unused values for Nos. 5-17 are for examples without gum. Examples with original gum command higher prices. Unused values of Nos. 1-4B and stamps after No. 17 are for examples with original gum as defined in the catalogue introduction.

Argentine Confederation

Symbolical of the Argentine Confederation
A1   A2

Unwmk.

1858, May 1   Litho.   Imperf.

1	A1	5c red	1.50	24.00
a.		Colon after "5"	1.75	32.50
b.		Colon after "V"	1.75	32.50
2	A1	10c green	2.50	57.50
f.		Diagonal half used as 5c on cover		800.00
3	A1	15c blue	16.00	160.00
c.		One-third used as 5c on cover		6,500.
		Nos. 1-3 (3)	20.00	241.50

There are nine varieties of Nos. 1, 2 and 3. Counterfeits and forged cancellations of Nos. 1-3 are plentiful.

1860, Jan.

4	A2	5c red	3.25	72.50
4A	A2	10c green	7.00	
4B	A2	15c blue	25.00	
		Nos. 4-4B (3)	35.25	

Nos. 4A and 4B were never placed in use. Some compositions of Nos. 4-4B contain 8 different types across the sheet. Other settings exist with minor variations. Counterfeits and forged cancellations of Nos. 4-4B are plentiful.

Argentine Republic

Seal of the Republic — A3

Broad "C" in "CENTAVOS," Accent on "U" of "REPUBLICA"

1862, Jan. 11

5	A3	5c rose	40.00	37.50
a.		5c rose lilac	87.50	35.00
6	A3	10c green	140.00	65.00
b.		Diagonal half used as 5c on cover		4,250.
7	A3	15c blue	275.00	225.00
a.		Without accent on "U"	7,000.	3,000.
b.		Tete beche pair	55,000.	
i.		15c ultramarine	425.00	325.00
j.		Diagonal third used as 5c on cover		5,000.

Only one used example of No. 7b is known. It has faults. Two unused examples are known. One is sound with original gum, the other is in a block, without gum, and has tiny faults.

Broad "C" in "CENTAVOS," No Accent on "U"

1863

7C	A3	5c rose	18.00	21.00
d.		5c rose lilac	100.00	110.00
m.		Worn plate (rose)	200.00	52.50
7F	A3	10c yellow green	350.00	140.00
g.		10c olive green	500.00	250.00
q.		10c green, ribbed paper	425.00	200.00
r.		Worn plate (green)	325.00	150.00
s.		Worn plate (olive green)	425.00	160.00

Narrow "C" in "CENTAVOS," No Accent on "U"

1864

7H	A3	5c rose red	160.00	32.50

The so-called reprints of 10c and 15c are counterfeits. They have narrow "C" and straight lines in shield. Nos. 7C and 7H have been extensively counterfeited.

Rivadavia Issue

Bernardino Rivadavia
A4   A5

Rivadavia — A6

1864-67   Engr.   Wmk. 84   Imperf.
Clear Impressions

8	A4	5c brown rose	1,300.	160.
a.		5c orange red ('67)	1,500.	160.
9	A5	10c green	2,000.	1,200.
10	A6	15c blue	7,500.	4,000.

Perf. 11½
Dull to Worn Impressions

11	A4	5c brown rose		
		('65)	30.00	12.00
11B	A4	5c lake ('65)	77.50	17.50
12	A5	10c green	80.00	30.00
a.		Half used as 5c on cover		900.00
c.		Horiz. pair, imperf vert.		1,750.
13	A6	15c blue	275.00	110.00

1867-72   Unwmk.   Imperf.

14	A4	5c carmine ('72)	250.	65.
15	A4	5c rose	200.	100.
15A	A5	10c green	4,000.	4,000.
16	A6	15c blue	2,000.	1,750.

Nos. 15A-16 issued without gum.

1867   Perf. 11½

17	A4	5c carmine	350.00	150.00

Nos. 14, 15 and 17 exist with part of papermaker's wmk. "LACROIX FRERES."

Rivadavia A7

Manuel Belgrano A8

Jose de San Martin — A9

Groundwork of Horizontal Lines

1867-68   Perf. 12

18	A7	5c vermilion	200.00	10.00
18A	A8	10c green	30.00	4.50
b.		Diag. half used as 5c on cover		750.00
19	A9	15c blue	65.00	15.00

Groundwork of Crossed Lines

20	A7	5c vermilion	10.50	.80
21	A9	15c blue	92.50	12.00

See Nos. 27, 33-34, 39 and types A19, A33, A34, A37. For surcharges and overprints see Nos. 30-32, 41-42, 47-51, O6-O7, O26.

Gen. Antonio G. Balcarce A10

Mariano Moreno A11

Carlos Maria de Alvear A12

Gervasio Antonio Posadas A13

Cornelio
Saavedra — A14

1873
22	A10	1c purple	5.00	2.00
a.		1c gray violet	6.25	2.00
23	A11	4c brown	5.00	.40
a.		4c red brown	17.50	2.00
24	A12	30c orange	100.00	16.00
a.		Vert. pair, imperf horiz.	4,000.	
25	A13	60c black	100.00	4.75
26	A14	90c blue	25.00	2.50
		Nos. 22-26 (5)	235.00	25.65

For overprints see Nos. O5, O12-O14, O19-O21, O25, O29.

1873

Laid Paper
27	A8	10c green	200.00	20.00

Nos. 18, 18A Surcharged in Black

Nos. 30-31   No. 32

1877, Feb.

Wove Paper
30	A7	1c on 5c vermilion	47.50	15.00
a.		Inverted surcharge	350.00	200.00
31	A7	2c on 5c vermilion	92.50	60.00
a.		Inverted surcharge	700.00	500.00
32	A8	8c on 10c green	125.00	30.00
b.		Inverted surcharge	500.00	425.00
		Nos. 30-32 (3)	265.00	105.00

Varieties also exist with double and triple surcharges, surcharge on reverse, 8c on No. 27, all made clandestinely from the original cliches of the surcharges.
Forgeries of these surcharges include the inverted and double varieties.

1876-77   *Rouletted*
33	A7	5c vermilion	150.00	60.00
34	A7	8c lake ('77)	25.00	.40

Belgrano   Dalmacio
A17   Vélez
                  Sarsfield
                  A18

San Martín — A19

1878   *Rouletted*
35	A17	16c green	8.00	1.10
36	A18	20c blue	10.00	3.00
37	A19	24c blue	17.50	3.00
		Nos. 35-37 (3)	35.50	7.10

See No. 56. For overprints see Nos. O9-O10, O15-O17, O22, O28.

Vicente
Lopez — A20   Alvear — A21

1877-80   *Perf. 12*
38	A20	2c yellow green	4.25	.90
39	A7	8c lake ('80)	4.25	.40
a.		8c brown lake	30.00	4.00
40	A21	25c lake ('78)	22.50	6.00
		Nos. 38-40 (3)	31.00	7.30

For overprints see Nos. O4, O11, O18, O24.

No. 18 Surcharged in Black

Large "P"   Small "P"
Wide "V"   Narrow "V"

1882
41	A7	½c on 5c ver	1.60	1.60
a.		Double surcharge	80.00	80.00
b.		Inverted surcharge	20.00	20.00
c.		"PROVISORIO" omitted	80.00	80.00
d.		Fraction omitted	50.00	
e.		"PROVISOBIO"	32.50	32.50
f.		Pair, one without surcharge	200.00	
g.		Small "P" in "PROVISORIO"	2.50	2.50
h.		As "a," small "P" in "PROVISORIO"	32.50	32.50
i.		As "b," small "P" in "PROVISORIO"	40.00	40.00
j.		As "d," small "P" in "PROVISORIO"	15.00	15.00

Perforated across Middle of Stamp
42	A7	½c on 5c ver	3.25	3.25
a.		"PROVISORIO"	40.00	40.00
b.		Large "P" in "PROVISORIO"	30.00	22.50

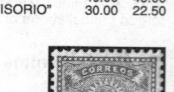

A23

1882   **Typo.**   *Perf. 12*
43	A23	½c brown	1.40	.80
a.		Imperf., pair	40.00	40.00
44	A23	1c red, perf. 14	3.50	1.00
a.		Perf. 12	9.00	4.25
45	A23	12c ultra, perf 14	45.00	8.75
a.		Perf. 12	55.00	8.75

Engr.
46	A23	12c grnsh blue, perf. 14	125.00	11.00
		Nos. 43-46 (4)	174.90	21.55

See type A29. For overprints see Nos. O2, O8, O23, O27.

No. 21 Surcharged in Red:

a   b

CUATRO
Centavos
1884 c

1884   **Engr.**   *Perf. 12*
47	A9 (a)	½c on 15c blue	1.90	1.50
a.		Groundwork of horiz. lines	100.00	80.00
b.		Inverted surcharge	27.50	20.00
48	A9 (b)	1c on 15c blue	16.00	13.00
a.		Groundwork of horiz. lines	10.00	6.50
b.		Inverted surcharge	80.00	57.50
c.		Double surcharge	40.00	32.50
d.		Triple surcharge	350.00	

Nos. 20-21 Surcharged in Black
49	A7 (a)	½c on 5c ver	4.00	3.25
a.		Inverted surcharge	160.00	110.00
b.		Date omitted	150.00	—
c.		Pair, one without surcharge	375.00	
d.		Double surcharge	550.00	
50	A9 (a)	½c on 15c blue	10.00	8.00
a.		Groundwork of horiz. lines	32.50	26.00
b.		Inverted surcharge	72.50	55.00
c.		Pair, one without surcharge	325.00	
51	A7 (c)	4c on 5c ver	10.00	6.50
a.		Inverted surcharge	26.00	20.00
b.		Double surcharge	325.00	200.00
c.		Pair, one without surcharge but with "4" in manuscript	550.00	350.00
d.		Pair, one without surcharge	250.00	
		Nos. 47-51 (5)	41.90	32.25

A29

1884-85   **Engr.**   *Perf. 12*
52	A29	½c red brown	1.00	.45
a.		Horiz. pair, imperf vert.	300.00	250.00
53	A29	1c rose red	5.25	.45
a.		Horiz. pair, imperf vert.	300.00	250.00
54	A29	12c deep blue	25.00	1.25
a.		12c grnish blue ('85)	30.00	1.25
b.		Horiz. pair, imperf vert.	300.00	250.00
		Nos. 52-54 (3)	31.25	2.15

For overprints see Nos. O1, O3, O9.

San Martin Type of 1878

1887   **Engr.**
56	A19	24c blue	17.50	1.40

Justo Jose de   Lopez — A31
Urquiza — A30

Miguel Juarez   Rivadavia
Celman   (Large head)
A32   A33

Rivadavia   Domingo F.
(Small head)   Sarmiento
A34   A35

Nicolas   San Martin
Avellaneda   A37
A36

Julio A. Roca   Belgrano
A37a   A37b

Manuel   Moreno
Dorrego   A39
A38

Bartolome
Mitre — A40

CINCO CENTAVOS.
A33 - Shows collar on left side only.
A34 - Shows collar on both sides. Lozenges in background larger and clearer than in A33.

1888-90   **Litho.**   *Perf. 11½*
57	A30	½c blue	.80	.45
b.		Vert. pair, imperf. horiz.	125.00	65.00
c.		Horiz. pair, imperf. vert.	125.00	65.00
58	A31	2c yel green	10.00	6.00
b.		Vert. pair, imperf. horiz.	80.00	
c.		Horiz. pair, imperf. vert.	200.00	
59	A32	3c blue green	1.75	.65
b.		Vert. pair, imperf. horiz.	80.00	
c.		Horiz. pair, imperf. btwn.	100.00	
d.		Vert. pair, imperf. btwn.	25.00	25.00
60	A33	5c carmine	8.00	.60
b.		Vert. pair, imperf. horiz.	100.00	
61	A34	5c carmine	12.50	1.25
b.		Vert. pair, imperf. horiz.		
			400.00	
62	A35	6c red	25.00	15.00
b.		Vert. pair, imperf. btwn.	80.00	
c.		Perf. 12	52.50	42.50
63	A36	10c brown	15.00	1.10
64	A37	15c orange	15.00	1.60
d.		Vert. pair, imperf. btwn.	600.00	
64A	A37a	20c green	12.00	1.25
64B	A37b	25c purple	15.00	2.00
65	A38	30c brown	21.00	2.50
b.		30c reddish choc brn	400.00	80.00
c.		Horiz. pair, imperf. btwn.	400.00	325.00
66	A39	40c sl, perf 12	25.00	3.00
a.		Perf. 11½	80.00	16.00
b.		Horiz. pair, imperf. btwn. (#66)		
			600.00	
67	A40	50c blue	100.00	8.25
		Nos. 57-67 (13)	261.05	43.65

In this issue there are several varieties of each value, the difference between them being in the relative position of the head to the frame.

Imperf., Pairs
57a	A30	½c	75.00	60.00
58a	A31	2c	55.00	
59a	A32	3c	35.00	25.00
61a	A34	5c		100.00
62a	A35	6c	55.00	
63a	A36	10c	55.00	
64c	A37	15c		200.00
65a	A38	30c	275.00	200.00

Urquiza   Velez
A41   Sarsfield
                       A42

 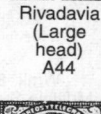

Miguel   Rivadavia
Juarez   (Large
Celman   head)
A43   A44

Sarmiento   Juan
A45   Bautista
                       Alberdi
                       A46

1888-89   **Engr.**   *Perf. 11½, 11½x12*
68	A41	½c ultra	.40	.25
a.		Vert. pair, imperf. horiz.		
b.		Imperf., pair	30.00	—
69	A42	1c brown	.90	.40
a.		Vert. pair, imperf. horiz.	65.00	
b.		Vert. pair, imperf. btwn.	—	
c.		Imperf., pair	30.00	
d.		Horiz. pair, imperf. btwn.	100.00	
70	A43	3c blue green	2.50	.75
71	A44	5c rose	2.75	.40
a.			40.00	—
72	A45	6c blue black	1.75	.55
b.		Perf. 11½x12	12.50	3.00

73	A46	12c blue	5.50	1.75
a.		Imperf., pair	30.00	
b.		bluish paper	8.00	2.00
c.		Perf. 11½	8.25	3.00
		Nos. 68-73 (6)	13.80	4.10

#69-70 exist with papermakers' watermarks. See #77, designs A50, A61. For surcharges see #83-84.

Jose Maria Paz
A48

Santiago Derqui
A49

Rivadavia (Small head)
A50

Avellaneda
A51

Moreno
A53

Mitre
A54

Posadas — A55

1890		Engr.	Perf. 11½	
75	A48	¼c green	.40	.30
76	A49	2c violet	.85	.20
a.		2c purple	.85	.20
b.		2c slate	1.25	.30
c.		Horiz. pair, imperf. btwn.	25.00	20.00
d.		Imperf., pair	35.00	
e.		Perf. 11½x12	5.00	.50
77	A50	5c carmine	2.00	.25
a.		Imperf., pair	50.00	25.00
b.		Perf. 11½x12	5.00	.30
c.		Vert. pair, imperf. btwn.	75.00	60.00
d.		Horiz. pair, imperf. btwn.	75.00	60.00
78	A51	10c brown	2.50	.40
b.		Imperf., pair	150.00	
c.		Vert. pair, imperf. btwn.	225.00	
80	A53	40c olive green	5.00	.80
a.		Imperf., pair	40.00	
b.		Horiz. pair, imperf. btwn.		250.00
81	A54	50c orange	5.00	.80
a.		Imperf., pair	60.00	
b.		Perf. 11½x12	16.00	1.60
82	A55	60c black	15.00	2.75
a.		Imperf., pair		
b.		Horiz. pair, imperf. btwn.	125.00	100.00
		Nos. 75-82 (7)	30.75	5.50

Type A50 differs from type A44 in having the head smaller, the letters of "Cinco Centavos" not as tall, and the curved ornaments at sides close to the first and last letters of "Republica Argentina."

Lithographed Surcharge on No. 73 in Black or Red

1890			Perf. 11½x12	
83	A46	¼c on 12c blue	.40	.40
a.		Perf. 11½	37.50	25.00
b.		Double surcharge	75.00	35.00
c.		Inverted surcharge	80.00	
84	A46	¼c on 12c blue (R)	.40	.40
a.		Double surcharge	52.50	52.50
b.		Perf. 11½	7.00	5.00

Surcharge is different on #83 and 84. Nos. 83-84 exist as pairs, one without surcharge. These were privately produced.

Rivadavia
A57

Jose de San Martin
A58

Gregorio Araoz de Lamadrid
A59

Admiral Guillermo Brown
A60

1891		Engr.	Perf. 11½	
85	A57	8c carmine rose	1.25	.25
a.		Imperf., pair	75.00	
86	A58	1p deep blue	40.00	7.50
87	A59	5p ultra	200.00	21.00
88	A60	20p green	300.00	60.00
		Nos. 85-88 (4)	541.25	88.75

A 10p brown and a 50p red were prepared but not issued. Values: 10p $1,500 for fine, 50p $1,000 with rough or somewhat damaged perfs.

Velez Sarsfield
A61

"Santa Maria," "Nina" and "Pinta"
A62

1890			Perf. 11½	
89	A61	1c brown	.80	.40
b.		Horiz. pair, imperf. btwn.		550.00

Type A61 is a re-engraving of A42. The figure "1" in each upper corner has a short horizontal serif instead of a long one pointing downward. In type A61 the first and last letters of "Correos y Telegrafos" are closer to the curved ornaments below than in type A42. Background is of horizontal lines (cross-hatching on No. 69).

1892, Oct. 12		Wmk. 85	Perf. 11½	
90	A62	2c light blue	6.00	3.00
a.		Double impression	190.00	
91	A62	5c dark blue	8.50	5.00

Discovery of America, 400th anniv. Counterfeits of Nos. 90-91 are litho.

Rivadavia
A63

Belgrano
A64

San Martin — A65

Perf. 11½, 12 and Compound

1892-95			Wmk. 85	
92	A63	½c dull blue	.35	.20
a.		½c bright ultra	50.00	25.00
93	A63	1c brown	.50	.20
94	A63	2c green	.60	.25
95	A63	3c orange ('95)	1.25	.20
96	A63	5c carmine	1.50	.25
b.		5c green (error)	650.00	650.00
98	A64	10c carmine rose	10.00	.40
99	A64	12c dp bl ('93)	7.50	.40
100	A64	16c gray	12.50	.55
101	A64	24c gray brown	12.50	.55
b.		Perf. 12	27.50	15.00
102	A64	50c blue green	18.00	.55
b.		Perf. 12	27.50	5.00
103	A65	1p lake ('93)	10.00	.75
a.		1p red brown	17.50	5.00
104	A65	2p dark green	21.00	2.25
a.		Perf. 12	110.00	37.50
105	A65	5p dark blue	37.50	2.75
		Nos. 92-105 (13)	133.20	9.30

The high values of this and succeeding issues are frequently punched with the word "INUTILIZADO," parts of the letters showing on each stamp. These punched stamps sell for only a small fraction of the catalogue values.

Reprints of No. 96b have white gum. The original stamp has yellowish gum. Value $125.

Imperf., Pairs

92b	A63	½c	55.00	—
93a	A63	1c	55.00	—
94a	A63	2c	27.50	—
96a	A63	5c	27.50	—
98a	A64	10c	55.00	—
99a	A64	12c	55.00	—
100a	A64	16c	55.00	—
101a	A64	24c	55.00	—
102a	A64	50c	55.00	—
103b	A65	1p	60.00	—
105a	A65	5p	140.00	—

Nos. 102a, 103b and 105a exist only without gum; the other imperfs are found with or without gum, and the values are the same for either condition.

Vertical Pairs, Imperf. Between

92c	A63	½c	125.00	
93b	A63	1c	100.00	
94b	A63	2c	50.00	
95a	A63	3c	250.00	—
96c	A63	5c	45.00	
98b	A64	10c	100.00	
99b	A64	12c	100.00	

Horizontal Pairs, Imperf. Between

93c	A63	1c	110.00	
94c	A63	2c	55.00	
96d	A63	5c	55.00	45.00
98d	A64	10c	110.00	

1896-97			Wmk. 86	
106	A63	½c slate	.50	.25
a.		½c gray blue	.50	.25
b.		½c indigo	.50	.25
107	A63	1c brown	.50	.25
108	A63	2c yellow green	.50	.25
109	A63	3c orange	.50	.25
110	A63	5c carmine	.50	.25
a.		Imperf., pair	100.00	
111	A64	10c carmine rose	8.00	.25
112	A64	12c deep blue	4.00	.25
113	A64	16c gray	10.00	.80
114	A64	24c gray brown	10.00	1.00
a.		Imperf., pair	100.00	
115	A64	30c orange ('97)	10.00	.60
116	A64	50c blue green	10.00	.60
117	A64	80c dull violet	18.00	.80
118	A65	1p lake	25.00	.80
119	A65	1p20c black ('97)	10.00	3.50
120	A65	2p dark green	16.00	8.00
121	A65	5p dark blue	90.00	10.00
a.		Perf. 12	325.00	90.00
		Nos. 106-121 (16)	213.50	27.85

Vertical Pairs, Imperf. Between

106c	A63	½c	200.00	
107a	A63	1c	125.00	
108a	A63	2c	125.00	
109a	A63	3c	200.00	
110b	A63	5c	125.00	125.00
112b	A64	12c	125.00	100.00

Horizontal Pairs, Imperf. Between

107b	A63	1c	125.00	
108b	A63	2c	125.00	
110c	A63	5c	125.00	80.00
111a	A64	10c	125.00	
112c	A64	12c	125.00	

Allegory, Liberty Seated
A66   A67

Perf. 11½, 12 and Compound

1899-1903				
122	A66	½c yellow brown	.35	.25
123	A66	1c green	.50	.25
124	A66	2c slate	.50	.25
125	A66	3c orange ('01)	.85	.40
126	A66	4c yellow ('03)	1.50	.50
127	A66	5c carmine rose	.50	.25
128	A66	6c black ('03)	1.00	.50
129	A66	10c dark green	1.50	.35
130	A66	12c dull blue	1.00	.50
131	A66	12c olive grn ('01)	1.00	.50
132	A66	15c sea green ('01)	2.75	.50
132B	A66	15c dull blue ('01)	3.00	.50
133	A66	16c orange	7.50	5.00
134	A66	20c claret	2.00	.25
135	A66	24c violet	3.50	.80
136	A66	30c rose	7.50	.50
137	A66	30c vermilion ('01)	3.75	.40
a.		30c scarlet	50.00	2.50
138	A66	50c brt blue	4.75	.40
139	A67	1p bl & blk, perf. 11½	14.00	.65
a.		Center inverted	1,500.	525.00
b.		Perf. 12	250.00	125.00
140	A67	5p orange & blk	57.50	7.00
		Punch cancellation		1.60
		Center inverted	2,750.	
141	A67	10p green & blk	50.00	9.25
		Punch cancellation		1.75
		Center inverted	3,600.	
		Punch cancellation		675.00
142	A67	20p red & black	200.00	21.00
		Punch cancellation		1.75
a.		Center invtd.(punch cancel)	2,000.	
		Nos. 122-142 (22)	364.95	50.00

Imperf., Pairs

122a	A66	½c	30.00	
123a	A66	1c	45.00	
124a	A66	2c	15.00	
125a	A66	3c	250.00	
127a	A66	5c	15.00	
128a	A66	6c	45.00	
129a	A66	10c	45.00	
132a	A66	15c	45.00	

Vertical Pairs, Imperf. Between

122b	A66	½c	10.00	10.00
123b	A66	1c	10.00	10.00
124b	A66	2c	5.00	5.00
125b	A66	3c	200.00	150.00
126a	A66	4c	250.00	200.00
127b	A66	5c	5.00	3.00
128b	A66	6c	12.00	10.00
129b	A66	10c	75.00	
132c	A66	15c	12.00	10.00

Horizontal Pairs, Imperf. Between

122c	A66	½c	30.00	20.00
123c	A66	1c	50.00	20.00
124c	A66	2c	5.00	
125c	A66	3c	225.00	150.00
126b	A66	4c	275.00	
127c	A66	5c	10.00	5.00
128c	A66	6c	17.50	10.00
129c	A66	10c	17.50	10.00
132d	A66	15c	35.00	20.00
138a	A66	50c	160.00	

River Port of Rosario
A68

1902, Oct. 26			Perf. 11½, 11½x12	
143	A68	5c deep blue	4.50	2.50
a.		Imperf., pair	95.00	
b.		Vert. pair, imperf. btwn.	95.00	
c.		Horiz. pair, imperf. btwn.	75.00	

Completion of port facilities at Rosario.

San Martin
A69   A70

1908-09		Typo.	Perf. 13½, 13½x12½	
144	A69	½c violet	.20	.20
145	A69	1c brnsh buff	.20	.20
146	A69	2c chocolate	.55	.20
147	A69	3c green	.70	.30
148	A69	4c redsh violet	1.40	.30
149	A69	5c carmine	.30	.20
150	A69	6c olive bister	.80	.25
151	A69	10c gray green	1.50	.20
152	A69	12c yellow buff	.40	.40
153	A69	12c dk blue ('09)	1.25	.20
154	A69	15c apple green	1.75	.85
155	A69	20c ultra	1.25	.20
156	A69	24c red brown	3.25	.60
157	A69	30c dull rose	5.00	.60
158	A69	50c black	4.75	.40
159	A70	1p sl bl & pink	11.00	1.75
		Nos. 144-159 (16)	34.30	6.85

The 1c blue was not issued. Value $250.
Wmk. 86 appears on ½, 1, 6, 20, 24 and 50c. Other values have similar wmk. with wavy rays.

Stamps lacking wmk. are from outer rows printed on sheet margin.

Pyramid of
May — A71

Nicolas
Rodriguez
Pena &
Hipolito
Vieytes — A72

Meeting at
Pena's
Home — A73

3c, Miguel de Azcuenaga (1754-1833) &
Father Manuel M. Alberti (1763-1811). 4c,
Viceroy's house & Fort Buenos Aires. 5c, Cornelio Saavedra (1759-1829). 10c, Antonio Luis
Beruti (1772-1842) & French distributing
badges. 12c, Congress building. 20c, Juan
Jose Castelli (1764-1812) & Domingo Matheu
(1765-1831). 24c, 1st council. 30c, Manuel
Belgrano (1770-1820) & Juan Larrea (1782-
1847). 50c, 1st meeting of republican government, May 25, 1810. 1p, Mariano Moreno
(1778-1811) & Juan Jose Paso (1758-1833).
5p, Oath of the Junta. 10p, Centenary Monument. 20p, Jose Francisco de San Martin
(1778-1850).

Inscribed "1810 1910"
Various Frames

1910, May 1		Engr.	Perf. 11½	
160	A71	½c bl & gray bl	.30	.20
161	A72	1c blue grn & blk	.30	.20
b.		Horiz. pair, imperf. btwn.	65.00	
162	A73	2c olive & gray	.20	.20
163	A72	3c green	.70	.20
164	A73	4c dk bl & grn	.70	.25
165	A71	5c carmine	.40	.20
166	A73	10c yel brn & blk	1.75	.20
167	A73	12c brt blue	1.40	.25
168	A72	20c gray brn & blk	3.25	.35
169	A73	24c org brn & bl	1.75	.90
170	A72	30c lilac & blk	1.75	.65
171	A71	50c car & blk	4.50	.90
172	A72	1p brt blue	10.00	3.50
173	A73	5p orange & vio	70.00	30.00
		Punch cancel		2.50
174	A71	10p orange & blk	90.00	65.00
		Punch cancel		3.00
175	A71	20p dp bl & ind	150.00	90.00
		Punch cancel		4.50
		Nos. 160-175 (16)	337.00	193.00

Centenary of the republic.

Center Inverted

160a	A71	½c	750.00	
161a	A72	1c	750.00	
162a	A73	2c	800.00	
164a	A73	4c	500.00	
167a	A73	12c	650.00	
171a	A71	50c	650.00	
173a	A73	5p	650.00	

Domingo F.
Sarmiento
A87

Agriculture
A88

1911, May 15	Typo.	Perf. 13½	
176 A87	5c gray brn & blk	.75	.50

Domingo Faustino Sarmiento (1811-88),
pres. of Argentina, 1868-74.

Wmk. 86, without Face

1911	Engr.	Perf. 12	
		Size: 19x25mm	
177 A88	5c vermilion	.40	.20
178 A88	12c deep blue	5.00	.20

Wmk. 86, with Face

1911		Typo.	Perf. 13½x12½	
		Size: 18x23mm		
179	A88	½c violet	.20	.20
180	A88	1c brown ocher	.20	.20
181	A88	2c chocolate	.20	.20
a.		Perf. 13½	4.25	1.75
b.		Imperf., pair	26.00	
182	A88	3c green	.40	.20
183	A88	4c brown violet	.35	.25
184	A88	10c gray green	.50	.20
185	A88	20c ultra	4.25	1.00
186	A88	24c red brown	5.25	3.50
187	A88	30c claret	1.75	.50
188	A88	50c black	8.00	.85
		Nos. 179-188 (10)	21.10	7.10

The 5c dull red is a proof. In this issue
Wmk. 86 comes: straight rays (4c, 20c, 24c)
and wavy rays (2c). All other values exist with
both forms.

Wmk. 87 (Horiz. or Vert.)

1912-14			Perf. 13½x12½	
189	A88	½c violet	.20	.20
190	A88	1c ocher	.20	.20
191	A88	2c chocolate	.30	.20
192	A88	3c green	.60	.20
193	A88	4c brown violet	.60	.20
194	A88	5c red	.20	.20
195	A88	10c deep green	1.40	.20
196	A88	12c deep blue	1.40	.20
197	A88	20c ultra	8.00	.70
198	A88	24c red brown	3.25	1.60
199	A88	30c claret	8.00	.60
200	A88	50c black	5.00	.60
		Nos. 189-200 (12)	29.15	5.10

See Nos. 208-212. For overprints see Nos.
OD1-OD8, OD47-OD54, OD102-OD108,
OD146-OD152, OD183-OD190, OD235-
OD241, OD281-OD284, OD318-OD323.

Perf. 13½

189a	A88	½c	.80	.25
190a	A88	1c	.80	.25
191a	A88	2c	.80	.20
192a	A88	3c	35.00	16.00
193a	A88	4c	1.60	.70
194a	A88	5c	.30	.20
196a	A88	12c	3.25	.80
197a	A88	20c	5.00	.70
		Nos. 189a-197a (8)	47.55	19.10

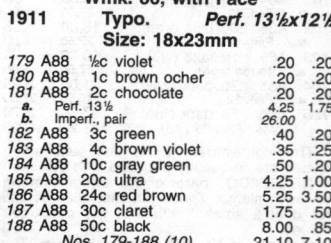

A89

1912-13			Perf. 13½	
201	A89	1p dull bl & rose	6.00	1.00
		Punch cancel		.30
202	A89	5p slate & ol grn	19.00	6.00
		Punch cancel		.60
203	A89	10p violet & blue	75.00	9.00
		Punch cancel		1.40
204	A89	20p blue & claret	175.00	60.00
		Punch cancel		2.00
		Nos. 201-204 (4)	275.00	76.00

1915	Unwmk.	Perf. 13½x12½	
208 A88	1c ocher	.50	.20
209 A88	2c chocolate	.50	.20
212 A88	5c red	.50	.20
	Nos. 208-212 (3)	1.50	.60

Only these denominations were printed on
paper without watermark.
Other stamps of the series are known
unwatermarked but they are from the outer
rows of sheets the other parts of which are
watermarked.

Francisco
Narciso de
Laprida
A90

Declaration of
Independence
A91

Jose de San Martin
A92   A92a

1916, July 9		Litho.	Wmk. 87	
		Perf. 13½, 13½x12½		
215	A90	½c violet	.20	.20
216	A90	1c buff	.25	.20
		Perf. 13½x12½		
217	A90	2c chocolate	.20	.20
218	A90	3c green	.45	.20
219	A90	4c red violet	.65	.20
		Perf. 13½		
220	A91	5c red	.30	.20
a.		Imperf., pair	40.00	
221	A91	10c gray green	1.50	.20
222	A92	12c blue	.65	.20
223	A92	20c ultra	1.00	.25
224	A92	24c red brown	1.60	.75
225	A92	30c claret	1.60	.40
226	A92	50c gray black	3.25	.50
227	A92a	1p sl bl & red	9.25	4.00
		Punch cancel		.50
228	A92a	5p black & gray grn	110.00	40.00
		Punch cancel		3.25
229	A92a	10p violet & blue	110.00	75.00
		Punch cancel		2.50
230	A92a	20p dull blue & cl	160.00	67.50
		Punch cancel		1.00
a.		Imperf., pair	650.00	
		Nos. 215-230 (16)	400.90	190.00

Cent. of Argentina's declaration of independence of Spain, July 9, 1816.

The watermark is either vert. or horiz. on
Nos. 215-220, 222; only vert. on No. 221, and
only horiz. on Nos. 223-230.

For overprints see #OD9, OD55-OD56,
OD109, OD153, OD191-OD192, OD285,
OD324.

A93

A94

A94a

Juan
Gregorio
Pujol — A95

1917		Perf. 13½, 13½x12½	
231 A93	½c violet	.20	.20
232 A93	1c buff	.25	.20
233 A93	2c brown	.25	.20
234 A93	3c lt green	.75	.20
235 A93	4c red violet	.80	.40
236 A93	5c red	.25	.20
a.	Imperf., pair	14.00	
237 A93	10c gray green	1.50	.20
	Perf. 13½		
238 A94	12c blue	1.00	.20
239 A94	20c ultra	1.50	.20
240 A94	24c red brown	4.50	2.00
241 A94	30c claret	4.50	.60
242 A94	50c gray black	4.00	.60
243 A94a	1p sl bl & red	4.00	.35
244 A94a	5p black & gray grn	20.00	3.00
	Punch cancel		1.50
245 A94a	10p violet & blue	47.50	9.25
	Punch cancel		1.00
246 A94a	20p dull bl & cl	77.50	15.00
	Punch cancel		.80
a.	Center inverted	1,200.	875.00
	Nos. 231-246 (16)	168.50	32.80

The watermark is either vert. or horiz. on
Nos. 231-236, 238; only vert. on No. 237, and
only horiz. on Nos. 239-246.

1918, June 15	Litho.	Perf. 13½	
247 A95	5c bister & gray	.70	.25

Cent. of the birth of Juan G. Pujol (1817-61),
lawyer and legislator.

		Perf. 13½, 13½x12½	
1918-19		Unwmk.	
248 A93	½c violet	.20	.20
249 A93	1c buff	.20	.20
a.	Imperf., pair	14.00	
250 A93	2c brown	.25	.20
251 A93	3c lt green	.25	.20
252 A93	4c red violet	.25	.20
253 A93	5c red	.20	.20
254 A93	10c gray green	1.10	.20
	Perf. 13½		
255 A94	12c blue	1.25	.20
256 A94	20c ultra	1.60	.20
257 A94	24c red brown	2.00	.50
258 A94	30c claret	2.50	.30
259 A94	50c gray black	5.50	.25
	Nos. 248-259 (12)	15.25	2.85

The stamps of this issue sometimes show
letters of papermakers' watermarks.
There were two printings, in 1918 and 1923,
using different ink and paper.

1920	Wmk. 88	Perf. 13½, 13½x12½	
264 A93	½c violet	.20	.20
265 A93	1c buff	.25	.20
266 A93	2c brown	.25	.20
267 A93	3c green	1.50	.30
268 A93	4c red violet	2.00	1.25
269 A93	5c red	.40	.20
270 A93	10c gray green	3.25	.20
	Perf. 13½		
271 A94	12c blue	1.75	.20
272 A94	20c ultra	2.50	.20
274 A94	30c claret	8.25	.70
275 A94	50c gray black	5.00	.90
	Nos. 264-275 (11)	25.35	4.55

See #292-300, 304-307A, 310-314, 318, 322.
For overprints see Nos. OD10-OD20,
OD57-OD71, OD74, OD110-OD121, OD154-
OD159, OD161-OD162, OD193-OD207,
OD209-OD211, OD242-OD252, OD254-
OD255, OD286-OD290, OD325-OD328,
OD330.

Belgrano's
Mausoleum
A96

Creation of
Argentine Flag
A97

Gen. Manuel
Belgrano — A98

1920, June 18		Perf. 13½	
280 A96	2c red	.35	.20
a.	Perf. 13½x12½	.35	.20
281 A97	5c rose & blue	.40	.20
282 A98	12c green & blue	.75	.75
	Nos. 280-282 (3)	1.50	1.15

Belgrano (1770-1820), Argentine general,
patriot and diplomat.

Gen. Justo
Jose de
Urquiza — A99

Bartolome
Mitre — A100

1920, Nov. 11			
283 A99	5c gray blue	.25	.20

Gen. Justo Jose de Urquiza (1801-70),
pres. of Argentina, 1854-60. See No. 303.

1921, June 26	Unwmk.		
284 A100	2c violet brown	.25	.20
285 A100	5c light blue	.25	.20

Bartolome Mitre (1821-1906), pres. of
Argentina, 1862-65.

Allegory, Pan-
America — A101

1921, Aug. 25   Perf. 13½

286	A101	3c violet	.55	.30
287	A101	5c blue	.80	.20
288	A101	10c vio brown	1.40	.35
289	A101	12c rose	2.00	.75
		Nos. 286-289 (4)	4.75	1.60

Inscribed   Inscribed
"Buenos   "Republica
Aires-Agosto   Argentina"
de 1921"   A103
A102

1921, Oct.   Perf. 13½x12½

290	A102	5c rose	.30	.20
a.		Perf. 13½	1.25	.20
291	A103	5c rose	1.50	.20
a.		Perf. 13½	2.50	.20

1st Pan-American Postal Cong., Buenos
Aires, Aug., 1921.
See Nos. 308-309, 319. For overprints see
Nos. OD72, OD160, OD208, OD253, OD329.

1920 Wmk. 89   Perf. 13½, 13½x12½

292	A93	½c violet	2.00	.75
293	A93	1c buff	5.00	.75
294	A93	2c brown	3.00	.75
297	A93	5c red	4.00	.75
298	A93	10c gray green	4.00	.40

Perf. 13½

299	A94	12c blue	3,000.	125.00
300	A94	20c ultra	12.00	.75
		Nos. 292-298,300 (6)	30.00	3.90

1920

303	A99	5c gray blue	350.00	225.00

Perf. 13½, 13½x12½

1922-23   Wmk. 90

304	A93	½c violet	.20	.20
305	A93	1c buff	.20	.20
306	A93	2c brown	.20	.20
307	A93	3c green	.40	.20
307A	A93	4c red violet	3.75	1.00
308	A102	5c rose	2.25	.20
309	A103	5c red	1.50	.20
310	A93	10c gray green	4.75	.30

Perf. 13½

311	A94	12c blue	.75	.20
312	A94	20c ultra	1.25	.20
313	A94	24c red brown	9.25	4.50
314	A94	30c claret	5.50	.50
		Nos. 304-314 (12)	30.00	8.00

Paper with Gray Overprint RA in Sun
Perf. 13½, 13½x12½

1922-23   Unwmk.

318	A93	2c brown	3.00	1.00
319	A103	5c red	2.00	.30

Perf. 13½

322	A94	20c ultra	15.00	1.50
		Nos. 318-322 (3)	20.00	2.80

San Martín
A104   A105
With Period after Value

1923, May   Litho.   Wmk. 90

323	A104	½c red violet	.20	.20
324	A104	1c buff	.30	.20
325	A104	2c dark brown	.30	.20
326	A104	3c lt green	.30	.20
327	A104	4c red brown	.30	.20
328	A104	5c red	.30	.20
329	A104	10c dull green	2.50	.20
330	A104	12c deep blue	.40	.20
331	A104	20c ultra	1.00	.20

332	A104	24c lt brown	2.50	1.50
333	A104	30c claret	7.75	.60
334	A104	50c black	4.00	.35

Without Period after Value
Wmk. 87   Perf. 13½

335	A105	1p blue & red	4.00	.20
336	A105	5p gray lilac & grn	16.00	1.75
		Punch cancel		.60
337	A105	10p claret & blue	55.00	10.50
		Punch cancel		1.00
338	A105	20p sl & brn lake	90.00	30.00
a.		Center inverted		
		Nos. 323-338 (16)	184.85	46.70

Nos. 335-338 and 353-356 canceled with
round or oval killers in purple (revenue cancellations) sell for one-fifth to one-half as much as
postally used copies.
For overprints see Nos. 399-404.

Design of 1923
Without Period after Value
Perf. 13½, 13½x12½

1923-24   Litho.   Wmk. 90

340	A104	½c red violet	.20	.20
341	A104	1c buff	.20	.20
342	A104	2c dk brown	.20	.20
343	A104	3c green	.20	.20
a.		Imperf., pair	8.00	
344	A104	4c red brown	.40	.20
345	A104	5c red	.20	.20
346	A104	10c dull green	.30	.20
347	A104	12c deep blue	.50	.20
348	A104	20c ultra	.65	.20
349	A104	24c lt brown	1.60	.70
350	A104	25c purple	.80	.20
351	A104	30c claret	1.60	.20
352	A104	50c black	1.60	.20
353	A105	1p blue & red	2.00	.20
354	A105	5p dk vio & grn	15.00	.75
		Punch cancel		.20
355	A105	10p claret & blue	32.50	3.25
		Punch cancel		.20
356	A105	20p slate & lake	47.50	7.50
		Punch cancel		.20
		Nos. 340-356 (17)	105.45	14.80

1931-33
Typographed

343b	A104	3c	1.40	.25
345a	A104	5c	2.50	.20
346a	A104	10c	4.00	.20
347a	A104	12c	8.50	1.50
348a	A104	20c	32.50	1.60
350a	A104	25c	20.00	.75
351a	A104	30c	15.00	.40
		Nos. 343b-351a (7)	83.90	4.90

The typographed stamps were issued only
in coils and have a rough impression with
heavy shading about the eyes and nose. Nos.
343 and 346 are known without watermark.
Nos. 341-345, 347-349, 351a may be found
in pairs, one with period.
See note after No. 338. See Nos. 362-368.
For overprints see Nos. OD21-OD33, OD75-
OD87, OD122-OD133, OD163-OD175,
OD212-OD226, OD256-OD268, OD291-
OD304, OD331-OD345.

Rivadavia — A106

1926, Feb. 8   Perf. 13½

357	A106	5c rose	.40	.20

Presidency of Bernardino Rivadavia, cent.

Rivadavia   San Martín
A108   A109

General Post   General Post
Office,   Office,
1926 — A110   1826 — A111

1926, July 1   Perf. 13½x12½

358	A108	3c gray green	.20	.20
359	A109	5c red	.20	.20

Perf. 13½

360	A110	12c deep blue	.90	.20
361	A111	25c chocolate	1.60	.20
a.		"1326" for "1826"	6.00	.75
		Nos. 358-361 (4)	2.90	.80

Centenary of the Post Office.
For overprints see #OD34, OD88, OD134,
OD227-OD228, OD269, OD305, OD346.

Type of 1923-31 Issue
Without Period after Value

1927   Wmk. 205   Perf. 13½x12½

362	A104	½c red violet	.25	.25
a.		Pelure paper	1.75	1.50
363	A104	1c buff	.25	.25
364	A104	2c dark brown	.25	.20
a.		Pelure paper	.35	.20
365	A104	5c red	.30	.20
a.		Period after value	3.50	1.90
b.		Pelure paper	.40	.20
366	A104	10c dull green	4.50	2.25
367	A104	20c ultra	18.00	2.25

Perf. 13½

368	A105	1p blue & red	35.00	7.00
		Nos. 362-368 (7)	58.55	12.40

Arms of
Argentina
and Brazil
A112

Wmk. RA in Sun (90)

1928, Aug. 27   Perf. 12½x13

369	A112	5c rose red	1.00	.25
370	A112	12c deep blue	1.50	.50

Cent. of peace between the Empire of Brazil
and the United Provinces of the Rio de la
Plata.

Allegory,   "Spain" and
Discovery of   "Argentina" — A114
the New
World — A113

"America"
Offering Laurels
to Columbus
A115

1929, Oct. 12   Litho.   Perf. 13½

371	A113	2c lilac brown	.85	.25
372	A114	5c light red	.85	.20
373	A115	12c dull blue	2.00	.75
		Nos. 371-373 (3)	3.70	1.20

Discovery of America by Columbus, 437th
anniv.

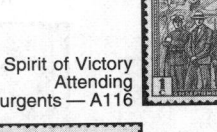

Spirit of Victory
Attending
Insurgents — A116

March of
the
Victorious
Insurgents
A117

Perf. 13½x12½ (A116), 12½x13 (A117)

1930

374	A116	½c violet gray	.20	.20
375	A116	1c myrtle green	.20	.20
376	A117	2c dull violet	.25	.20
377	A117	3c green	.30	.25

378	A116	4c violet	.25	.25
379	A116	5c rose red	.20	.20
380	A116	10c gray black	.70	.35
381	A117	12c dull blue	.50	.25
382	A117	20c ocher	.50	.25
383	A117	24c red brown	2.25	1.50
384	A117	25c green	2.50	1.50
385	A117	30c deep violet	4.50	2.00
386	A117	50c black	6.25	2.50
387	A117	1p sl bl & red	11.00	10.00
388	A117	2p black & org	22.50	10.00
389	A117	5p dull grn & blk	65.00	40.00
390	A117	10p dp red brn & dull blue	90.00	42.50
391	A117	20p yel grn & dl bl	225.00	100.00
392	A117	50p dk grn & vio	600.00	450.00
		Nos. 374-390 (17)	207.10	112.15

Revolution of 1930.
Nos. 387-392 with oval (parcel post) cancel-
lation sell for less.
For overprint see No. 405.

1931   Perf. 12½x13

393	A117	½c red violet	.20	.20
394	A117	1c gray black	1.25	.50
395	A117	3c green	.60	.30
396	A117	4c red brown	.35	.25
397	A117	5c red	.20	.20
a.		Plane omitted, top left corner	3.00	1.60
398	A117	10c dull green	1.25	.30
		Nos. 393-398 (6)	3.85	1.75

Revolution of 1930.

Stamps of 1924-25 Overprinted in Red or Green

1931, Sept. 6   Perf. 13½, 13½x12½

399	A104	3c green	.40	.40
400	A104	10c dull green	.60	.60
401	A104	30c claret (G)	4.50	2.50
402	A104	50c black	4.50	3.00

Overprinted in Blue

403	A105	1p blue & red	5.00	3.50
404	A105	5p dk violet & grn	70.00	20.00

No. 388 Overprinted in Blue

Perf. 12½x13

405	A117	2p black & orange	13.00	9.00
		Nos. 399-405 (7)	98.00	39.00

1st anniv. of the Revolution of 1930.
See Nos. C30-C34.

Refrigeration
Compressor — A118

Perf. 13½x12½

1932, Aug. 29   Litho.

406	A118	3c green	1.00	.50
407	A118	10c scarlet	2.00	.40
408	A118	12c gray blue	5.00	1.50
		Nos. 406-408 (3)	8.00	2.40

6th Intl. Refrigeration Congress.

Port of La Plata
A119

Pres. Julio A. Roca — A120

Municipal Palace
A121

Cathedral of La Plata — A122

Dardo Rocha
A123

Perf. 13½x13, 13x13½ (10c)
1933, Jan.

409	A119	3c green & dk brn	.40	.30
410	A120	10c orange & dk vio	.50	.20
411	A121	15c dk bl & dp bl	3.50	1.75
412	A122	20c violet & yel brn	1.60	1.00
413	A123	30c dk grn & vio brn	14.00	5.50
	Nos. 409-413 (5)		20.00	8.75

50th anniv. of the founding of the city of La Plata, Nov. 19th, 1882.

Christ of the Andes — A124

Buenos Aires Cathedral
A125

1934, Oct. 1   Perf. 13x13½, 13½x13

414	A124	10c rose & brown	.70	.20
415	A125	15c dark blue	1.40	.45

32nd Intl. Eucharistic Cong., Oct. 10-14.

"Liberty" with Arms of Brazil and Argentina
A126

Symbolical of "Peace" and "Friendship"
A127

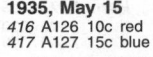

1935, May 15   Perf. 13x13½

416	A126	10c red	.85	.25
417	A127	15c blue	1.60	.50

Visit of Pres. Getulio Vargas of Brazil.

Belgrano A128

Sarmiento A129

Urquiza — A130

Louis Braille — A131

San Martin — A132

Brown — A133

Moreno A134

Alberdi A135

Nicolas Avellaneda A136

Rivadavia A137

Mitre A138

Bull (Cattle Breeding) A139

Martin Güemes A140

Agriculture A141

Merino Sheep (Wool) A142

Two types of A140:
Type I - Inscribed Juan Martin Guemes.
Type II - Inscribed Martin Güemes.

Perf. 13, 13½x13, 13x13½

1935-51		Litho.	Wmk. 90	
418	A128	½c red violet	.20	.20
419	A129	1c buff	.20	.20
a.		Typo.	.20	.20
420	A130	2c dark brown	.20	.20
421	A131	2½c black ('39)	.20	.20
422	A132	3c green	.20	.20
423	A132	3c lt gray ('39)	.20	.20
424	A134	3c lt gray ('46)	.20	.20
425	A133	4c lt gray	.20	.20
426	A133	4c sage green ('39)	.20	.20
427	A134	5c yel brn, typo.	.20	.20
a.		Tete beche pair, typo.	4.50	2.25
b.		Booklet pane of 8, typo.		
c.		Booklet pane of 4, typo.		
d.		Litho.	1.40	.20
428	A135	6c olive green	.20	.20
429	A136	8c orange ('39)	.20	.20
430	A137	10c car, typo.	.30	.20
431	A137	10c brown ('42)	.20	.20
a.		Typo.	.40	
432	A138	12c brown	.20	.20
433	A138	12c red ('39)	.20	.20
434	A139	15c slate bl ('36)	.85	.20
435	A139	15c pale ultra ('39)	.50	.20
436	A140	15c lt gray bl (II) ('42)	40.00	2.00
437	A140	20c lt ultra (I)	.60	.20

Sugar Cane A143

Oil Well (Petroleum) — A144

Map of South America A145   A146

Fruit — A147

Iguacu Falls (Scenic Wonders) A148

Grapes (Vineyards) A149

Cotton — A150

438	A140	20c lt ultra (II) ('36)	.35	.20
439	A140	20c bl gray (II) ('39)	.35	.20
439A	A139	20c dk bl & pale bl, ('42) 22x33mm	.85	.20
440	A139	20c blue ('51)	.20	.20
a.		Typo.	.20	.20
441	A141	25c car ('36)	.20	.20
442	A142	30c org brn ('36)	.50	.20
443	A143	40c dk vio ('36)	.40	.20
444	A144	50c red & org ('36)	.35	.20
445	A145	1p brn blk & lt bl ('36)	20.00	1.00
446	A146	1p brn blk & lt bl ('37)	13.00	.50
a.		Chalky paper	100.00	2.00
447	A147	2p brn lake & dk ultra ('36)	.85	.20
448	A148	5p ind & ol grn ('36)	6.00	.25
449	A149	10p brn lake & blk	35.00	2.00
450	A150	20p bl grn & brn ('36)	47.50	7.50
	Nos. 418-450 (34)		170.80	18.85

See Nos. 485-500, 523-540, 659, 668. For overprints see Nos. O37-O41, O43-O51, O53-O56, O58-O78, O108, O112, OD35-OD46, OD89-OD101, OD135-OD145, OD176-OD182C, OD229-OD234F, OD270-OD280, OD306-OD317, OD347-OD357.

No. 439A exists with attached label showing medallion. Value $42.50 unused, $22.50 used.

Souvenir Sheet

A151

Without Period after Value
1935, Oct. 17   Litho.   Imperf.

452	A151	Sheet of 4	52.50	30.00
a.		10c dull green	7.00	4.00

Phil. Exhib. at Buenos Aires, Oct. 17-24, 1935. The stamps were on sale during the 8 days of the exhibition only. Sheets measure 83x101mm.

Plaque — A152

1936, Dec. 1   Perf. 13x13½
453	A152	10c rose	.50	.25

Inter-American Conference for Peace.

Domingo Faustino Sarmiento A153

"Presidente Sarmiento" A154

1938, Sept. 5
454	A153	3c sage green	.50	.50
455	A153	5c red	.50	.50
456	A153	15c deep blue	1.00	.50
457	A153	50c orange	3.00	1.00
		Nos. 454-457 (4)	5.00	2.50

50th anniv. of the death of Domingo Faustino Sarmiento, pres., educator and author.

1939, Mar. 16
458	A154	5c greenish blue	.35	.20

Final voyage of the training ship "Presidente Sarmiento."

Allegory of the UPU — A155

Coat of Arms — A157

Post Office, Buenos Aires — A156

Iguacu Falls — A158

Bonete Hill, Nahuel Huapi Park — A159

Allegory of Modern Communications A160

Argentina, Land of Promise A161

Lake Frias, Nahuel Huapi Park — A162

Perf. 13x13½, 13½x13
1939, Apr. 1   Photo.
459	A155	5c rose carmine	.20	.20
460	A156	15c grnsh black	.40	.25
461	A157	20c brt blue	.40	.20
462	A158	25c dp blue grn	.85	.40
463	A159	50c brown	1.60	.65
464	A160	1p brown violet	1.90	.80
465	A161	2p magenta	8.75	5.25
466	A162	5p purple	35.00	16.00
		Nos. 459-466 (8)	49.10	23.75

Universal Postal Union, 11th Congress.

Souvenir Sheets

A163

A164

1939, May 12   Wmk. 90   *Imperf.*
467	A163	Sheet of 4	6.00	4.25
a.		5c rose carmine (A155)	1.25	.75
b.		20c bright blue (A157)	1.25	.75
c.		25c deep blue green (A158)	1.25	.75
d.		50c brown (A159)	1.25	.75
468	A164	Sheet of 4	6.00	4.25

Issued in four forms:
a.	Unsevered horizontal pair of sheets, type A163 at left, A164 at right	15.00	15.00
b.	Unsevered vertical pair of sheets, type A163 at top, A164 at bottom	15.00	15.00
c.	Unsevered block of 4 sheets, type A163 at left, A164 at right	52.50	52.50
d.	Unsevered block of 4 sheets, type A163 at top, A164 at bottom	52.50	52.50

11th Cong. of the UPU and the Argentina Intl. Phil. Exposition (C.Y.T.R.A.). No. 468 contains Nos. 467a-467d.

Family and New House A165

Perf. 13½x13
1939, Oct. 2   Litho.   Wmk. 90
469	A165	5c bluish green	.25	.20

1st Pan-American Housing Congress.

Bird Carrying Record A166

Head of Liberty and Arms of Argentina A167

Record and Winged Letter A168

Perf. 13x13½, 13½x13 (#472)
1939, Dec. 11   Photo.
470	A166	1.18p indigo	15.00	10.00
471	A167	1.32p bright blue	15.00	10.00
472	A168	1.50p dark brown	50.00	30.00
		Nos. 470-472 (3)	80.00	50.00

These stamps were issued for the recording and mailing of flexible phonograph records.

Map of the Americas — A169

1940, Apr. 14   *Perf. 13x13½*
473	A169	15c ultramarine	.40	.20

50th anniv. of the Pan American Union.

Souvenir Sheet

Reproductions of Early Argentine Stamps — A170

Wmk. RA in Sun (90)
1940, May 25   Litho.   *Imperf.*
474	A170	Sheet of 5	9.50	5.50
a.		5c dark blue (Corrientes A2)	1.10	.70
b.		5c red (Argentina A1)	1.10	.70
c.		5c dark blue (Cordoba #1)	1.10	.70
d.		5c red (Argentina A3)	1.10	.70
e.		10c dark blue (Buenos Aires A1)	1.10	.70

100th anniv. of the first postage stamp.

General Domingo French and Colonel Antonio Beruti A171

1941, Feb. 20   *Perf. 13½x13*
475	A171	5c dk gray blue & lt blue	.30	.20

Issued in honor of General French and Colonel Beruti, patriots.

Marco M. de Avellaneda A172

Statue of Gen. Julio Roca A173

1941, Oct. 3   *Perf. 13x13½*
476	A172	5c dull slate blue	.30	.20

Avellaneda, (1814-41), army leader and martyr.

1941, Oct. 19   Photo.   Wmk. 90
477	A173	5c dark olive green	.30	.20

Dedication of a monument to Lt. Gen. Julio Argentino Roca (1843-1914).

Carlos Pellegrini and Bank of the Nation A174

1941, Oct. 26   *Perf. 13½x13*
478	A174	5c brown carmine	.30	.20

Founding of the Bank of the Nation, 50th anniv.

Gen. Juan Lavalle — A175

1941, Dec. 5   *Perf. 13½x13*
479	A175	5c bright blue	.30	.20

Gen. Juan Galo de Lavalle (1797-1841).

National Postal Savings Bank A176

1942, Apr. 5   Litho.   *Perf. 13½x13*
480	A176	1c pale olive	.20	.20

Jose Manuel Estrada — A177

1942, July 13   *Perf. 13x13½*
481	A177	5c brown violet	.30	.20

Jose Estrada (1842-1894), writer and diplomat.

No. 481 exists with label, showing medallion, attached. Value, pair $10.

Types of 1935-51
Perf. 13, 13x13½, 13½x13
1942-50   Litho.   Wmk. 288
485	A128	½c brown violet	4.75	1.00
486	A129	1c buff ('50)	.20	.20
487	A130	2c dk brown ('50)	.20	.20
488	A132	3c lt gray	16.00	1.25
489	A134	3c lt gray ('49)	.20	.20
490	A137	10c red brn ('49)	.20	.20
491	A138	12c red	.20	.20
492	A140	15c lt gray blue (II)	.30	.20
493	A139	20c dk sl bl & pale bl	1.25	.20
494	A141	25c dull rose ('49)	.60	.20
495	A142	30c org brn ('49)	1.25	.20
496	A143	40c violet ('49)	8.00	.20
497	A144	50c red & org ('49)	8.00	.20
498	A146	1p brn blk & lt bl	6.50	.20
499	A147	2p brn lake & bl ('49)	13.00	.85
500	A148	5p ind & ol grn ('49)	50.00	4.50
		Nos. 485-500 (16)	110.65	10.00

No. 493 measures 22x33mm.

Post Office, Buenos Aires — A178

Proposed Columbus Lighthouse
A179

Inscribed: "Correos y Telegrafos."

1942, Oct. 5   Litho.   Perf. 13
503 A178 35c lt ultra   2.75 .20
    See Nos. 541-543.

1942, Oct. 12   Wmk. 288
504 A179 15c dull blue   5.00 .50

Wmk. 90
505 A179 15c dull blue   65.00 10.00
    450th anniv. of the discovery of America by Columbus.

Jose C. Paz — A180   Books and Argentine Flag — A181

1942, Dec. 15   Wmk. 288
506 A180 5c dark gray   .35 .20
    Cent. of the birth of Jose C. Paz, statesman and founder of the newspaper La Prensa.

1943, Apr. 1   Litho.   Perf. 13
507 A181 5c dull blue   .20 .20
    1st Book Fair of Argentina.

Arms of Argentina Inscribed "Honesty, Justice, Duty" — A182

1943-50   Wmk. 288   Perf. 13
Size: 20x26mm
508 A182 5c red ('50)   6.00 .20

Wmk. 90
509 A182 5c red   .25 .20
   a.   5c dull red, unsurfaced paper   3.00 .20
510 A182 15c green   .70 .20

Perf. 13x13½
Size: 22x33mm
511 A182 20c dark blue   1.10 .20
    Nos. 508-511 (4)   8.05 .80
    Change of political organization, 6/4/43.

Independence House, Tucuman A183   Liberty Head and Savings Bank A184

1943-51   Wmk. 90   Perf. 13
512 A183 5c blue green   1.00 .20

Wmk. 288
513 A183 5c blue green ('51)   .50 .20
    Restoration of Independence House.

1943, Oct. 25   Wmk. 90
514 A184 5c violet brown   .50 .20

Wmk. 288
515 A184 5c violet brown   45.00 3.00
    1st conference of National Postal Savings.

Port of Buenos Aires in 1800 — A185

1943, Dec. 11   Wmk. 90
516 A185 5c gray black   .20 .20
    Day of Exports.

Warship, Merchant Ship and Sailboat A186   Arms of Argentine Republic A187

1944, Jan. 31   Perf. 13
517 A186 5c blue   .20 .20
    Issued to commemorate Sea Week.

1944, June 4
518 A187 5c dull blue   .20 .20
    1st anniv. of the change of political organization in Argentina.

St. Gabriel A188   Cross at Palermo A189

1944, Oct. 11
519 A188 3c yellow green   .20 .20
520 A189 5c deep rose   .20 .20
    Fourth national Eucharistic Congress.

Allegory of Savings A190   Reservists A191

1944, Oct. 24
521 A190 5c gray   .20 .20
    20th anniv. of the National Savings Bank.

1944, Dec. 1
522 A191 5c blue   .20 .20
    Day of the Reservists.

Types of 1935-51
Perf. 13x13½, 13½x13
1945-47   Litho.   Unwmk.
523 A128 ½c brown vio ('46)   .20 .20
524 A129 1c yellow brown   .20 .20
525 A130 2c sepia   .20 .20
526 A132 3c lt gray (San Martin)   .40
527 A134 3c lt gray (Moreno) ('46)   .20 .20
528 A135 6c olive grn ('47)   .20 .20
529 A137 10c brown ('46)   1.25 .20
530 A140 15c lt gray bl (II)   .75
531 A139 20c dk sl bl & pale bl   1.25 .20
532 A141 25c dull rose   1.00 .20
533 A142 30c orange brown   1.00 .20
534 A143 40c violet   2.00 .20
535 A144 50c red & orange   3.00 .20
536 A146 1p brn blk & lt bl   3.00
537 A147 2p brown lake & bl   30.00 1.00
538 A148 5p ind & ol grn ('46)   50.00 4.00

539 A149 10p dp cl & int blk   10.00 2.00
540 A150 20p bl grn & brn ('46)   10.00 2.00
    Nos. 523-540 (18)   114.65 11.80
    No. 531 measures 22x33mm.

Post Office Type Inscribed: "Correos y Telecommunicaciones"

1945   Unwmk.   Perf. 13x13½
541 A178 35c lt ultra   2.50 .20

Wmk. 90
542 A178 35c lt ultra   1.25 .20

Wmk. 288
543 A178 35c lt ultra   .35 .20
    Nos. 541-543 (3)   4.10 .60

Bernardino Rivadavia
A192   A193

Mausoleum of Rivadavia A194

Perf. 13½x13
1945, Sept. 1   Litho.   Unwmk.
544 A192 3c blue green   .20 .20
545 A193 5c rose   .20 .20
546 A194 20c blue   .30 .20
    Nos. 544-546 (3)   .70 .60
    Cent. of the death of Bernardino Rivadavia, Argentina's first president.
    No. 546 exists with mute label attached. The pair sells for four times the price of the single stamp.

San Martin A195   Monument to Army of the Andes, Mendoza A196

1945-46   Wmk. 90   Typo. or Litho.
547 A195 5c carmine   .20 .20
   a.   Litho. ('46)   .20 .20

Wmk. 288
548 A195 5c carmine, litho.   125.00 20.00

Unwmk.
549 A195 5c carmine ('46)   .50 .20
   a.   Litho. ('46)   .20 .20
    For overprints see Nos. O42, O57.

1946, Jan. 14   Litho.   Perf. 13½x13
550 A196 5c violet brown   .20 .20
    Issued to honor the Unknown Soldier of the War for Independence.

A197   A198

1946, Apr. 12
551 A197 5c Franklin D. Roosevelt   .20 .20

1946, June 4   Perf. 13x13½
    Liberty Administering Presidential Oath.
552 A198 5c blue   .20 .20
    Inauguration of Pres. Juan D. Perón, 6/4/46.

Argentina Receiving Popular Acclaim A199

1946, Oct. 17   Perf. 13½x13
553 A199 5c rose violet   .20 .20
554 A199 10c blue green   .25 .20
555 A199 15c dark blue   .45 .20
556 A199 50c red brown   .70 .30
557 A199 1p carmine rose   1.40 .70
    Nos. 553-557 (5)   3.00 1.60
    First anniversary of the political organization change of Oct. 17, 1945.

Coin Bank and World Map — A200

1946, Oct. 31   Unwmk.
558 A200 30c dk rose car & pink   .60 .20
    Universal Day of Savings, October 31, 1946.

Argentine Industry — A201

International Bridge Connecting Argentina and Brazil A202

1946, Dec. 6   Perf. 13x13½
559 A201 5c violet brown   .20 .20
    Day of Argentine Industry, Dec. 6.

1947, May 21   Litho.   Perf. 13½x13
560 A202 5c green   .20 .20
    Opening of the Argentina-Brazil International Bridge, May 21, 1947.

Map of Argentine Antarctic Claims — A203   Justice — A204

1947-49   Unwmk.   Perf. 13x13½
561 A203 5c violet & lilac   .30 .20
562 A203 20c dk car rose & rose   .70 .20

Wmk. 90
563 A203 20c dk car rose & rose   2.00 .20

Wmk. 288
564 A203 20c dk car rose & rose ('49)   2.00 .20
Nos. 561-564 (4)   5.00 .80

1st Argentine Antarctic mail, 43rd anniv.

1947, June 4   **Unwmk.**
565 A204 5c brn vio & pale yel   .20 .20

1st anniversary of the Peron government.

Icarus Falling A205

1947, Sept. 25   *Perf. 13½x13*
566 A205 15c red violet   .20 .20

Aviation Week.

Training Ship Presidente Sarmiento — A206

1947, Oct. 5   *Perf. 13x13½*
567 A206 5c blue   .20 .20

50th anniv. of the launching of the Argentine training frigate "Presidente Sarmiento."

Cervantes and Characters from Don Quixote A207

Perf. 13½x13
1947, Oct. 12   **Photo.**   **Wmk. 90**
568 A207 5c olive green   .20 .20

400th anniv. of the birth of Miguel de Cervantes Saavedra, playwright and poet.

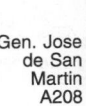

Gen. Jose de San Martin A208

Perf. 13½x13
1947-49   **Unwmk.**   **Litho.**
569 A208 5c dull green   .20 .20
Wmk. 288
570 A208 5c dull green ('49)   .20 .20

Transfer of the remains of Gen. Jose de San Martin's parents.

School Children — A209   Statue of Araucanian Indian — A210

1947-49   **Unwmk.**   *Perf. 13x13½*
571 A209 5c green   .20 .20
Wmk. 90
574 A209 20c brown   .35 .20

Wmk. 288
575 A209 5c green ('49)   .35 .20
Nos. 571-575 (3)   .90 .60

Argentine School Crusade for World Peace.

1948, May 21   **Wmk. 90**
576 A210 25c yellow brown   .30 .20

American Indian Day, Apr. 19.

Cap of Liberty — A211   Manual Stop Signal — A212

1948, July 16
577 A211 5c ultra   .20 .20

Revolution of June 4, 1943, 5th anniv.

1948, July 22
578 A212 5c chocolate & yellow   .20 .20

Traffic Safety Day, June 10.

Post Horn and Oak Leaves — A213   Argentine Farmers — A214

1948, July 22   **Unwmk.**
579 A213 5c lilac rose   .20 .20

200th anniversary of the establishment of regular postal service on the Plata River.

Perf. 13x13½
1948, Sept. 20   **Wmk. 288**
580 A214 10c red brown   .20 .20

Agriculture Day, Sept. 8, 1948.

Liberty and Symbols of Progress — A215

Perf. 13x13½
1948, Nov. 23   **Photo.**   **Wmk. 287**
581 A215 25c red brown   .20 .20

3rd anniversary of President Juan D. Peron's return to power, October 17, 1945.

Souvenir Sheets

A216

15c, Mail coach. 45c, Buenos Aires in 18th cent. 55c, 1st train, 1857. 85c, Sailing ship, 1767.

1948, Dec. 21   **Unwmk.**   *Imperf.*
582 A216   Sheet of 4   3.00 3.00
a.   15c dark green   .45 .45
b.   45c orange brown   .45 .45
c.   55c lilac brown   .45 .45
d.   85c ultramarine   .45 .45

A217

Designs: 85c, Domingo de Basavilibaso (1709-75). 1.05p, Postrider. 1.20p, Sailing ship, 1798. 1.90p, Courier in the Andes, 1772.

583 A217   Sheet of 4   14.00 11.00
a.   85c brown   3.00 2.50
b.   1.05p dark green   3.00 2.50
c.   1.20p dark blue   3.00 2.50
d.   1.90p red brown   3.00 2.50

200th anniversary of the establishment of regular postal service on the Plata River.

Winged Wheel — A218

Perf. 13½x13
1949, Mar. 1   **Wmk. 288**
584 A218 10c blue   .25 .20

Railroad nationalization, 1st anniv.

Liberty A219

1949, June 20   **Engr.**   **Wmk. 90**
585 A219 1p red & red violet   .40 .20

Ratification of the Constitution of 1949.

Allegory of the UPU A220

1949, Nov. 19
586 A220 25c dk grn & yel grn   .25 .20

75th anniv. of the UPU.

> **Catalogue values for unused stamps in this section, from this point to the end of the section, are for Never Hinged items.**

Gen. Jose de San Martin — A221

San Martin at Boulogne sur Mer — A222

Mausoleum of San Martin — A223

20c, 50c, 75c, Different portraits of San Martin. 1p, House where San Martin died.

Engr., Photo. (25c, 1p, 2p)
1950, Aug. 17   **Wmk. 90**   *Perf. 13½*
587 A221 10c indigo & dk pur   .20 .20
588 A221 20c red brn & dk brn   .20 .20
589 A222 25c brown   .20 .20
590 A221 50c dk green & ind   .40 .20
591 A221 75c choc & dk grn   .40 .20
a.   Souv. sheet of 4, #587, 588, 590, 591, imperf.   1.25 .80
592 A222 1p dark green   .85 .25
593 A223 2p dp red lilac   .75 .35
Nos. 587-593 (7)   3.00 1.60

Death cent. of General Jose de San Martin.

Map Showing Antarctic Claims — A224

1951, May 21   **Litho.**   *Perf. 13x13½*
594 A224 1p choc & lt blue   .70 .20

For overprint see No. O52.

Pegasus and Train A225

Communications Symbols — A226

Design: 25c, Ship and dolphin.

1951, Oct. 17   Photo.   Perf. 13½
595	A225	5c dark brown	.20 .20
596	A225	25c Prus green	.25 .20
597	A226	40c rose brown	.30 .20
		Nos. 595-597 (3)	.75 .60

Close of Argentine Five Year Plan.

Woman Voter
and "Argentina"
A227

1951, Dec. 14   Perf. 13½x13
598	A227	10c brown violet	.20 .20

Granting of women's suffrage.

Eva Peron
A228   A229

Litho. or Engraved (#605)

1952, Aug. 26   Wmk. 90   Perf. 13
599	A228	1c orange brown	.20 .20
600	A228	5c gray	.20 .20
601	A228	10c rose lilac	.20 .20
602	A228	20c rose pink	.20 .20
603	A228	25c dull green	.20 .20
604	A228	40c dull violet	.20 .20
605	A228	45c deep blue	.20 .20
606	A228	50c dull brown	.20 .20

Photo.
607	A229	1p dark brown	.25 .20
608	A229	1.50p deep green	1.50 .20
609	A229	2p brt carmine	.45 .20
610	A229	3p indigo	.75 .20
		Nos. 599-610 (12)	4.55 2.40

For overprints see Nos. O79-O85.

Inscribed: "Eva Peron"

1952-53   Perf. 13x13½
611	A229	1p dark brown	.30 .20
612	A229	1.50p deep green	1.10 .20
613	A229	2p brt car ('53)	1.10 .20
614	A229	3p indigo	2.75 .20

Engr.
Perf. 13½x13
Size: 30x40mm
615	A229	5p red brown	2.75 .35
616	A228	10p red	7.00 1.40
617	A229	20p green	11.00 4.00
618	A228	50p ultra	20.00 10.00
		Nos. 611-618 (8)	46.00 16.55

For overprints see Nos. O86-O93.

Indian Funeral
Urn — A230

1953, Aug. 28   Photo.   Perf. 13x13½
619	A230	50c blue green	.20 .20

Founding of Santiago del Estero, 400th anniv.

Rescue Ship "Uruguay" — A231

1953, Oct. 8   Perf. 13½
620	A231	50c ultra	.85 .20

50th anniv. of the rescue of the Antarctic expedition of Otto C. Nordenskjold.

Planting
Argentine Flag
in the Antarctic
A232

1954, Jan. 20   Engr.   Perf. 13½x13
621	A232	1.45p blue	1.25 .20

50th anniv. of Argentina's 1st antarctic p.o. and the establishing of the La Hoy radio p.o. in the South Orkneys.

Wired
Communications
A233

Television
A234

Perf. 13x13½, 13½x13

1954, Apr.   Photo.   Wmk. 90
622	A233	1.50p shown	.35 .25
623	A233	3p Radio	1.10 .30
624	A234	5p shown	1.40 .55
		Nos. 622-624 (3)	2.85 1.10

Intl. Plenipotentiary Conf. of Telecommunications, Buenos Aires, 1952.

Pediment,
Buenos Aires
Stock
Exchange
A235

1954, July 13   Perf. 13½x13
625	A235	1p dark green	.30 .20

Cent. of the establishment of the Buenos Aires Stock Exchange.

Eva
Peron — A236

1954   Wmk. 90
626	A236	3p dp car rose	2.00 .50

Wmk. 288
627	A236	3p dp car rose	225.00 40.00

2nd anniv. of the death of Eva Peron.

Jose de San
Martin — A237

Wheat — A238

Industry - A238a

Eva Peron
Foundation
Building
A239

Cliffs of Humahuaca — A240

Gen. Jose de
San
Martin — A241

Designs: 50c, Buenos Aires harbor. 1p, Cattle ranch (Ganaderia). 3p, Nihuil Dam. 5p, Iguacu Falls, vert. 20p, Mt. Fitz Roy, vert.

**Engraved (#632, 638-642),
Photogravure (#634-637)
Perf. 13½, 13x13½ (80c), 13½x13
(#639, 641-642)**

1954-59   Wmk. 90
628	A237	20c brt red, typo.	.20 .20
629	A237	20c red, litho. ('55)	1.00 .20
630	A237	40c red, litho. ('56)	.20 .20
631	A237	40c brt red, typo. ('55)	.25 .20
632	A239	50c blue ('56)	.30 .20
633	A239	50c bl, litho. ('59)	1.00 .20
634	A238	80c brown	.30 .20
635	A239	1p brown ('58)	.30 .20
636	A238a	1.50p ultra ('58)	.30 .20
637	A239	2p dk rose lake	.40 .20
638	A239	3p violet brn ('56)	.40 .20
639	A240	5p gray grn ('55)	8.00 .20
a.		Perf. 13½	10.00 .20
640	A240	10p yel grn ('55)	6.00 .80
641	A240	20p dull vio ('55)	12.00 .20
a.		Perf. 13½	15.00 .20
642	A241	50p ultra & ind ('55)	10.00 .20
a.		Perf. 13½	12.00 .20
		Nos. 628-642 (15)	40.65 3.60

See Nos. 699-700. For similar designs inscribed "Republica Argentina" see Nos. 823-827, 890, 935, 937, 940, 990, 995, 1039, 1044, 1048.

For overprints see Nos. O94-O106, O142, O153-O157.

Allegory
A242

1954, Aug. 26   Typo.   Perf. 13½
643	A242	1.50p slate black	.65 .20

Cent. of the establishment of the Buenos Aires Grain Exchange.

Clasped Hands
and Congress
Medal — A243

1955, Mar. 21   Photo.   Perf. 13½x13
644	A243	3p red brown	.80 .20

Issued to publicize the National Productivity and Social Welfare Congress.

Allegory of
Aviation — A244

Argentina
Breaking
Chains — A245

1955, June 18   Wmk. 90   Perf. 13½
645	A244	1.50p olive gray	.65 .20

Commercial aviation in Argentina, 25th anniv.

1955, Oct. 16   Litho.
647	A245	1.50p olive green	.30 .20

Liberation Revolution of Sept. 16, 1955.

Army Navy
and Air
Force
Emblems
A246

Perf. 13½x13
1955, Dec. 31   Photo.   Wmk. 90
648	A246	3p blue	.40 .20

"Brotherhood of the Armed Forces."

A247

1956, Feb. 3   Perf. 13½
649	A247	1.50p Justo Jose de Urquiza	.30 .20

Battle of Caseros, 104th anniversary.

A248

1956, July 28   Engr.   _Perf. 13½x13_
650 A248 2p Coin and die   .30 .20
75th anniversary of the Argentine Mint.

1856 Stamp of Corrientes
A249

Juan G. Pujol — A250

Design: 2.40p, Stamp of 1860-78.

1956, Aug. 21
651 A249 40c dk grn & blue   .20 .20
652 A249 2.40p brn & lil rose   .30 .20

Photo.
653 A250 4.40p brt blue   .65 .20
   _a._   Souv. sheet, #651-653, imperf.   2.25 2.00
   Nos. 651-653 (3)   1.15 .60

Centenary of Argentine postage stamps. No. 653a for the Argentine stamp cent. and Philatelic Exhib. for the Cent. of Corrientes Stamps, Oct. 12-21. The 4.40p is photo., the other two stamps and border litho. Colors of 40c and 2.40p differ slightly from engraved stamps.

Felling Trees, La Pampa
A251

Maté Herb and Gourd, Misiones — A252

1p, Cotton plant and harvest, Chaco.

1956, Sept. 1   _Perf. 13½_
654 A251 50c ultra   .20 .20
655 A251 1p magenta   .20 .20
656 A252 1.50p green   .25 .20
   Nos. 654-656 (3)   .65 .60
Elevation of the territories of La Pampa, Chaco and Misiones to provinces.

"Liberty"
A253

Florentino Ameghino
A254

Perf. 13½
1956, Sept. 15   Wmk. 90   Photo.
657 A253 2.40p lilac rose   .30 .20
1st anniv. of the Revolution of Liberation.

1956, Nov. 30
658 A254 2.40p brown   .30 .20
Issued to honor Florentino Ameghino (1854-1911), anthropologist.
For overprint see No. O110.

Adm. Brown Type of 1935-51
1956   Litho.   _Perf. 13_
Two types:
I.   Bust touches upper frame line of name panel at bottom.
II.   White line separates bust from frame line.
Size: 19½-20½x26-27mm
659 A133 20c dull purple (I)   .20 .20
   _a._   Type II   .20 .20
   _b._   Size 19½x25¼mm (I)   .20 .20
For overprint see No. O108.

Benjamin Franklin
A255

1956, Dec. 22   Photo.   _Perf. 13½_
660 A255 40c intense blue   .30 .20
250th anniv. of the birth of Benjamin Franklin.

Frigate "Hercules"
A256

Guillermo Brown
A257

1957, Mar. 2
661 A256   40c brt blue   .20 .20
662 A257 2.40p gray black   .35 .20
   Nos. 661-662,C63-C65 (5)   1.20 1.00
Admiral Guillermo (William) Brown (1777-1857), founder of the Argentine navy.

Roque Saenz Pena (1851-1914)
A258

Church of Santo Domingo, 1807
A259

1957, Apr. 1
663 A258 4.40p grnsh gray   .45 .20
Roque Saenz Pena, pres. 1910-14.

For overprint see No. O111.

"La Portena"
A260

1957, July 6   Wmk. 90
664 A259 40c brt blue green   .20 .20
150th anniv. of the defense of Buenos Aires.

1957, Aug. 31   Wmk. 90   _Perf. 13½_
665 A260 40c pale brown   .20 .20
Centenary of Argentine railroads.

Esteban Echeverria
A261

"Liberty"
A262

1957, Sept. 2   _Perf. 13x13½_
666 A261 2p claret   .25 .20
Esteban Echeverria (1805-1851), poet.
For overprint see No. O109.

1957, Sept. 28   _Perf. 13½_
667 A262 40c carmine rose   .20 .20
Constitutional reform convention.

Portrait Type of 1935-51
1957, Oct. 28   Litho.   _Perf. 13½_
Size: 16½x22mm
668 A128 5c Jose Hernandez   .20 .20
For overprint see No. O112.

Oil Derrick and Hands Holding Oil — A263

Perf. 13½
1957, Dec. 21   Wmk. 90   Photo.
669 A263 40c bright blue   .20 .20
50th anniv. of the national oil industry.

Museum, La Plata — A264

1958, Jan. 11
670 A264 40c dark gray   .20 .20
City of La Plata, 75th anniversary.

A265

A266

40c, Locomotive & arms of Argentina & Bolivia. 1p, Map of Argentine-Bolivian boundary & plane.

1958, Apr. 19   Wmk. 90   _Perf. 13½_
671 A265 40c slate & dp car   .30 .20
672 A266 1p dark brown   .30 .20
Argentine-Bolivian friendship. No. 671 for the opening of the Jacuiba-Santa Cruz railroad; No. 672, the exchange of presidential visits.

Symbols of the Republic
A267

1958, Apr. 30   Photo. & Engr.
673 A267 40c multicolored   .20 .20
674 A267 1p multicolored   .20 .20
675 A267 2p multicolored   .25 .20
   Nos. 673-675 (3)   .65 .60
Transmission of Presidential power.

Flag Monument — A268

1958, June 21   Litho.   Wmk. 90
676 A268 40c blue & violet bl   .20 .20
1st anniv. of the Flag Monument of Rosario.

Map of Antarctica — A269

1958, July 12   _Perf. 13½_
677 A269 40c car rose & blk   .50 .20
International Geophysical Year, 1957-58.

Stamp of Cordoba and Mail Coach
A270

1958, Oct. 18
678 A270 40c pale blue & slate   .20 .20
   Nos. 678,C72-C73 (3)   .65 .60
Centenary of Cordoba postage stamps.

"Slave" by Michelangelo and UN Emblem — A271

Engraved and Lithographed
1959, Mar. 14   Wmk. 90   _Perf. 13½_
679 A271 40c violet brn & gray   .20 .20
10th anniv. (in 1958) of the signing of the Universal Declaration of Human Rights.

Orchids and Globe — A272

1959, May 23   Photo.   Perf. 13½
680 A272 1p dull claret   .25 .20
1st International Horticulture Exposition.

Pope Pius XII — A273

1959, June 20   Engr.   Perf. 13½
681 A273 1p yellow & black   .20 .20
Pope Pius XII, 1876-1958.

William Harvey — A274

1959, Aug. 8   Litho.   Wmk. 90
1p, Claude Bernard. 1.50p, Ivan P. Pavlov.
682 A274 50c green   .20 .20
683 A274 1p dark red   .20 .20
684 A274 1.50p brown   .25 .20
    Nos. 682-684 (3)   .65 .60
21st Intl. Cong. of Physiological Sciences, Buenos Aires.

Type of 1958 and

Domestic Horse — A275

Jose de San Martin — A276

Tierra del Fuego A277

Inca Bridge, Mendoza — A278

Ski Jumper A279

Mar del Plata A280

Designs: 10c, Cayman. 20c, Llama. 50c, Puma. No. 690, Sunflower. 3p, Zapata Slope, Catamarca. 12p, 23p, 25p, Red Quebracho tree. 20p, Nahuel Huapi Lake. 22p, "Industry" (cogwheel and factory).
Two overall paper sizes for 1p, 5p:
  I - 27x37½mm or 37½x27mm.
  II - 27x39mm or 39x27mm.

Perf. 13x13½
1959-70   Litho.   Wmk. 90
685 A275 10c slate green   .20 .20
686 A275 20c dl red brn ('61)   .20 .20
687 A275 50c bister ('60)   .20 .20
688 A275 50c bis, typo. ('60)   .20 .20
689 A275 1p rose red   .20 .20

Perf. 13½
690 A278 1p brn, photo., I
    ('61)   .20 .20
  a.   Paper II ('69)   1.00 .20
690B A278 1p brown, I   .80 .20
691 A278 2p rose red ('61)   .25 .20
692 A276 2p red, typo. (19½ x 26mm) ('61)   .30 .20
  a.   Redrawn (19½ x 25mm)   4.75 .20
693 A277 3p dk bl, photo. ('60)   .20 .20
694 A276 4p red, typo ('62)   .20 .20
694A A276 4p red ('62)   .20 .20
695 A277 5p gray brn, photo., I   .40 .20
  e.   5p dark brown, paper II ('70)   8.00 .20
695A A276 8p ver ('65)   1.25 .20
695B A276 8p red ('65)   .30 .20
695C A276 10p ver ('66)   .65 .20
695D A276 10p red, typo. ('66)   .50 .20

Photo.
696 A278 10p lt red brn ('60)   .50 .20
697 A278 12p dk brn vio ('62)   .80 .20
697A A278 12p dk brn, litho. ('64)   8.00 .20
698 A278 20p Prus grn ('60)   2.75 .20
698A A276 20p red, typo. ('67)   .25 .20
699 A238a 22p ultra ('62)   1.50 .20
700 A238a 22p ultra, litho. ('62)   24.00 .20
701 A278 23p green ('65)   4.75 .20
702 A278 25p dp vio ('66)   1.25 .20
703 A278 25p pur, litho. ('66)   6.25 .20
704 A279 100p blue ('61)   8.00 .20
705 A280 300p dp vio ('62)   6.00 .20
    Nos. 685-705 (29)   70.50 5.80

See Nos. 882-887, 889, 892, 923-925, 928-930, 938, 987-989, 991.
For overprints and surcharges see Nos. 1076, C82-C83, O113-O118, O122-O124, O126-O141, O143-O145, O163.
The 300p remained on sale as a 3p stamp after the 1970 currency exchange.

Symbolic Sailboat — A281

1959, Oct. 3   Litho.   Perf. 13½
706 A281 1p blk, red & bl   .20 .20
Red Cross sanitary education campaign.

Child Playing with Doll — A282

1959, Oct. 17
707 A282 1p red & blk   .20 .20
Issued for Mother's Day, 1959.

Buenos Aires 1p Stamp of 1859 — A283

1959, Nov. 21   Wmk. 90   Perf. 13½
708 A283 1p gray & dk bl   .20 .20
Issued for the Day of Philately.

Bartolomé Mitre and Justo José de Urquiza — A284

1959, Dec. 12   Photo.   Perf. 13½
709 A284 1p purple   .20 .20
Treaty of San Jose de Flores, centenary.

WRY Emblem — A285

Abraham Lincoln — A286

1960, Apr. 7   Litho.   Wmk. 90
710 A285 1p bister & car   .20 .20
711 A285 4.20p apple grn & dp claret   .30 .20
World Refugee Year, July 1, 1959-June 30, 1960. See No. B25.

1960, Apr. 14   Photo.   Perf. 13½
712 A286 5p ultra   .40 .20
Sesquicentennial (in 1959) of the birth of Abraham Lincoln.

Cornelio Saavedra and Cabildo, Buenos Aires — A287

"Cabildo" and: 2p, Juan José Paso. 4.20p, Manuel Alberti and Miguel Azcuénaga. 10.70p, Juan Larrea and Domingo Matheu.

Perf. 13½
1960, May 28   Wmk. 90   Photo.
713 A287 1p rose lilac   .20 .20
714 A287 2p bluish grn   .20 .20
715 A287 4.20p gray & grn   .25 .20
716 A287 10.70p gray & ultra   .45 .20
    Nos. 713-716,C75-C76 (6)   1.65 1.20
150th anniversary of the May Revolution. Souvenir sheets are Nos. C75a and C76a.

Luis Maria Drago — A288

Juan Bautista Alberdi — A289

1960, July 8
717 A288 4.20p brown   .25 .20
Centenary of the birth of Dr. Luis Maria Drago, statesman and jurist.

1960, Sept. 10   Wmk. 90   Perf. 13½
718 A289 1p green   .20 .20
150th anniversary of the birth of Juan Bautista Alberdi, statesman and philosopher.

Map of Argentina and Antarctic Sector — A290

Caravel and Emblem A291

1960, Sept. 24   Litho.   Perf. 13½
719 A290 5p violet   .85 .25
National census of 1960.

1960, Oct. 1   Photo.
720 A291 1p dk olive grn   .20 .20
721 A291 5p brown   .45 .20
    Nos. 720-721,C78-C79 (4)   1.25 .80
8th Congress of the Postal Union of the Americas and Spain.

Virgin of Luján, Patroness of Argentina A292

Argentine Boy Scout Emblem A293

1960, Nov. 12   Wmk. 90   Perf. 13½
722 A292 1p dark blue   .20 .20
First Inter-American Marian Congress.

1961, Jan. 17   Litho.
723 A293 1p car rose & blk   .30 .20
International Patrol Encampment of the Boy Scouts, Buenos Aires.

"Shipment of Cereals," by Quinquela
Martin — A294

1961, Feb. 11   Photo.   Perf. 13½
724 A294 1p red brown   .30 .20
Export drive: "To export is to advance."

Naval Battle of San
Nicolás — A295

1961, Mar. 2   Perf. 13½
725 A295 2p gray   .30 .20
Naval battle of San Nicolas, 150th anniv.

Mariano
Moreno by
Juan de Dios
Rivera
A296

1961, Mar. 25   Perf. 13½
726 A296 2p blue   .20 .20
Mariano Moreno (1778-1811), writer, politician, member of the 1810 Junta.

Emperor Trajan   Rabindranath
Statue — A297   Tagore — A298

1961, Apr. 11
727 A297 2p slate green   .20 .20
Visit of Pres. Giovanni Gronchi of Italy to
Argentina, April 1961.

1961, May 13   Photo.   Perf. 13½
728 A298 2p purple, grysh   .20 .20
Centenary of the birth of Rabindranath
Tagore, Indian poet.

San Martin
Statue,
Madrid
A299

1961, May 24   Wmk. 90
729 A299 1p olive gray   .20 .20
Unveiling of a statue of General José de
San Martin in Madrid.

Manuel
Belgrano
A300

1961, June 17   Perf. 13½
730 A300 2p violet blue   .20 .20
Erection of a monument by Hector Rocha,
to General Manuel Belgrano in Buenos Aires.

Explorers,
Sledge and
Dog Team
A301

1961, Aug. 19   Photo.   Wmk. 90
731 A301 2p black   .70 .25
10th anniversary of the General San Martin
Base, Argentine Antarctic.

Spanish   Sarmiento Statue
Conquistador   by Rodin,
and   Buenos
Sword — A302   Aires — A303

1961, Aug. 19   Litho.
732 A302 2p red & blk   .20 .20
First city of Jujuy, 400th anniversary.

1961, Sept. 9   Photo.
733 A303 2p violet   .20 .20
Domingo Faustino Sarmiento (1811-88),
political leader and writer.

Symbol of
World Town
Planning
A304

1961, Nov. 25   Litho.   Perf. 13½
734 A304 2p ultra & yel   .20 .20
World Town Planning Day, Nov. 8.

Manuel Belgrano   Grenadier, Flag
Statue, Buenos   and Regimental
Aires — A305   Emblem — A306

1962, Feb. 24   Photo.
735 A305 2p Prus blue   .20 .20
150th anniversary of the Argentine flag.

1962, Mar. 31   Wmk. 90   Perf. 13½
736 A306 2p carmine rose   .20 .20
150th anniversary of the San Martin Grenadier Guards regiment.

Mosquito and
Malaria
Eradication
Emblem
A307

1962, Apr. 7   Litho.
737 A307 2p vermilion & blk .20 .20
WHO drive to eradicate malaria.

Church of the   Bust of Juan
Virgin of   Jufrè — A309
Luján — A308

1962, May 12   Perf. 13½
738 A308 2p org brn & blk   .20 .20
75th anniversary of the pontifical coronation
of the Virgin of Lujan.

1962, June 23   Photo.
739 A309 2p Prus blue   .20 .20
Founding of San Juan, 4th cent.

"Soaring into   Juan
Space" — A310   Vucetich — A311

1962, Aug. 18   Litho.   Perf. 13½
740 A310 2p maroon, blk & bl .20 .20
Argentine Air Force, 50th anniversary.

1962, Oct. 6   Photo.   Wmk. 90
741 A311 2p green   .20 .20
Juan Vucetich (1864-1925), inventor of the
Argentine system of fingerprinting.

Domingo F.   February 20th
Sarmiento   Monument, Salta
A312   A313

Design: 4p, Jose Hernandez.

1962-66   Photo.   Perf. 13½
742   A312 2p deep green   .65 .20
        Litho.
742A A312 2p lt green ('64) .55 .20
        Photo.
742B A312 4p dull red ('65) .45 .20
        Litho.
742C A312 4p rose red ('66) .60 .20
      Nos. 742-742C (4)   2.25 .80
      See No. 817-819. For overprints see Nos.
O119-O121, O125, O149.

1963, Feb. 23   Photo.   Wmk. 90
743 A313 2p dark green   .20 .20
150th anniversary of the Battle of Salta, War
of Independence.

Gear Wheels
A314

1963, Mar. 16   Litho.   Perf. 13½
744 A314 4p gray, blk & brt rose   .20 .20
Argentine Industrial Union, 75th anniv.

National College,   Child Draining
Buenos   Cup — A316
Aires — A315

1963, Mar. 16   Wmk. 90
745 A315 4p dull org & blk   .20 .20
National College of Buenos Aires, cent.

1963, Apr. 6
746 A316 4p multicolored   .20 .20
FAO "Freedom from Hunger" campaign.

Frigate "La
Argentina,"
1817, by
Emilio Biggeri
A317

1963, May 18   Photo.
747 A317 4p bluish green   .30 .20
Issued for Navy Day, May 17.

Seat of 1813
Assembly
and Official
Seal — A318

1963, July 13   Litho.   Perf. 13½
748 A318 4p lt blue & blk   .20 .20
150th anniversary of the 1813 Assembly.

Battle of
San
Lorenzo,
1813
A319

1963, Aug. 24
749 A319 4p grn & blk, grnsh   .20 .20
Sesquicentennial of the Battle of San
Lorenzo.

Queen
Nefertari
Offering
Papyrus
Flowers, Abu
Simbel
A320

1963, Sept. 14   Perf. 13½
750 A320 4p ocher, blk & bl grn   .30 .20
Campaign to save the historic monuments
in Nubia.

Government House, Buenos
Aires — A321

1963, Oct. 12   Wmk. 90   *Perf. 13½*
751 A321 5p rose & brown   .20 .20
Inauguration of President Arturo Illia.

"Science"
A322

Francisco de las
Carreras,
Supreme Court
Justice
A323

1963, Oct. 16   Litho.
752 A322 4p org brn, bl & blk   .20 .20
10th Latin-American Neurosurgery Congress.

1963, Nov. 23   Photo.   *Perf. 13½*
753 A323 5p bluish green   .20 .20
Centenary of judicial power.

Blackboards
A324

1963, Nov. 23   Litho.
754 A324 5p red, blk & bl   .20 .20
Issued to publicize "Teachers for America"
through the Alliance for Progress program.

Kemal Atatürk
A325

"Payador" by
Juan Carlos
Castagnino
A326

1963, Dec. 28   Photo.   *Perf. 13½*
755 A325 12p dark gray   .30 .20
25th anniversary of the death of Kemal Atatürk, president of Turkey.

1964, Jan. 25   Litho.
756 A326 4p ultra, blk & lt bl   .30 .20
Fourth National Folklore Festival.

Maps of South Georgia, South Orkney
and South Sandwich Islands
A327

4p, Map of Argentina & Antarctic claims,
vert.

1964, Feb. 22   Wmk. 90   *Perf. 13½*
Size: 33x22mm
757 A327 2p lt & dk bl & bister   1.25 .25
Size: 30x40mm
758 A327 4p lt & dk bl & ol grn   1.75 .30
    Nos. 757-758,C92 (3)   4.75 1.25
Argentina's claim to Antarctic territories,
60th anniv.

Jorge
Newbery in
Cockpit
A328

1964, Feb. 23   Photo.
759 A328 4p deep green   .20 .20
Newbery, aviator, 50th death anniv.

John F.
Kennedy
A329

1964, Apr. 14   Engr.   Wmk. 90
760 A329 4p claret & dk bl   .35 .20
President John F. Kennedy (1917-63).

José Brochero by
José
Cuello — A330

1964, May 9   Photo.   *Perf. 13½*
761 A330 4p light sepia   .20 .20
50th anniversary of the death of Father Jose
Gabriel Brochero.

Soldier of
Patricios
Regiment
A331

1964, May 29   Litho.   Wmk. 90
762 A331 4p blk, ultra & red   .40 .20
    Issued for Army Day. Later Army Day
stamps, inscribed "Republica Argentina," are
of type A340a.

Pope John
XXIII — A332

1964, June 27   Engr.
763 A332 4p orange & blk   .25 .20
Issued in memory of Pope John XXIII.

University of
Cordoba
Arms — A333

Pigeons and UN
Building,
NYC — A334

1964, Aug. 22   Litho.   Wmk. 90
764 A333 4p blk, ultra & yel   .20 .20
350th anniv. of the University of Cordoba.

1964, Oct. 24   *Perf. 13½*
765 A334 4p dk blue & lt blue   .20 .20
Issued for United Nations Day.

Joaquin V.
Gonzalez
A335

Julio Argentino
Roca
A336

1964, Nov. 14   Photo.
766 A335 4p dk rose carmine   .20 .20
    Centenary (in 1963) of the birth of Joaquin
V. Gonzalez, writer.

1964, Dec. 12   *Perf. 13½*
767 A336 4p violet blue   .20 .20
    General Julio A. Roca, (1843-1914), presi-
dent of Argentina, (1880-86, 1898-1904).

Market at
Montserrat
Square, by
Carlos
Morel — A337

1964, Dec. 19   Photo.
768 A337 4p sepia   .30 .20
19th century Argentine painter Carlos Morel.

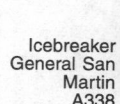

Icebreaker
General San
Martin
A338

2p, General Belgrano Base, Antarctica.

1965   *Perf. 13½*
769 A338 2p dull purple   .40 .20
770 A338 4p ultra   .50 .20
    Issued to publicize the natl. territory of
Tierra del Fuego, Antarctic and South Atlantic
Isles.
    Issue dates: 4p, Feb. 27; 2p, June 5.

Girl with Piggy
Bank — A339

1965, Apr. 3   Litho.
771 A339 4p red org & blk   .20 .20
National Postal Savings Bank, 50th anniv.

Sun and
Globe
A340

1965, May 29
772 A340 4p blk, org & dl bl   .25 .20
    Nos. 772,C98-C99 (3)   1.65 .90
International Quiet Sun Year, 1964-65.

Hussar of
Pueyrredon
Regiment
A340a

1965, June 5   Wmk. 90   *Perf. 13½*
773 A340a 8p dp ultra, blk & red   .50 .20
    Issued for Army Day. See Nos. 796, 838,
857, 893, 944, 958, 974, 1145.

Ricardo Rojas
(1882-1957)
A341

1965, June 26   Photo.
    Portraits: No. 775, Ricardo Guiraldes (1886-
1927). No. 776, Enrique Larreta (1873-1961).
No. 777, Leopoldo Lugones (1874-1938). No.
778, Roberto J. Payro (1867-1928).

774 A341 8p brown   .35 .20
775 A341 8p brown   .35 .20
776 A341 8p brown   .35 .20
777 A341 8p brown   .35 .20
778 A341 8p brown   .35 .20
    Nos. 774-778 (5)   1.75 1.00
    Issued to honor Argentine writers. Printed
se-tenant in sheets of 100 (10x10); 2 horizontal rows of each design with Guiraldes in top
rows and Rojas in bottom rows.

Hipolito
Yrigoyen
A342

1965, July 3   Litho.
779 A342 8p pink & black   .20 .20
    Hipolito Yrigoyen (1852-1933), president of
Argentina 1916-22, 1928-30.

Children Looking Through Window
A343

1965, July 24   **Photo.**
780 A343 8p salmon & blk   .25 .20
International Seminar on Mental Health.

Child's Funerary Urn and 16th Century Map
A344

1965, Aug. 7   **Litho.**
781 A344 8p lt grn, dk red, brn & ocher   .30 .20
City of San Miguel de Tucuman, 400th anniv.

Cardinal Cagliero — A345   Dante Alighieri — A346

1965, Aug. 21   **Photo.**
782 A345 8p violet   .20 .20
Juan Cardinal Cagliero (1839-1926), missionary to Argentina and Bishop of Magida.

1965, Sept. 16   **Wmk. 90**   **Perf. 13½**
783 A346 8p light ultra   .30 .20
Dante Alighieri (1265-1321), Italian poet.

Clipper "Mimosa" and Map of Patagonia
A347

1965, Sept. 25   **Litho.**
784 A347 8p red & black   .30 .20
Centenary of Welsh colonization of Chubut, and the founding of the city of Rawson.

Map of Buenos Aires, Cock and Compass Emblem of Federal Police
A348

1965, Oct. 30   **Photo.**   **Perf. 13½**
785 A348 8p carmine rose   .30 .20
Issued for Federal Police Day.

Child's Drawing of Children
A349

1965, Nov. 6   **Litho.**   **Wmk. 90**
786 A349 8p lt yel grn & blk   .30 .20
Public education law, 81st anniversary.

Church of St. Francis, Catamarca
A350

Ruben Dario
A351

1965, Dec. 8
787 A350 8p org yel & red brn   .20 .20
Brother Mamerto de la Asuncion Esquiu, preacher, teacher and official of 1885 Provincial Constitutional Convention.

Litho. and Photo.
1965, Dec. 22   **Perf. 13½**
788 A351 15p bl vio, *gray*   .20 .20
Ruben Dario (pen name of Felix Ruben Garcia Sarmiento, 1867-1916), Nicaraguan poet, newspaper correspondent and diplomat.

"The Orange Seller"
A352

Pueyrredon Paintings: No. 790, "Stop at the Grocery Store." No. 791, "Landscape at San Fernando" (sailboats). No. 792, "Bathing Horses at River Plata."

1966, Jan. 29   **Photo.**   **Perf. 13½**
789 A352 8p bluish green   .70 .40
790 A352 8p bluish green   .70 .40
791 A352 8p bluish green   .70 .40
792 A352 8p bluish green   .70 .40
   a.   Block of 4, #789-792 + 2 labels   2.80 1.60
Prilidiano Pueyrredon (1823-1870), painter.

Sun Yat-sen, Flags of Argentina and China — A353

1966, Mar. 12   **Wmk. 90**   **Perf. 13½**
793 A353 8p dk red brown   .70 .25
Dr. Sun Yat-sen (1866-1925), founder of the Republic of China.

Souvenir Sheet

Rivadavia Issue of 1864 — A354

Wmk. 90
1966, Apr. 20   **Litho.**   **Imperf.**
794 A354   Sheet of 3   .95 .95
   a.   4p gray & red brown   .20 .20
   b.   5p gray & green   .20 .20
   c.   8p gray & dark blue   .20 .20
2nd Rio de la Plata Stamp Show, Buenos Aires, Mar. 16-24.

People of Various Races and WHO Emblem
A355

1966, Apr. 23   **Perf. 13½**
795 A355 8p brown & black   .30 .20
Opening of the WHO Headquarters, Geneva.

Soldier Type of 1965

Army Day: 8p, Cavalryman, Guemes Infernal Regiment.

1966, May 28   **Litho.**
796 A340a 8p multicolored   .55 .30

Coat of Arms — A356

Arms: a, National. b, Buenos Aires. c, La Rioja. d, Catamarca. e, Cordoba. f, Corrientes. g, Chaco. h, Chubut. i, Entre Rios. j, Formosa. k, Jujuy. l, La Pampa. m, Federal Capital. n, Mendoza. o, Misiones. p, Neuquen. q, Salta. r, San Juan. s, San Luis. t, Santa Cruz. u, Santa Fe. v, Santiago del Estero. w, Tucuman. x, map of Rio Negro. y, Map of Tierra del Fuego, Antarctica, South Atlantic Islands.

1966, July 30   **Wmk. 90**   **Perf. 13½**
797   Sheet of 25   40.00
  a.-y.   A356 10p black & multi   1.00 .65
150th anniv. of Argentina's Declaration of Independence.

Three Crosses, Caritas Emblem
A357

1966, Sept. 10   **Litho.**   **Perf. 13½**
798 A357 10p ol grn, blk & lt bl   .25 .20
Caritas, charity organization.

Hilario Ascasubi (1807-75) — A358

Portraits: #800, Estanislao del Campo (1834-80). #801, Miguel Cane (1851-1905). #802, Lucio V. Lopez (1848-94). #803, Rafael Obligado (1851-1920). #804, Luis Agote (1868-1954), M.D. #805, Juan B. Ambrosetti (1865-1917), naturalist and archaeologist. #806, Miguel Lillo (1862-1931), botanist and chemist. #807, Francisco P. Moreno (1852-1919), naturalist and paleontologist. #808, Francisco J. Muñiz (1795-1871), physician.

1966		Photo.	Wmk. 90	
799	A358	10p dk blue green	.40	.35
800	A358	10p dk blue green	.40	.35
801	A358	10p dk blue green	.40	.35
802	A358	10p dk blue green	.40	.35
803	A358	10p dk blue green	.40	.35
804	A358	10p deep violet	.40	.35
805	A358	10p deep violet	.40	.35
806	A358	10p deep violet	.40	.35
807	A358	10p deep violet	.40	.35
808	A358	10p deep violet	.40	.35
		Nos. 799-808 (10)	4.00	3.50

Nos. 799-803 issued Sept. 17 to honor Argentine writers. Printed se-tenant in sheets of 100 (10x10); 2 horizontal rows of each portrait. Nos. 804-808 issued Oct. 22 to honor

Argentine scientists; 2 horizontal rows of each portrait. Scientists set has value at upper left, frame line with rounded corners.

Anchor
A359

1966, Oct. 8   **Litho.**
809 A359 4p multicolored   .25 .20
Argentine merchant marine.

Flags and Map of the Americas
A360

1966, Oct. 29   **Perf. 13½**
810 A360 10p gray & multi   .25 .20
7th Conference of American Armies.

Argentine National Bank — A361

1966, Nov. 5   **Photo.**
811 A361 10p brt blue green   .20 .20
75th anniv. of the Argentine National Bank.

La Salle Monument and College, Buenos Aires — A362

1966, Nov. 26   **Litho.**   **Perf. 13½**
812 A362 10p brown org & blk   .20 .20
75th anniv. of the Colegio de la Salle, Buenos Aires, and to honor Saint Jean Baptiste de la Salle (1651-1719), educator.

Map of Argentine Antarctica and Expedition Route — A363

1966, Dec. 10   **Wmk. 90**
813 A363 10p multicolored   .70 .45
1965 Argentine Antarctic expedition, which planted the Argentine flag on the South Pole. See No. 851.

Juan Martin de
Pueyrredon — A364

1966, Dec. 17   Photo.   Perf. 13½
814 A364 10p dull red brn   .20 .20
Issued to honor Juan Martin de Pueyrredon
(1777-1850), Governor of Cordoba and of the
United Provinces of the River Plate.

Gen. Juan de
Las
Heras — A365

1966, Dec. 17   Engr.
815 A365 10p black   .20 .20
Issued to honor Gen. Juan Gregorio de Las
Heras (1780-1866), Peruvian field marshal
and aide-de-camp to San Martin.

Inscribed "Republica Argentina"
Types of 1955-61 and

Guillermo
Brown — A366

Designs: 6p, Jose Hernandez. 50p, Gen.
Jose de San Martin. 500p, Red deer in forest.

Two overall paper sizes for 6p, 50p (No.
827) and 90p:
I - 27x37½mm
II - 27x39mm

Perf. 13½
1965-68   Wmk. 90   Photo.
817 A366 6p rose red, litho, I
             ('67)   1.25 .20
818 A366 6p rose red ('67)   2.25 .20
819 A366 6p brn, 15x22mm
             ('68)   .20 .20
823 A238a 43p dk car rose   6.25 .20
824 A238a 45p brn ('66)   4.25 .20
825 A238a 45p brn, litho ('67) 7.00 .20
826 A241 50p dk bl, 29x40mm   7.00 .20
827 A241 50p dk bl,
             22x31½mm, I
             ('67)   4.75 .20
  a.   Paper II   2.75 .20
828 A366 90p ol bis, I ('67) 3.00 .20
  a.   Paper II   12.00 .20

Trout Leaping
in National
Park — A366a

Engr.
829 A495   500p yellow grn
              ('66)   1.50   .50
829A A366a 1,000p vio bl ('68) 6.00 2.00
  Nos. 817-829A (11)   43.45 4.30
The 500p and 1,000p remained on sale as
5p and 10p stamps after the 1970 currency
exchange.
See Nos. 888, 891, 939, 941, 992, 1031,
1040, 1045-1047. For surcharge and overprints see Nos. 1077, O153-O158, O162.

Pre-Columbian
Pottery — A367

1967, Feb. 18   Litho.   Perf. 13½
830 A367 10p multicolored   .30 .20
20th anniv. of UNESCO.

"The Meal" by Fernando
Fader — A368

1967, Feb. 25   Photo.   Wmk. 90
831 A368 10p red brown   .30 .20
Issued in memory of the Argentine painter
Fernando Fader (1882-1935).

Col. Juana Azurduy
de Padilla (1781-
1862),
Soldier — A369

Famous Argentine Women: #833, Juana
Manuela Gorriti, writer. #834, Cecilia Grierson
(1858-1934), physician. #835, Juana Paula
Manso (1819-75), writer and educator. #836,
Alfonsina Storni (1892-1938), writer and
educator.

1967, May 13   Photo.   Perf. 13½
832 A369 6p dark brown   .30 .20
833 A369 6p dark brown   .30 .20
834 A369 6p dark brown   .30 .20
835 A369 6p dark brown   .30 .20
836 A369 6p dark brown   .30 .20
  Nos. 832-836 (5)   1.50 1.00
Printed se-tenant in sheets of 100 (10x10);
2 horizontal rows of each portrait.

Schooner
"Invincible,"
1811 — A370

1967, May 20   Litho.
837 A370 20p multicolored   .85 .35
Issued for Navy Day.

Soldier Type of 1965

Army Day: 20p, Highlander (Arribeños
Corps).

1967, May 27
838 A340a 20p multicolored   .70 .30

Souvenir Sheet

Manuel Belgrano and José
Artigas — A371

1967, June 22   Imperf.
839 A371   Sheet of 2   .40 .40
  a.   6p gray & brown   .20 .20
  b.   22p brown & gray   .25 .25
Third Rio de la Plata Stamp Show, Montevideo, Uruguay, June 18-25.

Peace Dove and   PADELAI
Valise — A372   Emblem — A373

1967, Aug. 5   Litho.   Perf. 13½
840 A372 20p multicolored   .25 .20
Issued for International Tourist Year 1967.

1967, Aug. 12   Litho.
841 A373 20p multicolored   .25 .20
75th anniv. of the Children's Welfare Association (Patronato de la Infancia-PADELAI).

Stagecoach
and Modern
City — A374

1967, Sept. 23 Wmk. 90 Perf. 13½
842 A374 20p rose, yel & blk   .25 .20
Centenary of Villa Maria, Cordoba.

San Martin by
Ibarra — A375

"Battle of Chacabuco" by P.
Subercaseaux — A376

1967, Sept. 30   Litho.
843 A375 20p blk brn & pale yel   .55 .20
Engr.
844 A376 40p blue black   .85 .20
Battle of Chacabuco, 150th anniversary.

Exhibition
Rooms — A377

1967, Oct. 11   Photo.
845 A377 20p blue gray   .20 .20
Government House Museum, 10th anniv.

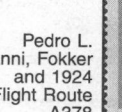

Pedro L.
Zanni, Fokker
and 1924
Flight Route
A378

1967, Oct. 21   Litho.   Perf. 13½
846 A378 20p multicolored   .30 .20
Issued for Aviation Week and to commemo-
rate the 1924 flight of the Fokker seaplane
"Province of Buenos Aires" from Amsterdam,
Netherlands, to Osaka, Japan.

Training
Ship
General
Brown,
by Emilio
Biggeri
A379

1967, Oct. 28   Wmk. 90
847 A379 20p multicolored   .85 .35
Issued to honor the Military Naval School.

Ovidio Lagos and
Front Page — A380

1967, Nov. 11   Photo.
848 A380 20p sepia   .20 .20
Centenary of La Capital, Rosario newspaper.

St. Barbara
A381

1967, Dec. 2   Perf. 13½
849 A381 20p rose red   .30 .20
St. Barbara, patron saint of artillerymen.

Portrait of his Wife, by Eduardo Sivori — A382

1968, Jan. 27 Photo. Perf. 13½
850 A382 20p blue green   .30 .20
Eduardo Sivori (1847-1918), painter.

Antarctic Type of 1966 and

Admiral Brown Scientific Station A383

Planes over Map of Antarctica — A384

6p, Map showing radio-postal stations 1966-67.

1968, Feb. 17 Litho. Wmk. 90
851 A363 6p multicolored   .40 .20
852 A383 20p multicolored   .60 .25
853 A384 40p multicolored   1.00 .30
  Nos. 851-853 (3)   2.00 .75
Issued to publicize Argentine research projects in Argentine Antarctica.

The Annunciation, by Leonardo da Vinci — A385   Man in Wheelchair and Factory — A386

1968, Mar. 23 Photo. Perf. 13½
854 A385 20p lilac rose   .20 .20
Issued for the Day of the Army Communications System and its patron saint, Gabriel.

1968, Mar. 23 Litho.
855 A386 20p green & black   .20 .20
Day of Rehabilitation of the Handicapped.

Children and WHO Emblem — A387

1968, May 11 Wmk. 90 Perf. 13½
856 A387 20p dk vio bl & ver   .20 .20
20th anniv. of WHO.

Soldier Type of 1965

Army Day: 20p, Uniform of First Artillery Regiment "General Iriarte."

1968, June 8 Litho.
857 A340a 20p multicolored   .75 .25

Frigate "Libertad," Painting by Emilio Biggeri — A388

1968, June 15 Wmk. 90
858 A388 20p multicolored   .75 .25
Issued for Navy Day.

Guillermo Rawson and Old Hospital A389

1968, July 20 Photo. Perf. 13½
859 A389 6p olive bister   .20 .20
Cent. of Rawson Hospital, Buenos Aires.

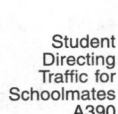

Student Directing Traffic for Schoolmates A390

1968, Aug. 10 Litho. Perf. 13½
860 A390 20p lt bl, blk, buff & car .20 .20
Traffic safety and education.

O'Higgins Joining San Martin at Battle of Maipu, by P. Subercaseaux — A391

1968, Aug. 15 Engr.
861 A391 40p bluish black   .65 .30
Sesquicentennial of the Battle of Maipu.

Osvaldo Magnasco (1864-1920), Lawyer, Professor of Law and Minister of Justice — A392

1968, Sept. 7 Photo. Perf. 13½
862 A392 20p brown   .25 .20

Grandmother's Birthday, by Patricia Lynch — A393

The Sea, by Edgardo Gomez — A394

1968, Sept. 21 Litho.
863 A393 20p multicolored   .25 .20
864 A394 20p multicolored   .25 .20
The designs were chosen in a competition among kindergarten and elementary school children.

Mar del Plata at Night A395

1968, Oct. 19 Litho. Perf. 13½
865 A395 20p black, ocher & bl   .25 .20
  Nos. 865,C113-C114 (3)   1.30 .70
4th Plenary Assembly of the Intl. Telegraph and Telephone Consultative Committee, Mar del Plata, Sept. 23-Oct. 25.

Frontier Gendarme A396   Patrol Boat A397

1968, Oct. 26
866 A396 20p multicolored   .30 .20
867 A397 20p blue, vio bl & blk .30 .20
No. 866 honors the Gendarmery; No. 867 the Coast Guard.

Aaron de Anchorena and Pampero Balloon A398

1968, Nov. 2 Photo.
868 A398 20p blue & multi   .30 .20
22nd Aeronautics and Space Week.

St. Martin of Tours, by Alfredo Guido — A399

1968, Nov. 9 Litho.
869 A399 20p lilac & dk brn   .20 .20
St. Martin of Tours, patron saint of Buenos Aires.

Municipal Bank Emblem A400

1968, Nov. 16
870 A400 20p multicolored   .20 .20
Buenos Aires Municipal Bank, 90th anniv.

Anniversary Emblem A401

1968, Dec. 14 Wmk. 90 Perf. 13½
871 A401 20p car rose & dk grn   .20 .20
ALPI (Fight Against Polio Assoc.), 25th anniv.

Shovel and State Coal Fields Emblem — A402   Pouring Ladle and Army Manufacturing Emblem — A403

1968, Dec. 21 Litho.
872 A402 20p orange, bl & blk   .25 .20
873 A403 20p dl vio, dl yel & blk .25 .20
Issued to publicize the National Coal and Steel industry at the Rio Turbio coal fields and the Zapla blast furnaces.

Woman Potter, by Ramon Gomez Cornet — A404

1968, Dec. 21 Photo. Perf. 13½
874 A404 20p carmine rose   .50 .40
Centenary of the Witcomb Gallery.

View of Buenos Aires and Rio de la Plata by Ulrico Schmidl A405

1969, Feb. 8 Litho. Wmk. 90
875 A405 20p yellow, blk & ver   .50 .35
Ulrico Schmidl (c. 1462-1554) who wrote "Journey to the Rio de la Plata and Paraguay."

Types of 1955-67

Designs: 50c, Puma. 1p, Sunflower. 3p, Zapata Slope, Catamarca. 5p, Tierra del Fuego. 6p, José Hernandez. 10p, Inca Bridge, Mendoza. 50p, José de San Martin. 90p, Guillermo Brown. 100p, Ski jumper.

Photo.; Litho. (50c, 3p, 10p)
1969-70 Wmk. 365 Perf. 13½
882 A275 50c bister ('70)   .70 .20
883 A277 5p brown   1.25 .20
884 A279 100p blue   26.00 1.40

Unwmk.

885	A278	1p brown ('70)	.65	.20
886	A277	3p dk blue ('70)	.65	.20
a.		Wmk. 90	5.25	.35
887	A277	5p brown ('70)	.75	.20
888	A366	6p red brn, 15x22mm ('70)	1.25	.20
889	A278	10p dull red ('70)	.50	.20
a.		Wmk. 90	475.00	47.50
890	A241	50p dk bl, 22x31½mm ('70)	1.75	.20
891	A366	90p ol brn, 22x32mm ('70)	3.50	.20
892	A279	100p blue ('70)	9.00	.30
		Nos. 882-892 (11)	46.00	3.50

For surcharges see Nos. 1076-1077.

Soldier Type of 1965

Army Day: 20p, Sapper (gastador) of Buenos Aires Province, 1856.

Wmk. 365

1969, May 31   Litho.   Perf. 13½
893	A340a	20p multicolored	.85	.35

Frigate Hercules, by Emilio Biggeri — A406

1969, May 31
894	A406	20p multicolored	1.00	.30

Issued for Navy Day.

"All Men are Equal" — A407   ILO Emblem — A408

1969, June 28   Wmk. 90
895	A407	20p black & ocher	.20	.20

International Human Rights Year.

1969, June 28   Litho.   Wmk. 365
896	A408	20p lt green & multi	.20	.20

50th anniv. of the ILO.

Pedro N. Arata (1849-1922), Chemist — A409   Radar Antenna, Balcarce Station and Satellite — A410

Portraits: No. 898, Miguel Fernandez (1883-1950), zoologist. No. 899, Angel P. Gallardo (1867-1934), biologist. No. 900, Cristobal M. Hicken (1875-1933), botanist. No. 901, Eduardo Ladislao Holmberg, M.D. (1852-1937), natural scientist.

1969, Aug. 9   Wmk. 365   Perf. 13½
897	A409	6p Arata	.40	.20
898	A409	6p Fernandez	.40	.20
899	A409	6p Gallardo	.40	.20

900	A409	6p Hicken	.40	.20
901	A409	6p Holmberg	.40	.20
		Nos. 897-901 (5)	2.00	1.00

Argentine scientists. See No. 778 note.

1969, Aug. 23   Wmk. 99
902	A410	20p yellow & blk	.30	.20

Communications by satellite through Intl. Telecommunications Satellite Consortium (INTELSAT). See No. C115.

Nieuport 28, Flight Route and Map of Buenos Aires Province A411

1969, Sept. 13   Litho.   Wmk. 90
903	A411	20p multicolored	.30	.20

50th anniv. of the first Argentine airmail service from El Palomar to Mar del Plata, flown Feb. 23-24, 1919, by Capt. Pedro L. Zanni.

Military College Gate and Emblem A412

1969, Oct. 4   Wmk. 365   Perf. 13½
904	A412	20p multicolored	.30	.20

Cent. of the National Military College, El Palomar (Greater Buenos Aires).

Gen. Angel Pacheco — A413

1969, Nov. 8   Photo.   Wmk. 365
905	A413	20p deep green	.25	.20

Gen. Angel Pacheco (1795-1869).

La Farola, Logotype of La Prensa — A414

1969, Nov. 8   Litho.   Perf. 13½

#907, Bartolomé Mitre & La Nacion logotype.
906	A414	20p orange, yel & blk	.70	.25
907	A414	20p brt green & blk	.70	.25

Cent. of newspapers La Prensa and La Nacion.

Julian Aguirre — A415

Musicians: No. 909, Felipe Boero. No. 910, Constantino Gaito. No. 911, Carlos Lopez Buchardo. No. 912, Alberto Williams.

Wmk. 365

1969, Dec. 6   Photo.   Perf. 13½
908	A415	6p Aguirre	.55	.30
909	A415	6p Boero	.55	.30
910	A415	6p Gaito	.55	.30
911	A415	6p Buchardo	.55	.30
912	A415	6p Williams	.55	.30
		Nos. 908-912 (5)	2.75	1.50

Argentine musicians. See No. 778 note.

Lt. Benjamin Matienzo and Nieuport Plane — A416

1969, Dec. 13   Litho.
913	A416	20p multicolored	.55	.35

23rd Aeronautics and Space Week.

High Power Lines and Map A417

Design: 20p, Map of Santa Fe Province and schematic view of tunnel.

1969, Dec. 13
914	A417	6p multicolored	.50	.20
915	A417	20p multicolored	1.00	.20

Completion of development projects: 6p for the hydroelectric dams on the Limay and Neuquen Rivers, the 20p the tunnel under Rio Grande from Sante Fe to Parana.

Lions Emblem A418

1969, Dec. 20   Wmk. 365   Perf. 13½
916	A418	20p black, emer & org	.60	.25

Argentine Lions Intl. Club, 50th anniv.

Madonna and Child, by Raul Soldi — A419

1969, Dec. 27   Litho.
917	A419	20p multicolored	.70	.30

Christmas 1969.

Manuel Belgrano, by Jean Gericault A420

The Creation of the Flag, Bas-relief by Jose Fioravanti — A421

Perf. 13½

1970, July 4   Unwmk.   Photo.
918	A420	20c deep brown	.35	.20

Litho.   Perf. 12½
919	A421	50c bister, blk & bl	.85	.50

Gen. Manuel Belgrano (1770-1820), Argentine patriot.

San Jose Palace A422

1970, Aug. 9   Litho.   Perf. 13½
920	A422	20c yellow grn & multi	.25	.20

Gen. Justo Jose de Urquiza (1801-70), pres. of Argentina, 1854-60.

Schooner "Juliet" — A423

1970, Aug. 8   Unwmk.
921	A423	20c multicolored	1.00	.40

Issued for Navy Day.

Receiver of 1920 and Waves A424

1970, Aug. 29
922	A424	20c lt blue & multi	.30	.20

50th anniv. of Argentine broadcasting.

Types of 1955-67 Inscribed "Republica Argentina" and Types A425, A426

Belgrano A425   Lujan Basilica A426

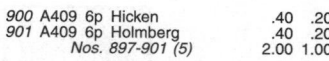

Designs: 1c, Sunflower. 3c, Zapata Slope, Catamarca. 5c, Tierra del Fuego. 8c, No. 931, Belgrano. 10c, Inca Bridge, Mendoza. 25c, 50c, 70c, Jose de San Martin. 65c, 90c, 1.20p, San Martin. 1p, Ski jumper. 1.15p, 1.80p, Adm. Brown.

1970-73   Photo.   Unwmk.   Perf. 13½

923	A278	1c dk green ('71)	.20	.20
924	A277	3c car rose ('71)	.20	.20
925	A277	5c blue ('71)	.20	.20
926	A425	6c deep blue	.20	.20
927	A425	8c green ('72)	.20	.20
928	A278	10c dull red ('71)	.40	.20
929	A278	10c brn, litho. ('71)	.50	.20
930	A278	10c org brn ('72)	.45	.20
931	A425	10c brown ('73)	.20	.20
932	A426	18c yel & dk brn, litho ('73)	.20	.20
933	A425	25c brown ('71)	.30	.20
934	A425	50c scarlet ('72)	1.25	.20
935	A241	65c brn, 22x31½mm, paper II ('71)	.65	.20
936	A425	70c dk blue ('73)	.30	.20
937	A241	90c emer, 22x31½mm ('72)	3.25	.20
938	A279	1p brn, 22½x29½mm ('71)	1.90	.20
939	A366	1.15p dk bl, 22½x32mm ('71)	1.10	.20
940	A241	1.20p org, 22x31½mm ('73)	1.10	.20
941	A366	1.80p brown ('73)	1.10	.20
		Nos. 923-941 (19)	13.70	3.80

The imprint "Casa de Moneda de la Nacion" (in capitals) appears on 3c, 5c, Nos. 928-929; 65c, 90c, 1p, 1.20p.

On type A425 only the 6c is inscribed "Ley 18.188" below denomination.

Fluorescent paper was used in printing the 25c, 50c, and 70c. The 3c, 5c, 8c, No. 931 and 65c were issued on both ordinary and fluorescent paper.

See Nos. 987-996, 1032-1038, 1042-1043, 1089-1107. For overprint and surcharge see Nos. 1010, 1078.

Soldier Type of 1965
Galloping messenger of Field Army, 1879.

1970, Oct. 17   Litho.   Perf. 13½
944 A340a 20c multicolored   .80 .25

Dome of Cathedral of Cordoba A430

1970, Nov. 7   Unwmk.
945 A430 50c gray & blk   .80 .20
Bishopric of Tucuman, 400th anniv. See #C131.

People Around UN Emblem A431

1970, Nov. 7
946 A431 20c tan & multi   .20 .20
25th anniversary of the United Nations.

State Mint and Medal A432

1970, Nov. 28   Unwmk.   Perf. 13½
947 A432 20c gold, grn & blk   .20 .20
Inauguration of the State Mint Building, 25th anniversary.

St. John Bosco and Dean Funes College A433

1970, Dec. 19   Litho.
948 A433 20c olive & blk   .20 .20
Honoring the work of the Salesian Order in Patagonia.

Nativity, by Horacio Gramajo Gutierrez — A434

1970, Dec. 19
949 A434 20c multicolored   .55 .35
Christmas 1970.

Argentine Flag, Map of Argentine Antarctica A435

1971, Feb. 20   Litho.   Perf. 13½
950 A435 20c multicolored   1.25 .50
Argentine South Pole Expedition, 5th anniv.

Phosphorescent Sorting Code and Albert Einstein — A436

1971, Apr. 30   Unwmk.   Perf. 13½
951 A436 25c multicolored   .50 .30
Electronics in postal development.

Symbolic Road Crossing A437

1971, May 29   Litho.
952 A437 25c blue & blk   .25 .20
Inter-American Regional Meeting of the Intl. Federation of Roads, Buenos Aires, 3/28-31.

Elias Alippi — A438

Actors: No. 954, Juan Aurelio Casacuberta. No. 955, Angelina Pagano. No. 956, Roberto Casaux. No. 957, Florencio Parravicini. See No. 778 note.

1971, May 29   Litho.
953	A438	15c Alippi	.35	.20
954	A438	15c Casacuberta	.35	.20
955	A438	15c Pagano	.35	.20
956	A438	15c Casaux	.35	.20
957	A438	15c Parravicini	.35	.20
		Nos. 953-957 (5)	1.75	1.00

Soldier Type of 1965
Army Day, May 29: Artilleryman, 1826.

1971, July 3   Unwmk.   Perf. 13½
958 A340a 25c multicolored   1.25 .50

Bilander "Carmen," by Emilio Biggeri — A439

1971, July 3
959 A439 25c multicolored   1.25 .25
Navy Day

Peruvian Order of the Sun A440

1971, Aug. 28
960 A440 31c multicolored   .30 .20
Sesquicentennial of Peru's independence.

Güemes in Battle, by Lorenzo Gigli A441

#962, Death of Güemes, by Antonio Alice.

1971, Aug. 28
Size: 39x29mm
961 A441 25c multicolored   .50 .30
Size: 84x29mm
962 A441 25c multicolored   .50 .30
Sesquicentennial of the death of Martin Miguel de Güemes, leader in Gaucho War, Governor and Captain General of Salta Province.

Stylized Tulip — A442

1971, Sept. 18
963 A442 25c tan & multi   .25 .20
3rd Intl. and 8th Natl. Horticultural Exhib.

Father Antonio Saenz, by Juan Gut — A443

1971, Sept. 18
964 A433 25c gray & multi   .25 .20
Sesquicentennial of University of Buenos Aires, and to honor Father Antonio Saenz, first Chancellor and Rector.

Fabricaciones Militares Emblem — A444

1971, Oct. 16   Unwmk.   Perf. 13½
965 A444 25c brn, gold, bl & blk   .25 .20
30th anniv. of military armament works.

Cars and Trucks A445

Design: 65c, Tree converted into paper.

1971, Oct. 16
966 A445 25c dull bl & multi   .50 .20
967 A445 65c green & multi   1.25 .50
Nos. 966-967,C134 (3)   2.35 .95
Nationalized industries.

Luis C. Candelaria and his Plane, 1918 — A446

1971, Nov. 27
968 A446 25c multicolored　.25 .20
25th Aeronautics and Space Week.

Observatory and Nebula of Magellan — A447

1971, Nov. 27
969 A447 25c multicolored　.25 .20
Cordoba Astronomical Observatory, cent.

Christ in Majesty A448

1971, Dec. 18　　**Litho.**
970 A448 25c blk & multi　.25 .20
Christmas 1971. Design is from a tapestry by Horacio Butler in Basilica of St. Francis, Buenos Aires.

Mother and Child, by J. C. Castagnino A449

1972, May 6　Unwmk.　Perf. 13½
971 A449 25c fawn & black　.25 .20
25th anniv. (in 1971) of UNICEF.

Mailman's Bag — A450

1972, Sept. 2　Litho.　Perf. 13½
972 A450 25c lemon & multi　.20 .20
Bicentenary of appointment of first Argentine mailman.

Adm. Brown Station, Map of Antarctica — A451

1972, Sept. 2
973 A451 25c blue & multi　.70 .35
10th anniv. (in 1971) of Antarctic Treaty.

Soldier Type of 1965

Army Day:　25c, Sergeant, Negro and Mulatto Corps, 1806-1807.

1972, Sept. 23
974 A340a 25c multicolored　.75 .35

Brigantine "Santisima Trinidad" — A452

1972, Sept. 23
975 A452 25c multicolored　.75 .35
Navy Day. See No. 1006.

A453

1972, Sept. 30　Litho.　Perf. 13½
976 A453 45c Oil pump　.90 .20
50th anniv. of the organ. of the state oil fields (Yacimientos Petroliferos Fiscales).

A454

1972, Sept. 30
977 A454 25c Sounding balloon　.25 .20
Cent. of Natl. Meteorological Service.

Trees and Globe — A455

1972, Oct. 14　　Perf. 13x13½
978 A455 25c bl, blk & lt bl　.70 .20
7th World Forestry Congress, Buenos Aires, Oct. 4-18.

Arms of Naval School, Frigate "Presidente Sarmiento" — A456

1972, Oct. 14
979 A456 25c gold & multi　.65 .35
Centenary of Military Naval School.

Early Balloon and Plane, Antonio de Marchi — A457

1972, Nov. 4　　Perf. 13½
980 A457 25c multicolored　.50 .30
Aeronautics and Space Week, and in honor of Baron Antonio de Marchi (1875-1934), aviation pioneer.

Bartolomé Mitre — A458

1972, Nov. 4　　Engr.
981 A458 25c dark blue　.50 .30
Pres. Bartolome Mitre (1821-1906), writer, historian, soldier.

Flower and Heart — A459

1972, Dec. 2　Litho.　Perf. 13½
982 A459 90c lt bl, ultra & blk　.60 .35
"Your heart is your health," World Health Day.

"Martin Fierro," by Juan C. Castignano A460

"Spirit of the Gaucho," by Vicente Forte — A461

1972, Dec. 2　Litho.　Perf. 13½
983 A460 50c multicolored　.30 .20
984 A461 90c multicolored　.65 .35
Intl. Book Year 1972, and cent. of publication of the poem, Martin Fierro, by Jose Hernandez (1834-86).

Iguacu Falls and Tourist Year Emblem — A462

1972, Dec. 16　　Perf. 13x13½
985 A462 45c multicolored　.30 .20
Tourism Year of the Americas.

King, Wood Carving, 18th Century A463

1972, Dec. 16　　Perf. 13½
986 A463 50c multicolored　.50 .25
Christmas 1972.

Types of 1955-73 Inscribed "Republica Argentina" and

Moon Valley, San Juan Province A463a

Designs: 1c, Sunflower. 5c, Tierra del Fuego. 10c, Inca Bridge, Mendoza. 50c, Lujan Basilica. 65c, 22.50p, San Martin. 1p, Ski jumper. 1.15p, 4.50p, Guillermo Brown. 1.80p, Manuel Belgrano.

Litho.; Photo. (1c, 65c, 1p)
Perf. 13½, 12½ (1.80p)

1972-75				Wmk. 365	
987	A278	1c dk green		.20	.20
988	A277	5c dark blue		.20	.20
989	A278	10c bister brn		.20	.20
989A	A426	50c dull pur ('75)		.20	.20
990	A241	65c gray brown		3.25	.20
991	A279	1p brown		1.40	.20
992	A366	1.15p dk gray bl		1.40	.20
993	A425	1.80p blue ('75)		.20	.20
994	A366	4.50p green ('75)		.65	.20
995	A241	22.50p vio bl ('75)		1.40	.20
996	A463a	50p multi ('75)		2.75	.30
		Nos. 987-996 (11)		11.85	2.30

Paper size of 1c is 27½x39mm; others of 1972, 37x27, 27x37mm.
Size of 22.50p, 50p: 26½x38½mm.
See Nos. 1050, 1108.

Cock (Symbolic of Police) — A464

1973, Feb. 3   Litho.   Unwmk.
997 A464 50c lt green & multi   .30 .20
Sesqui. of Federal Police of Argentina.

First Coin of Bank of Buenos Aires — A465

1973, Feb. 3   Perf. 13½
998 A465 50c purple, yel & brn   .20 .20
Sesquicentennial of the Bank of Buenos Aires Province.

DC-3 Planes Over Antarctica — A466

1973, Apr. 28   Litho.   Perf. 13½
999 A466 50c lt blue & multi   1.50 .60
10th anniversary of Argentina's first flight to the South Pole.

Rivadavia's Chair, Argentine Arms and Colors — A467

1973, May 19   Litho.   Perf. 13½
1000 A467 50c multicolored   .25 .20
Inauguration of Pres. Hector J. Campora, May 25, 1973.

San Martin, by Gil de Castro — A468

San Martin and Bolivar A469

1973, July 7   Litho.   Perf. 13½
1001 A468 50c lt green & multi   .35 .20
1002 A469 50c yellow & multi   .35 .20
Gen. San Martin's farewell to the people of Peru and his meeting with Simon Bolivar at Guayaquil July 26-27, 1822.

Eva Peron A470

1973, July 26   Litho.   Perf. 13½
1003 A470 70c black, org & bl   .20 .20
Maria Eva Duarte de Peron (1919-1952), political leader.

House of Viceroy Sobremonte, by Hortensia de Virgilion — A471

1973, July 28   Perf. 13x13½
1004 A471 50c blue & multi   .20 .20
400th anniversary of the city of Cordoba.

Woman, by Lino Spilimbergo A472

1973, Aug. 28   Litho.   Perf. 13½
1005 A472 70c multicolored   .70 .20
Philatelists' Day. See Nos. B60-B61.

Ship Type of 1972
Navy Day: 70c, Frigate "La Argentina."

1973, Oct. 27   Litho.   Perf. 13½
1006 A452 70c multicolored   .60 .35

New and Old Telephones — A473

1973, Oct. 27
1007 A473 70c brt blue & multi   .40 .20
Natl. telecommunications system, 25th anniv.

Plume Made of Flags of Participants A474

1973, Nov. 3   Perf. 13½
1008 A474 70c yellow bis & multi   .25 .20
12th Cong. of Latin Notaries, Buenos Aires.

No. 940 Overprinted

1973, Nov. 30   Photo.
1010 A241 1.20p orange   .85 .20
Assumption of presidency by Juan Peron, Oct. 12.

Virgin and Child, Window, La Plata Cathedral A476

Christmas: 1.20p, Nativity, by Bruno Venier, b. 1914.

1973, Dec. 15   Litho.   Perf. 13½
1011 A476 70c gray & multi   .35 .20
1012 A476 1.20p black & multi   .70 .35

The Lama, by Juan Batlle Planas — A477

Paintings: 50c, Houses in Boca District, by Eugenio Daneri, horiz. 90c, The Blue Grotto, by Emilio Pettoruti, horiz.

1974, Feb. 9   Litho.   Perf. 13½
1013 A477 50c multicolored   .30 .20
1014 A477 70c multicolored   .35 .20
1015 A477 90c multicolored   .60 .30
 Nos. 1013-1015,B64 (4)   1.55 .95
Argentine painters.

Mar del Plata A478

1974, Feb. 9
1016 A478 70c multicolored   .30 .20
Centenary of Mar del Plata.

Weather Symbols — A479

1974, Mar. 23   Litho.   Perf. 13½
1017 A479 1.20p multicolored   .35 .20
Cent. of intl. meteorological cooperation.

Justo Santa Maria de Oro — A480

1974, Mar. 23
1018 A480 70c multicolored   .20 .20
Bicentenary of the birth of Brother Justo Santa Maria de Oro (1772-1836), theologian, patriot, first Argentine bishop.

Belisario Roldan (1873-1922), Writer — A481

1974, June 29   Photo.   Unwmk.
1019 A481 70c bl & brn   .20 .20

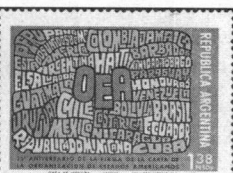

Poster with Names of OAS Members — A482

1974, June 29   Litho.
1020 A482 1.38p multicolored   .20 .20
Organization of American States, 25th anniv.

ENCOTEL Emblem — A483

1974, Aug. 10   Litho.   Perf. 13
1021 A483 1.20p blue, gold & blk   .40 .20
ENCOTEL, Natl. Post and Telegraph Press.

Flags of Argentina, Bolivia, Brazil, Paraguay, Uruguay A484

1974, Aug. 16   Perf. 13½
1022 A484 1.38p multicolored   .25 .20
6th Meeting of Foreign Ministers of Rio de la Plata Basin Countries.

El Chocon Hydroelectric Complex, Limay River — A485

Somisa Steel Mill, San Nicolas A486

Gen. Belgrano Bridge, Chaco-Corrientes — A487

Perf. 13½, 13x13½ (4.50p)
1974, Sept. 14
1023 A485 70c multicolored .40 .20
1024 A486 1.20p multicolored .60 .30
1025 A487 4.50p multicolored 2.00 .50
Nos. 1023-1025 (3) 3.00 1.00
Development projects.

Brigantine Belgrano, by Emilio Biggeri — A488

1974, Oct. 26 Litho. Perf. 13½
1026 A488 1.20p multicolored .60 .30
Departure into exile in Chile of General San Martin, Sept. 22, 1822.

Alberto R. Mascias and Bleriot Plane — A489

1974, Oct. 26 Unwmk.
1027 A489 1.20p multicolored .50 .25
a. Wmk 365
Air Force Day, Aug. 10, and to honor Alberto Roque Garcias (1878-1951), aviation pioneer.

Hussar, 1812, by Eleodoro Marenco A490

1974, Oct. 26
1028 A490 1.20p multicolored .50 .25
Army Day.

Post Horn and Flags A491

1974, Nov. 23 Unwmk. Perf. 13½
1029 A491 2.65p multicolored .85 .20
a. Wmk 365
Centenary of Universal Postal Union.

Franciscan Monastery — A492

1974, Nov. 23 Litho.
1030 A492 1.20p multicolored .40 .20
400th anniversary, city of Santa Fe.

Trout Type of 1968
1974 Engr. Unwmk.
1031 A366a 1000p vio bl 3.25 .80
Due to a shortage of 10p stamps a quantity of this 1,000p was released for use as 10p.

Types of 1954-73 Inscribed "Republica Argentina" and

Red Deer in Forest — A495

Congress Building — A497

Designs: 30c, 60c, 1.80p, Manuel Belgrano. 50c, Lujan Basilica. 1.20p, 2p, 6p, San Martin (16x22½mm). 2.70p, 7.50p, 22.50p, San Martin (22x31½mm). 4.50p, 13.50p, Guillermo Brown. 10p, Leaping trout.

1974-76 Unwmk. Photo. Perf. 13½
1032 A425 30c brown vio .20 .20
1033 A426 50c blk & brn red .20 .20
1034 A426 50c bister & bl .20 .20
1035 A425 60c ocher .20 .20
1036 A425 1.20p red .30 .20
1037 A425 1.80p deep blue .20 .20
1038 A425 2p dark purple .20 .20

1039 A241 2.70p dk bl, 22x31½mm .25 .20
1040 A366 4.50p green .85 .20
1041 A495 5p yel green .40 .20
1042 A425 6p red orange .20 .20
1043 A425 6p emerald .20 .20
1044 A241 7.50p grn, 22x31½mm .85 .20
1045 A366a 10p violet blue 1.00 .20
1046 A366 13.50p scar, 16x22½mm .85 .20
1047 A366 13.50p scar, 22x31½mm .85 .20
1048 A241 22.50p dp bl, 22x31½mm .75 .20
1049 A497 30p yel & dk red brn 1.10 .20
1050 A463a 50p multicolored 1.50 .20
Nos. 1032-1050 (19) 10.30 3.80

Issued: 10p, 5/74; 30c, 1.20p, 2.70p, 5/15/74; 5p, 11/20/74; 30p, 12/10/74; 2p, 3/1/75; 60c, 7.50p, 4/30/75; 4.50p, 7/21/75; 1.80p, #1042, 1047, 22.50p, 8/14/75; #1046, 10/10/75; #1034, 10/30/75; #1043, 11/6/75; 50p, 2/76.
Fluorescent paper was used in printing No. 1036, 2p, Nos. 1044 and 1047. The 30p was issued on both ordinary and fluorescent paper.
See No. 829. For type of A495 overprinted see No. 1144.

Miniature Sheet

A498

1974, Dec. 7 Litho. Perf. 13½
1052 A498 Sheet of 6 3.50 2.75
a. 1p Mariano Necochea .25 .20
b. 1.20p Jose de San Martin .25 .20
c. 1.70p Manuel Isidoro Suarez .35 .25
d. 1.90p Juan Pascual Pringles .40 .30
e. 2.70p Latin American flags .65 .35
f. 4.50p Jose Felix Bogado 1.10 .50
Sesqui. of Battles of Junin and Ayacucho.

Dove, by Vito Campanella — A499

St. Anne, by Raul Soldi — A500

1974, Dec. 21 Litho. Perf. 13½
1053 A499 1.20p multicolored .50 .20
1054 A500 2.65p multicolored .75 .30
Christmas 1974.

Boy Looking at Stamp — A501

1974, Dec. 21
1055 A501 1.70p black & yel .40 .20
World Youth Philately Year.

Space Monsters, by Raquel Forner — A502

Argentine modern art: 4.50p, Dream, by Emilio Centurion.

1975, Feb. 22 Litho. Perf. 13½
1056 A502 2.70p multi .90 .25
1057 A502 4.50p multi 1.75 .40

Indian Woman and Cathedral, Catamarca — A503

Tourist Publicity: #1059, Carved chancel and street scene. #1060, Grazing cattle and monastery yard. #1061, Painted pottery and power station. #1062, Farm cart and colonial mansion. #1063, Perito Moreno glacier and spinning mill. #1064, Lake Lapataia and scientific surveyor. #1065, Los Alerces National Park and oil derrick.

1975 Litho. Unwmk. Perf. 13½
1058 A503 1.20p shown .25 .20
1059 A503 1.20p Jujuy .25 .20
1060 A503 1.20p Salta .25 .20
1061 A503 1.20p Santiago del Estero .25 .20
1062 A503 1.20p Tucuman .25 .20
1063 A503 6p Santa Cruz .50 .20
1064 A503 6p Tierra del Fuego .50 .20
1065 A503 6p Chubut .50 .20
Nos. 1058-1065 (8) 2.75 1.60
Issue dates: 1.20p, Mar. 8; 6p, Dec. 20.

"We Have Been Inoculated" A504

1975, Apr. 26 Unwmk. Perf. 13½
1066 A504 2p multi .45 .25
Children's inoculation campaign (child's painting).

Hugo A. Acuña and South Orkney Station — A505

Designs: No. 1068, Francisco P. Moreno and Lake Nahuel Huapi. No. 1069, Lt. Col. Luis Piedra Buena and cutter, Luisito. No. 1070, Ensign José M. Sobral and Snow Hill House. No. 1071, Capt. Carlos M. Moyano and Cerro del Toro (mountain).

1975, June 28   **Litho.**   *Perf. 13*
1067	A505	2p grnsh bl & multi	.25	.20
1068	A505	2p yel grn & multi	.25	.20
1069	A505	2p lt vio & multi	.25	.20
1070	A505	2p gray bl & multi	.25	.20
1071	A505	2p pale grn & multi	.25	.20
		Nos. 1067-1071 (5)	1.25	1.00

Pioneers of Antarctica.

Frigate "25 de Mayo" A506

1975, Sept. 27   **Unwmk.**   *Perf. 13½*
1072 A506 6p multi   .40 .25

Navy Day 1975.

Eduardo Bradley and Balloon A507

1975, Sept. 27   **Wmk. 365**
1073 A507 6p multi   .40 .25

Air Force Day.

Declaration of Independence, by Juan M. Blanes — A508

1975, Oct. 25
1074 A508 6p multi   .30 .20

Sesquicentennial of Uruguay's declaration of independence.

Flame A509

1975, Oct. 17   **Unwmk.**
1075 A509 6p gray & multi   .30 .20

Loyalty Day, 30th anniversary of Pres. Peron's accession to power.

Nos. 886, 891 and 932 Surcharged

1975   **Lithographed, Photogravure**
1076	A277	6c on 3p	.20	.20
1077	A366	30c on 90p	.20	.20
1078	A426	5p on 18c	.35	.20
		Nos. 1076-1078 (3)	.75	.60

Issued: 6c, 10/30; 30c, 11/20; 5p, 10/24. The 6c also exists on No. 886a.

International Bridge, Flags of Argentina & Uruguay — A510

1975, Oct. 25   **Litho.**   **Wmk. 365**
1081 A510 6p multi   .35 .20

Opening of bridge connecting Colon, Argentina, and Paysandu, Uruguay.

Post Horn, Surcharged A511

1975, Nov. 8
1082 A511 10p on 20c multi   .45 .20

Introduction of postal code. Not issued without surcharge.

Nurse Holding Infant A512

1975, Dec. 13   **Litho.**   *Perf. 13½*
1083 A512 6p multi   .45 .20

Children's Hospital, centenary.

Nativity, Nueva Pompeya Church — A513

1975, Dec. 13   **Litho.**   **Unwmk.**
1084 A513 6p multicolored   .30 .20

Christmas 1975.

Types of 1970-75 and

Church of St. Francis, Salta — A515

Designs: 3p, No. 1099, 60p, 90p, Manuel Belgrano. 12p, 15p, 20p, 30p, No. 1100, 100p, 110p, 120p, 130p, San Martin. 15p, 70p, Guillermo Brown. 300p, Moon Valley (lower inscriptions italic). 500p, Adm. Brown Station, Antarctica.

1976-78   **Photo.**   **Unwmk.**   *Perf. 13½*
1089	A425	3p slate	.20	.20
1090	A425	12p rose red	.25	.20

             Perf. 12½x13
         Litho.   **Wmk. 365**
1091	A425	12p rose red	.20	.20
1092	A425	12p emerald	.20	.20

             Perf. 13½
         Photo.   **Unwmk.**
1093	A425	12p emer ('77)	.20	.20
1094	A425	15p rose red	.20	.20
1095	A425	15p vio bl ('77)	.20	.20
1097	A425	20p rose red ('77)	.35	.20
1098	A425	30p rose red ('77)	.35	.20
1099	A425	40p dp grn	.50	.20
1100	A425	40p rose red ('77)	.35	.20
1101	A425	60p dk bl ('77)	.70	.20
1102	A425	70p dk bl ('77)	1.00	.20
1103	A425	90p emer ('77)	1.00	.20
1104	A425	100p red	.75	.25
1105	A425	110p rose red ('78)	.50	.20
1106	A425	120p rose red ('78)	.60	.20
1107	A425	130p rose red ('78)	.70	.25

               Litho.
1108	A463a	300p multi	3.50	1.50
a.		Wmk 365		
1109	A515	500p multi ('77)	8.25	1.40
a.		Wmk 365		
1110	A515	1000p multi ('77)	10.00	2.00
		Nos. 1089-1110 (21)	30.00	8.70

Fluorescent paper was used in printing both 12p rose red, 15p rose red, 20p, 30p, 40p rose red, 100p, 110p, 120p, 130p.

No. 1099 and the 300p were issued on both ordinary and fluorescent paper.

See Nos. B73-B74.

A516

1976   **Photo.**   **Unwmk.**   *Perf. 13½*
1112	A516	12c gray & blk	.20	.20
1113	A516	50c gray & grn	.20	.20
1114	A516	1p red & blk	.20	.20
1115	A516	4p bl & blk	.20	.20
1116	A516	5p org & blk	.20	.20
1117	A516	6p dp brn & blk	.20	.20
1118	A516	10p gray & vio bl	.25	.20
1119	A516	27p lt grn & blk	.50	.20
1120	A516	30p lt bl & blk	.90	.20
1121	A516	45p yel & blk	.90	.20
1122	A516	50p dl grn & blk	1.25	.20
1123	A516	100p brt grn & red	1.60	.20

            Perf. 13x12½
1976   **Litho.**   **Wmk. 365**
1124	A516	5p org & blk	.20	.20
1125	A516	27p lt grn & blk	.50	.20
1126	A516	45p yel & blk	1.25	.20
		Nos. 1112-1126 (15)	8.55	3.00

The 1p, 6p, 10p, 50p and No. 1116 were issued on both ordinary and fluorescent paper.

Jet and Airlines Emblem — A517

            Perf. 13x13½
1976, Apr. 24   **Litho.**   **Unwmk.**
1130 A517 30p bl, lt bl & dk bl   1.00 .20

Argentine Airlines, 25th anniversary.

Frigate Heroina & Map of Falkland Islands — A518

1976, Apr. 26
1131 A518 6p multi   1.00 .40

Argentina's claim to Falkland Islands.

Louis Braille — A519

            Wmk. 365
1976, May 22   **Engr.**   *Perf. 13½*
1132 A519 19.70 deep blue   .30 .20

Sesquicentennial of the invention of the Braille system of writing for the blind by Louis Braille (1809-1852).

Private, 7th Infantry Regiment A520

1976, May 29   **Litho.**   **Unwmk.**
1133 A520 12p multi   .40 .20

Army Day.

Schooner Rio de la Plata, by Emilio Biggeri — A521

1976, June 19
1134 A521 12p multi   .40 .20

Navy Day.

Dr. Bernardo Houssay — A522

Argentine Nobel Prize Winners: 10p, Bernardo Houssay, medicine and physiology, 1947. 15p, Luis F. Leloir, chemistry, 1970. 20p, Carlos Saavedra Lamas, peace, 1936.

1976, Aug. 14   Litho.   Perf. 13½
1135 A522 10p org & blk   .25 .20
1136 A522 15p yel & blk   .30 .20
1137 A522 20p ocher & blk   .45 .25
　　Nos. 1135-1137 (3)   1.00 .65

Rio de la Plata International
Bridge — A523

1976, Sept. 18   Litho.   Perf. 13½
1138 A523 12p multi   .30 .20
　　Inauguration of International Bridge connecting Puerte Unzue, Argentina, and Fray Bentos, Uruguay.

Pipelines & Cooling Tower, Gen. Mosconi Plant A524

1976, Nov. 20   Litho.   Perf. 13½
1139 A524 28p multi   .40 .20

Pablo Teodoro Fels & Bleriot
Monoplane, 1910 — A525

1976, Nov. 20
1140 A525 15p multi   .30 .20
　　Air Force Day.

Nativity
A526

1976, Dec. 18   Litho.   Perf. 13½
1141 A526 20p multi   .65 .30
　　Christmas. Painting by Edith Chiapetto.

Water Conference
Emblem — A527

1977, Mar. 19   Litho.   Perf. 13½
1142 A527 70p multi   .70 .25
　　UN Water Conf., Mar del Plata, Mar. 14-25.

Dalmacio Velez Sarsfield — A528

1977, Mar. 19   Engr.
1143 A528 50p blk & red brn .70 .30
　　Dalmacio Velez Sarsfield (1800-1875), author of Argentine civil code.

Red Deer Type
of 1974
Surcharged

1977, July 30   Photo.   Perf. 13½
1144 A495 100p on 5p brn   1.40 .35
　　Sesquicentennial of Uruguayan postal service. Not issued without surcharge.

Soldier, 16th
Lancers
A529

1977, July 30
1145 A529 30p multi   .40 .20
　　Army Day.

Schooner Sarandi, by Emilio
Biggeri — A530

1977, July 30
1146 A530 30p multi   .40 .25
　　Navy Day.

Soccer Games'
Emblem
A531

　　70p, Argentina '78 emblem, flags & soccer field.

1977, May 14
1147 A531 30p multi   .40 .20
1148 A531 70p multi   .85 .40
　　11th World Cup Soccer Championship, Argentina, June 1-25, 1978.

The Visit, by
Horacio Butler
A532

Consecration,
by Miguel P.
Caride — A533

1977, Mar. 26   Litho.
1149 A532 50p multi   .50 .25
1150 A533 70p multi   .65 .40
　　Argentine artists.

Sierra de la Ventana — A534

　　Views: #1152, Civic Center, Santa Rosa. #1153, Skiers, San Martin de los Andes. #1154, Boat on Lake Fonck, Rio Negro.

1977, Oct. 8   Litho.   Perf. 13x13½
1151 A534 30p multi   .30 .20
1152 A534 30p multi   .30 .20
1153 A534 30p multi   .30 .20
1154 A534 30p multi   .30 .20
　　Nos. 1151-1154 (4)   1.20 .80

Guillermo
Brown, by R.
del
Villar — A535

1977, Oct. 8   Perf. 13½
1155 A535 30p multi   .40 .25
　　Adm. Guillermo Brown (1777-1857), leader in fight for independence, bicentenary of birth.

Jet
A536

Double-decker, 1926 — A537

1977   Litho.   Perf. 13½
1156 A536 30p multi   .25 .20
1157 A537 40p multi   .30 .20
　　50th anniversary of military plane production (30p); Air Force Day (40p).
　　Issue dates: 30p, Dec. 3; 40p, Nov. 26.

Adoration of
the
Kings — A538

1977, Dec. 17
1158 A538 100p multi   1.00 .30
　　Christmas 1977.

Historic City Hall,
Buenos
Aires — A539

Chapel of
Rio Grande
Museum,
Tierra del
Fuego
A540

　　5p, 20p, La Plata Museum. 10p, Independence Hall, Tucuman. 40p, City Hall, Salta. #1165, City Hall, Buenos Aires. 100p, Columbus Theater, Buenos Aires. 100p, Rosario. 200p, flag Monument, Rosario. 280p, 300p, Chapel of Rio Grande Museum, Tierra del Fuego. 480p, 520p, 800, Ruins of Jesuit Mission Church of San Ignacio, Misiones. 500p, Candonga Chapel, Cordoba. 1000p, G.P.O., Buenos Aires. 2000p, Civic Center, Bariloche, Rio Negro.

　　Three types of 10p: I. Nine vertical window bars; small imprint "E. MILIAVACA Dib." II. Nine bars; large imprint "E. MILIAVACA DIB." III. Redrawn; 5 bars; large imprint.

1977-81 Photo. Unwmk.   Perf. 13½
　　Size: 32x21mm, 21x32mm
1159 A540 5p gray & blk   .20 .20
1160 A540 10p lt ultra &
　　　　　blk, I   .20 .20
　a.   Type II   .20 .20
1161 A540 10p lt bl & blk,
　　　　　III   .20 .20
1162 A540 20p citron &
　　　　　blk, litho.   .20 .20
1163 A540 40p gray bl &
　　　　　blk   .25 .20
1164 A539 50p yel & blk   .30 .20
1165 A540 50p citron & blk   .20 .20
1166 A540 100p org & blk,
　　　　　litho.   .35 .20
　a.   Wmk. 365   92.50 24.00
1167 A540 100p red org &
　　　　　blk   .20 .20
1168 A540 100p turq & blk   .20 .20
1169 A539 200p lt bl & blk   .50 .25
1170 A540 280p rose & blk   14.00 .20
1171 A540 300p lemon &
　　　　　blk   .95 .20
1172 A540 480p org & blk   1.75 .25
1173 A540 500p yel grn &
　　　　　blk   1.75 .20
1174 A540 520p org & blk   1.75 .30
1175 A540 800p rose lil &
　　　　　blk   2.25 .30
1176 A540 1000p lem bis &
　　　　　blk   2.50 .40
1177 A540 1000p gold & blk,
　　　　　40x29mm   3.75 .40
1178 A540 2000p multi   2.25 .40
　　Nos. 1159-1178 (20)   33.75 4.90

　　#1161, 1163, 1165, 1167, 1169, 1171, 1173, 1176, 1177 were issued on both ordinary and fluorescent paper. No. 1174 was issued only on fluorescent paper. All others were issued only on ordinary paper.
　　Issued: #1164, 5/30/77; 280p, 12/15/77; #1160, 3/14/78; 480p, 5/22/78; 5p, 7/25/78; 20p, 500p, 9/8/78; #1166, 9/20/78; #1177, 9/28/78; 520p, 9/30/78; 300p, 10/5/78; 40p, 12/1/78; #1161/79; #1165, 1/8/79; 800p, 3/20/79; #1167, 4/25/79; 200p, 6/23/79; #1176, 12/15/79; 2000p, 6/25/80; #1168, 5/26/81.
　　For overprints see Nos. 1253, 1315.

Soccer Games' Emblem A544

1978, Feb. 10   Photo.   Perf. 13½
1179 A544 200p yel grn & bl   .85 .30
  a.   Wmk 365   100.00
11th World Cup Soccer Championship, Argentina, June 1-25.

View of El Rio, Rosario — A545

Designs (Argentina '78 Emblem and): 100p, Rio Tercero Dam, Cordoba. 150p, Cordillera Mountains, Mendoza. 200p, City Center, Mar del Plata. 300p, View of Buenos Aires.

1978, May 6   Litho.   Perf. 13
1180 A545 50p multi   .20 .20
1181 A545 100p multi   .30 .20
1182 A545 150p multi   .50 .20
1183 A545 200p multi   .50 .25
1184 A545 300p multi   1.10 .30
  Nos. 1180-1184 (5)   2.60 1.15
Sites of 11th World Cup Soccer Championship, June 1-25.

Children — A546

1978, May 20
1185 A546 100p multi   .35 .20
50th anniversary of Children's Institute.

Labor Day, by B. Quinquela Martin — A547

Design: No. 1187, Woman's torso, sculpture by Orlando Pierri.

1978, May 20   Perf. 13½
1186 A547 100p multi   .35 .20
1187 A547 100p multi   .35 .20

Argentina, Hungary, France, Italy and Emblem — A548

Stadium — A549

Teams and Argentina '78 Emblem: 200p, Poland, Fed. Rep. of Germany, Tunisia, Mexico. 300p, Austria, Spain, Sweden, Brazil. 400p, Netherlands, Iran, Peru, Scotland.

1978   Litho.   Perf. 13
1188 A548 100p multi   .30 .20
1189 A548 200p multi   .65 .20
1190 A548 300p multi   .95 .25
1191 A548 400p multi   1.25 .35
  Nos. 1188-1191 (4)   3.15 1.00

Souvenir Sheet
Lithographed and Engraved
Perf. 13½
1192 A549 700p buff & blk   2.50 1.40
11th World Cup Soccer Championship, Argentina, June 1-25. Issued: #1188-1191, 6/6; #1192, 6/3.

Stadium Type of 1978 Inscribed in Red: "ARGENTINA / CAMPEON"
Lithographed and Engraved
1978, Sept. 2   Perf. 13½
1193 A549 1000p bulf, blk & red   3.25 1.40
Argentina's victory in 1978 Soccer Championship. No. 1193 has margin similar to No. 1192 with Rimet Cup emblem added in red.

Young Tree Nourished by Old Trunk, UN Emblem — A550

1978 Sept. 2   Litho.
1194 A550 100p multi   .35 .25
Technical Cooperation among Developing Countries Conf., Buenos Aires, Sept. 1978.

Emblems of Buenos Aires & Bank — A551

1978, Sept. 16
1195 A551 100p multi   .35 .25
Bank of City of Buenos Aires, centenary.

General Savio & Steel Production — A552

1978, Sept. 16
1196 A552 100p multi   .35 .25
Gen. Manuel N. Savio (1892-1948), general manager of military heavy industry.

San Martin — A553

1978, Oct.   Engr.
1197 A553 2000p grnsh blk   6.25 1.10

1979   Wmk. 365
1198 A553 2000p grnsh blk   4.75 .35
Gen Jose de San Martin (1778-1850), soldier and statesman. See No. 1292.

Globe & Argentine Flag — A554

1978, Oct. 7   Litho.   Perf. 13½
1199 A554 200p multi   .70 .30
12th Intl. Cancer Cong., Buenos Aires, Oct. 5-11.

Chessboard, Queen & Pawn — A555

1978, Oct. 7
1200 A555 200p multi   2.00 .65
23rd National Chess Olympics, Buenos Aires, Oct. 25-Nov. 12.

Correct Positioning of Stamps A557

50p, Use correct postal code number.

1978   Photo.   Perf. 13½
1201 A557 20p ultra   .20 .20
1203 A557 50p carmine   .25 .20
No. 1201 issued on both ordinary and fluorescent paper.

A558

A559

1978-82   Photo.   Perf. 13½
1204 A558 150p bl & ultra   .35 .20
1205 A558 180p bl & ultra   .45 .20
1206 A558 200p bl & ultra   .30 .20
1207 A559 240p ol bis & bl ('79)   .40 .20
1208 A559 260p blk & lt bl ('79)   .40 .20
1209 A559 290p blk & lt bl ('79)   .45 .20
1210 A559 310p mag & bl ('79)   .50 .20
1211 A559 350p ver & bl ('79)   .65 .20
1212 A559 450p ultra & bl   .50 .20
1213 A559 600p grn & bl ('80)   .70 .25
1214 A559 700p blk & bl ('80)   .70 .25

1215 A559 800p red & bl ('81)   .65 .20
1216 A559 1100p gray & bl ('81)   .90 .20
1217 A559 1500p blk & bl ('81)   .35 .20
1218 A559 1700p grn & bl ('82)   .45 .20
  Nos. 1204-1218 (15)   7.75 3.10
No. 1204 issued on fluorescent and ordinary paper. No. 1206 issued only on fluorescent paper.
For overprint see No. 1338.

Balsa "24" A561

Ships: 200p, Tug Legador. 300p, River Parana tug No. 34. 400p, Passenger ship Ciudad de Parana.

1978, Nov. 4   Litho.   Perf. 13½
1220 A561 100p multi   .25 .20
1221 A561 200p multi   .50 .20
1222 A561 300p multi   .70 .30
  a.   Pair, #1221-1222   1.25
1223 A561 400p multi   .95 .40
  a.   Pair, #1220, 1223   1.25
  Nos. 1220-1223 (4)   2.40 1.10
20th anniversary of national river fleet. Issued on fluorescent paper.

View and Arms of Bahia Blanca A562

1978, Nov. 25   Litho.   Perf. 13½
1224 A562 20p multi   .50 .20
Sesquicentennial of Bahia Blanca.

"Spain," (Queen Isabella and Columbus) by Arturo Dresco — A563

1978, Nov. 25
1225 A563 300p multi   2.75 .30
Visit of King Juan Carlos and Queen Sofia of Spain to Argentina, Nov. 26.

Virgin and Child, San Isidro Cathedral A564

1978, Dec. 16
1226 A564 200p gold & multi   .55 .30
Christmas 1978.

Slope at Chacabuco, by Pedro
Subercaseaux — A565

Painting: 1000p, The Embrace of Maipu
(San Martin and O'Higgins), by Pedro Subercaseaux, vert.

1978, Dec. 16   Litho.   Perf. 13½
1227 A565 500p multi   1.00 .25
1228 A565 1000p multi   2.00 .40
José de San Martin, 200th birth anniversary.

Adolfo
Alsina
A566

Design: No. 1230, Mariano Moreno.

1979, Jan. 20
1229 A566 200p lt bl & blk   .30 .20
1230 A566 200p yel red & blk   .30 .20
Adolfo Alsina (1828-1877), political leader,
vice-president; Mariano Moreno (1778-1811),
lawyer, educator, political leader.

Argentina No. 37 and UPU
Emblem — A567

1979, Jan. 20
1231 A567 200p multi   .25 .20
Centenary of Argentina's UPU membership.

Still-life,
by
Carcova
A568

Painting: 300p, The Laundresses, by Faustino Brughetti.

1979, Mar. 3
1232 A568 200p multi   .45 .20
1233 A568 300p multi   .60 .20
Ernesto de la Carcova (1866-1927) and
Faustino Brughetti (1877-1956), Argentine
painters.

A569

1979, Mar. 3
1234 A569 200p Balcarce Earth
            station   .55 .25
Third Inter-American Telecommunications
Conference, Buenos Aires, March 5-9.

A570

1979
1235 A570 30p Stamp collecting   .20 .20
Printed on ordinary and fluorescent paper.

European
Olive — A571

1979, June 2   Litho.   Perf. 13½
1236 A571 100p shown   .25 .20
1237 A571 200p Tea   .55 .25
1238 A571 300p Sorghum   .85 .40
1239 A571 400p Common flax   1.10 .55
    Nos. 1236-1239 (4)   2.75 1.40

Laurel and
Regimental
Emblem
A572

1979, June 9
1240 A572 200p gold & multi   .40 .25
Founding of Subteniente Berdina Village in
memory of Sub-lieutenant Rodolfo Hernan
Berdina, killed by terrorists in 1975.

"75" and Automobile Club
Emblem — A573

1979, June 9
1241 A573 200p gold & multi   .40 .20
Argentine Automobile Club, 75th anniv.

Exchange Building and
Emblem — A574

1979, June 9
1242 A574 200p bl, blk & gold   .40 .20
Grain Exchange, 125th anniversary.

Cavalry Officer,
1817 — A575

1979, July 7   Litho.   Perf. 13½
1243 A575 200p multi   1.00 .30
Army Day.

Corvette Uruguay and Navy
Emblem — A576

#1245, Hydrographic service ship &
emblem.

1979   Perf. 13
1244 A576 250p multi   .85 .35
1245 A576 250p multi   .85 .35
Navy Day; Cent. of Naval Hydrographic Service. Issued: #1244, July 28; #1245, July 7.

Tree and
Man — A577

1979, July 28   Perf. 13½
1246 A577 250p multi   .60 .25
Protection of the Environment Day, June 5.

"Spad" Flying over Andes, and Vicente
Almandos Almonacid — A578

1979, Aug. 4
1247 A578 250p multi   .70 .25
Air Force Day.

Gen. Julio A. Roca Occupying Rio
Negro, by Juan M. Blanes — A579

1979, Aug. 4
1248 A579 250p multi   .70 .25
Conquest of Rio Negro Desert, centenary.

Rowland
Hill — A580

1979, Sept. 29   Litho.   Perf. 13½
1249 A580 300p gray red & blk   .55 .25
Sir Rowland Hill (1795-1879), originator of
penny postage.

Viedma
Navarez
Monument
A581

1979, Sept. 29
1250 A581 300p multi   .60 .25
Viedma and Carmen de Patagones towns,
bicentenary.

Pope Paul
VI — A582

Design: No. 1252, Pope John Paul I.

1979, Oct. 27   Engr.   Perf. 13½
1251 A582 500p black   1.00 .30
1252 A582 500p sepia   1.00 .30

No. 1169 Overprinted in Red: "75
ANIV. / SOCIEDAD/ FILATELICA / DE
ROSARIO"

1979, Nov. 10   Photo.   Perf. 13½
1253 A539 200p lt blue & blk   .60 .20
Rosario Philatelic Society, 75th anniversary.

A583

1979, Nov. 10   Litho.
1254 A583 300p multi   .70 .30
Frontier resettlement.

A584

1979, Dec. 1   Litho.   Perf. 13½
1255 A584 300p multi   .70 .30
Military Geographic Institute centenary.

Christmas 1979 — A585

1979, Dec. 1
1256 A585 300p multi   .55 .25

General Mosconi Birth
Centenary — A586

1979, Dec. 15   Engr.   Perf. 13½
1257 A586 1000p blk & bl   1.50 .25

Rotary
Emblem
and
Globe
A587

1979, Dec. 29   Litho.
1258 A587 300p multi   1.75 .35
Rotary International, 75th anniversary.

Child and IYC
Emblem
A588

Family, by Pablo Menicucci — A589

1979, Dec. 29
1259 A588 500p lt bl & sepia   .75 .20
1260 A589 1000p multi   1.50 .25
International Year of the Child.

Microphone, Waves, ITU
Emblem — A590

1980, Mar. 22   Litho.   Perf. 13x13½
1261 A590 500p multi   .95 .25
Regional Administrative Conference on
Broadcasting by Hectometric Waves for Area
2, Buenos Aires, Mar. 10-29.

Guillermo
Brown — A591

1980   Engr.   Perf. 13½
1262 A591 5000p black   4.50 .20
See No. 1372.

Argentine Red Cross
Centenary — A592

1980, Apr. 19   Litho.   Perf. 13½
1263 A592 500p multi   .50 .20

OAS Emblem
A593

1980, Apr. 19
1264 A593 500p multi   .55 .25
Day of the Americas, Apr. 14.

Dish Antennae, Balcarce — A594

1980, Apr. 26   Litho. & Engr.
1265 A594 300p shown   .40 .20
1266 A594 300p Hydroelectric Sta-
              tion, Salto
              Grande   .40 .20
1267 A594 300p Bridge, Zarate-
              Brazo Largo   .40 .20
      Nos. 1265-1267 (3)   1.20 .60

Capt. Hipolito Bouchard, Frigate
"Argentina" — A595

1980, May 31   Litho.   Perf. 13x13½
1268 A595 500p multicolored   .70 .30
Navy Day.

"Villarino," San Martin, by Theodore
Gericault — A596

1980, May 31
1269 A596 500p multicolored   .70 .30
Return of the remains of Gen. Jose de San
Martin to Argentina, centenary.

Buenos Aires Gazette, 1810,
Signature — A597

1980, June 7   Perf. 13½
1270 A597 500p multicolored   .55 .25
Journalism Day.

Miniature Sheet

Coaches in
Victoria
Square — A598

1980 June 14
1271   Sheet of 14   9.00 9.00
  a.-n. A598 500p any single   .60   .60
Buenos Aires, 400th anniv. No. 1271 shows
ceramic mural of Victoria Square by Rodolfo
Franco in continuous design. See No. 1285.

Gen. Pedro
Aramburu
A599

1980, July 12   Litho.   Perf. 13½
1272 A599 500p yel & blk   .55 .25
Gen. Pedro Eugenio Aramburu (1903-
1970), provisional president, 1955.

Army
Day
A600

1980, July 12
1273 A600 500p multicolored   .85 .30

Gen. Juan Gregorio de Las Heras
(1780-1866), Hero of 1817 War of
Independence — A601

Grandees of Argentina Bicentenary: No.
1275, Rivadavia. No. 1276, Brig. Gen Jose
Matias Zapiola (1780-1874), naval commander and statesman.

1980, Aug. 2   Litho.   Perf. 13½
1274 A601 500p tan & blk   .55 .25
1275 A601 500p multicolored   .55 .25
1276 A601 500p lt lilac & blk   .55 .25
      Nos. 1274-1276 (3)   1.65 .75

Avro "Gosport" Biplane, Maj. Francisco
de Artega — A602

1980, Aug. 16   Perf. 13
1277 A602 500p multicolored   .70 .25
Air Force Day. Arteaga (1882-1930) was first
director of Military Aircraft Factory where Avro
"Gosport" was built (1927).

University of La Plata, 75th
Anniversary — A603

1980, Aug. 16   Perf. 13½
1278 A603 500p multi   .55 .25

Souvenir Sheets

Emperor
Penguin
A604

South Orkneys Argentine
Base — A605

414

ARGENTINA

No. 1279 (A604): a, shown. b, Bearded penguin. c, Adelie penguins. d, Papua penguins.
e, Sea elephants. f, A605 shown. g, A606
shown. h, Fur seals. i, Giant petrels. j, Blue-
eyed cororants. k, Stormy petrels. m, Anarctic
doves.

1980, Sept. 27   Litho.   Perf. 13½
1279   Sheet of 12   11.00 11.00
 a.-m. A604 500p, any single   .75   .60
1280   Sheet of 12   11.00 11.00
 a. A605 500p Puerto Soledad   .75   .60
 b. A605 500p Building close   .75   .60

75th anniv. of Argentina's presence in the
South Orkneys and 150th anniv. of political
and military command in the Falkland Islands.
Nos. 1279-1280 each contain 12 stamps (4x3)
with landscape designs in center of sheets.
Silhouettes of Argentine exploration ships in
margins. #1280 contains #1279a-1279e,
1279h-1279m, 1280a-1280b.

Anti-smoking
Campaign
A608

1980, Oct. 11
1282 A608 700p multi   .90 .25

National
Census — A609

1980, Sept.
1283 A609 500p blk & bl   1.00 .20

Madonna and Child (Congress
Emblem) — A610

1980, Oct. 1   Litho.
1284 A610 700p multi   .85 .20

National Marian Cong., Mendoza, Oct. 8-12

Mural Type of 1980
Miniature Sheet

1980, Oct. 25
1285   Sheet of 14   9.00 9.00
 a.-n. A598 500p, any single   .60   .50

Buenos Aires, 400th anniv./Buenos Aires
'80 Stamp Exhib., Oct. 24-Nov. 2. No. 1285
shows ceramic mural Arte bajo la Ciudad by
Alfredo Guido in continuous design.

Technical
Military
Academy, 50th
Anniversary
A611

1980, Nov. 1
1286 A611 700p multi   .75 .20

Amateur Radio
Operation
A612

1980, Nov. 1
1287 A612 700p multi   .75 .20

Medal — A613

Lujan
Cathedral
Floor
Plan — A614

1980, Nov. 29   Litho.   Perf. 13½
1288 A613 700p multi   .75 .25
1289 A614 700p olive & brn   .75 .25

Christmas 1980. 150th anniv. of apparition
of Holy Virgin to St. Catherine Laboure, Paris
(No. 1288), 350th anniv. of apparition at Lujan.

150th Death
Anniversary of
Simon
Bolivar — A615

1980, Dec. 13
1290 A615 700p multi   .75 .25

Soccer Gold Cup Championship,
Montevideo, 1980 — A616

1981, Jan. 3   Litho.
1291 A616 1000p multi   1.10 .25

San Martin Type of 1978

1981, Jan. 20   Engr.   Perf. 13½
1292 A553 10,000p dark blue   7.25 .20

Landscape in Lujan, by Marcos
Tiglio — A617

Paintings: No. 1304, Expansion of Light
along a Straight Line, by Miguel Angel Vidal,
vert.

1981, Apr. 11   Litho.
1303 A617 1000p multi   .85 .30
1304 A617 1000p multi   .85 .30

Intl. Sports
Medicine
Congress, June
7-12 — A618

1981, June 6   Litho.   Perf. 13½
1305 A618 1000p bl & dk brn   .75 .20

Esperanza Base, Antarctica — A619

Cargo Plane, Map of Vice-Commodore
Marambio Island — A620

Perf. 13½, 13x13½ (No. 1308)
1981, June 13
1306 A619 1000p shown   1.40 .40
1307 A619 2000p Almirante Irizar 2.50 .55
1308 A620 2000p shown   2.50 .85
 Nos. 1306-1308 (3)   6.40 1.80

Antarctic Treaty 20th anniv.

Antique Pistols (Military Club
Centenary) — A621

1981, June 27   Perf. 13½
1309 A621 1000p Club building   .80 .20
1310 A621 2000p shown   .80 .20

Gen. Juan A.
Alvarez de
Arenales
(1770-1831)
A622

Famous Men: No. 1312, Felix G. Frias
(1816-1881), writer. No. 1313, Jose E.
Uriburu (1831-1914), statesman.

1981, Aug. 8   Litho.   Perf. 13½
1311 A622 1000p multi   .70 .20
1312 A622 1000p multi   .70 .20
1313 A622 1000p multi   .70 .20
 Nos. 1311-1313 (3)   2.10 .60

Naval Observatory Centenary — A623

1981, Aug. 15   Litho.   Perf. 13x13½
1314 A623 1000p multi   .75 .25

No. 1176 Overprinted in Red: "50
ANIV. DE LA ASOCIACION /
FILATELICA Y NUMISMATICA / DE
BAHIA BLANCA"

1981, Aug. 15   Photo.   Perf. 13½
1315 A540 1000p lem & blk   2.00 1.00

50th anniv. of Bahia Blanca Philatelic and
Numismatic Society.

St. Cayetano, Stained-glass Window,
Buenos Aires — A624

1981, Sept. 5   Litho.   Perf. 13½
1316 A624 1000p multi   .70 .20

St. Cayetano, founder of Teatino Order,
500th birth anniv.

Pablo Castaibert (1883-1909) and his
Monoplane (Air Force Day) — A625

1981, Sept. 5   Perf. 13x13½
1317 A625 1000p multi   .65 .20

Intl. Year
of the
Disabled
A626

1981, Sept. 10   Perf. 13½
1318 A626 1000p multi   .65 .20

22nd Latin-American Steelmakers'
Congress, Buenos Aires, Sept. 21-
23 — A627

1981, Sept. 19
1319 A627 1000p multi   .65 .20

Army Regiment
No. 1
(Patricios),
175th
Anniv. — A628

1981, Oct. 10   Litho.   Perf. 13½
1320 A628 1500p Natl. arms   .45 .20
1321 A628 1500p shown   .45 .20
  a.   Pair, #1320-1321   .90 .30

A629

San Martin as artillery Captain in Battle of Bailen, 1808.

1981, Oct. 5
1322   Sheet of 8 + 4 labels   4.75 1.75
  a.   A629 1000p multi   .35   .20
  b.   A629 1500p multi   .50   .20

Espamer '81 Intl. Stamp Exhib. (Americas, Spain, Portugal), Buenos Aires, Nov. 13-22.
No. 1322 contains 2 each se-tenant pairs with label between.

A630

1981, Oct. 5
1323 A630 1000p multi   2.25 .30

Anti-indiscriminate whaling.

Espamer '81
Emblem and
Ship
A631

1981
1324 A631 1300p multi   1.00 .40

No. 1324 Overprinted in Blue:
"CURSO SUPERIOR DE ORGANIZACIONES DE FILATELICOS-UPAE-BUENOS AIRES-1981"

1981, Nov. 7   Photo.   Perf. 13½
1325 A631 1300p multi   1.25 .20

Postal Administration philatelic training course.

Soccer Players
A632

Designs: Soccer players.

1981, Nov. 13   Litho.
1326   Sheet of 4 + 2 labels   7.25 7.25
  a.   A632 2000p multi   .50   .50
  b.   A632 3000p multi   .65   .65
  c.   A632 5000p multi   1.10 1.10
  d.   A632 15,000p multi   3.25 3.25

Espamer '81.

"Peso" Coin Centenary — A633

1981, Nov. 21
1327 A633 2000p Patacon, 1881   .40 .20
1328 A633 3000p Argentine Oro,
                     1881   .60 .20

Christmas
1981 — A634

1981, Dec. 12
1329 A634 1500p multi   .85 .25

Traffic
Safety
A635

1981, Dec. 19   Litho.
1330 A635 1000p Observe traffic
                     lights, vert.   .75 .40
1331 A635 2000p Drive carefully,
                     vert.   .75 .40
1332 A635 3000p Cross at white
                     lines   .75 .40
1333 A635 4000p Don't shine
                     headlights   1.50 .40
       Nos. 1330-1333 (4)   3.75 1.60

Francisco Luis
Bernardez,
Ciuda
Laura — A636

Writers and title pages from their works: 2000p, Lucio V. Mansilla, Excursion a los indios ranqueles. 3000p, Conrado Nale Roxlo, El Grillo. 4000p, Victoria Ocampo, Sur.

1982, Mar. 20   Litho.
1334 A636 1000p shown   .60 .20
1335 A636 2000p multi   .85 .20
1336 A636 3000p multi   1.25 .30
1337 A636 4000p multi   1.75 .30
       Nos. 1334-1337 (4)   4.45 1.00

No. 1218 Overprinted: "LAS / MALVINAS / SON/ ARGENTINAS"

1982, Apr. 17   Photo.   Perf. 13½
1338 A559 1700p green & blue   .50 .20

Argentina's claim on Falkland Islands.

Robert
Koch — A637

1982, Apr. 17   Litho.   Wmk. 365
1339 A637 2000p multi   .50 .25

TB bacillus centenary and 25th Intl. Tuberculosis Conference.

American
Airforces
Commanders'
22nd
Conf. — A638

1982, Apr. 17
1340 A638 2000p multi   .70 .30

Stone Carving, City Founder's
Signature (Don Hernando de
Lerma) — A639

1982, Apr. 17
1341 A639 2000p multi   .70 .30

Souvenir Sheet
1342 A639 5000p multi   2.00 2.00

City of Salta, 400th anniv. No. 1342 contains one 43x30mm stamp.

Naval Center Centenary — A640

1982, Apr. 24   Perf. 13x13½
1343 A640 2000p multi   .70 .30

Chorisia
Speciosa — A641

1982   Unwmk.   Photo.   Perf. 13½
1344 A641 200p   Zinnia
                     peruviana   .20 .20
1345 A641 300p   Ipomoea
                     purpurea   .20 .20
1346 A641 400p   Tillandsia
                     aeranthos   .20 .20
1347 A641 500p   shown   .20 .20
1348 A641 800p   Oncidium
                     bifolium   .20 .20
1349 A641 1000p Erythrina
                     crista-galli   .20 .20
1350 A641 2000p Jacaranda
                     mimosi-fo-
                     lia   .25 .20
1351 A641 3000p Bauhinia
                     candicans   .30 .20

1352 A641 5000p   Tecoma
                      stans   .50 .20
1353 A641 10,000p Tabebuia
                      ipe   1.00 .25
1354 A641 20,000p Passiflora
                      coerulea   2.25 .35
1355 A641 30,000p Aristolochia
                      littoralis   3.25 .50
1356 A641 50,000p Oxalis en-
                      neaphylla   5.25 .70
       Nos. 1344-1356 (13)   14.00 3.60

Nos. 1344-1346, 1348-1350 issued on fluorescent paper. Nos. 1353-1356 issued on ordinary paper. Others issued on both fluorescent and ordinary paper.
Issued: 500p, 2000p, 5000p, 10,000p, 5/22; 200p, 300p, 1000p, 20,000p, 9/25; 400p, 800p, 30,000p, 50,000p, 12/4; 3000p, 12/18.
See Nos. 1429-1443A, 1515-1527, 1683-1691. For overprint see No. 1382.

10th
Death
Anniv. of
Gen.
Juan C.
Sanchez
A641a

1982, May 29   Litho.   Wmk. 365
1364 A641a 5000p grn & blk   .90 .30

Luis Venet, First Commander — A641b

1982, June 12
1365 A641b 5000p org & blk   1.10 .45

Size: 83x28mm
1366 A641b 5000p Map   .75 .30
  a.   Pair, Nos. 1365-1366   2.00 2.00

153rd Anniv. of Malvinas Political and Military Command District.

Visit of Pope
John Paul II
A641c

1982, June 12
1367 A641c 5000p multi   1.75 .55

Organ Grinder,
by Aldo Severi
(b.
1928) — A641d

3000p, Still Life, by Santiago Cogorno (b. 1915).

1982, July 3   Wmk. 365
1368 A641d 2000p shown   .25 .20
1369 A641d 3000p multi   .40 .20

Guillermo Brown Type of 1980 and:

Jose de San Martin
A641e

Litho. and Engr.

1982   Unwmk.   Perf. 13½
1372 A591 30,000p blk & bl   3.25   .65
1376 A641e 50,000p sepia & car   6.50   .85

Issue dates: 30,000p, June; 50,000p, July.

Scouting Year
A641f

Wmk. 365

1982, Aug. 7   Litho.   Perf. 13½
1380 A641f 5000p multi   1.25   .20

Alconafta Fuel Campaign
A641g

1982, Aug. 7   Wmk. 365
1381 A641g 2000p multi   .30   .20

No. 1352 Overprinted: "50 ANIVERSARIO SOCIEDAD FILATELICA DE TUCUMAN"

1982, Aug. 7   Photo.   Unwmk.
1382 A641 5000p multi   1.50   1.25

Rio III Central Nuclear Power Plant, Cordoba
A642

Wmk. 365

1982, Sept. 4   Litho.   Perf. 13½
1383 A642 2000p shown   .30   .20
1384 A642 2000p Control room   .30   .20

Namibia Day — A643

1982, Sept. 4
1385 A643 5000p Map   .75   .20

Formosa Cathedral — A644

Churches and Cathedrals of the Northeast: 2000p, Our Lady of Itati, Corrientes, vert. 3000p, Resistencia Cathedral, Chaco, vert. 10,000p, St. Ignatius Church ruins, Misiones.

1982, Sept. 18   Litho. & Engr.
1386 A644 2000p dk grn & blk   .50   .50
1387 A644 3000p dk brn & brn   .50   .50
1388 A644 5000p dk bl & brn   1.00   .50
1389 A644 10,000p dp org & blk   1.50   .50
     Nos. 1386-1389 (4)   3.50   2.00

Tension Sideral, by Mario Alberto Agatiello
A645

Sculpture (Espamer '81 and Juvenex '82 Exhibitions): 3000p, Sugerencia II, by Eduardo Mac Entyre. 5000p, Storm, by Carlos Silva.

1982, Oct. 2   Litho.   Perf. 13½
1390 A645 2000p multi   .25   .20
1391 A645 3000p multi   .45   .20
1392 A645 5000p multi   .60   .20
     Nos. 1390-1392 (3)   1.30   .60

Sante Fe Bridge
A646

1982, Oct. 16   Litho. & Engr.
1393 A646 2000p bl & blk   .40   .20

2nd Southern Cross Games, Santa Fe and Rosario, Nov. 26-Dec. 5.

10th World Men's Volleyball Championship — A647

1982, Oct. 16   Litho.   Wmk. 365
1394 A647 2000p multi   .40   .30
1395 A647 5000p multi   .60   .30

Los Andes Newspaper Centenary — A648

Design: Army of the Andes Monument, Hill of Glory, Mendoza.

1982, Oct. 30
1396 A648 5000p multi   .50   .20

A649

1982, Oct. 30   Wmk. 365
1397 A649 5000p Signs   .55   .25

50th Anniv. of Natl. Roads, Administration.

A650

1982, Nov. 20   Litho.

La Plata City Cent.: No. 1400: a, Cathedral, diff. b, Head, top. c, Observatory. d, City Hall, diff. e, Head, bottom. f, University.

1398 A650 5000p Cathedral   .75   .20
1399 A650 5000p City Hall   .75   .20
1400   Sheet of 6   2.25   1.00
a.-f.   A650 2500p any single   .30   .20

Well, Natl. Hydrocarbon Congress Emblem — A651

1982, Nov. 20
1401 A651 5000p multi   .50   .20

Oil Discovery, Comodoro Rivadavia, 75th anniv.

Jockey Club of Buenos Aires Centenary
A652

#1403, Carlos Pellegrini, first president.

1982, Dec. 4   Litho.
1402 A652 5000p Emblem   .50   .20
1403 A652 5000p multi   .50   .20

Christmas
A653

1982, Dec. 18   Perf. 13½
1404 A653 3000p St. Vincent de Paul   1.50   .20

Size: 29x38mm
1405 A653 5000p St. Francis of Assisi   1.25   .20

Pedro B. Palacios (1854-1917), Writer — A654

Writers: 2000p, Leopoldo Marechal (1900-1970). 3000p, Delfina Bunge de Galvez (1881-1952). 4000p, Manuel Galvez (1882-1962). 5000p, Evaristo Carriego (1883-1912).

1983, Mar. 26   Litho.   Perf. 13½
1406 A654 1000p multi   .20   .20
1407 A654 2000p multi   .25   .20
1408 A654 3000p multi   .30   .20
1409 A654 4000p multi   .40   .20
1410 A654 5000p multi   .55   .20
a.   Strip of 5, #1406-1410   1.75   1.00

Recovery of the Malvinas (Falkland Islands) — A655

1983, Apr. 9   Litho.   Perf. 13½
1411 A655 20,000p Map, flag   1.50   .50

Telecommunications Systems — A656

1983, Apr. 16   Wmk. 365
1412 A656 5000p SITRAM   1.00   .50
1413 A656 5000p RED ARPAC   1.50   .50

Naval League Emblem
A657

1983, May 14   Litho.   Perf. 13½
1414 A657 5000p multi   .35   .20

Navy Day and 50th anniv. of Naval League.

Allegory, by Victor Rebuffo
A658

1983, May 14
1415 A658 5000p multi   .35   .20

Natl. Arts Fund, 25th Anniv.

75th Anniv. of Colon Opera House, Buenos Aires — A659

1983, May 28   **Wmk. 365**
1416 A659 5000p Main hall .70 .20
1417 A659 10000p Stage 1.00 .20

Protected Species — A660

1983, July 2   **Litho.**   **Perf. 13½**
1418 A660 1p Chrysocyon brachyturus .30 .20
1419 A660 1.50p Ozotocerus bezoarticus .50 .20
1420 A660 2p Myrmecophaga tridactyla .55 .20
1421 A660 2.50p Leo onca .65 .20
Nos. 1418-1421 (4) 2.00 .80

City of Catamarca, 300th Anniv. — A661

Foundation of the City of Catamarca, by Luis Varela Lezana (1900-1982).

1983, July 16   **Litho.**   **Perf. 13½**
1422 A661 1p multi .30 .20

Mamerto Esquiu (1826-1883) A662

1983, July 16
1423 A662 1p multi .30 .20

Bolivar, by Herrera Toro — A663

Bolivar, Engraving by Kepper — A664

Perf. 13 (A663), 13½ (A664)
1983   **Unwmk.**
1424 A663 1p multi .30 .20
1425 A664 2p black .60 .20
1426 A664 10p San Martin 3.00 1.50
Nos. 1424-1426 (3) 3.90 1.90

Issue dates: 1p, 2p, July 23. 10p, Aug. 20.
See Nos. 1457-1462B.

Gen. Toribio de Luzuriaga (1782-1842) A665

1983, Aug. 20   **Litho.**   **Perf. 13½**
1427 A665 1p multi .30 .20

50th Anniv. of San Martin National Institute A666

1983, Aug. 20   **Engr.**   **Unwmk.**
1428 A666 2p sepia .60 .20

Flower Type of 1982 in New Currency
1983-85   **Photo.**   **Perf. 13½**
1429 A641 5c like #1347 .20 .20
1430 A641 10c like #1349 .20 .20
1431 A641 20c like #1350 .20 .20
1432 A641 30c like #1351 .20 .20
1433 A641 40c Eichhornia crassipes .20 .20
1434 A641 50c like #1352 .20 .20
1435 A641 1p like #1353 .20 .20
1435A A641 1.80p Mutisia retusa .20 .20
1436 A641 2p like #1354 .25 .20
1437 A641 3p like #1355 .30 .20
1438 A641 5p like #1356 .55 .20
1439 A641 10p Alstroemeria aurantiaca 1.10 .80
1440 A641 20p like #1345 .55 .20
1441 A641 30p Embothrium coccineum 3.50 2.50
1442 A641 50p like #1346 1.10 .40
1443 A641 100p like #1348 1.60 .50
1443A A641 300p Cassia carnaval .80 .25
Nos. 1429-1443A (17) 11.35 6.85

Issued: 20p, 8/27/84; 50p, 10/19/84; 100p, 12/84; 300p, 6/15/85.
Nos. 1429, 1433, 1435A issued on fluorescent paper. Nos. 1443, 1443A issued on ordinary paper. Others issued on both ordinary and fluorescent paper.
For overprint and surcharge see #1489, 1530.

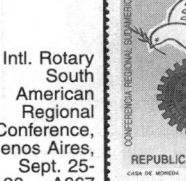

Intl. Rotary South American Regional Conference, Buenos Aires, Sept. 25-28 — A667

1983, Sept. 24   **Litho.**
1444 A667 1p multi .55 .25

9th Pan American Games, Caracas, Aug. 13-28 — A668

1983, Sept. 24
1445 A668 1p Track .30 .20
1446 A668 2p Emblem .65 .30

World Communications Year — A669

1983, Oct. 8   **Perf. 13½**
1447 A669 2p multi .60 .25

Squash Peddler by Antonio Berni (1905-1981) A670

2p, Figure in Yellow by Luis Seoane (1910-79).

1983, Oct. 15   **Perf. 13½**
1448 A670 1p multi .30 .20
1449 A670 2p multi .50 .25

World Communications Year — A671

Designs: 1p, Wagon, 18th cent. 2p, Post chaise, 19th cent. 4p, Steam locomotive, 1857. 5p, Tramway, 1910.

1983, Nov. 19   **Litho.**   **Perf. 13½**
1450 A671 1p multi .20 .20
1451 A671 2p multi .25 .20
1452 A671 4p multi .50 .20
1453 A671 5p multi .65 .25
Nos. 1450-1453 (4) 1.60 .85

World Communications Year — A672

1983, Nov. 26   **Litho.**   **Perf. 12½x12**
1454 A672 2p General Post Office .40 .20

Return to Elected Government A673

1983, Dec. 10   **Photo.**   **Perf. 13½**
1455 A673 2p Coin, 1813 .30 .20

Eudyptes Crestatus A674

Designs: b, Diomedea exulans. c, Diomedea melanophris. d, Eudyptes chrysolophus. e, Luis Piedra Buena. f, Carlos Maria Moyano. g, Luis Py. h, Augusto Lasserre. i, Phoebetria palpebrata. j, Hydrurga leptonyx. k, Lobodon carcinophagus. l, Leptonychotes weddelli.

1983, Dec. 10   **Litho.**
1456 Sheet of 12 4.50 2.25
a.-l. A674 2p any single .35 .20

Southern pioneers and fauna. Margin depicts various airplanes and emblems.

Bolivar Type of 1983

Famous men: 10p, Angel J. Carranza (1834-99), historian. No. 1458, 500p, Guillermo Brown. No. 1459, Estanislao del Campo (1834-80), poet. 30p, Jose Hernandez (1834-86), author. 40p, Vicente Lopez y Planes (1784-1856), poet and patriot. 50p, San Martin. 200p, Belgrano.

1983-85   **Litho. & Engr.**   **Perf. 13½**
1457 A664 10p pale bl & dk bl .50 .30
1458 A664 20p dk bl & blk 2.75 1.40
1459 A664 20p dl brn ol & ol blk .50 .30
1460 A664 30p pale bl & bluish blk .60 .30
1461 A664 40p lt bl grn & blk .90 .40
1462 A664 50p Prus & choc 1.10 .25
1462A A664 200p int bl & blk 3.00 .95
1462B A664 500p brn & int bl 2.00 .50
Nos. 1457-1462B (8) 11.35 4.40

Issued: #1458, 10/6; 10p, #1459, 30p, 40p, 3/23/85; 50p, 4/23/85; 200p, 11/2/85; 500p, 5/2/85.

Christmas 1983 — A675

Nativity Scenes: 2p, Tapestry, by Silke. 3p, Stained-glass window, San Carlos de Bariloche's Wayn Church, vert.

1983, Dec. 17   Litho.   Perf. 13½
1463 A675 2p multi .30 .20
1464 A675 3p multi .55 .30

Centenary of El Dia Newspaper A676

1984, Mar. 24   Litho.
1465 A676 4p Masthead, printing roll .40 .20

Alejandro Carbo Teachers' College Centenary — A677

1984, June 2   Litho.   Perf. 13½
1466 A677 10p Building .40 .25

1984 Olympics A678

#1468, Weightlifting, discus, shot put. #1469, Javelin, fencing. #1470, Bicycling, swimming.

1984, July 28   Litho.   Perf. 13½
1467 A678 5p shown .25 .20
1468 A678 5p multicolored .25 .20
1469 A678 10p multicolored .45 .25
1470 A678 10p multicolored .45 .25
    Nos. 1467-1470 (4) 1.40 .90

Rosario Stock Exchange Centenary A679

1984, Aug. 11
1471 A679 10p multicolored .45 .25

Wheat A680

1984, Aug. 11
1472 A680 10p shown .50 .25
1473 A680 10p Corn .50 .25
1474 A680 10p Sunflower .50 .25
    Nos. 1472-1474 (3) 1.50 .75

18th FAO Regional Conference for Latin America and Caribbean (No. 1472); 3rd Natl. Corn Congress (No. 1473); World Food Day (No. 1474).

Wildlife Protection — A681

1984, Sept. 22   Litho.   Perf. 13½
1475 A681 20p Hippocamelus bisulcus .40 .20
1476 A681 20p Vicugna vicugna .40 .20
1477 A681 20p Aburria jacutinga .40 .20
1478 A681 20p Mergus octosetaceus .40 .20
1479 A681 20p Podiceps gallardoi .40 .20
    Nos. 1475-1479 (5) 2.00 1.00

First Latin American Theater Festival, Cordoba, Oct. — A682

1984, Oct. 13   Litho.   Perf. 13½
1480 A682 20p Mask .25 .20

Intl. Eucharistic Congress, 50th Anniv. — A683

Apostles' Communion, by Fra Angelico.

1984, Oct. 13
1481 A683 20p multicolored .30 .20

Glaciares Natl. Park (UNESCO World Heritage List) — A684

1984, Nov. 17   Litho.
1482 A684 20p Sea .25 .20
1483 A684 30p Glacier .40 .20

City of Puerto Deseado Centenary — A685

1984, Nov. 17   Perf. 13½
1484 A685 20p shown .30 .20
1485 A685 20p Ushuaia centenary .30 .20

Childrens' Paintings, Christmas 1984 — A686

1984, Dec. 1   Litho.   Perf. 13½
1486 A686 20p Diego Aguero .30 .20
1487 A686 30p Leandro Ruiz .60 .20
1488 A686 50p Maria Castillo, vert. .60 .20
    Nos. 1486-1488 (3) 1.50 .60

No. 1439 Overprinted

1984, Dec. 1   Photo.   Perf. 13½
1489 A641 10p multicolored .40 .40

Buenos Aires Philatelic Center, 50th anniv.

Vista Del Jardin Zoologico, by Fermin Eguia — A687

Paintings: No. 1491, El Congreso Iluminado, by Francisco Travieso. No. 1492, Galpones (La Boca), by Marcos Borio.

1984, Dec. 15   Perf. 13½
1490 A687 20p multi .30 .20
1491 A687 20p multi, vert. .30 .20
1492 A687 20p multi, vert. .30 .20
    Nos. 1490-1492 (3) .90 .60

Gen. Martin Miguel de Guemes (1785-1821) — A688

1985, Mar. 23   Litho.   Perf. 13½
1493 A688 30p multicolored .25 .20

ARGENTINA '85 Exhibition — A689

First airmail service from: 20p, Buenos Aires to Montevideo, 1917. 40p, Cordoba to Villa Dolores, 1925. 60p, Bahia Blanca to Comodoro Rivadavia, 1929. 80p, Argentina to Germany, 1934. 100p, naval service to the Antarctic, 1952.

1985, Apr. 27
1494 A689 20p Bleriot Gnome .20 .20
1495 A689 40p Junker F-13L .30 .20
1496 A689 60p Latte 25 .50 .20
1497 A689 80p L.Z. 127 Graf Zeppelin .65 .30

1498 A689 100p Consolidated PBY Catalina .85 .40
    Nos. 1494-1498 (5) 2.50 1.30

Central Bank, 50th Anniv. A690

1985, June 1
1499 A690 80p Bank Bldg., Buenos Aires .55 .20

Jose A. Ferreyra (1889-1943), Director of Munequitas Portenas — A691

Famous directors and their films: No. 1501, Leopoldo Torre Nilsson (1924-1978), scene from Martin Fierro.

1985, June 1
1500 A691 100p shown .60 .20
1501 A691 100p multi .60 .20

Carlos Gardel (1890-1935), Entertainer A692

Paintings: No. 1502, Gardel playing the guitar on stage, by Carlos Alonso (b. 1929). No. 1503, Gardel in a wide-brimmed hat, by Hermegildo Sabat (b. 1933). No. 1504, Portrait of Gardel in an ornamental frame, by Aldo Severi (b. 1928) and Martiniano Arce (b. 1939).

1985, June 15
1502 A692 200p multi .95 .45
1503 A692 200p multi .95 .45
1504 A692 200p multi .95 .45
    Nos. 1502-1504 (3) 2.85 1.35

The Arrival, by Pedro Figari A693

A Halt on the Plains, by Prilidiano Pueyrredon — A693a

Oil paintings (details): 30c, The Wagon Square, by C. B. de Quiros. Illustration A693a is reduced.

1985, July 6   Litho.   Perf. 13½
1505 A693 20c multi 1.00 .25
1506 A693 30c multi 1.25 .25

Souvenir Sheet
Perf. 12

1507 A693a   Sheet of 2   2.50   2.50
    a.   20c Pilgrims, vert.   .30   .30
    b.   30c Wagon   .40   .40

ARGENTINA '85. No. 1507 contains 2 30x40mm stamps. See No. 1542.

Buenos Aires to Montevideo, 1917 Teodoro Fels Flight — A694

Historic flight covers: #1509, Villa Dolores to Cordoba, 1925. #1510, Buenos Aires to France, 1929 St. Exupery flight. #1511, Buenos Aires to Bremerhaven, 1934 Graf Zeppelin flight. #1512, 1st Antarctic flight, 1952.

1985, July 13   **Perf. 12x12½**
1508 A694 10c emer & multi   .40   .20
1509 A694 10c ultra & multi   .40   .20
1510 A694 10c lt choc & multi   .40   .20
1511 A694 10c chnt & multi   .40   .20
1512 A694 10c ap grn & multi   .40   .20
    Nos. 1508-1512 (5)   2.00   1.00

ARGENTINA '85.

Illuminated Fruit, by Fortunato Lacamera (1887-1951) — A695

Paintings: 20c, Woman with Bird, by Juan del Prete, vert.

1985, Sept. 7   **Perf. 13½**
1513 A695 20c multi   .85   .30
1514 A695 30c multi   1.00   .30

Flower Types of 1982-85

Designs: 1a, Begonia micranthera var. hieronymi. 5a, Gymnocalycium bruchii.

1985-88   **Photo.**   **Perf. 13½**
1515 A641 ½c like #1356   .20   .20
1516 A641 1c like #1439   .20   .20
1517 A641 2c like #1345   .20   .20
1518 A641 3c like #1441   .20   .20
1519 A641 5c like #1346   .25   .20
1520 A641 10c like #1348   .35   .20
1521 A641 20c like #1347   .80   .20
1522 A641 30c like #1443A   1.10   .25
1523 A641 50c like #1344   1.75   .30
1524 A641 1a multi   3.50   .65
1525 A641 2a multi   .40   .20
1526 A641 5a multi   6.75   3.00

Size: 15x23mm

1527 A641 8½c like #1349   .30   .20
    Nos. 1515-1527 (13)   16.00   6.00

Issued: ½c, 1c, 12/16; 2c, 8½c, 30c, 9/18; 3c, 5c, 10c, 50c, 1a, 9/7; 20c, 10/17; 5a, 3/21/87; 2a, 12/5/88.

No. 1435 Surcharged

1986, Nov. 4   **Photo.**   **Perf. 13½**
1530 A641 10c on 1p No. 1435   .20   .20

Folk Musical Instruments A699

1985, Sept. 14   **Litho.**   **Perf. 13½**
1531 A699 20c Frame drum   .55   .25
1532 A699 20c Long flute   .55   .25
1533 A699 20c Jew's harp   .55   .25

1534 A699 20c Pan flutes   .55   .25
1535 A699 20c Musical bow   .55   .25
    Nos. 1531-1535 (5)   2.75   1.25

Juan Bautista Alberdi (1810-1884), Historian, Politician A700

Famous men: Nicolas Avellaneda (1836-1885), President in 1874. 30c, Fr. Luis Beltran (1784-1827), military and naval engineer. 40c, Ricardo Levene (1885-1959), historian, author.

1985, Oct. 5
1536 A700 10c multi   .25   .20
1537 A700 20c multi   .45   .25
1538 A700 30c multi   .65   .30
1539 A700 40c multi   1.10   .45
    Nos. 1536-1539 (4)   2.45   1.20

Type of 1985 and

Skaters A701

Deception, by J. H. Rivoira — A702

1985, Oct. 19   **Litho.**   **Perf. 13½**
1540 A701 20c multi   .35   .30
1541 A702 30c multi   .50   .50

Size: 147x75mm
Imperf

1542 A693a 1a multi   1.90   1.50

IYY. No. 1542 is inscribed in silver with the UN 40th anniversary and IYY emblems.

Provincial Views — A703

#1543, Rock Window, Buenos Aires. #1544, Forclaz Windmill, Entre Rios. #1545, Lake Potrero de los Funes, San Luis. #1546, Mission church, north-east province. #1547, Penguin colony, Punta Tombo, Chubut. #1548, Water Mirrors, Cordoba.

1985, Nov. 23   **Perf. 13½**
1543 A703 10c multi   .25   .25
1544 A703 10c multi   .25   .25
1545 A703 10c multi   .25   .25
1546 A703 10c multi   .25   .25
1547 A703 10c multi   .25   .25
1548 A703 10c multi   .25   .25
    Nos. 1543-1548 (6)   1.50   1.50

Christmas 1985 — A704

Designs: 10c, Birth of Our Lord, by Carlos Cortes. 20c, Christmas, by Hector Viola.

1985, Dec. 7
1549 A704 10c multi   .25   .20
1550 A704 20c multi   .50   .45

Natl. Campaign for the Prevention of Blindness — A705

1985, Dec. 7
1551 A705 10c multi   .25   .20

Rio Gallegos City, Cent. — A716

1985, Dec. 21   **Litho.**   **Perf. 13½**
1552 A716 10c Church   .80   .40

Natl. Grape Harvest Festival, 50th Anniv. A717

1986, Mar. 15
1553 A717 10c multi   .25   .20
    Exists with Wmk. 265, Value $10.

Historical Architecture in Buenos Aires — A718

Designs: No. 1554, Valentin Alsina House, Italian Period, 1860-70. No. 1555, House on Cerrito Street, French influence, 1880-1900. No. 1556, House on the Avenida de Mayo y Santiago del Estero, Art Nouveau, 1900-10. No. 1557, Customs Building, academic architecture, 1900-15. No. 1558, Isaac Fernandez Blanco Museum, house of architect Martin Noel, natl. restoration, 1910-30. Nos. 1554-1556 vert.

1986, Apr. 19
1554 A718 20c multi   .40   .30
1555 A718 20c multi   .40   .30
1556 A718 20c multi   .40   .30
1557 A718 20c multi   .40   .30
1558 A718 20c multi   .40   .30
    Nos. 1554-1558 (5)   2.00   1.50

Antarctic Bases, Pioneers and Fauna — A719

Designs: a, Base, Jubany. b, Arctocephalus gazella. c, Otaria byronia. d, Gen. Belgrano Base. e, Daption capensis. f, Diomedia melanophris. g, Apterodytes patagonica. h, Macronectes giganteus. i, Hugo Alberto Acuna (1885-1953). j, Spheniscus magellanicus. k, Gallinago gallinage. l, Capt. Agustin del Castillo (1855-89).

1986, May 31
1559   Sheet of 12   9.00   9.00
    a.-l.   A719 10c any single   .75   .75

Famous People — A720

#1560, Dr. Alicia Moreau de Justo, human rights activist. #1561, Dr. Emilio Ravignani (1886-1954), historian. #1562, Indira Gandhi.

1986, July 5   **Litho.**   **Perf. 13½**
1560 A720 10c multi   .45   .25
1561 A720 10c multi   .45   .25
1562 A720 30c multi   1.10   .65
    Nos. 1560-1562 (3)   2.00   1.15

Statuary, Buenos Aires — A721

1986, July 5

20c, Fountain of the Nereids, by Dolores Lola Mora (1866-1936). 30c, Lamenting at Work, by Rogelio Yrurtia (1879-1950), horiz.

1563 A721 20c multi   .50   .45
1564 A721 30c multi   .80   .65

Famous Men — A722

#1565, Francisco N. Laprida (1786-1829), politician. #1566, Estanislao Lopez (1786-1838), brigadier general. #1567, Francisco Ramirez (1786-1821), general.

1986, Aug. 9   **Litho.**   **Perf. 13**
1565 A722 20c dl yel, brn & blk   .40   .40
1566 A722 20c dl yel, brn & blk   .40   .40
1567 A722 20c dl yel, brn & blk   .40   .40
    Nos. 1565-1567 (3)   1.20   1.20

Fr. Ceferino
Namuncura
(1886-1905)
A723

1986, Aug. 30   *Perf. 13½*
1568 A723 20c multi   .60 .40

Miniature Sheets

Natl. Team Victory, 1986 World Cup
Soccer Championships,
Mexico — A724

Designs: No. 1569a-1569d, Team. Nos.
1569e-1569h, Shot on goal. Nos. 1570a-
1570d, Action close-up. Nos. 1570e-1570h,
Diego Maradona holding soccer cup.

1986, Nov. 8   *Litho.*   *Perf. 13½*
1569 A724 Sheet of 8   10.00 10.00
   a.-h. 75c any single   1.10 1.10
1570 A724 Sheet of 8   10.00 10.00
   a.-h. 75c any single   1.10 1.10

San Francisco (Cordoba),
Cent. — A725

1986, Nov. 8
1571 A725 20c Municipal Building   .50 .45

Mutualism Day — A727

1986, Nov. 22
1573 A727 20c multi   .60 .45

Christmas — A728

Designs: 20c, Naif retable, by Aniko Szabo
(b. 1945). 30c, Everyone's Tree, by Franca
Delacqua (b. 1947).

1986, Dec. 13   *Litho.*   *Perf. 13½*
1574 A728 20c multicolored   .50 .35
1575 A728 30c multicolored   .60 .35

Santa Rosa de
Lima, 400th
Birth
Anniv. — A729

1986, Dec. 13
1576 A729 50c multicolored   1.75 .75

Rio Cuarto
Municipal
Building
A730

1986, Dec. 20
1577 A730 20c shown   .40 .25
1578 A730 20c Court Building, Cor-
     doba   .40 .25
Rio Cuarto City, bicent. Court Building, Cordoba, 50th anniv.

Antarctic
Treaty, 25th
Anniv. — A731

1987, Mar. 7   *Litho.*   *Perf. 13½*
1579 A731 20c Marine biologist   .35 .20
1580 A731 30c Ornithologist   .60 .25
Souvenir Sheet
Perf. 12
1581   Sheet of 2   3.00 3.00
   a.   A731 20c like No. 1579   .40 .20
   b.   A731 30c like No. 1580   .55 .25
No. 1581 contains 2 stamps, size: 40x50mm.

Natl. Mortgage Bank, Cent. — A732

1987, Mar. 21   *Perf. 13½*
1582 A732 20c multicolored   .65 .45

Natl. Cooperative Associations
Movement — A733

1987, Mar. 21
1583 A733 20c multicolored   .65 .45

Second State
Visit of Pope
John
Paul II — A734

Engr., Litho. (No. 1585)
1987, Apr. 4   *Perf. 13½*
1584 A734 20c shown   .35 .25
1585 A734 80c Papal blessing   1.40 .70
Souvenir Sheet
Perf. 12
1586 A734 1a like 20c   2.25 2.25
No. 1586 contains one 40x50mm stamp.

Intl.
Peace
Year
A735

30c, Pigeon, abstract sculpture by Victor
Kaniuka.

1987, Apr. 11   *Litho.*
1587 A735 20c multicolored   .35 .20
1588 A735 30c multicolored   .55 .35

Low Handicap
World Polo
Championships
A736

Polo Players, painting by Alejandro Moy.

1987, Apr. 11
1589 A736 20c multicolored   .75 .20

Miniature Sheet

ICOM
'86 — A737

Designs: a, Emblem. b, Family crest,
National History Museum, Buenos Aires. c, St.
Bartholomew, Enrique Larreta Museum of
Spanish Art, Buenos Aires. d, Zoomorphic
club, Patagonian Museum, San Carlos de
Bariloche. e, Supplication, anthropomorphic
sculpture, Natural Sciences Museum, La
Plata. f, Wrought iron lattice from the house of
J. Urquiza, president of the Confederation of
Argentina, Entre Rios History Museum,
Parana. g, St. Joseph, 18th cent. wood figu-
rine, Northern History Museum, Salta. h,
Funerary urn, Provincial Archaeological
Museum, Santiago del Estero.

1987, May 30
1590   Sheet of 8   3.50 3.50
   a.-h. A737 25c any single   .40 .30
Intl. Council of Museums, 14th general conf.

Natl. College of Monserrat, Cordoba,
300th Anniv. — A738

1987, July 4   *Imperf.*
1591 A738 1a multicolored   1.40 1.40
Monserrat '87 Philatelic Exposition.

Fight
Drug
Abuse
A739

The Proportions of Man, by da Vinci.

1987, Aug. 15   *Perf. 13½*
1592 A739 30c multicolored   .45 .20

Famous
Men
A740

Portraits and quotations: 20c, Jorge Luis
Borges (1899-1986), writer. 30c, Armando
Discepolo (1887-1971), playwright. 50c, Car-
los A. Pueyrredon (1887-1962), professor,
Legion of Honor laureate.

1987, Aug. 15
1593 A740 20c multicolored .30 .20
1594 A740 30c multicolored .50 .25
1595 A740 50c multicolored .75 .35
Nos. 1593-1595 (3) 1.55 .80

Pillar Boxes
A741   A742

1987   Photo.   Perf. 13½
1596 A741 (30c) yel, blk & dark
red 2.00 .30
Booklet with 10 stamps 20.00
1597 A742 (33c) lt blue grn, blk &
yel .85 .35

Issue dates: (30c), June 8; (33c), July 13.

The
Sower,
by Julio
Vanzo
A743

1987, Sept. 12
1598 A743 30c multicolored .35 .20
Argentine Agrarian Federation, 75th anniv.

10th Pan
American
Games,
Indianapolis,
Aug. 7-
25 — A744

1987, Sept. 26
1599 A744 20c Basketball .25 .20
1600 A744 30c Rowing .35 .20
1601 A744 50c Yachting .55 .20
Nos. 1599-1601 (3) 1.15 .60

Children
Playing
Doctor,
WHO
Emblem
A745

1987, Oct. 7
1602 A745 30c multi .35 .20
Vaccinate every child campaign.

Heroes of the
Revolution
A746

Signing
of the
San
Nicolas
Accord,
1852, by
Rafael
del Villar
A747

Independence anniversaries and historic
events: No. 1603, Maj.-Col. Ignacio Alvarez
Thomas (1787-1857). No. 1604, Col. Manuel
Crispulo Bernabe Dorrego (1787-1829). No.
1606, 18th cent. Spanish map of the Falkland
Isls., administered by Jacinto de Altolaguirre.

1987, Oct. 17
1603 A746 25c shown .30 .20
1604 A746 25c multi .30 .20
1605 A747 50c shown .55 .30
1606 A747 50c multi .55 .30
Nos. 1603-1606 (4) 1.70 1.00

Museum established in the House of the
San Nicholas Accord, 50th anniv. (#1605);
Jacinto de Altolaguirre (1754-1787), governor
the Malvinas Isls. for the King of Spain
(#1606).

Celedonio Galvan Moreno, 1st
Director — A748

1987, Nov. 21
1607 A748 50c multicolored .55 .40
Postas Argentinas magazine, 50th anniv.

LRA National
Radio, Buenos
Aires, 50th
Anniv. — A749

1987, Nov. 21
1608 A749 50c multicolored .55 .40

Natl.
Philatelic
Society,
Cent.
A750

1987, Nov. 21
1609 A750 1a Jose Marco del
Pont 1.10 .55

Christmas
A751

Tapestries: 50c, *Navidad*, by Alisia Frega.
1a, *Vitral*, by Silvina Trigos.

1987, Dec. 5
1610 A751 50c multicolored .55 .20
1611 A751 1a multicolored 1.10 .55

Natl. Parks — A752

1987, Dec. 19   Perf. 13x13½
1612 A752 50c Baritu .55 .35
1613 A752 50c Nahuel Huapi .55 .35
1614 A752 50c Rio Pilcomayo .55 .35
1615 A752 50c Tierra del Fuego .55 .35
1616 A752 50c Iguacu .55 .35
Nos. 1612-1616 (5) 2.75 1.75

See #1647-1651, 1715-1719, 1742-1746.

Landscapes in Buenos Aires Painted
by Jose Cannella — A753

1988-89   Litho.   Perf. 13½
1617 A753 5a Caminito 2.00 1.10
1618 A753 10a Viejo Al-
macen 4.00 2.25
1618A A753 10a like No.
1618 1.10 .50
1618B A753 50a like No.
1617 1.10 .50
c.   Wmk 365 125.00 20.00
Nos. 1617-1618B (4) 8.20 4.35

No. 1618 inscribed "Viejo Almacen"; No.
1618A inscribed "El Viejo Almacen."
Issue dates: 5a, #1618, 3/15; #1618A,
10/20; 50a, 5/30/89.
For overprint see No. 1635.

Minstrel
in a
Tavern,
by
Carlos
Morel
A754

Paintings: No. 1620, Interior of Curuzu, by
Candido Lopez.

1988, Mar. 19   Litho.   Perf. 13½
1619 A754 1a shown .60 .30
1620 A754 1a multicolored .60 .30

See Nos. 1640-1641.

Argentine-Brazilian Economic
Cooperation and Integration Program
for Mutual Growth — A755

1988, Mar. 19
1621 A755 1a multicolored .50 .25

Cities of Alta Gracia and Corrientes,
400th Annivs. — A756

1988, Apr. 9   Litho.   Perf. 13½
1622 A756 1a Alta Gracia Church .75 .40
1623 A756 1a Chapel of St. Anne,
Corrientes .75 .40

Labor Day — A757

Grain Carriers, a tile mosaic by Alfredo
Guido, Line D of Nueve de Julio station, Bue-
nos Aires subway: a, (UL). b, (UR). c, (LL). d,
(LR).

1988, May 21
1624 A757 Block of 4 3.00 2.00
a.-d.   50c any single .50 .50

1988 Summer
Olympics,
Seoul — A758

1988, July 16   Litho.   Perf. 13½
1625 A758 1a Running .30 .20
1626 A758 2a Soccer .75 .30
1627 A758 3a Field hockey 1.10 .50
1628 A758 4a Tennis 1.40 .65
Nos. 1625-1628 (4) 3.55 1.65

Mendoza Bank, Cent. — A759

Natl.
Gendarmerie,
Cent. — A760

1988, Aug. 13
1629 A759 2a multicolored .65 .45
1630 A760 2a multicolored .65 .45

Sarmiento and Cathedral School to
the North, Buenos Aires — A761

1988, Sept. 10   Litho.   Perf. 13½
1631 A761 3a multicolored .65 .45

Domingo Faustino Sarmiento (1811-1888),
educator, politician.

St. Cayetano, Patron of Workers
A762

El Amor, by Antonio Berni, Pacific Gallery, Buenos Aires — A763

1988, Sept. 10   **Litho.**
1632 A762 2a multicolored   .45   .45
1633 A762 3a Our Lady of Car-
     men, Cuyo   .70   .70

Souvenir Sheet
Perf. 12
1634 A763 5a multicolored   1.00 1.00
Liniers Philatelic Circle and the Argentine Western Philatelic Institution (IFADO), 50th anniv.
No. 1634 contains one 40x30mm stamp.

No. 1617 Ovptd. with Congress Emblem and:
"XXI CONGRESO DE LA SOCIEDAD INTERNACIONAL DE UROLOGIA"
1988, Oct. 29   **Litho.**   **Perf. 13½**
1635 A753 5a multicolored   3.50   .40
21st Congress of the Intl. Urology Soc.

Tourism
A763a

1988, Nov. 1   **Litho.**   **Perf. 13½**
1635A A763a 3a Purmamarca,
     Jujuy   .50   .25
Size: 28½x38mm
1635B A763a 20a Ushuaia   3.35 1.60

Buenos Aires Subway, 75th Anniv.
A764

1988, Dec. 17   **Litho.**   **Perf. 13½**
1636 A764 5a Train, c. 1913   1.10   .55

Christmas
A765

Frescoes in Ucrania Cathedral, Buenos Aires: No. 1637, *Virgin Patron.* No. 1638, *Virgin of Tenderness.*
1988, Dec. 17
1637 A765 5a multicolored   1.25   .50
1638 A765 5a multicolored   1.25   .50

St. John Bosco (1815-1888), Educator, and Church in Ushuaia — A766

1989, Apr. 8   **Litho.**   **Perf. 13½**
1639 A766 5a multicolored   .30   .20
Dated 1988.

Art Type of 1988
Paintings: No. 1640, *Blancos,* by Fernando Fader (1882-1935). No. 1641, *Rincon de los Areneros,* by Justo Lynch (1870-1953).
1989, Apr. 8
1640 A754 5a multicolored   .50   .20
1641 A754 5a multicolored   .50   .20

Holy Week
A767

Sculpture and churches: No. 1642, *The Crown of Thorns,* Calvary of Tandil, and Church of Our Lady Carmelite, Tandil. No. 1643, *Jesus the Nazarene* and Metropolitan Cathedral, Buenos Aires. No. 1644, *Jesus Encounters His Mother* (scene of the crucifixion), La Quebrada Village, San Luis. No. 1645, *Our Lady of Sorrow* and Church of Humahuaca, Jujuy.
1989, Apr. 22   **Litho.**   **Perf. 13½**
1642 A767 2a multicolored   .20   .20
1643 A767 2a multicolored   .20   .20
1644 A767 3a multicolored   .30   .20
1645 A767 3a multicolored   .30   .20
     Nos. 1642-1645 (4)   1.00   .80
Printed in sheets of 16+4 labels containing blocks of 4 of each design. Labels picture Jesus's arrival in Jerusalem (Palm Sunday).

Prevent Alcoholism — A768

1989, Apr. 22
1646 A768 5a multicolored   .30   .20

Natl. Park Type of 1987
1989, May 6   **Perf. 13x13½**
1647 A752 5a Lihue Calel   .70   .20
1648 A752 5a El Palmar   .70   .20
1649 A752 5a Calilegua   .70   .20
1650 A752 5a Chaco   .70   .20
1651 A752 5a Los Glaciares   .70   .20
     Nos. 1647-1651 (5)   3.50 1.00

Admission of Argentina to the ITU, Cent. — A769

1989, May 6   **Perf. 13½**
1652 A769 10a multicolored   .45   .20

World Model Aircraft Championships — A770

1989, May 27   **Litho.**   **Perf. 13½**
1653 A770 5a F1A glider   .20   .20
1654 A770 5a F1B rubber band
     motor   .20   .20
1655 A770 10a F1C gas motor   .35   .20
     Nos. 1653-1655 (3)   .75   .60

French Revolution, Bicent. — A771

Designs: 10a, "All men are born free and equal." 15a, French flag and *La Marianne,* by Gandon. 25a, *Liberty Guiding the People,* by Delacroix.
1989, July 1   **Litho.**   **Perf. 13½**
1656 A771 10a shown   .50   .20
1657 A771 15a multicolored   .50   .20
Souvenir Sheet
Perf. 12
1658 A771 25a multicolored   .25   .20
No. 1658 contains one 40x30mm stamp.

The Republic, a Bronze Bust in the Congreso de la Nacion, Buenos Aires — A772

1989, Aug. 12   **Litho.**   **Perf. 13½**
1659 A772 300a on 50a multi   .75   .50
Peaceful transition of power (presidential office). Not issued without surcharge.

Immigration to Argentina — A773

1989, Aug. 19   **Perf. 13½**
1660 A773 150a S.S. *Weser,*
     1889   .65   .35
1661 A773 200a Immigrant hotel,
     1889   .75   .45
Souvenir Sheet
Perf. 12
1662   Sheet of 2   1.60 1.60
  a.   A773 150a like No. 1660   .65   .35
  b.   A773 200a like No. 1661   .75   .45
No. 1662 contains 40c30mm stamps.

Famous Men
A774

Designs: No. 1663, Fr. Guillermo Furlong (1889-1974), historian, and title page of *The Jesuits.* No. 1664, Dr. Gregorio Alvarez (1889-1986), physician, and title page of *Canto a Chos Malal.* 200a, Brig.-Gen. Enrique Martinez (1789-1870) and lithograph *La Batalla de Maipu,* by Teodoro Gericault.
1989, Oct. 7   **Litho.**   **Perf. 13½**
1663 A774 150a multicolored   .35   .20
1664 A774 150a multicolored   .35   .20
1665 A774 200a multicolored   .35   .20
     Nos. 1663-1665 (3)   1.05   .60

America Issue — A775

Emblem of the Postal Union of the Americas and Spain (PUAS) and pre-Columbian art from Catamarca Province: 200a, Wooden mask from Atajo, Loma Morada. 300a, Urn of the Santa Maria Culture (Phase 3) from Punta de Balastro, Santa Maria Department.
1989, Oct. 14
1666 A775 200a multicolored   .50   .35
1667 A775 300a multicolored   .75   .50

Federal Police Week — A776

Children's drawings: No. 1668, Diego Molinari, age 13. No. 1669, Carlos Alberto Sarago, age 8. No. 1670, Roxana Andrea Osuna, age 7. No. 1671, Pablo Javier Quaglia, age 9.
1989, Oct. 28   **Litho.**   **Perf. 13½**
1668 A776 100a multi   .25   .20
1669 A776 100a multi   .25   .20
1670 A776 150a multi   .40   .20
1671 A776 150a multi   .40   .20
     Nos. 1668-1671 (4)   1.30   .80

Battle of Vuelta de Obligado, 1845 — A777

Illustration reduced.

1989, Dec. 2   **Litho.**   **Perf. 13x13½**
1672 A777 300a multicolored   .40   .20

Paintings — A778

Cristo de los Cerros, Sculpture by Chipo Cespedes A779

1989, Dec. 2   **Perf. 13½**
1673 A778 200a Gato Frias   .35 .20
1674 A778 200a Maria Carballido .35 .20
1675 A779 300a shown   .35 .20
   Nos. 1673-1675 (3)   1.05 .60
            Christmas.

Buenos Aires Port, Cent. — A780

Illustration reduced.

1990, Mar. 3   **Litho.**   **Perf. 13½**
1676 A780 Strip of 4   7.50 6.00
a.-d. 200a any single   1.25   .65

Aconcagua Intl. Fair, Mendoza — A781

Design: Aconcagua mountain, Los Horcones Lagoon and fair emblem. Illustration reduced.

1990, Mar. 3
1677 A781 Pair, #a.-b.   2.00 1.50

Natl. Savings and Insurance Fund, 75th Anniv. — A782

1990, May 5   **Litho.**   **Perf. 13½**
1678 A782 1000a multicolored   .35 .20

Miniature Sheet

1990 World Cup Soccer Championships, Italy — A783

Designs: a, Athlete's torso (striped jersey). b, Athlete's torso (solid jersey). c, Players' feet, soccer ball. d, Player (knee to waist).

1990, May 5
1679 A783 Sheet of 4   5.00 5.00
a.-d. 2500a multicolored   1.00 1.00

Carlos Pellegrini, Commercial High School Founder, Cent. — A784

1990, June 2   **Litho.**   **Perf. 13½**
1680 A784 2000a multicolored   .30 .20

Youth Against Drugs A785

1990, June 2
1681 A785 2000a multicolored   .30 .20

Intl. Literacy Year A786

1990, July 14   **Litho.**   **Perf. 13½**
1682 A786 2000a multicolored   .30 .20

Flower Type of 1982 in New Currency
1989-90   **Photo.**   **Perf. 13½**
1683 A641 10a like #1433   .20 .20
1684 A641 20a like #1435A   .20 .20
1685 A641 50a like #1354   .20 .20
1686 A641 100a like #1439   .20 .20
1687 A641 300a like #1345   .40 .20
1688 A641 500a like #1441   .65 .35
1689 A641 1000a like #1355   .20 .20
1690 A641 5000a like #1349   1.00 .70
1691 A641 10,000a like #1350 1.50 1.00
   Nos. 1683-1691 (9)   4.55 3.25

Issued: 20a, 100a, 300a, 8/1/89; 10a, 8/24/89; 50a, 8/30/89; 1000, 3/8/90; 5000a, 4/6/90; 10,000a, 7/2/90.

World Basketball Championships A787

1990, Aug. 11   **Litho.**   **Perf. 13½**
1703 A787 2000a multicolored 2.00 1.50
            Souvenir Sheet
               Perf. 12
1704 A787 5000a Jump ball   3.75 2.75

Postal Union of the Americas and Spain, 14th Congress — A788

1990, Sept. 15   **Litho.**   **Perf. 13½**
1705 A788 3000a Arms, seal   1.50 .75
1706 A788 3000a Sailing ships 1.50 .75
1707 A788 3000a Modern freighter 1.50 .75

1708 A788 3000a Van, cargo plane 1.50 .75
   Nos. 1705-1708 (4)   6.00 3.00

America Issue A789

1990, Oct. 13
1709 A789 3000a Iguacu Falls, hamelia erecta 1.50 .60
1710 A789 3000a Puerto Deseado, elephant seal 1.50 .60

Natl. Parks Type of 1987
1990, Oct. 27   **Perf. 13x13½**
1715 A752 3000a Lanin   1.50 .65
1716 A752 3000a Laguna Blanca 1.50 .65
1717 A752 3000a Perito Moreno 1.50 .65
1718 A752 3000a Puelo   1.50 .65
1719 A752 3000a El Rey   1.50 .65
   Nos. 1715-1719 (5)   7.50 3.25

Stamp Day A790

1990, Oct. 27   **Perf. 13½**
1720 A790 3000a multicolored 1.50 .60

Salvation Army, Cent. — A793

Designs: No. 1722, Natl. University of the Littoral, Santa Fe, cent.

1990, Dec. 1   **Litho.**   **Perf. 13½**
1721 A793 3000a multicolored 1.75 1.00
1722 A793 3000a multicolored 1.75 1.00
a. Pair, #1721-1722 + label 3.75 2.25

Miniature Sheets

Christmas — A794

Stained glass windows: No. 1723, The Immaculate Conception. No. 1724, The Nativity. No. 1725, Presentation of Jesus at the Temple.

1990, Dec. 1   **Perf. 13½x13**
            Sheets of 4
1723 A794 3000a #a.-d.   6.00 6.00
1724 A794 3000a #a.-d.   6.00 6.00
1725 A794 3000a #a.-d.   6.00 6.00

Landscapes — A795

Paintings: No. 1726, Los Sauces, by Atilio Malinverno. No. 1727, Paisaje, by Pio Collivadino, vert.

1991, May 4   **Litho.**   **Perf. 13½**
1726 A795 4000a multicolored 1.00 .85
1727 A795 4000a multicolored 1.00 .85

Return of Remains of Juan Manuel de Rosas (1793-1877) A796

1991, June 1   **Litho.**   **Perf. 13½**
1728 A796 4000a multicolored 1.00 .85

Swiss Confederation, 700th Anniv. — A797

1991, Aug. 3   **Litho.**   **Perf. 13½**
1729 A797 4000a multicolored   .95 .80

Miniature Sheet

Cartoons A798

Designs: a, Hernan, the Corsair by Jose Luis Salinas. b, Don Fulgencio by Lino Palacio. c, Medical Rules of Salerno by Oscar Esteban Conti. d, Buenos Aires Undershirt by Alejandro del Prado. e, Girls! by Jose A.G. Divito. f, Langostino by Eduardo Carlos Ferro. g, Mafalda by Joaquin Salvador Lavoro. h, Mort Cinder by Alberto Breccia.

1991, Aug. 3
1730 A798 4000a Sheet of 8, #a.-h. 7.75 7.50

City of La Rioja, 400th Anniv. — A799

1991, Sept. 14   Litho.   *Perf. 13½*
1731 A799 4000a multicolored   1.00 .85

First Balloon Flight over the Andes, 75th Anniv. — A800

Illustration reduced.

1991, Sept. 14
1732 A800 4000a multicolored   1.00 .85

America Issue A801

#1733, Magellan's caravel, Our Lady of Victory. #1734, Ships of Juan Diaz de Solis.

1991, Nov. 9   Litho.   *Perf. 13½*
1733 A801 4000a multicolored   1.00 .80
1734 A801 4000a multicolored   1.00 .80

Anniversaries — A802

Designs: a, J. Enrique Pestalozzi, founder of newspaper, Daily Argentinian. b, Leandro N. Alem, founder of Radical People's Party. c, Man with rifle, emblem of Argentine Federal Shooting Club. d, Dr. Nicasio Etchepareborda, emblem of College of Odontology. e, Dalmiro Huergo, emblem of Graduate School of Economics.

1991, Nov. 30
1735 A802 4000a Strip of 5, #a.-e.   5.00 4.00

Christmas — A803

Stained glass windows from Our Lady of Lourdes Basilica, Buenos Aires: Nos. 1736a-1736b, Top and bottom portions of Virgin of the Valley, Catamarca. Nos. 1736c-1736d, Top and bottom portions of Virgin of the Rosary of the Miracle, Cordoba.

1991, Nov. 30
1736 A803 4000a Block of 4, #a.-d.   5.00 3.50

Famous Men A804

Designs: a, Gen. Juan de Lavalle (1797-1841), Peruvian medal of honor. b, Brig. Gen. Jose Maria del Rosario Siriaco Paz (1791-1854), medal. c, Marco Manuel de Avellaneda (1813-1841), lawyer. d, Guillermo Enrique Hudson (1841-1922), author.

1991, Dec. 14   Litho.   *Perf. 13½*
1737 A804 4000a Block of 4, #a.-d.   5.00 3.50

Birds — A805

1991, Dec. 28
1738 A805 4000a Pterocnemia pennata   1.25 .85
1739 A805 4000a Morphnu guianensis   1.25 .85
1740 A805 4000a Ara chloroptera   1.25 .85
   Nos. 1738-1740 (3)   3.75 2.55

Miniature Sheet

Arbrafex '92, Argentina-Brazil Philatelic Exhibition — A806

Traditional costumes: a, Gaucho, woman. b, Gaucho, horse. c, Gaucho in store. d, Gaucho holding lariat.

1992   Litho.   *Perf. 13½*
1741 A806 38c Sheet of 4, #a.-d.   5.00 4.00

Natl. Parks Type of 1987

1992, Apr. 4   Litho.   *Perf. 13x13½*
1742 A752 38c Alerces   .75 .55
1743 A752 38c Formosa Nature Reserve   .75 .55
1744 A752 38c Petrified Forest   .75 .55
1745 A752 38c Arrayanes   .75 .55
1746 A752 38c Laguna de los Pozuelos   .75 .55
   Nos. 1742-1746 (5)   3.75 2.75

Mushrooms — A807

1992-94   Photo.   *Perf. 13½*
1748 A807 10c Psilocybe cubensis   .20 .20
1749 A807 25c Coprinus atramentarius   .50 .35
   a.   Wmk. 365   30.00 30.00
1750 A807 38c like #1748   .75 .55
1751 A807 48c like #1749   .95 .65
1752 A807 50c Suillus granulatus   1.00 .70
1753 A807 51c Morchella esculenta   1.00 .70
1754 A807 61c Amanita muscaria   1.25 .85
1755 A807 68c Coprinus comatus   1.25 .85
1756 A807 1p like #1754   2.00 1.40
1757 A807 1.25p like #1752   2.50 1.75
1758 A807 1.77p Stropharia oeruginosa   3.50 2.50
1759 A807 2p like #1753   4.00 2.75
   Nos. 1748-1759 (12)   18.90 13.25

No. 1758 not issued without overprint "Centro Filatelico de Neuquen y Rio Negro 50th Aniversario."

Issued: 38c, 4/4/92; 48c, 51c, 61c, 8/1/92; 1.77p, 11/7/92; 25c, 50c, 8/17/93; 1p, 2p, 8/26/93; 10c, 1/11/94; 68c, 1.25p, 10/10/92; #1749a, 1997.

See design A838.

Falkland Islands War, 10th Anniv. A808

1992, May 2   Litho.   *Perf. 13½*
1767 A808 38c Pucara 1A-58   .75 .55
1768 A808 38c Cruiser Gen. Belgrano   .75 .55
1769 A808 38c Soldier and truck   .75 .55
   Nos. 1767-1769 (3)   2.25 1.65

Miniature Sheet

Preserve the Environment — A809

a, Deer. b, Geese. c, Butterflies. d, Whale.

1992, June 6   Litho.   *Perf. 12*
1770 A809 38c Sheet of 4, #a.-d.   5.00 4.00

Paintings by Florencio Molina Campos — A810

1992, June 6   *Perf. 13½*
1771 A810 38c A La Sombra   .75 .55
1772 A810 38c Tileforo Areco, vert.   .75 .55

Famous Men A811

Designs: No. 1773, Gen. Lucio N. Mansilla (1792-1871). No. 1774, Jose Manuel Estrada (1842-1894), writer. No. 1775, Brig. Gen. Jose I. Garmendia (1842-1915).

1992, July 4   Litho.   *Perf. 13½*
1773 A811 38c multicolored   .75 .55
1774 A811 38c multicolored   .75 .55
1775 A811 38c multicolored   .75 .55
   Nos. 1773-1775 (3)   2.25 1.65

Fight Against Drugs — A812

1992, Aug. 1   *Perf. 13½x13*
1776 A812 38c multicolored   .75 .55

Col. Jose M. Calaza, 140th Birth Anniv. A813

1992, Sept. 5   Litho.   *Perf. 13½*
1777 A813 38c multicolored   .75 .55

Discovery of America, 500th Anniv. — A814

Designs: a, Columbus, castle, ship. b, Native drawings, Columbus.

1992, Oct. 10   Litho.   *Perf. 13½*
1778 A814 38c Pair, #a.-b.   1.50 1.50

Argentine Film Posters A815

1992, Nov. 7   Litho.   *Perf. 13½*
1779 A815 38c Dios Se Lo Pague, 1948   .75 .55
1780 A815 38c Las Aguas Bajan Turbias, 1952   .75 .55
1781 A815 38c Un Guapo Del 900, 1960   .75 .55
1782 A815 38c La Tregua, 1974   .75 .55
1783 A815 38c La Historia Oficial, 1984   .75 .55
   Nos. 1779-1783 (5)   3.75 2.75

Christmas
A816

1992, Nov. 28
1784 A816 38c multicolored   .75 .55

Miniature Sheet

Iberoprenfil '92 — A817

Lighthouses: a, Punta Mogotes. b, Rio
Negro. c, San Antonio. d, Cabo Blanco.

1992, Dec. 5
1785 A817 38c Sheet of 4, #a.-d. 5.00 3.00

Fight Against AIDS
A818   A819

1992, Dec. 12 Litho. Perf. 13½
1786 A818 10c multicolored   1.00 .30
1787 A819 26c multicolored   2.00 .50

Intl.
Space
Year
A820

1992, Dec. 19
1788 A820 38c multicolored   .75 .55

Souvenir Sheet

Miraculous Lord Crucifix, 400th Anniv.
of Arrival in America — A821

1992, Dec. 26   Perf. 12
1789 A821 76c multicolored   1.50 1.50

Jujuy City,
400th
Anniv. — A822

1993, Apr. 24 Litho. Perf. 13½
1790 A822 38c multicolored   .75 .55

Argentina Soccer Assoc.,
Cent. — A823

1993, Mar. 27
1791 A823 38c multicolored   .75 .55

Souvenir Sheet

Intl.
Philatelic
Exhibitions
A824

Designs: a, 38c, City Hall, Poznan, Poland.
b, 48c, Statue of Christ the Redeemer, Rio de
Janeiro, Brazil. c, 76c, Royal Palace, Bangkok,
Thailand.

1993, May 8 Litho. Perf. 12
1792 A824 Sheet of 3, #a.-c. 4.00 3.25
  Polska '93 (#1792a), Brasiliana '93
(#1792b), Bangkok '92 (#1792c).

Luis C. Candelaria's Flight Over
Andes Mountains, 75th Anniv. — A825

1993, June 26 Litho. Perf. 13x13½
1793 A825 38c multicolored   .75 .55
    Illustration reduced.

Order of San
Martin, 50th
Anniv. — A826

National
History
Academy,
Cent. — A827

1993, May 29   Perf. 13½
1794 A826 38c multicolored   .75 .55
1795 A827 38c multicolored   .75 .55

Armed Forces
Memorial
Day — A828

1993, June 12
1796 A828 38c Natl. Gendarme-
    rie   .75 .55
1797 A828 38c Coast Guard .75 .55

Paintings — A829

  #1798, Old House, by Norberto Russo.
#1799, Pa'las Casas, by Adriana Zaefferer.

1993, Aug. 14 Litho. Perf. 13½
1798 A829 38c multicolored   .75 .55
1799 A829 38c multicolored   .75 .55

Pato — A830

1993, Aug. 28 Litho. Perf. 12
1800 A830 1p multicolored   2.00 1.40

Nut-Bearing Trees — A831

  #1801, Enterolobium contortisiliquum.
#1802, Prosopis alba. #1803, Magnolia
grandiflora. #1804, Erythrina falcata. Illustration reduced.

1993, Sept. 25 Litho. Perf. 13x13½
1801 A831 75c multicolored   1.50 1.00
1802 A831 75c multicolored   1.50 1.00
1803 A831 1.50p multicolored 3.00 2.00
1804 A831 1.50p multicolored 3.00 2.00
    Nos. 1801-1804 (4) 9.00 6.00

America
Issue
A832

  Whales: 50c, Eubalaena australis. 75c,
Cephalorhynchus commersonii.

1993, Oct. 9   Perf. 13½
1805 A832 50c multicolored   1.00 .70
1806 A832 75c multicolored   1.50 1.10

Miniature Sheet

Christmas,
New
Year — A833

  Denomination at: a, UL. b, UR. c, LL. d, LR.

1993, Dec. 4 Litho. Perf. 13½
1807 A833 75c Sheet of 4, #a.-d. 6.00 6.00

Cave of the
Hands, Santa
Cruz — A834

1993, Dec. 18
1808 A834 1p multicolored   2.00 1.40

New Emblem, Argentine Postal
Service — A835

Illustration reduced.

1994, Jan. 8   *Perf. 11½*
1809 A835 75c multicolored   6.00 .75

A836

1994 World Cup Soccer
Championships, US — A837

Players from: 25c, Germany, 1990. 50c,
Brazil, 1970. 75c, 1.50p, Argentina, 1986. 1p,
Italy, 1982.

1994, June 11   Litho.   *Perf. 13½*
1810 A836 25c multicolored   .50 .20
1811 A836 50c multicolored   1.00 .70
1812 A836 75c multicolored   1.50 1.00
1813 A836 1p multicolored   2.00 1.40
     Nos. 1810-1813 (4)   5.00 3.30

Souvenir Sheet
Perf. 12

1814 A836 1.50p multicolored   3.00 3.00

No. 1814 contains one 40x50mm stamp
with continuous design.

1994, July 23   *Perf. 13½*
Drawings of championships by: No. 1815,
Julian Lisenberg. No. 1816, Matias Taylor,
vert. No. 1817, Torcuato S. Gonzalez Agote,
vert. No. 1818, Maria Paula Palma.

1815 A837 75c multicolored   1.50 1.00
1816 A837 75c multicolored   1.50 1.00
1817 A837 75c multicolored   1.50 1.00
1818 A837 75c multicolored   1.50 1.00
     Nos. 1815-1818 (4)   6.00 4.00

Issued in sheet containing a block of 4 of
each stamp + 4 labels.

A838

Molothrus Badius — A838a

1994-95   Litho.   *Perf. 13½*
1819 A838 10c like #1748   .20 .20
1820 A838 25c like #1749   .50 .35
1823 A838 50c like #1752   1.00 .70
1828 A838 1p like #1754   2.00 1.40

1832 A838   2p like #1753   4.00 2.75
1835 A838a 9.40p multicolored   19.00 13.00
     Nos. 1819-1835 (6)   26.70 18.40

See design A807.
Issued: 10c, 25c, 50c, 1p, 2p, 6/14/94;
9.40p, 4/12/95.
This is an expanding set. Numbers may
change.

Wildlife of
Falkland
Islands
A839

Designs: 25c, Melanodera melanodera. 50c,
Pygoscelis papua. 75c, Tachyeres
brachypterus. 1p, Mirounga leonina.

1994, Aug 6
1839 A839 25c multicolored   .50 .35
1840 A839 50c multicolored   1.00 .70
1841 A839 75c multicolored   1.50 1.00
1842 A839 1p multicolored   2.00 1.40
     Nos. 1839-1842 (4)   5.00 3.45

City of San
Luis, 400th
Anniv. — A840

1994, Aug. 20
1843 A840 75c multicolored   1.50 1.00

Province of
Tierra del
Fuego,
Antarctica and
South Atlantic
Islands
A841

1994, Aug. 20
1844 A841 75c multicolored   1.50 1.00

Argentine Inventors — A842

Designs: No. 1845, Ladislao Jose Biro
(1899-1985), ball point pen. No. 1846, Raul
Pateras de Pescara (1890-1966), helicopter.
No. 1847, Quirino Cristiani (1896-1984),
animated drawings. No. 1848, Enrique
Finochietto (1881-1948), surgical instruments.

1994, Oct. 1
1845 A842 75c multicolored   1.50 1.00
1846 A842 75c multicolored   1.50 1.00
1847 A842 75c multicolored   1.50 1.00
1848 A842 75c multicolored   1.50 1.00
  a.   Block of 4, #1845-1848   6.00 6.00

Issued in sheets containing 4 #1848a + 4
labels.

UNICEF
Christmas
A843

1994, Nov. 26   Litho.   *Perf. 11½*
1849 A843 50c shown   1.00 .70
1850 A843 75c Bell, bulb, star,
                  diff.   1.50 1.00

Take
Care of
Our
Planet
A844

Children's paintings: No. 1851, Boy, girl
holding earth, vert. No. 1852, Children outdoors, vert. No. 1853, World as house. No.
1854, People around "world" table.

1994, Dec. 3   *Perf. 13½*
1851 A844 25c multicolored   .50 .35
1852 A844 25c multicolored   .50 .35
1853 A844 50c multicolored   1.00 .70
1854 A844 50c multicolored   1.00 .70
     Nos. 1851-1854 (4)   3.00 2.10

Christmas — A845

1994, Dec. 10
1855 A845 50c Annunciation   1.00 .70
1856 A845 75c Madonna & Child   1.50 1.00

Nos. 1855-1856 each issued in sheets of 20
+ 5 labels.

12th Pan American Games, Mar del
Plata — A846

1995   Litho.   *Perf. 13½*
1857 A846 75c Running   1.50 1.00
1858 A846 75c Cycling   1.50 1.00
1859 A846 75c Diving   1.50 1.00
1860 A846 1.25p Gymnastics,
                  vert.   2.50 1.75
1861 A846 1.25p Soccer, vert.   2.50 1.75
     Nos. 1857-1861 (5)   9.50 6.50

Issued: No. 1857, 2/18; others, 3/11.

Natl. Constitution — A847

Design: 75c, Natl. Congress Dome, woman
from statue The Republic Triumphant.

1995, Apr. 8
1862 A847 75c multicolored   1.50 1.00

21st Intl. Book Fair — A848

Illustration reduced.

1995, Apr. 8
1863 A848 75c multicolored   1.50 1.00

Birds
A849

1995   Litho.   *Perf. 13½*
1876 A849 5p Carduelis
               magellanica   10.00 7.00
1880 A849 10p Zonotrichia
               capensis   20.00 14.00

Issued: 5p, 10p, 5/23/95. This is an
expanding set. Numbers may change.

A850

1995, Mar. 25   Litho.   Die Cut
Self-Adhesive
1883A A850 25c multicolored   8.00 .35
1884 A850 75c multicolored   2.00 1.00
  a.   Booklet pane, 2 #1883A, 6
         #1884   12.50
         Complete booklet, #1884a 50.00
  b.   Booklet pane, 4 #1883A, 12
         #1884   25.00
         Complete booklet, #1884b 80.00

Argentine Engineers' Center,
Cent. — A851

1995, June 3   *Perf. 13½*
1885 A851 75c multicolored   1.50 1.00

Jose Marti (1853-95) — A852

#1887, Antonio Jose de Sucre (1795-1830).

1995, Aug. 12   Litho.   *Perf. 13½*
1886 A852 1p multicolored   2.00 1.40
1887 A852 1p multicolored   2.00 1.40

Fauna — A853

1995, Sept. 1   Litho.   *Perf. 13½*
1888 A853 5c Ostrich   .20 .20
1889 A853 25c Penguin   .50 .35
1890 A853 50c Toucan   1.00 .70
1891 A853 75c Condor   1.50 1.00
1892 A853 1p Owl   2.00 1.40
1893 A853 2p Bigua   4.00 2.75
1894 A853 2.75p Tero   5.50 3.75

Booklet Stamps
Perf. 13½ on 2 or 3 Sides

1895	A853	25c Alligator	.50	.35
1896	A853	50c Fox	1.00	.70
1897	A853	75c Anteater	1.50	1.00
1898	A853	75c Deer	1.50	1.00
1899	A853	75c Whale	1.50	1.00
a.		Booklet pane, 1 each Nos. 1889-1891, 1895-1899	9.00	
		Complete booklet, #1899a	9.00	
		Nos. 1888-1899 (12)	20.70	14.20

See Nos. 1958, 2004-2004A.

Native Heritage — A854

a, Cave drawings, shifting sands. b, Stone mask. c, Anthropomorphous vessel. d, Woven textile.

1995, Sept. 9

1900	A854	75c Block of 4, #a.-d.	6.00	6.00

Sunflower, Postal Service Emblem — A855

1995, Oct. 7

1901	A855	75c multicolored	7.00	.75

Juan D. Peron (1895-1974) — A856

1995, Oct. 7

1902	A856	75c lt ol bis & dk bl	1.50	1.00

Miniature Sheet

Anniversaries — A857

Annivs: a, UN, 50th. b, ICAO, 50th (in 1994). c, FAO, 50th. d, ILO, 75th (in 1994).

1995, Oct. 14   *Perf. 12*

1903	A857	75c Sheet of 4, #a.-d.	6.00	6.00

Christmas and New Year — A858

Designs: Nos. 1904, 1908, Christmas tree, presents. No. 1905, "1996." No. 1906, Champagne glasses. No. 1907, Present.

1995, Nov. 25   **Litho.**   *Perf. 13½*

1904	A858	75c multicolored	1.50	1.00

Booklet Stamps
Perf. 13½ on 1 or 2 Sides

1905	A858	75c multicolored	1.50	1.00
1906	A858	75c multicolored	1.50	1.00
1907	A858	75c multicolored	1.50	1.00
1908	A858	75c multicolored	1.50	1.00
a.		Booklet pane, #1905-1908 + label	6.00	
		Complete booklet, #1908a	6.00	
		Nos. 1904-1908 (5)	7.50	5.00

No. 1908a is a continuous design. Ribbon extends from edge to edge on #1908 and stops at edge of package on #1905.

Miniature Sheet

Motion Pictures, Cent. — A859

Black and white film clips, director: a, The Battleship Potemkin, Sergei Eisenstein (Soviet Union). b, Casablanca, Michael Curtiz (US). c, Bicycle Thief, Vittorio De Sica (Italy). d, Limelights, Charles Chaplin (England). e, The 400 Blows, Francois Truffaut (France). f, Chronicle of the Lonely Child, Leonardo Favio (Argentina).

1995, Dec. 2   *Perf. 13½*

1909	A859	75c Sheet of 6, #a.-f.	9.00	9.00

The Sky — A860

1995, Dec. 16   *Perf. 13½ on 3 Sides*
Booklet Stamps

1910	A860	25c Dirigible	.50	.35
1911	A860	25c Kite	.50	.35
1912	A860	25c Hot air balloon	.50	.35
1913	A860	50c Balloons	1.00	.70
1914	A860	50c Paper airplane	1.00	.70
1915	A860	75c Airplane	1.50	1.00
1916	A860	75c Helicopter	1.50	1.00
1917	A860	75c Parachute	1.50	1.00
a.		Booklet pane, #1910-1917 + label	8.00	
		Complete booklet, No. 1917a	8.00	

Nos. 1910-1917 do not appear in Scott number order in No. 1917a, which has a continuous design.

America Issue A861

Postal vehicles from Postal & Telegraph Museum: #1918, Horse & carriage. #1919, Truck.

1995, Dec. 16   *Perf. 13½*

1918	A861	75c multicolored	1.50	1.00
1919	A861	75c multicolored	1.50	1.00

Olympic Games, Cent. A862

1996, Mar. 30   **Litho.**   *Perf. 13½*

1920	A862	75c Running	1.50	1.00
1921	A862	1p Discus	2.00	1.40

Physicians A863

Designs: a, Francisco J. Muniz (1795-1871). b, Ricardo Gutierrez (1838-96). c, Ignacio Pirovano (1844-95). d, Esteban L. Maradona (1895-1995).

1996, Apr. 20   **Litho.**   *Perf. 12*

1922	A863	50c Sheet of 4	4.00	4.00
a.-d.		Any single	1.00	1.00

Jerusalem, 3000th Anniv. — A864

7th cent. mosaic maps of city, denomination at: No. 1923, LL. No. 1924, LR.

1996, May 18   **Litho.**   *Perf. 13½*

1923	A864	75c multicolored	1.50	1.00
1924	A864	75c multicolored	1.50	1.00
a.		Pair, #1923-1924	5.00	3.00

No. 1924a is a continuous design and was issued in sheets of 8 + 4 labels.

Endangered Fauna — A865

1996, June 15   **Litho.**   *Perf. 13½*

1925	A865	75c Capybara	1.50	1.00
1926	A865	75c Guanaco	1.50	1.00
a.		Pair, #1925-1926	3.00	3.00

America Issue.

Summer Olympic Games A866

Designs: 75c, Torch bearer, Buenos Aires, candidate for 2004 Games. 1p, Men's eight with coxswain, Atlanta, 1996.

1996, July 6

1927	A866	75c multicolored	1.50	1.00
1928	A866	1p multicolored	2.00	1.40

National Parks — A867

Wildlife, national park: No. 1929, Mountain turkey, Diamante. No. 1930, Parrot, San Antonio Nature Reserve. No. 1931, Deer, Otamendi Natl. Reserve. No. 1932, Rabbit, El Leoncito Nature Reserve.

Illustration reduced.

1996, Aug. 24   **Litho.**   *Perf. 13x13½*

1929	A867	75c multicolored	1.50	1.00
1930	A867	75c multicolored	1.50	1.00
1931	A867	75c multicolored	1.50	1.00
1932	A867	75c multicolored	1.50	1.00
		Nos. 1929-1932 (4)	6.00	4.00

Central Post Office, Buenos Aires — A868

1996, Oct. 5   **Litho.**   *Die Cut*
Self-Adhesive
Size: 25x35mm

1933	A868	75c multicolored	1.50	1.50

Vignette of No. 1933 is broken by circular and rectangular die cut areas to guard against reuse.

See Nos. 1983-1984.

Carousel Figures — A869

#1934, Hand-carved decorative ornaments. #1935, Child on carousel horse. #1936, Carousel. #1937, Heads of horses. #1938, Child in airplane. #1939, Carousel pig. #1940, Boy in car.

1996, Oct. 5   *Perf. 13½ Horiz.*
Booklet Stamps

1934	A869	25c multicolored	.50	.50
1935	A869	25c multicolored	.50	.50
1936	A869	25c multicolored	.50	.50
1937	A869	50c multicolored	1.00	1.00
1938	A869	50c multicolored	1.00	1.00
1939	A869	50c multicolored	1.00	1.00
1940	A869	75c multicolored	1.50	1.50
a.		Booklet pane, #1934-1940	6.00	
		Complete booklet, #1940a	6.00	

Sequence of stamps in No. 1940a: No. 1940, 1934, 1937, 1935, 1938, 1936, 1939.

Port Belgrano Naval Base, Cent. — A870

Designs: 25c, LST "San Antonio." 50c, Corvette *Rosales*. 75c, Destroyer *Hercules*. 1p, Aircraft carrier, "25th of May."

1996-97   **Litho.**   *Perf. 13½*

1941	A870	25c multicolored	.50	.50
1942	A870	50c multicolored	1.00	1.00
1943	A870	75c multicolored	1.50	1.50
1944	A870	1p multicolored	2.00	2.00
		Nos. 1941-1944 (4)	5.00	5.00

Issued: 25c, 1p, 10/5/96; 50c, 75c, 2/1/97.

Christmas — A871

Tapestries: 75c, Nativity, by Gladys Angelica Rinaldi, vert. 1p, Candles, by Norma Bonet de Maekawa.

1996, Nov. 30   **Litho.**   **Perf. 13½**
1945 A871 75c multicolored   1.50   1.50
1946 A871 1p multicolored   2.00   2.00

Exploration of Antarctica — A872

Designs: 75c, Melchior Base. 1.25p, Icebreaker ARA Alte. Irizar.

1996, Nov. 30
1947 A872 75c multicolored   1.50   1.50
1948 A872 1.25p multicolored   2.50   2.50

National Gallery, Cent. A873

Paintings of women by: 75c, Paul Gauguin, vert. No. 1950, Edouard Monet, vert. No. 1951, Amedeo Modigliani, vert. 1.25p, Pablo Picasso.

1996, Dec. 14
1949 A873 75c multicolored   1.50   1.50
1950 A873 1p multicolored   2.00   2.00
1951 A873 1p multicolored   2.00   2.00
1952 A873 1.25p multicolored   2.50   2.50
   Nos. 1949-1952 (4)   8.00   8.00

Mining Industry — A874

1997, Feb. 1   **Litho.**   **Perf. 13½**
1953 A874 75c Granite   1.50   1.50
1954 A874 1.25p Borax   2.50   2.50

Traditional Costumes — A875

1997, Feb. 22   **Litho.**   **Perf. 13½**
1955 A875 75c multicolored   1.50   1.50
   America issue.

Repatriation of the Curved Sword of Gen. San Martin, Cent. — A876

1997, Mar. 15   **Litho.**   **Perf. 13½**
1956 A876 75c multicolored   1.50   1.50

29th Youth Rugby World Championships — A877

1997, Mar. 22
1957 A877 75c multicolored   1.50   1.50

Fauna Type of 1995

1997, Feb. 22   **Litho.**   **Perf. 13½**
1958 A853 10c Reddish sandpiper   .20   .20

Buenos Aires-Rio de Janeiro Regatta, 50th Anniv. — A879

1997, Apr. 5   **Litho.**   **Perf. 13½**
1960 A879 75c Fortuna II   1.50   1.50

Natl. History Museum, Cent. — A880

1997, May 17
1961 A880 75c multicolored   1.50   1.50

La Plata Natl. University, Cent. — A881

1997, May 17
1962 A881 75c multicolored   1.50   1.50

Lighthouses A882

a, Cabo Virgenes. b, Isla Pingüino. c, San Juan de Salvamento. d, Punta Delgada.

1997, May 31
1963 A882 75c Sheet of 4, #a.-d.   6.00   6.00

Ramón J. Cárcano (1860-1946), Developer of Postal and Telegraph System A883

1997, May 31
1964 A883 75c multicolored   1.50   1.50

Buenos Aires, Candidate for 2004 Summer Olympics — A884

1997, June 21
1965 A884 75c multicolored   1.50   1.50

First Electric Tram in Buenos Aires, Cent. A885

Designs: a, Lacroze Suburban Service Tram Co., 1912. b, Lacroze Urban Service Tram Co., 1907. c, Anglo Argentina Tram Co., 1930. d, Buenos Aires City Transportation Corp., 1942. e, Military Manufacture Tram, 1956. f, South Electric Tram, 1908.

1997, July 12
   Sheet of 6
1966 A885 75c #a.-f. + 2 labels   9.00   9.00

Monument to Joaquín V. González (1863-1923), La Rioja — A886

1997, Aug. 9
1967 A886 75c multicolored   1.50   1.50

Musicians and Composers A887

Paintings: No. 1968, Alberto Ginastera (1916-83), by Carlos Nine. No. 1969, Astor Piazzolla (1921-92), by Carlos Alonso. No. 1970, Anibal Troilo (1914-75), by Hermenegildo Sabat. No. 1971, Atahualpa Yupanqui (b. 1908), by Luis Scafati.

1997, Aug. 9
1968 A887 75c multicolored   1.50   1.50
1969 A887 75c multicolored   1.50   1.50
1970 A887 75c multicolored   1.50   1.50
1971 A887 75c multicolored   1.50   1.50
   Nos. 1968-1971 (4)   6.00   6.00

Argentine Authors — A888

#1972, Jorge Luis Borges (1899-1986), maze. #1973, Julio Cortázar (1914-84), hop scotch game.

1997, Aug. 30   **Litho.**   **Perf. 13**
1972 A888 1p multicolored   2.00   2.00
1973 A888 1p multicolored   2.00   2.00

Women's Political Rights Law, 50th Anniv. A889

1997, Sept. 6   **Litho.**   **Perf. 13½**
1974 A889 75c Eva Perón   3.00   1.50

Mercosur (Common Market of Latin America) A890

1997, Sept. 27   **Litho.**   **Perf. 13½**
1975 A890 75c multicolored   1.50   1.50
   See Bolivia #1019, Brazil #2646, Paraguay #2564, Uruguay #1681.

Launching of Frigate President Sarmiento, Cent. — A891

#1976, Painting of ship by Hugo Leban.

#1977: a, Ship. b, Ship's figurehead, vert.

1997, Oct. 4
1976 A891 75c multicolored   1.50 1.50
Souvenir Sheet
Perf. 12
1977 A891 75c Sheet of 2, #a.-b. 5.00 3.00
No. 1977 contains two 40x30mm stamps.

Ernesto "Che"
Guevara
(1928-67)
A892

1997, Oct. 18
1978 A892 75c multicolored   5.00 1.50

Ecology on Stamps — A893

Children's drawings: No. 1979, Animal, by J. Chiapparo, vert. No. 1980, Vicuna, by L.L. Portal, vert. No. 1981, Seal, by A. Lloren. No. 1982, Bird in flight, by J. Saccone.

1997, Nov. 8   **Litho.**   *Perf. 13½*
1979 A893 50c multicolored   1.00 1.00
1980 A893 50c multicolored   1.00 1.00
1981 A893 75c multicolored   1.50 1.50
1982 A893 75c multicolored   1.50 1.50
    Nos. 1979-1982 (4)   5.00 5.00

**Central Post Office, Buenos Aires,
Type of 1996**

1997, July 24   **Litho.**   *Die Cut*
Self-Adhesive
Size: 23x35mm
1983 A868 25c multicolored   .50   .50
1984 A868 75c multicolored   1.50 1.50
  a. Bklt. pane, 2 #1983, 6 #1984 10.00
         Complete booklet, #1984a   10.00
Nos. 1983-1984 are broken at both the top and bottom of each stamp by three lines of wavy die cutting.

Christmas — A893a

Nativity scene tapestries by: #1984B, 1984G, Mary José. #1984C, Elena Aguilar. #1984D, Silvia Pettachi. #1984E, Ana Escobar. #1984F, Alejandra Martinez. #1984H, Nidia Martinez.

1997, Nov. 22   **Litho.**   *Perf. 13½*
1984B A893a 75c multicolored   1.50 1.50
Booklet Stamps
Self-Adhesive
Size: 44x27mm
Die Cut
1984C A893a 25c multicolored   .50   .50
1984D A893a 25c multicolored   .50   .50
1984E A893a 50c multicolored   1.00 1.00
1984F A893a 50c multicolored   1.00 1.00
1984G A893a 75c multicolored   1.50 1.50
1984H A893a 75c multicolored   1.50 1.50
  i. Booklet pane, #1984C-
          1984H   6.00
Nos. 1984C-1984H are broken at upper right by three die cut chevrons.

Mother Teresa
(1910-97)
A893b

1997, Dec. 27
1984J A893b 75c multicolored   3.00 1.50

Dr. Bernardo A. Houssay (1887-1971),
1947 Nobel Prize Winner in
Medicine — A894

1998, Jan. 31   **Litho.**   *Perf. 13½*
1985 A894 75c multicolored   1.50 1.50

First Ascension of Mount Aconcagua,
Cent. — A895

Illustration reduced.

1998, Feb. 14   *Perf. 12*
1986 A895 1.25p multicolored   2.50 2.50

Founding of San Martin de los Andes,
Cent. — A896

1998, Mar. 14   **Litho.**   *Perf. 13½*
1987 A896 75c multicolored   1.50 1.50

Regimental
Quarters of
Gen. San
Martin's
Mounted
Grenadiers
A897

Designs: a, Statue. b, Large jar with painting of San Martin. c, Regimental seal. d, Regimental quarters.

1998, Mar. 21   **Litho.**   *Perf. 13½*
1988 A897 75c Block of 4, #a.-d. 6.00 6.00

Protection of
the Ozone
A898

1998, Mar. 28   **Litho.**   *Perf. 13½*
1989 A898 75c multicolored   1.50 1.50

America
Issue — A899

Letter carriers: #1990, Wearing white uniform. #1991, Carrying letter bag with shoulder strap.

1998, Apr. 4
1990 A899 75c multicolored   1.50 1.50
1991 A899 75c multicolored   1.50 1.50

Characters from Stories by Maria
Elena Walsh — A900

#1992, El Reino Del Reves. #1993, Zoo Loco. #1994, Dailan Kifki. #1995, Manuelita.

1998, Apr. 17   **Litho.**   *Die Cut*
Booklet Stamps
Self-Adhesive
1992 A900 75c multicolored   1.50 1.50
1993 A900 75c multicolored   1.50 1.50
1994 A900 75c multicolored   1.50 1.50
1995 A900 75c multicolored   1.50 1.50
  a. Complete booklet, #1992-1995 6.00

Historic
Chapels
A901

#1996, San Pedro de Fiambalá, Catamarca. #1997, Huacalera, Jujuy. #1998, Santo Domingo, La Rioja. #1999, Tumbaya, Jujuy.

1998, Apr. 25   **Litho.**   *Perf. 13x13½*
1996 A901 75c multicolored   1.50 1.50
1997 A901 75c multicolored   1.50 1.50
1998 A901 75c multicolored   1.50 1.50
1999 A901 75c multicolored   1.50 1.50
    Nos. 1996-1999 (4)   6.00 6.00

White Helmets, A Commitment to
Humanity — A902

1998, May 23   **Litho.**   *Perf. 13½*
2000 A902 1p multicolored   2.00 2.00

Beginning with No. 2001, many Argentine stamps are inscribed "Correo Official," but these are not Official stamps (i.e., for government use only).

1998 World Cup Soccer
Championships, France — A903

Stylized players representing: a, Argentina. b, Croatia. c, Jamaica. d, Japan.

1998, May 30
2001 A903 75c Block of 4, #a.-d. 6.00 6.00

Journalist's
Day — A904

1998, June 20
2002 A904 75c multicolored   1.50 1.50

Creation of Argentine Postal System,
250th Anniv. — A905

a, Corrientes design A2, peso coin. b, Building, post box.

1998, June 27
2003 A905 75c Pair, #a.-b.   3.00 3.00

Fauna Type of 1995

1998   **Litho.**   *Die Cut*
Self-Adhesive (#2004)
2004   A853 60c Picaflor   1.25 1.25
Perf. 13½
2004A A853 3.25p Tero   6.50 6.50
#2004 is broken at bottom right by 3 or 5 lines of wavy die cutting.
Issued: 60c, 12/12; 3.25p, 7/22.

Ruins, Mission
St. Ignacio
A906

1998, July 25   **Litho.**   *Perf. 13½*
2005 A906 75c multicolored   1.50 1.50
Mercosur.

Cattle
A907

1998, Aug. 1
2006	A907	25c Brahman	.50	.50
2007	A907	25c Aberdeen-Angus	.50	.50
2008	A907	50c Hereford	1.00	1.00
2009	A907	50c Criolla	1.00	1.00
2010	A907	75c Holland-Argentina	1.50	1.50
2011	A907	75c Shorthorn	1.50	1.50
	Nos. 2006-2011 (6)		6.00	6.00

Deception Island Base, Antarctica,
50th Anniv. — A908

1998, Aug. 15   Litho.   *Perf. 14½*
2012 A908 75c multicolored   1.50 1.50

State of
Israel,
50th
Anniv.
A909

1998, Sept. 5   Litho.   *Perf. 13½*
2013 A909 75c multicolored   1.50 1.50

Argentine-Japan Friendship Treaty,
Cent. — A910

1998, Oct. 3
2014 A910 75c multicolored   1.50 1.50

Post
Office
Building,
Buenos
Aires,
70th
Anniv.
A911

Designs: No. 2015, Building, clock, tile. No.
2016, Column ornamentation, tile, bench.

1998, Oct. 3
2015	A911	75c multicolored	1.50	1.50
2016	A911	75c multicolored	1.50	1.50
a.		Pair, #2015-2016	3.00	3.00

Cartoons — A912

Designs: a, Patoruzu, by Quinterno. b,
Matias, by Sendra. c, Clemente, by Caloi. d, El

Eternauta, by Oesterheld and López. e, Loco
Chavez, by Trillo and Altuna. f, Inodoro Pe-
reyra, by Fontanarrosa. g, Tia Vicenta, by Lan-
drú. h, Gaturro, by Nik.

1998, Oct. 17   Litho.   *Perf. 13¾x13¼*
2017 A912 75c Sheet of 8,
#a.-h.   12.00 12.00

Dr. Pedro de
Elizalde's
Children's
Hospital, 220th
Anniv. — A913

1998, Oct. 24   Litho.   *Perf. 13½*
2025 A913 15c multicolored   2.25 1.00

Raoul Wallenberg (1912-47),
Humanitarian — A914

1998, Nov. 21
2026 A914 75c multicolored   1.50 1.50

Espamer
'98 — A915

25c, Spanish flags, arms. 75c, 18th cent.
schooner. 75c+75c, Brigantine, gray sails.
1.25p+1.25p, Brigantine, white sails.

1998, Nov. 21   *Die Cut*
Booklet Stamps
Self-Adhesive
2027	A915	25c multicolored	.50	.50
2028	A915	75c multicolored	1.50	1.50
2029	A915	75c +75c multi	3.00	3.00
2030	A915	1.25p +1.25p multi	5.00	5.00
a.		Booklet pane, #2027-2030	15.00	

Nos. 2027-2030 are broken at top right of
each stamp by four lines of wavy die cutting.
No. 2030a is a complete booklet.

Organization of American States, 50th
Anniv. — A916

1998, Nov. 28   *Perf. 13½*
2031 A916 75c multicolored   1.50 1.50

Dinosaurs of Argentina — A917

Designs: a, Eoraptor. b, Gasparinisaura. c,
Giganotosaurus. d, Patagosaurus.

1998, Nov. 28
2032 A917 75c Sheet of 4, #a.-d. 9.00 6.00

Christmas
A918

1998, Dec. 5
2033 A918 75c multicolored   1.50 1.50

Newspaper
El Liberal,
Cent.
A919

1998, Dec. 5
2034 A919 75c Juan A. Figueroa 1.50 1.50

La Nueva
Provincia,
Daily
Newspaper,
Cent.
A920

1998, Dec. 12
2035 A920 75c Enrique Julio   1.50 1.50

Universal Declaration of Human
Rights, 50th Anniv. — A921

1998, Dec. 12
2036 A921 75c multicolored   1.50 1.50

Holocaust Memorial, Cathedral of
Buenos Aires — A922

1998, Dec. 12
2037 A922 75c multicolored   1.50 1.50

Southern
Cross — A923

Inscriptions: 8.75p, Sur postal express.
17.50p, Sur postal 24.

1999-2000   Litho.   *Die Cut*
Self-Adhesive
2038	A923	8.75p bl & silver	17.50	17.50
2039	A923	17.50p bl & gold	35.00	35.00

Issued: 8.75p, 7/1/99; 17.50p, 3/2/00. Nos.
2038-2039 are broken at right by five wavy
lines of die cutting.

National
Fund for
the Arts,
40th
Anniv.
A925

1999, Mar. 6   Litho.   *Perf. 13½*
2042 A925 75c multicolored   1.50 1.50

Intl.
Year of
the
Ocean
(in
1998)
A926

1999, Mar. 6
2043	A926	50c Penguin, vert.	1.00	1.00
2044	A926	75c Dolphins	1.50	1.50

Postmen — A927

Designs: 25c, Early postman, city scene.
50c, Early postman, people on bicycles, factory. 75c, Modern postman, city buildings.

1998-99   Litho.   *Die Cut*
Self-Adhesive
2045	A927	25c multicolored	.50	.50
2046	A927	75c multicolored	1.50	1.50
a.		Strip of 4, 1 #2045, 3 #2046	5.00	

Booklet Stamps
Serpentine Die Cut
2047	A927	25c multicolored	.50	.50
2048	A927	75c multicolored	1.50	1.50
a.		Bkt. pane, 2 #2047, 6 #2048	10.00	
		Complete booklet, #2048a	10.00	

Size: 21x27mm
Die Cut
2049	A927	25c multicolored	.50	.50
2050	A927	50c multicolored	1.00	1.00
2051	A927	75c multicolored	1.50	1.50
a.		Bkt. pane, 2 ea #2049-2051	6.00	
		Complete booklet, #2051a	6.00	

Nos. 2045-2048 are broken at lower right by
five lines of wavy die cutting. Nos. 2049-2051
are broken in center by five wavy lines of die
cutting. Nos. 2045-2046 have darker vignettes
than #2047-2048.
Issued: Nos. 2045-2048, 12/9/98. Nos.
2049-2051, 2/2/99.

25th
Book
Fair
A928

Designs: a, Book. b, Obelisk, readers.

1999, Apr. 17 Litho. *Perf. 13¾x13½*
2052 A928 75c Pair, a.-b.   3.00 3.00

Argentine Rugby Union, Cent. — A929

75c, Player, balls. 1.50p, Old, modern players.

1999, Apr. 24 Litho. Perf. 13¾x13½
2054 A929 75c multicolored 1.50 1.50
Souvenir Sheet
2055 A929 1.50p multi + 3 labels 3.00 3.00

Cafes of Buenos Aires — A930

Designs: a, Mug, Giralda Dairy. b, Two glasses, Homero Manzi Cafe. c, Hat hanging on rack, Ideal Sweet Shop. d, Cup and saucer, Tortoni Cafe.

Serpentine Die Cut
1999, Apr. 30 Litho.
Self-Adhesive
2056 Booklet pane of 4 6.00
  a. A930 25c multicolored .50 .50
  b.-c. A930 75c multi, each 1.50 1.50
  d. A930 1.25c multicolored 2.50 2.50
  Complete booklet, #2056 6.00

Argentine Olympic Committee, 75th Anniv. — A931

1999, May 15 Perf. 14x13¼
2057 A931 75c Pierre de Coubertin 1.50 1.50

Enrico Caruso (1873-1921), Opera Singer — A932

Designs: a, Portrait of Caruso. b, Singer, various musical instruments. c, Outside of Colon Theatre, Buenos Aires. d, Scene from opera, "El Matrero."

1999, May 15 Perf. 13½
2058 A932 75c Sheet of 4, #a.-d. 6.00 6.00

Famous Women A933

Designs: a, Rosario Vera Penaloza (1873-1950), educator. b, Julieta Lanteri (1862-1932), physician.

1999, June 5 Perf. 14x13¼
2059 A933 75c Pair, #a.-b. 3.00 3.00

Souvenir Sheets

Paintings from Natl. Museum of Art, Buenos Aires — A934

No. 2060: a, Anarchy of Year 20, by Luis Felipe Noé. b, Retrato de L.E.S., by Carlos Alonso.
No. 2061: a, Typical Orchestra, by Antonio Berni. b, Untitled, (Woman seated), by Aída Carballo.
Illustration reduced.

1999, June 5 Perf. 14
Sheets of 2
2060-2061 A934 75c #a.-b., each 3.00 3.00
  No. 2060b is 40x40mm, No. 2061a, 70x50mm, No. 2061b, 40x50mm.

Carrier Pigeon A935

1999, June 12 Perf. 13¾x13½
2062 A935 75c multicolored 1.50 1.50

Maps — A936

1999, June 12 Die Cut
Self-Adhesive
2063 A936 35c Local highway .70 .70
2064 A936 40c City street .80 .80
2065 A936 50c Regional highway 1.00 1.00
  Nos. 2063-2065 (3) 2.50 2.50

Nos. 2063-2065 are broken at lower left by five wavy lines of die cutting.

Dogs A937

Designs: a, 25c, Boxer. b, 25c, English sheepdog. c, 50c, Collie. d, 50c, St. Bernard. e, 75c, German shepherd. f, 75c, Siberian husky.

1999, July 24 Litho. Perf. 13½
2066 A937 Sheet of 6, #a.-f. 6.00 6.00

Natl. Telecommunications Day — A938

1999, July 24 Perf. 13½x13¾
2067 A938 75c multicolored 1.50 1.50

Justo José de Urquiza School, Concepcion del Uruguay, 150th Anniv. — A939

1999, Aug. 7 Perf. 13¾x13½
2068 A939 75c multicolored 1.50 1.50

Otto Krause Technical School, Buenos Aires, Cent. — A940

1999, Aug. 7 Perf. 13½x13¾
2069 A940 75c multicolored 1.50 1.50

Bethlehem 2000 Project — A941

1999, Aug. 21 Perf. 13½
2070 A941 75c multicolored 3.00 1.50

America Issue, A New Millennium Without Arms — A942

Perf. 13½x13¾, 13¾x13½
1999, Aug. 21
2071 A942 75c shown 1.50 1.50
2072 A942 75c Tree of hands, vert. 1.50 1.50

National Parks — A943

Parks and animals: No. 2073, Mburucuyá, coypu. No. 2074, Quebrada de Los Condoritos, condor. No. 2075, San Guillermo, vicuna. No. 2076, Sierra de las Quijadas, puma. No. 2077, Talampaya, gray fox.
Illustration reduced.

1999, Sept. 25 Litho. Perf. 14x13½
2073 A943 50c multicolored 1.00 1.00
2074 A943 50c multicolored 1.00 1.00
2075 A943 50c multicolored 1.00 1.00
2076 A943 75c multicolored 1.50 1.50
2077 A943 75c multicolored 1.50 1.50
  Nos. 2073-2077 (5) 6.00 6.00

Inter-American Development Bank, 40th Anniv. — A944

1999, Oct. 9 Litho. Perf. 13½x13¾
2078 A944 75c multi 1.50 1.50

UPU, 125th Anniv. A945

1999, Oct. 9 Perf. 13¾x13½
2079 A945 1.50p multi 3.00 3.00

Trees — A946

a, Nothofagus pumilio. b, Prosopis caldenia. c, Schinopsis balansae. d, Cordia trichotoma.

1999, Oct. 16 Perf. 13½x13¾
2080 A946 75c Strip of 4, #a-d 6.00 6.00

Sinking of A.R.A. Fournier, 50th Anniv. A947

1999, Oct. 16 Perf. 13¾x13½
2081 A947 75c multi 1.50 1.50

Aviation Anniversaries — A948

Designs: No. 2082, Late 25 airplane. No. 2083, Parachutists.

1999, Oct. 30 Perf. 13¾x13½
2082 A948 75c multi 1.50 1.50
2083 A948 75c multi 1.50 1.50

First Argentine airmail flight, 70th anniv. (#2082), Hundred consecutive jumps by Argentine Parachute Club, 50th anniv.

Souvenir Sheets

Millennium — A949

No. 2084: a, 75c, Head of soccer player. b, 50c, Machine as soccer player.
No. 2085: a, 50c, Cane, vert. b, 75c, Head of Jorge Luis Borges (1899-1986), writer.
No. 2086: a, 50c, Accordion player on bed, vert. b, 75c, Stylized tango dancers.

1999, Oct. 30　　　　　　**Perf. 14**
2084　A949　Sheet of 2, #a.-b.　2.50　2.50
2085　A949　Sheet of 2, #a.-b.　2.50　2.50
2086　A949　Sheet of 2, #a.-b.　2.50　2.50

Size of 75c stamps: 40x40mm.

Argentine Soccer Teams — A950

Designs: No. 2087, Banner and flags of River Plate team. No. 2088, Banner of Boca Juniors team, balloons.
River Plate team (red and white colors) - No. 2089: a, Stadium, emblem, soccer balls. b, Team on field. c, Fans. d, Emblem. e, Trophy. f, Banner in stadium. g, Player, ball.
Boca Juniors team (blue and yellow team colors) - No. 2090: a, Two players, ball. b, Emblem. c, Four players celebrating. d, Fans, balloons. e, Banner in stadium. f, Blurred shot of players in action. g, Blurred shot of players, diff.

1999　　　　　　**Perf. 13½x13¼**
2087　A950　75c multi　　　1.50　1.50
2088　A950　75c multi　　　1.50　1.50

Self-Adhesive
Die Cut
2089　Pane of 7　　　　　10.00
　a.　A950 25c multi　　　.50　.50
　b.-c.　A950 50c any single　1.00　1.00
　d.-f.　A950 75c any single　1.50　1.50
　g.　A950 1.50p multi　　3.00　3.00
2090　Pane of 7　　　　　10.00
　a.　A950 25c multi　　　.50　.50
　b.-c.　A950 50c any single　1.00　1.00
　d.-f.　A950 75c any single　1.50　1.50
　g.　A950 1.50p multi　　3.00　3.00

Issued: Nos. 2087-2088, 11/13; Nos. 2089-2090, 11/15.
Sizes: #2089a-2089f, 2090a-2090f, 37x27mm; #2089g, 2090g, 37x37mm.

Canonization of Brother Héctor Valdivielso Sáez — A951

1999, Nov. 20　　　　**Perf. 13¾x13½**
2091　A951　75c multi　　　1.50　1.50

Manuel Belgrano National Naval School, Bicent. A952

1999, Nov. 27
2092　A952　75c multi　　　1.50　1.50

Souvenir Sheet

Launch of Corvette Uruguay, 125th Anniv. — A953

1999, Nov. 27　　Litho.　　**Perf. 14**
2093　A953　1.50p multi　　　3.00　3.00

A954

Christmas A955

No. 2094, Figurines of Holy Family.
No. 2095: a, Magus. b, Bell. c, Two Magi, camels. d, Leaf. e, Angel with star. f, Nativity scene. g, Star. h, Ornaments.

1999, Dec. 4　　　　**Perf. 13¾x13½**
2094　A954　75c multi　　　1.50　1.50
　　　　　　Perf. 14
2095　　　　Sheet of 8　　　9.00　9.00
　a.-b.　A955 25c any single　.50　.50
　c.-d.　A955 50c any single　1.00　1.00
　e.-h.　A955 75c any single　1.50　1.50
Sizes: Nos. 2095a, 2095b, 2095g, 2095h, 30x30mm.

Viticulture — A956

Designs: a, 25c, Grape on vine. b, 50c, Bottoms of wine bottles. c, 50c, Cork and corkscrew. d, 25c, Glass of wine, wine bottle.
Illustration reduced.

2000, Feb. 26　　Litho.　　**Perf. 13¼**
2096　A956　Block of 4, #a-d　3.00　3.00

World Mathematics Year — A957

2000, Mar. 18　　　　**Perf. 13¾x13½**
2097　A957　75c multi　　　1.50　1.50

Birds A958

---

a, Leptotila verrauxi. b, Columba picazuro. c, Columbina picni. d, Zenaida auriculata.

2000, Mar. 18　　　　　**Die Cut**
　　　　Self-Adhesive
2098　Booklet of 4　　　　6.00
　a.-d.　A958 75c any single　1.50　1.50

Souvenir Sheet

Bangkok 2000 Stamp Exhibition — A959

Designs: a, 25c, Vanda coerulea. b, 75c, Erythrina crista-galli.
Illustration reduced.

2000, Mar. 25　　　　**Perf. 14**
2099　A959　Sheet of 2, #a-b　2.00　2.00

Miniature Sheet

Libraries — A960

Designs: a, 25c, National Public Library Protection Commission. b, 50c, Jujuy Public Library. c, 75c, Argentine Library for the Blind. d, Argentine National Library.
Illustration reduced.

Litho., Litho. & Embossed (#2100c)
2000, Apr. 15　　　　**Perf. 13½**
2100　A960　Sheet of 4, #a-d　5.00　5.00

Gen. Luis Maria Campos Military School, Cent. A961

2000, Apr. 29　　　**Perf. 13¾x13½**
2101　A961　75c multi　　　1.50　1.50

Discovery of Brazil, 500th Anniv. — A962

a, 75c, Pedro Cabral, 1558 map of Brazil coastline. b, 25c, Compass rose and ship.
Illustration reduced.

2000, Apr. 29
2102　A962　Pair, #a-b　　　2.00　2.00

Souvenir Sheet

The Stamp Show 2000, London — A963

Designs: a, 25c, Great Britain #1 and design A1, La Porteña, 1st locomotive in Argentina. b, 75c, Argentina No. 7, mail box.
Illustration reduced.

2000, May 20　　　　**Perf. 14**
2103　A963　Sheet of 2, #a-b　2.00　2.00

91st Intl. Convention of Rotary International, Buenos Aires — A964

2000, June 3　Litho.　**Perf. 13½x13¾**
2104　A964　75c multi　　　1.50　1.50

Stampin' the Future — A965

Children's Stamp Design Contest Winners: 25c, Rocío Casado. 50c, Carolina Cáceres, vert. 75c, Valeria A. Pizarro. 1p, Cristina Ayala Castro, vert.

Perf. 13½x13¼, 13¼x13½
2000, June 24
2105-2108　A965　Set of 4　　5.00　5.00

America Issue A966

AIDS Prevention: No. 2109, Handshake. No. 2110, Heart and hands.

2000, July 8　　　**Perf. 13¾x13½**
2109-2110　A966　75c Set of 2　3.00　3.00

Antoine de Saint-Exupéry (1900-44), Pilot, Writer — A967

#2111, 2115, Potez 25. #2112, 2116, Late 28. #2113, Saint-Exupéry. #2114, Henri Guillaumet, Vicente A. Almonacid and Jean Mermoz. #2117, Map of southern Argentina, tail of Late 25 plane. 1p, Nose of Late 25 plane, cover from 1st airmail flight to Trelew.

2000, July 29　　　　**Perf. 13½**
2111　A967　25c multi　　　.50　.50

2112	A967	50c multi	1.00 1.00

Booklet Stamps
Perf. 14
Size: 30x30mm

2113	A967	25c multi	.50 .50
2114	A967	50c multi	1.00 1.00

Size: 60x20mm

2115	A967	25c multi	.50 .50
2116	A967	50c multi	1.00 1.00
a.		Booklet pane, #2113-2116	3.00

Size: 40x30mm

2117	A967	50c multi	1.00 1.00
2118	A967	1p multi	2.00 2.00
a.		Booklet pane, #2117-2118	3.00
		Booklet, #2116a, 2118a	6.00
		Nos. 2111-2118 (8)	7.50 7.50

Argentine airmail service, 73rd anniv., Aerofila 2000 Philatelic Exhibition, Buenos Aires (No. 2118a).

President Arturo U. Illia (1900-82) A968

2000, Aug. 5 *Perf. 13½x13¼*
2119 A968 75c multi 1.50 1.50

José de San Martín (1778-1850) A969

2000, Aug. 26 *Perf. 13½*
2120 A969 75c multi 1.50 1.50

Dalmacio Vélez Sarsfield (1800-75), Writer of Civil Code — A970

Perf. 13½x13¼
2000, Sept. 23 Litho.
2121 A970 75c multi 1.50 1.50

2000 Summer Olympic, Sydney — A971

No. 2122: a, Windsurfing. b, Field hockey. c, Volleyball. d, Pole vault.
Illustration reduced.

2000, Sept. 23 *Perf. 13½*
2122 A971 75c Block of 4, #a-d 6.00 6.00

Horses A972

No. 2123: a, Argentine Petiso. b, Argentine Carriage Horse. c, Peruvian. d, Criolla. e, Argentine Saddle Horse. f, Argentine Polo.
No. 2124: a, Horse-drawn mail coach. b, Horse's head.

2000, Oct. 7 *Perf. 13¾x13½*

2123		Sheet of 6 + 2 labels	6.00 6.00
a.-b.	A972 25c Any single		.50 .50
c.-d.	A972 50c Any single		1.00 1.00
e.-f.	A972 75c Any single		1.50 1.50

Souvenir Sheet
Perf. 14

2124		Sheet of 2	2.00 2.00
a.	A972 25c multi		.50 .50
b.	A972 75c mutli		1.50 1.50

España 2000 Intl. Philatelic Exhibition.

Archaeological Artifacts — A973

Designs: 10c, Ceremonial hatchet, Santa Maria culture. 25c, Musical pipes. 50c, Loom, Mapuche culture. 60c, Poncho. 75c, Funerary mask, Tafi culture. 1p, Basket, Mbayá Indians. 2p, Drum, Mapuche culture. 3.25p, Ceremonial mask, Chané culture. 5p, Funerary urn, Belén culture. 9.40p, Rhea-feather costume.
Type A Syncopation (1st stamp #2125): On two longer sides, groups of 2 and 18 holes separated by a bracket-shaped hole equal in width to two holes.

Perf. 13½x13¾ Sync. Type A
2000 Litho.

2125	A973	10c multi	.20 .20
2126	A973	25c multi	.50 .50
2127	A973	50c multi	1.00 1.00
2128	A973	60c multi	1.25 1.25
2129	A973	75c multi	1.50 1.50
2130	A973	1p multi	2.00 2.00
2131	A973	2p multi	4.00 4.00
2132	A973	3.75p multi	7.50 7.50
2133	A973	5p multi	10.00 10.00
2134	A973	9.40p multi	19.00 19.00
		Nos. 2125-2134 (10)	46.95 46.95

Issued: 10c, 60c, 11/16; 25c, 50c, 75c, 9.40p, 10/26; 1p, 2p, 9/13; 3.25p, 5p, 8/30.

Natl. Atomic Energy Commission, 50th Anniv. A974

2000, Nov. 11 Litho. *Perf. 13½*
2135 A974 75c multi 1.50 1.50

Fileteado Art Style and the Tango — A975

No. 2136: a, Left side of Fileteado design. b, Right side of Fileteado design. c, Musicians. d, Tango dancers.
Illustration reduced.

2000, Nov. 11 *Perf. 13¾x13½*
2136 A975 75c Block of 4, #a-d 6.00 6.00

Organ Donation Campaign A976

2000, Nov. 25 *Perf. 13½*
2137 A976 75c multi 1.50 1.50

Christmas A977

2000, Nov. 25
2138 A977 75c multi 1.50 1.50

Medicinal Plants — A978

Designs: No. 2139, 75c, Mirabilis jalapa. No. 2140, 75c, Senna corymbosa. No. 2141, 75c, Eugenia uniflora. No. 2142, 75c, Commelina erecta.

2000, Nov. 25
2139-2142 A978 Set of 4 6.00 6.00

Pre-Columbian Art — A979

Various artifacts. Background colors: a, Bright orange. b, Red orange. c, Green. d, Red violet.
Illustration reduced.

2000, Dec. 9
2143 A979 75c Block of 4, #a-d 6.00 6.00

A979a

Serpentine Die Cut 11¼x11
2001, Feb. 6 Litho.
Self-Adhesive
Background Color

2143E	A979a	10c blue green	.20 .20
2143F	A979a	25c brt green	.50 .50
2143G	A979a	60c orange	1.25 1.25
2143H	A979a	75c red	1.50 1.50
2143I	A979a	1p blue	2.00 2.00
2143J	A979a	3p red brown	6.00 6.00
2143K	A979a	3.25p yel green	6.50 6.50
2143L	A979a	5.50p rose	11.00 11.00
		Nos. 2143E-2143L (8)	28.95 28.95

Nos. 2143E-2143L are broken at right by five die cut wavy lines. Sold at Unidad Postal outlets.

Miniature Sheet

Cenozoic Mammals — A980

No. 2144: a, Megaterio (Megatherium americanum). b, Gliptodonte (Doedicurus clavicaudatus). c, Macrauquenia (Macrauchenia patachonica). d, Toxodonte (Toxodon platensis).

2001, Mar. 10 *Perf. 13¾x13½*
2144 A980 75c Sheet of 4, #a-d 6.00 6.00

Antarctic Bases, 50th Anniv. — A981

Map and: No. 2145, 75c, Cormorant, Base Brown. No. 2146, 75c, Skua, Base San Martín.

Perf. 13¾x13½
2001, Mar. 24 Litho.
2145-2146 A981 Set of 2 3.00 3.00

Apiculture — A982

No. 2147: a, Bee on flower. b, Bees on honeycomb. c, Bees, apiarist, and hives. d, Honey, pollen.

2001, Apr. 7 *Perf. 13½x13¼*

2147		Block of 4	6.00 6.00
a.-d.	A982 75c Any single		1.50 1.50

Souvenir Sheet

Argentine Antarctic Institute, 50th Anniv. — A983

No. 2148: a, Scientist with fossils. b, Scientist with mapping equipment.

2001, Apr. 21			**Perf. 14**	
2148 A983	75c Sheet of 2, #a-b		3.00	3.00

Spain to Argentina Flight of Plus Ultra Seaplane, 75th Anniv. — A984

2001, Apr. 28		**Perf. 13¾x13½**		
2149 A984	75c multi		1.50	1.50

Art in Silver — A985

No. 2150: a, Bridle (Freno). b, Stirrups (Estribos). c, Spurs (Espuelas). d, Gaucho's ornament (Rastra).
Illustration reduced.

2001, May 19 Litho.		**Perf. 13¾x13½**		
2150 A985	75c Block of 4, #a-d		6.00	6.00

World Youth Soccer Championships — A986

Designs: No. 2151, 75c, Player kicking ball. No. 2152, 75c, Goalie catching ball.

2001, June 16				
2151-2152 A986	Set of 2		3.00	3.00

Souvenir Sheet

Belgica 2001 Intl. Stamp Exhibition, Brussels — A987

No. 2153: a, 25c, Washerwoman by the Banks of the Belgrano, by Prilidiano Pueyrredón. b, 75c, The Hay Harvest, by Pieter Breughel, the Elder.

2001, June 16			**Perf. 14**	
2153 A987	Sheet of 2, #a-b		2.00	2.00

2001 Census — A988

Perf. 13½x13¾ Syncopated			
2001, July 14			
2154 A988	75c multi	1.50	1.50

SAC-C Satellite, Birds and Flowers A989

2001, July 14		**Perf. 13¾x13½**		
2155 A989	75c multi		1.50	1.50

Environmental protection.

Bandoneón Recital - 1990, by Aldo Severi — A990

2001, July 28		**Perf. 13½x13¾**		
2156 A990	75c multi		1.50	1.50

The tango in art.

Souvenir Sheet

Phila Nippon '01, Japan — A991

No. 2157: a, Tango dancers, musical score. b, Kabuki dancer.

2001, July 28			**Perf. 14**	
2157 A991	75c Sheet of 2, #a-b		3.00	3.00

Miniature Sheet

Wild Cats — A992

No. 2158: a, 25c, Puma. b, 25c, Jaguar. c, 50c, Jaguarundi and young. d, 50c, Ocelot. e, 75c, Mountain cat. f, 75c, Huiña.

2001, July 28		**Perf. 13¾x13½**		
2158 A992	Sheet of 6, #a-f, +2 labels		6.00	6.00

Enrique Santos Discépolo (1901-51), Tango Lyricist — A993

2001, Aug. 4		**Perf. 13½x13¾**		
2159 A993	75c multi		1.50	1.50

America Issue - UNESCO World Heritage — A994

No. 2160 - Buildings and artifacts from Jesuit Block and Estancias of Cordoba: a, Denomination at UL. b, Denomination at UR.
Illustration reduced.

2001, Aug. 11		**Perf. 13¾x13½**		
2160 A994	75c Horiz. pair, #a-b		3.00	3.00

Prevention of Breast Cancer — A995

2001, Sept. 1		**Perf. 13½x13¾**		
2161 A995	75c multi		1.50	1.50

World Championship Race Cars of Juan Manuel Fangio — A996

No. 2162 - Cars and track layouts: a, Alfa Romeo 159 Alfetta, Barcelona, 1951. b, Mercedes-Benz W196, Reims, France, 1954. c, Lancia-Ferrari D50, Monte Carlo, Monaco, 1956. d, Maserati 250F, Nürburgring, Germany, 1957.
Illustration reduced.

2001, Oct. 6		**Perf. 13¾x13½**		
2162 A996	75c Block of 4, #a-d		6.00	6.00

Politicians A997

Designs: No. 2163, 75c, Roque Sáenz Peña (1851-1914). No. 2164, 75c, Justo José de Urquiza (1801-70).

2001, Oct. 20				
2163-2164 A997	Set of 2		3.00	3.00

Souvenir Sheet

Hafnia 01 Philatelic Exhibition, Copenhagen — A999

No. 2166: a, 25c, Argentine post rider, 18th cent. b, 75c, European post rider, 17th cent.

2001, Oct. 27 Litho.		**Perf. 14**		
2166 A999	Sheet of 2, #a-b		2.00	2.00

SEMI-POSTAL STAMPS

Samuel F. B. Morse — SP1

Globe — SP2

Landing of Columbus SP5

Map of Argentina SP6

Designs: 10c+5c, Alexander Graham Bell. 25c+15c, Rowland Hill.

Wmk. RA in Sun (90)				
1944, Jan. 5	**Litho.**		**Perf. 13**	
B1 SP1	3c +2c lt vio & sl bl		.35	.25
B2 SP2	5c +5c dl red & sl bl		.65	.20
B3 SP1	10c +5c org & slate bl		1.25	.70
B4 SP1	25c +15c red brn & sl bl		1.75	1.10
B5 SP5	1p +50c lt grn & sl bl		8.00	7.25
Nos. B1-B5 (5)			12.00	9.50

The surtax was for the Postal Employees Benefit Association.

1944, Feb. 17 Wmk. 90 Perf. 13

B6	SP6	5c +10c ol yel & slate	.75	.50
B7	SP6	5c +10c vio brn & slate	3.25	2.00
B8	SP6	5c +1p dl org & slate	9.00	6.50
B9	SP6	5c +20p dp bl & slate	22.50	15.00
		Nos. B6-B9 (4)	35.50	24.00

The surtax was for the victims of the San Juan earthquake.

Souvenir Sheets

National Anthem and Flag — SP7

Illustration reduced.

1944, July 17 Imperf.

B10	SP7	5c +1p vio brn & lt bl	1.90	1.90
B11	SP7	5c +50p bl blk & lt bl	350.00	250.00

Surtax for the needy in the provinces of La Rioja and Catamarca.

Catalogue values for unused stamps in this section, from this point to the end of the section, are for Never Hinged items.

Stamp Designing SP8

1950, Aug. 26 Photo. Perf. 13½

B12	SP8	10c +10c violet	.25	.25
		Nos. B12,CB1-CB5 (6)	20.45	15.65

Argentine Intl. Philatelic Exhibition, 1950.

Poliomyelitis Victim — SP9

1956, Apr. 14 Perf. 13½x13

B13	SP9	20c +30c slate	.30	.20

The surtax was for the poliomyelitis fund. Head in design is from Correggio's "Antiope," Louvre.

Stamp of 1858 and Mail Coach on Raft — SP10

Designs: 2.40p+1.20p, Album, magnifying glass and stamp of 1858. 4.40p+2.20p, Government seat of Confederation, Parana.

1958, Mar. 29 Litho. Perf. 13½

B14	SP10	40c +20c brt grn & dl pur	.30	.25
B15	SP10	2.40p +1.20p ol gray & bl	.40	.25
B16	SP10	4.40p +2.20p lt bl & dp claret	.60	.40
		Nos. B14-B16,CB8-CB12 (8)	5.80	4.55

Surtax for Intl. Centennial Philatelic Exhibition, Paraná, Entre Rios, Apr. 19-27.

View of Flooded Land — SP11

1958, Oct. 4 Photo. Perf. 13½

B17	SP11	40c +20c brown	.20	.20
		Nos. B17,CB13-CB14 (3)	1.25	1.15

The surtax was for flood victims in the Buenos Aires district.

Child Receiving Blood — SP12

1958, Dec. 20 Litho. Wmk. 90

B18	SP12	1p +50c blk & rose red	.20	.20

The surtax went to the Anti-Leukemia Foundation.

Runner SP13

1959, Sept. 5 Perf. 13½

Designs: 50c+20c, Basketball players, vert. 1p+50c, Boxers, vert.

B19	SP13	20c +10c emer & blk	.20	.20
B20	SP13	50c +20c yel & blk	.20	.20
B21	SP13	1p +50c mar & blk	.20	.20
		Nos. B19-B21,CB15-CB16 (5)	1.60	1.35

3rd Pan American Games, Chicago, Aug. 27-Sept. 7, 1959.

Condor — SP14

Birds: 50c+20c, Fork-tailed flycatchers. 1p+50c, Magellanic woodpecker.

1960, Feb. 6

B22	SP14	20c +10c dk bl	.20	.20
B23	SP14	50c +20c dp vio bl	.20	.20
B24	SP14	1p +50c brn & buff	.20	.20
		Nos. B22-B24,CB17-CB18 (5)	1.35	1.15

The surtax was for child welfare work. See Nos. B30, CB29.

Souvenir Sheet

Uprooted Oak Emblem — SP15

1960, Apr. 7 Wmk. 90 Imperf.

B25	SP15	Sheet of 2	1.25	1.25
a.		1p + 50c bister & carmine	.55	.55
b.		4.20p + 2.10p apple grn & dp claret	.55	.55

WRY, July 1, 1959-June 30, 1960. The surtax was for aid to refugees.

Jacaranda — SP16

Flowers: 1p+1p, Passionflower. 3p+3p, Orchid. 5p+5p, Tabebuia.

1960, Dec. 3 Photo. Perf. 13½

B26	SP16	50c +50c deep blue	.20	.20
B27	SP16	1p +1p bluish grn	.20	.20
B28	SP16	3p +3p henna grn	.30	.25
B29	SP16	5p +5p dark brn	.50	.35
		Nos. B26-B29 (4)	1.20	1.00

"TEMEX 61" (Intl. Thematic Exposition). For overprints see Nos. B31-B34.

Type of 1960

Bird: 4.20p+2.10p, Blue-eyed shag.

1961, Feb. 25 Wmk. 90 Perf. 13½

B30	SP14	4.20p +2.10p chestnut brn	.50	.30

Surtax for child welfare work. See #CB29.

Nos. B26-B29 Overprinted in Black, Brown, Blue or Red: "14 DE ABRIL DIA DE LAS AMERICAS"

1961, Apr. 15

B31	SP16	50c +50c deep blue	.20	.20
B32	SP16	1p +1p bluish grn (Brn)	.20	.20
B33	SP16	3p +3p henna brn (Bl)	.30	.25
B34	SP16	5p +5p dk brn (R)	.50	.35
		Nos. B31-B34 (4)	1.20	1.00

Day of the Americas, Apr. 14.

Cathedral, Cordoba SP17

Stamp of 1862 SP18

Flight into Egypt, by Ana Maria Moncalvo SP19

Design: 10p+10p, Cathedral, Buenos Aires.

Perf. 13½

1961, Oct. 21 Wmk. 90 Photo.

B35	SP17	2p +2p rose claret	.25	.20
B36	SP18	3p +3p green	.30	.20
B37	SP17	10p +10p brt blue	.90	.50
a.		Souvenir sheet of 3	1.75	1.10
		Nos. B35-B37 (3)	1.45	.90

1962 International Stamp Exhibition. No. B37a contains three imperf. stamps similar to Nos. B35-B37 in dark blue.

1961, Dec. 16 Litho.

B38	SP19	2p +1p lilac & blk brn	.20	.20
B39	SP19	10p +5p light & deep claret	.50	.20

The surtax was for child welfare.

Chalk-browed Mockingbird SP20

Design: 12p+6p, Rufous-collared sparrow.

1962, Dec. 29 Perf. 13½

B40	SP20	4p +2p bis, brn & bl grn	.90	.60
B41	SP20	12p +6p gray, yel, grn & brn	1.50	1.10

The surtax was for child welfare. See Nos. B44, B47, B48-B50, CB32, CB35-CB36.

Soccer — SP21

Perf. 13½

1963, May 18

B42	SP21	4p +2p multi	.25	.20
B43	SP21	12p +6p Horsemanship	.45	.35
a.		Dark carmine (jacket) omitted		
		Nos. B42-B43,CB31 (3)	1.25	1.05

4th Pan American Games, Sao Paulo.

Bird Type of 1962

Design: Vermilion flycatcher.

1963, Dec. 21 Litho.

B44	SP20	4p +2p blk, red, org & grn	.60	.30

The surtax was for child welfare. See No. CB32.

Fencers — SP22

4p+2p, National Stadium, Tokyo, horiz.

1964, July 18 Wmk. 90 Perf. 13½

B45	SP22	4p +2p red, ocher & brn	.20	.20
B46	SP22	12p +6p bl grn & blk	.40	.30
		Nos. B45-B46,CB33 (3)	1.10	1.00

18th Olympic Games, Tokyo, Oct. 10-25, 1964. See No. CB33.

Bird Type of 1962

Design: Red-crested cardinal.

1964, Dec. 23 Litho.

B47	SP20	4p +2p dk bl, red & grn	.60	.30

The surtax was for child welfare. See #CB35.

Bird Type of 1962
Inscribed "R. ARGENTINA"

Designs: 8p+4p, Lapwing. 10p+5p, Scarlet-headed marshbird, horiz. 20p+10p, Amazon kingfisher.

1966-67   **Perf. 13½**

B48	SP20	8p +4p blk, ol, brt grn & red	.80	.35
B49	SP20	10p +5p blk, bl, org & grn	.80	.55
B50	SP20	20p +10p blk, yel, bl & pink	.40	.35
		Nos. B48-B50,CB36,CB38-CB39 (6)	4.30	3.25

The surtax was for child welfare.
Issue dates: 8p+4p, Mar. 26, 1966. 10p+5p, Jan. 14, 1967. 20p+10p, Dec. 23, 1967.

Grandmother's Birthday, by Patricia Lynch; Lions Emblem — SP23

Perf. 12½x13½

1968, Dec. 14   **Litho.**   **Wmk. 90**

B51	SP23	40p + 20p multi	.45	.40

1st Lions Intl. Benevolent Phil. Exhib. Surtax for the Children's Hospital Benevolent Fund.

White-faced Tree Duck — SP24

1969, Sept. 20   **Wmk. 365**   **Perf. 13½**

B52	SP24	20p + 10p multi	.50	.35

Surtax for child welfare. See No. CB40.

Slender-tailed Woodstar (Hummingbird) SP25

1970, May 9   **Wmk. 365**   **Perf. 13½**

B53	SP25	20c + 10c multi	.45	.40

The surtax was for child welfare. See Nos. CB41, B56-B59, B62-B63.

Dolphinfish — SP26

1971, Feb. 20   **Unwmk.**   **Perf. 12½**
Size: 75x15mm

B54	SP26	20c + 10c multi	.50	.45

Surtax for child welfare. See No. CB42.

Children with Stamps, by Mariette Lydis — SP27

1971, Dec. 18   **Litho.**   **Perf. 13½**

B55	SP27	1p + 50p multi	.50	.30

2nd Lions Intl. Solidarity Stamp Exhib.

Bird Type of 1970

Birds: 25c+10c, Saffron finch. 65c+30c, Rufous-bellied thrush, horiz.

1972, May 6   **Unwmk.**   **Perf. 13½**

B56	SP25	25c + 10c multi	.30	.20
B57	SP25	65c + 30c multi	.45	.30

Surtax was for child welfare.

Bird Type of 1970

Birds: 50c+25c, Southern screamer (chaja). 90c+45c, Saffron-cowled blackbird, horiz.

1973, Apr. 28

B58	SP25	50c + 25c multi	.50	.30
B59	SP25	90c + 45c multi	.70	.50

Surtax was for child welfare.

Painting Type of Regular Issue

Designs: 15c+15c, Still Life, by Alfredo Guttero, horiz. 90c+90c, Nude, by Miguel C. Victorica, horiz.

1973, Aug. 28   **Litho.**   **Perf. 13½**

B60	A472	15c + 15c multi	.30	.20
B61	A472	90c + 90c multi	1.00	.70

Bird Type of 1970

Birds: 70c+30c, Blue seed-eater. 1.20p+60c, Hooded siskin.

1974, May 11   **Litho.**   **Perf. 13½**

B62	SP25	70c + 30c multi	.50	.35
B63	SP25	1.20p + 60c multi	.75	.40

Surtax was for child welfare.

Painting Type of 1974

Design: 70c+30c, The Lama, by Juan Batlle Planas.

1974, May 11   **Litho.**   **Perf. 13½**

B64	A477	70c + 30c multi	.30	.25

PRENFIL-74 UPU, Intl. Exhib. of Phil. Periodicals, Buenos Aires, Oct. 1-12.

Plushcrested Jay — SP28

Designs: 13p+6.50p, Golden-collared macaw. 20p+10p, Begonia. 40p+20p, Teasel.

1976, June 12   **Litho.**   **Perf. 13½**

B65	SP28	7p + 3.50p multi	.20	.20
B66	SP28	13p + 6.50p multi	.30	.20
B67	SP28	20p + 10p multi	.50	.30
B68	SP28	40p + 20p multi	1.00	.50
		Nos. B65-B68 (4)	2.00	1.20

Argentine philately.

Telegraph, Communications Satellite — SP29

Designs: 20p+10p, Old and new mail trucks. 60p+30p, Old, new packet boats. 70p+35p, Biplane and jet.

1977, July 16   **Litho.**   **Perf. 13½**

B69	SP29	10p + 5p multi	.25	.20
B70	SP29	20p + 10p multi	.50	.60
B71	SP29	60p + 30p multi	1.00	.85
B72	SP29	70p + 35p multi	1.25	.85
		Nos. B69-B72 (4)	3.00	2.50

Surtax was for Argentine philately.
No. B70 exists with wmk. 365.

Church of St. Francis Type, 1977,
Inscribed: "EXPOSICION ARGENTINA '77"

1977, Aug. 27

B73	A515	160p + 80p multi	2.50	2.00

Surtax was for Argentina '77 Philatelic Exhibition. Issued in sheets of 4.

No. B73 Overprinted with Soccer Cup Emblem

1978, Feb. 4   **Litho.**   **Perf. 13½**

B74	A515	160p + 80p multi	4.50	4.25
a.		Souvenir sheet of 4	20.00	19.00

11th World Cup Soccer Championship, Argentina, June 1-25.

Spinus Magellanicus SP30

Birds: #B76, Variable seedeater. #B77, Yellow thrush. #B78, Pyrocephalus rubineus. #B79, Great kiskadee.

1978, Aug. 5   **Litho.**   **Perf. 13½**

B75	SP30	50p + 50p multi	.90	.60
B76	SP30	100p + 100p multi	1.10	.90
B77	SP30	150p + 150p multi	1.40	1.25
B78	SP30	200p + 200p multi	1.75	1.75
B79	SP30	500p + 500p multi	8.50	7.25
		Nos. B75-B79 (5)	13.65	11.75

ARGENTINA '78, Inter-American Philatelic Exhibition, Buenos Aires, Oct. 27-Nov. 5. Nos. B75-B79 issued in sheets of 4 with marginal inscriptions commemorating Exhibition and 1978 Soccer Championship.

Caravel "Magdalena," 16th Century — SP31

Sailing Ships: 500+500p, 3 master "Rio de la Plata," 17th cent. 600+600p, Corvette "Descubierta," 18th cent. 1500+1500p, Naval Academy yacht "A.R.A. Fortuna," 1979.

1979, Sept. 8   **Litho.**   **Perf. 13½**

B80	SP31	400p +400p multi	4.00	2.25
B81	SP31	500p +500p multi	4.75	2.50
B82	SP31	600p +600p multi	6.00	3.25
B83	SP31	1500p +1500p multi	15.00	8.00
		Nos. B80-B83 (4)	29.75	16.00

Buenos Aires '80, Intl. Philatelic Exhibition, 10/24-11/2/80. Issued in sheets of 4.

Purmamarca Church SP32

Churches: 200p + 100p, Molinos. 300p + 150p, Animana. 400p + 200p, San Jose de Lules.

1979, Nov. 3   **Litho.**   **Perf. 13½**

B84	SP32	100p + 50p multi	.25	.20
B85	SP32	200p + 100p multi	.45	.20
B86	SP32	300p + 150p multi	.60	.20
B87	SP32	400p + 200p multi	.90	.25
		Nos. B84-B87 (4)	2.20	.85

Buenos Aires No. 3, Exhibition and Society Emblems — SP33

Argentine Stamps: 750p+750p, type A580. 1000p+1000p, No. 91. 2000p+2000p, type A588.

1979, Dec. 15   **Litho.**   **Perf. 13½**

B88	SP33	250p + 250p	.90	.75
B89	SP33	750p + 750p	2.25	1.75
B90	SP33	1000p + 1000p	3.00	2.50
B91	SP33	2000p + 2000p	6.00	5.00
		Nos. B88-B91 (4)	12.15	10.00

PRENFIL '80, Intl. Philatelic Literature and Publications Exhib., Buenos Aires, Nov. 7-16, 1980.

Minuet, by Carlos E. Pellegrini SP34

Paintings: 700p+350p, Media Cana, by Carlos Morel. 800p+400p, Cielito, by Pellegrini. 1000p+500p, El Gato, by Juan Leon Palliere.

1981, July 11   **Litho.**   **Perf. 13½**

B92	SP34	500p + 250p multi	.70	.35
B93	SP34	700p + 350p multi	1.00	.70
B94	SP34	800p + 400p multi	1.10	.90
B95	SP34	1000p + 500p multi	1.40	1.25
		Nos. B92-B95 (4)	4.20	3.20

Espamer '81 Intl. Stamp Exhib. (Americas, Spain, Portugal), Buenos Aires, Nov. 13-22.

Canal, by Beatrix Bongliani (b. 1933) — SP35

Tapestries: 1000p+500p, Shadows, by Silvia Sieburger, vert. 2000p+1000p, Interpretation of a Rectangle, by Silke R. de Haupt, vert. 4000p+2000p, Tilcara, by Tana Sachs.

1982, July 31   **Litho.**   **Perf. 13½**

B96	SP35	1000p + 500p multi	.20	.20
B97	SP35	2000p + 1000p multi	.40	.40
B98	SP35	3000p + 1500p multi	.60	.60
B99	SP35	4000p + 2000p multi	.80	.80
		Nos. B96-B99 (4)	2.00	2.00

Boy Playing
Marbles
SP36

1983, July 2   Litho.   Perf. 13½

B100	SP36	20c + 10c shown	.20	.20
B101	SP36	30c + 15c Jumping rope	.45	.20
B102	SP36	50c + 25c Hopscotch	.85	.20
B103	SP36	1p + 50c Flying kites	1.10	.50
B104	SP36	2p + 1p Spinning top	1.60	.65
		Nos. B100-B104 (5)	4.20	1.75

Surtax was for natl. philatelic associations.
See Nos. B106-B110.

Compass, 15th Cent. — SP37

ARGENTINA '85 Intl. Stamp Show: b, Arms of Spain, Argentina. c, Columbus' arms. d-f, Columbus' arrival at San Salvador Island. Nos. B105b-B105f in continuous design; ships shown on singles range in size, left to right, from small to large. Surtax was for exhibition.

1984, Apr. 28   Litho.   Perf. 13½

B105		Block of 6	3.75	3.75
a.-f.	SP37 5p + 2.50p, any single		.50	.25

Children's Game Type of 1983

1984, July 7   Litho.   Perf. 13½

B106	SP36	2p + 1p Blind Man's Buff	.20	.20
B107	SP36	3p + 1.50p The Loop	.30	.25
B108	SP36	4p + 2p Leap Frog	.35	.30
B109	SP36	5p + 2.50p Rolling the loop	.45	.35
B110	SP36	6p + 3p Ball Mold	.55	.45
		Nos. B106-B110 (5)	1.85	1.55

Butterflies — SP38

1985, Nov. 9   Litho.   Perf. 13½

B111	SP38	5c + 2c Rothschildia jacobaeae	.75	.20
B112	SP38	10c + 5c Heliconius erato phyllis	.75	.40
B113	SP38	20c + 10c Precis evarete hilaris	1.00	.75
B114	SP38	25c + 13c Cyanopepla pretiosa	1.50	1.00
B115	SP38	40c + 20c Papilio androgeus	2.00	1.50
		Nos. B111-B115 (5)	6.00	3.85

Children's Drawings — SP39

1986, Aug. 30   Litho.

B116	SP39	5c + 2c N. Pastor	.20	.20
B117	SP39	10c + 5c T. Valleistein	.35	.35

B118	SP39	20c + 10c J.M. Flores	.60	.60
B119	SP39	25c + 13c M.E. Pezzuto	.75	.75
B120	SP39	40c + 20c E. Diehl	1.10	1.10
		Nos. B116-B120 (5)	3.00	3.00

Surtax for natl. philatelic associations.

Miniature Sheets

Fresh-water Fish — SP40

No. B121: a, Metynnis maculatus. b, Cynolebias nigripinnis. c, Leporinus solarii. d, Aphyocharax rathbuni. e, Corydoras aeneus. f, Thoracocharax securis. g, Cynolebias melanotaenia. h, Cichlasoma facetum.
No. B122: a, Tetragonopterus argenteus. b, Hemigrammus caudovittatus. c, Astyanax bimaculatus. d, Gymnocorymbus ternetzi. e, Hoplias malabaricus. f, Aphyocharax rubripinnis. g, Apistogramma agassizi. h, Pyrrhulina rachoviana.

1987, June 27

B121	Sheet of 8	2.00	1.75
a.-h.	SP40 10c +5c, any single	.25	.20
B122	Sheet of 8	4.00	3.50
a.-h.	SP40 20c +10c, any single	.50	.40

PRENFIL '88, Intl. Philatelic Literature and Media Exhibition, Buenos Aires, Nov. 25-Dec. 2 — SP41

Locomotives and railroad car: No. B123, Yatay locomotive, 1888. No. B124, FCCA electric passenger car, 1914. No. B125, B-15 locomotive, 1942. No. B126, GT-22 No. 200 locomotive, 1988.

1988, June 4   Litho.   Perf. 13½

B123	SP41	1a +50c multi	.65	.50
B124	SP41	1a +50c multi	.65	.50
B125	SP41	1a +50c multi	.65	.50
B126	SP41	1a +50c multi	.65	.50
		Nos. B123-B126 (4)	2.60	2.00

Nos. B123-B125 each issued in sheets of 4.

Horses
SP42

Paintings: No. B127, The Waiting, by Gustavo Solari. No. B128, Mare and Foal, by E. Castro. No. B129, Saint Isidor, by Castro. No. B130, At Lagoon's Edge, by F. Romero Carranza. No. B131, Under the Tail, by Castro.

1988, Oct. 29   Litho.   Perf. 13½

B127	SP42	2a +1a multi	.70	.50
B128	SP42	2a +1a multi	.70	.50
B129	SP42	2a +1a multi	.70	.50
B130	SP42	2a +1a multi	.70	.50
B131	SP42	2a +1a multi	.70	.50
		Nos. B127-B131 (5)	3.50	2.50

PRENFIL
'88 — SP43

Covers of philatelic magazines.

1988, Nov. 26   Litho.   Perf. 13½

B132	SP43	1a +1a Cronaca Filatelica, Italy	.40	.30
B133	SP43	1a +1a CO-FI, Brazil	.40	.30
B134	SP43	1a +1a References de la Poste, France	.40	.30
B135	SP43	2a +2a Postas Argentinas	.65	.50
		Nos. B132-B135 (4)	1.85	1.40

Souvenir Sheet

ARBRAPEX '88 — SP44

Designs: No. B136a, Candel Delivery at San Ignacio, by Leonie Matthis, Cornelio Saavedra Museum, Buenos Aires. No. B136b, Immaculate Conception, a statue in the Isaac Fernandez Blanco Museum, Buenos Aires.

1988, Nov. 26   Perf. 12

B136	SP44 Sheet of 2	1.60	1.25
a.	2a +2a multi	.65	.50
b.	3a +3a multi	.95	.70

Fish
SP45

#B137, Diplomystes viedmensis. #B138, Haplochiton taeniatus. #B139, Percichthys trucha. #B140, Galaxias platei. #B141, Salmo fario.

1989, June 24   Litho.   Perf. 13½

B137	SP45	10a +5a multi	.25	.20
B138	SP45	10a +5a multi	.25	.20
B139	SP45	10a +5a multi	.25	.20
B140	SP45	10a +5a multi	.25	.20
B141	SP45	10a +5a multi	.25	.20
		Nos. B137-B141 (5)	1.25	1.00

Printed in sheets of 4.

Discovery of America 500th Anniv. (in 1992) and ESPAMER '90 — SP46

Documents and chronicles: No. B142, Columbus's coat of arms, Book of Privileges title page. No. B143, Illustration from New Chronicle and Good Government, by Guaman Poma de Ayala. No. B144, Illustration from Discovery and Conquest of Peru, by Pedro de Cieza de Leon. No. B145, Illustration from Travel to the River Plate, by Ulrico Schmidl.

1989, Sept. 16   Litho.   Perf. 13½
Yellow, Rose Violet & Black

B142	SP46	100a +50a	.90	.80
B143	SP46	150a +50a	.90	.80
B144	SP46	200a +100a	.90	.80
B145	SP46	250a +100a	.90	.80
		Nos. B142-B145 (4)	3.60	3.20

Designs: No. B146, Podisus nigripinnus. No. B147, Adalia bipunctata. No. B148, Nabis punctipennis. No. B149, Hippodamia convergens. No. B150, Calleida suturalis.

1990, June 30   Litho.   Perf. 13½

B146	SP47	1000a +500a multi	1.00	.85
B147	SP47	1000a +500a multi	1.00	.85
B148	SP47	1000a +500a multi	1.00	.85
B149	SP47	1000a +500a multi	1.00	.85
B150	SP47	1000a +500a multi	1.00	.85
		Nos. B146-B150 (5)	5.00	4.25

Printed in sheets of 4.

Souvenir Sheet

First Natl. Exposition of Aerophilately — SP48

a, Lieut. Marcos A. Zar, Macchi seaplane. b, Capt. Antonio Parodi, Ansaldo SVA biplane. Illustration reduced.

1990, July 14   Litho.   Perf. 12

B151	SP48 Sheet of 2	6.00	5.00
a.	2000a +2000a multi	3.00	2.50
b.	3000a +3000a multi	3.00	2.50

Souvenir Sheet

1992 Summer Olympics, Barcelona SP49

Designs: a, Shot put. b, High jump. c, Hurdles. d, Pole vault.

1990, Dec. 15   Litho.   Perf. 13½

B152	Sheet of 4	9.00	9.00
a.-d.	SP49 2000a +2000a multi	2.25	2.25

Espamer '91 Philatelic Exhibition.
See No. B155.

Souvenir Sheet

Discovery of America, 500th Anniv. (in 1992) — SP50

Voyage of Alesandro Malaspina, 1789-1794: a, Sailing ship. b, Malaspina. c, Indian, hut. d, Indian, horse, artist drawing.

1990, Oct. 13   Litho.   Perf. 13½

B153	Sheet of 4	6.00	6.00
a.-d.	SP50 2000a +1000a, any single	1.50	1.50

Espamer '91, Buenos Aires.

Souvenir Sheet

Race Cars and Drivers — SP51

Designs: a, Juan Manuel Fangio. b, Juan Manuel Bordeu. c, Carlos Alberto Reutemann. d, Oscar and Juan Galvez.

1991		Litho.	**Perf. 13½**	
B154	SP51	Sheet of 4	4.75	4.75
a.-d.		2500a +2500a, any single	1.25	1.25

Espamer '91.

Souvenir Sheet
1992 Summer Olympics Type of 1990

Women's gymnastics routines: a, Floor exercise. b, Uneven parallel bars. c, Balance beam. d, Rhythmic gymnastics.

1991, June 29		Litho.	**Perf. 13½**	
B155		Sheet of 4	4.75	4.75
a.-d.	SP49	2500a +2500a, any single	1.25	1.25

Espamer '91.

Iberoprenfil '92 — SP52

Designs: No. B156, Castor missile. No. B157, Satellite LUSAT 1.

1991, Dec. 28		Litho.	**Perf. 13½**	
B156	SP52	4000a +4000a multi	2.00	1.75
B157	SP52	4000a +4000a multi	2.00	1.75

Dinosaurs SP53

1992, May 2		Litho.	**Perf. 13½**	
B158	SP53	38c +38c Carnotaurus	2.00	2.00
B159	SP53	38c +38c Amargasaurus	2.00	2.00

Iberoprenfil '92, Buenos Aires — SP54

Paintings by Raul Soldi (b. 1905): No. B160, The Fiesta. No. B161, Church of St. Anne of Glew.

1992, Sept. 5		Litho.	**Perf. 13½**	
B160	SP54	76c +76c multi	3.50	3.50
B161	SP54	76c +76c multi	3.50	3.50

Parafil '92 — SP55

1992, Nov. 21		Litho.	**Perf. 13½**	
B162	SP55	76c +76c multi	3.00	3.00

2nd Argentine-Paraguayan Philatelic Exhibition, Buenos Aires.

Souvenir Sheet

Birds — SP56

a, Egretta thula. b, Amblyramphus holosericeus. c, Paroaria coronata. d, Chloroceryle amazona.

1993, July 17		Litho.	**Perf. 13½**	
B163	SP56	38c +38c Sheet of 4	8.00	8.00

Souvenir Sheet

Latin American Air Post Philatelic Exhibition — SP57

Designs: a, 25c+25c, Antoine de Saint-Exupery (1940-44), pilot, author. b, 75c+75c, "The Little Prince," vert. Illustration reduced.

1995, June 3		Litho.	**Perf. 12**	
B164	SP57	Sheet of 2, #a.-b.	7.00	7.00

For overprint see No. B180.

Souvenir Sheet

Exploration of Antarctica SP58

75c+25c, Transport ship ARA Bahia Aguirre. 1.25p+75c, Argentine Air Force Hercules C-130.

1995, July 8				
B165	SP58	Sheet of 2, #a.-b.	9.00	9.00

Aerofila '96 SP59

Historic airplanes, pilots: No. B166, "Plus ultra," Ramon Franco Bahamonde (1896-1938). No. B167, 14 Bis, Alberto Santos-Dumont (1873-1932). No. B168, Spirit of St. Louis, Charles A. Lindbergh (1902-1974). No. B169, Buenos Aires, Eduardo A. Olivero (1896-1966).

1996, July 13		Litho.	**Perf. 13½**	
B166	SP59	25c +25c multi	1.50	1.50
B167	SP59	25c +25c multi	1.50	1.50
B168	SP59	50c +50c multi	3.00	3.00
B169	SP59	50c +50c multi	3.00	3.00
		Nos. B166-B169 (4)	9.00	9.00

Ceramic Murals from Buenos Aires Subway SP60

1996, Sept. 21		Litho.	**Perf. 13½**	
B170	SP60	1p +50c Dragon	4.00	4.00
B171	SP60	1.50p +1p Bird	7.00	7.00

MEVIFIL '97, 1st Intl. Exhibition of Audio-Visual and Philatelic Information Media — SP61

Designs: No. B172, France Type A1. No. B173, Spain Type A3. No. B174, Argentina Type A4. No. B175, Buenos Aires Type A1.

1997, May 10		Litho.	**Perf. 13½**	
B172	SP61	50c +50c multi	2.00	2.00
B173	SP61	50c +50c multi	2.00	2.00
B174	SP61	50c +50c multi	2.00	2.00
B175	SP61	50c +50c multi	2.00	2.00
a.		Block of 4, #B172-B175	8.00	8.00

Issued in sheets of 16 stamps + 4 labels.

Trains — SP62

Designs: No. B176, Las Nubes (Train to the Clouds), Salta. No. B177, Historical train, Buenos Aires. No. B178, Old Patagonian Express, Rio Negro-Chubut. No. B179, Southern Fueguino Railway, Tierra Del Fuego. Illustration reduced.

1997, Sept. 6		Litho.	**Perf. 13**	
B176	SP62	50c +50c multi	2.00	2.00
B177	SP62	50c +50c multi	2.00	2.00
B178	SP62	50c +50c multi	2.00	2.00
B179	SP62	50c +50c multi	2.00	2.00
		Nos. B176-B179 (4)	8.00	8.00

No. B164 Ovptd. in Red Violet in Sheet Margin:

1997, Sept. 27		Litho.	**Perf. 12**	
B180	SP57	Sheet of 2, #a.-b.	7.00	7.00

Cartography — SP63

Maps of the Buenos Aires area from: 25c+25c, 1546. No. B182, 17th century. No. B183, 1910. 75c+75c, 1999.

		Perf. 13¾x13½		
1999, Nov. 20			**Litho.**	
B181	SP63	25c + 25c multi	1.00	1.00
B182	SP63	50c + 50c multi	2.00	2.00
B183	SP63	50c + 50c multi	2.00	2.00
B184	SP63	75c + 75c multi	3.00	3.00
a.		Block of 4, #B181-B184	12.00	12.00

Methods of Transportation — SP64

No. B185: a, Bicycle. b, Graf Zeppelin. c, Train. d, Trolley. Illustration reduced.

2000, Oct. 21		Litho.	**Perf. 14x13½**	
B185		Block of 4	8.00	8.00
a.	SP64	25c +25c multi	1.00	1.00
b.-c.	SP64	50c +50c Any single	2.00	2.00
d.	SP64	75c +75c multi	3.00	3.00

Cetaceans — SP65

No. B186: a, Burmeister's porpoise (Mariposa espinosa). b, River Plate dolphin. c, Minke whale. d, Humpback whale (Yubarta). Illustration reduced.

2001, Sept. 15		Litho.	**Perf. 14x13½**	
B186		Block of 4	8.00	8.00
a.	SP65	25c +25c multi	1.00	1.00
b.-c.	SP65	50c +50c Any single	2.00	2.00
d.	SP65	75c +75c multi	3.00	3.00

AIR POST STAMPS

Airplane Circles the Globe — AP1 / Eagle — AP2

Wings Cross the Sea — AP3

Condor on Mountain Crag — AP4

Perforations of Nos. C1-C37 vary from clean-cut to rough and uneven, with many skipped perfs.

Perf. 13x13½, 13½x13
1928, Mar. 1   Litho.   Wmk. 90
C1	AP1	5c lt red	1.25	.50
C2	AP1	10c Prus blue	2.25	1.00
C3	AP2	15c lt brown	2.25	.80
C4	AP1	18c lilac gray	3.00	2.75
a.		18c brown lilac	3.25	2.75
b.		Double impression	375.00	
C5	AP2	20c ultra	2.25	.80
C6	AP2	24c deep blue	3.50	2.75
C7	AP3	25c brt violet	3.50	1.50
C8	AP3	30c rose red	5.25	1.00
C9	AP4	35c rose	3.50	1.00
C10	AP1	36c bister brn	2.50	1.50
C11	AP4	50c gray black	4.00	.50
C12	AP2	54c chocolate	3.50	2.00
C13	AP2	72c yellow grn	4.75	2.00
a.		Double impression	300.00	
C14	AP3	90c dk brown	9.00	1.75
C15	AP3	1p slate bl & red	11.00	.65
C16	AP3	1.08p rose & dk bl	16.00	4.50
C17	AP3	1.26p dull vio & grn	20.00	8.00
C18	AP4	1.80p blue & lil rose	20.00	8.00
C19	AP4	3.60p gray & blue	42.50	19.00
		Nos. C1-C19 (19)	160.00	60.00

The watermark on No. C4a is larger than on the other stamps of this set, measuring 10mm across Sun.

Zeppelin First Flight

Air Post Stamps of 1928 Overprinted in Blue

1930, May
C20	AP2	20c ultra	10.00	5.00
C21	AP4	50c gray black	20.00	10.00
a.		Inverted overprint	475.00	
C22	AP3	1p slate bl & red	21.00	10.00
a.		Inverted overprint	650.00	
C23	AP4	1.80p blue & lil rose	55.00	25.00
C24	AP4	3.60p gray & blue	150.00	70.00
		Nos. C20-C24 (5)	256.00	120.00

Overprinted in Green
C25	AP2	20c ultra	10.00	6.00
C26	AP4	50c gray black	12.50	9.00
C27	AP3	90c dark brown	10.00	6.00
C28	AP3	1p slate bl & red	20.00	12.50
C29	AP4	1.80p blue & lil rose	600.00	400.00
a.		Thick paper	850.00	
		Nos. C25-C29 (5)	652.50	433.50

Air Post Stamps of 1928 Overprinted in Red or Blue

On AP1-AP2

On AP3-AP4

1931
C30	AP1	18c lilac gray	2.00	1.50
C31	AP2	72c yellow green	14.00	10.50
C32	AP3	90c dark brown	14.00	10.50
C33	AP4	1.80p bl & lil rose (Bl)	30.00	22.50
C34	AP4	3.60p gray & blue	57.50	40.00
		Nos. C30-C34 (5)	117.50	85.00

1st anniv. of the Revolution of 1930.

Zeppelin Issue
Nos. C1, C4, C4a, C14 Overprinted in Blue or Red

On AP1

On AP3

1932, Aug. 4
C35	AP1	5c lt red (Bl)	3.00	2.00
C36	AP1	18c lilac gray (R)	12.50	9.00
a.		18c brown lilac (R)	100.00	60.00
C37	AP3	90c dark brown (R)	32.50	26.00
		Nos. C35-C37 (3)	48.00	37.00

Plane and Letter — AP5

Mercury — AP6

Plane in Flight — AP7

Perf. 13½x13, 13x13½
1940, Oct. 23   Photo.   Wmk. 90
C38	AP5	30c deep orange	5.00	.20
C39	AP6	50c dark brown	7.50	.20
C40	AP5	1p carmine	1.75	.20
C41	AP7	1.25p deep green	.50	.20
C42	AP5	2.50p bright blue	1.25	.20
		Nos. C38-C42 (5)	16.00	1.00

Plane and Letter — AP8

Mercury and Plane — AP9

Perf. 13½x13, 13x13½
1942, Oct. 6   Litho.   Wmk. 90
C43	AP8	30c orange	.20	.20
C44	AP9	50c dull brn & buff	.40	.20

See Nos. C49-C52, C57, C61.

Plane over Iguaçu Falls — AP10

Plane over the Andes — AP11

Perf. 13½x13
1946, June 10   Unwmk.
C45	AP10	15c dull red brn	.25	.20
C46	AP11	25c gray green	.20	.20

See Nos. C53-C54.

Allegory of Flight AP12

Astrolabe — AP13

Perf. 13½x13, 13x13½
1946, Sept. 25   Litho.   Unwmk.
Surface-Tinted Paper
C47	AP12	15c sl grn, pale grn	.55	.20
C48	AP13	60c vio brn, ocher	.55	.35

Types of 1942
1946-48   Unwmk.   Perf. 13½x13
C49	AP8	30c orange	1.40	.20
C50	AP9	50c dull brn & buff	2.50	.20
C51	AP8	1p carmine ('47)	1.25	.20
C52	AP8	2.50p brt blue ('48)	5.50	.75
		Nos. C49-C52 (4)	10.65	1.35

Types of 1946
1948   Wmk. 90
C53	AP10	15c dull red brn	.20	.20
C54	AP11	25c gray green	.25	.20

Atlas (National Museum, Naples) — AP14

Map of Argentine Republic, Globe and Caliper — AP15

Perf. 13½x13, 13x13½
1948-49   Photo.   Wmk. 288
C55	AP14	45c dk brown ('49)	.35	.20
C56	AP15	70c dark green	.50	.25

4th Pan-American Reunion of Cartographers, Buenos Aires, Oct.-Nov., 1948.

Mercury Type of 1942
1949   Litho.   Perf. 13x13½
C57	AP9	50c dull brn & buff	.40	.20

Marksmanship Trophy — AP16

1949, Nov. 4   Photo.
C58	AP16	75c brown	.75	.20

World Rifle Championship, 1949.

Catalogue values for unused stamps in this section, from this point to the end of the section, are for Never Hinged items.

Douglas DC-3 and Condor AP17

Perf. 13x13½
1951, June 20   Wmk. 90
C59	AP17	20c dk olive grn	.20	.20

10th anniversary of the State air lines.

Douglas DC-6 and Condor — AP18

1951, Oct. 17   Perf. 13½
C60	AP18	20c blue	.20	.20

End of Argentine 5-year Plan.

Plane-Letter Type of 1942
1951   Litho.   Perf. 13½x13
C61	AP8	1p carmine	.40	.20

Jesus by Leonardo da Vinci (detail, "Virgin of the Rocks") AP19

Perf. 13½x13
1956, Sept. 29   Photo.   Wmk. 90
C62	AP19	1p dull purple	.35	.20

Issued to express the gratitude of the children of Argentina to the people of the world for their help against poliomyelitis.

Battle of Montevideo AP20

Leonardo
Rosales and
Tomas
Espora
AP21

Guillermo
Brown — AP22

Map of Americas
& Arms of
Buenos
Aires — AP23

1957, Mar. 2   Perf. 13½
C63 AP20 60c blue gray   .20 .20
C64 AP21 1p brt pink   .20 .20
C65 AP22 2p brown   .25 .20
   Nos. C63-C65 (3)   .65 .60
   Cent. of the death of Admiral Guillermo
Brown, founder of the Argentine navy.

1957, Aug. 16
C66 AP23 2p rose violet   .40 .20
   Issued to publicize the Inter-American Economic Conference in Buenos Aires.

AP24

1957, Aug. 31   Wmk. 90   Perf. 13½
C67 AP24 60c Modern jlcomotive   .20 .20
   Centenary of Argentine railroads.

AP25

1957, Sept. 14
C68 AP25 1p Globe, Flag,Compass
   Rose   .20 .20
C69 AP25 2p Key   .30 .20
   1957 International Congress for Tourism.

Birds
Carrying
Letters
AP26

1957, Nov. 6
C70 AP26 1p bright blue   .20 .20
   Issued for Letter Writing Week, Oct. 6-12.

Early Plane
AP27

1958, May 31   Perf. 13½
C71 AP27 2p maroon   .20 .20
   50th anniv. of the Argentine Aviation Club.

Stamp Anniv. Type

Designs: 80c, Stamp of Buenos Aires and view of the Plaza de la Aduana. 1p, Stamp of 1858 and "The Post of Santa Fe."

1958   Litho.   Perf. 13½
C72 A270 80c pale bis & sl bl   .20 .20
C73 A270 1p red org & dk bl   .25 .20
   Cent. of the 1st postage stamps of Buenos Aires & the Argentine Confederation.
   Issue dates: 80c, Oct. 18; 1p, Aug. 23.

Comet
Jet over
World
Map
AP29

1959, May 16   Perf. 13½
C74 AP29 5p black & olive   .35 .20
   Inauguration of jet flights by Argentine Airlines.

Type of Regular Issue, 1960.

"Cabildo" and: 1.80p, Mariano Moreno. 5p, Manuel Belgrano and Juan Jose Castelli.

Perf. 13½

1960, May 28   Wmk. 90   Photo.
C75 A287 1.80p red brown   .20 .20
   a.   Souvenir sheet of 3   .65 .40
C76 A287 5p buff & purple   .35 .20
   a.   Souvenir sheet of 3   1.25 .80
   Souvenir sheets are imperf. No. C75a contains one No. C75 and 1p and 2p resembling Nos. 713-714; stamps in reddish brown. No. C76a contains one No. C76 and 4.20p and 10.70p resembling Nos. 715-716; stamps are in green.

Symbolic of New
Provinces — AP30

1960, July 8   Litho.
C77 AP30 1.80p dp car & blue   .20 .20
   Elevation of the territories of Chubut, Formosa, Neuquen, Rio Negro and Santa Cruz to provinces.

Type of Regular Issue, 1960

1960, Oct. 1   Photo.   Perf. 13½
C78 A291 1.80p rose lilac   .20 .20
C79 A291 10.70p brt grnsh blue   .40 .20

UNESCO
Emblem
AP31

1962, July 14   Litho.
C80 AP31 13p ocher & brown   .40 .25
   15th anniv. of UNESCO.

Mail Coach
AP32

1962, Oct. 6   Wmk. 90   Perf. 13½
C81 AP32 5.60p gray brn & blk   .20 .20
   Mailman's Day, Sept. 14, 1962.

No. 695 and Type of 1959 Surcharged in Green

1962, Oct. 31   Photo.
C82 A277 5.60p on 5p brown   .30 .20
C83 A277 18p on 5p brn, grnsh   1.00 .20

UPAE
Emblem — AP33   Skylark — AP34

1962, Nov. 24   Photo.   Perf. 13½
C84 AP33 5.60p dark blue   .20 .20
   50th anniv. of the founding of the Postal Union of the Americas and Spain, UPAE.

1963, Feb. 9   Litho.
   Design: 11p, Super Albatros.
C85 AP34 5.60p blue & black   .20 .20
C86 AP34 11p blue, blk & red   .30 .20
   9th World Gliding Championships.

Symbolic
Plane
AP35

1963-65   Wmk. 90   Perf. 13½
C87 AP35 5.60p dk pur, car &
   brt grn   .40 .20
C88 AP35 7p black & bis
   ('64)   .55 .20
C88A AP35 7p black & bis
   ('65)   4.00 .55
C89 AP35 11p blk, dk pur &
   grn   .55 .25
C90 AP35 18p dk pur, red &
   vio bl   1.10 .35
C91 AP35 21p brown, red &
   gray   1.40 .55
   Nos. C87-C91 (6)   8.00 2.10
   "Argentina" reads down on No. C88, up on No. C88A. See Nos. C101-C104, C108-C111, C123-C126, C135-C141. For overprint and surcharges see Nos. C96, C146-C150.

Type of Regular Issue, 1964

Map of Falkland Islands (Islas Malvinas).

1964, Feb. 22   Perf. 13½
   Size: 33x22mm
C92 A327 18p lt & dk bl & ol grn   1.75 .70

UPU
Monument,
Bern, and UN
Emblem
AP36

1964, May 23   Engr.   Perf. 13½
C93 AP36 18p red & dk brown   .50 .25
   15th UPU Cong., Vienna, Austria, 5-6/64.

Discovery of
America,
Florentine
Woodcut
AP37

1964, Oct. 10   Litho.
C94 AP37 13p tan & black   .35 .30
   Day of the Race, Columbus Day.

Lt. Matienzo
Base,
Antarctica
AP38

1965, Feb. 27   Photo.   Perf. 13½
C95 AP38 11p salmon pink   .50 .25
   Issued to publicize the national territory of Tierra del Fuego, Antarctic and South Atlantic Isles.

No. C88A Overprinted in Silver: "PRIMERS / JORNADAS FILATELICAS / RIOPLATENSES"

1965, Mar. 17   Litho.
C96 AP35 7p black & bister   .25 .20
   1st Rio de la Plata Stamp Show, sponsored jointly by the Argentine and Uruguayan Philatelic Associations, Montevideo, Mar. 19-28.

ITU
Emblem — AP39   Ascending
Rocket — AP40

1965, May 11   Wmk. 90   Perf. 13½
C97 AP39 18p slate, blk & red   .40 .25
   Centenary of the ITU.

1965, May 29   Photo.   Perf. 13½
   Design: 50p, Earth with trajectories and magnetic field, horiz.
C98 AP40 18p vermilion   .40 .20
C99 AP40 50p dp violet blue   1.00 .50
   6th Symposium on Space Research, held in Buenos Aires, and to honor the Natl. Commission of Space Research.

Type of 1963-65 Inscribed "Republica Argentina" Reading Down

1965, Oct. 13   Litho.   Wmk. 90
C101 AP35 12p dk car rose &
   brn   1.40 .20
C102 AP35 15p vio blue & dk
   red   .85 .25
C103 AP35 27.50p dk bl grn &
   gray   1.40 .40
C104 AP35 30.50p dk brown &
   dk bl   2.00 .60
   Nos. C101-C104 (4)   5.65 1.45

Argentine Antarctica Map and Centaur Rocket AP41

1966, Feb. 19   *Perf. 13½*
C105 AP41 27.50p bl, blk & dp org   1.00 .75

Launchings of sounding balloons and of a Gamma Centaur rocket in Antarctica during February, 1965.

Sea Gull and Southern Cross AP42

1966, May 14   *Perf. 13½*
C106 AP42 12p Prus blue, blk & red   .30 .20

50th anniv. of the Naval Aviation School.

Blériot Plane Flown by Fels, 1917 — AP43

1967, Sept. 2   Litho.   *Perf. 13½*
C107 AP43 26p olive, bl & blk   .25 .20

Flight by Theodore Fels from Buenos Aires to Montevideo, Sept. 2, 1917, allegedly the 1st intl. airmail flight.

Type of 1963-65 Inscribed "Republica Argentina" Reading Down

1967, Dec. 20   *Perf. 13½*
C108 AP35 26p brown   .60 .25
C109 AP35 40p violet   4.50 .30
C110 AP35 68p blue green   3.00 .15
C111 AP35 78p ultra   1.25 .60
   Nos. C108-C111 (4)   9.35 1.60

Vito Dumas and Ketch "Legh II" AP44

1968, July 27   Litho.   Wmk. 90
C112 AP44 68p bl, blk, red & vio bl   .65 .40

Issued to commemorate Vito Dumas's one-man voyage around the world in 1943.

Type of Regular Issue and

Assembly Emblem — AP45

40p, Globe and map of South America.

1968, Oct. 19   Litho.   *Perf. 13½*
C113 A395 40p brt pink, lt bl & blk   .40 .20
C114 AP45 68p bl, lt bl, gold & blk   .65 .30

4th Plenary Assembly of the Intl. Telegraph and Telephone Consultative Committee, Mar del Plata, Sept. 23-Oct. 25.

Radar Antenna, Balcarce Station AP46

   Perf. 13½
1969, Aug. 23   Wmk. 90   Photo.
C115 AP46 40p blue gray   .70 .25

Communications by satellite through Intl. Telecommunications Consortium (INTELSAT).

Atucha Nuclear Center AP47

1969, Dec. 13   Litho.   Wmk. 365
C116 AP47 26p blue & multi   1.40 .80

Completion of Atucha Nuclear Center.

Type of 1963-65 Inscribed "Republica Argentina" Reading Down

1969-71   *Perf. 13½*
C123 AP35 40p violet   5.00 .30
C124 AP35 68p dk blue grn ('70)   2.00 .60
    Unwmk.
C125 AP35 26p yellow brn ('71)   .25 .20
C126 AP35 40p violet ('71)   2.75 .40
   Nos. C123-C126 (4)   10.00 1.50

Old Fire Engine and Fire Brigade Emblem AP48

1970, Aug. 8   Litho.   Unwmk.
C128 AP48 40c green & multi   .55 .30

Centenary of the Fire Brigade.

Education Year Emblem AP49

1970, Aug. 29   *Perf. 13½*
C129 AP49 68c blue & blk   .40 .25

Issued for International Education Year.

Fleet Leaving Valparaiso, by Antonio Abel — AP50

1970, Oct. 17   Litho.   *Perf. 13½*
C130 AP50 26c multicolored   1.00 .35

150th anniv. of the departure for Peru of the liberation fleet from Valparaiso, Chile.

Sumampa Chapel — AP51

1970, Nov. 7   Photo.
C131 AP51 40c multicolored   .95 .35

Bishopric of Tucuman, 400th anniversary.

Buenos Aires Planetarium — AP52

1970, Nov. 28   Litho.   *Perf. 13½*
C132 AP52 40c multicolored   .60 .25

Jorge Newbery and Morane Saulnier Plane AP53

1970, Dec. 19
C133 AP53 26c bl, blk, yel & grn   .40 .25

24th Aeronautics and Space Week.

Industries Type of Regular Issue
Design: 31c, Refinery.

1971, Oct. 16   Litho.   *Perf. 13½*
C134 A445 31c red, blk & yel   .60 .25

Type of 1963-65 Inscribed "Republica Argentina" Reading Down

1971-74   **Unwmk.**
C135 AP35 45c brown   3.25 .20
C136 AP35 68c red   .50 .20
C137 AP35 70c vio blue ('73)   .85 .20
C138 AP35 90c emerald ('73)   1.90 .20
C139 AP35 1.70p blue ('74)   .50 .25
C140 AP35 1.95p emerald ('74)   .50 .30
C141 AP35 2.65p dp claret ('74)   .50 .40
   Nos. C135-C141 (7)   8.00 1.75

Fluorescent paper was used for Nos. C135-C136, C138-C141. The 70c was issued on both papers.

Don Quixote, Drawing by Ignacio Zuloaga AP54

1975, Apr. 26   Photo.   *Perf. 13½*
C145 AP54 2.75p yellow, blk & red   .60 .35

Day of the Race and for Espana 75 Intl. Philatelic Exhibition, Madrid, Apr. 4-13.

No. C87 Surcharged

1975, Sept. 15   Litho.   Wmk. 90
C146 AP35 9.20p on 5.60p   .90 .20
C147 AP35 19.70p on 5.60p   1.25 .45
C148 AP35 100p on 5.60p   5.50 2.25
   Nos. C146-C148 (3)   7.65 2.90

No. C87 Surcharged

1975, Oct. 15
C149 AP35 9.20p on 5.60p   .70 .30
C150 AP35 19.70p on 5.60p   1.25 .60

Argentine State Airline, 50th Anniv. — AP55

1990, Sept. 15   *Perf. 13½*
C151 AP55 2500a Junkers JU52-3M   1.25 .90
C152 AP55 2500a Grumman SA-16   1.25 .90
C153 AP55 2500a Fokker F-27   1.25 .90
C154 AP55 2500a Fokker F-28   1.25 .90
   Nos. C151-C154 (4)   5.00 3.60

AIR POST SEMI-POSTAL STAMPS

Catalogue values for unused stamps in this section are for Never Hinged items.

Philatelic Exhibition Type

#CB1, Stamp engraving. #CB2, Proofing stamp die. #CB3, Sheet of stamps. #CB4, The letter. #CB5, Gen. San Martin.

   Perf. 13½
1950, Aug. 26   Wmk. 90   Photo.
CB1 SP8 45c + 45c vio bl   .40 .25
CB2 SP8 70c + 70c dk brn   .55 .40
  a.   Souv. sheet of 3, #B12, CB1, CB2, imperf.   3.00 3.00
CB3 SP8 1p + 1p cerise   1.50 1.50
CB4 SP8 2.50p + 2.50p ol gray   8.50 6.00
CB5 SP8 5p + 5p dull grn   9.25 7.25
   Nos. CB1-CB5 (5)   20.20 15.40

Argentine Intl. Philatelic Exhib., 1950.

Pieta by Michelangelo SPAP2

1951, Dec. 22   *Perf. 13½x13*
CB6 SPAP2 2.45p +7.55p grnsh blk   21.00 14.00

Surtax as for the Eva Peron Foundation.

Flower and Child's Head SPAP3

1958, Mar. 15   *Perf. 13½*
CB7 SPAP3 1p +50c deep claret   .30 .30

Surtax for National Council for Children.

Stamp of
1858 — SPAP4

1958, Mar. 29   Litho.   Wmk. 90
CB8   SPAP4   1p + 50c gray ol &
               bl   .40   .30
CB9   SPAP4   2p + 1p rose lilac
               & vio   .50   .40
CB10 SPAP4   3p + 1.50p green
               & brown   .60   .50
CB11 SPAP4   5p + 2.50p gray ol
               & car rose   1.00   .85
CB12 SPAP4   10p + 5p gray ol &
               brn   2.00 1.60
      Nos. CB8-CB12 (5)   4.50 3.65
The surtax was for the Intl. Centennial Phila-
telic Exhibition, Buenos Aires, Apr. 19-27.

Type of Semi-Postal Issue, 1958
Designs: 1p+50c, Flooded area. 5p+2.50p,
House and truck under water.

1958, Oct. 4   Photo.   Perf. 13½
CB13 SP11   1p + 50c dull purple   .25   .20
CB14 SP11   5p + 2.50p grnsh blue .80   .75
The surtax was for victims of a flood in the
Buenos Aires district.

Type of Semi-Postal Issue
1959, Sept. 5   Litho.   Perf. 13½
CB15 SP13   2p + 1p Rowing   .40   .25
CB16 SP13   3p + 1.50p Woman
              diver   .60   .50

Bird Type of Semi-Postal Issue
2p+1p, Rufous tinamou. 3p+1.50p, Rhea.

1960, Feb. 6   Perf. 13½
CB17 SP14   2p + 1p rose car & sal .30 .20
CB18 SP14   3p + 1.50p slate green .45 .35
The surtax was for child welfare work.
See No. CB29.

Buenos Aires
Market Place,
1810
SPAP5

6p+3p, Oxcart water carrier. 10.70p+5.30p,
Settlers landing. 20p+10p, The Fort.

1960, Aug. 20   Photo.   Wmk. 90
CB19 SPAP5   2 + 1p rose
               brown   .20   .20
CB20 SPAP5   6 + 3p gray   .35   .35
CB21 SPAP5   10.70 + 5.30p blue .60 .35
CB22 SPAP5   20 + 10p bluish
               grn   1.00   .85
      Nos. CB19-CB22 (4)   2.15 1.65
Inter-American Philatelic Exhibition
EFIMAYO 1960, Buenos Aires, Oct. 12-24,
held to for the sesquicentennial of the May
Revolution of 1910.
For overprints see Nos. CB25-CB28.

Seibo, National
Flower — SPAP6

1960, Sept. 10   Perf. 13½
#CB24, Copihue, Chile's national flower.
CB23 SPAP6   6 + 3p lilac rose   .35   .30
CB24 SPAP6   10.70 + 5.30p ver   .50   .40
The surtax was for earthquake victims in
Chile.

Nos. CB19-CB22 Overprinted: "DIA
DE LAS NACIONES UNIDAS 24 DE
OCTUBRE"
1960, Oct. 8
CB25 SPAP5   2 + 1p rose
               brown   .20   .20
CB26 SPAP5   6 + 3p gray   .30   .30
CB27 SPAP5   10.70 + 5.30p blue .50 .40
CB28 SPAP5   20 + 10p bluish
               green   .85   .75
      Nos. CB25-CB28 (4)   1.85 1.65
United Nations Day, Oct. 24, 1960.

Type of Semi-Postal Issue, 1960
Design: Emperor penguins.

1961, Feb. 25   Photo.   Wmk. 90
CB29 SP14   1.80p + 90c gray   .30   .20
The surtax was for child welfare work.

Stamp of   Crutch, Olympic
1862 — SPAP7   Torch and
                    Rings — SPAP8

1962, May 19   Litho.
CB30 SPAP7   6.50p + 6.50p Prus bl
               & grnsh bl   .70   .65
Opening of the "Argentina 62" Philatelic
Exhibition, Buenos Aires, May 19-29.

Type of Semi-Postal Issue, 1963
1963, May 18   Wmk. 90   Perf. 13½
CB31 SP21   11p + 5p Bicycling   .55   .50

Type of Semi-Postal Issue, 1962
1963, Dec. 21   Perf. 13½
CB32 SP20   11p + 5p Great kis-
              kadee   .70   .60
The surtax was for child welfare.

Type of Semi-Postal Issue, 1964
1964, July 18   Litho.
CB33 SP22   11p + 5p Sailboat   .50   .50

1964, Sept. 19   Litho.   Perf. 13½
CB34 SPAP8   18p + 9p bluish grn,
               blk, red & yel   .60   .60
13th "Olympic" games for the handicapped,
Tokyo, 1964.

Bird Type of Semi-Postal Issue, 1962
1964, Dec. 23   Litho.   Wmk. 90
CB35 SP20   18p + 9p Chilean
              swallow   .90   .75
The surtax was for child welfare.

**Bird Type of Semi-Postal Issue, 1962,
Inscribed "R. ARGENTINA"**
Design: Rufous ovenbird.

1966, Mar. 26   Perf. 13½
CB36 SP20   27.50p + 12.50p bl,
              ocher, yel &
              grn   .80   .70
The surtax was for child welfare.

Coat of Arms — SPAP9

1966, June 25   Litho.   Perf. 13½
CB37 SPAP9   10p + 10p multi   1.75 1.40
ARGENTINA '66 Philatelic Exhibition held in
connection with the sesquicentennial celebration of the Declaration of Independence, Buenos Aires, July 16-23. The surtax was for the
Exhibition. Issued in sheets of 4.

**Bird Type of Semi-Postal Issue, 1962,
Inscribed "R. ARGENTINA"**
Designs: 15p+7p, Blue and yellow tanager.
26p+13p, Toco toucan.

1967   Litho.   Wmk. 90
CB38 SP20   15p + 7p blk, bl, grn
              & yel   1.00   .90
CB39 SP20   26p + 13p blk, org,
              yel & bl   .50   .40
The surtax was for child welfare.
Issued: 15p+7p, Jan. 14; 26p+13p, Dec. 23.

Bird Type of Semi-Postal Issue, 1969
Design: 26p+13p, Lineated woodpecker.

1969, Sept. 20   Wmk. 365   Perf. 13½
CB40 SP24   26p + 13p multi   .50   .40
The surtax was for child welfare.

Bird Type of Semi-Postal Issue, 1970
Design: 40c+20c, Chilean flamingo.

1970, May 9   Litho.   Wmk. 365
CB41 SP25   40c + 20c multi   .45   .40
The surtax was for child welfare.

Fish Type of Semi-Postal Issue, 1971
Design: Pejerrey (atherinidae family).

**1971, Feb. 20   Unwmk.   Perf. 12½
Size: 75x15mm**
CB42 SP26   40c + 20c multi   .40   .40
The surtax was for child welfare.

OFFICIAL STAMPS

Regular Issues Overprinted in Black

1884-87		Unwmk.	Perf. 12, 14	
O1	A29	½c brown	12.00	10.00
O2	A23	1c red	8.00	6.00
b.		Perf. 12	40.00	32.50
O3	A29	1c red	.50	.35
b.		Double overprint	35.00	35.00
O4	A20	2c green	.50	.35
b.		Double overprint	75.00	
O5	A11	4c brown	.50	.35
O6	A7	8c lake	.50	.35
O7	A8	10c green	40.00	25.00
O8	A23	12c ultra (#45)	6.50	4.00
a.		Perf. 14	325.00	125.00
O9	A29	12c grnsh blue	.80	.65
O10	A19	24c blue	1.25	1.00
O11	A21	25c lake	16.00	12.50
O12	A12	30c orange	32.50	20.00
O13	A13	60c black	20.00	12.50
O14	A14	90c blue	20.00	16.00
b.		Double overprint	50.00	45.00
		Nos. O1-O14 (14)	159.05	109.05

Inverted Overprint

O1a	A29	½c	16.00	12.50
O2a	A23	1c Perf. 14	50.00	40.00
c.		Perf. 12	32.50	30.00
O3a	A29	1c	1.60	
O4a	A20	2c	65.00	40.00
O5a	A11	4c	40.00	32.50
O6a	A7	8c	60.00	60.00
O8b	A23	12c Perf. 12	12.50	
O9a	A29	12c	125.00	65.00
O10a	A19	24c	2.75	1.60
O13a	A13	60c	90.00	50.00
O14a	A14	90c	50.00	40.00

1884			Rouletted	
O15	A17	16c green	1.75	1.00
a.		Double overprint	16.00	
b.		Inverted overprint	125.00	
O16	A18	20c blue	8.00	7.00
a.		Inverted overprint	60.00	40.00
O17	A19	24c blue	1.25	1.00
a.		Inverted overprint	4.00	2.50
b.		Double ovpt., one inverted	250.00	
		Nos. O15-O17 (3)	11.00	9.00

Overprinted Diagonally in Red

1885			Perf. 12	
O18	A20	2c green	2.00	1.50
a.		Inverted overprint	40.00	32.50
O19	A11	4c brown	2.00	1.40
a.		Inverted overprint	40.00	32.50
b.		Double overprint	50.00	
O20	A13	60c black	20.00	16.00
O21	A14	90c blue	200.00	150.00

1885			Rouletted	
O22	A19	24c blue	17.50	12.50

On all of these stamps, the overprint is
found reading both upwards and downwards.
Counterfeits exist of No. O21 overprint and
others.

**Regular Issues Handstamped
Horizontally in Black**

1884			Perf. 12, 14	
O23	A23	1c red	50.00	17.00
a.		Perf. 12	150.00	100.00
O24	A20	2c green, diago-
	nal overprint	25.00	15.00
a.		Horizontal overprint	150.00	125.00
O25	A11	4c brown	10.00	8.00
O26	A7	8c lake	10.00	10.00
O27	A23	12c ultra	27.50	20.00

Overprinted Diagonally

O28	A19	24c bl, rouletted	20.00	15.00
O29	A13	60c black	15.00	10.00

Counterfeit overprints exist.

Liberty Head — O31

		Perf. 11½, 12 and Compound		
1901, Dec. 1			*Engr.*	
O31	O1	1c gray	.25	.20
b.		Vert. pair, imperf. horiz.	50.00	
c.		Horiz. pair, imperf. vert.	50.00	
O32	O1	2c orange brown	.30	.20
O33	O1	5c red	.40	.20
b.		Vert. pair, imperf. horiz.	50.00	
O34	O1	10c dark green	.50	.20
O35	O1	30c dark blue	4.00	1.00
O36	O1	50c orange	2.00	1.00
		Nos. O31-O36 (6)	7.45	2.80

Imperf, Pairs

O31a	O1	1c	40.00	
O32a	O1	2c	40.00	
O33a	O1	5c	50.00	
O34a	O1	10c	40.00	
O35a	O1	30c	65.00	
O36a	O1	50c	50.00	

**Regular Stamps of 1935-51
Overprinted in Black**

c

		Perf. 13x13½, 13½x13, 13		
1938-54		**Wmk. RA in Sun (90)**		
O37	A129	1c buff ('40)	.20	.20
O38	A130	2c dk brn ('40)	.20	.20
O39	A132	3c grn ('39)	.20	.20
O40	A132	3c lt gray ('39)	.20	.20
O41	A134	5c yel brn	.20	.20
O42	A195	5c car ('53)	.20	.20
O43	A137	10c carmine	.20	.20
O44	A137	10c brn ('39)	.20	.20

O45	A140	15c lt gray bl, type II ('47)	.20	.20
O46	A139	15c slate blue	.50	.20
O47	A139	15c pale ultra ('39)	.20	.20
O48	A139	20c blue ('53)	.30	.20
O49	A141	25c carmine	.20	.20
a.		Overprint 11mm	.20	.20
O49B	A143	40c dk violet	.90	.20
O50	A144	50c red & org	.20	.20
a.		Overprint 11mm	.25	.20
O51	A146	1p brn blk & lt bl ('40)	.20	.20
a.		Overprint 11mm	.25	.20
O52	A224	1p choc & lt bl ('51)	.20	.20
a.		Overprint 11mm	.20	.20
O53	A147	2p brn lake & dk ultra (ovpt. 11mm) ('54)	.70	.20
		Nos. O37-O53 (18)	5.20	3.60

Overprinted in Black on Stamps and Types of 1945-47
Perf. 13x13½, 13½x13

1945-46			Unwmk.	
O54	A130	2c sepia	2.75	.40
O55	A134	3c lt gray	2.25	.30
O56	A134	5c yel brn	.65	.20
O57	A195	5c dp car	.20	.20
O58	A137	10c brown	.20	.20
a.		Double overprint		
O59	A140	15c lt gray bl, type II	.20	.20
O61	A141	25c dull rose	.20	.20
O62	A144	50c red & org	.55	.20
O63	A146	1p brn blk & lt bl	.20	.20
O64	A147	2p brn lake & bl	.40	.20
O65	A148	5p ind & ol grn	.20	.20
O66	A149	10p dp cl & int blk	.45	.20
O67	A150	20p bl grn & brn	1.00	.30
		Nos. O54-O67 (13)	9.25	3.00

Overprinted in Black on Stamps and Types of 1942-50
Perf. 13, 13x13½

1944-51			Wmk. 288	
O73	A134	3c lt gray	1.10	.50
O74	A134	5c yellow brown	.20	.20
O75	A137	10c red brown	.20	.20
O76	A140	15c lt gray bl, type II	.25	.20
O77	A144	50c red & org (overprint 11 mm)	1.50	.50
O78	A146	1p brn blk & lt bl (overprint 11mm)	1.75	.40
		Nos. O73-O78 (6)	5.00	2.00

> Catalogue values for unused stamps in this section, from this point to the end of the section, are for Never Hinged items.

Nos. 600-606 Overprinted in Black

d

1953		Wmk. 90	Perf. 13	
O79	A228	5c gray	.20	.20
O80	A228	10c rose lilac	.20	.20
O81	A228	20c rose pink	.20	.20
O82	A228	25c dull green	.20	.20
O83	A228	40c dull violet	.20	.20
O84	A228	45c deep blue	.20	.20
O85	A228	50c dull brown	.20	.20

e

f

Nos. 611-617 Overprinted Type "e" in Blue
Perf. 13x13½, 13½x13

O86	A229	1p dk brown	.20	.20
O87	A229	1.50p dp green	.30	.20
O88	A229	2p brt carmine	.20	.20
O89	A229	3p indigo	.55	.25

Size: 30x40mm

O90	A229	5p red brown	.60	.45
O91	A228	10p red	2.75	1.75
O92	A229	20p green	30.00	20.00
		Nos. O79-O92 (14)	36.00	24.45

No. 612 Overprinted Type "f" in Blue

O93	A229	1.50p dp grn	1.00	.30

Regular Issues of 1954-59 Variously Overprinted in Black or Blue

g

h

Perf. 13½, 13x13½, 13½x13

1955-61		Litho.	Wmk. 90	
O94	A237(c)	20c red (#629)	.20	.20
O95	A237(c)	20c red (#629)	.20	.20
O96	A237(d)	40c red, ovpt. 15mm (#630)	.20	.20

Engr.

O97	A239(g)	50c bl (#632)	.20	.20

Photo.

O98	A239(h)	1p brn (#635)	.20	.20
O99	A239(e)	1p brn (Bl, #635)	.20	.20
O100	A239(e)	1p brn (Bk, #635)	.20	.20

Engr.

O101	A239(h)	3p vio brn (#638)	.20	.20
O102	A240(e)	5p gray grn (#639)	.20	.20
O103	A240(e)	10p yel grn (#640)	.50	.20
O104	A240(f)	20p dl vio (#641)	.75	.30
O105	A240(h)	20p dl vio (#641)	.75	.25
O106	A241(e)	50p ultra & ind (#642)	1.10	.20
		Nos. O94-O106 (13)	5.00	2.75

The overprints on #O99-O100 & O103-O104 are horizontal; that on #O106 is vertical. On #O106 overprint measures 23mm.
Issued: #O102, 1957; #O97, O101, O103, O105, 1958; #O98-O99, O104, 1959; #O100, 1960; #O106, 1961.

No. 659 Overprinted Type "d"

1957	Wmk. 90	Litho.	Perf. 13	
O108	A133	20c dl pur (ovpt. 15mm)	.20	.20

Nos. 666, 658 and 663 Variously Overprinted

1957		Photo.	Perf. 13x13½, 13½	
O109	A261(g)	2p claret	.20	.20
O110	A254(e)	2.40p brown	.20	.20
O111	A258(c)	4.40p grnsh gray	.25	.20
		Nos. O109-O111 (3)	.65	.60

Nos. 668, 685-687, 690-691, 693-705, 742, 742C and Types of 1959-65 Overprinted in black, Blue or Red Types "e," "g," or

i

j

k

m

n

Lithographed; Photogravure

1960-68		Perf. 13x13½, 13½		
O112	A128(g)	5c buff (vert.)	.20	.20
O113	A275(j)	10c sl grn	.20	.20
O114	A275(j)	20c dl red brn	.20	.20
O115	A275(i)	50c bister	.20	.20
O116	A278(k)	1p brn	.20	.20
O117	A278(j)	1p brn, photo. (vert. ovpt.)	.20	.20
O117A	A278(j)	1p brn, litho., (down)	.20	.20
O118	A276(j)	2p rose red	.20	.20
O119	A312(m)	2p dp grn	.25	.20
O120	A312(j)	2p brt grn (up)	.20	.20
O121	A312(j)	2p grn litho.	.20	.20
		(down)	.25	.20
O122	A277(e)	3p dk bl (horiz.)	.20	.20
O123	A277(j)	3p dk blue	.20	.20
O124	A276(j)	4p red, litho.	.20	.20
O125	A312(j)	4p rose red, litho. (down)	.20	.20
O126	A277(e)	5p brn (Bl) (horiz.)	.25	.20
O127	A277(e)	5p brn (Bk) (horiz.)	.25	.20
O128	A277(j)	5p sepia	.20	.20
O129	A277(e)	5p sepia (horiz. ovpt.)	.20	.20
O130	A276(j)	8p red	.20	.20
O131	A278(i)	10p lt red brn	.45	.20
O132	A278(j)	10p vermilion	.20	.20
O133	A278(j)	10p brn car (up)	.20	.20
O134	A278(m)	12p dk brn vio (horiz.)	.40	.20
O135	A278(k)	20p Prus grn	.50	.20
O136	A278(j)	20p Prus grn (up)	.40	.20
O137	A276(j)	20p red, litho.	.35	.20
O138	A276(m)	20p red, litho.(horiz.)	.25	.20
O139	A278(j)	23p grn (vert. ovpt.)	.50	.20
O140	A278(j)	25p dp vio, photo. (R) (up)	.50	.20
O141	A278(j)	25p pur, litho. (R) (down)	.50	.20
O142	A241(n)	50p dk blue	1.10	.20
O143	A279(m)	100p bl (horiz. ovpt.)	1.10	.35
O144	A279(m)	100p blue (up)	1.10	.35
O145	A280(x)	300p dp violet (horiz.)	2.25	.60
		Nos. O112-O145 (35)	14.00	7.70

The "m" overprint measures 15½mm on 2p; 14½mm on 12p, 100p and 300p; 13mm on 20p.
Issued: #O122, O127, O135, 1961; #O112-O114, O116, O118, 1962; #O124, 1963; #O119, O134, O143, 1964; #O117, O125, O130, O139, O144, 1965; #O120, O128, O132-O133, O136, O140, O142, O145, 1966;

#O121, O129, O137-O138, O141, 1967; #O117A, 1968.

Nos. 699, 823-825, 827-829, and Type of 1962 Overprinted in Black or Red Types "j," "m," or "o"

o

Inscribed: "Republica Argentina"
Litho., Photo., Engr.

1964-67		Wmk. 90	Perf. 13½	
O149	A312(j)	6p rose red (down)	.25	.20
O153	A238a(m)	22p ultra	.50	.20
O154	A238a(j)	43p dk car rose (down)	.75	.20
O155	A238a(j)	45p brn, photo. (up)	.75	.20
O156	A238a(j)	45p brn, litho. (up)	1.10	.20
O157	A241(j)	50p dk bl (up) (R)	2.25	.20
O158	A366(j)	90p ol bis (up)	2.75	.20
O162	A495(o)	500p yel grn	3.50	.80
		Nos. O149-O162 (8)	11.85	2.20

Issued: No. O153, 1964; No. O155, 1966; Nos. O149, O156-O162, 1967.

Type of 1959-67 Ovptd. Type "j"

1969	Litho.	Wmk. 365	Perf. 13½	
O163	A276	20p vermilion	.20	.20

Beginning with No. 2001, many Argentine stamps are inscribed "Correo Official," but are not official stamps.

OFFICIAL DEPARTMENT STAMPS

Regular Issues of 1911-37 Overprinted in Black

Type I

Type II

Ministry of Agriculture (M. A.)
Type I

1913-37				
		On Stamp of 1911		
OD1	A88	2c #181	.20	.20
		On Stamps of 1912-14		
OD2	A88	1c #190	.20	.20
OD3	A88	2c #191	.20	.20
OD4	A88	5c #194	.30	.20
OD5	A88	12c #196	.20	.20
		Nos. OD2-OD5 (4)	.90	.80
		On Stamps of 1915-16		
OD6	A88	1c #208	.20	.20
OD7	A88	2c #209	.20	.20
OD8	A88	5c #212	.20	.20
OD9	A91	5c #220	.20	.20
		Nos. OD6-OD9 (4)	.80	.80
		On Stamp of 1917		
OD10	A94	12c #238	.30	.20
		On Stamps of 1918-19		
OD11	A93	1c #249	.20	.20
OD12	A93	2c #250	.20	.20
OD13	A93	5c #253	.20	.20
OD14	A94	12c #255	.20	.20
OD15	A94	20c #256	.20	.20
		Nos. OD10-OD15 (6)	1.30	1.20

On Stamps of 1920

No.	Type	Denom	Cat. No.	Un	U
OD16	A93	1c	#265	.30	.25
OD17	A93	2c	#266	.50	.25
OD18	A93	5c	#269	.20	.20
Nos. OD16-OD18 (3)				1.00	.70

On Stamps of 1922-23

No.	Type	Denom	Cat. No.	Un	U
OD19	A94	12c	#311	1.00	.40
OD20	A94	20c	#312	25.00	

On Stamps of 1923

No.	Type	Denom	Cat. No.	Un	U
OD21	A104	1c	#324	.20	.20
OD22	A104	2c	#325	.25	.20
OD23	A104	5c	#328	.20	.20
OD24	A104	12c	#330	.20	.20
OD25	A104	20c	#331	.20	.20
Nos. OD21-OD25 (5)				1.05	1.00

On Stamps of 1923-31

No.	Type	Denom	Cat. No.	Un	U
OD26	A104	1c	#341	.20	.20
OD27	A104	2c	#342, I	.20	.20
a.			Type II	1.50	.75
OD28	A104	3c	#343	.20	.20
OD29	A104	5c	#345, II	.20	.20
a.			Type I	.20	.20
OD30	A104	10c	#346, II	.20	.20
OD31	A104	12c	#347	.20	.20
OD32	A104	20c	#348, I	.20	.20
a.			Type II	.20	.20
OD33	A104	30c	#351	.20	.20
Nos. OD26-OD33 (8)				1.60	1.60

On Stamp of 1926

No.	Type	Denom	Cat. No.	Un	U
OD34	A110	12c	#360	.20	.20

Type II
On Stamps of 1935-37

No.	Type	Denom	Cat. No.	Un	U
OD35	A129	1c	#419	.20	.20
OD36	A130	2c	#420	.20	.20
OD37	A132	3c	#422	.20	.20
OD38	A134	5c	#427	.20	.20
OD39	A137	10c	#430	.50	.20
OD40	A139	15c	#434	.50	.20
OD41	A140	20c	#437	.30	.20
OD42	A140	20c	#438	.20	.20
OD43	A141	25c	#441	.25	.20
OD44	A142	30c	#442	.20	.20
OD45	A145	1p	#445	2.50	1.50
OD46	A146	1p	#446	.50	.25
Nos. OD35-OD46 (12)				5.45	3.75

Ministry of War
(M. G.)
Type I
On Stamp of 1911

No.	Type	Denom	Cat. No.	Un	U
OD47	A88	2c	#181	.20	.20

On Stamps of 1912-14

No.	Type	Denom	Cat. No.	Un	U
OD48	A88	1c	#190	.20	.20
OD49	A88	2c	#191	.75	.20
OD50	A88	5c	#194	.20	.20
OD51	A88	12c	#196	.20	.20
Nos. OD48-OD51 (4)				1.35	.80

On Stamps of 1915-16

No.	Type	Denom	Cat. No.	Un	U
OD52	A88	1c	#208	6.00	.75
OD53	A88	2c	#209	.60	.20
OD54	A88	5c	#212	.75	.20
OD55	A91	5c	#220	1.00	.25
OD56	A92	12c	#222	1.00	.25
Nos. OD52-OD56 (5)				9.35	1.75

On Stamps of 1917

No.	Type	Denom	Cat. No.	Un	U
OD57	A93	1c	#232	.30	.20
OD58	A93	2c	#233	.40	.20
OD59	A93	5c	#236	.30	.20
OD60	A94	12c	#238	.60	.20
Nos. OD57-OD60 (4)				1.60	.80

On Stamps of 1918-19

No.	Type	Denom	Cat. No.	Un	U
OD61	A93	1c	#249	.20	.20
OD62	A93	2c	#250	.20	.20
OD63	A93	5c	#253	.20	.20
OD64	A94	12c	#255	.40	.20
OD65	A94	20c	#256	1.25	.20
Nos. OD61-OD65 (5)				2.25	1.00

On Stamps of 1920

No.	Type	Denom	Cat. No.	Un	U
OD66	A93	2c	#266	.40	.20
OD67	A93	5c	#269	.40	.20
OD68	A94	12c	#271	.35	.20
Nos. OD66-OD68 (3)				1.15	.60

On Stamp of 1920

No.	Type	Denom	Cat. No.	Un	U
OD69	A94	12c	#299	2.00	.25

On Stamps of 1922-23

No.	Type	Denom	Cat. No.	Un	U
OD70	A93	1c	#305	.75	.20
OD71	A93	2c	#306	1.50	.45
OD72	A103	5c	#309	.75	.20
OD73	A94	20c	#312	.30	.20
Nos. OD70-OD73 (4)				3.30	1.05

On Stamp of 1922-23

No.	Type	Denom	Cat. No.	Un	U
OD74	A93	2c	#318	5.00	.50

On Stamps of 1923

No.	Type	Denom	Cat. No.	Un	U
OD75	A104	1c	#324	.20	.20
OD76	A104	2c	#325	.20	.20
OD77	A104	5c	#328	.20	.20
OD78	A104	12c	#330	.20	.20
OD79	A104	20c	#331	1.00	.20
Nos. OD75-OD79 (5)				1.80	1.00

On Stamps of 1923-31

No.	Type	Denom	Cat. No.	Un	U
OD80	A104	1c	#341	1.25	.45
OD81	A104	2c	#342	.20	.20
OD82	A104	3c	#343, I	.20	.20
a.			Type II	.40	.20
OD83	A104	5c	#345, I	.20	.20
a.			Type II	.20	.20
OD84	A104	10c	#346, II	.20	.20
a.			Type I	.60	.20
OD85	A104	20c	#348, I	.40	.20
a.			Type II	.20	.20
OD86	A104	30c	#351, II	.20	.20
a.			Type I	1.00	.20
OD87	A105	1p	#353	2.00	.30
Nos. OD80-OD87 (8)				4.45	1.95

On Stamp of 1926

No.	Type	Denom	Cat. No.	Un	U
OD88	A109	5c	#359	.60	.20

Type II
On Stamps of 1935-37

No.	Type	Denom	Cat. No.	Un	U
OD89	A129	1c	#419	.20	.20
OD90	A130	2c	#420	.20	.20
OD91	A132	3c	#422	.20	.20
OD92	A134	5c	#427	.20	.20
OD93	A137	10c	#430	.20	.20
OD94	A139	15c	#434	.25	.20
OD95	A140	20c	#437	1.00	.20
OD96	A140	20c	#438	.25	.20
OD97	A141	25c	#441	.20	.20
OD98	A142	30c	#442	.20	.20
OD99	A144	50c	#444	.25	.20
OD100	A145	1p	#445	1.25	.50
OD101	A146	1p	#446	.50	.25
Nos. OD89-OD101 (13)				4.90	2.95

Ministry of Finance
(M. H.)
Type I
On Stamp of 1911

No.	Type	Denom	Cat. No.	Un	U
OD102	A88	2c	#181	.20	.20

On Stamps of 1912-14

No.	Type	Denom	Cat. No.	Un	U
OD103	A88	1c	#190	.20	.20
OD104	A88	2c	#191	.20	.20
OD105	A88	5c	#194	.20	.20
OD106	A88	12c	#196	.20	.20
Nos. OD103-OD106 (4)				.80	.80

On Stamps of 1915-16

No.	Type	Denom	Cat. No.	Un	U
OD107	A88	2c	#209	.20	.20
OD108	A88	5c	#212	.20	.20
OD109	A91	5c	#220	.20	.20
Nos. OD107-OD109 (3)				.60	.60

On Stamps of 1917

No.	Type	Denom	Cat. No.	Un	U
OD110	A93	2c	#233	.20	.20
OD111	A93	5c	#236	1.25	.20
OD112	A94	12c	#238	.20	.20
Nos. OD110-OD112 (3)				1.65	.60

On Stamps of 1918-19

No.	Type	Denom	Cat. No.	Un	U
OD113	A93	2c	#250		25.00
OD114	A93	5c	#253	.20	.20
OD115	A94	12c	#255	.45	.20
OD116	A94	20c	#256	.45	.20

On Stamps of 1920

No.	Type	Denom	Cat. No.	Un	U
OD117	A93	1c	#265	.75	.45
OD118	A93	2c	#266	1.25	.45
OD119	A93	5c	#269	.30	.20
OD120	A94	12c	#271	.60	.20
Nos. OD117-OD120 (4)				2.90	1.30

On Stamps of 1922-23

No.	Type	Denom	Cat. No.	Un	U
OD121	A94	20c	#312	12.50	2.50

On Stamps of 1923

No.	Type	Denom	Cat. No.	Un	U
OD122	A104	1c	#324	.75	.40
OD123	A104	2c	#325	.20	.20
OD124	A104	5c	#328	.20	.20
OD125	A104	12c	#330	.20	.20
OD126	A104	20c	#331	.20	.20
Nos. OD122-OD126 (5)				1.55	1.20

On Stamps of 1923-31

No.	Type	Denom	Cat. No.	Un	U
OD127	A104	3c	#343	7.00	1.50
OD128	A104	5c	#345	.20	.20
OD129	A104	10c	#346	.20	.20
OD130	A104	12c	#347	7.00	3.75
OD131	A104	20c	#348, I	.20	.20
a.			Type II	.35	.20
OD132	A104	30c	#351	.25	.20
OD133	A105	1p	#353	.40	.20
Nos. OD127-OD133 (7)				15.25	6.25

On Stamp of 1926

No.	Type	Denom	Cat. No.	Un	U
OD134	A110	12c	#360	12.50	12.50

Type II
On Stamps of 1935-37

No.	Type	Denom	Cat. No.	Un	U
OD135	A129	1c	#419	.20	.20
OD136	A130	2c	#420	.20	.20
OD137	A132	3c	#422	.20	.20
OD138	A134	5c	#427	.20	.20
OD139	A137	10c	#430	.20	.20
OD140	A139	15c	#434	.45	.20
OD141	A140	20c	#437	.20	.20
OD142	A140	20c	#438	.20	.20
OD143	A142	30c	#442	.20	.20
OD144	A145	1p	#445	2.00	1.00
OD145	A146	1p	#446	.50	.20
Nos. OD135-OD145 (11)				4.55	3.00

Ministry of the Interior
(M. I.)
Type I
On Stamp of 1911

No.	Type	Denom	Cat. No.	Un	U
OD146	A88	2c	#181	.25	.20

On Stamps of 1912-14

No.	Type	Denom	Cat. No.	Un	U
OD147	A88	1c	#190	.20	.20
OD148	A88	2c	#191	.20	.20
OD149	A88	5c	#194	.20	.20
OD150	A88	12c	#196	.20	.20
Nos. OD146-OD150 (5)				1.05	1.00

On Stamps of 1915-17

No.	Type	Denom	Cat. No.	Un	U
OD151	A88	2c	#209	.80	.30
OD152	A88	5c	#212	.75	.20
OD153	A91	5c	#220	.60	.20
OD154	A93	5c	#236	1.50	.20
Nos. OD151-OD154 (4)				3.65	.90

On Stamps of 1918-19

No.	Type	Denom	Cat. No.	Un	U
OD155	A93	2c	#250	.20	.20
OD156	A93	5c	#253	.20	.20

On Stamps of 1920

No.	Type	Denom	Cat. No.	Un	U
OD157	A93	1c	#265	3.75	1.25
OD158	A93	5c	#269	.75	.35

On Stamps of 1922-23

No.	Type	Denom	Cat. No.	Un	U
OD159	A93	2c	#306	12.50	12.50
OD160	A103	5c	#309	3.50	1.25
OD161	A94	12c	#311	1.25	.40
OD162	A94	20c	#312	1.25	.40
Nos. OD159-OD162 (4)				18.50	14.55

On Stamps of 1923

No.	Type	Denom	Cat. No.	Un	U
OD163	A104	1c	#324	.20	.20
OD164	A104	2c	#325	.20	.20
OD165	A104	5c	#328	.20	.20
OD166	A104	12c	#330	2.00	2.00
OD167	A104	20c	#331	.75	.20
Nos. OD163-OD167 (5)				3.35	2.80

On Stamps of 1923-31

No.	Type	Denom	Cat. No.	Un	U
OD168	A104	1c	#341	.20	.20
OD169	A104	2c	#342	.20	.20
OD170	A104	3c	#343, II	.20	.20
a.			Type I	1.25	.30
OD171	A104	5c	#345, I	.20	.20
a.			Type II	.20	.20
OD172	A104	10c	#346, II	.20	.20
OD173	A104	12c	#347	.30	.20
OD174	A104	20c	#348, II	.20	.20
a.			Type I	.75	.20
OD175	A104	30c	#351	.20	.20
Nos. OD168-OD175 (8)				1.70	1.60

Type II
On Stamps of 1935-37

No.	Type	Denom	Cat. No.	Un	U
OD176	A129	1c	#419	.20	.20
OD177	A130	2c	#420	.20	.20
OD178	A132	3c	#422	.20	.20
OD178A	A134	5c	#427	.20	.20
OD179	A137	10c	#430	.30	.20
OD180	A139	15c	#434	.30	.20
OD181	A140	20c	#437	.75	.20
OD182	A140	20c	#438	.20	.20
OD182A	A142	30c	#442	.20	.20
OD182B	A145	1p	#445	2.00	1.00
OD182C	A146	1p	#446	.55	.20
Nos. OD176-OD182C (11)				5.00	3.00

Ministry of Justice and Instruction
(M. J. I.)
Type I
On Stamp of 1911

No.	Type	Denom	Cat. No.	Un	U
OD183	A88	2c	#181	1.25	.20

On Stamps of 1912-14

No.	Type	Denom	Cat. No.	Un	U
OD184	A88	1c	#190	1.50	.20
OD185	A88	2c	#191	1.00	.20
OD186	A88	5c	#194	.45	.20
OD187	A88	12c	#196	.45	.20
Nos. OD184-OD187 (4)				3.40	.80

On Stamps of 1915-17

No.	Type	Denom	Cat. No.	Un	U
OD188	A88	1c	#208	.30	.20
OD189	A88	2c	#209	.30	.20
OD190	A88	5c	#212	1.00	.20
OD191	A91	5c	#220	.25	.20
OD192	A92	12c	#222	.75	.20
Nos. OD188-OD192 (5)				2.60	1.00

On Stamps of 1917

No.	Type	Denom	Cat. No.	Un	U
OD193	A93	1c	#232	.25	.20
OD194	A93	2c	#233	.75	.20
OD195	A93	5c	#236	.20	.20
OD196	A94	12c	#238	17.50	5.00
Nos. OD193-OD196 (4)				18.75	5.60

On Stamps of 1918-19

No.	Type	Denom	Cat. No.	Un	U
OD197	A93	1c	#249	.20	.20
OD198	A93	2c	#250	.20	.20
OD199	A93	5c	#253	.20	.20
OD200	A94	12c	#255	.20	.20
OD201	A94	20c	#256	.50	.20
Nos. OD197-OD201 (5)				1.30	1.00

On Stamps of 1920

No.	Type	Denom	Cat. No.	Un	U
OD202	A93	1c	#265	.25	.20
OD203	A93	2c	#266	.20	.20
OD204	A93	5c	#269	.20	.20
OD205	A94	12c	#271	.40	.20
Nos. OD202-OD205 (4)				1.05	.80

On Stamps of 1922-23

No.	Type	Denom	Cat. No.	Un	U
OD206	A93	1c	#305	.25	.20
OD207	A93	2c	#306	1.50	.50
OD208	A103	5c	#309	.20	.20
OD209	A94	12c	#311	10.00	1.75
OD210	A94	20c	#312	1.50	.35
Nos. OD206-OD210 (5)				13.50	3.00

On Stamps of 1922-23

No.	Type	Denom	Cat. No.	Un	U
OD211	A93	2c	#318	2.50	2.50

On Stamps of 1923

No.	Type	Denom	Cat. No.	Un	U
OD212	A104	1c	#324	.20	.20
OD213	A104	2c	#325	.20	.20
OD214	A104	5c	#328	.20	.20
OD215	A104	12c	#330	.20	.20
OD216	A104	20c	#331	.50	.20
Nos. OD212-OD216 (5)				1.30	1.00

On Stamps of 1923-31

No.	Type	Denom	Cat. No.	Un	U
OD217	A104	½c	#340	2.00	.75
OD218	A104	1c	#341, I	.20	.20
a.			Type II	.20	.20
OD219	A104	2c	#342	.20	.20
OD220	A104	3c	#343, I	.20	.20
a.			Type II	.20	.20
OD221	A104	5c	#345, I	.20	.20
a.			Type II	.20	.20
OD222	A104	10c	#346, II	.20	.20
a.			Type I	.30	.20
OD223	A104	12c	#347	.20	.20
OD224	A104	20c	#348, I	.20	.20
a.			Type II	.30	.20
OD225	A104	30c	#351	.20	.20
OD226	A105	1p	#353	.40	.50
Nos. OD217-OD226 (10)				4.00	2.85

On Stamps of 1926

No.	Type	Denom	Cat. No.	Un	U
OD227	A109	5c	#359	.20	.20
OD228	A110	12c	#360	.20	.20

Type II
On Stamps of 1935-37

No.	Type	Denom	Cat. No.	Un	U
OD229	A129	1c	#419	.20	.20
OD230	A130	2c	#420	.20	.20
OD231	A132	3c	#422	.20	.20
OD232	A134	5c	#427	.20	.20
OD233	A137	10c	#430	.20	.20
OD234	A139	15c	#434	.45	.20
OD234A	A140	20c	#437	.20	.20
OD234B	A140	20c	#438	.20	.20
OD234C	A141	25c	#441	.20	.20
OD234D	A142	30c	#442	.20	.20
OD234E	A145	1p	#445	1.00	.60
OD234F	A146	1p	#446	.30	.20
Nos. OD229-OD234F (12)				3.55	2.80

Ministry of Marine
(M. M.)
Type I
On Stamp of 1911

No.	Type	Denom	Cat. No.	Un	U
OD235	A88	2c	#181	.20	.20

On Stamps of 1912-14

No.	Type	Denom	Cat. No.	Un	U
OD236	A88	1c	#190	.20	.20
OD237	A88	2c	#191	.20	.20
OD238	A88	5c	#194	2.00	.20
OD239	A88	12c	#196	.20	.20
Nos. OD236-OD239 (4)				2.60	.80

On Stamps of 1915-16

No.	Type	Denom	Cat. No.	Un	U
OD240	A88	2c	#209	.60	.20
OD241	A88	5c	#212	.40	.20

On Stamps of 1917

No.	Type	Denom	Cat. No.	Un	U
OD242	A93	1c	#232	.20	.20
OD243	A93	2c	#233	.20	.20
OD244	A93	5c	#236	.20	.20
Nos. OD242-OD244 (3)				.60	.60

On Stamps of 1918-19

No.	Type	Denom	Cat. No.	Un	U
OD245	A93	1c	#249	.20	.20
OD246	A93	2c	#250	.20	.20
OD247	A93	5c	#253	.25	.20
OD248	A94	12c	#255	.25	.20
OD249	A94	20c	#256	3.00	.75
Nos. OD245-OD249 (5)				3.90	1.15

On Stamps of 1920

No.	Type	Denom	Cat. No.	Un	U
OD250	A93	1c	#265	.20	.20
OD251	A93	2c	#266	.20	.20
OD252	A93	5c	#269	.25	.20
Nos. OD250-OD252 (3)				.65	.60

On Stamps of 1922-23

No.	Type	Denom	Cat. No.	Un	U
OD253	A103	5c	#309	1.00	.20
OD254	A94	12c	#311	7.00	7.00
OD255	A94	20c	#312	7.00	1.50
Nos. OD253-OD254 (2)				8.00	7.20

On Stamps of 1923

No.	Type	Denom	Cat. No.	Un	U
OD256	A104	1c	#324	.20	.20
OD257	A104	2c	#325	.20	.20
OD258	A104	5c	#328	.30	.20
OD259	A104	12c	#330	.65	.20
OD260	A104	20c	#331	.65	.20
Nos. OD256-OD260 (5)				2.00	1.00

On Stamps of 1923-31

No.	Type	Denom	Cat. No.	Un	U
OD261	A104	1c	#341	.75	.25
OD262	A104	2c	#342	.20	.20
OD263	A104	3c	#343	.65	.20
OD264	A104	5c	#345, I	.20	.20
a.			Type II	.60	.20
OD265	A104	10c	#346	.60	.20
OD266	A104	20c	#348, II	.60	.20
a.			Type I	.75	.20
OD267	A104	30c	#351	1.00	.20
OD268	A105	1p	#353	11.00	3.00
Nos. OD261-OD268 (8)				15.00	4.45

On Stamp of 1926

No.	Type	Denom	Cat. No.	Un	U
OD269	A109	5c	#359	.50	.20

Type II
On Stamps of 1935-37

No.	Type	Denom	Cat. No.	Un	U
OD270	A129	1c	#419	.20	.20
OD271	A130	2c	#420	.20	.20
OD272	A132	3c	#422	.20	.20

OD273	A134	5c #427		.20	.20
OD274	A137	10c #430		.25	.20
OD275	A139	15c #434		.30	.20
OD276	A140	20c #437		.40	.20
OD277	A140	20c #438		.30	.20
OD278	A142	30c #442		.25	.20
OD279	A145	1p #445		3.25	1.00
OD280	A146	1p #446		.75	.20
		Nos. OD270-OD280 (11)		6.30	3.00

Ministry of Public Works (M. O. P.)
Type I
On Stamp of 1911

OD281	A88	2c #181	.30	.20

On Stamps of 1912-14

OD282	A88	1c #190	.30	.20
OD283	A88	5c #194	.20	.20
OD284	A88	12c #196	1.50	.35
		Nos. OD282-OD284 (3)	2.00	.75

On Stamps of 1916-19

OD285	A91	5c #220	10.00	1.00
OD286	A94	12c #238	25.00	
OD287	A94	20c #256	25.00	

On Stamps of 1920

OD288	A93	2c #266	6.00	2.50
OD289	A93	5c #269	2.00	.20
OD290	A94	12c #271	20.00	6.00
		Nos. OD288-OD290 (3)	28.00	8.70

On Stamps of 1923

OD291	A104	1c #324	.40	.20
OD292	A104	2c #325	.30	.20
OD293	A104	5c #328	.40	.20
OD294	A104	12c #330	.60	.20
OD295	A104	20c #331	1.00	.20
		Nos. OD291-OD295 (5)	2.70	1.00

On Stamps of 1923-31

OD296	A104	1c #341		.20	.20
OD297	A104	2c #342		.20	.20
OD298	A104	3c #343		.20	.20
OD299	A104	5c #345, I		.20	.20
a.		Type II		.20	.20
OD300	A104	10c #346		.20	.20
OD301	A104	12c #347		9.00	1.25
OD302	A104	20c #348, I		.20	.20
a.		Type II		2.50	.50
OD303	A104	30c #351		.40	.20
OD304	A105	1p #353		20.00	6.00
		Nos. OD296-OD304 (9)		30.60	8.65

On Stamp of 1926

OD305	A109	5c #359	.60	.20

Type II
On Stamps of 1935-37

OD306	A129	1c #419	.20	.20
OD307	A130	2c #420	.20	.20
OD308	A132	3c #422	.20	.20
OD309	A134	5c #427	.20	.20
OD310	A137	10c #430	.30	.20
OD311	A139	15c #434	.60	.20
OD312	A140	20c #437	.75	.20
OD313	A140	20c #438	.20	.20
OD314	A142	30c #442	.20	.20
OD315	A144	50c #444	.20	.20
OD316	A145	1p #445	2.00	1.00
OD317	A146	1p #446	.50	.25
		Nos. OD306-OD317 (12)	5.55	3.25

Ministry of Foreign Affairs and Religion (M. R. C.)
Type I
On Stamp of 1911

OD318	A88	2c #181	5.00	1.25

On Stamps of 1912-14

OD319	A88	1c #190	.20	.20
OD320	A88	2c #191	.20	.20
OD321	A88	5c #194	.40	.20
OD322	A88	12c #196	1.50	.25
		Nos. OD319-OD322 (4)	2.30	.85

On Stamps of 1915-19

OD323	A88	5c #212	.40	.20
OD324	A91	5c #220	.20	.20
OD325	A94	20c #256	2.00	.75
		Nos. OD323-OD325 (3)	2.60	1.15

On Stamps of 1920

OD326	A93	1c #265	.40	.20
OD327	A93	5c #269	.20	.20

On Stamps of 1922-23

OD328	A93	2c #306	9.00	3.50
OD329	A103	5c #309	27.50	
OD330	A93	10c #311	22.50	
		Nos. OD328-OD330 (3)	59.00	

On Stamps of 1923

OD331	A104	1c #324	.20	.20
OD332	A104	2c #325	.20	.20
OD333	A104	5c #328	.20	.20
OD334	A104	12c #330	.20	.20
OD335	A104	20c #331	.20	.20
		Nos. OD331-OD335 (5)	1.00	1.00

On Stamps of 1923-31

OD336	A104	½c #340	1.00	.50
OD337	A104	1c #341	.20	.20
OD338	A104	2c #342	.20	.20
OD339	A104	3c #343	.20	.20

OD340	A104	5c #345		.20	.20
OD341	A104	10c #346, II		.20	.20
a.		Type I		1.50	.20
OD342	A104	12c #347		.20	.20
OD343	A104	20c #348, I		.20	.20
a.		Type II		.20	.20
OD344	A104	30c #351, I		.20	.20
a.		Type II		.20	.20
OD345	A105	1p #353		.40	.20
		Nos. OD336-OD345 (11)		3.20	2.50

On Stamp of 1926

OD346	A110	12c #360	.20	.20

Type II
On Stamps of 1935-37

OD347	A129	1c #419		.20	.20
OD348	A130	2c #420		.20	.20
OD349	A132	3c #422		.20	.20
OD350	A134	5c #427		.20	.20
OD351	A137	10c #430		.20	.20
OD352	A139	15c #434		.20	.20
OD353	A140	20c #437		.20	.20
OD354	A140	20c #438		.20	.20
OD355	A142	30c #442		.20	.20
OD356	A145	1p #445		2.50	1.25
OD357	A146	1p #446		1.00	.50
		Nos. OD347-OD357 (11)		5.30	3.55

Buenos Aires

The central point of the Argentine struggle for independence. At intervals Buenos Aires maintained an independent government but after 1862 became a province of the Argentine Republic.

8 Reales = 1 Peso

Values of Buenos Aires Nos. 1-8 vary according to condition. Quotations are for fine copies. Very fine to superb specimens sell at much higher prices, and inferior or poor copies sell at reduced values, depending on the condition of the individual specimen.
Nos. 1-8 were issued without gum.

Steamship — A1

1858		Unwmk.	Typo.	Imperf.	
1	A1	1 (in) pesos lt brn		350.	250.
2	A1	2 (dos) pesos blue		175.	140.
b.		Diagonal half used as 1p on cover			7,500.
3	A1	3 (tres) pesos grn		1,500.	750.
a.		3p dark green		1,800.	825.
4	A1	4 (cuatro) pesos ver		4,750.	1,750.
a.		Half used as 2p on cover			15,000.
5	A1	5 (cinco) pesos org		4,250.	1,450.
a.		5p ocher		4,250.	1,450.
b.		5p olive yellow		4,250.	1,450.

Issued: #2-5, Apr. 29; #1, Oct. 26.

1858, Oct. 26					
6	A1	4 (cuatro) reales brown		250.	200.
a.		4r gray brown		250.	200.
b.		4r yellow brown		250.	200.

1859, Jan. 1					
7	A1	1 (in) pesos blue		160.	225.
b.		1p indigo		200.	250.
b.		Impression on reverse of stamp in blue		3,000.	
c.		Double impression		250.	300.
d.		Tete beche pair			65,000.
e.		Half used as 4r on cover			7,500.
8	A1	1 (to) pesos blue		350.	225.

Nos. 1, 2, 3 and 7 have been reprinted on very thick, hand-made paper. The same four stamps and No. 8 have been reprinted on thin, hard, white wove paper.
Counterfeits of Nos. 1-8 are plentiful.

Liberty Head — A2

1859, Sept. 3

9	A2	4r green, *bluish*	250.00	160.00
10	A2	1p blue	35.00	17.50
11	A2	2p vermilion, fine impression	350.00	160.00
a.		2p red, blurred impression	300.00	125.00
b.		Vert. half used as 1p on cover		2,000.

Both fine and blurred impressions of these stamps may be found. They have generally been called Paris and Local prints, respectively, but the opinion now obtains that the differences are due to the impression and that they do not represent separate issues. Values are for fine impressions, unless otherwise noted. Rough or blurred impressions sell for less.
Many shades exist of Nos. 1-11.

1862, Oct. 4

12	A2	1p rose	200.00	100.00
13	A2	2p blue	350.00	75.00

All three values have been reprinted in black, brownish black, blue and red brown on thin hard white paper. The 4r has also been reprinted in green on bluish paper.
Values are for fine impressions. Rough or blurred impressions sell for less.

CORDOBA

A province in the central part of the Argentine Republic.
100 Centavos = 1 Peso

Arms of Cordoba — A1

Unwmk.
1858, Oct. 28		Litho.	Imperf.
		Laid Paper	

1	A1	5c blue	125.
2	A1	10c black	2,500.

Cordoba stamps were printed on laid paper, but stamps from edges of the sheets sometimes do not show any laid lines and appear to be on wove paper. Counterfeits are plentiful.

CORRIENTES

The northeast province of the Argentine Republic.
1 Real M(oneda) C(orriente) = 12½ Centavos M.C. = 50 Centavos
100 Centavos Fuertes = 1 Peso Fuerte

Nos. 1-2 were issued without gum. Nos. 3-8 were issued both with and without gum (values the same).

A1   A2
Ceres

Unwmk.
1856, Aug. 21		Typo.	Imperf.	
1	A1	1r black, *blue*	85.00	175.00

No. 1 used is valued with pen cancellation.

Pen Stroke Through "Un Real"
1860, Feb. 8				
2	A1	(3c) black, *blue*	350.00	175.00

No. 2 used is valued with pen cancellation.

1860-78

3	A2	(3c) black, *blue*	9.50	30.00
4	A2	(2c) blk, *yel grn* ('64)	37.50	37.50
a.		(2c) black, *blue green*	92.50	110.00
5	A2	(2c) blk, *yel* ('67)	7.50	19.00
6	A2	(3c) blk, *dk bl* ('71)	3.00	19.00
7	A2	(3c) blk, *rose red* ('76)	100.00	50.00
a.		(3c) black, *lil rose* ('75)	140.00	80.00

8	A2	(3c) blk, *dk rose* ('79)		8.00	32.50
a.		(3c) black, *red vio* ('77)		60.00	35.00
		Nos. 3-8 (6)		165.50	188.00

Pen canceled examples of Nos. 3-8 that do not indicate the town of origin sell for much less.
Printed from settings of 8 varieties, 3 or 4 impressions constituting a sheet. Some impressions were printed inverted and tete beche pairs may be cut from adjacent impressions.
From Jan. 1 to Feb. 24, 1864, No. 4 was used as a 5 centavos stamp but copies so used can only be distinguished when they bear dated cancellations.
The reprints show numerous spots and small defects which are not found on the originals. They are printed on gray blue, dull blue, gray green, dull orange and light magenta papers.

ARMENIA

är-'mē-nē-ə

LOCATION — South of Russia bounded by Georgia, Azerbaijan, Iran and Turkey
GOVT. — Republic
AREA — 11,490 sq. mi.
POP. — 3,409,234 (est. 1999)
CAPITAL — Yerevan

With Azerbaijan and Georgia, Armenia made up the Transcaucasian Federation of Soviet Republics.
Stamps of Armenia were replaced in 1923 by those of Transcaucasian Federated Republics.
With the breakup of the Soviet Union on Dec. 26, 1991, Armenia and ten former Soviet republics established the Commonwealth of Independent States.

100 Kopecks = 1 Ruble
100 Luma = 1 Dram (1993)

Catalogue values for unused stamps in this country are for Never Hinged items, beginning with Scott 430 in the regular postage section.

Counterfeits abound of all overprinted and surcharged stamps.

Watermark

Wmk. 171-Diamonds

Perforations
Perforations are the same as the basic Russian stamps.

National Republic
Russian Stamps of 1902-19 Handstamped

At least thirteen types exist of both framed and unframed overprints ("a" and "c"). The device is the Armenian "H," initial of Hayasdan (Armenia). Inverted and double overprints are found.

Surcharged

Type I - Without periods (two types).
Type II - Periods after 1st "K" and "60."

Black Surcharge

1919 Unwmk. Perf. 14x14½

1	A14	60k on 1k orange (II)	2.50	.40
a.		Imperf. (I)	1.00	.25
b.		Imperf. (II)	1.00	.25

Violet Surcharge

2	A14	60k on 1k orange (II)	.50	.50

Handstamped in Violet—a

Perf.

6	A15	4k carmine	2.00	2.00
7	A14	5k claret, imperf.	7.50	7.50
a.		Perf.	5.00	5.00
9	A14	10k on 7k lt blue	5.00	1.25
10	A11	15k red brn & bl	3.00	.25
11	A8	20k blue & car	2.00	1.00
13	A11	35k red brn & grn	3.50	3.50
14	A8	50k violet & green	3.50	3.50
15	A14	60k on 1k orange (II)	2.00	2.00
a.		Imperf. (I)	1.90	2.00
b.		Imperf. (II)	8.50	9.00
18	A13	5r dk bl, grn & pale bl	3.50	4.25
a.		Imperf.	1.00	1.00
19	A12	7r dk green & pink	1.75	2.00
20	A13	10r scar, yel & gray	1.75	2.00

Handstamped in Black

31	A14	2k green, imperf.	1.00	.20
a.		Perf.	5.00	4.25
32	A14	3k red, imperf.	1.00	.20
a.		Perf.	5.00	2.00
33	A15	4k carmine	.20	.20
34	A14	5k claret	1.00	.20
a.		Imperf.	5.00	5.00
36	A15	10k dark blue	2.00	.65
37	A14	10k on 7k lt blue	.50	.20
38	A11	15k red brn & bl	.50	.20
a.		Imperf.	3.00	3.00
39	A8	20k blue & car	1.00	.20
40	A11	25k green & gray vio	1.00	.20
41	A11	35k red brn & grn	1.00	.20
42	A8	50k violet & green	1.00	.20
43	A14	60k on 1k orange (II)	2.50	2.50
43A	A11	70k brown & org		.30
a.		Imperf.		.30
44	A9	1r pale brn, dk brn & org	1.50	.30
a.		Imperf.	.50	.50
45	A12	3½r mar & lt grn, imperf.	5.00	.65
a.		Perf.	5.00	.85
46	A13	5r dk bl, grn & pale bl	.60	.65
a.		Imperf.	6.00	1.00
47	A12	7r dk green & pink	6.00	1.10
48	A13	10r scar, yel & gray	50.00	1.00

Handstamped in Violet—c

Unwmk. Perf.
Wove Paper

62	A14	2k green, imperf.	.40	.40
a.		Perf.	4.50	4.50
63	A14	3k red, imperf.	.25	.25
a.		Perf.	3.00	2.75
64	A15	4k carmine	.50	.50
65	A14	5k claret	3.00	.40
a.		Imperf.	3.00	.60
67	A15	10k dark blue	1.00	.85
68	A14	10k on 7k lt bl	1.00	.65
69	A11	15k red brn & bl	2.50	2.50
70	A8	20k blue & car	.40	.40
71	A11	25k grn & gray vio	1.00	1.00
72	A11	35k red brn & grn	1.50	1.50
73	A8	50k violet & grn	.50	.50
74	A14	60k on 1k org (II)	2.50	2.00
a.		Imperf. (I)	1.65	1.65
b.		Imperf. (II)	2.00	2.00
75	A9	1r pale brn, dk brn & org	.60	.60
a.		Imperf.	1.50	1.50
76	A12	3½r mar & lt grn, imperf.	.75	.75
a.		Perf.	1.00	1.00
77	A13	5r dk bl, grn & pale bl, imperf.	5.00	5.00
a.		Perf.	4.00	4.00
78	A12	7r dk green & pink	7.50	7.50
79	A13	10r scar, yel & gray	2.25	1.90

Imperf

85	A11	70k brown & org	5.00	2.00

Handstamped in Black

Perf.

90	A14	1k orange	10.00	4.50
a.		Imperf.	10.00	6.00
91	A14	2k green, imperf.	1.00	.20
a.		Perf.	7.50	2.50
92	A14	3k red, imperf.	1.00	.20
a.		Perf.	10.00	2.75

93	A15	4k carmine	.50	.50
94	A14	5k claret	1.00	.20
a.		Imperf.	3.00	.60
95	A14	7k light blue	15.00	15.00
96	A15	10k dark blue	12.00	12.00
97	A14	10k on 7k lt blue	.20	.20
98	A11	15k red brn & bl	.20	.20
99	A8	20k blue & car	.20	.20
100	A11	25k grn & gray vio	.50	.20
101	A11	35k red brn & grn	.20	.20
102	A8	50k violet & grn	.20	.20
102A	A14	60k on 1k org, imperf. (I)	.30	.30
b.		Imperf. (II)	.50	.50
c.		Imperf. (II)	2.50	1.25
103	A9	1r pale brn, dk brn & org	1.00	1.00
a.		Imperf.	.75	.75
104	A12	3½r maroon & lt grn	4.00	.50
a.		Imperf.	5.00	.30
105	A13	5r dk bl, grn & pale bl	2.50	2.50
a.		Imperf.	2.50	2.50
106	A12	7r dk green & pink	3.00	2.50
107	A13	10r scar, yel & gray	7.00	3.50

Imperf

113	A11	70k brown & org	1.00	.25

Handstamped in Violet or Black:

5r f **10r** g

Violet Surcharge, Type f

1920 Perf.

120	A14	3r on 3k red, imperf.	.85	.85
a.		Perf.	2.50	2.50
121	A15	5r on 3k red	3.75	3.25
122	A15	5r on 4k car	10.00	8.00
123	A14	5r on 5k claret, imperf.	10.00	10.00
a.		Perf.	10.00	8.00
124	A15	5r on 10k dk blue	10.00	8.00
125	A14	5r on 10k on 7k lt bl	10.00	8.00
126	A8	5r on 20k bl & car		

Imperf

127	A14	5r on 2k green	7.00	7.00
128	A11	5r on 35k red brn & grn	7.00	7.00

Black Surcharge, Type f or Type g (#130)

Perf.

130	A14	1r on 1k orange	.50	.50
a.		Imperf.	.75	.75
131	A14	3r on 3k red	.20	.20
a.		Imperf.	.20	.20
132	A15	3r on 4k carmine	3.00	3.00
133	A14	5r on 2k grn, imperf.	.20	.20
a.		Perf.	2.00	2.00
134	A14	5r on 3k red	5.00	5.00
a.		Imperf.	2.50	2.50
135	A15	5r on 4k carmine	.40	.40
a.		Imperf.	4.75	4.75
136	A14	5r on 5k claret	.50	.50
a.		Imperf.	.50	.50
137	A14	5r on 7k lt blue	2.00	2.00
138	A15	5r on 10k dk blue	.50	.50
139	A14	5r on 10k on 7k lt bl	.50	.50
140	A11	5r on 14k bl & rose	2.00	2.00
141	A11	5r on 15k red brn & blue	.50	.50
a.		Imperf.	2.00	2.00
142	A8	5r on 20k bl & car	.50	.50
a.		Imperf.	10.00	10.00
143	A11	5r on 20k on 14k bl & rose	12.00	12.00
144	A11	5r on 25k grn & gray vio	12.00	12.00

Black Surcharge, Type g or Type f (#148A, 151)

145	A14	10r on 1k org, imperf.	.90	.90
a.		Perf.	225.00	225.00
146	A14	10r on 3k red	175.00	175.00
147	A14	10r on 5k claret	15.00	15.00
a.		Imperf.	6.00	
148	A8	10r on 20k bl & car	15.00	15.00
148A	A11	10r on 25k grn & gray vio	8.00	8.00
149	A11	10r on 25k grn & gray vio	5.00	5.00
a.		Imperf.	8.00	8.00
150	A11	10r on 35k red brn & grn	.50	.50
151	A8	10r on 50k brn vio & grn	1.75	1.75
152	A8	10r on 50k brn vio & grn	.45	.45
152A	A11	10r on 70k brn & org, imperf.	3.00	3.00
b.		Perf.	200.00	200.00
152C	A8	25r on 20k bl & car	4.00	4.00
153	A11	25r on 25k grn & gray vio	2.00	2.00
154	A11	25r on 35k red brn & grn	2.00	2.00
a.		Imperf.	3.50	3.50

155	A8	25r on 50k vio & grn	4.00	4.00
a.		Imperf.	5.00	5.00
156	A11	25r on 70k brn & org	8.00	8.00
a.		Imperf.	5.00	5.00
157	A9	50r on 1r pale brn, dk brn & org, imperf.	1.00	1.00
a.		Perf.	5.00	5.00
158	A13	50r on 5r dk bl, grn & lt bl	10.00	10.00
a.		Imperf.	10.00	10.00
159	A12	100r on 3½r mar & lt grn	7.00	7.00
a.		Imperf.	7.00	7.00
160	A13	100r on 5r dk bl, grn & pale bl	10.00	10.00
a.		Imperf.	7.00	7.00
161	A12	100r on 7r dk grn & pink	35.00	35.00
a.		Imperf.	35.00	35.00
162	A13	100r on 10r scar, yel & gray	10.00	10.00

Wmk. Wavy Lines (168)
Perf. 11½
Vertically Laid Paper

163	A12	100r on 3½r blk & gray	100.00	100.00
164	A12	100r on 7r blk & yel	100.00	100.00

1920 Unwmk. Imperf.
Wove Paper

166	A14 (g)	1r on 60k on 1k org (I)	12.00	12.00
168	A14 (f)	5r on 1k orange	9.00	9.00
173	A11 (f)	5r on 35k red brn & grn	2.50	2.50
177	A11 (g)	50r on 70k brn & org	5.00	5.00
179	A12 (g)	50r on 3½r mar & lt grn	2.00	2.00
181	A9 (g)	100r on 1r pale brn, dk brn & org	4.00	4.00

Romanov Issues Surcharged Type g or Type f (#185-187, 190)
On Stamps of 1913

1920 Perf. 13½

184	A16	1r on 1k brn org	10.00	10.00
185	A18	3r on 3k rose red	15.00	15.00
186	A19	5r on 4k dull red	10.00	10.00
187	A22	5r on 14k blue grn	60.00	60.00
187A	A19	10r on 4k dull red	30.00	
187B	A26	10r on 35k gray vio & dk grn		
187C	A19	25r on 4k dull red	10.00	10.00
188	A26	25r on 35k gray vio & dk grn	2.75	2.75
189	A28	25r on 70k yel grn & brn	2.75	2.75
190	A31	50r on 3r dk vio	2.00	2.00
190A	A16	100r on 1k brn org	100.00	100.00
190B	A17	100r on 2k green	10.50	10.50
191	A30	100r on 2r brown	10.50	10.50
192	A31	100r on 3r dk vio	10.50	10.50

On Stamps of 1915, Type g
Thin Cardboard
Inscriptions on Back
Perf. 12

193	A21	100r on 10k blue	3.00	
194	A23	100r on 15k brn	3.00	
195	A24	100r on 20k ol	3.00	

On Stamps of 1916, Type f
Perf. 13½

196	A20	5r on 10k on 7k brown	5.00	5.00
197	A22	5r on 20k on 14k bl grn	8.00	8.00

Surch. Type f or Type g (#204-205A, 207-207C, 210-211) over Type c
Type c in Violet
Perf.

200	A15	5r on 4k car	1.00	1.00
201	A15	5r on 10k dk bl	1.00	1.00
202	A11	5r on 15k red brn & bl	2.00	2.00
203	A8	5r on 20k blue & car	1.75	1.75
204	A11	5r on 25k grn & gray vio	1.50	1.50
205	A11	5r on 35k red brn & grn	3.00	3.00
205A	A8	10r on 50k brn vio & grn	3.50	3.50

206	A8	25r on 50k brn vio & grn	150.00	150.00
207	A9	50r on 1r pale brn, dk brn & org, imperf.	3.50	3.50
a.		Perf.	25.00	25.00
207B	A12	100r on 3½r mar & lt grn	30.00	
207C	A12	100r on 7r dk grn & pink	9.00	

Imperf

208	A14	5r on 2k green	25.00	25.00
209	A14	5r on 5k claret	25.00	25.00
210	A11	25r on 70k brn & org	5.50	5.50
211	A13	100r on 5r dk bl, grn & pale bl	1.00	1.00

Surcharged Type g or Type f (212-213, 215, 219-219A, 221-222) over Type c
Type c in Black
Perf.

212	A14	5r on 7k lt bl	150.00	150.00
213	A14	5r on 10k on 7k lt bl	5.00	5.00
214	A11	5r on 15k red brn & bl	.50	.50
215	A8	5r on 20k blue & car	3.00	3.00
215A	A11	10r on 5r on 25k grn & gray vio	5.00	5.00
216	A11	10r on 35k red brn & grn	.50	.50
217	A8	10r on 50k brn vio & grn	1.00	1.00
217A	A9	50r on 1r pale brn, dk brn & org	1.00	1.00
b.		Imperf.	1.10	1.10
217C	A12	100r on 3½r mar & lt grn	1.50	1.50
218	A13	100r on 5r dk bl, grn & pale bl	10.00	10.00
a.		Imperf.	1.75	1.75
219	A12	100r on 7r dk grn & pink	15.00	15.00
219A	A13	100r on 10r scar, yel & gray	10.00	10.00

Imperf

220	A14	1r on 60k on 1k org (I)	20.00	20.00
221	A14	5r on 2k green	.80	.80
222	A14	5r on 5k claret	3.00	3.00
223	A11	10r on 70k brn & org	2.00	2.00
224	A11	5r on 70k brn & org	2.00	2.00

Surcharged Type g or Type f (#233) over Type a
Type a in Violet
Imperf

231	A9	50r on 1r pale brn, dk brn & org	140.00	140.00
232	A13	100r on 5r dk bl, grn & pale bl	10.50	

Type a in Black
Perf.

233	A8	5r on 20k blue & car	.80	.80
233A	A11	10r on 25k grn & gray vio	55.00	55.00
234	A11	10r on 35k red brn & grn	.90	.90
235	A12	100r on 3½r mar & lt grn	1.25	1.25
a.		Imperf.	1.50	1.50

Imperf

237	A14	5r on 2k green	125.00	125.00
237A	A11	10r on 70k brn & org		

Surcharged Type a and New Value
Type a in Violet
Perf.

238	A11	10r on 15k brn & blue	.80	.80

Type a in Black

239	A8	5r on 20k blue & car	3.00	3.00
239A	A8	10r on 20k blue & car	3.00	3.00
239B	A8	10r on 50k brn red & grn	7.50	

Imperf

240	A12	100r on 3½r mar & lt grn	1.90	1.90

Surcharged Type c and New Value
Type c in Black

1920			Perf.	
241	A15	5r on 4k red	1.75	1.75
242	A11	5r on 15k red brn & bl	1.00	1.00
243	A8	10r on 20k blue & car	1.75	1.75
243A	A11	10r on 25k grn & gray vio	1.00	1.00
244	A11	10r on 35k red brn & grn	1.00	1.00
a.		With additional surch. "5r"	1.50	1.50
245	A12	100r on 3½r mar & lt grn	1.50	1.50
		Imperf		
247	A14	3r on 3k red	4.75	4.75
248	A14	5r on 2k green	.30	.30
249	A9	50r on 1r pale brn, dk brn & org	.90	.90

Type c in Violet

| 249A | A14 | 5r on 2k green | 6.50 | |

Postal Savings Stamps Surcharged

A1   A2   A3

Perf. 14½x15
Wmk. 171

250	A1	60k on 1k red & buff	50.00	50.00
251	A2	1r on 1k red & buff	5.00	5.00
252	A3	5r on 5k green & buff	7.25	7.25
253	A3	5r on 10k brn & buff	30.00	3.00

Russian Semi-Postal Stamps of 1914-18 Surcharged with Armenian Monogram and New Values like Regular Issues
On Stamps of 1914
Unwmk. Perf.

255	SP5	25r on 1k red brn & dk grn, *straw*	60.00	60.00
256	SP5	25r on 3k mar & gray grn, *pink*	60.00	60.00
257	SP5	50r on 7 dk brn & dk grn, *buff*	20.00	20.00
258	SP5	100r on 1k red brn & dk grn, *straw*	25.00	25.00
259	SP5	100r on 3k mar & gray grn, *pink*	25.00	25.00
260	SP5	100r on 7k dk brn & dk grn, *buff*	25.00	25.00

On Stamps of 1915-19

261	SP5	25r on 1k org brn & gray	75.00	75.00
262	SP5	25r on 3k car & gray	30.00	30.00
263	SP5	50r on 10k dk bl & brn	25.00	25.00
264	SP5	100r on 1k org brn & gray	50.00	3.50
265	SP5	100r on 10k dk bl & brn	50.00	3.50

These surcharged semi-postal stamps were used for ordinary postage.

A set of 10 stamps in the above designs was prepared in 1920, but not issued. Value of set, $4. Exist with "SPECIMEN" overprint and imperf. Reprints exist.

Soviet Socialist Republic

Hammer and Sickle — A7

Mythological Monster — A8

Symbols of Soviet Republics on Designs from old Armenian Manuscripts A9

Ruined City of Ani — A10

Mythological Monster — A11

Soviet Symbols, Armenian Designs — A14

Armenian Soldier — A12

Mythological Monster A13

Mt. Alagöz and Plain of Shirak A15

Fisherman on River Aras — A16

Post Office in Erevan and Mt. Ararat A17

Ruin in City of Ani — A18   Street in Erevan — A19

Lake Sevan and Sevan Monastery — A20

Mythological Subject from old Armenian Monument — A21

Mt. Ararat — A22

1921		Unwmk.	Perf. 11½, Imperf.	
278	A7	1r gray green	.30	
279	A8	2r slate gray	.30	
280	A9	3r carmine	.30	
281	A10	5r dark brown	.30	
282	A11	25r gray	.30	.20
283	A12	50r red	.20	
284	A13	100r orange	.20	
285	A14	250r dark blue	.20	
286	A15	500r brown vio	.20	
287	A16	1000r sea green	.25	
288	A17	2000r bister	.75	
289	A18	5000r dark brown	.60	
290	A19	10,000r dull red	.60	
291	A20	15,000r slate blue	.60	
292	A21	20,000r lake	.60	
293	A22	25,000r gray blue	1.25	
294	A22	25,000r brown olive	6.50	
		Nos. 278-294 (17)	13.45	

Except the 25r, Nos. 278-294 were not regularly issued and used. Counterfeits exist. For surcharges see Nos. 347-390.

Russian Stamps of 1909-17 Surcharged

Wove Paper
Lozenges of Varnish on Face

1921, Aug.			Perf. 13½
295	A9	5000r on 1r	10.00
296	A12	5000r on 3½r	10.00
297	A13	5000r on 5r	10.00
298	A12	5000r on 7r	10.00
299	A13	5000r on 10r	10.00
		Nos. 295-299 (5)	50.00

Nos. 295-299 were not officially issued. Counterfeits abound.

A23   Mt. Ararat & Soviet Star — A24

Soviet Symbols — A25

Crane — A26

Peasant — A27

Harpy — A28

Peasant Sowing — A29

Soviet Symbols — A30

Forging — A31

Plowing
A32

1922   **Perf. 11½**

300	A23	50r green & red		.50
301	A24	300r slate bl & buff		.60
302	A25	400r blue & pink		.60
303	A26	500r vio & pale lil		.60
304	A27	1000r dull bl & pale bl		.60
305	A28	2000r black & gray		.85
306	A29	3000r black & grn		.85
307	A30	4000r black & lt brn		.85
308	A31	5000r blk & dull red		.75
309	A32	10,000r black & pale rose		.75
a.		Tête bêche pair		35.00
		Nos. 300-309 (10)		6.95

Nos. 300-309 were not issued without surcharge.

Stamps of types A23 to A32, printed in other colors than Nos. 300 to 309, are essays.

Nos. 300-309 with Handstamped Surcharge of New Values in Rose, Violet or Black

1922

310	10,000 on 50r (R)	45.00	60.00
311	10,000 on 50r (V)	8.50	11.00
312	10,000 on 50r	8.50	11.00
313	15,000 on 300r (R)	45.00	75.00
314	15,000 on 300r (V)	8.50	14.00
315	15,000 on 300r	8.50	14.00
316	25,000 on 400r (V)	8.50	14.00
317	25,000 on 400r	8.50	14.00
318	30,000 on 500r (R)	52.50	90.00
319	30,000 on 500r (V)	10.00	17.00
320	30,000 on 500r	10.00	17.00
321	50,000 on 1000r (R)	45.00	75.00
322	50,000 on 1000r (V)	8.50	14.00
323	50,000 on 1000r	8.50	14.00
324	75,000 on 3000r	11.00	20.00
325	100,000 on 2000r (R)	100.00	100.00
326	100,000 on 2000r (V)	20.00	20.00
327	100,000 on 2000r	20.00	20.00
328	200,000 on 4000r (V)	22.50	22.50
329	200,000 on 4000r	22.50	22.50
330	300,000 on 5000r (V)	30.00	45.00
331	300,000 on 5000r	30.00	45.00
332	500,000 on 10,000r (V)	30.00	30.00
333	500,000 on 10,000r	30.00	30.00
	Nos. 310-333 (24)	591.50	795.00

Forgeries exist.

Goose — A33

Armenian Woman at Well — A35

Armenian Village Scene A34

Mt. Ararat A36

Mt. Ararat A37

New Values in Gold Kopecks, Handstamped Surcharge in Black

1922   *Imperf.*

334	A33	1(k) on 250r rose	12.50	12.50
335	A33	1(k) on 250r gray	20.00	20.00
336	A34	2(k) on 500r rose	8.00	8.00
337	A34	3(k) on 500r gray	8.00	8.00
338	A35	4(k) on 1000r rose	8.00	8.00
339	A35	4(k) on 1000r gray	15.00	15.00
340	A36	5(k) on 2000r gray	8.00	8.00
341	A36	10(k) on 2000r rose	8.00	8.00
342	A37	15(k) on 5000r rose	52.50	52.50
343	A37	20(k) on 5000r gray	8.00	8.00
		Nos. 334-343 (10)	148.00	148.00

Nos. 334-343 were issued for postal tax purposes.

Nos. 334-343 exist without surcharge but are not known to have been issued in that condition. Counterfeits exist of both sets.

Regular Issue of 1921 Handstamped with New Values in Black or Red Short, Thick Numerals

1922   *Imperf.*

347	A8	2(k) on 2r (R)	50.00	50.00
350	A11	4(k) on 25r (R)	30.00	30.00
353	A13	10(k) on 100r (R)	20.00	20.00
354	A14	15(k) on 250r	10.00	10.00
355	A15	20(k) on 500r	15.00	15.00
a.		With "k" written in red	10.00	10.00
357	A22	50(k) on 25,000r bl (R)	12.00	12.00
358	A22	50(k) on 25,000r brn ol (R)	9.00	9.00
359	A22	50(k) on 25,000r brn ol		
		Nos. 347-358 (7)	146.00	146.00

       Perf. 11½

360	A7	1(k) on 1r, imperf.	25.00	25.00
a.		Perf.	15.00	15.00
361	A7	1(k) on 1r (R)	35.00	35.00
a.		Imperf.	40.00	40.00
362	A8	2(k) on 2r, imperf.	40.00	40.00
a.		Perf.	40.00	40.00
363	A15	2(k) on 500r	35.00	35.00
a.		Imperf.	50.00	50.00
364	A15	2(k) on 500r (R)	9.00	9.00
365	A11	4(k) on 25r, imperf.	25.00	25.00
a.		Perf.	25.00	25.00
366	A12	5(k) on 50r, imperf.	1.75	1.75
a.		Perf.	2.50	2.50
367	A13	10(k) on 100r	20.00	20.00
a.		Imperf.	20.00	20.00
368	A21	35(k) on 20,000r, imperf.	50.00	50.00
a.		With "k" written in violet	50.00	50.00
b.		Perf.	65.00	65.00
c.		As "a," perf.	65.00	65.00
d.		With "kop" written in violet, imperf.	65.00	65.00
		Nos. 360-368 (9)	240.75	240.75

Manuscript Surcharge in Red

       Perf. 11½

371	A14	1k on 250r dk bl	40.00	40.00

Handstamped in Black or Red Tall, Thin Numerals

       Imperf

377	A11	4(k) on 25r (R)	4.25	4.25
379	A13	10(k) on 100r	10.00	10.00
380	A15	20(k) on 500r	6.00	6.00
381	A22	50k on 25,000r bl	75.00	75.00
a.		Surcharged "50" only	50.00	50.00
382	A22	50k on 25,000r bl (R)	12.00	12.00
382A	A22	50k on 25,000r brn ol	24.00	24.00
		Nos. 377-382A (6)	131.25	131.25

On Nos. 381, 382 and 382A the letter "k" forms part of the surcharge.

       Perf. 11½

383	A7	1(k) on 1r (R)	50.00	50.00
a.		Imperf.		
384	A14	1(k) on 250r	1.75	1.75
385	A15	2(k) on 500r	8.00	8.00
a.		Imperf.	20.00	20.00
386	A15	2(k) on 500r (R)	20.00	20.00
387	A9	3(k) on 3r	20.00	20.00
a.		Imperf.	20.00	20.00
388	A21	3(k) on 20,000r, imperf.	10.00	10.00
a.		Perf.	50.00	50.00
389	A11	4(k) on 25r	2.50	2.50
a.		Imperf.	4.25	4.25
390	A12	5(k) on 50r, imperf.	10.00	10.00
a.		Perf.	15.00	15.00
		Nos. 383-390 (8)	122.25	122.25

> **Catalogue values for unused stamps in this section, from this point to the end of the section, are for Never Hinged items.**

Mt. Ararat — A45

a, 20k. b, 2r. c, 5r.

1992, May 28   Litho.   **Perf. 14**
430   A45   Strip of 3, #a.-c.   4.00   4.00

Souvenir Sheet
431   A45   7r Eagle & Mt. Ararat   45.00   45.00

AT & T Communications System in Armenia—A45a

1992, July 1   Litho.   **Perf. 13x13½**
431A   A45a   50k multicolored   4.50   3.50

A46

A47

1992 Summer Olympics, Barcelona: a, 40k, Ancient Greek wrestlers. b, 3.60r, Boxing. c, 5r, Weight lifting. d, 12r, Gymnastics.

1992, July 25   Litho.   **Perf. 14**
432   A46   Strip of 4, #a.-d.   3.50   3.50

1992-93   Litho.   **Perf. 14½, 15x14½**

20k, Natl. flag. 1r, Goddess Waroubini. Orgov radio telescope. 2r, Yerevan Airport. No. 436, Goddess Anahit. No. 437, Runic message, 7th cent B.C. 5r, UPU emblem. 20r, Silver cup.

433	A47	20k multicolored	.20	.20
434	A47	1r gray green	.20	.20
435	A47	2r blue	.30	.30
436	A47	3r brown	.50	.50
437	A47	3r bronze	.20	.20
438	A47	5r brown black	.75	.75
439	A47	20r gray	.20	.20
		Nos. 433-439 (7)	2.35	2.35

No. 435 is airmail. See Nos. 464-471, 521-524.

Issued: #436, 20k, 2r, 5r, 8/25/92; others, 5/12/93.

Religious Artifacts — A50   Yerevan '93 — A52

David of Sassoun, by Hakop Kojoian—A50a

Scenic Views — A51

1993, May 23   Litho.   **Perf. 14**

448	A50	40k Marker	.20	.20
449	A50	80k Gospel page	.30	.25
450	A50	3.60r Bas-relief, 13th cent.	1.10	.90
451	A50	5r Icon of the Madonna	1.75	1.50
		Nos. 448-451 (4)	3.35	2.85

Souvenir Sheet
    Perf. 14x13½
451A   A50a   12r multicolored   6.00   5.00

1993, May 24   **Perf. 14**

Designs (illustration reduced): 40k, Garni Canyon, vert. 80k, Shaki Waterfall, Zangezur, vert. 3.60r, Arpa River Canyon, vert. 5r, Lake Sevan. 12r, Mount Aragats.

452	A51	40k multicolored	.20	.20
453	A51	80k multicolored	.20	.20
454	A51	3.60r multicolored	.50	.50
455	A51	5r multicolored	.60	.60
456	A51	12r multicolored	1.50	1.50
		Nos. 452-456 (5)	3.00	3.00

1993, May 25   **Perf. 14½**

457	A52	10r multicolored	.50	.50
a.		Min. sheet of 6 + 2 labels	4.25	

For surcharges see Nos. 485-486.

Souvenir Sheet

Noah's Descent from Mt. Ararat, by Hovhannes Aivazovsky—A52a

1993, May 24   Litho.   **Perf. 14½**
458   A52a   7r multicolored   2.50   2.50

Religious Relics, Echmiadzin — A53

Designs: 3r, Wooden panel, descent from cross, 9th cent. 5r, Gilded silver reliquary for Holy Cross of Khotakerats. 12r, Cross depicting right hand of St. Karapet, 14th cent. 30r, Reliquary for arm of St. Thaddeus the Apostle, 17th cent. 50r, Gilded silver vessel for consecrated ointment, 1815.

1994, Aug. 4   Litho.   **Perf. 14x14½**

459	A53	3d multicolored	.20	.20
460	A53	5d multicolored	.20	.20
461	A53	12d multicolored	.30	.30

462 A53 30d multicolored .80 .80
463 A53 50d multicolored 1.25 1.25
   Nos. 459-463 (5) 2.75 2.75

Artifacts and Landmarks Type of 1993

Gods of Van (Urartu): 10 l, Shivini, god of the sun. 50 l, Tayshaba, god of elements. 10d, Khaldi, supreme god. 25d, Natl. arms.

1994   *Perf. 14½*
464 A47 10 l black & brown .20 .20
465 A47 50 l black & red brown .20 .20
469 A47 10d black & gray .50 .50
471 A47 25d red & bister 1.25 1.25
   Nos. 464-471 (4) 2.15 2.15

Issued: 10 l, 50 l, 10d, 25d, 8/4/94. This is an expanding set. Numbers may change.

A54

1994, Dec. 31 Litho.   *Perf. 14½x14*
479 A54 16d No. 1a .45 .45
First Armenian postage stamp, 75th anniv.

A54a   A54b

1994, Dec. 30 Litho.   *Perf. 14x14½*
480 A54a 30d Early printing press .50 .50
First Armenian periodical, 170th anniv.

1994, Dec. 30 Litho.   *Perf. 14x14½*
481 A54b 30d Natl. arms, stadium .55 .55
Natl. Olympic Committee.

A54c

1994, Dec. 30 Litho.   *Perf. 14x14½*
482 A54c 40d Olympic rings .75 .75
Intl. Olympic Committee, Cent.

A54d

1994, Dec. 31 Litho.   *Perf. 14x14½*
483 A54d 50d multi + label .85 .85
Ervand Otian (1869-1926)

A54e

1994, Dec. 31 Litho.   *Perf. 14½x14*
484 A54e 50d multi + label .85 .85
Levon Shant (1869-1951).

No. 457 Surcharged in Blue or Red Brown

a   b

1994, Sept. 10 Litho.   *Perf. 14*
485 A52(a) 40d on 10r (Bl) 1.60 1.60
486 A52(b) 40d on 10r (RB) 1.60 1.60
Yerevan '94.

A55   A56

Christianity in Armenia: 60d, Cross, 10th-11th cent. No. 488, Kings Abgar & Trdat, 1836. No. 489, St. Bartholomew, St. Thaddeus. 80d, St. Gregory, the Illuminator. 90d, Baptism of the Armenian people, 1892. 400d, Plan of Echmiadzin, c. 1660, engr. by Jakob Peeters.

1995, Apr. 3 Litho.   *Perf. 14x15*
487 A55 60d multicolored .55 .55
488 A55 70d multicolored .65 .65
489 A55 70d multicolored .65 .65
490 A55 80d multicolored .75 .75
491 A55 90d multicolored .85 .85
   Nos. 487-491 (5) 3.45 3.45
Souvenir Sheet
492 A55 400d multicolored 4.00 4.00
Nos. 488-489 are 45x44mm.

1995, Apr. 3
493 A56 150d gray & black 1.25 1.25
Vazgen I (1908-94), Catholikos of All Armenians.

Armenia Fund
A57

1995, Apr. 27   *Perf. 15x14*
494 A57 90d multicolored .80 .80

UN, 50th Anniv.
A58

1995, Apr. 28
495 A58 90d multicolored .80 .80

Cultural Artifacts — A59

Designs: 30d, Black polished pottery, 14th-13th cent. B.C. 60d, Silver cup, 5th cent. B.C. 130d, Gohar carpet, 1700 A.D.

1995, Apr. 27   *Perf. 15x14*
496 A59 30d multicolored .25 .25
497 A59 60d multicolored .50 .50
498 A59 130d multicolored 1.25 1.25
   Nos. 496-498 (3) 2.00 2.00

Birds — A60

1995, Apr. 27   *Perf. 14*
499 A60 40d Milvus milvus .50 .50
500 A60 60d Aquila chrysaetos .75 .75

End of World War II, 50th Anniv. A61

Designs: No. 501, P. Kitsook, 408th Armenian Rifle Division. No. 502, A. Sargissin, N. Safarian, 89th Taman Armenian Triple Order-Bearer Division. No. 503, B. Chernikov, N. Tavartkeladze, V. Penkovsky, 76th Armenian Alpine Rifle Red Banner (51st Guards) Division. No. 504, S. Zakian, H. Babayan, I. Lyudnikov, 390th Armenian Rifle Division. No. 505, A. Vasillian, M. Dobrovolsky, Y. Grechany, G. Sorokin, 409th Armenian Rifle Division.

No. 506, vert.: a, Marshal Hovhannes Baghramian. b, Adm. Hovhannes Issakov. c, Marshal Hamazasp Babajanian. d, Marshal Sergey Khoudyakov.

No. 507: Return of the Hero, by Mariam Aslamazian.

1995, Sept. 30 Litho.   *Perf. 15x14*
501 A61 60d multicolored .45 .45
502 A61 60d multicolored .45 .45
503 A61 60d multicolored .45 .45
504 A61 60d multicolored .45 .45
505 A61 60d multicolored .45 .45
   Nos. 501-505 (5) 2.25 2.25
Miniature Sheet
Perf. 15x14½
506 A61 60d Sheet of 4, #a.-d. 3.00 3.00
Souvenir Sheet
Perf. 15x14
507 A61 300d multicolored 3.75 3.75

Authors A62

Designs: No. 508, Ghevond Alishan (1820-1901). No. 509, Gregor Artsruni (1845-92), vert. No. 510, Franz Werfel (1890-1945).

1995, Oct. 5 Litho.   *Perf. 15x14*
508 A62 90d blue & black .75 .75
509 A62 90d multicolored .75 .75
510 A62 90d blue & maroon .75 .75
   Nos. 508-510 (3) 2.25 2.25

Nos. 508-510 issued with se-tenant label.

A64

Prehistoric artifacts: 40d, Four-wheeled carriages, 15th cent. BC. 60d, Bronze model of geocentric solar system, 11-10th cent. BC, vert. 90d, Tombstone, Red Tufa, 7-6th cent. BC, vert.

1995, Dec. 5   *Perf. 14½x15, 15x14½*
512 A64 40d multicolored .25 .25
513 A64 60d multicolored .60 .60
514 A64 90d multicolored .90 .90
   Nos. 512-514 (3) 1.75 1.75

A65

Christianity in Armenia — A66

Views of Yerevan: 60d, Brandy distillery, wine cellars. 80d, Abovian Street. 90d, Sports and concert complex. 100d, Baghramian Avenue. 120d, Republic Square. 400d, Panoramic photograph of Yerevan.

1995, Dec. 5   *Perf. 15x14*
515 A65 60d salmon & black .35 .35
516 A65 80d pale org & blk .45 .45
517 A65 90d buff & black .50 .50
Size: 61x24mm
518 A65 100d pale yel bis & blk .85 .85
519 A65 120d dull org & blk 1.10 1.10
   Nos. 515-519 (5) 3.25 3.25
Souvenir Sheet
520 A66 400d multicolored 3.50 3.50

No. 464 Surcharged in Green, Red, Blue Violet, or Red Brown

1996, Mar. 30 Litho.   *Perf. 14½*
521 A47 40d on 10l (G) 1.00 1.00
522 A47 100d on 10l (R) 2.50 2.50
523 A47 150d on 10l (BV) 3.50 3.50
524 A47 200d on 10l (RB) 5.00 5.00
   Nos. 521-524 (4) 12.00 12.00

Alexsandre Griboyedov (1795-1829), Writer — A67

1996, Apr. 24 Litho.   *Perf. 14x14½*
525 A67 90d multi + label .70 .70

Khrimian Hayrik (1820-1907), Catholicos of All Armenians — A68

1996, Apr. 30   **Perf. 14½x14**
526 A68 90d brown & blue   .70 .70
No. 526 is printed se-tenant with label.

Admiral Lazar Serbryakov (1795-1862) — A69

1996, Apr. 30
527 A69 90d multi + label   .70 .70

Armenian Red Cross, 75th Anniv. — A70

1996, May 3   **Perf. 14x14½**
528 A70 60d multicolored   .45 .45

Motion Pictures, Cent. A71

1996, May 3   **Perf. 14½x14**
529 A71 60d multicolored   .45 .45

Endangered Fauna — A72

1996, May 3   **Perf. 14**
530 A72 40d Carpa aegagrus   .30 .30
531 A72 60d Panthera pardus   .45 .45

1996 Summer Olympics, Atlanta — A73   Modern Olympic Games, Cent. — A74

Designs: a, 40d, Cyclist. b, 60d, Athletic event. c, 90d, Wrestling.

1996, July 25
532 A73 Strip of 3, #a.-c.   1.25 1.25

1996, July 25   **Perf. 14x14½**
533 A74 60d multicolored   .45 .45

Fridtjof Nansen (1861-1930), Arctic Explorer — A75

1996, May 20   **Litho.**   **Perf. 14x14½**
534 A75 90d multicolored   .60 .60

32nd Chess Olympiad, Yerevan — A76

#535, Petrosian-Botvinnik, World Championship match, Moscow, 1963. #536, Kasparov-Karpov, World Championship Match, Leningrad, 1986. #537, G. Kasparian, first prize winner, Contest of the Shakhmati v SSSR magazine, 1939. #538, 32nd Chess Olympiad, Yerevan.

1996, Sept. 15   **Litho.**   **Perf. 14**
535 A76 40d multicolored   .35 .35
536 A76 40d multicolored   .35 .35
537 A76 40d multicolored   .35 .35
538 A76 40d multicolored   .35 .35
   a. Booklet pane, #535-538   1.50
     Complete booklet, 2 #538a   3.00
   Nos. 535-538 (4)   1.40 1.40
No. 538a issued 9/24.

Tigran Petrosian, World Chess Champion, Chess House, Yerevan — A77

1996, Sept. 20   **Perf. 14x15**
539 A77 90d multicolored   .75 .75

Capra Aegagrus A78

World Wildlife Fund: 70d, Two running. 100d, One standing. 130d, One holding head down. 350d, Two facing forward.

1996, Oct. 20   **Litho.**   **Perf. 14½x14**
540 A78 70d multicolored   .40 .40
541 A78 100d multicolored   .50 .50
542 A78 130d multicolored   .75 .75
543 A78 350d multicolored   2.00 2.00
   a. Block of 4, #540-543   3.75 3.75
   b. Booklet pane, 2 #543a   7.50
     Complete booklet, #543b   7.50
Issued in sheets of 16 stamps.

Christianity in Armenia, 1700th Anniv. — A79

Armenian churches: No. 544, St. Catherine Church, St. Petersburg, 1780. No. 545, Church of the Holy Mother, Kishinev, 1803. No. 546, Church of the Holy Mother, Samarkand, 1903. No. 547, Armenian Church, Lvov,

1370. No. 548, St. Hripsime Church, Yalta, 1913.
   500d, Church of St. Gevorg of Etchmiadzin, Tbilisi, 1805.

1996   **Litho.**   **Perf. 14x15**
544 A79 100d multicolored   .50 .50
545 A79 100d multicolored   .50 .50
546 A79 100d multicolored   .50 .50
547 A79 100d multicolored   .50 .50
548 A79 100d multicolored   .50 .50
   Nos. 544-548 (5)   2.50 2.50
Souvenir Sheet
549 A79 500d multicolored   2.50 2.50

First Armenian Printing Press, Etchmiadzin, 225th Anniv. — A80

1997, Mar. 26   **Litho.**   **Perf. 15x14**
550 A80 70d multicolored   .35 .35

Armenian Entertainers — A81

#551, Folk singer, Jivani (1846-1909). #552, Arno Babajanian (1921-83), composer, vert.

1997, Mar. 26   **Perf. 15x14, 14x15**
551 A81 90d multicolored   .45 .45
552 A81 90d multicolored   .45 .45

Paintings from Natl. Gallery of Armenia A82

#553, "One of my Dreams," by Eghishe Tadevossian. #554, "Countryside," by Gevorg Bashinjaghian. #555, "Portrait of Natalia Tehumian," by Hakob Hovnatanian. #556, "Salomé," by Vardges Sureniants.

1997, May 28   **Litho.**   **Perf. 15x14**
553 A82 150d multi   .70 .70
554 A82 150d multi   .70 .70
555 A82 150d multi, vert.   .70 .70
556 A82 150d multi, vert.   .70 .70
   Nos. 553-556 (4)   2.80 2.80
See Nos. 573-575.

Rouben Mamulian (1897-1987), Motion Picture Director — A83

1997, Oct. 8   **Litho.**   **Perf. 15x14**
557 A83 150d multicolored   .70 .70

Moscow '97, World Philatelic Exhibition — A84

1997, Oct. 17   **Perf. 14x15**
558 A84 170d St. Basil's Cathedral   .80 .80

Eghishe Charents (1897-1937), Poet — A85

1997, Oct. 19   **Perf. 15x14**
559 A85 150d multicolored   .70 .70

A86   A87

Europa (Stories and Legends): 170d, Hayk, the Progenitor of the Armenians. 250d, Vahagn, the Dragon Slayer.

1997, Oct. 18   **Perf. 14x15**
560 A86 170d multicolored   .80 .80
561 A86 250d multicolored   1.10 1.10

1997, Dec. 19   **Litho.**   **Perf. 14**
562 A87 40d Iris lycotis   .20 .20
563 A87 170d Iris elegantissima   .85 .85

Religious Buildings A88   Christmas A89

#564, San Lazzaro, the Mekhitarian Congregation, Venice. #565, St. Gregory the Illuminator Cathedral, Anthelias. #566, St. Khach Armenian Church, Rostov upon Don. #567, St. James Monastery, Jerusalem. #568, Nercissian School, Tbilisi.
   500d, Lazarian Seminary, Moscow.

1997, Dec. 22   **Perf. 15x14, 14x15**
564 A88 100d multi, horiz.   .50 .50
565 A88 100d multi   .50 .50
566 A88 100d multi   .50 .50
567 A88 100d multi, horiz.   .50 .50
Size: 60x21mm
568 A88 100d multi, horiz.   .50 .50
   Nos. 564-568 (5)   2.50 2.50
Souvenir Sheet
569 A88 500d multicolored   2.50 2.50
Christianity in Armenia, 1700th anniv. (in 2001).

1997, Dec. 26   **Perf. 14x15**
570 A89 40d multicolored   .25 .25

Diana, Princess of Wales (1961-97) A90

1998, Apr. 8   **Litho.**   **Perf. 15x14**
571 A90 250d multicolored   1.00 1.00
No. 571 was issued in sheets of 5 + label.

Karabakh
Movement, 10th
Anniv. — A91

1998, Feb. 20   Litho.   Perf. 13½x14
572 A91 250d multicolored   1.00 1.00

Paintings from Natl. Gallery of
Armenia Type of 1997

#573, "Tartar Women's Dance," by Alexander Bazhbeouk-Melikian. #574, "Family. Generations," by Yervand Kochar. #575, "Spring in Our Yard," by Haroutiun Kalents.

1998, Feb. 21   Perf. 15x14, 14x15
573 A82 150d multi   .65 .65
574 A82 150d multi, vert.   .65 .65
575 A82 150d multi, vert.   .65 .65
   Nos. 573-575 (3)   1.95 1.95

1998 World Cup
Soccer
Championships,
France — A92

1998, June 10   Litho.   Perf. 14x15
576 A92 250d multicolored   1.10 1.10

National
Holidays
and
Festivals
A93

Europa: 170d, Couple jumping over fire, Trndez. 250d, Girls taking part in traditional ceremony, Ascension Day.

1998, June 24   Litho.   Perf. 15x14
577 A93 170d multicolored   .75 .75
578 A93 250d multicolored   1.25 1.25

Butterflies   National
A94   Costumes
                       A95

1998, June 26   Perf. 14
579 A94 170d Papilio alexanor   .75 .75
580 A94 250d Rethera komarovi   1.25 1.25

1998, July 16   Litho.   Perf. 14x13½
581 A95 170d Ayrarat   .75 .75
582 A95 250d Vaspurakan   1.10 1.10

See Nos. 591-592.

Christianity in
Armenia, 1700th
Anniv. (in
2001) — A96

Churches: a, St. Forty Children's, 1958, Milan. b, St. Sargis, London, 1923. c, St. Vardan Cathedral, 1968, New York. d, St.

Hovannes Cathedral, 1902, Paris. e, St. Gregory the Illuminator Cathedral, 1938, Buenos Aires.

1998, Sept. 25   Litho.   Perf. 11½
583 A96 100d Sheet of 5, #a.-e. 2.40 2.40

Memorial to
Armenian
Earthquake
Victims
A97

1998, Sept. 26   Perf. 15x14
584 A97 250d multicolored   1.10 1.10

No. 584 was issued in sheets of 8 + 2 labels.

Minerals
A98

1998, Oct. 23
585 A98 170d Pyrite   .75 .75
586 A98 250d Agate   1.10 1.10

See Nos. 616-617.

Valery Bryusov
(1873-1924),
Writer — A99

1998, Dec. 1   Perf. 14x15
587 A99 90d multicolored   .45 .45

Souvenir Sheet

Sergei Parajanov, Film Director, 75th
Birth Anniv. — A100

Illustration reduced.

1999, Apr. 19   Litho.   Perf. 14x14¾
588 A100 500d multicolored   2.25 2.25
 a.   IBRA 99 emblem in margin 2.25 2.25

State
Reserves
A101

1999, Apr. 22   Perf. 14¾x14¼
589 A101 170d Khosrov   .75 .75
590 A101 250d Kilijan   1.25 1.25

Europa.

National Costumes Type of 1998

1999, Apr. 20   Perf. 14x13½
591 A95 170d Karin   .75 .75
592 A95 250d Zangezour   1.25 1.25

Council of
Europe, 50th
Anniv. — A102

1999, June 12
593 A102 170d multicolored   .80 .80

Cilician
Ships
A103

1999, Aug. 12   Litho.   Perf. 14¾x14
Sail Colors
594 A103 170d orange & blue   .80 .80
595 A103 250d red & white   1.25 1.25

With PhilexFrance 99 Emblem at LR
596 A103 250d red & white   1.25 1.25
   Nos. 594-596 (3)   3.30 3.30

Domesticated
Animals — A104

1999, Aug. 19   Perf. 13¼x13¾
597 A104 170d Armenian gampr
              dog   .80 .80
598 A104 250d Van cat   1.25 1.25

**With China 1999 World Philatelic
Exhibition Emblem at LR**
599 A104 250d Van cat   1.25 1.25
   Nos. 597-599 (3)   3.30 3.30

Souvenir Sheet

First Pan-Armenian Games — A105

Illustration reduced.

1999, Aug. 28   Perf. 14¾x14
600 A105 250d multicolored   2.10 2.10

Souvenir Sheet

Christianity in Armenia, 1700th Anniv.
(in 2001) — A106

Churches: a, St. Gregory the Illuminator, Cairo. b, St. Gregory the Illuminator, Singapore. c, St. Khach, Suceava, Romania. d, St. Savior, Worcester, Mass. e, Church of the Holy Mother, Madras, India.

1999, Aug.   Litho.   Perf. 13¼x13¾
601 A106 70d Sheet of 5, #a.-e.
              + label   1.60 1.60

UPU, 125th
Anniv.
A107

1999, Oct.   Perf. 14¾x14¼
602 A107 270d multicolored   1.40 1.40

Politicians Assassinated Oct. 27,
1999 — A108

Designs: No. 603, Parliament Speaker Karen Demirchyan, Parliament building. No. 604, Prime Minister Vazgen Sargsyan, troops. 540d, Demirchyan, Sargsyan, Yuri Bakhshyan, Ruben Miroyan, Henrik Abrahamyan, Armenak Armenakyan, Leonard Petrossyan and Mikael Kotanyan.

**   Perf. 14¾x14¼**
2000, Feb. 21   Litho.
603 A108 250d multi   1.10 1.10
604 A108 250d multi   1.10 1.10
 a.   Sheet, 5 each #603-604   11.00 11.00

Imperf
Size: 60x44mm
605 A108 540d multi   2.50 2.50

Fish — A109

Designs: 50d, Salmo ischchan. 270d, Barbus goktschaicus.

2000, May 23   Litho.   Perf. 13¼x13¾
606 A109 50d multi   .25 .25
607 A109 270d multi   1.25 1.25

Fairy Tales
A110

2000, May 25   Perf. 14¾x14¼
608 A110 70d The Liar Hunter   .35 .35
609 A110 130d The King and the
              Peddler   .60 .60

Europa, 2000
Common Design Type

2000, June 19   Perf. 14¼x14¾
610 CD17 40d multi   .20 .20
611 CD17 500d multi   2.25 2.25

Christianity as State Religion, 1700th
Anniv. — A111

No. 612: a, St. Gayane Church, Vagharshapat. b, Etchmiadzin Cathedral, Vagharshapat. c, Church of the Holy Mother, Khor Virap. d, St. Shoghakat Church, Vagharshapat. e, St. Hripsime Church, Vagharshapat. Illustration reduced.

2000, July 10   Litho.   Perf. 13¼x13¾
612 A111 70d Sheet of 5, #a-e, +
              label   1.75 1.75

2000 Summer
Olympics,
Sydney — A112

Designs: 10d, Basketball. 30d, Tennis.
500d, Weight lifting.

2000, July 11   **Perf. 13½x13¾**
613-615 A112 Set of 3   2.50 2.50

Mineral Type of 1998

Designs: 170d, Quartz. 250d, Molybdenite.

2000, Sept. 4   **Perf. 14¾x14**
616-617 A98 Set of 2   1.90 1.90

A113   A114

2000, Sept. 11   **Perf. 14x14¾**
618 A113 270d multi   1.25 1.25

Nerses Shnorhali (1100-73), poet and
musician.

2000, Sept. 15
619 A114 170d multi   .80 .80

Christmas.

Avetik Issahakian (1875-1957),
Poet — A115

2000, Sept. 17   **Perf. 14¾x14**
620 A115 130d multi   .60 .60

Musical   Famous
Instruments   Armenians
A116   A117

Designs: 170d, Dhol. 250d, Duduk.

2000, Dec. 22   **Litho.**   **Perf. 14x13¼**
621-622 A116 Set of 2   1.90 1.90

2000, Dec. 23   **Perf. 14¾x14¼**
No. 623: a, Viktor Hambartsoumian (1908-
96), cosmologist. b, Abraham Alikhanov
(1904-70), physicist. c, Andranik Iossifian
(1905-93), engineer. d, Sargis Saltikov (1905-
83), metallurgist. e, Samuel Kochariants
(1909-87), nuclear weapons scientist. f, Atrem
Mikoyan (1905-70), aircraft designer. g, Norayr
Sissakian (1907-66), biologist. h, Ivan Knuny-
ants (1906-90), chemist. i, Nikoghayos
Yenikolopian (1924-93), chemist.
No. 624: a, Nikoghayos Adonts (1871-
1942), historian. b, Manouk Abeghian (1865-
1944), grammarian. c, Hovhannes Toumanian
(1869-1923), poet. d, Hrachya Ajarian (1876-
1953), linguist. e, Gevorg Emin (1918-98),
writer. f, Yervand Lalayan (1864-1931), anthropologist. g, Daniel Varoujan (1884-1915),
poet. h, Paruyr Sevak (1924-71), writer. i, William Saroyan (1908-81), writer.
No. 625: a, Hamo Beknazarian (1892-
1965), actor. b, Alexandre Tamanian (1878-
1936), architect. c, Vahram Papazian (1888-
1968), actor. d, Vassil Tahirov (1859-1938),
viticulturist. e, Leonid Yengibarian (1935-72),
mime. f, Haykanoush Danielian (1893-1958),
singer. g, Sergo Hambartsoumian (1910-83)
"Strongest man on Earth". h, Hrant Shahinian
(1923-96), gymnast. i, Toros Toramanian
(1864-1934), architectural historian.
No. 626: a, Komitas (1869-1935), composer. b, Aram Khachatourian (1903-78),
composer. c, Martiros Sarian (1880-1972),
artist. d, Avet Terterian (1929-94), composer.
e, Alexandre Spendiarian (1871-1928), composer. f, Arshile Gorky (1904-48), artist. g,
Minas Avetissian (1928-75), artist. h, Levon
Orbeli (1882-1958), physiologist. i, Hripsimeh
Simonian (1916-98), artist.

623		Booklet pane of 9	4.50	
a.-i.	A117	110d Any single	.50	.50
624		Booklet pane of 9	4.50	
a.-i.	A117	110d Any single	.50	.50
625		Booklet pane of 9	4.50	
a.-i.	A117	110d Any single	.50	.50
626		Booklet pane of 9	4.50	
a.-i.	A117	110d Any single	.50	.50
		Booklet, #623-626	18.00	

Record of Lamentations, by St. Grigor
Narekatzi, 1000th Anniv. — A119

2001, June 8   **Litho.**   **Perf. 14¾x14**
628 A119 25d multi   .20 .20

Europa
A120

Designs: 50d, Lake Sevan. 500d,
Spandarian Reservoir.

2001, June 9
629-630 A120 Set of 2   2.60 2.60

Armenian
Admission
to Council
of Europe
A121

2001, June 11
631 A121 240d multi   1.10 1.10

Worldwide Fund for Nature
(WWF) — A122

Sciurus persicus: a, 40d, On branch. b, 50d,
Eating. c, 80d, Close-up. d, 120d, Digging.
Illustration reduced.

Perf. 13¼x13¾
2001, Aug. 25   **Litho.**
632 A122   Block of 4, #a-d   2.10 2.10

AIR POST STAMPS

AP1   AP2

Design: 90d, Artiom Katsian (1886-1943),
world record holding pilot on range and altitude in 1909.

1995, Dec. 5   **Litho.**   **Perf. 14x15**
C1 AP1 90d multicolored   .75 .75

1996, Apr. 30   **Litho.**   **Perf. 14x14½**
C2 AP2 90d multicolored   .70 .70

Nelson Stepanian (1913-44), WWII fighter
ace.

ARUBA

ə-'rü-bə

LOCATION — West Indies, north of
Venezuela
AREA — 78 sq. mi.
POP. — 67,014
CAPITAL — Oranjestad

On Jan. 1, 1986 Aruba, formerly part
of Netherlands Antilles, achieved a separate status within the Kingdom of the
Netherlands.

100 Cents = 1 Gulden

Catalogue values for all unused
stamps in this country are for
Never Hinged items.

Used values are for CTO or stamps
removed from first day covers. Postally used examples sell for more.

Traditional
House — A1

Perf. 14x13

			Unwmk.	
1986-87		**Litho.**		
1	A1	5c shown	.20	.20
2	A1	15c King William III Tower	.20	.20
3	A1	20c Loading crane	.20	.20
4	A1	25c Lighthouse	.20	.20
5	A1	30c Snake	.30	.25
6	A1	35c Owl	.30	.25
7	A1	45c Shell	.30	.25
8	A1	55c Frog	.40	.35
9	A1	60c Water skier	.50	.45
10	A1	65c Net fishing	.60	.55
11	A1	75c Music box	.60	.55
12	A1	85c Pre-Columbian bisque pot	.65	.60
13	A1	90c Bulb cactus	.70	.65
14	A1	100c Grain	.75	.70
15	A1	150c Watapana tree	1.25	1.10
16	A1	250c Aloe plant	2.10	1.90
		Nos. 1-16 (16)	9.25	8.40

Issued: 5c, 30c, 60c, 150c, 1/1; 15c, 35c,
65c, 250c, 2/5; 20c, 45c, 75c, 100c, 4/7/87;
25c, 55c, 85c, 90c, 7/17/87.

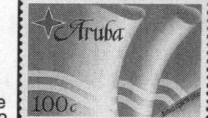

Independence
A2

1986, Jan. 1   **Perf. 14x13, 13x14**
18 A2 25c Map   .35 .30
19 A2 45c Coat of arms, vert.   .60 .55
20 A2 55c Natl. anthem, vert.   .70 .65
21 A2 100c Flag   1.00 .90
    Nos. 18-21 (4)   2.65 2.40

Intl. Peace
Year — A3

1986, Aug. 29   **Litho.**   **Perf. 14x13**
22 A3 60c shown   .75 .55
23 A3 100c Barbed wire   1.00 .80

Princess Juliana and Prince Bernhard, 50th Wedding Anniv. — A4

1987, Jan. 7   Photo.   Perf. 13x14
24 A4 135c multicolored   1.25 1.10

State Visit of Queen Beatrix and Prince Claus of the Netherlands A5

1987, Feb. 16   Litho.   Perf. 14x13
25 A5 55c shown   .55 .45
26 A5 60c Prince William-Alexander   .60 .50

Tourism — A6

1987, June 5   Litho.
27 A6 60c Beach and sea   .65 .60
28 A6 100c Rock and cacti   1.10 1.00

Aloe Vera Plant — A7   Coins — A8

1988, Jan. 27   Litho.   Perf. 13x14
29 A7 45c Field   .40 .40
30 A7 60c Plant   .60 .55
31 A7 100c Harvest   1.00 .90
    Nos. 29-31 (3)   2.00 1.85

1988, Mar. 16   Litho.   Perf. 13x14
32 A8 25c multicolored   .25 .25
33 A8 55c 50-cent   .50 .50
34 A8 65c 5 and 10-cent   .75 .70
35 A8 150c 1-florin   1.50 1.40
    Nos. 32-35 (4)   3.00 2.85

Love Issue — A9   A10

1988, May 4
36 A9 70c shown   .50 .45
37 A9 135c Seashells, coastal scenery   1.10 1.00

1988, Aug. 24
38 A10 35c shown   .40 .35
39 A10 100c Emblems   1.00 .90

Aruba, the 162nd member of the Intl. Olympic Committee (35c), 1988 Summer Olympics, Seoul (100c).

Carnival A11

1989, Jan. 5   Perf. 14x13
40 A11 45c Two children   .40 .40
41 A11 60c Girl   .60 .55
42 A11 100c Entertainer   1.00 .90
    Nos. 40-42 (3)   2.00 1.85

Maripampun, *Omphalophalmum Rubrum* — A12

1989, Mar. 16   Litho.   Perf. 14x13
43 A12 35c Leaves   .35 .30
44 A12 55c Pods   .55 .50
45 A12 200c Blossom   1.75 1.60
    Nos. 43-45 (3)   2.65 2.40

New Year 1990 — A13   UPU — A14

Dande band members playing instruments or singing: 25c, Violin, tambor, cuatro, marimba. 70c, Lead singer, guitar. 150c, Accordion, urri, guitar.

1989, Nov. 16   Litho.   Perf. 13x14
46 A13 25c multicolored   .25 .20
47 A13 70c multicolored   .60 .55
48 A13 150c multicolored   1.25 1.10
    Nos. 46-48 (3)   2.10 1.85

1989, June 8   Litho.   Perf. 13x14
49 A14 250c multicolored   2.25 2.00

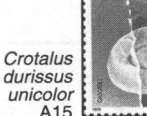

Crotalus durissus unicolor A15

1989, Aug. 24   Perf. 14x13
50 A15 45c shown   .45 .40
51 A15 55c multi, diff.   .50 .45
52 A15 60c multi, diff.   .65 .60
    Nos. 50-52 (3)   1.60 1.45

Snake species in danger of extinction.

Man Living in Harmony with Nature — A16

1990, Feb. 7   Perf. 13x14, 14x13
53 A16 45c The land   .45 .40
54 A16 55c shown   .55 .50
55 A16 100c The sea   1.00 .90
    Nos. 53-55 (3)   2.00 1.80

Environmental protection. #53, 55 horiz.

Marine Life — A17

Designs: 60c, Giant caribbean anemone, Pederson's cleaning shrimp. 70c, Queen angelfish, red and orange coral. 100c, Banded coral shrimp, fire sponge, yellow boring sponge.

A18   A19

1990, Apr. 4   Litho.   Perf. 14x13
56 A17 60c multicolored   .65 .60
57 A17 70c multicolored   .75 .70
58 A17 100c multicolored   1.10 1.00
    Nos. 56-58 (3)   2.50 2.30

1990, May 30   Litho.   Perf. 13x14
59 A18 35c multicolored   .30 .25
60 A18 200c Character trademark   1.75 1.60

World Cup Soccer Championships, Italy.

1990, Sept. 12
61 A19 45c Tools   .40 .35
62 A19 60c Stone figure   .60 .55
63 A19 100c Jar   1.00 .90
    Nos. 61-63 (3)   2.00 1.80

Archeological discoveries.

Landscapes A20

1991, Jan. 31   Litho.   Perf. 14x13
64 A20 55c Seashore   .50 .50
65 A20 65c Desert   .65 .60
66 A20 100c Cactus, ocean view   1.00 .90
    Nos. 64-66 (3)   2.15 2.00

Working Women — A21   Medicinal Plants — A22

Designs: 35c, Taking care of others. 70c, Housewife. 100c, Women in society.

1991, Mar. 28   Litho.   Perf. 13x14
67 A21 35c multicolored   .30 .25
68 A21 70c multicolored   .65 .60
69 A21 100c multicolored   .90 .80
    Nos. 67-69 (3)   1.85 1.65

Style of inscriptions varies.

1991, May 29
70 A22 65c Ocimum sanctum   .55 .55
71 A22 75c Jatropha gossypifolia   .65 .65
72 A22 95c Croton flavens   .90 .80
    Nos. 70-72 (3)   2.10 2.00

A23   A24

Aruban Handicrafts: 35c, Fish net, wood float, wooden needle. 250c, Straw hat, hat block.

1991, July 31   Litho.   Perf. 13x14
73 A23 35c lt bl, dk bl & blk   .30 .25
74 A23 250c pink, lil rose & blk   2.25 2.00

1991, Nov. 29   Litho.   Perf. 13x14
75 A24 35c Toucan   .35 .30
76 A24 70c People shaking hands   .65 .60
77 A24 100c Windmill   1.00 .90
    Nos. 75-77 (3)   2.00 1.80

Welcome to Aruba.

Aruba Postal Service, Cent. — A25

60c, Government decree, 1892, vert. 75c, First post office. 80c, Current post office.

Perf. 13x14, 14x13
1992, Jan. 31   Litho.
78 A25 60c multicolored   .60 .55
79 A25 75c multicolored   .75 .70
80 A25 80c multicolored   .85 .75
    Nos. 78-80 (3)   2.20 2.00

Equality Day — A26

1992, Mar. 25   Litho.   Perf. 14x13
81 A26 100c People of five races   .95 .80
82 A26 100c Woman, man, scales   .95 .80

Discovery of America, 500th Anniv. — A27

1992, July 30   Litho.   Perf. 13x14
83 A27 30c Columbus   .30 .25
84 A27 40c Sailing ship   .40 .35
85 A27 50c Natives, map   .55 .50
    Nos. 83-85 (3)   1.25 1.10

Natural Bridges in Aruba — A28

Designs: 70c, Seroe Colorado Bridge, south coast. 80c, Natural Bridge, north coast.

1992, Nov. 30   Litho.   Perf. 14x13
86 A28 70c multicolored   .70 .65
87 A28 80c multicolored   .80 .70

A29   A30

1993, Jan. 29   Litho.   Perf. 13x14
88 A29 200c multicolored   1.90 1.90

Express mail service.

1993, Mar. 31   Litho.   Perf. 13x14
Various rock formations found in Districts of Ayo and Casibari.

89 A30 50c multicolored   .50 .50
90 A30 60c multicolored   .60 .60
91 A30 100c multicolored   .90 .90
    Nos. 89-91 (3)   2.00 2.00

Folklore — A31

Sailing
Sports — A32

40c, String instruments, drum. 70c, Traditional music & games. 80c, Dera Gai song lyrics.

1993, May 28   Litho.   Perf. 13x14
92	A31	40c multicolored	.40	.40
93	A31	70c multicolored	.70	.70
94	A31	80c multicolored	.80	.80
		Nos. 92-94 (3)	1.90	1.90

1993, July 30   Litho.   Perf. 13x14
95	A32	50c Sailboating	.50	.50
96	A32	65c Land sailing	.65	.65
97	A32	75c Wind surfing	.75	.75
		Nos. 95-97 (3)	1.90	1.90

Iguana — A33

Perf. 14x13, 13x14
1993, Sept. 1   Litho.
98	A33	35c Young	.40	.40
99	A33	60c Almost grown	.60	.60
100	A33	100c Mature, vert.	1.00	1.00
		Nos. 98-100 (3)	2.00	2.00

Burrowing
Owl — A34

Perf. 14x13, 13x14
1994, Jan. 28   Litho.
101	A34	5c Two adults	.20	.20
102	A34	10c Two adults, young	.35	.30
103	A34	35c Adult with prey, vert.	.65	.55
104	A34	40c Adult, vert.	.80	.70
		Nos. 101-104 (4)	2.00	1.75

World Wildlife Fund.

A35

A36

Intl. Olympic Committee, Cent.: 90c, Baron Pierre de Coubertin (1863-1937), founder of modern Olympics.

1994, Mar. 29   Litho.   Perf. 13x14
105	A35	50c multicolored	.50	.45
106	A35	90c multicolored	.75	.65

1994, July 7   Litho.   Perf. 13x14
107	A36	65c shown	.60	.55
108	A36	150c Mascot, soccer ball	1.40	1.25

1994 World Cup Soccer Championships, US.

Wild Fruit — A37

Designs: 40c, Malpighia punicifolia. 70c, Cordia sebestena. 85c, Pithecellobium unguis-cati. 150c, Coccoloba uvifera.

1994, Sept. 28   Litho.   Perf. 13x14
109	A37	40c multicolored	.40	.35
110	A37	70c multicolored	.75	.65
111	A37	85c multicolored	.90	.80
112	A37	150c multicolored	1.50	1.40
		Nos. 109-112 (4)	3.55	3.20

Architectural
Landmarks
A38

Designs: 35c, Government building, 1888. 60c, Ecury residence, 1929, vert. 100c, Protestant Church, 1846, vert.

1995, Jan. 27   Litho.   Perf. 14x13
113	A38	35c multicolored	.35	.30

Perf. 13x14
114	A38	60c multicolored	.65	.60
115	A38	100c multicolored	1.00	.90
		Nos. 113-115 (3)	2.00	1.80

UN, 50th
Anniv. — A39

Interpaso
Horses — A40

Designs: 30c, Flags, sea, UN emblem, dove, text from UN charter. 200c, World with flags, doves, UN emblem.

1995, Mar. 29   Litho.   Perf. 13x14
116	A39	30c multicolored	.40	.35
117	A39	200c multicolored	2.00	1.90

1995, May 26   Perf. 14x13, 13x14
Designs: 25c, 10-time champion Casanova II, ribbons, horiz. 75c, Paso Fino, horiz. 80c, Horse doing figure 8. 90c, Girl on horse.
118	A40	25c multicolored	.25	.25
119	A40	75c multicolored	.70	.65
120	A40	80c multicolored	.75	.70
121	A40	90c multicolored	.85	.80
		Nos. 118-121 (4)	2.55	2.40

Vegetables — A41

1995, July 28   Litho.   Perf. 13x14
122	A41	25c Vigna sinensis	.25	.25
123	A41	50c Cucumis anguria	.50	.45
124	A41	70c Hibiscus esculentus	.70	.65
125	A41	85c Cucurbita moschata	.80	.75
		Nos. 122-125 (4)	2.25	2.10

Turtles — A42

1995, Sept. 27   Litho.   Perf. 14x13
126	A42	15c Hawksbill	.30	.20
127	A42	50c Green	.50	.35
128	A42	95c Loggerhead	.90	.70
129	A42	100c Leatherback	.95	.70
		Nos. 126-129 (4)	2.65	1.95

Separate Status,
10th Anniv. — A43

Statesmen and politicians: No. 130, Jan Hendrik Albert Eman (1887-1957). No. 131, Juan Enrique Irausquin (1904-62). No. 132, Cornelis Albert Eman (1916-67). No. 133, Gilberto Francois Croes (1938-85).

1996, Jan. 1   Litho.   Perf. 13x14
130	A43	100c multicolored	.90	.85
131	A43	100c multicolored	.90	.85
132	A43	100c multicolored	.90	.85
133	A43	100c multicolored	.90	.85
		Nos. 130-133 (4)	3.60	3.40

The 1986 date on No. 133 is in error.

America
Issue — A44

National dresswear: 65c, Woman wearing long, full dress, apron, vert. 70c, Man wearing hat, bow tie, white shirt, black pants, vert. 100c, Couple dancing.

Perf. 13x14, 14x13
1996, Mar. 25   Litho.
134	A44	65c multicolored	.75	.75
135	A44	70c multicolored	.80	.75
136	A44	100c multicolored	1.10	1.00
		Nos. 134-136 (3)	2.65	2.50

1996 Summer
Olympic
Games,
Atlanta — A45

1996, May 28   Litho.   Perf. 14x13
137	A45	85c Runners	.90	.85
138	A45	130c Cyclist	1.40	1.25

A46

A47

Famous Women: No. 139, Livia (Mimi) Ecury (1920-91), nurse. No. 140, Lolita Euson (1914-94), poet. No. 141, Laura Wernet-Paskel (1911-62), teacher.

1996, Sept. 27   Litho.   Perf. 13x14
139	A46	60c multicolored	.65	.65
140	A46	60c multicolored	.65	.65
141	A46	60c multicolored	.65	.65
		Nos. 139-141 (3)	1.95	1.95

1997, Jan. 23   Litho.   Perf. 13x14
Year of Papiamento 1997: 50c, Sign promoting use of Papiamento language, children playing on beach, people in water, boat. 140c, "Papiamento," sunrise.
142	A47	50c multicolored	.50	.45
143	A47	140c multicolored	1.25	1.40

Mailman on
Bicycle, 1936-
57
A48

America issue: 70c, Mailman handing mail to woman, jeep, 1957-88. 80c, Mailman on motor scooter placing mail in mailbox, 1995.

Aruban
Architectrue
A49

30c, Decorated cunucu house. 65c, Steps with "popchi's." 100c, Arends's Building, vert.

1997, March 27   Litho.   Perf. 14x13
144	A48	60c multicolored	.55	.55
145	A48	70c multicolored	.65	.55
146	A48	80c multicolored	.80	.65
		Nos. 144-146 (3)	2.00	1.75

1997, May 22   Litho.   Perf. 14x13
147	A49	30c multicolored	.30	.30
148	A49	65c multicolored	.70	.65

Perf. 13x14
149	A49	100c multicolored	1.00	.90
		Nos. 147-149 (3)	2.00	1.85

Marine Life — A50

Designs: a, Marlin jumping out of water, lighthouse. b, Dolphin jumping out of water, trees, plants on beach. c, Iguana on rock, beach. d, Dolphin, fish. e, Two dolphins, fish. f, Fish, turtles, owl on beach. g, Various fish among coral. h, Diver, shipwreck, fish, coral. i, Various fish.

1997, May 29   Litho.   Perf. 12½x13
150	A50	90c Sheet of 9, #a.-i.	9.00	9.00

PACIFIC 97.

Cruise
Tourism
A51

Designs: 35c, Ship at pier, tourists walking toward ship. 50c, Ship with gangway lowered, tourists. 150c, Ship out to sea, small boat.

1997, July 24   Litho.   Perf. 14x13
151	A51	35c multicolored	.40	.35
152	A51	50c multicolored	.55	.50
153	A51	150c multicolored	1.60	1.40
		Nos. 151-153 (3)	2.55	2.25

Aruban Wild
Flowers
A52

50c, Erythrina velutina. 60c, Cordia dentata. 70c, Tabebuia billbergii. 130c, Guaiacum officinale.

1997, Sept. 25
154	A52	50c multicolored	.55	.55
155	A52	60c multicolored	.70	.70
156	A52	80c multicolored	.80	.80
157	A52	130c multicolored	1.50	1.50
		Nos. 154-157 (4)	3.55	3.55

Fort Zoutman,
Bicent. — A53

1998, Jan. 13   Litho.   Perf. 14x13
158	A53	30c sepia & multi	.35	.35
159	A53	250c gray & multi	3.00	3.00

Total Solar Eclipse,
1998 — A54

1998, Feb. 26   Litho.   Perf. 13x14
160 A54 85c shown   1.10 1.10
161 A54 100c Map, track of
            eclipse   1.25 1.25

Native
Birds — A55

50c, Mimus gilvus. 60c, Falco sparverius.
70c, Icterus icterus. 150c, Coereba flaveola.

Perf. 14x13, 13x14
1998, July 10   Litho.
162 A55 50c multi   .55 .55
163 A55 60c multi, vert.   .70 .70
164 A55 70c multi, vert.   .80 .80
165 A55 150c multi   1.75 1.75
      Nos. 162-165 (4)   3.80 3.80

World Stamp
1998 — A56

1998, Sept. 8   Litho.   Perf. 14x13
166 A56 225c multicolored   2.50 2.50

Endangered
Animals
A57

Equus asinus: 40c, Two standing on hill.
65c, Three standing, rocks, cacti, tree. 100c,
Adult, foal standing among rocks, cacti.

1999, June 21   Litho.   Perf. 14x13
167 A57 40c multicolored   .45 .45
168 A57 65c multicolored   .75 .75
169 A57 100c multicolored   1.10 1.10
      Nos. 167-169 (3)   2.30 2.30

Cacti — A58

Designs: 50c, Opuntia wentiana. 60c,
Lemaireocereus griseus. 70c, Cephalocereus
lanuginosus. 75c, Cephalocereus lanuginosus
(in bloom).

1999, Mar. 31   Litho.   Perf. 14x13
170 A58 50c multicolored   .60 .60
171 A58 60c multicolored   .70 .70
172 A58 70c multicolored   .80 .80
173 A58 75c multicolored   .90 .90
      Nos. 170-173 (4)   3.00 3.00

Dogs — A59

Various dogs, background: 40c, Trees. 60c,
Cactus, aloe plant, rocks. 80c, Tree, sea.
165c, Sky, clouds.

1999, May 31   Litho.   Perf. 13x14
174 A59 40c multicolored   .45 .45
175 A59 60c multicolored   .75 .75
176 A59 80c multicolored   .90 .90
177 A59 165c multicolored   1.90 1.90
      Nos. 174-177 (4)   4.00 4.00

Discovery of
Aruba, 500th
Anniv. — A60

1999, Aug. 9   Litho.   Perf. 14x13
178 A60 150c shown   1.75 1.75
179 A60 175c Abstract paintings   2.00 2.00
   a. Souvenir sheet, #178-179   3.75 3.75

Natl. Library,
50th
Anniv. — A61

1999, Aug. 20
180 A61 70c shown   .80 .80
181 A61 100c Original building   1.10 1.10

Christmas - A62

Die Cut Perf. 13x13½
1999, Dec. 1
Self-Adhesive Coil Stamps   Litho.
182 A62 40c Magi on shore   .45 .45
183 A62 70c Magi in desert   .80 .80
184 A62 100c Holy Family   1.10 1.10
      Nos. 182-184 (3)   2.35 2.35

Tourist
Attractions
A62a

Reptiles
A63

Tourist Attractions: 25c, Guadirikiri Cave.
55c, Cactus landscape. 85c, Hooiberg. 500c,
Conchi. Reptiles: 40c, Norops lineatus. 60c,
Iguana iguana, vert. 75c, Leptodeira annulata,
vert. 150c, Cnemidophorus murinus.

2000   Litho.   Perf. 14x13, 13x14
185 A62a 25c multi   .30 .30
186 A63   40c multi   .45 .45
187 A62a 55c multi   .60 .60
188 A63   60c multi   .65 .65
189 A63   75c multi   .85 .85
190 A62a 85c multi   1.00 1.00
191 A63   150c multi   1.75 1.75
192 A62a 500c multi   5.75 5.75
      Nos. 185-192 (8)   11.35 11.35

Issued: 40c, 60c, 75c, 150c, 1/31; 25c, 55c,
85c, 500c, 6/5.

America
Issue,
Campaign
Against
AIDS — A64

Perf. 14x13, 13x14
2000, Mar. 2   Litho.
193 A64 75c Flags   .85 .85
194 A64 175c Ribbon on globe,
            vert.   2.00 2.00

Organization
Anniversaries
A65

Designs: 150c, Aruba Bank N.V., 75th
anniv. 165c, Alto Vista Church, 250th anniv.

2000, Apr. 20   Litho.   Perf. 14x13
195 A65 150c multi   1.60 1.60
196 A65 165c multi   1.90 1.90

Type of 2000

Animals: 5c, Cat. 15c, Shells. 30c, Tortoise.
35c, Mud house, vert. 50c, Rabbit. 100c,
Balashi gold smelter, vert. 200c, Parakeet.
250c, Rock crystals.

Perf. 14x13, 13x14 (#200, 202)
2001   Litho.
197 A63   5c multi   .20 .20
198 A62a 15c multi   .20 .20
199 A63   30c multi   .35 .35
200 A62a 35c multi   .40 .40
201 A63   50c multi   .55 .55
202 A62a 100c multi   1.10 1.10
203 A63   200c multi   2.25 2.25
204 A62a 250c multi   2.75 2.75
      Nos. 197-204 (8)   7.80 7.80

Issued: 5c, 30c, 50c, 200c, 1/31. 15c, 35c,
100c, 250c, 8/6.

Mascaruba,
40th
Anniv. — A66

Actors on stage and audience in: 60c: Background. 150c, Foreground.

2001, Mar. 26   Litho.   Perf. 14x13
205-206 A66 Set of 2   2.40 2.40

Classic Motor
Vehicles
A67

Designs: 25c, 1930 Ford Crown Victoria
Leatherback. 40c, 1933 Citroen Commerciale.
70c, 1948 Plymouth pickup truck. 75c, 1959
Ford Edsel.

2001, May 31
207-210 A67 Set of 4   2.40 2.40

Year of
Dialogue
Among
Civilizations
A68

2001, Oct. 9   Litho.   Perf. 14x13
211 A68 175c multi   2.00 2.00

SEMI-POSTAL STAMPS

Surtax for child welfare organizations unless otherwise stated.

Solidarity
SP1

1986, May 7   Litho.   Perf. 14x13
B1 SP1 30c + 10c shown   .35 .30
B2 SP1 35c + 15c Three ropes   .65 .55
B3 SP1 60c + 25c One rope   .90 .75
      Nos. B1-B3 (3)   1.90 1.60

Surtax for social and cultural projects.

SP2

1986, Oct. 29   Litho.   Perf. 14x13
B4 SP2 45c + 20c Boy, cater-
            pillar   .70 .70
B5 SP2 70c + 25c Boy, cocoon   .90 .90
B6 SP2 100c + 40c Girl, butter-
            fly   1.40 1.40
      Nos. B4-B6 (3)   3.00 3.00

Christmas
SP3

1987, Oct. 27   Litho.   Perf. 14x13
B7 SP3 25c +10c Boy on beach   .45 .45
B8 SP3 45c +20c Drawing
            Christmas tree   .65 .65
B9 SP3 70c +30c Child, creche
            figures   1.00 1.00
      Nos. B7-B9 (3)   2.10 2.10

Solidarity
SP4

YMCA emblem in various geometric
designs.

1988, Aug. 3   Litho.   Perf. 14x13
B10 SP4 45c +20c shown   .60 .60
B11 SP4 60c +25c multi, diff.   .80 .80
B12 SP4 100c +50c multi, diff.   1.40 1.40
      Nos. B10-B12 (3)   2.80 2.80

11th YMCA world council.
Surtax for social and cultural projects.

Children's
Toys — SP5

1988, Oct. 26   Perf. 13x14
B13 SP5 45c +20c Jacks   .50 .50
B14 SP5 70c +30c Top   .85 .85
B15 SP5 100c +50c Kite   1.25 1.25
      Nos. B13-B15 (3)   2.60 2.60

Children
SP6

1989, Oct. 26   Perf. 14x13
B16 SP6 45c +20c Baby spoon   .55 .55
B17 SP6 60c +30c Chasing a
            ball   .70 .70
B18 SP6 100c +50c Adult & child
            holding hands   1.25 1.25
      Nos. B16-B18 (3)   2.50 2.50

Solidarity
SP7

1990, July 25
B19 SP7 55c +25c shown   .75 .75
B20 SP7 100c +50c Family,
            house   1.40 1.40

Surtax for social and cultural projects.

SP8   SP9

Christmas song.

1990, Oct. 24   Litho.   Perf. 13x14
B21 SP8   45c +20c Wind surf-
     boards   .70   .70
B22 SP8   60c +30c shown   .90   .90
B23 SP8   100c +50c Kites, lizard   1.50 1.50
     Nos. B21-B23 (3)   3.10 3.10

1991, Oct. 25   Litho.   Perf. 13x14
Literacy: 45c+25c, Discovery of reading.
60c+35c, Pointing to letter. 100c+50c, Child
reading.
B24 SP9   45c +25c multi   .60   .60
B25 SP9   60c +35c multi   .80   .80
B26 SP9   100c +50c multi   1.25 1.25
     Nos. B24-B26 (3)   2.65 2.65

Solidarity SP10

55c+30c, Girl scouts, flag & emblem.
100c+50c, Hand holding cancer fund emblem,
people.

1992, May 27   Litho.   Perf. 14x13
B27 SP10   55c +30c multi   .80   .80
B28 SP10   100c +50c multi   1.50 1.50

Surtax for social and cultural projects.

Postal Services of Aruba, Cent. — SP11

Designs: 50c+30c, Heart. 70c+35c, Airplane, letters. 100c+55c, Pigeon with letter in
beak, vert.

1992, Oct. 30   Litho.   Perf. 14x13
B29 SP11   50c +30c multi   .80   .80
B30 SP11   70c +35c multi   1.00 1.00
     Perf. 13x14
B31 SP11   100c +50c multi   1.50 1.50
     Nos. B29-B31 (3)   3.30 3.30

Youth Foreign Study Programs SP12

Abstract designs of: 50c+30c, Landscapes.
75c+40c, Young man, scenes of other countries, vert. 100c+50c, Integrating cultures.

1993, Oct. 27   Perf. 14x13, 13x13
B32 SP12   50c +30c multi   .80   .80
B33 SP12   75c +40c multi   1.10 1.10
B34 SP12   100c +50c multi   1.50 1.50
     Nos. B32-B34 (3)   3.40 3.40

Solidarity SP13

Intl. Year of the Family: 50c+35c, Family
seated, reading, studying. 100c+50c, Family
playing in front of house.

1994, May 30   Litho.   Perf. 14x13
B35 SP13   50c +35c multi   .90   .90
B36 SP13   100c +50c multi   1.50 1.50

Surtax for social and cultural projects.

SP14

Designs: 50c+30c, Children on anchor with
umbrella. 80c+35c, Children inside Sun.
100c+50c, Child riding owl.

1994, Oct. 27   Litho.   Perf. 14x13
B37 SP14   50c +30c multi   .80   .80
B38 SP14   80c +35c multi   1.25 1.25
B39 SP14   100c +50c multi   1.50 1.50
     Nos. B37-B39 (3)   3.55 3.55

SP15   SP16

Children's drawings: 50c+25c, Children with
balloons, house. 70c+35c, Three people with
picnic basket on sunny day. 100c+50c, People
gardening on sunny day.

1995, Oct. 26   Litho.   Perf. 13x14
B40 SP15   50c +25c multi   .70   .70
B41 SP15   70c +35c multi   1.00 1.00
B42 SP15   100c +50c multi   1.40 1.40
     Nos. B40-B42 (3)   3.10 3.10

1996, July 26   Litho.   Perf. 13x14
El Sol Naciente Lodge, 75th Anniv.:
60c+30c, Masonic emblems. 100c+ 50c, Col-
umns, terrestrial and celestial globes.
B43 SP16   60c +30c multi   1.10 1.10
B44 SP16   100c +50c multi   1.90 1.90

Surtax for social and cultural projects
(Solidarity)

SP17

Cartoons: 50c+25c, Mother, baby rabbit
waiting at school bus stop. 70c+35c, Mother,
baby owl, outside school. 100c+50c, Children
flying kite.

1996, Oct. 24   Litho.   Perf. 14x13
B45 SP17   50c +25c multi   .95   .95
B46 SP17   70c +35c multi   1.25 1.25
B47 SP17   100c +50c multi   1.90 1.90
     Nos. B45-B47 (3)   4.10 4.10

SP18

Designs: 50c+25c, Girl sitting among aloe
plants. 70c+35c, Boy, butterfly, cactus, vert.
100c+50c, Girl swimming under water, fish,
coral.

Perf. 14x13, 13x14
1997, Oct. 23   Litho.
B48 SP18   50c +25c multi   .85   .85
B49 SP18   70c +35c multi   1.25 1.25
B50 SP18   100c +50c multi   1.60 1.60
     Nos. B48-B50 (3)   3.70 3.70

Solidarity SP19

Service Organizations: 60c+30c, Globe,
emblem of Lions Intl., wheelchair balanced on
map of Aruba. 100c+50c, Child reading book,

emblem of Rotary Intl., woman in rocking
chair.

1998, May 29   Litho.   Perf. 14x13
B51 SP19   60c +30c multi   1.20 1.20
B52 SP19   100c +50c multi   2.00 2.00

Surtax for social and cultural projects.

SP20

50c+25c, Girl performing traditional ribbon
dance. 80c+40c, Boy playing a cuarta.
100c+50c, Two boys playing basketball.

1998, Oct. 22   Litho.   Perf. 13x14
B53 SP20   50c +25c multi   .85   .85
B54 SP20   80c +40c multi   1.25 1.25
B55 SP20   100c +50c multi   1.75 1.75
     Nos. B53-B55 (3)   3.85 3.85

SP21

Designs: 60c+30c, Child on beach with man
with fishing net. 80c+40c, Adult reading to children. 100c+50c, Mother, child, vert.

Perf. 14x13, 13x13
1999, Oct. 21   Litho.
B56 SP21   60c +30c multi   1.00 1.00
B57 SP21   80c +40c multi   1.40 1.40
B58 SP21   100c +50c multi   1.75 1.75
     Nos. B56-B58 (3)   4.15 4.15

Solidarity SP22

75c+35c, Children on playground equipment. 100c+50c, Children playing in sand.

2000, Aug. 28   Litho.   Perf. 14x13
B59-B60 SP22 Set of 2   3.00 3.00

SP23

Children's art: 60c+30c, House with solar
collectors. 80c+40c, House, girl, garbage can.
100c+50c, Flying automobiles.

2000, Oct. 26
B61-B63 SP23 Set of 3   4.00 4.00

Child Welfare SP24

Intl. Volunteers Year: 40c+20c, Children at
crosswalk. 60c+30c, Boys walking dog.

100c+50c, Children depositing trash in can at
beach.

2001, Oct. 31   Litho.   Perf. 13x14
B64-B66 SP24 Set of 3   3.50 3.50

ASCENSION

ə-ˈsen͵t͵-shən

LOCATION — An island in the South
Atlantic Ocean, 900 miles from
Liberia
GOVT. — A part of the British Crown
Colony of St. Helena
AREA — 34 sq. mi.
POP. — 1,117 (1993)

In 1922 Ascension was placed under
the administration of the Colonial Office
and annexed to the British Crown Colony of St. Helena. The only post office
is at Georgetown.

12 Pence = 1 Shilling
20 Shillings = 1 Pound
100 Pence = 1 Pound (1971)

> **Catalogue values for unused
> stamps in this country are for
> Never Hinged items, beginning
> with Scott 50.**

Stamps and Types of St. Helena,
1912-22 Overprinted in Black or Red

1922		**Wmk. 4**	**Perf. 14**	
1	A9	½p green & blk	3.50	10.50
2	A10	1p green	4.00	10.50
3	A10	1½p rose red	13.00	42.50
4	A9	2p gray & blk	12.50	11.00
5	A9	3p ultra	11.00	14.00
6	A10	8p dl vio & blk	22.50	42.50
7	A10	2sh ultra & blk, *blue*	75.00	110.00
8	A10	3sh vio & blk	110.00	140.00
		Wmk. 3		
9	A9	1sh blk, *gray grn*	25.00	42.50
		(R)		
		Nos. 1-9 (9)	276.50	423.50

Seal of Colony — A3

1924-27	**Typo. Wmk. 4 Perf. 14**		
	Chalky Paper		
10	A3	½p black & gray	2.90	10.50
11	A3	1p green & blk	5.00	6.00
12	A3	1½p rose red	6.50	25.00
13	A3	2p bluish gray & gray	9.75	5.50
14	A3	3p ultra	6.75	10.50
15	A3	4p blk & gray, *yel*	42.50	70.00
16	A3	5p ol & lil ('27)	9.50	19.00
17	A3	6p rose lil & gray	42.50	75.00
18	A3	8p violet & gray	12.50	37.50
19	A3	1sh brown & gray	17.00	42.50
20	A3	2sh ultra & gray, *blue*	50.00	75.00
21	A3	3sh blk & gray, *blue*	70.00	77.50
		Nos. 10-21 (12)	274.90	454.00

View of Georgetown — A4

Map of
Ascension — A5

Sooty
Tern
Breeding
Colony
A9

1½p, Pier at Georgetown. 3p, Long Beach.
5p, Three Sisters. 5sh, Green Mountain.

1934, July 2   **Engr.**
23	A4	½p violet & blk	.85	.75
24	A5	1p lt grn & blk	1.60	1.10
25	A4	1½p red & black	1.60	2.10
26	A5	2p org & black	1.60	2.40
27	A4	3p ultra & blk	1.60	1.40
28	A5	5p blue & black	2.00	3.00
29	A5	8p dk brn & blk	3.75	4.50
30	A9	1sh carmine & blk	16.50	6.00
31	A5	2sh6p violet & blk	32.50	40.00
32	A4	5sh brown & blk	52.50	65.00
		Nos. 23-32 (10)	114.50	126.25

Common Design Types
pictured following the introduction.

Silver Jubilee Issue
Common Design Type
1935, May 6   **Perf. 11x12**
33	CD301	1½p car & dk blue	3.25	7.00
34	CD301	2p blk & ultra	10.00	20.00
35	CD301	5p ind & grn	16.00	22.50
36	CD301	1sh brn vio & ind	22.50	25.00
		Nos. 33-36 (4)	51.75	74.50

25th anniv. of the reign of King George V.

Coronation Issue
Common Design Type
1937, May 19   **Perf. 13½x14**
37	CD302	1p deep green	.30	.70
38	CD302	2p deep orange	.75	.40
39	CD302	3p bright ultra	.75	.50
		Nos. 37-39 (3)	1.80	1.60
		Set, never hinged	2.50	

Georgetown — A11

Designs: 1p, 2p, 4p, Green Mountain. 1½p,
2sh6p, Pier at Georgetown. 3p, 5sh, Long
Beach. 6p, 10sh, Three Sisters.

1938-49   **Perf. 13**
Center in Black
40	A11	½p violet ('44)	.35	1.60
		Never hinged	.65	
a.		Perf. 13½	1.75	1.25
		Never hinged	3.25	
		Perf. 13½		
41	A11	1p green	19.00	7.50
		Never hinged	35.00	
		Perf. 13		
41A	A11	1p org yel ('42)	.25	.55
		Never hinged	.40	
b.		Perf. 14 ('49)	.35	15.00
		Never hinged	.65	
c.		Perf. 13½	6.50	8.50
		Never hinged	12.50	
42	A11	1½p red ('44)	.40	.75
		Never hinged	.75	
a.		Perf. 14 ('49)	1.40	12.00
		Never hinged	2.75	
b.		Perf. 13½	1.75	1.40
		Never hinged	3.50	
43	A11	2p org ('44)	.40	.40
		Never hinged	.75	
a.		Perf. 14 ('49)	1.50	32.50
		Never hinged	2.00	
b.		Perf. 13½	1.60	1.00

		Never hinged		3.25
		Perf. 13½		
44	A11	3p ultra	55.00	25.00
		Never hinged	95.00	
		Perf. 13		
44A	A11	3p black ('44)	.35	.80
		Never hinged	.65	
c.		Perf. 13½('40)	7.50	.90
		Never hinged	14.00	
44B	A11	4p ultra ('44)	2.00	3.00
		Never hinged	4.00	
d.		Perf. 13½	6.00	3.00
		Never hinged	12.00	
		Perf. 13½		
45	A11	6p gray blue	4.50	1.25
		Never hinged	8.00	
a.		Perf. 13 ('44)	4.50	4.50
		Never hinged	8.00	
		Perf. 13		
46	A11	1sh dk brn ('44)	3.25	2.00
		Never hinged	4.25	
a.		Perf. 13½	6.75	1.40
		Never hinged	12.50	
47	A11	2sh6p car ('44)	17.00	30.00
		Never hinged	32.50	
a.		Perf. 13½	20.00	7.00
		Never hinged	37.50	
48	A11	5sh yel brn ('44)	25.00	25.00
		Never hinged	45.00	
a.		Perf. 13½	52.50	7.00
		Never hinged	100.00	
49	A11	10sh red vio ('44)	45.00	52.50
		Never hinged	62.50	
a.		Perf. 13½	52.50	45.00
		Never hinged	110.00	
b.		10sh brt analine red pur, perf 13	55.00	40.00
		Never hinged	110.00	

See Nos. 54-56.

> **Catalogue values for unused stamps in this section, from this point to the end of the section, are for Never Hinged items.**

Peace Issue
Common Design Type
Perf. 13½x14
1946, Oct. 21   **Engr.**   **Wmk. 4**
| 50 | CD303 | 2p deep orange | .40 | .50 |
| 51 | CD303 | 4p deep blue | .40 | .30 |

Silver Wedding Issue
Common Design Types
1948, Oct. 20   Photo.   Perf. 14x14½
| 52 | CD304 | 3p black | .50 | .50 |
Engraved; Name Typographed
Perf. 11½x11
| 53 | CD305 | 10sh red violet | 42.50 | 40.00 |
Type of 1938
Designs: 1p, Three Sisters. 1½p,
Georgetown Pier. 2p, Green Mountain.

Perf. 13
1949, June 1   Engr.   Wmk. 4
| 54 | A11 | 1p green & black | .45 | .40 |
Perf. 14
55	A11	1½p lilac rose & blk	.55	.75
a.		Perf. 13	.50	6.00
b.		1½p carmine & black	7.00	4.75
56	A11	2p red & black	.75	.75
		Nos. 54-56 (3)	1.75	1.90
Issue date: No. 55a, Feb. 25, 1953.

UPU Issue
Common Design Types
Engr.; Name Typo. on Nos. 58, 59
1949, Oct. 10   Perf. 13½, 11x11½
57	CD306	3p rose carmine	1.25	1.10
58	CD307	4p indigo	3.25	2.50
59	CD308	6p olive	3.50	3.00
60	CD309	1sh slate	6.25	6.00
		Nos. 57-60 (4)	14.25	12.60

Coronation Issue
Common Design Type
1953, June 2   Engr.   Perf. 13½x13
| 61 | CD312 | 3p gray & black | 1.50 | 1.50 |

Reservoir
A16

Designs: 1p, Map of Ascension. 1½p,
Georgetown. 2p, Map showing Ascension
between South America and Africa and cable
lines. 2½p, Mountain road. 3p, Yellow-billed
tropic bird. 4p, Longfinned tuna. 6p, Waves.

7p, Young green turtles. 1sh, Land crab.
2sh6p, Sooty tern (wideawake). 5sh, Perfect
Crater. 10sh, View from Northwest.

1956, Nov. 19   Wmk. 4   Perf. 13
Center in Black
62	A16	½p brown	.20	.25
63	A16	1p lilac rose	.35	.55
64	A16	1½p orange	.35	.55
65	A16	2p carmine	.55	.45
66	A16	2½p org brown	.65	.75
67	A16	3p blue	.90	.90
68	A16	4p turq blue	.85	1.25
69	A16	6p dark blue	1.10	.80
70	A16	7p olive	1.40	.90
71	A16	1sh scarlet	1.90	.80
72	A16	2sh6p brown violet	19.00	6.00
73	A16	5sh bright green	25.00	15.00
74	A16	10sh purple	50.00	32.50
		Nos. 62-74 (13)	102.25	60.70

Brown
Booby — A17

Birds: 1½p, Black tern. 2p, Fairy tern. 3p,
Red-billed tropic bird in flight. 4½p, Brown
noddy. 6p, Sooty tern. 7p, Frigate bird. 10p,
Blue-faced booby. 1sh, Yellow-billed tropic
bird. 1sh6p, Red-billed tropic bird. 2sh6p,
Madeiran storm petrel. 5sh, Red-footed booby
(brown phase). 10sh, Frigate birds. £1, Red-
footed booby (white phase).

Perf. 14x14½
1963, May 23   Photo.   Wmk. 314
75	A17	1p multicolored	.75	.25
a.		Booklet pane of 4	1.00	
76	A17	1½p multicolored	1.00	.50
a.		Booklet pane of 4	1.25	
b.		Blue omitted	70.00	
77	A17	2p multicolored	1.00	.25
a.		Booklet pane of 4	1.50	
78	A17	3p multicolored	1.00	.25
a.		Booklet pane of 4	1.75	
79	A17	4½p multicolored	1.00	.25
80	A17	6p multicolored	1.00	.25
a.		Booklet pane of 4	4.50	
81	A17	7p multicolored	1.00	.25
82	A17	10p multicolored	1.00	.25
83	A17	1sh multicolored	1.00	.25
84	A17	1sh6p multicolored	3.75	1.00
a.		Booklet pane of 4	7.50	
85	A17	2sh6p multicolored	5.50	6.75
86	A17	5sh multicolored	6.00	6.00
87	A17	10sh multicolored	11.00	6.75
88	A17	£1 multicolored	17.00	8.50
		Nos. 75-88 (14)	52.00	32.00

Freedom from Hunger Issue
Common Design Type
1963, June 4   Wmk. 314
| 89 | CD314 | 1sh6p car rose | 2.00 | 1.00 |

Red Cross Centenary Issue
Common Design Type
1963, Sept. 2   Litho.   Perf. 13
| 90 | CD315 | 3p black & red | .90 | .90 |
| 91 | CD315 | 1sh6p ultra & red | 6.00 | 6.00 |

ITU Issue
Common Design Type
Perf. 11x11½
1965, May 17   Wmk. 314
| 92 | CD317 | 3p mag & violet | .60 | .40 |
| 93 | CD317 | 6p grnsh bl & brn org | 1.60 | 1.10 |

Intl. Cooperation Year Issue
Common Design Type
1965, Oct. 25   Wmk. 314   Perf. 14½
| 94 | CD318 | 1p bl grn & claret | .50 | .50 |
| 95 | CD318 | 6p lt vio & green | 1.00 | 1.00 |

Churchill Memorial Issue
Common Design Type
1966, Jan. 24   Photo.   Perf. 14
Design in Black, Gold and Carmine Rose
96	CD319	1p bright blue	.35	.25
97	CD319	3p green	1.40	.85
98	CD319	6p brown	1.75	1.40
99	CD319	1sh6p violet	5.00	4.00
		Nos. 96-99 (4)	8.50	6.50

World Cup Soccer Issue
Common Design Type
1966, July 1   Litho.   Perf. 14
| 100 | CD321 | 3p multicolored | .70 | .50 |
| 101 | CD321 | 6p multicolored | 1.40 | 1.25 |

WHO Headquarters Issue
Common Design Type
1966, Sept. 20   Litho.   Perf. 14
| 102 | CD322 | 3p multicolored | 1.50 | .75 |
| 103 | CD322 | 1sh6p multicolored | 3.50 | 2.00 |

Apollo Satellite
Station,
Ascension — A18

Wmk. 314
1966, Nov. 7   Photo.   Perf. 14
104	A18	4p purple & black	.20	.20
105	A18	8p blue grn & black	.20	.20
106	A18	1sh3p brn ol & blk	.20	.20
107	A18	2sh6p brt grnsh blue & black	.40	.40
		Nos. 104-107 (4)	1.00	1.00

Opening of the Apollo communications sat-
ellite-earth station, part of the US Apollo
program.

UNESCO Anniversary Issue
Common Design Type
1967, Jan. 3   Litho.   Perf. 14
108	CD323	3p "Education"	.65	.75
109	CD323	6p "Science"	1.50	1.75
110	CD323	1sh6p "Culture"	5.00	4.00
		Nos. 108-110 (3)	7.15	6.50

BBC
Emblem
A19

Photo.; Gold Impressed
1967, Dec. 1   Wmk. 314   Perf. 14½
111	A19	1p ultra & gold	.20	.20
112	A19	3p dk green & gold	.20	.20
113	A19	6p brt purple & gold	.20	.20
114	A19	1sh6p brt red & gold	.35	.35
		Nos. 111-114 (4)	.95	.95

Opening of the British Broadcasting Company's South Atlantic Relay Station on Ascension Island.

Human Rights
Flame and
Chain — A20

Perf. 14½x14
1968, July 8   Litho.   Wmk. 314
115	A20	6p org, car & blk	.20	.20
116	A20	1sh6p gray, mag & blk	.30	.30
117	A20	2sh6p brt grn, plum & blk	.40	.40
		Nos. 115-117 (3)	.90	.90
International Human Rights Year.

Blackfish
A21

Fish: No. 119, Sailfish. 6p, Oldwife. 8p,
Leather jacks. 1sh6p, Yellowtails. 1sh9p, Tuna.
2sh3p, Mako sharks. 2sh11p, Rock hind
(jack).

Perf. 13x12½

1968-69		**Wmk. 314**		**Litho.**
118	A21	4p brt grnsh bl & blk	.25	.20
119	A21	4p red & multi	.30	.30
120	A21	6p yel olive & multi	.35	.35
121	A21	8p brt rose lil & multi	.50	.40
122	A21	1sh6p brown & multi	1.75	1.75
123	A21	1sh9p emer & multi	1.00	.90
124	A21	2sh3p ocher & multi	1.60	1.10
125	A21	2sh11p dp org & multi	3.25	3.00
		Nos. 118-125 (8)	9.00	8.00

Issue dates: No. 119, 6p, 1sh6p, 2sh11p, Mar. 3, 1969; others, Oct. 23, 1968.
See Nos. 130-133.

Arms of R.N.S. Rattlesnake A22

Coats of Arms of Royal Naval Ships: 9p, Weston. 1sh9p, Undaunted. 2sh3p, Eagle.

Perf. 14x14½

1969, Oct. 1		**Photo.**		**Wmk. 314**
126	A22	4p multicolored	.50	.45
127	A22	9p multicolored	.65	.55
128	A22	1sh9p multicolored	1.00	.70
129	A22	2sh3p multicolored	1.10	.80
a.		Min. sheet of 4, #126-129	7.00	7.00
		Nos. 126-129 (4)	3.25	2.50

See Nos. 134-137, 152-159, 166-169.

Fish Type of 1968

Deep-sea fish: 4p, Wahoo. 9p, Coalfish. 1sh9p, Dolphinfishes. 2sh3p, Soldierfish.

1970, Apr. 6		**Litho.**		**Perf. 14**
130	A21	4p bluish grn & multi	2.50	2.00
131	A21	9p org & multi	3.25	2.00
132	A21	1sh9p ultra & multi	3.50	2.50
133	A21	2sh3p gray & multi	3.50	2.50
		Nos. 130-133 (4)	12.75	9.00

Naval Arms Type of 1969

4p, Penelope. 9p, Carlisle. 1sh6p, Amphion. 2sh6p, Magpie.

Perf. 12½x12

1970, Sept. 7		**Photo.**		**Wmk. 314**
134	A22	4p ultra, gold & blk	1.25	.25
135	A22	9p lt blk, blk, gold & red	1.75	.50
136	A22	1sh6p grnsh bl, gold & blk	2.00	1.25
137	A22	2sh6p lt grnsh bl, gold & blk	2.50	2.00
a.		Miniature sheet of 4, #134-137	11.00	10.00
		Nos. 134-137 (4)	7.50	4.00

Decimal Currency Issue

Tycho Brahe's Observatory, Quadrant and Supernova, 1572 — A23

Man into Space: ½p, Chinese rocket, 1232, vert. 1p, Medieval Arab astronomers, vert. 2p, Galileo, his telescope and drawing of moon, 1609. 2½p, Isaac Newton, telescope and apple. 3½p, Harrison's chronometer and ship, 1735. 4½p, First American manned orbital flight (Project Mercury, 1962, vert.). 5p, Reflector of Palomar telescope and ring nebula in Lyra, Messier 57. 7½p, Jodrell Bank telescope. 10p, Mariner 7, 1969, and telescopic view of Mars. 12½p, Sputnik 2 and dog Laika, 1957. 15p, Astronaut walking in space, 1965 (Gemini 4; vert.). 50p, US astronauts and moon landing module, 1969. £1, Future space research station.

1971, Feb. 15		**Litho.**		**Perf. 14½**
138	A23	½p multicolored	.20	.20
a.		Booklet pane of 4	.50	
139	A23	1p multicolored	.20	.20
a.		Booklet pane of 4	.75	
140	A23	1½p multicolored	.25	.25
a.		Booklet pane of 4	1.00	
141	A23	2p multicolored	.30	.25
a.		Booklet pane of 4	1.90	

142	A23	2½p multicolored	.75	.60
a.		Booklet pane of 4	2.50	
143	A23	3½p multicolored	1.50	.60
a.		Booklet pane of 4	3.50	
144	A23	4½p multicolored	1.00	.60
145	A23	5p multicolored	.75	.60
146	A23	7½p multicolored	3.00	1.40
147	A23	10p multicolored	1.75	1.50
148	A23	12½p multicolored	4.75	1.75
149	A23	25p multicolored	5.50	2.00
150	A23	50p multicolored	4.75	2.25
151	A23	£1 multicolored	4.75	4.00
		Nos. 138-151 (14)	30.45	16.20

For overprints see Nos. 189-191.

Course of Quest — A25

Coats of Arms of Royal Naval Ships: 4p, Milford. 9p, Pelican. 15p, Oberon.

1971, Nov. 15		**Photo.**		**Perf. 13½x13**
152	A24	2p gold & multi	1.10	.20
153	A24	4p gold & multi	1.25	.45
154	A24	9p gold & multi	1.75	1.10
155	A24	15p gold & multi	1.90	1.75
a.		Souvenir sheet of 4, #152-155	7.00	7.00
		Nos. 152-155 (4)	6.00	3.50

Naval Arms Type of 1969

1½p, Lowestoft. 3p, Auckland. 6p, Nigeria. 17½p, Bermuda.

1972, May 22		**Litho.**		**Perf. 14x14½**
156	A22	1½p bl, gold & blk	.65	.65
157	A22	3p grnsh bl, gold & blk	.70	.70
158	A22	6p grn, gold, blk & bl	.80	.80
159	A22	17½p lil, gold, blk & red	1.60	1.60
a.		Miniature sheet of 4, #156-159	4.00	4.00
		Nos. 156-159 (4)	3.75	3.75

1972, Aug. 2			**Perf. 14**

Designs: 4p, Shackleton and "Quest", horiz. 7½p, Shackleton's cabin and Quest in pack ice, horiz. 11p, Shackleton statue, London, and memorial cairn, South Georgia.

160	A25	2½p multicolored	.65	.50
161	A25	4p multicolored	.70	.65
162	A25	7½p multicolored	.75	.70
163	A25	11p multicolored	.90	.90
a.		Souvenir sheet of 4, #160-163	3.75	3.75
		Nos. 160-163 (4)	3.00	2.75

Sir Ernest Henry Shackleton (1874-1922), explorer of Antarctica.

Silver Wedding Issue, 1972
Common Design Type

Design: Queen Elizabeth II, Prince Philip, land crab and shark.

1972, Nov. 20		**Photo.**		**Perf. 14x14½**
164	CD324	2p violet & multi	.20	.20
165	CD324	16p car rose & multi	.55	.55

Naval Arms Type of 1969

2p, Birmingham. 4p, Cardiff. 9p, Penzance. 13p, Rochester.

1973, May 28		**Litho.**		**Wmk. 314**
166	A22	2p blue & multi	2.25	1.40
167	A22	4p yel grn & multi	2.75	1.40
168	A22	9p lt blue & multi	3.50	1.60
169	A22	13p violet & multi	4.00	1.60
a.		Min. sheet of 4, #166-169	22.50	15.00
		Nos. 166-169 (4)	12.50	6.00

Turtles — A26

1973, Aug. 28				**Perf. 13½**
170	A26	4p Green	1.75	1.10
171	A26	9p Loggerhead	3.50	2.25
172	A26	12p Hawksbill	5.50	3.50
		Nos. 170-172 (3)	10.75	6.85

Light Infanty Marine Sergeant, 1900 — A27

Uniforms (Royal Marines): 6p, Private, 1816. 12p, Officer, Light Infantry, 1880. 20p, Color Sergeant, Artillery, 1910.

1973, Oct. 31				**Perf. 14½**
173	A27	2p multicolored	2.00	1.50
174	A27	6p lt green & multi	2.75	1.75
175	A27	12p lt blue & multi	3.25	2.50
176	A27	20p lt lilac & multi	3.75	2.75
		Nos. 173-176 (4)	11.75	8.50

Departure of the Royal Marines from Ascension, 50th anniv.

Princess Anne's Wedding Issue
Common Design Type

1973, Nov. 14				**Perf. 14**
177	CD325	2p ocher & multi	.20	.20
178	CD325	18p multicolored	.40	.40

Letter and UPU Emblem A29

UPU Cent.: 9p, Emblem and Mercury.

		Wmk. 314		
1974, Mar. 27		**Litho.**		**Perf. 14½**
179	A29	2p multicolored	.20	.20
180	A29	9p vio blue & multi	.50	.50

Young Churchill and Blenheim Palace A30

25p, Churchill and UN Headquarters, NYC.

1974, Nov. 30		**Litho.**		**Unwmk.**
181	A30	5p slate grn & multi	.20	.20
182	A30	25p purple & multi	.80	.80
a.		Souvenir sheet of 2, #181-182	2.00	2.25

Sir Winston Churchill (1874-1965).

Skylab over Photograph of Ascension Taken by Skylab 3 — A31

Skylab Space Station: 18p, Command module and photo of Ascension from Skylab 4.

1975, Mar. 20		**Wmk. 314**		**Perf. 14½**
183	A31	2p multicolored	.20	.20
184	A31	18p multicolored	.80	.80

US Air Force C-141A Starlifter — A32

Aircraft: 5p, Royal Air Force C-130 Hercules. 9p, Vickers VC-10. 24p, U.S. Air Force C-5A Galaxy.

				Perf. 13½x14
1975, June 19		**Litho.**		**Wmk. 314**
185	A32	2p multicolored	1.25	.55
186	A32	5p multicolored	1.50	.70
187	A32	9p multicolored	1.75	1.25
188	A32	24p multicolored	3.00	2.50
a.		Souvenir sheet of 4, #185-188	13.00	13.00
		Nos. 185-188 (4)	7.50	5.00

Wideawake Airfield, Ascension Island.

Nos. 144, 148-149 Overprinted

1975, Aug.		**Litho.**		**Perf. 14½**
189	A23	4½p multicolored	.25	.25
190	A23	12½p multicolored	.35	.35
191	A23	25p multicolored	.50	.50
		Nos. 189-191 (3)	1.10	1.10

Apollo Soyuz space test project (Russo-American cooperation), launching July 15; link-up, July 17.

HMS Peruvian and Zenobia Arriving Oct. 22, 1815 A33

Designs: 5p, Water Supply, Dampiers Drip. 9p, First Landing, Oct. 1815. 15p, The Garden on Green Mountain. All designs after paintings by Isobel McManus.

1975, Oct. 22		**Wmk. 373**		**Perf. 14½**
192	A33	2p lt blue & multi	.20	.20
193	A33	5p lt blue & multi	.30	.20
194	A33	9p red & multi	.45	.40
195	A33	15p red & multi	.90	.75
		Nos. 192-195 (4)	1.85	1.55

British occupation, 160th anniv.

Canaries A34

2p, Fairy tern, vert. 3p, Waxbills. 4p, Black noddy. 5p, Brown noddy. 6p, Common mynah. 7p, Madeira storm petrels. 8p, Sooty terns. 9p, White booby. 10p, Red-footed booby. 15p, Red-throated francolin. 18p, Brown booby. 25p, Red-billed bo'sun bird. 50p, Yellow-billed bo'sun bird. £1, Ascension frigatebird. £2, Boatswain Island Bird Sanctuary and birds.

		Perf. 14x14½, 14½x14
1976, Apr. 26		**Wmk. 373**
		Size: 35x27mm, 27x35mm

196	A34	1p multi	.40	1.25
197	A34	2p multi	.45	1.25
198	A34	3p multi	.45	1.25
199	A34	4p multi, vert.	.50	1.25
200	A34	5p multi	.60	1.25
201	A34	6p multi	.60	1.25
202	A34	7p multi, vert.	.60	1.25
203	A34	8p multi	.60	1.25
204	A34	9p multi, vert.	.60	1.25
205	A34	10p multi	.60	1.25
206	A34	15p multi, vert.	1.10	1.40

207	A34	18p multi, vert.	1.10	1.40
208	A34	25p multi	1.25	1.40
209	A34	50p multi	2.00	2.25
210	A34	£1 multi, vert.	2.40	2.75

Perf. 13½
Size: 46x33mm

| 211 | A34 | £2 multicolored | 4.75 | 6.00 |
| | | Nos. 196-211 (16) | 18.00 | 27.70 |

Great Britain Type A1 with Ascension Cancel — A35

9p, Ascension No. 1, vert. 25p, Freighter Southampton Castle.

1976, May 4   Perf. 13½x14, 14x13½

212	A35	5p lt brn, car & blk	.20	.20
213	A35	9p gray grn, grn & blk	.30	.30
214	A35	25p blue & multi	.50	.50
		Nos. 212-214 (3)	1.00	1.00

Festival of Stamps 1976. See Tristan da Cunha #208a for souvenir sheet that contains one each of Ascension #214, St. Helena #297 and Tristan da Cunha #208.

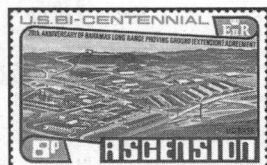

US Base A36

Designs: 9p, NASA Station, Devil's Ashpit. 25p, Viking satellite landing on Mars.

Wmk. 373
1976, July 4   Litho.   Perf. 13½

215	A36	8p black & multi	.40	.40
216	A36	9p black & multi	.50	.50
217	A36	25p black & multi	1.10	1.10
		Nos. 215-217 (3)	2.00	2.00

American Bicentennial. No. 215 also for the 20th anniv. of Bahamas Long Range Proving Ground (extension) Agreement.

Queen in Coronation Coach — A37

Designs: 8p, Prince Philip on Ascension Island, 1957, vert. 12p, Queen leaving Buckingham Palace in coronation coach.

Perf. 14x13½, 13½x14
1977, Feb. 7   Litho.   Wmk. 373

218	A37	8p multicolored	.20	.20
219	A37	12p multicolored	.25	.25
220	A37	25p multicolored	.45	.45
		Nos. 218-220 (3)	.90	.90

Reign of Queen Elizabeth II, 25th anniv.

Water Pipe in Tunnel — A38

5p, Breakneck Valley wells. 12p, Break tank in pipe line, horiz. 25p, Dam & reservoir, horiz.

1977, June 27   Litho.   Perf. 14½

221	A38	3p multicolored	.20	.20
222	A38	5p multicolored	.20	.20
223	A38	12p multicolored	.50	.30
224	A38	25p multicolored	1.00	.60
		Nos. 221-224 (4)	1.90	1.30

Water supplies constructed by Royal Marines, 1832 and 1881.

Mars Bay Site, 1877 A39

Designs: 8p, Mars Bay and instrument sites. 12p, Prof. and Mrs. Gill before their tent. 25p, Map of Ascension.

Perf. 13½x14
1977, Oct. 3   Litho.   Wmk. 373

225	A39	3p multicolored	.20	.20
226	A39	8p multicolored	.30	.25
227	A39	12p multicolored	.50	.45
228	A39	25p multicolored	1.00	.85
		Nos. 225-228 (4)	2.00	1.75

Centenary of visit of Prof. David Gill (1843-1914), astronomer, to Ascension.

Elizabeth II Coronation Anniversary Issue
Souvenir Sheet
Common Design Types
Unwmk.
1978, May 21   Litho.   Perf. 15

229		Sheet of 6	2.50	2.50
a.	CD326	25p Lion of England	.40	.40
b.	CD327	25p Elizabeth II	.40	.40
c.	CD328	25p Green turtle	.40	.40

No. 229 contains 2 se-tenant strips of Nos. 229a-229c, separated by horizontal gutter with commemorative and descriptive inscriptions and showing central part of coronation procession with coach.

East Crater (Broken Tooth) — A40

Volcanoes: 5p, Hollands Crater (Hollow Tooth). 12p, Bears Back. 15p, Green Mountain. 25p, Two Boats village.

1978, Sept. 4   Litho.   Perf. 14½

230	A40	3p multicolored	.20	.20
231	A40	5p multicolored	.20	.20
232	A40	12p multicolored	.40	.40
233	A40	15p multicolored	.50	.50
234	A40	25p multicolored	.80	.80
a.		Souvenir sheet, 2 each #230-234	4.25	5.00
b.		Strip of 5, #230-234	2.00	2.00

No. 234b shows panoramic view of volcanic terrain.

Resolution A41

Capt. Cook's voyages: 8p, Cook's chronometer. 12p, Green turtle. 25p, Cook after Flaxman/Wedgwood medallion.

Litho.; Litho. & Engr. (25p)
1979, Jan. 8   Perf. 11

235	A41	3p multicolored	.20	.20
236	A41	8p multicolored	.30	.25
237	A41	12p multicolored	.55	.40
238	A41	25p multicolored	1.10	.85
		Nos. 235-238 (4)	2.15	1.70

St. Mary's Church, Georgetown — A42

Designs: 12p, Old map of Ascension Island. 50p, Ascension, by Rembrandt.

Wmk. 373
1979, May 24   Litho.   Perf. 14½

239	A42	8p multicolored	.20	.20
240	A42	12p multicolored	.20	.20
241	A42	50p multicolored	.60	.60
		Nos. 239-241 (3)	1.00	1.00

Ascension Day.

Landing Cable at Comfortless Cove — A43

Eastern Telegraph Co., 80th anniv.: 8p, Cable Ship Anglia. 12p, Map showing cables across the Atlantic, vert. 15p, Cable-laying ship. 25p, Cable and earth station.

1979, Sept. 15

242	A43	3p rose car & black	.20	.20
243	A43	8p dk yel grn & black	.20	.20
244	A43	12p yel bister & black	.30	.30
245	A43	15p violet & black	.35	.35
246	A43	25p deep org & black	.55	.55
		Nos. 242-246 (5)	1.60	1.60

Ascension No. 45 — A44

1979, Dec. 17   Wmk. 373   Perf. 14

247	A44	3p shown	.20	.20
248	A44	8p No. 73	.20	.20
249	A44	12p No. 14	.20	.20
250	A44	50p Hill portrait, vert.	.55	1.35
		Nos. 247-250 (4)	1.15	1.35

Sir Rowland Hill (1795-1879), originator of penny postage.

Anogramma Ascensionis A45

1980, Feb. 18   Litho.   Perf. 14½

251	A45	3p shown	.20	.20
252	A45	6p Xiphopteris ascensionense	.20	.20
253	A45	8p Sporobolus caespitosus	.20	.20
254	A45	12p Sporobolus durus, vert.	.25	.25
255	A45	18p Dryopteris ascensionis, vert.	.40	.40
256	A45	24p Marattia purpurascens, vert.	.50	.50
		Nos. 251-256 (6)	1.75	1.75

17th Century Bottle Post, London 1980 Emblem A46

1980, May 1   Wmk. 373   Perf. 14

257	A46	8p shown	.20	.20
258	A46	12p 36-gun frigate, 19th century	.25	.25
259	A46	15p "Garth Castle," 1863	.30	.30
260	A46	50p "St. Helena," Lockheed C141	.85	.85
a.		Souvenir sheet of 4, #257-260	2.00	2.00
		Nos. 257-260 (4)	1.60	1.60

London 1980 Intl. Stamp Exhib., May 6-14.

Queen Mother Elizabeth Birthday
Common Design Type
1980, Aug. 11   Litho.   Perf. 14

| 261 | CD330 | 15p multicolored | .40 | .40 |

Lubbock's Yellowtail A47

1980, Sept. 15   Litho.   Perf. 13½x14

262	A47	3p shown	.20	.20
263	A47	10p Resplendent angelfish	.30	.30
264	A47	25p Hedgehog butterflyfish	.70	.70
265	A47	40p Marmalade razorfish	1.10	1.10
		Nos. 262-265 (4)	2.30	2.30

Tortoisen, by Thomas Maxon A48

Map of South Atlantic Ridge and Contintental Drift — A49

15p, Wideawake Fair, by Linton Palmer, 1866.

1980, Nov. 17   Perf. 13½, 14 (60p)

266	A48	10p multicolored	.20	.20
267	A48	15p multicolored	.35	.35
268	A49	60p multicolored	1.25	1.25
		Nos. 266-268 (3)	1.80	1.80

Royal Geographical Soc., 50th anniv.

Green Mountain Farm, 1881 — A50

Designs: 15p, Two Boats, 1881. 20p, Green Mountain and Two Boats farms, 1981. 30p, Green Mountain Farm, 1981.

1981, Feb. 15   Litho.   Perf. 14

269	A50	12p multicolored	.20	.20
270	A50	15p multicolored	.30	.30
271	A50	20p multicolored	.35	.35
272	A50	30p multicolored	.65	.65
		Nos. 269-272 (4)	1.50	1.50

Cable and Wireless Earth Station A51

1981, Apr. 27   Litho.   Perf. 14

273	Sheet of 10	3.75	3.75
a.	A51 15p multicolored	.35	.35

Flight of Columbia space shuttle. Gutter contains story of Ascension and space shuttle; margin shows craft and dish antenna.

Poinsettia — A52

1981, May 11   Wmk. 373   Perf. 13½

274	A52	1p shown	.20	.20
275	A52	2p Clustererd wax flower	.20	.20
276	A52	3p Kolanchoe, vert.	.20	.20
277	A52	4p Yellow pops	.20	.20
278	A52	5p Camel's foot creeper	.20	.20
279	A52	8p White oleander	.20	.20
280	A52	10p Ascension lily, vert.	.25	.25
281	A52	12p Coral plant, vert.	.30	.30
282	A52	15p Yellow allamanda	.40	.40
283	A52	20p Ascention euphorbia	.50	.50
284	A52	30p Flame of the forest, vert.	.85	.85
285	A52	40p Bougainvillea	1.00	1.00

Size: 42x53mm

286	A52	50p Solanum	1.25	1.25
287	A52	£1 Ladies petticoat	2.75	2.75
288	A52	£2 Red hibiscus	5.25	5.25
	Nos. 274-288 (15)		13.75	13.75

Nos. 275-276, 280, 282-283 and 287 also issued inscribed 1982.
For overprints see Nos. 321-322.

Linschoten's Map of Ascension, 1599 (Illustration reduced) — A53

Maxwell's Map of Ascension, 1793 — A54

Designs: Old maps of Ascension.

1981, May 22   Perf. 14½

289	A53	Sheet of 4	.60	.60
a.-d.	5p any single		.20	.20
290	A54	10p shown	.25	.25
291	A54	12p Maxwell, 1793, diff.	.35	.35
292	A54	15p Eckberg & Chapman, 1811	.40	.40
293	A54	40p Campbell, 1819	1.10	1.10
	Nos. 289-293 (5)		2.70	2.70

Royal Wedding Issue
Common Design Type

1981, July 22   Wmk. 373   Perf. 14

294	CD331	10p Bouquet	.20	.20
295	CD331	15p Charles	.30	.30
296	CD331	50p Couple	1.00	1.00
	Nos. 294-296 (3)		1.50	1.50

Nos. 294-296 each se-tenant with label.

Man Shining
Cannon — A55

1981, Sept. 14   Litho.   Perf. 14

297	A55	5p shown	.20	.20
298	A55	10p Mountain climbing	.20	.20
299	A55	15p First aid treatment	.35	.35
300	A55	40p Duke of Edinburgh	.80	.80
	Nos. 297-300 (4)		1.55	1.55

Duke of Edinburgh's Awards, 25th anniv.

Scouting
Year
A56

1982, Feb. 22   Litho.   Perf. 14

301	A56	10p Parallel rope walking	.25	.25
302	A56	15p 1st Ascension scout flag	.40	.40
303	A56	25p Radio operators	.60	.60
304	A56	40p Baden-Powell	.75	.75
a.	Souvenir sheet of 4		2.25	2.25
	Nos. 301-304 (4)		2.00	2.00

No. 304a contains stamps in designs of Nos. 301-304 (30x30mm, perf. 14½, diamondshape).

Sesquicentennial of Charles Darwin's
Visit — A57

1982, Apr. 19

305	A57	10p Portrait	.25	.25
306	A57	12p Pistols	.35	.35
307	A57	15p Rock crab	.40	.40
308	A57	40p Beagle	1.10	1.10
	Nos. 305-308 (4)		2.10	2.10

40th Anniv. of Wideawake
Airfield — A58

1982, June 15   Litho.   Perf. 14

309	A58	5p Fairey Swordfish	.60	.60
310	A58	10p North American B25C Mitchell	.80	.80
311	A58	15p Boeing EC-135N Aria	1.10	1.10
312	A58	50p Lockheed Hercules	1.60	1.60
	Nos. 309-312 (4)		4.10	4.10

Princess Diana Issue
Common Design Type
Perf. 14½x14

1982, July 1   Wmk. 373

313	CD333	12p Arms	.30	.30
314	CD333	15p Diana	.40	.40
315	CD333	25p Wedding	.60	.60
316	CD333	50p Portrait	1.25	1.25
	Nos. 313-316 (4)		2.55	2.55

Christmas and 50th Anniv. of BBC
Overseas Broadcasting — A59

Anniv. Emblem and: 5p, Bush House (London headquarters). 10p, Atlantic relay station. 25p, Lord Reith, first director general. 40p, King George V delivering Christmas address, 1932.

1982, Dec. 20   Litho.   Perf. 14

317	A59	5p multicolored	.20	.20
318	A59	10p multicolored	.30	.30
319	A59	15p multicolored	.70	.70
320	A59	40p multicolored	1.10	1.10
	Nos. 317-320 (4)		2.30	2.30

Nos. 282-283 Overprinted: "1st
PARTICIPATION / COMMONWEALTH
GAMES 1982"

1982   Litho.   Perf. 13½

321	A52	15p multicolored	.40	.40
322	A52	20p multicolored	.50	.50

12th Commonwealth Games, Brisbane, Australia, Sept. 30-Oct. 9.

A60

1983, Mar. 1   Perf. 14

323	A60	7p Marasmius echinosphaerus	.25	.25
324	A60	12p Chlorophyllum molybdites	.45	.45
325	A60	15p Leucocoprinus cepaestipes	.55	.55
326	A60	20p Lycoperdon marginatum	.75	.75
327	A60	50p Marasmiellus distantifolius	1.75	1.75
	Nos. 323-327 (5)		3.75	3.75

View of
Georgetown
A61

1983, May 12   Litho.   Perf. 14

328	A61	12p shown	.30	.30
329	A61	15p Farm, Green Mountain	.30	.30
330	A61	20p Boatswain Bird Isld.	.45	.45
331	A61	60p Telemetry Hill	1.10	1.10
	Nos. 328-331 (4)		2.15	2.15

See Nos. 359-362.

Manned Flight Bicentenary — A62

Military Aircraft.

1983, Aug. 1   Wmk. 373   Perf. 14

332	A62	12p Wessex Five helicopter	.75	.75
333	A62	15p Vulcan B2	.85	.85
334	A62	20p Nimrod MR2P	1.00	1.00
335	A62	60p Victor K2	1.75	1.75
	Nos. 332-335 (4)		4.35	4.35

Introduced
Species
A63

1983, Sept.   Litho.   Wmk. 373

336	A63	12p Iguanid	.30	.30
337	A63	15p Rabbit	.40	.40
338	A63	20p Cat	.50	.50
339	A63	60p Donkey	1.50	1.50
	Nos. 336-339 (4)		2.70	2.70

Tellina
Antonii
Philippi
A64

1983, Nov. 28   Litho.   Perf. 14½

340	A64	7p shown	.20	.20
341	A64	12p Nodipecten nodosus	.35	.35
342	A64	15p Cypraea lurida oceanica	.45	.45
343	A64	20p Nerita ascensionis gmelin	.60	.60
344	A64	50p Micromelo undatus	1.50	1.50
	Nos. 340-344 (5)		3.10	3.10

St. Helena Colony,
150th
Anniv. — A65

Designs: First issue inscribed Ascension instead of overprinted.

1984, Jan. 10   Litho.   Perf. 14

345	A65	12p No. 3	.30	.30
346	A65	15p No. 4	.40	.40
347	A65	20p No. 6	.50	.50
348	A65	60p No. 9	1.50	1.50
	Nos. 345-348 (4)		2.70	2.70

Souvenir Sheet

Visit of Prince
Andrew — A66

1984, Apr. 10   Perf. 14½x14

349	Sheet of 2		2.25	2.25
a.	A66 12p Andrew		.25	.25
b.	A66 70p In naval uniform		1.75	1.75

Lloyd's List Issue
Common Design Type

1984, May 28

351	CD335	12p Naval semaphore	.25	.25
352	CD335	15p "Southampton Castle"	.35	.35
353	CD335	20p Pier Head	.45	.45
354	CD335	70p Dane	1.50	1.50
	Nos. 351-354 (4)		2.55	2.55

1984
Coins and
Wildlife
A67

1984, June   Perf. 14

355	A67	12p One penny, yellowfin tuna	.45	.45
356	A67	15p Two pence, donkeys	.60	.60
357	A67	20p Fifty pence, green turtle	.70	.70
358	A67	70p One pound, sooty terns	1.75	1.75
	Nos. 355-358 (4)		3.50	3.50

View Type of 1983

1984, Oct.   Litho.   Wmk. 373

359	A61	12p Devil's Riding School	.25	.25
360	A61	15p St. Mary's Church	.35	.35

361	A61	20p	Two Boats Village	.50	.50
362	A61	70p	Ascension Isld.	1.75	1.75
		Nos. 359-362 (4)	2.85	2.85

Trees — A68

1985, Mar. 8   Litho.   Perf. 14½x14

363	A68	7p	Bermuda cypress	.50	.50
364	A68	12p	Norfolk Island pine	.55	.55
365	A68	15p	Screwpine	.65	.65
366	A68	20p	Eucalyptus	.80	.80
367	A68	65p	Spore tree	2.00	2.00
		Nos. 363-367 (5)	4.50	4.50

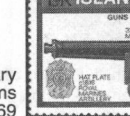

Military Firearms A69

Large guns and insignia: 12p, Thirty-two pounder small bore muzzle loader, c. 1820; Royal Marines hat plate, c. 1816. 15p, Seven-inch rifled muzzle loader, c. 1866; royal cipher. 20p, Seven-pounder rifled muzzle loader, c. 1877; Royal Artillery badge. 70p, HMS Hood 5.5-inch gun; ship crest.

1985, July 21   Wmk. 373   Perf. 14½

368	A69	12p	multicolored	.65	.65
369	A69	15p	multicolored	.75	.75
370	A69	20p	multicolored	.80	.80
371	A69	70p	multicolored	2.25	2.25
		Nos. 368-371 (4)	4.45	4.45

Queen Mother 85th Birthday
Common Design Type

12p, With Duke of York, Balmoral, 1924. 15p, With Princes Andrew and Edward. 20p, At Ascot. 70p, Christening of Prince Henry, Windsor Castle. 75p, Leaving the QEII, 1968.

Perf. 14½x14

1985, June 7   Wmk. 384

372	CD336	12p	multicolored	.25	.25
373	CD336	15p	multicolored	.30	.30
374	CD336	20p	multicolored	.40	.40
375	CD336	70p	multicolored	1.40	1.40
		Nos. 372-375 (4)	2.35	2.35

Souvenir Sheet

376	CD336	75p	multicolored	1.60	1.50

Intl. Youth Year, Girl Guides 75th Anniv. — A70

1985, Oct. 4   Wmk. 373

377	A70	12p	Guides' banner	.65	.65
378	A70	15p	First aid	.75	.75
379	A70	20p	Camping	.85	.85
380	A70	70p	Lady Baden-Powell	2.50	2.50
		Nos. 377-380 (4)	4.75	4.75

Wildflowers A71   Halley's Comet A72

Wmk. 384

1985, Dec. 6   Litho.   Perf. 14

381	A71	12p	Clerodendrum fragrans	.40	.40
382	A71	15p	Shell ginger	.45	.45
383	A71	20p	Cape daisy	.60	.60
384	A71	70p	Ginger lily	1.75	1.75
		Nos. 381-384 (4)	3.20	3.20

1986, Mar. 7

Designs: 12p, Newton's reflector telescope. 15p, Edmond Halley, Old Greenwich Observatory. 20p, Short's Gregorian telescope, comet, 1759. 70p, ICE space probe, Ascension satellite tracking station.

385	A72	12p	multicolored	.55	.55
386	A72	15p	multicolored	.65	.65
387	A72	20p	multicolored	.70	.70
388	A72	70p	multicolored	2.00	2.00
		Nos. 385-388 (4)	3.90	3.90

Queen Elizabeth II 60th Birthday
Common Design Type

Designs: 7p, Infant photograph, 1926. 15p, 1st worldwide Christmas broadcast, 1952. 20p, Garter Ceremony, Windsor Castle, 1983. 35p, Royal Tour, New Zealand, 1981. £1, Visiting Crown Agents' offices, 1983.

1986, Apr. 21   Perf. 14x14½

389	CD337	7p	scarlet, blk & sil	.20	.20
390	CD337	15p	ultra, blk & sil	.25	.25
391	CD337	20p	green & multi	.35	.35
392	CD337	35p	violet & multi	.65	.65
393	CD337	£1	rose vio & multi	1.75	1.75
		Nos. 389-393 (5)	3.20	3.20

For overprints see Nos. 431-435.

AMERIPEX '86 — A73

1986, May 22   Perf. 14½

394	A73	12p	No. 183	.35	.35
395	A73	15p	No. 260	.45	.45
396	A73	20p	No. 215	.55	.55
397	A73	70p	No. 310	2.00	2.00
		Nos. 394-397 (4)	3.35	3.35

Souvenir Sheet

398	A73	75p	Statue of Liberty, New York Harbor	2.25	2.25

Statue of Liberty, cent.

Royal Wedding Issue, 1986
Common Design Type

Designs: 15p, Couple kissing. 35p, Andrew in navy uniform, helicopter.

Wmk. 384

1986, July 23   Litho.   Perf. 14

399	CD338	15p	multicolored	.45	.45
400	CD338	35p	multicolored	1.00	1.00

Ships A74

1986, Oct. 14   Wmk. 384   Perf. 14½

401	A74	1p	Ganymede, c. 1811	.20	.20
402	A74	2p	Kangaroo, c. 1811	.20	.20
403	A74	4p	Trinculo, c. 1811	.20	.20
404	A74	5p	Daring, c. 1811	.20	.20
405	A74	9p	Thais, c. 1811	.25	.25
406	A74	10p	Pheasant, 1819	.35	.35
407	A74	15p	Myrmidon, 1819	.45	.45
408	A74	18p	Atholl, 1825	.55	.55
409	A74	20p	Medina, 1830	.60	.60
410	A74	25p	Saracen, 1840	.80	.80
411	A74	30p	Hydra, c. 1845	.90	.90
412	A74	50p	Sealark, 1840	1.40	1.40
413	A74	70p	Rattlesnake, 1868	1.90	1.90
414	A74	£1	Penelope, 1889	3.00	3.00
415	A74	£2	Monarch, 1897	6.00	6.00
		Nos. 401-415 (15)	17.00	17.00

For surcharges see Nos. 502-504.

Edible Bush Fruits A75

1987, Jan. 29   Perf. 14

416	A75	12p	Cape gooseberry	.35	.35
417	A75	15p	Prickly pear	.45	.45
418	A75	20p	Guava	.60	.60
419	A75	70p	Loquat	2.00	2.00
		Nos. 416-419 (4)	3.40	3.40

1st Manned Space Flight, 25th Anniv. — A76   Military Uniforms, 1815-20 — A77

1987, Mar. 30

420	A76	15p	Ignition	.45	.45
421	A76	18p	Lift-off	.55	.55
422	A76	25p	Reentry	.70	.70
423	A76	£1	Splashdown	3.00	3.00
		Nos. 420-423 (4)	4.70	4.70

Souvenir Sheet

424	A76	70p	Friendship 7 capsule	2.25	2.25

1987, June 29

Designs: a, Captains in full dress, 1st landing on Ascension. b, Surgeon and sailors at campsite. c, Seaman returning from Dampier's Drip with water supply. d, Midshipman at lookout post. e, Commander and surveyor.

425		Strip of 5	4.00	4.00
a.-e.	A77	25p multicolored	.80	.80

See Nos. 458, 474, 482, 507.

Butterflies A78

1987, Aug. 10   Perf. 14½

426	A78	15p	Painted lady	.60	.60
427	A78	18p	Monarch	.75	.75
428	A78	25p	Diadem	1.00	1.00
429	A78	£1	Long-tailed blue	3.75	3.75
		Nos. 426-429 (4)	6.10	6.10

See Nos. 436-439, 459-462.

Birds — A79

Designs: a, Ascension frigatebirds (males). b, Brown booby, frigatebird, white boobies. c, Frigatebird, white booby. d, Ascension frigatebirds (females). e, Adult frigatebird feeding young.

1987, Oct. 8   Wmk. 373   Perf. 14

430		Strip of 5	6.00	6.00
a.-e.	A79	25p any single	1.25	1.25

No. 430 has continuous design.
See No. 453.

Nos. 389-393 Ovptd. "40TH WEDDING ANNIVERSARY" in Silver

Perf. 14x14½

1987, Dec. 9   Litho.   Wmk. 384

431	CD337	7p	scar, blk & sil	.20	.20
432	CD337	15p	ultra, blk & sil	.40	.40
433	CD337	20p	green & multi	.65	.65
434	CD337	35p	violet & multi	1.00	1.00
435	CD337	£1	rose vio & multi	2.75	2.75
		Nos. 431-435 (5)	5.00	5.00

40th wedding anniv. of Queen Elizabeth II and Prince Philip.

Insects Type of 1987

1988, Jan. 18   Perf. 14½

436	A78	15p	Field cricket	.60	.60
437	A78	18p	Bush cricket	.75	.75
438	A78	25p	Ladybug	1.00	1.00
439	A78	£1	Burnished brass moth	4.00	4.00
		Nos. 436-439 (4)	6.35	6.35

Capt. William Bate (d. 1838), 1st Garrison Commander and Colonial Founder of Ascension A80

Designs: 9p, Bate's Memorial, St. Mary's Church. 15p, Commodore's Cottage, Cross Hill. 18p, North East or Bate's Cottage, 1833. 25p, Landmarks on map. 70p, Bate and 3 soldiers.

1988, Apr. 14   Litho.   Perf. 14

440	A80	9p	multicolored	.35	.35
441	A80	15p	multicolored	.55	.55
442	A80	18p	multicolored	.65	.65
443	A80	25p	multicolored	.90	.90
444	A80	70p	multicolored	2.25	2.25
		Nos. 440-444 (5)	4.70	4.70

Australia Bicentennial Emblem and Ships Named HMS Resolution — A81

1988, June 23   Litho.   Perf. 14

445	A81	9p	3-Masted square-rigger, 1667	.35	.35
446	A81	18p	3-Masted square-rigger, 1772	.65	.65
447	A81	25p	Navy cruiser, 1892	.90	.90
448	A81	65p	Battleship, 1916	2.25	2.25
		Nos. 445-448 (4)	4.15	4.15

Australia bicentennial.

Nos. 445-448 Overprinted

Wmk. 384

1988, July 30   Litho.   Perf. 14

449	A81	9p	multicolored	.35	.35
450	A81	18p	multicolored	.65	.65
451	A81	25p	multicolored	.90	.90
452	A81	65p	multicolored	2.25	2.25
		Nos. 449-452 (4)	4.15	4.15

SYDPEX '88, July 30-Aug. 7.

Bird Type of 1987

Behaviors of the wideawake tern, Sterna fuscata: a, Two adults, flock overhead. b, Nesting (two birds). c, Nesting (three birds). d, Adult and young. e, Tern flapping its wings.

1988, Aug. 15		**Perf. 14**	
453	Strip of 5	6.00	6.00
a.-e.	A79 25p any single	1.25	1.25

No. 453 has continuous design.

Lloyds of London, 300th Anniv.
Common Design Type

8p, Lloyd's Coffee House, Tower Street, 1688. 18p, Cable ship Alert, horiz. 25p, Satellite recovery in space, horiz. 65p, Ship Good Hope Castle on fire off Ascension, 1973.

Wmk. 373

1988, Oct. 17		**Litho.**	**Perf. 14**	
454	CD341	8p multicolored	.30	.30
455	CD341	18p multicolored	.60	.60
456	CD341	25p multicolored	.85	.85
457	CD341	65p multicolored	2.25	2.25
		Nos. 454-457 (4)	4.00	4.00

Military Uniforms Type of 1987

Uniforms of the Royal Marines: a, Marines arrive in Ascension (marines), 1821. b, Semaphore station (officer, marine), 1829. c, Octagonal tank (sergeant), 1831. d, Water pipe tunnel (officers), 1833. e, Constructing barracks (officer), 1834.

1988, Nov. 21			
458	Strip of 5	5.00	5.00
a.-e.	A77 25p multicolored	1.00	1.00

Insect Type of 1987

Wmk. 384

1989, Jan. 16		**Litho.**	**Perf. 14½**	
459	A78	15p Plume moth	.60	.60
460	A78	18p Green bottle	.70	.70
461	A78	25p Weevil	.95	.95
462	A78	£1 Paper wasp	3.75	3.75
		Nos. 459-462 (4)	6.00	6.00

Land Crabs, Gecarcinus Lagostoma — A82

1989, Apr. 17				
463	A82	15p multi	.50	.50
464	A82	18p multi, diff.	.65	.65
465	A82	25p multi, diff.	.90	.90
466	A82	£1 multi, diff.	3.50	3.50
		Nos. 463-466 (4)	5.55	5.55

Miniature Sheet

467		Sheet of 4	5.50	5.50
a.	A82	15p like No. 463	.50	.50
b.	A82	18p like No. 464	.65	.65
c.	A82	25p like No. 465	.85	.85
d.	A82	£1 like No. 466	3.50	3.50

Vignettes of Nos. 467a-467d do not have frame.

Moon Landing, 20th Anniv.
Common Design Type

Apollo 7: 15p, Tracking Station, Ascension Is. 18p, Launch, Cape Kennedy. 25p, Mission emblem. 70p, Expended Saturn IVB stage. £1, Lunar landing profile for the Apollo 11 mission.

1989, July 20		**Perf. 14x13½**	
	Size of Nos. 469-470: 29x29mm		
468	CD342	15p multicolored	.45	.45
469	CD342	18p multicolored	.55	.55
470	CD342	25p multicolored	.75	.75
471	CD342	70p multicolored	2.10	2.10
		Nos. 468-471 (4)	3.85	3.85

Souvenir Sheet

472	CD342	£1 multicolored	3.00	3.00

Souvenir Sheet

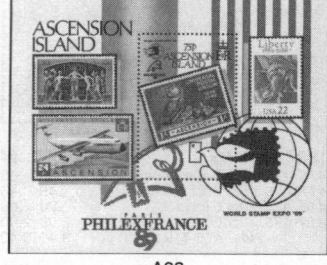

A83

1989, July 7		**Perf. 14x13½**	
473	A83 75p Emblems, No. 60	2.50	2.50

Miniature Sheet

World Stamp Expo '89, Washington, DC, and PHILEXFRANCE '89, Paris — A84

The Statue of Liberty and scenes from the centenary celebrations, 1986: a, Operation Sail. b, Face. c, Upper body. d, Three crown points. e, Ships in harbor, view of lower Manhattan. f, Ship in port, New York City.

1989, Aug. 21		**Wmk. 373**	
474	Sheet of 6	2.75	2.75
a.-f.	A84 15p any single	.45	.45

Devil's Ashpit Tracking Station A85

1989, Sept. 30		**Wmk. 384**	**Perf. 14**	
475		Sheet, 5 each #a.-b.	6.75	6.75
a.	A85 18p shown		.55	.55
b.	A85 25p US space shuttle launch		.80	.80

Termination of NASA tracking operations, begun in 1965, at the station.

Shells and Mollusks A86

Wmk. 384

1989, Nov. 6		**Litho.**	**Perf. 14**	
476	A86	8p *Strombus latus*	.30	.30
477	A86	18p *Tonna galea*	.60	.60
478	A86	25p *Harpa doris*	.85	.85
479	A86	£1 *Charonia variegata*	3.25	3.25
		Nos. 476-479 (4)	5.00	5.00

Donkeys — A87

Perf. 14 on 3 Sides
Booklet Stamps

1989, Nov. 17		**Litho.**	**Wmk. 384**	
480	A87 18p shown		.50	.50
a.	Booklet pane of 6		3.00	
481	A87 25p Green turtle		.75	.75
a.	Booklet pane of 4		3.00	

No. 480a sold for £1.

Military Type of 1987

Royal Navy equipment, c. 1815-1820: a, Seaman's pistol, hat, cutlass. b, Midshipman's belt buckle, button, sword, hat. c, Surgeon's hat, sword, instrument chest. d, Captain's hat, telescope, sword. e, Admiral's epaulet, megaphone, hat, pocket.

1990, Feb. 12		**Litho.**	**Perf. 14**	
482	Strip of 5		4.75	4.75
a.-e.	A77 25p any single		.95	.95

World Wildlife Fund — A88

Frigate birds (*Fregata aquila*): 9p, Family group. 10p, Chick. 11p, Male in flight. 15p, Female and immature in flight.

1990, Mar. 5		**Perf. 14½x14**	**Wmk. 373**	
483	A88	9p multicolored	1.25	1.00
484	A88	10p multicolored	1.50	1.25
485	A88	11p multicolored	1.75	1.50
486	A88	15p multicolored	2.50	2.00
		Nos. 483-486 (4)	7.00	5.75

Great Britain Nos. 1-2 A89

Exhibition emblem and: 18p, Early Ascension cancellations. 25p, Unloading mail at Wideawake Airfield. £1, Main P.O., Royal Mail van.

1990, May 3		**Litho.**	**Perf. 14**	
487	A89	9p shown	.30	.30
488	A89	18p multicolored	.60	.60
489	A89	25p multicolored	.85	.85
490	A89	£1 multicolored	3.25	3.25
		Nos. 487-490 (4)	5.00	5.00

Penny Black 150th anniv., Stamp World London '90.

Queen Mother, 90th Birthday
Common Design Types

1990, Aug. 4		**Wmk. 384**	**Perf. 14x15**	
491	CD343	25p Portrait, 1940	.85	.85
		Perf. 14½		
492	CD343	£1 King, Queen with soldiers	3.25	3.25

Garth Castle, 1910 — A90

Designs: 18p, RMS St. Helena, 1982. 25p, Launching new RMS St. Helena, 1989. 70p, Duke of York launching new RMS St. Helena. £1, New RMS St. Helena.

Wmk. 373

1990, Sept. 13		**Litho.**	**Perf. 14½**	
493	A90	9p multicolored	.35	.35
494	A90	18p multicolored	.65	.65
495	A90	25p multicolored	.90	.90
496	A90	70p multicolored	2.50	2.50
		Nos. 493-496 (4)	4.40	4.40

Souvenir Sheet

497	A90	£1 multicolored	3.50	3.50

See St. Helena Nos. 535-539, Tristan da Cunha Nos. 482-486.

Christmas — A91

Sculpture (8p) and paintings of Madonna and Child by: 8p, Felici. 18p, Unknown artist. 25p, Gebhard. 65p, Gritti.

1990, Oct. 24		**Perf. 14**	
498	A91	8p multicolored	.30	.30
499	A91	18p multicolored	.65	.65
500	A91	25p multicolored	.90	.90
501	A91	65p multicolored	3.25	3.25
		Nos. 498-501 (4)	5.10	5.10

Nos. 410, 412 & 414 Ovptd. in Silver "BRITISH FOR 175 YEARS"

1991, Feb. 5	**Wmk. 384**	**Perf. 14½**	
502	A74	25p on #410	1.00	1.00
503	A74	50p on #412	2.00	2.00
504	A74	£1 on #414	4.00	4.00
		Nos. 502-504 (3)	7.00	7.00

Elizabeth & Philip, Birthdays
Common Design Types

1991, June 18			
505	CD345	25p multicolored	.80	.80
506	CD346	25p multicolored	.80	.80
a.	Pair, #505-506 + label	1.60	1.60

Military Uniforms Type of 1987

Royal Marines Equipment 1821-1844: a, Officer's shako, epaulettes, belt plate, button. b, Officer's cap, sword, epaulettes, belt plate. c, Drum Major's shako with cords, staff. d, Sergeant's shako, chevrons, belt plate, canteen. e, Drummer's drum, sticks, shako.

1991, Aug. 1	**Wmk. 373**	**Perf. 14**	
507	A77	25p Strip of 5, #a.-e.	4.00	4.00

Atlantic Relay Station, 25th Anniv. A92

15p, BBC Atlantic relay station. 18p, English Bay transmitters. 25p, Satellite receiving station. 70p, Antenna support tower.

1991, Sept. 17		**Wmk. 384**	**Perf. 14½**	
508	A92	15p multi	.50	.50
509	A92	18p multi	.60	.60
510	A92	25p multi, vert.	.85	.85
511	A92	70p multi, vert.	2.50	2.50
		Nos. 508-511 (4)	4.45	4.45

Christmas A93

Designs: 8p, St. Mary's Church, exterior. 18p, St. Mary's Church, interior. 25p, Grotto of Our Lady of Ascension, exterior. 65p, Grotto of Our Lady of Ascension, interior.

1991, Oct. 1		**Perf. 14**	
512	A93	8p multicolored	.30	.30
513	A93	18p multicolored	.60	.60
514	A93	25p multicolored	.85	.85
515	A93	65p multicolored	2.25	2.25
		Nos. 512-515 (4)	4.00	4.00

Fish A94

Wmk. 373

1991, Dec. 10		**Litho.**		***Perf. 14***
516	A94	1p Blackfish	.20	.20
517	A94	2p Five finger	.20	.20
518	A94	4p Resplendent angelfish	.20	.20
519	A94	5p Silver fish	.20	.20
520	A94	9p Gurnard	.30	.30
521	A94	10p Blue dad	.35	.35
522	A94	15p Cunning fish	.50	.50
523	A94	18p Grouper	.60	.60
524	A94	20p Moray eel	.65	.65
525	A94	25p Hardback soldierfish	.85	.85
526	A94	30p Blue marlin	1.00	1.00
527	A94	50p Wahoo	1.65	1.65
528	A94	70p Yellowfin tuna	2.25	2.25
529	A94	£1 Blue shark	3.25	3.25
530	A94	£2.50 Bottlenose dolphin	8.50	8.50
		Nos. 516-530 (15)	20.70	20.70

Queen Elizabeth II's Accession to the Throne, 40th Anniv.
Common Design Type
Wmk. 373

1992, Feb. 6		**Litho.**		***Perf. 14***
531	CD349	9p multicolored	.30	.30
532	CD349	15p multicolored	.50	.50
533	CD349	18p multicolored	.60	.60
534	CD349	25p multicolored	.85	.85
535	CD349	70p multicolored	2.25	2.25
		Nos. 531-535 (5)	4.50	4.50

Discovery of America, 500th Anniv. — A95

Wmk. 373

1992, Feb. 18		**Litho.**		***Perf. 14***
536	A95	9p STV Eye of the Wind	.30	.30
537	A95	18p STV Soren Larsen	.60	.60
538	A95	25p Pinta, Santa Maria, & Nina	.85	.85
539	A95	70p Columbus, Santa Maria	2.25	2.25
		Nos. 536-539 (4)	4.00	4.00

World Columbian Stamp Expo '92, Chicago and Genoa '92 Intl. Philatelic Exhibitions.

Wideawake Airfield, 50th Anniv. — A96

Wmk. 373

1992, May 5		**Litho.**		***Perf. 14***
540	A96	15p Control tower	.50	.50
541	A96	18p Nose hangar	.60	.60
542	A96	25p Construction work	.85	.85
543	A96	70p Laying fuel pipeline	2.25	2.25
		Nos. 540-543 (4)	4.20	4.20

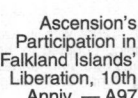

Ascension's Participation in Falkland Islands' Liberation, 10th Anniv. — A97

#548a, 15p + 3p like #544. b, 18p + 4p like #545. c, 25p + 5p like #546. d, 65p + 13p like #547.

Wmk. 373

1992, June 12		**Litho.**		***Perf. 14***
544	A97	15p Nimrod Mk.2	.50	.50
545	A97	18p VC10	.60	.60
546	A97	25p Wessex HU Mk.5 helicopter	.85	.85
547	A97	65p Vulcan B2	2.25	2.25
		Nos. 544-547 (4)	4.20	4.20

Souvenir Sheet

548	A97	Sheet of 4, #a.-d.	5.00	5.00

Surtax for Soldiers', Sailors' and Airmen's Families Association.

Children's drawings: 8p, Snowman, rocks, candle. 18p, Underwater Santa, Christmas tree. 25p, Hello, bells. 65p, Nativity Scene, angel.

Christmas A98

Wmk. 384

1992, Oct. 13		**Litho.**		***Perf. 14***
549	A98	8p multicolored	.30	.30
550	A98	18p multicolored	.70	.70
551	A98	25p multicolored	.95	.95
552	A98	65p multicolored	2.50	2.50
		Nos. 549-552 (4)	4.45	4.45

Yellow Canary — A99

Wmk. 373

1993, Jan. 12		**Litho.**		***Perf. 14½***
553	A99	15p Singing male	.40	.40
554	A99	18p Adult male, female	.55	.55
555	A99	25p Young calling for food	.80	.80
556	A99	70p Mixed flock	2.25	2.25
		Nos. 553-556 (4)	4.00	4.00

Royal Air Force, 75th Anniv.
Common Design Type

Designs: 20p, Sopwith Snipe. No. 558, Supermarine Southampton. 30p, Avro Anson. 70p, Vickers Wellington 1C.
No. 561a, Westland Lysander. b, Gloster Meteor. c, DeHavilland Comet. d, British Aerospace Nimrod.

Wmk. 373

1993, Apr. 1		**Litho.**		***Perf. 14***
557	CD350	20p multicolored	.60	.60
558	CD350	25p multicolored	.70	.70
559	CD350	30p multicolored	.85	.85
560	CD350	70p multicolored	2.25	2.25
		Nos. 557-560 (4)	4.40	4.40

Souvenir Sheet

561	CD350	25p Sheet of 4, #a.-d.	3.00	3.00

South Atlantic Cable Company, 25th Anniv. A100

Designs: 20p, Map showing cable route. 25p, Cable ship laying cable. 30p, Map of Ascension. 70p, Cable ship off Ascension.

Perf. 14x14½

1993, June 8		**Litho.**		**Wmk. 384**
562	A100	20p multicolored	.60	.60
563	A100	25p multicolored	.75	.75
564	A100	30p multicolored	.90	.90
565	A100	70p multicolored	2.00	2.00
		Nos. 562-565 (4)	4.25	4.25

Flowers A101

Perf. 14x14½

1993, Aug. 3		**Litho.**		**Wmk. 384**
566	A101	20p Lantana camara	.60	.60
567	A101	25p Moonflower	.75	.75
568	A101	30p Hibiscus	.90	.90
569	A101	70p Frangipani	2.00	2.00
		Nos. 566-569 (4)	4.25	4.25

Christmas A102

Designs: 12p, Child mailing Christmas card. 20p, Mail loaded onto Tristar. 25p, Plane in flight. 30p, Mail unloaded at Wideawake Airfield. 65p, Child reading card, Georgetown.

Perf. 14½x14

1993, Oct. 19		**Litho.**		**Wmk. 373**
570	A102	12p multicolored	.35	.35
571	A102	20p multicolored	.60	.60
572	A102	25p multicolored	.75	.75
573	A102	30p multicolored	.90	.90
574	A102	65p multicolored	2.00	2.00
		Nos. 570-574 (5)	4.60	4.60
a.		Souvenir sheet of 5, #570-574	4.50	4.50

Stamps from No. 574a show a continuous design, while Nos. 570-574 have white borders on sides.

Prehistoric Aquatic Reptiles — A103

1994, Jan. 25		**Wmk. 373**		***Perf. 14***
575	A103	12p Ichthyosaurus	.35	.35
576	A103	20p Metriorhynchus	.60	.60
577	A103	25p Mosasaurus	.75	.75
578	A103	30p Elasmosaurus	.90	.90
579	A103	65p Plesiosaurus	1.90	1.90
		Nos. 575-579 (5)	4.50	4.50

Ovptd. with Hong Kong '94 Emblem

1994, Feb. 18				
580	A103	12p on #575	.35	.35
581	A103	20p on #576	.60	.60
582	A103	25p on #577	.75	.75
583	A103	30p on #578	.90	.90
584	A103	65p on #579	1.90	1.90
		Nos. 580-584 (5)	4.50	4.50

Green Turtle A104

20p, Four on beach. 25p, Crawling in sand. #587, Crawling from sea. 65p, Swimming.
No. 589a, Side view, crawling from sea. b, Digging nest. c, Hatchlings heading to sea. d, Digging nest, diff.

1994, Mar. 22				
585	A104	20p multicolored	.60	.60
586	A104	25p multicolored	.75	.75
587	A104	30p multicolored	.90	.90
588	A104	65p multicolored	1.90	1.90
		Nos. 585-588 (4)	4.15	4.15

Souvenir Sheet

589	A104	30p Sheet of 4, #a.-d.	3.50	3.50

Civilian Ships A105

Ships serving during Falkland Islands War, 1982: 20p, Tug Yorkshireman. 25p, Minesweeper support RMS St. Helena. 30p, Oil tanker British ESK. 65p, Cruise liner Uganda, hospital ship.

1994, June 14				
590	A105	20p multicolored	.60	.60
591	A105	25p multicolored	.75	.75
592	A105	30p multicolored	.90	.90
593	A105	65p multicolored	1.90	1.90
		Nos. 590-593 (4)	4.15	4.15

Sooty Tern A106

1994, Aug. 16				
594	A106	20p Chick	.60	.60
595	A106	25p Juvenile	.75	.75
596	A106	30p Brooding adult	.90	.90
597	A106	65p Displaying male	1.90	1.90
		Nos. 594-597 (4)	4.15	4.15

Souvenir Sheet

598	A106	£1 Dread	3.00	3.00

Christmas A107

Donkeys: 12p, Mare with foal. 20p, Young adult. 25p, Foal. 30p, Adult, egrets. 65p, Adult.

1994, Oct. 11				***Perf. 14x14½***
599	A107	12p multicolored	.40	.40
600	A107	20p multicolored	.60	.60
601	A107	25p multicolored	.75	.75
602	A107	30p multicolored	.95	.95
603	A107	65p multicolored	2.00	2.00
		Nos. 599-603 (5)	4.70	4.70

Flowers A108

20p, Leonurus japonicus. 25p, Periwinkle. 30p, Four o'clock. 65p, Blood flower.

1995, Jan. 10				***Perf. 14***
604	A108	20p multi, vert.	.60	.60
605	A108	25p multi	.75	.75
606	A108	30p multi, vert.	.95	.95
607	A108	65p multi	2.00	2.00
		Nos. 604-607 (4)	4.30	4.30

Island Scenes, c. 1895 A109

Designs: 12p, Horse-drawn wagon, Two Boats, Green Mountain. 20p, Island stewards' store. 25p, Royal Navy headquarters, barracks. 30p, Police office. 65p, Pier head.

1995, Mar. 7		**Wmk. 384**		***Perf. 14½***
608	A109	12p sepia	.35	.35
609	A109	20p sepia	.60	.60
610	A109	25p sepia	.75	.75
611	A109	30p sepia	.90	.90
612	A109	65p sepia	2.00	2.00
		Nos. 608-612 (5)	4.60	4.60

End of World War II, 50th Anniv.
Common Design Types

Designs: 20p, 5.5-inch guns taken from HMS Hood, 1941. 25p, Fairey Swordfish, first aircraft to land at Ascension. 30p, HMS Dorsetshire patrolling South Atlantic. 65p, HMS Devonshire patrolling South Atlantic. £1, Reverse of War Medal, 1939-45.

1995, May 8 Wmk. 373 Perf. 14

613	CD351	20p multicolored	.60	.60
614	CD351	25p multicolored	.75	.75
615	CD351	30p multicolored	.90	.90
616	CD351	65p multicolored	2.00	2.00
		Nos. 613-616 (4)	4.25	4.25

Souvenir Sheet

617	CD352	£1 multicolored	3.00	3.00

Butterflies — A110

1995, Sept. 1 Wmk. 384

618	A110	20p Long-tailed blue	.60	.60
619	A110	25p Painted lady	.75	.75
620	A110	30p Diadem	.90	.90
621	A110	65p African monarch	2.00	2.00
		Nos. 618-621 (4)	4.25	4.25

Souvenir Sheet

622	A110	£1 Red admiral	3.00	3.00

Singapore '95 (#622).

Christmas A111

Designs based on children's drawings: 12p, Santa on boat. 20p, Santa on wall. 25p, Santa in chimney. 30p, Santa on dolphin. 65p, South Atlantic run.

1995, Oct. 10 Wmk. 373

623	A111	12p multicolored	.35	.35
624	A111	20p multicolored	.60	.60
625	A111	25p multicolored	.75	.75
626	A111	30p multicolored	.90	.90
627	A111	65p multicolored	2.00	2.00
		Nos. 623-627 (5)	4.60	4.60

Mollusks A112

12p, Cypraea lurida. 25p, Cypraea spurca. 30p, Harpa doris. 65p, Umbraculum umbraculum.

Wmk. 384
1996, Jan. 10 Litho. Perf. 14

628	A112	12p multicolored	.35	.35
629	A112	25p multicolored	.75	.75
630	A112	30p multicolored	.90	.90
631	A112	65p multicolored	2.00	2.00
a.		Strip of 4, #628-631	4.00	4.00

Queen Elizabeth II, 70th Birthday
Common Design Type

Various portraits of Queen, scenes of Ascension: 20p, St. Marys Church. 25p, The Residency. 30p, Roman Catholic Grotto. 65p, The Exiles Club.

Wmk. 384
1996, Apr. 22 Litho. Perf. 13½

632	CD354	20p multicolored	.65	.65
633	CD354	25p multicolored	.80	.80
634	CD354	30p multicolored	1.00	1.00
635	CD354	65p multicolored	2.00	2.00
		Nos. 632-635 (4)	4.45	4.45

CAPEX '96 A113

Island transport: 20p, US Army Jeep. 25p, 1924 Citreon 7.5HP two seater. 30p, 1930 Austin Ten-four Tourer. 65p, Series 1 Land Rover.

Wmk. 384
1996, June 8 Litho. Perf. 14

636	A113	20p multicolored	.65	.65
637	A113	25p multicolored	.80	.80
638	A113	30p multicolored	1.00	1.00
639	A113	65p multicolored	2.00	2.00
		Nos. 636-639 (4)	4.45	4.45

Birds and Their Young — A114

1p, Madeiran storm petrel. 2p, Red-billed tropicbird. 4p, Indian mynah. 5p, House sparrow. 7p, Common waxbill. 10p, White tern. 12p, Francolin. 15p, Brown noddy. 20p, Yellow canary. 25p, Black noddy. 30p, Red-footed booby. 40p, Yellow-billed tropicbird. 65p, Brown booby. £1, Masked booby. £2, Sooty tern. £3, Ascension frigate bird.

Wmk. 373
1996, Aug. 12 Litho. Perf. 13

640	A114	1p multicolored	.20	.20
641	A114	2p multicolored	.20	.20
642	A114	4p multicolored	.20	.20
643	A114	5p multicolored	.20	.20
644	A114	7p multicolored	.20	.20
645	A114	10p multicolored	.30	.30
646	A114	12p multicolored	.35	.35
647	A114	15p multicolored	.45	.45
648	A114	20p multicolored	.60	.60
649	A114	25p multicolored	.70	.70
650	A114	30p multicolored	.90	.90
651	A114	40p multicolored	1.10	1.10
652	A114	65p multicolored	1.90	1.90
a.		Sheet of 1, perf. 14	2.10	2.10
653	A114	£1 multicolored	3.00	3.00
a.		Souvenir sheet of 1	3.25	3.25
654	A114	£2 multicolored	6.00	6.00
655	A114	£3 multicolored	9.00	9.00
		Nos. 640-655 (16)	25.30	25.30

No. 652a for Hong Kong '97. Issued 2/3/97. No. 653a for return of Hong Kong to China. Issued 7/1/97.

BBC Atlantic Relay Station, 30th Anniv. A115

Various views of relay station: 20p, 25p, Towers. 30p, Towers, buildings. 65p, Satellite dish, towers, beach.

1996, Sept. 9 Wmk. 384 Perf. 14

656	A115	20p multicolored	.65	.65
657	A115	25p multicolored	.80	.80
658	A115	30p multicolored	1.00	1.00
659	A115	65p multicolored	2.00	2.00
		Nos. 656-659 (4)	4.45	4.45

Christmas A116

Santa Claus: 12p, On satellite dish. 20p, Playing golf. 25p, By beach. 30p, On RAF Tristar. 65p, Aboard RMS St. Helena.

Perf. 14x14½
1996, Sept. 23 Litho. Wmk. 373

660	A116	12p multicolored	.40	.40
661	A116	20p multicolored	.65	.65
662	A116	25p multicolored	.80	.80
663	A116	30p multicolored	1.00	1.00
664	A116	65p multicolored	2.00	2.00
		Nos. 660-664 (5)	4.85	4.85

UNICEF, 50th anniv.

A117

Wmk. 373
1997, Jan. 7 Litho. Perf. 14½

665	A117	20p Date palm	.65	.65
666	A117	25p Mauritius hemp	.80	.80
667	A117	30p Norfolk Island pine	1.00	1.00
668	A117	65p Dwarf palm	2.00	2.00
		Nos. 665-668 (4)	4.45	4.45

Hong Kong '97.

A118

Wmk. 373
1997, Apr. 1 Litho. Perf. 14½

Flag, ship or aircraft: 12p, Great Britain Red Ensign, tanker Maserk Ascension. 25p, RAF Ensign, Tristar. 30p, NASA emblem, Space Shuttle Atlantis. 65p, Royal Navy White Ensign, HMS Northumberland.

669	A118	12p multicolored	.40	.40
670	A118	25p multicolored	.80	.80
671	A118	30p multicolored	.95	.95
672	A118	65p multicolored	2.00	2.00
		Nos. 669-672 (4)	4.15	4.15

Herbs A119

Designs: a, Solanum sodomaeum. b, Ageratum conyzoides. c, Leonurus sibricus. d, Cerastium vulgatum. e, Commelina diffusa.

Perf. 14x14½
1997, June 7 Litho. Wmk. 373

673	A119	30p Strip of 5, #a.-e.	5.00	5.00

A120

Queen Elizabeth II and Prince Philip, 50th Wedding Anniv.: No. 674, Queen Elizabeth II. No. 675, Prince Philip playing polo. No. 676, Queen petting horse. No. 677, Prince Philip. No. 678, Prince Philip, Queen Elizabeth II. No. 679, Prince Harry, Prince William riding horses. £1.50, Queen Elizabeth, Prince Philip riding in open carriage.

Wmk. 384
1997, July 10 Litho. Perf. 13½

674	A120	20p multicolored	.65	.65
675	A120	20p multicolored	.65	.65
a.		Pair, #674-675	1.40	1.40
676	A120	25p multicolored	.85	.85
677	A120	25p multicolored	.85	.85
a.		Pair, #676-677	1.75	1.75
678	A120	30p multicolored	1.00	1.00
679	A120	30p multicolored	1.00	1.00
a.		Pair, #678-679	2.00	2.00
		Nos. 674-679 (6)	5.00	5.00

Souvenir Sheet

680	A120	£1.50 multicolored	4.75	4.75

Perf. 14 on 3 Sides
1997, Sept. 1 Litho. Wmk. 373
Booklet Stamps

681	A121	15p like #644	.50	.50
682	A121	35p like #648	1.10	1.10
a.		Booklet pane, 2 ea #681-682	3.25	
		Complete booklet, #682a	3.25	

 Birds — A121

Game Fish — A122

Perf. 14x14½
1997, Sept. 3 Litho. Wmk. 373

683	A122	12p Black marlin	.35	.35
684	A122	20p Atlantic sailfish	.65	.65
685	A122	25p Swordfish	.80	.80
686	A122	30p Wahoo	.95	.95
687	A122	£1 Yellowfin tuna	3.25	3.25
		Nos. 683-687 (5)	6.00	6.00

A123 A124

St. Mary's Church (Christmas): 15p, Interior view. 35p, Stained glass window, Madonna and Child. 40p, Stained glass window, Falklands, 1982. 50p, Stained glass window.

Wmk. 384
1997, Oct. 1 Litho. Perf. 14

688	A123	15p multicolored	.50	.50
689	A123	35p multicolored	1.10	1.10
690	A123	40p multicolored	1.25	1.25
691	A123	50p multicolored	1.75	1.75
		Nos. 688-691 (4)	4.60	4.60

Wmk. 373
1998, Feb. 10 Litho. Perf. 14

Insects: 15p, Cactoblastis cactorum. 35p, Teleonemia scrupulosa. 40p, Neltumius arizonensis. 50p, Algarobius prosopis.

692	A124	15p multicolored	.50	.50
693	A124	35p multicolored	1.10	1.10
694	A124	40p multicolored	1.25	1.25
695	A124	50p multicolored	1.60	1.60
		Nos. 692-695 (4)	4.45	4.45

Diana, Princess of Wales (1961-97)
Common Design Type

a, In polka-dotted dress. b, In yellow blouse. c, With longer hair style. d, Holding flowers.

Perf. 14½x14
1998, Mar. 31 Litho. Wmk. 373

696	CD355	35p Sheet of 4, #a.-d.	5.25	5.25

No. 696 sold for £1.40 + 20p, with surtax from international sales being donated to the Princess Diana Memorial Fund and surtax from national sales being donated to designated local charity.

Royal Air Force, 80th Anniv.
Common Design Type of 1993
Re-inscribed

15p, Fairey Fawn. 35p, Vickers Vernon. 40p, Supermarine Spitfire F-22. 50p, Bristol Britannia C2. No. 701: a, Blackburn Kangaroo. b, SE5a. c, Curtiss Kittyhawk III. d, Boeing Fortress II (B-17).

Wmk. 384
1998, Apr. 1   Litho.   Perf. 14
697 CD350 15p multicolored .70 .70
698 CD350 35p multicolored 1.60 1.60
699 CD350 40p multicolored 1.90 1.90
700 CD350 50p multicolored 2.25 2.25
Nos. 697-700 (4) 6.45 6.45

Souvenir Sheet
701 CD350 50p Sheet of 4, #a.-d. 6.75 6.75

Birds — A125

Island Sports — A126

Wmk. 373
1998, June 15   Litho.   Perf. 14
702 A125 15p Swallow .50 .50
703 A125 25p House martin .80 .80
704 A125 35p Cattle egret 1.10 1.10
705 A125 40p Swift 1.25 1.25
706 A125 50p Allen's gallinule 1.60 1.60
Nos. 702-706 (5) 5.25 5.25

Wmk. 373
1998, Aug. 17   Litho.   Perf. 14
707 A126 15p Cricket .50 .50
708 A126 35p Golf 1.10 1.10
709 A126 40p Soccer 1.25 1.25
710 A126 50p Trapshooting 1.60 1.60
Nos. 707-709 (3) 2.85 2.85

Christmas A127

Designs: 15p, Children's nativity play. 35p, Santa arriving on Ascension. 40p, Santa arriving at a party. 50p, Carol singers.

Wmk. 373
1998, Oct. 1   Litho.   Perf. 14
711 A127 15p multicolored .50 .50
712 A127 35p multicolored 1.10 1.10
713 A127 40p multicolored 1.25 1.25
714 A127 50p multicolored 1.60 1.60
Nos. 711-714 (4) 4.45 4.45

World War II Aircraft A128

15p, Curtiss C-46 Commando. 35p, Douglas C-47 Dakota. 40p, Douglas C-54 Skymaster. 50p, Consolidated Liberator Mk.V. £1.50, Consolidated Liberator LB-30.

Wmk. 373
1999, Jan. 20   Litho.   Perf. 14
715 A128 15p multicolored .50 .50
716 A128 35p multicolored 1.10 1.10
717 A128 40p multicolored 1.25 1.25
718 A128 50p multicolored 1.60 1.60
Nos. 715-718 (4) 4.45 4.45

Souvenir Sheet
719 A128 £1.50 multicolored 4.75 4.75
Winston Churchill, 125th birth anniv.

Australia '99, World Stamp Expo A129

Union Castle Mail Ships: 15p, SS Glengorm Castle. 35p, SS Gloucester Castle. 40p, SS Durham Castle. 50p, SS Garth Castle.

£1, HMS Endeavour.

Perf. 14½x14
1999, Mar. 5   Litho.   Wmk. 373
720 A129 15p multicolored .50 .50
721 A129 35p multicolored 1.10 1.10
722 A129 40p multicolored 1.25 1.25
723 A129 50p multicolored 1.60 1.60
Nos. 720-723 (4) 4.45 4.45

Souvenir Sheet
724 A129 £1 multicolored 3.25 3.25

World Wildlife Fund — A130

Fairy tern: No. 725, Two on branch. No. 726, One on branch. No. 727, Adult feeding chick. No. 728, Two in flight.

Wmk. 384
1999, Apr. 27   Litho.   Perf. 14½
725 A130 10p multicolored .35 .35
726 A130 10p multicolored .35 .35
727 A130 10p multicolored .35 .35
728 A130 10p multicolored .35 .35
  a. Sheet of 16, 4 each #725-728 5.75 5.75
Nos. 725-728 (4) 1.40 1.40

Wedding of Prince Edward and Sophie Rhys-Jones
Common Design Type
Perf. 13¾x14
1999, June 19   Litho.   Wmk. 384
729 CD356 50p Separate portraits 1.60 1.60
730 CD356 £1 Couple 3.25 3.25

1st Manned Moon Landing, 30th Anniv.
Common Design Type
Designs: 15p, Command and service modules. 35p, Moon from Apollo 11. 40p, Devil's Ashpit Tracking Station. 50p, Lunar module lifts off moon. £1.50, Looking at earth from moon.

Perf. 14x13¾
1999, July 20   Litho.   Wmk. 384
731 CD357 15p multicolored .50 .50
732 CD357 35p multicolored 1.10 1.10
733 CD357 40p multicolored 1.25 1.25
734 CD357 50p multicolored 1.60 1.60
Nos. 731-734 (4) 4.45 4.45

Souvenir Sheet
Perf. 14
735 CD357 £1.50 multicolored 4.75 4.75
No. 735 contains one 40mm circular stamp.

Queen Mother's Century
Common Design Type
Queen Mother: 15p, With King George VI, Winston Churchill. 35p, With Prince Charles. 40p, At Clarence House, 88th birthday. 50p, With drummers at Clarence House. £1.50, With Titanic.

Wmk. 384
1999, Aug. 20   Litho.   Perf. 13½
736-739 CD358 Set of 4 4.50 4.50

Souvenir Sheet
740 CD358 £1.50 black 5.00 5.00

Christmas A131

Wmk. 384
1999, Oct. 6   Litho.   Perf. 13¾
741 A131 15p 3 children .50 .50
742 A131 35p 2 children, hats 1.10 1.10
743 A131 40p 2 children, bed 1.25 1.25
744 A131 50p 4 children 1.75 1.75
Nos. 741-744 (4) 4.60 4.60

Cable and Wireless, Cent. A132

Perf. 13¼x13¾
1999, Dec. 13   Litho.   Wmk. 373
745 A132 15p CS Anglia .50 .50
746 A132 35p CS Cambria 1.10 1.10
747 A132 40p Map 1.25 1.25
748 A132 50p CS Colonia 1.60 1.60
Nos. 745-748 (4) 4.45 4.45

Souvenir Sheet
749 A132 £1.50 CS Seine 5.00 5.00

Turtle Project — A133

15p, Young turtles. 35p, Turtle, trail at left. 40p, Turtle with tracking device on beach. 50p, Turtle with tracking device heading to sea. No. 754: a, Turtle head, rock. b, Like 15p. c, Turtle on beach, sea. d, Turtle in surf.

2000, Mar. 8   Litho.   Perf. 13¾
750 A133 15p multi .50 .50
751 A133 35p multi 1.10 1.10
752 A133 40p multi 1.25 1.25
753 A133 50p multi 1.60 1.60
Nos. 750-753 (4) 4.45 4.45

Souvenir Sheet
Perf. 14
754 A133 25p Sheet of 4, #a-d 3.25 3.25
No. 754 contains four 40x26mm stamps.

Prince William, 18th Birthday
Common Design Type
William: 15p, As toddler, vert. 35p, Wearing suit and wearing cap, vert. 40p, Holding flowers, and in parka. 50p, In suit and in checked shirt.

Perf. 13¾x14¼, 14¼x13¾
2000, June 21   Litho.   Wmk. 373
Stamps With White Border
755 CD359 15p multi .45 .45
756 CD359 35p multi 1.00 1.00
757 CD359 40p multi 1.25 1.25
758 CD359 50p multi 1.50 1.50
Nos. 755-758 (4) 4.20 4.20

Souvenir Sheet
Stamps Without White Border
Perf. 14¼
759 Sheet of 5 4.50 4.50
  a. CD359 10p multi .30 .30
  b. CD359 15p multi .45 .45
  c. CD359 35p multi 1.00 1.00
  d. CD359 40p multi 1.25 1.25
  e. CD359 50p multi 1.50 1.50

Forts A134

Designs: 15p, 1815 fortifications. 35p, Fort Thornton, 1817. 40p, Fort Hayes, 1860. 50p, Fort Bedford, 1940.

Wmk. 373
2000, Aug. 14   Litho.   Perf. 14
760-763 A134 Set of 4 4.00 4.00

Christmas — A135

Carols: 15p, I Saw Three Ships. 25p, Silent Night. 40p, Away in a Manger. 90p, Hark, the Herald Angels Sing.

2000, Oct. 16   Wmk. 384
764-767 A135 Set of 4 5.00 5.00

Souvenir Sheet

New Year 2001 (Year of the Snake) — A136

Turtles: a, 25p, Green. b, 40p, Loggerhead. Illustration reduced.

Wmk. 373
2001, Feb. 1   Litho.   Perf. 14½
768 A136 Sheet of 2, #a-b 1.90 1.90
Hong Kong 2001 Stamp Exhibition.

Sinking of the Roebuck, Tercentenary A137

Designs: 15p, Capt. William Dampier. 35p, Drawing of the Roebuck, horiz. 40p, Cave dwelling at Dampier's Drip, horiz. 50p, Map.

2001, Feb. 25   Litho.   Perf. 14
769-772 A137 Set of 4 4.00 4.00

Discovery of Ascension Island, 500th Anniv. — A138

Designs: 15p, Alfonso de Albuquerque. 35p, Portuguese caravel. 40p, Cantino map. 50p, Rear admiral Sir George Cockburn.

Perf. 14¾x14¼
2001, Mar. 25   Litho.   Wmk. 384
773-776 A138 Set of 4 4.00 4.00

The Age of Victoria A139

Designs: 15p, Great Britain Type A1 with Ascension cancel, vert. 25p, Parade, 1901. 35p, HMS Phoebe. 40p, The Red Lion, 1863. 50p, Queen Victoria, vert. 65p, Sir Joseph Dalton Hooker, botanist. £1.50, Queen Victoria's Funeral.

Wmk. 373
2001, May 24   Litho.   Perf. 14
777-782 A139 Set of 6 6.50 6.50

Souvenir Sheet
783 A139 £1.50 multi 4.25 4.25

Souvenir Sheet

Belgica 2001 Intl. Stamp Exhibition, Brussels — A140

Ascension tourist sites: a, 35p, Islander Hostel. b, 35p, The Residency. c, 40p, The Red Lion. d, 40p, Turtle Ponds.

Wmk. 373

2001, June 9	Litho.		*Perf. 14¼*	
784	A140	Sheet of 4, #a-d	4.25	4.25

Birdlife International World Bird Festival A141

Ascension frigate bird: 15p, On rock with wings outstretched, vert. 35p, Chick, with mouth open, vert. 40p, Pair in flight. 50p, Close-up of bird.

Perf. 13¾x14¼, 14¼x13¾

2001, Oct. 1	Litho.		**Wmk. 373**	
785-788	A141	Set of 4	4.00	4.00

Souvenir Sheet

789		Sheet, #785-788, 789a, perf. 14¼	4.25	4.25
a.		A141 10p Two birds on rock	.25	.25

POSTAGE DUE STAMPS

Outline Map of Ascension — D1

1986		Litho.	*Perf. 15x14*	
J1	D1	1p beige & brown	.20	.20
J2	D1	2p orange & brown	.20	.20
J3	D1	5p org ver & brn	.20	.20
J4	D1	7p violet & black	.20	.30
J5	D1	10p ultra & black	.25	.35
J6	D1	25p pale green & blk	.60	.70
		Nos. J1-J6 (6)	1.65	1.95

AUSTRALIAN STATES

NEW SOUTH WALES

ˈnü saᴜth ˈwā͡əlz

LOCATION — Southeast coast of Australia in the South Pacific Ocean
GOVT. — British Crown Colony
AREA — 309,432 sq. mi.
POP. — 1,500,000 (estimated, 1900)
CAPITAL — Sydney

In 1901 New South Wales united with five other British colonies to form the Commonwealth of Australia. Stamps of Australia are now used.

12 Pence = 1 Shilling
20 Shillings = 1 Pound

Watermarks

Wmk. 12- Crown and Single-lined A

Wmk. 13- Large Crown and Double-lined A

Wmk. 49- Double-lined Numerals Corresponding with the Value

Wmk. 50- Single-lined Numeral

Wmk. 51- Single-lined Numeral

Wmk. 52- Single-lined Numeral

Wmk. 53- 5/-

Wmk. 54- Small Crown and NSW

Wmk. 55- Large Crown and NSW

Wmk. 56- NSW

Wmk. 57- 5/- NSW in Diamond

Wmk. 58- 20/- NSW in Circle

Wmk. 70- V and Crown

Wmk. 199- Crown and A in Circle

Values for unused stamps are for examples with original gum as defined in the catalogue introduction except for Nos. 1-20 which are rarely found with gum and are valued without gum. Very fine examples of Nos. 35-100, F3-F5, J1-J10 and O1-O40 will have perforations touching the framelines or design on one or more sides due to the narrow spacing of the stamps on the plates and imperfect perforation methods. Stamps with perfs clear of the design on all four sides are scarce and will command higher prices.

Seal of the Colony
A1   A2

A1 has no clouds. A2 has clouds added to the design, except in pos. 15.

			Engr.	Imperf.
1850		**Unwmk.**		
1	A1	1p red, *yelsh wove*	4,000.	400.
b.		1p red, *bluish wove*	4,000.	350.
2	A2	1p red, *yelsh wove*	2,500.	290.
b.		1p red, *yellowish laid*	4,000.	450.
c.		1p red, *bluish wove*	2,500.	275.
e.		1p red, *bluish laid*		450.
f.		Hill unshaded	4,250.	450.
g.		No clouds	4,250.	450.
h.		No trees	4,250.	450.

Twenty-five varieties.
Stamps from early impressions of the plate sell at considerably higher prices.
No. 1 was reproduced by the collotype process in a souvenir sheet distributed at the London International Stamp Exhibition 1950. The paper is white.

Plate I — A3   Plate II — A4

Plate I: Vertically lined background.
Plate I re-touched: Lines above and below "POSTAGE" and "TWO PENCE" deepened. Outlines of circular band around picture also deepened.
Plate II (First re-engraving of Plate I): Horizontally lined background; the bale on the left side is dated and there is a dot in the star in each corner.
Plate II retouched: Dots and dashes added in lower spandrels.

Plate I
Late (worn plate) Impressions

3	A3	2p blue, *yelsh wove*	1,675.	150.
a.		Early impressions	4,500.	360.

Twenty-four varieties.

Plate I, Retouched

4	A3	2p blue, *yelsh wove*	3,000.	275.

Twelve varieties.

Plate II
Late (worn plate) Impressions

5	A4	2p blue, *yelsh wove*	1,750.	160.
a.		2p blue, *bluish wove*	1,750.	160.
b.		2p blue, *grayish wove*	1,750.	160.
c.		"CREVIT" omitted	—	375.
d.		Pick and shovel omitted	—	290.
e.		No whip	3,000.	210.
h.		Early impressions	4,000.	225.

Plate II, Retouched

5F	A4	2p blue, *bluish wove*	2,350.	175.
g.		No whip		275.
i.		"CREVIT" omitted		375.

Eleven varieties.

Plate III
A5

Plate IV
A6

Plate III (Second re-engraving of Plate I): The bale is not dated and, with the exception of Nos. 7, 10 and 12, it is single-lined. There are no dots in the stars.

Plate IV (Third re-engraving of Plate I): The bale is double-lined and there is a circle in the center of each star.

1850-51

6	A5	2p bl, *grayish wove*	2,100.	175.
a.		Fan with 6 segments	—	350.
b.		Double-lined bale	—	225.
c.		No whip	—	250.
7	A6	2p blue, *bluish wove* ('51)	2,350.	150.
a.		2p ultra, *white laid*	2,900.	175.
b.		2p blue, *grayish wove*	2,350.	150.
c.		Fan with 6 segments	—	210.
d.		No clouds	—	210.

Twenty-four varieties.

Plate V — A7

A8

Plate V (Fourth re-engraving of Plate I): There is a pearl in the fan-shaped ornament below the central design.

1850-51

8	A7	2p blue, *grayish wove* ('51)	2,400.	150.
a.		2p ultra, *yellowish laid*	3,500.	290.
b.		Fan with 6 segments	—	250.
c.		Pick and shovel omitted	—	250.
9	A8	3p grn, *bluish wove*	2,400.	225.
a.		3p green, *yellowish wove*	3,750.	240.
b.		3p green, *yellowish laid*	4,650.	425.
c.		3p green, *bluish laid*	4,650.	425.
d.		No whip	—	350.

Twenty-four varieties of #8, twenty-five of #9.

Queen Victoria
A9   A10

TWO PENCE
Plate I - Background of wavy lines.
Plate II - Stars in corners.
Plate III (Plate I re-engraved) - Background of crossed lines.

SIX PENCE
Plate I - Background of fine lines.
Plate II (Plate I re-engraved) - Background of coarse lines.

1851   **Yellowish Wove Paper**

10	A9	1p carmine	1,675.	225.00
b.		No leaves to right of "SOUTH"	3,250.	360.00
c.		Two leaves to right of "SOUTH"	3,250.	425.00
d.		"WALE"	3,250.	425.00
11	A9	2p ultra, Plate I	750.00	90.00

1852   **Bluish Laid Paper**

12	A9	1p orange brown	3,000.	375.
a.		No leaves to right of "SOUTH"		550.
b.		Two leaves to right of "SOUTH"		625.
c.		"WALE"		625.

1852-55
Bluish or Grayish Wove Paper

13	A9	1p red	900.00	110.00
a.		1p carmine	1,000.	125.00
b.		No leaves to right of "SOUTH"		225.00
c.		Two leaves to right of "SOUTH"		290.00
d.		"WALE"		290.00

14	A9	2p blue, Plate I	650.00	30.00
a.		2p ultramarine	700.00	30.00
b.		2p slate	650.00	30.00
15	A10	2p blue, Plate II ('53)	1,050.	87.50
a.		"WAEES"	2,300.	450.00
16	A9	2p blue, Plate III ('55)	450.00	55.00
17	A9	3p green	1,250.	140.00
a.		"WACES"	1,500.	190.00
b.		"WACES"		350.00
18	A9	6p brown, Plate I	2,000.	250.00
a.		6p black brown	2,000.	250.00
b.		"WALLS"	4,250.	525.00
19	A9	6p brown, Plate II	2,000.	275.00
a.		6p bister brown	2,000.	275.00
20	A9	8p yellow ('53)	3,600.	600.00
a.		8p orange	3,600.	675.00
b.		No leaves to right of "SOUTH"		1,250.

The plates of the 1, 2, 3 and 8p each contained 50 varieties and those of the 6p 25 varieties.

The 2p, plate II, 6p, plate II, and 8p have been reprinted on grayish blue wove paper. The reprints of the 2p have the spandrels and background much worn. Most of the reprints of the 6p have no floreate ornaments to the right and left of "South." On all the values the wreath has been retouched.

Type of 1851 and:

A11   A12

A13   A14

1854-55   **Wmk. 49**

23	A9	1p orange	150.00	15.00
a.		No leaves to right of "SOUTH"	325.00	75.00
b.		Two leaves to right of "SOUTH"	425.00	110.00
c.		"WALE"	425.00	125.00
24	A9	2p blue	100.00	10.00
a.		2p ultramarine	100.00	10.00
25	A9	3p green	175.00	25.00
a.		"WACES"		110.00
b.		Watermarked "2"	2,750.	1,500.

Value for No. 25b is for copy with the design cut into.

26	A11	5p green	900.00	550.00
27	A12	6p sage green	425.00	32.50
28	A12	6p brown	450.00	32.50
a.		Watermarked "8"	1,650.	100.00
29	A12	6p gray	400.00	50.00
a.		Watermarked "8"	1,650.	100.00
30	A13	8p orange ('55)	4,750.	1,000.
a.		8p yellow	4,750.	1,000.
31	A14	1sh pale red brown	725.00	75.00
a.		1sh red	675.00	75.00
b.		Watermarked "8"	2,000.	160.00

See Nos. 38-42, 56, 58, 65, 67.
Nos. 38-42 exist with wide margins. Copies with perforations trimmed are often offered as Nos. 26, 30, and 30a.

A15   A16

1856

32	A15	1p red	140.00	20.00
a.		1p orange	140.00	20.00
b.		Printed on both sides	2,000.	2,000.
33	A15	2p blue	110.00	7.75
a.		Watermarked "1"		4,500.
b.		Watermarked "5"	550.00	300.00
c.		Watermarked "8"		1,500.
34	A15	3p green	750.00	80.00
a.		3p yellow green	725.00	75.00
b.		Watermarked "2"		3,600.
		Nos. 32-34 (3)	1,000.	107.75

The two known copies of No. 33c are in museums. Both are used.

The 1p has been reprinted in orange on paper watermarked Small Crown and NSW, and the 2p in deep blue on paper watermarked single lined "2." These reprints are usually overprinted "SPECIMEN."

See Nos. 34C-37, 54, 63, 90.

1859   **Litho.**

34C	A15	2p light blue	725.00

1860-63 **Engr. Wmk. 49** *Perf. 13*

35	A15	1p red	57.50	8.00
a.		1p orange	100.00	8.00
b.		Perf. 12x13		1,800.
c.		Perf. 12	90.00	15.00
36	A15	2p blue, perf. 12	100.00	10.00
a.		Watermarked "1"		3,250.
c.		Perf. 12x13	2,400.	225.00
37	A15	3p blue green	50.00	10.00
a.		3p yellow green	50.00	9.00
b.		3p deep green	50.00	10.00
c.		Watermarked "6"	90.00	12.50
d.		Perf. 12	600.00	45.00
38	A11	5p dark green	40.00	16.00
a.		5p yellow green	75.00	30.00
b.		Perf. 12	165.00	42.50
39	A12	6p brown, perf. 12	275.00	42.50
a.		6p gray, perf. 12	275.00	42.50
40	A12	6p violet	60.00	6.00
a.		6p aniline lilac	950.00	140.00
b.		Watermarked "5"	360.00	30.00
c.		Watermarked "12"	1,150.	20.00
e.		Perf. 12	275.00	18.00
41	A13	8p yellow	140.00	40.00
a.		8p orange	225.00	35.00
b.		Perf. 12	2,100.	575.00
42	A14	1sh rose	80.00	8.00
a.		1sh carmine	75.00	7.25
c.		Perf. 12	400.00	50.00
		Nos. 35-42 (8)	802.50	140.50

1864   **Wmk. 50**   *Perf. 13*

43	A15	1p red	45.00	15.00

1861-80   **Wmk. 53**   *Perf. 13*

44	A16	5sh dull violet	225.00	35.00
a.		5sh purple	200.00	35.00
b.		5sh dull violet, perf. 12	1,500.	360.00
c.		5sh purple, perf. 12	—	45.00
d.		5sh purple, perf. 10	225.00	42.50
e.		5sh purple, perf. 12x10	400.00	60.00

See No. 101. For overprint see No. O11.
Reprints are perf. 10 and overprinted "REPRINT" in black.

A17   A18

1862-65 **Typo.** **Unwmk.** *Perf. 13*

45	A17	1p red ('65)	90.00	30.00
a.		Perf. 14	72.50	50.00
46	A18	2p blue	55.00	2.75
a.		Perf. 14	67.50	32.50

1863-64   **Wmk. 50**   *Perf. 13*

47	A17	1p red	21.00	1.75
a.		Watermarked "2"	95.00	12.00
48	A18	2p blue	11.00	.55
a.		Watermarked "1"	140.00	5.00

1862   **Wmk. 49**   *Perf. 13*

49	A18	2p blue	50.00	7.50
a.		Watermarked "5"	125.00	16.00
b.		Perf. 12x13	550.00	
c.		Perf. 12	150.00	27.50

See Nos. 52-53, 61-62, 70-76.

A19   A20

1867, Sept. **Wmk. 51, 52** *Perf. 13*

50	A19	4p red brown	40.00	3.25
a.		Imperf.		
51	A20	10p lilac	11.00	3.50
a.		Imperf.		
b.		Horiz. pair, imperf. between	550.00	

See Nos. 55, 64, 91, 97, 117, 129.

A21   A22

A23

Typo.; Engr. (3p, 5p, 8p)
1871-84   **Wmk. 54**   *Perf. 13*

52	A17	1p red	6.00	.40
a.		Perf. 10	360.00	27.50
b.		Perf. 13x10	15.00	.40
c.		Horiz. pair imperf. between		550.00
53	A18	2p blue	7.25	.40
a.		Imperf.		
b.		Horiz. pair, imperf. vert.		725.00
c.		Perf. 10	360.00	35.00
d.		Perf. 13x10	7.25	.40
e.		Perf. 12x13		
f.		Perf. 11x12	240.00	37.50
54	A15	3p green ('74)	19.00	2.25
a.		Perf. 11	200.00	140.00
b.		Perf. 12	—	450.00
c.		Perf. 10x12	160.00	32.50
d.		Perf. 12x11	125.00	45.00
e.		Perf. 10	65.00	5.00
f.		Perf. 13x10	125.00	13.50
55	A19	4p red brown ('77)	55.00	6.00
a.		Perf. 10	275.00	45.00
b.		Perf. 13x10	75.00	3.50
56	A11	5p dk grn, perf. 10 ('84)	15.00	8.00
a.		Imperf.		
b.		Perf. 12	300.00	125.00
c.		Perf. 10x12	110.00	37.50
d.		Perf. 13x10		
57	A21	6p lilac ('72)	37.50	.90
a.		Imperf.		
b.		Perf. 13x10	50.00	1.60
c.		Perf. 10	300.00	13.50
58	A13	8p yellow ('77)	100.00	16.00
a.		Imperf.		
b.		Perf. 10	300.00	24.00
c.		Perf. 13x10	200.00	21.00

59	A22	9p on 10p red brown, perf. 12 (Bk)	12.50	4.00
a.		Double surcharge, blk & bl	175.00	
b.		Perf. 10x12	325.00	250.00
c.		Perf. 10	12.00	4.00
d.		Perf. 12x11	16.00	5.25
e.		Perf. 11x12	—	
f.		Perf. 13	22.00	5.50
g.		Perf. 11	35.00	7.25
h.		Perf. 10x11	45.00	10.50
60	A23	1sh black ('76)	75.00	2.75
a.		Imperf.		
b.		Perf. 13x10	250.00	5.00
c.		Perf. 10	275.00	12.00
d.		Perf. 11		
		Nos. 52-60 (9)	327.25	40.70

The surcharge on #59 measures 15mm.
See #66, 68. For overprints see #O1-O10.

Typo.; Engr. (3p, 5p, 8p)

1882-91		Wmk. 55	Perf. 11x12	
61	A17	1p red	5.00	.30
a.		Perf. 10	9.00	.30
b.		Perf. 10x13	125.00	5.50
c.		Perf. 10x12	300.00	75.00
d.		Perf. 12x11		140.00
e.		Perf. 10x11	550.00	140.00
f.		Perf. 11		175.00
g.		Perf. 13	725.00	360.00
62	A18	2p blue	11.00	.20
a.		Perf. 10	21.00	.30
b.		Perf. 13x10	80.00	2.25
c.		Perf. 12x10	550.00	125.00
d.		Perf. 12x10	360.00	90.00
e.		Perf. 11		125.00
f.		Perf. 12x11	360.00	120.00
g.		Perf. 11x10	550.00	140.00
h.		Perf. 10		250.00
63	A15	3p green	5.00	.75
a.		Imperf., pair	175.00	
b.		Vert. pair, imperf. btwn.	200.00	
c.		Imperf. vert., pair		
d.		Double impression		
e.		Perf. 10	6.50	.70
f.		Perf. 11	6.50	.70
g.		Perf. 12	8.00	.90
h.		Perf. 12x11	7.25	.90
i.		Perf. 10x12	30.00	3.00
m.		Perf. 10x11	18.00	1.40
n.		Perf. 12x10	30.00	3.25
64	A19	4p red brown	27.50	1.25
a.		Perf. 10	40.00	2.75
b.		Perf. 10x12	180.00	75.00
c.		Perf. 12	225.00	90.00
65	A11	5p dk blue green	7.25	.60
a.		Imperf., pair	200.00	
b.		Perf. 11	12.00	.65
c.		Perf. 10	12.00	.80
d.		Perf. 12	12.00	.80
e.		Perf. 10x12		27.50
f.		5p green, perf. 12x11	—	
g.		5p green, perf. 11x10	45.00	5.50
h.		5p green, perf. 12x10	75.00	3.25
i.		5p green, perf. 10x11	40.00	4.00
j.		5p green, perf. 11		
66	A21	6p lilac, perf. 10	37.50	.90
a.		Horiz. pair, imperf. between		750.00
b.		Perf. 10x12	32.50	1.40
c.		Perf. 11x12	72.50	11.00
d.		Perf. 12	85.00	9.00
e.		Perf. 11x10	55.00	1.75
f.		Perf. 11	85.00	7.25
g.		Perf. 10x13		325.00
67	A13	8p yellow, perf. 10	90.00	15.00
a.		Perf. 11	90.00	16.00
b.		Perf. 12	150.00	24.00
c.		Perf. 10x12	110.00	30.00
68	A23	1sh black	60.00	2.00
a.		Perf. 10x13		
b.		Perf. 10	57.50	2.00
c.		Perf. 11	200.00	11.00
d.		Perf. 10x12		
		Nos. 61-68 (8)	243.25	21.00

Nos. 63 and 65 exist with two types of watermark 55 - spacings of 1mm or 2mm between crown and NSW.
See No. 90. For surcharges and overprints see Nos. 92-94, O12-O19.

The 1, 2, 4, 6, 8p and 1sh have been reprinted on paper watermarked Large Crown and NSW. The 1, 2, 4p and 1sh are perforated 11x12, the 6p is perforated 10 and the 8p 11. All are overprinted "REPRINT," the 1sh in red and the others in black.

Perf. 11x12

1886-87		Typo.	Wmk. 56	
Bluish Revenue Stamp Paper				
70	A17	1p scarlet	5.50	1.25
a.		Perf. 10	16.00	4.00
71	A18	2p dark blue	14.00	2.25
a.		Perf. 10	57.50	5.00

For overprint, see No. O20.

A24

Perf. 12 (#73-75), 12x10 (#72, 75A) and Compound

1885-86				
"POSTAGE" in Black				
72	A24	5sh green & vio	400.00	72.50
a.		Perf. 10		
73	A24	10sh rose & vio	1,150.	225.00
74	A24	£1 rose & vio	2,500.	—
a.		Perf. 13		2,100.

"POSTAGE" in Blue
Bluish Paper

75	A24	10sh rose & vio	175.00	55.00
b.		Perf. 10	675.00	160.00
c.		Perf. 12x11		

White Paper

75A	A24	£1 rose & vio	3,400.	1,600.

For overprints, see Nos. O21-O23.
The 5sh with black overprint and the £1 with blue overprint have been reprinted on paper watermarked NSW. They are perforated 12x10 and are overprinted "REPRINT" in black.

1894		White Paper
"POSTAGE" in Blue		
76	A24	10sh rose & violet
a.		Double overprint

See No. 108B.

View of Sydney
A25

Emu
A26

Captain Cook — A27

Victoria and Coat of Arms — A28

Lyrebird
A29

Kangaroo
A30

1888-89		Wmk. 55	Perf. 11x12	
77	A25	1p violet	3.50	.20
a.		Perf. 12	4.50	.20
b.		Perf. 12x11½	16.00	.80
78	A26	2p blue	5.00	.20
a.		Imperf., pair	110.00	
b.		Perf. 12	7.50	.20
c.		Perf. 12x11½	11.50	.20
79	A27	4p brown	10.00	2.75
a.		Perf. 12	27.50	6.75
b.		Perf. 12	24.00	3.00
c.		Perf. 11	400.00	125.00
d.		Imperf.		
80	A28	6p carmine rose	20.00	3.25
a.		Perf. 12	19.00	7.50
b.		Perf. 12x11½	32.50	3.75
81	A29	8p red violet	14.50	2.25
a.		Perf. 12	14.50	2.50
b.		Perf. 12x11½	37.50	10.00
82	A30	1sh vio brown ('89)	17.50	1.00
a.		Imperf., pair	650.00	
b.		Perf. 12x11½	19.00	1.00
c.		Perf. 12	24.00	1.00
		Nos. 77-82 (6)	70.50	9.65

First British settlement in Australia, cent.
For overprints see Nos. O24-O29.

1888		Wmk. 56	Perf. 11x12	
83	A25	1p violet	12.00	1.25
84	A26	2p blue	60.00	6.00

See #104B-106C, 113-115, 118, 125-127, 130.

Map of Australia
A31

Governors Capt. Arthur Phillip (above) and Lord Carrington
A32

1888-89		Wmk. 53	Perf. 10	
85	A31	5sh violet ('89)	225.00	50.00
86	A32	20sh ultra	340.00	160.00

See #88, 120. For overprints see #O30-O31.

1890		Wmk. 57	Perf. 10	
87	A31	5sh violet	175.00	24.00
a.		Perf. 11	175.00	35.00
b.		Perf. 10x11	200.00	24.00
c.		Perf. 12	325.00	37.50

Perf. 11x12
Wmk. 58

88	A32	20sh ultra	200.00	75.00
a.		Perf. 11	225.00	75.00
b.		Perf. 10	275.00	110.00
c.		Perf. 12	310.00	110.00

For overprints see Nos. O32-O33.

"Australia"
A33

Victoria
A37

1890, Dec. 22		Wmk. 55	Perf. 11x12	
89	A33	2½p ultra	2.50	.45
a.		Perf. 12	10.00	.45
b.		Perf. 12x11½	60.00	90.00

For overprint see No. O35.

Type of 1856

1891	Engr.	Wmk. 52	Perf. 10	
90	A15	3p green	9.00	15.00
a.		Double impression		

Type of 1867

1893	Typo.		Perf. 11	
91	A20	10p lilac	13.50	5.50
a.		Perf. 10	14.50	6.75
b.		Perf. 11x10 or 10x11	22.50	10.00
c.		Perf. 12x11	160.00	22.50

Types of 1862-84 Surcharged in Black:

a   b

1891, Jan. 5		Wmk. 55	Perf. 11x12	
92	A17(a)	½p on 1p gray	2.75	3.00
a.		Imperf.		
b.		Surcharge omitted		
c.		Double surcharge	250.00	
93	A21(b)	7½p on 6p brown	5.00	3.00
a.		Perf. 10	5.00	2.50
b.		Perf. 11	5.00	2.50
c.		Perf. 12	5.50	3.00
d.		Perf. 10x12	5.50	3.00

Perf. 12x11½

94	A23(b)	12½p on 1sh red	10.00	7.50
a.		Perf. 11x12	11.00	7.50
b.		Perf. 10	11.00	8.00
c.		Perf. 11	11.50	8.00
d.		Perf. 12	13.50	7.50
		Nos. 92-94 (3)	17.75	13.50

For overprints see Nos. O34, O36-O37.

1892				
95	A37	½p slate	2.00	.20
a.		Perf. 12x11½	2.00	.20
b.		Perf. 12	2.00	.20
c.		Perf. 10	25.00	.90
d.		Perf. 10x12	90.00	9.50
e.		Perf. 11	100.00	8.00

See #102, 109, 121. For overprint see #O38.

Types of 1867-71

1897			Perf. 11x12	
96	A22	9p on 10p red brn (Bk)	8.00	4.50
a.		9p on 10p org brn (Bk)	8.00	4.50
b.		Surcharge omitted	—	
c.		Double surcharge	125.00	110.00
d.		Perf. 11	11.00	7.50
e.		Perf. 12	10.00	6.75
97	A20	10p violet	12.00	5.00
a.		Perf. 12x11½	12.00	5.00
b.		Perf. 11	18.00	5.00
c.		Perf. 12	13.50	5.50

The surcharge on No. 96 measures 13½mm.
For overprints see Nos. O39-O40.

Seal
A38

Victoria
A39

A40

ONE PENNY:
Die I - The first pearl in the crown at the left is merged into the arch, the shading under the fleur-de-lis is indistinct, and the "s" of "WALES" is open.
Die II - The first pearl is circular, the vertical shading under the fleur-de-lis is clear, and the "s" of "WALES" not so open.

2½ PENCE:
Die I - There are 12 radiating lines in the star on the Queen's breast.
Die II - There are 16 radiating lines in the star. The eye is nearly full of color.

1897			Perf. 12	
98	A38	1p rose red, II	2.25	.20
a.		Die I, perf. 11x12	2.75	.20
b.		Imperf., pair	—	
c.		Imperf. horiz., pair	300.00	
d.		Die I, perf. 12x11½	4.00	.20
e.		Die I, perf. 12	6.75	.60
f.		Die II, perf. 12x11½	1.60	.20
g.		Die II, perf. 11x12	2.75	.20
99	A39	2p deep blue	6.00	.20
a.		Perf. 11x12	2.50	.20
b.		Perf. 12x11½	2.50	.20
100	A40	2½p dp purple, II	6.75	1.10
a.		Die I, perf. 12x11	6.75	1.40
b.		Die I, perf. 11	7.50	2.00
c.		Die I, perf. 11½x12	9.50	1.10
d.		Die II, perf. 11x12	5.75	1.10
e.		Die II, perf. 11½x12	8.00	1.10
		Nos. 98-100 (3)	15.00	1.50

Sixtieth year of Queen Victoria's reign.
See Nos. 103-104, 110-112, 122-124.

Type of 1861

1897	Engr.	Wmk. 53	Perf. 11	
101	A16	5sh red violet	37.50	13.50
a.		Horiz. pair, imperf. btwn.	3,000.	
b.		Perf. 11x12 or 12x11	40.00	17.50
c.		Perf. 12	45.00	18.00

Perf. 12x11½, 11½x12

1899, Oct.		Typo.	Wmk. 55	
HALF PENNY:				
Die I - Narrow "H" in "HALF."				
102	A37	½p blue green, I	1.00	.20
a.		Imperf., pair	60.00	70.00
103	A39	2p ultra	1.60	.20
a.		Imperf., pair	57.50	
104	A40	2½p dk blue, II	2.75	.65
a.		Imperf., pair	90.00	
104B	A27	4p org brown	9.00	3.75
c.		Imperf., pair	275.00	
105	A28	6p emerald	67.50	20.00
a.		Imperf., pair	210.00	
106	A28	6p orange	11.00	1.25
a.		6p yellow	12.00	1.25
b.		Imperf., pair	175.00	
106C	A29	8p magenta	18.00	3.00
		Nos. 102-106C (7)	110.85	29.05

Lyrebird
A41

"Australia"
A42

1903			Perf. 12x11½	
107	A41	2sh6p blue green	42.50	16.00

See Nos. 119, 131.

1903 Wmk. 70 Perf. 12½

108	A42	9p org brn & ultra	10.00	2.50
a.		Perf. 11	675.00	375.00

See No. 128.

Type of 1885-86

1904 Wmk. 56 Perf. 11
Chalky Paper
"POSTAGE" in Blue

108B	A24	10sh brt rose & vio	225.00	75.00
c.		Perf. 12x11	150.00	40.00
d.		Perf. 12	150.00	60.00

The watermark (NSW) of No. 108B is 20x7mm, with rounded angles in "N" and "W." On No. 75, the watermark is 21x7mm, with sharp angles in the "N" and "W."

HALF PENNY:
Die II - Wide "H" in "HALF."

Perf. 11, 11x12½, 12x11½ and Compound

1905-06 Wmk. 12

109	A37	½p blue grn, II	1.50	.40
a.		½p blue green, I	2.50	.40
b.		Booklet pane of 12		
110	A38	1p car rose, II	1.50	.20
a.		Booklet pane of 6		
b.		Booklet pane of 12		
111	A39	2p deep ultra	1.75	.20
112	A40	2½p dk blue, II	3.25	1.40
113	A27	4p org brown	8.50	3.25
114	A28	6p orange	11.50	1.60
a.		6p yellow	13.00	1.60
b.		Perf. 11	225.00	
115	A29	8p magenta	18.00	3.50
117	A20	10p violet	12.50	3.50
118	A30	1sh vio brown	16.00	1.60
119	A41	2sh6p blue green	27.50	16.00

Wmk. 199

120	A32	20sh ultra	175.00	67.50
	Nos. 109-115,117-120 (11)		277.00	99.15

1906-07 Wmk. 13

121	A37	½p green, I	5.00	1.00
122	A38	1p rose, II	5.00	.75
123	A39	2p ultra	5.00	.75
124	A40	2½p blue, II	45.00	
125	A27	4p org brown	10.00	5.00
126	A28	6p orange	25.00	12.50
127	A29	8p red violet	25.00	15.00
128	A42	9p org brn & ultra, perf. 12x12½ ('06)	8.00	1.25
a.		Perf. 11	55.00	40.00
129	A20	10p violet	25.00	20.00
130	A30	1sh vio brown	25.00	5.00
131	A41	2sh6p blue green	50.00	30.00
	Nos. 121-131 (11)		228.00	
	Nos. 121-123,125-128,130-131 (9)			71.25

Portions of some of the sheets on which the above are printed show the watermark "COMMONWEALTH OF AUSTRALIA." Stamps may also be found from portions of the sheet without watermark.

SEMI-POSTAL STAMPS

SP1

Allegory of Charity — SP2

Illustrations reduced.

1897, June Wmk. 55 Perf. 11

B1	SP1	1p (1sh) grn & brn	37.50	37.50
B2	SP2	2½p (2sh6p) rose, bl & gold	200.00	200.00

Diamond Jubilee of Queen Victoria. The difference between the postal and face values of these stamps was donated to a fund for a home for consumptives.

REGISTRATION STAMPS

Queen Victoria — R1

Unwmk.

1856, Jan. 1 Engr. Imperf.

F1	R1	(6p) orange & blue	675.00	175.00
F2	R1	(6p) red & blue	675.00	150.00
a.		Frame printed on back	2,750.	2,000.

1860 Perf. 12, 13

F3	R1	(6p) orange & blue	350.00	45.00
F4	R1	(6p) red & blue	260.00	45.00

Nos. F1 to F4 exist also on paper with papermaker's watermark in sheet.

1863 Wmk. 49

F5	R1	(6p) red & blue	75.00	15.00

Fifty varieties.

Nos. F1-F2 were reprinted on thin white wove unwatermarked paper and on thick yellowish wove unwatermarked paper; the former are usually overprinted "SPECIMEN."

No. F4 was reprinted on thin white wove unwatermarked paper; perf. 10 and overprinted "REPRINT" in black.

POSTAGE DUE STAMPS

D1

Perf. 10, 11, 11½, 12 and Compound

1891-92 Typo. Wmk. 55

J1	D1	½p green, perf 10	3.25	2.50
J2	D1	1p green	4.50	.90
a.		Perf. 12	18.00	3.75
J3	D1	2p green	7.25	1.25
a.		Perf. 10x12	17.00	4.00
J4	D1	3p green	12.50	3.50
J5	D1	4p green	10.00	1.25
J6	D1	6p green, perf 10	17.50	3.25
J7	D1	8p green, perf 10	70.00	10.00
J8	D1	5sh green, perf 10	150.00	32.50
a.		Perf. 11	225.00	85.00

Perf. 12x10

J9	D1	10sh green	200.00	85.00
a.		Perf. 10	325.00	50.00
J10	D1	20sh green	250.00	125.00
a.		Perf. 10	350.00	80.00
b.		Perf. 12	325.00	
	Nos. J1-J10 (10)		725.00	265.15

Nos. J1-J5 exist on both ordinary and chalky paper.
Used values for Nos. J8-J10 are for c-t-o copies.

OFFICIAL STAMPS

Regular Issues Overprinted in Black or Red

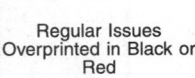

Perf. 10, 11, 12, 13 and Compound

1879-80 Wmk. 54

O1	A17	1p red	11.00	3.00
a.		Perf. 10	300.00	40.00
b.		Perf. 10x13	22.50	4.75
O2	A18	2p blue	15.00	3.00
a.		Perf. 11x12		225.00
b.		Perf. 10	225.00	40.00
O3	A15	3p green (R)	400.00	275.00
O4	A15	3p green	200.00	60.00
a.		Watermarked "6"		450.00
b.		Double overprint		
O5	A19	4p red brown	200.00	10.00
a.		Perf. 10x13	275.00	75.00
O6	A11	5p dark green	22.50	14.00
O7	A21	6p lilac	275.00	9.00
a.		Perf. 10	325.00	60.00
b.		Perf. 10x13		150.00

O8	A13	8p yellow (R)	1,000.	200.00
O9	A13	8p yellow		20.00
a.		Perf. 10	340.00	100.00
O10	A23	1sh black (R)	275.00	10.00
a.		Perf. 10		22.50
b.		Perf. 10x13		27.50

1880 Wmk. 53

O11	A16	5sh lilac, perf. 11	240.00	75.00
a.		Double overprint		1,600.
b.		Perf. 10	340.00	140.00
c.		Perf. 12x10	375.00	110.00
d.		Perf. 13	425.00	82.50
e.		Perf. 10x12		

1881 Wmk. 55

O12	A17	1p red	8.00	1.60
a.		Perf. 10x13		200.00
O13	A18	2p blue	7.50	1.00
a.		Perf. 10x13	325.00	90.00
O14	A15	3p green	6.50	3.25
a.		Double overprint		
b.		Perf. 12	225.00	125.00
c.		Perf. 11		
O15	A19	4p red brown	27.50	3.75
a.		Perf. 10x12	175.00	80.00
b.		Perf. 12	325.00	200.00
O16	A11	5p dark green	12.00	12.00
a.		Perf. 12	125.00	
b.		Perf. 10x12	—	
O17	A21	6p lilac	20.00	5.00
a.		Perf. 12		55.00
b.		Perf. 11x12	65.00	14.50
O18	A13	8p yellow	25.00	10.00
a.		Double overprint		
b.		Perf. 12	210.00	45.00
O19	A23	1sh black (R)	25.00	6.50
a.		Double overprint		190.00
b.		Perf. 10x13		65.00
c.		Perf. 11	22.50	7.00
	Nos. O12-O19 (8)		131.50	43.10

Beware of other red overprints on watermark 55 stamps.

1881 Wmk. 56

O20	A17	1p red	30.00	8.00

1887-90

O21	A24	10sh on #75		1,350.
O22	A24	£1 on #75A	5,500.	3,500.

No. 75 Overprinted O S

1889

O23	A24	10sh rose & vio	1,750.00	600.00
a.		Perf. 10	3,200.	2,000.

Overprinted

1888-89 Wmk. 55

O24	A25	1p violet	2.00	.30
a.		Overprinted "O" only		
O25	A26	2p blue	3.75	.30
O26	A27	4p red brown	10.00	3.00
O27	A28	6p carmine	8.00	4.00
O28	A29	8p red lilac	18.00	9.00
O29	A30	1sh vio brown	16.00	3.00
a.		Double overprint		
	Nos. O24-O29 (6)		57.75	19.60

Wmk. 53

O30	A31	5sh violet (R)	625.00	450.00
O31	A32	20sh ultra	1,500.	750.00

1890 Wmk. 57

O32	A31	5sh violet	150.00	65.00
a.		Perf. 12	575.00	125.00

Wmk. 58

O33	A32	20sh ultra	1,800.	550.00

Centenary of the founding of the Colony (Nos. O24-O33).

1891 Wmk. 55

O34	A17(a)	½p on 1p gray & black	50.00	45.00
a.		Double overprint		
O35	A33	2½p ultra	7.50	5.00
O36	A21(b)	7½p on 6p brn & black	32.50	30.00
O37	A23(b)	12½p on 1sh red & black	60.00	60.00
	Nos. O34-O37 (4)		150.00	140.00

1892

O38	A37	½p gray	5.50	8.00

1894 Wmk. 54

O39	A22	9p on 10p red brn	375.00	375.00

Wmk. 52

O40	A20	10p lilac, perf. 10	200.00	175.00
a.		Perf. 11x10	300.00	300.00

The official stamps became obsolete on Dec. 31, 1894. In Aug., 1895, sets of 32 varieties of "O.S." stamps, together with some envelopes and postal cards, were placed on sale at the Sydney post office at £2 per set.

These sets contained most of the varieties listed above and a few which are not known in the original issues. An obliteration consisting of the letters G.P.O. or N.S.W. in three concentric ovals was lightly applied to the center of each block of four stamps.

It is understood that the earlier stamps and many of the overprints were reprinted to make up these sets.

QUEENSLAND

'kwēnz-ˌland

LOCATION — Northeastern part of Australia
GOVT. — British Crown Colony
AREA — 670,500 sq. mi.
POP. —498,129 (1901)
CAPITAL — Brisbane

Originally a part of New South Wales, Queensland was constituted a separate colony in 1859. It was one of the six British Colonies that united in 1901 to form the Commonwealth of Australia.

12 Pence = 1 Shilling
20 Shillings = 1 Pound

Values for unused stamps are for examples with original gum as defined in the catalogue introduction. Very fine examples of Nos. 4-73, 84-125, 128-140, and F1-F3b will have perforations touching the design on at least one or more sides due to the narrow spacing of the stamps on the plates. Stamps with perfs clear of the design on all four sides are scarce and will command higher prices.

Watermarks

Wmk. 5- Small Star

Wmk. 6- Large Star

Wmk. 12- Crown and Single-lined A

Wmk. 13- Crown and Double-lined A

Wmk. 65- "Queensland Postage Stamps" in Sheet in Script Capitals

Wmks. 66 & 67- "Queensland" in Large Single-lined Roman Capitals in the Sheet and Short-pointed Star to Each Stamp (Stars Vary Slightly in Size and Shape)

Wmk. 68- Crown and Q

Wmk. 69- Large Crown and Q

There are two varieties of the watermark 68, differing slightly in the position and shape of the crown and the tongue of the "Q."

Wmk. 70- V and Crown

Queen Victoria — A1

Wmk. 6
			1860, Nov. 1 Engr.	Imperf.
1	A1	1p deep rose	3,000.	750.
2	A1	2p deep blue	5,750.	2,000.
3	A1	6p deep green	4,000.	750.

Clean-Cut Perf. 14 to 16
4	A1	1p deep rose	1,600.	225.
5	A1	2p deep blue	450.	90.00
a.	Horiz. pair, imperf between			
6	A1	6p deep green	475.	55.00

Clean-Cut Perf. 14 to 16
1860-61				Wmk. 5
6A	A1	2p blue	475.00	90.00
b.	Horiz. pair, imperf., vert		925.00	
6D	A1	3p brown ('61)	250.00	55.00
6E	A1	6p deep green	500.00	55.00
6F	A1	1sh gray violet	475.00	75.00

Regular Perf. 14
| 6H | A1 | 1p rose | 110.00 | 35.00 |
| 6I | A1 | 2p deep blue | 300.00 | 50.00 |

Rough Perf. 14 to 16
7	A1	1p deep rose	70.00	32.50
8	A1	2p blue	90.00	32.50
a.	Horiz. pair, imperf between	2,000.	
9	A1	3p brown ('61)	50.00	27.50
a.	Horiz. pair, imperf. vert.	1,800.	

10	A1	6p deep green	140.00	25.00
a.	6p yellow green		175.00	25.00
11	A1	1sh dull violet	360.00	77.50

Thick Yellowish Paper
Square Perf. 12½ to 13
1862-67				Unwmk.
12	A1	1p Indian red	300.00	65.00
13	A1	1p orange ('63)	55.00	13.50
a.	Perf. 13, round holes ('67)	55.00	13.50
b.	Horiz. pair, imperf. between		
c.	Imperf., pair	—	525.00
14	A1	2p deep blue	35.00	13.50
a.	2p pale blue	80.00	27.50
b.	Perf. 13, round holes ('67)	80.00	25.00
c.	Imperf., pair	—	550.00
e.	Horiz. pair, imperf. between		950.00
f.	Vert. pair, imperf between	1,150	
15	A1	3p brown ('63)	50.00	27.50
a.	Imperf.		
b.	Perf. 13, round holes ('67)	55.00	32.50
16	A1	6p yellow grn ('63)	72.50	13.50
a.	6p green	125.00	25.00
b.	Perf. 13, round holes ('67)	110.00	22.50
c.	Imperf., pair	—	550.00
d.	Horiz. pair, imperf. between		1,050.
17	A1	1sh gray ('63)	125.00	22.50
b.	Imperf. horizontally		
c.	Horiz. pair, imperf. between	—	1,100.
d.	Perf. 13, round holes ('67)		

White Wove Paper
1865		Wmk. 5	Rough Perf. 13	
18	A1	1p orange	60.00	18.00
a.	Horiz. pair, imperf. vert.	425.00	
19	A1	2p light blue	50.00	14.50
a.	Vert. pair, imperf. horiz.	875.00	
b.	Half used as 1p on cover		2,000.
20	A1	6p yellow green	125.00	22.50
		Nos. 18-20 (3)	235.00	55.00

Perf. 13, Round Holes
1866				Wmk. 65
21	A1	1p orange vermilion	140.00	25.00
22	A1	2p blue	50.00	16.00
b.	Diagonal half used as 1p on cover	—	

1866	Unwmk.	Litho.	Perf. 13	
23	A1	4p lilac	100.00	16.00
a.	4p slate	150.00	20.00
24	A1	5sh pink	225.00	55.00
b.	Vert. pair, imperf between		950.00

Wmk. 66, 67
1868-74		Engr.	Perf. 13	
25	A1	1p orange ('71)	40.00	4.50
26	A1	2p blue	40.00	2.50
27	A1	3p grnsh brn ('71)	90.00	5.00
a.	3p brown	80.00	5.00
b.	3p olive brown	80.00	5.50
28	A1	6p yel green ('71)	125.00	7.75
a.	6p deep green	160.00	14.50
30	A1	1sh grnsh gray ('72)	375.00	40.00
31	A1	1sh violet ('74)	225.00	20.00

Perf. 12
32	A1	1p orange	250.00	27.50
33	A1	2p blue	575.00	35.00
34	A1	3p brown	325.00	140.00
35	A1	6p deep green	850.00	45.00
36	A1	1sh violet	375.00	45.00

Perf. 13x12
36A	A1	1p orange		225.00
37	A1	2p blue	1,250.	50.00
37A	A1	3p brown		1,100.

The reprints are perforated 13 and the colors differ slightly from those of the originals.

1868-75		Wmk. 68	Perf. 13	
38	A1	1p orange	45.00	4.50
a.	Imperf pair	175.00	
39	A1	1p rose ('74)	50.00	8.00
40	A1	2p blue	37.50	4.25
b.	Imperf., pair	300.00	
41	A1	3p brown ('75)	65.00	14.00
42	A1	6p yel green ('69)	100.00	7.50
a.	6p apple green	125.00	9.00
b.	6p deep green	125.00	9.00
43	A1	1sh violet ('75)	175.00	30.00
		Nos. 38-43 (6)	472.50	68.25

No. 40 exists in vert. pair, imperf. btwn.

1876-78			Perf. 12	
44	A1	1p orange	35.00	4.50
a.	Imperf.	350.00	
45	A1	1p rose	45.00	10.00
46	A1	2p blue	22.50	1.40
47	A1	3p brown	60.00	9.00
48	A1	6p yellow green	140.00	4.50
a.	6p apple green	140.00	6.50
b.	6p deep green	140.00	7.00
49	A1	1sh violet	42.50	9.00
m.	Vert. pair, imperf between		
		Nos. 44-49 (6)	345.00	38.40

#44, 49 exist in vertical pairs, imperf. between.

Perf. 13x12
49B	A1	1p orange		150.00
49C	A1	2p blue	1,600.	250.00
49D	A1	4p yellow		300.00
49E	A1	6p deep green		300.00

Perf. 12½x13
| 49G | A1 | 1p orange vermilion | | 325.00 |
| 49H | A1 | 2p deep blue | | 350.00 |

The reprints are perforated 12 and are in paler colors than the originals.

1879		Unwmk.	Perf. 12	
50	A1	6p pale emerald	175.00	25.00
a.	Horiz. pair, imperf. vert.		650.00

A2

A3

1875-81	Litho.	Wmk. 68	Perf. 13	
50B	A1	4p yellow ('75)	800.00	42.50

Perf. 12
51	A1	4p buff ('76)	600.00	22.50
a.	4p yellow	600.00	24.00
52	A1	2sh pale blue ('81)	65.00	22.50
a.	2sh deep blue	75.00	22.50
b.	Imperf.		
53	A2	2sh6p lt red ('81)	110.00	40.00
54	A1	5sh orange brn ('81)	150.00	60.00
a.	5sh fawn	150.00	60.00
55	A1	10sh brown ('81)	325.00	110.00
a.	Imperf., pair	800.00	
56	A1	20sh rose ('81)	650.00	125.00
		Nos. 50B-56 (7)	2,700.	422.50

Nos. 53-56, 62-64, 74-83 with pen (revenue) cancellations removed are often offered as unused.

1879-81	Typo.	Wmk. 68	Perf. 12	
57	A3	1p rose red	13.50	1.75
a.	1p red orange	16.00	3.00
b.	1p brown orange	35.00	5.50
c.	"QOEENSLAND"	100.00	30.00
d.	Imperf.		
e.	Vert. pair, imperf. horiz.		325.00
58	A3	2p gray blue	26.00	1.25
a.	2p deep ultra	29.00	1.25
b.	Imperf.		
c.	"PENGE"	125.00	37.50
d.	"TW" joined	25.00	1.75
e.	Vert. pair, imperf. horiz.	450.00	
59	A3	4p orange yellow	100.00	10.00
a.	Imperf.		
60	A3	6p yellow green	62.50	4.50
61	A3	1sh pale violet ('81)	50.00	5.50
a.	1sh deep violet	52.50	4.50
		Nos. 57-61 (5)	252.00	23.00

The stamps of type A3 were electrotyped from plates made up of groups of four types, differing in minor details. Two dies were used for the 1p and 2p, giving eight varieties for each of those values.
Nos. 59-60 exist imperf. vertically.
For surcharge see No. 65.

Moire on Back
1878-79				Unwmk.
62	A3	1p brown org ('79)	375.00	55.00
a.	"QOEENSLAND"		1,800.
63	A3	2p deep ultra ('79)	450.00	27.50
a.	"PENGE"	4,250.	700.00
64	A1	1sh red violet	100.00	47.50
		Nos. 62-64 (3)	925.00	130.00

No. 57b
Surcharged
Vertically in Black

Half-penny

1881				Wmk. 68
65	A3	½p on 1p brn org	175.00	95.00
a.	"QOEENSLAND"	950.00	750.00

A4

A5

1882-83		Typo.	Perf. 12	
66	A4	1p pale red	5.25	.35
a.	1p rose	5.25	.35
b.	Imperf. pair		
67	A4	2p gray blue	8.00	.35
a.	2p deep blue		
b.	Imperf.		
68	A4	4p yellow ('83)	18.00	2.00
a.	"PENGE"	125.00	45.00
b.	Imperf., pair		

69	A4	6p yellow green	10.00	1.25
70	A4	1sh violet ('83)	19.00	2.25
		Nos. 66-70 (5)	60.25	6.20

There are eight minor varieties of the 1p, twelve of the 2p and four each of the other values. On the 1p there is a period after "PENNY." On all values the lines of shading on the neck extend from side to side.
Compare design A4 with A6, A10, A11, A15, A16.

1883			Perf. 9½x12	
71	A4	1p rose	140.00	25.00
72	A4	2p gray blue	310.00	50.00
73	A4	1sh pale violet	200.00	30.00
		Nos. 71-73 (3)	650.00	105.00

Beware of faked perfs.
See Nos. 94, 95, 100.

Wmk. 68 Twice Sideways
1882-85	Engr.		Perf. 12	
		Thin Paper		
74	A5	2sh ultra	60.00	22.50
75	A5	2sh6p vermilion	50.00	22.50
76	A5	5sh car rose ('85)	50.00	25.00
77	A5	10sh brown	95.00	42.50
78	A5	£1 dk grn ('83)	225.00	125.00
		Nos. 74-78 (5)	480.00	237.50

The 2sh, 5sh and £1 exist imperf.
There are two varieties of the watermark on Nos. 74-78, as in the 1879-81 issue.
Copies with revenue cancels sell for $3.25-6.50.

1886		Wmk. 69	Perf. 12	
		Thick Paper		
79	A5	2sh ultra	90.00	32.50
80	A5	2sh6p vermilion	40.00	22.50
81	A5	5sh car rose	37.50	30.00
82	A5	10sh dark brown	100.00	42.50
83	A5	£1 dark green	175.00	60.00
		Nos. 79-83 (5)	442.50	187.50

High value stamps with cancellations removed are offered as unused.
Copies with revenue cancels sell for $3.25-6.50.
See Nos. 126-127, 141-144.

A6

Redrawn
1887-89	Typo.	Wmk. 68	Perf. 12	
84	A6	1p orange	4.00	.35
85	A6	2p gray blue	8.00	.50
a.	2p deep ultra	11.50	.90
86	A6	2sh red brown ('89)	65.00	37.50

Perf. 9½x12
| 88 | A6 | 2p deep ultra | 225.00 | 90.00 |
| | | Nos. 84-88 (4) | 302.00 | 128.35 |

The 1p has no period after the value.
In the redrawn stamps the shading lines on the neck are not completed at the left, leaving an irregular white line along that side.
Variety "LA" joined exists on Nos. 84-86, 88, 90, 91, 93, 97, 98, 102.
On No. 88 beware of faked perfs.

A7

A8

1890-92			Perf. 12½, 13	
89	A7	½p green	4.00	1.10
90	A6	1p orange red	2.75	.20
a.	Imperf.	30.00	30.00
91	A6	2p gray blue	4.50	.20
92	A8	2½p rose carmine	10.00	1.10
93	A6	3p brown ('92)	9.00	2.00
94	A4	4p orange	16.00	1.75
a.	4p yellow	15.00	1.75
b.	"PENGE"	75.00	25.00
95	A4	6p green	11.00	1.75
96	A6	2sh red brown	40.00	12.50
		Nos. 89-96 (8)	97.25	20.60

The ½p and 3p exist imperf.

1895		Wmk. 69	Perf. 12½, 13	
		Thick Paper		
98	A6	1p orange	3.25	.45
99	A6	2p gray blue	3.25	.45

Perf. 12

100	A4	1sh pale violet	16.00	3.75
		Nos. 98-100 (3)	22.50	4.65

A9   A10

Moiré on Back

1895   **Unwmk.**   *Perf. 12½, 13*

101	A9	½p green	2.25	1.75
a.		Without moire	55.00	
102	A6	1p orange	2.25	1.00
a.		"PE" missing	110.00	75.00

Wmk. 68

103	A9	½p green	1.75	.75
a.		½p deep green	1.50	.75
b.		Printed on both sides	80.00	
104	A10	1p orange	3.25	.20
105	A10	2p gray blue	5.00	.35

Wmk. 69
Thick Paper

106	A9	½p green	2.25	1.00

1895-96   **Unwmk.**   **Thin Paper**
Crown and Q Faintly Impressed

107	A9	½p green	2.50	1.10
108	A10	1p orange	3.50	1.00
108A	A6	2p gray blue	11.00	

A11   A12

A13

1895-96   **Wmk. 68**

109	A11	1p red	7.50	.20
110	A12	2½p rose	12.00	3.50
111	A13	5p violet brown	14.00	3.50
111A	A11	6p yellow green		

A14   A15

A16   A17

A18   A19

TWO PENCE:
Type I - Point of bust does not touch frame.
Type II - First redrawing. The top of the crown, the chignon and the point of the bust touch the frame. The forehead is completely shaded.
Type III - Second redrawing. The top of crown does not touch the frame, though the chignon and the point of the bust do. The forehead and the bridge of the nose are not shaded.

1897-1900   *Perf. 12½, 13*

112	A14	½p deep green	3.50	3.50
a.		Perf. 12		110.00
113	A15	1p red	2.00	.20
a.		Perf. 12	2.75	.60
114	A16	2p gray blue (I)	2.00	.20
a.		Perf. 12	2.00	.20
115	A17	2½p rose	16.00	12.50
116	A17	2½p violet, *blue*	9.00	1.10
117	A15	3p brown	8.00	1.40
118	A15	4p bright yellow	8.00	1.40
119	A18	5p violet brown	7.50	1.40
120	A15	6p yellow green	8.00	1.75
121	A19	1sh lilac	12.50	1.60
a.		1sh light violet	14.50	1.75
122	A19	2sh turq blue	30.00	14.00
		Nos. 112-122 (11)	106.50	39.05

1898   *Serrated Roulette 13*

123	A15	1p scarlet	4.50	2.75
a.		Serrated and perf. 13	6.00	3.75
b.		Serrated in black	9.00	9.00
c.		Serrated without color and in black	9.00	11.00
d.		Same as "b," and perf. 13	80.00	80.00
e.		Same as "c," and perf. 13	100.00	85.00

Victoria   "Australia"
A20   A21

1899   **Typo.**   *Perf. 12, 12½, 13*

124	A20	½p blue green	1.75	.65

Unwatermarked stamps are proofs.

1903   **Wmk. 70**   *Perf. 12½*

NINE PENCE:
Type I- "QUEENSLAND" 18x1 ½mm.
Type II- "QUEENSLAND" 17½x1 ¼mm.

125	A21	9p org brn & ultra, II	13.00	2.50
a.		Type I	13.00	2.50

See No. 128.

Type of 1882
Perf. 12, 12½, 13

1906   **Litho.**   **Wmk. 68**

126	A5	5sh rose	125.00	75.00
127	A5	£1 dark green	400.00	125.00

1907   **Typo.** **Wmk. 13** *Perf. 12½*

128	A21	9p yel brn & ultra, I	13.50	3.00
a.		Type II	25.00	3.75
b.		Perf. 11, type II		225.00

1907   **Wmk. 68**   *Perf. 12½, 13*

129	A16	2p ultra, type II	8.00	2.50
129A	A18	5p dark brown	9.00	2.25
b.		5p olive brown	10.00	2.50

1907-09   **Wmk. 12**

130	A20	½p deep green	1.60	.90
131	A15	1p red	2.00	.20
a.		Imperf., pair	200.00	
132	A16	2p ultra, II	6.75	.20
133	A16	2p ultra, III	2.50	.20
134	A15	3p pale brown	10.00	1.25
135	A15	4p bright yellow	11.00	2.50
136	A15	4p gray black ('09)	12.00	2.00
137	A18	5p brown	7.75	2.50
a.		5p olive brown	12.50	3.25
138	A15	6p yellow green	11.00	2.25
139	A19	1sh violet	13.50	3.50
140	A19	2sh turquoise bl	32.50	11.00

Wmk. 12 Sideways
Litho.

141	A5	2sh6p deep orange	45.00	35.00
142	A5	5sh rose	50.00	35.00
143	A5	10sh dark brown	90.00	45.00
144	A5	£1 blue green	200.00	125.00
		Nos. 130-144 (15)	495.60	266.50

POSTAL FISCAL STAMPS

Authorised for postal use from Jan. 1, 1880. Authorization withdrawn July 1, 1892.

Used values are for examples with postal cancellations used from Jan. 1, 1880 through June 30, 1892.

Beware of copies with a pen cancellation removed and a fake postmark added.

Queen Victoria

		PF1	PF2	

1866-74 **Engr.** **Unwmk.** *Perf. 13*

AR1	PF1	1p blue	30.00	8.00
AR2	PF1	6p violet	30.00	35.00
AR3	PF1	1sh green	35.00	10.00
AR4	PF1	2sh brown	100.00	50.00
AR5	PF1	2sh 6p red	100.00	37.50
AR6	PF1	5sh yellow	300.00	75.00
AR7	PF1	6sh yellow		
AR8	PF1	10sh yel grn	400.00	175.00
AR9	PF1	20sh rose	500.00	175.00

Wmk. 68

AR10	PF1	1p blue	20.00	20.00
AR11	PF1	6p violet	27.50	30.00
AR12	PF1	6p blue	27.50	17.50
AR13	PF1	1sh green	35.00	17.50
AR14	PF1	2sh brown	100.00	35.00
AR15	PF1	5sh yellow	300.00	75.00
AR16	PF1	10sh yel grn	400.00	110.00
AR17	PF1	20sh rose	500.00	175.00

1872-73 **Wmk. 69** *Perf. 13*

AR18	PF2	1p lilac	12.00	8.00
AR19	PF2	6p brown	25.00	12.50
AR20	PF2	1sh green	35.00	15.00
AR21	PF2	2sh blue	50.00	12.50
AR22	PF2	2sh 6p ver	75.00	30.00
AR23	PF2	5sh org brn	125.00	30.00
AR24	PF2	10sh brown	300.00	85.00
AR25	PF2	20sh rose	500.00	150.00

Perf. 12

AR26	PF2	1p lilac	12.00	8.00
AR27	PF2	6p brown	25.00	12.50
AR28	PF2	2sh blue	50.00	12.50
AR29	PF2	2sh 6p ver	75.00	30.00
AR30	PF2	5sh org brn	125.00	30.00
AR31	PF2	10sh brown	300.00	85.00
AR32	PF2	20sh rose	500.00	150.00

Unwmk.
Perf. 13

AR33	PF2	1p lilac	15.00	10.00
AR34	PF2	6p lilac	75.00	37.50
AR35	PF2	6p brown	25.00	12.50
AR36	PF2	1sh green	35.00	15.00
AR37	PF2	2sh blue	55.00	60.00
AR38	PF2	2sh 6p ver	100.00	40.00
AR39	PF2	5sh org brn	150.00	50.00
AR40	PF2	10sh brown	300.00	100.00
AR41	PF2	20sh rose	500.00	125.00

Perf. 12

AR42	PF2	1p lilac	15.00	10.00
AR43	PF2	6p lilac	90.00	50.00
AR44	PF2	6p brown	50.00	40.00
AR45	PF2	1sh green	35.00	15.00
AR46	PF2	2sh blue	55.00	60.00
AR47	PF2	2sh 6p ver	100.00	40.00
AR48	PF2	5sh org brn	150.00	50.00
AR49	PF2	10sh brown	300.00	100.00
AR50	PF2	20sh rose	500.00	125.00

Queen Victoria — PF3

1878-79 **Engr.** **Unwmk.** *Perf. 12*

AR51	PF3	1p violet	50.00	15.00

Wmk. 68

AR52	PF3	1p violet	20.00	10.00

SEMI-POSTAL STAMPS

Queen Victoria,
Colors and
Bearers — SP1

SP2

1900, June 19   **Wmk. 68**

B1	SP1	1p red lilac	100.00	95.00
B2	SP2	2p deep violet	250.00	225.00

These stamps were sold at 1sh and 2sh respectively. The difference was applied to a patriotic fund in connection with the Boer War.

REGISTRATION STAMPS

R1

Clean-Cut Perf. 14 to 16

1861   **Wmk. 5**   **Engr.**

F1	R1	(6p) olive yellow	400.00	75.00
a.		Horiz. pair, imperf. vert.	4,000.	

Rough Perf. 14 to 16

F2	R1	(6p) dull yellow	50.00	35.00

1864   *Perf. 12½ to 13*

F3	R1	(6p) golden yellow	80.00	35.00
a.		Imperf.		
b.		Double impression	800.00	

The reprints are watermarked with a small truncated star and perforated 12.

SOUTH AUSTRALIA

ˈsauth ō-ˈstrāl-yə

LOCATION — Central part of southern Australia
GOVT. — British Colony
AREA — 380,070 sq. mi.
POP. — 358,346 (1901)
CAPITAL — Adelaide

South Australia was one of the six British colonies that united in 1901 to form the Commonwealth of Australia.

12 Pence = 1 Shilling
20 Shillings = 1 Pound

Values for unused stamps are for examples with original gum as defined in the catalogue introduction.

Very fine examples of Nos. 10-60 and O1-O60 will have perforations slightly cutting into the framelines or design on one or more sides due to the narrow spacing of the stamps on the plates.

Stamps with perfs clear on all sides are scarce to rare and will command higher to substantially higher prices.

Watermarks

Wmk. 6- Star with   Wmk. 7- Star with
Long Narrow   Short Broad
Points   Points

Wmk. 70- Crown and V

Wmk. 72- Crown and SA

Wmk. 73- Crown and SA, Letters Close

Wmk. 74- Crown and Single-lined A

Queen Victoria — A1

1855-56   Engr.   Wmk. 6   Imperf. London Print

1	A1	1p dark green	2,750.	375.
2	A1	2p dull carmine	600.	80.
3	A1	6p deep blue	2,000.	150.
4	A1	1sh violet ('56)	4,500.	

No. 4 was never put in use. Nos. 1 and 3 without watermark are proofs.

1856-59   Local Print

5	A1	1p deep yel grn ('58)	5,000.	550.00
a.		1p yellow green ('58)	4,500.	500.00
6	A1	2p blood red	1,400.	100.00
a.		Printed on both sides		750.00
b.		2p orange red ('56)	—	75.00
7	A1	2p pale red ('57)	650.00	40.00
a.		Printed on both sides		600.00
8	A1	6p slate blue ('57)	2,000.	150.00
9	A1	1sh orange ('57)	4,000.	375.00
a.		Printed on both sides		
b.		1sh red orange	—	425.00

1858-59   Rouletted

10	A1	1p yellow grn ('59)	475.00	45.00
a.		Horiz. pair, imperf. between		
b.		1p pale yellow green	475.00	50.00
11	A1	2p pale red ('59)	125.00	18.00
a.		Printed on both sides		600.00
12	A1	6p slate blue	375.00	27.50
13	A1	1sh orange ('59)	900.00	45.00
c.		Printed on both sides		1,000.

See #14-16, 19-20, 25-26, 28-29, 32, 35-36, 41-43, 47, 51-52, 69-70, 73, 113, 118. For overprints see #O1-O2, O5, O7, O9, O11-O13, O17, O20, O27, O30, O32, O39-O40, O42, O52, O76, O85.

A2   A3

Surcharge on #22-24, 34, 49-50

1860-69   Rouletted

14	A1	1p dull blue green	50.00	29.00
a.		1p deep green	225.00	65.00
b.		1p bright green	225.00	65.00
15	A1	1p sage green	55.00	27.50
16	A1	2p vermilion ('62)	50.00	4.00
a.		Horiz. pair, imperf. btwn.	700.00	300.00
b.		Rouletted and perf. all around		700.00
c.		Printed on both sides		500.00
18	A2	4p dull violet ('67)	65.00	19.00
19	A1	6p grnsh bl ('63)	65.00	4.00
20	A1	6p dull blue	90.00	6.00
a.		6p sky blue	125.00	6.50
b.		6p Prussian blue	550.00	50.00
c.		Horiz. pair, imperf btwn.		600.00
d.		6p ultramarine	60.00	3.75
e.		Horiz. pair, imperf. btwn. (#20f)	—	425.00
f.		6p indigo blue	—	52.50
g.		Rouletted and perf. all around (#20f)	—	350.00
21	A3	9p gray lilac ('69)	70.00	9.00
a.		Double impression		
c.		Rouletted and perf. all around	1,750.	275.00
22	A3	10p on 9p red org (Bl) ('66)	160.00	25.00
23	A3	10p on 9p yel (Bl) ('67)	190.00	22.50
24	A3	10p on 9p yel (Blk) ('69)	1,150.	32.50
a.		Inverted surcharge	—	2,400.
c.		Printed on both sides	—	800.
d.		Rouletted x perf. 10		
24E	A1	1sh red brown	125.00	13.00
f.		Vert. pair, imperf. btwn.		1,250.
25	A1	1sh lake brn ('65)	125.00	13.00
a.		Horiz. pair, imperf. btwn.	—	375.00
26	A1	1sh brown ('63)	140.00	17.50
a.		1sh chestnut ('64)	150.00	12.00
27	A2	2sh carmine ('67)	750.00	27.50
a.		Horiz. pair, imperf. btwn.		750.00

There are six varieties of the surcharge "TEN PENCE" in this and subsequent issues. Nos. 16b, 20g, 21c, 28a, 32c, 33a are rouletted remainders that were later perforated.

See #31, 33, 46, 48, 53, 63, 68, 72, 74, 112, 113B, 119-120. For surcharges & overprints see #34, 44-45, 49-50, 59, 67, 71, O4, O6, O8, O10, O16-O19, O18, O21, O26, O28-O29, O31, O33, O36-O38, O41, O41B, O43, O53. Compare with design A6a.

1867-72   Perf. 11½ to 12½xRoulette

28	A1	1p blue green	225.00	32.50
a.		Rouletted and perf. all around		650.00
29	A1	1p yellow green	140.00	20.00
31	A2	4p dull violet ('68)	1,500.	110.00
a.		4p purple ('69)	—	110.00
32	A1	6p Prus blue	450.00	21.00
a.		6p sky blue	500.00	17.50
c.		Printed on both sides		
d.		Rouletted and perf. all around		300.00
		6p indigo blue ('69)	475.00	25.00
33	A3	9p gray lilac ('72)		275.00
34	A3	10p on 9p yel (Bl) ('68)	800.00	35.00
a.		Printed on both sides	—	500.00
35	A1	1sh chestnut ('68)	275.00	30.00
36	A1	1sh lake brown ('69)	275.00	25.00

#44-45   3-PENCE

Perf. 10, 11½, 12½ and Compound 1867-74

41	A1	1p yellow green	45.00	17.50
42	A1	1p blue green	60.00	12.50
a.		Printed on both sides		
43	A1	2p vermilion		1,250.
44	A2	3p on 4p dp bl (Blk) ('70)	60.00	5.50
a.		3p on 4p ultra, black surcharge	125.00	5.50
b.		Surcharge omitted	20,000.	5,000.
c.		Double surcharge		4,500.
d.		Surcharged on both sides		3,250.
45	A2	3p on 4p sl bl (Red) ('70)	425.00	62.50
46	A2	4p dull violet	60.00	9.00
47	A1	6p dark blue	90.00	8.00
a.		6p sky blue	350.00	9.25
b.		Imperf. vert., pair		
48	A3	9p red lilac ('72)	47.50	5.00
a.		9p violet	110.00	5.50
b.		9p red violet	110.00	5.50
c.		Printed on both sides		350.00
49	A3	10p on 9p yel (Bl) ('68)	1,500.	26.00
50	A3	10p on 9p yel (Blk) ('69)	150.00	21.00
51	A1	1sh deep brown	150.00	12.00
52	A1	1sh red brown	100.00	12.00
a.		1sh chestnut	125.00	12.50
53	A2	2sh carmine	60.00	7.50
a.		Printed on both sides		
b.		Horiz. pair, imperf. vert.	400.00	

See Nos. 67, O14, O28, O36.

A6   A6a

1868   Typo.   Wmk. 72   Rouletted

54	A6a	2p orange red	65.00	4.00
a.		Imperf.		
b.		Printed on both sides		275.00
c.		Horiz. pair, imperf. btwn.		275.00

1869   Perf. 11½ to 12½xRoulette

55	A6a	2p orange red		150.00

1870   Perf. 10xRoulette

56	A6a	2p orange red	350.00	30.00

Perf. 10, 11½, 12½ and Compound 1868-75

57	A6	1p bl grn ('75)	24.00	4.50
58	A6a	2p orange red	13.00	1.00
a.		Printed on both sides		200.00
b.		Horiz. pair, imperf. btwn.		

Engr.

59	A3	10p on 9p yel (Bl)		1,500.

1869   Typo.   Wmk. 6   Rouletted

60	A6a	2p orange red	65.00	11.50
a.		Imperf.		
b.		Printed on both sides		

Perf. 11½ to 12½xRoulette

61	A6a	2p orange red		125.00

Perf. 11½ to 12½

61B   A6a   2p orange red

See #62, 64-66, 97-98, 105-106, 115-116, 133-134, 145-146. For surcharges & overprints see #75, O3, O22-O25, O34-O35, O44-O47, O49, O55-O56, O62-O63, O68-O69, O74, O78-O79.

1871   Wmk. 70   Perf. 10

62	A6a	2p orange red	75.00	16.00

Engr.

63	A2	4p dull violet	2,250.	350.00

Copies of the 4p from edge of sheet sometimes lack watermark.

Perf. 10, 11½, 12½ and Compound 1876-80   Typo.   Wmk. 73

64	A6	1p green	6.00	.50
65	A6a	2p orange	4.25	.50
66	A6a	2p blood red ('80)	225.00	7.50
		Nos. 64-66 (3)	235.25	8.50

See #97-98, 105-106, 115-116, 133-134, 145-146.

HALF-PENNY

No. 71   No. 75

8 PENCE

1876-84   Engr.   Wmk. 7

67	A2	3p on 4p ultra (Blk)	65.00	17.50
a.		3p on 9p deep blue		15.00
b.		Double surcharge		1,500.
68	A2	4p reddish violet	50.00	5.50
a.		4p dull violet	60.00	9.00
69	A1	6p deep blue	65.00	4.50
a.		Horiz. pair, imperf. vert.		
b.		Imperf.		
70	A1	6p pale ultra ('84)	40.00	2.25
71	A3	8p on 9p bister brn	65.00	5.50
a.		8p on 9p yellow brown	57.50	2.50
b.		8p on 9p gray brown ('80)	52.50	4.00
d.		Double surcharge		375.00
72	A3	9p rose lilac	12.00	5.50
a.		Printed on both sides		300.00
73	A1	1sh red brown	37.50	3.25
a.		1sh brown	40.00	2.50
b.		Horiz. pair, imperf. btwn.		300.00
74	A2	2sh carmine	35.00	4.50
a.		Horiz. pair, imperf. vert.		
b.		Imperf., pair	400.00	

For overprint see No. O41.

1882   Wmk. 73   Perf. 10   Black Surcharge

75	A6	½p on 1p green	10.50	4.00

A9

A10

A11

A12

Perf. 10, 11½, 12½ and Compound

1883-90   Typo.

76	A9	½p chocolate brown	2.25	.25
a.		½p red brown ('89)	2.25	.25
b.		½p bister brown	3.50	.25
78	A10	3p deep green ('86)	6.50	.75
a.		3p olive green ('90)	11.00	1.50
79	A11	4p violet ('90)	7.75	1.75
80	A12	6p blue ('87)	7.75	1.00
		Nos. 76-80 (4)	24.25	3.75

See #96, 100-101, 104, 108-109, 111. For surcharges & overprints see #94-95, 99, O48, O50-O51, O54, O57-O61, O64, O66-O67, O71, O73, O75, O81-O82.

A13

1886-96   Perf. 10, 11½ to 12½

81	A13	2sh6p violet	27.50	6.50
82	A13	5sh rose	40.00	16.00
83	A13	10sh green	100.00	25.00
84	A13	15sh buff	200.00	140.00
85	A13	£1 blue	160.00	60.00
86	A13	£2 red brown	475.00	150.00
87	A13	50sh rose red	600.00	200.00
88	A13	£3 olive green	825.00	
89	A13	£4 lemon	1,000.	
90	A13	£5 gray	2,700.	
90A	A13	£5 brown ('96)	2,600.	
91	A13	£10 bronze	3,000.	700.00
92	A13	£15 silver	6,500.	
93	A13	£20 lilac	8,250.	

For overprints see Nos. O83-O84.

#94, 99

#95

Perf. 10, 11½x12½ and Compound 1891   Brown Surcharge

94	A11	2½p on 4p green	8.00	1.40
a.		"½" nearer the "2"	30.00	20.00
b.		Pair, imperf. between		375.00
c.		Fraction bar omitted	90.00	80.00

Carmine Surcharge

95	A12	5p on 6p red brn	17.00	6.00
a.		No period after "D"	160.00	

See #99. For overprints see #O48, O57, O59.

Many stamps of the issues of 1855-91 have been reprinted; they are all on paper watermarked Crown and SA, letters wide apart, and are overprinted "REPRINT."

1893   Typo.   Perf. 15

96	A9	½p brown	3.00	.20
a.		Horiz. pair, imperf. btwn	125.00	
b.		Pair, perf. 12 btwn; perf. 15 around	200.00	50.00
97	A6	1p green	4.00	.20
98	A6a	2p orange	6.50	.20
a.		Vert. pair, imperf. between	225.00	
99	A11	2½p on 4p green	12.00	1.60
a.		"½" nearer the "2"	40.00	35.00
b.		Fraction bar omitted		
100	A11	4p gray violet	13.00	2.00
101	A12	6p blue	32.50	4.25
		Nos. 96-101 (6)	71.00	8.45

Kangaroo,
Palm — A16

Coat of
Arms — A17

1894, Mar. 1
102	A16	2½p blue violet	13.00	1.50
103	A17	5p dull violet	15.00	2.50

See Nos. 107, 110, 117, 135-136, 147, 151.
For overprints see Nos. O65, O70, O72, O80.

1895-97   *Perf. 13*
104	A9	½p pale brown	3.00	.25
105	A6	1p green	5.25	.50
a.		Vert. pair, imperf. between		
106	A6a	2p orange	4.25	.20
107	A16	2½p blue violet	7.50	.35
108	A10	3p olive green ('97)	5.00	.30
109	A11	4p bright violet	6.50	.35
110	A17	5p dull violet	7.00	.35
111	A12	6p blue	8.00	.40
		Nos. 104-111 (8)	46.50	2.70

Some authorities regard the so-called redrawn 1p stamps with thicker lettering (said to have been issued in 1897) as impressions from a new or cleaned plate.

Perf. 11½, 12½, Clean-Cut, Compound
1896   Engr.   Wmk. 7
112	A3	9p lilac rose	12.50	6.50
113	A1	1sh dark brown	26.00	5.50
a.		Horiz. pair, imperf. vert.		
c.		Horiz. pair, imperf. btwn.	180.00	
113B	A2	2sh carmine	32.50	8.00
		Nos. 112-113B (3)	71.00	20.00

Adelaide Post
Office — A18

1899   Typo.   Wmk. 73   *Perf. 13*
114	A18	½p yellow green	1.75	.25
115	A6	1p carmine	3.00	.25
a.		1p scarlet	2.75	.50
116	A6a	2p purple	2.25	.25
117	A16	2½p dark blue	7.00	.75
		Nos. 114-117 (4)	14.00	1.45

See #132, 144. For overprint see #O77.

Perf. 11½, 12½
1901   Engr.   Wmk. 72
118	A1	1sh dark brown	24.00	16.00
a.		1sh red brown	24.00	10.00
b.		Horiz. pair, imperf. vert.		
119	A2	2sh carmine	27.50	15.00

1902
120	A3	9p magenta	20.00	20.00

A19

A20

Perf. 11½, 12½ and Compound
1902-03   Typo.   Wmk. 73
121	A19	3p olive green	4.75	.75
122	A19	4p red orange	7.50	1.50
123	A19	6p blue green	6.50	1.50
124	A19	8p ultra (value 19mm long)	8.50	2.25
124A	A19	8p ultra (value 16½mm long) ('03)	13.00	3.00
b.		"EIGNT"	900.00	3,000.
125	A19	9p claret	8.50	2.25
a.		Pair, imperf. between	300.00	
126	A19	10p org buff	11.00	3.50
127	A19	1sh brown ('03)	12.00	3.00
a.		Horiz. or vert. pair, imperf. btwn.	700.00	
128	A19	2sh6p purple	32.50	9.00
129	A19	5sh rose	75.00	52.50

130	A19	10sh green ('03)	110.00	65.00
131	A19	£1 blue	275.00	150.00
		Nos. 121-131 (12)	564.25	294.25

1904   *Perf. 12x11½*
132	A18	½p yellow green	3.00	.55
133	A6	1p rose	6.50	.60
134	A6a	2p purple	6.50	.60
135	A16	2½p dark blue	14.00	1.50
136	A17	5p dull violet	11.00	1.75
		Nos. 132-136 (5)	41.00	5.00

1904-08   *Perf. 12 and 12x11½*
137	A20	6p blue green	8.25	1.75
138	A20	8p ultra ('06)	11.50	2.25
139	A20	9p claret	8.00	1.60
139A	A20	10p org buff ('07)	20.00	5.25
b.		Pair, imperf. between	325.00	225.00
140	A20	1sh brown	12.00	2.00
a.		Pair, imperf. between	250.00	
141	A20	2sh6p purple ('05)	55.00	8.25
142	A20	5sh scarlet	55.00	32.50
142B	A20	10sh green ('08)	140.00	125.00
143	A20	£1 deep blue	200.00	140.00
		Nos. 137-143 (9)	509.75	318.60

See Nos. 148-150, 152-157.

1906-12   Wmk. 74
144	A18	½p green	1.50	.20
145	A6	1p carmine	1.50	.20
146	A6a	2p purple	2.50	.20
a.		Horiz. pair, imperf. between		
147	A16	2½p dk blue ('11)	10.50	1.50
148	A20	3p ol grn (value 19mm long)	6.50	1.25
a.		Horiz. pair, imperf. between		
149	A20	3p ol grn (value 17mm long) ('09)	8.50	1.50
150	A20	4p red orange	9.75	1.75
151	A17	5p dull vio ('08)	8.50	2.00
152	A20	6p blue grn ('07)	7.50	1.10
a.		Vert. pair, imperf. between	240.00	
153	A20	8p ultra ('09)	15.00	5.50
154	A20	9p claret	15.00	3.00
a.		Vert. pair, imperf. between	195.00	
b.		Horiz. pair, imperf. between	225.00	
155	A20	1sh brown	11.00	3.00
a.		Pair, imperf. between	175.00	
156	A20	2sh6p purple ('09)	32.50	10.50
157	A20	5sh lt red ('12)	82.50	
		Nos. 144-157 (14)	212.75	31.70

OFFICIAL STAMPS

For Departments
Regular Issues Overprinted in Red, Black or Blue:

A. (Architect), A. G. (Attorney General), A. O. (Audit Office), B. D. (Barracks Department), B. G. (Botanical Gardens), B. M. (Bench of Magistrates), C. (Customs), C. D. (Convict Department), C. L. (Crown Lands), C. O. (Commissariat Officer), C. S. (Chief Secretary), C. Sgn. (Colonial Surgeon), C. P. (Commissioner of Police), C. T. (Commissioner of Titles), D. B. (Destitute Board), D. R. (Deed Registry), E. (Engineer), E. B. (Education Board), G. P. (Government Printer), G. S. (Government Storekeeper), G. T. (Goolwa Tramway), G. F. (Gold Fields), H. (Hospital), H. A. (House of Assembly), I. A. (Immigration Agent), I. E. (Intestate Estates), I. S. (Inspector of Sheep), L. A. (Lunatic Asylum), L. C. (Legislative Council), L. L. (Legislative Library), L. T. (Land Titles), M. (Military), M. B. (Marine Board), M. R. (Manager of Railways), M. R. G. (Main Roads Gambierton), N. T. (Northern Territory), O. A. (Official Assignee), P. (Police), P. A. (Protector of Aborigines), P. O. (Post Office), P. S. (Private Secretary), P. W. (Public Works), R. B. (Road Board), R. G. (Registrar General of Births, &c.), S. (Sheriff), S. C. (Supreme Court), S. G. (Surveyor General), S. M. (Stipendiary Magistrate), S. T. (Superintendent of Telegraph), T. (Treasurer), T. R. (Titles Registry), V. (Volunteers), V. A. (Valuator), V. N. (Vaccination), W. (Waterworks).

1868-74   Wmk. 6   *Rouletted*
O1	A1	1p green	
O2	A1	2p pale red	
O3	A6a	2p vermilion	
O4	A2	4p dull violet	
O5	A1	6p slate blue	
O6	A3	9p gray lilac	
O7	A1	1sh brown	
O8	A2	2sh carmine	

Perf. 11½ to 12½ x Roulette
O9	A1	1p green	
O10	A2	4p dull violet	
O11	A1	6p blue	
O12	A1	1sh brown	

Perf. 10, 11½, 12½ and Compound
O13	A1	1p green	
O14	A2	3p on 4p slate blue (Red)	
O16	A2	4p dull violet	
O17	A1	6p deep blue	

O18	A3	9p violet	
O19	A3	10p on 9p yellow (Blk)	
O20	A1	1sh brown	
O21	A2	2sh carmine	

Rouletted
Wmk. 72
O22	A6a	2p orange	

Perf. 10 x Roulette
O23	A6a	2p orange	

Perf. 10, 11½, 12½ and Compound
Wmk. 70
O24	A6a	2p orange	

Perf. 10
O25	A6a	2p orange	
O26	A2	4p dull violet	

For General Use

Overprinted in Black **O.S.**

Perf. 10, 11½, 12½ and Compound
1874   Wmk. 6
O27	A1	1p green	—	450.00
a.		Printed on both sides		
O28	A2	3p on 4p ultra		150.00
a.		No period after "S"		375.00
O29	A2	4p dull violet	27.50	9.50
a.		Inverted overprint		25.00
b.		No period after "S"		400.00
c.		Perf. 10	1,650.	
O30	A1	6p deep blue	55.00	9.50
a.		No period after "S"		22.50
O31	A3	9p violet	250.00	60.00
a.		No period after "S"	300.00	
O32	A1	1sh red brown	55.00	16.00
a.		Double overprint		27.50
b.		No period after "S"	110.00	40.00
O33	A2	2sh carmine	67.50	14.00
a.		Double overprint		
b.		No period after "S"		32.50

1874-75   Wmk. 72
O34	A6	1p blue green	100.00	27.50
a.		Inverted overprint		
O35	A6a	2p orange	14.00	1.40

1876-86   Wmk. 7
O36	A2	3p on 4p ultra		
O37	A2	4p dull violet	100.00	17.00
O38	A2	4p reddish vio	37.50	3.00
a.		Double overprint		
b.		Inverted overprint		
c.		Dbl. ovpt., one inverted		
O39	A1	6p dark blue	62.50	5.00
a.		Double overprint		37.50
b.		Inverted overprint		
O40	A1	6p ultramarine	57.50	4.50
a.		Double overprint		
b.		Inverted overprint		
O41	A3	8p on 9p yel brn	425.00	125.00
a.		Double overprint	750.00	
O41B	A3	9p violet	4,000.	
O42	A1	1sh red brown	45.00	5.00
a.		Inverted overprint	150.00	75.00
b.		Double overprint		
O43	A2	2sh carmine	110.00	8.00
a.		Double overprint		70.00
b.		Inverted overprint		75.00

1880-91   Wmk. 73
O44	A6	1p blue green	11.00	.50
a.		Inverted overprint		22.50
b.		Double overprint	35.00	20.00
c.		Dbl. ovpt., one inverted		
O45	A6	1p yellow green	12.00	.50
a.		Inverted overprint		10.00
O46	A6a	2p orange	11.00	.25
a.		Inverted overprint		
b.		Double overprint	70.00	25.00
c.		Overprinted sideways		
d.		Dbl. ovpt., one inverted		
e.		Dbl. ovpt., both inverted		57.50
O47	A6a	2p blood red	52.50	5.00
O48	A11	2½p on 4p green	35.00	9.50
a.		"½" nearer the "2"		75.00
b.		Double overprint		
c.		Pair, one without ovpt.		
		Nos. O44-O48 (5)	121.50	15.75

1882-90   *Perf. 10*
O49	A6	½p on 1p green	25.00	8.00
a.		Inverted overprint		
O50	A11	4p violet	21.00	1.90
O51	A12	6p blue	12.00	1.25
		Nos. O49-O51 (3)	58.00	11.15

Overprinted in Black **O.S.**

Perf. 10, 11½, 12½ and Compound
1891   Wmk. 7
O52	A1	1sh red brown	42.50	3.50
O53	A2	2sh carmine	100.00	10.00
a.		Double overprint		

1891-95   Wmk. 73
O54	A9	½p brown	12.00	2.50
O55	A6	1p blue green	12.00	.30
a.		Double overprint	80.00	

O56	A6a	2p orange	12.00	.30
O57	A11	2½p on 4p green	45.00	2.75
a.		"½" nearer the "2"	52.50	18.00
b.		Inverted overprint	100.00	
O58	A11	4p violet	17.50	1.25
O59	A12	5p on 6p red brn	55.00	2.50
O60	A12	6p blue	9.75	.75
a.		Double overprint		
		Nos. O54-O60 (7)	163.25	10.35

1893   *Perf. 15*
O61	A9	½p brown	15.00	1.75
O62	A6	1p green	11.00	.30
O63	A6a	2p orange	12.00	.20
a.		Inverted overprint		18.00
b.		Double overprint		32.50
O64	A11	4p gray violet	65.00	1.75
a.		Double overprint		21.00
O65	A17	5p dull violet	80.00	4.50
O66	A12	6p blue	20.00	.70
		Nos. O61-O66 (6)	203.00	9.20

1896   *Perf. 13*
O67	A9	½p brown	12.50	1.75
a.		Triple overprint		
O68	A6	1p green	16.00	.20
O69	A6a	2p orange	11.00	.20
O70	A16	2½p blue violet	60.00	1.40
O71	A11	4p brt violet	65.00	1.75
a.		Double overprint	30.00	40.00
O72	A17	5p dull violet	60.00	4.25
O73	A12	6p blue	25.00	.90
		Nos. O67-O73 (7)	249.50	10.45

On No. O67a, one overprint is upright, two sideways.

Same Overprint in Dark Blue
1891-95   *Perf. 10*
O74	A6	1p green	150.00	15.00
O75	A12	6p blue		

Black Overprint
Perf. 11½, 12½, Clean-Cut
1897   Wmk. 7
O76	A1	1sh brown	40.00	4.50
a.		Double overprint		

Overprinted in Black **O. S.**

1900   Wmk. 73   *Perf. 13*
O77	A18	½p yellow green	10.00	1.75
O78	A6	1p carmine rose	11.50	.20
a.		Inverted overprint		
b.		Double overprint		
O79	A6a	2p purple	11.50	.20
a.		Inverted ovpt.	40.00	
O80	A16	2½p dark blue	82.50	1.40
a.		Inverted overprint		30.00
O81	A11	4p violet	65.00	.70
a.		Inverted overprint	125.00	
O82	A12	6p blue	20.00	.75
		Nos. O77-O82 (6)	200.50	5.00

1901   *Perf. 10*
O83	A13	2sh6p violet	3,000.	2,000.
O84	A13	5sh rose	2,250.	2,250.

On Nos. O77-O82 the letters "O.S." are 11½mm apart; on Nos. O83-O84, 14½mm apart.

Overprinted in Black **O.S.**

1903   Wmk. 72   *Perf. 11½, 12½*
O85	A1	1sh red brown	40.00	25.00

Many of the official stamps are found with one or both the periods after "O.S." missing. This occurs more often in the later than in the earlier issues.

TASMANIA

taz-'mā-nē-ə

LOCATION — An island off the southeastern coast of Australia
GOVT. — British Colony
AREA — 26,215 sq. mi.
POP. — 172,475 (1901)
CAPITAL — Hobart

Tasmania was one of the six British colonies that united in 1901 to form the Commonwealth of Australia. The island was originally named Van Diemen's Land by its discoverer, Abel Tasman, the present name having been adopted in 1853. Stamps of Australia are now used.

12 Pence = 1 Shilling
20 Shillings = 1 Pound

Watermarks

Wmk. 6- Large Star

Wmk. 49-
Double-lined
Numeral

Wmk. 75-
Double-lined
Numeral

Wmk. 50-
Single-lined "2"

Wmk. 51-
Single-lined "4"

Wmk. 52- Single-
lined "10"

Wmk. 70- V and
Crown

Wmk. 13- Crown
& Double-lined A

Wmk. 76- TAS   Wmk. 77- TAS

Wmk. 78- Multiple TAS

Values for unused stamps are for examples with original gum as defined in the catalogue introduction except for Nos. 1-2a and 10 which are valued without gum as few examples exist with any remaining original gum. Very fine examples of Nos. 17-75a will have perforations touching the design on one or more sides due to the narrow spacing of the stamps on the plates. Stamps with perfs clear of the design on all four sides are scarce and command higher prices.

Queen Victoria
A1   A2

Unwmk.

1853, Nov. 1		**Engr.**		**Imperf.**
1	A1	1p blue	3,000.	750.00
2	A2	4p red orange	2,000.	300.00
a.		4p yellow orange	2,000.	300.00
		Cut to shape		15.00

Twenty-four varieties of each.

The 4p on vertically laid paper is believed to be a proof. Value, unused, $5,000.

The reprints are made from defaced plates and show marks across the face of each stamp. They are on thin and thick, unwatermarked paper and thin cardboard; only the first are perforated. Nearly all the reprints of Tasmania may be found with and without the overprint "REPRINT."

Nos. 1-47A with pen or revenue cancellations sell for a small fraction of the price of postally used specimens. Copies are found with pen cancellation removed.

Queen Victoria — A3

1855		**Wmk. 6**		**Wove Paper**
4	A3	1p dark carmine	4,500.	700.00
5	A3	2p green	1,800.	475.00
a.		2p deep green	1,800.	525.00
6	A3	4p deep blue	1,250.	85.00

1856-57				**Unwmk.**
7	A3	1p pale red	5,000.	500.00
8	A3	2p emerald ('57)	6,000.	750.00
9	A3	4p blue ('57)	650.00	85.00

1856				**Pelure Paper**
10	A3	1p brown red	3,000.	600.00

1857		**Wmk. 139, 49, 75**		
11	A3	1p carmine	80.00	24.00
a.		1p orange red	100.00	17.50
b.		1p brown red	275.00	20.00
c.		Double impression	200.00	125.00
12	A3	2p sage green	140.00	32.50
a.		2p yellow green	250.00	62.50
b.		2p green	—	35.00
13	A3	4p pale blue	100.00	13.00
b.		Printed on both sides		
		Nos. 11-13 (3)		320.00

See #17-19, 23-25, 29-31, 35-37, 39-41, 45-47A.

A4   A4a

1858				
14	A4	6p gray lilac	150.00	55.00
a.		6p red violet	600.00	150.00
b.		Double impression		200.00
15	A4	6p blue gray	300.00	50.00
16	A4a	1sh vermilion	400.00	55.00
		Nos. 14-16 (3)	850.00	160.00

No. 15 watermarked large star was not regularly issued.

1864				**Rouletted**
17	A3	1p carmine	300.00	100.00
a.		1p brick red		140.00
18	A3	2p yellow grn		375.00
19	A3	2p blue		140.00
21	A4	6p gray lilac		175.00
22	A4a	1sh vermilion		500.00

1864-69				**Perf. 10**
23	A3	1p brick red	50.00	20.00
a.		1p carmine	45.00	20.00
b.		1p orange red	50.00	20.00
24	A3	2p yellow green	275.00	65.00
a.		2p sage green	325.00	125.00
25	A3	4p blue	100.00	9.00
a.		Double impression		100.00
26	A4	6p lilac	175.00	15.00
a.		6p red lilac	350.00	60.00
27	A4	6p slate blue	225.00	50.00
28	A4a	1sh vermilion	100.00	17.50
a.		Horiz. pair, imperf. vert.		
		Nos. 23-28 (6)	925.00	176.50

1864-69				**Perf. 12, 12½**
29	A3	1p carmine	24.00	5.50
a.		1p orange red	40.00	16.00
b.		1p brick red	42.50	22.50
c.		Double impression		
d.		Wmkd. "2"		950.00
		As "d," pen cancel		125.00
30	A3	2p yellow green	125.00	35.00
a.		2p dark green	200.00	35.00
b.		2p sage green	250.00	100.00
31	A3	4p blue	65.00	11.00

		Perf. 11½, 12½		
32	A4	6p red lilac	25.00	11.00
a.		6p purple	75.00	21.00
b.		6p violet	110.00	17.50
d.		Horiz. pair, imperf. vert.		
e.		Double impression		100.00
33	A4	6p slate blue, perf. 12½	250.00	65.00
34	A4a	1sh vermilion	90.00	27.50
a.		Double impression		160.00
b.		Horiz. pair, imperf. vert.		
		Nos. 29-34 (6)	579.00	155.00

The reprints are on unwatermarked paper, perforated 11½, and on thin cardboard, imperforate and perforated.

		Pin-perf. 5½ to 9½, 13½ to 14½		
1867				
35	A3	1p carmine	350.00	77.50
36	A3	2p yellow green		275.00
37	A3	4p blue		160.00
38	A4	6p gray		150.00
38A	A4	6p red lilac		450.00
38B	A4a	1sh vermilion		—

		Oblique Roulette		
39	A3	1p carmine	675.00	275.00
40	A3	2p yellow green		400.00
41	A3	4p blue		325.00
42	A4	6p gray		550.00
43	A4	6p red lilac		575.00
44	A4a	1sh vermilion		750.00

1868				**Serrate Perf. 19**
45	A3	1p carmine	225.00	100.00
46	A3	2p yellow green		175.00
47	A3	4p blue	650.00	110.00
47A	A3	6p purple		500.00

Queen Victoria — A5

1870-71	**Typo.**	**Wmk. 50**		**Perf. 11½**
48	A5	2p blue green	35.00	3.25
a.		Imperf., pair		
b.		Perf. 12	45.00	5.00
d.		2p blue green	80.00	6.50
e.		As "d," perf. 12	40.00	5.00

See Nos. 49-75, 98, 108-109.

		Wmk. 51		
49	A5	1p rose ('71)	60.00	20.00
a.		Imperf., pair	600.00	210.00
50	A5	4p blue	725.00	300.00

		Wmk. 52		
51	A5	1p rose	40.00	9.00
a.		Imperf. pair	275.00	250.00
c.		Perf. 11½	1,000.	

52	A5	10p black	20.00	17.00
a.		Imperf. pair	125.00	
b.		Perf. 11½	25.00	20.00

The reprints are on unwatermarked paper. The 4p has also been reprinted on thin cardboard, imperf and perf.

1871-76		**Wmk. 76**		**Perf. 11½**
53	A5	1p rose	4.50	.60
a.		Imperf.		
c.		Perf. 12	65.00	9.00
53B	A5	1p vermilion ('73)	250.00	95.00
54	A5	2p dp grn ('72)	12.00	.60
a.		2p yellow green	125.00	1.25
b.		2p blue green	45.00	.60
c.		Imperf. pair		125.00
d.		2p green, perf. 12	450.00	140.00
e.		Double impression		
55	A5	3p brown	37.50	4.50
a.		3p purple brown	37.50	4.50
b.		As "a," imperf. pair		325.00
56	A5	3p indian red ('71)	37.50	4.50
a.		3p indian red	35.00	4.50
b.		Imperf. pair	125.00	
c.		Vert. pair, imperf. horiz.		
d.		Perf. 12	85.00	21.00
57	A5	4p dull yellow ('76)	40.00	7.50
a.		Perf. 12	225.00	15.00
58	A5	9p blue	20.00	7.50
a.		Imperf. pair	125.00	
b.		Perf. 12	40.00	40.00
59	A5	5sh bright violet	125.00	37.50
a.		Imperf.		
b.		Horiz. pair, imperf. vert.		
c.		Perf. 12	175.00	150.00
		Pen cancel		.30
		Nos. 53-59 (8)	526.50	157.70

The reprints are on unwatermarked paper, the 5sh has also been reprinted on thin cardboard; all are perforated.

1878		**Wmk. 77**		**Perf. 14**
60	A5	1p rose	4.50	.60
61	A5	2p deep green	4.50	.60
62	A5	8p violet brown	15.00	4.50
		Nos. 60-62 (3)	24.00	5.70

The 8p has been reprinted on thin unwatermarked paper, perforated 11½.

1880-83				**Perf. 12, 11½**
63	A5	3p indian red, perf. 12	9.00	2.00
a.		Imperf. pair	85.00	
b.		Horiz. pair, imperf. between	600.00	
c.		Perf. 11½	10.50	3.00
64	A5	4p lem, perf. 11½ ('83)	40.00	7.50
a.		4p olive yellow, perf. 11½	95.00	21.00
b.		Printed on both sides	210.00	
c.		Imperf.		
d.		4p deep yellow, perf. 12	75.00	22.50

Type of 1871
Surcharged in Black

1889				**Perf. 14**
65	A5	½p on 1p carmine	9.00	1.75
a.		"al" sideways in surcharge	825.00	500.00

No. 65 has been reprinted on thin cardboard, perforated 12, with the surcharge "Halfpenny" 19mm long.

1889-96				**Perf. 11½**
66	A5	1p red orange	2.25	.70
a.		½p yellow orange	2.25	.70
b.		Perf. 12	2.00	.85
67	A5	1p dull red	8.25	2.00
a.		1p vermilion	5.00	2.00
68	A5	1p car, perf. 12	8.25	3.25
a.		1p pink, perf. 12	27.50	5.00
b.		1p salmon rose, perf. 12	8.25	3.25
c.		Imperf. pair	92.50	92.50

				Perf. 12
69	A5	4p bister ('96)	18.00	8.25
70	A5	9p chalky bl ('96)	10.00	3.25
		Nos. 66-70 (5)	46.75	17.45

1891		**Wmk. 76**		**Perf. 11½**
71	A5	½p orange	16.00	8.25
a.		½p brown orange	16.00	8.25
b.		Imperf. pair	75.00	
c.		Perf. 12	35.00	9.25
72	A5	1p salmon rose	21.00	11.50
a.		1p carmine, perf. 12	40.00	20.00
73	A5	4p ol bis, perf. 12	15.00	6.50
		Nos. 71-73 (3)	52.00	26.25

See Nos. 98, 108-109.

Surcharged in Black

TASMANIA

1891 Wmk. 77 Perf. 11½
Surcharge 14mm High

74	A5	2½p on 9p lt blue	6.00	6.50
a.		Dbl. surcharge, one invtd.	210.00	200.00
b.		Imperf. pair	140.00	

Perf. 12
Surcharge 15mm High

75	A5	2½p on 9p lt blue	5.50	5.00
a.		Surcharged in blue		

No. 74 has been reprinted on thin unwatermarked paper, imperforate. There is also a reprint on thin cardboard, in deep ultramarine, with surcharge 16½mm high, and perforated 12.

A8

A9

1892-99 Typo. Perf. 14

76	A8	½p orange & vio	.85	.35
77	A9	2½p magenta	2.50	.65
78	A8	5p pale bl & brn	3.50	1.40
79	A8	6p blue vio & blk	3.50	1.50
80	A8	10p red brn & grn ('99)	6.75	5.50
81	A8	1sh rose & green	4.50	1.50
82	A8	2sh6p brown & blue	25.00	8.00
83	A8	5sh brn vio & red	37.50	17.00
84	A8	10sh brt vio & brn	75.00	45.00
85	A8	£1 green & yel	475.00	225.00
		Nos. 76-85 (10)	634.10	305.90

No. 80 shows the numeral on white tablet.
See #99, 110-111. For overprint see #AR35.

Lake Marion — A10

Mt. Wellington — A11

View of Hobart — A12

Tasman's Arch — A13

Spring River, Port Davey — A14

Russell Falls — A15

Mt. Gould and Lake St. Clair — A16

Dilston Falls — A17

1899-1900 Engr. Wmk. 78 Perf. 14

86	A10	½p dark green	5.00	1.75
87	A11	1p carmine	5.00	.60
88	A12	2p violet	5.50	.45
89	A13	2½p dark blue	11.00	5.00
90	A14	3p dark brown	8.50	1.75
91	A15	4p ocher	16.00	2.25
92	A16	5p ultramarine	16.00	7.50
93	A17	6p lake	20.00	6.50
		Nos. 86-93 (8)	87.00	25.80

See Nos. 94-97, 102-107, 114-117.

Perf. 11, 12½, 11x12½

1902-03 Litho., Typo. Wmk. 70

94	A10	½p green	2.25	.30
95	A11	1p carmine	5.50	.20
96	A11	1p dull red	5.00	.20
97	A12	2p violet	3.25	.20
98	A5	9p blue	9.00	3.00
a.		9p ultramarine	225.00	
b.		9p indigo	90.00	
c.		Perf. 11	7.25	3.50
99	A8	1sh rose & green	12.00	3.75
a.		Perf. 11	27.50	27.50
		Nos. 94-99 (6)	37.00	7.65

Nos. 94, 97 are litho., Nos. 96, 98-99 typo. No. 95 was printed both ways.

No. 78 Surcharged in Black

1904 Wmk. 77 Perf. 14

100	A8	1½p on 5p blue & brn	1.75	1.25

Perf. 11, 12, 12½ and Compound

1905-08 Typo. Wmk. 13

102	A10	½p dull green	2.00	.20
a.		Booklet pane of 12		
103	A11	1p carmine	2.00	.20
a.		Booklet pane of 18		
104	A12	2p violet	3.50	.20
105	A14	3p dark brown	7.00	2.00
106	A15	4p ocher	13.00	2.25
107	A17	6p lake	40.00	5.00
108	A5	8p violet brown	19.00	5.00
109	A5	9p blue	8.00	3.00
110	A8	1sh rose & green	13.00	2.50
111	A8	10sh brt vio & brn	100.00	62.50
a.		Perf. 11	175.00	
		Nos. 102-111 (10)	207.50	82.85

Nos. 104-107 also printed litho.

1911 Redrawn

114	A12	2p bright violet	3.50	.30
115	A15	4p dull yellow	16.00	8.00
116	A17	6p lake	17.00	8.00
		Nos. 114-116 (3)	36.50	16.30

The redrawn 2p measures 33½x25mm instead of 32½x24½mm. There are many slight changes in the clouds and other parts of the design.

The 4p is much lighter, especially the waterfall and trees above it. This appears to be a new or cleaned plate rather than a redrawn one.

In the redrawn 6p there are more colored lines in the waterfall and the river and more white dots in the trees.

No. 114 Surcharged in Red

1912

117	A12	1p on 2p bright violet	.85	.50

POSTAL FISCAL STAMPS

Authorised for postal use by Act of November 1, 1882. Authorization withdrawn Nov. 30, 1900.

Used values are for examples with postal cancellations used from Nov. 1, 1882 through Nov. 30, 1900.

Beware of copies with a pen cancellation removed and a fake postmark added.

PF1

PF2

St. George and the Dragon
PF3   PF4

1863-64 Engr. Wmk. 139 Imperf.

AR1	PF1	3p green	75.00	50.00
AR2	PF2	2sh 6p car	80.00	50.00
AR3	PF3	5sh green	75.00	55.00
AR4	PF3	5sh brown	200.00	150.00
AR5	PF4	10sh orange	175.00	150.00

For overprint see No. AR32.

Perf. 10

AR6	PF1	3p green	40.00	22.50
AR7	PF2	2sh 6p car	50.00	
AR8	PF3	5sh brown	75.00	
AR9	PF4	10sh orange	42.50	

Perf. 12

AR10	PF1	3p green	45.00	27.50
AR11	PF2	2sh 6p car	45.00	35.00
AR12	PF3	5sh green	32.50	27.50
AR13	PF3	5sh brown	80.00	
AR14	PF4	10sh orange	35.00	27.50

Perf. 12½

AR15	PF1	3p green	80.00	
AR16	PF2	2sh 6p car	80.00	
AR17	PF3	5sh brown	100.00	
AR18	PF4	10sh orange	70.00	

Perf. 11½

AR19	PF1	3p green		
AR20	PF2	2sh 6p car	42.50	32.50
AR21	PF3	5sh brown	32.50	22.50
AR22	PF4	10sh orange	55.00	40.00

Wmk. 77
Perf. 12

AR23	PF2	2sh 6p car	20.00	15.00

For overprint see No. AR33.

Duck-billed Platypus — PF5

1880 Engr. Wmk. 77 Perf. 14

AR24	PF5	1p slate	12.50	4.00
AR25	PF5	3p brown	12.50	3.00
AR26	PF5	6p lilac	65.00	2.50
AR27	PF5	1sh rose	75.00	6.00

For overprints see Nos. AR28-AR31.

**Nos. AR24-AR27, AR2, AR23, 85
Overprinted "REVENUE"**

1900, Nov. 15

AR28	PF5	1p slate	20.00	
AR29	PF5	3p brown	20.00	20.00
AR30	PF5	6p lilac	60.00	
AR31	PF5	1sh rose	100.00	
AR32	PF2	2sh 6p car (#AR2)		
AR33	PF2	2sh 6p car (#AR23)	200.00	
AR34	PF4	10sh orange		
AR35	A8	£1 grn & yel (#85)	200.00	150.00

Nos. AR28-AR35 were not supposed to be postally used. Because of imprecise terminology, postal use was tolerated until all postal use of revenues ceased on Nov. 30, 1900.

Other denominations and watermarks were overprinted after postal use was no longer allowed.

VICTORIA

vik-'tōr-ē-ə

LOCATION — In the extreme southeastern part of Australia
GOVT. — British Colony
AREA — 87,884 sq. mi.
POP. — 1,201,341 (1901)
CAPITAL — Melbourne

Victoria was one of the six former British colonies which united on Jan. 1, 1901, to form the Commonwealth of Australia.

12 Pence = 1 Shilling
20 Shillings = 1 Pound

Unused values for Nos. 1-16 are for stamps without gum as these stamps are seldom found with original gum. Otherwise, unused values are for stamps with original gum as defined in the catalogue introduction.

Very fine examples of all rouletted, perforated and serrate perforated stamps from Nos. 9-109 and F2 will have roulettes, perforations or serrate perforations touching the design. Examples clear on four sides range from scarce to rare and will command higher prices.

Watermarks

Wmk. 6—Large Star

Wmk. 80

Wmk. 50

Wmk. 80a

Wmk. 81

Wmk. 139

Wmk. 49

Wmk. 75

Wmk. 70—V and Crown   Wmk. 13—Crown & Double-lined A

Queen Victoria A1   Victoria on Throne A2

1850		Litho.	Unwmk.	Imperf.	
1	A1	1p dull red		700.00	75.00
a.		1p vermilion		600.00	125.00
2	A1	1p rose		375.00	70.00
a.		1p pink		400.00	85.00
3	A1	3p blue		475.00	50.00
a.		3p light blue		650.00	75.00
4	A1	3p indigo		625.00	50.00
		Nos. 1-4 (4)		2,175.00	245.00

Nos. 1-4 exist with and without frame line.

THREE TYPES OF 2p:
Type I - Border, two sets of nine wavy lines crisscrossing. Background, 22 groups of wavy triple lines below "VICTORIA."
Type II - Border, same. Background, 15 groups of wavy triple lines below "VICTORIA."
Type III - Border, two sets of five wavy lines crisscrossing. Background, same as type II.

5	A1	2p lilac, I		2,500.	250.00
a.		2p brn lilac, I		3,750.	325.00
6	A1	2p brn lilac, II		1,000.	90.00
a.		2p gray lilac, II		1,000.	90.00
7	A1	2p brn lilac, III		650.00	60.00
a.		2p gray lilac, III		700.00	100.00
b.		Value omitted, III			2,500.
8	A1	2p yel brn, III		650.00	65.00

			Rouletted 7		
9	A1	1p vermilion			2,250.
10	A1	3p blue			150.00
a.		3p deep blue		1,600.	190.00

			Perf. 12		
12	A1	3p blue		2,000.	110.00
		3p deep blue		2,000.	110.00

| 1852 | | Engr. | | Imperf. | |
| 14 | A2 | 2p reddish brown | | 160.00 | 22.50 |

#14 was reprinted on paper with watermark 70, imperf. & perf. 12½, overprinted "REPRINT."

1854				Litho.	
15	A2	2p gray brown		225.00	32.50
16	A2	2p brown lilac		200.00	30.00
a.		2p red lilac		175.00	20.00

Fifty varieties.

A3   A4

1854-58				Typo.	
17	A3	6p orange		175.00	25.00
a.		6p red orange		225.00	27.50

See Nos. 19-20, 22-24A, 26-28.

| | | | **Lithographed** | | |
| 18 | A4 | 1sh blue | | 575.00 | 22.50 |

See Nos. 21, 25.

| | | | **Typographed** | | |
| 19 | A3 | 2sh green | | 1,100. | 150.00 |

| 1857-58 | | | | Rouletted 7, 9½ | |
| 20 | A3 | 6p orange | | 525.00 | 60.00 |

| | | | **Lithographed** | | |
| 21 | A4 | 1sh blue | | 1,500. | 90.00 |

| | | | **Typographed** | | |
| 22 | A3 | 2sh green ('58) | | 3,500. | 300.00 |

			Small Serrate Perf. 19		
23	A3	6p orange		1,200.	100.00
			Large Serpentine Perf. 10½		
24	A3	6p orange		800.00	57.50
			Serrate x Serpentine Perf.		
24A	A3	6p orange			75.00

| 1859 | | Litho. | | Perf. 12 | |
| 25 | A4 | 1sh blue | | 140.00 | 17.50 |

| | | | **Typographed** | | |
| 26 | A3 | 2sh green | | 225.00 | 32.50 |

| 1861 | | Wmk. "SIX PENCE" (80) | | | |
| 27 | A3 | 6p black | | 260.00 | 57.50 |

		Wmk. Single-lined "2" (50)			
1864				Perf. 12, 13	
28	A3	2sh blue, green		250.00	8.50

A5

		Wmk. Large Star (6)			
1856, Oct.		Engr.		Imperf.	
29	A5	1p green		125.00	30.00
1858				Rouletted 5½-6½	
30	A5	6p blue		125.00	7.00

Nos. 29 and 30 have been reprinted on paper watermarked V and Crown. They are imperforate and overprinted "REPRINT."

A6   A7

1857-61		Typo.		Imperf.	
31	A6	1p yellow green		100.00	15.00
a.		Printed on both sides		900.00	
32	A6	4p vermilion		275.00	15.00
a.		Printed on both sides		900.00	
33	A6	4p rose		200.00	11.50

			Rouletted 7 to 9½		
34	A6	1p yellow green		325.00	125.00
35	A6	4p rose		525.00	40.00

| | | | **Perf. 12** | | |
| 36 | A6 | 1p yellow green | | 600.00 | 325.00 |

		Unwmk.		Imperf.	
37	A6	1p blue green		350.00	15.00
38	A6	2p lilac		275.00	15.00
39	A6	4p rose		500.00	40.00

Copies of No. 39 printed in dull carmine on thin paper are regarded as printer's waste and of little value. They are also found printed on both sides.

			Rouletted 7 to 9½		
40	A6	1p blue green		300.00	10.00
a.		1p yellow green		400.00	32.50
b.		Horiz. pair, imperf. btwn.			1,000.
41	A6	2p lilac		—	225.00
42	A6	4p rose		300.00	8.00
a.		Horiz. pair, imperf. btwn.			1,000.

			Perf. 12		
43	A6	1p blue green		160.00	10.00
a.		1p yellow green		200.00	15.00
b.		Horiz. pair, imperf. btwn.			650.00
44	A6	2p lilac			90.00
45	A6	4p rose		175.00	5.00
b.		Vert. pair, imperf. btwn.			

| | | | **Serrate Perf. 19** | | |
| 45A | A6 | 2p lilac | | 600.00 | 250.00 |

			Laid Paper		
			Imperf		
46	A6	4p rose		600.00	22.50

			Rouletted 5 to 7		
47	A6	2p violet		150.00	5.00
a.		2p brown lilac		225.00	8.00
b.		2p dark lilac		200.00	8.00
48	A6	4p rose		160.00	5.25

			Perf. 12		
49	A6	2p violet		240.00	14.00
50	A6	4p rose		150.00	11.00

		Wove Paper			
1860		Wmk. Value in Words (80)			
51	A6	1p yellow green		60.00	8.00
a.		Wmk. "FOUR PENCE" (error)			2,000.
52	A6	2p gray lilac		140.00	7.50
				400.00	24.00

| | | Wmk. "THREE PENCE" (80) | | | |
| 53 | A6 | 2p gray lilac | | 240.00 | 10.00 |

		Single-lined "2" (50)			
54	A6	2p lilac		160.00	16.00
a.		2p gray lilac		160.00	16.00
b.		2p brown lilac		160.00	16.00
c.		As "b," wmkd. single-lined "6"			4,500.

| 1860 | | Unwmk. | | Laid Paper | |
| 56 | A7 | 3p deep blue | | 350.00 | 45.00 |

		Wmk. Value in Words (80)			
		Perf. 11½ to 12			
1860-62				Wove Paper	
57	A7	3p blue		175.00	10.00
58	A7	3p claret		175.00	35.00
a.		Perf. 13		190.00	40.00
59	A7	4p rose		175.00	4.50
60	A7	6p orange		3,000.	325.00
61	A7	6p black		250.00	8.00

| | | Wmk. "FIVE SHILLINGS" (80) | | | |
| 62 | A7 | 4p rose | | 1,500. | 20.00 |

		Wmk. Single-lined "4" (80a)			
1863				Imperf.	
63	A7	4p rose		—	140.00

| | | | **Rouletted** | | |
| 64 | A7 | 4p rose | | 2,400. | 200.00 |

| | | | **Perf. 11½ to 12** | | |
| 65 | A7 | 4p rose | | 100.00 | 8.00 |

| 1863 | | Unwmk. | | Perf. 12 | |
| 66 | A7 | 4p rose | | 450.00 | 10.50 |

A8   A9

1861-63		Wmk. 80		Perf. 11½ to 12	
67	A8	1p green		90.00	9.00
68	A9	6p black		175.00	7.50

| | | Wmk. Double-lined "1" (139) | | | |
| 69 | A8 | 1p green | | 200.00 | 13.00 |

		Wmk. Single-lined Figures (50)			
70	A8	1p green		45.00	6.50
71	A9	6p black		175.00	6.50

The 1p and 6p of 1861-63 are known on paper without watermark but were probably impressions on the margins of watermarked sheets.

A10   A11

A12   A13

		Wmk. Single-lined Figures (50, 80a, 81)			
1863-67				Perf. 11½ to 13	
74	A10	1p green		70.00	4.00
a.		Double impression		900.00	
75	A10	2p gray lilac		75.00	4.00
a.		2p violet		50.00	2.75
76	A10	4p rose		110.00	3.00
a.		Double impression		900.00	
77	A11	6p blue		87.50	3.00
78	A10	8p orange		300.00	50.00
79	A12	10p brn, rose		150.00	4.50
80	A13	1sh blue, blue		150.00	3.00
		Nos. 74-80 (7)		942.50	71.50

See Nos. 81-82, 84-96, 99-101, 108-112, 115-119, 124-126, 144, 188. Compare design A11 design A54.

A14

		Wmk. Double-lined "1" (139)			
81	A10	1p green		95.00	5.00
82	A10	2p gray lilac		250.00	8.00
83	A14	3p lilac		200.00	35.00
84	A11	6p blue		65.00	6.00
		Nos. 81-84 (4)		610.00	54.00

See Nos. 97, 113, 155, 186. Compare design A14 with design A51.

| | | Wmk. Double-lined "2" (49) | | | |
| 85 | A11 | 6p blue | | | 3,250. |

		Wmk. Single-lined "4" (80a)			
86	A10	1p green		150.00	11.00
87	A10	2p gray lilac		200.00	7.00
88	A11	6p blue			1,500.

		Wmk. Double-lined "4" (75)			
89	A10	1p green		1,300.	150.00
90	A10	2p gray lilac		200.00	6.00
91	A10	4p rose		225.00	7.00
92	A11	6p blue		325.00	18.00

		Wmk. Single-lined "6" (50)			
93	A10	1p green		250.00	20.00
94	A10	2p gray lilac		225.00	5.75

		Wmk. Single-lined "8" (50)			
95	A10	1p green		225.00	15.00
96	A10	2p gray lilac		250.00	7.50
97	A14	3p lilac		200.00	30.00
99	A12	10p slate		600.00	125.00

		Wmk. "SIX PENCE" (80)			
100	A10	1p green		750.00	21.00
101	A11	6p blue		350.00	15.00

All values of the 1864-67 series except the 3p and 8p are known on unwatermarked paper. They are probably varieties from watermarked sheets which have been so placed on the printing press that some of the stamps escaped the watermark.

One copy of the 2p gray lilac, design A10, is reported to exist with only "PENCE" of watermark 80 showing. Some believe this is part of the "SIX PENCE" watermark.

1870		Wmk. "THREE PENCE" (80)			
108	A11	6p blue		225.00	6.25
		Wmk. "FOUR PENCE" (80)			
109	A11	6p blue		500.00	40.00

A15

1867-78		Wmk. (70)		Perf. 11½ to 13	
110	A10	1p green		60.00	2.00
111	A10	2p lilac		85.00	3.25
a.		2p gray lilac		62.50	2.00
112	A10	2p lilac, lilac		90.00	10.00
113	A14	3p red lilac		300.00	18.00
a.		3p lilac		350.00	20.00
114	A14	3p orange		22.50	2.00
a.		3p yellow		62.50	2.00
115	A10	4p rose		90.00	3.50
116	A11	6p blue		25.00	2.50
117	A11	6p ultra		27.50	2.50
a.		6p lilac blue		62.50	2.25
118	A10	8p brn, rose		125.00	5.00
119	A13	1sh bl, blue		250.00	10.00
120	A15	5sh bl, yel		1,700.	450.00
121	A15	5sh bl & rose		160.00	15.00
a.		Without blue line under crown		140.00	15.00
122	A15	5sh ultra & rose		175.00	20.00

See #126, 144, 188. For surcharge see #124.

See #191. Compare design A15 with design A58.

A16   A19

1870				Perf. 13	
123	A16	2p lilac		40.00	2.00
a.		Perf. 12		40.00	1.25

No. 110 Surcharged in $\frac{1}{2}$ $\frac{1}{2}$
Red

HALF

1873, July 19			**Perf. 13, 12**	
124	A10	½p on 1p green	35.00	10.00

No. 79 Surcharged **9**   **9**
in Blue

NINEPENCE

1871	**Wmk. Single-lined "10" (81)**			
125	A12	9p on 10p brn, *rose*	375.00	11.00
a.		Double surcharge		1,200.

1873-78				**Typo.**
126	A10	8p brown, *rose* ('78)	125.00	6.50
127	A19	9p brown, *rose*	125.00	6.50

For additional stamps of design A19, see Nos. 128-129, 174-175. Compare design A19 with design A55.

1875	**Wmk. V and Crown (70)**			
128	A19	9p brown, *rose*	140.00	11.00

8ᵈ   **8ᵈ**
No. 128 Surcharged
in Black

EIGHTPENCE

1876				
129	A19	8p on 9p brn, *rose*	175.00	14.00

A21   A22

A23

A24   A25

1873-81			**Perf. 13, 12**	
130	A21	½p rose ('74)	5.50	.35
131	A21	½p rose, *rose* ('78)	20.00	8.00
132	A22	1p grn ('75)	15.00	1.00
133	A22	1p grn, *gray* ('78)	90.00	60.00
134	A22	1p grn, *yel* ('78)	60.00	15.00
135	A23	2p violet	15.00	.25
136	A23	2p vio, *grnsh* ('78)	125.00	15.00
137	A23	2p vio, *buff* ('78)	125.00	15.00
137A	A23	2p vio, *lil* ('78)		350.00
138	A24	1sh bl, *bl* ('76)	55.00	4.00
139	A25	2sh bl, *grn* ('81)	175.00	20.00

See Nos. 140, 156A-159, 184, 189-190. Compare design A21 with design A46, A24 with A56, A25 with A57.

1878	**Double-lined Outer Oval**			
140	A23	2p violet	20.00	.25
a.		Imperf., pair		400.00
b.		Pair, imperf. btwn.		

A26   A27

A28

1881-83			**Perf. 12½**	
141	A26	1p green ('83)	14.00	.90
142	A27	2p brown	27.50	.25
143	A27	2p lilac	12.00	.20
144	A10	4p car rose	200.00	2.75
145	A28	4p car rose	40.00	1.50
		Nos. 141-145 (5)	293.50	5.60

See Nos. 156, 185, 187. Compare design A26 with design A47, A27 with A49, A28 with A52.

A29   A30

A31   A32

A33   A34

1884-86				
146	A29	½p rose	6.00	.40
147	A30	1p green	6.00	.20
148	A31	2p violet	4.75	.20
a.		2p lilac rose	10.50	.20
149	A30	3p bister	8.00	.50
a.		3p ocher	6.50	.50
150	A32	4p magenta	32.50	2.25
a.		4p violet (error)	4,000.	400.00
151	A30	6p gray blue	42.50	1.40
a.		6p ultramarine	35.00	1.40
152	A33	8p rose, *rose*	22.50	4.50
153	A34	1sh blue, *yel*	47.50	3.25
154	A33	2sh olive, *grn*	22.50	2.00
		Nos. 146-154 (9)	192.25	14.70

See Nos. 177-178, 192A. Compare designs A31-A32 with designs A37-A38.

Nos. 114, 145, 138-139 Overprinted "STAMP / DUTY" Vertically in Blue or Black

1885				
155	A14	3p orange (Bl)	60.00	21.00
156	A28	4p car rose (Bl)	50.00	12.50
156A	A24	1sh bl, *bl* (Bl)		1,250.
157	A24	1sh bl, *bl* (Bk)	95.00	22.50
158	A25	2sh bl, *grn* (Bk)	75.00	20.00
		Nos. 155-156,157-158 (4)	280.00	76.00

Reprints of 4p and 1sh have brighter colors than originals. They lack the overprint "REPRINT."

A35   A36

A37   A38

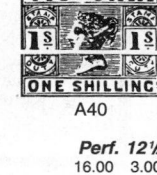

A39   A40

1886-87			**Perf. 12½**	
159	A35	½p lilac	16.00	3.00
160	A35	½p rose	4.50	.20
160A	A35	½p scarlet	5.00	.20
161	A36	1p green	5.00	.20
162	A37	2p violet	3.00	.20
a.		2p red lilac	2.00	.20
b.		Imperf.		
163	A38	4p red	6.00	.60
164	A39	6p blue	7.50	.40
165	A39	6p ultra	7.50	.20
166	A40	1sh lilac brown	22.50	1.50
		Nos. 159-166 (9)	77.00	6.50

See No. 180.

A41   A42

1889				
167	A41	1sh6p blue	110.00	62.50
168	A41	1sh6p orange	15.00	4.00

Southern Cross   Queen Victoria
A43   A44

1890-95			**Perf. 12½**	
169	A42	1p org brn	2.25	.20
a.		1p chocolate brown	2.75	.20
170	A42	1p yel brn	2.00	.20
171	A42	1p brn org, *pink* ('91)	1.60	.50
172	A43	2½p brn red, *yel*	6.00	.50
173	A44	5p choc ('91)	7.00	.50
174	A19	9p green ('92)	20.00	5.00
175	A19	9p rose red	13.00	1.50
a.		9p rose ('95)	13.00	1.50
176	A40	1sh deep claret	15.00	.50
a.		1sh red brown	13.00	.40
b.		1sh maroon	20.00	1.00
177	A33	2sh yel grn	25.00	10.00
178	A33	2sh emerald	20.00	6.00
		Nos. 169-178 (10)	111.85	24.90

In 1891 many stamps of the early issues were reprinted. They are on paper watermarked V and Crown, perforated 12, 12½, and overprinted "REPRINT."

See Nos. 181, 183, 192. Compare design A43 with design A50, A44 with A53.

A45

1897				
179	A45	1½p yellow green	4.00	1.75

See No. 182. Compare design A45 with design A48.

1899				
180	A35	½p emerald	5.00	.20
181	A42	1p brt rose	4.00	.20
182	A45	1½p red, *yel*	2.75	1.50
183	A43	2½p dark blue	6.50	1.25
		Nos. 180-183 (4)	18.25	3.15

1901				
184	A21	½p blue green	1.90	.50
a.		"VICTCRIA"	65.00	25.00
185	A27	2p violet	4.50	.20
186	A14	3p brown org	14.00	1.50
187	A28	4p bister	25.00	5.00
188	A11	6p emerald	9.00	2.75
189	A24	1sh orange yel	35.00	10.00
190	A25	2sh blue, *rose*	40.00	11.00
191	A15	5sh rose red & bl	60.00	20.00
		Nos. 184-191 (8)	189.40	50.95

1901				
192	A42	1p olive green	6.50	5.00
192A	A30	3p sage green	21.00	12.00

Nos. 192-192A were available for postal use until June 30, 1901, and thereafter restricted to revenue use.

A46   A47

A48

A49   A50

A51   A52

A53   A54

A55   A56

A57   A58

1901	**Perf. 11, 12½ and Compound**			
193	A46	½p blue green	1.50	.20
194	A47	1p rose red	1.25	.20
a.		1p rose	1.25	.20
195	A48	1½p red, *yellow*	2.25	.50
a.		Perf. 11	50.00	32.50
196	A49	2p violet	2.75	.20
197	A50	2½p blue	3.25	.20
198	A51	3p brown org	6.00	.30
199	A52	4p bister	6.00	.35
200	A53	5p chocolate	5.25	.25
201	A54	6p emerald	8.00	.50
202	A55	9p rose	10.00	.75
203	A56	1sh org yel	11.50	.75
204	A57	2sh blue, *rose*	21.00	2.25
205	A58	5sh rose red & bl	65.00	12.50
a.		5sh car & blue	65.00	9.00
		Nos. 193-205 (13)	143.75	18.95

See Nos. 209-229, 232.

King Edward VII
A59   A60

1901-05

206	A59	£1 deep rose	325.00 125.00
a.		Perf. 11 ('05)	325.00 140.00
208	A60	£2 dk blue ('02)	750.00 275.00
a.		Perf. 11 ('05)	850.00 600.00

See Nos. 230-231.

1903   **Redrawn**

209	A56	1sh yellow	15.00 1.40
a.		1sh orange	13.00 1.40

No. 209 has the network lighter than No. 203. In the latter the "P" and "E" of "POST-AGE" are in a position more nearly horizontal than on No. 209.

Perf. 11, 12x12½, 12½, 12½x11

1905-10   **Wmk. 13**

218	A46	½p blue green	1.25 .60
219	A47	1p rose red	1.00 .20
a.		1p carmine rose	2.00 .20
220	A49	2p violet	3.25 .20
a.		2p purple	3.25 .20
221	A50	2½p blue	3.50 .25
222	A51	3p brown org	4.50 .30
a.		3p dull yellow	5.25 .25
223	A52	4p bister	6.50 .40
224	A53	5p chocolate	6.00 .30
225	A54	6p emerald	8.25 .50
226	A55	9p orange brown	10.00 1.10
		9p brown rose	13.00 1.10
227	A55	9p car rose	10.00 1.10
228	A56	1sh yellow ('08)	10.00 1.00
229	A58	5sh org red & ultra	62.50 12.50
a.		5sh rose red & ultra	70.00 12.50
230	A59	£1 pale red ('07)	325.00 110.00
a.		£1 rose ('10)	325.00 100.00
231	A60	£2 dull blue	750.00 300.00
		Nos. 218-229 (12)	126.75 18.45

No. 220 Surcharged in Red

ONE PENNY

1912, July 1

232	A49	1p on 2p violet	.30 .20

POSTAL FISCAL STAMPS

On Jan. 1, 1884, all postage and fiscal stamps were made available for either purpose. Fiscal stamps became invalid after June 30, 1901.

Used values are for examples with postal cancellations used from Jan. 1, 1884 through June 30, 1901.

Beware of copies with a pen cancellation removed and a fake postmark added.

Stamps inscribed "Stamp Duty" that were issued primarily in postal rates in the normal postage stamp size are listed in the postage section (Nos. 146-178, 180-183, 192-192A). The stamps meeting primarily fiscal rates and in the larger fiscal stamp size, are listed here in the Postal-Fiscal section.

Stamps Inscribed "Stamp Statute"

Victoria — PF1   Coat of Arms — PF2

PF3

3p, denomination in center. Frames differ on design PF1.

Wmk. V and Crown (70)

1870-83   Typo.   Perf. 13

AR1	PF1	1p green	17.50	17.50
		Revenue cancel		2.00
a.		Perf. 12½	30.00	30.00
AR2	PF1	3p lilac	125.00	100.00
		Revenue cancel		45.00
AR3	PF1	4p red	125.00	75.00
		Revenue cancel		45.00
AR4	PF1	6p blue	50.00	15.00
		Revenue cancel		5.00
a.		Perf. 12	50.00	15.00
		Revenue cancel		5.00
AR5	PF1	1sh blue, *blue*	45.00	17.50
		Revenue cancel		6.00
a.		Perf. 12	50.00	22.50
		Revenue cancel		6.00
b.		Perf. 12½	45.00	17.50
		Revenue cancel		6.00
c.		Wmk. 50, perf. 13	40.00	17.50
		Revenue cancel		6.00
d.		Wmk. 50, perf. 12	65.00	22.50
		Revenue cancel		7.00
AR6	PF1	2sh blue, *grn*	65.00	42.50
		Revenue cancel		12.50
a.		Perf. 12	65.00	50.00
		Revenue cancel		12.50
b.		Wmk. 50, perf. 13	75.00	55.00
		Revenue cancel		12.50
c.		Wmk. 50, perf. 12	75.00	55.00
		Revenue cancel		12.50
AR7	PF2	2sh 6p orange, *yel*	125.00	55.00
		Revenue cancel		30.00
a.		Perf. 12	125.00	75.00
		Revenue cancel		30.00
b.		Perf. 12½	—	75.00
		Revenue cancel		30.00
AR8	PF1	5sh blue, *yel*	150.00	50.00
		Revenue cancel		30.00
a.		Perf. 12	175.00	
b.		Perf. 12½	150.00	50.00
		Revenue cancel		30.00
AR9	PF1	10sh brown, *rose*	600.00	125.00
		Revenue cancel		50.00
a.		Perf. 12		
b.		Wmk. 50, perf. 13	600.00	125.00
		Revenue cancel		50.00
c.		Wmk. 50, perf. 12		
AR10	PF1	£1 lilac, *yel*	350.00	100.00
		Revenue cancel		40.00
a.		Perf. 12	350.00	100.00
		Revenue cancel		40.00
b.		Perf. 12½	350.00	100.00
		Revenue cancel		40.00
AR11	PF3	£5 black, *grn*	3,000.	300.00
		Revenue cancel		70.00
a.		Perf. 12		
b.		Perf. 12½	3,000.	300.00
		Revenue cancel		70.00

Nos. AR1-AR12 distributed for postal use from Jan. 1, 1884 through Apr. 23, 1884.

No. AR1 Surcharged "½d/HALF"

1879-96

AR12	PF1	½p on 1p grn	75.00	50.00
		Revenue cancel		20.00

Stamps Inscribed "Stamp Duty"

PF4   PF5

PF6   PF7

PF8   PF9

PF10   PF11

PF12   PF13

PF14   PF15

PF16   PF17

PF18   PF23

PF19   PF24

PF20   PF25

PF21   PF26

PF22   PF27

PF28

Wmk. V and Crown (70)

1879-96   Litho.   Perf. 13

AR13	PF4	1p green	50.00	10.00
		Revenue cancel		4.00
a.		Perf. 12	50.00	10.00
		Revenue cancel		4.00
b.		Perf. 12½		
AR14	PF8	1sh 6p pink	125.00	20.00
		Revenue cancel		8.00
a.		Perf. 12	—	27.50
		Revenue cancel		8.00
b.		Perf. 12½		
AR15	PF11	3sh violet, *blue*	350.00	27.50
		Revenue cancel		8.00
a.		Perf. 12	—	40.00
		Revenue cancel		8.00
b.		Perf. 12½		
AR16	PF12	4sh orange	80.00	17.50
		Revenue cancel		4.00
a.		Perf. 12	80.00	17.50
		Revenue cancel		4.00
b.		Perf. 12½		
AR17	PF4	6sh green	250.00	27.50
		Revenue cancel		8.00
AR18	PF15	10sh brn, *pink*	350.00	60.00
		Revenue cancel		30.00
a.		Perf. 12		
b.		Perf. 12½		
AR19	PF16	15sh lilac	1,000.	125.00
		Revenue cancel		40.00
AR20	PF17	£1 orange	400.00	65.00
		Revenue cancel		15.00
a.		Perf. 12½	400.00	
AR21	PF18	£1 5sh pink	850.00	150.00
		Revenue cancel		100.00
AR22	PF19	£1 10sh olive	900.00	100.00
		Revenue cancel		40.00
AR23	PF20	35sh lilac	3,500.	
		Revenue cancel		200.00
AR24	PF21	£2 blue	—	90.00
		Revenue cancel		15.00
AR25	PF22	45sh violet	1,500.	125.00
		Revenue cancel		35.00
AR26	PF23	£5 rose	1,250.	275.00
		Revenue cancel		70.00
AR27	PF24	£6 blue, *pink*	—	500.00
		Revenue cancel		100.00
AR28	PF25	£7 violet, *blue*	—	500.00
		Revenue cancel		100.00
AR29	PF26	£8 scarlet, *yel*	—	650.00
		Revenue cancel		110.00
AR30	PF27	£9 green, *grn*	—	650.00
		Revenue cancel		110.00

Typo.

AR31	PF4	1p green	30.00	10.00
		Revenue cancel		4.00
a.		Perf. 12	30.00	10.00
		Revenue cancel		4.00
b.		Perf. 12½		
AR32	PF5	1p brown	8.00	2.00
		Revenue cancel		.75
a.		Perf. 12	8.00	3.00
		Revenue cancel		.75
b.		Perf. 12½		
AR33	PF6	6p blue	40.00	6.00
		Revenue cancel		2.50
a.		Perf. 12	50.00	6.00
		Revenue cancel		2.50
b.		Perf. 12½		
AR34	PF7	1sh blue, *blue*	65.00	6.00
		Revenue cancel		2.50
a.		Perf. 12	65.00	6.00
		Revenue cancel		2.50

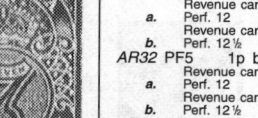

b.	Perf. 12½		65.00	6.00
	Revenue cancel			2.50
AR35	PF7	1sh blue, *yel,*		
		perf 12½	90.00	20.00
	Revenue cancel			10.00
AR36	PF8	1sh 6p pink	150.00	25.00
	Revenue cancel			10.00
AR37	PF9	2sh blue, *grn*	100.00	15.00
	Revenue cancel			7.50
a.	Perf. 12		125.00	17.50
	Revenue cancel			7.50
b.	Perf. 12½		—	20.00
	Revenue cancel			7.50
AR38	PF10	2sh 6p orange,		
		perf 12½	80.00	12.50
	Revenue cancel			2.00
AR39	PF11	3sh violet, *bl,*		
		perf 12½	200.00	22.50
	Revenue cancel			7.50
AR40	PF11	3sh bister	60.00	17.50
	Revenue cancel			7.50
AR41	PF12	4sh org, perf		
		12½	90.00	10.00
	Revenue cancel			2.50
AR42	PF13	5sh claret, *yel*	55.00	6.00
	Revenue cancel			2.00
a.	Perf. 12		70.00	12.50
	Revenue cancel			2.00
b.	Perf. 12½		55.00	12.50
	Revenue cancel			2.00
AR43	PF13	5sh car rose	85.00	10.00
	Revenue cancel			4.00
AR44	PF14	6sh green	90.00	25.00
	Revenue cancel			8.00
AR45	PF15	10sh brn, *pink*	—	60.00
	Revenue cancel			30.00
a.	Perf. 12			
b.	Perf. 12½			
AR46	PF15	10sh green	110.00	17.50
	Revenue cancel			10.00
AR47	PF16	15sh brown	350.00	45.00
	Revenue cancel			8.00
AR48	PF17	£1 org, *yel,*		
		perf 12½	375.00	65.00
	Revenue cancel			15.00
a.	Perf. 12		650.00	80.00
	Revenue cancel			15.00
AR49	PF18	£1 5sh pink	1,000.	90.00
	Revenue cancel			50.00
AR50	PF19	£1 10sh olive	700.00	80.00
	Revenue cancel			30.00
AR51	PF21	£2 blue	900.00	80.00
	Revenue cancel			15.00
a.	Perf. 12		—	100.00
	Revenue cancel			15.00
AR52	PF22	45sh gray lilac	2,500.	100.00
	Revenue cancel			30.00
AR53	PF23	£5 rose, perf.		
		12	—	250.00
	Revenue cancel			75.00
a.	perf. 12½		—	400.00
	Revenue cancel			100.00
AR54	PF28	£10 lilac	2,000.	100.00
	Revenue cancel			35.00
a.	Perf. 12		1,750.	110.00
	Revenue cancel			35.00

#AR49-AR52, AR54, used, are valued cto.

PF29

PF30

PF31

Wmk. V and Crown (70)

1879-1900		**Engr.**		**Perf. 12½**
AR55	PF29	£25 green	—	500.00
	Revenue cancel			65.00
a.	Perf. 13			
b.	Perf. 12			
AR56	PF30	£50 violet	—	500.00
	Revenue cancel			75.00
a.	Perf. 13			
AR57	PF31	£100 red	—	475.00
	Revenue cancel			125.00
a.	Perf. 13			
b.	Perf. 12			
	Revenue cancel			125.00
		Typo.		
AR58	PF29	£25 green	—	110.00
a.	Lithographed			
	Revenue cancel			50.00
AR59	PF30	£50 violet	—	150.00
a.	Lithographed			
	Revenue cancel			70.00
AR60	PF31	£100 red	—	225.00
a.	Lithographed			
	Revenue cancel			100.00

Nos. AR55-AR60, used, are valued cto.

PF32

1887-90				**Typo.**
AR61	PF32	£5 cl & ultra	1,250.	100.00
	Revenue cancel			25.00
AR62	PF32	£6 blue & yel	1,500.	125.00
	Revenue cancel			30.00
AR63	PF32	£7 blk & red	1,750.	150.00
	Revenue cancel			40.00
AR64	PF32	£8 org & lilac	1,900.	175.00
	Revenue cancel			45.00
AR65	PF32	£9 red & green	2,000.	200.00
	Revenue cancel			50.00

Nos. AR61-AR65, used, are valued cto.

SEMI-POSTAL STAMPS

SP1

Queen Victoria and Figure of Charity — SP2

Wmk. V and Crown (70)

1897, Oct.		**Typo.**		**Perf. 12½**
B1	SP1	1p deep blue	15.00	18.00
B2	SP2	2½p red brown	110.00	110.00

These stamps were sold at 1sh and 2sh6p respectively. The premium was given to a charitable institution.

Victoria Cross — SP3

Scout Reporting SP4

1900				
B3	SP3	1p brown olive	70.00	70.00
B4	SP4	2p emerald	140.00	140.00

These stamps were sold at 1sh and 2sh respectively. The premium was given to a patriotic fund in connection with the South African War.

REGISTRATION STAMPS

R1

		Unwmk.		
1854, Dec. 1		**Typo.**		**Imperf.**
F1	R1	1sh rose & blue	1,000.	100.00
1857				**Rouletted 7**
F2	R1	1sh rose & blue	5,000.	150.00

LATE FEE STAMP

LF1

		Unwmk.		
1855, Jan. 1		**Typo.**		**Imperf.**
I1	LF1	6p lilac & green	650.00	150.00

POSTAGE DUE STAMPS

D1

Wmk. V and Crown (70)

1890		**Typo.**		**Perf. 12½**
J1	D1	½p claret & blue	2.00	1.60
J2	D1	1p claret & blue	3.25	1.25
J3	D1	2p claret & blue	5.00	1.50
J4	D1	4p claret & blue	6.00	1.75
J5	D1	5p claret & blue	5.50	1.60
J6	D1	6p claret & blue	6.25	1.50
J7	D1	10p claret & blue	60.00	32.50
J8	D1	1sh claret & blue	35.00	5.00
J9	D1	2sh claret & blue	92.50	42.50
J10	D1	5sh claret & blue	140.00	90.00
	Nos. J1-J10 (10)		355.50	179.20
1891				
J11	D1	½p lake & blue	2.50	2.00
J12	D1	1p brown red & blue	4.25	1.25
J13	D1	2p brown red & blue	4.25	.90
J14	D1	4p lake & blue	6.50	4.50
	Nos. J11-J14 (4)		17.50	8.65
1894				
J15	D1	½p bl grn & rose	1.60	1.40
J16	D1	1p bl grn & rose	.70	.35
J17	D1	2p bl grn & rose	1.50	.30
J18	D1	4p bl grn & rose	3.50	1.25
J19	D1	5p bl grn & rose	4.00	2.25
J20	D1	6p bl grn & rose	4.00	2.50
J21	D1	10p bl grn & rose	10.00	8.50
J22	D1	1sh bl grn & rose	5.00	2.75
J23	D1	2sh green & rose	60.00	20.00
J24	D1	5sh green & rose	100.00	35.00
	Nos. J15-J24 (10)		190.30	74.30
1906				**Wmk. 13**
J25	D1	½p yel grn & rose	1.60	1.60
J26	D1	1p yel grn & rose	3.00	.65
J27	D1	2p yel grn & rose	6.50	1.50
J28	D1	4p yel grn & rose	13.00	10.00
	Nos. J25-J28 (4)		24.10	13.75

A 5p with wmk. 13 exists but was not issued.

WESTERN AUSTRALIA

ˈwes-tərn o-ˈstrāl-yə

LOCATION — Western part of Australia, occupying about a third of that continent
GOVT. — British Colony
AREA — 975,920 sq. mi.
POP. — 184,124 (1901)

CAPITAL — Perth

Western Australia was one of the six British colonies that united on January 1, 1901, to form the Commonwealth of Australia.

12 Pence = 1 Shilling
20 Shillings = 1 Pound

Unused values for Nos. 1-10 are for stamps without gum as these stamps are seldom found with original gum. Otherwise, unused values are for stamps with original gum as defined in the catalogue introduction.

Very fine examples of all rouletted and perforated stamps from Nos. 6-34 have roulettes or perforations touching the design. Examples clear on all four sides range from scarce to rare and will command higher prices.

Watermarks

Wmk. 82- Swan

Wmk. 70- V and Crown

Wmk. 13- Crown & Double-lined A

Wmk. 83- Crown and W A

Wmk. 74- Crown and Single-lined A

Swan

	A1	A2		
1854-57		**Engr.**	**Wmk. 82**	**Imperf.**
1	A1	1p black	750.	175.
			Litho.	
2	A2	2p brown, *red* ('57)	1,750.	450.
a.	2p brown, *deep red* ('57)		1,800.	750.
b.	Printed on both sides		2,000.	750.

See Nos. 4, 6-7, 9, 14-39, 44-52, 54, 59-61. For surcharges see Nos. 41, 55-56.

A3   A4

3	A3	4p blue	300.	150.
a.		Frame inverted		60,000.
		As "a," cut to shape		16,000.
b.		4p slate blue	1,250.	700.
4	A2	6p bronze ('57)	2,500.	600.
5	A4	1sh pale brown	400.	275.
a.		1sh dark brown	500.	375.
b.		1sh dark red brown	900.	400.
c.		1sh pale red brown		1,800.

Engraved
Rouletted

| 6 | A1 | 1p black | 1,400. | 400. |

Lithographed

7	A2	2p brown, *red* ('57)	3,250.	1,200.
a.		Printed on both sides		1,500.
8	A3	4p blue	1,400.	450.
9	A2	6p bronze ('57)	3,500.	800.
10	A4	1sh brown	1,500.	700.

The 1p, 2p, 4p and 6p are known with pin-perforation but this is believed to be unofficial. No. 7a is only recorded used and with pin perforations.

1860		**Engr.**		***Imperf.***
14	A1	2p vermilion	75.00	60.00
a.		2p pale orange	75.00	60.00
15	A1	4p blue	300.00	1,200.
16	A1	6p dull green	1,200.	600.00

Rouletted

17	A1	2p vermilion	450.00	175.00
a.		2p pale orange	400.00	160.00
18	A1	4p deep blue	2,250.	—
19	A1	6p dull green	1,750.	400.00

1861		**Clean-Cut Perf. 14 to 16**		
20	A1	1p rose	325.00	80.00
a.		Imperf.		
21	A1	2p blue	70.00	25.00
a.		Imperf., pair		
b.		Horiz. pair, imperf. vert.		
22	A1	4p vermilion	500.00	250.00
23	A1	6p purple brn	175.00	35.00
24	A1	1sh green	300.00	45.00
a.		Imperf.		

Rough Perf. 14 to 16

24B	A1	1p rose	200.00	27.50
24C	A1	6p pur brn, *bluish*	750.00	50.00
24D	A1	1sh deep green	1,200.	350.00

Perf. 14

25	A1	1p rose	140.00	45.00
25A	A1	2p blue	70.00	30.00
25B	A1	4p vermilion	200.00	100.00

		Unwmk.		**Perf. 13**
26	A1	1p lake	40.00	5.50
28	A1	6p violet	90.00	32.50

1865-79		**Wmk. 1**		**Perf. 12½**
29	A1	1p bister	40.00	2.00
30	A1	1p yel ocher	60.00	5.50
31	A1	2p yellow	45.00	.50
a.		2p bister (error) ('79)	7,500.	3,750.
32	A1	4p carmine	50.00	5.50
a.		Double impression	6,000.	
33	A1	6p violet	62.50	6.00
a.		6p lilac	125.00	6.00
b.		6p red lilac	125.00	6.00
c.		Double impression		
34	A1	1sh bright green	85.00	10.50
a.		1sh sage green	200.00	18.00
		Nos. 29-34 (6)	342.50	30.00

1872-78				**Perf. 14**
35	A1	1p bister	50.00	2.00
36	A1	1p yellow ocher	40.00	.50
37	A1	2p yellow	40.00	.40
38	A1	4p carmine	200.00	65.00
39	A1	6p lilac	80.00	4.00
		Nos. 35-39 (5)	410.00	71.90

A5   A8

1872				**Typo.**
40	A5	3p red brown	26.00	3.75
a.		3p brown	26.00	3.75

See #53, 92. For surcharges see #57, 69-72A.

No. 31 Surcharged in Green   ONE PENNY

1875		**Engr.**		**Perf. 12½**
41	A1	1p on 2p yellow	200.00	45.00
a.		Pair, one without surcharge		
b.		"O" of "ONE" omitted		
c.		Triple surcharge		

Forged surcharges exist.

1882		**Wmk. 2**		**Perf. 12**
44	A1	1p ocher yellow	85.00	1.60
46	A1	2p yellow	110.00	1.10
47	A1	4p carmine	160.00	27.50
48	A1	6p pale violet	275.00	27.50
		Nos. 44-48 (4)	630.00	57.70

1882				**Perf. 14**
49	A1	1p ocher yellow	14.00	.20
50	A1	2p yellow	18.00	.20
51	A1	4p carmine	72.50	11.50
52	A1	6p violet	47.50	2.50
a.		6p pale violet	80.00	2.50

Typographed

53	A5	3p brown	12.50	.45
a.		3p red brown	8.50	.70
		Nos. 49-53 (5)	164.50	14.85

1883		**Engr.**		**Perf. 12x14**
54	A1	1p ocher yellow	1,650.	300.00

Nos. 44 and 49 Surcharged in Red

1884				**Perf. 12**
55	A1	½p on 1p ocher yel	9.00	12.00

				Perf. 14
56	A1	½p on 1p ocher yel	13.00	15.00

No. 40 Surcharged in Green

1885		**Typo.**		**Wmk. 1**
57	A5	1p on 3p red brown	27.50	8.50
a.		1p on 3p brown	12.00	6.00
b.		"1" with straight top	27.50	11.00

Wmk. Crown and C A (2)

1885		**Typo.**		**Perf. 14**
58	A8	½p green		2.00 .20
		See No. 89.		

1888				**Engr.**
59	A1	1p rose	12.00	.70
60	A1	2p slate	30.00	2.00
61	A1	4p red brown	82.50	18.00
		Nos. 59-61 (3)	124.50	20.70

A9   A10

A11   A12

1890-93				**Typo.**
62	A9	1p carmine rose	10.00	.20
63	A10	2p slate	14.00	.20
64	A11	2½p blue	6.00	.75
65	A12	4p orange brown	6.00	.80
66	A12	5p bister	8.25	1.00
67	A12	6p violet	14.00	.80
68	A12	1sh olive green	16.00	2.25
		Nos. 62-68 (7)	74.25	6.00

See Nos. 73-74, 76, 80, 90, 94.

Nos. 40 and 53a Surcharged in Green

1893		**Wmk. Crown and C C (1)**		
69	A5	1p on 3p red brown	11.00	5.00
a.		1p on 3p brown	11.00	3.25

---

b.		Double surcharge	725.00	

Wmkd. Crown and C A (2)

| 70 | A5 | 1p on 3p brown | 40.00 | 9.00 |

Nos. 40a and 53a Surcharged in Green

1895		**Wmk. Crown and C C (1)**		
71	A5	½p on 3p brown	7.00	3.00
a.		Double surcharge	700.00	

Green and Red Surcharge

| 72 | A5 | ½p on 3p brown | 125.00 | |

Wmk. Crown and C A (2)

| 72A | A5 | ½p on 3p brown | | 75.00 |

After the supply of paper watermarked Crown and C C was exhausted, No. 72A was printed. Ostensibly this was to provide samples for Postal Union distribution, but a supply for philatelic demands was also made.

Types of 1890-93 and

A15

1899-1901		**Typo.**		**Wmk. 83**
73	A9	1p carmine rose	3.50	.20
74	A10	2p yellow	9.00	.20
75	A15	2½p blue ('01)	6.00	.20
		Nos. 73-75 (3)	18.50	.60

A16   A17

A18   A19

A20   A21

A22   Southern Cross — A23

Queen Victoria
A24   A25

Perf. 12½, 12x12½

1902-05				**Wmk. 70**
76	A9	1p car rose	6.50	.20
a.		1p salmon		
b.		Perf. 11	100.00	5.00
c.		Perf. 12½x11		175.00
77	A16	2p yellow	3.25	.20
a.		Perf. 11	125.00	5.50
b.		Perf. 12½x11		225.00
79	A17	4p orange brn	6.00	.80
a.		Perf. 11	375.00	110.00
80	A17	5p ol bis, perf 12½ ('05)	72.50	40.00
a.		Perf. 11	45.00	21.00
81	A18	8p pale yel grn	20.00	2.75
82	A19	9p orange	27.50	4.00
	a.	Perf. 11	60.00	40.00

83	A20	10p red	27.50	5.50
84	A21	2sh red, *yel*	42.50	8.25
		Perf. 11	125.00	55.00
85	A22	2sh6p dk bl, *rose*	40.00	7.75
86	A23	5sh blue green	70.00	19.00
87	A24	10sh violet	175.00	60.00
88	A25	£1 brown org	475.00	225.00
		Nos. 76-88 (12)	965.75	373.45

Perf. 12½, 12x12½

1905-12				**Wmk. 13**
89	A8	½p dp green ('10)	2.25	.35
90	A9	1p rose	3.00	.20
e.		Perf. 11	13.00	2.50
f.		Perf. 12½x11	200.00	82.50
91	A16	2p yellow	3.00	.20
a.		Perf. 11	11.00	4.50
b.		Perf. 12½x11	225.00	95.00
92	A5	3p brown	6.50	.40
a.		Perf. 11	12.00	2.75
b.		Perf. 12½x11	260.00	82.50
93	A17	4p orange brn	8.00	1.50
a.		4p bister brown	8.00	1.50
b.		Perf. 11	475.00	90.00
94	A12	5p olive bis	10.00	.70
		Perf. 11	25.00	8.50
95	A18	8p pale yel grn ('12)	16.00	17.00
96	A19	9p orange	21.00	3.00
b.		Perf. 11	65.00	55.00
97	A20	10p red orange	21.00	10.00
98	A23	5s blue green	140.00	40.00
		Nos. 89-98 (10)	230.75	73.35

For surcharge see No. 103.

A26   A27

1906-07		**Wmk. 83**		**Perf. 14**
99	A26	6p bright violet	18.00	.70
100	A27	1sh olive green	25.00	10.00

1912		**Wmk. 74**		**Perf. 11½x12**
101	A26	6p bright violet	11.00	3.00
102	A27	1sh gray green	22.50	4.00
a.		Perf. 12½		

No. 91 Surcharged

1912		**Wmk. 13**		**Perf. 12½**
103	A16	1p on 2p yellow		.75 .40

Stamps of Western Australia were replaced by those of Australia.

POSTAL FISCAL STAMPS

Postal use of the 1p telegraph stamp was authorized beginning Oct. 25, 1886.

Used values are for examples with postal cancellations.

Beware of copies with a pen cancellation removed and a fake postmark added.

PF1   PF2

1886		**Wmk. 1**		**Perf. 14**
AR1	PF1	1p bister	30.00	6.00

				Perf. 12½
AR2	PF1	1p bister	27.50	4.00

The 6p is known postally used but was not authorized.

Authorized for postal use by the Post and Telegraph Act of Sept. 5, 1893 were the current revenue stamps through the 1sh value.

Beware of copies with a pen cancellation removed and a fake postmark added.

Because the Act specified current stamps, postally used examples from the provisional issue of of 1881 are not included here.

1882		Wmk. 2		Perf. 14
AR3	PF2	1p purple	10.00	1.50
AR4	PF2	2p purple	100.00	35.00
AR5	PF2	3p purple	35.00	2.25
AR6	PF2	6p purple	40.00	4.00
AR7	PF2	1sh purple	75.00	5.50
		Wmk. 83		
AR8	PF2	1p purple	6.50	1.50
AR9	PF2	3p purple	27.50	2.25
AR10	PF2	6p purple	27.50	2.50
AR11	PF2	1sh purple	75.00	10.00

Nos. AR7, AR11 have a rectangular outer frame and a circular frame around the swan.

Higher values are known with postal cancels, some postally used, but these were not authorized.

AUSTRALIA

o-'străl-yə

LOCATION — Oceania, south of Indonesia, bounded on the west by the Indian Ocean
GOVT. — Self-governing dominion of the British Commonwealth
AREA — 2,967,909 sq. mi.
POP. — 17,892,423 (1996)
CAPITAL — Canberra

Australia includes the former British colonies of New South Wales, Victoria, Queensland, South Australia, Western Australia and Tasmania.

12 Pence = 1 Shilling
20 Shillings = 1 Pound
100 Cents = 1 Dollar (1966)

Catalogue values for unused stamps in this country are for Never Hinged items, beginning with Scott 197 in the regular postage section, Scott C6 in the air post section, Scott J71 in the postage due section, and all of the Australian Antarctic Territory.

Watermarks

Wmk. 8- Wide Crown and Wide A

Wmk. 9- Wide Crown and Narrow A

Wmk. 10- Narrow Crown and Narrow A

Wmk. 11- Multiple Crown and A

Wmk. 12- Crown and Single-lined A

Wmk. 13- Large Crown and Double-lined A

Wmk. 55- Large Crown and NSW

Wmk. 203- Small Crown and A Multiple

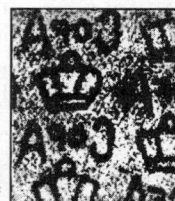
Wmk. 228- Small Crown and C of A Multiple

Kangaroo and Map — A1

Die I - The inside frameline has a break at left, even with the top of the letters of the denomination.
Die II - The frameline does not show a break.
Die III - The left inside frameline shows a break parallel to the face of the kangaroo.
Die IV - As Die III, with a break in the top outside frameline above the "ST" of "AUSTRALIA." The upper right inside frameline has an incomplete corner.
Dies are only indicated when there are more than one for any denomination.

1913 Typo. Wmk. 8 Perf. 11½, 12

1	A1	½p green	6.00	2.75
		Never hinged	10.00	
2	A1	1p car, die I	6.75	.75
		Never hinged	11.50	
h.		Die II	12.50	1.00
		Never hinged	22.50	
3	A1	2p gray	24.00	4.00
		Never hinged	45.00	
4	A1	2½p dark blue	27.50	12.50
		Never hinged	45.00	
5	A1	3p ol bis, die I	45.00	8.75
		Never hinged	95.00	
a.		Die II	150.00	47.50
		Never hinged	300.00	
6	A1	4p orange	47.50	21.00
		Never hinged	100.00	
7	A1	5p orange brown	40.00	30.00
		Never hinged	110.00	
8	A1	6p ultra (II)	45.00	18.00
		Never hinged	125.00	
b.		Die III	1,000.	300.00
9	A1	9p purple	42.50	22.50
		Never hinged	110.00	
10	A1	1sh blue green	45.00	15.00
		Never hinged	175.00	
11	A1	2sh brown	160.00	75.00
		Never hinged	500.00	
12	A1	5sh yellow & gray	250.00	140.00
		Never hinged	650.00	
13	A1	10sh pink & gray	600.00	425.00
		Never hinged	1,600.	
14	A1	£1 ultra & brown	1,300.	1,000.
		Never hinged	2,750.	
15	A1	£2 dp rose & blk	2,350.	1,550.
		Nos. 1-12 (12)	739.25	350.25

On No. 4 "2½d" is colorless in solid blue background.
See Nos. 38-59, 96-102, 121-129, 206.

King George V A2

Kookaburra (Kingfisher) A3

1913-14 Unwmk. Engr. Perf. 11

17	A2	1p carmine	4.25	4.25
		Never hinged	5.75	
a.		Vert. pair, imperf. between	2,000.	
18	A3	6p lake brown ('14)	70.00	35.00
		Never hinged	150.00	

See No. 95.

A4

ONE PENNY
Die I - Normal die, having outside the oval band with "AUSTRALIA" a white line and a heavy colored line.
Die Ia - As die I with a small white spur below the right serif at foot of the "1" in left tablet.
Die II - A heavy colored line between two white lines back of the emu's neck. A white scratch crossing the vertical shading lines at the lowest point of the bust.
TWO PENCE
Die I - The numeral "2" is thin. The upper curve is 1mm. across and a very thin line connects it with the foot of the figure.
Die II - The "2" is thicker than in die I. The top curve is 1½mm across and a strong white line connects it with the foot of the figure. There are thin vertical lines across the ends of the groups of short horizontal lines at each side of "TWO PENCE."
THREE PENCE
Die I - The ends of the thin horizontal lines in the background run into the solid color of the various parts of the design. The numerals are thin and the letters of "THREE PENCE" are thin and irregular.
Die II - The oval about the portrait, the shields with the numerals, etc., are outlined by thin white lines which separate them from the horizontal background lines. The numerals are thick and the letters of "THREE PENCE" are heavy and regular.
FIVE PENCE
Die I - The top of the flag of the "5" is slightly curved.
Die II - The top of the flag of the "5" is flat. There are thin white vertical lines across the ends of the short horizontal lines at each side of "FIVE PENCE."

1914-24 Typo. Wmk. 9 Perf. 14

19	A4	½p emerald ('15)	2.50	.40
		Never hinged	4.50	
a.		Thin "½" at right	1,400.	700.00
20	A4	½p orange ('23)	2.50	1.25
		Never hinged	3.50	
21	A4	1p red (I)	4.25	.20
		Never hinged	7.50	
a.		1p carmine rose (I)	8.25	.80
		Never hinged	20.00	
b.		1p red (Ia)	375.00	4.75
		Never hinged	500.00	
c.		1p carmine (II) ('18)	60.00	30.00
		Never hinged	95.00	
d.		1p scar (I), rough paper	18.00	1.00
e.		1p rose red (Ia), rough paper	250.00	20.00
f.		1p brt rose (Ia), rough paper	375.00	50.00
22	A4	1p vio (I) ('22)	4.50	.60
		Never hinged	8.00	
a.		1p red violet	6.50	1.50
		Never hinged	10.00	
23	A4	1p green (I) ('24)	3.50	.20
		Never hinged	4.50	
24	A4	1½p choc ('18)	5.00	.20
		Never hinged	8.00	
a.		1½p red brown	5.50	.20
		Never hinged	14.00	
b.		1½p black brown	4.50	.25
		Never hinged	7.50	
25	A4	1½p emerald ('23)	3.50	.20
		Never hinged	4.00	
26	A4	1½p scarlet ('24)	2.50	.20
		Never hinged	3.50	
27	A4	2p brn org (I) ('20)	10.00	.25
		Never hinged	17.00	
a.		2p orange (I) ('20)	12.00	.30
		Never hinged	19.00	
b.		Booklet pane of 6		
28	A4	2p red (I) ('22)	7.50	.20
		Never hinged	14.00	
29	A4	2p red brn (I) ('24)	15.00	3.75
		Never hinged	25.00	
30	A4	3p ultra (I) ('24)	25.00	2.25
		Never hinged	35.00	
31	A4	4p orange ('15)	40.00	2.25
		Never hinged	70.00	
a.		4p yellow	110.00	16.00
		Never hinged	250.00	
32	A4	4p violet ('21)	17.50	13.00
		Never hinged	25.00	
33	A4	4p lt ultra ('22)	45.00	4.50
		Never hinged	60.00	
34	A4	4p ol bis ('24)	27.50	4.00
		Never hinged	37.50	
35	A4	4½p violet ('24)	22.50	4.00
		Never hinged	35.00	
36	A4	5p org brn ('15)	18.00	3.00
		Never hinged	45.00	

37	A4	1sh4p lt blue ('20)	65.00	19.00
		Never hinged	125.00	
		Nos. 19-37 (19)	321.25	59.45

See Nos. 60-76, 113-120, 124.

1915 Perf. 11½, 12

38	A1	2p gray	45.00	11.00
		Never hinged	95.00	
39	A1	2½p dark blue	45.00	15.00
		Never hinged	110.00	
40	A1	6p ultra (II)	125.00	19.00
		Never hinged	275.00	
a.		Die III	900.00	250.00
41	A1	9p violet	125.00	32.50
		Never hinged	275.00	
42	A1	1sh blue green	125.00	20.00
		Never hinged	325.00	
43	A1	2sh brown	400.00	90.00
		Never hinged	900.00	
44	A1	5sh yellow & gray	700.00	225.00
		Never hinged	1,500.	
		Nos. 38-44 (7)	1,565.	412.50

1915-24 Wmk. 10

45	A1	2p gray (I)	25.00	6.00
		Never hinged	40.00	
a.		Die II, shiny paper	35.00	8.00
46	A1	2½p dark blue	25.00	10.00
		Never hinged	40.00	
a.		"1" of fraction omitted	10,000.	3,500.
47	A1	3p olive bister (I)	20.00	3.50
		Never hinged	35.00	
a.		Die II	80.00	25.00
b.		3p lt olive (IV)	35.00	10.00
48	A1	6p ultra (II)	50.00	7.00
		Never hinged	90.00	
a.		6p chalky blue (III)	65.00	7.00
c.		6p ultra (IV)	50.00	6.00
49	A1	6p yel brn (IV, '23)	20.00	2.50
		Never hinged	40.00	
50	A1	9p lilac (III)	40.00	12.00
		Never hinged	55.00	
a.		9p violet (II)	35.00	6.00
		Never hinged	55.00	
51	A1	1sh blue grn (II, '16)	35.00	4.50
		Never hinged	55.00	
b.		Die IV	35.00	3.00
52	A1	2sh brown ('16)	150.00	15.00
		Never hinged	350.00	
53	A1	2sh vio brn (II, '24)	50.00	25.00
		Never hinged	100.00	
54	A1	5sh yel & gray ('18)	190.00	80.00
		Never hinged	350.00	
55	A1	10sh brt pink & gray ('17)	400.00	150.00
		Never hinged	750.00	
56	A1	£1 ultra & brn ('16)	1,250.	700.00
		Never hinged	2,500.	
a.		£1 ultra & brn org ('16)	1,300.	700.00
57	A1	£1 gray (IV, '24)	450.00	275.00
		Never hinged	750.00	
58	A1	£2 dp rose & blk ('19)	2,250.	1,250.
		Never hinged	3,000.	
59	A1	£2 rose & vio brn ('24)	1,750.	1,200.
		Never hinged	2,750.	
		Nos. 45-54 (10)	605.00	165.50

Perf. 14, 14½, 14½x14

1918-23 Wmk. 11

60	A4	½p emerald	3.00	1.00
		Never hinged	4.25	
a.		Thin "½" at right	110.00	45.00
61	A4	1p rose (I)	25.00	9.00
		Never hinged	32.50	
62	A4	1p dl grn (I) ('24)	6.00	6.00
		Never hinged	9.00	
63	A4	1½p choc (I) ('19)	5.00	1.00
		Never hinged	11.00	
a.		1½p red brown ('19)	8.00	1.00
		Never hinged	15.00	
		Nos. 60-63 (4)	39.00	17.00

1924 Unwmk. Perf. 14

64	A4	1p green (I)	4.25	3.75
		Never hinged	5.50	
65	A4	1½p carmine	4.25	3.00
		Never hinged	6.75	

Perf. 14, 13½x12½

1926-30 Wmk. 203

66	A4	½p orange	1.40	1.00
		Never hinged	3.00	
a.		Perf. 14 ('27)	6.50	5.25
		Never hinged	8.50	
67	A4	1p green (I)	1.50	.35
		Never hinged	3.00	
a.		1p green (Ia)	47.50	60.00
		Never hinged	65.00	
b.		Perf. 14	2.75	.45
		Never hinged	4.50	
68	A4	1½p rose red ('27)	2.75	.20
		Never hinged	3.50	
c.		Perf. 14 ('26)	6.00	.65
		Never hinged	12.00	
69	A4	1½p red brn ('30)	4.00	2.00
		Never hinged	8.00	
70	A4	2p red brn (II, '28)	7.00	4.00
		Never hinged	10.50	
a.		Perf. 14 (I, '27)	27.50	20.00
		Never hinged	40.00	
71	A4	2p red (II) ('30)	4.00	.20
		Never hinged	12.50	
a.		2p red (I) ('30)	5.00	1.60
		Never hinged	12.00	
c.		Unwmkd. (II) ('31)	1,500.	1,000.

72	A4	3p ultra (I)	30.00 10.00
		Never hinged	55.00
a.		3p ultra (II) ('29)	17.50 2.00
		Never hinged	30.00
b.		Perf. 14	20.00 4.50
		Never hinged	37.50
73	A4	4p ol bis ('29)	16.00 2.00
		Never hinged	32.50
a.		Perf. 14 ('28)	42.50 22.50
		Never hinged	85.00
74	A4	4½p dk vio ('27)	17.00 3.75
		Never hinged	25.00
a.		Perf. 13½x12½ ('28)	47.50 13.00
		Never hinged	67.50
75	A4	5p brn buff (II) ('30)	17.50 4.50
		Never hinged	32.50
76	A4	1sh4p pale turq bl ('28)	85.00 20.00
		Never hinged	175.00
a.		Perf. 14 ('27)	125.00 70.00
		Never hinged	300.00
		Nos. 66-76 (11)	186.15 48.00

For surcharges & overprints see #106-107, O3-O4.

Parliament House, Canberra A5

Unwmk.

1927, May 9		**Engr.**	**Perf. 11**
94	A5	1½p brown red	.60 .20
		Never hinged	1.00
a.		Vert. pair, imperf. btwn.	2,750. 2,500.

Opening of Parliament House at Canberra.

Melbourne Exhibition Issue
Kookaburra Type of 1914

1928, Oct. 29			
95	A3	3p deep blue	3.75 3.00
		Never hinged	5.25
a.		Pane of 4	125.00 150.00
		Never hinged	190.00

No. 95a was issued at the Melbourne Intl. Phil. Exhib. No marginal inscription. Printed in sheets of 60 stamps (15 panes). No. 95 was printed in sheets of 120 and issued Nov. 2 throughout Australia.

Kangaroo-Map Type of 1913
Perf. 11½, 12

1929-30		**Wmk. 203**		**Typo.**
96	A1	6p brown	21.00	5.00
		Never hinged	30.00	
97	A1	9p violet	30.00	5.00
		Never hinged	70.00	
98	A1	1sh blue green	27.50	4.50
		Never hinged	65.00	
99	A1	2sh red brown	60.00	12.50
		Never hinged	140.00	
100	A1	5sh yel & gray	190.00	60.00
		Never hinged	325.00	
101	A1	10sh pink & gray	350.00	275.00
		Never hinged	600.00	
102	A1	£2 dl red & blk ('30)	1,800.	425.00
		Never hinged	3,750.	
		Nos. 96-102 (7)	2,903.	787.00

For overprint see No. O5.

Black Swan — A6

Unwmk.

1929, Sept. 28		**Engr.**	**Perf. 11**
103	A6	1½p dull red	.75 .75
		Never hinged	1.40

Centenary of Western Australia.

Capt. Charles Sturt — A7

1930, June 2			
104	A7	1½p dark red	.40 .20
		Never hinged	.45
105	A7	3p dark blue	3.50 3.00
		Never hinged	6.00

Capt. Charles Sturt's exploration of the Murray River, cent.

FIVE PENCE

Nos. 68 and 74a surcharged

1930	**Wmk. 203**		**Perf. 13½x12½**
106	A4	2p on 1½p rose red	.75 .25
		Never hinged	1.50
107	A4	5p on 4½p dark violet	5.00 5.00
		Never hinged	10.00

"Southern Cross" over Hemispheres A8

Perf. 11, 11½

1931, Mar. 19			**Unwmk.**
111	A8	2p dull red	.75 .20
		Never hinged	1.10
112	A8	3p blue	4.75 2.00
		Never hinged	8.00
		Nos. 111-112, C2 (3)	12.50 9.20

Trans-oceanic flights (1928-1930) of Sir Charles Edward Kingsford-Smith (1897-1935). See #C3 for similar design. For overprints see #CO1, O1-O2.

Types of 1913-23 Issues
Perf. 13½x12½

1931-36		**Typo.**		**Wmk. 228**
113	A4	½p orange ('32)	2.50	1.60
		Never hinged	3.00	
114	A4	1p green (I)	1.50	.20
		Never hinged	2.25	
115	A4	1½p red brn ('36)	6.00	4.50
		Never hinged	8.00	
116	A4	2p red (II)	1.75	.20
		Never hinged	2.50	
117	A4	3p ultra (II) ('32)	17.50	.30
		Never hinged	25.00	
118	A4	4p ol bis ('33)	17.50	.45
		Never hinged	26.00	
120	A4	5p brn buff (II) ('32)	12.00	.30
		Never hinged	20.00	

Perf. 11½, 12; 13½x12½ (1sh4p)

121	A1	6p yel brn ('36)	16.00	11.00
		Never hinged	25.00	
122	A1	9p violet ('32)	16.50	2.00
		Never hinged	40.00	
124	A4	1sh4p lt blue ('32)	60.00	6.00
		Never hinged	140.00	
125	A1	2sh red brn ('35)	4.00	.90
		Never hinged	6.00	
126	A1	5sh yel & gray ('32)	125.00	18.00
		Never hinged	250.00	
127	A1	10sh pink & gray ('32)	325.00	100.00
		Never hinged	650.00	
128	A1	£1 gray ('35)	450.00	165.00
		Never hinged	650.00	
129	A1	£2 dl rose & blk ('34)	2,000.	350.00
		Never hinged	3,000.	
		Nos. 113-129 (15)	3,405.	660.45

For redrawn 2sh see No. 206. For overprints see Nos. O6-O11.

Sydney Harbor Bridge — A9

Unwmk.

1932, Mar. 14		**Engr.**	**Perf. 11**
130	A9	2p red	1.90 .50
		Never hinged	2.25
131	A9	3p blue	4.00 3.00
		Never hinged	6.75
132	A9	5sh gray green	350.00 200.00
		Never hinged	575.00

Wmk. 228
Perf. 10½
Typo.

133	A9	2p red	1.60 .80
		Never hinged	2.75

Opening of the Sydney Harbor Bridge on Mar. 19, 1932.
Value for 5sh, used, is for CTO copies.
For overprints see Nos. O12-O13.

Kookaburra A14

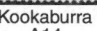

Male Lyrebird A16

1932, June 1			**Perf. 13½x12½**
139	A14	6p light brown	15.00 .50
		Never hinged	25.00

1932, Feb. 15		**Unwmk.**	**Perf. 11**
		Size: 21½x25mm	
141	A16	1sh green	37.50 .75
		Never hinged	75.00

See #175, 300. For overprint see #O14.

Yarra Yarra Tribesman, Yarra River and View of Melbourne A17

Wmk. 228

1934, July 2		**Engr.**	**Perf. 10½**
142	A17	2p vermilion	1.10 .30
		Never hinged	1.75
a.		Perf. 11½	3.75 .75
		Never hinged	6.50
143	A17	3p blue	2.75 2.50
		Never hinged	5.25
a.		Perf. 11½	4.25 2.50
		Never hinged	6.50
144	A17	1sh black	40.00 16.00
		Never hinged	67.50
a.		Perf. 11½	40.00 20.00
		Never hinged	72.50
		Nos. 142-144 (3)	43.85 18.80

Centenary of Victoria.

Merino Sheep — A18

1934, Nov. 1			**Perf. 11½**
147	A18	2p copper red, Die I	2.50 .20
		Never hinged	3.50
a.		Die II	20.00 1.50
148	A18	3p dark blue	10.00 6.00
		Never hinged	15.00
149	A18	9p dark violet	35.00 25.00
		Never hinged	67.50
		Nos. 147-149 (3)	47.50 31.20

Capt. John Macarthur (1767-1834), "father of the New South Wales woolen industry."
Two dies of 2p: I, shading on hill in background uneven from light to dark. II, shading is uniformly dark.

Cenotaph in Whitehall, London — A19

George V on His Charger "Anzac" — A20

1935, Mar. 18   *Perf. 13½x12½*
150 A19   2p red   .65   .20
    Never hinged   .90

Perf. 11
151 A19   1sh black   40.00   25.00
    Never hinged   70.00
   a.   Perf 13½x12½   1,000.
    Never hinged   1,400.

Anzacs' landing at Gallipoli, 20th anniv.

1935, May 2   *Perf. 11½*
152 A20   2p red   .75   .20
    Never hinged   2.00
153 A20   3p blue   3.00   2.25
    Never hinged   7.50
154 A20   2sh violet   37.50   30.00
    Never hinged   70.00
    Nos. 152-154 (3)   41.25   32.45

25th anniv. of the reign of King George V.

Amphitrite Joining Cables between Australia and Tasmania A21

1936, Apr. 1
157 A21   2p red   .35   .20
    Never hinged   .60
158 A21   3p dark blue   3.25   2.00
    Never hinged   5.25

Australia/Tasmania telephone link.

Proclamation Tree and View of Adelaide, 1936 — A22

1936, Aug. 3
159 A22   2p red   .40   .20
    Never hinged   1.10
160 A22   3p dark blue   3.25   3.25
    Never hinged   5.00
161 A22   1sh green   12.00   6.00
    Never hinged   20.00
    Nos. 159-161 (3)   15.65   9.45

Centenary of South Australia.

Gov. Arthur Phillip at Sydney Cove — A23

1937, Oct. 1   *Perf. 13x13½*
163 A23   2p red   .90   .20
    Never hinged   1.90
164 A23   3p ultra   2.75   1.60
    Never hinged   4.50
165 A23   9p violet   16.00   11.00
    Never hinged   25.00
    Nos. 163-165 (3)   19.65   12.80

150th anniversary of New South Wales.

Kangaroo A24

Queen Elizabeth A25

King George VI
A26   A27

Koala — A28

Merino Sheep — A29

Kookaburra (Kingfisher) A30

Platypus A31

Queen Elizabeth and King George VI in Coronation Robes
A32   A33

King George VI and Queen Elizabeth A34

Two Types of A25 and A26:
Type I - Highlighted background. Lines around letters of Australia Postage and numerals of value.
Type II - Background of heavy diagonal lines without the highlighted effect. No lines around letters and numerals.

Perf. 13½x14, 14x13½

				Engr.	**Wmk. 228**
1937-46					
166	A24	½p org, perf. 15x14 ('42)		.20	.20
		Never hinged		1.00	
a.		Perf. 13½x14 ('38)		.70	.25
		Never hinged		1.25	
167	A25	1p emerald (I)		.20	.20
		Never hinged		1.00	
168	A26	1½p dull red brn (II)		3.00	1.75
		Never hinged		4.50	
a.		Perf. 15x14 ('41)		4.25	3.50
		Never hinged		6.25	
169	A26	2p scarlet (I)		.30	.20
		Never hinged		1.00	
170	A27	3p ultramarine		12.00	.60
		Never hinged		30.00	
a.		3p dp ultra, thin paper ('38)		20.00	.80
		Never hinged		50.00	
171	A28	4p grn, perf. 15x14 ('42)		.85	.20
		Never hinged		1.25	
a.		Perf. 13½x14 ('38)		2.50	.20
		Never hinged		5.00	
172	A29	5p pale rose vio, perf. 14x15 ('46)		1.25	.50
		Never hinged		2.00	
a.		Perf. 14x13½ ('38)		2.50	.55
		Never hinged		4.00	
173	A30	6p vio brn, perf. 15x14 ('42)		.60	.20
		Never hinged		1.50	
a.		Perf. 13½x14		5.25	.85
		Never hinged		15.00	
b.		6p chocolate, perf. 15x14		1.00	1.50
		Never hinged		1.50	
174	A31	9p sep, perf. 14x15 ('43)		1.75	.20
		Never hinged		2.50	
a.		Perf. 14x13½ ('38)		3.75	.90
		Never hinged		7.25	
175	A16	1sh gray grn, perf. 15x14 ('41)		1.10	.20
		Never hinged		1.50	
a.		Perf. 13½x14		22.50	2.00
		Never hinged		47.50	

176	A27	1sh4p magenta ('38)		1.50	.50
		Never hinged		2.00	

Perf. 13½

177	A32	5sh dl red brn ('38)		5.00	2.50
		Never hinged		10.00	
178	A33	10sh dl gray vio ('38)		30.00	13.00
		Never hinged		45.00	
179	A34	£1 bl gray ('38)		60.00	27.50
		Never hinged		90.00	
		Nos. 166-179 (14)		117.75	47.75

No. 175 measures 17½x21½mm.
See #223A, 293, 295, 298, 300. For surch. & overprints see #190, M1, M4-M5, M7.

1938-42   *Perf. 15x14*

180	A25	1p emerald (II)		.55	.25
181	A25	1p dl red brn (II) ('41)		.50	.20
181B	A26	1½p bl grn (II) ('41)		.60	.20
182	A26	2p scarlet (II)		.60	.20
182B	A26	2p red vio (II) ('41)		.20	.20
183	A27	3p dk ultra ('40)		15.00	.75
		Never hinged		30.00	
183A	A27	3p dk vio brn ('42)		.20	.20
		Nos. 180-183A (7)		17.65	2.00
		Set, never hinged		40.00	

No. 183 differs from Nos. 170-170a in the shading lines on the king's left eyebrow which go downward, left to right, instead of the reverse. Also, more of the left epaulette shows.
For surcharges & ovpt. see #188-189, M3.

Coil Perforation

A special perforation was applied to stamps intended for use in coils to make separation easier. It consists of small and large holes (2 small, 10 large, 2 small) on the stamps' narrow side. Some of the stamps so perforated were sold in sheets.

This coil perforation may be found on Nos. 166, 181, 182, 182B, 193, 215, 223A, 231, 257, 315-316, 319, 319a and others.

Nurse, Sailor, Soldier and Aviator — A35

Perf. 13½x13

				Engr.	**Wmk. 228**
1940, July 15					
184	A35	1p green		1.00	.20
		Never hinged		2.00	
185	A35	2p red		1.00	.20
		Never hinged		2.00	
186	A35	3p ultra		4.00	3.00
		Never hinged		7.00	
187	A35	6p chocolate		12.50	10.00
		Never hinged		21.00	
		Nos. 184-187 (4)		18.50	13.40

Australia's participation in WWII.

No. 182 Surcharged in Blue

1941, Dec. 10   *Perf. 15x14*
188 A26   2½p on 2p red   .20   .20
    Never hinged   .25

No. 183 Surcharged in Blue and Yellow

189 A27   3½p on 3p dk ultra   .40   .35
    Never hinged   .50

No. 172a Surcharged in Purple

Perf. 14x13½
190 A29   5½p on 5p pale rose vio   4.00   4.00
    Never hinged   4.75
    Nos. 188-190 (3)   4.60   4.55

Queen Elizabeth
A36   A37

King George VI
A38   A39

George VI and Blue Wrens A40

Emu A41

1942-44   **Engr.**   *Perf. 15x14*

191	A36	1p brown vio ('43)		.20	.20
192	A37	1½p green		.20	.20
193	A38	2p lt rose vio ('44)		.20	.20
194	A39	2½p red		.20	.20
195	A40	3½p ultramarine		.20	.20
196	A41	5½p indigo		.35	.20
		Nos. 191-196 (6)		1.35	1.20
		Set, never hinged		1.75	

See #224-225. For overprint see #M2.

Catalogue values for unused stamps in this section, from this point to the end of the section, are for Never Hinged items.

Duke and Duchess of Gloucester A42

1945, Feb. 19   **Engr.**   *Perf. 14½*
197 A42   2½p brown red   .20   .20
198 A42   3½p bright ultra   .25   .25
199 A42   5½p indigo   .25   .25
    Nos. 197-199 (3)   .70   .70

Inauguration of the Duke of Gloucester as Governor General.

Official Crest and Inscriptions A43

Dove and Australian Flag A44

Angel of Peace; "Motherhood" and "Industry" A45

1946, Feb. 18   **Wmk. 228**   *Perf. 14½*
200 A43   2½p carmine   .20   .20
201 A44   3½p deep ultra   .20   .25
202 A45   5½p deep yellow green   .40   .35
    Nos. 200-202 (3)   .80   .80

End of WWII. See #1456-1458.

Sir Thomas Mitchell and Map of Queensland
A46

1946, Oct. 14
203	A46	2½p dark carmine	.20	.20
204	A46	3½p deep ultra	.20	.25
205	A46	1sh olive green	.80	.35
	Nos. 203-205 (3)		1.20	.80

Sir Thomas Mitchell's exploration of central Queensland, cent.

Kangaroo-Map Type of 1913 Redrawn

1945, Dec.	**Typo.**	**Perf. 11½**
206	A1	2sh dk red brown	4.00	3.50

The R and A of AUSTRALIA are separated at the base and there is a single line between the value tablet and "Two Shillings." On No. 125 the tail of the R touches the A, while two lines appear between value tablet and "Two Shillings." There are many other minor differences in the design.
For overprint see No. M6.

John Shortland A47

Pouring Steel A48

Loading Coal — A49

1947, Sept.	**Engr.**	**Perf. 14½x14**
207	A47	2½p brown red	.30	.20

		Perf. 14½		
208	A48	3½p deep blue	.25	.30
209	A49	5½p deep green	.35	.30
	Nos. 207-209 (3)		.90	.80

150th anniv. of the discovery of the Hunter River estuary, site of Newcastle by Lieut. John Shortland. By error the 2½p shows his father, Capt. John Shortland.

Princess Elizabeth — A50

Perf. 14x14½			
1947, Nov. 20		**Wmk. 228**	
210	A50	1p brown violet	.20	.20

See No. 215.

Hereford Bull A51

Crocodile A52

1948, Feb. 16		**Perf. 14½**	
211	A51	1sh3p violet brown	1.90	.70
212	A52	2sh chocolate	2.00	.50

See No. 302.

William J. Farrer — A53

Design: No. 214, Ferdinand von Mueller.

1948		**Perf. 14½x14**	
213	A53	2½p red	.20	.20
214	A53	2½p dark red	.20	.20

William J. Farrer (1845-1906), wheat researcher, and Ferdinand von Mueller (1825-1896), German-born botanist.
Issue dates: #213, July 12. #214, Sept. 13.

Elizabeth Type of 1947
1948, Aug.	**Unwmk.**	**Perf. 14x14½**
215	A50	1p brown violet	.20	.20

Scout in Uniform — A55

Arms of Australia — A56

1948, Nov. 15	**Engr.**	**Wmk. 228**
216	A55	2½p brown red	.20	.20

Pan-Pacific Scout Jamboree, Victoria, Dec. 29, 1948 to Jan. 9, 1949. See No. 249.

1949-50	**Wmk. 228**	**Perf. 14x13½**
218	A56	5sh dark red	3.50	.50
219	A56	10sh red violet	15.00	1.00
220	A56	£1 deep blue	35.00	4.00
221	A56	£2 green ('50)	100.00	15.00
	Nos. 218-221 (4)		153.50	20.50

Henry Hertzberg Lawson (1867-1922), Author and Poet — A57

Perf. 14½x14		
1949, June 17	**A57**	**Unwmk.**
222	A57	2½p rose brown	.20	.20

Outback Mail Carrier and Plane — A58

1949, Oct. 10			
223	A58	3½p violet blue	.25	.20

UPU, 75th anniv.

Types of 1938, 1942-44 & A59

Aborigine A59

John Forrest A60

1948-50	**Unwmk.**	**Perf. 14½x14**
223A	A24	½p orange ('49)	.20	.20
224	A37	1½p green ('49)	.25	.20
225	A38	2p lt rose violet	.30	.20

		Wmk. 228		
226	A59	8½p dark brown ('50)	.50	.40
	Nos. 223A-226 (4)		1.25	1.00

Issued: 2p, Dec.; ½p, Sept.; 1½p, 8/29; 8½p, 8/14.
See Nos. 248, 303.

1949, Nov. 28		**Wmk. 228**	
227	A60	2½p brown red	.20	.20

Forrest (1847-1918), explorer & statesman.

New South Wales A61

Victoria A62

First stamp designs.

Perf. 14½x14		
1950, Sept. 27		**Unwmk.**
228	A61	2½p rose brown	.25	.20
229	A62	2½p rose brown	.25	.20
a.	Pair, #228-229		.65	.40

Cent. of Australian adhesive postage stamps. Issued in sheets of 160 stamps containing alternate copies of Nos. 228 and 229.

Elizabeth A63

George VI A64

A65

A66

1950-51	**Engr.**	**Unwmk.**
230	A63	1½p deep green	.30	.20
231	A63	2p yellow grn ('51)	.20	.20
232	A64	2½p violet brn ('51)	.20	.20
233	A64	3p dull green ('51)	.30	.20
	Nos. 230-233 (4)		1.00	.80

Issued: 1½p, 6/19; 2p, 3/28; 2½p, 5/23; 3p, 11/14.

1950-52		**Wmk. 228**	
234	A64	2½p red	.20	.20
235	A64	3p red ('51)	.20	.20
236	A65	3½p red brown ('51)	.30	.20
237	A65	4½p scarlet ('52)	.40	.35
238	A65	6½p choc ('52)	.30	.30
238A	A65	6½p blue green ('52)	.40	.20
239	A66	7½p deep blue ('51)	.45	.30
	Nos. 234-239 (7)		2.25	1.75

Issued: 2½p, 4/12; 3p, 2/28; 7½p, 10/31; 3½p, 11/28; 4½p, #238, 2/20; #238A, 4/9.

A67

Founding of the Commonwealth of Australia, 50th Anniv. — A68

Designs: No. 240, Sir Edmund Barton. No. 241, Sir Henry Parkes. 5½p, Duke of York opening first Federal Parliament. 1sh6p, Parliament House, Canberra.

Perf. 14½x14		
1951, May 1	**Engr.**	**Unwmk.**
240	A67	3p carmine	.40	.20
241	A67	3p carmine	.40	.20
a.	Pair, #240, 241		.80	.65
242	A68	5½p deep blue	.40	.70
243	A68	1sh6p red brown	1.25	.90
	Nos. 240-243 (4)		2.45	2.00

Edward Hammond Hargraves A69

King George VI A70

Design: No. 245, Charles Joseph Latrobe (1801-1875), first governor of Victoria.

1951, July 2			
244	A69	3p rose brown	.25	.20
245	A69	3p rose brown	.25	.20
a.	Pair, #244, 245		.65	.65

Discovery of gold in Australia, cent. (No. 244); Establishment of representative government in Victoria, cent. (No. 245). Sheets contain alternate rows of Nos. 244 and 245.

1952, Mar. 19	**Wmk. 228**	**Perf. 14½**
247	A70	1sh½p slate blue	1.60	.25

Aborigine Type of 1950 Redrawn Size: 20½x25mm

248	A59	2sh6p dark brown	3.25	.40

Portrait as on A59; lettering altered and value repeated at lower left. See No. 303.

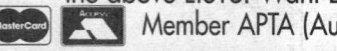
Scout Type of 1948
Dated "1952-53"
Perf. 14x14½

1952, Nov. 19   Wmk. 228
249 A55 3½p red brown   .20 .20
Pan-Pacific Scout Jamboree, Greystanes, Dec. 30, 1952, to Jan. 9, 1953.

Modern Dairy, Butter Production — A71

Perf. 14½

1953, Feb. 11   Unwmk.   Typo.
250 A71 3p shown   .75 .20
251 A71 3p Wheat   .75 .20
252 A71 3p Beef   .75 .20
  a. Strip of 3, #250-252   4.50 4.50
253 A71 3½p shown   .75 .20
254 A71 3½p Wheat   .75 .20
255 A71 3½p Beef   .75 .20
  a. Strip of 3, #253-255   3.25 3.25
  Nos. 250-255 (6)   4.50 1.20
Both the 3p and 3½p were printed in panes of 50 stamps: 17 Butter, 17 Wheat and 16 Beef. The stamps were issued to encourage food production.

Queen Elizabeth II — A72

Perf. 14½x14
1953-54   Unwmk.   Engr.
256 A72 1p purple   .20 .20
256A A72 2½p deep blue ('54) .25 .20
257 A72 3p dark green   .25 .20

Wmk. 228
258 A72 3½p dark red   .25 .20
258B A72 6½p orange ('54)   .90 .20
  Nos. 256-258B (5)   1.85 1.00
Issued: 3½p, 4/21; 3p, 6/17; 1p, 8/19; 2½p, 6½p, 6/23.
See Nos. 292, 296.

Coronation Issue

Queen Elizabeth II A73

1953, May 25   Unwmk.
259 A73 3½p rose red   .25 .20
260 A73 7½p violet   .70 .45
261 A73 2sh dull green   2.25 1.10
  Nos. 259-261 (3)   3.20 1.75

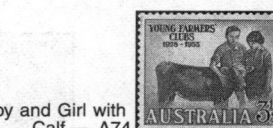
Boy and Girl with Calf — A74

1953, Sept. 3   Perf. 14½
262 A74 3½p dp green & red brn .25 .20
Official establishment of Young Farmers' Clubs, 25th anniv.

Lieut. Gov. David Collins A75

Tasmania Stamp of 1853 A77

Sullivan Cove, Hobart A76

#264, Lieut. Gov. William Paterson (facing left).

1953, Sept. 23   Perf. 14½x14
263 A75 3½p red brown   .35 .20
264 A75 3½p red brown   .35 .20
  a. Pair, #263-264   1.25 1.10
265 A76 2sh green   3.00 2.50
  Nos. 263-265 (3)   3.70 2.90
Settlement in Tasmania, 150th anniv. Sheets contain alternate rows of Nos. 263 and 264.

1953, Nov. 11   Perf. 14½
266 A77 3p red   .20 .20
Tasmania's first postage stamps, cent.

Elizabeth II and Duke of Edinburgh — A78

Elizabeth II — A79

Telegraph Pole and Key — A80

1954, Feb. 2   Perf. 14½x14, 14x14½
267 A78 3½p rose red   .20 .20
268 A79 7½p purple   .30 .80
269 A78 2sh green   1.50 1.00
  Nos. 267-269 (3)   2.00 2.00
Visit of Queen Elizabeth II and the Duke of Edinburgh, 1954.

1954, Apr. 7   Engr.   Perf. 14
270 A80 3½p dark red   .25 .20
Inauguration of the telegraph in Australia, cent.

Red Cross and Globe — A81

Swan — A82

1954, June 9   Perf. 14½x14
271 A81 3½p deep blue & red   .20 .20
Australian Red Cross Society.

1954, Aug. 2   Unwmk.   Perf. 14½
274 A82 3½p black   .20 .20
Western Australia's first postage stamp, cent.

Diesel and Early Steam Locomotives A83

1954, Sept. 13   Perf. 14x14½
275 A83 3½p red brown   .20 .20
Centenary of Australian railroads.

Antarctic Flora and Fauna and Map — A84

1954, Nov. 17   Perf. 14
276 A84 3½p black   .20 .20
Australia's interest in the Antarctic continent.

Olympic Circles and Arms of Melbourne — A85

1954, Dec. 1
277 A85 2sh dark blue   2.50 1.50
16th Olympic Games to be held in Melbourne Nov.-Dec. 1956. See No. 286.

Globe, Flags and Rotary Emblem — A86

1955, Feb. 23   Perf. 14x14½
278 A86 3½p carmine   .20 .20
Rotary International, 50th anniv.

Elizabeth II — A87

Top of US Monument, Canberra — A88

1955, Mar. 9   Wmk. 228   Perf. 14½
279 A87 1sh½p dk gray blue   3.50 .25
See No. 301.

1955, May 4   Unwmk.   Perf. 14x14½
280 A88 3½p deep ultra   .20 .20
Friendship between Australia and the US.

Cobb and Company Mail Coach A89

1955, July 6   Perf. 14½x14
281 A89 3½p dark brown   .20 .20
282 A89 2sh brown   2.50 1.90
Pioneers of Australia's coaching era.

World Map, YMCA Emblem A90

Engr. and Typo.
1955, Aug. 10   Perf. 14
283 A90 3½p Prus green & red   .20 .20
Centenary of YMCA.

Florence Nightingale and Modern Nurse — A91

Queen Victoria — A92

1955, Sept. 21 Engr. Perf. 14x14½
284 A91 3½p red violet   .20 .20
Centenary of Florence Nightingale's work in the Crimea and of the founding of modern nursing.

1955, Oct. 17   Perf. 14½
285 A92 3½p green   .20 .20
South Australia's first postage stamps, cent.

Olympic Type of 1954
1955, Nov. 30 Unwmk. Perf. 14
286 A85 2sh deep green   2.50 1.50
16th Olympic Games at Melbourne, Nov. 22-Dec. 8, 1956.

Queen Victoria, Queen Elizabeth II and Badges of Victoria, New South Wales and Tasmania — A93

1956, Sept. 26   Perf. 14½x14
287 A93 3½p brown carmine   .25 .20
Centenary of responsible government in Victoria, New South Wales and Tasmania.

Melbourne Coat of Arms — A94

Southern Cross, Olympic Torch — A95

Collins Street, Melbourne A96

Design: 2sh, Melbourne across Yarra River.

1956, Oct. 31 Engr. Perf. 14½, 14
288 A94 4p dark carmine   .30 .20
289 A95 7½p ultramarine   .55 .40
Photo.
Perf. 14x14½
290 A96 1sh multicolored   .70 .45
Perf. 12x11½
Granite Paper
291 A96 2sh multicolored   .95 .95
    Nos. 288-291 (4)   2.50 2.00
16th Olympic Games, Melbourne, 11/22-12/8.
A lithographed souvenir sheet incorporating reproductions of Nos. 288-291 in reduced size was of private origin and not postally valid.

Types of 1938-55 and

Queen Elizabeth II — A97

Perf. 14½x14, 14x15, 15x14, 14½
1956-57   Engr.   Unwmk.
292 A72 3½p dark red   1.00 .20
293 A28 4p green   1.60 .20
294 A97 4p claret ('57)   .30 .20
  a. Booklet pane of 6 ('57) 7.50
295 A30 6p brown violet   2.75 .20
296 A72 6½p orange   1.75 .20
297 A97 7½p violet ('57)   3.00 .40
298 A31 9p sepia   9.00 .55
299 A97 10p gray blue ('57) 2.75 .20
300 A16 1sh gray green   6.00 .30
301 A87 1sh7p redsh brn ('57) 4.50 .30
302 A52 2sh chocolate   12.00 .25
303 A59 2sh6p brown ('57)   9.00 .25
    Nos. 292-303 (12)   53.65 3.25
No. 300 measures 17½x21½mm. No. 303 measures 20½x25mm and is the redrawn type of 1952.
Issued: 3½p, 7/2; 2sh, 7/21; #293, 6p, 8/18; 6½p, Sept. 9p, 1sh, 12/13; 2sh6p, 1/30; 10p, 3/6; #294, 1sh7p, 3/13; 7½p, 11/13.

South Australia Coat of Arms — A99

1957, Apr. 17 Unwmk. Perf. 14½
304 A99 4p brown red   .20 .20
Centenary of responsible government in South Australia.
There are two types of No. 304.

Caduceus and Map of Australia A100

1957, Aug. 21   Perf. 14½x14
305 A100 7p violet blue   .60 .20
Royal Flying Doctor Service of Australia.

Star of Bethlehem and Praying Child A101

1957, Nov. 6   Engr.
306 A101 3½p dull rose   .25 .20
307 A101 4p pale purple   .25 .20
    Christmas.

Canberra War Memorial, Sailor and Airman A102

#309, As #308 with soldier and service woman. Printed in alternate rows in sheet.

1958, Feb. 10   Unwmk.
308 A102 5½p brown carmine   1.25 .75
309 A102 5½p brown carmine   1.25 .75
  a. Pair, #308-309   3.50 3.50

Sir Charles Kingsford-Smith and "Southern Cross" — A103

1958, Aug. 27   Perf. 14x14½
310 A103 8p brt violet blue 1.00 .90
1st air crossing of the Tasman Sea, 30th anniv. See New Zealand No. 321.

Broken Hill Mine — A104

1958, Sept. 10   Perf. 14½x14
311 A104 4p brown   .25 .20
Broken Hill mining field, 75th anniv.

Nativity — A105

1958, Nov. 5   Perf. 14½x15
312 A105 3½p dark red   .20 .20
313 A105 4p dark purple   .25 .20
    Christmas.

A106

A107

A108

A109

A110

Platypus A111

Tasmanian Tiger A112

Flannel Flower — A113

Aboriginal Stockman Cutting Out a Steer A114

Designs: 3p, Queen Elizabeth II facing right. 6p, Banded anteater. 8p, Tiger cat. 9p, Kangaroos. 11p, Rabbit bandicoot. 1sh6p, Christmas bells (flower). 2sh3p, Wattle (flower). 2sh5p, Banksia (flower). 3sh, Waratah (flower).

FIVE PENCE
Die I - Four short lines inside "5" at right of ball; six short lines left of ball; full length line above ball is seventh from bottom. Odd numbered horizontal rows in each sheet are in Die I.
Die II - Five short lines inside "5" at right of ball; seven at left; full length line above ball is eighth from bottom. Even numbered horizontal rows in each sheet are in Die II.

Perf. 14½x14, 14x14½, 14½
1959-64   Engr.   Unwmk.
314 A106 1p dull violet   .20 .20
315 A107 2p red brown   .55 .20
316 A108 3p bluish green   .20 .20
317 A108 3½p dark green   .20 .20
318 A109 4p carmine   1.90 .20
  a. Booklet pane of 6   25.00
319 A110 5p dark blue (I)   .90 .20
  a. 5p dark blue (II)   .90 .20
  b. Booklet pane of 6 ('60) 11.00
320 A111 6p chocolate   2.10 .20
321 A111 8p red brown   .80 .20
322 A111 9p brown black   1.90 .20
323 A111 11p dark blue   1.40 .20
324 A111 1sh slate green   3.75 .20
325 A112 1sh2p dk purple   1.40 .20
326 A113 1sh6p red, yellow   2.75 .60
327 A113 2sh dark blue   1.40 .20
328 A113 2sh3p green, yel   1.40 .20
328A A113 2sh3p yellow grn   5.25 1.00
329 A113 2sh6p brown, yellow 6.50 .40
330 A113 3sh crimson   1.60 .35
Wmk. 228
331 A114 5sh red brown   21.00 1.00
    Nos. 314-331 (19)   55.20 6.15
Issued: 1p, 4p, 2/2; 3½p, 3/18; 2sh, 4/8; 3p, 5/20; 3sh, 7/15; 1sh, #328, 9/9; 5p, 10/1; 9p, 10/21; 1sh6p, 2/3/60; 2sh5p, 3/16/60; 8p, 5/11/60; 6p, 9/30/60; 11p, 5/3/61; 5sh, 7/26/61; 2p, 1sh2p, 3/21/62; #328A, 10/28/64.

Luminescent Printings
Paper with an orange red phosphorescence (surface coating), was used for some printings of the Colombo Plan 1sh, No. 340, the Churchill 5p, No. 389, and several regular postage stamps. These include 2p, 3p, 6p, 8p, 9p, 11p, 1sh2p, 1sh6p and 2sh3p (Nos. 315, 316, 365, 367, 321, 368, 323, 325, 369, 328A).
Stamps printed only on phosphorescent paper include the Monash 5p, Hargrave 5p, ICY 2sh3p and Christmas 5p (Nos. 388, 390-393) and succeeding commemoratives; the 2sh, 2sh6p and 3sh regular birds (Nos. 370, 372, 373); and most of the regular series in decimal currency.
Ink with a phosphorescent content was used in printing most of the 5p red, No. 366, almost all of the 5p red booklets, No. 366a, most of the decimal 4c regular, No. 397, and its booklet pane, No. 397a, and all of No. 398.

Postmaster Isaac Nichols Boarding Vessel to Receive Mail — A115

1959, Apr. 22   Perf. 14½x14
332 A115 4p dark gray blue   .25 .20
First post office, Sydney, 150th anniv.

Parliament House, Brisbane, and Queensland Arms — A116

1959, June 5   Perf. 14x14½
333 A116 4p dk green & violet .25 .20
Cent. of Queensland self-government.

Approach of the Magi — A117

1959, Nov. 4 **Perf. 15x14½**
334 A117 5p purple .25 .20
Christmas.

Girl Guide and Lord Baden-Powell — A118

1960, Aug. 18 **Perf. 14½x14**
335 A118 5p dark blue .30 .20
50th anniversary of the Girl Guides.

The Overlanders by Sir Daryl Lindsay — A119

1960, Sept. 21 **Perf. 14½**
336 A119 5p lilac rose .30 .20
Exploration of Australia's Northern Territory, cent.

Melbourne Cup and Archer, 1861 Winner — A120

1960, Oct. 12 **Unwmk.**
337 A120 5p sepia .30 .20
Centenary of the Melbourne Cup.

Queen Victoria A121 **Open Bible and Candle A122**

1960 Nov. 2 **Engr.** **Perf. 14½**
338 A121 5p dark green .20 .20
Centenary of the first Queensland stamps.

1960, Nov. 9 **Unwmk.**
339 A122 5p maroon .20 .20
Christmas; beginning of 350th anniv. year of the publication of the King James translation of the Bible.

Colombo Plan Emblem — A123

1961, June 30 **Perf. 14x14½**
340 A123 1sh red brown .75 .20
Colombo Plan for the peaceful development of South East Asia countries, 10th anniv.

Dame Nellie Melba, by Sir Bertram Mackennal — A124

1961, Sept. 20 **Perf. 14½**
341 A124 5p deep blue .30 .20
Dame Nellie Melba, singer, birth cent.

Page from Book of Hours, 15th Century A125

John McDouall Stuart — A126

1961, Nov. 8 **Perf. 14½x14**
342 A125 5p reddish brown .30 .20
Christmas; end of the 350th anniv. year of the publication of the King James translation of the Bible.

1962, July 25 **Unwmk.** **Perf. 14½**
345 A126 5p carmine .30 .20
First south-north crossing of Australia by John McDouall Stuart, cent.

Nurse and Rev. Flynn's Grave — A127

1962, Sept. 5 **Photo.** **Perf. 13½**
346 A127 5p multicolored .30 .20
a. Red omitted 400.00
Australian Inland Mission founded by Rev. John Flynn, 50th anniv.

Woman and Globe — A128 **Madonna and Child — A129**

1962, Sept. 26 **Engr.** **Perf. 14x14½**
347 A128 5p dark green .30 .20
World Conf. of the Associated Country Women of the World, Melbourne, Oct. 2-12.

1962, Oct. 17 **Perf. 14½**
348 A129 5p deep violet .30 .20
Christmas.

View of Perth and Kangaroo Paw — A130

Arms of Perth A131

1962, Nov. 1 **Photo.** **Perf. 14**
349 A130 5p multicolored .30 .20
a. Red omitted 750.00
Perf. 14½x14
350 A131 2sh3p blk, red & ultra 4.00 4.00
British Empire and Commonwealth Games, Perth, Nov. 22-Dec. 1.

Elizabeth II — A132 **Elizabeth II and Prince Philip — A133**

1963, Feb. 18 **Engr.** **Perf. 14½**
351 A132 5p dark green .30 .20
352 A133 2sh3 red brown 4.00 4.00
Visit of Elizabeth II and Prince Philip.

Walter Burley Griffin and Arms of Canberra A134

Red Cross Centenary Emblem — A135

1963, Mar. 8 **Unwmk.** **Perf. 14½x14**
353 A134 5p dark green .35 .20
50th anniv. of Canberra; Walter Burley Griffin, American architect, who laid out plan for Canberra.

1963, May 8 **Photo.** **Perf. 13½x13**
354 A135 5p dk blue, red & gray .35 .20
Centenary of the International Red Cross.

Explorers Blaxland, Lawson and Wentworth Looking West from Mt. York — A136

1963, May 28 **Engr.** **Perf. 14½x14**
355 A136 5p dark blue .30 .20
1st crossing of the Blue Mts., 150th anniv.

Globe, Ship, Plane and Map of Australia A137

1963, Aug. 28 **Unwmk.**
356 A137 5p red .35 .20
Importance of exports to Australian economy.

Elizabeth II A138 **Black-backed Magpie and Eucalyptus A139**

Abel Tasman and Ship — A144

George Bass, Whaleboat — A145

Designs: 6p, Yellow-tailed thornbill, horiz. 1sh6p, Galah on tree stump. 2sh, Golden whistler. 2sh5p, Blue wren and bracken fern. 2sh6p, Scarlet robin, horiz. 3sh, Straw-necked ibis. 5sh, William Dampier and "Roebuck" sailing ship. 7sh6p, Capt. James Cook. 10sh, Matthew Flinders and three-master "Investigator." £2, Admiral Philip Parker King.

Perf. 15x14
1963-65 **Unwmk.** **Engr.**
365 A138 5p green .55 .20
a. Booklet pane of 6 ('64) 20.00
b. Pair, imperf. btwn. 1.50 1.50
366 A138 5p red .45 .20
a. Booklet pane of 6 25.00
Photo.
Perf. 13½
367 A139 6p multi .70 .20
a. Vert. pair, imperf. btwn.
368 A139 9p multi .90 2.40
369 A139 1sh6p multi .65 1.25
370 A139 2sh multi 1.50 .40
371 A139 2sh5p multi 2.25 3.00
372 A139 2sh6p multi 4.25 2.75
a. Red omitted 1,500.
373 A139 3sh multi 4.25 1.50
Engr.
Perf. 14½x14, 14½x15
374 A144 4sh violet blue 2.50 .50
Wmk. 228
375 A145 5sh red brown 3.50 1.10
376 A144 7sh6p olive green 16.50 14.00
377 A144 10sh deep claret 26.00 4.00
378 A145 £1 purple 30.00 13.00
379 A145 £2 brn blk 55.00 65.00
Nos. 365-379 (15) 149.00 109.50

No. 365a was printed in sheets of 288 which were sold intact by the Philatelic Bureau. These sheets have been broken to obtain pairs and blocks which are imperf. between (see No. 365b).
Issued: #365, 4sh, 10/9/63; 10sh, £1, 2/26/64; 9p, 1sh6p, 2sh5p, 3/11/64; 6p, 8/19/64; 7sh6p, £2, 8/26/64; 5sh, 11/25/64; 2sh, 2sh6p, 3sh, 4/21/65; #366, 6/30/65.
See Nos. 400-401, 406-417, 1727-1728.

Star of Bethlehem — A146

1963, Oct. 25 **Unwmk.** **Perf. 14½**
380 A146 5p blue .20 .20
Christmas.

Cable Around World and Under Sea — A147

1963, Dec. 3 **Photo.** **Perf. 13½**
381 A147 2sh3p gray, ver, blk & blue 4.50 3.50
Opening of the Commonwealth Pacific (telephone) cable service (COMPAC). See New Zealand No. 364.

Bleriot 60 Plane, 1914 — A148

1964, July 1   Engr.   Perf. 14½x14
382 A148 5p olive green   .20   .20
383 A148 2sh3p red   5.25   4.25

50th anniv. of the first air mail flight in Australia; Maurice Guillaux, aviator.

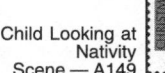

Child Looking at Nativity Scene — A149

1964, Oct. 21   Photo.   Perf. 13½
384 A149 5p bl, blk, red & buff   .20   .20
  a.   Red omitted   475.00
  b.   Black omitted   600.00

Christmas.

No. 384a used is valued on cover. The red ink can be removed from No. 384 by bleaching.

"Simpson and His Donkey" by Wallace Anderson — A150

1965, Apr. 14   Engr.   Perf. 14x14½
385 A150 5p olive bister   .25   .20
386 A150 8p dark blue   1.25   .90
387 A150 2sh3p rose claret   4.50   4.00
        Nos. 385-387 (3)   6.00   5.10

50th anniv. of the landing of the Australian and New Zealand Army Corps (ANZAC) at Gallipoli, Turkey, Apr. 25, 1915. Private John Simpson Kirkpatrick saved the lives of many wounded soldiers. The statue erected in his honor stands in front of Melbourne's Shrine of Remembrance.

Radio Mast and Satellite Orbiting Earth A151

Winston Churchill A152

1965, May 10   Photo.   Perf. 13½
388 A151 5p multicolored   .20   .20
  a.   Black ("5d") and pylon) omitted   850.00

ITU, cent.

1965, May 24
389 A152 5p lt blue, gray & blk   .25   .20

Sir Winston Spencer Churchill (1874-1965), statesman and WWII leader.
See New Zealand No. 371.

John Monash and Transmission Tower — A153

Lawrence Hargrave and Sketch for 1902 Seaplane A154

1965, June 23   Photo.   Perf. 13½
390 A153 5p red, yel, blk & brn   .25   .20

Birth cent. of General Sir John Monash (1865-1931), soldier, Vice-Chancellor of University of Melbourne and chairman of the Victoria state electricity commission.

1965, Aug. 4   Unwmk.   Perf. 13½
391 A154 5p multicolored   .25   .20
  a.   Purple (5d) omitted   225.00

50th anniv. of the death of Lawrence Hargrave (1850-1915), aviation pioneer.

ICY Emblem — A155

Nativity — A156

1965, Sept. 1   Photo.   Perf. 13½
392 A155 2sh3p lt blue & green   2.75   2.50

International Cooperation Year.

1965, Oct. 20   Unwmk.   Perf. 13½
393 A156 5p multicolored   .30   .20
  a.   Gold omitted   1,000.
  b.   Ultramarine omitted   475.00

Christmas.

Types of 1963-65 and

Elizabeth II — A157

Humbug Fish — A158

Designs: No. 400, Yellow-tailed thornbill, horiz. 6c, blue-faced honeyeater, horiz. 8c, Coral fish. 9c, Hermit crab. 10c Anemone fish. 13c, Red-necked avocet. 15c, Galah on tree stump. 20c, Golden whistler. 24c Azure kingfisher, horiz. 25c, Scarlet robin, horiz. 30c Straw-necked ibis. 40c Abel Tasman and ship. 50c, William Dampier and "Roebuck" sailing ship. 75c, Capt. James Cook. $1, Matthew Flinders and three-master "Investigator." $2, George Bass and whaleboat. $4, Admiral Philip Parker King.

Perf. 14½x14 (A157); 13½ (A158, A139)

Engr. (A157), Photo. (A158, A139)
1966-71
394 A157 1c red brown   .25   .20
395 A157 2c olive green   .65   .20
396 A157 3c Prus green   .65   .20
397 A157 4c red   .20   .20
  a.   Booklet pane of 5 + label   30.00
398 A157 5c on 4c red ('67)
                                     .30   .20
  a.   Booklet pane of 5 + label
                                    5.50
399 A157 5c dk blue ('67)   .65   .20
  a.   Booklet pane of 5 + label   11.00
400 A139 5c lt grn, blk, brn & yel
                                     .25   .20
401 A139 6c gray, blk, lem & bl   .70   .30
401A A157 6c orange ('70)   .50   .20
402 A158 7c brn, ver, blk & gray .75   .20
402A A157 7c dp rose lilac ('71)   .65   .20
403 A158 8c multicolored   .75   .30
404 A158 9c multicolored   .75   .20
405 A158 10c lt brn, blk, org & bl .75   .20
406 A139 13c lt bl grn, blk, gray & red
                                    1.60   .20
  a.   Red omitted   1,000.
  b.   Gray omitted   750.00
407 A139 15c lt grn, blk, gray & rose
                                    1.40   .60
  a.   Gray omitted   1,500.

408 A139 20c pink, blk, yel & gray 2.75   .20
  a.   Yellow omitted   900.00
409 A139 24c tan, blk, vio bl & org .80   .85
410 A139 25c gray, grn, blk & red 3.25   .20
  a.   Red omitted   1,100.
411 A139 30c lt grn, buff, blk & red 11.00 .55
  a.   Red omitted   900.00

Engr.
Perf. 14½x14, 14½x15
412 A144 40c violet blue   4.50   .20
413 A145 50c brown red   6.25   .20
414 A144 75c olive green   .90   .70
415 A144 $1 deep claret   1.60   .20
  a.   Perf 15x14   75.00 15.00
416 A145 $2 purple   6.75   .45
417 A145 $4 sepia   5.00   4.50
        Nos. 394-417 (26)   53.60 11.85

No. 398 issued in booklets only.
Booklet panes of 10 of No. 399, and of 5 No. 400, are torn from sheets. They were issued for the use of "Australian Defence Forces," as the covers read, in Viet Nam.
Issued: #398, 399, 9/29/67; #401A, 9/28/70; #402A, 10/1/71; #415a, 1973; others, 2/14/66.

Coil Stamps
1966-67   Photo.   Perf. 15 Horiz.
418 A157 3c emerald, blk & buff   .40   .35
419 A157 4c org red, blk & buff   .60   .20
420 A157 5c blue, black & buff   .75   .20
        Nos. 418-420 (3)   1.75   .75

Issued: 5c, 9/29/67; others, 2/14/66.

Rescue A159

1966, July 6   Photo.   Perf. 13½
421 A159 4c blue, ultra & black   .25   .20

Royal Life Saving Society, 75th anniv.

Adoration of the Shepherds A160

1966, Oct. 19   Photo.   Perf. 13½
422 A160 4c olive & black   .25   .20

Christmas.

Dutch Sailing Ship, 17th Century — A161

Hands Reaching for Bible — A162

1966, Oct. 24   Photo.   Perf. 13½
423 A161 4c bl, blk, dp org & gold .25   .20

350th anniv. of Dirk Hartog's discovery of the Australian west coast, and his landing on the island named after him.

1967, Mar. 7   Photo.   Perf. 13½
424 A162 4c multicolored   .25   .20

British and Foreign Bible Soc., 150th anniv.

Combination Lock and Antique Keys — A163

1967, Apr. 5   Photo.   Perf. 13½
425 A163 4c emerald, blk & lt blue .25   .20

150th anniv. of banking in Australia (Bank of New South Wales).

Lions Intl., 50th Anniv. — A164

1967, June 7   Photo.   Perf. 13½
426 A164 4c ultra, black & gold   .25   .20

YWCA Emblems and Flags A165

1967, Aug. 21   Photo.   Perf. 13½
427 A165 4c dk blue, lt bl & lilac .25   .20

World Council Meeting of the YWCA, Monash University, Victoria, Aug. 14-Sept. 1.

Seated Women Symbolizing Obstetrics and Gynecology, Female Symbol A166

1967, Sept. 20   Photo.   Perf. 13½
428 A166 4c lilac, dk blue & blk .25   .20

5th World Congress of Gynecology and Obstetrics, Sydney, Sept. 23-30.

Gothic Arches and Christmas Bell Flower A167

Cross, Stars of David and Yin Yang Forming Mandala — A168

1967   Photo.   Perf. 13½
429 A167 5c multicolored   .25   .20
430 A168 25c multicolored   2.25   2.25

Christmas.
Issue dates: 5c, Oct. 18; 25c, Nov. 27.

Satellite Orbiting Earth — A169

Satellite and Antenna, Moree, N.S.W. — A170

Design: 20c, World weather map connecting Washington, Moscow and Melbourne, and computer and teleprinter tape spools.

1968, Mar. 20 Photo. *Perf. 13½*

431 A169 5c dull yel, red, bl & dk blue .25 .20
432 A169 20c blue, blk & red 3.00 3.00
433 A170 25c Prus blue, blk & lt green 3.50 3.50
Nos. 431-433 (3) 6.75 6.70

Use of satellites for weather observations and communications.

Kangaroo Paw, Western Australia A171

Sturt's Desert Rose, Northern Territory A171a

State Flowers: 13c, Pink heath, Victoria. 15c, Tasmanian blue gum, Tasmania. 20c, Sturt's desert pea, South Australia. 25c, Cooktown orchid, Queensland. 30c, Waratah, New South Wales.

1968, July 10 Photo. *Perf. 13½*
Flowers in Natural Colors

434 A171 6c bister & dk brn .75 .20
435 A171 13c lt grnsh blue .90 .20
436 A171 15c dk brn & yel 1.25 .25
437 A171 20c lemon & black 3.50 .20
438 A171 25c light ultra 2.75 .20
439 A171 30c chocolate .85 .20
Nos. 434-439 (6) 10.00 1.25

A 1971 reprinting of No. 439 shows more areas of white in the pink petals. This is scarcer than the first printing.

Coil Stamps

1970-75 *Perf. 14½ Horiz.*

Designs: 5c, Golden wattle, national flower. 7c, 10c, Sturt's desert pea.

439A A171a 2c dk grn & multi .20 .20
i. Lettering and value bolder .20 .20
439B A171a 4c gray & multi .50 .40
439C A171a 5c gray & multi .20 .20
439D A171a 6c gray & multi 1.10 .50
h. Green omitted 400.00
439E A171a 7c blk, red & grn .35 .20
f. Green omitted 150.00
439G A171a 10c blk, red & grn .30 .20
Nos. 439A-439G (6) 2.65 1.70

Issued: 4c, 5c, 4/27; 6c, 10/28; 2c, 7c, 10/1/71; 10c, 1/15/75; #439Ai, 11/73.

Soil Testing Through Chemistry & by Computer A172

Hippocrates & Hands Holding Hypodermic A173

1968, Aug. 6 Photo. *Perf. 13½*

440 A172 5c multicolored .25 .20
441 A173 5c multicolored .25 .20

9th Intl. Congress of Soil Science, University of Adelaide, Aug. 6-16 (No. 440); General Assembly of World Medical Associations, Sydney, Aug. 6-9 (No. 441). Nos. 440-441 printed in sheets of 100 in two separate panes of 50 connected by a gutter. Each sheet contains 10 gutter pairs.

Runner and Aztec Calendar Stone — A174

Symbolic House and Money — A175

Design: 25c, Aztec calendar stone and Mexican flag, horiz.

1968, Oct. 2

442 A174 5c multicolored .20 .20
443 A174 25c multicolored 2.25 2.00

19th Olympic Games, Mexico City, Oct. 12-27. Nos. 442-443 printed in sheets of 100 in two separate panes of 50 connected by a gutter. Each sheet contains 10 gutter pairs.

1968, Oct. 16

444 A175 5c multicolored .25 .20

11th Triennial Congress of the Intl. Union of Building Societies and Savings Associations, Sydney, Oct. 20-27.

View of Bethlehem and Church Window — A176

1968, Oct. 23 Photo. *Perf. 13½*

445 A176 5c lt bl, red, grn & gold .20 .20
a. Red omitted 350.00

Christmas.

Edgeworth David (1858-1934), Geologist A177

Sir Edmund Barton (1849-1920) A178

Reginald C. and John R. Duigan, Aviators — A179

Famous Australians: #447, Caroline Chisholm (1808-77), social worker, reformer. #448, Albert Namatjira (1902-59), aborigine, artist. #449, Andrew Barton (Banjo) Paterson (1864-1941), poet, writer.

1968, Nov. 6 Engr. *Perf. 15x14*

446 A177 5c green, *greenish* .80 .20
a. Booklet pane of 5 + label 4.00
447 A177 5c purple, *pink* .80 .20
a. Booklet pane of 5 + label 4.00
448 A177 5c dark brown, *buff* .80 .20
a. Booklet pane of 5 + label 4.00
449 A177 5c indigo, *lt blue* .80 .20
a. Booklet pane of 5 + label 4.00
Nos. 446-449 (4) 3.20 .80

1969, Oct. 22 Engr. *Perf. 15x14*

Prime Ministers: #451, Alfred Deakin (1856-1919). #452, John C. Watson (1867-1941). #453, Sir George H. Reid (1845-1918).

450 A178 5c indigo, *greenish* .80 .20
a. Booklet pane of 5 + label 4.00
451 A178 5c indigo, *greenish* .80 .20
a. Booklet pane of 5 + label 4.00
452 A178 5c indigo, *greenish* .80 .20
a. Booklet pane of 5 + label 4.00
453 A178 5c indigo, *greenish* .80 .20
a. Booklet pane of 5 + label 4.00
Nos. 450-453 (4) 3.20 .80

1970, Nov. 16 Engr. *Perf. 15x14*

Famous Australians: #455, Lachlan Macquarie (1761-1824), Governor of New South Wales. #456, Adam Lindsay Gordon (1833-70), poet. #457, Edward John Eyre (1815-1901), explorer.

454 A179 6c dark blue .80 .20
a. Booklet pane of 5 + label 4.00
455 A179 6c dark brown, *salmon* .80 .20
a. Booklet pane of 5 + label 4.00
456 A179 6c magenta, *brt pink* .80 .20
a. Booklet pane of 5 + label 4.00
457 A179 6c brown red, *salmon* .80 .20
a. Booklet pane of 5 + label 4.00
Nos. 454-457 (4) 3.20 .80

Nos. 446-457 were issued in booklet panes only; all stamps have 1 or 2 straight edges.

Macquarie Lighthouse — A180

1968, Nov. 27 Engr. *Perf. 14½x13½*

458 A180 5c indigo, *buff* .35 .20

Macquarie Lighthouse, Outer South Head, Sydney, 150th anniv.

Surveyor George W. Goyder and Assistants, 1869; Building in Darwin, 1969 — A181

1969, Feb. 5 Photo. *Perf. 13½*

459 A181 5c black brn & dull yel .20 .20

First permanent settlement of the Northern Territory of Australia, cent.

Melbourne Harbor Scene A182

1969, Feb. 26 Photo. *Perf. 13½*

460 A182 5c dull blue & multi .20 .20

6th Biennial Conference of the Intl. Assoc. of Ports and Harbors, Melbourne, March 3-8.

Overlapping Circles A183

1969, June 5 Photo. *Perf. 13½*

461 A183 5c gray, vio bl, bl & gold .20 .20

ILO, 50th anniv.

Sugar Cane — A184

Primary industries: 15c, Eucalyptus (timber). 20c, Wheat. 25c, Ram, ewe, lamb (wool).

1969, Sept. 17 *Perf. 13½x13*

462 A184 7c blue & multi .75 .75
463 A184 15c emerald & multi 3.75 3.50
464 A184 20c org brn & multi 1.40 .60
465 A184 25c gray, black & yel 1.25 .70
Nos. 462-465 (4) 7.15 5.55

Nativity — A185

Tree of Life — A186

Perf. 13½x13, 13x13½
1969, Oct. 15 Photo.

466 A185 5c multicolored .20 .20
467 A186 25c multicolored 2.75 2.75

Christmas.

Vickers Vimy Flown by Ross Smith, England to Australia A187

#469, B.E. 2E plane, automobile, spectators. #470, Ford truck, surveyors Lieuts. Hudson Fysh & P.J. McGinness.

1969, Nov. 12 *Perf. 13x13½*

468 A187 5c bl, blk, cop red & ol .60 .35
469 A187 5c bl, blk, cop red & ol .60 .35
470 A187 5c cop red, black & ol .60 .35
a. Strip of 3, #468-470 3.50 3.00
Nos. 468-470 (3) 1.80 1.05

1st England to Australia flight by Capt. Ross Smith & Lieut. Keith Smith, 50th anniv.

No. 470a has various combinations possible.

Diesel Locomotive and New Track Linking Melbourne, Sydney and Brisbane with Perth A188

1970, Feb. 11 Photo. *Perf. 13x13½*

471 A188 5c multicolored .25 .20

Completion of the standard gauge railroad between Sydney and Perth.

EXPO '70 Australian Pavilion A189

Design: 20c, Southern Cross and Japanese inscription: "From the country of the south with warm feeling."

1970, Mar. 16 Photo. *Perf. 13x13½*

472 A189 5c bl, blk, red & brnz .25 .20
473 A189 20c red & black 1.00 .45

EXPO '70 Intl. Exhib., Osaka, Japan, Mar. 15-Sept. 13.

Queen Elizabeth II and Prince Philip A190

Australian Flag — A191

1970, Mar. 31
474 A190 5c yel bister & black .25 .20
475 A191 30c vio blue & multi 2.25 2.00

Visit of Queen Elizabeth II, Prince Philip and Princess Anne to Australia.

Steer, Alfalfa and Native Spear Grass A192

1970, Apr. 13 Photo. Perf. 13x13½
476 A192 5c emerald & multi .25 .20

11th Intl. Grasslands Congress, Surfers Paradise, Queensland, Apr. 13-23.

Capt. James Cook and "Endeavour" — A193

#478, Sextant, "Endeavour." #479, "Endeavour," landing party, kangaroo. #480, Daniel Charles Solander, Sir Joseph Banks, Cook, map, botanical drawing. #481, Cook taking possession with Union Jack; "Endeavour," coral. 30c, Cook, "Endeavour," sextant, kangaroo, aborigines.

1970, Apr. 20 Perf. 13½x13
Size: 24x35½mm
477 A193 5c org brn & multi .40 .20
478 A193 5c org brn & multi .40 .20
479 A193 5c org brn & multi .40 .20
480 A193 5c org brn & multi .40 .20
481 A193 5c org brn & multi .40 .20
a. Strip of 5, #477-481 2.00 2.00
Size: 62x29mm
482 A193 30c org brn & multi 2.50 2.50
a. Souv. sheet, #477-482, imperf 9.00 9.00
Nos. 477-482 (6) 4.50 3.50

Cook's discovery and exploration of the eastern coast of Australia, 200th anniv.
No. 481a has continuous design.
No. 482a with brown marginal overprint "Souvenir Sheet ANPEX 1970. . ." is of private origin.

Snowy Mountains Hydroelectric Project A194

Designs: 8c, Ord River hydroelectric project (dam, cotton plant and boll). 9c, Bauxite and aluminum production (mine, conveyor belt and aluminum window frame). 10c, Oil and natural gas (off-shore drilling rig and pipelines).

1970, Aug. 31 Photo. Perf. 13½x13
483 A194 7c multicolored 1.60 .40
484 A194 8c multicolored .25 .20
485 A194 9c multicolored .25 .20
486 A194 10c multicolored 1.10 .20
Nos. 483-486 (4) 3.20 1.00

Australian economic development.

Flame Symbolizing Democracy and Freedom of Speech — A195

1970, Oct. 2 Photo. Perf. 13½x13
487 A195 6c green & multi .25 .20

16th Commonwealth Parliamentary Assoc. Conference, Canberra, Oct. 2-9.

Herd of Illawarra Shorthorns and Laboratory A196

1970, Oct. 7 Perf. 13x13½
488 A196 6c multicolored .25 .20

18th Intl. Dairy Cong., Sydney, Oct. 12-16.

 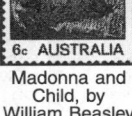

Madonna and Child, by William Beasley A197

UN Emblem, Dove and Symbols A198

1970, Oct. 14 Perf. 13½x13
489 A197 6c multicolored .25 .20

Christmas.

1970, Oct. 19
490 A198 6c blue & multi .25 .20

25th anniversary of the United Nations.

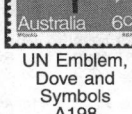

Qantas Boeing 707, and Avro 504 — A199

30c, Sunbeam Dyak powered Avro 504 on ground and Qantas Boeing 707 in the air.

1970, Nov. 2 Perf. 13½x13
491 A199 6c multicolored .20 .20
492 A199 30c multicolored 1.40 1.40

Qantas, Australian overseas airlines, 50th anniv.

Japanese Noh Actor, Australian Dancer and Chinese Opera Character — A200

15c, Chinese pipe, trumpet, Australian aboriginal didgeridoo, Thai fiddle, Indian double oboe, Tibetan drums. 20c, Red Sea dhow, Chinese junk, Australian lifeguard's surfboat, Malaysian & South Indian river boats.

1971, Jan. 6 Photo. Perf. 13½x13
493 A200 7c multicolored .50 .55
494 A200 15c multicolored .80 .90
495 A200 20c multicolored .70 .80
Nos. 493-495 (3) 2.00 2.25

Link between Australia and Asia; 28th Intl. Congress of Orientalists, Canberra, Jan. 6-12.

Southern Cross A201

1971, Apr. 21 Photo. Perf. 13x13½
496 A201 6c multicolored .25 .20

Australian Natives Assoc., cent.

Symbolic Market Graphs — A202

Rotary Emblem A203

1971, May 5 Perf. 13½x13
497 A202 6c silver & multi .25 .20

Centenary of Sydney Stock Exchange.

1971, May 17 Perf. 13½x13
498 A203 6c multicolored .25 .20

First Intl. Rotary Convention held in Australia, Sydney, May 16-20.

DH-9A, Australian Mirage Jet Fighters A204

RSPCA Centenary A205

1971, June 9 Perf. 13½x13
499 A204 6c multicolored .35 .20

Royal Australian Air Force, 50th anniv.

1971, July 5 Photo. Perf. 13½x13
Designs: 12c, Man and lamb (animal science). 18c, Kangaroo (fauna conservation). 24c, Seeing eye dog (animals' aid to man).
500 A205 6c blk, brown & org .25 .20
501 A205 12c blk, dk grn & yel .75 .20
502 A205 18c brown & multi .95 .30
503 A205 24c blue & multi 1.25 .50
Nos. 500-503 (4) 3.20 1.20

Royal Society for Prevention of Cruelty to Animals in Australia, cent.

Longnecked Tortoise, Painted on Bark — A206

Aboriginal Art: 25c, Mourners' body paintings, Warramunga tribe. 30c, Cave painting, Western Arnhem Land, vert. 35c, Graveposts, Bathurst and Melville Islands, vert.

Perf. 13x13½, 13½x13
1971, Sept. 29
504 A206 20c multicolored .65 .25
505 A206 25c multicolored .65 .45
506 A206 30c multicolored .90 .35
507 A206 35c multicolored .65 .40
Nos. 504-507 (4) 2.85 1.45

Three Kings and Star — A207

1971, Oct. 13 Photo. Perf. 13½x13
508 Block of 7 35.00
a. A207 7c brt grn, dk bl (Kings) & lil 6.25 .30
b. A207 7c lil, red brn, grn & dk bl 4.50 .20
c. A207 7c red brown & lilac 1.25 .20
d. A207 7c lilac, red brn & brt grn 2.00 .20
e. A207 7c red brown & dark blue 2.10 .20
f. A207 7c lilac, green & dk blue 14.00 1.40
g. A207 7c brt grn, dk bl & lilac (Kings) 2.50 .20

Christmas. Nos. 508a-508g printed se-tenant in sheets of 50. Each sheet contains 2 green crosses formed by 4 No. 508g and three No. 508a.

Andrew Fisher (1862-1928) A208

Cameo Brooch A209

Prime Ministers: No. 515, Joseph Cook (1860-1947). No. 516, William Morris Hughes (1864-1952). No. 517, Stanley Melbourne Bruce (1883-1967).

1972, Mar. 8 Engr. Perf. 15x14
514 A208 7c dark blue .50 .20
a. Booklet pane of 5 + label 2.50
515 A208 7c dark red .50 .20
a. Booklet pane of 5 + label 2.50
516 A208 7c dark blue .50 .20
a. Booklet pane of 5 + label 2.50
517 A208 7c dark red .50 .20
a. Booklet pane of 5 + label 2.50
Nos. 514-517 (4) 2.00 .80

Nos. 514-517 were issued in booklets only; all stamps have one or two straight edges.

1972, Apr. 18 Photo. Perf. 13½
518 A209 7c multicolored .25 .20

Country Women's Assoc., 50th anniv.

Apple and Banana A210

1972, June 14
519 A210 20c shown 1.75 1.75
520 A210 25c Rice 1.75 1.75
521 A210 30c Fish 1.75 1.75
522 A210 35c Cattle 3.50 3.50
Nos. 519-522 (4) 8.75 8.75

Worker in Sheltered Workshop — A211

18c, Amputee assembling electrical circuit. 24c, Boy wearing Toronto splint, playing ball.

1972, Aug. 2 Perf. 13½x13
523 A211 12c grn & brn .25 .20
524 A211 18c org & ol, horiz. 1.25 .20
525 A211 24c brn & ultra .50 .20
Nos. 523-525 (3) 2.00 .60

Rehabilitation of the handicapped.

Overland Telegraph Line — A212

1972, Aug. 22 Photo. Perf. 13x13½
526 A212 7c dk red, blk & lemon .25 .20
Centenary of overland telegraph line.

Athlete, Olympic Rings — A213

1972, Aug. 28 Perf. 13½x13
527 A213 7c shown .20 .20
528 A213 7c Swimming .20 .20
529 A213 7c Rowing .20 .20
530 A213 35c Equestrian 4.50 4.00
Nos. 527-530 (4) 5.10 4.60
20th Olympic Games, Munich, 8/26-9/11.

Abacus, Numerals, Computer Circuits A214

1972, Oct. 16 Photo. Perf. 13x13½
531 A214 7c multicolored .20 .20
10th Intl. Congress of Accountants.

19th Cent. Combine Harvester A215

Perf. 13½x13, 13x13½
1972, Nov. 15 Photo.
532 A215 5c Pioneer family, vert. .20 .20
533 A215 10c Water pump, vert. .45 .20
534 A215 15c shown .30 .20
535 A215 40c Pioneer house .65 .20
536 A215 50c Cobb & Co. coach 1.10 .20
537 A215 60c Early Morse key, vert. 1.00 .45
538 A215 80c Paddle-wheel steamer 1.10 .45
Nos. 532-538 (7) 4.80 1.90
Australian pioneer life.

Jesus and Children A216

Dove, Cross and "Darkness into Light" — A217

Metric Conversion, Mass — A218

Perf. 14½x14, 13½x13
1972, Nov. 29
539 A216 7c tan & multi .35 .20
540 A217 35c blue & multi 7.50 7.50
Christmas.

1973, Mar. 7 Photo. Perf. 14x14½
Metric conversion: No. 542, Temperature, horiz. No. 543, Length. No. 544, Volume.
541 A218 7c pale vio & multi .80 .20
542 A218 7c yellow & multi .80 .20
543 A218 7c yel green & multi .80 .20
544 A218 7c brt rose & multi .80 .20
Nos. 541-544 (4) 3.20 .80
Conversion to metric system.

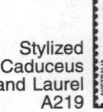

Stylized Caduceus and Laurel A219

1973, Apr. 4 Photo. Perf. 14½x14
545 A219 7c dk bl, emer & lil rose .25 .20
WHO, 25th anniv.

Dame Mary Gilmore, Writer A220

Shipping Industry A221

Famous Australians: #547, William Charles Wentworth, explorer. #548, Sir Isaac Isaacs, lawyer, 1st Australian-born Governor-General. #549, Marcus Clarke, writer.

Engr. & Litho.
1973, May 16 Perf. 15x14
546 A220 7c bister & black 1.00 .20
547 A220 7c bister & black 1.00 .20
548 A220 7c black & violet 1.00 .20
549 A220 7c black & violet 1.00 .20
a. Block of 4, #546-549 4.00 1.00

1973, June 6 Photo. Perf. 13½x13
Designs: 25c, Iron ore and steel. 30c, Truck convoy (beef road). 35c, Aerial mapping.
550 A221 20c ultra & multi 2.00 1.50
551 A221 25c red & multi 2.00 1.50
552 A221 30c ol brn & multi 2.00 1.50
553 A221 35c olive & multi 2.75 1.75
Nos. 550-553 (4) 8.75 6.25
Australian economic development.

Banded Coral Shrimp A222

Chrysoprase A223

Helichrysum Thomsonii A223a

Wombat A224

Radio Astronomy A225

Red Gums of the Far North, by Hans Heysen — A226

Coming South (Immigrants), by Tom Roberts — A226a

Paintings: $1, Sergeant of Light Horse, by George Lambert. No. 575, On the Wallaby Track. $4, Shearing the Rams, by Tom Roberts. No. 577, McMahon's Point, by Arthur Streeton. No. 578, Mentone.

Perf. 14x15, 15x14 (A222, A223, A223a); Perf. 14x14½ (A224); Perf. 13x13½ (A225, A226, $1)
1973-84 Photo.
554 A222 1c shown .20 .20
555 A222 2c Fiddler crab .20 .20
556 A222 3c Coral crab .20 .20
557 A222 4c Mauve stinger .20 .20
558 A223 6c shown .20 .20
559 A223 7c Agate .20 .20
560 A223 8c Opal .20 .20
561 A223 9c Rhodonite .20 .20
562 A223 10c Star sapphire ('74) .20 .20
563 A225 11c Atomic absorption spectrophotometry ('75) .55 .25
564 A223a 18c shown ('75) .50 .20
565 A224 20c shown ('74) .40 .20
566 A225 24c shown ('75) 1.00 .40
567 A224 25c Spiny anteater ('74) 1.25 .35
568 A224 30c Brushtail possum ('74) .70 .20
569 A225 33c Immunology ('75) 1.00 1.00
570 A223a 45c Callistemon teretifolius, horiz. ('75) .65 .25
571 A225 48c Oceanography ('75) 1.75 1.10
572 A224 75c Feather-tailed glider ('74) 1.25 .75
573 A226a $1 multi ('74) 1.50 .25
574 A226 $2 shown ('74) 2.75 .30
575 A226 $2 multi ('81) 2.50 .30
576 A226 $4 multi ('74) 5.00 2.25

Litho.
Perf. 14½
577 A226a $5 multi ('79) 6.00 2.00
578 A226 $5 multi ('84) 6.00 1.25
579 A226a $10 shown ('77) 12.00 3.25
Nos. 554-579 (26) 46.60 16.10

Issued: 1c-9c, 7/11; 20c, 25c, 30c, 75c, 2/13; $1, #574, $4, 4/24; 10c, 10/16; 11c, 24c, 33c, 48c, 5/14; 18c, 45c, 8/27; $10, 10/19; #577, 3/14; #575, 6/17; #578, 4/4.

No. 560 Surcharged in Red

Perf. 15x14
580 A223 9c on 8c multi ('74) .20 .20

Hand Protecting Playing Children A227

1973, Sept. 5 Photo. Perf. 13x13½
581 A227 7c bis brn, grn & plum .25 .20
50th anniv. of Legacy, an ex-servicemen's organization concerned with the welfare of widows and children of servicemen.

Baptism of Christ A228

The Good Shepherd A229

1973, Oct. 3 Perf. 14x14½
582 A228 7c gold & multi .30 .20
a. Perf. 14x15 3.50 2.50

Perf. 13½
583 A229 30c gold & multi 2.50 2.50
Christmas.

Buchanan's Hotel, Townsville A230

St. James' Church, Sydney — A231

Designs: 7c, Opera House, Sydney. 40c, Como House, Melbourne.

1973, Oct. 17 Photo. Perf. 14½x14
584 A230 7c lt blue & ultra .40 .20
a. Perf. 15x14 4.00 .80
585 A230 10c bister & black .60 .35

Perf. 13x13½, 13½x13
586 A230 40c dl pink, gray & blk .75 .75
587 A231 50c gray & multi 2.00 1.50
Nos. 584-587 (4) 3.75 2.80
Australian architecture; opening of the Sydney Opera House, Oct. 14, 1973 (No. 584).

Radio and Gramophone Speaker A232

1973, Nov. 21 Photo. Perf. 13½x13
588 A232 7c dull blue, blk & brn .25 .20
Broadcasting in Australia, 50th anniv.

Supreme Court Judge on Bench A233

Australian Football A234

1974, May 15 Photo. Perf. 14x14½
589 A233 7c multicolored .25 .20

150th anniv. of the proclamation of the Charter of Justice in New South Wales and Van Diemen's Land (Australia's Third Charter).

1974, July 24 Photo. Perf. 14x14½
590 A234 7c shown .35 .20
591 A234 7c Cricket .35 .20
592 A234 7c Golf .35 .20
593 A234 7c Surfing .35 .20
594 A234 7c Tennis .35 .20
595 A234 7c Bowls, horiz. .35 .20
596 A234 7c Rugby, horiz. .35 .20
Nos. 590-596 (7) 2.45 1.40

Carrier Pigeon A235

Designs: 30c, Carrier pigeons, vert.

1974, Oct. 9 Photo. Perf. 14½x14
597 A235 7c multicolored .25 .20
a. Perf. 15x14 .75 .20

Perf. 13½x13
598 A235 30c multicolored 1.00 1.00

UPU, cent. A booklet containing a strip of 5 each of Nos. 597-598 was produced and sold for $4 Australian by the National Stamp Week Promotion Council with government approval.

William Charles Wentworth A236

Adoration of the Kings, by Dürer A237

Typo. & Litho.
1974, Oct. 9 Perf. 14x15
599 A236 7c bister & black .35 .20
a. Perf. 14x14½ .90 .25

Sesquicentennial of 1st Australian independent newspaper. W. C. Wentworth and Dr. Robert Wardell were the editors and the "A" is type from masthead of "The Australian."

1974, Nov. 13 Engr. Perf. 14x14½
Christmas: 35c, Flight into Egypt, by Albrecht Dürer.
600 A237 10c buff & black .25 .20
601 A237 35c buff & black .90 .90

Pre-school Education A238

Correspondence Schools — A239

Science Education A240

Advanced Education — A241

Perf. 13x13½, 13½x13
1974, Nov. 20 Photo.
602 A238 5c multicolored .25 .20
603 A239 11c multicolored .35 .25
604 A240 15c multicolored .40 .30
605 A241 60c multicolored 1.00 .95
Nos. 602-605 (4) 2.00 1.70

"Avoid Pollution" A242

"Road Safety" — A243

Design: No. 607, "Avoid bush fires."

1975, Jan. 29 Photo. Perf. 14½x14
606 A242 10c multicolored .30 .20
a. Perf. 15x14 7.50 3.75
607 A242 10c multicolored .30 .20
a. Perf. 15x14 1.50 1.00

Perf. 14x14½
608 A243 10c multicolored .30 .20
Nos. 606-608 (3) .90 .60

Environmental dangers.

Symbols of Womanhood, Sun, Moon A244

Joseph B. Chifley (1885-1951) A245

1975, Mar. 12 Photo. Perf. 14x14½
609 A244 10c dk vio blue & grn .25 .20
International Women's Year.

1975, Mar. 26
610 A245 10c shown .20 .20
611 A245 10c John Curtin, 1885-1945 .20 .20
612 A245 10c Arthur W. Fadden, 1895-1973 .20 .20
613 A245 10c Joseph A. Lyons, 1879-1939 .20 .20
614 A245 10c Earle Page, 1880-1963 .20 .20

615 A245 10c John H. Scullin, 1876-1953 .20 .20
Nos. 610-615 (6) 1.20 1.20
Australian Prime Ministers.

Australian Postal Commission A246

Design: No. 617, Australian Telecommunications Commission.

1975, July 1 Photo. Perf. 14½x14
616 A246 10c red, black & gray .40 .20
a. Perf. 15x14 .50 .20
617 A246 10c yel, black & gray .40 .20
a. Pair, #616-617 .95 .75
b. Perf. 15x14 .50 .20
c. Pair, #616a, 617b 1.25 1.00

Formation of Australian Postal and Telecommunications Commissions. Printed checkerwise.

Edith Cowan, Judge and Legislator A247

Truganini, Last Tasmanian Aborigine A248

Portraits: No. 619, Louisa Lawson (1848-1920), journalist. No. 620, Ethel Florence (Henry Handel) Richardson (1870-1946), novelist. No. 621, Catherine Spence (1825-1910), teacher, journalist, voting reformer. No. 622, Emma Constance Stone (1856-1902), first Australian woman physician.

1975, Aug. 6 Photo. Perf. 14x14½
618 A247 10c olive grn & multi .30 .30
a. Perf. 14x15 .35 .35
619 A247 10c yel bister & multi .30 .30
a. Perf. 14x15 .35 .35
620 A248 10c olive & multi .30 .30
a. Perf. 14x15 .35 .35
621 A248 10c gray & multi .30 .30
a. Perf. 14x15 .35 .35
622 A247 10c violet & multi .30 .30
a. Perf. 14x15 .35 .35
623 A248 10c brown & multi .30 .30
a. Perf. 14x15 .35 .35
Nos. 618-623 (6) 1.80 1.80

Famous Australian women.

Spirit House (PNG) and Sydney Opera House — A249

Bird in Flight and Southern Cross A250

1975, Sept. 16 Photo. Perf. 13½
624 A249 18c multicolored .40 .20
625 A250 25c multicolored .75 .55

Papua New Guinea independence, Sept. 16, 1975.

Adoration of the Kings — A251

"The Light Shineth in the Darkness" A252

1975, Oct. 29 Photo. Perf. 14½x14
626 A251 15c multicolored .30 .20
627 A252 45c silver & multi 1.50 1.50

Christmas.

Australian Coat of Arms A253

Type I - Kangaroo: eye is dot, right paw has 1 toe, left foot has 1 toe. Emu: feet have 1 toe.
Type II - Kangaroo: eye is line, right paw has 3 toes, left foot has 2 toes. Emu: feet have 2 toes.
Other differences exist.

1976, Jan. 5 Photo. Perf. 14½x14
628 A253 18c multicolored, type I .40 .20
a. Type II .75 .25

"Williams' Coffin" Telephone, 1878 — A254

1976, Mar. 10 Photo. Perf. 13½
629 A254 18c buff & multi .35 .20
Centenary of first telephone call by Alexander Graham Bell, Mar. 10, 1876.

John Oxley A255

Designs: Australian explorers.

1976, June 9 Photo. Perf. 13½
630 A255 18c shown .25 .20
631 A255 18c Hamilton Hume and William Hovell .25 .20
632 A255 18c John Forrest .25 .20
633 A255 18c Ernest Giles .25 .20
634 A255 18c Peter Warburton .25 .20
635 A255 18c William Gosse .25 .20
Nos. 630-635 (6) 1.50 1.20

Survey Rule, Graph, Punched Tape — A256

1976, June 15 Perf. 15x14
636 A256 18c multicolored .30 .20
Commonwealth Scientific and Industrial Research Organization, 50th anniv.

Soccer Goalkeeper A257

Olympic Rings and: No. 638, Woman gymnast, vert. 25c, Woman diver, vert. 40c, Bicycling.

Perf. 13x13½, 13½x13

1976, July 14			**Photo.**	
637	A257	18c multicolored	.30	.20
638	A257	18c multicolored	.30	.20
639	A257	25c multicolored	.45	.40
640	A257	40c multicolored	.65	.50
	Nos. 637-640 (4)		1.70	1.30

21st Olympic Games, Montreal, Canada, July 17-Aug. 1.

Richmond Bridge, Tasmania A258

Mt. Buffalo, Victoria — A259

Designs: 25c, Broken Bay, New South Wales. 35c, Wittenoom Gorge, Western Australia. 70c, Barrier Reef, Queensland. 85c, Ayers Rock, Northern Territory.

Perf. 14½x14, 14x14½

1976, Aug. 25			**Photo.**	
641	A258	5c multicolored	.25	.20
642	A258	25c multicolored	.35	.20
643	A258	35c multicolored	.30	.30
644	A259	50c multicolored	.50	.25
645	A259	70c multicolored	.60	.35
646	A258	85c multicolored	1.00	.80
	Nos. 641-646 (6)		3.00	2.10

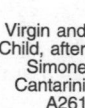

Blamire Young and Australia No. 59 — A260

1976, Sept. 27		**Photo.**	**Perf. 13½**	
647	A260	18c apple grn & multi	.35	.20

Miniature Sheet

648		Sheet of 4	1.60	1.50
a.	A260	18c yellow & dark brown	.35	.35
b.	A260	18c rose, dk brown & yel	.35	.35
c.	A260	18c bl, dk brn, rose & yel	.35	.35

Natl. Stamp Week, Sept. 27-Oct. 3. Blamire Young (1862-1935), designer of Australia's 1st issue. No. 648 shows different stages of 4-color printing. The 4th stamp in sheet is identical with No. 647.

Virgin and Child, after Simone Cantarini A261

Holly, Toy Koala, Christmas Tree and Decoration, Partridge A262

1976, Nov. 1		**Photo.**	**Perf. 14½x14**	
649	A261	15c brt car & lt blue	.30	.20

Perf. 13½

650	A262	45c multicolored	.80	.75

Christmas.

John Gould (1804-1881) Ornithologist A263

Famous Australians: No. 652, Thomas Laby (1880-1946), nuclear scientist. No. 653, Sir Baldwin Spencer (1860-1929), anthropologist (aborigines). No. 654, Griffith Taylor (1880-1963), geographer and arctic explorer.

1976, Nov. 10			**Perf. 15x14**	
651	A263	18c shown	.30	.20
652	A263	18c Laby	.30	.20
653	A263	18c Spencer	.30	.20
654	A263	18c Taylor	.30	.20
	Nos. 651-654 (4)		1.20	.80

Violinists — A264

1977, Jan. 19		**Photo.**	**Perf. 14x14½**	
655	A264	20c shown	.25	.20
656	A264	30c Dramatic scene	.30	.20
657	A264	40c Dancer	.55	.40
658	A264	60c Opera singer	.70	.20
	Nos. 655-658 (4)		1.80	1.00

Performing arts in Australia.

Elizabeth II A265

Wicket Keeper, Slip Fieldsman A266

Design: 45c, Elizabeth II and Prince Philip.

1977, Feb. 2				
659	A265	18c multicolored	.30	.20
660	A265	45c multicolored	.75	.75

Reign of Queen Elizabeth II, 25th anniv.

1977, Mar. 9		**Photo.**	**Perf. 13½**	

Cricket match, 19th century: No. 662, Umpire and batsman. No. 663, Two fieldsmen. No. 664, Batsman and umpire. No. 665, Bowler and fieldsman. 45c, Batsman facing bowler.

661	A266	18c gray & multi	.30	.25
662	A266	18c gray & multi	.30	.25
663	A266	18c gray & multi	.30	.25
664	A266	18c gray & multi	.30	.25
665	A266	18c gray & multi	.30	.25
a.		Strip of 5, #661-665	1.50	1.50
666	A266	45c gray & multi	.80	.75
	Nos. 661-666 (6)		2.30	2.00

Parliament House, Canberra A267

1977, Apr. 13			**Perf. 14½x14**	
667	A267	18c multicolored	.40	.20

Parliament House, Canberra, 50th anniv.

Trade Union Workers A268

1977, May 9		**Photo.**	**Perf. 13**	
668	A268	18c multicolored	.35	.20

Australian Council of Trade Unions (ACTU), 50th anniv.

Surfing Santa — A269

Virgin and Child — A270

1977, Oct. 31		**Photo.**	**Perf. 14x14½**	
669	A269	15c multicolored	.35	.20

Perf. 13½x13

670	A270	45c multicolored	.75	.75

Christmas.

Australian Flag — A271

1978, Jan. 26		**Photo.**	**Perf. 13x13½**	
671	A271	18c multicolored	.35	.20

Australia Day, 190th anniversary of first permanent settlement in New South Wales.

Harry Hawker and Sopwith "Camel" A272

Australian Aviators and their Planes: No. 673, Bert Hinkler and Avro Avian. No. 674, Charles Kingsford-Smith and Fokker "Southern Cross." No. 675, Charles Ulm and "Southern Cross."

1978, Apr. 19		**Litho.**	**Perf. 15½**	
672	A272	18c ultra & multi	.30	.20
673	A272	18c blue & multi	.30	.20
674	A272	18c orange & multi	.30	.20
675	A272	18c yellow & multi	.30	.20
a.		Souv. sheet, 2 each #674-675, imperf.	1.60	1.60
	Nos. 672-675 (4)		1.20	.80

No. 675a for 50th anniv. of first Trans-Pacific flight from Oakland, Cal., to Brisbane.

Beechcraft Baron Landing A273

1978, May 15		**Photo.**	**Perf. 13½**	
676	A273	18c multicolored	.30	.20

Royal Flying Doctor Service, 50th anniv.

Illawarra Flame Tree A274

Sturt's Desert Rose, Map of Australia A275

Australian trees: 25c, Ghost gum. 40c, Grass tree. 45c, Cootamundra wattle.

1978, June 1				
677	A274	18c multicolored	.20	.20
678	A274	25c multicolored	.60	.60
679	A274	40c multicolored	.70	.70
680	A274	45c multicolored	.65	.65
	Nos. 677-680 (4)		2.15	2.15

1978, June 19		**Litho.**	**Perf. 15½**	
681	A275	18c multicolored	.35	.20

Establishment of Government of the Northern Territory.

Hooded Dotterel — A276

Australian birds: 20c, Little grebe. 25c, Spur-wing Plover. 30c, Pied oystercatcher. 55c, Lotus bird.

1978		**Photo.**	**Perf. 13½**	
682	A276	5c multicolored	.20	.20
683	A276	20c multicolored	.25	.20
684	A276	25c multicolored	.35	.20
685	A276	30c multicolored	.40	.30
686	A276	55c multicolored	.70	.50
	Nos. 682-686 (5)		1.90	1.40

Issued: Nos. 683, 686, July 3; others, July 17. See Nos. 713-718, 732-739, 768.

Australia No. 95 on Album Page — A277

1978, Sept. 25		**Litho.**	**Perf. 15½**	
687	A277	20c multicolored	.30	.20
a.		Miniature sheet of 4	1.25	1.25

National Stamp Week; 50th anniv. of Melbourne Intl. Phil. Exhib.; Oct. 1928.

Virgin and Child, by Simon Marmion — A278

1978			**Perf. 15**	

Paintings from National Gallery, Victoria: 15c, Virgin and Child, after Van Eyck. 55c, Holy Family, by Perino del Vaga.

688	A278	15c multicolored	.20	.20
689	A278	25c multicolored	.50	.50
690	A278	55c multicolored	.80	.80
	Nos. 688-690 (3)		1.50	1.50

Christmas. Issued: 25c, 10/3; others, 11/1.

Tulloch
A279

Race horses: 35c, Bernborough, vert. 50c,
Phar Lap, vert. 55c, Peter Pan.

Perf. 15x14, 14x15

1978, Oct. 18			Photo.	
691	A279	20c multicolored	.25	.20
692	A279	35c multicolored	.45	.50
693	A279	50c multicolored	.65	.65
694	A279	55c multicolored	.65	.65
	Nos. 691-694 (4)		2.00	2.00

Australian horse racing.

Flag Raising at
Sydney
Cove — A280

1979, Jan. 26	Litho.	Perf. 15½		
695	A280	20c multicolored	.35	.20

Australia Day, Jan. 26.

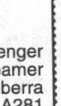

Passenger
Steamer
Canberra
A281

Ferries and Murray River Steamers: 35c,
M.V. Lady Denman. 50c, P.S. Murray River
Queen. 55c, Hydrofoil Curl Curl.

1979, Feb. 14	Photo.	Perf. 13½		
696	A281	20c multicolored	.30	.20
697	A281	35c multicolored	.50	.40
698	A281	50c multicolored	.75	.65
699	A281	55c multicolored	.85	.85
	Nos. 696-699 (4)		2.40	2.10

Port
Campbell
A282

Designs: Australian National Parks.

1979, Apr. 9	Litho.	Perf. 15½		
700	A282	20c shown	.30	.20
701	A282	20c Uluru	.30	.20
702	A282	20c Royal	.30	.20
703	A282	20c Flinders Ranges	.30	.20
704	A282	20c Namburg	.30	.20
a.	Strip of 5, #700-704		1.50	
705	A282	20c Girraween, vert.	.30	.20
706	A282	20c Mount Field, vert.	.30	.20
a.	Pair, #705-706		.60	
	Nos. 700-706 (7)		2.10	1.40

Double
Fairlie
A283

Australian steam locomotives: 35c, Puffing
Billy. 50c, Pichi Richi. 55c, Zig Zag.

Perf. 13½, 15x14 (20c)

1979, May 16			Photo.	
707	A283	20c multicolored	.20	.20
708	A283	35c multicolored	.40	.30
709	A283	50c multicolored	.75	.60
710	A283	55c multicolored	.80	.80
	Nos. 707-710 (4)		2.15	1.90

"Black Swan"
A284

1979, June 6	Photo.	Perf. 13½		
711	A284	20c multicolored	.35	.20

150th anniversary of Western Australia.

Children
Playing, IYC
Emblem
A285

1979, Aug. 13	Litho.	Perf. 13½x13		
712	A285	20c multicolored	.30	.20

International Year of the Child.

Bird Type of 1978

Australian birds: 1c, Zebra finch. 2c, Crimson finch. 15c, Forest kingfisher, vert. 20c,
Eastern yellow robin. 40c, Lovely wren, vert.
50c, Flame robin, vert.

1979, Sept. 17	Photo.	Perf. 13½		
713	A276	1c multicolored	.20	.20
714	A276	2c multicolored	.20	.20
715	A276	15c multicolored	.30	.20
716	A276	20c multicolored	.30	.20
717	A276	40c multicolored	.50	.20
718	A276	50c multicolored	.70	.20
	Nos. 713-718 (6)		2.20	1.20

Christmas
Letters, Flag-
wrapped
Parcels — A286

Trout
Fishing — A287

Christmas: 15c, Nativity, icon. 55c,
Madonna and Child, by Buglioni.

1979	Litho.	Perf. 13		
719	A286	15c multicolored	.20	.20
720	A286	25c multicolored	.30	.30
721	A286	55c multicolored	.90	.90
	Nos. 719-721 (3)		1.40	1.40

Issue dates: 25c, Sept. 24. Others, Nov. 1.

1979, Oct. 24	Photo.	Perf. 14x14½		

Sport fishing: 35c, Angler. 50c, Black marlin
fishing. 55c, Surf fishing.

722	A287	20c multicolored	.25	.20
723	A287	35c multicolored	.45	.45
724	A287	50c multicolored	.70	.45
725	A287	55c multicolored	.75	.70
	Nos. 722-725 (4)		2.15	1.80

Matthew
Flinders,
Map of
Australia
A288

1980, Jan. 23	Litho.	Perf. 13½		
726	A288	20c multicolored	.30	.20

Australia Day, Jan. 28.

Dingo
A289

1980, Feb. 20	Litho.	Perf. 13½x13		
727	A289	20c shown	.30	.20
728	A289	25c Border collie	.35	.35
729	A289	35c Australian terrier	.60	.40
730	A289	50c Australian cattle dog	.80	.70
731	A289	55c Australian kelpie	.65	.65
	Nos. 727-731 (5)		2.70	2.30

Bird Type of 1978
Perf. 13½, 14x15 (22c), 13x12½ (28c, 60c)

1980		Litho., Photo. (22c)		
732	A276	10c Golden-shoulder parrot, vert.	.20	.20
a.	Perf. 14½x14		1.50	.50
733	A276	22c White-tailed king-fisher, vert.	.30	.20
734	A276	28c Rainbow bird, vert.	.45	.20
735	A276	35c Regent bower bird, vert.	.45	.20
736	A276	45c Masked woodswal-low	.95	.20
a.	Perf. 14x14½		2.50	1.75
737	A276	60c King parrot, vert.	.75	.25
738	A276	80c Rainbow pitta	1.00	.45
739	A276	$1 Western magpie, vert.	1.25	.30
	Nos. 732-739 (8)		5.35	2.00

Issued: #733, 734, 737, 3/31; others, 7/1.

Queen Elizabeth II,
54th
Birthday — A290

1980, Apr. 21	Litho.	Perf. 13x13½		
740	A290	22c multicolored	.35	.20

Wanderer
A291

High Court
Building,
Canberra
A292

1980, May 7	Litho.	Perf. 13x13½		
741		Strip of 5	1.25	1.00
a.	A291	22c shown	.25	.20
b.	A291	22c Stealing sheep	.25	.20
c.	A291	22c Squatter on horseback	.25	.20
d.	A291	22c Three troopers	.25	.20
e.	A291	22c Wanderer's ghost	.25	.20

"Waltzing Matilda", poem by Andrew Barton
Patterson (1864-1941). No. 741 in continuous
design.

1980, May 19				
742	A292	22c multicolored	.35	.20

Opening of High Court of Australia Building,
Canberra, May 26.

Salvation
Army
Officers
A294

Perf. 13x13½, 13½x12½

1980, Aug. 11				
747	A294	22c shown	.30	.20
748	A294	22c St. Vincent de Paul Society, vert.	.30	.20
749	A294	22c Meals on Wheels, vert.	.30	.20
750	A294	22c "Life. Be in it." (Jog-gers, bicyclists)	.30	.20
	Nos. 747-750 (4)		1.20	.80

Mailman c.
1900 — A295

Holy Family, by
Prospero
Fontana — A296

1980, Sept. 29	Litho.	Perf. 13x13½		
751	A295	22c Mailbox	.30	.20
752	A295	22c shown	.30	.20
753	A295	22c Mail truck	.30	.20
754	A295	22c Mailman, mailbox	.30	.20
755	A295	22c Mailman, diff.	.30	.20
a.	Souvenir sheet of 3		1.00	1.00
b.	Strip of 5, #751-755		1.50	1.00

Natl. Stamp Week, Sept. 29-Oct. 5. #755a
contains stamps similar to #751, 753, 755.
No. 755a overprinted "SYDPEX 80" was privately produced.

1980			Perf. 13x13½	

Christmas: 15c, Virgin Enthroned, by Justin
O'Brien. 60c, Virgin and Child, by Michael
Zuern the Younger, 1680.

756	A296	15c multicolored	.25	.20
757	A296	28c multicolored	.45	.45
758	A296	60c multicolored	.90	.65
	Nos. 756-758 (3)		1.60	1.30

Issued: 15c, 60c, Nov. 3; 28c, Oct. 1.

CA-6
Wackett
Trainer,
1941 — A297

Designs: Australian military training planes.

1980, Nov. 19			Perf. 13½x14	
759	A297	22c shown	.30	.30
760	A297	40c Winjeel, 1955	.60	.60
761	A297	45c Boomerang, 1944	.65	.50
762	A297	60c Nomad, 1975	1.00	.60
	Nos. 759-762 (4)		2.55	2.00

Bird Type of 1978

1980, Nov. 17	Litho.	Perf. 13½		
768	A276	18c Spotted catbird, vert.	.35	.20

Flag on Map
of Australia
A298

1981, Jan. 21				
771	A298	22c multicolored	.35	.20

Australia Day, Jan. 21.

Jockey Darby
Munro (1913-
1966), by Tony
Rafty — A299

Australian sportsmen (Caricatures by Tony
Rafty): 35c, Victor Trumper (1877-1915),
cricket batsman. 55c, Norman Brookes (1877-
1968), tennis player. 60c, Walter Lindrum
(1898-1960), billiards player.

1981, Feb. 18			Perf. 14x13½	
772	A299	22c multicolored	.25	.20
773	A299	35c multicolored	.45	.40
774	A299	55c multicolored	.65	.65
775	A299	60c multicolored	.75	.75
	Nos. 772-775 (4)		2.10	2.00

Australia
No. C2 and
Cover
A300

Perf. 13x13½, 13½x13

1981, Mar. 25   **Litho.**
776 A300 22c Australia No. C2,
     vert.   .30 .25
777 A300 60c shown   .90 .80
Australia-United Kingdom official airmail
service, 50th anniv.

Map of
Australia,
APEX
Emblem
A301

1981, Apr. 6   **Photo.**   **Perf. 13x13½**
778 A301 22c multicolored   .30 .20
50th anniv. of APEX (young men's service
club).

Queen
Elizabeth's
Personal Flag
of Australia
A302

1981, Apr. 21   **Perf. 13**
779 A302 22c multicolored   .35 .20
Queen Elizabeth II, 55th birthday.

License Inspected,
Forrest Creek, by
S.T. Gill — A303

Gold Rush Era (Sketches by S.T. Gill): No.
781, Puddling. No. 782, Quality of Washing
Stuff. No. 783, Diggers on Route to Deposit
Gold.

1981, May 20   **Photo.**   **Perf. 13x13½**
780 A303 22c multicolored   .30 .20
781 A303 22c multicolored   .30 .20
782 A303 22c multicolored   .30 .20
783 A303 22c multicolored   .30 .20
     Nos. 780-783 (4)   1.20 .80

Lace
Monitor — A303a

Tasmanian
Tiger — A304

Two Types of A304:
Type I - Indistinct line at right of ear, stripes
even with base of tail.
Type II - Heavy line at right of ear, stripes
longer.

1981-83   **Litho.**
784 A303a 1c shown   .20 .20
785 A303a 3c Corroboree frog   .20 .20
786 A304 5c Queensland
     hairy-nosed
     wombat, vert.   .20 .20
787 A303a 15c Eastern snake-
     necked tortoise   .20 .20
788 A304 24c Type I   .35 .20
   a.   Shown, type II   .35 .20
789 A304 25c Greater bilby,
     vert.   .35 .20

790 A303a 27c Blue Mountains
     tree frog   .35 .20
791 A304 30c Bridled nail-
     tailed wallaby,
     vert.   .35 .20
792 A303a 40c Smooth knob-
     tailed gecko   .45 .25
793 A304 50c Leadbeater's
     opossum   .65 .40
794 A304 55c Stick-nest rat,
     vert.   .75 .40
795 A303a 65c Yellow-faced
     whip snake   .80 .45
796 A303a 70c Crucifix toad   .90 .55
797 A303a 75c Eastern water
     dragon   .90 .55
798 A303a 85c Centralian blue-
     tongued lizard   1.00 .65
799 A303a 90c Freshwater croc-
     odile   1.10 .70
800 A303a 95c Thorny devil   1.25 .75
     Nos. 784-800 (17)   10.00 6.30
Perfs: 1c, 70c, 85c, 95c, 13½; 3c, 15c, 27c,
40c, 50c, 65c, 75c, 90c, 12½x13; 5c, 25c, 30c,
55c, 13x12½; 24c, 13x13½.
Issued: 24c, 7/1/81; 5c, 25c, 30c, 50c, 55c,
7/15/81; 3c, 27c, 65c, 75c, 4/19/82; 15c, 40c,
90c, 6/16/82. 1c, 70c, 85c, 95c, 2/2/83.

1982-84   **Perf. 14x14½, 14½x14**
785a A303a 3c ('84)   .30 .20
786a A304 5c ('84)   1.00 .20
787a A303a 15c ('84)   .70 .25
789a A304 25c ('83)   1.10 .20
790a A303a 27c   .75 .25
792a A303a 40c ('84)   2.00 .30
793a A304 50c ('83)   1.25 .40
795a A303a 65c ('84)   1.40 .60
797a A303a 75c ('84)   1.50 .60
     Nos. 785a-797a (9)   10.00 3.20

Prince
Charles and
Lady Diana
A305

1981, July 29   **Litho.**   **Perf. 13**
804 A305 24c multicolored   .40 .20
805 A305 60c multicolored   1.10 .75
Royal Wedding.

Fungi — A306

Intl. Year of the
Disabled — A307

1981, Aug. 19   **Litho.**   **Perf. 13**
806 A306 24c Cortinarius cin-
     nabarinus   .25 .20
807 A306 35c Coprinus comatus   .40 .40
808 A306 55c Armillaria lute-
     obubalina   .75 .60
809 A306 60c Cortinarius austro-
     venetus   .90 .80
     Nos. 806-809 (4)   2.30 2.00

1981, Sept. 16   **Perf. 14x13½**
810 A307 24c multicolored   .40 .20

Christmas Bush
for His Adorning
A308

Globe
A309

Christmas (Carols by William James and
John Wheeler): 30c, The Silver Stars are in
the Sky. 60c, Noeltime.

1981   **Litho.**   **Perf. 13x13½**
811 A308 18c multicolored   .35 .20
812 A308 30c multicolored   .50 .35
813 A308 60c multicolored   1.25 1.00
     Nos. 811-813 (3)   2.10 1.55
Issue dates: 30c, Sept. 28; others, Nov. 2.

1981, Sept. 30
814 A309 24c multicolored   .35 .20
815 A309 60c multicolored   1.00 .90
Commonwealth Heads of Government
Meeting, Melbourne, Sept. 30-Oct. 7.

Yacht — A310

1981, Oct. 14   **Litho.**   **Perf. 13x13½**
816 A310 24c Ocean racer   .35 .20
817 A310 35c Lightweight sharp-
     ie   .50 .60
818 A310 55c 12-Meter   .75 .60
819 A310 60c Sabot   .90 .80
     Nos. 816-819 (4)   2.50 2.20

Australia
Day, Jan. 26
A311

1982, Jan. 20   **Litho.**   **Perf. 13x13½**
820 A311 24c multicolored   .40 .20

Sperm Whale
A312

1982, Feb. 17   **Perf. 13x13½, 13½x13**
821 A312 24c shown   .35 .20
822 A312 35c Southern right
     whale, vert.   .60 .60
823 A312 55c Blue whale, vert.   .90 .75
824 A312 60c Humpback whale   1.00 1.00
     Nos. 821-824 (4)   2.85 2.55

Elizabeth II, 56th
Birthday — A313

Roses — A314

1982, Apr. 21   **Perf. 13½**
825 A313 27c multicolored   .40 .20

1982, May 19   **Perf. 13x13½**
826 A314 27c Marjorie Atherton   .30 .30
827 A314 40c Imp   .55 .50
828 A314 65c Minnie Watson   .80 .80
829 A314 75c Satellite   .90 .85
     Nos. 826-829 (4)   2.55 2.45

50th Anniv.
of Australian
Broadcasting
Commission
A315

1982, June 16   **Perf. 13½x13**
830 A315 27c Announcer,
     microphone   .45 .25
831 A315 27c Emblem   .45 .25
   a.   Pair, #830-831   .90 .50
#830-831 se-tenant in continuous design.

Alice Springs
Post Office,
1872 — A316

1982, Aug. 4   **Perf. 13½x14, 14x13½**
832 A316 27c shown   .30 .20
833 A316 27c Kingston, 1869   .30 .20
834 A316 27c York, 1893   .30 .20
835 A316 27c Flemington, 1890,
     vert.   .30 .20
836 A316 27c Forbes, 1881, vert.   .30 .20
837 A316 27c Launceston, 1889,
     vert.   .30 .20
838 A316 27c Rockhampton,
     1892, vert.   .30 .20
     Nos. 832-838 (7)   2.10 1.40

Christmas — A317

1st Australian Christmas cards, 1881. 21c,
horiz.

1982   **Litho.**   **Perf. 14½**
839 A317 21c multicolored   .25 .20
840 A317 35c multicolored   .50 .30
841 A317 75c multicolored   1.00 .90
     Nos. 839-841 (3)   1.75 1.40
Issue dates: 35c, Sept. 15; others, Nov. 1.

12th Commonwealth Games,
Brisbane, Sept. 30-Oct. 9 — A318

1982, Sept. 22   **Litho.**   **Perf. 14x14½**
842 A318 27c Archery   .45 .20
843 A318 27c Boxing   .45 .20
844 A318 27c Weightlifting   .45 .20
   a.   Souvenir sheet of 3, #842-844   1.50 1.40
845 A318 75c Pole vault   .90 .90
     Nos. 842-845 (4)   2.25 1.50

Natl. Stamp
Week
A319

1982, Sept. 27   **Perf. 13x13½**
846 A319 27c No. 132   .40 .20

A320   A321

Design: Gurgurr (Moon Spirit), Bark Painting
by Yirawala Gunwinggu Tribe.

1982, Oct. 12   **Perf. 14½**
847 A320 27c multicolored   .40 .20
Opening of Natl. Gallery, Canberra.

Perf. 12½x13½
1982, Nov. 17   **Photo.**
Designs: Various eucalypts (gum trees).
848 A321 1c Pink-flowered mar-
     ri   .20 .20
849 A321 2c Gungurru   .20 .20
850 A321 3c Red-flowering gum   1.00 1.00

851 A321 10c Tasmanian blue
    gum   1.00 1.00
852 A321 27c Forrest's marlock   .75 .75
  a.   Bklt. pane, #850-851, 2 #848-
    849, 3 #852 + label   5.00
  b.   Bklt. pane, 2 ea #848-849, 852   2.10
    Bklt. pane, 2 ea #848-852 (5)   3.15 3.15
    Nos. 848-852 issued in booklets only.

Mimi Spirits
Singing and
Dancing, by
David
Milaybuma
A322

Aboriginal Bark Paintings: Music and dance
of the Mimi Spirits, Gunwinggu Tribe.

1982, Nov. 17   **Litho.**   **Perf. 13½x14**
853 A322 27c shown   .40 .20
854 A322 40c Lofty Nabardayal   .65 .65
855 A322 65c Jimmy Galareya   1.00 .75
856 A322 75c Dick Nguleingulei
    Murrumurru   1.10 1.00
    Nos. 853-856 (4)   3.15 2.65

Historic Fire
Engines
A323

1983, Jan. 12   **Perf. 13½x14**
857 A323 27c Shand Mason
    Steam, 1891   .40 .25
858 A323 40c Hotchkiss, 1914   .65 .65
859 A323 65c Ahrens-Fox PS2,
    1929   1.00 1.00
860 A323 75c Merryweather
    Manual, 1851   1.10 1.00
    Nos. 857-860 (4)   3.15 2.90

Australia
Day — A324

1983, Jan. 26   **Litho.**   **Perf. 14½**
861 A324 27c Sirius   .45 .25
862 A324 27c Supply   .45 .25
  a.   Pair, #861-862   .90 .75

A325   A326

1983, Feb. 2   **Perf. 14x13½**
863 A325 27c multicolored   .40 .20

Australia-New Zealand Closer Economic
Relationship agreement (ANZCER).

1983, Mar. 9   **Litho.**   **Perf. 14½**
864 A326 27c Equality, dignity   .45 .20
865 A326 27c Social justice, co-
    operation   .45 .20
866 A326 27c Liberty, freedom   .45 .20
867 A326 75c Peace, harmony   1.25 1.25
    Nos. 864-867 (4)   2.60 1.85

Commonwealth day.

Queen
Elizabeth II,
57th Birthday
A327

1983, Apr. 20   **Perf. 14½**
868 A327 27c Britannia   .40 .20

World Communications Year — A328

1983, May 18   **Litho.**   **Perf. 13½x14**
869 A328 27c multicolored   .45 .20

50th Anniv.
of Australian
Jaycees
Youth
Organization
A329

1983, June 8
870 A329 27c multicolored   .40 .20

St. John
Ambulance
Cent. — A330

Regent
Skipper — A331

1983, June 8   **Perf. 13½x14**
871 A330 27c multicolored   .40 .20

1983   **Perf. 13½, 14½x14 (30c)**
872 A331 4c shown   .20 .20
873 A331 10c Cairn's birdwing   .20 .20
874 A331 20c Macleay's swal-
    lowtail   .30 .20
875 A331 27c Ulysses   .45 .20
875A A331 30c Chlorinda hair-
    streak   .50 .20
876 A331 35c Blue tiger   .55 .20
877 A331 45c Big greasy   .60 .20
878 A331 60c Wood white   .85 .30
879 A331 80c Amaryllis azure   1.00 .40
880 A331 $1 Sword grass
    brown   1.25 .20
    Nos. 872-880 (10)   5.90 2.30

Issue dates: 30c, Oct. 24; others, June 15.

The Sentimental
Bloke, by C.J.
Dennis,
1909 — A332

Folktale scenes: a, The bloke. b, Doreen -
the intro. c, The stror at coot. d, Hitched. e,
The mooch of life.

1983, Aug. 3   **Perf. 14½**
881   Strip of 5   1.75 1.50
  a.-e.   A332 27c multi, any single   .35 .30

Kookaburra
Bird Wearing
Santa
Hat — A333

1983   **Litho.**   **Perf. 13½x14**
882 A333 24c Nativity   .35 .35
883 A333 35c multicolored   .50 .35
884 A333 85c Holiday beach
    scene   1.25 .60
    Nos. 882-884 (3)   2.10 1.30

Christmas. Issued: #883, 9/14; #882, 884,
11/2.

Inland
Explorers — A334

Clay sculptures by Dianne Quinn: No. 885,
Ludwig Leichhardt (1813-48). No. 886, William
John Wills (1834-61), Robert O'Hara Burke
(1821-61). No. 887, Paul Edmund de
Strzelecki (1797-1873). No. 888, Alexander
Forrest (1849-1901).

1983, Sept. 26   **Perf. 14½**
885 A334 30c multicolored   .35 .20
886 A334 30c multicolored   .35 .20
887 A334 30c multicolored   .35 .20
888 A334 30c multicolored   .35 .20
    Nos. 885-888 (4)   1.40 .80

Australia
Day — A335

1984, Jan. 26   **Litho.**   **Perf. 13½x14**
889 A335 30c Cooks' Cottage   .30 .20

50th Anniv. of Official Air Mail
Service — A336

Pilot Charles Ulm (1898-1934); his plane,
"Faith in Australia," and different flight covers.

1984, Feb. 22   **Litho.**   **Perf. 13½**
890 A336 45c Australia-New Zea-
    land   .75 .60
891 A336 45c Australia-Papua
    New Guinea   .75 .60
  a.   Pair, #890-891   1.50 1.50

Thomson,
1898 — A337

Australian-made vintage cars: b, Tarrant,
1906. c, Australian Six, 1919. d, Summit,
1923. e, Chic, 1924.

1984, Mar. 14   **Perf. 14½**
892   Strip of 5   1.75 1.50
  a.-e.   A337 30c any single   .35 .25

Queen
Elizabeth II,
58th Birthday
A338

1984, Apr. 18   **Perf. 14½**
893 A338 30c multicolored   .30 .20

Clipper Ships
A339

1984, May 23   **Perf. 14x13½, 13½x14**
894 A339 30c Cutty Sark, 1869,
    vert.   .35 .30
895 A339 45c Orient, 1853   .55 .55
896 A339 75c Sobraon, 1866   .90 .90

897 A339 85c Thermopylae,
    1868, vert.   1.10 1.10
    Nos. 894-897 (4)   2.90 2.85

Freestyle
Skiing — A340

Coral
Hopper — A341

1984, June 6   **Litho.**   **Perf. 14½**
898 A340 30c shown   .40 .20
899 A340 30c Slalom, horiz.   .40 .20
900 A340 30c Cross-country,
    horiz.   .40 .20
901 A340 30c Downhill   .40 .20
    Nos. 898-901 (4)   1.60 .80

Perf. 13½, 14x14½ (30c, 33c)
1984-86   **Litho.**
902 A341 2c shown   .20 .20
903 A341 3c Jimble   .20 .20
904 A341 5c Tasseled an-
    glerfish   .20 .20
905 A341 10c Stonefish   .20 .20
906 A341 20c Red handfish   .25 .20
907 A341 25c Orange-tipped
    cowrie   .45 .25
908 A341 30c Choat's wrasse   .55 .25
909 A341 33c Leafy sea dragon   .45 .20
910 A341 40c Red velvet fish   .55 .20
911 A341 45c Texile cone shell   .65 .30
912 A341 50c Blue-lined surge-
    onfish   .90 .50
913 A341 55c Bennett's nudi-
    branch   1.00 .50
914 A341 60c Lionfish   .85 .40
915 A341 65c Stingray   .95 .40
916 A341 70c Blue-ringed octo-
    pus   1.00 .50
917 A341 80c Pineapple fish   1.10 .55
918 A341 85c Regal angelfish   1.50 .95
919 A341 90c Crab-eyed goby   1.25 .55
920 A341 $1 Crown of thorns
    starfish   1.50 .60
    Nos. 902-920 (19)   13.75 7.20

Issued: 2c, 25c, 30c, 50c, 55c, 6/18;
33c, 1/20/85; 5c, 20c, 40c, 80c, 90c, 6/12/85;
3c, 10c, 45c, 60c, 65c, 70c, $1, 6/11/86.

1984
Summer
Olympics
A342

Event stages.

Perf. 13½x14, 14x13½
1984, July 25
922 A342 30c Start (facing down)   .45 .20
923 A342 30c Competing (facing
    right)   .45 .20
924 A342 30c Finish, vert.   .45 .20
    Nos. 922-924 (3)   1.35 .60

Ausipex '84
A343

Christmas
A344

#926: a, Victoria #3. b, New South Wales
#1. c, Tasmania #1. d, South Australia #1. e,
Western Australia #1. f, Queensland #3.

1984   **Litho.**   **Perf. 14½**
925 A343 30c No. 2   .45 .20

Souvenir Sheet
926   Sheet of 7   3.50 3.00
  a.-f.   A343 30c any single   .50 .20

#926 contains #925, 926a-926f. Issue
dates: #925, Aug. 22; #926, Sept. 21.

1984   Litho.   Perf. 14x13½
927 A344 24c Angel and Child .30 .25
928 A344 30c Veiled Virgin and
                Child .35 .25
929 A344 40c Angel .50 .40
930 A344 50c Three Kings .65 .45
931 A344 85c Madonna and
                Child 1.10 1.00
        Nos. 927-931 (5) 2.90 2.35
Stained-glass windows. Issue dates: 40c,
Sept. 17; others, Oct. 30.

European
Settlement
Bicentenary
A345

Design: No. 932, Bicentennial Emblem.
Rock paintings: No. 933, Stick figures,
Cobar Region, New South Wales. No. 934,
Bunjil's Cave, Grampians, Western Victoria.
No. 935, Quinkan Gallery, Cape York, Queens-
land. No. 936, Wandjina Spirit and Snake
Babies, Gibb River, Western Australia. No.
937, Rock Python, Western Australia. No. 938,
Silver Barramundi, Kakadu Natl. Park, North-
ern Territory. 85c, Rock Possum, Kakadu Natl.
Park.

1984, Nov. 7   Litho.   Perf. 14½
932 A345 30c multicolored .40 .25
933 A345 30c multicolored .40 .25
934 A345 30c multicolored .40 .25
935 A345 30c multicolored .40 .25
936 A345 30c multicolored .40 .25
937 A345 30c multicolored .40 .25
938 A345 30c multicolored .40 .25
939 A345 85c multicolored 1.10 .60
        Nos. 932-939 (8) 3.90 2.35

Settlement of
Victoria
Sesquicentenary
A346

1984, Nov. 19
940 A346 30c Helmeted honeyeater .45 .20
941 A346 30c Leadbeater's possum .45 .20
    a.   Pair, #940-941 .90

Australia
Day — A347

1985, Jan. 25   Litho.
942 A347 30c Musgrave Ranges,
                by Sidney Nolan .45 .20
    a.   Pair, #942 tete-beche 1.25
943 A347 30c The Walls of China,
                by Russell Drys-
                dale .45 .20
    a.   Pair, #942-943 .90
    b.   Pair, #943 tete-beche 1.25

Intl. Youth
Year — A348

1985, Feb. 13   Litho.   Perf. 14x13½
944 A348 30c multicolored .40 .20

Royal Victorian   District Nursing
Volunteer   Service
Artillery   Centenary
A349   A350

Colonial military uniforms: b, Western Australian Pinjarrah Cavalry. c, New South Wales
Lancers. d, New South Wales Contingent to
the Sudan. e, Victorian Mounted Rifles.

1985, Feb. 25   Perf. 14½
945   Strip of 5 1.75 1.60
    a.-e. A349 33c any single .35 .35

1985, Mar. 13   Perf. 14½
946 A350 33c multicolored .40 .20

Australian Cockatoo — A351

Perf. 14 Horiz. on 1 or 2 sides
1985, Mar. 13
947 A351 1c apple grn, yel & buff .50 .50
948 A351 33c apple grn, yel, & lt
                grnsh blue .45 .20
    a.   Bkt. pane, 1 #947, 3 #948 2.75
        Issued in booklets only.

Queen Elizabeth II,
59th
Birthday — A352

1985, Apr. 10   Perf. 13
949 A352 33c Abel Tasman, ex-
                plorer .55 .30
950 A352 33c The Eendracht .55 .30
951 A352 33c William Dampier .55 .30
952 A352 90c Globe and hand 1.50 .90
    a.   Souvenir sheet of 4, #949-952 3.50 3.50
        Nos. 949-952 (4) 3.15 1.80

Queen Elizabeth II,
59th
Birthday — A353

1985, Apr. 22   Perf. 14x13½
953 A353 33c Queen's Badge, Or-
                der of Australia .45 .20

A354   A356

1985, May 15   Litho.   Perf. 14x13
954 A354 33c Soil .45 .30
955 A354 50c Air .65 .50
956 A354 80c Water 1.00 .70
957 A354 90c Energy 1.10 .90
        Nos. 954-957 (4) 3.20 2.40
Environmental conservation.

1985, July 17   Litho.   Perf. 14½
Illustrations from classic children's books: a,
Elves & Fairies, by Annie Rentoul. b, The
Magic Pudding, text and illustrations by Nor-
man Lindsay. c, Ginger Meggs, by James
Charles Bancks. d, Blinky Bill, by Dorothy
Wall. e, Snugglepot and Cuddlepie, by May
Gibbs.
960   Strip of 5 1.75 1.25
    a.-e. A356 33c any single .35 .20

Electronic
Mail — A357

1985, Sept. 18   Litho.
961 A357 33c multicolored .40 .20

Christmas
A358

Angel in a ship, detail from a drawing by
Albrecht Durer (1471-1528).

1985, Sept. 18   Litho.
962 A358 45c multicolored .45 .35
        See Nos. 967-970.

Coastal
Shipwrecks
A359

Salvaged antiquities: 33c, Astrolabe from
Batavia, 1629. 50c, German beardman (Bel-
larmine) jug from Vergulde Draeck, 1656. 90c,
Wooden bobbins from Batavia, and scissors
from Zeewijk, 1727. $1, Silver buckle from
Zeewijk.

1985, Oct. 2   Litho.   Perf. 13
963 A359 33c multicolored .40 .20
964 A359 50c multicolored .60 .60
965 A359 90c multicolored 1.25 1.00
966 A359 $1 multicolored 1.75 .80
        Nos. 963-966 (4) 4.00 2.60

Christmas Type of 1985
Illustrations by Scott Hartshorne.

1985, Nov. 1   Litho.   Perf. 14
967 A358 27c Angel with trumpet .30 .20
968 A358 33c Angel with bells .40 .25
969 A358 55c Angel with star .70 .65
970 A358 90c Angel with orna-
                ment 1.10 1.10
        Nos. 967-970 (4) 2.50 2.20

Australia   AUSSAT — A361
Day — A360

1986, Jan. 24   Litho.   Perf. 14½
971 A360 33c Aboriginal painting .40 .20

1986, Jan. 24
Various communications satellites.
972 A361 33c multicolored .35 .20
973 A361 80c multicolored 1.10 .75

South
Australia,
Sesquicent.
A362

1986, Feb. 12   Perf. 13½x14
974 A362 33c Sailing ship Buffalo .50 .20
975 A362 33c City Sign, sculpture
                by O.H. Hajek .50 .20
    a.   Pair, #974-975 1.00 .60

Cook's New
Holland
Expedition
A363

1986, Mar. 12   Perf. 13
976 A363 33c Hibiscus mer-
                ankensis .35 .25
977 A363 33c Banksia serrata .35 .25
978 A363 50c Dillenia alata .60 .60
979 A363 80c Corria reflexa .90 .70
980 A363 90c Parkinson 1.00 .90
981 A363 90c Banks 1.00 1.00
        Nos. 976-981 (6) 4.20 3.70
Australian bicentennial. Sydney Parkinson
(d. 1775), artist. Sir Joseph Banks (1743-
1820), naturalist.

Halley's   Elizabeth II, 60th
Comet — A364   Birthday — A365

1986, Apr. 9   Perf. 14x13½
982 A364 33c Radio telescope, tra-
                jectory diagram .45 .20

1986, Apr. 21   Perf. 14½
983 A365 33c multicolored .45 .20

Horses
A366

1986, May 21
984 A366 33c Brumbies .45 .25
985 A366 80c Stock horse mus-
                tering 1.10 .65
986 A366 90c Show-jumping 1.25 .95
987 A366 $1 Australian pony 1.40 .95
        Nos. 984-987 (4) 4.20 2.80

Click Go the
Shears, Folk
Song — A366a

Lines from the song: b, Old shearer stands.
c, Ringer looks around. d, Boss of the board.
e, Tar-boy is there. f, Shearing is all over.

1986, July 21   Litho.   Perf. 14½
987A   Strip of 5 2.75 1.50
    b.-f.   A366a 33c, any single .55 .20
Amalgamated Shearers' Union, predeces-
sor of the Australian Workers' Union, cent.

Australia
Bicentennial
A367

Settling of Botany Bay penal colony: No. 988, King George III, c. 1767, by A. Ramsay. No. 989, Lord Sydney, secretary of state, 1783-1789, by Gilbert Stuart. No. 990, Capt. Arthur Phillip, 1st penal colony governor, by F. Wheatley, 1786. $1, Capt. John Hunter, governor, 1795-1800, by W. B. Bennett, 1815.

1986, Aug. 6   **Litho.**   **Perf. 13**
988	A367	33c multicolored	.50	.30
989	A367	33c multicolored	.50	.30
990	A367	33c multicolored	.50	.30
991	A367	$1 multicolored	1.50	1.00
		Nos. 988-991 (4)	3.00	1.90

Wildlife
A368

Alpine
Wildflowers
A369

Designs: a, Red kangaroo. b, Emu. c, Koala. d, Kookaburra. e, Platypus.

1986, Aug. 13   **Perf. 14½x14**
992		Strip of 5	2.00	1.25
a.-e.	A368 36c any single		.40	.20

Rouletted 9½ Vert. on 1 or 2 sides
1986, Aug. 25
Booklet Stamps
993	A369	3c Royal bluebell	.45	.45
994	A369	5c Alpine marsh marigold	1.00	1.00
995	A369	25c Mount Buffalo sunray	1.00	.75
996	A369	36c Silver snow daisy	.90	.20
a.	Bklt. pane, #993, #994, 2 #996		3.25	
b.	Bklt. pane, #993, #995, 2 #996		3.25	
		Nos. 993-996 (4)	3.35	2.40

Orchids — A370

America's Cup
Triumph
'83 — A371

1986, Sept. 18   **Perf. 14½**
997	A370	36c Elythranthera emarginata	.50	.20
998	A370	55c Dendrobium nindii	.80	.60
999	A370	90c Caleana major	1.40	1.00
1000	A370	$1 Thelymitra variegata	1.50	1.10
		Nos. 997-1000 (4)	4.20	2.90

1986, Sept. 26   **Perf. 14x13½**
1001	A371	36c Australia II crossing finish line	.60	.25
1002	A371	36c Trophy	.60	.25
1003	A371	36c Boxing kangaroo	.60	.25
		Nos. 1001-1003 (3)	1.80	.75

Intl. Peace
Year — A372

1986, Oct. 22   **Litho.**   **Perf. 14x13½**
1004	A372	36c multicolored	.50	.20

Christmas
A373

Kindergarten nativity play: No. 1005, Holy Family, vert. No. 1006, Three Kings, vert. No. 1007, Angels. No. 1008a, Angels, peasants. No. 1008b, Holy Family, angels, vert. No. 1008c, Shepherd, angels, vert. No. 1008d, Three Kings. No. 1008e, Shepherds.

1986, Nov. 3   **Litho.**
1005	A373	30c multicolored	.50	.20
a.	Perf 14x13½		1.00	.50
1006	A373	36c multicolored	.60	.25
1007	A373	60c multicolored	1.00	.65
		Nos. 1005-1007 (3)	2.10	1.10

Souvenir Sheet
1008		Sheet of 5	2.50	2.50
a.-e.	A373 30c any single		.50	.50

Perfs: Nos. 1005-1006, 1008c, 15x14½; Nos. 1007, 1008a 1008e, 14½x15. No. 1008b, 15x14½x15x15; No. 1008d, 14½x15x14½x14½.

Australia
Day — A374

1987, Jan. 23   **Litho.**   **Perf. 13½x14**
1009	A374	36c Flag, circuit board	.45	.20
1010	A374	36c Made in Australia campaign emblem	.45	.20

America's
Cup — A375

Fruits — A376

Views of yachts racing.

1987, Jan. 28   **Perf. 15x14½**
1011	A375	36c multicolored	.40	.20
1012	A375	55c multicolored	.60	.55
1013	A375	90c multicolored	1.10	.90
1014	A375	$1 multicolored	1.40	.95
		Nos. 1011-1014 (4)	3.50	2.60

1987, Feb. 11   **Perf. 14x13½**
1015	A376	36c Melons, grapes	.45	.30
1016	A376	65c Tropical fruit	.80	.60
1017	A376	90c Pears, apples, oranges	1.10	.90
1018	A376	$1 Berries, peaches	1.25	.95
		Nos. 1015-1018 (4)	3.60	2.75

Agricultural
Shows — A377

1987, Apr. 10   **Litho.**   **Perf. 14x13½**
1019	A377	36c Livestock	.45	.20
1020	A377	65c Produce	.80	.60
1021	A377	90c Carnival	1.10	.90
1022	A377	$1 Farmers	1.25	.95
		Nos. 1019-1022 (4)	3.60	2.65

Queen
Elizabeth II,
61st Birthday
A378

1987, Apr. 21   **Perf. 13½x14**
1023	A378	36c multicolored	.45	.20

First Fleet
Leaving
England
A379

Continuous design: No. 1024a, Convicts awaiting transportation. b, Capt. Arthur Phillip, Mrs. Phillip, longboat on shore. c, Sailors relaxing and working. d, Longboats heading from and to fleet. 4e, Fleet in harbor.

No. 1025a, Longboat approaching Tenerife, The Canary Isls. b, Fishing in Tenerife Harbor. $1, Fleet, dolphins.

1987   **Perf. 13**
1024		Strip of 5	4.00	4.00
a.-e.	A379 36c any single		.80	.20
1025		Pair	1.00	1.00
a.-b.	A379 36c any single		.50	.20
1026	A379	$1 multicolored	1.50	1.50
		Nos. 1024-1026 (3)	6.50	6.50

Australia bicent.; departure of the First Fleet, May 13, 1787; arrival at Tenerife, June 1787.
Issued: #1024, 5/13; #1025-1026, 6/3.

1987, Aug. 6

First Fleet arrives at Rio de Janeiro, Aug. 1787: a, Whale, storm in the Atlantic. b, Citrus grove. c, Market. d, Religious procession. e, Fireworks over harbor.

1027		Strip of 5	1.75	1.75
a.-e.	A379 36c any single		.35	.20

No. 1027 has a continuous design.

1987, Oct. 13

First Fleet arrives at Cape of Good Hope, Oct. 1787: No. 1028a, British officer surveys livestock and supplies, Table Mountain. No. 1028b, Ships anchored in Table Bay. No. 1029, Fishermen pull in nets as the Fleet approaches the Cape.

1028		Pair	.90	.90
a.-b.	A379 37c any single		.45	.20
1029	A379	$1 multicolored	1.25	.50

No. 1028 has a continuous design.

1988, Jan. 26

Arrival of the First Fleet, Sydney Cove, Jan. 1788: a, Five aborigines on shore. b, Four aborigines on shore. c, Kangaroos. d, White cranes. e, Flag raising.

1030		Strip of 5	2.25	2.25
a.-e.	A379 37c any single		.45	.20

Printed se-tenant in a continuous design.

The Early
Years: Sydney
Cove and
Parramatta
Colonies
A380

Details from panorama "View of Sydney from the East Side of the Cove," 1808, painted by convict artist John Eyre to illustrate The Present Picture of New South Wales, published in London in 1811, and paintings in British and Australian museums: a, Government House, 1790, Sydney, by midshipman George Raper. b, Government Farm, Parramatta, 1791, attributed to the Port Jackson Painter. c, Parramatta Road, 1796, attributed to convict

artist Thomas Watling. d, The Rocks and Sydney Cove, 1800, an aquatint engraving by Edward Dayes. e, Sydney Hospital, 1803, by George William Evans, an explorer and surveyor-general of New South Wales. Printed se-tenant in a continuous design.

1988, Apr. 13   **Litho.**   **Perf. 13**
1031		Strip of 5	2.50	2.50
a.-e.	A380 37c any single		.50	.20

Australia Bicentennial.

The Man from
Snowy River,
1890, Ballad by
A.B. Paterson
A381

Fauna
A382

Excerpts: a, At the station. b, Mountain bred. c, Terrible descent. d, At their heels. e, Brought them back.

1987, June 24   **Perf. 14x13½**
1034		Strip of 5	2.25	2.25
a.-e.	A381 36c any single		.45	.30

Printed se-tenant in a continuous design.

1987, July 1   **Perf. 14½x14**

Designs: a, Possum. b, Cockatoo. c, Wombat. d, Rosella. e, Echidna.
1035		Strip of 5	1.75	1.75
a.-e.	A382 37c any single		.35	.20

Printed se-tenant in a continuous design.

Technology — A383

1987, Aug. 19   **Perf. 14½**
1036	A383	37c Bionic ear	.40	.20
1037	A383	53c Microchips	.55	.30
1038	A383	63c Robotics	.70	.35
1039	A383	68c Zirconia ceramics	.75	.35
		Nos. 1036-1039 (4)	2.40	1.20

Children
A384

1987, Sept. 16
1040	A384	37c Crayfishing	.35	.20
1041	A384	55c Cat's cradle	.55	.30
1042	A384	90c Eating meat pies	.80	.45
1043	A384	$1 Playing with a joey	1.00	.50
		Nos. 1040-1043 (4)	2.70	1.45

Christmas
A385

Carolers: a, Woman, two girls. b, Man, two girls. c, Four children. d, Man, two women, boy. e, Six youths. 37c, three women, two men. Nos. 1044a-1044e are vert.

1987, Nov. 2   **Litho.**   **Perf. 14½**
1044		Strip of 5	2.00	2.00
a.-e.		A385 30c any single	.40	.20

Perf. 13½x14
1045	A385	37c multicolored	.45	.20
1046	A385	63c shown	.80	.30
		Nos. 1044-1046 (3)	3.25	2.50

Carols by Candlelight, Christmas Eve, Sidney Myer Bowl, Melbourne.

Aboriginal Crafts — A386

Designs: 3c, Spearthrower, Western Australia. 15c, Shield, New South Wales. No. 1049, Basket, Queensland. No. 1050, Bowl, Central Australia. No. 1051, Belt, Northern Territory.

Perf. 15½ Horiz.

1987, Oct. 13   **Photo.**
1047	A386	3c multicolored	1.25	1.25
1048	A386	15c multicolored	1.90	1.25
1049	A386	37c multicolored	1.10	.35
a.		Bklt. pane, 2 ea #1047, 1049	4.50	
1050	A386	37c multicolored	1.25	.35
1051	A386	37c multicolored	1.25	.35
a.		Bklt. pane, #1048, 3 #1050, 2 #1051	9.00	
		Nos. 1047-1051 (5)	6.75	3.55

Issued only in booklets.

Caricature of Australian Koala and American Bald Eagle — A387

1988, Jan. 26   **Perf. 13**
1052	A387	37c multicolored	.55	.20

Australia bicentennial. See No. 1086 and US No. 2370.

Living Together — A388

Cartoons.

1988   **Perf. 14**
1053	A388	1c Religion	.20	.20
1054	A388	2c Industry	.20	.20
1055	A388	3c Local government	.20	.20
1056	A388	4c Trade unions	.20	.20
1057	A388	5c Parliament	.20	.20
1058	A388	10c Transportation	.20	.20
1059	A388	15c Sports	.20	.20
1060	A388	20c Commerce	.30	.20
1061	A388	25c Housing	.35	.20
1062	A388	30c Welfare	.45	.20
1063	A388	37c Postal services	.55	.20
a.		Booklet pane of 10	5.50	
1063B	A388	39c Tourism	.55	.20
c.		Booklet pane of 10	5.50	
1064	A388	40c Recreation	.60	.20
1065	A388	45c Health	.70	.25
1066	A388	50c Mining	.75	.30
1067	A388	53c Primary industry	.80	.30
1068	A388	55c Education	.85	.30
1069	A388	60c Armed Forces	.95	.35
1070	A388	63c Police	1.00	.35
1071	A388	65c Telecommunications	1.00	.35
1072	A388	68c The media	1.10	.40
1073	A388	70c Science and technology	1.10	.40
1074	A388	75c Visual arts	1.10	.45
1075	A388	80c Performing arts	1.25	.45
1076	A388	90c Banking	1.40	.50
1077	A388	95c Law	1.50	.55

1078	A388	$1 Rescue and emergency services	1.50	.55
		Nos. 1053-1078 (27)	19.20	8.10

Issued: 1c, 2c, 3c, 5c, 30c, 40c, 55c, 60c, 63c, 65c, 68c, 75c, 95c, 3/16; 39c, 9/28; others, 2/17.

Queen Elizabeth II, 62nd Birthday A389

1988, Apr. 21   **Perf. 14½**
1079	A389	37c multicolored	.60	.20

EXPO '88, Brisbane, Apr. 30-Oct. 30 — A390

1988, Apr. 29   **Perf. 13**
1080	A390	37c multicolored	.60	.20

Opening of Parliament House, Canberra A391

1988, May 9   **Perf. 14½**
1081	A391	37c multicolored	.60	.20

Australia Bicentennial A392

Designs: No. 1082, Colonist, clipper ship. No. 1083, British and Australian parliaments, Queen Elizabeth II. No. 1084, Cricketer W.G. Grace. No. 1085, John Lennon (1940-1980), William Shakespeare (1564-1616) and Sydney Opera House. #1083a, 1085a have continuous design picturing flag of Australia.

1988, June 21   **Litho.**   **Perf. 13**
1082	A392	37c multicolored	.80	.20
1083	A392	37c multicolored	.80	.20
a.		Pair, #1082-1083	1.75	.75
1084	A392	$1 multicolored	2.25	.55
1085	A392	$1 multicolored	2.25	.55
a.		Pair, #1084-1085	4.75	2.50
		Nos. 1082-1085 (4)	6.10	1.50

See Great Britain Nos. 1222-1225.

Caricature Type of 1988

Design: Caricature of an Australian koala and New Zealand kiwi.

1988, June 21   **Litho.**   **Perf. 13½**
1086	A387	37c multicolored	.60	.20

Australia bicentennial. See New Zealand No. 907.

"Dream" Lore on Art of the Desert A393

Aboriginal paintings from Papunya Settlement in the Flinders University Art Museum: 37c, Bush Potato Country, by Turkey Tolsen Tjupurrula with by David Corby Tjapaltjarri. 55c, Courtship Rejected, by Limpi Puntungka Tjapangati. 90c, Medicine Story, anonymous. $1, Ancestor Dreaming, by Tim Leura Tjapaltjarri.

1988, Aug. 1   **Litho.**   **Perf. 13**
1087	A393	37c multicolored	.60	.20
1088	A393	55c multicolored	.90	.75
1089	A393	90c multicolored	1.50	.50
1090	A393	$1 multicolored	1.60	.55
		Nos. 1087-1090 (4)	4.60	2.00

1988 Summer Olympics, Seoul — A394

1988, Sept. 14   **Perf. 14½**
1091	A394	37c Basketball	.60	.20
1092	A394	65c Running	1.10	.90
1093	A394	$1 Rhythmic gymnastics	1.60	.55
		Nos. 1091-1093 (3)	3.30	1.65

34th Commonwealth Parliamentary Conference, Canberra — A395

1988, Sept. 19
1094	A395	37c Scepter and mace	.60	.20

Works in the Contemporary Decorative Arts Collection at the Natl. Gallery — A396

Roulette 9 Horiz.

1988, Sept. 28   **Litho.**
1095	A396	2c "Australian Fetish," by Peter Tully	2.50	2.50
1096	A396	5c Vase by Colin Levy	2.50	2.50
1097	A396	39c Teapot by Frank Bauer	.75	.35
a.		Bklt. pane of 3 (2c, 2 39c)	4.50	
b.		Bklt. pane of 6 (5c, 5 39c)	6.25	
		Nos. 1095-1097 (3)	5.75	5.35

Nos. 1095-1097 issued in booklets only.

Views — A397

1988, Oct. 17   **Photo.**   **Perf. 13**
1098	A397	39c The Desert	.65	.25
1099	A397	55c The Top End	.90	.30
1100	A397	65c The Coast	1.10	.40
1101	A397	70c The Bush	1.10	.40
		Nos. 1098-1101 (4)	3.75	1.35

Christmas A398

Children's design contest winning drawings: 32c, Nativity scene, by Danielle Hush, age 7. 39c, Koala wearing a Santa hat, by Kylie Courtney, age 6. 63c, Cockatoo wearing a Santa hat, by Benjamin Stevenson, age 10.

1988, Oct. 31   **Perf. 13½x13**
1102	A398	32c multicolored	.55	.20
1103	A398	39c multicolored	.65	.20
1104	A398	63c multicolored	1.10	.55
		Nos. 1102-1104 (3)	2.30	.95

Sir Henry Parkes (1815-1896), Advocate of the Federation of the Six Colonies — A399

1989, Jan. 25   **Litho.**   **Perf. 14x13½**
1105	A399	39c multicolored	.70	.20

Australia Day.

Sports — A400

1989, Feb. 13   **Perf. 14x14½**
1106	A400	1c Bowls	.20	.20
a.		Perf. 13¼x13¾ ('90)	.20	.20
1107	A400	2c Bowling	.20	.20
a.		Perf. 13¼x13¾ ('91)	.20	.20
1108	A400	3c Football	.20	.20
1109	A400	39c Fishing	.70	.20
a.		Booklet pane of 10	7.00	
d.		Perf. 13¼x13¾ on 3 or 4 sides ('90)	.70	.20
e.		Booklet pane of 10, #1109d	7.00	
1109B	A400	41c Cycling	.60	.20
c.		Booklet pane of 10	6.25	
1110	A400	55c Kite-flying	.95	.30
1111	A400	70c Cricket	1.25	.40
1112	A400	$1.10 Golf	2.00	.65

#1109d also exists perfed on 4 sides from sheets. These are scarcer

1990-94
1114	A400	5c Kayaking, canoeing	.20	.20
a.		Perf. 13¼x13¾	.20	.20
1115	A400	10c Windsurfing	.20	.20
a.		Perf. 13¼x13¾	.30	.20
1116	A400	20c Tennis	.30	.20
a.		Perf. 13¼x13¾	.30	.20
1117	A400	65c Rock climbing	1.00	.35
a.		Perf. 13¼x13¾	1.00	1.00
1118	A400	$1 Running	1.50	.55
a.		Perf. 13¼x13¾	3.75	2.00

Issued: #1114a, 1115a, 1116a, 1117a, 1118, 1/17/90; #1118a, 1/91; #1115, 1117, 2/92; #1116, 7/93; #1114, 3/94.

1990, Aug. 27
1119	A400	43c Skateboarding	.65	.20
a.		Booklet pane of 10	6.75	

Perf. 13½
1120	A400	$1.20 Hang-gliding	1.90	.50

1991, Aug. 22   **Perf. 14x14½**
1121	A400	75c Netball	1.10	.40
1122	A400	80c Squash	1.25	.40
1123	A400	85c Diving	1.25	.40
1124	A400	90c Soccer	1.40	.45
		Nos. 1106-1124 (19)	16.85	6.20

For self-adhesive stamps see #1185-1186.

Botanical Gardens — A401

Designs: $2, Nooroo, New South Wales. $5, Mawarra, Victoria. $10, Palm House, Adelaide Botanical Garden. $20, A View of the Artist's House and Garden in Mills Plains, Van Diemen's Land by John Glover.

1989-90   Litho. & Engr.   Perf. 14
1132 A401 $2 multicolored   2.50 1.00
  a. Perf. 13¼x13¾ ('91)   2.00 1.00
1133 A401 $5 multicolored   6.00 2.00
  a. Perf. 13¼x13¾   6.75 2.00
1134 A401 $10 multicolored   12.00 2.00
Perf. 14½x14
1135 A401 $20 multicolored   19.00 8.00
  Nos. 1132-1135 (4)   39.50 13.00

Issued: $10, 4/12; $2, $5, 9/13; $20, 8/15/90.

Sheep A402

1989, Feb. 27   Perf. 13½x14
1136 A402 39c Merino   .55 .20
1137 A402 39c Poll Dorset   .55 .20
1138 A402 85c Polwarth   1.25 .50
1139 A402 $1 Corriedale   1.40 .75
  Nos. 1136-1139 (4)   3.75 1.65

World Sheep and Wool Congress, Tasmania, Feb. 27-Mar. 6.

Queen Elizabeth II, 63rd Birthday — A403

1989, Apr. 21   Litho.   Perf. 14½
1140 A403 39c Statue by John Dowie   .65 .20

Colonial Australia A404

Pastoral Era: a, Immigrant ship in port, c. 1835. b, Pioneer's hut, wool bales in dray. c, Squatter's homestead. d, Shepherds. e, Explorers.

1989, May 10
1141 Strip of 5   2.50 1.10
  a.-e. A404 39c any single   .50 .20

Stars of Stage and Screen — A405

Performers and directors: 39c, Gladys Moncrieff and Roy Rene, the stage, 1920's. 85c, Charles Chauvel and Chips Rafferty, talking films. $1, Nellie Stewart and James Cassius Williamson, the stage, 1890's. $1.10, Lottie Lyell and Raymond Longford, silent films.

1989, July 12   Litho.   Perf. 14½
1142 A405 39c multicolored   .50 .20
  a. Perf. 14x13½ ('90)   5.00 5.00
1143 A405 85c multicolored   1.00 1.00
1144 A405 $1 multicolored   1.25 .50
1145 A405 $1.10 multicolored   1.40 .55
  Nos. 1142-1145 (4)   4.15 2.25

Impressionist Paintings A406

Paintings by Australian artists: No. 1146, Impression for Golden Summer, by Sir Arthur Streeton. No. 1147, All on a Summer's Day, by Charles Conder, vert. No. 1148, Petit Dejeuner, by Frederick McCubbin. No. 1149, Impression, by Tom Roberts.

Perf. 13½x14, 14x13½
1989, Aug. 23   Litho.
1146 A406 41c shown   .60 .20
1147 A406 41c multicolored   .60 .20
1148 A406 41c multicolored   .60 .20
1149 A406 41c multicolored   .60 .20
  Nos. 1146-1149 (4)   2.40 .80

The Urban Environment — A407

1989, Sept. 1   Litho.   Perf. 15½
Booklet Stamps
1150 A407 41c Freeways   .70 .70
1151 A407 41c Architecture   .70 .70
1152 A407 41c Commuter train   .70 .70
  a. Bkt. pane, 2 ea #1150, 1152, 3 #1151   5.00
  Nos. 1150-1152 (3)   2.10 2.10

No. 1152a sold for $3.

Australian Youth Hostels, 50th Anniv. A408

1989, Sept. 13   Perf. 14½
1153 A408 41c multicolored   .65 .20

Street Cars — A409

Designs: No. 1154, Horse-drawn tram, Adelaide, 1878. No. 1155, Steam tram, Sydney, 1884. No. 1156, Cable car, Melbourne, 1886. No. 1157, Double-deck electric tram, Hobart, 1893. No. 1158, Combination electric tram, Brisbane, 1901.

1989, Oct. 11   Litho.   Perf. 13½x14
1154 A409 41c multicolored   .65 .20
1155 A409 41c multicolored   .65 .20
1156 A409 41c multicolored   .65 .20
  a. Perf. 14½ on 3 sides   1.25 1.25
  b. Booklet pane of 10, #1156a   12.50
1157 A409 41c multicolored   .65 .20
1158 A409 41c multicolored   .65 .20
  Nos. 1154-1158 (5)   3.25 1.00

Purchase of booklet containing No. 1156b included STAMPSHOW '89 admission ticket and a Melbourne one-day transit pass. Sold for $8.

Christmas A410   Radio Australia, 50th Anniv. A411

Illuminations: 36c, Annunciation, from the Nicholai Joseph Foucault Book of Hours, c. 1510-20. 41c, Annunciation to the Shepherds, from the Wharncliffe Hours, c. 1475. 80c, Adoration of the Magi, from Parisian Book of Hours, c. 1490-1500.

1989, Nov. 1   Perf. 14x13½
1159 A410 36c multicolored   .45 .20
  a. Booklet pane of 10   4.50
Perf. 15x14½
1160 A410 41c multicolored   .55 .20
1161 A410 80c multicolored   1.00 .60
  Nos. 1159-1161 (3)   2.00 1.00

1989, Nov. 1   Perf. 14x13½
1162 A411 41c multicolored   .65 .20

Australia Day A412   Special Occasions A413

1990, Jan. 17   Litho.   Perf. 15x14½
1163 A412 41c Golden wattle   .65 .20

1990, Feb. 7   Perf. 14x13½
1164 A413 41c Thinking of You   .65 .20
  a. Booklet pane of 10   6.50
  b. Perf. 14½ on 3 sides   .65 .20
  c. Booklet pane of 10, #1164b   6.50
  See No. 1193.

Women Practicing Medicine in Australia, Cent. A414

1990, Feb. 7   Perf. 14½x15
1165 A414 41c Constance Stone   .65 .20

Dr. Constance Stone, Australia's first woman doctor.

A415   A416

Fauna of the High Country.

1990, Feb. 21   Perf. 14x13½
1166 A415 41c Greater glider   .55 .20
1167 A415 65c Spotted-tailed quoll   .80 .50
1168 A415 70c Mountain pygmy-possum   1.00 .60
1169 A415 80c Brush-tailed rock-wallaby   1.25 .70
  Nos. 1166-1169 (4)   3.60 2.00

1990, Mar. 14
1170 A416 41c Quit smoking   .55 .20
1171 A416 41c Don't drink and drive   .55 .20

1172 A416 41c Eat right   .55 .20
1173 A416 41c Medical check-ups   .55 .20
  Nos. 1170-1173 (4)   2.20 .80
  Community health.

A417   A418

Scenes from WW II, 1940-41: #1174, Anzacs at the front. #1175, Women working in factories, aircraft at the ready. 65c, Veterans and memorial parade. $1, Helicopters picking up wounded, cemetery. $1.10, Anzacs reading mail from home, 5 women watching departure of 2 ships.

1990, Apr. 12   Litho.   Perf. 14½
1174 A417 41c shown   .55 .20
1175 A417 41c multicolored   .55 .20
1176 A417 65c multicolored   .80 .55
1177 A417 $1 multicolored   1.25 .65
1178 A417 $1.10 multicolored   1.40 .70
  Nos. 1174-1178 (5)   4.55 2.30

Australia and New Zealand Army Corps (ANZAC).

1990, Apr. 19   Perf. 14½
1179 A418 41c multicolored   .60 .20

Queen Elizabeth's 64th birthday.

Penny Black, 150th Anniv. A419

Stamps on stamps: a, New South Wales #44. b, South Australia #4. c, Tasmania #2. d, Victoria #120. e, Queensland #111A. f, Western Australia #3a.

1990, May 1   Perf. 13½x14
1180 Block of 6   4.00 1.25
  a.-f. A419 41c any single   .65 .20
  g. Souvenir sheet of 6   4.25 3.75

The Gold Rush — A420

a, Off to the diggings. b, The diggings. c, Panning for gold. d, Commissioner's tent. e, Gold escort.

1990, May 16   Perf. 13
1181 Strip of 5   2.50 2.50
  a.-e. A420 41c any single   .50 .20

Cooperation in Antarctic Research A421

1990, June 13   Litho.   Perf. 14½x14
1182 A421 41c Glaciology   .60 .20
1183 A421 $1.10 Krill (marine biology)   1.60 .55
  a. Min. sheet of 2, #1182-1183   2.25 2.25
  b. #1183a overprinted   3.75 3.75

No. 1183 is overprinted in gold, in sheet margin only, for NZ 1990 International Stamp Exhibition, Auckland, Aug. 24-Sept. 2, 1990. See Russia Nos. 5902-5903.

Colonial
Australia
A422

Boom Time: a, Land boom. b, Building
boom. c, Investment boom. d, Retail boom. e,
Factory boom.

1990, July 12   Litho.   Perf. 13
1184   Strip of 5   2.50 2.50
  a.-e. A422 41c any single   .50   .25

Sports Type of 1989
1990-91   Typo.   Die Cut Perf. 11½
         Self-Adhesive
1185 A400 41c Cycling   .75   .65
1186 A400 43c Skateboarding   .70   .20
  a.   Litho.   .70   .20

Blue background has large dots on No.
1186 and smaller dots on No. 1186a. No.
1186 is on waxed paper backing printed with 0
to 4 koalas. No. 1186a is on plain paper backing printed with one kangaroo.
  Issued: 41c, 5/16; #1186, 8/27; #1186a,
1991.
  This is an expanding set. Numbers will
change if necessary.

Salmon Gums by
Robert
Juniper — A423

43c, The Blue Dress by Brian Dunlop.

         Perf. 15½ Vert.
1990, Sept. 3   Litho.
         Booklet Stamps
1191 A423 28c multicolored   2.25 1.75
  a.   Perf. 14½ vert.   2.25 1.75
1192 A423 43c multicolored   .65   .50
  a.   Bkt. pane, #1191, 4 #1192   3.25
  b.   Perf. 14½ vert.   .65   .50
  c.   Bkt. pane, #1191a, 4 #1192b   3.25

Thinking Of You Type
1990, Sept. 3   Perf. 14½
1193 A413 43c multicolored   .50   .20
  a.   Booklet pane of 10   5.00

Christmas
A424

1990, Oct. 31   Litho.   Perf. 14½
1194 A424 38c Kookaburras   .60   .20
  a.   Booklet pane of 10   6.25
1195 A424 43c Nativity, vert.   .70   .20
1196 A424 80c Opossum   1.40   .60
         Nos. 1194-1196 (3)   2.70 1.00

Local Government in
Australia, 150th
Anniv. — A425

1990, Oct. 31
1197 A425 43c Town Hall, Ade-
             laide   .70   .20

Flags
A426

1991, Jan. 10   Litho.   Perf. 14½
1199 A426 43c National flag   .55   .20
1200 A426 90c White ensign   1.10   .55
1201 A426 $1 Air Force en-
             sign   1.25   .65
1202 A426 $1.20 Red ensign   1.40   .75
         Nos. 1199-1202 (4)   4.30 2.15

Australia Day.

Water
Birds — A427

1991, Feb. 14
1203 A427 43c Black swan   .55   .20
1204 A427 43c Black-necked
             stork, vert.   .55   .20
1205 A427 85c Cape Barren
             goose, vert.   1.00 1.00
1206 A427 $1 Chestnut teal   1.10   .60
         Nos. 1203-1206 (4)   3.20 2.00

Women's
Wartime
Services,
50th Anniv.
A428

50th Anniv: #1208, Siege of Tobruk. $1.20,
Australian War Memorial, Canberra.

1991, Mar. 14   Litho.   Perf. 14½
1207 A428 43c shown   .55   .20
1208 A428 43c multicolored   .55   .20
1209 A428 $1.20 multicolored   1.40   .70
         Nos. 1207-1209 (3)   2.50 1.10

Queen Elizabeth II's
65th
Birthday — A429

1991, Apr. 11   Litho.   Perf. 14½
1210 A429 43c multicolored   .55   .20

Insects
A430

1991, Apr. 11
1211 A430 43c Hawk moth   .55   .20
1212 A430 43c Cotton harlequin
             bug   .55   .20
1213 A430 80c Leichhardt's
             grasshopper   1.00   .60
1214 A430 $1 Jewel beetle   1.10   .70
         Nos. 1211-1214 (4)   3.20 1.70

Australian
Photography, 150th
Anniv. — A431

Designs: No. 1215a, Bondi, by Max Dupain,
1939. No. 1215b, Gears for the Mining Industry, Vickers Ruwolt Melbourne, by Wolfgang
Sievers, 1967. 70c, Wheel of Youth, by Harold

Cazneaux, 1929. $1.20, Teacup Ballet, by
Olive Cotton, 1935.

1991, May 13   Litho.   Perf. 14½
1215   Pair   1.10   .40
  a.-b. A431 43c any single   .55   .20
1216 A431 70c blk, olive & cl   .90   .50
1217 A431 $1.20 blk, gray & Prus
             bl   1.40   .75
         Nos. 1215-1217 (3)   3.40 1.65

Golden Days of   Pets — A433
Radio — A432

1991, June 13   Litho.   Perf. 14½
1218 A432 43c Music & variety
             shows   .70   .20
1219 A432 43c Soap operas   .70   .20
1220 A432 85c Quiz shows   1.25 1.25
1221 A432 $1 Children's stories   1.50   .65
         Nos. 1218-1221 (4)   4.15 2.30

1991, July 25   Litho.   Perf. 14½
1222 A433 43c Puppy   .65   .20
1223 A433 43c Kitten   .65   .20
1224 A433 70c Pony   1.10   .40
1225 A433 $1 Cockatoo   1.50   .60
         Nos. 1222-1225 (4)   3.90 1.40

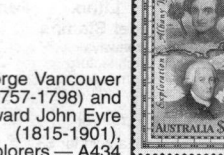

George Vancouver
(1757-1798) and
Edward John Eyre
(1815-1901),
Explorers — A434

1991, Sept. 26   Litho.   Perf. 14½
1226 A434 $1.05 multicolored   1.60   .55
  a.   Souvenir sheet of 1   1.60 1.60
  b.   As "a," overprinted in gold   2.75 2.75

Vancouver's visit to Western Australia,
200th anniv. and Eyre's journey to Albany,
Western Australia, 150th anniv.
  No. 1226b overprinted in sheet margin with
show emblem and: "PHILANIPPON / WORLD
STAMP / EXHIBITION / TOKYO / 16-24 NOV
1991" followed by Japanese inscription.
  Issue date: #1226b, Nov. 16.

Australian
Literature of
the 1890's
A435

Designs: 43c, Seven Little Australians by
Ethel Turner. 75c, On Our Selection by Steele
Rudd. $1, Clancy of the Overflow by A.B.
"Banjo" Paterson, vert. $1.20, The Drover's
Wife by Henry Lawson, vert.

1991, Oct. 10
1227 A435 43c multicolored   .65   .20
1228 A435 75c multicolored   1.10   .50
1229 A435 $1 multicolored   1.60   .65
1230 A435 $1.20 multicolored   1.90   .80
         Nos. 1227-1230 (4)   5.25 2.15

Christmas
A436

1991, Nov. 1
1231 A436 38c Shepherd   .50   .20
  a.   Booklet pane of 20   10.00
1232 A436 43c Baby Jesus   .55   .20
1233 A436 90c Wise man,
             camel   1.10   .45
         Nos. 1231-1233 (3)   2.15   .85

Thinking of
You — A437

1992, Jan. 2   Litho.   Perf. 14½x15
1234 A437 45c Wildflowers   .50   .25
  a.   Booklet pane of 10   5.00

Threatened
Species — A438

#1235: a, Parma wallaby. b, Ghost bat. c,
Long-tailed dunnart. d, Little pygmy possum.
e, Dusky hopping mouse. f, Squirrel glider.

1992, Jan. 2   Litho.   Perf. 14x14½
1235   Block of 6   4.00 3.50
  a.-f. A438 45c any single   .65   .25

         Die Cut
         Perf. 11½
         Self-Adhesive
         Size: 31x22mm

1241 A438 45c like #1235a   .65   .25
  a.   Typo.   .65   .25
1242 A438 45c like #1235b   .65   .25
  a.   Typo.   .65   .25
1243 A438 45c like #1235c   .65   .25
  a.   Typo.   .65   .25
1244 A438 45c like #1235d   .65   .25
  a.   Typo.   .65   .25
1245 A438 45c like #1235e   .65   .25
  a.   Typo.   .65   .25
1246 A438 45c like #1235f   .65   .25
  a.   Typo.   .65   .25
  b.   Bkt. pane, 2 each #1241-
          1244, 1 each #1245-1246   6.25
  c.   Pane of 5, #1242-1246   3.25
  d.   Strip of 6, #1241-1246   4.00
  e.   Strip of 6, #1241a-1246a   4.00
  f.   #1246c overprinted   4.00
  g.   As "f," no die cutting   190.00

Litho. stamps are sharper in appearance
than typo. stamps, most notably on the black
lettering. Nos. 1246b and 1246c have tagging
bars which make the right portion of the
stamps appear toned.
  No. 1246f - overprinted in Gold on sheet
margin of No. 1246c with emblem of "WORLD
COLUMBIAN / STAMP EXPO '92 / MAY 22-
31, 1992 - CHICAGO." Issued in May.
  See Nos. 1271-1293, 1406-1417.

Wetlands
A439

         Perf. 14½ Horiz.
1992, Jan. 2   Photo.
         Booklet Stamps
1247 A439 20c Noosa River,
             Queensland   .55   .45
  a.   Perf. 14 horiz.   .55   .55
1248 A439 45c Lake Eildon, Vic-
             toria   .55   .45
  a.   Bkt. pane, #1247, 4 #1248   2.75
          Complete booklet, #1248a   2.75
  b.   Perf. 14 horiz.   .55   .55
  c.   Bkt. pane, #1247a, 4 #1248b   2.75
          Complete booklet, #1248c   2.75

Sailing Ships
A440

         Perf. 14½x15, 15x14½
1992, Jan. 15   Litho.
1249 A440 45c Young Endeav-
             our   .70   .20
1250 A440 45c Britannia, vert.   .70   .20
1251 A440 $1.05 Akarana, vert.   1.60   .60
1252 A440 $1.20 John Louis   1.75   .70
  a.   Sheet of 4, #1249-1252   4.75 4.75
  b.   As "a," overprinted   5.50 5.50
  c.   As "a," overprinted   7.50 7.50
         Nos. 1249-1252 (4)   4.75 1.70

Australia Day. Discovery of America, 500th
anniv. (No. 1252a).
  Overprint in gold on sheet margin of No.
1252b contains emblem and "WORLD

COLUMBIAN / STAMP EXPO '92 / MAY 22-31, 1992-CHICAGO." No. 1252b issued in May.

Overprint in gold on sheet margin of No. 1252c contains emblem and "GENOVA '92 / 18-27 SEPTEMBER." No. 1252c issued in Sept.

Australian Battles, 1942 — A441

1992, Feb. 19   Litho.   Perf. 14½

1253	A441	45c Bombing of Darwin	.55	.20
1254	A441	75c Milne Bay	.80	.60
1255	A441	75c Kokoda Trail	.80	.60
1256	A441	$1.05 Coral Sea	1.25	.80
1257	A441	$1.20 El Alamein	1.40	.95
		Nos. 1253-1257 (5)	4.80	3.15

Intl. Space Year — A442

1992, Mar. 19

1258	A442	45c Helix Nebula	.65	.20
1259	A442	$1.05 The Pleiades	1.50	.65
1260	A442	$1.20 Spiral Galaxy NGC 2997	1.60	.70
a.		Sheet of 3, #1258-1260	3.75	3.75
b.		As "a," overprinted	5.00	5.00
		Nos. 1258-1260 (3)	3.75	1.55

Overprint on sheet margin of No. 1260b contains emblem of "WORLD COLUMBIAN / STAMP EXPO '92 / MAY 22-31, 1992-CHICAGO." No. 1260b issued in May.

Queen Elizabeth II, 66th Birthday A443

1992, Apr. 9   Perf. 14x14½

1261	A443	45c Wmk. 228 & #258	.65	.20

Vineyard Regions A444

Designs: No. 1262, Hunter Valley New South Wales. No. 1263, North Eastern Victoria. No. 1264, Barossa Valley South Australia. No. 1265, Coonawarra South Australia. No. 1266, Margaret River Western Australia.

1992, Apr. 9

1262	A444	45c multicolored	.65	.20
1263	A444	45c multicolored	.65	.20
1264	A444	45c multicolored	.65	.20
1265	A444	45c multicolored	.65	.20
1266	A444	45c multicolored	.65	.20
		Nos. 1262-1266 (5)	3.25	1.00

Land Care — A445

a, Salt action. b, Farm planning. c, Erosion control. d, Tree planting. e, Dune care.

1992, June 11   Litho.   Perf. 14½x14

1267		Strip of 5	2.75	2.25
a.-e.	A445	45c Any single	.55	.20

1992 Summer Olympics and Paralympics, Barcelona A446

1992, July 2   Perf. 14½

1268	A446	45c Cycling	.50	.20
1269	A446	$1.20 Weight lifting	1.40	.60
1270	A446	$1.20 High jump	1.40	.60
		Nos. 1268-1270 (3)	3.30	1.40

Threatened Species Type of 1992

1992-98   Litho.   Perf. 14x14½

1271	A438	30c Saltwater crocodile	.40	.20
1272	A438	35c Echidna	.50	.20
1273	A438	40c Platypus	.55	.20
1274	A438	45c Kangaroo	.65	.20
1275	A438	45c Adult kangaroo with joey	.65	.20
1276	A438	45c Two adult kangaroos	.65	.20
a.		Sheet of 3, #1274-1276	2.10	1.00
1277	A438	45c Four koalas	.65	.20
1278	A438	45c Koala walking	.65	.20
1279	A438	45c Koala in tree	.65	.20
a.		Block of 6, #1274-1279	4.00	1.40
b.		Souv. sheet, #1274-1279	4.00	4.00
1280	A438	50c Koala	.70	.25
1281	A438	60c Common brushtail possum	.85	.30
1282	A438	70c Kookaburra	.95	.35
a.		"Australia 70c" in brn ('96)	.95	.35
1283	A438	85c Pelican	1.25	.40
1284	A438	90c Eastern gray kangaroo	1.25	.40
1285	A438	95c Common wombat	1.40	.45
1286	A438	$1.20 Pink cockatoo	1.60	.55
a.		"Australia $1.20" in brown ('98)	1.65	.55
1287	A438	$1.35 Emu	2.00	.65
		Nos. 1271-1287 (17)	15.35	5.15

PHILAKOREA '94 (#1279b).

On No. 1279a Australia and denomination are orange, "KANGAROO" is 9mm long, and date is 1½mm long. Date is 1mm long and "KANGAROO" 8mm long on Nos. 1279d and 1279f.

"Australia" and denominations on Nos. 1282, 1286 are in orange.

No. 1276a inscribed in sheet margin with "CHINA '96 - 9th Asian International Exhibition" in Chinese and English and exhibition emblems.

No. 1282a comes from 3 Koala or 1 Kangaroo and 1 Koala printing. No. 1286a comes from 1 Kangaroo printing.

Issued: 35c, 50c, 60c, 95c, 8/13; 40c, 70c, 90c, $1.20, 8/12/93; 30c, 85c, $1.35, 3/10/94; 45c, 5/12/94; #1279b, 8/94; #1282a, 3/96; #1276a, 5/18/96; #1286a, 12/98.

1996   Litho.   Perf. 14x14½

1274a	A438	45c brown panel	.60	.20
b.		Bright orange panel	.60	.20
1275a	A438	45c brown panel	.60	.20
b.		Bright orange panel	.60	.20
1276b	A438	45c brown panel	.60	.20
c.		Bright orange panel	.60	.20
1277a	A438	45c brown panel	.60	.20
b.		Bright orange panel	.60	.20
1278a	A438	45c brown panel	.60	.20
b.		Bright orange panel	.60	.20
1279c	A438	45c brown panel	.60	.20
d.		Block, #1274a-1275a, 1276b, 1277a-1278a, 1279c	4.00	1.40
e.		Bright orange panel	.60	1.40
f.		Block, #1274b-1275b, 1276c, 1277b-1278b, 1279e	4.00	1.40

On No. 1279a Australia and denomination are orange, "KANGAROO" is 9mm long, and date is 1½mm long. Date is 1mm long and "KANGAROO" 8mm long on Nos. 1279d and 1279f. No. 1279d comes from 2 Koala printing. No. 1279f comes from 3 Koala printing.

Die Cut Perf. 11

1994, May 12   **Litho.**
Self-Adhesive

1288	A438	45c like #1274	.65	.20
1289	A438	45c like #1275	.65	.20
1290	A438	45c like #1276	.65	.20
1291	A438	45c like #1277	.65	.20
1292	A438	45c like #1278	.65	.20
1293	A438	45c like #1279	.65	.20
a.		Bkl. pane, #1290, 1293, 2 each #1288-1289, 1291-1292	6.50	
b.		Strip of 6, #1288-1293	4.00	

Opening of Sydney Harbor Tunnel, August 29 — A447

Sydney Harbor Bridge and Tunnel: a, Left side. b, Right side.

1992, Aug. 28   Litho.   Perf. 14½

1296	A447	45c Pair, #a.-b.	1.25	.45
c.		Pair, #d.-e., perf 15½	1.25	.45

Buildings in Western Australia Goldfield Towns A448

#1297, Warden's Courthouse, Coolgardie. #1298, Post Office, Kalgoorlie. $1.05, York Hotel, Kalgoorlie. $1.20, Town Hall, Kalgoorlie.

1992, Sept. 17   Litho.   Perf. 14x14½

1297	A448	45c multicolored	.50	.20
1298	A448	45c multicolored	.50	.20
1299	A448	$1.05 multicolored	1.10	.50
1300	A448	$1.20 multicolored	1.25	.60
		Nos. 1297-1300 (4)	3.35	1.50

Sheffield Shield Cricket Competition, Cent. — A449

Cricket match, 1890s: 45c, Bowler. $1.20, Batsman, wicket keeper.

1992, Oct. 15   Litho.   Perf. 14½

1301	A449	45c multicolored	.60	.20
1302	A449	$1.20 multicolored	1.60	.55

Christmas A450

Designs: 40c, Children dressed as Mary and Joseph with baby carriage. 45c, Boy jumping from bed Christmas morning. $1, Boy and girl singing Christmas carol.

1992, Oct. 30   Litho.   Perf. 14x14½

1303	A450	40c multicolored	.45	.45
a.		Booklet pane of 20	9.00	
1304	A450	45c multicolored	.60	.20
1305	A450	$1 multicolored	1.25	.45
		Nos. 1303-1305 (3)	2.30	1.10

Watercolor Paintings by Albert Namatjira A451

Designs: No. 1306a, Ghost Gum, Central Australia. b, Across the Plain to Mount Giles.

1993, Jan. 14   Litho.   Perf. 14x15

1306	A451	45c Pair, #a.-b.	1.25	.40

Australia Day.

Dreamings A452

Aboriginal paintings: 45c, Wild Onion Dreaming, by Pauline Nakamarra Woods. 75c, Yam Plants, by Jack Wunuwun, vert. 85c, Goose Egg Hunt, by George Milpurrurru, vert. $1, Kalumpiwarra-Ngulalintji, by Rover Thomas.

1993, Feb. 4   Perf. 14x14½, 14½x14   Litho.

1307	A452	45c red & multi	.55	.20
1308	A452	75c org yel & multi	.80	.30
1309	A452	85c buff & multi	.90	.35
1310	A452	$1 salmon & multi	1.00	.45
		Nos. 1307-1310 (4)	3.25	1.30

World Heritage Sites in Australia — A453

1993, Mar. 4   Litho.   Perf. 14½x14

1311	A453	45c Uluru (Ayers Rock)	.55	.20
1312	A453	85c Fraser Island	.90	.40
1313	A453	95c Shark Bay	1.00	.40
1314	A453	$2 Kakadu	2.00	.85
		Nos. 1311-1314 (4)	4.45	1.85

See Nos. 1485-1488.

World War II Ships A454

45c, Cruiser HMAS Sydney II. 85c, Corvette HMAS Bathurst. $1.05, Destroyer HMAS Arunta. $1.20, Hospital Ship Centaur.

1993, Apr. 7   Litho.   Perf. 14x14½

1315	A454	45c multicolored	.60	.20
1316	A454	85c multicolored	.90	.35
1317	A454	$1.05 multicolored	1.10	.60
1318	A454	$1.20 multicolored	1.40	.65
		Nos. 1315-1318 (4)	4.00	1.80

A455   A456

1993, Apr. 7   Perf. 14½x14

1319	A455	45c multicolored	.55	.20

Queen Elizabeth II, 67th birthday.

1993, May 7   Litho.   Perf. 14½x14

Designs based on 19th cent. trade union banners: #1320, Baker, shoe maker. #1321, Stevedore, seamstresses. $1, Blacksmith, telephone operator, cook. $1.20, Carpenters.

1320	A456	45c multicolored	.50	.20
1321	A456	45c multicolored	.50	.20
1322	A456	$1 multicolored	1.00	.55
1323	A456	$1.20 multicolored	1.25	.65
		Nos. 1320-1323 (4)	3.25	1.60

Working life in the 1890s.

Trains A457

#1324, Centenary Special, Tasmania. #1325, Spirit of Progress. #1326, Western Endeavour. #1327, Silver City Comet. #1328, Kuranda Tourist Train. #1329, The Ghan.

1324 A457 45c multicolored   .60   .40
1325 A457 45c multicolored   .60   .40
1326 A457 45c multicolored   .60   .40
1327 A457 45c multicolored   .60   .40
1328 A457 45c multicolored   .60   .40
1329 A457 45c multicolored   .60   .40
  a. Block of 6, #1324-1329   3.75 3.75

Die Cut Perf. 12x11½
Self-Adhesive
1330 A457 45c like No. 1324   .60   .20
1331 A457 45c like No. 1325   .60   .20
1332 A457 45c like No. 1326   .60   .20
1333 A457 45c like No. 1327   .60   .20
1334 A457 45c like No. 1328   .60   .20
1335 A457 45c like No. 1329   .60   .20
  a. Strip of 6, #1330-1335   3.75
  b. Bklt. pane, #1332, 1335, 2 ea
    #1330-1331, 1333-1334   6.00

Aboriginal Art — A458

Aboriginal paintings: 45c, Black Cockatoo Feather, by Fiona Foley, vert. 75c, Ngarrgooroon Country, by Hector Jandany. $1, Ngak Ngak, by Ginger Riley. $1.05, Untitled work, by Robert Cole, vert.

Perf. 14½x14, 14x14½
1993, July 1   **Litho.**
1336 A458 45c henna brown & multi   .60   .20
1337 A458 75c brown & multi   1.00   .30
1338 A458 $1 gray & multi   1.25   .55
1339 A458 $1.05 olive & multi   1.40   .60
  Nos. 1336-1339 (4)   4.25 1.65

Dame Enid Lyons, MP, and Sen. Dorothy Tangney A459

No. 1340, Stylized globe, natl. arms, Inter-Parliamentary Conf. emblem.

1993, Sept. 2   **Litho.**   *Perf. 14½*
1340 A459 45c multicolored   .60   .20
1341 A459 45c multicolored   .60   .20
  a. Pair, #1340-1341   1.25   .40

90th Inter-Parliamentary Union Conference (#1340). First women in Australian Federal Parliament, 50th anniv. (#1341). Nos. 1340-1341 printed in panes of 25 with 16 #1340 and 9 #1341. Panes with 16 #1341 and 9 #1340 were issued Nov. 19, but were available only through Philatelic Agency.

A460   A461

Dinosaurs: #1342, 1348, Ornithocheirus. #1343, 1349, Leaellynasaura. #1344, Allosaurus. #1345, Timimus. #1346, Muttaburrasaurus. #1347, Minmi.

1993, Oct. 1   *Perf. 14x14½, 14½x14*
1342 A460 45c multi, horiz.   .60   .20
1343 A460 45c multi   .60   .20
1344 A461 45c multi   .60   .20
1345 A461 45c multi   .60   .20
Size: 29x50mm
1346 A461 75c multi   .95   .35
1347 A461 $1.05 multi horiz.   1.40   .60
  a. Souvenir sheet of 6, #1342-1347   4.75 4.75
  b. As "a," overprinted   5.50 5.50
  c. As "a," overprinted   5.50 5.50
  Nos. 1342-1347 (6)   4.75 1.75

Self-Adhesive
Die Cut Perf. 11½
1348 A460 45c multi horiz.   .60   .20
1349 A460 45c multi   .60   .20
  a. Bklt. pane, 5 each #1348-1349   6.00

Overprint in gold on sheet margin of No. 1347b contains "BANGKOK 1993" show emblem and "WORLD PHILATELIC / EXHIBITION / BANGKOK 1-10 OCTOBER 1993."
Overprint in gold on sheet margin of No. 1347c contains dinosaur and "Sydney / STAMP & COIN / SHOW / 15-17 October 1993."

Christmas — A462

1993, Nov. 1   **Litho.**   *Perf. 14½x14*
1354 A462 40c Goodwill   .50   .20
  a. Booklet pane of 20   10.50
1355 A462 45c Joy   .60   .20
1356 A462 $1 Peace   1.25   .45
  Nos. 1354-1356 (3)   2.35   .85

Australia Day — A463

Landscape paintings: 45c, Shoalhaven River Bank-Dawn, by Arthur Boyd. 85c, Wimmera (from Mt. Arapiles), by Sir Sidney Nolan. $1.05, Lagoon, Wimmera, by Nolan. $2, White Cockatoos in Paddock with Flame Trees, by Boyd, vert.

Perf. 14½x14, 14x14½
1994, Jan. 13   **Litho.**
1357 A463 45c multicolored   .65   .20
1358 A463 85c multicolored   1.25   .40
1359 A463 $1.05 multicolored   1.50   .50
1360 A463 $2 multicolored   3.00 1.00
  Nos. 1357-1360 (4)   6.40 2.10

See #1418-1421, 1476-1479, 1572-1574.

Royal Life Saving Society, Cent. A464

1994, Jan. 20   **Litho.**   *Perf. 14x14½*
1361 A464 45c Vigilance   .55   .20
1362 A464 45c Education   .55   .20
1363 A464 95c Drill   1.10   .45
1364 A464 $1.20 Fitness   1.40   .55
  Nos. 1361-1364 (4)   3.60 1.40

Die Cut Perf. 11½
Self-Adhesive
1365 A464 45c like #1361   .65   .20
1366 A464 45c like #1362   .65   .20
  a. Pair, #1365-1366   1.40
  b. Booklet pane, 5 #1366a   7.00

Thinking of You — A465

1994, Feb. 3   **Litho.**   *Perf. 14½x14*
1367 A465 45c Rose   .50   .20
1368 A465 45c Tulips   .50   .20
1369 A465 45c Poppies   .50   .20
  a. Pair, #1368-1369   1.00   .40
  b. Booklet pane, 5 #1369a   5.00
  Nos. 1367-1369 (3)   1.50   .60

A466   A467

1994, Apr. 8   **Litho.**   *Perf. 14½*
1370 A466 45c multicolored   .50   .20
Queen Elizabeth II, 68th birthday.

1994, Apr. 8   *Perf. 14½x14*
1371 A467 95c multicolored   1.00   .45
Opening of Friendship Bridge, Thailand-Laos.

Intl. Year of the Family A468

Children's paintings of their families: 45c, Bobbie Lea Blackmore. 75c, Kathryn Teoh. $1, Maree McCarthy.

1994, Apr. 14   **Litho.**   *Perf. 14x14½*
1372 A468 45c multicolored   .55   .20
1373 A468 75c multicolored   .90   .30
1374 A468 $1 multicolored   1.25   .50
  Nos. 1372-1374 (3)   2.70 1.00

Australian Women's Right to Vote, Cent. A469

1994, June 9   **Litho.**   *Perf. 14x14½*
1375 A469 45c multicolored   .50   .20

Bunyips Folklore Creatures A470

Types of Bunyips: No. 1376, Aboriginal legend. No. 1377, Nature Spirit. 90c, Berkeley's Creek. $1.35, Natural history.

1994, July 14   **Litho.**   *Perf. 14x14½*
1376 A470 45c multicolored   .55   .20
1377 A470 45c multicolored   .55   .20
  a. Pair, #1376-1377   1.00   .40
1378 A470 90c multicolored   1.00   .40
1379 A470 $1.35 multicolored   1.60   .65
  Nos. 1376-1379 (4)   3.70 1.45

World War II Prime Ministers A471

Designs: a, Robert Menzies. b, Arthur Fadden. c, John Curtin. d, Francis (Frank) Forde. e, Joseph Benedict (Ben) Chifley.

1994, Aug. 11
1380   Strip of 5   2.75 1.10
  a.-e. A471 45c any single   .55   .20

Aviation Pioneers — A472

Designs: No. 1381, Lawrence Hargrave, box kites. No. 1382, Ross and Keith Smith, Vickers Vimy. $1.35, Ivor McIntyre, Stanley Globe, Fairey IIID A10-3 seaplane. $1.80, Freda Thompson, DeHavilland Moth Major.

1994, Aug. 29   **Engr.**   *Perf. 12*
1381 A472 45c multicolored   .55   .20
1382 A472 45c multicolored   .55   .20
1383 A472 $1.35 multicolored   1.60   .65
1384 A472 $1.80 multicolored   2.00   .85
  Nos. 1381-1384 (4)   4.70 1.90

First England-Australia flight within 30-day time span (#1382). First aerial circumnavigation of Australia (#1383). First woman to fly solo from England-Australia (#1384).

A473   Australian Zoo Animals — A474

Perf. 14x14½, 14½x14
1994, Sept. 28   **Litho.**
1385 A473 45c Scarlet macaw   .65   .40
1386 A473 45c Cheetah, vert.   .65   .40
1387 A474 45c Fijian crested iguana   .65   .40
1388 A474 45c Orangutan   .65   .40
Size: 50x30mm
Perf. 14½x14
1389 A473 $1 Asian elephant   1.50 1.50
  a. Souv. sheet of 5, #1385-1389, perf. 14½   4.25 4.25
  b. As "a," ovptd.   6.00 6.00
  c. As "a," ovptd.   6.00 6.00
  d. As "a," ovptd.   6.00 6.00
  e. As "a," ovptd.   6.00 6.00
  Nos. 1385-1389 (5)   4.10 3.10

Self-Adhesive
Die Cut Perf. 11½
1390 A473 45c like #1385   1.00   .25
1391 A473 45c like #1386   1.00   .25
  a. Bklt. pane, 6 #1390, 4 #1391   10.00

Overprint in gold on sheet margin:
No. 1389b, show emblem and "Brisbane Stamp Show Zoos / October 21-23, 1994."
No. 1389c, show emblem and "SYDNEY / STAMP / AND / COIN / SHOW / 30/9/94 TO 2/10/94."
No. 1389d, show emblem and "Stampshow '94 Melbourne October 27-30 / National/State Centennial Exhibition 1894-1994."
No. 1389e, show emblem and "STAMP SHOW 94 / Fremantle Convention Centre / 5-6 November 1994."

Christmas A475

Details from Adoration of the Magi, by Giovanni Toscani: 40c, Madonna and Child, vert. 45c, One of Magi, horse and groom. $1, Joseph receiving frankincense from Magi. $1.80, Entire painting.

1994, Oct. 31   **Litho.**   *Perf. 14½x14*
1392 A475 40c multicolored   .60   .20
  a. Booklet pane of 20   12.00
  Complete booklet, #1392a   12.00
Perf. 14x14½
1393 A475 45c multicolored   .70   .25
1394 A475 $1 multicolored   1.60   .40
Size: 50x30mm
1395 A475 $1.80 multicolored   2.75   .80
  Nos. 1392-1395 (4)   5.65 1.65

50th Sydney-Hobart Yacht Race — A476

Designs: a, Yachts bow-on, Sydney Opera House, Harbor Bridge. b, Two yachts abeam.

1994, Oct. 31   **Perf. 14½**
1396		Pair	1.40	.50
a.-b.	A476	45c any single	.70	.25

Self-Adhesive
Die Cut Perf. 11½
1397	A476	45c like #1396a	1.10	.25
1397A	A476	45c like #1396b	1.10	.25

A477

Die Cut Perf. 17
1994, Nov. 2   **Litho.**
Self-Adhesive
Booklet Stamps
Background Color
1398	A477	45c bluish green	.70	.70
1399	A477	45c blue	.70	.70
1400	A477	45c purple	.70	.70
1401	A477	45c yellow green	.70	.70
1402	A477	45c pale yel green	.70	.70
1403	A477	45c pale red brown	.70	.70
1404	A477	45c rose	.70	.70
1405	A477	45c orange yellow	.70	.70
a.		Booklet pane of 20	14.00	
		Nos. 1398-1405 (8)	5.60	5.60

No. 1405a contains 3 each #1399, 1401, 1403, 1405 and 2 each #1398, 1400, 1402, 1404. No. 1405a was sold in ATM machines, at the Natl. Philatelic Center, and Australian Philatelic Bureau.

Two printings differ slightly in shade and advertisement on back of pane.

Australia Day Type of 1994

Paintings: No. 1418, Back Verandah, by Russell Drysdale. No. 1419, Skull Springs Country, by Guy Grey-Smith. $1.05, Outcamp, by Robert Juniper. $1.20, Kite Flying, by Ian Fairweather.

1995, Jan. 12   **Litho.**   **Perf. 15x14½**
1418	A463	45c multicolored	.70	.25
1419	A463	45c multicolored	.70	.25
1420	A463	$1.05 multicolored	1.60	.40
1421	A463	$1.20 multicolored	1.75	.45
		Nos. 1418-1421 (4)	4.75	1.35

St. Valentine's Day — A478

Various designs: a, Red heart. b, Red & gold heart. c, Gold heart.

1995, Feb. 6   **Litho.**   **Perf. 14½x14**
1422		Strip of 3	2.10	.75
a.-c.	A478	45c any single	.70	.25

See No. 1480.

Endeavour A479

#1423: a, Captain Cook's Endeavour. b, Replica.

1995, Feb. 9   **Litho.**   **Perf. 14x14½**
1423		Pair	1.40	.50
a.-b.	A479	45c any single	.70	.25

Booklet Stamps
Size: 44x26mm
Perf. 14 Horiz.
1424	A479	20c like #1423a	1.00	1.00
1425	A479	45c like #1423b	.70	.25
a.		Bklt. pane, #1424, 4 #1425	3.25	
		Complete booklet, #1425a	3.25	

Natl. Trust, 50th Anniv. A480

Designs: No. 1426a, Coalport plate, Regency style bracket clock. No. 1426b, 15th-16th cent. x-frame Italian style chair, 19th cent. Steiner doll. $1, Advance Australia teapot, neo-classical parian-ware statuette. $2, China urn, silver bowl.

1995, Mar. 16   **Engr.**   **Perf. 14x14½**
1426		Pair	1.40	.50
a.-b.	A480	45c any single	.70	.25
1427	A480	$1 red brn & bl	1.50	.50
1428	A480	$2 blue & green	3.00	1.00
		Nos. 1426-1428 (3)	5.90	2.00

Opals — A481

1995, Apr. 5   **Litho.**   **Perf. 14½x14**
1429	A481	$1.20 Light opal	1.75	.90
1430	A481	$2.50 Black opal	3.75	1.90

Nos. 1429-1430 each contain a holographic image. Soaking in water may affect the hologram.
See Nos. 1554-1555.

A482   A483

1995, Apr. 20   **Litho.**   **Perf. 14½**
1431	A482	45c multicolored	.65	.20

Queen Elizabeth II, 69th birthday.

1995, Apr. 20   **Litho.**   **Perf. 14½x14**

Famous Australians from World War II.
1432	A483	45c Sir Edward Dunlop	.65	.40
1433	A483	45c Mrs. Jessie Vasey	.65	.40
1434	A483	45c Tom Derrick	.65	.40
1435	A483	45c Rawdon Hume Middleton	.65	.40
a.		Block of 4, #1432-1435	2.60	1.00

Self-Adhesive
Die Cut Perf. 11½
1436	A483	45c like #1432	.65	.20
1437	A483	45c like #1433	.65	.20
1438	A483	45c like #1434	.65	.20
1439	A483	45c like #1435	.65	.20
a.		Booklet pane, 4 #1436, 2 each #1437-1439	6.50	
b.		Strip of 4, #1436-1439	3.00	
		Nos. 1432-1439 (8)	5.20	2.40

See Nos. 1452-1455.

UN, 50th Anniv. A484

1995, May 11   **Litho.**   **Perf. 14x14½**
1440	A484	45c + label, multi	.65	.20
a.		Block of 4 + 4 labels	2.75	.90

No. 1440 was issued se-tenant with label in blocks of 4 + 4 labels in four designs. In alternating rows, labels appear on left or right side of stamp.

A485   A486

Poster, scene from: No. 1441, The Story of the Kelly Gang, 1906. No. 1442, On Our Selection, 1932. No. 1443, Jedda, 1955. No. 1444, Picnic at Hanging Rock, 1970s. No. 1445, Strictly Ballroom, 1992.

1995, June 8   **Litho.**   **Perf. 14½x14**
1441	A485	45c multicolored	.65	.40
1442	A485	45c multicolored	.65	.40
1443	A485	45c multicolored	.65	.40
1444	A485	45c multicolored	.65	.40
1445	A485	45c multicolored	.65	.40
a.		Strip of 5, #1441-1445	3.25	1.25

Self-Adhesive
Die Cut Perf. 11½
1446	A485	45c like #1441	.65	.20
1447	A485	45c like #1442	.65	.20
1448	A485	45c like #1443	.65	.20
1449	A485	45c like #1444	.65	.20
1450	A485	45c like #1445	.65	.20
a.		Strip of 5, #1446-1450	3.50	
b.		Bklt. pane, 2 ea #1446-1450	6.50	

Motion Pictures, cent.
By its nature No. 1450b constitutes a complete booklet. The peelable backing serves as a booklet cover.

1995, July 13   **Litho.**   **Perf. 14½x14**

People with Disabilities: No. 1451a, Person flying kite from wheelchair. b, Blind person playing violin, guide dog.
1451		Pair	1.25	.95
a.-b.	A486	45c any single	.60	.20

Famous Australians from World War II Type of 1995

1995, Aug. 10   **Litho.**   **Perf. 14x14½**
1452	A483	45c Leon Goldsworthy	.65	.25
1453	A483	45c Len Waters	.65	.25
1454	A483	45c Ellen Savage	.65	.25
1455	A483	45c Percy Collins	.65	.25
a.		Block of 4, #1452-1455	2.60	2.25

Peace Types of 1946
Perf. 14x14½, 14½x14
1995, Aug. 10   **Engr.**
1456	A43	45c red brown	.65	.20
1457	A45	45c dark green	.65	.20
1458	A44	$1.50 dark blue	2.25	2.00
		Nos. 1456-1458 (3)	3.55	2.40

End of World War II, 50th anniv.

Wildlife A487

Designs: a, Koalas. b, Pandas.

1995, Sept. 1   **Litho.**   **Perf. 14**
1459		Pair	1.25	.95
a.-b.	A487	45c any single	.60	.20
c.		Souv. sheet #1459a, perf. 11x11½	.60	.20
d.		Souv. sheet #1459b, perf. 11x11½	.60	.60
e.		#1459c Ovptd. in sheet margin	1.00	1.00
f.		#1459d Ovptd. in sheet margin	1.00	1.00

Overprints read: No. 1459e: "AUSTRALIAN STAMP EXHIBITION." No. 1459f: "INTERNATIONAL STAMP & COIN EXPO. / BEIJING '95."
Issued: No. 1459f, 9/14/95.
See People's Republic of China Nos. 2597-2598.

Australian Medical Discoveries A488

Designs: No. 1461a, Joseph Slattery, Thomas Lyle, Walter Filmer, x-ray pioneers. No. 1461b, Jean Macnamara, Macfarlane Burnet, viruses and immunology. No. 1461C, Fred Hollows, eye care, vert. $2.50, Howard Florey, co-discoverer of penicillin, vert.

1995, Sept. 7   **Perf. 14x14½, 14½x14**
1461		Pair	1.25	.95
a.-b.	A488	45c any single	.60	.20
1461C	A488	45c multicolored	.60	.20
1461D	A488	$2.50 multicolored	3.75	3.75
		Nos. 1461-1461D (3)	5.60	4.90

No. 1461D exists in sheetlets of 10.

The World Down Under A489

Designs: Nos. 1462a, 1465a, Flatback turtle. Nos. 1462b, 1465b, Flame angelfish, nudibranch. Nos. 1463a, 1465c, Potato cod, giant maori wrasse. Nos. 1463b, 1465d, Giant trevally. Nos. 1464a, 1465e, Black marlin. Nos. 1464b, 1465f, Mako & tiger sharks.

1995, Oct. 3   **Litho.**   **Perf. 14x14½**
1462		Pair	1.25	.80
a.-b.	A489	45c any single	.60	.80
1463		Pair	1.25	.80
a.-b.	A489	45c any single	.60	.80
1464		Pair	1.25	.80
a.-b.	A489	45c any single	.60	.80
		Nos. 1462-1464 (3)	3.75	2.40

Miniature Sheet of 6
1465	A489	45c #a.-f.	4.00	3.75
g.		Ovptd. in sheet margin	4.50	
h.		Ovptd. in sheet margin	4.50	
i.		Ovptd. in sheet margin	4.50	
j.		Ovptd. in sheet margin	4.50	
k.		Ovptd. in sheet margin	4.50	

Nos. 1462-1464 have pale blue border on three sides. No. 1465 is a continuous design and does not have the pale border. Fish on No. 1465 are printed with additional phosphor ink producing a glow-in-the-dark effect under ultraviolet light.

Overprints in gold in sheet margin of No. 1465 include show emblems and text:
No. 1465g: "ADELAIDE / STAMP AND / COLLECTIBLES / FAIR / 14/10/95 - 15/10/95."
No. 1465h: "SYDNEY / CENTREPOINT 95 / STAMPSHOW."
No. 1465i: "Brisbane Stamp Show / 20-22 October 1995."
No. 1465j: "Melbourne Stamp & Coin Fair / 27-29 October 1995."
No. 1465k: "Swanpex WA / 28-29 October 1995."

Booklet Stamps
Self-Adhesive
Die Cut Perf. 11½
1466	A489	45c like #1462a	.65	.20
1467	A489	45c like #1462b	.65	.20
1468	A489	45c like #1463a	.65	.20
1469	A489	45c like #1463b	.65	.20
1470	A489	45c like #1464a	.65	.20
1471	A489	45c like #1464b	.65	.20
a.		Booklet pane, #1470-1471, 2 each #1466-1469	6.50	
b.		Strip of 6, #1466-1471	4.50	

By its nature, No. 1471a constitutes a complete booklet. The peelable backing serves as a booklet cover.

Christmas — A490

Stained glass windows, Our Lady Help of Christians Church, Melbourne: 40c, Madonna and Child. 45c, Angel carrying banner. $1, Three rejoicing angels.

1995, Nov. 1   **Litho.**   *Perf. 14½x14*
1472	A490	40c multicolored	.60	.30
1473	A490	45c multicolored	.65	.30
1474	A490	$1 multicolored	1.50	.75
		Nos. 1472-1474 (3)	2.75	1.35

Booklet Stamp
Self-Adhesive
Die Cut Perf. 11½

1475	A490	40c multicolored	.60	.30
a.		Booklet pane of 20	12.00	

Madonna and Child on No. 1475 are printed with additional phosphor ink giving parts of the stamp a rough texture.

By its nature, No. 1475a constitutes a complete booklet. The peelable backing serves as a booklet cover, which also contains 20 labels. The complete booklet is available with backing showing two different advertisements.

Australia Day Type of 1994

Paintings by Australian women: 45c, West Australian Banksia, by Margaret Preston, vert. 85c, The Babe is Wise, by Lina Bryans, vert. $1, The Bridge in Curve, by Grace Cossington Smith. $1.20, Beach Umbrellas, by Vida Lahey.

Perf. 14x14½, 14½x14

1996, Jan. 16   **Litho.**
1476	A463	45c multicolored	.65	.20
1477	A463	85c multicolored	1.25	.40
1478	A463	$1 multicolored	1.50	.50
1479	A463	$1.20 multicolored	1.75	.60
		Nos. 1476-1479 (4)	5.15	1.70

Heart and Roses
A491

1996, Jan. 30   *Perf. 14x14½*
1480	A491	45c gold & multi	.65	.20

See No. 1422.

Military Aviation
A492

#1481, Firefly, Sea Fury. #1482, Beaufighter, Kittyhawk. #1483, Hornet. #1484, Kiowa.

1996, Feb. 26   **Litho.**   *Perf. 14x14½*
1481	A492	45c multicolored	.70	.20
1482	A492	45c multicolored	.70	.20
1483	A492	45c multicolored	.70	.20
1484	A492	45c multicolored	.70	.20
a.		Block of 4, #1481-1484	2.80	2.50

Australian World Heritage Sites Type of 1993

Designs: 45c, Tasmanian Wilderness. 75c, Willandra Lakes. 95c, Fossil Cave, Naracoorte. $1, Lord Howe Island.

1996, Mar. 14   **Litho.**   *Perf. 14½x14*
1485	A453	45c multicolored	.70	.20
1486	A453	75c multicolored	1.25	.40
1487	A453	95c multicolored	1.40	.45
1488	A453	$1 multicolored	1.50	.50
		Nos. 1485-1488 (4)	4.85	1.55

Indonesian Bear Cuscus — A493

No. 1489, Australian Spotted Cuscus.

1996, Mar. 22
1489	A493	45c multicolored	.70	.20
1490	A493	45c multicolored	.70	.20
a.		Pair, Nos. 1489-1490	1.40	.95
b.		Souvenir sheet, No. 1490a	1.40	1.40

No. 1490a has continuous design.
No. 1490b exists overprinted "WORLD PHILATELIC YOUTH EXHIBITION /

PAMERAN FILATELI REMAJA DUNIA / INDONESIA '96." These were sold at the show, but apparently were never sold by the philatelic agency.

See Indonesia Nos. 1640-1642.

Queen Elizabeth II, 70th Birthday
A494

Litho. & Engr.
1996, Apr. 11   *Perf. 14x14½*
1491	A494	45c multicolored	.70	.20

North Melbourne Kangaroos
A495

Brisbane Bears
A496

Sydney Swans — A497

Carlton Blues — A498

Adelaide Crows — A499

Fitzroy Lions — A500

Richmond Tigers — A501

St. Kilda Saints — A502

Melbourne Demons — A503

Collingwood Magpies — A504

Fremantle Dockers — A505

Footscray Bulldogs — A506

West Coast Eagles A507

Essendon Bombers A508

Geelong Cats — A509

Hawthorn Hawks — A510

1996, Apr. 23   **Litho.**   *Perf. 14½x14*
1492	A495	45c multicolored	.70	.70
1493	A496	45c multicolored	.70	.70
1494	A497	45c multicolored	.70	.70
1495	A498	45c multicolored	.70	.70
1496	A499	45c multicolored	.70	.70
1497	A500	45c multicolored	.70	.70
1498	A501	45c multicolored	.70	.70
1499	A502	45c multicolored	.70	.70
1500	A503	45c multicolored	.70	.70
1501	A504	45c multicolored	.70	.70
1502	A505	45c multicolored	.70	.70
1503	A506	45c multicolored	.70	.70
1504	A507	45c multicolored	.70	.70
1505	A508	45c multicolored	.70	.70
1506	A509	45c multicolored	.70	.70
1507	A510	45c multicolored	.70	.70
a.		Min. sheet of 16, #1492-1507	11.25	

Booklet Stamps
Self-Adhesive
Serpentine Die Cut 11½

1508	A495	45c multicolored	.70	.20
a.		Booklet pane of 10	7.00	
1509	A496	45c multicolored	.70	.20
a.		Booklet pane of 10	7.00	
1510	A497	45c multicolored	.70	.20
a.		Booklet pane of 10	7.00	
1511	A498	45c multicolored	.70	.20
a.		Booklet pane of 10	7.00	
1512	A499	45c multicolored	.70	.20
a.		Booklet pane of 10	7.00	
1513	A500	45c multicolored	.70	.20
a.		Booklet pane of 10	7.00	
1514	A501	45c multicolored	.70	.20
a.		Booklet pane of 10	7.00	
1515	A502	45c multicolored	.70	.20
a.		Booklet pane of 10	7.00	
1516	A503	45c multicolored	.70	.20
a.		Booklet pane of 10	7.00	
1517	A504	45c multicolored	.70	.20
a.		Booklet pane of 10	7.00	
1518	A505	45c multicolored	.70	.20
a.		Booklet pane of 10	7.00	
1519	A506	45c multicolored	.70	.20
a.		Booklet pane of 10	7.00	
1520	A507	45c multicolored	.70	.20
a.		Booklet pane of 10	7.00	
1521	A508	45c multicolored	.70	.20
a.		Booklet pane of 10	7.00	
1522	A509	45c multicolored	.70	.20
a.		Booklet pane of 10	7.00	
1523	A510	45c multicolored	.70	.20
a.		Booklet pane of 10	7.00	

By their nature, Nos. 1508a-1523a are complete booklets. The peelable paper backing serves as a booklet cover.

Australian Football League, cent.

Flora and Fauna — A511

Designs: 5c, Leadbeater's possum. 10c, Powerful owl. 20c, Saltwater crocodile, Kangkong flower. 25c, Northern dwarf tree frog, red lily. No. 1528, Little kingfisher. No. 1529, Jacana. No. 1530, Jabiru. No. 1531, Brolga. $1, Big greasy butterfly, water lily. $2, Blackwood wattle. $5, Mountain ash, fern. $10, Kakadu Wetlands during lightning storm, great egret, red lily.

Perf. 14x14½, 14½x14 (#1535)

1996-99   **Litho.**
1524	A511	5c multi	.20	.40
1525	A511	10c multi	.20	.40
1526	A511	20c multi	.30	.40
1527	A511	25c multi	.40	.40
1528	A511	45c multi	.70	.40
1529	A511	45c multi	.70	.40
1530	A511	45c multi	.70	.40
1531	A511	45c multi	.70	.40
a.		Block of 4, #1528-1531	3.00	3.00
b.		Souvenir sheet of 2, #1530-1531	1.20	
1532	A511	$1 multi	1.00	1.00
1533	A511	$2 multi	2.00	2.00

Size: 30x50mm
1534	A511	$5 multi, vert.	5.00	5.00

Size: 50x30mm
1535	A511	$10 multi	9.00	9.00
a.		Souvenir sheet of 1	12.00	10.00
b.		As "a," ovptd. in sheet margin	27.50	25.00
c.		As "a," ovptd in sheet margin	11.00	11.00
		Nos. 1524-1535 (12)	20.90	20.20

Self-Adhesive
Serpentine Die Cut 11½, 11¼ (#1539i)

1536	A511	45c like #1529	.70	.20
1537	A511	45c like #1528	.70	.20
1538	A511	45c like #1531	.70	.20
1539	A511	45c like #1530	.70	.20
a.		Booklet pane, 3 ea #1536, #1538, 2 ea #1537, #1539	7.00	
b.		Strip of 4, #1536-1539	2.80	
h.		Sheet of 5, #1537-1539, 2 #1536	3.50	
i.		Booklet pane, 5 each #1536-1539	14.00	

Serpentine Die Cut 12½x13
1539C	A511	45c like #1529	.70	.20
1539D	A511	45c like #1528	.70	.20
1539E	A511	45c like #1531	.70	.20
1539F	A511	45c like #1530	.70	.20
g.		Strip of 4, #1539C-1539F	2.80	

Nos. 1536-1539 are booklet stamps.

No. 1531b is inscribed in sheet margin with Shanghai '97 emblem and "International Stamp & Coin Exposition Shanghai '97" in Chinese and English.

No. 1535b is overprinted in silver in sheet margin with PACIFIC 97 emblem and "Australia Post Exhibition Sheet No. 4."

No. 1535c is overprinted in copper in sheet margin with "PHILA NIPPON '01" and show emblem. Issued: No. 1535c, 8/1/01.

By its nature No. 1539a is a complete booklet. The peelable backing serves as a booklet cover.

Issued: 5c, 10c, $2, $5, 5/9/96; 20c, 25c, $1, $10, #1538a, 4/10/97; #1528-1531, 1536-1539, 6/2/97; #1531b, 11/17/97; #1539C-1539F, 11/13/99; No. 1539i, 9/1/98.

No. 1539i is a complete booklet.

See Nos. 1734-1746E, 1984-1995.

Modern Olympic Games, Cent.
A512

#1540, Edwin Flack, 1st Australian gold medalist, runners. #1541, Fanny Durack, 1st Australian woman gold medalist, swimmers. $1.05, Paralympics, Atlanta.

Litho. & Engr.
1996, June 6   *Perf. 14x14½*
1540	A512	45c multicolored	.70	.20
1541	A512	45c multicolored	.70	.20
a.		Pair, #1540-1541	1.40	1.25
1542	A512	$1.05 multicolored	1.60	1.60
		Nos. 1540-1542 (3)	3.00	2.00

Transfer of Olympic Flag from Atlanta to Sydney
A513

1996, July 22   **Litho.**
1543	A513	45c multicolored	.70	.20

Issued in sheets of 10.

Children's Book Council, 50th Anniv. A514

Covers from "Book of the Year" books: No. 1544, "Animalia." No. 1545, "Greetings from Sandy Beach." No. 1546, "Who Sank the Boat?" No. 1547, "John Brown, Rose and the Midnight Cat."

1996, July 4   Litho.   Perf. 14x14½

1544	A514 45c multicolored	.70	.45
1545	A514 45c multicolored	.70	.45
1546	A514 45c multicolored	.70	.45
1547	A514 45c multicolored	.70	.45
a.	Block of 4, #1544-1547	2.80	2.50

Serpentine Die Cut 11½
Self-Adhesive

1548	A514 45c like #1544	.70	.20
1549	A514 45c like #1546	.70	.20
1550	A514 45c like #1547	.70	.20
1551	A514 45c like #1545	.70	.20
a.	Booklet pane, 4 #1548, 2 each #1549-1551	7.00	
b.	Strip of 4, #1548-1551	2.80	

By its nature, No. 1551a is a complete booklet. The peelable paper backing serves as a booklet cover.

National Council of Women, Cent. — A515

Designs: 45c, Margaret Windeyer (1866-1939), honorary life president. $1, Rose Scott (1847-1925), founding executive member.

1996, Aug. 8   Litho.   Perf. 14½x14

1552	A515 45c claret & yellow	.70	.20
1553	A515 $1 blue & yellow	1.50	1.50

Gems Type of 1995
1996, Sept. 5   Litho.   Perf. 14½x14

1554	A481 45c Pearl	.70	.20
1555	A481 $1.20 Diamond	1.90	1.90

No. 1555 contains a round foil design. Soaking in water may affect the design.

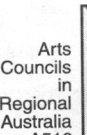

Arts Councils in Regional Australia A516

Silhouettes of performing artists, outdoor scene: 20c, Ballet dancer, violinist, field, bales, trees. 45c, Violinist, hand holding flower, dancer, tree in field.

Perf. 14 Horiz.
1996, Sept. 12   Litho.
Booklet Stamps

1556	A516 20c multicolored	1.25	1.00
1557	A516 45c multicolored	.70	.20
a.	Bklt. pane, #1556, 4 #1557	3.25	
	Complete booklet, #1557a	3.25	

A517   Pets — A518

1996-97   Perf. 14x14½, 14½x14

1558	A517 45c Cockatoo	.70	.40
1559	A517 45c Ducks, vert.	.70	.40
1560	A517 45c Dog, cat, vert.	.70	.40
a.	Pair, #1559-1560	1.40	1.40

1561	A518 45c Dog, puppy	.70	.40
1562	A518 45c Kittens	.70	.40
a.	Pair, #1561-1562	1.40	1.40

Size: 29x49mm

1563	A518 45c Pony mare, foal	.70	.40
a.	Souvenir sheet, #1558-1563	4.25	4.25
b.	As "a," ovptd.	4.25	4.25
c.	As "a," ovptd.	4.25	4.25
d.	As "a," ovptd.	4.25	4.25
e.	As "a," ovptd.	4.25	4.25
f.	As "a," ovptd.	4.25	4.25
g.	As "a," ovptd.	4.25	4.25
h.	As "a," ovptd.	4.25	4.25
	Nos. 1558-1563 (6)	4.20	2.20

Self-Adhesive
Serpentine Die Cut 11½

1564	A518 45c like #1561	.70	.20
1565	A518 45c like #1562	.70	.20
a.	Bklt. pane, 6 #1564, 4 #1565	7.00	

No. 1563a is a continuous design.
Overprints in gold on sheet margin: No. 1563b, show emblem and "10TH ASIAN INTERNATIONAL PHILATELIC EXHIBITION 1996" in Chinese and English. No. 1563c, pets emblem and, "ASDA CENTREPOINT '96 STAMP AND COIN SHOW / 5-7 October 1996." No. 1563d, pets emblem and "ST PETERS STAMP & COLLECTIBLE FAIR / 12-13 OCTOBER 1996." No. 1563e, pets emblem and "MELBOURNE '96 NATIONAL PHILATELIC EXHIBITION / 17-20 OCTOBER 1996." No. 1563f, pets emblem and "QUEENSLAND SPRING STAMP AND COIN SHOW / 25-27 OCTOBER 1996." No. 1563g, pets emblem and "SWANPEX '96 / 26-27 OCTOBER 1996." No. 1563h: Hong Kong '97 emblem and "11TH ASIAN INTERNATIONAL STAMP EXHIBITION / 12-16 FEBRUARY 1997."
By its nature, No. 1565a is a complete booklet. The peelable paper backing serves as a booklet cover.
Issued: Nos. 1558-1563, 1563a, 1564-1465, 10/1/96; Nos. 1563b-1563g, 10/3/96; No. 1563h, 2/12/97.

Baron Ferdinand von Mueller (1825-96), Botanist — A519

1996, Oct. 9   Perf. 14

1566	A519 $1.20 multicolored	1.90	1.90

See Germany No. 1949.

Christmas — A520

1996, Nov. 1   Perf. 14½x14

1567	A520 40c Madonna and Child	.65	.20
1568	A520 45c Wise man	.70	.20
1569	A520 $1 Shepherd boy, lamb	1.50	.30
	Nos. 1567-1569 (3)	2.85	.70

Self-Adhesive
Serpentine Die Cut 12

1570	A520 40c like #1567	.65	.20
a.	Booklet pane of 20	13.00	

By its nature, No. 1570a is a complete booklet. The peelable paper backing serves as a booklet cover.

Exploration of Australian Coast & Christmas Island by Willem de Vlamingh, 300th Anniv.— A521

Portrait of a Dutch Navigator, by Jan Verkolje.

1996, Nov. 1   Perf. 14x14½

1571	A521 45c multicolored	.70	.20
a.	Pair, #1571 & Christmas Is. #404	1.40	1.40

Australia Day Type of 1994

Paintings: 85c, Landscape '74, by Fred Williams. 90c, The Balcony 2, by Brett Whiteley. $1.20, Fire Haze at Gerringong, by Lloyd Rees.

1997, Jan. 16   Litho.   Perf. 14½x14

1572	A463 85c multicolored	1.25	.40
1573	A463 90c multicolored	1.40	.45
1574	A463 $1.20 multicolored	1.90	.60
	Nos. 1572-1574 (3)	4.55	1.45

Sir Donald Bradman, Cricketer A522

1997, Jan. 23   Litho.   Perf. 14½

1575	A522 45c Portrait	.70	.40
1576	A522 45c At bat	.70	.40
a.	Pair, No. 1575-1576	1.40	1.40

See #1634-1646, 1719-1722, 1800-1807, 1933-1936, 1941-1942.

Greetings — A523

1997, Jan. 29   Perf. 14½x14

1577	A523 45c Rose	.70	.20

Serpentine Die Cut 11½
Booklet Stamp
Self-Adhesive

1578	A523 45c like #1577	.70	.20
a.	Booklet pane of 10	7.00	

By its nature, No. 1578a is a complete booklet. The peelable paper backing, which also contains 12 labels, serves as a booklet cover.

Classic Cars — A524

#1579, 1934 Ford Coupe Utility. #1580, 1948 GMH Holden 48-215 (FX). #1581, 1958 Austin Lancer. #1582, 1962 Chrysler Valiant R Series.

1997, Feb. 27   Litho.   Perf. 14x14½

1579	A524 45c multicolored	.70	.40
a.	Booklet pane of 4	3.00	
1580	A524 45c multicolored	.70	.40
a.	Booklet pane of 4	3.00	
1581	A524 45c multicolored	.70	.40
a.	Booklet pane of 4	3.00	
1582	A524 45c multicolored	.70	.40
a.	Booklet pane of 4	3.00	
b.	Block of 4, #1579-1582	3.00	1.60
	Complete booklet, #1579a, 1580a, 1581a, 1582a	16.00	

Complete booklet contains 2 postal cards and 16 self-adhesive labels.

Serpentine Die Cut 12
Booklet Stamps
Self-Adhesive

1583	A524 45c like #1579	.70	.20
1584	A524 45c like #1580	.70	.20
1585	A524 45c like #1581	.70	.20
1586	A524 45c like #1582	.70	.20
a.	Bklt. pane, 2 ea #1583, 1585, 3 ea #1584, 1586	7.00	
b.	Strip of 4, #1583-1586	3.00	

By its nature, No. 1586a is a complete booklet. The peelable backing serves as a booklet cover. The backing for No. 1586b is inscribed with a 3x8mm black vertical box and "SNP CAMBEC."

Circuses in Australia, 150th Anniv. — A525

#1591, Queen of the Arena, May Wirth (1894-1978). #1592, Wizard of the Wire, Con Colleano (1899-1973). #1593, Clowns. #1594, Tumblers.

1997, Mar. 13   Litho.   Perf. 14½x14

1591	A525 45c multicolored	.70	.20
1592	A525 45c multicolored	.70	.20
1593	A525 45c multicolored	.70	.20
1594	A525 45c multicolored	.70	.20
a.	Block of 4, #1591-1594	3.00	3.00

Queen Elizabeth II, 71st Birthday, 50th Wedding Anniv. A526

1997, Apr. 17   Engr.   Perf. 14x14½

1595	A526 45c Design A50	.70	.20

A527   A528

1997, Apr. 17   Perf. 14½x14

1596	A527 45c multicolored	.70	.20

Lions Clubs of Australia, 50th anniv.

1997, May 8   Litho.   Perf. 14½x14

Dolls and Teddy Bears: No. 1597, Doll wearing red hat. No. 1598, Bear standing. No. 1599, Doll wearing white dress holding teddy bear. No. 1600, Doll in brown outfit. No. 1601, Teddy bear seated.

1597	A528 45c multicolored	.70	.20
1598	A528 45c multicolored	.70	.20
1599	A528 45c multicolored	.70	.20
1600	A528 45c multicolored	.70	.20
1601	A528 45c multicolored	.70	.20
a.	Strip of 5, #1597-1601	3.50	3.50

Emergency Services A529

#1602, Disaster victim evacuated. #1603, Police rescue hiker. $1.05, Rapid response saves home. $1.20, Ambulance dash saves life.

1997, July 10   Litho.   Perf. 14x14½

1602	A529 45c multicolored	.70	.20
1603	A529 45c multicolored	.70	.20
a.	Pair, #1602-1603	1.40	.40
1604	A529 $1.05 multicolored	1.60	1.60
1605	A529 $1.20 multicolored	1.75	1.75
	Nos. 1602-1605 (4)	4.75	3.75

Arrival of Merino Sheep in Australia, Bicent. A530

Designs: No. 1606, George Peppin, Junior (1827-76), breeder, Merino sheep. No. 1607, "Pepe" chair, uses of wool.

1997, Aug. 7　Litho.　Perf. 14x14½

1606	A530	45c multicolored	.70 .20
1607	A530	45c multicolored	.70 .20
a.		Pair, #1606-1607	1.40 1.40

Scenes from "The Dreaming," Animated Stories for Children A531

Designs: 45c, Dumbi the Owl. $1, The Two Willy-Willies. $1.20, How Brolga Became a Bird. $1.80, Tuggan-Tuggan.

1997, Aug. 21　　　　　　Perf. 14½

1608	A531	45c multicolored	.70 .20
1609	A531	$1 multicolored	1.50 .40
1610	A531	$1.20 multicolored	1.75 .45
1611	A531	$1.80 multicolored	2.75 .70
		Nos. 1608-1611 (4)	6.70 1.75

Prehistoric Animals — A532

#1612, Rhoetosaurus brownei. #1613, Mcnamaraspis kaprios. #1614, Ninjemys oweni. #1615, Paracyclotosaurus davidi. #1616, Woolungasaurus glendowerensis.

1997, Sept. 4　Litho.　Perf. 14½x14

1612	A532	45c multicolored	.65 .40
1613	A532	45c multicolored	.65 .40
1614	A532	45c multicolored	.65 .40
1615	A532	45c multicolored	.65 .40
1616	A532	45c multicolored	.65 .40
a.		Strip of 5, #1612-1616	3.25 3.25

Printed in sheets of 10 stamps.

A533　　　Nocturnal Animals — A534

Perf. 14½x14, 14x14½

1997, Oct. 1　　　　　　Litho.

1617	A533	45c Barking owl	.65 .40
1618	A533	45c Spotted-tailed quoll	.65 .40
a.		Pair, #1617-1618	1.40 1.40
1619	A534	45c Platypus	.65 .40
1620	A534	45c Brown antechinus	.65 .40
1621	A534	45c Dingo	.65 .40
a.		Strip of 3, #1619-1621	2.00 2.00

Size: 49x29mm

1622	A534	45c Yellow-bellied glider	.65 .45
a.		Souvenir sheet, #1617-1622	4.00 4.00
		Nos. 1617-1622 (6)	3.90 2.45

No. 1622a is printed with additional phosphor ink revealing a glow-in-the-dark spider and web under ultraviolet light.

Size: 21x32mm

Serpentine Die Cut Perf. 11½

Self-Adhesive

1623	A533	45c like #1617	.65 .20
1624	A533	45c like #1618	.65 .20
a.		Booklet pane, 5 each #1623-1624	6.50
b.		Pair, #1623-1624	1.40

By its nature No. 1624a is a complete booklet. The peelable paper backing serves as a booklet cover.

Breast Cancer Awareness A535

1997, Oct. 27　Litho.　Perf. 14x14½

1625	A535	45c multicolored	.65 .20

Christmas A536

Children in Christmas Nativity pageant: 40c, Angels. 45c, Mary holding Baby Jesus. $1, Three Wise Men.

1997, Nov. 3

1626	A536	40c multicolored	.60 .20
1627	A536	45c multicolored	.65 .20
1628	A536	$1 multicolored	1.40 .45
		Nos. 1626-1628 (3)	2.65 .85

Booklet Stamps

Serpentine Die Cut Perf. 11½

Self-Adhesive

1629	A536	40c multicolored	.60 .20
a.		Booklet pane of 20	12.00

By its nature No. 1629a is a complete booklet. The peelable paper backing serves as a booklet cover, which also contains 20 labels.

Maritime Heritage — A537

1998, Jan. 15　Litho.　Perf. 14½x14

1630	A537	45c Flying Cloud	.60 .20
a.		Sheet of 10	6.00 2.00
1631	A537	85c Marco Polo	1.10 .35
a.		Sheet of 2, #1631 perf. 13½ & Canada #1779, perf. 13	1.75 1.75
1632	A537	$1 Chusan	1.25 .40
1633	A537	$1.20 Heather Belle	1.60 .50
		Nos. 1630-1633 (4)	4.55 1.45

Australia '99 (#1630a). World Stamp Expo. (#1631a).
See Canada #1779a.
Issued: #1630a, 6/17/98; #1631a, 3/19/99.

Legends Type of 1997

Olympians: No. 1634: a, Betty Cuthbert. b, Cuthbert running. c, Herb Elliott. d, Elliott running. e, Dawn Fraser. f, Fraser swimming. g, Marjorie Jackson. h, Jackson running. i, Murray Rose. j, Rose swimming. k, Shirley Strickland. l, Strickland clearing hurdle.

1998, Jan. 21　　　　　　Perf. 14x14½

Size: 34x27mm

1634		Sheet of 12	7.25 7.25
a.-l.	A522	any single	.60 .40

Booklet Stamps

Self-Adhesive

Serpentine Die Cut 11½

Size: 34x25mm

1635	A522	45c like #1634a	.60 .20
1636	A522	45c like #1634b	.60 .20
1637	A522	45c like #1634c	.60 .20
1638	A522	45c like #1634d	.60 .20
1639	A522	45c like #1634e	.60 .20
1640	A522	45c like #1634f	.60 .20
1641	A522	45c like #1634g	.60 .20
1642	A522	45c like #1634h	.60 .20
1643	A522	45c like #1634i	.60 .20
1644	A522	45c like #1634j	.60 .20
1645	A522	45c like #1634k	.60 .20
1646	A522	45c like #1634l	.60 .20
a.		Bklt. pane of 12, #1635-1646	7.25

By its nature, No. 1646a is a complete booklet. The peelable backing serves as a booklet cover.

Greetings — A538

1998, Feb. 12　Litho.　Perf. 14½x14

1647	A538	45c Champagne roses	.60 .20

Booklet Stamp

Self-Adhesive

Serpentine Die Cut 11½

1648	A538	45c like #1647	.60 .20
a.		Booklet pane of 10	6.00

By its nature No. 1648a is a complete booklet. The peelable paper backing, which contains 12 labels, serves as a booklet cover.

Queen Elizabeth II, 72nd Birthday A539

1998, Apr. 9　Litho.　Perf. 14x14½

1649	A539	45c multicolored	.60 .20

Royal Australian Navy Fleet Air Arm, 50th Anniv. A540

1998, Apr. 9

1650	A540	45c multicolored	.60 .20

Farming in Australia A541

Designs: No. 1651, Sheep for producing wool. No. 1652, Sheaves of wheat. No. 1653, Herding cattle on horseback. No. 1654, Harvesting sugar cane. No. 1655, Dairy cattle, man on motorcycle.

1998, Apr. 21

1651	A541	45c multicolored	.60 .40
1652	A541	45c multicolored	.60 .40
1653	A541	45c multicolored	.60 .40
1654	A541	45c multicolored	.60 .40
1655	A541	45c multicolored	.60 .40
a.		Strip of 5, #1651-1655	3.00 3.00

Booklet Stamps

Self-Adhesive

Serpentine Die Cut 11½

Size: 37x25mm

1656	A541	45c like #1651	.60 .20
1657	A541	45c like #1652	.60 .20
1658	A541	45c like #1653	.60 .20
1659	A541	45c like #1654	.60 .20
1660	A541	45c like #1655	.60 .20
a.		Bklt. pane, 2 ea #1656-1660	6.00

The peelable backing of No. 1660a serves as a booklet cover.

Heart Health A542

1998, May 4　Litho.　Perf. 14x14½

1661	A542	45c multicolored	.60 .20

Rock and Roll in Australia A543

a, "The Wild One," by Johnny O'Keefe, 1958. b, "Oh Yeah Uh Huh," by Col Joye and the Joye Boys, 1959. c, "He's My Blonde-headed Stompie Wompie Real Gone Surfer Boy," by Little Pattie, 1963. d, "Shakin' All Over," by Normie Rowe, 1965. e, "She's So Fine," by The Easybeats, 1965. f, "The Real Thing," by Russell Morris, 1969. g, "Turn Up Your Radio," by The Masters Apprentices, 1970. h, "Eagle Rock," by Daddy Cool, 1971. i, "Most People I Know Think That I'm Crazy," by Billy Thorpe & the Aztecs, 1972. j, "Horror Movie," by Skyhooks, 1974. k, "It's a Long Way to the Top," by AC/DC, 1975. l, "Howzat," by Sherbet, 1976.

1998, May 26

1662	A543	Sheet of 12	7.25 7.50
a.-l.		45c any single	.60 .60

Coil Stamps

Self-Adhesive

Serpentine Die Cut 11½

Size: 37x25mm

1663	A543	45c like #1662a	.60 .20
1664	A543	45c like #1662b	.60 .20
1665	A543	45c like #1662d	.60 .20
1666	A543	45c like #1662d	.60 .20
1667	A543	45c like #1662e	.60 .20
1668	A543	45c like #1662f	.60 .20
1669	A543	45c like #1662g	.60 .20
1670	A543	45c like #1662h	.60 .20
1671	A543	45c like #1662i	.60 .35
1672	A543	45c like #1662j	.60 .20
1673	A543	45c like #1662k	.60 .20
1674	A543	45c like #1662l	.60 .20
a.		Strip of 12 + label	7.25

Endangered Birds — A544

World Wildlife Fund: #1675, Helmeted honeyeater. #1676, Orange-bellied parrot. #1677, Red-tailed black cockatoo. #1678, Gouldian finch.

1998, June 25　　　　　　Perf. 14x14½

1675	A544	5c multicolored	.20 .20
1676	A544	5c multicolored	.20 .20
a.		Pair, #1675-1676	.20 .20
1677	A544	45c multicolored	.60 .20
1678	A544	45c multicolored	.60 .20
a.		Pair, #1677-1678	1.25 1.25

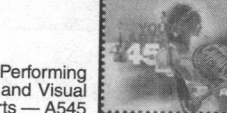

Performing and Visual Arts — A545

Young people: No. 1679, Playing French horn. No. 1680, Dancing.

1998, July 16　Litho.　Perf. 14x14½

1679	A545	45c multicolored	.60 .20
1680	A545	45c multicolored	.60 .20
a.		Pair, #1679-1680	1.25 1.25

Orchids — A546

Designs: 45c, Phalaenopsis rosenstromii. 85c, Arundina graminifolia. $1, Grammatophyllum speciosum. $1.20, Dendrobium phalaenopsis.

1998, Aug. 6　Litho.　Perf. 14½x14

1681	A546	45c multicolored	.60 .20
1682	A546	85c multicolored	1.00 .35
1683	A546	$1 multicolored	1.25 .40

1684	A546	$1.20 multicolored	1.50	.50
a.		Souvenir sheet, #1681-1684	4.50	4.50
		Nos. 1681-1684 (4)	4.35	1.45

See Singapore Nos. 858-861b.

The Teapot of Truth, by Cartoonist Michael Leunig
A547

#1685, Angel carrying teapot, bird with flower. #1686, Birds perched on heart-shaped vine. #1687, Characters using their heads to pour tea into cup. $1, Stylized family. $1.20, Stylized teapot with face & legs.

1998, Aug. 13   *Perf. 14x14½*

1685	A547	45c multicolored	.60	.20
a.		Booklet pane of 4	2.50	
1686	A547	45c multicolored	.60	.20
a.		Booklet pane of 4	2.50	
1687	A547	45c multicolored	.60	.20
a.		Booklet pane of 4	2.50	

Size: 30x25mm

1688	A547	$1 multicolored	1.25	1.25
a.		Booklet pane of 2	2.50	
1689	A547	$1.20 multicolored	1.50	1.50
a.		Booklet pane of 2	3.00	
b.		Complete booklet, #1685a, 1686a, 1687a, 1688a, 1689a, 1 postal card & 16 self-adhesive labels	14.00	
		Nos. 1685-1689 (5)	4.55	3.35

A548   A549

Butterflies,

1998, Sept. 3   *Litho.*   *Perf. 14½x14*

1690	A548	45c Red lacewing	.55	.55
1691	A548	45c Dull oakblue	.55	.55
1692	A548	45c Meadow argus	.55	.55
1693	A548	45c Ulysses	.55	.55
1694	A548	45c Common red-eye	.55	.55
a.		Strip of 5, #1690-1694	2.75	2.75
b.		Souv. sheet of 5, #1690-1694	3.00	3.00

No. 1694b for China 1999 World Philatelic Exhibition. Issued 8/21/99.

Self-Adhesive
Serpentine Die Cut 11½

1695	A548	45c like #1690	.55	.20
1696	A548	45c like #1691	.55	.20
1697	A548	45c like #1692	.55	.20
1698	A548	45c like #1693	.55	.20
1699	A548	45c like #1694	.55	.20
a.		Strip of 5, #1695-1699	2.75	

1998, Sept. 10

#1700, Sextant, map of Bass Strait. #1701, Telescope, map of Van Diemen's Land (Tasmania).

1700	A549	45c multicolored	.55	.20
1701	A549	45c multicolored	.55	.20
a.		Pair, #1700-1701	1.10	1.10

Circumnavigation of Tasmania by George Bass (1771-c. 1803) and Matthew Flinders (1774-1814), bicent.

A550   Marine
                      Life — A551

#1702, Fiery squid. #1703, Manta ray. #1704, Bottlenose dolphin. #1705, Weedy seadragon. #1706, Southern right whale. #1707, White pointer shark.

Perf. 14½x14, 14x14½

1998, Oct. 1   *Litho.*

1702	A550	45c multi	.55	.30
1703	A550	45c multi, horiz.	.55	.30
1704	A551	45c multi	.55	.30
1705	A551	45c multi	.55	.30
a.		Pair, #1704-1705	1.10	1.10

Size: 50x30mm

1706	A551	45c multi, horiz.	.55	.20
1707	A551	45c multi	.55	.20
a.		Souvenir sheet, #1702-1707	3.50	3.50
		Nos. 1702-1707 (6)	3.30	1.60

Booklet Stamps
Self-Adhesive
Serpentine Die Cut Perf. 11½

1708	A551	45c like #1704	.55	.20
1709	A551	45c like #1705	.55	.20
a.		Bklt. pane, 5 ea #1708-1709	5.50	

No. 1709a is a complete booklet. The peel-able paper backing serves as a booklet cover. Nos. 1708-1709 also exist in coils.

Universal Declaration of Human Rights, 50th Anniv. — A552

1998, Oct. 22   *Litho.*   *Perf. 14½x14*

1712	A552	45c multicolored	.60	.20

Christmas
A553

40c, Magi. 45c, Nativity. $1, Journey to Bethlehem.

1998, Nov. 2   *Perf. 14x14½*

1713	A553	40c multicolored	.50	.20
1714	A553	45c multicolored	.60	.20
1715	A553	$1 multicolored	1.25	.45
		Nos. 1713-1715 (3)	2.35	.85

Booklet Stamp
Self-Adhesive
Serpentine Die Cut Perf. 11½

1716	A553	40c multicolored	.50	.20
a.		Booklet pane of 20	10.00	

No. 1716a is a complete booklet.

Nationality and Citizenship Act, 50th Anniv.
A554

1999, Jan. 14   *Litho.*   *Perf. 14x14½*

1717	A554	45c multicolored	.55	.20

Die Cut Perf. 11¾
Self-Adhesive

1718	A554	45c multicolored	.55	.20

Legends Type of 1997

Designs: Nos. 1719, 1721, Arthur Boyd, artist. Nos. 1720, 1722, "Nebuchadnezzar on Fire Falling over a Waterfall," by Boyd.

1999, Jan. 22   *Litho.*   *Perf. 14x14½*

1719	A522	45c multicolored	.60	.30
1720	A522	45c multicolored	.60	.30
a.		Pair, #1719-1720	1.25	1.25

Booklet Stamps
Self-Adhesive
Serpentine Die Cut Perf. 11½

1721	A522	45c multicolored	.60	.20
1722	A522	45c multicolored	.60	.20
a.		Bklt. pane, 5 ea #1721-1722	6.00	

No. 1722a is a complete booklet.

Love — A555

1999, Feb. 4   *Perf. 14x14½*

1723	A555	45c Red roses	.60	.40

Booklet Stamp
Self-Adhesive
Serpentine Die Cut Perf. 11½

1724	A555	45c like #1723	.60	.20
a.		Booklet pane of 10	6.00	

No. 1724a is a complete booklet.

Intl. Year of Older Persons
A556

Designs: No. 1725, Woman walking with girl, man up close. No. 1726, Woman up close, man playing soccer by boy.

1999, Feb. 11   *Perf. 14x14½*

1725	A556	45c multicolored	.60	.30
1726	A556	45c multicolored	.60	.30
a.		Pair, #1725-1726	1.25	1.25

Early Navigators Type of 1963

#1727: a, like #374. b, like #376. c, like #377.
#1728: a, like #375. b, like #379. c, like #378.

Perf. 14x14½, 14½x14

1999, Mar. 19   *Litho.*

1727		Sheet of 3	1.75	1.75
a.-c.		A144 45c any single	.55	.55
d.		As #1727, imperf.	16.00	16.00
e.		As #1727, perfin "A99" in sheet margin	42.50	42.50
1728		Sheet of 3	1.75	1.75
a.-c.		A144 45c any single	.55	.55
d.		As #1728, imperf.	16.00	16.00
e.		As #1728, perfin "A99" in sheet margin	42.50	42.50

Australia '99, World Stamp Expo. Nos. 1727e-1728e were made from Nos. 1727d-1728d at Australia '99. Examples with the perforating and "A99" inverted were intentionally misperfed personally by patrons of the show.

Sailing Ships — A557

1999, Mar. 19   *Perf. 14½x14*

1729	A557	45c Polly Woodside	.60	.20
a.		Souvenir sheet of 2, #1729, Ireland #1169		
1730	A557	85c Alma Doepel	1.10	.35
1731	A557	$1 Enterprize	1.25	.40
1732	A557	$1.05 Lady Nelson	1.40	.45

Australia '99, World Stamp Expo (#1729a). No. 1729 was issued in sheets of 20 with a se-tenant label showing Australia '99 logo. Panes of 10 #1729 with labels were sold only at the show, where patrons could have their photos printed on the label.

Olympic Torch — A558

1999, Mar. 22

1733	A558	$1.20 #289	1.60	.55

Flora & Fauna Type of 1996

Flowers: #1734, 1743, 1746B, Correa reflexa. #1735, 1744, 1746C, Hibbertia scandens. #1736, 1745, 1746D, Ipomoea pes-

---

caprae. #1737, 1746, 1746E, Wahlenbergia stricta.
70c, Humpback whales, zebra volute. #1739, Brahminy kite, checkerboard helmet shell. #1740, Fraser Island, chambered nautilus. $1.05, Loggerhead turtle, baler. $1.20, White-bellied sea eagle, Campbell's stromb.

1999   *Litho.*   *Perf. 14x14½*

1734	A511	45c multicolored	.60	.40
1735	A511	45c multicolored	.60	.40
1736	A511	45c multicolored	.60	.40
1737	A511	45c multicolored	.60	.40
a.		Block of 4, #1734-1737	2.40	2.40
1738	A511	70c multicolored	.90	.30
1739	A511	90c multicolored	1.10	.40
1740	A511	90c multicolored	1.10	.40
a.		Pair, #1739-1740	2.25	2.25
1741	A511	$1.05 multicolored	1.40	.45
1742	A511	$1.20 multicolored	1.50	.50
		Nos. 1734-1742 (9)	8.40	3.65

Booklet Stamps
Serpentine Die Cut 11, 11¼
(#1742Df)
Self-Adhesive

1742A	A511	45c like #1734	.60	.20
1742B	A511	45c like #1735	.60	.20
1742C	A511	45c like #1736	.60	.20
1742D	A511	45c like #1737	.60	.20
e.		Booklet pane, 3 each #1742A, 1742C, 2 each #1742B, 1742D	6.00	
f.		Booklet pane, 5 each #1742A-1742D	12.00	
g.		Strip of 4, #1743-1746	2.40	

Die Cut perf. 12½x12¾

1743	A511	45c like #1734	.60	.20
1744	A511	45c like #1735	.60	.20
1745	A511	45c like #1736	.60	.20
1746	A511	45c like #1737	.60	.20
a.		Booklet pane, 3 each #1743, 1745, 2 each #1744, 1746	6.00	

Nos. 1742De, 1746a are complete booklets.

Coil Stamps
Serpentine Die Cut 11½

1746B	A511	45c like #1734	.60	.20
1746C	A511	45c like #1735	.60	.20
1746D	A511	45c like #1736	.60	.20
1746E	A511	45c like #1737	.60	.20
f.		Strip of 4, #1746B-1746E	2.40	
h.		Pane, #1746B, 1746D-1746E, 2 #1746C	3.00	

Issued: #1738-1742, 7/8; others, 4/8.
No. 1742Df is a complete booklet.

Queen Mother and Queen Elizabeth II — A559

1999, Apr. 15   *Perf. 14x14½*

1747	A559	45c multicolored	.60	.20

Queen Elizabeth II, 73rd birthday.

Children's Television Programs — A560

Designs: #1748, 1753, "Here's Humphrey." #1749, 1754, "Bananas in Pajamas." #1750, 1755, "Mr. Squiggle." #1751, 1756, Teddy bears from "Play School." #1752, 1757, Clock, dog, boy from "Play School."

1999, May 6   *Litho.*   *Perf. 14½x14*

1748	A560	45c multicolored	.60	.40
1749	A560	45c multicolored	.60	.40
1750	A560	45c multicolored	.60	.40
1751	A560	45c multicolored	.60	.40
1752	A560	45c multicolored	.60	.40
a.		Strip of 5, #1748-1752	3.00	3.00

Self-Adhesive
Serpentine Die Cut 11½x11¼
1753	A560	45c like #1748	.60	.20
1754	A560	45c like #1749	.60	.20
1755	A560	45c like #1750	.60	.20
1756	A560	45c like #1751	.60	.20
1757	A560	45c like #1752	.60	.20
a.		Bklt. pane, 2 ea #1753-1757	6.00	

No. 1757a is a complete booklet.

Perth Mint, Cent. A561

1999, May 13   Litho.   Perf. 14¼x14
1758	A561	$2 gold & multi	2.50	1.25

Test Rugby in Australia, Cent. A562

#1759, 1763, Kicking ball, vert. #1760, 1764, Catching ball. $1, Diving with ball. $1.20, Being tackled.

1999, June 8   Perf. 14½x14
1759	A562	45c multi	.60	.40
1760	A562	45c multi, vert.	.60	.40
a.		Pair, #1759-1760	1.25	.40

Perf. 14x14½
1761	A562	$1 multi	1.25	.40
1762	A562	$1.20 multi	1.50	.55

Serpentine Die Cut 11½
Self-Adhesive
Coil Stamps
1763	A562	45c like #1759	.60	.20
1764	A562	45c like #1760	.60	.20
a.		Pair, #1763-1764	1.25	

Snowy Mountains Hydroelectric Projects, 50th Anniv. A563

#1765, Rock bolters at Tumut 2 Power Station Hall, driller at Tooma-Tumut Tunnel. #1766, English class for migrant workers at Cooma. #1767, Eucumbene Dam, Tumut 2 Tailwater Tunnel. #1768, Island Bend Dam, German carpenters.

1999, Aug. 12   Litho.   Perf. 14x14½
1765	A563	45c multicolored	.60	.20
1766	A563	45c multicolored	.60	.20
1767	A563	45c multicolored	.60	.20
1768	A563	45c multicolored	.60	.20
a.		Block of 4, #1765-1768	2.40	2.40

Self-Adhesive
Coil Stamps
Litho.
Serpentine Die Cut 11¾
1769	A563	45c Like #1765	.60	.60
1770	A563	45c Like #1766	.60	.60
1771	A563	45c Like #1767	.60	.60
1772	A563	45c Like #1768	.60	.60
a.		Strip of 4, #1769-1772	2.40	

Greetings A564

1999, Sept. 1   Litho.   Perf. 14½x14
1773	A564	45c Teddy bear	.60	.20
1774	A564	45c Birthday cake	.60	.20
1775	A564	45c Roses, rings	.60	.20
1776	A564	45c Pen, letter	.60	.20

1777	A564	45c Christmas ornament	.60	.20
1778	A564	$1 Koala	1.25	.40
		Nos. 1773-1778 (6)	4.25	1.40

Nos. 1773-1778 each were printed with a se-tenant label at right in sheets of 20. Size of label is 24mm wide on No. 1777, 17mm on others. Labels were inscribed with phrases appropriate to the stamp design, or blank, upon which Australia Post printed photographs, sent to them through special orders. See No. 1926.

2000 Olympic Games, Sydney — A565

1999, Sept. 14   Litho.   Perf. 14½x14
1779	A565	45c multicolored	.60	.20

Sydney Design 99, Intl. Design Congress A566

Designs: 45c, Australia Post emblem. 90c, Embryo chair. $1.35, Possum skin textile design. $1.50, Storey Hall, Royal Melbourne Institute of Technology.

1999, Sept. 16   Litho.   Perf. 14x14½
1780	A566	45c multicolored	.60	.20
1781	A566	90c multicolored	1.10	.40
1782	A566	$1.35 multicolored	1.75	.60
1783	A566	$1.50 multicolored	2.00	.65
		Nos. 1780-1783 (4)	5.45	1.85

Pond Fauna — A567

Designs: Nos. 1784, 1790c, Roth's tree frog. Nos. 1785, 1790d, Dragonfly. Nos. 1786, 1790b, Sacred kingfisher. Nos. 1787, 1790f, Magnificent tree frog. Nos. 1788, 1790e, 1791, Northern dwarf tree frog. Nos. 1789, 1790a, 1792, Javelin frog.
No. 1793, Sacred kingfisher. No. 1794, Magnificent tree frog.

1999, Oct. 1   Litho.   Perf. 14x14½
1784	A567	45c multicolored	.60	.20
1785	A567	45c multicolored	.60	.20
a.		Pair, #1784-1785	1.25	1.25

Size: 26x38mm
Perf. 14½x14
1786	A567	45c multicolored	.60	.20
1787	A567	45c multicolored	.60	.20
a.		Pair, #1786-1787	1.25	1.25

Size: 24x30mm
1788	A567	50c multicolored	.70	.25
1789	A567	50c multicolored	.70	.25
a.		Pair, #1788-1789	1.40	1.40
		Nos. 1784-1789 (6)	3.80	1.30

Souvenir Sheet
Perf. 14½
1790	A567	Sheet of 6, #a-f	4.00	4.00
g.		Ovptd. in sheet margin	4.00	4.00

No. 1790d has foil impression on dragonfly's wings.
No. 1790 with overprints for Victorian and South Australian Philatelic Congresses in 1999 are unofficial.
No. 1790g issued 3/25/00 overprinted in sheet margin "BANGKOK 2000 / 25 March - 3 April 2000" and show emblem.

Self-Adhesive
Serpentine Die Cut 11¼
Size: 24x30mm
1791	A567	50c multicolored	.70	.25
1792	A567	50c multicolored	.70	.25
a.		Bklt. pane, 5 ea #1791-1792	7.00	

Nos. 1791-1792 are booklet stamps. No. 1792a is a complete booklet.

Die Cut Perf. 11¾
Size: 26x38mm
1793	A567	45c multi	.60	.20
1794	A567	45c multi	.60	.20
a.		Pair, #1793-1794	1.20	

Christmas A568

1999, Nov. 1   Perf. 14½x14
1795	A568	40c Madonna and child, vert.	.50	.20

Perf. 14x14½
1796	A568	$1 Tree	1.25	.40

Booklet Stamp
Self-Adhesive
Serpentine Die Cut 11¾
1797	A568	40c Like #1795	.50	.20
a.		Booklet pane of 20	10.00	

Celebrate 2000 — A569

1999, Nov. 1   Litho.   Perf. 14½x14
1798	A569	45c multicolored	.60	.20

No. 1798 has a holographic image. Soaking in water may affect hologram. No. 1798 printed with a se-tenant label at right in sheets of 20. Labels were inscribed "Celebrate 2000" or blank, upon which Australia Post printed photographs, sent to them through special orders.
Sheets of 10 stamps plus 10 photo labels have been available at special events. These have the sheet selvage inscribed for each event. Most of these have been available only at the event and exist in very limited quantities.

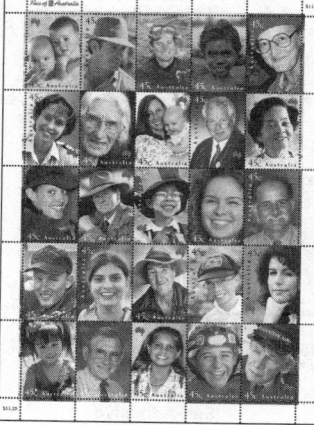

Faces of Australia — A570

Ordinary people: a, Nicholle and Meghan Triandis, baby twins. b, David Willis, cattleman with hat. c, Natasha Bramley, with snorkel gear. d, Cyril Watson, Aboriginal boy. e, Mollie Dowdall, with red hat. f, Robin Dicks, in khaki uniform. g, Mary Simons, with gray hair. h, Peta and Samantha Nieuwerth, mother and daughter. i, Dr. John Matthews, with stethoscope. j, Edith Dizon-Fitzsimmons, with large earrings. k, Philippa Weir, with brown hat. l, John Thurgar, with suit, tie and hat. m, Miguel Alzona, with large, multicolored hat. n, Rachael Thomson, girl with wavy hair. o, Necip Akarsu, with mustache. p, Justin Allan, with HMAS Brisbane cap. q, Wadad Dennaoui, with checked blouse. r, Jack Laity, with hat and jacket. s, Kelsey Stubbin, with Australia cap. t, Gianna Rossi, with hand on chin. u, Paris Hansch, young girl. v, Donald George Whatham, in shirt and tie. w, Stacey Coull, Aboriginal girl in patterned blouse. x, Alex Payne, with bicycle helmet. y, John Lodge, with Salvation Army hat.

2000, Jan. 1   Litho.   Perf. 14¾x13¾
1799		Sheet of 25	14.50	14.50
a.-y.		A570 45c Any single	.55	.40

Legends Type of 1997
Aging veterans of World War I: Nos. 1800, 1804, Walter Parker. Nos. 1801, 1805, Roy Longmore. Nos. 1802, 1806, Alec Campbell. Nos. 1803, 1807, 1914-15 Star.

2000, Jan. 21   Litho.   Perf. 14x14¾
Size: 34x25mm
1800	A522	45c multi	.55	.25
1801	A522	45c multi	.55	.25
1802	A522	45c multi	.55	.25
1803	A522	45c multi	.55	.25
a.		Block of 4, #1800-1803	2.20	1.00

Self-Adhesive
Die Cut Perf. 11¾
1804	A522	45c multi	.55	.25
1805	A522	45c multi	.55	.25
1806	A522	45c multi	.55	.25
1807	A522	45c multi	.55	.25
a.		Complete booklet, 2 each #1804-1806, 4 #1807	5.50	

A571   A572

2000, Feb. 24   Litho.   Perf. 14¾x14
Arts festivals.
1808	A571	45c Perth	.55	.25
1809	A571	45c Adelaide	.55	.25
1810	A571	45c Sydney	.55	.25
1811	A571	45c Melbourne	.55	.25
1812	A571	45c Brisbane	.55	.25
a.		Strip of 5, #1808-1812	2.75	1.25

2000, Mar. 23   Litho.   Perf. 14¾x14
Gardens: #1813, 1818, 1823, Coast banksia, false sarsaparailla, swamp bloodwood (denomination at UR). #1814, 1819, 1824, Swamp bottlebrush, Eastern spinebill (denomination at UL). #1815, 1820, 1825, Canna X generalis varieties (denomination at LL). #1816, 1821, 1826, Pond, roses, purple swamphen (denomination at UR). #1817, 1822, 1927, Pond, hibiscus, nerium oleander (denomination at UL).
1813	A572	45c multi	.55	.25
1814	A572	45c multi	.55	.25
1815	A572	45c multi	.55	.25
1816	A572	45c multi	.55	.25
1817	A572	45c multi	.55	.25
a.		Horiz. strip, #1813-1817	2.75	1.25

Booklet Stamps
Self-Adhesive
Serpentine Die Cut 11½x11¼
Pale Green Frames
1818	A572	45c multi	.55	.25
1819	A572	45c multi	.55	.25
1820	A572	45c multi	.55	.25
1821	A572	45c multi	.55	.25
1822	A572	45c multi	.55	.25
a.		Booklet, 2 each #1818-1822	5.50	
		Nos. 1818-1822 (5)	2.75	1.25

Coil Stamps
Self-Adhesive
Serpentine Die Cut 11¾
Pale Green Frames
1823	A572	45c multi	.55	.25
1824	A572	45c multi	.55	.25
1825	A572	45c multi	.55	.25
1826	A572	45c multi	.55	.25
1827	A572	45c multi	.55	.25
a.		Strip of 5, #1823-1827	2.75	

Queen Elizabeth II, 74th Birthday A573

2000, Apr. 13   Litho.   Perf. 14x14¾
1828	A573	45c multi	.55	.25

Korean War, 50th Anniv. A574

2000, Apr. 18
1829 A574 45c multi .55 .25

Daisy — A575

Australia on Globe, Southern Cross — A576

Kangaroo and Flag — A577

Sand, Sea and Sky — A578

Rainforest A579

2000, May 11 **Perf. 14½x14**
1830 A575 45c multi + label .55 .25
1831 A576 45c multi + label .55 .25
1832 A577 45c multi + label .55 .25
a. Sheet of 10 + 10 labels 10.50 10.50
1833 A578 45c multi + label .55 .25
1834 A579 45c multi + label .55 .25
    Nos. 1830-1834 (5) 2.75 1.25

Nos. 1830-1834 each issued in sheets of 20 stamps and labels, with and without decorative selvage.
Sheets containing 10 No. 1831 with margins and ten labels that could be personalized were sold for $12, $2 of which was donated to volunteer organizations of the purchaser's choice. Volunteer organizations could purchase these sheets and offer them for resale in fundraising projects.
No. 1832a sold for $16. Sheet has decorative selvage and labels showing stock photo.

The Move Towards Federation — A580

Designs: No. 1835, Taking the vote. No. 1836, Waiting for the results. No. 1837, The fair new nation. No. 1838, Queen Victoria.

2000, May 22 **Perf. 14¾x14**
1835 A580 45c multi .55 .25
1836 A580 45c multi .55 .25
a. Pair, #1835-1836 1.10 .50

Size: 30x50mm
Perf. 14x14½
1837 A580 $1.50 multi 1.90 .95
1838 A580 $1.50 multi 1.90 .95
a. Pair, #1837-1838 3.80 1.90
b. Souvenir sheet, #1836a, 1838a 5.00 2.40
c. As "b," with marginal inscription for The Stamp Show 2000, London 5.00 2.40
    Nos. 1835-1838 (4) 4.90 2.40

Tourist Attractions — A581

Designs: 50c, Sydney Opera House. $1, Nandroya Falls. $1.50, Sydney Harbour Bridge. $2, Cradle Mountain. $3, The Pinnacles. $4.50, Flinders Ranges. $5, Twelve Apostles. $10, Devils Marbles.

2000, June 20 Litho. Perf. 14½x14
1839 A581 50c multi .60 .30
1840 A581 $1 multi 1.25 .60
1841 A581 $1.50 multi 1.90 .95
1842 A581 $2 multi 2.50 1.25
1843 A581 $3 multi 3.75 1.90

Size: 56x25mm
Perf. 14x14½
1844 A581 $4.50 multi 5.50 2.75
1845 A581 $5 multi 6.00 3.00
1846 A581 $10 multi 12.00 6.00
    Nos. 1839-1846 (8) 33.50 16.75
    See No. 1925, 1979-1983.

2000 Paralympics, Sydney — A582

#1847, 1855, Wheelchair tennis. #1848, 1856, Amputee running. #1849, 1853, Wheelchair basketball. #1850, 1852, Cycling for the visually impaired. #1851, 1854, Amputee shot put.

2000, July 3 Litho. Perf. 14¾x14
1847 A582 45c multi .55 .25
1848 A582 45c multi .55 .25
a. Pair, #1847-1848 1.10 .50
1849 A582 49c multi .60 .30
1850 A582 49c multi .60 .30
1851 A582 49c multi .60 .30
a. Strip of 3, #1849-1851 1.80 .90

Booklet Stamps
Self-Adhesive
Die Cut Perf. 11½x11¾
1852 A582 49c multi .60 .30
1853 A582 49c multi .60 .30
1854 A582 49c multi .60 .30
a. Bklt., 4 ea #1852-1853, 2 #1854 6.00

Coil Stamps
Self-Adhesive
Serpentine Die Cut 11¾
1855 A582 45c multi .55 .25
1856 A582 45c multi .55 .25
a. Pair, #1855-1856 1.10

Australian Victoria Cross, Cent. — A583

#1857, Sir Neville Howse. #1858, Sir Arthur Roden Cutler. #1859, Victoria Cross. #1860, Edward Kenna. #1861, Keith Payne.

2000, July 24 Litho. Perf. 14¾x14
1857 A583 45c multi .55 .25
1858 A583 45c multi .55 .25
1859 A583 45c multi .55 .25
1860 A583 45c multi .55 .25
1861 A583 45c multi .55 .25
a. Horiz. strip of 5, #1857-1861 2.75 1.25

Olympic Sports — A584

#1862a, 1869, Water polo. #1862b, 1870, Women's field hockey. #1862c, 1863, Swimming. #1862d, 1865, Basketball. #1862e, 1866, Triathlon cycling. #1862f, 1871, Equestrian. #1862g, 1872, Tennis. #1862h, 1864, Rhythmic gymnastics. #1862i, 1867, Runner. #1862j, 1868, Rowing.

2000, Aug. 17 Litho. Perf. 14¾x14
1862 Sheet of 10 5.00 2.50
a.-j. A584 45c Any single .50 .25
k. As #1862, with inscription added in sheet margin 5.00 5.00

No. 1862k was issued 9/15/00 and has additional multicolored inscription in upper sheet margin reading "15-28 / September / 2000 / OLYMPHILEX 2000" and show emblem.

Booklet Stamps
Self-Adhesive
Serpentine Die Cut 11½x11¼
1863 A584 45c multi .50 .25
1864 A584 45c multi .50 .25
1865 A584 45c multi .50 .25
1866 A584 45c multi .50 .25
1867 A584 45c multi .50 .25
1868 A584 45c multi .50 .25
1869 A584 45c multi .50 .25
1870 A584 45c multi .50 .25
1871 A584 45c multi .50 .25
1872 A584 45c multi .50 .25
a. Booklet, #1863-1872 5.00

Sydney and Athens — A585

Olympic torch, flag and: 45c, Parthenon. $1.50, Sydney Opera House.

2000, Sept. 15 Litho. Perf. 14½x14
1873 A585 45c multi + label .50 .25
1874 A585 $1.50 multi + label 1.60 .80
    See Greece Nos. 1968-1969.

Australian Gold Medalists at 2000 Olympics A586

Cathy Freeman Lighting Olympic Flame — A587

#1875, 1891, Ian Thorpe. #1876, 1892, Men's 4x100-meter freestyle swimming team. #1877, 1893, Michael Diamond. #1878, 1894, Three day event equestrian team. #1879, 1895, Susie O'Neill. #1880, 1896, Men's 4x200-meter freestyle swimming team. #1881, 1897, Simon Fairweather. #1882, 1898, Brett Aitken, Scott McGrory. #1883, 1899, Grant Hackett. #1884, 1900, Women's water polo team. #1885, 1901, Natalie Cook, Kerri Pottharst. #1886, 1902, Cathy Freeman. #1887, 1903, Lauren Burns. #1888, 1904, Women's field hockey team. #1889, 1905, Jenny Armstrong, Belinda Stowell. #1890, 1906, Tom King, Mark Turnbull.

2000 Digitally Printed Perf. 14¼
1875 A586 45c multi .50 .25
1876 A586 45c multi .50 .25
1877 A586 45c multi .50 .25

1878 A586 45c multi .50 .25
1879 A586 45c multi .50 .25
1880 A586 45c multi .50 .25
1881 A586 45c multi .50 .25
1882 A586 45c multi .50 .25
1883 A586 45c multi .50 .25
1884 A586 45c multi .50 .25
1885 A586 45c multi .50 .25
1886 A586 45c multi .50 .25
1887 A586 45c multi .50 .25
1888 A586 45c multi .50 .25
1889 A586 45c multi .50 .25
1890 A586 45c multi .50 .25

Litho.
1891 A586 45c multi .50 .25
1892 A586 45c multi .50 .25
1893 A586 45c multi .50 .25
1894 A586 45c multi .50 .25
1895 A586 45c multi .50 .25
1896 A586 45c multi .50 .25
1897 A586 45c multi .50 .25
1898 A586 45c multi .50 .25
1899 A586 45c multi .50 .25
1900 A586 45c multi .50 .25
1901 A586 45c multi .50 .25
1902 A586 45c multi .50 .25
1903 A586 45c multi .50 .25
1904 A586 45c multi .50 .25
1905 A586 45c multi .50 .25
1906 A586 45c multi .50 .25
1907 A587 45c multi .50 .25
    Nos. 1875-1907 (33) 16.50 8.25

Issued: #1875, 1876, 1891, 1892, 9/17; #1877, 1893, 9/18; #1878-1880, 1894-1896, 9/20; #1881, 1897, 9/21; #1882, 1898, 9/22; #1883, 1884, 1899, 1900, 9/24; #1885, 1886, 1901, 1902, 9/26; #1887, 1903, 9/28; #1888, 1904, 9/30; #1889, 1890, 1905, 1906, 10/1; #1907, 10/10.
#1875-1890 have shinier appearance than #1891-1906. Olympic rings, flag stars and flag edge on #1875-1890 has a more ragged appearance than #1891-1906, which have crisp details.
#1875-1907 printed in sheets of 10. Sheets of #1875-1890 have rouletted right margin and one of six red animal imprints in lower right margin representing where the sheets were made (Platypus, Sydney; Kookaburra, Canberra; Koala, Brisbane; Swan, Perth; Kangaroo, Adelaide; Opossum, Melbourne). Sheets of #1875-1890 were placed on sale at 67 outlets within 24 hours of the awarding of the medals to the athletes. Sheets of #1891-1906, which have a straight-edged right margin and a red Australia map imprint in lower right margin, gradually became available nationwide as stocks were printed and shipped.
A sheet containing Nos. 1891-1907 and 8 labels was available only in the Australia Post annual collection. Value, $8.50.

Space — A588

#1908, 1914a, Flight crew. #1909, 1914b, Robots, vert. #1910, 1914c, 1915, 1917, Astronaut, vert. #1911, 1914d, 1916, 1918, Terrain, vert. #1912, 1914e, Spacecraft. #1913, 1914f, Launch site, vert.

Perf. 14x14½, 14½x14
2000, Oct. 3 Litho.
1908 A588 45c multi .50 .25
1909 A588 45c multi .50 .25

Size: 26x38mm
1910 A588 45c multi .50 .25
1911 A588 45c multi .50 .25
a. Pair, #1910-1911 1.00 .50

Size: 50x30mm
1912 A588 45c multi .50 .25

Size: 30x50mm
1913 A588 45c multi .50 .25
    Nos. 1908-1913 (6) 3.00 1.50

Souvenir Sheet
Litho. with Translucent Foil
Perf. 14½
1914 Sheet of 6 3.00 1.50
a.-f. A588 45c any single .50 .25
g. As #1914, ovptd. in margin in gold 3.00 1.50

Booklet Stamps
Litho.
Self-Adhesive
Serpentine Die Cut 11½x11¼
1915 A588 45c multi .50 .25
1916 A588 45c multi .50 .25
a. Booklet, 5 each #1915-1916 5.00

Coil Stamps
Serpentine Die Cut 11½

1917	A588 45c multi	.50	.25
1918	A588 45c multi	.50	.25
a.	Pair, #1917-1918	1.00	.50

Nos. 1915-1918 have pink and gray frames. No 1914g overprinted with emblem of Hong Kong 2001 Stamp Exhibition. Issued 2/1/01.

2000 Paralympics, Sydney — A589

Designs: No. 1919, Paralympics emblem. No. 1920, Runner with torch.

2000, Oct. 18   Litho.   Perf. 14½x14

1919	A589 45c multi + label	.50	.25
1920	A589 45c multi + label	.50	.25

Siobhan Paton, Paralympian of the Year — A590

2000, Oct. 31   Perf. 14¼

1921	A590 45c multi	.50	.25

Christmas — A591

40c, Madonna and child. 45c, Manger.

2000, Nov. 1   Litho.   Perf. 14½x14

1922	A591 40c multi	.45	.20
1923	A591 45c multi	.50	.25
a.	Souvenir sheet, #1922-1923	.95	.45

Booklet Stamp
Serpentine Die Cut 11¾

1924	A591 40c multi	.45	.20
a.	Booklet of 20 + 20 stickers	9.00	

Tourist Attractions Type of 2000
2000, Nov. 1   Perf. 14½x14

1925	A581 80c Byron Bay	.85	.45

No. 1778 Overprinted in Dark Blue

2001, Jan.   Litho.   Perf. 14½x14

1926	A564 $1 multi + label	1.10	.40

Federation of Australia, Cent. — A592

Designs: Nos. 1927, 1931, Federation Arch, Sydney. Nos. 1928, 1932, Sir Edmund Barton, first prime minister. No. 1929, National celebrations, horiz (50x30mm). No. 1930, State banquet (30x50mm).

Perf. 14¾x14, 14x14¾
2001, Jan. 1   Litho.

1927	A592 49c multi	.55	.25
1928	A592 49c multi	.55	.25
a.	Pair, #1927-1928	1.10	.50
1929	A592 $2 multi	2.25	1.10
1930	A592 $2 multi	2.25	1.10
a.	Souvenir sheet, #1927-1930, perf. 14½	5.75	2.75

Self-Adhesive
Booklet Stamps
Serpentine Die Cut 11½x11

1931	A592 49c multi	.55	.55
1932	A592 49c multi	.55	.55
a.	Booklet, 5 each # 1931-1932	5.50	
	Nos. 1927-1932 (6)	6.70	3.80

Australian Legends Type of 1997
Slim Dusty, musician: Nos. 1933, 1935, With guitar. Nos. 1934, 1936, Wearing blue shirt.

2001, Jan. 25   Perf. 14x14¾
Size: 34x26mm

1933	A522 45c multi	.50	.25
1934	A522 45c multi	.50	.25
a.	Pair, #1933-1934	1.00	.50

Self-Adhesive
Booklet Stamps
Serpentine Die Cut 11x11½

1935	A522 45c multi	.50	.50
1936	A522 45c multi	.50	.50
a.	Booklet, 5 each #1935-1936	5.00	
	Nos. 1933-1936 (4)	2.00	1.50

Australian Army, Cent. A593

Rising Sun badge and: No. 1937, Light Horse Brigade, 1940, soldiers in New Guinea, 1943. No. 1938, Soldier in UN peacekeeping mission carrying Rwandan child, 1995, soldiers on commando officer selection course, 1997.

2001, Feb. 15   Perf. 14x14¾

1937	A593 45c multi	.50	.25
1938	A593 45c multi	.50	.25
a.	Pair, #1937-1938	.50	.25

Opening of National Museum, Canberra A594

Designs: No. 1939, Museum floor plan. No. 1940, Pangk (wallaby sculpture), by George MacNaught and Joe Ngallametta.

2001, Mar. 8

1939	A594 49c multi	.50	.25
1940	A594 49c multi	.50	.25
a.	Pair, #1939-1940	1.00	.50

Australian Legends Type of 1997
Similar to Nos. 1575-1576, but with cropped designs and "1908-2001" inscription added.

2001, Mar. 13   Perf. 14¼

1941	A522 45c Like #1575	.45	.25
1942	A522 45c Like #1576	.45	.25
a.	Pair, #1941-1942	.90	.50

Rock Music A595

Designs: Nos. 1943a, 1953, Khe Sanh, by Cold Chisel, 1978. Nos. 1943b, 1952, Down Under, by Men at Work, 1981. Nos. 1943c, 1951, Power and the Passion, by Midnight Oil, 1983. Nos. 1943d, 1950, Original Sin, by INXS. Nos. 1943e, 1949, You're the Voice, by John Farnham, 1986. Nos. 1943f, 1948, Don't Dream It's Over, by Crowded House, 1986. Nos. 1943g, 1947, Treaty, by Yothu Yindi, 1991. Nos. 1943h, 1946, Tomorrow, by Silverchair, 1994. Nos. 1943i, 1945, Confide in Me, by Kylie Minogue, 1994. Nos. 1943j, 1944, Truly, Madly, Deeply, by Savage Garden, 1997.

2001, Mar. 20   Litho.   Perf. 14x14¾

1943	Sheet of 10	4.50	4.50
a.-j.	A595 45c Any single	.45	.25

Self-Adhesive
Serpentine Die Cut 11¼x11½

1944	A595 45c multi	.45	.45
1945	A595 45c multi	.45	.45
1946	A595 45c multi	.45	.45
1947	A595 45c multi	.45	.45
1948	A595 45c multi	.45	.45
1949	A595 45c multi	.45	.45
1950	A595 45c multi	.45	.45
1951	A595 45c multi	.45	.45
1952	A595 45c multi	.45	.45
1953	A595 45c multi	.45	.45
a.	Horiz. strip of 10, #1944-1953	4.50	
b.	Booklet, #1944-1953	4.50	

Queen Elizabeth II, 75th Birthday — A596

2001, Apr. 12   Litho.   Perf. 14¾x14

1954	A596 45c multi	.45	.25

Flower — A597

Balloons — A598

Streamers — A599

Kangaroos — A600

Bayulu Banner — A601

Litho., Litho with Hologram (#1957)
2001, Apr. 24   Perf. 14½x14

1955	A597 45c multi + label	.45	.25
1956	A598 45c multi + label	.45	.25
1957	A599 45c multi + label	.45	.25
1958	A600 $1 multi + label	1.00	.50
1959	A601 $1.50 multi + label	1.60	.80
	Nos. 1955-1959 (5)	3.95	2.05

Federal Parliament, Cent. — A602

Designs: No. 1960, The Opening of the First Federal Parliament, 9 May 1901, by Charles Nuttall. No. 1961, Opening of the First Parliament of the Commonwealth of Australia by H.R.H. The Duke of Cornwall and York (Later King George V), May 9, 1901, by Tom Roberts.

2001, May 3   Litho.   Perf. 14¼

1960	A602 45c multi	.45	.25
a.	Souvenir sheet of 1	.45	.25
1961	A602 $2.45 multi	2.60	1.25
a.	Souvenir sheet of 1	2.60	1.25

Outback Services A603

Designs: Nos. 1962, 1967, 1972, Telecommunications. Nos. 1963, 1968, 1973, Transport. Nos. 1964, 1969, 1974, School of the Air.

Nos. 1965, 1970, 1975, Postal service. Nos., 1966, 1971, 1976, Royal flying Doctor Service.

2001, June 5   *Perf. 14x14½*

1962	A603 45c multi	.45	.25
1963	A603 45c multi	.45	.25
1964	A603 45c multi	.45	.25
1965	A603 45c multi	.45	.25
1966	A603 45c multi	.45	.25
a.	Horiz. strip, #1962-1966	2.25	2.25

Self-Adhesive
Coil Stamps
Serpentine Die Cut 11¼

1967	A603 45c multi	.45	.45
1968	A603 45c multi	.45	.45
1969	A603 45c multi	.45	.45
1970	A603 45c multi	.45	.45
1971	A603 45c multi	.45	.45
a.	Horiz. strip, #1967-1971	2.25	

Booklet Stamps
Serpentine Die Cut 11¾

1972	A603 45c multi	.45	.45
1973	A603 45c multi	.45	.45
1974	A603 45c multi	.45	.45
1975	A603 45c multi	.45	.45
1976	A603 45c multi	.45	.45
a.	Booklet, 2 each #1972-1976	4.50	
	Nos. 1962-1976 (15)	6.75	5.75

Dragon Boat Races A604

Dragon boats and: 45c, Hong Kong Convention and Exhibition Center. $1, Sydney Opera House.

2001, June 25   *Perf. 14x14½*

1977	A604 45c multi	.45	.25
1978	A604 $1 multi	1.00	.50
a.	Souvenir sheet, #1977-1978	1.45	.75

See Hong Kong Nos. 938-939.

Tourist Attraction Type of 2000

Designs: 50c, Blue Mountains. $1, Murrumbidgee River. $1.50, Port Douglas. $20, Uluru.

Litho., Litho with Foil Application ($20)

2001, July 12   *Perf. 14½x14*

1979	A581 50c multi	.50	.25
1980	A581 $1 multi	1.00	.50
1981	A581 $1.50 multi	1.50	.75

Size: 56x25mm
Perf. 14x14½

1982	A581 $20 multi	20.00	10.00
	Nos. 1979-1982 (4)	23.00	11.50

Booklet Stamp
Self-Adhesive
Serpentine Die Cut 11¼x10½

1983	A581 50c multi	.50	.50
a.	Booklet, 10 #1983	5.00	

Flora & Fauna Type of 1996

Birds: Nos. 1984, 1988, 1992, Variegated fairy wren. Nos. 1985, 1989, 1993, Painted firetail. Nos. 1986, 1990, 1994, Crimson chat. Nos. 1987, 1991, 1995, Budgerigar.

2001, Aug. 9   **Litho.**   *Perf. 14x14½*

1984	A511 45c multi	.50	.25
1985	A511 45c multi	.50	.25
1986	A511 45c multi	.50	.25
1987	A511 45c multi	.50	.25
a.	Block of 4, #1984-1987	2.00	2.00

Self-Adhesive
Coil Stamps
Die Cut Perf. 12½x12¾

1988	A511 45c multi	.50	.50
1989	A511 45c multi	.50	.50
1990	A511 45c multi	.50	.50
1991	A511 45c multi	.50	.50
a.	Horiz. strip of 4, #1988-1991	2.00	

Booklet Stamps
Serpentine Die Cut 11¼

1992	A511 45c multi	.50	.50
1993	A511 45c multi	.50	.50
1994	A511 45c multi	.50	.50
1995	A511 45c multi	.50	.50
a.	Booklet pane, #1993, 1995	1.00	
b.	Booklet pane, #1992-1995, rouletted at bottom	2.00	
	Booklet, #1995a, #1995b	5.00	
c.	Booklet pane, #1992-1995, rouletted at side	2.00	
	Booklet, 5 #1995c	10.00	
	Nos. 1984-1995 (12)	6.00	5.00

Daniel Solander (1733-82), Botanist on Endeavour A605

Designs: 45c, Barringtonia calyptrata and Solander. $1.50, Cachlospermum gillivraei and Endeavour.

2001, Aug. 16   **Litho. & Engr.**
Perf. 12½x12¾

1996	A605 45c multi	.50	.25
1997	A605 $1.50 multi	1.60	.80

See Sweden No. 2419.

Commonwealth Heads of Government Meeting, Brisbane — A606

2001, Sept. 4   **Litho.**   *Perf. 14½x14*

1998	A606 45c Southern Cross	.45	.25
1999	A606 45c Australia on globe	.45	.25
a.	Pair, #1998-1999	.90	.50

Christmas — A607

2001, Sept. 4   *Perf. 14½x14*

2000	A607 40c Christmas tree	.40	.20
2001	A607 80c Star	.80	.40

2001, Sept. 4   **Stamp + Label**   *Perf. 14½x14*

Birds of Prey — A608

Designs: No. 2002, Wedge-tailed eagle. No. 2003, Nankeen kestrel. No. 2004, Red goshawk, vert. No. 2005, Spotted harrier, vert.

Perf. 14x14½, 14½x14

2001, Sept. 11

2002	A608 49c multi	.50	.25
2003	A608 49c multi	.50	.25
a.	Pair, #2002-2003	1.00	.50
2004	A608 98c multi	.95	.50
2005	A608 98c multi	.95	.50
a.	Pair, #2004-2005	1.90	1.00
	Nos. 2002-2005 (4)	2.90	1.50

Caricatures of Australian Wildlife by Roland Harvey — A609

Designs: Nos. 2006, 2012, Bilby and antechinus musicians, dancing cockatoo. Nos. 2007, 2013, Koala with birthday cake. Nos. 2008, 2014, Ring-tailed possums with drinks and food. Nos. 2009, 2015, Bilbies, crocodile, emu, koala and gifts. Nos. 2010, 2016, Wombat and ladder. Nos. 2011, 2017, Wallabies, echidnas, platypus and ladder.

2001, Oct. 2   *Perf. 14½x14*

2006	A609 45c multi	.45	.25
2007	A609 45c multi	.45	.25
2008	A609 45c multi	.45	.25
a.	Horiz. strip of 3, #2006-2008	1.35	.75
b.	Souvenir sheet, #2006-2008	1.35	.75
2009	A609 45c multi	.45	.25
2010	A609 45c multi	.45	.25

2011	A609 45c multi	.45	.25
a.	Horiz. strip, #2009-2011	1.35	.75
b.	Souvenir sheet, #2009-2011	1.35	.75

Self-Adhesive
Serpentine Die Cut 11½x11

2012	A609 45c multi	.45	.45
2013	A609 45c multi	.45	.45
2014	A609 45c multi	.45	.45
2015	A609 45c multi	.45	.45
2016	A609 45c multi	.45	.45
2017	A609 45c multi	.45	.45
a.	Coil strip, 2012-2017	2.70	
b.	Booklet, #2014-2015, 2 each #2012-2013, 2016-2017	4.50	
	Nos. 2006-2017 (12)	5.40	4.20

Christmas — A610

Illuminations from the Wharncliffe Hours, by Maitre Francois: 40c, Adoration of the Magi. 45c, Flight into Egypt.

2001, Nov. 1   *Perf. 14½x14*

2018	A610 40c multi	.40	.20
2019	A610 45c multi	.45	.25

Self-Adhesive
Serpentine Die Cut 11½x11¼

2020	A610 40c multi	.40	.40
a.	Booklet of 20 + 20 labels	8.00	

AIR POST STAMPS

Airplane over Bush Lands — AP1

Unwmk.

1929, May 20   **Engr.**   *Perf. 11*

C1	AP1 3p deep green	6.50	3.75
	Never hinged	12.50	
a.	Booklet pane of 4 ('30)	125.00	

Kingsford-Smith Type of 1931

1931, Mar. 19

C2	A8 6p gray violet	7.00	7.00
	Never hinged	10.00	

AP3

1931, Nov. 4

C3	AP3 6p olive brown	15.00	12.00
	Never hinged	22.50	

For overprint see No. CO1.

Mercury and Hemispheres AP4

1934, Dec. 1   *Perf. 11*

C4	AP4 1sh6p violet brown	20.00	3.00
	Never hinged	55.00	

Perf. 13x13½

1937, Oct. 22   **Wmk. 228**

C5	AP4 1sh6p violet brown	7.50	.25
	Never hinged	12.50	

> Catalogue values for unused stamps in this section, from this point to the end of the section, are for Never Hinged items.

Mercury and Globe — AP5

1949, Sept. 1   *Perf. 14½*

C6	AP5 1sh6p sepia	1.75	.20

1956, Dec. 6   **Unwmk.**

C7	AP5 1sh6p sepia	16.00	.85

Super-Constellation over Globe — AP6

1958, Jan. 6   *Perf. 14½x14*

C8	AP6 2sh dark violet blue	2.50	1.75

Inauguration of Australian "Round the World" air service.

AIR POST OFFICIAL STAMP

No. C3 Overprinted

Perf. 11, 11½

1931, Nov. 17   **Unwmk.**

CO1	AP3 6p olive brown	22.50	22.50
	Never hinged	27.50	

Issued primarily for official use, but to prevent speculation, a quantity was issued for public distribution.

POSTAGE DUE STAMPS

Very fine examples of Nos. J1-J38 will have perforations touching the design on one or more sides due to the narrow spacing of the stamps on the plates. Stamps with perfs clear of the design on all four sides are scarce and will command higher prices.

D1   D2

1902 Typo. Wmk. 55 Perf. 11½, 12

J1	D1 ½p emerald	3.00	4.00
J2	D1 1p emerald	12.00	6.00
a.	Perf. 11	750.00	300.00
J3	D1 2p emerald	25.00	7.00
J4	D1 3p emerald	25.00	18.00
J5	D1 4p emerald	37.50	11.00
J6	D1 6p emerald	50.00	9.00
J7	D1 8p emerald	87.50	75.00
J8	D1 5sh emerald	160.00	70.00
	Nos. J1-J8 (8)	400.00	200.00

The 1p, 2p and 4p, type D1, exist also in perforations compounding 11 with 11½ & 12.

Perf. 11½, 12, 11 and 11 Compound with 11½, 12

1902-04

J9	D2 ½p emerald	7.25	8.50
a.	Perf. 11	140.00	100.00
J10	D2 1p emerald	4.50	2.75
a.	Perf. 11	75.00	35.00
b.	Perf 11½, 12	150.00	80.00
J11	D2 2p emerald	15.00	3.50
a.	Perf. 11	110.00	25.00
b.	Perf 11½, 12		85.00
J12	D2 3p emerald	55.00	8.75
a.	Perf. 11	175.00	65.00
J13	D2 4p emerald	50.00	6.00
a.	Perf. 11	120.00	32.50
J14	D2 5p emerald	50.00	16.00
a.	Perf. 11	160.00	32.50
b.	Perf 11½, 12 compound with 11	60.00	16.00

J15	D2	6p emerald	72.50	18.00
J16	D2	8p emerald	125.00	40.00
J17	D2	10p emerald	87.50	15.00
a.		Perf 11½, 12 compound with 11	100.00	16.00
J18	D2	1sh emerald	57.50	14.00
a.		Perf. 11	175.00	40.00
b.		Perf. 11½, 12 compound with 11	80.00	18.00
J19	D2	2sh emerald	110.00	25.00
a.		Perf 11½, 12 compound with 11	120.00	35.00
J20	D2	5sh emerald	225.00	22.50
a.		Perf. 11	425.00	125.00

Perf. 11

J21	D2	10sh emerald	2,250.	1,500.
J22	D2	20sh emerald	3,750.	2,750.
		Nos. J9-J20 (12)	859.25	180.00

Perf. 11½, 12 Compound with 11

1906   Wmk. 12

J23	D2	½p emerald	14.00	7.00
J24	D2	1p emerald	30.00	2.50
a.		Perf. 11	850.00	350.00
J25	D2	2p emerald	50.00	4.00
J26	D2	3p emerald	375.00	200.00
J27	D2	4p emerald	77.50	20.00
a.		Perf. 11	1,300.	600.00
J28	D2	6p emerald	225.00	20.00
		Nos. J23-J28 (6)	771.50	253.50

1907   Wmk. 13   Perf. 11½x11

J29	D2	½p emerald	24.00	65.00
J30	D2	1p emerald	70.00	37.50
J31	D2	2p emerald	125.00	92.50
J32	D2	4p emerald	200.00	95.00
J33	D2	6p emerald	240.00	110.00
		Nos. J29-J33 (5)	659.00	400.00

 D3   D4

Perf. 11 (2sh, 10sh, 20sh), 11½x11 (1sh, 5sh)

1908-09   Wmk. 12

J34	D3	1sh emer ('09)	110.00	16.00
J35	D3	2sh emerald	1,100.	1,100.
J36	D3	5sh emerald	250.00	52.50
J37	D3	10sh emerald	1,900.	2,250.
J38	D3	20sh emerald	5,500.	6,000.

Perf. 11, 12x12½, 12½, 14

1909   Wmk. 13

J39	D4	½p green & car	13.50	26.00
J40	D4	1p green & car	13.50	4.00
a.		Perf 11	1,500.	600.00
J41	D4	2p green & car	22.50	3.50
a.		Perf 11	6,000.	1,500.
J42	D4	3p green & car	22.50	12.50
J43	D4	4p green & car	21.00	4.50
J44	D4	6p green & car	26.00	7.25
a.		Perf 11	6,000.	3,000.
J45	D4	1sh green & car	29.00	4.00
J46	D4	2sh green & car	67.50	13.50
J47	D4	5sh green & car	87.50	15.00
J48	D4	10sh green & car	240.00	150.00
J49	D4	£1 green & car	460.00	275.00
		Nos. J39-J49 (11)	1,003.	515.25

1922-25   Wmk. 10   Perf. 14, 11 (4p)

J50	D4	½p grn & car ('23)	6.50	1.75
J51	D4	1p green & car	6.50	1.90
J52	D4	1½p yellow green & rose ('25)	3.75	3.25
J53	D4	2p green & car	8.00	3.75
J54	D4	3p green & car	15.00	2.75
J55	D4	4p green & car	19.00	2.25
J56	D4	6p green & car	22.50	13.00
		Nos. J50-J56 (7)	81.25	28.65

No. J55 exists perf 14.

1931-37   Wmk. 228   Perf. 11, 14

J57	D4	½p yel green & rose ('34)	12.50	11.50
J58	D4	1p yel grn & rose	7.75	1.00
J59	D4	2p yel grn & rose	9.00	.50
J60	D4	3p yel green & rose ('37)	72.50	57.50
J61	D4	4p yel green & rose ('34)	6.75	1.90
J62	D4	6p yel green & rose ('36)	310.00	225.00
J63	D4	1sh yel green & rose ('34)	50.00	26.00
		Nos. J57-J63 (7)	468.50	323.40

 D5

Engraved; Value Typo.

1938   Perf. 14½x14

J64	D5	½p green & car	.75	1.25
J65	D5	1p green & car	5.00	.50
J66	D5	2p green & car	4.50	.50
J67	D5	3p green & car	15.00	3.50
J68	D5	4p green & car	4.50	.25
J69	D5	6p green & car	45.00	17.50
J70	D5	1sh green & car	20.00	7.50
		Nos. J64-J70 (7)	94.75	31.00

> **Catalogue values for unused stamps in this section, from this point to the end of the section, are for Never Hinged items.**

Type of 1938 Value Tablet Redrawn

 Original   Redrawn

Pence denominations: "D" has melon-shaped center in redrawn tablet. The redrawn 3p differs slightly, having semi-melon-shaped "D" center, with vertical white stroke half filling it.
1sh. 1938: Numeral "1" narrow, with six background lines above.
1sh. 1947: Numeral broader, showing more white space around dotted central ornament. Three lines above.

1946-57   Wmk. 228

J71	D5	½p grn & car ('56)	2.75	1.40
J72	D5	1p grn & car ('47)	1.40	.25
J73	D5	2p green & car	.85	1.00
J74	D5	3p green & car	4.50	.35
J75	D5	4p grn & car ('52)	5.50	.50
J76	D5	5p grn & car ('48)	8.25	1.25
J77	D5	6p grn & car ('47)	8.25	.65
J78	D5	7p grn & car ('53)	5.50	3.00
J79	D5	8p grn & car ('57)	13.50	11.50
J80	D5	1sh grn & car ('47)	13.50	1.25
		Nos. J71-J80 (10)	64.00	21.15

1953-54
White Tablet, Carmine Numeral

J81	D5	1sh grn & car ('54)	9.00	5.00
J82	D5	2sh green & car	12.50	10.00
J83	D5	5sh green & car	17.50	2.50
		Nos. J81-J83 (3)	39.00	17.50

Issued: 2sh, 5sh, Aug. 26; 1sh, Feb. 17.

Redrawn Type of 1947-57

Two Types of Some Pence Values:
Type I - Background lines touch numeral, "D" and period.
Type II - Lines do not touch numeral, etc. Second engraving of 1sh has sharper and thicker lines.
The ½p type II has 7 dots under the "2."
The 8p type II has distinct lines in centers of "8" and between "8" and "D."

Engr.; Value Typo.

1958-60   Unwmk.   Perf. 14½x14

J86	D5	½p grn & car, II	2.25	1.10
a.		Six dots under the "2"	3.75	.95
J87	D5	1p grn & car, II	2.25	.40
a.		Type I	2.50	1.50
J88	D5	3p grn & car, II	1.50	.75
J89	D5	4p grn & car, I	4.00	4.00
a.		Type II ('59)	3.00	6.00
J90	D5	5p grn & car, I	11.50	6.00
a.		Type II ('59)	57.50	25.00
J91	D5	6p grn & car, II	2.40	1.75
J92	D5	8p grn & car, II	8.75	15.00
a.		Indistinct lines	15.00	15.00
J93	D5	10p grn & car, II	4.00	3.25

White Tablet, Carmine Numeral

J94	D5	1sh green & car	4.75	2.50
a.		2nd redrawing ('60)	9.00	.60
J95	D5	2sh grn & car	19.00	5.50
		Nos. J86-J95 (10)	60.40	40.25

Issued: 1sh, 9/8/58; 10p, 12/9/59; 2sh, 3/8/60; 3p, 6p, 5/25/60; others, 2/27/58.

MILITARY STAMPS

Nos. 166, 191, 183A, 173, 175, 206 and 177 Overprinted in Black:

 a   b

 c

Perf. 14½x14, 15x14, 11½, 13½x13

1946-47   Wmk. 228

M1	A24(a)	½p orange	2.10	2.00
		Never hinged	3.25	
M2	A36(b)	1p brown vio	1.75	1.50
		Never hinged	2.75	
a.		Blue overprint	100.00	67.50
		Never hinged	125.00	
M3	A27(b)	3p dk vio brn	1.40	1.50
		Never hinged	2.25	
a.		Double overprint	500.00	
M4	A30(a)	6p brn violet	10.50	6.75
		Never hinged	16.00	
M5	A16(a)	1sh gray green	10.50	8.00
		Never hinged	16.00	
M6	A1 (c)	2sh dk red brn	30.00	32.50
		Never hinged	40.00	
M7	A32(c)	5sh dl red brn	77.50	87.50
		Never hinged	110.00	
		Nos. M1-M7 (7)	133.75	139.75

"B.C.O.F." stands for "British Commonwealth Occupation Force."
Forged overprints of Nos. M6-M7 exist.
Issued: #M1-M3, 10/11/46; #M4-M7, 5/8/47.

OFFICIAL STAMPS

Perforated Initials
In 1913-31, postage stamps were perforated "OS" for federal official use. The Scott Standard Catalogues do not list officials with perforated initials, but listings for these Australian stamps will be found in the *Scott Classic Specialized Catalogue*.

Overprinted Official stamps are comparatively more difficult to find well centered than the basic issues on which they are printed. This is because poorly centered sheets that had been discarded were purposely chosen to save money.

Overprinted   O S

On Regular Issue of 1931
1931, May 4   Unwmk.   Perf. 11, 11½

O1	A8	2p dull red	60.00	22.50
O2	A8	3p blue	175.00	35.00

These stamps were issued primarily for official use but to prevent speculation a quantity was issued for public distribution.
Used values are for cto copies.
Counterfeit overprints exist.

On Regular Issues of 1928-32
1932   Wmk. 203   Perf. 13½x12½

O3	A4	2p red, II	10.00	.90
O4	A4	4p olive bister	30.00	6.00

Perf. 11½, 12

O5	A1	6p brown	67.50	35.00

1932-33   Wmk. 228   Perf. 13½x12½

O6	A4	½p orange	6.00	1.25
a.		Inverted overprint	3,000.	1,500.
O7	A4	1p green, I	2.00	.75
O8	A4	2p red, II	5.00	.60
a.		Inverted overprint		2,250.
O9	A4	3p ultra, II ('33)	14.00	7.50
O10	A4	5p brown buff	42.50	21.00
a.		Wmk. 203		

Perf. 11½, 12

O11	A1	6p yellow brown	35.00	25.00
a.		Inverted overprint		
		Nos. O6-O11 (6)	104.50	56.10

1932   Unwmk.   Perf. 11, 11½

O12	A9	2p red	5.50	4.50
O13	A9	3p blue	18.00	18.00
O14	A16	1sh gray green	55.00	32.50
		Nos. O12-O14 (3)	78.50	55.00

AUSTRALIAN ANTARCTIC TERRITORY

> **Catalogue values for all unused stamps in this section are for Never Hinged items.**

All stamps are also valid for postage in Australia.

Edgeworth David, Douglas Mawson and A.F. McKay (1908-09 South Pole Expedition) — A1

Australian Explorers and Map of Antarctica — A2

Designs: 8p, Loading weasel (snow truck). 1sh, Dog team and iceberg, vert. 2sh3p, Emperor penguins and map, vert.

Perf. 14½, 14½x14, 14x14½

1957-59   Engr.   Unwmk.

L1	A1	5p brown	.60	.20
L2	A2	8p dark blue	3.00	2.00
L3	A2	1sh dark green	3.00	1.75
L4	A2	2sh ultra ('57)	1.40	.55
L5	A2	2sh3p green	7.00	3.50
		Nos. L1-L5 (5)	15.00	8.00

Nos. L1 and L2 were printed as 4p and 7p stamps and surcharged typographically in black and dark blue before issuance.
Sizes of stamps: No. L2, 34x21mm; Nos. L3, L5, 21x34mm; No. L4, 43½x25½mm.

1961, July 5   Perf. 14½

L6	A1	5p dark blue	1.10	.20

The denomination on No. L6 is not within a typographed circle, but is part of the engraved design.

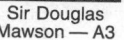 Sir Douglas Mawson — A3   Lookout and Iceberg — A4

1961, Oct. 18

L7	A3	5p dark green	.40	.20

50th anniv. of the 1911-14 Australian Antarctic Expedition.

Perf. 13½x13, 13x13½

1966-68   Photo.   Unwmk.

Designs: 1c, Aurora australis and camera dome. 2c, Banding penguins. 5c, Branding of elephant seals. 7c, Measuring snow strata. 10c, Wind gauges. 15c, Weather balloon. 20c,

Helicopter. 25c, Radio operator. 50c, Ice compression tests. $1, "Mock sun" (parahelion) and dogs. 20c, 25c, 50c and $1 horizontal.

L8	A4	1c multicolored	.70	.35
L9	A4	2c multicolored	3.00	.80
L10	A4	4c multicolored	.95	.90
L11	A4	5c multicolored	2.75	1.75
L12	A4	7c multicolored	.80	.80
L13	A4	10c multicolored	1.00	.90
L14	A4	15c multicolored	5.00	2.00
L15	A4	20c multicolored	6.25	2.50
L16	A4	25c multicolored	3.00	3.00
L17	A4	50c multicolored	4.75	5.50
L18	A4	$1 multicolored	26.00	14.00
	Nos. L8-L18 (11)		54.20	32.50

Issued: 5c, 9/25/68; others, 9/28/66.
Nos. L8-L18 are on phosphorescent helecon paper. Fluorescent orange is one of the colors used in printing the 10c, 15c, 20c and 50c.

Sastrugi Snow Formation A5

1971, June 23 Photo. Perf. 13x13½
L19	A5	6c shown	.75	.75
L20	A5	30c Pancake ice	4.25	4.25

10th anniv. of the Antarctic Treaty pledging peaceful uses of and scientific cooperation in Antarctica.

Capt. Cook, Sextant, Azimuth Compass A6

Design: 35c, Chart of Cook's circumnavigation of Antarctica, and "Resolution."

1972, Sept. 13 Photo. Perf. 13x13½
L21	A6	7c bister & multi	1.50	1.00
L22	A6	35c buff & multi	4.00	4.00

Bicentenary of Capt. James Cook's circumnavigation of Antarctica.

Plankton and Krill Shrimp — A7

Mawson's D.H. Gipsy Moth, 1931 — A8

Food Chain (Essential for Survival): 7c, Adelie penguin feeding on krill shrimp. 9c, Leopard seal pursuing fish, horiz. 10c, Killer whale hunting seals, horiz. 20c, Wandering albatross, horiz. $1, Sperm whale attacking giant squid.
Explorers' Aircraft: 8c, Rymill's DH Fox Moth returning to Barry Island. 25c, Hubert Wilkins Lockheed Vega, horiz. 30c, Lincoln Ellsworth's Northrop Gamma. 35c, Lars Christensen's Avro Avian and Framnes Mountains, horiz. 50c, Richard Byrd's Ford Tri-Motor dropping US flag over South Pole.

Perf. 13½x13, 13x13½
1973, Aug. 15
L23	A7	1c multicolored	.20	.20
L24	A8	5c multicolored	.20	.20
L25	A7	7c multicolored	1.40	.60
L26	A8	8c multicolored	.30	.30
L27	A7	9c multicolored	.25	.25
L28	A7	10c multicolored	3.00	1.25
L29	A7	20c multicolored	.35	.35
L30	A8	25c multicolored	.35	.35
L31	A8	30c multicolored	.35	.35
L32	A8	35c multicolored	.30	.45
L33	A8	50c multicolored	1.25	.85
L34	A7	$1 multicolored	2.25	.85
	Nos. L23-L34 (12)		10.20	6.00

Adm. Byrd, Plane, Mountains A9

Design: 20c, Adm. Byrd, Floyd Bennett trimotored plane, map of Antarctica.

1979, June 20 Litho. Perf. 15½
L35	A9	20c multicolored	.50	.50
L36	A9	55c multicolored	1.00	.95

50th anniv. of first flight over South Pole by Richard Byrd (1888-1957).

"S.Y. Nimrod" A10

2c, 5c, 22c, 25c, 40c, 55c, $1 are vertical. No. L41 actually pictures the S.S. Morning.

Perf. 13½x13, 13x13½
1974-81 Litho.
L37	A10	1c S.Y. Aurora	.20	.20
L38	A10	2c R.Y. Penola	.20	.20
L39	A10	5c M.V. Thala Dan	.20	.20
L40	A10	10c H.M.S. Challenger	.20	.20
L41	A10	15c shown	.95	.95
L42	A10	15c S.Y. Nimrod, stern view	.25	.20
L43	A10	20c R.R.S. Discovery II	.30	.30
L44	A10	22c R.Y.S. Terra Nova	.30	.30
L45	A10	25c S.S. Endurance	.40	.35
L46	A10	30c S.S. Fram	.50	.50
L47	A10	35c M.S. Nella Dan	.45	.40
L48	A10	40c M.S. Kista Dan	.50	.50
L49	A10	45c L'Astrolabe	.55	.55
L50	A10	50c S.S. Norvegia	.70	.70
L51	A10	55c S.Y. Discovery	.80	.80
L52	A10	$1 H.M.S. Resolution	1.25	.65
	Nos. L37-L52 (16)		7.75	7.00

A11   A12

1982, May 5 Litho. Perf. 14x13½
L53	A11	27c Mawson, landscape	.35	.35
L54	A11	75c Mawson, map	1.25	1.25

Sir Douglas Mawson (1882-1958), explorer.

1983, Apr. 6 Litho. Perf. 14½
Local Wildlife: a, Light-mantled sooty albatross. b, Macquarie Isld. shags. c, Elephant seals. d, Royal penguins. e, Antarctic prions.
L55		Strip of 5, multi	3.00	3.50
a.-e.	A12	27c, any single	.60	.70

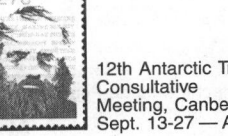

12th Antarctic Treaty Consultative Meeting, Canberra, Sept. 13-27 — A13

1983, Sept. 7 Litho. Perf. 14½
L56	A13	27c multicolored	.50	.50

South Magnetic Pole Expedition, 75th Anniv. A14

1984, Jan. 16
L57	A14	30c Prismatic compass	.50	.50
L58	A14	85c Aneroid barometer	1.25	1.50

Dog Team, Mawson Station A15

1984-87 Litho. Perf. 14½x15
L60	A15	2c Summer afternoon	.20	.20
L61	A15	5c shown	.20	.20
L62	A15	10c Evening	.20	.20
L63	A15	15c Prince Charles Mts.	.20	.20
L64	A15	20c Morning	.30	.30
L65	A15	25c Sea ice, iceberg	.40	.40
L66	A15	30c Mt. Coates	.50	.50
L67	A15	33c Iceberg Alley, Mawson	.50	.50
L68	A15	36c Winter evening	.50	.50
L69	A15	45c Brash ice, vert.	.65	.65
L70	A15	60c Midwinter shadows	.85	.85
L71	A15	75c Coastline	1.10	1.10
L72	A15	85c Landing field	1.40	1.40
L73	A15	90c Pancake ice, vert.	1.25	1.25
L74	A15	$1 Emperor penguins, Auster Rookery	1.50	1.50
	Nos. L60-L74 (15)		9.75	9.75

Issued: 5, 25, 30, 75, 85c, 7/18/84; 15, 33, 45, 90c, $1, 8/7/85; 2, 10, 20, 36, 60c, 3/11/87.

Antarctic Treaty, 25th Anniv. — A16

1986, Sept. 17 Litho. Perf. 14x13½
L75	A16	36c multicolored	.85	.75

Environment, Conservation and Technology A17

No. L76: a, Hour-glass dolphins and the Nella Dan. b, Emperor penguins and Davis Station. c, Crabeater seal and helicopters. d, Adelie penguins and snow-ice transport vehicle. e, Gray-headed albatross and photographer.

1988, July 20 Litho. Perf. 13
L76		Strip of 5	4.50	3.00
a.-e.	A17	37c any single	1.00	.75

Paintings by Sir Sidney Nolan (b. 1917) — A18

1989, June 14 Litho. Perf. 14x13½
L77	A18	39c Antarctica	.65	.65
L78	A18	39c Iceberg Alley	.65	.65
L79	A18	60c Glacial Flow	1.00	1.00
L80	A18	80c Frozen Sea	1.40	1.40
	Nos. L77-L80 (4)		3.70	3.70

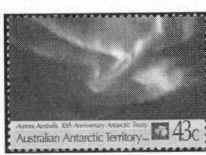

Aurora Australis A19

Design: $1.20, Research ship Aurora Australis.

1991, June 20 Litho. Perf. 14½
L81	A19	43c multicolored	.50	.50
L82	A19	$1.20 multicolored	1.75	1.75

Antarctic Treaty, 30th anniv. (No. L81).

Regional Wildlife A20

Perf. 14x14½, 14½x14
1992-93 Litho.
L83	A20	45c Adelie penguin	.60	.45
L84	A20	75c Elephant seal	.95	.70
L85	A20	85c Northern giant petrel	1.10	.75
L86	A20	95c Weddell seal	1.25	.90
L86A	A20	$1 Royal penguins	1.25	.90
L87	A20	$1.20 Emperor penguin, vert.	1.50	1.00
L88	A20	$1.40 Fur seals	1.60	1.40
L89	A20	$1.50 King penguins, vert.	1.90	1.40
	Nos. L83-L89 (8)		10.15	7.50

Issued: $1, $1.40, $1.50, 1/14/93; others, 5/14/92.

The Last Huskies A21

1994, Jan. 13 Litho. Perf. 14½
L90	A21	45c Dog up close, vert.	.65	.35
L91	A21	75c Sled team	1.10	.90
L92	A21	85c Dog seated, vert.	1.25	1.00
L93	A21	$1.05 Three dogs	1.50	1.25
	Nos. L90-L93 (4)		4.50	3.50

Whales & Dolphins A22

1995, June 15 Litho. Perf. 14½
L94	A22	45c Humpback whale	.70	.45
L95	A22	45c Hourglass dolphin, vert.	.70	.45
L96	A22	45c Minke whale, vert.	.70	.45
a.		Pair, #L95-L96	1.40	1.10
L97	A22	$1 Killer whale	1.40	1.50
a.		Souvenir sheet of 4, #L94-L97	3.50	3.50
b.		As "a," overprinted	8.00	8.00
c.		As "a," overprinted	8.00	8.00
	Nos. L94-L97 (4)		3.50	1.85

No. L97b is overprinted in gold in sheet margin with Singapore '95 emblem and: "Australia Post Exhibition Sheet No. 2," in both Chinese and English, with "Singapore 95 World Stamp Exhibition."
No. L97c is overprinted in gold in sheet margin with exhibition emblem, "Australian Post Exhibition Sheet No. 3" and "CAPEX '96 WORLD PHILATELIC EXHIBITION / EXPOSITION PHILATELIQUE MONDIALE"
Issued: #L97b, 9/1/95; #L97c, 6/15/96.

Landscapes, by Christian Clare Robertson — A23

#L98, Rafting sea ice. #L99, Shadow on the Plateau. $1, Ice cave. $1.20, Twelve Lake.

1996, May 16 Litho. Perf. 14½x14
L98	A23	45c multicolored	.70	.55
L99	A23	45c multicolored	.70	.55
a.		Pair, Nos. L98-L99	1.40	1.25
L100	A23	$1 multicolored	1.60	1.10
L101	A23	$1.20 multicolored	1.90	1.45
	Nos. L98-L101 (4)		4.90	3.45

Australian Natl. Antarctic Research Expeditions, 50th Anniv. A24

Designs: No. L102, Apple field huts. No. L103, Inside an apple hut. 95c, Summer surveying. $1.05, Sea ice research. $1.20, Remote field camp.

1997, May 15 Litho. Perf. 14x14½

L102	A24	45c multicolored	.60	.45
L103	A24	45c multicolored	.60	.45
a.		Pair, #L102-L103	1.25	1.00
L104	A24	95c multicolored	.95	.90
L105	A24	$1.05 multicolored	1.10	1.00
L106	A24	$1.20 multicolored	1.25	1.10
		Nos. L102-L106 (5)	4.50	3.90

Modes of Transportation A25

Designs: No. L107, Snowmobile. No. L108, Ship, "Aurora Australis." $1, Helicopter airlifting a four-wheel drive ATV, vert. $2, Antarctic Hagglunds (rubber-tracked vehicles with fiberglass cabins), vert.

Perf. 14x14½, 14½x14

1998, Mar. 5   Litho.

L107	A25	45c multicolored	.55	.55
L108	A25	45c multicolored	.55	.55
a.		Pair, #L107-L108	1.25	1.00
L109	A25	$1 multicolored	1.40	1.25
L110	A25	$2 multicolored	2.50	1.50
		Nos. L107-L110 (4)	5.00	3.85

Preservation of Huts used During Mawson's Antarctic Expedition A26

#L111, Photograph of Mawson, sailing ship Aurora. #L112, Photograph, "Home of the Blizzard," by Frank Hurley. 90c, Photograph, "Huskie Team," by Xavier Mertz. $1.35, Huts restoration.

1999, May 13 Litho. Perf. 14x14½

L111	A26	45c multicolored	.50	.50
L112	A26	45c multicolored	.50	.50
a.		Pair, #L111-L112	1.25	1.00
L113	A26	90c multicolored	1.25	1.25
L114	A26	$1.35 multicolored	1.75	1.75
		Nos. L111-L114 (4)	4.00	4.00

Penguins A27

2000, July 24 Litho. Perf. 13¾x14½

L115	A27	45c Emperor penguins	.55	.25
L116	A27	45c Adélie penguins	.55	.25
a.		Pair, #L115-L116	1.10	.50

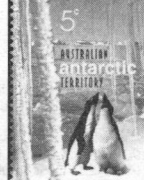

Australians in the Antarctic, Cent. — A28

No. L117: a, Penguins and icicles. b, Louis Bernacchi, physicist. c, Nimrod. d, Scientists at South Magnetic Pole. e, Griffith Taylor and Frank Debenham, geologists. f, First radio used in Antarctica. g, First flight over Antarctica. h, Sir Douglas Mawson, explorer. i, BANZARE (British, Australian and New Zealand Antarctic Research Expedition). j, Australia's claim to territory. k, Establishment of ANARE (Australian National Antarctic Research Expeditions). l, Transport. m, Aurora

Australis. n, Climate research. o, Cold-weather clothing. p, Nella Dan. q, First women on Antarctica. r, Communications. s, Tourism. t, Satellite view of Antarctica.

2001, May 17 Litho. Perf. 14¾x14

L117		Sheet of 20	4.50	4.50
a.-e.		A28 5c Any single	.20	.20
f.-j.		A28 10c Any single	.20	.20
k.-o.		A28 25c Any single	.25	.25
p.-t.		A28 45c Any single	.50	.25

Worldwide Frund for Nature (WWF) — A29

No. L118: a, Leopard seal and pup on ice. b, Leopard seal and penguin on ice. c, Penguins, two leopard seals in water. d, Penguins, leopard seal in water.

2001, Sept. 11 Litho. Perf. 14x14½

L118	A29	Block of 4	1.80	1.00
a.-d.		45c Any single	.45	.25

AUSTRIA

'os-trē-ə

LOCATION — Central Europe
GOVT. — Republic
AREA — 32,378 sq. mi.
POP. — 8,139,299 (1999 est.)
CAPITAL — Vienna

Before 1867 Austria was an absolute monarchy, which included Hungary and Lombardy-Venetia. In 1867 the Austro-Hungarian Monarchy was established, with Austria and Hungary as equal partners. After World War I, in 1918, the different nationalities established their own states and only the German-speaking parts remained, forming a republic under the name "Deutschosterreich" (German Austria), which name was shortly again changed to "Austria." In 1938 German forces occupied Austria, which became part of the German Reich. After the liberation by Allied troops in 1945, an independent republic was re-established.

60 Kreuzer = 1 Gulden
100 Neu-Kreuzer = 1 Gulden (1858)
100 Heller = 1 Krone (1899)
100 Groschen = 1 Schilling (1925)
100 Cents = 1 Euro (2002)

> Catalogue values for unused stamps in this country are for Never Hinged items, beginning with Scott 432 in the regular postage section, Scott B165 in the semi-postal section, Scott C47 in the airpost section, Scott J175 in the postage due section, and Scott 4N1 in the AMG section.

Unused stamps without gum sell for about one-third or less of the values quoted.

Watermarks

Wmk. 91 - "BRIEF-MARKEN" In Double-lined Capitals Across the Middle of the Sheet

Wmk. 140 - Crown

Issues of the Austrian Monarchy (including Hungary)

Coat of Arms — A1

NINE KREUZER
Type I. One heavy line around coat of arms center. On the 9kr the top of "9" is about on a level with "Kreuzer" and not near the top of the label. Each cliche has the "9" in a different position.
Type IA. As type I, but with 1¼mm between "9" and "K."
Type II. One heavy line around coat of arms center. On the 9kr the top of "9" is much higher than the top of the word "Kreuzer" and nearly touches the top of the label.
Type III. As type II, but with two, thinner, lines around the center.

Wmk. K.K.H.M. in Sheet or Unwmk.
1850   Typo.   Imperf.

The stamps of this issue were at first printed on a rough hand-made paper, varying in thickness and having a watermark in script letters K.K.H.M., the initials of Kaiserlich Königliches Handels-Ministerium (Imperial and Royal Ministry of Commerce), vertically in the gutter between the panes. Parts of these letters show on margin stamps in the sheet. From 1854 a thick, smooth machine-made paper without watermark was used.

Thin to Thick Paper

1	A1	1kr yellow	1,100.	75.00
a.		Printed on both sides	1,900.	125.00
b.		1kr orange	1,450.	100.00
c.		1kr brown orange	2,150.	375.00
2	A1	2kr black	950.00	60.00
a.		Ribbed paper	—	1,850.
b.		2kr gray black	1,250.	72.50
d.		Half used as 1kr on cover		25,000.
3	A1	3kr red	650.00	3.00
a.		Ribbed paper	2,600.	95.00
b.		Laid paper	—	
c.		Printed on both sides		7,500.
4	A1	6kr brown	650.00	4.25
a.		Ribbed paper		1,500.
d.		Diagonal half used as 3kr on cover		11,500.
5	A1	9kr blue, type II	1,200.	10.00
a.		9kr blue, type I	1,350.	10.50
b.		9kr blue, type IA	13,500.	1,000.
c.		Laid paper, type III		8,750.
d.		Printed on both sides, type II		7,500.

1854

Machine-made Paper, Type III

1d	A1	1kr yellow	875.00	70.00
2c	A1	2kr black	1,100.	55.00
3e	A1	3kr red	300.00	2.10
f.		3kr red, type I	2,650.	32.50
4b	A1	6kr brown	550.00	4.50
5e	A1	9kr blue	625.00	2.25

In 1852-54, Nos. 1 to 5, rouletted 14, were used in Tokay and Homonna. A 12kr blue exists, but was not issued.
The reprints are type III in brighter colors, some on paper watermarked "Briefmarken" in the sheet.
For similar design see Lombardy-Venetia A1.

Emperor Franz Josef
A2   A3   A4
A5   A6

1858-59   Embossed   Perf. 14½

Two Types of Each Value.
Type I. Loops of the bow at the back of the head broken, except the 2kr. In the 2kr, the "2" has a flat foot, thinning to the right. The frame line in the UR corner is thicker than the line below. In the 5kr the top frame line is unbroken.
Type II. Loops complete. Wreath projects further at top of head. In the 2kr, the "2" has a more curved foot of uniform thickness, with a shading line in the upper and lower curves. The frame line UR is thicker than the line below. In the 5kr the top frame line is broken.

6	A2	2kr yellow, type II	675.00	42.50
a.		2kr yellow, type I	1,750.	350.00
b.		2kr orange, type II	1,800.	225.00
c.		Half used as 1kr on cover		25,000.
7	A3	3kr black, type II	1,900.	175.00
a.		3kr black, type I	1,100.	225.00
8	A3	3kr green, type II ('59)	925.00	125.00
9	A4	5kr red, type II	225.00	.85
a.		5kr red, type I	350.00	11.50
b.		5kr red, type II with type I frame	400.00	20.00
10	A5	10kr brown, type II	550.00	2.50
a.		10kr brown, type I	625.00	27.50
b.		Half used as 5kr on cover		11,000.
11	A6	15kr blue, type II	525.00	1.75
a.		Type I	1,050.	12.50
b.		Half used as 7kr on cover		

The reprints are of type II and are perforated 10½, 11, 12, 12½ and 13. There are also imperforate reprints of Nos. 6 to 8.
For similar designs see Lombardy-Venetia A2-A6.

Franz Josef — A7   Coat of Arms — A8

1860-61   Embossed   Perf. 14

12	A7	2kr yellow	300.00	25.00
a.		Half used as 1kr on cover		12,500.
13	A7	3kr green	275.00	22.50
14	A7	5kr red	175.00	.75
15	A7	10kr brown	275.00	1.75
a.		Half used as 5kr on cover		5,500.
16	A7	15kr blue	275.00	1.00

The reprints are perforated 9, 9½, 10, 10½, 11, 11½, 12, 12½, 13 and 13½.
There are also imperforate reprints of the 2 and 3kr.

For similar design see Lombardy-Venetia A7. For overprints see Poland Nos. J11-J12.

1863

17	A8	2kr yellow	450.00	80.00
a.		Half used as 1kr on cover		12,500.
18	A8	3kr green	350.00	75.00
19	A8	5kr rose	300.00	7.00
20	A8	10kr blue	775.00	8.25
21	A8	15kr yellow brown	950.00	10.00

For similar design see Lombardy-Venetia A1.

Wmk. 91, or, before July 1864, Unwmkd.

1863-64   Perf. 9½

22	A8	2kr yellow ('64)	125.00	10.00
a.		Ribbed paper		325.00
b.		Half used as 1kr on cover		12,500.
23	A8	3kr green ('64)	125.00	10.00
a.		Ribbed paper		350.00
24	A8	5kr rose	45.00	.40
25	A8	10kr blue	140.00	2.50
a.		Half used as 5kr on cover		11,000.
26	A8	15kr yellow brown	140.00	1.50
		Nos. 22-26 (5)	575.00	24.40

The reprints are perforated 10½, 11½, 13 and 13½. There are also imperforate reprints of the 2 and 3kr.

Issues of Austro-Hungarian Monarchy

From 1867 to 1871 the independent postal administrations of Austria and Hungary used the same stamps.

A9

A10

5 kr:

Type I. In arabesques in lower left corner, the small ornament at left of the curve nearest the figure "5" is short and has three points at bottom.

Type II. The ornament is prolonged within the curve and has two points at bottom. The corresponding ornament at top of the lower left corner does not touch the curve (1872).

Type III. Similar to type II but the top ornament is joined to the curve (1881). Two different printing methods were used for the 1867-74 issues. The first produced stamps on which the hair and whiskers were coarse and thick, from the second they were fine and clear.

1867-72   Wmk. 91   Typo.   Perf. 9½
Coarse Print

27	A9	2kr yellow	85.00	1.75
a.		Half used as 1kr on cover		12,500.
28	A9	3kr green	80.00	2.00
29	A9	5kr rose, type II	50.00	.20
a.		5kr rose, type I	55.00	.20
b.		Perf. 10½, type II	125.00	
c.		Cliché of 3kr in plate of 5kr		52,500.
30	A9	10kr blue	160.00	2.25
a.		Half used as 5kr on cover		15,000.
31	A9	15kr brown	140.00	4.25
32	A9	25kr lilac	20.00	12.50
b.		25kr brown violet	125.00	32.50

Perf. 12

33	A10	50kr light brown	27.50	90.00
a.		50kr pale red brown	275.00	100.00
b.		50kr brownish rose	325.00	175.00
c.		Pair, imperf. btwn., vert. or horizontal	700.00	1,000.

Issues for Austria only
1874-80   Perf. 9½
Fine Print

34	A9	2kr yellow ('76)	7.00	.75
35	A9	3kr green ('76)	32.50	.50
36	A9	5kr rose, type III	10.00	.20
37	A9	10kr blue ('75)	67.50	.40
38	A9	15kr brown ('77)	5.00	4.00
39	A9	25kr gray lil ('78)	1.10	110.00

Perf. 9

34a	A9	2kr	175.00	40.00
35a	A9	3kr	140.00	20.00
36a	A9	5kr	50.00	2.25
37a	A9	10kr	275.00	25.00
38a	A9	15kr	350.00	70.00

Perf. 10½

34b	A9	2kr	40.00	2.75
35b	A9	3kr	60.00	1.75
36b	A9	5kr	9.00	.75
37b	A9	10kr	140.00	2.25
38b	A9	15kr	175.00	16.00

Perf. 12

34c	A9	2kr	175.00	87.50
35c	A9	3kr	160.00	14.00
36c	A9	5kr	35.00	3.25
37c	A9	10kr	325.00	90.00
38c	A9	15kr	425.00	125.00
40	A10	50kr brown ('80)	16.00	100.00

Perf. 13

34d	A9	2kr	210.00	210.00
35d	A9	3kr	140.00	25.00
36d	A9	5kr	70.00	12.50
37d	A9	10kr	175.00	60.00
38d	A9	15kr	425.00	275.00
40a	A10	50kr	21.00	140.00

Perf. 9x10½

34e	A9	2kr	225.00	40.00
35e	A9	3kr	175.00	35.00
36e	A9	5kr	62.50	19.00
37e	A9	10kr	200.00	50.00

Various compound perforations exist.

Values are for stamps that do not show the watermark. Stamps showing the watermark often sell for more.

For similar designs see Offices in the Turkish Empire A1-A2.

A11

Perf. 9, 9½, 10, 10½, 11½, 12, 12½
1883
Inscriptions in Black

41	A11	2kr brown	5.50	.50
42	A11	3kr green	4.75	.30
43	A11	5kr rose	11.00	.25
a.		Vert. pair, imperf. btwn.	250.00	350.00
44	A11	10kr blue	4.25	.35
45	A11	20kr gray	55.00	3.25
46	A11	50kr red lilac	300.00	52.50

The last printings of Nos. 41-46 are watermarked "ZEITUNGS-MARKEN" instead of "BRIEF-MARKEN." Values are for stamps that do not show watermark. Stamps with watermarks that are identifiable as being from "BRIEF-MARKEN" sheets often sell for slightly more, while those with watermarks identifying stamps from "ZEITUNGS-MARKEN" sheets often sell for considerably more.

The 5kr has been reprinted in a dull red rose, perforated 10½.

For similar design see Offices in the Turkish Empire A3.

For surcharges see Offices in the Turkish Empire Nos. 15-19.

A12

A13

Perf. 9 to 13½, also Compound
1890-96   Unwmk.
Granite Paper
Numerals in black, Nos. 51-61

51	A12	1kr dark gray	1.25	.25
a.		Pair, imperf. between	160.00	350.00
52	A12	2kr light brown	.25	.25
53	A12	3kr gray green	.40	.25
a.		Pair, imperf. between	175.00	425.00
54	A12	5kr rose	.40	.25
a.		Pair, imperf. between	160.00	325.00
55	A12	10kr ultramarine	.75	.25
a.		Pair, imperf. between	210.00	425.00
56	A12	12kr claret	2.00	.35
a.		Pair, imperf. between		
57	A12	15kr lilac	1.40	.35
a.		Pair, imperf. between	210.00	425.00
58	A12	20kr olive green	30.00	2.00
59	A12	24kr gray blue	2.00	1.25
a.		Pair, imperf. between	225.00	425.00
60	A12	30kr dark brown	2.50	.65
61	A12	50kr violet	5.00	7.50

Engr.

62	A13	1gld dark blue	1.50	2.25
63	A13	1gld pale lilac ('96)	35.00	3.50
64	A13	2gld carmine	3.50	12.50
65	A13	2gld gray green ('96)	15.00	27.50
		Nos. 51-65 (15)	100.95	59.10

Nearly all values of the 1890-1907 issues are found with numerals missing in one or more corners, some with numerals printed on the back.

For surcharges see Offices in the Turkish Empire Nos. 20-25, 28-31.

A14

Perf. 9 to 13½, also Compound
1891   Typo.
Numerals in black

66	A14	20kr olive green	2.25	.25
67	A14	24kr gray blue	4.50	.75
68	A14	30kr brown	2.25	.25
a.		Pair, imperf. between	225.00	350.00
b.		Perf. 9	90.00	32.50
69	A14	50kr violet	2.75	.40
		Nos. 66-69 (4)	11.75	1.65

For surcharges see Offices in the Turkish Empire Nos. 26-27.

A15

A16

A17

A18

Perf. 10½ to 13½ and Compound
1899
Without Varnish Bars
Numerals in black, Nos. 70-82

70	A15	1h lilac	.55	.20
b.		Imperf.	110.00	200.00
c.		Perf. 10½	15.00	4.50
d.		Numerals inverted	375.00	950.00
71	A15	2h dark gray	2.50	.50
72	A15	3h bister brown	5.00	.20
b.		"3" in lower right corner sideways		1,100.
73	A15	5h blue green	7.25	.20
c.		Perf. 10½	10.50	2.75
74	A15	6h orange	.40	.20
75	A16	10h rose	8.00	.20
b.		Perf. 10½	300.00	125.00
76	A16	20h brown	.60	.20
77	A16	25h ultramarine	50.00	.30
78	A16	30h red violet	14.50	2.25
b.		Horiz. pair, imperf. between	275.00	
80	A17	40h green	25.00	2.50
81	A17	50h gray blue	16.00	3.50
b.		All four "50's" parallel		1,600.
82	A17	60h brown	35.00	1.00
b.		Horiz. pair, imperf. btwn.	275.00	—
c.		Perf. 10½	50.00	1.50

Engr.

83	A18	1k carmine rose	2.25	.20
a.		1k carmine	5.00	.20
b.		Vert. pair, imperf. btwn.	275.00	300.00
84	A18	2k gray lilac	45.00	.40
a.		Vert. pair, imperf. btwn.	275.00	500.00
85	A18	4k gray green	4.00	10.00
		Nos. 70-85 (15)	216.05	21.85

For surcharges see Offices in Crete Nos. 1-7, Offices in the Turkish Empire Nos. 32-45.

1901   With Varnish Bars

70a	A15	1h lilac	1.75	.40
71a	A15	2h dark gray	1.75	.35
72a	A15	3h bister brown	.35	.20
73a	A15	5h blue green	.20	.20
74a	A15	6h orange	.20	.20
75a	A16	10h rose	.25	.20
76a	A16	20h brown	.65	.20
77a	A16	25h ultra	.85	.20
78a	A16	30h red violet	1.75	.90
79	A17	35h green	.85	.40
80a	A17	40h green	1.60	3.25

81a	A17	50h gray blue	4.00	6.75
82a	A17	60h brown	2.00	.65
		Nos. 70a-78a,79,80a-82a (13)	16.20	13.90

The diagonal yellow bars of varnish were printed across the face to prevent cleaning.

A19

A20

A21

Perf. 12½ to 13½ and Compound
1905-07   Typo.
Colored Numerals
Without Varnish Bars

86	A19	1h lilac	.20	.35
87	A19	2h dark gray	.20	.20
88	A19	3h bister brown	.20	.20
89	A19	5h dk blue green	8.50	.20
90	A19	5h yellow grn ('06)	.40	.20
91	A19	6h deep orange	.40	.20
92	A20	10h carmine ('06)	.45	.20
93	A20	12h violet ('07)	1.00	.65
94	A20	20h brown ('06)	2.75	.20
95	A20	25h ultra	3.50	.35
96	A20	30h red violet ('06)	6.00	.25

Black Numerals

97	A20	10h carmine	10.50	.20
98	A20	20h brown	35.00	1.75
99	A20	25h ultra	32.50	2.75
100	A20	30h red violet	52.50	1.50

White Numerals

101	A21	35h green	2.25	.25
102	A21	40h deep violet	2.25	.75
103	A21	50h dull blue	2.75	2.25
104	A21	60h yellow brown	2.75	.60
105	A21	72h rose	2.75	1.60
		Nos. 86-105 (20)	166.85	14.65

For surcharges see Offices in Crete #8-14.

1904
With Varnish Bars

86a	A19	1h lilac	.55	1.00
87a	A19	2h dark gray	1.60	.55
88a	A19	3h bister brown	1.75	.20
89a	A19	5h dk blue green	3.50	.20
91a	A19	6h deep orange	7.75	.30
97a	A20	10h carmine	2.25	.20
98a	A20	20h brown	32.50	.75
99a	A20	25h ultra	35.00	.75
100a	A20	30h red violet	40.00	1.50
101a	A21	35h green	32.50	.60
102a	A21	40h deep violet	30.00	3.50
103a	A21	50h dull blue	30.00	7.00
104a	A21	60h yellow brown	35.00	1.10
105a	A21	72h rose	1.10	1.10
		Nos. 86a-105a (14)	253.50	18.75

Stamps of the 1901, 1904 and 1905 issues perf. 9 or 10½, also compound with 12½, were not sold at any post office, but were supplied only to some high-ranking officials. This applies also to the contemporary issues of Austrian Offices Abroad.

Karl VI — A22

Franz Josef — A23

Schönbrunn Castle — A24

Franz Josef — A25

Designs: 2h, Maria Theresa. 3h, Joseph II. 5h, 10h, 25h, Franz Josef. 6h, Leopold II. 12h, Franz I. 20h, Ferdinand I. 30h, Franz Josef as youth. 35h, Franz Josef in middle age. 60h, Franz Josef on horseback. 1k, Franz Josef in royal robes. 5k, Hofburg, Vienna.

			Typo.	Perf. 12½
1908-13				
110	A22	1h gray black	.30	.65
111	A22	2h blue vio ('13)	.20	.45
a.		2h violet	.20	.20
112	A22	3h magenta	.20	.20
113	A22	5h yellow green	.20	.20
a.		Booklet pane of 6	25.00	
114	A22	6h buff	.60	.60
b.		6h orange brown ('13)	1.50	1.25
115	A22	10h rose	.20	.20
a.		Booklet pane of 6	75.00	
116	A22	12h scarlet	1.50	1.40
117	A22	20h chocolate	1.60	.20
118	A22	25h ultra ('13)	1.40	.25
a.		25h deep blue	2.50	.25
119	A22	30h olive green	3.75	.30
120	A22	35h slate	3.50	.35
		Engr.		
121	A23	50h dark green	.65	.20
a.		Vert. pair, imperf. btwn.	190.00	275.00
b.		Horiz. pair, imperf. btwn.	190.00	275.00
122	A23	60h deep carmine	.35	.20
a.		Vert. pair, imperf. btwn.	275.00	325.00
b.		Horiz. pair, imperf. btwn.	275.00	325.00
123	A23	72h dk brown ('13)	1.75	.30
124	A23	1k purple	12.00	.20
a.		Vert. pair, imperf. btwn.	190.00	275.00
b.		Horiz. pair, imperf. btwn.	190.00	275.00
125	A24	2k lake & ol grn	18.00	.35
126	A24	5k bister & dk vio	35.00	4.00
127	A25	10k blue, bis & dp brn	160.00	50.00
		Nos. 110-127 (18)	241.20	60.05
		Set, never hinged	540.00	

Definitive set issued for the 60th year of the reign of Emperor Franz Josef.

The 1h-35h exist on both ordinary (1913) and chalk-surfaced (1908) paper.

All values exist imperforate. They were not sold at any post office, but presented to a number of high government officials. This applies also to all imperforate stamps of later issues, including semi-postals, etc., and those of the Austrian Offices Abroad.

Litho. forgeries of No. 127 exist.

For overprint and surcharge see #J47-J48.

For similar designs see Offices in Crete A5-A6, Offices in the Turkish Empire A16-A17.

Birthday Jubilee Issue

Similar to 1908 Issue, but designs enlarged by labels at top and bottom bearing dates "1830" and "1910"

				Typo.
1910				
128	A22	1h gray black	4.00	6.25
129	A22	2h violet	5.00	7.75
130	A22	3h magenta	4.50	6.75
131	A22	5h yellow green	.20	.20
132	A22	6h buff	2.50	5.00
133	A22	10h rose	.20	.20
134	A22	12h scarlet	3.00	6.50
135	A22	20h chocolate	5.50	6.25
136	A22	25h deep blue	1.25	1.25
137	A22	30h olive green	3.25	4.50
138	A22	35h slate	3.25	4.50
		Engr.		
139	A23	50h dark green	4.50	8.00
140	A23	60h deep carmine	4.50	8.00
141	A23	1k purple	4.50	9.00
142	A24	2k lake & ol grn	125.00	190.00
143	A24	5k bister & dk vio	92.50	150.00

144	A25	10k blue, bis & dp brn	175.00	275.00
		Nos. 128-144 (17)	438.65	689.15
		Set, never hinged	725.00	

80th birthday of Emperor Franz Josef. All values exist imperforate. Litho. forgeries of Nos. 142-144 exist.

Austrian Crown — A37

Franz Josef — A38

A39

Coat of Arms — A40

				Typo.
1916-18				
145	A37	3h brt violet	.20	.20
146	A37	5h lt green	.20	.20
a.		Booklet pane of 6	14.00	
b.		Booklet pane of 4 + 2 labels	27.50	
147	A37	6h deep orange	.25	.65
148	A37	10h magenta	.20	.20
a.		Booklet pane of 6	27.50	
149	A37	12h light blue	.30	1.10
150	A38	15h rose red	.40	.20
a.		Booklet pane of 6	15.00	
151	A38	20h chocolate	3.25	.20
152	A38	25h blue	5.00	.40
153	A38	30h slate	4.50	.65
154	A39	40h olive green	.20	.20
155	A39	50h blue green	.20	.20
156	A39	60h deep blue	.20	.20
157	A39	80h orange brown	.20	.20
158	A39	90h red violet	.20	.20
159	A39	1k car, yel ('18)	.30	.20
		Engr.		
160	A40	2k dark blue	.55	.20
161	A40	3k claret	9.00	.90
162	A40	4k deep green	1.75	1.75
163	A40	10k deep violet	21.00	35.00
		Nos. 145-163 (19)	47.90	42.85
		Set, never hinged	110.00	

Stamps of type A38 have two varieties of the frame. Stamps of type A40 have various decorations about the shield.

Nos. 145-163 exist imperf. Value, set $400.

				Ordinary Paper
1917				
164	A40	2k light blue	.75	.50
165	A40	3k carmine rose	10.00	.75
166	A40	4k yellow green	1.10	1.10
167	A40	10k violet	90.00	70.00
		Nos. 164-167 (4)	101.85	72.35
		Set, never hinged	225.00	

Nos. 164-167 exist imperf. Value, set $250.

See Nos. 172-175 (granite paper). For overprints and surcharges see Nos. 181-199, C1-C3, J60-J63, N1-N5, N10-N19, N33-N37, N42-N51. Western Ukraine 2-7, 11-15, 19-28, 57-58, 85-89, 94-103, N3-N14, NJ13.

Emperor Karl I — A42

				Typo.
1917-18				
168	A42	15h dull red	.20	.20
a.		Booklet pane of 6	14.00	
169	A42	20h dk green ('18)	.20	.20
a.		20h green ('17)	.55	.20
170	A42	25h blue	.70	.20
171	A42	30h dull violet	.75	.20
		Nos. 168-171 (4)	1.85	.80
		Set, never hinged	5.75	

Nos. 168-171 exist imperf. Value, set $40.

For overprints and surcharges see Nos. N6-N9, N20, N38-N41, N52, N64. Western Ukraine 1, 8, 16-18, 90-93, N15-N18.

				Engr.
1918-19				
Granite Paper				
172	A40	2k light blue	.20	.45
a.		Perf. 11½	450.00	525.00
		Never hinged, #172a	750.00	
173	A40	3k carmine rose	.25	1.10
174	A40	4k yellow green ('19)	4.00	13.50
175	A40	10k lt violet ('19)	7.50	16.00
		Nos. 172-175 (4)	11.95	31.05
		Set, never hinged	17.50	

Issues of the Republic

Austrian Stamps of 1916-18 Overprinted

			Unwmk.	Perf. 12½
1918-19				
181	A37	3h bright violet	.20	.20
182	A37	5h light green	.20	.20
183	A37	6h deep orange	.20	1.10
184	A37	10h magenta	.20	.20
185	A37	12h light blue	.25	1.25
186	A42	15h dull red	.20	1.00
187	A42	20h deep green	.20	.20
188	A42	25h blue	.20	.20
189	A42	30h dull violet	.20	.20
190	A39	40h olive green	.20	.20
191	A39	50h deep green	.45	1.10
192	A39	60h deep blue	.45	1.75
193	A39	80h orange brown	.20	.20
a.		Inverted overprint	200.00	
		Never hinged, #193a	275.00	
194	A39	90h red violet	.20	.45
195	A39	1k carmine, yel	.20	.25
		Granite Paper		
196	A40	2k light blue	.20	.20
a.		Pair, imperf. between	240.00	
		Never hinged, #196a	325.00	
b.		Perf. 11½	65.00	62.50
		Never hinged, #196b	100.00	
197	A40	3k carmine rose	.30	.75
198	A40	4k yellow green	.80	1.90
a.		Perf. 11½	16.00	25.00
		Never hinged, #198a	27.50	
199	A40	10k deep violet	7.25	17.50
		Nos. 181-199 (19)	12.10	28.85
		Set, never hinged	20.00	

Nos. 181, 182, 184, 187-191, 194, 197 and 199 exist imperforate.

Post Horn — A43

Coat of Arms — A44

Allegory of New Republic — A45

			Typo.	Perf. 12½
1919-20				
Ordinary Paper				
200	A43	3h gray	.20	.20
201	A44	5h yellow green	.20	.20
202	A44	5h gray ('20)	.20	.20
203	A43	6h orange	.20	.45
204	A44	10h deep rose	.20	.20
205	A44	10h red ('20)	.20	.20
a.		Thick grayish paper ('20)	.20	.20
206	A43	12h grnsh blue	.20	.65
207	A43	15h bister ('20)	.20	.55
a.		Thick grayish paper ('20)	.20	.20
208	A45	20h dark green	.20	.20
a.		20h yellow green	.20	.20
b.		As "a," thick grysh paper ('20)	.50	2.00
209	A44	25h blue	.20	.20
210	A43	25h violet ('20)	.20	.20
211	A45	30h dark brown	.20	.20
212	A45	40h violet	.20	.20
213	A44	40h with lake ('20)	.20	.60
214	A44	45h olive green	.20	.60
215	A45	50h dark blue	.20	.20
a.		Thick grayish paper ('20)	.25	.55
216	A43	60h olive green ('20)	.20	.20
217	A44	1k carmine, yel	.20	.20
218	A44	1k light blue ('20)	.20	.20
		Nos. 200-218 (19)	3.80	5.25
		Set, never hinged	4.25	

All values exist imperf. (For regularly issued imperfs, see Nos. 227-235.)

For overprints and surcharge see Nos. B11-B19, B30-B38, J102, N21, N27, N53, N58, N65, N71.

Parliament Building A46

			Engr.	Perf. 12½, 11½
1919-20				
Granite Paper				
219	A46	2k ver & blk	.25	.55
a.		Center inverted	3,650.	
220	A46	2½k olive bis ('20)	.20	.25
221	A46	3k blue & blk brn	.20	.20
222	A46	4k carmine & blk	.20	.20
a.		Center inverted	1,750.	1,400.
223	A46	5k black ('20)	.20	.20
a.		Perf. 11½x12½	45.00	67.50
224	A46	7½k plum	.20	.35
a.		Perf. 11½	110.00	160.00
b.		Perf. 11½x12½	75.00	125.00
225	A46	10k olive grn & blk brn	.20	.35
a.		Perf. 11½x12½	125.00	175.00
b.		Perf. 11½	14.50	25.00
226	A46	20k lil & red ('20)	.20	.45
a.		Center inverted	10,500.	6,250.
b.		Perf. 11½	62.50	110.00
		Nos. 219-226 (8)	1.65	2.55
		Set, never hinged	2.10	

A number of values exist imperforate between. Values, $300 to $400 a pair.

See No. 248. For overprints and surcharge see Nos. B23-B29, B43-B49, N30, N60, N74.

			Typo.	Imperf.
1920				
Ordinary Paper				
227	A44	5h yellow green	.20	.50
228	A44	5h gray	.20	.20
229	A44	10h deep rose	.20	.20
230	A44	10h red	.20	.20
231	A43	15h bister	.20	.20
232	A43	25h violet	.20	.20
233	A45	30h dark brown	.20	.20
234	A45	40h violet	.20	.20
235	A43	60h olive green	.20	.20
		Nos. 227-235 (9)		2.10
		Set, never hinged	1.80	

Arms

A47 A48

			Typo.	Perf. 12½
1920-21				
Ordinary Paper				
238	A47	80h rose	.20	.20
239	A47	1k black brown	.20	.20
241	A47	1½k green ('21)	.20	.20
242	A47	2k blue	.20	.30
243	A48	3k yel grn & dk grn ('21)	.20	.30
244	A48	4k red & claret ('21)	.20	.20
245	A48	5k vio & claret ('21)	.20	.20
246	A48	7½k yel & brn ('21)	.20	.25
247	A48	10k ultra & blue ('21)	.20	.20
		Nos. 238-247 (9)	1.80	2.05
		Set, never hinged	2.25	

Nos. 238-245, 247 exist on white paper of good quality and on thick grayish paper of inferior quality; No. 246 only on white paper.

For overprints and surcharges see Nos. B20-B22, B39-B42, N22-N23, N31, N54-N55, N61-N62, N66-N67.

				Engr.
1921				
248	A46	50k dk violet, yel	.35	.80
		Never hinged	.60	
a.		Perf. 11½	15.00	50.00
		Never hinged	25.00	

Symbols of Agriculture A49

Symbols of Labor and Industry A50

1922-24 — Typo. — Perf. 12½

250	A49	½k olive bister	.20	.60
251	A50	1k brown	.20	.20
252	A50	2k cobalt blue	.20	.20
253	A49	2½k orange brown	.20	.20
254	A50	4k dull violet	.20	1.00
255	A50	5k gray green	.20	.20
256	A49	7½k gray violet	.20	.20
257	A50	10k claret	.20	.20
258	A49	12½k green	.20	.20
259	A49	15k bluish green	.20	.20
260	A50	20k dark blue	.20	.20
261	A50	25k claret	.20	.20
262	A50	30k pale gray	.20	.20
263	A50	45k pale red	.20	.20
264	A50	50k orange brown	.20	.20
265	A50	60k yellow green	.20	.20
266	A50	75k ultramarine	.20	.20
267	A50	80k yellow	.20	.20
268	A49	100k gray	.20	.20
269	A49	120k brown	.20	.20
270	A49	150k orange	.20	.20
271	A49	160k light green	.20	.20
272	A49	180k red	.20	.20
273	A49	200k pink	.20	.20
274	A49	240k dark violet	.20	.20
275	A49	300k light blue	.20	.20
276	A49	400k deep green	.85	.90
a.		400k gray green	.85	.30
277	A49	500k yellow	.20	.20
278	A49	600k slate	.20	.20
279	A49	700k brown ('24)	.70	.20
280	A49	800k violet ('24)	.80	1.50
281	A50	1000k violet ('23)	.55	.20
282	A50	1200k car rose ('23)	.35	.45
283	A50	1500k orange ('24)	1.00	.20
284	A50	1600k slate ('23)	2.75	2.75
285	A50	2000k dp bl ('23)	3.50	1.50
286	A50	3000k lt blue ('23)	11.00	1.75
287	A50	4000k dk bl, *bl* ('24)	5.00	2.10
		Nos. 250-287 (38)	32.10	17.65
		Set, never hinged	92.50	

Nos. 250-287 exist imperf. Value, set $500.
For overprints & surcharges see #N24-N26, N28-N29, N32, N56, N59, N63, N68-N70, N72-N73.

Symbols of Art and Science — A51

1922-24 — Engr. — Perf. 12½

288	A51	20k dark brn	.20	.20
a.		Perf. 11½	1.10	1.25
		Never hinged, #288a	1.60	
289	A51	25k blue	.20	.20
a.		Perf. 11½	1.00	2.50
		Never hinged, #289a	1.90	
290	A51	50k brown red	.20	.20
a.		Perf. 11½	2.25	3.50
		Never hinged, #290a	3.75	
b.		Vert. pair, imperf. btwn.	200.00	250.00
		Never hinged	250.00	
291	A51	100k deep grn	.20	.20
a.		Perf. 11½	5.50	7.00
		Never hinged, #291a	8.00	
b.		Vert. pair, imperf. btwn.	—	375.00
292	A51	200k dark violet	.20	.20
a.		Perf. 11½	8.00	13.50
		Never hinged, #292a	12.00	
b.		Vert. pair, imperf. btwn.	300.00	
		Never hinged	375.00	
293	A51	500k dp orange	.20	1.00
294	A51	1000k blk vio, *yel*	.20	.20
a.		Perf. 11½	160.00	250.00
		Never hinged, #294a	400.00	
b.		Vert. pair, imperf. btwn.	240.00	
		Never hinged	300.00	
c.		Horiz. pair, imperf. btwn.	300.00	
		Never hinged	375.00	
295	A51	2000k olive grn, *yel*	.20	.20
a.		Vert. pair, imperf. btwn.	275.00	
		Never hinged	325.00	
296	A51	3000k claret brn ('23)	8.00	.65
297	A51	5000k gray black ('23)	1.50	1.50

Granite Paper

298	A51	10,000k red brown ('24)	3.25	4.00
		Nos. 288-298 (11)	14.35	8.55
		Set, never hinged	35.00	

On Nos. 281-287, 291-298 "kronen" is abbreviated to "k" and transposed with the numerals.
Nos. 288-298 exist imperf. Value, set $375.

Numeral A52

Fields Crossed by Telegraph Wires A53

White-Shouldered Eagle — A54

Church of Minorite Friars — A55

1925-27 — Typo. — Perf. 12

303	A52	1g dark gray	.20	.20
304	A52	2g claret	.35	.20
305	A52	3g scarlet	.70	.20
306	A52	4g grnsh blue ('27)	1.10	.20
307	A52	5g brown orange	1.50	.20
308	A52	6g ultramarine	1.25	.20
309	A52	7g chocolate	1.50	.20
310	A52	8g yellow green	5.75	.20
311	A53	10g orange	.35	.20
312	A53	12g blue	.35	.20
313	A53	15g red lilac	.35	.20
314	A53	16g dark blue	.35	.20
315	A53	18g olive green	1.10	.55
316	A54	20g dark violet	.35	.20
317	A54	24g carmine	.70	.40
318	A54	30g dark brown	.55	.20
319	A54	40g ultramarine	1.10	.20
320	A54	45g yellow brown	1.25	.20
321	A54	50g gray	1.50	.25
322	A54	80g turquoise blue	3.25	4.50

Perf. 12½

Engr.

323	A55	1s deep green	15.00	1.40
a.		1s light green	210.00	8.25
		Never hinged, #323a	625.00	
324	A55	2s brown rose	6.25	10.00
		Nos. 303-324 (21)	44.45	20.10
		Set, never hinged	140.00	

#303-305, 307-324 exist imperf. Value, set $400.
For type A52 surcharged see Nos. B118.

Güssing — A56

National Library, Vienna — A57

15g, Hochosterwitz. 16g, 20g, Durnstein. 18g, Traunsee. 24g, Salzburg. 30g, Seewiesen. 40g, Innsbruck. 50g, Worthersee. 60g, Hohenems. 2s, St. Stephen's Cathedral, Vienna.

1929-30 — Typo. — Perf. 12½
Size: 25½x21½mm

326	A56	10g brown orange	.90	.20
327	A56	10g bister ('30)	.90	.20
328	A56	15g violet brown	.70	1.25
329	A56	16g dark gray	1.75	.20
330	A56	18g blue green	.40	.45
331	A56	20g dark gray ('30)	.40	.20
332	A56	24g maroon	4.25	6.00
333	A56	24g lake ('30)	6.50	.45
334	A56	30g dark violet	4.25	.20
335	A56	40g dark blue	7.25	.20
336	A56	50g gray violet ('30)	27.50	.20
337	A56	60g olive green	22.50	.25

Engr.
Size: 21x26mm

338	A57	1s black brown	5.25	.25
a.		Horiz. pair, imperf. btwn.	240.00	
		Never hinged	300.00	
b.		Vert. pair, imperf. btwn.	240.00	
		Never hinged	300.00	

339	A57	2s dark green	9.25	8.75
a.		Horiz. pair, imperf. btwn.	240.00	
		Never hinged	300.00	
		Nos. 326-339 (14)	91.80	18.80
		Set, never hinged	290.00	

Type of 1929-30 Issue
Designs: 12g, Traunsee. 64g, Hohenems.

1932 — Perf. 12
Size: 21x16½mm

340	A56	10g olive brown	.80	.20
341	A56	12g blue green	1.50	.20
342	A56	18g blue green	1.40	2.10
343	A56	20g dark gray	1.10	.20
344	A56	24g carmine rose	5.25	.20
345	A56	24g dull violet	3.50	.20
346	A56	30g dark violet	17.50	.20
347	A56	30g carmine rose	4.25	.20
a.		Vert. pair, imperf. btwn.	40.00	
		Never hinged, #347a	50.00	
348	A56	40g dark blue	19.00	.90
349	A56	40g dark violet	6.25	.30
350	A56	50g gray violet	24.00	.30
351	A56	50g dull blue	5.75	.30
352	A56	60g gray green	52.50	2.50
353	A56	64g gray green	12.00	.30
		Nos. 340-353 (14)	154.80	8.10
		Set, never hinged	500.00	

For overprints and surcharges see Nos. B87-B92, B119-B121.

Burgenland A67

Tyrol A68

Costumes of various districts: 3g, Burgenland. 4g, 5g, Carinthia. 6g, 8g, Lower Austria. 12g, 20g, Upper Austria. 24g, 25g, Salzburg. 30g, 35g, Styria. 45g, Tyrol. 60g, Vorarlberg bridal couple. 64g, Vorarlberg. 1s, Viennese family. 2s, Military.

1934-35 — Typo. — Perf. 12

354	A67	1g dark violet	.20	.20
355	A67	3g scarlet	.20	.20
356	A67	4g olive green	.20	.20
357	A67	5g red violet	.20	.20
358	A67	6g ultramarine	.20	.25
359	A67	8g green	.20	.20
360	A67	12g dark brown	.20	.20
361	A67	20g yellow brown	.20	.20
362	A67	24g grnsh blue	.20	.20
363	A67	25g violet	.20	.25
364	A67	30g maroon	.20	.20
365	A67	35g rose carmine	.30	.45

Perf. 12½

366	A68	40g slate gray	.40	.25
367	A68	45g brown red	.35	.20
368	A68	60g ultramarine	.60	.35
369	A68	64g brown	.75	.20
370	A68	1s deep violet	.90	.55
371	A68	2s dull green	35.00	65.00

Designs Redrawn
Perf. 12 (6g), 12½ (2s)

372	A67	6g ultra ('35)	.20	.20
373	A68	2s emerald ('35)	3.25	5.25
		Nos. 354-373 (20)	43.95	74.75
		Set, never hinged	110.00	

The design of No. 358 looks as though the man's ears were on backwards, while No. 372 appears correctly.
On No. 373 there are seven feathers on each side of the eagle instead of five.
Nos. 354-373 exist imperf. Value, set $375.
For surcharges see Nos. B128-B131.

Dollfuss Mourning Issue

Engelbert Dollfuss — A85

1934-35 — Engr. — Perf. 12½

374	A85	24g greenish black	.40	.30
		Never hinged	1.25	
375	A85	24g indigo ('35)	.75	.70
		Never hinged	2.50	

"Mother and Child," by Joseph Danhauser A86

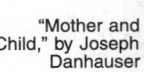

"Madonna and Child," after Painting by Dürer — A87

1935, May 1

376	A86	24g dark blue	.40	.20
		Never hinged	1.00	
a.		Vert. pair, imperf. btwn.	200.00	
		Never hinged	250.00	
b.		Horiz. pair, imperf. btwn.	190.00	
		Never hinged	240.00	

Mother's Day. Nos. 376-377 exist imperf. Value, each $150.

1936, May 5   Photo.
377 A87 24g violet blue   .20 .30
    Never hinged   .55

Mother's Day.

Farm
Workers — A88

Design: 5s, Factory workers.

1936, June   Engr.   Perf. 12½
378 A88 3s red orange   12.50 17.50
    Never hinged   24.00
379 A88 5s brown black   30.00 42.50
    Never hinged   45.00

Nos. 378-379 exist imperf. Value, set $210.

Engelbert
Dollfuss
A90

Mother and
Child — A91

1936, July 25
380 A90 10s dark blue   675.00 800.00
    Never hinged   900.00

Second anniv. of death of Engelbert Dollfuss, chancellor. Exists imperf. Value, $1,750.

1937, May 5   Photo.   Perf. 12
381 A91 24g henna brown   .20 .25
    Never hinged   .55

Mother's Day. Exists imperf. Value, $140.

S.S.
Maria
Anna
A92

Steamships: 24g, Uranus, 64g, Oesterreich.

1937, June 9
382 A92 12g red brown   .60 .35
383 A92 24g deep blue   .60 .35
384 A92 64g dark green   .60 .80
   Nos. 382-384 (3)   1.80 1.50
   Set, never hinged   5.00

Cent. of steamship service on Danube River. Exist imperf. Value, set $350.

First
Locomotive,
"Austria"
A95

Designs: 25g, Modern steam locomotive. 35g, Modern electric train.

1937, Nov. 22
385 A95 12g black brown   .20 .20
386 A95 25g dark violet   .65 1.00
387 A95 35g brown red   1.60 2.25
   Nos. 385-387 (3)   2.45 3.45
   Set, never hinged   7.00

Centenary of Austrian railways. Exist imperf. Value, set $90.

Rose and Zodiac
Signs — A98

1937   Engr.   Perf. 13x12½
388 A98 12g dark green   .20 .20
389 A98 24g dark carmine   .20 .20
   Set, never hinged   .40

For Use in Vienna, Lower Austria and Burgenland
Germany Nos. 509-511 and 511B
Overprinted in Black

a   b

1945   Unwmk.   Perf. 14
390 A115(a) 5pf dp yellow green   .20 .20
391 A115(b) 6pf purple   .20 .20
392 A115(a) 8pf red   .20 .20
393 A115(b) 12pf carmine   .20 .20
   Nos. 390-393 (4)   .80 .80
   Set, never hinged   .80

Nos. 390-393 exist with overprint inverted or double.
Germany No. 507, the 3pf, with overprint "a" was prepared, not issued, but sold to collectors after the definitive Republic issue had been placed in use. Value $30, hinged, $60, never hinged.

German Semi-Postal Stamps, #B207, B209, B210, B283 Surcharged in Black

c

d

1945   Perf. 14, 14x13½, 13½x14
394 SP181(c) 5pf on 12pf + 88pf   .50 1.50
395 SP184(d) 6pf on 6pf + 14pf   2.50 11.00
396 SP242(d) 8pf on 42pf + 108pf   .50 1.50
397 SP183(d) 12pf on 3pf + 7pf   .50 1.50
   Nos. 394-397 (4)   4.00 15.50
   Set, never hinged   10.00

The surcharges are spaced to fit the stamps.

Stamps of Germany, Nos. 509 to 511, 511B, 519 and 529 Overprinted

e   f

1945   Typo.   Perf. 14
Size: 18½x22½mm
398 A115(e) 5pf dp yel grn   .25 .45
399 A115(f) 5pf dp yel grn   4.00 7.75
400 A115(e) 6pf purple   .20 .35
401 A115(e) 8pf red   .20 .35
402 A115(e) 12pf carmine   .20 .35

Engr.
Size: 21½x26mm
403 A115(e) 30pf olive green   6.25 10.00
   a.   Thin bar at bottom   15.00 17.50
   a.   Never hinged   25.00
404 A118(e) 42pf brt green   15.00 32.50
   a.   Thin bar at bottom   15.00 27.50
   a.   Never hinged   25.00
   Nos. 398-404 (7)   26.10 51.75
   Set, never hinged   55.00

On Nos. 403a and 404a, the bottom bar of the overprint is 2½mm wide, and, as the overprint was applied in two operations, "Osterreich" is usually not exactly centered in its diagonal slot. On Nos. 403 and 404, the bottom bar is 3mm wide, and "Osterreich" is always well centered.
Germany Nos. 524-527 (the 1m, 2m, 3m and 5m), overprinted with vertical bars and "Osterreich" similar to "e" and "f," were prepared, not issued, but sold to collectors after the definitive Republic issue had been placed in use. Value for set, $70 hinged, $150 ever hinged.
Counterfeits exist of Nos. 403-404, 403a-404a and 1m-5m overprints.

For Use in Styria
Stamps of Germany Nos. 506 to 511, 511A, 511B, 514 to 523 and 529
Overprinted in Black

1945   Unwmk.   Typo.   Perf. 14
Size: 18½x22½mm
405 A115 1pf gray black   1.50 3.00
406 A115 3pf lt brown   1.50 3.00
407 A115 4pf slate   5.00 10.00
408 A115 5pf dp yel grn   1.00 2.00
409 A115 6pf purple   .20 .35
410 A115 8pf red   .70 1.60
411 A115 10pf dark brown   1.50 3.25
412 A115 12pf carmine   .20 .30

Engr.
413 A115 15pf brown lake   .75 1.75
414 A115 16pf pck green   14.00 18.00
415 A115 20pf blue   2.75 5.25
416 A115 24pf org brn   10.00 18.00

Size: 22½x26mm
417 A115 25pf brt ultra   1.00 2.75
418 A115 30pf olive green   1.00 2.00
419 A115 40pf brt red violet   1.25 2.25
420 A118 42pf brt green   2.00 3.50
421 A115 50pf myrtle green   1.40 3.50
422 A115 60pf dk red brown   2.25 4.75
423 A115 80pf indigo   2.00 3.75
   Nos. 405-423 (19)   50.00 89.00
   Set, never hinged 110.00

Overprinted on Nos. 524-527
Perf. 12½, 14
424 A116 1m dk slate grn   7.50 20.00
   a.   Perf. 12½   100.00
425 A116 2m violet   7.50 25.00
   a.   Perf. 14   12.00 45.00
426 A116 3m copper red   25.00 55.00
   a.   Perf. 14   125.00
427 A116 5m dark blue   225.00 525.00
   a.   Perf. 14   575.00
   Nos. 424-427 (4)   265.00 625.00
   Set, never hinged   450.00

On the preceding four stamps the innermost vertical lines are 10½mm apart; on the pfennig values 6½mm apart.
Counterfeits exist of Nos. 405-427 overprints.

Germany Nos. 524 to 527 Overprinted in Black

Perf. 14
428 A116 1m dk slate grn   10.50 22.50
429 A116 2m violet   10.50 27.50

Perf. 12½
430 A116 3m copper red   21.00 60.00
431 A116 5m dark blue   140.00 450.00
   a.   Perf. 14   600.00
   Nos. 428-431 (4)   182.00 560.00
   Set, never hinged   375.00

On the preceding four stamps, "Osterreich" is thinner, measuring 16mm. On the previous set of 23 values it measures 18mm.
Counterfeits exist of Nos. 428-431 overprints.

Catalogue values for unused stamps in this section, from this point to the end of the section, are for Never Hinged items.

For Use in Vienna, Lower Austria and Burgenland

Coat of Arms
A99   A100

Typographed or Lithographed
1945, July 3   Unwmk.   Perf. 14x13½
Size: 21x25mm
432 A99 3pf brown   .20 .20
433 A99 4pf slate   .20 .20
434 A99 5pf dark green   .20 .20
435 A99 6pf deep violet   .20 .20
436 A99 8pf orange brown   .20 .20
437 A99 10pf deep brown   .20 .20
438 A99 12pf rose carmine   .20 .20
439 A99 15pf orange red   .20 .20
440 A99 16pf dull blue green   .20 .35

Perf. 14
Size: 24x28½mm
441 A99 20pf light blue   .20 .20
442 A99 24pf orange   .20 .20
443 A99 25pf dark blue   .20 .20
444 A99 30pf deep gray grn   .20 .20
445 A99 38pf ultramarine   .20 .20
446 A99 40pf brt red vio   .20 .20
447 A99 42pf sage green   .20 .20
448 A99 50pf blue green   .20 .60
449 A99 60pf maroon   .20 .20
450 A99 80pf dull lilac   .20 .60

Engr.   Perf. 14x13½
451 A100 1m dark green   .20 .60
452 A100 2m dark purple   .20 .60
453 A100 3m dark violet   .20 .60
454 A100 5m brown red   .20 .60
   Nos. 432-454 (23)   4.60 6.75

Nos. 432, 433, 437, 439, 440, 443, 446, 448, 449 are typographed. Nos. 434, 435, 441, 442 are lithographed; the other values exist both ways.
For overprint see No. 604.

For General Use

Lermoos, Winter
Scene — A101   The Prater
Woods,
Vienna — A105

Hochosterwitz,
Carinthia
A106   Lake Constance
A110

Dürnstein, Lower Austria A124

Designs: 4g, Eisenerz surface mine. 5g, Leopoldsberg, near Vienna. 6g, Hohensalzburg, Salzburg Province. 12g, Wolfgang See, near Salzburg. 15g, Forchtenstein Castle, Burgenland. 16g, Gesäuse Valley. 24g, Hóldrichs Mill, Lower Austria. 25g, Oetz Valley Outlet, Tyrol. 30g, Neusiedler Lake, Burgenland. 35g, Belvedere Palace, Vienna. 38g, Langbath Lake. 40g, Mariazell, Styria. 42g, Traunkirchen. 45g, Hartenstein Castle. 50g, Silvretta Mountains, Vorarlberg. 60g, Railroad viaducts near Semmering. 70g, Waterfall of Bad-Gastein, Salzburg. 80g, Kaiser Mountains, Tyrol. 90g, Wayside Shrine, Traøss, Styria. 2s, St. Christof am Arlberg, Tyrol. 3s, Heiligenblut, Carinthia. 5s, Schönbrunn, Vienna.

1945-46   Photo.   Unwmk.   *Perf. 14x13½*

455	A101	3g sapphire	.20	.20
456	A101	4g dp orange ('46)	.20	.20
457	A101	5g dk carmine rose	.20	.20
458	A101	6g dk slate green	.20	.20
459	A105	8g golden brown	.20	.20
460	A106	10g dark green	.20	.20
461	A106	12g dark brown	.20	.20
462	A106	15g dk slate bl ('46)	.20	.20
463	A106	16g chnt brn ('46)	.20	.20

Perf. 13½x14

464	A110	20g dp ultra ('46)	.20	.20
465	A110	24g dp yellow grn ('46)	.20	.20
466	A110	25g gray black ('46)	.20	.20
467	A110	30g dark red	.20	.20
468	A110	35g brown red ('46)	.20	.20
469	A110	38g brn olive ('46)	.20	.20
470	A110	40g gray	.20	.20
471	A110	42g brn org ('46)	.20	.20
472	A110	45g dark blue ('46)	.20	.25
473	A110	50g dark blue ('46)	.20	.20
474	A110	60g dark violet	.20	.20
a.		Imperf., pair	50.00	60.00
475	A110	70g Prus blue ('46)	.20	.25
476	A110	80g brown	.20	.40
477	A110	90g Prussian green	1.10	1.10
478	A124	1s dk red brn ('46)	.75	.75
479	A124	2s blue gray ('46)	2.75	2.75
480	A124	3s dk slate grn ('46)	.75	.80
481	A124	5s dark red ('46)	1.50	1.75
		Nos. 455-481 (27)	11.25	11.85

See Nos. 486-488, 496-515. For overprints and surcharges see Nos. 492-493, B166, B280, B287.

No. 461 Overprinted in Carmine

1946, Sept. 26

482	A106	12g dark brown	.20	.20

Meeting of the Soc. for Cultural and Economic Relations with the USSR, Vienna, Sept. 26-29.

City Hall Park, Vienna A128   Hochosterwitz, Carinthia A129

1946-47   Photo.   Unwmk.   *Perf. 14x13½*

483	A128	8g deep plum	.20	.20
484	A128	8g olive brown	.20	.20
a.		8g dark olive green		
485	A129	10g dk brn vio ('47)	.20	.20

Perf. 13½x14

486	A110	30g blue gray ('47)	.20	.20
487	A110	50g brown violet ('47)	.20	.20
488	A110	60g violet blue ('47)	2.00	1.10
		Nos. 483-488 (6)	3.00	2.10

See No. 502.

Franz Grillparzer A130

1947   Engr.   *Perf. 14x13½*

489	A130	18g chocolate	.20	.20

Photo.

490	A130	18g dk violet brn	.20	.20

Death of Grillparzer, dramatic poet, 75th anniv.
A second printing of No. 490 on thicker paper has a darker frame and clearer delineation of the portrait.
Issue dates: #489, Feb. 10; #490, Mar. 31.

Franz Schubert — A131

1947, Mar. 31   Engr.

491	A131	12g dark green	.20	.20

150th birth anniv. of Franz Schubert, musician and composer.

Nos. 469 and 463 Surcharged in Brown

1947, Sept. 1   Photo.   *Perf. 14*

492	A110	75g on 38g brown ol	.20	.80
493	A106	1.40s on 16g chnt brn	.20	.20

The surcharge on No. 493 varies from brown to black brown.

Symbols of Global Telegraphic Communication A132

1947, Nov. 5   Engr.   *Perf. 14x13½*

495	A132	40g dark violet	.20	.20

Centenary of the telegraph in Austria.

Scenic Type of 1946
1946, Aug.   Photo.   *Perf. 13½x14*

496	A124	1s dark brown	1.25	.50
497	A124	2s dark blue	7.00	2.75
498	A124	3s dark slate green	2.25	.75
499	A124	5s dark red	32.50	8.00
		Nos. 496-499 (4)	43.00	12.00

On Nos. 478 to 481 the upper and lower panels show a screen effect. On Nos. 496 to 499 the panels appear to be solid color.

Scenic Types of 1945-46
1947-48   Photo.   *Perf. 14x13½*

500	A101	3g bright red	.20	.20
501	A101	5g bright red	.20	.20
502	A106	10g bright red	.20	.20
503	A106	15g brt red ('48)	1.40	1.25

Perf. 13½x14

504	A110	20g bright red	.50	.20
505	A110	30g bright red	.75	.20
506	A110	40g bright red	.75	.20
507	A110	50g bright red	1.00	.20
508	A110	60g brt red ('48)	6.50	1.25
509	A110	70g brt red ('48)	3.50	.20
510	A110	80g brt red ('48)	3.50	.20
511	A110	90g brt red ('48)	3.75	.25
512	A124	1s dark violet	.80	.20
513	A124	2s dark violet	1.10	.20
514	A124	3s dk violet ('48)	9.00	1.00
515	A124	5s dk violet ('48)	11.00	1.50
		Nos. 500-515 (16)	44.15	7.45

Carl Michael Ziehrer (1843-1922), Composer A133

#517, Adalbert Stifter (1805-68), novelist. #518, Anton Bruckner (1824-96), composer. 60g, Friedrich von Amerling (1803-87), painter.

1948-49   Engr.

516	A133	20g dull green	.35	.20
517	A133	40g chocolate	5.00	2.50
518	A133	40g dark green	5.00	4.00
519	A133	60g rose brown	.65	.30
		Nos. 516-519 (4)	11.00	7.00

Issue dates: 20g, Jan. 21, No. 517, Sept. 6, No. 518, Sept. 3, 1949, 60g, Jan. 26.

Vorarlberg, Montafon Valley — A134   Costume of Vienna, 1850 — A135

Austrian Costumes: 3g, Tyrol, Inn Valley. 5g, Salzburg, Pinzgau. 10g, Styria, Salzkammergut. 15g, Burgenland, Lutzmannsburg. 25g, Vienna, 1850. 30g, Salzburg, Pongau. 40g, Vienna, 1840. 45g, Carinthia, Lesach Valley. 50g, Vorarlberg, Bregenzer Forest. 60g, Carinthia, Lavant Valley. 70g, Lower Austria, Wachau. 75g, Styria, Salzkammergut. 80g, Styria, Enns Valley. 90g, Central Styria. 1s, Tyrol, Puster Valley. 1.20s, Lower Austria, Vienna Woods. 1.40s, Upper Austria, Inn District. 1.45s, Wilten. 1.50s, Vienna, 1853. 1.60s, Vienna, 1830. 1.70s, East Tyrol, Kals. 2s, Upper Austria, Ischl. 1820. 2.40s, Kitzbuhel. 2.50s, Upper Steiermark, 1850. 2.70s, Little Walser Valley. 3s, Burgenland. 3.50s, Lower Austria, 1850. 4.50s, Gail Valley. 5s, Ziller Valley. 7s, Steiermark, Sulm Valley.

1948-52   Unwmk.   *Perf. 14x13½*

			Photo.	
520	A134	3g gray ('50)	.60	.50
521	A134	5g dk grn ('49)	.25	.20
522	A134	10g deep blue	.25	.20
523	A134	15g brown	.60	.20
524	A134	20g yellow green	.20	.20
525	A134	25g brown ('49)	.20	.20
526	A134	30g dk car rose	2.50	.20
527	A134	30g dk vio ('50)	.60	.20
528	A134	40g violet	2.50	.20
529	A134	40g green ('49)	.20	.20
530	A134	45g violet blue	2.25	.40
531	A134	50g org brn ('49)	.60	.20
532	A134	60g scarlet	.20	.20
533	A134	70g brt bl grn ('49)	.20	.20
534	A134	75g blue	3.75	.40
535	A134	80g car rose ('49)	.35	.20
536	A134	90g brn vio ('49)	22.50	.30
537	A134	1s ultramarine	4.00	.20
538	A134	1s rose red ('50)	62.50	.20
539	A134	1s dk grn ('51)	.20	.20
540	A134	1.20s violet ('49)	.40	.20
541	A134	1.40s brown	2.50	.20
542	A134	1.45s dk car ('51)	1.00	.20
543	A134	1.50s ultra ('51)	.60	.20
544	A134	1.60s org red ('49)	.20	.20
545	A134	1.70s vio bl ('50)	2.50	.55
546	A134	2s blue green	.40	.20
547	A134	2.20s slate ('52)	4.75	.20
548	A134	2.40s blue ('51)	1.00	.20
549	A134	2.50s brown ('52)	4.50	.20
550	A134	2.70s dk brn ('51)	.45	.45
551	A134	3s brn car ('49)	1.90	.20
552	A134	3.50s dull grn ('51)	9.75	.20
553	A134	4.50s brn vio ('51)	.60	.40
554	A134	5s dark red vio	1.00	.20
555	A134	7s olive ('52)	1.50	.20

Engr.

556	A135	10s gray ('50)	27.50	5.00
		Nos. 520-556 (37)	165.00	13.80

In 1958-59, 21 denominations of this set were printed on white paper, differing from the previous grayish paper with yellowish gum.

Pres. Karl Renner — A136

1948, Nov. 12   *Perf. 14x13½*

557	A136	1s deep blue	1.90	1.10

Founding of the Austrian Republic, 30th anniv. See Nos. 573, 636.

Franz Gruber and Josef Mohr A137

1948, Dec. 18   *Perf. 13½x14*
558 A137 60g red brown   4.25 4.00
  130th anniv. of the hymn "Silent Night, Holy Night".

Symbolical of Child Welfare — A138

1949, May 14   Photo.   *Perf. 14x13½*
559 A138 1s bright blue   11.50 1.25
  1st year of activity of UNICEF in Austria.

Johann Strauss, the Younger — A139

1949   **Engr.**
  30g, Johann Strauss, the elder. #561, Johann Strauss, the younger. #562, Karl Millöcker.

560	A139 30g violet brown	2.25	1.65
561	A139 1s dark blue	2.75	1.10
562	A139 1s dark blue	12.00	6.25
	Nos. 560-562 (3)	17.00	9.00

  Johann Strauss, the elder (1804-49), Johann Strauss, the younger (1825-99), and Karl Millöcker (1842-1899), composers. See #574.

Esperanto Star, Olive Branches — A140

St. Gebhard — A141

1949, June 25   **Photo.**
563 A140 20g blue green   1.00 .50
  Austrian Esperanto Congress at Graz.

1949, Aug. 6   **Engr.**
564 A141 30g dark violet   1.50 1.25
  St. Gebhard (949-995), Bishop of Vorarlberg.

Letter, Roses and Post Horn A142

  UPU, 75th Anniv.: 60g, Plaque. 1s, "Austria," wings and monogram.

1949, Oct. 8   *Perf. 13½x14*
565	A142 40g dark green	3.75	1.60
566	A142 60g dk carmine	3.75	1.65
567	A142 1s dk violet blue	6.50	4.75
	Nos. 565-567 (3)	14.00	8.00

Moritz Michael Daffinger — A143

Andreas Hofer — A144

  30g, Alexander Girardi. #569, Daffinger. #570, Hofer. #571, Josef Madersperger.

1950   **Unwmk.**   *Perf. 14x13½*
568	A144 30g dark blue	1.50	.75
569	A143 60g red brown	6.00	3.25
570	A144 60g dark violet	10.50	6.50
571	A144 60g purple	4.50	2.25
	Nos. 568-571 (4)	22.50	12.75

  Alexander Girardi (1850-1918), actor; Moritz Michael Daffinger (1790-1849), painter; Andreas Hofer (1767-1810), patriot; Josef Madersperger (1768-1850), inventor.
  Issue dates: 30g, Dec. 5; No. 569, Jan. 25; No. 570, Feb. 20; No. 571, Oct. 2.

Austrian Stamp of 1850 — A146

1950, May 20   *Perf. 14½*
572 A146 1s black, *straw*   1.60 .90
  Centenary of Austrian postage stamps.

Renner Type of 1948
Frame and Inscriptions Altered
1951, Mar. 3
573 A136 1s black, *straw*   1.40 .20
  In memory of Pres. Karl Renner, 1870-1950.

Strauss Type of 1949
Portrait: 60g, Joseph Lanner.
1951, Apr. 12
574 A139 60g dk blue green   3.50 1.10
  Joseph Lanner (1801-43), composer.

Martin Johann Schmidt — A147

Boy Scout Emblem — A148

1951, June 28   Engr.   *Perf. 14x13½*
575 A147 1sh brown red   4.50 2.00
  150th death anniv. of Martin Johann Schmidt, painter.

1951, Aug. 3   **Engr. and Litho.**
576 A148 1sh dk grn, ocher & pink   3.50 2.75
  7th World Scout Jamboree, Bad Ischl-St. Wolfgang, Aug. 3-13, 1951.

Wilhelm Kienzl — A149

Josef Schrammel A150

  Design: 1s, Karl von Ghega.

1951-52   **Engr.**   **Unwmk.**
577	A149 1s deep green ('52)	6.50	1.10
578	A149 1.50s indigo	3.00	.90
579	A150 1.50s violet blue ('52)	6.50	1.10
	Nos. 577-579 (3)	16.00	3.10

  Ghega (1802-60), civil engineer; Kienzl (1857-1941), composer; Schrammel (1852-95), composer. See #582.
  Issued: 1s, 3/2; #578, 10/3; #579, 3/3.

Breakfast Pavilion, Schönbrunn A151

1952, May 24   *Perf. 13½x14*
580 A151 1.50s dark green   5.75 1.00
  Vienna Zoological Gardens, 200th anniv.

Globe as Dot Over "i" — A152

School Girl — A153

1952, July 1   *Perf. 14x13½*
581 A152 1.50s dark blue   5.00 .65
  Formation of the Intl. Union of Socialist Youth Camp, Vienna, July 1-10, 1952.

Type Similar to A150
  Portrait: 1s, Nikolaus Lenau.

1952, Aug. 13
582 A150 1s deep green   6.00 1.10
  Nikolaus Lenau, pseudonym of Nikolaus Franz Niembsch von Strehlenau (1802-50), poet.

1952, Sept. 6
583 A153 2.40s dp violet blue   9.00 1.75
  Issued to stimulate letter-writing between Austrian and foreign school children.

Hugo Wolf — A154

Pres. Theodor Körner — A155

1953, Feb. 21   Engr.   *Perf. 14x13½*
587 A154 1.50s dark blue   6.00 .70
  Hugo Wolf, composer, 50th death anniv.

1953, Apr. 24
588 A155 1.50s dk violet blue   6.00 .70
  80th birthday of Pres. Theodor Körner. See Nos. 591, 614.

State Theater, Linz, and Masks A156

1953, Oct. 17   *Perf. 13½x14*
589 A156 1.50s dark gray   14.00 1.50
  State Theater at Linz, 150th anniv.

Child and Christmas Tree — A157

Karl von
Rokitansky
A158

1953, Nov. 30   *Perf. 14x13½*
590 A157 1s dark green   1.40   .20
See No. 597.

Type Similar to A155
Portrait: 1.50s, Moritz von Schwind.

1954, Jan. 21   *Perf. 14x13½*
591 A155 1.50s purple   12.00 1.10
Moritz von Schwind, painter, 150th birth
anniv.

1954, Feb. 19
592 A158 1.50s purple   14.00 1.40
Karl von Rokitansky, physician, 150th birth
anniv. See No. 595.

Esperanto
Star and
Wreath
A159

Engr. and Photo.
1954, June 5   *Perf. 13½x14*
593 A159 1s dk brown & emer   4.50 .20
Esperanto movement in Austria, 50th anniv.

A160

1954, Aug. 4   Engr.   *Perf. 14x13½*
594 A160   1s dark blue green 10.00 1.75
300th birth anniv. of Johann Michael
Rottmayr von Rosenbrunn, painter.

Type Similar to A158
Portrait: 1.50s, Carl Auer von Welsbach.

1954, Aug. 4
595 A158 1.50s violet blue   30.00 1.50
25th death anniv. of Carl Auer von Welsbach (1858-1929), chemist.

2nd Intl. Congress
for Catholic
Church Music,
Vienna, Oct. 4-
10 — A161

1954, Oct. 2   Unwmk.
Organ, St. Florian Monastery and Cherub.
596 A161 1s brown   2.25 .20

Christmas Type of 1953
1954, Nov. 30
597 A157 1s dark blue   2.75 .25

Arms of
Austria and
Official
Publication
A162

1954, Dec. 18   Engr.
598 A162 1s salmon & black   2.25 .20
Austria's State Printing Plant, 150th anniv.,
and Wiener Zeitung, government newspaper,
250th year of publication.

Parliament
Building
A163

Designs: 1s, Western railroad station,
Vienna. 1.45s, Letters forming flag. 1.50s,
Public housing, Vienna. 2.40s, Limberg dam.

1955, Apr. 27   *Perf. 13½x14*
599 A163   70g rose violet   1.50 .20
600 A163   1s deep ultra   5.50 .20
601 A163   1.45s scarlet   8.25 1.75
602 A163   1.50s brown   17.50 .20
603 A163   2.40s dk blue green   8.25 3.00
    Nos. 599-603 (5)   41.00 5.35
10th anniv. of Austria's liberation.

Type of 1945
Overprinted in
Blue

1955, May 15   *Perf. 14x13½*
604 A100 2s blue gray   2.00 .20
Signing of the state treaty with the US,
France, Great Britain and Russia, 5/15/55.

Workers of
Three
Races
Climbing
Globe
A164

1955, May 20   *Perf. 13½x14*
605 A164 1s indigo   2.00 1.60
4th congress of the Intl. Confederation of
Free Trade Unions, Vienna, May.

Burgtheater,
Vienna
A165

Design: 2.40s, Opera House, Vienna.

1955, July 25
606 A165 1.50s light sepia   3.00 .20
607 A165 2.40s dark blue   4.00 1.25
Re-opening of the Burgtheater and Opera
House in Vienna.

Symbolic of
Austria's
Desire to
Join the
UN — A166

1955, Oct. 24   Unwmk.
608 A166 2.40s green   14.00 1.40
Tenth anniversary of UN.

Wolfgang
Amadeus Mozart,
Birth
Bicent. — A167

1956, Jan. 21   *Perf. 14x13½*
609 A167 2.40s slate blue   3.75 .50

Symbolic of
Austria's Joining
the UN — A168

1956, Feb. 20
610 A168 2.40s chocolate   11.00 1.10
Austria's admission to the UN.

Globe
Showing
Energy of
the Earth
A169

1956, May 8   *Perf. 13½x14*
611 A169 2.40s deep blue   10.00 1.40
Fifth Intl. Power Conf., Vienna, June 17-23.

Map of Europe
and City
Maps — A170

Photo. and Typo.
1956, June 8   *Perf. 14x13½*
612 A170 1.45s lt grn blk & red   2.50 .50
23rd Intl. Housing and Town Planning Congress, Vienna, July 22-28.

J.B. Fischer von Erlach, Architect, 300th Birth Anniv. — A171

1956, July 20   Engr.
613 A171 1.50s brown   1.25 1.10

Körner Type of 1953
1957, Jan. 11
614 A155 1.50s gray black   1.50 1.25

Death of Pres. Theodor Körner.

Dr. Julius Wagner-Jauregg, Psychiatrist, Birth Cent. — A172

1957, Mar. 7   Perf. 14x13½
615 A172 2.40s brn violet   3.25 1.25

Anton Wildgans, Poet, 25th Death Anniv. — A173

1957, May 3   Unwmk.
616 A173 1s violet blue   .30 .20

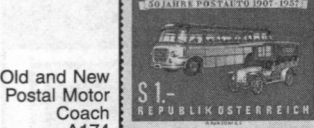

Old and New Postal Motor Coach A174

1957, June 14   Perf. 13½x14
617 A174 1s black, yellow   .30 .20

Austrian Postal Motor Coach Service, 50th anniv.

Gasherbrum II and Glacier A175

1957, July 27
618 A175 1.50s gray blue   .35 .20

Austrian Karakorum Expedition, which climbed Mount Gasherbrum II on July 7, 1956.

A176   A177

Designs: 20g, Farmhouse at Mörbisch. 50g, Heiligenstadt, Vienna. 1s, Mariazell. 1.40s, County seat, Klagenfurt. 1.50s, Rabenhof Building, Erdberg, Vienna. 1.80s, The Mint, Hall, Tyrol. 2s, Christkindl Church. 3.40s, Steiner Gate, Krems. 4s, Vienna Gate,

Hainburg. 4.50s, Schwechat Airport, Vienna. 5.50s, Chur Gate, Feldkirch. 6s, County seat, Graz. 6.40s, "Golden Roof," Innsbruck. 10s, Heidenreichstein Castle.

1957-61   Litho.   Perf. 14x13½
     Size: 20x25mm
618A A176 20g violet blk ('61)   .20 .20
619 A176 50g bluish blk ('59)   .20 .20
     Engr.
620 A176 1s chocolate   1.25 .20
     Typo.
621 A176 1s chocolate   1.75 .20
     Litho.
622 A176 1s choc ('59)   .90 .20
622A A176 1.40s brt greenish bl ('60)   .30 .20
623 A176 1.50s rose lake ('58)   .50 .20
624 A176 1.80s brt ultra ('60)   .30 .20
625 A176 2s dull blue ('58)   6.00 .20
626 A176 3.40s yel grn ('60)   .90 .75
627 A176 4s brt red lil ('60)   .75 .20
627A A176 4.50s dl green ('60)   1.00 .50
628 A176 5.50s grnsh gray ('60)   .55 .20
629 A176 6s brt vio ('60)   1.00 .20
629A A176 6.40s brt blue ('60)   1.00 .90
     Engr.
     Size: 22x28mm
630 A177 10s dk bl grn   3.00 .45
   Nos. 618A-630 (16)   19.60 5.00

Of the three 1s stamps above, Nos. 620 and 621 have two names in imprint (designer H. Strohofer, engraver G. Wimmer). No. 622 has only Strohofer's name.
Values for Nos. 618A-624, 626-630 are for stamps on white paper. Most denominations also come on grayish paper with yellowish gum.
See Nos. 688-702.

1960-65   Photo.   Perf. 14½x14
     Size: 17x21mm
630A A176 50g slate ('64)   .20 .20
     Size: 18x21½mm
630B A176 1s chocolate   .20 .20
     Size: 17x21mm
630C A176 1.50s dk car ('65)   .20 .20
   Nos. 630A-630C (3)   .60 .60

Nos. 630A-630C issued in sheets and coils.

Graukogel, Badgastein A180

1958, Feb. 1   Engr.   Perf. 14x13½
631 A180 1.50s dark blue   .25 .20

Intl. Ski Federation Alpine championships, Badgastein, Feb. 2-7.

Plane over Map of Austria A181

1958, Mar. 27   Perf. 13½x14
632 A181 4s red   .45 .20

Re-opening of Austrian Airlines.

Mother and Daughter — A182

1958, May 8   Unwmk.   Perf. 14x13½
633 A182 1.50s dark blue   .25 .20

Issued for Mother's Day.

Walther von der Vogelweide A183

1958, July 17   Litho. and Engr.
634 A183 1.50s multicolored   .25 .20

3rd Austrian Song Festival, Vienna, 7/17-20.

Oswald Redlich (1858-1944), Historian — A184

1958, Sept. 17   Engr.
635 A184 2.40s ultramarine   .45 .20

Renner Type of 1948
1958, Nov. 12
636 A136 1.50s deep green   .45 .25

Austrian Republic, 40th anniv.

Giant "E" on Map — A185

1959, Mar. 9
637 A185 2.40s emerald   .35 .20

Idea of a United Europe.

Cigarette Machine and Trademark of Tobacco Monopoly — A186

1959, May 8   Unwmk.   Perf. 13½
638 A186 2.40s dark olive bister   .30 .20

Austrian tobacco monopoly, 175th anniv.

Capercaillie A188

Animals: 1.50s, Roe buck. 2.40s, Wild boar. 3.50s, Red deer, doe and fawn.

1959, May 20   Engr.
640 A188 1s rose violet   .30 .20
641 A188 1.50s blue violet   .65 .20
642 A188 2.40s dk bl green   .45 .40
643 A188 3.50s dark brown   .35 .20
   Nos. 640-643 (4)   1.75 1.00

Congress of the Intl. Hunting Council, Vienna, May 20-24.

Joseph Haydn (1732-1809), Composer A189

1959, May 30   Unwmk.
644 A189 1.50s violet brown   .45 .20

Coat of Arms, Tyrol — A190

1959, June 13   Perf. 14x13½
645 A190 1.50s rose red   .25 .20

Fight for liberation of Tyrol, 150th anniv.

Antenna, Zugspitze — A191

1959, June 19   Perf. 13½
646 A191 2.40s dk bl grn   .30 .20

Inauguration of Austria's relay system.

Field Ball Player — A192

1s, Runner. 1.80s, Gymnast on vaulting horse. 2s, Woman hurdler. 2.20s, Hammer thrower.

1959-70   Engr.   Perf. 14x13½
647 A192 1s lilac   .20 .20
648 A192 1.50s blue green   .50 .20
648A A192 1.80s carmine ('62)   .45 .35
648B A192 2s rose lake ('70)   .25 .20
648C A192 2.20s bluish blk ('67)   .25 .20
   Nos. 647-648C (5)   1.65 1.15

Archduke Johann — A187

1959, May 11   Perf. 14x13½
639 A187 1.50s deep green   .25 .20

Archduke Johann of Austria, military leader and humanitarian, death cent.

Orchestral Instruments
A193

Litho. and Engr.
1959, Aug. 19   **Perf. 14x13½**
649 A193 2.40s dull bl & blk   .30 .20
World tour of the Vienna Philharmonic Orchestra.

Family Fleeing over Mountains
A194

1960, Apr. 7   **Engr.**   **Perf. 13½x14**
650 A194 3s Prussian green   .65 .25
WRY, July 1, 1959-June 30, 1960.

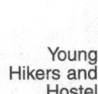

President Adolf Schärf — A195

1960, Apr. 20   **Perf. 14x13½**
651 A195 1.50s gray olive   .65 .20
Pres. Adolf Scharf, 70th birthday.

Young Hikers and Hostel
A196

1960, May 20   **Perf. 13½x14**
652 A196 1s carmine rose   .25 .20
Youth hiking; youth hostel movement.

Anton Eiselsberg, Surgeon, Birth Cent. — A197

Litho. and Engr.
1960, June 20   **Perf. 14x13½**
653 A197 1.50s buff & dk brn   .70 .20

Gustav Mahler (1860-1911), Composer
A198

1960, July 7   **Engr.**
654 A198 1.50s chocolate   .70 .20

Jakob Prandtauer, Architect, 300th Birth Anniv. — A199

1960, July 16   **Unwmk.**
655 A199 1.50s Melk Abbey   .70 .20

Gross Glockner Mountain Road, 25th Anniv. — A200

1960, Aug. 3
656 A200 1.80s dark blue   .70 .50

Ionic Capital — A201

1960, Aug. 29   **Perf. 14x13½**
657 A201 3s black   1.40 .75
Europa: Idea of a United Europe.

Griffen, Carinthia
A202

1960, Oct. 10   **Engr.**   **Perf. 13½x14**
658 A202 1.50s slate green   .30 .20
40th anniv. of the plebiscite which kept Carinthia with Austria.

Flame and Broken Chain — A203

1961, May 8   **Unwmk.**   **Perf. 14x13½**
659 A203 1.50s scarlet   .30 .20
Victims in Austria's fight for freedom.

First Austrian Mail Plane, 1918
A204

1961, May 15   **Perf. 13½x14**
660 A204 5s violet blue   .70 .30
Airmail Phil. Exhib., LUPOSTA 1961, Vienna, May.

Transportation by Road, Rail and Waterway
A205

Engraved and Typographed
1961, May 29   **Perf. 13½**
661 A205 3s rose red & olive   .45 .30
13th European Conference of Transportation ministers, Vienna, May 29-31.

Society of Creative Artists, Künstlerhaus, Vienna, Cent. — A206

Designs: 1s, Mountain Mower, by Albin Egger-Lienz. 1.50s, The Kiss, by August von Pettenkofen. 3s, Girl, by Anton Romako. 5s, Ariadne's Triumph, by Hans Makart.

1961, June 12   **Engr.**   **Perf. 13½x14**
Inscriptions in Red Brown
662 A206   1s rose lake   .20 .20
663 A206 1.50s dull violet   .25 .25
664 A206   3s olive green   .75 .70
665 A206   5s blue violet   .45 .40
    Nos. 662-665 (4)   1.65 1.55

Sonnblick Mountain and Observatory
A207

1961, Sept. 1   **Perf. 14x13½**
666 A207 1.80s violet blue   .40 .30
Sonnblick meteorological observatory, 75th anniv.

Mercury and Globe — A208

1961, Sept. 18
667 A208 3s black   .70 .40
Intl. Banking Congress, Vienna, Sept. 1961. English inscription listing UN financial groups.

Coal Mine Shaft — A209

Designs: 1.50s, Generator. 1.80s, Iron blast furnace. 3s, Pouring steel. 5s, Oil refinery.

1961, Sept. 15   **Engr.**   **Perf. 14x13½**
668 A209   1s black   .20 .20
669 A209 1.50s green   .25 .20
670 A209 1.80s dark car rose   .55 .40
671 A209   3s bright lilac   .70 .50
672 A209   5s blue   .90 .70
    Nos. 668-672 (5)   2.60 2.00
15th anniversary of nationalized industry.

Arms of Burgenland
A210

1961, Oct. 9   **Engr. and Litho.**
673 A210 1.50s blk, yel & dk red   .35 .20
Burgenland as part of the Austrian Republic, 40th anniv.

Franz Liszt (1811-86), Composer
A211

1961, Oct. 20   **Engr.**
674 A211 3s dark brown   .55 .40

Parliament
A212

1961, Dec. 18   **Perf. 13½x14**
675 A212 1s brown   .20 .20
Austrian Bureau of Budget, 200th anniv.

Kaprun-Mooserboden Reservoir — A213

Hydroelectric Power Plants: 1.50s, Ybbs-Persenbeug dam and locks. 1.80s, Lünersee dam and reservoir. 3s, Grossraming dam. 4s, Bisamberg transformer plant. 6.40s, St. Andrä power plant.

1962, Mar. 26   **Unwmk.**
676 A213   1s violet blue   .20 .20
677 A213 1.50s red lilac   .25 .20
678 A213 1.80s green   .40 .35
679 A213   3s brown   .40 .35
680 A213   4s rose red   .40 .35
681 A213 6.40s gray   1.25 1.10
    Nos. 676-681 (6)   2.90 2.55
Nationalization of the electric power industry, 15th anniv.

Johann Nestroy — A214

1962, May 25   **Perf. 14x13½**
682 A214 1s violet   .20 .20

Johann Nepomuk Nestroy, Viennese playwright, author and actor, death cent.

Friedrich Gauermann (1807-1862), Landscape Painter — A215

1962, July 6   **Engr.**
683 A215 1.50s intense blue   .20 .20

Scout Emblem and Handshake A216

1962, Oct. 5
684 A216 1.50s dark green   .35 .20

Austria's Boy Scouts, 50th anniv.

Lowlands Forest A217

1.50s, Deciduous forest. 3s, Fir & larch forest.

1962, Oct. 12   **Perf. 13½x14**
685 A217   1s greenish gray   .20 .20
686 A217   1.50s reddish brown   .25 .25
687 A217   3s dk slate green   .90 .70
    Nos. 685-687 (3)   1.35 1.15

Buildings Types of 1957-61

Designs: 30g, City Hall, Vienna. 40g, Porcia Castle, Spittal on the Drau. 60g, Tanners' Tower, Wels. 70g, Residenz Fountain, Salzburg. 80g, Old farmhouse, Pinzgau. 1s, Romanesque columns, Millstatt Abbey. 1.20s, Kornmesser House, Bruck on the Mur. 1.30s, Schatten Castle, Feldkirch, Vorarlberg. 2s, Dragon Fountain, Klagenfurt. 2.20s, Beethoven House, Vienna. 2.50s, Danube Bridge, Linz. 3s, Swiss Gate, Vienna. 3.50s, Esterhazy Palace, Eisenstadt. 8s, City Hall, Steyr. 20s, Melk Abbey.

1962-70   **Litho.**   **Perf. 14x13½**
    Size: 20x25mm
688 A176   30g greenish gray   .50 .20
689 A176   40g rose red   .20 .20
690 A176   60g violet brown   .35 .20
691 A176   70g dark blue   .25 .20
692 A176   80g yellow brown   .35 .20
693 A176   1s brown ('70)   .20 .20
694 A176   1.20s red lilac   .40 .20
695 A176   1.30s green ('67)   .20 .20
696 A176   2s dk blue ('68)   .25 .20
697 A176   2.20s green   1.40 .20
698 A176   2.50s violet   .80 .20
699 A176   3s bright blue   .65 .20
700 A176   3.50s rose carmine   .80 .20
701 A176   8s claret ('65)   1.00 .20

Perf. 13½
Engr.
    Size: 28x36½mm
702 A177   20s rose claret ('63)   2.50 .35
    Nos. 688-702 (15)   9.85 3.15

Values for Nos. 688-702 are for stamps on white paper. Some denominations also come on grayish paper with yellowish gum.

Electric Locomotive and Train of 1837 — A218

Lithographed and Engraved

1962, Nov. 9   **Perf. 13½x14**
703 A218 3s buff & black   .90 .40

125th anniversary of Austrian railroads.

Postillions and Postal Clerk, 1863 — A219

1963, May 7   **Photo.**   **Perf. 14x13½**
704 A219 3s dk brn & citron   .70 .40

First Intl. Postal Conference, Paris, cent.

Hermann Bahr, Poet, Birth Cent. — A220

Lithographed and Engraved

1963, July 19   **Perf. 14x13½**
705 A220 1.50s blue & black   .25 .20

St. Florian Statue, Kefermarkt, Contemporary and Old Fire Engines — A221

1963, Aug. 30   **Unwmk.**
706 A221 1.50s brt rose & blk   .25 .20

Austrian volunteer fire brigades, cent.

Factory, Flag and "ÖGB" on Map of Austria A222

1963, Sept. 23   **Litho.**   **Perf. 13½x14**
707 A222 1.50s gray, red & dk brn   .25 .20

5th Congress of the Austrian Trade Union Federation (ÖGB), Sept. 23-28.

Arms of Austria and Tyrol A223

1963, Sept. 27   **Unwmk.**
708 A223 1.50s tan, blk, red & yel   .25 .20

Tyrol's union with Austria, 600th anniv.

Prince Eugene of Savoy (1663-1736), Austrian General — A224

1963, Oct. 18   **Engr.**   **Perf. 14x13½**
709 A224 1.50s violet   .25 .20

Intl. Red Cross, Cent. — A225

1963, Oct. 25   **Engr. and Photo.**
710 A225 3s blk, sil & red   .50 .20

Slalom A226

Sports: 1.20s, Biathlon (skier with rifle). 1.50s, Ski jump. 1.80s, Women's figure skating. 2.20s, Ice hockey. 3s, Tobogganing. 4s, Bobsledding.

Photo. and Engr.

1963, Nov. 11   **Perf. 13½x14**
711 A226   1s multi   .20 .20
712 A226   1.20s multi   .20 .20
713 A226   1.50s multi   .20 .20
714 A226   1.80s multi   .25 .20
715 A226   2.20s multi   .40 .20
716 A226   3s multi   .30 .20
717 A226   4s multi   .55 .35
    Nos. 711-717 (7)   2.10 1.60

9th Winter Olympic Games, Innsbruck, Jan. 29-Feb. 9, 1964.

Baroque Creche by Josef Thaddäus Stammel — A227

1963, Nov. 29   **Engr.**   **Perf. 14x13½**
718 A227 2s dark Prus green   .25 .20

Flowers A228

1964, Apr. 17   **Litho.**   **Perf. 14**
719 A228   1s Nasturtium   .20 .20
720 A228   1.50s Peony   .20 .20
721 A228   1.80s Clematis   .25 .20
722 A228   2.20s Dahlia   .35 .20
723 A228   3s Morning glory   .40 .25
724 A228   4s Hollyhock   .50 .35
    Nos. 719-724 (6)   1.90 1.40

Vienna Intl. Garden Show, Apr. 16-Oct. 11.

St. Mary Magdalene and Apostle — A229

1964, May 21   **Engr.**   **Perf. 13½**
725 A229 1.50s bluish black   .25 .20

Romanesque art in Austria. The 12th century stained-glass window is from the Weitensfeld Church, the bust of the Apostle from the portal of St. Stephen's Cathedral, Vienna.

Pallas Athena and National Council Chamber — A230

Engr. and Litho.

1964, May 25   **Perf. 14x13½**
726 A230 1.80s black & emer   .30 .20

2nd Parliamentary and Scientific Conf., Vienna.

The Kiss, by Gustav Klimt A231

1964, June 5   **Litho.**   **Perf. 13½**
727 A231 3s multicolored   .35 .25

Re-opening of the Vienna Secession, a museum devoted to early 20th century art (art nouveau).

Brother of Mercy and Patient — A232

1964, June 11   **Engr.**   **Perf. 14x13½**
728 A232 1.50s dark blue   .25 .20

Brothers of Mercy in Austria, 350th anniv.

"Bringing the News of Victory at Kunersdorf" by Bernardo Bellotto — A233

"The Post in Art": 1.20s, Changing Horses at Relay Station, by Julius Hörmann. 1.50s, The Honeymoon Trip, by Moritz von Schwind. 1.80s, After the Rain, by Ignaz Raffalt. 2.20s, Mailcoach in the Mountains, by Adam Klein. 3s, Changing Horses at Bavarian Border, by Friedrich Gauermann. 4s, Postal Sleigh (Truck) in the Mountains, by Adalbert Pilch. 6.40s, Saalbach Post Office, by Adalbert Pilch.

1964, June 15   **Perf. 13½x14**
729	A233	1s rose claret	.20	.20
730	A233	1.20s sepia	.20	.20
731	A233	1.50s violet blue	.20	.20
732	A233	1.80s brt violet	.20	.20
733	A233	2.20s black	.20	.20
734	A233	3s dl car rose	.30	.20
735	A233	4s slate green	.35	.20
736	A233	6.40s dull claret	.80	.45
	Nos. 729-736 (8)		2.45	1.85

15th UPU Cong., Vienna, May-June 1964.

Workers — A234

1964, Sept. 4   **Perf. 14x13½**
737 A234 1s black   .20 .20
Centenary of Austrian Labor Movement.

Common Design Types pictured following the introduction.

Europa Issue, 1964
Common Design Type
1964, Sept. 14   **Litho.**   **Perf. 12**
Size: 21x36mm
738 CD7 3s dark blue   .50 .20

Emblem of Radio Austria and Transistor Radio Panel A235

1964, Oct. 1   **Photo.**   **Perf. 13½**
739 A235 1s black brn & red   .20 .20
Forty years of Radio Austria.

6th Congress of the Intl. Graphic Federation, Vienna, Oct. 12-17 — A236

Litho. and Engr.
1964, Oct. 12   **Perf. 14x13½**
740 A236 1.50s Old printing press   .20 .20

Dr. Adolf Schärf (1890-1965), Pres. of Austria (1957-65) A237

Pres. Adolf Schärf, Schärf Student Center.

Typo. and Engr.
1965, Apr. 20   **Perf. 12**
741 A237 1.50s bluish black   .20 .20

Ruins and New Buildings — A238

1965, Apr. 27   **Engr.**   **Perf. 14x13½**
742 A238 1.80s carmine lake   .20 .20
Twenty years of reconstruction.

Oldest Seal of Vienna University — A239

Photo. and Engr.
1965, May 10   **Perf. 14x13½**
743 A239 3s gold & red   .35 .20
University of Vienna, 600th anniv.

St. George, 16th Century Wood Sculpture A240

1965, May 17   **Engr.**
744 A240 1.80s bluish black   .25 .20
Art of the Danube Art School, 1490-1540, exhibition, May-Oct. 1965. The stamp background shows an engraving by Albrecht Altdorfer.

ITU Emblem, Telegraph Key and TV Antenna — A241

1965, May 17   **Unwmk.**
745 A241 3s violet blue   .35 .20
ITU, cent.

Ferdinand Raimund — A242

Portraits: No. 746, Dr. Ignaz Philipp Semmelweis. No. 747, Bertha von Suttner. No. 749, Ferdinand Georg Waldmüller.

1965   **Engr.**   **Perf. 14x13½**
746	A242	1.50s violet	.30	.20
747	A242	1.50s bluish black	.30	.20
748	A242	3s dark brown	.55	.20
749	A242	3s greenish blk	.55	.20
	Nos. 746-749 (4)		1.70	.80

Semmelweis (1818-65), who discovered the cause of puerperal fever and introduced antisepsis in obstetrics (#746). 60th anniv. of the awarding of the Nobel Prize for Peace to von Suttner (1843-1914), pacifist and author

(#747). Raimund (1790-1836), actor and playwright (#748). Waldmüller (1793-1865), painter (#749).
Issue dates: No. 746, Aug. 13; No. 747, Dec. 1; No. 748, June 1; No. 749, Aug. 23.

4th Gymnaestrada, Intl. Athletic Meet, Vienna, July 20-24 — A243

1.50s, Male gymnasts with practice bars. 3s, Dancers with tambourines.

1965, July 20   **Photo. and Engr.**
750 A243 1.50s gray & black   .20 .20
751 A243 3s bister & blk   .35 .25

Red Cross and Strip of Gauze — A244

1965, Oct. 1   **Litho.**   **Perf. 14x13½**
752 A244 3s black & red   .35 .20
20th Intl. Red Cross Conference, Vienna.

Austrian Flag and Eagle with Mural Crown — A245

1965, Oct. 7   **Photo. and Engr.**
753 A245 1.50s gold, red & blk   .20 .20
50th anniv. of the Union of Austrian Towns.

Austrian Flag, UN Headquarters and Emblem A246

Lithographed and Engraved
1965, Oct. 25   **Unwmk.**   **Perf. 12**
754 A246 3s blk, brt bl & red   .45 .20
Austria's admission to the UN, 10th anniv.

University of Technology, Vienna A247

1965, Nov. 8   **Engr.**   **Perf. 13½x14**
755 A247 1.50s violet   .20 .20
Vienna University of Technology, 150th anniv.

Map of Austria with Postal Zone Numbers — A248

1966, Jan. 14   **Photo.**   **Perf. 12**
756 A248 1.50s yel, red & blk   .20 .20
Introduction of postal zone numbers, 1/1/66.

PTT Building, Emblem and Churches of Sts. Maria Rotunda and Barbara — A249

Lithographed and Engraved
1966, Mar. 4   **Perf. 14x13½**
757 A249 1.50s blk, dull yellow   .20 .20
Headquarters of the Post and Telegraph Administration, cent.

Maria von Ebner Eschenbach (1830-1916), Novelist, Poet — A250

1966, Mar. 11   **Engr.**
758 A250 3s plum   .35 .20

Ferris Wheel, Prater — A251

1966, Apr. 19   **Engr.**   **Perf. 14x13½**
759 A251 1.50s slate green   .20 .20
Opening of the Prater (park), Vienna, to the public by Emperor Joseph II, 200th anniv.

Josef Hoffmann (1870-1956), Architect A252

1966, May 6   **Unwmk.**   **Perf. 12**
760 A252 3s dark brown   .35 .20

Wiener Neustadt Arms — A253

Photo. and Engr.
1966, May 27   *Perf. 14*
761 A253 1.50s multicolored   .20 .20
Wiener Neustadt Art Exhib., centered around the time and person of Frederick III (1440-93).

Austrian Eagle and Emblem of National Bank — A254

1966, May 27   *Perf. 14*
762 A254 3s gray grn, dk brn & dk green   .35 .20
Austrian National Bank, 150th anniv.

Puppy — A255

Litho. and Engr.
1966, June 16   *Perf. 12*
763 A255 1.80s yellow & black   .25 .20
120th anniv. of the Vienna Humane Society.

Alpine Flowers — A256

1.50s, Columbine. 1.80s, Turk's cap. 2.20s, Wulfenia carinthiaca. 3s, Globeflowers. 4s, Fire lily. 5s, Pasqueflower.

1966, Aug. 17   Litho.   *Perf. 13½*
Flowers in Natural Colors
764	A256	1.50s dark blue	.20	.20
765	A256	1.80s dark blue	.25	.20
766	A256	2.20s dark blue	.35	.20
767	A256	3s dark blue	.50	.30
768	A256	4s dark blue	.50	.35
769	A256	5s dark blue	.50	.35
		Nos. 764-769 (6)	2.30	1.60

Fair Building A257

1966, Aug. 26   Engr.   *Perf. 13½x13*
770 A257 3s violet blue   .35 .20
First International Fair at Wels.

Peter Anich (1723-1766), Tirolean Cartographer and Books — A258

1966, Sept. 1   *Perf. 14x13½*
771 A258 1.80s black   .20 .20

Sick Worker and Health Emblem — A259

1966, Sept. 19   Engr. and Litho.
772 A259 3s black & vermilion   .35 .20
15th Occupational Medicine Congress, Vienna, Sept. 19-24.

Theater Collection: "Eunuchus" by Terence from a 1496 Edition A260

Designs: 1.80s, Map Collection: Title page of Geographia Blavania (Cronus, Hercules and celestial sphere). 2.20s, Picture Archive and Portrait Collection: View of Old Vienna after a watercolor by Anton Stutzinger. 3s, Manuscript Collection: Illustration from the 15th century "Livre du Cuer d'Amours Espris" of the Duke René d'Anjou.

Photogravure and Engraved
1966, Sept. 28   *Perf. 13½x14*
773	A260	1.50s multicolored	.20	.20
774	A260	1.80s multicolored	.20	.20
775	A260	2.20s multicolored	.25	.20
776	A260	3s multicolored	.35	.20
		Nos. 773-776 (4)	1.00	.80

Austrian National Library.

Young Girl A261   Strawberries A262

Litho. and Engr.
1966, Oct. 3   *Perf. 14x13½*
777 A261 3s light blue & black   .35 .20
"Save the Child" society, 10th anniv.

1966, Nov. 25   Photo.   *Perf. 13½x13*
778	A262	50g shown	.20	.20
779	A262	1s Grapes	.20	.20
780	A262	1.50s Apple	.20	.20
781	A262	1.80s Blackberries	.25	.20
782	A262	2.20s Apricots	.25	.20
783	A262	3s Cherries	.35	.25
		Nos. 778-783 (6)	1.45	1.25

Coat of Arms of University of Linz — A263

Photo. and Engr.
1966, Dec. 9   *Perf. 14x13½*
784 A263 3s multi   .35 .20
Inauguration of the Universary of Linz, Oct. 8, 1966.

Vienna Ice Skating Club, Cent. — A264

Photo. and Engr.
1967, Feb. 3   *Perf. 14x13½*
785 A264 3s Skater, 1866   .35 .20

Ballet Dancer — A265

1967, Feb. 15   Engr.   *Perf. 11½x12*
786 A265 3s deep claret   .35 .20
a.   Perf. 12   1.25 1.10
"Blue Danube" waltz by Johann Strauss, cent.

Dr. Karl Schönherr (1867-1943), Poet, Playwright and Physician — A266

1967, Feb. 24   Engr.   *Perf. 14x13½*
787 A266 3s gray brown   .35 .20

Ice Hockey Goalkeeper A267

Photogravure and Engraved
1967, Mar. 17   *Perf. 13½x14*
788 A267 3s pale grn & dk bl   .35 .20
Ice Hockey Championships, Vienna, Mar. 18-29.

Violin, Organ and Laurel — A268

1967, Mar. 28   Engr.   *Perf. 13½*
789 A268 3.50s indigo   .40 .20
Vienna Philharmonic Orchestra, 125th anniv.

Motherhood, Watercolor by Peter Fendi — A269

1967, Apr. 28   Litho.   *Perf. 14*
790 A269 2s multicolored   .25 .20
Mother's Day.

Gothic Mantle Madonna A270

1967, May 19   Engr.   *Perf. 13½x14*
791 A270 3s slate   .35 .20
"Austrian Gothic," art exhibition, Krems, 1967. The Gothic wood carving is from Frauenstein in Upper Austria.

Medieval Gold Cross A271   Swan, Tapestry by Oscar Kokoschka A272

Litho. and Engr.
1967, June 9   *Perf. 13½*
792 A271 3.50s Prus grn & multi   .40 .20
Salzburg Treasure Chamber; exhibition at Salzburg Cathedral, June 12-Sept. 15.

1967, June 9   Photo.
793 A272 2s multicolored   .25 .20
Nibelungen District Art Exhibition, Pöchlarn, celebrating the 700th anniversary of Pöchlarn as a city. The design is from the border of the Amor and Psyche tapestry at the Salzburg Festival Theater.

View and Arms of Vienna A273

Engraved and Photogravure
1967, June 12   *Perf. 13x13½*
794 A273 3s black & red   .35 .20
10th Europa Talks, "Science and Society in Europe," Vienna, June 13-17.

Prize Bull "Mucki" A274

1967, Aug. 28 Engr. Perf. 13½
795 A274 2s deep claret .35 .20
Centenary of the Ried Festival and the Agricultural Fair.

Potato Beetle A275

Engraved and Photogravure
1967, Aug. 29 Perf. 13½x14
796 A275 3s black & multi .35 .20
6th Intl. Congress for Plant Protection, Vienna.

First Locomotive Used on Brenner Pass A276

1967, Sept. 23 Photo. Perf. 12
797 A276 3.50s tan & slate grn .45 .20
Centenary of railroad over Brenner Pass.

Christ in Glory — A277

1967, Oct. 9 Perf. 13½
798 A277 2s multicolored .25 .20
Restoration of the Romanesque (11th century) frescoes in the Lambach monastery church.

Main Gate to Fair, Prater, Vienna A278

1967, Oct. 24 Photo. Perf. 13½x14
799 A278 2s choc & buff .25 .20
Congress of Intl. Trade Fairs, Vienna, Oct., 1967.

Medal Showing Minerva and Art Symbols — A279

Litho. & Engr.
1967, Oct. 25 Perf. 13½
800 A279 2s dk brn, dk bl & yel .25 .20
Vienna Academy of Fine Arts, 275th anniv. The medal was designed by Georg Raphael Donner (1693-1741) and is awarded as an artist's prize.

Frankfurt Medal for Reformation, 1717 — A280

1967, Oct. 31 Engr. Perf. 14x13½
801 A280 3.50s blue black .40 .20
450th anniversary of the Reformation.

Mountain Range and Stone Pines A281

1967, Nov. 7 Perf. 13½
802 A281 3.50s green .40 .20
Centenary of academic study of forestry.

Land Survey Monument, 1770 — A282

1967, Nov. 7 Photo.
803 A282 2s olive black .25 .20
150th anniversary of official land records.

St. Leopold, Window, Heiligenkreuz Abbey — A283

1967, Nov. 15 Engr. & Photo.
804 A283 1.80s multicolored .25 .20
Margrave Leopold III (1075-1136), patron saint of Austria.

Tragic Mask and Violin — A284

1967, Nov. 17 Perf. 13½
805 A284 3.50s bluish lil & blk .40 .20
Academy of Music and Dramatic Art, 150th anniv.

Nativity from 15th Century Altar — A285

1967, Nov. 27 Engr. Perf. 14x13½
806 A285 2s green .25 .20
Christmas.
The design shows the late Gothic carved center panel of the altar in St. John's Chapel in Nonnberg Convent, Salzburg.

Innsbruck Stadium, Alps and FISU Emblem — A286

1968, Jan. 22 Engr. Perf. 13½
807 A286 2s dark blue .25 .20
Winter University Games under the auspices of FISU (Fédération Internationale du Sport Universitaire), Innsbruck, Jan. 21-28.

Camillo Sitte (1843-1903), Architect, City Planner — A287

1968, Apr. 17 Perf. 13½
808 A287 2s black brown .25 .20

Mother and Child — A288

1968, May 7
809 A288 2s slate green .25 .20
Mother's Day.

Cup and Serpent Emblem — A289

1968, May 7 Photo.
810 A289 3.50s dp plum, gray & gold .40 .20
Bicentenary of the Veterinary College.

Bride with Lace Veil — A290

1968, May 24 Engr. Perf. 12
811 A290 3.50s blue black .40 .20
Embroidery industry of Vorarlberg, cent.

Horse Race A291

1968, June 4 Perf. 13½
812 A291 3.50s sepia .40 .20
Centenary of horse racing at Freudenau, Vienna.

Dr. Karl Landsteiner A292

1968, June 14 Perf. 14x13½
813 A292 3.50s dark blue .40 .20
Birth cent. of Dr. Karl Landsteiner (1868-1943), pathologist, discoverer of the four main human blood types.

Peter Rosegger (1843-1918), Poet and Writer — A293

1968, June 26
814 A293 2s slate green .25 .20

Angelica Kauffmann, Self-portrait A294

1968, July 15 Engr. Perf. 14x13½
815 A294 2s intense black .25 .20
"Angelica Kauffmann and her Contemporaries," art exhibitions, Bregenz, July 28-Oct. 13, and Vienna, Oct. 22, 1968-Jan. 6, 1969.

Bronze Statue of Young Man, 1st Century B.C. — A295

1968, July 15 Litho. & Engr.
816 A295 2s grnsh gray & blk .25 .20
20 years of excavations on Magdalene Mountain, Carinthia.

Bishop, Romanesque Bas-relief — A296

1968, Sept. 20   Engr.   Perf. 14x13½
817 A296 2s blue gray   .25   .20
Graz-Seckau Bishopric, 750th anniv.

Koloman Moser (1868-1918), Stamp Designer, Painter — A297

Engr. & Photo.
1968, Oct. 18   Perf. 12
818 A297 2s black brn & ver   .25   .20

Intl. Human Rights Year — A298

1968, Oct. 18   Photo.   Perf. 14x13½
819 A298 1.50s gray, dp car & dk green   .30   .20

Republic of Austria, 50th Anniv. — A299

#820, Pres. Karl Renner and States' arms. #821, Coats of arms of Austria and Austrian states. #822, Article I of Austrian Constitution and States' coats of arms.

Engr. & Photo.
1968, Nov. 11   Perf. 13½
820 A299 2s black & multi   .35   .30
821 A299 2s black & multi   .35   .30
822 A299 2s black & multi   .35   .30
        Nos. 820-822 (3)   1.05   .90

Hymn "Silent Night, Holy Night," 150th Anniv. — A300

Crèche, Memorial Chapel, Oberndorf-Salzburg.

1968, Nov. 29   Engr.   Perf. 14x13½
823 A300 2s slate green   .25   .20
Christmas.

Angels, from Last Judgment by Troger (Röhrenbach-Greillenstein Chapel) — A301

Baroque Frescoes: No. 825, Vanquished Demons, by Paul Troger, Altenburg Abbey. No. 826, Sts. Peter and Paul, by Troger, Melk Abbey. No. 827, The Glorification of Mary, by Franz Anton Maulpertsch, Maria Treu Church, Vienna. No. 828, St. Leopold Carried into Heaven, by Maulpertsch, Ebenfurth Castle Chapel. No. 829, Symbolic figures from The Triumph of Apollo, by Maulpertsch, Halbthurn Castle.

Engr. & Photo.
1968, Dec. 11   Perf. 13½x14
824 A301 2s multicolored   .30   .30
825 A301 2s multicolored   .30   .30
826 A301 2s multicolored   .30   .30
827 A301 2s multicolored   .30   .30
828 A301 2s multicolored   .30   .30
829 A301 2s multicolored   .30   .30
        Nos. 824-829 (6)   1.80 1.80

St. Stephen — A302

Statues in St. Stephen's Cathedral, Vienna: No. 831, St. Paul. No. 832, Mantle Madonna. No. 833, St. Christopher. No. 834, St. George and the Dragon. No. 835, St. Sebastian.

1969, Jan. 28   Engr.   Perf. 13½
830 A302 2s black   .30   .30
831 A302 2s rose claret   .30   .30
832 A302 2s gray violet   .30   .30
833 A302 2s slate violet   .30   .30
834 A302 2s slate green   .30   .30
835 A302 2s dk red brn   .30   .30
        Nos. 830-835 (6)   1.80 1.80
500th anniversary of Diocese of Vienna.

Parliament and Pallas Athena Fountain, Vienna A303

1969, Apr. 8   Engr.   Perf. 13½
836 A303 2s greenish black   .25   .20
Interparliamentary Union Conf., Vienna, 4/7-13.

Europa Issue, 1969
Common Design Type
1969, Apr. 28   Photo.   Perf. 12
837 CD12 2s gray grn, brick red & blue   .25   .20

Council of Europe Emblem A304

1969, May 5
838 A304 3.50s gray, ultra, blk & yel   .45   .25
20th anniversary of Council of Europe.

Frontier Guards — A305

Engr. & Photo.
1969, May 14   Perf. 12
839 A305 2s sepia & red   .25   .20
Austrian Federal Army.

Don Giovanni, by Mozart A306

Cent. of Vienna Opera House: a, Don Giovanni, Mozart. b, Magic Flute, Mozart. c, Fidelio, Beethoven. d, Lohengrin, Wagner. e, Don Carlos, Verdi. f, Carmen, Bizet. g, Rosencavalier, Richard Strauss. h, Swan Lake, Ballet by Tchaikovsky.

1969, May 23   Perf. 13½
840 A306 Sheet of 8   4.00 4.00
a.-h.   2s, any single   .35   .35
Centenary of Vienna Opera House.
No. 840 contains 8 stamps arranged around gold and red center label showing Opera House. Printed in sheets containing 4 Nos. 840 with wide gutters between.

Emperor Maximilian I Exhibition, Innsbruck, May 30-Oct. 5 — A307

Gothic armor of Maximilian I.

1969, June 4   Engr.
841 A307 2s bluish black   .25   .20

19th Cong. of the Intl. Org. of Municipalities, Vienna — A308

1969, June 16   Photo.   Perf. 13½
Oldest Municipal Seal of Vienna.
842 A308 2s tan, red & black   .25   .20

SOS Children's Villages in Austria, 20th Anniv. — A309

Girl's head and village house.

Engraved and Photogravure
1969, June 16   Perf. 13½x14
843 A309 2s yel grn & sepia   .25   .20

ILO, 50th Anniv. — A310

1969, Aug. 22   Photo.   Perf. 13x13½
Hands holding wrench, and UN emblem.
844 A310 2s deep green   .25   .20

Year of Austrians Living Abroad, 1969 — A311

Austria's flag and shield circling the world.

Engraved and Lithographed
1969, Aug. 22   Perf. 14x13½
845 A311 3.50s slate & red   .40   .20

Etching Collection in the Albertina, Vienna, Bicent. — A312

Etchings: No. 846, Young Hare, by Dürer. No. 847, El Cid Killing a Bull, by Francisco de Goya. No. 848, Madonna with the Pomegranate, by Raphael. No. 849, The Painter, by Peter Brueghel. No. 850, Rubens' Son Nicolas, by Rubens. No. 851, Self-portrait, by Rembrandt. No. 852, Lady Reading, by Francois Guerin. No. 853, Wife of the Artist, by Egon Schiele.

Engraved and Photogravure
1969, Sept. 26   Perf. 13½
Gray Frame, Buff Background
846 A312 2s black & brown   .30   .30
847 A312 2s black   .30   .30
848 A312 2s black   .30   .30
849 A312 2s black   .30   .30
850 A312 2s black & salmon   .30   .30
851 A312 2s black   .30   .30
852 A312 2s black & salmon   .30   .30
853 A312 2s black   .30   .30
        Nos. 846-853 (8)   2.40 2.40

President Franz Jonas — A313

1969, Oct. 3
854 A313 2s gray & vio blue   .25   .20
70th birthday of Franz Jonas, Austrian Pres.

Post Horn, Globe and Lightning A314

1969, Oct. 17   **Perf. 13½x14**
855 A314 2s multicolored   .25 .20

Union of Postal and Telegraph employees, 50th anniv.

Savings Box, about 1450 — A315

1969, Oct. 31   Photo.   Perf. 13x13½
856 A315 2s silver & slate green   .25 .20

The importance of savings.

Madonna, by Albin Egger-Lienz A316

Engr. & Photo.
1969, Nov. 24   **Perf. 12**
857 A316 2s dp claret & pale yel   .25 .20

Christmas.

Josef Schöffel — A317

1970, Feb. 6   Engr.   Perf. 14x13½
858 A317 2s dull purple   .25 .20

60th death anniv. of Josef Schöffel, (1832-1910), who saved the Vienna Woods.

St. Klemens M. Hofbauer — A318

Engraved and Photogravure
1970, Mar. 13   **Perf. 14x13½**
859 A318 2s dk brn & lt tan   .25 .20

150th death anniv. St. Klemens Maria Hofbauer (1751-1820); Redemptorist preacher in Poland and Austria, canonized in 1909.

Chancellor Leopold Figl — A319

Belvedere Palace, Vienna — A320

1970, Apr. 27   Engr.   Perf. 13½
860 A319 2s dark olive gray   .25 .20
861 A320 2s dark rose brown   .25 .20

25th anniversary of Second Republic.

European Nature Conservation Year, 1970 — A321

1970, May 19   Engr.   Perf. 13½
862 A321 2s Krimml waterfalls   .30 .20

Leopold Franzens University, Innsbruck, 300th Anniv. — A322

Litho. & Engr.
1970, June 5   **Perf. 13½**

St. Leopold on oldest seal of Innsbruck University.

863 A322 2s red & black   .30 .20

Organ, Great Hall, Music Academy — A323

Photo. & Engr.
1970, June 5   **Perf. 14**
864 A323 2s gold & deep claret   .25 .20

Vienna Music Academy Building, cent.

Tower Clock, 1450-1550 A324

Old Clocks from Vienna Horological Museum: #866, Lyre clock, 1790-1815. #867, Pendant clock 1600-50. #868, Pendant watch, 1800-30. #869, Bracket clock, 1720-60. #870, French column clock, 1820-50.

1970
865 A324 1.50s buff & sepia   .25 .25
866 A324 1.50s greenish & grn   .25 .25
867 A324 2s pale bl & dk bl   .30 .30
868 A324 2s pale rose & lake   .30 .30
869 A324 3.50s buff & brown   .50 .50
870 A324 3.50s pale lil & brn vio   .50 .50
    Nos. 865-870 (6)   2.10 2.10

Issued: #865, 867, 869, 6/22; others, 10/23.

The Beggar Student, by Carl Millöcker — A325

Operettas: No. 872, Fledermaus, by Johann Strauss. No. 873, The Dream Waltz, by Oscar Strauss. No. 874, The Bird Seller, by Carl Zeller. No. 875, The Merry Widow, by Franz Lehar. No. 876, Two Hearts in Three-quarter Time, by Robert Stolz.

1970   Photo. & Engr.   Perf. 13½
871 A325 1.50s pale grn & grn   .25 .25
872 A325 1.50s yel & vio blue   .25 .25
873 A325 2s pale rose & vio
       brn   .30 .30
874 A325 2s pale grn & sep   .30 .30
875 A325 3.50s pale bl & ind   .50 .50
876 A325 3.50s beige & slate   .50 .50
    Nos. 871-876 (6)   2.10 2.10

Issued: #871, 873, 875, 7/3; others 9/11.

Bregenz Festival Stage — A326

1970, July 23   **Photo.**
877 A326 3.50s dark blue & buff   .40 .20

25th anniversary of Bregenz Festival.

Salzburg Festival Emblem — A327

1970, July 27   **Perf. 14**
878 A327 3.50s blk, red, gold &
       gray   .40 .20

50th anniversary of Salzburg Festival.

A328

1970, Aug. 31   **Engr.**
879 A328 3.50s dark gray   .45 .20

13th General Assembly of the World Veterans Federation, Aug. 28-Sept. 4. The head of St. John is from a sculpture showing the Agony in the Garden in the chapel of the Parish Church in Ried. It is attributed to Thomas Schwanthaler (1634-1702).

Thomas Koschat (1845-1914), Carinthian Song Composer A329

1970, Sept. 16   **Perf. 14x13½**
880 A329 2s chocolate   .25 .20

Mountain Scene A330

1970, Sept. 16   Photo.   Perf. 14x13½
881 A330 2s vio bl & pink   .25 .20

Hiking and mountaineering in Austria.

Alfred Cossmann (1870-1951), Engraver — A331

1970, Oct. 2   Engr.   Perf. 14x13½
882 A331 2s dark brown   .25 .20

Arms of Carinthia — A332

Photo. & Engr.
1970, Oct. 2   **Perf. 14**
883 A332 2s ol, red, gold, blk & sil   .25 .20

Carinthian plebiscite, 50th anniversary.

UN Emblem A333

1970, Oct. 23   Litho.   Perf. 14x13½
884 A333 3.50s lt blue & blk   .50 .20

25th anniversary of the United Nations.

Adoration of the Shepherds, Carving from Garsten Vicarage A334

1970, Nov. 27   Engr.   Perf. 13½x14
885 A334 2s dk violet blue   .25 .20

Christmas.

Karl Renner
(1870-1950),
Austrian
Pres. — A335

1970, Dec. 14   Engr.   Perf. 14x13½
886 A335 2s deep claret   .25 .20

Beethoven, by
Georg
Waldmüller
A336

Photo. & Engr.
1970, Dec. 16   Perf. 13½
887 A336 3.50s black & buff   .50 .20
Ludwig van Beethoven (1770-1827), composer, birth bicentenary.

Enrica Handel-
Mazzetti (1871-
1955), Novelist,
Poet — A337

1971, Jan. 11   Engr.   Perf. 14x13½
888 A337 2s sepia   .25 .20

"Watch
Out for
Children!"
A338

1971, Feb. 18   Photo.   Perf. 13½
889 A338 2s blk, red brn & brt grn .25 .20
Traffic safety.

Saltcellar,
by
Benvenuto
Cellini
A339

Art Treasures: 1.50s, Covered vessel, made
of prase, gold and precious stones, Florentine,
1580. 2s, Emperor Joseph I, ivory statue by
Matthias Steinle, 1693.

Photo. & Engr.
1971, Mar. 22   Perf. 14
890 A339 1.50s gray & slate grn   .20 .20
891 A339 2s gray & dp plum   .25 .20
892 A339 3.50s gray, blk & bister .55 .35
         Nos. 890-892 (3)   1.00 .75

Emblem of
Austrian
Wholesalers'
Organization
A340

1971, Apr. 16   Photo.   Perf. 13½
893 A340 3.50s multicolored   .45 .20
Intl. Chamber of Commerce, 23rd Congress, Vienna, Apr. 17-23.

Jacopo de
Strada, by
Titian — A341

Paintings in Vienna Museum: 2s, Village
Feast, by Peter Brueghel, the Elder. 3.50s,
Young Venetian Woman, by Albrecht Dürer.

1971, May 6   Engr.   Perf. 13½
894 A341 1.50s rose lake   .25 .20
895 A341 2s greenish black   .25 .20
896 A341 3.50s deep brown   .50 .35
         Nos. 894-896 (3)   1.00 .75

Seal of Paulus
of
Franchenfordia,
1380 — A342

Photo. & Engr.
1971, May 6   Perf. 13½x14
897 A342 3.50s dk brn & bister   .40 .20
Congress commemorating the centenary of
the Austrian Notaries' Statute, May 5-8.

St.   August
Matthew — A343   Neilreich — A344

1971, May 27   Perf. 12½x13½
898 A343 2s brt rose lil & brn   .25 .20
Exhibition of "1000 Years of Art in Krems."
The statue of St. Matthew is from the Lentl
Altar, created about 1520 by the Master of the
Pulkau Altar.

1971, June 1   Engr.   Perf. 14x13½
899 A344 2s brown   .25 .20
August Neilreich (1803-71), botanist.

Singer with
Lyre — A345

Photo. & Engr.
1971, July 1   Perf. 13½x14
900 A345 4s lt bl, vio bl & gold   .50 .30
Intl. Choir Festival, Vienna, July 1-4.

Coat of Arms of
Kitzbuhel — A346

1971, Aug. 23   Perf. 14
901 A346 2.50s gold & multi   .35 .20
700th anniversary of the town of Kitzbuhel.

Vienna Stock Exchange — A347

1971, Sept. 1   Engr.   Perf. 13½x14
902 A347 4s reddish brown   .55 .20
Bicentenary of the Vienna Stock Exchange.

First and
Latest
Exhibition
Halls
A348

1971, Sept. 6   Photo.   Perf. 13½x13
903 A348 2.50s dp rose lilac   .35 .20
Vienna Intl. Fair, 50th anniv.

Trade Union
Emblem — A349

1971, Sept. 20   Perf. 14x13½
904 A349 2s gray, buff & red   .25 .20
Austrian Trade Union Assoc., 25th anniv.

Arms of
Burgenland
A350

1971, Oct. 1
905 A350 2s dk bl, gold, red & blk .25 .20
50th anniv. of Burgenland joining Austria.

Marcus
Car — A351

Photo. & Engr.
1971, Oct. 1   Perf. 14
906 A351 4s pale green & blk   .50 .25
Austrian Automobile, Motorcycle and Touring Club, 75th anniv.

Europa
Bridge — A352

1971, Oct. 8   Engr.   Perf. 14x13½
907 A352 4s violet blue   .50 .25
Opening of highway over Brenner Pass.

Styria's
Iron
Mountain
A353

Designs: 2s, Austrian Nitrogen Products,
Ltd., Linz. 4s, United Austrian Iron and Steel
Works, Ltd. (VOEST), Linz Harbor.

1971, Oct. 15   Perf. 13½
908 A353 1.50s reddish brown   .25 .20
909 A353 2s bluish black   .30 .20
910 A353 4s dk slate grn   .45 .35
         Nos. 908-910 (3)   1.00 .75
25 years of nationalized industry.

High-speed Train
on Semmering
A354

1971, Oct. 21   Perf. 14
911 A354 2s claret   .25 .20
Inter-city rapid train service.

Trout Fisherman
A355

1971, Nov. 15   Perf. 13½
912 A355 2s dark red brn   .25 .20

Dr. Erich Tschermak-Seysenegg
(1871-1962), Botanist — A356

Photo. & Engr.
1971, Nov. 15   Perf. 14x13½
913 A356 2s pale ol & dk pur   .25 .20

Infant Jesus as Savior, by Dürer — A357

1971, Nov. 26   *Perf. 13½*
914 A357 2s gold & multi   .25 .20

Christmas.

Franz Grillparzer, by Moritz Daffinger — A358

Litho. & Engr.
1972, Jan. 21   *Perf. 14x13½*
915 A358 2s buff, gold & blk   .30 .20

Death cent. of Franz Grillparzer (1791-1872), dramatic poet.

Fountain, Main Square, Friesach — A359

Designs: 2s, Fountain, Heiligenkreuz Abbey. 2.50s, Leopold Fountain, Innsbruck.

1972, Feb. 23   **Engr.**   *Perf. 14x13½*
916 A359 1.50s rose lilac   .25 .20
917 A359 2s brown   .25 .20
918 A359 2.50s olive   .30 .25
    Nos. 916-918 (3)   .80 .65

Cardiac Patient and Monitor A360

1972, Apr. 11   *Perf. 13½x14*
919 A360 4s violet brown   .55 .25

World Health Day.

Conference of European Post and Telecommunications Ministers, Vienna, Apr. 11-14 — A361

St. Michael's Gate, Royal Palace, Vienna.

1972, Apr. 11   *Perf. 14x13½*
920 A361 4s violet blue   .55 .25

Gurk (Carinthia) Diocese, 900th Anniv. — A362

Photo. & Engr.
1972, May 5   *Perf. 14*
921 A362 2s Sculpture, Gurk Cathedral   .30 .20

. The design is after the central column supporting the sarcophagus of St. Hemma in Gurk Cathedral.

City Hall, Congress Emblem A363

1972, May 23   **Litho. & Engr.**
922 A363 4s red, blk & yel   .55 .20

9th Intl. Congress of Public and Cooperative Economy, Vienna, May 23-25.

Power Line in Carnic Alps — A364

2.50s, Power Station, Semmering. 4s, Zemm Power Station (lake in Zillertaler Alps).

1972, June 28   *Perf. 13½x14*
923 A364 70g gray & violet   .20 .20
924 A364 2.50s gray & red brn   .30 .30
925 A364 4s gray & slate   .50 .50
    Nos. 923-925 (3)   1.00 1.00

Nationalization of the power industry, 25th anniv.

Runner with Olympic Torch — A365

Engr. & Photo.
1972, Aug. 21   *Perf. 14x13½*
926 A365 2s sepia & red   .25 .20

Olympic torch relay from Olympia, Greece, to Munich, Germany, passing through Austria.

St. Hermes, by Conrad Laib — A366

1972, Aug. 21   **Engr.**
927 A366 2s violet brown   .25 .20

Exhibition of Late Gothic Art, Salzburg.

Pears A367

1972, Sept.   *Perf. 14*
928 A367 2.50s dk blue & multi   .30 .20

World Congress of small plot Gardeners, Vienna, Sept. 7-10.

Souvenir Sheet

Spanish Riding School, Vienna, 400th Anniv. — A368

1972, Sept. 12   *Perf. 13½*
929   Sheet of 6   2.75 2.75
a. A368 2s Spanish walk   .25 .25
b. A368 2s Piaffe   .25 .25
c. A368 2.50s Levade   .30 .30
d. A368 2.50s On long rein   .30 .30
e. A368 4s Capriole   .50 .50
f. A368 4s Courbette   .50 .50

Arms of University of Agriculture A369

Photo. & Engr.
1972, Oct. 17   *Perf. 14x13½*
930 A369 2s black & multi   .25 .20

University of Agriculture, Vienna, cent.

Church and Old University — A370

1972, Nov. 7   **Engr.**
931 A370 4s red brown   .55 .20

Paris Lodron University, Salzburg, 350th anniv.

Carl Michael Ziehrer — A371

1972, Nov. 14
932 A371 2s rose claret   .25 .20

50th death anniv. of Carl Michael Ziehrer (1843-1922), composer.

Virgin and Child, Wood, 1420-30 A372

Photo. & Engr.
1972, Dec. 1   *Perf. 13½*
933 A372 2s olive & chocolate   .25 .20

Christmas.

Racing Sleigh, 1750 A373

Designs: 2s, Coronation landau, 1824. 2.50s, Imperial state coach, 1763.

1972, Dec. 12
934 A373 1.50s pale gray & brn   .20 .20
935 A373 2s pale gray & sl grn   .30 .20
936 A373 2.50s pale gray & plum   .35 .25
    Nos. 934-936 (3)   .85 .65

Collection of historic state coaches and carriages in Schönbrunn Palace.

Map of Austrian Telephone System A374

1972, Dec. 14   **Photo.**   *Perf. 14*
937 A374 2s yellow & blk   .25 .20

Completion of automation of Austrian telephone system.

"Drugs are Death" A375

1973, Jan. 26   **Photo.**   *Perf. 13½x14*
938 A375 2s scarlet & multi   1.50 .45

Fight against drug abuse.

Alfons Petzold (1882-1923), Poet — A376

1973, Jan. 26   **Engr.**   *Perf. 14x13½*
939 A376 2s reddish brn   .25 .20

Theodor Körner (1873-1957), Austrian Pres. — A377

Photo. & Engr.
1973, Apr. 24   *Perf. 14x13½*
940 A377 2s gray & deep claret   .25 .20

Douglas DC-9
A378

1973, May 14   *Perf. 13½x14*
941 A378 2s vio bl & rose red   .30 .20
First intl. airmail service, Vienna to Kiev, Mar. 31, 1918, 55th anniv.; Austrian Aviation Corporation, 50th anniv.; Austrian Airlines, 15th anniv.

Otto Loewi (1873-1961), Pharmacologist, Nobel Laureate — A379

1973, June 4   Engr.   Perf. 14x13½
942 A379 4s deep violet   .55 .20

"Support" — A380

1973, June 25
943 A380 2s dark blue   .25 .20
Federation of Austrian Social Insurance Institutes, 25th anniv.

Europa Issue 1973

Post Horn and Telephone
A381

1973, July 9   Photo.   Perf. 14
944 A381 2.50s ocher, blk & yel   .30 .20

Dornbirn Fair Emblem
A382

1973, July 27   Perf. 13½x14
945 A382 2s multicolored   .30 .20
Dornbirn Trade Fair, 25th anniversary.

23rd Intl. Military Pentathlon Championships, Wiener Neustadt, Aug. 13-18 — A383

1973, Aug. 13   Engr.   Perf. 14x13½
946 A383 4s Hurdles   .50 .20

Leo Slezak (1873-1946), Operatic Tenor — A384

1973, Aug. 17   Perf. 14
947 A384 4s dark brown   .50 .20

Gate, Vienna Hofburg, and ISI Emblem — A385

Photogravure and Engraved
1973, Aug. 20   Perf. 14x13½
948 A385 2s gray, dk brn & ver   .25 .20
39th Congress of Intl. Statistical Institute, Vienna, Aug. 20-30.

Tegetthoff off Franz Josef Land, by Julius Prayer A386

1973, Aug. 30   Engr.   Perf. 13½x14
949 A386 2.50s Prussian grn   .30 .20
Discovery of Franz Josef Land by an Austrian North Pole expedition, cent.

Academy of Science, by Canaletto A387

1973, Sept. 4
950 A387 2.50s violet   .30 .20
Intl. meteorological cooperation, cent.

Arms of Viennese Tanners — A388

Photo. & Engr.
1973, Sept. 4   Perf. 14
951 A388 4s red & multi   .55 .20
13th Congress of the Intl. Union of Leather Chemists' Societies, Vienna, Sept. 1-7.

Max Reinhardt (1873-1943), Theatrical Director — A389

1973, Sept. 7   Engr.   Perf. 13x13½
952 A389 2s rose magenta   .25 .20

Trotter A390

1973, Sept. 28   Perf. 13½
953 A390 2s green   .30 .20
Centenary of Vienna Trotting Association.

Ferdinand Hanusch(1866-1923), Secretary of State — A391

1973, Sept. 28   Perf. 14x13½
954 A391 2s rose brown   .25 .20

Police Radio Operator A392

1973, Oct. 2   Perf. 13½x14
955 A392 4s violet blue   .50 .20
50th anniv. of Intl. Criminal Police Org. (INTERPOL).

Josef Petzval's Photographic Lens — A393

Litho. & Engr.
1973, Oct. 8   Perf. 14
956 A393 2.50s blue & multi   .30 .20
EUROPHOT Photographic Cong., Vienna.

Emperor's Spring, Hell Valley A394

Photo. & Engr.
1973, Oct. 23   Perf. 13½x14
957 A394 2s sepia, blue & red   .25 .20
Vienna's first mountain spring water supply system, cent.

Almsee, Upper Austria — A395

Hofburg and Prince Eugene Statue, Vienna — A395a

Designs: 50g, Farmhouses, Zillertal, Tirol. 1s, Kahlenbergerdorf. 1.50s, Bludenz, Vorarlberg. 2s, Inn Bridge, Alt Finstermunz. 2.50s, Murau, Styria. 3s, Bischofsmütze, Salzburg. 3.50s, Easter Church, Oberwart. 4.50s, Windmill, Retz. 5s, Aggstein Castle, Lower Austria. 6s, Lindauer Hut, Vorarlberg. 6.50s, Holy Cross Church, Villach, Carinthia. 7s, Falkenstein Castle, Carinthia. 7.50s, Hohensalzburg. 8s, Votive column, Reiteregg, Styria. 10s, Lake Neusiedl, Burgenland. 11s, Old Town, Enns. 16s, Openair Museum, Bad Tatzmannsdorf. 20s, Myra waterfalls.

Photo. & Engr.
1973-78   Perf. 13½x14
Size: 23x29mm

958	A395	50g gray & slate green	.20	.20
959	A395	1s brn & dk brown	.20	.20
960	A395	1.50s rose & brown	.25	.20
961	A395	2s gray bl & dk blue	.30	.20
962	A395	2.50s vio & dp violet	.35	.20
963	A395	3s lt ultra & vio blue	.45	.20
963A	A395	3.50s dl org & brown	.50	.20
964	A395	4s brt lil & pur	.55	.20
965	A395	4.50s brt grn & bl green	.60	.20
966	A395	5s lilac & vio	.65	.20
967	A395	6s dp rose & dk violet	.80	.20
968	A395	6.50s bl grn & indigo	.90	.20
969	A395	7s sage grn & sl green	.95	.20
970	A395	7.50s lil rose & claret	1.00	.25
971	A395	8s dl red & dp brown	1.10	.20
972	A395	10s gray grn & dk green	1.40	.20
973	A395	11s ver & dk carmine	1.60	.20
974	A395	16s bister & brown	2.25	.60
975	A395	20s ol bis & ol grn	2.75	1.25
976	A395a	50s gray vio & vio bl	6.75	2.50
Nos. 958-976 (20)			23.55	7.80

Issued: #960-963, 1974; #958-959, 967, 976, 1975; #965, 971, 973, 1976; #968, 970, 974-975, 1977; #963A, 1978. See #1100-1109.

Nativity — A396

1973, Nov. 30   Perf. 14
977 A396 2s multicolored   .30 .20
Christmas. Design from 14th century stained-glass window.

Pregl — A397

1973, Dec. 12 Engr. *Perf. 14x13½*
978 A397 4s deep blue   .50 .20
  50th anniv. of the awarding of the Nobel prize for chemistry to Fritz Pregl (1869-1930).

Radio Austria, 50th Anniv. — A398

1974, Jan. 14 Photo. *Perf. 14x13½*
979 A398 2.50s Telex Machine   .30 .20

Hugo Hofmannsthal(1874-1929), Poet and Playwright — A399

1974, Feb. 1 Engr. *Perf. 14*
980 A399 4s violet blue   .50 .20

Anton Bruckner and Bruckner House A400

1974, Mar. 22 Engr. *Perf. 14*
981 A400 4s brown   .50 .20
  Founding of Anton Bruckner House (concert hall), Linz, and birth of Anton Bruckner (1824-1896), composer, 150th anniv.

Vegetables A401

Photo. & Engr.
1974, Apr. 18 *Perf. 14*
982 A401 2s shown   .30 .20
983 A401 2.50s Fruits   .35 .30
984 A401 4s Flowers   .50 .50
  Nos. 982-984 (3)   1.15 1.00
  Intl. Garden Show, Vienna, Apr. 18-Oct. 14.

Seal of Judenburg A402

1974, Apr. 24 Photo. *Perf. 14x13½*
985 A402 2s plum & multi   .30 .20
  750th anniversary of Judenburg.

Karl Kraus(1874-1936), Poet and Satirist — A403

1974, Apr. 6   Engr.
986 A403 4s dark red   .50 .20

St. Michael, by Thomas Schwanthaler A404

1974, May 3
987 A404 2.50s slate green   .30 .20
  Exhibition of the works by the Schwanthaler Family of sculptors, (1633-1848), Reichersberg am Inn, May 3-Oct. 13.

A405

Europa: King Arthur, from tomb of Maximilian I

1974, May 8   *Perf. 13½*
988 A405 2.50s ocher & slate blue .30 .20

Austrian Automobile Assoc., 75th Anniv. — A406

De Dion Bouton motor tricycle.

Photo. & Engr.
1974, May 17 *Perf. 14x13½*
989 A406 2s gray & vio brn   .30 .20

Satyr's Head, Terracotta A407

1974, May 22 *Perf. 13½x14*
990 A407 2s org brn, gold & blk   .30 .20
  Exhibition, "Renaissance in Austria," Schallaburg Castle, May 22-Nov. 14.

Road Transport Union Emblem — A408

1974, May 24 Photo. *Perf. 14x13½*
991 A408 4s deep orange & blk   .50 .20
  14th Congress of the Intl. Road Transport Union, Innsbruck.

Franz Anton Maulbertsch (1724-96), Painter — A409

1974, June 7 Engr. *Perf. 14x13½*
992 A409 2s Self-portrait   .25 .20

Gendarmes, 1824 and 1974 A410

1974, June 7 Photo. *Perf. 13½x14*
993 A410 2s red & multi   .25 .20
  125th anniversary of Austrian gendarmery.

Fencing A411

Photo. & Engr.
1974, June 14 *Perf. 13½*
994 A411 2.50s red org & blk   .30 .20

Transportation Symbols — A412

1974, June 18 Photo. *Perf. 14x13½*
995 A412 4s lt ultra & multi   .50 .20
  European Conference of Transportation Ministers, Vienna, June 18-21.

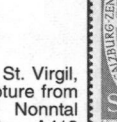

St. Virgil, Sculpture from Nonntal Church — A413

1974, June 28 Engr. *Perf. 13½x14*
996 A413 2s violet blue   .25 .20
  Consecration of the Cathedral of Salzburg by Scotch-Irish Bishop Feirgil (St. Virgil), 1200th anniv. Salzburg was a center of Christianization in the 8th century.

Franz Jonas and Austrian Eagle — A414

1974, June 28
997 A414 2s black   .25 .20
  Jonas (1899-1974), Austrian Pres., 1965-1974.

Franz Stelzhamer   Diver
A415   A416

1974, July 12 Engr. *Perf. 14x13½*
998 A415 2s indigo   .25 .20
  Franz Stelzhamer (1802-1874), poet who wrote in Upper Austrian vernacular, death cent.

Photo. & Engr.
1974, Aug. 16 *Perf. 13x13½*
999 A416 4s blue & sepia   .50 .20
  13th European Swimming, Diving and Water Polo Championships, Vienna, Aug. 18-25.

Ferdinand Ritter von Hebra — A417

1974, Sept. 10 Engr. *Perf. 14x13½*
1000 A417 4s brown   .50 .20
  30th Meeting of the Assoc. of German-speaking Dermatologists, Graz, Sept. 10-14. Dr. von Hebra (1816-1880) was a founder of modern dermatology.

Arnold Schonberg A418

1974, Sept. 13 *Perf. 13½x14*
1001 A418 2.50s purple   .30 .20
  Schönberg (1874-1951), composer.

Radio Station, Salzburg A419

1974, Oct. 1   Photo.
1002 A419 2s multicolored   .25 .20
50th anniversary of Austrian broadcasting.

Edmund Eysler (1874-1949), Composer A420

1974, Oct. 4   Engr.   Perf. 14x13½
1003 A420 2s dark olive   .25 .20

Mailman, Mail Coach and Train, UPU Emblem A421

4s, Mailman, jet, truck, 1974, & UPU emblem.

1974, Oct. 9   Photo.   Perf. 13½
1004 A421 2s deep claret & lil   .25 .20
1005 A421 4s dark blue & gray   .50 .20
Centenary of Universal Postal Union.

Gauntlet Protecting Rose A422

1974, Oct. 23   Photo.   Perf. 13½x14
1006 A422 2s multicolored   .25 .20
Environment protection.

Austrian Sports Pool Emblem A423

1974, Oct. 23   Photo.   Perf. 13½x14
1007 A423 70g multicolored   .20 .20
Austrian Sports Pool (lottery), 25th anniv.

Carl Ditters von Dittersdorf (1739-1799), Composer A424

1974, Oct. 24   Engr.   Perf. 14x13½
1008 A424 2s Prussian green   .25 .20

Virgin and Child, Wood, c. 1600 — A425

1974, Nov. 29   Photo. & Engr.
1009 A425 2s brown & gold   .35 .20
Christmas.

Franz Schmidt (1874-1939), Composer A426

1974, Dec. 18
1010 A426 4s gray & black   .55 .20

European Architectural Heritage Year — A427

Photo. & Engr.
1975, Jan. 24   Perf. 13½
1011 A427 2.50s St. Christopher   .40 .20
The design shows part of a wooden figure from central panel of the retable in the Kefermarkt Church, 1490-1497.

Safety Belt and Skeleton Arms — A428

1975, Apr. 1   Photo.   Perf. 14x13½
1012 A428 70g violet & multi   .20 .20
Introduction of obligatory use of automobile safety belts.

Stained Glass Window, Vienna City Hall — A429

1975, Apr. 2   Perf. 14
1013 A429 2.50s multicolored   .30 .20
11th meeting of the Council of European Municipalities, Vienna, Apr. 2-5.

Austria as Mediator A430

1975, May 2   Litho.   Perf. 14
1014 A430 2s blk & bister   .30 .20
2nd Republic of Austria, 30th anniv.

National Forests, 50th Anniv. — A431

1975, May 6   Engr.
1015 A431 2s green   .35 .20

High Priest, by Michael Pacher — A432

Europa Issue 1975
Photo. & Engr.
1975, May 27   Perf. 14x13½
1016 A432 2.50s black & multi   .40 .20
Design is detail from painting "The Marriage of Joseph and Mary," by Michael Pacher (c. 1450-1500).

Gosaukamm Funicular — A433

1975, June 23   Perf. 14x13½
1017 A433 2s slate & red   .30 .20
4th Intl. Funicular Cong., Vienna, 6/23-27.

Josef Misson and Mühlbach am Manhartsberg — A434

1975, June 27   Perf. 13½x14
1018 A434 2s choc & redsh brn   .25 .20
Josef Misson (1803-1875), poet who wrote in Lower Austrian vernacular, death cent.

Setting Sun and "P" — A435

1975, Aug. 27   Litho.   Perf. 14x13½
1019 A435 1.50s org, blk & bl   .20 .20
Austrian Assoc. of Pensioners 25th anniv. meeting, Vienna, Aug. 1975.

Ferdinand Porsche (1875-1951), Engineer, Auto Maker A436

Photo. & Engr.
1975, Sept. 3   Perf. 13½x14
1020 A436 1.50s gray & purple   .25 .20

Leo Fall (1873-1925), Composer A437

1975, Sept. 16   Engr.   Perf. 14x13½
1021 A437 2s violet   .25 .20

10th World Judo Championships, Vienna — A438

1975, Oct. 20   Photo.   Perf. 14x13½
1022 A438 2.50s Judo Throw   .30 .20

Heinrich Angeli (1840-1925), Painter — A439

1975, Oct. 21   Engr.   Perf. 14x13½
1023 A439 2s rose lake   .30 .20

Johann Strauss and Dancers A440

Photo. & Engr.
1975, Oct. 24   Perf. 13½x14
1024 A440 4s ocher & sepia   .55 .20
Johann Strauss (1825-1899), composer.

Stylized Musician
Playing a
Viol — A441

1975, Oct. 30   Perf. 14x13½
1025 A441 2.50s silver & vio bl   .35 .20
Vienna Symphony Orchestra, 75th anniv.

Symbolic
House — A442

1975, Oct. 31   Photo.
1026 A442 2s multicolored   .25 .20
Austrian building savings societies, 50th
anniv.

Fan with
"Hanswurst"
Scene, 18th
Century
A443

1975, Nov. 14 Photo. Perf. 13½x14
1027 A443 1.50s green & multi   .20 .20
Salzburg Theater bicentenary.

Virgin and Child,
from 15th Century
Altar — A444

Photo. & Engr.
1975, Nov. 28   Perf. 13x13½
1028 A444 2s gold & dull purple   .25 .20
Christmas.

"The Spiral
Tree," by
Hundertwasser
A445

Photo., Engr. & Typo.
1975, Dec. 11   Perf. 13½x14
1029 A445 4s multicolored   .65 .25
Austrian modern art. Friedenstreich
Hundertwasser is the pseudonym of Friedrich
Stowasser (1928-2000).

Old
Burgtheater
A446

#1030b, Grand staircase, new Burgtheater.

Perf. 14 (pane), 13½x14 (stamps)
1976, Apr. 8   Engr.
1030   Pane of 2 + label   1.10 1.10
a. A446 3s violet blue   .30   .30
b. A446 3s deep brown   .30   .30
Bicentenary of Vienna Burgtheater. Label
(head of Pan) and inscription in vermilion.

Dr. Robert Barany
(1876-1936),
Winner of Nobel
Prize for
Medicine,
1914 — A447

Photo. & Engr.
1976, Apr. 22   Perf. 14x13½
1031 A447 3s blue & brown   .45 .20

Ammonite
A448

1976, Apr. 30 Photo. Perf. 13½x14
1032 A448 3s red & multi   .45 .20
Vienna Museum of Natural History, Centenary Exhibition.

Carinthian Dukes'
Coronation
Chair — A449

Photo. & Engr.
1976, May 6   Perf. 14x13½
1033 A449 3s grnsh blk & org   .45 .20
Millennium of Carinthia.

Siege of Linz,
17th Century
Etching — A450

1976, May 14
1034 A450 4s blk & gray grn   .55 .20
Upper Austrian Peasants' War, 350th anniv.

Skittles
A451

1976, May 14   Perf. 13½x14
1035 A451 4s black & org   .55 .20
11th World Skittles Championships, Vienna.

Duke Heinrich
II, Stained-glass
Window — A452

1976, May 14   Perf. 14
1036 A452 3s multicolored   .45 .20
Babenberg Exhibition, Lilienfeld.

St. Wolfgang,
from Pacher
Altar — A453

1976, May 26 Engr. Perf. 13½
1037 A453 6s bright violet   .75 .40
Intl. Art Exhibition at St. Wolfgang.

Europa Issue 1976

Tassilo Cup,
Kremsmunster,
777 — A454

Photo. & Engr.
1976, Aug. 13   Perf. 14x13½
1038 A454 4s ultra & multi   .60 .20

Timber Fair
Emblem — A455

1976, Aug. 13   Photo.
1039 A455 3s green & multi   .35 .20
Austrian Timber Fair, Klagenfurt, 25th anniv.

Constantin
Economo, M.D.
(1876-1931),
Neurologist
A456

1976, Aug. 23   Engr.
1040 A456 3s dark red brown   .35 .20

Administrative Court, by Salomon
Klein — A457

1976, Oct. 25 Engr. Perf. 13½x14
1041 A457 6s deep brown   .80 .30
Austrian Central Administrative Court, cent.

Souvenir Sheet

Coats of Arms of
Austrian
Provinces — A458

Millennium of Austria: a, Lower Austria. b,
Upper Austria. c, Styria. d, Carinthia. e, Tyrol.
f, Voralberg. g, Salzburg. h, Burgenland. i,
Vienna.

Photo. & Engr.
1976, Oct. 25   Perf. 14
1042   Sheet of 9   3.00 3.00
a.-i. A458 2s any single   .30   .30

"Cancer"
A459

1976, Nov. 17 Photo. Perf. 14x13½
1043 A459 2.50s multicolored   .35 .20
Fight against cancer.

UN Emblem and
Bridge — A460

1976, Nov. 17
1044 A460 3s blue & gold   .45 .20
UN Industrial Development Org. (UNIDO),
10th anniv.

Punched Tape,
Map of Europe
A461

1976, Nov. 17   Perf. 14
1045 A461 1.50s multicolored   .20 .20
Austrian Press Agency (APA), 30th anniv.

Viktor
Kaplan,
Kaplan
Turbine
A462

Photo. & Engr.
1976, Nov. 26   Perf. 13½x14
1046 A462 2.50s multicolored   .35 .20
Viktor Kaplan (1876-1934), inventor of
Kaplan turbine, birth centenary.

Nativity, by Konrad von Friesach, c. 1450
A463

1976, Nov. 26 ***Perf. 13½***
1047 A463 3s multicolored .40 .20

Christmas.

Augustin, the Piper — A464

Photo. & Engr.

1976, Dec. 29 ***Perf. 13½***
1048 A464 6s multicolored .75 .25

Modern Austrian art.

Rainer Maria Rilke (1875-1926), Poet — A465

Vienna City Synagogue — A466

1976, Dec. 29 Engr. ***Perf. 14x13½***
1049 A465 3s deep violet .40 .20

1976, Dec. 29 Photo. ***Perf. 13½***
1050 A466 1.50s multicolored .20 .20

Sesquicentennial of Vienna City Synagogue.

Nikolaus Joseph von Jacquin (1727-1817), Botanist — A467

1977, Feb. 16 Engr. ***Perf. 14x13½***
1051 A467 4s chocolate .55 .20

Oswald von Wolkenstein (1377-1445), Poet — A468

Photo. & Engr.

1977, Feb. 16 ***Perf. 14***
1052 A468 3s multicolored .35 .20

Handball
A469

1977, Feb. 25 Photo. ***Perf. 13½x14***
1053 A469 1.50s multicolored .20 .20

World Indoor Handball Championships, Austria, Feb. 5-Mar. 6.

Alfred Kubin (1877-1959), Illustrator and Writer — A470

1977, Apr. 12 Engr. ***Perf. 14x13½***
1054 A470 6s dk violet blue .70 .25

Great Spire, St. Stephen's Cathedral
A471

Designs: 3s, Heathen Tower and Frederick's Gable. 4s, Interior view with Albertinian Choir.

1977, Apr. 22 Engr. ***Perf. 13½***
1055 A471 2.50s dark brown .35 .20
1056 A471 3s dark blue .40 .25
1057 A471 4s rose lake .50 .35
Nos. 1055-1057 (3) 1.25 .80

Restoration and re-opening of St. Stephen's Cathedral, Vienna, 25th anniversary.

Fritz Hermanovsky-Orlando (1877-1954), Poet and Artist — A472

Photo. & Engr.

1977, Apr. 29 ***Perf. 13½x14***
1058 A472 6s Prus green & gold .70 .25

Intl. Atomic Energy Agency (IAEA), 20th Anniv. — A473

1977, May 2 Photo. ***Perf. 14***
1059 A473 3s IAEA Emblem .35 .20

Schwanenstadt, 350th Anniv. — A474

1977, June 10 Photo. ***Perf. 14x13½***
1060 A474 3s Town arms .35 .20

Europa Issue 1977

Attersee, Upper Austria — A475

1977, June 10 Engr. ***Perf. 14***
1061 A475 6s olive green .90 .30

Globe, by Vincenzo Coronelli, 1688 — A476

Photo. & Engr.

1977, June 29 ***Perf. 14***
1062 A476 3s black & buff .35 .20

5th Intl. Symposium of the Coronelli World Fed. of Friends of the Globe, Austria, June 29-July 3.

Kayak Race
A477

1977, July 15 Photo. ***Perf. 13½x14***
1063 A477 4s multicolored .50 .20

3rd Kayak Slalom White Water Race on Lieser River, Spittal.

The Good Samaritan, by Francesco Bassano
A478

1977, Sept. 16 Photo. & Engr.
1064 A478 1.50s brown & red .20 .20

Workers' Good Samaritan Org., 50th anniv.

Papermakers' Coat of Arms — A479

1977, Oct. 10 ***Perf. 14x13½***
1065 A479 3s multicolored .35 .20

17th Conf. of the European Committee of Pulp and Paper Technology (EUCEPA), Vienna.

Man with Austrian Flag Lifting Barbed Wire — A480

1977, Nov. 3 ***Perf. 14***
1066 A480 2.50s slate & red .35 .20

Honoring the martyrs for Austria's freedom.

"Austria," First Steam Locomotive in Austria — A481

Designs: 2.50s, Steam locomotive 214. 3s, Electric locomotive 1044.

Photo. & Engr.

1977, Nov. 17 ***Perf. 13½***
1067 A481 1.50s multicolored .20 .20
1068 A481 2.50s multicolored .35 .20
1069 A481 3s multicolored .45 .20
Nos. 1067-1069 (3) 1.00 .60

140th anniversary of Austrian railroads.

Christmas — A482

Virgin and Child, wood statue, Mariastein, Tyrol.

1977, Nov. 25 ***Perf. 14x13½***
1070 A482 3s multicolored .30 .20

Modern Austrian Art — A483

1977, Dec. 2 ***Perf. 13½x14***

The Danube Maidens, by Wolfgang Hutter.

1071 A483 6s multicolored .75 .20

Egon Friedell (1878-1938), Writer and Historian
A484

1978, Jan. 23 Photo. & Engr.
1072 A484 3s lt blue & blk .40 .20

Subway Train A485

1978, Feb. 24   Photo.
1073 A485 3s multicolored   .45 .20
New Vienna subway system.

Biathlon Competition A486

1978, Feb. 28   Photo. & Engr.
1074 A486 4s multicolored   .45 .20
Biathlon World Championships, Hochfilzen, Tyrol, Feb. 28-Mar. 5.

Leopold Kunschak (1871-1953), Political Leader — A487

1978, Mar. 13   Engr.   Perf. 14x13½
1075 A487 3s violet blue   .40 .20

Coyote, Aztec Feather Shield A488

1978, Mar. 13   Photo.   Perf. 13½x14
1076 A488 3s multicolored   .40 .20
Ethnographical Museum, 50th anniv. exhibition.

Alpine Farm, Woodcut by Suitbert Lobisser — A489

1978, Mar. 23   Engr.   Perf. 13½
1077 A489 3s dark brown, *buff*   .40 .20
Lobisser (1878-1943), graphic artist.

Capercaillie, Hunting Bag, 1730, and Rifle, 1655 — A490

Photo. & Engr.
1978, Apr. 28   Perf. 13½
1078 A490 6s multicolored   .75 .35
Intl. Hunting Exhibition, Marchegg.

Europa Issue 1978

Riegersburg, Styria — A491

1978, May 3   Engr.
1079 A491 6s deep rose lilac   .75 .35

Parliament, Vienna, and Map of Europe — A492

1978, May 3   Photo.   Perf. 14x13½
1080 A492 4s multicolored   .45 .20
3rd Interparliamentary Conference for European Cooperation and Security, Vienna.

Admont Pietà, c. 1410 — A493

1978, May 26   Photo. & Engr.
1081 A493 2.50s ocher & black   .25 .20
Gothic Art in Styria Exhibition, St. Lambrecht, 1978.

Ort Castle, Gmunden — A494

1978, June 9
1082 A494 3s multicolored   .30 .20
700th anniversary of Gmunden City.

Child with Flowers and Fruit — A495

Photo. & Engr.
1978, June 30   Perf. 14x13½
1083 A495 6s gold & multi   .85 .35
25 years of Social Tourism.

Lehar and his Home, Bad Ischl — A496

1978, July 14   Engr.   Perf. 14x13½
1084 A496 6s slate   .75 .30
International Lehar Congress, Bad Ischl. Franz Lehar (1870-1948), operetta composer.

Congress Emblem A497

1978, Aug. 21   Photo.   Perf. 13½x14
1085 A497 1.50s black, red & yel   .20 .20
Cong. of Intl. Fed. of Building Construction and Wood Workers, Vienna, Aug. 20-24.

Ottokar of Bohemia and Rudolf of Hapsburg A498

1978, Aug. 25   Photo. & Engr.
1086 A498 3s multicolored   .35 .20
Battle of Durnkrut and Jedenspeigen (Marchfeld), which established Hapsburg rule in Austria, 700th anniversary.

First Documentary Reference to Villach, "ad pontem uillah" — A499

1978, Sept. 8   Litho.   Perf. 13½x14
1087 A499 3s multicolored   .35 .20
1100th anniversary of Villach, Carinthia.

Seal of Graz, 1440 — A500

Photo. & Engr.
1978, Sept. 13   Perf. 14x13½
1088 A500 4s multicolored   .50 .25
850th anniversary of Graz.

Emperor Maximilian Fishing — A501

1978, Sept. 15   Perf. 14x13½
1089 A501 4s multicolored   .50 .20
World Fishing Championships, Vienna, Sept. 1978.

"Aid to the Handicapped" — A502

1978, Oct. 2   Photo.   Perf. 13½x14
1090 A502 6s orange brn & blk   .75 .30

Symbolic Column — A503

1978, Oct. 9   Photo.   Perf. 13½
1091 A503 2.50s orange, blk & gray   .30 .20
9th Intl. Congress of Concrete and Prefabrication Industries, Vienna, Oct. 8-13.

Grace, by Albin Egger-Lienz A504

1978, Oct. 27   Perf. 13½x14
1092 A504 6s multicolored   .75 .30
European Family Congress, Vienna, Oct. 26-29.

Lise Meitner (1878-1968), Physicist, and Atom Symbol — A505

1978, Nov. 7   Engr.   Perf. 14x13½
1093 A505 6s dark violet   .75 .30

Viktor Adler, by Anton Hanak A506

Photo. & Engr.
1978, Nov. 10   Perf. 13½x14
1094 A506 3s vermilion & black   .40 .20
Viktor Adler (1852-1918), leader of Social Democratic Party, 60th death anniversary.

Franz Schubert, by Josef Kriehuber A507

1978, Nov. 17   **Engr.**   *Perf. 14*
1095 A507 6s reddish brown   .65 .35
Franz Schubert (1797-1828), composer.

Virgin and Child, Wilhering Church — A508

Photo. & Engr.
1978, Dec. 1   *Perf. 12½x13½*
1096 A508 3s multicolored   .35 .20
Christmas.

Archduke Johann Shelter, Grossglockner — A509

1978, Dec. 6   *Perf. 13½x14*
1097 A509 1.50s gold & dk vio bl   .20 .20
Austrian Alpine Club, centenary.

Modern Austrian Art — A510

Adam, by Rudolf Hausner.

1978, Dec. 6   **Photo.**   *Perf. 13½x14*
1098 A510 6s multicolored   .75 .35

Universal Declaration of Human Rights, 30th Anniv. — A511

1978, Dec. 6   *Perf. 14x13½*
1099 A511 6s Bound Hands   .75 .30

Type of 1973
Designs: 20g, Freistadt, Upper Austria. 3s, Bishofsmutze, Salzburg. 4.20s, Hirschegg, Kleinwalsertal. 5.50s, Peace Chapel, Stoderzinken. 5.60s, Riezlern, Kleinwalsertal. 9s, Asten Carinthia. 12s, Kufstein Fortress. 14s, Weiszsee, Salzburg.

Photo. & Engr.
1978-83   *Perf. 13½x14*
    Size: 23x29mm
1100 A395 20g vio bl & dk bl   .20 .20
    Size: 17x21mm
1102 A395 3s lt ultra & vio bl   .45 .20

    Size: 23x29mm
1104 A395 4.20s blk & grysh bl   .55 .20
1105 A395 5.50s lilac & pur   .75 .20
1106 A395 5.60s yel grn & ol grn   .75 .20
1107 A395   9s rose & car   1.25 .45
1108 A395 12s ocher & vio brn   1.75 .20
1109 A395 14s lt green &
               green   2.00 .20
    Nos. 1100-1109 (8)   7.70 1.85
Issued: 3s, 12/7/78; 4.20s, 6/22/79; 20g, 6/27/80; 12s, 10/3/80; 14s, 1/27/82; 5.50s, 5.60s, 7/1/82; 9s, 2/9/83.

Child and IYC Emblem A512

Photo. & Engr.
1979, Jan. 16   *Perf. 14*
1110 A512 2.50s dk blue, blk & brn   .30 .20
International Year of the Child.

CCIR Emblem A513

1979, Jan. 16   **Photo.**   *Perf. 13½x14*
1111 A513 6s multicolored   .75 .30
Intl. Radio Consultative Committee (CCIR) of the ITU, 50th anniv.

Air Rifle, Air Pistol and Club Emblem A514

Photo. & Engr.
1979, Mar. 7   *Perf. 13½*
1112 A514 6s multicolored   .75 .30
Austrian Shooting Club, cent., and European Air Rifle and Air Pistol Championships, Graz.

Figure Skater — A515

1979, Mar. 7   **Photo.**   *Perf. 14x13½*
1113 A515 4s multicolored   .55 .25
World Ice Skating Championships, Vienna.

Steamer Franz I A516

Designs: 2.50s, Tugboat Linz. 3s, Passenger ship Theodor Körner.

1979, Mar. 13   **Engr.**   *Perf. 13½*
1114 A516 1.50s violet blue   .20 .20
1115 A516 2.50s sepia   .30 .20
1116 A516   3s magenta   .35 .20
    Nos. 1114-1116 (3)   .85 .60
1st Danube Steamship Company, 150th anniv.

Fashion Design, by Theo Zasche, 1900 — A517

Photo. & Engr.
1979, Mar. 26   *Perf. 13x13½*
1117 A517 2.50s multicolored   .30 .20
50th Intl. Fashion Week, Vienna.

Wiener Neustadt Cathedral, 700th Anniv. — A518

1979, Mar. 27   **Engr.**   *Perf. 13½*
1118 A518 4s violet blue   .50 .25

Teacher and Pupils, by Franz A. Zauner — A519

Photo. & Engr.
1979, Mar. 30   *Perf. 14x13½*
1119 A519 2.50s multicolored   .30 .20
Education of the deaf in Austria, 200th anniv.

Population Chart and Baroque Angel — A520

1979, Apr. 6
1120 A520 2.50s multicolored   .30 .20
Austrian Central Statistical Bureau, 150th anniv.

Laurenz Koschier — A521

Europa Issue, 1979
1979, May 4
1121 A521 6s ocher & purple   .80 .30

Diesel Motor — A522

1979, May 4   **Photo.**
1122 A522 4s multicolored   .45 .20
13th CIMAC Congress (Intl. Org. for Internal Combustion Machines).

Arms of Ried, Schärding and Braunau — A523

Photo. & Engr.
1979, June 1   *Perf. 14x13½*
1123 A523 3s multicolored   .30 .20
200th anniversary of Innviertel District.

Flood and City — A524

1979, June 1   *Perf. 13½x14*
1124 A524 2.50s multicolored   .30 .20
Control and eliminate water pollution.

Arms of Rottenmann A525

Photo. & Engr.
1979, June 22   *Perf. 14x13½*
1125 A525 3s multicolored   .30 .20
700th anniversary of Rottenmann.

Jodok Fink (1853-1929), Governor of Vorarlberg A526

1979, June 29   **Engr.**   *Perf. 14*
1126 A526 3s brown carmine   .40 .20

Arms of Wels, Returnees' Emblem, "Europa Sail" — A527

1979, July 6 Photo. Perf. 14x13½
1127 A527 4s yellow grn & blk   .45 .20
5th European Meeting of the Intl. Confederation of Former Prisoners of War, Wels, July 6-8.

Symbolic Flower, Conference Emblem — A528

1979, Aug. 20 Litho. Perf. 14x13½
1128 A528 4s turq blue   .45 .20
UN Conf. for Science and Technology, Vienna, Aug. 20-31.

Donaupark, UNIDO and IAEA Emblems A529

1979, Aug. 24 Engr. Perf. 13½x14
1129 A529 6s grayish blue   .75 .30
Opening of the Donaupark Intl. Center in Vienna, seat of the UN Industrial Development Org. (UNIDO) and the Intl. Atomic Energy Agency (IAEA).

Diseased Eye and Blood Vessels A530

1979, Sept. 10 Photo. Perf. 14
1130 A530 2.50s multicolored   .35 .20
10th World Congress of Intl. Diabetes Federation, Vienna, Sept. 9-14.

View of Stanz Valley through East Portal of Arlberg Tunnel A531

1979, Sept. 14 Photo. & Engr.
1131 A531 4s multicolored   .45 .20
16th World Road Cong., Vienna, 9/16-21.

Steam Printing Press A532

Photo. & Engr.
1979, Sept. 18 Perf. 13½x14
1132 A532 3s multicolored   .40 .20
Austrian Government Printing Office, 175th anniv.

Richard Zsigmondy (1865-1929), Chemist — A533

1979, Sept. 21 Engr. Perf. 14x13½
1133 A533 6s multicolored   .75 .30

"Save Energy" A534

1979, Oct. 1 Photo. Perf. 14x13½
1134 A534 2.50s multicolored   .30 .20

Festival and Convention Center, Bregenz (Model) — A535

1979, Oct. 1 Engr. Perf. 14
1135 A535 2.50s purple   .30 .20

Lions International Emblem A536

1979, Oct. 11 Photo. & Engr.
1136 A536 4s multicolored   .45 .25
25th Lions Europa Forum, Vienna, 10/11-13.

A537

Photo. & Engr.
1979, Oct. 19 Perf. 13½x14
1137 A537 2.50s Wilhelm Exner   .30 .20
Centenary of Technological Handicraft Museum, founded by Wilhelm Exner.

Modern Austrian Art — A538

1979, Oct. 23 Litho. Perf. 13½x14
The Compassionate Christ, by Hans Fronius.
1138 A538 4s olive & ol blk   .50 .25

Locomotive and Arms — A539

1979, Oct. 24 Photo. Perf. 13½x14
1139 A539 2.50s multicolored   .30 .20
Raab-Odenburg-Ebenfurt railroad, cent.

August Musger — A540

Photo. & Engr.
1979, Oct. 30 Perf. 14x13½
1140 A540 2.50s bl gray & blk   .30 .20
August Musger (1868-1929), developer of slow-motion film technique.

Nativity, St. Barbara's Church A541

1979, Nov. 30 Perf. 13½x14
1141 A541 4s multicolored   .45 .25
Christmas.

Arms of Baden — A542

1980, Jan. 25 Perf. 14
1142 A542 4s multicolored   .45 .25
Baden, 500th anniversary.

Fight Rheumatism A543

1980, Feb. 21 Perf. 13½
1143 A543 2.50s red & aqua   .30 .20

Austrian Exports — A544

1980, Feb. 21 Photo. Perf. 14x13½
1144 A544 4s dark blue & red   .45 .25

Austrian Red Cross Centenary A545

1980, Mar. 14 Photo. Perf. 13½x14
1145 A545 2.50s multicolored   .30 .20

Rudolph Kirchschlager A546

Photo. & Engr.
1980, Mar. 20 Perf. 14x13½
1146 A546 4s sepia & red   .45 .25

Robert Hamerling (1830-1889), Poet — A547

1980, Mar. 24 Engr. Perf. 13½x14
1147 A547 2.50s olive green   .35 .20

Seal of Hallein — A548

Photo. & Engr.
1980, Apr. 30 Perf. 14x13½
1148 A548 4s red & black   .45 .25
Hallein, 750th anniversary.

Empress Maria Theresa (1717-80) A549

Paintings by: 2.50s, Andreas Moller. 4s, Martin van Meytens. 6s, Josef Ducreux.

1980, May 13 Engr. Perf. 13½
1149 A549 2.50s violet brown   .30 .25
1150 A549 4s dark blue   .45 .40
1151 A549 6s rose lake   .65 .65
Nos. 1149-1151 (3)   1.40 1.30

Flags of Austria and Four Powers A550

1980, May 14 Photo. Perf. 13½x14
1152 A550 4s multicolored   .45 .25
State Treaty, 25th anniversary.

St. Benedict, by Meinrad Guggenbichler A551

1980, May 16   Engr.   Perf. 14½
1153 A551 2.50s olive green   .30 .20
Congress of Benedictine Order of Austria.

Hygeia by Gustav Klimt — A552

1980, May 20   Photo.   Perf. 14
1154 A552 4s multicolored   .45 .25
Academic teaching of hygiene, 175th anniv.

Aflenz Ground Satellite Receiving Station Inauguration A553

1980, May 30   Photo.   Perf. 14
1155 A553 6s multicolored   .85 .30

Steyr, Etching, 1693 A554

Photo. & Engr.
1980, June 4   Perf. 13½
1156 A554 4s multicolored   .45 .25
Millennium of Steyr.

Worker, Oil Drill Head — A555

1980, June 12
1157 A555 2.50s multicolored   .30 .20
Austrian oil production, 25th anniversary.

Seal of Innsbruck, 1267 A556

1980, June 23   Perf. 13½x14½
1158 A556 2.50s multicolored   .35 .20
Innsbruck, 800th anniversary.

Duchy of Styria, 800th Anniv. — A557

Perf. 14½x13½
1980, June 23   Photo.
1159 A557 4s Duke's hat   .45 .20

Leo Ascher (1880-1942), Composer A558

1980, Aug. 18   Engr.   Perf. 14
1160 A558 3s dark purple   .45 .20

Bible Illustration, Book of Genesis — A559

1980, Aug. 25   Perf. 13½
1161 A559 4s multicolored   .45 .25
10th Intl. Cong. of the Org. for Old Testament Studies.

Europa Issue 1980

Robert Stolz (1880-1975), Composer A560

1980, Aug. 25   Engr.   Perf. 14x13½
1162 A560 6s red brown   .85 .30

Old and Modern Bridges A561

1980, Sept. 1   Photo.   Perf. 13½
1163 A561 4s multicolored   .45 .25
11th Congress of the Intl. Assoc. for Bridge and Structural Engineering, Vienna.

Moon Figure, by Karl Brandstätter A562

Photo. & Engr.
1980, Oct. 10   Perf. 14x13½
1164 A562 4s multicolored   .45 .25

Customs Service, Sesquicentennial A563

1980, Oct. 13   Photo.
1165 A563 2.50s multicolored   .30 .20

Gazette Masthead, 1810 A564

1980, Oct. 23   Photo.   Perf. 13½
1166 A564 2.50s multicolored   .30 .20
Official Gazette of Linz, 350th anniversary.

Waidhofen Town Book Title Page, 14th Century — A565

Photo. & Engr.
1980, Oct. 24   Perf. 14
1167 A565 2.50s multicolored   .30 .20
Waidhofen on Thaya, 750th anniversary.

Federal Austrian Army, 25th Anniversary A566

1980, Oct. 24   Photo.   Perf. 13½x14
1168 A566 2.50s grnsh black & red   .30 .20

Alfred Wegener A567

1980, Oct. 31   Engr.
1169 A567 4s violet blue   .55 .25
Alfred Wegener (1880-1930), scientist, formulated theory of continental drift.

Robert Musil (1880-1942), Poet — A568

1980, Nov. 6   Perf. 14x13½
1170 A568 4s dark red brown   .55 .25

Christmas — A569

Nativity, stained glass window, Klagenfurt.

Photo. & Engr.
1980, Nov. 28   Perf. 13½
1171 A569 4s multicolored   .55 .25

25th Anniversary of Social Security A570

1981, Jan. 19   Litho.   Perf. 13½x14
1172 A570 2.50s multicolored   .30 .20

Niebelungen Saga, 1926, by Dachauer — A571

1981, Apr. 6   Engr.   Perf. 14x13½
1173 A571 3s sepia   .40 .20
Wilhelm Dachauer (1881-1951), artist and engraver.

Machinist in Wheelchair A572

1981, Apr. 6   Photo. & Engr.
1174 A572 6s multicolored   .75 .35
Rehabilitation Intl., 3rd European Regional Conf.

Sigmund Freud (1856-1939), Psychoanalyst A573

1981, May 6   Engr.
1175 A573 3s rose violet   .40 .20

Congress, Vienna — A574

1981, May 11   Photo.
1176 A574 4s multicolored   .55 .25

Kuenringer Exhibition, Zwettl Monastery A575

Azzo (founder of House of Kuenringer) and his followers, bear-skin manuscript.

1981, May 15   **Photo. & Engr.**
1177 A575 3s multicolored   .35 .20

Europa — A576

1981, May 22   **Photo.**
1178 A576 6s Maypole   .80 .35

Telephone Service Centenary A577

Photo. and Engr.
1981 May 29   *Perf. 13½x14*
1179 A577 4s multicolored   .45 .25

Seibersdorf Research Center, 25th Anniv. — A578

1981, June 29   **Photo.**   *Perf. 13½*
1180 A578 4s multicolored   .45 .25

The Frog King (Child's Drawing) A579

1981, June 29   *Perf. 13½x14*
1181 A579 3s multicolored   .35 .20

Town Hall and Town Seal of 1250 A580

Photo. & Engr.
1981, July 17   *Perf. 13½x14*
1182 A580 4s multicolored   .45 .25
St. Veit an der Glan, 800th anniv.

Johann Florian Heller (1813-1871), Pioneer of Urinalysis — A581

1981, Aug. 31   *Perf. 14x13½*
1183 A581 6s red brown   .75 .35
11th Intl. Clinical Chemistry Congress.

Ludwig Boltzmann (1844-1906), Physicist — A582

1981, Sept. 4   **Engr.**   *Perf. 14x13½*
1184 A582 3s dark green   .45 .20

Intl. Pharmaceutical Federation World Congress, Vienna — A583

Photo. & Engr.
1981, Sept. 7   *Perf. 14*
1185 A583 6s Scale   .75 .35

Otto Bauer, Politician, Birth Centenary A584

1981, Sept. 7   **Photo.**   *Perf. 14x13½*
1186 A584 4s multicolored   .45 .25

Escher's Impossible Cube — A585

1981, Sept. 14
1187 A585 4s dk blue & brt blue   .45 .25
10th Intl. Mathematicians' Cong., Innsbruck.

Kneeling Virgin, Detail of Coronation of Mary Altarpiece, St. Wolfgang, 500th Anniv. — A586

1981, Sept. 25   **Engr.**   *Perf. 14x13½*
1188 A586 3s dark blue   .35 .20

South-East Fair, Graz, 75th Anniv. A587

1981, Sept. 25   **Photo.**   *Perf. 13½x14*
1189 A587 4s multicolored   .45 .25

Holy Trinity, 12th Cent. Byzantine Miniature A588

1981, Oct. 5
1190 A588 6s multicolored   .75 .35
16th Intl. Byzantine Congress.

Hans Kelsen (1881-1973), Co-author of Federal Constitution A589

1981, Oct. 9   **Engr.**
1191 A589 3s dark carmine   .35 .20

Edict of Tolerance Bicen. — A590

Photo. & Engr.
1981, Oct. 9   *Perf. 14*
1192 A590 4s Joseph II   .45 .25

World Food Day A591

1981, Oct. 16   **Photo.**   *Perf. 13½*
1193 A591 6s multicolored   .75 .35

Between the Times, by Oscar Asboth A592

1981, Oct. 22   **Litho.**   *Perf. 13½x14*
1194 A592 4s multicolored   .55 .25

Intl. Catholic Workers' Day — A593

Photo. & Engr.
1981, Oct. 23   *Perf. 14x13½*
1195 A593 3s multicolored   .35 .20

Baron Josef Hammer-Purgstall, Founder of Oriental Studies, 125th Death Anniv. — A594

Photo. & Engr.
1981, Nov. 23   *Perf. 14*
1196 A594 3s multicolored   .35 .20

Julius Raab (1891-1964), Politician A595

1981, Nov. 27   **Engr.**   *Perf. 13½*
1197 A595 6s rose lake   .75 .35

Nativity, Corn Straw Figures A596

1981, Nov. 27   **Photo. & Engr.**
1198 A596 4s multicolored   .50 .20
Christmas.

Stefan Zweig (1881-1942), Poet — A597

1981, Nov. 27   **Engr.**   *Perf. 14x13½*
1199 A597 4s dull violet   .50 .20

800th Anniv. of St. Nikola on the Danube A598

1981, Dec. 4   **Photo. & Engr.**
1200 A598 4s multicolored   .55 .20

Vienna Emergency Medical Service Centenary A599

1981, Dec. 9   **Photo.**   *Perf. 13½x14*
1201 A599 3s multicolored   .35 .20

Schladming-Haus Alpine World Skiing
Championship — A600

1982, Jan. 27   **Perf. 14**
1202 A600 4s multicolored   .45 .20

Dorotheum
(State Auction
Gallery),
275th
Anniv. — A601

Photo. & Engr.
1982, Mar. 12   **Perf. 14**
1203 A601 4s multicolored   .45 .20

Water Rescue
Service, 25th
Anniv. — A602

1982, Mar. 19 Photo.   Perf. 14x13½
1204 A602 5s multicolored   .60 .30

St. Severin and
the End of the
Roman Era
Exhibition — A603

Photo. & Engr.
1982, Apr. 23   **Perf. 14x13½**
1205 A603 3s St. Severin   .35 .20

Intl. Kneipp
Hydropathy
Congress,
Vienna — A604

1982, May 4   **Perf. 14**
1206 A604 4s multicolored   .55 .20

Printing in
Austria, 500th
Anniv. — A605

1982, May 7
1207 A605 4s Printers' guild arms   .55 .20

5th European
Urology Soc.
Cong.,
Vienna — A606

Design: Urine analysis, Canone di Avicenna
manuscript.

1982, May 12   **Photo.**
1208 A606 6s multicolored   .75 .35

St. Francis of
Assisi, 800th Birth
Anniv. — A607

1982, May 14   **Photo. & Engr.**
1209 A607 3s multicolored   .35 .20

Haydn and His
Time Exhibition,
Rohrau — A608

1982, May 19 Engr.   Perf. 13½
1210 A608 3s olive green   .35 .20

25th World Milk
Day — A609

1982, May 25 Photo.   Perf. 14x13½
1211 A609 7s multicolored   .90 .40

800th Anniv of
Gfohl (Market
Town) — A610

Photo. & Engr.
1982, May 28   **Perf. 14**
1212 A610 4s multicolored   .45 .20

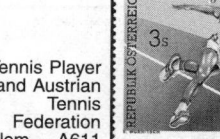

Tennis Player
and Austrian
Tennis
Federation
Emblem — A611

1982, June 11
1213 A611 3s multicolored   .35 .20

900th Anniv.
of City of
Langenlois
A612

Photo. & Engr.
1982, June 11   **Perf. 13½x14**
1214 A612 4s multicolored   .45 .20

800th Anniv. of
City of
Weiz — A613

1982, June 18 Photo.   Perf. 14x13½
1215 A613 4s Arms   .45 .20

Ignaz Seipel
(1876-1932),
Statesman
A614

1982, July 30 Engr.   Perf. 14x13½
1216 A614 3s brown violet   .35 .20

Europa Issue 1982

Sesquicentennial of Linz-Freistadt-
Budweis Horse-drawn
Railroad — A615

1982, July 30   **Perf. 13½**
1217 A615 6s brown   .90 .35

Mail Bus Service,
75th
Anniv. — A616

1982, Aug. 6 Photo.   Perf. 14x13½
1218 A616 4s multicolored   .50 .20

Rocket Lift-
off — A617

1982, Aug. 9   **Perf. 14**
1219 A617 4s multicolored   .50 .20
2nd UN Conference on Peaceful Uses of
Outer Space, Vienna, Aug. 9-21.

Geodesists'
Day — A618

Photo. & Engr.
1982, Sept. 1   **Perf. 13½x14**
1220 A618 3s Tower, Office of
        Standards   .35 .20

Protection of
Endangered
Species — A619

1982, Sept. 9   **Perf. 14**
1221 A619 3s Bustard   .50 .25
1222 A619 4s Beaver   .60 .30
1223 A619 6s Capercaillie   .90 .45
        Nos. 1221-1223 (3)   2.00 1.00

10th Anniv.
of Intl.
Institute for
Applied
Systems
Analysis,
Vienna
A620

1982, Oct. 4   **Photo.**
1224 A620 3s Laxenburg Castle   .35 .20

St.
Apollonia
(Patron
Saint of
Dentists)
A621

1982, Oct. 11   **Photo. & Engr.**
1225 A621 4s multicolored   .45 .20
70th Annual World Congress of Dentists.

Emmerich
Kalman (1882-
1953),
Composer
A622

1982, Oct. 22 Engr.   Perf. 13½
1226 A622 3s dark blue   .35 .20

Max Mell (1882-
1971),
Poet — A623

1982, Nov. 10 Photo. Perf. 14x13½
1227 A623 3s multicolored   .35 .20

Christmas
A624

Design: Christmas crib, Damuls Church, Vorarlberg, 1630.

Photo. & Engr.
1982, Nov. 25   *Perf. 13½*
1228 A624 4s multicolored   .45 .20

Centenary of St. George's College, Istanbul — A625

1982, Nov. 26   **Litho.**   *Perf. 14*
1229 A625 4s Bosporus   .45 .20

Portrait of a Girl, by Ernst Fuchs — A626

1982, Dec. 10   **Photo. & Engr.**
1230 A626 4s multicolored   .45 .20

Postal Savings Bank Centenary A627

Photo. & Engr.
1983, Jan. 12   *Perf. 14*
1231 A627 4s Bank   .55 .20

Hildegard Burjan (1883-1933), Founder of Caritas Socialis A628

1983, Jan. 28   **Engr.**
1232 A628 4s rose lake   .55 .20

World Communications Year — A629

1983, Feb. 18   **Photo.**   *Perf. 13½x14*
1233 A629 7s multicolored   .95 .40

75th Anniv. Children's Friends Org. — A630

Photo. & Engr.
1983, Feb. 23   *Perf. 14x13½*
1234 A630 4s multicolored   .55 .20

Josef Matthias Hauer (1883-1959), Composer A631

1983, Mar. 18   **Engr.**   *Perf. 14*
1235 A631 3s deep lilac rose   .40 .20

25th Anniv. of Austrian Airlines A632

1983, Mar. 31   **Photo.**   *Perf. 13½x14*
1236 A632 6s multicolored   .85 .35

Work Inspection Centenary A633

1983, Apr. 8   **Photo.**   *Perf. 13½*
1237 A633 4s multicolored   .55 .20

Upper Austria Millennium Provincial Exhibition — A634

1983, Apr. 28   **Photo.**   *Perf. 13½*
1238 A634 3s Wels Castle, by Matthaus Merian   .40 .20

Gottweig Monastery, 900th Anniv. — A635

Photo. & Engr.
1983, Apr. 29   *Perf. 13½*
1239 A635 3s multicolored   .40 .20

7th World Pacemakers Symposium A636

1983, Apr. 29   **Photo.**   *Perf. 14x13½*
1240 A636 4s multicolored   .55 .20

Catholic Students' Org. A637

1983, May 20   **Photo.**   *Perf. 14*
1241 A637 4s multicolored   .55 .20

Weitra, 800th Anniv. A638

Photo. & Engr.
1983, May 20   *Perf. 13½*
1242 A638 4s multicolored   .55 .20

Granting of Town Rights to Hohenems, 650th Anniv. — A639

1983, May 27   **Photo.**   *Perf. 14*
1243 A639 4s multicolored   .55 .20

25th Anniv. of Stadthall, Vienna A640

1983, June 24   **Photo.**   *Perf. 14*
1244 A640 4s multicolored   .55 .20

Viktor Franz Hess (1883-1964), 1936 Nobel Prize Winner in Physics — A641

1983, June 24   **Engr.**   *Perf. 14x13½*
1245 A641 6s dark green   .95 .35
Europa.

Kiwanis Intl. Convention, Vienna — A642

1983, July 1   **Photo.**   *Perf. 13½*
1246 A642 5s multicolored   .70 .30

7th World Congress of Psychiatry, Vienna — A643

1983, July 11   **Photo.**   *Perf. 14*
1247 A643 4s Emblem, St. Stephen's Cathedral   .55 .20

Baron Carl von Hasenauer (1833-1894), Architect A644

1983, July 20   **Engr.**   *Perf. 13½x14*
1248 A644 3s Natural History Museum, Vienna   .45 .20

27th Intl. Chamber of Commerce Professional Competition, Linz — A645

1983, Aug. 16   **Photo.**
1249 A645 4s Chamber building   .55 .20

13th Intl. Chemotherapy Congress, Vienna, Aug. 28-Sept. 2 — A646

1983, Aug. 26
1250 A646 5s Penicillin test on cancer   .70 .30

Catholics'
Day — A647

1983, Sept. 9 Photo. *Perf. 14x13½*
1251 A647 3s multicolored .40 .20

Visit of Pope
John
Paul II — A648

Photo. & Engr.
1983, Sept. 9 *Perf. 13½*
1252 A648 6s multicolored .90 .35

Souvenir Sheet

Battle of 1683 to Relieve Vienna, by
Frans Geffel — A649

1983, Sept. 9 *Perf. 14*
1253 A649 6s multicolored .95 .50
300th anniv. of Vienna's rescue from Turkey.

Vienna Rathaus
Centenary
A650

1983, Sept. 23 *Perf. 13½x14*
1254 A650 4s multicolored .55 .20

Karl von
Terzaghi
(1883-1963),
Founder of
Scientific
Subterranean
Engineering
A651

1983, Oct. 3 **Engr.**
1255 A651 3s dark blue .40 .20

10th
Trade
Unions
Federal
Congress,
Oct. 3-8
A652

1983, Oct. 3 Photo. *Perf. 13½*
1256 A652 3s black & red .40 .20

Evening Sun in
Burgenland, by
Gottfried
Kumpf — A653

Photo. & Engr.
1983, Oct. 7 *Perf. 13½x14*
1257 A653 4s multicolored .55 .20

Modling-Hinterbruhl Electric Railroad
Centenary — A654

1983, Oct. 21 **Photo.**
1258 A654 3s multicolored .40 .20

Provincial Museum of Upper Austria
Sesquicentennial — A655

1983, Nov. 4 **Photo. & Engr.**
1259 A655 4s Francisco-Carolinum
Museum .55 .20

Creche,
St.
Andreas
Parish
Church,
Kitzbuhel
A656

1983, Nov. 25 *Perf. 14*
1260 A656 4s multicolored .55 .20
Christmas.

Parliament Bldg.
Vienna, 100th
Anniv. — A657

1983, Dec. 2 **Engr.**
1261 A657 4s slate blue .55 .20

Altar Ppicture, St.
Nikola/Pram
Church — A658

1983, Dec. 6 Photo. *Perf. 14x13½*
1262 A658 3s multicolored .40 .20

Wolfgang Pauli
(1900-58),
Physicist, Nobel
Laureate — A659

1983, Dec. 15 Engr. *Perf. 14½x13½*
1263 A659 6s dark red brn .90 .35

Gregor Mendel (1822-1884), Genetics
Founder — A660

Photo. & Engr.
1984, Jan. 5 *Perf. 13½*
1264 A660 4s multicolored .55 .20

Anton Hanak (1875-1934),
Sculptor — A661

1984, Jan. 5
1265 A661 3s red brown & blk .40 .20

50th Anniv. of 1934 Uprising — A662

1984, Feb. 10 Photo. *Perf. 14*
1266 A662 4.50s Memorial, Woel-
lersdorf .65 .30

Wernher von
Reichersberg
Family, Bas-relief,
15th
Cent. — A663

Photo. & Engr.
1984, Apr. 25 *Perf. 14x13½*
1267 A663 3.50s brown & blue .50 .25
900th anniv. of Reichersberg Monastery.

Tobacco
Monopoly
Bicentenary
A665

1984, May 4 *Perf. 13½*
1269 A665 4.50s Cigar wrapper, tobacco plant .65 .30

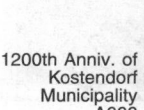

1200th Anniv. of
Kostendorf
Municipality
A666

1984, May 4
1270 A666 4.50s View, arms .65 .20

Automobile
Engineers
World
Congress
A667

1984, May 4 Photo. *Perf. 13½x14*
1271 A667 5s Wheel bearing cross-
section .70 .30

Europa
(1959-1984)
A668

1984, May 4 *Perf. 13½*
1272 A668 6s multicolored .90 .35

Archduke Johann
(1782-1859), by
S. von Carolsfeld
A669

Photo. & Engr.
1984, May 11 *Perf. 14*
1273 A669 4.50s multicolored .65 .30

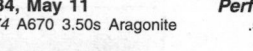

Ore and Iron
Provincial
Exhibition
A670

1984, May 11 *Perf. 13½*
1274 A670 3.50s Aragonite .50 .20

Era of Emperor
Francis Joseph
Exhibition
A671

Design: Cover of Viribus Unitis, publ. by
Max Herzig, 1898.

1984, May 18
1275 A671 3.50s red & gold .50 .20

City of Vocklabruck, 850th Anniv. — A672

Photo. & Engr.
1984, May 30   *Perf. 14x13½*
1276 A672 4.50s Tower, arms   .65 .30

Museum of Carinthia, Cent. — A673

1984, June 1   *Perf. 13½*
Dionysius, Virinum mosaic.
1277 A673 3.50s multicolored   .50 .20

Erosion Prevention Systems Centenary A674

1984, June 5   **Engr.**   *Perf. 14*
1278 A674 4.50s Stone reinforcement wall   .65 .30

Tyrol Provincial Celebration, 1809-1984 A675

Art Exhibition: Meeting of Imperial Troops with South Tyrolean Reserves under Andreas Hofer near Sterzing in April 1809, by Ludwig Schnorr von Carolsfeld, 1830.

Photo. & Engr.
1984, June 5   *Perf. 14x13½*
1279 A675 3.50s multicolored   .50 .20

Ralph Benatzky (1884-1957), Composer A676

1984, June 5   **Engr.**
1280 A676 4s violet brown   .55 .25

Christian von Ehrenfels (1859-1932), Philosopher A677

1984, June 22   **Photo.**   *Perf. 14*
1281 A677 3.50s multicolored   .50 .20

25th Anniv. of Minimundus (Model City) A678

1984, June 22   *Perf. 13½x14*
1282 A678 4s Eiffel Tower, Tower of Pisa, ferris wheel   .55 .25

Blockheide Eibenstein Nature Park A679

1984   **Photo. & Engr.**
1283 A679 4s shown   .55 .25
1284 A679 4s Lake Neusiedl   .55 .25
   Issued: #1283, June 29; #1284, Aug. 13.
   See #1349-1354, 1492-1496, 1744, 1777, 1813, 1843.

Monasteries and Abbeys A679a

Designs: 3.50s, Geras Monastery, Lower Austria. 4s, Stams. 4.50s, Schlagl. 5s, Benedictine Abbey of St. Paul Levanttal. 6s, Rein-Hohenfurth.

1984-85   *Perf. 14*
1285 A679a 3.50s multicolored   .50 .20
1286 A679a 4s multicolored   .50 .20
1287 A679a 4.50s multicolored   .65 .30
1288 A679a 5s multicolored   .65 .30
1288A A679a 6s multicolored   .90 .35
   Nos. 1285-1288A (5)   3.20 1.35
   Issued: 3.50s, 4/27/84; 4s, 9/28/84; 4.50s, 5/18/84; 5s, 9/27/85; 6s, 10/4/84.
   See Nos. 1361-1365, 1464A-1468.

Schanatobel Railroad Bridge — A680

Railroad Anniversaries: 3.50s, Arlberg centenary. 4.50s, Tauern, 75th.

1984, July 6   *Perf. 14*
1289 A680 3.50s shown   .50 .20
1290 A680 4.50s Falkenstein Bridge   .65 .20

Balloon Flight in Austria Bicent. — A681

1984, July 6   **Photo.**
1291 A681 6s Johan Stuwer's balloon   .90 .35

Intl. Lawyers' Congress, Vienna — A682

1984, Aug. 31   **Photo. & Engr.**
1292 A682 7s Vienna Palace of Justice, emblem   .95 .45

7th European Anatomy Congress, Innsbruck — A683

1984, Sept. 3   **Photo.**
1293 A683 6s Josef Hyrtl, anatomist   .90 .35

A684

1984, Oct. 12
1294 A684 4s Window, by Karl Korab   .55 .20

Johannes of Gmunden, Mathematician, 600th Birth Anniv. — A685

1984, Oct. 18
1295 A685 3.50s Clock (Immset Uhr), 1555   .50 .20

Concordia Press Club, 125th Anniv. — A686

1984, Nov. 9   **Photo.**   *Perf. 13½*
1296 A686 4.50s Quill   .65 .30

Fanny Eissler, Dancer, Death Centenary — A687

1984, Nov. 23   **Photo. & Engr.**
1297 A687 4s multicolored   .55 .30

Christmas A688

Design: Christ is Born, Aggsbacher Altar, Herzogenburg Monastery.

1984, Nov. 30   *Perf. 14*
1298 A688 4.50s multicolored   .65 .20

Karl Franzens University, Graz, 400th Anniv. — A689

1985, Jan. 4   *Perf. 14x13½*
1299 A689 3.50s Seal   .50 .20

Dr. Lorenz Bohler, Surgeon, Birth Cent. — A690

1985, Jan. 15   **Engr.**
1300 A690 4.50s dk rose lake   .60 .20

Nordic Events, Ski Championships, Seefeld — A691

1985, Jan. 17   **Photo.**   *Perf. 13½*
1301 A691 4s Ski jumper, cross country racer   .55 .20

Linz Diocese Bicentenary A692

1985, Jan. 25
1302 A692 4.50s Linz Cathedral interior .60 .20

Alban Berg (1885-1935), Composer A693

1985, Feb. 8 **Engr.**
1303 A693 6s bluish black .80 .25

Vocational Training Inst., 25th Anniv. A694

1985, Feb. 15 Photo. Perf. 13½x14
1304 A694 4.50s multicolored .60 .20

City of Bregenz, Bimillennium A695

1985, Feb. 22 **Perf. 14x13½**
1305 A695 4s multicolored .55 .20

Austrian Registration Labels Cent. A696

1985, Mar. 15 **Perf. 13½x14**
1306 A696 4.50s Label, 1885 .60 .20

Josef Stefan (1835-1893), Physicist — A697

Photo. & Engr.
1985, Mar. 22 **Perf. 14x13½**
1307 A697 6s buff, dl red brn & dk brn .80 .25

St. Leopold Exhibition, Klosterneuburg A698

St. Leopold 16th-17th cent. embroidery.

1985, Mar. 29
1308 A698 3.50s multicolored .50 .20

Liberation From German Occupation, 40th Anniv. — A699

1985, Apr. 26 **Photo.**
1309 A699 4.50s multicolored .60 .20

Painter Franz von Defregger (1835-1921) A700

1985, Apr. 26
1310 A700 3.50s Fairy tale teller .50 .20

Europa Issue 1985

Johann Joseph Fux (1660-1741), Composer, Violin and Trombone A701

Photo. & Engr.
1985, May 3 **Perf. 13½**
1311 A701 6s lil gray & dk brn .90 .25

Boheimkirchen (Market Town) Millennium — A702

1985, May 10 **Perf. 14**
1312 A702 4.50s View, coat of arms .60 .20

European Free Trade Assoc., 25th Anniv. — A703

Mercury staff, flags of member and affiliate nations.

1985, May 10 Photo. Perf. 13½
1313 A703 4s multicolored .55 .20

St. Polten Diocese, Bicent. — A704

1985, May 15 **Photo. & Engr.**
Episcopal residence gate, St. Polten diocese arms.
1314 A704 4.50s multicolored .60 .20

The Gumpp Family of Builders, Innsbruck — A705

Perf. 14½x13½
1985, May 17 **Photo.**
1315 A705 3.50s multicolored .50 .20

Garsten Market Town Millennium A706

Design: 17th century engraving by George Matthaus Fischer (1628-1696).

Photo. & Engr.
1985, June 7 **Perf. 13½x14**
1316 A706 4.50s multicolored .60 .20

UN, 40th Anniv. A707

Perf. 13½x14½
1985, June 26 **Photo.**
1317 A707 4s multicolored .55 .20
Austrian membership, 30th anniv.

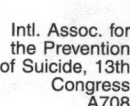

Intl. Assoc. for the Prevention of Suicide, 13th Congress A708

Photo. & Engr.
1985, June 28 **Perf. 14**
1318 A708 5s brn, lt ap grn & yel .70 .30

Souvenir Sheet

Year of the Forest — A709

1985, June 28 **Perf. 13½**
1319 A709 6s Healthy and damaged woodland 1.00 .35

Kurhaus, Bad Ischl Operetta Activities Emblem A710

1985, July 5 **Perf. 14**
1320 A710 3.50s multicolored .50 .20
Bad Ischl Festival, 25th anniv.

Intl. Competition of Fire Brigades, Vocklabruck A711

1985, July 18 Photo. Perf. 14x13½
1321 A711 4.50s Fireman, emblem .60 .20

Grossglockner Alpine Motorway, 50th Anniv. — A712

Photo. & Engr.
1985, Aug. 2 **Perf. 13½**
1322 A712 4s View of Fuschertorl .55 .20

World Chess Federation Congress, Graz — A713

1985, Aug. 28 Photo. Perf. 13½
1323 A713 4s Checkered globe, emblem .55 .20

The Legendary Foundation of Konigstetten by Charlemagne, by Auguste Stephan, c. 1870 — A714

Photo. & Engr.
1985, Aug. 30   *Perf. 14*
1324 A714 4.50s multicolored   .60 .20
Konigstetten millennium.

Hofkirchen-Taufkirchen-Weibern Municipalities, 1200th Anniv. — A715

1985, Aug. 30   *Perf. 13½x14*
1325 A715 4.50s View of Weiburn, municipal arms   .60 .20

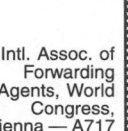

Dr. Adam Politzer (1835-1923), Physician A716

1985, Sept. 12   **Engr.**   *Perf. 14*
1326 A716 3.50s blue violet   .50 .20
Politzer pioneered aural therapy for auditory disorders.

Intl. Assoc. of Forwarding Agents, World Congress, Vienna — A717

1985, Oct. 7   **Photo.**   *Perf. 13½*
1327 A717 6s multicolored   .85 .35

Carnival Figures Riding High Bicycles, By Paul Flora A718

Photo. & Engr.
1985, Oct. 25   *Perf. 14*
1328 A718 4s multicolored   .55 .20

St. Martin on Horseback A719

1985, Nov. 8   **Photo.**
1329 A719 4.50s multicolored   .60 .30
Eisenstadt Diocese, 25th anniv.

Creche, Marble Bas-relief, Salzburg — A720

Photo. & Engr.
1985, Nov. 29   *Perf. 13½*
1330 A720 4.50s gold, dl vio & buff   .60 .30
Christmas.

Hanns Horbiger (1860-1931), Inventor A721

1985, Nov. 29   *Perf. 14*
1331 A721 3.50s gold & sepia   .50 .20

Aqueduct, Hundsau Brook, Near Gostling A722

1985, Nov. 29   *Perf. 13½x14½*
1332 A722 3.50s red, bluish blk & brt ultra   .50 .20
Vienna Aqueduct, 75th anniv.

Chateau de la Muette, Paris Headquarters — A723

1985, Dec. 13
1333 A723 4s sep, rose lil & gold   .55 .25
Org. for Economic Cooperation and Development, 25th anniv.

Johann Bohm (1886-1959), Pres. Austrian Trade Fed. — A724

1986, Jan. 24   **Photo.**   *Perf. 14*
1334 A724 4.50s blk, ver & grayish black   .65 .30

Intl. Peace Year — A725

     Perf. 13½x14½
1986, Jan. 24   **Photo.**
1335 A725 6s multicolored   .85 .35

Digital Telephone Service Introduction A726

1986, Jan. 29   **Photo.**
1336 A726 5s Push-button keyboard   .75 .30

Johann Georg Albrechtsberger (b. 1736), Composer — A727

Photo. & Engr.
1986, Jan. 31   *Perf. 13½x14½*
1337 A727 3.50s Klosterneuburg organ   .50 .20

Korneuberg, 850th Anniv. — A728

1986, Feb. 7   **Photo.**   *Perf. 14*
1338 A728 5s multicolored   .75 .30

Self-portrait, by Oskar Kokoschka (b.1886) — A729

     Perf. 14½x13½
1986, Feb. 28   **Photo.**
1339 A729 4s multicolored   .60 .30

Admission to Council of Europe, 30th Anniv. — A730

1986, Feb. 28   **Photo.**   *Perf. 13x13½*
1340 A730 6s multicolored   .85 .35

Clemens Holzmeister (b. 1886), Architect, Salzburg Festival Theater, 1926 — A731

Photo. & Engr.
1986, Mar. 27   *Perf. 13½*
1341 A731 4s sepia & redsh brn   .60 .30

3rd Intl. Geotextile Congress, Vienna A732

1986, Apr. 7   **Photo.**   *Perf. 13½x14½*
1342 A732 5s multicolored   .75 .30

Prince Eugen and Schlosshof Castle A733

Photo. & Engr.
1986, Apr. 21   *Perf. 14*
1343 A733 4s multicolored   .60 .30
Prince Eugen Exhibition, Schlosshof and Niederweiden.

St. Florian Monastery, Upper Austria A734

1986, Apr. 24
1344 A734 4s multicolored   .60 .30
The World of Baroque provincial exhibition, St. Florian.

Herberstein Castle, Arms of Styria A735

1986, May 2   *Perf. 13½x14½*
1345 A735 4s multicolored   .60 .30

Europa 1986 — A736

1986, May 2   *Perf. 13½*
1346 A736 6s Pasque flower   .85 .45

Wagner, Scene from Opera Lohengrin — A737

1986, May 21
1347 A737 4s multicolored   .60 .30
Intl. Richard Wagner Congress, Vienna.

Antimonite A738

1986, May 23   *Perf. 13½x14½*
1348 A738 4s multicolored   .60 .30
Burgenland Provincial Minerals Exhibition.

Scenery Type of 1984

1986-89		Photo. & Engr.	Perf. 14	
1349	A679	5s Martinswall, Tyrol	.65	.35
1350	A679	5s Tschauko Falls, Carinthia	.65	.35
1351	A679	5s Dachstein Ice Caves	.80	.45
1352	A679	5s Gauertal, Montafon	.80	.45
1353	A679	5s Krimmler Waterfalls	.80	.60
1354	A679	5s Lusthauswasser	.80	.60
		Nos. 1349-1354 (6)	4.50	2.80

Issued: #1351, 6/11/87; #1352, 8/21/87; #1353, 8/19/88; #1354, 9/1/89.

Waidhofen on Ybbs Township, 800th Anniv. — A739

1986, June 20	Photo.	Perf. 13½	
1355 A739	4s multicolored	.50	.30

Salzburg Local Railway, Cent. A740

1986, Aug. 8	Photo.	Perf. 14	
1356 A740	4s multicolored	.55	.30

Seals of Dukes Leopold Of Austria, Otakar of Styria, and Georgenberg Church — A741

1986, Aug. 14	Photo. & Engr.		
1357 A741	5s multicolored	.70	.30

Georgenberg Treaty, 800th anniv.

Julius Tandler (1869-1936), Social Reformer A742

1986, Aug. 22			
1358 A742	4s multicolored	.60	.30

Sonnblick Observatory, Cent. A743

1986, Aug. 27	Photo. & Engr.	Perf. 13½x14½	
1359 A743	4s Observatory, 1886	.60	.30

Discovery of Mandrake Root — A744

1986, Aug. 27	Perf. 14½x13½	
1360 A744	5s multicolored	.75	.30

European Assoc. for Anesthesiology, 7th cong.

Monasteries and Abbeys Type of 1984

Designs: 5.50s, St. Gerold's Provostry, Vorarlberg. 7s, Loretto Monastery, Burgenland. 7.50s, Dominican Convent, Vienna. 8s, Zwettl Monastery. 10s, Wilten Monastery.

1986-88		Photo. & Engr.	Perf. 14	
1361	A679a	5.50s multicolored	.80	.60
1362	A679a	7s multicolored	1.10	.90
1363	A679a	7.50s multicolored	1.10	.85
1364	A679a	8s multicolored	1.40	1.00
1365	A679a	10s multicolored	1.75	1.25
		Nos. 1361-1365 (5)	6.15	4.60

Issued: 5.50s, 9/12/86; 7.50s, 10/3; 7s, 8/14/87; 8s, 5/27/88; 10s, 3/18/88.

Otto Stoessl (d. 1936), Writer — A745

1986, Sept. 3	Photo. & Engr.	Perf. 14	
1366 A745	4s multicolored	.60	.30

Vienna Fire Brigade, 300th Anniv. — A746

1986, Sept. 3	Photo.	
1367 A746	4s Fireman, 1686	.60	.30

Silk Viennese Hunting Tapestry A747

1986, Sept. 3	Photo. & Engr.	Perf. 14	
1368 A747	5s multicolored	.75	.40

Intl. conf. on Oriental Carpets, Vienna, Budapest.

A748

1986, Oct. 10	Photo. & Engr.	Perf. 14	
1369 A748	5s Minister at pulpit	.70	.40

Protestant Act, 25th anniv., and Protestant Patent of Franz Josef I ensuring religious equality, 125th anniv.

Disintegration, by Walter Schmogner A749

1986, Oct. 17	Perf. 13½x14	
1370 A749	4s multicolored	.60	.30

Franz Liszt, Composer, and Birthplace, Burgenland A750

1986, Oct. 17	Perf. 13½	
1371 A750	5s green & sepia	.70	.40

Souvenir Sheet

European Security Conference, Vienna — A751

Illustration reduced.

1986, Nov. 4	Perf. 13½x14	
1372 A751	6s Vienna	.95	.65

Strettweg Cart, 7th Cent. B.C. A752

1986, Nov. 26	Photo. & Engr.	Perf. 14	
1373 A752	4s multicolored	.65	.30

Joanneum Styrian Land Museum, 175th anniv.

Christmas A753

Design: The Little Crib, bas-relief by Schwanthaler (1740-1810), Schlierbach Monastery.

1986, Nov. 28		
1374 A753	5s gold & rose lake	.80	.40

Federal Chamber of Commerce, 40th Anniv. — A754

1986, Dec. 2	Photo.	
1375 A754	5s multicolored	.80	.40

Industry A755

1986-91			Perf. 14x13½	
1376	A755	4s Steel workers	.80	.30
1377	A755	4s Office worker, computer	.80	.35
1378	A755	4s Lab assistant	.80	.30
1378A	A755	4.50s Textile worker	.80	.60
1379	A755	5s Bricklayer	.80	.60
		Nos. 1376-1379 (5)	4.00	2.15

Issued: #1376, 12/4/86; #1377, 10/5/87; #1378, 10/21/88; 5s, 10/10/89; 4.50s, 10/11/91.

This is an expanding set. Numbers will change if necessary.

The Educated Eye, by Arnulf Rainer — A756

1987, Jan. 13	Photo.	Perf. 13½x14	
1386 A756	5s multicolored	.80	.40

Adult education in Vienna, cent.

The Large Blue Madonna, by Anton Faistauer (1887-1970) — A757

Paintings: 6s, Self-portrait, 1922, by A. Paris Gütersloh (1887-1973).

1987, Jan. 29		Perf. 14	
1387 A757	4s multicolored	.55	.20
1388 A757	6s multicolored	.90	.40

Europa 1987 — A758

1987, Apr. 6	Photo. & Engr.	Perf. 13½x14	
1389 A758	6s Hundertwasser House	.95	.55

World Ice Hockey Championships,
Vienna — A759

Perf. 13½x14½
1987, Apr. 17 Photo.
1390 A759 5s multicolored .80 .60

Opening of
the Austria
Center,
Vienna
A760

1987, Apr. 22
1391 A760 5s multicolored .80 .60

Salzburg
City Charter,
700th Anniv.
A761

1987, Apr. 24
1392 A761 5s multicolored .80 .60

Work-Men-Machines, Provincial
Exhibition, Upper Austria — A762

Photo. & Engr.
1987, Apr. 29 **Perf. 14**
1393 A762 4s Factory, 1920 .65 .50

Equal Rights for
Men and
Women — A763

1987, Apr. 29 Photo. **Perf. 13½**
1394 A763 5s multicolored .80 .60

Adele Block-
Bauer I,
Abstract by
Gustav
Klimt — A764

Photo. & Engr.
1987, May 8 **Perf. 13½**
1395 A764 4s multicolored .65 .50

The Era of Emperor Franz Joseph, provincial exhibition, Lower Austria.

Arthur Schnitzler
(1862-1931),
Poet — A765

1987, May 15 **Perf. 14½x13½**
1396 A765 6s multicolored 1.00 .75

Von
Raitenau,
View of
Salzburg
A766

1987, May 15 **Perf. 14**
1397 A766 4s multicolored .65 .50
Prince Archbishop Wolf Dietrich von
Raitenau, patron of baroque architecture in
Salzburg, provincial exhibition.

Lace,
Lustenau
Municipal
Arms
A767

1987, May 22
1398 A767 5s multicolored .80 .60
Lustenau, 1100th anniv.

Souvenir Sheet

Austrian Railways
Sesquicentenary — A768

1987, June 5 Photo. **Perf. 13½**
1399 A768 6s multicolored 1.00 .75

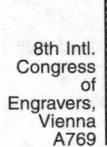

8th Intl.
Congress
of
Engravers,
Vienna
A769

Photo. & Engr.
1987, June 17 **Perf. 14**
1400 A769 5s gray, gray brn & dull
rose .80 .60

Dr. Karl Josef
Bayer (1847-
1904),
Chemist — A770

1987, June 22 **Perf. 14x13½**
1401 A770 5s multicolored .80 .60
Eighth Intl. Light Metals Congress, June 22-
26, Leoben and Vienna; Bayer Technique for
producing aluminum oxide from bauxite, cent.

Shipping on
Achensee,
Cent. — A771

1987, June 26 Photo.
1402 A771 4s multicolored .65 .50

Ombudsmen's
Office, 10th
Anniv. — A772

1987, July 1
1403 A772 5s Palais Rottal, Vienna .80 .60

Dr. Erwin
Schrodinger
(1887-1961), 1933
Nobel Laureate in
Physics — A773

1987, Aug. 11 **Photo. & Engr.**
1404 A773 5s dull olive bister,
choc & buff .80 .60

Freistadt
Exhibitions,
125th
Anniv.
A774

1987, Aug. 11 **Perf. 14x14½**
1405 A774 5s multicolored .80 .60

Arbing, 850th
Anniv. — A775

1987, Aug. 21 **Perf. 13½**
1406 A775 5s multicolored .80 .60

1987 World
Cycling
Championships,
Villach to
Vienna — A776

1987, Aug. 25 **Perf. 14**
1407 A776 5s multicolored .80 .60

World
Congress of
Savings
Banks,
Vienna
A777

Perf. 13½x14½
1987, Sept. 9 Photo.
1408 A777 5s multicolored .80 .60

Johann
Michael
Haydn
(1737-1806),
Composer
A778

Perf. 13½x14½
1987, Sept. 14 Engr.
1409 A778 4s dull violet .65 .50

Paul
Hofhaymer
(1459-1537),
Composer
A779

Photo. & Engr.
1987, Sept. 11 **Perf. 14**
1410 A779 4s gold, blk & ultra .65 .50

Bearded
Vulture — A780

1987, Sept. 25
1411 A780 4s multicolored .65 .50
Innsbruck Zoo, 25th anniv.

Baumgottinnen, by Arnulf
Neuwirth — A781

1987, Oct. 9 **Perf. 14x13½**
1412 A781 5s multicolored .80 .60
Modern Art.

Gambling Monopoly, 200th Anniv. — A782

Perf. 14½x13½
1987, Oct. 30 Photo.
1413 A782 5s Lottery drum .80 .60

Christoph Willibald Gluck (1714-1787), Composer A784

Photo. & Engr.
1987, Nov. 13 **Perf. 14**
1415 A784 5s cream & blk .90 .65

Oskar Helmer (b. 1887), Politician — A785

1987, Nov. 13
1416 A785 4s multicolored .70 .50

Joseph Mohr (1792-1848) and Franz Gruber (1787-1863), Opening Bars of "Silent Night, Holy Night" — A786

1987, Nov. 27
1417 A786 5s multicolored .90 .65
Christmas.

Intl. Education Congress of Salesian Fathers — A787

Photo. & Engr.
1988, Jan. 12 **Perf. 13½**
1418 A787 5s St. John Bosco, children .90 .65

Ernst Mach (1838-1916), Physicist — A788

Photo. & Engr.
1988, Feb. 19 **Perf. 14½x13½**
1419 A788 6s multicolored 1.10 .80

Village with Bridge (1904), by Franz von Zulow (1883-1963), Painter — A789

1988, Feb. 25 Photo. Perf. 14½x14
1420 A789 4s multicolored .70 .50

Biedermeier Provincial Exhibition, Vormarz in Vienna — A790

Painting: Confiscation, by Ferdinand Georg Waldmuller (1793-1865).

Photo. & Engr.
1988, Mar. 11 **Perf. 14**
1421 A790 4s multicolored .70 .50

Anschluss of March 11, 1938 — A791

1988, Mar. 11 Photo. Perf. 13½
1422 A791 5s gray olive, brn blk & ver .85 .65

No. 2 Aigen Steam Locomotive, 1887 A792

1988, Mar. 22 **Perf. 13½x14½**
1423 A792 4s shown .70 .50
1424 A792 5s Electric train, Josepsplatz .85 .65
Muhlkreis Railway, cent. (4s); Vienna Local Railway, cent. (5s).

World Wildlife Fund — A793

Photo. & Engr.
1988, Apr. 15 **Perf. 13½x14**
1425 A793 5s Bee eater .90 .65

Styrian Provincial Exhibition on Glass and Coal, Barnbach A794

1988, Apr. 29 **Perf. 13½**
1426 A794 4s Frosted glass .70 .50

Intl. Red Cross, 125th Anniv. — A795

1988, May 6 Photo. Perf. 14
1427 A795 12s grn, brt red & blk 2.25 1.75

Gothic Silver Censer — A796

1988, May 6 Photo. & Engr.
1428 A796 4s multicolored .70 .50
Art and Monasticism at the Birth of Austria, lower Austrian provincial exhibition, Seitenstetten.

Europa 1988 A797

Communication and transportation.

1988, May 13 Photo.
1429 A797 6s multicolored 1.10 .80

Mattsee Monastery and Lion of Alz — A798

1988, May 18 Photo. & Engr.
1430 A798 4s multicolored .70 .50
Provincial exhibition at Mattsee Monastery: Bavarian Tribes in Salzburg.

Weinberg Castle A799

Perf. 13½x14½
1988, May 20 Photo.
1431 A799 4s multicolored .70 .50
Upper Austrian provincial exhibition: Weinberg Castle.

Odon von Horwath (1901-1938), Dramatist — A800

Photo. & Engr.
1988, June 1 **Perf. 14½x13½**
1432 A800 6s olive bis & slate grn 1.10 .80

Stockerau Festival, 25th Anniv. — A801

1988, June 17 **Perf. 14**
1433 A801 5s Stockerau Town Hall .80 .60

Tauern Motorway Opening — A802

1988, June 24 Photo. Perf. 13½x14
1434 A802 4s multicolored .65 .50

Brixlegg, 1200th Anniv. A803

Photo. & Engr.
1988, July 1 **Perf. 13½x14½**
1435 A803 5s multicolored .80 .60

View of Klagenfurt, Engraving by Matthaus Merian (1593-1650) — A804

Photo. & Engr.
1988, Aug. 12 **Perf. 14**
1436 A804 5s multicolored .80 .60
Carinthian Postal Service, 400th Anniv.

Brixen-im-Thale, 1200th Anniv. — A805

1988, Aug. 12
1437 A805 5s multicolored .80 .60

Feldkirchen, 1100th Anniv. — A806

1988, Sept. 2   *Perf. 13½*
1438 A806 5s multicolored   .80 .60

Feldbach, 800th Anniv. A807

1988, Sept. 15   **Photo. & Engr.**
1439 A807 5s multicolored   .80 .60

Ansfelden, 1200th Anniv. — A808

1988, Sept. 23   *Perf. 14*
1440 A808 5s multicolored   .80 .60

Exports A809

1988, Oct. 18   **Photo.**   *Perf. 14x13½*
1441 A809 8s multicolored   3.50 3.00

No. 1441 has a holographic image. Soaking in water may affect the hologram.

Vienna Concert Hall, 75th Anniv. A810

Photo. & Engr.
1988, Oct. 19   *Perf. 13½*
1442 A810 5s multicolored   .80 .60

The Watchmen, by Giselbert Hoke — A811

1988, Oct. 21   *Perf. 14*
1443 A811 5s multicolored   .80 .60

Social Democrats Unification Party Congress, Cent. — A812

1988, Nov. 11   **Photo.**   *Perf. 14½x14*
1444 A812 4s multicolored   .65 .50

Leopold Schonbauer (1888-1963), Physician — A813

Photo. & Engr.
1988, Nov. 11   *Perf. 14½x13½*
1445 A813 4s multicolored   .65 .50

Christmas A814

Nativity painting from St. Barbara's Church.

1988, Nov. 25   *Perf. 14*
1446 A814 5s multicolored   .80 .60

Benedictine Monastery, Melk, 900th Anniv. — A815

Design: Fresco by Paul Troger.

1989, Mar. 17   **Photo. & Engr.**
1447 A815 5s multicolored   .80 .60

Madonna and Child, by Lucas Cranach (1472-1553) A816

1989, Mar. 17   *Perf. 14½x13½*
1448 A816 4s multicolored   .60 .50

Diocese of Innsbruck, 25th anniv.

Marianne Hainisch (1839-1936), Women's Rights Activist — A817

1989, Mar. 24   *Perf. 14x13½*
1449 A817 6s multicolored   .95 .70

Glider Plane and Parachutist A818

1989, Mar. 31   **Photo.**   *Perf. 14*
1450 A818 6s multicolored   1.00 .75

World Gliding Championships, Wiener Neustadt, and World Parachuting Championships, Damuls.

Bruck an der Leitha Commune, 750th Anniv. — A819

Painting by Georg Matthaus Vischer (1628-1696).

1989, Apr. 21
1451 A819 5s multicolored   .85 .60

Die Malerei, 1904, by Rudolf Jettmar (1869-1939) A820

Perf. 14½x13½
1989, Apr. 21   **Photo.**
1452 A820 5s multicolored   .85 .60

Holy Trinity Church, Stadl-Paura A821

1989, Apr. 26   **Photo. & Engr.**
1453 A821 5s multicolored   .85 .60

Michael Prunner (1669-1739), baroque architect.

Eduard Suess (1831-1914), Structural Geologist and Map — A822

Portrait by J. Krieher (1800-1876).

1989, Apr. 26
1454 A822 6s multicolored   1.00 .75

Ludwig Wittgenstein (1889-1951), Philosopher A823

1989, Apr. 26
1455 A823 5s multicolored   .85 .60

Styrian Provincial Exhibition, Judenburg A824

Design: Judenberg, 17th cent., an engraving by Georg Matthaus Vischer.

1989, Apr. 28   *Perf. 14x13½*
1456 A824 4s multicolored   .70 .50

Industrial Technology Exhibition, Pottenstein — A825

1989, Apr. 28   **Photo.**   *Perf. 13½*
1457 A825 4s Steam engine   .70 .50

Radstadt Township, 700th Anniv. A826

1989, May 3   **Photo.**   *Perf. 13½x14½*
1458 A826 5s multicolored   .85 .60

Europa 1989 A827

1989, May 5
1459 A827 6s Toy boat   1.00 .75

Monastery Church at Lambach, 900th Anniv. — A828

Photo. & Engr.
1989, May 19   *Perf. 14*
1460 A828 4s multicolored   .70 .50

Paddle Steamer *Gisela* A829

1989, May 19 Photo. *Perf. 13½*
1461 A829 5s multicolored .85 .60
Shipping on the Traunsee, 150th anniv.

St. Andra im Lavanttal, 650th Anniv. A830

Period cityscape by Matthaus Merian.

1989, May 26 Photo. & Engr.
1462 A830 5s multicolored .85 .60

Richard Strauss (1864-1949), Composer A831

Photo. & Engr.
1989, June 1 *Perf. 14½x13½*
1463 A831 6s dark brn, gold & red brn 1.00 .75

Achensee Railway, Cent. A832

1989, June 8 Photo. *Perf. 13½*
1464 A832 5s multicolored .85 .60

Monastery Type of 1984

Design: 50g, Vorau Abbey, Styria. 1s, Monastery of Mehrerau, Vorarlberg. 1.50s, Monastery of the German Order in Vienna. 2s, Bendictine Monastery, Michaelbeuern. 11s, Engelszell Abbey. 12s, Monastery of the Hospitalers, Eisenstadt. 17s, St. Peter, Salzburg. 20s, Wernberg Monastery.

1989-92 Photo. & Engr. *Perf. 14*
1464A A679a 50g multi .20 .20
1465 A679a 1s multi .20 .20
1465A A679a 1.50s multi .30 .20
1466 A679a 2s multi .35 .25
1467 A679a 11s multi 1.90 1.40
1467A A679a 12s multi 2.25 1.75
1468 A679a 17s multi 2.75 2.00
1469 A679a 20s multi 2.75 2.00
 Nos. 1464A-1469 (8) 10.70 8.00

 Issued: 1s, 9/1/89; 17s, 6/29/89; 11s, 3/9/90; 50g, 10/12/90; 20s, 5/3/91; 2s, 9/27/91; 1.50s, 10/23/92; 12s, 6/17/92.
 This is an expanding set. Numbers will change if necessary.

Interparliamentary Union, Cent. — A833

Photo. & Engr.
1989, June 30 *Perf. 14*
1475 A833 6s Parliament, Vienna 1.00 .75

Social Security in Austria, Cent. — A834

1989, Aug. 1 Photo.
1476 A834 5s multicolored .70 .50

UN Offices in Vienna, 10th Anniv. A835

1989, Aug. 23
1477 A835 8s multicolored 1.10 .85

Wildalpen, 850th Anniv. A836

Photo. & Engr.
1989, Sept. 15 *Perf. 13½x14*
1478 A836 5s Foundry, coat of arms .80 .60

33rd Congress of the Association for Quality Assurance (EOQC) — A837

1989, Sept. 18 Photo. *Perf. 14x13½*
1479 A837 6s multicolored .90 .70

14th World Congress of the Soc. for Criminal Law (AIDP) A838

Photo. & Engr.
1989, Oct. 2 *Perf. 13½*
1480 A838 6s Justice Palace, Vienna .90 .70

Lebensbaum, by Ernst Steiner — A839

1989, Oct. 10 *Perf. 13½x14*
1481 A839 5s multicolored .80 .60

Georg Trakl (1887-1914), Expressionist Poet — A840

1989, Nov. 6 Photo. *Perf. 14½x13½*
1482 A840 4s Trakl .60 .45
1483 A840 4s Anzengruber .60 .45
 Ludwig Anzengruber (1839-1889), playwright and novelist.

Alfred Fried (1864-1921), Pacifist, Publisher and 1911 Nobel Laureate — A841

1989, Nov. 10 Photo. & Engr.
1484 A841 6s multicolored .90 .70

Parish Church Christ Child, by Johann Carl Reslfeld A842

1989, Dec. 1 *Perf. 13½x14½*
1485 A842 5s multicolored .75 .60
 Christmas.

Postal Communications in Europe, 500th Anniv. — A843

The Young Post Rider, an Engraving by Albrecht Durer

Photo. & Engr.
1990, Jan. 12 *Perf. 14*
1486 A843 5s multicolored .80 .60
 See Belgium No. 1332, Germany No. 1592, Berlin No. 9N584 and German Democratic Republic No. 2791.

Hahnenkamm Alpine Competition, Kitzbuhel, 50th Anniv. — A844

Perf. 13½x14½
1990, Jan. 12 Photo.
1487 A844 5s multicolored .80 .60

Salomon Sulzer (1804-90), Cantor and Composer A845

Perf. 14½x13½
1990, Jan. 17 Photo.
1488 A845 4.50s multicolored .70 .55

Friedrich Emich (1860-1940), Chemist — A846

1990, Jan. 22 Photo. & Engr.
1489 A846 6s claret & pale green .95 .70

Miniature from the *Market Book of Grein*, by Ulrich Schreier, c. 1490 A847

1990, Mar. 9 *Perf. 14*
1490 A847 5s sepia, buff & gray .80 .60
 City of Linz, 500th anniv.

University Seals — A848

1990, Apr. 6
1491 A848 5s multicolored .85 .65
 625th Anniv. of Vienna University and 175th anniv. of Vienna Technical University.

Scenery Type of 1984

1990-97 *Perf. 14*
1492 A679 5s Styrian Vineyards .85 .65
1493 A679 5s Obir Caverns .95 .70
1494 A679 5s Natural Bridge, Vorarlberg .90 .75
1495 A679 6s Wilder Kaiser Mountain, Tyrol 1.25 .95
1496 A679 6s Peggau Cave, Styria 1.00 .80
1497 A679 6s Moorland, swamp, Heidenreichstein 1.25 1.00
1498 A679 6s Hohe Tauern Natl. Park 1.25 1.00
1499 A679 6s Nussberg Vineyards 1.00 .80
 Nos. 1492-1499 (8) 8.45 6.65

 Issued: #1492, 4/27; #1493, 3/26/91; #1494, 2/5/92; #1495, 2/19/93; #1496, 4/29/94; #1497, 5/19/95; #1498, 3/29/96; #1499, 2/21/97.

Anthering, 1200th Anniv. — A849

Church and municipal arms.

1990, Apr. 27 Photo. *Perf. 14x13½*
1500 A849 7s multicolored 1.25 1.00

Labor Day, Cent. — A850

1990, Apr. 30   Photo.   *Perf. 13½*
1501 A850 4.50s multicolored   .80   .60

Seckau Abbey, 850th Anniv. — A851

1990, May 4   Engr.   *Perf. 14x13½*
1502 A851 4.50s bluish black   .80   .60

Ebene Reichenau Post Office A852

1990, May 4   Photo.   *Perf. 13½x14*
1503 A852 7s multicolored   1.25 1.00

Hans Makart (1840-84), Self-Portrait A853

Self Portrait: 5s, Egon Schiele (1890-1918).

Photo. & Engr.
1990, May 29   *Perf. 14*
1504 A853 4.50s multicolored   .80   .60
1505 A853 5s multicolored   .85   .65

Ferdinand Raimund (1790-1836), Actor — A854

1990, June 1   Photo.   *Perf. 14x13½*
1506 A854 4.50s multicolored   .80   .60

Christ Healing the Sick by Rembrandt A855

Photo. & Engr.
1990, June 5   *Perf. 14*
1507 A855 7s multicolored   1.25 1.00
2nd Intl. Christus Medicus Cong., Bad Ischl.

Hardegg, 700th Anniv. — A856

Photo. & Engr.
1990, June 8   *Perf. 13½x14*
1508 A856 4.50s multicolored   .80   .60

Oberdrauburg, 750th Anniv. — A857

1990, June 8   Photo.
1509 A857 5s multicolored   .85   .65

Gumpoldskirchen, 850th Anniv. — A858

Photo. & Engr.
1990, June 15   *Perf. 13½*
1510 A858 5s multicolored   .85   .65

Mathias Zdarsky (1856-1940), Alpine Skier — A859

1990, June 20   *Perf. 14x13½*
1511 A859 5s multicolored   .85   .65

Telegraph, 1880, Anton Tschechow, 1978 — A860

1990, June 28   Photo.   *Perf. 14*
1512 A860 9s multicolored   1.50 1.10
Modern shipbuilding in Austria, 150th anniv.

Joseph Friedrich Perkonig (1890-1959), Poet — A861

Photo. & Engr.
1990, Aug. 3   *Perf. 14x13½*
1513 A861 5s gold & brown   .85   .65

Herr des Regenbogens, by Robert Zeppel-Sperl A862

Photo. & Engr.
1990, Aug. 30   *Perf. 13½x14*
1514 A862 5s gold & brown   .85   .65

European Dialysis and Transplantation Society, 27th Congress — A863

1990, Sept. 4   Photo.   *Perf. 14*
1515 A863 7s multicolored   1.25 1.00

Franz Werfel (1890-1945), Writer — A864

Photo. & Engr.
1990, Sept. 11   *Perf. 14x13½*
1516 A864 5s multicolored   .95   .70

Austrian Forces in UN Peace Keeping Forces, 30th Anniv. A865

1990, Sept. 20   Photo.   *Perf. 13½*
1517 A865 7s multicolored   1.25 1.00

Federal and State Arms A866

1990, Sept. 24   Photo. & Engr.
1518 A866 5s multicolored   .95   .70
Federalism in Austria.

Mining Univ., Leoben, 150th Anniv. — A867

Photo & Engr.
1990, Oct. 22   *Perf. 14*
1519 A867 4.50s blk, bl grn & red   .85   .65

Karl Freiherr von Vogelsang (1818-90), Politician — A868

Photo. & Engr.
1990, Nov. 8   *Perf. 14x13½*
1520 A868 4.50s multicolored   .85   .65

Metalworkers and Miners Trade Union, Cent. — A869

1990, Nov. 16   *Perf. 14*
1521 A869 5s multicolored   .95   .70

3rd World Curling Championships A870

1990, Nov. 23   Photo.   *Perf. 14x13½*
1522 A870 7s multicolored   1.40 1.00

Palmhouse at Schonbrunn — A871

1990, Nov. 30   *Perf. 14*
1523 A871 5s multicolored   .95   .70

Christmas A872

Altar in Klosterneuburg Abbey by the Master from Verdun.

Photo. & Engr.
1990, Nov. 23   *Perf. 13½*
1524 A872 5s multicolored   .95   .70

Franz Grillparzer (1791-1872), Dramatic Poet — A873

Photo. & Engr.
1991, Jan. 15   *Perf. 14x13½*
1525 A873 4.50s multicolored   .85   .65

Alpine Skiing World Championship,
Saalbach-Hinterglemm — A874

1991, Jan. 21   *Perf. 13½*
1526 A874 5s multicolored   .95 .70

Bruno Kreisky
(1911-90),
Chancellor
A875

1991, Jan. 21 Photo. *Perf. 14x13½*
1527 A875 5s multicolored   .95 .70

Friedrich Freiherr von Schmidt (1825-
1891), Architect — A876

1991, Jan. 21   *Perf. 14*
1528 A876 7s multicolored   1.40 1.00

Visual
Arts
A877

Designs: 4.50s, Donner Fountain, Vienna,
by Raphael Donner (1693-1741), sculptor. 5s,
Kitzbuhel in Winter, by Alfons Walde (1891-
1958), painter. 7s, Vienna Stock Exchange,
Theophil Hansen (1813-1891), architect.

1991, Feb. 8
1529 A877 4.50s multicolored   .85 .65
1530 A877 5s multicolored   .95 .70
1531 A877 7s multicolored   1.40 1.00
    Nos. 1529-1531 (3)   3.20 2.35
See No. 1543.

Marie von
Ebner
Eschenbach
(1830-1916),
Poet
A878

1991, Mar. 12 Engr. *Perf. 13½x14½*
1532 A878 4.50s rose violet   .85 .65

Miniature Sheet

Wolfgang
Amadeus Mozart
(1756-1791),
Composer
A879

Design: b, Magic Flute Fountain, Vienna.

1991, Mar. 22   *Perf. 13½*
1533   Sheet of 2 + label   1.75 1.25
  a.-b. A879 5s any single   .80 .60

Spittal an
der Drau,
800th
Anniv.
A880

1991, Apr. 11   *Perf. 14*
1534 A880 4.50s multicolored   .75 .60

Europa
A881

1991, May 3   Photo.   *Perf. 14*
1535 A881 7s ERS-1 satellite   1.10 .80

Garden
Banquet
by
Anthony
Bays
A882

1991, May 10   Photo.   *Perf. 13½*
1536 A882 5s multicolored   .75 .60
Vorarlberg Provincial Exhibition, Hohenems.

Museum
of
Military
History,
Cent.
A883

7s, Interior of Museum of Art History.

Photo. & Engr.
1991, May 24   *Perf. 13½*
1537 A883 5s multicolored   .95 .80
1538 A883 7s multicolored   1.25 1.00
Museum of Art History, Cent. (#1538).

Grein,
500th
Anniv.
A884

1991, May 24   Photo.   *Perf. 14*
1539 A884 4.50s multicolored   .90 .45

Tulln, 1200th
Anniv.
A885

1991, May 24   *Perf. 13½x14*
1540 A885 5s multicolored   .95 .80

Completion of
Karawanken
Tunnels — A886

1991, May 31   *Perf. 14x13½*
1541 A886 7s multicolored   1.25 1.00

5th Anniv.
of St.
Polten as
Provincial
Capital of
Lower
Austria
A887

1991, July 5   Photo.   *Perf. 14*
1542 A887 5s multicolored   .80 .65

Visual Arts Type of 1991
Design: 4.50s, Karlsplatz Station of Vienna
Subway by Otto Wagner (1841-1918),
Architect.

1991, July 12   Photo. & Engr.
1543 A877 4.50s multicolored   .75 .60

Rowing and Junior Canoeing World
Championships, Vienna — A888

1991, Aug. 20 Photo. *Perf. 13½x14*
1544 A888 5s multicolored   .85 .70

European Congress of
Radiologists — A889

1991, Sept. 13   *Perf. 14*
1545 A889 7s multicolored   1.10 .95

Paracelsus (1493-
1541),
Physician — A890

1991, Sept. 27   *Perf. 14x13½*
1546 A890 4.50s multicolored   .75 .60

Joint Austrian-
Soviet Space
Mission
A891

1991, Oct. 2   *Perf. 14*
1547 A891 9s multicolored   1.50 1.25

Austrian Folk
Festivals
A892

4.50s, Almabtrieb, Tyrol. 5s, Winzerkrone,
Vienna. 7s, Ernte-Monstranz, Styria.

1991, Oct. 4   Photo. & Engr.
1548 A892 4.50s multicolored   .75 .60
1549 A892 5s multicolored   .85 .70
1550 A892 7s multicolored   1.10 .95
    Nos. 1548-1550 (3)   2.70 2.25

See #1577-1579, 1619-1621, 1633-1635,
1671-1673, 1694, 1705-1706, 1714, 1730,
1741, 1752-1753, 1762, 1778, 1799-1800,
1805-1806, 1824, 1836-1838.

The General by
Rudolph
Pointner
A893

Photo. & Engr.
1991, Oct. 11   *Perf. 13½x14*
1551 A893 5s multicolored   .85 .70

Birth of Christ, Baumgartenberg
Church — A894

1991, Nov. 29
1552 A894 5s multicolored   .85 .70
Christmas.

Julius Raab,
Politician, Birth
Cent. — A895

1991, Nov. 29   *Perf. 14x13½*
1553 A895 4.50s red brn & brn   .75 .60

1992
Winter
and
Summer
Olympic
Games
A897

1992, Jan. 14   **Photo.**   *Perf. 14*
1555 A897 7s multicolored   1.25 1.00

Trade Union of Clerks in Private
Enterprises, Cent. — A898

1992, Jan. 14
1556 A898 5.50s multicolored   .95 .80

8th Natural Run
Toboggan World
Championships
A899

1992, Jan. 29   *Perf. 14x13½*
1557 A899 5s multicolored   .90 .75

George Saiko,
Poet, Birth
Cent. — A900

1992, Feb. 5   **Engr.**   *Perf. 14x13½*
1558 A900 5.50s brown   .95 .80

Worker's Sports,
Cent. — A901

1992, Feb. 5   **Photo.**   *Perf. 14*
1559 A901 5.50s multicolored   .95 .80

Souvenir Sheet

Vienna Philharmonic Orchestra, 150th
Anniv. — A902

Photo. & Engr.
1992, Mar. 27   *Perf. 14*
1560 A902 5.50s multicolored   .95 .80

Scientists
A903

Designs: 5s, Franz Joseph Muller von
Reichenstein (1742-1825), discoverer of tellu-
rium. 5.50s, Dr. Paul Kitaibel (1757-1817), botanist. 6s, Christian Johann Doppler (1803-
1853), physicist. 7s, Richard Kuhn (1900-
1967), chemist.

1992, Mar. 27   **Photo.**
1561 A903   5s multicolored   .80 .70
1562 A903 5.50s multicolored   .95 .80
1563 A903   6s multicolored   1.00 .85
1564 A903   7s multicolored   1.25 .95
   Nos. 1561-1564 (4)   4.00 3.30

Railway
Workers
Union,
Cent.
A904

1992, Apr. 2   *Perf. 14x13½*
1565 A904 5.50s black & red   .95 .80

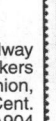

Norbert Hanrieder
(1842-1913),
Poet — A905

Photo. & Engr.
1992, Apr. 30   *Perf. 14x13½*
1566 A905 5.50s purple & buff   .95 .80

Carl Zeller
(1842-1898)
and Karl
Millocker
(1842-1899),
Operetta
Composers
A906

Photo. & Engr.
1992, Apr. 30   *Perf. 14*
1567 A906 6s multicolored   1.00 .85

LD Steel
Mill, 40th
Anniv.
A907

1992, May 8   **Photo.**   *Perf. 14x13½*
1568 A907 5s multicolored   .85 .70

Discovery
of
America,
500th
Anniv.
A908

Photo. & Engr.
1992, May 8   *Perf. 14*
1569 A908 7s multicolored   1.25 .95
   Europa.

Austro-Swiss Treaty on Regulation of
Rhine River, Cent. — A909

1992, May 8   **Photo.**   *Perf. 13½x14*
1570 A909 7s multicolored   1.25 .95

Protection of the
Alps — A910

1992, May 22   *Perf. 14x13½*
1571 A910 5.50s multicolored   .95 .80

Dr. Anna Dengel
(1892-1980),
Physician — A911

1992, May 22   **Photo. & Engr.**
1572 A911 5.50s multicolored   .95 .80

Sebastian Rieger
(1867-1953),
Poet — A912

1992, May 22   **Engr.**
1573 A912 5s red brown   .85 .70

Lienz,
750th
Anniv.
A913

1992, June 17   **Photo.**   *Perf. 14x13½*
1574 A913 5s Town Hall   .90 .70

Intl. Congress
of Austrian
Society of
Surgeons
A914

Photo. & Engr.
1992, June 17   *Perf. 14*
1575 A914 6s multicolored   1.10 .90

Dr. Kurt
Waldheim,
President of
Austria, 1986-
92 — A915

1992, June 22   *Perf. 14x13½*
1576 A915 5.50s multicolored   .95 .75

Folk Festivals Type of 1991

Designs: 5s, Marksman's target, Lower Austria. 5.50s, Peasant's chest, Carinthia. 7s,
Votive icon, Vorarlberg.

Photo. & Engr.
1992, Sept. 18   *Perf. 14*
1577 A892   5s multicolored   .90 .70
1578 A892 5.50s multicolored   .95 .75
1579 A892   7s multicolored   1.25 1.00
   Nos. 1577-1579 (3)   3.10 2.45

Marchfeld
Canal — A917

1992, Oct. 9   **Photo.**   *Perf. 13½x14*
1580 A917 5s multicolored   .90 .70

5th Intl. Ombudsman Conference,
Vienna — A918

Photo & Engr.
1992, Oct. 9   *Perf. 14*
1581 A918 5.50s multicolored   .95 .75

The
Clearance
of
Seawater,
by Peter
Pongratz
A919

1992, Oct. 9
1582 A919 5.50s multicolored   .95 .75

Academy of Fine Arts, 300th Anniv. — A920

Photo. & Engr.

1992, Oct. 23   *Perf. 14*
1583 A920 5s red & blue   1.00 .85

Birth of Christ, by Johann Georg Schmidt A921

1992, Nov. 27   *Perf. 14x13½*
1584 A921 5.50s multicolored   1.10 .90
Christmas.

Veit Koniger, Sculptor, Death Bicent. A922

Photo. & Engr.

1992, Nov. 27   *Perf. 14*
1585 A922 5s multicolored   1.00 .80

Herman Potocnik, Theoretician of Geosynchronous Satellite Orbit, Birth Cent. — A923

1992, Nov. 27   **Photo.**
1586 A923 10s multicolored   2.00 1.60

Famous Buildings A924

5s, Statues & dome of Imperial Palace, Vienna, designed by Joseph Emanuel Fischer von Erlach. 5.50s, Kinsky Palace, designed by Lukas von Hildebrandt. 7s, Vienna State Opera, designed by Eduard van der Null & August Siccard von Siccardsburg.

1993, Jan. 22   **Photo. & Engr.**
1587 A924   5s multicolored   1.00 .80
1588 A924   5.50s multicolored   1.10 .90
1589 A924   7s multicolored   1.40 1.10
    Nos. 1587-1589 (3)   3.50 2.80

Joseph Emanuel Fischer von Erlach, 300th birth anniv. (#1587). Johann Lukas von Hildebrandt, 325th birth anniv. (#1588). Eduard van der Null, August Siccard von Siccardsburg, 125th death anniv. (#1589).

Radio Dispatched Medical Service, 25th Anniv. — A925

1993, Feb. 19   **Photo.**
1590 A925 5s multicolored   1.00 .80

Typewriter Made by Peter Mitterhofer (1822-1893) A926

1993, Feb. 19   *Perf. 13½x14*
1591 A926 17s multicolored   3.50 2.75

Popular Entertainers — A927

Strada del Sole, by Rainhard Fendrich.

1993, Mar. 19   **Photo.**   *Perf. 14*
1592 A927 5.50s multicolored   1.00 .80
   See Nos. 1626, 1639.

Charles Sealsfield (1793-1864), Writer A928

Photo. & Engr.

1993, Mar. 19   *Perf. 13½x14*
1593 A928 10s multicolored   1.75 1.40

Rights of the Child — A930

1993, Apr. 16   **Photo.**   *Perf. 13½x14*
1595 A930 7s multicolored   1.25 1.00

Flying Harlequin, by Paul Flora A931

1993, Apr. 16   **Photo. & Engr.**
1596 A931 7s multicolored   1.25 1.00
    Europa.

Monastery of Admont — A932

Designs: 1s, Detail of abbesse's crosier, St. Gabriel Abbey, Styria. 5.50s, Death, wooden statue by Josef Stammel (1695-1765). 6s, Stained glass, Mariastern-Gwiggen Monastery. 7s, Marble lion, Franciscan Monastery, Salzburg. 8s, Gothic entry, Wilhering Monastery, Upper Austria. 7.50s, Cupola fresco, by Paul Troger, Monastery of Altenburg. 10s, Altarpiece, St. Peregrinus praying, Maria Luggau Monastery. 20s, Crosier, Fiecht Monastery. 26s, Sculpture of Mater Dolorosa, Franciscan Monastery, Schwaz, Tirol. 30s, Madonna of Scottish Order, Schottenstift Monastery, Vienna.

Perf. 14x13½, 13½x14 (8s, 26s), 14 (1s, 30s)

1993-95   **Photo. & Engr.**
1599 A932 1s multicolored   .20 .20
1603 A932 5.50s multicolored   1.00 .75

Perf. 14

1606 A932   6s multicolored   1.10 .90
1606A A932   7s multicolored   1.25 1.00
1607 A932   7.50s multicolored   1.25 1.00
1608 A932   8s multicolored   1.60 1.25
1609 A932   10s multicolored   1.75 1.40
1613 A932   20s multicolored   3.50 1.75
1613A A932   26s multicolored   5.25 4.25
1614 A932   30s multicolored   5.50 4.50
   Nos. 1599-1614 (10)   22.40 17.00

Issued: 5.50s, 4/16; 6s, 9/17; 20s, 10/8; 7.50s, 4/4/94; 10s, 8/26/94; 30s, 10/7/94; 7s, 11/18/94; 8s, 9/15/95; 26s, 10/6/95; 1s, 4/28/95.

This is an expanding set. Numbers may change.

Peter Rosegger (1843-1918), Writer — A933

1993, May 5   **Photo.**   *Perf. 14x13½*
1617 A933 5.50s green & black   1.00 .80

Lake Constance Steamer Hohentwiel A934

1993, May 5   **Photo.**   *Perf. 14*
1618 A934 6s multicolored   1.10 .85
   See Germany #1786, Switzerland #931.

Folk Festivals Type of 1991

Designs: 5s, Corpus Christi Day Procession, Upper Austria. 5.50s, Blockdrawing, Burgenland. 7s, Cracking whip when snow is melting, Salzburg.

Photo. & Engr.

1993, June 11   *Perf. 14*
1619 A892   5s multicolored   .90 .70
1620 A892   5.50s multicolored   1.00 .80
1621 A892   7s multicolored   1.25 1.00
   Nos. 1619-1621 (3)   3.15 2.50

UN Conference on Human Rights, Vienna A935

1993, June 11   **Photo.**
1622 A935 10s multicolored   1.75 1.40

Franz Jagerstatter (1907-1943), Resistance Fighter — A936

1993, Aug. 6   **Photo.**   *Perf. 14x13½*
1623 A936 5.50s multicolored   1.00 .80

Schafberg Railway, Cent. A937

1993, Aug. 6   *Perf. 13½x14*
1624 A937 6s multicolored   1.10 .90

Self-portrait with Puppet, by Rudolf Wacker (1893-1939) A938

Photo. & Engr.

1993, Aug. 6   *Perf. 14*
1625 A938 6s multicolored   1.10 .90

Popular Entertainers Type of 1993

Design: 5.50s, Granny, by Ludwig Hirsch.

1993, Sept. 3   **Photo.**   *Perf. 14*
1626 A927 5.50s multicolored   1.00 .80

Vienna Mens' Choral Society, 150th Anniv. A940

1993, Sept. 17   **Photo.**   *Perf. 14*
1627 A940 5s multicolored   .90 .75

Easter, by Max Weiler — A941

Photo. & Engr.

1993, Oct. 8   *Perf. 13½x14*
1628 A941 5.50s multicolored   1.00 .80

99 Heads, by Hundertwasser — A942

1993, Oct. 8
1629 A942 7s multicolored   1.25   1.00
Council of Europe Conference, Vienna.

Austrian Republic, 75th Anniv. — A943

Design: 5.50s, Statue of Pallas Athena.

Photo. & Engr.
1993, Nov. 12   *Perf. 13½x14*
1630 A943 5.50s multicolored   1.00   .80

Trade Unions in Austria, Cent. — A944

1993, Nov. 12   **Photo.**   *Perf. 14*
1631 A944 5.50s multicolored   1.00   .80

Birth of Christ, by Master of the Krainburger Altar — A945

Photo. & Engr.
1993, Nov. 26   *Perf. 13½x14*
1632 A945 5.50s multicolored   1.00   .80
Christmas.

Folklore and Customs Type of 1991
Antiques: 5.50s, Dolls, cradle, Vorarlberg. 6s, Sled, Steiermark. 7s, Godparent's bowl, Upper Austria.

Photo. & Engr.
1994, Jan. 28   *Perf. 14*
1633 A892 5.50s multicolored   1.00   .80
1634 A892 6s multicolored   1.10   .90
1635 A892 7s multicolored   1.25   1.00
    Nos. 1633-1635 (3)   3.35   2.70

1994 Winter Olympics, Lillehammer, Norway — A946

1994, Feb. 9
1636 A946 7s multicolored   1.25   1.00

Vienna Mint, 800th Anniv. A947

1994, Feb. 18
1637 A947 6s multicolored   1.10   .90

Lying Lady, by Herbert Boeckl (1894-1966) — A948

1994, Mar. 18   **Photo.**   *Perf. 14x13½*
1638 A948 5.50s multicolored   .95   .70

Popular Entertainers Type of 1993
Design: 6s, Rock Me Amadeus, by Falco.

1994, Mar. 18   *Perf. 14*
1639 A927 6s multicolored   1.00   .80

Wiener Neustadt, 800th Anniv. — A949

1994, Mar. 18
1640 A949 6s multicolored   1.00   .80

Lake Rudolph, Teleki-Hohnel Expedition — A950

Photo. & Engr.
1994, May 27   *Perf. 14x13½*
1641 A950 7s multicolored   1.25   1.00
Europa.

Daniel Gran, 300th Birth Anniv. A951

Fresco: 20s, Allegory of Theology, Jurisprudence and Medicine.

1994, May 27
1642 A951 20s multicolored   3.50   2.75

Carinthian Summer Festival, 25th Anniv. — A952

Design: 5.50s, Scene from The Prodigal Son.

Photo. & Engr.
1994, June 17   *Perf. 14*
1643 A952 5.50s lake & gold   .95   .75

Railway Centennials — A953

1994   **Photo. & Engr.**   *Perf. 14*
1647 A953 5.50s Gailtal   .95   .75
1648 A953 6s Murtal   1.00   .80
    Issued: 5.50s, 6s, 6/17/94.

Hermann Gmeiner, 75th Birth Anniv. — A954

1994, June 17   *Perf. 14x13½*
1656 A954 7s multicolored   1.25   1.00

Karl Seitz (1869-1950) Politician A955

1994, Aug. 12   **Photo.**   *Perf. 14*
1657 A955 5.50s multicolored   1.00   .80

Karl Bohm (1894-1981), Conductor A956

Photo. & Engr.
1994, Aug. 26   *Perf. 14x13½*
1658 A956 7s gold & dk blue   1.25   1.00

Ethnic Minorities in Austria A957

1994, Sept. 9   **Photo.**   *Perf. 13½*
1659 A957 5.50s multicolored   1.00   .80

Franz Theodor Csokor (1885-1969), Writer — A958

7s, Joseph Roth (1894-1939), writer.

1994, Sept. 9   *Perf. 14x13½*
1660 A958 6s multicolored   1.00   .80
1661 A958 7s multicolored   1.25   1.00

Savings Banks in Austria, 175th Anniv. — A959

Photo. & Engr.
1994, Oct. 7   *Perf. 14x13½*
1662 A959 7s Coin bank   1.25   1.00

Modern Art — A960

1994, Oct. 7   *Perf. 13½x14*
Design: 6s, "Head," by Franz Ringel.
1663 A960 6s multicolored   1.10   .90

Austrian Working Environment — A961

1994, Nov. 18   **Photo.**   *Perf. 14*
1664 A961 6s Stewardess, child   1.10   .90
    See Nos. 1690, 1703, 1736, 1773, 1828, 1859.

Richard Coudenhove Kalergi, Founder of PanEuropean Union, Birth Cent. — A962

Photo. & Engr.
1994, Nov. 18   *Perf. 13½*
1665 A962 10s multicolored   1.90   1.50

Birth of Christ, by Anton Wollenek A963

1994, Nov. 25   *Perf. 14*
1666 A963 6s multicolored   1.10   .90
    Christmas.

Membership in European Union — A964

1995, Jan. 13   Photo.   Perf. 14
1667 A964 7s multicolored   1.25 1.00

Adolf Loos (1870-1933), Architect A965

1995, Jan. 13
1668 A965 10s House, Vienna   1.90 1.50

Official Representation for Workers, 75th Anniv. — A966

1995, Feb. 24   Perf. 14x13½
1669 A966 6s multicolored   1.10 .90

Austrian Gymnastics and Sports Assoc., 50th Anniv. — A967

1995, Feb. 24
1670 A967 6s multicolored   1.10 .90

Folklore and Customs Type of 1991
Designs: 5.50s, Belt, Gailtal, Carinthia. 6s, Vineyard watchman's costume, Vienna. 7s, Bonnet, Wachau, Lower Austria.

Photo. & Engr.
1995, Mar. 24   Perf. 14
1671 A892 5.50s multicolored   1.10 .90
1672 A892   6s multicolored   1.25 1.00
1673 A892   7s multicolored   1.40 1.10
     Nos. 1671-1673 (3)   3.75 3.00

Second Republic, 50th Anniv. — A968

1995, Apr. 27
1674 A968 6s State seal   1.25 1.00

History of Mining & Industry A969

Design: Blast furnaces, old Heft ironworks.

1995, Apr. 28   Perf. 13½x14
1675 A969 5.50s multicolored   1.10 .90
Carinthian Provincial Exhibition.

Nature Lovers Club, Cent. — A970

1995, Apr. 28   Perf. 14
1676 A970 5.50s multicolored   1.10 .90

Europa — A971

1995, May 19   Perf. 14
1677 A971   7s multicolored   1.50 1.25

1995 Conference of Ministers of Transportation, Vienna — A972

1995, May 26   Photo.   Perf. 14
1678 A972 7s multicolored   1.40 1.25

Bregenz Festival, 50th Anniv. A973

1995, June 9
1679 A973 6s multicolored   1.25 1.00

St. Gebhard (949-995) A974

Stained glass window, by Martin Hausle.

1995, June 9
1680 A974 7.50s multicolored   1.50 1.25

UN, 50th Anniv. — A975

1995, June 26   Photo.   Perf. 14
1681 A975 10s multicolored   2.00 2.00

Josef Loschmidt (1821-95), Chemist — A976

Photo. & Engr.
1995, June 26   Perf. 14x13½
1682 A976 20s multicolored   4.00 4.00

Salzburg Festival, 75th Anniv. — A977

Photo. & Engr.
1995, Aug. 18   Perf. 13½x14
1683 A977 6s multicolored   1.25 1.00

Kathe Leichter, Resistance Member, Birth Cent. — A978

1995, Aug. 18   Perf. 14x13½
1684 A978 6s buff, black & red   1.25 1.00

Europaisches Landschaftsbild, by Adolf Frohner — A979

1995, Aug. 18
1685 A979 6s multicolored   1.25 1.00

Operetta Composers A980

Designs: 6s, Franz von Suppe (1819-95), scene from "The Beautiful Galathea." 7s, Nico Dostal (b. 1895), scene from "The Hungarian Wedding."

1995, Sept. 15   Perf. 14
1686 A980 6s multicolored   1.25 1.00
1687 A980 7s multicolored   1.40 1.10
     See Croatia No. 253.

University of Klagenfurt, 25th Anniv. — A981

1995, Oct. 6   Photo.   Perf. 14
1688 A981 5.50s multicolored   1.10 .90

Carinthian Referendum, 75th Anniv. — A982

1995, Oct. 6   Photo. & Engr.
1689 A982 6s multicolored   1.25 1.00

Austria Working Environment Type of 1994
1995, Oct. 20
1690 A961 6s Post office official 1.25 1.00

Composers A983

6s, Anton von Webern (1883-1945). 7s, Ludwig van Beethoven (1770-1827).

1995, Oct. 20   Perf. 13½x14
1691 A983 6s orange & blue   1.25 1.00
1692 A983 7s orange & red   1.40 1.10

Christmas A984

1995, Dec. 1   Photo. & Engr.   Perf. 13½
1693 A984 6s Christ Child   1.25 1.00

Folklore and Customs Type of 1991
Design: Roller and Scheller in "Procession of Masked Groups in Imst," Tyrol.

Photo. & Engr.
1996, Feb. 9   Perf. 14
1694 A892 6s multicolored   1.25 1.00

Maria Theresa Academy, 250th Anniv. — A985

1996, Feb. 9
1695 A985 6s multicolored   1.25 1.00

1996 World Ski Jumping Championships A986

1996, Feb. 9 Photo.
1696 A986 7s multicolored 1.40 1.10

New Western Pier, Vienna Intl. Airport A987

1996, Mar. 28 Photo. *Perf. 14*
1697 A987 7s multicolored 1.40 1.10

A988

6s, Mother with Child, by Peter Fendi (1796-1842). 7s, Self-portrait, by Leopold Kupelwieser (1795-1862).

1996, Mar. 29
1698 A988 6s multicolored 1.25 1.00
1699 A988 7s multicolored 1.40 1.10

Anton Bruckner (1824-96), Composer, Organist A989

Photo. & Engr.
1996, Apr. 26 *Perf. 14*
1700 A989 5.50s Organ, music 1.10 .90

Georg Matthäus Vischer, 300th Death Anniv. A990

1996, Apr. 26
1701 A990 10s Kollmitz Castle 2.00 1.50

City of Klagenfurt, 800th Anniv. — A991

1996, May 3
1702 A991 6s Ancient square 1.25 1.00

Austrian Working Environment Type of 1994
1996, May 17
1703 A961 6s Chef, waitress 1.25 1.00

Paula von Preradovic, Author A992

1996, May 17 *Perf. 13½x14*
1704 A992 7s black, gray & buff 1.40 1.10
Europa.

Folklore and Customs Type of 1991
Designs: 5.50s, Corpus Christi poles, Salzburg. 7s, Tyrolian riflemen.

Photo. & Engr.
1996, June 21 *Perf. 14*
1705 A892 5.50s multicolored 1.00 .80
1706 A892 7s multicolored 1.25 1.00

1996 Summer Olympic Games, Atlanta — A993

1996, June 21
1707 A993 10s multicolored 1.90 1.50

Burgenland Province, 75th Anniv. — A994

1996, Sept. 20
1708 A994 6s multicolored 1.10 .90

Austrian Mountain Rescue Service, Cent. — A995

1996, Sept. 27
1709 A995 6s multicolored 1.10 .90

Austria Millenium A996

Designs: a, Deed by Otto III. b, Empress Maria Theresa, Josef II. c, Duke Henry II. d, 1848 Revolution. e, Rudolf IV. f, Dr. Karl Renner, 1st Republic. g, Emperor Maximilian I. h, State Treaty of 1955, 2nd Republic. i, Imperial Crown of Rudolf II. j, Austria, Europe.

Photo. & Engr.
1996, Oct. 25 *Perf. 14*
1710 Sheet of 10 19.00 19.00
 a.-b. A996 6s any single 1.10 1.10
 c.-f. A996 7s any single 1.25 1.25
 g.-h. A996 10s any single 1.90 1.90
 i.-j. A996 20s any single 3.80 3.80

Power Station, by Reinhard Artberg A997

1996, Nov. 22
1711 A997 7s multicolored 1.25 1.25

UNICEF, 50th Anniv. — A998

1996, Nov. 22 Photo.
1712 A998 10s multicolored 1.90 1.90

Christmas A999

1996, Nov. 29 **Photo. & Engr.**
1713 A999 6s multicolored 1.25 1.00

Folklore and Customs Type of 1991
Epiphany Carol Singers, Burgenland.

Photo. & Engr.
1997, Jan. 17 *Perf. 14*
1714 A892 7s multicolored 1.25 1.00

Theodor Kramer, Poet, Birth Cent. — A1000

1997, Jan. 17
1715 A1000 5.50s deep blue 1.00 .80

Austrian Academy of Sciences, 150th Anniv. — A1001

1997, Feb. 21 Photo. *Perf. 14*
1716 A1001 10s multicolored 1.75 1.40

Austrian Electricity Board, 50th Anniv. A1002

1997, Mar. 21
1717 A1002 6s multicolored 1.00 .80

The Cruel Lady of Forchtenstein Castle, Burgenland A1003

Photo. & Engr.
1997, Mar. 21 *Perf. 14*
1718 A1003 7s multicolored 1.10 .95
See #1731, 1733, 1745-1746, 1763, 1775, 1794, 1802, 1804, 1810-1811.

Erich Wolfgang Korngold (1897-1957), Composer A1004

1997, Mar. 21
Design: Scene from opera, "The Dead City."
1719 A1004 20s bl, blk & gold 3.25 1.60

Vienna Rapid, Austrian Soccer Champions — A1005

1997, Apr. 25 Photo. *Perf. 14*
1720 A1005 7s multicolored 1.25 1.00
See #1754, 1779, 1807, 1839.

Deer Feeding in Wintertime A1006

1997, Apr. 25
1721 A1006 7s multicolored 1.25 1.00
See #1747, 1782, 1808, 1835.

St. Peter Canisius (1521-97) A1007

1997, Apr. 25　　　*Photo. & Engr.*
1722 A1007 7.50s Canisius Altar,
　　　　　　　　Innsbruck　　1.25 1.10

Composers — A1008

Designs: 6s, Johannes Brahms (1833-
1897). 10s, Franz Schubert (1797-1828).

1997, May 9
1723 A1008　6s gold & vio bl　1.00　.80
1724 A1008　10s purple & gold　1.75 1.40

Stamp
Day — A1009

1997, May 9　　　　　*Perf. 13½*
1725 A1009 7s "A" and "E"　　1.25 1.00
　See #B357-B362, 1765, 1791, 1818. The
1st letters spell "Briefmarke," the 2nd
"Philatelie."

Child's View of
"Town Band of
Bremen"
A1010

1997, May 23　　　　　*Photo.*
1726 A1010 7s multicolored　1.25 1.00
　　　　Europa.

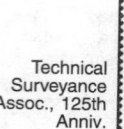

Technical
Surveyance
Assoc., 125th
Anniv.
A1011

1997, June 13　*Photo.*　*Perf. 14*
1727 A1011 7s multicolored　1.40 1.10

Railways
A1012

Designs: 6s, Hochschneeberg Cog Railway.
7.50s, Wiener Neustadt-Odenburg Railway.

1997, June 13　　*Photo. & Engr.*
1728 A1012　6s multicolored　1.25　.95
1729 A1012　7.50s multicolored　1.50 1.25

Folklore and Customs Type of 1991
　　　　Photo. & Engr.
1997, July 11　　　　　*Perf. 14*
1730 A892 6.50s Marching
　　　　　　band, Tyrol　1.25　1.00

Stories and Legends Type
Design: Dragon of Klagenfurt.
1997, July 11
1731 A1003 6.50s multicolored　1.25 1.00

Karl Heinrich
Waggerl, Birth
Cent. — A1013

1997, July 11
1732 A1013 7s multicolored　1.40 1.00

Stories and Legends Type of 1997
　Design: Danube water nymph rescuing fer-
ryman, Upper Austria.
　　　　Photo. & Engr.
1997, Sept. 19　　　　*Perf. 14*
1733 A1003 14s multicolored　2.75 2.10

1997 Orthopedics Congress,
Vienna — A1014

1997, Sept. 19　*Photo.*　*Perf. 14*
1734 A1014 8s Adolph Lorenz　1.60 1.25

Vienna
Agricultural
University,
125th Anniv.
A1015

1997, Sept. 19
1735 A1015 9s multicolored　1.75 1.40

**Austrian Working Environment Type
of 1994**
　　　　Photo. & Engr.
1997, Oct. 17　　　　　*Perf. 14*
1736 A961　6.50s Nurse, patient　1.25 1.00

"House in Wind," by Helmut
Schickhofer — A1016

1997, Oct. 17
1737 A1016 7s multicolored　1.40 1.00

Blind Persons
Assocs. in
Austria,
Cent. — A1017

Photo. & Embossed
1997, Oct. 17
1738 A1017 7s multicolored　1.40 1.00
　#1738 has embossed Braille inscription.

Dr. Thomas
Klestil, Pres. of
Austria, 65th
birthday — A1018

Photo. & Engr.
1997, Oct. 31　　　*Perf. 14x13½*
1739 A1018 7s multicolored　1.40 1.00

Oskar Werner
(1922-84),
Actor — A1019

1997, Oct. 31　　　　　*Perf. 14*
1740 A1019 7s multicolored　1.40 1.00

Folklore and Customs Type of 1991
　Upper Austria tower wind players, Steyr.
　　　　Photo. & Engr.
1997, Nov. 21　　　　　*Perf. 14*
1741 A892 6.50s multicolored　1.25 1.00

Light For All Relief Organization, 25th
Anniv. — A1020

1997, Nov. 28　*Photo.*　*Perf. 14*
1742 A1020 7s multicolored　1.40 1.00

Christmas
A1021

Photo. & Engr.
1997, Nov. 28　　　　　*Perf. 14*
1743 A1021 7s Mariazell Madon-
　　　　　　na　　　1.40 1.00

Scenery Type of 1984
　Kalkalpen Natl. Park, Upper Austria.
　　　　Photo. & Engr.
1998, Jan. 23　　　　　*Perf. 14*
1744 A679 7s multicolored　1.10　.85

Stories and Legends Type of 1997
　Designs: 9s, The Charming Augustin. 13s,
Pied Piper from Korneuburg.
1998, Jan. 23
1745 A1003　9s multicolored　1.40 1.00
1746 A1003　13s multicolored　2.00 1.50

Hunting and Environment Type
1998, Feb. 6　　　　　*Photo.*
1747 A1006 9s Black cocks　1.40 1.00

1998 Winter Olympic Games,
Nagano — A1022

1998, Feb. 6　　　*Photo. & Engr.*
1748 A1022 14s multicolored　2.25 1.60

Lithographic
Printing,
Bicent.
A1023

　Portrait of Aloys Senefelder (1771-1834),
inventor of lithography, on printing stone.

1998, Mar. 13　*Litho.*　*Perf. 13½*
1749 A1023 7s multicolored　1.40 1.00

Joseph Binder
(1898-1972),
Graphic
Artist — A1024

1998, Mar. 13　*Photo.*　*Perf. 14*
1750 A1024 7s Poster　1.40 1.00

Wiener
Secession, Cent.
(Assoc. of Artists
in Austria-
Viennese
Secession)
A1025

1998, Mar. 13　　　*Photo. & Engr.*
1751 A1025 8s multicolored　1.60 1.25

Folklore and Customs Type of 1991
　6.50s, Fiacre, Vienna. 7s, Samson figure,
Palm Sunday Donkey Procession, Tyrol.

1998, Apr. 3
1752 A892　6.50s multicolored　1.25　.95
1753 A892　7s multicolored　1.40 1.00

Soccer Champions Type of 1997
1998, Apr. 17　　　　　*Photo.*
1754 A1005 7s Austria-Memphis
　　　　　　Club　　　1.40 1.00

Salzburg
Archdiocese,
1200th Anniv.
A1026

1998, Apr. 17　　　*Photo. & Engr.*
1755 A1026 7s multicolored　　1.40 1.00

St. Florian, Patron Saint of Fire Brigades A1027

1998, Apr. 17   Photo.
1756 A1027 7s multicolored   1.40 1.00

Railway Centennials A1028

No. 1757, Ybbs Railway. No. 1758, Pöstlingberg Railway. No. 1759, Pinzgau Railway.

1998   Photo. & Engr.   Perf. 14
1757 A1028 6.50s multicolored   1.25 1.00
1758 A1028 6.50s multicolored   1.25 1.00
1759 A1028 6.50s multicolored   1.25 1.00
   Nos. 1757-1759 (3)   3.75 3.00
Issued: #1757, 5/15; #1758, 6/12; #1759, 7/17.

Ferdinandeum, Federal Museum of Tyrol, 175th Anniv. A1029

1998, May 15
1760 A1029 7s multicolored   1.40 1.00

Vienna Festival Weeks — A1030

1998, May 15
1761 A1030 7s Townhall   1.40 1.00
   Europa.

Folklore and Customs Type of 1991
Samson figure & the Zwergin, Lungau district, Salzburg.

1998, June 5
1762 A892 6.50s multicolored   1.25 1.00

Stories and Legends Type of 1997
Design: 25s, Saint Konrad collecting spring water in his handkerchief, Ems Castle.

1998, June 5
1763 A1003 25s multicolored   5.00 3.75

Christine Lavant, Poet, 25th Death Anniv. A1031

1998, June 5   Photo.
1764 A1031 7s multicolored   1.40 1.00

Stamp Day Type of 1997
Photo. & Engr.
1998, June 12   Perf. 13½
1765 A1009 7s "R" and "L"   1.40 1.00

See #1725, 1791,1818, B357-B362. The 1st letters spell "Briefmarke," the 2nd "Philatelie."

Austrian Presidency of the European Union — A1032

1998, July 1   Photo.   Perf. 13½x14
1766 A1032 7s multicolored   1.40 1.00

The People's Opera, Vienna, 50th Anniv. & Franz Lehar (1870-1948), Composer — A1033

1998, Sept. 10   Photo.   Perf. 14
1767 A1033 6.50s multicolored   1.25 .85

Elizabeth, Empress of Austria (1837-98) A1034

1998, Sept. 10   Photo. & Engr.
1768 A1034 7s multicolored   1.40 .90

Vienna University for Commercial Sudies, Cent. — A1035

1998, Sept. 10   Photo.
1769 A1035 7s multicolored   1.40 .90

Hans Kudlich, Emancipator of Peasants, 175th Birth Anniv. A1036

Photo. & Engr.
1998, Oct. 23   Perf. 14
1770 A1036 6.50s multicolored   1.25 .90

"My Garden," by Hans Staudacher A1037

1998, Oct. 23
1771 A1037 7s multicolored   1.25 .90

City of Eisenstadt, 350th Anniv. — A1038

1998, Oct. 23
1772 A1038 7s multicolored   1.25 .90

Austrian Working Environment Type of 1994
Photo. & Engr.
1998, Nov. 6   Perf. 14
1773 A961 6.50s Reporter, photographer   1.10 .85

Christmas A1039

1423 Fresco from Tainach/Tinje Church, Carinthia.

1998, Nov. 27
1774 A1039 7s multicolored   1.25 .85

Stories and Legends Type of 1997
The Dark Maiden of Hardegg Castle.

Photo. & Engr.
1999, Feb. 19   Perf. 14
1775 A1003 8s multicolored   1.25 .85

1999 Nordic Skiing World Championships, Mt. Dachstein, Ramsau A1040

1999, Feb. 19
1776 A1040 7s multicolored   1.10 .85

Scenery Type of 1984
Bohemian Forest, Upper Austria.

Photo. & Engr.
1999, Mar. 19   Perf. 14
1777 A679 7s multicolored   1.10 .85

Folklore and Customs Type of 1991
Traditional walking pilgrimage to Mariazell.

1999, Mar. 19
1778 A892 6.50s multicolored   1.00 .75

Soccer Champions Type of 1997
Design: Soccer Club SK Puntigamer Sturm Graz.

1999, Apr. 16   Photo.   Perf. 14
1779 A1005 7s multicolored   1.10 .85

Schönnbrun Palace, UNESCO World Heritage Site — A1041

Photo. & Engr.
1999, Apr. 16   Perf. 14
1780 A1041 13s multicolored   2.00 1.50
   See No. 1845.

Austrian Patent Office, Cent. — A1042

1999, Apr. 16
1781 A1042 7s multicolored   1.10 .85

Hunting and Environment Type of 1997
1999, May 7   Litho.   Perf. 14
1782 A1006 6.50s Partridges   1.00 .75

Austrian General Sport Federation, 50th Anniv. A1043

1999, May 7   Engr.   Perf. 14
1783 A1043 7s multicolored   1.10 .80

Council of Europe, 50th Anniv. A1044

1999, May 7   Photo.   Perf. 13½x14
1784 A1044 14s multicolored   2.25 1.60

Karl Jenschke (1899-1969), Automobile Designer A1045

1999, May 28
1785 A1045 7s Steyr automobile   1.10 .80

564

AUSTRIA

Marble Relief
of St. Martin
A1046

Photo. & Engr.
1999, May 28   *Perf. 14*
1786 A1046 8s multicolored   1.25 .95
    See Nos. 1787, 1817, 1830, 1851-1852.

Religious Art Type
Design: 9s, St. Anne, Mary and Jesus.
Photo. & Engr.
1999, Sept. 17   *Perf. 13¾*
1787 A1046 9s multicolored   1.40 1.10

Austrian Social
Welfare
Service, 125th
Anniv.
A1047

1999, June 4   Litho.   *Perf. 13¾*
1788 A1047 7s multicolored   1.10 .80

Johann
Strauss,
the
Younger
(1825-99),
Composer
A1048

8s, Johann Strauss, the Elder (1804-49).

1999, June 4   **Photo. & Engr.**
1789 A1048 7s multicolored   1.10 .80
1790 A1048 8s multicolored   1.25 .95

Stamp Day Type of 1997
1999, June 18   *Perf. 13½*
1791 A1009 7s "K" and "I"   1.10 .80
    See #1725, 1765, 1818, B357-B362. The
1st letters spell "Briefmarke," the 2nd
"Philatelie."

Donau-Auen Natl. Park — A1049

1999, June 18   *Perf. 13¾*
1792 A1049 7s multicolored   1.10 .80
    Europa.

Natl.
Gendarmery,
150th
Anniv. — A1050

1999, June 18
1793 A1050 7s multicolored   1.10 .80

Stories and Legends Type of 1997
Design: The Holy Notburga.
Photo. & Engr.
1999, Aug. 27   *Perf. 13¾x14*
1794 A1003 20s multicolored   3.25 2.50

Graz Opera
House, 100th
Anniv. — A1051

Photo. & Engr.
1999, Sept. 17   *Perf. 13¾*
1795 A1051 6.50s multicolored   1.00 .75

International Year of Older
Persons — A1052

1999, Sept. 17   *Perf. 13¾*
1796 A1052 7s multicolored   1.10 .85

Federation of
Austrian Trade
Unions, 14th
Congress
A1053

1999, Oct. 15   Litho.   *Perf. 13¾*
1797 A1053 6.50s multicolored   1.00 .75

"Caffee Girardi,"
by Wolfgang
Herzig — A1054

Photo. & Engr.
1999, Oct. 22   *Perf. 13¾x14*
1798 A1054 7s multicolored   1.10 .85

Folklore & Customs Type of 1991
7s, The Pummerin, Bell in St. Stephen's
Cathedral, Vienna. 8s, Pumpkin Festival,
Lower Austria.
1999   **Photo. & Engr.**   *Perf. 13¾*
1799 A892 7s multicolored   1.10 .85
1800 A892 8s multicolored   1.25 .95
    Issued: 8s, 10/22; 7s, 11/12.

National
Institute of
Geology,
150th
Anniv
A1055

Photo. & Engr.
1999, Nov. 12   *Perf. 13¾x14*
1801 A1055 7s multicolored   1.10 .85

Stories & Legends Type of 1997
Design: 32s, Discovery of Erzberg.
Photo. & Engr.
1999, Nov. 12   *Perf. 13¾x14*
1802 A1003 32s multicolored   5.00 3.75

Christmas
A1056

Photo. & Engr.
1999, Nov. 26   *Perf. 13¾*
1803 A1056 7s Pinkafeld creche   1.10 .85

Stories & Legends Type of 1997
Design: 10s, House of the Basilisk, Vienna.
Photo. & Engr.
2000, Jan. 21   *Perf. 13¾x14*
1804 A1003 10s multi   1.40 1.00
  a.   Souvenir sheet of 1   13.00 9.50
    No. 1804a was sold only with the purchase
of an 80s ticket to the Vienna Intl. Philatelic
Exhibition.

Folklore & Customs Type of 1991
Designs: 6.50s, Schleicherlaufen Festival,
Telfs. 7s, Carrying miniature churches, Bad
Eisenkappel.
2000   **Photo. & Engr.**   *Perf. 13¾*
1805 A892 6.50s multi   .90 .65
1806 A892 7s multi   1.00 .75
    Issued: 6.50s, 1/21; 7s, 2/11.

Soccer Champions Type of 1997
Design: Tirol Soccer Club.
2000, Mar. 3   Photo.   *Perf. 13¾*
1807 A1005 7s multi   1.00 .75

Hunting and Environment Type of 1997
2000, Mar. 3   *Perf. 14x14¼*
1808 A1006 7s Ibex   1.00 .75

Intl. Gardening
Exhibition,
Graz — A1057

Photo. & Embossed
2000, Mar. 3   *Perf. 13½x13¾*
1809 A1057 7s multi   1.00 .75

Stories & Legends Type of 1997
Designs: 22s, The Witch's Ride. 23s, The
Bread Loaf Monument.
2000   **Photo. & Engr.**   *Perf. 13¾x14*
1810 A1003 22s multi   3.00 2.25
1811 A1003 23s multi   3.00 2.25
    Issued: 22s, 4/28. 23s, 6/16.

First Ascent of
Grossglockner,
Bicent.
A1058

2000, Apr. 28   *Perf. 13¾*
1812 A1058 7s multi   .95 .70

Scenery Type of 1984
Design: Sonnblick Glacier, Granatspitze,
Weissee, Salzburg.
2000, May 9   *Perf. 13¾x14*
1813 A679 7s multi   .95 .70

Europa, 2000
Common Design Type
2000, May 9   Photo.   *Perf. 14¼x13½*
1814 CD17 7s multi   .95 .70

Klagenfurt
Airport, 75th
Anniv.
A1059

2000, May 19   *Perf. 13¾*
1815 A1059 7s multi   .95 .70

Protection of Historical Monuments,
150th Anniv. — A1060

Photo. & Engr.
2000, May 19   *Perf. 14x13¼*
1816 A1060 8s multi   1.10 .80

Religious Art Type of 1999
Design: 9s, Illustration of St. Malachy from
book, *The Life of Bishop Malachy.*
2000, May 19   *Perf. 13¾*
1817 A1046 9s multi   1.25 .90

Stamp Day Type of 1997
2000, May 30   *Perf. 13½*
1818 A1009 7s "E" and "E"   .95 .70
    See #1725, 1765, 1791, B357-B362. The
1st letters spell "Briefmarke," the 2nd
"Philatelie."

Austrian
Postage
Stamps, 150th
Anniv.
A1061

2000, May 30   *Perf. 13¾*
1819 A1061 7s Nos. 5, 1818   .95 .70

Children's
Television
Character,
Confetti
A1062

2000, May 31
1820 A1062 7s multi   .95 .70
    See No. 1841.

Blue Blues, by Friedensreich Hundertwasser (1928-2000), Artist — A1063

Colors of seven solid vertical panels at top: a, Silver. b, Red. c, Red violet. d, Black.

2000, June 2
1821   Sheet of 4   4.00 3.00
a.-d.   A1063 7s Any single   .95   .70

Discovery of Human Blood Types, Cent. — A1064

Perf. 13¾x13½
2000, June 16   **Photo.**
1822 A1064 8s multi   1.10 .80

Scheduled Motorized Vehicle Passenger Transportation, Cent. — A1065

Photo. & Engr.
2000, June 16   *Perf. 14*
1823 A1065 9s multi   1.25 .90

Folklore & Customs Type of 1991
7s, Intl. meeting of rafters, Carinthia.

Photo. & Engr.
2000, Aug. 25   *Perf. 13¾*
1824 A892 7s multi   .85 .65

Vienna Philharmonic Orchestra, Cent. — A1066

2000, Sept. 15
1825 A1066 7s multi   .85 .65

Hallstatt-Dachstein and Salzkammergut World Heritage Site — A1067

World Heritage Site Type of 1999
Hallstatt-Dachstein and Salzkammergut

2000, Sept. 15
1826 A1067 7s multi   .85 .65

2000 Summer Olympics, Sydney — A1068

2000, Sept. 15   *Perf. 14x13¾*
1827 A1068 9s multi   1.10 .80

Working Environment Type of 1994
2000, Sept. 29
1828 A961 6.50s Papermaker,
               printer   .80 .60

Turf Turkey, by Ida Szigethy A1069

2000, Oct. 13   *Perf. 13¾*
1829 A1069 7s multi   .85 .65

Religious Art Type of 1999
Design: 8s, Illuminated text, Codex 965.

2000, Oct. 13
1830 A1046 8s multi   1.00 .75

Association of Austrian Adult Education Centers, 50th Anniv. A1070

Photo. & Engr.
2000, Nov. 24   *Perf. 13¾*
1831 A1070 7s multi   .95 .75

Vaccinations in Austria, Bicent. — A1071

2000, Nov. 24   *Perf. 14¼x13½*
1832 A1071 7s multi   .95 .75

Christmas A1072

Altar sidewing, St. Martin's Church, Ludesch.

2000, Dec. 1   *Perf. 13¾*
1833 A1072 7s multi   .95 .75

2001 Alpine Skiing World Championships, St. Anton am Arlberg — A1073

2000, Dec. 15   *Perf. 14x13¾*
1834 A1073 7s multi   .95 .75

Hunting & Environment Type of 1997
2001, Feb. 16   Photo.   *Perf. 14x14¼*
1835 A1006 7s Ducks   .90 .65

Folklore & Customs Type of 1991
Designs: No. 1836, Lenten altar cloths, Eastern Tyrol. No. 1837, Water disk shooting, Prebersee. No. 1838, Boat Mill, Mureck.

Photo. & Engr.
2001, May 4   *Perf. 13¾*
1836 A892 7s multi   .90 .65
1837 A892 7s multi   .95 .65
1838 A892 8s multi   1.10 .85

   Issued: No. 1836, 5/4/01. No. 1838, 3/30/01. No. 1837, 8/24/01.

Soccer Champions Type of 1997
**2001, Mar. 30   Photo.   *Perf. 13¾*
1839 A1005 7s Wustenrot Salz-
               burg   .90 .65

Zilltertal Railway, Cent. A1074

Photo. & Engr.
2001, Mar. 30   *Perf. 13¾*
1840 A1074 7s multi   .90 .65

Children's Television Character Type of 2000
**2001, Apr. 20   Photo.   *Perf. 13¾*
1841 A1062 7s Rolf Rüdiger   .90 .65

Salzburg Airport, 75th Anniv. A1075

Photo. & Engr.
2001, Apr. 20   *Perf. 13½x14¼*
1842 A1075 14s multi   1.90 1.40

Scenery Type of 1984
Design: Bärenschützkamm, Styria.

Photo. & Engr.
2001, May 4   *Perf. 13¾*
1843 A679 7s multi   .90 .65

Europa A1076

**2001, May 18   Photo.   *Perf. 13¾*
1844 A1076 15s multi   1.90 1.40

UNESCO World Heritage Type of 1999
Design: Semmering Railway.

Photo. & Engr.
2001, June 8   *Perf. 13¾*
1845 A1041 35s multi   4.50 3.50

Austrian Aero Club, Cent. — A1077

2001, June 8   *Perf. 13¾x14*
1846 A1077 7s multi   .90 .65

UN High Commissioner for Refugees, 50th Anniv. — A1078

2001, June 8   *Perf. 14x13¾*
1847 A1078 21s multi   2.60 2.00

7th IVV Hiking Olympics A1079

**2001, June 22   Photo.   *Perf. 13¾*
1848 A1079 7s multi   .90 .65

Military Post Offices Abroad A1080

2001, June 22
1849 A1080 7s multi   .90 .65

Conversion of East-West Railway to Four Tracks A1081

Photo. & Engr.
2001, Aug. 31   *Perf. 13¾*
1850 A1081 7s multi   .95 .65

Religious Art Type of 1999
Designs: 7s, Church vestment cut from Turkish tent, 1683. 10s, Pluvial.

**2001   Photo. & Engr.   *Perf. 13¾*
1851 A1046 7s multi   .95 .65
1852 A1046 10s multi   1.40 .95

   Issued: 7s, 10/5; 10s, 9/14.

Johann Nestroy (1801-62), Playwright A1082

2001, Sept. 14

1853	A1082	7s multi	.95	.65

The Continents (Detail), by Helmut Leherb — A1083

2001, Sept. 14

1854	A1083	7s multi	.95	.65

Joseph Ritter von Führich (1800-76), Painter — A1084

2001, Sept. 14 ***Perf. 14***

1855	A1084	8s multi	1.10	.75

Leopold Ludwig Döbler (1801-64), Magician A1085

2001, Oct. 5

1856	A1085	7s multi	.95	.65

Meteorology and Geodynamics Institute, 150th Anniv. — A1086

2001, Oct. 5

1857	A1086	12s multi	1.60	1.10

Cat King, by Manfred Deix — A1087

2001, Oct. 5 ***Perf. 13¾***

1858	A1087	19s multi	2.50	1.60

Working Environment Type of 1994

2001, Oct. 16 ***Perf. 14***

1859	A961	7s Public servants	.95	.65

Christmas A1088

Photo. & Engr.

2001, Nov. 30 ***Perf. 14***

1860	A1088	7s multi	.90	.65

SEMI-POSTAL STAMPS

Issues of the Monarchy

Emperor Franz Josef — SP1

Perf. 12½

1914, Oct. 4 **Typo.** **Unwmk.**

B1	SP1	5h green	.20	*.30*
B2	SP1	10h rose	.20	*.35*
		Set, never hinged	1.10	

Nos. B1-B2 were sold at an advance of 2h each over face value. Exist imperf.; value, set $50.

The Firing Step — SP2

1915, May 1

Designs: 5h+2h, Cavalry. 10h+2h, Siege gun. 20h+3h, Battleship. 35h+3h, Airplane.

B3	SP2	3h + 1h violet brn	.20	*.40*
B4	SP2	5h + 2h green	.20	.20
B5	SP2	10h + 2h deep rose	.20	.20
B6	SP2	20h + 3h Prus blue	.45	*2.10*
B7	SP2	35h + 3h ultra	2.10	*4.25*
		Nos. B3-B7 (5)	3.15	*7.15*
		Set, never hinged	9.00	

Exist imperf. Value, set $110.

Issues of the Republic

Types of Austria, 1919-20, Overprinted in Black

1920, Sept. 16 ***Perf. 12½***

B11	A44	5h gray, *yellow*	.45	*1.25*
B12	A44	10h red, *pink*	.35	*1.00*
B13	A43	15h bister, *yel*	.25	*.75*
B14	A45	20h dark grn, *bl*	.25	*.60*
B15	A43	25h violet, *pink*	.25	*.65*
B16	A45	30h brown, *buff*	1.25	*2.50*
B17	A45	40h carmine, *yel*	.25	*.70*
B18	A45	50h dark bl, *blue*	.25	*.55*
B19	A43	60h ol grn, *azure*	1.10	*1.25*
B20	A47	80h red	.30	*.65*
B21	A47	1k orange brown	.35	*.75*
B22	A47	2k pale blue	.35	*.75*

Granite Paper

Imperf

B23	A46	2½k brown red	.35	*.90*
B24	A46	3k dk blue & green	.45	*1.10*
B25	A46	4k carmine & violet	.55	*1.40*
B26	A46	5k blue	.60	*1.10*
B27	A46	7½k yellow green	.60	*1.10*
B28	A46	10k gray grn & red	.60	*1.25*
B29	A46	20k lilac & orange	.65	*1.75*
		Nos. B11-B29 (19)	9.20	*20.00*
		Set, never hinged	19.00	

Carinthia Plebiscite. Sold at three times face value for the benefit of the Plebiscite Propaganda Fund.

Nos. B11-B19 exist imperf. Value, set $125.

Types of Regular Issues of 1919-21 Overprinted

1921, Mar. 1 ***Perf. 12½***

B30	A44	5h gray, *yellow*	.25	*.45*
B31	A44	10h orange brown	.25	*.45*
B32	A43	15h gray	.25	*.45*
B33	A45	20h green, *yellow*	.25	*.45*
B34	A43	25h blue, *yellow*	.25	*.45*
B35	A45	30h violet, *bl*	.45	*.90*
B36	A45	40h org brn, *pink*	.50	*1.25*
B37	A45	50h green, *blue*	1.10	*2.10*
B38	A43	60h lilac, *yellow*	.35	*.90*
B39	A47	80h pale blue	.40	*.80*
B40	A47	1k red org, *blue*	.35	*.75*
B41	A47	1½k green, *yellow*	.20	*.40*
B42	A47	2k lilac brown	.20	*.40*

Overprinted

B43	A46	2½k light blue	.25	*.45*
B44	A46	3k ol grn & brn red	.25	*.45*
B45	A46	4k lilac & orange	.70	*1.50*
B46	A46	5k olive green	.25	*.55*
B47	A46	7½k brown red	.25	*.65*
B48	A46	10k blue & olive grn	.25	*.65*
B49	A46	20k car rose & vio	.45	*1.00*
		Nos. B30-B49 (20)	7.20	*15.00*
		Set, never hinged	13.00	

Nos. B30-B49 were sold at three times face value, the excess going to help flood victims. Exists imperf. Value, set $175.

Franz Joseph Haydn — SP9

Musicians: 5k, Mozart. 7½k, Beethoven. 10k, Schubert. 25k, Anton Bruckner. 50k, Johann Strauss (son). 100k, Hugo Wolf.

1922, Apr. 24 **Engr.** ***Perf. 12½***

B50	SP9	2½k brown, perf. 11½	6.00	*10.50*
a.		Perf. 12½	7.25	*12.00*
		Never hinged	17.50	
B51	SP9	5k dark blue	1.10	*1.50*
B52	SP9	7½k black	1.40	*2.50*
a.		Perf. 11½	90.00	*140.00*
		Never hinged	150.00	
B53	SP9	10k dark violet	1.90	*3.00*
a.		Perf. 11½	2.50	*5.25*
		Never hinged	5.50	
B54	SP9	25k dark green	3.75	*6.50*
a.		Perf. 11½	4.25	*8.25*
		Never hinged	10.50	
B55	SP9	50k claret	2.10	*3.00*
B56	SP9	100k brown olive	7.00	*8.75*
a.		Perf. 11½	8.00	*17.50*
		Never hinged	21.00	
		Nos. B50-B56 (7)	23.25	*35.75*
		Set, never hinged	47.50	

These stamps were sold at 10 times face value, the excess being given to needy musicians.

All values exist imperf. on both regular and handmade papers. Value, set $325.

A 1969 souvenir sheet without postal validity contains reprints of the 5k in black, 7½k in claret and 50k in dark blue, each overprinted "NEUDRUCK" in black at top. It was issued for the Vienna State Opera Centenary Exhibition.

View of Bregenz — SP16

Designs: 120k, Mirabelle Gardens, Salzburg. 160k, Church at Eisenstadt. 180k, Assembly House, Klagenfurt. 200k, "Golden Roof," Innsbruck. 240k, Main Square, Linz. 400k, Castle Hill, Graz. 600k, Abbey at Melk. 1000k, Upper Belvedere, Vienna.

1923, May 22 ***Perf. 12½***

Various Frames

B57	SP16	100k dk green	2.75	*5.50*
B58	SP16	120k deep blue	2.50	*5.00*
B59	SP16	160k dk violet	2.50	*5.00*
B60	SP16	180k red violet	2.50	*5.00*
B61	SP16	200k lake	2.50	*5.00*
B62	SP16	240k red brown	2.50	*5.00*
B63	SP16	400k dark brown	2.50	*5.00*
B64	SP16	600k olive brn	2.75	*7.00*
B65	SP16	1000k black	4.00	*8.75*
		Nos. B57-B65 (9)	24.50	*51.25*
		Set, never hinged	55.00	

Nos. B57-B65 were sold at five times face value, the excess going to needy artists.

All values exist imperf. on both regular and handmade papers. Value, set $325.

Feebleness SP25

Siegfried Slays the Dragon SP30

Designs: 300k+900k, Aid to industry. 500k+1500k, Orphans and widow. 600k+1800k, Indigent old man. 1000k+3000k, Alleviation of hunger.

1924, Sept. 6 **Photo.**

B66	SP25	100k + 300k yel green	3.25	*6.25*
B67	SP25	300k + 900k red brn	4.50	*8.25*
B68	SP25	500k + 1500k brn vio	4.50	*8.25*
B69	SP25	600k + 1800k pck bl	4.50	*13.00*
B70	SP25	1000k + 3000k brn org	7.50	*14.50*
		Nos. B66-B70 (5)	24.25	*50.25*
		Set, never hinged	45.00	

The surtax was for child welfare and anti-tuberculosis work. Set exists imperf. Value, $325.

1926, Mar. 8 **Engr.**

Designs: 8g+2g, Gunther's voyage to Iceland. 15g+5g, Brunhild accusing Kriemhild. 20g+5g, Nymphs telling Hagen the future. 24g+6g, Rudiger von Bechelaren welcomes the Nibelungen. 40g+10g, Dietrich von Bern vanquishes Hagen.

B71	SP30	3g + 2g olive blk	1.10	.65
B72	SP30	8g + 2g indigo	.30	*.35*
B73	SP30	15g + 5g dk claret	.30	*.35*
B74	SP30	20g + 5g olive grn	.45	*.75*
B75	SP30	24g + 6g dk violet	.45	*.75*
B76	SP30	40g + 10g red brn	3.00	*3.75*
		Nos. B71-B76 (6)	5.60	*6.60*
		Set, never hinged	12.00	

Nibelungen issue.

Nos. B71-B76 were printed in two sizes: 27½x28½mm and 28½x27½mm.

The surtax was for child welfare. Set exists imperf. Value, $250.

Pres. Michael Hainisch SP36

Pres. Wilhelm Miklas SP37

1928, Nov. 5

B77	SP36	10g dark brown	5.00	9.00
B78	SP36	15g red brown	5.00	9.00
B79	SP36	30g black	5.00	9.00
B80	SP36	40g indigo	5.00	9.00
	Nos. B77-B80 (4)		20.00	36.00
	Set, never hinged		30.00	

Tenth anniversary of Austrian Republic. Sold at double face value, the premium aiding war orphans and children of war invalids.
Set exists imperf. Value $350.

1930, Oct. 4

B81	SP37	10g light brown	7.50	14.50
B82	SP37	20g red	7.50	14.50
B83	SP37	30g brown violet	7.50	14.50
B84	SP37	40g indigo	7.50	14.50
B85	SP37	50g dark green	7.50	14.50
B86	SP37	1s black brown	7.50	14.50
	Nos. B81-B86 (6)		45.00	87.00
	Set, never hinged		80.00	

Nos. B81-B86 were sold at double face value. The excess aided the anti-tuberculosis campaign and the building of sanatoria in Carinthia.
Set exists imperf. Value, $425.

Regular Issue of 1929-30 Overprinted in Various Colors

1931, June 20

B87	A56	10g bister (Bl)	32.50	42.50
B88	A56	20g dk gray (R)	32.50	42.50
B89	A56	30g dk violet (Gl)	32.50	42.50
B90	A56	40g dk blue (Gl)	32.50	42.50
B91	A56	50g gray vio (O)	32.50	42.50
B92	A57	1s black brn (Bk)	32.50	42.50
	Nos. B87-B92 (6)		195.00	255.00
	Set, never hinged		475.00	

Rotary convention, Vienna.
Nos. B87 to B92 were sold at double their face values. The excess was added to the beneficent funds of Rotary International.
Exists imperf.

Ferdinand Raimund — SP38

Poets: 20g, Franz Grillparzer. 30g, Johann Nestroy. 40g, Adalbert Stifter. 50g, Ludwig Anzengruber. 1s, Peter Rosegger.

1931, Sept. 12

B93	SP38	10g dark violet	12.00	21.00
B94	SP38	20g gray black	12.00	21.00
B95	SP38	30g orange red	12.00	21.00
B96	SP38	40g dull blue	12.00	21.00
B97	SP38	50g gray green	12.00	21.00
B98	SP38	1s yellow brown	12.00	21.00
	Nos. B93-B98 (6)		72.00	126.00
	Set, never hinged		110.00	

Nos. B93-B98 were sold at double face value. The surtax aided unemployed young people.
Set exists imperf. Value, $425.

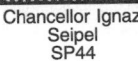

Chancellor Ignaz Seipel SP44 — Ferdinand Georg Waldmüller SP45

1932, Oct. 12   *Perf. 13*

B99	SP44	50g ultra	9.00	17.50
	Never hinged		16.00	

Msgr. Ignaz Seipel, Chancellor of Austria, 1922-29. Sold at double face value, the excess aiding wounded veterans of World War I.
Exists imperf. Value, $150.

1932, Nov. 21

Artists: 24g, Moritz von Schwind. 30g, Rudolf von Alt. 40g, Hans Makart. 64g, Gustav Klimt. 1s, Albin Egger-Lienz.

B100	SP45	12g slate green	17.00	30.00
B101	SP45	24g dp violet	17.00	30.00
B102	SP45	30g dark red	17.00	30.00
B103	SP45	40g dark gray	17.00	30.00
B104	SP45	64g dark brown	17.00	30.00
B105	SP45	1s claret	17.00	30.00
	Nos. B100-B105 (6)		102.00	180.00
	Set, never hinged		160.00	

Nos. B100 to B105 were sold at double their face values. The surtax was for the assistance of charitable institutions.
Set exists imperf. Value, $575.

Mountain Climbing SP51

Designs: 24g, Ski gliding. 30g, Walking on skis. 50g, Ski jumping.

1933, Jan. 9   Photo.   *Perf. 12½*

B106	SP51	12g dark green	7.00	11.50
B107	SP51	24g dark violet	67.50	95.00
B108	SP51	30g brown red	12.50	17.50
B109	SP51	50g dark blue	67.50	95.00
	Nos. B106-B109 (4)		154.50	219.00
	Set, never hinged		300.00	

Meeting of the Intl. Ski Federation, Innsbruck, Feb. 8-13.
These stamps were sold at double their face value. The surtax was for the benefit of "Youth in Distress."
#B106-B109 exist imperf. Value $1,200.

Stagecoach, after Painting by Moritz von Schwind — SP55

1933, June 23   Engr.   *Perf. 12½*
Ordinary Paper

B110	SP55	50g deep ultra	150.00	190.00
	Never hinged		225.00	
a.		Granite paper	300.00	425.00
	Never hinged		450.00	

Sheets of 25.
Nos. B110 and B110a exist imperf. Values $675 and $1,300.

Souvenir Sheet
Perf. 12
Granite Paper

B111		Sheet of 4	2,000.	2,750.
	Never hinged		2,500.	
a.	SP55	50g deep ultra	400.	550.
	Never hinged		525.	

Intl. Phil. Exhib., Vienna, 1933. In addition to the postal value of 50g the stamp was sold at a premium of 50g for charity and of 1.60s for the admission fee to the exhibition.
Size of No. B111: 126x103mm.
A 50g dark red in souvenir sheet, with dark blue overprint ("NEUDRUCK WIPA 1965"), had no postal validity.
Even though the margins No. B111 have no gum, the sheet sells for a premium when definitely never hinged.

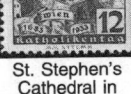

St. Stephen's Cathedral in 1683 — SP56

Marco d'Aviano, Papal Legate — SP57

Designs: 30g, Count Ernst Rudiger von Starhemberg. 40g, John III Sobieski, King of Poland. 50g, Karl V, Duke of Lorraine. 64g, Burgomaster Johann Andreas von Liebenberg.

1933, Sept. 6   Photo.   *Perf. 12½*

B112	SP56	12g dark green	21.00	27.50
B113	SP57	24g dark violet	19.00	26.00
B114	SP57	30g brown red	19.00	26.00
B115	SP57	40g blue black	27.50	42.50
B116	SP57	50g dark blue	19.00	26.00
B117	SP57	64g olive brown	24.00	37.50
	Nos. B112-B117 (6)		129.50	185.50
	Set, never hinged		250.00	

Deliverance of Vienna from the Turks, 250th anniv., and Pan-German Catholic Congress, Sept. 6, 1933.
The stamps were sold at double their face value, the excess being for the aid of Catholic works of charity.
Set exists imperf. Value, $850.

Types of Regular Issue of 1925-30 Surcharged:

a

b

c

1933, Dec. 15

B118	A52(a)	5g + 2g ol grn	.25	.55
B119	A56(b)	12g + 3g lt blue	.25	.70
B120	A56(b)	24g + 6g brn org	.25	.60
B121	A57(c)	1s + 50g org red	25.00	40.00
	Nos. B118-B121 (4)		25.75	41.85
	Set, never hinged		42.50	

Winterhelp. Exists imperf. Value, set $525.

Anton Pilgram — SP62

Architects: 24g, J. B. Fischer von Erlach. 30g, Jakob Prandtauer. 40g, A. von Siccardsburg & E. van der Null. 60g, Heinrich von Ferstel. 64g, Otto Wagner.

1934, Dec. 2   Engr.   *Perf. 12½*
Thick Yellowish Paper

B122	SP62	12g black	9.00	15.00
B123	SP62	24g dull violet	9.00	15.00
B124	SP62	30g carmine	9.00	15.00
B125	SP62	40g brown	9.00	15.00
B126	SP62	60g blue	9.00	15.00
B127	SP62	64g dull green	9.00	15.00
	Nos. B122-B127 (6)		54.00	90.00
	Set, never hinged		82.50	

Exist imperf. Value, set $425.
Nos. B124-B127 exist in horiz. pairs imperf. between. Value, each $160.
These stamps were sold at double their face value. The surtax on this and the following issues was devoted to general charity.

Types of Regular Issue of 1934 Surcharged in Black:

a   b

1935, Nov. 11   *Perf. 12, 12½*

B128	A67(a)	5g + 2g emerald	.45	.90
B129	A67(a)	12g + 3g blue	.75	1.00
B130	A67(a)	24g + 6g lt brown	.45	.90
B131	A68(b)	1s + 50g ver	24.00	35.00
	Nos. B128-B131 (4)		25.65	37.80
	Set, never hinged		45.00	

Winterhelp. Set exists imperf. Value, $125.

Prince Eugene of Savoy — SP68

Slalom Turn — SP74

Military Leaders: 24g, Field Marshal Laudon. 30g, Archduke Karl. 40g, Field Marshal Josef Radetzky. 60g, Admiral Wilhelm Tegetthoff. 64g, Field Marshal Franz Conrad Hotzendorff.

1935, Dec. 1   *Perf. 12½*

B132	SP68	12g brown	9.00	15.00
B133	SP68	24g dark green	9.00	15.00
B134	SP68	30g claret	9.00	15.00
B135	SP68	40g slate	9.00	15.00
B136	SP68	60g deep ultra	9.00	15.00
B137	SP68	64g dark violet	9.00	15.00
	Nos. B132-B137 (6)		54.00	90.00
	Set, never hinged		82.50	

These stamps were sold at double their face value. Set exists imperf. Value, $450.

1936, Feb. 20   Photo.

Designs: 24g, Jumper taking off. 35g, Slalom turn. 60g, Innsbruck view.

B138	SP74	12g Prus green	2.50	3.00
B139	SP74	24g dp violet	4.50	4.50
B140	SP74	35g rose car	22.50	37.50
B141	SP74	60g sapphire	22.50	37.50
	Nos. B138-B141 (4)		52.00	82.50
	Set, never hinged		90.00	

Ski concourse issue. These stamps were sold at twice face value. Set exists imperf. Value, $450.

St. Martin of Tours — SP78

Designs: 12g+3g, Medical clinic. 24g+6g, St. Elizabeth of Hungary. 1s+1s, "Flame of Charity."

1936, Nov. 2   Unwmk.

B142	SP78	5g + 2g dp green	.25	.40
B143	SP78	12g + 3g dp violet	.25	.40
B144	SP78	24g + 6g dp blue	.25	.40
B145	SP78	1s + 1s dk car	5.50	11.00
	Nos. B142-B145 (4)		6.25	12.20
	Set, never hinged		10.50	

Winterhelp. Set exists imperf. Value, $175.

Josef Ressel — SP82

Nurse and Infant — SP88

Inventors: 24g, Karl von Ghega. 30g, Josef Werndl. 40g, Carl Auer von Welsbach. 60g, Robert von Lieben. 64g, Viktor Kaplan.

1936, Dec. 6   Engr.

B146	SP82	12g dk brown	2.10	4.50
B147	SP82	24g dk violet	2.10	4.50
B148	SP82	30g dp claret	2.10	4.50
B149	SP82	40g gray violet	2.10	4.50

B150	SP82	60g vio blue	2.10	4.50
B151	SP82	64g dk slate green	2.10	4.50
		Nos. B146-B151 (6)	12.60	27.00
		Set, never hinged	24.00	

These stamps were sold at double their face value. Exists imperf. Value, set $350.

1937, Oct. 18   Photo.

12g+3g, Mother and child. 24g+6g, Nursing the aged. 1s+1s, Sister of Mercy with patient.

B152	SP88	5g + 2g dk green	.20	.35
B153	SP88	12g + 3g dk brown	.20	.35
B154	SP88	24g + 6g dk blue	.20	.35
B155	SP88	1s + 1s dk carmine	3.00	6.75
		Nos. B152-B155 (4)	3.60	7.80
		Set, never hinged	6.25	

Winterhelp. Set exists imperf. Value, $90.

Gerhard van Swieten — SP92

The Dawn of Peace — SP101

Physicians: 8g, Leopold Auenbrugger von Auenbrugg. 12g, Karl von Rokitansky. 20g, Joseph Skoda. 24g, Ferdinand von Hebra. 30g, Ferdinand von Arlt. 40g, Joseph Hyrtl. 60g, Theodor Billroth. 64g, Theodor Meynert.

1937, Dec. 5   Engr.   Perf. 12½

B156	SP92	5g choc	1.90	4.00
B157	SP92	8g dk red	1.90	4.00
B158	SP92	12g brown blk	1.90	4.00
B159	SP92	20g dk green	1.90	4.00
B160	SP92	24g dk violet	1.90	4.00
B161	SP92	30g brown car	1.90	4.00
B162	SP92	40g dp olive grn	1.90	4.00
B163	SP92	60g indigo	1.90	4.00
B164	SP92	64g brown vio	1.90	4.00
		Nos. B156-B164 (9)	17.10	36.00
		Set, never hinged	29.00	

These stamps were sold at double their face value. Set exists imperf. Value, $550.

> **Catalogue values for unused stamps in this section, from this point to the end of the section, are for Never Hinged items.**

1945, Sept. 10   Photo.   Perf. 14
B165	SP101	1s + 10s dk green	.85	1.40

No. 467 Surcharged in Black

1946, June 25
B166	A110	30g + 20g dk red	3.00	5.00

First anniversary of United Nations.

Pres. Karl Renner SP102

1946   Engr.   Perf. 13½x14

B167	SP102	1s + 1s dk slate grn	2.00	4.00
B168	SP102	2s + 2s dk blue vio	2.00	4.00
B169	SP102	3s + 3s dk purple	2.00	4.00
B170	SP102	5s + 5s dk vio brn	2.00	4.00
		Nos. B167-B170 (4)	8.00	16.00

See Nos. B185-B188.

Nazi Sword Piercing Austria — SP103

Sweeping Away Fascist Symbols — SP104

Designs: 8g+6g, St. Stephen's Cathedral in Flames. 12g+12g, Pleading hand in concentration camp. 30g+30g, Hand choking Nazi serpent. 42g+42g, Hammer breaking Nazi pillar. 1s+1s, Oath of allegiance. 2s+2s, Austrian eagle and burning swastika.

Unwmk.
1946, Sept. 16   Photo.   Perf. 14

B171	SP103	5g + (3g) dk brown	.45	.65
B172	SP104	6g + (4g) dk slate grn	.30	.55
B173	SP104	8g + (6g) orange red	.30	.55
B174	SP104	12g + (12g) slate blk	.30	.55
B175	SP104	30g + (30g) violet	.30	.55
B176	SP104	42g + (42g) dull brn	.30	.55
B177	SP104	1s + 1s dk red	.45	.65
B178	SP104	2s + 2s dk car rose	.60	.65
		Nos. B171-B178 (8)	3.00	4.70

Anti-fascist propaganda.

Race Horse with Foal SP111

Various Race Horses.

1946, Oct. 20   Engr.   Perf. 13½x14
B179	SP111	16g + 16g rose brown	2.00	3.00
B180	SP111	24g + 24g dk purple	2.00	3.00
B181	SP111	60g + 60g dk green	2.00	3.00
B182	SP111	1s + 1s dk blue gray	2.00	3.00
B183	SP111	2s + 2s yel brown	2.00	3.00
		Nos. B179-B183 (5)	10.00	15.00

Austria Prize race, Vienna.

St. Ruprecht's Church, Vienna — SP116

1946, Oct. 30   Perf. 14x13½
B184	SP116	30g + 70g dark red	.35	.70

Founding of Austria, 950th anniv. The surtax aided the Stamp Day celebration.

Renner Type of 1946
Souvenir Sheets
1946, Sept. 5   Imperf.

B185		Sheet of 8	500.00	900.00
a.		SP102 1s+1s dk slate grn	55.00	100.00
B186		Sheet of 8	500.00	900.00
a.		SP102 2s+2s dk blue vio	55.00	100.00
B187		Sheet of 8	500.00	900.00
a.		SP102 3s+3s dark purple	55.00	100.00
B188		Sheet of 8	500.00	900.00
a.		SP102 5s+5s dk vio brown	55.00	100.00

1st anniv. of Austria's liberation. Sheets of 8 plus center label showing arms.

Statue of Rudolf IV the Founder — SP118

Designs: 5g+20g, Tomb of Frederick III. 6g+24g, Main pulpit. 8g+32g, Statue of St. Stephen. 10g+40g, Madonna of the Domestics statue. 12g+48g, High altar. 30g+1.20s, Organ, destroyed in 1945. 50g+1.80s, Anton Pilgram statue. 1s+5s, Cathedral from northeast. 2s+10s, Southwest corner of cathedral.

1946, Dec. 12   Engr.   Perf. 14x13½

B189	SP118	3g + 12g brown	.25	.50
B190	SP118	5g + 20g dk vio brown	.25	.50
B191	SP118	6g + 24g dk blue	.25	.50
B192	SP118	8g + 32g dk grn	.25	.50
B193	SP118	10g + 40g dp blue	.40	.75
B194	SP118	12g + 48g dk vio	.45	.80
B195	SP118	30g + 1.20s car	1.10	1.90
B196	SP118	50g + 1.80s dk bl	1.25	2.00
B197	SP118	1s + 5s brn vio	1.75	3.25
B198	SP118	2s + 10s vio brn	3.50	7.50
		Nos. B189-B198 (10)	9.45	18.20

The surtax aided reconstruction of St. Stephen's Cathedral, Vienna.

Reaping Wheat — SP128

Designs: 8g+2g, Log raft. 10g+5g, Cement factory. 12g+8g, Coal mine. 18g+12g, Oil derricks. 30g+10g, Textile machinery. 35g+15g, Iron furnace. 60g+20g, Electric power lines.

1947, Mar. 23   Perf. 14x13½

B199	SP128	3g + 2g yel brown	.40	.50
B200	SP128	8g + 2g dk bl grn	.40	.50
B201	SP128	10g + 5g slate blk	.40	.50
B202	SP128	12g + 8g dark pur	.40	.50
B203	SP128	18g + 12g ol green	.40	.50
B204	SP128	30g + 10g deep cl	.40	.50
B205	SP128	35g + 15g crimson	.40	.50
B206	SP128	60g + 20g dk blue	.40	.50
		Nos. B199-B206 (8)	3.20	4.00

Vienna International Sample Fair, 1947.

Race Horse and Jockey SP136

1947, June 29   Perf. 13½x14
B207	SP136	60g + 20g deep blue, pale pink	.20	.20

Cup of Corvinus SP137

Prisoner of War — SP147

Designs: 8g+2g, Statue of Providence, Vienna. 10g+5g, Abbey at Melk. 12g+8g, Picture of a Woman, by Kriehuber. 18g+12g, Children at the Window, by Waldmuller. 20g+10g, Entrance, Upper Belvedere Palace. 30g+10g, Nymph Egeria, Schönbrunn Castle. 35g+15g, National Library, Vienna. 48g+12g, "Workshop of a Printer of Engravings," by Schmutzer. 60g+20g, Girl with Straw Hat, by Amerling.

1947, June 20   Perf. 14x13½

B208	SP137	3g + 2g brown	.30	.40
B209	SP137	8g + 2g dk blue grn	.30	.40
B210	SP137	10g + 5g dp claret	.30	.40
B211	SP137	12g + 8g dk purple	.30	.40
B212	SP137	18g + 12g golden brn	.30	.40
B213	SP137	20g + 10g sepia	.30	.40
B214	SP137	30g + 10g dk yel grn	.30	.40
B215	SP137	35g + 15g deep car	.30	.40
B216	SP137	48g + 12g dk brn vio	.30	.40
B217	SP137	60g + 20g dp blue	.30	.40
		Nos. B208-B217 (10)	3.00	4.00

1947, Aug. 30

12g+8g, Prisoners' Mail. 18g+12g, Prison camp visitor. 35g+15g, Family reunion. 60g+20g, "Industry" beckoning. 1s+40g, Sower.

B218	SP147	8g + 2g dk green	.20	.30
B219	SP147	12g + 8g dk vio brn	.20	.30
B220	SP147	18g + 12g black brn	.20	.30
B221	SP147	35g + 15g rose brn	.20	.30
B222	SP147	60g + 20g dp blue	.20	.30
B223	SP147	1s + 40g redsh brn	.20	.30
		Nos. B218-B223 (6)	1.20	1.80

Olympic Flame and Emblem — SP153

1948, Jan. 16   Engr.
B224	SP153	1s + 50g dark blue	.35	.35

The surtax was used to help defray expenses of Austria's 1948 Olympics team.

Laabenbach Bridge Neulengbach SP154

Designs: 20g+10g, Dam, Vermunt Lake. 30g+10g, Danube Port, Vienna. 40g+20g, Mining, Erzberg. 45g+20g, Tracks, Southern Railway Station, Vienna. 60g+30g, Communal housing project, Vienna. 75g+35g, Gas Works, Vienna. 80g+40g, Oil refinery. 1s+50g, Gesäuse Highway, Styria. 1.40s+70g, Parliament Building, Vienna.

1948, Feb. 18   Perf. 14x13½

B225	SP154	10g + 5g slate blk	.20	.20
B226	SP154	20g + 10g lilac	.20	.20
B227	SP154	30g + 10g dull grn	.50	.50
B228	SP154	40g + 20g ol brn	.20	.20
B229	SP154	45g + 20g dk blue	.20	.20
B230	SP154	60g + 30g dk red	.20	.20
B231	SP154	75g + 35g dk vio brn	.20	.20
B232	SP154	80g + 40g vio brn	.20	.20
B233	SP154	1s + 50g dp blue	.20	.20
B234	SP154	1.40s + 70g dp car	.50	.50
		Nos. B225-B234 (10)	2.60	2.60

The surtax was for the Reconstruction Fund.

Violet — SP155

Hans Makart — SP156

Designs: 20g+10g, Anemone. 30g+10g, Crocus. 40g+20g, Yellow primrose. 45g+20g, Pasqueflower. 60g+30g, Rhododendron. 75g+35g, Dogrose. 80g+40g, Cyclamen. 1s+50g, Alpine Gentian. 1.40s+70g, Edelweiss.

1948, May 14   Engr. & Typo.

B235	SP155	10g + 5g multi	.35	.25
B236	SP155	20g + 10g multi	.20	.20
B237	SP155	30g + 10g multi	2.50	2.00
B238	SP155	40g + 20g multi	.50	.25
B239	SP155	45g + 20g multi	.20	.20
B240	SP155	60g + 30g multi	.20	.20
B241	SP155	75g + 35g multi	.20	.20
B242	SP155	80g + 40g multi	.30	.20
B243	SP155	1s + 50g multi	.40	.30
B244	SP155	1.40s + 70g multi	.65	.55
	Nos. B235-B244 (10)		5.50	4.35

1948, June 15   Unwmk.   Engr.

Designs: 20g+10g, Künstlerhaus, Vienna. 40g+20g, Carl Kundmann. 50g+25g, A. S. von Siccardsburg. 60g+30g, Hans Cannon. 1s+50g, William Unger. 1.40s+70g, Friedrich von Schmidt.

B245	SP156	20g + 10g dp yel green	6.25	5.00
B246	SP156	30g + 15g dark brown	3.00	1.90
B247	SP156	40g + 20g ind	3.00	1.90
B248	SP156	50g + 25g dk vio	3.50	2.75
B249	SP156	60g + 30g dk red	3.50	2.75
B250	SP156	1s + 50g blue	6.25	5.00
B251	SP156	1.40s + 70g red brown	8.50	7.50
	Nos. B245-B251 (7)		34.00	26.80

Kunstlerhaus, home of the leading Austrian Artists Association, 80th anniv.

St. Rupert — SP157

Easter — SP158

Designs: 30g+15g, Cathedral and Fountain. 40g+20g, Facade of Cathedral. 50g+25g, Cathedral from South. 60g+30g, Abbey of St. Peter. 80g+40g, Inside Cathedral. 1s+50g, Salzburg Cathedral and Castle. 1.40s+70g, Madonna by Michael Pacher.

1948, Aug. 6   Perf. 14x13½

B252	SP157	20g + 10g dp grn	6.00	5.50
B253	SP157	30g + 15g red brn	2.50	2.50
B254	SP157	40g + 20g sl blk	1.90	1.75
B255	SP157	50g + 25g choc	.40	.40
B256	SP157	60g + 30g dk red	.40	.40
B257	SP157	80g + 40g dk brn vio	.40	.40
B258	SP157	1s + 50g dp blue	.75	.50
B259	SP157	1.40s + 70g dk grn	1.50	1.25
	Nos. B252-B259 (8)		13.85	12.70

The surtax was to aid in the reconstruction of Salzburg Cathedral.

1949, Apr. 13   Unwmk.

Designs: 60g+20g, St. Nicholas Day. 1s+25g, Birthday. 1.40s+35g, Christmas.

Inscribed: "Gluckliche Kindheit"

B260	SP158	40g + 10g brn vio	17.00	12.50
B261	SP158	60g + 20g brn red	17.00	12.50
B262	SP158	1s + 25g dp ultra	17.00	12.50
B263	SP158	1.40s + 35g dk	17.00	12.50
	Nos. B260-B263 (4)		68.00	50.00

The surtax was for Child Welfare.

Arms of Austria, 1230 — SP159

SP160

1949, Aug. 17   Engr. & Photo.

B264	SP159	40g + 10g 1230	7.00	6.00

Engraved and Typographed

B265	SP159	60g + 15g 1450	7.00	6.00
B266	SP159	1s + 25g 1600	7.00	6.00
B267	SP159	1.60s + 40g 1945	7.00	6.00
	Nos. B264-B267 (4)		28.00	24.00

Surtax was for returned prisoners of war.

1949, Dec. 3   Engr.

Laurel Branch, Stamps and Magnifier

B268	SP160	60g + 15g dark red	2.25	1.50

Stamp Day, Dec. 3-4.

Arms of Austria and Carinthia SP161

Carinthian with Austrian Flag — SP162

Design: 1.70s+40g, Casting ballot.

1950, Oct. 10   Photo.   Perf. 14x13½

B269	SP161	60g + 15g	25.00	18.00
B270	SP162	1s + 25g	35.00	20.00
B271	SP162	1.70s + 40g	40.00	30.00
	Nos. B269-B271 (3)		100.00	68.00

Plebiscite in Carinthia, 30th anniv.

Collector Examining Cover — SP163

Miner and Mine — SP164

1950, Dec. 2   Engr.

B272	SP163	60g + 15g blue grn	8.50	6.00

Stamp Day.

1951, Mar. 10   Unwmk.

60g+15g, Mason holding brick and trowel. 1s+25g, Bridge builder with hook and chain. 1.70s+40g, Electrician, pole and insulators.

B273	SP164	40g + 20g dark brown	13.00	11.00
B274	SP164	60g + 15g dk grn	13.00	11.00
B275	SP164	1s + 25g red brown	13.00	11.00
B276	SP164	1.70s + 40g vio bl	13.00	11.00
	Nos. B273-B276 (4)		52.00	44.00

Issued to publicize Austrian reconstruction.

Laurel Branch and Olympic Circles SP165

1952, Jan. 26   Perf. 13½x14

B277	SP165	2.40s + 60g grnsh black	15.00	13.00

The surtax was used to help defray expenses of Austria's athletes in the 1952 Olympic Games.

Cupid as Postman SP166

1952, Mar. 10   Perf. 14x13½

B278	SP166	1.50s + 35g dark brn car	17.50	16.00

Stamp Day.

Sculpture, "Christ, The Almighty" SP167

1952, Sept. 6   Perf. 13½x14

B279	SP167	1s + 25g grnsh gray	11.00	9.00

Austrian Catholic Conv., Vienna, 9/11-14.

Type of 1945-46 Overprinted in Gold

1953, Aug. 29   Unwmk.

B280	A124	1s + 25g on 5s dl bl	2.50	2.00

60th anniv. of labor unions in Austria.

Bummerlhaus Steyr — SP168

Globe and Philatelic Accessories SP169

Designs: 1s+25g, Johannes Kepler. 1.50s+40g, Lutheran Bible, 1st edition. 2.40s+60g, Theophil von Hansen. 3s+75g, Reconstructed Lutheran School, Vienna.

1953, Nov. 5   Engr.   Perf. 14x13½

B281	SP168	70g + 15g vio brn	.30	.30
B282	SP168	1s + 25g dk gray blue	.30	.30
B283	SP168	1.50s + 40g choc	.90	.90
B284	SP168	2.40s + 60g dk grn	2.50	2.25
B285	SP168	3s + 75g dk pur	6.00	5.75
	Nos. B281-B285 (5)		10.00	9.50

The surtax was used toward reconstruction of the Lutheran School, Vienna.

1953, Dec. 5

B286	SP169	1s + 25g chocolate	5.00	3.75

Stamp Day.

Type of 1945-46 with Denomination Replaced by Asterisks

Overprinted in Brown

1954, Feb. 19   Perf. 13½x14

B287	A124	1s + 20g blue gray	.20	.20

Surtax for aid to avalanche victims.

Patient Under Sun Lamp — SP170

Designs: 70g+15g, Physician using microscope. 1s+25g, Mother and children. 1.45s+35g, Operating room. 1.50s+35g, Baby on scale. 2.40s+60g, Nurse.

1954   Engr.   Perf. 14x13½

B288	SP170	30g + 10g pur	1.50	1.10
B289	SP170	70g + 15g dk brn	.25	.25
B290	SP170	1s + 25g dk bl	.30	.25
B291	SP170	1.45s + 35g dk bl green	.45	.40
B292	SP170	1.50s + 35g dk red	5.00	4.50
B293	SP170	2.40s + 60g dk red brown	6.00	5.50
		Nos. B288-B293 (6)	13.50	12.00

The surtax was for social welfare.

Early Vienna-Ulm Ferryboat SP171

1954, Dec. 4   Perf. 13½x14

B294	SP171	1s + 25g dk gray grn	4.50	4.00

Stamp Day.

"Industry" Welcoming Returned Prisoner of War SP172

1955, June 29

B295	SP172	1s + 25g red brn	2.00	1.50

Surtax for returned prisoners of war and relatives of prisoners not yet released.

Collector Looking at Album — SP173

1955, Dec. 3   Perf. 14x13½

B296	SP173	1s + 25g vio brn	3.00	2.75

Stamp Day. The surtax was for the promotion of Austrian philately.

Ornamental Shield and Letter — SP174

1956, Dec. 1   Engr.

B297	SP174	1s + 25g scarlet	2.75	2.50

Stamp Day. See note after No. B296.

Arms of Austria, 1945 — SP175

Engr. & Typo.
1956, Dec. 21   Perf. 14x13½

B298	SP175	1.50s + 50g on 1.60s + 40g gray & red	.25	.20

The surtax was for Hungarian refugees.

New Post Office, Linz 2 SP176

Design: 2.40s+60g, Post office, Kitzbuhel.

1957-58   Engr.   Perf. 13½x14

B299	SP176	1s + 25g dk sl grn	2.75	2.50
B300	SP176	2.40s + 60g blue	.65	.60

Stamp Day. See note after B296. Issue dates: 1s, Nov. 30, 1957. 2.40s, Dec. 6, 1957. See No. B303.

Roman Carriage from Tomb at Maria Saal SP177

Litho. & Engr.
1959, Dec. 5   Perf. 13½x14

B301	SP177	2.40s + 60g pale lil & blk	.55	.50

Stamp Day.

Progressive Die Proof under Magnifying Glass SP178

1960, Dec. 2   Engr.   Perf. 13½x14

B302	SP178	3s + 70g vio brn	.85	.70

Stamp Day.

Post Office Type of 1957
Design: 3s+70g, Post Office, Rust.

1961, Dec. 1   Unwmk.   Perf. 13½

B303	SP176	3s + 70g dk bl grn	.90	.70

Stamp Day. See note after No. B296.

Hands of Stamp Engraver at Work SP179

1962, Nov. 30   Perf. 13½x14

B304	SP179	3s + 70g dull pur	1.25	.90

Stamp Day.

Railroad Exit, Post Office Vienna 101 SP180

1963, Nov. 29   Litho. & Engr.

B305	SP180	3s + 70g tan & blk	.80	.80

Stamp Day.

View of Vienna, North SP181

Designs: Various view of Vienna with compass indicating direction.

1964, July 20   Litho.   Perf. 13½x14

B306	SP181	1.50s + 30g ("N")	.20	.20
B307	SP181	1.50s + 30g ("NO")	.20	.20
B308	SP181	1.50s + 30g ("O")	.20	.20
B309	SP181	1.50s + 30g ("SO")	.20	.20
B310	SP181	1.50s + 30g ("S")	.20	.20
B311	SP181	1.50s + 30g ("SW")	.20	.20
B312	SP181	1.50s + 30g ("W")	.20	.20
B313	SP181	1.50s + 30g ("NW")	.20	.20
		Nos. B306-B313 (8)	1.60	1.60

Vienna Intl. Phil. Exhib. (WIPA 1965).

Post Bus Terminal, St. Gilgen, Wolfgangsee — SP182

1964, Dec. 4   Unwmk.   Perf. 13½

B314	SP182	3s + 70g multi	.45	.45

Stamp Day.

Wall Painting, Tomb at Thebes — SP183

Development of Writing: 1.80s+50g, Cuneiform writing on stone tablet and man's head from Assyrian palace. 2.20s+60g, Wax tablet with Latin writing, Corinthian column. 3s+80g, Gothic writing on sealed letter, Gothic window from Munster Cathedral. 4s+1s, Letter with seal and postmark and upright desk. 5s+1.20s, Typewriter.

Litho. & Engr.
1965, June 4   Perf. 14x13½

B315	SP183	1.50s + 40g multi	.20	.20
B316	SP183	1.80s + 50g multi	.20	.20
B317	SP183	2.20s + 60g multi	.35	.35
B318	SP183	3s + 80g multi	.20	.20
B319	SP183	4s + 1s multi	.45	.45
B320	SP183	5s + 1.20s multi	.60	.60
		Nos. B315-B320 (6)	2.00	2.00

Vienna Intl. Phil. Exhib., WIPA, June 4-13.

Mailman Distributing Mail SP184

1965, Dec. 3   Engr.   Perf. 13½x14

B321	SP184	3s + 70g blue grn	.40	.35

Stamp Day.

Letter Carrier, 16th Century — SP185

Litho. & Engr.
1966, Dec. 2   Perf. 13½

B322	SP185	3s + 70g multi	.40	.35

Stamp Day. Design is from Ambras Heroes' Book, Austrian National Library.

Letter Carrier, 16th Century Playing Card — SP186

Engr. & Photo.
1967, Dec. 1   Perf. 13x13½

B323	SP186	3.50s + 80g multi	.40	.35

Stamp Day.

Mercury, Bas-relief from Purkersdorf SP187

1968, Nov. 29   Engr.   Perf. 13½

B324	SP187	3.50s + 80g slate green	.40	.35

Stamp Day.

Unken Post Station Sign, 1710 — SP188

Engr. & Photo.
1969, Dec. 5   Perf. 12

B325	SP188	3.50s + 80g tan, red & blk	.40	.35

Stamp Day. Design is from a watercolor by Friedrich Zeller.

Saddle, Bag, Harness and Post Horn — SP189

Engr. & Litho.
1970, Dec. 4   Perf. 13½x14

B326	SP189	3.50s + 80g gray blk & yel	.40	.35

Stamp Day.

"50 Years" SP190

Engr. & Photo.
1971, Dec. 3   Perf. 13½

B327	SP190	4s + 1.50s gold & red brn	.60	.45

50th anniversary of the Federation of Austrian Philatelic Societies.

Local Post
Carrier — SP191

1972, Dec. 1 Engr. Perf. 14x13½
B328 SP191 4s + 1s olive green .60 .45
Stamp Day.

Gabriel, by Lorenz
Luchsperger, 15th
Century — SP192

1973, Nov. 30
B329 SP192 4s + 1s maroon .60 .45
Stamp Day.

Mail Coach
Leaving Old PTT
Building — SP193

1974, Nov. 29 Engr. Perf. 14x13½
B330 SP193 4s + 2s violet blue .70 .70
Stamp Day.

Alpine
Skiing,
Women's
SP194

Designs: 1.50s+70g, Ice hockey. 2s+90g,
Ski jump. 4s+1.90s, Bobsledding.

1975, Mar. 14 Photo. Perf. 13½x14
B331 SP194 1s + 50g multi .25 .25
B332 SP194 1.50s + 70g multi .30 .30
B333 SP194 2s + 90g multi .35 .35
B334 SP194 4s + 1.90s multi .70 .70
  Nos. B331-B334 (4) 1.60 1.60

1975, Nov. 14
Designs: 70g+30g, Figure skating, pair.
2s+1s, Cross-country skiing. 2.50s+1s, Luge.
4s+2s, Biathlon.

B335 SP194 70g + 30g multi .20 .20
B336 SP194 2s + 1s multi .30 .30
B337 SP194 2.50s + 1s multi .40 .40
B338 SP194 4s + 2s multi .70 .70
  Nos. B335-B338 (4) 1.60 1.60

12th Winter Olympic Games, Innsbruck,
Feb. 4-15, 1976.

Austria Nos. 5,
250,
455 — SP195

Photo. & Engr.
1975, Nov. 28 Perf. 14
B339 SP195 4s + 2s multi .65 .65
Stamp Day; 125th anniv. of Austrian stamps.

Postilion's
Gala Hat
and Horn
SP196

1976, Dec. 3 Perf. 13½x14
B340 SP196 6s + 2s blk & lt vio .80 .80
Stamp Day.

Emanuel
Herrmann
SP197

1977, Dec. 2 Perf. 14x13½
B341 SP197 6s + 2s multi .80 .80
Stamp Day. Emanuel Herrmann (1839-
1902), economist, invented postal card. Austria issued first postal card in 1869.

Post Bus,
1913
SP198

1978, Dec. 1 Photo. Perf. 13½x14
B342 SP198 10s + 5s multi 1.40 1.40
Stamp Day.

Heroes'
Square,
Vienna
SP199

Photo. & Engr.
1979, Nov. 30 Perf. 13½
B343 SP199 16s + 8s multi 2.75 2.50

No. B343 Inscribed "2. Phase"
1980, Nov. 21
B344 SP199 16s + 8s multi 2.75 2.50

Souvenir Sheet
1981, Feb. 20
B345 SP199 16s + 8s multi 3.00 2.50
WIPA 1981 Phil. Exhib., Vienna, May 22-31.
No. B345 contains one stamp without
inscription.

Mainz-Weber Mailbox, 1870 — SP200

1982, Nov. 26 Photo. & Engr.
B346 SP200 6s + 3s multi 1.00 1.00
Stamp Day.

Boy
Examining
Cover
SP201

Photo. & Engr.
1983, Oct. 21 Perf. 14
B347 SP201 6s + 3s multi 1.10 1.10
Stamp Day. See Nos. B349-B352, B354-
B355.

World Winter Games for the
Handicapped — SP202

1984, Jan. 5 Photo. Perf. 13½x13
B348 SP202 4s + 2s Downhill skier .75 .75

Stamp Day Type of 1983
Designs: No. B349, Seschemnofer III burial
chamber detail, pyramid of Cheops, Gizeh.
No. B350, Roman messenger on horseback.
No. B351, Nuremberg messenger, 16th cent.
No. B352, The Postmaster (detail), 1841, litho-
graph by Carl Schuster.

1984-87 Photo. & Engr. Perf. 14
B349 SP201 6s + 3s multi 1.25 1.25
B350 SP201 6s + 3s multi 1.25 1.25
B351 SP201 6s + 3s multi 1.25 1.25
B352 SP201 6s + 3s multi 1.40 1.40
  Nos. B349-B352 (4) 5.15 5.15

Issue: #B349, 11/30/84; #B350, 11/28/85;
#B351, 11/28/86; #B352, 11/19/87.

4th World Winter Sports
Championships for the Disabled,
Innsbruck — SP203

1988, Jan. 15 Photo. Perf. 13½
B353 SP203 5s + 2.50s multi 1.10 1.10

Stamp Day Type of 1983
Designs: No. B354, Railway mail car. No.
B355, Hansa-Brandenburg CI mail plane.

1988-89 Photo. & Engr. Perf. 14
B354 SP201 6s +3s multi 1.40 1.40
B355 SP201 6s +3s multi 1.40 1.40
Issued: #B354, Nov. 17; #B355, May 24,
1989.

Stamp
Day — SP204

1990, May 25 Photo. Perf. 13½
B356 SP204 7s +3s multi 1.75 1.75

SP205

SP205a

1991, May 29 Photo. & Engr.
B357 SP205 7s +3s B & P 1.75 1.75
1992, May 22
B358 SP205 7s +3s R & H 1.75 1.75
1993, May 5
B359 SP205 7s +3s I & I 1.75 1.75
1994, May 27
B360 SP205 7s +3s E & L 1.75 1.75
1995, May 26
B361 SP205a 10s +5s F & A 3.00 3.00
1996, May 17
B362 SP205a 10s +5s M & T 3.00 3.00
  Nos. B357-
  B362,1725,1765,1791 (9) 16.75 15.80
Stamp Day. The 1st letters spell
"Briefmarke," the 2nd "Philatelie."
For "A" & "E," see #1725; "R" & "L," #1765;
"K" & "I," #1791; "E" & "E," #1818.

Special
Olympics
Winter
Games
SP206

1993, Mar. 19 Photo. Perf. 13½x14
B367 SP206 6s +3s multi 1.75 1.75

Vienna Intl. Postage Stamp Exhibition
(WIPA), 2000 — SP207

#B368, #5, postman on bicycle. #B369,
#339, early mail truck. #B370, #525, airplane,
service vehicles.

1997-2000 Photo. & Engr. Perf. 14
B368 SP207 27s +13s multi 6.75 6.75
B369 SP207 32s +13s multi 7.50 7.50
B370 SP207 32s +16s multi 7.50 7.50
  a. Souvenir sheet, #B368-
    B370 + label 19.00 19.00
  Nos. B368-B370 (3) 21.75 21.75
Stamps from #B370a are dated "2000."
Issued: #B368, 5/23; #B369, 11/6/98;
#B370, 9/17/99. #B370a, 2000.

Stamp Day — SP208

Illustration reduced.

Photo. & Engr.

2001, May 18   **Perf. 13¾**
B371 SP208 20s +10s multi + label   4.00 4.00

AIR POST STAMPS

Issues of the Monarchy

Types of Regular Issue of 1916 Surcharged

1918, Mar. 30 Unwmk. Perf. 12½

C1	A40	1.50k on 2k lilac	2.00	3.75
C2	A40	2.50k on 3k ocher	10.00	22.50
a.		Inverted surcharge	1,100.	
		Never hinged		
b.		Perf. 11½	325.00	425.00
		Never hinged	600.00	
c.		Perf. 12½x11½	27.50	45.00
		Never hinged	52.50	

Overprinted

C3	A40	4k gray	5.25	11.00
		Nos. C1-C3 (3)	17.25	37.25
		Set, never hinged	32.50	

Set exists imperf. Value, $200.
Nos. C1-C3 also exist without surcharge or overprint. Value, set perf.; $300; imperf., $275.
Nos. C1-C3 were printed on grayish and on white paper.
A 7k on 10k red brown was prepared but not regularly issued. Value, perf. or imperf., $300.

Issues of the Republic

Hawk — AP1

Wilhelm Kress — AP2

1922-24 Typo. Perf. 12½

C4	AP1	300k claret	.30	1.25
C5	AP1	400k green ('24)	4.50	12.50
C6	AP1	600k bister	.20	.90
C7	AP1	900k brn orange	.20	.90

Engr.

C8	AP2	1200k brn violet	.20	.90
C9	AP2	2400k slate	.20	.90
C10	AP2	3000k dp brn ('23)	2.50	7.00
C11	AP2	4800k dark bl ('23)	2.50	7.00
		Nos. C4-C11 (8)	10.60	31.35
		Set, never hinged	22.50	

Set exists imperf. Value, $250.

Plane and Pilot's Head — AP3

Airplane Passing Crane — AP4

1925-30 Typo. Perf. 12½

C12	AP3	2g gray brown	.35	.90
C13	AP3	5g red	.20	.25
a.		Horiz. pair, imperf. btwn.	250.00	
		Never hinged	300.00	
C14	AP3	6g dark blue	.80	1.40
C15	AP3	8g yel green	.90	1.60
C16	AP3	10g dp org ('26)	.90	1.60
a.		Horiz. pair, imperf. btwn.	250.00	
		Never hinged	300.00	
C17	AP3	15g red vio ('26)	.35	.80
a.		Horiz. pair, imperf. btwn.	300.00	
		Never hinged	375.00	
C18	AP3	20g org brn ('30)	10.00	6.25
C19	AP3	25g blk vio ('30)	4.00	7.75
C20	AP3	30g bister ('26)	7.00	8.25
C21	AP3	50g bl gray ('26)	12.50	12.50
C22	AP3	80g dk grn ('30)	1.90	3.50

Photo.

C23	AP4	10g orange red	.80	2.50
a.		Horiz. pair, imperf. btwn.	250.00	
		Never hinged	300.00	
C24	AP4	15g claret	.55	1.40
C25	AP4	30g brn violet	.70	2.50
C26	AP4	50g gray black	.75	2.75
C27	AP4	1s deep blue	6.00	6.25
C28	AP4	2s dark green	1.50	3.50
a.		Vertical pair, imperf. btwn.	250.00	
		Never hinged	300.00	
C29	AP4	3s red brn ('26)	42.50	52.50
C30	AP4	5s indigo ('26)	11.50	22.50

Size: 25½x32mm

C31	AP4	10s blk brown, gray ('26)	9.00	17.50
		Nos. C12-C31 (20)	112.20	156.20
		Set, never hinged	225.00	

Exists imperf. Value, set $800.

Airplane over Güssing Castle — AP5

Airplane over the Danube — AP6

Designs (each includes plane): 10g, Maria-Worth. 15g, Durnstein. 20g, Hallstatt. 25g, Salzburg. 30g, Upper Dachstein and Schladminger Glacier. 40g, Lake Wetter. 50g, Arlberg. 60g, St. Stephen's Cathedral. 80g, Church of the Minorites. 2s, Railroad viaduct, Carinthia. 3s, Gross Glockner mountain. 5s, Aerial railway. 10s, Seaplane and yachts.

1935, Aug. 16 Engr. Perf. 12½

C32	AP5	5g rose violet	.20	.40
C33	AP5	10g red orange	.20	.20
C34	AP5	15g yel green	.60	1.25
C35	AP5	20g gray blue	.20	.30
C36	AP5	25g violet brn	.20	.30
C37	AP5	30g brn orange	.20	.35
C38	AP5	40g gray green	.20	.35
C39	AP5	50g light sl bl	.20	.45
C40	AP5	60g black brn	.30	.65
C41	AP5	80g light brown	.35	.80
C42	AP6	1s rose red	.30	.70
C43	AP6	2s olive green	1.75	4.00
C44	AP6	3s yellow brn	7.00	15.00
C45	AP6	5s dark green	4.50	11.00
C46	AP6	10s slate blue	42.50	80.00
		Nos. C32-C46 (15)	58.70	115.75
		Set, never hinged	87.50	

Set exists imperf. Value, $275.

> Catalogue values for unused stamps in this section, from this point to the end of the section, are for Never Hinged items.

Windmill, Neusiedler Lake Shore — AP20

1s, Roman arch, Carnuntum. 2s, Town Hall, Gmund. 3s, Schieder Lake, Hinterstoder. 4s, Praegraten, Eastern Tyrol. 5s, Torsäule, Salzburg. 10s, St. Charles Church, Vienna.

1947 Unwmk. Perf. 14x13½

C47	AP20	50g black brown	.20	.20
C48	AP20	1s dark brn vio	.30	.25
C49	AP20	2s dark green	.35	.40
C50	AP20	3s chocolate	2.25	2.75
C51	AP20	4s dark green	1.40	2.00
C52	AP20	5s dark blue	1.40	2.00
C53	AP20	10s dark blue	.75	1.50
		Nos. C47-C53 (7)	6.65	9.10

Rooks AP27

Birds: 1s, Barn swallows. 2s, Blackheaded gulls. 3s, Great cormorants. 5s, Buzzard. 10s, Gray heron. 20s, Golden eagle.

1950-53 Perf. 13½x14

C54	AP27	60g dark bl vio	2.50	1.10
C55	AP27	1s dark vio blue ('53)	17.50	15.00
C56	AP27	2s dark blue ('53)	15.00	6.00
C57	AP27	3s dk slate green ('53)	100.00	65.00
C58	AP27	5s red brn ('53)	100.00	65.00
C59	AP27	10s gray vio ('53)	45.00	30.00
C60	AP27	20s brn blk ('52)	10.00	4.00
		Nos. C54-C60 (7)	290.00	186.10
		Set, hinged	180.00	

Value at lower left on Nos. C59 and C60.
No. C60 exists imperf.

Etrich "Dove" AP28

Designs: 3.50s, Twin-engine jet airliner. 5s, Four-engine jet airliner.

1968, May 31 Engr. Perf. 13½x14

C61	AP28	2s olive bister	.30	.25
C62	AP28	3.50s slate green	.50	.40
C63	AP28	5s dark blue	.75	.60
		Nos. C61-C63 (3)	1.55	1.25

IFA WIEN 1968 (International Air Post Exhibition), Vienna, May 30-June 4.

POSTAGE DUE STAMPS

Issues of the Monarchy

D1

D2

Perf. 10 to 13½

1894-95 Typo. Wmk. 91

J1	D1	1kr brown	1.60	1.40
a.		Perf. 13½	26.00	30.00
J2	D1	2kr brown ('95)	3.50	2.00
a.		Pair, imperf. btwn.	175.00	210.00
J3	D1	3kr brown	2.75	1.00
J4	D1	5kr brown	2.50	1.40
a.		Perf. 13½	16.00	15.00
b.		Pair, imperf. btwn.	160.00	175.00
J5	D1	6kr brown ('95)	2.50	5.00
J6	D1	7kr brown ('95)	.80	4.50
a.		Vert. pair, imperf. btwn.	250.00	300.00
b.		Horiz. pair, imperf. btwn.	275.00	
J7	D1	10kr brown	4.00	.50
J8	D1	20kr brown	.80	4.50
J9	D1	50kr brown	35.00	55.00
		Nos. J1-J9 (9)	53.45	74.30

Values for Nos. J1-J9 are for stamps that do not show the watermark. Stamps showing the watermark often sell for more.
See Nos. J204-J231.

1899-1900 Imperf.

J10	D2	1h brown	.20	.40
J11	D2	2h brown	.25	.50
J12	D2	3h brown ('00)	.20	.40
J13	D2	4h brown	1.75	1.40

J14	D2	5h brown ('00)	2.25	1.10
J15	D2	6h brown	.30	.85
J16	D2	10h brown	.25	.40
J17	D2	12h brown	.40	.25
J18	D2	15h brown	.40	1.40
J19	D2	20h brown	17.00	3.00
J20	D2	40h brown	.80	2.50
J21	D2	100h brown	4.00	2.25
		Nos. J10-J21 (12)	27.80	16.45

Perf. 10½, 12½, 13½ and Compound

J22	D2	1h brown	.55	.20
J23	D2	2h brown	.45	.20
J24	D2	3h brown ('00)	.40	.20
J25	D2	4h brown	.20	.20
J26	D2	5h brown ('00)	.40	.20
J27	D2	6h brown	.40	.20
J28	D2	10h brown	.45	.20
J29	D2	12h brown	2.25	.65
J30	D2	15h brown	2.25	.80
J31	D2	20h brown	.60	.30
J32	D2	40h brown	1.00	.75
J33	D2	100h brown	20.00	1.25
		Nos. J22-J33 (12)	29.15	5.15

Nos. J10-J33 exist on unwmkd. paper.
For surcharges see Offices in the Turkish Empire Nos. J1-J5.

D3

1908-13 Unwmk. Perf. 12½

J34	D3	1h carmine	1.00	1.00
J35	D3	2h carmine	.25	.20
d.		Half used as 1h on cover		65.00
J36	D3	4h carmine	.20	.20
c.		Half used as 2h on cover		65.00
J37	D3	6h carmine	.20	.20
J38	D3	10h carmine	.25	.20
c.		Half used as 5h on cover		55.00
J39	D3	14h carmine ('13)	3.25	1.75
J40	D3	20h carmine	4.75	.20
c.		Half used as 10h on cover		65.00
J41	D3	25h carmine ('10)	4.50	3.50
J42	D3	30h carmine	5.00	.20
J43	D3	50h carmine	17.50	.25
J44	D3	100h carmine	16.00	.45
		Nos. J34-J44 (11)	52.90	8.20

All values exist on ordinary paper, #J34-J38, J40, J42-J44 on chalky paper and #J34-J38, J40, J44 on thin ordinary paper. In most cases, values are for the least expensive stamp of the types. Some of the expensive types sell for considerably more.
All values exist imperf.
See Offices in the Turkish Empire type D3.

1911, July 16

J45	D3	5k violet	45.00	9.00
J46	D3	10k violet	175.00	2.75

Regular Issue of 1908 Overprinted or Surcharged in Carmine or Black:

1916, Oct. 21

J47	A22	1h gray (C)	.20	.20
a.		Pair, one without overprint	125.00	
J48	A22	15h on 2h vio (Bk)	.20	.35
		Set, never hinged	.25	

D4

D5

1916, Oct. 1

J49	D4	5h rose red	.20	.20
J50	D4	10h rose red	.20	.20
J51	D4	15h rose red	.20	.20
J52	D4	20h rose red	.20	.20
J53	D4	25h rose red	.30	.65
J54	D4	30h rose red	.20	.25
J55	D4	40h rose red	.20	.30
J56	D4	50h rose red	.90	1.50

J57	D5	1k ultramarine	.25	.20
a.		Horiz. pair, imperf. btwn.	325.00	350.00
J58	D5	5k ultramarine	1.60	2.25
J59	D5	10k ultramarine	2.25	1.10
		Nos. J49-J59 (11)	6.50	7.05
		Set, never hinged		17.00

Exists imperf. Value, set $80.
For overprints see J64-J74, Western
Ukraine Nos. 54-55, NJ1-NJ6, Poland Nos. J1-
J10.

Type of Regular Issue of 1916
Surcharged

1917

J60	A38	10h on 24h blue	1.10	.40
J61	A38	15h on 36h violet	.30	.20
J62	A38	20h on 54h orange	.20	.30
J63	A38	50h on 42h chocolate	.20	.20
		Nos. J60-J63 (4)	1.80	1.10
		Set, never hinged		5.00

All values of this issue are known imperforate, also without surcharge, perforated and
imperforate.
For overprints see Western Ukraine Nos.
57-58.

Issues of the Republic

Postage Due
Stamps of 1916
Overprinted

1919

J64	D4	5h rose red	.20	.20
a.		Inverted overprint	225.00	225.00
J65	D4	10h rose red	.20	.20
J66	D4	15h rose red	.25	.35
J67	D4	20h rose red	.25	.35
J68	D4	25h rose red	8.75	13.50
J69	D4	30h rose red	.20	.25
J70	D4	40h rose red	.25	.60
J71	D4	50h rose red	.30	1.25
J72	D5	1k ultramarine	3.50	8.00
J73	D5	5k ultramarine	8.00	10.50
J74	D5	10k ultramarine	7.25	3.50
		Nos. J64-J74 (11)	29.15	38.70
		Set, never hinged		67.50

#J64, J65, J67, J70 exist imperf.

D6   D7

1920-21   *Perf. 12½*

J75	D6	5h bright red	.20	.30
J76	D6	10h bright red	.20	.20
J77	D6	15h bright red	.20	1.10
J78	D6	20h bright red	.20	.20
J79	D6	25h bright red	.20	.90
J80	D6	30h bright red	.20	.25
J81	D6	40h bright red	.20	.20
J82	D6	50h bright red	.20	.20
J83	D6	80h bright red	.20	.25
J84	D7	1k ultramarine	.20	.20
J85	D7	1½k ultra ('21)	.20	.20
J86	D7	2k ultra ('21)	.20	.20
J87	D7	3k ultra ('21)	.20	.50
J88	D7	4k ultra ('21)	.20	.55
J89	D7	5k ultramarine	.20	.20
J90	D7	8k ultra ('21)	.20	.60
J91	D7	10k ultramarine	.20	.25
J92	D7	20k ultra ('21)	.20	1.10
		Nos. J75-J92 (18)		7.40
		Set, never hinged		3.60

Nos. J84 to J92 exist on white paper and on
grayish white paper. They also exist imperf.;
value, set $85.

Imperf

J93	D6	5h bright red	.20	.35
J94	D6	10h bright red	.20	.20
J95	D6	15h bright red	.20	.90
J96	D6	20h bright red	.20	.20

J97	D6	25h bright red	.20	.90
J98	D6	30h bright red	.20	.60
J99	D6	40h bright red	.20	.35
J100	D6	50h bright red	.20	.60
J101	D6	80h bright red	.20	.35
		Nos. J93-J101 (9)		4.45
		Set, never hinged		1.80

No. 207a Surcharged in
Dark Blue

1921, Dec.   *Perf. 12½*

J102	A43	7½k on 15h bister	.20	.20
		Never hinged	.20	
a.		Inverted surcharge	250.00	350.00
		Never hinged	350.00	

D8   D9

D10

1922

J103	D8	1k reddish buff	.20	.25
J104	D8	2k reddish buff	.20	.25
J105	D8	4k reddish buff	.20	.50
J106	D8	5k reddish buff	.20	.25
J107	D8	7½k reddish buff	.20	.70
J108	D8	10k blue green	.20	.25
J109	D8	15k blue green	.20	.50
J110	D8	20k blue green	.20	.35
J111	D8	25k blue green	.20	.80
J112	D8	40k blue green	.20	.30
J113	D8	50k blue green	.20	.90
		Nos. J103-J113 (11)		5.05
		Set, never hinged		2.20

Issue date: Nos. J108-J113, June 2.

1922-24

J114	D9	10k cobalt blue	.20	.30
J115	D9	15k cobalt blue	.20	.35
J116	D9	20k cobalt blue	.20	.45
J117	D9	50k cobalt blue	.20	.35
J118	D10	100k plum	.20	.20
J119	D10	150k plum	.20	.20
J120	D10	200k plum	.20	.20
J121	D10	400k plum	.20	.20
J122	D10	600k plum ('23)	.20	.35
J123	D10	800k plum	.20	.20
J124	D10	1,000k plum ('23)	.20	.20
J125	D10	1,200k plum ('23)	.20	2.50
J126	D10	1,500k plum ('24)	.20	.25
J127	D10	1,800k plum ('24)	1.50	5.25
J128	D10	2,000k plum ('23)	.30	.85
J129	D10	3,000k plum ('24)	5.75	12.00
J130	D10	4,000k plum ('24)	3.75	9.75
J131	D10	6,000k plum ('24)	6.75	16.00
		Nos. J114-J131 (18)	20.65	49.60
		Set, never hinged		40.00

Value, Nos. J103-J131 imperf, $225.

D11   D12

1925-34   *Perf. 12½*

J132	D11	1g red	.20	.20
J133	D11	2g red	.20	.20
J134	D11	3g red	.20	.20
J135	D11	4g red	.20	.20
J136	D11	5g red ('27)	.20	.20
J137	D11	6g red	.20	.45
J138	D11	8g red	.20	.20
J139	D11	10g dark blue	.20	.20
J140	D11	12g dark blue	.20	.20
J141	D11	14g dark blue ('27)	.20	.20
J142	D11	15g dark blue	.20	.20
J143	D11	16g dark blue ('29)	.20	.20
J144	D11	18g dark blue ('34)	1.10	3.50
J145	D11	20g dark blue	.20	.20
J146	D11	23g dark blue	.20	.20
J147	D11	24g dark blue ('32)	1.10	.20

J148	D11	28g dark blue ('27)	.90	.30
J149	D11	30g dark blue	.20	.20
J150	D11	31g dark blue ('29)	1.10	.25
J151	D11	35g dark blue ('30)	1.10	.20
J152	D11	39g dark blue ('32)	1.40	.20
J153	D11	40g dark blue	1.25	1.75
J154	D11	60g dark blue	.85	1.10
J155	D12	1s dark green	5.50	1.10
J156	D12	2s dark green	27.50	3.50
J157	D12	5s dark green	77.50	32.50
J158	D12	10s dark green	45.00	4.25
		Nos. J132-J158 (27)	167.35	52.10
		Set, never hinged		425.00

Issues of 1925-27 imperf, value, set $425.
Issued: 3g, 2s-10s, Dec; 5g, 28g, 1/1; 14g,
June; 31g, 2/1; 35g, Jan; 24g, 39g, Sept; 16g,
May; 18g, 6/25; others, 6/1.

Coat of Arms

D13   D14

1935, June 1

J159	D13	1g red	.20	.20
J160	D13	2g red	.20	.20
J161	D13	3g red	.20	.20
J162	D13	5g red	.20	.20
J163	D13	10g blue	.20	.20
J164	D13	12g blue	.20	.20
J165	D13	15g blue	.20	.40
J166	D13	20g blue	.20	.20
J167	D13	24g blue	.20	.20
J168	D13	30g blue	.20	.20
J169	D13	39g blue	.20	.20
J170	D13	60g blue	.75	.90
J171	D14	1s green	.75	.30
J172	D14	2s green	1.25	.70
J173	D14	5s green	2.75	2.50
J174	D14	10s green	3.75	.60
		Nos. J159-J174 (16)	11.45	7.40
		Set, never hinged		42.50

On #J163-J170, background lines are horiz.
Nos. J159-J174 exist imperf. Value, set
$125.

> **Catalogue values for unused
> stamps in this section, from this
> point to the end of the section, are
> for Never Hinged items.**

D15

1945   **Unwmk.**   **Typo.**   *Perf. 10½*

J175	D15	1g vermilion	.20	.20
J176	D15	2g vermilion	.20	.20
J177	D15	3g vermilion	.20	.20
J178	D15	5g vermilion	.20	.20
J179	D15	10g vermilion	.20	.20
J180	D15	12g vermilion	.20	.20
J181	D15	20g vermilion	.20	.20
J182	D15	24g vermilion	.20	.20
J183	D15	30g vermilion	.20	.20
J184	D15	60g vermilion	.20	.20
J185	D15	1s violet	.20	.35
J186	D15	2s violet	.20	.45
J187	D15	5s violet	.20	.20
J188	D15	10s violet	.20	.20
		Nos. J175-J188 (14)	2.80	3.20

Issued: 1g-60g, Sept. 10; 1s-10s, Sept. 24.

Occupation Stamps of
the Allied Military
Government
Overprinted in Black

1946   *Perf. 11*

J189	OS1	3g deep orange	.35	.30
J190	OS1	5g bright green	.35	.30
J191	OS1	6g red violet	.35	.30
J192	OS1	8g rose pink	.35	.30
J193	OS1	10g light gray	.35	.30
J194	OS1	12g pale buff brown	.40	.30
J195	OS1	15g rose red	.40	.30
J196	OS1	20g copper brown	.40	.30
J197	OS1	25g deep blue	.40	.30
J198	OS1	30g bright violet	.40	.30
J199	OS1	40g light ultra	.40	.30
J200	OS1	60g light olive grn	.40	.30
J201	OS1	1s dark violet	.50	.40

J202	OS1	2s yellow	.50	.40
J203	OS1	5s deep ultra	.70	.60
		Nos. J189-J203 (15)	6.25	5.00

Nos. J189-J203 were issued by the Renner
Government. Inverted overprints exist on
about half of the denominations.
Issued: 3g-60g, Apr. 23; 1s-5s, May 20.

Type of 1894-95
Inscribed "Republik Osterreich"

1947   **Typo.**   *Perf. 14*

J204	D1	1g chocolate	.20	.20
J205	D1	2g chocolate	.20	.20
J206	D1	3g chocolate	.20	.20
J207	D1	5g chocolate	.20	.20
J208	D1	8g chocolate	.20	.20
J209	D1	10g chocolate	.20	.20
J210	D1	12g chocolate	.20	.20
J211	D1	15g chocolate	.20	.20
J212	D1	16g chocolate	.20	.40
J213	D1	17g chocolate	.20	.40
J214	D1	18g chocolate	.20	.40
J215	D1	20g chocolate	.50	.20
J216	D1	24g chocolate	.30	.30
J217	D1	30g chocolate	.20	.20
J218	D1	36g chocolate	.50	.60
J219	D1	40g chocolate	.20	.20
J220	D1	42g chocolate	.50	.60
J221	D1	48g chocolate	.50	.60
J222	D1	50g chocolate	.55	.20
J223	D1	60g chocolate	.20	.20
J224	D1	70g chocolate	.20	.20
J225	D1	80g chocolate	3.75	1.75
J226	D1	1s blue	.20	.20
J227	D1	1.15s blue	2.50	.20
J228	D1	1.20s blue	3.00	1.00
J229	D1	2s blue	.40	.40
J230	D1	5s blue	.40	.40
J231	D1	10s blue	.40	.40
		Nos. J204-J231 (28)	16.50	10.55

Issue dates: 1g, 20g, 50g, 80g, 1.15s,
1.20s, Sept. 25, others, Aug. 14.

D16   D17

1949-57

J232	D16	1g carmine	.20	.20
J233	D16	2g carmine	.20	.20
J234	D16	4g carmine ('51)	1.00	.20
J235	D16	5g carmine	2.25	.20
J236	D16	8g carmine ('51)	2.75	1.50
J237	D16	10g carmine	.20	.20
J238	D16	20g carmine	.20	.20
J239	D16	30g carmine	.20	.20
J240	D16	40g carmine	.20	.20
J241	D16	50g carmine	.20	.20
J242	D16	60g carmine ('50)	7.50	.20
J243	D16	63g carmine ('57)	4.75	4.00
J244	D16	70g carmine	.20	.20
J245	D16	80g carmine	.20	.20
J246	D16	90g carmine ('50)	.20	.20
J247	D16	1s purple	.20	.20
J248	D16	1.20s purple	.35	.20
J249	D16	1.35s purple	.30	.20
J250	D16	1.40s purple ('51)	.45	.20
J251	D16	1.50s purple ('53)	.20	.20
J252	D16	1.65s purple ('50)	.40	.20
J253	D16	1.70s purple	.40	.20
J254	D16	2s purple	.35	.20
J255	D16	2.50s purple ('51)	.45	.20
J256	D16	3s purple	1.00	.20
J257	D16	4s purple ('51)	1.00	.45
J258	D16	5s purple	1.75	.20
J259	D16	5s purple	1.75	.20
		Nos. J232-J259 (28)	29.85	11.00

Issued: 60g, 90g, 1.65s, 8/7; 4g, 8g, 1.40s,
2.50s-4s, 12/4; 1.50s, 2/18; 63g, 4/30; others,
11/17.

1985-89   **Photo.**   *Perf. 14*
Background Color

J260	D17	10g brt yel ('86)	.20	.20
J261	D17	20g pink ('86)	.20	.20
J262	D17	50g orange ('86)	.20	.20
J263	D17	1s lt blue ('86)	.20	.20
J264	D17	2s pale brn ('86)	.30	.20
J265	D17	3s violet ('86)	.40	.30
J266	D17	5s ocher	.60	.40
J267	D17	10s pale grn ('89)	1.50	1.10
		Nos. J260-J267 (8)	3.60	2.80

Issue dates: 5s, Dec. 12. 20g, 1s, 3s, Mar.
19. 10g, 50g, 2s, Oct. 3. 10s, June 30.

MILITARY STAMPS

Issues of the Austro-Hungarian Military Authorities for the Occupied Territories in World War I

See Bosnia and Herzegovina for similar designs inscribed "MILITARPOST" instead of "FELDPOST."

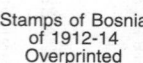

Stamps of Bosnia of 1912-14 Overprinted

		1915	Unwmk.	Perf. 12½	
M1	A23	1h olive green		.20	.35
M2	A23	2h bright blue		.20	.35
M3	A23	3h claret		.20	.35
M4	A23	5h green		.20	.20
M5	A23	6h dark gray		.20	.35
M6	A23	10h rose carmine		.20	.20
M7	A23	12h deep ol grn		.25	.45
M8	A23	20h orange brn		.30	.55
M9	A23	25h ultramarine		.25	.45
M10	A23	30h orange red		2.75	5.25
M11	A24	35h myrtle grn		2.25	4.25
M12	A24	40h dark violet		2.25	4.25
M13	A24	45h olive brown		2.50	4.50
M14	A24	50h slate blue		2.25	4.25
M15	A24	60h brn violet		.30	3.25
M16	A24	72h dark blue		2.25	4.25
M17	A25	1k brn vio, straw		2.50	5.25
M18	A25	2k dk gray, blue		2.25	4.25
M19	A26	3k car, green		20.00	32.50
M20	A26	5k dk vio, gray		18.00	27.50
M21	A25	10k dk ultra, gray		160.00	210.00
		Nos. M1-M21 (21)		219.30	312.75
		Set, never hinged		325.00	

Exists imperf. Value, set $275.
Nos. M1-M21 also exist with overprint double, inverted and in red. These varieties were made by order of an official but were not regularly issued.

M1 M2
Emperor Franz Josef

Perf. 11½, 12½ and Compound

		1915-17		Engr.	
M22	M1	1h olive green		.20	.20
M23	M1	2h dull blue		.20	.20
M24	M1	3h claret		.20	.20
M25	M1	5h green		.20	.20
a.		Perf. 11½		42.50	60.00
		Never hinged		75.00	
b.		Perf. 11½x12½		55.00	100.00
		Never hinged		110.00	
c.		Perf. 12½x11½		77.50	110.00
		Never hinged		140.00	
M26	M1	6h dark gray		.20	.20
M27	M1	10h rose carmine		.20	.20
M28	M1	10h gray bl ('17)		.20	.20
M29	M1	12h dp olive grn		.20	.20
M30	M1	15h car rose ('17)		.20	.20
a.		Perf. 11½		7.00	15.00
		Never hinged		12.50	
M31	M1	20h orange brn		.30	.35
M32	M1	20h ol green ('17)		.30	.35
M33	M1	25h ultramarine		.20	.20
M34	M1	30h vermilion		.20	.35
M35	M1	35h dark green		.30	.50
M36	M1	40h dark violet		.30	.50
M37	M1	45h olive brown		.25	.50
M38	M1	50h myrtle green		.25	.50
M39	M1	60h brown violet		.25	.50
M40	M1	72h dark blue		.25	.50
M41	M1	80h org brn ('17)		.20	.25
M42	M1	90h magenta ('17)		.70	1.10
M43	M2	1k brn vio, straw		1.40	2.10
M44	M2	2k dk gray, blue		1.10	1.00
M45	M2	3k car, green		.80	1.75
M46	M2	4k dark violet, gray ('17)		.80	2.75
M47	M2	5k dk vio, gray		18.00	27.50
M48	M2	10k dk ultra, gray		2.75	6.00
		Nos. M22-M48 (27)		30.15	48.50
		Set, never hinged		65.00	

#M22-M48 exist imperf. Value, set $125.

Emperor Karl I
M3 M4

		1917-18		Perf. 12½	
M49	M3	1h grnsh blue ('18)		.20	.20
a.		Perf. 11½		3.25	5.25
		Never hinged		6.00	
M50	M3	2h red org ('18)		.20	.20
M51	M3	3h olive gray		.20	.20
a.		Perf. 11½		12.00	19.00
		Never hinged		22.50	
b.		Perf. 11½x12½		21.00	35.00
		Never hinged		40.00	
M52	M3	5h olive green		.20	.20
M53	M3	6h violet		.20	.20
M54	M3	10h orange brn		.20	.20
M55	M3	12h blue		.20	.20
a.		Perf. 11½		2.00	4.25
		Never hinged		4.25	
M56	M3	15h bright rose		.20	.20
M57	M3	20h red brown		.20	.20
M58	M3	25h ultramarine		.30	.30
M59	M3	30h slate		.20	.20
M60	M3	40h olive bister		.20	.20
a.		Perf. 11½		1.25	2.10
		Never hinged		2.25	
M61	M3	50h deep green		.20	.20
a.		Perf. 11½		5.00	9.00
		Never hinged		10.00	
M62	M3	60h car rose		.20	.20
M63	M3	80h dull blue		.20	.20
M64	M3	90h dk violet		.40	.50
M65	M4	2k rose, straw		.20	.20
a.		Perf. 11½		2.00	3.50
		Never hinged		3.50	
M66	M4	3k green, blue		.80	1.75
M67	M4	4k rose, green		13.50	16.00
a.		Perf. 11½		25.00	35.00
		Never hinged		37.50	
M68	M4	10k dl vio, gray		2.00	4.25
a.		Perf. 11½		10.00	19.00
		Never hinged		16.00	
		Nos. M49-M68 (20)		20.00	25.80
		Set, never hinged		35.00	

Nos. M49-M68 exist imperf. Value, set $45.
See No. M82. For surcharges and overprints see Italy Nos. N1-N19, Poland Nos. 30-40, Romania Nos. 1N1-1N17, Western Ukraine Nos. 34-53, 75-81.

Emperor Karl I — M5

		1918	Typo.	Perf. 12½
M69	M5	1h grnsh blue		18.00
M70	M5	2h orange		9.00
M71	M5	3h olive gray		7.00
M72	M5	5h yellow green		.25
M73	M5	10h dark brown		.25
M74	M5	20h red		.70
M75	M5	25h blue		.70
M76	M5	30h bister		67.50
M77	M5	45h dark slate		67.50
M78	M5	50h deep green		45.00
M79	M5	60h violet		90.00
M80	M5	80h rose		45.00
M81	M5	90h brown violet		1.75

			Engr.	
M82	M4	1k ol bister, blue		.25
		Nos. M69-M82 (14)		352.90
		Set, never hinged		750.00

Nos. M69-M82 were on sale at the Vienna post office for a few days before the Armistice signing. They were never issued at the Army Post Offices. They exist imperf.; value, set $450.
For surcharges see Italy Nos. N20-N33.

MILITARY SEMI-POSTAL STAMPS

Emperor Karl I — MSP7
Empress Zita — MSP8

	Perf. 12½x13		
1918, July 20		**Unwmk.**	**Typo.**
MB1	MSP7 10h gray green	.25	.55
MB2	MSP8 20h magenta	.25	.55
MB3	MSP7 45h blue	.25	.55
	Nos. MB1-MB3 (3)	.75	1.65
	Set, never hinged		2.10

Nos. M69-M82 were on sale at the Vienna post office for a few days before the Armistice signing. They were never issued at the Army Post Offices. They exist imperf.; value, set $450. These stamps were sold at a premium of 10h each over face value. The surtax was for "Karl's Fund."
For overprints see Poland Nos. 27-29, Western Ukraine Nos. 31-33.
Exist imperf. Value, set $8.

MILITARY NEWSPAPER STAMPS

Mercury — MN1

		1916	Unwmk.	Typo.	Perf. 12½
MP1	MN1	2h blue		.20	.20
a.		Perf. 11½		1.40	1.60
		Never hinged		1.75	
b.		Perf. 12½x11½		150.00	200.00
		Never hinged		250.00	
MP2	MN1	6h orange		.50	.80
MP3	MN1	10h carmine		.60	.80
MP4	MN1	20h brown		.40	.80
a.		Perf. 11½		1.90	5.00
		Never hinged		5.00	
		Nos. MP1-MP4 (4)		1.70	2.60
		Set, never hinged		3.25	

Exist imperf. Values, Nos. MP2-MP3, $1 each, Nos. MP1, MP4, $18 each.
For surcharges see Italy Nos. NP1-NP4.

NEWSPAPER STAMPS

From 1851 to 1866, the Austrian Newspaper Stamps were also used in Lombardy-Venetia.

Values for unused stamps 1851-67 are for fine copies with original gum. Specimens without gum sell for about a third or less of the figures quoted.

Issues of the Monarchy

Mercury - N1

Three Types
Type I - The "G" has no crossbar.
Type II - The "G" has a crossbar.
Type IIa - as type II but the rosette is deformed. Two spots of color in the "G."

		1851-56	Unwmk.	Typo.	Imperf.
		Machine-made Paper			
P1	N1	(0.6kr) bl, type IIa		175.00	75.00
a.		Blue, type I		250.00	110.00
b.		Ribbed paper		625.00	160.00
c.		Blue, type II		600.00	250.00
P2	N1	(6kr) yel, type I		—	7,000.
P3	N1	(30kr) rose, type I		—	9,000.
P4	N1	(6kr) scar, type II ('56)		67,500.	40,000.

From 1852 No. P3 and from 1856 No. P2 were used as 0.6 kreuzer values.
Values for Nos. P2-P3 unused are for stamps without gum. Pale shades sell at considerably lower values.
Originals of Nos. P2-P3 are usually in pale colors and poorly printed. Values are for stamps clearly printed and in bright colors. Numerous reprints of Nos. P1-P4 were made between 1866 and 1904. Those of Nos. P2-P3 are always well printed and in much deeper colors. All reprints are in type I, but occasionally show faint traces of a crossbar on "G" of "ZEITUNGS."

N2 N3

Two Types of the 1858-59 Issue
Type I - Loops of the bow at the back of the head broken.
Type II - Loops complete. Wreath projects further at top of head.

		1858-59		Embossed	
P5	N2	(1kr) blue, type I		650.00	550.00
P6	N2	(1kr) lilac, type II ('59)		875.00	275.00

		1861			
P7	N3	(1kr) gray		175.00	125.00
a.		(1kr) gray lilac		625.00	175.00
b.		(1kr) deep lilac		2,500.	575.00

The embossing on the reprints of the 1858-59 and 1861 issues is not as sharp as on the originals.

N4

Wmk. 91, or, before July 1864, Unwmkd.

		1863			
P8	N4	(1.05kr) gray		45.00	15.00
a.		Tete beche pair		125,000.	
b.		(1.05kr) gray lilac		75.00	17.50

Values are for stamps that do not show the watermark. Stamps showing the watermark often sell for more.
The embossing of the reprints is not as sharp as on the originals.

Mercury
N5 N6

Three Types
Type I - Helmet not defined at back, more or less blurred. Two thick short lines in front of wing of helmet. Shadow on front of face not separated from hair.
Type II - Helmet distinctly defined. Four thin short lines in front of wing. Shadow on front of face clearly defined from hair.
Type III - Outer white circle around head is open at top (closed on types I and II). Greek border at top and bottom is wider than on types I and II.

		1867-73	Typo.	Wmk. 91	
		Coarse Print			
P9	N5	(1kr) vio, type I		37.50	4.00
a.		(1kr) violet, type II ('73)		125.00	18.00

		1874-76			
		Fine Print			
P9B	N5	(1kr) violet, type III ('76)		.55	.20
c.		(1kr) gray lilac, type I ('76)		90.00	25.00
d.		(1kr) violet, type II		27.50	5.00
e.		Double impression, type III		175.00	

Stamps of this issue, except No. P9c, exist in many shades, from gray to lilac brown and deep violet. Stamps in type III exist also privately perforated or rouletted.

		1880			
P10	N6	½kr blue green		4.50	.85

Nos. P9B and P10 also exist on thicker paper without sheet watermark and No. P10 exists with unofficial perforation.

N7

1899   Unwmk.   *Imperf.*
Without Varnish Bars

P11	N7	2h dark blue	.20	.20
P12	N7	6h orange	2.00	1.75
P13	N7	10h brown	.80	.75
P14	N7	20h rose	1.75	1.75
		Nos. P11-P14 (4)	4.75	4.45

1901
With Varnish Bars

P11a	N7	2h dark blue	.60	.20
P12a	N7	6h orange	8.50	11.50
P13a	N7	10h brown	10.50	6.75
P14a	N7	20h rose	19.00	26.00
		Nos. P11a-P14a (4)	38.60	44.45

Nos. P11 to P14 were re-issued in 1905.

Mercury   N8   N9

1908   *Imperf.*

P15	N8	2h dark blue	1.40	.20
a.		Tete beche pair	250.00	300.00
P16	N8	6h orange	2.50	.30
P17	N8	10h carmine	2.50	.30
P18	N8	20h brown	2.75	.25
		Nos. P15-P18 (4)	9.15	1.05

All values are found on chalky, regular and thin ordinary paper. They exist privately perforated.

1916   *Imperf.*

P19	N9	2h brown	.20	.20
P20	N9	4h green	.30	.85
P21	N9	6h dark blue	.25	.70
P22	N9	10h orange	.35	.85
P23	N9	30h claret	.30	.80
		Nos. P19-P23 (5)	1.40	3.40
		Set, never hinged	2.75	

Issues of the Republic

Newspaper Stamps of 1916 Overprinted

1919

P24	N9	2h brown	.20	.20
P25	N9	4h green	.25	.70
P26	N9	6h dark blue	.20	.70
P27	N9	10h orange	.25	.90
P28	N9	30h claret	.20	.50
		Nos. P24-P28 (5)	1.10	3.00
		Set, never hinged	1.75	

Mercury   N10   N11

1920-21   *Imperf.*

P29	N10	2h violet	.20	.20
P30	N10	4h brown	.20	.20
P31	N10	5h slate	.20	.20
P32	N10	6h turq blue	.20	.20
P33	N10	8h green	.20	.30
P34	N10	9h yellow ('21)	.20	.20
P35	N10	10h red	.20	.20
P36	N10	12h blue	.20	.30
P37	N10	15h lilac ('21)	.20	.20
P38	N10	18h blue grn ('21)	.20	.25
P39	N10	20h orange	.20	.25
P40	N10	30h yellow brn ('21)	.20	.20
P41	N10	45h green ('21)	.20	.35
P42	N10	60h claret	.20	.20
P43	N10	72h chocolate ('21)	.20	.45
P44	N10	90h violet ('21)	.20	.55
P45	N10	1.20k red ('21)	.20	.65
P46	N10	2.40k yellow grn ('21)	.20	.55
P47	N10	3k gray ('21)	.20	.40
		Nos. P29-P47 (19)	3.80	5.85
		Set, never hinged	4.00	

Nos. P37-P40, P42, P44 and P47 exist also on thick gray paper.

1921-22

P48	N11	45h gray	.20	.25
P49	N11	75h brown org ('22)	.20	.35
P50	N11	1.50k ol bister ('22)	.20	.50
P51	N11	1.80k gray blue ('22)	.20	.55
P52	N11	2.25k light brown	.20	.75
P53	N11	3k dull green ('22)	.20	.55
P54	N11	6k claret ('22)	.20	.65
P55	N11	7.50k bister	.20	.85
		Nos. P48-P55 (8)	1.60	4.45
		Set, never hinged	1.75	

Nos. P24-P55 exist privately perforated.

NEWSPAPER TAX STAMPS

Values for unused stamps 1853-59 are for copies in fine condition with gum. Specimens without gum sell for about one-third or less of the figures quoted.

Issues of the Monarchy

NT1   NT2

Unwmk.
1853, Mar. 1   Typo.   *Imperf.*

PR1	NT1	2kr green	1,450.	50.00

The reprints are in finer print than the more coarsely printed originals, and on a smooth toned paper.

Values for Nos. PR2-PR9 are for stamps that do not show the watermark. Stamps showing the watermark often sell for more.

Wmk. 91, or, before July 1864, Unwmkd.

1858-59

Two Types.
Type I - The banderol on the Crown of the left eagle touches the beak of the eagle.
Type II - The banderol does not touch the beak.

PR2	NT2	1kr blue, type II		
		('59)	30.00	5.50
a.		1kr blue, type I	675.00	140.00
b.		Printed on both sides, type II		—
PR3	NT2	2kr brown, type II		
		('59)	22.50	6.75
a.		2kr red brown, type II	350.00	150.00
PR4	NT2	4kr brn, type I	400.00	850.00

Nos. PR2a, PR3a, and PR4 were printed only on unwatermarked paper. Nos. PR2 and PR3 exist on unwatermarked and watermarked paper.

Nos. PR2 and PR3 exist in coarse and (after 1874) in fine print, like the contemporary postage stamps.

The reprints of the 4kr brown are of type II and on a smooth toned paper.

Issue date: 4kr, Nov. 1.

See Lombardy-Venetia for the 1kr in black and the 2kr, 4fk in red.

NT3   NT4

1877   Redrawn

PR5	NT3	1kr blue	12.50	1.40
a.		1kr pale ultramarine		1,600.
PR6	NT3	2kr brown	14.00	6.75

In the redrawn stamps the shield is larger and the vertical bar has eight lines above the white square and nine below, instead of five.

Nos. PR5 and PR6 exist also watermarked "WECHSEL" instead of "ZEITUNGS-MARKEN."

1890, June 1

PR7	NT4	1kr brown	9.00	1.00
PR8	NT4	2kr green	10.00	1.60

#PR5-PR8 exist with private perforation.

NT5

Perf. 13, 12½
1890, June 1   Wmk. 91

PR9	NT5	25kr carmine	90.00 200.00

Nos. PR1-PR9 did not pay postage, but were a fiscal tax, collected by the postal authorities on newspapers.

SPECIAL HANDLING STAMPS

(For Printed Matter Only)
Issues of the Monarchy

Mercury
SH1

1916   Unwmk.   *Perf. 12½*

QE1	SH1	2h claret, *yel*	.60	1.60
QE2	SH1	5h dp green, *yel*	.60	1.60
		Set, never hinged	3.50	

SH2

1917   *Perf. 12½*

QE3	SH2	2h claret, *yel*	.20	.30
a.		Pair, imperf. between	175.00	275.00
		Never hinged	200.00	
b.		Perf. 11½x12½	55.00	95.00
		Never hinged	110.00	
c.		Perf. 12½x11½	80.00	150.00
		Never hinged	160.00	
d.		Perf. 11½	1.25	2.50
		Never hinged	2.50	
QE4	SH2	5h dp green, *yel*	.20	.30
a.		Pair, imperf. between	160.00	250.00
		Never hinged	175.00	
b.		Perf. 11½x12½	45.00	87.50
		Never hinged	95.00	
c.		Perf. 12½x11½	70.00	140.00
		Never hinged	140.00	
d.		Perf. 11½	1.25	2.50
		Never hinged	2.50	
		Set, never hinged	.60	

Nos. QE1-QE4 exist imperforate.

Issues of the Republic

Nos. QE3 and QE4 Overprinted

1919

QE5	SH2	2h claret, *yel*	.20	.20
a.		Inverted overprint	325.00	
		Never hinged	375.00	
b.		Perf. 11½x12½	5.25	10.50
		Never hinged	8.00	
c.		Perf. 12½x11½	65.00	160.00
		Never hinged	125.00	
d.		Perf. 11½	.30	1.10
		Never hinged	.65	
QE6	SH2	5h deep green,	.20	.20
a.		Perf. 11½x12½	2.25	3.75
		Never hinged	2.75	
b.		Perf. 12½x11½	25.00	45.00
		Never hinged	37.50	
c.		Perf. 11½	.20	.70
		Never hinged	.45	
		Set, never hinged	.40	

Nos. QE5 and QE6 exist imperforate.

SH3

Dark Blue Surcharge
1921

QE7	SH3	50h on 2h claret, *yel*	.20	.20
		Never hinged	.20	

SH4

1922   *Perf. 12½*

QE8	SH4	50h lilac, *yel*	.20	1.75
		Never hinged	.20	

#QE5-QE8 exist in vertical pairs, imperf between. No. QE8 exists imperf.

OCCUPATION STAMPS

Issued under Italian Occupation
Issued in Trieste

Austrian Stamps of 1916-18 Overprinted

1918   Unwmk.   *Perf. 12½*

N1	A37	3h bright vio	1.00	1.00
a.		Double overprint	30.00	30.00
b.		Inverted overprint	30.00	30.00
N2	A37	5h light grn	1.00	1.00
a.		Inverted overprint	30.00	30.00
c.		Double overprint	30.00	
N3	A37	6h dp orange	1.40	1.40
N4	A37	10h magenta	4.00	2.50
a.		Inverted overprint	30.00	30.00
N5	A37	12h light bl	2.00	2.00
a.		Double overprint	30.00	30.00
N6	A42	15h dull red	1.00	1.00
a.		Inverted overprint	30.00	30.00
b.		Double overprint	30.00	30.00
N7	A42	20h dark green	1.00	1.00
a.		Inverted overprint	30.00	30.00
c.		Double overprint	67.50	
N8	A42	25h deep blue	6.75	6.75
a.		Inverted overprint	125.00	125.00
N9	A42	30h dl violet	2.00	2.00
N10	A39	40h olive grn	85.00	85.00
N11	A39	50h dark green	7.00	6.75
N12	A39	60h deep blue	19.00	18.00
N13	A39	80h orange brn	11.00	12.00
a.		Inverted overprint	—	
N14	A39	1k car, *yel*	11.00	12.00
a.		Double overprint	67.50	
N15	A40	2k light bl	200.00	200.00
		Never hinged	400.00	
N16	A40	4k yellow grn	400.00	400.00
		Never hinged	800.00	

Handstamped

N17	A40	10k dp violet	25,000.	25,000.
		Never hinged	27,500.	

Granite Paper

N18	A40	2k light blue	300.00	
		Never hinged	600.00	
N19	A40	3k car rose	250.00	250.00
		Never hinged	500.00	
		Nos. N1-N14 (14)	153.15	152.40
		Set, never hinged, #N1-N14	300.00	

Some authorities question the authenticity of No. N18. Counterfeits of Nos. N10, N15-N19 are plentiful.

Italian Stamps of 1901-18 Overprinted

Wmk. 140   *Perf. 14*

N20	A42	1c brown	1.50	2.00
a.		Inverted overprint	20.00	20.00
N21	A43	2c orange brn	1.50	2.00
a.		Inverted overprint	17.00	17.00
N22	A48	5c green	.70	1.00
a.		Inverted overprint	35.00	35.00
b.		Double overprint	85.00	
N23	A48	10c claret	.70	1.00
a.		Inverted overprint	47.50	47.50
b.		Double overprint	85.00	
N24	A50	20c brn orange	.90	1.25
a.		Inverted overprint	67.50	67.50
b.		Double overprint	85.00	85.00
N25	A49	25c blue	1.00	1.75
a.		Inverted overprint	85.00	85.00
N26	A49	40c brown	8.00	10.00
a.		Inverted overprint	95.00	95.00
N27	A45	45c olive grn	2.50	3.50
a.		Inverted overprint	95.00	95.00
N28	A49	50c violet	3.50	4.75
N29	A49	60c brown car	42.50	55.00
a.		Inverted overprint	190.00	
b.		Double overprint		

N30	A46	1 l brn & green	14.50	21.00
a.		Inverted overprint		
		Nos. N20-N30 (11)	77.30	103.25
		Set, never hinged	150.00	

Italian Stamps of 1901-18 Surcharged

N31	A48	5h on 5c green	1.00	1.50
		Never hinged	2.00	
a.		"5" omitted	85.00	85.00
b.		Inverted surcharge	85.00	85.00
N32	A50	20h on 20c brn org	1.00	1.50
		Never hinged	2.00	
a.		Double surcharge	85.00	85.00

Issued in the Trentino

Austrian Stamps of 1916-18 Overprinted

		1918	**Unwmk.**	**Perf. 12½**
N33	A37	3h bright vio	4.00	3.00
a.		Double overprint	67.50	67.50
b.		Inverted overprint	55.00	55.00
N34	A37	5h light grn	3.50	1.75
a.		"8 nov. 1918"	*1,750.*	
b.		Inverted overprint	55.00	55.00
N35	A37	6h dp orange	50.00	40.00
N36	A37	10h magenta	3.50	2.00
a.		"8 nov. 1918"	95.00	95.00
N37	A37	12h light blue	140.00	110.00
N38	A42	15h dull red	4.00	3.00
N39	A42	20h dark green	2.00	2.00
a.		"8 nov. 1918"	110.00	110.00
b.		Double overprint	67.50	67.50
c.		Inverted overprint	22.50	22.50
N40	A42	25h deep blue	35.00	30.00
N41	A42	30h dl violet	12.00	10.00
N42	A39	40h olive grn	45.00	40.00
N43	A39	50h dark green	27.50	22.50
a.		Inverted overprint	110.00	110.00
N44	A39	60h deep blue	40.00	35.00
a.		Double overprint	110.00	110.00
N45	A39	80h orange brn	55.00	45.00
N46	A39	90h red violet	1,250.	1,000.
N47	A39	1k car, *yel*	55.00	45.00
N48	A40	2k light blue	375.00	290.00
N49	A40	4k yel green	*1,750.*	*1,500.*
N50	A40	10k dp violet		

Granite Paper

N51	A40	2k light blue	475.00	
		Never hinged	675.00	

Counterfeits of Nos. N33-N51 are plentiful.

Italian Stamps of 1901-18 Overprinted

		Wmk. 140	**Perf. 14**
N52	A42	1c brown	1.00	3.50
a.		Inverted overprint	55.00	55.00
b.		Double overprint	55.00	
N53	A43	2c orange brn	1.00	3.50
a.		Inverted overprint	55.00	55.00
b.		Double overprint	55.00	55.00
N54	A48	5c green	1.00	3.50
a.		Inverted overprint	55.00	55.00
b.		Double overprint	55.00	55.00
N55	A48	10c claret	1.00	3.50
a.		Inverted overprint	75.00	75.00
b.		Double overprint	55.00	55.00
N56	A50	20c brn orange	1.00	3.50
a.		Inverted overprint	75.00	75.00
N57	A49	40c brown	55.00	35.00
N58	A45	45c olive grn	25.00	35.00
a.		Double overprint	140.00	140.00
N59	A49	50c violet	25.00	35.00
N60	A46	1 l brn & green	25.00	35.00
a.		Double overprint	140.00	140.00
		Nos. N52-N60 (9)	135.00	157.50

Italian Stamps of 1906-18 Surcharged

N61	A48	5h on 5c green	1.00	1.75
N62	A48	10h on 10c claret	1.00	1.75
a.		Inverted overprint	67.50	67.50
N63	A50	20h on 20c brn org	1.00	1.75
a.		Double surcharge	67.50	67.50
		Nos. N61-N63 (3)	3.00	5.25

General Issue

Italian Stamps of 1901-18 Surcharged

1919

N64	A42	1c on 1c brown	.90	1.25
a.		Inverted surcharge	17.00	17.50
N65	A43	2c on 2c org brn	.90	1.25
a.		Double surcharge	175.00	
b.		Inverted surcharge	13.50	13.50
N66	A48	5c on 5c green	.85	.45
a.		Inverted surcharge	40.00	40.00
b.		Double surcharge	67.50	
N67	A48	10c on 10c claret	.90	.45
a.		Inverted surcharge	40.00	40.00
b.		Double surcharge	67.50	67.50
N68	A50	20c on 20c brn org	.90	.45
a.		Double surcharge	87.50	87.50
N69	A49	25c on 25c blue	.85	1.00
a.		Double surcharge	87.50	
N70	A49	40c on 40c brown	.90	2.00
a.		"ccrona"	100.00	100.00
N71	A45	45c on 45c ol grn	.90	2.00
a.		Inverted surcharge	110.00	110.00
N72	A49	50c on 50c violet	.90	2.00
N73	A49	60c on 60c brn car	.90	3.00
a.		"00" for "60"	125.00	125.00

Surcharged

N74	A46	1cor on 1 l brn & grn	1.75	3.00
		Nos. N64-N74 (11)	10.65	16.85

Surcharges similar to these but differing in style or arrangement of type were used in Dalmatia.

OCCUPATION STAMPS SPECIAL DELIVERY STAMPS

Issued in Trieste

Special Delivery Stamp of Italy of 1903 Overprinted

		1918	**Wmk. 140**	**Perf. 14**
NE1	SD1	25c rose red	30.00	37.50
		Never hinged	60.00	
a.		Inverted overprint	125.00	125.00

General Issue

Special Delivery Stamps of Italy of 1903-09 Surcharged

1919

NE2	SD1	25c on 25c rose	1.10	1.75
a.		Double surcharge	67.50	67.50
NE3	SD2	30c on 30c bl & rose	1.50	2.40

OCCUPATION POSTAGE DUE STAMPS

Issued in Trieste

Postage Due Stamps of Italy, 1870-94, Overprinted

		1918	**Wmk. 140**	**Perf. 14**
NJ1	D3	5c buff & mag	.25	.45
a.		Inverted overprint	13.50	13.50
b.		Double overprint	150.00	
NJ2	D3	10c buff & mag	.35	.50
a.		Inverted overprint	67.50	67.50
NJ3	D3	20c buff & mag	.75	1.10
a.		Double overprint	150.00	
b.		Inverted overprint	67.50	67.50

NJ4	D3	30c buff & mag	2.00	3.00
NJ5	D3	40c buff & mag	22.50	30.00
a.		Inverted overprint	200.00	200.00
NJ6	D3	50c buff & mag	50.00	67.50
a.		Inverted overprint	240.00	250.00
NJ7	D3	1 l buff & mag	150.00	200.00
		Nos. NJ1-NJ7 (7)	225.85	302.55

General Issue

Postage Due Stamps of Italy, 1870-1903 Surcharged

1919

Buff & Magenta

NJ8	D3	5c on 5c	.50	.70
a.		Inverted overprint	19.00	19.00
NJ9	D3	10c on 10c	.50	.70
a.		Center and surcharge invtd.	125.00	125.00
NJ10	D3	20c on 20c	.70	1.00
a.		Double overprint	140.00	140.00
NJ11	D3	30c on 30c	.85	1.50
NJ12	D3	40c on 40c	.85	1.50
NJ13	D3	50c on 50c	.85	1.50

Surcharged

NJ14	D3	1cor on 1 l bl & mag	.85	1.50
NJ15	D3	2cor on 2 l bl & mag	45.00	80.00
NJ16	D3	5cor on 5 l bl & mag	45.00	80.00
		Nos. NJ8-NJ16 (9)	95.10	168.40

A. M. G. ISSUE FOR AUSTRIA

Catalogue values for unused stamps in this section are for Never Hinged items.

Issued jointly by the Allied Military Government of the US and Great Britain, for civilian use in areas under American, British and French occupation. (Upper Austria, Salzburg, Tyrol, Vorarlberg, Styria and Carinthia).

OS1

		1945	**Unwmk.**	**Litho.**	**Perf. 11**
4N1	OS1	1g aquamarine	.25	.35
4N2	OS1	3g deep orange	.25	.35
4N3	OS1	4g buff	.25	.35
4N4	OS1	5g bright green	.25	.35
4N5	OS1	6g red violet	.35	.35
4N6	OS1	8g rose pink	.25	.35
4N7	OS1	10g light gray	.25	.35
4N8	OS1	12g pale buff brown	.35	.35
4N9	OS1	15g rose red	.35	.35
4N10	OS1	20g copper brown	.35	.35
4N11	OS1	25g deep blue	.25	.35
4N12	OS1	30g bright violet	.25	.35
4N13	OS1	40g light ultra	.25	.35
4N14	OS1	60g light olive grn	.25	.35
4N15	OS1	1s dark violet	.35	.45
4N16	OS1	2s yellow	.35	.55
4N17	OS1	5s deep ultra	.55	.75

For Nos. 4N2, 4N4-4N17 overprinted "PORTO" see Nos. J189-J203.

AUSTRIAN OFFICES ABROAD

These stamps were on sale and usable at all Austrian post-offices in Crete and in the Turkish Empire.

100 Centimes = 1 Franc

OFFICES IN CRETE

Used values are italicized for stamps often found with false cancellations.

Stamps of Austria of 1899-1901 Issue, Surcharged in Black:

a　　b

c　　d

		1903-04	**Unwmk.**	**Perf. 12½, 13½**
		On Nos. 73a, 75a, 77a, 81a		
		Granite Paper		
		With Varnish Bars		
1	A15(a)	5c on 5h blue green	1.50	3.50
2	A16(b)	10c on 10h rose	.80	3.75
3	A16(b)	25c on 25h ultra	40.00	24.00
4	A17(c)	50c on 50h gray blue	7.50	100.00
		On Nos. 83, 83a, 84, 85		
		Without Varnish Bars		
5	A18(d)	1fr on 1k car rose	2.50	95.00
a.		1fr on 1k carmine	4.00	95.00
b.		Horiz. or vert. pair, imperf. between	200.00	
6	A18(d)	2fr on 2k ('04)	9.00	240.00
7	A18(d)	4fr on 4k ('04)	10.00	475.00
		Nos. 1-7 (7)	71.30	

Surcharged on Austrian Stamps of 1904-05

1905

		On Nos. 89, 97		
		Without Varnish Bars		
8a	A19(a)	5c on 5h blue green	50.00	35.00
9	A20(b)	10c on 10h car	1.25	9.00
		On Nos. 89a, 97a, 99a, 103a		
		With Varnish Bars		
8	A19(b)	5c on 5h bl grn	4.00	5.50
9a	A20(b)	10c on 10h carmine	19.00	22.50
10	A20(b)	25c on 25h ultra	1.25	85.00
11	A21(b)	50c on 50h dl bl	1.50	350.00

Surcharged on Austrian Stamps and Type of 1906-07

		1907		**Perf. 12½, 13½**
		Without Varnish Bars		
12	A19(a)	5c on 5h yel green (#90)	1.10	4.00
13	A20(b)	10c on 10h car (#92)	1.50	27.50
14	A20(b)	15c on 15h vio	1.50	27.50
		Nos. 12-14 (3)	4.10	59.00

A5　　A6

		1908	**Typo.**	**Perf. 12½**
15	A5	5c green, *yellow*	.40	.60
16	A5	10c scarlet, *rose*	.45	.80
17	A5	15c brown, *buff*	.55	4.50
18	A5	25c dp blue, *blue*	11.00	5.00
		Engr.		
19	A6	50c lake, *yellow*	2.00	22.50
20	A6	1fr brown, *gray*	2.75	32.50
a.		Vert pair, imperf. btwn.	210.00	
		Nos. 15-20 (6)	17.15	65.90

Nos. 15-18 are on paper colored on the surface only. All values exist imperforate.

60th year of the reign of Emperor Franz Josef, for permanent use.

Paper Colored Through

1914					Typo.
21	A5	10c rose, *rose*		1.75	900.00
22	A5	25c ultra, *blue*		.80	110.00

Nos. 21 and 22 exist imperforate.

OFFICES IN THE TURKISH EMPIRE

From 1863 to 1867 the stamps of Lombardy-Venetia (Nos. 15 to 24) were used at the Austrian Offices in the Turkish Empire.

100 Soldi = 1 Florin
40 Paras = 1 Piaster

Values for unused stamps are for copies with gum. Specimens without gum sell for about one-third or less of the figures quoted.

Used values are italicized for stamps often found with false cancellations.

For similar designs in Kreuzers, see early Austria.

A1 A2

Two different printing methods were used, as in the 1867-74 issues of Austria. They may be distinguished by the coarse or fine lines of the hair and whiskers and by the paper, which is more transparent on the later issue.

1867		Typo.	Wmk. 91	Perf. 9½
		Coarse Print		
1	A1	2sld orange	1.75	22.50
a.		2sld yellow	50.00	27.50
2	A1	3sld green	100.00	40.00
a.		3sld dark green	125.00	70.00
3	A1	5sld red	90.00	11.00
a.		5sld carmine	110.00	14.50
4	A1	10sld blue	95.00	1.75
a.		10sld light blue	110.00	2.50
b.		10sld dark blue	100.00	3.00
5	A1	15sld brown	16.00	6.50
a.		15sld dark brown	50.00	21.00
b.		15sld reddish brown	17.50	10.00
c.		15sld gray brown	45.00	9.00
6	A1	25sld violet	12.50	30.00
a.		25sld brown violet	16.00	35.00
b.		25sld gray lilac	50.00	35.00
7	A2	50sld brn, perf. 10½	1.00	42.50
a.		Perf. 12	80.00	65.00
b.		Perf. 13	250.00	
k.		Perf. 9	25.00	50.00
l.		50sld pale red brn, perf. 12	55.00	60.00
m.		Vert. pair, imperf. btwn.	300.00	650.00
n.		Horiz. pair, imperf. btwn.	300.00	750.00
o.		Perf. 10½x9	60.00	100.00

	Perf. 9, 9½, 10½ and Compound		
1876-83			
	Fine Print		
7C	A1	2sld yellow ('83)	.20	1,300.
7D	A1	3sld green ('78)	1.00	20.00
7E	A1	5sld red ('78)	.40	15.00
7F	A1	10sld blue	65.00	1.00
7I	A1	15sld org brn ('81)	9.00	125.00
7J	A1	25sld gray lilac ('83)	.50	275.00
	Nos. 7C-7J (6)		76.10	

The 10 soldi has been reprinted in deep dull blue, perforated 10½.

A3

1883			*Perf. 9½, 10, 10½*
8	A3	2sld brown	.20	110.00
9	A3	3sld green	1.00	25.00
10	A3	5sld red	.20	16.00
11	A3	10sld blue	.75	.50
12	A3	20sld gray, perf. 10	1.00	60.00
a.		Perf. 9½	5.00	6.75
13	A3	50sld red lilac	1.40	16.00
	Nos. 8-13 (6)		4.55	

No. 9 Surcharged

10 PARAS ON 3 SOLDI:
Type I - Surcharge 16½mm across. "PARA" about ½mm above bottom of "10." 2mm space between "10" and "P"; 1½mm between "A" and "10." Perf. 9½ only.
Type II - Surcharge 15¼ to 16mm across. "PARA" on same line with figures or slightly higher or lower. 1½mm space between "10" and "P"; 1mm between "A" and "10." Perf. 9½ and 10.

1886			*Perf. 9½ and 10*
14	A3	10pa on 3sld green, type II	.30	5.50
a.		Surcharge type I	175.00	325.00
b.		Inverted surcharge, type I		1,850.

Surcharge on Austria #42-46

1888				
15	A11	10pa on 3kr grn	3.00	7.50
a.		"01 PARA 10"		400.00
16	A11	20pa on 5kr rose	.50	7.25
17	A11	1pi on 10kr blue	45.00	1.10
a.		Perf. 13½		225.00
b.		Double surcharge		275.00
18	A11	2pi on 20kr gray	1.50	4.00
19	A11	5pi on 50kr vio	2.00	15.00
	Nos. 15-19 (5)		52.00	34.85

Austria Nos. 52-55, 58, 61 Surcharged

1890-92		Unwmk.	*Perf. 9 to 13½*
		Granite Paper	
20	A12	8pa on 2kr brn ('92)	.20	.50
a.		Perf. 9½	10.00	13.50
21	A12	10pa on 3kr green	.65	.50
22	A12	20pa on 5kr rose	.25	.50
23	A12	1pi on 10kr ultra	.35	.20
24	A12	2pi on 20kr ol grn	5.50	25.00
25	A12	5pi on 50kr violet	11.00	60.00
	Nos. 20-25 (6)		17.95	86.70

See note after Austria No. 65 on missing numerals, etc.

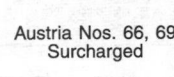

Austria Nos. 66, 69 Surcharged

1891			*Perf. 10 to 13½*
26	A14	2pi on 20kr green	4.25	1.25
a.		Perf. 9½	110.00	70.00
27	A14	5pi on 50kr violet	2.50	2.50

Two types of the surcharge on No. 26 exist.

Austria Nos. 62-65 Surcharged

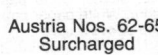

1892			*Perf. 10½, 11½*
28	A13	10pi on 1gld blue	10.00	22.50
29	A13	20pi on 2gld car	12.00	35.00
a.		Double surcharge		

1896			*Perf. 10½, 11½, 12½*
30	A13	10pi on 1gld pale lilac	12.00	19.00
31	A13	20pi on 2gld gray grn	37.50	60.00

Austria Nos. 73, 75, 77, 81, 83-85 Surcharged

#32-35   #36-38

			Perf. 10½, 12½, 13½ and Compound
1900			
		Without Varnish Bars	
32	A15	10pa on 5h bl grn	4.00	.80
33	A16	20pa on 10h rose	5.00	.75
b.		Perf. 12½x10½	250.00	85.00
34	A16	1pi on 25h ultra	3.00	.25
35	A17	2pi on 50h gray bl	7.25	3.25
36	A18	5pi on 1k car rose	1.00	.30
a.		5pi on 1k carmine	1.10	.90
b.		Horiz. or vert. pair, imperf. btwn.		110.00
37	A18	10pi on 2k gray lil	2.50	2.25
38	A18	20pi on 4k gray grn	2.00	6.00
	Nos. 32-38 (7)		24.75	13.60

In the surcharge on Nos. 37 and 38 "piaster" is printed "PIAST."

1901			
		With Varnish Bars	
32a	A15	10pa on 5h blue green	1.75	2.25
33a	A16	20pa on 10h rose	2.25	160.00
34a	A16	1pi on 25h ultra	1.50	.45
35a	A17	2pi on 50h gray blue	3.25	5.25
	Nos. 32a-35a (4)		8.75	

A4 A5

A6

1906			*Perf. 12½ to 13½*
		Without Varnish Bars	
39	A4	10pa dark green	11.00	2.50
40	A5	20pa rose	.80	.65
41	A6	1pi ultra	.35	.25
42	A6	2pi gray blue	.80	.65
	Nos. 39-42 (4)		12.95	4.05

1903			**With Varnish Bars**
39a	A4	10pa dark green	4.25	1.50
40a	A5	20pa rose	2.25	.40
41a	A5	1pi ultra	1.60	.25
42a	A6	2pi gray blue	125.00	2.25

1907			
		Without Varnish Bars	
43	A4	10pa yellow green	.50	1.40
45	A5	30pa violet	.50	2.75

A7 A8

1908		Typo.	*Perf. 12½*
46	A7	10pa green, *yellow*	.20	.25
47	A7	20pa scarlet, *rose*	.25	.25
48	A7	30pa brown, *buff*	.30	.50
49	A7	1pi deep bl, *blue*	11.00	.20
50	A7	60pa vio, *bluish*	.55	3.00
		Engr.	
51	A8	2pi lake, *yellow*	.35	.20
52	A8	5pi brown, *gray*	.60	.80
53	A8	10pi green, *yellow*	.80	1.50
54	A8	20pi blue, *gray*	1.50	3.50
	Nos. 46-54 (9)		15.55	10.20

Nos. 46-50 are on paper colored on the surface only. 60th year of the reign of Emperor Franz Josef I, for permanent use. All values exist imperforate.

1913-14			Typo.
		Paper Colored Through	
57	A7	20pa rose, *rose* ('14)	.70	325.00
58	A7	1pi ultra, *blue*	.35	.45

Nos. 57 and 58 exist imperforate.

POSTAGE DUE STAMPS

Type of Austria D2 Surcharged

D2

Black Surcharge

1902		Unwmk.	*Perf. 12½, 13½*
J1	D2	10pa on 5h green	1.10	2.75
J2	D2	20pa on 10h green	1.10	2.75
J3	D2	1pi on 20h green	1.75	3.25
J4	D2	2pi on 40h green	1.75	3.25
J5	D2	5pi on 100h green	2.75	2.75
	Nos. J1-J5 (5)		8.45	14.75

Shades of Nos. J1-J5 exist, varying from yellowish green to dark green.

D3

1908		Typo.	*Perf. 12½*
J6	D3	¼pi green	3.00	5.50
J7	D3	½pi green	1.50	5.50
J8	D3	1pi green	2.00	5.50
J9	D3	1½pi green	.80	12.50
J10	D3	2pi green	2.00	13.50
J11	D3	5pi green	2.00	8.00
J12	D3	10pi green	16.00	100.00
J13	D3	20pi green	16.00	110.00
J14	D3	30pi green	13.00	11.50
	Nos. J6-J14 (9)		56.30	272.00

Nos. J6-J14 exist in distinct shades of green and on thick chalky, regular and thin ordinary paper. Values are for the least expensive variety. For comprehensive listings, see Scott Classic Specialized Catalogue.

No. J6-J14 exist imperforate.
Forgeries exist.

LOMBARDY-VENETIA

Formerly a kingdom in the north of Italy forming part of the Austrian Empire. Milan and Venice were the two principal cities. Lombardy was annexed to Sardinia in 1859, and Venetia to the kingdom of Italy in 1866.

100 Centesimi = 1 Lira
100 Soldi = 1 Florin (1858)

Unused examples without gum of Nos. 1-24 are worth approximately 20% of the values given, which are for stamps with original gum as defined in the catalogue introduction.

For similar designs in Kreuzers, see early Austria.

Coat of Arms — A1

15 CENTESIMI:
Type I- "5" is on a level with the "1." One heavy line around coat of arms center.
Type II- As type I, but "5" is a trifle sideways and is higher than the "1."
Type III- As type II, but two, thinner, lines around center.
45 CENTESIMI:
Type I- Lower part of "45" is lower than "Centes." One heavy line around coat of arms center. "45" varies in height and distance from "Centes."
Type II- One heavy line around coat of arms center. Lower part of "45" is on a level with lower part of "Centes."
Type III- As type II, but two, thinner, lines around center.

Wmk. K.K.H.M. in Sheet or Unwmkd.

1850   **Typo.**   **Imperf.**

Thick to Thin Paper

1	A1	5c buff	2,500.	125.00
a.		Printed on both sides	8,500.	225.00
b.		5c yellow	5,000.	575.00
c.		5c orange	2,750.	225.00
d.		5c lemon yellow		1,500.
3	A1	10c black	2,500.	125.00
a.		10c gray black	2,650.	125.00
4	A1	15c red, type III	1,200.	5.00
b.		15c red, type I	2,500.	20.00
c.		Ribbed paper, type II	—	750.00
d.		Ribbed paper, type III	12,500.	190.00
f.		15c red, type II	1,300.	29.00
5	A1	30c brown	3,100.	12.00
a.		Ribbed paper	4,900.	125.00
6	A1	45c blue, type III	10,500.	30.00
a.		45c blue, type I	11,000.	50.00
b.		Ribbed paper, type I	—	375.00
c.		45c blue, type II		90.00

1854

Machine-made Paper, Type III

3c	A1	10c black	6,000.	225.00
4g	A1	15c pale red	700.	3.50
5b	A1	30c brown	3,100.	10.00
6d	A1	45c blue	8,000.	42.50

See note about the paper of the 1850 issue of Austria. *The reprints are type III, in brighter colors.*

A2   A3

A4   A5

A6

Two Types of Each Value.

Type I- Loops of the bow at the back of the head broken.

Type II- Loops complete. Wreath projects further at top of head.

1858-62	**Embossed**		**Perf. 14½**	
7	A2	2s yel, type II	650.	110.00
a.		2s yellow, type I	3,900.	525.00
8	A3	3s black, type II	6,500.	140.00
a.		3s black, type I	2,600.	275.00
b.		Perf. 16, type I		1,000.
c.		Perf. 15x16 or 16x15, type I	4,600.	400.00
9	A3	3s grn, type II ('62)	500.	90.00
10	A4	5s red, type II	275.	5.00
a.		5s red, type I	875.	12.50
b.		Printed on both sides, type II		6,000.
11	A5	10s brown, type II	2,250.	10.00
a.		10s brown, type I	500.	42.50
12	A6	15s blue, type II	2,500.	24.00
a.		15s blue, type I	3,900.	90.00
b.		Printed on both sides, type II		15,000.

The reprints are of type II and are perforated 10½, 11, 11½, 12, 12½ and 13. There are also imperforate reprints of Nos. 7-9.

A7

A8

1861-62			**Perf. 14**	
13	A7	5s red	2,750.	3.50
14	A7	10s brown ('62)	4,150.	32.50

The reprints are perforated 9, 9½, 10½, 11, 12, 12½ and 13. There are also imperforate reprints of the 2 and 3s.

The 2, 3 and 15s of this type exist only as reprints.

1863

15	A8	2s yellow	160.00	150.00
16	A8	3s green	2,250.	90.00
17	A8	5s rose	2,750.	15.00
18	A8	10s blue	5,250.	75.00
19	A8	15s yellow brown	3,500.	175.00

1864-65		**Wmk. 91**	**Perf. 9½**	
20	A8	2s yellow ('65)	210.00	450.00
21	A8	3s green	32.50	22.50
22	A8	5s rose	4.75	3.50
23	A8	10s blue	30.00	11.00
24	A8	15s yellow brown	350.00	100.00

Nos. 15-24 reprints are perforated 10½ and 13. There are also imperforate reprints of the 2s and 3s.

NEWSPAPER TAX STAMPS

From 1853 to 1858 the Austrian Newspaper Tax Stamp 2kr green (No. PR1) was also used in Lombardy-Venetia, at the value of 10 centesimi.

NT1

Type I - The banderol of the left eagle touches the beak of the eagle.
Type II - The banderol does not touch the beak.

1858-59	**Unwmk. Typo.**		**Imperf.**	
PR1	NT1	1kr black, type I ('59)	3,250.	2,900.
PR2	NT1	2kr red, type II ('59)	325.00	55.00
a.		Watermark 91	400.00	100.00
PR3	NT1	4kr red, type I	100,000.	3,250.

The reprints are on a smooth toned paper and are all of type II.

AZERBAIJAN

‚a-zər-‚bī-'jän

(Azerbaidjan)

LOCATION — Southernmost part of Russia in Eastern Europe, bounded by Georgia, Dagestan, Caspian Sea, Iran and Armenia.
GOVT. — A Soviet Socialist Republic
AREA — 33,430 sq. mi.
POP. — 7,908,224 (1999 est)
CAPITAL — Baku

With Armenia and Georgia, Azerbaijan made up the Transcaucasian Federation of Soviet Republics.

Stamps of Azerbaijan were replaced in 1923 by those of Transcaucasian Federated Republics.

With the breakup of the Soviet Union on Dec. 26, 1991, Azerbaijan and ten former Soviet republics established the Commonwealth of Independent States.

100 Kopecks = 1 Ruble
100 Giapiks = 1 Manat (1992)

Catalogue values for unused stamps in this country are for Never Hinged items, beginning with Scott 350 in the regular postage section, and Scott C1 in the air post section.

National Republic

Standard Bearer — A1

Farmer at Sunset — A2

Baku — A3

Temple of Eternal Fires — A4

1919	**Unwmk.**	**Litho.**	**Imperf.**	
1	A1	10k multicolored	.20	.30
2	A1	20k multicolored	.20	.30
3	A2	40k green, yellow & blk	.20	.30
4	A2	60k red, yellow & blk	.25	.35
5	A2	1r blue, yellow & blk	.35	.50
6	A3	2r red, bister & blk	.35	.50
7	A3	5r blue, bister & blk	.45	.85
8	A3	10r olive grn, bis & blk	.65	.95
9	A4	25r blue, red & black	1.10	12.50
10	A4	50r ol grn, red & black	1.40	1.75
		Nos. 1-10 (10)	5.15	18.30

The two printings of Nos. 1-10 are distinguished by the grayish or thin white paper. Both have yellowish gum. White paper copies are worth five times the above values.
For surcharges see Nos. 57-64, 75-80.

Soviet Socialist Republic

Symbols of Labor — A5

Oil Well — A6

Bibi Eibatt Oil Field — A7

Khan's Palace, Baku — A8

Globe and Workers — A9

Maiden's Tower, Baku — A10

Goukasoff House — A11

Blacksmiths — A12

Hall of Judgment, Baku — A13

1922

15	A5	1r gray green	.20	.35
16	A6	2r olive black	.50	.50
17	A7	5r gray brown	.20	.35
18	A9	10r gray	.50	.65
19	A9	25r orange brown	.20	.40
20	A10	50r violet	.20	.40
21	A11	100r dull red	.35	.50
22	A12	150r blue	.35	.50
23	A9	250r violet & buff	.35	.50
24	A13	400r dark blue	.35	.50
25	A12	500r gray vio & blk	.35	.50
26	A13	1000r dk blue & rose	.35	.60
27	A8	2000r blue & black	.35	.50
28	A7	3000r brown & blue	.35	.50
a.		Tete beche pair	15.00	15.00
29	A11	5000r black, ol grn	.60	.75
		Nos. 15-29 (15)	5.20	7.50

Counterfeits exist of Nos. 1-29. They generally sell for more than genuine copies.
For overprints and surcharges see Nos. 32-41, 43, 45-55, 65-72, 300-304, 307-333.

Nos. 15, 17, 23, 28, 27 Handstamped from Metal Dies in a Numbering Machine

1922

32	A5	10,000r on 1r	9.25	9.25
33	A7	17,500r on 5r	11.00	11.50
34	A9	33,000r on 250r	5.75	5.75
35	A7	50,000r on 3000r	5.75	5.75
36	A8	66,000r on 2000r	12.50	11.50
		Nos. 32-36 (5)	44.25	43.75

Same Surcharges on Regular Issue and Semi-Postal Stamps of 1922

1922-23

36A	A7	500r on 5r	100.00	100.00
37	A6	1000r on 2r	20.00	15.00
38	A8	2000r on 10r	10.00	4.00
39	A8	5000r on 2000r	7.50	3.00
40	A11	15,000r on 5000r	12.00	10.00
41	A5	20,000r on 1r	15.00	9.00
42	SP1	25,000r on 500r	35.00	
43	A7	50,000r on 5r	30.00	12.50
44	SP2	50,000r on 1000r	26.00	
45	A11	50,000r on 5000r	5.00	4.50
45A	A8	60,000r on 2000r	30.00	14.00
46	A11	70,000r on 5000r	20.00	20.00
47	A6	100,000r on 2r	15.00	15.00
48	A8	200,000r on 10r	10.00	10.00
49	A9	200,000r on 25r	15.00	15.00
50	A7	300,000r on 3000r	20.00	5.00
51	A8	500,000r on 2000r	15.00	10.00

Revalued

52	A7	500r on #33	250.00	250.00
53	A11	15,000r on #46	250.00	250.00
54	A7	300,000r on #35	250.00	250.00
55	A8	500,000r on #36	250.00	250.00

The surcharged semi-postal stamps were used for regular postage.

Same Surcharges on Stamps of 1919

57	A1	25,000r on 10k	.70	1.00
58	A1	50,000r on 20k	.70	1.00
59	A2	75,000r on 40k	1.75	2.50
60	A2	100,000r on 60k	.70	.95
61	A2	200,000r on 1r	.70	.95
62	A3	300,000r on 2r	.95	1.10
63	A3	500,000r on 5r	1.00	1.10
64	A2	750,000r on 40k	3.50	2.75
		Nos. 57-64 (8)	10.00	11.35

Handstamped from Settings of Rubber Type in Black or Violet

100000 | 200.000

Nos. 65-66, 71-80 | Nos. 67-70

On Stamps of 1922

65	A6	100,000r on 2r	12.00	12.00
66	A8	200,000r on 10r	13.00	14.00
67	A8	200,000r on 10r (V)	17.50	15.00
68	A9	200,000r on 25r (V)	15.00	11.00
a.		Black surcharge	26.00	27.50
69	A7	300,000r on 3000r (V)	25.00	25.00

70	A8	500,000r on 2000r (V)	20.00	20.00
a.		Black surcharge	27.50	29.00
72	A11	1,500,000r on 5000r (V)	16.00	15.00
a.		Black surcharge	16.00	15.00

On Stamps of 1919

75	A1	50,000r on 20k	2.50	
76	A2	75,000r on 40k	2.50	
77	A2	100,000r on 60k	2.50	
78	A2	200,000r on 1r	2.50	.20
79	A3	300,000r on 2r	2.50	
80	A3	500,000r on 5r	2.50	
		Nos. 75-80 (6)	15.00	.20

Inverted and double surcharges of Nos. 32-80 sell for twice the normal price.
Counterfeits exist of Nos. 32-80.

Baku Province
Regular and Semi-Postal Stamps of 1922 Handstamped in Violet or Black
БАКИНСКОИ П. К.

The overprint reads "Bakinskoi P(ochtovoy) K(ontory)," meaning Baku Post Office.

		1922 Unwmk.	Imperf.
300	A5	1r gray green	42.50
301	A7	5r gray brown	42.50
302	A12	150r blue	42.50
303	A9	250r violet & buff	42.50
304	A13	400r dark blue	42.50
305	SP1	500r bl & pale bl	42.50
306	SP2	1000r brown & bis	42.50
307	A8	2000r blue & black	42.50
308	A7	3000r brown & blue	42.50
309	A11	5000r black, ol grn	42.50
		Nos. 300-309 (10)	425.00

Stamps of 1922 Handstamped in Violet
БАКИНСКАГО Г.-П.-Т.О.№1

Ovpt. reads: Baku Post, Telegraph Office No. 1.

1924

Overprint 24x2mm

312	A12	150r blue	50.00
313	A9	250r violet & buff	50.00
314	A13	400r dark blue	50.00
317	A8	2000r blue & black	50.00
318	A7	3000r brn & blue	50.00
319	A11	5000r black, ol grn	50.00

Overprint 30x3½mm

323	A12	150r blue	50.00
324	A9	250r violet & buff	50.00
325	A13	400r dark blue	50.00
328	A8	2000r blue & black	50.00
329	A7	3000r brn & blue	50.00
330	A11	5000r black, ol grn	50.00

Overprinted on Nos. 32-33, 35

331	A5	10,000r on 1r	50.00
332	A7	15,000r on 5r	50.00
333	A7	50,000r on 3000r	50.00
		Nos. 312-333 (15)	750.00

The overprinted semipostal stamps were used for regular postage.
A 24x2mm handstamp on #17, B1-B2, and 30x3½mm on #15, 17, B1-B2, was of private origin.

Catalogue values for unused stamps in this section, from this point to the end of the section, are for Never Hinged items.

Flag, Map — A20

Unwmk.
1992, Mar. 26 — Litho. — Perf. 14

350	A20	35k multicolored	1.25	1.25

Caspian Sea — A21

1992, May 7 — Perf. 12

351	A21	25g on 15k multi	.25	.25
a.		Booklet pane of 12	3.00	
		Complete booklet, #351a	3.00	
352	A21	35g on 15k multi	.30	.30
353	A21	50g on 15k multi	.40	.40
354	A21	1.50m on 15k multi	1.25	1.25
355	A21	2.50m on 15k multi	2.25	2.25
		Nos. 351-355 (5)	4.45	4.45

Nos. 351-355 are overprinted or sucharged on a National Park series prepared for the Soviet Union with one stamp for each republic. Not issued without surcharge. Value, $4.
For additional surcharges see Nos. 435, 501-504.

Iran-Azerbaijan Telecommunications — A21a

1992 — Photo. — Perf. 13x13½

355A	A21a	15g multicolored	1.60	1.60

See Iran No. 2544.
For surcharges see Nos. 403-406.

Horses A22

1993, Feb. 1 — Litho. — Perf. 13

356	A22	20g shown	.20	.20
357	A22	30g Kabarda	.20	.20
358	A22	50g Qarabair	.20	.20
359	A22	1m Don	.20	.20
360	A22	2.50m Yakut	.45	.45
361	A22	5m Orlov	.75	.75
362	A22	10m Diliboz	1.75	1.75
		Nos. 356-362 (7)	3.75	3.75

Perf. 12½
Souvenir Sheet

362A	A22	8m Qarabag	1.75	1.75

For overprints see Nos. 629-636.

Maiden's Tower — A23

Government Building — A24

1992-93 — Litho. — Perf. 12½x12

363	A23	10g blk & blue grn	.20	.20
365	A23	20g black & red	.20	.20
367	A23	50g black & blue grn	.20	.20
368	A23	50g black & yellow	.35	.35
370	A23	1m black & rose lilac	.20	.20
372	A23	1.50m black & blue	1.00	1.00
373	A23	2.50m black & yellow	.35	.35
374	A23	5m black & green	.65	.65
		Nos. 363-374 (8)	3.15	3.15

Issued: 10g, 20g, 1.50m, 5m, #367, Dec. 20; #368, 1m, 2.50m, 5m, June 20, 1993.
For surcharges see Nos. 550-557.
This is an expanding set. Numbers may change.

1993, Oct. 12 — Litho. — Perf. 12½

375	A24	25g yellow & black	.20	.20
376	A24	30g green & black	.20	.20
377	A24	50g blue & black	.25	.25
378	A24	1m red & black	.50	.50
		Nos. 375-378 (4)	1.15	1.15

For surcharges see No. 407-414.

Flowers — A25

1993, Aug. 12 — Litho. — Perf. 12½

379	A25	25g Tulipa eichleri	.20	.20
380	A25	50g Puschkinia scilloides	.20	.20
381	A25	1m Iris elegantissima	.20	.20
382	A25	1.50m Iris acutiloba	.25	.25
383	A25	5m Tulipa florenskyii	.80	.80
384	A25	10m Iris reticulata	1.50	1.50
		Nos. 379-384 (6)	3.15	3.15

Souvenir Sheet
Perf. 13

385	A25	10m Muscari elecostomum	1.50	1.50

No. 385 contains one 32x40mm stamp.

Fish A26

25g, Acipenser guldenstadti. 50g, Acipenser stellatus. 1m, Rutilus frisii kutum. 1.50m, Rutilus rutilus caspicus. 5m, Salmo trutta caspius. No. 391, Alosa kessleri. #392, Huso huso.

1993, Aug. 27 — Perf. 12½

386	A26	25g multicolored	.20	.20
387	A26	50g multicolored	.20	.20
388	A26	1m multicolored	.20	.20
389	A26	1.50m multicolored	.25	.25
390	A26	5m multicolored	.80	.80
391	A26	10m multicolored	1.50	1.50
		Nos. 386-391 (6)	3.15	3.15

Souvenir Sheet
Perf. 13

392	A26	10m multicolored	1.50	1.50

No. 392 contains one 40x32mm stamp.

Pres. Heydar A. Aliyev — A27

Design: No. 394, Map of Nakhichevan.

1993, Sept. 12 — Litho. — Perf. 12½x13

393	A27	25m multicolored	1.25	1.25
394	A27	25m multicolored	1.25	1.25
a.		Pair, #393-394	2.50	2.50
b.		Souv. sheet, #393-394, perf. 12	32.50	
c.		Souv. sheet, #393-394, perf. 12	5.50	

Name on map spelled "Naxcivan" on #394c. It is spelled "Haxcivan" on #394-394b. No. 394c issued Sept. 20, 1993.

Historic Buildings, Baku — A28

Style of tombs: 2m, Fortress, 13th-14th cent. 4m, Moorish gate, 15th cent. 8m, Oriental-style columns, 15th cent.

1994, Jan. 17   Litho.   Perf. 11
395	A28	2m red, silver & black	.20 .20
396	A28	4m green, silver & black	.35 .35
397	A28	8m blue, silver & black	.75 .75
		Nos. 395-397 (3)	1.30 1.30

A29

1994, Jan. 17   Perf. 12½
398	A29	5m Natl. Colors, Star, Crescent	.45 .45
399	A29	8m Natl. coat of arms	.75 .75

A30

1994, Jan. 17   Perf. 12½
400	A30	10m multi + label	.60 .60

Mohammed Fizuli (1494-1556), poet.

Mammed Amin Rasulzade (1884-1955), 1st President — A31

Jalil Mamedkulizade, Writer, 125th Birth Anniv. — A32

1994, May 21   Perf. 12½, 13 (#402)
401	A31	15m blk, yel & brown	1.00 1.00
402	A32	20m black, blue & gold	1.00 1.00

No. 402 printed se-tenant with label.

No. 355A Surcharged

No. 351 Surcharged

1994, Jan. 18   Photo.   Perf. 13x13½
403	A21a	2m on 15g	.20 .20
404	A21a	20m on 15g	.35 .35
405	A21a	25m on 15g	.45 .45
406	A21a	50m on 15g	1.00 1.00
		Nos. 403-406 (4)	2.00 2.00

5 m.

Nos. 375-378 Surcharged

1994, Feb. 22   Litho.   Perf. 12½
407	A24	5m on 1m #375	.20 .20
408	A24	10m on 30g #377	.20 .20
409	A24	15m on 30g #377	.20 .20
a.		Pair, #408-409	.30 .30
410	A24	20m on 50g #378	.25 .25
411	A24	25m on 1m #375	.30 .30
a.		Pair, #407, 411	.45 .45
412	A24	40m on 50g #378	.40 .40
a.		Pair, #410, 412	.65 .65
413	A24	50m on 25g #376	.45 .45
414	A24	100m on 25g #376	1.00 1.00
a.		Pair, #413-414	1.50 1.50
		Nos. 407-414 (8)	3.00 3.00

Baku Oil Fields — A33

Designs: 15m, Temple of Eternal Fires. 20m, Oil derricks. 25m, Early tanker. 50m, Ludwig Nobel, Robert Nobel, Petr Bilderling, Alfred Nobel.

1994, June 10   Photo.   Perf. 13
415	A33	15m multicolored	.30 .30
416	A33	20m multicolored	.40 .40
417	A33	25m multicolored	.45 .45
418	A33	50m multicolored	1.00 1.00
a.		Souvenir sheet of 1	1.00 1.00
		Nos. 415-418 (4)	2.15 2.15

See Turkmenistan Nos. 39-43.

Minerals — A34

Posthorn — A35

1994, June 15   Litho.   Perf. 13
419	A34	5m Laumontite	.30 .30
420	A34	10m Epidot calcite	.55 .55
421	A34	15m Andradite	.80 .80
422	A34	20m Amethyst	1.10 1.10
a.		Souvenir sheet, #420-423 + 2 labels, perf. 12	2.75 2.75
		Nos. 419-422 (4)	2.75 2.75

1994, June 28   Litho.   Perf. 12½
426	A35	5m black & red	.20 .20
427	A35	10m black & green	.20 .20
428	A35	20m black & blue	.20 .20
429	A35	25m black & yellow	.25 .25
431	A35	40m black & brown	.40 .40
		Nos. 426-431 (5)	1.25 1.25

For surcharges see Nos. 487-489A.

400 M.

No. 351 Surcharged

1994, Oct. 17   Unwmk.   Perf. 12
435	A21	400m on 25g multi	.85 .85

Souvenir Sheet

Pres. Heydar A. Aliyev — A36

Illustration reduced.

1994, Oct. 28   Litho.   Perf. 14
436	A36	150m multicolored	2.25 2.25

Ships of the Caspian Sea A37

Designs: a, Tugboat, "Captain Racebov." b, "Azerbaijan." c, Balt Ro Ro line, "Merkuri I." d, Tanker, "Tovuz." e, Tanker.

1994, Oct. 28
437	A37	50m Strip of 5, #a.-e.	1.75 1.75

Issued in sheets of 15 stamps. The background of the sheet shows a nautical chart, giving each stamp a different background.

1994 World Cup Soccer Championships, US — A38

Various soccer plays. Denominations: 5m, 10m, 20m, 25m, 30m, 50m, 80m.

1994, June 17   Litho.   Perf. 13
438-444	A38	Set of 7	3.50 3.50

Souvenir Sheet
445	A38	100m multicolored	1.50 1.50

No. 445 contains one 32x40mm stamp and is a continuous design.

Dinosaurs — A39

Designs: 5m, Coelophysis, segisaurus. 10m, Pentaceratops, tyrannosaurids. 20m, Segnosaurus, oviraptor. 25m, Albertosaurus, corythosaurus. 30m, Iguanodons. 50m, Stegosaurus, allosaurus. 80m, Tyrannosaurus, saurolophus. 100m, Phobetor.

1994, Sept. 15
446-452	A39	Set of 7	3.50 3.50

Souvenir Sheet
Perf. 12½
453	A39	100m multicolored	1.50 1.50

No. 453 contains one 40x32mm stamp and is a continuous design.

Lyrurus Mlokosiewickzi — A40

a, 50m, Female on nest. b, 80m, Female on mountain cliff. c, 100m, 2 males. d, 120m, Male.

1994, Dec. 15   Litho.   Perf. 12½
454	A40	Block of 4, #a.-d.	3.25 3.25

World Wildlife Fund.

Raptors A41

10m, Haliaeetus albicilla. 15m, Aguila heliaca. 20m, Aguila rapax. 25m, Gypaetus barbatus, vert. 50m, Falco cherrug, vert. 100m, Aguila chrysaetos.

1994, Nov. 15   Litho.   Perf. 13
458-462	A41	Set of 5	3.50 3.50

Souvenir Sheet
Perf. 12½
463	A41	100m multicolored	1.50 1.50

No. 463 contains one 40x32mm stamp and is a continuous design.

Cats A42

Designs: 10m, Felis libica, vert. 15m, Felis otocolobus, vert. 20m, Felis lyns. 25m, Felis pardus. 50m, Panthera tigrus. 100m, Panthera tigrus adult and cub, vert.

1994, Dec. 14   Perf. 13
464-468	A42	Set of 5	3.50 3.50

Souvenir Sheet
469	A42	100m multicolored	1.50 1.50

No. 469 contains one 32x40mm stamp and is a continuous design.
For overprints see Nos. 637-642.

Butterflies A43

Designs: 10m, Parnassius apollo. 25m, Zegris menestho. 50m, Manduca atropos. 60m, Pararge adrastoides.

1995, Jan. 23   Litho.   Perf. 14
470	A43	10m multicolored	.20 .20
471	A43	25m multicolored	.40 .40
472	A43	50m multicolored	.80 .80
473	A43	60m multicolored	1.00 1.00
a.		Souvenir sheet of 4, #470-473	2.50 2.50
		Nos. 470-473 (4)	2.40 2.40

Intl. Olympic Committee, Cent. — A44

Designs: No. 474, Pierre de Coubertin. No. 475, Discus. No. 476, Javelin.

1994, Dec. 15   Litho.   Perf. 12
474-476 A44 100m Set of 3   2.00 2.00

A45   A46

1994 Winter Olympic medalists, Lillehammer: 10m, Aleksei Urnamov, Russia, figure skating, 25, Nancy Kerrigan, US, figure skating. 40m Bonnie Blair, US, speed skating, horiz. 50m, Takanori Kano, Japan, ski jumping, horiz. 80m, Philip Laros, Canada, freestyle skiing. 100m, Four-man bobsled, Germany.

200m, Katja Seizinger, skiing, Germany, vert.

1995, Feb. 10   Litho.   Perf. 14
478-483 A45 Set of 6   2.00 2.00
Souvenir Sheet
484 A45 200m multicolored   1.75 1.75

1995, Feb. 21
Women in space - #485: a, Mary Kliv, US. b, Valentina Tereshkova, Russia. c, Tamara Cernigan, US. d, Wendy Lourens, US.
#486: a, Meg Jamison, US. b, Kitty Coleman, US. c, Ellen Sulman, US. d, M.I. Weber, US.

Miniature Sheets of 4
485-486 A46 100m each, #a.-d.   2.50
First manned moon landing, 25th anniv. (in 1994).

Nos. 426-428 Surcharged

1995   Litho.   Perf. 12½
487 A35 100m on 5m #426   .20 .20
488 A35 250m on 10m #427   .40 .40
488A A35 400m on 25m No. 429   .50 .50
489 A35 500m on 20m #428   .65 .65
489A A35 900m on 40m No. 431   1.10 1.10
Nos. 487-489A (5)   2.85 2.85
Issued: #488A, 7/7; #487-488, 489, 2/28.

Mushrooms — A47

Designs: 100m, Gymnopilus spectabilis. 250m, Fly agaris. 300m, Lepiota procera. 400m, Hygrophorus spectosus. 500m, Fly agaris, diff.

1995, Sept. 1   Litho.   Perf. 14
490-493 A47 Set of 4   3.50 3.50
Souvenir Sheet
494 A47 500m multicolored   1.50 1.50

Singapore '95 — A48

Orchids: 100m, Paphiopedilum argus, paphiopedilum barbatum. 250m, Maxillaria

picta. 300m, Laeliocattleya. 400m, Dendrobium nobile. 500m, Cattleya gloriette.

1995, Sept. 1
495-498 A48 Set of 4   3.50 3.50
Souvenir Sheet
499 A48 500m multicolored   1.50 1.50

UN, 50th Anniv. A49

Design: 250m, Azerbaijan Pres. Heydar A. Aliyev, UN Sec. Gen. Boutros Boutros-Ghali.

1995, Sept. 15
500 A49 250m multicolored   2.00 2.00

Nos. 352-355 Surcharged

1995   Litho.   Perf. 12
501 A21 200m on 2.50m #355   .30 .30
502 A21 600m on 35g #352   .85 .85
503 A21 800m on 50g #353   1.10 1.10
504 A21 1000m on 1.50m #354   1.40 1.40
Nos. 501-504 (4)   3.65 3.65

Uzeyir Hacibeyov (1885-1948) A50

400m, Oglu Iskenderov (1895-1965).

1995, June 30 Litho. Perf. 12x12½
505 A50 250m silver gray & black   .60 .60
506 A50 400m gold bister & brn   .90 .90

Balloons and Airships A51

100m, First hydrogen balloon, 1784. 150m, 1st motorized balloon, 1883. 250m, First elliptical balloon, 1784. 300m, 1st Scott Baldwin dirigible, 1904. 400m, US Marine balloon, 1917. 500m, Pedal-powered dirigible, 1909. 800m, 1st rigid dirigible designed by Hugo Eckener, 1924.

1995, July 20   Litho.   Perf. 13
507 A51 100m multi, vert.   .20 .20
508 A51 150m multi, vert.   .30 .30
509 A51 250m multi   .45 .45
510 A51 300m multi   .55 .55
511 A51 400m multi   .75 .75
512 A51 500m multi   .90 .90
Nos. 507-512 (6)   3.15 3.15
Souvenir Sheet
513 A51 800m multicolored   1.50 1.50

Marine Life A52

50m, Loligo vulgaris. 100m, Orchistoma pileus. 150m, Pegea confoederata. 250m, Polyorchis karafutoensis. 300m, Agalma okeni.
500m, Corolla spectabillis.

1995, June 2   Litho.   Perf. 13
514 A52 50m multi   .20 .20
515 A52 100m multi   .40 .40
516 A52 150m multi   .50 .50
517 A52 250m multi, vert.   .90 .90
518 A52 300m multi, vert.   1.10 1.10
Nos. 514-518 (5)   3.10 3.10
Souvenir Sheet
519 A52 500m multicolored   1.50 1.50

Turtles A53

Designs: 50m, Chelus fimbriatus. 100m, Caretta caretta. 150m, Geochelone pardalis. 250m, Geochelone elegans. 300m, Testudo hermanni.
500m, Macroclemys temmincki.

1995, June 12   Litho.   Perf. 13
520 A53 50m multicolored   .20 .20
521 A53 100m multicolored   .40 .40
522 A53 150m multicolored   .50 .50
523 A53 250m multicolored   .90 .90
524 A53 300m multicolored   1.10 1.10
Nos. 520-524 (5)   3.10 3.10
Souvenir Sheet
525 A53 500m multicolored   1.50 1.50

1998 World Cup Soccer Championships, France — A54

Various soccer plays.

1995, Sept. 30   Litho.   Perf. 12½
526 A54 100m orange & multi   .40 .40
527 A54 150m green & multi   .60 .60
528 A54 250m yel org & multi   .90 .90
529 A54 300m yellow & multi   1.10 1.10
530 A54 400m blue & multi   1.50 1.50
Nos. 526-530 (5)   4.50 4.50
Souvenir Sheet
Perf. 13
531 A54 600m multicolored   2.25 2.25

Domestic Cats — A55

1995, Oct. 30   Perf. 12½
532 A55 100m Persian   .20 .20
533 A55 150m Chartreux   .30 .30
534 A55 250m Somali   .45 .45
535 A55 300m Longhair Scottish fold   .55 .55
536 A55 400m Cumric   .75 .75
537 A55 500m Turkish angora   .90 .90
Nos. 532-537 (6)   3.15 3.15
Souvenir Sheet
538 A55 800m Birman   1.50 1.50
No. 538 contains one 32x40mm stamp.

Fauna and Flora — A56

Designs: 100m, Horse. 200m, Muscari elecostomum, vert. 250m, Huso huso. 300m, Aquila chrysaetos. 400m, Panthera tigris. 500m, Lyrurus miokosiewickzi, facing right. 1000m, Lyrurus miokosiewickzi, facing left.

1995, Nov. 30
539 A56 50m multicolored   .20 .20
540 A56 200m multicolored   .30 .30
541 A56 250m multicolored   .30 .30
542 A56 300m multicolored   .40 .40
543 A56 400m multicolored   .50 .50
544 A56 500m multicolored   .60 .60
545 A56 1000m multicolored   1.50 1.50
Nos. 539-545 (7)   3.80 3.80

John Lennon (1940-80) A57

1995, Dec. 8   Perf. 14½
546 A57 500m multicolored   .60 .60
Issued in sheet of 16 plus label.

Miniature Sheet

Locomotives — A58

Designs: No. 547a, 4-4-0, America. b, J3 Hudson, US. c, 2-8-2. d, 2-6-2, Germany. e, 2-8-2, Germany. f, 2-6-2, Italy. g, G-C5, Japan. h, 2-10-2 QJ, China. i, 0-10-0, China.
500m, Electric passenger train, vert.

1996, Feb. 1   Perf. 14
547 A58 100m Sheet of 9, #a.-i.   6.00 6.00
Souvenir Sheet
548 A58 500m multicolored   3.00 3.00

Dr. M. Topcubasov, Surgeon — A59

1996, Feb. 1
549 A59 300m multicolored   1.50 1.50

Nos. 363, 365, 367-368, 370, 372-374 Surcharged

1995, Jan. 4   Litho.   Perf. 12½x12
550 A23 250m on 10g #363   .40 .40
551 A23 250m on 20g #365   .40 .40
552 A23 250m on 50g #368   .40 .40
553 A23 250m on 1.50m #372   .40 .40
554 A23 500m on 50g #367   .75 .75
555 A23 500m on 1m #370   .75 .75
556 A23 500m on 2.50m #373   .75 .75
557 A23 500m on 5m #374   .75 .75
Nos. 550-557 (8)   4.60 4.60

1996 Olympic Games, Atlanta A60

1996, Apr. 9   Litho.   Perf. 14
568 A60 50m Carl Lewis   .20 .20
569 A60 100m Muhammed Ali   .40 .40
570 A60 150m Li Ning   .60 .60
571 A60 200m Said Aouita   .80 .80
572 A60 250m Olga Korbut   1.00 1.00

573 A60 300m Nadia Comaneci 1.25 1.25
574 A60 400m Greg Louganis 1.50 1.50
Nos. 568-574 (7) 5.75 5.75

Souvenir Sheet

575 A60 500m Nazim Hüsey-
nov, vert. 2.00 2.00

Husein
Aliyev
(1911-91),
Artist
A61

Paintings: 100m, Water bird, swamp. 200m,
Landscape.

1996, Apr. 16   Litho.   Perf. 14
576 A61 100m multicolored .75 .75
577 A61 200m multicolored 1.50 1.50
  a. Pair, #576-577 + label 2.25 2.25

No. 577a issued in sheets of 6 stamps.

Resid Behbudov (1915-89),
Singer — A62

1996, Apr. 22   Perf. 12½
578 A62 100m multicolored 1.25 1.25

A63

1996, Mar. 20
579 A63 250m multicolored 1.25 1.25

Novruz Bayrami, natl. holiday.

A64

1996, May 28   Litho.   Perf. 14
580 A64 250m multicolored 1.25 1.25

Independence, 5th anniv.

A65

1996, Apr. 22   Litho.   Perf. 12½
581 A65 100m multicolored 1.25 1.25

Yusif Memmedeliyev (1905-95), chemist.

A66

1996, June 7   Perf. 14
Jerusalem, 3000th Anniv.: a, 100m, Wailing
Wall. b, 250m, Inside cathedral. c, 300m,
Dome of the Rock.
  500m, Windmill.

582 A66 Sheet of 3, #a.-c. 3.50 3.50

Souvenir Sheet

583 A66 500m multicolored 3.00 3.00

For overprints see Nos. 643-644.

Dogs
A67

Designs: 50m, German shepherd. 100m,
Basset hound. 150m, Collie. 200m, Bull terrier. 300m, Boxer. 400m, Cocker spaniel.
  500m, Sharpei.

1996, June 18   Perf. 13
584-589 A67 Set of 6 5.00 5.00

Souvenir Sheet

590 A67 500m multicolored 2.50 2.50

Birds — A68

Designs: 50m, Tetraenura regia. 100m,
Coliuspasser macrourus. 150m, Oriolus
xanthornus. 200m, Oriolus oriolus. 300m,
Sturnus vulgaris. 400m, Serinus mozambicus.
  500m, Merops apiaster.

1996, June 19   Perf. 13
591-596 A68 Set of 6 5.00 5.00

Souvenir Sheet

597 A68 500m multicolored 2.50 2.50

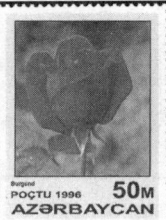

Roses — A69

Designs: 50m, Burgundy. 100m, Virgo.
150m, Rose gaujard. 200m, Luna. 300m, Lady
rose. 400m, Landora.
  500m, Lougsor, horiz.

1996, June 19
598-603 A69 Set of 6 5.00 5.00

Souvenir Sheet

604 A69 500m multicolored 2.50 2.50

A70   A71

1996, July 8   Litho.   Perf. 14
605 A70 500m multicolored 1.25 1.25

UNICEF, 50th anniv.

1996, July 22
Competing teams: 100m, Spain, Bulgaria.
150m, Romania, France. 200m, Czech
Republic, Germany. 250m, England, Israel.
300m, Croatia, Turkey. 400m, Italy, Russia.
  500m, Trophy cup.

606-611 A71 Set of 6 3.25 3.25

Souvenir Sheet

612 A71 500m multicolored 1.50 1.50

Euro '96, European Soccer Championships,
Great Britain.

Ships
A72

Ship, home country: 100m, Chinese junk.
150m, Danmark, Denmark. 200m, Nippon
Maru, Japan. 250m, Mircea, Romania. 300m,
Kruzenshtern, Russia. 400m, Ariadne,
Germany.
  500m, Tovarishch, Russia, vert.

1996, Aug. 26   Litho.   Perf. 14
613-618 A72 Set of 6 4.00 4.00

Souvenir Sheet

619 A72 500m multicolored 3.00 3.00

For overprints see Nos. 645-651.

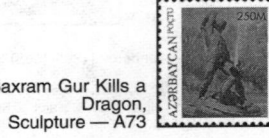

Baxram Gur Kills a
Dragon,
Sculpture — A73

1997, Mar. 6   Litho.   Perf. 13½x13
620 A73 250m black & yellow .45 .45
621 A73 400m black & vermilion .60 .60
622 A73 500m black & green .75 .75
623 A73 1000m black & purple 1.50 1.50
  Nos. 620-623 (4) 3.30 3.30

See No. 671.

Famous Personalities — A74

#624, Mamed-Kerim Ogli Aliyev (1897-
1962), politician. #625, Illyas Efendiyev (1914-
96), writer. #626, Fatali Xan-Xoyskiy (1875-
1920), politician. #627, Nariman Narimanov
(1870-1925), politician, writer.

1997, Mar. 25   Litho.   Perf. 14
Background Color
624 A74 250m tan 1.10 1.10
625 A74 250m gray blue 1.10 1.10
626 A74 250m pale red 1.10 1.10
627 A74 250m pale olive 1.10 1.10
  Nos. 624-627 (4) 4.40 4.40

Qobustan
Prehistoric
Art — A75

Rock carvings: a, Oxen. b, Large horned
animals. c, Six figures.

1997, May 19   Litho.   Perf. 14
628 A75 500m Sheet of 3, #a.-c. 4.25 4.25

For overprint see No. 674.

#356-362A, 464-469 Ovptd. in Red

1997, June 2   Litho.   Perf. 13
Denominations as Before
629-635 A22 Set of 7 8.00 8.00

Souvenir Sheet

636 A22 8m multicolored 5.00 5.00

Location of overprint varies. No. 636 is
ovptd. both on stamp and in sheet margin.

1997, June 2
Denominations as Before
637-641 A42 Set of 5 6.00 6.00

Souvenir Sheet

642 A42 100m multicolored 5.00 5.00

Location of overprint varies. No. 642 is
ovptd. both on stamp and in sheet margin.

Nos. 582-583, 613-619 Ovptd.

1997, June 2   Perf. 14
643 A66 Sheet of 3, #a.-c. 5.00 5.00

Souvenir Sheet

644 A66 500m multicolored 5.00 5.00

Size and location of overprint varies. Overprint appears both on stamp and in sheet
margin.

1997, June 2   Perf. 14
Denominations as Before
645-650 A72 Set of 6 5.00 5.00

Souvenir Sheet

651 A72 500m multicolored 5.00 5.00

Location of overprint varies. No. 651 is
ovptd. both on stamp and in sheet margin.

Grimm's
Fairy
Tales — A76

Bremen Musical: No. 652: a, Dog. b, Dancing horse, cat. c, Rooster.
500m, Animals looking through window at treaure chest, man.

1997, July 1   Perf. 13½x14
652 A76 250m Sheet of 3, #a.-c.   2.00 2.00
Souvenir Sheet
653 A76 500m multicolored   1.40 1.40

Caspian Seals
A77

Designs: a, Seal looking right. b, Mountain top, seal looking forward. c, Seal, seagull. d, Seal looking left. e, Seal looking forward. f, Small seal.
500m, Mother nursing pup.

1997, July 1
654 A77 250m Sheet of 6, #a.-f.   4.25 4.25
Souvenir Sheet
655 A77 500m multicolored   1.40 1.40

Traditional Musical Instruments — A77a

1997, Aug. 4   Litho.   Perf. 14
656 A77a 250m Qaval   .75 .75
657 A77a 250m Tanbur   .75 .75
658 A77a 500m Cenq   1.50 1.50
        Nos. 656-658 (3)   3.00 3.00

A78   A79

Azerbaijan Oil Industry: a, Early oil derricks, building. b, Off-shore oil drilling platform.

1997, Aug. 18   Perf. 14½
Souvenir Sheet
659 A78 500m Sheet of 2, #a.-b.   3.00 3.00

1997, Sept. 12   Perf. 14x13½
660 A79 250m Hagani Shirvany, poet   1.00 1.00

Issued in sheets of 4 + 5 labels.

Mosques
A80

#661, Ashaqi mechet Qovqar-agi, Shusha, 1874-75. #662, Momuna-Zatun, Naxcivan, 1187. #663, Taza-pir, Baku (1905-14).

1997, Sept. 18   Litho.   Perf. 14
661 A80 250m multicolored   .85 .85
662 A80 250m multicolored   .85 .85
663 A80 250m multicolored   .85 .85
        Nos. 661-663 (3)   2.55 2.55

H.C. Rasul Beyov (1917-1984), Communications Official — A81

1997, Oct. 6   Litho.   Perf. 14
664 A81 250m multicolored   2.00 2.00

1998 World Cup Soccer Championships, France — A82

Winning team photos: No. 665: a, Italy, 1938. b, Argentina, 1986. c, Uruguay, 1980. d, Brazil, 1994. e, England, 1966. f, Germany, 1990.
1500m, Tofiq Bahramov, "Golden Whistle" prize winner, 1966, vert.

1997, Oct. 15
665 A82 250m Sheet of 6, #a.-f.   5.00 5.00
Souvenir Sheet
666 A82 1500m multicolored   4.00 4.00

A83   A84

Figure skaters: No. 667: a, Katarina Witt, Germany. b, Elvis Stojko, Canada. c, Midori Ito, Japan. d, Silhouettes of various winter sports against natl. flag. e, Hand holding Olympic torch. f, Kristi Yamaguchi, US. g, John Curry, England. h, Lu Chen, China.
No. 668, Gordeyeva and Grinkov, Russia.

1997   Litho.   Perf. 14
667 A83 250m Sheet of 8, #a.-h.   2.50 2.50
Souvenir Sheet
668 A83 500m multicolored   .65 .65

1998 Winter Olympic Games, Nagano.

1998, Feb. 4   Perf. 13½
Diana, Princess of Wales (1961-97): No. 669, Wearing black turtleneck. No. 670, Wearing violet dress.
669 A84 400m multicolored   .50 .50
670 A84 400m multicolored   .50 .50

#669-670 were each issued in sheets of 6.

Sculpture Type of 1997
1998, Mar. 23   Litho.   Perf. 13½x13
671 A73 100m blk & bright pink   1.00 1.00

Hasan Aliyev, Ecologist, 90th Birth Anniv. A85

1998, Apr. 3   Perf. 14
672 A85 500m multicolored   1.00 1.00

Souvenir Sheet

Pres. Heydar Aliyev, 75th Birthday — A86

Illustration reduced.

1998, May 10   Perf. 13½
673 A86 500m multicolored   2.00 2.00

No. 628 Ovptd.

1998, May 13   Perf. 14
674 A75 500m Sheet of 3, #a.-c.   4.00 4.00
Additional inscription in sheet margin reads "ISRAEL 98 - WORLD STAMP EXHIBITION / TEL-AVIV 13-21 MAY 1998."

Musicians A87

#675, Gara Garayev. #676, Ashig Hasgar. #677, Sayid Mohammadhusein.

1998, June 7   Litho.   Perf. 14
675 A87 250m multicolored   .50 .50
676 A87 250m multicolored   .50 .50
677 A87 250m multicolored   .50 .50
        Nos. 675-677 (3)   1.50 1.50

Bul-Bul, Singer, Birth Cent. — A88

1998, July 7
678 A88 500m multicolored   1.00 1.00

Disney Characters at World Rapid Chess Championship — A89

250m, Minnie, Mickey.
No. 679: a, Minnie, Mickey. b, Goofy. c, Donald. d, Pluto. e, Minnie. f, Daisy. g, Goofy, Donald. h, Mickey.
#680, Donald, Mickey. #681, Minnie, Mickey.

1998   Perf. 13½
678A A89 250m multicolored   .50 .50
Perf. 13½x14
679 A89 500m Sheet of 8, #a.-h. 8.00 8.00
Souvenir Sheets
680-681 A89 4000m each   8.00 8.00
Issued: 250m, 12/28; others, 11/13.

New Year Holiday A90

Europa: 1000m, Woman rolling dough. 3000m, Men performing at holiday festival.

1998, Dec. 29   Litho.   Perf. 13x12½
682 A90 1000m multicolored   .50 .50
683 A90 3000m multicolored   1.50 1.50

Nos. 682-683 Ovptd.

1999, Apr. 27   Litho.   Perf. 13x12½
684 A90 1000m on #682   .50 .50
685 A90 3000m on #683   1.50 1.50

A91   A92

Europa: 1000m, Rose flamingo, Gizilagach Natl. Park. 3000m, Deer, Girkan Natl. Park.

1999, Apr. 28   Perf. 12½x12¾
686 A91 1000m multicolored   .50 .50
687 A91 3000m multicolored   1.50 1.50

1999, Aug. 3   Litho.   Perf. 11¼x11¾
Towers: 1000m, Dord Kundge, 14th cent. 3000m, Danravy, 13th cent.
688 A92 1000m black & blue   .45 .45
689 A92 3000m black & red   1.40 1.40

See Nos. 701-702, 717-718.

A93   A95

A94

Naxçivan Autonomous Republic, 75th anniv.: a, Pres. Heydar Aliyev, flag. b, Map of Naxçivan.

1999, Oct. 9   ***Perf. 12***
690 A93 1000m Pair, #a.-b.   .90 .90
  c. Souvenir sheet, pair, #a.-b.   .90 .90

1999, Oct. 20   ***Perf. 12½x12***
691 A94 250m multicolored   .20 .20
Gafar Gabbarli (1899-1934), playwright.

Souvenir Sheet
Perf. 14¾x14½ (a), 14½x13¾ (b-d)
1999, Oct. 30
80th anniv. of Azerbaijan postage stamps: a, #1. b, #3. c, #7. d, #10. b-d horiz.
692 A95 500m Sheet of 4, #a.-d.   1.00 1.00

A96   A98

A97

Baku Caravansary: No. 693, Inner courtyard. No. 694, Facade, camels.

1999, Dec. 29 **Litho.** ***Perf. 13***
693-694 A96 500m Set of 2   2.10 2.10

1999, Dec. 29   ***Perf. 12***
695 A97 1000m multi   1.10 1.10
Council of Europe, 50th anniv.

1999, Dec. 29
Azerbaijan flag, UPU emblem and: a, 250m, Dove. b, 3000m, Computer, satellite.
696 A98 Pair, #a.-b.   2.25 2.25
UPU, 125th anniv.

Souvenir Sheet

Epic Legend Kitabi Dede Gorgud, 1300th Anniv. A99

Designs: a, Beyrek fights with camel. b, Wounded Tural on horseback. c, Gazan Khan sleeping, horse.

1999, Dec. 29   ***Perf. 12¼x11¾***
697 A99 1000m Sheet of 3, #a.-c.   2.50 2.50

Europa, 2000
Common Design Type
2000, Feb. 7 **Litho.** ***Perf. 12¾x13***
698 CD17 1000m multi   1.00 1.00
699 CD17 3000m multi   3.00 3.00

Souvenir Sheet

Baku Transportation — A100

Designs: a, Phaeton. b, Horse-drawn tram. c, Electric tram. d, Trolleybus.
Illustration reduced.

2000, Feb. 15 **Litho.** ***Perf. 12½x12***
700 A100 500m Sheet of 4, #a-d 2.75 2.75

Tower Type of 1999
100m, Ramany Castle, 14th cent., horiz.
250m, Nardaran Castle, 14th cent., horiz.
2000, May 5 **Litho.** ***Perf. 11¾x11¼***
701 A92 100m black & orange   .25 .25
702 A92 250m black & green   .65 .65

World Meteorological Organization, 50th Anniv. — A101

2000, May 5   ***Perf. 12***
703 A101 1000m multi   1.00 1.00

Worldwide Fund for Nature — A102

Aythya nyroca: a, One in flight. b, Two on rocks, three in water. c, One on rocks, three in water. d, One in water, three in flight.
Illustration reduced.

2000, May 5   ***Perf. 12½x12***
704 A102 500m Block of 4, #a-d 2.00 2.00

2000 Summer Olympics, Sydney — A103

Designs: a, Wrestling. b, Weight lifting. c, Boxing. d, Running.
Illustration reduced.

2000, May 5   ***Perf. 12x12½***
705 A103 500m Block of 4, #a-d 2.00 2.00

Souvenir Sheet

Phasianus Colchicus — A104

Illustration reduced.

2000, June 21 **Litho.** ***Perf. 13½x13***
706 A104 2000m multi   3.25 3.25

Fruit A105

No. 707: a, Cydonia oblonga. b, Punica granatum. c, Persica L. d, Ficus carica.

2000, June 21   ***Perf. 13x13¼***
707   Sheet of 4   3.25 3.25
  a.-d. A105 500m Any single .80 .80

Rasul Rza (1911-81), Poet A106

2000, Sept. 28 **Litho.** ***Perf. 13x13¼***
708 A106 250m multi   .40 .40

Reptiles A107

No. 709: a, Vipera lebetina. b, Laserta saxcola. c, Vipera xanthina. d, Phrynocephalus mystaceus.
No. 710, Natrix tessellata, Phrynocephalus helioscopus, vert.

2000, Sept. 28   ***Perf. 13½x13***
709   Sheet of 4   3.25 3.25
  a.-d. A107 500m Any single .80 .80

Souvenir Sheet
Perf. 13x13½
710 A107 500m multi   .80 .80

Sabit Rahman (1910-70), Writer A108

2000, Nov. 17   ***Perf. 13x13¼***
711 A108 1000m multi   1.60 1.60

Intl. Year for the Culture of Peace — A109

2000, Nov. 17   ***Perf. 13¼x13***
712 A109 3000m multi   4.75 4.75

Souvenir Sheet

2000 Olympic Medalists — A110

No. 713: a, Namig Abdullaev, 54kg freestyle wrestling gold medalist. b, Zemfira Meftahaddinova, women's skeet shooting gold medalist. c, Vugar Alakbarov, middleweight boxing bronze medalist.

2001, Jan. 26 **Litho.** ***Perf. 13½x13¾***
713 A110 1000m Sheet of 3, #a-c 2.60 2.60
Dated 2000.

Europa — A111

Caspian Sea and: 1000m, Seal. 3000m, Sturgeon, crab, jellyfish.

              Perf. 13½x13¼
2001, Mar. 28   **Litho.**
714-715 A111 Set of 2   5.00 5.00
715a   Pane, 4 each #714-715 20.00
Stamps in the middle two columns of No. 715a are tete beche. No. 715a was sold with booklet cover, but unattached to it.

Admission of Azerbaijan to Council of Europe A112

2001, Apr. 25   ***Perf. 13¼x13½***
716 A112 1000m multi   1.10 1.10

Tower Type of 1999
Designs: 100m, Sheki, 18th cent., horiz. 250m, Sheki, 12th-13th cent., horiz.
2001, July 27   ***Perf. 14x13¾***
717 A92 100m black & lilac   .30 .30
718 A92 250m black & yellow   .80 .80

Souvenir Sheet

UN High Commissioner for Refugees, 50th Anniv. — A113

2001, Aug. 22   ***Perf. 13¼x13½***
719 A113 3000m multi   2.25 2.25

Souvenir Sheet

Nasir ad-Din at-Tusi (1201-74), Scientist — A114

2001, Sept. 7   **Perf. 13¼**
720 A114 3000m multi   2.25 2.25

SEMI-POSTAL STAMPS

Carrying Food to Sufferers SP1

1922   **Unwmk.**   **Imperf.**
B1 SP1 500r blue & pale blue   .40 .75

For overprint and surcharge see Nos. 42, 305.

Widow and Orphans — SP2

1922
B2 SP2 1000r brown & bister   .50 1.25
     Counterfeits exist.
For overprint and surcharge see #44, 306.

Russian stamps of 1909-18 were privately overprinted as above in red, blue or black by a group of Entente officers working with Russian soldiers returning from Persia. Azerbaijan was not occupied by the Allies. There is evidence that existing covers (some seemingly postmarked at Baku, dated Oct. 19, 1917, and at Tabriz, Russian Consulate, Apr. 25, 1917) are fakes.

AIR POST STAMP

Catalogue values for all stamps in this section are for never hinged items.

Eagle — AP1

1995, Oct. 16   **Litho.**   **Perf. 14**
C1 AP1 2200m multicolored   1.50 1.50

AZORES

ˈā-ˌzōrz

LOCATION — Group of islands in the North Atlantic Ocean, due west of Portugal
AREA — 922 sq. mi.
POP. — 253,935 (1930)
CAPITAL — Ponta Delgada

Azores stamps were supplanted by those of Portugal in 1931.
In 1934-45, #RA5-RA11, RAJ1-RAJ4, and many stamps between #155-223 were used for regular postage in Portugal.
The Azores were declared an autonomous, or self-governing, region of Portugal in 1976. See Portugal for issues since 1980.

1000 Reis = 1 Milreis
100 Centavos = 1 Escudo (1912)

Stamps of Portugal Overprinted in Black or Carmine

a

A second type of this overprint has a broad "O" and open "S."

1868   **Unwmk.**   **Imperf.**
1	A14	5r black	3,150.	1,600.
2	A14	10r yellow	13,000.	7,750.
3	A14	20r bister	175.00	125.00
4	A14	50r green	175.00	125.00
5	A14	80r orange	200.00	140.00
6	A14	100r lilac	200.00	140.00

The reprints are on thick chalky white wove paper, ungummed, and on thin ivory paper with shiny white gum. Value $20 each.

1868-70   **Perf. 12½**
5 REIS:
Type I - The "5" at the right is 1mm from end of label.
Type II - The "5" is 1½mm from end of label.
7	A14	5r black (C)	65.00	50.00
8	A14	10r yellow	87.50	50.00
a.		Inverted overprint	250.00	
9	A14	20r bister	65.00	45.00
10	A14	25r rose	65.00	8.00
a.		Inverted overprint		
11	A14	50r green	190.00	140.00
12	A14	80r orange	190.00	140.00
13	A14	100r lilac	190.00	140.00
14	A14	120r blue	160.00	90.00
15	A14	240r violet	575.00	300.00

The reprints are on thick chalky white paper ungummed, perf 13½, and on thin ivory paper with shiny white gum, perf 13½. Value $15 each.

1871-75   **Perf. 12½, 13½**
21	A15	5r black (C)	12.00	6.00
a.		Inverted overprint	45.00	
23	A15	10r yellow	26.00	12.50
a.		Inverted overprint		
b.		Double overprint	60.00	
24	A15	20r bister	25.00	12.50
25	A15	25r rose	15.00	3.00
a.		Inverted overprint		
b.		Double overprint	35.00	
c.		Perf. 14	150.00	55.00
d.		Dbl. impression of stamp		

26	A15	50r green	80.00	30.00
27	A15	80r orange	95.00	50.00
28	A15	100r lilac	80.00	40.00
a.		Perf. 14	160.00	100.00
29	A15	120r blue	150.00	82.50
a.		Inverted overprint		
30	A15	240r violet	800.00	500.00

Nos. 21-29 exist with overprint "b."

The reprints are of type "b." They are on thick chalky white paper ungummed, perf 13½, and also on thin white paper with shiny white gum and perforated 13½.

Overprinted in Black

b

1875-80
15 REIS:
Type I - The figures of value, 1 and 5, at the right in upper label are close together.
Type II - The figures of value at the right in upper label are spaced.
31	A15	10r blue green	150.00	100.00
32	A15	10r yellow green	100.00	60.00
33	A15	15r lilac brown	15.00	11.50
a.		Inverted overprint	125.00	
34	A15	50r blue	140.00	60.00
35	A15	150r blue	160.00	100.00
36	A15	150r yellow	190.00	125.00
37	A15	300r violet	80.00	50.00

The reprints have the same papers, gum and perforations as those of the preceding issue.

Black Overprint

1880   **Perf. 12½, 13½**
38	A17	25r gray	125.00	30.00
39	A18	25r red lilac	47.50	6.00
a.		25r gray	47.50	6.00
b.		Double overprint		

Overprinted in Carmine or Black

1881-82
40	A16	5r black (C)	21.00	7.50
41	A23	25r brown ('82)	45.00	5.00
a.		Double overprint		
42	A19	50r blue	150.00	30.00
		Nos. 40-42 (3)	216.00	42.50

Reprints of Nos. 38, 39, 39a, 40 and 42 have the same papers, gum and perforations as those of preceding issues.

Overprinted in Red or Black

c

1882-85   **Perf. 11½, 12½, 13½**
15, 20 REIS
Type I - The figures of value are some distance apart and close to the end of the label.
Type II - The figures are closer together and farther from the end of the label. On the 15 reis this is particularly apparent in the upper right figures.
43	A16	5r black (R)	25.00	10.00
44	A21	5r slate	15.00	3.00
a.		Double overprint		
c.		Inverted overprint		
45	A15	10r green	75.00	50.00
a.		Inverted overprint		
46	A22	10r green	25.00	10.00
a.		Double overprint		
47	A15	15r lilac brn	60.00	35.00
b.		Inverted overprint		
48	A15	20r bister	90.00	50.00
a.		Inverted overprint		
49	A15	20r carmine	110.00	80.00
a.		Double overprint	160.00	
50	A23	25r brown	19.00	3.00
51	A15	50r blue	775.00	550.00
52	A24	50r blue	24.00	3.00
a.		Double overprint		
53	A15	80r yellow	55.00	37.50
a.		80r orange	67.50	42.50
b.		Double overprint		
54	A15	100r lilac	100.00	62.50
55	A15	150r blue	900.00	600.00
56b	A15	150r yellow	55.00	37.50
57b	A15	300r violet	55.00	52.50

This set was issued on both ordinary and enamel surfaced papers. Nos. 51 and 55 exist only on ordinary paper, Nos. 44, 46, 49 and 53

---

only on surfaced paper, and the other values on both types of paper. Values for Nos. 56b and 57b are for copies printed on surfaced paper. Copies on ordinary paper are worth more.

For specialized listings of this issue and other early Azores stamps, see the Scott Classic Specialized Catalogue.

Reprints of the 1882-85 issues have the same papers, gum and perforations as those of preceding issues.

Red Overprint
58	A21	5r slate	20.00	4.00
59	A24a	500r black	160.00	110.00
60	A15	1000r black	110.00	82.50

1887   **Black Overprint**
61	A25	20r pink	25.00	10.00
a.		Inverted overprint	—	—
b.		Double overprint	—	—
62	A26	25r lilac rose	25.00	2.00
a.		Inverted overprint	—	—
b.		Double ovpt., one invtd.	—	—
63	A26	25r red violet	25.00	2.00
a.		Double overprint	—	—
64	A24a	500r red violet	125.00	75.00
a.		Perf. 13½	400.00	200.00
		Nos. 61-64 (4)	200.00	89.00

Nos. 58-64 inclusive have been reprinted on thin white paper with shiny white gum and perforated 13½.

Prince Henry the Navigator Issue

Portugal Nos. 97-109 Overprinted

1894, Mar. 4   **Perf. 14**
65	A46	5r orange yel	2.75	2.00
a.		Inverted overprint	45.00	45.00
66	A46	10r violet rose	2.75	2.00
a.		Double overprint	—	—
b.		Inverted overprint	—	—
67	A46	15r brown	3.25	2.50
68	A46	20r violet	3.50	2.50
a.		Double overprint	—	—
69	A47	25r green	4.00	3.00
a.		Double overprint	50.00	50.00
b.		Inverted overprint	50.00	50.00
70	A47	50r blue	10.00	4.25
71	A47	75r dp carmine	19.00	6.00
72	A47	80r yellow grn	21.00	6.00
73	A47	100r lt brn, pale buff	21.00	5.00
a.		Double overprint	—	—
74	A48	150r lt car, pale rose	30.00	10.00
75	A48	300r dk bl, sal buff	32.50	17.50
76	A48	500r brn vio, pale lil	60.00	25.00
77	A48	1000r gray blk, yelsh	110.00	45.00
a.		Double overprint	500.00	400.00
		Nos. 65-77 (13)	319.75	130.75

St. Anthony of Padua Issue

Portugal Nos. 132-146 Overprinted in Red or Black

1895, June 13   **Perf. 12**
78	A50	2½r black (R)	2.50	1.10
79	A51	5r brown yel	7.50	2.50
80	A51	10r red lilac	7.75	3.50
81	A51	15r red brown	11.50	5.00
82	A51	20r gray lilac	12.50	6.50
83	A51	25r green & vio	8.00	2.50
84	A52	50r blue & brn	25.00	12.00
85	A52	75r rose & brn	35.00	27.50
86	A52	80r lt grn & brn	40.00	30.00
87	A52	100r choc & blk	42.50	29.00
88	A53	150r vio rose & bis	80.00	80.00
89	A53	200r blue & bis	97.50	70.00
90	A53	300r slate & bis	110.00	82.50
91	A53	500r vio brn & grn	175.00	110.00
92	A53	1000r violet & grn	275.00	190.00
		Nos. 78-92 (15)	929.75	652.10

7th cent. of the birth of Saint Anthony of Padua.

Common Design Types pictured following the introduction.

Vasco da Gama Issue
Common Design Types

1898, Apr. 1   *Perf. 14, 15*

93	CD20	2½r blue green	2.75	1.00
94	CD21	5r red	2.75	1.10
95	CD22	10r gray lilac	5.00	2.00
96	CD23	25r yellow green	5.00	2.00
97	CD24	50r dark blue	8.00	6.00
98	CD25	75r violet brown	16.00	9.50
99	CD26	100r bister brown	20.00	9.50
100	CD27	150r bister	32.50	20.00
		Nos. 93-100 (8)	92.00	51.10

For overprints and surcharges see Nos. 141-148.

King Carlos — A28   King Manuel II — A29

1906   **Typo.**   *Perf. 11½x12*

101	A28	2½r gray	.35	.30
a.		Inverted overprint	25.00	25.00
102	A28	5r orange yel	.35	.30
a.		Inverted overprint	25.00	25.00
103	A28	10r yellow grn	.35	.30
104	A28	20r gray vio	.50	.45
105	A28	25r carmine	.35	.30
106	A28	50r ultra	4.50	3.00
107	A28	75r brown, *straw*	1.50	.80
108	A28	100r dk blue, *bl*	1.50	.90
109	A28	200r red lilac, *pnksh*	1.60	.90
110	A28	300r dk blue, *rose*	5.00	3.25
111	A28	500r black, *blue*	11.00	9.00
		Nos. 101-111 (11)	27.15	19.50

"Acores" and letters and figures in the corners are in red on the 2½, 10, 20, 75 and 500r and in black on the other values.

1910, Apr. 1   *Perf. 14x15*

112	A29	2½r violet	.40	.30
113	A29	5r black	.40	.35
114	A29	10r dk green	.70	.50
115	A29	15r lilac brn	.70	.50
116	A29	20r carmine	.90	.75
117	A29	25r violet brn	.40	.35
a.		Perf. 11½	2.40	1.10
118	A29	50r blue	2.40	1.00
119	A29	75r bister brn	2.40	1.00
120	A29	80r slate	2.40	1.00
121	A29	100r brown, *lt grn*	3.00	2.50
122	A29	200r green, *sal*	3.00	2.50
123	A29	300r black, *blue*	2.40	1.00
124	A29	500r olive & brown	7.00	6.00
125	A29	1000r blue & black	15.00	12.00
		Nos. 112-125 (14)	41.10	31.75

The errors of color 10r black, 15r dark green, 25r black and 50r carmine are considered to be proofs.

Stamps of 1910 Overprinted in Carmine or Green

1910

126	A29	2½r violet	.30	.25
a.		Inverted overprint	9.00	9.00
127	A29	5r black	.25	.25
a.		Inverted overprint	9.00	9.00
128	A29	10r dk green	.30	.25
a.		Inverted overprint	9.00	9.00
129	A29	15r lilac brn	1.25	.90
a.		Inverted overprint	9.00	9.00
130	A29	20r carmine (G)	1.25	.90
a.		Inverted overprint	16.00	16.00
b.		Double overprint	16.00	16.00
131	A29	25r violet brn	.25	.25
a.		Perf. 11½	50.00	42.50
132	A29	50r blue	1.00	.80
133	A29	75r bister brn	1.00	.70
a.		Double overprint	9.00	9.00
134	A29	80r slate	1.00	.70
135	A29	100r brown, *grn*	.90	.70
136	A29	200r green, *sal*	.90	.70
137	A29	300r black, *blue*	2.50	1.40
138	A29	500r olive & brn	3.25	1.75
139	A29	1000r blue & blk	7.50	4.00
		Nos. 126-139 (14)	21.65	13.55

Vasco da Gama Issue Overprinted or Surcharged in Black:

d

e

f

1911   *Perf. 14, 15*

141	CD20(d)	2½r bl grn	.50	.35
142	CD21(e)	15r on 5r red	.50	.35
143	CD23(e)	25r yellow grn	.50	.35
144	CD24(d)	50r dk blue	1.50	1.00
145	CD25(d)	75r violet brn	1.25	1.10
146	CD27(e)	80r on 150r bister	1.25	1.10
147	CD26(d)	100r yellow brn	1.40	1.20
a.		Double surcharge	21.00	21.00
148	CD22(f)	1000r on 10r lil	14.00	9.00
		Nos. 141-148 (8)	20.90	14.50

Postage Due Stamps of Portugal Overprinted or Surcharged in Black "ACORES" and

g

h

1911   *Perf. 12*

149	D1	5r black	1.00	.75
150	D1	10r magenta	2.00	.75
a.		"Acores" double	16.00	12.00
151	D1	20r orange	3.50	2.00
152	D1	200r brn, *buff*	16.00	14.00
a.		"Acores" inverted		
153	D1	300r on 50r slate	15.00	12.50
154	D1	500r on 100r car, *pink*	15.00	12.50
		Nos. 149-154 (6)	52.50	42.50

Ceres Issue of Portugal Overprinted in Black or Carmine

With Imprint

1912-31   *Perf. 12x11½, 15x14*

155	A64	¼c olive brown	.35	.25
a.		Inverted overprint	9.00	7.00
156	A64	½c black (C)	.35	.25
157	A64	1c deep green	.70	.50
a.		Inverted overprint	9.00	
158	A64	1c dp brn ('18)	.35	.25
a.		Inverted overprint	12.00	
159	A64	1½c choc ('13)	.70	.50
a.		Inverted overprint	9.00	
160	A64	1½c dp grn ('18)	.35	.25
a.		Inverted overprint	12.00	
161	A64	2c carmine	.50	.35
a.		Inverted overprint	14.00	
162	A64	2c orange ('18)	.35	.30
a.		Inverted overprint	18.00	
163	A64	2½c violet	.35	.30
164	A64	3c rose ('18)	.35	.30
165	A64	3c dull ultra ('25)	.25	.20

166	A64	3½c lt grn ('18)	.35	.30
167	A64	4c lt grn ('19)	.35	.30
168	A64	4c orange ('30)	.65	.45
169	A64	5c dp blue	.35	.30
170	A64	5c yel brn ('18)	.50	.30
171	A64	5c ol brn ('23)	.35	.30
172	A64	5c blk brn ('30)	2.40	1.75
173	A64	6c dull rose ('20)	.35	.30
174	A64	6c choc ('25)	.35	.30
175	A64	6c red brn ('31)	.25	.20
176	A64	7½c yel brn	4.75	2.00
177	A64	7½c dp bl ('18)	1.25	.75
178	A64	8c slate ('13)	.50	.40
179	A64	8c bl grn ('22)	.50	.30
180	A64	8c orange ('25)	.75	.55
181	A64	10c org brn	.85	.50
182	A64	12c bl gray ('20)	1.90	1.00
183	A64	12c dp grn ('22)	.65	.50
184	A64	13½c chlky bl ('20)	1.90	*1.00*
185	A64	14c dk bl, *yel* ('20)	1.75	*1.00*
186	A64	15c plum ('13)	12.00	3.50
187	A64	15c blk (R) ('23)	.35	.30
188	A64	16c brt ultra ('24)	.75	.50
189	A64	16c dp bl ('30)	2.00	*1.50*
190	A64	20c vio brn, *grn* ('13)	8.00	4.00
191	A64	20c choc ('20)	.60	.45
192	A64	20c dp grn ('23)	.80	.60
a.		Double overprint	15.00	15.00
193	A64	20c gray ('24)	.55	.35
194	A64	24c grnsh bl ('21)	.60	.30
195	A64	25c salmon ('23)	.40	.30
196	A64	30c brn, *pink* ('13)	45.00	30.00
197	A64	30c brn, *yel* ('19)	1.75	1.00
198	A64	30c gray brn ('21)	1.25	1.00
199	A64	32c dp grn ('25)	3.25	2.00
200	A64	36c red ('21)	.60	.30
201	A64	40c dp blue ('23)	.75	.50
202	A64	40c blk brn ('24)	1.40	.60
203	A64	40c brt grn ('30)	1.10	.50
204	A64	48c brt rose ('24)	2.50	1.00
205	A64	48c dull pink ('31)	6.25	6.00
206	A64	50c org, *sal* ('13)	5.25	1.00
207	A64	50c yellow ('23)	1.25	1.00
208	A64	50c bister ('30)	2.50	1.75
209	A64	50c red brn ('31)	2.00	1.50
210	A64	60c blue ('21)	1.00	.70
211	A64	64c pale ultra ('24)	3.00	1.00
212	A64	64c brown rose ('31)	45.00	45.00
213	A64	75c dull rose ('23)	6.00	4.00
214	A64	75c car rose ('30)	2.00	1.25
215	A64	80c dull rose ('21)	1.25	.65
216	A64	80c violet ('24)	1.25	.90
217	A64	80c dk grn ('31)	1.50	1.25
218	A64	90c chlky bl ('21)	2.00	.75
219	A64	96c dp rose ('26)	8.25	4.50
220	A64	1e dp grn, *bl*	4.75	1.50
221	A64	1e violet ('21)	2.00	.75
222	A64	1e gray vio ('24)	2.00	1.00
223	A64	1e brn lake ('30)	12.50	10.00
224	A64	1.10e yel brn ('21)	2.00	1.25
225	A64	1.20e yel grn ('21)	2.50	1.00
226	A64	1.20e buff ('24)	5.00	1.75
227	A64	1.25e dk blue ('30)	1.50	.75
228	A64	1.50e blk vio ('23)	3.00	1.75
229	A64	1.50e lilac ('25)	8.00	1.75
230	A64	1.60e dp bl ('25)	2.75	1.75
231	A64	2e slate grn ('21)	4.25	2.00
232	A64	2.40e apple grn ('26)	80.00	50.00
233	A64	3e lil pink ('26)	80.00	55.00
234	A64	3.20e gray grn ('25)	10.00	4.50
235	A64	5e emer ('24)	20.00	12.00
236	A64	10e pink ('24)	40.00	20.00
237	A64	20e pale turq ('25)	125.00	75.00
		Nos. 155-237 (83)	602.70	377.65

For same overprint on surcharged stamps see Nos. 300-306. For same design without imprint see Nos. 307-313.

Castello-Branco Issue

Stamps of Portugal, 1925, Overprinted in Black or Red

1925, Mar. 29   *Perf. 12½*

238	A73	2c orange	.20	.20
239	A73	3c green	.20	.20
240	A73	4c ultra (R)	.20	.20
241	A73	5c scarlet	.20	.20
242	A74	10c pale blue	.20	.20
243	A74	16c red orange	.25	.25
244	A75	25c car rose	.25	.25
245	A75	32c green	.45	.40
246	A75	40c grn & blk (R)	.45	.40
247	A74	48c red brn	1.00	.90
248	A76	50c blue green	1.00	.75
249	A76	64c orange brn	1.00	.75
250	A76	75c gray blk (R)	1.00	.75
251	A75	80c brown	1.00	.75
252	A75	96c car rose	1.10	.90
253	A77	1.50e dk bl, *bl* (R)	1.10	.90
254	A77	1.60e indigo (R)	1.25	1.00
255	A77	2e dk grn, *grn* (R)	1.90	1.50
256	A77	2.40e red, *org*	2.40	1.60
257	A77	3.20e blk, *grn* (R)	4.50	3.50
		Nos. 238-257 (20)	19.65	15.60

First Independence Issue

Stamps of Portugal, 1926, Overprinted in Red

1926, Aug. 13   *Perf. 14, 14½*
Center in Black

258	A79	2c orange	.25	.25
259	A80	3c ultra	.25	.25
260	A79	4c yellow grn	.25	.25
261	A80	5c black brn	.25	.25
262	A79	6c ocher	.25	.25
263	A80	15c dk green	.50	.50
264	A81	20c dull violet	.50	.50
265	A82	25c scarlet	.50	.50
266	A81	32c deep green	.50	.50
267	A82	40c yellow brn	.50	.50
268	A82	50c olive bis	1.25	1.10
269	A82	75c red brown	1.40	1.25
270	A83	1e black violet	1.75	1.50
271	A84	4.50e olive green	6.00	5.00
		Nos. 258-271 (14)	14.15	12.60

The use of these stamps instead of those of the regular issue was obligatory on Aug. 13th and 14th, Nov. 30th and Dec. 1st, 1926.

Second Independence Issue

Same Overprint on Stamps of Portugal, 1927, in Red

1927, Nov. 29
Center in Black

272	A86	2c lt brown	.25	.25
273	A87	3c ultra	.25	.25
274	A86	4c orange	.25	.25
275	A88	5c dk brown	.25	.25
276	A89	6c orange brn	.25	.25
277	A87	15c black brn	.25	.25
278	A86	25c gray	1.00	.90
279	A89	32c blue grn	1.00	.90
280	A90	40c yellow grn	.60	.50
281	A90	96c red	2.50	2.00
282	A88	1.60e myrtle grn	2.50	2.10
283	A91	4.50e bister	6.50	5.00
		Nos. 272-283 (12)	15.60	12.90

Third Independence Issue

Same Overprint on Stamps of Portugal, 1928, in Red

1928, Nov. 27
Center in Black

284	A93	2c lt blue	.25	.25
285	A94	3c lt green	.25	.25
286	A95	4c lake	.25	.25
287	A96	5c olive grn	.25	.25
288	A97	6c orange brn	.25	.25
289	A94	15c slate	.50	.40
290	A95	16c dk violet	.65	.50
291	A93	25c ultra	.65	.50
292	A97	32c dk green	.65	.55
293	A96	40c olive brn	.65	.55
294	A94	50c red orange	1.25	1.10
295	A94	80c lt gray	1.25	1.10
296	A97	96c carmine	2.25	1.75
297	A96	1e claret	2.25	1.75
298	A93	1.60e dk blue	2.25	1.75
299	A98	4.50e yellow	6.00	5.00
		Nos. 284-299 (16)	19.60	16.20

A31
A32

1929-30   *Perf. 12x11½, 15x14*

300	A31	4c on 25c pink ('30)	.60	.50
301	A31	4c on 60c dp blue	1.10	.80
302	A31	10c on 25c pink	1.10	.80
303	A31	12c on 25c pink	1.10	.80
304	A31	15c on 25c pink	1.10	.80
305	A31	20c on 25c pink	1.75	1.50
306	A31	40c on 1.10e yel brn	4.00	3.00
		Nos. 300-306 (7)	10.75	8.20

Black or Red Overprint

1930   *Perf. 14*
Without Imprint at Foot

307	A32	4c orange	.65	.40
308	A32	5c dp brown	2.10	1.75
309	A32	10c vermilion	1.10	.75

310	A32	15c black (R)	1.10	.75
311	A32	40c brt green	1.10	.60
312	A32	80c violet	11.00	8.75
313	A32	1.60e dk blue	3.00	1.10
		Nos. 307-313 (7)	20.05	14.10

POSTAGE DUE STAMPS

D2   D3

Portugal Nos. J7-J13 Overprinted in Black

1904   **Unwmk.**   **Perf. 12**

J1	D2	5r brown	.80	.55
J2	D2	10r orange	.90	.55
J3	D2	20r lilac	1.40	.90
J4	D2	30r gray green	1.40	.90
a.		Double overprint		
J5	D2	40r gray violet	2.40	1.25
J6	D2	50r carmine	4.00	2.25
J7	D2	100r dull blue	5.00	3.75
		Nos. J1-J7 (7)	15.90	10.15

Same Overprinted in Carmine or Green (Portugal Nos. J14-J20)

1911

J8	D2	5r brown	.50	.40
J9	D2	10r orange	.50	.40
J10	D2	20r lilac	.75	.50
J11	D2	30r gray green	.75	.50
J12	D2	40r gray violet	1.25	1.00
J13	D2	50r carmine (G)	6.00	5.00
J14	D2	100r dull blue	2.50	2.00
		Nos. J8-J14 (7)	12.25	9.80

Portugal Nos. J21-J27 Overprinted in Black

1918

J15	D3	½c brown	.45	.20
a.		Inverted overprint	4.00	
b.		Double overprint	4.00	
J16	D3	1c orange	.45	.20
a.		Inverted overprint	4.00	
b.		Double overprint	4.00	
J17	D3	2c red lilac	.45	.20
a.		Inverted overprint	4.00	
b.		Double overprint	4.00	
J18	D3	3c green	.45	.20
a.		Inverted overprint	4.00	
b.		Double overprint	4.00	
J19	D3	4c gray	.45	.20
a.		Inverted overprint	4.00	
b.		Double overprint	4.00	
J20	D3	5c rose	.45	.20
a.		Double overprint	4.00	
J21	D3	10c dark blue	.45	.20
		Nos. J15-J21 (7)	3.15	1.40

Stamps and Type of Portugal Postage Dues, 1921-27, Overprinted in Black

1922-24   **Perf. 11½x12**

J30	D3	½c gray green ('23)	.25	.20
J31	D3	1c gray green ('23)	.35	.25
J32	D3	2c gray green ('23)	.35	.25
J33	D3	3c gray green ('24)	.55	.25
J34	D3	8c gray green ('24)	.55	.25
J35	D3	10c gray green ('24)	.55	.25
J36	D3	12c gray green ('24)	.55	.25
J37	D3	16c gray green ('24)	.60	.25
J38	D3	20c gray green	.60	.25
J39	D3	24c gray green	.60	.25
J40	D3	32c gray green ('24)	.60	.25
J41	D3	36c gray green	.60	.30
J42	D3	40c gray green ('24)	.60	.30
J43	D3	48c gray green ('24)	.60	.30
J44	D3	50c gray green	.60	.30
J45	D3	60c gray green	.65	.30
J46	D3	72c gray green	.65	.30
J47	D3	80c gray green ('24)	3.25	2.00
J48	D3	1.20e gray green	3.25	2.00
		Nos. J30-J48 (19)	15.75	8.50

NEWSPAPER STAMPS

Newspaper Stamps of Portugal, Nos. P1, P1a, Overprinted Types b & c in Black or Red and:

N3

Perf. 11½, 12½ and 13½
1876-88   **Unwmk.**

P1	N1	2½r (a) olive	8.00	3.50
a.		Inverted overprint	—	
P2	N1	2½r (b) olive ('82)	3.00	1.00
a.		Inverted overprint	—	
b.		Double overprint	—	
P3	N3	2r black ('85)	3.00	2.00
a.		Inverted overprint	—	
b.		Double overprint, one inverted	—	
P4	N1	2½r (b) bister ('82)	3.00	1.00
a.		Double overprint	5.00	
P5	N3	2r black (R) ('88)	10.00	6.00
		Nos. P1-P5 (5)	27.00	13.50

Reprints of the newspaper stamps have the same papers, gum and perforations as reprints of the regular issues. Value $2 each.

PARCEL POST STAMPS

Portugal Nos. Q1-Q17 Overprinted Like Nos. 155-237 in Black or Red

1921-22   **Unwmk.**   **Perf. 12**

Q1	PP1	1c lilac brown	.35	.25
a.		Inverted overprint	4.00	
Q2	PP1	2c orange	.35	.25
a.		Inverted overprint	4.00	
Q3	PP1	5c light brown	.35	.25
a.		Inverted overprint	5.00	
b.		Double overprint	5.00	
Q4	PP1	10c red brown	.45	.25
a.		Inverted overprint	5.00	
b.		Double overprint	5.00	
Q5	PP1	20c gray blue	.45	.25
a.		Inverted overprint	5.00	
b.		Double overprint	5.00	
Q6	PP1	40c carmine	.45	.25
a.		Double overprint	6.50	
Q7	PP1	50c black (R)	.65	.50
Q8	PP1	60c dark blue (R)	.65	.50
Q9	PP1	70c gray brown	2.10	1.10
a.		Double overprint	5.00	
Q10	PP1	80c ultra	2.10	1.10
Q11	PP1	90c light violet	2.10	1.10
Q12	PP1	1e light green	2.10	1.10
Q13	PP1	2e pale lilac	3.50	2.00
Q14	PP1	3e olive	6.25	2.10
Q15	PP1	4e ultra	7.50	2.10
Q16	PP1	5e gray	7.50	4.00
Q17	PP1	10e chocolate	24.00	11.50
		Nos. Q1-Q17 (17)	60.85	28.60

POSTAL TAX STAMPS

These stamps represent a special fee for the delivery of postal matter on certain days in the year. The money derived from their sale is applied to works of public charity.

Nos. 114 and 157 Overprinted in Carmine

1911-13   **Unwmk.**   **Perf. 14x15**

RA1	A29	10r dark green	1.00	.55

The 20r of this type was for use on telegrams.

Perf. 15x14

RA2	A30	1c deep green	3.00	1.90

The 2c of this type was for use on telegrams.

Postal Tax Stamp of Portugal, No. RA4, Overprinted Like Nos. 155-237 in Black

1915   **Perf. 12**

RA3	PT2	1c carmine	.40	.25

The 2c of this type was for use on telegrams.

Postal Tax Stamp of 1915 Surcharged

1924

RA4	PT1	15c on 1c rose	.70	.45

Comrades of the Great War Issue

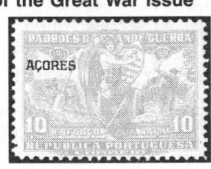

Postal Tax Stamps of Portugal, 1925, Overprinted

1925, Apr. 8   **Perf. 11**

RA5	PT3	10c brown	.75	.55
RA6	PT3	10c green	.75	.55
RA7	PT3	10c rose	.75	.55
RA8	PT3	10c ultra	.75	.55
		Nos. RA5-RA8 (4)	3.00	2.20

The use of Nos. RA5-RA11 in addition to the regular postage was compulsory on certain days. If the tax represented by these stamps was not prepaid, it was collected by means of Postal Tax Due Stamps.

Pombal Issue
Common Design Types

1925   **Perf. 12½**

RA9	CD28	20c dp grn & blk	.75	.55
RA10	CD29	20c dp grn & blk	.75	.55
RA11	CD30	20c dp grn & blk	.75	.55
		Nos. RA9-RA11 (3)	2.25	1.65

POSTAL TAX DUE STAMPS

Postal Tax Due Stamp of Portugal Overprinted like Nos. RA5-RA8
1925, Apr. 8   **Unwmk.**   **Perf. 11x11½**

RAJ1	PTD1	20c brown orange	.75	.45

See note after No. RA8.

Pombal Issue
Common Design Types

1925, May 8   **Perf. 12½**

RAJ2	CD28	40c dp grn & blk	.75	.55
RAJ3	CD29	40c dp grn & blk	.75	.55
RAJ4	CD30	40c dp grn & blk	.75	.55
		Nos. RAJ2-RAJ4 (3)	2.25	1.65

See note after No. RA8.

BAHAMAS
bə-'hä-məs

LOCATION — A group of about 700 islands and 2,000 rocks in the West Indies, off the coast of Florida. Only 30 islands are inhabited.
GOVT. — Independent state in British Commonwealth
AREA — 5,382 sq. mi.
POP. — 283,705 (1999 est.)
CAPITAL — Nassau

The principal island, on which the capital is located, is New Providence. The Bahamas obtained internal self-government on January 7, 1964, and independence on July 10, 1973.

12 Pence = 1 Shilling
20 Shillings = 1 Pound
100 Cents = 1 Dollar (1966)

Catalogue values for unused stamps in this country are for Never Hinged items, beginning with Scott 130, and Scott C1 in the air post section.

Values for unused stamps are for examples with original gum as defined in the catalogue introduction. Very fine examples of Nos. 2-26 will have perforations touching the design or frameline on at least one side due to the narrow spacing of the stamps on the plates. Stamps with perfs clear of the design or framelines on all four sides are extremely scarce and will command higher prices.

Pen cancellations usually indicate revenue use. Such stamps sell for much less than postally canceled copies. Beware of stamps with revenue or pen cancellations removed and forged postal cancellations added.

Queen Victoria
A1   A2

1859-60		**Unwmk. Engr.**		**Imperf.**
1	A1	1p dull lake ('60)	50.	1,400.
a.		1p reddish lake	4,500.	2,000.
b.		1p brownish lake	4,500.	2,250.

Most unused copies of #1 are remainders, and false cancellations are plentiful. #1a and 1b are on thicker paper than #1.

1861		**Rough Perf. 14 to 16**		
2	A1	1p lake	925.	275.
a.		Clean-cut perf. ('60)	3,250.	750.
3	A2	4p dull rose	1,600.	500.
a.		Imperf. between, pair	20,000.	
4	A2	6p gray lilac	3,150.	575.
a.		Pale lilac	3,250.	575.

1862		**Engr.**		**Perf. 11½, 12**
5	A1	1p lake	1,100.	175.
a.		Pair, imperf. between	4,750.	
6	A2	4p dull rose	3,000.	375.
7	A2	6p gray violet	9,000.	475.

No. 5a was not issued in the Bahamas. It is unique and faulty.
Nos. 5-7 exist with perf. 11½ or 12 compound with 11.

Perf. 13				
8	A1	1p brown lake	650.	125.
a.		1p carmine lake	750.	150.
9	A2	4p rose	2,750.	400.
10	A2	6p gray violet	3,250.	425.
a.		6p dull violet	3,250.	500.

Queen Victoria — A3

1863-65		**Typo. Wmk. 1**		**Perf. 12½**
11	A1	1p lake	85.00	70.00
a.		1p brown lake	95.00	70.00
b.		1p rose lake	95.00	70.00
12	A1	1p vermilion	65.00	50.00
a.		1p rose red	70.00	55.00
b.		1p red	70.00	55.00
13	A2	4p rose	375.00	70.00
a.		4p rose lake	400.00	90.00
b.		4p bright rose	250.00	70.00
14	A2	6p dk violet	160.00	80.00
a.		6p violet	250.00	100.00
b.		6p rose lilac	5,250.	3,500.
c.		6p lilac	325.00	75.00
15	A3	1sh green ('65)	2,500.	300.00

For surcharge see No. 26.

1863-81				**Perf. 14**
16	A1	1p vermilion	45.00	20.00
17	A1	1p car lake (anil.)	1,500.	
18	A2	4p rose	375.00	50.00
a.		4p deep rose ('76)	400.00	50.00
b.		4p dull rose	1,650.	50.00
19	A3	1sh green ('80)	7.50	7.50
a.		1shp dark green	160.00	45.00

Some copies of No. 16 show a light aniline appearance and care should be taken not to confuse these with No. 17. All known used copies of No. 17 bear fiscal cancels.

1882-98				**Wmk. 2**
20	A1	1p vermilion	350.00	65.00
21	A2	4p rose	800.00	65.00
22	A3	1sh green	30.00	17.50
23	A3	1sh blue grn ('98)	35.00	22.50
		Perf. 12		
24	A1	1p vermilion	40.00	22.50
25	A2	4p rose	500.00	60.00

No. 14a Surcharged in Black

1883		**Wmk. 1**		**Perf. 12½**
26	A2	4p on 6p violet	575.	425.
a.		Inverted surcharge	12,500.	7,250.

The surcharge, being handstamped, is found in various positions. Counterfeit overprints exist.

Queen Victoria — A5   Queen's Staircase — A6

1884-90		**Typo. Wmk. 2**		**Perf. 14**
27	A5	1p carmine rose	6.00	2.00
a.		1p pale rose	50.00	10.00
b.		1p car (aniline)	3.00	6.00
28	A5	2½p ultra	8.25	5.00
a.		2½p dull blue	55.00	15.00
29	A5	4p yellow	8.25	5.00
30	A5	6p violet	5.00	25.00
31	A5	5sh olive green	60.00	70.00
32	A5	£1 brown	325.00	275.00
		Revenue cancellation		55.00
		Nos. 27-32 (6)	412.50	379.00

Cleaned fiscally used copies of No. 32 are often found with postmarks of small post offices added. Dangerous forged postmarks exist, especially dated "AU 29 94."

1901-03		**Engr.**		**Wmk. 1**
33	A6	1p carmine & blk	6.00	4.00
34	A6	5p org & blk ('03)	10.00	42.50
35	A6	2sh ultra & blk ('03)	24.00	45.00
36	A6	3sh green & blk ('03)	27.50	55.00
		Nos. 33-36 (4)	67.50	146.50

See Nos. 48, 58-62, 71, 78, 81-82.

Edward VII   George V
A7   A8

1902		**Wmk. 2**		**Typo.**
37	A7	1p carmine rose	2.25	2.25
38	A7	2½p ultra	7.00	1.75
39	A7	4p orange	13.50	45.00
40	A7	6p bister brn	6.00	15.00
41	A7	1sh gray blk & car	17.50	42.50
42	A7	5sh violet & ultra	52.50	70.00
43	A7	£1 green & blk	325.00	300.00
		Nos. 37-43 (7)	423.75	476.50

Beware of forged postmarks, especially dated "2 MAR 10."

1906-11		**Wmk. 3**		
44	A7	½p green	4.50	2.00
45	A7	1p car rose	22.50	1.75
46	A7	2½p ultra ('07)	22.50	22.50
47	A7	6p bister brn ('11)	35.00	50.00
		Nos. 44-47 (4)	84.50	76.25

1911-16				**Engr.**
48	A6	1p red & gray blk ('16)	4.00	2.40
a.		1p carmine & black	13.50	3.00

For overprints see Nos. B1-B2.

1912-19				**Typo.**
49	A8	½p green	.85	6.00
50	A8	1p car rose (ani-line)	2.75	.45
50A	A8	2p gray ('19)	2.10	2.75
51	A8	2½p ultra	4.25	16.00
52	A8	4p orange	2.50	11.00
53	A8	6p bister brn	1.75	3.75
		Chalky Paper		
54	A8	1sh black & car	2.75	8.00
55	A8	5sh violet & ultra	35.00	57.50
56	A8	£1 dull grn & blk	225.00	260.00
		Nos. 49-56 (9)	276.95	365.45

1917-19				**Engr.**
58	A6	3p reddish pur, buff	4.50	4.25
59	A6	3p brown & blk ('19)	2.50	5.00
60	A6	5p violet & blk	3.25	9.00
61	A6	2sh ultra & black	25.00	42.50
62	A6	3sh green & black	45.00	47.50
		Nos. 58-62 (5)	80.25	108.25

Peace Commemorative Issue

King George V and Seal of Bahamas — A9

1920, Mar. 1		**Engr.**		**Perf. 14**
65	A9	½p gray green	.90	4.50
66	A9	1p deep red	2.75	1.10
67	A9	2p gray	3.25	6.75
68	A9	3p brown	3.25	9.00
69	A9	1sh dark green	22.50	32.50
		Nos. 65-69 (5)	32.65	53.85

Types of 1901-12
Typo., Engr. (A6)

1921-34				**Wmk. 4**
70	A8	½p green ('24)	.45	.40
71	A6	1p car & black	.90	1.00
72	A8	1p car rose	1.00	.20
73	A8	1½p fawn ('34)	2.25	1.40
74	A8	2p gray ('27)	1.00	2.75
75	A8	2½p ultra ('22)	.80	2.75
76	A8	3p violet, yel ('31)	5.50	15.00
77	A8	4p yellow ('24)	1.60	5.25
78	A6	5p red vio & gray blk ('29)	6.50	35.00
79	A8	6p bister brn ('22)	1.40	3.00
80	A8	1sh blk & red ('26)	3.25	7.25
81	A6	2sh ultra & blk ('22)	30.00	50.00
82	A6	3sh grn & blk ('24)	50.00	65.00
83	A8	5sh vio & ultra ('24)	30.00	55.00
84	A8	£1 grn & blk ('26)	160.00	275.00
		Nos. 70-84 (15)	294.65	519.00

The 3p, 1sh, 5sh and £1 are on chalky paper.

Seal of Bahamas — A10

1930, Jan. 2		**Engr.**		**Perf. 12**
85	A10	1p red & black	1.90	2.50
86	A10	3p dp brown & blk	3.50	13.50
87	A10	5p dk vio & blk	3.50	13.50

88	A10	2sh ultra & black	20.00	40.00
89	A10	3sh dp green & blk	37.50	70.00
			66.40	139.50

The dates on the stamps commemorate important events in the history of the colony. The 1st British occupation was in 1629. The Bahamas were ceded to Great Britain in 1729 and a treaty of peace was signed by that country, France and Spain.

Type of 1930 Issue
Without Dates at Top

1931-46				
90	A10	2sh ultra & black ('43)	5.75	2.50
a.		2sh ultra & slate purple	19.00	22.50
91	A10	3sh dp green & blk ('46)	5.50	2.25
a.		3sh deep grn & slate purple	27.50	22.50

Nos. 90a-91a are on thick paper with yellowish gum, Nos. 90-91 are on thin white paper with colorless gum.
For overprints see Nos. 126-127.

Common Design Types pictured following the introduction.

Silver Jubilee Issue
Common Design Type

1935, May 6				**Perf. 13½x14**
92	CD301	1½p car & blue	1.00	2.00
93	CD301	2½p blue & brn	4.50	7.00
94	CD301	6p ol grn & lt bl	6.25	10.00
95	CD301	1sh brt vio & ind	6.50	8.25
		Nos. 92-95 (4)	18.25	27.25
		Set, never hinged	30.00	

Flamingos in Flight
A11

1935, May 22				**Perf. 12½**
96	A11	8p car & ultra	5.50	3.25
		Never hinged	9.00	

Coronation Issue
Common Design Type

1937, May 12				**Perf. 13½x14**
97	CD302	½p dp green	.20	.20
98	CD302	1½p brown	.30	.65
99	CD302	2½p brt ultra	.65	.70
		Nos. 97-99 (3)	1.15	1.55
		Set, never hinged	1.75	

George VI — A12

Sea Gardens, Nassau
A13

Fort Charlotte
A14

Flamingos in Flight
A15

1938-46		**Typo. Wmk. 4**		**Perf. 14**
100	A12	½p green	.20	.80
101	A12	1p carmine	4.00	4.50
101A	A12	1p gray ('41)	.25	.55
102	A12	1½p red brown	.60	1.00
103	A12	2p gray	12.00	5.75
103B	A12	2p carmine ('41)	.35	.55
c.		"TWO PENCE" double		4,500.
104	A12	2½p ultra	1.90	1.90
104A	A12	2½p lt violet ('43)	.60	.65
b.		"2½ PENNY" double	2,000.	
		Never hinged	2,500.	

105	A12	3p lt violet	7.50	8.00
105A	A12	3p ultra ('43)	.40	.90

Engr.

Perf. 12½

106	A13	4p red org & bl	.60	.80
107	A14	6p blue & ol grn	.45	.80
108	A15	8p car & blk	2.75	1.90

Typo.

Perf. 14

109	A12	10p yel org ('46)	1.00	.55
110	A12	1sh blk & brt red	4.00	.60
112	A12	5sh pur & ultra	11.00	11.00
113	A12	£1 bl grn & blk	37.50	42.50
		Nos. 100-113 (17)	85.10	82.75
		Set, never hinged	143.65	

#110-113 printed on chalky & ordinary paper.
See the Classic Specialized Catalogue for listings of varieties.

See Nos. 154-156. For overprints see Nos. 116-125, 128-129.

No. 104 Surcharged in Black

3d.

1940, Nov. 28   **Perf. 14**

115	A12	3p on 2½p ultra	.45	.55
		Never hinged		.80

Stamps of 1931-42 Overprinted in Black

1942, Oct. 12   **Perf. 14, 12½, 12**

116	A12	½p green	.20	.55
117	A12	1p gray	.20	.55
118	A12	1½p red brown	.20	.55
119	A12	2p carmine	.20	.60
120	A12	2½p ultra	.20	.60
121	A12	3p ultra	.20	.60
122	A13	4p red org & blue	.25	.80
123	A14	6p blue & ol grn	.35	1.60
124	A15	8p car & ultra	.50	.65
125	A12	1sh black & car	2.25	3.50
126	A10	2sh dk ultra & blk	5.50	9.50
127	A10	3sh dp grn & sl pur	3.00	8.00
128	A12	5sh lilac & ultra	8.50	12.50
129	A12	£1 green & black	20.00	25.00
		Nos. 116-129 (14)	41.55	65.00
		Set, never hinged	64.50	

450th anniv. of the discovery of America by Columbus.
Nos. 125, 128-129 printed on chalky and ordinary paper.
Two printings of the basic stamps were overprinted, the first with dark gum, the second with white gum.
For shades, see the *Scott Classic Catalogue.*

Catalogue values for unused stamps in this section, from this point to the end of the section, are for Never Hinged items.

Peace Issue
Common Design Type

Perf. 13½x14

1946, Nov. 11   **Engr.**   **Wmk. 4**

130	CD303	1½p brown	.20	.35
131	CD303	3p deep blue	.20	.35

Infant Welfare Clinic A16

Designs: 1p, Modern agriculture. 1½p, Sisal. 2p, Native straw work. 2½p, Modern dairying. 3p, Fishing fleet. 4p, Out island settlement. 6p, Tuna fishing. 8p, Paradise Beach. 10p, Modern hotel. 1sh, Yacht racing. 2sh, Water skiing. 3sh, Shipbuilding. 5sh, Modern transportation. 10sh, Modern salt production. £1, Parliament Building.

1948, Oct. 11   **Unwmk.**   **Perf. 12**

132	A16	½p orange	.30	.80
133	A16	1p olive green	.30	.30
134	A16	1½p olive bister	.35	.70

135	A16	2p vermilion	.30	.35
136	A16	2½p red brown	.60	.65
137	A16	3p brt ultra	.75	.75
138	A16	4p gray black	.55	.75
139	A16	6p emerald	1.60	.75
140	A16	8p violet	.65	.75
141	A16	10p rose car	.70	.65
142	A16	1sh olive brn	1.25	1.00
143	A16	2sh claret	5.25	7.50
144	A16	3sh brt blue	7.00	7.50
145	A16	5sh purple	7.50	5.50
146	A16	10sh dk gray	8.75	8.00
147	A16	£1 red orange	10.00	12.50
		Nos. 132-147 (16)	45.85	48.45

300th anniv., in 1947, of the settlement of the colony.

Silver Wedding Issue
Common Design Type

Perf. 14x14½

1948, Dec. 1   **Wmk. 4**   **Photo.**

148	CD304	1½p red brown	.20	.20

Engr.; Name Typo.

Perf. 11½x11

149	CD305	£1 gray green	30.00	35.00

UPU Issue
Common Design Types

Engr.; Name Typo. on #151 & 152

1949, Oct. 10   **Perf. 13½, 11x11½**

150	CD306	2½p violet	.30	.35
151	CD307	3p indigo	1.25	1.50
152	CD308	6p blue gray	.90	1.25
153	CD309	1sh rose car	1.50	1.50
		Nos. 150-153 (4)	3.95	4.60

George VI Type of 1938

Perf. 13½x14

1951-52   **Wmk. 4**   **Typo.**

154	A12	½p claret ('52)	.80	2.25
a.		Wmk. 4a (error)	2,000.	
155	A12	2p green	.90	.75
156	A12	3p rose red ('52)	.70	2.75
		Nos. 154-156 (3)	2.40	5.75

Coronation Issue
Common Design Type

1953, June 3   **Engr.**   **Perf. 13½x13**

157	CD312	6p blue & black	.60	.60

Infant Welfare Clinic A17

Designs: 1p, Modern Agriculture. 1½p, Out island settlement. 2p, Native strawwork. 3p, Fishing fleet. 4p, Water skiing. 5p, Modern dairying. 6p, Modern transportation. 8p, Paradise Beach. 10p, Modern hotels. 1sh, Yacht racing. 2sh, Sisal. 2sh6p, Shipbuilding. 5sh, Tuna fishing. 10sh, Modern salt production. £1, Parliament Building.

1954, Jan. 1   **Perf. 11x11½**

158	A17	½p red org & blk	.20	1.40
159	A17	1p org brn & ol grn	.20	.30
a.		Booklet pane of 4	.55	
160	A17	1½p black & blue	.20	.55
a.		Booklet pane of 4	.70	
161	A17	2p dk grn & brn org	.20	.30
a.		Booklet pane of 4	.70	
162	A17	3p dp car & blk	.45	.70
163	A17	4p lil rose & bl green	.25	.25
a.		Booklet pane of 4	1.75	
164	A17	5p dp ultra & brn	1.00	2.10
165	A17	6p blk & aqua	1.25	.20
a.		Booklet pane of 4	5.50	
166	A17	8p rose vio & blk	.50	.35
a.		Booklet pane of 4	2.50	
167	A17	10p ultra & blk	.25	.20
168	A17	1sh ol brn & ultra	.50	.20
169	A17	2sh blk & brn org	1.40	.50
170	A17	2sh6p dp bl & blk	2.50	1.90
171	A17	5sh dp org & emer	13.00	.70
172	A17	10sh grnsh blk & black	14.00	2.40
173	A17	£1 vio & grnsh black	14.50	6.25
		Nos. 158-173 (16)	50.40	18.30

See No. 203. For types overprinted or surcharged see Nos. 181-182, 185-200, 202.

Queen Elizabeth II — A18

Wmk. 314

1959, June 10   **Engr.**   **Perf. 13**

174	A18	1p dk red & black	.20	.20
175	A18	2p green & black	.20	.20
176	A18	6p blue & black	.30	.30
177	A18	10p brown & black	.55	.55
		Nos. 174-177 (4)	1.25	1.25

Cent. of the 1st postage stamp of Bahamas.

Christ Church Cathedral, Nassau — A19

Perf. 14x13

1962, Jan. 30   **Photo.**   **Unwmk.**

178	A19	8p shown	.45	.45
179	A19	10p Public library	.45	.45

Centenary of the city of Nassau.

Freedom from Hunger Issue
Common Design Type

Perf. 14x14½

1963, June 4   **Wmk. 314**

180	CD314	8p sepia	1.00	1.00
a.		"8d," "BAHAMAS" omitted	875.00	

Nos. 166-167 Overprinted: "BAHAMAS TALKS/ 1962"

Perf. 11x11½

1963, July 15   **Wmk. 4**

181	A17	8p rose vio & black	.75	.75
182	A17	10p ultra & black	1.50	1.50

Meeting of Pres. Kennedy and Prime Minister Harold Macmillan, Dec. 1962.

Red Cross Centenary Issue
Common Design Type

Wmk. 314

1963, Sept. 2   **Litho.**   **Perf. 13**

183	CD315	1p black & red	.20	.20
184	CD315	10p ultra & red	2.00	2.25

Type of 1954 Overprinted: "NEW CONSTITUTION/ 1964"

Designs as Before

Perf. 11x11½

1964, Jan. 7   **Engr.**   **Wmk. 314**

185	A17	½p red org & blk	.20	.75
186	A17	1p org brn & ol green	.20	.20
187	A17	1½p black & blue	.55	.75
188	A17	2p dk grn & brn org	.20	.20
189	A17	3p dp car & blk	1.10	1.00
190	A17	4p lil rose & bl green	.30	.45
191	A17	5p dp ultra & brn	.30	1.25
192	A17	6p blk & aqua	1.50	.25
193	A17	8p rose vio & blk	.55	.25
194	A17	10p ultra & black	.25	.20
195	A17	1sh ol brn & ultra	1.00	.20
196	A17	2sh blk & brn org	1.10	1.40
197	A17	2sh6p dp bl & blk	2.25	2.25
198	A17	5sh dp org & emer	5.00	2.50
199	A17	10sh grnsh blk & black	5.25	4.25
200	A17	£1 vio & grnsh black	6.25	14.50
		Nos. 185-200 (16)	26.00	30.40

Shakespeare Issue
Common Design Type

Perf. 14x14½

1964, Apr. 23   **Photo.**   **Wmk. 314**

201	CD316	6p greenish blue	.35	.30

Type of 1954 Surcharged with Olympic Rings, New Value and Bars

Perf. 11x11½

1964, Oct. 1   **Engr.**   **Wmk. 314**

202	A17	8p on 1sh ol brn & ultra	.45	.45

18th Olympic Games, Tokyo, Oct. 10-25.

Queen Type of 1954

1964, Oct. 6   **Wmk. 314**

203	A17	2p dk grn & brn org	.50	.50

½p. BAHAMAS

Out Island Regatta A21

Designs: ½p, Colony badge. 1½p, Princess Margaret Hospital. 2p, High School. 3p, Flamingo. 4p, Liner "Queen Elizabeth." 6p, Island development. 8p, Yachting. 10p, Public Square, Nassau. 1sh, Sea Garden, Nassau. 2sh, Cannons at Fort Charlotte. 2sh6p, Sea plane and jetliner. 5sh, 1914 Williamson film project and 1939 underwater post office. 10sh, Conch shell. £1, Columbus' flagship.

Engr. and Litho.

1965, Jan. 7   **Perf. 13½x13**

204	A21	½p multi, *bluish*	.20	1.00
205	A21	1p multi	.20	.65
206	A21	1½p multi	.20	1.40
a.		Booklet pane of 4	.40	
207	A21	2p multi	.20	.20
a.		Booklet pane of 4	.45	
208	A21	3p multi	1.40	.20
a.		Booklet pane of 4	.55	
209	A21	4p multi	1.90	1.50
a.		Booklet pane of 4	2.50	
210	A21	6p multi	.20	.20
a.		Booklet pane of 4	1.25	
211	A21	8p multi	.30	.25
a.		Booklet pane of 4	1.75	
212	A21	10p multi	.20	.20
213	A21	1sh multi, *grnsh*	.30	.20
214	A21	2sh multi, *grnsh*	.65	1.00
215	A21	2sh6p multi	1.50	2.40
216	A21	5sh multi	1.75	.80
217	A21	10sh multi	10.00	2.75
218	A21	£1 multi	11.00	7.25
		Nos. 204-218 (15)	30.00	20.00

Booklet panes were issued Mar. 23, 1965.
See Nos. 252-266. For surcharges see Nos. 221, 230-244.

ITU Issue
Common Design Type

Perf. 11x11½

1965, May 17   **Litho.**   **Wmk. 314**

219	CD317	1p emerald & org	.20	.20
220	CD317	2sh lilac & olive	1.40	1.40

9d.

No. 211 Surcharged

BAHAMAS

Engr. & Litho.

1965, July 12   **Perf. 13½x13**

221	A21	9p on 8p multi	.40	.30

Intl. Cooperation Year Issue
Common Design Type

Wmk. 314

1965, Oct. 25   **Litho.**   **Perf. 14½**

222	CD318	½p blue grn & claret	.20	.20
223	CD318	1sh lt violet & grn	.50	.75

Churchill Memorial Issue
Common Design Type

1966, Jan. 24   **Photo.**   **Perf. 14**

224	CD319	½p multicolored	.20	.20
225	CD319	2p multicolored	.40	.20
226	CD319	10p multicolored	.75	1.00
227	CD319	1sh multicolored	.75	1.50
		Nos. 224-227 (4)	2.10	2.90

Royal Visit Issue
Common Design Type Inscribed "Royal Visit / 1966"

1966, Feb. 4   **Litho.**   **Perf. 11x12**

228	CD320	6p violet blue	.65	.65
229	CD320	1sh dk car rose	1.75	1.75

2c

Nos. 204-218 Surcharged

Engr. & Litho.

1966, May 25   **Wmk. 314**

Perf. 13½x13

230	A21	1c on ½p multi	.20	.20
231	A21	2c on 1p multi	.20	.20
232	A21	3c on 2p multi	.20	.20
233	A21	4c on 3p multi	.20	.20

234 A21	5c on 4p multi	.20	.20
a.	Surch. omitted, vert. strip of 7-10	2,700.	
235 A21	8c on 6p multi	.20	.20
236 A21	10c on 8p multi	.25	.25
237 A21	11c on 1½p multi	.35	.25
238 A21	12c on 10p multi	.40	.30
239 A21	15c on 1sh multi	.50	.35
240 A21	22c on 2sh multi	1.40	1.25
241 A21	50c on 2sh6p multi	1.40	1.25
242 A21	$1 on 5sh multi	2.50	2.50
243 A21	$2 on 10sh multi	5.50	5.00
244 A21	$3 on £1 multi	8.00	7.50
	Nos. 230-244 (15)	20.75	19.00

The denominations are next to the bars instead of below on Nos. 232, 235-240; the length of the bars varies to cover old denomination.

No. 234a, if single, is identical with No. 209, but distinguishable if in vertical strip of 7 to 10. No. 234 was printed in sheets of 100 (10x10); No. 209 in sheets of 60 (10x6).

World Cup Soccer Issue
Common Design Type

1966, July 1		**Litho.**	**Perf. 14**
245 CD321	8c multicolored	.25	.25
246 CD321	15c multicolored	.40	.40

WHO Headquarters Issue
Common Design Type

1966, Sept. 20		**Litho.**	**Perf. 14**
247 CD322	11c multicolored	.40	.40
248 CD322	15c multicolored	.60	.60

UNESCO Anniversary Issue
Common Design Type

1966, Dec. 1		**Litho.**	**Perf. 14**
249 CD323	3c "Education"	.20	.20
250 CD323	15c "Science"	.45	.45
251 CD323	$1 "Culture"	2.10	2.10
	Nos. 249-251 (3)	2.75	2.75

Type of 1965
Values in Cents and Dollars
Engr. & Litho.

1967, May 25   **Perf. 13½x13**

1c, Colony badge. 2c, Out Island Regatta. 3c, High School. 4c, Flamingo. 5c, Liner "Oceanic." 8c, Island development. 10c, Yachting. 11c, Princess Margaret Hospital. 12c, Public Square, Nassau. 15c, Sea Garden, Nassau. 22c, Cannon at Fort Charlotte. 50c, Sea plane, jetliner. $1, 1914 Williamson film project, 1939 underwater post office. $2, Conch shell. $3, Columbus' flagship.

252 A21	1c brown & multi	.20	2.50
253 A21	2c grn, slate & bl	.20	.65
254 A21	3c grn, indigo & vio	.20	.20
255 A21	4c ultra, blue & red	3.75	.50
256 A21	5c pur, bl & indigo	.85	3.00
257 A21	8c dk brn, bl & dl grn	.20	.20
258 A21	10c car rose, bl & pur	.25	.75
259 A21	11c bl, grn & rose red	.20	.85
260 A21	12c ol grn, bl & lt brn	.20	.20
261 A21	15c rose & multi	.50	.20
262 A21	22c rose red, brn & bl	.60	.70
263 A21	50c emer, ol & bl	1.75	.80
264 A21	$1 sep, brn org & dk blue	1.75	.65
265 A21	$2 green & multi	11.50	3.25
266 A21	$3 pur, bl & brn org	3.25	2.10
	Nos. 252-266 (15)	25.40	16.55

Nos. 252-266 are on toned paper. Printings on very white, untinted paper appeared between late 1969 and May, 1971. Value, set $500.

Seal of Bahamas, Queen Elizabeth II and Lord Baden-Powell — A22

60th anniv. of world Scouting: 15c, Scout emblem and portraits as on 3c.

Perf. 14x13½

1967, Sept. 1		**Photo.**	**Wmk. 314**
267 A22	3c multicolored	.25	.20
268 A22	15c multicolored	.70	.20

Human Rights Flame and Globe A23

Intl. Human Rights Year: 12c, Human rights flame and scales of justice. $1, Human rights flame and Seal of Bahamas.

1968, May 13		**Litho.**	**Perf. 14**
269 A23	3c multicolored	.20	.20
270 A23	12c multicolored	.40	.40
271 A23	$1 multicolored	1.40	1.40
	Nos. 269-271 (3)	2.00	2.00

Golf — A24

Tourist Publicity: 11c, Yachting. 15c, Horse racing. 50c, Water skiing.

1968, Aug. 20		**Unwmk.**	**Perf. 13½**
272 A24	5c multicolored	1.40	1.40
273 A24	11c multicolored	.95	.95
274 A24	15c multicolored	1.40	1.40
275 A24	50c multicolored	2.00	2.00
	Nos. 272-275 (4)	5.75	5.75

Olympic Monument and Sailboat — A25

Olympic Monument, San Salvador Island, Bahamas, and: 11c, Long jump. 50c, Running. $1, Sailing.

1968, Sept. 30		**Photo.**	**Perf. 14½x14**
276 A25	5c multicolored	.40	.40
277 A25	11c multicolored	.60	.60
278 A25	50c multicolored	.85	.85
279 A25	$1 multicolored	2.40	2.40
	Nos. 276-279 (4)	4.25	4.25

19th Olympic Games, Mexico City, 10/12-27.

Legislative Building — A26

Designs: 10c, Bahamas mace and Big Ben, London, vert. 12c, Local straw market, vert. 15c, Horse-drawn surrey.

Perf. 14½

1968, Nov. 1		**Unwmk.**	**Litho.**
280 A26	3c brt blue & multi	.20	.20
281 A26	10c yel, blk & blue	.25	.25
282 A26	12c brt rose & multi	.25	.25
283 A26	15c green & multi	.30	.30
	Nos. 280-283 (4)	1.00	1.00

14th Commonwealth Parliamentary Conf., Nassau, Nov. 1-8.

$100 Coin with Queen Elizabeth II and Landing of Columbus — A27

Gold Coins with Elizabeth II on Obverse: 12c, $50 coin and Santa Maria flagship. 15c, $20 coin and Nassau Harbor Lighthouse. $1, $10 coin and Fort.

Engr. on Gold Paper

1968, Dec. 2		**Unwmk.**	**Perf. 13½**
284 A27	3c dark red	.50	.50
285 A27	12c dark green	.75	.75
286 A27	15c lilac	.90	.90
287 A27	$1 black	2.25	2.25
	Nos. 284-287 (4)	4.40	4.40

First gold coinage in the Bahamas.

Bahamas Postal Card and Airplane Wing — A28

Design: 15c, Seaplane, 1929.

Perf. 14½x14

1969, Jan. 30		**Litho.**	**Unwmk.**
288 A28	12c multicolored	.80	.80
289 A28	15c multicolored	.95	.95

50th anniv. of the 1st flight from Nassau, Bahamas, to Miami, Fla., Jan. 30, 1919.

Game Fishing Boats A29

Designs: 11c, Paradise Beach. 12c, Sunfish sailboats. 15c, Parade on Rawson Square.

1969, Aug. 26		**Litho.**	**Wmk. 314**
290 A29	3c multicolored	.20	.20
291 A29	11c multicolored	.60	.60
292 A29	12c multicolored	.65	.65
293 A29	15c multicolored	.80	.80
a.	Souvenir sheet of 4, #290-293	3.50	3.50
	Nos. 290-293 (4)	2.25	2.25

Tourist publicity.

Holy Family, by Nicolas Poussin — A30

Paintings: 3c, Adoration of the Shepherds, by Louis Le Nain. 12c, Adoration of the Kings, by Gerard David. 15c, Adoration of the Kings, by Vincenzo Foppa.

1969, Oct. 15		**Photo.**	**Perf. 12**
294 A30	3c red & multi	.25	.25
295 A30	11c emerald & multi	.35	.35
296 A30	12c ultra & multi	.40	.40
297 A30	15c multicolored	.50	.50
	Nos. 294-297 (4)	1.50	1.50

Christmas.

Girl Guides, Globe and Flags A31

Designs: 12c, Yellow elder and Brownie emblem. 15c, Ranger emblem.

1970, Feb. 23		**Wmk. 314**	**Perf. 14½**
298 A31	3c vio blue, yel & red	.20	.20
299 A31	12c dk brn, grn & yel	.60	.60
300 A31	15c vio bl, bluish grn & yel	.80	.80
	Nos. 298-300 (3)	1.60	1.60

60th anniversary of the Girl Guides.

Opening of UPU Headquarters, Bern — A32

1970, May 20		**Litho.**	**Perf. 14½**
301 A32	3c vermilion & multi	.20	.20
302 A32	15c orange & multi	.55	.55

Bus and Globe A33

Globe and: 11c, Train. 12c, Sailboat and ship. 15c, Plane.

1970, July 14		**Perf. 13½x13**
303 A33	3c orange & multi	.50	.50
304 A33	11c emerald & multi	1.50	1.50
305 A33	12c multicolored	1.50	1.50
306 A33	15c blue & multi	1.50	1.50
a.	Souvenir sheet of 4, #303-306	9.00	9.00
	Nos. 303-306 (4)	5.00	5.00

Issued to promote good will through worldwide travel and tourism.

People, Palms and Flamingo — A34

15c, Red Cross Headquarters, Nassau & marlin.

1970, Aug. 18		**Perf. 14x14½**
307 A34	3c multicolored	.75	.50
308 A34	15c multicolored	.75	1.00

Centenary of British Red Cross Society.

Nativity by G. B. Pittoni — A35

Christmas: 11c, Holy Family, by Anton Raphael Mengs. 12c, Adoration of the Shepherds, by Giorgione. 15c, Adoration of the Shepherds, School of Seville.

Perf. 12½x13

1970, Nov. 3   Litho.   Wmk. 314
309	A35	3c multicolored	.25	.25
310	A35	11c red org & multi	.35	.35
311	A35	12c emerald & multi	.35	.35
312	A35	15c blue & multi	.55	.55
a.		Souv. sheet of 4, #309-312 + 3 labels	2.00	2.00
		Nos. 309-312 (4)	1.50	1.50

International Airport — A36

2c, Breadfruit. 3c, Straw market. 4c, 6c, Hawksbill turtle. 5c, Grouper. 8c, Yellow elder. 10c, Bahamian sponge boat. 11c, Flamingos. 7c, 12c, Hibiscus. 15c, Bonefish. 18c, 22c, Royal poinciana. 50c, Post office, Nassau. $1, Pineapple, vert. $2, Crayfish, vert. $3, "Junkanoo" (costumed drummer), vert.

Wmk. 314 Upright (Sideways on $1, $2, $3)

1971   Perf. 14½x14, 14x14½
313	A36	1c blue & multi	.20	.20
314	A36	2c red & multi	.20	.20
315	A36	3c lilac & multi	.20	.20
316	A36	4c brown & multi	1.50	5.25
317	A36	5c dp org & multi	.60	.40
318	A36	6c brown & multi	.40	.80
319	A36	7c green & multi	1.75	2.50
320	A36	8c yel & multi	.55	.95
321	A36	10c red & multi	.50	.20
322	A36	11c red & multi	2.25	1.75
323	A36	12c green & multi	1.75	1.90
324	A36	15c gray & multi	.50	.35
325	A36	18c multicolored	.60	.40
326	A36	22c green & multi	2.50	7.50
327	A36	50c multicolored	1.25	1.40
328	A36	$1 red & multi	5.75	1.50
329	A36	$2 blue & multi	4.00	3.25
330	A36	$3 vio bl & multi	3.50	6.25
		Nos. 313-330 (18)	28.00	35.00

See Nos. 398-401, 426-443.

Wmk. 314 Sideways (Upright on $1, $2, $3)

1973
317a	A36	5c	9.75	9.75
320a	A36	8c	2.75	2.75
327a	A36	50c	2.00	2.00
328a	A36	$1	2.00	2.00
329a	A36	$2	2.00	2.00
330a	A36	$3	3.00	3.00
		Nos. 317a-330a (6)	21.50	21.50

1976   Wmk. 373
313a	A36	1c	.20	.20
314a	A36	2c	.20	.20
315a	A36	3c	.20	.20
317b	A36	5c	.20	.20
320b	A36	8c	.20	.20
321a	A36	10c	.20	.20
327b	A36	50c	1.25	1.25
328b	A36	$1	2.50	2.50
329b	A36	$2	4.75	4.75
330b	A36	$3	7.50	7.50
		Nos. 313a-330b (10)	17.20	17.20

Snowflake with Peace Signs — A37

Christmas: 11c, "Peace on Earth" with doves. 15c, Christmas wreath around old Bahamas coat of arms. 18c, Star of Bethlehem over palms.

Perf. 14x14½

1971   Photo.   Wmk. 314
331	A37	3c dp lil rose, gold & org	.20	.20
332	A37	11c violet & gold	.35	.35
333	A37	15c gold embossed & multi	.35	.35
334	A37	18c brt bl, gold & vio bl	.40	.40
a.		Souv. sheet of #331-334, perf 15	2.00	2.00
		Nos. 331-334 (4)	1.30	1.30

High Jump, Arms of Bahamas — A38

Olympic Rings, Compass, Arms of Bahamas and: 11c, Bicycling. 15c, Running. 18c, Sailing.

1972, June 27   Litho.   Perf. 13x13½
335	A38	10c lt violet & multi	.40	.40
336	A38	11c ocher & multi	.50	.50
337	A38	15c yel green & multi	.70	.70
338	A38	18c blue & multi	.95	.95
a.		Souvenir sheet of 4, #335-338	3.25	3.25
		Nos. 335-338 (4)	2.55	2.55

20th Olympic Games, Munich, 8/26-9/10.

Shepherd and Star of Bethlehem — A39

Designs: 6c, Bells. 15c, Holly and monstrance. 20c, Poinsettia.

1972, Oct. 3   Wmk. 314   Perf. 14
339	A39	3c gold & multi	.20	.20
340	A39	6c black & multi	.20	.20
341	A39	15c black & multi	.30	.30
342	A39	20c gold & multi	.55	.55
a.		Souvenir sheet of 4, #339-342	2.00	2.50
		Nos. 339-342 (4)	1.25	1.25

Christmas. Gold on 15c is embossed.

Souvenir Sheet

Map of Bahama Islands — A40

1972, Nov. 1   Litho.   Perf. 15
343	A40	Sheet of 4	3.75	4.75
a.		11c blue & multi	.35	.35
b.		15c blue & multi	.45	.45
c.		18c blue & multi	.55	.55
d.		50c blue & multi	1.50	1.50

Tourism Year of the Americas.

Silver Wedding Issue, 1972
Common Design Type

Design: Queen Elizabeth II, Prince Philip, mace and galleon.

Perf. 14x14½

1972, Nov. 13   Photo.   Wmk. 314
344	CD324	11c car rose & multi	.25	.25
345	CD324	18c violet & multi	.45	.45

Weather Satellite, WMO Emblem — A41

1973, Apr. 3   Litho.   Perf. 14
346	A41	15c shown	.60	.40
347	A41	18c Weather radar	.80	.60

Intl. meteorological cooperation, cent.

Clarence A. Bain — A42

Independence: 11c, New Bahamian coat of arms. 15c, New flag and Government House. $1, Milo B. Butler, Sr.

1973   Wmk. 314   Perf. 14½x14
348	A42	3c lilac & multi	.20	.20
349	A42	11c lt blue & multi	.30	.30
350	A42	15c lt green & multi	.50	.50
351	A42	$1 yel & multi	1.25	1.25
a.		Souvenir sheet of 4, #348-351	2.75	2.75
		Nos. 348-351 (4)	2.25	2.25

Issued: #348-350, 7/10; #351, 351a, 8/1.

Virgin in Prayer, by Sassoferrato — A43

1973, Oct. 16   Litho.   Perf. 14

Christmas: 11c, Virgin and Child with St. John, by Filippino Lippi. 15c, Choir of Angels, by Marmion. 18c, The Two Trinities, by Murillo.
352	A43	3c blue & multi	.20	.20
353	A43	11c multicolored	.35	.35
354	A43	15c gray grn & multi	.35	.35
355	A43	18c lil rose & multi	.55	.55
a.		Souvenir sheet of 4, #352-355	1.75	2.00
		Nos. 352-355 (4)	1.45	1.45

Agriculture, Science and Medicine — A44

18c, Symbols of engineering, art, and law.

1974, Feb. 5   Litho.   Perf. 13½x14
356	A44	15c dull grn & multi	.40	.40
357	A44	18c multicolored	.60	.60

University of the West Indies, 25th anniv.

UPU Emblem — A45

Designs: 13c, UPU emblem, vert. 14c, UPU emblem. 18c, UPU monument, Bern, vert.

1974, Apr. 23   Perf. 14
358	A45	3c multicolored	.20	.20
359	A45	13c multicolored	.35	.35
360	A45	14c olive bis & multi	.35	.35
361	A45	18c multicolored	.40	.40
a.		Souvenir sheet of 4, #358-361	1.50	2.00
		Nos. 358-361 (4)	1.30	1.30

Centenary of Universal Postal Union.

Roseate Spoonbills, Trust Emblem — A46

Protected Birds (National Trust Emblem and): 14c, White-crowned pigeons. 21c, White-tailed tropic birds. 36c, Bahamian parrot.

1974, Sept. 10   Litho.   Perf. 14
362	A46	13c multicolored	1.25	.60
363	A46	14c multicolored	1.25	.50
364	A46	21c multicolored	1.50	.90
365	A46	36c multicolored	1.90	3.75
a.		Souvenir sheet of 4, #362-365	8.50	10.00
		Nos. 362-365 (4)	5.90	5.75

Bahamas National Trust, 15th anniv.

Holy Family, by Jacques de Stella — A47

Christmas: 10c, Virgin and Child, by Girolamo Romanino. 12c, Virgin and Child with St. John and St. Catherine, by Andrea Previtali. 21c, Virgin and Child with Angels, by Previtali.

1974, Oct. 29   Wmk. 314   Perf. 13
366	A47	8c black & multi	.25	.25
367	A47	10c green & multi	.35	.35
368	A47	12c red & multi	.35	.35
369	A47	21c ultra & multi	.55	.55
a.		Souvenir sheet of 4, #366-369	2.00	2.25
		Nos. 366-369 (4)	1.50	1.50

Anteos Maerula — A48

1975, Feb. 4   Litho.   Perf. 14x13½
370	A48	3c shown	.25	.25
371	A48	14c Eurema nicippe	1.00	.70
372	A48	18c Papilio andraemon	1.25	1.00
373	A48	21c Euptoieta hegesia	1.50	1.40
a.		Souvenir sheet of 4, #370-373	7.00	6.00
		Nos. 370-373 (4)	4.00	3.35

Sheep Raising — A49

Designs: 14c, Electric reel fishing, vert. 18c, Growing food. 21c, Crude oil refinery, vert.

Unwmk.

1975, May 27   Litho.   Perf. 14
374	A49	3c dull grn & multi	.20	.20
375	A49	14c green & multi	.20	.20
376	A49	18c brown & multi	.30	.25
377	A49	21c vio bl & multi	.90	.45
a.		Souvenir sheet of 4, #374-377	1.50	1.50
		Nos. 374-377 (4)	1.60	1.10

Economic diversification.

Rowena Rand,
Staff and
Chrismon — A50

Plant and IWY
Emblem — A51

Wmk. 373

1975, July 22   Litho.   Perf. 14
378 A50 14c multicolored   .35 .40
379 A51 18c multicolored   .40 .60

International Women's Year.

Adoration of the Shepherds, by
Perugino — A52

Christmas: 8c, 18c, Adoration of the Kings,
by Ghirlandaio. 21c, like 3c.

1975, Dec. 2   Litho.   Perf. 13½
380 A52 3c dk green & multi   .20   .20
381 A52 8c dk violet & multi   .20   .20
382 A52 18c purple & multi   .55   .55
383 A52 21c maroon & multi   .60   .60
  a.   Souvenir sheet of 4, #380-383   2.25 2.50
       Nos. 380-383 (4)   1.55 1.55

Telephones, 1876 and 1976 — A53

Designs: 16c, Radio-telephone link, Dele-
porte, Nassau (radar). 21c, Alexander Graham
Bell. 25c, Communications satellite.

1976, Mar. 23   Litho.   Perf. 14
384 A53 3c multicolored   .20   .20
385 A53 16c multicolored   .40   .40
386 A53 21c multicolored   .50   .50
387 A53 25c multicolored   .65   .65
       Nos. 384-387 (4)   1.75 1.75

Centenary of first telephone call by Alexander Graham Bell, Mar. 10, 1876.

Bicycling and
Olympic
Rings — A54

Olympic Rings and: 16c, Long jump. 25c,
Sailing. 40c, Boxing.

1976, July 13   Litho.   Perf. 14
388 A54 8c magenta & blue   .25   .25
389 A54 16c orange & brn   .40   .40
390 A54 25c magenta & blue   .60   .60
391 A54 40c orange & brn   1.10 1.10
  a.   Souvenir sheet of 4, #388-391   2.75 2.75
       Nos. 388-391 (4)   2.35 2.35

21st Olympic Games, Montreal, Canada,
July 17-Aug. 1.

John
Murray,
Earl of
Dunmore
A55

Design: 16c, Map of US and Bahamas.

1976, June 1   Wmk. 373   Perf. 14
392 A55 16c multicolored   .50   .50
393 A55 $1 multicolored   2.00 2.00
  a.   Souvenir sheet of 4, #393   8.00 9.00

American Bicentennial.

Virgin and
Child,
Filippo
Lippi — A56

Christmas: 21c, Adoration of the Shep-
herds, School of Seville. 25c, Adoration of the
Kings, by Vincenzo Foppa. 40c, Virgin and
Child, by Vivarini.

1976, Oct. 19   Litho.   Perf. 14½x14
394 A56 3c brt blue & multi   .20   .20
395 A56 21c dp org & multi   .30   .30
396 A56 25c emerald & multi   .30   .30
397 A56 40c red lilac & multi   .50   .50
  a.   Souvenir sheet of 4, #394-397 1.75 1.75
       Nos. 394-397 (4)   1.30 1.30

Type of 1971

16c, Hibiscus. 21c, Breadfruit. 25c, Hawksbill turtle. 40c, Bahamian sponge boat.

1976, Nov. 2   Litho.   Wmk. 373
398 A36 16c emerald & multi   .55   .40
399 A36 21c vermilion & multi   .65 1.00
400 A36 25c brown & multi   .75   .50
401 A36 40c vermilion & multi   2.50   .75
       Nos. 398-401 (4)   4.45 2.65

Elizabeth II Seated under Gold
Canopy — A57

16c, Coronation. 21c, Taking and signing of
oath. 40c, Queen holding orb and scepter.

1977, Feb. 7   Perf. 12
402 A57 8c silver & multi   .20   .20
403 A57 16c silver & multi   .30   .30
404 A57 21c silver & multi   .30   .30
405 A57 40c silver & multi   .45   .45
  a.   Souvenir sheet of 4, #402-405 2.05 2.55
       Nos. 402-405 (4)   1.25 1.25

Reign of Queen Elizabeth II, 25th anniv.
For surcharges see Nos. 412-415. \

Featherduster — A58

Marine Life: 8c, Porkfish. 16c, Elkhorn coral.
21c, Soft coral and sponge.

1977, May 24   Litho.   Perf. 13½
406 A58 3c multicolored   .20   .20
407 A58 8c multicolored   .30   .30
408 A58 16c multicolored   .80   .80
409 A58 21c multicolored   1.00 1.00
  a.   Souv. sheet of 4, #406-409, perf 14½ 2.50 3.00
       Nos. 406-409 (4)   2.30 2.30

Campfire
and
Shower
A59

1977, Sept. 27   Litho.   Wmk. 373
410 A59 16c shown   .60   .50
411 A59 21c Boating   .75   .60

6th Caribbean Jamboree, Kingston,
Jamaica, Aug. 5-14.

Nos. 402-405a Overprinted: "Royal
Visit / October 1977"

1977, Oct. 19   Litho.   Perf. 12
412 A57 8c silver & multi   .20   .20
413 A57 16c silver & multi   .30   .30
414 A57 21c silver & multi   .40   .40
415 A57 40c silver & multi   .80   .80
  a.   Souvenir sheet of 4   2.25 2.75
       Nos. 412-415 (4)   1.70 1.70

Caribbean visit of Queen Elizabeth II, Oct.
19-20.

Virgin and
Child — A60

Crèche Figurines: 16c, Three Kings. 21c,
Adoration of the Kings. 25c, Three Kings.

1977, Oct. 25   Litho.   Perf. 13½
416 A60 3c gold & multi   .20   .20
417 A60 16c gold & multi   .40   .40
418 A60 21c gold & multi   .50   .50
419 A60 25c gold & multi   .60   .60
  a.   Souv. sheet, #416-419, perf 14½ 1.90 1.90
       Nos. 416-419 (4)   1.70 1.70

Christmas.

Nassau Public
Library — A61

Litho.
Perf. 14½x14
1978, Mar. 28

Architectural Heritage: 8c, St. Matthew's
Church.
16c, Government House. 18c, The Hermitage, Cat Island.

420 A61 3c black & yel green   .20   .20
421 A61 8c black & lt blue   .20   .20
422 A61 16c black & lilac rose   .25   .25
423 A61 18c black & salmon   .35   .35
  a.   Souvenir sheet of 4, #420-423 1.10 1.10
       Nos. 420-423 (4)   1.00 1.00

Scepter, St.
Edward's Crown,
Orb — A62

Perf. 14x13½
1978, June 27   Litho.   Wmk. 373
424 A62 16c shown   .30   .30
425 A62 $1 Elizabeth II   1.00 1.10
  a.   Souvenir sheet of 2, #424-425 2.25 2.25

Coronation of Queen Elizabeth II, 25th anniv.

Type of 1971

Designs as before and: 16c, Hibiscus. 25c,
Hawksbill turtle.

Perf. 14½x14, 14x14½
1978, June   Unwmk.
426 A36 1c blue & multi   .20   .20
430 A36 5c dp org & multi   .20   .20
436 A36 16c brt grn & multi   .40   .40
439 A36 25c brown & multi   .60   .60
440 A36 50c lemon & multi   1.10 1.10
441 A36 $1 lemon & multi   2.50 2.50
442 A36 $2 blue & multi   4.75 4.75
443 A36 $3 vio bl & multi   7.25 7.25
       Nos. 426-443 (8)   17.00 17.00

Angels and
Palms
A63

Christmas: 5c, Coat of arms within wreath,
and sailing ships.

Perf. 14x14½
1978, Nov. 14   Litho.   Wmk. 373
444 A63 5c car, pink & gold   .20   .20
445 A63 21c ultra, dk bl & gold   .30   .30
  a.   Souvenir sheet of 2, #444-445 2.50 2.50

Baby Walking, IYC
Emblem — A64

IYC Emblem and: 16c, Children playing
leapfrog. 21c, Girl skipping rope. 25c, Building
blocks with "IYC" and emblem.

Perf. 13½x13
1979, May 15   Litho.   Wmk. 373
446 A64 5c multicolored   .20   .20
447 A64 16c multicolored   .25   .25
448 A64 21c multicolored   .35   .35
449 A64 25c multicolored   .40   .40
  a.   Souv. sheet, #446-449, perf 14 1.10 1.10
       Nos. 446-449 (4)   1.20 1.20

International Year of the Child.

Rowland Hill and Penny Black — A65

21c, Stamp printing press, 1840, Bahamas
#7. 25c, Great Britain #27 with 1850's Nassau
cancellation, Great Britain #29. 40c, Early
mailboat, Bahamas #1.

1979, Aug. 14   Perf. 13½x14
450 A65 10c multicolored   .20   .20
451 A65 21c multicolored   .35   .35
452 A65 25c multicolored   .40   .40
453 A65 40c multicolored   .65   .65
  a.   Souvenir sheet of 4, #450-453 1.75 1.75
       Nos. 450-453 (4)   1.60 1.60

Sir Rowland Hill (1795-1879), originator of
penny postage.

Commonwealth Plaque over Map of
Bahamas — A66

Designs: 21c, Parliament buildings. 25c,
Legislative chamber. $1, Senate chamber.

1979, Sept. 27   Litho.   Perf. 13½

454	A66	16c multicolored	.25	.25
455	A66	21c multicolored	.35	.35
456	A66	25c multicolored	.40	.40
457	A66	$1 multicolored	1.60	1.60
a.		Souvenir sheet of 4, #454-457	2.75	2.75
		Nos. 454-457 (4)	2.60	2.60

Parliament of Bahamas, 250th anniv.

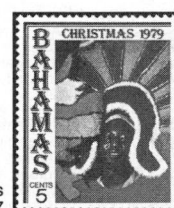

Headdress
A67

Christmas: Goombay Carnival costumes.

1979, Nov. 6   Litho.   Perf. 13

458	A67	5c multicolored	.20	.20
459	A67	10c multicolored	.20	.20
460	A67	16c multicolored	.25	.25
461	A67	21c multicolored	.30	.30
462	A67	25c multicolored	.40	.40
463	A67	40c multicolored	.65	.65
a.		Souv. sheet, 458-463, perf 13½	2.00	2.00
		Nos. 458-463 (6)	2.00	2.00

Columbus'
Landing,
1492
A68

1980, July 9   Litho.   Perf. 15

464	A68	1c shown	.20	.20
465	A68	3c Blackbeard	.20	.20
466	A68	5c Articles, 1647, Eleuthera map	.20	.20
467	A68	10c Ceremonial mace	.20	.20
468	A68	12c Col. Andrew Deveaux	.25	.25
469	A68	15c Slave trading, Vendue House	.30	.30
470	A68	16c Shipwreck salvage, 19th cent.	.30	.30
471	A68	18c Blockade runner, 1860s	.35	.35
472	A68	21c Bootlegging, 1919-1929	.40	.40
473	A68	25c Pineapple cultivation	.25	.25
474	A68	40c Sponge clipping	.75	.75
475	A68	50c Victoria & Colonial Hotels	1.00	1.00
476	A68	$1 Modern agriculture	2.00	2.00
477	A68	$2 Ship, jet	3.75	3.75
478	A68	$3 Central Bank, Arms	5.75	5.75
479	A68	$5 Prince Charles, Prime Minister Pindling	9.50	9.50
		Nos. 464-479 (16)	25.40	25.40

For overprints and surcharges see Nos. 496-499, 532-535.

1985, Nov. 6   Wmk. 384

464a	A68	1c	.20	.20
465a	A68	3c	.20	.20
467a	A68	10c	.20	.20
473a	A68	25c	.50	.50
		Nos. 464a-473a (4)	1.10	1.10

Virgin and Child, Straw Figures — A69

1980, Oct. 28   Litho.   Perf. 14½

480	A69	5c shown	.20	.20
481	A69	21c Three kings	.35	.35
482	A69	25c Angel	.40	.40
483	A69	$1 Christmas tree	1.60	1.60
a.		Souvenir sheet of 4, #480-483	2.50	2.50
		Nos. 480-483 (4)	2.55	2.55

Christmas.

Man with
Crutch,
Sun
Rays
A70

1981, Feb. 10   Litho.   Perf. 14½

484	A70	5c shown	.20	.20
485	A70	$1 Man in wheelchair	1.50	1.50
a.		Souvenir sheet of 2, #484-485	1.75	1.75

International Year of the Disabled.

Grand
Bahama
Tracking
Station
A71

Satellite Views: 20c, Bahamas. 25c, Eleuthera. 50c, Andros and New Providence.

Wmk. 373
1981, Apr. 21   Litho.   Perf. 13½

486	A71	10c multi	.20	.20
487	A71	20c multi, vert.	.35	.35
488	A71	25c multi	.45	.45
489	A71	50c multi, vert.	.90	.90
a.		Souvenir sheet of 4, #486-489	2.00	2.75
		Nos. 486-489 (4)	1.90	1.90

Prince
Charles and
Lady
Diana — A72

Wmk. 373
1981, July 22   Litho.   Perf. 14½

490	A72	30c shown	.50	.50
491	A72	$2 Charles, Prime Minister	3.50	3.50
a.		Souvenir sheet of 2, #490-491	5.00	5.75

Royal wedding.

Bahama
Ducks
A73

Wmk. 373
1981, Aug. 25   Litho.   Perf. 14

492	A73	5c shown	.25	.25
493	A73	20c Reddish egrets	1.00	1.00
494	A73	25c Brown boobies	1.00	1.00
495	A73	$1 West Indian tree ducks	2.50	2.50
a.		Souvenir sheet of 4, #492-495	5.25	5.25
		Nos. 492-495 (4)	4.75	4.75

See Nos. 514-517.

Nos. 466-467, 473, 475 Overprinted:
"COMMONWEALTH FINANCE
MINISTERS' MEETING 21-23
SEPTEMBER 1981"

1981, Sept.   Litho.   Perf. 15

496	A68	5c multicolored	.20	.20
497	A68	10c multicolored	.20	.20
498	A68	25c multicolored	.40	.40
499	A68	50c multicolored	.85	.85
		Nos. 496-499 (4)	1.65	1.65

World
Food Day
A74

Perf. 13x13½
1981, Oct. 16   Wmk. 373

500	A74	5c Chickens	.20	.20
501	A74	20c Sheep	.40	.40
502	A74	30c Lobster	.60	.60
503	A74	50c Pigs	1.00	1.00
a.		Souvenir sheet of 4, #500-503	2.25	2.75
		Nos. 500-503 (4)	2.20	2.20

Christmas — A75

Wmk. 373
1981, Nov. 23   Litho.   Perf. 14

504		Sheet of 9	5.00	5.00
a.	A75	5c Father Christmas	.20	.20
b.	A75	5c shown	.20	.20
c.	A75	5c St. Nicholas, Holland	.20	.20
d.	A75	25c Lussibruden, Sweden	.40	.40
e.	A75	25c Mother and child	.40	.40
f.	A75	25c King Wenceslas, Czechoslovakia	.40	.40
g.	A75	30c Mother and child	.45	.45
h.	A75	30c Mother and child standing	.45	.45
i.	A75	$1 Christkindl angel, Germany	1.75	1.75

TB
Bacillus
Centenary
A76

1982, Feb. 3   Litho.   Perf. 14

505	A76	5c Koch	.20	.20
506	A76	16c X-ray	.30	.30
507	A76	21c Microscopes	.40	.40
508	A76	$1 Mantoux test	1.90	1.90
a.		Souv. sheet of #505-508, perf 14½	3.50	4.00
		Nos. 505-508 (4)	2.80	2.80

Flamingoes
A77

Designs: a, Females. b, Males. c, Nesting. d, Juvenile birds. e, Immature birds. No. 509 in continuous design.

Wmk. 373
1982, Apr. 28   Litho.   Perf. 14

509		Strip of 5, multicolored	4.00	4.00
a.-e.		A77 25c any single	.80	.80

Princess Diana Issue
Common Design Type

1982, July 1   Litho.   Perf. 14

510	CD333	16c Arms	.25	.25
511	CD333	25c Diana	.40	.40
512	CD333	40c Wedding	.60	.60
513	CD333	$1 Portrait	1.50	1.50
		Nos. 510-513 (4)	2.75	2.75

Bird Type of 1981
Wmk. 373

1982, Aug. 18   Litho.   Perf. 14

514	A73	10c Bat	.20	.20
515	A73	16c Hutia	.30	.30
516	A73	21c Racoon	.35	.35
517	A73	$1 Dolphins	1.75	1.75
a.		Souvenir sheet of 4, #514-517	3.25	3.25
		Nos. 514-517 (4)	2.60	2.60

28th
Commonwealth
Parliamentary
Conference
A78

Perf. 14x13½
1982, Oct. 16   Litho.   Wmk. 373

518	A78	5c Plaque	.20	.20
519	A78	25c Assoc. arms	.50	.50
520	A78	40c Natl. arms	.80	.80
521	A78	50c House of Assembly	1.00	1.00
		Nos. 518-521 (4)	2.50	2.50

Christmas
A79

Designs: 5c, Wesley Methodist Church, Baillou Hill Road. 12c, Centerville Seventh Day Adventist Church. 15c, Church of God of Prophecy, East Street. 21c, Bethel Baptist Church, Meeting Street. 25c, St. Francis Xavier Catholic Church, West Hill Street. $1, Holy Cross Anglican Church, Highbury Park.

1982, Nov. 3   Perf. 14

522	A79	5c multicolored	.20	.20
523	A79	12c multicolored	.25	.25
524	A79	15c multicolored	.30	.30
525	A79	21c multicolored	.40	.40
526	A79	25c multicolored	.50	.50
527	A79	$1 multicolored	1.90	1.90
		Nos. 522-527 (6)	3.55	3.55

A80

1983, Mar. 14   Litho.

528	A80	5c Lynden O. Pindling	.20	.20
529	A80	25c Flags	.40	.40
530	A80	35c Map	.55	.55
531	A80	$1 Ocean liner	1.60	1.60
		Nos. 528-531 (4)	2.75	2.75

Commonwealth Day.

Nos. 469-472 Surcharged

1983, Apr. 5   Litho.   Perf. 15

532	A68	20c on 15c multi	.30	.30
533	A68	31c on 21c multi	.55	.55
534	A68	35c on 16c multi	.65	.65
535	A68	80c on 18c multi	1.50	1.50
		Nos. 532-535 (4)	3.00	3.00

30th Anniv. of
Customs
Cooperation
Council — A81

Perf. 14x13½
1983, May 31   Wmk. 373

536	A81	31c Officers, ship	.50	.50
537	A81	$1 Officers, jet	1.60	1.60

10th Anniv. of Independence A82

1983, July 6   Litho.   Perf. 14
538 A82 $1 Flag raising   1.50 1.50
   a. Souvenir sheet, perf. 12   1.50 1.50

Local Butterflies A83

1983, Aug. 24   Perf. 14½x14
539 A83 5c Carters skipper   .25 .25
540 A83 25c Giant southern
       white   .90 .90
541 A83 31c Large orange
       sulphur   1.10 1.10
542 A83 50c Flambeau   1.75 1.75
   a. Souvenir sheet of 4   4.25 4.25
      Nos. 539-542 (4)   4.00 4.00

No. 542a contains Nos. 539-542, perf. 14 and perf. 14½x14.

American Loyalists Arrival Bicentenary — A84

Paintings by Alton Lowe.

1983, Sept. 28   Perf. 14
543 A84 5c Loyalist Dreams   .20 .20
544 A84 31c New Plymouth,
       Abaco   .55 .55
545 A84 35c New Plymouth Hotel   .60 .60
546 A84 50c Island Hope   .90 .90
   a. Souvenir sheet of 4, #543-546   2.25 2.25
      Nos. 543-546 (4)   2.25 2.25

Christmas — A85   125th Anniv. of
                Bahamas
                Stamps — A86

Children's designs: 5c, Christmas Bells, by Monica Pinder. 20c, The Flamingo by Cory Bullard. 25c, The Yellow Hibiscus with Christmas Candle by Monique A. Bailey. 31c, Santa goes a Sailing by Sabrina Seiler, horiz. 35c, Silhouette scene with Christmas trees by James Blake. 50c, Silhouette scene with Pelicans, by Erik Russell, horiz.

1983, Nov. 1   Perf. 14
547 A85 5c multicolored   .20 .20
548 A85 20c multicolored   .30 .30
549 A85 25c multicolored   .40 .40
550 A85 31c multicolored   .50 .50
551 A85 35c multicolored   .60 .60
552 A85 50c multicolored   .80 .80
      Nos. 547-552 (6)   2.80 2.80

1984, Feb. 22   Litho.   Perf. 14
553 A86 5c No. 3   .20 .20
554 A86 $1 No. 1   1.60 1.60

Lloyd's List Issue
Common Design Type
Wmk. 373
1984, Apr. 25   Litho.   Perf. 14½
555 CD335 5c Trent   .20 .20
556 CD335 31c Orinoco   .55 .55
557 CD335 35c Nassau Harbor   .60 .60
558 CD335 50c Container ship
       Oropesa   .85 .85
      Nos. 555-558 (4)   2.20 2.20

1984 Summer Olympics A87

1984, June 20 Litho. Perf. 14x14½
559 A87 5c Running   .20 .20
560 A87 25c Discus   .40 .40
561 A87 31c Boxing   .50 .50
562 A87 $1 Basketball   1.60 1.60
   a. Souvenir sheet of 4, #559-562   2.75 2.75
      Nos. 559-562 (4)   2.70 2.70

Flags of Bahamas and Caribbean Community — A88

Wmk. 373
1984, July 4   Litho.   Perf. 14
563 A88 50c multicolored   .90 .90

Conference of Heads of Government of Caribbean Community, 5th Meeting.

Allen's Cay Iguana A89

1984, Aug. 15   Perf. 14
564 A89 5c shown   .20 .20
565 A89 25c Curly-tailed lizard   .60 .60
566 A89 35c Greenhouse frog   .80 .80
567 A89 50c Atlantic green turtle   1.00 1.00
   a. Souvenir sheet of 4, #564-567   3.00 3.00
      Nos. 564-567 (4)   2.60 2.60

25th Anniv. of   Christmas — A91
Natl. Trust — A90

Wildlife: a, Calliphlox evelynae. b, Megaceryle alcyon, Eleutherodactylus planirostris. c, Phoebis sennae, Phoenicopterus ruber, Himantopus himantopus, Phoebus sennae. d, Urbanus proteus, Chelonia mydas. e, Pandion haliaetus.
Continuous design.

1984, Aug. 15   Litho.   Perf. 14
568   Strip of 5   5.25 5.25
   a.-e. A90 31c any single   1.10 1.10

1984, Nov. 7   Litho.   Perf. 13½x13
Madonna and Child Paintings.
569 A91 5c Titian   .20 .20
570 A91 31c Anais Colin   .55 .55
571 A91 35c Elena Caula   .60 .60
   a. Souvenir sheet of 3, #569-571   1.40 1.40
      Nos. 569-571 (3)   1.35 1.35

Girl Guides, 75th Anniv., Intl. Youth Year A92

1985, Feb. 22   Litho.   Perf. 14
572 A92 5c Brownies   .20 .20
573 A92 25c Camping   .35 .35
574 A92 31c Girl Guides   .50 .50
575 A92 35c Rangers   .55 .55
   a. Souvenir sheet of 4, #572-575   1.60 1.60
      Nos. 572-575 (4)   1.60 1.60

Audubon Birth Bicentenary — A93

Wmk. 373
1985, Apr. 24   Litho.   Perf. 14
576 A93 5c Killdeer   .20 .20
577 A93 31c Mourning dove,
       vert.   .85 .85
578 A93 35c Mourning doves,
       diff., vert.   .90 .90
579 A93 $1 Killdeers, diff.   2.50 2.50
      Nos. 576-579 (4)   4.45 4.45

Queen Mother 85th Birthday
Common Design Type
Perf. 14½x14
1985, June 7   Litho.   Wmk. 384
580 CD336 5c Portrait, 1927   .20 .20
581 CD336 25c At christening
       of Peter Phil-
       lips   .40 .40
582 CD336 35c Portrait, 1985   .60 .60
583 CD336 50c Holding Prince
       Henry   .80 .80
      Nos. 580-583 (4)   2.00 2.00

Souvenir Sheet
584 CD336 $1.25 In a pony and
       trap   2.00 2.00

UN and UN Food and Agriculture Org., 40th Annivs. — A94

Wmk. 373
1985, Aug. 26   Litho.   Perf. 14
585 A94 25c Wheat, emblems   .40 .40

Commonwealth Heads of Government Meeting, 1985 — A95

1985, Oct. 16   Wmk. 373   Perf. 14½
586 A95 31c Queen Elizabeth II   .50 .50
587 A95 35c Flag, Commonwealth
       emblem   .55 .55

Christmas A96

Paintings by Alton Roland Lowe: 5c, Grandma's Christmas Bouquet. 25c, Junkanoo Romeo and Juliet, vert. 31c, Bunce Girl, vert. 35c, Home for Christmas.

1985, Nov. 5   Perf. 13
588 A96 5c multicolored   .20 .20
589 A96 25c multicolored   .50 .50
590 A96 31c multicolored   .60 .60
591 A96 35c multicolored   .60 .60
   a. Souv. sheet, #588-591, perf 14   2.00 2.00
      Nos. 588-591 (4)   2.00 2.00

Queen Elizabeth II 60th Birthday
Common Design Type
Designs: 10c, Age 1, 1927. 25c, Coronation, Westminster Abbey, 1953. 35c, Giving speech, royal visit, Bahamas. 40c, At Djakova, Yugoslavia, state visit, 1972. $1, Visiting Crown Agents, 1983.

1986, Apr. 21   Wmk. 384   Perf. 14½
592 CD337 10c scar, blk & sil   .20 .25
593 CD337 25c ultra & multi   .35 .45
594 CD337 35c green & multi   .45 .60
595 CD337 40c violet & multi   .55 .65
596 CD337 $1 rose vio & multi   1.25 1.75
      Nos. 592-596 (5)   2.80 3.70

AMERIPEX '86 — A97

1986, May 19   Perf. 14
597 A97 5c Nos. 464, 471   .20 .20
598 A97 25c Nos. 288-289   .45 .45
599 A97 31c No. 392   .55 .55
600 A97 50c No. 489a   .90 .90
601 A97 $1 Statue of Liberty,
       vert.   1.75 1.75
   a. Souvenir sheet of one   1.75 1.75
      Nos. 597-601 (5)   3.85 3.85

Statue of Liberty, cent.

Royal Wedding Issue, 1986
Common Design Type
Designs: 10c, Formal engagement. $1, Andrew in dress uniform.

1986, July 23   Perf. 14½x14
602 CD338 10c multicolored   .20 .20
603 CD338 $1 multicolored   1.60 1.60

Fish A98

1986-87   Wmk. 384   Perf. 14
604 A98 5c Rock beauty   .20 .20
605 A98 10c Stoplight par-
       rotfish   .20 .20
606 A98 15c Jacknife fish   .25 .25
607 A98 20c Flamefish   .30 .30
608 A98 25c Swissguard
       basslet   .35 .35
609 A98 30c Spotfin butterf-
       lyfish   .40 .40
610 A98 35c Queen trigger-
       fish   .50 .50
611 A98 40c Four-eyed but-
       terflyfish   .55 .55
612 A98 45c Fairy basslet   .65 .65
613 A98 50c Queen angelfish   .70 .70
614 A98 60c Blue chromis   .85 .85
615 A98 $1 Spanish hogfish   1.40 1.40
616 A98 $2 Harlequin bass   7.00 7.00
617 A98 $3 Blackbar
       soldierfish   6.50 6.50
618 A98 $5 Pygmy angelfish   7.25 7.25
618A A99 $10 Red hind ('87)   16.00 16.00
      Nos. 604-618A (16)   43.10 43.10

Nos. 605, 608, 611-613, 615, 617-618 exist inscribed "1990." Nos. 611, 615, 616 "1988." Issue dates: $10, Jan. 2, others, Aug. 5.

1987, June 25   Wmk. 373
604a   5c   .20 .20
605a   10c   .20 .20
606a   15c   .25 .25
611a   40c   .55 .55
612a   45c   .65 .65
613a   50c   .70 .70
614a   60c   .85 .85
615a $1   1.40 1.40
616a $2   2.75 2.75
      Nos. 604a-616a (9)   7.55 7.55

Nos. 604a-616a dated 1987. No. 605a "1988." No. 604a "1989."

Christ Church
Cathedral — A99

Wmk. 373

1986, Sept. 16   Litho.   Perf. 14½
619 A99 10c View, 19th cent.   .20   .20
620 A99 40c View, 1986   .65   .65
  a.   Souvenir sheet of 2, #619-620   .85   .85

City of Nassau, Diocese of Nassau and the
Bahamas and Christ Church, 125th anniv.

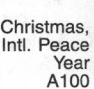

Christmas,
Intl. Peace
Year
A100

Wmk. 384

1986, Nov. 4   Litho.   Perf. 14
621 A100 10c Nativity   .20   .20
622 A100 40c Flight to Egypt   .65   .65
623 A100 45c Children praying   .75   .75
624 A100 50c Exchanging gifts   .80   .80
  a.   Souvenir sheet of 4, #621-624   2.50   2.50
      Nos. 621-624 (4)   2.40   2.40

Pirates of the
Caribbean — A101

A102

Wmk. 373

1987, June 2   Litho.   Perf. 14½
625 A101 10c Anne Bonney   .25   .25
626 A101 40c Blackbeard (d.
        1718)   .90   .90
627 A101 45c Capt. Edward En-
        gland   1.00   1.00
628 A101 50c Capt. Woodes
        Rogers (c. 1679-
        1732)   1.25   1.25
      Nos. 625-628 (4)   3.40   3.40

Souvenir Sheet
629 A102 $1.25 Map of the Ba-
        hamas   2.75   2.75

Paintings of
Lighthouses
by Alton
Roland Lowe
A103

1987, Mar. 31   Wmk. 384
630 A103 10c Great Isaac   .30   .30
631 A103 40c Bird Rock   1.25   1.25
632 A103 45c Castle Is.   1.50   1.50
633 A103 $1 Hole in the Wall   3.25   3.25
      Nos. 630-633 (4)   6.30   6.30

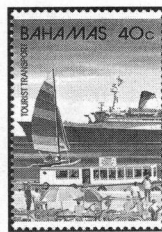

Tourist
Transportation
A104

Ships: No. 634a, Cruise ship, sailboat. b,
Cruise ships, tugboat, speedboat. c, Pleasure
boat leaving harbor, sailboat. d, Pleasure boat
docked, sailboats. e, Sailboats.
Aircraft: No. 635a, Bahamasair plane. b,
Bahamasair and Pan Am aircraft. c, Aircraft,
radar tower. d, Control tower, aircraft. e, Helicopter, planes.

1987, Aug. 26   Wmk. 373   Perf. 14
634   Strip of 5   3.75   3.75
  a.-e.   A104 40c any single   .75   .75
635   Strip of 5   3.75   3.75
  a.-e.   A104 40c any single   .75   .75

Orchids
Painted by
Alton Roland
Lowe
A105

1987, Oct. 20   Wmk. 384   Perf. 14½
636 A105 10c Cattleyopis lindenii   .20   .20
637 A105 40c Encyclia lucayana   .65   .65
638 A105 45c Encyclia hodgeana   .75   .75
639 A105 50c Encyclia lleidae   .80   .80
  a.   Souvenir sheet of 4, #636-639   2.50   2.50
      Nos. 636-639 (4)   2.40   2.40

Christmas.

Discovery of
America, 500th
Anniv. (in
1992) — A106

10c, Ferdinand & Isabella. 40c, Columbus
before the Talavera Committee. 45c, Lucayan
village. 50c, Lucayan potters. $1.50, Map, c.
1500.

Perf. 14x14½
1988, Feb. 23   Litho.   Wmk. 373
640 A106   10c multicolored   .20   .20
641 A106   40c multicolored   .65   .65
642 A106   45c multicolored   .75   .75
643 A106   50c multicolored   .80   .80
      Nos. 640-643 (4)   2.40   2.40

Souvenir Sheet
644 A106 $1.50 multicolored   3.00   3.00

See #663-667, 688-692, 725-729, 749-753,
762.

World
Wildlife
Fund
A107

Whistling ducks, Dendrocygna arborea.

1988, Apr. 29   Perf. 14½
645 A107   5c Ducks in flight   .75   .25
646 A107 10c Among marine
        plants   1.50   .50
647 A107 20c Adults, ducklings   3.00   1.00
648 A107 45c Wading   6.25   2.25
      Nos. 645-648 (4)   11.50   4.00

Abolition of
Slavery,
150th Anniv.
A108

1988, Aug. 9   Perf. 14
649 A108 10c African hut   .20   .20
650 A108 40c Basket weavers in
        hut, Grantstown   .80   .80

1988
Summer
Olympics,
Seoul
A109

Games emblem and details of painting by
James Martin: 10c, Olympic flame, high jump,
hammer throw, basketball and gymnastics.
40c, Swimming, boxing, weight lifting, fencing
and running. 45c, Gymnastics, shot put and
javelin. $1, Running, cycling and gymnastics.

Wmk. 384
1988, Aug. 30   Litho.   Perf. 14
651 A109 10c multicolored   .20   .20
652 A109 40c multicolored   .80   .80
653 A109 45c multicolored   .90   .90
654 A109 $1 multicolored   2.00   2.00
  a.   Souvenir sheet of 4, #651-654   4.00   4.00
      Nos. 651-654 (4)   3.90   3.90

Lloyds of London, 300th Anniv.
Common Design Type

Designs: 10c, Lloyds List No. 560, 1740.
40c, Freeport Harbor, horiz. 45c, Space shuttle over the Bahamas, horiz. $1, Supply ship
Yarmouth Castle on fire.

1988, Oct. 4   Wmk. 373
655 CD341 10c multicolored   .20   .20
656 CD341 40c multicolored   .80   .80
657 CD341 45c multicolored   .90   .90
658 CD341 $1 multicolored   2.00   2.00
      Nos. 655-658 (4)   3.90   3.90

Christmas
Carols — A110

Designs: 10c, O' Little Town of Bethlehem.
40c, Little Donkey. 45c, Silent Night. 50c,
Hark! The Herald Angels Sing.

1988, Nov. 21   Wmk. 384   Perf. 14½
659 A110 10c multicolored   .20   .20
660 A110 40c multicolored   .80   .80
661 A110 45c multicolored   .90   .90
662 A110 50c multicolored   1.00   1.00
  a.   Souvenir sheet of 4, #659-662   2.90   2.90
      Nos. 659-662 (4)   2.90   2.90

Discovery of America Type

Design: 10c, Columbus as chartmaker. 40c,
Development of the caravel. 45c, Navigational
tools. 50c, Arawak artifacts. $1.50, Caravel
under construction, an illumination from the
Nuremburg Chronicles, 15th cent.

1989, Jan. 25   Litho.   Wmk. 373
Perf. 14½x14
663 A106 10c multicolored   .20   .20
664 A106 40c multicolored   .80   .80
665 A106 45c multicolored   .90   .90
666 A106 50c multicolored   1.00   1.00
      Nos. 663-666 (4)   2.90   2.90

Souvenir Sheet
667 A106 $1.50 multicolored   3.00   3.00

Hummingbirds
A111

Wmk. 384
1989, Mar. 29   Litho.   Perf. 14½
668 A111 10c Cuban emerald   .20   .20
669 A111 40c Ruby-throated   .80   .80
670 A111 45c Bahama woodstar   .90   .90
671 A111 50c Rufous   1.00   1.00
      Nos. 668-671 (4)   2.90   2.90

Intl. Red Cross and Red Crescent
Organizations, 125th Annivs. — A112

1989, May 31   Perf. 14x14½
672 A112 10c Water safety   .20   .20
673 A112 $1 Dunant, Battle of
        Solferino   2.00   2.00

Moon Landing, 20th Anniv.
Common Design Type

Apollo 8: 10c, Apollo Communications System, Grand Bahama Is. 40c, James Lovell Jr.,
William Anders and Frank Borman. 45c, Mission emblem. $1, The Rising Earth (photo-
graph). $2, Astronaut practicing lunar surface
activities at Manned Spacecraft Center, Houston, in training for Apollo 11 mission.

1989, July 20   Perf. 14x13½
Size of Nos. 674-675: 29x29mm
674 CD342 10c multicolored   .20   .20
675 CD342 40c multicolored   .80   .80
676 CD342 45c multicolored   .90   .90
677 CD342 $1 multicolored   2.00   2.00
      Nos. 674-677 (4)   3.90   3.90

Souvenir Sheet
678 CD342 $2 multicolored   4.00   4.00

Christmas
A113

Designs: 10c, Church of the Nativity, Bethlehem. 40c, Basilica of the Annunciation, Nazareth. 45c, By the Sea of Galilee, Tabgha. $1,
Church of the Holy Sepulcher, Jerusalem.

Perf. 14½x14
1989, Oct. 16   Wmk. 373
679 A113 10c multicolored   .20   .20
680 A113 40c multicolored   .80   .80
681 A113 45c multicolored   .90   .90
682 A113 $1 multicolored   2.00   2.00
  a.   Souvenir sheet of 4, #679-682   4.00   4.00
      Nos. 679-682 (4)   3.90   3.90

World
Stamp
Expo '89
A114

Expo emblem and: 10c, Earth, #359. 40c,
UPU Headquarters, #301. 45c, US Capitol,
#601. $1, Passenger jet, #150. $2, Washing-
ton, DC, on map.

1989, Nov. 17   Wmk. 384   Perf. 14
683 A114 10c multicolored   .20   .20
684 A114 40c multicolored   .80   .80
685 A114 45c multicolored   .90   .90
686 A114 $1 multicolored   2.00   2.00
      Nos. 683-686 (4)   3.90   3.90

Souvenir Sheet
Perf. 14½x14
687 A114 $2 multicolored   4.00 4.00

No. 687 contains one 31x38mm stamp.

Discovery of America Type of 1988
10c, Caravel launch. 40c, Provisioning ships. 45c, Shortening sails. 50c, Lucayan fishermen. $1.50, Columbus's fleet departing from Cadiz.

Perf. 14½x14
1990, Jan. 24   Litho.   Wmk. 373
688	A106	10c multicolored	.30	.25
689	A106	40c multicolored	1.25	1.00
690	A106	45c multicolored	1.50	1.25
691	A106	50c multicolored	1.75	1.50
		Nos. 688-691 (4)	4.80	4.00

Souvenir Sheet
692 A106 $1.50 multicolored   5.00 5.00

Organization of American States, Cent. — A115

1990, Mar. 14   Wmk. 384   Perf. 14
693 A115 40c multicolored   .80 .80

Souvenir Sheet

Stamp World London '90 — A116

Aircraft: a, Spitfire I. b, Hurricane IIc.

1990, May 3   Wmk. 384
694 A116   Sheet of 2   4.00 4.00
a.-b. $1 any single   2.00 2.00

For surcharge see No. B3.

Intl. Literacy Year A117

10c, Teacher helping student. 40c, Children reading to each other. 50c, Children reading aloud.

1990, June 27   Wmk. 384   Perf. 14
695	A117	10c multicolored	.20	.20
696	A117	40c multicolored	.80	.80
697	A117	50c multicolored	1.00	1.00
		Nos. 695-697 (3)	2.00	2.00

Queen Mother, 90th Birthday
Common Design Types
1990, Aug. 4   Perf. 14x15
698 CD343   40c Portrait, c. 1938   .80 .80
Perf. 14½
699 CD344 $1.50 At garden party, 1938   3.00 3.00

Bahamian Parrot — A118

1990, Sept. 26   Wmk. 373   Perf. 14
700	A118	10c shown	.30	.25
701	A118	40c In flight	1.25	1.00
702	A118	45c Head	1.50	1.25
703	A118	50c On branch	1.75	1.50
		Nos. 700-703 (4)	4.80	4.00

Souvenir Sheet
704 A118 $1.50 On branch, diff.   4.50 4.50

Christmas A119

Birds — A120

Wmk. 373
1990, Nov. 5   Litho.   Perf. 13½
705	A119	10c Angel appears to Mary	.20	.20
706	A119	40c Nativity	.80	.80
707	A119	45c Angel appears to shepherds	.90	.90
708	A119	$1 Three kings	2.00	2.00
a.		Souvenir sheet of 4, #705-708	3.90	3.90
		Nos. 705-708 (4)	3.90	3.90

Wmk. 384
1991, Feb. 4   Litho.   Perf. 14
709	A120	5c Green heron	.20	.20
710	A120	10c Turkey vulture	.20	.20
711	A120	15c Osprey	.30	.30
712	A120	20c Clapper rail	.40	.40
713	A120	25c Royal tern	.50	.50
714	A120	30c Key West quail dove	.60	.60
715	A120	40c Smooth-billed ani	.80	.80
716	A120	45c Burrowing owl	.90	.90
717	A120	50c Hairy woodpecker	1.00	1.00
718	A120	55c Mangrove cuckoo	1.10	1.10
719	A120	60c Bahama mockingbird	1.25	1.25
720	A120	70c Red-winged blackbird	1.40	1.40
721	A120	$1 Thick-billed vireo	2.00	2.00
722	A120	$2 Bahama yellowthroat	4.00	4.00
723	A120	$5 Stripe-headed tanager	10.00	10.00
724	A120	$10 Greater Antillean bullfinch	20.00	20.00
		Nos. 709-724 (16)	44.65	44.65

Issued: $10, July 1; others, Feb. 4.

1993   Wmk. 373
710a		10c	.20	.20
713a		25c	.50	.50
714a		30c	.60	.60
715a		40c	.80	.80
718a		55c	1.10	1.10
723a		$5	10.00	10.00
		Nos. 710a-723a (6)	13.20	13.20

Nos. 710a-723a dated 1993. 40c, 55c exist dated 1995.
Issued: 40c, 12/31/93; others, 9/23/93.

Discovery of America Type
Designs: 15c, Columbus practices celestial navigation. 40c, The fleet in rough seas. 55c, Natives on the beach. 60c, Map of voyage. $1.50, Pinta's crew sights land.

Perf. 14½x14
1991, Apr. 9   Litho.   Wmk. 384
725	A106	15c multicolored	.30	.30
726	A106	40c multicolored	.80	.80
727	A106	55c multicolored	1.10	1.10
728	A106	60c multicolored	1.25	1.25
		Nos. 725-728 (4)	3.45	3.45

Souvenir Sheet
729 A106 $1.50 multicolored   3.00 3.00

Elizabeth & Philip, Birthdays
Common Design Types
Wmk. 384
1991, June 17   Litho.   Perf. 14½
730	CD346	15c multicolored	.30	.30
731	CD345	$1 multicolored	2.00	2.00
a.		Pair, #730-731 + label	2.30	2.30

Hurricane Awareness — A121

Designs: 15c, Weather radar image of Hurricane Hugo. 40c, Anatomy of hurricane rotating around eye. 55c, Flooding caused by Hurricane David. 60c, Lockheed WP-3D Orion.

1991, Aug. 28   Wmk. 384   Perf. 14
732	A121	15c multicolored	.30	.30
733	A121	40c multicolored	.80	.80
734	A121	55c multicolored	1.10	1.10
735	A121	60c multicolored	1.25	1.25
		Nos. 732-735 (4)	3.45	3.45

Christmas A122

Designs: 15c, The Annunciation. 55c, Mary and Joseph traveling to Bethlehem. 60c, Angel appearing to shepherds. $1, Adoration of the Magi.

1991, Oct. 28   Wmk. 373   Perf. 14
736	A122	15c multicolored	.30	.30
737	A122	55c multicolored	1.10	1.10
738	A122	60c multicolored	1.25	1.25
739	A122	$1 multicolored	2.00	2.00
a.		Souvenir sheet of 4, #736-739	4.75	4.75
		Nos. 736-739 (4)	4.65	4.65

Majority Rule, 25th Anniv. A123

Designs: 15c, First Progressive Liberal Party cabinet. 40c, Signing of Independence Constitution. 55c, Handing over constitutional instrument, vert. 60c, First Bahamian Governor-General, Sir Milo Butler, vert.

Wmk. 373
1992, Jan. 10   Litho.   Perf. 14
740	A123	15c multicolored	.35	.35
741	A123	40c multicolored	1.00	1.00
742	A123	55c multicolored	1.25	1.25
743	A123	60c multicolored	1.50	1.50
		Nos. 740-743 (4)	4.10	4.10

Queen Elizabeth II's Accession to the Throne, 40th Anniv.
Common Design Type
Wmk. 373
1992, Feb. 6   Litho.   Perf. 14
744	CD349	15c multicolored	.30	.30
745	CD349	40c multicolored	.70	.70
746	CD349	55c multicolored	1.00	1.00
747	CD349	60c multicolored	1.10	1.10
748	CD349	$1 multicolored	1.90	1.90
		Nos. 744-748 (5)	5.00	5.00

Discovery of America Type
Designs: 15c, Lucayans first sight of fleet. 40c, Approaching Bahamas coastline. 55c, Lucayans about to meet Columbus. 60c, Columbus gives thanks for safe arrival. $1.50, Monument to Columbus' landing.

Perf. 14½x14
1992, Mar. 17   Litho.   Wmk. 384
749	A106	15c multicolored	.30	.30
750	A106	40c multicolored	.75	.75
751	A106	55c multicolored	1.00	1.00
752	A106	60c multicolored	1.10	1.10
		Nos. 749-752 (4)	3.15	3.15

Souvenir Sheet
753 A106 $1.50 multicolored   2.75 2.75

Templeton, Galbraith and Hansberger Ltd. Building — A124

Wmk. 384
1992, Apr. 22   Litho.   Perf. 14½
754 A124 55c multicolored   1.00 1.00

Templeton Prize for Progress in Religion, 20th Anniv.

1992 Summer Olympics, Barcelona A125

Perf. 14½x14
1992, June 2   Wmk. 373
755	A125	15c Pole vault	.30	.30
756	A125	40c Javelin	.75	.75
757	A125	55c Hurdling	1.00	1.00
758	A125	60c Basketball	1.10	1.10
		Nos. 755-758 (4)	3.15	3.15

Souvenir Sheet
759 A125 $2 Sailing   3.75 3.75

Intl. Conference on Nutrition — A126

15c, Drought-affected earth, starving child. 55c, Hand holding plant, stalks of grain.

Perf. 14½x13
1992, Aug. 11   Litho.   Wmk. 373
760	A126	15c multicolored	.30	.30
761	A126	55c multicolored	1.00	1.00

Discovery of America Type
Souvenir Sheet
Perf. 14x13½
1992, Oct. 12   Litho.   Wmk. 384
762 A106 $2 Coming ashore   3.75 3.75

Christmas A127

1992, Nov. 2   Wmk. 373   Perf. 14
763	A127	15c The Annunciation	.30	.30
764	A127	55c Nativity Scene	1.00	1.00
765	A127	60c Angel, shepherds	1.10	1.10
766	A127	70c The Magi	1.25	1.25
a.		Souvenir sheet of 4, #763-766	3.75	3.75
		Nos. 763-766 (4)	3.65	3.65

The Contract, Farm Labor Program, 50th Anniv. A128

Bahamian, American flags and: 15c, Silhouette of worker's head. 55c, Onions. 60c, Citrus fruits. 70c, Apples.

Perf. 14x14½

1993, Mar. 16   Litho.   Wmk. 384
767	A128	15c	multicolored	.30 .30
768	A128	55c	multicolored	1.00 1.00
769	A128	60c	multicolored	1.10 1.10
770	A128	70c	multicolored	1.25 1.25
		Nos. 767-770 (4)		3.65 3.65

Royal Air Force, 75th Anniv.
Common Design Type

Designs: 15c, Westland Wapiti. 40c, Gloster Gladiator. 55c, DeHavilland Vampire. 70c, English Electric Lightning.
No. 775a, Avro Shackleton. b, Fairey Battle. c, Douglas Boston. d, DeHavilland DH9a.

Wmk. 373

1993, Apr. 1   Litho.   Perf. 14
771	CD350	15c	multicolored	.25 .25
772	CD350	40c	multicolored	.70 .70
773	CD350	55c	multicolored	.95 .95
774	CD350	70c	multicolored	1.25 1.25
		Nos. 771-774 (4)		3.15 3.15

Souvenir Sheet of 4
775	CD350	60c #a.-d.	4.50 4.50

Coronation of Queen Elizabeth II, 40th Anniv. A129

Wmk. 373

1993, June 2   Litho.   Perf. 13½
776	A129	15c	Nos. 424-425	.30 .30
777	A129	55c	No. 157	1.00 1.00
778	A129	60c	Nos. 402-403	1.10 1.10
779	A129	70c	Nos. 404-405	1.25 1.25
		Nos. 776-779 (4)		3.65 3.65

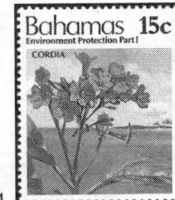

A130

Natl. symbols: 15c, Lignum vitae. 55c, Yellow elder. 60c, Blue marlin. 70c, Flamingo.

1993, July 8   Litho.   Perf. 14
780	A130	15c	multicolored	.30 .30
781	A130	55c	multicolored	1.00 1.00
782	A130	60c	multicolored	1.10 1.10
783	A130	70c	multicolored	1.25 1.25
		Nos. 780-783 (4)		3.65 3.65

Independence, 20th anniv.

A131

1993, Sept. 8   Litho.   Perf. 14

Wildflowers.
784	A131	15c	Cordia	.25 .25
785	A131	55c	Seaside morning glory	1.10 1.10

786	A131	60c	Poinciana	1.25 1.25
787	A131	70c	Spider lily	1.40 1.40
		Nos. 784-787 (4)		4.00 4.00

Christmas A132

1993, Nov. 1   Litho.   Perf. 14
788	A132	15c	Angel, Mary	.30 .30
789	A132	55c	Shepherds, angel	1.00 1.00
790	A132	60c	Holy family	1.10 1.10
791	A132	70c	Three wise men	1.25 1.25
		Nos. 788-791 (4)		3.65 3.65

Souvenir Sheet
792	A132	$1 Madonna and Child	1.90 1.90

Intl. Year of the Family A133

Wmk. 384

1994, Feb. 18   Litho.   Perf. 13½
793	A133	15c	shown	.30 .30
794	A133	55c	Children studying	1.00 1.00
795	A133	60c	Son, father fishing	1.10 1.10
796	A133	70c	Children, grand- mother	1.25 1.25
		Nos. 793-796 (4)		3.65 3.65

Hong Kong '94.

Royal Visit — A134

Designs: 15c, Bahamas, United Kingdom flags. 55c, Royal Yacht Britannia. 60c, Queen Elizabeth II. 70c, Prince Philip, Queen.

Perf. 14x13½

1994, Mar. 7   Wmk. 373
797	A134	15c	multicolored	.30 .30
798	A134	55c	multicolored	1.00 1.00
799	A134	60c	multicolored	1.10 1.10
800	A134	70c	multicolored	1.25 1.25
		Nos. 797-800 (4)		3.65 3.65

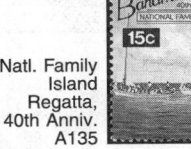

Natl. Family Island Regatta, 40th Anniv. A135

Designs: 15c, 55c, 60c, 70c, Various sailing boats at sea. $2, Beached yacht, vert.

Wmk. 373

1994, Apr. 27   Litho.   Perf. 14
801	A135	15c	multicolored	.30 .30
802	A135	55c	multicolored	1.00 1.00
803	A135	60c	multicolored	1.10 1.10
804	A135	70c	multicolored	1.25 1.25
		Nos. 801-804 (4)		3.65 3.65

Souvenir Sheet
805	A135	$2 multicolored	3.75 3.75

Intl. Olympic Committee, Cent. — A136

Flag, Olympic rings, and: 15c, Nos. 276-279, horiz. 55c, Nos. 388-391. 60c, Nos. 559-562, horiz. 70c, Nos. 755-758.

Wmk. 373

1994, May 31   Litho.   Perf. 14
806	A136	15c	multicolored	.30 .30
807	A136	55c	multicolored	1.00 1.00
808	A136	60c	multicolored	1.10 1.10
809	A136	70c	multicolored	1.25 1.25
		Nos. 806-809 (4)		3.65 3.65

Souvenir Sheet

First Recipients of the Order of the Caribbean Community — A137

Illustration reduced.

Perf. 13x14

1994, July 5   Litho.   Wmk. 373
810	A137	$2 multicolored	4.00 4.00

A138   A139

Butterfly, flower: 15c, Canna skipper, canna. 55c, Cloudless sulphur, cassia. 60c, White peacock, passion flower. 70c, Devillier's swallowtail, calico flower.

1994, Aug. 16   Litho.   Perf. 14
811	A138	15c	multicolored	.25 .25
812	A138	55c	multicolored	1.10 1.10
813	A138	60c	multicolored	1.25 1.25
814	A138	70c	multicolored	1.40 1.40
		Nos. 811-814 (4)		4.00 4.00

1994, Sept. 13   Perf. 13½x14

Marine Life: a, Cuban hogfish, Spanish hogfish. b, Tomate, squirrelfish. c, French angelfish. d, Queen angelfish. e, Rock beauty. $2, Rock beauty, queen angelfish.
815	A139	40c Strip of 5, #a.-e.	4.00 4.00

Souvenir Sheet
816	A139	$2 multicolored	4.00 4.00

Christmas — A140

Wmk. 384

1994, Oct. 31   Litho.   Perf. 14
817	A140	15c	Angel	.25 .25
818	A140	55c	Holy family	1.10 1.10
819	A140	60c	Shepherds	1.25 1.25
820	A140	70c	Magi	1.40 1.40
		Nos. 817-820 (4)		4.00 4.00

Souvenir Sheet
821	A140	$2 Christ Child, vert.	3.75 3.75

College of the Bahamas, 20th Anniv. — A141

Designs: 15c, Lion. 70c, Queen Elizabeth II, college facade.

Wmk. 373

1995, Feb. 8   Litho.   Perf. 14
822	A141	15c	multicolored	.30 .30
823	A141	70c	multicolored	1.40 1.40

End of World War II, 50th Anniv.
Common Design Types

Designs: 15c, Bahamian soldiers on parade. 55c, Neutrality patrols flown by PBY-5A flying boats. 60c, Bahamian women in all three services. 70c, B-24 Liberator, Bahamians in RAF. $2, Reverse of War Medal 1939-45.

Wmk. 373

1995, May 8   Litho.   Perf. 13½
824	CD351	15c	multicolored	.25 .25
825	CD351	55c	multicolored	1.10 1.10
826	CD351	60c	multicolored	1.25 1.25
827	CD351	70c	multicolored	1.40 1.40
		Nos. 824-827 (4)		4.00 4.00

Souvenir Sheet
Perf. 14
828	CD352	$2 multicolored	4.00 4.00

Kirtland's Warbler — A142

#829: a, 25c, Female feeding young. b, 25c, Immature bird feeding, prior to migration. c, 15c, Female at nest. d, 15c, Singing male. $2, Female on branch overlooking lake.

1995, June 7   Litho.   Perf. 13½
829	A142	Strip of 4, #a.-d.	1.90 1.90

Souvenir Sheet
Perf. 13
830	A142	$2 multicolored	4.00 4.00

World Wildlife Fund (#829). No. 830 contains one 42x28mm stamp and has continuous design.

Tourism A143

Designs: 15c, Eleuthera Cliffs. 55c, Clarence Town, Long Island. 60c, Albert Lowe Museum. 70c, Yachting.

Wmk. 384

1995, July 18   Litho.   Perf. 14½
831	A143	15c	multicolored	.25 .25
832	A143	55c	multicolored	1.10 1.10
833	A143	60c	multicolored	1.25 1.25
834	A143	70c	multicolored	1.40 1.40
		Nos. 831-834 (4)		4.00 4.00

Designs: 15c, Pig, poultry farming. 55c, Horticultural methods. 60c, Healthy eating. 70c, Sustainable fishing.

FAO, 50th Anniv. A144

Perf. 13½x13

1995, Sept. 5	Litho.	Wmk. 373	
835 A144 15c multicolored		.25	.25
836 A144 55c multicolored		1.10	1.10
837 A144 60c multicolored		1.25	1.25
838 A144 70c multicolored		1.40	1.40
Nos. 835-838 (4)		4.00	4.00

UN, 50th Anniv.
Common Design Type

Designs: 15c, Sikorsky S-55, UNEF, Sinai, 1957. 55c, Ferret armored car, UNEF, Sinai, 1957. 60c, Fokker F-27, UNAMIC/UNTAC, Cambodia, 1991-93. 70c, Lockheed Hercules.

	Wmk. 373		
1995, Oct. 25	Litho.	Perf. 14	
839 CD353 15c multicolored		.25	.25
840 CD353 55c multicolored		1.10	1.10
841 CD353 60c multicolored		1.25	1.25
842 CD353 70c multicolored		1.40	1.40
Nos. 839-842 (4)		4.00	4.00

Christmas — A145

Designs: 15c, St. Agnes Anglican Church. 55c, Church of God. 60c, Sacred Heart Roman Catholic Church. 70c, Salem Union Baptist Church.

1995, Nov. 17			
843 A145 15c multicolored		.25	.25
844 A145 55c multicolored		1.10	1.10
845 A145 60c multicolored		1.25	1.25
846 A145 70c multicolored		1.40	1.40
Nos. 843-846 (4)		4.00	4.00

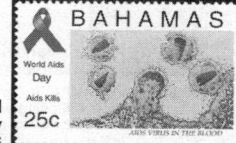

World AIDS Day A146

1995, Dec. 1			
847 A146 25c Virus in blood		.50	.50
848 A146 70c Scientific research		1.40	1.40

Shells A147

Designs: 5c, Sunrise tellin. 10c, Queen conch. 15c, Angular triton. 20c, True tulip. 25c, Reticulated cowrie-helmet. 30c, Sand dollar. 40c, Lace short-frond murex. 45c, Inflated sea biscuit. 50c, West Indian top shell (magpie). 55c, Spiny oyster. 60c, King helmet. 70c, Lion's paw. $1, Crown cone. $2, Atlantic partridge tun. $5, Wide-mouthed purpura. $10, Triton's trumpet.

1996	Litho.	Wmk. 373	Perf. 14	
849 A147 5c multicolored			.20	.20
850 A147 10c multicolored			.20	.20
851 A147 15c multicolored			.30	.30
852 A147 20c multicolored			.40	.40
853 A147 25c multicolored			.50	.50
854 A147 30c multicolored			.60	.60
855 A147 40c multicolored			.80	.80
856 A147 45c multicolored			.90	.90
857 A147 50c multicolored			1.00	1.00
858 A147 55c multicolored			1.10	1.10
859 A147 60c multicolored			1.25	1.25
860 A147 70c multicolored			1.40	1.40
a. Souvenir sheet of 1			1.40	1.40

861 A147 $1 multicolored		2.00	2.00
a. Souvenir sheet of 1		2.00	2.00
862 A147 $2 multicolored		4.00	4.00
863 A147 $5 multicolored		10.00	10.00
864 A147 $10 multicolored		20.00	20.00
Nos. 849-864 (16)		44.65	44.65

No. 860a issued 6/20/97 for return of Hong Kong to China.
No. 861a issued 2/3/97 for Hong Kong '97.
Nos. 849-864 exist dated "1997."
Nos. 849-853, 855, 857, 859, 861-864 exist dated "1999."
Issued: $10, 7/1; others, 1/2.
See Nos. 962-964.

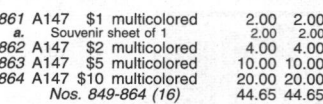

Radio, Cent. A148

Designs: 15c, East Goodwin Lightship, Marconi apparatus suspended from masthead. 55c, Arrest of Dr. Crippen, newspaper headline telling of wireless message from SS Montrose. 60c, SS Philadelphia, first readable transatlantic messages. 70c, Yacht Elettra, Guglielmo Marconi.
$2, SS Titantic, SS Carpathia.

1996, Feb. 4	Litho.	Perf. 13½	
865 A148 15c multicolored		.25	.25
866 A148 55c multicolored		1.10	1.10
867 A148 60c multicolored		1.25	1.25
868 A148 70c multicolored		1.40	1.40
Nos. 865-868 (4)		4.00	4.00

Souvenir Sheet

869 A148 $2 multicolored		4.00	4.00

A149 A150

	Wmk. 384		
1996, June 25	Litho.	Perf. 13½	
870 A149 15c Swimming		.25	.25
871 A149 55c Track		1.10	1.10
872 A149 60c Basketball		1.25	1.25
873 A149 70c Long jump		1.40	1.40
Nos. 870-873 (4)		4.00	4.00

Souvenir Sheet

874 A149 $2 Javelin, 1896		4.00	4.00

Modern Olympic Games, cent.

	Wmk. 384		
1996, Sept. 3	Litho.	Perf. 14	

Reptiles: 15c, Green anole. 55c, Fowl snake. 60c, Inagua freshwater turtle. 70c, Acklins rock iguana.

875 A150 15c multicolored		.25	.25
876 A150 55c multicolored		1.10	1.10
877 A150 60c multicolored		1.25	1.25
878 A150 70c multicolored		1.40	1.40
a. Souvenir sheet, #875-878		4.00	4.00
Nos. 875-878 (4)		4.00	4.00

Environmental protection.

Christmas A151

Designs: 15c, Angel Gabriel and Mary. 55c, Mary and Joseph. 60c, Shepherds. 70c, Magi. $2, Presentation at the Temple.

	Wmk. 373		
1996, Nov. 4	Litho.	Perf. 14	
879 A151 15c multicolored		.25	.25
880 A151 55c multicolored		1.10	1.10
881 A151 60c multicolored		1.25	1.25
882 A151 70c multicolored		1.40	1.40
Nos. 879-882 (4)		4.00	4.00

Souvenir Sheet

883 A151 $2 multicolored		4.00	4.00

Archives Dept., 25th Anniv. — A152

Perf. 14½x14

1996, Dec. 9	Litho.	Wmk. 384	
884 A152 55c shown		1.10	1.10

Souvenir Sheet
Perf. 14x13½

885 A152 $2 Building, horiz.		4.00	4.00

Queen Elizabeth II and Prince Philip, 50th Wedding Anniv. — A153

Designs: No. 886, Queen. No. 887, Grenadier Guards. No. 888, Prince Philip. No. 889, Queen reviewing Grenadier Guards. No. 890, Prince holding trophy, Queen opening jewel box. No. 891, Prince on polo pony.
$2, Queen, Prince riding in open carriage, horiz.

	Wmk. 373		
1997, July 9	Litho.	Perf. 13	
886 A153 50c multicolored		1.00	1.00
887 A153 50c multicolored		1.00	1.00
a. Pair, #886-887		2.00	2.00
888 A153 60c multicolored		1.25	1.25
889 A153 60c multicolored		1.25	1.25
a. Pair, #888-889		2.50	2.50
890 A153 70c multicolored		1.40	1.40
891 A153 70c multicolored		1.40	1.40
a. Pair, #890-891		2.80	2.80
Nos. 886-891 (6)		7.30	7.30

Souvenir Sheet

892 A153 $2 multicolored		4.00	4.00

Intl. Year of the Reefs A154

Various pictures of marine life and coral.

Perf. 14x14½

1997, Sept. 3	Litho.	Wmk. 384	
893 A154 15c multicolored		.25	.25
894 A154 55c multicolored		1.10	1.10
895 A154 60c multicolored		1.25	1.25
896 A154 70c multicolored		1.40	1.40
Nos. 893-896 (4)		4.00	4.00

Christmas — A155

Perf. 13x13½

1997, Oct. 6	Litho.	Wmk. 373	
897 A155 15c Angel		.25	.25
898 A155 55c Madonna & Child		1.10	1.10
899 A155 60c Shepherd		1.25	1.25
900 A155 70c Magi		1.40	1.40
Nos. 897-900 (4)		4.00	4.00

Souvenir Sheet

901 A155 $2 Christ Child		4.00	4.00

Diana, Princess of Wales (1961-97)
Common Design Type

Various portraits: 902: a, 55c. b, 60c. c, 70c.

Perf. 14½x14

1998, Mar. 31	Litho.	Wmk. 373	
901A CD355 15c multicolored		.30	.30

Sheet of 4

902 CD355 #a.-c., 901A		4.00	4.00

Organization of American States, 50th Anniv. — A156

Map of North and South America, national flags, and: 15c, "New Vision" paper. 55c, Building.

1998, Apr. 14		Perf. 13½x14	
903 A156 15c multicolored		.30	.30
904 A156 55c multicolored		1.10	1.10

University of the West Indies, 50th Anniv. — A157

1998, Apr. 14			
905 A157 55c multicolored		1.10	1.10

Universal Declaration of Human Rights, 50th Anniv. — A158

1998, Apr. 14			
906 A158 55c multicolored		1.10	1.10

Royal Air Force, 80th Anniv.
Common Design Type of 1993
Re-Inscribed

Designs: 15c, Handley Page Hyderabad. 55c, Hawker Demon. 60c, Gloster Meteor F.8. 70c, Lockheed Neptune MR.1.
No. 911: a, Sopwith Camel. b, Short 184. c, Supermarine Spitfire PR.19. d, North American Mitchell III.

1998, Apr. 1			
907 CD350 15c multicolored		.25	.25
908 CD350 55c multicolored		1.10	1.10
909 CD350 60c multicolored		1.25	1.25
910 CD350 70c multicolored		1.40	1.40
Nos. 907-910 (4)		4.00	4.00

Souvenir Sheet

911 CD350 50c Sheet of 4, #a.-d.		4.00	4.00

Independence, 25th Anniv. — A159

15c, Supreme Court Building. 55c, Nassau Library. 60c, Government House. 70c, Gregory Arch.
$2, Exuma-Family Island Regatta, George Town.

Wmk. 373

| | | | | **1998, July 10** | **Litho.** | **Perf. 13½** |

912	A159	15c multicolored	.25	.25
913	A159	55c multicolored	1.10	1.10
914	A159	60c multicolored	1.25	1.25
915	A159	70c multicolored	1.40	1.40
		Nos. 912-915 (4)	4.00	4.00

Souvenir Sheet

| 916 | A159 | $2 multicolored | 4.00 | 4.00 |

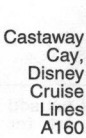

Castaway Cay, Disney Cruise Lines
A160

1998, Aug. 1   **Perf. 14**

917	A160	55c Daytime	1.10	1.10
918	A160	55c Nighttime	1.10	1.10
a.		Pair, #917-918	2.25	2.25
b.		Bklt. pane, 5 each #917-918	11.00	
		Complete booklet, #918b	11.00	

MS Ryndam, Half Moon Cay — A161

1998, Aug. 19   **Perf. 13½x13**

| 919 | A161 | 55c multicolored | 1.10 | 1.10 |

Roses A162

Wmk. 373

| | | | | **1998, Sept. 8** | **Litho.** | **Perf. 14** |

920	A162	55c Yellow cream	1.10	1.10
921	A162	55c Big red	1.10	1.10
922	A162	55c Seven sisters	1.10	1.10
923	A162	55c Barrel pink	1.10	1.10
924	A162	55c Island beauty	1.10	1.10
a.		Bklt. pane, 2 each #920-924	11.00	
		Complete booklet, #924a	11.00	
		Nos. 920-924 (5)	5.50	5.50

Souvenir Sheet

| 925 | A162 | 55c like #924 | 1.10 | 1.10 |

No. 925 has parts of other roses extending into center left and upper left area of stamp.

Intl. Year of the Ocean — A163

Wmk. 373

| | | | | **1998, Nov. 24** | **Litho.** | **Perf. 14** |

| 926 | A163 | 15c Killer whale | .30 | .30 |
| 927 | A163 | 55c Tropical fish | 1.10 | 1.10 |

Christmas A164

1998, Dec. 11

928	A164	15c The Annunciation	.25	.25
929	A164	55c Shepherds, star	1.10	1.10
930	A164	60c Magi	1.25	1.25
931	A164	70c Flight into Egypt	1.40	1.40
		Nos. 928-931 (4)	4.00	4.00

Souvenir Sheet

| 932 | A164 | $2 Nativity scene | 4.00 | 4.00 |

Timothy Gibson, Composer of Natl. Anthem A165

1998   **Litho.**   **Wmk. 373**   **Perf. 13½**

| 933 | A165 | 60c multicolored | 1.25 | 1.25 |

Independence, 25th anniv.

National Trust, 40th Anniv. — A166

Flamingos on the beach: a, One chick, adults. b, Two chicks, adults. c, One chick spreading wings, adults. d, Six in flight over others. e, Three ascending into flight.

Wmk. 384

| | | | | **1999, Feb. 9** | **Litho.** | **Perf. 14** |

| 934 | A166 | 55c Strip of 5, #a.-e. | 5.50 | 5.50 |

No. 934 is a continuous design.
See Nos. 940, 961, 969.

Australia '99, World Stamp Expo A167

Maritime history: 15c, Arawak Indians. 55c, Santa Maria. 60c, Blackbeard's ship, Queen Anne's Revenge. 70c, Banshee running Union blockade, US Civil War.
$2, American invasion of Fort Nassau, 1776.

Perf. 14x14½

| | | | | **1999, Mar. 9** | | **Wmk. 373** |

935	A167	15c multicolored	.25	.25
936	A167	55c multicolored	1.10	1.10
937	A167	60c multicolored	1.25	1.25
938	A167	70c multicolored	1.40	1.40
		Nos. 935-938 (4)	4.00	4.00

Souvenir Sheet

| 939 | A167 | $2 multicolored | 4.00 | 4.00 |

National Trust, 40th Anniv. Type

Marine life: a, Dolphin. b, Large fish, four in background. c, Several fish, coral. d, Turtle, fish, coral. e, Lobster, coral.

Wmk. 384

| | | | | **1999, Apr. 6** | **Litho.** | **Perf. 14** |

| 940 | A166 | 55c Strip of 5, #a.-e. | 5.50 | 5.50 |

No. 940 is a continuous design.

Bahamas Historical Society, 40th Anniv. A168

1999, June 9   **Litho.**   **Perf. 13**

| 941 | A168 | $1 multicolored | 2.00 | 2.00 |

1st Manned Moon Landing, 30th Anniv.
Common Design Type

15c, Ascent module in assembly area. 65c, Apollo command & service module. 70c, Descent stage. 80c, Module turns to dock with service module.
$2, Looking at earth from moon.

Perf. 14x13¾

| | | | | **1999, July 20** | **Litho.** | **Wmk. 384** |

942	CD357	15c multicolored	.30	.30
943	CD357	65c multicolored	1.25	1.25
944	CD357	70c multicolored	1.40	1.40
945	CD357	80c multicolored	1.60	1.60
		Nos. 942-945 (4)	4.55	4.55

Souvenir Sheet
Perf. 14

| 946 | CD357 | $2 multicolored | 4.00 | 4.00 |

No. 946 contains one 40mm circular stamp 40mm.

UPU, 125th Anniv. A170

Wmk. 384

| | | | | **1999, Aug. 17** | **Litho.** | **Perf. 13½** |

947	A170	15c Mail Packet Delaware	.30	.30
948	A170	65c S.S. Atlantis	1.25	1.25
949	A170	70c M.V. Queen of Bermuda	1.40	1.40
950	A170	80c USS Saufley	1.60	1.60
		Nos. 947-950 (4)	4.55	4.55

Queen Mother's Century
Common Design Type

Queen Mother: 15c, At Hertfordshire Hospital. 65c, With Princess Elizabeth. 70c, With Prince Andrew. 80c, With Irish Guards.
$2, With brother David and 1966 British World Cup team members.

Wmk. 373

| | | | | **1999, Aug.** | **Litho.** | **Perf. 13½** |

951	CD358	15c multicolored	.30	.30
952	CD358	65c multicolored	1.25	1.25
953	CD358	70c multicolored	1.40	1.40
954	CD358	80c multicolored	1.60	1.60
		Nos. 951-954 (4)	4.55	4.55

Souvenir Sheet

| 955 | CD358 | $2 multicolored | 4.00 | 4.00 |

Environmental Protection — A171

15c, Turtle pond. 65c, Green turtles, limestone cliffs. 70c, Barracudas. 80c, Sea fans on reef.
$2, Atlantic bottlenose dolphin.

Wmk. 373

| | | | | **1999, Sept. 21** | **Litho.** | **Perf. 13¾** |

956	A171	15c multicolored	.30	.30
957	A171	65c multicolored	1.25	1.25
958	A171	70c multicolored	1.40	1.40
959	A171	80c multicolored	1.60	1.60
		Nos. 956-959 (4)	4.55	4.55

Souvenir Sheet

| 960 | A171 | $2 multicolored | 4.00 | 4.00 |

National Trust Type of 1999

Designs: a, Tern. b, Heron. c, Hummingbird, orange flower. d, Duck. e, Parrot.

Wmk. 384

| | | | | **1999, Oct. 8** | **Litho.** | **Perf. 14¼** |

| 961 | A166 | 65c Strip of 5, #a.-e. | 6.50 | 6.50 |

Shell Type of 1996

1999		**Litho.**	**Wmk. 373**	**Perf. 14**
962	A147	35c Like #854	.70	.70
963	A147	65c Like #856	1.25	1.25
964	A147	80c Like #858	1.60	1.60
		Nos. 962-964 (3)	3.55	3.55

Christmas A172

People in various Junkanoo costumes.

Perf. 14½x14¼

| | | | | **1999, Oct. 25** | **Litho.** | **Wmk. 373** |

965	A172	15c multicolored	.30	.30
966	A172	65c multicolored	1.25	1.25
967	A172	70c multicolored	1.40	1.40
968	A172	80c multicolored	1.60	1.60
		Nos. 965-968 (4)	4.55	4.55

National Trust Type of 1999

Designs: a, Orchid. b, Rodent. c, Hummingbird, red flowers. d, Lizard. e, Hibiscus.

Wmk. 384

| | | | | **1999, Oct. 8** | **Litho.** | **Perf. 14¼** |

| 969 | A166 | 65c Strip of 5, #a.-e. | 6.50 | 6.50 |

Historic Fishing Villages A173

15c, New Plymouth. 65c, Cherokee Sound. 70c, Hope Town. 80c, Spanish Wells.

Perf. 13¼x13

| | | | | **2000, Jan. 25** | **Litho.** | **Wmk. 373** |

970	A173	15c multi	.30	.30
971	A173	65c multi	1.25	1.25
972	A173	70c multi	1.40	1.40
973	A173	80c multi	1.60	1.60
		Nos. 970-973 (4)	4.55	4.55

Souvenir Sheet

1999 World Champions in Women's 4x100-Meter Relay Race — A174

Illustration reduced.

Wmk. 373

| | | | | **2000, Feb. 22** | **Litho.** | **Perf. 14½** |

| 974 | A174 | $2 multi | 4.00 | 4.00 |

Bush Medicine Plants A175

Perf. 14¼x14½

| | | | | **2000, May 2** | | **Wmk. 373** |

975	A175	15c Prickly pear	.30	.30
976	A175	65c Buttercup	1.25	1.25
977	A175	70c Shepherd's needle	1.40	1.40
978	A175	80c Five fingers	1.60	1.60
		Nos. 975-978 (4)	4.55	4.55

The Stamp Show 2000, London A176

Battle of Britain, 60th anniv.: 15c, Quick turnaround, rearm and refuel. 65c, Squadron leader R. Stanford-Tuck in Hurricane 1. 70c, Melee. 80c, Tally ho.
$2, Airplanes in flight.

2000, May 22　　　**Perf. 13¼x13½**

979	A176	15c multi	.30	.30
980	A176	65c multi	1.25	1.25
981	A176	70c multi	1.40	1.40
982	A176	80c multi	1.60	1.60

Nos. 979-982 (4)　　4.55　4.55

Souvenir Sheet

983　A176　$2 multi　　　4.00　4.00

Souvenir Sheet

Bahamas Cooperatives — A177

Illustration reduced.

2000, June 27　**Litho.**　**Perf. 14**
984　A177　$2 multi　　　4.00　4.00

2000 Summer Olympics, Sydney A178

15c, Swimming. 65c, Triple jump. 70c, Women's 4x100 meter relay. 80c, Yachting.

2000, July 17　　　**Perf. 14¼x14½**
985-988　A178　Set of 4　　4.50　4.50

Christmas A179

Orchids: 15c, Cockle-shell orchid. 65c, Pleated encyclia. 70c, Pine pink. 80c, Graceful encyclia.

2000, Nov. 7　　　**Perf. 14½x14¼**
989-992　A179　Set of 4　　4.50　4.50

Bahamas Humane Society, 76th Anniv. A180

Designs: 15c, Education. 65c, Fund raising. 70c, Veterinary care. 80c, Animal rescue.

Wmk. 373
2000, Dec. 12　**Litho.**　**Perf. 14**
993-996　A180　Set of 4　　4.75　4.75

Early Settlements A181

Designs: 15c, Meadow St., Inagua. 65c, Bain Town. 70c, Hope Town, Abaco. 80c, The Blue Hills.

Wmk. 373
2001, Feb. 6　**Litho.**　**Perf. 14¼**
997-1000　A181　Set of 4　　4.75　4.75

Sir Lynden Pindling (1930-2000), Prime Minister — A182

Pindling and: 15c, Microphone. 65c, Flag.

2001, Mar. 22　　　**Perf. 14½x14¼**

1001-1002	A182	Set of 2	1.60	1.60
1001a		Inscribed "10th July, 1973"	.30	.30

No. 1001 is inscribed "10th July, 1972." Issued: No. 1001a, 8/6/01.

Edible Wild Fruits A183

Designs: 15c, Cocoplum. 65c, Guana berry. 70c, Mastic. 80c, Seagrape.

2001, May 15　　　**Perf. 14¼x14½**
1003-1006　A183　Set of 4　　4.75　4.75

Birds and Eggs A184

Designs: 5c, Reddish egret. 10c, Purple gallinule. 15c, Antillean nighthawk. 20c, Wilson's plover. 25c, Killdeer. 30c, Bahama woodstar. 40c, Bahama swallow. 50c, Bahama mockingbird. 60c, Black-cowled oriole. 65c, Great lizard cuckoo. 70c, Audubon's shearwater. 80c, Gray kingbird. $1, Bananaquit. $2, Yellow warbler. $5, Antillean bullfinch. $10, Roseate spoonbill.

Wmk. 373
2001, July 1　**Litho.**　**Perf. 14**

1007	A184	5c multi	.20	.20
1008	A184	10c multi	.20	.20
1009	A184	15c multi	.30	.30
1010	A184	20c multi	.40	.40
1011	A184	25c multi	.50	.50
1012	A184	30c multi	.60	.60
1013	A184	40c multi	.80	.80
1014	A184	50c multi	1.00	1.00
1015	A184	60c multi	1.25	1.25
1016	A184	65c multi	1.25	1.25
1017	A184	70c multi	1.40	1.40
1018	A184	80c multi	1.60	1.60
1019	A184	$1 multi	2.00	2.00
1020	A184	$2 multi	4.00	4.00
1021	A184	$5 multi	10.00	10.00
1022	A184	$10 multi	20.00	20.00

Nos. 1007-1022 (16)　45.50　45.50

Visits of Royal Navy Ships A185

HMS: 15c, Norfolk, 1933. 25c, Scarborough, 1930s. 50c, Bahamas, 1944. 65c, Battleaxe, 1979. 70c, Invincible, 1997. 80c, Norfolk, 2000.

Wmk. 373
2001, Aug. 21　**Litho.**　**Perf. 14**
1023-1028　A185　Set of 6　　6.25　6.25

Christmas — A186

Paintings: 15c, The Adoration of the Shepherds, by Peter Paul Rubens. 65c, Adoration of the Magi, by Rubens and Anthony Van Dyck. 70c, The Holy Virgin in the Wreath of Flowers, by Rubens and Jan Breughel. 80c, The Holy Virgin Adored by Angels, by Rubens.

2001, Nov. 6
1029-1032　A186　Set of 4　　4.75　4.75

SEMI-POSTAL STAMPS

No. 48 Overprinted in Red

1917, May 18　**Wmk. 3**　**Perf. 14**
B1　A6　1p car & black　　.40　1.60

Type of 1911 Overprinted in Red

1919, Jan. 1

B2	A6	1p red & black	.40	2.25
a.		Double overprint		1,600.

This stamp was originally scheduled for release in 1918.

Souvenir Sheet

No. 694 Surcharged

HURRICANE RELIEF +$1

Wmk. 384
1992, Nov. 16　**Litho.**　**Perf. 14**
B3　A116　Sheet of 2, #a.-b.　8.00　8.00

AIR POST STAMPS

Catalogue values for all unused stamps in this section are for Never Hinged items.

Manned Flight Bicentenary — AP1

Airplanes.

Wmk. 373
1983, Oct. 13　**Litho.**　**Perf. 14**

C1	AP1	10c Consolidated Catalina	.50	.20
a.		Without emblem ('85)	.20	.20
b.		Without emblem, wmk. 384 ('86)	.20	.20
C2	AP1	25c Avro Tudor IV	.65	.40
a.		Without emblem ('85)	.45	.45
b.		Without emblem, wmk. 384 ('86)	.45	.45
C3	AP1	31c Avro Lancastrian	.75	.55
a.		Without emblem ('85)	.55	.55
C4	AP1	35c Consolidated Commodore	.60	.60
a.		Without emblem ('85)	.85	.65

Nos. C1-C4 (4)　2.50　1.75

Aircraft AP2

1987, July 7

C5	AP2	15c Bahamasair Boeing 737	1.50	.90
C6	AP2	40c Eastern Boeing 757	2.10	1.50
C7	AP2	45c Pan Am Airbus A300 B4	2.10	1.50
C8	AP2	50c British Airways Boeing 747	2.10	1.50

Nos. C5-C8 (4)　7.80　5.40

SPECIAL DELIVERY STAMPS

No. 34 Overprinted

1916　**Wmk. 1**　**Perf. 14**

E1	A6	5p orange & black	6.50	27.50
a.		Double overprint	750.00	1,000.
b.		Inverted overprint	1,100.	1,250.
c.		Double ovpt., one invtd.	1,250.	1,250.
d.		Pair, one without overprint	18,000.	27,500.

The No. E1 overprint exists in two types. Type I (illustrated) is much scarcer. Type II shows "SPECIAL" farther right, so that the letter "I" is slightly right of the vertical line of the "E" below it.

Type of Regular Issue of 1903 Overprinted

1917, July 2   Wmk. 3
E2 A6 5p orange & black   .80 5.00

No. 60 Overprinted in Red

1918
E3 A6 5p violet & black   .60 1.75

WAR TAX STAMPS

Stamps of 1912-18 Overprinted

1918, Feb. 21   Wmk. 3   Perf. 14
MR1	A8	½p green	8.00	30.00
a.		Double overprint	1,600.	1,100.
b.		Inverted overprint	1,850.	1,300.
MR2	A8	1p car rose	.80	.90
a.		Double overprint	2,000.	1,250.
b.		Inverted overprint	1,250.	1,300.
MR3	A6	3p brown, yel	3.75	3.50
a.		Inverted overprint	1,750.	1,100.
b.		Double overprint	1,400.	1,400.
MR4	A8	1sh black & red	75.00	110.00
a.		Double overprint	7,500.	
		Nos. MR1-MR4 (4)	87.55	144.40

Same Overprint on No. 48a

1918, July 10
MR5	A6	1p car & black	3.50	5.50
a.		Double overprint	1,500.	1,600.
b.		Double ovpt., one invtd.	1,500.	
c.		Inverted overprint	1,600.	1,350.

Nos. 49-50, 54 Overprinted in Black or Red

MR6	A8	½p green	1.60	1.60
MR7	A8	1p car rose	.65	.30
a.		Watermarked sideways	600.00	
MR8	A8	1sh black & red (R)	7.00	2.50
		Nos. MR6-MR8 (3)	9.25	4.40

Nos. 58-59 Overprinted

1918-19
MR9	A6	3p brown, yel	.90	3.25
MR10	A6	3p brown & blk ('19)	.90	3.75

Nos. 49-50, 54 Overprinted in Red or Black

1919, July 14
MR11	A8	½p green (R)	.30	1.25
MR12	A8	1p car rose	1.10	1.40
MR13	A8	1sh black & red (R)	10.00	24.00
		Nos. MR11-MR13 (3)	11.40	26.65

No. 59 Overprinted

MR14 A6 3p brown & black   .80 5.75

BAHRAIN

bä-'rān

LOCATION — An archipelago in the Persian Gulf, including the islands of Bahrain, Muharraq, Sitra, Nebi Saleh, Kasasifeh and Arad.
GOVT. — Independent sheikdom
AREA — 255 sq. mi.
POP. — 629,090 (1999 est.)
CAPITAL — Manama

Bahrain was a British-protected territory until it became an independent state on August 15, 1971.

12 Pies = 1 Anna
16 Annas = 1 Rupee
100 Naye Paise = 1 Rupee (1957)
1000 Fils = 1 Dinar (1966)

> **Catalogue values for unused stamps in this country are for Never Hinged items, beginning with Scott 62 in the regular postage section and Scott MR2 in the postal tax section.**

Indian Postal Administration
Stamps of India, 1926-32, Overprinted in Black

BAHRAIN a

Wmk. Multiple Stars (196)
1933, Aug. 10   Perf. 14
1	A46	3p gray	2.50	.40
2	A47	½a green	7.00	3.00
3	A48	9p dark green	3.50	.85
4	A48	1a dark brown	6.50	2.25
5	A60	1a3p violet	3.50	.65
6	A60	2a vermilion	9.25	7.00
7	A51	3a blue	17.50	35.00
8	A70	3a6p deep blue	3.50	.50
9	A61	4a olive green	17.00	35.00
10	A54	8a red violet	5.25	.90
11	A55	12a claret	7.00	1.50

Overprinted in Black

b

BAHRAIN

12	A56	1r green & brown	15.00	7.50
13	A56	2r brn org & car rose	30.00	35.00
14	A56	5r dk violet & ultra	85.00	110.00
		Nos. 1-14 (14)	212.50	239.55

Stamps of India, 1926-32, Overprinted Type "a" in Black

1934
15	A72	1a dark brown	8.00	.30
16	A51	3a carmine rose	4.50	.35
17	A52	4a olive green	3.60	.35
		Nos. 15-17 (3)	16.10	1.00

India Nos. 138, 111, 111a Overprinted Type "a" in Black

1935-37   Perf. 13½x14, 14
18	A71	½a green	3.75	.50
19	A49	2a vermilion	32.50	7.00
a.		Small die ('37)	42.50	.25

India Stamps of 1937 Overprinted Type "a" in Black

1938-41   Wmk. 196   Perf. 13½x14
20	A80	3p slate	6.50	2.50
21	A80	½a brown	2.75	.20
22	A80	9p green	2.25	2.00
23	A80	1a carmine	2.00	.20

24	A81	2a scarlet	6.00	.90
26	A81	3a yel grn ('41)	12.50	4.25
27	A81	3a6p ultra	4.00	2.50
28	A81	4a dk brn ('41)	110.00	50.00
30	A81	8a bl vio ('40)	130.00	35.00
31	A81	12a car lake ('40)	95.00	42.50

Overprinted Type "b" in Black
32	A82	1r brn & slate	2.50	1.25
33	A82	2r dk brn & dk vio	12.00	2.00
34	A82	5r dp ultra & dk grn	32.50	13.00
35	A82	10r rose car & dk vio ('41)	60.00	25.00
36	A82	15r dk grn & brn ('41)	42.50	42.50
37	A82	25r dk vio & bl vio ('41)	90.00	70.00
		Nos. 20-37 (16)	610.50	294.30
		Set, never hinged	525.00	

India Stamps of 1941-43 Overprinted Type "a" in Black

1942-44   Wmk. 196   Perf. 13½x14
38	A83	3p slate	.90	.55
39	A83	½a rose vio ('44)	3.25	.85
40	A83	9p lt green ('43)	10.00	10.00
41	A83	1a car rose ('44)	3.25	.45
42	A84	1a3p bister ('43)	7.50	11.25
43	A84	1½a dk pur ('43)	4.50	3.25
45	A84	2a scarlet ('43)	3.25	1.40
46	A84	3a violet ('43)	12.25	3.75
47	A84	3½a ultra	3.25	11.25
48	A85	4a chocolate	1.75	1.25
49	A85	6a peacock blue	9.00	7.50
50	A85	8a blue vio ('43)	3.00	1.75
51	A85	12a car lake	4.50	3.25
		Nos. 38-51 (13)	66.40	56.50
		Set, never hinged	65.00	

British Postal Administration
See Oman (Muscat) for similar stamps with surcharge of new value only.

Great Britain Nos. 258 to 263, 243 and 248 Surcharged in Black

BAHRAIN

c

½
ANNA

1948-49   Wmk. 251   Perf. 14½x14
52	A101	½a on ½p green	.35	.60
53	A101	1a on 1p vermilion	.35	.75
54	A101	1½a on 1½p lt red brn	.35	.80
55	A101	2a on 2p lt orange	.35	.20
56	A101	2½a on 2½p ultra	.45	1.75
57	A101	3a on 3p violet	.35	.20
58	A102	6a on 6p rose lilac	.35	.20
59	A103	1r on 1sh brown	1.40	.50

Great Britain Nos. 249A, 250 and 251A Surcharged in Black

BAHRAIN

2 RUPEES

Wmk. 259   Perf. 14
60	A104	2r on 2sh6p yel grn	4.50	4.25
61	A104	5r on 5sh dull red	6.50	6.00
61A	A105	10r on 10sh ultra	55.00	37.50
		Nos. 52-61A (11)	69.95	52.75
		Set, never hinged	70.00	

Surcharge bars at bottom on No. 61A.
Issued: 10r, 7/4/49; others, 4/1/48.

> **Catalogue values for unused stamps in this section, from this point to the end of the section, are for Never Hinged items.**

Silver Wedding Issue
Great Britain Nos. 267 and 268 Surcharged in Black

BAHRAIN
2½
ANNAS

Perf. 14½x14, 14x14½
1948, Apr. 26   Wmk. 251
62	A109	2½a on 2½p	.45	.25
63	A110	15r on £1	37.50	45.00

Three bars obliterate the original denomination on No. 63.

Olympic Issue
Great Britain Nos. 271 to 274 Surcharged "BAHRAIN" and New Value in Black

1948, July 29   Perf. 14½x14
64	A113	2½a on 2½p brt ultra	.50	.90
a.		Double surcharge	750.00	1,250.
65	A114	3a on 3p dp vio	.50	1.60
66	A115	6a on 6p red vio	1.40	2.00
67	A116	1r on 1sh dk brn	1.40	2.00
		Nos. 64-67 (4)	3.80	6.50

A square of dots obliterates the original denomination on No. 67.

UPU Issue
Great Britain Nos. 276 to 279 Surcharged "BAHRAIN", New Value and Square of Dots in Black

1949, Oct. 10   Photo.   Perf. 14½x14
68	A117	2½a on 2½p brt ultra	.50	1.60
69	A118	3a on 3p brt vio	.80	2.25
70	A119	6a on 6p red vio	.75	2.50
71	A120	1r on 1sh brown	1.90	1.40
		Nos. 68-71 (4)	3.95	7.75

Great Britain Nos. 280, 281, 283-285 Surcharged Type "c" in Black

1950-51   Wmk. 251
72	A101	½a on ½p lt org	.55	.55
73	A101	1a on 1p ultra	1.40	.30
74	A101	1½a on 1½p green	1.40	7.50
75	A101	2a on 2p lt red brn	.55	.30
76	A101	2½a on 2½p ver	1.40	7.50
77	A102	4a on 4p ultra	1.40	1.40

═ BAHRAIN

Great Britain Nos. 286-288 Surcharged in Black

2 RUPEES

Three types of surcharge on No. 78: Type I, "2" level with "RUPEES;" Type II, "2" raised higher than "RUPEES," 15mm between "BAHRAIN" and "2 RUPEES;" Type III, as type II, but 16mm between "BAHRAIN" and "2 RUPEES."

Perf. 11x12
Wmk. 259
78	A121	2r on 2sh6p green, type I ('51)	20.00	5.25
a.		2r on 2sh6p, type II ('53)	60.00	30.00
b.		2r on 2sh6p, type III ('55)	675.00	70.00
79	A121	5r on 5sh dl red	15.00	7.00
80	A122	10r on 10sh ultra	25.00	
		Nos. 72-80 (9)	66.70	29.80

Longer bars, at lower right, on No. 80.
Issued: 4a, Nov. 2, 1950; others, May 3, 1951.

Stamps of Great Britain, 1952-54, Surcharged "BAHRAIN" and New Value in Black or Dark Blue

1952-54   Wmk. 298   Perf. 14½x14
81	A126	½a on ½p red org ('53)	.25	.25
a.		"½" omitted	175.00	200.00
82	A126	1a on 1p ultra	.25	.20
83	A126	1½a on 1½p grn	.25	.25
84	A126	2a on 2p red brn	.25	.25
85	A127	2½a on 2½p scar	.55	1.00
86	A127	3a on 3p dk pur (Dk Bl)	1.00	.25
87	A128	4a on 4p ultra	5.00	.50
88	A129	6a on 6p lil rose	3.50	.45
89	A132	12a on 1sh3p dk grn	3.50	.75
90	A131	1r on 1sh6p dk bl	3.50	1.00
		Nos. 81-90 (10)	18.05	4.90

Issued: #83, 85, 12/5; #81-82, 84, 8/31/53; #87, 89-90, 11/2/53; #86, 88, 1/18/54.

Six stamps of this design picturing Sheik Sulman bin Hamad Al Kalifah were for local use in 1953-57.

Six stamps of similar design (same sheik, "Bahrain" vertical at left) were issued in 1961 for local use.

Coronation Issue
Great Britain Nos. 313-316 Surcharged "BAHRAIN" and New Value in Black

Perf. 14½x14

1953, June 3			**Wmk. 298**
92	A134	2½a on 2½p scar	1.00	1.00
93	A135	4a on 4p brt ultra	1.75	2.50
94	A136	12a on 1sh3p dk grn	2.50	3.00
95	A137	1r on 1sh6p dk bl	6.00	3.00
	Nos. 92-95 (4)		11.25	9.50

Squares of dots obliterate the original denominations on Nos. 94-95.

Great Britain Nos. 309-311 Surcharged "BAHRAIN" and New Value in Black

1955 Wmk. 308 Engr. Perf. 11x12			
96	A133	2r on 2sh6p dk brn	3.00	1.25
97	A133	5r on 5sh crimson	9.50	3.50
98	A133	10r on 10sh brt ultra	20.00	5.00
	Nos. 96-98 (3)		32.50	9.75

Three slightly different types of surcharge are found on the 2r; two on 5r and 10r.

Great Britain Nos. 317, 323, 325, 332-333 Surcharged "BAHRAIN" and New Value

Perf. 14½x14

			Photo.
1956-57 Wmk. 308			
99	A126	½a on ½p red org	.20	.20
100	A128	4a on 4p ultra	5.00	13.00
101	A129	6a on 6p lil rose	.45	.40
102	A132	12a on 1sh3p dk green	6.75	8.50
103	A131	1r on 1sh6p dk bl ('57)	7.50	.20
	Nos. 99-103 (5)		19.90	22.30

Great Britain Nos. 317-325, 328, 332 Surcharged "BAHRAIN" and New Value

1957, Apr. 1			
104	A129	1np on 5p lt brown	.20	.20
105	A126	3np on ½p red org	.25	1.10
106	A126	6np on 1p ultra	.25	1.10
107	A126	9np on 1½p green	.25	1.10
108	A126	12np on 2p red brn	.30	.40
109	A127	15np on 2½p scar, type I	.35	.20
a.	Type II		.40	1.25
110	A127	20np on 3p dk pur	.25	.20
111	A128	25np on 4p ultra	.65	1.25
112	A129	40np on 6p lil rose	.65	.20
113	A130	50np on 9p dp ol grn	3.00	2.75
114	A132	75np on 1sh3p dk grn	1.75	.30
	Nos. 104-114 (11)		7.90	8.80

The arrangement of the surcharge varies on different values: there are three bars through value on No. 113.

Jubilee Jamboree Issue
Great Britain Nos. 334-336 Surcharged "BAHRAIN," New Value and Square of Dots in Black

Perf. 14½x14

1957, Aug. 1 Photo. Wmk. 308			
115	A138	15np on 2½p scar	.20	.30
116	A138	25np on 4p ultra	.30	.30
117	A138	75np on 1sh3p dk grn	.40	.40
	Nos. 115-117 (3)		.90	1.00

Great Britain No. 357 Surcharged "BAHRAIN/ NP 15 NP" in Black

1960 Wmk. 322 Perf. 14½x14			
118	A127	15np on 2½p scar, type II	3.00	9.00

Sheik Sulman bin Hamad Al Khalifah

A1   A2

Perf. 14½x14

1960, July 1 Photo. Unwmk.			
119	A1	5np lt ultra	.20	.20
120	A1	15np orange	.20	.20
121	A1	20np lt violet	.20	.20
122	A1	30np olive bister	.20	.20
123	A1	40np gray	.20	.20
124	A1	50np emerald	.20	.20
125	A1	75np red brown	.30	.20

Engr.

Perf. 13x13½

126	A2	1r gray	1.50	.25
127	A2	2r carmine	2.75	1.60
128	A2	5r ultra	4.50	2.25
129	A2	10r olive green	11.00	3.50
	Nos. 119-129 (11)		21.25	9.00

Sheik Isa bin Sulman Al Khalifah A3

Bahrain Airport A4

Designs: 5r, 10r, Deep water jetty.

1964, Feb. 22 Photo. Perf. 14½x14			
130	A3	5np ultra	.20	.20
131	A3	15np orange	.20	.20
132	A3	20np brt purple	.20	.20
133	A3	30np brown olive	.20	.20
134	A3	40np slate	.20	.20
135	A3	50np emerald	.30	.20
136	A3	75np chestnut	.60	.25

Engr.

Perf. 13½x13

137	A4	1r black	4.00	1.00
138	A4	2r rose red	6.00	1.00
139	A4	5r violet blue	9.00	6.00
140	A4	10r dull green	11.00	6.00
	Nos. 130-140 (11)		31.90	15.45

Bahrain Postal Administration

Sheik Isa bin Sulman Al Khalifah — A5

Sheik and Bahrain International Airport — A6

Pearl Divers — A7

Bab al Bahrain, Suq Al-Khamis Mosque, Sheik, Emblem, etc. — A8

Designs: 50f, 75f, Pier, Mina Sulman harbor. 200f, Falcon and horse race. 500f, "Hospitality," pouring coffee and Sheik's Palace.

Perf. 14½x14

1966, Jan. 1 Photo. Unwmk.			
141	A5	5f green	.20	.20
142	A5	10f dark red	.20	.20
143	A5	15f ultra	.20	.20
144	A5	20f magenta	.20	.20

Perf. 13½x14

145	A6	30f green & black	.20	.20
146	A6	40f blue & black	.30	.20
147	A6	50f dp car rose & blk	.40	.20
148	A6	75f violet & black	.50	.25

Perf. 14½x14

149	A7	100f dk blue & yel	1.75	.75
150	A7	200f dk green & org	7.75	1.50
151	A7	500f red brown & yel	5.75	2.50
152	A8	1d multicolored	11.00	6.00
	Nos. 141-152 (12)		28.45	12.40

Produce, Date Palm, Ship, Truck and Plane A9

Map of Bahrain and WHO Emblem A10

1966, Mar. 28 Litho. Perf. 13x13½			
153	A9	10f red & blue green	.30	.30
154	A9	20f green & vio	.65	.65
155	A9	40f olive bis & lt bl	1.25	1.25
156	A9	200f vio blue & pink	6.25	6.25
	Nos. 153-156 (4)		8.45	8.45

6th Bahrain Trade Fair & Agricultural Show.

1968, June Unwmk. Perf. 13½x14			
157	A10	20f gray & black	.50	.50
158	A10	40f blue grn & black	2.00	1.40
159	A10	150f dp rose & black	7.50	5.50
	Nos. 157-159 (3)		10.00	7.40

20th anniv. of the WHO.

Isa Town A11

1968, Nov. 18 Litho. Perf. 14½			
160	A11	50f shown	1.60	1.60
161	A11	80f Market	2.50	2.50
162	A11	120f Stadium	4.25	4.25
163	A11	150f Mosque	6.75	6.75
	Nos. 160-163 (4)		15.10	15.10

Education Symbol — A12

1969, Apr. Litho. Perf. 13			
164	A12	40f multicolored	1.25	1.25
165	A12	60f multicolored	2.50	2.00
166	A12	150f multicolored	6.25	4.25
	Nos. 164-166 (3)		10.00	7.50

50th anniversary of education in Bahrain.

Map of Arabian Gulf, Radar and Emblem A13

Designs: 40f, 150f, Radar installation and emblem of Cable & Wireless Ltd., vert.

Perf. 14x13½, 13½x14

1969, July 14 Litho.			
167	A13	20f lt green & multi	1.75	1.00
168	A13	40f vio blue & multi	3.75	2.25
169	A13	100f ocher & multi	8.50	5.25
170	A13	150f rose lilac & multi	13.50	9.00
	Nos. 167-170 (4)		27.50	17.50

Opening of the satellite earth station (connected through the Indian Ocean satellite Intelsat III) at Ras Abu Jarjur, July 14.

Municipal Building, Arms and Map of Bahrain A14

1970, Feb. 23 Litho. Perf. 12x12½			
171	A14	30f blue & multi	2.75	2.75
172	A14	150f multicolored	10.00	10.00

2nd Conf. of the Arab Cities' Org.

Copper Bull's Head A15

Conf. Emblem and: 80f, Gateway to Qalat al Bahrain, 7th cent. B.C. 120f, Aerial view of grave mounds, Bahrain. 150f, Dilmun seal, 2000 B.C.

1970, Mar. 1 Photo. Perf. 14½			
173	A15	60f multicolored	2.25	2.00
174	A15	80f multicolored	3.50	2.25
175	A15	120f multicolored	4.25	3.50
176	A15	150f multicolored	5.00	4.25
	Nos. 173-176 (4)		15.00	12.00

3rd Intl. Asian Archaeological Conf., Bahrain.

Vickers VC 10, Big Ben and Minaret A16

1970, Apr. 5 Litho. Perf. 14½x14			
177	A16	30f multicolored	1.40	.85
178	A16	60f multicolored	3.00	1.90
179	A16	120f multicolored	5.50	6.25
	Nos. 177-179 (3)		9.90	9.00

1st flight to London from the Arabian Gulf Area by Gulf Aviation Company.

Intl. Education Year Emblem A17

120f, Education Year emblem & students.

1970, Nov. 1 Litho. Perf. 14½x14			
180	A17	60f blk, blue & org	3.00	3.00
181	A17	120f multicolored	6.00	6.00

Independent State

Government House, Manama — A18

UN Emblem and Sails — A19

Designs: 30f, "Freedom" with dove and torch, and globe. 120f, 150f, Bahrain coat of arms.

1971, Oct. 2   Photo.   Perf. 14½x14
182	A18	30f gold & multi	1.60	1.60
183	A18	60f gold & multi	3.25	3.25
184	A18	120f gold & multi	6.50	6.50
185	A18	150f gold & multi	8.25	8.25
	Nos. 182-185 (4)		19.60	19.60

Declaration of Bahrain independence, Aug. 15, 1971.

Perf. 14x14½, 14½x14
1972, Feb. 1   Litho.
30f, 60f, Dhow with sails showing UN and Arab League emblems, horiz. 150f, as 120f.
186	A19	30f multicolored	2.50	2.50
187	A19	60f red, gray & multi	6.00	6.00
188	A19	120f dull blue & multi	12.50	12.50
189	A19	150f multicolored	14.00	14.00
	Nos. 186-189 (4)		35.00	35.00

Bahrain's admission to the Arab League and the United Nations.

"Your Heart is your Health" — A20

1972, Apr. 7   Litho.   Perf. 14½x14
190	A20	30f black & multi	3.75	3.75
191	A20	60f gray & multi	7.50	7.50

World Health Day.

UN and FAO Emblems A21

1973, May 12   Litho.   Perf. 12½x13
192	A21	30f org red, pur & grn	3.75	3.75
193	A21	60f ocher, brn & grn	6.50	6.50

World Food Programs, 10th anniversary.

People of Various Races, Human Rights Flame — A22

1973, Nov.   Litho.   Perf. 14x14½
194	A22	30f blue, blk & brn	4.00	4.00
195	A22	60f lake, blk & brn	7.75	7.75

25th anniversary of the Universal Declaration of Human Rights.

Flour Mill A23

60f, Intl. Airport. 120f, Sulmaniya Medical Center. 150f, ALBA aluminum smelting plant.

1973, Dec. 16   Photo.   Perf. 14½
196	A23	30f multicolored	1.00	1.00
197	A23	60f multicolored	1.75	1.75
198	A23	120f multicolored	3.50	3.50
199	A23	150f multicolored	4.25	4.25
	Nos. 196-199 (4)		10.50	10.50

National Day.

Letters and UPU Emblem — A24

Carrier Pigeon and UPU Emblem A25

60f, UPU emblem & letters. 150f, Like 120f.

1974, Feb. 4   Litho.   Perf. 13½
200	A24	30f blue & multi	1.00	1.00
201	A24	60f emerald & multi	1.75	1.75

Perf. 12½x13½
202	A25	120f ultra & multi	3.00	3.00
203	A25	150f yellow & multi	4.25	4.25
	Nos. 200-203 (4)		10.00	10.00

Bahrain's admission to UPU.

Traffic Signals — A26

1974, May 4   Litho.   Perf. 14½
204	A26	30f org brown & multi	2.75	2.75
205	A26	60f brt blue & multi	6.25	6.25

International Traffic Day.

Jet, Globe, Mail Coach and UPU Emblem — A27

1974, Sept. 1   Photo.   Perf. 14x14½
206	A27	30f multicolored	.75	.75
207	A27	60f multicolored	1.50	1.50
208	A27	120f multicolored	3.25	3.25
209	A27	150f multicolored	4.00	4.00
	Nos. 206-209 (4)		9.50	9.50

Centenary of Universal Postal Union.

National Day Emblem, Sitra Power Station — A28

National Day: 120f, 150f, Bahrain dry dock.

1974, Dec. 16   Litho.   Perf. 14½
210	A28	30f blue & multi	.85	.85
211	A28	60f green & multi	1.40	1.40
212	A28	120f lil rose & multi	3.50	3.50
213	A28	150f ver & multi	4.25	4.25
	Nos. 210-213 (4)		10.00	10.00

Perf. 14½x14
Woman's Silk Gown

A29

Photo.; Gold Embossed
1975, Feb. 1
Design: Various women's costumes.
214	A29	30f blue grn & multi	.65	.65
215	A29	60f vio blue & multi	1.10	1.10
216	A29	120f rose red & multi	2.75	2.75
217	A29	150f multicolored	3.50	3.50
	Nos. 214-217 (4)		8.00	8.00

Pendant — A30

Designs: Various jewelry.

1975, Apr. 1   Photo.   Perf. 14½x14
218	A30	30f olive & multi	.60	.60
219	A30	60f dp pur & multi	1.40	1.40
220	A30	120f dp car & multi	2.75	2.75
221	A30	150f dp blue & multi	3.50	3.50
	Nos. 218-221 (4)		8.25	8.25

Woman Planting Flower, IWY Emblem — A31

1975, July 28   Litho.   Perf. 14½
60f, Educated woman holding IWY emblem.
222	A31	30f multicolored	1.50	1.50
223	A31	60f multicolored	3.50	3.50

International Women's Year.

Miniature Sheet

Arabian Stallion — A32

Arabian horses: a, Brown head. b, White mare. c, Mare and foal. d, White head. e, White mare. f, Mare and stallion. g, Bedouins on horseback. #224a, 224b, 224d are vert.

Perf. 14x14½, 14½x14
1975, Sept. 1   Photo.
224		Sheet of 8	52.50	32.50
a.-h.	A32 60f any single		5.25	3.50

Flag of Bahrain — A33

Map of Bahrain — A34

Sheik Isa — A35

1976-80   Litho.   Perf. 14½
225	A33	5f red & ultra	.20	.20
226	A33	10f red & green	.20	.20
227	A33	15f red & black	.20	.20
228	A33	20f red & brown	.20	.20
228A	A34	25f gray & blk ('79)	.20	.20
229	A34	40f blue & black	.25	.25
229A	A34	50f yel grn & blk ('79)	.30	.30
230	A34	60f dl grn & blk ('77)	.35	.35
231	A34	80f rose lil & blk	.45	.45
232	A34	100f lt red brn & blk ('77)	.55	.55
233	A34	150f org & black	.85	.85
234	A34	200f yel & black	1.10	1.10

Engr.   Perf. 12x12½
235	A35	300f lt grn & grn	1.60	1.60
236	A35	400f pink & red brn	2.25	2.25
237	A35	500f lt bl & dk bl	2.75	2.75
238	A35	1d gray & sepia	5.50	5.00
239	A35	2d rose & vio ('80)	11.50	9.25
240	A35	3d buff & brn ('80)	17.00	14.00
	Nos. 225-240 (18)		45.45	39.70

A later printing of the 100f-200f, and possibly others, has a larger printers imprint at bottom.

Concorde at London Airport — A36

#245, Concorde at Bahrain Airport. #246, Concorde over London to Bahrain map. #247, Concorde on runway at night.

1976, Jan. 22   Photo.   Perf. 13x14
244	A36	80f gold & multi	2.25	2.25
245	A36	80f gold & multi	2.25	2.25
246	A36	80f gold & multi	2.25	2.25
247	A36	80f gold & multi	2.25	2.25
a.	Souvenir sheet of 4		11.00	11.00
b.	Block of 4, #244-247		9.00	9.00

1st commercial flight of supersonic jet Concorde, London to Bahrain, Jan. 21. No. 247a contains 4 stamps with simulated perfs.

Soldier, Flag and Arms of Bahrain — A37

1976, Feb. 5   Litho.   Perf. 14½
248	A37	40f yellow & multi	2.00	2.00
249	A37	80f lt blue & multi	4.00	4.00

Defense Force Day.

Sheik Isa, King Khalid, Bahrain and Saudi Flags A38

1976, Mar. 23 Litho. Perf. 14½
250 A38 40f gold & multi   1.75 1.75
251 A38 80f silver & multi   3.00 3.00
Visit of King Khalid of Saudi Arabia.

New Housing, Housing Ministry's Seal — A39

1976, Dec. 16 Litho. Perf. 14½
252 A39 40f rose & multi   1.60 1.60
253 A39 80f blue & multi   3.25 3.25
National Day.

APU Emblem A40

1977, Apr. 12 Litho. Perf. 14½
254 A40 40f silver & multi   1.50 1.50
255 A40 80f rose & multi   3.00 3.00
Arab Postal Union, 25th anniversary.

Miniature Sheet

Dogs on Beach and Dhow A41

Saluki dogs: b, Dog and camels. c, Dog and gazelles. d, Dog and Ruler's Palace. e, Dog's head. f, Heads of two dogs. g, Dog in dunes. h, Playing dogs.

1977, July Photo. Perf. 14x14½
256   Sheet of 8   28.00 28.00
a.-h.   A41 80f any single   2.75 2.75

Students and Candle A42

1977, Sept. 8 Litho. Perf. 14½
257 A42 40f multicolored   1.50 1.50
258 A42 80f multicolored   3.00 3.00
International Literacy Day.

Shipyard and Flags A43

1977, Dec. 16 Litho. Perf. 14½
259 A43 40f multicolored   1.50 1.50
260 A43 80f multicolored   3.00 3.00
Inauguration of Arab Shipbuilding and Repair Yard Co.

Antenna, ITU Emblem A44

1978, May 17 Litho. Perf. 14½
261 A44 40f yellow & multi   1.50 1.50
262 A44 80f silver & multi   3.00 3.00
10th World Telecommunications Day.

Ghanja Dhow — A45

Dhows of the Arabian Gulf. #267-270 vertical.

Perf. 14x14½, 14½x14
1979, June 16 Photo.
263 A45 100f shown   3.25 3.25
264 A45 100f Zarook   3.25 3.25
265 A45 100f Shu'ai   3.25 3.25
266 A45 100f Jaliboot   3.25 3.25
267 A45 100f Baghla   3.25 3.25
268 A45 100f Sambuk   3.25 3.25
269 A45 100f Boom   3.25 3.25
270 A45 100f Kotia   3.25 3.25
a.   Block of 8, #263-270   40.00 40.00

Learning to Walk — A46

IYC Emblem and: 100f, Hands surrounding girl, UN emblem.

1979 Litho. Perf. 14½
271 A46 50f multicolored   1.50 1.50
272 A46 100f multicolored   3.00 3.00
International Year of the Child.

Hegira, 1,500th Anniv. — A47

1980 Photo. Perf. 13x13½
273 A47 50f multicolored   .65 .65
274 A47 100f multicolored   1.25 1.25
a.   Miniature sheet of 1   6.00 6.00
275 A47 150f multicolored   2.00 2.00
276 A47 200f multicolored   2.75 2.75
Nos. 273-276 (4)   6.65 6.65

Falcon A48

Designs: Falcons.

Perf. 13½x14, 14x13½
1980, Nov. 1 Photo.
277   Block of 8   17.50 15.00
a.-h.   A48 100f any single   1.75 1.75

IYD Emblem, Sheik Isa A49

1981, Mar. 21 Litho. Perf. 14½
278 A49 50f multicolored   1.60 1.60
279 A49 100f multicolored   3.25 3.25
International Year of the Disabled.

50th Anniversary of Electricity in Bahrain — A50

1981, Apr. 26 Litho. Perf. 14½
280 A50 50f multicolored   1.60 1.60
281 A50 100f multicolored   3.25 3.25

Stone Cutting — A51

1981, July 1 Photo. Perf. 14x13½
282 A51 50f shown   .75 .75
283 A51 100f Pottery   1.25 1.25
284 A51 150f Weaving   2.75 2.75
285 A51 200f Basket making   3.00 3.00
Nos. 282-285 (4)   7.75 7.75

Hegira (Pilgrimage Year) — A52

Designs: Various mosques.

1981, Oct. 1 Photo. Perf. 14x13½
286 A52 50f multicolored   .80 .80
287 A52 100f multicolored   1.60 1.60
288 A52 150f multicolored   2.25 2.25
289 A52 200f multicolored   3.25 3.25
Nos. 286-289 (4)   7.90 7.90

Sheik Isa, 20th Anniv. of Coronation A53

1981, Dec. 16 Photo. Perf. 14x13½
290 A53 15f multicolored   .25 .25
291 A53 50f multicolored   .80 .80
292 A53 100f multicolored   1.75 1.75
293 A53 150f multicolored   2.50 2.50
294 A53 200f multicolored   3.50 3.50
Nos. 290-294 (5)   8.80 8.80

Wildlife in al Areen Park — A54

Designs: a, Gazelle. b, Oryx. c, Dhub lizard. d, Arabian hares. e, Oryxes. f, Reems.

1982, Mar. 1 Photo. Perf. 13½x14
295   Sheet of 6   14.00 14.00
a.-f.   A54 100f any single   2.25 2.25

3rd Session of Gulf Supreme Council, Nov. — A55

1982, Nov. 9 Litho. Perf. 14½
296 A55 50f blue & multi   .85 .85
297 A55 100f green & multi   2.25 2.25

Opening of Madinat Hamad Housing Development — A56

1983, Dec. 1 Litho. Perf. 14½
298 A56 50f multicolored   .85 .85
299 A56 100f multicolored   2.25 2.25

Al Khalifa Dynasty Bicentenary — A57

Sheiks or Emblems: a, 500fr, Isa bin Sulman. b, Emblem (tan & multi). c, Isa bin Ali, 1869-1932. d, Hamad bin Isa, 1932-42. e, Sulman bin Hamad, 1942-61. f, Emblem (pale green & multi). g, Emblem (lemon & multi). h, Emblem (light blue & multi). i, Emblem (gray & multi).

1983, Dec. 16 Litho. Perf. 14½
300   Sheet of 9   9.00 9.00
a.-i.   A57 100f any single   .80 .80
Souvenir Sheet
301 A57 500f multicolored   8.50 8.50
No. 301 contains one stamp 60x38mm.

Gulf Co-operation Council Traffic Week — A58

1984, Apr. 30 Litho. Perf. 14½
302 A58 15f multicolored   .30 .30
303 A58 50f multicolored   1.00 1.00
304 A58 100f multicolored   2.00 2.00
Nos. 302-304 (3)   3.30 3.30

1984
Summer
Olympics
A59

1984, Sept. 15   *Perf. 14½*
305	A59	15f Hurdles	.25	.25
306	A59	50f Equestrian	.80	.80
307	A59	100f Diving	1.60	1.60
308	A59	150f Fencing	2.00	2.00
309	A59	200f Shooting	3.50	3.50
		Nos. 305-309 (5)	8.15	8.15

Postal
Service
Cent.
A60

1984, Dec. 8   **Photo.**   *Perf. 12x11½*
310	A60	15f multicolored	.40	.40
311	A60	50f multicolored	1.25	1.25
312	A60	100f multicolored	2.25	2.25
		Nos. 310-312 (3)	3.90	3.90

Miniature Sheet

Coastal Fish — A61

1985, Feb. 10   **Photo.**   *Perf. 13½x14*
313		Sheet of 10	12.00	12.00
a.-j.	A61	100f any single	1.40	1.40

1st Arab
Gulf
States
Week for
Social
Work
A62

1985, Oct. 15   **Litho.**   *Perf. 14½*
314	A62	15f multicolored	.25	.25
315	A62	50f multicolored	.85	.85
316	A62	100f multicolored	1.90	1.90
		Nos. 314-316 (3)	3.00	3.00

Intl.
Youth
Year
A63

1985, Nov. 16
317	A63	15f multicolored	.25	.25
318	A63	50f multicolored	.85	.85
319	A63	100f multicolored	1.90	1.90
		Nos. 317-319 (3)	3.00	3.00

Bahrain-Saudi Arabia Causeway
Opening — A64

1986, Nov.   **Litho.**   *Perf. 14½*
320	A64	15f Causeway, aerial view	.25	.25
321	A64	50f Island	.85	.85
322	A64	100f Causeway	1.90	1.90
		Nos. 320-322 (3)	3.00	3.00

Sheik Isa, 25th
Anniv. as the
Emir — A65

1986, Dec. 16
323	A65	15f multicolored	.25	.25
324	A65	50f multicolored	.85	.85
325	A65	100f multicolored	1.90	1.90
a.		Souvenir sheet of 3, #323-325	7.50	5.50
		Nos. 323-325 (3)	3.00	3.00

WHO,
40th
Anniv.
A66

1988, Apr. 30   **Litho.**   *Perf. 14½*
326	A66	50f multicolored	.50	.50
327	A66	150f multicolored	1.40	1.40

Opening
of
Ahmed
Al Fateh
Islamic
Center
A67

1988, June 2   **Litho.**   *Perf. 14½*
328	A67	50f multicolored	.50	.50
329	A67	150f multicolored	1.40	1.40

1988 Summer Olympics, Seoul — A68

1988, Sept. 17   **Litho.**   *Perf. 14½*
330	A68	50f Running	.30	.30
331	A68	80f Equestrian	.45	.45
332	A68	150f Fencing	.80	.80
333	A68	200f Soccer	1.10	1.10
		Nos. 330-333 (4)	2.65	2.65

Gulf Cooperation Council Supreme
Council 9th Regular Session,
Bahrain — A69

1988, Dec. 19   **Litho.**   *Perf. 14½*
334	A69	50f multicolored	.50	.50
335	A69	150f multicolored	1.40	1.40

Miniature Sheets

Camels — A70

No. 336: a, Close-up of head, rider in background. b, Camel kneeling at rest. c, Two adults, calf. d, Three adults. e, Camel facing right. f, Mount and rider (facing left).

No. 337: a, Man walking in front of camel, oil well. b, Man walking in front of camel. c, Oil well, camel's head. d, Mount and rider (facing

forward). e, Mount and rider (facing right). f, Two dromedaries at a run.
Nos. 337a-337f vert.

Perf. 13½x14, 14x13½

1989, June 15
336		Sheet of 6	6.00	6.00
a.-f.	A70	150f any single	1.00	1.00
337		Sheet of 6	6.00	6.00
a.-f.	A70	150f any single	1.00	1.00

Sheik Isa — A71

1989, Dec. 16   **Litho.**   *Perf. 13½x14*
338	A71	25f multicolored	.20	.20
339	A71	40f multicolored	.25	.25
340	A71	50f multicolored	.30	.30
341	A71	60f multicolored	.35	.35
342	A71	75f multicolored	.45	.45
343	A71	80f multicolored	.50	.50
344	A71	100f multicolored	.60	.60
345	A71	120f multicolored	.75	.75
346	A71	150f multicolored	.90	.90
347	A71	200f multicolored	1.25	1.25
a.		Souv. sheet of 10, #338-347	6.00	6.00
		Nos. 338-347 (10)	5.55	5.55

Houbara (Bustard) — A72

Designs: a, Two birds facing right. b, Two birds facing each other. c, Chicks. d, Adult, chick. e, Adult, facing right, vert. f, In flight. g, Adult facing right. h, Chick, facing left, vert. i, Adult facing left. j, Adult male, close-up. k, Courtship display. l, Two birds facing left.

1990, Feb. 17   **Photo.**   *Perf. 14*
348		Sheet of 12	11.00	11.00
a.-l.	A72	150f any single	.90	.90

 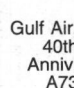

Gulf Air,
40th
Anniv.
A73

1990, Mar. 24   **Litho.**   *Perf. 14½*
360	A73	50f multicolored	.30	.30
361	A73	80f multicolored	.50	.50
362	A73	150f multicolored	.95	.95
363	A73	200f multicolored	1.25	1.25
		Nos. 360-363 (4)	3.00	3.00

Chamber of Commerce, 50th
Anniv. — A74

1990, May 26
364	A74	50f multicolored	.30	.30
365	A74	80f multicolored	.50	.50
366	A74	150f multicolored	.95	.95
367	A74	200f multicolored	1.25	1.25
		Nos. 364-367 (4)	3.00	3.00

Intl.
Literacy
Year
A75

1990, Sept. 8   **Litho.**   *Perf. 14½*
368	A75	50f multicolored	.30	.30
369	A75	80f multicolored	.50	.50
370	A75	150f multicolored	.95	.95
371	A75	200f multicolored	1.25	1.25
		Nos. 368-371 (4)	3.00	3.00

Miniature Sheet

Indigenous
Birds — A76

a, Galerida cristata. b, Upupa epops. c, Pycnonotus leucogenys. d, Streptopelia turtur. e, Streptopelia decaocto. f, Falco tinnunculus. g, Passer domesticus, horiz. h, Lanius excubitor, horiz. i, Psittacula krameri.

1991, Sept. 15   **Litho.**   *Perf. 14½*
372		Sheet of 9	9.00	9.00
a.-i.	A76	150f any single	1.10	1.10

See Nos. 382, 407.

Coronation of Sheik Isa, 30th
Anniv. — A77

Design: Nos. 374, 376, 378, 380, 381a, Portrait at left, leaves.

Litho. & Embossed

1991, Dec. 16   *Perf. 14½*
373	A77	50f multicolored	.35	.35
374	A77	50f multicolored	.35	.35
375	A77	80f multicolored	.55	.55
376	A77	80f multicolored	.55	.55
377	A77	150f multicolored	1.10	1.10
378	A77	150f multicolored	1.10	1.10
379	A77	200f multicolored	1.50	1.50
380	A77	200f multicolored	1.50	1.50
		Nos. 373-380 (8)	7.00	7.00

Souvenir Sheet
Perf. 14x14½
381		Sheet of 2	7.50	7.50
a.-b.	A77	500f any single	3.75	3.75

No. 381 contains 41x31mm stamps.

Indigenous Birds Type of 1991
Miniature Sheet

#382: a, Ciconia ciconia. b, Merops apiaster. c, Sturnus vulgaris. d, Hypocolius ampelinus. e, Cuculus canorus. f, Turdus viscivorus. g, Coracias garrulus. h, Carduelis carduelis. i, Lanius collurio. j, Turdus iliacus, horiz. k, Motacilla alba, horiz. l, Oriolus oriolus, horiz. m, Erithacus rubecula. n, Luscinia luscinia. o, Muscicapa striata. p, Hirundo rustica.

1992, Mar. 21   **Litho.**   *Perf. 14½*
382		Sheet of 16	13.50	13.50
a.-p.	A76	150f any single	.80	.80

Miniature Sheet

Horse
Racing
A78

Designs: No. 383a, Horses leaving starting gate. b, Trainers leading horses. c, Horses racing around turn. d, Horses in stretch racing by flags. e, Two horses racing by grandstand. f, Five horses galloping. g, Two brown horses racing. h, Black horse, gray horse racing.

1992, May 22
383		Sheet of 8	7.25	7.25
a.-h.	A78	150f any single	.90	.90

1992 Summer Olympics,
Barcelona — A79

1992, July 25   Litho.   Perf. 14½
384	A79	50f Equestrian	.35	.35
385	A79	80f Running	.60	.60
386	A79	150f Judo	1.10	1.10
387	A79	200f Cycling	1.40	1.40
		Nos. 384-387 (4)	3.45	3.45

Bahrain
Intl.
Airport,
60th
Anniv.
A80

1992, Oct. 27   Litho.   Perf. 14½
388	A80	50f multicolored	.35	.35
389	A80	80f multicolored	.55	.55
390	A80	150f multicolored	1.00	1.00
391	A80	200f multicolored	1.25	1.25
		Nos. 388-391 (4)	3.15	3.15

Children's Art — A81

Designs: 50f, Girl jumping rope, vert. 80f, Women in traditional dress, vert. 150f, Women stirring kettle. 200f, Fishermen.

1992, Nov. 28   Litho.   Perf. 14½
392	A81	50f multicolored	.30	.30
393	A81	80f multicolored	.50	.50
394	A81	150f multicolored	.95	.95
395	A81	200f multicolored	1.25	1.25
		Nos. 392-395 (4)	3.00	3.00

Inauguration of Expansion of
Aluminum Bahrain — A82

50f, Ore funicular. 80f, Smelting pot. 150f, Mill. 200f, Cylindrical aluminum ingots.

1992, Dec. 16
396	A82	50f multicolored	.30	.30
397	A82	80f multicolored	.50	.50
398	A82	150f multicolored	.95	.95
399	A82	200f multicolored	1.25	1.25
		Nos. 396-399 (4)	3.00	3.00

Bahrain
Defense
Force, 25th
Anniv.
A83

Designs: 50f, Artillery forces, vert. 80f, Fighters, tanks, and ship, vert. 150f, Frigate. 200f, Jet fighter.

Perf. 13½x13, 13x13½
1993, Feb. 5   Litho.
400	A83	50f multicolored	.30	.30
401	A83	80f multicolored	.50	.50
402	A83	150f multicolored	.95	.95
403	A83	200f multicolored	1.25	1.25
		Nos. 400-403 (4)	3.00	3.00

World Meteorology Day — A84

Designs: 50f, Satellite image of Bahrain, vert. 150f, Infrared satellite map of world. 200f, Earth, seen from space, vert.

1993, Mar. 23   Litho.   Perf. 14½
404	A84	50f multicolored	.45	.45
405	A84	150f multicolored	1.40	1.40
406	A84	200f multicolored	1.75	1.75
		Nos. 404-406 (3)	3.60	3.60

Bird Type of 1991
Miniature Sheet

Designs: a, Ardea purpurea. b, Gallinula chloropus. c, Phalacrocorax nigrogularis. d, Dromas ardeola. e, Alcedo atthis. f, Vanellus vanellus. g, Haematopus ostralegus, horiz. h, Nycticorax nycticorax. i, Sterna caspia, horiz. j, Arenaria interpres, horiz. k, Rallus aquaticus, horiz. l, Anas platyrhychos, horia. m, Larus fuscus, horiz.

1993, May 22   Litho.   Perf. 14½
407		Sheet of 13 + 2 labels	11.00	11.00
	a.-m.	A76 150f any single	.85	.85

Gazella Subgutturosa Marica — A85

1993, July 24   Litho.   Perf. 14½
408	A85	25f Calf	.20	.20
409	A85	50f Female standing	.30	.30
410	A85	50f Female walking	.30	.30
411	A85	150f Male	.95	.95
		Nos. 408-411 (4)	1.75	1.75

World Wildlife Federation.

Wild
Flowers — A86

Designs: a, Lycium shawii. b, Alhagi maurorum. c, Caparis spinosa. d, Cistanche phelypae. e, Asphodelus tenuifolius. f, Limonium axillare. g, Cynomorium coccineum. h, Calligonum polygonoides.

1993, Oct. 16   Litho.   Perf. 13½x13
412	A86	150f Sheet of 8, #a.-h.	6.50	6.50

A87

1994, Jan. 22   Litho.   Perf. 14½
Background Color
413	A87	50f yellow	.30	.30
414	A87	80f blue green	.50	.50
415	A87	150f purple	.95	.95
416	A87	200f blue	1.25	1.25
		Nos. 413-416 (4)	3.00	3.00

Intl. Year of the Family.

A88

Butterflies: No. 417a, Lepidochrysops arabicus. b, Ypthima bolanica. c, Eurema brigitta. d, Precis limnoria. e, Aglais urticae. f, Colotis protomedia. g, Salamis anacardii. h, Byblia ilithyia.
No. 418a, Papilio machaon. b, Agrodiaetus loewii. c, Vanessa cardui. d, Papilio demoleus. e, Hamanumida daedalus. f, Funonia orithya. g, Funonia chorimine. h, Colias croceus.

Perf. 13½x13, 13x13½
1994, Mar. 21   Litho.
417	A88	50f Sheet of 8, #a.-h.	2.50	2.50
418	A88	150f Sheet of 8, #a.-h.	7.50	7.50

No. 418 is horiz.

A89

1994, May 8   Litho.   Perf. 14½
419	A89	50f lilac & multi	.30	.30
420	A89	80f yellow & multi	.50	.50
421	A89	150f salmon & multi	.95	.95
422	A89	200f green blue & multi	1.25	1.25
		Nos. 419-422 (4)	3.00	3.00

Intl. Red Cross & Red Crescent Societies, 75th anniv.

1994 World Cup Soccer
Championships, US — A90

Designs: 50f, Goalkeeper. 80f, Heading ball. 150f, Dribbling ball. 200f, Slide tackle.

1994, June 17   Litho.   Perf. 14
423	A90	50f multicolored	.30	.30
424	A90	80f multicolored	.50	.50
425	A90	150f multicolored	.95	.95
426	A90	200f multicolored	1.25	1.25
		Nos. 423-426 (4)	3.00	3.00

Bahrain's First Satellite Earth Station,
25th Anniv. — A91

1994, July 14
427	A91	50f blue & multi	.30	.30
428	A91	80f yellow & multi	.50	.50
429	A91	150f violet & multi	.95	.95
430	A91	200f pink, yellow & multi	1.25	1.25
		Nos. 427-430 (4)	3.00	3.00

Education in
Bahrain, 75th
Anniv. — A92

1994, Nov. 19   Litho.   Perf. 14½
431	A92	50f yellow & multi	.30	.30
432	A92	80f buff & multi	.50	.50
433	A92	150f salmon & multi	.95	.95
434	A92	200f pink & multi	1.25	1.25
		Nos. 431-434 (4)	3.00	3.00

Gulf
Cooperation
Council
Supreme
Council, 15th
Regular
Session,
Bahrain — A93

1994, Dec. 19   Perf. 14
435	A93	50f blue green & multi	.30	.30
436	A93	80f brown & multi	.50	.50
437	A93	150f lilac rose & multi	.95	.95
438	A93	200f blue & multi	1.25	1.25
		Nos. 435-438 (4)	3.00	3.00

Date
Palm
A94

Designs: 80f, Flowering stage. 100f, Dates beginning to ripen. 200f, Dates up close. 250f, Trees from distance.
500f, Pitcher, basket of dates.

1995, Mar. 21   Litho.   Perf. 14
439	A94	80f multicolored	.50	.50
440	A94	100f multicolored	.60	.60
441	A94	200f multicolored	1.25	1.25
442	A94	250f multicolored	1.50	1.50
		Nos. 439-442 (4)	3.85	3.85

Souvenir Sheet
443	A94	500f multicolored	3.00	3.00

No. 443 contains one 65x48mm stamp.

Fight
Against
Polio
A95

1995, Apr. 22   Litho.   Perf. 13x13½
444	A95	80f pink & multi	.40	.40
445	A95	200f blue & multi	1.00	1.00
446	A95	250f lt brown & multi	1.40	1.40
		Nos. 444-446 (3)	2.80	2.80

World Health Day.

1st Natl.
Industries
Exhibition
A96

1995, May 15
447	A96	80f blue green & multi	.40	.40
448	A96	200f lilac & multi	1.00	1.00
449	A96	250f lt brown & multi	1.40	1.40
		Nos. 447-449 (3)	2.80	2.80

FAO, 50th Anniv. A97

Fields of various crops.

1995, June 17   Litho.   Perf. 14
450 A97 80f lilac & multi   .40 .40
451 A97 200f blue & multi   1.00 1.00
452 A97 250f lt pink & multi   1.40 1.40
Nos. 450-452 (3)   2.80 2.80

Arab League, 50th Anniv. — A98

1995, Sept. 14   Litho.   Perf. 14½
453 A98 80f pink & multi   .40 .40
454 A98 200f blue & multi   1.10 1.10
455 A98 250f yellow & multi   1.40 1.40
Nos. 453-455 (3)   2.90 2.90

UN, 50th Anniv. A99

1995, Oct. 24   Litho.   Perf. 14½
456 A99 80f yellow & multi   .40 .40
457 A99 100f green & multi   .55 .55
458 A99 200f pink & multi   1.10 1.10
459 A99 250f blue & multi   1.40 1.40
Nos. 456-459 (4)   3.45 3.45

Miniature Sheet

Traditional Architecture — A100

Example of architecture, detail: a, Tower with balcony. b, Arched windows behind balcony. c, Double doors under arch. d, Four rows of square windows above row of arched windows. e, Door flanked by two windows. f, Three windows.

1995, Nov. 20   Litho.   Perf. 14½
460 A100 200f Sheet of 6, #a.-f.   6.50 6.50

National Day — A101

1995, Dec. 16   Litho.   Perf. 14½
461 A101 80f blue & multi   .40 .40
462 A101 100f green & multi   .55 .55
463 A101 200f violet & multi   1.10 1.10
464 A101 250f blue grn & multi   1.40 1.40
Nos. 461-464 (4)   3.45 3.45

Public Library, 50th Anniv. — A102

1996, Mar. 23   Litho.   Perf. 14
465 A102 80f pink & multi   .40 .40
466 A102 200f green & multi   1.10 1.10
467 A102 250f blue & multi   1.40 1.40
Nos. 465-467 (3)   2.90 2.90

Pearl Diving — A103

Designs: 80f, Group of divers on ship, three in water. 100f, Five divers in water, ship. 200f, Diver underneath water. 250f, Diver being pulled up, underwater scene.
500f, Lantern, weight, scales, pearls, knife. Illustration reduced.

1996, May 8   Litho.   Perf. 14
468 A103 80f multicolored   .40 .40
469 A103 100f multicolored   .55 .55
470 A103 200f multicolored   1.10 1.10
471 A103 250f multicolored   1.40 1.40
Nos. 468-471 (4)   3.45 3.45

Souvenir Sheet
Perf. 14½
472 A103 500f multicolored   2.75 2.75
No. 472 contains one 70x70mm stamp.

1996 Summer Olympics, Atlanta — A104

1996, July 19   Litho.   Perf. 14
473 A104 80f olive & multi   .40 .40
474 A104 100f pink & multi   .55 .55
475 A104 200f blue grn & multi   1.10 1.10
476 A104 250f orange & multi   1.40 1.40
Nos. 473-476 (4)   3.45 3.45

Interpol, Intl. Criminal Police Organization — A105

1996, Sept. 25   Litho.   Perf. 14
477 A105 80f blue & multi   .40 .40
478 A105 100f yellow & multi   .55 .55
479 A105 200f pink & multi   1.10 1.10
480 A105 250f green & multi   1.40 1.40
Nos. 477-480 (4)   3.45 3.45

Aluminum Production in Bahrain, 25th Anniv. — A106

1996, Nov. 20   Litho.   Perf. 14
481 A106 80f bister & multi   .40 .40
482 A106 100f orange & multi   .55 .55
483 A106 200f blue & multi   1.10 1.10
484 A106 250f green & multi   1.40 1.40
Nos. 481-484 (4)   3.45 3.45

Accession to the Throne by Sheik Isa Bin Salman Al Khalifa, 35th Anniv. — A107

1996, Dec. 16
485 A107 80f gray & multi   .40 .40
486 A107 100f green & multi   .55 .55
487 A107 200f pink & multi   1.10 1.10
488 A107 250f blue & multi   1.40 1.40
Nos. 485-488 (4)   3.45 3.45

Bahrain Refinery, 60th Anniv. — A108

1997, Jan. 15   Litho.   Perf. 14
489 A108 80f red & multi   .45 .45
490 A108 200f blue & multi   1.10 1.10
491 A108 250f yellow & multi   1.25 1.25
Nos. 489-491 (3)   2.80 2.80

Pure Strains of Arabian Horses, Amiri Stud A109

Designs: a, Musannaan, Al-Jellabieh, Rabdaan. b, Kuheilaan weld umm zorayr. c, Al-Jellaby. d, Musannaan. e, Kuheilaan aladiyat. f, Kuheilaan aafas. g, Al-Dhahma. h, Mlolshaan. i, Al-Kray. j, Krush. k, Al Hamdaany. l, Hadhfaan. m, Rabda. n, Al-Suwaitieh. o, Al-Obeyah. p, Al-Shuwaimeh. q, Al-Ma'anaghieh. r, Al-Tuwaisah. s, Wadhna. t, Al-Saqlawieh. u, Al-Shawafah.

1997, Apr. 23   Litho.   Perf. 14x14½
492 A109 200f Sheet of 21, #a.-u.   22.50 22.50

9th Men's Junior World Volleyball Championship — A110

1997, Aug. 21   Litho.   Perf. 14x14½
493 A110 80f brown & multi   .45 .45
494 A110 100f green & multi   .55 .55
495 A110 200f gray brn & multi   1.10 1.10
496 A110 250f blue & multi   1.25 1.25
Nos. 493-496 (4)   3.35 3.35

Montreal Protocol on Substances that Deplete Ozone Layer, 10th Anniv. — A111

1997, Sept. 16   Litho.   Perf. 14½
497 A111 80f yellow & multi   .45 .45
498 A111 100f purple & multi   .55 .55
499 A111 200f red & multi   1.10 1.10
500 A111 250f green & multi   1.25 1.25
Nos. 497-500 (4)   3.35 3.35

Sheikh Isa Bin Salman Bridge A112

Designs: 80f, Pylon, supports. 200f, Center of bridge. 250f, 500f, Entire span.

1997, Dec. 28   Litho.   Perf. 13x13½
501 A112 80f multicolored   .45 .45
502 A112 200f multicolored   1.10 1.10
Size: 76x26mm
503 A112 250f multicolored   1.25 1.25
Nos. 501-503 (3)   2.80 2.80

Souvenir Sheet
504 A112 500f multicolored   2.75 2.75

Inuaguration of Urea Plant, GPIC (Refinery) Complex — A113

Designs: 80f, View of plant from Persian Gulf. 200f, Plant facilities. 250f, Aerial view.

1998, Mar. 3   Litho.   Perf. 13x13½
505 A113 80f multicolored   .45 .45
506 A113 200f multicolored   1.10 1.10
507 A113 250f multicolored   1.25 1.25
Nos. 505-507 (3)   2.80 2.80

World Health Organization, 50th Anniv. — A114

1998, May 11   Litho.   Perf. 14
508 A114 80f orange & multi   .45 .45
509 A114 200f green & multi   1.10 1.10
510 A114 250f gray & multi   1.25 1.25
Nos. 508-510 (3)   2.80 2.80

1998 World Cup Soccer
Championships, France — A115

Designs: 200f, Soccer balls, world maps,
vert. 250f, Players, globe, vert.

1998, June 10
511	A115	80f multicolored	.45	.45
512	A115	200f multicolored	1.10	1.10
513	A115	250f multicolored	1.25	1.25
		Nos. 511-513 (3)	2.80	2.80

14th
Arabian
Gulf
Soccer
Cup,
Bahrain
A116

Design: 200f, 250f, Soccer ball.

1998, Oct. 30　　Litho.　　Perf. 14
514	A116	80f shown	.45	.45
515	A116	200f pale violet & multi	1.10	1.10
516	A116	250f bister & multi	1.25	1.25
		Nos. 514-516 (3)	2.80	2.80

Grand
Competition
for Holy Koran
Recitation
A117

1999, Jan. 9　　Litho.　　Perf. 14
517	A117	100f gray olive & multi	.55	.55
518	A117	200f yellow & multi	1.10	1.10
519	A117	250f green & multi	1.25	1.25
		Nos. 517-519 (3)	2.90	2.90

Isa Bin Salman Al-Khalifa (1933-99),
Emir of Bahrain — A118

Natl. flag, map and: 100f, 500f, Emir holding
sword, vert. 250f, Portrait up close, vert.

Perf. 13¼ (#520, 522), 14¼ (#521)
1999, June 5　　　　　　Litho.
520	A118	100f multicolored	.55	.55
521	A118	200f multicolored	1.10	1.10
522	A118	250f multicolored	1.25	1.25
		Nos. 520-522 (3)	2.90	2.90

Souvenir Sheet
Perf. 14½x13
523	A118	500f multicolored	3.00	3.00

Nos. 520, 522 are 31x50mm. No. 523 contains one 67x102mm stamp.

Intl. Year of
Older
Persons
A119

1999, Oct. 9　　Litho.　　Perf. 13x13½
524	A119	100f multi	.55	.55
525	A119	200f multi, diff.	1.10	1.10
526	A119	250f multi, diff.	1.25	1.25
		Nos. 524-526 (3)	2.90	2.90

Bahrain Stock Exchange, 10th
Anniv. — A120

1999, Nov. 24　　Litho.　　Perf. 14¼
527	A120	100f shown	.55	.55
528	A120	200f Statues	1.10	1.10
529	A120	250f Globe	1.25	1.25
		Nos. 527-529 (3)	2.90	2.90

Hamad Bin Isa Al-
Khalifa, Emir of
Bahrain — A121

Emir Hamad: 100f, 500f, Receiving flag
from late Emir. 200f, And flag. 250f, And map.

1999, Dec. 16　　Litho.　　Perf. 14½
531	A121	100f multi	.55	.55
532	A121	200f multi	1.10	1.10
533	A121	250f multi	1.25	1.25
		Nos. 531-533 (3)	2.90	2.90

Souvenir Sheet
Perf. 13¼x12¾
534	A121	500f multi	2.50	2.50

Dilmun
Culture
Exhibition
A122

Map of Bahrain and: 100f, Bull's head, seal.
200f, Bull's head. 250f, Seal.

2000, Feb. 26　　Litho.　　Perf. 14¼
535	A122	100f multi	.55	.55
536	A122	200f multi	1.10	1.10
537	A122	250f multi	1.25	1.25
		Nos. 535-537 (3)	2.90	2.90

Gulf Air,
50th
Anniv.
A123

Map of Bahrain and: 100f, Emblem, world
map. 200f, Emblem. 250f, Birds.

2000, Mar. 24
538	A123	100f multi	.55	.55
539	A123	200f multi	1.10	1.10
540	A123	250f multi	1.25	1.25
		Nos. 538-540 (3)	2.90	2.90

Made in Bahrain Exhibition — A124

2000, May 9　　　　　　Perf. 14½
541	A124	100f shown	.55	.55
542	A124	200f Emblem, diff.	1.10	1.10
543	A124	250f Oil refinery	1.25	1.25
		Nos. 541-543 (3)	2.90	2.90

Souvenir Sheet

Passage
Through
Time
A125

Designs: a, Minarets, fort, flag on dhow's
stern. b, Dhows, oil refinery. c, Minaret, date
picker. d, Satellite dishes, fort, flag. e, Bridge,
pool. f, Woman, jar, dhows. g, Dhows, coffee
pot. h, Man with falcon, horse and rider. i,
Pearl divers. j, Oyster shuckers. k, Men casting nets. l, Men repairing nets.

Litho. with Foil Application
2000, Oct. 9　　　　　　Perf. 14¼
544		Sheet of 12	12.00	12.00
a.-d.	A125	100f Any single	.50	.50
e.-h.	A125	200f Any single	1.10	1.10
i.-l.	A125	250f Any single	1.40	1.40

21st Supreme Council Session of the
Gulf Co-operation Council — A126

Designs: 100f, Emblem. 200f, Flags.

2000, Dec. 30　　Litho.　　Perf. 14¼
545-546	A126	Set of 2	1.60	1.60

Beit al-Quran, Manama — A127

Designs: 100f, Stained-glass window. 200f,
Building illuminated at dusk. 250f, Building
during day.
　500f, Building during day, stained-glass window, building illuminated at dusk.

2001, Feb. 18　　Litho.　　Perf. 14¼
547-549	A127	Set of 3	3.00	3.00

Size: 170x80mm
Imperf
550	A127	500f multi	2.60	2.60

Housing and Agriculture Ministry, 25th
Anniv. — A128

Various buildings: 100f, 150f, 200f, 250f.

2001, Apr. 28　　　　　　Perf. 14¼
551-554	A128	Set of 4	3.75	3.75

WAR TAX STAMPS

WT1　　　　　　　WT2

1973, Oct. 21　　Litho.　　Perf. 14½
MR1	WT1	5f sky blue	125.00	65.00

Catalogue values for all unused
stamps in this section, from this
point to the end of the section, are
for Never Hinged items.

1974　　　　　　Litho.　　Perf. 14½
MR2	WT2	5f light blue	1.75	.25
a.		Perf. 14½x13½	2.50	

No. MR2a was issued around 1988.

BANGKOK

ˈbaŋˌkäk

LOCATION — Capital of Siam
(Thailand)

Stamps were issued by Great Britain
under rights obtained in the treaty of
1855. These were in use until July 1,
1885, when the stamps of Siam were
designated as the only official postage
stamps to be used in the kingdom.

100 Cents = 1 Dollar

Excellent counterfeits of Nos. 1-22
are plentiful.

Stamps of Straits
Settlements Overprinted
in Black

1882　　　　Wmk. 1　　Perf. 14
1	A2	2c brown	2,400.	1,250.
2	A2	4c rose	2,000.	1,200.
b.		Double overprint		6,750.
3	A6	5c brown violet	240.00	275.00
4	A6	6c violet	175.00	125.00
5	A3	8c yel orange	1,800.	175.00
6	A7	10c slate	325.00	140.00
7	A3	12c blue	800.00	425.00
8	A3	24c green	625.00	140.00
9	A4	30c claret	35,000.	22,500.
10	A5	96c olive gray	4,400.	2,450.

See note after No. 20.

1882-83　　　　　　Wmk. 2
11	A2	2c brown	425.00	325.00
12	A2	2c rose ('83)	50.00	40.00
a.		Inverted overprint	18,000.	9,000.
b.		Double overprint	2,400.	2,400.
c.		Triple overprint	9,000.	
13	A2	4c rose	450.00	275.00
14	A2	4c brown ('83)	67.50	65.00
a.		Double overprint	3,150.	
15	A6	5c ultra ('83)	200.00	150.00
16	A2	6c violet ('83)	140.00	100.00
17	A3	8c yel orange	125.00	60.00
a.		Inverted overprint	16,000.	9,000.
18	A7	10c slate	140.00	80.00
19	A3	12c violet brn ('83)	240.00	140.00
20	A3	24c green	3,500.	2,250.

Double overprints must have two clear
impressions. Partial double overprints exist on
a number of values of these issues. They sell
for a modest premium over catalogue value
depending on how much of the impression is
present.

1883　　　　　　Wmk. 1
21	A5	2c on 32c pale red	2,000.	2,000.

On Straits Settlements No. 9
1885 **Wmk. 38**
22 A7 32c on 2a yel
(B+B) 36,000. 45,000.

BANGLADESH
ˌbäŋ-glə-ˈdesh

LOCATION — In southern, central Asia, touching India, Burma, and the Bay of Bengal
GOVT. — Republic in the British Commonwealth
AREA — 55,598 sq. mi.
POP. — 127,117,967 (1999 est.)
CAPITAL — Dhaka (Dacca)

Bangladesh, formerly East Pakistan, broke away from Pakistan in April 1971, proclaiming its independence. It consists of 14 former eastern districts of Bengal and the former Sylhet district of Assam province of India.

100 Paisas = 1 Rupee
100 Paisas (Poishas) = 1 Taka (1972)

> Catalogue values for all unused stamps in this country are for Never Hinged items.

Various stamps of Pakistan were handstamped locally for use in Bangladesh from March 26, 1971 until April 30, 1973.

Map of Bangladesh A1 — Sheik Mujibur Rahman A2

Designs: 20p, "Dacca University Massacre." 50p, "A Nation of 75 Million People." 1r, Flag of Independence (showing map). 2r, Ballot box. 3r, Broken chain. 10r, "Support Bangladesh" and map.

Perf. 14x14½
1971, July 29 Litho. Unwmk.
1 A1 10p red, dk pur & lt bl .20 .20
2 A1 20p bl, grn, red & yel .20 .20
3 A1 50p dp org, gray & brn .20 .20
4 A1 1r red, emer & yel .25 .20
5 A1 2r lil rose, lt & dk bl .40 .30
6 A1 3r blue, emer & grn .50 .40
7 A2 5r dp org, tan & blk .75 .75
8 A1 10r gold, dk bl & lil rose 1.00 1.50
Nos. 1-8 (8) 3.50 3.75

A set of 15 stamps of types A1 and A2 in new paisa-taka values and colors was rejected by Bangladesh officials and not issued. Bangladesh representatives in England released these stamps, which were not valid, on Feb. 1, 1972.
Imperfs of Nos. 1-8 were in the Format International liquidation. They are not errors.

Nos. 1-8 Overprinted in Black or Red — BANGLADESH LIBERATED বাংলাদেশের মুক্তি

1971, Dec. 20
9 A1 10p multicolored .20 .20
10 A1 20p multicolored .20
11 A1 50p multicolored .25
12 A1 1r multicolored .50
13 A1 2r multicolored .75
14 A1 3r multicolored 1.10
15 A2 5r multicolored (R) 1.50 1.25
16 A1 10r multicolored 2.50 2.50
Nos. 9-16 (8) 7.00

Liberation of Bangladesh.
The 10p, 5r and 10r were issued in Dacca, but Nos. 10-14 were not put on sale in Bangladesh.

Monument — A3

1972, Feb. 21 Litho. Perf. 13
32 A3 20p green & rose .50 .35
Language Movement Martyrs.

"Independence" A4

1972, Mar. 26 Photo. Perf. 13
33 A4 20p maroon & red .20 .20
34 A4 60p dark blue & red .25 .35
35 A4 75p purple & red .30 .45
Nos. 33-35 (3) .75 1.00
First anniversary of independence.

Doves of Peace — A5 — Flower Growing from Ruin — A6

1972, Dec. 16 Litho. Perf. 13
36 A5 20p ocher & multi .20 .20
37 A5 60p lilac & multi .25 .40
38 A5 75p yellow green & multi .30 .40
Nos. 36-38 (3) .75 1.00
Victory Day, Dec. 16.

1973, Mar. 25 Litho. Perf. 13
39 A6 20p ocher & multi .20 .20
40 A6 60p brown & multi .40 .40
41 A6 1.35t violet blue & multi .75 1.10
Nos. 39-41 (3) 1.35 1.70
Martyrs of the war of liberation.

Embroidered Quilt — A7

Hilsa — A8

Court of Justice — A9

Designs: 3p, Jute field. 5p, Jack fruit. 10p, Farmer plowing with ox team. 20p, Hibiscus rosenensis. 25p, Tiger. 60p, Bamboo and water lilies. 75p, Women picking tea. 90p, Handicrafts. 2t, Collecting date palm juice, vert. 5t, Net fishing. 10t, Sixty-dome Mosque.

Perf. 14x14½, 14½x14
1973, Apr. 30 Litho.
Size: 21x28mm, 28x21mm
42 A7 2p black .20 .20
43 A7 3p bright green .20 .20
44 A7 5p light brown .20 .20
45 A7 10p black .20 .20

46 A7 20p olive .70 .30
47 A7 25p red lilac 1.90 .60
48 A8 50p rose lilac 1.50 .50
49 A7 60p gray .70 .25
50 A7 75p orange 1.25 .45
51 A7 90p red brown 1.25 .45
Taka Expressed as "TA"
Size: 35x22mm
52 A9 1t violet 3.50 1.25
53 A9 2t greenish gray 4.50 1.50
54 A9 5t grayish blue 6.00 2.00
55 A9 10t rose 6.50 2.25
Nos. 42-55 (14) 28.60 10.35
See Nos. 82-85, 95-106, 165-176, 356. For overprints see Nos. O1-O10, O13.

Human Rights Flame A10 — Family, Chart, Map of Bangladesh A11

1973, Dec. 10 Litho. Perf. 13x13½
56 A10 10p multi & multi .20 .20
57 A10 1.25t violet & multi .40 .40
25th anniversary of the Universal Declaration of Human Rights.

1974, Feb. 10 Litho. Perf. 13½
58 A11 20p blue grn & multi .20 .20
59 A11 25p brt blue & multi .20 .20
60 A11 75p red & multi .45 .45
Nos. 58-60 (3) .85 .85
First census in Bangladesh.
For overprints see Nos. 194-196.

Copernicus, Heliocentric System — A12

Flag and UN Headquarters A13

1974, July 22 Litho. Perf. 13½
61 A12 25p violet, blk & org .20 .20
62 A12 75p emerald, blk & org .60 .60
Nicolaus Copernicus (1473-1543), Polish astronomer.

1974, Sept. 25 Litho. Perf. 13½
63 A13 25p lilac & multi .20 .20
64 A13 1t blue & multi .50 .50
Admission of Bangladesh to the UN.

A14 — A15

Designs: 25p, 1.75t, UPU emblem. 1.25t, 5t, Mail runner. 25p, 1.25t, country and denomination appear on a yellow background, 1.75t, 5t, blue background.

1974, Oct. 9 Perf. 13½
65 A14 25p multicolored .20 .20
66 A14 1.25t multicolored .20 .20
67 A14 1.75t multicolored .30 .25
68 A14 5t multicolored .85 1.10
a. Souv. sheet of 4, #65-68, imperf. 60.00
Nos. 65-68 (4) 1.55 1.75

1974, Nov. 4 Litho.
69 A15 25p Royal bengal tiger .50 .25
70 A15 50p Tiger cub 1.25 .75
71 A15 2t Swimming tiger 2.75 3.00
Nos. 69-71 (3) 4.50 4.00
"Save the Tiger," World Wildlife Fund.

Type of 1973
Taka Expressed in Bengali
1974-75 Perf. 14½x14, 14x14½
Size: 35x22mm
82 A9 1t violet 1.50 .20
83 A9 2t grayish green 2.50 1.00
84 A9 5t grayish blue ('75) 5.00 .80
85 A9 10t rose ('75) 11.00 7.50
Nos. 82-85 (4) 20.00 9.50
See Nos. 350-356. For overprints see Nos. O11-O12, O14.

Family — A16 — Children — A17

Family A18

1974, Dec. 30 Litho. Perf. 14
86 A16 25p ocher & multi .20 .20
87 A17 70p claret & multi .30 .30
88 A18 1.25t multicolored .50 .50
Nos. 86-88 (3) 1.00 1.00
Family planning. The numerals on No. 87 look like "90" but mean "70."

Betbunia Satellite Earth Station — A19

1975, June 14 Litho. Perf. 14
89 A19 25p red, black & silver .20 .20
90 A19 1t vio blue, blk & silver .60 .60
Opening of Betbunia Satellite Earth Station.

Allegory, IWY Emblem A20

1975, Dec. 31 Litho. Perf. 15
91 A20 50p rose & multi .20 .20
92 A20 2t lt lilac & multi .70 .70
International Women's Year.

Types of 1973 Redrawn

1976-77   Litho.   Perf. 15x14½

Size: 18x23mm, 23x18mm

95	A7	5p green	.20 .20
96	A7	10p black	.20 .20
97	A7	20p olive green	.50 .20
98	A7	25p rose lilac	1.00 .20
99	A9	50p rose lilac	1.00 .20
100	A7	60p gray	.50 .25
101	A7	75p olive	.80 1.00
102	A7	90p red brown	.50 .25

Taka Expressed in Bengali

Size: 32x20mm, 20x32mm

103	A9	1t violet	1.25 .20
104	A9	2t greenish gray	6.50 .30
105	A9	5t grayish blue	4.00 2.00
106	A9	10t rose ('77)	9.00 2.00
		Nos. 95-106 (12)	25.45 7.00

For overprints see Nos. O16-O25.

Telephones, 1876 and 1976 — A21

Alexander Graham Bell — A22

1976, Mar. 10   Litho.   Perf. 15

107	A21	2.25t multicolored	.25 .25
108	A22	5t multicolored	.75 .75

Centenary of first telephone call by Alexander Graham Bell, Mar. 10, 1876.

Eye and Healthful Food A23

1976, Apr. 7   Litho.   Perf. 15

109	A23	30p yellow & multi	.35 .35
110	A23	2.25t orange & multi	1.60 1.60

World Health Day: Foresight prevents blindness.

Liberty Bell A24

Designs: 2.25t, Statue of Liberty, New York Skyline. 5t, Mayflower. 10t, Mt. Rushmore, presidents' heads.

1976, May 29   Photo.   Perf. 13½x14

111	A24	30p multicolored	.20 .20
112	A24	2.25t multicolored	.25 .25
113	A24	5t multicolored	.75 .75
114	A24	10t multicolored	.75 .75
a.		Souv. sheet, #111-114, perf 13	3.50 3.50
		Nos. 111-114 (4)	1.95 1.95

American Bicentennial. Sheet exists imperf.

Weaver, Chemist, Farmer, Student and Emblem — A25

1976, July 29   Litho.   Perf. 15

115	A25	30p multicolored	.20 .20
116	A25	2.25t multicolored	.40 .40

25th anniversary of Colombo Plan. For overprint see No. 252.

Hurdles — A26

Montreal Olympic Emblem and: 30p, Running, horiz. 1t, High jump. 2.25t, Swimming, horiz. 3.50t, Gymnastics. 5t, Soccer.

1976, Nov. 29   Litho.   Perf. 15

117	A26	25p multicolored	.20 .20
118	A26	30p multicolored	.20 .20
119	A26	1t multicolored	.20 .20
120	A26	2.25t multicolored	.35 .35
121	A26	3.50t multicolored	.60 .60
122	A26	5t multicolored	1.10 1.10
		Nos. 117-122 (6)	2.65 2.65

21st Olympic Games, Montreal, Canada, July 17-Aug. 1.

Coronation Ceremony — A27

Designs: 2.25t, Queen Elizabeth II. 10t, Queen and Prince Philip.

1977, Feb. 7   Perf. 14x15

123	A27	30p multicolored	.20 .20
124	A27	2.25t multicolored	.20 .20
125	A27	10t multicolored	.55 .55
a.		Souv. sheet, #123-125, perf 14½	1.00 1.50
		Nos. 123-125 (3)	.95 .95

25th anniv. of the reign of Elizabeth II.

Qazi Nazrul Islam — A28

Nazrul A29

1977, Aug. 29   Litho.   Perf. 14

126	A28	40p lt green & black	.20 .20
127	A29	2.25t multicolored	.35 .35

Qazi Nazrul Islam (1899-1976), natl. poet.

Pigeon Carrying Letter A30

1977, Sept. 29   Litho.   Perf. 14

128	A30	30p multicolored	.20 .20
129	A30	2.25t multicolored	.25 .25

Asian-Oceanic Postal Union (AOPU), 15th anniversary.

Leopard A31

40p and 1t are vert.

1977, Nov. 9   Litho.   Perf. 13

130	A31	40p Asiatic black bear	.20 .20
131	A31	1t Axis deer	.35 .20
132	A31	2.25t shown	.70 .20
133	A31	3.50t Gayal	.75 .35
134	A31	4t Elephant	1.40 .50
135	A31	5t Bengal tiger	1.60 .75
		Nos. 130-135 (6)	5.00 2.20

Campfire, Tent, Scout Emblem — A32

Designs: 3.50t, Emblem, first aid, signaling, horiz. 5t, Scout emblem and oath.

1978, Jan. 22   Litho.   Perf. 13

136	A32	40p multicolored	.25 .25
137	A32	3.50t multicolored	1.00 1.00
138	A32	5t multicolored	1.75 1.75
		Nos. 136-138 (3)	3.00 3.00

1st National Boy Scout Jamboree, Jan. 22. For overprint see No. 269.

Champac — A33

Flowers and Flowering Trees: 1t, Pudding pipe tree. 2.25t, Flamboyant tree. 3.50t, Water lilies. 4t, Butea. 5t, Anthocephalus indicus.

1978, Mar. 31   Litho.   Perf. 13

139	A33	40p multicolored	.20 .20
140	A33	1t multicolored	.50 .50
141	A33	2.25t multicolored	.85 .85
142	A33	3.50t multicolored	1.10 1.10
143	A33	4t multicolored	1.25 1.25
144	A33	5t multicolored	1.40 1.40
		Nos. 139-144 (6)	5.30 5.30

For overprints see Nos. 259A-259F.

Crown, Scepter and Staff of State — A34

Designs: 3.50t, Royal family on balcony. 5t, Queen Elizabeth II and Prince Philip. 10t, Queen in coronation regalia, Westminster Abbey.

1978, May 20   Perf. 14

145	A34	40p multicolored	.20 .20
146	A34	3.50t multicolored	.20 .20
147	A34	5t multicolored	.25 .30
148	A34	10t multicolored	.50 .65
a.		Souv. sheet, #145-148, perf 14½	1.40 1.40
		Nos. 145-148 (4)	1.15 1.35

Coronation of Queen Elizabeth II, 25th anniv. For overprint see No. 228B.

Alan Cobham's DH50, 1926 — A35

Planes: 2.25t, Capt. Hans Bertram's Junkers W33 Atlantis, 1932-33. 3.50t, Wright brothers' plane. 5t, Concorde.

1978, June 15   Litho.   Perf. 13

149	A35	40p multicolored	.20 .20
150	A35	2.25t multicolored	1.00 .90
151	A35	3.50t multicolored	1.50 1.25
152	A35	5t multicolored	3.00 2.50
		Nos. 149-152 (4)	5.70 4.85

75th anniversary of powered flight.

Holy Kaaba, Mecca — A37

Design: 3.50t, Pilgrims at Mt. Arafat, horiz.

1978, Nov. 9   Litho.   Perf. 13

154	A37	40p multicolored	.20 .20
155	A37	3.50t multicolored	.75 .75

Pilgrimage to Mecca.

Jasim Uddin, Poet A38

1979, Mar. 14   Litho.   Perf. 14

156	A38	40p multicolored	.30 .40

Rowland Hill — A39

Moulana Bhashani — A40

Hill and Stamps of Bangladesh: 3.50t, No. 1, horiz. 10t, No. 66, horiz.

1979, Aug. 27   Litho.   Perf. 14
157 A39 40p multicolored   .20   .20
158 A39 3.50t multicolored   .35   .35
159 A39 10t multicolored   1.10   1.10
  a.   Souvenir sheet of 3, #157-159   2.75   2.75
         Nos. 157-159 (3)   1.65   1.65

Sir Rowland Hill (1795-1879), originator of penny postage.

1979, Nov. 17   Perf. 12½
160 A40 40p multicolored   .55   .55

Moulana Abdul Hamid Khan Bhashani (1880-1976), philosopher and statesman.

A41

IYC Emblem and: 40p, Boys and Hoops. 3.50t, Boys flying kites. 5t, Children jumping.

1979, Dec. 17   Litho.   Perf. 14x14½
161 A41 40p multicolored   .20   .20
162 A41 3.50t multicolored   .45   .45
163 A41 5t multicolored   .65   .65
  a.   Souv. sheet, #161-163, perf 14½ 2.50   2.50
         Nos. 161-163 (3)   1.30   1.30

International Year of the Child.

Type of 1973

Designs: 5p, Lalbag Fort. 10p, Fenchungan Fertilizer Factory, vert. 15p, Pineapple. 20p, Gas well. 25p, Jute on boat. 30p, Banana tree. 40p, Baitul Mukarram Mosque. 50p, Baitul Mukarram Mosque. 80p, Garh excavations. 1ta, Dotara (musical instrument.) 2t, Karnaphuli Dam.

1979-82   Photo.   Perf. 14½
Size: 18x23mm, 23x18mm
165 A7   5p brown ('79)   .20   .20
166 A7   10p Prus blue   .20   .20
167 A7   15p yellow org ('81)   .20   .20
168 A7   20p dk carmine ('79)   .30   .20
169 A7   25p dk blue ('82)   .35   .20
170 A7   30p lt olive grn ('80)   1.25   .20
171 A8   40p rose magenta ('79)   .45   .20
172 A9   50p black & gray ('81)   2.50   1.00
173 A7   80p dk brown ('80)   .25   .20
174 A7   1t red lilac ('81)   3.50   .25
175 A7   2t brt ultra ('81)   .75   1.25
         Nos. 165-175 (11)   9.95   4.10

For overprints see Nos. O27-O36.

A42

1980, Feb. 23   Litho.   Perf. 14

Rotary Intl., 75th Anniv.: 40p, Rotary emblem, diff.

179 A42 40p multicolored   .20   .20
180 A42 5t ultra & gold   .90   .90

For overprints see Nos. 285-286.

Canal Digging A43

1980, Mar. 27   Litho.   Perf. 14
181 A43 40p multicolored   .40   .30

Sher-e-Bangla A.K. Fazlul Huq (1873-1962), Natl. Leader — A44

1980, Apr. 27   Litho.   Perf. 14
182 A44 40p multicolored   .30   .30

Early Mail Transport, London 1980 Emblem — A45

1980, May 5
183 A45 1t shown   .20   .20
184 A45 10t Modern mail trans-
           port   1.40   1.40
  a.   Souvenir sheet of 2, #183-184 1.50   2.00

London 80 Intl. Stamp Exhib., May 6-14.

Dome of the Rock — A46

Adult Education — A47

1980, Aug. 21   Litho.   Perf. 14½
185 A46 50p violet rose   .75   .30

For the families of Palestinians.

1980, Aug. 23   Perf. 13½
186 A47 50p multicolored   .35   .30

Beach Scene A48

1980, Sept. 27   Litho.   Perf. 14
187 A48 50p shown   .20   .20
188 A48 5t Beach scene, diff.   .80   1.00
  a.   Souvenir sheet of 2, #187-188 1.25   1.50
  b.   Pair, #187-188   1.25   1.25

World Tourism Conference, Manila, Sept. 27. No. 188b has continuous design. For overprints see Nos. 243-244.

Hegira (Pilgrimage Year) — A49

1980, Nov. 11   Photo.   Perf. 14
189 A49 50p multicolored   .25   .25

A50

Design: Deer and Boy Scout emblem.

1981, Jan. 1   Litho.   Perf. 14
190 A50 50p multicolored   .20   .20
191 A50 5t multicolored   1.40   1.90

5th Asia-Pacific and 2nd Bangladesh Scout Jamboree, 1980-1981.

A51

1980, Dec. 9   Litho.   Perf. 14
192 A51 50p multicolored   .20   .20
193 A51 2t multicolored   .35   .20

Begum Roquiah (1880-1932), educator.

Nos. 58-60 Overprinted:
2nd / CENSUS / 1981

1981, Mar. 6   Perf. 13½
194 A11 20p multicolored   .20   .20
195 A11 25p multicolored   .20   .20
196 A11 75p multicolored   .20   .20
         Nos. 194-196 (3)   .60   .60

A52

1981, Mar. 16   Litho.   Perf. 14
197 A52 1t multicolored   .20   .20
198 A52 15t multicolored   2.10   2.50
  a.   Souvenir sheet of 2, #197-198 3.25   3.25

Queen Mother Elizabeth, 80th birthday (1980).

A53

1981, Mar. 26
199 A53 50p Citizen Holding Rifle
           & Flag   .20   .20
200 A53 2t People, map   .40   .40

10th anniversary of independence.

UN Conference on Least-developed Countries, Paris — A54

1981, Sept. 1   Litho.   Perf. 14x13½
201 A54 50p multicolored   .40   .20

Birth Centenary of Kemal Ataturk (First President of Turkey) — A55

1981, Nov. 10   Litho.   Perf. 14
202 A55 50p Portrait   .50   .50
203 A55 1t Portrait, diff.   .70   .70

Intl. Year of the Disabled A56

1981, Dec. 26   Litho.   Perf. 14
204 A56 50p Sign language, vert.   .40   .40
205 A56 2t Amputee   1.25   1.25

World Food Day, Oct. 16 — A57

1981, Dec. 31   Litho.   Perf. 13½x14
206 A57 50p multicolored   .50   .65

A58

1982, May 22   Litho.   Perf. 13½x14
207 A58 50p Boat hauling rice
           straw   .50   .65

10th Anniv. of UN Conf. on Human Environment. For overprint see No. 281.

A59

1982, Oct. 9
208 A59 50p multicolored .60 .75
Dr. Kazi Motahar Hossain, educator and statistician.

Scouting Year A60

1982, Oct. 21   Litho.   Perf. 14
209 A60 50p Emblem, knots .75 .50
210 A60 2t Baden-Powell, vert. 2.75 3.25

Capt. Mohiuddin Jahangir A61

Liberation Heroes (Tablet Color): b, Sepoy Hamidur Rahman (pale green). c, Sepoy Mohammed Mustafa Kamal (rose claret). d, Mohammad Ruhul Amin (yellow). e, M. Matiur Rahman (olive bister). f, Lance-Naik Munshi Abdur Rob (brown orange). g, Lance-Naik Nur Mouhammad (bright yellow green).

1982, Dec. 16   Litho.   Perf. 14
211　　　Strip of 7 2.00 2.25
a.-g.　A61 50p multicolored .30 .30

Metric System A62

1983, Jan. 10   Litho.   Perf. 14
212 A62 50p Mail scale, vert. .50 .50
213 A62 2t Weights, measures 1.75 1.75

TB Bacillus Centenary A63

1983, Feb. 20   Litho.   Perf. 14
214 A63 50p Koch 1.25 1.25
215 A63 1t Slides, microscope 2.25 2.25

A64

1983, Mar. 14   Litho: Perf. 14
216 A64 1t Open stage theater .20 .20
217 A64 3t Boat race .20 .20
218 A64 10t Snake dance .60 .60
219 A64 15t Tea garden 1.00 1.00
　　　Nos. 216-219 (4) 2.00 2.00
　　　Commonwealth Day.

Jnantapash Shahidullah (1885-1969), Educator and Linguist — A65

1983, July 10   Litho.   Perf. 14
220 A65 50p multicolored .95 .95

Birds A66

1983, Aug. 17   Litho.   Perf. 14
221 A66 50p Copsychus saulari 1.25 .65
222 A66 2t Halcyon smyrnensis, vert. 2.00 2.00
223 A66 3.75t Dinopium benghalense, vert. 2.25 2.25
224 A66 5t Carina scutulota 3.00 3.00
a.　Souvenir sheet of 4, #221-224 11.00 11.00
　　　Nos. 221-224 (4) 8.50 7.90
　　　No. 224a sold for 13t.

Local Fish A67

1983, Oct. 31   Litho.   Perf. 14
225 A67 50p Macrobrachium rosengergii .60 .25
226 A67 2t Stromateus cinereus 1.90 1.40
227 A67 3.75t Labeo rohita 2.25 1.75
228 A67 5t Anabas testudineus 2.75 2.25
a.　Souv. sheet of 4, #225-228, imperf. 7.50 7.50
　　　Nos. 225-228 (4) 7.50 5.65
　　　No. 228a sold for 13t.

No. 148 Ovptd. "Nov. '83/Visit of Queen" in Red

1983, Nov. 14   Litho.   Perf. 14
228B A34 10t multicolored 5.25 5.25

Hall A69

1983, Dec. 5   Litho.   Perf. 14
232 A69 50p Sangsad Bhaban .20 .20
233 A69 5t Shait Gumbaz 2.25 2.25
14th Islamic Foreign Ministers Conference.

A70

Perf. 11½x12½, 12½x11½
1983, Dec. 21
234 A70 5p Mailboat .20 .20
235 A70 10p Dacca P.O. counter .20 .20
236 A70 15p IWTA Terminal .20 .20
237 A70 20p Sorting mail .20 .20
238 A70 25p Mail delivery .20 .20
239 A70 30p Postman at mailbox .20 .20
240 A70 50p Mobile post office .20 .20

Size: 30½x18½mm
Perf. 12x11½
241 A70 1t Kamalapur Railway Station .25 .25
242 A70 2t Zia Intl. Airport .50 .50
242A A70 5t Khulna P.O. 1.25 1.25
　　　Nos. 234-242A (10) 3.40 3.40
　　　Nos. 235-237, 239-242A horiz.
Nos. 234-240 reprinted on cream paper.
See #270-271. For overprints see #O37-O46, O48, O51-O52.

No. 188b Overprinted in Red in English

or Bengali

1984, Feb. 1   Litho.   Perf. 14
243 A48 50p Beach Scene .25 .25
244 A48 5t Beach Scene, diff. 2.25 2.25
a.　Pair, #243-244 2.50 2.50
1st Bangladesh Natl. Philatelic Exhibition, 1984. No. 244a has continuous design.

A71

1984, May 17   Perf. 14½
245　　50p Girl examining stamp album .25 .25
246　　7.50t Boy updating collection 2.00 2.00
a.　Souvenir sheet of 2, #245-246 4.00 4.00
b.　A71 Pair, #245-246 2.25 2.25
c.　As "a," overprinted 9.25 9.25
　　　#246a sold for 10t.
Overprint in sheet margin of No. 246c reads: "SILVER JUBILEE / BANGLADESH POSTAGE STAMPS 1971-96."

Dacca Zoo — A72

1984, July 17   Litho.   Perf. 14
247 A72 1t Sarus crane, gavial 1.40 1.40
248 A72 2t Peafowl, royal Bengal tiger 2.75 2.75

Postal Life Insurance, Cent. — A73

1984, Dec. 3
249 A73 1t Chicken hawk, hen .40 .40
250 A73 5t Beneficiaries 1.90 1.90

Abbasudin Ahmad, Bengali Singer — A74

1984, Dec. 24
251 A74 3t multicolored 1.10 1.10

No. 116 Ovptd. for KHULNAPEX '84 Stamp Exhibition

1984, Dec. 29   Litho.   Perf. 15
252 A25 2.25t multicolored 1.10 1.10

1984 Summer Olympics, Los Angeles A75

1984, Dec. 31   Perf. 14
253 A75 1t Bicycling 1.25 .25
254 A75 5t Field hockey 2.50 2.50
255 A75 10t Volleyball 3.50 3.50
　　　Nos. 253-255 (3) 7.25 6.25

Islamic Development Bank, 9th Annual Congress, Dacca — A76

1985, Feb. 2
256 A76 1t Farmer .40 .40
257 A76 5t Four Asian races 1.90 1.90

UN Child Survival Campaign A77

1985, Mar. 14
258 A77 1t Breastfeeding .30 .30
259 A77 10t Growth monitoring 2.75 2.75

Nos. 139-144 Ovptd. in Bengali for Local Elections

1985, May 16 Litho. Perf. 13
259A A33 40p multicolored .20 .20
259B A33 1t multicolored .20 .20
259C A33 2.25t multicolored .25 .25
259D A33 3.50t multicolored .35 .35
259E A33 4t multicolored .45 .45
259F A33 5t multicolored .55 .55
  Nos. 259A-259F (6) 2.00 2.00

UN Decade for Women — A78

1985, July 18 Perf. 14
260 A78 1t shown .20 .20
261 A78 10t Technology 1.60 1.60

UN, 40th Anniv. A79

1985, Sept. 15
262 A79 1t UN building .20 .20
263 A79 10t World map, natl. flag 1.25 1.25
  11th anniv. of UN admission.

Intl. Youth Year — A80

1985, Nov. 2 Litho. Perf. 14
264 A80 1t Scissors, pencil .20 .20
265 A80 5t Hammer, wrenches .70 .70

Seven Doves, Council Emblem — A81

1985, Dec. 8 Litho. Perf. 14
266 A81 1t shown .20 .20
267 A81 5t Flags, lotus blossom .80 .80
  1st South Asian Regional Council Summit, SARC, Dacca.

Shilpacharya Zainul Abedin (1914-1976), Founder, Dacca College of Art — A82

1985, Dec. 28
268 A82 3t multicolored 1.00 1.00

No. 138 Overprinted Reading Up

1985, Dec. 29 Perf. 13
269 A32 5t multicolored 2.75 2.25
  3rd Natl. Scout Jamboree.
  The overprint comes in two types.

Postal Services Type of 1983-84
1986-93 Litho. Perf. 12x11½
  Size: 30½x19mm
270 A70 3t Sorting machine .30 .30
  Perf. 12x12½
  Size: 33½x22½mm
271 A70 4t Chittagong Port .55 .55
  Issued: 3t, Jan. 11, 1986; 4t, Apr. 22, 1993.
  For overprint see No. O46.
  This is an expanding set. Numbers will change if necessary.

Fishing Net, by Safiuddin Ahmed A83

  Paintings by Bengali artists: 5t, Happy Return, by Quamrul Hassan. 10t, Levelling the Plowed Field, by Zainul Abedin.

1986, Apr. 6 Litho. Perf. 14
275 A83 1t multicolored .20 .20
276 A83 5t multicolored .55 .55
277 A83 10t multicolored 1.10 1.10
  Nos. 275-277 (3) 1.85 1.85

1986 World Cup Soccer Championships, Mexico — A84

1986, June 29 Perf. 15x14
278 A84 1t Stealing the ball .30 .30
279 A84 10t Goal 3.00 3.00
  Souvenir Sheet
  Imperf
279A A84 20t multicolored 5.25 5.25
  No. 279A contains one stamp 62x45mm with simulated perfs.

Gen. M.A.G. Osmani (1918-1984), Liberation Forces Commander-in-Chief — A85

1986, Sept. 10 Litho. Perf. 14
280 A85 3t multicolored 1.50 1.50

No. 207 Ovptd.

1986, Dec. 3 Litho. Perf. 13½x14
281 A58 50p on #207 1.75 2.00

Intl. Peace Year — A86

A87

1986, Dec. 25 Litho. Perf. 12x12½
282 A86 1t shown .50 .25
283 A86 10t City ruins, flower 4.00 4.00
  Souvenir Sheet
284 A87 20t shown 2.50 2.50

Nos. 179-180 Ovptd. or Surcharged "CONFERENCE FOR DEVELOPMENT '87"

1987, Jan. 12 Perf. 14
285 A42 1t on 40p multicolored .20 .20
286 A42 5t multicolored .65 .65

Language Movement, 35th Anniv. — A88

Illustration reduced.

1987, Feb. 21 Perf. 12½x12
287 3t Protestors 1.00 1.00
288 3t Memorial 1.00 1.00
  a. A88 Pair, Nos. 287-288 2.00 2.00

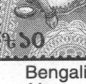

World Health Day — A89   Bengali New Year — A90

1987, Apr. 7 Perf. 11½x12
289 A89 1t Child immunization 2.50 2.50
  See No. 318.

1987, Apr. 16 Perf. 12x12½
290 A90 1t Bengali script, embroidery .20 .20
291 A90 10t shown .75 .75

Jute Carpet A91

Exports: 1t, Jute shika (wall hanging, bowlholder and mats), vert. 10t, Table lamp and shade, vert.

Perf. 12x12½, 12½x12
1987, May 18 Litho.
292 A91 1t multicolored .20 .20
293 A91 5t shown .35 .35
294 A91 10t multicolored .75 .75
  Nos. 292-294 (3) 1.30 1.30

Ustad Ayet Ali Khan (1884-1967), Composer, and Surbahar A92

1987, Sept. 8 Perf. 12x12½
295 A92 5t multicolored .80 .80

Palanquin A93

Transportation.

1987, Oct. 24   Litho.   Perf. 12½x12
296 A93 2t shown   .20 .20
297 A93 3t Bicycle rickshaw   .30 .30
298 A93 5t Paddle steamer   .55 .55
299 A93 7t Train   .75 .75
300 A93 10t Ox cart   1.25 1.25
         Nos. 296-300 (5)   3.05 3.05
         For overprint see No. 424.

Hossain Shahid
Suhrawardy
(1893-1963),
Politician — A94

1987, Dec. 5   Litho.   Perf. 12x12½
301 A94 3t multicolored   .40 .40

Intl. Year of Shelter for the
Homeless — A95

Illustration reduced.

1987, Dec. 15   Perf. 12½x12
302 5t Homeless people   .50 .50
303 5t Prosperous community   .50 .50
  a. A95 Pair, Nos. 302-303   1.00 1.00

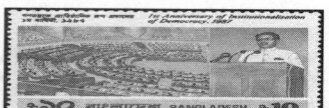

Natl. Democracy, 1st Anniv. — A96

Design: Pres. Hossain Mohammed Ershad
addressing parliament.

1987, Dec. 31
304 A96 10t multicolored   1.90 1.90

Woman
Tending
Crop
A97

1988, Jan. 26
305 A97 3t shown   .35 .35
306 A97 5t Milking cow, village   .50 .50

Intl. Fund for Agricultural Development
(IFAD) Seminar on Loans for Women in Rural
Areas.

1988 Summer Olympics, Seoul — A98

1988 Summer Games emblem and Sports:
a, Basketball. b, Weight lifting. c, Women's
tennis. d, Shooting. e, Boxing.

1988, Sept. 29   Litho.   Perf. 11½
307   Strip of 5   3.00 2.50
  a.-e. A98 5t any single   .60 .50

Historical
Sites
A99

Designs: 1t, Shait Gumbaz Mosque (inte-
rior), Bagerhat. 4t, Paharpur Monastery. 5t,
Kantanagar Temple, Dinajpur. 10t, Lalbag
Fort, Dacca.

1988, Oct. 9   Perf. 12½x12
308 A99 1t multicolored   .20 .20
309 A99 4t multicolored   .20 .20
310 A99 5t multicolored   .25 .25
311 A99 10t multicolored   .50 .35
         Nos. 308-311 (4)   1.15 1.00

Qudrat-i-Khuda
(1900-1977),
Scientist — A100

1988, Nov. 3   Perf. 12x12½
312 A100 5t multicolored   .55 .55

Asia Cup
Cricket — A101

1988, Nov. 27
313   Strip of 3   3.25 3.25
  a. A101 1t Wicketkeeper   .20 .20
  b. A101 5t Batsman   .95 .95
  c. A101 10t Bowler   2.00 2.00

Intl. Red Cross
and Red
Crescent
Organizations,
125th
Annivs. — A102

1988, Oct. 26   Litho.   Perf. 12x12½
314 A102 5t Emblems, Dunant   .60 .60
315 A102 10t Blood donation   1.25 1.25

Dacca G.P.O., 25th Anniv. — A103

1988, Dec. 6   Perf. 12
316 A103 1t Exterior   .20 .20
317 A103 5t Sales counter   .65 .65

World Health Day Type of 1987
1988, Jan. 16   Litho.   Perf. 11½x12
318 A89 25p Oral rehydration   .70 .70

32nd Meeting of
the Colombo
Plan Consultative
Committee,
Dacca — A104

1988, Nov. 29   Perf. 12x12½
319 A104 3t multicolored   .25 .25
320 A104 10t multicolored   .75 .75

No. 191 Ovptd.

No. 277 Overprinted

1989, Dec. 29   Litho.   Perf. 14
321 A50 5t multicolored   1.25 1.25
         5th Natl. Rover Moot (Scouting).

1989, Mar. 1
322 A83 10t multicolored   1.10 1.10
         4th Asiatic Exposition.

A106

1989, Mar. 13   Litho.   Perf. 12x12½
324 A106 10t multicolored   .85 .85
         Police academy, Sardah, 75th anniv.

A107

1989, Mar. 7   Litho.   Perf. 12x12½
Modernizing water supply services.
325 A107 10t multicolored   .85 .85
         12th Natl. Science & Technology Week.

A108

French Revolution, Bicent. — A109

Scenes from the revolution: 5t, Close-up of
revolutionaries destroying the Bastille, vert.
No. 326b, Liberty guiding the people. No.
326c, Women's march on Versailles, vert. No.
327a, Celebration of the Federation on the
Champ de Mars. No. 327b, Storming of the
Bastille. 25t, Montage of scenes, #326a-326c.

1989, July 12   Perf. 14
326   Sheet of 3 + label   2.25 2.25
  a.   A108 5t multicolored   .45 .45
  b.-c. A108 10t any single   .90 .90
                             Perf. 14x15
327   Strip of 2 + label   2.25 2.25
  a.-b. A109 17t any single   1.10 1.10
                         Size: 152x88mm
                             Imperf
328   A108 25t multicolored   2.25 2.25
         Nos. 326-328 (3)   6.75 6.75
Labels picture the revolution anniv. emblem.

Rural Development in Asia and the
Pacific (CIRDAP), 10th Anniv. — A110

Illustration reduced.

1989, Aug. 10   Litho.   Perf. 12½x12
329   5t multi   .50 .50
330   10t multi   1.00 1.00
  a.   Pair, Nos. 329-330   1.50 1.50

Child
Survival
A111

1989, Aug. 22
331 A111 1t shown   .20 .20
332 A111 10t Women and chil-
         dren, diff.   .90 .90
         SOS Children's Village, 40th anniv.

Involvement of
the Bangladesh
Army in UN
Peace-keeping
Operations, 1st
Anniv. — A112

1989, Sept. 12   Perf. 12x12½
333 A112 4t shown   .65 .65
334 A112 10t Camp, two soldiers   1.60 1.60

2nd Asian
Poetry Festival,
Dacca — A113

1989, Nov. 17   Litho.   Perf. 12x12½
335 A113 2t multicolored   .20 .20
336 A113 10t multicolored   .90 .90

State
Printing
Office
A114

1989, Dec. 7   *Perf. 13½*
337 A114 10t multicolored   1.25 1.25

Bangladesh Television, 25th
Anniv. — A115

1989, Dec. 25 Litho.   *Perf. 12½x12*
338 A115 5t shown   .50 .50
339 A115 10t Emblem, flowers,
      diff.   1.00 1.00

World
Wildlife
Fund
A116

Various gavials, *(Gavialis gangeticus).*

1990, Jan. 31 Litho.   *Perf. 14*
340 A116 50p shown   .20 .20
341 A116 2t Reptile's jaws   .55 .55
342 A116 4t 4 reptiles   1.00 1.00
343 A116 10t 2 reptiles resting   2.75 2.75
    a.   Block of 4, #340-343   4.50 4.50

A117

1990, Feb. 2   *Perf. 14*
344 A117 6t multicolored   .85 .85

Natl. Population Day.

A118

1990, May 6   *Perf. 14*
345 A118 7t shown   1.60 1.60
346 A118 10t Penny Black, No.
      230   2.50 2.50

Penny Black, 150th anniv.

Justice Syed Mahbub Murshed, (1911-
1979) — A119

1990, Apr. 3 Litho.   *Perf. 12½x12*
347 A119 5t multicolored   1.10 1.10

Intl. Literacy
Year — A120

Design: 10t, Boy teaching girl to write.

1990, Apr. 10   *Perf. 12x12½*
348 A120 6t multicolored   1.40 1.40
349 A120 10t multicolored   2.00 2.00

Type of 1973 Redrawn and:

Loading Cargo
Plane — A121

Curzon
Hall — A122

Fertilizer
Plant — A123

Postal
Academy,
Rajshahi
A124

Salimullah
Hall — A125

Bangla
Academy — A126

Designs: No. 356, Sixty-dome Mosque
(English inscription at LR).

1989-99   *Perf. 12x11½, 12, 12x12½*
350 A121 3t multicolored   .20 .20
    a.   Perf. 14¼x14   .20 .20
351 A122 5t gray blk & red brn   .25 .25
    a.   Perf. 14¼   .25 .25
352 A123 10t carmine   .50 .50
353 A124 20t multicolored   1.10 1.10

       Perf. 14½x14
354 A125 6t blue gray & yel   .55 .55

       Perf. 14x14½
355 A126 2t brown & green   .20 .20

     Perf. 14¼
    Size: 35x22 mm
    Taka Expressed in Bengali
356 A9 10t rose   .50 .50
    Nos. 350-356 (7)   3.30 3.30

   Issued: 5t, 3/31; 3t, 4/30; 10t, 20t, 7/8; 6t,
1/30/91; 2t, 12/3/93; No. 356, 3/18/99; #351a,
8/31/99.
   No. 356 is very similar to No. 85 but differs
in several ways: the inscription "Sixty-Dome
Mosque" has been enlarged and moved from
the upper left of the vignette to the lower right;
a Bengali inscription has been added in its
place at upper left; and the entire design has
been lightened condiderably, especially in the
skyline of the mosque.
   For overprints see Nos. O47A-O47B, O50.
   This is an expanding set. Numbers will
change.

World Cup Soccer Championships,
Italy — A133

1990, June 12 Litho.   *Perf. 14*
362 A133 8t shown   2.00 2.00
363 A133 10t Soccer player,
      diff.   3.50 3.50

    Size: 115x79mm
      Imperf
364 A133 25t Colosseum, soc-
      cer ball   7.50 7.50
    Nos. 362-364 (3)   13.00 13.00

Fruits — A134

1990, July 16   *Perf. 12x12½*
365 A134 1t Mangifera indica   .20 .20
366 A134 2t Psidium guayava   .35 .35
367 A134 3t Citrullus vulgaris   .50 .50
368 A134 4t Carica papaya   .70 .70
369 A134 5t Artocarpus heter-
      ophyllus   .90 .90
370 A134 10t Averrhoa carambo-
      la   1.75 1.75
    Nos. 365-370 (6)   4.40 4.40

UN Conference on Least Developed
Nations, Paris — A135

1990, Sept. 3 Litho.   *Perf. 14*
371 A135 10t multicolored   1.90 1.90

Asia-Pacific Postal Training Center,
20th Anniv. — A136

Illustration reduced.

1990, Sept. 10   *Perf. 13½x14*
372   2t multicolored   .50 .50
373   6t multicolored   1.50 1.50
    a.   A136 Pair, #372-373   2.00 2.00

   No. 373a has continuous design.

11th
Asian
Games,
Beijing
A137

1990, Sept. 22   *Perf. 14*
374 A137 2t Rowing   .40 .40
375 A137 4t Kabaddi   .85 .85
376 A137 8t Wrestling   1.75 1.75
377 A137 10t Badminton   2.00 2.00
    Nos. 374-377 (4)   5.00 5.00

Lalan Shah,
Poet — A138

1990, Oct. 17 Litho.   *Perf. 14*
378 A138 6t multicolored   1.40 1.40

UN Development Program, 40th
Anniv. — A139

1990, Oct. 24 Litho.   *Perf. 14*
379 A139 6t multicolored   1.25 1.25

A139a   A140

1990, Nov. 29 Litho.   *Perf. 14½x14*
379A A139a 2t brown   .40 .40

   Immunization program. See No. 560.
   For surcharge see O47.

1990, Dec. 24 Litho.   *Perf. 13½x12*
   Butterflies.
380 A140 6t Danaus chrysippus   1.50 1.50
381 A140 6t Precis almana   1.50 1.50
382 A140 10t Ixias pyrene   2.50 2.50
383 A140 10t Danaus plexippus   2.50 2.50
    a.   Block of 4, #380-383   8.00 8.00

UN
Decade
Against
Drugs
A141

1991, Jan 1 Litho.   *Perf. 14x13½*
384 A141 2t Drugs, map   .75 .75
385 A141 4t shown   1.50 1.50

Third National
Census — A142

1991, Mar. 12   Litho.   Perf. 14
386 A142 4t multicolored   .80   .80

Independence, 20th Anniv. — A143

Designs: a, Invincible Bangla statue. b,
Freedom Fighter statue. c, Mujibnagar Memo-
rial. d, Eternal flame. e, National Martyrs'
Memorial.

1991, Mar. 26   Perf. 13½
387 A143 4t Strip of 5, #a.-e.   2.75   2.75

No. 387 printed in continuous design.

A144

Pres. Ziaur
Rahman, 10th
Death
Anniv. — A145

1991, May 30   Perf. 14
388 A144 50p multicolored   .20   .20
389 A145 2t multicolored   .90   .90
 a.   Souvenir sheet of 2, #388-389   1.75   1.75

No. 389a sold for 10t.

Endangered Animals — A146

1991, June 16   Perf. 12
390 A146 2t Petaurista petauris-
           ta   .40   .40
391 A146 4t Presbytis entellus,
           vert.   .75   .75
392 A146 6t Buceros bicornis,
           vert.   1.10   1.10
 a.   Pair, #391-392   1.85   1.85
393 A146 10t Manis crassi-
           caudata   1.75   1.75
 a.   Pair, #390, 393   2.15   2.15
      Nos. 390-393 (4)   4.00   4.00

Kaikobad (1857-
1951),
Poet — A147

1991, July 21   Litho.   Perf. 14
394 A147 6t multicolored   .85   .85

Rabindranath Tagore, Poet, 50th
Anniv. of Death — A148

1991, Aug. 7
395 A148 4t multicolored   .85   .85

Blood and Eye
Donations
A149

1991, Sept. 19
396 A149 3t shown   1.00   .60
397 A149 5t Blind man and eye   1.50   1.25

Sandhani, Medical Students Association,
14th anniversary.

Shahid
Naziruddin,
Leader of
Democratic
Movement, 1st
Anniv. of
Death — A150

1991, Oct. 10
398 A150 2t multicolored   .80   .80

Shaheed Noor
Hossain, 4th
Death
Anniv. — A151

1991, Nov. 10   Litho.   Perf. 14
399 A151 2t multicolored   .80   .80

Archaeological Treasures of
Mainamati — A152

Designs: a, Bronze Stupa with images of
Buddha. b, Bowl and pitcher. c, Ruins of

Salban Vihara Monastery. d, Gold coins. e,
Terra-cotta plaque.

1991, Nov. 26   Litho.   Perf. 13½
400 A152 4t Strip of 5, #a.-e.   5.00   5.00

Mass
Uprising,
First
Anniv.
A153

1991, Dec. 6   Perf. 14
401 A153 4t multicolored   .80   .80

Miniature Sheets

Independence,
20th
Anniv. — A154

Martyred intellectuals who died in 1971 -
No. 402: a, A.N.M. Munier Chowdhury. b,
Ghyasuddin Ahmad. c, S.M.A. Rashidul
Hasan. d, Muhammad Anwar Pasha. e, Dr.
Md. Mortaza. f, Shahid Saber. g, Fazlur
Rahman Khan. h, Ranada Prasad Saha. i,
Adhyaksha Joges Chandra Ghose. j, Santosh
Chandra Bhattacharyya.
  No. 403: a, Dr. Gobinda Chandra Deb. b,
A.N.M. Muniruzzaman. c, Mufazzal Haider
Chaudhury. d, Dr. Abdul Alim Choudhury. e,
Sirajuddin Hossain. f, Shahidulla Kaiser. g,
Altaf Mahmud. h, Dr. Jyotirmay Guha
Thakurta. i, Dr. Md. Abul Khair. j, Dr. Serajul
Haque Khan.
  No. 404: a, Dr. Mohammad Fazle Rabbi. b,
Mir Abdul Quyyum. c, A.N.M. Golam Mostafa.
d, Dhirendranath Dutta. e, S.A. Mannan (Ladu
Bhai). f, Nizamuddin Ahmad. g, Abul Bashar
Chowdhury. h, Selina Parveen. i, Dr. Abul
Kalam Azad. j, Saidul Hassan.
  No. 404K: l, LCDR. Moazzam Hussain. m,
Muhammad Habibur Rahman. n, Khandoker
Abu Taleb. o, Moshiur Rahman. p, Md. Abdul
Muktadir. q, Nutan Chandra Sinha. r, Syed
Nazmul Haque. s, Dr. Mohammed Amin
Uddin. t, Dr. N.A.M. Faizul Mohee. u, Sukha
Ranjan Somaddar.

1991-93   Litho.   Perf. 13½
          Sheets of 10
402 A154 2t #a.-j. + 5 labels   1.90   1.90
403 A154 2t #a.-j. + 5 labels   1.90   1.90
404 A154 2t #a.-j. + 5 labels   1.90   1.90
              Perf. 14½
404K A154 2t #l.-u. + 5 labels   3.00   3.00

  Issued: #402-404, 12/14/91; #404K,
12/14/93.
  See Nos. 470-471, 499-500, 534-535, 558-
559, 568-569, 595, 627-628.

Shrimp — A155

Illustration reduced.

1991, Dec. 31   Perf. 14
405 A155 6t Penaeus monodon   1.25   1.25
406 A155 6t Metapenaeus monoceros   1.25   1.25
 a.   A155 Pair, #405-406   2.50   2.50

Shaheed
Mirze Abu
Raihan
Jaglu, 5th
Death
Anniv.
A156

1992, Feb. 8   Litho.   Perf. 14x13½
407 A156 2t multicolored   .95   .95

World Environment Day — A157

Design: 4t, Scenes of environmental protection and pollution control, vert.

1992, June 5   Litho.   Perf. 14
408 A157 4t multicolored   .45   .45
409 A157 10t multicolored   1.10   1.10

Nawab
Sirajuddaulah of
Bengal (1733-
1757)
A158

1992, July 2   Litho.   Perf. 14
410 A158 10t multicolored   1.00   1.00

Syed Ismail
Hossain Sirajee
(1880-1931),
Social Reformer
A159

1992, July 17
411 A159 4t multicolored   .80   .80

Tree
Week — A160

1992, July 17   Litho.   Perf. 14
412 A160 2t Couple planting tree,
           horiz.   .50   .50
413 A160 4t Birds, trees   1.00   1.00

1992
Summer
Olympics,
Barcelona
A161

Olympic rings and: a, 4t, Rowing. b, 6t,
Hands holding Olympic torch. c, 10t, Peace
doves. d, 10t, Clasped hands.

1992, July 25   Perf. 14
414 A161 Block of 4, #a.-d.   2.75   2.75

The Star
Mosque,
18th Cent.
A162

1992, Oct. 29   Litho.   Perf. 14½x14
415 A162 10t multicolored   1.10   1.10

Masnad-E-Ala
Isa Khan, 393rd
Anniv. of
Death — A163

1992, Sept. 15   *Perf. 14x14½*
416 A163 4t multicolored   .80 .80

7th SAARC
Summit,
Dacca — A164

1992, Dec. 5
417 A164 6t Flags of members   .50 .50
418 A164 10t Emblem   .85 .85

1992 Bangladesh Natl. Philatelic
Exhibition — A165

Designs: No. 419a, Elephant and mahout,
ivory work, 19th cent. b, Post rider, mail box
and postman delivering mail to villager.

1992, Sept. 26   *Perf. 14½x14*
419 A165 10t Pair, #a.-b. + label   2.50 2.50
    c.   Souv. sheet, imperf.   2.75 2.75
    No. 419c contains one strip of No. 419 with
simulated perforations and sold for 25t.

1992 Intl. Conference on Nutrition,
Rome — A166

1992, Dec. 5
420 A166 4t multicolored   .55 .55

Meer Nisar Ali Titumeer (1782-
1831) — A167

1992, Nov. 19   **Litho.**   *Perf. 14½x14*
421 A167 10t multicolored   1.00 1.00

Archaeological Relics,
Mahasthan — A168

Relics from 3rd century B.C.-15th century
A.D.: No. 422a, Terracotta seal and head. b,
Terracotta hamsa. c, Terracotta Surya image.
d, Gupta stone columns.

1992, Nov. 30   **Litho.**   *Perf. 14½x14*
422 A168 10t Strip of 4, #a.-d.   4.00 4.00

Canal Digging — A169

a, Workers digging canal. b, Completed
project.
Illustration reduced.

1993, Mar. 31   **Litho.**   *Perf. 14½x14*
423 A169 2t Pair, #a.-b.   1.40 1.40

No. 300 Overprinted

1992, Aug. 18   **Litho.**   *Perf. 12½x12*
424 A93 10t multicolored   1.10 1.10

Syed Abdus
Samad (1895-
1964), Soccer
Player — A170

1993, Feb. 2   *Perf. 14x14½*
425 A170 2t multicolored   .80 .80

A171

1993, Apr. 14
426 A171 2t multicolored   .70 .70
Completion of 14th cent. Bengali era.

Haji Shariat
Ullah (1770-
1839), Social
Reformer,
Religious and
Political
Leader — A172

1993, Mar. 10   **Litho.**   *Perf. 14x14½*
427 A172 2t multicolored   .70 .70

World
Health
Day
A173

1993, Apr. 7   *Perf. 14½x14, 14x14½*
428 A173 6t Prevent accidents   1.25 .75
429 A173 10t Prevent violence,
vert.   1.50 1.50

Compulsory Primary
Education — A174

1993, May 26
430 A174 2t Slate, chalk, books   .40 .40
431 A174 2t Hand writing, children, vert.   .40 .40

Nawab Sir Salimullah (1871-1915),
Social Reformer — A175

1993, June 7   **Litho.**   *Perf. 14½x14*
432 A175 4t multicolored   .55 .55

Fishing
Industry
A176

1993, Aug. 15   **Litho.**   *Perf. 14½x14*
433 A176 2t multicolored   .55 .55

Tomb of Sultan Ghiyasuddin Azam
Shah — A177

1993, Dec. 30   **Litho.**   *Perf. 14½x14*
434 A177 10t multicolored   1.10 1.10

Scenic
Views
A178

Designs: No. 435, Sunderban. No. 436,
Madhabkunda Waterfall, vert. No. 437, River,
mountains, vert. No. 438, Beach, Kuakata.

1993, Oct. 30   *Perf. 14½x14, 14x14½*
435 A178 10t multicolored   1.25 1.25
436 A178 10t multicolored   1.25 1.25
437 A178 10t multicolored   1.25 1.25
438 A178 10t multicolored   1.25 1.25
    a.   Souv. sheet, #435-438, im-
perf   5.00 5.00
    Nos. 435-438 (4)   5.00 5.00
#438a sold for 50t and has simulated perfs.

6th Asian Art
Biennial,
Bangladesh
A179

1993, Nov. 7   **Litho.**   *Perf. 14x14½*
439 A179 10t multicolored   .85 .85

Foy's
Lake
A180

1993, Nov. 6   *Perf. 14½x14*
440 A180 10t multicolored   1.10 1.10
Tourism month.

14th Asian
Pacific, 5th
Bangladesh Natl.
Scout Jamboree
A181

1994, Jan. 5   *Perf. 14x14½*
441 A181 2t multicolored   .55 .55

Oral Rehydration
Solution, 25th
Anniv. — A182

1994, Feb. 5   **Litho.**   *Perf. 13½x14*
442 A182 2t multicolored   .55 .55

6th SAF
Games,
Dhaka
A183

1993, Dec. 6   *Perf. 14x13½, 13½x14*
443 A183 2t Shot put   .30 .30
444 A183 4t Runners, vert.   .65 .65

Mosques
A184

Mosques: 4t, Interior, Chhota Sona,
Nawabgonj. No. 446, Exterior, Chhota Sona.
No. 447, Exterior, Baba Adam's, Munshigonj.

1994, Mar. 30   **Litho.**   *Perf. 14x13½*
445 A184 4t multicolored   .30 .30
446 A184 6t multicolored   .50 .50
447 A184 6t multicolored   .50 .50
    Nos. 445-447 (3)   1.30 1.30
For overprint see No. 509.

ILO, 75th Anniv. A185

Designs: 4t, People, oxen working in fields. 10t, Man rotating gearwheel, vert.

Perf. 14x13½, 13½x14
1994, Apr. 11 **Litho.**
448 A185 4t multicolored .40 .40
449 A185 10t multicolored 1.00 1.00

Bangla Era, 15th Cent. — A186

1994, Apr. 14 **Perf. 13½x14**
450 A186 2t multicolored .55 .55

Traditional Festivals A187

1994, May 12 **Perf. 14x13½**
451 A187 4t Folk Festival .40 .40
452 A187 4t Baishakhi Festival .40 .40

Intl. Year of the Family — A188

1994, May 15 **Perf. 13½x14**
453 A188 10t multicolored 1.50 1.50

Tree Planting Campaign A189

1994, June 15 Litho. Perf. 13½x14
454 A189 4t Family planting trees .55 .55
455 A189 6t Hands, seedlings .80 .80

1994 World Cup Soccer Championships, US — A190

Soccer player's uniform colors: a, Red, yellow & blue. b, Yellow, green, & red.

1994, June 17 Litho. Perf. 14½
456 A190 20t Pair, #a.-b. + label 4.25 4.25
Complete booklet, #456 11.50

Jamuna Multi-Purpose Bridge — A191

1994, July 24 **Perf. 14½x14**
457 A191 4t multicolored .40 .40

Birds — A192

Designs: 4t, Oriolus xanthornus. No. 459, Gallus gallus. No. 460, Dicrurus paradiseus. No. 461, Dendrocitta vagabunda.

1994, Aug. 31 **Perf. 14x14½**
458 A192 4t multicolored .50 .50
459 A192 6t multicolored .75 .75
460 A192 6t multicolored .75 .75
461 A192 6t multicolored .75 .75
a. Souvenir sheet, #458-461 2.75 2.75
Nos. 458-461 (4) 2.75 2.75

No. 461a sold for 25t.

Dr. Mohammad Ibrahim (1911-89), Pioneer in Treatment of Diabetes — A193

1994, Sept. 6 Litho. Perf. 14x14½
462 A193 2t multicolored .40 .40

Nawab Faizunnessa Chowdhurani (1834-1903), Social Reformer A194

1994, Sept. 23 **Perf. 14x14½**
463 A194 2t multicolored .40 .40

12th Asian Games, Hiroshima, Japan A195

1994, Oct. 2 **Perf. 14½x14**
464 A195 4t multicolored .55 .55

Shells A196

Designs: No. 465, White, pink pearls, oysters. No. 466, Snail, three other shells. No. 467, Scallop, other shells. No. 468, Spiral shaped shells, vert.

Perf. 14½x14, 14x14½
1994, Oct. 30 **Litho.**
465 A196 6t multicolored .60 .60
466 A196 6t multicolored .60 .60
467 A196 6t multicolored .60 .60
468 A196 6t multicolored .60 .60
Nos. 465-468 (4) 2.40 2.40

Democracy Demonstration, Death of Dr. Shamsul Alam Khan Milon, 4th Anniv. — A197

1994, Nov. 27 **Perf. 14½x14**
469 A197 2t multicolored .40 .40

Martyred Intellectual Type of 1991
Miniature Sheets of 8
Martyred intellectuals who died in 1971: No. 470: a, Dr. Harinath Dey. b, Dr. Lt. Col. A.F. Ziaur Rahman. c, Mamum Mahmud. d, Mohsin Ali Dewan. e, Dr. Lt. Col. N.A.M. Jahangir. f, Shah Abdul Majid. g, Muhammad Akhter. h, Meherunnesa.
No. 471: a, Dr. Kasiruddin Talukder. b, Fazlul Haque Choudhury. c, Md. Shamsuzzaman. d, A.K.M. Shamsuddin. e, Lt. Mohammad Anwarul Azim. f, Nurul Amin Khan. g, Mohammad Sadeque. h, Md. Araz Ali.

1994, Dec. 14 **Perf. 14½**
470 A154 2t #a.-h. + 4 labels 1.25 1.25
471 A154 2t #a.-h. + 4 lables 1.25 1.25

Vegetables A199

1994, Dec. 24 Perf. 14x14½, 14½x14
472 A199 4t Diplazium esculentum .25 .25
473 A199 4t Momordica charantia .25 .25
474 A199 6t Lagenaria siceraria .50 .50
475 A199 6t Trichosanthes dioica .50 .50
476 A199 10t Solanum melongena .85 .85
477 A199 10t Cucurbita maxima .85 .85
Nos. 472-477 (6) 3.20 3.20

Nos. 472-476 are vert.

World Tourism Organization, 20th Anniv. — A200

1995, Jan. 2 **Perf. 14½x14**
478 A200 10t multicolored .95 .95

Intl. Trade Fair, Dhaka A201

Designs: 4t, Trade products. 6t, Factories, emblems of industry.

1995, Jan. 7 Litho. Perf. 14x14½
479 A201 4t multicolored .30 .30
480 A201 6t multicolored .60 .60

Bangladesh Rifles, Bicent. — A202

1995, Jan. 10 Litho. Perf. 14½x14
481 A202 2t shown .30 .30
482 A202 4t Building, battalion .60 .60

Fight Against Cancer — A203

1995, Apr. 7 Litho. Perf. 14x14½
483 A203 2t multicolored .40 .40

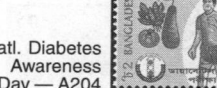

Natl. Diabetes Awareness Day — A204

1995, Feb. 28 **Perf. 14**
484 A204 2t multicolored .55 .55

For overprint see No. O49.

Munshi Mohammad Meherullah (1861-1907), Educator A205

1995, June 7 Litho. Perf. 14x14½
485 A205 2t multicolored .55 .55

FAO, 50th Anniv. — A206

1995, Oct. 16 Litho. Perf. 14
486 A206 10t multicolored .90 .90

UN, 50th Anniv. A207

UN emblem, "50," and: 2t, Dove of peace, UN headquarters. No. 488, "1945," earth from space, "1995." No. 489, Hands of different nationalities clasping, UN headquarters.

1995, Oct. 24 **Perf. 14½x14**
487 A207 2t multicolored .20 .20
488 A207 10t multicolored 1.00 1.00
489 A207 10t multicolored 1.00 1.00
Nos. 487-489 (3) 2.20 2.20

Flowers — A208

#490, Bombax ceiba. #491, Lagerstroemia speciosa. #492, Gloriosa superba. #493, Canna indica. #494, Bauhinia purpurea. #495, Passiflora incarnata.

1995, Oct. 9   *Perf. 14½x14, 14x14½*
490	A208	6t multicolored	.65	.65
491	A208	6t multi, vert.	.65	.65
492	A208	10t multi, vert.	.85	.85
493	A208	10t multi, vert.	.85	.85
494	A208	10t multi, vert.	.85	.85
495	A208	10t multi, vert.	.85	.85
		Nos. 490-495 (6)	4.70	4.70

Shaheed Khandaker Mosharraf Hossain A208a

1995, Oct. 16   Litho.   *Perf. 13¾x14¼*
496	A208a	2t multi	

No. 496 was removed from sale shortly after release.

18th Eastern Regional Conference on Tuberculosis and Respiratory Diseases, Dhaka — A209

1995, Oct. 29   Litho.   *Perf. 14½x14*
497	A209	6t multicolored	.55	.55

South Asian Assoc. for Regional Cooperation (SAARC), 10th Anniv. — A210

1995, Dec. 8   Litho.   *Perf. 14x14½*
498	A210	2t multicolored	.70	.70

Martyred Intellectual Type of 1991
Sheets of 8

Martyred intellectuals who died in 1971 - #499: a, Shaikh Habibur Rahman. b, Dr. Major Naimul Islam. c, Md. Shahidullah. d, Ataur Rahman Khan Khadim. e, A.B.M. Ashraful Islam Bhuiyan. f, Dr. Md. Sadat Ali. g, Sarafat Ali. h, M.A. Sayeed.

No. 500: a, Abdul Ahad. b, Lt. Col. Mohammad Abdul Qadir. c, Mozammel Hoque Chowdhury. d, Rafiqul Haider Chowdhury. e, Dr. Azharul Haque. f, A.K. Shamsuddin. g, Anudwaipayan Bhattacharjee. h, Lutfunnahar Helena.

1995, Dec. 14   Litho.   *Perf. 14½x14*
499	A154	2t #a.-h. + 4 labels	1.50	1.50
500	A154	2t #a.-h. + 4 labels	1.50	1.50

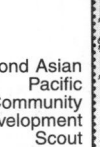

Second Asian Pacific Community Development Scout Camp — A211

1995, Dec. 18   Litho.   *Perf. 14x14½*
501	A211	2t multicolored	.55	.55

Volleyball, Cent. — A212

1995, Dec. 25
502	A212	6t multicolored	.55	.55

Traditional Costumes — A213

Designs: No. 503, Man in punjabi and lungi, vert. No. 504, Woman in sari, vert. No. 505, Christian bride and groom, vert. No. 506, Muslim bridal couple, vert. No. 507, Hindu bridal couple. No. 508, Buddhist bridal couple.

1995, Dec. 25   *Perf. 14x14½, 14x14½*
503	A213	6t multicolored	.60	.60
504	A213	6t multicolored	.60	.60
505	A213	10t multicolored	1.00	1.00
506	A213	10t multicolored	1.00	1.00
507	A213	10t multicolored	1.00	1.00
508	A213	10t multicolored	1.00	1.00
		Nos. 503-508 (6)	5.20	5.20

No. 446 Ovptd. in Red

1995   Litho.   *Perf. 14x13½*
509	A184	6t multicolored	1.50	1.50

Shaheed Amanullah Mohammad Asaduzzaman (1942-69) A214

1996, Jan. 20   *Perf. 14x14½*
510	A214	2t multicolored	.50	.50

1996 World Cup Cricket Championships — A215

1996, Feb. 14   *Perf. 14x14½, 14½x14*
511	A215	4t Pitching, vert.	.60	.60
512	A215	6t At bat, vert.	.85	.85
513	A215	10t shown	1.40	1.40
		Nos. 511-513 (3)	2.85	2.85

Independence, 25th Anniv. — A216

Designs: No. 514, Natl. Martyrs' Memorial. No. 515, Industrial development. No. 516, 1971 Destruction of war. No. 517, Educational development. No. 518, Development in communication. No. 519, Development in health.

1996, Mar. 26   Litho.   *Perf. 14x14½*
514	A216	4t multicolored	.35	.35
515	A216	4t multicolored	.35	.35
516	A216	4t multicolored	.35	.35
517	A216	4t multicolored	.35	.35
518	A216	4t multicolored	.35	.35
519	A216	4t multicolored	.35	.35
		Nos. 514-519 (6)	2.10	2.10

Michael Madhusudan Dutt (1824-73), Writer — A217

1996, June 29   Litho.   *Perf. 14x14½*
520	A217	4t multicolored	.60	.60

1996 Summer Olympic Games, Atlanta A218

1996, July 19   Litho.   *Perf. 14*
521	A218	4t Gymnast, vert.	.60	.60
522	A218	6t Judo, vert.	.90	.90
523	A218	10t High jumper	1.40	1.40
524	A218	10t Runners	1.40	1.40
a.		Souvenir sheet, #521-524	7.00	7.00
		Nos. 521-524 (4)	4.30	4.30

No. 524a sold for 50t.

Sheikh Mujibur Rahman (1920-75), Prime Minister — A219

Design: No. 527, Maulana Mohammad Akrum Khan (1868-1968).

1996   Litho.   *Perf. 14x14½*
526	A219	4t multicolored	.60	.60
527	A219	4t multicolored	.60	.60

Issued: No. 526, 8/15/96, No. 527, 8/18/96.

Ustad Alauddin Khan (1862-1972), Musician — A220

1996, Sept. 6   Litho.   *Perf. 14x14½*
528	A220	4t multicolored	.20	.20

Children's Paintings A221

Perf. 14x14½, 14½x14

1996, Oct. 9   Litho.
529	A221	2t Kingfisher, vert.	.45	.45
530	A221	4t River Crossing	.95	.95

Jailed, 21st Death Anniv. — A222

a, Syed Nazrul Islam. b, Tajuddin Ahmad. c, M. Monsoor Ali. d, A.H.M. Quamaruzzaman.

1996, Nov. 3   Litho.   *Perf. 14x14½*
531	A222	4t Block of 4, #a.-d.	2.00	2.00

UNICEF, 50th Anniv. — A223

Designs: 4t, Children receiving food, medicine, aid. 10t, Mother holding infant.

1996, Dec. 11
532	A223	4t multicolored	.65	.65
533	A223	10t multicolored	1.60	1.60

Martyred Intellectual Type of 1991

Martyred intellectuals who died in 1971: No. 534: a, Dr. Jekrul Haque. b, Munshi Kabiruddin Ahmed. c, Md. Abdul Jabbar. d, Mohammad Amir. e, A.K.M. Shamsul Huq Khan. f, Dr. Siddique Ahmed. g, Dr. Soleman Khan. h, S.B.M. Mizanur Rahman.

No. 535: a, Aminuddin. b, Md. Nazrul Islam. c, Zahirul Islam. d, A.K. Lutfor Rahman. e, Afsar Hossain. f, Abul Hashem Mian. g, A.T.M. Alamgir. h, Baser Ali.

1996, Dec. 14   Litho.   *Perf. 14½x14*
Sheets of 8
534	A154	2t #a.-h. + 4 labels	2.25	2.25
535	A154	2t #a.-h. + 4 labels	2.25	2.25

Victory Day, 25th Anniv. A224

Designs: 4t, People celebrating, natl. flag. 6t, Soldiers, monument, vert.

1996, Dec. 16 ***Perf. 14½x14, 14x14½***
536 A224 4t multicolored .65 .65
537 A224 6t multicolored 1.00 1.00

Paul Harris (1868-1947), Founder of Rotary Intl. — A225

1997, Feb. 18 Litho. ***Perf. 14x14½***
538 A225 4t multicolored .40 .40

Sheikh Mujibur Rahman's Mar. 7 Speech, 26th Anniv. — A226

1997, Mar. 7 ***Perf. 12½***
539 A226 4t multicolored .40 .40

Sheikh Mujibur Rahman (1920-75) A227

1997, Mar. 17 ***Perf. 14x14½***
540 A227 4t multicolored .40 .40

Independence, 25th Anniv. (in 1996) — A228

1997, Mar. 26 Litho. ***Perf. 12½***
541 A228 4t multi .40 .40

Heinrich von Stephan (1831-97) A229

1997, Apr. 8 Litho. ***Perf. 14x14½***
542 A229 4t multicolored .40 .40

Livestock A230

1997, Apr. 10 Litho. ***Perf. 14½x14***
543 A230 4t Goat .35 .35
544 A230 4t Sheep .35 .35
545 A230 6t Cow .50 .50
546 A230 6t Buffalo .50 .50
Nos. 543-546 (4) 1.70 1.70

Paintings — A231

Designs: 6t, "Tilling the Field-2," by S.M. Sultan (1923-94). 10t, "Three Women," by Quamrul Hassan (1921-88).

1997, June 26 Litho. ***Perf. 12½***
547 A231 6t multicolored .60 .60
548 A231 10t multicolored .95 .95

6th Intl. Cricket Council Trophy Championship, Malaysia — A232

1997, Sept. 4
549 A232 10t multicolored 1.00 1.00

Ancient Mosques A233

Designs: 4t, Kusumba Mosque, Naogaon, 1558. 6t, Atiya Mosque, Tangail, 1609. 10t, Bagha Mosque, Rajshahi, 1523.

1997, Sept. 4 Litho. ***Perf. 14½x14***
550 A233 4t multicolored .25 .25
551 A233 6t multicolored .35 .35
552 A233 10t multicolored .60 .60
Nos. 550-552 (3) 1.20 1.20

Abdul Karim Sahitya Visharad (1871-1953), Scholar — A234

1997, Oct. 11 ***Perf. 14x14½***
553 A234 4t multicolored .25 .25

9th Asia-Pacific, 7th Bangladesh Rover Moot '97 — A235

1997, Oct. 25 ***Perf. 14x14½***
554 A235 2t multicolored .35 .35

Armed Forces, 25th Anniv. A236

1997, Nov. 11 ***Perf. 14½x14***
555 A236 2t multicolored .20 .20

East Bengal Regiment, 50th Anniv. A237

1998, Feb. 15
556 A237 2t multicolored .20 .20

Mohammad Mansooruddin (1904-87) A238

1998, Feb. 4 ***Perf. 14x14½***
557 A238 4t multicolored .25 .25

Martyred Intellectual Type of 1991
Sheets of 8 + 4 Labels

Martyred intellectuals who died in 1971: No. 558: a, Dr. Shamsuddin Ahmed. b, Mohammad Salimullah. c, Mohiuddin Haider. d, Abdur Rahim. e, Nitya Nanda Paul. f, Abdul Jabber. g, Dr. Humayun Kabir. h, Khaja Nizamuddin Bhuiyan.

No. 559: a, Gulam Hossain. b, Ali Karim. c, Md. Moazzem Hossain. d, Rafiqul Islam. e, M. Nur Hussain. f, Captain Mahmood Hossain Akonda. g, Abdul Wahab Talukder. h, Dr. Hasimoy Hazra.

1997, Dec. 14
558-559 A154 2t #a.-h., each 1.00 1.00

Immunization Type of 1990

1998, Jan. 22 ***Perf. 14½x14***
560 A139a 1t green .20 .20

For overprint see No. O53.

Bulbul Chowdhury (1919-54), Dancer — A239

1998, May 17 ***Perf. 14x14½***
561 A239 4t multicolored .25 .25

Opening of the Bangabandhu Bridge — A240

Designs: 4t, East approach road. 6t, West approach road. 8t, River training works. 10t, Bangabandhu Bridge.

1998, June 23 ***Perf. 14***
562 A240 4t multicolored .25 .25
563 A240 6t multicolored .35 .35
564 A240 8t multicolored .45 .45
565 A240 10t multicolored .55 .55
Nos. 562-565 (4) 1.60 1.60

1998 World Cup Soccer Championships, France — A241

1998, June 10
566 A241 6t Trophy .35 .35
567 A241 18t Player, trophy 1.00 1.00

Martyred Intellectual Type of 1991
Sheets of 8 + 4 Labels

Martyred intellectuals who died in 1971 - No. 568: a, Md. Khorshed Ali Sarker. b, Abu Yakub Mahfuz. c, S.M. Nurul Huda. d, Nazmul Hoque Sarker. e, Md. Taslim Uddin. f, Gulam Mostafa. g, A. H. Nurul Alam. h, Timir Kanti Dev.

No. 569: a, Altaf Hossain. b, Aminul Hoque. c, S.M. Fazlul Hoque. d, Mozammel Ali. e, Syed Akbar Hossain. f, Sk. Abdus Salam. g, Abdur Rahman. h, Dr. Shyamal Kanti Lala.

1998, Dec. 14 Litho. ***Perf. 14½x14***
568-569 A154 2t #a.-h., set of 2 1.75 1.75

Princess Diana (1961-97) — A242

Diana: a, 8t, In hat. b, 18t, In black dress. c, 22t, In blue dress.
Illustration reduced.

1998, June 6 Litho. ***Perf. 14¼***
570 A242 Horiz. strip of 3, #a-c 2.25 2.25

World Solar Program, 1996-2005 A243

Perf. 13¾x14¼
1998, Sept. 24 **Litho.**
571 A243 10t multi .55 .55

World Habitat Day — A244

1998, Oct. 5
572 A244 4t multi .65 .65

Intl. Fund for
Agricultural
Development,
20th
Anniv. — A245

Sunflower and: 6t, Farmers, "20." 10t, Vegetables, pickers.

1998, Oct. 17
573 A245 6t multi   .35 .35
574 A245 10t multi   .55 .55

Wills Intl. Cup
Cricket Matches
A246

1998, Oct. 28
575 A246 6t multi   .35 .35

Begum Rokeya (1880-1932), Author,
Educator — A247

1998, Dec. 9 Litho.   Perf. 14¼x13¾
576 A247 4t multi   .20 .20

Universal
Declaration of
Human Rights,
50th
Anniv. — A248

1998, Dec. 10   Perf. 13¾x14¼
577 A248 10t multi   .50 .50

UN
Peacekeeping,
50th
Anniv. — A249

1998, Dec. 30   Perf. 13¾x14¼
578 A249 10t multi   .50 .50

Qazi Nazrul Islam (1899-1976),
Poet — A250

1998, Dec. 31   Perf. 14¼
579 A250 6t multi   .35 .35

Sixth National
Scout Jamboree
A251

1999, Feb. 6   Perf. 13¾x14¼
580 A251 2t multi   .20 .20

Surjya Sen (1894-1934), Anti-Colonial
Leader — A252

1999, Mar. 22   Perf. 14¼x13¾
581 A252 4t multi   .20 .20

Dr. Fazlur
Rahman Khan
(1929-82),
Architect of
Sears Tower,
Chicago — A253

1999, Apr. 13   Perf. 13¾x14¼
582 A253 4t multi   .20 .20

ICC Cricket
World Cup,
England — A254

Designs: 8t, Emblems. 10t, Bangladesh
flag, cricket ball, tiger.

1999, May 11   Perf. 13¾x14¼
583 A254 8t multi   .45 .45
584 A254 10t multi   .55 .55
  a. Souv. sheet, #583-584, perf 14¼ 1.75 1.75
      No. 584a sold for 30t.

Mother Teresa
(1910-97)
A255

1999, Sept. 5
585 A255 4t multi   .25 .25

Admission to
UN, 25th
Anniv. — A256

1999, Sept. 13
586 A256 8t multi   .40 .40

Shaheed
Mohammad
Maizuddin
(1930-84)
A257

1999, Sept. 27
587 A257 2t multi   .20 .20

Intl. Year of
Older
Persons — A258

1999, Oct. 1
588 A258 6t multi   .30 .30

World
Habitat
Day
A259

1999, Oct. 4   Perf. 14¼x13¾
589 A259 4t multi   .20 .20

UPU,
125th
Anniv.
A260

1999, Oct. 9   Perf. 14¼x13¾
590 A260 4t Truck   .20 .20
591 A260 4t Motorcycle   .20 .20
592 A260 6t Boat   .35 .35
593 A260 6t Airplanes   .35 .35
  a. Souv. sheet, #590-593, perf 14¼ 1.40 1.40
      Nos. 590-593 (4)   1.10 1.10
      No. 593a sold for 25t.

Sir Jagadis
Chandra Bose
(1858-1937),
Physicist
A261

1999   Perf. 13¾x14¼
594 A261 4t multi   .20 .20

Martyred Intellectual Type of 1991

Martyred intellectuals who died in 1971 -
No. 595: a, Dr. Mohammad Shafi. b, Maulana
Kasimuddin Ahmed. c, Quazi Ali Imam. d,
Sultanuddin Ahmed. e, A. S. M. Ershadullah. f,
Mohammad Fazlur Rahman. g, Dr. Capt. A. K.
M. Farooq. h, Mohammad Latafot Hossain
Joarder.

1999, Dec. 14   Litho.   Perf. 14¼
595 A154 2t Sheet of 8, #a-d, +
          4 labels   1.90 1.90

A number has been reserved for an additional sheet in this set.

Millennium — A262

Designs: 4t, Natl. Martyr's Memorial, flag.
6t, Satellite, computer, satellite dish, Bangabandhu Bridge, vert.

**   Perf. 14¼x13¾, 13¾x14¼**
2000, Jan. 1   Litho.
597-598 A262 Set of 2   .50 .50

Fifth Cub
Camporee
A263

2000, Feb. 13   Perf. 13¾x14¼
599 A263 2t multi   .20 .20

Jibanananda
Das (1899-
1954),
Poet — A264

2000, Feb. 17
600 A264 4t multi   .20 .20

Dr. Muhammad
Shamsuzzoha
(1934-69),
Educator
A265

2000, Feb. 18
601 A265 4t multi   .20 .20

Intl. Mother Language Day — A266

Martyrs: #602, Abul Barkat (1927-52). #603, Abdul Jabbar (1919-52). #604, Shafiur Rahman (1918-52). #605, Rafiq Uddin Ahmad (1926-52).

2000, Feb. 21
602-605 A266 4t Set of 4 .80 .80

World Meteorological Organization, 50th Anniv. — A267

2000, Mar. 23
606 A267 10t multi .50 .50

ICC Cricketnext.com Cricket Week — A268

2000, Apr. 8
607 A268 6t multi .30 .30

Insects — A269

Designs: 2t, Wasp. 4t, Grasshopper. 6t, Apis indica. 10t, Bombyx mori.

2000, May 18 *Perf. 14¼*
608-611 A269 Set of 4 1.10 1.10

Fauna A270

Designs: No. 612, 4t, Gekko gecko. No. 613, 4t, Hystrix indica. No. 615, 6t, Python molurus. No. 616, 6t, Varanus bengalensis.

2000, May 18 *Perf. 14¼x13¾*
612-615 A270 Set of 4 1.00 1.00

7th Pepsi Asia Cricket Cup — A271

2000, May 28 *Perf. 13¾x14¼*
616 A271 6t multi .30 .30

Birds A272

#617, 4t, Amaurornis phoenicurus. #618, 4t, Gallicrex cinerea. #619, 6t, Phalacrocorax niger, vert. #620, 6t, Ardeola grayii, vert.

Perf. 14¼x13¾, 13¾x14¼
2000, July 15
617-620 A272 Set of 4 1.00 1.00

2000 Summer Olympics, Sydney — A273

Shot putters: 6t, Woman. 10t, Man.

2000, Sept. 18 *Perf. 13¾x14¼*
621-622 A273 Set of 2 .80 .80

Bangladesh - People's Republic of China Diplomatic Relations, 25th Anniv. — A274

2000, Oct. 4 *Litho. Perf. 12½*
623 A274 6t multi .30 .30

Idrakpur Fort, Munshigonj — A275

Vajrasattva Bhojavihara Mainamati, Comilla — A276

Perf. 14¼x13¾, 13¾x14¼
2000, Nov. 5 *Litho.*
624 A275 4t multi .20 .20
625 A276 6t multi .35 .35

Intl. Volunteers Year (in 2001) — A277

2000, Dec. 5 Litho. *Perf. 13¾x14¼*
626 A277 6t multi .30 .30

Martyred Intellectuals Type of 1991

Martyred intellectuals who died in 1971 - No. 627, 2t: a, M. A. Gofur. b, Faizur Rahman Ahmed. c, Muslimuddin Miah. d, Sgt. Shamsul Karim Khan. e, Bhikku Zinananda. f, Abdul Jabber. g, Sekander Hayat Chowdhury. h, Chishty Shah Helalur Rahman.
No. 628, 2t: a, Birendra Nath Sarker. b, A. K. M. Nurul Haque. c, Sibendra Nath Mukherjee. d, Zahir Raihan. e, Ferdous Dowla Bablu. f, Capt. A. K. M. Nurul Absur. g, Mizanur Rahman Miju. h, Dr. Shamshad Ali.

2000 Litho. *Perf. 12½*
Sheets of 8, #a-h, + 4 labels
627-628 A154 Set of 2 1.75 1.75

Hason Raza (1854-1922) A278

2000 ? *Perf. 13¾x14¼*
629 A278 6t multi .35 .35

2001 Census — A279

2001 Litho. *Perf. 13¾x14¼*
630 A279 4t multi .25 .25

UN High Commissioner for Refugees, 50th Anniv. (in 2001) — A280

Perf. 13¾x14¼
2000, Dec. 14 *Litho.*
631 A280 10t multi .45 .45

Peasant Women, by Rashid Chowdhury A282

2001, Apr. 1 Litho. *Perf. 13¾x14¼*
633 A282 10t multi .45 .45

Houses of Worship — A283

No. 634: a, Lalbagh Kella Mosque. b, Uttara Ganabhavan, Natore. c, Armenian Church, Armanitola. d, Panam Nagar, Sonargaon. Illustration reduced.

2001 *Perf. 14¼x13¾*
634 A283 6t Block of 4, #a-d 2.75 2.75

OFFICIAL STAMPS

Nos. 42-47, 49-50, 52, 82-84 and 54 Overprinted in Black or Red

Perf. 14x14½, 14½x14
1973-75				**Litho.**
O1	A7	2p black (R)	.20	.20
O2	A7	3p brt green	.20	.20
O3	A7	5p lt brown	.20	.20
O4	A7	10p black (R)	.20	.20
O5	A7	20p olive	1.10	.20
O6	A7	25p red lilac	3.00	.20
O8	A7	60p gray (R)	3.00	.20
O9	A7	75p orange ('74)	1.10	.20
O10	A9	1t violet (#52)	12.00	3.25
O11	A9	1t violet (#82)	2.25	.35
O12	A9	2t grayish grn ('74)	3.75	1.25
O13	A9	5t gray blue (#54)	5.25	4.50
O14	A9	5t grysh bl (#84) ('75)	6.50	5.00
		Nos. O1-O14 (13)	38.75	16.00

Issue date: Apr. 30, 1973.

Nos. 95-101, 103-105 Overprinted "SERVICE" in Black or Red

1976 Litho.		*Perf. 15x14½, 14½x15*		
O16	A7	5p green	.30	.30
O17	A7	10p black (R)	.30	.30
O18	A7	20p olive	.30	.30
O19	A7	25p rose	.30	.30
O20	A8	50p rose lilac	.40	.40
O21	A7	60p gray (R)	.50	.50
O22	A7	75p olive	.55	.55

Perf. 15
O23	A9	1t violet	.85	.85
O24	A9	2t greenish gray	1.60	1.60
O25	A9	5t grayish blue	4.25	4.25
		Nos. O16-O25 (10)	9.35	9.35

Nos. 165-169, 171-175 Ovptd. "SERVICE"

1979-82		**Photo.**	*Perf. 14½*	
O27	A7	5p brown	.20	.20
O28	A7	10p Prussian blue	.20	.20
O29	A7	15p yellow orange	.20	.20
O30	A7	20p dk carmine	.20	.20
O31	A7	25p dk blue ('82)	.25	.25
O32	A9	40p rose magenta	.45	.45
O33	A9	50p gray ('81)	.55	.55
O34	A7	80p dark brown	.80	.80
O35	A7	1t red lilac ('81)	1.10	1.10
O36	A7	2t brt ultra ('81)	1.90	1.90
		Nos. O27-O36 (10)	5.85	5.85

#234-242, 271 Ovptd. "Service" in Red, Diagonally Up on #O43A, 1t, 2t, 4t

1983-93		*Perf. 11½x12½, 12½x11½*		
O37	A70	5p bluish green	.20	.20
O38	A70	10p deep magenta	.20	.20
O39	A70	15p blue	.20	.20
O40	A70	20p dark gray	.20	.20
O41	A70	25p slate	.20	.20
O42	A70	30p gray brown	.20	.20
O43	A70	50p yellow brown	.20	.20
O43A	A70	50p yellow brown		

Size: 30½x28½mm

Perf. 12x11½
O44	A70	1t ultramarine	.30	.30
O45	A70	2t Prussian blue	.60	.60

Perf. 12

O46	A70	4t blue	1.40	1.40
	Nos. O37-O46 (11)		3.90	3.90

Issued: 4t, 7/27/92; #O43A, 1993(?); others, 12/21/83.

No. 379A Ovptd. in Red

1990 Litho. Perf. 14½x14

O47	A139a	2t brown		

No. 350 Ovptd. "Service" Diagonally in Red

1994, July 16 Litho. Perf. 12x11½

O47A	A122	3t multicolored	11.50	11.50

No. 354 Ovptd. in Red

1992, Nov. 22 Litho. Perf. 14½x14

O47B	A125	6t blue gray & yel	6.75	6.75

No. 241 Ovptd. in Red

1992, Sept. 16 Litho. Perf. 12x11½

O48	A70	1t ultramarine	.20	.20

No. 484 Ovptd. in Red

1996 Litho. Perf. 14

O49	A204	2t multicolored	2.75	2.75

No. 351 Ovptd. in Blue

1997? Litho. Perf. 12

O50	A122	5t multicolored	.30	.30

Bengali overprint reads from top to bottom.

Nos. 235, 237 Ovptd. in Black সার্ভিস or Red

1997? Perf. 12½x11½

O51	A70	10p on #235	.65	.65
O52	A70	20p on #237 (R)	1.25	1.25

No. 560 Ovptd. in Red

1998 Litho. Perf. 14½x14

O53	A139a	1t green	.20	.20

BARBADOS

bär-'bā-⸗dŏs

LOCATION — A West Indies island east of the Windwards
GOVT. — Independent state in the British Commonwealth
AREA — 166 sq. mi.
POP. — 266,100 (1997 est.)
CAPITAL — Bridgetown

The British colony of Barbados became an independent state on November 30, 1966.

4 Farthings = 1 Penny
12 Pence = 1 Shilling
20 Shillings = 1 Pound
100 Cents = 1 Dollar (1950)

Catalogue values for unused stamps in this country are for Never Hinged items, beginning with Scott 207 in the regular postage section, Scott B2 in the semipostal section and Scott J1 in the postage due section.

Watermarks

Wmk. 5- Small Star   Wmk. 6- Large Star

Values for unused stamps are for examples with original gum as defined in the catalogue introduction. Very fine examples of Nos. 10-42a, 44-59a will have perforations touching the design on at least one side due to the narrow spacing of the stamps on the plates and imperfect perforation methods. Stamps with perfs clear of the design on all four sides are extremely scarce and will command higher prices.

Britannia
A1   A2

1852-55 Unwmk. Engr. Imperf.
Blued Paper

1	A1	(½p) deep green	100.00	300.00
a.		(½p) yellow green	9,000.	700.00
2	A1	(1p) dark blue	16.50	65.00
a.		(1p) blue	25.00	175.00
3	A1	(2p) slate blue	15.00	
a.		(2p) grayish slate	200.00	1,100.
b.		As "a," vert. half used as 1p on cover		6,750.
4	A1	(4p) brn red ('55)	62.50	275.00
			194.00	

No. 3 was not placed in use. Beware of color changelings of Nos. 2-3 that may resemble No. 3a. Certificates of authenticity are required for Nos. 3a and 3b.
Use of #3b was authorized from 8/4-9/21/1854.

1855-58
White Paper

5	A1	(½p) deep green ('58)	85.50	175.00
a.		(½p) yellow green ('57)	400.00	100.00
6	A1	(1p) blue	20.00	50.00
a.		(1p) pale blue	55.00	60.00

It is believed that the (4p) brownish red on white paper exists only as No. 17b.

1859

8	A2	6p rose red	625.00	100.00
9	A2	1sh black	150.00	60.00

Pin-perf. 14

10	A1	(½p) pale yel grn	2,250.	350.00
11	A1	(1p) blue	2,250.	140.00

Pin-perf. 12½

12	A1	(½p) pale yel grn	5,500.	550.
12A	A1	(1p) blue	16,000.	1,250.

Pin-perf. 14x12½

12B	A1	(½p) pale yel grn	—	3,250.

1861 Clean-Cut Perf. 14 to 16

13	A1	(½p) dark blue grn	65.00	9.00
14	A1	(1p) pale blue	575.00	45.00
a.		(1p) blue		45.00
b.		Half used as ½p on cover		3,150.

Rough Perf. 14 to 16

15	A1	(½p) green	10.50	8.00
a.		(½p) blue green	60.00	75.00
b.		Imperf., pair	450.00	
16	A1	(1p) blue	24.00	3.00
a.		Diagonal half used as ½p on cover		1,750.
b.		Imperf., pair	500.00	450.00
17	A1	(4p) rose red	62.50	27.50
a.		(4p) brown red	90.00	35.00
b.		As "a," imperf., pair	850.00	
c.		(4p) rose red, imperf., pair	675.00	
18	A1	(4p) vermilion	175.00	60.00
a.		Imperf., pair	800.00	
19	A2	6p rose red	175.00	11.00
20	A2	6p orange ver	55.00	15.00
a.		6p vermilion	67.50	12.00
b.		Imperf., pair	400.00	800.00
21	A2	1sh brownish black	45.00	3.75
b.		Horiz. pair, imperf. btwn.	5,250.	
c.		1sh blue (error)	13,500.	

No. 21c was never placed in use. All copies are pen-marked (some have been removed) and have clipped perfs on one or more sides. Use of #14b, 16a was authorized from 4/63-11/66.

Perf. 11 to 13

22	A1	(½p) deep green	6,500.	
23	A1	(1p) blue	2,000.	

Nos. 22 and 23 were never placed in use.

1870 Wmk. 6 Rough Perf. 14 to 16

24	A1	(½p) green	80.00	10.00
a.		Imperf., pair (#24)	750.00	
b.		(½p) yellow green	110.00	40.00
25	A1	(1p) blue	1,200.	40.00
a.		Imperf., pair	1,500.	
26	A1	(4p) dull red	700.00	80.00
27	A2	6p vermilion	650.00	50.00
28	A2	1sh black	250.00	17.50

1871 Wmk. 5

29	A1	(1p) blue	90.00	3.00
30	A1	(4p) rose red	750.00	30.00
31	A2	6p vermilion	400.00	22.50
32	A2	1sh black	125.00	10.00

Clean-Cut Perf. 14½ to 16

33	A1	(1p) blue	190.00	3.00
a.		Diagonal half used as ½p on cover		1,500.
34	A2	6p vermilion	600.00	50.00
35	A2	1sh black	120.00	9.00

Perf. 11 to 13x14½ to 16

36	A1	(½p) blue green	225.00	27.50
37	A1	(4p) vermilion	475.00	80.00

1873 Perf. 14

38	A2	3p claret	475.00	110.00

Wmk. 6
Clean-Cut Perf. 14½ to 16

39	A1	(½p) blue green	190.00	17.50
40	A1	(4p) rose red	800.00	140.00
41	A2	6p vermilion	575.00	60.00
a.		Imperf., pair	75.00	1,500.
42	A2	1sh black	100.00	12.00
a.		Horiz. pair, imperf. btwn.	4,250.	

Britannia — A3

1873 Wmk. 5 Perf. 15½x15

43	A3	5sh dull rose	1,000.	375.00

For surcharged bisects see Nos. 57-59.

1874 Wmk. 6 Perf. 14

44	A2	½p blue green	22.50	7.50
45	A2	1p blue	67.50	3.50

Clean-Cut Perf. 14½ to 16

45A	A2	1p blue		12,000.

1875 Wmk. 1 Perf. 12½

46	A2	½p yellow green	35.00	3.00
47	A2	4p scarlet	175.00	9.00
48	A2	6p orange	550.00	70.00
49	A2	1sh purple	425.00	15.00
	Nos. 46-49 (4)		1,185.	

1875-78 Perf. 14

50	A2	½p yel green ('76)	8.00	2.00
51	A2	1p ultramarine	45.00	.75
a.		1p gray blue	45.00	.75
b.		Half used as ½p on cover		1,400.
c.		Watermarked sideways		1,500.
52	A2	3p violet ('78)	85.00	9.00
53	A2	4p rose red	85.00	6.00
a.		4p scarlet	140.00	
b.		As "a," perf. 14x12½	4,750.	
54	A2	4p lake	450.00	5.00
55	A2	6p chrome yel	95.00	3.25
a.		6p yellow	300.00	16.00
56	A2	1sh purple ('76)	125.00	5.00
a.		1sh violet	2,500.	40.00
b.		1sh dull mauve	350.00	4.50
c.		Half used as 6p on cover		4,500.

#48, 49, 55, 56 have the watermark sideways.
No. 53b was never placed in use.

A4   A5

Large Surcharge, ("1" 7mm High, "D" 2¾mm High)

1878 Wmk. 5 Perf. 15½x15
Slanting Serif

57	A4	1p on half of 5sh	4,000.	650.
a.		Unsevered pair	16,000.	2,250.
b.		Unsevered horiz. pair, #57 + 58		3,500.
d.		Unsevered horiz. pair, #57 + 58, imperf. between		—
e.		Unsevered horiz. pair, #57 + 59, imperf. between	25,000.	8,500.

Straight Serif

58	A4	1p on half of 5sh	4,500.	950.
a.		Unsevered pair		3,750.

Small Surcharge, ("1" 6mm, "D" 2½mm High)

59	A5	1p on half of 5sh	5,250.	950.00
a.		Unsevered pair	17,000.	3,750.

On Nos. 57, 58 and 59 the surcharge is found reading upwards or downwards.
The perforation, which divides the stamp into halves, measures 11½ to 13.
The old denomination has been cut off the bottom of the stamps.

Queen Victoria — A6

1882-85 Typo. Wmk. 2 Perf. 14

60	A6	½p green	5.25	.80
61	A6	1p carmine rose	4.75	.50
a.		1p rose	47.50	1.75
b.		Half used as ½p on cover		900.00
62	A6	2½p dull blue	52.50	.75
a.		2½p ultramarine	70.00	1.50
63	A6	3p magenta	3.00	8.75
a.		3p lilac	85.00	26.00
64	A6	4p slate	175.00	2.00
65	A6	4p brown ('85)	2.75	1.00
66	A6	6p olive gray	52.50	25.00
67	A6	1sh orange brown	17.00	18.00
68	A6	5sh bister	125.00	175.00
	Nos. 60-68 (9)		437.75	231.80

No. 65 Surcharged in HALF-PENNY Black

1892

69	A6	½p on 4p brown	1.75	2.50
a.		Without hyphen	9.00	15.00
b.		Double surcharge		
c.		Double surch., red & black	500.00	1,050.
d.		As "c," without hyphen	1,350.	1,350.

A8   Badge of Colony — A9

1892-1903 Wmk. 2

70	A8	1f sl & car ('96)	1.60	.20
71	A8	½p green	1.90	.20
72	A8	1p carmine rose	3.50	.20

73	A8	2p sl & org ('99)	6.00	.70
74	A8	2½p ultramarine	12.50	.20
75	A8	5p olive brn	5.25	3.50
76	A8	6p vio & car	9.50	1.50
77	A8	8p org & ultra	2.75	15.00
78	A8	10p bl grn & car	6.00	35.00
79	A8	2sh6p slate & org	35.00	35.00
80	A8	2sh6p pur & grn ('03)	55.00	97.50
		Nos. 70-80 (11)	139.00	159.00

See Nos. 90-101. For surcharge see No B1.

Victoria Jubilee Issue

1897				Wmk. 1
81	A9	1f gray & car	1.25	.30
82	A9	½p gray green	1.75	.30
83	A9	1p carmine rose	2.00	.35
84	A9	2½p ultra	4.25	.70
85	A9	5p dk olive brn	8.50	9.25
86	A9	6p vio & car	12.00	14.00
87	A9	8p org & ultra	7.00	15.00
88	A9	10p bl grn & car	30.00	35.00
89	A9	2sh6p slate & org	35.00	42.50
		Nos. 81-89 (9)	101.75	117.40

Bluish Paper

81a	A9	1f gray & car	24.00	27.50
82a	A9	½p gray green	25.00	27.50
83a	A9	1p carmine rose	32.50	35.00
84a	A9	2½p ultra	35.00	40.00
85a	A9	5p dk olive brn	210.00	225.00
86a	A9	6p vio & car	125.00	150.00
87a	A9	8p org & ultra	125.00	140.00
88a	A9	10p bl grn & car	175.00	200.00
89a	A9	2sh6p slate & org	100.00	110.00
		Nos. 81a-89a (9)	851.50	930.00

Badge Type of 1892-1903

1904-10				Wmk. 3
90	A8	1f gray & car	5.50	1.25
91	A8	1f brown ('09)	3.25	.25
92	A8	½p green	9.50	.20
93	A8	1p carmine rose	9.25	.20
94	A8	1p carmine ('09)	8.75	.20
95	A8	2p gray ('09)	5.00	7.75
96	A8	2½p ultramarine	8.00	.40
97	A8	6p vio & car	8.00	12.50
98	A8	6p dl vio & vio ('10)	6.25	12.00
99	A8	8p org & ultra	52.50	27.50
100	A8	1sh blk, grn ('10)	6.50	12.00
101	A8	2sh6p pur & green	27.50	55.00
		Nos. 90-101 (12)	150.00	129.25

Nelson Centenary Issue

Lord Nelson Monument — A10

1906		Engr.		Wmk. 1
102	A10	1f gray & black	2.00	.60
103	A10	½p green & black	3.00	.40
104	A10	1p car & black	3.50	.25
105	A10	2p org & black	4.00	4.25
106	A10	2½p ultra & black	5.00	4.00
107	A10	6p lilac & black	15.00	19.00
108	A10	1sh rose & black	17.50	32.50
		Nos. 102-108 (7)	50.00	61.00

See Nos. 110-112.

The "Olive Blossom" A11

1906, Aug. 15				Wmk. 3
109	A11	1p blk, green & blue	9.00	1.00

Tercentenary of the 1st British landing.

Nelson Type of 1906

1907, July 6				Wmk. 3
110	A10	1f gray & black	4.25	2.25
111	A10	2p org & black	15.00	17.00
112	A10	2½p ultra & black	8.25	16.00
a.		2½p indigo & black	750.00	1,000.
		Nos. 110-112 (3)	27.50	35.25

A12

A13

King George V — A14

1912				Typo.
116	A12	¼p brown	.40	.85
117	A12	½p green	1.50	.20
a.		Booklet pane of 6		
118	A12	1p carmine	3.00	.20
a.		1p scarlet	12.50	2.00
b.		Booklet pane of 6		
119	A12	2p gray	1.60	8.25
120	A12	2½p ultramarine	1.00	.25
121	A13	3p violet, yel	1.00	8.25
122	A13	4p blk & scar, yel	1.00	9.50
123	A13	6p vio & red vio	6.00	7.00
124	A14	1sh black, green	4.00	6.50
125	A14	2sh vio & ultra, bl	24.00	26.00
126	A14	3sh grn & violet	47.50	52.50
		Nos. 116-126 (11)	91.00	119.50

Seal of the Colony — A15

1916-18				Engr.
127	A15	¼p brown	.30	.25
128	A15	½p green	.75	.20
129	A15	1p red	1.00	.20
130	A15	2p gray	3.50	10.00
131	A15	2½p ultramarine	.85	.75
132	A15	3p violet, yel	2.25	2.50
133	A15	4p red, yel	.60	5.00
134	A15	4p red & blk ('18)	.85	2.50
135	A15	6p claret	1.50	2.25
136	A15	1sh black, green	3.50	5.00
137	A15	2sh violet, blue	15.00	8.50
138	A15	3sh dark violet	32.50	70.00
139	A15	3sh dk vio & grn ('18)	15.00	30.00
a.		3sh bright vio & grn ('18)	150.00	175.00
		Nos. 127-139 (13)	77.60	137.15

Nos. 134 and 139 are from a re-engraved die. The central medallion is not surrounded by a line and there are various other small alterations.

Victory Issue

Victory

A16   A17

1920, Sept. 9				Wmk. 3
140	A16	¼p bister & black	.25	.55
141	A16	½p yel green & blk	.80	.20
a.		Booklet pane of 2		
142	A16	1p org red & blk	2.25	.20
a.		Booklet pane of 2		
143	A16	2p gray & black	2.00	4.25
144	A16	2½p ultra & dk bl	2.40	6.50
145	A16	3p red lilac & blk	2.40	3.25
146	A16	4p gray grn & blk	2.40	3.50
147	A16	6p orange & blk	3.00	6.50
148	A17	1sh yel green & blk	7.50	14.00
149	A17	2sh brown & blk	17.00	18.00
150	A17	3sh orange & blk	20.00	22.00
		Nos. 140-150 (11)	60.00	78.95

1921, Aug. 22				Wmk. 4
151	A16	1p orange red & blk	14.00	.20
		Nos. 140-151 (12)	74.00	79.15

A18

A19

1921-24				Wmk. 4
152	A18	¼p brown	.20	.20
153	A18	½p green	.35	.20
154	A18	1p carmine	.30	.20
155	A18	2p gray	1.25	.20
156	A18	2½p ultramarine	.95	4.00
158	A18	6p claret	1.50	3.50
159	A18	1sh blk, emer ('24)	30.00	55.00
160	A18	2sh dk vio, blue	13.00	12.50
161	A18	3sh dark violet	13.00	30.00

				Wmk. 3
162	A18	3p violet, yel	.75	4.00
163	A18	4p red, yel	.70	7.75
164	A18	1sh black, green	4.00	7.00
		Nos. 152-164 (12)	66.00	124.55

1925-35		Wmk. 4		Perf. 14
165	A19	¼p brown	.20	.20
166	A19	½p green	.20	.20
a.		Perf. 13½x12½ ('32)	5.00	.20
b.		Booklet pane of 10		
167	A19	1p carmine	.20	.20
a.		Perf. 13½x12½ ('32)	4.50	.30
b.		Booklet pane of 10		
168	A19	1½p org, perf. 13½x12½ ('32)	.75	.60
a.		Booklet pane of 6		
b.		Perf. 14	3.50	.80
169	A19	2p gray	.50	1.25
170	A19	2½p ultramarine	.50	.50
a.		Perf. 13½x12½ ('32)	4.50	2.00
171	A19	3p vio brn, yel	.60	.45
172	A19	3p red brn, yel ('35)	6.00	6.00
173	A19	4p red, yel	.80	.80
174	A19	6p claret	.80	.80
175	A19	1sh blk, emerald	1.50	2.50
a.		Perf. 13½x12½ ('32)	37.50	22.50
176	A19	1sh brn blk, yel grn ('32)	4.25	7.50
177	A19	2sh violet, bl	5.00	4.00
178	A19	2sh6p car, blue ('32)	15.00	17.50
179	A19	3sh dark violet	8.00	12.50
		Nos. 165-179 (15)	44.30	55.00

Charles I and George V — A20

1927, Feb. 17				Perf. 12½
180	A20	1p carmine lake	1.25	.75

Tercentenary of the settlement of Barbados.

Common Design Types pictured following the introduction.

Silver Jubilee Issue
Common Design Type

1935, May 6				Perf. 11x12
186	CD301	1p car & dk bl	.25	.25
187	CD301	1½p blk & ultra	1.25	3.25
188	CD301	2½p ultra & brn	1.00	2.00
189	CD301	1sh brn vio & ind	6.50	9.50
		Nos. 186-189 (4)	9.00	15.00
		Set, never hinged	20.00	

Coronation Issue
Common Design Type

1937, May 14				Perf. 13½x14
190	CD302	1p carmine	.20	.20
191	CD302	1½p brown	.20	.20
192	CD302	2½p bright ultra	.40	.40
		Nos. 190-192 (3)	.80	.80
		Set, never hinged	1.25	

A21

1938-47		Perf. 13-14 & Compound		
193	A21	½p green	3.00	.20
b.		Perf. 14	45.00	1.40
c.		Booklet pane of 10		
193A	A21	½p bister ('42)	.20	.20
194	A21	1p carmine	7.75	.20
b.		Perf. 13½x13	150.00	3.00
c.		Booklet pane of 10		
194A	A21	1p green ('42)	.20	.20
d.		Perf. 13½x13	2.00	.50
195	A21	1½p red orange	.20	.20
c.		Perf. 14	3.50	.50
d.		Booklet pane of 6		
195A	A21	2p rose lake ('41)	.20	2.25
195B	A21	2p bright rose red ('43)	.20	.35
e.		Perf. 14	.20	1.00

196	A21	2½p ultramarine	.25	.35
197	A21	3p brown	.25	1.10
b.		Perf. 14	.25	
197A	A21	3p deep bl ('47)	.20	1.00
198	A21	4p black	.20	.20
a.		Perf. 14	.30	.30
199	A21	6p violet	.40	.20
199A	A21	8p red vio ('46)	.25	1.10
200	A21	1sh brn olive	.50	.20
a.		1sh olive green	7.50	1.40
201	A21	2sh6p brown vio	3.25	.80
201A	A21	5sh indigo ('41)	1.50	3.00
		Nos. 193-201A (16)	18.50	11.55
		Set, never hinged	30.00	

For surcharge see No. 209.

Kings Charles I, George VI Assembly Chamber and Mace A22

1939, June 27		Engr.		Wmk. 4
				Perf. 13½x14
202	A22	½p deep green	1.40	.35
203	A22	1p scarlet	1.40	.20
204	A22	1½p deep orange	1.40	.45
205	A22	2½p ultramarine	1.40	2.50
206	A22	3p yellow brown	1.40	1.50
		Nos. 202-206 (5)	7.00	5.00
		Set, never hinged	10.00	

Tercentenary of the General Assembly.

> Catalogue values for unused stamps in this section, from this point to the end of the section, are for Never Hinged items.

Peace Issue
Common Design Type

1946, Sept. 18				
207	CD303	1½p deep orange	.20	.20
208	CD303	3p brown	.20	.20

Nos. 195e, 195B, Surcharged in Black **ONE PENNY**

1947, Apr. 21				Perf. 14
209	A21	1p on 2p brt rose red	1.00	1.00
a.		Double surcharge		
b.		Perf. 13½x13	2.00	2.00

The existence of No. 209a has been questioned by specialists. The editors would like to see authenticated evidence of its existence.

Silver Wedding Issue
Common Design Types

				Perf. 14x14½
1948, Nov. 24		Photo.		Wmk. 4
210	CD304	1½p orange	.20	.20

Engraved; Name Typographed
Perf. 11½x11

211	CD305	5sh dark blue	10.00	8.00

UPU Issue
Common Design Types

1949, Oct. 10			Perf. 13½, 11x11½
212	CD306	1½p red orange	.35	.35
213	CD307	3p indigo	.55	.55
214	CD308	4p gray	1.00	1.00
215	CD309	1sh olive	1.40	1.40
		Nos. 212-215 (4)	3.30	3.30

Dover Fort — A23

Admiral Nelson Statue — A24

Designs: 2c, Sugar cane breeding. 3c, Public buildings. 6c, Casting net. 8c, Intercolonial schooner. 12c, Flying Fish. 24c, Old Main Guard Garrison. 48c, Cathedral. 60c, Careenage. $1.20, Map. $2.40, Great Seal, 1660.

Perf. 11x11½ (A23), 13x13½ (A24)

		1950, May 1 Engr.	Wmk. 4	
216	A23	1c slate	.20	.20
217	A23	2c emerald	.20	.20
218	A23	3c slate & brown	.20	.20
219	A24	4c carmine	.30	.30
220	A23	6c blue	.35	.30
221	A23	8c choc & blue	.60	.40
222	A23	12c olive & aqua	1.25	.75
223	A23	24c gray & red	1.40	.60
224	A24	48c violet	4.00	2.75
225	A23	60c brn car & bl grn	2.50	3.00
226	A24	$1.20 olive & car	9.00	5.25
227	A23	$2.40 gray	21.00	13.00
		Nos. 216-227 (12)	41.00	27.35

University Issue
Common Design Types

1951, Feb. 16   **Perf. 14x14½**

228	CD310	3c turq bl & choc	.25	.20
229	CD311	12c ol brn & turq bl	1.00	.75

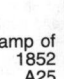

Stamp of 1852 A25

Perf. 13½

		1952, Apr. 15 Wmk. 4	Engr.	
230	A25	3c slate bl & dp grn	.20	.20
231	A25	4c rose pink & bl	.25	.60
232	A25	12c emer & slate bl	.30	.60
233	A25	24c gray blk & red brn	.50	.50
		Nos. 230-233 (4)	1.25	1.90

Centenary of Barbados postage stamps.

Coronation Issue
Common Design Type

1953, June 4   **Perf. 13½x13**

234	CD312	4c red orange & black	.30	.20

Harbor Police A26

Designs as in 1950 with portrait of Queen Elizabeth II. $2.40, Great Seal, 1660 ("E II R").

Perf. 11x11½ (horiz.), 13x13½ (vert.)

		1953-57	Engr.	
235	A23	1c slate ('53)	.20	.65
236	A23	2c grnsh blue & deep org	.20	.35
237	A23	3c emerald & blk	.80	.45
238	A24	4c orange & gray	.20	.20
239	A26	5c dp car & dp bl	.70	.35
240	A23	6c red brown	.40	.35
241	A23	8c brt blue & blk	1.60	.35
242	A23	12c brn ol & aqua	.80	.20
243	A23	24c gray & red ('56)	.35	.20
244	A24	48c violet ('56)	4.00	.90
245	A23	60c brown car & blue grn ('56)	15.00	4.50
246	A24	$1.20 ol & car ('56)	14.50	2.25
247	A23	$2.40 gray ('57)	5.75	1.10
		Nos. 235-247 (13)	44.50	11.85

See Nos. 257-264.

West Indies Federation
Common Design Type

Perf. 11½x11

		1958, Apr. 23	Wmk. 314	
248	CD313	3c green	.20	.20
249	CD313	6c blue	.40	1.00
250	CD313	12c carmine rose	.50	.40
		Nos. 248-250 (3)	1.10	1.60

Deep Water Harbor, Bridgetown A27

1961, May 6   **Engr.**   **Perf. 11x11½**

251	A27	4c orange & black	.25	.30
252	A27	8c ultra & black	.30	.50
253	A27	24c black & pink	.45	.50
		Nos. 251-253 (3)	1.00	1.30

Deep Water Harbor at Bridgetown opening.

Scout Emblem and Map of Barbados — A28

Perf. 11½x11

		1962, Mar. 9	Wmk. 314	
254	A28	4c orange & black	.30	.20
255	A28	12c gray & blue	.75	.25
256	A28	$1.20 greenish gray & carmine rose	1.25	2.25
		Nos. 254-256 (3)	2.30	2.70

50th anniv. of the founding of the Boy Scouts of Barbados.

Queen Types of 1953-57
Perf. 11x11½, 13x13½

		1964-65	Engr.	Wmk. 314
257	A23	1c slate	.25	1.75
258	A24	4c orange & gray	.35	.45
259	A23	8c brt bl & blk ('65)	.50	.30
260	A23	12c brn ol & aqua ('65)	.60	
261	A23	24c gray & red	.60	.45
262	A24	48c violet	2.50	1.75
263	A23	60c brn car & bl grn	6.50	3.50
264	A23	$2.40 gray ('65)	4.00	2.00
		Nos. 257-264 (8)	15.30	
		Nos. 257-259,261-264 (7)		10.20

The 12c was never put on sale in Barbados.

ITU Issue
Common Design Type
Perf. 11x11½

		1965, May 17	Litho.	Wmk. 314
265	CD317	2c lilac & ver	.20	.20
266	CD317	48c yellow & gray	1.50	1.50

Sea Horse A29

Designs: 1c, Deep sea coral. 2c, Lobster. 4c, Sea urchin. 5c, Staghorn coral. 6c, Butterflyfish. 8c, File shell. 12c, Balloonfish. 15c, Angelfish. 25c, Brain coral. 35c, Brittle star. 50c, Flyingfish. $1, Queen conch shell. $2.50, Fiddler crab.

Wmk. 314 Upright

		1965, July 15	Photo.	Perf. 14x13½
267	A29	1c dk blue, pink & black	.25	.25
268	A29	2c car rose, sepia & orange	.25	.20
269	A29	3c org, brn & sep ("Hippocanpus")	.50	.65
270	A29	4c ol grn & dk bl	.20	.20
a.		Imperf., pair	300.00	150.00
271	A29	5c lil, brn & pink	.35	.35
272	A29	6c greenish bl, yel & blk	.50	.25
273	A29	8c ultra, orange, red & black	.30	.20
274	A29	12c rose lil, yel & blk	.40	.20
275	A29	15c red, yel & blk	.90	.55
276	A29	25c yel brn & ultra	1.10	.55
277	A29	35c grn, rose brn & blk	1.75	.20
278	A29	50c yel brn & ultra	2.25	.45
279	A29	$1 gray & multi	3.25	1.40
280	A29	$2.50 lt bl & multi	3.25	2.50
		Nos. 267-280 (14)	15.25	7.95

		1966-69	Wmk. 314 Sideways	

Design: $5, "Dolphin" (coryphaena hippurus).

267a	A29	1c	.20	.20
268a	A29	2c ('67)	.20	.20
269A	A29	3c ("Hippocampus") ('67)	.20	.20
270b	A29	4c	.20	.20
271a	A29	5c	.20	.20
272a	A29	6c ('67)	.20	.20
273a	A29	8c ('67)	.25	.20
274a	A29	12c ('67)	.35	.20
275a	A29	15c	.50	.35
276a	A29	25c	.60	.50
277a	A29	35c	.85	.60
278a	A29	50c	1.25	1.10
279a	A29	$1	2.50	1.90
280a	A29	$2.50	6.25	6.00
280B	A29	$5 dk ol & multi ('69)	12.50	12.50
		Nos. 267a-280B (15)	26.25	24.60

For surcharge see No. 327.

Churchill Memorial Issue
Common Design Type

		1966, Jan. 24	Wmk. 314	Perf. 14
281	CD319	1c multicolored	.20	.20
282	CD319	4c multicolored	.20	.20
283	CD319	25c multicolored	1.00	1.00
284	CD319	35c multicolored	1.40	1.40
		Nos. 281-284 (4)	2.80	2.80

Royal Visit Issue
Common Design Type

		1966, Feb. 4	Litho.	Perf. 11x12
285	CD320	3c violet blue	.20	.20
286	CD320	35c dark car rose	1.75	1.75

UNESCO Anniversary Issue
Common Design Type

		1967, Jan. 6	Litho.	Perf. 14
287	CD323	4c "Education"	.20	.20
288	CD323	12c "Science"	.55	.55
289	CD323	25c "Culture"	1.40	1.40
		Nos. 287-289 (3)	2.15	2.15

Arms of Barbados — A30

Policeman and Anchor Monument — A31

Designs: 25c, Hilton Hotel, horiz. 35c, Garfield Sobers, captain of Barbados and West Indies Cricket Team. 50c, Pine Hill Dairy, horiz.

		1966, Dec. 2	Unwmk.	Photo.
290	A30	4c multicolored	.20	.20
291	A30	25c multicolored	.35	.35
292	A30	35c multicolored	.50	.50
293	A30	50c multicolored	.75	.75
		Nos. 290-293 (4)	1.80	1.80

Barbados' independence, Nov. 30, 1966.

		1967, Oct. 16	Litho.	Perf. 13½x14

Designs: 25c, Policeman with telescope. 35c, Police motor launch, horiz. 50c, Policemen at Harbor Gate.

294	A31	4c multicolored	.20	.20
295	A31	25c multicolored	.30	.30
296	A31	35c multicolored	.50	.50
297	A31	50c multicolored	.80	.80
		Nos. 294-297 (4)	1.80	1.80

Centenary of Bridgetown Harbor Police.
For surcharge see No. 322.

Independence Arch — A32

1st Anniv. of Independence: 4c, Sir Winston Scott, Governor-General, vert. 35c, Treasury Building. 50c, Parliament Building.

		1967, Dec. 4	Photo.	Unwmk.
298	A32	4c multicolored	.20	.20
299	A32	25c multicolored	.25	.25
300	A32	35c multicolored	.40	.40
301	A32	50c multicolored	.60	.60
		Nos. 298-301 (4)	1.45	1.45

UN Building, Santiago, Chile — A33

		1968, Feb. 27		Perf. 14½x14
302	A33	15c multicolored	.20	.20

20th anniv. of the UN Economic Commission for Latin America.

Radar Antenna on Top of Old Sugar Mill, Sugar Cane — A34

Designs: 25c, Caribbean Meteorological Institute, Barbados, horiz. 50c, HARP gun used in High Altitude Research Program, at Paragon in Christ Church, Barbados.

		1968, June 4	Photo.	Unwmk.
303	A34	3c violet & multi	.20	.20
304	A34	25c vermilion & multi	.30	.30
305	A34	50c orange & multi	.70	.70
		Nos. 303-305 (3)	1.20	1.20

World Meteorological Day.

Girl Scout at Campfire, Lady Baden-Powell and Queen Elizabeth II — A35

Lady Baden-Powell, Queen Elizabeth II and: 25c, Pax Hill Headquarters. 35c, Girl Scout badge.

Perf. 14x14½

		1968, Aug. 29	Photo.	Unwmk.
306	A35	3c dp ultra, blk & gold	.20	.20
307	A35	25c bluish green, black & gold	.35	.35
308	A35	35c org yel, blk & gold	.70	.70
		Nos. 306-308 (3)	1.25	1.25

Barbados Girl Scouts' 50th anniv.

Human Rights Flame and Escape to Freedom A36

Designs: 4c, Human Rights flame, hands, and broken chain. 25c, Human Rights flame, family and broken chain.

Perf. 11x11½
1968, Dec. 10   Litho.   Unwmk.
309 A36 4c violet, gray grn &
            red brown   .20 .20
310 A36 25c org, blk & blue   .40 .40
311 A36 35c greenish blue, blue,
            blk & org   .55 .55
    Nos. 309-311 (3)   1.15 1.15

International Human Rights Year.

In the Paddock A37

Horse Racing: 25c, "They're off!" 35c, On the flat. 50c, The Finish.

1969, Mar. 15   Litho.   Perf. 14½
312 A37 4c multicolored   .20 .20
313 A37 25c multicolored   .25 .25
314 A37 35c multicolored   .35 .35
315 A37 50c multicolored   .55 .55
    a. Souvenir sheet of 4, #312-315 2.50 3.00
    Nos. 312-315 (4)   1.35 1.35

Map of Caribbean — A38

Design: 12c, 50c, "Strength in Unity," horiz.

Perf. 14x14½, 14½x14
1969, May 6   Photo.   Wmk. 314
316 A38 5c brown & multi   .20 .20
317 A38 12c ultra & multi   .20 .20
318 A38 25c green & multi   .30 .30
319 A38 50c magenta & multi   .65 .65
    Nos. 316-319 (4)   1.35 1.35

1st anniv. of CARIFTA (Caribbean Free Trade Area).

ILO Emblem A39

Perf. 14x13
1969, Aug. 5   Litho.   Unwmk.
320 A39 4c bl grn, brt grn & blk .20 .20
321 A39 25c red brn, brt mag & red .40 .40

50th anniv. of the ILO.

No. 294 Surcharged   **ONE CENT**

1969, Aug. 30   Perf. 13½x14
322 A31 1c on 4c multicolored   .35 .35

Barbados Boy Scout Emblem — A40

Designs: 25c, Sea Scouts rowing in Bridgetown harbor. 35c, Campfire. 50c, Various Scouts in front of National Headquarters and Training Center, Hazelwood.

Perf. 13½x13
1969, Dec. 16   Litho.   Unwmk.
323 A40 5c multicolored   .20 .20
324 A40 25c multicolored   .50 .50
325 A40 35c multicolored   .65 .65
326 A40 50c multicolored   1.00 1.00
    a. Souvenir sheet of 4, #323-326 10.00 12.00
    Nos. 323-326 (4)   2.35 2.35

Attainment of independence by the Barbados Boy Scout Assoc.

No. 271a Surcharged   **4 x**

Wmk. 314 Sideways
1970, Mar. 11   Photo.   Perf. 14x13½
327 A29 4c on 5c multicolored   .20 .20

This locally applied surcharge exists in several variations: double, triple, on back, in pair with one missing, etc.

Lion at Gun Hill — A41

Barbados Museum A42

2c, Trafalgar Fountain. 3c, Montefiore Drinking Fountain. 4c, St. James' Monument. 5c, St. Ann's Fort. 6c, Old Sugar Mill, Morgan Lewis. 8c, Cenotaph. 10c, South Point Lighthouse. 15c, Sharon Moravian Church. 25c, George Washington House. 35c, St. Nicholas Abbey. 50c, Bowmanston Pumping Station. $1, Queen Elizabeth Hospital. $2.50, Modern sugar factory. $5, Seawell Intl. Airport.

Wmk. 314 Upright (A41), Sideways (A42)
Perf. 12½x13, 13x12½
1970, May 4   Photo.
328 A41 1c bl grn & multi   .20 .20
329 A41 2c crimson & multi   .20 .20
330 A41 3c blue & multi   .20 .20
331 A41 4c yellow & multi   .20 .20
332 A41 5c dp org & multi   .20 .20
333 A41 6c dull yel & multi   .20 .20
334 A41 8c dp blue & multi   .20 .20
335 A41 10c red & multi   .20 .20
336 A42 12c ultra & multi   .20 .20
337 A42 15c yellow & multi   .20 .20
338 A42 25c orange & multi   .40 .40
339 A42 35c pink & multi   .55 .55
340 A42 50c bl grn & multi   .65 .65
341 A42 $1 emerald & multi   1.40 1.40
342 A42 $2.50 ver & multi   3.50 3.50
343 A42 $5 yellow & multi   6.50 6.50
    Nos. 328-343 (16)   15.00 15.00

Nos. 328-332, 334-343 were reissued in 1971 on glazed paper.

Wmk. 314 Sideways (A41), Upright (A42)
1972-74
331a A41 4c   .20 .20
332a A41 5c   .20 .20
333a A41 6c   .20 .20
334a A41 8c   .20 .20
335a A41 10c ('74)   .25 .25
336a A42 12c   .25 .25
337a A42 15c   .30 .30
338a A42 25c   .55 .55
339a A42 35c   .85 .85
340a A42 50c   1.25 1.25
341a A42 $1   2.50 2.50
342a A42 $2.50 ('73)   6.50 6.50
343a A42 $5 ('73)   13.00 13.00
    Nos. 331a-343a (13)   26.25 26.25

For surcharge, see No. 391.

Primary Education, UN and Education Year Emblems — A43

UN and Education Year Emblems and: 5c, Secondary education (student with microscope). 25c, Technical education (men working with power drill). 50c, University building.

1970, June 26   Litho.   Perf. 14
344 A43 4c multicolored   .20 .20
345 A43 5c multicolored   .20 .20
346 A43 25c multicolored   .35 .35
347 A43 50c multicolored   .75 .75
    Nos. 344-347 (4)   1.50 1.50

UN, 25th anniv., and Intl. Education Year.

Minnie Root A44

Flowers: 1c, Barbados Easter lily, vert. 10c, Eyelash orchid. 25c, Pride of Barbados, vert. 35c, Christmas hope.

1970, Aug. 24   Litho.   Wmk. 314
Flowers in Natural Colors
348 A44 1c green   .20 .20
349 A44 5c deep magenta   .20 .20
350 A44 10c dark blue   .45 .25
351 A44 25c brt orange brown   1.25 .55
352 A44 35c blue   1.75 .90
    a. Souvenir sheet of 5   3.00 2.25
    Nos. 348-352 (5)   3.85 2.10

No. 352a contains 5 imperf. stamps similar to Nos. 348-352 with simulated perforations.

Christ Carrying Cross — A45

Easter: 10c, 50c, Resurrection, by Benjamin West, St. George's Anglican Church. 35c like 4c, Window from St. Margaret's Anglican Church, St. John.

1971, Apr. 7   Wmk. 314   Perf. 14
353 A45 4c purple & multi   .20 .20
354 A45 10c silver & multi   .20 .20
355 A45 35c brt blue & multi   .50 .50
356 A45 50c gold & multi   .80 .80
    Nos. 353-356 (4)   1.70 1.70

Sailfish Craft A46

Tourism: 5c, Tennis. 12c, Horseback riding. 25c, Water-skiing. 50c, Scuba diving.

1971, Aug. 17   Perf. 14x14½
357 A46 1c multicolored   .20 .20
358 A46 5c multicolored   .20 .20
359 A46 12c multicolored   .20 .20
360 A46 25c multicolored   .50 .50
361 A46 50c multicolored   1.00 1.00
    Nos. 357-361 (5)   2.10 2.10

Samuel Jackman Prescod — A47

1971, Sept. 26   Perf. 14
362 A47 3c orange & multi   .20 .20
363 A47 35c ultra & multi   .65 .65

Samuel Jackman Prescod (1806-1871), 1st black member of Barbados Assembly.

Coat of Arms A48

15c, 50c, Flag and map of Barbados.

1971, Nov. 23
364 A48 4c light blue & multi   .20 .20
365 A48 15c multicolored   .30 .30
366 A48 25c yel green & multi   .45 .45
367 A48 50c blue & multi   .90 .90
    Nos. 364-367 (4)   1.85 1.85

5th anniv. of independence.

Telegraphy, 1872 and 1972 — A49

Designs: 10c, "Stanley Angwin" off St. Lawrence Coast. 35c, Earth station and Intelsat 4. 50c, Mt. Misery tropospheric scatter station.

1972, Mar. 28   Litho.   Perf. 14
368 A49 4c purple & multi   .20 .20
369 A49 10c emerald & multi   .25 .25
370 A49 35c red & multi   .55 .55
371 A49 50c orange & multi   .85 .85
    Nos. 368-371 (4)   1.85 1.85

Centenary of telecommunications to and from Barbados.

Lord Baden-Powell, Charles W. Springer, George B. Burton — A50

5c, Map of Barbados and Combermere School, vert. 25c, Photograph of 1922 troop. 50c, Flags of various Boy Scout troops.

1972, Aug. 1
372 A50 5c ultra & multi   .20 .20
373 A50 15c ultra & multi   .40 .40
374 A50 25c ultra & multi   .60 .60
375 A50 50c ultra & multi   1.10 1.10
    Nos. 372-375 (4)   2.30 2.30

60th anniv. of Barbados Boy Scouts and 4th Caribbean Jamboree.

Bookmobile, Open Book — A51

Intl. Book Year: 15c, Visual aids truck. 25c, Central Library, Bridgetown. $1, Codrington College.

1972, Oct. 31   Litho.   Wmk. 314
376 A51 4c brt pink & multi   .20 .20
377 A51 15c dull org & multi   .25 .25
378 A51 25c buff & multi   .40 .40
379 A51 $1 lt violet & multi   1.90 1.90
    Nos. 376-379 (4)   2.75 2.75

Pottery Wheels A52

Barbados pottery industry: 15c, Kiln. 25c, Finished pottery, Chalky Mount. $1, Pottery on sale at market.

1973, Mar. 1   Wmk. 314   Perf. 14

380	A52	5c dull red & multi	.20	.20
381	A52	15c olive grn & multi	.20	.20
382	A52	25c gray & multi	.35	.35
383	A52	$1 yellow & multi	1.40	1.40
		Nos. 380-383 (4)	2.15	2.15

First Flight in Barbados, Wright Box
Kite, 1911 — A53

Aircraft: 15c, First flight to Barbados, De
Havilland biplane, 1928. 25c, Passenger
plane, 1939. 50c, Vickers VC-10 over control
tower, 1973.

1973, July 25   Perf. 12½x12

384	A53	5c blue & multi	.20	.20
385	A53	15c vio blue & multi	.40	.40
386	A53	25c multicolored	.65	.65
387	A53	50c blue & multi	1.40	1.40
		Nos. 384-387 (4)	2.65	2.65

Chancellor Sir Hugh Wooding — A54

Designs: 25c, Sherlock Hall, Cave Hill Campus. 35c, Cave Hill Campus.

1973, Dec. 11   Perf. 13x14

388	A54	5c dp orange & multi	.20	.20
389	A54	25c red brown & multi	.40	.40
390	A54	35c multicolored	.60	.60
		Nos. 388-390 (3)	1.20	1.20

25th anniv. of the Univ. of the West Indies.

No. 338a Surcharged

1974, Apr. 30   Photo.   Perf. 13x12½

391	A42	4c on 25c multi	.20	.20
	a.	"4c." omitted		20.00

Old
Sailboat
A55

Designs: 35c, Rowboat. 50c, Motor-pow-
ered fishing boat. $1, Trawler "Calamar."

1974, June 11   Wmk. 314   Perf. 14

392	A55	15c blue & multi	.25	.25
393	A55	35c multicolored	.50	.50
394	A55	50c vio blue & multi	.70	.70
395	A55	$1 blue & multi	1.40	1.40
	a.	Souvenir sheet of 4, #392-395	3.00	3.75
		Nos. 392-395 (4)	2.85	2.85

Fishing boats of Barbados.

Fire Orchid — A56

Orchids. 1c, 20c, 25c, $2.50, $5 horizontal.

**Wmk. 314 Sideways; Upright (1c,
20c, 25c, $1, $10)**

1974-77   Photo.   Perf. 14

396	A56	1c Cattleya gas- kelliana alba	.20	.20
397	A56	2c shown	.20	.20
398	A56	3c Rose Marie	.20	.20
399	A56	4c Fiery red orchid	.20	.20
400	A56	5c Schomburgkia humboltii	.20	.20
401	A56	8c Dancing dolls	.20	.20
402	A56	10c Spider orchids	.20	.20
403	A56	12c Dendrobium aggregatum	.25	.20
404	A56	15c Lady slippers	.40	.35
404C	A56	20c Spathoglottis	.45	.40
405	A56	25c Eyelash	.75	.65
406	A56	35c Bletia patula	.80	.65
406B	A56	45c Sunset Glow	1.10	.85
407	A56	50c Sunset Glow	1.10	.85

Perf. 14½x14, 14x14½

408	A56	$1 Ascocenda red gem	2.00	1.50
409	A56	$2.50 Brassolaelio- cattleya nug- get	4.75	3.75
410	A56	$5 Caularthron bicornutum	9.50	8.00
411	A56	$10 Moon orchid	17.50	15.00
		Nos. 396-411 (18)	40.00	33.50

Issued: 20c, 45c, 5/3/77; others, 9/16/74.
For surcharge see No. B2.

**Wmk. 314 Upright; Sideways (1c,
25c, $1)**

1976   Perf. 14

396a	A56	1c multicolored	.20	.20
397a	A56	2c multicolored	.20	.20
398a	A56	3c multicolored	.20	.20
399a	A56	4c multicolored	.25	.20
402a	A56	10c multicolored	.45	.40
404a	A56	15c multicolored	.80	.70
405a	A56	25c multicolored	1.00	.90
406a	A56	35c multicolored	1.50	1.25

Perf. 14½x14

408a	A56	$1 multicolored	4.00	3.50
		Nos. 396a-408a (9)	8.60	7.55

1975   Wmk. 373   Perf. 14

396b	A56	1c multicolored	.20	.20
397b	A56	2c multicolored	.20	.20
398b	A56	3c multicolored	.20	.20
399b	A56	4c multicolored	.25	.25
400b	A56	5c multicolored	.20	.20
402b	A56	10c multicolored	.20	.20
403b	A56	12c multicolored	.25	.20
404b	A56	15c multicolored	.50	.45
406c	A56	45c multicolored	1.10	.90

Perf. 14½x14, 14x14½

408b	A56	$1 multicolored	2.00	1.90
409b	A56	$2.50 multicolored	5.00	4.50
410b	A56	$5 multicolored	10.00	9.50
411b	A56	$10 multicolored	18.00	18.00
		Nos. 396b-411b (13)	38.10	36.75

UPU Emblem, Barbados
No. 64 — A57

Cent. of the UPU: 35c, Letters encircling
globe. 50c, Barbados coat of arms. $1, Map of
Barbados, sailing ship and jet.

1974, Oct. 9   Litho.   Perf. 14½

412	A57	8c brt rose, org & gray	.20	.20
413	A57	35c red, blk, & ocher	.45	.45
414	A57	50c vio blue, bl & sil	.65	.65
415	A57	$1 ultra, blk & brn	1.25	1.25
	a.	Souvenir sheet of 4, #412-415	3.00	3.00
		Nos. 412-415 (4)	2.55	2.55

Yacht Britannia off Barbados — A58

Royal Visit, Feb. 1975: 35c, $1, Palms and
sunset.

1975, Feb. 18

416	A58	8c brown & multi	.20	.20
417	A58	25c blue & multi	.40	.40
418	A58	35c purple & multi	.60	.60
419	A58	$1 violet & multi	1.60	1.60
		Nos. 416-419 (4)	2.80	2.80

St. Michael's
Cathedral — A59

Designs: 15c, Bishop Coleridge. 50c, All
Saint's Church. $1, St. Michael, stained glass
window, St. Michael's Cathedral.

Wmk. 314

1975, July 29   Litho.   Perf. 14

420	A59	5c blue & multi	.20	.20
421	A59	15c blue & multi	.20	.20
422	A59	50c green & multi	.60	.60
423	A59	$1 multicolored	1.00	1.00
	a.	Souvenir sheet of 4, #420-423	2.25	2.75
		Nos. 420-423 (4)	2.00	2.00

Anglican Diocese in Barbados,
sesquicentennial.

Pony
Float
A60

Designs: 25c, Stiltsman (band and mas-
queraders). 35c, Maypole dancing. 50c,
Cuban dancers.

1975, Nov. 18   Litho.   Wmk. 373

424	A60	8c yellow & multi	.20	.20
425	A60	25c buff & multi	.30	.30
426	A60	35c ultra & multi	.40	.40
427	A60	50c orange & multi	.65	.65
	a.	Souvenir sheet of 4, #424-427	1.75	1.75
		Nos. 424-427 (4)	1.55	1.55

Crop-over (harvest) festival.

Sailing Ship, 17th
Cent. — A61

Coat of
Arms — A62

350th Anniv. of 1st Settlement: 10c,
Bearded fig tree and fruit. 25c, Ogilvy's 17th
cent. map. $1, Capt. John Powell.

1975, Dec. 17   Wmk. 373   Perf. 13½

428	A61	4c lt blue & multi	.20	.20
429	A61	10c lt blue & multi	.20	.20
430	A61	25c yellow & multi	.55	.50
431	A61	$1 dk red & multi	1.90	1.60
	a.	Souvenir sheet of 4, #428-431	3.00	2.75
		Nos. 428-431 (4)	2.85	2.50

Coil Stamps

1975, Dec.   Unwmk.   Perf. 15x14

432	A62	5c light blue	.20	.20
433	A62	25c violet	.25	.25

Map of
West
Indies,
Bats,
Wicket
and Ball
A63

Prudential
Cup — A64

1976, July 7   Litho.   Perf. 14

438	A63	25c lt blue & multi	.85	.50
439	A64	45c lilac rose & black	1.10	1.00

World Cricket Cup, won by West Indies
Team, 1975.

Map of South Carolina settled by
Barbadians — A65

American Bicentennial: 25c, George Washington and map of Bridge Town area. 50c,
Declaration of Independence. $1, Masonic
emblem and Prince Hall, founder and Grand
Master of African Grand Lodge, Boston, 1790-
1807.

1976, Aug. 17   Wmk. 373   Perf. 13½

440	A65	15c multicolored	.20	.20
441	A65	25c multicolored	.35	.35
442	A65	50c multicolored	.65	.65
443	A65	$1 multicolored	1.40	1.40
		Nos. 440-443 (4)	2.60	2.60

Mailman
with
Bicycle
A66

PO Act, 125th anniv.: 35c, Mailman on
motor scooter. 50c, Cover with Barbados No.
2. $1, Mail truck.

1976, Oct. 19   Litho.   Perf. 14

444	A66	8c rose red, blk & bis	.20	.20
445	A66	35c multicolored	.40	.40
446	A66	50c vio blue & multi	.60	.60
447	A66	$1 red & multi	1.10	1.10
		Nos. 444-447 (4)	2.30	2.30

Coast
Guard
Vessels
A67

Designs: 15c, Bank note, reverse, showing
Barbados Parliament. 25c, National anthem by
Van Roland Edwards (music) and Irvine
Burgie (lyrics). $1, Independence Day parade.

1976, Nov. 30   Perf. 13x13½

448	A67	5c multicolored	.20	.20
449	A67	15c multicolored	.20	.20
450	A67	25c yel, brown & blk	.25	.25
451	A67	$1 multicolored	1.00	1.00
	a.	Souvenir sheet of 4, #448-451	2.00	2.00
		Nos. 448-451 (4)	1.65	1.65

10th anniv. of independence.

Queen Knighting
Garfield Sobers,
1957 Visit — A68

Designs: 50c, Queen arriving at Westminster Abbey. $1, Queen leaving coach.

1977, Feb. 7   **Perf. 14x13½**
452 A68 15c silver & multi   .20   .20
453 A68 50c silver & multi   .55   .55
454 A68 $1 silver & multi   1.25   1.25
       Nos. 452-454 (3)   2.00   2.00

25th anniv. of the reign of Queen Elizabeth II. See Nos. 467-469.

Underwater Park — A69

Beauty of Barbados: 35c, Royal palms, vert. 50c, Underwater caves. $1, Stalagmite in Harrison's Cave, vert.

1977, May 3   Wmk. 373   Perf. 14
455 A69   5c multicolored   .20   .20
456 A69 35c multicolored   .50   .50
457 A69 50c multicolored   .65   .65
458 A69 $1 multicolored   1.40   1.40
   a. Souvenir sheet of 4, #455-458 2.75   2.75
       Nos. 455-458 (4)   2.75   2.75

House of   Charles I Handing
Commons   Charter to
Maces — A70   Carlisle — A71

Designs: 25c, Speaker's chair. 50c, Senate Chamber. $1, Sam Lord's Castle, horiz.

1977, Aug. 2   Litho.   Perf. 13½
459 A70 10c red brown & yel   .20   .20
460 A70 25c slate grn & org   .30   .30
461 A70 50c dk green, grn & yel   .60   .60
462 A70 $1 dk & lt blue & org   1.10   1.10
       Nos. 459-462 (4)   2.20   2.20

13th Regional Conference of Commonwealth Parliamentary Association.

Perf. 13½x13, 13x13½
1977, Oct. 11   Litho.   Wmk. 373
Designs: 12c, Charter scroll. 45c, Charles I and Earl of Carlisle. $1, Map of Barbados, by Richard Ligon, 1657, horiz.

463 A71 12c buff & multi   .20   .20
464 A71 25c buff & multi   .30   .30
465 A71 45c buff & multi   .55   .55
466 A71 $1 buff & multi   1.10   1.10
       Nos. 463-466 (4)   2.15   2.15

350th anniv. of charter granting Barbados to the Earl of Carlisle.

Silver Jubilee Type, 1977, Inscribed: "ROYAL VISIT"

1977, Oct. 31 Unwmk.   Roulette 5
Self-adhesive
467 A68 15c silver & multi   .20   .20
468 A68 50c silver & multi   .60   .60
469 A68 $1 silver & multi   1.10   1.10
       Nos. 467-469 (3)   1.90   1.90

Caribbean visit of Queen Elizabeth II. Printed on peelable paper backing inscribed in ultramarine multiple rows: "SILVER JUBILEE

ROYAL VISIT BARBADOS." Printed with die-cut label inscribed in black "BEND & PEEL" attached at left of stamp. Sheets of 50 stamps and 50 labels.

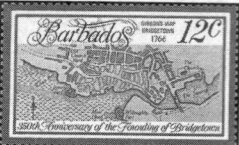

Gibson's Map of Bridgetown,
1766 — A72

25c, Bridgetown, engraving by S. Copens, 1695. 45c, Trafalgar Square, Bridgetown, drawing by J. M. Carter, 1835. $1, The Bridges, 1978.

Wmk. 373
1978, Mar. 1   Litho.   Perf. 14½
470 A72 12c gold & multi   .20   .20
471 A72 25c gold & multi   .25   .25
472 A72 45c gold & multi   .45   .45
473 A72 $1 gold & multi   .85   .85
       Nos. 470-473 (4)   1.75   1.75

350th anniv. of founding of Bridgetown.

Elizabeth II Coronation Anniv. Issue
Souvenir Sheet
Common Design Types

1978, Apr. 21 Unwmk.   Perf. 15
474   Sheet of 6   3.00   3.00
   a. CD326 50c Griffin of Edward III   .50   .50
   b. CD327 50c Elizabeth II   .50   .50
   c. CD328 50c Pelican   .50   .50

No. 474 contains 2 se-tenant strips of Nos. 474a-474c, separated by horizontal gutter with commemorative and descriptive inscriptions and showing central part of coronation with coach.

Freak
Bridge
Hand
A73

10c, World Bridge Fed. emblem. 45c, Central American and Caribbean Bridge Fed. emblem. $1, Map of Caribbean, cards.

Wmk. 373
1978, June 6   Litho.   Perf. 14½
475 A73   5c multicolored   .20   .20
476 A73 10c multicolored   .20   .20
477 A73 45c multicolored   .50   .50
478 A73 $1 multicolored   1.00   1.00
   a. Souvenir sheet of 4, #475-478 1.50   1.50
       Nos. 475-478 (4)   1.90   1.90

7th Regional Bridge Tournament, Dover Centre, Barbados, June 5-14.

Girl Guides' Camp — A74

Designs: 28c, Girl Guides helping children and handicapped. 50c, Badge with "60," vert. $1, Badge with initials, vert.

1978, Aug. 1   Litho.   Perf. 13½
479 A74 12c multicolored   .20   .20
480 A74 28c multicolored   .30   .30
481 A74 50c multicolored   .50   .50
482 A74 $1 multicolored   1.00   1.00
       Nos. 479-482 (4)   2.00   2.00

Girl Guides of Barbados, 60th anniv.

Garment
Industry
A75

Industries of Barbados: 28c, Cooper, vert. 45c, Blacksmith, vert. 50c, Wrought iron industry.

1978, Nov. 14   Litho.   Perf. 14
483 A75 12c multicolored   .20   .20
484 A75 28c multicolored   .30   .30
485 A75 45c multicolored   .40   .40
486 A75 50c multicolored   .50   .50
       Nos. 483-486 (4)   1.40   1.40

Early Mail
Steamer
A76

Ships: 25c, Q.E.II in Deep Water Harbour. 50c, Ra II (raft) nearing Barbados. $1, Early mail steamer.

1979, Feb. 8   Litho.   Perf. 13x13½
487 A76 12c multicolored   .20   .20
488 A76 25c multicolored   .30   .30
489 A76 50c multicolored   .50   .50
490 A76 $1 multicolored   1.00   1.00
       Nos. 487-490 (4)   2.00   2.00

Barbados
No. 235
A77

28c, Barbados #430, vert. 45c, Penny Black and Maltese postmark, vert. 50c, Barbados #21b.

Wmk. 373
1979, May 8   Litho.   Perf. 14
491 A77 12c multicolored   .20   .20
492 A77 28c multicolored   .20   .20
493 A77 45c multicolored   .30   .30
       Nos. 491-493 (3)   .70   .70

Souvenir Sheet
494 A77 50c multicolored   .40   .40

Sir Rowland Hill (1795-1879), originator of penny postage.

Birds — A78   Launcher
                   Transported
                   through
                   Barbados — A79

1979-81 Photo. Wmk. 373   Perf. 14
495   A78 1c Grass
                canaries   .20   .20
496   A78 2c Rain birds   .20   .20
497   A78 5c Sparrows   .20   .20
498   A78 8c Frigate birds   .20   .20
499   A78 10c Cattle egrets   .20   .20
500   A78 12c Green gaulins   .20   .20
501   A78 20c Hummingbirds   .20   .20
502   A78 25c Ground doves   .25   .25
503   A78 28c Blackbirds   .30   .30
504   A78 35c Green-throat-
                ed caribs   .40   .40
505   A78 45c Wood doves   .55   .55
506   A78 50c Ramiers   .65   .65
506A A78 55c Black-breast-
                ed plover
                ('81)   .80   .80
507   A78 70c Yellow breasts   .80   .80
508   A78 $1 Pee whistlers   1.25   1.25
509   A78 $2.50 Christmas
                birds   3.25   3.25
510   A78 $5 Kingfishers   7.00   7.00
511   A78 $10 Red-seal coot   14.00 14.00
       Nos. 495-511 (18)   30.70 30.65

Issue dates: 55c, Sept. 1; others, Aug. 7. See #570-572. For surcharges see #563-565.

1979, Oct. 9   Photo.
Designs: 10c, Gun on landing craft, Foul Bay, horiz. 20c, Firing of 16-inch launcher by day. 28c, Bath Earth Station and Intelsat IV-A, horiz. 45c, Intelsat over Caribbean, horiz. 50c, Intelsat IV-A over Atlantic, and globe. $1, Lunar landing module, horiz.

512 A79 10c multicolored   .20   .20
513 A79 12c multicolored   .20   .20
514 A79 20c multicolored   .20   .20
515 A79 28c multicolored   .20   .20
516 A79 45c multicolored   .30   .30
517 A79 50c multicolored   .35   .35
       Nos. 512-517 (6)   1.45   1.45

Souvenir Sheet
518 A79 $1 multicolored   .85   .85

Space exploration. No. 518 commemorates 10th anniversary of first moon landing.

Family, IYC
Emblem — A80

IYC Emblem and: 28c, Children holding hands and map of Barbados. 45c, Boy and teacher. 50c, Children playing. $1, Boy and girl flying kite.

1979, Nov. 27   Litho.   Perf. 14
519 A80 12c multicolored   .20   .20
520 A80 28c multicolored   .20   .20
521 A80 45c multicolored   .30   .30
522 A80 50c multicolored   .35   .35
523 A80 $1 multicolored   .65   .65
       Nos. 519-523 (5)   1.70   1.70

Map of Barbados, Anniversary
Emblem — A81

Rotary Intl., 75th Anniv.: 28c, Map of district 404. 50c, 75th anniv. emblem. $1, Paul P. Harris, founder.

1980, Feb. 19   Litho.   Perf. 13½
524 A81 12c multicolored   .20   .20
525 A81 28c multicolored   .20   .20
526 A81 50c multicolored   .35   .35
527 A81 $1 multicolored   .65   .65
       Nos. 524-527 (4)   1.40   1.40

A82

A83

12c, Regiment volunteer, artillery company, 1909. 35c, Drum major. 50c, Sovereign's, regimental flags. $1, e, Women's corps.

Wmk. 373
1980, Apr. 8 Litho. *Perf. 14½*
528 A82 12c multicolored .20 .20
529 A82 35c multicolored .20 .20
530 A82 50c multicolored .35 .35
531 A82 $1 multicolored .65 .65
Nos. 528-531 (4) 1.40 1.40
Barbados Regiment, 75th anniv.

Souvenir Sheets
Wmk. 373
1980, May 6 Litho. *Perf. 14*
Early mailman, London 1980 emblem. The vignette is a different color for each stamp.
532 Sheet of 6 1.10 1.10
a.-f. A83 28c any single .20 .20
533 Sheet of 6 2.25 2.25
a.-f. A83 50c any single .35 .35
London 80 Intl. Stamp Exhib., May 6-14.

Underwater Scenes — A84

1980, Sept. 30 Litho. *Perf. 13½*
534 A84 12c multicolored .20 .20
535 A84 28c multicolored .25 .25
536 A84 50c multicolored .40 .40
537 A84 $1 multicolored .75 .75
a. Souvenir sheet of 4, #534-537 1.50 1.50
Nos. 534-537 (4) 1.60 1.60

Bathsheba Railroad Station — A85

1981, Jan. 13 Litho. *Perf. 14½*
538 A85 12c shown .20 .20
539 A85 28c Cab stand, The Green .20 .20
540 A85 45c Mule-drawn tram .30 .30
541 A85 70c Horse-drawn bus .50 .50
542 A85 $1 Fairchild St. railroad station .65 .65
Nos. 538-542 (5) 1.85 1.85
See Nos. 577-580.

Visually Handicapped Girl at Typewriter — A86

1981, May 19 Litho. *Perf. 14*
543 A86 10c shown .20 .20
544 A86 25c Sign language alphabet, vert. .20 .20
545 A86 45c Blind people crossing street, vert. .30 .30
546 A86 $2.50 Baseball game 1.60 1.60
Nos. 543-546 (4) 2.30 2.30
International Year of the Disabled.

Royal Wedding Issue
Common Design Type
Wmk. 373
1981, July 22 Litho. *Perf. 13½*
547 CD331 28c Bouquet .20 .20
548 CD331 50c Charles .35 .35
549 CD331 $2.50 Couple 1.60 1.60
Nos. 547-549 (3) 2.15 2.15

4th Caribbean Arts Festival (CARIFESTA), July 19-Aug. 3 — A87

1981, Aug. 11 Litho. *Perf. 14½*
550 A87 15c Landship maneuver .20 .20
551 A87 20c Yoruba dancer .20 .20
552 A87 40c Tuk band .30 .30
553 A87 55c Frank Collymore (sculpture) .40 .40
554 A87 $1 Barbados Harbor (painting) .75 .75
Nos. 550-554 (5) 1.85 1.85

Hurricane Gladys, View from Apollo A88

1981, Sept. 29 Litho. *Perf. 14*
555 A88 35c Satellite view over Barbados .30 .30
556 A88 50c shown .40 .40
557 A88 60c Police watch .50 .50
558 A88 $1 Spotter plane .80 .80
Nos. 555-558 (4) 2.00 2.00

Harrison's Cave — A89

Perf. 14x14½
1981, Dec. 1 Litho. Wmk. 373
559 A89 10c Twin Falls .20 .20
560 A89 20c Rotunda Room Stream .20 .20
561 A89 55c Rotunda Room formation .35 .35
562 A89 $2.50 Cascade Pool 1.60 1.60
Nos. 559-562 (4) 2.35 2.35

Nos. 503, 505, 507 Surcharged
1982, Feb. 1 Photo. *Perf. 14*
563 A78 15c on 28c multi .20 .20
564 A78 40c on 45c multi .40 .40
565 A78 60c on 70c multi .60 .60
Nos. 563-565 (3) 1.20 1.20

Black Belly Sheep A90

1982, Feb. 9 Litho.
566 A90 40c Ram .40 .40
567 A90 50c Ewe .50 .50
568 A90 60c Ewe, lambs .60 .60
569 A90 $1 Pair, #566-569 1.00 1.00
Nos. 566-569 (4) 2.50 2.50

Bird Type of 1979
Wmk. 373
1982, Mar. 1 Photo. *Perf. 14*
570 A78 15c like #503 .20 .20
571 A78 40c like #506 .40 .40
572 A78 60c like #507 .60 .60
Nos. 570-572 (3) 1.20 1.20

Transportation Type
1982, Apr. 6 Litho. *Perf. 14½*
577 A85 20c Lighter .20 .20
578 A85 35c Rowboat .35 .35
579 A85 55c Speightstown schooner .55 .55
580 A85 $2.50 Inter-colonial schooner 2.50 2.50
Nos. 577-580 (4) 3.60 3.60
Early marine transport.

Visit of Pres. Ronald Reagan — A92

1982, Apr. 8 Litho. *Perf. 14*
581 A92 20c Barbados Flag, arms .20 .20
582 A92 20c US Flag, arms .20 .20
a. Pair, Nos. 581-582 .40 .40
583 A92 55c like #581 .55 .50
584 A92 55c like #582 .55 .50
a. Pair, Nos. 583-584 1.10 1.10
Nos. 581-584 (4) 1.50 1.40
Printed in sheets of 8 with gutter showing Pres. Reagan and Prime Minister Tom Adams.

Princess Diana Issue
Common Design Type
1982, July 1 Litho. *Perf. 14½*
585 CD333 20c Arms .20 .20
586 CD333 60c Diana .45 .45
587 CD333 $1.20 Wedding .90 .90
588 CD333 $2.50 Portrait 1.75 1.75
Nos. 585-588 (4) 3.30 3.30

Scouting Year — A93 Washington's 250th Birth Anniv. — A94

1982, Sept. 7 Wmk. 373 *Perf. 14*
589 A93 15c Helping woman .20 .20
590 A93 40c Sign, emblem, flag, horiz. .45 .45
591 A93 55c Religious service, horiz. .55 .55
592 A93 $1 Flags 1.00 1.00
Nos. 589-592 (4) 2.20 2.20

Souvenir Sheet
1982, Nov. 2 *Perf. 13½x13*
593 A93 $1.50 Laws 1.60 1.60
594 A94 10c Arms .20 .20
595 A94 55c Washington's house, Barbados .55 .55
596 A94 60c Taking command .60 .60
597 A94 $2.50 Taking oath 2.50 2.50
Nos. 594-597 (4) 3.85 3.85

A95

1983, Mar. 14 Litho. *Perf. 14*
598 A95 15c Map, globe .20 .20
599 A95 40c Beach .40 .40
600 A95 60c Sugar cane harvest .60 .60
601 A95 $1 Cricket game 1.00 1.00
Nos. 598-601 (4) 2.20 2.20
Commonwealth day.

Gulf Fritillary A96

Perf. 13½x13
1983, Feb. 8 Wmk. 373
602 A96 20c shown .25 .25
603 A96 40c Monarch .45 .45
604 A96 55c Mimic .60 .60
605 A96 $2.50 Hanno Blue 3.00 3.00
Nos. 602-605 (4) 4.30 4.30

Manned Flight Bicentenary — A97

1983, June 14 Litho. *Perf. 14*
606 A97 20c US Navy dirigible .30 .30
607 A97 40c Douglas DC-3 .85 .85
608 A97 55c Vickers Viscount 1.25 1.25
609 A97 $1 Lockheed TriStar 2.50 2.50
Nos. 606-609 (4) 4.90 4.90

Nash 600, 1941 A98

1983, Aug. 9 Litho. *Perf. 14*
610 A98 25c shown .25 .25
611 A98 45c Dodge, 1938 .50 .50
612 A98 75c Ford Model AA, 1930 .75 .75
613 A98 $2.50 Dodge Four, 1918 2.50 2.50
Nos. 610-613 (4) 4.00 4.00

A99 A100

1983, Aug. 30 Litho. *Perf. 14*
614 A99 20c Players .20 .20
615 A99 65c Emblem, map .65 .65
616 A99 $1 Cup 1.00 1.00
Nos. 614-616 (3) 1.85 1.85
World Cup Table Tennis Championship.

1983, Nov. 1 *Perf. 14*
Christmas: 10c, 25c, Angel with lute, painting details. $2, The Virgin and Child, by Masaccio.
617 A100 10c multicolored .20 .20
618 A100 25c multicolored .25 .25

Souvenir Sheet
619 A100 $2 multicolored 2.00 2.00

Barbados Museum, Golden Jubilee A101

Museum Paintings: 45c, by Richard Day. 75c, St. Ann's Garrison in Barbados by W.S. Hedges. $2.50, Needham's Point, Carlisle Bay.

1983, Nov. 1 *Perf. 14*
620 A101 45c multicolored .45 .45
621 A101 75c multicolored .75 .75
622 A101 $2.50 multicolored 2.50 2.50
Nos. 620-622 (3) 3.70 3.70

1984 Olympics, Los Angeles A102

1984, Apr. 3 Litho. *Perf. 14*
623 A102 50c Track & field .50 .50
624 A102 65c Shooting .65 .65
625 A102 75c Sailing .75 .75

626	A102	$1 Bicycling		1.00	1.00
a.		Souvenir sheet of 4, #623-626		3.00	3.00
		Nos. 623-626 (4)		2.90	2.90

Lloyd's List Issue
Common Design Type

1984, Apr. 25   Litho.   **Perf. 14½**

627	CD335	45c World map		.45	.45
628	CD335	50c Bridgetown Harbor		.50	.50
629	CD335	75c Philosopher		.75	.75
630	CD335	$1 Sea Princess		1.00	1.00
		Nos. 627-630 (4)		2.70	2.70

Souvenir Sheet

1984 UPU Congress — A103

Illustration reduced.

1984, June 6   Litho.   **Perf. 13½**

631	A103	$2 #213, UPU emblem	2.00	2.00

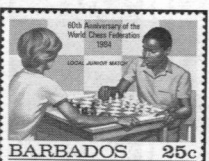

World Chess Fed., 60th Anniv. A104

1984, Aug. 8   **Perf. 14x14½**

632	A104	25c Junior match	.30	.30
633	A104	45c Knights	.50	.50
634	A104	65c Queens	.75	.75
635	A104	$2 Rooks	2.25	2.25
		Nos. 632-635 (4)	3.80	3.80

Christmas — A105

1984, Oct. 24   Litho.   **Perf. 14**

636	A105	50c Poinsettia	.50	.50
637	A105	65c Snow-on-the-mountain	.65	.65
638	A105	75c Christmas candle	.75	.75
639	A105	$1 Christmas hope	1.00	1.00
		Nos. 636-639 (4)	2.90	2.90

Marine Life A106

1985   Litho.   **Wmk. 373**   **Perf. 14**

640	A106	1c Bristle worm	.20	.20
641	A106	2c Spotted trunk fish	.20	.20
642	A106	5c Coney fish	.20	.20
643	A106	10c Pink-tipped anemone	.20	.20
645	A106	20c Christmas tree worm	.30	.30
646	A106	25c Hermit crab	.35	.35
648	A106	35c Animal flower	.50	.50
649	A106	40c Vase sponge	.60	.60
650	A106	45c Spotted moray	.65	.65
651	A106	50c Ghost crab	.75	.75
653	A106	65c Flaming tongue snail	.95	.95
654	A106	75c Sergeant major fish	1.10	1.10
656	A106	$1 Caribbean warty anemone	1.50	1.50
657	A106	$2.50 Green turtle	3.75	3.75
658	A106	$5 Rock beauty	7.25	7.25
659	A106	$10 Elkhorn coral	15.00	15.00
		Nos. 640-659 (16)	33.50	33.50

Issued: 10c, 20c, 25c, 50c, $2.50, $5, 2/26; 5c, 35c, 40c, 65c, $10, 4/9; 1c, 2c, 45c, 75c, $1, 5/7.
Exist inscribed "1987," etc.

1986 (?)   **Wmk. 384**

640a	A106	1c	.20	.20
641a	A106	2c	.20	.20
642a	A106	5c	.20	.20
643a	A106	10c	.20	.20
645a	A106	20c	.30	.30
646a	A106	25c	.35	.35
648a	A106	35c	.45	.45
649a	A106	40c	.60	.60
650a	A106	45c	.65	.65
651a	A106	50c	.75	.75
653a	A106	65c	.95	.95
654a	A106	75c	1.10	1.10
656a	A106	$1	1.50	1.50
657a	A106	$2.50	3.75	3.75
658a	A106	$5	7.25	7.25
659a	A106	$10	15.00	15.00
		Nos. 640a-659a (16)	33.45	33.45

Some inscribed "1986." Also exist with "1987," "1988," and with no date.

Queen Mother 85th Birthday
Common Design Type

Perf. 14½x14

1985, June 7   Litho.   **Wmk. 384**

660	CD336	25c At Buckingham Palace, 1930	.25	.25
661	CD336	65c With Lady Diana, 1981	.65	.65
662	CD336	75c At the docks	.75	.75
663	CD336	$1 Holding Prince Henry	1.00	1.00
		Nos. 660-663 (4)	2.65	2.65

Souvenir Sheet

664	CD336	$2 Opening the Garden Center, Syon House	2.00	2.00

Audubon Birth Bicentenary — A107

Illustrations of North American bird species. Nos. 666-668 vert.

Wmk. 373

1985, Aug. 6   Litho.   **Perf. 14**

665	A107	45c Falco peregrinus	.60	.60
666	A107	65c Dendroica discolor	.90	.90
667	A107	75c Ardea herodias	1.10	1.10
668	A107	$1 Dendroica petechia	1.40	1.40
		Nos. 665-668 (4)	4.00	4.00

Satellite Orbiting Earth A108

1985, Sept. 10

669	A108	75c multicolored	.75	.75

INTELSAT, Intl. Telecommunications Satellite Consortium, 20th anniv.

Royal Barbados Police, 150th Anniv. — A109

1985, Nov. 19

670	A109	25c Traffic Dept.	.25	.25
671	A109	50c Police Band	.50	.50
672	A109	65c Dog Force	.65	.65
673	A109	$1 Mounted Police	1.00	1.00
		Nos. 670-673 (4)	2.40	2.40

Souvenir Sheet

674	A109	$2 Band on parade, horiz.	2.00	2.00

Queen Elizabeth II 60th Birthday
Common Design Type

Designs: 25c, Age 2. 50c, Senate House opening, University College of the West Indies, Jamaica, 1953. 65c, With Prince Philip, Caribbean Tour, 1985. 75c, Banquet, state visit to Sao Paulo, Brazil, 1968. $2, Visiting Crown Agents, 1983.

Perf. 14x14½

1986, Apr. 21   Litho.   **Wmk. 384**

675	CD337	25c scar, blk & sil	.20	.20
676	CD337	50c ultra & multi	.45	.45
677	CD337	65c green & multi	.60	.60
678	CD337	75c violet & multi	.70	.70
679	CD337	$2 rose vio & multi	1.90	1.90
		Nos. 675-679 (5)	3.85	3.85

EXPO '86, Vancouver — A110

1986, May 2   **Perf. 14**

680	A110	50c Trans-Canada North Star	.50	.50
681	A110	$2.50 Lady Nelson	2.50	2.50

AMERIPEX '86 — A111

1986, May 22   **Wmk. 373**

682	A111	45c No. 441	.45	.45
683	A111	50c No. 442	.50	.50
684	A111	65c No. 558	.65	.65
685	A111	$1 Nos. 583-584	1.00	1.00
		Nos. 682-685 (4)	2.60	2.60

Souvenir Sheet

686	A111	$2 Statue of Liberty, NY Harbor	2.00	2.00

Statue of Liberty, cent.

Royal Wedding Issue, 1986
Common Design Type

Designs: 45c, Informal portrait. $1, Andrew in navy uniform.

Perf. 14½x14

1986, July 23   Litho.   **Wmk. 384**

687	CD338	45c multicolored	.45	.45
688	CD338	$1 multicolored	1.00	1.00

Electrification of Barbados, 75th Anniv. A112

10c, Transporting utility poles, 1923. 25c, Heathfield ladder, 1935. 65c, Transport fleet, 1941. $2, Bucket truck, 1986.

Wmk. 384

1986, Sept. 16   Litho.   **Perf. 14**

689	A112	10c multi	.20	.20
690	A112	25c multi, vert.	.25	.25
691	A112	65c multi	.65	.65
692	A112	$2 multi, vert.	2.00	2.00
		Nos. 689-692 (4)	3.10	3.10

Christmas — A113

Church windows and flowers.

1986, Oct. 28   **Wmk. 373**

693	A113	25c Alpinia purpurata	.25	.25
694	A113	50c Anthurium andraeanum	.50	.50
695	A113	75c Heliconia rostrata	.75	.75
696	A113	$2 Heliconia psittacorum	2.00	2.00
		Nos. 693-696 (4)	3.50	3.50

Natl. Special Olympics, 10th Anniv. A114

1987, Mar. 27   **Wmk. 373**   **Perf. 14**

697	A114	15c Shot put	.20	.20
698	A114	45c Wheelchair race	.45	.45
699	A114	65c Girl's long jump	.65	.65
700	A114	$2 Emblem, creed	2.00	2.00
		Nos. 697-700 (4)	3.30	3.30

CAPEX '87 — A115

1987, June 12

701	A115	25c Barn swallow	.35	.35
702	A115	50c Yellow warbler	.75	.75
703	A115	65c Audubon's shearwater	.90	.90
704	A115	75c Black-whiskered vireo	1.10	1.10
705	A115	$1 Scarlet tanager	1.50	1.50
		Nos. 701-705 (5)	4.60	4.60

Natl. Scouting Movement, 75th Anniv. — A116

1987, July 24   **Perf. 14x14½**

706	A116	10c Scout sign	.20	.20
707	A116	25c Campfire	.25	.25
708	A116	65c Merit badges, etc.	.65	.65
709	A116	$2 Marching band	2.00	2.00
		Nos. 706-709 (4)	3.10	3.10

Bridgetown Synagogue Restoration A117

1987, Oct. 6   **Wmk. 384**   **Perf. 14½**

710	A117	50c Exterior	.65	.65
711	A117	65c Interior	.85	.85
712	A117	75c Ten Commandments, vert.	1.00	1.00
713	A117	$1 Marble laver, vert.	1.40	1.40
		Nos. 710-713 (4)	3.90	3.90

Natl. Independence, 21st
Anniv. — A118

E.W. Barrow (1920-87), Father of
Independence — A119

25c, Coat of arms, seal of the colony. 45c, Natl. flag. Union Jack. 65c, Silver dollar, penny. $2, Old and new regimental flags, Queen Elizabeth's colors.

1987, Nov. 24   Litho.   Perf. 14½

714	A118	25c multicolored	.25	.25
715	A118	45c multicolored	.45	.45
716	A118	65c multicolored	.65	.65
717	A118	$2 multicolored	2.00	2.00
		Nos. 714-717 (4)	3.35	3.35

Souvenir Sheet

718	A119	$1.50 multicolored	1.50	1.50

Cricket
A120

Bat, wicket posts, ball, 18th cent. belt buckle and batters: 15c, E.A. "Manny" Martindale. 45c, George Challenor. 50c, Herman C. Griffith. 75c, Harold Austin. $2, Frank Worrell.

1988   Litho.   Wmk. 373   Perf. 14

719	A120	15c multicolored	.20	.20
720	A120	45c multicolored	.45	.45
720A	A120	50c multicolored	.50	.50
721	A120	75c multicolored	.75	.75
722	A120	$2 multicolored	2.00	2.00
		Nos. 719-722 (5)	3.90	3.90

The 50c was originally printed with the wrong photograph but was not issued. Copies of the error have appeared on the market.
Issued: No. 720A, July 11; others, June 6.

Lizards — A121

1988, June 13

723	A121	10c Kentropyx borckianus	.20	.20
724	A121	50c Hemidactylus mabouia	.60	.60
725	A121	65c Anolis extremus	.75	.75
726	A121	$2 Gymnophthalmus underwoodii	2.25	2.25
		Nos. 723-726 (4)	3.80	3.80

1988 Summer
Olympics,
Seoul — A122

Wmk. 373

1988, Aug. 2   Litho.   Perf. 14½

727	A122	25c Cycling	.25	.25
728	A122	45c Running	.45	.45
729	A122	75c Swimming	.75	.75
730	A122	$2 Yachting	2.00	2.00
a.		Souvenir sheet of 4, #727-730	3.50	3.50
		Nos. 727-730 (4)	3.45	3.45

Lloyds of London, 300th Anniv.
Common Design Type

40c, Royal Exchange, 1774. 50c, Sugar mill (windmill), horiz. 65c, Container ship Author, horiz. $2, Sinking of the Titanic, 1912.

1988, Oct. 18   Litho.   Perf. 14

731	CD341	40c multicolored	.40	.40
732	CD341	50c multicolored	.50	.50
733	CD341	65c multicolored	.65	.65
734	CD341	$2 multicolored	2.00	2.00
		Nos. 731-734 (4)	3.55	3.55

Harry Bayley
Observatory,
25th Anniv.
A123

Designs: 25c, Observatory, crescent Moon, Venus and Harry Bayley. 65c, Observatory and constellations. 75c, Andromeda Galaxy and telescope. $2, Orion Constellation.

1988, Nov. 28   Wmk. 384   Perf. 14½

735	A123	25c multicolored	.25	.25
736	A123	65c multicolored	.65	.65
737	A123	75c multicolored	.75	.75
738	A123	$2 multicolored	2.00	2.00
		Nos. 735-738 (4)	3.65	3.65

Commercial Aviation, 50th
Anniv. — A124

Designs: 25c, Caribbean Airline Liat BAe748. 65c, Pan American DC-8. 75c, Two British Airways Concordes, Grantley Adams Intl. Airport. $2, Two Caribbean Air Cargo Boeing 707-351c.

1989, Mar. 20   Litho.   Perf. 14

739	A124	25c multicolored	.25	.25
740	A124	65c multicolored	.65	.65
741	A124	75c multicolored	.75	.75
742	A124	$2 multicolored	2.00	2.00
		Nos. 739-742 (4)	3.65	3.65

Parliament,
350th Anniv.
A125

1989, July 19   Litho.   Perf. 13½

743	A125	25c Assembly chamber	.25	.25
744	A125	50c The Speaker	.50	.50
745	A125	75c Parliament, c. 1882	.75	.75
746	A125	$2.50 Queen in Parliament	2.50	2.50
		Nos. 743-746 (4)	4.00	4.00

See No. 752.

Wildlife Preservation — A126

1989, Aug. 1   Perf. 14x13½

747	A126	10c Wild hare, vert.	.20	.20
748	A126	50c Red-footed tortoise	.80	.80
749	A126	65c Green monkey, vert.	1.00	1.00
750	A126	$2 Toad	3.00	3.00
		Nos. 747-750 (4)	5.00	5.00

Souvenir Sheet

751	A126	$1 Mongoose, vert.	2.00	2.00

Parliament Anniv. Type of 1989
Souvenir Sheet

1989, Oct. 9   Wmk. 373   Perf. 13½

752	A125	$1 The Mace	1.00	1.00

35th Commonwealth Parliamentary Conf.

Wild
Plants — A127

World Stamp
Expo '89,
Washington,
DC — A128

1989-92   Wmk. 373   Perf. 14½

753	A127	2c Bread'n cheese	.20	.20
754	A127	5c Scarlet cordia	.20	.20
755	A127	10c Columnar cactus	.20	.20
756	A127	20c Spiderlily	.20	.20
757	A127	25c Rock balsam	.25	.25
758	A127	30c Hollyhock	.30	.30
758A	A127	35c Red sage	.35	.35
759	A127	45c Yellow shakshak	.45	.45
760	A127	50c Whitewood	.50	.50
761	A127	55c Bluebell	.55	.55
762	A127	65c Prickly sage	.65	.65
763	A127	70c Seaside samphire	.70	.70
764	A127	80c Flat-hand dildo	.80	.80
764A	A127	90c Herringbone	.90	.90
765	A127	$1.10 Lent tree	1.10	1.10
766	A127	$2.50 Rodwood	2.50	2.50
767	A127	$5 Cowitch	5.00	5.00
768	A127	$10 Maypole	10.00	10.00
		Nos. 753-768 (18)	24.85	24.85

Issued: 35c, 90c, June 9, 1992 (inscribed 1991); others, Nov. 1.
Nos. 754-756, 763, 765 exist inscribed "1991."
For overprints see Nos. 788-790.

1990   Litho.   Wmk. 384

753a	A127	2c	.20	.20
754a	A127	5c	.20	.20
755a	A127	10c	.20	.20
756a	A127	20c	.20	.20
757a	A127	25c	.25	.25
759a	A127	45c	.40	.40
760a	A127	50c	.45	.45
762a	A127	65c	.60	.60
766a	A127	$2.50	2.25	2.25
767a	A127	$5	4.50	4.50
768a	A127	$10	9.00	9.00
		Nos. 753a-768a (11)	18.25	18.25

Inscribed 1990.

1989, Nov. 17   Wmk. 384   Perf. 14

Water sports.

769	A128	25c Water skiing	.25	.25
770	A128	50c Yachting	.50	.50
771	A128	65c Scuba diving	.65	.65
772	A128	$2.50 Surfing	2.50	2.50
		Nos. 769-772 (4)	3.90	3.90

Horse
Racing
A129

Wmk. 373

1990, May 3   Litho.   Perf. 14

773	A129	25c Bugler, jockeys	.25	.25
774	A129	45c Parade ring	.45	.45
775	A129	75c In the straight	.75	.75
776	A129	$2 Winner, vert.	2.00	2.00
		Nos. 773-776 (4)	3.45	3.45

Barbados
No. 2 — A130

Stamps on stamps: No. 778, Barbados #61. 65c, Barbados #73. $2.50, Barbados #121. No. 781a, Great Britain #1. No. 781b, Barbados #108.

1990, May 3

777	A130	25c shown	.25	.25
778	A130	50c multicolored	.50	.50
779	A130	65c multicolored	.65	.65
780	A130	$2.50 multicolored	2.50	2.50
		Nos. 777-780 (4)	3.90	3.90

Souvenir Sheet

781		Sheet of 2	1.00	1.00
a.-b.	A130	50c any single	.50	.50

Stamp World London '90.

Queen Mother, 90th Birthday
Common Design Types

1990, Aug. 8   Wmk. 384   Perf. 14x15

782	CD343	75c At age 23	.75	.75

Perf. 14½

783	CD344	$2.50 Engagement portrait, 1923	2.50	2.50

Insects
A131

Wmk. 373

1990, Oct. 16   Litho.   Perf. 14

784	A131	50c Dragonfly	.50	.50
785	A131	65c Black hardback beetle	.65	.65
786	A131	75c Green grasshopper	.75	.75
787	A131	$2 God-horse	2.00	2.00
		Nos. 784-787 (4)	3.90	3.90

Nos. 757, 764 and
766 Overprinted

1990, Nov. 21   Perf. 14½

788	A127	25c on No. 757	.25	.25
789	A127	80c on No. 764	.80	.80
790	A127	$2.50 on No. 766	2.50	2.50
		Nos. 788-790 (3)	3.55	3.55

Christmas — A132

1990, Dec. 4   Perf. 14

791	A132	20c Christmas star	.20	.20
792	A132	50c Nativity scene	.50	.50
793	A132	$1 Stained glass window	1.00	1.00
794	A132	$2 Angel	2.00	2.00
		Nos. 791-794 (4)	3.70	3.70

Yellow Warbler A133

1991, Mar. 4

795	A133	10c shown	.25	.25
796	A133	20c Male, female, nest	.55	.55
797	A133	45c Female, chicks	1.25	1.25
798	A133	$1 Male, fledgling	2.75	2.75
		Nos. 795-798 (4)	4.80	4.80

World Wildlife Fund.

Fishing A134

Perf. 13½x14, 14x13½

1991, June 18   Litho.   Wmk. 373

799	A134	5c Daily catch, vert.	.20	.20
800	A134	50c Line fishing	.50	.50
801	A134	75c Cleaning fish	.80	.80
802	A134	$2.50 Game fishing, vert.	2.50	2.50
		Nos. 799-802 (4)	4.00	4.00

Freemasonry in Barbados, 250th Anniv. — A135

Designs: 25c, Masonic Building, Bridgetown. 65c, Compass and square. 75c, Royal arch jewel. $2.50, Columns, apron and centenary badge.

1991, Sept. 17   Perf. 14

803	A135	25c multicolored	.25	.25
804	A135	65c multicolored	.65	.65
805	A135	75c multicolored	.75	.75
806	A135	$2.50 multicolored	2.50	2.50
		Nos. 803-806 (4)	4.15	4.15

Butterflies A136

1991, Nov. 15   Wmk. 384

807	A136	20c Polydamus swallowtail	.25	.25
808	A136	50c Long-tailed skipper, vert.	.65	.65
809	A136	65c Cloudless sulphur	.85	.85
810	A136	$2.50 Caribbean buckeye, vert.	3.25	3.25
		Nos. 807-810 (4)	5.00	5.00

Souvenir Sheet

811	A136	$4 Painted lady	6.00	6.00

Phila Nippon '91.

Independence, 25th Anniv. — A137

Governor-General Dame Nita Barrow and: 10c, Students in classroom. 25c, Barbados Workers Union headquarters. 65c, Building industry. 75c, Agriculture. $1, Inoculations given at health clinic. $2.50, Gordon Greenidge, Desmond Haynes, cricket players (no portrait).

1991, Nov. 20   Wmk. 373

812	A137	10c multicolored	.20	.20
813	A137	25c multicolored	.25	.25
814	A137	65c multicolored	.65	.65
815	A137	75c multicolored	.75	.75
816	A137	$1 multicolored	1.00	1.00
		Nos. 812-816 (5)	2.85	2.85

Souvenir Sheet

817	A137	$2.50 multi, vert.	2.40	2.50

Easter — A138

Wmk. 384

1992, Apr. 7   Litho.   Perf. 14

818	A138	35c Christ carrying cross	.35	.35
819	A138	70c Christ on cross	.70	.70
820	A138	90c Christ taken down from cross	.95	.95
821	A138	$3 Christ risen	3.00	3.00
		Nos. 818-821 (4)	5.00	5.00

Flowering Trees — A139

Perf. 14x13½

1992, June 9   Litho.   Wmk. 373

822	A139	10c Cannon ball	.20	.20
823	A139	30c Golden shower	.30	.30
824	A139	80c Frangipani	.80	.80
825	A139	$1.10 Flamboyant	1.10	1.10
		Nos. 822-825 (4)	2.40	2.40

Orchids A140

Designs: 55c, Epidendrum "Costa Rica." 65c, Cattleya guttaca. 70c, Laeliacattleya "Splashing Around." $1.40, Phalaenopsis "Kathy Saegert."

1992, Sept. 8   Perf. 13½x14

826	A140	55c multicolored	.55	.55
827	A140	65c multicolored	.65	.65
828	A140	70c multicolored	.70	.70
829	A140	$1.40 multicolored	1.40	1.40
		Nos. 826-829 (4)	3.30	3.30

For overprints see Nos. 838-841.

Transport and Tourism A141

Designs: 5c, Mini Moke, Gun Hill Signal Station, St. George. 35c, Tour bus, Bathsheba Beach, St. Joseph. 90c, BWIA McDonnell Douglas MD 83, Grantley Adams Airport. $2, Cruise ship Festivale, deep water harbor, Bridgetown.

Wmk. 373

1992, Dec. 15   Perf. 14½

830	A141	5c multicolored	.20	.20
831	A141	35c multicolored	.35	.35
832	A141	90c multicolored	.90	.90
833	A141	$2 multicolored	2.00	2.00
		Nos. 830-833 (4)	3.45	3.45

Cacti and Succulents A142

Wmk. 373

1993, Feb. 9   Litho.   Perf. 14

834	A142	10c Barbados gooseberry	.20	.20
835	A142	35c Night-blooming cereus	.40	.40
836	A142	$1.40 Aloe	1.40	1.40
837	A142	$2 Scrunchineel	2.00	2.00
		Nos. 834-837 (4)	4.00	4.00

Nos. 826-829 Ovptd. "WORLD ORCHID CONFERENCE 1993" on 2 or 4 lines

Perf. 13½x14

1993, Apr. 1   Litho.   Wmk. 373

838	A140	55c on #826 multi	.55	.55
839	A140	65c on #827 multi	.65	.65
840	A140	70c on #828 multi	.70	.70
841	A140	$1.40 on #829 multi	1.40	1.40
		Nos. 838-841 (4)	3.30	3.30

Royal Air Force, 75th Anniv.
Common Design Type

Designs: 10c, Hawker Hunter. 30c, Handley Page Victor. 70c, Hawker Typhoon. $3, Hawker Hurricane.

No. 846a, Armstrong Whitworth Siskin 3a. b, Supermarine S.6B. c, Supermarine Walrus. d, Hawker Hart.

1993, Apr. 1   Perf. 14

842	CD350	10c multicolored	.20	.20
843	CD350	30c multicolored	.30	.30
844	CD350	70c multicolored	.70	.70
845	CD350	$3 multicolored	3.00	3.00
		Nos. 842-845 (4)	4.20	4.20

Souvenir Sheet

846	CD350	50c Sheet of 4, #a.-d.	2.00	2.00

Cannon A143

Designs: 5c, 18-pounder Culverin, 1625, Denmark Fort. 45c, 6-pounder Commonwealth gun, 1649-1660, St. Ann's Fort. $1, 9-pounder Demi-culverin, 1691, The Main Guard. $2.50, 32-pounder Demi-cannon, 1693-94, Charles Fort.

Wmk. 373

1993, June 8   Perf. 13

847	A143	5c multicolored	.20	.20
848	A143	45c multicolored	.45	.45
849	A143	$1 multicolored	1.00	1.00
850	A143	$2.50 multicolored	2.50	2.50
		Nos. 847-850 (4)	4.15	4.15

Barbados Museum, 60th Anniv. — A144

Designs: 10c, Shell box, carved figure. 75c, Map, print of three people. 90c, Silver cup, print of soldier. $1.10, Map.

Wmk. 373

1993, Sept. 14   Litho.   Perf. 14

851	A144	10c multicolored	.20	.20
852	A144	75c multicolored	.75	.75
853	A144	90c multicolored	.95	.95
854	A144	$1.10 multicolored	1.10	1.10
		Nos. 851-854 (4)	3.00	3.00

A145

Prehistoric Aquatic Reptiles: a, Plesiosaurus. b, Ichthyosaurus. c, Elasmosaurus. d, Mosasaurus. e, Archelon. Continuous design.

Wmk. 373

1993, Oct. 28   Litho.   Perf. 13

855	A145	90c Strip of 5, #a.-e.	5.00	5.00

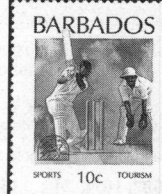

A146

Wmk. 384

1994, Jan. 11   Litho.   Perf. 14

856	A146	10c Cricket	.20	.20
857	A146	35c Motor racing	.35	.35
858	A146	50c Golf	.50	.50
859	A146	70c Run Barbados 10k	.70	.70
860	A146	$1.40 Swimming	1.40	1.40
		Nos. 856-860 (5)	3.15	3.15

Sports & tourism.

No. 822 exists inscribed "1996"; Nos. 872-877, 880, 885 "1997."

Migratory Birds A147

Wmk. 373

1994, Feb. 18   Litho.   Perf. 14

861	A147	10c Whimbrel	.20	.20
862	A147	35c American golden plover	.35	.35
863	A147	70c Ruddy turnstone	.70	.70
864	A147	$3 Tricolored heron	3.00	3.00
		Nos. 861-864 (4)	4.25	4.25

Hong Kong '94.

1st UN Conference of Small Island Developing States — A148

1994, Apr. 25   Perf. 14x14½

865	A148	10c Bathsheba	.20	.20
866	A148	65c Pico Tenneriffe	.65	.65
867	A148	90c Ragged Point Lighthouse	.90	.90
868	A148	$2.50 Consett Bay	2.50	2.50
		Nos. 865-868 (4)	4.25	4.25

Order of the Caribbean Community A149

First award recipients: No. 869, Sir Shridath Ramphal, statesman, Guyana. No. 870, Derek

Walcott, writer, Nobel Laureate, St. Lucia. No. 871, William Demas, economist, Trinidad and Tobago.

Wmk. 373

		1994, July 4	Litho.	Perf. 14	
869	A149	70c multicolored		.70	.70
870	A149	70c multicolored		.70	.70
871	A149	70c multicolored		.70	.70
		Nos. 869-871 (3)		2.10	2.10

Ships A150

Designs: 5c, Dutch Flyut, 1695. 10c, Geestport, 1994. 25c, HMS Victory, 1805. 30c, Royal Viking Queen, 1994. 35c, HMS Barbados, 1945. 45c, Faraday, 1924. 50c, USCG Hamilton, 1974. 65c, HMCS Saguenay, 1939. 70c, Inanda, 1928. 80c, HMS Rodney, 1944. 90c, USS John F. Kennedy, 1982. $1.10, William & John, 1627. $5, USCG Champlain, 1931. $10, Artist, 1877.

Wmk. 373

		1994, Aug. 16	Litho.	Perf. 14	
872	A150	5c multicolored		.20	.20
873	A150	10c multicolored		.20	.20
874	A150	25c multicolored		.25	.25
875	A150	30c multicolored		.30	.30
876	A150	35c multicolored		.35	.35
877	A150	45c multicolored		.45	.45
878	A150	50c multicolored		.50	.50
879	A150	65c multicolored		.65	.65
880	A150	70c multicolored		.70	.70
881	A150	80c multicolored		.80	.80
882	A150	90c multicolored		.90	.90
883	A150	$1.10 multicolored		1.10	1.10
884	A150	$5 multicolored		5.00	5.00
885	A150	$10 multicolored		10.00	10.00
		Nos. 872-885 (14)		21.40	21.40

Nos. 872-885 are not dated. Nos. 872-877, 880, 882, 885 exist inscribed "1997." Nos. 872-873, 877, 880 exist inscribed "1998." Nos. 873, 877, 885 exist inscribed "1999."

1996			Wmk. 384		
872a	A150	5c		.20	.20
873a	A150	10c		.20	.20
875a	A150	30c		.30	.30
876a	A150	35c		.35	.35
877a	A150	45c		.45	.45
878a	A150	50c		.50	.50
879a	A150	65c		.65	.65
880a	A150	70c		.70	.70
881a	A150	80c		.80	.80
882a	A150	90c		.90	.90
883a	A150	$1.10		1.10	1.10
884a	A150	$5		5.00	5.00
		Nos. 872a-884a (12)		11.15	11.15

Inscribed (1996."
Issued: Nos. 875a-877a, 879a-882a, 9/1/96; others, May.

West India Regiment, Bicent. — A151

Designs: 30c, 2nd Regiment, 1860. 50c, 4th Regiment, Light Company, 1795. 70c, 3rd Regiment, drum major, 1860. $1, 5th Regiment, undress, working dress, 1815. $1.10, 1st, 2nd Regiments, Review Order, 1874.

Perf. 15x14

		1995, Feb. 21	Litho.	Wmk. 373	
886	A151	30c multicolored		.30	.30
887	A151	50c multicolored		.50	.50
888	A151	70c multicolored		.70	.70
889	A151	$1 multicolored		1.00	1.00
890	A151	$1.10 multicolored		1.10	1.10
		Nos. 886-890 (5)		3.60	3.60

End of World War II
Common Design Type

10c, Barbadians serving in the Middle East. 35c, Lancaster bomber. 55c, Spitfire fighter. $2.50, SS Davisian sunk off Barbados, July 10, 1940.

$2, Reverse of War Medal 1939-45.

Wmk. 373

		1995, May 8	Litho.	Perf. 14	
891	CD351	10c multicolored		.20	.20
892	CD351	35c multicolored		.30	.30
893	CD351	55c multicolored		.55	.55
894	CD351	$2.50 multicolored		2.50	2.50
		Nos. 891-894 (4)		3.55	3.55

Souvenir Sheet

895	CD352	$2 multicolored		2.50	2.50

Combermere School, 300th Anniv. — A152

Designs: 5c, Scouting, Combermere 1st Barbados, 1912. 20c, Violin, sheet music. 35c, Cricket, Sir Frank Worrell, vert. 90c, Frank Collymore, #553. $3, Landscape.

Wmk. 373

		1995, July 25	Litho.	Perf. 14	
896	A152	5c multicolored		.20	.20
897	A152	20c multicolored		.20	.20
898	A152	35c multicolored		.35	.35
899	A152	$3 multicolored		3.00	3.00
		Nos. 896-899 (4)		3.75	3.75

Souvenir Sheet

900		Sheet of 5, #896-899, 900a		4.50	4.50
a.		A152 90c multicolored		.90	.90

UN, 50th Anniv.
Common Design Type

Designs: 30c, Douglas C-124 Globemaster, Korea 1950-53. 45c, Royal Navy Sea King helicopter. $1.40, Wessex helicopter, UNFICYP, Cyprus 1964. $2, Gazelle helicopter, UNFICYP, Cyprus 1964.

Wmk. 373

		1995, Oct. 24	Litho.	Perf. 14	
901	CD353	30c multicolored		.30	.30
902	CD353	45c multicolored		.45	.45
903	CD353	$1.40 multicolored		1.40	1.40
904	CD353	$2 multicolored		2.00	2.00
		Nos. 901-904 (4)		4.15	4.15

Water Lilies — A153

Wmk. 373

		1995, Dec. 19	Litho.	Perf. 14	
905	A153	10c Blue beauty		.20	.20
906	A153	65c White water lily		.65	.65
907	A153	70c Sacred lotus		.70	.70
908	A153	$3 Water hyacinth		3.00	3.00
		Nos. 905-908 (4)		4.55	4.55

Barbados Philatelic Society, Cent. A154

Magnifiying glass, tongs, and: 10c, #70. 55c, #109. $1.10, #148. $1.40, #192.

Wmk. 373

		1996, Jan. 30	Litho.	Perf. 14	
909	A154	10c multicolored		.20	.20
910	A154	55c multicolored		.55	.55
911	A154	$1.10 multicolored		1.10	1.10
912	A154	$1.40 multicolored		1.40	1.40
		Nos. 909-912 (4)		3.25	3.25

A155

Modern Olympic Games, Cent. — A156

		1996, Apr. 2	Litho.	Perf. 14	
913	A155	20c Soccer		.20	.20
914	A155	30c Relay race		.30	.30
915	A155	55c Basketball		.55	.55
916	A155	$3 Rhythmic gymnastics		3.00	3.00
		Nos. 913-916 (4)		4.05	4.05

Souvenir Sheet

917	A156	$2.50 Discus thrower		2.50	2.50

Olymphilex '96 (No. 917).

CAPEX '96 A157

Transportation links with Canada: 10c, Canadian Airlines DC10. 90c, Air Canada Boeing 767. $1, Air Canada 320 Airbus. $1.40, Canadian Airlines Boeing 767.

Wmk. 373

		1996, June 7	Litho.	Perf. 14	
918	A157	10c multicolored		.20	.20
919	A157	90c multicolored		.90	.90
920	A157	$1 multicolored		1.00	1.00
921	A157	$1.40 multicolored		1.40	1.40
		Nos. 918-921 (4)		3.50	3.50

Chattel Houses A158

House features: 35c, Shed roof, lattice work. 70c, Pedimented porch, carved wooden trim. $1.10, Decorative, elegant porch. $2, Hip roof, bell pelmet window hoods.

1996, June 7

922	A158	35c multicolored		.35	.35
923	A158	70c multicolored		.70	.70
924	A158	$1.10 multicolored		1.10	1.10
925	A158	$2 multicolored		2.00	2.00
		Nos. 922-925 (4)		4.15	4.15

Christmas A159

Children's paintings: 10c, Going to Church on Christmas morning. 30c, The Tuk Band. 55c, Caroling on Christmas. $2.50, Decorated houses.

Wmk. 373

		1996, Nov. 12	Litho.	Perf. 14½	
926	A159	10c multicolored		.20	.20
927	A159	30c multicolored		.30	.30
928	A159	55c multicolored		.55	.55
929	A159	$2.50 multicolored		2.50	2.50
		Nos. 926-929 (4)		3.55	3.55

UNICEF, 50th anniv.

Hong Kong '97 — A160

Dogs: 10c, Doberman pinscher. 30c, German shepherd. 90c, Japanese akita. $3, Irish red setter.

Perf. 14x14½

		1997, Feb. 12	Litho.	Wmk. 373	
930	A160	10c multicolored		.20	.20
931	A160	30c multicolored		.30	.30
932	A160	90c multicolored		.90	.90
933	A160	$3 multicolored		3.00	3.00
		Nos. 930-933 (4)		4.40	4.40

Visit of US Pres. Clinton to Barbados, May 1997 A161

35c, Barbados flag, arms. 90c, US flag, arms.

		1997, May 9	Litho.	Perf. 14	
934	A161	35c multicolored		.35	.35
935	A161	90c multicolored		.90	.90
a.		Pair, #934-935		1.25	1.25

Issued in sheets of 8 stamps + 2 labels.

Shells — A162

5c, Measled cowry. 35c, Trumpet triton. 90c, Scotch bonnet. $2, West Indian murex. $2.50, Sea bottom with miscellaneous shells.

		1997, July 29	Litho.	Perf. 14	
936	A162	5c multicolored		.20	.20
937	A162	35c multicolored		.35	.35
938	A162	90c multicolored		.90	.90
939	A162	$2 multicolored		1.90	1.90
		Nos. 936-939 (4)		3.35	3.35

Souvenir Sheet

940	A162	$2.50 multicolored		2.40	2.40

Public Library, 150th Anniv. A163

Designs: 10c, Lucas manuscripts. 30c, Storytelling to children. 70c, Bookmobile. $3, Information technology.

		1997, Oct. 1	Litho.	Perf. 14	
941	A163	10c multicolored		.20	.20
942	A163	30c multicolored		.30	.30
943	A163	70c multicolored		.70	.70
944	A163	$3 multicolored		3.10	3.10
		Nos. 941-944 (4)		4.30	4.30

Fruit — A164

1997, Dec. 16   Litho.   Perf. 14½
945 A164   35c Barbados cherry   .35   .35
946 A164   40c Sugar apple   .40   .40
947 A164 $1.15 Soursop   1.10   1.10
948 A164 $1.70 Papaya   1.60   1.60
    Nos. 945-948 (4)   3.45   3.45

Souvenir Sheet

Sir Grantley
Adams, Birth
Cent. — A165

a, Natl. Arms. b, Grantley Adams. c, Natl.
flag.

1998, Apr. 27   Litho.   Perf. 13
949 A165 $1 Sheet of 3, #a.-c.   3.00   3.00

Diana, Princess of Wales (1961-97)
Common Design Type of 1998

Portraits wearing: a, Blue hat. b, Red suit
jacket. c, Tiara. d, Black and white.

1998, May   Perf. 14½x14
950 CD355 $1.15 Sheet of 4,
    #a.-d.   6.50   6.50

Organization of American States, 50th
Anniv. — A166

Designs: 15c, Beach during storm, beach
during sunny day. $1, Dancers in native cos-
tumes. $2.50, Judge reading at podium, statue
of justice.

1998, June 30   Litho.   Perf. 14
951 A166   15c multicolored   .20   .20
952 A166 $1 multicolored   .95   .95
953 A166 $2.50 multicolored   2.50   2.50
    Nos. 951-953 (3)   3.65   3.65

University of
West Indies,
50th Anniv.
A167

1998, July 20   Perf. 14½
954 A167   40c Frank Worrell
    Hall   .40   .40
955 A167 $1.15 Graduation   1.10   1.10
956 A167 $1.40 Plaque, hum-
    mingbird   1.40   1.40
957 A167 $1.75 Quadrangle   1.75   1.75
    Nos. 954-957 (4)   4.65   4.65

Tourism
A168

1998, Dec. 1   Litho.   Perf. 14
958 A168   10c Catamaran, vert.   .20   .20
959 A168   45c Jolly Roger   .45   .45
960 A168   70c Atlantis submarine   .70   .70
961 A168 $2 MV Harbor Master,
    vert.   2.00   2.00
    Nos. 958-961 (4)   3.35   3.35

Australia '99, World Stamp
Expo — A169

Illustration reduced.

1999, Mar. 19   Litho.   Perf. 14
962 A169 $4 Sailboat   3.50   3.50

Piping
Plover
A170

World Wildlife Fund: 10c, Juvenile in shallow
water. 45c, Female with eggs. 50c, Fledglings
in nest, male, female. 70c, Male.

1999, Apr. 27   Litho.   Perf. 14
963 A170   10c multicolored   .20   .20
964 A170   45c multicolored   .45   .45
965 A170   50c multicolored   .50   .50
966 A170   70c multicolored   .70   .70
    Nos. 963-966 (4)   1.85   1.85

**1st Manned Moon Landing, 30th
Anniv.**
Common Design Type

Designs: 40c, Astronaut training. 45c, First
stage separation. $1.15, Lunar module. $1.40,
Docking with service module.
$2.50, Looking at earth from moon.

Perf. 14x13¾
1999, July 20   Litho.   Wmk. 384
967 CD357   40c multicolored   .40   .40
968 CD357   45c multicolored   .45   .45
969 CD357 $1.15 multicolored   1.10   1.10
970 CD357 $1.40 multicolored   1.40   1.40
    Nos. 967-970 (4)   3.35   3.35

Souvenir Sheet
Perf. 14
971 CD357 $2.50 multicolored   2.50   2.50

No. 971 contains one 40mm circular stamp.

Rabbits
A171

Designs: a, Rabbit running. b, Rabbit profile.
c, Rabbit nursing young. d, Two rabbits leaping. e, Two rabbits at rest.

Perf. 14x14½
1999, Aug. 21   Litho.   Wmk. 373
972 A171   70c Strip of 5, #a.-e.   3.50   3.50
China 1999 World Philatelic Exhibition.

UPU,
125th
Anniv.
A172

1999, Oct. 11   Litho.   Perf. 14
973 A172   10c Mail coach   .20   .20
974 A172   45c Mail van   .45   .45
975 A172 $1.75 Airplane   1.75   1.75
976 A172 $2 Computers   2.00   2.00
    Nos. 973-976 (4)   4.40   4.40

Souvenir Sheet

Millennium — A173

Illustration reduced.

Wmk. 373
2000, Feb. 8   Litho.   Perf. 14
977 A173 $3 multi   3.00   3.00

100th Test Cricket
Match at Lord's
Ground — A174

Designs: 45c, Sir Conrad Hunte. 90c, Malcolm Marshall. $2, Sir Garfield St. A. Sobers.
$2.50, Lord's Ground, horiz.

Wmk. 373
2000, May 22   Litho.   Perf. 14
978 A174   45c multi   .45   .45
979 A174   90c multi   .90   .90
980 A174 $2 multi   2.00   2.00
    Nos. 978-980 (3)   3.35   3.35

Souvenir Sheet
981 A174 $2.50 multi   2.50   2.50
The Stamp Show 2000, London (#981).

Sites in
Barbados
A175

5c, Drax Hall House. 10c, Reaping sugar
cane. 40c, Needham's Point Lighthouse. 45c,
Port St. Charles. 65c, Synagogue. 70c,
Bridgetown port. 90c, Harrison's Cave. $1.15,
Villa Nova. $1.40, Cricket at Kensington Oval.
$1.75, Sunbury House. $2, Bethel Methodist
Church. $3, Barbados Wildlife Reserve. $5,
Royal Westmoreland golf course. $10, Gran-
tley Adams Intl. Airport.

Wmk. 373
2000, May 22   Litho.   Perf. 14
982 A175   5c multi   .20   .20
983 A175   10c multi   .20   .20
984 A175   40c multi, vert.   .40   .40
985 A175   45c multi   .45   .45
986 A175   65c multi   .65   .65
987 A175   70c multi   .70   .70
988 A175   90c multi   .90   .90
989 A175 $1.15 multi   1.10   1.10
990 A175 $1.40 multi   1.40   1.40
991 A175 $1.75 multi   1.75   1.75
992 A175 $2 multi   2.00   2.00
993 A175 $3 multi, vert.   3.00   3.00
994 A175 $5 multi, vert.   5.00   5.00
995 A175 $10 multi   10.00   10.00
    Nos. 982-995 (14)   27.75   27.75

World Stamp Expo 2000,
Anaheim — A176

25c, Golf equipment. 40c, Golfer on golf
ball. $1.40, Golfer at tee. $2, Golfer putting.

Perf. 14½x14¼
2000, July 7   Litho.   Wmk. 373
996-999 A176   Set of 4   4.00   4.00

Vintage Cars
A177

Designs: 10c, 1947 Bentley Mk VI. 30c,
Vanden Plas Princess. 90c, 1952 Austin Atlantic. $3, 1950 Bentley Special.

Perf. 14¼x14½
2000, Nov. 7   Wmk. 373
1000-1003 A177   Set of 4   4.25   4.25

Souvenir Sheet

Hong Kong 2001 Stamp
Exhibition — A178

Wmk. 373
2001, Feb. 1   Litho.   Perf. 13¼
1004 A178 $3 Thread snake   3.00   3.00

Deep Sea Creatures — A179

No. 1005: a, Lizard fish. b, Goldentail
moray. c, Blackbar soldierfish. d, Golden
zoanthid. e, Sponge brittle star. f, Magnificent
feather duster. g, Bearded fireworm. h, Lima
shell. i, Yellow tube sponge.

Wmk. 373
2001, May 31   Litho.   Perf. 13½
1005 A179   45c Sheet of 9, #a-i   4.00   4.00

Phila
Nippon
'01, Japan
A180

Various kites: 10c, 65c, $1.40, $1.75.

2001, Aug. 1   Perf. 14
1006-1009 A180   Set of 4   4.00   4.00

George
Washington's
Visit to
Barbados,
250th
Anniv. — A181

Designs: 45c, Washington, ship, trunk,
dockworker. 50c, Washington, ship, palm
trees. $1.15, Washington, Declaration of Inde-
pendence. $2.50, Fort at Needham's Point.
$3, Portrait of Washington.

Wmk. 373

2001, Nov. 2	Litho.		*Perf. 13¼*	
1010-1013	A181	Set of 4	4.75	4.75

Souvenir Sheet

| 1014 | A181 | $3 multi | 3.00 | 3.00 |

SEMI-POSTAL STAMPS

No. 73 Surcharged in Red

Kingston Relief Fund.
1d.

			Perf. 14	
1907, Jan. 25		Typo.		*Wmk. 2*
B1	A8	1p on 2p sl & org	1.75	2.50
a.		No period after 1d	15.00	17.50
b.		Inverted surcharge	1.75	2.50
c.		Inverted surcharge, no period after 1d	15.00	17.50
d.		Double surcharge	600.00	650.00
e.		Dbl. surch., both invtd.	600.00	

Catalogue values for unused stamps in this section, from this point to the end of the section, are for Never Hinged items.

No. 406 Surcharged

1979, May 29	Photo.		Wmk. 314	
B2	A56	28c + 4c on 35c multi	.30	.30

The surtax was for victims of the eruption of Mt. Soufrière.

POSTAGE DUE STAMPS

Catalogue values for unused stamps in this section are for Never Hinged items.

D1

			Perf. 14	
1934-47	Typo.		Wmk. 4	
J1	D1	½p green ('35)	.75	.75
J2	D1	1p black	1.40	1.40
a.		Half used as ½p on cover		750.00
J3	D1	3p dk car rose ('47)	22.50	22.50
		Nos. J1-J3 (3)	24.65	24.65

A 2nd die of the 1p was introduced in 1947. Use of J2a was authorized from Mar. 1934 through Feb. 1935. Some examples have "½d" written on the bisect in black or red ink.

1950

J4	D1	1c green	.20	.20
J5	D1	2c black	.40	.40
J6	D1	6c carmine rose	1.50	1.75
		Nos. J4-J6 (3)	2.10	2.35

Values are for 1953 chalky paper printing.

Wmk. 4a (error)

J4a	D1	1c green	140.00	
J5a	D1	2c black	190.00	
J6a	D1	6c carmine rose	110.00	
		Nos. J4a-J6a (3)	440.00	

			Perf. 14	
1965, Aug. 3		Wmk. 314		
J7	D1	1c green	.30	.30
J8	D1	2c black	.35	.35
J9	D1	6c carmine rose	.65	.65
a.		Wmk. sideways, perf 14x13½	2.25	2.25
		Nos. J7-J9 (3)	1.30	1.30

Issued: No. J9a, 2/4/74.

Wmk. 314 Sideways

			Perf. 13x13½	
1974, Dec. 4				
J8b	D1	2c	1.50	1.50
J9b	D1	6c	1.50	1.50

D2

Designs: Each stamp shows different stylized flower in background.

			Perf. 13½x14	
1976, May 12	Litho.		Wmk. 373	
J10	D2	1c brt pink & mag	.20	.20
J11	D2	2c lt & dk vio blue	.20	.20
J12	D2	5c yellow & brown	.20	.20
J13	D2	10c lilac & purple	.20	.20
J14	D2	25c yel green & dk grn	.30	.30
J15	D2	$1 rose & red	.90	.90
		Nos. J10-J15 (6)	2.00	2.00

			Perf. 15x14	
1985, July				
J10a	D2	1c	.20	.20
J11a	D2	2c	.20	.20
J12a	D2	5c	.20	.20
J13a	D2	10c	.20	.20
J14a	D2	25c	.20	.20
		Nos. J10a-J14a (5)	1.00	1.00

WAR TAX STAMP

No. 118 Overprinted **WAR TAX**

			Perf. 14	
1917		Wmk. 3		
MR1	A12	1p carmine	.20	.20
a.		Imperf., pair	4,000.	

BARBUDA

bär-'büd-ə

LOCATION — Northernmost of the Leeward Islands, West Indies
GOVT. — Dependency of Antigua
AREA — 63 sq. mi.
POP. — 1,500 (1995 est.)
See Antigua.

12 Pence = 1 Shilling

Catalogue values for unused stamps in this country are for Never Hinged items, beginning with Scott 12 in the regular postage section, and Scott B1 in the semi-postal section.

Watermark

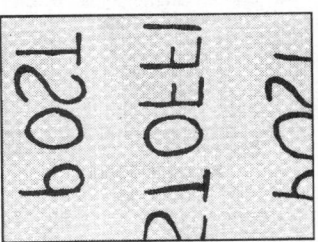

Wmk. 380- "POST OFFICE"

Leeward Islands Stamps and Types of 1912-22 Overprinted in Black or Red

Die II

For description of dies I and II, see back of this section of the Catalogue.

			Perf. 14	
1922, July 13		Wmk. 4		
1	A5	½p green	1.50	7.00
2	A5	1p rose red	1.50	7.00
3	A5	2p gray	1.60	6.50
4	A5	2½p ultramarine	1.60	7.00
5	A5	6p vio & red vio	3.00	15.00
6	A5	2sh vio & ultra, bl	13.50	45.00
7	A5	3sh green & violet	30.00	67.50
8	A5	4sh blk & scar (R)	35.00	67.50

Wmk. 3

9	A5	3p violet, yel	1.50	9.00
10	A5	1sh blk, emer(R)	3.00	7.50
11	A5	5sh grn & red, yel	85.00	125.00
		Nos. 1-11 (11)	177.20	364.00

Catalogue values for unused stamps in this section, from this point to the end of the section, are for Never Hinged items.

Map — B1

Fish — B2

			Unwmk.	
1968-70	Litho.		*Perf. 14*	
12	B1	½c blk, salmon pink & red brn	.20	.20
13	B1	1c blk, org & brt org	.20	.20
14	B1	2c blk, brt pink & brt rose	.20	.20
15	B1	3c blk, yel & org yel	.20	.20
16	B1	4c blk, lt grn & brt grn	.20	.20
17	B1	5c blk, bl grn & brt bl grn	.20	.20
18	B1	6c blk, lt lil & red lil	.20	.20
19	B1	10c blk, lt bl & dk bl	.20	.20
20	B1	15c blk, dl grn & grn	.20	.20
21	B2	20c Great barracuda	.75	1.25
22	B2	25c Great amberjack	.30	.25
23	B2	35c French angelfish	.40	.40
24	B2	50c Porkfish	.55	.55
25	B2	75c Striped parrotfish	.80	.80
26	B2	$1 Longspine squirrelfish	1.10	1.10
27	B2	$2.50 Catalufa	2.75	2.75
28	B2	$5 Blue chromis	5.00	6.00
		Nos. 12-28 (17)	13.45	14.90

Issued: ½c-15c, 11/19/68; 20c, 7/22/70; 25c-75c, 2/5/69; others, 3/6/69. For surcharge see No. 80.

1968 Summer Olympics, Mexico City — B3

Designs: 25c, Running, Aztec calendar stone. 35c, High jumping, Aztec statue. 75c, Yachting, Aztec lion mask. $1, Soccer, Aztec carved stone.

1968, Dec. 20

29	B3	25c multicolored	.40	.20
30	B3	35c multicolored	.50	.25
31	B3	75c multicolored	.75	.40
		Nos. 29-31 (3)	1.65	.85

Souvenir Sheet

| 32 | B3 | $1 multicolored | 2.50 | 3.00 |

The Ascension, by Orcagna — B4

1969, Mar. 24

33	B4	25c blue & black	.20	.25
34	B4	35c dp carmine & blk	.20	.35
35	B4	75c violet & black	.25	.40
		Nos. 33-35 (3)	.65	1.00

Easter.

3rd Caribbean Boy Scout Jamboree — B5

1969, Aug. 7

36	B5	25c Flag ceremony	.40	.45
37	B5	35c Campfire	.50	.60
38	B5	75c Rowing	.65	.75
		Nos. 36-38 (3)	1.55	1.80

The Sistine Madonna, by Raphael — B6

1969, Oct. 20

39	B6	½c multicolored	.20	.20
40	B6	25c multicolored	.20	.20
41	B6	35c multicolored	.20	.20
42	B6	75c multicolored	.20	.25
		Nos. 39-42 (4)	.80	.85

Christmas.

English Monarchs — B7

#43, William I. #44, William II. #45, Henry I. #46, Stephen. #47, Henry II. #48, Richard I. #49, John. #50, Henry III. #51, Edward I. #52, Edward II. #53, Edward III. #54, Richard II. #55, Henry IV. #56, Henry V. #57, Henry VI. #58, Edward IV. #59, Edward V. #60, Richard III. #61, Henry VII. #62, Henry VIII. #63, Edward VI. #64, Lady Jane Grey. #65, Mary I. #66, Elizabeth I. #67, James I. #68, Charles I. #69, Charles II. #70, James II. #71, William III. #72, Mary II. #73, Anne. #74, George I. #75, George II. #76, George III. #77, George IV. #78, William IV. #79, Victoria.

			Perf. 14½x14	
1970-71				
43-79	B7	35c Set of 37	3.75	4.50

Issued: 1970, #43, 2/16; #44, 3/2; #45, 3/16; #46, 4/4; #47, 4/15; #48, 5/1; #49, 5/15; #50, 6/1; #51, 6/15; #52, 7/1; #53, 7/15; #54, 8/1; #55, 8/15; #56, 9/1; #57, 9/15; #58, 10/1; #59, 10/15; #60, 11/2; #61, 11/16; #62, 12/1; #63, 12/15.
1971; #64, 1/2; #65, 1/15; #66, 2/1; #67, 2/15; #68, 3/1; #69, 3/15; #70, 4/1; #71, 4/15; #72, 5/1; #73, 5/15; #74, 6/1; #75, 6/15; #76, 7/1; #77, 7/15; #78, 8/2; #79, 8/16.

See Nos. 622-627 for other Monarchs.

No. 12 Surcharged

1970, Feb. 26 ***Perf. 14***
80 B1 20c on 1/2c multicolored .25 .25

Easter — B8

1970, Mar. 16
81 B8 25c Carrying Cross .20 .20
82 B8 35c Descent from cross .20 .25
83 B8 75c Crucifixion .20 .30
a. Strip of 3, #81-83 .70 .70

Charles Dickens B9

1970, July 10
84 B9 20c Oliver Twist .20 .20
85 B9 75c Old Curiosity Shop .35 .40

Christmas — B10

Designs: 20c, Madonna of the Meadow, by Giovanni Bellini. 50c, Madonna, Child and Angels from Wilton Diptych. 75c, Nativity, by Piero della Francesca.

1970, Oct. 15
86 B10 20c multicolored .20 .20
87 B10 50c multicolored .20 .20
88 B10 75c multicolored .20 .25
Nos. 86-88 (3) .60 .65

British Red Cross, Cent. B11

1970, Dec. 21
89 B11 20c Patient in wheelchair, vert. .20 *.25*
90 B11 35c shown .25 *.35*
91 B11 75c Child care .35 *.60*
Nos. 89-91 (3) .80 *1.20*

Easter — B12

Details from the Mond Crucifixion, by Raphael.

1971, Apr. 7
92 B12 35c Angel .20 *.40*
93 B12 50c Crucifixion .20 *.50*
94 B12 75c Angel, diff. .25 *.60*
a. Strip of 3, #92-94 .75 *1.50*

Martello Tower B13

1971, May 10
95 B13 20c shown .20 .20
96 B13 25c Sailboats .20 .20
97 B13 50c Hotel bungalows .20 .20
98 B13 75c Government House, mystery stone .20 .20
Nos. 95-98 (4) .80 .80

Christmas — B14

Paintings: ½c, The Granduca Madonna, by Raphael. 35c, The Ansidei Madonna, by Raphael. 50c, The Virgin and Child, by Botticelli. 75c, The Madonna of the Trees, by Bellini.

1971, Oct. 4
99 B14 ½c multicolored .20 .20
100 B14 35c multicolored .20 .20
101 B14 50c multicolored .20 .20
102 B14 75c multicolored .25 .25
Nos. 99-102 (4) .85 .85

A set of four stamps for Durer (20c, 35c, 50c, 75c) was not authorized.

All stamps are types of Antigua or overprinted on stamps of Antigua unless otherwise specified. Many of the "BARBUDA" overprints are vertical.

Nos. 321-322 Ovptd. "BARBUDA"

1973, Nov. 14 ***Perf. 13½***
103 A65 35c multicolored 7.25 7.25
104 A65 $2 multicolored 2.25 2.25

Nos. 313-315a Ovptd. in Red "BARBUDA"

1973, Nov. 26 ***Perf. 13½x14***
105 A63 20c multicolored .20 .25
106 A63 35c multicolored .30 .50
107 A63 75c multicolored .40 .75
Nos. 105-107 (3) .90 1.50

Souvenir Sheet

108 Sheet of 4, #105-107, 108a 1.75 1.75
a. A63 5c multicolored

Carnival, 1973.

Nos. 307, 309, 311, 311a Ovptd. "BARBUDA"

Perf. 14x13½

1973, Nov. 26 **Wmk. 314**
109 A53 ½c multicolored .20 .20
110 A53 20c multicolored .20 .20
111 A53 75c multicolored .45 .25
Nos. 109-111 (3) .85 .65

Souvenir Sheet

112 Sheet of 5, #109-111, 112a-112b + label 2.75 2.75
a. A53 10c multicolored
b. A53 35c multicolored

Nos. 241a, 242-243, 244a, 245-248, 249a, 250-254, 255a, 256, 256a, 257 Ovptd. "BARBUDA"

Wmk. 314 Sideways, Upright

1973-74 ***Perf. 14***
113 A51 ½c multicolored .20 .20
114 A51 1c multicolored .20 .25
115 A51 2c multicolored .25 .25
116 A51 3c multicolored .25 .20
117 A51 4c multicolored .30 .25
118 A51 5c multicolored .40 .35
119 A51 6c multicolored .40 .35
120 A51 10c multicolored .45 .40
121 A51 15c multicolored .45 .40
122 A51 20c multicolored .55 .50
123 A51 25c multicolored .55 .50
124 A51 35c multicolored .55 .60
125 A51 50c multicolored .55 .60
126 A51 75c multicolored .55 .60
127 A51 $1 multicolored .55 .60
128 A51 $2.50 multicolored 1.25 1.25
a. Wmk. upright 9.25 10.00
129 A51 $5 multicolored 1.25 2.25
Nos. 113-129 (17) 8.70 9.55

Issue dates: ½c, 3c, 15c, $1, $2.50, Feb. 18, 1974. Others, Nov. 26.

Nos. 316-320a Ovptd. in Silver or Red "BARBUDA"

Perf. 14½

1973, Dec. 11 **Photo.** **Unwmk.**
130 A64 3c multicolored .20 .20
131 A64 5c multicolored .20 .20
132 A64 20c multicolored .20 .20
133 A64 35c multicolored (R) .20 .20
134 A64 $1 multicolored (R) .20 .20
Nos. 130-134 (5) 1.00 1.00

Souvenir Sheet

135 Sheet of 5 + label 6.50 7.50
a. A64 35c multicolored (S)
b. A64 $1 multicolored (S)

No. 135 contains Nos. 130-132, 135a-135b.

Nos. 323-324a Ovptd. "BARBUDA"

1973, Dec. 16 **Litho.** ***Perf. 13½***
136 A65 35c multicolored .25 .25
137 A65 $2 multicolored 1.25 1.25
a. Souvenir sheet of 2, #136-137 5.25 6.25

Nos. 325-328 Ovptd. "BARBUDA"

1974, Feb. 18 **Wmk. 314**
138 A66 5c multicolored .20 .20
139 A66 20c multicolored .20 .20
140 A66 35c multicolored .20 .20
141 A66 75c multicolored .20 .20
Nos. 138-141 (4) .80 .80

Nos. 329-333 Ovptd. "BARBUDA"

1974, May 1 ***Perf. 14x13½***
142 A53 ½c multicolored .20 .20
143 A53 10c multicolored .20 .20
144 A53 20c multicolored .25 .20
145 A53 35c multicolored .35 .25
146 A53 75c multicolored .50 .40
Nos. 142-146 (5) 1.50 1.25

No. 333a exists with overprint.

Nos. 334-340 Ovptd. Type "a" or "b" and No. 340 "BARBUDA" in Red

a & b

1974, July 15 **Unwmk.** ***Perf. 14½***

Se-tenant Pairs Overprinted Type "a" on Left Stamp, Type "b" on Right Stamp

148 A67 ½c multicolored .20 .20
149 A67 1c multicolored .20 .20
150 A67 2c multicolored .20 .20
151 A67 5c multicolored .40 .40
152 A67 20c multicolored 1.25 1.25
153 A67 35c multicolored 2.25 2.25
154 A67 $1 multicolored 6.50 6.50
Nos. 148-154 (7) 11.00 11.00

Souvenir Sheet

Perf. 13

155 Sheet of 7 + label 7.00 7.00
a. A67 ½c multicolored .20 .20
b. A67 1c multicolored .20 .20
c. A67 2c multicolored .20 .20
d. A67 5c multicolored .20 .20
e. A67 20c multicolored 1.00 1.00
f. A67 35c multicolored 1.50 2.00
g. A67 $1 multicolored 3.50 3.50

UPU, cent.

Nos. 341-344a Ovptd. "BARBUDA"

1974, Aug. 14 **Wmk. 314** ***Perf. 14***
156 A68 5c multicolored .20 .20
157 A68 20c multicolored .20 .20
158 A68 35c multicolored .20 .20
159 A68 75c multicolored .20 .20
a. Souvenir sheet of 4, #156-159 1.00 1.00
Nos. 156-159 (4) .80 .80

Nos. 345-348a Ovptd. "BARBUDA" and

World Cup Soccer Championships — B16

Various soccer plays.

1974, Sept. 2 **Unwmk.** ***Perf. 15, 14***
160 A69 5c multicolored .20 .20
161 A69 35c multicolored .20 .20
162 B16 35c multicolored .20 .20
163 A69 75c multicolored .20 .20
164 A69 $1 multicolored .25 .25
a. Souv. sheet of 4, #160-161, 163-164 + 2 labels, perf. 13½ 1.25 1.25
165 B16 $1.20 multicolored .25 .25
166 B16 $2.50 multicolored .35 .45
a. Souv. sheet of 3, #162, 165-166 1.25 1.25
Nos. 160-166 (7) 1.65 1.75

UPU, Cent. — B17

1974, Sept. 30 ***Perf. 14x13½***
167 B17 35c Ship letter, 1833 .20 .20
168 B17 $1.20 #1, 2 on FDC .25 .30
169 B17 $2.50 Airplane, map .40 .50
a. Souvenir sheet of 3, #167-169 1.75 1.75
Nos. 167-169 (3) .85 1.00

Greater Amberjack B18

1974-75 ***Perf. 14x14½, 14½x14***
170 B18 ½c Oleander, rose bay .20 *.55*
171 B18 1c Blue petrea .30 *.55*
172 B18 2c Poinsettia .30 *.55*
173 B18 3c Cassia tree .30 *.55*
174 B18 4c shown 2.75 .55
175 B18 5c Holy Trinity School .30 .20
176 B18 6c Snorkeling .30 *.40*
177 B18 10c Pilgrim Holiness Church .30 .25
178 B18 15c New Cottage Hospital .30 .25
179 B18 20c Post Office & Treasury .30 .25
180 B18 25c Island jetty & boats .60 .40
181 B18 35c Martello Tower .60 .40

Size: 39x25mm

Perf. 14

182 B18 50c Warden's House .60 .40
183 B18 75c Inter-island air service 2.00 1.40
184 B18 $1 Tortoise 1.40 1.10

Size: 45x29mm

Perf. 13½x14

185 B18 $2.50 Spiny lobster 1.60 *2.40*
186 B18 $5 Frigate birds 7.00 3.50
a. Perf. 14x15 12.00 17.50

Size: 34x47mm

187 B18 $10 Hibiscus 4.00 *6.25*
Nos. 170-187 (18) 23.15 *19.95*

Nos. 170-173, 180, 187 vert.

Issued: 4c, 5c, 6c, 10c, 15c, 20c, 25c, 35c, 75c, 10/15/74; ½c, 1c, 2c, 3c, 50c, $1, $2.50, #186, 1/6/75; #186a, 7/24/75; $10, 9/19/75.

For overprints see Nos. 213-214.

Nos. 349-352a Ovptd. "BARBUDA" in
Red and

Winston Churchill, Birth Cent. — B19

1974   **Perf. 14½, 13½x14**

188	A70	5c multicolored	.20	.20
189	B19	5c Making broadcast	.20	.20
190	A70	35c multicolored	.30	.20
191	B19	35c Portrait	.20	.20
192	A70	75c multicolored	.50	.50
193	B19	75c Painting	.25	.25
194	A70	$1 multicolored	.75	.70
a.		Souv. sheet of 4, #188, 190, 192, 194	7.50	9.00
195	B19	$1 Victory sign	.35	.30
a.		Souv. sheet of 4, #189, 191, 193, 195	1.25	1.75
		Nos. 188-195 (8)	2.75	2.55

Issue dates: Nos. 188, 190, 192, 194, Oct.
15, others, Nov. 20. For overprints see Nos.
213-214.

Nos. 353-360a Ovptd. "BARBUDA"

1974, Nov. 25   **Perf. 14½**

196	A71	½c multicolored	.20	.20
197	A71	1c multicolored	.20	.20
198	A71	3c multicolored	.20	.20
199	A71	5c multicolored	.20	.20
200	A71	20c multicolored	.20	.20
201	A71	35c multicolored	.20	.20
202	A71	35c multicolored	.20	.20
203	A71	75c multicolored	.20	.20
a.		Souv. sheet, #200-203, perf 13½	1.00	1.25
		Nos. 196-203 (8)	1.60	1.60

Nos. 369-373a Ovptd. "BARBUDA"

1975, Mar. 17

204	A72	5c multicolored	.20	.20
205	A72	15c multicolored	.35	.25
206	A72	50c multicolored	.50	.35
207	A72	50c multicolored	.70	.60
208	A72	$1 multicolored	.75	.70
a.		Souv. sheet of 5, #204-208 + label, perf. 13½x14	2.50	3.00
		Nos. 204-208 (5)	2.50	2.10

Stamps from No. 208a are 43x28mm.

Battle
of the
Saints
B20

1975, May 30   **Perf. 13½x14**

209	B20	35c shown	1.00	1.00
210	B20	50c Two ships	1.25	1.25
211	B20	50c Ships firing	1.50	1.50
212	B20	95c Sailors abandoning ship	1.75	2.00
		Nos. 209-212 (4)	5.50	5.50

Barbuda No. 186a Ovptd.

a

b

1975, July 2   **Perf. 14x15**

213	B18	(a) $5 multicolored	6.50	6.50
214	B18	(b) $5 multicolored	6.50	6.50

Overprint "a" is in 1st and 3rd vertical rows,
"b" 2nd and 4th. The 5th row has no overprint.
This can be collected se-tenant either as Nos.
213, 214 or 213, 214 and 186a.

Military
Uniforms — B21

Designs: 35c, Officer of 65th Foot, 1763.
50c, Grenadier, 27th Foot, 1701-1710. 75c,
Officer of 21st Foot, 1793-1796. 95c, Officer,
Royal Regiment of Artillery, 1800.

1975, Sept. 17   **Perf. 14**

215	B21	35c multicolored	.50	.50
216	B21	50c multicolored	.75	.75
217	B21	75c multicolored	1.25	1.25
218	B21	95c multicolored	1.50	1.50
		Nos. 215-218 (4)	4.00	4.00

Barbuda Nos. 189, 191, 193, 195
Ovptd.
"30th ANNIVERSARY /
UNITED NATIONS / 1945 - 1975"

1975, Oct. 24   **Perf. 13½x14**

219	B19	5c multicolored	.20	.20
220	B19	35c multicolored	.20	.20
221	B19	75c multicolored	.20	.20
222	B19	$1 multicolored	.20	.25
		Nos. 219-222 (4)	.80	.85

Nos. 394-401a Ovptd. "BARBUDA"

1975, Nov. 17   **Perf. 14**

223	A77	½c multicolored	.20	.20
224	A77	1c multicolored	.20	.20
225	A77	2c multicolored	.20	.20
226	A77	3c multicolored	.20	.20
227	A77	5c multicolored	.20	.20
228	A77	10c multicolored	.20	.20
229	A77	35c multicolored	.20	.20
230	A77	$2 multicolored	.20	.20
a.		Souvenir sheet of 4, #227-230	1.75	2.00
		Nos. 223-230 (8)	1.60	1.60

Nos. 402-404 Ovptd. "BARBUDA"

1975, Dec. 15   **Perf. 14**

231	A78	5c multicolored	1.10	1.10
232	A78	35c multicolored	2.25	2.25
233	A78	$2 multicolored	4.25	4.25
		Nos. 231-233 (3)	7.60	7.60

American
Revolution,
Bicent.
B22

Details from Surrender of Cornwallis at
Yorktown, by Trumbull: No. 234a, British
officers. b, Gen. Benjamin Lincoln. c, Washington, Allied officers.
The Battle of Princeton: No. 235a, Infantry.
b, Battle. c, Cannon fire.
Surrender of Burgoyne at Saratoga by
Trumbull: No. 236a, Mounted officer. b, Washington, Burgoyne. c, American officers.
Signing the Declaration of Independence,
by Trumbull: No. 237a, Delegates to Continental Congress. b, Adams, Sherman, Livingston,
Jefferson and Franklin. c, Hancock, Thomson,
Read, Dickinson, and Rutledge. Strips of 3
have continuous designs.

1976, Mar. 8   **Perf. 13½x13**

234	B22	15c Strip of 3, #a.-c.	.30	.30
235	B22	35c Strip of 3, #a.-c.	1.00	1.00
d.		Souvenir sheet, #234-235	1.50	1.50
236	B22	$1 Strip of 3, #a.-c.	1.25	1.25
237	B22	$2 Strip of 3, #a.-c.	2.25	2.25
d.		Souvenir sheet, #236-237	3.75	3.75

See Nos. 244-247.

Birds
B23

1976, June 30   **Perf. 13½x14**

238	B23	35c Bananaquits	1.10	.60
239	B23	50c Blue-hooded euphonia	1.10	.70

240	B23	75c Royal tern	1.50	.90
241	B23	95c Killdeer	1.75	1.00
242	B23	$1.25 Glossy cowbird	1.75	1.00
243	B23	$2 Purple gallinule	1.75	1.25
		Nos. 238-243 (6)	8.95	5.45

Barbuda #234-237 With Inscription
Added at Top Across the Three Stamps
in Blue
"H.M. Queen Elizabeth" "Royal Visit
6th July 1976" "H.R.H. Duke of
Edinburgh"

1976, Aug. 12   **Perf. 13½x14**
     Size: 38x31mm

244	B22	15c Strip of 3, #a.-c.	.30	.30
245	B22	35c Strip of 3, #a.-c.	.50	.50
d.		Souvenir sheet of 2, #244-245	1.25	1.25
246	B22	$1 Strip of 3, #a.-c.	.75	.75
247	B22	$2 Strip of 3, #a.-c.	1.25	1.25
d.		Souvenir sheet, #246-247	3.00	3.00

Nos. 244-247 are perforated on outside
edges; imperf. vertically within.

Nos. 448-452 Ovptd. "BARBUDA"

1976, Dec. 2   **Perf. 14**

248	A85	8c multicolored	.20	.20
249	A85	10c multicolored	.20	.20
250	A85	15c multicolored	.20	.20
251	A85	50c multicolored	.20	.20
252	A85	$1 multicolored	.20	.20
		Nos. 248-252 (5)	1.00	1.00

Nos. 431-437 Ovptd. "BARBUDA"

1976, Dec. 28   **Perf. 15**

253	A82	½c yellow & multi	.20	.20
254	A82	1c purple & multi	.20	.20
255	A82	2c emerald & multi	.20	.20
256	A82	15c brt blue & multi	.20	.20
257	A82	30c olive & multi	.20	.20
258	A82	$1 orange & multi	.20	.20
259	A82	$2 red & multi	.20	.20
a.		Souv. sheet of 4, #256-259, perf 13½	2.25	2.25
		Nos. 253-259 (7)	1.40	1.40

Telephone, Cent. — B24

1977, Jan. 31   **Perf. 14**

260	B24	75c shown	.20	.20
261	B24	$1.25 Satellite dish, television	.25	.35
262	B24	$2 Satellites in earth orbit	.40	.60
a.		Souv. sheet, #260-262, perf 15	1.25	1.50
		Nos. 260-262 (3)	.85	1.15

Coronation of
Queen
Elizabeth II,
25th
Anniv. — B25

Designs: Nos. 263a, St. Margaret's Church,
Westminster. b, Westminster Abbey entrance.
c, Westminster Abbey.
Nos. 264a, Riders on horseback. b, Coronation coach. c, Team of horses. Strips of 3 have
continuous designs.

1977, Feb. 7   **Perf. 13½x13**

263	B25	75c Strip of 3, #a.-c.	.45	.45
264	B25	$1.25 Strip of 3, #a.-c.	.60	.60

Souvenir Sheet

265	B25	Sheet of 6	1.25	1.25

Nos. 263a-264c se-tenant with labels. No.
265 contains Nos. 263a-264c with silver
borders.

Nos. 405-422 Ovptd. "BARBUDA"

1977, Apr. 4   **Perf. 15**

266	A79	½c multicolored	.20	.20
267	A79	1c multicolored	.30	.20
268	A79	2c multicolored	.30	.20
269	A79	3c multicolored	.30	.20
270	A79	4c multicolored	.30	.20
271	A79	5c multicolored	.30	.20
272	A79	6c multicolored	.30	.20
273	A79	10c multicolored	.30	.20
274	A79	15c multicolored	.30	.20
275	A79	20c multicolored	.30	.25
276	A79	25c multicolored	.30	.25
277	A79	35c multicolored	.35	.30
278	A79	50c multicolored	.40	.40
279	A79	75c multicolored	.40	.40
280	A79	$1 multicolored	.50	.50

     Perf. 13½x14

281	A80	$2.50 multicolored	1.25	1.40
282	A80	$5 multicolored	2.25	2.50
283	A80	$10 multicolored	5.50	6.00
		Nos. 266-283 (18)	13.85	13.80

For overprints see Nos. 506-516.

Nos. 459-464 Ovptd. "BARBUDA"

1977, Apr. 4   **Perf. 13½x14, 12**

284	A87	10c multicolored	.20	.20
285	A87	30c multicolored	.20	.20
286	A87	50c multicolored	.20	.25
287	A87	90c multicolored	.25	.35
288	A87	$2.50 multicolored	.50	1.00
		Nos. 284-288 (5)	1.35	2.00

Souvenir Sheet

289	A87	$5 multicolored	1.40	1.50

A booklet of self-adhesive stamps contains
one pane of six rouletted and die cut 50c
stamps in design of 90c (silver overprint), and
one pane of one die cut $5 (gold overprint) in
changed colors. Panes have marginal
inscriptions.
For overprints see Nos. 312-317.

Nos. 465-471a Ovptd. "BARBUDA"

1977, June 13   **Perf. 14**

290	A88	½c multicolored	.20	.20
291	A88	1c multicolored	.20	.20
292	A88	2c multicolored	.20	.20
293	A88	10c multicolored	.20	.20
294	A88	30c multicolored	.45	.45
295	A88	50c multicolored	.75	.75
296	A88	$2 multicolored	1.50	1.50
a.		Souvenir sheet of 3, #294-296	4.00	4.00
		Nos. 290-296 (7)	3.50	3.50

Overprint is slightly smaller on No. 296a.

Nos. 472-476a Ovptd. "BARBUDA"

1977, Aug. 12   **Perf. 14**

297	A89	10c multicolored	.20	.20
298	A89	30c multicolored	.20	.20
299	A89	50c multicolored	.20	.20
300	A89	90c multicolored	.20	.20
301	A89	$1 multicolored	.20	.30
a.		Souvenir sheet of 4, #298-301	1.75	1.75
		Nos. 297-301 (5)	1.00	1.10

Royal
Visit
B26

1977, Oct. 27   **Perf. 14½**

302	B26	50c Royal yacht Britannia	.20	.20
303	B26	$1.50 Jubliee emblem	.20	.25
304	B26	$2.50 Flags	.30	.40
a.		Souvenir sheet of 3, #302-304	2.00	2.00
		Nos. 302-304 (3)	.70	.85

Nos. 483-489 Ovptd. "BARBUDA"

1977, Nov. 15   **Perf. 14**

305	A90	½c multicolored	.20	.20
306	A90	1c multicolored	.20	.20
307	A90	2c multicolored	.20	.20
308	A90	8c multicolored	.20	.20
309	A90	10c multicolored	.20	.20
310	A90	25c multicolored	.20	.20
311	A90	$2 multicolored	.20	.20
a.		Souvenir sheet of 4, #308-311	1.60	1.60
		Nos. 305-311 (7)	1.40	1.40

Nos. 477-482 Ovptd. "BARBUDA" in
Black

1977, Dec. 20   **Perf. 12**

312	A87	10c multicolored	.20	.20
313	A87	30c multicolored	.20	.20
314	A87	50c multicolored	.20	.20
315	A87	90c multicolored	.25	.25
316	A87	$2.50 multicolored	.40	.40
		Nos. 312-316 (5)	1.25	1.25

Nos. 312-316 exist with blue overprint.

1977, Nov. 28   **Perf. 13½x14**

312a	A87	10c multicolored	.20	.20
313a	A87	30c multicolored	.20	.20
314a	A87	50c multicolored	.20	.20
315a	A87	90c multicolored	.25	.25
316a	A87	$2.50 multicolored	.40	.40
		Nos. 312a-316a (5)	1.25	1.25

Souvenir Sheet

317	A87	$5 multicolored	2.00	2.00

Overprint of Nos. 312a-316a differs from
that on Nos. 312-316.

Anniversaries — B27

First navigable airships, 75th anniv: No. 318a, Zeppelin LZ1. b, German Naval airship L31. c, Graf Zeppelin. d, Gondola on military airship.

Soviet space program, 20th anniv: No. 319a, Sputnik, 1957. b, Vostok rocket, 1961. c, Voskhod rocket, 1964. d, Space walk, 1965.

Lindbergh's Atlantic crossing, 50th anniv: No. 320a, Fueling for flight. b, New York take-off. c, Spirit of St. Louis. d, Welcome in England.

Coronation of Queen Elizabeth II, 25th anniv: No. 321a, Lion of England. b, Unicorn of Scotland. c, Yale of Beaufort. d, Falcon of Plantagenets.

Rubens, 400th birth anniv: No. 322a, Two lions. b, Daniel in the Lion's Den. c, Two lions lying down. d, Lion at Daniel's feet. Block of 4 has continuous design.

1977, Dec. 29 Perf. 14½x14
Blocks of 4
318	B27	75c #a.-d.	1.25	1.25
319	B27	95c #a.-d.	1.50	1.50
320	B27	$1.25 #a.-d.	1.60	1.60
321	B27	$2 #a.-d.	2.00	2.00
322	B27	$5 #a.-d.	2.00	2.00
e.		Min. sheet, #318-322 + 4 labels	8.00	8.00
		Nos. 318-322 (5)	8.35	8.35

Nos. 490-494a Ovptd. "BARBUDA"
1978, Feb. 15 Perf. 13x13½
323	A91	10c multicolored	.20	.20
324	A91	15c multicolored	.20	.20
325	A91	50c multicolored	.25	.25
326	A91	90c multicolored	.35	.35
327	A91	$2 multicolored	.50	.50
a.		Souv. sheet, #324-327, perf 14	4.75	3.50
		Nos. 323-327 (5)	1.50	1.50

Pieta, by Michelangelo — B28

Works by Michelangelo: 95c, Holy Family. $1.25, Libyan Sibyl. $2, The Flood.

1978, Mar. 23 Perf. 13½x14
328	B28	75c multicolored	.20	.20
329	B28	95c multicolored	.20	.20
330	B28	$1.25 multicolored	.20	.20
331	B28	$2 multicolored	.20	.20
a.		Souvenir sheet of 4, #328-331	2.25	2.25
		Nos. 328-331 (4)	.80	.80

Nos. 495-502 Ovptd. "BARBUDA"
1978, Mar. 23 Perf. 14
332	A92	½c multicolored	.20	.20
333	A92	1c multicolored	.20	.20
334	A92	2c multicolored	.20	.20
335	A92	10c multicolored	.20	.20
336	A92	50c multicolored	.35	.35
337	A92	90c multicolored	.40	.40
338	A92	$2 multicolored	1.00	1.00
		Nos. 332-338 (7)	2.55	2.55

Souvenir Sheet
339	A92	$2.50 multicolored	1.75	1.75

Nos. 503-507 Ovptd. "BARBUDA"
1978, May 22 Perf. 14½
340	A93	10c multicolored	.20	.20
341	A93	50c multicolored	.40	.40
342	A93	90c multicolored	.70	.70
343	A93	$2 multicolored	1.25	1.25
		Nos. 340-343 (4)	2.55	2.55

Souvenir Sheet
344	A93	$2.50 multicolored	2.25	2.25

Coronation of Queen Elizabeth II, 25th Anniv. — B29

Crowns: No. 345a, St. Edward's. b, Imperial State. No. 346a, Queen Mary's. b, Queen Mother's. No. 347a, Queen Consort's. b, Queen Victoria's.

1978, June 2 Perf. 15
Miniature Sheets of Two Each Plus Two Labels
345	B29	75c Sheet of 4	1.00	1.00
346	B29	$1.50 Sheet of 4	1.50	1.50
347	B29	$2.50 Sheet of 4	2.50	2.50

Souvenir Sheet
Perf. 14½
348	B29	Sheet of 6, #345a-347b	2.50	2.50

Nos. 508-514 Ovptd. in Black or Deep Rose Lilac "BARBUDA"
1978 Perf. 14
349	A94	10c multicolored	.20	.20
350	A94	30c multicolored	.20	.20
351	A94	50c multicolored	.25	.25
352	A94	90c multicolored	.40	.40
353	A94	$2.50 multicolored	.95	.95
		Nos. 349-353 (5)	2.00	2.00

Souvenir Sheet
354	A94	$5 multicolored	2.00	2.00

Self-adhesive
355		Souvenir booklet	7.50	7.50
a.	A95	Bkt. pane, 3 each 25c and 50c, die cut, rouletted (DRL)	2.00	2.00
b.	A95	$5 Bkt. pane of 1, die cut	5.00	5.00

Issued: #349-354, June 2; #355, Oct. 12.

Nos. 515-518 Ovptd. "BARBUDA"
1978, Sept. 12 Perf. 15
356	A96	10c multicolored	.20	.20
357	A96	15c multicolored	.20	.20
358	A96	$3 multicolored	1.00	1.00
		Nos. 356-358 (3)	1.40	1.40

Souvenir Sheet
359		Sheet of 4	1.50	1.50
a.	A96	25c multicolored	.20	.20
b.	A96	30c multicolored	.20	.20
c.	A96	50c multicolored	.25	.25
d.	A96	$2 multicolored	.75	.75

Nos. 519-523 Ovptd. "BARBUDA"
1978, Nov. 20 Perf. 14
360	A97	25c multicolored	.35	.35
361	A97	50c multicolored	.55	.55
362	A97	90c multicolored	.80	.80
363	A97	$2 multicolored	1.40	1.40
		Nos. 360-363 (4)	3.10	3.10

Souvenir Sheet
364	A97	$2.50 multicolored	2.75	2.75

Flora and Fauna B30

1978, Nov. 20 Perf. 15
365	B30	25c Blackbar soldierfish	2.25	2.25
366	B30	50c Painted lady	3.75	3.75
367	B30	75c Dwarf poinciana	2.75	2.75
368	B30	95c Zebra butterfly	3.75	3.75
369	B30	$1.25 Bougainvillea	2.50	2.50
		Nos. 365-369 (5)	15.00	15.00

Nos. 524-527 Ovptd. in Silver "BARBUDA"
1978, Nov. 20 Perf. 14
370	A98	8c multicolored	.20	.20
371	A98	25c multicolored	.20	.20
372	A98	$2 multicolored	.85	.85
		Nos. 370-372 (3)	1.25	1.25

Souvenir Sheet
373	A98	$4 multicolored	2.50	2.50

Events and Annivs. B31

Designs: 75c, 1978 World Cup Soccer Championships, vert. 95c, Wright Brothers 1st powered flight, 75th anniv. $1.25, First Trans-Atlantic balloon flight, Aug. 1978. $2, Coronation of Elizabeth II, 25th anniv., vert.

1978, Dec. 20 Perf. 14
374	B31	75c multicolored	.40	.40
375	B31	95c multicolored	.50	.50
376	B31	$1.25 multicolored	.75	.75
377	B31	$2 multicolored	.90	.90
a.		Souv. sheet, #374-377, imperf	5.00	5.00
		Nos. 374-377 (4)	2.55	2.55

No. 377a has simulated perfs.

Nos. 528-532 Ovptd. in Bright Blue "BARBUDA" and

Sir Rowland Hill, Death Cent. B32

1979, Apr. 4
378	A99	25c multicolored	.20	.20
379	A99	50c multicolored	.35	.35
380	B32	75c Sir Rowland Hill, vert.	.40	.40
381	B32	95c Mail coach, 1840	.50	.50
382	A99	$1 multicolored	.65	.65
383	B32	$1.25 London's first pillar box, 1855	.70	.70
384	B32	$2 St. Martin's Post Office, London, vert.	1.10	1.10
a.		Souvenir sheet of 4, #380-381, 383-384, imperf.	2.75	2.75
385	A99	$2 multicolored	1.40	1.40
		Nos. 378-385 (8)	5.30	5.30

Souvenir Sheet
386	A99	$2.50 multicolored	2.00	2.00

No. 384a has simulated perfs.
For overprints see Nos. 423-426.

Nos. 533-536 Ovptd. "BARBUDA"
1979, Apr. 16
387	A100	10c multicolored	.20	.20
388	A100	50c multicolored	.30	.30
389	A100	$4 multicolored	.90	.90
		Nos. 387-389 (3)	1.40	1.40

Souvenir Sheet
390	A100	$2.50 multicolored	1.00	1.00

Intl. Civil Aviation Organization, 30th Anniv. — B33

1979, May 24 Perf. 13½x14
391	B33	75c Passengers leaving 747	.30	.40
392	B33	95c Air traffic controllers	.40	.50
393	B33	$1.25 Plane on runway	.50	.60
a.		Block of 3, #391-393 + label	1.50	1.50

Nos. 537-541 Ovptd. "BARBUDA"
1979, May 24 Perf. 14
394	A101	25c multicolored	.30	.30
395	A101	50c multicolored	.50	.50
396	A101	90c multicolored	1.00	1.00
397	A101	$2 multicolored	1.50	1.50
		Nos. 394-397 (4)	3.30	3.30

Souvenir Sheet
398	A101	$5 multicolored	2.75	2.75

Nos. 542-546 Ovptd. "BARBUDA"
1979, Aug. 1 Perf. 14½
399	A102	30c multicolored	.30	.30
400	A102	50c multicolored	.40	.40
401	A102	90c multicolored	.55	.55
402	A102	$3 multicolored	1.50	1.50
		Nos. 399-402 (4)	2.75	2.70

Souvenir Sheet
403	A102	$2.50 multicolored	1.60	1.60

Nos. 547-551 Ovptd. "BARBUDA"
1979, Aug. 1 Perf. 14
404	A103	25c multicolored	.40	.40
405	A103	50c multicolored	1.10	.50
406	A103	90c multicolored	1.10	.65
407	A103	$3 multicolored	2.25	1.75
		Nos. 404-407 (4)	4.85	3.30

Souvenir Sheet
408	A103	$2.50 multicolored	2.50	2.50

Intl. Year of the Child — B34

Details of the Christ Child from various paintings by Durer: 25c, 1512. 50c, 1516. 75c, 1526. $1.25, 1502.

1979, Sept. 24 Perf. 14x13½
409	B34	25c multicolored	.20	.20
410	B34	50c multicolored	.20	.20
411	B34	75c multicolored	.25	.25
412	B34	$1.25 multicolored	.35	.35
a.		Souvenir sheet of 4, #409-412	1.50	1.50
		Nos. 409-412 (4)	1.00	1.00

Nos. 552-556 Ovptd. "BARBUDA"
1979, Nov. 21 Perf. 14
413	A104	8c multicolored	.20	.20
414	A104	25c multicolored	.25	.25
415	A104	50c multicolored	.40	.25
416	A104	$4 multicolored	1.40	1.40
		Nos. 413-416 (4)	2.25	2.05

Souvenir Sheet
Perf. 12x12½
417	A104	$3 multicolored	1.40	1.40

Nos. 557-561 Ovptd. "BARBUDA"
1980, Mar. 18
418	A105	10c multicolored	.20	.20
419	A105	25c multicolroed	.20	.20
420	A105	$1 multicolored	.30	.30
421	A105	$2 multicolored	.45	.45
		Nos. 418-421 (4)	1.15	1.15

Souvenir Sheet
422	A105	$3 multicolored	1.50	2.00

Nos. 571A-571D Overprinted "BARBUDA" in Dark Blue
1980, May 6 Perf. 12
423	A99	25c multicolored	.30	.20
424	A99	50c multicolored	.35	.40
425	A99	$1 multicolored	.70	.75
426	A99	$2 multicolored	2.25	1.65
		Nos. 423-426 (4)	3.60	3.00

First Moon Landing, 10th Anniv. — B35

1980, May 21 Perf. 13½x14
427	B35	75c Crew badge	.45	.45
428	B35	95c Plaque left on moon	.50	.50
429	B35	$1.25 Lunar, command modules	.60	.60
430	B35	$2 Lunar module	.95	.95
a.		Souvenir sheet of 4, #427-430	2.75	2.75
		Nos. 427-430 (4)	2.50	2.50

American Widgeon B36

1980, June 16 Perf. 14½x14
431	B36	1c shown	.55	.40
432	B36	2c Snowy plover	.55	.40
433	B36	4c Rose-breasted grosbeak	.65	.40
434	B36	6c Mangrove cuckoo	.65	.40
435	B36	10c Adelaide's warbler	.65	.40
436	B36	15c Scaly-breasted thrasher	.65	.40
437	B36	20c Yellow-crowned night heron	.75	.40
438	B36	25c Bridled quail dove	.75	.40
439	B36	35c Carib grackle	.75	.40
440	B36	50c Northern pintail	.75	.40
441	B36	75c Black-whiskered vireo	.75	.45

442 B36	$1 Blue-winged teal	1.10	.75

Perf. 14x14½

443 B36	$1.50 Green-throated carib	1.40	1.00
444 B36	$2 Red-necked pigeon	2.00	1.40
445 B36	$2.50 Stolid flycatcher	2.75	1.60
446 B36	$5 Yellow-bellied sapsucker	3.25	3.25
447 B36	$7.50 Caribbean elaenia	4.75	4.75
448 B36	$10 Great egret	6.50	6.50
Nos. 431-448 (18)		29.20	23.70

Nos. 443-448 vert.

Nos. 572-578 Ovptd. "BARBUDA"

1980, July 29   Perf. 13½x14, 14x13½

449 A106a	10c multicolored	.20	.20
450 A106a	30c multicolored	.20	.20
451 A106a	50c multicolored	.35	.35
452 A106a	90c multicolored	.50	.50
453 A106a	$1 multicolored	.50	.50
454 A106a	$4 multicolored	2.25	2.25
Nos. 449-454 (6)		4.00	4.00

Souvenir Sheet
Perf. 14

455 A106a	$5 multicolored	3.50	3.50

Nos. 579-583 Ovptd. "BARBUDA"

1980, Sept. 8   Perf. 14

456 A107	30c multicolored	.20	.20
457 A107	50c multicolored	.25	.25
458 A107	90c multicolored	.30	.30
459 A107	$3 multicolored	.75	.75
Nos. 456-459 (4)		1.50	1.50

Souvenir Sheet

460 A107	$5 multicolored	2.00	2.00

Nos. 584-586 Optd. "BARBUDA"

1980, Oct. 6

461 A108	10c multicolored	.25	.25
462 A108	$2.50 multicolored	1.75	1.75

Souvenir Sheet
Perf. 12

463 A108	$3 multicolored	2.50	2.50

Nos. 587-591 Ovptd. "BARBUDA"

1980, Dec. 8   Perf. 14

464 A109	10c multicolored	2.00	.90
465 A109	30c multicolored	2.50	1.00
466 A109	$1 multicolored	3.50	2.50
467 A109	$2 multicolored	4.00	4.75
Nos. 464-467 (4)		12.00	9.15

Souvenir Sheet

468 A109	$2.50 multicolored	5.50	5.50

Nos. 602-606 Ovptd. "BARBUDA"

1981, Jan. 26

469 A111	25c multicolored	1.00	.25
470 A111	50c multicolored	1.25	.35
471 A111	90c multicolored	1.75	.50
472 A111	$3 multicolored	3.25	1.00
Nos. 469-472 (4)		7.25	2.10

Souvenir Sheet

473 A111	$2.50 multicolored	2.25	2.25

Famous Women — B37

1981, Mar. 9   Perf. 14x13½

474 B37	50c Florence Nightingale	.25	.25
475 B37	90c Marie Curie	.60	.60
476 B37	$1 Amy Johnson	.55	.55
477 B37	$4 Eleanor Roosevelt	.75	.75
Nos. 474-477 (4)		2.15	2.15

Walt Disney Characters at Sea — B38

1981, May 15   Perf. 13½x14

478 B38	10c Goofy	1.25	.35
479 B38	20c Donald Duck	1.50	.45
480 B38	25c Mickey Mouse	1.90	.65
481 B38	30c Goofy fishing	1.90	.75
482 B38	35c Goofy sailing	1.90	.75
483 B38	40c Mickey fishing	2.10	1.00
484 B38	75c Donald Duck boating	2.25	1.25
485 B38	$1 Minnie Mouse	2.50	1.75
486 B38	$2 Chip 'n Dale	4.00	2.50
Nos. 478-486 (9)		19.30	9.45

Souvenir Sheet

487 B38	$2.50 Donald Duck, diff.	15.00	15.00

Nos. 618-622 Ovptd. "BARBUDA"

1981, June 9   Perf. 14

488 A112	10c multicolored	.20	.20
489 A112	50c multicolored	.50	.50
490 A112	90c multicolored	1.00	1.00
491 A112	$4 multicolored	2.75	2.75
Nos. 488-491 (4)		4.45	4.45

Souvenir Sheet
Perf. 14x14½

492 A112	$5 multicolored	5.00	5.00

Miniature Sheets

Royal Wedding — B39

a-b, $1, L & R sides of Buckingham Palace.
c-d, $1.50, L & R sides of Caernarvon Castle.
e-f, $4, L & R sides of Highgrove House.

1981, July 27   Perf. 11x11½
Sheets of 6, #a-f

493 B39	blk & salmon	4.00	4.00
494 B39	blk & purple	4.00	4.00
495 B39	blk & gray grn	4.00	4.00

Souvenir Sheet
Perf. 11½x11

496 B39	$5 St. Paul's Cathedral, vert.	1.25	1.25

Stamps of same denomination have continuous design. For surcharges see #592-594.

Common Design Types
pictured following the introduction.

Nos. 623-627 Ovptd. in Black or Silver "BARBUDA"

1981, Aug. 14   Perf. 14

497 CD331	25c multicolored	.20	.20
498 CD331	50c multicolored	.25	.25
499 CD331	$4 multicolored	.80	.80
Nos. 497-499 (3)		1.25	1.25

Souvenir Sheet

500 CD331	$5 multicolored	1.50	1.50

Self-adhesive

501 CD331	Booklet	10.00	10.00
a.	Pane of 6 (2x25c, 2x$1, 2x$2), Charles, die cut, rouletted (S)	5.00	5.00
b.	Pane of 1, $5 Couple, die cut (S)	5.00	5.00

Issued: #497-500, Aug. 24; #501, Oct. 12.
For surcharge see No. B1.

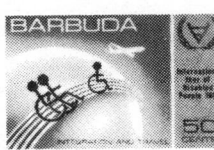

Intl. Year of the Disabled B40

1981, Sept. 14   Perf. 14

502 B40	50c Travel	.45	.45
503 B40	90c Braille, sign language	.45	.45
504 B40	$1 Helping hands	.55	.55
505 B40	$4 Mobility aids	.80	.80
Nos. 502-505 (4)		2.25	2.25

Nos. 607-617 Ovptd. "BARBUDA"

1981, Nov. 1   Perf. 15

506 A79	6c multicolored	.20	.20
507 A79	10c multicolored	.20	.20
508 A79	20c multicolored	.20	.20
509 A79	25c multicolored	.25	.20
510 A79	35c multicolored	.40	.30
511 A79	50c multicolored	.50	.40
512 A79	75c multicolored	.75	.60
513 A79	$1 multicolored	1.00	.75

Perf. 13½x14

514 A80	$2.50 multicolored	2.50	1.90
515 A80	$5 multicolored	5.00	3.75
516 A80	$10 multicolored	9.50	7.50
Nos. 506-516 (11)		20.50	16.00

Nos. 628-632 Ovptd. "BARBUDA"

1981, Dec. 14   Perf. 15

517 A113	10c multicolored	.60	.20
518 A113	50c multicolored	1.25	.50
519 A113	90c multicolored	1.90	.90
520 A113	$2.50 multicolored	3.25	2.50
Nos. 517-520 (4)		7.00	4.10

Souvenir Sheet

521 A113	$5 multicolored	4.50	4.50

Nos. 643-647 Ovptd. "BARBUDA"

1981, Dec. 14

522 A116	10c multicolored	.20	.20
523 A116	50c multicolored	.55	.55
524 A116	90c multicolored	1.00	1.00
525 A116	$2 multicolored	2.25	2.25
Nos. 522-525 (4)		4.00	4.00

Souvenir Sheet

526 A116	$4 multicolored	3.00	3.00

Nos. 638-642 Ovptd. in Black or Silver "BARBUDA"

1981, Dec. 22

527 A115	8c multi	.20	.20
528 A115	30c multi	.25	.25
529 A115	$1 multi (S)	.50	.50
530 A115	$3 multi	1.40	1.40
Nos. 527-530 (4)		2.35	2.35

Souvenir Sheet

531 A115	$5 multi	2.25	2.25

Birth of Prince William — B41

Various portraits.

1982, June 21   Wmk. 380   Perf. 14

532 B41	$1 buff & multi	.65	.65
533 B41	$2.50 lt pink & multi	1.25	1.25
534 B41	$5 lt lilac & multi	2.75	2.75
Nos. 532-534 (3)		4.65	4.65

Souvenir Sheet

535 B41	$5 Couple	4.00	4.00

See Nos. 540-543.

The overprint on stamps of Antigua, from here on, read "BARBUDA MAIL" in one or two lines.

#672-675 Ovptd. in Black or Silver
Perf. 14½x14

1982, Oct. 12   Unwmk.

536 CD332	90c multi	.65	.65
537 CD332	$1 multi (S)	.75	.75
538 CD332	$4 multi (S)	3.00	3.00
Nos. 536-538 (3)		4.40	4.40

Souvenir Sheet

539 CD332	$5 multi	4.25	4.25

Barbuda Nos. 532-535 Inscribed "Twenty First Birthday Greetings to H.R.H. The Princess of Wales"

Various portraits.

1982, July 1   Perf. 14x14½
Wmk. 380

540 B41	$1 lt grn & multi	1.25	.50
541 B41	$2.50 pale sal & multi	2.00	1.50
542 B41	$5 lt bl & multi	3.25	3.00
Nos. 540-542 (3)		6.50	5.00

Souvenir Sheet

543 B41	$4 Couple	3.50	3.50

#663-666 Ovptd. in Black or Silver
Perf. 14½x14

1982, Aug. 30   Unwmk.

544 CD332	90c multi	.75	.75
545 CD332	$1 multi (S)	.85	.85
546 CD332	$4 multi	3.25	3.25
Nos. 544-546 (3)		4.85	4.85

Souvenir Sheet

547 CD332	$5 multi	6.00	6.00

Nos. 676-683 Overprinted

1982, Dec. 6   Perf. 15

551 A121	10c multicolored	.20	.20
552 A121	25c multicolored	.25	.25
553 A121	45c multicolored	1.00	1.00
554 A121	60c multicolored	.35	.35
555 A121	$1 multicolored	1.10	1.10
556 A121	$3 multicolored	1.10	1.10
Nos. 551-556 (6)		4.00	4.00

Souvenir Sheets

557 A121	$4 on #682	2.75	2.75
558 A121	$4 on #683	2.75	2.75

Nos. 684-688 Overprinted

1982, Dec. 6   Perf. 14

559 A122	10c multicolored	.20	.20
560 A122	30c multicolored	.30	.30
561 A122	75c multicolored	.75	.75
562 A122	$4 multicolored	1.75	1.75
Nos. 559-562 (4)		3.00	3.00

Souvenir Sheet

563 A122	$5 multicolored	3.00	3.00

Nos. 689-693 Overprinted

1983, Mar. 14   Perf. 14½

564 A123	45c multicolored	.25	.25
565 A123	50c multicolored	.35	.35
566 A123	60c multicolored	.40	.40
567 A123	$4 multicolored	3.00	3.00
Nos. 564-567 (4)		4.00	4.00

Souvenir Sheet

568 A123	$5 multicolored	4.00	4.00

Nos. 694-697 Overprinted

1983, Mar. 14   Perf. 14

569 A124	25c multicolored	.55	.55
570 A124	45c multicolored	.70	.70
571 A124	60c multicolored	1.00	1.00
572 A124	$3 multicolored	3.25	3.25
Nos. 569-572 (4)		5.50	5.50

Nos. 698-702 Overprinted

1983, Apr. 12

573 A125	15c multicolored	1.00	1.00
574 A125	50c multicolored	2.50	2.50
575 A125	60c multicolored	2.00	2.00
576 A125	$3 multicolored	3.75	3.75
Nos. 573-576 (4)		9.25	9.25

Souvenir Sheet

577 A125	$5 multicolored	4.00	4.00

First Manned Balloon Flight, Bicent. — B43

1983, June 13

578 B43	$1 Vincenzo Lunardi, 1785	.50	.50
579 B43	$1.50 Montgolfier brothers, 1783	.75	.75
580 B43	$2.50 Blanchard & Jeffries, 1785	1.25	1.25
Nos. 578-580 (3)		2.50	2.50

Souvenir Sheet

581 B43	$5 Graf Zeppelin, 1928	3.25	3.25

Nos. 703-707 Overprinted

1983, July 4   **Perf. 15**

582	A126	15c multicolored	1.00	.35
583	A126	50c multicolored	4.00	1.50
584	A126	60c multicolored	4.50	1.60
585	A126	$3 multicolored	5.00	4.00
		Nos. 582-585 (4)	14.50	7.45

Souvenir Sheet

586	A126		8.50	8.50

Nos. 726-730 Overprinted

1983, Sept. 12

587	A128	30c multicolored	1.00	1.00
588	A128	50c multicolored	1.25	1.25
589	A128	60c multicolored	1.50	1.50
590	A128	$4 multicolored	5.25	5.25
		Nos. 587-590 (4)	9.00	9.00

Souvenir Sheet

591	A128	$5 multicolored	6.50	6.50

Barbuda Nos. 493-495 Surcharged 45c on $1, 50c on $1.50, or 60c on $4

1983, Oct. 21   **Perf. 11½x11**

592	B39	Sheet of 6, #493	7.50	7.50
593	B39	Sheet of 6, #494	7.50	7.50
594	B39	Sheet of 6, #495	7.50	7.50

Nos. 708-725 Overprinted

1983, Oct. 28   **Perf. 14**

595	A127	1c multicolored	.20	.20
596	A127	2c multicolored	.20	.20
597	A127	3c multicolored	.20	.20
598	A127	5c multicolored	.20	.20
599	A127	10c multicolored	.25	.25
600	A127	15c multicolored	.50	.50
601	A127	20c multicolored	.60	.60
602	A127	25c multicolored	.60	.60
603	A127	30c multicolored	.75	.75
604	A127	40c multicolored	.85	.85
605	A127	45c multicolored	.95	.95
606	A127	50c multicolored	1.10	1.10
607	A127	60c multicolored	1.10	1.10
608	A127	$1 multicolored	1.50	1.50
609	A127	$2 multicolored	2.25	2.25
610	A127	$2.50 multicolored	2.75	2.75
611	A127	$5 multicolored	4.00	4.00
612	A127	$10 multicolored	6.00	6.00
		Nos. 595-612 (18)	24.00	24.00

Nos. 731-735 Overprinted

1983, Oct. 28   **Perf. 14**

613	A129	10c multicolored	.20	.20
614	A129	30c multicolored	.20	.20
615	A129	$1 multicolored	.75	.75
616	A129	$4 multicolored	3.00	3.00
		Nos. 613-616 (4)	4.15	4.15

Souvenir Sheet

617	A129	$5 multicolored	4.50	4.50

#736-739 Ovptd. in Black or Silver

1983, Dec. 14   **Perf. 14**

618	A130	15c multicolored (S)	.20	.20
619	A130	50c multicolored (S)	.45	.45
620	A130	60c multicolored	.50	.50
621	A130	$3 multicolored	2.75	2.75
		Nos. 618-621 (4)	3.90	3.90

Members of Royal Family — B44

1984, Feb. 14   **Perf. 14½x14**

622	B44	$1 Edward VII	.75	1.00
623	B44	$1 George V	.75	1.00
624	B44	$1 George VI	.75	1.00
625	B44	$1 Elizabeth II	.75	1.00
626	B44	$1 Prince Charles	.75	1.00
627	B44	$1 Prince William	.75	1.00
		Nos. 622-627 (6)	4.50	6.00

Nos. 740-744 Overprinted and

1984 Summer Olympics, Los Angeles B45

1984   **Perf. 15, 13½ (B45)**

628	A131	25c multicolored	.20	.20
629	A131	50c multicolored	.40	.40
630	A131	90c multicolored	.45	.45
631	B45	$1.50 Olympic Stadium, Athens	1.10	1.10
632	B45	$2.50 Olympic Stadium, Los Angeles	1.90	1.90
633	A131	$3 multicolored	2.50	2.50
634	B45	$5 Torch bearer	4.00	4.00
a.		Souv. sheet of 1, perf. 15	3.75	3.75
		Nos. 628-634 (7)	10.55	10.55

Souvenir Sheet

635	A131	$5 multicolored	3.75	3.75

Issue dates: A131, Apr. 26, B45, July 27.

Nos. 755-759 Overprinted

1984, July 12   **Perf. 15**

636	A133	15c multicolored	.80	.80
637	A133	50c multicolored	1.00	1.00
638	A133	60c multicolored	1.25	1.25
639	A133	$3 multicolored	2.50	2.50
		Nos. 636-639 (4)	5.55	5.55

Souvenir Sheet

640	A133	$5 multicolored	5.00	5.00

Nos. 745-749 Overprinted

1984, July 12

641	A132	45c multicolored	1.50	.40
642	A132	50c multicolored	1.50	.45
643	A132	60c multicolored	1.75	.50
644	A132	$4 multicolored	4.25	3.50
		Nos. 641-644 (4)	9.00	4.85

Souvenir Sheet

645	A132	$5 multicolored	6.50	6.50

#760-767 Ovptd. in Black or Silver

1984, Oct. 1   **Perf. 14**

646	A134	10c multicolored (S)	.20	.20
647	A134	20c multicolored	.20	.20
648	A134	30c multicolored	.25	.25
649	A134	40c multicolored	.30	.30
650	A134	90c multicolored (S)	.70	.70
651	A134	$1.10 multicolored (S)	.90	.90
652	A134	$1.50 multicolored (S)	1.25	1.25
653	A134	$2 multicolored	1.60	1.60
		Nos. 646-653 (8)	5.40	5.40

Nos. 768-772 Overprinted

1984, Oct. 1

654	A135	40c multicolored	.35	.35
655	A135	50c multicolored	.40	.40
656	A135	60c multicolored	.50	.50
657	A135	$3 multicolored	2.75	2.75
		Nos. 654-657 (4)	4.00	4.00

Souvenir Sheet

658	A135	$5 multicolored	4.25	4.25

Nos. 773-778 Overprinted

1984, Nov. 21   **Perf. 15**

659	A136	40c multicolored	.40	.40
660	A136	50c multicolored	.50	.50
661	A136	60c multicolored	.60	.60
662	A136	$2 multicolored	2.00	2.00
663	A136	$3 multicolored	3.00	3.00
		Nos. 659-663 (5)	6.50	6.50

Souvenir Sheet

664	A136	$5 multicolored	5.00	5.00

Nos. 782-791 Overprinted in Silver

1984   **Perf. 15**

665	A137a	15c multicolored	.20	.20
666	A137a	25c multicolored	.20	.20
667	A137a	50c multicolored	.40	.40
668	A137a	60c multicolored	.50	.50
669	A137a	70c multicolored	.55	.55
670	A137a	90c multicolored	.75	.75
671	A137a	$3 multicolored	2.50	2.50
672	A137a	$4 multicolored	3.25	3.25
		Nos. 665-672 (8)	8.35	8.35

Souvenir Sheets

673	A137a	$5 #790	4.50	4.50
674	A137a	$5 #791, horiz.	4.50	4.50

Issued: Correggio, 11/21; Degas, 11/30.

Nos. 779-781 Overprinted

1984, Nov. 30

675	A137	$1 multicolored	.80	.80
676	A137	$5 multicolored	4.00	4.00

Souvenir Sheet

677	A137	$5 multicolored	4.50	4.50

Nos. 819-827 Overprinted

1985, Feb. 18

678	A139	60c multicolored	.45	.45
679	A139	60c multicolored	.45	.45
680	A139	60c multicolored	.45	.45
681	A139	60c multicolored	.45	.45
682	A139	$1 multicolored	.75	.75
683	A139	$1 multicolored	.75	.75
684	A139	$1 multicolored	.75	.75
685	A139	$1 multicolored	.75	.75
		Nos. 678-685 (8)	4.80	4.80

Souvenir Sheet

686	A139	$5 multicolored	4.50	4.50

Queen Mother (Lady Elizabeth Bowes-Lyon), 1907 — B46

1985, Feb. 26   **Perf. 14x14½**

687	B46	15c shown	.20	.20
688	B46	45c Duchess of York, 1926	.35	.35
689	B46	50c Coronation, 1937	.40	.40
690	B46	60c Queen Mother	.50	.50
691	B46	90c Wearing tiara	.70	.70
692	B46	$2 Wearing blue hat	1.60	1.60
693	B46	$3 With children	2.50	2.50
		Nos. 687-693 (7)	6.25	6.25

For overprints see Nos. 724-728, 733, 735.

Nos. 828-834 Overprinted

1985, May 10   **Perf. 15**

694	A140	25c multicolored	.20	.20
695	A140	30c multicolored	.25	.25
696	A140	50c multicolored	.40	.40
697	A140	90c multicolored	.70	.70
698	A140	$1 multicolored	.80	.80
699	A140	$3 multicolored	2.50	2.50
		Nos. 694-699 (6)	4.85	4.85

Souvenir Sheet

700	A140	$5 multicolored	4.00	4.00

Audubon, Birth Bicentenary — B47

1985, Apr. 4   **Perf. 14**

701	B47	45c Roseate tern	.40	.40
702	B47	50c Mangrove cuckoo	.45	.45
703	B47	60c Yellow-crowned night heron	.55	.55
704	B47	$5 Brown pelican	4.50	4.50
		Nos. 701-704 (4)	5.90	5.90

Nos. 845-849, 910-913 Ovptd. in Black or Silver

1985-86   **Perf. 15, 12½x12**

705	A143	60c on #910 (S)	.50	.50
706	A143	90c on #845	.70	.70
707	A143	90c on #911 (S)	.70	.70
708	A143	$1 on #846	.80	.80
709	A143	$1.50 on #847	1.25	1.25
710	A143	$1.50 on #912	1.25	1.25
711	A143	$3 on #848	2.50	2.50
712	A143	$3 on #913	2.50	2.50
		Nos. 705-712 (8)	10.20	10.20

Souvenir Sheet

713	A143	$5 on #849	4.50	4.50

Issue dates: Nos. 706, 708-709, 711, 713, July 18, 1985. Others, Dec. 1986.

Nos. 850-854 Overprinted

1985, July 18   **Perf. 14**

714	A144	25c multicolored	.25	.25
715	A144	60c multicolored	.50	.50
716	A144	95c multicolored	.80	.80
717	A144	$4 multicolored	3.50	3.50
		Nos. 714-717 (4)	5.05	5.05

Souvenir Sheet

718	A144	$5 multicolored	4.50	4.50

Nos. 840-844 Overprinted

1985, Aug. 2

719	A142	10c multicolored	.20	.20
720	A142	30c multicolored	.30	.30
721	A142	60c multicolored	.50	.50
722	A142	$4 multicolored	3.75	3.75
		Nos. 719-722 (4)	4.75	4.75

Souvenir Sheet

723	A142	$5 multicolored	4.50	4.50

Barbuda Nos. 687-693 Ovptd. "4TH AUG 1900-1985" and Antigua Nos. 866A-870 Ovptd. "BARBUDA / MAIL" in Silver or Black

Perf. 14, 12x12½ (#729, 731, 736)

1985-86

724	B46	15c multi	.20	.20
725	B46	45c multi	.35	.35
726	B46	50c multi	.40	.40
727	B46	60c multi	.50	.50
728	B46	90c multi	.70	.70
729	A148	90c multi	.70	.70
730	A148	$1 multi (S)	.80	.80
731	A148	$1 like #730	.80	.80
732	A148	$1.50 multi (S)	1.25	1.25
733	B46	$2 multi	1.60	1.60
734	A148	$2.50 multi	2.00	2.00
735	B46	$3 multi	2.50	2.50
736	A148	$3 multi	2.50	2.50
		Nos. 724-736 (13)	14.30	14.30

Souvenir Sheet

737	A148	$5 multi	4.50	4.50

Queen Mother's 85th birthday.

Issue dates: 15c, 45c, 50c, 60c, No. 728, $2, No. 735, Aug. 2. No. 730, $1.50, $2.50, Nov. 8. Others, Dec. 1986. Nos. 729, 731, 736 issued in sheets of 5 plus label.

Nos. 835-839 Overprinted

1985, Aug. 30   **Perf. 15**

738	A141	15c multicolored	.20	.20
739	A141	50c multicolored	.40	.40
740	A141	60c multicolored	.45	.45
741	A141	$3 multicolored	2.50	2.50
		Nos. 738-741 (4)	3.55	3.55

Souvenir Sheet

742	A141	$5 multicolored	4.00	4.00

Nos. 855-859 Overprinted

1985, Aug. 30   **Perf. 14**

743	A145	30c multicolored	.25	.25
744	A145	90c multicolored	.70	.70
745	A145	$1.50 multicolored	1.25	1.25
746	A145	$3 multicolored	2.50	2.50
		Nos. 743-746 (4)	4.70	4.70

Souvenir Sheet

747	A145	$5 multicolored	4.25	4.25

Nos. 860-861 Overprinted

1985, Nov. 25   **Perf. 14**

748	A146	$2 yellow green	1.60	1.60

Souvenir Sheet

749	A146	$5 deep brown	4.00	4.00

#871-875 Ovptd. in Black or Silver

1985, Nov. 25

750	A149	15c multi (S)	.20	.20
751	A149	45c multi	.40	.40
752	A149	60c multi	.55	.55
753	A149	$3 multi (S)	3.00	3.00
		Nos. 750-753 (4)	4.15	4.15

Souvenir Sheet

754	A149	$5 multi	4.50	4.50

Nos. 862-866 Overprinted

1986, Feb. 17

755	A147	25c multicolored	.20	.20
756	A147	50c multicolored	.40	.40
757	A147	60c multicolored	.50	.50
758	A147	$3 multicolored	2.50	2.50
		Nos. 755-758 (4)	3.60	3.60

Souvenir Sheet

759	A147	$5 multicolored	4.00	4.00

Nos. 886-889 Overprinted

1986, Feb. 17   **Perf. 14½**

760	A152	60c multicolored	.50	.50
761	A152	$1 multicolored	.80	.80
762	A152	$4 multicolored	3.25	3.25
		Nos. 760-762 (3)	4.55	4.55

Souvenir Sheet

763	A152	$5 multicolored	4.00	4.00

Nos. 876-880 Overprinted

1986, Mar. 10   **Perf. 14**

764	A150	25c multicolored	.20	.20
765	A150	50c multicolored	.40	.40
766	A150	$1 multicolored	.80	.80
767	A140	$3 multicolored	2.50	2.50
		Nos. 764-767 (4)	3.90	3.90

Souvenir Sheet

768	A150	$5 multicolored	4.00	4.00

Nos. 881-885 Overprinted

1986, Mar. 10		Perf. 14		
769	A151	15c multicolored	.20	.20
770	A151	45c multicolored	.35	.35
771	A151	60c multicolored	.50	.50
772	A151	$3 multicolored	2.50	2.50
		Nos. 769-772 (4)	3.55	3.55

Souvenir Sheet

773	A151	$5 multicolored	4.00	4.00

Nos. 905-909 Overprinted

1986, Apr. 4		Perf. 15		
774	A156	10c multicolored	.20	.20
775	A156	25c multicolored	.20	.20
776	A156	60c multicolored	.50	.50
777	A156	$4 multicolored	3.25	3.25
		Nos. 774-777 (4)	4.15	4.15

Souvenir Sheet

778	A156	$5 multicolored	4.00	4.00

B48 BARBUDA $1

1986, Apr. 21				
779	B48	$1 Shaking hands	.80	.80
780	B48	$2 Talking with woman	1.60	1.60
781	B48	$2.50 With officer	2.00	2.00
		Nos. 779-781 (3)	4.40	4.40

Souvenir Sheet

Perf. 13½x14

782	B48	$5 Portraits	4.00	4.00

No. 782 contains one 34x27mm stamp.

Nos. 925-928 Overprinted in Silver or Black

1986, Aug. 12				
783	CD339	60c multi	.50	.50
784	CD339	$1 multi	.80	.80
785	CD339	$4 multi	3.25	3.25
		Nos. 783-785 (3)	4.55	4.55

Souvenir Sheet

786	CD339	$5 multi (Bk)	4.00	4.00

Nos. 920-924 Overprinted and

$1 Halley's Comet Barbuda B49

1986		Perf. 14, 15 (B49)		
787	A158	5c multicolored	.20	.20
788	A158	10c multicolored	.20	.20
789	A158	60c multicolored	.50	.50
790	B49	$1 shown	.85	.85
791	B49	$2.50 Early telescope, dish antenna, vert.	2.00	2.00
792	A158	$4 multicolored	3.25	3.25
793	B49	$5 World map, comet	4.00	4.00
		Nos. 787-793 (7)	11.00	11.00

Souvenir Sheet

794	A159	$5 multicolored	4.00	4.00

Issued: #790-791, 793, 7/10; others, 9/22.

Nos. 901-904 Overprinted

1986, Aug. 12		Perf. 13½x14		
795	A155	40c multicolored	.30	.30
796	A155	$1 multicolored	.80	.80
797	A155	$3 multicolored	2.50	2.50
		Nos. 795-797 (3)	3.60	3.60

Souvenir Sheet

Perf. 14x13½

798	A155	$5 multicolored	4.00	4.00

Nos. 915-919 Overprinted

1986, Aug. 28		Perf. 14		
799	A157	30c multicolored	.25	.25
800	A157	60c multicolored	.50	.50
801	A157	$1 multicolored	.80	.80
802	A157	$4 multicolored	3.25	3.25
		Nos. 799-802 (4)	4.80	4.80

Souvenir Sheet

803	A157	$5 multicolored	4.00	4.00

See Nos. 848-851.

Nos. 934-938 Overprinted

1986, Aug. 28		Litho.	Perf. 15	
804	A161	25c multicolored	.20	.20
805	A161	50c multicolored	.40	.40
806	A161	$1 multicolored	.80	.80
807	A161	$3 multicolored	2.50	2.50
		Nos. 804-807 (4)	3.90	3.90

Souvenir Sheet

808	A161	$5 multicolored	4.00	4.00

Nos. 939-942 Ovptd. in Silver

1986, Sept. 22		Perf. 14		
809	CD340	45c multicolored	.40	.40
810	CD340	60c multicolored	.60	.60
811	CD340	$4 multicolored	4.00	4.00
		Nos. 809-811 (3)	5.00	5.00

Souvenir Sheet

812	CD340	$5 multicolored	5.00	5.00

Nos. 943-947 Overprinted in Silver or Black

1986, Nov. 10		Perf. 15		
813	A162	15c multicolored	.20	.20
814	A162	45c multicolored	.30	.30
815	A162	60c multicolored	.45	.45
816	A162	$3 multicolored	2.25	2.25
		Nos. 813-816 (4)	3.20	3.20

Souvenir Sheet

817	A162	$5 multi (Bk)	4.00	4.00

Nos. 948-957 Overprinted

1986, Nov. 10				
818	A163	10c multicolored	.20	.20
819	A163	15c multicolored	.20	.20
820	A163	50c multicolored	.40	.40
821	A163	60c multicolored	.45	.45
822	A163	70c multicolored	.50	.50
823	A163	$1 multicolored	.75	.75
824	A163	$3 multicolored	2.25	2.25
825	A163	$4 multicolored	3.00	3.00
		Nos. 818-825 (8)	7.75	7.75

Souvenir Sheets

826	A163	$4 multicolored	3.25	3.25
827	A163	$5 multicolored	4.00	4.00

Nos. 958-962 Overprinted

1986, Nov. 28				
828	A164	10c multicolored	.20	.20
829	A164	50c multicolored	.40	.40
830	A164	$1 multicolored	.75	.75
831	A164	$4 multicolored	3.00	3.00
		Nos. 828-831 (4)	4.35	4.35

Souvenir Sheet

832	A164	$5 multicolored	4.00	4.00

Nos. 929-933 Overprinted

1987, Jan. 12		Perf. 14		
833	A160	30c multicolored	.30	.30
834	A160	60c multicolored	.55	.55
835	A160	$1 multicolored	.90	.90
836	A160	$3 multicolored	2.75	2.75
		Nos. 833-836 (4)	4.50	4.50

Souvenir Sheet

837	A160	$5 multicolored	4.00	4.00

Nos. 968-972A Overprinted

1987, Jan. 12				
838	A165	10c multicolored	.20	.20
839	A165	15c multicolored	.20	.20
840	A165	50c multicolored	.40	.40
841	A165	60c multicolored	.50	.50
842	A165	70c multicolored	.55	.55
843	A165	$1 multicolored	.80	.80
844	A165	$3 multicolored	2.50	2.50
845	A165	$4 multicolored	3.25	3.25
		Nos. 838-845 (8)	8.40	8.40

Souvenir Sheets

846	A165	$5 multi (#972)	4.00	4.00
847	A165	$5 multi (#972A)	4.00	4.00

Automobile, cent.

Nos. 963-966 Overprinted

1987, Mar. 10				
848	A157	30c multicolored	.25	.25
849	A157	60c multicolored	.45	.45
850	A157	$1 multicolored	.75	.75
851	A157	$4 multicolored	3.00	3.00
		Nos. 848-851 (4)	4.45	4.45

See Nos. 799-802.

Nos. 1000-1004 Overprinted

1987, Apr. 23		Perf. 15		
852	A170	30c multicolored	.25	.25
853	A170	60c multicolored	.45	.45
854	A170	$1 multicolored	.75	.75
855	A170	$3 multicolored	2.25	2.25
		Nos. 852-855 (4)	3.70	3.70

Souvenir Sheet

856	A171	$5 multicolored	5.00	5.00

Nos. 1005-1014 Overprinted

1987, July 1		Perf. 14		
857	A172	15c multicolored	.20	.20
858	A173	30c multicolored	.25	.25
859	A172	40c multicolored	.30	.30
860	A172	50c multicolored	.40	.40
861	A172	60c multicolored	.45	.45
862	A172	$1 multicolored	.75	.75
863	A173	$2 multicolored	1.50	1.50
864	A173	$3 multicolored	2.25	2.25
		Nos. 857-864 (8)	6.10	6.10

Souvenir Sheets

865	A172	$5 multicolored	4.00	4.00
866	A173	$5 multicolored	4.00	4.00

Nos. 1025-1034 Overprinted

1987, July 28		Perf. 15		
867	A175	10c multicolored	.20	.20
868	A175	15c multicolored	.20	.20
869	A175	30c multicolored	.25	.25
870	A175	50c multicolored	.40	.40
871	A175	60c multicolored	.50	.50
872	A175	70c multicolored	.55	.55
873	A175	90c multicolored	.70	.70
874	A175	$1.50 multicolored	1.25	1.25
875	A175	$2 multicolored	1.60	1.60
876	A175	$3 multicolored	2.25	2.25
		Nos. 867-876 (10)	7.90	7.90

SHORE CRAB
Marine Life B50
BARBUDA 5c

1987, July 28				
877	B50	5c Shore crab	.20	.20
878	B50	10c Sea cucumber	.20	.20
879	B50	15c Stop light parrotfish	.20	.20
880	B50	25c Banded coral shrimp	.20	.20
881	B50	35c Spotted drum	.25	.25
882	B50	60c Thorny star-fish	.45	.45
883	B50	75c Atlantic trumpet triton	.55	.55
884	B50	90c Feather-star, yellow beaker sponge	.65	.65
885	B50	$1 Blue gorgonian, vert.	.75	.75
886	B50	$1.25 Slender filefish, vert.	.90	.90
887	B50	$5 Barred hamlet, vert.	3.75	3.75
888	B50	$7.50 Fairy basslet, vert.	5.50	5.50
889	B50	$10 Fire coral, butterfly fish, vert.	7.50	7.50
		Nos. 877-889 (13)	21.10	21.10

For surcharges see Nos. 1133-1134.

#1048-1052 Ovptd. in Silver or Black

1987, Oct. 12		Perf. 14		
890	A178	10c multicolored	.20	.20
891	A178	60c multicolored	.50	.50
892	A178	$1 multicolored	.80	.80
893	A178	$3 multicolored	2.25	2.25
		Nos. 890-893 (4)	3.75	3.75

Souvenir Sheet

894	A178	$5 multi (Bk)	4.00	4.00

1988 Summer Olympics, Seoul.

#990-999 Ovptd. in Black or Silver

1987, Oct. 12		Perf. 13½x14		
895	A169	10c multicolored	.20	.20
896	A169	30c multicolored	.25	.25
897	A169	40c multicolored	.30	.30
898	A169	60c multicolored	.50	.50
899	A169	90c multicolored	.70	.70
900	A169	$1 multicolored (S)	.80	.80
901	A169	$3 multicolored	2.25	2.25
902	A169	$4 multicolored	3.00	3.00
		Nos. 895-902 (8)	8.00	8.00

Size: 110x95mm

Imperf

903	A169	$5 multicolored	4.00	4.00
904	A169	$5 multicolored (S)	4.00	4.00

#1015-1024 Ovptd. in Silver or Black

1987, Nov. 5		Perf. 14		
905	A174	15c multicolored	.20	.20
906	A174	25c multicolored	.25	.25
907	A174	45c multicolored	.35	.35
908	A174	50c multicolored (Bk)	.40	.40
909	A174	60c multicolored	.50	.50
910	A174	90c multicolored	.70	.70
911	A174	$1 multicolored	.80	.80
912	A174	$2 multicolored	1.60	1.60
913	A174	$3 multicolored (Bk)	2.25	2.25
914	A174	$5 multicolored	4.00	4.00
		Nos. 905-914 (10)	11.05	11.05

#1040-1047 Ovptd. in Black or Silver

1987, Nov. 5				
915	A177	15c multicolored	.45	.30
916	A177	30c multicolored	1.00	.60
917	A177	45c multicolored	.50	.40
918	A177	50c multicolored	.55	.45
919	A177	60c multicolored	1.50	1.00
920	A177	$1 multicolored	1.00	.75
921	A177	$2 multicolored	1.50	1.25
922	A177	$3 multicolored (S)	3.50	3.00
		Nos. 915-922 (8)	10.00	7.75

Nos. 1035-1039 Overprinted

1987, Dec. 8				
923	A176	30c multicolored	.25	.25
924	A176	60c multicolored	.50	.50
925	A176	$1 multicolored	.80	.80
926	A176	$3 multicolored	2.25	2.25
		Nos. 923-926 (4)	3.80	3.80

Souvenir Sheet

927	A176	$5 multicolored	4.00	4.00

Nos. 1063-1067 Overprinted

1988, Jan. 12				
928	A181	45c multicolored	.30	.30
929	A181	60c multicolored	.45	.45
930	A181	$1 multicolored	.75	.75
931	A181	$4 multicolored	3.00	3.00
		Nos. 928-931 (4)	4.50	4.50

Souvenir Sheet

932	A181	$5 multicolored	4.00	4.00

Nos. 1083-1091 Overprinted

1988, Mar. 25				
933	A184	25c multicolored	.20	.20
934	A184	30c multicolored	.25	.25
935	A184	40c multicolored	.30	.30
936	A184	45c multicolored	.35	.35
937	A184	50c multicolored	.40	.40
938	A184	60c multicolored	.50	.50
939	A184	$1 multicolored	.80	.80
940	A184	$2 multicolored	1.60	1.60
		Nos. 933-940 (8)	4.40	4.40

Souvenir Sheet

941	A184	$5 multicolored	4.00	4.00

Nos. 1058-1062 Ovptd. in Silver

1988, May 6				
942	A180	15c multicolored	.20	.20
943	A180	45c multicolored	.35	.35
944	A180	60c multicolored	.50	.50
945	A180	$4 multicolored	3.25	3.25
		Nos. 942-945 (4)	4.30	4.30

Souvenir Sheet

946	A180	$5 multicolored	4.00	4.00

Nos. 1068-1072 Overprinted

1988, July 4				
947	A182	25c multicolored	.20	.20
948	A182	60c multicolored	.50	.50
949	A182	$2 multicolored	1.60	1.60
950	A182	$3 multicolored	2.25	2.25
		Nos. 947-950 (4)	4.55	4.55

Souvenir Sheet

951	A182	$5 multicolored	4.00	4.00

Nos. 1073-1082 Overprinted

1988, July 4				
952	A183	10c multicolored	.20	.20
953	A183	15c multicolored	.20	.20
954	A183	50c multicolored	.40	.40
955	A183	60c multicolored	.50	.50
956	A183	70c multicolored	.55	.55
957	A183	80c multicolored	.80	.80
958	A183	$3 multicolored	2.25	2.25
959	A183	$4 multicolored	3.25	3.25
		Nos. 952-959 (8)	8.15	8.15

Souvenir Sheets

960	A183	$5 multi (#1081)	4.00	4.00
961	A183	$5 multi (#1082)	4.00	4.00

Nos. 1092-1101 Overprinted

1988, July 25				
962	A185	10c multicolored	.20	.20
963	A185	30c multicolored	.25	.25
964	A185	45c multicolored	.40	.40
965	A185	60c multicolored	.55	.55
966	A185	90c multicolored	.75	.75
967	A185	$1 multicolored	.85	.85
968	A185	$3 multicolored	2.50	2.50
969	A185	$4 multicolored	3.50	3.50
		Nos. 962-969 (8)	9.00	9.00

Souvenir Sheets

970	A185	$5 multi (#1100)	4.00	4.00
971	A185	$5 multi (#1101)	4.00	4.00

Nos. 1102-1111 Overprinted

1988, July 25   *Perf. 13½x14*

972	A187	30c multicolored	.25	.25
973	A187	40c multicolored	.30	.30
974	A187	45c multicolored	.35	.35
975	A187	50c multicolored	.40	.40
976	A187	$1 multicolored	.80	.80
977	A187	$2 multicolored	1.60	1.60
978	A187	$3 multicolored	2.25	2.25
979	A187	$4 multicolored	3.25	3.25
		Nos. 972-979 (8)	9.20	9.20

Souvenir Sheets

980	A187	$5 multi (#1110)	4.00	4.00
981	A187	$5 multi (#1111)	4.00	4.00

Nos. 1053-1057 Overprinted

1988, Aug. 25   *Perf. 15*

982	A179	10c multicolored	.20	.20
983	A179	60c multicolored	.45	.45
984	A179	$1 multicolored	.75	.75
985	A179	$3 multicolored	2.25	2.25
		Nos. 982-985 (4)	3.65	3.65

Souvenir Sheet

986	A179	$5 multicolored	4.00	4.00

Nos. 1112-1116 Overprinted

1988, Aug. 25

987	A188	30c multicolored	.25	.25
988	A188	60c multicolored	.50	.50
989	A188	$1 multicolored	.80	.80
990	A188	$3 multicolored	2.25	2.25
		Nos. 987-990 (4)	3.80	3.80

Souvenir Sheet

991	A188	$5 multicolored	4.00	4.00

Nos. 1127-1136 Overprinted

1988, Sept. 16   *Perf. 14*

992	A190	10c multicolored	.20	.20
993	A190	30c multicolored	.25	.25
994	A190	50c multicolored	.40	.40
995	A190	90c multicolored	.60	.60
996	A190	$1 multicolored	.75	.75
997	A190	$2 multicolored	1.60	1.60
998	A190	$3 multicolored	2.25	2.25
999	A190	$4 multicolored	3.00	3.00
		Nos. 992-999 (8)	9.05	9.05

Souvenir Sheets

1000	A191	$5 multi (#1135)	4.00	4.00
1001	A191	$5 multi (#1136)	4.00	4.00

Nos. 1140-1144 Overprinted

1988, Sept. 16

1002	A192	40c multicolored	.30	.30
1003	A192	60c multicolored	.50	.50
1004	A192	$1 multicolored	.80	.80
1005	A192	$3 multicolored	2.25	2.25
		Nos. 1002-1005 (4)	3.85	3.85

Souvenir Sheet

1006	A192	$5 multicolored	4.00	4.00

Nos. 1145-1162 Overprinted

1988-90

1007	A193	1c multicolored	.20	.20
1008	A193	2c multicolored	.20	.20
1009	A193	3c multicolored	.20	.20
1010	A193	5c multicolored	.20	.20
1011	A193	10c multicolored	.20	.20
1012	A193	15c multicolored	.20	.20
1013	A193	20c multicolored	.20	.20
1014	A193	25c multicolored	.20	.20
1015	A193	30c multicolored	.25	.25
1016	A193	40c multicolored	.30	.30
1017	A193	45c multicolored	.35	.35
1018	A193	50c multicolored	.40	.40
1019	A193	60c multicolored	.50	.50
1020	A193	$1 multicolored	.80	.80
1021	A193	$2 multicolored	1.60	1.60
1022	A193	$2.50 multicolored	2.00	2.00
1023	A193	$5 multicolored	4.00	4.00
1024	A193	$10 multicolored	8.00	8.00
1025	A193	$20 multi ('90)	16.00	16.00
		Nos. 1007-1025 (19)	35.80	35.80

Issue dates: $20, May 4, others Dec. 8.

Nos. 1162A-1167 Overprinted

1989, Apr. 28

1026	A194	1c multicolored	.20	.20
1027	A194	2c multicolored	.20	.20
1028	A194	3c multicolored	.20	.20
1029	A194	4c multicolored	.20	.20
1030	A194	30c multicolored	.25	.25
1031	A194	60c multicolored	.50	.50
1032	A194	$1 multicolored	.80	.80
1033	A194	$4 multicolored	3.25	3.25
		Nos. 1026-1033 (8)	5.60	5.60

Souvenir Sheet

1034	A194	$5 multicolored	4.00	4.00

Nos. 1175-1176 Overprinted

1989, May 24

1035	A196	$1.50 Strip of 4, #a.-d.	4.75	4.75

Souvenir Sheet

1036	A196	$6 multicolored	4.75	4.75

Nos. 1177-1186 Overprinted

1989, May 29

1037	A197	10c multicolored	.20	.20
1038	A197	30c multicolored	.35	.35
1039	A197	40c multicolored	.50	.50
1040	A197	60c multicolored	.70	.70
1041	A197	$1 multicolored	1.25	1.25
1042	A197	$2 multicolored	2.25	2.25
1043	A197	$3 multicolored	3.50	3.50
1044	A197	$4 multicolored	4.75	4.75
		Nos. 1037-1044 (8)	13.50	13.50

Souvenir Sheets

1045	A197	$7 multi (#1185)	5.50	5.50
1046	A197	$7 multi (#1186)	5.50	5.50

Nos. 1187-1196 Overprinted

1989, Sept. 18

1047	A198	25c multicolored	.20	.20
1048	A198	45c multicolored	.30	.30
1049	A198	50c multicolored	.40	.40
1050	A198	60c multicolored	.45	.45
1051	A198	75c multicolored	.55	.55
1052	A198	90c multicolored	.65	.65
1053	A198	$3 multicolored	2.25	2.25
1054	A198	$4 multicolored	3.00	3.00
		Nos. 1047-1054 (8)	7.80	7.80

Souvenir Sheets

1055	A198	$6 multi (#1195)	4.50	4.50
1056	A198	$6 multi (#1196)	4.50	4.50

Nos. 1197-1206 Overprinted

1989, Dec. 14   *Perf. 14x13½*

1057	A199	25c multicolored	.20	.20
1058	A199	45c multicolored	.30	.30
1059	A199	50c multicolored	.40	.40
1060	A199	60c multicolored	.45	.45
1061	A199	$1 multicolored	.75	.75
1062	A199	$2 multicolored	1.50	1.50
1063	A199	$3 multicolored	2.25	2.25
1064	A199	$4 multicolored	3.00	3.00
		Nos. 1057-1064 (8)	8.85	8.85

Souvenir Sheets

1065	A199	$5 multi (#1205)	3.75	3.75
1066	A199	$5 multi (#1206)	3.75	3.75

Nos. 1217-1222 Overprinted

1989, Dec. 20   *Perf. 14*

1067	A201	15c multicolored	.20	.20
1068	A201	25c multicolored	.20	.20
1069	A201	$1 multicolored	.75	.75
1070	A201	$4 multicolored	3.00	3.00
		Nos. 1067-1070 (4)	4.15	4.15

Souvenir Sheets

1071	A201	$5 multi (#1221)	3.75	3.75
1072	A201	$5 multi (#1222)	3.75	3.75

Nos. 1264-1273 Overprinted

1989, Dec. 20

1073	A208	10c multicolored	.20	.20
1074	A208	25c multicolored	.20	.20
1075	A208	30c multicolored	.25	.25
1076	A208	50c multicolored	.40	.40
1077	A208	60c multicolored	.45	.45
1078	A208	70c multicolored	.50	.50
1079	A208	$4 multicolored	3.00	3.00
1080	A208	$5 multicolored	3.75	3.75
		Nos. 1073-1080 (8)	8.75	8.75

Souvenir Sheets

1081	A208	$5 multi (#1272)	3.75	3.75
1082	A208	$5 multi (#1273)	3.75	3.75

Nos. 1223-1232 Overprinted

1990, Feb. 21

1083	A202	10c multicolored	.20	.20
1084	A202	25c multicolored	.20	.20
1085	A202	50c multicolored	.40	.40
1086	A202	60c multicolored	.45	.45
1087	A202	75c multicolored	.55	.55
1088	A202	$1 multicolored	.75	.75
1089	A202	$3 multicolored	2.25	2.25
1090	A202	$4 multicolored	3.00	3.00
		Nos. 1083-1090 (8)	7.80	7.80

Souvenir Sheets

1091	A202	$6 multi (#1231)	4.50	4.50
1092	A202	$6 multi (#1232)	4.50	4.50

Nos. 1233-1237 Overprinted

1990, Mar. 30

1093	A203	25c multicolored	.20	.20
1094	A203	45c multicolored	.30	.30
1095	A203	60c multicolored	.45	.45
1096	A203	$4 multicolored	3.00	3.00
		Nos. 1093-1096 (4)	3.95	3.95

Souvenir Sheet

1097	A203	$5 multicolored	3.75	3.75

Nos. 1258-1262 Overprinted

1990, Mar. 30

1098	A206	10c multicolored	.20	.20
1099	A206	45c multicolored	.30	.30
1100	A206	$1 multicolored	.75	.75
1101	A206	$4 multicolored	3.00	3.00
		Nos. 1098-1101 (4)	4.25	4.25

Souvenir Sheet

1102	A206	$5 multicolored	3.75	3.75

Nos. 1275-1284 Overprinted

1990, June 6

1103	A210	10c multicolored	.20	.20
1104	A210	20c multicolored	.20	.20
1105	A210	25c multicolored	.20	.20
1106	A210	45c multicolored	.30	.30
1107	A210	60c multicolored	.45	.45
1108	A210	$2 multicolored	1.50	1.50
1109	A210	$3 multicolored	2.25	2.25
1110	A210	$4 multicolored	3.00	3.00
		Nos. 1103-1110 (8)	8.10	8.10

Souvenir Sheets

1111	A210	$5 multi (#1283)	3.75	3.75
1112	A210	$5 multi (#1284)	3.75	3.75

Nos. 1285-1294 Overprinted

1990, July 12

1113	A211	15c multicolored	.20	.20
1114	A211	45c multicolored	.30	.30
1115	A211	50c multicolored	.40	.40
1116	A211	60c multicolored	.45	.45
1117	A211	$1 multicolored	.75	.75
1118	A211	$2 multicolored	1.50	1.50
1119	A211	$3 multicolored	2.25	2.25
1120	A211	$5 multicolored	3.75	3.75
		Nos. 1113-1120 (8)	9.60	9.60

Souvenir Sheets

1121	A211	$6 multi (#1293)	4.50	4.50
1122	A211	$6 multi (#1294)	4.50	4.50

Nos. 1295-1304 Overprinted

1990, Aug. 14

1123	A212	10c multicolored	.20	.20
1124	A212	15c multicolored	.20	.20
1125	A212	50c multicolored	.40	.40
1126	A212	60c multicolored	.45	.45
1127	A212	$1 multicolored	.75	.75
1128	A212	$2 multicolored	1.50	1.50
1129	A212	$3 multicolored	2.25	2.25
1130	A212	$4 multicolored	3.00	3.00
		Nos. 1123-1130 (8)	8.75	8.75

Souvenir Sheets

1131	A212	$5 multi (#1303)	3.75	3.75
1132	A212	$5 multi (#1304)	3.75	3.75

Barbuda Nos. 888-889 Surcharged "1st Anniversary / Hurricane Hugo / 16th September, 1989-1990"

1990, Sept. 17   *Perf. 15*

1133	A50	$5 on $7.50	3.75	3.75
1134	A50	$7.50 on $10	5.50	5.50

Nos. 1324-1328 Overprinted

1990, Oct. 12   *Perf. 14*

1135	A217	15c multicolored	.20	.20
1136	A217	35c multicolored	.30	.30
1137	A217	75c multicolored	.55	.55
1138	A217	$3 multicolored	2.25	2.25
		Nos. 1135-1138 (4)	3.30	3.30

Souvenir Sheet

1139	A217	$6 multicolored	4.50	4.50

No. 1313 Ovptd. in Silver Miniature Sheet

1990, Dec. 14

1140	A215	45c Sheet of 20, #a.-t.	6.75	6.75

Nos. 1360-1369 Overprinted

1990, Dec. 14   *Perf. 14x13½, 13½x14*

1141	A221	25c multicolored	.20	.20
1142	A221	30c multicolored	.25	.25
1143	A221	40c multicolored	.30	.30
1144	A221	60c multicolored	.45	.45
1145	A221	$1 multicolored	.75	.75
1146	A221	$2 multicolored	1.50	1.50
1147	A221	$4 multicolored	3.00	3.00
1148	A221	$5 multicolored	3.75	3.75
		Nos. 1141-1148 (8)	10.20	10.20

Souvenir Sheets

1149	A221	$6 multi (#1368)	4.50	4.50
1150	A221	$6 multi (#1369)	4.50	4.50

Nos. 1305-1308 Overprinted

1991, Feb. 4   *Perf. 15x14*

1151	A213	45c green	.35	.35
1152	A213	60c bright rose	.45	.45
1153	A213	$5 bright ultra	3.75	3.75
		Nos. 1151-1153 (3)	4.55	4.55

Souvenir Sheet

1154	A213	$6 black	4.50	4.50

Nos. 1309-1312 Overprinted

1991, Feb. 4   *Perf. 13½*

1155	A214	50c red & deep grn	.40	.40
1156	A214	75c red & vio brn	.60	.60
1157	A214	$4 red & brt ultra	3.00	3.00
		Nos. 1155-1157 (3)	4.00	4.00

Souvenir Sheet

1158	A214	$6 red & black	4.50	4.50

Birds — B52

1991, Mar. 25   Litho.   *Perf. 14*

1164	B52	60c Troupial	.45	.45
1168	B52	$2 Christmas bird	1.50	1.50
1169	B52	$4 Rose-breasted grosbeak	3.00	3.00
1171	B52	$7 Stolid flycatcher	5.25	5.25
		Nos. 1164-1171 (4)	10.20	10.20

This is an expanding set. Numbers will change.

Nos. 1329-1333 Overprinted

1991, Apr. 23   Litho.   *Perf. 14*

1173	A218	50c multicolored	.40	.40
1174	A218	75c multicolored	.55	.55
1175	A218	$1 multicolored	.75	.75
1176	A218	$5 multicolored	3.75	3.75
		Nos. 1173-1176 (4)	5.45	5.45

Souvenir Sheet

1177	A218	$6 multicolored	4.50	4.50

Nos. 1350-1359 Overprinted

1991, Apr. 23

1178	A220	10c multicolored	.20	.20
1179	A220	25c multicolored	.20	.20
1180	A220	50c multicolored	.40	.40
1181	A220	60c multicolored	.45	.45
1182	A220	$1 multicolored	.75	.75
1183	A220	$2 multicolored	1.50	1.50
1184	A220	$3 multicolored	2.25	2.25
1185	A220	$4 multicolored	3.00	3.00
		Nos. 1178-1185 (8)	8.75	8.75

Souvenir Sheets

1186	A220	$6 multi (#1358)	4.50	4.50
1187	A220	$6 multi (#1359)	4.50	4.50

Nos. 1370-1379 Overprinted

1991, June 21   *Perf. 14x13½*

1188	A222	10c multicolored	.20	.20
1189	A222	45c multicolored	.35	.35
1190	A222	50c multicolored	.40	.40
1191	A222	60c multicolored	.45	.45
1192	A222	$1 multicolored	.75	.75
1193	A222	$2 multicolored	1.50	1.50
1194	A222	$3 multicolored	2.25	2.25
1195	A222	$4 multicolored	3.00	3.00
		Nos. 1188-1195 (8)	8.90	8.90

Souvenir Sheets

1196	A222	$6 multi (#1378)	4.50	4.50
1197	A222	$6 multi (#1379)	4.50	4.50

Nos. 1380-1390 Overprinted

1991, July 25   Litho.   *Perf. 14*

1198	A223	10c multicolored	.20	.20
1199	A223	15c multicolored	.20	.20
1200	A223	25c multicolored	.20	.20
1201	A223	45c multicolored	.35	.35
1202	A223	50c multicolored	.40	.40
1203	A223	$1 multicolored	.75	.75
1204	A223	$2 multicolored	1.50	1.50
1205	A223	$4 multicolored	3.00	3.00
1206	A223	$5 multicolored	3.75	3.75
		Nos. 1198-1206 (9)	10.35	10.35

Souvenir Sheets

1207	A223	$6 multi (#1389)	4.50	4.50
1208	A223	$6 multi (#1390)	4.50	4.50

Nos. 1411-1420 Overprinted

1991, Aug. 26   Litho.   *Perf. 14*

1209	A226	10c multicolored	.20	.20
1210	A226	15c multicolored	.20	.20
1211	A226	45c multicolored	.35	.35
1212	A226	60c multicolored	.45	.45
1213	A226	$1 multicolored	.75	.75
1214	A226	$2 multicolored	1.50	1.50
1215	A226	$4 multicolored	3.00	3.00
1216	A226	$5 multicolored	3.75	3.75
		Nos. 1209-1216 (8)	10.20	10.20

Souvenir Sheets

1217	A226	$6 multi (#1419)	4.50	4.50
1218	A226	$6 multi (#1420)	4.50	4.50

Nos. 1401-1410 Overprinted

1991, Oct. 18				
1219	A225	10c multicolored	.20	.20
1220	A225	35c multicolored	.25	.25
1221	A225	50c multicolored	.40	.40
1222	A225	75c multicolored	.55	.55
1223	A225	$1 multicolored	.75	.75
1224	A225	$2 multicolored	1.50	1.50
1225	A225	$4 multicolored	3.00	3.00
1226	A225	$5 multicolored	3.75	3.75
		Nos. 1219-1226 (8)	10.40	10.40
		Souvenir Sheets		
1227	A225	$6 multi (#1409)	4.50	4.50
1228	A225	$6 multi (#1410)	4.50	4.50

Nos. 1446-1455 Overprinted

1991, Nov. 18				
1229	CD347	10c multicolored	.20	.20
1230	CD347	15c multicolored	.20	.20
1231	CD347	20c multicolored	.20	.20
1232	CD347	40c multicolored	.30	.30
1233	CD347	$1 multicolored	.85	.85
1234	CD347	$2 multicolored	1.50	1.50
1235	CD347	$4 multicolored	3.00	3.00
1236	CD347	$5 multicolored	3.75	3.75
		Nos. 1229-1236 (8)	10.00	10.00
		Souvenir Sheets		
1237	CD347	$4 multi (#1454)	3.00	3.00
1238	CD347	$4 multi (#1455)	3.00	3.00

Nos. 1503-1510 Overprinted

1991, Dec. 24			**Perf. 12**	
1239	A238	10c multicolored	.20	.20
1240	A238	30c multicolored	.25	.25
1241	A238	40c multicolored	.30	.30
1242	A238	60c multicolored	.45	.45
1243	A238	$1 multicolored	.80	.80
1244	A238	$3 multicolored	2.25	2.25
1245	A238	$4 multicolored	3.00	3.00
1246	A238	$5 multicolored	3.75	3.75
		Nos. 1239-1246 (8)	11.00	11.00

Nos. 1421-1435 Overprinted

1992, Feb. 20			**Perf. 13½**	
1249	A227	5c multicolored	.20	.20
1250	A227	10c multicolored	.20	.20
1251	A227	15c multicolored	.20	.20
1252	A227	25c multicolored	.20	.20
1253	A227	30c multicolored	.25	.25
1254	A227	40c multicolored	.30	.30
1255	A227	50c multicolored	.40	.40
1256	A227	75c multicolored	.55	.55
1257	A227	$2 multicolored	1.50	1.50
1258	A227	$3 multicolored	2.25	2.25
1259	A227	$4 multicolored	3.00	3.00
1260	A227	$5 multicolored	3.75	3.75
		Nos. 1249-1260 (12)	12.80	12.80
		Size: 102x76mm		
		Imperf		
1261	A227	$5 multi (#1433)	3.75	3.75
1262	A227	$5 multi (#1434)	3.75	3.75
1263	A227	$6 multi	4.50	4.50

Nos. 1476-1483 Overprinted

1992, Apr. 7		**Litho.**	**Perf. 14**	
1264	A231	10c multicolored	.20	.20
1265	A231	15c multi, vert.	.20	.20
1266	A231	45c multi, vert.	.35	.35
1267	A231	60c multi, vert.	.45	.45
1268	A231	$1 multi	.75	.75
1269	A231	$2 multi	1.50	1.50
1270	A231	$4 multi	3.00	3.00
1271	A231	$5 multi, vert.	3.75	3.75
		Nos. 1264-1271 (8)	10.20	10.20

Nos. 1484-1485 Overprinted

1992, Apr. 7		**Litho.**	**Perf. 14**	
		Souvenir Sheets		
1272	A231	$6 multi (#1484)	5.00	5.00
1273	A231	$6 multi (#1485)	5.00	5.00

Nos. 1551-1560 Overprinted

1992, Apr. 16		**Litho.**	**Perf. 14x13½**	
1274	A242	10c multicolored	.20	.20
1275	A242	15c multicolored	.20	.20
1276	A242	30c multicolored	.25	.25
1277	A242	40c multicolored	.35	.35
1278	A242	$1 multicolored	.85	.85
1279	A242	$2 multicolored	1.60	1.60
1280	A242	$4 multicolored	3.25	3.25
1281	A242	$4 multicolored	4.25	4.25
		Nos. 1274-1281 (8)	10.95	10.95
		Souvenir Sheets		
1282	A242	$6 multi (#1559)	5.00	5.00
1283	A242	$6 multi (#1560)	5.00	5.00

Nos. 1489-1492 Overprinted

1992, June 19		**Litho.**	**Perf. 14**	
1284	A234	75c multi	.55	.55
1285	A234	$2 multi, vert.	1.50	1.50
1286	A234	$3.50 multi	2.75	2.75
		Nos. 1284-1286 (3)	4.80	4.80
		Souvenir Sheet		
1287	A234	$5 multi, vert.	4.25	4.25

Nos. 1493-1494 Overprinted

1992, June 19				
1288	A235	$1.50 multi	1.10	1.10
1289	A235	$4 multi	3.00	3.00

Nos. 1495-1496 Overprinted

1992, June 19				
1290	A236	$2 multi	1.50	1.50
1291	A236	$2.50 multi, vert.	1.90	1.90

Nos. 1499-1502 Overprinted

1992, June 19				
1292	A237	25c multicolored	.20	.20
1293	A237	$2 multicolored	1.50	1.50
1294	A237	$3 multicolored	2.25	2.25
1295	A237	$4 multicolored	3.50	3.50
		Nos. 1292-1295 (4)	7.45	7.45

Nos. 1571-1578 Overprinted

1992, Oct. 12		**Litho.**	**Perf. 14**	
1296	A244	15c multicolored	.20	.20
1297	A244	30c multicolored	.25	.25
1298	A244	40c multicolored	.30	.30
1299	A244	$1 multicolored	.75	.75
1300	A244	$2 multicolored	1.50	1.50
1301	A244	$4 multicolored	3.00	3.00
		Nos. 1296-1301 (6)	6.00	6.00
		Souvenir Sheets		
1302	A244	$6 multi	4.50	4.50
1303	A244	$6 multi	4.50	4.50

Nos. 1599-1600 Overprinted

1992, Oct. 12			**Perf. 14½**	
1304	A247	$1 multicolored	.75	.75
1305	A247	$2 multicolored	1.50	1.50

Nos. 1513-1518 Overprinted

1992, Nov. 3			**Perf. 14**	
1306	CD348	10c multicolored	.20	.20
1307	CD348	30c multicolored	.25	.25
1308	CD348	$1 multicolored	.80	.80
1309	CD348	$5 multicolored	3.75	3.75
		Nos. 1306-1309 (4)	5.00	5.00
		Souvenir Sheets		
1310	CD348	$6 multi (#1517)	4.50	4.50
1311	CD348	$6 multi (#1518)	4.50	4.50

Nos. 1541-1550 Ovptd. "BARBUDA / MAIL"

1992, Dec. 8				
1312	A241	10c multicolored	.20	.20
1313	A241	15c multicolored	.20	.20
1314	A241	30c multicolored	.25	.25
1315	A241	50c multicolored	.40	.40
1316	A241	$1 multicolored	.75	.75
1317	A241	$2 multicolored	1.50	1.50
1318	A241	$4 multicolored	3.00	3.00
1319	A241	$5 multicolored	3.75	3.75
		Nos. 1312-1319 (8)	10.05	10.05
		Souvenir Sheets		
1320	A241	$6 multi (#1549)	5.50	5.50
1321	A241	$6 multi (#1550)	5.50	5.50

Nos. 1609-1618 Ovptd. "BARBUDA MAIL"

1992, Dec. 8		**Litho.**	**Perf. 13½x14**	
1322	A251	10c multicolored	.20	.20
1323	A251	25c multicolored	.20	.20
1324	A251	30c multicolored	.25	.25
1325	A251	40c multicolored	.30	.30
1326	A251	60c multicolored	.45	.45
1327	A251	$1 multicolored	.75	.75
1328	A251	$4 multicolored	3.00	3.00
1329	A251	$5 multicolored	3.75	3.75
		Nos. 1322-1329 (8)	8.90	8.90
		Souvenir Sheets		
1330	A251	$6 multi (#1616)	5.50	5.50
1331	A251	$6 multi (#1617)	5.50	5.50

No. 1601 Ovptd. "BARBUDA MAIL"

1992		**Litho.**	**Perf. 14**	
		Souvenir Sheet		
1332	A248	$6 multicolored	4.50	4.50

Nos. 1519-1528 Ovptd.

1993, Jan. 25		**Litho.**	**Perf. 14**	
1333	A239	10c multicolored	.20	.20
1334	A239	15c multicolored	.20	.20
1335	A239	30c multicolored	.30	.30
1336	A239	40c multicolored	.35	.35
1337	A239	$1 multicolored	.90	.90
1338	A239	$2 multicolored	1.75	1.75
1339	A239	$4 multicolored	3.50	3.50
1340	A239	$5 multicolored	4.50	4.50
		Nos. 1332-1339 (8)	11.70	11.70
		Souvenir Sheets		
1341	A239	$6 multi (#1527)	5.50	5.50
1342	A239	$6 multi (#1528)	5.50	5.50

Nos. 1561-1570 Ovptd.

1993, Mar. 22		**Litho.**	**Perf. 13**	
1343	A243	10c multicolored	.20	.20
1344	A243	15c multicolored	.20	.20
1345	A243	30c multicolored	.25	.25
1346	A243	40c multicolored	.30	.30
1347	A243	$1 multicolored	.80	.80
1348	A243	$2 multicolored	1.50	1.50
1349	A243	$4 multicolored	3.00	3.00
1350	A243	$5 multicolored	3.75	3.75
		Nos. 1343-1350 (8)	10.00	10.00
		Imperf		
		Size: 120x95mm		
1351	A243	$6 multi (#1569)	5.50	5.50
1352	A243	$6 multi (#1570)	5.50	5.50

Nos. 1589-1598 Ovptd.

1993, May 10		**Litho.**	**Perf. 14**	
1353	A246	10c multicolored	.20	.20
1354	A246	25c multicolored	.20	.20
1355	A246	45c multicolored	.35	.35
1356	A246	60c multicolored	.45	.45
1357	A246	$1 multicolored	.75	.75
1358	A246	$2 multicolored	1.50	1.50
1359	A246	$4 multicolored	3.00	3.00
1360	A246	$5 multicolored	3.75	3.75
		Nos. 1353-1360 (8)	10.20	10.20
		Souvenir Sheets		
1361	A246	$6 multi (#1597)	5.50	5.50
1362	A246	$6 multi (#1598)	5.50	5.50

Nos. 1603-1608 Ovptd.

1993, June 29		**Litho.**	**Perf. 14**	
1363	A250	10c multicolored	.20	.20
1364	A250	25c multicolored	.25	.25
1365	A250	30c multicolored	.30	.30
1366	A250	40c multicolored	.35	.35
1367	A250	60c multicolored	.55	.55
1368	A250	$1 multicolored	.90	.90
1369	A250	$4 multicolored	3.50	3.50
1370	A250	$5 multicolored	4.50	4.50
		Nos. 1363-1370 (8)	10.55	10.55
		Souvenir Sheets		
1371	A250	$6 multi (#1607)	5.50	5.50
1372	A250	$6 multi (#1608)	5.50	5.50

Nos. 1619-1632 Ovptd.

1993, Aug. 16		**Litho.**	**Perf. 14**	
1373	A252	10c multicolored	.20	.20
1374	A252	40c multicolored	.30	.30
1375	A253	45c multicolored	.35	.35
1376	A252	75c multicolored	.60	.60
1377	A252	$1 multicolored	.75	.75
1378	A252	$1.50 multicolored	1.10	1.10
1379	A252	$2 multicolored	1.50	1.50
1380	A253	$2 multi (#1626)	1.50	1.50
1381	A253	$2 multi (#1627)	1.50	1.50
1382	A252	$2.25 multicolored	1.75	1.75
1383	A252	$3 multicolored	2.25	2.25
1384	A252	$4 multi (#1630)	3.00	3.00
1385	A253	$4 multi (#1631)	3.00	3.00
1386	A252	$6 multicolored	4.50	4.50
		Nos. 1373-1386 (14)	22.30	22.30

Numbers have been reserved for four souvenir sheets in this set.

Nos. 1650-1659 Ovptd.

1993, Sept. 21		**Litho.**	**Perf. 14**	
1391	A256	15c multicolored	.20	.20
1392	A256	25c multicolored	.20	.20
1393	A256	30c multicolored	.25	.25
1394	A256	40c multicolored	.35	.35
1395	A256	$1 multicolored	.75	.75
1396	A256	$2 multicolored	1.50	1.50
1397	A256	$4 multicolored	3.00	3.00
1398	A256	$5 multicolored	3.75	3.75
		Nos. 1391-1398 (8)	10.00	10.00
		Souvenir Sheets		
1399	A256	$6 multi (#1658)	6.50	6.50
1400	A256	$6 multi (#1659)	6.50	6.50

No. 1660 Ovptd.

1993, Nov. 11		**Litho.**	**Perf. 14**	
1401	A257	$1 Sheet of 12, #a.-l.	9.00	9.00

Numbers have been reserved for two souvenir sheets in this set.

Nos. 1697-1710 Ovptd.

1994, Mar. 3		**Litho.**	**Perf. 14**	
1404-1415	A267	$2 Set of 12	18.00	18.00
		Souvenir Sheets		
1416-1417	A267	$6 each	4.50	4.50

Nos. 1676-1678 Ovptd.

1994, Apr. 21		**Litho.**	**Perf. 14**	
1418	A260	40c multicolored	.30	.30
1419	A260	$3 multicolored	2.25	2.25
		Souvenir Sheet		
1420	A260	$6 multicolored	4.50	4.50

Nos. 1679-1682 Ovptd.

1994, Apr. 21				
1421-1423	A261	Set of 3	4.50	4.50
		Souvenir Sheet		
1424	A261	$6 multicolored	4.50	4.50

Nos. 1683-1685 Ovptd.

1994, Apr. 21				
1425	A262	40c multicolored	.30	.30
1426	A262	$4 multicolored	3.25	3.25
		Souvenir Sheet		
1427	A262	$5 multicolored	3.75	3.75

Nos. 1686-1688 Ovptd.

1994, Apr. 21				
1428	A263	30c multicolored	.25	.25
1429	A263	$4 multicolored	3.25	3.25
		Souvenir Sheet		
1430	A263	$6 multicolored	4.50	4.50

Nos. 1692-1693 Ovptd.

1994, Apr. 21				
1431	A265	$5 multicolored	4.00	4.00
		Souvenir Sheet		
1432	A265	$6 multicolored	4.50	4.50

Nos. 1694-1696 Ovptd.

1994, Apr. 21				
1433	A266	15c multicolored	.20	.20
1434	A266	$5 multicolored	4.00	4.00
		Souvenir Sheet		
1435	A266	$6 multicolored	4.50	4.50

Nos. 1732-1735 Ovptd.

1994, Apr. 21				
1436-1439	A270	Set of 4	1.10	1.10

Nos. 1711-1720 Ovptd.

1994, June 15				
1440-1446	A268	Set of 7	12.00	12.00
		Souvenir Sheets		
1447-1449	A268	$6 each	4.50	4.50

Nos. 1736-1741 Ovptd.

1994, June 15				
1450-1453	A271	30c Set of 4	7.25	7.25
		Souvenir Sheets		
1454-1455	A271	$6 each	4.50	4.50

Nos. 1689-1691 Ovptd.

1994, Sept. 21		**Litho.**	**Perf. 14**	
1456	A264	$1 multicolored	.75	.75
1457	A264	$3 multicolored	2.25	2.25
		Souvenir Sheet		
1458	A264	$6 multicolored	4.50	4.50

Nos. 1786-1795 Ovptd.

1994, Sept. 21		**Litho.**	**Perf. 14**	
1459-1466	A279	Set of 8	10.00	10.00
		Souvenir Sheets		
1467-1468	A279	$6 each	4.50	4.50

Nos. 1776-1779 Ovptd.

1994, Nov. 3		**Litho.**	**Perf. 14**	
1469	A277	$1.50 multi (#1776)	9.00	9.00
1470	A277	$1.50 multi (#1777)	9.00	9.00
		Souvenir Sheets		
1471	A277	$1.50 multi (#1778)	1.10	1.10
1472	A277	$1.50 multi (#1779)	1.10	1.10

Nos. 1835-1842 Ovptd.

1995, Jan. 12		**Litho.**	**Perf. 14**	
1473-1478	A291	Set of 6	8.50	8.50
		Souvenir Sheets		
1479	A291	$6 multi (#1841)	4.50	4.50
1480	A291	$6 multi (#1842)	4.50	4.50

Nos. 1857-1866 Ovptd.

1995, Jan. 12		**Litho.**	**Perf. 14**	
1481-1488	A295	Set of 8	6.75	6.75
		Souvenir Sheets		
		Perf. 13½x14		
1489	A295	$6 multi (#1865)	4.50	4.50
1490	A295	$6 multi (#1866)	4.50	4.50

Nos. 1829-1834 Ovptd.

1996, Feb. 14		**Litho.**	**Perf. 14**	
1491	A290	75c multi (#1829)	5.50	5.50
1492	A290	75c multi (#1830)	5.50	5.50
1493	A290	75c multi (#1831)	5.50	5.50
		Souvenir Sheets		
1494	A290	$6 multi (#1832)	5.50	5.50
1495	A290	$6 multi (#1833)	5.50	5.50
1496	A290	$6 multi (#1834)	5.50	5.50

644

BARBUDA

Nos. 1867-1881 Ovptd.
1995 Litho. *Perf. 14½x14*
1497 A296 15c multi (#1867) .20 .20
1498 A296 25c multi (#1868) .20 .20
1499 A296 35c multi (#1869) .30 .30
1500 A296 40c multi (#1870) .35 .35
1501 A296 45c multi (#1871) .40 .40
1502 A296 60c multi (#1872) .55 .55
1503 A296 65c multi (#1873) .60 .60
1504 A296 70c multi (#1873) .65 .65
1505 A296 75c multi (#1874) .70 .70
1506 A296 90c multi (#1875) .80 .80
1507 A296 $1.20 multi (#1876) 1.10 1.10
1508 A296 $2 multi (#1877) 1.75 1.75
1509 A296 $5 multi (#1878) 4.50 4.50
1510 A296 $10 multi (#1879) 9.00 9.00
1511 A296 $20 multi (#1880) 18.00 18.00
Nos. 1497-1511 (15) 39.10 39.10

Nos. 1806-1808 Ovptd.
1996, Jan. 22 *Perf. 14*
1512 A281 50c Sheet of 9, #a.-i. 3.50 3.50
Souvenir Sheets
1513 A281 $6 multi (#1807) 4.50 4.50
1514 A281 $6 multi (#1808) 4.50 4.50

Nos. 1949-1956 Ovptd.
1996, Jan. 22 *Perf. 13½x14*
1515-1520 A314 Set of 6 6.75 6.75
Souvenir Sheets
1521 A314 $5 multi (#1955) 3.75 3.75
1522 A314 $6 multi (#1956) 4.50 4.50

Nos. 1810-1813 Ovptd.
1995, Sept. 29 Litho. *Perf. 14*
1546-1548 A283 Set of 3 4.00 4.00
Souvenir Sheet
1549 A283 $6 multi (on #1813) 5.50 5.50

End of World War II, 50th Anniv. — B53

Design: German bombers over St. Paul's Cathedral, London.

1995, Nov. 13 Litho. *Perf. 13*
1550 B53 $8 multicolored 6.00 6.00
For overprints and surcharges see #1639, B3.

Queen Elizabeth, the Queen Mother, 95th Birthday B54

1995, Nov. 20
1551 B54 $7.50 multicolored 5.50 5.50
For overprints and surcharges see #1638, B2.

United Nations, 50th Anniv. — B55

1995, Nov. 27
1552 B55 $8 New York City 6.00 6.00
For surcharge see #B4.

Nos. 1848, 1851, 1854-1856 Ovptd.
1996, Feb. 14 Litho. *Perf. 14*
1553 A294 15c multi (#1848) .20 .20
1554 A294 $1 multi (#1851) .75 .75
1555 A294 $4 multi (#1854) 3.00 3.00
Nos. 1553-1555 (3) 3.95 3.95
Souvenir Sheets
1556 A294 $6 multi (#1855) 4.50 4.50
1557 A294 $6 multi (#1856) 4.50 4.50

Nos. 1882-1890 Ovptd.
1996, June 13 Litho. *Perf. 14*
1558-1563 A297 Set of 6 7.50 7.50
1564 A297 75c Sheet of 12, #a-l 8.25 8.25
Souvenir Sheets
1565 A297 $6 multi (#1889) 5.50 5.50
1566 A297 $6 multi (#1890) 5.50 5.50

Nos. 1891-1898 Ovptd.
1996, July 16 *Perf. 14*
1567-1572 A298 Set of 6 7.00 7.00
Souvenir Sheets
1573 A298 $6 multi (#1897) 5.00 5.00
1574 A298 $6 multi (#1898) 5.00 5.00

Nos. 1930-1933 Ovptd.
1996, Sept. 10
1575-1576 A310 Strip of 3, #a.-c., each 3.00 3.00
Souvenir Sheets
1577 A310 $6 multi (#1932) 5.00 5.00
1578 A310 $6 multi (#1933) 5.00 5.00

Nos. 1945-1948 Ovptd.
1996, Oct. 25 Litho. *Perf. 14*
1579 A313 $1 Sheet of 9, #a.-i. (#1945) 8.00 8.00
1580 A313 $1 Sheet of 9, #a.-i. (#1946) 8.00 8.00
Souvenir Sheets
1581 A313 $6 multi (#1947) 5.25 5.25
1582 A313 $6 multi (#1948) 5.25 5.25

Nos. 2001-2002 Ovptd.
1996, Nov. 14 *Perf. 13½x14*
1583 A323 $2 Strip of 3, #a.-c. 5.25 5.25
Souvenir Sheet
1584 A323 $6 multicolored 5.25 5.25

Nos. 2018-2025 Ovptd.
1997, Jan. 28 Litho. *Perf. 13½x14*
1585-1590 A328 Set of 6 6.50 6.50
Souvenir Sheets
1591 A328 $6 multi (#2024) 5.50 5.50
1592 A328 $6 multi (#2025) 5.50 5.50

Nos. 1905-1906 Ovptd.
1997, Feb. 24 *Perf. 14*
1593 A301 Strip of 3, #a.-c. 2.50 2.50
Souvenir Sheet
1594 A301 $6 multicolored 5.50 5.50

Nos. 1907-1908 Ovptd.
1997, Feb. 24
1595 A302 $5 multicolored 4.50 4.50
Souvenir Sheet
1596 A302 $6 multicolored 5.50 5.50

Nos. 1899-1902 Ovptd.
Sheets of 6 or 8 + Label
1997, Apr. 4 Litho. *Perf. 14*
1597 A299 $1.20 #a.-f. 6.50 6.50
1598 A299 $1.20 #a.-h. 8.50 8.50
Souvenir Sheets
1599 A299 $3 multicolored 2.75 2.75
1600 A299 $6 multicolored 5.50 5.50

Nos. 1903-1904 Ovptd.
1997 Litho. *Perf. 14*
1601 A300 Strip of 3, #a.-c. 2.50 2.50
Souvenir Sheet
1602 A300 $6 multicolored 5.50 5.50

Nos. 1909-1910 Ovptd.
1997 *Perf. 13½x14*
1603 A303 $1.50 Strip or block of 4, #a.-d. 5.50 5.50
Souvenir Sheet
1604 A303 $6 multicolored 5.50 5.50

Nos. 1913-1917 Ovptd.
1997 Litho. *Perf. 14*
1605-1608 A305 Set of 4 5.00 5.00
Souvenir Sheet
1609 A305 $6 multicolored 5.50 5.50

Nos. 1918-1919 Ovptd.
1997
1610 A306 45c Sheet of 12, #a-l 4.75 4.75
Souvenir Sheet
1611 A306 $6 multicolored 5.50 5.50

Nos. 1928-1929 Ovptd.
1997
1612 A309 75c Sheet of 12, #a-l 8.00 8.00
Souvenir Sheet
1613 A309 $6 multicolored 5.50 5.50

Nos. 1934-1942 Ovptd.
1997, May 30 Litho. *Perf. 14*
1614-1619 A311 Set of 6 7.50 7.50
Sheet of 9
1620 A311 $1.20 #a.-i. 8.25 8.25
Souvenir Sheets
1621 A311 $6 multi (#1941) 4.50 4.50
1621A A311 $6 multi (#1942) 4.50 4.50

Nos. 1911-1912 Ovptd.
1997 Litho. *Perf. 14*
1622 A304 75c Sheet of 12, #a-l 8.00 8.00
Souvenir Sheet
1623 A304 $6 multicolored 5.50 5.50

Nos. 1943-1944 Ovptd.
1997
1624 A312 75c Sheet of 12, #a-l 8.00 8.00
Souvenir Sheet
1625 A312 $6 multicolored 5.50 5.50

Nos. 1967-1970 Ovptd.
1997
1626-1627 A317 75c Strips of 4, #a.-d., each 2.75 2.75
Souvenir Sheets
1628 A317 $6 multi (#1969) 5.50 5.50
1629 A317 $6 multi (#1970) 5.50 5.50

Nos. 1970A-1974 Ovptd.
1997, Nov. 3 Litho. *Perf. 14*
1629A-1629F A318 Set of 6 2.50 2.50
Sheets of 6
1629G A318 $1.20 #k.-p. (#1971) 5.50 5.50
1629H A318 $1.50 #q.-v. (#1972) 6.75 6.75
Souvenir Sheets
1629I A318 $6 multi (#1973) 4.50 4.50
1629J A318 $6 multi (#1974) 4.50 4.50

Nos. 2111-2118 Ovptd.
1997 Litho. *Perf. 14*
1630-1635 A345 Set of 6 5.25 5.25
Souvenir Sheets
1636 A345 $6 multi (#2117) 4.50 4.50
1637 A345 $6 multi (#2118) 4.50 4.50

Nos. 2069-2070 Ovptd.
1997, Nov. 3 Litho. *Perf. 14*
Sheet of 6
1637A A337 $1 #c.-h. (#2069) 4.50 4.50
Souvenir Sheet
1637B A337 $6 multi (#2070) 4.50 4.50

Nos. 1550-1551 Ovptd. in Gold
"Golden Wedding of
H.M. Queen Elizabeth II
and H.R.H. Prince Phillip
1947-1997"
1997, July 25 Litho. *Perf. 13*
1638 B54 $7.50 on #1551 5.50 5.50
1639 B53 $8 on #1550 6.00 6.00

Nos. 1983-1986 Ovptd.
1998 Litho. *Perf. 14*
1640 A320 75c Vert. strip, #a.-d. (#1983) 2.75 2.75
1641 A320 75c Vert. strip, #a.-d. (#1984) 2.75 2.75
Souvenir Sheets
1643 A320 $5 multicolored 4.50 4.50
1644 A320 $6 multicolored 5.50 5.50

Nos. 2003-2004 Ovptd.
1998 Litho. *Perf. 14*
1645 A324 60c Block of 4, #a.-d. 2.00 2.00
Souvenir Sheet
1646 A324 $6 multi 5.25 5.25

Nos. 2094-2102 Ovptd.
1998
1647-1652 A342 Set of 6 5.75 5.75
1653 A342 $1 Sheet of 8 + label 6.75 6.75
Souvenir Sheets
1654 A342 $6 multi (#2101) 5.25 5.25
1655 A342 $6 multi (#2102) 5.25 5.25

Nos. 2005-2008 Ovptd.
1998 Litho. *Perf. 14*
1656-1658 A325 Set of 3 2.50 2.50
Souvenir Sheet
1659 A325 $6 multicolored 5.25 5.25

Nos. 2009-2012 Ovptd.
1998
1660-1662 A326 Set of 3 2.50 2.50
Souvenir Sheet
1663 A326 $6 multicolored 5.25 5.25

Nos. 2119-2122 Ovptd.
1998 Litho. *Perf. 14*
Sheets of 6
1664 A346 $1.65 #a.-f. (#2119) 8.50 8.50
1665 A346 $1.65 #a.-f. (#2120) 8.50 8.50
Souvenir Sheets
1666 A346 $6 multi (#2121) 5.25 5.25
1667 A346 $6 multi (#2122) 5.25 5.25

Nos. 2037-2038 Ovptd.
1998 Litho. *Perf. 14*
Sheet of 9
1668 A330 $1 #a.-i. (#2037) 7.75 7.75
Souvenir Sheet
1669 A330 $6 multi (#2038) 5.25 5.25

Nos. 2063-2064 Ovtpd.
1998
Sheet of 9
1670 A334 $1 #a.-i. (#2063) 7.75 7.75
Souvenir Sheet
1671 A334 $6 multi (#2064) 5.25 5.25

Nos. 2039-2047 Ovptd.
1998 Litho. *Perf. 14*
1672-1675 A331 Set of 4 4.75 4.75
Sheets of 9
1676 A331 $1.10 #a.-i. (#2043) 8.50 8.50
1677 A331 $1.10 #a.-i. (#2044) 8.50 8.50
Souvenir Sheets
1678-1680 A331 $6 each (#2045-2047) 5.25 5.25

Nos. 2140-2148 Ovptd.
1998
1681-1688 A349 Set of 8 6.50 6.50
Souvenir Sheet
1689 A349 $6 multi (#2148) 5.25 5.25

Nos. 2211-2219 Ovptd.
1998
1690-1696 A366 Set of 7 5.00 5.00
Souvenir Sheets
1697 A366 $6 multi (#2218) 5.25 5.25
1698 A366 $6 multi (#2219) 5.25 5.25

Nos. 2058-2062 Ovptd.
1998 Litho. *Perf. 14*
Sheets of 6
1699 A333 $1.20 #a.-f. (#2058) 5.50 5.50
1700 A333 $1.65 #a.-f. (#2059) 7.50 7.50
Souvenir Sheets
1701-1703 A333 $6 each (#2060-2062) 4.50 4.50

Nos. 2067-2068 Ovptd.
1999 Litho. *Perf. 14*
1704 A336 $1.75 Strip of 3, #a.-c. 5.50 5.50
Souvenir Sheet
1705 A336 $6 multi (#2068) 6.50 6.50

Nos. 2071-2072 Ovptd.
1999 *Perf. 13½x14*
1706 A338 $1.75 Sheet of 3, #a.-c. 4.25 4.25
Souvenir Sheet
1707 A338 $6 multi (#2072) 4.75 4.75

Nos. 2084-2093 Ovptd.

1999		**Litho.**	**Perf. 14**	
1708-1713	A341	Set of 6	4.25	4.25
		Sheets of 8		
1714	A341	$1.65 #a.-h. (#2090)	5.00	5.00
1715	A341	$1.65 #a.-h.,(#2091)	5.00	5.00
		Souvenir Sheets		
1716-1717	A341	$6 each (#2092-2093)	4.50	4.50

Nos. 2065-2066 Ovptd.

1999		**Litho.**	**Perf. 14**	
1718	A335	$1.75 multicolored	1.40	1.40
		Souvenir Sheet		
1719	A335	$6 multicolored	4.75	4.75

Nos. 2075-2083 Ovptd.

1999				
1720-1725	A340	Set of 6	4.00	4.00
		Sheet of 6		
1726	A340	$1.75 #a.-f.	8.00	8.00
		Souvenir Sheets		
1727	A340	$6 multi (#2082)	4.50	4.50
1728	A340	$6 multi (#2083)	4.50	4.50

No. 2184 Ovptd.

1999				
1729	A358	$1.20 multicolored	.90	.90

Nos. 2107-2110 Ovptd.

1999		**Litho.**	**Perf. 14**	
		Sheets of 6		
1730	A344	$1.65 #a.-f. (#2107)	7.50	7.50
1731	A344	$1.65 #a.-f. (#2108)	7.50	7.50
		Souvenir Sheets		
1732	A344	$6 brown (#2109)	4.50	4.50
1733	A344	$6 brown (#2110)	4.50	4.50

Nos. 2133-2139 Ovptd.

1999				
1734-1739	A348	Set of 6	4.25	4.25
		Souvenir Sheet		
1740	A348	$6 multi (#2139)	4.50	4.50

Nos. 2155-2161 Ovptd.

1999				
1741-1746	A351	Set of 6	3.25	3.25
		Souvenir Sheet		
1747	A351	$6 multi (#2161)	4.50	4.50

Nos. 2295-2301 Ovptd.

1999			**Perf. 13¾**	
1748-1753	A383	Set of 6	5.50	5.50
		Souvenir Sheet		
1754	A383	$6 multi (#2301)	4.50	4.50

Nos. 2103-2106 Ovptd.

2000		**Litho.**	**Perf. 14**	
		Sheets of 6		
1755	A343	$1.65 #a-f (#2103)	7.50	7.50
1756	A343	$1.65 #a-f (#2104)	7.50	7.50
		Souvenir Sheets		
1757	A343	$6 multi (#2105)	4.50	4.50
1758	A343	$6 multi (#2106)	4.50	4.50

Nos. 2123-2132 Ovptd.

2000				
1759-1764	A347	Set of 6	5.50	5.50
		Sheets of 6		
1765	A347	$1.65 #a-f (#2129)	7.50	7.50
1766	A347	$1.65 #a-f (#2130)	7.50	7.50
		Souvenir Sheets		
1767	A347	$6 multi (#2131)	4.50	4.50
1768	A347	$6 multi (#2132)	4.50	4.50

Nos. 2166-2170 Ovptd.

2000		**Litho.**	**Perf. 14x14½**	
		Sheets of 3		
1769	A353	$1.75 #a-c (#2166)	4.00	4.00
1770	A353	$1.75 #a-c (#2167)	4.00	4.00
		Souvenir Sheets		
1771	A353	$6 multi (#2168)	4.50	4.50
1772	A353	$6 multi (#2169)	4.50	4.50
1773	A353	$6 multi (#2170)	4.50	4.50

Nos. 2172-2175 Ovptd.

2000			**Perf. 14**	
		Sheets of 6		
1774	A355	$1.65 #a-f (#2172)	7.50	7.50
1775	A355	$1.65 #a-f (#2173)	7.50	7.50
		Souvenir Sheets		
1776	A355	$6 multi (#2174)	4.50	4.50
1777	A355	$6 multi (#2175)	4.50	4.50

Nos. 2194-2197 Ovptd.

2000				
1778-1780	A361	Set of 3	2.50	2.50
		Souvenir Sheet		
1781	A361	$6 multi	4.50	4.50

No. 2198 Ovptd.

2000			**Perf. 13½**	
1782	A362	$1 multi	.75	.75

SEMI-POSTAL STAMP

> Catalogue values for unused stamps in this section are for Never Hinged items.

Barbuda No. 501 Crudely Surcharged

S. Atlantic Fund + 50c

1982, June 28
Self-Adhesive

B1	CD331	Booklet	16.00

Nos. 1550-1552 Surcharged
"HURRICANE RELIEF" in Silver

1995, Nov.		**Litho.**	**Perf. 13**	
B2	B54	$7.50 +$1 on #1551	6.25	6.25
B3	B53	$8 +$1 on #1550	6.75	6.75
B4	B55	$8 +$1 on #1552	6.75	6.75
		Nos. B2-B4 (3)	19.75	19.75

BASUTOLAND

bə-'sü-tə-,land

LOCATION — An enclave in the state of South Africa
GOVT. — British Crown Colony
AREA — 11,716 sq. mi.
POP. — 733,000 (est. 1964)
CAPITAL — Maseru

The Colony, a former independent native state, was annexed to the Cape Colony in 1871. In 1883 control was transferred directly to the British Crown. Stamps of the Cape of Good Hope were used from 1871 to 1910 and those of the Union of South Africa from 1910 to 1933. Basutoland became the independent state of Lesotho on Oct. 4, 1966.

12 Pence = 1 Shilling
100 Cents = 1 Rand (1961)

> Catalogue values for unused stamps in this country are for Never Hinged items, beginning with Scott 29 in the regular postage section and Scott J1 in the postage due section.

George V — A1   George VI — A2

Crocodile and River Scene

Perf. 12½

1933, Dec. 1		**Engr.**	**Wmk. 4**	
1	A1	½p emerald	.60	1.25
2	A1	1p carmine	.70	.60
3	A1	2p red violet	.90	.60
4	A1	3p ultra	.80	1.00
5	A1	4p slate	1.90	6.25
6	A1	6p yellow	2.10	1.50
7	A1	1sh red orange	2.25	5.00
8	A1	2sh6p dk brown	18.00	50.00
9	A1	5sh violet	50.00	62.50
10	A1	10sh olive green	100.00	125.00
		Nos. 1-10 (10)	177.25	253.70
		Set, never hinged	325.00	

Common Design Types
pictured following the introduction.

Silver Jubilee Issue
Common Design Type

1935, May 4			**Perf. 13½x14**	
11	CD301	1p car & blue	.60	.35
12	CD301	2p gray blk & ultra	.90	1.00
13	CD301	3p blue & brown	3.25	2.75
14	CD301	6p brt vio & indigo	3.25	2.75
		Nos. 11-14 (4)	8.00	6.85
		Set, never hinged	12.50	

Coronation Issue
Common Design Type

1937, May 12			**Perf. 13½x14**	
15	CD302	1p carmine	.35	.30
16	CD302	2p rose violet	.50	.55
17	CD302	3p bright ultra	.60	.55
		Nos. 15-17 (3)	1.45	1.40
		Set, never hinged	1.90	

1938, Apr. 1			**Perf. 12½**	
18	A2	½p emerald	.30	.30
19	A2	1p rose car	.30	.20
20	A2	1½p light blue	.30	.20
21	A2	2p rose lilac	.30	.30
22	A2	3p ultra	.35	.35
23	A2	4p gray	.45	1.25
24	A2	6p yel ocher	.50	.65
25	A2	1sh red orange	.75	.90
26	A2	2sh6p black brown	2.75	2.75
27	A2	5sh violet	11.00	11.00
28	A2	10sh olive green	15.00	17.00
		Nos. 18-28 (11)	32.00	34.90
		Set, never hinged	55.00	

> Catalogue values for unused stamps in this section, from this point to the end of the section, are for Never Hinged items.

Peace Issue

South Africa Nos. 100-102 Overprinted

Basic stamps inscribed alternately in English and Afrikaans.

1945, Dec. 3		**Wmk. 201**	**Perf. 14**	
29	A42	1p rose pink & choc, pair	.35	.35
a.		Single, English	.20	.20
b.		Single, Afrikaans	.20	.20
30	A43	2p vio & slate blue, pair	.35	.35
a.		Single, English	.20	.20
b.		Single, Afrikaans	.20	.20
31	A43	3p ultra & dp ultra, pair	.40	.40
a.		Single, English	.20	.20
b.		Single, Afrikaans	.20	.20
		Nos. 29-31 (3)	1.10	1.10

King George VI — A3

King George VI and Queen Elizabeth A4

Princess Margaret Rose and Princess Elizabeth A5

Royal British Family A6

Perf. 12½

1947, Feb. 17		**Wmk. 4**	**Engr.**	
35	A3	1p red	.20	.20
36	A4	2p green	.20	.20
37	A5	3p ultra	.20	.20
38	A6	1sh dark violet	.20	.20
		Nos. 35-38 (4)	.80	.80

Visit of the British Royal Family, 3/11-12/47.

Silver Wedding Issue
Common Design Types

1948, Dec. 1		**Photo.**	**Perf. 14x14½**	
39	CD304	1½p brt ultra	.20	.20

Engr.; Name Typo.
Perf. 11½

40	CD305	10sh dk brn ol	40.00	30.00

UPU Issue
Common Design Types
Engr.; Name Typo. on 3p, 6p
Perf. 13½, 11x11½

1949, Oct. 10		**Wmk. 4**		
41	CD306	1½p blue	.50	.40
42	CD307	3p indigo	1.00	1.00
43	CD308	6p orange yel	1.25	1.10
44	CD309	1sh red brown	1.25	1.00
		Nos. 41-44 (4)	4.00	3.50

Coronation Issue
Common Design Type

1953, June 3		**Engr.**	**Perf. 13½x13**	
45	CD312	2p red violet & black	.30	.30

Qiloane Hill — A7   Shearing Angora Goats — A8

Designs: 1p, Orange River. 2p, Mosotho horseman. 3p, Basuto household. 4½p, Maletsunyane falls. 6p, Herdboy with lesiba. 1sh, Pastoral scene. 1sh3p, Plane at Lancers Gap. 2sh6p, Old Fort Leribe. 5sh, Mission cave house.

1954, Oct. 18		**Wmk. 4**	**Perf. 13½**	
46	A7	½p dk brown & gray	.20	.20
47	A7	1p grn & gray blk	.20	.20
48	A7	2p org & dp blue	.55	.20
49	A7	3p car & ol green	.75	.25
50	A7	4½p dp blue & ind	.65	.20
51	A7	6p dk grn & org brn	1.40	.20
52	A7	1sh rose vio & dk ol green	1.75	.25
53	A7	1sh3p aqua & brown	12.50	4.25
54	A7	2sh6p lilac rose & dp ultra	8.25	4.75
55	A7	5sh dp car & black	4.25	7.75
56	A8	10sh dp ol & black	17.00	22.50
		Nos. 46-56 (11)	47.50	40.75

See Nos. 72-82, 87-91. For surcharges see Nos. 57, 61-71.

No. 48 Surcharged

1959, Aug. 1				
57	A7	½p on 2p org & dp blue	.20	.20

Chief Moshoeshoe (Moshesh) — A9

Designs: 1sh, Council chamber. 1sh3p, Mosotho on horseback.

Perf. 13x13½
1959, Dec. 15   **Wmk. 314**

58	A9	3p lt yel, grn & blk	.20	.20
59	A9	1sh green & pink	.20	.20
60	A9	1sh3p orange & ultra	.30	.30
		Nos. 58-60 (3)	.70	.70

Institution of the Basutoland National Council.

Nos. 46-56 Surcharged with New Value

2½c 2½c 3½c 3½c
I   II   I   II

5c 5c 10c 10c
I   II   I   II

12½c 12½c
I   II

25c 25c 25c
I   II   III

50c 50c R1 R1 R1
I   II   I   II   III

1961, Feb. 14   **Wmk. 4**   **Perf. 13½**

61	A7	½c on ½p	.20	.20
a.		Double surcharge	300.00	
62	A7	1c on 1p	.20	.20
63	A7	2c on 2p	.20	.20
a.		Inverted surcharge	100.00	
64	A7	2½c on 3p (II)	.20	.20
a.		Type I	.20	.20
b.		Inverted surcharge (II)	1,750.	1,000.
65	A7	3½c on 4½p (I)	.20	.20
a.		Type II	3.00	4.50
66	A7	5c on 6p (II)	.20	.20
a.		Type I	.20	.20
67	A7	10c on 1sh (I)	.20	.20
a.		Type II	75.00	85.00
68	A7	12½c on 1sh3p (II)	.40	.20
a.		Type I	.40	.20
69	A7	25c on 2sh6p (I)	.20	.20
a.		Type II	25.00	10.00
b.		Type III	.65	.65
70	A7	50c on 5sh (II)	.75	1.40
a.		Type I	1.25	1.50
71	A8	1r on 10sh (III)	6.00	6.00
a.		Type I	20.00	7.50
b.		Type II	9.00	20.00
		Nos. 61-71 (11)	8.75	9.20

Surcharge types on Nos. 64-71 are numbered chronologically.

Types of 1954
Value in Cents and Rands

Designs: ½c, Qiloane Hill. 1c, Orange River. 2c, Mosotho horseman. 2½c, Basuto household. 3½c, Maletsunyane Falls. 5c, Herdboy with lesiba. 10c, Pastoral scene. 12½c, Plane at Lancers Gap. 25c, Old Fort Leribe. 50c, Mission cave house. 1r, Shearing Angora goats.

1961-63   **Wmk. 4**   **Engr.**   **Perf. 13½**

72	A7	½c dk brn & gray ('62)	.20	.20
73	A7	1c dp grn & gray blk ('62)	.20	.35
74	A7	2c org & dp bl ('62)	.50	1.60
75	A7	2½c car & ol grn	.85	.20
76	A7	3½c dp bl & ind ('62)	.30	1.25
77	A7	5c dk grn & org brn ('62)	.40	.55
78	A7	10c rose vio & dk ol ('62)	.40	.35
79	A7	12½c aqua & brn ('62)	9.75	6.50
80	A7	25c lilac rose & dp ultra ('62)	6.00	5.50
81	A7	50c dp car & blk ('62)	9.75	10.00
		Perf. 11½		
82	A8	1r dp cl & blk ('63)	19.00	11.00
		Nos. 72-82 (11)	47.35	37.50

See Nos. 87-91. For overprints on stamps and types see Lesotho Nos. 5-14, 20a.

Freedom from Hunger Issue
Common Design Type
Perf. 14x14½
1963, June 4   **Photo.**   **Wmk. 314**

83	CD314	12½c lilac	.50	.40

Red Cross Centenary Issue
Common Design Type
1963, Sept. 2   **Litho.**   **Perf. 13**

84	CD315	2½c black & red	.20	.20
85	CD315	12½c ultra & red	.70	.70

Queen Type of 1961-63
1964   **Engr.**   **Perf. 13½**

87	A7	1c grn & gray blk	.20	.20
88	A7	2½c car & ol green	.20	.20
89	A7	5c dk green & org brn	.35	.35
90	A7	12½c aqua & brown	3.00	1.75
91	A7	50c dp car & black	7.25	10.00
		Nos. 87-91 (5)	11.00	12.50

Mosotho Woman and Child — A10

Designs: 3½c, Maseru border post. 5c, Mountains. 12½c, Legislative Building.

Perf. 14x13½
1965, May 10   **Photo.**   **Wmk. 314**

97	A10	2½c ultra & multi	.20	.20
98	A10	3½c blue & bister	.20	.20
99	A10	5c blue & ocher	.20	.20
100	A10	12½c lt blue, blk & buff	.40	.40
		Nos. 97-100 (4)	1.00	1.00

Attainment of self-government.

ITU Issue
Common Design Type
1965, May 17   **Litho.**   **Perf. 11x11½**

101	CD317	1c ver & red lilac	.20	.20
102	CD317	20c grnsh bl & org brn	.85	.65

Intl. Cooperation Year Issue
Common Design Type
1965, Oct. 25   **Wmk. 314**   **Perf. 14½**

103	CD318	½c blue grn & cl	.20	.20
104	CD318	12½c lt vio & green	.90	.70

Churchill Memorial Issue
Common Design Type
1966, Jan. 24   **Photo.**   **Perf. 14**
Design in Black, Gold and Carmine Rose

105	CD319	1c bright blue	.20	.20
106	CD319	2½c green	.20	.20
107	CD319	10c brown	.50	.50
108	CD319	22½c violet	1.25	1.25
		Nos. 105-108 (4)	2.15	2.15

POSTAGE DUE STAMPS

Catalogue values for all unused stamps in this section are for Never Hinged items.

D1

1933-38   **Wmk. 4**   **Typo.**   **Perf. 14**

J1	D1	1p dark red ('38)	.40	1.00
a.		1p dark carmine	1.00	1.50
b.		Wmk. 4a (error)	67.50	
J2	D1	2p lt violet	.30	1.00
a.		Wmk. 4a (error)	67.50	

Nos. J1-J2 valued on chalky paper. For surcharge see No. J7.

Coat of Arms — D2

1956, Dec. 1

J3	D2	1p carmine	.35	.25
J4	D2	2p dark purple	.35	.25

Nos. J2-J4 Surcharged with New Value

1961

J5	D2	1c on 1p carmine	.20	.20
J6	D2	1c on 2p dk purple	.20	.20
J7	D1	5c on 2p lt violet	3.00	3.00
a.		Wmk. 4a (error)	275.00	
J8	D2	5c on 2p dark pur ("5" 7½mm high)	3.60	3.60
a.		"5" 3½mm high	17.50	25.00
		Nos. J5-J8 (4)	3.60	3.60

Value in Cents
1964   **Wmk. 314**   **Perf. 14**

J9	D2	1c carmine	2.25	2.25
J10	D2	5c dark purple	2.25	2.25

For overprints see Lesotho Nos. J1-J2.

OFFICIAL STAMPS

Nos. 1-3 and 6 Overprinted "OFFICIAL"

1934   **Wmk. 4**   **Engr.**   **Perf. 12½**

O1	A1	½p emerald	3,500.	3,500.
O2	A1	1p carmine	1,400.	1,000.
O3	A1	2p red violet	850.00	500.00
O4	A1	6p yellow	9,000.	4,500.

Counterfeits exist.

BATUM

LOCATION — A seaport on the Black Sea

Batum is the capital of Adzhar, a territory which, in 1921, became an autonomous republic of the Georgian Soviet Socialist Republic.

Stamps of Batum were issued under the administration of British forces which occupied Batum and environs between December, 1918, and July, 1920, following the Treaty of Versailles.

100 Kopecks = 1 Ruble

Counterfeits exist of Nos. 1-65.

Basic Russian Designs

A8   A11   A14

A15   A19

A1

1919   **Unwmk.**   **Litho.**   **Imperf.**

1	A1	5k green	4.00	5.50
2	A1	10k ultramarine	4.00	5.50
3	A1	50k yellow	1.50	2.00
4	A1	1r red brown	1.75	2.50
5	A1	3r violet	6.50	7.50
6	A1	5r brown	7.50	9.00
		Nos. 1-6 (6)	25.25	32.00

For overprints and surcharges see #13-20, 51-65.

Russian Stamps of 1909-17 Surcharged

1919   **On Stamps of 1917**

7	A14	10r on 1k orange	25.00	27.50
8	A14	10r on 3k red	12.50	15.00

On Stamp of 1909-12
Perf. 14x14½

9	A14	10r on 5k claret	225.00	225.00

On Stamp of 1917

10	A14	10r on 10k on 7k light blue	200.00	200.00
		Nos. 7-10 (4)	462.50	467.50

БАТУМ. ОБ.

Russian Stamps of 1909-13 Surcharged

Коп 35 Коп

1919

11	A15	35k on 4k carmine	1,650.	2,900.
12	A19	35k on 4k dull red	6,500.	7,750.

This surcharge was intended for postal cards. A few cards which bore adhesive stamps were also surcharged.

Values are for stamps off card and without gum.

Type of 1919 Issue Overprinted

1919   **Unwmk.**   **Imperf.**

13	A1	5k green	5.75	6.00
14	A1	10k dark blue	5.75	6.00
15	A1	25k orange	5.75	6.00
16	A1	1r pale blue	2.75	5.00
17	A1	2r salmon pink	.80	.90
18	A1	3r violet	.80	.90
19	A1	5r brown	1.25	1.25
a.		"CCUPATION"	225.00	250.00
20	A1	7r dull red	2.50	3.00
		Nos. 13-20 (8)	25.35	29.55

Russian Stamps of 1909-17 Surcharged in Various Colors:

10r & 50r   15r

On Stamps of 1917
1919-20   **Imperf.**

21	A14	10r on 3k red	22.50	20.00
22	A14	15r on 1k org (R)	45.00	40.00
23	A14	15r on 1k org (Bk)	67.50	60.00
24	A14	15r on 1k org (V)	45.00	40.00
25	A14	50r on 1k org	275.00	275.00
26	A14	50r on 2k green	350.00	350.00

On Stamps of 1909-17
Perf. 14x14½

27	A14	50r on 2k green	400.00	375.00
28	A14	50r on 3k red	850.00	825.00
29	A15	50r on 4k car	600.00	575.00
30	A14	50r on 5k claret	375.00	350.00
31	A15	50r on 10k dk blue (R)	950.00	900.00
32	A11	50r on 15k red brn & blue	375.00	375.00

Surcharged

On Stamps of 1909-17

33	A14	25r on 5k cl (Bk)	45.00	45.00
34	A14	25r on 5k cl (Bl)	45.00	45.00
35	A14	25r on 10k on 7k lt blue (Bk)	80.00	80.00
36	A14	25r on 10k on 7k lt blue (Bl)	45.00	45.00
37	A11	25r on 20k on 14k bl & rose (Bk)	67.50	67.50
38	A11	25r on 20k on 14k bl & rose (Bl)	50.00	45.00
39	A11	25r on 25k grn & gray vio (Bk)	100.00	90.00
40	A11	25r on 25k grn & gray vio (Bl)	100.00	90.00

41	A8	25r on 50k vio & green (Bk)	45.00	45.00
42	A8	25r on 50k vio & green (Bl)	50.00	50.00
43	A14	50r on 2k green	70.00	70.00
44	A14	50r on 3k red	70.00	70.00
45	A15	50r on 4k car	100.00	90.00
46	A14	50r on 5k claret	100.00	90.00

On Stamps of 1917

Imperf

47	A14	50r on 2k green	250.00	240.00
48	A14	50r on 3k red	325.00	325.00
49	A14	50r on 5k claret	950.00	900.00

On Stamp of 1913

Perf. 13½

50	A19	50r on 4k dull red (Bl)	67.50	67.50

Nos. 3, 13 and 15 Surcharged in Black or Blue:

1920   *Imperf.*

51	A1	25r on 5k green	24.00	24.00
52	A1	25r on 5k grn (Bl)	30.00	30.00
53	A1	25r on 25k orange	17.00	17.00
54	A1	25r on 25k org (Bl)	65.00	65.00
55	A1	50r on 50k yellow	15.00	15.00
56	A1	50r on 50k yel (Bl)	60.00	60.00
		Nos. 51-56 (6)	211.00	211.00

The surcharges on Nos. 21-56 inclusive are handstamped and are known double, inverted, etc.

Tree Type of 1919 Overprinted Like Nos. 13-20

1920

57	A1	1r orange brown	.60	3.25
58	A1	2r gray blue	.65	3.25
59	A1	3r rose	.75	3.25
60	A1	5r black brown	.65	3.25
61	A1	7r yellow	.65	3.25
62	A1	10r dark green	.60	3.25
63	A1	15r violet	.80	4.25
64	A1	25r vermilion	.75	4.00
65	A1	50r dark blue	.90	6.25
		Nos. 57-65 (9)	6.35	34.00

The variety "BPITISH" occurs on #57-65.

BECHUANALAND

ˌbech-ˈwä-nə-ˌland

(British Bechuanaland)

LOCATION — Southern Africa
GOVT. — A British Crown Colony, annexed in 1895 to the Cape of Good Hope Colony which became a province in the Union of South Africa.
AREA — 51,424 sq. mi.
POP. — 84,210 (1904)
CAPITAL — Mafeking

12 Pence = 1 Shilling
20 Shillings = 1 Pound

Watermarks

Wmk. 29- Orb   Wmk. 14- VR in Italics

Cape of Good Hope   **British**
Stamps of 1871-85   **Bechuanaland**
Overprinted

1886   **Wmk. 1**   *Perf. 14*

Black Overprint

1	A6	4p blue	50.00	57.50

Wmk. 2

Black Overprint

3	A6	3p claret	30.00	37.50

Red Overprint

4	A6	½p black	10.00	14.50
a.		Double overprint in red & blk	850.00	

Wmk. Anchor (16)

Black Overprint

5	A6	½p black	6.50	10.00
a.		"ritish"	1,800.	1,800.
b.		Double overprint	2,500.	
6	A6	1p rose	9.00	8.50
b.		"ritish"	2,100.	1,600.
7	A6	2p bister	27.50	10.00
a.		"ritish"	4,500.	4,000.
b.		Double overprint		1,500.
8	A6	6p violet	70.00	35.00
9	A3	1sh green	210.00	140.00
a.		"ritish"	11,500.	8,500.

There is no period after Bechuanaland in the genuine stamps.

Black Ovpt. on Great Britain #111

1887   **Wmk. 30**

10	A54	½p vermilion	1.10	1.25
a.		Double overprint	2,250.	

For overprints see Bechuanaland Protectorate Nos. 51-53.

A1

A2   A3

1887   **Typo.**   **Wmk. 29**

Country Name in Black

11	A1	1p lilac	14.00	3.50
12	A1	2p lilac	57.50	1.75
13	A1	3p lilac	3.25	5.00
14	A1	4p lilac	35.00	2.50
15	A1	6p lilac	45.00	14.50

Wmk. 14

16	A2	1sh green	30.00	5.00
17	A2	2sh green	45.00	35.00
18	A2	2sh6p green	57.50	47.50
19	A2	5sh green	80.00	140.00
		Pen cancellation		4.00
20	A2	10sh green	175.00	325.00
		Pen cancellation		22.50

Wmk. 29

21	A3	£1 lilac	900.00	750.00
		Pen cancellation		37.50
22	A3	£5 lilac	2,750.	1,350.
		Pen cancellation		175.00

The corner designs and central oval differs on No. 22.
For overprints see Bechuanaland Protectorate Nos. 54-58, 60-66. For surcharges see Nos. 23-28, 30, Cape of Good Hope No. 171.

1d.

Nos. 11-12, 14-16 Surcharged

1888

Country Name in Black

Black Surcharge

23	A1	1p on 1p lilac	7.00	5.50
a.		Double surcharge		

24	A1	6p on 6p lilac	80.00	12.00

Red Surcharge

25	A1	2p on 2p lilac	15.00	3.00
a.		"2" with curved tail	190.00	150.00
26	A1	4p on 4p lilac	200.00	275.00

Green Surcharge

27	A1	2p on 2p lilac		2,500.

Blue Surcharge

27A	A1	6p on 6p lilac		5,750.

Wmk. 14

Black Surcharge

28	A2	1sh on 1sh green	125.00	70.00

British

One Half-Penny

Bechuanaland   No. 29   No. 30

Green Ovpt. on Cape of Good Hope #41

1889   **Wmk. 16**

29	A4	½p black	4.75	17.50

Vertical overprint, double overprints one inverted or double, and varieties such as "British" omitted probably are from printers waste.

Wmk. 29

Black Surcharge on No. 13

30	A1	½p on 3p lilac & blk	125.00	140.00

Cape of Good Hope Nos. 43-44 Overprinted in Black

1891   **Wmk. 16**

31	A4	1p rose	10.00	9.00
a.		Horiz. pair, one without overprint	1,750.	
b.		"British" omitted		1,000.
c.		"Bechuanaland" omitted	1,050.	
32	A4	2p bister	3.00	3.00
a.		Without period	200.00	250.00

See Nos. 38-39.

Stamps of Great Britain Overprinted in Black

1891-94   **Wmk. 30**

33	A40	1p lilac	5.25	1.00
34	A56	2p green & car	5.00	3.50
35	A59	4p brown & green	2.50	.75
36	A62	6p violet, rose	2.75	1.75
37	A65	1sh green ('94)	11.50	15.00
		Nos. 33-37 (5)	27.00	22.00

For surcharges see Cape of Good Hope Nos. 172, 176-177.

Cape of Good Hope Nos. 43-44 Overprinted Like Nos. 31-32 but Reading Down

1893-95   **Wmk. 16**

38	A6	1p rose	2.50	2.75
a.		No dots over the "i's" of "British"	75.00	75.00
b.		"British" omitted	1,000.	
c.		As "a," reading up		1,275.
d.		Pair, one without overprint		
39	A6	2p bister ('95)	4.75	2.75
a.		Double overprint	900.00	800.00
b.		No dots over the "i's" of "British"	125.00	110.00
c.		"British" omitted	425.00	425.00
d.		As "b," reading up		

Cape of Good Hope No. 42 Overprinted

"BECHUANALAND" 16mm Long Overprint Lines 13mm Apart

1897

40	A6	½p light green	2.50	7.00

"BECHUANALAND" 15mm Long Overprint Lines 10½mm Apart

41	A6	½p light green	9.00	35.00

"BECHUANALAND" 15mm Long Overprint Lines 13½mm Apart

42	A6	½p light green	20.00	65.00
		Nos. 40-42 (3)	31.50	107.00

BECHUANALAND PROTECTORATE

ˌbech-ˈwä-nə-ˌland prə-ˈtek-tə-ˌrət

LOCATION — In central South Africa, north of the Republic of South Africa, east of South-West Africa and bounded on the north and east by Angola and Southern Rhodesia
GOVT. — British Protectorate
AREA — 222,000 sq. mi.
POP. — 540,400 (1964)

Bechuanaland Protectorate became the independent republic of Botswana, Sept. 30, 1966.

12 Pence = 1 Shilling
20 Shillings = 1 Pound
100 Cents = 1 Rand (1961)

> Catalogue values for unused stamps in this country are for Never Hinged items, beginning with Scott 137 in the regular postage section and Scott J7 in the postage due section.

Additional Overprint in Black on Bechuanaland No. 10

Protectorate   a   b

Protectorate
c

1888-90   **Wmk. 30**   *Perf. 14*

51	A54(a)	½p vermilion	175.00	225.00
a.		Double overprint	725.00	
52	A54(b)	½p ver ('89)	3.00	25.00
a.		Double overprint	300.00	
53	A54(c)	½p vermilion	150.00	175.00
a.		Inverted overprint	65.00	85.00
b.		Double overprint	80.00	110.00
c.		As "a," double	500.00	500.00

For surcharge see No. 68.

Bechuanaland Nos. 16-20 Overprinted Type "b" in Black

Wmk. 14

Country Name in Black

54	A2	1sh green	65.00	52.50
a.		First "o" omitted	3,250.	3,000.
55	A2	2sh green	575.00	850.00
a.		First "o" omitted	7,500.	—
56	A2	2sh6p green	600.00	800.00
a.		First "o" omitted	7,500.	
57	A2	5sh green	1,200.	1,750.
a.		First "o" omitted	10,000.	
58	A2	10sh green	3,250.	5,000.
a.		First "o" omitted	15,000.	

Bechuanaland Nos. 11-15 Overprinted Type "b" and Surcharged in Black

1888   **Wmk. 29**

Country Name in Black

60	A1	1p on 1p lilac	7.00	14.00
a.		Short "1"	300.00	325.00
61	A1	2p on 2p lilac	22.50	17.50
a.		"2" with curved tail	450.00	400.00
63	A1	3p on 3p lilac	100.00	160.00
64	A1	4p on 4p lilac	275.00	275.00
a.		Small "4"	2,500.	2,400.
65	A1	6p on 6p lilac	62.50	42.50

In #60 the "1" is 2½mm high; in #60a, 2mm.

Value Surcharged in Red

66	A1	4p on 4p lilac	65.00	37.50

Cape of Good Hope Type of 1886
Overprinted in Green

1889   Wmk. 16
67	A6	½p black	3.75	32.50
a.		Double overprint	400.00	500.00
b.		"Bechuanaland" omitted	725.00	

Black Surcharge on Bechuanaland Protectorate No. 52
Wmk. 30
68	A54	4p on ½p ver	17.50	3.50
a.		Inverted surcharge		4,500.

Stamps of Great Britain 1881-87, Overprinted in Black

1897, Oct.
69	A54	½p vermilion	1.00	2.00
70	A40	1p lilac	3.75	.50
71	A56	2p green & car	2.75	4.25
72	A58	3p violet, yel	5.00	7.75
73	A59	4p brown & green	12.00	10.00
74	A62	6p violet, rose	20.00	10.00
		Nos. 69-74 (6)	44.50	34.50

For surcharges see Cape of Good Hope Nos. 167-170, 173-175.

Same on Great Britain No. 125

1902, Feb. 25
75	A54	½p blue green	1.50	2.00

Stamps of Great Britain, 1902, Overprinted in Black

1904-12
76	A66	½p gray green ('06)	1.75	1.75
77	A66	1p car ('05)	6.00	.65
78	A66	2½p ultra	5.50	4.50
79	A74	1sh scar & grn ('12)	37.50	100.00
		Nos. 76-79 (4)	50.75	106.90

Same on Great Britain No. 143

1908
80	A66	½p pale yel green	3.25	3.50

Bechuanaland

Transvaal No. 274 Overprinted

Protectorate

1910   Wmk. 3
81	A27	6p brn org & blk	175.00	325.00

This stamp was issued for fiscal use, although it is known postally used.

Great Britain No. 154 Overprinted Like Nos. 76-79

1912, Sept.   Wmk. 30   Perf. 15x14
82	A81	1p scarlet	1.10	.90

Great Britain Stamps of 1912-13 Overprinted Like Nos. 76-79
Wmk. Crown and GvR (33)

1914-24
83	A82	½p green	1.10	1.60
84	A83	1p scarlet	2.50	.55
85	A84	1½p red brn ('20)	2.00	2.75
86	A85	2p orange (I)	2.25	3.75
a.		2p orange (II) ('24)	32.50	5.50
87	A86	2½p ultra	3.25	15.00
88	A87	3p bluish violet	5.50	11.00
89	A88	4p slate green	5.75	12.50
90	A89	6p dull violet	6.25	14.00
91	A90	1sh bister	8.50	16.00
		Nos. 83-91 (9)	37.10	77.15

The dies of No. 86 are the same as in Great Britain 1912-13 issue.

Overprinted   BECHUANALAND PROTECTORATE
Wmk. 34   Perf. 11x12
92	A91	2sh6p dk brown	90.00	200.00
a.		2sh6p light brown ('16)	90.00	200.00
93	A91	5sh rose car	140.00	325.00
a.		5sh carmine ('20)	250.00	350.00

Nos. 92, 93 were printed by Waterlow Bros. & Layton; Nos. 92a, 93a were printed by Thomas De La Rue & Co.

Same Overprint On Retouched Stamps of 1919

1920-23
94	A91	2sh6p gray brown	85.00	150.00
95	A91	5sh car rose	110.00	225.00

Great Britain Stamps of 1924 Overprinted like Nos. 76-79
Wmk. Crown and Block GvR Multiple (35)

1925-26   Perf. 15x14
96	A82	½p green	1.50	2.00
97	A83	1p scarlet	2.00	1.00
99	A85	2p deep org (II)	2.50	1.25
101	A87	3p violet	3.25	6.50
102	A88	4p slate green	4.25	27.50
103	A89	6p dull violet	30.00	40.00
104	A90	1sh bister	10.00	27.50
		Nos. 96-104 (7)	53.50	105.75

George V
A11

George VI, Cattle and Baobab Tree
A12

Perf. 12½

1932, Dec. 12   Engr.   Wmk. 4
105	A11	½p green	.85	.20
106	A11	1p carmine	.85	.20
107	A11	2p red brown	.85	.20
108	A11	3p ultra	.85	.50
109	A11	4p orange	1.25	4.25
110	A11	6p red violet	2.50	2.00
111	A11	1sh blk & ol grn	6.00	3.50
112	A11	2sh black & org	27.50	21.00
113	A11	2sh6p black & car	26.00	32.50
114	A11	3sh black & red vio	42.50	45.00
115	A11	5sh black & ultra	55.00	55.00
116	A11	10sh blk & red brown	77.50	110.00
		Nos. 105-116 (12)	241.65	274.35

Common Design Types pictured following the introduction.

Silver Jubilee Issue
Common Design Type

1935, May 4   Perf. 11x12
117	CD301	1p car & blue	.60	1.10
118	CD301	2p black & ultra	1.25	1.60
119	CD301	3p ultra & brown	1.75	2.10
120	CD301	6p brown vio & ind	2.40	2.75
		Nos. 117-120 (4)	6.00	7.55

Coronation Issue
Common Design Type

1937, May 12   Perf. 13½x14
121	CD302	1p carmine	.20	.20
122	CD302	2p brown	.20	.20
123	CD302	3p bright ultra	.25	.25
		Nos. 121-123 (3)	.65	.65
		Set, never hinged	1.50	

1938, Apr. 1   Perf. 12½
124	A12	½p green	.70	1.00
125	A12	1p rose car	.20	.20
126	A12	1½p light blue	5.00	.75
127	A12	2p brown	.20	.30
128	A12	3p ultra	.20	.20
129	A12	4p orange	.50	2.25
130	A12	6p rose violet	1.60	3.75
131	A12	1sh blk & ol grn	1.60	3.00
133	A12	2sh6p black & car	8.00	9.00

135	A12	5sh black & ultra	17.50	9.75
136	A12	10sh black & brn	8.00	18.00
		Nos. 124-136 (11)	43.50	49.50
		Set, never hinged	67.50	

Catalogue values for unused stamps in this section, from this point to the end of the section, are for Never Hinged items.

Peace Issue

South Africa Nos. 100-102 Overprinted

Basic stamps inscribed alternately in English and Afrikaans.

1945, Dec. 3   Wmk. 201   Perf. 14
137	A42	1p rose pink & choc, pair	.30	.30
a.		Single, English	.20	.20
b.		Single, Afrikaans	.20	.20
138	A43	2p vio & slate blue, pair	.40	.40
a.		Single, English	.20	.20
b.		Single, Afrikaans	.20	.20
139	A43	3p ultra & dp ultra, pair	.50	.50
a.		Single, English	.25	.25
b.		Single, Afrikaans	.25	.25
		Nos. 137-139 (3)	1.20	1.20

World War II victory of the Allies.

Royal Visit Issue
Types of Basutoland, 1947
Perf. 12½

1947, Feb. 17   Wmk. 4   Engr.
143	A3	1p red	.20	.20
144	A4	2p green	.20	.20
145	A5	3p ultra	.20	.20
146	A6	1sh dark violet	.30	.30
		Nos. 143-146 (4)	.90	.90

Visit of the British Royal Family, 4/17/47.

Silver Wedding Issue
Common Design Types

1948, Dec. 1   Photo.   Perf. 14x14½
147	CD304	1½p brt ultra	.20	.20

Engr.; Name Typo.
Perf. 11½x11
148	CD305	10sh gray black	26.00	32.50

UPU Issue
Common Design Types
Engr.; Name Typo. on 3p and 6p

1949, Oct. 10   Perf. 13½, 11x11½
149	CD306	1½p blue	.25	.25
150	CD307	3p indigo	.35	.35
151	CD308	6p red lilac	.80	.80
152	CD309	1sh olive	1.50	1.50
		Nos. 149-152 (4)	2.90	2.90

Coronation Issue
Common Design Type

1953, June 3   Engr.   Perf. 13½x13
153	CD312	2p brown & black	.30	.30

Elizabeth II — A13

Victoria, Elizabeth II and Water Hole — A14

1955-58   Perf. 13x13½
154	A13	½p green	.25	.25
155	A13	1p rose car	.25	.25
156	A13	2p brown	.25	.25
157	A13	3p ultra	.35	.35
158	A13	4p orange ('58)	4.25	4.25
159	A13	4½p indigo	1.25	1.25
160	A13	6p rose violet	.90	.90
161	A13	1sh blk & ol grn	1.50	1.50
162	A13	1sh3p blk & rose vio	2.00	6.50
163	A13	2sh6p black & car	5.50	10.50

164	A13	5sh black & ultra	10.50	16.00
165	A13	10sh black & brn	24.00	30.00
		Nos. 154-165 (12)	51.00	72.00

For surcharges see Nos. 169-179.

Perf. 14½x14

1960, Jan. 21   Photo.   Wmk. 314
166	A14	1p brown & black	.20	.20
167	A14	3p car rose & black	.20	.20
168	A14	6p ultra & black	.30	.30
		Nos. 166-168 (3)	.70	.70

Proclamation of the Protectorate, 75th anniv.

Nos. 155-165 Surcharged

1c 1c 3½c 3½c 3½c
I II I II III

5c 5c R1 R1
I II I II

Perf. 13x13½

1961, Feb. 14   Wmk. 4   Engr.
169		1c on 1p (I)	.20	.20
a.		Type II	.20	.20
170		2c on 2p	.20	.20
171		2½c on 3p	.20	.20
a.		Pair, one without surcharge	700.00	
172		2½c on 3p	.90	.90
173		3½c on 4p (III)	.20	.20
a.		Type I	.50	.50
b.		Type II	1.60	1.60
174		5c on 6p (II)	.25	.25
a.		Type I	.75	.75
175		10c on 1sh	.30	.30
a.		Pair, one without surcharge	700.00	
176		12½c on 1sh3p ("12½c" 11¼mm wide)	.55	.55
a.		"12½c" 12½mm wide	.75	.75
177		25c on 2sh6p	.80	.80
178		50c on 5sh	1.90	1.90
179		1r on 10sh (II, "R1" at lower center)	4.50	4.50
a.		Type II, "R1" at lower left	6.50	6.50
b.		Type I	300.00	110.00
		Nos. 169-179 (11)	10.00	10.00

Nos. 173a and 173b are found in the same sheet; each comes with "3½c" in both wide and narrow settings.

Surch. types are numbered chronologically.

African Golden Oriole — A15   Baobab Tree — A16

Designs: 2c, African hoopoe. 2½c, Scarlet-chested sunbird. 3½c, Cape widow bird (Yellow bishop). 5c, Swallow-tailed bee-eater. 7½c, Gray hornbill. 10c, Red-headed weaver. 12½c, Brown-hooded kingfisher. 20c, Woman musician. 35c, Woman grinding corn. 50c, Bechuana ox. 1r, Lion. 2r, Police camel patrol.

Perf. 14x14½, 14½x14

1961, Oct. 2   Photo.   Wmk. 314
180	A15	1c lilac, blk & yel	.20	.20
181	A15	2c pale ol, blk & org	.20	.20
182	A15	2½c bis, blk, grn & dp car	.25	.20
183	A15	3½c pink, blk & yel	.35	.25
184	A15	5c dl org, blk, grn & bl	.45	.30
185	A15	7½c yel grn, blk, red & brn	.65	.40
186	A15	10c aqua & multi	.90	.50
187	A15	12½c gray, yel, red & blue	1.10	.55
188	A16	20c gray & brn	1.40	1.10
189	A16	25c yel & dk brn	2.50	1.40
190	A16	35c dp org & ultra	2.75	1.75
191	A16	50c lt ol grn & sep	4.00	2.75
192	A15	1r ocher & black	8.25	5.25
193	A15	2r blue & brn	16.00	10.50
		Nos. 180-193 (14)	39.00	25.35

Freedom from Hunger Issue
Common Design Type

1963, June 4   Perf. 14x14½
194	CD314	12½c green	.50	.50

Red Cross Centenary Issue
Common Design Type

1963, Sept. 2   Litho.   *Perf. 13*
195 CD315 2½c black & red   .20 .20
196 CD315 12½c ultra & red   .80 .80

Shakespeare Issue
Common Design Type

1964, Apr. 23 Photo. *Perf. 14x14½*
197 CD316 12½c red brown   .30 .30

Notwani River Dam, Gaberones Water
Supply — A17

Wmk. 314

1965, Mar. 1   Photo.   *Perf. 14½*
198 A17 2½c dark red & gold   .20 .20
199 A17 5c deep ultra & gold   .20 .20
200 A17 12½c brown & gold   .30 .30
201 A17 25c emerald & gold   .55 .55
   Nos. 198-201 (4)   1.25 1.25

Internal self-government, Mar. 1, 1965.

ITU Issue
Common Design Type
Perf. 11x11½

1965, May 17   Litho.   Wmk. 314
202 CD317 2½c ver & dl yel   .20 .20
203 CD317 12½c red lil & pale brn   .70 .70

Intl. Cooperation Year Issue
Common Design Type

1965, Oct. 25   *Perf. 14½*
204 CD318 1c bl grn & claret   .20 .20
205 CD318 12½c lt vio & grn   .75 .75

Churchill Memorial Issue
Common Design Type

1966, Jan. 24 Photo. *Perf. 14*
Design in Black, Gold and Carmine Rose
206 CD319 1c bright blue   .20 .20
207 CD319 2½c green   .20 .20
208 CD319 12½c brown   .75 .75
209 CD319 20c violet   1.10 1.10
   Nos. 206-209 (4)   2.25 2.25

Haslar Smoke Generator — A18

Wmk. 314

1966, June 1 Photo. *Perf. 14½*
210 A18 2½c shown   .20 .20
211 A18 5c Bugler   .20 .20
212 A18 15c Gun site   .40 .40
213 A18 35c Regimental cap
   badge   .85 .85
   Nos. 210-213 (4)   1.65 1.65

25th anniv. of the Bechuanaland Pioneers
and Gunners.

POSTAGE DUE STAMPS

Postage Due Stamps
of Great Britain
Overprinted

On Stamp of 1914-22

1926   Wmk. 33   *Perf. 14x14½*
J1 D1 1p carmine   3.75 60.00
On Stamps of 1924-30
Wmk. 35
J2 D1 ½p emerald   3.75 45.00

Overprinted

J3 D1 2p black brown   6.50 80.00
   Nos. J1-J3 (3)   14.00 185.00
   Set, never hinged   30.00

D2

1932   Wmk. 4   Typo.   *Perf. 14½*
J4 D2 ½p olive green   6.00 30.00
J5 D2 1p carmine rose   6.00 8.00
J6 D2 2p dull violet   8.00 35.00
   Nos. J4-J6 (3)   20.00 73.00
   Set, never hinged   30.00

> **Catalogue values for unused stamps in this section, from this point to the end of the section, are for Never Hinged items.**

Nos. J4-J6 Surcharged

Type I   Type II

1961, Feb. 14
J7 D2 1c on 1p car rose, II   .20 .20
 a.   Type I   .30 .30
 b.   Double surcharge, II   140.00
J8 D2 2c on 2p dull vio, II   .30 .30
 a.   Type I   .35 .35
J9 D2 5c on ½p ol green, I   .50 .50
   Nos. J7-J9 (3)   1.00 1.00

Nos. J7, J7a, J8 and J8a are on chalky
paper. Nos. J7 and J8 printed on ordinary
paper sell for much more.

Denominations in Cents

1961   Wmk. 4   *Perf. 14*
J10 D2 1c carmine rose   .20 .20
J11 D2 2c dull violet   .20 .20
J12 D2 5c olive green   .40 1.25
   Nos. J10-J12 (3)   .80 1.65

BELARUS
ˌbē-lə-ˈrüs

(Byelorussia)

(White Russia)

LOCATION — Eastern Europe,
bounded by Russia, Latvia, Lithuania
and Poland
GOVT. — Independent republic, member of the Commonwealth of Independent States
AREA — 80,134 sq. mi.
POP. — 10,401,784 (1999 est.)
CAPITAL — Minsk

With the breakup of the Soviet Union
on Dec. 26, 1991, Belarus and ten former Soviet republics established the
Commonwealth of Independent States.

100 Kopecks = 1 Ruble

> **Catalogue values for all unused stamps in this country are for Never Hinged items.**

Five denominations, perf and imperf, of
this design produced in 1920 were not
put in use and were probably
propaganda labels. They are common.
Numerous forgeries exist.

Cross of
Ephrosinia of
Polotsk — A1

1992, Mar. 20   Litho.   *Perf. 12x12½*
1 A1 1r multicolored   .35 .20
   For surcharge see No. 230.

R.R.
Schurma
(1892-1978),
Composer
A2

1992, Apr. 10   Photo.   *Perf. 12x11½*
2 A2 20k blue & black   .25 .20
   For surcharge see No. 203.

Arms of Polotsk — A3

Designs: No. 13, Stag jumping fence. No.
14, Man's head, sword.

1992-94   Photo.   *Perf. 12x11½*
11 A3 2r shown   .20 .20
   Perf. 12x12½
12 A3 25r Minsk   .20 .20
13 A3 700r Grodno   .20 .20
14 A3 700r Vitebsk   .20 .20
   Nos. 11-14 (4)   .80 .80

Issued: 2r, 6/9/92; 25r, 11/11/93; #13, 14,
10/17/94.
This is an expanding set. Numbers will
change if necessary.

National
Symbols
A4

No. 15, Natl. arms. No. 16, Map, flag.

1992, Aug. 31   Litho.   *Perf. 12x12½*
15 A4 5r black, red & yellow   .50 .40
16 A4 5r multicolored   .50 .40
   For surcharges see Nos. 55-58, 61-64.

No. 1 Overprinted

Cross of Ephrosinia of Polotsk — A5

A5 illustration reduced.

1992, Sept. 25 Litho. *Perf. 12x12½*
17 A1 1r on #1 multi   .20 .20
Souvenir Sheet
Perf. 12
18 A5 5r multicolored   .90 .75

Orthodox Church in Belarus, 1000th anniv.
No. 18, imperf, was issued Feb. 15, 1993.
For surcharges see Nos. 59-60, 65-66.

Buildings
A6

Designs: No. 19, Church of Boris Gleb,
Grodno, 12th cent. No. 20, World Castle, 16th
cent. No. 21, Nyasvizh Castle, 16th-19th cent.
No. 22, Kamyanets Tower, 12th-13th cent,
vert. No. 23, Church of Ephrosinia of Polotsk,
12th cent., vert. No. 24, Calvinist Church, Zaslaw, 16th cent., vert.

1992, Oct. 15   Litho.   *Perf. 12*
19 A6 2r multicolored   .20 .20
20 A6 2r multicolored   .20 .20
21 A6 2r multicolored   .20 .20
22 A6 2r multicolored   .20 .20
23 A6 2r multicolored   .20 .20
24 A6 2r multicolored   .20 .20
   Nos. 19-24 (6)   1.20 1.20

Centuries of construction are in Roman
numerals.

Natl. Arms — A7

1992-94   Litho.   *Perf. 12x12½*
25 A7 30k light blue   .20 .20
26 A7 45k olive green   .20 .20
27 A7 50k green   .20 .20
28 A7 1r brown   .20 .20
29 A7 2r red brown   .20 .20
30 A7 3r org yellow   .20 .20
31 A7 5r blue   .20 .20
32 A7 10r red   .35 .25
33 A7 15r violet   .25 .25
34 A7 25r yellow green   .40 .30
35 A7 50r bright pink   .25 .25
36 A7 100r henna brown   .25 .25
37 A7 150r plum   .40 .40
38 A7 200r blue green   .20 .20
39 A7 300r salmon pink   .20 .20
40 A7 600r light lilac   .20 .20
40A A7 1000r rose carmine   .25 .25
40B A7 3000r gray blue   .40 .30
   Nos. 25-40B (18)   4.50 4.20

Issued: 30k, 45k, 50k, 11/10; 1r-3r, 10r,
1/4/93; 5r, 15r, 25r, 2/9/93; 50r, 100r, 150r,
6/16/93; 200r-3,000r, 12/28/94; others, 1992.
For surcharges see #141-142, 211A-212.

Ceramics
A8

Designs: No. 41, Pitcher and bowl. No. 42, Four pieces on tree branches. No. 43, Two large pitchers. No. 44, One large pitcher.

1992, Dec. 24   Litho.   Perf. 11½
41	A8	1r multicolored	.20	.20
42	A8	1r multicolored	.20	.20
43	A8	1r multicolored	.20	.20
44	A8	1r multicolored	.20	.20
		Nos. 41-44 (4)	.80	.80

M. I. Garetzky (1893-1938), Writer — A9

1993, June 22   Photo.   Perf. 12x11½
45	A9	50r magenta	.25	.25

Straw Figures
A10

Designs: 5r, Chickens. 10r, Child, mother, vert. 15r, Woman, vert. 25r, Man with scythe, woman with rake, vert.

Perf. 12x11½, 11½x12
1993, Apr. 22   Litho.
47	A10	5r multicolored	.20	.20
48	A10	10r multicolored	.25	.20
49	A10	15r multicolored	.25	.20
50	A10	25r multicolored	.30	.20
		Nos. 47-50 (4)	1.00	.80

First World Congress of White Russians — A11

1993, July 8   Litho.   Perf. 12
51	A11	50r multicolored	.90	.90

Europa — A12

Paintings by Chagall: No. 52, Promenade, vert. No. 53, Man Over Vitebsk. 2500r, Allegory.

1993, Oct. 12   Litho.   Perf. 14
52	A12	1500r multicolored	2.75	2.75
53	A12	1500r multicolored	2.75	2.75
a.		Pair, #52-53	6.00	6.00
		Souvenir Sheet		
54	A12	2500r multicolored	45.00	45.00

Nos. 15-16, 18 Surcharged

a

"b" overprint is the same as "a," but with "WINTER PRE-OLYMPICS GAMES LIL-LEHAMMER, NORWAY" in five lines at top. Size and location of surcharge varies.

1993, Oct. 15   Litho.   Perf. 12x12½
55	A4(a)	1500r on 5r #15	3.50	3.50
56	A4(b)	1500r on 5r #15	3.50	3.50
a.		Pair, #55-56	7.00	7.00
57	A4(a)	1500r on 5r #16	3.50	3.50
58	A4(b)	1500r on 5r #16	3.50	3.50
a.		Pair, #57-58	7.00	7.00
		Nos. 55-58 (4)	14.00	14.00
		Souvenir Sheets		
		Perf. 12		
59	A5(a)	1500r on 5r #18	3.50	3.50
60	A5(b)	1500r on 5r #18	3.50	3.50

No. 59 exists imperf. The status of No. 60 is in question.

Nos. 15-16, 18 Surcharged

c

"d" overprint is the same as "c," but with "WORLD CUP/USA 94" at top. Size and location of surcharge varies.

1993, Oct. 15   Litho.   Perf. 12x12½
61	A4(c)	1500r on 5r #15	3.50	3.50
62	A4(d)	1500r on 5r #15	3.50	3.50
a.		Pair, #61-62	7.00	7.00
63	A4(c)	1500r on 5r #16	3.50	3.50
64	A4(d)	1500r on 5r #16	3.50	3.50
a.		Pair, #63-64	7.00	7.00
		Nos. 61-64 (4)	14.00	14.00
		Souvenir Sheets		
		Perf. 12		
65	A5(c)	1500r on 5r #18	3.50	3.50
66	A5(d)	1500r on 5r #18	3.50	3.50

The status of Nos. 65-66 are in question.

Stansilavski Church
A13

1993, Nov. 24   Litho.   Perf. 12
67	A13	150r multicolored	.35	.35

For surcharge see No. 242.

Famous People
A14

Designs: 50r, Kastus Kalinovsky, led 1863 independence movement. No. 69, Prince Rogvold of Polotsk, map of Polotsk. No. 70, Princess Rogneda, daughter of Rogvold, fortress. 100r, Statue of Simon Budny (1530-93), writer and printer, vert.

1993   Perf. 12x12½, 12½x12
68	A14	50r multicolored	.20	.20
69	A14	75r multicolored	.20	.20
70	A14	75r multicolored	.25	.25
71	A14	100r multicolored	.35	.35
		Nos. 68-71 (4)	1.00	1.00

Issued: 50r, 12/29; 75r, 12/30; 100r, 12/31.

Nos. 27, 29, 30 Surcharged

1994, Feb. 1   Photo.   Perf. 12x12½
72	A7	15r on 30k light green	.20	.20
73	A7	25r on 45k olive green	.20	.20
74	A7	50r on 50k green	.20	.20
		Nos. 72-74 (3)	.60	.60

Birds — A15

1994, Jan. 19   Litho.   Perf. 11½
75	A15	20r Aguila chrysaetos	.20	.20
76	A15	40r Cygnus olor	.20	.20
77	A15	40r Alcedo atthis	.20	.20
a.		Block of 3, #75-77 + label	.60	.60

See #87-89. For surcharge see #303.

Six World Wildlife Fund labels with 1000r denominations depicting 3 different animals and 3 different birds exist. They were not valid for postage.

Liberation of Soviet Areas, 50th Anniv.
A16

Battle maps and: a, Katyusha rockets, liberation of Russia. b, Fighter planes, liberation of Ukraine. c, Combined offensive, liberation of Belarus.

1994, July 3   Litho.   Perf. 12
78	A16	500r Block of 3 + label	.80	.75

See Russia No. 6213, Ukraine No. 195.

1994 Winter Olympics, Lillehammer
A17

1994, Aug. 30   Litho.   Perf. 12x12½
79	A17	1000r Speed skating	.20	.20
80	A17	1000r Women's figure skating	.20	.20
81	A17	1000r Hockey	.20	.20
82	A17	1000r Cross-country skiing	.20	.20
83	A17	1000r Biathlon	.20	.20
		Nos. 79-83 (5)	1.00	1.00

Painters — A18

Designs: No. 84, Farmer, oxen in field, by Ferdinand Rushchyts. No. 85, Knight on horseback, by Jasev Drazdovich. No. 86, Couple walking up path, by Petra Sergievich. Illustration reduced

1994, July 18   Litho.   Perf. 12
84	A18	300r multicolored	.20	.20
85	A18	300r multicolored	.20	.20
86	A18	300r multicolored	.20	.20
		Nos. 84-86 (3)	.60	.60

For overprint see No. 127.

Bird Type of 1994

1994, Sept. 30   Perf. 11½
87	A15	300r like #75	.20	.20
88	A15	400r like #76	.20	.20
89	A15	400r like #77	.20	.20
		Nos. 87-89 (3)	.60	.60

Ilya Yefimovich Repin (1844-1930), Ukrainian Painter — A19

#90, Self-portrait. #91, Repin Museum.

1994, Oct. 31   Litho.   Perf. 12x12½
90		1000r multicolored	.40	.30
91		1000r multicolored	.40	.30
a.	A19	Pair, #90-91	.80	.60

Churches
A20

Designs: No. 92, Sacred Consolidated Church, Sinkavitsch, 16th cent. No. 93, Sts. Peter and Paul Cathedral, Gomel, 19th cent.

1994, Oct. 20   Litho.   Perf. 12
92	A20	700r multicolored	.20	.20
93	A20	700r multicolored	.20	.20

Kosciuszko Uprising, Bicent. (in 1994) — A21

Battle scene and: No. 94, Tomasz Vaishetcki (1754-1816). No. 95, Jakov Jasinski (1761-94). No. 96, Tadeusz Kosziuszko (1746-1817). No. 97, Mikhail K. Aginski (1765-1833).

1995, Jan. 11   Perf. 12½x12
94	A21	600r multicolored	.20	.20
95	A21	600r multicolored	.20	.20
96	A21	1000r multicolored	.30	.30
97	A21	1000r multicolored	.30	.30
		Nos. 94-97 (4)	1.00	1.00

End of World War II, 50th Anniv. — A22

1995, May 4   Litho.   Perf. 13½
98   A22   180r multicolored   .20   .20
99   A22   600r multicolored   .20   .20

A23   A24

1995, May 7   Perf. 14
100   A23   600r A Popov   .20   .20
Radio, cent. Exists imperf.

1995-96   Litho.   Perf. 13x14
102   A24   180r olive brown & red   .20   .20
103   A24   200r gray green & bister   .20   .20
105   A24   280r green & blue   .20   .20
109   A24   600r plum & bister   .20   .20
      Nos. 102-109 (4)   .80   .80
No. 102 exists imperf.
Issued: 180r, 5/10/95; 280r, 5/18/95; 600r, 8/29/95; 200r, 1/30/96.
This is an expanding set. Numbers may change.

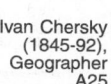

Ivan Chersky (1845-92), Geographer A25

1995, May 15   Litho.   Perf. 13½x14
113   A25   600r multicolored   .20   .20
Exists imperf.

A26

Traditional Costumes: 600r, Woman wearing shawl, coat, ankle length skirt, man with long coat. 1200r, Woman wearing shawl & apron holding child, man wearing vest, knickers.

1995, July 13   Litho.   Perf. 14½x14
114   A26   180r multicolored   .20   .20
115   A26   600r multicolored   .20   .20
116   A26   1200r multicolored   .25   .25
      Nos. 114-116 (3)   .65   .65
See Nos. 164-167, 214-216.

A27

1995, July 20   Perf. 12
World Wildlife Fund: Various pictures of a beaver.
117   A27   300r multi   .20   .20
118   A27   450r multi   .20   .20
119   A27   450r multi, horiz.   .20   .20
120   A27   800r multi, horiz.   .40   .40
      Nos. 117-120 (4)   1.00   1.00

A28   A29

1995, Aug. 29   Litho.   Perf. 14
121   A28   600r Book Fair   .20   .20
Exists imperf.

1995, Oct. 3   Litho.   Perf. 14
122   A29   600r Natl. arms   .20   .20
123   A29   600r Flag   .20   .20
New national symbols. Exist imperf.

UN, 50th Anniv. — A30

1995, Oct. 24   Litho.   Perf. 13½x14
124   A30   600r bister, black & blue   .20   .20
Exists imperf.

Churches A31

Designs: No. 125, Mstislav, 17th-19th cent. No. 126, Kamai, 17th cent.

1995, Nov. 21   Perf. 14
125   A31   600r multicolored   .20   .20
126   A31   600r multicolored   .20   .20

No. 84 Ovptd.

1995, Dec. 27   Litho.   Perf. 12
127   A18   300r multicolored   .20   .20

P. V. Sukhi (1895-1975), Airplane Designer A32

1995, Dec. 27   Perf. 13½
128   A32   600r multicolored   .20   .20

Wildlife A33

1000r, Lynx lynx. #130, Capreolus capreolus. #131, Ursus arctos. 3000r, Alces alcest. 5000r, Bison bonasus. 10,000r, Cervus elaphus, vert.

1995-96   Litho.   Perf. 14
129   A33   1000r multi   .20   .20
130   A33   2000r multi, vert.   .30   .30
131   A33   2000r multi   .30   .30
132   A33   3000r multi, vert.   .45   .45
133   A33   5000r multi   .75   .75
      Nos. 129-133 (5)   2.00   2.00

Souvenir Sheet
Imperf
134   A33   10,000r multicolored   1.25   1.25
Issued: #129-133, 2/6/96; #134, 12/29/95.

Famous People — A34

Designs: 600r, L. Sapega (1557-1633), statesman. 1200r, K. Semyanovitch (1600-51), military scholar. 1800r, S. Polotzki (1629-80), writer. Illustration reduced.

1995, Dec. 30   Litho.   Perf. 12
135   A34   600r multicolored   .20   .20
136   A34   1200r multicolored   .20   .20
137   A34   1800r multicolored   .30   .30
      Nos. 135-137 (3)   .70   .70

Miniature Sheet

Butterflies A35

Designs: No. 138a, Apatura iris. b, Lopinga achine. c, Callimorpha dominula. d, Catocala fraxini. e, Papilio machaon. f, Parnassius apollo. g, Ammobiota hebe. h, Colias palaeno. No. 139, Proserpinus proserpina. No. 140, Vacciniina optilete.

1996, Mar. 29   Litho.   Perf. 14
138   A35   300r Sheet of 8, #a.-h.   7.50   7.50

Souvenir Sheets
139-140   A35   1000r each   3.25   3.25
Inscribed 1995.

Nos. 28, 34 Surcharged in Green or Red

1996   Litho.   Perf. 12x12½
141   A7   (B) on 1r #28 (G)   .20   .20
142   A7   (A) on 25r #34 (R)   .20   .20
Nos. 141-142 were valued at 200r and 400r, respectively, on day of issue.
Issued: #141, 2/28/96; #142, 3/13/96.

Souvenir Sheet

Beaver — A36

Illustration reduced.

1996, Mar. 26   Litho.   Perf. 12½x12
143   A36   1200r multicolored   .35   .35

Kondrat Krapiva (1896-1991), Writer A37

1996, Mar. 5   Litho.   Perf. 14x14½
144   A37   1000r multicolored   .20   .20

Chernobyl Disaster, 10th Anniv. A38

Radiation symbol and: a, Eye. b, Leaf showing contamination. c, Boarded-up window.

1996, Apr. 10   Litho.   Perf. 14
145   A38   1000r Block of 3, #a.-c. + label   .50   .50

Coat of Arms — A39

1996, May 6   Litho.   Perf. 13½
146   A39   100r blue & black   .20   .20
147   A39   500r green & black   .20   .20
148   A39   600r ver & black   .20   .20
149   A39   1000r org & black   .20   .20
150   A39   1500r dp lil rose & blk   .20   .20
151   A39   1800r violet & black   .20   .20
152   A39   2200r rose vio & blk   .20   .20
153   A39   3300r yellow & blk   .30   .20
154   A39   5000r grn bl & blk   .50   .35
155   A39   10,000r ap grn & blk   1.00   .60
156   A39   30,000r brn & black   3.00   2.00
157   A39   50,000r red brn & blk   4.50   3.00
      Nos. 146-157 (12)   10.70   7.55
See Nos. 182, 196-201.

Agreement with Russia A40

1996, June 14   Perf. 13½x14
158   A40   1500r multicolored   .25   .25

1996 Summer Olympic Games, Atlanta A41

1996, July 15   Litho.   Perf. 14
159   A41   3000r Rhythmic gymnastics   .30   .30
160   A41   3000r Discus   .30   .30

161 A41 3000r Wrestling .30 .30
162 A41 3000r Weight lifting .30 .30
Nos. 159-162 (4) 1.20 1.20

Souvenir Sheet
Imperf

163 A41 5000r Shooting, vert. .75 .75
No. 163 has simulated perforations.

Regional Costume Type of 1995

Couples in traditional 19th cent. costumes: 1800r, Kapilska-Kletzky region. 2200r, David-Gorodok-Turai region. 3300r, Kobrin region. 5000r, Naralyan region.

1996, Aug. 13 Litho. *Perf. 14*
164 A26 1800r multicolored .20 .20
165 A26 2200r multicolored .25 .25
166 A26 3300r multicolored .30 .30
Nos. 164-166 (3) .75 .75

Souvenir Sheet
Imperf

167 A26 5000r multicolored .75 .75

Medicinal Plants — A42

No. 168, Sanguisorba officinaus. No. 169, Acorus calamus. 2200r, Potentilla erecta. 3300r, Frangula alnus. 5000r, Menyanthes trifoliata.

1996, Aug. 15 *Perf. 14x13½*
168 A42 1500r multicolored .20 .20
169 A42 1500r multicolored .20 .20
170 A42 2200r multicolored .20 .20
171 A42 3300r multicolored .30 .30
Nos. 168-171 (4) .90 .90

Souvenir Sheet
Imperf

172 A42 5000r multicolored .75 .75

Birds A44
Ardea cinerea

No. 173: a, Ardea cinerea. b, Ciconia nigra. c, Phalacrocorax caroo. d, Ciconia ciconia. e, Larus ridibundus. f, Gallinago gallinago. g, Chlidonias leucopterus. h, Remiz pendulinus. i, Botaurus stellaris. j, Fulica atra. k, Ixobrychus minutus. l, Alcedo atthts.
No. 174: a, Anas crecca. b, Anas strepera. c, Anas acuta. d, Anas platyrhynchos. e, Aythya marila. f, Clangula hyemalis. g, Anas clypeata. h, Anas querquedula. i, Anas penelope. j, Arthya nyroca. k, Bucephala clangula. l, Mergus merganser. m, Mergus albellus. n, Aythya fuligula. o, Mergus serrator. p, Aythya ferina.
No. 175, Aythya ferina, diff. No. 176, Gallinago gallinago, diff.

1996, Sept. 10 Litho. *Perf. 14*
173 A44 400r Sheet of 12, #a.-l. 5.00 5.00
174 A44 400r Sheet of 16, #a.-p. 5.00 5.00

Souvenir Sheets
175-176 A44 1000r each 3.25 3.25

Grammar Book, 1596 — A45

1996, Sept. 19 Litho. *Perf. 14x13½*
177 A45 1500r multicolored .25 .25

Churches A46

1996, Sept. 24 *Perf. 14x14½*
178 A46 3300r Pinsk .40 .40
179 A46 3300r Mogilev, 17th cent. .40 .40

Mikola Shchakatskin (1896-1940), Art Critic — A47

1996, Oct. 16
180 A47 2000r multicolored .25 .25

Minsk Telephone Station, Cent. A48

1996, Nov. 14
181 A48 2000r multicolored .25 .25

Natl. Arms Type of 1996
1996, Nov. 21 Litho. *Perf. 13½x14*
182 A39 200r gray green & black .20 .20

Pres. Aleksandr G. Lukashenka, Natl. Flag — A49

1996, Dec. 6 Litho. *Perf. 13½*
183 A49 2500r multicolored .25 .25

Famous Men — A50

Designs: No. 184, Kyril Turovski (1130-81), Bishop of Turov. No. 185, Mikola Gusovski (1470-1533), writer. No. 186, Mikolaj Radziwil (1515-65), chancellor of Lithuania.

1996, Dec. 17 *Perf. 13½*
184 A50 3000r multicolored .30 .30
185 A50 3000r multicolored .30 .30
186 A50 3000r multicolored .30 .30
Nos. 184-186 (3) .90 .90

New Year — A51

1500r, Christmas tree, buildings in Minsk.

1996, Dec. 21 *Perf. 14*
187 A51 1500r multicolored .20 .20
188 A51 2000r multicolored, vert. .20 .20

Natl. Museum of Art, Minsk — A52

Icons: No. 189, Madonna and Child, Smolensk, 16th cent. No. 190, Paraskeva, 16th cent. No. 191, Ilya, 17th cent. No. 192, Three saints, 18th cent.
5000r, Birth of Christ, by Peter Yacijevitsch, 1649.

1996, Dec. 26 *Perf. 13½*
189 A52 3500r multicolored .40 .40
190 A52 3500r multicolored .40 .40
191 A52 3500r multicolored .40 .40
192 A52 3500r multicolored .40 .40
Nos. 189-192 (4) 1.60 1.60

Souvenir Sheet
Imperf

193 A46 5000r multicolored .75 .75

Georgi K. Zhukov (1896-1974), Soviet Marshal A53

1997, Jan. 3 *Perf. 13½*
194 A53 2000r multicolored .30 .30

Kupala Natl. Theater, Minsk — A54

1997, Jan. 3 *Perf. 13½x14*
195 A54 3500r multicolored .40 .40

Coat of Arms Type of 1996
1997 Litho. *Perf. 13½x14*
196 A39 400r lt brown & black .20 .20
197 A39 800r dull blue & black .20 .20
198 A39 1500r brt blue & black .45 .45
199 A39 2000r apple green & black .60 .60
200 A39 2500r dk blue & black .45 .45
201 A39 3000r brown & black .45 .45

Issued: 400r, 2000r, 1/9; 1500r, 1/16; 800r, 2500r, 3000r, 9/22.

V.K. Byalynitsky-Birulya (1872-1957), Painter — A55

1997, Feb. 26 *Perf. 14*
202 A55 2000r multicolored .30 .30

No. 2 Surcharged in Gray

1997, Mar. 10 Photo. *Perf. 12x11½*
203 A2 3500r on 20k bl & blk .50 .50

Fish — A56

2000r, Salmo trutta. 3000r, Vimba vimba. #206, Thymallus thymallus. #207, Barbus barbus.
5000r, Acipenser ruthenus.

1997, Apr. 10 Litho. *Perf. 13½x14*
204 A56 2000r multicolored .25 .25
205 A56 3000r multicolored .30 .30
206 A56 4500r multicolored .50 .50
207 A56 4500r multicolored .50 .50
Nos. 204-207 (4) 1.55 1.55

Souvenir Sheet
208 A56 5000r multicolored .75 .75

Intl. Conference on Sustainable Development of Countries with Economies in Transition — A57

Designs: 3000r, Earth with "SOS" formed in atmosphere. 4500r, Hand above flora and fauna.

1997, Apr. 16 *Perf. 14x14½*
209 A57 3000r multicolored .40 .40
210 A57 4500r multicolored .60 .60
a. Pair, #209-210 + label 1.00 1.00

Entry into UPU, 50th Anniv. — A58

1997, May 13 *Perf. 14½x14*
211 A58 3000r multicolored .50 .50

Nos. 28-29 Surcharged in Violet Blue

1997 Litho. *Perf. 12x12½*
211A A7 100r on 1r brown 5.00 5.00
212 A7 100r on 2r red brown .20 .20

Issued: 2r, 5/22.

World War II Liberation Day, July 3 — A59

1997, June 26   *Perf. 14½x14*
213 A59 3000r multicolored   .90   .90

Traditional Costume Type

Men and women in 19th cent. costumes, regions: 2000r, Dzisna. 3000r, Navagrudak. 4500r, Byhau.

1997, July 10
214 A26 2000r multicolored   .55   .55
215 A26 3000r multicolored   .85   .85
216 A26 4500r multicolored   1.25   1.25
   Nos. 214-216 (3)   2.65   2.65

Book Printing in Belarus, 480th Anniv. — A60

#217, Text, Vilnius period. #218, Text, Prague period. 4000r, F. Skorina (1488-1535), Polatsk period. 7500r, F. Skorina, Krakow period.

1997, Sept. 7   *Perf. 13½*
217 A60 3000r shown   .85   .85
218 A60 3000r gray, black & red   .85   .85
219 A60 4000r gray, black & red   1.10   1.10
220 A60 7500r gray, black & red   2.00   2.00
   Nos. 217-220 (4)   4.80   4.80

Pinsk Jesuit College A61

1997, Sept. 13   *Perf. 14x14½*
221 A61 3000r multicolored   .85   .85

National Library, 75th Anniv. A62

1997, Sept. 15
222 A62 3000r multicolored   .90   .90

Belarus School for the Blind, Cent. A63

1997, Sept. 28   **Litho.**   *Perf. 14x14¼*
223 A63 3000r multicolored   .45   .45

Intl. Children's Day — A64

1997, Sept. 28   **Litho.**   *Perf. 14x14½*
224 A64 3000r multicolored   .85   .85

Fight Against AIDS — A65

1997, Oct. 14   *Perf. 14½x14*
225 A65 4000r multicolored   1.10   1.10

Farm Tractors A66

3300r, Belarus "1221." 4400r, First wheel tractor, 1953. #228, Belarus "952." #229, Belarus "680."

1997, Oct. 16   *Perf. 14x14½*
226 A66 3300r multicolored   1.00   1.00
227 A66 4400r multicolored   1.25   1.25
228 A66 7500r multicolored   2.00   2.00
229 A66 7500r multicolored   2.00   2.00
   a.   Sheet, 2 ea #226-229 + label   13.00   13.00
   Nos. 226-229 (4)   6.25   6.25

No. 1 Surcharged

1997, Dec. 8   **Litho.**   *Perf. 12x12½*
230 A1 3000r on 1r multi   .45   .45

Holiday Greetings A68

1997, Dec. 23   **Litho.**   *Perf. 14x14¼*
231 A68 1400r New Year   .20   .20
232 A68 4400r Christmas   .50   .50

1998 Winter Olympic Games, Nagano — A69

Designs: a, 2000r, Cross country skiing. b, 3300r, Ice hockey. c, 4400r, Biathlon. d, 7500r, Freestyle skiing.

1998, Feb. 3   **Litho.**   *Perf. 13½*
233 A69   Block of 4, #a.-d.   2.50

P.M. Mascherov (1918-80), Author — A70

1998, Feb. 12   **Litho.**   *Perf. 13½*
234 A70 2500r multicolored   .30   .30

Minsk Automobile Plant — A71

Dump trucks: 1400r, 1947 MAZ-205. 2000r, 1968 MAZ-503B. 3000r, 1977 MAZ-5549. 4400r, 1985 MAZ-5551. 7500r, 1994 MAZ-5516.

1998, Apr. 23   **Litho.**   *Perf. 13½*
235 A71 1400r multicolored   .20   .20
236 A71 2000r multicolored   .25   .25
237 A71 3000r multicolored   .40   .40
238 A71 4400r multicolored   .55   .55
239 A71 7500r multicolored   .95   .95
   a.   Souvenir sheet, #235-239 + label   2.50   2.50
   Nos. 235-239 (5)   2.35   2.35

 (A72)   A73

A72   A73

1998, May 5   **Litho.**   *Perf. 14*
240 A72 15,000r multicolored   1.00   1.00

Europa. Town of Nesvizh, 775th Anniv.

1998, May 20   **Litho.**   *Perf. 14*
241 A73 8600r multicolored   1.10   1.10

Adam Mickiewicz (1798-1855), poet.

No. 67 Surcharged in Silver with Post Horn, New Value and Cyrillic Text

1998, May 22   *Perf. 12*
242 A13 8600r on 150r multi   1.10   1.10

St. Petersburt-Mahilyou Post Route, 225th anniv.

A74   A75

Songbirds from Red Book of Belarus: 1500r, Luscinia svecica. 3200r, Remiz pendulinus. 3800r, Acrocephalus paludicola. 5300r, Locustella luscinioides. 8600r, Parus cyanus.

1998, May 29   *Perf. 14*
243 A74 1500r multicolored   .20   .20
244 A74 3200r multicolored   .40   .40
245 A74 3800r multicolored   .50   .50
246 A74 5300r multicolored   .65   .65
247 A74 8600r multicolored   1.10   1.10
   a.   Sheet, 2 each #243-247   5.75   5.75
   Nos. 243-247 (5)   2.85   2.85

1998   *Perf. 13½x14*

Mills, Musical Instruments: 100r, Water-powered mill. 200r, Windmill. 500r, Stork. 1000r, Bison. 2000r, Christmas Star. 3200r, Dulcimer. 5000r, Church, Synkovichy. 5300r, Hurdy-gurdy. 10,000r, Flaming wheel.

248 A75 100r green & black   .20   .20
249 A75 200r brown & black   .20   .20
250 A75 500r bl, lt blu & blk   .20   .20
251 A75 1000r grn, lt grn & blk   .20   .20
252 A75 2000r bl, lt bl & blk   .20   .20
253 A75 3200r ap grn & blk   1.00   1.00
254 A75 5000r bl, lt bl & blk   .20   .20
255 A75 5300r bis, blk & buff   1.75   1.75
256 A75 10,000r org, lt org & blk   .30   .30
   Nos. 248-256 (9)   4.25   4.25

Issued: 100r, 200r, 7/1; 3200r, 5300r, 6/23; 2000r, 10,000r, 8/5;
See Nos. 282-288, 331-335, 338-339, 361.

Belarussian Auto Works (BelAZ), 50th Anniv. — A76

Designs: 1500r, Front end loader. Large quarry truck models: 3200r, #75131. 3800r, #75303. 5300r, #75483. 8600r, #755.

1998, Aug. 12   *Perf. 14x14½*
259 A76 1500r multicolored   .20   .20
260 A76 3200r multicolored   .20   .20
261 A76 3800r multicolored   .20   .20
262 A76 5300r multicolored   .20   .20
263 A76 8600r multicolored   .20   .20
   a.   Sheet of 5, #259-263 + label   .80   .80

A77

Mushrooms: 2500r, Morchella esculenta. 3800r, Morchella conica. 4600r, Macrolepiota rhacodes. 5800r, Marcrolepiota procera. 9400r, Coprinus comatus.

1998, Sept. 10   **Litho.**   *Perf. 14¼x14*
264 A77 2500r multicolored   .20   .20
265 A77 3800r multicolored   .20   .20
266 A77 4600r multicolored   .20   .20
267 A77 5800r multicolored   .20   .20
268 A77 9400r multicolored   .25   .25
   Nos. 264-268 (5)   1.05   1.05

Tete beche pairs

264a A77 2500r   .20   .20
265a A77 3800r   .20   .20
266a A77 4600r   .20   .20
267a A77 5800r   .30   .30
268a A77 9400r   .50   .50

See Nos. 316-320.

A78

Wooden Sculptures: 3400r, Naversha, 12-13th cent. 3800r, Archangel Michael, 1470-1480. 5800r, Prophet Zacharias, 1642-1646. 9400r, Madonna and Child, 16th cent.

1998, Oct. 6   *Perf. 13½*
269 A78 3400r multicolored   .20   .20
270 A78 3800r multicolored   .20   .20
271 A78 5800r multicolored   .20   .20
272 A78 9400r multicolored   .25   .25
   Nos. 269-272 (4)   .85   .85

World Stamp Day — A79

1998, Oct. 9 **Perf. 14x14½**
273 A79 5500r multicolored .20 .20

Paintings from Natl. Art Museum — A80

3000r, "Kalozha" (church), by V.K. Tsvirko (1913-93). 3500r, "Corner Living Room," by S.U. Zhukovsky (1875-1944). 5000r, "Winter Dream," by V.K. Byalynitsky-Birulya (1872-1957). 5500r, "Portrait of a Girl," by I.I. Alyashkevich (1777-1830). 10,000r, "Woman with a Bowl of Fruit," by I.F. Hrutski (1810-85).

1998, Oct. 20 **Perf. 13½**
274 A80 3000r multi .20 .20
275 A80 3500r multi .20 .20
276 A80 5000r multi .20 .20
277 A80 5500r multi, vert. .20 .20
278 A80 10,000r multi, vert. .30 .20
Nos. 274-278 (5) 1.10 1.00

A81   A82

1998, Nov. 25 **Perf. 14½x14**
279 A81 7100r multicolored .20 .20
Universal Declaration of Human Rights, 50th anniv.

1998, Nov. 30
Christmas and New Year: No. 280, Girl wearing short yellow coat, rabbit, log cabin. No. 281, Rabbit, girl wearing long fur-trimmed pink coat, hat.

280 A82 5500r multicolored .20 .20
281 A82 5500r multicolored .20 .20
a. Pair, #280-281 .20 .20

Type of 1998

Designs: 800r, Church. 1500r, Dulcimer. 3000r, Hurdy-gurdy. 30,000r, Water-powered mill. 50,000r, Windmill. 100,000r, Exhibition center, Minsk, horiz. 500,000r, Dancers.

Perf. 13½x14, 14x13½
1998-99 **Litho.**
282 A75 800r red lil, pale lil & blk .20 .20
283 A75 1500r golden brn, buff & blk .20 .20
284 A75 3000r yel, pale yel & blk .20 .20
285 A75 30,000r Prus bl, lt bl & blk .25 .25
286 A75 50,000r org, pale org & blk .40 .40
287 A75 100,000r brt pink & blk .80 .80
288 A75 500,000r brn & blk 3.50 3.50
Nos. 282-288 (7) 5.55 5.55

Issued: 800r, 2/5/99; 1500r, 3000r, 12/22/98; 30,000r, 50,000r, 4/14/99; 100,000r, 4/22/99; 500,000r, 6/25/99.

Statues of Aleksander Pushkin and Adam Mickiewicz, St. Petersburg — A95

1999, Jan. 20 **Litho.** **Perf. 13½**
294 A95 15,300r multi .20 .20

Trucks Made In Minsk — A96

10,000r, Model 8007. 15,000r, Model 543M rocket launcher. No. 297, Model 7907. No. 298, Model 543m with radar. No. 299: a, 50,000r, Model 7917. b, 150,000r, Model 74135.

1999, Feb. 23
295 A96 10,000r multi .20 .20
296 A96 15,000r multi .20 .20
297 A96 30,000r multi .30 .30
298 A96 30,000r multi .30 .30
Nos. 295-298 (4) 1.00 1.00
Souvenir Sheet
299 A96 Sheet of 6, #295-298, 299a, 299b + 3 labels 3.25 3.25

No. 295 printed in sheets of 8. See Nos. 322-323.

Glassware in National History and Culture Museum A97

1999, Mar. 4
300 A97 30,000r Goblet .30 .30
301 A97 30,000r Three pieces .30 .30
302 A97 100,000r Lamp .90 .90
Nos. 300-302 (3) 1.50 1.50

No. 77a Surcharged in Red

1999, Apr. 26 **Litho.** **Perf. 11½**
303 A15 150,000r on No. 77a 1.40 1.40

Europa — A98

Nature Reserves: No. 304, Berezina, 1925. No. 305, Belovezhskaya Forest, 1939.

1999, Apr. 27 **Litho.** **Perf. 13½**
304 A98 150,000r multicolored 1.25 1.25
305 A98 150,000r multicolored 1.25 1.25

Regional Architecture — A99

1999, June 10 **Litho.** **Perf. 13½**
306 A99 50,000r Well .40 .40
307 A99 50,000r House .40 .40
308 A99 100,000r Windmill .80 .80
Nos. 306-308 (3) 1.60 1.60

No. 306 printed in sheets of 8.

Paintings A100

30,000r, Portrait of Y. M. Pen, by A. M. Brazer. 60,000r, St. Anthony's Church, Vitebsk, by S. B. Yudovin. No. 311, Street in Vitebsk, by Y. M. Pen. No. 312, House in Vitebsk, by M. P. Michalap, horiz. 200,000r, Etching by Marc Chagall.

1999, July 2
309 A100 30,000r multi .20 .20
310 A100 60,000r multi .45 .45
311 A100 100,000r multi .70 .70
312 A100 100,000r multi .70 .70
Nos. 309-312 (4) 2.05 2.05
Souvenir Sheet
313 A100 200,000r multi 1.40 1.40

V. M. Karvat (1958-96), Hero — A101

1999, Aug. 12
314 A101 25,000r multi .20 .20

UPU, 125th Anniv. — A102

Designs: a, Minsk post office, 1954. b, First Minsk post office, 1800.

1999, Aug. 20
315 A102 150,000r Pair, #a.-b. 2.10 2.10

Mushroom Type of 1998

Designs: 30,000r, Flammulina velutipes. 50,000r, Kuehneromyces mutabilis. 75,000r, Lyophyllum connatum. 100,000r, Lyophyllum decastes. 150,000r, Armillariella mellea.

1999, Aug. 21 **Perf. 14¼x14**
316 A77 30,000r multi .20 .20
a. Tete beche pair .40 .40
317 A77 50,000r multi .35 .35
a. Tete beche pair .70 .70
318 A77 75,000r multi .55 .55
a. Tete beche pair 1.10 1.10
319 A77 100,000r multi .70 .70
a. Tete beche pair 1.40 1.40
Nos. 316-319 (4) 1.80 1.80
Souvenir Sheet
320 A77 150,000r multi 1.10 1.10
a. Tete beche pair 2.25 2.25

Left margin of No. 320 is perforated, and sheet contains two labels.

Re-annexation of Western Belarus from Poland, 60th Anniv. — A103

1999, Sept. 17 **Litho.** **Perf. 13½x14**
321 A103 29,000r multi .20 .20

Truck Type of 1999

51,000r, MAZ-6430. 86,000r, MAZ-4370.

1999, Nov. 15 **Litho.** **Perf. 13½**
322 A96 51,000r multi .20 .20
323 A96 86,000r multi .35 .35

Children's Art — A104

1999, Nov. 25
324 A104 32,000r shown .20 .20
325 A104 59,000r Girl, vert. .25 .25

New Year A105

No. 326: a, Bear, snow-covered trees. b, People, snowman.

1999, Nov. 30 **Perf. 14x14¼**
326 A105 30,000r Pair, #a-b, + central label .25 .25

Christianity, 2000th Anniv. — A106

Designs: 50r, Spaso-Preobrazhenskaya Church, Polotsk. 75r, St. Atistratig Cathedral, Slutsk. 100r, Rev, Serafim Sorovsky Church, Beloozersk.

2000, Jan. 1 **Perf. 14¼x14**
327 A106 50r multi .20 .20
328 A106 75r multi .30 .30
329 A106 100r multi .40 .40
Nos. 327-329 (3) .90 .90

Souvenir Sheet

Christianity, 2000th Anniversary — A107

Designs: a, Mother of God mosaic, St. Sofia, Cathedral, Kiev, 11th cent. b, Christ Pantocrator fresco, Church of the Savoior's Transfiguration, Polotsk, 12th cent. c, Volodymyr Madonna, Tretiakov Gallery, Moscow, 12th cent.

2000, Jan. 5   *Perf. 12x12¼*
330 A107 100r Sheet of 3, #a-c   1.25 1.25
See Ukraine No. 370, Russia No. 6568.

Type of 1998 and

Kryzhachok Dancers — A108

2000   **Litho.**   *Perf. 13½x14*
331 A75 1r Bison .20 .20
332 A75 2r Christmas star .20 .20
333 A75 3r Hurdy-gurdy .20 .20
334 A75 5r Church, Synkovichy .20 .20
335 A75 10r Flaming wheel .20 .20
336 A108 A Kupala folk holiday .20 .20
337 A108 20r Kryzhachok dancers .20 .20
338 A75 30r Water-powered mill .20 .20
339 A75 50r Windmill .20 .20
Nos. 332-339 (8) 1.60 1.60

Booklet Stamp
Self-Adhesive
Serpentine Die Cut 5¾
340 A108 20r red & black .20 .20
a. Booklet pane of 18 1.50
Booklet #340a 1.50

No. 336 sold for 19r on day of issue.
No. 340 has a line below the country name.
Nos. 337 and 364 have lines of microprinting below the country name.
See Nos. 364-368.
Issued: 1r, 5r, 10r, 1/6; #340, 1/14; 2r, 30r, 1/29; 3r, A, #337, 3/10; 50r, 4/6.

Sukhoi Fighter Aircraft A109

Designs: Nos. 341, 344a, Su-24. Nos. 342, 344b, Su-25. Nos. 343, 344c, Su-27.

2000, Feb. 23 Litho.   *Perf. 14x14¼*
341 A109 50r multicolored .25 .25
342 A109 50r multicolored .25 .25
343 A109 50r multicolored .25 .25
Nos. 341-343 (3) .75 .75

Souvenir Sheet
344 Sheet of 3 + label 2.25 2.25
a.-c. A109 150r Any single .75 .75

Birds — A110

Designs: No. 345, Mergellus albelius. No. 346, Burhinus oedicnemus. 75r, Lagopus lagopus. 100r, Aquila pomarina, vert.

Perf. 13½x13¾, 13¾x13½
2000, Mar. 22
345 A110 50r multi .25 .25
346 A110 50r multi .25 .25
347 A110 75r multi .35 .35
348 A110 100r multi .50 .50
Nos. 345-348 (4) 1.35 1.35

Partisan Madonna of Minsk, by M. Savitsky — A111

2000, Apr. 27   *Perf. 13½*
349 A111 100r multi .45 .45
End of World War II, 55th anniv.

Europa, 2000
Common Design Type
2000, May 9   *Perf. 14x13½*
350 CD17 250r multi .85 .85
a. Tete beche pair 1.70 1.70

Ballet — A112

Designs: 100r, Male dancer lifting female dancer. 150r, Dancer with crown.

2000, May 25 Litho.   *Perf. 13¾x13½*
351 A112 100r multi .45 .45

Souvenir Sheet
352 A112 150r multi + label .70 .70

UN High Commissioner for Refugees, 50th Anniv. — A113

2000, Aug. 23 Litho.   *Perf. 13½x14*
353 A113 50r multi .25 .25

Worldwide Fund for Nature (WWF) — A114

Lynx lynx: No. 354, 100r, Close-up of head. No. 355, 100r, On tree. No. 356, 150r, On snow. No. 357, 150r, Adult and young.

2000, Aug. 25   *Perf. 14x13½*
354-357 A114 Set of 4 1.75 1.75
357a Sheet, 2 each #354-357 3.75 3.75

Intl. Year of Culture of Peace A115

2000, Sept. 5 Litho.   *Perf. 13½x14*
358 A115 100r multi .30 .30

2000 Summer Olympics, Sydney — A116

No. 359: a, Gymnast on rings. b, Kayak. c, Rhythmic gymnastics.
Illustration reduced.

2000, Sept. 10 Litho.   *Perf. 14x13½*
359 A116 100r Strip of 3, #a-c 1.00 1.00

Souvenir Sheet
360 A116 400r Runner + label 1.40 1.40

Type of 1998
100r, Exhibition center, Minsk, horiz.

2000   **Litho.**   *Perf. 14x13½*
361 A75 100r brt pink & blk .30 .30
Issued: 100r, 10/18/00.

Type of 2000
Designs: 20r, Kryzhachok dancers. 30r, Water-powered mill. B, Dazhynki Crop Festival. A, Kupala folk holiday. 50r, Windmill.

Serpentine Die Cut 5¾
2000, Nov. 8   **Litho.**
Self-Adhesive
364 A108 20r red & black .20 .20
365 A108 30r green & black .20 .20
366 A108 B yel & black .20 .20
367 A108 A blue & black .20 .20
368 A108 50r brown & black .20 .20
Nos. 364-368 (5) 1.00 1.00

No. 364 has a line of microprinting below country name, No. 340 has hairline. Nos. 366-367 sold for 34r and 39r respectively on day of issue. Nos. 364-368 each issued in sheets of 24.

A117

A118

A119

Minerals — A120

2000, Nov. 22 Litho.   *Perf. 14x14¼*
371 A117 200r multi .60 .60
372 A118 200r multi .60 .60
373 A119 200r multi .60 .60
374 A120 200r multi .60 .60
Nos. 371-374 (4) 2.40 2.40

New Year 2001 — A121

2000, Nov. 28 Litho.   *Perf. 14x13½*
375 A121 200r multi .60 .60

Christmas — A122

2000, Dec. 5
376 A122 100r multi .30 .30

A123

Children's Art Contest Winners A124

2000, Dec. 26   *Perf. 13½*
377 A123 100r multi .30 .30
378 A124 100r multi .30 .30

St. Euphrosyne of Polotsk, 900th Anniv. of Birth — A125

Illustration reduced.

2001, Jan. 5 Litho.   *Imperf.*
379 A125 500r multi 1.40 1.40

Brest Arms — A126

Gomel Arms — A127

2001, Jan. 10   *Perf. 14¼x14*

380	A126	200r multi	.55	.55
381	A127	200r multi	.55	.55

BELGIAN CONGO

ˈbel-jən ˈkäŋˌɡō

LOCATION — Central Africa
GOVT. — Belgian colony
AREA — 902,082 sq. mi. (estimated)
POP. — 12,660,000 (1956)
CAPITAL — Léopoldville

Congo was an independent state, founded by Leopold II of Belgium, until 1908 when it was annexed to Belgium as a colony. In 1960 it became the independent Republic of the Congo. See Congo Democratic Republic and Zaire.

100 Centimes = 1 Franc

> Catalogue values for unused stamps in this country are for Never Hinged items, beginning with Scott 187 in the regular postage section, Scott B32 in the semi-postal section, Scott C17 in the airpost section, and Scott J8 in the postage due section.

Independent State

A1   A2

King Leopold II — A3

1886   Unwmk.   Typo.   *Perf. 15*

1	A1	5c green	8.50	21.00
2	A1	10c rose	4.00	5.00
3	A2	25c blue	42.50	35.00
4	A3	50c olive green	6.50	6.50
5	A1	5fr lilac	325.00	260.00
a.		Perf. 14	825.00	
b.		5fr deep lilac	725.00	475.00

Counterfeits exist.
For surcharge see No. Q1.

King Leopold II — A4

1887-94

6	A4	5c grn ('89)	.75	.75
7	A4	10c rose ('89)	1.25	1.25
8	A4	25c blue ('89)	1.25	1.25
9	A4	50c reddish brown	45.00	21.00
10	A4	50c gray ('94)	2.50	16.00
11	A4	5fr violet	900.00	375.00
12	A4	5fr gray ('92)	110.00	95.00
13	A4	10fr buff ('91)	400.00	275.00

The 25fr and 50fr in gray were not issued. Values, each $20.
Counterfeits exist of Nos. 10-13, 25fr and 50fr, unused, used, genuine stamps with faked cancels and counterfeit stamps with genuine cancels.
For surcharges see Nos. Q3-Q6.

Port Matadi — A5

River Scene on the Congo, Stanley Falls — A6

Inkissi Falls — A7

Railroad Bridge on M'pozo River — A8

Hunting Elephants A9

Bangala Chief and Wife — A10

1894-1901   Engr.   *Perf. 12½ to 15*

14	A5	5c pale bl & blk	13.00	13.00
15	A5	5c red brn & blk ('95)	3.25	1.40
16	A5	5c grn & blk ('00)	1.75	.50
17	A6	10c red brn & blk	13.00	13.00
18	A6	10c grnsh bl & blk ('95)	1.50	1.40
a.		Center inverted	1,850.	2,250.
19	A6	10c car & blk ('00)	3.25	.75
20	A7	25c yel org & blk	3.50	2.40
21	A7	25c lt bl & blk ('00)	3.00	1.40
22	A8	50c grn & blk	1.40	1.40
23	A8	50c ol & blk ('00)	3.00	.75
24	A9	1fr lilac & blk	20.00	12.00
a.		1fr rose lilac & black	240.00	24.00
25	A9	1fr car & blk ('01)	210.00	5.00
26	A10	5fr lake & blk	40.00	25.00
a.		5fr carmine rose & black	87.50	37.50
		Nos. 14-26 (13)	316.65	78.00

For overprints see #31-32, 34, 36-37, 39.

Climbing Oil Palms — A11

Congo Canoe A12

1896

27	A11	15c ocher & blk	3.75	.75
28	A12	40c bluish grn & blk	3.75	3.00

For overprints see Nos. 33, 35.

Congo Village A13

River Steamer on the Congo A14

1898

29	A13	3.50fr red & blk	140.00	85.00
a.		Perf. 14x12	360.00	240.00
30	A14	10fr yel grn & blk	90.00	24.00
a.		Center inverted	25,000.	
b.		Perf. 12	525.00	25.00
c.		Perf. 12x14	325.00	—
		As "c," pen canceled		14.50

For overprints see Nos. 38, 40.

Belgian Congo

Overprinted **CONGO BELGE**

1908

31	A5	5c green & blk	7.25	7.25
a.		Handstamped	2.50	1.75
32	A6	10c car & blk	12.00	12.00
a.		Handstamped	2.50	1.75
33	A11	15c ocher & blk	7.25	7.25
a.		Handstamped	5.50	3.50
34	A7	25c lt blue & blk	3.75	2.50
a.		Handstamped	7.25	3.50
c.		Double overprint (#34)	190.00	
35	A12	40c bluish grn & blk	2.50	2.50
a.		Handstamped	7.25	5.50
36	A8	50c olive & blk	4.25	2.50
a.		Handstamped	4.25	3.50
b.		Inverted overprint (#36)	500.00	
37	A9	1fr car & blk	20.00	2.50
a.		Handstamped	26.00	7.25
38	A13	3.50fr red & blk	25.00	20.00
a.		Handstamped	160.00	110.00
39	A10	5fr car & blk	42.50	24.00
a.		Handstamped	60.00	42.50
40	A14	10fr yel grn & blk	85.00	21.00
a.		Perf. 14½	240.00	—
b.		Handstamped	125.00	47.50
c.		Handstamped, perf. 14	290.00	225.00
		Nos. 31-40 (10)	209.50	101.50

Most of the above handstamps are also found inverted and double.
Values for handstamped overprints are for those applied locally.
Counterfeits of the handstamped overprints exist.

Port Matadi A15

River Scene on the Congo, Stanley Falls — A16

Climbing Oil Palms — A17

Railroad Bridge on M'pozo River — A18

1909   *Perf. 14*

41	A15	5c green & blk	.75	.75
42	A16	10c carmine & blk	.75	.50
43	A17	15c ocher & blk	25.00	15.00
44	A18	50c olive & blk	3.00	2.50
		Nos. 41-44 (4)	29.50	18.75

Port Matadi A19

River Scene on the Congo, Stanley Falls — A20

Climbing Oil Palms — A21

Inkissi Falls — A22

Congo Canoe A23

Railroad Bridge on M'pozo River — A24

Hunting Elephants A25

Congo Village A26

Bangala Chief and Wife — A27

River Steamer on the Congo A28

1910-15   Engr.   *Perf. 14, 15*

45	A19	5c green & blk	.75	.25
46	A20	10c carmine & blk	.60	.25
47	A21	15c ocher & blk	.50	.25
48	A21	15c grn & blk ('15)	.35	.25
a.		Booklet pane of 10	14.00	
49	A22	25c blue & blk	1.50	.35
50	A23	40c bluish grn & blk	2.25	2.25
51	A23	40c brn red & blk ('15)	4.25	2.40
52	A24	50c olive & blk	3.50	2.00
53	A24	50c brn lake & blk ('15)	6.00	2.40
54	A25	1fr carmine & blk	3.50	2.75
55	A25	1fr ol bis & blk ('15)	2.25	.85

56	A26	3fr red & blk	16.00	12.00
57	A27	5fr carmine & blk	24.00	24.00
58	A27	5fr ocher & blk ('15)	1.75	.85
59	A28	10fr green & blk	20.00	20.00
		Nos. 45-59 (15)	87.20	70.85

Nos. 48, 51, 53, 55 and 58 exist imperforate.
For overprints and surcharges see Nos. 64-76, 81-86, B5-B9.

Port Matadi
A29

Stanley Falls, Congo River — A30

Inkissi Falls — A31

TEN CENTIMES.
Type I - Large white space at top of picture and two small white spots at lower edge. Vignette does not fill frame.
Type II - Vignette completely fills frame.

1915

60	A29	5c green & blk	.20	.20
a.		Booklet pane of 10	7.50	
61	A30	10c car & blk (II)	.20	.20
a.		10c carmine & black (I)	.20	.20
d.		Booklet pane of 10 (II)	14.00	
62	A31	25c blue & blk	.85	.25
a.		Booklet pane of 10	65.00	
		Nos. 60-62 (3)	1.25	.65

Nos. 60 to 62 exist imperforate.
For surcharges see Nos. 77-80, 87, B1-B4.

Stamps of 1910 Issue Surcharged in Red or Black

1921

64	A23	5c on 40c bluish grn & blk (R)	.25	.25
65	A19	10c on 5c grn & blk (R)	.25	.25
66	A24	15c on 50c ol & blk (R)	.25	.25
67	A21	25c on 10c ocher & blk (R)	1.50	1.00
68	A20	30c on 10c car & blk	.35	.35
69	A22	50c on 25c bl & blk (R)	1.40	.90
		Nos. 64-69 (6)	4.00	3.00

The position of the new value and the bars varies on Nos. 64 to 69.

Overprinted

1921

70	A25	1fr carmine & blk	.75	.75
a.		Double overprint	20.00	
71	A26	3fr red & blk	2.50	2.50
72	A27	5fr carmine & blk	4.75	4.75
73	A28	10fr green & blk (R)	4.25	2.50
		Nos. 70-73 (4)	12.25	10.50

Belgian Surcharges

Nos. 51, 53, 60-62 Surcharged in Black or Red

1922

74	A24	5c on 50c	.35	.30
75	A29	10c on 5c (R)	.35	.25
76	A23	25c on 40c (R)	2.00	.30
77	A30	30c on 10c (II)	.20	.20
a.		30c on 10c (I)	.20	.20
b.		Double surcharge	4.75	4.75
78	A31	50c on 25c (R)	.40	.20
		Nos. 74-78 (5)	3.30	1.30

No. 74 has the surcharge at each side.

Congo Surcharges
Nos. 60, 51 Surcharged in Red or Black:

a

B

1922

80	A29	10c on 5c (R)	.55	.55
a.		Inverted surcharge	17.50	17.50
b.		Double surcharge	4.75	
c.		Double surch., one invtd.	40.00	
d.		Pair, one without surcharge	42.50	
e.		On No. 45	125.00	125.00
81	A23	25c on 40c	.70	.35
a.		Inverted surcharge	17.50	17.50
b.		Double surcharge	5.50	
c.		"25c" double		
d.		25c on 5c, No. 60	100.00	100.00

Nos. 55, 58 Surcharged with vertical bars over original values

1922

84	A25	10c on 1fr (R)	.55	.55
a.		Double surcharge	14.00	
b.		Inverted surcharge	17.50	17.50
85	A27	25c on 5fr	1.50	1.50

Nos. 68, 77 Handstamped **0,25**

86	A20	25c on 30c on 10c	7.00	8.50
87	A30	25c on 30c on 10c (II)	7.00	8.50

Nos. 86-87 exist with handstamp surcharge inverted.
Counterfeit handstamped surcharges exist.

Ubangi Woman — A32

Watusi Cattle — A44

Designs: 10c, Baluba woman. 15c, Babuende woman. No. 90, 40c, 1.25fr, 1.50fr, 1.75fr, Ubangi man. 25c, Basketmaking. 30c, 35c, Nos. 101, 102, Carving wood. 50c, Archer. Nos. 92, 100, Weaving. 1fr, Making pottery. 3fr, Working rubber. 5fr, Making palm oil. 10fr, African elephant.

1923-27 Engr. Perf. 12

88	A32	5c yellow	.20	.20
89	A32	10c green	.20	.20
90	A32	15c olive brn	.20	.20
91	A32	20c olive grn ('24)	.20	.20
92	A44	20c green ('26)	.20	.20
93	A44	25c red brown	.25	.20
94	A44	30c rose red ('24)	.45	.45
95	A44	30c olive grn ('25)	.20	.20
96	A44	35c green ('27)	.45	.35

97	A32	40c violet ('25)	.20	.20
98	A44	50c gray blue	.25	.20
99	A44	50c buff ('25)	.30	.20
100	A44	75c red orange	.25	.20
101	A44	75c gray bl ('25)	.40	.25
102	A44	75c salmon red ('26)	.20	.20
103	A44	1fr bister brn	.55	.20
104	A44	1fr dl blue ('25)	.35	.20
105	A44	1fr rose red ('27)	.85	.20
106	A32	1.25fr dl blue ('26)	.30	.20
107	A32	1.50fr dl blue ('26)	.30	.20
108	A32	1.75fr dl blue ('27)	3.75	3.25
109	A44	3fr gray brn ('24)	4.00	2.25
110	A44	5fr gray ('24)	10.00	4.75
111	A44	10fr gray blk ('24)	17.50	8.50

1925-26

112	A44	45c dk vio ('26)	.40	.25
113	A44	60c carmine rose	.40	.20
		Nos. 88-113 (26)	42.35	23.65

For surcharges see Nos. 114, 136-138, 157.

No. 107 Surcharged

1927, June 14

114	A32	1.75fr on 1.50fr dl bl	.30	.20

Sir Henry Morton Stanley — A45

1928, June 30 Perf. 14

115	A45	5c gray blk	.20	.20
116	A45	10c dp violet	.20	.20
117	A45	20c orange red	.35	.25
118	A45	35c green	1.00	.75
119	A45	40c red brown	.40	.20
120	A45	60c black brn	.40	.20
121	A45	1fr carmine	.40	.20
122	A45	1.60fr dk gray	4.00	3.25
123	A45	1.75fr dp blue	1.60	.80
124	A45	2fr dk brown	1.10	.30
125	A45	2.75fr red violet	4.50	.45
126	A45	3.50fr rose lake	1.40	.75
127	A45	5fr slate grn	1.10	.30
128	A45	10fr violet blue	1.60	.75
129	A45	20fr claret	6.75	2.25
		Nos. 115-129 (15)	25.00	10.85

Sir Henry M. Stanley (1841-1904), explorer.

Nos. 118, 121-123, 125-126 Surcharged in Red, Blue or Black

1931, Jan. 15

130	A45	40c on 35c	.50	.40
131	A45	1.25fr on 1fr (Bl)	.40	.20
132	A45	2fr on 1.60fr	.80	.30
133	A45	2fr on 1.75fr	.75	.30
134	A45	3.25fr on 2.75fr (Bk)	2.25	2.00
135	A45	3.25fr on 3.25fr (Bk)	3.00	2.10

Nos. 96, 108, 112 Surcharged in Red

Perf. 12½, 12

136	A44	40c on 35c grn	3.25	3.00
137	A44	50c on 45c dk vio	2.00	1.10

Surcharged

138	A32	2(fr) on 1.75fr dl bl	8.50	7.50
		Nos. 130-138 (9)	21.45	16.90

View of Sankuru River — A46

Flute Players — A50

Designs: 15c, Kivu Kraal. 20c, Sankuru River rapids. 25c, Uele hut. 50c, Musicians of Lake Leopold II. 60c, Batetelas drummers. 75c, Mangbetu woman. 1fr, Domesticated elephant of Api. 1.25fr, Mangbetu chief. 1.50fr, 2fr, Village of Mondimbi. 2.50fr, Okapi. 4fr, Canoes at Stanleyville. 5fr, Woman preparing cassava. 10fr, Baluba chief. 20fr, Young woman of Irumu.

1931-37 Engr. Perf. 11½

139	A46	10c gray brn ('32)	.20	.20
140	A46	15c gray ('32)	.20	.20
141	A46	20c brn lil ('32)	.20	.20
142	A46	25c dp blue ('32)	.20	.20
143	A50	40c dp grn ('32)	.20	.20

144	A46	50c violet ('32)	.20 .20
b.		Booklet pane of 8	6.25
145	A50	60c vio brn ('32)	.20 .20
146	A50	75c rose ('32)	.20 .20
b.		Booklet pane of 8	1.25
147	A50	1fr rose red ('32)	.20 .20
148	A50	1.25fr red brown	.20 .20
b.		Booklet pane of 8	1.25
149	A46	1.50fr dk ol gray ('37)	.20 .20
b.		Booklet pane of 8	6.00
150	A46	2fr ultra ('37)	.20 .20
151	A46	2.50fr dp blue ('37)	.30 .20
b.		Booklet pane of 8	8.50
152	A46	3.25fr gray blk ('32)	.45 .30
153	A50	4fr dl vio ('32)	.20 .20
154	A50	5fr dp vio ('32)	.50 .25
155	A50	10fr red ('32)	.50 .40
156	A50	20fr blk brn ('32)	1.50 1.25
		Nos. 139-156 (18)	5.85 5.00

No. 109
Surcharged in
Red

1932, Mar. 15   **Perf. 12**

157	A44	3.25fr on 3fr gray brn	2.75 2.25

King Albert Memorial Issue

King Albert — A62

1934, May 7   **Photo.**   **Perf. 11½**

158	A62	1.50fr black	.65 .35

Leopold I,
Leopold II,
Albert I,
Leopold III
A63

1935, Aug. 15   **Engr.**   **Perf. 12½x12**

159	A63	50c green	.70 .40
160	A63	1.25fr dk carmine	.70 .20
161	A63	1.50fr brown vio	.70 .20
162	A63	2.40fr brown org	1.75 1.60
163	A63	2.50fr lt blue	1.75 .80
164	A63	4fr brt violet	1.75 1.10
165	A63	5fr black brn	1.75 1.25
		Nos. 159-165 (7)	9.10 5.55

Founding of Congo Free State, 50th anniv.
For surcharges see Nos. B21-B22.

Molindi
River — A64

Bamboos — A65

Suza River — A66

Rutshuru
River — A67

Karisimbi
A68

Mitumba
Forest
A69

1937-38   **Photo.**   **Perf. 11½**

166	A64	5c purple & blk	.20 .20
167	A65	90c car & brn	.40 .30
168	A66	1.50fr dp red brn & blk	.20 .20
169	A67	2.40fr ol blk & brn	.20 .20
170	A68	2.50fr dp ultra & blk	.30 .20
171	A69	4.50fr dk grn & brn	.30 .20
172	A69	4.50fr car & sep	.20 .20
		Nos. 166-172 (7)	1.80 1.50

National Parks.
No. 172 was issued in sheets of four measuring 140x111mm. It was sold by subscription, the subscription closing Oct. 20, 1937. Value, $1.60.
Nos. 166-171 were issued Mar. 1, 1938. See #B26. For surcharges see #184, 186.

King Albert
Memorial,
Leopoldville — A70

1941, Feb. 7   **Litho.**   **Perf. 11**

173	A70	10c lt gray	.20 .20
174	A70	15c brown vio	.25 .20
175	A70	25c lt blue	.30 .20
176	A70	50c lt violet	.25 .20
177	A70	75c rose pink	.95 .30
178	A70	1.25fr gray	.30 .20
179	A70	1.75fr orange	.95 .45
180	A70	2.50fr carmine	.65 .20
181	A70	2.75fr vio blue	.95 .60
182	A70	5fr lt olive grn	4.00 1.50
183	A70	10fr rose red	2.75 1.75
		Nos. 173-183 (11)	11.55 5.80

Exist imperforate.
For surcharge see No. 185.

Nos. 168, 179, 169 Surcharged in
Blue or Black

Nos. 184, 186   No. 185

1941-42   **Perf. 11½, 11**

184	A66	5c on 1.50fr (Bl)	.20 .20
a.		Inverted surcharge	14.00 14.00
185	A70	75c on 1.75fr ('42)	.35 .35
a.		Inverted surcharge	14.00 14.00
186	A67	2.50(fr) on 2.40fr ('42)	.85 .70
a.		Double surcharge	27.50 27.50
b.		Inverted surcharge	14.00 14.00
		Nos. 184-186 (3)	1.40 1.25

> **Catalogue values for unused stamps in this section, from this point to the end of the section, are for Never Hinged items.**

A71

Oil Palms — A72

Congo
Woman — A73

Askari — A75

Leopard
A74

Okapi
A76

Inscribed "Congo Belge Belgisch Congo"

1942, May 23   **Engr.**   **Perf. 12½**

187	A71	5c red	.20 .20
188	A72	10c olive grn	.20 .20
189	A72	15c brown car	.20 .20
190	A72	20c dp ultra	.20 .20
191	A72	25c brown vio	.20 .20
192	A72	30c blue	.20 .20
193	A72	50c dp green	.20 .20
194	A72	60c chestnut	.20 .20
195	A73	75c dl lil & blk	.20 .20
196	A73	1fr dk brn & blk	.20 .20
197	A73	1.25fr rose red & blk	.20 .20
198	A74	1.75fr dk gray brn	.75 .35
199	A74	2fr ocher	.75 .20
200	A74	2.50fr carmine	.75 .20
201	A75	3.50fr dk ol grn	.35 .20
202	A75	5fr orange	.70 .20
203	A75	6fr brt ultra	.50 .20
204	A75	7fr black	.60 .20
205	A75	10fr dp brown	.75 .20
206	A76	20fr plum & blk	8.00 .65
		Nos. 187-206 (20)	15.35 4.60

Same Inscribed "Belgisch Congo Congo Belge"

207	A72	10c olive grn	.20 .20
208	A72	15c brown car	.20 .20
209	A72	20c dp ultra	.20 .20
210	A72	25c brown vio	.20 .20
211	A72	30c blue	.20 .20
212	A72	50c dp green	.20 .20
213	A72	60c chestnut	.20 .20
214	A73	75c dl lil & blk	.20 .20
215	A73	1fr dk brn & blk	.20 .20
216	A73	1.25fr rose red & blk	.20 .20
217	A73	1.75fr dk gray brn	.75 .35
218	A74	2fr ocher	.75 .20
219	A74	2.50fr carmine	.75 .20
220	A75	3.50fr dk ol grn	.30 .20
221	A75	5fr orange	.55 .20
222	A75	6fr brt ultra	.55 .20
223	A75	7fr black	.55 .20
224	A75	10fr dp brown	.65 .20
225	A76	20fr plum & blk	7.00 .65
		Nos. 207-225 (19)	13.85 4.40

Miniature sheets of Nos. 193, 194, 197, 200, 211, 214, 217 and 219 were printed in 1944 by the Belgian Government in London and given to the Belgian political review, Message, which distributed them to its subscribers, one a month. Value per sheet, about $12.50.
Remainders of these eight miniature sheets received marginal overprints in various colors in 1950, specifying a surtax of 100fr per sheet and paying tribute to the UPU. These sheets, together with four of Ruanda-Urundi, were

sold by the Committee of Cultural Works (and not at post offices) in sets of 12 for 1,217.15 francs. Set value, about $325.
Nos. 187-227 imperforate had no franking value.
For surcharges see Nos. B34-B37.

Congo
Woman — A77

Askari — A78

1943, Jan. 1

226	A77	50fr ultra & blk	6.50 .40
227	A78	100fr car & blk	7.50 .60

Slaves and Arab
Guards
A79

Auguste
Lambermont
A80

Design: 10fr, Leopold II.

Perf. 13x11½, 12½x12

1947   **Engr.**   **Unwmk.**

228	A79	1.25fr black brown	.25 .20
229	A80	3.50fr dark blue	.40 .20
230	A80	10fr red orange	.75 .20
		Nos. 228-230 (3)	1.40 .60

50th anniv. of the abolition of slavery in Belgian Congo. See Nos. 261-262.

Baluba Carving of
Former King — A82

Carved Figures and Masks of Baluba Tribe: 10c, 50c, 2fr, "Ndoha," figure of tribal king. 15c, 70c, 1.20fr, 2.50fr, "Tshimanyi," an idol. 20c, 75c, 1.60fr, 3.50fr, "Buangakokoma," statue of kneeling beggar. 25c, 1fr, 2.40fr, 5fr, "Mbuta," sacred double cup, carved with two faces, Man and Woman. 40c, 1.25fr, 6fr, 8fr, "Ngadimuashi," female mask. 1.50fr, 3fr, 10fr, 50fr, "Buadi-Muadi," mask with squared features. 6.50fr, 20fr, 100fr, "Mbowa," executioner's mask with buffalo horns.

1947-50   **Perf. 12½**

231	A82	10c dp org ('48)	.20 .20
232	A82	15c ultra ('48)	.20 .20
233	A82	20c brt bl ('48)	.20 .20
234	A82	25c rose car ('48)	.20 .20
235	A82	40c violet ('48)	.20 .20
236	A82	50c olive brn	.20 .20
237	A82	70c yel grn ('48)	.20 .20
238	A82	75c magenta ('48)	.20 .20
239	A82	1fr yel org & dk vio	1.50 .20
240	A82	1.20fr gray & brn ('50)	.20 .20
241	A82	1.25fr lt bl grn & mag ('48)	.30 .20
242	A82	1.50fr ol & mag ('50)	14.00 1.10
243	A82	1.60fr bl gray & brt bl ('50)	.40 .20

244	A82	2fr org & mag ('48)	.20	.20
245	A82	2.40fr bl grn & dk grn ('50)	.30	.20
246	A82	2.50fr brn red & bl grn	.30	.20
247	A82	3fr lt ultra & ind ('49)	4.25	.20
248	A82	3.50fr lt bl & blk ('48)	3.50	.20
249	A82	5fr bis & mag ('48)	1.25	.20
250	A82	6fr brn org & ind ('48)	1.40	.20
251	A82	6.50fr red org & red brn ('49)	1.90	.20
252	A82	8fr gray bl & dk grn ('50)	1.25	.20
253	A82	10fr pale vio & red brn ('48)	4.00	.20
254	A82	20fr red org & vio brn	1.90	.20
255	A82	50fr dp org & blk ('48)	3.75	.20
256	A82	100fr crim & blk brn	4.00	.30
		Nos. 231-256 (26)	46.00	6.20

Railroad Train and Map — A83

1948, July 1   Unwmk.   Perf. 13½
257 A83 2.50fr dp bl & grn   1.00 .20
50th anniv. of railway service in the Congo.

Globe and Ship A84

1949, Nov. 21   Perf. 11½
Granite Paper
258 A84 4fr violet blue   .85 .20
75th anniv. of the UPU.

Allegorical Figure and Map — A85

1950, Aug. 12   Perf. 12x12½
259 A85 3fr blue & indigo   1.75 .20
260 A85 6.50fr car rose & blk brn   2.00 .25
Establishment of Katanga Province, 50th anniv.

Portrait Type of 1947
1.50fr, Cardinal Lavigerie. 3fr, Baron Dhanis.

Perf. 12½x12
1951, June 25   Unwmk.
261 A80 1.50fr purple   2.00 .25
262 A80 3fr black brown   2.00 .20

Littonia — A86   St. Francis Xavier — A86a

1952-53   Photo.   Perf. 11½
Granite Paper
Flowers in Natural Colors
Size: 21x25½mm
263 A86 10c Dissotis   .20 .20
264 A86 15c Protea   .20 .20
265 A86 20c Vellozia   .20 .20

266	A86	25c shown	.20	.20
267	A86	40c Ipomoea	.20	.20
268	A86	50c Angraecum	.20	.20
269	A86	60c Euphorbia	.20	.20
270	A86	75c Ochna	.20	.20
271	A86	1fr Hibiscus	.20	.20
272	A86	1.25fr Protea ('53)	.65	.45
273	A86	1.50fr Schrizoglossum	.20	.20
274	A86	2fr Ansellia	.25	.20
275	A86	3fr Costus	.25	.20
276	A86	4fr Nymphaea	.30	.20
277	A86	5fr Thunbergia	.45	.20
278	A86	6.50fr Thonningia	.55	.20
279	A86	7fr Gerbera	.55	.20
280	A86	8fr Gloriosa ('53)	.90	.20
281	A86	10fr Silene ('53)	1.60	.20
282	A86	20fr Aristolochia	1.40	.20

Size: 22x32mm
283 A86 50fr Eulophia ('53)   7.00 .45
284 A86 100fr Crytosepalum ('53)   11.00 1.00
Nos. 263-284 (22)   26.90 5.70
Nos. 264, 269 and 270 with additional surcharges are varieties of Congo Democratic Republic Nos. 324, 327 and 328.

1953, Jan. 5   Engr.   Perf. 12½x13
285 A86a 1.50fr ultra & gray blk   .50 .30
400th death anniv. of St. Francis Xavier.

Canoe on Lake Kivu — A87

1953, Jan. 5   Perf. 14
286 A87 3fr car & blk   1.25 .20
287 A87 7fr dp bl & brn org   1.25 .25
Issued to publicize the Kivu Festival, 1953.

Royal Colonial Institute Jubilee Medal A88

Design: 6.50fr, Same with altered background and transposed inscriptions.

1954, Dec. 27   Photo.   Perf. 13½
288 A88 4.50fr indigo & gray   1.10 .30
289 A88 6.50fr dk grn & brn   .90 .20
25th anniv. of the founding of the Belgian Royal Colonial Institute.

King Baudouin and Tropical Scene A89

Designs: King and various views.

Inscribed "Congo Belge-Belgisch Congo"
Engr.; Portrait Photo.
1955, Feb. 15   Unwmk.   Perf. 11½
Portrait in Black
290 A89 1.50fr rose car   5.25 .90
291 A89 3fr green   3.50 .80
292 A89 4.50fr ultra   3.50 .55
293 A89 6.50fr dp claret   5.25 .25

Inscribed "Belgisch Congo-Congo Belge"
294 A89 1.50fr rose car   5.25 .90
295 A89 3fr green   3.50 .80
296 A89 4.50fr ultra   3.50 .55
297 A89 6.50fr deep claret   5.25 .25
Nos. 290-297 (8)   35.00 5.00

Map of Africa and Emblem of Royal Touring Club — A90

1955, July 26   Engr.   Perf. 11½
Inscription in French
298 A90 6.50fr vio blue   3.25 .25
Inscription in Flemish
299 A90 6.50fr vio blue   3.25 .25
5th International Congress of African Tourism, Elisabethville, July 26-Aug. 4. Nos. 298-299 printed in alternate rows.

Kings of Belgium A91

1958, July 1   Unwmk.   Perf. 12½
300 A91 1fr rose vio   .25 .20
301 A91 1.50fr ultra   .25 .20
302 A91 3fr rose car   .25 .20
303 A91 5fr green   .70 .20
304 A91 6.50fr brn red   .45 .20
305 A91 10fr dl vio   .65 .20
Nos. 300-305 (6)   2.55 1.30
Belgium's annexation of Congo, 50th anniv.

Roan Antelope — A92

Black Buffaloes A93

20c, White rhinoceros. 40c, Giraffe. 50c, Thick-tailed bushbaby. 1fr, Gorilla. 2fr, Black-and-white colobus (monkey). 3fr, Elephants. 5fr, Okapis. 6.50fr, Impala. 8fr, Giant pangolin. 10fr, Eland and zebras.

1959, Oct. 15   Photo.   Perf. 11½
Granite Paper
306 A92 10c bl & brn   .20 .20
307 A93 20c red org & slate   .20 .20
308 A92 40c brn & bl   .20 .20
309 A93 50c brt ultra, red & sep   .20 .20
310 A92 1fr brn, grn & blk   .20 .20
311 A93 1.50fr blk & org yel   .20 .20
312 A92 2fr crim, blk & brn   .20 .20
313 A93 3fr blk, gray & lil rose   .25 .20
314 A92 5fr brn, dk brn & brt grn   .40 .20
315 A93 6.50fr bl, brn & org yel   .45 .20
316 A92 8fr org brn, ol bis & lil   .50 .30
317 A93 10fr multi   .60 .20
Nos. 306-317 (12)   3.60 2.50

Madonna and Child — A94

1959, Dec. 1   Unwmk.   Perf. 11½
318 A94 50c golden brn, ocher & red brn   .20 .20
319 A94 1fr dk bl, pur & red brn   .20 .20
320 A94 2fr gray, brt bl & red brn   .20 .20
Nos. 318-320 (3)   .60 .60

Map of Africa and Symbolic Honeycomb A95

1960, Feb. 19   Unwmk.   Perf. 11½
Inscription in French
321 A95 3fr gray & red   .25 .20
Inscription in Flemish
322 A95 3fr gray & red   .25 .20
Commission for Technical Co-operation in Africa South of the Sahara (C. C. T. A.), 10th anniv.

SEMI-POSTAL STAMPS

Types of 1910-15 Issues Surcharged in Red

1918, May 15   Unwmk.   Perf. 14, 15
B1 A29 5c + 10c grn & bl   .20 .20
B2 A30 10c + 15c car & bl (I)   .20 .20
B3 A21 15c + 20c bl grn & bl   .20 .20
B4 A31 25c + 25c dp bl & pale bl   .20 .25
B5 A23 40c + 40c brn red & bl   .35 .45
B6 A24 50c + 50c brn lake & bl   .35 .45
B7 A25 1fr + 1fr ol bis & bl   1.50 2.00
B8 A27 5fr + 5fr och & bl   8.25 11.00
B9 A28 10fr + 10fr grn & bl   77.50 105.00
Nos. B1-B9 (9)   88.75 119.75
The position of the cross and the added value varies on the different stamps.
Perf 15 stamps are worth approximately twice the values shown.
Nos. B1-B9 exist imperforate.

SP1

Design: #B11 inscribed "Belgisch Congo."

1925, July 8   Perf. 12½
B10 SP1 25c + 25c carmine & blk   .20 .25
B11 SP1 25c + 25c carmine & blk   .20 .25
a.   Pair, Nos. B10-B11   .40 .50
Colonial campaigns in 1914-1918.
The surtax helped erect at Kinshasa a monument to those who died in World War I.

Nurse Weighing Child — SP3

First Aid Station SP5

20c+10c, Missionary & Child. 60c+30c, Congo hospital. 1fr+50c, Dispensary service. 1.75fr+75c, Convalescent area. 3.50fr+1.50fr, Instruction on bathing infant. 5fr+2.50fr, Operating room. 10fr+5fr, Students.

1930, Jan. 16   Engr.   Perf. 11½

B12	SP3	10c + 5c ver	.30	.30
B13	SP3	20c + 10c dp brn	.40	.40
B14	SP5	35c + 15c dp grn	.70	.70
B15	SP5	60c + 30c dl vio	.85	.85
B16	SP3	1fr + 50c dk car	1.40	1.40
B17	SP5	1.75fr + 75c dp bl	2.10	2.10
B18	SP5	3.50fr + 1.50fr rose lake	5.00	5.00
B19	SP5	5fr + 2.50fr red brn	4.25	4.25
B20	SP5	10fr + 5fr gray blk	5.00	5.00
		Nos. B12-B20 (9)	20.00	20.00

The surtax was intended to aid welfare work among the natives, especially the children.

Nos. 161, 163 Surcharged "+50c" in Blue or Red

1936, May 15   Perf. 12½x12

B21	A63	1.50fr + 50c (Bl)	2.50	3.00
B22	A63	2.50fr + 50c (R)	2.00	2.00

Surtax was for the King Albert Memorial Fund.

Queen Astrid with Congolese Children — SP12

1936, Aug. 29   Photo.   Perf. 12½

B23	SP12	1.25fr + 5c dark brown	.40	.35
B24	SP12	1.50fr + 10c dull rose	.40	.35
B25	SP12	2.50fr + 25c dark blue	.60	.60
		Nos. B23-B25 (3)	1.40	1.30

Issued in memory of Queen Astrid. The surtax was for the aid of the National League for Protection of Native Children.

National Park Type of 1937-38 Souvenir Sheet

1938, Oct. 3   Perf. 11½

Star in Yellow

B26		Sheet of 6	18.00	18.00
a.	A64	5c ultra & light brown	3.00	3.00
b.	A65	90c ultra & light brown	3.00	3.00
c.	A66	1.50fr ultra & light brown	3.00	3.00
d.	A67	2.40fr ultra & light brown	3.00	3.00
e.	A68	2.50fr ultra & light brown	3.00	3.00
f.	A69	4.50fr ultra & light brown	3.00	3.00

Intl. Tourist Cong. A surtax of 3.15fr was for the benefit of the Congo Tourist Service.

Marabou Storks and Vultures — SP14

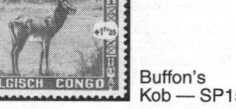

Buffon's Kob — SP15

Designs: 1.50fr+1.50fr, Pygmy chimpanzees. 4.50fr+4.50fr, Dwarf crocodiles. 5fr+5fr, Lioness.

1939, June 6   Photo.   Perf. 14

B27	SP14	1fr + 1fr dp cl	5.50	5.50
B28	SP15	1.25fr + 1.25fr car	5.50	5.50
B29	SP15	1.50fr + 1.50fr brt pur	7.50	7.50
B30	SP14	4.50fr + 4.50fr sl grn	5.50	5.50
B31	SP15	5fr + 5fr brown	6.00	6.00
		Nos. B27-B31 (5)	30.00	30.00

Surtax for the Leopoldville Zoological Gardens.

Sold in full sets by subscription.

> **Catalogue values for unused stamps in this section, from this point to the end of the section, are for Never Hinged items.**

Lion of Belgium and Inscription "Belgium Shall Rise Again" — SP19

1942, Feb. 17   Engr.   Perf. 12½

B32	SP19	10fr + 40fr brt grn	1.50	1.75
B33	SP19	10fr + 40fr vio bl	1.50	1.75

Nos. 193, 216, 198 and 220 Surcharged in Red

a

b

c

1945

B34	A72 (a)	50c + 50fr	2.00	3.25
B35	A73 (b)	1.25fr + 100fr	2.00	3.25
B36	A74 (c)	1.75fr + 100fr	2.00	3.50
B37	A75 (b)	3.50fr + 100fr	2.00	3.50
		Nos. B34-B37 (4)	8.00	13.50

The surtax was for the Red Cross. Sold in full sets by subscription.

Mozart at Age 7 — SP20

Queen Elisabeth and Sonata by Mozart — SP21

Perf. 11½

1956, Oct. 10   Unwmk.   Engr.

B38	SP20	4.50fr + 1.50fr brt lil	2.00	2.00
B39	SP21	6.50fr + 2.50fr ultra	3.00	3.00

200th anniv. of the birth of Wolfgang Amadeus Mozart.

The surtax was for the Pro-Mozart Committee.

Nurse and Children SP22

4.50fr+50c, Patient receiving injection. 6.50fr+40c, Patient being bandaged.

1957, Dec. 10   Photo.   Perf. 13x10½
Cross in Carmine

B40	SP22	3fr + 50c dk bl	.90	.85
B41	SP22	4.50fr + 50c dk grn	.80	.75
B42	SP22	6.50fr + 50c red brn	1.00	.95
		Nos. B40-B42 (3)	2.70	2.55

The surtax was for the Red Cross.

High Jump SP23

1960, May 2   Unwmk.   Perf. 13½

B43	SP23	50c + 25c shown	.20	.25
B44	SP23	1.50fr + 50c Hurdles	.20	.25
B45	SP23	2fr + 1fr Soccer	.20	.30
B46	SP23	3fr + 1.25fr Javelin	.75	.90
B47	SP23	6.50fr + 3.50fr Discus	1.00	1.25
		Nos. B43-B47 (5)	2.35	2.95

17th Olympic Games, Rome, Aug. 25-Sept. 11. The surtax was for the youth of Congo.

AIR POST STAMPS

Wharf on Congo River AP1

Congo "Country Store" AP2

View of Congo River AP3

Stronghold in the Interior — AP4

Unwmk.

1920, July 1   Engr.   Perf. 12

C1	AP1	50c orange & blk	.20	.20
C2	AP2	1fr dull vio & blk	.20	.20
C3	AP3	2fr blue & blk	.50	.20
C4	AP4	5fr green & blk	.90	.40
		Nos. C1-C4 (4)	1.80	1.00

Kraal AP5

Porters on Safari AP6

1930, Apr. 2

C5	AP5	15fr dk brn & blk	1.90	.75
C6	AP6	30fr brn vio & blk	2.25	.75

Fokker F VII over Congo AP7

1934, Jan. 22   Perf. 13½x14

C7	AP7	50c gray black	.20	.20
C8	AP7	1fr dk carmine	.20	.20
a.		Booklet pane of 8	5.25	
C9	AP7	1.50fr green	.20	.20
C10	AP7	3fr brown	.20	.20
C11	AP7	4.50fr brt ultra	.25	.20
a.		Booklet pane of 8	10.00	
C12	AP7	5fr red brown	.20	.20
C13	AP7	15fr brown vio	.40	.25
C14	AP7	30fr red orange	.70	.60
C15	AP7	50fr violet	2.00	.95
		Nos. C7-C15 (9)	4.35	3.00

The 1fr, 3fr, 4.50fr, 5fr, 15fr exist imperf.

No. C10 Surcharged in Blue with New Value and Bars

1936, Mar. 25

C16	AP7	3.50fr on 3fr brown	.20	.20

> **Catalogue values for unused stamps in this section, from this point to the end of the section, are for Never Hinged items.**

No. C9 Surcharged in Black

1942, Apr. 27

C17	AP7	50c on 1.50fr green	.35	.20
a.		Inverted surcharge	6.50	6.50

POSTAGE DUE STAMPS

In 1908-23 regular postage stamps handstamped "TAXES" or "TAX," usually boxed, were used in lieu of postage due stamps.

D1

1923-29(?) Typo. Unwmk. Perf. 14

J1	D1	5c black brown	.20	.20
J2	D1	10c rose red	.20	.20
J3	D1	15c violet	.20	.20
J4	D1	30c green	.25	.20
J5	D1	50c ultramarine	.30	.30
J6	D1	50c blue	.30	.30
J7	D1	1fr gray	.45	.25
		Nos. J1-J7 (7)	1.90	1.65

> **Catalogue values for unused stamps in this section, from this point to the end of the section, are for Never Hinged items.**

D2   D3

1943			Perf. 14x14½	
J8	D2	10c olive green	.20	.20
J9	D2	20c dark ultramarine	.20	.20
J10	D2	50c green	.20	.20
J11	D2	1fr dark brown	.20	.20
J12	D2	2fr yellow orange	.20	.20
		Nos. J8-J12 (5)	1.00	1.00

1943			Perf. 12½	
J8a	D2	10c olive green	.30	.30
J9a	D2	20c dark ultramarine	.30	.30
J10a	D2	50c green	.30	.30
J11a	D2	1fr dark brown	.45	.45
J12a	D2	2fr yellow orange	.45	.45
		Nos. J8a-J12a (5)	1.80	1.80

1957		Engr.	Perf. 11½	
J13	D3	10c olive brown	.20	.20
J14	D3	20c claret	.20	.20
J15	D3	50c green	.20	.20
J16	D3	1fr light blue	.30	.25
J17	D3	2fr vermilion	.40	.25
J18	D3	4fr purple	.60	.35
J19	D3	6fr violet blue	.75	.45
		Nos. J13-J19 (7)	2.65	1.90

PARCEL POST STAMPS

PP1   PP2

PP3

Handstamped Surcharges on Nos. 5, 11-12

1887-93		Unwmk.	Perf. 15	
Blue-Black Surcharge				
Q1	PP1	3.50fr on 5fr lilac	1,000.	750.00
Black Surcharge				
Q3	PP2	3.50fr on 5fr vio	850.00	500.00
Q4	PP3	3.50fr on 5fr vio ('88)	575.00	325.00
a.		Blue surcharge	625.00	375.00
Q6	PP3	3.50fr on 5fr gray ('93)	95.00	72.50
		Never hinged	125.00	

Nos. Q1, Q3-Q4, Q4a and Q6 are known with inverted surcharge, No. Q1 with double surcharge and No. Q6 in pair with unsurcharged stamp. These varieties sell for somewhat more than the normal surcharges. Genuine stamps with counterfeit surcharges, counterfeit stamps with counterfeit surcharges, and both with counterfeit cancels exist.

BELGIUM

'bel-jəm

LOCATION — Western Europe, bordering the North Sea
GOVT. — Constitutional Monarchy
AREA — 11,778 sq. mi.
POP. — 10,192,264 (1998 est.)
CAPITAL — Brussels

100 Centimes = 1 Franc
100 Cents = 1 Euro (2002)

Catalogue values for unused stamps in this country are for Never Hinged items, beginning with Scott 322 in the regular postage section, Scott B370 in the semi-postal section, Scott C8 in the airpost section, Scott CB1 in the airpost semi-postal section, Scott J40 in the postage due section, Scott M1 in the military stamp section, Scott O36 in the officials section, and Scott Q267 in the parcel post section.

Watermark

Wmk. 96 (No Frame)

King Leopold I
A1 A2

Wmk. Two "L's" Framed (96)

1849 Engr. *Imperf.*

1	A1 10c brown	*2,250.*	75.00
a.	10c red brown	*3,500.*	475.00
b.	10c bister brown	*2,500.*	125.00
2	A1 20c blue	*2,850.*	57.50
a.	20c milky blue	*3,250.*	160.00
b.	20c greenish blue	*3,500.*	290.00

The reprints are on thick and thin wove and thick laid paper unwatermarked.

A pale blue shade exists that is often confused with the milky blue.

A souvenir sheet containing reproductions of the 10c, 20c and 40c of 1849-51 with black burelage on back was issued Oct. 17, 1949, for the cent. of the 1st Belgian stamps. It was sold at BEPITEC 1949, an intl. stamp exhib. at Brussels, and was not valid.

1849-50

3	A2 10c brown ('50)	*2,000.*	90.00
4	A2 20c blue ('50)	*1,750.*	52.50
5	A2 40c carmine rose	*1,650.*	425.00

Nos. 3-5 were printed on both thick and thin paper and sell for about the same prices.

Wmk. Two "L's" Without Frame (96)

1851-54

6	A2 10c brown	525.00	9.00
a.	Ribbed paper ('54)	900.00	50.00
7	A2 20c blue	575.00	8.50
a.	Ribbed paper ('54)	900.00	47.50
8	A2 40c car rose	*2,850.*	100.00
a.	Ribbed paper ('54)	*3,500.*	260.00

Nos. 6-8 were printed on both thin and thick paper and sell for about the same prices.

Nos. 6a, 7a, 8a must have regular and parallel ribs covering the whole stamp.

1858-61 Unwmk.

9	A2 1c green ('61)	*225.00*	125.00
10	A2 10c brown	375.00	7.50
11	A2 20c blue	400.00	7.50
12	A2 40c vermilion	*2,400.*	70.00

Nos. 9 and 13 were valid for postage on newspapers and printed matter only.

Nos. 10-12 were printed in two sizes: 21mm high (with a 16½mm high oval) and 22mm high (with a 17¼mm high oval). The 22mm high stamps were issued in 1861. The 21mm high stamps sell for more.

Reprints of Nos. 9 to 12 are on thin wove paper. The colors are brighter than those of the originals. They were made from the dies and show lines outside the stamps.

1863-65 *Perf. 14½*

13	A2 1c green ('65)	35.00	25.00
14	A2 10c brown ('65)	47.50	3.25
15	A2 20c blue ('65)	50.00	3.25
16	A2 40c car rose ('65)	325.00	25.00
	Nos. 13-16 (4)	457.50	56.50

Values for Nos. 13-16 are for copies with perfs cutting into design.

Nos. 13-16 also come perf 12½ and 12½x13, which were issued in 1863. Values differ. See the Scott Classic Specialized Catalogue.

King Leopold I - A3a
A3

A4

A4a

A5

London Print

1865 Typo. *Perf. 14*

17	A5 1fr pale violet	1,300.	110.00

Brussels Print

Thick or Thin Paper

1865-67 *Perf. 15*

18	A3 10c slate ('67)	125.00	1.50
b.	Pair, imperf. between		—
19	A3a 20c blue ('67)	175.00	1.50
20	A4 30c brown ('67)	425.00	11.00
b.	Pair, imperf. between	*1,100.*	
21	A4a 40c rose ('67)	450.00	20.00
22	A5 1fr violet	1,200.	90.00

Nos. 18-22 also come perf. 14½x14, issued in 1865-66. Values differ. See the Scott Classic Specialized Catalogue. Nos. 18b and 20b are from the earlier printings.

The reprints are on thin paper, imperforate and ungummed.

Coat of Arms — A6

1866-67 *Imperf.*

23	A6 1c gray	250.00	150.00

Perf. 15, 14½x14

24	A6 1c gray	45.00	16.00
25	A6 2c blue ('67)	140.00	90.00
26	A6 5c brown	150.00	90.00
	Nos. 23-26 (4)	585.00	346.00

Nos. 23-26 were valid for postage on newspapers and printed matter only.

Values are for perf. 15 stamps. Values for 14½x14 differ. See the Scott Classic Specialized Catalogue.

Counterfeits exist.

Reprints of Nos. 24-26 are on thin paper, imperforate and with or without gum.

Imperf. varieties of 1869-1912 (between Nos. 28-105) generally are without gum.

A7

A8

A9

A10

A11

A12

A13

A14

King Leopold II — A15

1869-70 *Perf. 15*

28	A7 1c green	6.50	.30
29	A7 2c ultra ('70)	20.00	1.50
30	A7 5c buff ('70)	45.00	.75
31	A7 8c lilac ('70)	80.00	50.00
32	A8 10c green	20.00	.40
33	A9 20c lt ultra ('70)	140.00	.90
34	A10 30c buff ('70)	80.00	4.00
35	A11 40c brt rose ('70)	110.00	6.00
36	A12 1fr dull lilac ('70)	350.00	17.00
a.	1fr rose lilac	350.00	20.00
	Nos. 28-36 (9)	851.50	80.85

The frames and inscriptions of Nos. 30, 31 and 42 differ slightly from the illustration.

Minor "broken letter" varieties exist on several values.

Nos. 28-30, 32-33, 35-38 also were printed in aniline colors. These are not valued separately.

See Nos. 40-43, 49-51, 55.

1875-78

37	A13 25c olive bister	140.00	1.25
a.	25c ocher	140.00	1.50
38	A14 50c gray	210.00	8.50
	Roller cancel		12.50
a.	50c gray black	325.00	55.00
b.	50c deep black	1,750.	225.00
39	A15 5fr dp red brown	*1,500.*	1,250.
	Roller cancel		575.00
a.	5fr pale brown ('78)	*3,750.*	1,250.
	Roller cancel		575.00

Dangerous counterfeits of No. 39 exist.

Printed in Aniline Colors

1881 *Perf. 14*

40	A7 1c gray green	20.00	.60
41	A7 2c lt ultra	17.50	2.50
42	A7 5c orange buff	57.50	1.10
a.	5c red orange	57.50	1.10
43	A8 10c gray green	30.00	.80
44	A13 25c olive bister	75.00	2.50
	Nos. 40-44 (5)	200.00	7.50

See note following No. 36.

A16

A17

A18

A19

1883

45	A16 10c carmine	27.50	2.50
46	A17 20c gray	150.00	7.75
47	A18 25c blue	260.00	35.00
	Roller cancel		15.00
48	A19 50c violet	260.00	35.00
	Roller cancel		15.00
	Nos. 45-48 (4)	697.50	80.25

A20

A21

A22

1884-85 *Perf. 14*

49	A7 1c olive green	13.50	.85
50	A7 1c gray	4.00	.30
51	A7 5c green	32.50	.40
52	A20 10c rose, *bluish*	10.00	.40
a.	Grayish paper	11.00	.50
c.	Yellowish paper	*200.00*	35.00
53	A21 25c blue, *pink* ('85)	11.00	.75
54	A22 1fr brown, *grnsh*	*600.00*	17.50

The frame and inscription of No. 51 differ slightly from the illustration.

See note after No. 36.

A23

A24

A25

A26

1886-91

55	A7	2c purple brn ('88)	12.50	1.50
56	A23	20c olive, *grnsh*	140.00	1.25
57	A24	35c vio brn, *brnsh* ('91)	18.00	3.00
58	A25	50c bister, *yelsh*	9.50	2.25
59	A26	2fr violet, *pale lil*	90.00	40.00
		Roller cancel		6.00
		Nos. 55-59 (5)	270.00	48.00

Values quoted for Nos. 60-107 are for stamps with label attached. Stamps without label sell for much less.

Coat of Arms
A27

King Leopold
A28

1893-1900

60	A27	1c gray	1.10	.20
61	A27	2c yellow	1.25	1.10
a.		Wmkd. coat of arms in sheet ('95)	—	—
62	A27	2c violet brn ('94)	1.60	.30
63	A27	2c red brown ('98)	3.25	.50
64	A27	5c yellow grn	7.75	.30
65	A28	10c orange brn	5.00	.30
66	A28	10c brt rose ('00)	3.50	.40
67	A28	20c olive green	22.50	.60
68	A28	25c ultra	20.00	.50
a.		No ball to "5" in upper left corner	32.50	12.50
69	A28	35c violet brn	25.00	1.50
a.		35c red brown	42.50	2.40
70	A28	50c bister	62.50	20.00
71	A28	50c gray ('97)	57.50	2.50
72	A28	1fr car, *lt grn*	75.00	20.00
73	A28	1fr orange ('00)	90.00	5.00
74	A28	2fr lilac, *rose*	90.00	70.00
75	A28	2fr lilac ('00)	150.00	13.50
		Nos. 60-75 (16)	615.95	136.70

Antwerp Exhibition Issue

Arms of Antwerp — A29

1894

76	A29	5c green, *rose*	4.75	3.25
77	A29	10c carmine, *bluish*	3.75	2.50
78	A29	25c blue, *rose*	1.00	1.00
		Nos. 76-78 (3)	9.50	6.75

Brussels Exhibition Issue

St. Michael and Satan
A30   A31

1896-97   **Perf. 14x14½**

79	A30	5c deep violet	1.00	.60
80	A31	10c orange brown	8.50	3.50
81	A31	10c lilac brown	.50	.35
		Nos. 79-81 (3)	10.00	4.45

A32

A33

A34

A35

A36

A37

A38

A39

Two types of 1c:
I - Periods after "Dimanche" and "Zondag" in label.
II - No period after "Dimanche." Period often missing after "Zondag."

1905-11   **Perf. 14**

82	A32	1c gray (I) ('07)	1.50	.20
a.		Type II ('08)	2.00	.60
83	A32	2c red brown ('07)	14.50	5.75
84	A32	5c green ('07)	11.50	.60
85	A33	10c dull rose	1.75	.60
86	A34	20c olive grn	26.00	1.00
87	A35	25c ultra	12.00	.85
a.		25c deep blue ('11)	13.50	2.00
88	A36	35c red brn	27.50	2.40
89	A37	50c bluish gray	95.00	4.00
90	A38	1fr yellow orange	110.00	8.00
91	A39	2fr violet	75.00	22.50
		Bar cancellation		5.00
		Nos. 82-91 (10)	374.75	45.90

A40   A41

Lion of Belgium — A42

A43   King
Albert I — A44

1912

92	A40	1c orange	.20	.20
93	A41	2c orange brn	.25	.45
94	A42	5c green	.20	.20
95	A43	10c red	.75	.40
96	A43	20c olive grn	16.00	4.00
97	A43	35c bister brn	1.00	.70
98	A43	40c green	16.00	14.50
99	A43	50c gray	1.00	.80
100	A43	1fr orange	4.00	3.00
101	A43	2fr violet	17.50	17.50
102	A44	5fr plum	80.00	25.00
		Nos. 92-102 (11)	136.90	66.75

Counterfeits exist of Nos. 97-102. Those of No. 102 are common.
For overprints see Nos. Q49-Q50, Q52, Q55-Q55A, Q57-Q60.

A45

1912-13

Larger Head

103	A45	10c red	.40	.20
a.		Without engraver's name	.20	.25
104	A45	20c olive grn ('13)	.40	.40
a.		Without engraver's name	2.00	2.00
105	A45	25c ultra	.25	.40
a.		With engraver's name	4.25	3.00
107	A45	40c green ('13)	.50	.60
		Nos. 103-107 (4)	1.55	1.60

For overprints see #Q51, Q53-Q54, Q56.

Albert I
A46

Cloth Hall of Ypres
A47

Bridge of
Dinant — A48

Library of
Louvain — A49

Scheldt
River at
Antwerp
A50

Anti-slavery
Campaign in
the Congo
A51

King Albert I
at Furnes
A52

Kings of
Belgium
Leopold I,
Albert I,
Leopold II
A53

1915-20   **Typo.**   **Perf. 14, 14½**

108	A46	1c orange	.20	.20
109	A46	2c chocolate	.20	.20
110	A46	3c gray blk ('20)	.30	.20
111	A46	5c green	1.00	.20
112	A46	10c carmine	.90	.20
113	A46	15c purple	1.50	.20
114	A46	20c red violet	3.00	.20
115	A46	25c blue	.50	.40

Engr.

116	A47	35c brn org & blk	.50	.30
117	A48	40c green & black	1.00	.30
a.		Vert. pair, imperf. btwn.		
118	A49	50c car rose & blk	4.50	.30
119	A50	1fr violet	32.50	1.00
120	A51	2fr slate	21.00	2.00
121	A52	5fr deep blue	275.00	125.00
		Telegraph or railroad cancel		55.00
122	A53	10fr brown	20.00	25.00
		Nos. 108-122 (15)	362.10	150.70

Two types each of the 1c, 10c and 20c; three of the 2c and 15c; four of the 5c, differing in the top left corner.
See No. 138. For surcharges see Nos. B34-B47.

Perron of
Liege
(Fountain)
A54

King Albert in
Trench Helmet
A55

1919   **Perf. 11½**

| 123 | A54 | 25c deep blue | 2.40 | .35 |
| a. | | Sheet of 10 | 5,500. | 5,750. |

Perf. 11, 11½, 11½x11, 11x11½
1919

Size: 18½x22mm

| 124 | A55 | 1c lilac brn | .20 | .20 |
| 125 | A55 | 2c olive | .20 | .20 |

Size: 22x26

126	A55	5c green	.20	.20
127	A55	10c carmine, 22x26¾mm	.25	.25
a.		Size: 22½x26mm	1.00	.60
128	A55	15c gray vio, 22x26¾mm	.30	.30
a.		Size: 22½x26mm	2.40	.60
129	A55	20c olive blk	1.10	1.10
130	A55	25c deep blue	1.60	1.60
131	A55	35c bister brn	3.00	3.00
132	A55	40c red	5.00	5.00
133	A55	50c red brn	9.50	10.00
134	A55	1fr lt orange	40.00	40.00
135	A55	2fr violet	375.00	375.00

Size: 28x33½mm

136	A55	5fr car lake	100.00	100.00
137	A55	10fr claret	110.00	110.00
		Nos. 124-137 (14)	646.35	646.85
		Set, never hinged	1,150.	

Type of 1915 Inscribed: "FRANK" instead of "FRANKEN"

1919, Dec.   **Perf. 14, 15**

| 138 | A52 | 5fr deep blue | 1.75 | 1.25 |
| | | Never hinged | 3.00 | |

Town Hall at
Termonde — A56

1920   **Perf. 11½**

139	A56	65c cl & blk, 27x22mm	.75	.20
		Never hinged	1.50	
a.		Center inverted	57,500.	
b.		Size: 26¼x22½mm	5.75	2.40
		Never hinged	13.50	

For surcharge see No. 143.

Nos. B48-B50
Surcharged in Red
or Black

1921   **Perf. 12**

140	SP6	20c on 5c + 5c (R)	.60	.25
a.		Inverted surcharge	525.00	525.00
		Never hinged	1,000.	
141	SP7	20c on 10c + 5c	.40	.25
142	SP8	20c on 5c + 15c (R)	.60	.25
a.		Inverted surcharge	525.00	525.00
		Never hinged	1,000.	

No. 139
Surcharged in
Red

143	A57	55c on 65c cl & blk	1.50	.35
a.		Pair, one without surcharge	2.25	.85
		Nos. 140-143 (4)	3.10	1.10
		Set, never hinged	8.50	

A58   A59

1922-27   **Typo.**   **Perf. 14**

144	A58	1c orange	.20	.20
145	A58	2c olive ('26)	.20	.20
146	A58	3c fawn	.20	.20
147	A58	5c gray	.20	.20
148	A58	10c blue grn	.20	.20
149	A58	15c plum ('23)	.20	.20
150	A58	20c black brn	.20	.20

151	A58	25c magenta	.20	.20
a.		25c dull violet ('23)	.50	.20
152	A58	30c vermilion	.50	.20
153	A58	30c rose ('25)	.35	.20
154	A58	35c red brown	.35	.30
155	A58	35c blue grn ('27)	.80	.35
156	A58	40c rose	.50	.20
157	A58	50c bister ('25)	.50	.20
158	A58	60c olive brn ('27)	3.00	.20
159	A58	1.25fr dp blue ('26)	1.10	1.10
160	A58	1.50fr brt blue ('26)	1.60	.45
161	A58	1.75fr ultra ('27)	1.40	.20
a.		Tete beche pair	5.00	5.00
c.		Bklt. pane of 4 + 2 labels	40.00	
		Nos. 144-161 (18)	11.70	5.00
		Set, never hinged	27.50	

See Nos. 185-190. For overprints and surcharges see #191-195, 197, B56, O1-O6.

1921-25   **Engr.**

11, 11x11½, 11½, 11½x11, 11½x12, 11½x12½, 12½

162	A59	50c dull blue	.30	.20
163	A59	75c scarlet ('22)	.25	.25
164	A59	75c ultra ('24)	.45	.20
165	A59	1fr black brn ('22)	.80	.20
166	A59	1fr dk blue ('25)	.60	.20
167	A59	2fr dk green ('22)	.90	.25
168	A59	5fr brown vio ('23)	13.50	15.00
169	A59	10fr magenta ('22)	9.00	6.50
		Nos. 162-169 (8)	25.80	22.80
		Set, never hinged	52.50	

No. 162 measures 18x20¾mm and was printed in sheets of 100.

Philatelic Exhibition Issues

1921, May 26   **Perf. 11½**

170	A59	50c dark blue	3.50	3.50
		Never hinged	4.75	
a.		Sheet of 25	200.00	175.00
		Never hinged	225.00	

No. 170 measures 17½x21¼mm, was printed in sheets of 25 and sold at the Philatelic Exhibition at Brussels.

The sheet normally has pin holes and a cancellation-like marking in the margin. These are considered unused and the condition valued here.

Souvenir Sheet

1924, May 24   **Perf. 11½**

171		Sheet of 4	140.00	140.00
		Never hinged	260.00	
a.	A59	5fr red brown	10.00	10.00
		Never hinged	12.00	

Sold only at the Intl. Phil. Exhib., Brussels. Sheet size: 130x145mm.

The sheet normally has pin holes and a cancellation-like marking in the margin. These are considered unused and the condition valued here.

Kings Leopold I and Albert I — A60

1925, June 1   **Perf. 14**

172	A60	10c dp green	7.25	7.25
173	A60	15c dull vio	3.75	4.50
174	A60	20c red brown	3.75	4.50
175	A60	25c grnsh black	3.75	4.50
176	A60	30c vermilion	3.75	4.50
177	A60	35c lt blue	3.75	4.50
178	A60	40c brnsh blk	3.75	4.50
179	A60	50c yellow brn	3.75	4.50
180	A60	75c dk blue	3.75	4.50
181	A60	1fr dk violet	6.50	6.50
182	A60	2fr ultra	4.00	4.00
183	A60	5fr blue blk	3.75	4.50
184	A60	10fr dp rose	6.50	8.00
		Nos. 172-184 (13)	58.00	66.25
		Set, never hinged	125.00	

75th anniv. of Belgian postage stamps.
Nos. 172-184 were sold only in sets and only by The Administration of Posts, not at post offices.

A61

1926-27   **Typo.**

185	A61	75c dk violet	.75	.70
186	A61	1fr pale yellow	.60	.35
187	A61	1fr rose red ('27)	1.00	.20
a.		Tete beche pair	7.50	4.50
c.		Bklt. pane 4 + 2 labels	25.00	
188	A61	2fr Prus blue	2.50	.45
189	A61	5fr emerald ('27)	27.50	1.60
190	A61	10fr dk brown ('27)	60.00	7.75
		Nos. 185-190 (6)	92.35	11.05
		Set, never hinged	250.00	

For overprints and surcharge see Nos. 196, Q174-Q175.

Stamps of 1921-27
Surcharged in Carmine,
Red or Blue

1927

191	A58	3c on 2c olive	.20	.20
192	A58	10c on 15c plum (R)	.20	.20
193	A58	35c on 40c rose (Bl)	.45	.20
194	A58	1.75fr on 1.50fr brt bl	2.25	.80
		Nos. 191-194 (4)	3.10	1.40
		Set, never hinged	3.75	

Nos. 153, 185 and 159
Surcharged in Black

1929, Jan. 1

195	A58	5c on 30c rose	.20	.20
196	A61	5c on 75c dk violet	.20	.20
197	A58	5c on 1.25fr dp blue	.20	.20
		Nos. 195-197 (3)	.60	.60
		Set, never hinged	.65	

The surcharge on Nos. 195-197 is a precancelation which alters the value of the stamp to which it is applied.

Values for precanceled stamps in unused column are for those which have not been through the post and have original gum. Values in second column are for postally used, gumless stamps.

A63   A64

1929-32   **Typo.**   **Perf. 14**

198	A63	1c orange	.20	.20
199	A63	2c emerald ('31)	.45	.45
200	A63	3c red brown	.20	.20
201	A63	5c slate	.20	.20
c.		Bklt. pane of 4 + 2 labels	8.25	
202	A63	10c olive grn	.20	.20
c.		Bklt. pane of 4 + 2 labels	4.50	
203	A63	20c brt violet	1.00	.25
204	A63	25c rose red	.45	.20
c.		Bklt. pane of 4 + 2 labels	8.25	
205	A63	35c green	.60	.20
c.		Bklt. pane of 4 + 2 labels	9.75	
206	A63	40c red vio ('30)	.30	.20
c.		Bklt. pane of 4 + 2 labels	9.75	
207	A63	50c dp blue	.45	.20
c.		Bklt. pane of 4 + 2 labels	8.25	
208	A63	60c rose ('30)	2.00	.20
c.		Bklt. pane of 4 + 2 labels	30.00	
209	A63	70c org brn ('30)	1.10	.20
c.		Bklt. pane of 4 + 2 labels	22.50	
210	A63	75c dk blue ('30)	2.00	.20
211	A63	75c dp brown ('32)	6.00	.20
b.		Bklt. pane of 4 + 2 labels	100.00	
		Nos. 198-211 (14)	15.15	3.10
		Set, never hinged	55.00	

For overprints and surcharges see Nos. 225-226, 240-241, 254-256, 309, O7-O15.

Tete Beche Pairs

201a	A63	5c	.60	.60
202a	A63	10c	.30	.30
204a	A63	25c	1.75	1.75
205a	A63	35c	2.75	2.75
206a	A63	40c	2.75	2.75
207a	A63	50c	2.25	2.25
208a	A63	60c	8.00	7.50
209a	A63	70c	6.00	5.00
210a	A63	75c	9.00	8.50
211a	A63	75c	27.50	25.00
		Nos. 201a-211a (10)	60.90	56.40
		Set, never hinged	110.00	

Tete-beche gutter pairs also exist.

Perf. 14½, 14x14½
1929, Jan. 25   **Engr.**

212	A64	10fr dk brown	15.00	4.00
213	A64	20fr dk green	85.00	20.00
214	A64	50fr red violet	13.50	13.50
a.		Perf. 14½	37.50	40.00
215	A64	100fr brownish lake	13.50	13.50
a.		Perf. 14½	37.50	40.00
		Nos. 212-215 (4)	127.00	51.00
		Set, never hinged	275.00	

Peter Paul   Zenobe
Rubens — A65   Gramme — A66

1930, Apr. 26 Photo. Perf. 12½x12

216	A65	35c blue green	.40	.20
217	A66	35c blue green	.40	.20
		Set, never hinged	2.10	

No. 216 issued for the Antwerp Exhibition, No. 217 the Liege Exhibition.

Leopold I, by   Leopold II, by
Jacques de   Joseph
Winn3 — A67   Lempoels — A68

Design: 1.75fr, Albert I.

1930, July 1 Engr. Perf. 11½

218	A67	60c brown violet	.20	.20
219	A68	1fr carmine	1.10	1.10
220	A68	1.75fr dk blue	2.75	1.25
		Nos. 218-220 (3)	4.05	2.55
		Set, never hinged	10.00	

Centenary of Belgian independence.
For overprints see Nos. 222-224.

Antwerp Exhibition Issue
Souvenir Sheet

Arms of
Antwerp
A70

1930, Aug. 9   **Perf. 11½**

221	A70	4fr Sheet of 1	87.50	87.50
		Never hinged	140.00	
a.		Single stamp	55.00	40.00

Size: 142x141mm. Inscription in lower margin "ATELIER DU TIMBRE-1930-ZEGELFABRIEK." Each purchaser of a ticket to the Antwerp Phil. Exhib., Aug. 9-15, was allowed to purchase one stamp. The ticket cost 6 francs.

The sheet normally has pin holes and a cancellation-like marking in the margin. These are considered unused and the condition valued here.

Nos. 218-220
Overprinted in Blue
or Red

1930, Oct.

222	A67	60c brown vio (Bl)	2.00	2.00
223	A68	1fr carmine (Bl)	8.25	7.75
224	A68	1.75fr dk blue (R)	14.50	14.50
		Nos. 222-224 (3)	24.75	24.25
		Set, never hinged	55.00	

50th meeting of the administrative council of the Intl. Labor Bureau at Brussels.

The names of the painters and the initials of the engraver have been added at the foot of these stamps.

Stamps of 1929-30 Surcharged in Blue or Black:

1931, Feb. 20   Perf. 14

225	A63	2c on 3c red brown (Bl)	.20	.20
226	A63	10c on 60c rose (Bk)	.50	.20
		Set, never hinged	3.75	

The surcharge on No. 226 is a precancellation which alters the denomination. See note after No. 197.

King Albert
A71   A71a

1931, June 15   Photo.

227	A71	1fr brown carmine	.50	.20
		Never hinged	1.00	

1932, June 1

228	A71a	75c bister brown	1.25	.20
		Never hinged	5.00	
a.		Tete beche pair	6.75	6.75
		Never hinged	17.50	
c.		Bklt. pane 4 + 2 labels	27.50	

See No. 257. For overprint see No. O18.

A72

1931-32   Engr.

229	A72	1.25fr gray black	.75	.50
230	A72	1.50fr brown vio	1.25	.50
231	A72	1.75fr dp blue	.80	.20
232	A72	2fr red brown	1.10	.20
233	A72	2.45fr dp violet	1.90	.40
234	A72	2.50fr black brn ('32)	10.00	.50
235	A72	5fr dp green	18.00	1.10
236	A72	10fr claret	45.00	12.50
		Nos. 229-236 (8)	78.80	15.90
		Set, never hinged	250.00	

Nos. 206 and 209 Surcharged as No. 226, but dated "1932"

1932, Jan. 1

240	A63	10c on 40c red vio	2.50	.30
241	A63	10c on 70c org brn	2.00	.20
		Set, never hinged	13.50	

See note after No. 197.

Gleaner   Mercury
A73   A74

1932, June 1   Typo.   Perf. 13½x14

245	A73	2c pale green	.35	.35
246	A74	5c dp orange	.20	.20
247	A73	10c olive grn	.25	.20
a.		Tete beche pair	4.00	4.00
		Never hinged	5.75	
c.		Bklt. pane 4 + 2 labels	15.00	

248	A74	20c brt violet	1.00	.20
249	A73	25c deep red	.60	.20
a.		Tete beche pair	3.50	3.50
		Never hinged	5.00	
250	A74	35c dp green	2.40	.20
c.		Bklt. pane 4 + 2 labels	15.00	
		Nos. 245-250 (6)	4.80	1.35
		Set, never hinged	14.50	

For overprints see Nos. O16-O17.

Auguste Piccard's
Balloon — A75

1932, Nov. 26   Engr.   Perf. 11½

251	A75	75c red brown	3.50	.30
252	A75	1.75fr dk blue	13.50	2.10
253	A75	2.50fr dk violet	17.00	11.50
		Nos. 251-253 (3)	34.00	13.90
		Set, never hinged	97.50	

Issued in commemoration of Prof. Auguste Piccard's two ascents to the stratosphere.

Nos. 206 and 209 Surcharged as No. 226, but dated "1933"

1933, Nov.   Perf. 14

254	A63	10c on 40c red vio	14.00	4.00
255	A63	10c on 70c org brn	12.50	1.50
		Set, never hinged	65.00	

No. 206 Surcharged as No. 226, but dated "1934"

1934, Feb.

256	A63	10c on 40c red vio	12.50	1.50
		Never hinged	35.00	

For Nos. 254 to 256 see note after No. 197.
Regummed copies of Nos. 254-256 abound.

King Albert Memorial Issue
Type of 1932 with Black Margins

1934, Mar. 10   Photo.

257	A71a	75c black	.30	.20
		Never hinged	.60	

Congo
Pavilion — A76

Designs: 1fr, Brussels pavilion. 1.50fr, "Old Brussels." 1.75fr, Belgian pavilion.

1934, July 1   Perf. 14x13½

258	A76	35c green	.75	.30
259	A76	1fr dk carmine	1.25	.40
260	A76	1.50fr brown	5.00	.80
261	A76	1.75fr blue	5.00	.30
		Nos. 258-261 (4)	12.00	1.80
		Set, never hinged	45.00	

Brussels Intl. Exhib. of 1935.

King Leopold III
A80   A81

1934-35   Perf. 13½x14

262	A80	70c olive blk ('35)	.35	.20
a.		Tete beche pair	1.50	1.00
c.		Bklt. pane 4 + 2 labels	6.25	
263	A80	75c brown	.65	.25

Perf. 14x13½

264	A81	1fr rose car ('35)	3.25	.35
		Nos. 262-264 (3)	4.25	.80
		Set, never hinged	10.00	

For overprint see No. O19.

Coat of Arms — A82

1935-48   Typo.   Perf. 14

265	A82	2c green ('37)	.20	.20
266	A82	5c orange	.20	.20
267	A82	10c olive bister	.20	.20
a.		Tete beche pair	.30	.25
		Never hinged	.50	
b.		Bklt. pane 4 + 2 labels	4.50	
268	A82	15c dk violet	.20	.20
269	A82	20c lilac	.20	.20
270	A82	25c carmine rose	.20	.20
a.		Tete beche pair	.30	.40
		Never hinged	.55	
c.		Bklt. pane 4 + 2 labels	4.50	
271	A82	25c yel org ('46)	.20	.20
272	A82	30c brown	.20	.20
273	A82	35c green	.20	.20
a.		Tete beche pair	.30	.30
		Never hinged	.50	
c.		Bklt. pane 4 + 2 labels	3.00	
274	A82	40c red vio ('38)	.20	.20
275	A82	50c blue	.40	.20
276	A82	60c slate ('41)	.20	.20
277	A82	65c red lilac ('46)	.25	.20
278	A82	70c lt blue grn ('45)	.25	.25
279	A82	75c lilac rose ('45)	.25	.20
280	A82	80c green ('48)	3.50	.40
281	A82	90c dull vio ('46)	.20	.20
282	A82	1fr red brown ('45)	.20	.20
		Nos. 265-282 (18)	7.25	3.85
		Set, never hinged	17.00	

Several stamps of type A82 exist in various shades.

Nos. 265, 361 were privately overprinted and surcharged "+10FR." by the Association Belgo-Americaine for the dedication of the Bastogne Memorial, July 16, 1950. The overprint is in six types.

See design O1. For overprints and surcharges see Nos. 312-313, 361-364, 390-394, O20-O22, O24, O26-O28, O33.

A83   A83a

Perf. 14, 14x13½, 11½

1936-51   Photo.

Size: 17½x21¾mm

283	A83	70c brown	.30	.20
a.		Tete beche pair	.80	.80
		Never hinged	1.40	
c.		Bklt. pane 4 + 2 labels	7.50	

Size: 20¾x24mm

284	A83a	1fr rose car	.30	.20
285	A83a	1.20fr dk brown ('51)	.80	.20
286	A83a	1.50fr brt red vio ('43)	.40	.30
287	A83a	1.75fr dp ultra ('43)	.20	.20
288	A83a	1.75fr dk car ('50)	.20	.20
289	A83a	2fr dk pur ('43)	1.00	1.00
290	A83a	2.25fr grnsh blk ('43)	.25	.20
291	A83a	2.50fr org red ('51)	1.75	.30
292	A83a	3.25fr chestnut ('43)	.20	.20
293	A83a	5fr dp green ('43)	1.00	.40
		Nos. 283-293 (11)	6.40	3.40
		Set, never hinged	17.00	

Nos. 287-288, 290-291, 293 inscribed "Belgie-Belgique."

See designs A85, A91. For overprints and surcharges see #314, O23, O25, O29, O31, O34.

A84   A85

1936-51   Engr.   Perf. 14x13½

294	A84	1.50fr rose lilac	.60	.35
295	A84	1.75fr dull blue	.20	.20
296	A84	2fr dull vio	.40	.30
297	A84	2.25fr gray vio ('41)	.25	.25
298	A84	2.45fr black	32.50	.70
299	A84	2.50fr ol blk ('40)	2.00	.25
300	A84	3.25fr org brn ('41)	.30	.20
301	A84	3fr dull green	2.40	.20
302	A84	10fr vio brn	.60	.20
a.		10fr light brown	1.00	.20
		Never hinged	3.00	
303	A84	20fr vermilion	1.00	.30

Perf. 11½

304	A84	3fr yel brn ('51)	.55	.20
305	A84	4fr bl, bluish ('50)	4.75	.20
a.		White paper	5.50	.20
306	A84	6fr brt rose car ('51)	2.75	.20
307	A84	10fr brn vio ('51)	.55	.20
308	A84	20fr red ('51)	1.10	.20
		Nos. 294-308 (15)	49.95	4.25
		Set, never hinged	150.00	

See No. 1159. For overprint and surcharges see Nos. 316-317, O32.

No. 206 Surcharged as No. 226, but dated "1937"

1937   Unwmk.   Perf. 14

309	A63	10c on 40c red vio	.20	.20
		Never hinged	.30	

See note after No. 197.

1938-41   Photo.   Perf. 13½x14

310	A85	75c olive gray	.25	.20
a.		Tete beche pair	.75	.80
		Never hinged	1.50	
c.		Bklt. pane 4 + 2 labels	6.75	
311	A85	1fr rose pink ('41)	.20	.20
a.		Tete beche pair	.25	.25
		Never hinged	.40	
b.		Booklet pane of 6	2.25	
c.		Bklt. pane 4 + 2 labels	2.25	
		Set, never hinged	.80	

For overprints and surcharges see Nos. 315, O25, O30, O35.

Nos. 272, 274, 283, 310, 299, 298 Surcharged in Blue, Black, Carmine or Red

a   b

c

1938-42

312	A82 (a)	10c on 30c (Bl)	.20	.20
313	A82 (a)	10c on 40c (Bl)	.20	.20
314	A83 (b)	10c on 70c (Bk)	.20	.20
315	A85 (b)	50c on 75c (C)	.20	.20
316	A84 (c)	2.25fr on 2.50fr (C)	.45	.45
317	A84 (c)	2.50fr on 2.45fr (R)	11.00	2.00
		Nos. 312-317 (6)	12.25	1.45
		Set, never hinged	26.00	

Issue date: No. 317, Oct. 31, 1938.

Basilica and   Water Exhibition
Bell   Buildings — A87
Tower — A86

Designs: 1.50fr, Albert Canal and Park. 1.75fr, Eygenbilsen Cut in Albert Canal.

1938, Oct. 31   Perf. 14x13½, 13½x14

318	A86	35c dk blue grn	.20	.20
319	A87	1fr rose red	.45	.30
320	A87	1.50fr vio brn	1.10	.60
321	A87	1.75fr ultra	1.25	.20
		Nos. 318-321 (4)	3.00	1.30
		Set, never hinged	11.00	

Intl. Water Exhibition, Liège, 1939.

Catalogue values for unused stamps in this section, from this point to the end of the section, are for Never Hinged items.

Lion Rampant
A90

Leopold III,
Crown and V
A91

1944   Unwmk.   Photo.   Perf. 12½
Inscribed: "Belgique-Belgie"

322	A90	5c	chocolate	.20 .20
323	A90	10c	green	.20 .20
324	A90	25c	lt blue	.20 .20
325	A90	35c	brown	.20 .20
326	A90	50c	lt bl grn	.20 .20
327	A90	75c	purple	.20 .20
328	A90	1fr	vermilion	.20 .20
329	A90	1.25fr	chestnut	.20 .20
330	A90	1.50fr	orange	.45 .40
331	A90	1.75fr	brt ultra	.20 .20
332	A90	2fr	aqua	3.75 1.90
333	A90	2.75fr	dp mag	.20 .20
334	A90	3fr	claret	.75 .60
335	A90	3.50fr	sl blk	.75 .60
336	A90	5fr	dk olive	6.75 4.75
337	A90	10fr	black	1.25 1.10
		Nos. 322-337 (16)		15.70 11.35

Inscribed: "Belgie-Belgique"

338	A90	5c	chocolate	.20 .20
339	A90	10c	green	.20 .20
340	A90	25c	lt bl	.20 .20
341	A90	35c	brown	.20 .20
342	A90	50c	lt bl grn	.20 .20
343	A90	75c	purple	.20 .20
344	A90	1fr	vermilion	.20 .20
345	A90	1.25fr	chestnut	.20 .20
346	A90	1.50fr	orange	.30 .45
347	A90	1.75fr	brt ultra	.20 .20
348	A90	2fr	aqua	2.00 2.00
349	A90	2.75fr	dp magenta	.20 .20
350	A90	3fr	claret	.65 .75
351	A90	3.50fr	slate blk	.65 .75
352	A90	5fr	dark olive	5.75 5.00
353	A90	10fr	black	1.00 1.25
		Nos. 338-353 (16)		12.35 12.20

1944-57   Perf. 14x13½

354	A91	1fr	brt rose red	.35 .20
355	A91	1.50fr	magenta	.50 .20
356	A91	1.75fr	dp ultra	.50 .55
357	A91	2fr	dp vio	1.50 .20
358	A91	2.25fr	grnsh blk	.55 .65
359	A91	3.25fr	chnt brn	.75 .20
360	A91	5fr	dk bl grn	3.00 .20
a.		Perf. 11½ ('57)		75.00 .20
		Nos. 354-360 (7)		7.15 2.20

Nos. 355, 357, 359 inscribed "Belgique-
Belgie."
For surcharges see Nos. 365-367 and foot-
note following No. 367.

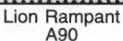

Stamps of 1935-41
Overprinted in Red

1944   Perf. 14

361	A82	2c	pale green	.20 .20
362	A82	15c	indigo	.20 .20
363	A82	20c	brt violet	.20 .20
364	A82	60c	slate	.25 .20
		Nos. 361-364 (4)		.85 .80

See note following No. 282.

Nos. 355, 357, and 360
Surcharged Typographically   −10%
in Black or Carmine

1946   Perf. 14x13½

365	A91	On 1.50fr	magenta	.40 .20
366	A91	On 2fr	dp vio (C)	1.50 .45
367	A91	On 5fr	dk bl grn (C)	2.00 .30
		Nos. 365-367 (3)		3.90 .95

To provide denominations created by a
reduction in postal rates, the Government produced #365-367 by typographed surcharge.
Also, each post office was authorized on May
20, 1946, to surcharge its stock of 1.50fr, 2fr
and 5fr stamps "-10 percent." Hundreds of
types and sizes of this surcharge exist, both
hand-stamped and typographed. These
include the "1,35," "1,80" and "4,50" applied at
Ghislenghien.

M. S. Prince
Baudouin — A92

2.25fr, S.S. Marie Henriette. 3.15fr, S.S.
Diamant.

1946, June 15   Photo.   Unwmk.

368	A92	1.35fr	brt bluish grn	.20 .20
369	A92	2.25fr	slate green	.30 .20
370	A92	3.15fr	slate black	.30 .20
		Nos. 368-370 (3)		.80 .60

Centenary of the steamship line between
Ostend and Dover.
#368 exists in two sizes: 21¼x18¼mm and
21x17mm. #369-370 are 24½x20mm.

Capt. Adrien de
Gerlache — A95

Belgica and
Explorers
A96

1947, June   Perf. 14x13½, 11½

371	A95	1.35fr	crimson rose	.45 .20
372	A96	2.25fr	gray black	2.75 2.00

50th anniv. of Capt. Adrien de Gerlache's
Antarctic Expedition.

Joseph A. F.
Plateau — A97

1947, June   Perf. 14x13½

373	A97	3.15fr	deep blue	.80 .20

Issued to mark the World Film and Fine Arts
Festival, Brussels, June, 1947.

Chemical
Industry — A98

Industrial
Arts — A99

Agriculture
A100

Textile Industry
A102

Communications Center — A101

Iron
Manufacture
A103

Photogravure (#374-376, 378),
Typographed (#377, 380), Engraved

1948   Unwmk.   Perf. 11½

374	A98	60c	blue grn	.85 .20
375	A98	1.20fr	brown	2.25 .20
376	A99	1.35fr	red brown	.85 .20
377	A100	1.75fr	brt red	1.60 .20
378	A99	1.75fr	dk gray grn	1.10 .20
379	A101	2.25fr	gray blue	2.00 1.75
380	A100	2.50fr	dk car rose	6.75 .20
381	A101	3fr	brt red vio	9.00 .30
382	A102	3.15fr	deep blue	2.00 .20
383	A102	4fr	brt ultra	8.25 .20
384	A103	6fr	blue green	13.00 .20
385	A103	6.30fr	brt red vio	4.00 3.75
		Nos. 374-385 (12)		51.65 7.60

See Nos. O42-O46.

Leopold I — A104

1949, July 1   Engr.   Perf. 14x13½

386	A104	90c	dk green	1.10 .55
387	A104	1.75fr	brown	.90 .20
388	A104	3fr	red	3.50 3.00
389	A104	4fr	deep blue	5.00 1.25
		Nos. 386-389 (4)		10.50 5.00

Cent. of Belgium's 1st postage stamps.
See note on souvenir sheet below No. 2.

Stamps of 1935-45
Precanceled and
Surcharged in Black

1949   Perf. 14

390	A82	5c on 15c	dk vio	.20 .20
391	A82	5c on 30c	brown	.20 .20
392	A82	5c on 40c	red vio	.20 .20
393	A82	20c on 70c	lt bl grn	.30 .35
394	A82	20c on 75c	lil rose	.20 .20

Similar Surcharge and
Precancellation in Black on Nos.
B455-B458
Perf. 14x13½

395	SP251	10c on #B455		3.50 3.00
396	SP251	40c on #B456		1.10 .85
397	SP251	80c on #B457		.65 .50
398	SP251	1.20fr on #B458		2.25 1.50
		Nos. 390-398 (9)		8.60 7.00

See note after No. 197.

St. Mary
Magdalene, from
Painting by Gerard
David — A105

1949, July 15   Photo.   Perf. 11

399	A105	1.75fr	dark brown	.70 .35

Gerard David Exhibition at Bruges, 1949.

Allegory
of UPU
A106

1949, Oct. 1   Engr.   Perf. 11½

400	A106	4fr	deep blue	4.50 2.50

75th anniv. of the UPU.

Symbolical of
Pension Fund
A107

Lion Rampant
A108

Perf. 11½

1950, May 1   Unwmk.   Photo.

401	A107	1.75fr	dark brown	.50 .25

General Pension Fund founding, cent.

1951, Feb. 15   Engr.   Perf. 11½

402	A108	20c	blue	.25 .20

1951-75   Typo.   Perf. 13½x14
Size: 17½x21mm

403	A108	2c	org brn ('60)	.20 .20
404	A108	3c	brt lil ('60)	.20 .20
405	A108	5c	pale violet	.20 .20
406	A108	5c	brt pink ('74)	.20 .20
407	A108	10c	red orange	.20 .20
408	A108	15c	brt pink ('59)	.20 .20
409	A108	20c	claret	.20 .20
410	A108	25c	green	1.75 .25
411	A108	25c	lt bl grn ('66)	.20 .20
412	A108	30c	gray grn ('57)	.20 .20
413	A108	40c	brown olive	.20 .20
414	A108	50c	ultra	.20 .20
a.		50c light blue		.20 .20
415	A108	60c	lilac rose	.20 .20
416	A108	65c	violet brn	12.50 .55
417	A108	75c	bluish lilac	.20 .20
418	A108	80c	emerald	.75 .20
419	A108	90c	deep blue	.75 .20
420	A108	1fr	rose	.20 .20
421	A108	2fr	emerald ('73)	.20 .20
422	A108	2.50fr	brown ('70)	.20 .20
423	A108	3fr	brt pink ('70)	.20 .20
424	A108	4fr	brt rose lil ('74)	.25 .20
425	A108	4.50fr	blue ('74)	.30 .20
426	A108	5fr	brt lilac ('75)	.30 .20

Size: 17x20½mm

427	A108	1.50fr	dk sl grn ('69)	.20 .20

Perf. 13½x13

428	A108	2fr	emerald ('68)	.20 .20

Photo.   Perf. 11½
Size: 20½x24mm

429	A108	50c	light blue ('61)	.45 .20
430	A108	60c	lilac rose ('66)	1.10 .70
431	A108	1fr	carmine rose ('59)	.20 .20

Perf. 13½x12½
Size: 17½x22mm

432	A108	50c	lt blue ('75)	.20 .20
a.		Booklet pane of 4 (#432, 784 and 2 #787) + labels		1.00
b.		Booklet pane of 4 (#432 and 3 #787) + labels		1.50
433	A108	1fr	rose ('69)	2.00 .90
434	A108	2fr	emerald ('72)	.50 .30
e.		Booklet pane of 6 (4 #434 + 2 #475)		5.50
f.		Booklet pane of 5 (#434, 4 #476 + label)		8.00
		Nos. 403-434 (32)		24.85 8.10

Counterfeits exist of No. 416. Nos. 429, 431
also issued in coils with black control number
on back of every fifth stamp. Nos. 432-434
issued in booklet panes only. No. 432 has one
straightedge, and stamps in the pane are tete-
beche. Each pane has 2 labels showing Belgian postal emblem and a large selvage with
postal code instructions.

Nos. 433-434 have 1 or 2 straight-edges.
Panes have a large selvage with inscription or
map of Belgium showing postal zones.

See designs A386, O5. For surcharges see
Nos. 477-478, 563-567.

Francois de Tassis (Franz von Taxis) — A109

Portraits: 1.75fr, Jean-Baptiste of Thurn & Taxis. 2fr, Baron Leonard I. 2.50fr, Count Lamoral I. 3fr, Count Leonard II. 4fr, Count Lamoral II. 5fr, Prince Eugene Alexander. 5.75fr, Prince Anselme Francois. 8fr, Prince Alexander Ferdinand. 10fr, Prince Charles Anselme. 20fr, Prince Charles Alexander.

1952, May 14　Engr.　Perf. 11½
Laid Paper

435	A109	80c olive grn	.75	.30
436	A109	1.75fr red org	.75	.30
437	A109	2fr violet brn	1.50	.40
438	A109	2.50fr carmine	2.25	1.65
439	A109	3fr olive bis	2.00	1.00
440	A109	4fr ultra	3.00	.85
441	A109	5fr red brn	4.00	1.75
442	A109	5.75fr blue vio	6.75	2.25
443	A109	8fr gray	12.50	2.75
444	A109	10fr rose vio	22.50	4.50
445	A109	20fr brown	60.00	22.50
	Nos. 435-445,B514 (12)		291.00	213.25

13th UPU Cong., Brussels, 1952.

King Baudouin
A110　　　　A111

1952-58　Engr.　Perf. 11½
Size: 21x24mm

446	A110	1.50fr gray green	.55	.20
447	A110	2fr crimson	.40	.20
448	A110	4fr ultra	3.50	.20

Size: 24½x35mm

449	A110	50fr gray brn	1.75	.20
a.		50fr violet brown	35.00	.60
450	A110	100fr rose red ('58)	5.00	.25

1953-72　Photo.　Perf. 11½

451	A111	1.50fr gray	.25	.20
452	A111	2fr rose carmine	6.75	.20
453	A111	2fr green	.25	.20
454	A111	2.50fr red brn ('57)	.60	.20
a.		2.50fr orange brown ('70)	.25	.20
455	A111	3fr rose lil ('58)	.40	.20
456	A111	3.50fr brt yel grn ('58)	.75	.20
457	A111	4fr brt ultra	.50	.20
458	A111	4.50fr dk red brn ('62)	3.00	.20
459	A111	5fr violet ('57)	1.25	.20
460	A111	6fr dp pink ('58)	.75	.20
461	A111	6.50fr gray ('60)	62.50	13.00
462	A111	7fr blue ('60)	.90	.20
463	A111	7.50fr grysh brn ('58)	47.50	12.50
464	A111	8fr bluish gray ('58)	1.25	.20
465	A111	8.50fr claret ('58)	15.00	.30
466	A111	9fr gray ('58)	47.50	.75
467	A111	12fr lt bl grn ('66)	.90	.25
468	A111	30fr red org ('58)	5.50	.20

Redrawn

469	A111	2.50fr org brn ('71)	.35	.20
470	A111	4.50fr brown ('72)	2.25	.60
471	A111	7fr blue ('71)	.60	.20

Perf. 13½x12½
Size: 17½x22mm

472	A111	1.50fr gray ('70)	.60	.30
b.		Bklt. pane of 10	6.50	
c.		Bklt. pane, 3 #472, 3 #475	15.00	
473	A111	2.50fr org brn ('70)	5.00	4.00
h.		Bklt. pane, 1 #473, 5 #475	16.00	
474	A111	3fr lilac rose ('69)	.60	.20
a.		Bklt. pane of 5 + label	25.00	
b.		Bklt. pane, 2 #433, 6 #474	18.00	
475	A111	3.50fr brt yel grn ('70)	.60	.25
476	A111	4.50fr dull red brn ('72)	.60	.35
	Nos. 446-476 (31)		217.35	36.55

Nos. 451, 453, 454a, 455, 456, 458 also issued in coils with black control number on back of every fifth stamp. These coils, except for No: 451, are on luminescent paper.

On Nos. 469-471, the 2, 4 and 7 are 3mm high. The background around the head is white. On Nos. 454, 458, 462 the 2, 4 and 7 are 2½mm high and the background is tinted.

Nos. 472-476 issued in booklets only and have 1 or 2 straight-edges. All panes have a large selvage with inscription or map.

See designs M1, O3.

Luminescent Paper

Stamps issued on both ordinary and luminescent paper include: Nos. 307-308, 430-431, 449-451, 453-460, 462, 464, 467-468, 472, 643-644, 650-651, 837, Q385, Q410.

Stamps issued only on luminescent paper include: Nos. 433, 454a, 472b, 473-474, 649, 652-658, 664-670, 679-682, 688-690, 694-696, 698-703, 705-711, 713-726, 729-747, 751-754, 756-757, 759, 761-762, 764, 766, 769, 772, 774, 778, 789, 791-793, 795, 797-799, 801-807, 809-811, 814-818, 820-834, 836, 838-848.

See note after No. 857.

Nos. 416 and 419 Surcharged and Precanceled in Black

1954, Jan. 1　Unwmk.　Perf. 13½x14

477	A108	20c on 65c vio brn	1.75	.30
478	A108	20c on 90c dp blue	1.75	.20

See note after No. 197.

Map and Rotary Emblem A112

80c, Mermaid and Mercury holding emblem. 4fr, Rotary emblem and two globes.

1954, Sept. 10　Engr.　Perf. 11½

479	A112	20c red	.25	.20
480	A112	80c dark green	.65	.30
481	A112	4fr ultra	1.40	.50
	Nos. 479-481 (3)		2.30	1.00

5th regional conf. of Rotary Intl. at Ostend. No. 481 for Rotary 50th Anniv. (in 1955).

A souv. sheet containing one each, imperf., was sold for 500 francs. It was not valid for postage. Value, $200.

The Rabot and Begonia — A113

Designs: 2.50fr, The Oudeburg and azalea. 4fr, "Three Towers" and orchid.

1955, Feb. 15　Photo.

482	A113	80c brt carmine	.85	.35
483	A113	2.50fr black brn	5.25	2.75
484	A113	4fr dk rose brn	5.00	.90
	Nos. 482-484 (3)		11.10	4.00

Ghent Intl. Flower Exhibition, 1955.

Homage to Charles V as a Child, by Albrecht de Vriendt A114

Charles V, by Titian — A115

4fr, Abdication of Charles V, by Louis Gallait.

1955, Mar. 25　Unwmk.　Perf. 11½

485	A114	20c rose red	.25	.20
486	A115	2fr dk gray green	1.90	.20
487	A114	4fr blue	5.00	1.25
	Nos. 485-487 (3)		7.15	1.65

Charles V Exhibition, Ghent, 1955.

Emile Verhaeren, by Montald Constant — A116

1955, May 11　Engr.

488	A116	20c dark gray	.20	.20

Birth cent. of Verhaeren, poet.

Allegory of Textile Manufacture A117

1955, May 11

489	A117	2fr violet brown	1.00	.20

2nd Intl. Textile Exhibition, Brussels, June 1955.

"The Foolish Virgin" by Rik Wouters — A118

1955, June 10

490	A118	1.20fr olive green	1.10	1.10
491	A118	2fr violet	1.60	.20

3rd biennial exhibition of sculpture, Antwerp, June 11-Sept. 10, 1955.

"Departure of Volunteers from Liege, 1830" by Charles Soubre — A119

1955, Sept. 10　Photo.

492	A119	20c grnsh slate	.20	.20
493	A119	2fr chocolate	.90	.20

Exhibition "The Romantic Movement in Liege Province," Sept. 10-Oct. 31, 1955; and 125th anniv. of Belgium's independence from the Netherlands.

Pelican Giving Blood to Young — A120

1956, Jan. 14　Engr.

494	A120	2fr brt carmine	.35	.20

Blood donor service of the Belgian Red Cross.

Buildings of Tournai, Ghent and Antwerp — A121

1956, July 14　Photo.

495	A121	2fr brt ultra	.30	.20

The Scheldt exhibition (Scaldis) at Tournai, Ghent and Antwerp, July-Sept. 1956.

Europa Issue

"Rebuilding Europe" — A122

1956, Sept. 15　Engr.

496	A122	2fr lt green	1.75	.20
497	A122	4fr purple	8.75	.70

Issued to symbolize the cooperation among the six countries comprising the Coal and Steel Community.

Train on Map of Belgium and Luxembourg A123

1956, Sept. 29

498	A123	2fr dark blue	.45	.20

Issued to mark the electrification of the Brussels-Luxembourg railroad.

Edouard Anseele — A124

1956, Oct. 27

499	A124	20c violet brown	.20	.20

Cent. of the birth of Edouard Anseele, statesman, and in connection with an exhibition held in his honor at Ghent.

"The Atom" and Exposition Emblem — A125

1957-58   **Unwmk.**
500	A125	2fr carmine rose	.25	.20
501	A125	2.50fr green ('58)	.40	.20
502	A125	4fr brt violet blue	.95	.45
503	A125	5fr claret ('58)	.85	.50
		Nos. 500-503 (4)	2.45	1.10

1958 World's Fair at Brussels.

Emperor Maximilian I Receiving Letter — A126

1957, May 19
504	A126	2fr claret	.40	.20

Day of the Stamp, May 19, 1957.

Sikorsky S-58 Helicopter A127

1957, June 15
505	A127	4fr gray grn & brt bl	.80	.45

100,000th passenger carried by Sabena helicopter service, June 15, 1957.

Zeebrugge Harbor A128

1957, July 6
506	A128	2fr dark blue	.40	.20

50th anniv. of the completion of the port of Zeebrugge-Bruges.

Leopold I Entering Brussels, 1831 — A129

Leopold I Arriving at Belgian Border A130

1957, July 17   **Photo.**
507	A129	20c dk gray grn	.20	.20
508	A130	2fr lilac	.50	.20

126th anniv. of the arrival in Belgium of King Leopold I.

Boy Scout and Girl Scout Emblems A131

Design: 4fr, Robert Lord Baden-Powell, painted by David Jaggers, vert.

1957, July 29   **Unwmk.**   **Perf. 11½**   **Engr.**
509	A131	80c gray	.25	.20
510	A131	4fr light green	1.00	.45

Cent. of the birth of Lord Baden-Powell, founder of the Boy Scout movement.

"Kneeling Woman" by Lehmbruck — A132

1957, Aug. 20   **Photo.**
511	A132	2.50fr dk blue grn	1.10	.85

4th Biennial Exposition of Sculpture, Antwerp, May 25-Sept. 15.

"United Europe" — A133

1957, Sept. 16   **Engr.**   **Perf. 11½**
512	A133	2fr dk violet brn	1.00	.20
513	A133	4fr dark blue	1.90	.45

Europa: United Europe for peace and prosperity.

Queen Elisabeth Assisting at Operation, by Allard L'Olivier A134

Perf. 11½
1957, Nov. 23   **Unwmk.**   **Engr.**
514	A134	30c rose lilac	.20	.20

50th anniv. of the founding of the Edith Cavell-Marie Depage and St. Camille schools of nursing.

Post Horn and Historic Postal Insignia A135

1958, Mar. 16   **Photo.**   **Perf. 11½**
515	A135	2.50fr gray	.25	.20

Postal Museum Day.

United Nations Issue

International Labor Organization A136

Allegory of UN — A137

Designs: 1fr, FAO. 2fr, World Bank. 2.50fr, UNESCO. 3fr, UN Pavilion. 5fr, ITU. 8fr, Intl. Monetary Fund. 11fr, WHO. 20fr, UPU.

Perf. 11½
1958, Apr. 17   **Unwmk.**   **Engr.**
516	A136	50c gray	.90	1.40
517	A136	1fr claret	.30	.45
518	A137	1.50fr dp ultra	.30	.45
519	A137	2fr gray brown	.85	1.25
520	A136	2.50fr olive grn	.30	.45
521	A136	3fr grnsh blue	.85	1.25
522	A137	5fr rose lilac	.55	.90
523	A136	8fr red brown	1.00	1.60
524	A136	11fr dull lilac	1.25	2.00
525	A136	20fr car rose	1.60	2.50
		Nos. 516-525,C15-C20 (16)	10.20	14.70

World's Fair, Brussels, Apr. 17-Oct. 19. Postally valid only from the UN pavilion at the Brussels Fair. Proceeds went toward financing the UN exhibits.

Eugène Ysaye A138

1958, Sept. 1
526	A138	30c dk blue & plum	.20	.20

Ysaye (1858-1931), violinist, composer.

Common Design Types pictured in section at front of book.

Europa Issue, 1958
Common Design Type
1958, Sept. 13   **Photo.**
Size: 24½x35mm
527	CD1	2.50fr brt red & blue	.20	.20
528	CD1	5fr brt blue & red	.35	.35

Issued to show the European Postal Union at the service of European integration.

Universal Declaration of Human Rights, 10th Anniv. — A140

Infant and UN Emblem.

1958, Dec. 10   **Engr.**
529	A140	2.50fr blue gray	.30	.20

Charles V , Jean-Baptiste of Thurn and Taxis — A141

1959, Mar. 15   **Unwmk.**
530	A141	2.50fr green	.35	.20

Issued for the Day of the Stamp. Design from painting by J.-E. van den Bussche.

NATO Emblem — A142

1959, Apr. 3   **Photo.**   **Perf. 11½**
531	A142	2.50fr dp red & dk bl	.45	.45
532	A142	5fr emerald & dk bl	1.25	1.40

10th anniv. of NATO. See No. 720.

City Hall, Audenarde — A143

1959, Aug. 17   **Engr.**
533	A143	2.50fr deep claret	.30	.20

Pope Adrian VI, by Jan van Scorel — A144

1959, Aug. 31   **Perf. 11½**
534	A144	2.50fr dark red	.20	.20
535	A144	5fr Prus blue	.55	.55

500th anniv. of the birth of Pope Adrian VI.

Europa Issue, 1959
Common Design Type
1959, Sept. 19   **Photo.**
Size: 24x35½mm
536	CD2	2.50fr dark red	.20	.20
537	CD2	5fr brt grnsh blue	.45	.45

Boeing 707 A146

Engraved and Photogravure
1959, Dec. 1   **Perf. 11½**
538	A146	6fr dk bl gray & car	1.75	.80

Inauguration of jet flights by Sabena Airlines.

Countess of Taxis — A147

1960, Mar. 21   **Engr.**   **Perf. 11½**
539	A147	3fr dark blue	.85	.20

Alexandrine de Rye, Countess of Taxis, Grand Mistress of the Netherlands Posts, 1628-1645, and day of the stamp, Mar. 21, 1960. The painting of the Countess is by Nicholas van der Eggermans.

24th Ghent Intl. Flower Exhibition — A148

1960, Mar. 28   **Unwmk.**
540 A148 40c Indian azalea   .20   .20
541 A148 3fr Begonia   .90   .20
542 A148 6fr Anthurium, bromelia   1.00   .90
   Nos. 540-542 (3)   2.10 1.30

Steel Workers, by Constantin Meunier — A149

Design: 3fr, The sower, field and dock workers, from "Monument to Labor," Brussels, by Constantin Meunier, horiz.

Engraved and Photogravure
1960, Apr. 30   *Perf. 11½*
543 A149 40c claret & brt red   .20   .20
544 A149 3fr brown & brt red   .85   .25
   Socialist Party of Belgium, 75th anniv.

Congo River Boat Pilot — A150

Designs: 40c, Medical team. 1fr, Planting tree. 2fr, Sculptors. 2.50fr, Shot put. 3fr, Congolese officials. 6fr, Congolese and Belgian girls playing with doll. 8fr, Boy pointing on globe to independent Congo.

1960, June 30   **Photo.**   *Perf. 11½*
   Size: 35x24mm
545 A150   10c bright red   .30   .20
546 A150   40c rose claret   .45   .20
547 A150   1fr brt lilac   .85   .75
548 A150   2fr gray green   .95   .85
549 A150 2.50fr blue   .85   .75
550 A150   3fr dk bl gray   1.00   .45
   Size: 51x35mm
551 A150   6fr violet bl   3.00 1.90
552 A150   8fr dk brown   5.00 4.00
   Nos. 545-552 (8)   12.40 9.10
   Independence of Congo.

Europa Issue, 1960
Common Design Type
1960, Sept. 17
   Size: 35x24½mm
553 CD3 3fr claret   .60   .20
554 CD3 6fr gray   1.25   .40

Children Examining Stamp and Globe — A152

1960, Oct. 1   **Photo.**   *Perf. 11½*
555 A152   40c bis & blk + label   .20   .20
   Promoting stamp collecting among children.

H. J. W. Frère-Orban A153

Engraved and Photogravure
1960, Oct. 17   **Unwmk.**
   Portrait in Brown
556 A153   10c orange yel   .20   .20
557 A153   40c blue grn   .20   .20
558 A153 1.50fr brt violet   .70   .70
559 A153   3fr red   1.10   .20
   Nos. 556-559 (4)   2.20 1.30
   Centenary of Communal Credit Society.

King Baudouin and Queen Fabiola A154

1960, Dec. 13   **Photo.**   *Perf. 11½*
   Portraits in Dark Brown
560 A154 40c green   .20   .20
561 A154 3fr red lilac   .30   .20
562 A154 6fr dull blue   1.25   .60
   Nos. 560-562 (3)   1.75 1.00
   Wedding of King Baudouin and Dona Fabiola de Mora y Aragon, Dec. 15, 1960.

Nos. 412, 414 Surcharged

1961-68   **Typo.**   *Perf. 13½x14*
563 A108 15c on 30c gray grn   .20   .20
564 A108 15c on 50c blue ('68)   .20   .20
565 A108 20c on 30c gray grn   .20   .20
   Nos. 563-565 (3)   .60   .60

No. 412 Surcharged and Precanceled

1961
566 A108 15c on 30c gray grn   .90   .20
567 A108 20c on 30c gray grn   1.90 1.40
   See note after No. 197.

Nicolaus Rockox, by Anthony Van Dyck — A155

Engraved and Photogravure
1961, Mar. 18   *Perf. 11½*
568 A155 3fr bister, blk & brn   .35   .20
   400th anniv. of the birth of Nicolaus Rockox, mayor of Antwerp.

Seal of Jan Bode, Alderman of Antwerp, 1264 — A156

1961, Apr. 16   **Photo.**
569 A156 3fr buff & brown   .35   .20
   Issued for Stamp Day, April 16.

Senate Building, Brussels, Laurel and Sword A157

Engraved and Photogravure
1961, Sept. 14   **Unwmk.**   *Perf. 11½*
570 A157 3fr brn & Prus grn   .30   .20
571 A157 6fr dk brn & dk car   2.75 1.00
   50th Conference of the Interparliamentary Union, Brussels, Sept. 14-22.

Europa Issue, 1961
Common Design Type
1961, Sept. 16   **Photo.**
572 CD4 3fr yel grn & dk grn   .25   .20
573 CD4 6fr org brn & blk   .35   .20

Atomic Reactor Plant, BR2, Mol — A159

Designs: 3fr, Atomic Reactor BR3, vert. 6fr, Atomic Reactor plant BR3.

1961, Nov. 8   **Unwmk.**   *Perf. 11½*
574 A159 40c dk blue grn   .20   .20
575 A159 3fr red lilac   .20   .20
576 A159 6fr bright blue   .35   .25
   Nos. 574-576 (3)   .75   .65
   Aatomic nuclear research center at Mol.

Horta Museum — A160

1962, Feb. 15   **Engr.**
577 A160 3fr red brown   .25   .20
   Baron Victor Horta (1861-1947), architect.

Postrider, 16th Century A161

Engraved and Photogravure
1962, Mar. 25   *Perf. 11½*
   Chalky Paper
578 A161 3fr brn & slate grn   .30   .20
   Stamp Day. See No. 677.

Gerard Mercator (Gerhard Kremer, 1512-1594), Cartographer — A162

Engraved and Photogravure
1962, Apr. 14   **Unwmk.**
579 A162 3fr sepia & gray   .30   .20

Bro. Alexis-Marie Gochet (1835-1910), Geographer, Educator — A163

1962, May 19   **Engr.**   *Perf. 11½*
   Portrait: 3fr, Canon Pierre-Joseph Triest (1760-1836), educator and founder of hospitals and orphanages.
580 A163 2fr dark blue   .30   .20
581 A163 3fr golden brown   .30   .20

Europa Issue, 1962
Common Design Type
1962, Sept. 15   **Photo.**
582 CD5 3fr dp car, citron & blk   .25   .20
583 CD5 6fr olive, citron & blk   .35   .35

Hand with Barbed Wire and Freed Hand — A165

1962, Sept. 16   **Engr. & Photo.**
584 A165 40c lt blue & blk   .20   .20
   Issued in memory of concentration camp victims.

Adam, by Michelangelo, Broken Chain and UN Emblem — A166

1962, Nov. 24   *Perf. 11½*
585 A166 3fr gray & blk   .25   .20
586 A166 6fr lt redsh brn & dk brn   .40   .30
   UN Declaration of Human Rights.

Henri Pirenne (1862-1935), Historian — A167

1963, Jan. 15   **Engr.**
587 A167 3fr ultramarine   .35   .20

Swordsmen and Ghent Belfry A168

3fr, Modern fencers. 6fr, Arms of the Royal and Knightly Guild of St. Michael, vert.

Engraved and Photogravure
1963, Mar. 23　Unwmk.　Perf. 11½
588 A168 1fr brn red & pale bl .20 .20
589 A168 3fr dk vio & yel grn .20 .20
590 A168 6fr gray, blk, red, bl & gold .30 .25
　Nos. 588-590 (3) .70 .65
350th anniv. of the granting of a charter to the Ghent guild of fencers.

Stagecoach A169

1963, Apr. 7
591 A169 3fr gray & ocher .25 .20
Stamp Day. See No. 678.

Hotel des Postes, Paris, Stagecoach and Stamp, 1863 A170

Perf. 11½
1963, May 7　Unwmk.　Engr.
592 A170 6fr dk brn, gray & yel grn .40 .35
Cent. of the 1st Intl. Postal Conf., Paris, 1863.

"Peace," Child in Rye Field — A171

1963, May 8　Engr. & Photo.
593 A171 3fr grn, blk, yel & brn .20 .20
594 A171 6fr buff, blk, brn & org .35 .25
May 8th Movement for Peace. (On May 8, 1945, World War II ended in Europe).

Allegory and Shields of 17 Member Nations A172

1963, June 13　Unwmk.　Perf. 11½
595 A172 6fr blue & black .40 .30
10th anniversary of the Conference of European Transport Ministers.

Seal of Union of Belgian Towns — A173

1963, June 17
596 A173 6fr grn, red, blk & gold .40 .35
Intl. Union of Municipalities, 50th anniv.

Caravelle over Brussels National Airport A174

Photogravure and Engraved
1963, Sept. 1　Unwmk.　Perf. 11½
597 A174 3fr green & gray .25 .20
40th anniversary of SABENA airline.

Europa Issue, 1963
Common Design Type
1963, Sept. 14　　　Photo.
Size: 35x24mm
598 CD6 3fr blk, dl red & lt brn .60 .20
599 CD6 6fr blk, lt bl & lt brn 1.60 .35

Jules Destrée A176

Design: No. 601, Henry Van de Velde.

Perf. 11½
1963, Nov. 16　Unwmk.　Engr.
600 A176 1fr rose lilac .20 .20
601 A176 1fr green .20 .20
Jules Destrée (1863-1936), statesman and founder of the Royal Academy of French Language and Literature, and of Henry Van de Velde (1863-1957), architect.
No. 600 incorrectly inscribed "1864."

Development of the Mail, Bas-relief — A177

1963, Nov. 23　Engr. & Photo.
602 A177 50c dl red, slate & blk .20 .20
Postal checking service, 50th anniv.

Dr. Armauer G. Hansen A178

Fight Against Leprosy: 2fr, Leprosarium. 5fr, Father Joseph Damien.

1964, Jan. 25　Unwmk.　Perf. 11½
603 A178 1fr brown org & blk .20 .20
604 A178 2fr brown org & blk .20 .20
605 A178 5fr brown org & blk .25 .20
　a.　Souvenir sheet of 3, #603-605 1.90 1.90
　Nos. 603-605 (3) .65 .60
No. 605a sold for 12fr.

Andreas Vesalius (1514-64), Anatomist — A179

Jules Boulvin (1855-1920), Mechanical Engineer A180

Design: 2fr, Henri Jaspar (1870-1939), statesman and lawyer.

Engraved and Photogravure
1964, Mar. 2　Unwmk.　Perf. 11½
606 A179 50c pale grn & blk .20 .20
607 A180 1fr pale grn & blk .20 .20
608 A180 2fr pale grn & blk .20 .20
　Nos. 606-608 (3) .60 .60

Postilion of Liege, 1830-40 — A181

1964, Apr. 5　Engr.　Perf. 11½
609 A181 3fr black .20 .20
Issued for Stamp Day 1964.

Arms of Ostend A182

1964, May 16　　Photo.
610 A182 3fr ultra, ver, gold & blk .20 .20
Millennium of Ostend.

Flame, Hammer and Globe — A183

1fr, "SI" and globe. 2fr, Flame over wavy lines.

1964, July 18　Unwmk.　Perf. 11½
611 A183 50c dark blue & red .20 .20
612 A183 1fr dark blue & red .20 .20
613 A183 2fr dark blue & red .20 .20
　Nos. 611-613 (3) .60 .60
Centenary of the First Socialist International, founded in London, Sept. 28, 1864.

Europa Issue, 1964
Common Design Type
1964, Sept. 12　Photo.　Perf. 11½
Size: 24x35½mm
614 CD7 3fr yel grn, dk car & gray .25 .20
615 CD7 6fr car rose, yel grn & bl .40 .40

Benelux Issue

King Baudouin, Queen Juliana and Grand Duchess Charlotte — A185

1964, Oct. 12
616 A185 3fr olive, lt grn & mar .20 .20
20th anniv. of the customs union of Belgium, Netherlands and Luxembourg.

Hand, Round & Pear-shaped Diamonds — A186

1965, Jan. 23　Unwmk.　Perf. 11½
617 A186 2fr ultra, dp car & blk .20 .20
Diamond Exhibition "Diamantexpo," Antwerp, July 10-28, 1965.

Symbols of Textile Industry — A187

1965, Jan. 25　　Photo.
618 A187 1fr blue, red & blk .20 .20
Eighth textile industry exhibition "Textirama," Ghent, Jan. 29-Feb. 2, 1965.

Vriesia — A188

Designs: 2fr, Echinocactus. 3fr, Stapelia.

1965, Feb. 13　Engr. & Photo.
619 A188 1fr multicolored .20 .20
620 A188 2fr multicolored .20 .20
621 A188 3fr multicolored .20 .20
　a.　Souvenir sheet of 3, #619-621 1.75 1.75
　Nos. 619-621 (3) .60 .60
25th Ghent International Flower Exhibition, Apr. 24-May 3, 1965.
#621a was issued Apr. 26 and sold for 20fr.

Paul Hymans (1865-1941), Belgian Foreign Minister, First President of the League of Nations — A189

1965, Feb. 24　Engr.　Perf. 11½
622 A189 1fr dull purple .20 .20

August Kekulé,
Benzene
Ring — A209

1966, July 9
672 A209 3fr brt blue & blk   .20 .20
August Friedrich Kekule (1829-96), chemistry professor at University of Ghent (1858-67).

No. 663
Overprinted with
Red and Blue
Emblem

1966, July 11   **Photo.**
673 A205 3fr multicolored   .20 .20
19th Intl. P.T.T. Cong., Brussels, July 11-15.

Rik Wouters (1882-
1916), Self-portrait
A210

1966, Sept. 6   **Photo.**   *Perf. 11½*
674 A210 60c multicolored   .20 .20

Europa Issue, 1966
Common Design Type
1966, Sept. 24   **Engr.**   *Perf. 11½*
Size: 24x34mm
675 CD9 3fr brt green   .20 .20
676 CD9 6fr brt rose lilac   .30 .30

Types of
1962-1963
Overprinted
in Black and
Red

1966, Nov. 11   **Engr. & Photo.**
677 A161 60c sepia & grnsh gray   .20 .20
678 A169 3fr sepia & pale bister   .20 .20
75th anniv., Royal Fed. of Phil. Circles of Belgium. Overprint shows emblem of F.I.P.

Lions
Emblem — A214

1967, Jan. 14   *Perf. 11½*
679 A214 3fr gray, blk & bl   .20 .20
680 A214 6fr lt green, blk & vio   .30 .20
Lions Club Intl., 50th anniv.

Pistol by
Leonhard
Cleuter
A215

1967, Feb. 11   **Photo.**
681 A215 2fr dp car, blk & cream   .20 .20
Fire Arms Museum in Liege.

International
Tourist Year
Emblem
A216

1967, Feb. 11
682 A216 6fr ver, ultra & blk   .30 .20
International Tourist Year, 1967.

Birches and
Trientalis
A217

Design: No. 684, Dunes, beach grass, privet and blue thistles.

1967, Mar. 11   **Photo.**   *Perf. 11½*
683 A217 1fr multicolored   .20 .20
684 A217 1fr multicolored   .20 .20
Issued to publicize the nature preserves at Hautes Fagnes and Westhoek.

Paul Emile Janson(1872-1944),
Lawyer, Statesman — A218

1967, Apr. 15   **Engr.**   *Perf. 11½*
685 A218 10fr blue   .35 .20

Postilion
A219

1967, Apr. 16   **Photo. & Engr.**
686 A219 3fr rose red & claret   .20 .20
Issued for Stamp Day, 1967.

Inscribed: "FITCE"
1967, June 24   *Perf. 11½*
687 A219 10fr ultra, sep & emer   .40 .30
Issued to commemorate the meeting of the Federation of Common Market Telecommunications Engineers, Brussels, July 3-8.

Europa Issue, 1967
Common Design Type
1967, May 2   **Photo.**
Size: 24x35mm
688 CD10 3fr blk, lt bl & red   .20 .20
689 CD10 6fr blk, grnsh gray & yel   .30 .30

Flax, Shuttle and
Mills — A221

1967, June 3   **Photo.**   *Perf. 11½*
690 A221 6fr tan & multi   .30 .20
Belgian linen industry.

Old Kursaal, Ostend — A222

1967, June 3   **Engr. & Photo.**
691 A222 2fr dk brn, lt bl & yel   .20 .20
700th anniversary of Ostend as a city.

Charles Plisnier
and Lodewijk de
Raet Foundations
A223

Designs: #692, Caesar Crossing Rubicon, 15th Century Tapestry. #693, Emperor Maximilian Killing a Boar, 16th cent. tapestry.

1967, Sept. 2   **Photo.**   *Perf. 11½*
692 A223 1fr multicolored   .20 .20
693 A223 1fr multicolored   .20 .20

Universities of
Ghent and Liège,
150th
Anniv. — A224

Arms of Universities: #694, Ghent. #695, Liege.

Engraved and Photogravure
1967, Sept. 30   *Perf. 11½*
694 A224 3fr gray & multi   .20 .20
695 A224 3fr gray & multi   .20 .20

Princess Margaret
of York — A225

1967, Sept. 30   **Photo.**
696 A225 6fr multicolored   .30 .25
British Week, Sept. 28-Oct. 2.

"Virga Jesse,"
Hasselt — A226

1967, Nov. 11   **Engr.**   *Perf. 11½*
697 A226 1fr slate blue   .20 .20
Christmas, 1967.

Hand Guarding
Worker — A227

1968, Feb. 3   **Photo.**   *Perf. 11½*
698 A227 3fr multicolored   .20 .20
Issued to publicize industrial safety.

Military Mailman,
1916, by James
Thiriar — A228

Engraved and Photogravure
1968, Mar. 17   *Perf. 11½*
699 A228 3fr sepia, lt bl & brn   .20 .20
Issued for Stamp Day, 1968.

View of Grammont
and Seal of
Baudouin
VI — A229

Historic Sites: 3fr, Theux-Franchimont fortress, sword and seal. 6fr, Neolithic cave and artifacts, Spiennes. 10fr, Roman oil lamp and St. Medard's Church, Wervik.

1968, Apr. 13   **Photo.**   *Perf. 11½*
700 A229 2fr bl, blk, lil & rose   .20 .20
701 A229 3fr orange, blk & car   .20 .20
702 A229 6fr ultra, ind & bis   .25 .20
703 A229 10fr tan, blk, yel & gray   .35 .30
    Nos. 700-703 (4)   1.00 .90

Stamp of 1866, No.
23 — A230

1968, Apr. 13   **Engr.**   *Perf. 13*
704 A230 1fr black   .20 .20
Centenary of the Malines Stamp Printery.

Europa Issue, 1968
Common Design Type
1968, Apr. 27 Photo. *Perf. 11½*
Size: 35x24mm
705 CD11 3fr dl grn, gold & blk .20 .20
706 CD11 6fr carmine, sil & blk .35 .25

St. Laurent Abbey, Liège — A232

Designs: 3fr, Gothic Church, Lisseweghe. No. 709. Barges in Zandvliet locks. No. 710, Ship in Neuzen lock, Ghent Canal. 10fr, Ronquieres canal ship lift.

Engraved and Photogravure
1968, Sept. 7 *Perf. 11½*
707 A232 2fr ultra, gray ol & sep .20 .20
708 A232 3fr ol bis, gray & sep .20 .20
709 A232 6fr ind, brt bl & sep .30 .20
710 A232 6fr black, grnsh bl & ol .25 .20
711 A232 10fr bister, brt bl & sep .50 .30
Nos. 707-711 (5) 1.45 1.10

No. 710 issued Dec. 14 for opening of lock at Neuzen, Netherlands.

Christmas Candle — A233

1968, Dec. 7 *Perf. 11½*
712 A233 1fr multicolored .20 .20
Christmas, 1968.

St. Albertus Magnus — A234

1969, Feb. 15 Engr. *Perf. 11½*
713 A234 2fr sepia .20 .20
The Church of St. Paul in Antwerp (16th century) was destroyed by fire in Apr. 1968.

Ruins of Aulne Abbey, Gozee — A235

1969, Feb. 15 Engr. & Photo.
714 A235 3fr brt pink & blk .20 .20
Aulne Abbey was destroyed in 1794 during the French Revolution.

The Travelers, Roman Sculpture — A236

1969, Mar. 15 Engr. *Perf. 11½*
715 A236 2fr violet brown .20 .20
2,000th anniversary of city of Arlon.

Broodjes Chapel, Antwerp — A237

1969, Mar. 15 Engr. & Photo.
716 A237 3fr gray & blk .20 .20
150th anniv. of public education in Antwerp.

Post Office Train — A238

1969, Apr. 13 Photo. *Perf. 11½*
717 A238 3fr multicolored .20 .20
Issued for Stamp Day.

Europa Issue, 1969
Common Design Type
1969, Apr. 26
Size: 35x24mm
718 CD12 3fr lt grn, brn & blk .20 .20
719 CD12 6fr sal, rose car & blk .30 .30

NATO Type of 1959 Redrawn and Dated "1949-1969"
1969, May 31 *Perf. 11½*
720 A142 6fr org brn & ultra .30 .30
20th anniv. of NATO. No. 720 inscribed Belgique-Belgie and OTAN-NAVO.

Construction Workers, by F. Leger — A240

1969, May 31
721 A240 3fr multicolored .20 .20
50th anniversary of the ILO.

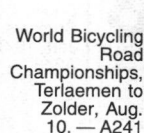

World Bicycling Road Championships, Terlaemen to Zolder, Aug. 10. — A241

1969, July 5 Photo. *Perf. 11½*
722 A241 6fr Bicyclist .30 .25

Ribbon in Benelux Colors — A242

1969, Sept. 6 Photo. *Perf. 11½*
723 A242 3fr blk, red, ultra & yel .20 .20
Signing of the customs union of Belgium, Netherlands & Luxembourg, 25th anniv.

Annevoie Garden and Pascali Rose A243

No. 725, Lochristi Garden and begonia.

1969, Sept. 6
724 A243 2fr multicolored .20 .20
725 A243 2fr multicolored .20 .20

Armstrong, Collins, Aldrin and Map Showing Tranquillity Base — A245

1969, Sept. 20 Photo.
726 A245 6fr black .30 .25
See note after Algeria #427. See #B846.

Wounded Veteran — A246

1969, Oct. 11 Engr. *Perf. 11½*
727 A246 1fr blue gray .20 .20
Natl. war veterans' aid organization (O.N.I.G.). The design is similar to type SP10.

Mailman — A247

1969, Oct. 18 Photo.
728 A247 1fr deep rose & multi .20 .20
Issued to publicize youth philately. Design by Danielle Saintenoy, 14.

Kennedy Tunnel Under the Schelde, Antwerp A248

6fr, Three highways crossing near Loncin.

1969, Nov. 8 Engr. *Perf. 11½*
729 A248 3fr multicolored .25 .20
730 A248 6fr multicolored .30 .30
Issued to publicize the John F. Kennedy Tunnel under the Schelde and the Walloon auto route and interchange near Loncin.

Henry Carton de Wiart, by Gaston Geleyn — A249

1969, Nov. 8
731 A249 6fr sepia .30 .20
Count de Wiart (1869-1951), statesman.

The Census at Bethlehem (detail), by Peter Brueghel A250

1969, Dec. 13 Photo.
732 A250 1.50fr multicolored .20 .20
Christmas, 1969.

Symbols of Bank's Activity, 100fr Coin A251

1969, Dec. 13 Engr. & Photo.
733 A251 3.50fr lt ultra, blk & sil .20 .20
50th anniv. of the Industrial Credit Bank (Societe nationale de credit a l'industrie).

Camellia — A252

1970, Jan. 31 Photo. *Perf. 11½*
734 A252 1.50fr shown .20 .20
735 A252 2.50fr Water lily .20 .20
736 A252 3.50fr Azalea .20 .20
a. Souvenir sheet of 3, #734-736 2.00 2.00
Nos. 734-736 (3) .60 .60
Ghent Int'l Flower Exhibition. No. 736a was issued Apr. 25 and sold for 25fr.

Beeches in Botanical Garden — A253

1970, Mar. 7 Engr. & Photo.
737 A253 3.50fr shown .20 .20
738 A253 7fr Birches .30 .30
European Nature Conservation Year.

Youth Stamp Day — A254

1970, Apr. 4 Photo.
739 A254 1.50fr Mailman .20 .20

New UPU Headquarters and
Monument, Bern — A255

1970, Apr. 12   Engr. & Photo.
740 A255 3.50fr grn & lt grn   .30 .20
    Opening of the new UPU Headquarters,
Bern.

Europa Issue, 1970
Common Design Type
1970, May 1   Photo.   Perf. 11½
Size: 35x24mm
741 CD13 3.50fr rose cl, yel & blk   .20 .20
742 CD13   7fr ultra, pink & blk   .40 .30

Cooperative Alliance Emblem — A257

1970, June 27   Photo.   Perf. 11½
743 A257 7fr black & org   .30 .20
    Intl. Cooperative Alliance, 75th anniv.

Ship in
Ghent
Terneuzen
Lock,
Zelzate
A258

Design: No. 745, Clock Tower, Virton, vert.

1970, June 27   Engr. & Photo.
744 A258 2.50fr indigo & lt bl   .20 .20
745 A258 2.50fr dk pur & ocher   .20 .20

King
Baudouin — A259

1970-80   Engr.   Perf. 11½
746 A259 1.75fr green ('71)   .25 .20
747 A259 2.25fr gray grn ('72) .35 .20
748 A259 2.50fr gray grn ('74) .20 .20
749 A259   3fr emerald ('73)   .20 .20
750 A259 3.25fr violet brn ('75) .20 .20
751 A259 3.50fr orange brn   .25 .20
752 A259 3.50fr brown ('71)   .25 .20
753 A259   4fr blue ('72)   .35 .20
754 A259 4.50fr brown ('72)   .25 .20
755 A259 4.50fr grnsh bl ('74) .25 .20
756 A259   5fr lilac ('72)   .25 .20
757 A259   6fr rose car ('72) .30 .20
758 A259 6.50fr vio blk ('74)   .35 .20
759 A259   7fr ver ('71)   .35 .20
760 A259 7.50fr brt pink ('75) .35 .20
761 A259   8fr black ('72)   .35 .20
762 A259   9fr ol bis ('71)   .60 .20
763 A259   9fr red brn ('80)   .45 .20
764 A259   10fr rose car ('71) .50 .20
765 A259   11fr gray ('76)   .50 .20
766 A259   12fr Prus bl ('72)   .60 .20
767 A259   13fr slate ('75)   .70 .20
768 A259   14fr gray grn ('76) .65 .20
769 A259   15fr lt vio ('71)   .70 .20
770 A259   16fr green ('77)   .70 .20
771 A259   17fr dull mag ('75) .80 .20
772 A259   18fr steel bl ('71) 1.00 .20
773 A259   18fr grnsh bl ('80) .90 .20
774 A259   20fr vio bl ('71)   1.00 .20
775 A259   22fr black ('74)   1.40 1.10
776 A259   22fr lt grn ('79)   1.10 .20
777 A259   25fr lilac ('75)   1.25 .20
778 A259   30fr ocher ('72)   1.50 .20
779 A259   35fr emer ('80)   1.50 .20
780 A259   40fr dk blue ('77)   2.00 .20
781 A259   45fr brown ('80)   2.25 .20

Perf. 12½x13½
Photo.
Size: 22x17mm
782 A259   3fr emerald ('73)   1.00 .75
  a.   Booklet pane of 4 (#782 and
       3 #783) + labels   10.00
783 A259   4fr blue ('73)   .60 .50
784 A259 4.50fr grnsh bl ('75)   .40 .30
785 A259   5fr lilac ('73)   .25 .20
  a.   Booklet pane of 4 + labels 2.75
786 A259   6fr carmine ('78)   .30 .20
787 A259 6.50fr dull pur ('75)   .45 .20
788 A259   8fr gray ('78)   .35 .20
       Nos. 746-788 (43)   27.95 10.45

    No. 751 issued Sept. 7, 1970, King
Baudouin's 40th birthday, and is inscribed
"1930-1970." Dates are omitted on other
stamps of type A259.
    Nos. 754, 756 also issued in coils in 1973
and Nos. 757, 761 in 1978, with black control
number on back of every fifth stamp.
    Nos. 782-788 issued in booklets only. Nos.
782, 784 have one straight-edge. Nos. 786,
788 have two. The rest have one or two.
Stamps in the panes are tete-beche. Each
pane has two labels showing Belgian Postal
emblem with a large selvage with postal code
instructions. Nos. 786, 788 not luminescent.
    See designs M2, O4. See Nos. 432a, 432b,
977a, 977b.

UN Headquarters,
NY — A260

1970, Sept. 12   Engr. & Photo.
789 A260 7fr dk brn & Prus bl   .30 .20
    25th anniversary of the United Nations.

25th International
Fair at Ghent, Sept.
12-27 — A261

1970, Sept. 19
790 A261 1.50fr Fair emblem   .20 .20

Queen
Fabiola — A262

1970, Sept. 19
791 A262 3.50fr lt blue & blk   .20 .20
    Issued to publicize the Queen Fabiola Foun-
dation for Mental Health.

The Mason, by
Georges
Minne — A263

1970, Oct. 17   Perf. 11½
792 A263 3.50fr dull yel & sep   .20 .20
50th anniv. of the National Housing Society.

Man, Woman and City — A264

1970, Oct. 17   Photo.
793 A264 2.50fr black & multi   .20 .20
    Social Security System, 25th anniv.

Madonna with the
Grapes, by Jean
Gossaert — A265

1970, Nov. 14   Engr.   Perf. 11½
794 A265 1.50fr dark brown   .20 .20
         Christmas 1970.

Arms of
Eupen,
Malmédy
and Saint-
Vith
A266

Engraved and Photogravure
1970, Dec. 12   Perf. 11½
795 A266 7fr sepia & dk brn   .30 .20
    The 50th anniversary of the return of the
districts of Eupen, Malmédy and Saint-Vith.

Automatic
Telephone — A267

1971, Jan. 16   Photo.   Perf. 11½
796 A267 1.50fr multicolored   .20 .20
    Automatization of Belgian telephone system.

50th
Automobile
Show,
Brussels,
Jan. 19-31
A268

1971, Jan. 16
797 A268 2.50fr "Auto"   .20 .20

Belgian Touring
Club, 75th
Anniv. — A269

1971, Feb. 13
798 A269 3.50fr Club emblem   .20 .20

Tournai
Cathedral
A270

1971, Feb. 13   Engr.
799 A270 7fr bright blue   .30 .20
    Cathedral of Tournai, 8th centenary.

"The Letter Box,"
by T.
Lobrichon — A271

1971, Mar. 13   Engr.   Perf. 11½
800 A271 1.50fr dark brown   .20 .20
         Youth philately.

Albert I, Jules Destrée and
Academy — A272

Engraved and Photogravure
1971, Apr. 17   Perf. 11½
801 A272 7fr gray & blk   .30 .20
    Founding of the Royal Academy of Lan-
guage and French Literature, 50th anniv.

Stamp Day — A273

1971, Apr. 25
802 A273 3.50fr Mailman   .20 .20

Europa Issue, 1971
Common Design Type
1971, May 1   Photo.
Size: 35x24mm
803 CD14 3.50fr olive & blk   .25 .20
804 CD14   7fr dk ol grn & blk   .35 .20

Radar
Ground
Station
A275

1971, May 15   Photo.   Perf. 11½
805 A275 7fr multicolored   .30 .20
    3rd World Telecommunications Day.

Antarctic Explorer, Ship and Penguins — A276

1971, June 19 **Photo.** *Perf. 11½*
806 A276 10fr multicolored .50 .50

Tenth anniversary of the Antarctic Treaty pledging peaceful uses of and scientific cooperation in Antarctica.

Abbey of Notre Dame, Orval, 900th Anniv. — A277

1971, June 26 **Engr.** *Perf. 11½*
807 A277 2.50fr Orval Abbey .20 .20

Georges Hubin (1863-1947), Socialist Leader, Minister of State — A278

1971, June 26 **Engr. & Photo.**
808 A278 1.50fr vio bl & blk .20 .20

Mr. and Mrs. Goliath, the Giants of Ath — A279

View of Ghent A280

1971, Aug. 7 **Photo.**
809 A279 2.50fr multicolored .20 .20

Engr.
810 A280 2.50fr gray brown .20 .20

Test Tubes and Insulin Molecular Diagram — A281

1971, Aug. 7 **Photo.**
811 A281 10fr lt gray & multi .40 .30

50th anniversary of the discovery of insulin.

Family and "50" — A283

1971, Sept. 11 **Photo.**
812 A283 1.50fr green & multi .20 .20

Belgian Large Families League, 50th anniv.

Achaemenidaen Tomb, Buzpar, and Persian Coat of Arms — A284

Engraved and Photogravure
1971, Oct. 2 *Perf. 11½*
813 A284 7fr multicolored .30 .20

2500th anniversary of the founding of the Persian empire by Cyrus the Great.

Dr. Jules Bordet (1870-1945), Serologist, Immunologist A285

Portrait: No. 815, Stijn Streuvels(1871-1945), Novelist (pen name Frank Lateur).

1971, Oct. 2 **Engr.**
814 A285 3.50fr slate green .20 .20
815 A285 3.50fr dark brown .20 .20

Flight into Egypt, Anonymous A286

1971, Nov. 13 **Photo.**
816 A286 1.50fr multicolored .20 .20

Christmas 1971.

Federation of Belgian Industries (FIB), 25th Anniv. — A287

1971, Nov. 13
817 A287 3.50fr black, ultra & gold .20 .20

International Book Year 1972 — A288

1972, Feb. 19
818 A288 7fr bister, blk & bl .30 .20

Coins of Belgium and Luxembourg A289

1972, Feb. 19 **Engr. & Photo.**
819 A289 1.50fr orange, blk & sil .20 .20

Economic Union of Belgium and Luxembourg, 50th anniversary.

Traffic Signal and Road Signs — A290

1972, Feb. 19 **Photo.**
820 A290 3.50fr blue & multi .20 .20

Via Secura (road safety), 25th anniversary.

Belgica '72 Emblem A291

1972, Mar. 27
821 A291 3.50fr choc, bl & lil .20 .20

International Philatelic Exhibition, Brussels, June 24-July 9.

"Your Heart is your Health" — A292

1972, Mar. 27
822 A292 7fr blk, gray, red & bl .25 .20

World Health Day.

Auguste Vermeylen (1872-1945), Flemish Writer, Educator — A293

Portrait, by Isidore Opsomer.

1972, Mar. 27
823 A293 2.50fr multicolored .20 .20

Stamp Day 1972 — A294

1972, Apr. 23
824 A294 3.50fr Astronaut on Moon .20 .20

Europa Issue 1972
Common Design Type
1972, Apr. 29
Size: 24x35mm
825 CD15 3.50fr light blue & multi .20 .20
826 CD15 7fr rose & multi .40 .30

"Freedom of the Press" — A296

1972, May 13 **Photo.** *Perf. 11½*
827 A296 2.50fr multicolored .20 .20

50th anniv. of the BELGA news information agency and 25th Congress of the Intl. Federation of Newspaper Editors (F.I.E.J.), Brussels, May 15-19.

Freight Cars with Automatic Coupling A297

1972, June 3
828 A297 7fr blue & multi .30 .20

Intl. Railroad Union, 50th anniv.

View of Couvin — A298

No. 830, Aldeneik Church, Maaseik, vert.

1972, June 24 **Engr.** *Perf. 13½x14*
829 A298 2.50fr bl, vio brn & sl grn .20 .20
830 A298 2.50fr dk brown & bl .20 .20

Beatrice, by Gustave de Smet — A299

1972, Sept. 9 **Photo.** *Perf. 11½*
831 A299 3fr multicolored .20 .20

Youth philately.

Radar Station,
Intelsat 4 — A300

1972, Sept. 16
832 A300 3.50fr lt bl, sil & blk　.20　.20
Opening of the Lessive satellite earth station.

Frans Masereel(1889-1972), Wood
Engraver — A301

1972, Oct. 21
833 A301 4.50fr Self-portrait　.20　.20

Adoration of the
Kings, by Felix
Timmermans
A302

1972, Nov. 11　Photo.　Perf. 11½
834 A302 3.50fr black & multi　.20　.20
Christmas 1972.

Maria
Theresa,
Anonymous
A303

1972, Dec. 16　Photo.　Perf. 11½
835 A303 2fr multicolored　.20　.20
200th anniversary of the Belgian Academy
of Science, Literature and Art, founded by
Empress Maria Theresa.

WMO Emblem, Meteorological
Institute, Ukkel — A304

1973, Mar. 24　Photo.　Perf. 11½
836 A304 9fr blue & multi　.40　.20
Cent. of intl. meteorological cooperation.

Natl. Industrial Fire
Prevention
Campaign — A305

1973, Mar. 24
837 A305 2fr "Fire"　.20　.20

Man and WHO
Emblem — A306

1973, Apr. 7
838 A306 8fr dk red, ocher & blk　.30　.25
25th anniv. of WHO.

Europa Issue 1973
Common Design Type
1973, Apr. 28
Size: 35x24mm
839 CD16 4.50fr org brn, vio bl &
　　　　　　yel　.25　.20
840 CD16 8fr olive, dk bl & yel　.55　.45

Thurn and Taxis
Courier — A308

Engraved and Photogravure
1973, Apr. 28　　　　　Perf. 11½
841 A308 4.50fr black & red brn　.20　.20
Stamp Day.

Arrows Circling
Globe — A309

1973, May 12　　　　　Photo.
842 A309 3.50fr dp ocher & multi　.20　.20
5th International Telecommunications Day.

Workers'
Sports
Exhibition
Poster,
Ghent, 1913
A310

1973, May 12
843 A310 4.50fr multicolored　.20　.20
60th anniversary of the International Workers' Sports Movement.

Fair Emblem
A311

1973, May 12　Photo.　Perf. 11½
844 A311 4.50fr multicolored　.20　.20
25th International Fair, Liege, May 12-27.

DC-10 and 1923 Biplane over
Brussels Airport — A312

Design: 10fr, Tips biplane, 1908.

1973, May 19　　　Engr. & Photo.
845 A312 8fr gray bl, blk & ultra　.30　.20
846 A312 10fr grn, lt bl & blk　.45　.35
50th anniv. of SABENA, Belgian airline (8fr)
and 25th anniv. of the "Vieilles Tiges" Belgian
flying pioneers' society (10fr).

Adolphe Sax and
Tenor Saxophone
A313

1973, Sept. 15　　　　　Photo.
847 A313 9fr green, blk & bl　.40　.20
Adolphe Sax (1814-1894), inventor of
saxophone.

Fresco from
Bathhouse,
Ostend — A314

1973, Sept. 15
848 A314 4.50fr multicolored　.25　.20
Year of the Spa.

St. Nicholas Church,
Eupen — A315

#850, Town Hall, Leau. #851, Aarshot
Church. #852, Chimay Castle. #853, Gem-
menich Border: Belgium, Germany, Netherlands. #854, St. Monan and church, Nas-
sogne. #855, Church tower, Dottignes. #856,
Grand-Place, Sint-Truiden.

1973-75　　　Engr.　　　Perf. 13
849 A315　2fr plum, sep & lt
　　　　　　vio　.20　.20
850 A315　3fr black, lt bl & mar　.50　.20
851 A315　3fr brn blk & yel　.30　.20
852 A315　4fr grnsh blk &
　　　　　　grnsh bl　.35　.20
853 A315　4fr grnsh blk & bl　.40　.20
854 A315　4fr grnsh blk & bl　.40　.20

855 A315　4.50fr multicolored　.50　.20
856 A315　5fr multicolored　.50　.20
　　　Nos. 849-856 (8)　3.15　1.60
Nos. 851, 855 not luminescent. Nos. 850,
852-854, 856 horiz.

Charley, by Henri
Evenepoel — A316

1973, Oct. 13　Photo.　Perf. 11½
857 A316 3fr multicolored　.20　.20
Youth philately.

Luminescent Paper
Starting with No. 858, all stamps are
on luminescent paper unless otherwise
noted.

Jean-Baptiste Moens — A317

1973, Oct. 13　　　Engr. & Photo.
858 A317 10fr multi + label　.40　.20
50th anniversary of the Belgian Stamp Dealers' Association. Printed in sheets of 12
stamps and 12 labels showing association
emblem.

Adoration of the
Shepherds, by
Hugo van der
Goes — A318

1973, Nov. 17　Engr.　Perf. 11½
859 A318 4fr blue　.20　.20
Christmas 1973.

Louis Pierard, by
M. I. Ianchelevici
A319

1973, Nov. 17　　　Engr. & Photo.
860 A319 4fr vermilion & buff　.25　.20
Louis Pierard (1886-1952), journalist, member of Parliament.

Highway, Automobile Club Emblem A320

1973, Nov. 17 **Photo.**
861 A320 5fr yellow & multi .25 .20
Flemish Automobile Club, 50th anniv.

Early Microphone, Emblem of Radio Belgium — A321

1973, Nov. 24 **Engr. & Photo.**
862 A321 4fr blue & black .20 .20
50th anniversary of Radio Belgium.

Felicien Rops (1833-1898), Painter, Engraver A323

Engraved and Photogravure
1973, Dec. 8 **Perf. 11½**
863 A323 7fr Self-portrait .30 .20

King Albert, (1875-1934) A324

1974, Feb. 16 **Photo.** **Perf. 11½**
864 A324 4fr Prus green & blk .25 .20

Sun, Bird, Flowers and Girl — A325

1974, Mar. 25 **Photo.** **Perf. 11½**
865 A325 3fr violet & multi .20 .20
Protection of the environment.

NATO Emblem A326

1974, Apr. 20 **Photo.** **Perf. 11½**
866 A326 10fr dp to lt blue .45 .25
25th anniversary of the signing of the North Atlantic Treaty.

Hubert Krains — A327

1974, Apr. 27 **Engr. & Photo.**
867 A327 5fr black & gray .20 .20
Stamp Day.

Europa Issue 1974

"Destroyed City," by Ossip Zadkine — A328

Design: 10fr, Solidarity, by Georges Minne.

1974, May 4
868 A328 5fr black & red .25 .20
869 A328 10fr black & ultra .60 .30

Children A329

1974, May 18 **Photo.** **Perf. 11½**
870 A329 4fr lt blue & multi .20 .20
10th Lay Youth Festival.

Planetarium, Brussels A330

Soleilmont Abbey Ruins — A331

4fr, Pillory, Braine-le-Chateau. 7fr, Fountain, Ghent (procession symbolic of Chamber of Rhetoric). 10fr, Belfry, Bruges, vert.

Engr. and Photo.
1974, June 22 **Perf. 11½**
871 A330 3fr sky blue & blk .20 .20
872 A330 4fr lilac rose & blk .20 .20
873 A331 5fr lt green & blk .30 .20
874 A331 7fr dull yellow & blk .35 .20
875 A330 10fr black, blue & brn .45 .20
Nos. 871-875 (5) 1.50 1.00
Historic buildings and monuments.

"BENELUX" A332

1974, Sept. 7 **Photo.** **Perf. 11½**
876 A332 5fr bl grn, dk grn & lt bl .25 .20
30th anniversary of the signing of the customs union of Belgium, Netherlands and Luxembourg.

Jan Vekemans, by Cornelis de Vos — A333

1974, Sept. 14
877 A333 3fr multicolored .20 .20
Youth philately.

Leon Tresignies, Willebroek Canal Bridge A334

1974, Sept. 28 **Engr. & Photo.**
878 A334 4fr brn & ol grn .20 .20
60th death anniversary of Corporal Leon Tresignies (1886-1914), hero of World War I.

Montgomery Blair, UPU Emblem A335

10fr, Heinrich von Stephan, UPU emblem.

1974, Oct. 5 **Perf. 11½**
879 A335 5fr green & blk .20 .20
880 A335 10fr brick red & blk .40 .30
Centenary of Universal Postal Union.

Symbolic Chart — A336

1974, Oct. 12 **Photo.** **Perf. 11½**
881 A336 7fr multicolored .30 .20
Central Economic Council, 25th anniv.

Rotary Emblem A337

1974, Oct. 19
882 A337 10fr multicolored .40 .20
Rotary International of Belgium.

Wild Boar (Regimental Emblem) — A338

1974, Oct. 26
883 A338 3fr multicolored .20 .20
Granting of the colors to the Ardennes Chasseurs Regiment, 40th anniversary.

Angel, by Van Eyck Brothers — A341

1974, Nov. 16 **Perf. 11½**
884 A341 4fr rose lilac .20 .20
Christmas 1974. The Angel shown is from the triptyque "The Mystical Lamb" in the Saint-Bavon Cathedral, Ghent.

Adolphe Quetelet, by J. Odevaere — A342

1974, Dec. 14 **Engr. & Photo.**
885 A342 10fr black & buff .40 .20
Death centenary of Adolphe Quetelet (1796-1874), statistician, astronomer and Secretary of Royal Academy of Brussels.

Themabelga, International Thematic Stamp Exhibition, Brussels, Dec. 13-21, 1975 — A343

1975, Feb. 15 **Photo.** **Perf. 11½**
912 A343 6.50fr Themabelga emblem .30 .20

Ghent Intl. Flower Exhib., Apr. 26-May 5 — A344

1975, Feb. 22
913 A344 4.50fr Neoregelia carolinae .25 .20
Photogravure and Engraved
914 A344 5fr Coltsfoot .25 .20
915 A344 6.50fr Azalea .30 .20
Nos. 913-915 (3) .80 .60

Charles Buls Normal School for Boys, Brussels, Cent. — A345

1975, Mar. 15 **Perf. 11½**
School emblem, man Leading boy.
916 A345 4.50fr black & multi .20 .20

Davids Foundation Emblem A346

1975, Mar. 22   **Photo.**
917 A346 5fr yellow & multi   .25 .20

Centenary of the Davids Foundation, a Catholic organization for the promotion of Flemish through education and books.

King Albert (1875-1934) A347

1975, Apr. 5   **Engr. & Photo.**
918 A347 10fr black & maroon   .45 .25

Mailman, 1840, by James Thiriar — A348

1975, Apr. 19   **Engr.**   **Perf. 11½**
919 A348 6.50fr dull magenta   .30 .20

Stamp Day 1975.

St. John, from Last Supper, by Bouts — A349

Europa: 10fr, Woman's Head, detail from "Trial by Fire," by Dirk Bouts.

1975, Apr. 26   **Engr. & Photo.**
920 A349 6.50fr black, grn & blue   .35 .20
921 A349 10fr black, ocher & red   .60 .30

Liberation of Concentration Camps, 30th Anniv. — A350

Concentration Camp Symbols: "B" denoted political prisoners, "KG" prisoners of war.

1975, May 3   **Photo.**
922 A350 4.50fr multicolored   .20 .20

Hospice of St. John, Bruges A351

Church of St. Loup, Namur — A352

Design: 10fr, Martyrs' Square, Brussels.

1975, May 12   **Engr.**   **Perf. 11½**
926 A351 4.50fr deep rose lilac   .25 .20
927 A352 5fr slate green   .25 .20
928 A351 10fr bright blue   .50 .30
   Nos. 926-928 (3)   1.00 .70

European Architectural Heritage Year.

Library, Louvain University, Ryckmans and Cerfaux A355

1975, June 7   **Photo.**   **Perf. 11½**
931 A355 10fr dull blue & sepia   .40 .20

25th anniversary of Louvain Bible Colloquium, founded by Professors Gonzague Ryckmans (1887-1969) and Lucien Cerfaux (1883-1968).

"Metamorphose" by Pol Mara — A356

1975, June 14
932 A356 7fr multicolored   .30 .20
Queen Fabiola Mental Health Foundation.

Marie Popelin, Palace of Justice, Brussels — A357

1975, June 21   **Engr. & Photo.**
933 A357 6.50fr green & claret   .30 .20
International Women's Year 1975. Marie Popelin (1846-1913), first Belgian woman doctor of law.

Assia, by Charles Despiau — A358

1975, Sept. 6   **Perf. 11½**
934 A358 5fr yellow grn & blk   .25 .20
Middelheim Outdoor Museum, 25th anniv.

Cornelia Vekemans, by Cornelis de Vos — A359

1975, Sept. 20   **Photo.**
935 A359 4.50fr multicolored   .20 .20
Youth philately.

Map of Schelde-Rhine Canal — A360

1975, Sept. 20
936 A360 10fr multicolored   .45 .25
Opening of connection between the Schelde and Rhine, Sept. 23, 1975.

National Bank, W. F. Orban, Founder A361

Photogravure and Engraved
1975, Oct. 11   **Perf. 12½x13**
937 A361 25fr multicolored   1.00 .30
Natl. Bank of Belgium, 125th anniv.

Edmond Thieffry and Plane, 1925 A362

1975, Oct. 18   **Perf. 11½**
938 A362 7fr black & lilac   .30 .20
First flight Brussels to Kinshasa, Congo, 50th anniversary.

"Seat of Wisdom" St. Peter's, Louvain — A363

1975, Nov. 8   **Perf. 11½**
939 A363 6.50fr blue, blk & grn   .30 .20
University of Louvain, 550th anniversary.

Angels, by Rogier van der Weyden A364

1975, Nov. 15
940 A364 5fr multicolored   .25 .20
Christmas 1975.

Willemsfonds Emblem — A365

1976, Feb. 21   **Photo.**   **Perf. 11½**
941 A365 5fr multicolored   .25 .20
Willems Foundation, which supports Flemish language and literature, 125th anniv.

American Bicentennial Emblem — A366

1976, Mar. 13   **Photo.**   **Perf. 11½**
942 A366 14fr multi+label   .60 .30
American Bicentennial. Black engraved inscription on labels commemorates arrival of first Walloon settlers in Nieu Nederland.

Cardinal Mercier — A367

1976, Mar. 20   **Engr.**
943 A367 4.50fr brt rose lilac   .20 .20
Desire Joseph Cardinal Mercier (1851-1926), professor at Louvain University, spiritual and patriotic leader during World War I.

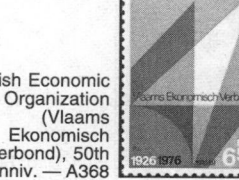

Flemish Economic Organization (Vlaams Ekonomisch Verbond), 50th Anniv. — A368

1976, Apr. 3   **Photo.**   **Perf. 11½**
944 A368 6.50fr multicolored   .30 .20

General Post Office, Brussels A369

1976, Apr. 24   **Engr.**   **Perf. 11½**
945 A369 6.50fr sepia   .30 .20
Stamp Day.

Potter's Hands A370

Europa: 6.50fr, Basket maker, vert.

1976, May 8   Photo.
946 A370 6.50fr multicolored   .45 .20
947 A370 14fr multicolored   .65 .40

Truck on Road A371

1976, May 8
948 A371 14fr black, yel & red   .65 .35
15th Intl. Road Union Cong., Brussels, May 9-13.

Queen Elisabeth (1876-1965) A372

1976, May 24   Perf. 11½
949 A372 14fr green   .60 .30

Ardennes Draft Horses A373

1976, June 19
950 A373 5fr multicolored   .25 .20
Ardennes Draft Horses Assoc., 50th anniv.

Souvenir Sheets

King Baudouin — A374

1976, June 26
951 A374   Sheet of 3   2.50 .50
   a.   4.50fr gray   .70 .70
   b.   6.50fr ocher   .70 .70
   c.   10fr brick red   .70 .70
952 A374   Sheet of 2   3.50 3.50
   a.   20fr yellow green   .85 .85
   b.   30fr Prussian blue   .85 .85

25th anniv. of the reign of King Baudouin. No. 951 sold for 30fr, No. 952 for 70fr. The surtax went to a new foundation for the improvement of living conditions in honor of the King.

Electric Train and Society Emblem — A375

1976, Sept. 11   Photo.   Perf. 11½
953 A375 6.50fr multi   .30 .20
Natl. Belgian Railroad Soc., 50th anniv.

William of Nassau, Prince of Orange — A376

1976, Sept. 11   Engr.
954 A376 10fr slate green   .40 .20
400th anniv. of the pacification of Ghent.

New Subway Train A377

1976, Sept. 18   Photo.
955 A377 6.50fr multi   .30 .20
Opening of first line of Brussels subway.

Young Musician, by W. C. Duyster — A378

1976, Oct. 2   Photo.   Perf. 11½
956 A378 4.50fr multi   .20 .20
Young musicians and youth philately.

Charles Bernard — A379

St. Jerome in the Mountains, by Le Patinier — A380

Blind Leading the Blind, by Breughel the Elder A381

#958, Fernand Victor Toussaint van Boelaere. #959, St. Jerome in the Mountains, by Le Patinier, vert.

1976, Oct. 16   Engr.
957 A379   5fr violet   .20 .20
958 A379   5fr red brn & sepia   .20 .20
959 A381   6.50fr dark brown   .30 .20
960 A381   6.50fr slate green   .30 .20
   Nos. 957-960 (4)   1.00 .80

Charles Bernard (1875-1961), French-speaking journalist; Toussaint van Boelaere (1875-1947), Flemish journalist; No. 959, Charles Plisnier Belgian-French Cultural Society. No. 960, Assoc. for Language Promotion.

Remouchamps Caves — A382

Hunnegem Priory, Gramont, and Madonna A383

Designs: No. 963, River Lys and St. Martin's Church. No. 964, Ham-sur-Heure Castle.

1976, Oct. 23   Engr.   Perf. 13
961 A382 4.50fr multi   .20 .20
962 A383 4.50fr multi   .20 .20
963 A383   5fr multi   .25 .20
964 A383   5fr multi   .25 .20
   Nos. 961-964 (4)   .90 .80

Tourism. #961-962 are not luminescent.

Nativity, by Master of Flemalle — A384

1976, Nov. 20   Perf. 11½
965 A384 5fr violet   .25 .20
Christmas 1976.

Rubens' Monogram — A385

1977, Feb. 12   Photo. & Engr.
966 A385 6.50fr lilac & blk   .30 .20
Peter Paul Rubens (1577-1640), painter.

Heraldic Lion — A386

1977-85   Typo.   Perf. 13½x14
     Size: 17x20mm
967 A386   50c brn ('80)   .20 .20
   a.   50c orange brown ('85)   .20 .20
968 A386   1fr brt lil   .20 .20
   a.   1fr bright rose lilac ('84)   .20 .20
969 A386   1.50fr gray ('78)   .20 .20
970 A386   2fr yel ('78)   .20 .20
970A A386   2.50fr yel grn ('81)   .20 .20
971 A386   2.75fr Prus bl ('80)   .30 .20
972 A386   3fr vio ('78)   .30 .20
   a.   3fr dull violet ('84)   .20 .20
973 A386   4fr red brn ('80)   .25 .20
   a.   4fr rose brown ('85)   .25 .20
974 A386   4.50fr lt ultra   .30 .20
975 A386   5fr grn ('80)   .30 .20
   a.   5fr emerald green ('84)   .20 .20
976 A386   6fr dl red brn   .35 .20
   a.   6fr light red brown ('85)   .35 .20
   Nos. 967-976 (11)   2.80 2.20

1978, Aug.   Photo.   Perf. 13½x12½
     Size: 17x22mm
     Booklet Stamps
977 A386 1fr brt lilac   .20 .20
   a.   Bklt. pane, #977-978, 2 #786   1.50
   b.   Bklt. pane, #977, 979, 2 #788   2.00
978 A386 2fr yellow   .30 .30
979 A386 3fr violet   .50 .50
   Nos. 977-979 (3)   1.00 1.00

Each pane has 2 labels showing Belgian Postal emblem, also a large selvage with zip code instructions. No. 977-979 not luminescent.
See Nos. 1084-1088, design O5.

Anniversary Emblem A387

1977, Mar. 14   Photo.   Perf. 11½
982 A387 6.50fr sil & multi   .30 .20
Royal Belgian Association of Civil and Agricultural Engineers, 50th anniversary.

Birds and Lions Emblem A388

1977, Mar. 28
983 A388 14fr multi   .60 .30
Belgian District #112 of Lions Intl., 25th anniv.

Pillar Box, 1852 — A389

1977, Apr. 23   Engr.
984 A389 6.50fr slate green   .45 .20
Stamp Day 1977.

Gileppe Dam, Jalhay A390

Europa: 14fr, War Memorial, Yser at Nieuport.

1977, May 7   Photo.   Perf. 11½
985 A390 6.50fr multi   .40 .20
986 A390 14fr multi   .90 .20

Mars and Mercury Association Emblem — A391

1977, May 14
987 A391 5fr multi   .25 .20
Mars and Mercury Association of Reserve and Retired Officers, 50th anniversary.

Prince de Hornes Coat of Arms — A392   Conversion of St. Hubertus — A394

Battle of the Golden Spur, from Oxford Chest — A393

Designs: 6.50fr, Froissart writing book, vert.

1977, June 11 Engr. Perf. 11½
988 A392 4.50fr violet ..... .30 .20
989 A393 5fr red ..... .35 .20
990 A393 6.50fr dark brown ..... .40 .25
991 A393 14fr slate green ..... .75 .35
Nos. 988-991 (4) 1.80 1.00

300th anniv. of the Principality of Overijse (4.50fr); 675th anniv. of the Battle of the Golden Spur (5fr); 600th anniv. of publication of 1st volume of the Chronicles of Jehan Froissart (6.50fr); 1250th anniv. of the death of St. Hubertus (14fr).

Rubens, Self-portrait A395

1977, June 25 Photo.
992 A395 5fr multi ..... .25 .20
a. Souvenir sheet of 3 ..... 1.25 .90

Peter Paul Rubens (1577-1640), painter. Stamps in #992a are 37¼mm high; #992, 35¼mm. #992a sold for 20fr.

Open Book, from The Lamb of God, by Van Eyck Brothers — A396

1977, Sept. 3 Photo. Perf. 11½
993 A396 10fr multi ..... .45 .25

Intl. Federation of Library Associations (IFLA), 50th Anniv. Cong., Brussels, Sept. 5-10.

Gymnast and Soccer Player — A397

6.50fr, Fencers in wheelchairs, horiz. 10fr, Basketball players. 14fr, Hockey players.

1977, Sept. 10
994 A397 4.50fr multi ..... .25 .20
995 A397 6.50fr multi ..... .35 .20
996 A397 10fr multi ..... .60 .20
997 A397 14fr multi ..... .80 .30
Nos. 994-997 (4) ..... 2.00 .90

Workers' Gymnastics and Sports Center, 50th anniversary (4.50fr); sport for the Handicapped (6.50fr); 20th European Basketball Championships (10fr); First World Hockey Cup (14fr).

Europalia 77 Emblem — A398

1977, Sept. 17
998 A398 5fr gray & multi ..... .25 .20

5th Europalia Arts Festival, featuring German Federal Republic, Belgium, Oct.-Nov. 1977.

The Egg Farmer, by Gustave De Smet — A399

1977, Oct. 8 Engr. & Photo.
999 A399 4.50fr bister & blk ..... .25 .20

Publicity for Belgian eggs.

Mother and Daughter with Album, by Constant Cap A400

1977, Oct. 15 Engr.
1000 A400 4.50fr dark brown ..... .25 .20

Youth Philately.

Bailiff's House, Gembloux — A401

Market Square, St. Nicholas A402

#1002, St. Aldegonde Church & Cultural Center. #1004, Statue and bridge, Liège.

1977, Oct. 22
1001 A401 4.50fr multi ..... .25 .20
1002 A401 4.50fr multi ..... .25 .20
1003 A402 5fr multi ..... .25 .20
1004 A402 5fr multi ..... .25 .20
Nos. 1001-1004 (4) ..... 1.00 .80

Tourism. Nos. 1001-1004 not luminescent. See Nos. 1017-1018, 1037-1040.

Nativity, by Rogier van der Weyden — A403

1977, Nov. 11 Engr.
1005 A403 5fr rose red ..... .30 .20

Christmas 1977.

Symbols of Transportation and Map — A404

Campidoglio Palace, Rome, and Map — A406

Designs: #1007, European Parliament, Strasbourg, Emblem, vert. #1009, Paul-Henri Spaak and map of 19 European member countries.

1978, Mar. 18 Photo. Perf. 11½
1006 A404 10fr blue & multi ..... .60 .20
1007 A404 10fr blue & multi ..... 1.10 .20
1008 A406 14fr blue & multi ..... .65 .55
1009 A406 14fr blue & multi ..... .65 .55
Nos. 1006-1009 (4) 3.00 1.50

European Action: 25th anniversary of the European Transport Ministers' Conference; 1st general elections for European Parliament; 20th anniversary of the signing of the Treaty of Rome; Paul Henri Spaak (1899-1972), Belgian statesman who worked for the establishment of European Community.

Grimbergen Abbey — A407

1978, Apr. 1 Engr.
1010 A407 4.50fr red brown ..... .25 .20

850th anniversary of the Premonstratensian Abbey at Grimbergen.

Ostend Chamber of Commerce and Industry, 175th Anniv. — A408

1978, Apr. 8 Photo.
1011 A408 8fr Emblem ..... .50 .20

No. 39 with First Day Cancel — A409

1978, Apr. 15
1012 A409 8fr multicolored ..... .35 .20

Stamp Day.

Europa Issue

Pont des Trous, Tournai A410

8fr, Antwerp Cathedral, by Vaclav Hollar.

Photogravure and Engraved
1978, May 6 Perf. 11½
1013 A410 8fr multi, vert. ..... .50 .20
1014 A410 14fr multi ..... .75 .30

Virgin of Ghent, Porcelain Plaque — A411

Paul Pastur Workers' University, Charleroi — A412

1978, Sept. 16 Photo. Perf. 11½
1015 A411 6fr multicolored ..... .40 .20
1016 A412 8fr multicolored ..... .55 .20

Municipal education in Ghent, 150th anniversary; Paul Pastur Workers' University, Charleroi, 75th anniv. #1015-1016 are not luminescent.

Types of 1977 and

Tourist Guide, Brussels A413

#1017, Jonathas House, Enghien. #1018, View of Wetteren and couple in local costume. #1020, Prince Carnival, Eupen-St. Vith.

1978, Sept. 25 Photo. & Engr.
1017 A401 4.50fr multi ..... .20 .20
1018 A402 4.50fr multi ..... .20 .20
1019 A413 6fr multi ..... .25 .20
1020 A413 6fr multi ..... .25 .20
Nos. 1017-1020 (4) ..... .90 .80

Tourism. #1017-1020 are not luminescent.

Royal Flemish Engineer's Organization, 50th Anniv. — A414

1978, Oct. 7 Photo.
1021 A414 8fr Emblem ..... .35 .20

Young Philatelist A415

1978, Oct. 14 Engr. Perf. 11½
1022 A415 4.50fr dk violet ..... .25 .20

Youth philately.

Nativity, Notre Dame, Huy — A416

1978, Nov. 18 Engr. Perf. 11½
1023 A416 6fr black ..... .30 .20

Christmas 1978.

Tyll Eulenspiegel,
Lay Action
Emblem — A417

1979, Mar. 3   Photo.   Perf. 11½
1024 A417 4.50fr multi   .30 .20
10th anniversary of Lay Action Centers.

European
Parliament
Emblem — A418

1979, Mar. 3
1025 A418 8fr multicolored   .50 .20
European Parliament, first direct elections,
June 7-10.

St. Michael
Banishing
Lucifer — A419

1979, Mar. 17   Photo. & Engr.
1026 A419 4.50fr rose red & blk .20 .20
1027 A419   8fr brt green & blk .30 .20
Millennium of Brussels.

NATO
Emblem and
Monument
A420

1979, Mar. 31   Photo.
1028 A420 3fr multicolored   1.75 .45
NATO, 30th anniv.

Prisoner's
Head — A421

1979, Apr. 7   Photo. & Engr.
1029 A421 6fr orange & blk   .25 .20
25th anniversary of the National Political
Prisoners' Monument at Breendonk.

Belgium No.
Q2 — A422

1979, Apr. 21   Photo.   Perf. 11½
1030 A422 8fr multicolored   .50 .20
Stamp Day 1979.

Mail
Coach
and Truck
A423

Europa: 14fr, Chappe's heliograph, Intelsat
satellite and dish antenna.

1979, Apr. 28   Photo. & Engr.
1031 A423 8fr multicolored   .45 .20
1032 A423 14fr multicolored   .90 .40

Chamber of
Commerce
Emblem — A424

1979, May 19   Photo.   Perf. 11½
1033 A424 8fr multicolored   .35 .20
Verviers Chamber of Commerce and Industry, 175th anniversary.

"50" Emblem
A425

1979, June 9   Photo.   Perf. 11½
1034 A425 4.50fr gold & ultra   .30 .20
Natl. Fund for Professional Credit, 50th
anniv.

Merchants,
Roman Bas-
relief
A426

1979, June 9
1035 A426 10fr multicolored   .60 .20
Belgian Chamber of Trade and Commerce,
50th anniversary.

"Tintin" as
Philatelist
A427

1979, Sept. 29   Photo.   Perf. 11½
1036 A427 8fr multicolored   1.10 .20
Youth philately.

Tourism Types of 1977

Designs: No. 1037, Belfry, Thuin. No. 1038,
Royal Museum of Central Africa, Tervuren. No.
1039, St. Nicholas Church and cattle, Ciney.
No. 1040, St. John's Church and statue of Our
Lady, Poperinge.

Perf. 11½ (A401), 13 (A402)
1979, Oct. 22   Photo. & Engr.
1037 A401 5fr multicolored   .20 .20
1038 A402 5fr multicolored   .20 .20
1039 A401 6fr multicolored   .35 .20
1040 A402 6fr multicolored   .35 .20
   Nos. 1037-1040 (4)   1.10 .80

Francois Auguste   Piano, String
Gevaert   Instruments
A429   A430

Design: 6fr, Emmanuel Durlet.

1979, Nov. 3   Perf. 11½
1041 A429 5fr brown   .35 .20
1042 A429 6fr brown   .40 .20
1043 A430 14fr brown   .90 .35
   Nos. 1041-1043 (3)   1.65 .75
Francois Auguste Gevaert (1828-1908),
musicologist and composer; Emmanuel Durlet
(1893-1977), pianist; Queen Elisabeth Musical
Chapel Foundation, 40th anniv.

Virgin and Child,
Notre Dame,
Foy — A431

1979, Nov. 24   Photo. & Engr.
1044 A431 6fr lt grnsh blue   .30 .20
Christmas 1979.

Independence, 150th
Anniversary — A432

1980, Jan. 26   Photo.   Perf. 11½
1045 A432 9fr purple   .40 .20

Frans van
Cauwelaert (1880-
1961), Minister of
State — A433

1980, Feb. 25   Engr.
1046 A433 5fr gray   .25 .20

Ghent Flower
Show, Apr. 19-
27 — A434

1980, Mar. 10   Photo.
1047 A434   5fr Spring flowers .25 .20
1048 A434 6.50fr Summer flowers .30 .20
1049 A434   9fr Autumn flowers .45 .20
   Nos. 1047-1049 (3)   1.00 .60

P.T.T., 50th
Anniv.
A435

1980, Apr. 14   Photo.   Perf. 11½
1050 A435 10fr multicolored   .45 .25

Belgium No.
C4 — A436

1980, Apr. 21
1051 A436 9fr multicolored   .50 .20
Stamp Day.

Europa — A437

9fr, St. Benedict, by Hans Memling. 14fr,
Margaret of Austria (1480-1530).

1980, Apr. 28
1052 A437 9fr multicolored   .45 .20
1053 A437 14fr multicolored   .70 .25

4th
Interparliamentary
Conf. for European
Cooperation &
Security, Brussels,
May 12-18 — A438

1980, May 10   Photo.   Perf. 11½
1054 A438 5fr Palais des Nations,
          Brussels   .25 .20

Golden
Carriage,
1780, Mons
A439

Tourism: #1056, Canal landscape, Damme.

1980, May 17
1055 A439 6.50fr multi   .30 .20
1056 A439 6.50fr multi   .30 .20

Souvenir Sheet

Royal Mint Theater, Brussels — A440

Photo. & Engr.
1980, May 31   Perf. 11½
1057 A440 50fr black   3.25 3.25
150th anniv. of independence. Sold for 75fr.

King Baudouin, 50th Birthday — A441

1980, Sept. 6   **Photo.**   **Perf. 11½**
1058 A441 9fr rose claret   .40 .20

View of Chiny A442

Portal and Court, Diest — A443

1980   **Engr.**   **Perf. 13**
1059 A442 5fr multicolored   .25 .20
1060 A443 5fr multicolored   .25 .20
Tourism. #1059-1060 are not luminescent.
Issued: #1059, 9/27; #1060, 12/13.
See #1072-1075, 1120-1125.

Emblem of Belgian Heart League A444

1980, Oct. 4   **Photo.**   **Perf. 11½**
1061 A444 14fr blue & magenta   .55 .25
Heart Week, Oct. 20-25.

Rodenbach Statue, Roulers — A445

1980, Oct. 11
1062 A445 9fr multicolored   .40 .20
Albrecht Rodenbach (1856-1880), poet.

Youth Philately — A446

1980, Oct. 27   **Photo.**   **Perf. 11½**
1063 A446 5fr multicolored   .25 .20

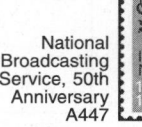

National Broadcasting Service, 50th Anniversary A447

1980, Nov. 10
1064 A447 10fr gray & blk   .45 .25

Garland and Nativity, by Daniel Seghers, 17th Century A448

1980, Nov. 17
1065 A448 6.50fr multicolored   .40 .20
Christmas 1980.

Baron de Gerlache, by F.J. Navez — A449

1981, Mar. 16   **Photo.**   **Perf. 11½**
1066 A449 6fr multicolored   .35 .20
1067 A449 9fr multicolored   .55 .20

Photogravure and Engraved
1068 A450 50fr multicolored   3.00 .55
Sesquicentennial of Chamber of Deputies, Senate and Dynasty.

Leopold I, By Geefs A450

9fr, Baron de Stassart, by F.J. Navez.

Tchantchès and Op-Signoorke, Puppets — A451

Photogravure and Engraved
1981, May 4   **Perf. 11½**
1069 A451 9fr shown   .40 .20
1070 A451 14fr d'Artagnan and Woltje   .65 .35
Europa.

Impression of M.A. de Cock (Founder of Post Museum) — A452

1981, May 18   **Photo.**
1071 A452 9fr multicolored   .40 .20
Stamp Day.

Tourism Types of 1980

#1072, Virgin and Child statue, Our Lady's Church, Tongre-Notre Dame. #1073, Egmont Castle, Zottegem. #1074, Eau d'Heure River. #1075, Tongerlo Abbey, Antwerp.

1981, June 15   **Engr.**   **Perf. 11½**
1072 A442 6fr multi   .35 .20
1073 A442 6fr multi   .35 .20
1074 A443 6.50fr multi   .35 .20
1075 A443 6.50fr multi   .35 .20
   Nos. 1072-1075 (4)   1.40 .80

Soccer Player — A453

1981, Sept. 5   **Photo.**   **Perf. 11½**
1076 A453 6fr multicolored   .35 .20
Soccer in Belgium centenary; Royal Antwerp Soccer Club.

E. Remouchamps, Founder — A454

1981, Sept. 5   **Photo. & Engr.**
1077 A454 6.50fr multi   .40 .20
Walloon Language and Literature Club 125th anniv.

Audit Office Sesquicentennial — A455

1981, Sept. 12   **Engr.**
1078 A455 10fr tan & dk brn   .60 .25

French Horn A456

1981, Sept. 12   **Photo.**
1079 A456 6.50fr multi   .40 .20
Vredekring (Peace Circle) Band of Antwerp centenary.

Souvenir Sheet

Pieta, by Ben Genaux — A457

1981, Sept. 19   **Photo.**   **Perf. 11½**
1080 A457 20fr multicolored   1.75 1.40
Mining disaster at Marcinelle, 25th anniv. Sold for 30fr.

Mausoleum of Marie of Burgundy and Charles the Bold, Bruges — A458

1981, Oct. 10   **Photo. & Engr.**
1081 A458 50fr multi   2.75 .60

Youth Philately — A459

1981, Oct. 24   **Photo.**
1082 A459 6fr multi   .30 .20

Type of 1977 and

A459a

A460

King Baudouin A460a

Photo. and Engr.; Photo.

1980-86   **Perf. 13½x14, 11½**
1084 A386 65c brt rose   .20 .20
1085 A386 1fr on 5fr grn   .20 .20
1086 A386 7fr brt rose   .30 .20
1087 A386 8fr grnsh bl   .35 .20
1088 A386 9fr dl org   .50 .20
1089 A459a 10fr blue   .40 .20
1090 A459a 11fr dl red   .45 .20
1091 A459a 12fr grn   .65 .20
1092 A459a 13fr scar   .55 .20
1093 A459a 15fr red org   1.25 .25
1094 A459a 20fr dk bl   .85 .20
1095 A459a 22fr lilac   1.60 .60
1096 A459a 23fr gray grn   1.25 .30
1097 A459a 30fr brown   1.25 .20
1098 A459a 40fr red org   1.75 .20
1099 A460 50fr lt grnsh bl & bl   2.10 .20
1100 A460a 50fr tan & dk brn   2.10 .20
1101 A460 65fr pale lil & blk   2.75 .60

1102 A460 100fr lt bis brn &
        dk bl   4.25 .40
1103 A460a 100fr lt bl & dk bl   4.25 .25
    Nos. 1084-1103 (20)   27.00 5.20

Issued: 65c, 4/14/80; 1fr, 5/3/82; 7fr,
5/17/82; 8fr, 5/9/83; 9fr, 2/11/85; 65fr, No.
1099, 1102, 11/5/81; 10fr, 11/15/82; 11fr,
4/5/83; 12fr, 1/23/84; 15fr, 22fr, 30fr, No. 1100,
3/26/84; 20fr, 40fr, No. 1103, 6/12/84; 23fr,
2/25/85; 13fr, 3/10/86. See #1231-1234.

Max Waller,
Movement
Founder — A461

Designs: 6.50fr, The Spirit Drinkers, by Gustave van de Woestyne. 9fr, Fernand Severin,
poet, 50th death anniv. 10fr, Jan van Ruus-
broec, Flemish mystic, 500th birth anniv. 14fr,
Thought and Man TV series, 25th anniv.

1981, Nov. 7
1104 A461   6fr multi   .30 .20
1105 A461   6.50fr multi   .35 .20
1106 A461   9fr multi   .50 .20
1107 A461   10fr multi   .80 .25
1108 A461   14fr multi   .75 .35
    Nos. 1104-1108 (5)   2.70 1.20
La Jeune Belgique cultural movement cent.
(6fr).

Nativity, 16th Cent.
Engraving — A466

1981, Nov. 21
1109 A466   6.50fr multi   .30 .20
    Christmas 1981.

Royal Conservatory of Music
Sesquicentennial — A467

Design: 9fr, Judiciary sesquicentennial.

1982, Jan. 25   Photo.   Perf. 11½
1110 A467   6.50fr multi   .30 .20
1111 A467   9fr multi   .40 .20

A468

1982, Mar. 1
1112 A468   6fr Cyclotron   .35 .20
1113 A468   14fr Galaxy, tele-
            scope   .85 .35
1114 A468   50fr Koch   3.00 .65
    Nos. 1112-1114 (3)   4.20 1.20
Radio-isotope production, Natl. Radio-ele-
ments Institute, Fleurus (6fr); Royal Belgian
Observatory (14fr); centenary of TB bacillus
discovery (50fr).

Joseph Lemaire
(1882-1966),
Minister of
State — A469

1982, Apr. 17   Photo.   Perf. 11½
1115 A469   6.50fr multi   .30 .20

Europa
1982
A470

1982, May 1
1116 A470   10fr Universal suffrage   .50 .20
1117 A470   17fr Edict of Tolerance,
            1781   .80 .40

Stamp Day — A471

1982, May 22   Photo. & Engr.
1118 A471   10fr multi   .50 .20

67th World
Esperanto
Congress,
Anvers
A472

1982, June 7   Photo.   Perf. 11½
1119 A472   12fr Tower of Babel   .60 .30

Tourism Type of 1980

Designs: No. 1120, Tower of Gosselies. No.
1121, Zwijveke Abbey, Dendermonde. No.
1122, Stavelot Abbey. No. 1123, Villers-la-
Ville Abbey ruins. No. 1124, Geraardsbergen
Abbey entrance. No. 1125, Beveren Pillory.

1982, June 21   Photo. & Engr.
1120 A443   7fr lt bl & blk   .50 .20
1121 A443   7fr lt grn & blk   .50 .20
1122 A442   7.50fr tan & dk brn .55 .25
1123 A442   7.50fr lt vio & pur .55 .25
1124 A443   7.50fr slate & blk   .55 .25
1125 A443   7.50fr beige & blk   .55 .25
    Nos. 1120-1125 (6)   3.20 1.40

Self Portrait, by
L.P. Boon (b.
1912) — A473

Designs: 10fr, Adoration of the Shepherds,
by Hugo van der Goes (1440-1482). 12fr, The
King on His Throne, carving by M. de Ghelder-
ode (1898-1962). 17fr, Madonna and Child, by
Pieter Paulus (1881-1959).

1982, Sept. 13   Photo.   Perf. 11½
1126 A473   7fr multicolored   .50 .20
1127 A473   10fr multicolored   .60 .20
1128 A473   12fr multicolored   .70 .35
1129 A473   17fr multicolored   1.00 .35
    Nos. 1126-1129 (4)   2.80 1.10

Abraham Hans,
Writer (1882-1932)
A474

1982, Sept. 27   Photo.   Perf. 11½
1130 A474   17fr multicolored   1.10 .35

Youth
Philately and
Scouting
A475

1982, Oct. 2   Photo.   Perf. 11½
1131 A475   7fr multicolored   .50 .20

Grand Orient
Lodge of Belgium
Sesquicentennial
A476

1982, Oct. 16   Photo. & Engr.
1132 A476   10fr Man taking oath .60 .20

Cardinal
Joseph
Cardijn
(1882-1967)
A477

1982, Nov. 13   Photo.
1133 A477   10fr multicolored   .50 .20

St. Francis of
Assisi (1182-1226)
A478

1982, Nov. 27
1134 A478   20fr multicolored   .90 .30

Horse-drawn
Trolley
A479

1983, Feb. 12   Photo.   Perf. 11½
1135 A479   7.50fr shown   .40 .25
1136 A479   10fr Electric trolley .50 .25
1137 A479   50fr Trolley, diff. 2.50 .50
    Nos. 1135-1137 (3)   3.40 1.00

Intl. Fed. for
Periodical
Press, 24th
World
Congress,
Brussels,
May 11-13
A480

1983, Mar. 19   Photo.   Perf. 11½
1138 A480   20fr multicolored   1.00 .25

Homage to
Women
A481

1983, Apr. 16
1139 A481   8fr Operator   .45 .20
1140 A481   11fr Homemaker   .55 .20
1141 A481   20fr Executive   1.00 .25
    Nos. 1139-1141 (3)   2.00 .65

Stamp
Day — A482

1983, Apr. 23
1142 A482   11fr multicolored   .60 .20

Procession
of the
Precious
Blood,
Bruges
A483

1983, Apr. 30   Photo.   Perf. 11½
1143 A483   8fr multi   .60 .20

Europa 1983 — A484

Paintings by P. Delvaux. 11fr vert.

1983, May 14
1144 A484   11fr Common Man   .65 .20
1145 A484   20fr Night Train   1.25 .45

Manned
Flight
Bicentenary
A485

1983, June 11   Photo.   Perf. 11½
1146 A485   11fr Balloon over city .65 .20
1147 A485   22fr Country   1.40 .45

Our Lady's
Church,
Hastiere
A486

1983, June 25
1148 A486   8fr shown   .40 .20
1149 A486   8fr Landen   .40 .20
1150 A486   8fr Park, Mouscron .40 .20
1151 A486   8fr Wijnendale Castle,
            Torhout   .40 .20
    Nos. 1148-1151 (4)   1.60 .80

Tineke Festival, Heule — A487

1983, Sept. 10   **Photo.**
1152 A487 8fr multi   .40 .20

Enterprise Year Emblem A488

1983, Sept. 24
1153 A488 11fr multicolored   .55 .20

European year for small and medium-sized enterprises and craft industry.

Youth Philately — A489

1983, Oct. 10   **Photo.**   **Perf. 11½**
1154 A489 8fr multicolored   .40 .20

Belgian Exports A490

1983, Oct. 24   **Perf. 11½**
1155 A490 10fr Diamond industry   .55 .20
1156 A490 10fr Metallurgy   .55 .20
1157 A490 10fr Textile industry   .55 .20
     Nos. 1155-1157 (3)   1.65 .60
     See Nos. 1161-1164.

Hendrik Conscience (1812-1883), Novelist — A491

1983, Nov. 7
1158 A491 20fr multicolored   1.00 .25

Leopold III Type of 1936
1983, Dec. 12   **Engr.**   **Perf. 12x11½**
1159 A84 11fr black   .55 .20

Leopold III memorial (1901-1983), King 1934-1951.

Free University of Brussels, Sesqui. — A492

Photogravure and Engraved
1984, Jan. 14   **Perf. 11½**
1160 A492 11fr multicolored   .55 .20

Exports Type of 1983
1984, Jan. 28   **Photo.**
1161 A490 11fr Chemicals   .55 .20
1162 A490 11fr Food   .55 .20
1163 A490 11fr Transportation
     equipment   .55 .20
1164 A490 11fr Technology   .55 .20
     Nos. 1161-1164 (4)   2.20 .80

King Albert I, 50th Death Anniv. — A494

1984, Feb. 11   **Photo. & Engr.**
1165 A494 8fr tan & dk brn   .40 .20

1984 Summer Olympic Games — A495

1984, Mar. 3   **Photo.**
     Souvenir Sheet
1166   Sheet of 2   2.00 2.00
  a.   A495 10fr Archery   .55 .55
  b.   A495 24fr Dressage   1.40 1.40
     See Nos. B1029-B1030.

Family, Globe, Birds — A496

1984, Mar. 24   **Photo.**   **Perf. 11½**
1167 A496 12fr multicolored   .60 .20

"Movement without a Name" peace org.

St. John Bosco Canonization A497

1984, Apr. 7
1168 A497 8fr multicolored   .40 .20

Europa (1959-84) A498

1984, May 5   **Photo.**   **Perf. 11½**
1169 A498 12fr black & red   .75 .20
1170 A498 22fr black & ultra   1.40 .30

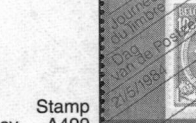

Stamp Day — A499

1984, May 19
1171 A499 12fr No. 52   .60 .20

2nd European Parliament Elections A500

1984, May 26
1172 A500 12fr multicolored   .60 .20

Royal Military School, 150th Anniv. — A501

1984, June 9   **Photo.**   **Perf. 11½**
1173 A501 22fr Hat   1.10 .25

Notre-Dame de la Chappelle, Brussels A502

Churches: No. 1175, St. Martin's, Montignyle-Tilleul. No. 1176, Tielt, vert.

     Perf. 11½x12, 12x11½
1984, June 23   **Photo. & Engr.**
1174 A502 10fr multicolored   .55 .20
1175 A502 10fr multicolored   .55 .20
1176 A502 10fr multicolored   .55 .20
     Nos. 1174-1176 (3)   1.65 .60

50th Anniv. of Chirojeugd (Christian Youth Movement) A503

1984, Sept. 15   **Photo.**   **Perf. 11½**
1177 A503 10fr Emblem   .50 .20

Affligem Abbey A504

1984, Oct. 6   **Photo. & Engr.**
1178 A504 8fr Averbode, vert.   .40 .25
1179 A504 22fr Chimay, vert.   1.25 .25
1180 A504 24fr Rochefort, vert.   1.25 .40
1181 A504 50fr shown   2.50 .50
     Nos. 1178-1181 (4)   5.40 1.40

Youth Philately A505

1984, Oct. 20   **Photo.**
1182 A505 8fr Postman smurf   .45 .20

Arthur Meulemans (1884-1966), Composer — A506

1984, Nov. 17   **Photo. & Engr.**
1183 A506 12fr multi   .60 .20

St. Norbert, 850th Death Anniv. — A507

1985, Jan. 14   **Photo. & Engr.**
1184 A507 22fr sepia & beige   1.10 .30

Europalia '85 — A508

1985, Jan. 21   **Photo.**
1185 A508 12fr Virgin of Louvain   .65 .20

Belgian Assoc. of Professional Journalists, Cent. A509

1985, Feb. 11   **Photo.**
1186 A509 9fr multicolored   .40 .20

Ghent Flower Festival, Orchids — A510

Photogravure and Engraved
1985, Mar. 18   **Perf. 11½**
1187 A510 12fr Vanda coerules   .70 .20
1188 A510 12fr Phalaenopsis   .70 .20
1189 A510 12fr Suphrolaelio cat-
     tlea riffe   .70 .20
     Nos. 1187-1189 (3)   2.10 .60

Visit of Pope John Paul II A511

1985, Apr. 1   **Photo.**
1190 A511 12fr multicolored   .60 .20

Belgian Worker's Party Cent. A512

1985, Apr. 15   **Photo.**
1191 A512 9fr Chained factory
gate .40 .20
1192 A512 12fr Broken wall, red
flag .60 .20

Jean de Bast (1883-1975), Engraver A513

1985, Apr. 22   **Engr.**
1193 A513 12fr blue black .60 .20
Stamp Day.

Public Transportation Year — A514

Design: 9fr, Steam tram locomotive Type 18, 1896. 12fr, Locomotive Elephant and tender, 1835. 23fr, Type 23 tank engine, 1904. 24fr, Type I Pacific locomotive, 1935. 50fr, Type 27 electric locomotive, 1975.

1985, May 6   **Photo.**
1194 A514 9fr multicolored .35 .20
1195 A514 12fr multicolored .50 .20
1196 A514 23fr multicolored .85 .35
1197 A514 24fr multicolored 1.10 .40
Nos. 1194-1197 (4) 2.80 1.15
Souvenir Sheet
1198 A514 50fr multicolored 2.75 2.00

Europa 1985 A515

1985, May 13   **Photo.**
1199 A515 12fr Cesar Franck at
organ, 1887 .80 .20
1200 A515 23fr Folk figures 1.50 .25

26th Navigation Congress, Brussels A516

1985, June 10   **Photo.**   **Perf. 11½**
1201 A516 23fr Zeebruge Harbor 1.25 .25
1202 A516 23fr Projected lock at
Strepy-Thieu 1.25 .25

St. Martin's Church, Marcinelle A517

Tourism: No. 1203, Church of the Assumption of Our Lady, Avernas-le-Baudouin, vert. No. 1204, Church of the Old Beguinage, Tongres, vert. No. 1206, Private residence, Puyenbroeck.

1985, June 24   **Perf. 11½**
1203 A517 12fr multicolored .60 .20
1204 A517 12fr multicolored .60 .20
1205 A517 12fr multicolored .60 .20
1206 A517 12fr multicolored .60 .20
Nos. 1203-1206 (4) 2.40 .80

Queen Astrid (1905-1935) A518

1985, Sept. 2   **Perf. 11½**
1207 A518 12fr brown .60 .20

Baking Pies for the Mattetart of Geraardsbergen A519

Folk events: 24fr, Children dancing, centenary of the St. Lambert de Hermalle-Argenteau Le Rouges youth organization.

1985, Sept. 16
1208 A519 12fr multicolored .60 .20
1209 A519 24fr multicolored .95 .30

Liberation from German Occupation, 40th Anniv. — A520

Allegories: 9fr, Dove, liberation of concentration camps. 23fr, Battle of Ardennes. 24fr, Destroyer, liberation of the River Scheldt estuary.

1985, Sept. 30   **Photo.**   **Perf. 11½**
1210 A520 9fr multicolored .50 .25
1211 A520 23fr multicolored 1.25 .65
1212 A520 24fr multicolored 1.25 .70
Nos. 1210-1212 (3) 3.00 1.60

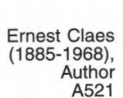

Ernest Claes (1885-1968), Author A521

1985, Oct. 7
1213 A521 9fr Portrait, book character .50 .25

Intl. Youth Year — A522

1985, Oct. 21
1214 A522 9fr Nude in repose, angel .50 .25

King Baudouin & Queen Fabiola, 25th Wedding Anniv. — A523

1985, Dec. 9
1215 A523 12fr multicolored .50 .40

Birds — A524

Photo. (50c-2fr, No. 1220, 4.50fr-6fr, No. 1229, 10fr), Typo. (Others)
1985-91   **Perf. 11½**
1216 A524 50c Roitelet huppe .20 .20
1217 A524 1fr Pic epeichette .20 .20
1218 A524 2fr Moineau friquet .20 .20
1219 A524 3fr Gros bec .20 .20
1220 A524 3fr Bruant des
roseax .25 .20
1221 A524 3.50fr Rouge gorge .25 .20
1222 A524 4fr Gorge bleue .25 .20
1223 A524 4.50fr Traquet Patre .35 .20
1224 A524 5fr Sittele torche-
pot .35 .20
1225 A524 6fr Bouvreuil .40 .20
1226 A524 7fr Mesange bleue .45 .20
1227 A524 8fr Martin-pecheur .45 .20
1228 A524 9fr Chardonneret .35 .20
1229 A524 9fr Grive
musicienne .65 .20
1230 A524 10fr Pinson .65 .20
Nos. 1216-1230 (15) 5.15 3.00

Issued: 7fr, 9/7/87; 5fr, 6fr, 9/12/88; 4fr, 4/17/89; 2fr, 12/4/89; 1fr, 1/8/90; 10fr, 1/15/90; 50c, #1220, 1229, 9/30/91; others, 9/30/85.
See #1432-1447, 1627, 1641, 1645, 1651, 1660, 1676, 1696, 1700, 1702-1703, 1714-1715. For stamps denominated in Francs and Euros, see Nos. 1785-1790A, 1836-1840..

King Type of 1981
1986-90   **Photo.**   **Perf. 11½**
1231 A459a 14fr black .80 .20
1232 A459a 24fr dk grysh
green 1.10 .30
1233 A459a 25fr blue black 1.40 .25
1234 A460a 200fr sage grn &
dl gray grn 9.00 .75
Nos. 1231-1234 (4) 12.30 1.50
Issued: 24fr, 4/7/86; 200fr, 11/3/86; 14fr, 1/15/90; 25fr, 2/19/90.

Congo Stamp Cent. — A525

1986, Jan. 27   **Photo.**   **Perf. 11½**
1236 A525 10fr Belgian Congo #3 .40 .20
See Zaire No. 1230.

Carnival Cities of Aalst and Binche A526

Folklore: masks, giants.

1986, Feb. 3
1237 A526 9fr Aalst Belfry .50 .20
1238 A526 12fr Binche Gilles .60 .20

Intl. Peace Year — A527

1986, Mar. 10
1239 A527 23fr Emblem, dove 1.25 .35

Stamp Day — A528

1986, Apr. 21   **Photo.**   **Perf. 11½**
1240 A528 13fr Artifacts .65 .40

Europa 1986 A529

1986, May 5
1241 A529 13fr Fish .65 .40
1242 A529 24fr Flora 1.40 .85

Dogs — A530

1986, May 26   **Photo.**   **Perf. 11½**
1243 A530 9fr Malines sheep-
dog .65 .30
1244 A530 13fr Tervueren sheepdog .85 .45
1245 A530 24fr Groenendael
sheepdog 1.60 .80
1246 A530 26fr Flemish cattle
dog 1.60 .85
Nos. 1243-1246 (4) 4.70 2.40

St. Ludger's Church, Zele — A531

#1248, Waver Town Hall. #1249, Nederzwalm Canal. #1250, Chapel of Our Lady of the Dunes, Bredene. #1251, Licot Castle, Viroinval. #1252, Eynenbourg Castle, La Calamine.

1986, June 30   **Photo. & Engr.**
1247 A531 9fr multi .60 .30
1248 A531 9fr multi .60 .30
1249 A531 13fr multi, horiz. .80 .45
1250 A531 13fr multi, horiz. .80 .45
1251 A531 13fr multi, horiz. .80 .45
1252 A531 13fr multi, horiz. .80 .45
Nos. 1247-1252 (6) 4.40 2.40

Youth Philately A532

1986, Sept. 1   Photo.   *Perf. 11½*
1253 A532 9fr dl ol grn, blk & dk
red   .50 .30

Cartoon Exhibition, Knokke.

Famous Men — A533

Designs: 9fr, Constant Permeke, painter, sculptor. 13fr, Baron Michel-Edmond de Selys Longchamps, scientist. 24fr, Felix Timmermans, writer. 26fr, Maurice Careme, poet.

1986, Sept. 29
1254 A533 9fr multicolored   .50 .30
1255 A533 13fr multicolored   .75 .45
1256 A533 24fr multicolored   1.40 .80
1257 A533 26fr multicolored   1.50 .90
     Nos. 1254-1257 (4)   4.15 2.45

Royal Academy for Dutch Language and Literature, Cent. A534

1986, Oct. 6   Engr.
1258 A534 9fr dark blue   .50 .30

Natl. Beer Industry A535

Perf. 12½x11½
1986, Oct. 13   Photo.
1259 A535 13fr Glass, barley, hops   .70 .50

Provincial Law and Councils, 150th Anniv. A536

1986, Oct. 27   *Perf. 11½*
1260 A536 13fr Stylized map   .70 .50

Christian Trade Union, Cent. A537

1986, Dec. 13   Photo.   *Perf. 11½*
1261 A537 9fr shown   .45 .35
1262 A537 13fr design reversed   .65 .50

Flanders Technology Intl. — A538

1987, Mar. 2   Photo.
1263 A538 13fr multi   .70 .50

EUROPALIA '87, Austrian Cultural Events — A539

Design: Woman, detail of a fresco by Gustav Klimt, Palais Stoclet, Brussels.

1987, Apr. 4   Photo.   *Perf. 11½*
1264 A539 13fr multicolored   .70 .50

Stamp Day 1987 — A540

Portrait: Jakob Wiener (1815-1899), 1st engraver of Belgian stamps.

1987, Apr. 11   Photo. & Engr.
1265 A540 13fr lt greenish blue &
sage grn   .70 .50

Folklore A541

1987, Apr. 25   Photo.
1266 A541 9fr Penitents procession, Veurne   .45 .35
1267 A541 13fr Play of John and Alice, Wavre   .65 .50

Europa 1987 — A542

Modern architecture: 13fr, Louvain-la-Neuve Church. 24fr, Regional Housing Assoc. Tower, St. Maartensdal at Louvain.

1987, May 9   Photo.
1268 A542 13fr multicolored   .85 .55
1269 A542 24fr multicolored   1.50 1.00

Statue of Andre-Ernest Gretry (1741-1813), French Composer A543

1987, May 23
1270 A543 24fr multicolored   1.50 1.00
Wallonie Royal Opera, Liege, 20th anniv.

Tourism — A544

#1271, Statues of Jan Breydel and Pieter de Conin, Bruges. #1272, Boondael Chapel, Brussels. #1273, Windmill, Keerbergen.

#1274, St. Christopher's Church, Racour. #1275, Virelles Lake, Chimay.

1987, June 13
1271 A544 13fr multicolored   1.00 .55
1272 A544 13fr multicolored   1.00 .55
1273 A544 13fr multicolored   1.00 .55
1274 A544 13fr multicolored   1.00 .55
1275 A544 13fr multicolored   1.00 .55
     Nos. 1271-1275 (5)   5.00 2.75

Royal Belgian Rowing Assoc., Cent. — A545

European Volleyball Championships A546

1987, Sept. 5
1276 A545 9fr multicolored   .50 .40
1277 A546 13fr multicolored   .75 .55

Foreign Trade Year — A547

1987, Sept. 12
1278 A547 13fr multi   .75 .55

Belgian Social Reform, Cent. A548

1987, Sept. 19
1279 A548 26fr Leisure, by P. Paulus   1.40 1.10

Youth Philately A549

1987, Oct. 3
1280 A549 9fr multi   .50 .40

Newspaper Centennials A550

1987, Dec. 12
1281 A550 9fr Le Soir   .55 .40
1282 A550 9fr Hett Lattste Nieuws, vert.   .55 .40

The Sea — A551

Designs: a, Lighthouse, trawler, rider and mount. b, Trawler, youths playing volleyball on beach. c, Cruise ship, sailboat, beach and cabana. d, Shore, birds.

1988, Feb. 6   Photo.   *Perf. 11½*
1283   Strip of 4 + label   2.50 1.75
a.-d. A551 10fr any single   .60 .45
   No. 1283 has a continuous design.

Dynamism of the Regions A552

1988, Mar. 5   Photo.   *Perf. 11½*
1284 A552 13fr Operation Athena   .80 .60
1285 A552 13fr Flanders Alive Campaign   .80 .60

Stamp Day — A553

Painting: 19th Cent. Postman, by James Thiriar.

1988, Apr. 16   Photo. & Engr.
1286 A553 13fr buff & sepia   .80 .60

Europa 1988 — A554

1988, May 9   Photo.   *Perf. 11½*
Transport and communication.

1287 A554 13fr Satellite dish   1.10 .60
1288 A554 24fr Non-polluting combustion engine   1.90 1.10

Tourism A555

Designs: No. 1289, Romanesque watchtower, ca. 12th-13th cent., Amay, vert. No. 1290, Our Lady of Hanswijk Basilica, 988, Mechelen, vert. No. 1291, St. Sernin's Church, 16th cent., Waimes. No. 1292, Old Town Hall, 1637, and village water pump, 1761, Peer, vert. No. 1293, Our Lady of Bon-Secours Basilica, 1892, Peruwelz.

Photo. & Engr.
1988, June 20   *Perf. 11½*
1289 A555 9fr beige & blk   .50 .40
1290 A555 9fr lt blue & blk   .50 .40
1291 A555 9fr pale blue grn & blk   .50 .40

1292 A555 13fr pale pink & blk .75 .55
1293 A555 13fr pale gray & blk .75 .55
Nos. 1289-1293 (5) 3.00 2.30
Our Lady of Hanswijk Basilica millennium (No. 1290); Waimes village, 1100th anniv. (No. 1291).

Jean Monnet (1888-1979), French Economist — A556

1988, Sept. 12 *Perf. 11½*
1294 A556 13fr black .70 .50

Tapestry in the Hall of the Royal Academy of Medicine — A557

Academies building and: No. 1296, Lyre, quill pen, open book and atomic symbols.

1988, Sept. 17 Photo.
1295 A557 9fr shown .50 .40
1296 A557 9fr multi .50 .40
Royal Academy of Medicine (#1295); Royal Academy of Science, Literature and Fine Arts (#1296).

Cultural Heritage A558

Artifacts: 9fr, Statue and mask in the Antwerp Ethnographical Museum. 13fr, Sarcophagus, St. Martin's Church, Trazegnies. 24fr, Church organ, Geraardsbergen. 26fr, Shrine, St. Hadelin's Church, Vise.

1988, Sept. 24
1297 A558 9fr multi .50 .40
1298 A558 13fr multi .70 .50
1299 A558 24fr multi 1.25 1.00
1300 A558 26fr multi 1.40 1.00
Nos. 1297-1300 (4) 3.85 2.90

Youth Philately A559

1988, Oct. 10
1301 A559 9fr multi .50 .40

Natl. Postal Savings Bank, 75th Anniv. A560

1988, Nov. 7
1302 A560 13fr multi .70 .50

Christmas 1988 and New Year 1989 A561

1988, Nov. 21
1303 A561 9fr Winter landscape .50 .40

Royal Mounted Guard, 50th Anniv. A562

1988, Dec. 12
1304 A562 13fr multi .75 .55

Printing Presses A563

9fr, J. Moretus I, Antwerp Museum, vert. 24fr, Stanhope, Printing Museum, Brussels, vert. 26fr, Litho Krause, Royal Museum, Mariemont.

1988, Dec. 19 Engr.
1305 A563 9fr bl blk & blk .50 .40
1306 A563 24fr dark red brn 1.40 1.10
1307 A563 26fr grn & slate grn 1.50 1.25
Nos. 1305-1307 (3) 3.40 2.75

Lace A564

1989, Mar. 20 Photo.
1308 A564 9fr Marche-en-Famenne .50 .40
1309 A564 13fr Brussels .70 .50
1310 A564 13fr Brugge .70 .50
Nos. 1308-1310 (3) 1.90 1.40

Stamp Day A565

1989, Apr. 24 Photo. & Engr.
1311 A565 13fr Mail coach, post chaise .75 .55

Europa 1989 — A566

Children's toys.

1989, May 8 Photo.
1312 A566 13fr Marbles, horiz. .75 .50
1313 A566 24fr Jumping-jack 1.40 1.00

Royal Academy of Fine Arts, Antwerp, 325th Anniv. — A567

1989, May 22 *Perf. 11½*
1314 A567 13fr multi .75 .50

European Parliament 3rd Elections — A568

Illustration reduced.

1989, June 5 Photo.
1315 A568 13fr Brussels .75 .50

Declaration of Rights of Man and the Citizen, Bicent. — A569

1989, June 12 *Perf. 11½*
1316 A569 13fr multi + label .75 .50

Tourism A570

#1317, St. Tillo's Church, Izegem. #1318, Logne Castle, Ferrieres. #1319, St. Laurentius's Church, Lokeren. #1320, Antoing Castle, Antoing.

1989, June 26 Photo. & Engr.
1317 A570 9fr multi .50 .40
1318 A570 9fr multi, vert. .50 .40
1319 A570 13fr multi, vert. .75 .50
1320 A570 13fr multi, vert. .75 .50
Nos. 1317-1320 (4) 2.50 1.80

Ducks — A571

1989, Sept. 4 Photo. *Perf. 12*
Booklet Stamps
1321 A571 13fr Mallard (8a) 1.10 .50
1322 A571 13fr Winter teal (8b) 1.10 .50
1323 A571 13fr Shoveller (8c) 1.10 .50
1324 A571 13fr Pintail (8d) 1.10 .50
a. Bklt. pane of 4, #1321-1324 4.50
Complete booklet, #1324a 4.50

Shigefusa Uesugi, a Seated Japanese Warrior, 13th Cent. A572

1989, Sept. 18 *Perf. 11½*
1325 A572 24fr multicolored 1.50 .50
Europalia.

Education League, 125th Anniv. — A573

1989, Sept. 25
1326 A573 13fr multicolored .80 .20

Treaty of London, 150th Anniv. — A574

1989, Oct. 2 Photo.
1327 A574 13fr Map of Limburg Provinces .80 .20
See Netherlands No. 750.

Mr. Nibbs — A575

1989, Oct. 9 *Perf. 11½*
1328 A575 9fr multicolored .60 .20
Youth philately promotion.

Christmas, New Year 1990 A576

1989, Nov. 20 Photo.
1329 A576 9fr Salvation Army band .60 .20

Fr. Damien (1840-89), Missionary, Molokai Is. Leper Colony, Hawaii A577

1989, Nov. 27 Photo.
1330 A577 24fr multicolored 1.50 .50

Father Adolf
Daens — A578

1989, Dec. 11   **Photo. & Engr.**
1331 A578 9fr pale & dk grn   .55   .20

*The Young Post
Rider,* an
Engraving by
Albrecht
Durer — A579

Ghent Flower
Festival — A580

1990, Jan. 12   **Photo. & Engr.**
1332 A579 14fr buff & red blk   .75   .55
Postal communications in Europe, 500th
anniv.
See Austria No. 1486, Germany No. 1592,
Berlin No. 9N584 and German Democratic
Republic No. 2791.

1990, Mar. 3   **Photo.**
1333 A580 10fr *Iris florentina*   .50   .40
1334 A580 14fr *Cattleya har-
     risoniana*   .75   .55
1335 A580 14fr *Lilium bulbiferum*   .75   .55
    Nos. 1333-1335 (3)   2.00 1.50

Intl. Women's Day — A581

1990, Mar. 12   **Photo.**   **Perf. 11½**
1336 A581 25fr Emilienne
     Brunfaut
                    1.45 1.00

Wheelchair
Basketball — A582

Sports.

1990, Mar. 19
1337 A582 10fr multicolored   .60   .40
1338 A582 14fr multicolored   .80   .60
1339 A582 25fr shown   1.40 1.00
    Nos. 1337-1339 (3)   2.80 2.00
Special Olympics (10fr); and 1990 World
Cup Soccer Championships, Italy (14fr).

Natl. Water
Supply
Soc., 75th
Anniv.
A583

1990, Apr. 2
1340 A583 14fr Water means life   .80   .60

Postman Roulin, by
Van Gogh — A584

1990, Apr. 9
1341 A584 14fr multicolored   .80   .60
    Stamp Day.

Labor Day,
Cent.
A585

1990, Apr. 30
1342 A585 25fr multicolored   1.40 1.00

Europa
1990
A586

Post offices.

1990, May 7   **Photo. & Engr.**
1343 A586 14fr Ostend 1   .80   .60
1344 A586 25fr Liege 1, vert.   1.40 1.00

18-Day Campaign, 1940 — A587

1990, May 14   **Photo.**   **Perf. 11½**
1345 A587 14fr Lys Monument,
     Courtrai   .80   .60
  Resistance of German occupation.

Stamp Collecting Promotion Type of
1988
Souvenir Sheet

Various flowers from *Sixty Roses for a
Queen,* by P.J. Redoute (1759-1840): a, *Rose
tricolore.* b, Belle Rubaree. c, *Mycrophylla.* d,
Amelie rose. e, Adelaide rose. f, Helene rose.

1990, June 2   **Photo. & Engr.**
1346   Sheet of 6   40.00 40.00
a.-c. SP487 14fr any single   1.40 1.40
d.-f. SP487 25fr any single   2.50 2.50
BELGICA '90, Brussels, June 2-10. sold for
220fr.

Battle of Waterloo, 1815 — A588

Design: Marshal Ney leading the French
cavalry. Illustration reduced.

1990, June 18   **Photo.**
1352 A588 25fr multi + label   1.60 1.10

Tourism
A589

1990, July 9
1353 A589 10fr Antwerp   .60   .45
1354 A589 10fr Dendermonde   .60   .45
1355 A589 14fr Gerpinnes, vert.   .80   .60
1356 A589 14fr Lommel   .80   .60
1357 A589 14fr Watermael   .80   .60
    Nos. 1353-1357 (5)   3.60 2.70

A590   A590a

King
Baudouin
A590b

1990-92   **Photo.**   **Perf. 11½**
1364 A590 14fr multicolored   .80   .20
1365 A590a 15fr rose car   .75   .20
1366 A590a 28fr blue green   1.75   .40
1367 A590b 100fr slate green   5.00   .40
    Nos. 1364-1367 (4)   8.30 1.20
   Issue dates: 14fr, Sept. 7; 15fr, Apr. 1; 28fr,
Aug. 3, 1992; 100fr, Sept. 14, 1992.

Fish
A591

Designs: No. 1383, Perch (Perche). No.
1384, Minnow (Vairon). No. 1385, Bitterling
(Bouviere). No. 1386, Stickleback (Epinoche).

1990, Sept. 8   **Perf. 12**
1383 A591 14fr multicolored   1.25   .60
1384 A591 14fr multicolored   1.25   .60
1385 A591 14fr multicolored   1.25   .60
1386 A591 14fr multicolored   1.25   .60
a.   Bklt. pane of 4, #1383-1386   5.00
    Complete booklet, #1386a   5.00

Youth
Philately
A592

1990, Oct. 13   **Perf. 11½**
1387 A592 10fr multicolored   .60   .45

St. Bernard, 900th
Birth
Anniv. — A593

1990, Nov. 5   **Photo & Engr.**
1388 A593 25fr black & buff   1.50 1.10

Winter
Scene by
Jozef
Lucas
A594

1990, Nov. 12   **Photo.**
1389 A594 10fr   .60   .40
    Christmas.

Self-Portrait
A595

Paintings by David Teniers (1610-1690).

1990, Dec. 3
1390 A595 10fr shown   .60   .40
1391 A595 14fr Dancers   .80   .60
1392 A595 25fr Bowlers   1.40 1.10
    Nos. 1390-1392 (3)   2.80 2.10

A596

Designs: 14fr, The Sower by Constantin
Meunier (1831-1905). 25fr, Brabo Fountain by
Jef Lambeaux (1852-1908).

            Photo. & Engr.
1991, Mar. 18   **Perf. 11½**
1393 A596 14fr buff & blk   .80   .60
1394 A596 25fr lt bl & dk bl   1.50 1.10

A597

1991, Apr. 8   **Photo.**   **Perf. 11½**
1395 A597 10fr Rhythmic gym-
      nastics   .65   .50
1396 A597 10fr Korfball   .65   .50
   No. 1395, European Youth Olympics. No.
1396, Korfball World Championships.

Stamp Printing Office, Mechlin — A598

1991, Apr. 22
1397 A598 14fr multicolored .90 .65
Stamp Day.

Liberal Trade Union, Cent. A599

1991, Apr. 29
1398 A599 25fr blue & lt blue 1.50 1.10

Europa A600

1991, May 6
1399 A600 14fr Olympus-1 satellite .90 .65
1400 A600 25fr Hermes space shuttle 1.50 1.10

Rerum Novarum Encyclical, Cent. A601

1991, May 13 Photo. Perf. 11½
1401 A601 14fr multicolored .85 .65

Princess Isabel & Philip le Bon — A602

1991, May 27 Photo. Perf. 11½
1402 A602 14fr multicolored .85 .65
Europalia '91. See Portugal No. 1861.

Tourism A603

Designs: No. 1403, Neptune's Grotto, Couvin. No. 1404, Dieleghem Abbey, Jette. No. 1405, Town Hall, Niel, vert. No. 1406, Nature Reserve, Hautes Fagnes. No. 1407, Legend of giant Rolarius, Roeselare, vert.

1991, June 17 Photo. & Engr.
1403 A603 14fr multicolored .85 .65
1404 A603 14fr multicolored .85 .65
1405 A603 14fr multicolored .85 .65
1406 A603 14fr multicolored .85 .65
1407 A603 14fr multicolored .85 .65
Nos. 1403-1407 (5) 4.25 3.25

King Baudouin, Coronation, 40th Anniv. and 60th Birthday A604

1991, June 24 Photo.
1408 A604 14fr multicolored .85 .65

Royal Academy of Medicine, 150th Anniv. — A605

Photo. & Engr.
1991, Sept. 2 Perf. 11½
1409 A605 10fr multicolored .65 .50

The English Coast at Dover by Alfred W. Finch (1854-1930) A606

1991, Sept. 9 Photo.
1410 A606 25fr multicolored 1.50 1.10
See Finland Nos. 868-869.

Mushrooms — A607

#1411, Amanita phalloides (13A). #1412, Amanita rubescens (13B). #1413, Boletus erythropus (13C). #1414, Hygrocybe persistens (13D).

1991, Sept. 16 Photo. Perf. 12
Booklet Stamps
1411 A607 14fr multicolored 1.25 .75
1412 A607 14fr multicolored 1.25 .75
1413 A607 14fr multicolored 1.25 .75
1414 A607 14fr multicolored 1.25 .75
a. Bklt. pane of 4, #1411-1414 5.00
Complete booklet, #1414a 5.00

Doctors Without Borders A608

Design: No. 1415, Amnesty Intl.

1991, Sept. 23 Perf. 11½
1415 A608 25fr multicolored 1.50 1.10
1416 A608 25fr multicolored 1.50 1.10

Telecom '91 — A609

1991, Oct. 7 Photo. Perf. 11½
1417 A609 14fr multicolored .90 .70
6th World Forum and Exposition on Telecommunications, Geneva, Switzerland.

Youth Philately — A610

Cartoon characters: No. 1418, Blake and Mortimer, by Edgar P. Jacobs (16a). No. 1419, Cori the ship boy, by Bob De Moor (16b). No. 1420, Cities of the Fantastic, by Francois Schuiten (16c). No. 1421, Boule and Bill, by Jean Roba (16d).

1991, Oct. 14 Perf. 12
Booklet Stamps
1418 A610 14fr multicolored 1.25 .90
1419 A610 14fr multicolored 1.25 .90
1420 A610 14fr multicolored 1.25 .90
1421 A610 14fr multicolored 1.25 .90
a. Bklt. pane of 4, #1418-1421 5.00
Complete booklet, #1421a 5.00

Belgian Newspapers, Cent. — A611

1991, Nov. 4 Photo. Perf. 11½
1422 A611 10fr Gazet Van Antwerpen .65 .50
1423 A611 10fr Het Volk .65 .50

Icon of Madonna and Child, Chevetogne Abbey A612

1991, Nov. 25 Photo. Perf. 11½
1424 A612 10fr multicolored .65 .50
Christmas.

Wolfgang Amadeus Mozart, Death Bicent. — A613

1991, Dec. 2 Photo. Perf. 11½
1425 A613 25fr multicolored 1.75 1.25

A614

1992, Feb. 10 Photo. Perf. 11½
1426 A614 14fr Fire fighting .80 .60

Belgian Resistance in WWII — A615

1992, Feb. 24
1427 A615 14fr multicolored .80 .60

Belgian Carpet Industry — A616

Antwerp Diamond Club, Cent. A617

Design: 14fr, Chef's hat, cutlery.

1992, Mar. 9
1428 A616 10fr multicolored .55 .40
1429 A616 14fr multicolored .80 .60
1430 A617 27fr multicolored 1.50 1.10
Nos. 1428-1430 (3) 2.85 2.10
Belgian Association of Master Chefs.

Expo '92, Seville A618

1992, Mar. 23
1431 A618 14fr multicolored .80 .60

Bird Type of 1985
1992-96		**Photo.**	**Perf.**	**11½**
1432	A524	1fr Sizerin flamme	.20	.20
1433	A524	2fr Merle noir	.20	.20
1434	A524	2fr Grive mauvis	.20	.20
1435	A524	4fr Gobe mouche noir	.30	.25
1436	A524	4fr Bergeronette grise	.25	.20
1437	A524	5fr Etourneau sansonnet	.35	.20
1438	A524	5fr Hirondelle de cheminee	.30	.20
1439	A524	5.50fr Geai des chenes	.30	.25
1440	A524	6fr Cincle plongeur	.35	.20
1441	A524	6.50fr Phragmite des jongs	.45	.30
1442	A524	7fr Loriot	.45	.20
1443	A524	8fr Mesange charbonniere	.45	.20
1444	A524	10fr Verdier	.60	.20
1445	A524	11fr Troglodyte mignon	.65	.20
1446	A524	13fr Moineau domestique	.70	.20

1446A A524 14fr Pouillot fitis .95 .25
1447 A524 16fr Jaseur boreal .90 .25
   Nos. 1432-1447 (17) 7.60 3.70
  Issued: 11fr, 4/1/92; 1fr, 2fr, 6fr, 8fr, 10fr, 6/92; 4fr, 5fr, 7fr, 9/7/92; 5.50fr, 9/27/93; 13fr, 16fr, 1/3/94; 6.50fr, 10/3/94; 14fr, 12/18/95; #1435A, 5/6/96; #1433A, 1434, 7/1/96.
  See No. 1838 for similar stamp with additional Euro denomination.

Jean Van Noten (1903-1982), Stamp Designer — A619

Photo. & Engr.
1992, Apr. 13   **Perf. 11½**
1448 A619 15fr ver & black .90 .70
   Stamp Day.

Abstract Painting by Jo Delahaut — A620

#1449, Witte Magie No. 6, by Roger Raveel.

1992, Apr. 27   **Photo.**   **Perf. 11½**
1449 A620 15fr multi, vert. .85 .65
1450 A620 15fr multi .85 .65

Discovery of America, 500th Anniv. — A621

1992, May 4
1451 A621 15fr shown .85 .65
1452 A621 28fr 500, globe, astrolabe 1.60 1.25
   Europa.

Fight Racism — A622

1992, May 18   **Photo.**   **Perf. 11½**
1453 A622 15fr black, gray & pink .90 .70

Paintings from Orsay Museum, Paris — A623

Paintings by Belgian artists: 11fr, The Hamlet, by Jacob Smits. 15fr, The Bath, by Alfred Stevens. 30fr, The Man at the Helm, by Theo Van Rysselberghe.

1992, June 15   **Photo.**   **Perf. 11½**
1454 A623 11fr multicolored .65 .50
1455 A623 15fr multicolored .90 .70
1456 A623 30fr multicolored 1.75 1.40
   Nos. 1454-1456 (3) 3.30 2.60

Tourism — A624

Designs: No. 1457, Manneken Pis Fountain, Brussels. No. 1458, Landcommander Castle Alden Biesen, Bilzen, horiz. No. 1459, Building facade, Andenne. No. 1460, Fools' Monday Carnival, Renaix, horiz. No. 1461, Great Procession, Tournai, horiz.

Photo. & Engr.
1992, July 6   **Perf. 11½**
1457 A624 15fr multicolored .90 .70
1458 A624 15fr multicolored .90 .70
1459 A624 15fr multicolored .90 .70
1460 A624 15fr multicolored .90 .70
1461 A624 15fr multicolored .90 .70
   Nos. 1457-1461 (5) 4.50 3.50
  Village of Andenne, 1300th anniv. (#1459). Grand Procession of Tournai, 900th anniv. (#1461).

Animals — A625

1992, Sept. 7   **Photo.**   **Perf. 12**
Booklet Stamps
1462 A625 15fr Polecat (13a) 1.10 .80
1463 A625 15fr Squirrel (13b) 1.10 .80
1464 A625 15fr Hedgehog (13c) 1.10 .80
1465 A625 15fr Dormouse (13d) 1.10 .80
  a.   Bklt. pane of 4, #1462-1465 4.50
     Complete booklet, #1465a 4.50

Brabant Revolution — A626

Design: 15fr, Troops fighting and Henri Van der Noot, Jean Andre Van der Meersch, and Jean Francois Vonck, rebel leaders.

Photo. & Engr.
1992, Sept. 21   **Perf. 11½**
1466 A626 15fr multicolored .90 .70

Arms of Thurn and Taxis — A627

1992, Oct. 5   **Photo.**   **Perf. 11½**
1467 A627 15fr multicolored .90 .70

Gaston Lagaffe, by Andre Franquin A628

1992, Oct. 12
1468 A628 15fr multicolored .90 .70
   Youth philately.

Single European Market — A629

1992, Oct. 26
1469 A629 15fr multicolored .90 .70

Antwerp Zoo, 150th Anniv. — A630

1992, Nov. 16
1470 A630 15fr Okapi .90 .70
1471 A630 30fr Tamarin 1.75 1.75

The Brussels Place Royale in Winter, by Luc De Decker A631

1992, Nov. 23
1472 A631 11fr multicolored .70 .50
   Christmas.

History A632

Designs: 11fr, Council of Leptines, 1250th anniv. 15fr, 28fr, Missale Romanum of Matthias Corvinus (Matyas Hunyadi, King of Hungary) (diff. details). 30fr, Battles of Neerwinden (1693, 1793).

1993, Mar. 15   **Photo.**   **Perf. 11½**
1473 A632 11fr multicolored .65 .50
1474 A632 15fr multicolored .90 .70
1475 A632 30fr multicolored 1.75 1.40
   Nos. 1473-1475 (3) 3.30 2.60
Souvenir Sheet
1476 A632 28fr multicolored 1.75 1.25
  Size of No. 1474, 80x28mm. No. 1476 contains one 55x40mm stamp.
  See Hungary No. 3385-3386.

A633

A634

Antwerp, Cultural City of Europe A635

Designs: No. 1477, Panoramic view of Antwerp (illustration reduced). No. 1478, Antwerp Town Hall, designed by Cornelis Floris. No. 1479, Woman's Head and Warrior's Torso, by Jacob Jordaens. No. 1480, St. Job's Altar (detail), Schoonbroek. No. 1481, Angels on stained glass window, Mater Dei Chapel of Institut Marie-Josee, by Eugeen Yoors, vert.

1993, Mar. 22
1477 A633 15fr multicolored .90 .70
1478 A634 15fr multicolored .90 .70
1479 A635 15fr gray & multi .90 .70
1480 A635 15fr green & multi .90 .70
1481 A635 15fr blue & multi .90 .70
   Nos. 1477-1481 (5) 4.50 3.50
    Antwerp '93.

Stamp Day — A636

1993, Apr. 5
1482 A636 15fr No. 74 .90 .70

Contemporary Paintings — A637

Europa: 15fr, Florence 1960, by Gaston Bertrand. 28fr, De Sjees, by Constant Permeke.

1993, Apr. 26   **Photo.**   **Perf. 11½**
1483 A637 15fr multicolored .90 .70
1484 A637 28fr multicolored 1.75 1.40

Butterflies — A638

1993, May 10
1485 A638 15fr Vanessa atalanta .90 .70
1486 A638 15fr Apatura iris .90 .70
1487 A638 15fr Inachis io .90 .70
1488 A638 15fr Aglais urticae .90 .70
   Nos. 1485-1488 (4) 3.60 2.80

Alumni Assoc. (UAE), Free University of Brussels, 150th Anniv. A639

1993, May 17
1489 A639 15fr blue & black .90 .70

Europalia '93 — A640

1993, May 24
1490 A640 15fr Mayan statuette .90 .70

Folklore A641

Designs: 11fr, Ommegang Procession, Brussels. 15fr, Royal Moncrabeau Folk Group, Namur. 28fr, Stilt walkers of Merchtem, vert.

1993, June 7   Photo.   Perf. 11½
1491 A641 11fr multicolored .65 .50
1492 A641 15fr multicolored .90 .70
1493 A641 28fr multicolored 1.60 1.25
     Nos. 1491-1493 (3) 3.15 2.45

Tourism A642

Castles: No. 1494, La Hulpe. No. 1495, Cortewalle (Beveren). No. 1496, Jehay. No. 1497, Arenberg (Heverlee), vert. No. 1498, Raeren.

Photo. & Engr.
1993, June 21   Perf. 11½
1494 A642 15fr pale green & blk .90 .70
1495 A642 15fr pale lilac & black .90 .70
1496 A642 15fr pale blue & black .90 .70
1497 A642 15fr pale brn & black .90 .70
1498 A642 15fr pale olive & blk .90 .70
     Nos. 1494-1498 (5) 4.50 3.50

Intl. Triennial Exhibition of Tournai A643

1993, July 5   Photo.   Perf. 11½
1499 A643 15fr black, blue & red .90 .70

Belgian Presidency of European Community Council A644

1993, Aug. 9   Photo.   Perf. 11½
1500 A644 15fr multicolored .90 .70

Rene Magritte (1898-1967), Artist — A645

1993, Aug. 9
1501 A645 30fr multicolored 1.75 1.40

King Baudouin (1930-1993) — A646

1993, Aug. 17   Photo.   Perf. 11½
1502 A646 15fr black & gray .90 .70

European House Cats — A647

1993, Sept. 6   Photo.   Perf. 12
Booklet Stamps
1503 A647 15fr Brown & white (10a) 1.00 .70
1504 A647 15fr Black & white (10b) 1.00 .70
1505 A647 15fr Gray tabby (10c) 1.00 .70
1506 A647 15fr Calico (10d) 1.00 .70
     a.   Booklet pane of 4, #1503-1506 4.00
          Complete booklet, #1506a 4.00

Publication of De Humani Corporis Fabrica, by Andreas Vesalius, 1543 — A648

1993, Oct. 4   Photo.   Perf. 11½
1507 A648 15fr multicolored .90 .70

Air Hostess Natacha, by Francois Walthery — A649

1993, Oct. 18
1508 A649 15fr multicolored .85 .65
     Youth philately.

Publication of "Faux Soir," 50th Anniv. — A650

1993, Nov. 8   Photo.   Perf. 11½
1509 A650 11fr multicolored .60 .45

Notre-Dame de la Chapelle, Brussels A651

1993, Nov. 22   Photo.   Perf. 11½
1510 A651 11fr multicolored .65 .50
     Christmas, New Year.

Children, Future Decisionmakers — A652

1993, Dec. 13   Photo.   Perf. 11½
1511 A652 15fr multicolored .90 .70

A653

A654

A655   A655a

King Albert II

1993-98   Photo.   Perf. 11½
1519 A653 16fr lt gray & multi .65 .20
1520 A653 16fr lt & dk bl grn .70 .20
1521 A655 16fr multi .75 .20
1521A A655 16fr blue .75 .20
1521B A655 17fr blue .75 .20
1521C A655 18fr olive black .75 .25
1521D A655 19fr dp gray vio .75 .30
1522 A653 20fr cream & brn 1.00 .40
1522A A655 20fr brown .90 .40
1523 A653 25fr sepia 1.00 .25
1524 A653 28fr claret 1.00 .30
1526 A653 30fr red lilac 1.10 .25
1526A A655 32fr violet blue 1.25 .25
1527 A653 32fr cream & org brn 1.25 .25
1527A A655 34fr dk bl gray 1.40 .40
1527B A655 36fr dk sl bl 1.50 .30
1528 A653 40fr pink & car 1.75 .30
1529 A653 50fr green 2.25 .35
1530 A655 50fr green 2.50 .40
1533 A654 100fr multi 4.50 .50
1535 A654 200fr multi 10.00 2.50
     Nos. 1519-1535 (21) 36.50 8.30

Coil Stamp
1536 A655a 19fr deep gray vio 1.25 .30

Issued: #1519, 12/15/93; #1520, 1/17/94; 30fr, 2/4/94; #1527, 3/7/94; 50fr, 4/18/94; #1522, 6/6/94; 40fr, 6/20/94; 100fr, 10/3/94; 200fr, 5/2/95; #1521, 6/6/96; #1521A, 1530, 28fr, 9/2/96; 17fr, 12/16/96; 34fr, 36fr, 2/10/97; 18fr, 4/7/97; #1521D, 7/7/97; 25fr, 4/20/98; #1536, 8/10/98; #1522A, 10/19/98; #1526a, 11/9/98.
This is an expanding set. Numbers will change.

Paintings A656

Designs: No. 1537, The Malleable Darkness, by Octave Landuyt. No. 1538, Ma Toute Belle, by Serge Vandercam, vert.

1994, Jan. 31   Photo.   Perf. 11½
1537 A656 16fr multicolored .90 .70
1538 A656 16fr multicolored .90 .70

Airplanes A657

13fr, Hanriot-Dupont HD-1. 15fr, Spad XIII. 30fr, Schreck FBA-H. 32fr, Stampe-Vertongen SV-4B.

1994, Feb. 28
1539 A657 13fr multicolored .70 .50
1540 A657 15fr multicolored .85 .65
1541 A657 30fr multicolored 1.60 1.25
1542 A657 32fr multicolored 1.75 1.40
     Nos. 1539-1542 (4) 4.90 3.80

Daily Newspapers — A658

No. 1543, "Le Jour-Le Courier," cent., vert. No. 1544, "La Wallonie," 75th anniv.

1994, Mar. 21   Photo.   Perf. 11½
1543 A658 16fr multicolored .95 .70
1544 A658 16fr multicolored .95 .70

Fall of the Golden Calf (Detail), by Fernand Allard l'Olivier — A659

1994, Mar. 28
1545 A659 16fr multicolored .95 .70
     Charter of Quaregnon, cent.

Stamp Day — A660

1994, Apr. 11   Photo.   Perf. 11½
1546 A660 16fr No. 102 .95 .70

History A661

Scenes from Brabantse Yeesten, 15th cent. illuminated manuscript: 13fr, Reconciliation between John I and Arnold, squire of

Wezemaal. 16fr, Tournament at wedding of Charles the Bold and Margaret of York. 30fr, Battle of Woeringen.

1994, Apr. 25
1547	A661	13fr multicolored	.75 .55
1548	A661	16fr multicolored	.95 .70
1549	A661	30fr multicolored	1.75 1.25
		Nos. 1547-1549 (3)	3.45 2.50

No. 1549 is 81x28mm.

Europa — A662

Designs: 16fr, Abbe Georges Lemaitre (1894-1966), proposed "big-bang" theory of origins of universe. 30fr, Gerardus Mercator (1512-94), cartographer, astronomer.

1994, May 9   Photo.   Perf. 11½
1550	A662	16fr multicolored	.95 .70
1551	A662	30fr multicolored	1.75 1.25

Papal Visit A663

#1552, Father Damien (1840-89). #1553, St. Mutien-Marie (1841-1917), Christian educator.

1994, May 16   Perf. 11½x12
1552	A663	16fr multicolored	.95 .70
1553	A663	16fr multicolored	.95 .70

Tourism A664

Churches: No. 1554, St. Peter's, Bertem. No. 1555, St. Bavo's, Kanegem, vert. No. 1556, Royal St. Mary's, Schaarbeek. No. 1557, St. Gery's, Aubechies. No. 1558, Sts. Peter and Paul, Saint-Severin, Condroz, vert.

1994, June 13   Photo.   Perf. 11½
1554	A664	16fr multicolored	.95 .70
1555	A664	16fr multicolored	.95 .70
1556	A664	16fr multicolored	.95 .70
1557	A664	16fr multicolored	.95 .70
1558	A664	16fr multicolored	.95 .70
		Nos. 1554-1558 (5)	4.75 3.50

Guillaume Lekeu (1870-94), Composer A665

Design: No. 1560, Detail of painting by Hans Memling (c.1430-94).

1994, Aug. 16   Photo.   Perf. 11½
1559	A665	16fr multicolored	1.10 .75
1560	A665	16fr multicolored	1.10 .75

Liberation of Belgium, 50th Anniv. — A666

Design: 16fr, General Crerar, Field Marshal Montgomery, Gen. Bradley, Belgium landscape. Illustration reduced.

1994, Sept. 5   Photo.   Perf. 11x11½
1561	A666	16fr multicolored	.95 .70

Wildflowers — A667

Designs: No. 1562, Caltha palustris. No. 1563, Cephalanthera damasonium. No. 1564, Calystegia soldanella. No. 1565, Epipactis helleborine.

1994, Sept. 26   Photo.   Perf. 12
Booklet Stamps
1562	A667	16fr multi (14a)	1.10 .75
1563	A667	16fr multi (14b)	1.10 .75
1564	A667	16fr multi (14c)	1.10 .75
1565	A667	16fr multi (14d)	1.10 .75
a.		Booklet pane of 4, #1562-1565	4.50
		Complete booklet, #1565a	4.50

Cubitus the Dog, by Luc Dupanloup — A668

1994, Oct. 10   Perf. 11½
1566	A668	16fr multicolored	1.10 .75

Youth philately.

Georges Simenon (1903-89), Writer A669

Photo. & Engr.
1994, Oct. 17   Perf. 11½
1567	A669	16fr multicolored	1.10 .75

See France No. 2443, Switzerland No. 948.

Christmas A670

1994, Dec. 5   Photo.   Perf. 11½
1568	A670	13fr multicolored	.85 .65

Anniversaries and Events — A671

#1569, August Vermeylen Fund, 50th anniv. #1570, Belgian Touring Club, cent. #1571, Assoc. of Belgian Enterprises, cent. #1572, Dept. of Social Security, 50th anniv.

1995, Feb. 13   Perf. 11½
1569	A671	16fr multicolored	1.10 .75
1570	A671	16fr multicolored	1.10 .75
1571	A671	16fr multicolored	1.10 .75
1572	A671	16fr multicolored	1.10 .75
		Nos. 1569-1572 (4)	4.40 3.00

Flowers of Ghent A672

1995, Mar. 6
1573	A672	13fr Hibiscus rosa-sinensis	.95 .65
1574	A672	16fr Rhododendron simsii	1.10 .75
1575	A672	30fr Fuchsia hybrida	2.25 1.60
		Nos. 1573-1575 (3)	4.30 3.00

Games — A673

1995, Mar. 20
1576	A673	13fr Crossword puzzles	.95 .70
1577	A673	16fr Chess	1.10 .75
1578	A673	30fr Scrabble	2.25 1.60
1579	A673	34fr Cards	2.50 1.75
		Nos. 1576-1579 (4)	6.80 4.80

Stamp Day — A674

1995, Apr. 10   Photo. & Engr.
1580	A674	16fr Frans de Troyer	1.10 .75

Peace & Freedom A675

Europa: 16fr, Broken barbed wire, prison guard tower. 30fr, Mushroom cloud, "Never again."

1995, Apr. 24   Photo.   Perf. 11½
1581	A675	16fr multicolored	1.10 .75
1582	A675	30fr multicolored	2.25 1.75

Liberation of concentration camps, 50th anniv. (#1581). Nuclear Non-Proliferation Treaty, 25th anniv. (#1582).

Battle of Fontenoy, 250th Anniv. — A676

16fr, Irish soldiers, Cross of Fontenoy.

1995, May 15   Photo.   Perf. 11½
1583	A676	16fr multicolored	1.10 .75

See Ireland No. 967.

UN, 50th Anniv. A677

1995, May 22   Photo.   Perf. 11½
1584	A677	16fr multicolored	1.10 .75

"Sauvagemont, Maransart," by Pierre Alechinsky — A678

No. 1586: "Telegram-style," by Pol Mara.

1995, June 6
1585	A678	16fr multicolored	1.10 .75
1586	A678	16fr multicolored	1.10 .75

Tourism A679

Architectural designs: No. 1587, Cauchie house, Brussels, by Paul Cauchie (1875-1952). No. 1588, De Vijf Werelddelen, corner building, Antwerp, by Frans Smet-Verhas (1851-1925). No. 1589, House, Liege, by Paul Jaspar (1859-1945).

1995, June 26
1587	A679	16fr multicolored	1.10 .75
1588	A679	16fr multicolored	1.10 .75
1589	A679	16fr multicolored	1.10 .75
		Nos. 1587-1589 (3)	3.30 2.25

Sailing Ships — A680

1995, Aug. 21   Photo.   Perf. 12
Booklet Stamps
1590	A680	16fr Mercator	1.00 .70
1591	A680	16fr Kruzenstern	1.00 .70
1592	A680	16fr Sagres II	1.00 .70
1593	A680	16fr Amerigo Vespucci	1.00 .70
a.		Booklet pane of 4, #1590-1593	4.00
		Complete booklet, #1593a	4.00

Classic Motorcycles A681

1995, Sept. 25   Photo.   Perf. 11½
1594	A681	13fr 1908 Minerva	.90 .65
1595	A681	16fr 1913 FN, vert.	1.10 .80
1596	A681	30fr 1929 La Mondiale	2.00 1.50
1597	A681	32fr 1937 Gillet, vert.	2.25 1.60
		Nos. 1594-1597 (4)	6.25 4.55

Comic Character, Sammy, by Arthur Berckmans A682

1995, Oct. 9 Photo. Perf. 11½
1598 A682 16fr multicolored 1.10 .80
Youth philately.

King's Day A683

16fr, King Albert II and Queen Paola.

1995, Nov. 15 Photo. Perf. 11½
1599 A683 16fr multicolored 1.10 .80

Christmas — A684

13fr, Nativity scene from "Breviary," book of devotions, c. 1500.

1995, Nov. 20
1600 A684 13fr multicolored .90 .70

Liberal Party, 150th Anniv. — A685

1996, Mar. 4 Photo. Perf. 11½
1601 A685 16fr multicolored 1.10 .80

Portrait of Emile Mayrisch (1862-1928), by Théo Van Rysselberghe (1862-1926) — A686

1996, Mar. 2
1602 A686 (A) multicolored 1.10 .80
No. 1602 was valued at 16fr on day of issue.
See Luxembourg No. 939.

Oscar Bonnevalle, Stamp Designer — A687

1996, Apr. 1
1603 A687 16fr multicolored 1.10 .80
Stamp Day.

Insects A688

#1604, Sympetrum sanguineum. #1605, Bombus terrestris. #1606, Lucanus cervus. #1607, Melolontha melolontha. #1608, Gryllus campestris. #1609, Coccinella septempunctata.

1996, Apr. 1 Photo. Perf. 12
Booklet Stamps
1604 A688 16fr multicolored 1.10 .80
1605 A688 16fr multicolored 1.10 .80
1606 A688 16fr multicolored 1.10 .80
1607 A688 16fr multicolored 1.10 .80
1608 A688 16fr multicolored 1.10 .80
1609 A688 16fr multicolored 1.10 .80
a. Booklet pane, #1604-1609 6.60
Complete booklet, #1609a 6.60

Famous Women A689

Europa: 16fr, Yvonne Nevejean (1900-87), saved Jewish children during World War II. 30fr, Marie Gevers (1883-1975), poet.

1996, May 6 Photo. Perf. 11½
1610 A689 16fr multicolored 1.10 .80
1611 A689 30fr multicolored 2.00 1.50

Tourism — A690

Designs: No. 1612, Grotto of Han-Sur-Lesse, horiz. No. 1613, Village of Begijnendijk as separate community, bicent.

1996, June 10 Photo. Perf. 11½
1612 A690 16fr multicolored 1.10 .80
1613 A690 16fr multicolored 1.10 .80

Architecture in Brussels — A691

#1614, La Maison du Roi (Grand Place). #1615, Galeries Royales Saint-Hubert. #1616, Le Palais d'Egmont, Le Petit Sablon, horiz. #1617, Le Cinquantenaire, horiz.

1996, June 10
1614 A691 16fr multi (7a) 1.10 .80
1615 A691 16fr multi (7b) 1.10 .80
1616 A691 16fr multi (7c) 1.10 .80
1617 A691 16fr multi (7d) 1.10 .80
Nos. 1614-1617 (4) 4.40 3.20

Auto Races at Spa, Cent. A692

1996, July 1
1618 A692 16fr 1900 German 6CV 1.10 .80
1619 A692 16fr 1925 Alfa Romeo P2 1.10 .80
1620 A692 16fr 1939 Mercedes Benz W154 1.10 .80
1621 A692 16fr 1967 Ferrari 330P 1.10 .80
Nos. 1618-1621 (4) 4.40 3.20

Paintings of Historical Figures — A693

Portraits from town hall triptych, Zierikzee, Netherlands: No. 1622, Philip I, the Handsome (1478-1506). No. 1623, Juana of Castile, the Mad (1479-1555).

1996, Sept. 2 Photo. Perf. 11½
1622 A693 16fr multicolored 1.10 .80
1623 A693 16fr multicolored 1.10 .80

Paintings from National Gallery, London — A694

14fr, Reading Man, by Rogier Van Der Weyden (1399-1464). 16fr, Susanna Fourment, by Peter Paul Rubens (1577-1640). 30fr, A Man in a Turban, by Jan Van Eyck (1390-1441).

1996, Sept. 2
1624 A694 14fr multicolored .90 .70
1625 A694 16fr multicolored 1.10 .80
1626 A694 30fr multicolored 2.00 1.50
Nos. 1624-1626 (3) 4.00 3.00

Bird Type of 1985
1996, Oct. 7 Photo. Perf. 11½
1627 A524 6fr Tarin des aulnes .40 .20

Comic Character, Cloro, by Raymond Macherot — A695

1996, Oct. 7
1628 A695 16fr multicolored 1.10 .80
Youth Philately.

Almanac of Mons, by Fr. Charles Letellier, 150th Anniv. A696

1996, Oct. 7
1629 A696 16fr multicolored 1.10 .80

Music and Literature A697

#1630, Arthur Grumiaux (1921-86), violinist. #1631, Flor Peeters (1903-86), organist. #1632, Christian Dotremont (1922-79), poet, artist. #1633, Paul Van Ostaijen (1896-1928), writer.

Photo. & Engr.
1996, Oct. 28 Perf. 11½
1630 A697 16fr multicolored 1.10 .80
1631 A697 16fr multicolored 1.10 .80
1632 A697 16fr multicolored 1.10 .80
1633 A697 16fr multicolored 1.10 .80
Nos. 1630-1633 (4) 4.40 3.20

Christmas and New Year — A698

Scenes from Christmas Market: a, Decorated trees, rooftops. b, Lighted greeting signs. c, Church. d, Selling desert items. e, Selling Nativity scenes. f, Selling meat. g, Santa ringing bell. h, Man smoking pipe, people with presents. i, People shopping.

1996, Nov. 18 Photo. Perf. 11½
1634 A698 14fr Sheet of 9, #a.-i. 8.25 6.25

Catholic Faculty University, Mons, Cent. A699

1997, Jan. 20 Photo. Perf. 11½
1635 A699 17fr multicolored 1.10 .80

Opera at Theatre Royal de la Monnaie, Brussels — A700

#1636, Marie Sasse (1834-1907), soprano. #1637, Ernest Van Dijck (1861-1923), tenor. #1638, Hector Dufranne (1870-1951), baritone. #1639, Clara Clairbert (1899-1970), soprano.

1997, Feb. 10
1636 A700 17fr multicolored 1.00 .75
1637 A700 17fr multicolored 1.00 .75
1638 A700 17fr multicolored 1.00 .75
1639 A700 17fr multicolored 1.00 .75
Nos. 1636-1639 (4) 4.00 3.00

Eastern Cantons — A701

Illustration reduced.

1997, Feb. 10   Photo.   Perf. 11½
1640 A701 17fr multicolored   1.00   .75

Bird Type of 1985
1997, Mar. 10
1641 A524 15fr Mesange boreale   .90   .25

UN Peace-Keeping Forces — A702

1997, Mar. 10
1642 A702 17fr multicolored   1.00   .75

Stories and Legends A703

Europa: 17fr, "De Bokkenrijders" (The Goat Riders). 30fr, Jean de Berneau.

1997, Mar. 10   Photo.   Perf. 11½
1643 A703 17fr multicolored   1.00   .75
1644 A703 30fr multicolored   1.75 1.25

Bird Type of 1985
1997, Apr. 7
        Size: 35x25mm
1645 A524 150fr Pie bavarde, horiz.   8.50 2.50
See No. 1840 for similar stamp with additional Euro denomination.

Constant Spinoy (1924-93), Stamp Engraver — A704

1997, Apr. 7   Photo. & Engr.
1646 A704 17fr multicolored   1.00   .75
        Stamp Day.

Intl. Flower Show, Liege — A705

1997, Apr. 21   Photo.
1647 A705 17fr multicolored   1.00   .75

Paintings by Paul Delvaux (1897-1994) A706

Details or entire paintings: 15fr, Woman with garland of leaves in hair. 17fr, Nude, horiz. 32fr, Woman wearing hat, trolley.

1997, Apr. 21
1648 A706 15fr multicolored   .85   .65
1649 A706 17fr multicolored   1.00   .75
1650 A706 32fr multicolored   1.75 1.40
     Nos. 1648-1650 (3)   3.60 2.80

Bird Type of 1985
1997, May 7   Photo.   Perf. 11½
1651 A524 3fr Alouette des champs   .25   .20

Queen Paola, 60th Birthday A707

1997, May 26
1652 A707 17fr Belvedere Castle   1.00   .75
     See Italy No. 2147.

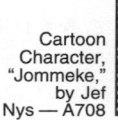

Cartoon Character, "Jommeke," by Jef Nys — A708

1997, May 26
1653 A708 17fr multicolored   1.00   .75

World Congress of Rose Societies — A709

Roses: No. 1654, Rosa damascena coccinea. No. 1655, Rosa sulfurea. No. 1656, Rosa centifolia.

1997, July 7   Photo.   Perf. 11½
1654 A709 17fr multicolored   1.25   .90
1655 A709 17fr multicolored   1.25   .90
1656 A709 17fr multicolored   1.25   .90
     Nos. 1654-1656 (3)   3.75 2.70

Churches — A710

No. 1657, Basilica of St. Martin, Halle. No. 1658, Notre Dame Church, Laeken, horiz. No. 1659, Basilica of St. Martin, Liège.

1997, July 7   Photo. & Engr.
1657 A710 17fr multicolored   1.25   .90
1658 A710 17fr multicolored   1.25   .90
1659 A710 17fr multicolored   1.25   .90
     Nos. 1657-1659 (3)   3.75 2.70

Bird Type of 1985
1997, Sept. 1   Photo.   Perf. 11½
1660 A525 7fr Bergeronnette printaniere   .40   .30

Bees and Apiculture — A711

#1661, Queen, workers. #1662, Development of the larvae. #1663, Bee exiting cell. #1664, Bee collecting nectar. #1665, Two bees. #1666, Two bees on honeycomb.

1997, Sept. 1   Photo.   Perf. 12
        Booklet Stamps
1661 A711 17fr multi (15a)   1.00   .75
1662 A711 17fr multi (15b)   1.00   .75
1663 A711 17fr multi (15c)   1.00   .75
1664 A711 17fr multi (15d)   1.00   .75
1665 A711 17fr multi (15e)   1.00   .75
1666 A711 17fr multi (15f)   1.00   .75
  a.   Booklet pane of 6, #1661-1666   6.00
     Complete booklet, #1666a   6.00

Craftsmen A712

1997, Sept. 1   Perf. 11½
1667 A712 17fr Stone cutter   .75   .60
1668 A712 17fr Mason   .75   .60
1669 A712 17fr Carpenter   .75   .60
1670 A712 17fr Blacksmith   .75   .60
     Nos. 1667-1670 (4)   3.00 2.40

Antarctic Expedition by the Belgica, Cent. — A713

1997, Sept. 22   Photo.   Perf. 11½
1671 A713 17fr multicolored   1.00   .75

Royal Museum of Central Africa, Cent. — A714

No. 1672, Mask, Shaba, Congo. No. 1673, Outside view of museum, horiz. 34fr, Dish Bearer sculpture, Buli area, Congo.

1997, Sept. 22   Photo.   Perf. 11½
1672 A714 17fr multicolored   1.00   .75
1673 A714 17fr multicolored   1.00   .75
1674 A714 34fr multicolored   2.00 1.50
     Nos. 1672-1674 (3)   4.00 3.00
     No. 1673 is 25x73mm.

"Fairon," by Pierre Grahame — A715

Bird Type of 1985
1997, Oct. 25   Photo.   Perf. 11½
Christmas.
1675 A715 15fr multicolored   .90   .70

Bird Type of 1985
1997, Dec. 1   Photo.   Perf. 11½
1676 A524 15fr Mesange boreale, horiz.   .90   .25
No. 1676 issued in coil rolls with every fifth stamp numbered on reverse.

Rhododendron A716

Serpentine Die Cut 13½ on 2 or 3 Sides
1997, Dec. 1
       Booklet Stamp
       Self-Adhesive
1677 A716 (17fr) multicolored   1.00   .25
  a.   Booklet pane of 10   10.00
By its nature, No. 1677a is a complete booklet. The peelable backing serves as a booklet cover.
     Compare with design A757.

"Thalys" High Speed Train — A717

1998, Jan. 19   Photo.   Perf. 11½
1678 A717 17fr multicolored   1.00   .75

Woman Suffrage in Belgium, 50th Anniv. — A718

1998, Jan. 19
1679 A718 17fr multicolored   1.00   .75

Gerard Walschap (1898-1989), Poet, Playwright — A719

#1681, Norge (1898-1990), writer

1998, Feb. 16   Photo.   Perf. 11½
1680 A719 17fr multicolored   .95   .70
1681 A719 17fr multicolored   .95   .70

Paintings, by René Magritte (1898-1967) — A720

#1682, "La Magie Noire (Black Magic)," nude woman. #1683, "La Corde Sensible (Heartstring)," cloud over champagne glass. #1684, "Le Chateau des Pyrenees (Castle of the Pyranees)," castle atop floating rock.

1998, Mar. 9   Photo.   Perf. 11½

1682	A720	17fr multi, vert.	.95	.70
1683	A720	17fr multi	.95	.70
1684	A720	17fr multi, vert.	.95	.70
		Nos. 1682-1684 (3)	2.85	2.10

Belgian Artists — A721

Details or entire paintings: No. 1685, "La Foire aux Amours," by Félicien Rops (1833-98). No. 1686, "Hospitality for the Strangers," by Gustave van de Woestijne (1881-1947). No. 1687, Self-portrait, "The Man with the Beard," by Felix de Boeck (1898-1995). No. 1688, "Black Writing Mixed with Colors," by Karel Appel & Christian Cotremont of COBRA.

1998, Mar. 9   Perf. 12
Booklet Stamps

1685	A721	17fr multicolored	.95	.70
1686	A721	17fr multicolored	.95	.70
1687	A721	17fr multicolored	.95	.70
1688	A721	17fr multicolored	.95	.70
a.		Booklet pane, #1685-1688	3.80	
		Complete booklet, #1688a	3.80	

Museum of Fine Arts, Ghent, bicent. (#1686). COBRA art movement of painters and poets, 50th anniv. (#1688).

Sabena Airlines, 75th Anniv. — A722

1998, Apr. 20   Photo.   Perf. 11½

1689	A722	17fr multicolored	.95	.70

Belgian Stamp Dealers' Assoc., 75th Anniv. A723

1998, Apr. 20

1690	A723	17fr multicolored	.95	.70

"The Return," by René Magritte (1898-1967) — A724

1998, Apr. 20

1691	A724	17fr multicolored	.95	.70

See France No. 2637.

Wildlife A725

1998, Apr. 20

1692	A725	17fr Vulpes vulpes	.95	.70
1693	A725	17fr Cervus elaphus	.95	.70
1694	A725	17fr Sus scrofa	.95	.70
1695	A725	17fr Capreolus capreolus	.95	.70
		Nos. 1692-1695 (4)	3.80	2.80

"Souvenir Sheets"
Starting in 1998, items looking like souvenir sheets have appeared in the market. The 1998 item is similar to No. 1695. The 1999 item is similar to No. 1725. These have no postal value.

Bird Type of 1985

1998, May 4   Photo.   Perf. 11½

1696	A524	1fr Mesange huppee	.20	.20

Edmund Struyf (1911-96), Founder of Pro-Post, Assoc. for Promotion of Philately — A726

1998, May 4   Photo. & Engr.

1697	A726	17fr multicolored	.95	.70

Stamp Day.

Natl. Festivals A727

1998, May 4   Photo.   Perf. 11½

1698	A727	17fr Torhout & Werchter Rock Festival	.95	.70
1699	A727	17fr Wallonia Festival	.95	.70

Europa.

Bird Type of 1985

1998, July 6   Photo.   Perf. 11½

1700	A524	7.50fr Pie-grieche grise	.45	.20

See No. 1837 for similar stamp with additional Euro denomination.

European Heritage Days — A728

a, Logo. b, Bourla Theatre, Antwerp. c, La Halle, Durbuy. d, Halletoren, Kortrijk. e, Louvain Town Hall. f, Perron, Liège. g, Royal Theatre, Namur. h, Aspremont-Lynden Castle, Rekem. i, Neo-Gothic kiosk, Sint-Niklaas. j, Chapelle Saint Vincent, Tournai. k, Villers-la-Ville Abbey. l, Saint Gilles Town Hall, Brussels.

1998, July 6

1701	A728	17fr Sheet of 12, #a.-l.	11.00	8.50

Bird Type of 1985

1998   Photo.   Perf. 11½

1702	A524	9fr Pic vert	.50	.20
1703	A524	10fr Turtle dove	.60	.20

Issued: 9fr, 8/10; 10fr, 9/28/98.

Free Thinking A729

1998, Aug. 10   Photo.   Perf. 11½

1704	A729	17fr multicolored	1.00	.75

Philips van Marnix van Sint-Aldegonde (1540-98), Author — A730

1998, Aug. 10

1705	A730	17fr multicolored	1.00	.75

Mniszech Palace (Belgian Embassy), Warsaw, Bicent. A731

Photo. & Engr.   Perf. 11½
1998, Sept. 28

1706	A731	17fr multicolored	1.00	.75

See Poland No. 3420.

Contemporary Belgium Films — A732

1998, Sept. 28   Photo.

1707	A732	17fr "Le Huitieme Jour"	1.00	.75
1708	A732	17fr "Daens"	1.00	.75

Cartoon Characters, "Chick Bill" and "Ric Hochet" — A733

1998, Oct. 19   Photo.   Perf. 11½

1709	A733	17fr multicolored	1.00	.75

Youth philately.

Assoc. of Space Explorers, 14th World Congress, Brussels — A734

1998, Oct. 19

1710	A734	17fr multicolored	1.00	.75

World Post Day A735

1998, Oct. 19   Photo.   Perf. 11½

1711	A735	34fr blue & dark blue	2.00	1.50

World Assoc. for the Development of Philately.

FGTB-ABVV Trade Union, Cent. — A736

Center panel of triptych by Constant Draz (1875-)

1998, Nov. 9   Photo.   Perf. 11½

1712	A736	17fr multicolored	1.00	.75

Christmas and New Year — A737

1998, Nov. 9

1713	A737	(17fr) multicolored	1.00	.75

Bird Type of 1985

1998-99   Photo.   Perf. 11½

1714	A524	16fr Mesange noire	.85	.65
1715	A524	21fr Grive litorne, horiz.	1.10	.85

No. 1715 also issued in coils with number on reverse of every 5th stamp.
Issued: 16fr, 1/25/99; 21fr, 12/14/98.
See No. 1839 for similar stamp with additional Euro denomination.

A738   A739

Greetings Stamps: No. 1716, Burning candle. No. 1717, Stork carrying a heart. No. 1718, Wristwatch. No. 1719, Four leaf clover with one leaf a heart. No. 1720, Two doves. No. 1721, Heart with arrow through it. No. 1722, Heart-shaped head on woman. No. 1723, Heart-shaped head on man.

1999, Jan. 25   Photo.   Perf. 12
Booklet Stamps

1716	A738	(17fr) multicolored	1.00	.75
1717	A738	(17fr) multicolored	1.00	.75
1718	A738	(17fr) multicolored	1.00	.75
1719	A738	(17fr) multicolored	1.00	.75
1720	A738	(17fr) multicolored	1.00	.75
1721	A738	(17fr) multicolored	1.00	.75
1722	A738	(17fr) multicolored	1.00	.75
1723	A738	(17fr) multicolored	1.00	.75
a.		Booklet pane, #1716-1723	8.00	
		Complete booklet, #1723a	8.00	

Nos. 1716-1717, 1719-1720 each also issued in sheets of 20 on July 1.

1999, Feb. 22 Photo. *Perf. 11½*

Owls.

1724	A739	17fr	Tyto alba	.90	.70
1725	A739	17fr	Athene noctua	.90	.70
1726	A739	17fr	Strix aluco	.90	.70
1727	A739	17fr	Asio otus	.90	.70
			Nos. 1724-1727 (4)	3.60	2.80

NATO, 50th Anniv. A740

1999, Mar. 15

1728	A740	17fr	Leopard tank	.90	.70
1729	A740	17fr	F16 fighter	.90	.70
1730	A740	17fr	Frigate Wande-laar	.90	.70
1731	A740	17fr	Hospital tent	.90	.70
1732	A740	17fr	General staff	.90	.70
			Nos. 1728-1732 (5)	4.50	3.50

UPU, 125th Anniv. A741

1999, Mar. 15

1733	A741	34fr	multicolored	1.90	1.40

National Parks and Nature Reserves A742

Europa: No. 1734, De Bunt, near town of Hamme. No. 1735, Harchies-Hensies-Pommeroeul.

1999, Apr. 12

1734	A742	17fr	multicolored	.90	.70
1735	A742	17fr	multicolored	.90	.70

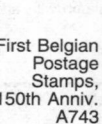

First Belgian Postage Stamps, 150th Anniv. A743

Photo. & Engr.

1999, Apr. 26 *Perf. 11½*

1736	A743	17fr	No. 1	.95	.70
1737	A743	17fr	No. 2	.95	.70
a.			Pair, #1736-1737	1.80	1.40

Painting, "My Favorite Room," by James Ensor (1860-1949) — A744

Designs: No. 1739, Woman Eating Oysters, vert. 30fr, Triumph Over Death, vert. 32fr, Old Lady With Masks, vert.

1999, May 17 Photo. *Perf. 11½*

1738	A744	17fr	multicolored	.95	.70
1739	A744	17fr	multicolored	.95	.70
1740	A744	30fr	multicolored	1.75	1.40
1741	A744	32fr	multicolored	1.90	1.50
			Nos. 1738-1741 (4)	5.55	4.30

See Israel No. 1365A.
Issued: #1738, 5/17; #1739-1741, 9/11.

Tourism — A745

#1742, Giants at Geraardsbergen Fair, vert. #1743, Cart d'Or procession of the Confrérie de la Miséracordie, Mons.

1999, June 7 Photo. *Perf. 11½*

1742	A745	17fr	multi (10a)	.95	.70
1743	A745	17fr	multi (10b)	.95	.70

Belgian Chocolate A746

1999, June 7

1744	A746	17fr	Bean picker	.95	.70
1745	A746	17fr	Candy maker	.95	.70
1746	A746	17fr	Consumer	.95	.70
			Nos. 1744-1746 (3)	2.85	2.10

King Albert and Queen Paola, 40th Wedding Anniv. — A747

1999, July 2 Photo. *Perf. 11½*

1747	A747	17fr	multicolored	.95	.70

Royalty Type of Semi-Postal Stamps
Souvenir Sheet

Kings: a, 50fr, Leopold I. b, 32fr, Leopold II. c, 17fr, Albert I. d, 17fr, Leopold III. e, 32fr, Baudouin. f, 50fr, Albert II.

Photo. & Engr.

1999, Sept. 29 *Perf. 11½*

1748	SP514		Sheet of 6, #a.-f.	15.00	15.00

Bruphila '99. No. 1748 sold for 300fr.

Nobel Laureates in Peace — A750

Designs: 17fr, Henri La Fontaine (1854-1943). 21fr, Auguste Beernaert (1829-1912).

Photo. & Engr.

1999, Sept. 30 *Perf. 11½*

1749	A750	17fr	red & gold	.90	.70
1750	A750	21fr	blue & gold	1.10	.85

See Sweden Nos. 2357-2358.

King Albert II
A751   A752

1999-2001 Photo. *Perf. 11¾x11½*

1752	A751	17fr	multicolored	.90	.25
1753	A751	17fr	prus blue	.80	.25
1754	A751	19fr	blue	.95	.25
1755	A751	20fr	yel brown	.90	.25
1756	A751	23fr	violet	1.00	.25
1757	A751	25fr	brown	1.10	.30
1759	A751	30fr	vio black	1.40	.35
1760	A751	32fr	green	1.50	.30
1761	A751	34fr	gray blue	1.50	.35
1763	A751	36fr	brown	1.60	.40

Engr.

Perf. 11½

1766	A753	50fr	blue	2.25	.55

Photo. *Perf. 11½*

1768	A754	100fr	multi	4.50	1.10

Engr.

1769	A753	200fr	claret	8.75	2.25
			Nos. 1752-1769 (13)	27.15	6.85

No. 1756 issued in coils.
Issued: 17fr, 10/4; 19fr, 1/24/00; 30fr, 4/3/00; 32fr, 6/19/00; 23fr, 9/4/00; 50fr, 9/11/00; No. 1753, 11/18/00; 36fr, 12/4/00; ; 20fr, 25fr, 34fr, 100fr, 200fr, 3/26/01.
This is an expanding set. Numbers may change.

Youth Philately — A756

Comic strips: a, Corentin, by Paul Cuvelier (16a). b, Jerry Spring, by Jijé (16b). c, Gil Jourdan, by Maurice Tillieux (16c). d, La Patrouille des Castors, by Mitacq (16d). e, Entrance hall of Belgian Comic Strip Museum (16e). f, Hassan & Kadour, by Jacques Laudy (16f). g, Buck Danny, by Victor Hubinon (16g). h, Tif et Tondu, by Fernand Dineur (16h). i, Les Timour, by Sirius (16i).

1999, Oct. 2 Photo. *Perf. 11½*

1771	A756	17fr	Sheet of 9, #a.-i.	7.75	6.00

Geranium — A757   Tulip — A758

Die Cut 10x9¾ on 2 or 3 sides

1999-2000 Photo.

Self-Adhesive
Booklet Stamps

1772	A757	(17fr)	multi	.85	.20
a.			Complete booklet, 10 #1772	8.50	
1773	A758	(21fr)	multi	1.00	.25
a.			Booklet, 10 #1773	10.00	

Die Cut Perf. 11¼
Coil Stamps

1774	A757	(17fr)	multi	.85	.20

Photo.

Serpentine Die Cut 14

1775	A758	(21fr)	multi	1.00	.25

Nos. 1774-1775 are on a waxed backing paper larger than the stamp.
Issued: No. 1773, 4/17/00; others, 11/22/99.

Christmas — A762

1999, Nov. 8 Photo. *Perf. 11½*

1776	A762	17fr	multi	.85	.65

Wedding of Prince Philippe and Mathilde d'Udekem d'Acoz, Dec. 4 — A763

1999, Nov. 29

1777	A763	17fr	shown	.85	.65

Souvenir Sheet

1778	A763	21fr	Couple, diff.	1.00	.80

The 20th Century — A764

No. 1779: a, Pope John XXIII. b, King Baudouin. c, Willy Brandt. d, John F. Kennedy. e, Mahatma Gandhi. f, Dr. Martin Luther King, Jr. g, Lenin. h, Che Guevara. i, Golda Meir. j, Nelson Mandela. k, Jesse Owens, Modern Olympic Games. l, Soccer. m, Tour de France. n, Edith Piaf. o, The Beatles. p, Charlie Chaplin. q, Tourism. r, Youth movements. s, Tinitin comic strips. t, Philately.

1999, Dec. 6 Photo. *Perf. 11½*

1779			Sheet of 20	17.00	17.00
a.-t.	A764	17fr	Any single	.85	.65

Numbers have been reserved for additional items in this set.

The 20th Century A764a

No. 1780: a, Yser front, World War I. b, Concentration camps. c, First atomic bomb. d, Yalta Conference. e, United Nations. f, Decolonization. g, Vietnam War. h, Collapse of the Berlin Wall. i, Peace movements. j, Middle East conflict. k, Rene Magritte, artist. l, Le Corbusier, architect. m, Bertolt Brecht, dramatist. n, James Joyce, novelist. o, Anne Teresa de Keersmaeker, choreographer. p, Bela Bartók, composer. q, Andy Warhol, artist. r, Maria Callas, opera singer. s, Henry Moore, sculptor. t, Toots Thielemans, Charlie Parker, jazz musicians.

2000, Nov. 20 Photo. *Perf. 11½*

1780			Sheet of 20	16.00	16.00
a.-t.	A764a	17fr	Any single	.80	.50

Numbers have been reserved for additional itmes in this set.

Year 2000 A765

2000, Jan. 3 Photo. *Perf. 11¾x11½*

1783	A765	17fr	multi	.85	.65

Brussels, 2000 European City of Culture — A766

Brussels skyline and: a, Seven people. b, Harmonica player, dancer. c, Airplane, train, ships.

2000, Jan. 24 **Photo.** **Perf. 11½**
1784	Strip of 3 + 2 labels	2.60	2.00
a.-c.	A766 17fr any single	.85	.65

Bird Type of 1985
Without "F" and
With Euro denomination

2000 **Photo.** **Perf. 11¾**
1785	A524	1fr Beccroisé des sapins	.20	.20
1786	A524	2fr Grimpereau des jardins	.20	.20
1787	A524	3fr Pipit parlouse	.20	.20
1788	A524	5fr Pinson du nord	.20	.20
1789	A524	10fr Pouillot siffleur	.45	.20
1790	A524	16fr Pie grièche écorcheur	.80	.20
1790A	A524	16fr Pie grièche écoucheur, horiz.	.70	.20
		Nos. 1785-1790A (7)	2.75	1.40

No. 1790A issued in coils.
Issued: #1790, 1/24; 1fr, 2fr, 3fr, 5fr, 5/8; 10fr, 9/11; #1790A, 9/4.

Holy Roman Emperor Charles V (1500-58) — A767

2000, Feb. 21 **Photo.** **Perf. 11½**
1791	A767	17fr shown	.80	.60
1792	A767	21fr At age 40	1.00	.75

Souvenir Sheet
1793	A767	34fr In armor	1.60	1.25
a.		Ovptd. in margin	1.60	1.25

No. 1793a was issued 10/6/00 and overprint in margin reads "ESPAÑA 2000 / Exposición Mundial de Filatelia / Madrid 6-14/X/2000." See Spain Nos. 3026-3028.

World Mathematics Year — A768

2000, Feb. 21
1794	A768	17fr multi	.80	.60

Stampin' The Future Children's Stamp Design Contest Winner — A769

2000, Feb. 21
1795	A769	17fr multi	.80	.60

European Soccer Championships, Belgium and Netherlands — A770

Illustration reduced.

2000, Mar. 27
1796	A770	Pair + label	1.75	1.25
a.		17fr Players	.80	.60
b.		21fr Ball	.95	.65

Serpentine Die Cut 10x9¾ on 3 sides
Booklet Stamp
Self-Adhesive
Size: 21x27mm

1797	A770	(17fr) Players, diff.	.80	.60
a.		Booklet, 10 #1797	8.00	

Worldwide Fund for Nature — A771

Endangered amphibians and reptiles: No. 1798, Vipera berus. No. 1799, Lacerta agilis, vert. No. 1800, Hyla arborea, vert. No. 1801, Salamandra salamandra.

Perf. 11¾x11½, 11½x11¾

2000, Mar. 27 **Photo.**
1798	A771	17fr multi	.80	.60
1799	A771	17fr multi	.80	.60
1800	A771	17fr multi	.80	.60
1801	A771	17fr multi	.80	.60
		Nos. 1798-1801 (4)	3.20	2.40

Stamp Day — A772

2000, Apr. 3 **Photo.** **Perf. 11½**
1802	A772	17fr multi	.80	.60

Franz von Taxis — A773

Illustration reduced.

2000, Apr. 3
1803	A773	17fr multi + label	.80	.60

Postal system in Europe, 500th anniv., Belgica 2001 Stamp Exhibition.

Ghent Flower Show A774

Designs: 16fr, Iris spuria. 17fr, Rhododendron, horiz. 21fr, Begonia.

2000, Apr. 17
1804	A774	16fr multi	.75	.55
1805	A774	17fr multi	.80	.60
1806	A774	21fr multi	.95	.70
		Nos. 1804-1806 (3)	2.50	1.85

Prince Philippe's Fund A775

2000, Apr. 17
1807	A775	17fr multi	.80	.60

2000 Summer Olympics and Paralympics, Sydney A776

Designs: 17fr, Belgian Olympic team emblem. No. 1809, Taekwondo. No. 1810, Wheelchair racer, horiz.
30fr+7fr, Swimmer in triathlon, horiz.

2000, May 8 **Photo.**
1808	A776	17fr multi	.80	.60
1809	A776	17fr +4fr multi	.95	.95
1810	A776	17fr +4fr multi	.95	.95
		Nos. 1808-1810 (3)	2.70	2.50

Souvenir Sheet
1811	A776	30fr +7fr multi	1.60	1.60

Olymphilex 2000 (No. 1811).

Opening of Musical Instrument Museum, Brussels — A777

No. 1812, Harpsichord (15a). No. 1813, Violin (15b). No. 1814, Lutes (15c). No. 1815, Treble viol (15d). No. 1816, Trumpets (15e). No. 1817, Johann Sebastian Bach (15f).

2000, May 8 **Photo.** **Perf. 11¾**
Booklet Stamps
1812	A777	(17fr) multi	.80	.60
1813	A777	(17fr) multi	.80	.60
1814	A777	(17fr) multi	.80	.60
1815	A777	(17fr) multi	.80	.60
1816	A777	(17fr) multi	.80	.60
1817	A777	(17fr) multi	.80	.60
a.		Booklet pane, #1812-1817	5.00	
		Booklet, #1817a	5.00	

Europa, 2000
Common Design Type

2000, May 9 **Perf. 11½**
1818	CD17	(21fr) multi	1.00	.75

UNESCO World Heritage Sites A778

Designs: No. 1819, Flemish Béguinages. No. 1820, Grand-Place, Brussels. No. 1821, Boat lifts, Canal du Centre.

2000, June 19 **Perf. 11½x11¾**
1819	A778	17fr multi	.80	.60
1820	A778	17fr multi	.80	.60
1821	A778	17fr multi	.80	.60
		Nos. 1819-1821 (3)	2.40	1.80

Tourism A779

Churches and their organs: No. 1822, Norbertine Abbey Church, Grimbergen. No. 1823, Collégiale Sainte Waudru, Mons. No. 1824, O.-L.-V. Hemelvaartkerk, Ninove. No. 1825, St. Peter's Church, Bastogne.

2000, June 19 **Perf. 11½**
1822	A779	17fr multi	.80	.60
1823	A779	17fr multi	.80	.60
1824	A779	17fr multi	.80	.60
1825	A779	17fr multi	.80	.60
		Nos. 1822-1825 (4)	3.20	2.40

A780

2000, Sept. 4 **Photo.** **Perf. 11¾**
1826	A780	17fr multi	.75	.50

European Postal Services, 500th Anniv., Belgica 2001 Stamp Exhibition. #1826 issued in coils.

Youth Philately — A781

2000, Sept. 11 **Perf. 11¾x11½**
1827	A781	17fr multi	.75	.50

Hainault Flower Show A782

2000, Sept. 11 **Perf. 11½x11¾**
1828	A782	17fr multi	.75	.50

Violets — A783

Die Cut Perf. 10x9¾ on 2 or 3 Sides
2000, Sept. 11 **Photo.**
Booklet Stamp
Self-Adhesive
1829	A783	(17fr) multi	.80	.25
a.		Booklet, 10 #1829	8.00	

Contemporary Art — A784

#831, Bing of the Ferro Lusto X, by Panamarenko. #1832, Construction, by Anne-Mie Van Kerckhoven. #1833, Belgique Eternelle, by J. & L. Charlier. #1834, Roses from series "Les Belles de Nuit," by Marie-Jo Lafontaine.

Perf. 11½x11¾, 11¾x11½

2000, Oct. 16   **Photo.**

1831	A784	17fr multi (21a)		.75	.50
1832	A784	17fr multi (21b), vert.		.75	.50
1833	A784	17fr multi (21c)		.75	.50
1834	A784	17fr multi (21d)		.75	.50
		Nos. 1831-1834 (4)		3.00	2.00

Christmas — A785

2000, Nov. 20   **Photo.**   **Perf. 11½**

1835	A785	17fr multi	.80	.50

Bird Type of 1985
Without F and With Euro Denomination

2000-2001   **Photo.**   **Perf. 11¾**

1836	A524	50c	Roitelet huppe	.20	.20
1837	A524	7.50fr	Pie-grieche grise	.35	.20
1838	A524	8fr	Mesange charbon-niere	.40	.20
1838A	A524	16fr	Sterne pier-regarin	.70	.20
1839	A524	21fr	Grive litorne, horiz.	.95	.25

Perf. 11½x11¾
Size: 35x25mm

1840	A524	150fr Pie bavarde, horiz.	6.75	1.75
		Nos. 1836-1840 (6)	9.35	2.80

Issued: 8fr, 12/4/00. 50c, 7.50fr, 21fr, 150fr, 3/26/01; 16fr, 6/9/01. Numbers have been reserved for additional stamps in this set.

Holy Year 2000 — A786

Illustration reduced.

Photo. & Engr.

2000, Dec. 27   **Perf. 11½**

1841	A786	17fr multi+ label	.80	.50

Royalty Type of Semi-Postal Stamps
Souvenir Sheet

Queens: a, 50fr, Louise-Marie. b, 32fr, Marie-Henriette. c, 17fr, Elisabeth. d, 17fr, Astrid. e, 32fr, Fabiola. f, 50fr, Paola.

Photo. & Engr.

2001, Feb. 12   **Perf. 11½**

1842	SP514	Sheet of 6, #a-f	14.00	14.00

No. 1842 sold for 300fr.

Ze´nobe Gramme (1826-1901), Electrical Engineer — A787

2001, Mar. 19   **Photo.**

1843	A787	17fr multi	.80	.50

Catholic University of Louvain, 575th Anniv. — A788

2001, Mar. 19

1844	A788	17fr multi	.80	.50

Europa — A789

2001, Apr. 23   **Photo.**   **Perf. 11½**

1845	A789	21fr multi	.95	.70

Musical and Literary Personalities — A790

Designs: No. 1846, Willem Elsschot (1882-1960), writer. No. 1847, Albert Ayguesparse (1900-96), writer.
21fr, Queen Elisabeth (1876-1965), patron of Queen Elisabeth Intl. Music Competition, horiz.

2001, Apr. 23   **Photo.**   **Perf. 11½**

1846	A790	17fr multi	.80	.50
1847	A790	17fr multi	.80	.50

Souvenir Sheet

1848	A790	21fr multi	.95	.70

Queen Elisabeth Intl. Music Competition, 50th anniv. (No. 1848).

A791

European Posts, 500th Anniv. — A792

Designs: No. 1849, Franz von Taxis, 16th cent. postrider. No. 1850, 17th cent. postman on road near Brussels. No. 1851, 18th cent. postman, quill pen, postal notice. No. 1852, 19th cent. postman, train, Belgium #2 on cover. No. 1853, 20th cent. postman, motorcycle, airplanes, mailboxes.
Illustration A791 reduced.

Perf. 11¾x11½

2001, June 9   **Photo.**
Stamp + label

1849	A791	17fr multi	.75	.50
1850	A792	17fr multi	.75	.50
1851	A792	17fr multi	.75	.50
1852	A792	17fr multi	.75	.50
1853	A792	17fr multi	.75	.50
		Nos. 1849-1853 (5)	3.75	2.50

Nos. 1849-1853 each printed in sheets of 10 stamps + 10 labels. Ten different labels are on the sheet containing No. 1853.

European Posts Type of 2001
Souvenir Sheet

Design: 150fr, 21st cent. postwoman, Belgica 2001 emblem.

2001, June 9   **Photo.**   **Perf. 11½**

1854	A792	150fr multi	13.00	13.00

No. 1854 contains one 38x48mm stamp without an attached label, and sold for 300fr, with the surtax going to Pro Post for the promotion of philately.

Houses of Worship — A793

Designs: 17fr, Hassan II Mosque, Casablanca, Morocco. 34fr, Koekelberg Basilica.

2001, June 10   Photo.   *Perf. 11½*
1855	A793 17fr multi	.75	.50
1856	A793 34fr multi	1.50	1.10

See Morocco Nos.

Muse´es Royaux des Beaux Arts, Brussels, 200th Anniv. — A794

No. 1857: a, Winter Landscape With Skaters, by Pieter Breughel the Elder. b, Study of a Negro's Head, by Peter Paul Rubens. c, Sunday, by Frits Van den Berghe. d, Mussel Triumph II, by Marcel Broodthaers.

2001, June 11   Photo.   *Perf. 12*
1857	Booklet pane of 4	3.00	
a.-d.	A794 17fr Any single	.75	.50
	Booklet, #1857	3.00	

Ancient Chinese Receptacles A795

Designs: 17fr, Earthenware vase. 34fr, Porcelain coffee pot.

2001, June 12   Photo.   *Perf. 11½*
1858	A795 17fr multi	.75	.50
1859	A795 34fr multi	1.50	1.10

See People's Republic of China Nos. 3108-3109.

Youth Philately — A796

2001, June 13
1860	A796 17fr multi	.75	.50

Belgian Chairmanship of European Union A797

2001, June 15
1861	A797 17fr multi	.75	.50

Tourism — A798

Town hall belfries: No. 1862, Binche. No. 1863, Dixmude.

2001, Aug. 6   *Perf. 11½x11¾*
1862	A798 17fr multi	.80	.50
1863	A798 17fr multi	.80	.50

Farmsteads — A799

2001, Aug. 6   *Perf. 11¾x11½*
1864	A799 17fr Damme	.80	.50
1865	A799 17fr Beauvechain	.80	.50
1866	A799 17fr Leuven	.80	.50
1867	A799 17fr Honnelles	.80	.50
1868	A799 17fr Hasselt	.80	.50
	Nos. 1864-1868 (5)	4.00	2.50

Stam and Pilou, Mascots of Stampilou Youth Philatelic Club — A800

2001, Oct. 8   Photo.   *Die Cut*
Self-Adhesive
Booklet Stamp
1869	A800 (17fr) multi	.75	.50
a.	Booklet of 5 + 5 labels	3.75	

Stamp Day.

SEMI-POSTAL STAMPS

Values quoted for Nos. B1-B24 are for stamps with label attached. Copies without label sell for one-tenth or less.

St. Martin of Tours Dividing His Cloak with a Beggar
SP1   SP2

Unwmk.
1910, June 1   Typo.   *Perf. 14*
B1	SP1 1c gray	.75	.75
B2	SP1 2c purple brn	6.50	6.50
B3	SP1 5c peacock blue	1.90	1.90
B4	SP1 10c brown red	1.90	1.90
B5	SP2 1c gray green	1.90	1.90
B6	SP2 2c violet brn	5.00	5.00
B7	SP2 5c peacock blue	2.25	2.25
B8	SP2 10c carmine	2.25	2.25
	Nos. B1-B8 (8)	22.45	22.45
	Set, never hinged	65.00	

Overprinted "1911" in Black
1911, Apr. 1
B9	SP1 1c gray	20.00	16.00
a.	Inverted overprint		
B10	SP1 2c purple brn	57.50	42.50
B11	SP1 5c peacock blue	6.50	5.25
B12	SP1 10c brown red	6.50	5.25
B13	SP2 1c gray green	30.00	24.00
B14	SP2 2c violet brn	25.00	21.00
B15	SP2 5c peacock blue	6.50	5.25
B16	SP2 10c carmine	6.50	5.25
	Nos. B9-B16 (8)	158.50	124.50
	Set, never hinged	600.00	

Overprinted "CHARLEROI-1911"
1911, June
B17	SP1 1c gray	3.50	2.50
B18	SP1 2c purple brn	11.00	10.00
B19	SP1 5c peacock blue	6.50	6.50
B20	SP1 10c brown red	6.50	6.50
B21	SP2 1c gray green	3.50	2.50
B22	SP2 2c violet brn	11.00	9.00
B23	SP2 5c peacock blue	6.50	6.50
B24	SP2 10c carmine	6.50	6.50
	Nos. B17-B24 (8)	55.00	50.00
	Set, never hinged	175.00	

Nos. B1-B24 were sold at double face value, except the 10c denominations which were sold for 15c. The surtax benefited the national anti-tuberculosis organization.

King Albert I — SP3

1914, Oct. 3   *Litho.*
B25	SP3 5c green & red	15.00	15.00
B26	SP3 10c red	1.50	1.50
B27	SP3 20c violet & red	45.00	45.00
	Nos. B25-B27 (3)	61.50	61.50
	Set, never hinged	125.00	

Counterfeits of Nos. B25-B27 abound. Probably as many as 90% of the stamps on the market are counterfeits. Values are for genuine examples.

Merode Monument — SP4

1914, Oct. 3
B28	SP4 5c green & red	.00	3.00
B29	SP4 10c red	5.00	5.00
B30	SP4 20c violet & red	75.00	75.00
	Nos. B28-B30 (3)	80.00	83.00
	Set, never hinged	175.00	

Counterfeits of Nos. B28-B30 abound. Probably as many as 90% of the stamps on the market are counterfeits. Values are for genuine examples.

King Albert I — SP5

1915, Jan. 1   *Perf. 12, 14*
B31	SP5 5c green & red	5.00	3.00
a.	Perf. 12x14	16.00	12.00
B32	SP5 10c rose & red	20.00	6.00
B33	SP5 20c violet & red	25.00	14.00
a.	Perf. 14x12	500.00	250.00
b.	Perf. 12	50.00	32.50
	Nos. B31-B33 (3)	50.00	23.00

Nos. B25-B33 were sold at double face value. The surtax benefited the Red Cross.

Types of Regular Issue of 1915 Surcharged in Red:

Nos. B34-B40   Nos. B41-B43

Nos. B44-B47

1918, Jan. 15   Typo.   *Perf. 14*
B34	A46 1c + 1c dp orange	.50	.50
B35	A46 2c + 2c brown	.60	.60
B36	A46 5c + 5c blue grn	1.40	1.40
B37	A46 10c + 10c red	2.25	2.25
B38	A46 15c + 15c brt violet	3.25	3.25
B39	A46 20c + 20c plum	7.50	7.50
B40	A46 25c + 25c ultra	7.50	7.50
	Engr.		
B41	A47 35c + 35c lt vio & blk	10.00	10.00
B42	A48 40c + 40c dull red & blk	10.00	10.00
B43	A49 50c + 50c turq blue & blk	12.00	12.00
B44	A50 1fr + 1fr bluish slate	35.00	35.00
B45	A51 2fr + 2fr dp gray grn	100.00	100.00
B46	A52 5fr + 5fr brown	250.00	250.00
B47	A53 10fr + 10fr dp blue	500.00	500.00
	Nos. B34-B47 (14)	940.00	940.00

Discus Thrower — SP6   Racing Chariot — SP7

Runner — SP8

1920, May 20   Engr.   *Perf. 12*
B48	SP6 5c + 5c dp green	1.40	1.40
B49	SP7 10c + 5c carmine	1.40	1.40
B50	SP8 15c + 15c dk brown	3.00	3.00
	Nos. B48-B50 (3)	5.80	5.80

7th Olympic Games, 1920. Surtax benefited wounded soldiers.
For surcharges see Nos. 140-142.

Allegory: Asking Alms from the Crown SP9 — Wounded Veteran SP10

1922, May 20
B51 SP9 20c + 20c brown 1.40 1.40

1923, July 5
B52 SP10 20c + 20c slate gray 1.75 1.75

Surtax on #B51-B52 was to aid wounded veterans.

SP11 — SP12

St. Martin, by Van Dyck SP13 — SP14

1925, Dec. 15 Typo. Perf. 14
B53 SP11 15c + 5c dull vio & red .50 .20
B54 SP11 30c + 5c gray & red .25 .20
B55 SP11 1fr + 10c chalky blue & red 1.25 1.40
Nos. B53-B55 (3) 2.00 1.80

Surtax for the Natl. Anti-Tuberculosis League.

1926, Feb. 10
B56 SP12 30c + 30c bluish grn (red surch.) .50 .50
B57 SP13 1fr + 1fr lt blue 7.25 7.25
B58 SP14 1fr + 1fr lt blue 1.10 1.25
Nos. B56-B58 (3) 8.85 9.00

The surtax aided victims of the Meuse flood.

Lion and Cross of Lorraine — SP15

Queen Elisabeth and King Albert SP16

1926, Dec. 6 Typo. Perf. 14
B59 SP15 5c + 5c dk brown .25 .20
B60 SP15 20c + 5c red brown .45 .40
B61 SP15 50c + 5c dull violet .30 .20

Engr. Perf. 11½
B62 SP16 1.50fr + 25c dk blue .75 .70
B63 SP16 5fr + 1fr rose red 6.50 6.00
Nos. B59-B63 (5) 8.25 7.50

Surtax was used to benefit tubercular war veterans.

Boat Adrift SP17

1927, Dec. 15 Engr. Perf. 11½, 14
B64 SP17 25c + 10c dk brn .70 .70
B65 SP17 35c + 10c yel grn .70 .70
B66 SP17 60c + 10c dp violet .60 .40
B67 SP17 1.75fr + 25c dk blue 1.50 2.00
B68 SP17 5fr + 1fr plum 4.50 4.75
Nos. B64-B68 (5) 8.00 8.55

The surtax on these stamps was divided among several charitable associations.

Ogives of Orval Abbey — SP18

Monk Carving Capital of Column — SP19

Ruins of Orval Abbey SP20

Design: 60c+15c, 1.75fr+25c, 3fr+1fr, Countess Matilda recovering her ring.

1928, Sept. 15 Photo. Perf. 11½
B69 SP18 5c + 5c red & gold .20 .20
B70 SP18 25c + 5c dk vio & gold .25 .20

Engr.
B71 SP19 35c + 15c dp grn .70 .70
B72 SP19 60c + 15c red brn .45 .20
B73 SP19 1.75fr + 25c dk blue 1.90 1.25
B74 SP19 2fr + 40c dp vio 15.00 12.50
B75 SP19 3fr + 1fr red 13.50 12.00

Perf. 14
B76 SP20 5fr + 5fr rose lake 9.00 9.00
B77 SP20 10fr + 10fr blk brn 9.00 9.00
Nos. B69-B77 (9) 45.00 45.10

Surtax for the restoration of the ruined Orval Abbey.
For overprints see Nos. B84-B92.

St. Waudru, Mons — SP22 — St. Rombaut, Malines — SP23

Designs: 25c + 15c, Cathedral of Tournal. 60c + 15c, St. Bavon, Ghent. 1.75fr + 25c, St. Gudule, Brussels. 5fr + 5fr, Louvain Library.

1928, Dec. 1 Photo. Perf. 14, 11½
B78 SP22 5c + 5c carmine .20 .20
B79 SP22 25c + 15c ol brn .25 .25

Engr.
B80 SP23 35c + 10c dp grn 1.00 1.00
B81 SP23 60c + 15c red brn .30 .30
B82 SP23 1.75fr + 25c vio bl 7.00 7.00
B83 SP23 5fr + 5fr red vio 14.00 14.00
Nos. B78-B83 (6) 22.75 22.75

The surtax was for anti-tuberculosis work.

Nos. B69-B77 with this overprint in blue or red were privately produced. They were for the laying of the 1st stone toward the restoration of the ruined Abbey of Orval. Value, set, $650.
Forgeries of the overprint exist.

Waterfall at Coo — SP28

Bayard Rock, Dinant — SP29

Designs: 35c+10c, Menin Gate, Ypres. 60c+15c, Promenade d'Orleans, Spa. 1.75fr+25c, Antwerp Harbor. 5fr+5fr, Quai Vert, Bruges.

1929, Dec. 2 Engr. Perf. 11½
B93 SP28 5c + 5c red brn .20 .25
B94 SP29 25c + 15c gray blk .65 .60
B95 SP28 35c + 10c green .80 .95
B96 SP28 60c + 15c rose lake .55 .50
B97 SP28 1.75fr + 25c dp blue 4.50 4.50

Perf. 14
B98 SP29 5fr + 5fr dl vio 27.50 27.50
Nos. B93-B98 (6) 34.20 34.30

Bornhem — SP34 — Beloeil — SP35

Gaesbeek SP36

25c + 15c, Wynendaele. 70c + 15c, Oydonck. 1fr + 25c, Ghent. 1.75fr + 25c, Bouillon.

1930, Dec. 1 Photo. Perf. 14
B99 SP34 10c + 5c violet .25 .30
B100 SP34 25c + 15c olive brn .60 .60

Engr.
B101 SP35 40c + 10c brn vio .80 1.00
B102 SP35 70c + 15c gray blk .55 .55
B103 SP35 1fr + 25c rose lake 3.50 3.50
B104 SP35 1.75fr + 25c dp bl 4.50 2.75
B105 SP36 5fr + 5fr gray grn 27.50 32.50
Nos. B99-B105 (7) 37.70 41.20

Prince Leopold SP41 — Queen Elisabeth SP42

Philatelic Exhibition Issue
Souvenir Sheet
1931, July 18 Photo. Perf. 14
B106 SP41 2.45fr + 55c car brn 140.00 140.00
a. Single stamp 60.00

Sold exclusively at the Brussels Phil. Exhib., July 18-21, 1931. Size: 122x159mm. Surtax for the Veterans' Relief Fund.
The sheet normally has pin holes and a cancellation-like marking in the margin. These are considered unused and the condition valued here.

1931, Dec. 1 Engr.
B107 SP42 10c + 5c red brn .30 .50
B108 SP42 25c + 15c dk vio 1.10 1.25
B109 SP42 50c + 10c dk grn .95 1.10
B110 SP42 75c + 15c blk brn .90 .70
B111 SP42 1fr + 25c rose lake 6.75 6.00
B112 SP42 1.75fr + 25c ultra 4.75 4.00
B113 SP42 5fr + 5fr brn vio 55.00 55.00
Nos. B107-B113 (7) 69.75 68.55

The surtax was for the National Anti-Tuberculosis League.

Désiré Cardinal Mercier — SP43 — Mercier Protecting Children and Aged at Malines — SP44

Mercier as Professor at Louvain University — SP45

Mercier in Full Canonicals, Giving His Blessing SP46

1932, June 10 Photo. Perf. 14½x14
B114 SP43 10c + 10c dk violet .40 .60
B115 SP43 50c + 30c brt violet 2.25 2.50
B116 SP43 75c + 25c olive brn 2.25 2.25
B117 SP43 1fr + 2fr brown red 6.00 6.00

Engr. Perf. 11½
B118 SP44 1.75fr + 75c dp blue 70.00 82.50
B119 SP45 2.50fr + 2.50fr dk brn 70.00 70.00
B120 SP44 3fr + 4.50fr dull grn 70.00 70.00
B121 SP45 5fr + 20fr vio brn 80.00 82.50

B122 SP46 10fr + 40fr brn
lake 175.00 *210.00*
Nos. B114-B122 (9) 475.90 *526.35*

Honoring Cardinal Mercier and to obtain funds to erect a monument to his memory. Exist with privately produced black overprint "Braine-L'Alleud 17-7-33 Collegio Card. Mercier." Value, set, $850.

Belgian Infantryman SP47

Sanatorium at Waterloo SP48

1932, Aug. 4   Perf. 14½x14
B123 SP47 75c + 3.25fr red
brn 55.00 55.00
B124 SP47 1.75fr + 4.25fr dk
blue 55.00 55.00

Honoring Belgian soldiers who fought in WWI and to obtain funds to erect a natl. monument to their glory.

1932, Dec. 1   Photo.   Perf. 13½x14
B125 SP48 10c + 5c dk
vio .30 *.90*
B126 SP48 25c + 15c red
vio 1.00 *1.25*
B127 SP48 50c + 10c red
brn 1.00 *1.25*
B128 SP48 75c + 15c ol
brn 1.00 *.80*
B129 SP48 1fr + 25c dp
red 13.00 10.50
B130 SP48 1.75fr + 25c dp
blue 10.50 9.25
B131 SP48 5fr + 5fr gray
grn 85.00 *90.00*
Nos. B125-B131 (7) 111.80 *113.95*

Surtax for the assistance of the Natl. Anti-Tuberculosis Society at Waterloo.

View of Old Abbey SP49

Ruins of Old Abbey — SP50

Count de Chiny Presenting First Abbey to Countess Matilda SP56

Restoration of Abbey in XVI and XVII Centuries SP57

Abbey in XVIII Century, Maria Theresa and Charles V — SP58

Madonna and Arms of Seven Abbeys SP60

Designs: 25c+15c, Guests, courtyard, 50c+25c, Transept. 75c+50c, Bell Tower. 1fr+1.25fr, Fountain. 1.25fr+1.75fr, Cloisters. 5fr+20fr, Duke of Brabant placing 1st stone of new abbey.

1933, Oct. 15   Perf. 14
B132 SP49 5c + 5c dull
grn 35.00 40.00
B133 SP50 10c + 15c ol
grn 32.50 35.00
B134 SP49 25c + 15c dk
brn 32.50 35.00
B135 SP50 50c + 25c red
brn 32.50 35.00
B136 SP50 75c + 50c dp
grn 32.50 35.00
B137 SP50 1fr + 1.25fr
cop red 32.50 35.00
B138 SP49 1.25fr + 1.75fr
gray blk 32.50 35.00
B139 SP56 1.75fr + 2.75fr
blue 37.50 40.00
B140 SP57 2fr + 3fr mag 37.50 40.00
B141 SP58 2.50fr + 5fr dull
grn 37.50 40.00
B142 SP56 5fr + 20fr vio 40.00 40.00
       Perf. 11½
B143 SP60 10fr + 40fr bl 225.00 225.00
Nos. B132-B143 (12) 607.50 *635.00*

The surtax was for a fund to aid in the restoration of Orval Abbey. Counterfeits exist.

"Tuberculosis Society" SP61

Peter Benoit SP62

1933, Dec. 1   Engr.   Perf. 14x13½
B144 SP61 10c + 5c blk .85 .85
B145 SP61 25c + 15c vio 3.00 3.00
B146 SP61 50c + 10c red
brn 2.25 2.25
B147 SP61 75c + 15c blk
brn 9.25 9.00
B148 SP61 1fr + 25c cl 10.50 10.50
B149 SP61 1.75fr + 25c vio
bl 12.50 12.50
B150 SP61 5fr + 5fr lilac 115.00 115.00
Nos. B144-B150 (7) 153.35 *153.10*

The surtax was for anti-tuberculosis work.

1934, June 1   Photo.
B151 SP62 75c + 25c olive brn 5.50 5.50

The surtax was to raise funds for the Peter Benoit Memorial.

King Leopold III
SP63   SP64

1934, Sept. 15
B152 SP63 75c + 25c ol blk 18.00 17.00
   a.   Sheet of 20 750.00 750.00
B153 SP64 1fr + 25c red
vio 17.00 16.00
   a.   Sheet of 20 750.00 750.00

The surtax aided the National War Veterans' Fund. Sold for 4.50fr a set at the Exhibition of War Postmarks 1914-18, held at Brussels by the Royal Philatelic Club of Veterans. The

---

price included an exhibition ticket. Sold at Brussels post office Sept. 18-22. No. B152 printed in sheets of 20 (4x5) and 100 (10x10). No. B153 printed in sheets of 20 (4x5) and 150 (10x15).

1934, Sept. 24
B154 SP63 75c + 25c violet 1.25 1.25
B155 SP64 1fr + 25c red brn 7.00 7.00

The surtax aided the National War Veterans' Fund. No. B154 printed in sheets of 100 (10x10); No. B155 in sheets of 150 (10x15). These stamps remained in use one year.

Crusader SP65

1934, Nov. 17   Engr.   Perf. 13½x14
Cross in Red
B156 SP65 10c + 5c blk 1.25 1.25
B157 SP65 25c + 15c brn 1.75 1.75
B158 SP65 50c + 10c dull
grn 1.75 1.75
B159 SP65 75c + 15c vio .85 .85
B160 SP65 1fr + 25c
rose 8.50 8.50
B161 SP65 1.75fr + 25c ul-
tra 7.50 7.50
B162 SP65 5fr + 5fr brn
vio 105.00 105.00
Nos. B156-B162 (7) 126.60 *126.60*

The surtax was for anti-tuberculosis work.

Prince Baudouin, Princess Josephine and Prince Albert SP66

1935, Apr. 10   Photo.
B163 SP66 35c + 15c dk grn .85 .75
B164 SP66 70c + 30c red brn .85 .60
B165 SP66 1.75fr + 50c dk blue 3.00 *3.50*
Nos. B163-B165 (3) 4.70 *4.85*

Surtax was for Child Welfare Society.

Stagecoach — SP67

Franz von Taxis — SP68

Queen Astrid — SP69

1935, Apr. 27
B166 SP67 10c + 10c ol blk .60 .65
B167 SP67 25c + 25c bis brn 1.90 1.75
B168 SP67 35c + 25c dk green 2.50 2.25
Nos. B166-B168 (3) 5.00 *4.65*

Printed in sheets of 10. Value, set of 3, $175.

Souvenir Sheet
1935, May 25   Engr.   Perf. 14
B169 SP68 5fr + 5fr grnsh
blk 125.00 125.00
   a.   Single stamp 65.00

Sheets measure 91½x117mm. Nos. B166-B169 were issued for the Brussels Philatelic Exhibition (SITEB). The sheet normally has pin holes and a cancellation-like marking in the margin. These are considered unused and the condition valued here.

1935   Photo.   Perf. 11½
Borders in Black
B170 SP69 10c + 5c ol blk .20 .20
B171 SP69 25c + 15c brown .20 *.30*
B172 SP69 35c + 5c dk green .20 *.25*
B173 SP69 50c + 10c rose lil .65 .55
B174 SP69 70c + 5c gray blk .20 .20
B175 SP69 1fr + 25c red .90 .70
B176 SP69 1.75fr + 25c blue 2.00 1.50
B177 SP69 2.45fr + 55c dk vio 2.50 *2.75*
Nos. B170-B177 (8) 6.85 *6.45*

Queen Astrid Memorial issue. The surtax was divided among several charitable organizations.
Issued: #B174, 10/31; others, 12/1.

Borgerhout Philatelic Exhibition Issue
Souvenir Sheet

Town Hall, Borgerhout — SP70

1936, Oct. 3
B178 SP70 70c + 30c pur brn 50.00 35.00
   a.   Single stamp 25.00

Sheet measures 115x126mm. The sheet normally has pin holes and a cancellation-like marking in the margin. These are considered unused and the condition valued here.

Town Hall and Belfry of Charleroi SP71

Prince Baudouin SP72

Charleroi Youth Exhibition
Souvenir Sheet
1936, Oct. 18   Engr.
B179 SP71 2.45fr + 55c gray
blue 42.50 40.00
   a.   Single stamp 25.00

Sheet measures 95x120mm. The sheet normally has pin holes and a cancellation-like marking in the margin. These are considered unused and the condition valued here.

1936, Dec. 1   Photo.   Perf. 14x13½
B180 SP72 10c + 5c dk brown .20 .20
B181 SP72 25c + 5c violet .20 *.25*
B182 SP72 35c + 5c dk green .20 *.25*
B183 SP72 50c + 5c vio brn .30 *.35*
B184 SP72 70c + 5c ol grn .20 .20
B185 SP72 1fr + 25c cerise .65 .45
B186 SP72 1.75fr + 25c ultra 1.10 .65
B187 SP72 2.45fr + 2.55fr vio
rose 3.00 *4.00*
Nos. B180-B187 (8) 5.85 *6.35*

The surtax was for the assistance of the National Anti-Tuberculosis Society.

1937, Jan. 10
B188 SP72 2.45fr + 2.55fr slate 1.50 1.50

Intl. Stamp Day. Surtax for the benefit of the Brussels Postal Museum, the Royal Belgian Phil. Fed. and the Anti-Tuberculosis Soc.

Queen Astrid and
Prince Baudouin
SP73

Queen Mother
Elisabeth
SP74

1937, Apr. 15   **Perf. 11½**

B189	SP73	10c + 5c magenta	.20	.20
B190	SP73	25c + 5c ol blk	.20	.25
B191	SP73	35c + 5c dk grn	.20	.25
B192	SP73	50c + 5c violet	.50	.55
B193	SP73	70c + 5c slate	.20	.30
B194	SP73	1fr + 25c dk car	.65	.60
B195	SP73	1.75fr + 25c dp ultra	1.10	1.10
B196	SP73	2.45fr + 1.55fr dk brn	2.75	2.75
		Nos. B189-B196 (8)	5.80	6.00

The surtax was to raise funds for Public Utility Works.

1937, Sept. 15   **Perf. 14x13½**

B197	SP74	70c + 5c int black	.30	.30
B198	SP74	1.75fr + 25c brt ultra	.70	.70

Souvenir Sheet
Perf. 11½

B199	Sheet of 4	26.00	15.00
a.	SP74 1.50fr+2.50fr red brn	3.75	3.25
b.	SP74 2.45fr+3.55fr red vio	3.25	2.00

Issued for the benefit of the Queen Elisabeth Music Foundation in connection with the Eugene Ysaye intl. competition.
No. B199 contains two se-tenant pairs of Nos. B199a and B199b. Size: 111x145mm. On sale one day, Sept. 15, at Brussels.
The sheet normally has pin holes and a cancellation-like marking in the margin. These are considered unused and the condition valued here.

Princess Josephine-
Charlotte
SP75

1937, Dec. 1   **Perf. 14x13½**

B200	SP75	10c + 5c sl grn	.20	.20
B201	SP75	25c + 5c lt brn	.20	.20
B202	SP75	35c + 5c yel grn	.20	.20
B203	SP75	50c + 5c ol gray	.40	.35
B204	SP75	70c + 5c brn red	.20	.20
B205	SP75	1fr + 25c red	.70	.55
B206	SP75	1.75fr + 25c vio bl	.85	.70
B207	SP75	2.45fr + 2.55fr mag	3.25	3.50
		Nos. B200-B207 (8)	6.00	5.90

King Albert Memorial Issue
Souvenir Sheet

King Albert Memorial — SP76

1938, Feb. 17   **Perf. 11½**

B208	SP76	2.45fr + 7.55fr brn vio	13.00	11.00

Dedication of the monument to King Albert.
The sheet normally has pin holes and a cancellation-like marking in the margin. These are considered unused and the condition valued here.

King
Leopold III
in Military
Plane
SP77

1938, Mar. 15

B209	SP77	10c + 5c car brn	.20	.30
B210	SP77	35c + 5c dp grn	.35	.90
B211	SP77	70c + 5c gray blk	.65	.50
B212	SP77	1.75fr + 25c ultra	1.50	1.40
B213	SP77	2.45fr + 2.55fr pur	3.50	3.00
		Nos. B209-B213 (5)	6.20	6.10

The surtax was for the benefit of the National Fund for Aeronautical Propaganda.

Basilica of
Koekelberg
SP78

Interior View of the
Basilica of
Koekelberg
SP79

1938, June 1   **Photo.**

B214	SP78	10c + 5c lt brn	.20	.20
B215	SP78	35c + 5c grn	.20	.20
B216	SP78	70c + 5c gray grn	.20	.20
B217	SP78	1fr + 25c car	.65	.55
B218	SP78	1.75fr + 25c ultra	.65	.65
B219	SP78	2.45fr + 2.55fr brn vio	2.75	3.50

Engr.

B220	SP79	5fr + 5fr dl grn	11.00	10.50
		Nos. B214-B220 (7)	15.65	15.80

Souvenir Sheet

1938, July 21   **Engr.**   **Perf. 14**

B221	SP79	5fr + 5fr lt vio	14.00	14.00

The surtax was for a fund to aid in completing the National Basilica of the Sacred Heart at Koekelberg.
Nos. B214, B216 and B218 are different views of the exterior of the Basilica.
The sheet normally has pin holes and a cancellation-like marking in the margin. These are considered unused and the condition valued here.

Stamps of 1938 Surcharged in Black:

Nos. B222-B223

No. B224

1938, Nov. 10   **Perf. 11½**

B222	SP78	40c on 35c+5c grn	.35	.40
B223	SP78	75c on 70c+5c gray grn	.50	.60
B224	SP78	2.50 +2.50fr on 2.45+2.55fr	4.50	5.00
		Nos. B222-B224 (3)	5.35	6.00

Prince Albert of
Liege — SP81

1938, Dec. 10   **Photo.**   **Perf. 14x13½**

B225	SP81	10c + 5c brown	.20	.20
B226	SP81	30c + 5c mag	.20	.30
B227	SP81	40c + 5c olive gray	.20	.30
B228	SP81	75c + 5c slate grn	.20	.20
B229	SP81	1fr + 25c dk car	.55	.75
B230	SP81	1.75fr + 25c ultra	.55	.75
B231	SP81	2.50fr + 2.50fr dp grn	3.50	5.50
B232	SP81	5fr + 5fr brn lake	11.00	8.50
		Nos. B225-B232 (8)	16.40	16.50

Henri Dunant
SP82

Florence
Nightingale
SP83

Queen Mother
Elisabeth and
Royal
Children — SP84

Queen
Astrid — SP86

King
Leopold and
Royal
Children
SP85

Queen Mother Elisabeth and Wounded
Soldier — SP87

1939, Apr. 1   **Photo.**   **Perf. 11½**
Cross in Carmine

B233	SP82	10c + 5c brn	.20	.20
B234	SP83	30c + 5c brn car	.30	.30
B235	SP84	40c + 5c ol gray	.20	.30
B236	SP84	75c + 5c slate blk	.40	.20
B237	SP84	1fr + 25c brt rose	1.90	1.10
B238	SP85	1.75fr + 25c brt ultra	.60	.80
B239	SP86	2.50fr + 2.50fr dl vio	1.25	1.60
B240	SP87	5fr + 5fr gray grn	4.25	5.50
		Nos. B233-B240 (8)	9.10	10.00

75th anniversary of the founding of the International Red Cross Society.

Rubens'
House,
Antwerp
SP88

"Albert and Nicolas
Rubens" — SP89

Arcade,
Rubens'
House
SP90

"Helena Fourment
and Her
Children" — SP91

Rubens and
Isabelle
Brandt — SP92

Peter Paul
Rubens — SP93

"The Velvet
Hat" — SP94

"Descent
from the
Cross"
SP95

1939, July 1

B241	SP88	10c + 5c brn	.20	.20
B242	SP89	40c + 5c brn car	.20	.20
B243	SP90	75c + 5c ol blk	.35	.35
B244	SP91	1fr + 25c rose	1.40	1.40
B245	SP92	1.50fr + 25c sep	1.60	1.60
B246	SP93	1.75fr + 25c dp ultra	2.50	2.50
B247	SP94	2.50fr + 2.50fr brt red vio	8.25	8.25
B248	SP95	5fr + 5fr slate gray	10.50	10.50
		Nos. B241-B248 (8)	25.00	25.00

Issued to honor Peter Paul Rubens. The surtax was used to restore Rubens' home in Antwerp.

"Martin van Nieuwenhove" by Hans Memling (1430?-1495), Flemish Painter — SP96

1939, July 1

B249 SP96 75c + 75c olive blk   2.75   2.75

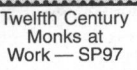

Twelfth Century Monks at Work — SP97

Reconstructed Tower Seen through Cloister — SP98

Monks Laboring in the Fields SP99

Orval Abbey, Aerial View SP100

Bishop Heylen of Namur, Madonna and Abbot General Smets of the Trappists — SP101

King Albert I and King Leopold III and Shrine — SP102

1939, July 20

B250	SP97	75c + 75c ol blk	2.50	2.75
B251	SP98	1fr + 1fr rose red	1.60	1.60
B252	SP99	1.50fr + 1.50fr dl brn	1.60	1.60
B253	SP100	1.75fr + 1.75fr saph	1.60	1.60
B254	SP101	2.50fr + 2.50fr brt red vio	7.25	6.50
B255	SP102	5fr + 5fr brn car	7.25	7.25
		Nos. B250-B255 (6)	21.80	21.30

The surtax was used for the restoration of the Abbey of Orval.

Bruges SP103   Furnes SP104

Belfries: 30c+5c, Thuin. 40c+5c, Lierre. 75c+5c, Mons. 1.75fr+25c, Namur. 2.50fr+2.50fr, Alost. 5fr+5fr, Tournai.

1939, Dec. 1   **Photo.**   **Perf. 14x13½**

B256	SP103	10c + 5c ol gray	.20	.25
B257	SP103	30c + 5c brn org	.25	.35
B258	SP103	40c + 5c brt red vio	.40	.45
B259	SP103	75c + 5c olive blk	.20	.25

Engr.

B260	SP104	1fr + 25c rose car	1.00	1.25
B261	SP104	1.75fr + 25c dk blue	1.00	1.25
B262	SP104	2.50fr + 2.50fr dp red brn	7.25	8.00
B263	SP104	5fr + 5fr pur	10.00	11.00
		Nos. B256-B263 (8)	20.30	22.80

Mons SP111   Ghent SP112

Coats of Arms: 40c+10c, Arel. 50c+10c, Bruges. 75c+15c, Namur. 1fr+25c, Hasselt. 1.75fr+50c, Brussels. 2.50fr+2.50fr, Antwerp. 5fr+5fr, Liege.

1940-41   **Typo.**   **Perf. 14x13½**

B264	SP111	10c + 5c multi	.20	.20
B265	SP111	30c + 5c multi	.20	.20
B266	SP111	40c + 10c multi	.20	.20
B267	SP112	50c + 10c multi	.20	.20
B268	SP112	75c + 15c multi	.20	.20
B269	SP112	1fr + 25c multi	.30	.30
B270	SP112	1.75fr + 50c multi	.45	.40
B271	SP112	2.50fr + 2.50fr multi	1.25	1.25
B272	SP111	5fr + 5fr multi	1.50	1.50
		Nos. B264-B272 (9)	4.50	4.45

Nos. B264, B269-B272 issued in 1941. Surtax for winter relief. See No. B279.

Queen Elisabeth Music Chapel SP120

Bust of Prince Albert of Liege — SP121

1940, Nov.   **Photo.**   **Perf. 11½**

B273	SP120	75c + 75c slate	1.25	1.25
B274	SP120	1fr + 1fr rose red	1.25	1.25
B275	SP121	1.50fr + 1.50fr Prus grn	1.25	1.25
B276	SP121	1.75fr + 1.75fr ultra	1.25	1.25
B277	SP120	2.50fr + 2.50fr brn org	2.50	2.50
B278	SP121	5fr + 5fr red vio	3.00	3.00
		Nos. B273-B278 (6)	10.50	10.50

The surtax was for the Queen Elisabeth Music Foundation. Nos. B273-B278 were not authorized for postal use, but were sold to advance subscribers either mint or canceled to order. See Nos. B317-B318.

Arms Types of 1940-41
Souvenir Sheets
Perf. 14x13½, Imperf.

1941, May   **Typo.**
Cross and City Name in Carmine
Arms in Color of Stamp

B279		Sheet of 9	13.00	13.00
a.	SP111	10c + 5c slate	1.10	1.25
b.	SP112	30c + 5c emerald	1.10	1.25
c.	SP111	40c + 10c chocolate	1.10	1.25
d.	SP112	50c + 10c light violet	1.10	1.25
e.	SP111	75c + 15c dull purple	1.10	1.25
f.	SP112	1fr + 25c carmine	1.10	1.25
g.	SP111	1.75fr + 50c dull blue	1.10	1.25
h.	SP112	2.50fr + 2.50fr ol gray	1.10	1.25
i.	SP111	5fr + 5fr dull violet	4.00	4.25

The sheets measure 106x148mm. The surtax was used for relief work.

Painting SP123   Sculpture SP124

Monks Studying Plans of Orval Abbey — SP128

Designs: 40c+60c, 2fr+3.50fr, Monk carrying candle. 50c+65c, 1.75fr+2.50fr, Monk praying. 75c+1fr, 3fr+5fr, Two monks singing.

1941, June   **Photo.**   **Perf. 11½**

B281	SP123	10c + 15c brn org	.35	.40
B282	SP124	30c + 30c ol gray	.35	.40
B283	SP124	40c + 60c dp brn	.35	.40
B284	SP124	50c + 65c vio	.35	.40
B285	SP124	75c + 1fr brt red vio	.35	.40
B286	SP124	1fr + 1.50fr rose red	.35	.40
B287	SP123	1.25fr + 1.75fr dp yel grn	.35	.40
B288	SP123	1.75fr + 2.50fr dp ultra	.35	.40
B289	SP123	2fr + 3.50fr red vio	.35	.40
B290	SP124	2.50fr + 4.50fr dl red brn	.35	.40
B291	SP124	3fr + 5fr dk ol grn	.35	.40
B292	SP128	5fr + 10fr grnsh blk	1.25	1.25
		Nos. B281-B292 (12)	5.10	5.65

The surtax was used for the restoration of the Abbey of Orval.

Maria Theresa SP129   Charles the Bold SP130

Portraits (in various frames): 35c+5c, Charles of Lorraine. 50c+10c, Margaret of Parma. 60c+10c, Charles V. 1fr+15c, Johanna of Castile. 1.50fr+1fr, Philip the Good. 1.75fr+1.75fr, Margaret of Austria. 3.25fr+3.25fr, Archduke Albert. 5fr+5fr, Archduchess Isabella.

1941-42   **Photo.**

B293	SP129	10c + 5c ol blk	.20	.20
B294	SP129	35c + 5c dl grn	.20	.20
B295	SP129	50c + 10c brn	.20	.20
B296	SP129	60c + 10c pur	.20	.20
B297	SP129	1fr + 15c brt car rose	.20	.20
B298	SP129	1.50fr + 1fr red vio	.20	.20

B299	SP129	1.75fr + 1.75fr ryl bl	.20	.20
B300	SP130	2.25fr + 2.25fr dl red brn	.30	.30
B301	SP129	3.25fr + 3.25fr lt brn	.35	.45
B302	SP129	5fr + 5fr sl grn	.40	.45
		Nos. B293-B302 (10)	2.45	2.60

Souvenir Sheet

Archduke Albert and Archduchess Isabella — SP139

B302A	SP139	Sheet of 2 ('42)	6.00	6.00
b.		3.25fr+6.75fr turquoise blue	2.25	2.25
c.		5fr+10fr dark carmine	2.25	2.25

The surtax was for the benefit of National Social Service Work among soldiers' families.

Souvenir Sheets

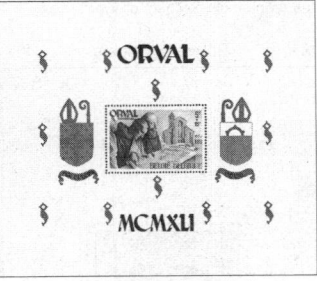

Monks Studying Plans of Orval Abbey — SP140

1941, Oct.   **Photo.**   **Perf. 11½**
Inscribed "Belgie-Belgique"

B303 SP140 5fr + 15fr ultra   7.00   7.00

Inscribed "Belgique-Belgie"
Imperf

B304 SP140 5fr + 15fr ultra   7.00   7.00

Surtax for the restoration of Orval Abbey. No. B304 exists perforated.

In 1942 these sheets were privately trimmed and overprinted "1142 1942" and ornament.

St. Martin Statue, Church of Dinant SP141   Lennik, Saint-Quentin SP142

St. Martin's Church, Saint-Trond SP146

Statues of St. Martin: 50c+10c, 3.25fr+3.25fr, Beck, Limburg. 60c+10c, 2.25fr+2.25fr, Dave on the Meuse. 1.75fr+50c, Hal, Brabant.

1941-42 Photo. Perf. 11½

B305	SP141	10c + 5c chest	.20	.20
B306	SP142	35c + 5c dk bl grn	.20	.20
B307	SP142	50c + 10c vio	.20	.20
B308	SP142	60c + 10c dp brn	.20	.20
B309	SP142	1fr + 15c car	.20	.20
B310	SP141	1.50fr + 25c sl grn	.20	.20
B311	SP142	1.75fr + 50c dk ultra	.30	.30
B312	SP142	2.25fr + 2.25fr red vio	.30	.30
B313	SP142	3.25fr + 3.25fr brn vio	.30	.30
B314	SP146	5fr + 5fr dk ol grn	.45	.45

Nos. B305-B314 (10) 2.55 2.55

Souvenir Sheets
Inscribed "Belgie-Belgique"

B315 SP146 5fr + 20fr vio brn ('42) 12.50 12.50

Inscribed "Belgique-Belgie"
Imperf

B316 SP146 5fr + 20fr vio brn ('42) 12.50 12.50

In 1956, the Bureau Europeen de la Jeunesse et de l'Enfance privately overprinted Nos. B315-B316: "Congres Europeen de l'education 7-12 Mai 1956," in dark red and dark green respectively. A black bar obliterates "Winterhulp-Secours d'Hiver."

Souvenir Sheets

Queen Elisabeth Music Chapel — SP147

1941, Dec. 1 Photo. Perf. 11½
Inscribed "Belgique-Belgie"
B317 SP147 10fr + 15fr ol blk 4.50 4.00

Inscribed "Belgie-Belique"
B318 SP147 10fr + 15fr ol blk 4.50 4.00

The surtax was for the Queen Elisabeth Music Foundation. These sheets were perforated with the monogram of Queen Elisabeth in 1942.
In 1954 Nos. B317-B318 were overprinted for the birth cent. of Edgar Tinel, composer. These overprinted sheets were not postally valid.

Jean Bollandus SP148 — Christophe Plantin SP156

Designs: 35c+5c, Andreas Vesalius. 50c+10c, Simon Stevinus. 60c+10c, Jean Van Helmont. 1fr+15c, Rembert Dodoens. 1.75fr+50c, Gerardus Mercator. 3.25fr+3.25fr, Abraham Ortelius. 5fr+5fr, Justus Lipsius.

1942, May 15 Photo. Perf. 14x13½
B319	SP148	10c + 5c dl brn	.20	.20
B320	SP148	35c + 5c gray grn	.20	.20
B321	SP148	50c + 10c fawn	.20	.20
B322	SP148	60c + 10c grnsh blk	.20	.20

Engr.
B323	SP148	1fr + 15c brt rose	.20	.20
B324	SP148	1.75fr + 50c dl bl	.20	.20
B325	SP148	3.25fr + 3.25fr lil rose	.20	.20
B326	SP148	5fr + 5fr vio	.25	.25

Perf. 13½x14
B327 SP156 10fr + 30fr red org .95 1.00
Nos. B319-B327 (9) 2.60 2.65

The surtax was used to help fight tuberculosis.
No. B327 was sold by subscription at the Brussels Post Office, July 1-10, 1942.

Belgian Prisoner — SP158

1942, Oct. 1 Perf. 11½
B331 SP158 5fr + 45fr olive gray 5.50 5.50

The surtax was for prisoners of war. Value includes a brown inscribed label which alternates with the stamps in the sheet.

SP159 — SP164

SP162

SP168

Various Statues of St. Martin.

1942-43
B332	SP159	10c + 5c org	.20	.20
B333	SP159	35c + 5c dk bl grn	.20	.20
B334	SP159	50c + 10c dp brn	.20	.20
B335	SP162	60c + 10c blk	.20	.20
B336	SP159	1fr + 15c brt rose	.20	.20
B337	SP164	1.50fr + 25c grnsh blk	.20	.20
B338	SP164	1.75fr + 50c dk bl	.20	.20
B339	SP162	2.25fr + 2.25fr brn	.30	.25
B340	SP162	3.25fr + 3.25fr brt red vio	.35	.30
B341	SP168	5fr + 10fr hn brn	.50	.45
B342	SP168	10fr + 20fr rose brn & vio brn ('43)	.65	.65

Inscribed "Belgique-Belgie"
B343 SP168 10fr + 20fr gldn brn & vio brn ('43) .65 .65
Nos. B332-B343 (12) 3.85 3.70

The surtax was for winter relief.
Issue dates: Nos. B332-B341, Nov. 12, 1942; Nos. B342-B343, Apr. 3, 1943.

Prisoners of War — SP170

#B345, 2 prisoners with package from home.

1943, May Photo. Perf. 11½
B344 SP170 1fr + 30fr ver 2.50 2.50
B345 SP170 1fr + 30fr brn rose 2.50 2.50

The surtax was used for prisoners of war.

Roof Tiler SP172 — Coppersmith SP173

Statues in Petit Sablon Park, Brussels: 35c+5c, Blacksmith. 60c+10c, Gunsmith. 1fr+15c, Armsmith. 1.75fr+75c, Goldsmith. 3.25fr+3.25fr, Fishdealer. 5fr+25fr, Watchmaker.

1943, June 1
B346	SP172	10c + 5c chnt brn	.20	.20
B347	SP172	35c + 5c grn	.20	.20
B348	SP173	50c + 10c dk brn	.20	.20
B349	SP173	60c + 10c slate	.20	.20
B350	SP173	1fr + 15c dl rose brn	.20	.20
B351	SP173	1.75fr + 75c ultra	.20	.20
B352	SP173	3.25fr + 3.25fr red vio	.30	.40
B353	SP173	5fr + 25fr dk pur	.50	.55

Nos. B346-B353 (8) 2.00 2.15

Surtax for the control of tuberculosis.

"O" SP180

"ORVAL" — SP185

1943, Oct. 9
B354	SP180	50c + 1fr "O"	.50	.50
B355	SP180	60c + 1.90fr "R"	.30	.25
B356	SP180	1fr + 3fr "V"	.30	.25
B357	SP180	1.75fr + 5.25fr "A"	.30	.25
B358	SP180	3.25fr + 16.75fr "L"	.40	.40
B359	SP185	5fr + 30fr dp brn	.75	.75

Nos. B354-B359 (6) 2.55 2.40

Surtax aided restoration of Orval Abbey.

St. Leonard Church, Leau SP186

St. Martin Church, Courtrai — SP190 — Basilica of St. Martin, Angre — SP191

Notre Dame, Hal — SP193

St. Martin SP194

35c+5c, St. Martin Church, Dion-le-Val. 50c+15c, St. Martin Church, Alost. 60c+20c, St. Martin Church, Liege. 3.25fr+11.75fr, St. Martin Church, Loppem. No. B369, St. Martin, beggar & Meuse landscape.

1943-44
B360	SP186	10c + 5c dp brn	.20	.20
B361	SP186	35c + 5c dk bl grn	.20	.20
B362	SP186	50c + 15c ol blk	.30	.30
B363	SP186	60c + 20c brt red vio	.30	.40
B364	SP190	1fr + 1fr rose brn	.40	.40
B365	SP191	1.75fr + 4.25fr dp ultra	.90	.60
B366	SP186	3.25fr + 11.75fr red lil	.90	.65
B367	SP193	5fr + 25fr dk bl	1.25	1.25
B368	SP194	10fr + 30fr gray grn ('44)	.90	.90
B369	SP194	10fr + 30fr blk brn ('44)	.90	.90

Nos. B360-B369 (10) 6.25 5.80

Surtax for winter relief.

Catalogue values for unused stamps in this section, from this point to the end of the section, are for Never Hinged items.

"Daedalus and Icarus" SP196 — Sir Anthony Van Dyck, Self-portrait SP200

Paintings by Van Dyck: 50c+2.50fr, "The Good Samaritan." 60c+3.40fr, Detail of "Christ Healing the Paralytic." 1fr+5fr, "Madonna and Child." 5fr+30fr, "St. Sebastian."

1944, Apr. 16 Photo. Perf. 11½
Crosses in Carmine
B370 SP196 35c + 1.65fr dk sl grn .40 .30
B371 SP196 50c + 2.50fr grnsh blk .40 .30

B372 SP196	60c + 3.40fr blk brn		.40	.30
B373 SP196	1fr + 5fr dk car		.60	.45
B374 SP200	1.75fr + 8.25fr int bl		.75	.60
B375 SP196	5fr + 30fr cop brn		.75	.60
Nos. B370-B375 (6)			3.30	2.55

The surtax was for the Belgian Red Cross.

Jan van Eyck — SP202

Godfrey of Bouillon — SP203

Designs: 50c+25c, Jacob van Maerlant. 60c+40c, Jean Joses de Dinant. 1fr+50c, Jacob van Artevelde. 1.75fr+4.25fr, Charles Joseph de Ligne. 2.25fr+8.25fr, Andre Gretry. 3.25fr+11.25fr, Jan Moretus-Plantin. 5fr+35fr, Jan van Ruysbroeck.

1944, May 31

B376 SP202	10c + 15c dk pur		.40	.25
B377 SP203	35c + 15c green		.40	.25
B378 SP203	50c + 25c chnt brn		.40	.25
B379 SP203	60c + 40c ol blk		.40	.25
B380 SP203	1fr + 50c rose		.40	.25
B381 SP203	1.75fr + 4.25fr ultra		.40	.25
B382 SP203	2.25fr + 8.25fr grnsh blk		1.00	.55
B383 SP203	3.25fr + 11.25fr dk brn		.40	.25
B384 SP203	5fr + 35fr sl bl		.70	.70
Nos. B376-B384 (9)			4.50	3.00

The surtax was for prisoners of war.

Sons of Aymon Astride Bayard SP211

Brabo Slaying the Giant Antigoon SP212

Till Eulenspiegel Singing to Nele SP214

50c+10c, St. Hubert converted by stag with crucifix. 1fr+15fr, St. George slaying the dragon. 1.75fr+5.25fr, Genevieve of Brabant with son & roe-deer. 3.25fr+11.75fr, Tchantches wrestling with the Saracen. 5fr+25fr, St. Gertrude rescuing the knight with the cards.

1944, June 25

B385 SP211	10c + 5c choc		.20	.20
B386 SP212	35c + 5c dk bl grn		.20	.20
B387 SP211	50c + 10c dl vio		.20	.20
B388 SP214	60c + 10c blk brn		.20	.20
B389 SP214	1fr + 15c rose brn		.20	.20
B390 SP214	1.75fr + 5.25fr ultra		.20	.30
B391 SP211	3.25fr + 11.75fr grnsh blk		.35	.50
B392 SP211	5fr + 25fr dk bl		.45	.70
Nos. B385-B392 (8)			2.00	2.50

The surtax was for the control of tuberculosis.

Nos. B385-B389 were overprinted "Breen-donk+10fr." in 1946 by the Union Royale Philatelique for an exhibition at Brussels. They had no postal validity.

Union of the Flemish and Walloon Peoples in their Sorrow — SP219

Union in Reconstruction — SP220

Perf. 11½

1945, May 1   **Unwmk.**   **Photo.**

B395 SP219	1fr + 30fr carmine		1.25	.90
B396 SP220	1¾fr + 30fr brt ultra		1.25	.90

1945, July 21

Size: 34½x23½mm

B397 SP219	1fr + 9fr scarlet		.25	.20
B398 SP220	1fr + 9fr car rose		.25	.20
Nos. B395-B398 (4)			3.00	2.20

Surtax for the postal employees' relief fund.

Prisoner of War SP221

Reunion SP222

Awaiting Execution SP223

Symbolical Figures "Recovery of Freedom" SP225

Design: 70c+30c, 3.50fr+3.50fr, Member of Resistance Movement.

1945, Sept. 10

B399 SP221	10c + 15c orange		.20	.20
B400 SP222	20c + 20c dp pur		.20	.20
B401 SP223	60c + 25c sepia		.20	.20
B402 SP221	70c + 30c dp yel grn		.20	.20
B403 SP221	75c + 50c org brn		.20	.20
B404 SP222	1fr + 75c brt bl grn		.25	.20
B405 SP223	1.50fr + 1fr brt red		.25	.20
B406 SP221	3.50fr + 3.50fr brt bl		1.10	1.00
B407 SP225	5fr + 40fr brown		.90	.90
Nos. B399-B407 (9)			3.50	3.30

The surtax was for the benefit of prisoners of war, displaced persons, families of executed victims and members of the Resistance Movement.

Arms of West Flanders — SP226

Arms of Provinces: 20c+20c, Luxembourg. 60c+25c, East Flanders. 70c+30c, Namur. 75c+50c, Limburg. 1fr+75c, Hainaut. 1.50fr+1fr, Antwerp. 3.50fr+1.50fr, Liege. 5fr+45fr, Brabant.

1945, Dec. 1

B408 SP226	10c + 15c sl blk & sl gray		.20	.20
B409 SP226	20c + 20c rose car & rose		.20	.20
B410 SP226	60c + 25c dk brn & pale brn		.20	.20
B411 SP226	70c + 30c dk grn & lt grn		.20	.20
B412 SP226	75c + 50c org brn & pale org brn		.20	.20
B413 SP226	1fr + 75c pur & lt pur		.20	.20
B414 SP226	1.50fr + 1fr car & rose		.20	.20
B415 SP226	3.50fr + 1.50fr dp bl & gray bl		.30	.20
B416 SP226	5fr + 45fr dp mag & cer		2.25	1.90
Nos. B408-B416 (9)			4.00	3.50

The surtax was for tuberculosis prevention.

Father Joseph Damien — SP227

Father Damien Comforting Leper — SP229

Leper Colony, Molokai Island, Hawaii SP228

Perf. 11½

1946, July 15   **Unwmk.**   **Photo.**

B417 SP227	65c + 75c dk blue		1.00	.65
B418 SP228	1.35fr + 2fr brown		1.00	.65
B419 SP229	1.75fr + 18fr rose brn		1.60	1.10

The surtax was for the erection of a museum in Louvain.

Symbols of Wisdom and Patriotism SP230

"In Memoriam" SP232

François Bovesse SP231

1946, July 15

B420 SP230	65c + 75c violet		1.00	.65
B421 SP231	1.35fr + 2fr dk org brn		1.40	.80
B422 SP232	1.75fr + 18fr car rose		1.90	1.10

The surtax was for the erection of a "House of the Fine Arts" at Namur.

Emile Vandervelde SP233

Sower SP235

Vandervelde, Laborer and Family — SP234

1946, July 15

B423 SP233	65c + 75c dk sl grn		1.25	.65
B424 SP234	1.35fr + 2fr dk vio bl		1.40	.80
B425 SP235	1.75fr + 18fr dp car		1.90	1.10
Nos. B417-B425 (9)			12.45	7.50

The surtax was for the Emile Vanderveide Institute, to promote social, economic and cultural activities.

For surcharges see Nos. CB4-CB12.

Pepin of Herstal — SP236

Malines — SP241

1fr+50c, Charlemagne. 1.50fr+1fr, Godfrey of Bouillon. 3.50fr+1.50fr, Robert of Jerusalem. #B430-B431, Baldwin of Constantinople.

1946, Sept. 15 Engr.   **Perf. 11½x11**

B426 SP236	75c + 25c grn		.60	.35
B427 SP236	1fr + 50c vio		.90	.50
B428 SP236	1.50fr + 1fr plum		1.25	.65
B429 SP236	3.50fr + 1.50fr brt bl		1.50	.75
B430 SP236	5fr + 45fr red vio		12.00	7.00
B431 SP236	5fr + 45fr red org		15.00	7.75
Nos. B426-B431 (6)			31.25	17.00

The surtax on Nos. B426-B429 was for the benefit of former prisoners of war, displaced persons, the families of executed patriots, and former members of the Resistance Movement.

The surtax on Nos. B430-B431 was divided among several welfare, national celebration and educational organizations.

Issue dates: Nos. B426-B429, Apr. 15; No. B430, Sept. 15; No. B431, Nov. 15.

See Nos. B437-B441, B465-B466, B472-B476.

1946, Dec. 2   **Perf. 11½**

Coats of Arms: 90c+60c, Dinant. 1.35fr+1.15fr, Ostend. 3.15fr+1.85fr, Verviers. 4.50fr+45.50fr, Louvain.

B432 SP241	65c + 35c rose car		.50	.50
B433 SP241	90c + 60c lem		.50	.50
B434 SP241	1.35fr + 1.15fr dp grn		.50	.50
B435 SP241	3.15fr + 1.85fr bl		1.50	1.25

B436 SP241 4.50fr + 45.50fr
                dk vio brn   13.00 12.00
    Nos. B432-B436 (5)   16.00 14.75

The surtax was for anti-tuberculosis work.
See Nos. B442-B446.

Type of 1946

Designs: 65c+35c, John II, Duke of Brabant.
90c+60c, Count Philip of Alsace.
1.35fr+1.15fr, William the Good. 3.15fr+1.85fr,
Bishop Notger of Liege. 20fr+20fr, Philip the
Noble.

1947, Sept. 25   Engr.   Perf. 11½x11
B437 SP236 65c + 35c Prus
                grn   .60   .50
B438 SP236 90c + 60c yel
                              1.00   .75
B439 SP236 1.35fr + 1.15fr car 1.40 1.10
B440 SP236 3.15fr + 1.85fr ul-
                tra   2.00   1.60
B441 SP236 20fr + 20fr red
                vio   52.50 42.50
    Nos. B437-B441 (5)   57.50 46.45

The surtax was for victims of World War II.

Arms Type of 1946 Dated "1947"

Coats of Arms: 65c+35c, Nivelles. 90c+60c,
St. Trond. 1.35fr+1.15fr, Charleroi.
3.15fr+1.85fr, St. Nicolas. 20fr+20fr, Bouillon.

1947, Dec. 15   Perf. 11½
B442 SP241 65c + 35c org   .80   .65
B443 SP241 90c + 60c dp cl   .70   .65
B444 SP241 1.35fr + 1.15fr dk
                brn   1.00   .70
B445 SP241 3.15fr + 1.85fr dp
                bl   2.50   1.75
B446 SP241 20fr + 20fr dk
                grn   20.00 12.50
    Nos. B442-B446 (5)   25.00 16.25

The surtax was for anti-tuberculosis work.

St. Benedict and
King
Totila — SP247

Achel Abbey
SP248

3.15fr+2.85fr, St. Benedict, legislator &
builder. 10fr+10fr, Death of St. Benedict.

1948, Apr. 5   Photo.
B447 SP247 65c + 65c red
                brn   1.25   .55
B448 SP248 1.35fr + 1.35fr
                gray   1.75   .55
B449 SP247 3.15fr + 2.85fr dp
                ultra   2.50   1.90
B450 SP247 10fr + 10fr brt
                red vio   12.50 10.00
    Nos. B447-B450 (4)   18.00 13.00

The surtax was to aid the Abbey of the Trap-
pist Fathers at Achel.

St. Begga and
Chevremont
Castle — SP249

Chevremont
Basilica and
Convent
SP250

3.15fr+2.85fr, Madonna of Chevremont &
Chapel. 10fr+10fr, Madonna of Mt. Carmel.

1948, Apr. 5   Unwmk.
B451 SP249 65c + 65c bl
                grn   1.00   .55
B452 SP250 1.35fr + 1.35fr dk
                car rose   1.60   .55
B453 SP249 3.15fr + 2.85fr dp
                bl   2.25   1.90
B454 SP249 10fr + 10fr dp
                brn   12.00 10.00
    Nos. B451-B454 (4)   16.85 13.00

The surtax was to aid the Basilica of the
Carmelite Fathers of Chèvremont.

Anseele Monument
Showing French
Inscription — SP251

90c+60c, View of Ghent. 1.35fr+1.15fr, Van
Artevelde monument, Ghent. 3.15fr+1.85fr,
Anseele Monument, Flemish inscription.

1948, June 21   Perf. 14x13½
B455 SP251 65c + 35c
                rose red   2.75   1.10
B456 SP251 90c + 60c
                gray   3.50   1.90
B457 SP251 1.35fr + 1.15fr
                hn brn   2.25   1.50
B458 SP251 3.15fr + 1.85fr
                brt bl   8.50   5.00
    a. Souv. sheet, #B455-B458 140.00 55.00
    Nos. B455-B458 (4)   17.00   9.50

Issued to honor Edouard Anseele, states-
man, founder of the Belgian Socialist Party.
No. B458a sold for 50fr.
For surcharges see Nos. 395-398.

Statue "The
Unloader"
SP252

Underground
Fighter
SP253

1948, Sept. 4   Perf. 11½x11
B460 SP252 10fr + 10fr gray
                grn   35.00 19.00
B461 SP253 10fr + 10fr red
                brn   20.00 11.00

The surtax was used toward erection of
monuments at Antwerp and Liege.

Portrait Type of 1946 and

Double Barred
Cross — SP254

Designs: 4fr+3.25fr, Isabella of Austria.
20fr+20fr, Archduke Albert of Austria.

1948, Dec. 15   Photo.   Perf. 13½x14
B462 SP254 20c + 5c dk sl grn .50   .20
B463 SP254 1.20fr + 30c mag   1.25   .70
B464 SP254 1.75fr + 25c red   1.75   .60

**   Engr.   Perf. 11½x11**
B465 SP236 4fr + 3.25fr ultra 9.50   6.50
B466 SP236 20fr + 20fr Prus
                grn   42.50 30.00
    Nos. B462-B466 (5)   55.50 38.00

The surtax was divided among several
charities.

Souvenir Sheets

Rogier van der Weyden
Paintings — SP255

Paintings by van der Weyden (No. B466A):
90c, Virgin and Child. 1.75fr, Christ on the
Cross. 4fr, Mary Magdalene.
Paintings by Jordaens (No. B466B): 90c,
Woman Reading. 1.75fr, The Flutist. 4fr, Old
Woman Reading Letter.

1949, Apr. 1   Photo.   Perf. 11½
B466A SP255 Sheet of 3   125.00 110.00
    c.   90c deep brown   37.50   32.50
    d.   1.75fr deep rose lilac 37.50 32.50
    e.   4fr dark violet blue 37.50 32.50
B466B SP255 Sheet of 3   125.00 110.00
    f.   90c dark violet   37.50   32.50
    g.   1.75fr red   37.50   32.50
    h.   4fr blue   37.50   32.50

The surtax went to various cultural and philanthropic organizations. Sheets sold for 50fr
each.
Gum on Nos. B466A-B466B is irregularly
applied.

Guido
Gezelle — SP256

1949, Nov. 15   Photo.   Perf. 14x13½
B467 SP256 1.75fr + 75c Prus
                grn   2.50   1.75

50th anniversary of the death of Guido
Gezelle, poet. The surtax was for the Guido
Gezelle Museum, Bruges.

Portrait Type of 1946 and

Arnica — SP257

Designs: 65c+10c, Sand grass. 90c+10c,
Wood myrtle. 1.20fr+30c, Field poppy.
1.75fr+25c, Philip the Good. 3fr+1.50fr,
Charles V. 4fr+2fr, Maria-Christina. 6fr+3fr,
Charles of Lorraine. 8fr+4fr, Maria-Theresa.

1949, Dec. 20   Typo.   Perf. 13½x14
B468 SP257 20c + 5c multi   .50   .50
B469 SP257 65c + 10c multi 1.25   1.10
B470 SP257 90c + 10c multi 2.00   1.50
B471 SP257 1.20fr + 30c multi 2.50 1.75

**   Engr.   Perf. 11½x11**
B472 SP236 1.75fr + 25c red
                org   1.40   .80
B473 SP236 3fr + 1.50fr dp
                claret   10.00   6.75
B474 SP236 4fr + 2fr ultra 10.00   8.00
B475 SP236 6fr + 3fr choc 16.00 11.00
B476 SP236 8fr + 4fr dl grn 16.00   8.75
    Nos. B468-B476 (9)   59.65 40.15

The surtax was apportioned among several
welfare organizations.

Arms of
Belgium and
Great
Britain — SP258

British
Memorial — SP260

Design: 2.50fr+50c, British tanks at Hertain.

**   Perf. 13½x14, 11½**
1950, Mar. 15   Engr.
B477 SP258 80c + 20c grn   1.50   1.00
B478 SP258 2.50fr + 50c red 5.00 3.75
B479 SP258 4fr + 2fr dp bl 9.25   6.25
    Nos. B477-B479 (3)   15.75 11.00

6th anniv. of the liberation of Belgian territory by the British army.

Hurdling
SP261

Relay Race
SP262

Designs: 90c+10c, Javelin throwing. 4fr+2fr,
Pole vault. 8fr+4fr, Foot race.

**   Perf. 14x13½, 13½x14**
1950, July 1   Engr.   Unwmk.
B480 SP261 20c + 5c brt
                grn   .40   .20
B481 SP261 90c + 10c vio
                brn   2.75   1.50
B482 SP262 1.75fr + 25c car 5.25 1.75
    a.   Souvenir sheet of 1 45.00 35.00
B483 SP261 4fr + 2fr lt bl 27.50 17.00
B484 SP261 8fr + 4fr dp
                grn   29.00 18.00
    Nos. B480-B484 (5)   64.90 38.45

Issued to publicize the European Athletic
Games, Brussels, August 1950.
The margins of No. B482a were trimmed in
April, 1951, and an overprint ("25 Francs pour
le Fonds Sportif-25e Foire Internationale Bruxelles") was added in red in French and in black
in Flemish by a private committee. These pairs
of altered sheets were sold at the Brussels
Fair.

Gentian — SP263

Sijsele
Sanatorium
SP264

Tombeek
Sanatorium
SP265

Designs: 65c+10c, Cotton Grass. 90c+10c,
Foxglove. 1.20fr+30c, Limonia. 4fr+2fr, Jauche
Sanatorium.

1950, Dec. 20   Typo.   Perf. 14x13½
B485 SP263 20c + 5c multi   .80   .40
B486 SP263 65c + 10c multi 1.50   .85
B487 SP263 90c + 10c multi 1.60   1.10
B488 SP263 1.20fr + 30c multi 2.75 2.25

Perf. 11½
Engr.
Cross in Red

B489	SP264	1.75fr + 25c car	2.50	1.40
B490	SP264	4fr + 2fr blue	13.00	7.00
B491	SP265	8fr + 4fr bl grn	21.00	15.00
		Nos. B485-B491 (7)	43.15	28.00

The surtax was for tuberculosis prevention and other charitable purposes.

Chemist
SP266

Allegory of Peace
SP268

Colonial Instructor and Class SP267

1951, Mar. 27   Unwmk.

B492	SP266	80c + 20c grn	1.40	1.00
B493	SP267	2.50fr + 50c vio brn	9.50	5.00
B494	SP268	4fr + 2fr dp bl	10.50	6.00
		Nos. B492-B494 (3)	21.40	12.00

Surtax for the reconstruction fund of the UNESCO.

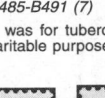

Monument to Political Prisoners — SP269

Fort of Breendonk SP270

8fr+4fr, Monument: profile of figure on pedestal.

1951, Aug. 20   Photo.   Perf. 11½

B495	SP269	1.75fr + 25c blk brn	2.50	1.75
B496	SP270	4fr + 2fr bl & sl gray	17.00	14.00
B497	SP269	8fr + 4fr dk bl grn	22.50	17.00
		Nos. B495-B497 (3)	42.00	32.75

The surtax was for the erection of a national monument.

Queen Elisabeth — SP271

1951, Sept. 22

B498	SP271	90c + 10c grnsh gray	1.75	.75
B499	SP271	1.75fr + 25c plum	2.25	1.50
B500	SP271	3fr + 1fr green	21.00	9.25
B501	SP271	4fr + 2fr gray bl	24.00	12.00
B502	SP271	8fr + 4fr sepia	30.00	14.00
		Nos. B498-B502 (5)	79.00	37.50

The surtax was for the Queen Elisabeth Medical Foundation.

Cross, Sun Rays and Dragon — SP272

Beersel Castle SP273

Horst Castle — SP274

Castles: 4fr+2fr, Lavaux St. Anne. 8fr+4fr, Veves.

1951, Dec. 17   Engr.   Unwmk.

B503	SP272	20c + 5c red	.25	.20
B504	SP272	65c + 10c dp ultra	.85	.60
B505	SP272	90c + 10c sep	.90	.80
B506	SP272	1.20fr + 30c rose vio	1.25	.90
B507	SP273	1.75fr + 75c red brn	1.75	1.50
B508	SP274	3fr + 1fr yel grn	12.00	7.50
B509	SP273	4fr + 2fr blue	14.00	8.50
B510	SP274	8fr + 4fr gray	19.00	11.00
		Nos. B503-B510 (8)	50.00	31.00

The surtax was for anti-tuberculosis work. See Nos. B523-B526, B547-B550.

Main Altar SP275

Basilica of the Sacred Heart Koekelberg SP276

Procession Bearing Relics of St. Albert of Louvain — SP277

1952, Mar. 1   Photo.   Perf. 11½

B511	SP275	1.75fr + 25c blk brn	1.50	1.25
B512	SP276	4fr + 2fr indigo	11.00	7.50

Engr.

B513	SP277	8fr + 4fr vio brn	15.00	9.25
a.		Souv. sheet, #B511-B513	250.00	125.00
		Nos. B511-B513 (3)	27.50	18.00

25th anniv. of the Cardinalate of J. E. Van Roey, Primate of Belgium. The surtax was for the Basilica. No. B513a sold for 30fr.

Beaulieu Castle, Malines SP278

August Vermeylen SP279

1952, May 14   Engr.
Laid Paper

B514	SP278	40fr + 10fr lt grnsh bl	175.00	175.00

Issued on the occasion of the 13th Universal Postal Union Congress, Brussels, 1952.

Perf. 11½
1952, Oct. 24   Unwmk.   Photo.

Portraits: 80c+40c, Karel Van de Woestijne. 90c+45c, Charles de Coster. 1.75fr+75c, M. Maeterlinck. 4fr+2fr, Emile Verhaeren. 8fr+4fr, Hendrik Conscience.

B515	SP279	65c + 30c pur	1.75	.90
B516	SP279	80c + 40c dk grn	3.75	1.10
B517	SP279	90c + 45c se-pia	2.75	1.25
B518	SP279	1.75fr + 75c cer	3.75	1.75
B519	SP279	4fr + 2fr bl vio	30.00	19.00
B520	SP279	8fr + 4fr dk brn	30.00	21.00
		Nos. B515-B520 (6)	72.00	45.00

1952, Nov. 15

4fr, Emile Verhaeren. 8fr, Hendrik Conscience.

B521	SP279	4fr (+ 9fr) blue	100.00	67.50
B522	SP279	8fr (+ 9fr) dk car rose	100.00	67.50

On Nos. B521-B522, the denomination is repeated at either side of the stamp. The surtax is expressed on se-tenant labels bearing quotations of Verhaeren (in French) and Conscience (in Flemish). Value is for stamp with label.

A 9-line black overprint was privately applied to these labels: "Conference Internationale de la Musique Bruxelles UNESCO International Music Conference Brussels 1953*"

Type of 1951 Dated "1952," and

Arms of Malmédy — SP281

Castle Ruins, Burgreuland SP282

Designs: 4fr+2fr, Vesdre Dam, Eupen. 8fr+4fr, St. Vitus, patron saint of Saint-Vith.

1952, Dec. 15   Engr.

B523	SP272	20c + 5c red brn	.40	.40
B524	SP272	80c + 20c grn	.85	.60
B525	SP272	1.20fr + 30c lil rose	1.75	1.00
B526	SP272	1.50fr + 50c ol brn	1.75	1.00
B527	SP281	2fr + 75c car	3.25	2.25
B528	SP282	3fr + 1.50fr choc	14.00	8.75
B529	SP281	4fr + 2fr blue	12.00	8.00
B530	SP281	8fr + 4fr vio brn	21.00	11.00
		Nos. B523-B530 (8)	55.00	33.00

The surtax on Nos. B523-B530 was for anti-tuberculosis and other charitable works.

Walthère Dewé SP283

Princess Josephine-Charlotte SP284

1953, Feb. 16   Photo.

B531	SP283	2fr + 1fr brn car	3.25	1.75

The surtax was for the construction of a memorial to Walthère Dewé, Underground leader in World War II.

1953, Mar. 14   Cross in Red

B532	SP284	80c + 20c ol grn	1.25	.70
B533	SP284	1.20fr + 30c brn	1.75	.80
B534	SP284	2fr + 50c rose lake	1.25	1.25
a.		Booklet pane of 8	80.00	65.00
B535	SP284	2.50fr + 50c crim	14.00	6.75
B536	SP284	4fr + 1fr brt blue	9.25	5.25
B537	SP284	5fr + 2fr sl grn	11.00	6.75
		Nos. B532-B537 (6)	38.50	21.50

The surtax was for the Belgian Red Cross.

The selvage of No. B534a is inscribed in French. Value for selvage inscribed in Dutch, $150.

Boats at Dock SP285

Bridge and Citadel, Namur — SP286

Allegory — SP287

Designs: 1.20fr+30c, Bridge at Bouillon. 2fr+50c, Antwerp waterfront. 4fr+2fr, Wharf at Ghent. 8fr+4fr, Meuse River at Freyr.

1953, June 22   Unwmk.   Perf. 11½

B538	SP285	80c + 20c grn	1.00	.90
B539	SP285	1.20fr + 30c redsh brn	1.75	1.60
B540	SP285	2fr + 50c sep	2.25	2.00
B541	SP286	2.50fr + 50c dp mag	11.00	8.50
B542	SP286	4fr + 2fr vio bl	16.00	8.50
B543	SP286	8fr + 4fr gray blk	20.00	8.50
		Nos. B538-B543 (6)	52.00	30.00

The surtax was used to promote tourism in the Ardenne-Meuse region and for various cultural works.

1953, Oct. 26   Engr.

B544	SP287	80c + 20c grn	3.50	2.50
B545	SP287	2.50fr + 1fr rose car	32.50	24.00
B546	SP287	4fr + 1.50fr blue	37.50	30.00
		Nos. B544-B546 (3)	73.50	56.50

The surtax was for the European Bureau of Childhood and Youth.

Type of 1951 Dated "1953," and

Ernest Malvoz — SP288

Robert Koch SP289

Portraits: 3fr+1.50fr, Carlo Forlanini. 4fr+2fr, Leon Charles Albert Calmette.

1953, Dec. 15

B547	SP272	20c + 5c blue	.50	.50
B548	SP272	80c + 20c rose vio	1.00	.60
B549	SP272	1.20fr + 30c choc	1.25	.80
B550	SP272	1.50fr + 50c dk gray	1.75	1.00
B551	SP288	2fr + 75c dk grn	3.00	1.60
B552	SP288	3fr + 1.50fr dk red	13.00	8.50
B553	SP288	4fr + 2fr ultra	11.00	7.00
B554	SP289	8fr + 4fr choc	17.50	10.00
	Nos. B547-B554 (8)		49.00	30.00

The surtax was for anti-tuberculosis and other charitable works.

King Albert I Statue — SP290

Albert I Monument, Namur SP291

9fr+4.50fr, Cliffs of Marche-les-Dames.

1954, Feb. 17   Photo.

B555	SP290	2fr + 50c chnt brn	2.50	1.75
B556	SP291	4fr + 2fr blue	15.00	11.00
B557	SP290	9fr + 4.50fr ol blk	22.50	12.00
	Nos. B555-B557 (3)		40.00	24.75

20th anniv. of the death of King Albert I. The surtax aided in the erection of the monument pictured on #B556.

Political Prisoners' Monument SP292

Camp and Fort, Breendonk SP293

Design: 9fr+4.50fr, Political prisoners' monument (profile).

1954, Apr. 1   Unwmk.   Perf. 11½

B558	SP292	2fr + 1fr red	12.50	7.00
B559	SP293	4fr + 2fr dk brn	30.00	17.50
B560	SP292	9fr + 4.50fr ol grn	32.50	17.50
	Nos. B558-B560 (3)		75.00	42.00

The surtax was used toward the creation of a monument to political prisoners.

Gatehouse and Gateway SP294

Nuns in Courtyard SP295

Our Lady of the Vine SP296

2fr+1fr, Swans in stream. 7fr+3.50fr, Nuns at well. 8fr+4fr, Statue above door.

1954, May 15

B561	SP294	80c + 20c dk bl grn	1.00	.75
B562	SP294	2fr + 1fr crim	11.00	1.50
B563	SP295	4fr + 2fr violet	16.00	9.25
B564	SP295	7fr + 3.50fr lil rose	35.00	22.50
B565	SP295	8fr + 4fr brown	32.50	19.00
B566	SP296	9fr + 4.50fr gray bl	55.00	30.00
	Nos. B561-B566 (6)		150.50	83.00

The surtax was for the Friends of the Beguinage of Bruges.

Child's Head — SP297

"The Blind Man and the Paralytic," by Antoine Carte SP298

1954, Dec. 1   Engr.

B567	SP297	20c + 5c dk grn	.50	.50
B568	SP297	80c + 20c dk gray	1.00	.90
B569	SP297	1.20fr + 30c org brn	1.50	1.00
B570	SP297	1.50fr + 50c pur	1.75	1.60
B571	SP298	2fr + 75c rose car	7.25	3.50
B572	SP298	4fr + 1fr brt blue	16.00	9.50
	Nos. B567-B572 (6)		28.00	17.00

The surtax was for anti-tuberculosis work.

Ernest Solvay SP299

Jean-Jacques Dony — SP300

Portraits: 1.20fr+30c, Egide Walschaerts. 25fr+50c, Leo H. Baekeland. 3fr+1fr, Jean-Etienne Lenoir. 4fr+2fr, Emile Fourcault and Emile Gobbe.

        Perf. 11½

1955, Oct. 22   Unwmk.   Photo.

B573	SP299	20c + 5c brn & dk brn	.40	.35
B574	SP300	80c + 20c vio	1.00	.50
B575	SP299	1.20fr + 30c ind	1.10	.65
B576	SP300	2fr + 50c dp car	4.00	2.50
B577	SP300	3fr + 1fr dk grn	12.50	6.25
B578	SP299	4fr + 2fr brown	12.50	6.25
	Nos. B573-B578 (6)		31.50	16.50

Issued in honor of Belgian scientists.
The surtax was for the benefit of various cultural organizations.

"The Joys of Spring" by E. Canneel SP301

Einar Holböll SP302

Portraits: 4fr+2fr, John D. Rockefeller. 8fr+4fr, Sir Robert W. Philip.

1955, Dec. 5   Unwmk.   Perf. 11½

B579	SP301	20c + 5c red lil	.70	.30
B580	SP301	80c + 20c green	1.00	.65
B581	SP301	1.20fr + 30c redsh brn	1.40	.80
B582	SP301	1.50fr + 50c vio bl	1.40	1.00
B583	SP302	2fr + 50c car	8.50	4.75
B584	SP302	4fr + 2fr ultra	17.50	10.00
B585	SP302	8fr + 4fr ol gray	21.00	12.50
	Nos. B579-B585 (7)		51.50	30.00

The surtax was for anti-tuberculosis work.

Palace of Charles of Lorraine — SP303

Queen Elisabeth and Sonata by Mozart — SP304

Design: 2fr+1fr, Mozart at age 7.

1956, Mar. 5   Engr.

B586	SP303	80c + 20c steel bl	1.00	1.00
B587	SP303	2fr + 1fr rose lake	4.25	3.00
B588	SP304	4fr + 2fr dull pur	6.75	3.75
	Nos. B586-B588 (3)		12.00	7.75

200th anniversary of the birth of Wolfgang Amadeus Mozart, composer.

The surtax was for the benefit of the Pro-Mozart Committee in Belgium.

Queen Elisabeth — SP305

1956, Aug. 16   Photo.

B589	SP305	80c + 20c slate grn	1.00	1.00
B590	SP305	2fr + 1fr deep plum	2.75	1.50
B591	SP305	4fr + 2fr brown	4.25	2.50
	Nos. B589-B591 (3)		8.00	5.00

Issued in honor of the 80th birthday of Queen Elisabeth. The surtax went to the Queen Elisabeth Foundation. See No. 659.

Ship with Cross — SP306

Infant on Scales SP307

Rehabilitation SP308

Design: 4fr+2fr, X-Ray examination.

1956, Dec. 17   Engr.

B592	SP306	20c + 5c redsh brn	.35	.30
B593	SP306	80c + 20c grn	.75	.60
B594	SP306	1.20fr + 30c dl lil	.90	.60
B595	SP306	1.5fr + 50c lt sl bl	.95	.90
B596	SP307	2fr + 50c ol grn	2.25	1.60
B597	SP307	4fr + 2fr dl pur car	11.00	6.25
B598	SP308	8fr + 4fr dp car	11.00	7.25
	Nos. B592-B598 (7)		27.20	17.50

The surtax was for anti-tuberculosis work.

Charles Plisnier and Albrecht Rodenbach SP309

80c+20c, Emiel Vliebergh & Maurice Wilmotte. 1.20fr+30c, Paul Pastur & Julius Hoste. 2fr+50c, Lodewijk de Raet & Jules Destree. 3fr+1fr, Constantin Meunier & Constant Permeke. 4fr+2fr, Lieven Gevaert & Edouard Empain.

        Perf. 11½

1957, June 8   Unwmk.   Photo.

B599	SP309	20c + 5c brt vio	.40	.35
B600	SP309	80c + 20c lt red brn	.55	.35
B601	SP309	1.20f + 30c blk brn	.65	.60
B602	SP309	2fr + 50c claret	1.60	.95
B603	SP309	3fr + 1fr dk ol grn	2.25	1.75
B604	SP309	4fr + 2fr vio bl	3.25	2.50
	Nos. B599-B604 (6)		8.70	6.50

The surtax was for the benefit of various cultural organizations.

BELGIUM

709

Dogs and Antarctic Camp SP310

1957, Oct. 18 — Engr. — Perf. 11½

B605	SP310	5fr + 2.50fr gray, org & vio brn	3.00	2.25
a.		Sheet of 4, #B605b	140.00	125.00
b.		Blue, slate & red brown	30.00	25.00

Surtax for Belgian Antarctic Expedition, 1957-58.

Gen. Patton's Grave and Flag SP311

Gen. George S. Patton, Jr. — SP312

Designs: 2.50fr+50c, Memorial, Bastogne. 3fr+1fr, Gen. Patton decorating Brig. Gen. Anthony C. McAuliffe. 6fr+3fr, Tanks of 1918 and 1944.

1957, Oct. 28 — Photo.

Size: 36x25mm, 25x36mm

B606	SP311	1fr + 50c dk gray	1.25	.90
B607	SP311	2.50fr + 50c ol grn	1.75	1.50
B608	SP311	3fr + 1fr red brn	2.75	1.60
B609	SP312	5fr + 2.50fr grysh bl	6.25	5.00

Size: 53x35mm

B610	SP311	6fr + 3fr pale brn car	10.00	6.00
		Nos. B606-B610 (5)	22.00	15.00

The surtax was for the General Patton Memorial Committee and Patriotic Societies.

Adolphe Max — SP313

1957, Nov. 10 — Engr.

B611	SP313	2.50fr + 1fr ultra	1.25	.75

18th anniversary of the death of Adolphe Max, mayor of Brussels. The surtax was for the national "Adolphe Max" fund.

"Chinels," Fosses SP314

"Op Signoorken," Malines SP315

Infanta Isabella Shooting Crossbow SP316

Legends: 1.50fr+50c, St. Remacle and the wolf. 2fr+1fr, Longman and the pea soup. 5fr+2fr, The Virgin with Inkwell, vert. 6fr+2.50fr, "Gilles" (clowns), Binche.

1957, Dec. 14 — Engr. & Photo.

B612	SP314	30c + 20c	.20	.30
B613	SP315	1fr + 50c	.40	.30
B614	SP314	1.50fr + 50c	.80	.50
B615	SP315	2fr + 1fr	1.10	1.00
B616	SP315	2.50fr + 1fr	1.25	.90
B617	SP316	5fr + 2fr	3.25	2.25
B618	SP316	6fr + 2.50fr	4.50	3.25
		Nos. B612-B618 (7)	11.50	8.50

The surtax was for anti-tuberculosis work. See Nos. B631-B637.

Benelux Gate SP317

Designs: 1fr+50c, Civil Engineering Pavilion. 1.50fr+50c, Ruanda-Urundi Pavilion. 2.50fr+1fr, Belgium 1900. 3fr+1.50fr, Atomium. 5fr+3fr, Telexpo Pavilion.

Perf. 11½

1958, Apr. 15 — Unwmk. — Engr.

Size: 35½x24½mm

B619	SP317	30c + 20c multi	.20	.20
B620	SP317	1fr + 50c multi	.20	.20
B621	SP317	1.50fr + 50c multi	.25	.25
B622	SP317	2.50fr + 1fr multi	.45	.45
B623	SP317	3fr + 1.50fr multi	.90	.50

Size: 49x33mm

B624	SP317	5fr + 3fr multi	1.10	.50
		Nos. B619-B624 (6)	3.10	2.10

World's Fair, Brussels, Apr. 17-Oct. 19.

Marguerite van Eyck by Jan van Eyck — SP318

Christ Carrying Cross, by Hieronymus Bosch SP319

Paintings: 1.50fr+50c, St. Donatien, Jan Gossart. 2.50fr+1fr, Self-portrait, Lambert Lombard. 3fr+1.50fr, The Rower, James Ensor. 5fr+3fr, Henriette, Henri Evenepoel.

1958, Oct. 30 — Photo. — Perf. 11½
Various Frames in Ocher and Brown

B625	SP318	30c + 20c dk ol grn	.25	.30
B626	SP319	1fr + 50c mar	.75	.70
B627	SP318	1.50fr + 50c vio bl	1.00	.75
B628	SP318	2.50fr + 1fr dk brn	2.00	1.25
B629	SP319	3fr + 1.50fr dl red	2.75	2.00
B630	SP318	5fr + 3fr brt bl	5.25	5.00
		Nos. B625-B630 (6)	12.00	10.00

The surtax was for the benefit of various cultural organizations.

Type of 1957

Legends: 40c+10c, Elizabeth, Countess of Hoogstraten. 1fr+50c, Jean de Nivelles. 1.50fr+50c, St. Evermare play, Russon. 2fr+1fr, The Penitents of Furnes. 2.50fr+1fr, Manger and "Pax." 5fr+2fr, Sambre-Meuse

procession. 6fr+2.50fr, Our Lady of Peace and "Pax," vert.

Engraved and Photogravure

1958, Dec. 6 — Unwmk. — Perf. 11½

B631	SP314	40c + 10c ultra & brt grn	.30	.20
B632	SP315	1fr + 50c gray brn & org	.40	.30
B633	SP315	1.50fr + 50c cl & brt grn	.60	.35
B634	SP314	2fr + 1fr brn & red	.70	.50
B635	SP316	2.50fr + 1fr vio brn & bl grn	2.50	1.90
B636	SP316	5fr + 2fr cl & bl	3.75	3.00
B637	SP316	6fr + 2.50fr bl & rose red	4.75	4.50
		Nos. B631-B637 (7)	13.00	10.75

The surtax was for anti-tuberculosis work.

"Europe of the Heart" SP320

1959, Feb. 25 — Photo. — Unwmk.

B638	SP320	1fr + 50c red lil	.55	.30
B639	SP320	2.50fr + 1fr dk grn	.95	.90
B640	SP320	5fr + 2.50fr dp brn	1.25	1.10
		Nos. B638-B640 (3)	2.75	2.30

The surtax was for aid for displaced persons.

Allegory of Blood Transfusion SP321

Henri Dunant and Battlefield at Solferino — SP322

Design: 2.50fr+1fr, 3fr+1.50fr, Red Cross, broken sword and drop of blood, horiz.

1959, June 10 — Photo. — Perf. 11½

B641	SP321	40c + 10c	.60	.30
B642	SP321	1fr + 50c	1.10	.45
B643	SP321	1.50fr + 50c	1.40	.60
B644	SP321	2.50fr + 1fr	1.90	1.10
B645	SP321	3fr + 1.50fr	4.75	2.50
B646	SP322	5fr + 3fr	7.25	3.25
		Nos. B641-B646 (6)	17.00	8.20

Cent. of the Intl. Red Cross idea. Surtax for the Red Cross and patriotic organizations.

Philip the Good — SP323

Arms of Philip the Good SP324

Designs: 1fr+50c, Charles the Bold. 1.50fr+50c, Emperor Maximilian of Austria. 2.50fr+1fr, Philip the Fair. 3fr+1.50fr, Charles V. Portraits after miniatures by Simon Bening (c. 1483-1561).

1959, July 4 — Engr.

B647	SP323	40c + 10c multi	.50	.35
B648	SP323	1fr + 50c multi	.80	.50
B649	SP323	1.50fr + 50c multi	.95	.75
B650	SP323	2.50fr + 1fr multi	1.25	1.40
B651	SP323	3fr + 1.50fr multi	3.25	3.00
B652	SP324	5fr + 3fr multi	5.25	4.00
		Nos. B647-B652 (6)	12.00	10.00

The surtax was for the Royal Library, Brussels.
Portraits show Grand Masters of the Order of the Golden Fleece.

Whale, Antwerp SP325

Carnival, Stavelot SP326

Designs: 1fr+50c, Dragon, Mons. 2fr+50c, Prince Carnival, Eupen. 3fr+1fr, Jester and cats, Ypres. 6fr+2fr, Holy Family, horiz. 7fr+3fr, Madonna, Liége, horiz.

Engraved and Photogravure

1959, Dec. 5 — Perf. 11½

B653	SP325	40c + 10c cit, Prus bl & red	.45	.40
B654	SP325	1fr + 50c ol & grn	.75	.60
B655	SP325	2fr + 50c lt brn, org & cl	.50	.40
B656	SP326	2.50fr + 1fr gray, pur & ultra	.80	.60
B657	SP326	3fr + 1fr gray, mar & yel	1.75	1.25
B658	SP326	6fr + 2fr ol, brt bl & hn brn	3.25	2.50
B659	SP326	7fr + 3fr chlky bl & org yel	5.00	4.25
		Nos. B653-B659 (7)	12.50	10.00

The surtax was for anti-tuberculosis work.

Child Refugee — SP327

Designs: 3fr+1.50fr, Man. 6fr+3fr, Woman.

1960, Apr. 7 — Engr.

B660	SP327	40c + 10c rose claret	.20	.20
B661	SP327	3fr + 1.50fr gray brn	.65	.50
B662	SP327	6fr + 3fr dk bl	1.60	1.10
a.		Souvenir sheet of 3	50.00	45.00
		Nos. B660-B662 (3)	2.45	1.80

World Refugee Year, 7/1/59-6/30/60.
No. B662a contains Nos. B660-B662 with colors changed: 40c+10c, dull purple; 3fr+1.50fr, red brown; 6fr+3fr, henna brown.

Parachutists and Plane
SP328

Designs: 2fr+50c, 2.50fr+1fr, Parachutists coming in for landing, vert 3fr+1fr, 6fr+2fr, Parachutist walking with parachute.

Photogravure and Engraved
1960, June 13 Perf. 11½
Multicolored

B663	SP328	40c + 10c	.20	.20
B664	SP328	1fr + 50c	.80	.55
B665	SP328	2fr + 50c	2.75	1.25
B666	SP328	2.50fr+1fr	3.00	2.00
B667	SP328	3fr + 1fr	3.00	2.00
B668	SP328	6fr + 2fr	6.25	4.00
	Nos. B663-B668 (6)		16.00	10.00

The surtax was for various patriotic and cultural organizations.

Mother and Child, Planes and Rainbow
SP329

Designs: 40c+10c, Brussels Airport, planes and rainbow. 6fr+3fr, Rainbow connecting Congo and Belgium, and planes, vert.

Perf. 11½
1960, Aug. 3 Unwmk. Photo.
Size: 35x24mm

B669	SP329	40c + 10c grnsh blue	.20	.20
B670	SP329	3fr + 1.50fr brt red	2.50	2.25

Size: 35x52mm

B671	SP329	6fr + 3fr violet	3.75	3.00
	Nos. B669-B671 (3)		6.45	5.45

The surtax was for refugees from Congo.

Infant, Milk Bottle and Mug — SP330

UNICEF: 1fr+50c, Nurse and children of 3 races. 2fr+50c, Refugee woman carrying gift clothes. 2.50fr+1fr, Negro nurse weighing infant. 3fr+1fr, Children of various races dancing. 6fr+2fr, Refugee boys.

Photogravure and Engraved
1960, Oct. 8 Perf. 11½

B672	SP330	40c + 10c gldn brn, yel & bl grn	.20	.20
B673	SP330	1fr + 50c ol gray, mar & slate	1.40	.75
B674	SP330	2fr + 50c vio, pale brn & brt grn	1.50	1.10
B675	SP330	2.50fr + 1fr dk red, sep & lt bl	1.75	1.40
B676	SP330	3fr + 1fr bl grn, red org & dl vio	.95	.85
B677	SP330	6fr + 2fr ultra, emer & brn	3.75	3.25
	Nos. B672-B677 (6)		9.55	7.55

Tapestry
SP331

Belgian handicrafts: 1fr+50c, Cut crystal vases, vert. 2fr+50c, Lace, vert. 2.50fr+1fr, Metal plate & jug. 3fr+1fr, Diamonds. 6fr+2fr, Ceramics.

1960, Dec. 5 Perf. 11½
Multicolored

B678	SP331	40c + 10c	.25	.25
B679	SP331	1fr + 50c	1.00	1.00
B680	SP331	2fr + 50c	2.00	1.50
B681	SP331	2.50fr+1fr	2.50	2.25
B682	SP331	3fr + 1fr	1.25	1.00
B683	SP331	6fr + 2fr	5.00	4.00
	Nos. B678-B683 (6)		12.00	10.00

The surtax was for anti-tuberculosis work.

Jacob Kats and Abbe Nicolas Pietkin SP332

Portraits: 1fr+50c, Albert Mockel and J. F. Willems. 2fr+50c, Jan van Rijswijck and Xavier M. Neujean. 2.50fr+1fr, Joseph Demarteau and A. Van de Perre. 3fr+1fr, Canon Jan-Baptist David and Albert du Bois. 6fr+2fr, Henri Vieuxtemps and Willem de Mol.

1961, Apr. 22 Unwmk. Perf. 11½
Multicolored
Portraits in Gray Brown

B684	SP332	40c + 10c	.25	.25
B685	SP332	1fr + 50c	1.50	1.00
B686	SP332	2fr + 50c	1.75	1.50
B687	SP332	2.50fr + 1fr	2.75	1.50
B688	SP332	3fr + 1fr	2.75	2.50
B689	SP332	6fr + 2fr	5.00	4.25
	Nos. B684-B689 (6)		14.00	11.00

The surtax was for the benefit of various cultural organizations.

White Rhinoceros
SP333

Animals: 1fr+50c, Przewalski horses. 2fr+50c, Okapi. 2.50fr+1fr, Giraffe, horiz. 3fr+1fr, Lesser panda, horiz. 6fr+2fr, European elk, horiz.

Perf. 11½
1961, June 5 Unwmk. Photo.
Multicolored

B690	SP333	40c + 10c	.20	.25
B691	SP333	1fr + 50c	.90	.90
B692	SP333	2fr + 50c	1.40	1.25
B693	SP333	2.50fr + 1fr	1.10	1.10
B694	SP333	3fr + 1fr	1.00	1.00
B695	SP333	6fr + 2fr	2.25	1.50
	Nos. B690-B695 (6)		6.85	6.00

The surtax was for various philanthropic organizations.

Antonius Cardinal Perrenot de Granvelle — SP334

Designs: 3fr+1.50fr, Arms of Cardinal de Granvelle. 6fr+3fr, Tower and crosier, symbolic of collaboration between Malines and the Archbishopric.

1961, July 29 Engr.

B696	SP334	40c + 10c mag, car & brn	.20	.20
B697	SP334	3fr + 1.50fr multi	.65	.50
B698	SP334	6fr + 3fr mag pur & bis	1.25	1.10
	Nos. B696-B698 (3)		2.10	1.80

400th anniv. of Malines as an Archbishopric.

Mother and Child by Pierre Paulus — SP335

Plaintings: 1fr+50c, Mother Love, Francois-Joseph Navez. 2fr+50c, Motherhood, Constant Permeke. 2.50fr+1fr, Madonna and Child, Rogier van der Weyden. 3fr+1fr, Madonna with Apple, Hans Memling. 6fr+2fr, Madonna of the Forget-me-not, Peter Paul Rubens.

1961, Dec. 2 Photo. Perf. 11½
Gold Frame

B699	SP335	40c + 10c dp brn	.20	.20
B700	SP335	1fr + 50c brt bl	.40	.30
B701	SP335	2fr + 50c rose red	.60	.40
B702	SP335	2.50fr + 1fr mag	.85	.75
B703	SP335	3fr + 1fr vio bl	1.00	.85
B704	SP335	6fr + 2fr dk sl grn	1.75	1.50
	Nos. B699-B704 (6)		4.80	4.00

The surtax was for anti-tuberculosis work.

Castle of the Counts of Male — SP336

Designs: 90c+10c, Royal library, horiz. 1fr+50c, Church of Our Lady, Tongres. 2fr+50c, Collegiate Church, Soignies, horiz. 2.50fr+1fr, Church of Our Lady, Malines. 3fr+1fr, St. Denis Abbey, Broqueroi. 6fr+2fr, Cloth Hall, Ypres, horiz.

1962, Mar. 12 Engr. Perf. 11½

B705	SP336	40c + 10c brt grn	.20	.20
B706	SP336	90c + 10c lil rose	.20	.20
B707	SP336	1fr + 50c dl vio	.40	.45
B708	SP336	2fr + 50c violet	.70	.60
B709	SP336	2.50fr + 1fr red brn	1.00	.85
B710	SP336	3fr + 1fr bl grn	1.00	.85
B711	SP336	6fr + 2fr car rose	1.50	1.40
	Nos. B705-B711 (7)		5.00	4.55

The surtax was for various cultural and philanthropic organizations.

Andean Cock of the Rock — SP337

Birds: 1fr+50c, Red lory. 2fr+50c, Guinea touraco. 2.50fr+1fr, Keel-billed toucan. 3fr+1fr, Great bird of paradise. 6fr+2fr, Congolese peacock.

Engraved and Photogravure
1962, June 23 Unwmk. Perf. 11½

B712	SP337	40c + 10c multi	.20	.20
B713	SP337	1fr + 50c multi	.45	.25
B714	SP337	2fr + 50c multi	.50	.40
B715	SP337	2.50fr + 1fr multi	.55	.45
B716	SP337	3fr + 1fr multi	1.10	.95
B717	SP337	6fr + 2fr multi	2.00	1.75
	Nos. B712-B717 (6)		4.80	4.00

The surtax was for various philanthropic organizations.

Handicapped Child — SP338

Handicapped Children: 40c+10c, Reading Braille. 2fr+50c, Deaf-mute girl with earphones and electronic equipment, horiz. 2.50fr+1fr, Child with ball (cerebral palsy). 3fr+1fr, Girl with crutches (polio). 6fr+2fr, Sitting boys playing ball, horiz.

1962, Sept. 22 Photo.

B718	SP338	40c + 10c choc	.20	.20
B719	SP338	1fr + 50c rose red	.30	.30
B720	SP338	2fr + 50c brt lil	.55	.65
B721	SP338	2.50fr + 1fr dl grn	.65	.65
B722	SP338	3fr + 1fr dk blue	.80	.80
B723	SP338	6fr + 2fr dk brn	1.50	1.25
	Nos. B718-B723 (6)		4.00	3.80

The surtax was for various institutions for handicapped children.

Queen Louise-Marie SP339

Belgian Queens: No. B725, like No. B724 with "ML" initials. 1fr+50c, Marie-Henriette. 2fr+1fr, Elisabeth. 3fr+1.50fr, Astrid. 8fr+2.50fr, Fabiola.

1962, Dec. 8 Photo. & Engr.
Gray, Black & Gold

B724	SP339	40c + 10c ("L")	.20	.20
B725	SP339	40c + 10c ("ML")	.20	.20
B726	SP339	1fr + 50c	.50	.50
B727	SP339	2fr + 1fr	.85	.85
B728	SP339	3fr + 1.50fr	.95	.85
B729	SP339	8fr + 2.50fr	1.40	1.00
	Nos. B724-B729 (6)		4.10	3.60

The surtax was for anti-tuberculosis work.

British War Memorial (Porte de Menin), Ypres SP340

1962, Dec. 26 Engr. Perf. 11½

B730	SP340	1fr + 50c multi	.50	.50

Millennium of the city of Ypres. Issued in sheets of eight.

Peace Bell Ringing over Globe — SP341

Engraved and Photogravure
1963, Feb. 18 Unwmk. Perf. 11½

B731	SP341	3fr + 1.50fr multi	1.50	1.50
a.		Sheet of 4	7.25	7.25
B732	SP341	6fr + 3fr multi	.75	.75

The surtax was for the installation of the Peace Bell (Bourdon de la Paix) at Koekelberg Basilica and for the benefit of various cultural organizations.

#B731 was issued in sheets of 4, #B732 in sheets of 30.

The Sower by
Brueghel — SP342

Designs: 3fr+1fr, The Harvest, by Brueghel,
horiz. 6fr+2fr, "Bread," by Anton Carte, horiz.

1963, Mar. 21   *Perf. 11½*
B733 SP342 2fr +1fr multi   .20 .20
B734 SP342 3fr +1fr multi   .40 .30
B735 SP342 6fr +2fr multi   .55 .50
    Nos. B733-B735 (3)   1.15 1.00
FAO "Freedom from Hunger" campaign.

Speed
Racing — SP343

2fr+1fr, Bicyclists at check point, horiz.
3fr+1.50fr, Team racing, horiz. 6fr+3fr, Pace
setters.

          Perf. 11½
1963, July 13   Unwmk.   Engr.
B736 SP343 1fr + 50c multi   .20 .20
B737 SP343 2fr + 1fr bl, car, blk
              & ol gray   .20 .20
B738 SP343 3fr + 1.50fr multi   .35 .35
B739 SP343 6fr + 3fr multi   .50 .50
    Nos. B736-B739 (4)   1.25 1.25
80th anniversary of the founding of the Belgian Bicycle League. The surtax was for athletes at the 1964 Olympic Games.

Princess Paola with
Princess
Astrid — SP344

Prince Albert and Family — SP345

Designs: 40c+10c, Prince Philippe. 2fr+50c,
Princess Astrid. 2.50fr+1fr, Princess Paola.
6fr+2fr, Prince Albert.

1963, Sept. 28   Photo.
B740 SP344 40c + 10c   .20 .20
B741 SP344 1fr + 50c   .35 .30
B742 SP344 2fr + 50c   .45 .40
B743 SP344 2.50fr + 1fr   .45 .40
B744 SP345 3fr + 1fr brn &
              multi   .45 .45
B745 SP345 3fr + 1fr yel
              grn & mul-
              ti   1.50 1.40
  a. Booklet pane of 8   17.00 17.00
B746 SP344 6fr + 2fr   .90 .85
    Nos. B740-B746 (7)   4.30 4.00
    Cent. of the Intl, Red Cross. No. B745
issued in booklet panes of 8, which are in two
forms: French and Flemish inscriptions in top
and bottom margins transposed. Value the
same.

Daughter of
Balthazar Gerbier,
Painted by
Rubens — SP346

Jesus, St. John and Cherubs by
Rubens — SP347

Portraits (Rubens' sons): 1fr+40c, Nicolas, 2
yrs. old. 2fr+50c, Franz. 2.50fr+1fr, Nicolas, 6
yrs. old. 3fr+1fr, Albert.

Photogravure and Engraved
1963, Dec. 7 Unwmk. Perf. 11½
B747 SP346 50c + 10c   .20 .20
B748 SP346 1fr + 40c   .20 .20
B749 SP346 2fr + 50c   .20 .20
B750 SP346 2.50fr + 1fr   .45 .45
B751 SP346 3fr + 1fr   .35 .35
B752 SP347 6fr + 2fr   .45 .45
    Nos. B747-B752 (6)   1.85 1.85
    The surtax was for anti-tuberculosis work.
See No. B771.

John Quincy Adams and Lord
Gambier Signing Treaty of Ghent, by
Amédée Forestier — SP348

1964, May 16 Photo. Perf. 11½
B753 SP348 6fr + 3fr dk blue   .75 .75
Signing of the Treaty of Ghent between the
US and Great Britain, Dec. 24, 1814.

Philip van
Marnix — SP349

Portraits: 3fr+1.50fr, Ida de Bure Calvin.
6fr+3fr, Jacob Jordaens.

1964, May 30   Engr.
B754 SP349 1fr + 50c blue gray   .20 .20
B755 SP349 3fr + 1.50fr rose pink .25 .25
B756 SP349 6fr + 3fr redsh brn   .45 .45
    Nos. B754-B756 (3)   .90 .90
    Issued to honor Protestantism in Belgium.
The surtax was for the erection of a Protestant
church.

Foot Soldier,
1918 — SP350

Designs: 2fr+1fr, Flag bearer, Guides Regiment, 1914. 3fr+1.50fr, Trumpeter of the Grenadiers and drummers, 1914.

1964, Aug. 1 Photo. Perf. 11½
B757 SP350 1fr + 50c multi   .20 .20
B758 SP350 2fr + 1fr multi   .25 .25
B759 SP350 3fr + 1.50fr multi .25 .25
    Nos. B757-B759 (3)   .70 .70
50th anniversary of the German aggression
against Belgium in 1914. The surtax aided
patriotic undertakings.

Battle of
Bastogne — SP351

6fr+3fr, Liberation of the estuary of the
Escaut.

1964, Aug. 1   Unwmk.
B760 SP351 3fr + 1fr multi   .20 .20
B761 SP351 6fr + 3fr multi   .30 .30
    Belgium's Resistance and liberation of
World War II. The surtax was to help found an
International Student Center at Antwerp and
to aid cultural undertakings.

Souvenir Sheets

Rogier van der Weyden
Paintings — SP352

Descent From the Cross — SP353

1964, Sept. 19 Photo. Perf. 11½
B762 SP352 Sheet of 3   2.25 2.25
  a.   1fr Philip the Good   .50 .50
  b.   2fr Portrait of a Lady   .50 .50
  c.   3fr Man with Arrow   .50 .50

                Engr.
B763 SP353 8fr red brown   2.25 2.25
Rogier van der Weyden (Roger de La Pasture, 1400-64). The surtax went to various cultural organizations. #B762 sold for 14fr, #B763
for 16fr.

Ancient View of the Pand — SP354

3fr+1fr, Present view of the Pand from Lys
River.

1964, Oct. 10   Photo.
B764 SP354 2fr + 1fr blk, grnsh bl
              & ultra   .40 .40
B765 SP354 3fr + 1fr lil rose, bl &
              dk brn   .40 .40
    The surtax was for the restoration of the
Pand Dominican Abbey in Ghent.

Type of 1963 and

Child of Charles I,
Painted by Van
Dyck — SP355

Designs: 1fr+40c, William of Orange with his
bride, by Van Dyck. 2fr+1fr, Portrait of a small
boy with dogs by Erasmus Quellin and Jan
Fyt. 3fr+1fr, Alexander Farnese by Antonio
Moro. 4fr+2fr, William II, Prince of Orange by
Van Dyck. 6fr+3fr, Artist's children by Cornelis
De Vos.

1964, Dec. 5 Engr. Perf. 11½
B766 SP355 50c + 10c rose clar-
              et   .20 .20
B767 SP355 1fr + 40c car rose .20 .20
B768 SP355 2fr + 1fr vio brn   .20 .20
B769 SP355 3fr + 1fr gray   .20 .20
B770 SP355 4fr + 2fr vio bl   .25 .25
B771 SP347 6fr + 3fr brt pur   .25 .25
    Nos. B766-B771 (6)   1.30 1.30
The surtax was for anti-tuberculosis work.

Liberator, Shaking
Prisoner's Hand,
Concentration
Camp — SP356

Designs: 1fr+50c, Prisoner's hand reaching
for the sun. 3fr+1.50fr, Searchlights and tank
breaking down barbed wire, horiz. 8fr+5fr,
Rose growing amid the ruins, horiz.

Engraved and Photogravure
1965, May 8 Unwmk. Perf. 11½
B772 SP356 50c + 50c tan, blk &
              buff   .20 .20
B773 SP356 1fr + 50c multi   .20 .20
B774 SP356 3fr + 1.50fr dl lil &
              blk   .25 .25
B775 SP356 8fr + 5fr multi   .35 .35
    Nos. B772-B775 (4)   1.00 1.00
    20th anniv. of the liberation of the concen-
tration camps for political prisoners and pris-
oners of war.

Stoclet
House,
Brussels
SP357

Stoclet House: 6fr+3fr, Hall with marble
foundation, vert. 8fr+4fr, View of house from
garden.

1965, June 21
B776 SP357 3fr + 1fr slate & tan .25 .25
B777 SP357 6fr + 3fr sepia   .30 .30
B778 SP357 8fr + 4fr vio brn &
              tan   .45 .45
    Nos. B776-B778 (3)   1.00 1.00
    Austrian architect Josef Hoffmann (1870-
1956), builder of the art nouveau residence of
Adolphe Stoclet, engineer and financier.

Jackson's
Chameleon
SP358

Animals from Antwerp Zoo: 2fr+1fr, Common iguanas. 3fr+1.50fr, African monitor.
6fr+3fr, Komodo monitor. 8fr+4fr, Nile softshell
turtle.

1965, Oct. 16   Photo.   Perf. 11½

B779	SP358	1fr + 50c multi	.20 .20
B780	SP358	2fr + 1fr multi	.20 .20
B781	SP358	3fr + 1.50fr multi	.25 .25
B782	SP358	6fr + 3fr multi	.45 .45
	Nos. B779-B782 (4)		1.10 1.10

Miniature Sheet

B783	SP358	8fr + 4fr multi	1.75 1.75

The surtax was for various cultural and philanthropic organizations. No. B783 contains one stamp, size: 52x35mm.

Boatmen's and Archers' Guild Halls SP359

Buildings on Grand-Place, Brussels: 1fr+40c, Brewers' Hall. 2fr+1fr, "King of Spain." 3fr+1.50fr, "Dukes of Brabant." 10fr+4.50fr, Tower of City Hall and St. Michael.

1965, Dec. 4   Engr.   Perf. 11½
Size: 35x24mm

B784	SP359	50c + 10c ultra	.20 .20
B785	SP359	1fr + 40c bl grn	.20 .20
B786	SP359	2fr + 1fr rose cl	.20 .20
B787	SP359	3fr + 1.50fr violet	.20 .20

Size: 24x44mm

B788	SP359	10fr + 4.50fr sep & gray	.30 .30
	Nos. B784-B788 (5)		1.10 1.10

The surtax was for anti-tuberculosis work.

Souvenir Sheets

Queen Elisabeth — SP360

Design: No. B790, Types of 1931 and 1956.

1966, Apr. 16   Photo.   Perf. 11½

B789	SP360	Sheet of 2 + label	1.50 1.50
a.		SP74 3fr dk brn & gray grn	.60 .60
b.		SP87 3fr dk brn, yel grn & gold	.60 .60
B790	SP360	Sheet of 2 + label	1.50 1.50
a.		SP42 3fr dk brn & dl bl	.60 .60
b.		SP304 3fr dk brn & gray	.60 .60

The surtax went to various cultural organizations. Each sheet sold for 20fr.

Luminescent Paper
was used in printing Nos. B789-B790, B801-B806, B808-B809, B811-B823, B825-B831, B833-B835, B837-B840, B842-B846, B848-B850, B852-B854, B856-B863, and from B865 onward unless otherwise noted. In many cases the low value of the set is not on luminescent paper. This will not be noted.

Diver — SP361

Design: 10fr+4fr, Swimmer at start.

1966, May 9   Engr.

B791	SP361	60c + 40c Prus grn, ol & org brn	.20 .20
B792	SP361	10fr + 4fr ol grn, org brn & mag	.40 .40

Issued to publicize the importance of swimming instruction.

Minorites' Convent, Liège — SP362

Designs: 1fr+50c, Val-Dieu Abbey, Aubel. 2fr+1fr, View and seal of Huy. 10fr+4.50fr, Statue of Ambiorix by Jules Bertin, and tower, Tongeren.

1966, Aug. 27   Engr.   Perf. 11½

B793	SP362	60c + 40c multi	.20 .20
B794	SP362	1fr + 50c multi	.20 .20
B795	SP362	2fr + 1fr multi	.20 .20
B796	SP362	10fr + 4.50fr multi	.40 .40
	Nos. B793-B796 (4)		1.00 1.00

The surtax was for various patriotic and cultural organizations.

Surveyor and Dog Team SP363

3fr+1.50fr, Adrien de Gerlache, "Belgica." 6fr+3fr, Surveyor, weather balloon, ship. 10fr+5fr, Penguins, "Magga Dan" (ship used for 1964, 1965 and 1966 expeditions).

1966, Oct. 8   Engr.   Perf. 11½

B797	SP363	1fr + 50c bl grn	.20 .20
B798	SP363	3fr + 1.50fr pale vio	.20 .20
B799	SP363	6fr + 3fr dk car	.35 .35
	Nos. B797-B799 (3)		.75 .75

Souvenir Sheet
Engraved and Photogravure

B800	SP363	10fr + 5fr dk gray, sky bl & dk red	.70 .70

Belgian Antarctic expeditions. #B800 contains one 52x35mm stamp.

Boy with Ball and Dog — SP364

Designs: 2fr+1fr, Girl skipping rope. 3fr+1.50fr, Girl and boy blowing soap bubbles. 6fr+3fr, Girl and boy rolling hoops, horiz. 8fr+3.50fr, Four children at play and cat, horiz.

1966, Dec. 3   Perf. 11½

B801	SP364	1fr + 1fr pink & blk	.20 .20
B802	SP364	2fr + 1fr lt bluish grn & blk	.20 .20
B803	SP364	3fr + 1.50fr lt vio & blk	.20 .20
B804	SP364	6fr + 3fr pale sal & dk brn	.25 .25
B805	SP364	8fr + 3.50fr lt yel grn & dk brn	.30 .30
	Nos. B801-B805 (5)		1.15 1.15

The surtax was for anti-tuberculosis work.

Souvenir Sheet

Refugees — SP365

1fr, Boy receiving clothes. 2fr, Tibetan children. 3fr, African mother and children.

1967, Mar. 11   Photo.   Perf. 11½

B806	SP365	Sheet of 3	1.25 1.25
a.		1fr black & yellow	.30 .30
b.		2fr black & blue	.30 .30
c.		3fr black & orange	.40 .40

Issued to help refugees around the world. Sheet has black border with Belgian P.T.T. and UN Refugee emblems. Sold for 20fr.

Robert Schuman SP366

Colonial Brotherhood Emblem SP368

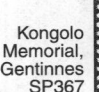

Kongolo Memorial, Gentinnes SP367

1967, June 24   Engr.   Perf. 11½

B807	SP366	2fr + 1fr gray blue	.25 .25

Engraved and Photogravure

B808	SP367	5fr + 2fr brn & olive	.30 .30
B809	SP368	10fr + 5fr multi	.45 .35

Robert Schuman (1886-1963), French statesman, one of the founders of European Steel and Coal Community, 1st pres. of European Parliament (2fr+1fr); Kongolo Memorial, erected in memory of missionary and civilian victims in the Congo (5fr+2fr); a memorial for African Troops, Brussels (10fr+5fr).

Preaching Fool from "Praise of Folly" by Erasmus SP369

Erasmus, by Quentin Massys SP370

Designs: 2fr+1fr, Exhorting Fool from Praise of Folly. 5fr+2fr, Thomas More's Family, by Hans Holbein, horiz. 6fr+3fr, Pierre Gilles (Aegidius), by Quentin Massys.

Photogravure and Engraved (SP369); Photogravure (SP370)

1967, Sept. 2   Unwmk.   Perf. 11

B810	SP369	1fr + 50c tan, blk, bl & car	.20 .20
B811	SP369	2fr + 1fr tan, blk & car	.20 .20
B812	SP370	3fr + 1.50fr multi	.20 .20
B813	SP369	5fr + 2fr tan, blk & car	.20 .20
B814	SP370	6fr + 3fr multi	.20 .20
	Nos. B810-B814 (5)		1.00 1.00

Issued to commemorate Erasmus (1466(?)-1536), Dutch scholar and his era.

Souvenir Sheet

Pro-Post Association Emblem — SP371

Engraved and Photogravure
1967, Oct. 21   Perf. 11½

B815	SP371	10fr + 5fr multi	.75 .75

Issued to publicize the POSTPHILA Philatelic Exhibition, Brussels, Oct. 21-29.

Detail from Brueghel's "Children's Games" SP372

Designs: Various Children's Games. Singles of Nos. B816-B821 arranged in 2 rows of 3 show complete painting by Pieter Brueghel.

1967, Dec. 9   Photo.   Perf. 11½

B816	SP372	1fr + 50c multi	.20 .20
B817	SP372	2fr + 50c multi	.20 .20
B818	SP372	3fr + 1fr multi	.20 .20
B819	SP372	5fr + 3fr multi	.30 .30
B820	SP372	10fr + 4fr multi	.40 .40
B821	SP372	13fr + 6fr multi	.60 .60
	Nos. B816-B821 (6)		1.90 1.90

Queen Fabiola Holding Refugee Child from Congo — SP373

6fr+3fr, Queen Elisabeth & Dr. Depage.

1968, Apr. 27   Photo.   Perf. 11½
Cross in Red

B822	SP373	6fr + 3fr sepia & gray	.25 .25
B823	SP373	10fr + 5fr sepia & gray	.45 .45

The surtax was for the Red Cross.

Woman Gymnast and Calendar Stone SP374

Yachting and "The Swimmer" by Andrien — SP375

Designs: 2fr+1fr, Weight lifter and Mayan motif. 3fr+1.50fr, Hurdler, colossus of Tula and animal head from Kukulkan. 6fr+2fr, Bicyclists and Chichen Itza Temple.

Engraved and Photogravure
1968, May 27   Perf. 11½

B824	SP374	1fr + 50c multi	.20 .20
B825	SP374	2fr + 1fr multi	.20 .20
B826	SP374	3fr + 1.50fr multi	.20 .20

B827 SP374 6fr + 2fr multi .25 .25

Photo.

B828 SP375 13fr + 5fr multi .50 .50
Nos. B824-B828 (5) 1.35 1.35

Issued to publicize the 19th Olympic Games, Mexico City, Oct. 12-27.

"Explosion" SP376

Designs (Paintings by Pol Mara): 12fr+5fr, "Fire." 13fr+5fr, "Tornado."

1968, June 22 Photo.

B829 SP376 10fr + 5fr multi .40 .40
B830 SP376 12fr + 5fr multi .65 .65
B831 SP376 13fr + 5fr multi .70 .70
Nos. B829-B831 (3) 1.75 1.75

The surtax was for disaster victims.

Undulate Triggerfish SP377

Tropical Fish: 3fr+1.50fr, Angelfish. 6fr+3fr, Turkeyfish (Pterois volitans). 10fr+5fr, Orange butterflyfish.

1968, Oct. 19 Engr. & Photo.

B832 SP377 1fr + 50c multi .20 .20
B833 SP377 3fr + 1.50fr multi .20 .20
B834 SP377 6fr + 3fr multi .30 .30
B835 SP377 10fr + 5fr multi .40 .40
Nos. B832-B835 (4) 1.10 1.10

King Albert and Queen Elisabeth Entering Brussels SP378

Tomb of the Unknown Soldier and Eternal Flame, Brussels — SP379

Designs: 1fr+50c, King Albert, Queen Elisabeth and Crown Prince Leopold on balcony, Bruges, vert. 6fr+3fr, King and Queen entering Liège.

1968, Nov. 9 Photo. Perf. 11½

B836 SP378 1fr + 50c multi .20 .20
B837 SP378 3fr + 1.50fr multi .20 .20
B838 SP378 6fr + 3fr multi .30 .30

Engraved and Photogravure

B839 SP379 10fr + 5fr multi .40 .40
Nos. B836-B839 (4) 1.10 1.10

50th anniv. of the victory in World War I.

Souvenir Sheet

The Painter and the Amateur, by Peter Brueghel — SP380

1969, May 10 Engr. Perf. 11½

B840 SP380 10fr + 5fr sepia 1.10 1.10

Issued to publicize the POSTPHILA 1969 Philatelic Exhibition, Brussels, May 10-18.

Huts, by Ivanka D. Pancheva, Bulgaria — SP381

Children's Drawings and UNICEF Emblem: 3fr+1.50fr, "My Art" (Santa Claus), by Claes Patric, Belgium. 6fr+3fr, "In the Sun" (young boy), by Helena Rejchlova, Czechoslovakia. 10fr+5fr, "Out for a Walk" by Phillis Sporn, US, horiz.

1969, May 31 Photo. Perf. 11½

B841 SP381 1fr + 50c multi .20 .20
B842 SP381 3fr + 1.50fr multi .20 .20
B843 SP381 6fr + 3fr multi .35 .35
B844 SP381 10fr + 5fr multi .50 .50
Nos. B841-B844 (4) 1.25 1.25

The surtax was for philanthropic purposes.

Msgr. Victor Scheppers SP382

1969, July 5 Engr.

B845 SP382 6fr + 3fr rose claret .45 .45

Msgr. Victor Scheppers (1802-77), prison reformer and founder of the Brothers of Mechlin (Scheppers).

Moon Landing Type of 1969
Souvenir Sheet

Design: 20fr+10fr, Armstrong, Collins and Aldrin and moon with Tranquillity Base, vert.

1969, Sept. 20 Photo. Perf. 11½

B846 A245 20fr + 10fr indigo 3.00 3.00

See note after No. 726.

Heads from Alexander the Great Tapestry, 15th Century — SP383

Designs from Tapestries: 3fr+1.50fr, Fiddler from "The Feast," c. 1700. 10fr+4fr, Head of beggar from "The Healing of the Paralytic," 16th century.

1969, Sept. 20

B847 SP383 1fr + 50c multi .20 .20
B848 SP383 3fr + 1.50fr multi .20 .20
B849 SP383 10fr + 4fr multi .45 .45
Nos. B847-B849 (3) .85 .85

The surtax was for philanthropic purposes.

Bearded Antwerp Bantam SP384

1969, Nov. 8 Engr. & Photo.

B850 SP384 10fr + 5fr multi .70 .70

Angel Playing Lute — SP385

Designs from Stained Glass Windows: 1.50fr+50c, Angel with trumpet, St. Waudru's, Mons. 7fr+3fr, Angel with viol, St. Jacques', Liege. 9fr+4fr, King with bagpipes, Royal Art Museum, Brussels.

1969, Dec. 13 Photo.

Size: 24x35mm

B851 SP385 1.50fr + 50c multi .20 .20
B852 SP385 3.50fr + 1.50fr multi .20 .20
B853 SP385 7fr + 3fr multi .35 .35

Size: 35x52mm

B854 SP386 9fr + 4fr multi .50 .50
Nos. B851-B854 (4) 1.25 1.25

The surtax was for philanthropic purposes.

Farm and Windmill, Open-air Museum, Bokrijk SP386

Belgian Museums: 3.50fr+1.50fr, Stage Coach Inn, Courcelles. 7fr+3fr, "The Thresher of Trevires," Gallo-Roman sculpture, Gaumais Museum, Virton. 9fr+4fr, "The Sovereigns," by Henry Moore, Middelheim Museum, Antwerp.

Engraved and Photogravure

1970, May 30 Perf. 11½

B855 SP386 1.50fr + 50c multi .20 .20
B856 SP386 3.50fr + 1.50fr multi .25 .25
B857 SP386 7fr + 3fr multi .35 .35
B858 SP386 9fr + 4fr multi .40 .40
Nos. B855-B858 (4) 1.20 1.20

The surtax went to various culture organizations.

"Resistance" SP387

Design: 7fr+3fr, "Liberation of Camps." The designs were originally used as book covers.

1970, July 4 Photo. Perf. 11½

B859 SP387 3.50fr + 1.50fr blk, gray grn & dp car .20 .20
B860 SP387 7fr + 3fr blk, lil & dp car .40 .40

Honoring the Resistance Movement and 25th anniv. of the liberation of concentration camps.

Fishing Rod and Reel SP388

Design: 9fr+4fr, Hockey stick and puck, vert.

1970, Sept. 19 Engr. & Photo.

B861 SP388 3.50fr + 1.50fr multi .30 .30
B862 SP388 9fr + 4fr multi .50 .50

Souvenir Sheet

Belgium Nos. 31, 36, 39 — SP389

1970, Oct. 10 Perf. 11½

B863 SP389 Sheet of 3 4.75 4.75
a. 1.50fr + 50c black & dull lilac 1.40 1.40
b. 3.50fr + 1.50fr black & lilac 1.40 1.40
c. 9fr + 4fr black & red brown 1.40 1.40

BELGICA 72 International Philatelic Exhibition, Brussels, June 24-July 9.

Camille Huysmans (1871-1968) SP390

3.50fr+1.50fr, Joseph Cardinal Cardijn (1882-1967). 7fr+3fr, Maria Baers (1883-1959). 9fr+4fr, Paul Pastur (1866-1938).

1970, Nov. 14 Perf. 11½

Portraits in Sepia

B864 SP390 1.50fr + 50c car rose .20 .20
B865 SP390 3.50fr + 1.50fr lilac .20 .20
B866 SP390 7fr + 3fr green .40 .40
B867 SP390 9fr + 4fr blue .50 .50
Nos. B864-B867 (4) 1.30 1.30

"Anxious City" (Detail) by Paul Delvaux SP391

7fr+3fr, "The Memory," by Rene Magritte.

1970, Dec. 12   **Photo.**
B868 SP391   3.50fr + 1.50fr multi   .20   .20
B869 SP391   7fr + 3fr multi   .40   .40

Notre Dame du Vivier, Marche-les-Dames — SP392

7fr+3fr, Turnhout Beguinage and Beguine.

1971, Mar. 13   **Perf. 11½**
B870 SP392   3.50fr + 1.50fr multi   .20   .20
B871 SP392   7fr + 3fr multi   .40   .40

The surtax was for philanthropic purposes.

Red Cross — SP393

1971, May 22   **Photo.**   **Perf. 11½**
B872 SP393   10fr + 5fr crim & blk   .75   .75

Belgian Red Cross.

Discobolus and Munich Cathedral — SP394

1971, June 19   **Engr. & Photo.**
B873 SP394   7fr + 3fr bl & blk   .40   .40

Publicity for the 20th Summer Olympic Games, Munich 1972.

Festival of Flanders — SP395

1971, Sept. 11   **Photo.**   **Perf. 11½**

Design: 7fr+3fr, Wallonia Festival.

B874 SP395   3.50fr + 1.50fr multi   .20   .20
B875 SP395   7fr + 3fr multi   .40   .40

Attre Palace — SP396

Steen Palace, Elewijt — SP397

Design: 10fr+5fr, Royal Palace, Brussels.

1971, Oct. 23   **Engr.**
B876 SP396   3.50fr + 1.50fr sl grn .30   .30
B877 SP397   7fr + 3fr red brn   .50   .50
B878 SP396   10fr + 5fr vio bl   .70   .70
   Nos. B876-B878 (3)   1.50 1.50

Surtax was for BELGICA 72, International Philatelic Exposition.

Ox Fly, tabanus bromius SP398

Insects: 1.50fr+50c, Luna moth, vert. 7fr+3fr, Wasp, polistes gallicus. 9fr+4fr, Tiger beetle, vert.

1971, Dec. 11   **Photo.**   **Perf. 11½**
B879 SP398   1.50fr + 50c multi   .20   .20
B880 SP398   3.50fr + 1.50fr multi   .20   .20
B881 SP398   7fr + 3fr multi   .40   .40
B882 SP398   9fr + 4fr multi   .60   .60
   Nos. B879-B882 (4)   1.40 1.40

Surtax was for philanthropic purposes.

Leopold I on #1 — SP399

2fr+1fr, Leopold I on #5. 2.50fr+1fr, Leopold II on #45. 3.50fr+1.50fr, Leopold II on #48. 6fr+3fr, Albert I on #135. 7fr+3fr, Albert I on #214. 10fr+5fr, Albert I on #231. 15fr+7.50fr, Leopold III on #290. 20fr+10fr, King Baudouin on #718.

Engraved and Photogravure
1972, June 24   **Perf. 11½**
B883 SP399   1.50fr + 50c   .20   .20
B884 SP399   2fr + 1fr   .20   .20
B885 SP399   2.50 + 1fr   .20   .20
B886 SP399   3.50fr + 1.50fr   .30   .30
B887 SP399   6fr + 3fr   .50   .50
B888 SP399   7fr + 3fr   .70   .70
B889 SP399   10fr + 5fr   .90   .90
B890 SP399   15fr + 7fr   1.10 1.10
B891 SP399   20fr + 10fr   2.00 2.00
   Nos. B883-B891 (9)   6.10 6.10

Belgica 72, Intl. Philatelic Exhibition, Brussels, June 24-July 9. Nos. B883-B891 issued in sheets of 10 and of 20 (2 tete beche sheets with gutter between). Sold in complete sets.

Epilepsy Emblem — SP400

1972, Sept. 9   **Photo.**   **Perf. 11½**
B892 SP400   10fr + 5fr multi   .55   .55

The surtax was for the William Lennox Center for epilepsy research and treatment.

Gray Lag Goose — SP401

Designs: 4.50fr+2fr, Lapwing. 8fr+4fr, Stork. 9fr+4.50fr, Kestrel, horiz.

1972, Dec. 16   **Photo.**   **Perf. 11½**
B893 SP401   2fr + 1fr multi   .25   .25
B894 SP401   4.50fr + 2fr multi   .30   .30
B895 SP401   8fr + 4fr multi   .60   .60
B896 SP401   9fr + 4.50fr multi   .60   .60
   Nos. B893-B896 (4)   1.75 1.75

Bijloke Abbey, Ghent — SP402

4.50fr+2fr, St. Ursmer Collegiate Church, Lobbes. 8fr+4fr, Park Abbey, Heverle. 9fr+4.50fr, Abbey, Floreffe.

1973, Mar. 24   **Engr.**   **Perf. 11½**
B897 SP402   2fr + 1fr sl grn   .20   .20
B898 SP402   4.50fr + 2fr brown   .25   .25
B899 SP402   8fr + 4fr rose lil   .50   .50
B900 SP402   9fr + 4.50fr brt bl   .60   .60
   Nos. B897-B900 (4)   1.55 1.55

Basketball SP403

1973, Apr. 7   **Photo. & Engr.**
B901 SP403   10fr + 5fr multi   .60   .60

First World Basketball Championships of the Handicapped, Bruges, Apr. 16-21.

Dirk Martens' Printing Press — SP404

Lady Talbot, by Petrus Christus — SP405

Hadrian and Marcus Aurelius Coins SP406

Council of Malines, by Coussaert — SP407

Designs: 3.50fr+1.50fr, Head of Amon and Tutankhamen's cartouche. 10fr+5fr, Three-master of Ostend Merchant Company.

Photogravure and Engraved; Photogravure (#B906)
1973, June 23   **Perf. 11½**
B902 SP404   2fr + 1fr multi   .20   .20
B903 SP404   3.50fr + 1.50fr multi   .20   .20
B904 SP405   4.50fr + 2fr multi   .20   .20
B905 SP406   8fr + 4fr multi   .60   .60
B906 SP407   8fr + 4fr multi   .85   .85
B907 SP407   10fr + 5fr multi   1.50 1.50
   Nos. B902-B907 (6)   3.55 3.55

500th anniv. of 1st book printed in Belgium (#B902); 50th anniv. of Queen Elisabeth Egyptological Foundation (#B903); 500th anniv. of death of painter Petrus Christus (#B904); Discovery of Roman treasure at Lut-tre-Liberchies (#B905); 500th anniv. of Great Council of Malines (#B906); 250th anniv. of the Ostend Merchant Company (#B907).

No. B902 is not luminescent.

Queen of Hearts — SP408

Old Playing Cards: #B909, King of Clubs. #B910, Jack of Diamonds. #B911, King of Spades.

1973, Dec. 8   **Photo.**   **Perf. 11½**
B908 SP408   5fr + 2.50fr multi   .40   .40
B909 SP408   5fr + 2.50fr multi   .40   .40
B910 SP408   5fr + 2.50fr multi   .40   .40
B911 SP408   5fr + 2.50fr multi   .40   .40
   a.   Strip of 4, #B908-B911   1.60 1.60

Surtax was for philanthropic purposes.

Symbol of Blood Donations SP409

Design: 10fr+5fr, Traffic lights, Red Cross (symbolic of road accidents).

1974, Feb. 23   **Photo.**   **Perf. 11½**
B912 SP409   4fr + 2fr multi   .25   .25
B913 SP409   10fr + 5fr multi   .55   .55

The Red Cross as blood collector and aid to accident victims.

Armand Jamar, Self-portrait SP410

Designs: 5fr+2.50fr, Anton Bergmann and view of Lierre. 7fr+3.50fr, Henri Vieuxtemps and view of Verviers. 10fr+5fr, James Ensor, self-portrait, and masks.

1974, Apr. 6   **Photo.**   **Perf. 11½**
                 Size: 24x35mm
B914 SP410   4fr + 2fr multi   .25   .25
B915 SP410   5fr + 2.50fr multi   .30   .30
B916 SP410   7fr + 3.50fr multi   .40   .40
                 Size: 35x52mm
B917 SP410   10fr + 5fr multi   .65   .65
   Nos. B914-B917 (4)   1.60 1.60

Van Gogh, Self-portrait and House at Cuesmes — SP411

1974, Sept. 21   Photo.   Perf. 11½
B918 SP411 10fr + 5fr multi   .55   .55
Opening of Vincent van Gogh House at Cuesmes, where he worked as teacher.

Gentian — SP412

Spotted Cat's Ear — SP414

Badger SP413

Design: 7fr+3.50fr, Beetle.

1974, Dec. 8   Photo.   Perf. 11½
B919 SP412 4fr + 2fr multi   .25   .25
B920 SP413 5fr + 2.50fr multi   .30   .30
B921 SP413 7fr + 3.50fr multi   .40   .40
B922 SP414 10fr + 5fr multi   .60   .60
    Nos. B919-B922 (4)   1.55 1.55

Pesaro Palace, Venice SP415

St. Bavon Abbey, Ghent SP416

Virgin and Child, by Michelangelo SP417

1975, Apr. 12   Engr.   Perf. 11½
B923 SP415 6.50fr + 2.50fr brn   .35   .35
B924 SP416 10fr + 4.50 vio brn   .60   .60
B925 SP417 15fr + 6.50fr brt bl   .80   .80
    Nos. B923-B925 (3)   1.75 1.75
Surtax was for various cultural organizations.

Frans Hemerijckx and Leprosarium, Kasai — SP418

1975, Sept. 13   Photo.   Perf. 11½
B926 SP418 20fr + 10fr multi   1.40 1.40
Dr. Frans Hemerijckx (1902-1969), tropical medicine and leprosy expert.

Emile Moyson SP419

Beheading of St. Dympna SP420a

Hand Reading Braille SP420

#B928, Dr. Ferdinand Augustin Snellaert.

1975, Nov. 22   Engr.   Perf. 11½
B927 SP419 4.50fr + 2fr lilac   .25   .25
B928 SP419 6.50fr + 3fr green   .35   .35

Engraved and Photogravure
B929 SP420 10fr + 5fr multi   .50   .50

Photo.
B930 SP420a 13fr + 6fr multi   .70   .70
    Nos. B927-B930 (4)   1.80 1.80
Emile Moyson (1838-1868), freedom fighter for the rights of Flemings and Walloons; Dr. Snellaert (1809-1872), physician and Flemish patriot; Louis Braille (1809-1852), sesquicentennial of invention of Braille system of writing for the blind; St. Dympna, patron saint of Geel, famous for treatment of mentally ill.

The Cheese Vendor — SP421

Designs (THEMABELGA Emblem and): No. B932, Potato vendor. No. B933, Basket carrier. No. B934, Shrimp fisherman with horse, horiz. No. B935, Knife grinder, horiz. No. B936, Milk vendor with dog cart, horiz.

1975, Dec. 13   Engr. & Photo.
B931 SP421 4.50fr + 1.50fr multi   .20   .20
B932 SP421 6.50fr + 3fr multi   .30   .30
B933 SP421 6.50fr + 3fr multi   .30   .30
B934 SP421 10fr + 5fr multi   .45   .45
B935 SP421 10fr + 5fr multi   .45   .45
B936 SP421 30fr + 15fr multi   1.50 1.50
    Nos. B931-B936 (6)   3.20 3.20
THEMABELGA Intl. Topical Philatelic Exhib., Brussels, Dec. 13-21. Issued in sheets of 10 (5x2).

Blackface Fund Collector — SP422

1976, Feb. 14   Photo.   Perf. 11½
B937 SP422 10fr + 5fr multi   .55 .55
"Conservatoire Africain" philanthropic soc., cent., and to publicize the Princess Paola creches.

Swimming and Olympic Emblem SP423

Montreal Olympic Games Emblem and: 5fr+2fr, Running, vert. 6.50fr+2.50fr, Equestrian.

1976, Apr. 10   Photo.   Perf. 11½
B938 SP423 4.50fr + 1.50fr multi   .20   .20
B939 SP423 5fr + 2fr multi   .25   .25
B940 SP423 6.50fr + 2.50fr multi   .45   .45
    Nos. B938-B940 (3)   .90   .90
21st Olympic Games, Montreal, Canada, July 17-Aug. 1.

Queen Elisabeth Playing Violin SP424

Perf. 11½
1976, May 1   Engr.   Photo.
B941 SP424 14fr + 6fr blk & cl   .95   .95
Queen Elisabeth International Music Competition, 25th anniversary.

Souvenir Sheet

Jan Olieslagers, Bleriot Monoplane, Aero Club Emblem — SP425

Engraved and Photogravure
1976, June 12   Perf. 11½
B942 SP425 25fr + 10fr multi   2.25 2.25
Royal Belgian Aero Club, 75th anniversary, and Jan Olieslagers (1883-1942), aviation pioneer.

Adoration of the Shepherds (detail), by Rubens — SP426

Rubens Paintings (Details): 4.50fr, Descent from the Cross. No. B945, The Virgin with the Parrot. No. B946, Adoration of the Kings. No. B947, Last Communion of St. Francis. 30fr+15fr, Virgin and Child.

1976, Sept. 4   Photo.   Perf. 11½
Size: 35x52mm
B943 SP426 4.50fr + 1.50fr multi   .35   .35
Size: 24x35mm
B944 SP426 6.50fr + 3fr multi   .55   .55
B945 SP426 6.50fr + 3fr multi   .55   .55
B946 SP426 10fr + 5fr multi   .85   .85
B947 SP426 10fr + 5fr multi   .85   .85
Size: 35x52mm
B948 SP426 30fr + 15fr multi   1.75 1.75
    Nos. B943-B948 (6)   4.90 4.90
Peter Paul Rubens (1577-1640), Flemish painter, 400th birth anniversary.

Dwarf, by Velazquez SP427

1976, Nov. 6   Photo.   Perf. 11½
B949 SP427 14fr + 6fr multi   .80   .80
Surtax was for the National Association for the Mentally Handicapped.

Dr. Albert Hustin SP428

Red Cross and Rheumatism Year Emblem SP429

1977, Feb. 19   Photo.   Perf. 11½
B950 SP428 6.50fr + 2.50 multi   .40   .40
B951 SP429 14fr + 7fr multi   .75   .75
Belgian Red Cross.

Bordet Atheneum, Empress Maria Theresa SP430

Conductor and Orchestra, by E. Tytgat SP431

Lucien Van Obbergh, Stage SP432

Humanistic Society Emblem SP433

Camille Lemonnier SP434

Design: No. B953, Marie-Therese College, Herve, and coat of arms.

1977, Mar. 21   Photo.   Perf. 11½

B952	SP430	4.50fr + 1fr multi	.20	.20
B953	SP430	4.50fr + 1fr multi	.20	.20
B954	SP431	5fr + 2fr multi	.25	.25
B955	SP432	6.50fr + 2fr multi	.30	.30
B956	SP433	6.50fr + 2fr blk & red	.30	.30

Engr.

B957	SP434	10fr + 5fr slate bl	.50	.50
	Nos. B952-B957 (6)		1.75	1.75

Bicentenaries of the Jules Bordet Atheneum, Brussels, and the Marie-Therese College, Herve (#B952-B953); 50th anniv. of the Brussels Philharmonic Soc., and Artists' Union (#B954-B955); 25th anniv. of the Flemish Humanistic Organization (#B956); 75th anniv. of the French-speaking Belgian writers' organization (#957).

Young Soccer Players — SP435

1977, Apr. 18   Photo.

B958	SP435	10fr + 5fr multi	.55	.55

30th Intl. Junior Soccer Tournament.

Albert-Edouard Janssen, Financier — SP436

Famous Men: No. B960, Joseph Wauters (1875-1929), editor of Le Peuple, and newspaper. No. B961, Jean Capart (1877-1947), Egyptologist, and hieroglyph. No. B962, August de Boeck (1865-1937), composer, and score.

1977, Dec. 3   Engr.   Perf. 11½

B959	SP436	5fr + 2.50fr brown	.30	.30
B960	SP436	5fr + 2.50fr red	.30	.30
B961	SP436	10fr + 5fr magenta	.55	.55
B962	SP436	10fr + 5fr blue gray	.55	.55
	Nos. B959-B962 (4)		1.70	1.70

Abandoned Child SP437

Checking Blood Pressure SP438

De Mick Sanatorium, Brasschaat — SP439

1978, Feb. 18   Photo.   Perf. 11½

B963	SP437	4.50fr + 1.50fr multi	.20	.20
B964	SP438	5fr + 3fr multi	.40	.40
B965	SP439	10fr + 5fr multi	.60	.60
	Nos. B963-B965 (3)		1.20	1.20

Help for abandoned children (No. B963); fight against hypertension (No. B964); fight against tuberculosis (No. B965).

Actors and Theater SP440

Karel van de Woestijne SP441

Designs: No. B967, Harquebusier, Harquebusier Palace and coat of arms. 10fr+5fr, John of Austria and his signature.

Engraved and Photogravure
1978, June 17   Perf. 11½

B966	SP440	6fr + 3fr multi	.40	.40
B967	SP440	6fr + 3fr multi	.40	.40

Engr.

B968	SP441	8fr + 4fr black	.45	.45
B969	SP441	10fr + 5fr black	.55	.55
	Nos. B966-B969 (4)		1.80	1.80

Cent. of Royal Flemish Theater, Brussels (#B966); 400th anniv. of Harquebusiers' Guild of Vise, Liege (#967); Karel van de Woestijne (1878-1929), poet (#B968); 400th anniv. of signing of Perpetual Edict by John of Austria (#969).

Lake Placid '80 and Belgian Olympic Emblems — SP442

Moscow '80 Emblem and: 8fr+3.50fr, Kremlin Towers, Belgian Olympic Committee emblem. 7fr+3fr, Runners from Greek vase, Lake Placid '80 emblem, Olympic rings. 14fr+6fr, Olympic flame, Lake Placid '80, Belgian emblems, Olympic rings.

1978, Nov. 4   Photo.   Perf. 11½

B970	SP442	6fr + 2.50fr multi	.30	.30
B971	SP442	8fr + 3.50fr multi	.45	.45

Souvenir Sheet

B972		Sheet of 2	1.50	1.50
a.		SP442 7fr + 3fr multi	.55	.55
b.		SP442 14fr + 6fr multi	.90	.90

Surtax was for 1980 Olympic Games.

Great Synagogue, Brussels — SP443

Dancers SP444

Father Pire, African Village SP445

1978, Dec. 2   Engr.   Perf. 11½

B973	SP443	6fr + 2fr sepia	.45	.45

Photo.

B974	SP444	8fr + 3fr multi	.35	.35
B975	SP445	14fr + 7fr multi	.65	.65
	Nos. B973-B975 (3)		1.45	1.45

Centenary of Great Synagogue of Brussels; Flemish Catholic Youth Action Organization, 50th anniversary; Nobel Peace Prize awarded to Father Dominique Pire for his "Heart Open to the World" movement, 20th anniversary.

Young People Giving First Aid — SP446

Skull with Bottle, Cigarette, Syringe — SP447

1979, Feb. 10   Photo.   Perf. 11½

B976	SP446	8fr + 3fr multi	.35	.35
B977	SP447	16fr + 8fr multi	.85	.85

Belgian Red Cross.

Beatrice Soetkens with Statue of Virgin Mary SP448

Details from Tapestries, 1516-1518, Showing Legend of Our Lady of Sand: 8fr+3fr, Francois de Tassis accepting letter from Emperor Frederick III (beginning of postal service). 14fr+7fr, Arrival of statue, Francois de Tassis and Philip the Fair. No. B981, Statue carried in procession by future Emperor Charles V and his brother Ferdinand. No. B982, Ship carrying Beatrice Soetkens with statue to Brussels, horiz.

1979, May 5   Photo.   Perf. 11½

B978	SP448	6fr + 2fr multi	.25	.25
B979	SP448	8fr + 3fr multi	.40	.40
B980	SP448	14fr + 7fr multi	.65	.65
B981	SP448	20fr + 10fr multi	1.10	1.10
	Nos. B978-B981 (4)		2.40	2.40

Souvenir Sheet

B982	SP448	20fr + 10fr multi	.90	.90

The surtax was for festivities in connection with the millennium of Brussels.

Notre Dame Abbey, Brussels — SP449

Designs: 8fr+3fr, Beauvoorde Castle. 14fr+7fr, 1st issue of "Courrier de L'Escaut" and Barthelemy Dumortier, founder. 20fr+10fr, Shrine of St. Hermes, Renaix.

Engraved and Photogravure
1979, Sept. 15   Perf. 11½

B983	SP449	6fr + 2fr multi	.35	.35
B984	SP449	8fr + 3fr multi	.50	.50
B985	SP449	14fr + 7fr multi	.60	.60
B986	SP449	20fr + 10fr multi	1.10	1.10
	Nos. B983-B986 (4)		2.55	2.55

50th anniv. of restoration of Notre Dame de la Cambre Abbey; historic Beauvoorde Castle, 15th cent. sesquicentennial of the regional newspaper "Le Courrier de L'Escaut"; 850th anniv. of the consecration of the Collegiate Church of St. Hermes, Renaix.

Grand-Hornu Coal Mine — SP450

1979, Oct. 22   Engr.   Perf. 11½

B987	SP450	10fr + 5fr blk	.55	.55

Henry Heyman SP451

Veterans Organization Medal SP452

Boy and IYC Emblem — SP453

1979, Dec. 8   Photo.   Perf. 11½

B988	SP451	8fr + 3fr multi	.45	.45
B989	SP452	10fr + 5fr multi	.55	.55
B990	SP453	16fr + 8fr multi	.75	.75
	Nos. B988-B990 (3)		1.75	1.75

Henri Heyman (1879-1958), Minister of State; Disabled Veterans' Organization, 50th anniv.; Intl. Year of the Child.

Ivo Van Damme, Olympic Rings — SP454

1980, May 3   Photo.   Perf. 11½
B991   SP454   20fr + 10fr multi   1.10   1.10

Ivo Van Damme (1954-1976), silver medalist, 800-meter race, Montreal Olympics, 1976. Surtax was for Van Damme Memorial Foundation.

Queen Louis-Marie, King Leopold I — SP455

150th Anniversary of Independence (Queens and Kings): 9fr+3fr, Marie Henriette. Leopold II. 14fr+6fr, Elisabeth, Albert I. 17fr+8fr, Astrid, Leopold III. 25fr+10fr, Fabiola, Baudouin.

Photogravure and Engraved
1980, May 31   Perf. 11½
B992   SP455   6.50 + 1.50fr multi   .30   .30
B993   SP455   9 + 3fr multi   .50   .50
B994   SP455   14 + 6fr multi   .70   .70
B995   SP455   17 + 8fr multi   1.00   1.00
B996   SP455   25 + 10fr multi   1.25   1.25
      Nos. B992-B996 (5)   3.75   3.75

Miner, by Constantine Meunier SP456

Seal of Bishop Notger, First Prince-Bishop — SP457

9fr+3fr, Brewer, 16th century, from St. Lambert's reliquary, vert. 25fr+10fr, Virgin and Child, 13th century, St. John's Collegiate Church, Liege.

1980, Sept. 13   Photo.   Perf. 11½
B997   SP456   9 + 3fr multi   .35   .35
B998   SP456   17 + 6fr multi   .70   .70
B999   SP456   25 + 10fr multi   1.10   1.10
      Nos. B997-B999 (3)   2.15   2.15
Souvenir Sheet
B1000   SP457   20 + 10fr multi   1.25   1.25
Millennium of the Principality of Liege.

Visual and Oral Handicaps SP458

Intl. Year of the Disabled: 10fr+5fr, Cerebral handicap, vert.

1981, Feb. 9   Photo.   Perf. 11½
B1001   SP458   10 + 5fr multi   .70   .70
B1002   SP458   25 + 10fr multi   1.60   1.60

Dove with Red Cross Carrying Globe SP459

Design: 10fr+5fr, Atomic model, vert.

1981, Apr. 6   Photo.   Perf. 11½
B1003   SP459   10 + 5fr multi   .70   .70
B1004   SP459   25 + 10fr multi   1.60   1.60
Red Cross and: 15th Intl. Radiology Congress, Brussels, June 24-July 1 (#B1003); intl. disaster relief (#B1004).

Ovide Decroly SP460

1981, June 1   Photo.   Perf. 11½
B1005   SP460   35 + 15fr multi   2.00   2.00
Ovide Decroly (1871-1932), developer of educational psychology.

Mounted Police Officer — SP461

Anniversaries: 9fr+4fr, Gendarmerie (State Police Force), 150th. 20fr+7fr, Carabineers Regiment, 150th. 40fr+20fr, Guides Regiment.

1981, Dec. 7   Photo.   Perf. 11½
B1006   SP461   9 + 4fr multi   .60   .60
B1007   SP461   20 + 7fr multi   1.25   1.25
B1008   SP461   40 + 20fr multi   2.75   2.75
      Nos. B1006-B1008 (3)   4.60   4.60

Billiards — SP462

1982, Mar. 29   Photo.   Perf. 11½
B1009   SP462   6 + 2fr shown   .40   .40
B1010   SP462   9 + 4fr Cycling   .60   .60
B1011   SP462   10 + 5fr Soccer   .70   .70
B1012   SP462   50 + 14fr Yachting   3.00   3.00
      Nos. B1009-B1012 (4)   4.70   4.70
Souvenir Sheet
B1013   Sheet of 4   5.00   5.00
a.   SP462 25fr like #B1009   1.40   1.40
b.   SP462 25fr like #B1010   1.40   1.40
c.   SP462 25fr like #B1011   1.40   1.40
d.   SP462 25fr like #B1012   1.40   1.40
#B1013 shows designs in changed colors.

Christmas SP463

1982, Nov. 6
B1014   SP463   10 + 1fr multi   .60   .45
Surtax was for tuberculosis research.

Belgica '82 Intl. Stamp Exhibition, Brussels, Dec. 11-19 SP464

Messengers (Prints). #B1016-B1018 vert.

Photogravure and Engraved
1982, Dec. 11   Perf. 11½
B1015   SP464   7 + 2fr multi   .40   .40
B1016   SP464   7.50 + 2.50fr multi   .45   .45
B1017   SP464   10 + 3fr multi   .55   .55
B1018   SP464   17 + 7fr multi   1.10   1.10
B1019   SP464   20 + 9fr multi   1.25   1.25
B1020   SP464   25 + 10fr multi   1.50   1.50
      Nos. B1015-B1020 (6)   5.25   5.25
Souvenir Sheet
B1021   SP464   50 + 25fr multi   6.00   6.00
No. B1021 contains one 48x37mm stamp.

50th Anniv. of Catholic Charities — SP465

1983, Jan. 22   Photo.   Perf. 11½
B1022   SP465   10 + 2fr multi   .65   .65

Mountain Climbing — SP466

1983, Mar. 7   Photo.
B1023   SP466   12 + 3fr shown   .80   .80
B1024   SP466   20 + 5fr Hiking   1.25   1.25
Surtax was for Red Cross.

Madonna by Jef Wauters — SP467

1983, Nov. 21   Photo.   Perf. 11½
B1025   SP467   11 + 1fr multi   .60   .60

Rifles Uniform — SP468

1983, Dec. 5   Photo.   Perf. 11½
B1026   SP468   8 + 2fr shown   .50   .50
B1027   SP468   11 + 2fr Lancers uniform   .75   .75
B1028   SP468   50 + 12fr Grenadiers uniform   3.50   3.50
      Nos. B1026-B1028 (3)   4.75   4.75

Type of 1984
1984, Mar. 3   Photo.   Perf. 11½
B1029   A495   8 + 2fr Judo, horiz.   .55   .55
B1030   A495   12 + 3fr Wind surfing   .85   .85

50th Anniv. of Natl. Lottery SP469

1984, Mar. 31   Photo.   Perf. 11½
B1031   SP469   12 + 3fr multi   .75   .75

Brussels Modern Art Museum Opening SP470

Paintings: 8fr+2fr, Les Masques Singuliers, by James Ensor. 12fr+3fr, Empire des Lumieres, by Rene Magritte. 22fr+5fr, The End, by Jan Cox. 50fr+13fr, Rhythm No. 6, by Jo Delahaut.

1984, Sept. 1   Photo.
B1032   SP470   8 + 2fr multi   .60   .60
B1033   SP470   12 + 3fr multi   .90   .90
B1034   SP470   22 + 5fr multi   1.60   1.60
B1035   SP470   50 + 13fr multi   3.75   3.75
      Nos. B1032-B1035 (4)   6.85   6.85

Child with Parents — SP471

1984, Nov. 3   Photo.
B1036   SP471   10 + 2fr shown   .60   .60
B1037   SP471   12 + 3fr Siblings   .75   .75
B1038   SP471   15 + 3fr Merry-go-round   .85   .85
      Nos. B1036-B1038 (3)   2.20   2.20
Surtax was for children's programs.

Christmas 1984 SP472

1984, Dec. 1
B1039   SP472   12 + 1fr Three Kings   .75   .75

Belgian Red Cross Blood Transfusion Service, 50th Anniv. — SP473

1985, Mar. 4   Photo.   Perf. 11½
B1040   SP473   9 + 2fr Tree   .60   .60
B1041   SP473   23 + 5fr Hearts   1.40   1.40
Surtax was for the Belgian Red Cross.

Solidarity SP474

Castles.

1985, Nov. 4   Photo. & Engr.
B1042 SP474 9 + 2fr Trazegnies   .60   .60
B1043 SP474 12 + 3fr Laarne   .80   .80
B1044 SP474 23 + 5fr Turnhout   1.40   1.40
B1045 SP474 50 + 12fr Colonster   3.50   3.50
Nos. B1042-B1045 (4)   6.30   6.30

Christmas 1985, New Year 1986 — SP475

Painting: Miniature from the Book of Hours, by Jean duc de Berry.

1985, Nov. 25   Photo.
B1046 SP475 12 + 1fr multi   .70   .70

King Baudouin Foundation SP476

1986, Mar. 24   Photo.
B1047 SP476 12 + 3fr Emblem   .80   .80
Surtax for the foundation.

Madonna SP477

Adoration of the Mystic Lamb, St. Bavon Cathedral Altarpiece, Ghent — SP478

Paintings by Hubert van Eyck (c. 1370-1426).

1986, Apr. 5   Photo.   Perf. 11½
B1048 SP477 9 + 2fr shown   .65   .65
B1049 SP477 13 + 3fr Christ in Majesty   .95   .95
B1050 SP477 24 + 6fr St. John the Baptist   1.75   1.75
Nos. B1048-B1050 (3)   3.35   3.35

Souvenir Sheet
B1051 SP478 50 + 12fr multi   5.25   5.25
Surtax for cultural organizations.

Antique Automobiles SP479

1986, Nov. 3   Photo.
B1052 SP479 9 + 2fr Lenoir, 1863   .65   .65
B1053 SP479 13 + 3fr Pipe de Tourisme, 1911   .90   .90
B1054 SP479 24 + 6fr Minerva 22 HP, 1930   1.75   1.75
B1055 SP479 26 + 6fr FN 8 Cylinder, 1931   1.90   1.90
Nos. B1052-B1055 (4)   5.20   5.20

Christmas 1986, New Year 1987 SP480

1986, Nov. 24   Photo.
B1056 SP480 13 + 1fr Village in winter   .75   .75

Natl. Red Cross — SP482

Nobel Prize winners for physiology (1938) and medicine (1974): No. B1058, Corneille Heymans (1892-1968). No. B1059, A. Claude (1899-1983).

Photogravure and Engraved
1987, Feb. 16   Perf. 11½
B1058 SP482 13 + 3fr dk brn & red   .90   .90
B1059 SP482 24 + 6fr dk brn & red   1.60   1.60

European Conservation Year — SP483

1987, Mar. 16   Photo.
B1060 SP483 9 + 2fr Bee orchid   .65   .65
B1061 SP483 24 + 6fr Horseshoe bat   1.60   1.60
B1062 SP483 26 + 6fr Peregrine falcon   1.75   1.75
Nos. B1060-B1062 (3)   4.00   4.00

Castles — SP484

1987, Oct. 17   Photo. & Engr.
B1063 SP484 9 + 2fr Rixensart   .60   .60
B1064 SP484 13 + 3fr Westerlo   .90   .90
B1065 SP484 26 + 5fr Fallais   1.75   1.75
B1066 SP484 50 + 12fr Gaasbeek   3.50   3.50
Nos. B1063-B1066 (4)   6.75   6.75

Christmas 1987 — SP485

Painting: Holy Family, by Rev. Father Lens.

1987, Nov. 14   Photo.
B1067 SP485 13 + 1fr multi   .85   .85

White and Yellow Cross of Belgium, 50th Anniv. — SP486

1987, Dec. 5
B1068 SP486 9 + 2fr multi   .70   .70

Promote Philately — SP487

Various flowers from Sixty Roses for a Queen, by P. J. Redoute (1759-1840).

1988, Apr. 25   Photo.   Perf. 11½
B1069 SP487 13 + 3fr shown   1.00   1.00
B1070 SP487 24 + 6fr multi, diff.   1.75   1.75

Souvenir Sheet
B1071 SP487 50 + 12fr multi, diff.   3.75   3.75
See #B1081-B1083, B1089-B1091, 1346.

1988 Summer Olympics, Seoul — SP488

1988, June 6   Photo.   Perf. 11½
B1072 SP488 9fr + 2fr Table tennis   .65   .65
B1073 SP488 13fr + 3fr Cycling   .95   .95

Souvenir Sheet
B1074 SP488 50fr + 12fr Marathon runners   3.70   3.70

Solidarity — SP489

1988, Oct. 24   Photo.   Perf. 12x11½
B1075 SP489 9fr + 2fr Jacques Brel   .60   .60
B1076 SP489 13fr + 3fr Jef Denyn   .90   .90
B1077 SP489 26fr + 6fr Fr. Ferdinand Verbiest   1.75   1.75
Nos. B1075-B1077 (3)   3.25   3.25

Belgian Red Cross SP490

Paintings: No. B1078, Crucifixion of Christ, by Rogier van der Weyden (c. 1399-1464). No. B1079, Virgin and Child, by David (c. 1460-

1523). B1089, The Good Samaritan, by Denis van Alsloot.

1989, Feb. 20   Photo.   Perf. 11½
B1078 SP490 9fr + 2fr multi   .60   .60
B1079 SP490 13fr + 3fr multi   .90   .90
B1080 SP490 24fr + 6fr multi   1.60   1.60
Nos. B1078-B1080 (3)   3.10   3.10

Stamp Collecting Promotion Type of 1988

Various flowers from Sixty Roses for a Queen, by P.J. Redoute (1759-1840) and inscriptions: No. B1081, "Centfeuille unique melee de rouge." No. B1082, "Bengale a grandes feuilles." No. B1083, Aeme vibere (tea roses).

1989, Apr. 17
B1081 SP487 13fr + 5fr multi   1.00   1.00
B1082 SP487 24fr + 6fr multi   1.60   1.60

Souvenir Sheet
B1083 SP487 50fr + 17fr multi   3.75   3.75

Solidarity SP491

Royal Greenhouses of Laeken.

1989, Oct. 23
B1084 SP491 9fr + 3fr Exterior   .60   .60
B1085 SP491 13fr + 4fr Interior, vert.   .85   .85
B1086 SP491 24fr + 5fr Dome exterior, vert.   1.40   1.40
B1087 SP491 26fr + 6fr Dome interior, vert.   1.50   1.50
Nos. B1084-B1087 (4)   4.35   4.35

Queen Elisabeth Chapelle Musicale, 50th Anniv. — SP492

1989, Nov. 6
B1088 SP492 24fr + 6fr G clef   1.50   1.50

Stamp Collecting Promotion Type of 1988

Various flowers from Sixty Roses for a Queen, by P.J. Redoute (1759-1840): No. B1089, Bengale desprez. No. B1090, Bengale philippe. No. B1091, Maria leonida.

1990, Feb. 5
B1089 SP487 14fr + 7fr multi   1.10   1.10
B1090 SP487 25fr + 12fr multi   2.00   2.00

Souvenir Sheet
B1091 SP487 50fr + 20fr multi   3.75   3.75

Youth and Music — SP493

14fr+3fr, Beethoven & Lamoraal, Count of Egmont (1522-1568). 25fr+6fr, Joseph Cantre (1890-1957), drawing & sculpture.

1990, Oct. 6
B1092 SP493 10fr + 2fr multi   .70   .70
B1093 SP493 14fr + 3fr multi   1.00   1.00
B1094 SP493 25fr + 6fr multi   1.75   1.75
Nos. B1092-B1094 (3)   3.45   3.45

King Baudouin & Queen Fabiola, 30th Wedding Anniv. — SP494

1990, Dec. 10
B1095 SP494 50fr +15fr multi   4.25 4.25

Belgian Red Cross SP495

Details from paintings: No. B1096, The Temptation of St. Anthony by Hieronymus Bosch. No. B1097, The Annunciation by Dirk Bouts.

1991, Feb. 25,   Photo.   *Perf. 11½*
B1096 SP495 14fr +3fr multi   1.10 1.10
B1097 SP495 25fr +6fr multi   2.00 2.00

Belgian Film Personalities — SP496

10fr+2fr, Charles Dekeukeleire (1905-71), producer. 14fr+3fr, Jacques Ledoux (1921-88), film conservationist. 25fr+6fr, Jacques Feyder (1899-1948), director.

1991, Oct. 28   Photo.   *Perf. 11½*
B1098 SP496 10fr +2fr multi   .75 .75
B1099 SP496 14fr +3fr multi   1.10 1.10
B1100 SP496 25fr +6fr multi   1.90 1.90
   Nos. B1098-B1100 (3)   3.75 3.75

1992 Winter and Summer Olympics, Albertville and Barcelona SP497

1992, Jan. 20   Photo.   *Perf. 11½*
B1101 SP497 10fr +2fr Speed skating   .75 .75
B1102 SP497 10fr +2fr Baseball   .75 .75
B1103 SP497 14fr +3fr Women's tennis, horiz.   1.10 1.10
B1104 SP497 25fr +6fr Skeet shooting   1.90 1.90
   Nos. B1101-B1104 (4)   4.50 4.50

Folk Legends SP498

11fr + 2fr, Proud Margaret. 15fr + 3fr, Gustine Maca & the Witches. 28fr + 6fr, Reynard the Fox.

1992, June 22   Photo.   *Perf. 11½*
B1105 SP498 11fr +2fr multi   .80 .80
B1106 SP498 15fr +3fr multi   1.10 1.10
B1107 SP498 28fr +6fr multi   2.00 2.00
   Nos. B1105-B1107 (3)   3.90 3.90

Belgian Red Cross SP499

Paintings: 15fr + 3fr, Man with the Pointed Hat, by Adriaen Brouwer (1605-1638). 28fr + 7fr, Nereid and Triton, by Peter Paul Rubens, horiz.

1993, Feb. 15   Photo.   *Perf. 11½*
B1108 SP499 15fr +3fr multi   1.10 1.10
B1109 SP499 28fr +7fr multi   2.10 2.10

Fight Against Cancer SP500

1993, Sept. 20   Photo.   *Perf. 11½*
B1110 SP500 15fr +3fr multi   1.10 1.10

Intl. Olympic Committee, Cent. — SP501

#B1112, Soccer players. #B1113, Figure skater.

1994, Feb. 14   Photo.   *Perf. 11½*
B1111 SP501 16fr +3fr multi   1.00 1.00
B1112 SP501 16fr +3fr multi   1.00 1.00
B1113 SP501 16fr +3fr multi   1.00 1.00
   Nos. B1111-B1113 (3)   3.00 3.00

1994 World Cup Soccer Championships, Los Angeles (#B1112). 1994 Winter Olympics, Lillehammer, Norway (#B1113).

Porcelain — SP502

Designs: No. B1114, Tournai plate, Museum of Mariemont-Morlanweiz. No. B1115, Etterbeek cup, saucer, Municipal Museum, Louvain. 50fr+11fr, Delft earthenware jars, Pharmacy Museum of Maaseik.

1994, June 27   Photo.   *Perf. 11½*
B1114 SP502 16fr +3fr multi   1.10 1.10
B1115 SP502 16fr +3fr multi   1.10 1.10
   Souvenir Sheet
B1116 SP502 50fr +11fr multi   3.50 3.50
No. B1116 contains one 49x38mm stamp.

Solidarity SP503

Design: 16fr+3fr, Hearing-impaired person.

1994, Nov. 14   Photo.   *Perf. 11½*
B1117 SP503 16fr +3fr multi   1.25 1.25

Museums — SP504

#B1118, Natl. Flax Museum, Kortrijk. #B1119, Natl. Water & Fountain Museum, Genval. 34fr+6fr, Intl. Carnival and Mask Museum, Binche.

1995, Jan. 30   Photo.   *Perf. 11½*
B1118 SP504 16fr +3fr multi   1.25 1.25
B1119 SP504 16fr +3fr multi   1.25 1.25
   Souvenir Sheet
B1120 SP504 34fr +6fr multi   2.75 2.75
Surtax for promotion of philately.

"Souvenir Sheets"
   Beginning in 1995 items looking like souvenir sheets have appeared in the market. The 1995 one has the design used for No. B1120. The 1996 one has the design similar to the one used for No. B1128. The 1997 one has the design used for No. B1131. These have no postal value.

Royal Belgian Soccer Assoc., Cent. SP505

1995, Aug. 21   Photo.   *Perf. 11½*
B1121 SP505 16fr +4fr multi   1.40 1.40

Belgian Red Cross SP506

#B1122, Princess Astrid, chairwoman of Belgian Red Cross. #B1123, Wilhelm C. Röntgen (1845-1923), discoverer of the X-ray. #B1124, Louis Pasteur (1822-95), scientist.

1995, Sept. 11
B1122 SP506 16fr +3fr multi   1.25 1.25
B1123 SP506 16fr +3fr multi   1.25 1.25
B1124 SP506 16fr +3fr multi   1.25 1.25
   Nos. B1122-B1124 (3)   3.75 3.75

Solidarity — SP507

1995, Nov. 6   Photo.   *Perf. 11½*
B1125 SP507 16fr +4fr multi   1.25 1.25
Surtax for fight against AIDS.

Museums — SP508

#B1126, Museum of Walloon Life, Liège. #B1127, Natl. Gin Museum, Hasselt. 34fr+6fr, Butchers' Guild Hall Museum, Antwerp.

1996, Feb. 19   Photo.   *Perf. 11½*
B1126 SP508 16fr +4fr multi   1.25 1.25
B1127 SP508 16fr +4fr multi   1.25 1.25
   Souvenir Sheet
B1128 SP508 34fr +6fr multi   2.50 2.50

Modern Olympic Games, Cent. SP509

1996, July 1   Photo.   *Perf. 11½*
B1129 SP509 16fr +4fr Table tennis   1.25 1.25
B1130 SP509 16fr +4fr Swimming   1.25 1.25
   Souvenir Sheet
B1131 SP509 34fr +6fr High jump   2.50 2.50
No. B1131 contains one 49x38mm stamp.

UNICEF, 50th Anniv. SP510

1996, Nov. 18   Photo.   *Perf. 11½*
B1132 SP510 16fr +4fr multi   1.40 1.40

Museums SP511

#B1133, Deportation and Resistance Museum, Mechlin. #B1134, Iron Museum, Saint Hubert. 41fr+9fr, Horta Museum, Saint Gilles.

1997, Jan. 20   Photo.   *Perf. 11½*
B1133 SP511 17fr +4fr multi   1.25 1.25
B1134 SP511 17fr +4fr multi   1.25 1.25
   Souvenir Sheet
B1135 SP511 41fr +9fr multi   3.00 3.00
Surtax for "Pro-Post" association.

Judo — SP512

1997, May 5   Photo.   *Perf. 11½*
B1136 SP512 17fr +4fr Men's (10a)   1.25 1.25
B1137 SP512 17fr +4fr Women's (10b)   1.25 1.25
Surtax for Belgian Olympic Committee.

Solidarity — SP513

1997, Oct. 25
B1138 SP513 17fr +4fr multi   1.25 1.25
Surtax for Multiple Sclerosis research.

King Leopold
III — SP514

32fr+15fr, King Baudouin I. 50fr+25fr, King
Albert II.

1998, Feb. 16   Engr.   Perf. 11½
B1139 SP514 17fr +8fr dk grn   1.50 1.50
B1140 SP514 32fr +15fr dk brn
    blk   2.75 2.75
Souvenir Sheet
B1141 SP514 50fr +25fr dk vio
    brn   4.50 4.50
See #B1146-B1148, 1748, B1154-B1156,
1842, B1158-B1160.

Sports
SP515

1998, June 8   Photo.   Perf. 11½
B1142 SP515 17fr +4fr Pelota   1.25 1.25
B1143 SP515 17fr +4fr Handball   1.25 1.25
Souvenir Sheet
B1144 SP515 30fr +7fr Soccer   2.00 2.00
1998 World Cup Soccer Championships,
France (#B1144).

Assist the
Blind — SP516

Photo. & Embossed
1998, Nov. 9   Perf. 11½
B1145 SP516 17fr +4fr multi   1.25 1.25
Face value is indicated in Braille.

Royalty Type of 1998
Designs: 17fr+8fr, King Albert I. 32fr+15fr,
King Leopold II. 50fr+25fr, King Leopold I.

1999, Jan. 25   Engr.   Perf. 11½
B1146 SP514 17fr +8fr deep
    green   1.50 1.50
B1147 SP514 32fr +15fr black   2.75 2.75
Souvenir Sheet
B1148 SP514 50fr +25fr deep
    brown   4.50 4.50

Motorcycles — SP517

1999, May 17   Photo.
B1149 SP517 17fr +4fr Speed
    race   1.10 1.10
B1150 SP517 17fr +4fr Trial, vert. 1.10 1.10
Souvenir Sheet
B1151 SP517 30fr +7fr
    Motocross,
    vert.   2.00 2.00

Solidarity
SP518

#1152, First aid. #1153, Dental care, vert.

1999, Nov. 8   Photo.   Perf. 11½
B1152 SP518 17fr +4fr multi   1.00 1.00
B1153 SP518 17fr +4fr multi   1.00 1.00

Royalty Type of 1998
Queens: 17fr + 8fr, Astrid (1905-35). 32fr
+15fr, Fabiola (b. 1928). 50fr +25fr, Paola (b.
1937).

Photo. & Engr.
2000, Jan. 24   Perf. 11½
B1154 SP514 17fr +8fr green   1.25 1.25
B1155 SP514 32fr +15fr black   2.25 2.25
Souvenir Sheet
B1156 SP514 50fr +25fr claret   3.75 3.75

Red
Cross/Red
Crescent
SP519

2000, Mar. 27   Photo.   Perf. 11½
B1157 SP519 17fr +4fr multi   .95 .95

Royalty Type of 1998
Queens: 17fr+8fr, Elisabeth (1876-1965).
32fr+15fr, Marie-Henriette (1836-1902).
50fr+25fr, Louise-Marie (1812-50).

Photo. & Engr.
2001, Feb. 12   Perf. 11½
B1158 SP514 17fr +8fr green   1.10 1.10
B1159 SP514 32fr +15fr black   2.25 2.25
Souvenir Sheet
B1160 SP514 50fr +25fr brown   3.50 3.50

Sports
SP520

World championship meets: No. B1161,
Cycle track racing, Antwerp. No. B1162, Artis-
tic gymnastics, Ghent.

2001, June 14   Photo.   Perf. 11½
B1161 SP520 17fr +4fr multi   .90 .90
B1162 SP520 17fr +4fr multi   .90 .90

Red Cross
Volunteers
SP521

2001, Sept. 10
B1163 SP521 17fr +4fr multi   .95 .95

AIR POST STAMPS

Fokker
FVII/3m over
Ostend
AP1

Designs: 1.50fr, Plane over St. Hubert. 2fr,
over Namur. 5fr, over Brussels.

Perf. 11½
1930, Apr. 30   Unwmk.   Photo.
C1 AP1 50c blue   .40 .40
C2 AP1 1.50fr black brn   2.25 2.50
C3 AP1 2fr deep green   2.00 .55
C4 AP1 5fr brown lake   1.75 .95
    Nos. C1-C4 (4)   6.40 4.40
    Set, never hinged   20.00
      Exist imperf.

1930, Dec. 5
C5 AP1 5fr dark violet   25.00 25.00
    Never hinged   45.00
Issued for use on a mail carrying flight from
Brussels to Leopoldville, Belgian Congo, start-
ing Dec. 7.
    Exists imperf.

#C2, C4 Surcharged in Carmine or
Blue

1935, May 23
C6 AP1 1fr on 1.50fr (C)   .55 .40
C7 AP1 4fr on 5fr (Bl)   7.50 7.00
    Set, never hinged 25.00

> **Catalogue values for unused
> stamps in this section, from this
> point to the end of the section, are
> for Never Hinged items.**

DC-4
Skymaster,
Sabena
Airline
AP5

1946, Apr. 20   Engr.   Perf. 11½
C8 AP5 6fr blue   .75 .25
C9 AP5 8.50fr violet brn   1.00 .35
C10 AP5 50fr yellow grn   5.00 .60
  a. Perf. 12x11½ ('54)   325.00 1.00
C11 AP5 100fr gray   8.25 .80
  a. Perf. 12x11½ ('54)   65.00 1.10
    Nos. C8-C11 (4)   15.00 2.00

Evolution of Postal
Transportation — AP6

1949, July 1
C12 AP6 50fr dark brown   42.50 15.00
Centenary of Belgian postage stamps.

Glider — AP7

Design: 7fr, "Tipsy" plane.

1951, June 18   Photo.   Perf. 13½
C12A   Strip of 2 + label   60.00 40.00
  b. AP7 6fr dark blue   20.00 14.00
  c. AP7 7fr carmine rose   20.00 14.00
For the 50th anniv. of the Aero Club of
Belgium. The strip sold for 50fr.

1951, July 25   Perf. 13½
C13 AP7 6fr sepia   4.50 .20
C14 AP7 7fr Prus green   3.50 .95

UN Types of Regular Issue, 1958
Designs: 5fr, ICAO. 6fr, World Meteorologi-
cal Organization. 7.50fr, Protection of Refu-
gees. 8fr, General Agreement on Tariffs and
Trade. 9fr, UNICEF. 10fr, Atomic Energy
Agency.

Perf. 11½
1958, Apr. 17   Unwmk.   Engr.
C15 A137 5fr dull blue   .25 .30
C16 A136 6fr yellow grn   .30 .45
C17 A137 7.50fr lilac   .30 .30
C18 A136 8fr sepia   .30 .30
C19 A137 9fr carmine   .40 .50
C20 A136 10fr redsh brown   .75 .60
    Nos. C15-C20 (6)   2.30 2.45
World's Fair, Brussels, Apr. 17-Oct. 19. See
note after No. 476.

AIR POST SEMI-POSTAL STAMPS

> **Catalogue values for unused
> stamps in this section are for
> Never Hinged items.**

American Soldier in Combat — SPAP1

Perf. 11x11½
1946, June 15   Unwmk.   Engr.
CB1 SPAP1 17.50fr + 62.50fr dl
    brn   2.00 .90
CB2 SPAP1 17.50fr + 62.50fr dl
    gray grn   2.00 .90
Surtax for an American memorial at
Bastogne.
An overprint, "Hommage a Roosevelt," was
privately applied to Nos. CB1-CB2 in 1947 by
the Association Belgo-Americaine.
In 1950 another private overprint was
applied, in red, to Nos. CB1-CB2. It consists of
"16-12-1944, 25-1-1945, Dedication July 16,
1950" and outlines of the American eagle
emblem and the Bastogne Memorial. Similar
overprints were applied to Nos. 265 and 345.

Flight
Allegory
SPAP2

1946, Sept. 7   **Perf. 11½**
CB3 SPAP2 2fr + 8fr brt vio   .60 1.00

The surtax was for the benefit of aviation.

Nos. B417-B425 Surcharged in
Various Arrangements in Red or Dark
Blue

Type I   Type II

Type I- Top line "POSTE AERIENNE"
Type II- Top line "LUCHTPOST"

1947, May 18   Photo.   Perf. 11½
Type I
CB4 SP227 1fr + 2fr (R)   .60   .90
CB5 SP228 1.50fr + 2.50fr   .60   .90
CB6 SP229 2fr + 45fr   .60   .90
CB7 SP230 1fr + 2fr (R)   .60   .90
CB8 SP231 1.50fr + 2.50fr   .60   .90
CB9 SP232 2fr + 45fr   .60   .90
CB10 SP233 1fr + 2fr (R)   .60   .90
CB11 SP234 1.50fr + 2.50fr (R) .60   .90
CB12 SP235 2fr + 45fr   .60   .90

Type II
CB4A SP227 1fr + 2fr (R)   .60   .90
CB5A SP228 1.50fr + 2.50fr   .60   .90
CB6A SP229 2fr + 45fr   .60   .90
CB7A SP230 1fr + 2fr (R)   .60   .90
CB8A SP231 1.50fr + 2.50fr   .60   .90
CB9A SP232 2fr + 45fr   .60   .90
CB10A SP233 1fr + 2fr (R)   .60   .90
CB11A SP234 1.50fr + 2.50fr (R) .60   .90
CB12A SP235 2fr + 45fr   .60   .90
    Nos. CB4-CB12A (18)   10.80 16.20

Issued for CIPEX, NYC. In 1948 Nos. CB4-
CB12 and CB4A-CB12A were punched with
the letters "IMABA," and the inscription "Imaba
du 21 au 29 aout 1948" was applied to the
backs. Value $20.

Helicopter
Leaving
Airport
SPAP3

1950, Aug. 7
CB13 SPAP3 7fr + 3fr blue   9.00 5.25

Surtax for the Natl. Aeronautical Committee.

SPECIAL DELIVERY STAMPS

From 1874 to 1903 certain hexagonal
telegraph stamps were used as special
delivery stamps.

Town Hall,
Brussels — SD1

Eupen — SD2

2.35fr, Street in Ghent. 3.50fr, Bishop's Palace, Liege. 5.25fr, Notre Dame Cathedral,
Antwerp.

1929   Unwmk.   Photo.   Perf. 11½
E1 SD1 1.75fr dark blue   .80   .30
E2 SD1 2.35fr carmine   1.50   .45
E3 SD1 3.50fr dark violet   10.00   9.00
E4 SD1 5.25fr olive green   5.50   5.25

1931
E5 SD2 2.45fr dark green   11.00   2.50
    Nos. E1-E5 (5)   28.80 17.50

No. E5 Surcharged in **2$^{Fr}_{50}$**
Red

1932
E6 SD2 2.50fr on 2.45fr dk grn   9.00 1.25

POSTAGE DUE STAMPS

D1   D2

1870   Unwmk.   Typo.   Perf. 15
J1 D1 10c green   3.75 2.00
J2 D1 20c ultra, thin paper   30.00 3.75

In 1909 many bisects of Nos. J1-J2 were
created. The 10c bisect used as 5c on piece
sells for $3.50.

No. J2 was also printed on thicker paper
and in aniline ink on thin paper.

1895-09   **Perf. 14**
J3 D2 5c yellow grn   .20   .20
J4 D2 10c orange brn   17.50   1.75
J5 D2 10c carmine ('00)   .20   .20
J6 D2 20c olive green   .20   .20
J7 D2 30c pale blue ('09) .30   .25
J8 D2 50c yellow brn   17.50   5.00
J9 D2 50c gray ('00)   .75   .45
J10 D2 1fr carmine   20.00 11.50
J11 D2 1fr ocher ('00)   6.50   5.00
    Nos. J3-J11 (9)   63.15 24.55

1916   **Redrawn**
J12 D2 5c blue grn   25.00   7.00
J13 D2 10c carmine   42.50 11.00
J14 D2 20c dp gray grn   42.50 15.00
J15 D2 30c brt blue   6.00   5.00
J16 D2 50c gray   125.00 60.00
    Nos. J12-J16 (5)   241.00 98.00

In the redrawn stamps the lions have a
heavy, colored outline. There is a thick vertical
line at the outer edge of the design on each
side.

D3   D4

1919   **Perf. 14**
J17 D3 5c green   .40   .50
J18 D3 10c carmine   .95   .35
J19 D3 20c gray green   7.25   1.25
J20 D3 30c bright blue   1.40   .40
J21 D3 50c gray   2.75   .50
    Nos. J17-J21 (5)   12.75   3.00

The 5c, 10c, 20c and 50c values also exist
perf 14x15.

1922-32   **Perf. 14x13½**
J22 D4 5c dk gray   .20   .20
J23 D4 10c green   .20   .20
J24 D4 20c deep brown   .20   .20
J25 D4 30c ver ('24)   .65   .20
  a.   30c rose red   1.00   .45
J26 D4 40c red brn ('25)   .25   .20
J27 D4 50c ultra   1.90   .20
J28 D4 70c red brn ('29)   .30   .20
J29 D4 1fr violet ('25)   .45   .20
J30 D4 1fr rose lilac ('32) .55   .20
J31 D4 1.20fr ol grn ('29) .65   .45
J32 D4 1.50fr ol grn ('32) .65   .45
J33 D4 2fr violet ('29)   .75   .20
J34 D4 3.50fr dp blue ('29) 1.00 .25
    Nos. J22-J34 (13)   7.75   3.15

1934-46   **Perf. 14x13½**
J35 D4 35c green ('35)   .40   .45
J36 D4 50c slate   .20   .20
J37 D4 60c carmine ('38)   .40   .30
J38 D4 80c slate ('38)   .30   .20
J39 D4 1.40fr gray ('35)   .65   .45
J39A D4 3fr org brn ('46) 1.50   .60
J39B D4 7fr brt red vio ('46) 2.25 3.25
    Nos. J35-J39B (7)   5.70   5.45

See Nos. J54-J61.

> **Catalogue values for unused
> stamps in this section, from this
> point to the end of the section, are
> for Never Hinged items.**

D5   D6

1945   Typo.   Perf. 12½
Inscribed "TE BETALEN" at Top
J40 D5 10c gray olive   .20   .20
J41 D5 20c ultramarine   .20   .20
J42 D5 30c carmine   .20   .20
J43 D5 40c black violet   .20   .20
J44 D5 50c dl bl grn   .20   .20
J45 D5 1fr sepia   .20   .20
J46 D5 2fr red orange   .20   .20

Inscribed "A PAYER" at Top
J47 D5 10c gray olive   .20   .20
J48 D5 20c ultramarine   .20   .20
J49 D5 30c carmine   .20   .20
J50 D5 40c black vio   .20   .20
J51 D5 50c dl bl grn   .20   .20
J52 D5 1fr sepia   .20   .20
J53 D5 2fr red orange   .20   .20
    Nos. J40-J53 (14)   2.80   2.80

Type of 1922-32

1949-53   Typo.   Perf. 14x13½
J54 D4 65c emerald   7.00   3.75
J55 D4 1.60fr lilac rose ('53) 14.00 6.50
J56 D4 1.80fr red   15.00   6.50
J57 D4 2.40fr gray lilac ('53) 9.00 4.00
J58 D4 4fr deep blue ('53) 11.00   .50
J59 D4 5fr red brown   3.50   .40
J60 D4 8fr lilac rose   7.25   3.75
J61 D4 10fr dark violet   7.25   3.75
    Nos. J54-J61 (8)   74.00 29.15

Numerals 6½mm or More High
1966-70   **Photo.**
J62 D6 1fr brt pink   .20   .20
J63 D6 2fr blue green   .20   .20
J64 D6 3fr blue   .20   .20
J65 D6 5fr purple   .25   .20
J66 D6 6fr bister brn   .40   .25
J67 D6 7fr red org ('70)   .45   .30
J68 D6 20fr slate grn   1.50   1.00
    Nos. J62-J68 (7)   3.20   2.35

Printed on various papers.

Numerals 4½-5½mm High
1985-87   Photo.   Perf. 14x13½
J69 D6 1fr lilac rose   .20   .20
J70 D6 2fr dull blue grn   .20   .20
J71 D6 3fr greenish blue   .20   .20
J72 D6 4fr green   .20   .20
J73 D6 5fr lt violet   .25   .20
J74 D6 7fr brt orange   .35   .30
J75 D6 8fr pale gray   .40   .30
J76 D6 9fr rose lake   .45   .35
J77 D6 10fr lt red brown   .50   .40
J78 D6 20fr lt olive grn 1.10   1.10
    Nos. J69-J78 (10)   3.85   3.45

Printed on various papers.
Issue dates: 3fr, 4fr, 8fr-10fr, Mar. 25, 1985.
2fr, 20fr, 1986. 1fr, 5fr, 7fr, 1987.
This is an expanding set. Numbers will
change again if necessary.

MILITARY STAMPS

> **Catalogue values for unused
> stamps in this section are for
> Never Hinged items.**

King Baudouin
M1   M2

1967, July 17   Photo.   Perf. 11
Unwmk.
M1 M1 1.50fr greenish gray   .25 .25

1971-75   Engr.   Perf. 11½
M2 M2 1.75fr gray green   .50 .45
M3 M2 2.25fr gray green ('72) .30 .30
M4 M2 2.50fr gray green ('74) .20 .20
M5 M2 3.25fr vio brown ('75) .25 .20
    Nos. M2-M5 (4)   1.25 1.15

#M1-M3 are luminescent, #M4-M5 are not.

MILITARY PARCEL POST STAMP

Type of Parcel Post Stamp of 1938
Surcharged with New Value and "M"
in Blue.

1939   Unwmk.   Perf. 13½
MQ1 PP19 3fr on 5.50fr copper red .30 .20

OFFICIAL STAMPS

For franking the official
correspondence of the Administration
of the Belgian National Railways.

Most examples of Nos. O1-O25 in the
marketplace are counterfeits. Values
are for genuine examples.

Regular Issue of 1921-
27 Overprinted in Black

1929-30   Unwmk.   Perf. 14
O1 A58 5c gray   .20   .20
O2 A58 10c blue green   .30   .40
O3 A58 35c blue green   .40   .30
O4 A58 60c olive green   .45   .30
O5 A58 1.50fr brt blue   8.00   6.25
O6 A58 1.75fr ultra ('30) 1.75   .20
    Nos. O1-O6 (6)   11.10   9.45

Same Overprint, in Red or Black, on
Regular Issues of 1929-30

1929-31
O7 A63 5c slate (R)   .25   .35
O8 A63 10c olive grn (R) .50   .40
O9 A63 25c rose red (Bk) 1.50   .85
O10 A63 35c dp green (R) 1.75   .50
O11 A63 40c red vio (Bk) 1.25   .45
O12 A63 50c dp blue (R) ('31) .80 .35
O13 A63 60c rose (Bk)   6.00   6.00
O14 A63 70c orange brn (Bk) 4.25 1.25
O15 A63 75c black vio (R)
         ('31)   4.00   .85
    Nos. O7-O15 (9)   20.30 11.00

Overprinted on Regular Issue of
1932

1932
O16 A73 10c olive grn (R) .50   .60
O17 A74 35c dp green   9.00   .75
O18 A71a 75c bister brn (R) 1.50 .30
    Nos. O16-O18 (3)   11.00   1.65

Overprinted on No. 262 in Red

1935   **Perf. 13½x14**
O19 A80 70c olive black   2.75   .25

Regular Stamps of 1935-36 Overprinted in Red

1936-38   Perf. 13½, 13½x14, 14

O20	A82	10c olive bister	.20	.35
O21	A82	35c green	.25	.40
O22	A82	50c dark blue	.45	.35
O23	A83	70c brown	1.50	.65

Overprinted in Black or Red on Regular Issue of 1938

Perf. 13½x14

O24	A82	40c red violet (Bk)	.30	.35
O25	A85	75c olive gray (R)	.65	.30
		Nos. O20-O25 (6)	3.35	2.40

Regular Issues of 1935-41 Overprinted in Red or Dark Blue

1941-44   Perf. 14, 14x13½, 13½x14

O26	A82	10c olive bister	.20	.20
a.		Inverted overprint		40.00
O27	A82	40c red violet	.55	.75
O28	A82	50c dark blue	.20	.20
a.		Inverted overprint		
O29	A83a	1fr rose car (Bl)	.45	.35
O30	A85	1fr rose pink (Bl)	.20	.20
O31	A83a	2.25fr grnsh blk ('44)	.30	.50
O32	A84	2.25fr gray violet	.45	.70
		Nos. O26-O32 (7)	2.35	2.90

Nos. O21, O23 and O25 Surcharged with New Values in Black or Red

1942

O33	A82	10c on 35c green	.20	.35
O34	A83	50c on 70c brown	.20	.20
O35	A85	50c on 75c ol gray (R)	.20	.20
		Nos. O33-O35 (3)	.60	.75

Counterfeits exist on Nos. O26-O35.

> **Catalogue values for unused stamps in this section, from this point to the end of the section, are for Never Hinged items.**

O1   O2

1946-48   Unwmk.   Perf. 14

O36	O1	10c olive bister	.25	.20
O37	O1	20c brt violet	2.00	.50
O38	O1	50c dk blue	.25	.20
O39	O1	65c red lilac ('48)	3.25	.75
O40	O1	75c lilac rose	.25	.20
O41	O1	90c brown violet	4.25	.35
		Nos. O36-O41 (6)	10.25	2.20

Types A99, A101 and A102 with "B" Emblem Added to Design

1948   Perf. 11½

O42	A99	1.35fr red brown	4.25	.75
O43	A99	1.75fr dk gray green	4.75	.25
O44	A101	3fr brt red violet	25.00	3.50
O45	A102	3.15fr deep blue	11.00	7.00
O46	A102	4fr brt ultra	20.00	13.00
		Nos. O42-O46 (5)	65.00	24.50

1953-66   Typo.   Perf. 13½x14

O47	O2	10c orange	.65	.20
O48	O2	20c red lilac	.80	.25
O49	O2	30c gray green ('58)	.80	.55
O50	O2	40c olive gray	.50	.20
O51	O2	50c light blue	.75	.20
O51A	O2	60c lilac rose ('66)	1.10	.55
O52	O2	65c red lilac	27.50	21.00
O53	O2	80c emerald	4.50	.70
O54	O2	90c deep blue	6.00	.85
O55	O2	1fr rose	.40	.20
		Nos. O47-O55 (10)	43.00	24.70

See Nos. O66, O68.

King Baudouin
O3   O4

1954-70   Photo.   Perf. 11½

O56	O3	1.50fr gray	.30	.20
O57	O3	2fr rose red	37.50	.25
O58	O3	2fr blue grn ('59)	.30	.20
O59	O3	2.50fr red brown ('58)	27.50	.75
O60	O3	3fr red lilac ('58)	1.25	.20
O61	O3	3.50fr yel green ('70)	.75	.20
O62	O3	4fr brt blue	.90	.25
O63	O3	6fr car rose ('58)	1.50	.60
		Nos. O56-O63 (8)	70.00	2.65

Type of 1953-66 Redrawn

1970-75   Typo.   Perf. 13½x14

O66	O2	1.50fr grnsh gray ('75)	.20	.20
O68	O2	2.50fr brown	.20	.20

1971-73   Engr.   Perf. 11½

O71	O4	3.50fr org brn ('73)	.25	.25
O72	O4	4.50fr brown ('73)	.25	.25
O73	O4	7fr red	.40	.50
O74	O4	15fr violet	.75	.30
		Nos. O71-O74 (4)	1.65	1.30

Nos. O71-O74 are on luminescent paper.

1974-80

O75	O4	3fr yellow grn	1.50	1.00
O76	O4	4fr blue	1.50	.50
O77	O4	4.50fr grnsh bl ('75)	.30	.20
O78	O4	5fr lilac	.30	.20
O79	O4	6fr carmine ('78)	.35	.20
O80	O4	6.50fr black ('76)	.40	.35
O81	O4	8fr bluish blk ('78)	.50	.25
O82	O4	9fr lt red brn ('80)	.55	.25
O83	O4	10fr rose carmine	.60	.25
O84	O4	25fr lilac ('76)	1.50	.50
O85	O4	30fr org brn ('78)	1.75	.50
		Nos. O75-O85 (11)	9.25	4.20

Heraldic Lion — O5

1977-82   Typo.   Perf. 13½x14

O87	O5	50c brown ('82)	.20	.20
O92	O5	1fr lilac ('82)	.20	.20
O94	O5	2fr orange ('82)	.20	.20
O95	O5	4fr red brown	.25	.20
O96	O5	5fr green ('80)	.25	.20
		Nos. O87-O96 (5)	1.10	1.00

NEWSPAPER STAMPS

Most examples of Nos. P1-P40 in the marketplace are counterfeits. Values are for genuine examples.

Parcel Post Stamps of 1923-27 Overprinted

Perf. 14½x14, 14x14½

1928   Unwmk.

P1	PP12	10c vermilion	.25	.40
P2	PP12	20c turq blue	.25	.40
P3	PP12	40c olive grn	.25	.40
P4	PP12	60c orange	.70	.90
P5	PP12	70c dk brown	.45	.40
P6	PP12	80c violet	.60	.70
P7	PP12	90c slate	2.25	2.00
P8	PP13	1fr brt blue	.90	.60
a.		1fr ultramarine	12.00	5.00
P10	PP13	2fr olive grn	1.50	.60
P11	PP13	3fr orange red	1.60	.90
P12	PP13	4fr rose	2.25	1.10
P13	PP13	5fr violet	2.25	1.00
P14	PP13	6fr bister brn	4.50	1.75
P15	PP13	7fr orange	5.00	2.25
P16	PP13	8fr dk brown	6.00	2.75
P17	PP13	9fr red violet	10.00	3.00
P18	PP13	10fr blue green	9.00	2.75
P19	PP13	20fr magenta	15.00	7.00
		Nos. P1-P8,P10-P19 (18)	62.75	28.90

Parcel Post Stamps of 1923-28 Overprinted

1929-31

P20	PP12	10c vermilion	.25	.20
P21	PP12	20c turq blue	.25	.20
P22	PP12	40c olive green	.30	.20
a.		Inverted overprint		
P23	PP12	60c orange	.55	.35
P24	PP12	70c dk brown	.55	.20
P25	PP12	80c violet	.60	.25
P26	PP12	90c gray	2.00	1.00
P27	PP13	1fr ultra	.60	.25
a.		1fr bright blue	4.00	2.50
P28	PP13	1.10fr org brn ('31)	6.25	1.40
P29	PP13	1.50fr gray vio ('31)	6.25	1.90
P30	PP13	2fr olive green	2.00	.25
P31	PP13	2.10fr sl gray ('31)	17.00	12.00
P32	PP13	3fr orange red	2.25	.45
P33	PP13	4fr rose	2.25	.70
P34	PP13	5fr violet	3.00	.55
P35	PP13	6fr bister brn	3.75	1.00
P36	PP13	7fr orange	3.75	1.00
P37	PP13	8fr dk brown	3.75	1.00
P38	PP13	9fr red violet	5.25	1.50
P39	PP13	10fr blue green	3.75	1.10
P40	PP13	20fr magenta	13.00	4.50
		Nos. P20-P40 (21)	77.35	30.00

PARCEL POST AND RAILWAY STAMPS

> Values for used Railway Stamps (Chemins de Fer) stamps are for copies with railway cancellations. Railway Stamps with postal cancellations sell for twice as much.

Coat of Arms — PP1

1879-82   Unwmk.   Typo.   Perf. 14

Q1	PP1	10c violet brown	57.50	5.75
Q2	PP1	20c blue	175.00	17.50
Q3	PP1	25c green ('81)	225.00	10.00
Q4	PP1	50c carmine	1,250.	10.00
Q5	PP1	80c yellow	1,350.	57.50
Q6	PP1	1fr gray ('82)	175.00	16.00

Used copies of Nos. Q1-Q6 with pinholes, a normal state, sell for approximately one third the values given.

Most of the stamps of 1882-1902 (Nos. Q7 to Q28) are without watermark. Twice in each sheet of 100 stamps they have one of three watermarks: (1) A winged wheel and "Chemins de Fer de l'Etat Belge," (2) Coat of Arms of Belgium and "Royaume de Belgique," (3) Larger Coat of Arms, without inscription.

PP2

1882-94   Perf. 15½x14¼

Q7	PP2	10c brown ('86)	20.00	1.50
Q8	PP2	15c gray ('94)	8.75	7.25
Q9	PP2	20c blue ('86)	65.00	7.00
Q10	PP2	25c yel grn ('91)	72.50	4.25
Q11	PP2	50c carmine	72.50	2.50
Q12	PP2	80c brnsh buff	72.50	.90
Q13	PP2	80c lemon	75.00	1.60
Q14	PP2	1fr lavender	350.00	3.00
Q15	PP2	2fr yel buff ('94)	210.00	67.50

Counterfeits exist.

PP3

Name of engraver below frame

1895-97

Numerals in Black, except 1fr, 2fr

Q16	PP3	10c red brown ('96)	11.00	.60
Q17	PP3	15c gray	11.00	7.00
Q18	PP3	20c blue	17.50	5.00
Q19	PP3	25c green	17.50	1.25
Q20	PP3	50c carmine	25.00	.80
Q21	PP3	60c violet ('96)	50.00	1.00
Q22	PP3	80c ol yel ('96)	50.00	1.40
Q23	PP3	1fr lilac brown	175.00	3.00
Q24	PP3	2fr yel buff ('97)	200.00	15.00

Counterfeits exist.

1901-02

Numerals in Black

Q25	PP3	30c orange	21.00	2.00
Q26	PP3	40c green	26.00	1.75
Q27	PP3	70c blue	50.00	1.40
a.		Numerals omitted	750.00	
b.		Numerals printed on reverse	750.00	
Q28	PP3	90c red	65.00	2.00
		Nos. Q25-CQ28 (4)	162.00	7.15

Winged Wheel PP4

Without engraver's name

1902-14   Perf. 15

Q29	PP3	10c yel brn & slate	.20	.20
Q30	PP3	15c slate & vio	.20	.20
Q31	PP3	20c ultra & yel brn	.20	.20
Q32	PP3	25c yel grn & red	.20	.20
Q33	PP3	30c orange & bl grn	.20	.20
Q34	PP3	35c bister & bl grn ('12)	.35	.20
Q35	PP3	40c blue grn & vio	.20	.20
Q36	PP3	50c pale rose & vio	.20	.20
Q37	PP3	55c lilac brn & ultra ('14)	.35	.20
Q38	PP3	60c violet & red	.20	.20
Q39	PP3	70c blue & red	.20	.20
Q40	PP3	80c lemon & vio brn	.20	.20
Q41	PP3	90c red & yel grn	.20	.20
Q42	PP4	1fr vio brn & org	.20	.20
Q43	PP4	1.10fr rose & blk ('06)	.20	.20
Q44	PP4	2fr ocher & bl grn	.20	.20
Q45	PP4	3fr black & ultra	.35	.20
Q46	PP4	4fr yel grn & red ('13)	1.25	.70
Q47	PP4	5fr org & bl grn ('13)	.55	.55
Q48	PP4	10fr ol yel & brn vio ('13)	.90	.55
		Nos. Q29-Q48 (20)	6.55	5.20

Regular Issues of 1912-13 Handstamped in Violet

1915   Perf. 14

Q49	A42	5c green	160.00	160.00
Q50	A43	10c red	800.00	800.00
Q51	A43	10c red	175.00	175.00
a.		With engraver's name	750.00	750.00
Q52	A43	20c olive grn	1,200.	1,200.
Q53	A45	20c olive grn	200.00	200.00
a.		With engraver's name	750.00	750.00
Q54	A45	25c ultra	200.00	200.00
a.		With engraver's name	750.00	750.00
Q55	A43	35c bister brn	250.00	250.00
Q55A	A40	40c green	1,750.	1,750.
Q56	A45	40c green	250.00	250.00
Q57	A43	50c gray	250.00	250.00
Q58	A43	1fr orange	200.00	200.00
Q59	A43	2fr violet	1,650.	1,650.
Q60	A44	5fr plum	3,500.	3,500.

Excellent forgeries of this overprint exist.

PP5

PP6

1916   Litho.   Perf. 13½

Q61	PP5	10c pale blue	1.10	.20
Q62	PP5	15c olive grn	1.40	.50
Q63	PP5	20c red	2.25	.50
Q64	PP5	25c lt brown	2.25	.50
Q65	PP5	30c lilac	1.40	.50
Q66	PP5	35c gray	1.40	.45
Q67	PP5	40c orange yel	3.00	1.50
Q68	PP5	50c bister	2.25	.45
Q69	PP5	55c brown	3.00	2.25
Q70	PP5	60c gray vio	2.25	.45
Q71	PP5	70c green	2.25	.45
Q72	PP5	80c red brown	2.25	.45
Q73	PP5	90c blue	2.25	.45
Q74	PP5	1fr gray	2.25	.45
Q75	PP6	1.10fr ultra (Franken)	27.50	21.00
Q76	PP6	2fr red	25.00	.45
Q77	PP6	3fr violet	25.00	.45
Q78	PP6	4fr emerald	45.00	1.50
Q79	PP6	5fr brown	45.00	3.00
Q80	PP6	10fr orange	45.00	1.50
		Nos. Q61-Q80 (20)	241.80	37.00

Type of 1916 Inscribed "FRANK" instead of "FRANKEN"

1920

Q81	PP6	1.10fr ultra	2.00	.45

PP7   PP8

1920   Perf. 14

Q82	PP7	10c blue grn	1.75	.75
Q83	PP7	15c olive grn	1.75	1.10
Q84	PP7	20c red	1.75	.75
Q85	PP7	25c gray brn	2.50	.75
Q86	PP7	30c red vio	27.00	22.50
Q87	PP7	40c pale org	11.00	.75
Q88	PP7	50c bister	9.00	.75
Q89	PP7	55c pale brown	5.50	4.50
Q90	PP7	60c dk violet	10.00	.75
Q91	PP7	70c green	18.00	1.10
Q92	PP7	80c red brown	40.00	1.50
Q93	PP7	90c dull blue	10.00	.75
Q94	PP7	1fr gray	85.00	1.50
Q95	PP8	1.10fr ultra	26.00	2.00
Q96	PP8	1.20fr dk green	11.00	.75
Q97	PP8	1.40fr black brn	11.00	.75
Q98	PP8	2fr vermilion	110.00	1.25
Q99	PP8	3fr red vio	125.00	.85
Q100	PP8	4fr yel grn	125.00	.75
Q101	PP8	5fr bister brn	125.00	.75
Q102	PP8	10fr brown org	125.00	.75
		Nos. Q82-Q102 (21)	881.25	45.30

PP9

PP10

Types PP7 and PP9 differ in the position of the wheel and the tablet above it.
Types PP8 and PP10 differ in the bars below "FR".
There are many other variations in the designs.

1920-21   Typo.

Q103	PP9	10c carmine	.30	.20
Q104	PP9	15c yel grn	.30	.20
Q105	PP9	20c blue grn	.70	.20

Q106	PP9	25c ultra	.65	.20
Q107	PP9	30c chocolate	.85	.20
Q108	PP9	35c orange brn	.90	.30
Q109	PP9	40c orange	1.10	.20
Q110	PP9	50c rose	1.10	.20
Q111	PP9	55c yel ('21)	4.50	3.25
Q112	PP9	60c dull rose	1.10	.20
Q113	PP9	70c emerald	3.00	.40
Q114	PP9	80c violet	2.25	.20
Q115	PP9	90c lemon	37.50	21.00
Q116	PP9	90c claret	4.50	.40
Q117	PP10	1fr buff	4.50	.35
Q118	PP10	1fr red brown	4.00	.30
Q119	PP10	1.10fr ultra	1.60	.45
Q120	PP10	1.20fr orange	6.25	.30
Q121	PP10	1.40fr yellow	10.00	1.75
Q122	PP10	1.60fr turq blue	18.00	.70
Q123	PP10	1.60fr emerald	40.00	.70
Q124	PP10	2fr pale rose	26.00	.30
Q125	PP10	3fr dp rose	24.00	.30
Q126	PP10	4fr emerald	24.00	.30
Q127	PP10	5fr lt violet	17.50	.30
Q128	PP10	10fr lemon	110.00	9.00
Q129	PP10	10fr dk brown	22.50	.30
Q130	PP10	15fr dp rose ('21)	22.50	.30
Q131	PP10	20fr dk blue ('21)	325.00	3.00
		Nos. Q103-Q131 (29)	714.60	45.50

PP11

1922   Engr.   Perf. 11½

Q132	PP11	2fr black	4.00	.20
Q133	PP11	3fr brown	37.50	.20
Q134	PP11	4fr green	9.00	.20
Q135	PP11	5r claret	9.00	.20
Q136	PP11	10fr yel brown	10.00	.20
Q137	PP11	15fr rose red	10.00	.20
Q138	PP11	20fr blue	67.50	.25
		Nos. Q132-Q138 (7)	147.00	1.50

PP12

PP13

Perf. 14x13½, 13½x14

1923-40   Typo.

Q139	PP12	5c red brn	.20	.25
Q140	PP12	10c vermilion	.20	.20
Q141	PP12	15c ultra	.20	.30
Q142	PP12	20c turq blue	.20	.20
Q143	PP12	30c brn vio ('27)	.20	.20
Q144	PP12	40c olive grn	.20	.20
Q145	PP12	50c mag ('27)	.20	.20
Q146	PP12	60c orange	.20	.20
Q147	PP12	70c dk brn ('24)	.20	.20
Q148	PP12	80c violet	.20	.20
Q149	PP12	90c sl ('27)	1.25	.20
Q150	PP13	1fr ultra	.35	.20
Q151	PP13	1fr brt blue ('28)	.55	.20
Q152	PP13	1.10fr orange	3.00	.30
Q153	PP13	1.50fr turq blue	3.25	.30
Q154	PP13	1.70fr dp brown ('31)	.75	.60
Q155	PP13	1.80fr claret	4.25	.60
Q156	PP13	2fr olive grn ('24)	.35	.20
Q157	PP13	2.10fr gray grn	7.50	.85
Q158	PP13	2.40fr dp violet	4.00	.85
Q159	PP13	2.70fr gray ('24)	12.00	.75
Q160	PP13	3fr org red	.45	.20
Q161	PP13	3.30fr brn ('24)	12.50	.75
Q162	PP13	4fr rose ('24)	.55	.20
Q163	PP13	5fr vio ('24)	.90	.20
Q163A	PP13	5fr brn vio ('40)	.45	.30
Q164	PP13	6fr bis brn ('27)	.50	.20
Q165	PP13	7fr org ('27)	.90	.20
Q166	PP13	8fr dp brown ('27)	.75	.20
Q167	PP13	9fr red vio ('27)	2.50	.20

Q168	PP13	10fr blue grn ('27)	1.10	.20
Q168A	PP13	10fr blk ('40)	4.00	3.75
Q169	PP13	20fr mag ('27)	1.90	.20
Q170	PP13	30fr turq grn ('31)	6.00	.40
Q171	PP13	40fr gray ('31)	55.00	.75
Q172	PP13	50fr bis ('27)	9.00	.30
		Nos. Q139-Q172 (36)	135.80	15.25

See Nos. Q239-Q262. For overprints see Nos. Q216-Q238. Stamps overprinted "Bagages Reisgoed" are revenues.

No. Q158 Surcharged

1924

Green Surcharge

Q173	PP13	2.30fr on 2.40fr violet	3.00	.50
a.		Inverted surcharge	57.50	

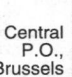

Type of Regular Issue of 1926-27 Overprinted

1928   Perf. 14

Q174	A61	4fr buff	6.50	.90
Q175	A61	5fr bister	6.50	1.10
		Set, never hinged	40.00	

Central P.O., Brussels
PP15

1929-30   Engr.   Perf. 11½

Q176	PP15	3fr black brn	1.40	.20
Q177	PP15	4fr gray	1.40	.20
Q178	PP15	5fr carmine	1.40	.20
Q179	PP15	6fr vio brn ('30)	22.50	25.00
		Nos. Q176-Q179 (4)	26.70	25.60
		Set, never hinged	100.00	

No. Q179 Surcharged in Blue

1933

Q180	PP15	4(fr) on 6fr vio brn	25.00	.25
		Never hinged	90.00	

Modern Locomotive
PP16

1934   Photo.   Perf. 13½x14

Q181	PP16	3fr dk green	10.00	2.50
Q182	PP16	4fr red violet	3.00	.20
Q183	PP16	5fr dp rose	9.50	.20
		Nos. Q181-Q183 (3)	22.50	2.90
		Set, never hinged	120.00	

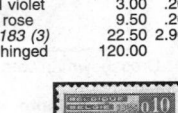

Modern Railroad Train — PP17

Old Railroad Train — PP18

1935   Engr.   Perf. 14x13½, 13½x14

Q184	PP17	10c rose car	.30	.20
Q185	PP17	20c violet	.35	.20
Q186	PP17	30c black brn	.45	.30
Q187	PP17	40c dk blue	.55	.20
Q188	PP17	50c orange red	.55	.20
Q189	PP17	60c green	.65	.20
Q190	PP17	70c ultra	.70	.20
Q191	PP17	80c olive blk	.65	.20
Q192	PP17	90c rose lake	.85	.45
Q193	PP18	1fr brown vio	.85	.20
Q194	PP18	2fr gray blk	2.00	.20
Q195	PP18	3fr red org	2.50	.20
Q196	PP18	4fr violet brn	3.00	.20
Q197	PP18	5fr plum	3.25	.20
Q198	PP18	6fr dp green	3.50	.20
Q199	PP18	7fr dp violet	17.00	.20
Q200	PP18	8fr olive blk	17.00	.20
Q201	PP18	9fr dk blue	17.00	.20
Q202	PP18	10fr car lake	17.00	.20
Q203	PP18	20fr green	90.00	.20
Q204	PP18	30fr violet	90.00	2.00
Q205	PP18	40fr black brn	90.00	2.50
Q206	PP18	50fr rose car	100.00	2.00
Q207	PP18	100fr ultra	250.00	45.00
		Nos. Q184-Q207 (24)	708.15	55.85
		Set, never hinged	1,750.	

Centenary of Belgian State Railway.

Winged Wheel
PP19

Surcharge in Red or Blue

1938   Photo.   Perf. 13½

Q208	PP19	5fr on 3.50fr dk grn	6.50	.45
Q209	PP19	5fr on 4.50fr rose vio (Bl)	.20	.20
Q210	PP19	6fr on 5.50fr cop red (Bl)	.30	.20
a.		Half used as 3fr on piece		1.50
		Nos. Q208-Q210 (3)	7.00	.85
		Set, never hinged	50.00	

Nos. Q208-Q210 exist without surcharge. Value, set, $550.
See Nos. MQ1, Q297-Q299.

Symbolizing Unity Achieved Through Railroads
PP20

1939   Engr.   Perf. 13½x14

Q211	PP20	20c redsh brn	3.50	3.75
Q212	PP20	50c vio bl	3.50	3.75
Q213	PP20	2fr rose red	3.50	3.75
Q214	PP20	9fr slate grn	3.50	3.75
Q215	PP20	10fr dk vio	3.50	3.75
		Nos. Q211-Q215 (5)	17.50	18.75
		Set, never hinged	22.50	

Railroad Exposition and Cong. held at Brussels.

Parcel Post Stamps of 1925-27 Overprinted in Blue or Carmine

Perf. 14½x14, 14x14½

1940   Unwmk.

Q216	PP12	10c vermilion	.20	.20
Q217	PP12	20c turq bl (C)	.20	.20
Q218	PP12	30c brn vio	.20	.20
Q219	PP12	40c ol grn (C)	.20	.20
Q220	PP12	50c magenta	.20	.20
Q221	PP12	60c orange	.20	.25
Q222	PP12	70c dk brn	.20	.20
Q223	PP12	80c vio (C)	.20	.20
Q224	PP12	90c slate	.25	.25
Q225	PP13	1fr ultra (C)	.25	.20
Q226	PP13	2fr ol grn (C)	.20	.20
Q227	PP13	3fr org red	.25	.20

Q228	PP13	4fr rose	.25	.20
Q229	PP13	5fr vio (C)	.25	.20
Q230	PP13	6fr bis brn	.35	.25
Q231	PP13	7fr orange	.35	.20
Q232	PP13	8fr dp brn	.35	.20
Q233	PP13	9fr red vio	.35	.20
Q234	PP13	10fr bl grn (C)	.35	.25
Q235	PP13	20fr magenta	.60	.25
Q236	PP13	30fr turq grn (C)	1.10	.75
Q237	PP13	40fr gray (C)	1.40	2.00
Q238	PP13	50fr bister	1.60	1.10
	Nos. Q216-Q238 (23)		9.55	8.10
	Set, never hinged		16.00	

Types of 1923-40

1941

Q239	PP12	10c dl olive	.20	.20
Q240	PP12	20c lt vio	.20	.20
Q241	PP12	30c fawn	.20	.20
Q242	PP12	40c dull blue	.20	.20
Q243	PP12	50c lt grn	.20	.20
Q244	PP12	60c gray	.20	.20
Q245	PP12	70c chalky grn	.20	.20
Q246	PP12	80c orange	.20	.20
Q247	PP12	90c rose lilac	.20	.20
Q248	PP13	1fr lt yel grn	.20	.20
Q249	PP13	2fr vio brn	.40	.20
Q250	PP13	3fr slate	.45	.20
Q251	PP13	4fr dl olive	.50	.20
Q252	PP13	5fr rose lilac	.50	.20
Q253	PP13	5fr black	.85	.30
Q254	PP13	6fr org ver	.75	.20
Q255	PP13	7fr lilac	.75	.20
Q256	PP13	8fr chalky grn	.75	.20
Q257	PP13	9fr blue	.90	.20
Q258	PP13	10fr rose lilac	.90	.20
Q259	PP13	20fr milky blue	2.00	.20
Q260	PP13	30fr orange	4.50	.35
Q261	PP13	40fr rose	5.00	.35
Q262	PP13	50fr brt red vio	6.75	.20
	Nos. Q239-Q262 (24)		27.00	5.30
	Set, never hinged		90.00	

Adjusting Tie Plates — PP21

Engineer at Throttle — PP22

Freight Station Interior — PP23

Signal and Electric Train — PP24

1942   **Engr.**   **Perf. 14x13½**

Q263	PP21	9.20fr red org	.60	.85
Q264	PP22	12.30fr dp grn	.60	.90
Q265	PP23	14.30fr dk car	.80	1.25

Perf. 11½

Q266	PP24	100fr ultra	20.00	17.00
	Nos. Q263-Q266 (4)		22.00	20.00
	Set, never hinged		25.00	

> **Catalogue values for unused stamps in this section, from this point to the end of the section, are for Never Hinged items.**

PP25

PP26

PP27

1945-46   **Photo.**   **Unwmk.**

Q267	PP25	10c ol blk ('46)	.30	.20
Q268	PP25	20c dp vio	.30	.20
Q269	PP25	30c chnt brn ('46)	.30	.20
Q270	PP25	40c dp bl ('46)	.30	.20
Q271	PP25	50c peacock grn	.30	.20
Q272	PP25	60c blk ('46)	.30	.20
Q273	PP25	70c emer ('46)	.45	.25
Q274	PP25	80c orange	.75	.20
Q275	PP25	90c brn vio ('46)	.30	.20
Q276	PP26	1fr bl grn ('46)	.30	.20
Q277	PP26	2fr blk brn	.30	.20
Q278	PP26	3fr grnsh blk ('46)	2.00	.20
Q279	PP26	4fr dark blue	.45	.20
Q280	PP26	5fr sepia	.50	.20
Q281	PP26	6fr dk ol grn ('46)	2.25	.20
Q282	PP26	7fr dk vio ('46)	.75	.25
Q283	PP26	8fr red org	.75	.20
Q284	PP26	9fr dp bl ('46)	.90	.20
Q285	PP27	10fr dk red ('46)	3.25	.20
Q286	PP27	10fr sepia ('46)	1.60	.25
Q287	PP27	20fr dk yel grn ('46)	.75	.20
Q288	PP27	30fr dp vio	1.00	.20
Q289	PP27	40fr rose pink	.90	.20
Q290	PP27	50fr brt bl ('46)	12.00	.20
	Nos. Q267-Q290 (24)		31.00	5.00

Mercury — PP28

1945-46   **Perf. 13½x13**

Q291	PP28	3fr emer ('46)	.25	.25
Q292	PP28	5fr ultra	.20	.20
Q293	PP28	6fr red	.20	.20

Inscribed "Belgique-Belgie"

Q294	PP28	3fr emer ('46)	.25	.25
Q295	PP28	5fr ultra	.20	.20
Q296	PP28	6fr red	.20	.20
	Nos. Q291-Q296 (6)		1.30	1.30

Winged Wheel Type of 1938
Carmine Surcharge

1946   **Perf. 13½x14**

Q297	PP19	8fr on 5.50fr brn	.65	.20
Q298	PP19	10fr on 5.50fr dk bl	.75	.20
Q299	PP19	12fr on 5.50fr vio	1.10	.20
	Nos. Q297-Q299 (3)		2.50	.60

Railway Crossing PP29

1947   **Engr.**   **Perf. 12½**

Q300	PP29	100fr dark green	7.00	.25

Crossbowman with Train — PP30

1947   **Photo.**   **Perf. 11½**

Q301	PP30	8fr dark olive brn	1.00	.20
Q302	PP30	10fr gray & blue	1.10	.25
Q303	PP30	12fr dark violet	1.60	.45
	Nos. Q301-Q303 (3)		3.70	.90

Surcharged with New Value and Bars in Carmine

1948

Q304	PP30	9fr on 8fr	1.25	.20
Q305	PP30	11fr on 10fr	1.25	.25
Q306	PP30	13.50fr on 12fr	2.00	.25
	Nos. Q304-Q306 (3)		4.50	.70

Delivery of Parcel — PP31

1948

Q307	PP31	9fr chocolate	6.50	.20
Q308	PP31	11fr brown car	7.00	.20
Q309	PP31	13.50fr gray	10.50	.25
	Nos. Q307-Q309 (3)		24.00	.65

Locomotive of 1835 PP32

Various Locomotives.
Lathe Work in Frame Differs

1949   **Engr.**   **Perf. 12½**

Q310	PP32	½fr dark brown	.60	.20
Q311	PP32	1fr carmine rose	.70	.20
Q312	PP32	2fr deep ultra	.95	.20
Q313	PP32	3fr dp magenta	2.00	.20
Q314	PP32	4fr blue green	2.75	.20
Q315	PP32	5fr orange red	2.75	.20
Q316	PP32	6fr brown vio	3.00	.25
Q317	PP32	7fr yellow grn	4.00	.20
Q318	PP32	8fr grnsh blue	5.00	.20
Q319	PP32	9fr yellow brn	6.00	.25
Q320	PP32	10fr citron	7.25	.20
Q321	PP32	20fr orange	11.00	.20
Q322	PP32	30fr blue	15.00	.20
Q323	PP32	40fr lilac rose	21.00	.25
Q324	PP32	50fr violet	21.00	.30
Q325	PP32	100fr red	65.00	.20

Engraved; Center Typographed

Q326	PP32	10fr car rose & blk	9.00	.80
	Nos. Q310-Q326 (17)		177.00	4.30

See No. Q337.

1949   **Engr.**

Design: Electric locomotive.

Q327	PP32	60fr black brown	20.00	.20

Opening of Charleroi-Brussels electric railway line, Oct. 15, 1949.

Mailing Parcel Post PP33

Sorting PP34

Loading PP35

1950-52   **Perf. 12, 12½**

Q328	PP33	11fr red orange	6.00	.20
Q329	PP33	12fr red vio ('51)	20.00	1.50
Q330	PP34	13fr dk blue grn	6.00	.20
Q331	PP34	15fr ultra ('51)	15.00	.30
Q332	PP35	16fr gray	6.00	.20
Q333	PP33	17fr brown ('52)	8.00	.20
Q334	PP35	18fr brt car ('51)	16.00	.45
Q335	PP35	20fr brn org ('52)	8.00	.20
	Nos. Q328-Q335 (8)		85.00	3.25

For surcharges see Nos. Q338-Q340.

Mercury and Winged Wheel — PP36

1951

Q336	PP36	25fr dark blue	10.00	8.50

25th anniv. of the founding of the Natl. Soc. of Belgian Railroads.

Type of 1949

Design: Electric locomotive.

1952   **Unwmk.**   **Perf. 11½**

Q337	PP32	300fr red violet	150.00	.50

Nos. Q331, Q328 and Q334 Surcharged with New Value and "X" in Red, Blue or Green

1953   **Perf. 12**

Q338	PP34	13fr on 15fr (R)	60.00	3.00
Q339	PP33	17fr on 11fr (Bl)	35.00	2.25
Q340	PP35	20fr on 18fr (G)	30.00	2.50
	Nos. Q338-Q340 (3)		125.00	7.75

Electric Train, 1952 PP37

1953   **Engr.**

Q341	PP37	200fr dk yel grn & vio brn	250.00	4.00
Q342	PP37	200fr dk green	225.00	1.00

No. Q341 was issued to commemorate the opening of the railway link connecting Brussels North and South Stations, Oct. 4, 1952.

New North Station, Brussels — PP38

Chapelle Station, Brussels PP39

Designs: No. Q348, 15fr, Congress Station. 10fr, 20fr, 30fr, 40fr, 50fr, South Station. 100fr, 200fr, 300fr, Central Station.

1953-57   **Unwmk.**   **Perf. 11½**

Q343	PP38	1fr bister	.30	.20
Q344	PP38	2fr slate	.40	.20
Q345	PP38	3fr blue grn	.60	.20
Q346	PP38	4fr orange	.80	.20
Q347	PP38	5fr red brn	.80	.20
Q348	PP38	5fr dk red brn	10.00	.25
Q349	PP38	6fr rose vio	1.10	.20
Q350	PP38	7fr brt green	1.10	.20
Q351	PP38	8fr rose red	1.40	.20
Q352	PP38	9fr brt grnsh bl	2.00	.20
Q353	PP38	10fr lt grn	2.25	.20
Q354	PP38	15fr dl red	13.00	.20
Q355	PP38	20fr blue	4.00	.20
Q356	PP39	30fr purple	6.25	.20
Q357	PP39	40fr brt purple	8.00	.20
Q358	PP39	50fr lilac rose	10.00	.20
Q359	PP39	60fr brt purple	20.00	.20
Q360	PP39	80fr brown vio	30.00	.20
Q361	PP39	100fr emerald	18.00	.20
Q361A	PP39	200fr brt vio bl	95.00	1.60
Q361B	PP39	300fr lilac rose	175.00	2.25
	Nos. Q343-Q361B (21)		400.00	7.70

Issued: #Q347, 20fr, 30fr, 1953; 80fr, 1955; 200fr, 1956; 300fr, 1957; others, 1954.
See Nos. Q407, Q431-Q432.

Electric Train — PP40

1954

Q362	PP40	13fr chocolate	14.00	.20
Q363	PP40	18fr dark blue	17.00	.20
Q364	PP40	21fr lilac rose	18.00	.45
		Nos. Q362-Q364 (3)	49.00	.85

Nos. Q362-Q364 Surcharged with New Value and "X" in Blue, Red or Green

1956

Q365	PP40	14fr on 13fr (B)	8.00	.20
Q366	PP40	19fr on 18fr (R)	8.25	.25
Q367	PP40	22fr on 21fr (G)	8.75	.45
		Nos. Q365-Q367 (3)	25.00	.90

Mercury and Winged Wheel — PP41

1957   Engr.   *Perf. 11½*

Q368	PP41	14fr brt green	7.75	.20
Q369	PP41	19fr olive gray	8.00	.20
Q370	PP41	22fr carmine rose	8.75	.30
		Nos. Q368-Q370 (3)	24.50	.70

Nos. Q369-Q370 Surcharged with New Value and "X" in Pink or Green

1959

Q371	PP41	20fr on 19fr (P)	22.50	.35
Q372	PP41	20fr on 22fr (G)	27.50	.55

Old North Station, Brussels PP42

1959   Engr.   *Perf. 11½*

Q373	PP42	20fr olive green	12.50	.20

See Nos. Q381, Q383. For surcharges see Nos. Q378, Q382, Q384.

Diesel and Electric Locomotives and Association Emblem PP43

1960   Unwmk.   *Perf. 11½*

Q374	PP43	20fr red	42.50	30.00
Q375	PP43	50fr dark blue	42.50	30.00
Q376	PP43	60fr red lilac	42.50	30.00
Q377	PP43	70fr emerald	42.50	30.00
		Nos. Q374-Q377 (4)	170.00	120.00

Intl. Assoc. of Railway Congresses, 75th anniv.

No. Q373 Surcharged with New Value and "X" in Red

1961

Q378	PP42	24fr on 20fr ol grn	60.00	.25

South Station, Brussels — PP44

1962   Unwmk.   *Perf. 11½*

Q379	PP44	24fr dull red	6.25	.25

No. Q379 Surcharged with New Value and "X" in Light Green

1963

Q380	PP44	26fr on 24fr dl red	6.50	.25

Type of 1959

Design: 26fr, Central Station, Antwerp.

1963   Engr.   *Perf. 11½*

Q381	PP42	26fr blue	6.25	1.75

No. Q381 Surcharged in Red

1964, Apr. 20

Q382	PP42	28fr on 26fr blue	6.25	.25

Type of 1959

Design: 28fr, St. Peter's Station, Ghent.

1965   Engr.   *Perf. 11½*

Q383	PP42	28fr red lilac	6.25	1.40

Nos. Q383 Surcharged with New Value and "X" in Green

1966

Q384	PP42	35fr on 28fr red lil	6.25	.20

Arlon Railroad Station PP45

Perf. 11½

1967, Aug.   Unwmk.   Engr.

Q385	PP45	25fr bister	10.00	.20
Q386	PP45	30fr blue green	5.00	.20
Q387	PP45	35fr deep blue	7.00	.35
		Nos. Q385-Q387 (3)	22.00	.75

See #Q408. For surcharges see #Q410-Q412.

Electric Train PP46

Designs: 2fr, 3fr, 4fr, 5fr, 6fr, 7fr, 8fr, 9fr, like 1fr. 10fr, 20fr, 30fr, 40fr, Train going right. 50fr, 60fr, 70fr, 80fr, 90fr, Train going left. 100fr, 200fr, 300fr, Diesel train.

1968-73   Engr.   *Perf. 11½*

Q388	PP46	1fr olive bis	.20	.20
Q389	PP46	2fr slate	.25	.20
Q390	PP46	3fr blue green	.55	.20
Q391	PP46	4fr orange	.55	.20
Q392	PP46	5fr brown	.65	.20
Q393	PP46	6fr plum	.55	.20
Q394	PP46	7fr brt green	.65	.20
Q395	PP46	8fr carmine	.85	.20
Q396	PP46	9fr blue	1.40	.20
Q397	PP46	10fr green	2.75	.20
Q398	PP46	20fr dk blue	1.60	.20
Q399	PP46	30fr dk purple	4.00	.20
Q400	PP46	40fr brt lilac	5.50	.20
Q401	PP46	50fr brt pink	6.75	.20
Q402	PP46	60fr brt violet	8.25	.30
Q402A	PP46	70fr dp bister ('73)	6.75	.30
Q403	PP46	80fr dk brown	6.75	.20
Q403A	PP46	90fr yel grn ('73)	5.50	.30
Q404	PP46	100fr emerald	11.00	.25
Q405	PP46	200fr violet blue	13.00	.50
Q406	PP46	300fr lilac rose	22.50	1.25
		Nos. Q388-Q406 (21)	100.00	5.90

See No. Q409.

Types of 1953-68

10fr, Congress Station, Brussels. 40fr, Arlon Station. 500fr, Electric train going left.

1968, June   Engr.   *Perf. 11½*

Q407	PP38	10fr gray	1.50	.20
Q408	PP45	40fr vermilion	22.50	.20
Q409	PP46	500fr yellow	30.00	1.90
		Nos. Q407-Q409 (3)	54.00	2.30

Nos. Q385, Q387 and Q408 Surcharged with New Value and "X"

1970, Dec.

Q410	PP45	37fr on 25fr bister	45.00	3.00
Q411	PP45	48fr on 35fr dp bl	13.00	5.00
Q412	PP45	53fr on 40fr ver	15.00	6.00
		Nos. Q410-Q412 (3)	73.00	14.00

Ostend Station PP47

1971, Mar.   Engr.   *Perf. 11½*

Q413	PP47	32fr bis & blk	2.50	2.25
Q414	PP47	37fr gray & blk	2.50	2.50
Q415	PP47	42fr bl & blk	4.00	3.00
Q416	PP47	44fr brt rose & blk	4.50	3.00
Q417	PP47	46fr vio & blk	4.50	3.00
Q418	PP47	50fr brick red & blk	5.25	3.25
Q419	PP47	52fr sep & blk	5.25	3.25
Q420	PP47	54fr yel grn & blk	5.75	3.25
Q421	PP47	61fr grnsh bl & blk	5.75	4.00
		Nos. Q413-Q421 (9)	40.00	27.50

Nos. Q413-Q416, Q419-Q421 Surcharged with New Value and "X"

1971, Dec. 15

Denomination in Black

Q422	PP47	34fr on 32fr bister	2.00	.55
Q423	PP47	40fr on 37fr gray	2.50	.70
Q424	PP47	47fr on 44fr brt rose	2.75	.80
Q425	PP47	53fr on 42fr blue	3.25	.85
Q426	PP47	56fr on 52fr sepia	3.25	1.00
Q427	PP47	59fr on 54fr yel grn	3.25	1.00
Q428	PP47	66fr on 61fr grnsh blue	4.00	1.10
		Nos. Q422-Q428 (7)	21.00	6.00

Track, Underpinning of Railroad Car and Emblems — PP48

1972, Mar.   Photo.

Q429	PP48	100fr emer, red & blk	10.00	1.10

Centenary of International Railroad Union.

Congress Emblem PP49

1974, Apr.   Photo.   *Perf. 11½*

Q430	PP49	100fr yel, blk & red	8.00	1.25

4th International Symposium on Railroad Cybernetics, Washington, DC, Apr. 1974.

Type of 1953-1957

1975, June 1   Engr.   *Perf. 11½*

Q431	PP38	20fr emerald	1.75	.20
Q432	PP38	50fr blue	3.75	.55

Railroad Tracks PP50

1976, June 10   Photo.   *Perf. 11½*

Q433	PP50	20fr ultra & multi	3.00	.20
Q434	PP50	50fr brt grn & multi	1.75	.50
Q435	PP50	100fr dp org & multi	4.00	1.00
Q436	PP50	150fr brt lil & multi	6.25	1.75
		Nos. Q433-Q436 (4)	15.00	3.45

Railroad Station — PP51

1977   Photo.   *Perf. 11½*

Q437	PP51	1000fr multi	40.00	10.00

See note following No. Q465.

Freight Car — PP52

Designs: 1fr-9fr, Freight car. 10fr-40fr, Hopper car. 50fr-90fr, Maintenance car. 100fr-500fr, Liquid fuel car.

1980, Dec. 16   Engr.   *Perf. 11½*

Q438	PP52	1fr bis brn & blk	.20	.20
Q439	PP52	2fr claret & blk	.20	.20
Q440	PP52	3fr brt grn & blk	.20	.20
Q441	PP52	4fr grnsh blk & blk	.20	.20
Q442	PP52	5fr sepia & blk	.20	.20
Q443	PP52	6fr dp org & blk	.35	.20
Q444	PP52	7fr purple & blk	.40	.20
Q445	PP52	8fr black	.40	.20
Q446	PP52	9fr green & blk	.45	.20
Q447	PP52	10fr yel bis & blk	.50	.20
Q448	PP52	20fr grnsh bl & blk	1.10	.20
Q449	PP52	30fr bister & blk	2.25	.35
Q450	PP52	40fr lt lil & blk	2.50	.40
Q451	PP52	50fr dk brn & blk	2.75	.55
Q452	PP52	60fr olive & blk	2.75	.70
Q453	PP52	70fr vio bl & blk	3.50	.75
Q454	PP52	80fr vio brn & blk	4.00	.85
Q455	PP52	90fr lil rose & blk	5.00	.95
Q456	PP52	100fr crim rose & blk	5.25	1.00
Q457	PP52	200fr brn & blk	10.00	2.00
Q458	PP52	300fr ol gray & blk	14.00	3.00
Q459	PP52	500fr dl pur & blk	25.00	5.25
		Nos. Q438-Q459 (22)	81.20	18.00

Train in Station — PP53

1982   Engr.   *Perf. 11½*

Q460	PP53	10fr red & blk	1.75	.25
Q461	PP53	20fr green & blk	1.25	.50
Q462	PP53	50fr sepia & blk	4.25	.75
Q463	PP53	100fr blue & blk	7.25	2.75
		Nos. Q460-Q463 (4)	14.50	4.25

Electric Locomotives PP54

1985, May 3   Photo.   *Perf. 11½*

Q464	PP54	250fr BB-150	11.00	2.00
Q465	PP54	500fr BB-120	24.00	10.00

Seven limited edition souvenir sheets exist. These include souvenir sheets of 4 of #Q437,

Q464-Q465 with French or Flemish inscriptions, and a bilingual sheet with one each of #Q437, Q464-Q465.

Stylized Castle, Gabled Station and Electric Rail Car — PP55

1987, Oct. 12	Engr.	Perf. 11½		
Q466	PP55	10fr dk red & blk	.50	.40
Q467	PP55	20fr dk grn & blk	1.00	.75
Q468	PP55	50fr dk brn & blk	2.50	1.90
Q469	PP55	100fr dk lil & blk	5.25	3.75
Q470	PP55	150fr dark olive bister & blk	7.75	5.75
Nos. Q466-Q470 (5)			17.00	12.55

High Speed Trains PP56

1996, June 2	Litho.	Perf. 11½		
Q471	PP56	100fr shown	6.00	4.50
Q472	PP56	300fr Train going left	18.50	13.50

Electric Trains PP57

Designs: 50fr, Passenger railcars. 100fr, End car. 200fr, Front car.

1997, Oct. 14	Photo.	Perf. 11½		
Q473	PP57	50fr multicolored	2.75	2.10
Q474	PP57	100fr multicolored	5.50	4.25
Q475	PP57	200fr multicolored	11.00	8.50
Nos. Q473-Q475 (3)			19.25	14.85

Electric Trains PP58

Designs: No. Q476, Eurostar (yellow & white train). No. Q477, Thalys (red & white train). 160fr, Eurostar, Thalys side by side.

1998	Photo.	Perf. 11½		
Q476	PP58	80fr multicolored	4.75	3.50
Q477	PP58	80fr multicolored	4.75	3.50
Q478	PP58	160fr multicolored	9.50	7.25
Nos. Q476-Q478 (3)			19.00	14.25

Agents — PP59

50fr, Male agent. 75fr, Female agent. 100fr, Female agent on platform, man in train. 125fr, Male agent on platform, woman in train.

		Perf. 11¾x11½		
1999, Sept. 25		Photo.		
Q479	PP59	50fr multi	2.40	1.75
Q480	PP59	75fr multi	3.75	2.75
Q481	PP59	100fr multi	5.00	3.75
Q482	PP59	125fr multi	6.00	4.50
Nos. Q479-Q482 (4)			17.15	12.75

Train Cars — PP60

Designs: 20fr, Gray tanker. 30fr, Red tanker. 50fr, Silver and blue tanker. 150fr, Locomotive, horiz.

2000, Oct. 20	Photo.	Perf. 11½		
Q483	PP60	20fr multi	.85	.65
Q484	PP60	30fr multi	1.25	.95
Q485	PP60	50fr multi	2.10	1.60
Nos. Q483-Q485 (3)			4.20	3.20

Souvenir Sheet

Q486	PP60	150fr multi	6.25	6.25

Belgian Natl. Railway Company, 75th Anniv. — PP61

No. Q487: a, 1938 Type 12 locomotive No. 12004. b, 1971 Series 06 dual engine No. 671. c, 1991 Series 03 threefold engine No. 328.

2001, May 7	Photo.	Perf. 11¾x11½		
Q487		Horiz. strip of 3 + 2 labels	2.25	1.50
a.-c.		PP61 17fr Any single	.75	.50

ISSUED UNDER GERMAN OCCUPATION

German Stamps of 1906-11 Surcharged

Nos. N1-N6

Nos. N7-N9

Wmk. Lozenges (125)

1914-15		Perf. 14, 14½		
N1	A16	3c on 3pf brown	.45	.20
N2	A16	5c on 5pf green	.40	.20
N3	A16	10c on 10pf car	.50	.20
N4	A16	25c on 20pf ultra	.50	.25
N5	A16	50c on 40pf lake & blk	2.50	1.25
N6	A16	75c on 60pf mag	.90	1.25
N7	A16	1fr on 80pf lake & blk, rose	2.50	1.75
N8	A17	1fr25c on 1m car	20.00	12.50
N9	A21	2fr50c on 2m gray bl	18.00	15.00
Nos. N1-N9 (9)			45.75	32.60
Set, never hinged			160.00	

German Stamps of 1906-18 Surcharged

Nos. N10-N21   No. N22

Nos. N23-N25

1916-18				
N10	A22	2c on 2pf drab	.25	.25
N11	A16	3c on 3pf brn	.35	.25
N12	A16	5c on 5pf grn	.35	.25
N13	A22	8c on 7½pf org	.65	.35
N14	A16	10c on 10pf car	.25	.20
N15	A22	15c on 15pf yel brn	.65	.25
N16	A22	15c on 15pf dk vio	.65	.45
N17	A16	20c on 25pf org & blk, yel	.35	.35
N18	A16	25c on 20pf ultra	.35	.25
a.		25c on 20pf blue	.40	.25
N19	A16	40c on 30pf org & blk, buff	.40	.30
N20	A16	50c on 40pf lake & blk	.35	.30
N21	A16	75c on 60pf mag	1.00	12.50
N22	A16	1fr on 80pf lake & blk, rose	2.00	2.50
N23	A17	1fr25c on 1m car	2.00	2.50
N24	A21	2fr50c on 2m gray bl	27.50	25.00
a.		2fr50c on 1m car (error)		3,500.
N25	A20	6fr25c on 5m sl & car	40.00	37.50
Nos. N10-N25 (16)			77.10	82.75
Set, never hinged			145.00	

A similar series of stamps without "Belgien" was used in parts of Belgium and France while occupied by German forces. See France Nos. N15-N26.

BELIZE

bə-'lēz

LOCATION — Central America bordering on Caribbean Sea to east, Mexico to north, Guatemala to west
GOVT. — Independent state
AREA — 8,867 sq. mi.
POP. — 219,296 (1996 est.)
CAPITAL — Belmopan

Belize was known as British Honduras until 1973. The former British colony achieved independence in September 1981.

100 Cents = 1 Dollar

Catalogue values for all unused stamps in this country are for Never Hinged items.

Fish-Animal Type of British Honduras Regular Issue 1968-72 Overprinted in Black on Silver Panel

Wmk. 314 (½c, 5c, $5), Unwmkd.				
1973, June 1	Litho.	Perf. 13x12½		
312	A37	½c multi (#235)	.20	.20
313	A37	1c multi (#214)	.20	.20
314	A37	2c multi (#215)	.20	.20
315	A37	3c multi (#216)	.20	.20
316	A37	4c multi (#217)	.20	.20
317	A37	5c multi (#238)	.20	.20
318	A37	10c multi (#219)	.20	.20
319	A37	15c multi (#220)	.20	.20
320	A37	25c multi (#221)	.30	.30
321	A37	50c multi (#222)	.50	.65
322	A37	$1 multi (#223)	.90	1.25
323	A37	$2 multi (#224)	2.00	2.40
324	A37	$5 multi (#240)	5.50	4.00
Nos. 312-324 (13)			10.80	10.20

No. 315 with silver panel omitted exists canceled. Nos. 313 and 319 exist with silver panel double.

Common Design Types pictured following the introduction.

Princess Anne's Wedding Issue
Common Design Type

1973, Nov. 14	Wmk. 314	Perf. 14		
325	CD325	26c blue grn & multi	.20	.25
326	CD325	50c ocher & multi	.35	.50

Crana A50

1974, Jan. 1	Litho.	Perf. 13½		
327	A50	½c shown	.20	.20
328	A50	1c Jewfish	.20	.20
329	A50	2c White-lipped peccary	.20	.20
330	A50	3c Grouper	.20	.20
331	A50	4c Collared anteater	.20	.20
332	A50	5c Bonefish	.20	.20
333	A50	10c Paca	.20	.20
334	A50	15c Dolphinfish	.20	.20
335	A50	25c Kinkajou	.25	.25
336	A50	50c Muttonfish	.55	.55
337	A50	$1 Tayra	1.00	1.00
338	A50	$2 Great barracudas	2.00	2.00
339	A50	$5 Mountain lion	5.25	5.25
Nos. 327-339 (13)			10.65	10.65

Stag, Mayan Pottery A51

Designs: Mayan pottery decorations.

1974, May 1		Perf. 14½		
340	A51	3c shown	.20	.20
341	A51	6c Fire snake	.20	.20
342	A51	16c Mouse	.20	.20
343	A51	26c Eagle	.30	.30
344	A51	50c Parrot	.65	.65
Nos. 340-344 (5)			1.55	1.55

Parides Arcas A52

Designs: Butterflies of Belize.

Wmk. 314 Sideways				
1974-77		Perf. 14		
345	A52	½c shown	.20	.20
346	A52	1c Thecla regalis	.20	.20
347	A52	2c Colobura dirce	.20	.20
348	A52	3c Catonephele numilia	.20	.20
349	A52	4c Battus belus	.20	.20
350	A52	5c Callicore patelina	.35	.20
351	A52	10c Callicore astala	.70	.35
Perf. 14x15; 14 (26, 35c)				
352	A52	15c Nessaea aglaura	.80	.50
a.		Watermark upright ('75)	.70	.40
353	A52	16c Prepona pseudojoiceyi	.45	.25
354	A52	25c Papilio thoas	1.10	.65
a.		Watermark upright ('77)	.80	.45
355	A52	26c Hamadryas arethusa	7.00	7.50
356	A52	50c Thecla bathildis	2.25	1.25
a.		Watermark upright ('77)	1.00	.60
357	A52	$1 Caligo uranus	2.25	1.25
358	A52	$2 Heliconius sapho	4.25	2.40
359	A52	$5 Eurytides philolaus	13.00	7.50
a.		Watermark upright ('75)	11.00	6.00
360	A52	$10 Philaethria dido	21.00	12.00
Nos. 345-360 (16)			54.15	34.85

Issue dates: No. 355A, July 25, 1977; No. 360, Jan. 2, 1975; others Sept. 2, 1974.
For surcharges & overprint see #380, 386, 395.

1975-78		Wmk. 373		
345a	A52	½c multicolored	.20	.20
347a	A52	2c multi ('77)	.20	.20
348a	A52	3c multi ('77)	.20	.20
349a	A52	4c multi ('77)	.25	.25
350a	A52	5c multi ('77)	.30	.30
351a	A52	10c multicolored	.65	.65
352b	A52	15c multi ('77)	.90	.90

354b A52 25c multi ('78) 1.25 1.25
355A A52 35c Parides arcas ('77) 2.00 2.00
  Nos. 345a-355A (9) 5.95 5.95

For overprints and surcharges see Nos. 395-396, 424, 426-427.

Churchill and Coronation Coach of Queen Elizabeth II — A53

$1, Churchill & Williamsburg, VA Liberty Bell.

Wmk. 373
1974, Nov. 30   Litho.   Perf. 14
363 A53 50c multicolored .20 .20
364 A53 $1 multicolored .35 .35

Sir Winston Churchill (1874-1965).

Mayan Urn — A54

Designs: Various Mayan vessels.

1975, June 2   Wmk. 314   Perf. 14
365 A54 3c lt green & multi .20 .20
366 A54 6c lt blue & multi .20 .20
367 A54 16c dull yel & multi .20 .20
368 A54 26c lilac & multi .25 .25
369 A54 50c lt brown & multi .50 .50
  Nos. 365-369 (5) 1.35 1.35

Musicians A55

Christmas: 26c, Nativity (Thatched hut and children). 50c, Drummers, vert. $1, Map of Belize, star, fleeing family, vert.

Perf. 14x14½, 14½x14
1975, Nov. 17   Litho.   Wmk. 314
370 A55 6c multicolored .20 .20
371 A55 26c multicolored .20 .20
372 A55 50c multicolored .30 .30
373 A55 $1 multicolored .60 .60
  Nos. 370-373 (4) 1.30 1.30

William Wrigley, Jr., Sapodilla Tree — A56

Bicentennial Emblem and: 35c, Charles Lindbergh and "Spirit of St. Louis." $1, John Lloyd Stephens and Mayan temple.

1976, Mar. 29   Wmk. 373   Perf. 14½
374 A56 10c multicolored .20 .20
375 A56 35c multicolored .25 .25
376 A56 $1 multicolored .65 .65
  Nos. 374-376 (3) 1.10 1.10

American Bicentennial.

Bicycling A57

Wmk. 373
1976, July 17   Litho.   Perf. 14½
377 A57 35c shown .20 .20
378 A57 45c Running .20 .20
379 A57 $1 Shooting .45 .45
  Nos. 377-379 (3) .85 .85

21st Olympic Games, Montreal, Canada, July 17-Aug. 1.

No. 355 Surcharged with New Value and Bar
Wmk. 314
1976, Aug. 30   Litho.   Perf. 14
380 A52 20c on 26c multi 2.00 1.10

Map of West Indies, Bats, Wicket and Ball A57a

Prudential Cup — A57b

Unwmk.
1976, Oct. 18   Litho.   Perf. 14
381 A57a 35c lt blue & multi .60 .60
382 A57b $1 lilac rose & blk 1.40 1.40

World Cricket Cup, won by West Indies Team, 1975.

Royal Visit, 1975 A58

Designs: 35c, Rose window and Queen's head. $2, Queen surrounded by bishops.

1977, Feb. 7   Litho.   Perf. 13½x14
383 A58 10c multicolored .20 .20
384 A58 35c multicolored .20 .20
385 A58 $2 multicolored .60 .60
  Nos. 383-385 (3) 1.00 1.00

25th anniv. of the reign of Elizabeth II.

No. 352 Surcharged with New Value and Bar
1977   Wmk. 314   Perf. 14x15
386 A52 5c on 15c multi 1.90 1.90

The first setting has the "5c" close to the the right edge of the block (varies). The second, and more common, setting has about 7mm from the right edge to the "5c."

Red-capped Manakin — A59

Designs: Birds of Belize.

Wmk. 373
1977, Sept. 3   Litho.   Perf. 14½
387 A59 8c shown .85 .60
388 A59 10c Hooded oriole .75 .30
389 A59 25c Blue-crowned motmot 1.40 .60
390 A59 35c Slaty-breasted tinamou 1.75 .75
391 A59 45c Ocellated turkey 2.00 1.25
392 A59 $1 White hawk 3.25 5.50
  a. Souvenir sheet of 6, #387-392 10.00 12.50
  Nos. 387-392 (6) 10.00 9.00

See Nos. 398-403, 416-421, 500-501. For overprints and surcharges see No. 502.

Medical Laboratory A60

Design: $1, Mobile medical unit and children receiving treatment.

1977, Dec. 2   Perf. 13½
393 A60 35c multicolored .25 .25
394 A60 $1 multicolored .65 .65
  a. Souvenir sheet of 2, #393-394 1.10 1.50

Pan American Health Org., 75th anniv.

Nos. 351 and 355A Overprinted in Gold: "BELIZE DEFENCE FORCE / 1ST JANUARY 1978"
Wmk. 314, 373
1978, Feb. 15   Litho.   Perf. 14
395 A52 10c multicolored .60 .60
396 A52 35c multicolored 1.25 1.25

Elizabeth II Coronation Anniversary Issue
Common Design Types
Souvenir Sheet
1978, Apr. 21   Unwmk.   Perf. 15
397   Sheet of 6 1.25 1.25
  a. CD326 75c White lion of Mortimer .20 .20
  b. CD327 75c Elizabeth II .20 .20
  c. CD328 75c Jaguar (Maya god) .20 .20

No. 397 contains 2 se-tenant strips of Nos. 397a-397c, separated by horizontal gutter with commemorative and descriptive inscriptions and showing central part of coronation procession with coach.

Bird Type of 1977
Wmk. 373
1978, July 31   Litho.   Perf. 14½
398 A59 10c White-crowned parrot .65 .65
399 A59 25c Crimson-collared tanager 1.00 1.00
400 A59 35c Citreoline trogon 1.50 1.50
401 A59 45c Sungrebe 1.60 1.60
402 A59 50c Muscovy duck 1.75 1.75
403 A59 $1 King vulture 2.50 2.50
  a. Souvenir sheet of 6, #398-403 9.00 11.00
  Nos. 398-403 (6) 9.00 9.00

Russelia Sarmentosa A61

Wild Flowers and Ferns: 15c, Lygodium polymorphum. 35c, Heliconia aurantiaca. 45c, Adiantum tetraphyllum. 50c, Angelonia ciliaris. $1, Thelypteris obliterata.

1978, Oct. 16   Litho.   Perf. 14x13½
404 A61 10c multicolored .30 .30
405 A61 15c multicolored .35 .35
406 A61 35c multicolored .35 .35
407 A61 45c multicolored .35 .35
408 A61 50c multicolored .35 .35
409 A61 $1 multicolored .70 .70
  Nos. 404-409 (6) 2.40 2.40

Christmas.

Internal Airmail Service, 1937 — A62

Mail Service: 10c, MV Heron, 1949. 35c, Dugout canoe on river, 1920. 45c, Stann Creek railroad, 1910. 50c, Mounted courier, 1882. $2, RMS Eagle, 1856, and "paid" cancel.

Perf. 13½x14
1979, Jan. 15   Litho.   Wmk. 373
410 A62 5c multicolored .30 .30
411 A62 10c multicolored .30 .30
412 A62 35c multicolored .30 .30
413 A62 45c multicolored .45 .45
414 A62 50c multicolored .45 .45
415 A62 $2 multicolored 1.75 1.75
  Nos. 410-415 (6) 3.55 3.55

Centenary of membership in UPU.

Bird Type of 1977
1979, Apr. 16   Unwmk.   Perf. 14½
416 A59 10c Boat-billed heron .25 .25
417 A59 25c Gray-necked wood rail .70 .70
418 A59 35c Lineated woodpecker .80 .80
419 A59 45c Blue gray tanager 1.00 1.00
420 A59 50c Laughing falcon 1.25 1.25
421 A59 $1 Long-tailed hermit 2.50 2.50
  a. Souvenir sheet of 6, #416-421 6.50 6.50
  Nos. 416-421 (6) 6.50 6.50

Nos. 477, 354b, 595, 355A, 599, 651 Surcharged with New Value and Bar

$1.25

1979-83   Litho.   Perf. 14
422 A67 10c on 15c multi 4.00 4.00
423 A67 10c on 15c multi
424 A52 10c on 25c multi 2.00 1.50
424A A67 10c on 35c multi 30.00
  b. Round obliterator 30.00
425 A76 10c on 35c multi
426 A52 15c on 35c multi 50.00
427 A52 15c on 35c multi 2.00 2.00
428 A76 $1.25 on $2 multi 6.00 4.00
429 A81 $1.25 on $2 multi 5.00 3.00

No. 422 has a square the width of the "10c" obliterating the old value. No. 423 has a rectangle that is wider than the "10c."
No. 424A has a square obliterator.
No. 426 has "15c" at top of stamp, No. 427 has "15c" at right of rectangle. Type differs.
No. 429 has rectangular obliterator with new value at top of stamp.
Many errors exist from printer's waste.
Issued: #426, 3/79; #427, 6/79; #424, 3/31/80; #422, 8/22/81; #423, 1/28/83; #425, 4/15/83; #428-429, 6/9/83.

Used Stamps
Postally used copies are valued the same as unused. CTO's are of minimal value. Most used stamps from No. 430-679 exist CTO. Most of these appeared on the market after the contract was canceled and were not authorized. The cancellations are printed and the paper differs from the issued stamps.

Imperforate Stamps
Stamps from No. 430-679 exist imperforate in small quantities.

Queen Elizabeth II, 25th Anniv. of
Coronation — A63

Designs: 25c, No. 439, Paslow Bldg.,
#397c. 50c, Parliament, London, #397a. 75c,
Coronation coach. $1, Queen on horseback,
vert. $2, Prince of Wales, vert. $3, Queen and
Prince Philip, vert. $4, Queen Elizabeth II, por-
trait, vert. No. 437, St. Edward's Crown, vert.
No. 438a, $5, Princess Anne on horseback,
Montreal Olympics, vert. No. 438b, $10,
Queen, Montreal Olympics, vert.

Unwmk.

1979, May 31		**Litho.**	**Perf. 14**	
430	A63	25c multicolored	1.25	
431	A63	50c multicolored	1.75	
432	A63	75c multicolored	2.40	
433	A63	$1 multicolored	3.00	
434	A63	$3 multicolored	3.25	
435	A63	$3 multicolored	3.25	
436	A63	$4 multicolored	3.50	
437	A63	$5 multicolored	4.00	
		Nos. 430-437 (8)	22.40	

Souvenir Sheets

438	A63	Sheet of 2, #a.-b.	15.00	
439	A63	$15 multicolored	15.00	

Powered Flight, 75th Anniv. — A64

1979, July 30				
440	A64	4c Safety, 1909	.50	
441	A64	25c Boeing 707	1.50	
442	A64	50c Concorde	3.75	
443	A64	75c Handley Page		
		W8b, 1922	2.10	
444	A64	$1 AVRO F, 1912	2.10	
445	A64	$1.50 Cody, 1910	3.00	
446	A64	$2 Triplane Roe II,		
		1909	3.00	
447	A64	$3 Santos-Dumont,		
		1906	3.00	
448	A64	$4 Wright Brothers		
		Flyer, 1903	3.75	
		Nos. 440-448 (9)	22.70	

Souvenir Sheets
Perf. 14½

449		Sheet of 2	15.00	
a.	A64	$5 Dunne D.5, 1910	7.50	
b.	A64	$5 Great Britain #581	7.50	
450	A64	$10 Belize Airways		
		Jet	15.00	

Sir Rowland Hill, death cent., "75th anniv."
of ICAO.

1980 Summer
Olympics,
Moscow — A65

1979, Oct. 10			**Perf. 14**	
451	A65	25c Handball	.60	
452	A65	50c Weight lifting	.85	
453	A65	75c Track	1.25	
454	A65	$1 Soccer	1.60	
455	A65	$2 Sailing	2.25	
456	A65	$3 Swimming	2.50	
457	A65	$4 Boxing	3.25	
458	A65	$5 Cycling	6.50	
		Nos. 451-458 (8)	18.80	

Souvenir Sheets
Perf. 14½

459		Sheet of 2	12.00	
a.	A65	$5 Track, diff.	4.00	
b.	A65	$10 Boxing, diff.	8.00	
460	A65	$15 Cycling, diff.	12.00	

1980 Winter
Olympics,
Lake
Placid — A66

1979, Dec. 4			**Perf. 14**	
461	A66	25c Torch	.20	
462	A66	50c Slalom skiing	.40	
463	A66	75c Figure skating	.65	
464	A66	$1 Downhill skiing	.85	
465	A66	$2 Speed skating	1.75	
466	A66	$3 Cross country ski-		
		ing	2.50	
467	A66	$4 Biathlon	3.50	
468	A66	$5 Olympic medals	4.25	
		Nos. 461-468 (8)	14.10	

Souvenir Sheets
Perf. 14½

469		Sheet of 2	10.50	
a.	A66	$5 Torch bearers	3.50	
b.	A66	$10 Medals, diff.	7.00	
470	A66	$15 Torch, diff.	10.50	

See Nos. 503-512.

Cypraea
Zebra
A67

1980, Jan. 7		**Litho.**	**Perf. 14**	
471	A67	1c shown	.65	.20
472	A67	2c Macrocallista		
		maculata	.80	.20
473	A67	3c Arca zebra, vert.	.95	.20
474	A67	4c Chama macer-		
		ophylla, vert.	.95	.20
475	A67	5c Latirus cariniferus	.95	.20
476	A67	10c Conus spurius,		
		vert.	1.10	.20
477	A67	15c Murex cabritii,		
		vert.	1.60	.20
478	A67	20c Atrina rigida	1.75	.20
479	A67	25c Chlamys imbri-		
		cata, vert.	1.75	.20
480	A67	35c Conus granulatus	2.00	.20
481	A67	45c Tellina radiata,		
		vert.	2.25	.20
482	A67	50c Leucozonia nas-		
		sa	2.25	.20
483	A67	85c Tripterotyphis tri-		
		angularis	3.50	.20
484	A67	$1 Strombus gigas,		
		vert.	3.75	.20
485	A67	$2 Strombus gallus,		
		vert.	5.75	.30
486	A67	$5 Fasciolaria tulipa	8.75	.75
487	A67	$10 Arene cruentata	11.00	1.25
		Nos. 471-487 (17)	49.75	5.10

Souvenir Sheets

488	A67	Sheet of 2, 85c, $5	15.00	10.00
489	A67	Sheet of 2, $2, $10	30.00	20.00

Stamps in Nos. 488-489 have different color
border and are of a slightly different size than
the sheet stamps.
The 10c, 50c, 85c, $1 exist dated 1981.
For overprints and surcharges see Nos.
422-423, 424A, 572-589, 592-593.

Intl. Year of
the
Child — A68

Various children. No. 498a, Three children.
No. 498b, Madonna and Child by Durer. No.
499, Children before Christmas tree.

1980, Mar. 15		**Litho.**	**Perf. 14**	
490	A68	25c multicolored	.50	
491	A68	50c multicolored	.80	
492	A68	75c multicolored	1.10	
493	A68	$1 multicolored	1.10	
494	A68	$1.50 multicolored	1.75	
495	A68	$2 multicolored	2.00	
496	A68	$3 multicolored	2.50	
497	A68	$4 multicolored	2.75	
		Nos. 490-497 (8)	12.50	

Souvenir Sheets
Perf. 13½

498	A68	$5 Sheet of 2, #a.-		
		b.	10.00	
499	A68	$10 multicolored	10.00	

No. 498 contains two 35x54mm stamps. No.
499 contains one 73x110mm stamp.

Bird Type of 1977
Souvenir Sheets

1980, June 16		**Unwmk.**	**Perf. 13½**	
500		Sheet of 6	42.50	25.00
a.	A59	10c Jabiru	6.00	3.75
b.	A59	25c Barred antshrike	6.75	3.75
c.	A59	35c Royal flycatcher	7.25	3.75
d.	A59	45c White-necked puffbird	7.25	4.00
e.	A59	50c Ornate hawk-eagle	7.25	4.00
f.	A59	$1 Golden-masked tanager	7.75	5.25
g.		Sheet of 12	85.00	70.00
501		Sheet of 2	30.00	30.00
a.	A59	$2 Jabiru	12.50	12.50
b.	A59	$3 Golden-masked tanager	17.50	17.50

No. 500g contains 2 each Nos. 500a-500f
with gutter between; inscribed "Protection of
Environment" and "Wildlife Protection."

No. 500 Overprinted or Surcharged
with Exhibition Emblem

1980, Oct. 3		**Litho.**	**Perf. 13½**	
502		Sheet of 6	37.50	37.50
a.	A59	10c multicolored	5.50	2.75
b.	A59	25c multicolored	6.00	3.00
c.	A59	35c multicolored	6.00	3.00
d.	A59	40c on 45c multi	6.50	3.25
e.	A59	40c on 50c multi	6.50	3.25
f.	A59	40c on $1 multi	6.50	3.25

ESPAMER '80 Stamp Exhibition, Madrid,
Spain, Oct. 3-12.

1980 Winter Olympics, Lake
Placid — A69

Events and winning country: 25c, Men's
speed skating, US. 50c, Ice hockey, US. 75c,
No. 512, Men's figure skating, Great Britain.
$1, Alpine skiing, Austria. $1.50, Women's
giant slalom, Germany. $2, Women's speed
skating, Netherlands. $3, Cross country ski-
ing, Sweden. $5, Men's giant slalom, Sweden.
Nos. 511a ($5), 511b ($10), Speed skating,
US.

1980, Aug. 20		**Litho.**	**Perf. 14**	
503	A69	25c multi + label	.25	
504	A69	50c multi + label	.50	
505	A69	75c multi + label	.75	
506	A69	$1 multi + label	.95	
507	A69	$1.50 multi + label	1.50	
508	A69	$2 multi + label	1.90	
509	A69	$3 multi + label	3.00	
510	A69	$5 multi + label	4.75	
		Nos. 503-510 (8)	13.60	

Souvenir Sheets
Perf. 14½

511	A69	Sheet of 2, #a.-b.	6.50	
512	A69	$10 multicolored	13.00	

Nos. 503-510 issued with se-tenant label.

Intl. Year of the
Child — A70

Nos. 513-521: Scenes from Sleeping
Beauty. $8, Detail from Paumgartner Family
Altarpiece by Albrecht Durer.

1980, Nov. 24			**Perf. 14**	
513	A70	35c multicolored	1.25	
514	A70	40c multicolored	1.50	
515	A70	50c multicolored	1.75	
516	A70	75c multicolored	1.90	
517	A70	$1 multicolored	2.10	
518	A70	$1.50 multicolored	3.00	
519	A70	$3 multicolored	4.25	
520	A70	$4 multicolored	4.25	
		Nos. 513-520 (8)	20.00	

Souvenir Sheets
Perf. 14½

521		Sheet of 2	14.00	
a.	A70	$5 Marriage	7.00	
b.	A70	$5 Couple on horseback	7.00	
522	A70	$8 multicolored	11.00	

Nos. 513-520 issued with se-tenant label.

Queen Mother Elizabeth, 80th
Birthday — A71

1980, Dec. 12
523 A71 $1 multicolored　　3.50

Souvenir Sheet
Perf. 14½

524 A71 $5 multicolored　　11.00

No. 524 contains one 46x31mm stamp.
No. 523 issued in sheet of 6.

Christmas — A72

1980, Dec. 30		**Litho.**	**Perf. 14**	
525	A72	25c Annunciation	.60	
526	A72	50c Bethlehem	.95	
527	A72	75c Holy Family	1.25	
528	A72	$1 Nativity	1.40	
529	A72	$1.50 Flight into		
		Egypt	1.90	
530	A72	$2 Shepards	2.25	
531	A72	$3 With angel	2.75	
532	A72	$4 Adoration	3.00	
		Nos. 525-532 (8)	14.10	

Souvenir Sheets
Perf. 14½

533	A72	$5 Nativity	6.50	
534	A72	$10 Madonna &		
		Child	13.00	

Nos. 525-532 each issued in sheets of 20 +
10 labels. The 2nd and 5th vertical rows consist of labels.

Nos. 529, 532, 534 Surcharged **$2**

1981, May 22
535	A72	$1 on $1.50 multi	3.00
536	A72	$2 on $4 multi	3.50

Souvenir Sheet
Perf. 14½
537	A72	$2 on $10 multi	4.50

Location of overprint and surcharge varies.

Intl. Rotary Club — A73

Designs: 25c, Paul P. Harris, founder. 50c, No. 546, Rotary, project emblem. $1, No. 545b, 75th anniv. emblem. $1.50 Diploma, horiz. $2, No. 545a, Project Hippocrates. $3, 75th anniv. project emblems, horiz. No. 544, Hands reach out, horiz.

1981, May 26 — **Perf. 14**
538	A73	25c multicolored	1.25
539	A73	50c multicolored	2.00
540	A73	$1 multicolored	2.75
541	A73	$1.50 multicolored	4.00
542	A73	$2 multicolored	4.75
543	A73	$3 multicolored	5.50
544	A73	$5 multicolored	7.00
		Nos. 538-544 (7)	27.25

Souvenir Sheets
Perf. 14½
545		Sheet of 2	25.00
a.		A73 $5 multicolored	8.00
b.		A73 $10 multicolored	16.00
546	A73	$10 multicolored	17.50

Originally scheduled to be issued Mar. 30, the set was postponed and issued without a 75c stamp. Supposedly some of the 75c were sold to the public.
For overprints and surcharges see Nos. 563-571, 590-591.

Royal Wedding of Prince Charles and Lady Diana — A74

1981, July 16 — **Perf. 13½x14**
548	A74	50c Coat of Arms	.50
549	A74	$1 Prince Charles	1.00
550	A74	$1.50 Couple	1.50

Size: 25x43mm
Perf. 13½
551	A74	50c like No. 548	.50
552	A74	$1 like No. 549	1.00
553	A74	$1.50 like No. 550	1.50
		Nos. 548-553 (6)	6.00

Miniature Sheet
Perf. 14½
554		Sheet of 3, #554a-554c	3.00
a.		A74 $3 like No. 550	1.00
b.		A74 $3 like No. 548	1.00
c.		A74 $3 like No. 549	1.00

Nos. 551-553 issued in sheets of 6 + 3 labels. No. 554 contains three 35x50mm stamps.
For overprints see Nos. 659-665.

1984 Olympics — A75

1981, Sept. 14 — **Perf. 14**
555	A75	85c Track	1.75
556	A75	$1 Cycling	4.50
557	A75	$1.50 Boxing	3.00
558	A75	$2 Emblems	3.50
559	A75	$3 Baron Coubertin	4.50
560	A75	$5 Torch, emblems	5.25
		Nos. 555-560 (6)	22.50

Souvenir Sheets
Perf. 13½
561		Sheet of 2	24.00
a.		A75 $5 like No. 559	8.00
b.		A75 $10 like No. 560	16.00

Perf. 14½
562	A75	$15 like No. 558	24.00

No. 561 contains two 35x54mm stamps. No. 562 contains one 46x68mm stamp.
Nos. 561-562 exist with gold background.

Nos. 538-546 Overprinted in Black or Gold

1981, Sept. 21 — **Perf. 14**
563	A73	25c multicolored (G)	1.40
564	A73	50c multicolored	1.75
565	A73	$1 multicolored	2.10
566	A73	$1.50 multicolored	2.75
567	A73	$2 multicolored (G)	3.25
568	A73	$3 multicolored	3.75
569	A73	$5 multicolored	5.00
		Nos. 563-569 (7)	20.00 .00

Souvenir Sheets
Perf. 14½
570	A73	Sheet of 2, #a.-	
		b. (G)	15.00
571	A73	$10 multicolored	15.00

Size of overprint varies.

Nos. 471-483, 485-489 Overprinted

1981, Sept. 21
572	A67	1c multicolored	.70
573	A67	2c multicolored	.70
574	A67	3c multicolored	.90
575	A67	4c multicolored	.90
576	A67	5c multicolored	.90
577	A67	10c multicolored	1.10
578	A67	15c multicolored	1.75
579	A67	20c multicolored	1.75
580	A67	25c multicolored	2.00
581	A67	35c multicolored	2.00
582	A67	45c multicolored	2.40
583	A67	50c multicolored	2.40
584	A67	85c multicolored	3.50
585	A67	$2 multicolored	6.25
586	A67	$5 multicolored	7.25
587	A67	$10 multicolored	10.50
		Nos. 572-587 (16)	45.00 .00

Souvenir Sheets
588	A67	Sheet of 2, #488	17.50
589	A67	Sheet of 2, #489	17.50

Size and style of overprint varies, italic on horiz. stamps, upright on vert. stamps and upright capitals on souvenir sheets.
The 10c is dated 1981. Less than 16 sheets dated 1980 were also overprinted.

Nos. 541, 545 Surcharged

$1

1981, Nov. 13 — **Perf. 14**
590	A73	$1 on $1.50 multi	5.00

Souvenir Sheet
Perf. 14½
591		Sheet of 2	8.00
a.		A73 $1 on $5 multicolored	4.00
b.		A73 $1 on $10 multicolored	4.00

Espamer '81.

Nos. 488, 489 Surcharged in Red

$1

1981, Nov. 14 — **Perf. 14½**
Souvenir Sheets
592		Sheet of 2	10.00
a.		A67 $1 on 85c	5.00
b.		A67 $1 on $5	5.00
593		Sheet of 2	10.00
a.		A67 $1 on $2	5.00
b.		A67 $1 on $10	5.00

Independence — A76

1981-82 — **Perf. 14**
594	A76	10c Flag	1.50
595	A76	35c Map, vert.	3.00
596	A76	50c Black orchid, vert.	8.00
597	A76	85c Tapir	2.50
598	A76	$1 Mahogany tree, vert.	2.50
599	A76	$2 Keel-billed toucan	11.50
		Nos. 594-599 (6)	29.00

Souvenir Sheet
Perf. 14½
600	A76	$5 like 10c	16.00

Issued: 50c-$2, 12/18; 10c, 35c, $5, 2/10/82.
For surcharges see Nos. 425, 428, 616.

1982 World Cup Soccer Championships, Spain — A77

1981, Dec. 28 — **Perf. 14**
601	A77	10c Uruguay '30, '50	1.00
602	A77	25c Italy '34, '38	1.75
603	A77	50c Germany '54, '74	2.25
604	A77	$1 Brazil '58, '62, '70	2.75
605	A77	$1.50 Argentina '78	3.50
606	A77	$2 England '66	3.75
		Nos. 601-606 (6)	15.00

Souvenir Sheets
Perf. 14½
607	A77	$2 Emblem	5.00
608	A77	$3 Player	5.00

No. 608 contains one 46x78mm stamp.
For surcharge see No. 617.

Sailing Ships A78

1982, Mar. 15 — **Perf. 14**
609	A78	10c Man of war, 19th cent.	2.50
610	A78	25c Madagascar, 1837	3.75
611	A78	35c Whitby, 1838	4.25
612	A78	50c China, 1838	4.75
613	A78	85c Swiftsure, 1850	6.00
614	A78	$2 Windsor Castle, 1857	8.75
		Nos. 609-614 (6)	30.00

Souvenir Sheet
Perf. 14½
615	A78	$5 19th cent. ships	30.00

Nos. 599 and 606 Surcharged

1982, Apr. 28
616	A76	$1 on $2 multi	4.00
617	A77	$1 on $2 multi	4.00

Essen '82 Philatelic Exhibition.

Princess of Wales, 21st Birthday — A79

Various portraits.

1982, May 20 — **Perf. 13½x14**
618	A79	50c multicolored	.50
619	A79	$1 multicolored	1.00
620	A79	$1.50 multicolored	1.50

Size: 25x42mm
Perf. 13½
621	A79	50c like No. 618	.50
622	A79	$1 like No. 619	1.00
623	A79	$1.50 like No. 620	1.50
		Nos. 618-623 (6)	6.00

Souvenir Sheet
Stamp Size: 31x47mm
Perf. 14½
624	A79	$3 Sheet of 3, #a.-c. like #618-620	4.00

Nos. 618-620 also exist with gold borders, size: 30x45mm.

Overprinted in
Silver

1982, Oct. 21   *Perf. 13½x14*
628 A79 50c multicolored   .35
629 A79 $1 multicolored   .45
630 A79 $1.50 multicolored   .60

Size: 25x42mm
Perf. 13½
631 A79 50c multicolored   .35
632 A79 $1 multicolored   .45
633 A79 $1.50 multicolored   .60
     Nos. 628-633 (6)   2.80

Souvenir Sheet
Perf. 14½
634 A79 $3 Sheet of 3, #a.-
         c.   8.50

Size of overprint varies. The overprint exists
on the gold bordered stamps. No. 634 exists
with a second type of overprint.

Boy
Scouts
A80

1982, Aug. 31   *Perf. 14*
638 A80 10c Building camp fire   .95
639 A80 25c Bird watching   1.75
640 A80 35c Playing guitar   1.40
641 A80 50c Hiking   1.50
642 A80 85c Flag, scouts   2.00
643 A80 $2 Salute   2.40
     Nos. 638-643 (6)   10.00

Souvenir Sheets
Perf. 14½
644 A80 $2 Scout holding
            flag, vert.   6.00
645 A80 $3 Lord Baden Pow-
            ell, vert.   6.00

Scouting, 75th anniv. and Lord Baden Powell, 125th birth anniv.
For overprints see Nos. 653-658.

Marine Life — A81

1982, Sept. 20   *Perf. 14*
646 A81 10c Gorgonia
            ventalina   2.25
647 A81 35c Carpilius coral-
            linus   3.75
648 A81 50c Plexaura flexuosa   4.25
649 A81 85c Condylactis gi-
            gantea   4.50
650 A81 $1 Stenopus his-
            pidus   5.75
651 A81 $2 Abudefduf saxa-
            tilis   7.00
     Nos. 646-651 (6)   27.50

Souvenir Sheet
Perf. 14½
652 A81 $5 Scyllarides aequi-
            noctialis   32.50

For surcharge see No. 429.

Nos. 638-643 Ovptd. in Gold:
BELGICA 82
INT. YEAR OF THE CHILD
SIR ROWLAND HILL 1795 1879
Picasso CENTENARY OF BIRTH
and Emblems

1982, Oct. 1   *Perf. 14*
653 A80 10c Building camp fire   2.50
654 A80 25c Bird watching   4.25
655 A80 35c Playing guitar   3.75
656 A80 50c Hiking   4.25
657 A80 85c Flag, scouts   6.75
658 A80 $2 Salute   11.00
     Nos. 653-658 (6)   32.50

Overprint is different on Nos. 654-655.
Sheets include labels with native Christmas
themes.

Nos. 548-554 Overprinted in Gold
Similar to Nos. 628-634

1982, Oct. 25   *Perf. 13½x14*
659 A74 50c Coat of Arms   1.40
660 A74 $1 Prince Charles   2.75
661 A74 $1.50 Couple   4.25

Size: 25x43mm
Perf. 13½
662 A74 50c like No. 659   1.40
663 A74 $1 like No. 660   2.75
664 A74 $1.50 like No. 661   4.25
     Nos. 659-664 (6)   16.80

Miniature Sheet
Perf. 14½
665   Sheet of 3, #665a-665c   14.00
   a.   A74 $3 like No. 661   3.50
   b.   A74 $3 like No. 659   3.50
   c.   A74 $3 like No. 660   3.50

Nos. 662-664 issued in sheets of 6 plus 3
labels. No. 665 contains three 35x50mm
stamps. Size and style of overprint varies.

Visit by
Pope
John
Paul II
A82

1983, Mar. 7   *Perf. 13½*
666 A82 50c Belize Cathedral   1.90

Souvenir Sheet
Perf. 14½
667 A82 $2.50 Pope John Paul II   4.75

No. 667 contains one 30x47mm stamp.
No. 666 issued in sheet of 6.

Commonwealth Day — A83

1983, Mar. 14   *Perf. 13½*
668 A83 35c Map, vert.   .30
669 A83 50c Maya Stella   .40
670 A83 85c Supreme Court
            Bldg.   .80
671 A83 $2 University Center   2.00
     Nos. 668-671 (4)   3.50

Issued in miniature sheets of 4. Other formats are suspect.

First Manned Flight, Bicent. — A84

1983, May 16   *Perf. 14*
672 A84 10c Flying boat, 1670   .20
673 A84 25c Flying machine,
            1709   .20
674 A84 50c Airship Guyton de
            Morveau   .30
675 A84 85c Dirigible   .50

---

676 A84 $1 Clement Bayard   .60
677 A84 $1.50 Great Britain R-34   .95
     Nos. 672-677 (6)   2.75

Souvenir Sheets
Perf. 14½
678 A84 $3 Nassau Balloon   1.65
679 A84 $3 Montgolfier Broth-
            ers balloon, vert.   1.65

"Errors"
Many   "errors,"   including
imperforates, exist of Nos. 680-898.
These unauthorized varieties were
printed without the knowledge of the
Belize postal service. There may be
large quantities of them.

Mayan Monuments — A85

1983, Nov. 14   Litho.   *Perf. 13½x14*
680 A85 10c Altun Ha   .20   .20
681 A85 15c Xunantunich   .20   .20
682 A85 75c Cerros   .60   .60
683 A85 $2 Lamanai   1.40   1.40
     Nos. 680-683 (4)   2.40   2.40

Souvenir Sheet
684 A85 $3 Xunantunich, diff.   2.75   2.75

World Communications Year — A86

1983, Nov. 28   *Perf. 14*
685 A86 10c Belmopan Earth
            Station   .20   .20
686 A86 15c Telstar 2   .20   .20
687 A86 75c UPU monument   .75   .75
688 A86 $2 Mail boat   2.00   2.00
     Nos. 685-688 (4)   3.15   3.15

Jaguar,
World
Wildlife
Fund
Emblem
A87

1983, Dec. 9
689 A87 5c Sitting   .20   .20
690 A87 10c Standing   .20   .20
691 A87 85c Swimming   1.10   1.10
692 A87 $1 Walking   1.40   1.40
     Nos. 689-692 (4)   2.90   2.90

Souvenir Sheet
693 A87 $3 Sitting in tree   3.25   3.25

No. 693 contains one stamp 45x28mm.

Christmas — A88

Scenes from mass celebrated by Pope John
Paul II during visit, Mar.

1983, Dec. 22
694 A88 10c multicolored   .20   .20
695 A88 15c multicolored   .20   .20
696 A88 75c multicolored   .75   .75
697 A88 $2 multicolored   2.00   2.00
     Nos. 694-697 (4)   3.15   3.15

Souvenir Sheet
698 A88 $3 multicolored   3.25   3.25

Foureye Butterflyfish — A89

1984, Feb. 27   *Perf. 15*
699 A89 1c shown   .20   .20
700 A89 2c Cushion star   .20   .20
701 A89 3c Flower coral   .20   .20
702 A89 4c Fairy basslets   .20   .20
703 A89 5c Spanish hogfish   .20   .20
704 A89 6c Star-eyed hermit
            crab   .20   .20
705 A89 10c Sea fans, fire
            sponge   .20   .20
706 A89 15c Blueheads   .20   .20
707 A89 25c Blue-striped grunt   .25   .25
708 A89 50c Coral crab   .50   .50
709 A89 60c Tube sponge   .60   .60
710 A89 75c Brain coral   .75   .75
711 A89 $1 Yellow-tail snap-
            per   1.00   1.00
712 A89 $2 Common lettuce
            slug   2.00   2.00
713 A89 $5 Yellow damselfish   5.00   5.00
714 A89 $10 Rock beauty   10.00 10.00
     Nos. 699-714 (16)   21.70 21.70

For overprints and surcharge see Nos. 715-
716, 762A-762C, 922.
The 50c, 60c, 75c, $1 exist inscribed "1986."

1988, July   *Perf. 13½*
705a A89 10c   .20   .20
706a A89 15c   .25   .25
707a A89 25c   .50   .50
708a A89 50c   .60   .60
709a A89 60c   .95   .95
711a A89 $1
     Nos. 705a-711a (6)   2.70   2.70

Nos. 705, 708 Overprinted: "VISIT OF
THE LORD / ARCHBISHOP OF
CANTERBURY / 8th-11th MARCH
1984"

1984, Mar. 8
715 A89 10c multicolored   .20   .20
716 A89 50c multicolored   .60   .60

1984 Summer Olympics — A90

1984, Apr. 30   *Perf. 13½x14*
717 A90 25c Shooting   .25   .25
718 A90 75c Boxing   .75   .75
719 A90 $1 Running   1.10   1.10
720 A90 $2 Bicycling   1.90   1.90
     Nos. 717-720 (4)   4.00   4.00

Souvenir Sheet
721 A90 $3 Discus   2.25   2.25

1984 Summer Olympics — A91

1984, Apr. 30   Litho.   *Perf. 14½*
Booklet Stamps
722 A91 5c Running   .20   .20
   a.   Booklet pane of 4   .30
723 A91 20c Javelin   .25   .25
   a.   Booklet pane of 4   1.10
724 A91 25c Shot put   .35   .35
   a.   Booklet pane of 4   1.50
725 A91 $2 Torch   2.50   2.50
   a.   Booklet pane of 4   10.50
     Nos. 722-725 (4)   3.30   3.30

Ausipex '84 — A92

1984, Sept. 26   Litho.   Perf. 15

726 A92	15c Br. Honduras #3	.20	.20
727 A92	30c Bath-Bristol mail coach, 1784	.30	.30
728 A92	65c Penny Black, Rowland Hill	.65	.65
729 A92	75c Railroad Pier, Commerce Bight	.75	.75

Perf. 14

730 A92	$2 Royal Exhibition Bldgs.	2.00	2.00
	Nos. 726-730 (5)	3.90	3.90

Souvenir Sheet

731 A92	$3 Australia #132, Br. Hond. #3	3.00	3.00

House of Tudor, 500th Anniv. — A93

White-fronted Parrot — A94

1984, Oct. 15   Perf. 14

732 A93	50c Queen Victoria	.35	.35
733 A93	50c Prince Albert	.35	.35
a.	Sheet of 4, 2 each, #732-733	1.50	
734 A93	75c King George VI	.55	.55
735 A93	75c Queen Elizabeth	.55	.55
a.	Sheet of 4, 2 each, #734-735	2.25	
736 A93	$1 Prince Charles	.75	.75
737 A93	$1 Princess Diana	.75	.75
a.	Sheet of 4, 2 each, #736-737	3.00	
	Nos. 732-737 (6)	3.30	3.30

Souvenir Sheet

738	Sheet of 2	2.00	2.00
a.	A93 $1.50 Prince Philip	1.00	1.00
b.	A93 $1.50 Queen Elizabeth II	1.00	1.00

1984, Nov. 1   Perf. 11

Parrots: b, White-capped. c, Red-lored. d, Mealy. b, d, horiz.

739	Block of 4	4.00	4.00
a.-d.	A94 $1 any single	1.00	1.00

Miniature Sheet
Perf. 14

740 A94	$3 Scarlet macaw	3.00	3.00

No. 740 contains one 48x32mm stamp.

Mayan Artifacts — A95

1984, Nov. 30   Perf. 15

741 A95	25c Incense holder, 1450	.25	.25
742 A95	75c Cylindrical vase, 675	.75	.75
743 A95	$1 Tripod vase, 500	1.00	1.00
744 A95	$2 Kinich Ahau (sun god)	2.00	2.00
	Nos. 741-744 (4)	4.00	4.00

Girl Guides 75th Anniv., Intl. Youth Year A96

1985, Mar. 15   Litho.   Perf. 15

745 A96	25c Gov.-Gen. Gordon	.25	.25
746 A96	50c Camping	.50	.50
747 A96	90c Map reading	.90	.90
748 A96	$1.25 Students in laboratory	1.25	1.25

749 A96	$2 Lady Baden-Powell	2.00	2.00
	Nos. 745-749 (5)	4.90	4.90

Each stamp shows the scouting and IYY emblems.
For overprints see Nos. 777-781.

Audubon Birth Bicentenary — A97

Illustrations by Audubon. 10c, 25c, 75c, $1, $5 vert.

Perf. 14, 15 ($1)

1985, May 30-1988   Litho.

750 A97	10c White-tailed kite	.20	.20
751 A97	15c Cuvier's kinglet	.20	.20
752 A97	25c Painted bunting	.35	.35
752A A97	60c like #752 ('88)		
753 A97	75c Belted kingfisher	1.00	1.00
754 A97	$1 Northern cardinal	1.40	1.40
755 A97	$3 Long-billed curlew	4.00	4.00
	Nos. 750-752,753-755 (6)	7.15	7.15

Souvenir Sheet
Perf. 13½x14

756 A97	$5 Portrait of Audubon, 1826, by John Syme	5.00	5.00

No. 756 contains one 38x51mm stamp.

Queen Mother, 85th Birthday — A98

Designs: 10c, The Queen Consort and Princess Elizabeth, 1928. 15c, Queen Mother, Elizabeth. 75c, Queen Mother waving a greeting. No. 760, Royal family photograph, christening of Prince Henry. $2, Holding the infant Prince Henry. No. 762, Queen Mother, diff.

1985, June 20

757 A98	10c shown	.20	.20
758 A98	15c multicolored	.20	.20
759 A98	75c multicolored	.75	.75
760 A98	$5 multicolored	5.00	5.00
	Nos. 757-760 (4)	6.15	6.15

Souvenir Sheets

761 A98	$2 multicolored	1.75	1.75
762 A98	$5 multicolored	4.25	4.25

Nos. 761-762 contain one 38x51mm stamp.
For overprints see Nos. 771-776.

Nos. 705-706, 708 Ovptd.:
INAUGURATION OF
NEW GOVERNMENT
21st. DECEMBER 1984

1985, June 24   Perf. 15

762A A89	10c multicolored	.30	.30
762B A89	15c multicolored	.45	.45
762C A89	50c multicolored	1.25	1.25
	Nos. 762A-762C (3)	2.00	2.00

Miniature Sheet

Commonwealth Stamp Omnibus, 50th Anniv. — A99

British Honduras Nos. 111-112, 127, 129, 143, 194, 307 and Belize Nos. 326, 385 and 397b on: a, George V and Queen Mary in an open carriage. b, George VI and Queen Consort Elizabeth crowned. c, Civilians celebrating the end of WWII. d, George VI and Queen Consort at mass service. e, Elizabeth II wearing robes of state and the imperial crown. f, Winston Churchill, WWII fighter planes. g, Bridal photograph of Elizabeth II and Prince Philip. h, Bridal photograph of Princess Anne

and Capt. Mark Phillips. i, Elizabeth II. j, Imperial crown.

1985, July 25   Perf. 14½x14

763	Sheet of 10	5.00	5.00
a.-j.	A99 50c any single	.50	.50

Souvenir Sheet
Perf. 14

764 A99	$5 Elizabeth II coronation photograph	5.00	5.00

No. 764 contains one 38x51mm stamp.
For overprints see Nos. 796-797.

British Post Office, 350th Anniv. A100

1985, Aug. 1   Perf. 15

765 A100	10c Postboy, letters	.20	.20
766 A100	15c Packet, privateer	.20	.20
767 A100	25c Duke of Marlborough	.25	.25
768 A100	75c Diana	.75	.75
769 A100	$1 Falmouth P.O. packet	1.00	1.00
770 A100	$3 S. S. Conway	3.00	3.00
	Nos. 765-770 (6)	5.40	5.40

Nos. 757-762 Ovptd. in Silver
"COMMONWEALTH SUMMIT /
CONFERENCE, BAHAMAS / 16th-
22nd OCTOBER 1985"

1985, Sept. 5   Litho.   Perf. 15

771 A98	10c multicolored	.20	.20
772 A98	15c multicolored	.20	.20
773 A98	75c multicolored	.75	.75
774 A98	$5 multicolored	5.00	5.00
	Nos. 771-774 (4)	6.15	6.15

Souvenir Sheets

775 A98	$2 multicolored	1.90	1.90
776 A98	$5 multicolored	4.75	4.75

Nos. 745-749 Ovptd. "80th
ANNIVERSARY OF / ROTARY
INTERNATIONAL"

1985, Sept. 25   Perf. 15

777 A96	25c multicolored	.25	.25
778 A96	50c multicolored	.50	.50
779 A96	90c multicolored	.90	.90
780 A96	$1.25 multicolored	1.25	1.25
781 A96	$2 multicolored	2.00	2.00
	Nos. 777-781 (5)	4.90	4.90

Royal Visit — A101

1985, Oct. 9   Perf. 15x14½

782 A101	25c Royal and natl. flags	.25	.25
783 A101	75c Elizabeth II	.75	.75

Size: 81x38mm

784 A101	$4 Britannia	4.00	4.00
a.	Strip of 3, #782-784	5.00	
	Nos. 782-784 (3)	5.00	5.00

Souvenir Sheet
Perf. 13½x14

785 A101	$5 Elizabeth II, diff.	5.00	5.00

No. 785 contains one 38x51mm stamp.

Disneyland, 30th Anniv. A102

Characters from "It's a Small World."

1985, Nov. 1   Perf. 11

786 A102	1c Royal Canadian Mounted Police	.20	.20
787 A102	2c American Indian	.20	.20
788 A102	3c Inca of the Andes	.20	.20
789 A102	4c Africa	.20	.20
790 A102	5c Far East	.20	.20
791 A102	6c Belize	.20	.20
792 A102	50c Balkans	.50	.50
793 A102	$1.50 Saudi Arabia	1.50	1.50
794 A102	$3 Japan	3.00	3.00
	Nos. 786-794 (9)	6.20	6.20

Souvenir Sheet
Perf. 14

795 A102	$4 Montage	4.00	4.00

Christmas.

Nos. 763-764 Ovptd. "PRE 'WORLD
CUP FOOTBALL' / MEXICO 1986"

1985, Dec. 20   Perf. 14½x14

796	Sheet of 10	5.00	5.00
a.-j.	A99 50c, any single	.50	.50

Souvenir Sheet

797 A99	$5 multicolored	5.00	5.00

Women in Folk Costumes — A103

1986, Jan. 15   Perf. 15

798 A103	5c India	.20	.20
799 A103	10c Maya	.20	.20
800 A103	15c Garifuna	.20	.20
801 A103	25c Creole	.30	.30
802 A103	50c China	.65	.65
803 A103	75c Lebanon	1.00	1.00
804 A103	$1 Europe	1.25	1.25
805 A103	$2 South America	2.50	2.50
	Nos. 798-805 (8)	6.30	6.30

Souvenir Sheet
Perf. 14

806 A103	$5 Maya, So. America	6.25	6.25

No. 806 contains one 38x51mm stamp.

Miniature Sheet

A104

Easter — A105

Papal arms, crucifix and: a, Pius X. b, Benedict XV. c, Pius XI. d, Pius XII. e, John XXIII. f, Paul VI. g, John Paul I. h, John Paul II. No. 573, John Paul II saying mass in Belize.

1986, Apr. 15   Litho.   Perf. 11

807	Sheet of 8 + label	6.25	6.25
a.-h.	A104 50c, any single	.80	.80

Souvenir Sheet
Perf. 14

808 A105	$4 multi	6.50	6.50

No. 807 contains center label picturing the Vatican, and papal crest.

Queen Elizabeth II, 60th Birthday — A106

A107

1986, Apr. 21   **Perf. 14**
809   Strip of 3   1.50 1.50
  a. A106 25c Age 2   .25   .25
  b. A106 50c Coronation   .50   .50
  c. A106 75c Riding horse   .75   .75
810   A106 $3 Wearing crown jewels   3.00 3.00

Souvenir Sheet

811   A107 $4 Portrait   3.25 3.25

A108

Halley's Comet — A109

1986, Apr. 30
812   Strip of 3   .75   .75
  a. A108 10c Planet-A probe   .20   .20
  b. A108 15c Sighting, 1910   .20   .20
  c. A108 50c Giotto probe   .50   .50
813   Strip of 3   3.75 3.75
  a. A108 75c Weather bureau   .75   .75
  b. A108 $1 US space telescope, shuttle   1.00 1.00
  c. A108 $2 Edmond Halley   2.00 2.00

Souvenir Sheet

814   A109 $4 Computer graphics   4.00 4.00

Miniature Sheet

US Presidents — A111

1986, May   **Perf. 11**
815   Sheet of 6 + 3 labels   3.75 3.75
  a. A110 10c George Washington   .20   .20
  b. A110 20c John Adams   .20   .20
  c. A110 30c Thomas Jefferson   .25   .25
  d. A110 50c James Madison   .40   .40
  e. A110 $1.50 James Monroe   1.10 1.10
  f. A110 $2 John Quincy Adams   1.60 1.60

Souvenir Sheet
Perf. 14

816   A111 $4 Washington   4.00 4.00

No. 815 contains 3 center labels picturing the great seal of the US.
Issue dates: #815, May 5; #816, May 7.

A112

Statue of Liberty, Cent. — A113

Designs: 25c, Bartholdi, statue. 50c, Statue, US centennial celebration, Philadelphia, 1876. 75c, Statue close-up, flags, 1886 unveiling. $3, Flags, statue close-up. $4, Statue, New York City skyline.

1986, May 15   **Perf. 14**
817   Strip of 3   4.00 4.00
  a. A112 25c multicolored   .25   .25
  b. A112 75c multicolored   .75   .75
  c. A112 $3 multicolored   3.00 3.00
818   A112 50c multicolored   .50   .50

Souvenir Sheet

819   A113 $4 multicolored   4.00 4.00

A114

AMERIPEX '86, Chicago, May 22-June 1 — A115

1986, May 22
820   Strip of 3   .75   .75
  a. A114 10c British Honduras No. 3   .20   .20
  b. A114 15c Stamp of 1981   .20   .20
  c. A114 50c US No. C3a   .50   .50
821   Strip of 3   3.75 3.75
  a. A114 75c USS Constitution   .75   .75
  b. A114 $1 Liberty Bell   1.00 1.00
  c. A114 $2 White House   2.00 2.00

Souvenir Sheet

822   A115 $4 Capitol Building   3.50 3.50

For overprints see Nos. 835-837.

1986 World Cup Soccer Championships, Mexico — A116

Designs: 25c, England vs. Brazil. 50c, Mexican player, Mayan statues. 75c, Belize players. $3, Aztec calendar stone, Mexico. $4, Flags composing soccer balls.

1986, June 16   **Litho.**   **Perf. 11**
823   A116 25c multicolored   .25   .25
824   A116 50c multicolored   .50   .50
825   A116 75c multicolored   .75   .75
826   A116 $3 multicolored   3.00 3.00
        Nos. 823-826 (4)   4.50 4.50

Souvenir Sheet
Perf. 14

827   A116 $4 multicolored   4.00 4.00

Nos. 823-826 printed in sheets of 8 plus label picturing Azteca Stadium, 2 each value per sheet.

Nos. 823-827 Overprinted
"ARGENTINA - /WINNERS 1986"

1986, Aug. 15
828   A116 25c multicolored   .25   .25
829   A116 50c multicolored   .50   .50
830   A116 75c multicolored   .75   .75
831   A116 $3 multicolored   3.00 3.00
        Nos. 828-831 (4)   4.50 4.50

Souvenir Sheet

832   A116 $4 multicolored   4.00 4.00

A117

Wedding of Prince Andrew and Sarah Ferguson A118

1986, July 23   **Perf. 14x14½**
833   Strip of 3   3.25 3.25
  a. A117 25c Sarah   .20   .20
  b. A117 75c Andrew   .60   .60
  c. A117 $3 Couple   2.25 2.25

Souvenir Sheet
Perf. 14½

834   Sheet of 2   4.00 4.00
  a. A118 $1 Sarah, diff.   1.00 1.00
  b. A118 $3 Andrew, diff.   3.00 3.00

Size of No. 833c: 92x41mm.

Nos. 820-822 Ovptd. with
STOCKHOLMIA '86 Emblems

1986, Aug. 28   **Litho.**   **Perf. 14**
835   Strip of 3   .75   .75
  a. A114 10c multicolored   .20   .20
  b. A114 15c multicolored   .20   .20
  c. A114 50c multicolored   .50   .50
836   Strip of 3   3.75 3.75
  a. A114 75c multicolored   .75   .75
  b. A114 $1 multicolored   1.00 1.00
  c. A114 $2 multicolored   2.00 2.00

Souvenir Sheet

837   A115 $4 multicolored   4.00 4.00

A119

Intl. Peace Year — A120

Children.

1986, Oct. 3   **Litho.**   **Perf. 14**
838   A119 25c Infant   .25   .25
839   A119 50c Caucasians   .50   .50
840   A119 75c Oriental   .75   .75
841   A119 $3 Indian, caucasian   3.00 3.00
        Nos. 838-841 (4)   4.50 4.50

Souvenir Sheet

842   A120 $4 shown   4.00 4.00

Nos. 838-841 printed se-tenant in sheets of 8 (2 each) plus center label.

Fungi — A121

Toucans — A122

1986, Oct. 30   **Perf. 14**
843   A121 5c Amanita lilloi   .20   .20
844   A122 10c Keel-billed toucan .20   .20
845   A121 20c Boletellus cubensis .30   .30
846   A122 25c Collared aracari   .40   .40
847   A121 75c Psilocybe caerulescens   1.25 1.25
848   A122 $1 Emerald toucanet   1.50 1.50
849   A122 $1.25 Crimson-rumped toucan   1.75 1.75
850   A121 $2 Russula puiggarii   3.00 3.00
        Nos. 843-850 (8)   8.60 8.60

Stamps of the same design printed in sheets of 8 plus center label picturing Audubon Society emblem.

Christmas
A123

Disney characters.

1986, Nov. 14   **Perf. 11**

851		Sheet of 9	6.50	6.50
a.	A123	2c Jose Carioca	.20	.20
b.	A123	3c Carioca, Panchito, Donald	.20	.20
c.	A123	4c Daisy	.20	.20
d.	A123	5c Mickey, Minnie	.20	.20
e.	A123	6c Carioca playing music	.20	.20
f.	A123	50c Panchito, Donald	.65	.65
g.	A123	65c Donald, Carioca	.90	.90
h.	A123	$1.35 Donald	1.75	1.75
i.	A123	$2 Goofy	2.75	2.75

Souvenir Sheet
Perf. 14

| 852 | A123 | $4 Donald | 6.00 | 6.00 |

Marriage of Queen Elizabeth II and the Duke of Edinburgh, 40th Anniv. — A124

A125

1987, Oct. 7   **Litho.**   **Perf. 15**

853	A124	25c Elizabeth, 1947	.20	.20
854	A124	75c Couple, c. 1980	.55	.55
855	A124	$1 Elizabeth, 1986	.75	.75
856	A124	$4 Wearing robes of Order of the Garter	3.00	3.00
		Nos. 853-856 (4)	4.50	4.50

Souvenir Sheet
Perf. 14

| 857 | A125 | $6 shown | 6.00 | 6.00 |

A126

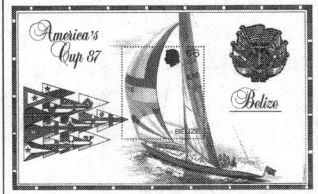

America's Cup 1986-87 — A127

Yachts that competed in the 1987 finals.

1987, Oct. 21   **Perf. 15**

858	A126	25c America II	.25	.25
859	A126	75c Stars and Stripes	.75	.75
860	A126	$1 Australia II	1.00	1.00
861	A126	$4 White Crusader	4.00	4.00
		Nos. 858-861 (4)	6.00	6.00

Souvenir Sheet
Perf. 14

| 862 | A127 | $6 Australia II sails | 6.00 | 6.00 |

Woodcarvings by Sir George Gabb (b. 1928) — A128

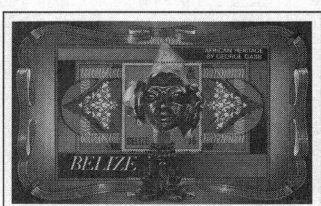

A129

1987, Nov. 4   **Perf. 15**

863	A128	25c Mother and Child	.20	.20
864	A128	75c Standing Form	.60	.60
865	A128	$1 Love-Doves	.80	.80
866	A128	$4 Depiction of Music	3.25	3.25
		Nos. 863-866 (4)	4.85	4.85

Souvenir Sheet
Perf. 14

| 867 | A129 | $6 African Heritage | 4.50 | 4.50 |

A130

Indigenous Primates — A131

1987, Nov. 11   **Perf. 15**

868	A130	25c Black spider monkey	.25	.25
869	A130	75c Male black howler	.75	.75
870	A130	$1 Spider monkeys	1.00	1.00
871	A130	$4 Howler monkeys	4.00	4.00
		Nos. 868-871 (4)	6.00	6.00

Souvenir Sheet
Perf. 14

| 872 | A131 | $6 Black spider, diff. | 6.00 | 6.00 |

Natl. Girl Guides Movement, 50th Anniv. — A132

Lady Olave Baden-Powell, Founder — A133

1987, Nov. 25   **Perf. 15**

873	A132	25c Flag-bearers	.25	.25
874	A132	75c Camping	.75	.75
875	A132	$1 On parade, camp	1.00	1.00
876	A132	$4 Olave Baden-Powell	4.00	4.00
		Nos. 873-876 (4)	6.00	6.00

Souvenir Sheet
Perf. 14

| 877 | A133 | $6 Lady Olave, diff. | 6.00 | 6.00 |

Intl. Year of Shelter for the Homeless A134

1987, Dec. 3   **Perf. 15**

878	A134	25c Tent dwellings	.25	.25
879	A134	75c Urban slum	.75	.75
880	A134	$1 Tents, diff.	1.00	1.00
881	A134	$4 Construction	4.00	4.00
		Nos. 878-881 (4)	6.00	6.00

Orchids A135

Illustrations from Reichenbachia, published by Henry F. Sander in 1886: 1c, Laelia euspatha. 2c, Cattleya citrina. 3c, Masdevallia bachousiana. 4c, Cypripedium tautzianum. 5c, Trichopilia suavis alba. 6c, Odontoglossum hebraicum. 7c, Cattleya trianaei schroederiana. 10c, Saccolabium giganteum. 30c, Cattleya warscewiczii. 50c, Chysis bractescens. 70c, Cattleya rochellensis. $1, Laelia elegans schilleriana. $1.50, Laelia anceps percivaliana. #895, $3, Laelia gouldiana.
#896, $3, Odontoglossum roezlii. $5, Cattleya dowiana aurea.

1987, Dec. 16   **Litho.**   **Perf. 14**

| 882-895 | A135 | Set of 14 | 11.00 | 11.00 |

Miniature Sheets

| 896-897 | A135 | Set of 2 | 8.00 | 8.00 |

Nos. 882-887 and 889-894 printed in blocks of six. Sheets of 14 contain 2 blocks of Nos. 882-887 plus 2 No. 888 and center label or 2 blocks of Nos. 889-894 plus center strip containing 2 No. 895 and center label. Center labels picture various illustrations from Reichenbachia.
Nos. 896-897 contain one 44x51mm stamp.

Miniature Sheet

Easter A136

Stations of the Cross (in sequential order): a, Jesus condemned to death. b, Carries the cross. c, Falls the first time. d, Meets his mother, Mary. e, Cyrenean takes up the cross. f, Veronica wipes Jesus's face. g, Falls the second time. h, Consoles the women of Jerusalem. i, Falls the third time. j, Stripped of his robes. k, Nailed to the cross. l, Dies. m, Taken down from the cross. n, Laid in the sepulcher.

1988, Mar. 21   **Perf. 14**

| 898 | | Sheet of 14 + label | 5.75 | 5.75 |
| a.-n. | A136 | 40c, any single | .40 | .40 |

A $6 souvenir sheet was prepared but not issued.

1988 Summer Olympics, Seoul — A137

1988, Aug. 15   **Litho.**   **Perf. 14**

899	A137	10c Basketball	.20	.20
900	A137	25c Volleyball	.25	.25
901	A137	60c Table tennis	.60	.60
902	A137	75c Diving	.75	.75
903	A137	$1 Judo	1.00	1.00
904	A137	$2 Field hockey	2.00	2.00
		Nos. 899-904 (6)	4.80	4.80

Souvenir Sheet

| 905 | A137 | $3 Women's gymnastics | 3.00 | 3.00 |

Intl. Red Cross, 125th Anniv. A138

1988, Nov. 18   **Litho.**   **Perf. 14**

906	A138	60c Travelling nurse, 1912	.60	.60
907	A138	75c Hospital ship, ambulance boat, 1937	.75	.75
908	A138	$1 Ambulance, 1956	1.00	1.00
909	A138	$2 Ambulance plane, 1940	2.00	2.00
		Nos. 906-909 (4)	4.35	4.35

Indigenous Small Animals — A139

1989   **Litho.**   **Wmk. 384**   **Perf. 14**

| 910 | A139 | 10c Gibnut (agouti) | .25 | .25 |

Unwmk.

911	A139	25c Four-eyed opossum, vert.	.65	.65
a.		Wmk. 384	.65	.65
912	A139	50c Ant bear	1.40	1.40
913	A139	60c like 10c	1.60	1.60
914	A139	75c Antelope	2.00	2.00
915	A139	$2 Peccary	5.50	5.50
		Nos. 910-915 (6)	11.40	11.40

Issued: 10c, 7/23; #911a, 12/6; others, 2/24.

Moon Landing, 20th Anniv.
Common Design Type

Apollo 9: 25c, Command service and lunar modules docked in space. 50c, Command service module. 75c, Mission emblem. $1, First manned lunar module in space. $5, Apollo 11 command service module.

Perf. 14x13½

1989, July 20   **Wmk. 384**
Size of Nos. 680-681: 29x29mm

916	CD342	25c multicolored	.20	.20
917	CD342	50c multicolored	.45	.45
918	CD342	75c multicolored	.65	.65
919	CD342	$1 multicolored	.90	.90
		Nos. 916-919 (4)	2.20	2.20

Souvenir Sheet

| 920 | CD342 | $5 multi | 5.00 | 5.00 |

No. 920 Overprinted

WORLD STAMP EXPO '89™
United States Postal Service
Nov. 17 — 20 and
Nov. 24 — Dec. 3, 1989
Washington Convention Center
Washington, DC

1989, Nov. 17   Perf. 14x13½
921 CD342 $5 multicolored   5.00 5.00
           World Stamp Expo '89.

No. 704 Surcharged

                                       5c

1989, Nov. 15   Perf. 15
922 A89 5c on 6c multi   2.00

Christmas
A140

Old churches.

Wmk. 384
1989, Dec. 13   Litho.   Perf. 14
927 A140 10c Wesley   .20 .20
928 A140 25c Baptist   .25 .25
929 A140 60c St. John's Cathe-
              dral   .60 .60
930 A140 75c St. Andrew's Pres-
              byterian   .75 .75
931 A140 $1 Holy Redeemer
              Cathedral   1.00 1.00
     Nos. 927-931 (5)   2.80 2.80

A141

Wmk. 373
1990, Mar. 1   Litho.   Perf. 14

Birds and Butterflies: 5c, Piranga leucoptera, Catonephele numilia female. 10c, Ramphastos sulfuratus, Nessaea aglaura. 15c, Fregata magnificens, Eurytides philolaus. 25c, Jabiru mycteria, Heliconius sapho. 30c, Ardea herodias, Colobura dirce. 50c, Icterus galbula, Hamadryas arethusia. 60c, Ara macao, Thecla regalis. 75c, Cyanerpes cyaneus, Callicore patelina. $1, Pulsatrix perspicillata, Caligo uranus. $2, Cyanocorax yncas, Philaethria dido. $5, Cathartes aura, Battus belus. $10, Pandion haliaetus, Papilio thoas.

932 A141   5c multicolored   .20 .20
933 A141 10c multicolored   .20 .20
934 A141 15c multicolored   .20 .20
935 A141 25c multicolored   .25 .25
936 A141 30c multicolored   .30 .30
937 A141 50c multicolored   .50 .50
938 A141 60c multicolored   .60 .60
939 A141 75c multicolored   .75 .75
940 A141 $1 multicolored   1.00 1.00
941 A141 $2 multicolored   2.00 2.00
942 A141 $5 multicolored   5.00 5.00
943 A141 $10 multicolored   10.00 10.00
     Nos. 932-943 (12)   21.00 21.00

The 10c exists inscribed "1993".
For overprints and surcharge see Nos. 944, 1021, 1030.

No. 940 Overprinted in Gold:
"FIRST DOLLAR / COIN / 1990"
1990, Mar. 1
944 A141 $1 multicolored   1.00 1.00

Turtles
A142

Wmk. 373
1990, Aug. 8   Litho.   Perf. 14
945 A142 10c Green   .20 .20
946 A142 25c Hawksbill   .25 .25
947 A142 60c Loggerhead   .60 .60
948 A142 75c Loggerhead, diff. .75 .75
949 A142 $1 Bocatora   1.00 1.00
950 A142 $2 Hicatee   2.00 2.00
     Nos. 945-950 (6)   4.80 4.80

Battle of
Britain,
50th
Anniv.
A143

Aircraft.
1990, Sept. 15 Wmk. 384 Perf. 13½
951 A143 10c Fairey Battle   .20 .20
952 A143 25c Bristol Beaufort .25 .25
953 A143 60c Bristol Blenheim .60 .60
954 A143 75c Armstrong-Whit-
              worth Whitley   .75 .75
955 A143 $1 Vickers-Armstrong
              Wellington   1.00 1.00
956 A143 $2 Handley-Page
              Hampden   2.00 2.00
     Nos. 951-956 (6)   4.80 4.80

Orchids — A144

1990, Nov. 1   Wmk. 384   Perf. 14
957 A144 25c Cattleya bowringi-
              ana   .25 .25
958 A144 50c Rhyncholaelia
              digbyana   .50 .50
959 A144 60c Sobralia
              macrantha   .60 .60
960 A144 75c Chysis bractes-
              cens   .75 .75
961 A144 $1 Vanilla planifolia 1.00 1.00
962 A144 $2 Epidendrum poly-
              anthum   2.00 2.00
     Nos. 957-962 (6)   5.10 5.10

Christmas.

Indigenous Fauna — A145

1991, Apr. 10
963 A145 25c Iguana   .25 .25
964 A145 50c Crocodile   .50 .50
965 A145 60c Manatee   .60 .60
966 A145 75c Boa constrictor .75 .75
967 A145 $1 Tapir   1.00 1.00
968 A145 $2 Jaguar   2.00 2.00
     Nos. 963-968 (6)   5.10 5.10

Elizabeth & Philip, Birthdays
Common Design Types
1991, June 17   Perf. 14½
969 CD345 $1 multicolored   1.00 1.00
970 CD346 $1 multicolored   1.00 1.00
  a.   Pair, #969-970 + label 2.00 2.00

Hurricanes — A146

1991, July 31 Wmk. 373   Perf. 14
971 A146 60c Weather radar   .60 .60
972 A146 75c Weather observa-
              tion station   .75 .75
973 A146 $1 Scene after hurri-
              cane   1.00 1.00
974 A146 $2 Hurricane Gilbert 2.00 2.00
     Nos. 971-974 (4)   4.35 4.35

Independence, 10th Anniv. — A147

Famous Men: 25c, Thomas V. Ramos (1887-1955). 60c, Sir Isaiah Morter (1860-1924). 75c, Antonio Soberanis (1897-1975). $1, Santiago Ricalde (1920-1975).

1991, Sept. 4   Wmk. 384
975 A147 25c multicolored   .30 .30
976 A147 60c multicolored   .65 .65
977 A147 75c multicolored   .80 .80
978 A147 $1 multicolored   1.10 1.10
     Nos. 975-978 (4)   2.85 2.85

Folktales
A148

Christmas.

Wmk. 373
1991, Nov. 6   Litho.   Perf. 14
979 A148 25c Anansi   .30 .30
980 A148 50c Jack-O-Lantern   .55 .55
981 A148 60c Tata Duende, vert. .65 .65
982 A148 75c Xtabai   .80 .80
983 A148 $1 Warrie Massa,
              vert.   1.10 1.10
984 A148 $2 Old Heg   2.25 2.25
     Nos. 979-984 (6)   5.65 5.65
     See Nos. 999-1002.

Orchids — A149

Easter: 25c, Gongora quinquenervis. 50c, Oncidium sphacelatum. 60c, Encyclia bractescens. 75c, Epidendrum ciliare. $1, Psygmorchis pusilla. $2, Galeandra batemanii.

1992, Apr. 1
985 A149 25c multicolored   .30 .30
986 A149 50c multicolored   .55 .55
987 A149 60c multicolored   .65 .65
988 A149 75c multicolored   .80 .80
989 A149 $1 multicolored   1.10 1.10
990 A149 $2 multicolored   2.25 2.25
     Nos. 985-990 (6)   5.65 5.65

Famous
Belizeans
A150

Designs: 25c, Gwendolyn Lizarraga, MBE (1901-75). 60c, Rafael Fonseca, CMG, OBE

(1921-78). 75c, Vivian Seay, MBE (1881-1971). $1, Samuel A. Haynes (1898-1971).

1992, Aug. 26   Perf. 13x12½
991 A150 25c multicolored   .30 .30
992 A150 60c multicolored   .65 .65
993 A150 75c multicolored   .80 .80
994 A150 $1 multicolored   1.10 1.10
     Nos. 991-994 (4)   2.85 2.85
     See Nos. 1013-1016.

Discovery of America, 500th
Anniv. — A151

Mayan ruins, modern buildings: 25c, Xunantunich, National Assembly. 60c, Altun Ha, Supreme Court Building. 75c, Santa Rita, Tower Hill Sugar Factory. $5, Lamanai, The Citrus Company.

Perf. 13½x14
1992, Oct. 1   Litho.   Wmk. 384
995 A151 25c multicolored   .30 .30
996 A151 60c multicolored   .65 .65
997 A151 75c multicolored   .80 .80
998 A151 $5 multicolored   5.50 5.50
     Nos. 995-998 (4)   7.25 7.25

Folklore Type of 1991
Christmas.
Perf. 13x12½
1992, Nov. 16   Litho.   Wmk. 373
999 A148 25c Hashishi Pampi   .25 .25
1000 A148 60c Cadejo   .60 .60
1001 A148 $1 La Sucia, vert. 1.00 1.00
1002 A148 $5 Sisimito   5.00 5.00
     Nos. 999-1002 (4)   6.85 6.85

Royal Air Force, 75th Anniv.
Common Design Type
Designs: 25c, Aerospatiale Puma. 50c, British Aerospace Harrier. 60c, DeHavilland Mosquito. 75c, Avro Lancaster. $1, Consolidated Liberator. $3, Short Stirling.

Wmk. 373
1993, Apr. 1   Litho.   Perf. 14
1003 CD350 25c multicolored   .25 .25
1004 CD350 50c multicolored   .50 .50
1005 CD350 60c multicolored   .65 .65
1006 CD350 75c multicolored   .80 .80
1007 CD350 $1 multicolored   1.00 1.00
1008 CD350 $3 multicolored   3.25 3.25
     Nos. 1003-1008 (6)   6.45 6.45

1993 World
Orchid
Conference,
Glasgow — A152

Perf. 14½x14
1993, Apr. 24   Litho.   Wmk. 384
1009 A152 25c Lycaste aromati-
              ca   .30 .30
1010 A152 60c Sobralia decora .65 .65
1011 A152 $1 Maxillaria alba 1.10 1.10
1012 A152 $2 Brassavola
              nodosa   2.25 2.25
     Nos. 1009-1012 (4)   4.30 4.30

Famous Belizeans Type of 1992
Designs: 25c, Herbert Watkin Beaumont (1880-1978). 60c, Dr. Selvyn Walford Young (1899-1977). 75c, Cleopatra White (1898-1987). $1, Dr. Karl Heusner (1872-1960).

Wmk. 384
1993, Aug. 11   Litho.   Perf. 14
1013 A150 25c multicolored   .30 .30
1014 A150 60c multicolored   .65 .65
1015 A150 75c multicolored   .85 .85
1016 A150 $1 multicolored   1.10 1.10
     Nos. 1013-1016 (4)   2.90 2.70

Christmas — A153

Wmk. 373

1993, Nov. 3		**Litho.**	***Perf. 14***
1017 A153	25c	Boom and chime band	.30 .30
1018 A153	60c	John Canoe dance	.65 .65
1019 A153	75c	Cortez dance	.80 .80
1020 A153	$2	Maya Musical Group	2.25 2.25
		Nos. 1017-1020 (4)	4.00 4.00

No. 940 Ovptd. with Hong Kong '94 Emblem

Wmk. 373

1994, Feb. 18		**Litho.**	***Perf. 14***
1021 A141	$1	multicolored	1.10 1.10

Royal Visit — A154

Designs: 25c, Belize, United Kingdom Flags. 60c, Queen Elizabeth II wearing hat. 75c, Queen. $1, Queen, Prince Philip.

		Perf. 14½x14	
1994, Feb. 24		**Litho.**	**Wmk. 373**
1022 A154	25c	multicolored	.30 .30
1023 A154	60c	multicolored	.65 .65
1024 A154	75c	multicolored	.80 .80
1025 A154	$1	multicolored	1.10 1.10
		Nos. 1022-1025 (4)	2.85 2.85

Bats A155

Wmk. 384

1994, May 30		**Litho.**	***Perf. 14***
1026 A155	25c	Insect feeder	.25 .25
1027 A155	60c	Fruit feeder	.60 .60
1028 A155	75c	Fish feeder	.75 .75
1029 A155	$2	Common vampire	2.00 2.00
		Nos. 1026-1029 (4)	3.60 3.60

No. 939 Surcharged

Wmk. 373

1994, Aug. 18		**Litho.**	***Perf. 14***
1030 A141	10c on 75c multi		.20 .20

Christmas A156

Orchids: 25c, Cycnoches chlorochilon. 60c, Brassavolas cucullata. 75c, Sobralia mucronata. $1, Nidema Boothii.

1994, Nov. 7			**Wmk. 384**
1031 A156	25c	multicolored	.25 .25
1032 A156	60c	multicolored	.60 .60
1033 A156	75c	multicolored	.75 .75
1034 A156	$1	multicolored	1.00 1.00
		Nos. 1031-1034 (4)	2.60 2.60

For overprints see Nos. 1051-1054.

Insects A157

Wmk. 373

1995, Jan. 11		**Litho.**	***Perf. 14***
1035 A157	5c	Ground beetle	.20 .20
1036 A157	10c	Harlequin beetle	.20 .20
1037 A157	15c	Giant water bug	.20 .20
1038 A157	25c	Peanut-head bug	.25 .25
1039 A157	30c	Coconut weevil	.30 .30
1040 A157	50c	Mantis	.50 .50
1041 A157	60c	Tarantula wasp	.60 .60
1042 A157	75c	Rhinoceros beetle	.75 .75
1043 A157	$1	Metallic wood borer	1.00 1.00
1044 A157	$2	Dobson fly	2.00 2.00
1045 A157	$5	Click beetle	5.00 5.00
1046 A157	$10	Long-horned beetle	10.00 10.00
		Nos. 1035-1046 (12)	21.00 21.00

Nos. 1035-1046 exist inscribed "1996." For overprints see Nos. 1063-1066.

End of World War II, 50th Anniv.
Common Design Type

Designs: 25c, War Memorial Cenotaph. 60c, Remembrance Sunday. 75c, British Honduras Forestry Unit. $1, Wellington Bomber.

		Wmk. 373	
1995, May 8		**Litho.**	***Perf. 13½***
1047 CD351	25c	multicolored	.30 .30
1048 CD351	60c	multicolored	.65 .65
1049 CD351	75c	multicolored	.80 .80
1050 CD351	$1	multicolored	1.10 1.10
		Nos. 1047-1050 (4)	2.85 2.85

Nos. 1031-1034 Ovptd. in Blue

1995, Sept. 1	**Wmk. 384**		***Perf. 14***
1051 A156	25c on No. 1031		.25 .25
1052 A156	60c on No. 1032		.60 .60
1053 A156	75c on No. 1033		.75 .75
1054 A156	$1 on No. 1034		1.00 1.00
		Nos. 1051-1054 (4)	2.60 2.60

UN, 50th Anniv.
Common Design Type

Designs: 25c, M113 Light reconnaissance vehicle. 60c, Sultan, armored command vehicle. 75c, Leyland/DAF 8x4 "Drops" vehicle. $2, Warrior infantry combat vehicle.

		Wmk. 384	
1995, Oct. 24		**Litho.**	***Perf. 14***
1055 CD353	25c	multicolored	.25 .25
1056 CD353	60c	multicolored	.60 .60
1057 CD353	75c	multicolored	.75 .75
1058 CD353	$2	multicolored	2.00 2.00
		Nos. 1055-1058 (4)	3.60 3.60

Christmas A158

Doves: 25c, Blue ground. 60c, White-fronted. 75c, Ruddy ground. $1, White-winged.

1995, Nov. 6			**Wmk. 373**
1059 A158	25c	multicolored	.25 .25
1060 A158	60c	multicolored	.60 .60
1061 A158	75c	multicolored	.75 .75
1062 A158	$1	multicolored	1.00 1.00
		Nos. 1059-1062 (4)	2.60 2.60

Nos. 1037, 1039-1040, 1044 Ovptd.

Wmk. 373

1996, May 17		**Litho.**	***Perf. 14***
1063 A157	15c on #1037		.20 .20
1064 A157	30c on #1039		.30 .30
1065 A157	50c on #1040		.50 .50
1066 A157	$2 on #1044		2.00 2.00
		Nos. 1063-1066 (4)	3.00 3.00

CAPEX '96 A159

Trains: 25c, Unloading banana train onto freighter, Commerce Bight Pier. 60c, Engine No. 1, Stann Creek Station. 75c, Mahogany log train, Hunslet 0-6-0 Side Tank Engine No. 4. $3, LMS Jubilee Class 4-6-0 Locomotive No. 5602 "British Honduras."

		Perf. 13½x13	
1996, June 6		**Litho.**	**Wmk. 373**
1067 A159	25c	multicolored	.25 .25
1068 A159	60c	multicolored	.60 .60
1069 A159	75c	multicolored	.75 .75
1070 A159	$3	multicolored	3.00 3.00
		Nos. 1067-1070 (4)	4.60 4.60

Christmas — A160

Orchids: 25c, Epidendrum stamfordianum. 60c, Oncidium carthagenense. 75c, Oerstedella verrucosa. $1, Coryanthes speciosa.

		Wmk. 373	
1996, Nov. 6		**Litho.**	***Perf. 14***
1071 A160	25c	multicolored	.25 .25
1072 A160	60c	multicolored	.60 .60
1073 A160	75c	multicolored	.75 .75
1074 A160	$1	multicolored	1.00 1.00
		Nos. 1071-1074 (4)	2.60 2.60

Hong Kong '97 A161

Cattle: 25c, Red poll. 60c, Brahman. 75c, Longhorn. $1, Charbray.

		Wmk. 373	
1997, Feb. 12		**Litho.**	***Perf. 14***
1075 A161	25c	multicolored	.30 .30
1076 A161	60c	multicolored	.70 .70
1077 A161	75c	multicolored	.85 .85
1078 A161	$1	multicolored	1.10 1.10
		Nos. 1075-1078 (4)	2.95 2.95

Snakes — A162   Howler Monkeys — A163

25c, Coral snake. 60c, Green vine snake. 75c, Yellow-jawed tommygoff. $1, Speckled racer.

		Wmk. 373	
1997, May 28		**Litho.**	***Perf. 14***
1079 A162	25c	multicolored	.30 .30
1080 A162	60c	multicolored	.65 .65
1081 A162	75c	multicolored	.80 .80
1082 A162	$1	multicolored	1.10 1.10
		Nos. 1079-1082 (4)	2.85 2.85

Wmk. 373

1997, Aug. 13		**Litho.**	***Perf. 14***

World Wildlife Fund: 10c, Adult male. 25c, Female feeding. 60c, Female with infant. 75c, Juvenile feeding.

1083 A163	10c	multicolored	.20 .20
1084 A163	25c	multicolored	.25 .25
1085 A163	60c	multicolored	.60 .60
1086 A163	75c	multicolored	.75 .75
		Nos. 1083-1086 (4)	1.80 1.80

Christmas A164

Orchids: 25c, Maxillaria elatior. 60c, Dimerandra emarginata. 75c, Macradenia brassavolae. $1, Ornithocephalus gladiatus.

		Wmk. 373	
1997, Nov. 21		**Litho.**	***Perf. 14***
1087 A164	25c	multicolored	.25 .25
1088 A164	60c	multicolored	.65 .65
1089 A164	75c	multicolored	.80 .80
1090 A164	$1	multicolored	1.10 1.10
		Nos. 1087-1090 (4)	2.80 2.80

Diana, Princess of Wales (1961-97)
Common Design Type

Designs: a, Up close portrait, smiling. b, Wearing evening dress. c, Up close portrait, serious. d, Holding bouquet of flowers.

		Perf. 14½x14	
1998, Mar. 31		**Litho.**	**Wmk. 373**
1091 CD355	$1	Sheet of 4, #a.-d.	4.50 4.50

University of West Indies, 50th Anniv. A165

		Wmk. 373	
1998, July 22		**Litho.**	***Perf. 13***
1092 A165	$1	multicolored	1.00 1.00

Organization of American States, 50th Anniv. A166

Designs: 25c, Children working computers, connecting high schools to the internet. $1, Map of Central America, Inter American Drug Abuse Control Commission.

1998, July 22

1093	A166	25c multicolored	.25	.25
1094	A166	$1 multicolored	1.00	1.00

Battle of St. George's Cay, Bicent. A167

Views of Old Belize from St. George, vert: No. 1095, Woman, child beside small boat. No. 1096, Soldiers at dock, cannon. No. 1097, Cannon balls, cannon, boats in water.

25c, Bayman gun flats. 60c, Bayman sloops. 75c, Schooners. $1, HMS Merlin. $2, Spanish flagship.

1998, Aug. 5 — Perf. 13½

1095	A167	10c multicolored	.20	.20
1096	A167	10c multicolored	.20	.20
1097	A167	10c multicolored	.20	.20
a.		Strip of 3, #1095-1097	.30	.30
1098	A167	25c multicolored	.25	.25
1099	A167	60c multicolored	.60	.60
1100	A167	75c multicolored	.75	.75
1101	A167	$1 multicolored	1.00	1.00
1102	A167	$2 multicolored	2.00	2.00
		Nos. 1095-1102 (8)	5.20	5.20

A168

Christmas - Flowers: 25c, Brassia maculata. 60c, Encyclia radiata. 75c, Stanhopea ecornuta. $1, Isochilus carnosiflorus.

1998, Nov. 4 — Perf. 14

1103	A168	25c multicolored	.25	.25
1104	A168	60c multicolored	.60	.60
1105	A168	75c multicolored	.75	.75
1106	A168	$1 multicolored	1.00	1.00
		Nos. 1103-1106 (4)	2.60	2.60

A169

1999, Mar. 17 — Perf. 13

Easter - Orchids: 10c, Eucharis grandiflora. 25c, Hippeastrum puniceum. 60c, Zephyranthes citrina. $1, Hymenocallis littoralis.

1107	A169	10c multicolored	.15	.15
1108	A169	25c multicolored	.25	.25
1109	A169	60c multicolored	.60	.60
1110	A169	$1 multicolored	1.00	1.00
		Nos. 1107-1110 (4)	2.00	2.00

UPU, 125th Anniv. A170

1999, Oct. 18 — Perf. 13¼

1111	A170	25c Bicycle	.25	.25
1112	A170	60c Truck	.60	.60
1113	A170	75c Mailship "Dee"	.75	.75
1114	A170	$1 Airplane	1.00	1.00
		Nos. 1111-1114 (4)	2.60	2.60

Christmas — A171

Designs: 25c, Holy Family with Jesus and St. John, by school of Peter Paul Rubens. 60c, The Holy Family with St. John, by unknown artist. 75c, Madonna with Child, St. John and Angel, by unknown artist. $1, Madonna with Child and St. John by Andrea da Salerno.

1999, Dec. 6 — Perf. 14

1115	A171	25c multicolored	.25	.25
1116	A171	60c multicolored	.60	.60
1117	A171	75c multicolored	.75	.75
1118	A171	$1 multicolored	1.00	1.00
		Nos. 1115-1118 (4)	2.60	2.60

Fauna A172

2000, Feb. 15 — Wmk. 373 — Litho. — Perf. 14

1119	A172	5c Iguana	.20	.20
1120	A172	10c Gibnut	.20	.20
1121	A172	15c Howler monkey	.20	.20
1122	A172	25c Ant bear	.25	.25
1123	A172	30c Hawksbill turtle	.30	.30
1124	A172	50c Antelope	.50	.50
1125	A172	60c Jaguar	.60	.60
1126	A172	75c Manatee	.75	.75
1127	A172	$1 Crocodile	1.00	1.00
1128	A172	$2 Tapir	2.00	2.00
1129	A172	$5 Collared peccary	5.00	5.00
1130	A172	$10 Boa constrictor	10.00	10.00
		Nos. 1119-1130 (12)	21.00	21.00

Fruits A173

2000, Apr. 19 — Wmk. 373 — Litho. — Perf. 14

1131	A173	25c Mango	.25	.25
1132	A173	60c Cashew	.60	.60
1133	A173	75c Papaya	.75	.75
1134	A173	$1 Banana	1.00	1.00
		Nos. 1131-1134 (4)	2.60	2.60

People's United Party, 50th Anniv. A174

10c, Birth of party politics, 9/29/50. 25c, People gain voting rights, 4/28/54. 60c, Self-government, 1/1/64. 75c, Building the new capital Belmopan, 1967-70. $1, Independence, 9/21/81.

Perf. 13¼x13¾

2000, Sept. 18 — Litho. — Wmk. 373

1135-1139	A174 Set of 5	3.00 3.00

Christmas A175

Orchids: 25c, Bletia purpurea. 60c, Cyrtopodium punctata. 75c, Cycnoches egertonianum. $1, Catasetum integerrimum.

Perf. 14½x14¼

2000 — Litho. — Wmk. 373

1140-1143	A175 Set of 4	2.60 2.60

Independence, 20th Anniv. — A176

Designs: 25c, Education. 60c, Shrimp farming. 75c, Privassion Cascade, vert. $2, Map, vert.

Wmk. 373

2001, Oct. 3 — Litho. — Perf. 14

1144-1147	A176 Set of 4	3.75 3.75

SEMI-POSTAL STAMPS

World Cup Soccer Championship — SP1

Designs: 20c+10c, 30c+15c, Scotland vs. New Zealand (diff.). 40c+20c, Kuwait vs. France. 60c+30c, Italy vs. Brazil. No. B5, France vs. Northern Ireland. $1.50+75c, Austria vs. Chile. No. B7, Italy vs. Germany, vert. $2+$1, England vs. France, vert.

1982, Dec. 10 — Litho. — Perf. 14

B1	SP1	20c +10c multi	.25	.25
B2	SP1	30c +15c multi	.35	.35
B3	SP1	40c +20c multi	.45	.45
B4	SP1	60c +30c multi	.75	.75
B5	SP1	$1 +50c multi	3.00	3.00
B6	SP1	$1.50 +75c multi	5.00	5.00
		Nos. B1-B6 (6)	9.80	9.80

Souvenir Sheets — Perf. 14½

B7	SP1	$1 +50c multi	3.50	3.50
B8	SP1	$2 +$1 multi	6.00	6.00

Nos. B7-B8 each contain one 50x70mm stamp.

POSTAGE DUE STAMPS

Numeral — D2

Each denomination has different border.

1976, July 1 — Litho. — Wmk. 373

J6	D2	1c green & red	.20	.20
J7	D2	2c violet & rose lil	.20	.20
J8	D2	5c ocher & brt grn	.20	.20
J9	D2	15c brown org & yel grn	.30	.30
J10	D2	25c slate grn & org	.50	.50
		Nos. J6-J10 (5)	1.40	1.40

CAYES OF BELIZE

Catalogue values for all unused stamps in this country are for Never Hinged items.

Spiny Lobster A1

Perf. 14½x14, 14x14½

1984, May 30 — Litho. — Unwmk.

1	A1	1c shown	.20	.20
2	A1	2c Blue crab	.20	.20
3	A1	5c Red-footed booby	.20	.20
4	A1	10c Brown pelican	.20	.20
5	A1	25c White-tailed deer	.20	.20
6	A1	25c Lighthouse, English Caye	.20	.20
7	A1	75c Spanish galleon, Santa Yaga, c. 1750	.55	.55
8	A1	$3 Map of Ambergris Caye, vert.	2.25	2.25
a.		Souvenir booklet	7.50	
9	A1	$5 Jetty, windsurfers	3.75	3.75
		Nos. 1-9 (9)	7.75	7.75

No. 8a contains four panes. One has one $3 stamp, one has a block of four 25c stamps, two have blocks of four 75c stamps but different text. The stamps are larger than Nos. 6-8, have slightly different colors and are perf. 14½.

The $1 stamp was not issued. Eighteen sheets of 40 were sold for postage by accident.

Lloyd's List Issue
Common Design Type

1984, June 6 — Perf. 14½x14

10	CD335	25c Queen Elizabeth 2	.20	.20
11	CD335	75c Lutine Bell	.55	.55
12	CD335	$1 Loss of the Fishburn	.75	.75
13	CD335	$2 Trafalgar Sword	1.50	1.50
		Nos. 10-13 (4)	3.00	3.00

1984 Summer Olympics, Los Angeles — A2

1984, Oct. 5 — Perf. 15

14	A2	10c Yachting	.20	.20
15	A2	15c Windsurfing	.20	.20
16	A2	75c Swimming	.75	.75
17	A2	$2 Kayaking	2.00	2.00
		Nos. 14-17 (4)	3.15	3.15

No. 17 inscribed Canoeing.

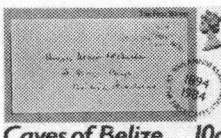

First Cayes Stamps, 90th Anniv. A3

1984, Nov. 5

18	A3	10c 1895 cover	.20	.20
19	A3	15c Sydney Cuthbert	.20	.20
20	A3	75c Cuthbert's steam yacht	.55	.55
21	A3	$2 British Honduras #133	1.50	1.50
		Nos. 18-21 (4)	2.45	2.45

Audubon Birth Bicentenary — A4

Illustrations by Audubon.

1985, May 20 — Perf. 14

22	A4	25c Blue-winged teal	.20	.20
23	A4	75c Semipalmated sandpiper	.55	.55
24	A4	$1 Yellow-crowned night heron, vert.	.75	.75
25	A4	$3 Common gallinule	2.25	2.25
		Nos. 22-25 (4)	3.75	3.75

Shipwrecks — A5

a, Oxford, c. 1675. b, Santa Yaga, 1780. c, No. 27, Comet, 1822. d, Yeldham, 1800.

1985, June 5   **Perf. 15**
26 A5 $1 Strip of 4+label, #a.-d.   4.00 4.00
Souvenir Sheet
Perf. 13½x14
27 A5 $5 multicolored   5.00 5.00
No. 27 contains one 38x51mm stamp. No. 26 has continuous design.

collecting accessories

12¼"   1¾"   11¾"

MINT SHEET BINDERS & PAGES

Keep those mint sheets intact in a handsome, 3-ring binder. Just like the cover album, the Mint Sheet album features the "D" ring mechanism on the right hand side of binder so you don't have to worry about damaging your stamps when turning the pages. Mint Sheet binder available in four colors.

ITEM		RETAIL
MBRD	Mint Sheet Binder - Red	$9.95
MBBL	Mint Sheet Binder - Blue	$9.95
MBGY	Mint Sheet Binder - Gray	$9.95
MBBK	Mint Sheet Binder - Black	$9.95
MS1	Mint Sheet Pages (25 per pack)	$5.95

STOCK PAGE BINDER AND SLIPCASE
Keep all your stock pages neat and tidy with binder and accompanying slipcase. Available in two colors.

ITEM	COLOR	RETAIL
SSBSRD	Red	$19.95
SSBSBL	Blue	$19.95

COVER BINDERS & PAGES
Padded, durable, 3-ring binder will hold up to 100 covers. Features the "D" ring mechanism on the right hand side of album so you don't have to worry about creasing or wrinkling covers when opening or closing binder.
Cover pages sold separately.

ITEM		RETAIL
CBRD	Cover Binder - Red	$7.95
CBBL	Cover Binder - Blue	$7.95
CBGY	Cover Binder - Gray	$7.95
CBBK	Cover Binder - Black	$7.95
T2	Cover Pages Black (25 per pack)	$4.95
T2C	Cover Pages Clear (25 per pack)	$4.95

9½"   2"   9¾"

These collecting accessories and others are available from your favorite stamp dealer or direct from:

1-800-572-6885
P.O. Box 828, Sidney OH 45365-0828
www.amosadvantage.com

AMOS
HOBBY PUBLISHING

Publishers of *Coin World, Linn's Stamp News* and *Scott Publishing Co.*

BENIN

bə-'nin

French Colony

LOCATION — West Coast of Africa
GOVT. — French Possession
AREA — 8,627 sq. mi.
POP. — 493,000 (approx.)
CAPITAL — Benin

In 1895 the French possessions known as Benin were incorporated into the colony of Dahomey and postage stamps of Dahomey superseded those of Benin. Dahomey took the name Benin when it became a republic in 1975.

100 Centimes = 1 Franc

> Catalogue values for unused stamps in this country are for Never Hinged items, beginning with Scott 342 in the regular postage section, Scott C240 in the airpost section, Scott J44 in the postage due section, and Scott Q8 in the parcel post section.

Watermark

Wmk. 385

Handstamped on Stamps of French Colonies

1892   **Unwmk.**   **Perf. 14x13½**
Black Overprint

1	A9	1c blk, *bluish*	110.00	95.00
2	A9	2c brn, *buff*	90.00	75.00
3	A9	4c claret, *lav*	35.00	30.00
4	A9	5c grn, *grnsh*	13.00	12.00
5	A9	10c blk, *lavender*	57.50	45.00
6	A9	15c blue	20.00	9.00
7	A9	20c red, *grn*	160.00	150.00
8	A9	25c blk, *rose*	70.00	40.00
9	A9	30c brn, *yelsh*	140.00	100.00
10	A9	35c blk, *orange*	140.00	100.00
11	A9	40c red, *straw*	110.00	90.00
12	A9	75c car, *rose*	275.00	225.00
13	A9	1fr brnz grn, *straw*	300.00	275.00

Red Overprint

14	A9	15c blue	70.00	45.00

Blue Overprint

15	A9	5c grn, *grnsh*	1,750.	750.00
15A	A9	15c blue	1,750.	750.00

For inverted and double overprints see the *Scott Classic Specialized Catalogue.* The overprints of Nos. 1-15A are of four types, three without accent mark on "E." They exist diagonal.
Counterfeits exist of Nos. 1-19.

Additional Surcharge in Red or Black

1892

16	A9	01c on 5c grn, *grnsh*	225.	175.
a.		Double surcharge	600.	600.

17	A9	40c on 15c blue	140.	60.
a.		Double surcharge		2,500.
18	A9	75c on 15c blue	625.	425.
19	A9	75c on 15c bl (Bk)	2,500.	1,900.

Counterfeits exist.

Navigation and Commerce
A3   A4

1893   **Typo.**   **Perf. 14x13½**
Name of Colony in Blue or Carmine

20	A3	1c blk, *bluish*	2.00	1.75
21	A3	2c brn, *buff*	2.75	2.10
22	A3	4c claret, *lav*	2.75	2.50
23	A3	5c grn, *grnsh*	4.00	3.00
24	A3	10c blk, *lavender*	4.50	3.00
25	A3	15c blue, quadrille paper	22.50	14.00
26	A3	20c red, *grn*	11.00	8.00
27	A3	25c blk, *rose*	29.00	18.00
28	A3	30c brn, *bis*	12.50	11.00
29	A3	40c red, *straw*	3.75	3.00
30	A3	50c car, *rose*	3.50	2.50
31	A3	75c vio, *org*	7.00	6.00
32	A3	1fr brnz grn, *straw*	42.50	35.00
		Nos. 20-32 (13)	147.75	109.85

Perf. 13½x14 stamps are counterfeits.

1894   **Perf. 14x13½**

33	A4	1c blk, *bluish*	2.00	1.50
34	A4	2c brn, *buff*	2.00	1.50
35	A4	4c claret, *lav*	2.00	1.50
36	A4	5c grn, *grnsh*	2.50	1.50
37	A4	10c blk, *lavender*	3.50	2.50
38	A4	15c bl, quadrille paper	5.50	2.50
39	A4	20c red, *grn*	5.00	4.00
40	A4	25c blk, *rose*	6.50	3.00
41	A4	30c brn, *bis*	4.00	3.50
42	A4	40c red, *straw*	12.00	7.00
43	A4	50c car, *rose*	16.00	8.00
44	A4	75c vio, *org*	10.00	8.00
45	A4	1fr brnz grn, *straw*	3.00	2.00
		Nos. 33-45 (13)	74.00	46.50

Perf. 13½x14 stamps are counterfeits.

PEOPLE'S REPUBLIC OF BENIN

LOCATION — West Coast of Africa
GOVT. — Republic.
AREA — 43,483 sq. mi.
POP. — 6,305,567 (1999 est.)
CAPITAL — Porto Novo (Cotonou is the seat of government)

The Republic of Dahomey proclaimed itself the People's Republic of Benin on Nov. 30, 1975. See Dahomey for stamps issued before then.

> Catalogue values for unused stamps in this section are for Never Hinged items.

Allamanda Cathartica — A83

Flowers: 35fr, Ixora coccinea. 45fr, Hibiscus. 60fr, Phaemeria magnifica.

Unwmk.
1975, Dec. 8   **Photo.**   **Perf. 13**

342	A83	10fr lilac & multi	.20	.20
343	A83	35fr gray & multi	.25	.20
344	A83	45fr multi	.35	.25
345	A83	60fr blue & multi	.40	.30
		Nos. 342-345 (4)	1.20	.95

For surcharges see Nos. 612, 618, 719, 723, 788.

Flag Bearers, Arms of Benin — A84

1976, Apr. 30   **Litho.**   **Perf. 12**

Design: 60fr, Speaker, wall with "PRPB," flag and arms of Benin. 100fr, Flag and arms of Benin.

346	A84	50fr ocher & multi	.30	.20
347	A84	60fr ocher & multi	.30	.20
348	A84	100fr multi	.55	.40
		Nos. 346-348 (3)	1.15	.80

Proclamation of the People's Republic of Benin. Nov. 30, 1975.

A.G. Bell, Satellite and 1876 Telephone — A85

1976, July 9   **Litho.**   **Perf. 13**

349	A85	200fr lilac, red & brn	1.10	.45

Centenary of first telephone call by Alexander Graham Bell, Mar. 10, 1876.

Dahomey Nos. 277-278 Surcharged

1976, July 19   **Photo.**   **Perf. 12½x13**

350	A57	50fr on 1fr multi	.30	.20
351	A57	60fr on 2fr multi	.40	.20

For overprint & surcharge see #654A, 711.

African Jamboree, Nigeria 1976 — A86

1976, Aug. 16   **Litho.**   **Perf. 12½x13**

352	A86	50fr Scouts Cooking	.30	.20
353	A86	70fr Three scouts	.40	.30

Blood Bank, Cotonou — A87

Designs: 50fr, Accident and first aid station. 60fr, Blood donation.

1976, Sept. 24   **Litho.**   **Perf. 13**

354	A87	5fr multicolored	.20	.20
355	A87	50fr multicolored	.30	.20
356	A87	60fr multicolored	.35	.25
		Nos. 354-356 (3)	.85	.65

National Blood Donors Day.

A88

A89

1976, Oct. 4   **Litho.**   **Perf. 13x12½**

357	A88	20fr Manioc	.20	.20
358	A88	30fr Corn	.30	.20
359	A88	60fr Cacao	.30	.20
360	A88	150fr Cotton	.80	.60
		Nos. 357-360 (4)	1.60	1.20

Natl. agricultural production campaign.
For surcharge see No. 565.

1976, Oct. 25

361	A89	50fr Classroom	.30	.20

Third anniversary of KPARO newspaper, used in local language studies.

Roan Antelope — A90

Flags, Wall, Broken Chains — A91

Penhari National Park: 30fr, Buffalo. 50fr, Hippopotamus, horiz. 70fr, Lion.

1976, Nov. 8   **Photo.**

362	A90	10fr multicolored	.20	.20
363	A90	30fr multicolored	.20	.20
364	A90	60fr multicolored	.30	.20
365	A90	70fr multicolored	.40	.25
		Nos. 362-365 (4)	1.10	.85

1976, Nov. 30   **Litho.**   **Perf. 12½**

150fr, Corn, raised hands with weapons.

366	A91	40fr multicolored	.20	.20
367	A91	150fr multicolored	.80	.60

First anniversary of proclamation of the People's Republic of Benin.

Table Tennis, Map of Africa (Games' Emblem) — A92

Design: 50fr, Stadium, Cotonou.

1976, Dec. 26   Litho.   Perf. 13
368 A92 10fr multi .20 .20
369 A92 50fr multi .30 .20
West African University Games, Cotonou, Dec. 26-31.

Europafrica Issue

Planes over Africa and Europe — A93

1977, May 13   Litho.   Perf. 13
370 A93 200fr multi .70 .55
For surcharge see No. 590.

Snake A94

1977, June 13   Litho.   Perf. 13x13½
371 A94 2fr shown .20 .20
372 A94 3fr Tortoise .20 .20
373 A94 5fr Zebus .20 .20
374 A94 10fr Cats .20 .20
Nos. 371-374 (4) .80 .80

Patients at Clinic A95

1977, Aug. 2   Litho.   Perf. 12½
375 A95 100fr multi .60 .40
World Rheumatism Year.

Karate, Map of Africa — A96

Designs: 100fr, Javelin, map of Africa, Benin Flag, horiz. 150fr, Hurdles.

1977, Aug. 30   Litho.   Perf. 12½
376 A96 90fr multi .35 .20
377 A96 100fr multi .45 .35
378 A96 150fr multi .60 .45
a. Souvenir sheet of 3, #376-378 2.00 2.00
Nos. 376-378 (3) 1.40 1.00
2nd West African Games, Lagos, Nigeria.
For surcharge see No. 925.

Chairman Mao — A97

Lister and Vaporizer — A98

1977, Sept. 9   Litho.   Perf. 13x12½
379 A97 100fr multicolored .50 .40
Mao Tse-tung (1893-1976), Chinese communist leader.

1977, Sept. 20   Engr.   Perf. 13
Designs: 150fr, Scalpels and flames, symbols of antisepsis, and Red Cross.
380 A98 150fr multi .75 .60
381 A98 210fr multi 1.25 .80
Joseph Lister (1827-1912), surgeon, founder of antiseptic surgery.
For surcharges see Nos. 560, 566, 919.

Guelege Mask, Ethnographic Museum, Porto Novo — A99

Designs: 50fr, Jar, symbol of unity, emblem of King Ghezo, Historical Museum, Abomey, vert. 210fr, Abomey Museum.

1977, Oct. 17   Perf. 13
382 A99 50fr red & multi .30 .20
383 A99 60fr blk, bl & bister .35 .25
384 A99 210fr multi 1.25 .80
Nos. 382-384 (3) 1.90 1.25
For surcharge see Nos. 562, 920.

Atacora Falls — A100

Mother and Child, Owl of Wisdom — A101

Tourist Publicity: 60fr, Pile houses, Ganvie, horiz. 150fr, Round huts, Savalou.

1977, Oct. 24   Litho.   Perf. 12½
385 A100 50fr multi .30 .25
386 A100 60fr multi .40 .25
387 A100 150fr multi 1.00 .70
a. Souvenir sheet of 3, #385-387 2.00 2.00
Nos. 385-387 (3) 1.70 1.20

1977, Dec. 3   Photo.
150fr, Chopping down magical tree, horiz.
388 A101 60fr multi .35 .25
389 A101 150fr multi .80 .60
Campaign against witchcraft.
For surcharge see No. 576.

Battle Scene — A102

1978, Jan. 16   Litho.   Perf. 12½
390 A102 50fr multi .50 .20
Victory of people of Benin over imperialist forces.

Map, People and Houses of Benin — A103

1978, Feb. 1
391 A103 50fr multi .45 .20
General population and dwelling census.

Alexander Fleming, Microscope and Penicillin — A104

1978, Mar. 12   Litho.   Perf. 13
392 A104 300fr multi 2.00 1.10
Alexander Fleming (1881-1955), 50th anniversary of discovery of penicillin.

Abdoulaye Issa, Weapons and Fighters A105

1978, Apr. 1   Perf. 12½x13
393 A105 100fr red, blk & gold .65 .40
First anniversary of death of Abdoulaye Issa and National Day of Benin's Youth.

Ed Hadj Omar and Horseback Rider — A106

Design: 90fr, L'Almamy Samory Toure (1830-1900) and horseback riders.

1976, Apr. 10   Perf. 13x12½
394 A106 90fr red & multi .60 .35
395 A106 100fr multi .65 .40
African heroes of resistance against colonialism.

ITU Emblem, Satellite, Landscape — A107

1978, May 17   Litho.   Perf. 13
396 A107 100fr multi .65 .40
10th World Telecommunications Day.

Soccer Player, Stadium, Argentina '78 Emblem — A108

Designs (Argentina '78 Emblem and): 300fr, Soccer players and ball, vert. 500fr, Soccer player, globe with ball on map.

1978, June 1   Litho.   Perf. 12½
397 A108 200fr multi 1.50 .70
398 A108 300fr multi 2.00 1.10
399 A108 500fr multi 3.50 1.75
a. Souvenir sheet of 3 7.00 7.00
Nos. 397-399 (3) 7.00 3.55
11th World Cup Soccer Championship, Argentina, June 1-25. No. 399a contains 3 stamps similar to Nos. 397-399 in changed colors.
For surcharges see #591, 593, 595.

Nos. 397-399a Overprinted in Red Brown:
a. FINALE / ARGENTINE: 3 / HOLLANDE: 1
b. CHAMPION / 1978 / ARGENTINE
c. 3e BRESIL / 4e ITALIE

1978, June 25   Litho.   Perf. 12½
400 A108 (a) 200fr multi 1.40 .75
401 A108 (b) 300fr multi 2.00 1.10
402 A108 (c) 500fr multi 3.50 1.75
a. Souvenir sheet of 3 7.00 7.00
Nos. 400-402 (3) 6.90 3.60
Argentina's victory in 1978 Soccer Championship.
For surcharge, see #596.

Games' Flag over Africa, Basketball Players — A109

Designs: 60fr, Map of Africa, volleyball players. 80fr, Map of Benin, bicyclists.

1978, July 13   Perf. 13x12½
403 A109 50fr lt bl & multi .35 .20
404 A109 60fr ultra & multi .40 .25
405 A109 80fr multi .55 .35
a. Souvenir sheet of 3 1.40 1.40
Nos. 403-405 (3) 1.30 .80
3rd African Games, Algiers, July 13-28. No. 405a contains 3 stamps in changed colors similar to Nos. 403-405.

Martin Luther
King, Jr. — A110

1978, July 30   *Perf. 12½*
406 A110 300fr multi   2.00 1.10
Martin Luther King, Jr. (1929-1968), American civil rights leader.
For surcharge see No. 592.

Kanna Taxi,
Oueme
A111

60fr Leatherworker & goods. 70fr, Drummer
& tom-toms. 100fr, Metalworker & calabashes.

1978, Aug. 26
407 A111 50fr multi   .35   .20
408 A111 60fr multi   .40   .25
409 A111 70fr multi   .45   .30
410 A111 100fr multi   .65   .40
     Nos. 407-410 (4)   1.85 1.15
Getting to know Benin through its provinces.

Map of Italy and Exhibition
Poster — A112

1978, Aug. 26   *Litho.*   *Perf. 13*
411 A112 200fr multi   1.40   .70
Riccione 1978 Philatelic Exhibition.
For overprint see No. 537.

Poultry
Breeding — A113

1978 Oct. 5   *Photo.*   *Perf. 12½x13*
412 A113 10fr Turkeys   .20   .20
413 A113 20fr Ducks   .20   .20
414 A113 50fr Chicken   .35   .35
415 A113 60fr Guinea fowl   .40   .40
     Nos. 412-415 (4)   1.15 1.15

Royal Messenger, UPU
Emblem — A114

UPU Emblem and: 60fr, Boatsman, ship &
car. 90fr, Special messenger & plane.

1978, Oct. 16 *Perf. 13x12½, 12½x13*
416 A114 50fr multi   .35   .35
417 A114 60fr multi, vert.   .40   .40
418 A114 90fr multi, vert.   .60   .60
     Nos. 416-418 (3)   1.35 1.35
Centenary of change of "General Postal
Union" to "Universal Postal Union."
For surcharge see No. 1009.

Raoul
Follereau
A115

1978, Dec. 17   *Litho.*   *Perf. 12½*
419 A115 200fr multi   1.75 1.75
Raoul Follereau (1903-1977), apostle to the
lepers and educator of the blind.

IYC
Emblem
A116

Intl. Year of the Child: 20fr, Glove as balloon
carrying childern. 50fr, Children of various
races surrounding globe.

1979, Feb. 20   *Litho.*   *Perf. 12x13*
420 A116 10fr multi   .20   .20
421 A116 20fr multi   .20   .20
422 A116 50fr multi   .35   .35
     Nos. 420-422 (3)   .75   .75

Hydrangea — A117

Flowers: 25fr, Assangokan. 30fr, Geranium.
40fr, Water lilies, horiz.

Perf. 13x12½, 12½x13
1979, Feb. 28   *Litho.*
423 A117 20fr multi   .20   .20
424 A117 25fr multi   .20   .20
425 A117 30fr multi   .20   .20
426 A117 40fr mutli   .25   .25
     Nos. 423-426 (4)   .85   .85

Emblem:
Map of
Africa and
Members'
Flags
A118

60fr, Map of Benin & flags. 80fr, OCAM flag
& map of Africa showing member states.

1979, Mar. 20   *Litho.*   *Perf. 12x13*
427 A118 50fr multi   .40   .40
428 A118 60fr multi   .45   .45
429 A118 80fr multi   .65   .65
     Nos. 427-429 (3)   1.50 1.50
OCAM Summit Conf., Cotonou, Mar. 20-28.
For overprints see Nos. 434-436.

Tower,
Waves,
Satellite,
ITU
Emblem
A119

1979, May 17   *Litho.*   *Perf. 12½*
430 A119 50fr multi   .40   .40
World Telecommunications Day.

Bank Building
and Sculpture
A120

1979, May 26   *Litho.*
431 A120 50fr multi   .35   .35
Opening of Headquarters of West African
Savings Bank in Dakar.

Guelede Mask, Abomey Tapestry,
Malaconotus Bird — A121

Design: 50fr, Jet, canoe, satellite, UPU and
exhibition emblems.

1979, June 8   *Litho.*   *Perf. 13*
432 A121 15fr multi   .20   .20
                   Engr.
433 A121 50fr multi   .35   .35
Philexafrique II, Libreville, Gabon, June 8-
17. Nos. 432, 433 each printed in sheets of 10
with 5 labels showing exhibition emblem.

Nos. 427-429 Overprinted: "26 au 28
juin 1979" and Dots
1979, June 26
434 A118 50fr multi   .35   .35
435 A118 60fr multi   .40   .40
436 A118 80fr multi   .55   .55
     Nos. 434-436 (3)   1.30 1.30
2nd OCAM Summit Conf., June 26-28.

Olympic
Flame, and
Emblems
A122

Pre-Olympic Year: 50fr, High jump.

1979, July 1   *Litho.*
437 A122 10fr multi   .20   .20
438 A122 50fr multi   .35   .35

Antelope
A123

Animals: 10fr, Giraffes, map of Benin, vert
20fr, Chimpanzee. 50fr, Elephants, map of
Benin, vert.

1979, Oct. 1   *Litho.*   *Perf. 13*
439 A123 5fr multi   .20   .20
440 A123 10fr multi   .20   .20
441 A123 20fr multi   .25   .25
442 A123 50fr multi   .35   .35
     Nos. 439-442 (4)   1.00 1.00

Map of
Africa,
Emblem
and
Jet — A124

1979, Dec. 12   *Litho.*   *Perf. 12½*
443 A124 50fr multi   .35   .35
444 A124 60fr multi   .40   .40
ASECNA (Air Safety Board), 20th anniv.

Mail
Services
A125

50fr, Post Office and headquarters, vert.

1979, Dec. 19   *Litho.*   *Perf. 13*
445 A125 50fr multi   .35   .35
446 A125 60fr multi   .40   .40
Office of Posts and Telecommunications,
20th anniversary.

Lenin and Globe — A126

1980, Apr. 22   *Litho.*   *Perf. 12½*
447 A126 50fr shown   .25   .25
448 A126 150fr Lenin in library   .75   .75
Lenin, 110th birth anniversary.

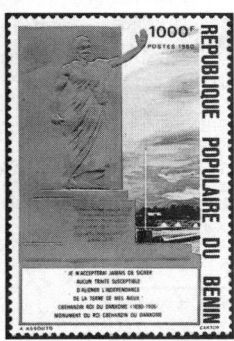

Monument to King Behanzin A126a

Litho. & Embossed

1980, May 31   *Perf. 12½*
448A   A126a 1000fr gold & multi   5.50 5.50
    For overprint see No. Q10A.

Cotonou Club Emlem — A127

1980, Feb. 23   **Litho.**   *Perf. 12½*
449   A127   90fr shown   .50   .50
450   A127   200fr Rotary emblem
           on globe, horiz.   1.25 1.25
    Rotary International, 75th anniversary.
    For surcharge see No. 915.

Galileo, Astrolabe — A128

1980, Apr. 2
451   A128   70fr shown   .45 .45
452   A128   100fr Copernicus, solar
           system   .65 .65
    Discovery of Pluto, 50th anniversary.

Abu Simbel, UNESCO Emblem — A129

1980, Apr. 15   *Perf. 13*
453   A129   50fr Column, vert.   .35   .35
454   A129   60fr Ramses II, vert.   .40   .40
455   A129   150fr shown   1.00 1.00
     Nos. 453-455 (3)   1.75 1.75
    UNESCO campaign to save Nubian monuments, 20h anniversary.

Monument, Martyrs' Square, Cotonou A130

Designs: Various monuments in Martyrs' Square. Cotonou. 60fr, 70fr, 100fr, horiz.

1980, May 2   *Perf. 12½x13, 13x12½*
456   A130   50fr multi   .35   .35
457   A130   60fr multi   .40   .40
458   A130   70fr multi   .45   .45
459   A130   100fr multi   .65   .65
     Nos. 456-459 (4)   1.85 1.85
    For surcharge see No. 539.

Musical Instruments — A131

1980, May 20   *Perf. 12½*
460   A131   5fr Assan, vert.   .20   .20
461   A131   10fr Tinbo   .20   .20
462   A131   15fr Tam-tam sato,
           vert.   .20   .20
463   A131   20fr Kora   .20   .20
464   A131   30fr Gangan   .20   .20
465   A131   50fr Sinhoun   .35   .35
     Nos. 460-465 (6)   1.35 1.35

First Non-stop Flight, Paris-New York — A132

1980, June 2   **Litho.**   *Perf. 12½*
466   A132   90fr shown   .60 .60
467   A132   100fr Dieudonne Coste,
           Maurice Bellonte   .65 .65
    For surcharge see No. 564.

Lunokhod I on the Moon — A133

1980, June 15   **Engr.**   *Perf. 13*
468   A133   90fr multi   .60 .60
    Lunokhod I Soviet unmanned moon mission, 10th anniv. See #C290.

Olympic Flame and Mischa, Moscow '80 Emblem — A134

1980, July 16   **Litho.**   *Perf. 12½*
469   A134   50fr shown   .35   .35
470   A134   60fr Equestrian, vert.   .40   .40
471   A134   70fr Judo   .50   .50
472   A134   200fr Flag, sports,
           globe, vert.   1.40 1.40
473   A134   300fr Weight lifting,
           vert.   2.25 2.25
     Nos. 469-473 (5)   4.90 4.90
    22nd Summer Olympic Games, Moscow, July 19-Aug. 3.
    For surcharges see Nos. 559, 561.

Telephone and Rising Sun A135

World Telecommunications Day: 50fr, Farmer on telephone, vert.

1980, May 17   **Litho.**   *Perf. 12½*
474   A135   50fr multi   .35   .35
475   A135   60fr multi   .40   .40

Cotonou West African Community Village A136

Designs: View of Cotonou.

1980, July 26   *Perf. 13x13½*
476   A136   50fr multi   .35   .35
477   A136   60fr multi   .40   .40
478   A136   70fr multi   .45   .45
     Nos. 476-478 (3)   1.20 1.20
    For surcharge see No. 540.

Agbadja Dancers — A137

Designs: Dancers and muscians.

1980, Aug. 1   *Perf. 12½*
479   A137   30fr multi   .20   .20
480   A137   50fr multi   .30   .30
481   A137   60fr multi   .40   .40
     Nos. 479-481 (3)   .90   .90

Fisherman A138   Philippines under Magnifier A139

Designs: 5fr, Throwing net. 15fr, Canoe and shore fishing. 20fr, Basket traps. 50fr, Hauling net. 60fr, River fishing. All horiz.

1980, Sept. 1
482   A138   5fr multi   .20   .20
483   A138   10fr multi   .20   .20
484   A138   15fr multi   .20   .20
485   A138   20fr multi   .20   .20
486   A138   50fr multi   .35   .35
487   A138   60fr multi   .40   .40
     Nos. 482-487 (6)   1.55 1.55
    For surcharge see No. 535.

Perf. 13x13½, 13x½x13

1980, Sept. 27
World Tourism Conference, Manila, Sept. 27: 60fr, Emblem on flag, hand pointing to Manila on globe, horiz.

488   A139   50fr multi   .35   .35
489   A139   60fr multi   .40   .40
    For surcharge see No. 557.

A140

1980, Oct. 1   *Perf. 12½*
490   A140   40fr Othreis materna   .25   .25
491   A140   50fr Othreis fullonia   .35   .35
492   A140   200fr Oryctes sp.   1.40 1.40
     Nos. 490-492 (3)   2.00 2.00

A141

Photo.
Perf. 13½

1980, Oct. 24
493   A141   75fr multi   .50 .50
    African Postal Union, 5th Anniv.

A142

1980, Nov. 4   *Perf. 12½x13*
494   A142   30fr shown   .25   .25
495   A142   50fr Freed prisoner   .35   .35
496   A142   60fr Man holding torch   .40   .40
     Nos. 494-496 (3)   1.00 1.00
    Declaration of human rights, 30th anniv.

A143

1980, Dec. 1   **Litho.**   *Perf. 13*
    Self-portrait, by Vincent van Gogh, 1888.
497   A143   100fr shown   .75 .75
498   A143   300fr Facteur Roulin   2.25 2.25
    Vincent van Gogh (1853-1890), artist.
    For surcharge see No. 579.

Offenbach and Scene from Orpheus in the Underworld — A144

1980, Dec. 15   **Engr.**
499 A144 50fr shown   .40 .40
500 A144 60fr Paris Life   .45 .45

Jacques Offenbach (1819-1880), composer.

Kepler and Satellites — A145

1980, Dec. 20
501 A145 50fr Kepler, diagram, vert.   .35 .35
502 A145 60fr shown   .40 .40

Johannes Kepler (1571-1630), astronomer.

Intl. Year of the Disabled — A146

1981, Apr. 10   **Litho.**   **Perf. 12½**
503 A146 115fr multi   .75 .75
For surcharge see No. 582.

20th Anniv. of Manned Space Flight — A147

1981, May 30   **Perf. 13**
504 A147 500fr multi   3.50 3.50
For surcharges see Nos. 580, 790.

13th World Telecommunications Day — A148

1981, May 30   **Litho.**   **Perf. 12½**
505 A148 115fr multi   .75 .75
For surcharge see No. 583.

Amaryllis A149

1981, June 20   **Perf. 12½**
506 A149 10fr shown   .20 .20
507 A149 20fr Eischornia crassipes, vert.   .25 .25
508 A149 80fr Parkia biglobosa, vert.   .55 .55
Nos. 506-508 (3)   1.00 1.00
For surcharge see No. 542.

Benin Sheraton Hotel A150

1981, July
509 A150 100fr multi   .65 .65
For surcharge see No. 541.

Guinea Pig — A151

1981, July 31   **Perf. 13x13½**
510 A151 5fr shown   .20 .20
511 A151 60fr Cat   .40 .40
512 A151 80fr Dogs   .55 .55
Nos. 510-512 (3)   1.15 1.15
For surcharges see Nos. 536, 543, 563.

World UPU Day — A152

1981, Oct. 9   **Engr.**   **Perf. 13**
513 A152 100fr red brn & blk   .65 .65

25th Intl. Letter Writing Week, Oct. 6-12 — A153

1981, Oct. 15
514 A153 100fr dk bl & pur   .65 .65
For surcharge see No. 558.

West African Economic Community A154

1981, Nov. 20   **Litho.**   **Perf. 12½**
515 A154 60fr multi   .40 .40

West African Rice Development Assoc. 10th Anniv. — A155

1981, Dec. 10   **Perf. 13x13½**
516 A155 60fr multi   .40 .40

TB Bacillus Centenary A156

1982, Mar. 1   **Litho.**   **Perf. 13**
517 A156 115fr multi   1.25 1.25
For surcharge see No. 584.

West African Economic Community, 5th Summit Conference A157

1982, May 27   **Perf. 12½**
518 A157 60fr multi   .40 .40

1982 World Cup — A158

1982, June 1   **Perf. 13**
519 A158 90fr Players   .65 .65
520 A158 300fr Flags on leg   2.25 2.25
For overprints and surcharges see #523-524, 594, 789.

France No. B349 Magnified, Map of France — A159

1982, June 11
521 A159 90fr multi   .60 .60
For surcharge see No. 916.

PHILEXFRANCE '82 Stamp Exhibition, Paris, June 11-21.

George Washington — A160

1982, Mar. 10   **Litho.**   **Perf. 14**
522 A160 200fr Washington, flag, map   1.00 1.00
For surcharge see No. 577.

Nos. 519-520 Overprinted with Finalists Names

1982, Aug. 16   **Perf. 12½**
523 A158 90fr multi   .60 .60
524 A158 300fr multi   2.00 2.00

Italy's victory in 1982 World Cup.
For surcharge see No. 811.

Bluethroat A161

1982, Sept. 1   **Perf. 14x14½, 14½x14**
525 A161 5fr Daoelo gigas, vert.   .20 .20
526 A161 10fr shown   .20 .20
527 A161 15fr Swallow, vert.   .20 .20
528 A161 20fr Kingfisher, weaver bird, vert.   .20 .20
529 A161 30fr Great sedge warbler   .25 .25
530 A161 60fr Common warbler   .50 .50
531 A161 80fr Owl, vert.   .65 .65
532 A161 100fr Cockatoo, vert.   .80 .80
Nos. 525-532 (8)   3.00 3.00

ITU Plenipotentiaries Conference, Nairobi, Sept. — A162

1982, Sept. 26   **Perf. 13**
533 A162 200fr Map   1.00 1.00
For surcharge see No. 585.

13th World UPU Day — A163

1982, Oct. 9   **Engr.**   **Perf. 13**
534 A163 100fr Monument   .65 .65

Nos. 482, 510, 411 Overprinted in Red or Blue:
#535 "Croix Rouge / 8 Mai 1982"
#536 "UAPT 1982"
#537 "RICCONE 1982"
Perf. 13, 12½, 13x13½
1982, Nov.   **Litho.**
535 A138 60fr on 5fr multi   .40 .40
536 A151 60fr on 5fr multi   .40 .40
537 A112 200fr multi (Bl)   1.40 1.40
Nos. 535-537 (3)   2.20 2.20

Visit of French Pres. Francois Mitterand A164

1983, Jan. 15   **Litho.**   **Perf. 12½x13**
538 A164 90fr multi   .60 .60
For surcharge see No. 917.

Nos. 458, 476, 508-509, 512
Surcharged
Perf. 13x12½, 13x13½, 12½

1983 Litho.
539 A130 60fr on 70fr multi .40 .40
540 A136 60fr on 50fr multi .40 .40
541 A150 60fr on 100fr multi .40 .40
542 A149 75fr on 80fr multi .50 .50
543 A151 75fr on 80fr multi .50 .50
  Nos. 539-543 (5) 2.20 2.20

Seme Oil Rig — A165

1983, Apr. 28 Litho. *Perf. 13x12½*
544 A165 125fr multi .80 .80

World Communications Year — A166

1983, May 17 Litho. *Perf. 13*
545 A166 185fr multi 1.00 1.00
  For surcharge see No. 898.

Riccione '83, Stamp Show — A167

1983, Aug. 27 Litho. *Perf. 13*
546 A167 500fr multi 3.25 3.25
  For surcharge see No. 922.

Benin Red Cross, 20th Anniv. A168

1983, Sept. 5 Photo. *Perf. 13*
547 A168 105fr multi .70 .70
  For surcharge see No. 581.

Handicrafts A169

Designs: 75fr, Handcarved lion chairs and table. 90fr, Natural tree table and stools. 200fr, Monkeys holding jar.

1983, Sept. 18 Litho. *Perf. 13*
548 A169 75fr multi .40 .40
549 A169 90fr multi .50 .50
550 A169 200fr multi 1.10 1.10
  Nos. 548-550 (3) 2.00 2.00
  For surcharge see No. 578.

14th UPU Day — A170

1983, Oct. 9 Engr. *Perf. 13*
551 A170 125fr multi .80 .80
  For surcharge see No. 575.

Religious Movements A171

1983, Oct. 31 Litho. *Perf. 14x15*
552 A171 75fr Zangbeto .35 .35
553 A171 75fr Egoun .35 .35

Plaited Hair Styles — A172

1983, Nov. 14
554 A172 30fr Rockcoco .25 .25
555 A172 75fr Serpent .35 .35
556 A172 90fr Songas .40 .40
  Nos. 554-556 (3) 1.00 1.00

Stamps of 1976-81 Surcharged

1983, Nov.
557 A139 5fr on 50fr #488 .20 .20
558 A153 10fr on 100fr #514 .20 .20
559 A134 15fr on 200fr #472 .20 .20
560 A98 15fr on 210fr #381 .20 .20
561 A134 25fr on 70fr #471 .20 .20
562 A99 25fr on 210fr #384 .20 .20
563 A151 75fr on 5fr #510 .35 .35
564 A132 75fr on 100fr #467 .35 .35
565 A88 75fr on 150fr #360 .35 .35
566 A98 75fr on 150fr #380 .35 .35
  Nos. 557-566 (10) 2.60 2.60

Alfred Nobel (1833-96) A173

1983, Dec. 19 Litho. *Perf. 15x14*
567 A173 300fr multi 1.40 1.40
  For surcharge see No. 923.

Council of Unity — A174

1984, May 29 Litho. *Perf. 12*
568 A174 75fr multi .35 .35
569 A174 90fr multi .40 .40
  For surcharge see No. 918.

1984 UPU Congress A175

1984, June 18 Litho. *Perf. 13*
570 A175 90fr multi .40 .40

Abomey Calavi Earth Station A176

1984, June 29 Litho. *Perf. 12½x13*
571 A176 75fr Satellite dish .35 .35

Traditional Costumes A177

1984, July 2 Litho. *Perf. 13½x13*
572 A177 5fr Koumboro .20 .20
573 A177 10fr Taka .20 .20
574 A177 20fr Toko .20 .20
  Nos. 572-574 (3) .60 .60

Nos. 389, 498, 503-505, 517, 522, 533, 547, 550 and 551 Surcharged

1984, Sept.
575 A170 5fr on 125fr #551 .20 .20
576 A101 5fr on 150fr #389 .20 .20
577 A160 10fr on 200fr #522 .20 .20
578 A169 10fr on 200fr #550 .20 .20
579 A143 15fr on 300fr #498 .20 .20
580 A147 40fr on 500fr #504 .25 .25
581 A168 75fr on 105fr #547 .35 .35
582 A146 75fr on 115fr #503 .35 .35
583 A148 75fr on 115fr #505 .35 .35
584 A156 75fr on 115fr #517 .35 .35
585 A162 75fr on 200fr #533 .35 .35
  Nos. 575-585 (11) 3.00 3.00

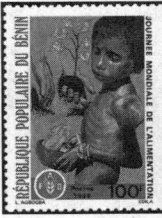

World Food Day — A178

1984, Oct. 16 Litho. *Perf. 12½*
586 A178 100fr Malnourished child .30 .30

Dinosaurs A179

1984, Dec. 14 Litho. *Perf. 13½*
587 A179 75fr Anatosaurus .25 .25
588 A179 90fr Brontosaurus .25 .25

Cultural & Technical Cooperation Agency, 15th Anniv. — A180

1985, Mar 20 Litho. *Perf. 13*
589 A180 300fr Emblem, globe, hands, book .90 .90

Stamps of 1977-82 Surcharged

1985, Mar.
590 A93 75fr on 200fr No. 370 .20 .20
591 A108 75fr on 200fr No. 397 .20 .20
592 A110 75fr on 300fr No. 406 .20 .20
593 A108 75fr on 300fr No. 398 .20 .20
594 A158 90fr on 300fr No. 520 .25 .25
595 A108 90fr on 500fr No. 399 .25 .25
596 A108 90fr on 500fr No. 402 .25 .25
  Nos. 590-596 (7) 1.55 1.55

End of World War II, 40th Anniv. — A180a

1985, May Litho. *Perf. 12*
596A A180a 100fr multicolored

Traditional Dances A181

1985, June 1 Litho. *Perf. 15x14½*
597 A181 75fr Teke, Borgou Tribe .20 .20
598 A181 100fr Tipen'ti, L'Atacora Tribe .30 .30

Intl. Youth Year — A182

1985, July 16 *Perf. 13½*
599 A182 150fr multi .45 .45

1986 World Cup Soccer Championships, Mexico — A183

1985, July 22 *Perf. 13x12½*
600 A183 200fr multi .60 .60

Beginning with Scott 601, Benin again surcharged stamps of Dahomey with a variety of surcharges. While the listings that follow contain more than 80 surcharged stamps, the Scott editors still need to examine more than 60 other stamps, in order to list all of those that are currently known to exist.

The size and location of the surcharge varies from stamp to stamp. The type face used in the surcharge may also vary from issue to issue.

a

b

c

55 f

République
Populaire
du Bénin

d

REPUBLIQUE
DU BENIN

80 F

e

DU BENIN

5 F.

f

g

h

i

j

Dahomey No. 336 Surcharged with Black Bars and New Value
1985, Aug.   **Perf. 12½**
601 A78(a) 15fr on 40fr multi   .20 .20

ASECNA Airlines, 25th Anniv. — A184
1985, Sept. 16   **Perf. 13**
602 A184 150fr multi   .45 .45

PHILEXAFRICA '85, Lome — A187
1985, Nov. 16   **Perf. 13**
605 A187 250fr #569, labor emblem   .90 .90
606 A187 250fr #C252, Gabon #366, magnified stamp   .90 .90
  a. Pair, Nos. 605-606 + label   1.80 1.80

Audubon Birth Bicent. — A188
1985, Oct. 17   **Litho.**   **Perf. 14x15**
607 A188 150fr Skua gull   .55 .55
608 A188 300fr Oyster catcher   1.10 1.10

Mushrooms and Toadstools
A189
1985, Oct. 17
609 A189 35fr Boletus edible   .20 .20
610 A189 40fr Amanite phalloide .20 .20
611 A189 100fr Brown chanterelle .40 .40
       Nos. 609-611 (3)   .80 .80

Dahomey #282, 292, Benin #343 Surcharged
1986, Mar.   **Photo.**
612 A83(b) 75fr on 35fr #343   .25 .25
613 A57(c) 90fr on 70fr #282   .35 .35
614 A60(b) 90fr on 140fr #292   .40 .40
       Nos. 612-614 (3)   1.00 1.00

African Parliamentary Union, 10th Anniv. — A190
1986, May 8   **Litho.**   **Perf. 13x12½**
615 A190 100fr multi   .40 .40
  9th Conference, Cotonou, May 8-10.

Halley's Comet — A191
1986, May 30   **Perf. 12½x12**
616 A191 205fr multi   1.50 1.50
  For surcharge see No. 809.

Dahomey No. 283, Benin No. 344
Surcharged
Engraved, Photogravure
1986, June   **Perf. 13**
617 A58(b) 100fr on 40fr #283   .40 .40
618 A83(b) 150fr on 45fr #344   .55 .55

1986 World Cup Soccer Championships, Mexico — A192
1986, June 29   **Litho.**
619 A192 500fr multi   1.75 1.75
  For surcharge see No. 792.

Fight against Desert Encroachment — A193
1986, July 16   **Perf. 13½**
620 A193 150fr multi   .55 .55

King Behanzin
A194

Amazon
A194a

1986-88   **Engr.**   **Perf. 13**
621 A194   40fr black   .20 .20
622 A194a 100fr brt blue   .40 .40
623 A194   125fr maroon   .60 .60
624 A194a 150fr violet   .60 .60
625 A194   190fr dark ultra   .90 .90
627 A194   220fr dark grn   1.00 1.00
       Nos. 621-627 (6)   3.70 3.70

Issued: 100fr, 150fr, 8/1; others, 10/1/88.
See No. 636. For surcharge see No. 787.

Flowers — A195

Perf. 13x12½, 12½x13
1986, Sept. 1   **Litho.**
631 A195 100fr Haemanthus   .40 .40
632 A195 205fr Hemerocalle, horiz. .90 .90
  For surcharge see No. 1061F.

Butterflies
A196

1986, Sept. 15

#633, Day peacock, little tortoiseshell, morio. #634, Aurora, machaon and fair lady.

633 A196 150fr shown .60 .60
634 A196 150fr multi .60 .60

Dahomey Nos. 290, 307 Overprinted

1985, Oct. 15
Perfs. & Printing Methods as Before

634A A67(b) 50fr on #307
634B A60(d) 150fr on 100fr
#290

Statue of Liberty, Cent. — A197

1986, Oct. 28   Litho.   Perf. 12½
635 A197 250fr multi .90 .90

King Behanzin — A198

1986, Oct. 30   Perf. 13½
636 A198 440fr multi 1.60 1.60

Behanzin, leader of resistance movement against French occupation (1886-1894). For surcharge see No. 921.

Brazilian Cultural Week, Cotonou — A200

1987, Jan. 17   Perf. 12½
638 A200 150fr multi .90 .90

Rotary Intl. District 910 Conference, Cotonou, Apr. 23-25 — A201

1987, Apr. 23   Litho.   Perf. 13½
639 A201 300fr Center for the Blind, Cotonou 1.75 1.75

Automobile Cent. — A202

Modern car and: 150fr, Steam tricycle, by De Dion-Bouton and Trepardoux, 1887. 300fr, Gas-driven Victoria, by Daimler, 1886.

1987, July 1   Perf. 12½
640 A202 150fr multi .90 .90
641 A202 300fr multi 1.75 1.75

For surcharge see No. 679B.

Snake Temple Baptism — A203

1987, July 20   Perf. 13½
642 A203 100fr multi .55 .55

Shellfish A204

1987, July 24   Perf. 12½
643 A204 100fr crayfish .55 .55
644 A204 150fr crab .90 .90

G. Hansen, R. Follerau — A205

1987, Sept. 4   Perf. 13
645 A205 200fr Cure Leprosy 1.10 1.10

Beginning of Benin Revolution, 15th Anniv. — A205a

1987, Oct. 28   Litho.   Perf. 12x12½
645A A205a 100fr multicolored

Locust Control A206

1987, Dec. 7   Litho.   Perf. 12½x13
646 A206 100fr multi .70 .70

Christmas 1987 A207

1987, Dec. 21   Perf. 13
647 A207 150fr multi 1.10 1.10

Dahomey Nos. 268, 284 Ovptd. or Surchd.

1987   Engr.   Perf. 13
647A A58(b) 15fr on 100fr #284
647B A53(b) 40fr on #268

See Nos. C362, C369.

Intl. Red Cross and Red Crescent Organizations, 125th Anniv. — A208

1988, May 25   Litho.   Perf. 13½
648 A208 200fr multi 1.25 1.25

A209

1988, July 11   Perf. 12½
649 A209 200fr multi 1.25 1.25

Martin Luther King, Jr. (1929-68), American civil rights leader.

A210

1988, May 25   Litho.   Perf. 13½
650 A210 125fr multi .90 .90

Organization of African Unity, 25th anniv.

WHO, 40th Anniv. — A211

1988, Sept. 1   Litho.   Perf. 13x12½
651 A211 175fr multi 1.10 1.10

Alma Ata Declaration, 10th anniv.; Health Care for All on Earth by the Year 2000. For surcharge see No. 786.

Ganvie Lake Village — A212

1988, Sept. 4   Perf. 13½
652 A212 125fr shown .85 .85
653 A212 190fr Boatman, village, diff. 1.25 1.25

A213

1988, Aug. 14   Perf. 12½
654 A213 125fr multi .90 .90

1st Benin Scout Jamboree, Aug. 12-19.

Benin No. 351, Dahomey Nos. 296, 328 Surcharged

1988
Printing Method & Perfs as Before

654A A57(d) 10fr on 60fr on 2fr #351
654B A62(d) 10fr on 65fr #296
654E A74(d) 150fr on 200fr #328

A214

1988, Dec. 30   Litho.   Perf. 13

Ritual Offering to Hebiesso, God of Thunder and Lightning.

655 A214 125fr multicolored .80 .80

Dahomey Nos. 161, 247, 302, 333, 339, 341 Surcharged

1988   Photo.   Perf. 12½x13
655A A19(d) 5fr on 3fr #161
655C A82(d) 30fr on 150fr #341
655D A76(d) 25fr on 100fr #333
655E A45(b) 50fr on 45fr #247
655F A81(d) 55fr on 200fr #339
655G A65(b) 65fr on 85fr #302

These are part of a set of 10. Another set of 19 surcharges also is known to exist. The editors need to see the rest of these stamps before listings can be created.

Rural Development Council, 30th Anniv. — A214a

1989, May 29   Litho.   Perf. 15x14
655K A214a 75fr multicolored

World Wildlife Fund — A216

Roseate terns, *Sterna dougalli.*

1989, Jan. 30   Litho.   *Perf. 13*
657 A216 10fr Three terns   .50   .25
658 A216 15fr Feeding on fish   .50   .25
659 A216 50fr Perched   1.50   .75
660 A216 125fr In flight   3.00   1.25
    Nos. 657-660 (4)   5.50   2.50

Eiffel Tower
Cent. — A217

1989, Apr. 24   Litho.   *Perf. 13x12½*
661 A217 190fr multi   1.10   1.10

PHILEXFRANCE '89, French
Revolution Bicent. — A218

Design: Bastille, emblems, Declaration of
Human Rights and Citizenship, France No.
B252-B253.

1989, July 7   *Perf. 13*
662 A218 190fr multicolored   1.10   1.10

Electric
Corp. of
Benin, 20th
Anniv.
A219

1989, Oct.   Litho.   *Perf. 12½x13*
663 A219 125fr multicolored   .80   .80

Fish
A220

1989, Sept. 22   *Perf. 13½*
664 A220 125fr Lote   .80   .80
665 A220 190fr Pike, salmon   1.25   1.25

Death of King
Glele,
Cent. — A221

1989, Dec. 16   Litho.   *Perf. 13½*
666 A221 190fr multicolored   1.25   1.25

Christmas
A222

1989, Dec. 25   *Perf. 13*
667 A222 200fr Holy family   1.40   1.40

Benin Posts & Telecommunications,
Cent. — A223

1990, Jan. 1   *Perf. 13½*
668 A223 125fr multicolored   .80   .80

Fruits and
Flora
A224

1990, Jan. 23   Litho.   *Perf. 11½*
669 A224 60fr Oranges   .40   .40
670 A224 190fr Kaufmann Tulips,
     vert.   1.40   1.40
671 A224 250fr Cashews, vert.   1.75   1.75
    Nos. 669-671 (3)   3.55   3.55
      Dated 1989.

Moon
Landing,
20th Anniv.
A225

1990, Jan. 23
672 A225 190fr multicolored   1.40   1.40
      Dated 1989.

World Cup Soccer Championships,
Italy — A226

1990, June 8   Litho.   *Perf. 12½*
673 A226 125fr shown   1.00   1.00
674 A226 190fr Character trade-
     mark, vert.   1.50   1.50
    For overprint see No. 676.

Post, Telephone
& Telegraph
Administration in
Benin,
Cent. — A227

1990, July 1   *Perf. 13*
675 A227 150fr multicolored   1.25   1.25

No. 673 Overprinted

1990   Litho.   *Perf. 12½*
676 A226 125fr multicolored   1.00   1.00

Charles de Gaulle (1890-
1970) — A228

1990, Nov. 22   Litho.   *Perf. 13*
677 A228 190fr multicolored   1.50   1.50
      See No. 689.

Galileo
Probe and
Jupiter
A229

1990, Dec. 1
678 A229 100fr multicolored   .75   .75
    For overprint see No. 681.

A230

1990, Dec. 25   Litho.   *Perf. 12½x13*
679 A230 200fr multicolored   1.75   1.75
      Christmas.

Benin No. 641 Surcharged

1990
Perf. & Printing Method as Before
679B A202(e) 190fr on 300fr
        #641

A230a   A231

1990   Litho.   *Perf. 11½x12*
679C A230a 125fr multicolored
    National People's Congress.

1991, Sept. 3   Litho.   *Perf. 13½*
680 A231 125fr multicolored   1.00   1.00
    Independence, 31st anniv.

No. 678 Ovptd. in Red

1991   *Perf. 13*
681 A229 100fr multicolored   .85   .85

French Open Tennis Championships,
Cent. — A232

1991   *Perf. 13½*
682 A232 125fr multicolored   1.00   1.00

African Tourism Year — A233

1991
683 A233 190fr multicolored   1.60 1.60

Christmas
A234

1991, Dec. 2   Litho.   Perf. 13½
684 A234 125fr multicolored   1.00 1.00

Dancer of
Guelede — A235

1991, Dec. 2
685 A235 190fr multicolored   1.60 1.60

Wolfgang
Amadeus Mozart,
Death
Bicent. — A236

1991, Dec. 2
686 A236 1000fr multicolored   6.00 6.00
     For surcharge see No. 793.

Discovery
of America,
500th
Anniv.
A237

1000fr, Columbus coming ashore, horiz.

1992, Apr. 24   Litho.   Perf. 13
687 A237 500fr blk, blue &
            brn   3.00 3.00
688 A237 1000fr multicolored   6.00 6.00
  a. Souvenir sheet, #687-688   9.00 9.00

De Gaulle Type of 1990
1992   Litho.   Perf. 13
689 A228 300fr like #677   2.25 2.25

Intl. Conference
on Nutrition,
Rome — A238

1992, Dec. 5   Litho.   Perf. 13
690 A238 190fr multicolored   1.60 1.60
     For surcharge see 928.

Dahomey Nos. 160, 266, 303, 311,
327, 334, 338, C161 Surcharged or
Overprinted (#690A)
1992
Perfs. & Printing Methods as Before
690A A66(e)   5fr on #303
690E A80(f)   35fr on #338
690F A19(e) 125fr on 2fr
                     #160
690G AP54(f) 125fr on 65fr
                     #C161
690H A77(f) 125fr on 65fr
                     #334 (G)
690I CD137(e) 125fr on 100fr
                     #311
690J A52(f) 190fr on 45fr
                     #266
690K A74(f) 125fr on 100fr
                     #327

Visit of Pope
John Paul II,
Feb. 3-5 — A239

Ouidah 92, First
Festival of Voodoo
Culture — A240

1993, Feb. 3   Litho.   Perf. 13x12½
691 A239 190fr multicolored   1.50 1.50

1993, Feb. 8   Perf. 13½
692 A240 125fr multicolored   1.00 1.00

Well of
Possotome,
Eurystome
A241

1993, May 25   Litho.   Perf. 12½
693 A241 125fr multicolored   1.00 1.00

OAU,
30th
Anniv.
A242

1993, June 7   Litho.   Perf. 13½
694 A242 125fr multicolored   1.00 1.00

John F. Kennedy — A243

1993, June 24   Perf. 13
695 A243 190fr shown   1.50 1.50
696 A243 190fr Martin Luther
            King, vert.   1.50 1.50
  Assassinations of Kennedy, 30th anniv.
(#695), and King, 25th anniv. (#696).

Dahomey Nos. 161, 173, 175, 277,
335 Overprinted or Surcharged
1993
Perfs. & Printing Methods as Before
697 A21(e)   5fr on #175
700 A19(f)   10fr on 3fr #161
701 A77(f)   10fr on 100fr #335
703 A57(f)   20fr on 1fr #277
704 A21(f)   25fr on 1fr #173

Benin Nos. 343, 345, 350, Dahomey
Nos.
169, 226-227, 249, 276, 295, 283,
286, 319, 333
Surcharged or Overprinted (#711, 713)
1994-95
707 A38(f)   5fr on 1fr #226
709 A71(f)   25fr on #319
710 A59(e)   40fr on #286
711 A57(e)   50fr on 1fr #350
712 A58(e)   80fr on 40fr #283
713 A76(g) 100fr on #333
715 A38(f) 135fr on 3fr #227
718 A62(e) 135fr on 30fr #295
719 A83(g) 135fr on 35fr #343
720 A56(h) 135fr on 40fr multi
722 A20(e) 135fr on 60fr #169
723 A83(g) 135fr on 60fr #345
725 A45(e) 200fr on 100fr #249

UNESCO
Conference on The
Slave
Route — A244

Perf. 13x13½, 12¾x12½ (#731)
1994   Litho.
729 A244 200fr multicolored
730 A244 300fr multicolored
731 A245 135fr multi

Intl. Year of
the Family
A246

1994   Litho.   Perf. 12½
732 A246 200fr multicolored

1994 World Cup
Soccer
Championships,
US — A247

1994   Litho.   Perf. 13x13½
733 A247 300fr multicolored

1996 Summer Olympics,
Atlanta — A248

Perf. 12½x13, 13x12½
1995, Apr. 30   Litho.
734 A248 45fr Water polo   .35 .35
735 A248 50fr Javelin   .40 .40
736 A248 75fr Weight lifting .60 .60
737 A248 100fr Tennis   .75 .75

---

738 A248 135fr Baseball   1.10 1.10
739 A248 200fr Synchronized
             swimming   1.50 1.50
     Nos. 734-739 (6)   4.70 4.70
Souvenir Sheet
740 A248 300fr Diving   3.50 3.50
  Nos. 735-740 are vert. No. 740 contains one
32x40mm stamp.

Dogs
A249

1995, Aug. 23   Litho.   Perf. 12½
741 A249 40fr German shep-
             herd   .30 .30
742 A249 50fr Beagle   .40 .40
743 A249 75fr Great dane   .55 .55
744 A249 100fr Boxer   .75 .75
745 A249 135fr Pointer   1.10 1.10
746 A249 200fr Fox terrier   1.50 1.50
     Nos. 741-746 (6)   4.60 4.60
Souvenir Sheet
747 A249 300fr Schnauzer   5.00 5.00

Ships
A250

  Designs: 40fr, Steam driven paddle boat,
1788. 50fr, Paddle steamer Charlotte, 1802.
75fr, Transatlantic steamship, Citta de
Catania. 100fr, Hovercraft Mountbatten SR-
N4. 135fr, QE II. 200fr, Japanese experimental
atomic energy ship, Mutsu-NEF.
  300fr, Paddle-steamer Savannah, 1819.

1995, May 20
748 A250 40fr multicolored   .30 .30
749 A250 50fr multicolored   .40 .40
750 A250 75fr multicolored   .55 .55
751 A250 100fr multicolored .75 .75
752 A250 135fr multicolored 1.10 1.10
753 A250 200fr multicolored 1.50 1.50
     Nos. 748-753 (6)   4.60 4.60
Souvenir Sheet
754 A250 300fr multicolored 3.50 3.50
  No. 754 contains one 40x32mm stamp.

Primates
A251

1995, June 30
755 A251 50fr Pan troglodytes   .40 .40
756 A251 75fr Mandrillus sphinx .55 .55
757 A251 100fr Colobus   .75 .75
758 A251 135fr Macaca sylvanus 1.10 1.10
759 A251 200fr Comopithecus
             hamadryas   1.50 1.50
     Nos. 755-759 (5)   4.30 4.30
Souvenir Sheet
760 A251 300fr Papio cy-
             nocephalus   3.50 3.50
  No. 760 contains one 32x40mm stamp.

Domestic
Cats
A252

1995, July 30   Litho.   Perf. 12½x13

761	A252	40fr Shorthair tabby	.30 .30
762	A252	50fr Ruddy red	.40 .40
763	A252	75fr White longhair	.55 .55
764	A252	100fr Seal color point	.75 .75
765	A252	135fr Tabby point	1.10 1.10
766	A252	200fr Black shorthair	1.50 1.50
		Nos. 761-766 (6)	4.60 4.60

Souvenir Sheet

767	A252	300fr Cat in basket	3.50 3.50

No. 767 contains one 40x32mm stamp.

Flowers — A253

Designs: 40fr, Dracunculus vulgaris. 50fr, Narcissus watieri. 75fr, Amaryllis belladonna. 100fr, Nymphaea capensis. 135fr, Chrysanthemum carinatum. 200fr, Iris tingitana.

1995, Oct. 15   Litho.   Perf. 12½

768	A253	40fr multicolored	.30 .30
769	A253	50fr multicolored	.40 .40
770	A253	75fr multicolored	.60 .60
771	A253	100fr multicolored	.85 .85
772	A253	135fr multicolored	1.10 1.10
773	A253	200fr multicolored	1.75 1.75
		Nos. 768-773 (6)	5.00 5.00

Wild Animals A254

50fr, Panthera leo. 75fr, Syncerus caffer. 100fr, Pan troglodytes. 135fr, Aepyceros melampus. 200fr, Geosciurus inaurus. 300fr, Loxodonta, vert.

Perf. 13x12½, 12½x13

1995, Sept. 20

774	A254	50fr multicolored	.40 .40
775	A254	75fr multicolored	.60 .60
776	A254	100fr multicolored	.85 .85
777	A254	135fr multicolored	1.10 1.10
778	A254	200fr multicolored	1.75 1.75
		Nos. 774-778 (5)	4.70 4.70

Souvenir Sheet

779	A254	300fr multicolored	3.50 3.50

Nos. 774-777 are vert. No. 779 contains one 32x40mm stamp.

Birds Feeding Their Chicks — A255

Designs: 40fr, Cocothraustes cocothraustes. 50fr, Streptopelia chinensis. 75fr, Falco peregrinus. 100fr, Dendroica fusca. 135fr, Larus ridibundus. 200fr, Pelecanus onocrotalus.

1995, Aug. 28   Perf. 12½x13

780	A255	40fr multicolored	.30 .30
781	A255	50fr multicolored	.40 .40
782	A255	75fr multicolored	.60 .60
783	A255	100fr multicolored	.85 .85
784	A255	135fr multicolored	1.10 1.10
785	A255	200fr multicolored	1.75 1.75
		Nos. 780-785 (6)	5.00 5.00

Benin Nos. 344, 504, 520,
619, 627, 651, 686
and Dahomey No. 291 Surcharged

1994-95

Printing Method and Perfs as Before

786	A211	25fr on 175fr #651	
787	A194	50fr on 220fr #627	
788	A83(h)	150fr on 45fr #344	
789	A158	150fr on 90fr #519	
790	A147	150fr on 500fr #504	
791	A60(f)	200fr on 135fr #291	
792	A192	200fr on 500fr #619	
793	A236	250fr on 1000fr #686	

Natl. Arms — A256

1995   Litho.   Perf. 12½

793A	A256	135fr yellow & multi	1.00 1.00
793B	A256	150fr yel grn & multi	1.10 1.10
794	A256	200fr multicolored	

See Nos. 948-951. For surcharge see No. 1021A.

Orchids — A257

Designs: 40fr, Angraecum sesquipedale. 50fr, Polystachya virginea. 75fr, Disa uniflora. 100fr, Ansellia africana. 135fr, Angraecum eichlerianum. 200fr, Jumellea confusa.

1995, Nov. 10   Litho.   Perf. 12½

795	A257	40fr multicolored	.30 .30
796	A257	50fr multicolored	.40 .40
797	A257	75fr multicolored	.55 .55
798	A257	100fr multicolored	.75 .75
799	A257	135fr multicolored	1.00 1.00
800	A257	200fr multicolored	1.50 1.50
		Nos. 795-800 (6)	4.50 4.50

Butterflies A258

Designs: 40fr, Graphium policenes. 50fr, Vanessa atalanta. 75fr, Polymmatus icarus. 100fr, Danaus chrysipus. 135fr, Cynthia cardui. 200fr, Argus celbulina. 1000fr, Charaxes jasius.

1996, Mar. 10

801	A258	40fr multicolored	.30 .30
802	A258	50fr multicolored	.40 .40
803	A258	75fr multicolored	.55 .55
804	A258	100fr multicolored	.75 .75
805	A258	135fr multicolored	1.10 1.10
806	A258	200fr multicolored	1.50 1.50
		Nos. 801-806 (6)	4.60 4.60

Souvenir Sheet

807	A258	1000fr multicolored	4.50 4.50

CHINA '96, Beijing A259

Designs: a, 40fr, Dancer in traditional Chinese costume. b, 50fr, Exhibition emblem. c, 75fr, Water lily. d, 100fr, Temple of Heaven.

1996, Apr. 8

808	A259	Block of 4, #a.-d.	3.75 3.75

Benin Nos. 523, 616 and
Dahomey No. 306
Surcharged or Overprinted (#810)

1996?

Perfs. & Printing Methods as Before

809	A191	5fr on 205fr #616	
810	A67(g)	35fr on #306	
811	A158	150fr on 90fr #523	

15th Lions Intl. District Convention — A260

1996   Litho.   Perf. 12½

811A	A260	100fr multicolored	.35 .35
811B	A260	135fr green & multi	1.10 1.10
812	A260	150fr yellow & multi	1.10 1.10
813	A260	200fr red & multi	1.50 1.50
		Nos. 811A-813 (4)	4.05 4.05

For surcharge see No. 1021B.
Issued: #811A, 12/27; others, 5/2.

La Francoponie Conference — A261

1995, Dec. 2   Litho.   Perf. 12½

814	A261	150fr pink & multi	.90 .90
815	A261	200fr blue & multi	1.25 1.25

Cats — A262

1995, Nov. 2   Litho.   Perf. 13

816	A262	40fr Lynx lynx	.30 .30
817	A262	50fr Felis concolor	.40 .40
818	A262	75fr Acinonyx jubatus	.50 .50
819	A262	100fr Panthera pardus	.70 .70
820	A262	135fr Panthera tigris	.95 .95
821	A262	200fr Panthera leo	1.40 1.40
		Nos. 816-821 (6)	4.25 4.25

1998 World Cup Soccer Championships, France — A263

Various soccer players.

1996, Feb. 10   Litho.   Perf. 13

822	A263	40fr multicolored	.30 .30
823	A263	50fr multicolored	.40 .40
824	A263	75fr multicolored	.55 .55
825	A263	100fr multicolored	.75 .75
826	A263	135fr multicolored	1.10 1.10
827	A263	200fr multicolored	1.50 1.50
		Nos. 822-827 (6)	4.60 4.60

Souvenir Sheet

Perf. 12½

828	A263	1000fr multicolored	4.50 4.50

No. 828 contains one 32x40mm stamp.

1996 Summer Olympic Games, Atlanta — A264

1996, Jan. 28   Litho.   Perf. 13

829	A264	40fr Diving	.30 .30
830	A264	50fr Tennis	.40 .40
831	A264	75fr Running	.55 .55
832	A264	100fr Gymnastics	.75 .75
833	A264	135fr Weight lifting	1.10 1.10
834	A264	200fr Shooting	1.50 1.50
		Nos. 829-834 (6)	4.60 4.60

Souvenir Sheet

835	A264	1000fr Water polo	4.50 4.50

No. 835 contains one 32x40mm stamp.

Christmas Paintings — A265

Entire paintings or details: 40fr, Holy Family Under the Oak Tree, by Raphael. 50fr, The Holy Family, by Raphael. 75fr, St. John the Baptist as a Child, by Murillo. 100fr, The Virgin of Balances, by Leonardo da Vinci. 135fr, The Virgin and the Infant, by Gerard David. 200fr, Adoration of the Magi, by Juan Batista Mayno. 1000fr, Rest on the Flight into Egypt, by Murillo.

1996, May 5   Litho.   Perf. 13

836	A265	40fr multicolored	.30 .30
837	A265	50fr multicolored	.40 .40
838	A265	75fr multicolored	.60 .60
839	A265	100fr multicolored	.75 .75
840	A265	135fr multicolored	1.10 1.10
841	A265	200fr multicolored	1.60 1.60
		Nos. 836-841 (6)	4.75 4.75

Souvenir Sheet

842	A265	1000fr multicolored	4.75 4.75

No. 842 contains one 40x32mm stamp.

Wild Cats — A266

Designs: 40fr, Leptailurus serval. 50fr, Profelis temmincki. 75fr, Leopardus pardalis. 100fr, Lynx rufus. 135fr, Prionailurus bengalensis. 200fr, Felis euphtilura. 1000fr, Neofelis nebulosa.

1996, June 10   Litho.   Perf. 12x12½

843	A266	40fr multicolored	.30 .30
844	A266	50fr multicolored	.40 .40
845	A266	75fr multicolored	.60 .60
846	A266	100fr multicolored	.75 .75
847	A266	135fr multicolored	1.10 1.10
848	A266	200fr multicolored	1.60 1.60
		Nos. 843-848 (6)	4.75 4.75

Souvenir Sheet

Perf. 12½

849	A266	1000fr multicolored	4.75 4.75

No. 849 contains one 32x40mm stamp.

Sailing
Ships
A267

1996, May 27   Perf. 13x12½
850 A267   40fr Thermopylae   .30   .30
851 A267   50fr 5-masted bark   .40   .40
852 A267   75fr Nightingale   .60   .60
853 A267 100fr Opium clipper   .75   .75
854 A267 135fr The Torrens   1.10 1.10
855 A267 200fr English clipper   1.60 1.60
    Nos. 850-855 (6)   4.75 4.75

Souvenir Sheet
Perf. 13
856 A267 1000fr Opium clipper,
                diff.   4.75 4.75
No. 856 contains one 32x40mm stamp.
For No. 850 surcharge see No. 1209.

Olymphilex
'96 — A268

1996, July 2   Perf. 13
857 A268   40fr Running   .30   .30
858 A268   50fr Kayaking   .40   .40
859 A268   75fr Gymnastics   .60   .60
860 A268 100fr Soccer   .75   .75
861 A268 135fr Tennis   1.10 1.10
862 A268 200fr Baseball   1.50 1.50
    Nos. 857-862 (6)   4.65 4.65

Souvenir Sheet
863 A268 1000fr Basketball   4.75 4.75
No. 863 contains one 32x40mm stamp.

Modern Olympic Games,
Cent. — A269

a, 40fr, Gold medal, woman hurdler. b, 50fr,
Runner, Olympic flame. c, 75fr, Pierre de
Coubertin, map of US. d, 100fr, Map of US,
"1996."

1996, June 20
864 A269 Block of 4, #a.-d.   4.00 4.00
No. 864 is a continuous design.

Horses
A270

Various horses.

1996, Aug. 10   Litho.   Perf. 13
865 A270   40fr multi, vert.   .30   .30
866 A270   50fr multi, vert.   .40   .40
867 A270   75fr multi, vert.   .55   .55
868 A270 100fr multi, vert.   .75   .75
869 A270 135fr multi, vert.   1.10 1.10
870 A270 200fr multicolored   1.50 1.50
    Nos. 865-870 (6)   4.60 4.60

Flowering
Cacti — A271

40fr, Parodia subterranea. 50fr,
Astrophytum senile. 75fr, Echinocereus mela-
nocentrus. 100fr, Turbinicarpus kinkerianus.
135fr, Astrophytum capricorne. 200fr, Nel-
loydia grandiflora.

1996, July 25
871 A271   40fr multicolored   .30   .30
872 A271   50fr multicolored   .40   .40
873 A271   75fr multicolored   .55   .55
874 A271 100fr multicolored   .75   .75
875 A271 135fr multicolored   1.10 1.10
876 A271 200fr multicolored   1.50 1.50
    Nos. 871-876 (6)   4.60 4.60
For No. 873 surcharge see No. 1210.

Mushrooms
A272

Designs: 40fr, Stropharia cubensis. 50fr,
Psilocybe zapotecorum. 75fr, Psilocybe mexi-
cana. 100fr, Conocybe siligineoides. 135fr,
Psilocybe caerulescens mazatecorum. 200fr,
Psilocybe caerulescens nigripes.
 1000fr, Psilocybe aztecorum, horiz.

1996, Sept. 30
877 A272   40fr multicolored   .30   .30
878 A272   50fr multicolored   .40   .40
879 A272   75fr multicolored   .55   .55
880 A272 100fr multicolored   .75   .75
881 A272 135fr multicolored   1.10 1.10
882 A272 200fr multicolored   1.50 1.50
    Nos. 877-882 (6)   4.60 4.60

Souvenir Sheet
Perf. 12½
883 A272 1000fr multicolored   4.50 4.50
No. 883 contains one 40x32mm stamp.

Prehistoric Animals — A273

1996, Aug. 30   Perf. 12½
884 A273   40fr Longisquama,
                vert.   .30   .30
885 A273   50fr Dimophodon,
                vert.   .40   .40
886 A273   75fr Dunkleosteus   .55   .55
887 A273 100fr Eryops   .75   .75
888 A273 135fr Peloneustes   1.10 1.10
889 A273 200fr Deinonychus   1.50 1.50
    Nos. 884-889 (6)   4.60 4.60

Birds — A274

Designs: 40fr, Campephilus principalis. 50fr,
Picathartes oreas. 75fr, Strigops habroptilus.
100fr, Amazona vittata. 135fr, Nipponia nippon. 200fr, Gymnogyps californianus.
 1000fr, Paradisea rudolphi.

1996, Sept. 10
890 A274   40fr multicolored   .30   .30
891 A274   50fr multicolored   .40   .40
892 A274   75fr multicolored   .55   .55
893 A274 100fr multicolored   .75   .75
894 A274 135fr multicolored   1.10 1.10
895 A274 200fr multicolored   1.50 1.50
    Nos. 890-895 (6)   4.60 4.60

Souvenir Sheet
896 A274 1000fr multicolored   4.50 4.50
No. 896 contains one 32x40mm stamp.

Dahomey No. 235 Overprinted
Benin No. 545 Surcharged

199?
Perfs. & Printing Methods as Before
897 A40(e)   30fr on #235
898 A166   75fr on 185fr #545

Dahomey Nos. 208, 239-241, 257-258,
261, 269, 274, 283, 320, 326, 334-
336, 337 Surcharged or Overprinted
(#899)

1996?
Perfs. & Printing Methods as Before
899 A77(f)   100fr on #335
900 A79(e)   125fr on 150fr #337
901 A77(h)   135fr on 65fr #334
902 A42(e)   150fr on 30fr #239
903 A43(h)   150fr on 30fr #241
904 A48(h)   150fr on 30fr #257
905 A50(h)   150fr on 30fr #261
906 CD132(h)   150fr on 40fr #269
907 A58(h)   150fr on 40fr #283
908 A71(e)   150fr on 40fr #320
909 A24(e)   150fr on 40fr #326
910 A78(e)   150fr on 40fr #336
911 A32(e)   150fr on 50fr #208
912 A42(e)   150fr on 70fr #240
913 A48(h)   150fr on 70fr #258
914 A55(h)   150fr on 200fr #274

Benin Nos. 381, 384, 449, 521, 538,
546, 567, 569, 636, Surcharged

1996?
Perfs. & Printing Methods as Before
915 A127   10fr on 90fr #449
916 A159   10fr on 90fr #521
917 A164   10fr on 90fr #538
918 A174   10fr on 90fr #569
919 A98   40fr on 210fr #381
920 A99   40fr on 210fr #384
921 A198   75fr on 440fr #636
922 A167 100fr on 500fr #546
923 A173 125r on 300fr #567

Obliterator on No. 922 has either one or two
bars. Pairs of No. 922 exist with each stamp
having a different obliterator.

No. 690 Surcharged
1995   Method and Perf. as Before
928 A238 150fr on 190fr #690

Benin No. 376 Surcharged
1995
Perfs. & Printing Methods as Before
925 A96   10fr on 90fr #376

Ungulates — A275

Designs: 40fr, Aepyceros melampus. 50fr,
Kobus ellipsiprymnus. 75fr, Caffer caffer.
100fr, Connochaetes taurinus. 135fr, Okapia
johnstoni. 200fr, Tragelaphus strepsiceros.

1996, Oct. 15   Litho.   Perf. 12½x12
930 A275   40fr multicolored   .30   .30
931 A275   50fr multicolored   .40   .40
932 A275   75fr multicolored   .55   .55
933 A275 100fr multicolored   .75   .75
934 A275 135fr multicolored   1.10 1.10
935 A275 200fr multicolored   1.50 1.50
    Nos. 930-935 (6)   4.60 4.60

Marine Mammals — A276

Designs: 40fr, Delphinapterus leucas. 50fr,
Tursiops truncatus. 75fr, Belaenoptera muscu-
lus. 100fr, Eubalaena australis. 135fr,
Gramphidelphis griseus. 200fr, Orcinus orca.

1996, Nov. 5   Perf. 13
936 A276   40fr multicolored   .30   .30
937 A276   50fr multicolored   .40   .40
938 A276   75fr multicolored   .55   .55
939 A276 100fr multicolored   .75   .75
940 A276 135fr multicolored   1.10 1.10
941 A276 200fr multicolored   1.50 1.50
    Nos. 936-941 (6)   4.60 4.60

Fish
A277

1996, Dec. 4   Litho.   Perf. 12½
942 A277   50fr Pomacanthidae,
                vert.   .40   .40
943 A277   75fr Acanthuridae   .55   .55
944 A277 100fr Carangidae   .75   .75
945 A277 135fr Chaetodontidae   1.10 1.10
946 A277 200fr Chaetodontidae,
                diff.   1.50 1.50
    Nos. 942-946 (5)   4.30 4.30

Souvenir Sheet
947 A277 1000fr Scaridae   4.50 4.50
No. 947 contains one 40x32mm stamp.

Coat of Arms Type of 1995
1996-97   Perf. 12½
948 A256 100fr multicolored   .45   .45
949 A256 135fr lt yellow & multi   .55   .55
950 A256 150fr lt bl grn & multi   .60   .60
951 A256 200fr lt orange & multi   .85   .85
    Nos. 949-951 (3)   2.00 2.00
#949-951 have "Republique du Benin" at
bottom.
 Issued: 100fr, 12/27/96; 135fr, 150fr, 200fr,
5/15/97.
For surcharge see No. 1021A.

Military
Uniforms — A278

Regiments of European infantry: 135fr,
Grenadier, Glassenapp. 150fr, Officer, Von
Groben. 200fr, Musketeer, Comte Dohna.
270fr, Bombardier. 300fr, Gendarme. 400fr,
Dragoon, Mollendorf.
 1000fr, Soldiers, flag, horses, vert.

1997, Feb. 20
952 A278 135fr multicolored   .55   .55
953 A278 150fr multicolored   .60   .60
954 A278 200fr multicolored   .80   .80
955 A278 270fr multicolored   1.10 1.10
956 A278 300fr multicolored   1.25 1.25
957 A278 400fr multicolored   1.60 1.60
    Nos. 952-957 (6)   5.90 5.90

Souvenir Sheet
Perf. 13
958 A278 1000fr multicolored 4.00 4.00

No. 958 contains one 32x40mm stamp.

Trains
A279

135fr, Steam turbine, Reid Maclead, 1920. 150fr, Experimental high speed, 1935. 200fr, Renard Argent, 1935. 270fr, Class No. 21-C-6, 1941. 300fr, Diesel, 1960. 400fr, Diesel, 1960, diff.
1000fr, Coronation Scot, 1937.

1997, Mar. 26   Litho.   Perf. 13
959	A279	135fr	multicolored	.50	.50
960	A279	150fr	multicolored	.55	.55
961	A279	200fr	multicolored	.75	.75
962	A279	270fr	multicolored	1.00	1.00
963	A279	300fr	multicolored	1.10	1.10
964	A279	400fr	multicolored	1.50	1.50
	Nos. 959-964 (6)			5.40	5.40

Souvenir Sheet
965 A279 1000fr multicolored 3.75 3.75

No. 965 contains one 40x32mm stamp.

1998 World Cup Soccer Championship, France — A280

Various soccer plays.

1997, Apr. 9   Perf. 12½x13
966	A280	135fr	multicolored	.50	.50
967	A280	150fr	multicolored	.55	.55
968	A280	200fr	multicolored	.75	.75
969	A280	270fr	multicolored	1.00	1.00
970	A280	300fr	multi, horiz.	1.10	1.10
971	A280	400fr	multi, horiz.	1.50	1.50
	Nos. 966-971 (6)			5.40	5.40

Souvenir Sheet
972 A280 1000fr multicolored 3.75 3.75

No. 972 contains one 40x32mm stamp.

Orchids — A281

Phalaenopsis: 135fr, Penetrate. 150fr, Golden sands. 200fr, Sun spots. 270fr, Fuscata. 300fr, Christi floyd. 400fr, Cayanne.
1000fr, Janet kuhn.

1997, June 9   Litho.   Perf. 12½x13
973	A281	135fr	multicolored	.50	.50
974	A281	150fr	multicolored	.55	.55
975	A281	200fr	multicolored	.70	.70
976	A281	270fr	multicolored	1.00	1.00
977	A281	300fr	multicolored	1.10	1.10
978	A281	400fr	multicolored	1.40	1.40
	Nos. 973-978 (6)			5.25	5.25

Souvenir Sheet
Perf. 12½
979 A281 1000fr multicolored 3.60 3.60

No. 979 contains one 32x40mm stamp.

Dogs — A282

Designs: 135fr, Irish setter. 150fr, Saluki. 200fr, Doberman pinscher. 270fr, Siberian husky. 300fr, Basenji. 400fr, Boxer.
1000fr, Rhodesian ridgeback.

1997, May 30   Perf. 13
980	A282	135fr	multicolored	.50	.50
981	A282	150fr	multicolored	.55	.55
982	A282	200fr	multicolored	.70	.70
983	A282	270fr	multicolored	1.00	1.00
984	A282	300fr	multicolored	1.10	1.10
985	A282	400fr	multicolored	1.40	1.40
	Nos. 980-985 (6)			5.25	5.25

Souvenir Sheet
Perf. 12½
986 A282 1000fr multicolored 3.60 3.60

No. 986 contains one 32x40mm stamp.

Antique Automobiles — A283

1997, July 5   Litho.   Perf. 13x12½
987	A283	135fr	1905 Buick	.45	.45
988	A283	150fr	1903 Ford	.50	.50
989	A283	200fr	1913 Stanley	.70	.70
990	A283	270fr	1911 Stoddar-Dayton	.90	.90
991	A283	300fr	1934 Cadillac	1.00	1.00
992	A283	400fr	1931 Cadillac	1.40	1.40
	Nos. 987-992 (6)			4.95	4.95

Souvenir Sheet
Perf. 13
993 A283 1000fr 1928 Ford 3.40 3.40

No. 993 contains one 40x32mm stamp.

Songbirds — A284

Designs: 135fr, Pyrrhula pyrrhula. 150fr, Carduelis spinus. 200fr, Turdus torquatus. 270fr, Parus cristatus. 300fr, Nucifraga caryocatactes. 400fr, Luscinia megarhynchos.
1000fr, Motacilla flava.

1997, July 30   Perf. 13x12½
994	A284	135fr	multicolored	.45	.45
995	A284	150fr	multicolored	.50	.50
996	A284	200fr	multicolored	.70	.70
997	A284	270fr	multicolored	.90	.90
998	A284	300fr	multicolored	1.00	1.00
999	A284	400fr	multicolored	1.40	1.40
	Nos. 994-999 (6)			4.95	4.95

Souvenir Sheet
Perf. 12½
1000 A284 1000fr multicolored 3.40 3.40

No. 1000 contains one 32x40mm stamp.

Flowering Cactus — A285

Designs: 135fr, Faucaria lupina. 150fr, Conophytum bilobun. 200fr, Lithops aucampiae. 270fr, Lithops helmutii. 300fr, Stapelia grandiflora. 400fr, Lithops fulviceps.
1000fr, Pleiospilos willowmorensis.

1997, Aug. 30   Litho.   Perf. 13x12½
1001	A285	135fr	multicolored	.45	.45
1002	A285	150fr	multicolored	.50	.50
1003	A285	200fr	multicolored	.70	.70
1004	A285	270fr	multicolored	.90	.90
1005	A285	300fr	multicolored	1.00	1.00
1006	A285	400fr	multicolored	1.25	1.25
	Nos. 1001-1006 (6)			4.80	4.80

Souvenir Sheet
Perf. 12½
1007 A285 1000fr multicolored 3.40 3.40

No. 1007 contains one 32x40mm stamp.

Benin No. 418 Surcharged

1995
Perfs. & Printing Methods as Before
1009 A114 10fr on 90fr #418

Benin Nos. 813, 948 Surcharged
Printing Methods and Perfs as before

1997-99 (?)
1021A A256 135fr on 100fr #948
1021B A260 135fr on 200fr #813

Early Locomotives — A286

Designs: 135fr, Puffing Billy, 1813. 150fr, La Fusée, 1829. 200fr, Royal George, 1827. 270fr, Nouveauté, 1829. 300fr, Locomotion, 1825, vert. 400fr, Sans Pareil, 1829, vert.
1000fr, Trevithick locomotive.

1997, Dec. 3   Litho.   Perf. 13
1022	A286	135fr	multicolored	.45	.45
1023	A286	150fr	multicolored	.50	.50
1024	A286	200fr	multicolored	.70	.70
1025	A286	270fr	multicolored	.95	.95
1026	A286	300fr	multicolored	1.00	1.00
1027	A286	400fr	multicolored	1.40	1.40
	Nos. 1022-1027 (6)			5.00	5.00

Souvenir Sheet
1028 A286 1000fr multicolored 3.50 3.50

No. 1028 contains one 40x32mm stamp.

Mushrooms
A287

Designs: 135fr, Amanita caesarea. 150fr, Cortinarius collinitus. 200fr, Amanita bisporigera. 270fr, Amanita rubescens. 300fr, Russula virescens. 400fr, Amanita inaurata.
1000fr, Amanita muscaria.

1997, Nov. 5   Litho.   Perf. 13
1029	A287	135fr	multicolored	.40	.40
1030	A287	150fr	multicolored	.55	.55
1031	A287	200fr	multicolored	.70	.70
1032	A287	270fr	multicolored	.95	.95
1033	A287	300fr	multicolored	1.00	1.00
1034	A287	400fr	multicolored	1.40	1.40
	Nos. 1029-1034 (6)			5.00	5.00

Souvenir Sheet
1035 A287 1000fr multicolored 3.50 3.50

No. 1035 contains one 32x40mm stamp.

Assoc. of African Petroleum Producers, 10th Anniv. — A288

1997, Oct. 20   Litho.   Perf. 13
1036	A288	135fr	green & multi		
1037	A288	200fr	orange & multi		
1038	A288	300fr	blue & multi		
1039	A288	500fr	yellow & multi	1.75	1.75

Old Sailing Vessels — A289

Designs: 135fr, Egyptian. 150fr, Greek. 200fr, Assyrian-Phoenician. 270fr, Roman. 300fr, Norman. 400fr, Mediterranean.
1000fr, English.

1997, Sept. 10   Litho.   Perf. 12½
1040	A289	135fr	multicolored	.50	.50
1041	A289	150fr	multicolored	.55	.55
1042	A289	200fr	multicolored	.75	.75
1043	A289	270fr	multicolored	1.00	1.00
1044	A289	300fr	multicolored	1.10	1.10
1045	A289	400fr	multicolored	1.50	1.50
	Nos. 1040-1045 (6)			5.40	5.40

Souvenir Sheet
1046 A289 1000fr multicolored 3.75 3.75

No. 1046 contains one 32x40mm stamp.

Fish
A290

Designs: 135fr, Epinephelus fasciatus. 150fr, Apogon victoriae. 200fr, Scarus gibbus. 270fr, Pygoplites diacanthus. 300fr, Cirrhilabrus punctatus. 400fr, Cirrhitichthys oxycephalus.
1000fr, Bodianus bilunulatus.

1997, Sept. 15   Litho.   Perf. 12½
1047	A290	135fr	multicolored	.50	.50
1048	A290	150fr	multicolored	.55	.55
1049	A290	200fr	multicolored	.75	.75
1050	A290	270fr	multicolored	1.00	1.00
1051	A290	300fr	multicolored	1.10	1.10
1052	A290	400fr	multicolored	1.50	1.50
	Nos. 1047-1052 (6)			5.40	5.40

Souvenir Sheet
Perf. 13
1053 A290 1000fr multicolored 3.75 3.75

No. 1053 contains one 40x32mm stamp.

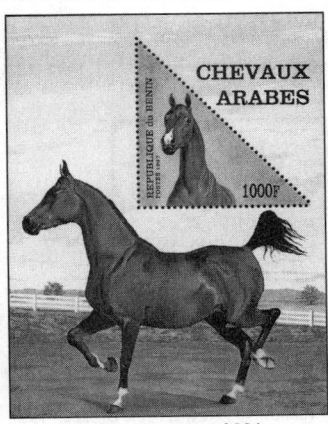

Arabian Horse — A291

Various horses. Denominations and background colors: d, 135fr, green. e, 150fr, red brown. f, 200fr, yellow. g, 270fr, orange brown. h, 300fr, tan. i, 400fr, olive green.

1997, May 25		**Litho.**	**Perf. 12½**	
1053A	A291	Pair, #d.-e.	1.00	1.00
1053B	A291	Pair, #f.-g.	1.60	1.60
1053C	A291	Pair, #h.-i.	2.50	2.50
		Nos. 1053A-1053C (3)	5.10	5.10

Souvenir Sheet

1054	A291	1000fr multicolored	3.50	3.50

Mushrooms A292

135fr, Tephrocybe carbonaria. 150fr, Suillus luteus. 200fr, Pleurotus ostreatus. 270fr, Hohenbuehelia geogenia. 300fr, Tylopilus felleus. 400fr, Lepiota leucothites. 1000fr, Gymnopilus junonius.

1998, Apr. 28		**Litho.**	**Perf. 12½**	
1055	A292	135fr multicolored	.45	.45
1056	A292	150fr multicolored	.50	.50
1057	A292	200fr multicolored	.65	.65
1058	A292	270fr multicolored	.90	.90
1059	A292	300fr multicolored	1.00	1.00
1060	A292	400fr multicolored	1.40	1.40
		Nos. 1055-1060 (6)	4.90	4.90

Souvenir Sheet

1061	A292	1000fr multicolored	3.50	3.50

No. 632 Surcharged

1998	**Method and Perf. as Before**		
1061F	A195(h) 150fr on 205fr		
	#632		

Fire Fighting Apparatus — A293

135fr, Philadelphia Double Deck, 1885. 150fr, Veteran, 1850. 200fr, Merry Weather, 1894. 270fr, Horse-drawn wagon, 19th cent. 300fr, 1948 Jeep. 400fr, Chevrolet 6400. 1000fr, 1952 American-La France-Foamite Corp.

1998, Apr. 30		**Litho.**	**Perf. 12¾**	
1062	A293	135fr multicolored	.45	.45
1063	A293	150fr multicolored	.50	.50
1064	A293	200fr multicolored	.65	.65
1065	A293	270fr multicolored	.90	.90
1066	A293	300fr multicolored	1.00	1.00
1067	A293	400fr multicolored	1.40	1.40
		Nos. 1062-1067 (6)	4.90	4.90

Souvenir Sheet

1068	A293	1000fr multicolored	3.50	3.50

No. 1068 contains one 40x32mm stamp.

Minerals — A294

#1069a, 135fr, Uranifere. #1069b, 150fr, Quartz. #1070a, 200fr, Aragonite. #1070b, 270fr, Malachite. #1071a, 300fr, Turquoise. #1071b, 400fr, Corundum. 1000fr, Marble.

1998, June 5		**Litho.**	**Perf. 12½**	
1069	A294	Pair, #a.-b.	1.00	1.00
1070	A294	Pair, #a.-b.	1.60	1.60
1071	A294	Pair, #a.-b.	2.50	2.50
		Nos. 1069-1071 (3)	5.10	5.10

Souvenir Sheet

1072	A294	1000fr multicolored	3.50	3.50

Locomotives — A295

Designs: 135fr, Red 0-6-0. 150fr, 0-4-4. 200fr, Brown 0-6-0. 270fr, Purple 0-6-0. 300fr, Blue 0-6-0. 1000fr, "Helvetia" 0-6-0. 1000fr, "Shelby Steel" 0-6-0.

1998, June 30		**Litho.**	**Perf. 12¾**	
1073	A295	135fr multicolored	.45	.45
1074	A295	150fr multicolored	.50	.50
1075	A295	200fr multicolored	.65	.65
1076	A295	270fr multicolored	.90	.90
1077	A295	300fr multicolored	1.00	1.00
1078	A295	400fr multicolored	1.40	1.40
		Nos. 1073-1078 (6)	4.90	4.90

Souvenir Sheet

Perf. 13

1079	A295	1000fr multicolored	3.50	3.50

No. 1079 contains one 40x32mm stamp.

Diana, Princess of Wales (1961-97) — A296

Portraits: a, 135fr. b, 150fr. c, 200fr. d, 270fr. e, 300fr. f, 400fr. g, 500fr. h, 600fr. i, 700fr.

1998, July 10		**Litho.**	**Perf. 12½**	
1083	A296	Sheet of 9, #a.-i.	11.50	11.50

Dahomey No. 302 Surcharged

1997?

Perfs. & Printing Method as Before

1084	A65(h) 35fr on 85fr #302	

Dinosaurs — A297

No. 1085: a, 135fr, Sordes. b, 150fr, Scaphognatus. c, 200fr, Dsungaripterus. d, 270fr, Brontosaurus. e, 300fr, Diplodocus. f, 400fr, Coelurus, Baryonyx. g, 500fr, Kronosaurus, Ichthyosaurus. h, 600fr, Ceratosaurus. i, 700f, Yangchuansaurus.

1998, July 25		**Litho.**	**Perf. 12¾**	
1085	A297	Sheet of 9, #a-i	9.50	9.50

Python Regius A298

Various views of python: a, 135fr. b, 150fr. c, 200fr. d, 2000fr.

1999, Apr. 27		**Litho.**	**Perf. 13**	
1086	A298	Strip of 4, #a.-d.	8.75	8.75

World Wildlife Fund.

Dogs — A299

1998, July 31		**Litho.**	**Perf. 12¾**	
1087	A299	135fr Beagle	.40	.40
1088	A299	150fr Dalmatian	.45	.45
1089	A299	200fr Dachshund	.60	.60
1090	A299	270fr Cairn terrier	.80	.80
1091	A299	300fr Shih Tzu	.85	.85
1092	A299	400fr Pug	1.10	1.10
		Nos. 1087-1092 (6)	4.20	4.20

Souvenir Sheet

Perf. 13

1093	A299	1000fr Springer spaniel, horiz.	3.00	3.00

No. 1093 contains one 40x32mm stamp.

Cats A300

135fr, Abyssinian. 150fr, Striped shorthair. 200fr, Siamese. 270fr, Red striped cat. 300fr, Gray cat with black stripes. 400fr, Manx. 1000fr, Cat with orange, black and white fur.

Perf. 12¼x12½, 12½x12¼

1998, Aug. 10			**Litho.**	
1094	A300	135fr multi, vert.	.45	.45
1095	A300	150fr multi, vert.	.50	.50
1096	A300	200fr multi, vert.	.65	.65
1097	A300	270fr multi	.90	.90
1098	A300	300fr multi	1.00	1.00
1099	A300	400fr multi	1.25	1.25
		Nos. 1094-1099 (6)	4.75	4.75

Souvenir Sheet

Perf. 13

1100	A300	1000fr multicolored	3.25	3.25

No. 1100 contains one 40x32mm stamp.

Antique Automobiles — 1101

Designs: 135fr, 1910 Bugatti 13. 150fr, 1903 Clément. 200fr, 1914 Stutz Bearcat. 270fr, 1907 Darracq. 300fr, 1913 Napier. 400fr, 1911 Pierce-Arrow. 1000fr, 1904 Piccolo, vert.

1998, Oct. 12			**Perf. 12¾**	
1101	A301	135fr multi	.40	.40
1102	A301	150fr multi	.45	.45
1103	A301	200fr multi	.60	.60
1104	A301	270fr multi	.80	.80
1105	A301	300fr multi	.85	.85
1106	A301	400fr multi	1.10	1.10
		Nos. 1101-1106 (6)	4.20	4.20

Souvenir Sheet

Perf. 12¾x12½

1107	A301	1000fr multi	3.00	3.00

No. 1107 contains one 32x40mm stamp.

Butterflies A301a

Designs: 135fr, Parnassius apollo. 150fr, Anthocharis cardamines. 200fr, Nymphalis antiopa. 250fr, Parage aegeria. 300fr, Palaeochrysophanus hippothoe. 400fr, Carterocephalus palaemon. 1000fr, Aglais urticae.

1998, Dec. 10		**Litho.**	**Perf. 12¾**	
1107A-1107F	A301a	Set of 6	3.75	3.75

Souvenir Sheet

Perf. 13

1107G	A301a	1000fr multi	2.50	2.50

No. 1107G contains one 40x32mm stamp.

African Wildlife — A302

Designs: 50fr, Ceratotherium simun. 100fr, Hipotragus niger. No. 1110, Phacochoerus aethiopicus. No. 1111, Hyaena brunnea. No. 1112, Colobus guereza. No. 1113, Hippopotamus amphibius. No. 1114, Cyncerus caffer caffer. No. 1115, Equus zebra. No. 1116, Acinonyx jubatus. No. 1117, Panthera leo leo. 400fr, Lycaon pictus. 500fr, Perodicticus potto.

Perf. 12¼x12½

1999, Mar. 10			**Litho.**	
1108	A302	50fr gray	.20	.20
1109	A302	100fr brt violet	.35	.35
1110	A302	135fr gray green	.45	.45
1111	A302	135fr black	.45	.45
1112	A302	150fr gray blue	.50	.50
1113	A302	150fr emerald	.50	.50
1114	A302	200fr dull brown	.65	.65
1115	A302	200fr blue	.65	.65
1116	A302	300fr henna brown	1.00	1.00
1117	A302	300fr brown	1.00	1.00
1118	A302	400fr red brown	1.40	1.40
1119	A302	500fr deep bister	1.60	1.60
		Nos. 1108-1119 (12)	8.75	8.75

Birds — A303

Designs: 135fr, Chloebia gouldiae. 150fr, Sicalis flaveola. 200fr, Quelea quelea. 270fr, Euplectes afer. 300fr, Paroaria coronata. 400fr, Emberiza flaviventris. 1000fr, Mandingoa nitidula.

1999, Jan. 30   Litho.   *Perf. 12¾*
1120-1125 A303   Set of 6   3.75   3.75

Souvenir Sheet
Perf. 12½
1126 A303 1000fr multi   2.60   2.60
No. 1126 contains one 32x40mm stamp.

Orchids
A304

Designs: 50fr, Brassocattleya cliftonii. 100fr, Wilsonara. 150fr, Cypripedium paeony. 300fr, Cymbidium babylon. 400fr, Cattleya. 500fr, Miltonia minx.

1999, Apr. 25   Litho.   *Perf. 12¾*
1127 A304   50fr multi   .20   .20
1128 A304   100fr multi   .35   .35
1129 A304   150fr multi   .50   .50
1130 A304   300fr multi   1.00   1.00
1131 A304   400fr multi   1.40   1.40
1132 A304   500fr multi   1.60   1.60
Nos. 1127-1132 (6)   5.05   5.05

Souvenir Sheet
Perf. 13
1133 A304 1000fr Miltonia (isis)   3.25   3.25
No. 1133 contains one 28x36mm stamp.

Chess Players
A305

Designs: 135fr, Mikhail Tal. 150fr, Emanuel Lasker. 200fr, José Raul Capablanca. 270fr, Alexander Alekhine. 300fr, Max Euwe. 400fr, Mikhail Botvinnik. 1000fr, Wilhelm Steinitz.

1999, Mar. 28   Litho.   *Perf. 12¾*
1134-1139 A305   Set of 6   3.75   3.75

Souvenir Sheet
Perf. 13
1140 A305 1000fr multi   2.60   2.60
No. 1140 contains one 32x40mm stamp.

Ancient
Sailing
Ships
A306

Designs: 135fr, Ceylonese canot. 150fr, Tanka-tim. 200fr, Sampan. 270fr, Polynesian canot. 300fr, Japanese junk. 400fr, Dacca-pulwar. 1000fr, Chinese junk.

1999, Feb. 15   Litho.   *Perf. 12¾*
1141-1146 A306   Set of 6   3.75   3.75

Souvenir Sheet
Perf. 12½
1147 A306 1000fr multi   2.50   2.50
No. 1147 contains one 40x32mm stamp.

Fish -
A307

Designs: 135fr, Notopterus chitala. 150fr, Puntius filamentosus. 200fr, Epaizeorhynchos bicolor. 270fr, Rasbora maculata. 300fr, Pristolepis fasciatus. 400fr, Betta splendens. 1000fr, Trichogaster trichopterus.

1999, May 10   Litho.   *Perf. 12½x12¼*
1148   A307   135fr multi
1149   A307   150fr multi
1150   A307   200fr multi
1151   A307   270fr multi
1152   A307   300fr multi
1153   A307   400fr multi

Souvenir Sheet
Perf. 13x13¼
1154   A307 1000fr multi
No. 1154 contains one 40x32mm stamp.

Grand Prix de
l'Amitie — A308

1999   Litho.   *Perf. 13½x13*
1155   A308   150fr multi
1156   A308   200fr multi
1157   A308   300fr multi
1157A   A308   500fr multi
The editors would like to examine any additional stamps that may have been issued in this set.

Grand Prix de l'Amitie Type of 1999
1999   Litho.   *Perf. 13½x13*
1158   A308 1000fr multi
Numbers have been reserved for two additional stamps in this set. The editors would like to examine any examples.

Early Steam
Vehicles
A309

Designs: 135fr, 1786 tricycle made by A. Murdock. 150fr, 1800 locomotive made by Richard Trevithick. 200fr, 1803 locomotive made by Trevithick. 270fr, 1811 locomotive made by John Blenkinsop. 300fr, 1829 locomotive, Stourbridge Lion. 400fr, 1830 locomotive, Tom Thumb. 1000fr, 1760 locomotive made by Isaac Newton, horiz.

1999, June 18   Litho.   *Perf. 12¾*
1159-1164 A309   Set of 6   3.75   3.75

Souvenir Sheet
Perf. 13
1165 A309 1000fr multi   2.50   2.50
No. 1165 contains one 40x32 mm stamp.

Council of
the
Entente,
40th Anniv.
A310

1999   Litho.   *Perf. 13x13½*
1167 A310   150fr multi
1168 A310   200fr multi
The editors suspect other stamps in this set have been issued and would like to examine them.

block>

Snakes
A311

Designs: 135fr, Elaphe longissima. 150fr, Pituophis melanoleucus. 200fr, Natrix natrix. 270fr, Oxybelis fulgidus. 300fr, Epicrates subflavus. 400fr, Crotalus atrox. 1000fr, Vipera berus.

1999, July 18   Litho.   *Perf. 12¾*
1170-1175 A311   Set of 6   3.75   3.75

Souvenir Sheet
Perf. 13
1176 A311 1000fr multi   2.60   2.60
No. 1176 contains one 40x32mm stamp.

China 1999 World Philatelic
Exhibition — A312

No. 1177: a, 50fr, Rocket testing, 14th cent. b, 100fr, Jiuquan space launch center. c, 135fr, DFH-3 communications satellite. d, 150fr, Launch of a foreign satellite. e, 200fr, Long March rocket CZ-2C. f, 300fr, Ship Yuan Wang. g, 400fr, Satellite dish. h, 500fr, Cacheted stamped covers.

1999, Aug. 22   *Perf. 12½*
1177 A312   Sheet of 8, #a-h   5.75   5.75

SOS Children's Villages, 50th
Anniv. — A313

Denominations and panel colors: 135fr, Light green. 200fr, Pink. 300fr, Light blue. 500fr, Yellow.

1999, Oct. 15   Litho.   *Perf. 12¾*
1178-1181 A313   Set of 4   3.50   3.50
For No. 1180 surcharge see No. 1208.

Souvenir Sheet

Manchester United, 1999 English
Soccer Champions — A314

No. 1182: a, 135fr, Players celebrating on platform. b, 200fr, Players in action. c, 300fr,

Players celebrating. d, 400fr, Stadium. e, 500fr, Trophies. f, 1000fr, Player with trophy.

1999, Oct. 15   *Perf. 13¼*
1182 A314   Sheet of 6, #a-f
          7.75   7.75

New Year
2000 (Year
of the
Dragon)
A315

Various dragons with frame colors of: 135fr, Buff. 150fr, Blue green. 200fr, Tan. 270fr, Pink. 300fr, Blue. 400fr, Light green. 1000fr, Lilac.

2000   *Perf. 12¾x12½*
1183-1188 A315   Set of 6   4.25   4.25

Souvenir Sheet
Perf. 12½
1189 A315 1000fr multi   3.00   3.00
No. 1189 contains one 28x36mm stamp.

Wild
Cats
A316

Designs: 135fr, Acinonyx jubatus. 150fr, Panthera onca. 200fr, Panthera uncia. 270fr, Panthera pardus. 300fr, Felis concolor. 400fr, Panthera tigris. 1000fr, Panthera leo.

Perf. 12½x12¼
1999, Sept. 28   Litho.
1190-1195 A316   Set of 6   3.75   3.75

Souvenir Sheet
1196 A316 1000fr multi   2.60   2.60

Cacti — A317

Designs: 135fr, Mammillaria lenta. 150fr, Oehmea nelsonii. 200fr, Neobesseya rosiflora. 270fr, Opuntia gosseliniana. 300fr, Parodia nivosa. 400fr, Rebutia senilis. 1000fr, Opuntia retrorsa, vert. Illustration reduced.

1999, Oct. 10   Litho.   *Perf. 12¼*
1197-1202 A317   Set of 6   3.75   3.75

Souvenir Sheet
Perf. 12½
1203 A317 1000fr multi   2.50   2.50
No. 1203 contains one 32x40mm rectangular stamp.

Birds
A318

No. 1204: a, 135fr, Estrilda locustella. b, 150fr, Estrilda melanotis.
No. 1205: a, 200fr, Pytelia melba. b, 270fr, Uraeginthus bengalensis.
No. 1206: a, 300fr, Pyromelana orix. b, 400fr, Ploceus cucullatus.
1000fr, Steganura paradisea.

1999, Dec. 7   Litho.   Perf. 12¼
Pairs, #a-b
1204-1206 A318   Set of 3   3.75 3.75
Souvenir Sheet
1207 A318 1000fr multi   2.60 2.60

No. 1180 Surcharged
Method and Perf. as Before
2000 ?
1208 A313 135fr on 300fr #1180

Nos. 850, 873 Surcharged
Methods and Perfs. as Before
2000 ?
1209 A267 135fr on 40fr #850
1210 A271 150fr on 75fr #873

Dogs — A319

Designs: 135fr, Alaskan malamute. 150fr, Shar-pei. 200fr, Boston terrier. 270fr, Pug. 300fr, St. Bernard. 400fr, Siberian husky. 1000fr, Golden retriever.

2000   Litho.   Perf. 12¾
1211-1216 A319   Set of 6   3.75 3.75
Souvenir Sheet
Perf. 12½
1217 A319 1000fr multi   2.50 2.50
No. 1217 contains one 32x40mm stamp.

AIR POST STAMPS
PEOPLE'S REPUBLIC

Catalogue values for unused stamps in this section are for Never Hinged items.

Nativity, by Aert van Leyden — AP84

Christmas: 85fr, Adoration of the Kings, by Rubens, vert. 140fr, Adoration of the Shepherds, by Charles Lebrun. 300fr, The Virgin with the Blue Diadem, by Raphael, vert.

1975, Dec. 19   Litho.   Perf. 13
C240 AP84 40fr gold & multi   .20 .20
C241 AP84 85fr gold & multi   .40 .20
C242 AP84 140fr gold & multi   .60 .25
C243 AP84 300fr gold & multi   1.40 .65
  Nos. C240-C243 (4)   2.60 1.30
For surcharges see Nos. C362, C367, C407, C432.

Slalom, Innsbruck Olympic Emblem — AP85

Innsbruck Olympic Games Emblem and: 150fr, Bobsledding, vert. 300fr, Figure skating, pairs.

1976, June 28   Litho.   Perf. 12½
C244 AP85 60fr multi   .25 .20
C245 AP85 150fr multi   .65 .25
C246 AP85 300fr multi   1.25 .55
  Nos. C244-C246 (3)   2.15 1.00
12th Winter Olympic Games, Innsbruck, Austria, Feb. 4-15.

Dahomey Nos. C263-C265
Overprinted or Surcharged:
"POPULAIRE / DU BENIN" and Bars
1976, July 4   Engr.   Perf. 13
C247 AP86 135fr multi   .55 .25
C248 AP86 210fr on 300fr multi   .90 .35
C249 AP86 380fr on 500fr multi 1.50 .65
  Nos. C247-C249 (3)   2.95 1.25
The overprint includes a bar covering "DU DAHOMEY" in shades of brown; "POPULAIRE DU BENIN" is blue on Nos. C247-C248, red on No. C249. The surcharge and bars over old value are blue on No. C248, red, brown on No. C249.

Long Jump
AP86

Designs (Olympic Rings and): 150fr, Basketball, vert. 200fr, Hurdles.

1976, July 16   Photo.   Perf. 13
C250 AP86 60fr multi   .30 .20
C251 AP86 150fr multi   .85 .30
C252 AP86 200fr multi   1.25 .45
  a. Souv. sheet of 3, #C250-C252   3.00 3.00
  Nos. C250-C252 (3)   2.40 .95
21st Olympic Games, Montreal, Canada, July 17-Aug 1.

Konrad Adenauer and Cologne Cathedral — AP87

Design: 90fr, Konrad Adenauer, vert.

1976, Aug. 27   Engr.   Perf. 13
C253 AP87 90fr multi   .60 .25
C254 AP87 250fr multi   1.75 .70
Konrad Adenauer (1876-1967), German Chancellor, birth centenary.
For surcharge see No. C289B.

Children's Heads and Flying Fish
(Dahomey Type A32) — AP88

210fr, Lion cub's head, Benin design A3, vert.

1976, Sept. 13
C255 AP88 60fr Prus bl & vio bl .35 .20
C256 AP88 210fr multi   1.10 .45
JUVAROUEN 76, Intl. Youth Phil. Exhib., Rouen, France, Apr. 25-May 2.
For surcharges see Nos. C300, C494.

Apollo 14
Emblem and
Blast-off — AP89

270fr, Landing craft and man on moon.

1976, Oct. 18   Engr.   Perf. 13
C257 AP89 130fr multi   .45 .30
C258 AP89 270fr multi   1.00 .65
Apollo 14 Moon Mission, 5th anniversary.
For surcharges see Nos. C312, C454.

Annunciation, by Master of Jativa — AP90

Christmas: 60fr, Nativity, by Gerard David. 270fr, Adoration of the Kings, Dutch School. 300fr, Flight into Egypt, by Gentile Fabriano, horiz.

1976, Dec. 20   Litho.   Perf. 12½
C259 AP90 50fr gold & multi   .25 .20
C260 AP90 60fr gold & multi   .35 .20
C261 AP90 270fr gold & multi   1.50 .60
C262 AP90 300fr gold & multi   1.60 1.00
  Nos. C259-C262 (4)   3.70 2.00
For surcharges see Nos. C310, C321, C484.

Gamblers and Lottery
Emblem — AP91

1977, Mar. 13   Litho.   Perf. 13
C263 AP91 50fr multi   .25 .20
National lottery, 10th anniversary.

Sassenage Castle, Grenoble — AP92

1977, May 16   Perf. 12½
C264 AP92 200fr multi   .80 .60
10th anniv. of Intl. French Language Council.
For surcharge see No. C334.

Concorde, Supersonic Plane — AP93

Designs: 150fr, Zeppelin. 300fr, Charles A. Lindbergh and Spirit of St. Louis. 500fr, Charles Nungesser and François Coli, French aviators lost over Atlantic, 1927.

1977, July 25   Engr.   Perf. 13
C265 AP93 80fr ultra & red   .40 .35
C266 AP93 150fr multi   .80 .60
C267 AP93 300fr multi   1.60 1.25
C268 AP93 500fr multi   2.50 2.00
  Nos. C265-C268 (4)   5.30 4.20
Aviation history.
For overprint and surcharges see Nos. C274, C316, C336.

Soccer Player — AP94

200fr, Soccer players and Games' emblem.

1977, July 28   Litho.   Perf. 12½x12
C269 AP94 60fr multi   .35 .20
C270 AP94 200fr multi   1.10 .80
World Soccer Cup elimination games.
For surcharges see Nos. C289A, C308.

Miss Haverfield, by Gainsborough — AP95

Designs: 150fr, Self-portrait, by Rubens. 200fr, Anguish, man's head by Da Vinci.

1977, Oct. 3   Engr.   Perf. 13
C271 AP95 100fr sl grn & mar   .55 .40
C272 AP95 150fr red brn & dk brn .80 .60
C273 AP95 200fr brn & red   1.10 .80
  Nos. C271-C273 (3)   2.45 1.80
For surcharges see Nos. C309, C317.

No. C265 Overprinted: "1er VOL COMMERCIAL / 22.11.77 PARIS NEW-YORK"

1977, Nov. 22   Engr.   Perf. 13
C274 AP93 80fr ultra & red   .40 .35
Concorde, 1st commercial flight, Paris to NY.

Viking on Mars — AP96

150fr, Isaac Newton, apple globe, stars. 200fr, Vladimir M. Komarov, spacecraft and earth. 500fr, Dog Laika, rocket and space.

1977, Nov. 28   Perf. 13
C275 AP96 100fr multi   .55 .40
C276 AP96 150fr multi   .80 .60
C277 AP96 200fr multi   1.10 .80
C278 AP96 500fr multi   2.75 2.00
    Nos. C275-C278 (4)   5.20 3.80
Operation Viking on Mars; Isaac Newton (1642-1727); 10th death anniv. of Russian cosmonaut Vladimir M. Komarov; 20th anniv. of 1st living creature in space.
For surcharges see Nos. C301, C314.

Monument, Red Star Place, Cotonou AP97

Lithographed; Gold Embossed
1977 Nov. 30   Perf. 12½
C279 AP97 500fr multi   1.75 1.10

Suzanne Fourment, by Rubens AP98

380fr, Nicholas Rubens, by Rubens.

1977, Dec. 12   Engr.   Perf. 13
C280 AP98 200fr multi   1.10 .80
C281 AP98 380fr claret & ocher 2.00 1.40
For surcharges see Nos. C311, C313, C483.

Parthenon and UNESCO Emblem — AP99

Designs: 70fr, Acropolis and frieze showing Pan-Athenaic procession, vert. 250fr, Parthenon and frieze showing horsemen, vert.

1978, Sept. 22   Litho.   Perf. 12½x12
C282 AP99 70fr multi   .35 .20
C283 AP99 250fr multi   1.25 .80
C284 AP99 500fr multi   2.75 1.50
    Nos. C282-C284 (3)   4.35 2.50
Save the Parthenon in Athens campaign.
For surcharge see No. C338.

Philexafrique II—Essen Issue
Common Design Types
Designs: No. C285, Buffalo and Dahomey #C33. No. C286, Wild ducks and Baden #1.

1978, Nov. 1   Litho.   Perf. 12½
C285 CD138 100fr multi   .65 .40
C286 CD139 100fr multi   .65 .40
a.   Pair, #C285-C286   1.30 1.00

Wilbur and Orville Wright and Flyer — AP100

1978, Dec. 28   Engr.   Perf. 13
C287 AP100 500fr multi   3.50 2.00
75th anniversary of 1st powered flight.
For surcharge see No. C339.

Cook's Ships, Hawaii, World Map — AP101

Design: 50fr, Battle at Kowrowa.

1979, June 1   Engr.   Perf. 13
C288 AP101 20fr multi   .20 .20
C289 AP101 50fr multi   .45 .45
Capt. James Cook (1728-1779), explorer.

No. C253, C269 Surcharged

1979
Perfs. & Printing Method as Before
C289A AP94 50fr on 60fr #C269
C289B AP87 50fr on 90fr multi

Lunokhod Type of 1980
1980, June 15   Engr.   Perf. 13
    Size: 27x48mm
C290 A133 210fr multi   1.40 1.40
For surcharges see Nos. C305, C450.

Soccer Players — AP102

1981, Mar. 31   Litho.   Perf. 13
C291 AP102 200fr Ball, globe .90 .90
C292 AP102 500fr shown   2.50 2.50
ESPANA '82 World Soccer Cup eliminations.
    For surcharges see Nos. C335, C455, Q10B.

Prince Charles and Lady Diana, London Bridge — AP103

1981, July 29   Litho.   Perf. 12½
C293 AP103 500fr multi   3.00 3.00
Royal wedding.
For surcharges see Nos. C323, C500.

Three Musicians, by Pablo Picasso (1881-1973) — AP104

Perf. 12½x13, 13x12½
1981, Nov. 2   Litho.
C294 AP104 300fr Dance, vert. 2.00 2.00
C295 AP104 500fr shown   3.50 3.50
For surcharges see Nos. C320, C340.

1300th Anniv. of Bulgaria AP105

1981, Dec. 2   Litho.   Perf. 13
C296 AP105 100fr multi   .60 .60

Visit of Pope John Paul II — AP106

1982, Feb. 17   Litho.   Perf. 13
C297 AP106 80fr multi   .55 .55

20th Anniv. of John Glenn's Flight — AP107

1982, Feb. 21   Litho.   Perf. 13
C298 AP107 500fr multi   3.00 3.00
For surcharge see No. C315.

Scouting Year AP108

1982, June 1   Perf. 12½
C299 AP108 105fr multi   .70 .70
For surcharge see No. C324.

Nos. C256, C275 Surcharged
1982, Nov.   Engr.   Perf. 13
C300 AP88 50fr on 210fr multi .35 .35
C301 AP96 50fr on 100fr multi .35 .35

Monet in Boat, by Claude Monet (1832-1883) — AP109

1982, Dec. 6   Litho.   Perf. 13x12½
C302 AP109 300fr multi   2.00 2.00
For surcharge see No. C326.

Christmas 1982 AP110

Virgin and Child Paintings.

1982, Dec. 20   Perf. 12½x13
C303 AP110 200fr Matthias Grunewald 1.25 1.25
C304 AP110 300fr Correggio   1.75 1.75
For surcharges see Nos. C325, C337.

No. C290 Surcharged
1983   Engr.   Perf. 13
C305 A133 75fr on 210fr multi .50 .50

Bangkok '83 Stamp Exhibition AP111

1983, Aug. 4   Photo.   Perf. 13
C306 AP111 300fr multi   1.50 1.50
For surcharge see No. C322.

Christmas 1983 AP112

1983, Dec. 26   Litho.   *Perf. 12½x13*
C307 AP112 200fr Loretto Madonna, by Raphael .65 .65
For surcharge see No. C319.

Types of 1976-82 Surcharged
1983, Nov.
C308 AP94 10fr on 200fr C270 .20 .20
C309 AP95 15fr on 200fr C273 .20 .20
C310 AP90 15fr on 270fr C261 .20 .20
C311 AP98 20fr on 200fr C280 .20 .20
C312 AP89 25fr on 270fr C258 .20 .20
C313 AP96 25fr on 200fr C277 .20 .20
C314 AP96 30fr on 200fr C277 .20 .20
C315 AP107 40fr on 500fr C298 .20 .20
C316 AP93 75fr on 150fr C266 .40 .40
C317 AP95 75fr on 150fr C272 .40 .40
Nos. C308-C317 (10) 2.40 2.40

Summer Olympics — AP113

1984, July 16   Litho.   *Perf. 13x13½*
C318 AP113 300fr Sam the Eagle, mascot 1.00 1.00

Nos. C262, C293-C294, C299, C302-C303, C306-C307 Surcharged
1984, Sept.
C319 AP112 15fr on 200fr multi .20 .20
C320 AP104 15fr on 300fr multi .20 .20
C321 AP90 25fr on 300fr multi .20 .20
C322 AP111 25fr on 300fr multi .20 .20
C323 AP103 40fr on 500fr multi .20 .20
C324 AP108 75fr on 105fr multi .25 .25
C325 AP110 90fr on 200fr multi .30 .30
C326 AP109 90fr on 300fr multi .30 .30
Nos. C319-C326 (8) 1.85 1.85

Christmas 1984 AP114

1984, Dec. 17   Litho.   *Perf. 12½x13*
C327 AP114 500fr Virgin and Child, by Murillo 1.50 1.50
For surcharge see No. C486.

Ships — AP115

1984, Dec. 28   Litho.   *Perf. 13*
C328 AP115 90fr Sidon merchant ship .30 .30
C329 AP115 125fr Wavertree, vert. .40 .40

Benin-S.O.M. Postal Convention AP116

Wmk. 385
1985, Apr. 15   Litho.   *Perf. 13½*
C330 AP116 75fr Benin arms .25 .25
C331 AP116 75fr Sovereign Order of Malta .25 .25
a. Pair, #C330-C331 .45 .45

PHILEXAFRICA III, Lome — AP117

1985, June 24   *Perf. 13*
C332 AP117 200fr Oil platform .60 .60
C333 AP117 200fr Soccer players .60 .60
a. Pair, #C332-C333 + label 1.25 1.25
For surcharges see Nos. C485-C485A.

Stamps of 1977-82 Surcharged
1985, Mar.
C334 AP92 75fr on 200fr #C264 .20 .20
C335 AP102 75fr on 200fr #C291 .20 .20
C336 AP93 75fr on 300fr #C267 .20 .20
C337 AP110 75fr on 300fr #C304 .20 .20
C338 AP99 90fr on 500fr #C284 .25 .25
C339 AP100 90fr on 500fr #C287 .25 .25
C340 AP104 90fr on 500fr #C295 .25 .25
Nos. C334-C340 (7) 1.55 1.55

Dahomey Stamps of 1971-75 Surcharged
1985, Aug.
C341 AP87(i) 25fr on 40fr #C266 .20 .20
C342 AP49(a) 40fr #C142 .20 .20
C343 AP56(i) 75fr on 85fr #C164 .20 .20
C344 AP60(a) 75fr on 100fr #C173 .20 .20
C345 AP64(i) 75fr on 125fr #C186 .20 .20
C346 AP56(i) 90fr on 20fr #C163 .25 .25
C347 A61(i) 90fr on 150fr #C153 .25 .25
C348 AP49(a) 90fr on 200fr #C143 .25 .25
C349 AP78(j) 90fr on 200fr #C237 .25 .25
C350 AP78(j) 150fr #C236 .45 .45
Nos. C341-C350 (10) 2.45 2.45

Christmas — AP118

1985, Dec. 20   Litho.   *Perf. 13x12½*
C351 AP118 500fr multi 1.75 1.75
For surcharge see No. C449.

Dahomey Nos. C34-C37, C84, C131 Surcharged or Overprinted
1986   Photo.   Perfs. as before
C352 AP33(b) 75fr on 70fr #C84 .25 .25
C353 AP14(b) 75fr on 100fr #C34 .25 .25
C354 AP15(b) 75fr on 200fr #C35 .25 .25
C355 AP15(b) 90fr on 250fr #C36 .35 .35
C356 AP45(b) 100fr #C131 .40 .40
C357 AP14(b) 150fr on 500fr #C37 .50 .50
Nos. C352-C357 (6) 2.00 2.00
Issued: 75fr, 90fr, Mar; 100fr, 150fr, June.

Dahomey Nos. C82, C139, C141, C146 Surcharged
1986
Perfs. & Printing Methods as Before
C357A AP33(d) 15fr on 45fr #C82
C357B AP48(d) 25fr on 200fr #C141 (S)
C357D AP48(d) 100fr on #C139
C357E CD135(d) 100fr on #C146

Christmas — AP119

1986, Dec. 24   Litho.   *Perf. 13x12½*
C358 AP119 300fr multi 1.25 1.25

Air Africa, 25th Anniv. AP120

1986, Dec. 30   *Perf. 12½*
C359 AP120 100fr multi .40 .40

Intl. Agricultural Development Fund (FIDA), 10th Anniv. — AP121

1987, Dec. 14   Litho.   *Perf. 13½*
C360 AP121 500fr multi 3.50 3.50

Christmas — AP122

1988, Dec. 23   Litho.   *Perf. 13x12½*
C361 AP122 500fr Adoration of the Magi, storyteller 3.25 3.25

No. C241 Surcharged
1989, Apr. 24   Litho.   *Perf. 13*
C362 AP84(b) 15fr on 85fr multi .20 .20

Dahomey Nos. C37, C53, C152, C156, C165, C175, C182, C234 Benin No. C242 Surcharged or Overprinted

République Populaire du Bénin

1987
Perfs. & Printing Methods as Before
C363 AP77 20fr on 250fr #C234
C364 AP48(b) 25fr on 150fr #C175 (S&B)
C365 AP63(b) 40fr on 15fr #C182
C366 AP48(b) 40fr on 100fr #C152
C367 AP84(b) 50fr on 140fr #C242
C368 AP14(b) 50fr on 500fr #C37
C369 AP22(b) 80fr on #C53
C370 AP56(b) 80fr on 150fr #C165
C373 AP52(b) 100fr on #C156

Dahomey Nos. C140, C144, C158, C166, C177, C185, C188 C191, C195, C207, C262 Surcharged

1988
Perfs. & Printing Methods as Before
C374 AP50(d) 10fr on 500fr #C144
C375 AP64(d) 10fr on 65fr #C185
C376 AP72(d) 15fr on 150fr #C207
C377 AP67(d) 25fr on 200fr #C191
C378 AP61(d) 40fr on 35fr #C195
C380 AP53(d) 70fr on 250fr #C158
C381 AP48(d) 100fr on #C140
C382 AP65(d) 100fr on #C188
C384 AP61(f) 125fr on #C177
C385 AP86(d) 125fr on 75fr #C262
C386 AP57(d) 150fr on 100fr #C166

Dahomey Nos. C181, C196, C208 Surcharged

1988
Perfs. & Printing Methods as Before
C388 AP61(d) 25fr on 100fr #C196
C390 AP62 40fr on 100fr #C181
C391 AP73(d) 40fr on 150fr #C208

Dahomey Nos. C108, C147-C148, C162, C167, C178, C187, C194

1992
Perfs. & Printing Methods as Before
C394 AP51(f) 70fr on #C148
C395 AP55(f) 100fr on #C162
C396 AP68(g) 100fr on #C194
C397 AP51(f) 125fr on 40fr #C147
C398 A52(f) 125fr on 70fr #C108
C400 AP64a(e) 125fr on 100fr #C187
C401 AP61(f) 190fr on 140fr #C178
C402 AP58(f) 190fr on 150fr #C167

Dahomey Nos. C145, C149-C150, C182, C189, C198, C257, C264-C265 Surcharged Benin No. C241 Surcharged

1993
Perfs. & Printing Methods as Before
C403 AP51(e) 5fr on 100fr #C149
C404 AP50(f) 10fr on 100fr #C145
C405 AP51(f) 20fr on 200fr #C150
C406 AP83(f) 20fr on 500fr #C257
C407 AP84(e) 25fr on 85fr #C241
C409 AP63(f) 30fr on 15fr #C182
C410 AP61(f) 30fr on 200fr #C198
C411 AP66(b) 35fr on #C189
C412 AP86(g) 300fr on #C264

Dahomey Nos. C14, C31, C34, C54, C101, C110, C128, C144, C151, C153, C155, C197, C222, C234, C250, C254-C256, C261, Benin C242 Surcharged or Overprinted

1994-95?
Perfs. & Printing Methods as Before
C414 AP52(e) 15fr on 40fr #C155
C415 AP83(f) 25fr on 200fr #C256
C416 AP83(f) 35fr on #C255
C417 AP49(g) 50fr on #C101
C418 AP48(b) 75fr on 40fr #C151
C419 AP4(g) 100fr on #C14
C420 AP22(h) 100fr #C54
C421 AP50(g) 125fr on 50fr #C144
C422 AP75(e) 125fr on 65fr #C222
C425 AP21(f) 135fr on 45fr #C110
C429 AP43(e) 135fr on 70fr #C128
C430 AP81(f) 135fr on 250fr #C250
C432 AP84(f) 150fr on 140fr #C242
C433 A61(b) 150fr on #C153
C434 AP61(f) 150fr on #C197
C435 AP13(e) 200fr on 100fr #C31
C436 AP14(e) 200fr on 100fr #C34
C445 AP61(e) 200fr on 250fr #C234
C446 AP61(e) 200fr on 250fr #C254
C447 AP85(f) 300fr on #C261

Dahomey No. C37, Benin No. C351 Surcharged

1994-95
Printing Method and Perfs as Before
C449 AP118 200fr on 500fr #C351

Benin No. C290 Surcharged
Dahomey Nos. C206, C257
Surcharged

1996
Perfs. & Printing Methods as Before

C450	A133	40fr on 210fr	#C290
C451	AP83(f)	200fr on 500fr	#C257
C452	AP72(f)	1000fr on 150fr	#C206

Dahomey No. C265 Surcharged
Benin Nos. C258, C292 Surcharged

1996
Perfs. & Printing Methods as Before

C453	AP86(g)	25fr on 500fr	#C265
C454	AP89	35fr on 270fr	#C258
C455	AP102	100fr on 500fr	#C292

Dahomey Nos. C61, C74, C85, C88,
C94, C106, C109, C111, C113, C115,
C120, C124-C125, C130, C135-C136,
C138, C142-C143, C150, C157, C204-
C205, C207-C208, C260, C263
Surcharged

1996?
Perfs. & Printing Methods as Before

C456	AP48(e)	70fr on 100fr	#C138
C457	AP34(h)	150fr on #C88	
C458	AP21(e)	150fr on #C115	
C459	AP72(e)	150fr on #C207	
C460	AP73(h)	150fr on #C208	
C461	AP34(e)	150fr on 30fr #C85	
C462	AP31(e)	150fr on 30fr #C74	
C463	AP21(e)	150fr on 30fr #C109	
C464	AP40(e)	150fr on 40fr on 30fr #C120	
C465	AP47(e)	150fr on 40fr #C136	
C466	AP49(e)	150fr on 40fr #C142	
C467	CD128(h)	150fr on 50fr #C94	
C468	AP38(h)	150fr on 50fr #C106	
C469	AP71(e)	150fr on 50fr #C204	
C470	AP54(h)	150fr on 70fr #C124	
C471	CD124(h)	150fr on 100fr #C61	
C472	AP21(e)	150fr on 100fr #C113	
C473	AP53(e)	150fr on 100fr #C157	
C474	AP84(e)	150fr on 100fr #C260	
C475	AP21(e)	150fr on 110fr #C111	
C476	AP44(e)	150fr on 110fr #C130	
C477	AP54(e)	150fr on 120fr #C125	
C478	AP86(g)	150fr on 135fr #C263	
C479	AP46(e)	150fr on 200fr #C135	
C480	AP49(e)	150fr on 200fr #C143	
C481	AP51(e)	150fr on 200fr #C150	
C482	AP71(e)	150fr on 200fr #C205	

Benin Nos. C261, C281, C327, C332-
C333 Surcharged
Dahomey Nos. C201, C127, C175
Surcharged

1996-97?
Perfs. & Printing Methods as Before

C483	AP98	30fr on 380fr #C281	
C484	AP90	35fr on 270fr #C261	
C485	AP117	125fr on 200fr #C332	
C485A	AP117	125fr on 200fr #C333	
C486	AP114	200fr on 500fr #C327	
C488	AP43(h)	150fr on 40fr #C127	
C489	AP70(f)	150fr on 50fr #C201	
C490	AP48(e)	200fr on 150fr #C175	

No. C256 Surcharged
Method and Perf. as Before
1996 ?

C494	AP88	40fr on 210fr #C256	

Benin #C293 Surcharged
Dahomey #C147, C250 Surcharged
Type f

1995-97?
Perf. & Printing Methods as Before

C500	AP103	150fr on 500fr #C293	
C503	AP51(e)	135fr on 40fr #C147	
C509	AP81(f)	150fr on 250fr #C250	

Dahomey Nos. #C86, C126, C70
Surcharged

1995-99?
Perfs. & Printing Methods as Before

C513	AP34(h)	35fr on 45fr #C86	
C515	AP42(h)	35fr on 100fr on 200fr #C126	
C516	AP29(h)	35fr on 100fr #C70	

Dahomey No. C105 Surcharged
Method and Perf. as Before
1997 ?

C523	A51(h)	35fr on 100fr #C105	

POSTAGE DUE STAMPS

French Colony
Handstamped in Black on Postage
Due Stamps of French Colonies

BENIN

1894   **Unwmk.**   **Imperf.**

J1	D1	5c black	125.00	45.00
J2	D1	10c black	125.00	45.00
J3	D1	20c black	125.00	45.00
J4	D1	30c black	125.00	45.00
		Nos. J1-J4 (4)	500.00	180.00

Nos. J1-J4 exist with overprint in various positions.

> **Catalogue values for unused stamps in this section are for Never Hinged items.**

People's Republic

Pineapples
D6

Mail
Delivery
D7

Designs: 20fr, Cashew, vert. 40fr, Oranges. 50fr, Akee. 80fr, Mail delivery by boat.

1978, Sept. 5   **Photo.**   **Perf. 13**

J44	D6	10fr multicolored	.20	.20
J45	D6	20fr multicolored	.20	.20
J46	D6	40fr multicolored	.30	.20
J47	D6	50fr multicolored	.45	.25
		Engr.		
J48	D7	60fr multi	.30	.25
J49	D7	80fr multi	.45	.30
		Nos. J44-J49 (6)	1.90	1.40

PARCEL POST STAMPS

> **Catalogue values for unused stamps in this section are for Never Hinged items.**

Nos. 448-448A, 459, 473, C292
Overprinted or Surcharged "Colis
Postaux"

Perfs. and Printing Methods as Before

1982, Nov.

Q8	A126	100fr on 150fr	.40	.20
Q9	A130	100fr multi	.40	.20
Q10	A134	300fr multi	1.25	.60
Q10A	A126a	1000fr multi	5.50	5.50
Q10B	AP102	5000fr on 500fr	27.50	27.50
		Nos. Q8-Q10B (5)	35.05	34.00

Dahomey No. C205 Surcharged

1989   **Photo.**   **Perf. 12½x13**

Q11	AP71	500fr on 200fr multi	3.25	3.25

BERMUDA

bər-'myü-də

LOCATION — A group of about 150 small islands of which only 20 are inhabited, lying in the Atlantic Ocean about 580 miles southeast of Cape Hatteras.
GOVT. — British Crown Colony
AREA — 20.5 sq. mi.
POP. — 62,471 (1999 est.)
CAPITAL — Hamilton

Bermuda achieved internal self-government in 1968.

4 Farthings = 1 Penny
12 Pence = 1 Shilling
20 Shillings = 1 Pound
100 Cents = 1 Dollar (1970)

> **Catalogue values for unused stamps in this country are for Never Hinged items, beginning with Scott 131.**

POSTMASTER STAMPS

PM1

1848-54   **Unwmk.**   **Imperf.**

X1	PM1	1p blk, *bluish* (1848)	125,000.
a.		Dated 1849	135,000.
X2	PM1	1p red, *bluish* (1856)	175,000.
a.		Dated 1854	225,000.
X3	PM1	1p red (1853)	160,000.

PM2

1860

X4	PM2	(1p) red, *yellowish*	100,000.

Same inscribed "HAMILTON"

1861

X5	PM2	(1p) red, *bluish*	130,000.

Nos. X1-X3 were produced and used by Postmaster William B. Perot of Hamilton. No. X4 is attributed to Postmaster James H. Thies of St. George's.

Only a few of each stamp exist. Values reflect actual sales figures for stamps in the condition in which they are found.

GENERAL ISSUES

Values for unused stamps are for examples with original gum as defined in the catalogue introduction. Very fine examples of Nos. 1-1a, 2-15b will have perforations touching the design (or framelines where applicable) on at least one side due to the narrow spacing of the stamps on the plates. Stamps with perfs clear of the design on all four sides are scarce and will command higher prices.

Queen Victoria
A1   A2

A3   A4

A5

1865-74   **Typo.**   **Wmk. 1**   **Perf. 14**

1	A1	1p rose red	80.00	2.50
b.		Imperf.	22,500.	13,750.
2	A2	2p blue ('66)	225.00	17.50
3	A3	3p buff ('73)	425.00	60.00
4	A4	6p brown lilac	900.	100.00
5	A4	6p lilac ('74)	21.00	16.00
6	A5	1sh green	250.00	42.50
		Nos. 1-6 (6)	2,001.	238.50

See Nos. 7-9, 19-21, 23, 25. For surcharges see Nos. 10-15.
No. 1b is a proof.

1882-1903   **Perf. 14x12½**

7	A3	3p buff	160.00	55.00
8	A4	6p violet ('03)	15.00	20.00
9	A5	1sh green ('94)	20.00	110.00
a.		Vert. strip of 3, perf. all around & imperf. btwn.	13,000.	15,000.
		Nos. 7-9 (3)	195.00	185.00

Handstamped
Diagonally

1874   **Perf. 14**

10	A5	3p on 1sh green	1,400.	950.

Handstamped
Diagonally

11	A1	3p on 1p rose	12,500.	—
12	A5	3p on 1sh green	2,250.	900.
a.		"P" with top like "R"	2,250.	1,100.

No. 11 is stated to be an essay, but a few copies are known used. Nos. 10-12 are found with double or partly double surcharges.

Surcharged in Black

One Penny.

1875

13	A2	1p on 2p blue	700.00 375.00
a.		Without period	11,000. 7,250.
14	A3	1p on 3p buff	450.00 350.00
15	A5	1p on 1sh green	500.00 300.00
a.		Inverted surcharge	— 17,500.
b.		Without period	13,750. 8,750.

A6   A7

1880   Wmk. 1

16	A6	½p brown	2.25 3.75
17	A7	4p orange	15.00 2.50

See Nos. 18, 24.

A8   A9

1883-1904   Wmk. 2

18	A6	½p dp gray grn ('93)	2.50 2.50
a.		½p green ('92)	2.25 .75
19	A1	1p aniline car ('89)	7.50 .30
a.		1p dull rose	125.00 4.00
b.		1p rose red	70.00 3.00
c.		1p carmine rose ('86)	45.00 .90
20	A2	2p blue ('86)	50.00 3.50
21	A2	2p brn pur ('98)	3.00 2.50
a.		2p aniline pur ('93)	11.00 4.00
22	A8	2½p ultra ('84)	6.00 .50
a.		2½p deep ultra	12.00 2.25
23	A3	3p gray ('86)	20.00 6.00
24	A7	4p brown org ('04)	27.50 55.00
25	A5	1sh olive bister ('93)	16.00 15.00
a.		1sh yellow brown	15.00 14.00
		Nos. 18-25 (8)	132.50 85.30

Black Surcharge

1901

26	A9	1f on 1sh gray	.80 .50

Dry Dock — A10

1902-03

28	A10	½p gray grn & blk ('03)	8.00 2.25
29	A10	1p car rose & brown	7.00 .35
30	A10	3p ol grn & violet	2.50 3.50
		Nos. 28-30 (3)	17.50 6.10

1906-10   Wmk. 3

31	A10	¼p pur & brn ('08)	1.40 1.40
32	A10	½p gray grn & blk	16.00 1.50
33	A10	½p green ('09)	10.00 2.25
34	A10	1p car rose & brn	20.00 .20
35	A10	1p carmine ('08)	16.00 .90
36	A10	2p orange & gray	6.75 10.00
37	A10	2½p blue & brown	12.50 11.50
38	A10	2½p ultra ('10)	11.00 8.50
39	A10	4p vio brn & blue ('09)	2.75 14.00
		Nos. 31-39 (9)	96.40 50.25

Caravel   King George V
A11   A12

1910-20   Engr.   Perf. 14

40	A11	¼p brown	1.40 2.25
41	A11	½p yel green	1.10 .30
a.		½p dark green	5.75 1.25
42	A11	1p rose red (I)	12.50 .35
a.		1p carmine (I)	42.50 7.00
43	A11	2p gray	2.75 7.00
44	A11	2½p ultra (I)	3.25 .55
45	A11	3p violet, yel	1.60 5.50
46	A11	4p red, yellow	4.25 10.00
47	A11	6p claret	10.00 7.00
48	A11	1sh blk, green	3.50 4.50
a.		1sh black, olive	4.00 11.50

Typographed
Chalky Paper

49	A12	2sh ultra & dl vio, bl ('20)	16.00 45.00
50	A12	2sh6p red & blk, bl ('26)	25.00 65.00
51	A12	4sh car & black ('20)	55.00 125.00
52	A12	5sh red & grn, yellow	45.00 75.00
53	A12	10sh red & grn, green	140.00 300.00
54	A12	£1 black & vio, red	350.00 500.00
		Nos. 40-54 (15)	671.35 1,147.

Types I of 1p and 2½p are illustrated above Nos. 81-97.

The 1p was printed from two plates, the 2nd of which, #42a, exists only in carmine on opaque paper with a bluish tinge. Compare #MR1 (as #42) and MR2 (as #42a).

Revenue cancellations are found on Nos. 52-54.

See Nos. 81-97.

Seal of the Colony and King George V A13

1920-21   Wmk. 3   Ordinary Paper

55	A13	¼p brown	2.25 12.00
56	A13	½p green	2.25 6.25
57	A13	2p gray	9.25 27.50

Chalky Paper

58	A13	3p vio & dl vio, yel	8.50 24.00
59	A13	4p red & blk, yellow	9.25 24.00
60	A13	1sh blk, gray grn	12.50 37.50

Ordinary Paper
Wmk. 4

67	A13	1p rose red	2.75 .25
68	A13	2½p ultra	9.25 8.50

Chalky Paper

69	A13	6p red vio & dl vio	19.00 50.00
		Nos. 55-60, 67-69 (9)	75.00 190.00

Issued: 6p, 1/19/21; others, 11/11/20.

King George V A14

1921, May 12   Engr.

71	A14	¼p brown	.45 2.75
72	A14	½p green	3.50 4.50
73	A14	1p carmine	2.50 .25

Wmk. 3

74	A14	2p gray	6.00 20.00
75	A14	2½p ultra	6.00 2.25
76	A14	3p vio, orange	4.25 11.50
77	A14	4p scarlet, org	8.00 15.00
78	A14	6p claret	8.50 32.50
79	A14	1sh blk, green	16.00 35.00
		Nos. 71-79 (9)	55.20 123.75

Tercentenary of "Local Representative Institutions" (Nos. 55-79).

Types of 1910-20 Issue

Types of 1p: **1d** **1d** **1d**
               I   II   IIi

Types of 2½p: **2½d** **2½d**
                 I   II

Three types of the 1d value: type I, figure "1" has pointed serifs, scroll at top left very weak; type II, thick "1" with square serifs, scroll weak; type III, thinner "1" with long square serifs,

---

scroll complete with strong line. Two types of the 2½d value: type I, small "d," short, thick figures of value; type II, larger "d," taller, thinner figures of value.

1922-34   Wmk. 4

81	A11	¼p brown ('28)	.30 .75
82	A11	½p green	.20 .20
83	A11	1p car, III ('28)	7.50 .30
a.		1p carmine, II ('26)	17.50 1.00
b.		1p carmine, I	15.00 .60
84	A11	1½p red brown ('34)	3.00 .30
85	A11	2p gray ('23)	1.00 .30
86	A11	2½p ap grn ('23)	1.00 1.00
87	A11	2½p ultra, II ('32)	2.00 .35
a.		2½p ultra, I ('26)	2.25 .50
88	A11	3p ultra ('24)	14.00 20.00
89	A11	3p vio, yellow ('26)	.80 .60
90	A11	4p red, yellow ('24)	1.00 1.00
91	A11	6p claret ('24)	.80 .80
92	A11	1sh blk, emer ('27)	5.00 5.00
93	A11	1sh brn blk, yel grn ('34)	30.00 40.00

Chalky Paper

94	A12	2sh ultra & vio, bl ('27)	30.00 40.00
a.		2sh bl & dp vio, dp bl ('31)	40.00 50.00
95	A12	2sh 6p red & blk, bl ('27)	40.00 37.50
a.		2sh6p pale org ver & blk, gray bl ('30)	2,750. 2,250.
b.		2sh6p dp ver & blk, deep blue ('31)	70.00 80.00
96	A12	10sh red & grn, emer ('24)	150.00 175.00
a.		10sh dp red & pale grn, dp emer ('31)	125.00 200.00
97	A12	12sh 6p ocher & gray blk ('32)	300.00 350.00
		Nos. 81-97 (17)	586.60 673.80

Revenue cancellations are found on Nos. 94-97.

For the 12sh6p with "Revenue" on both sides, see #AR1.

Common Design Types pictured following the introduction.

Silver Jubilee Issue
Common Design Type

1935, May 6   Perf. 11x12

100	CD301	1p car & dk bl	.40 .35
101	CD301	1½p blk & ultra	.60 1.10
102	CD301	2½p ultra & brn	1.00 .55
103	CD301	1sh brn vio & ind	10.50 13.00
		Nos. 100-103 (4)	12.50 15.00
		Set, never hinged	14.00

Hamilton Harbor — A15

Yacht "Lucie" — A17

South Shore — A16

Grape Bay — A18

Typical Cottage — A19

Scene at Par-la-Ville — A20

1936-40   Perf. 12
105	A15	½p blue green	.20	.20
106	A16	1p car & black	.20	.20
107	A16	1½p choc & black	.65	.40
108	A17	2p lt bl & blk	3.00	2.00
109	A17	2p brn blk & turq bl ('38)	29.00	8.75
109A	A17	2p red & ultra ('40)	1.00	1.00
110	A18	2½p dk bl & lt bl	.65	.25
111	A19	3p car & black	1.75	1.25
112	A20	6p vio & rose lake	.50	.20
113	A18	1sh deep green	2.75	8.25
114	A15	1sh6p brown	.30	.25
		Nos. 105-114 (11)	40.00	22.75
		Set, never hinged	65.00	

No. 108, blue border and black center.
No. 109, black border, blue center.

Coronation Issue
Common Design Type
1937, May 14   Perf. 13½x14
115	CD302	1p carmine	.25	.20
116	CD302	1½p brown	.30	.20
117	CD302	2½p bright ultra	.55	.35
		Nos. 115-117 (3)	1.10	.75
		Set, never hinged	1.50	

Hamilton Harbor — A21

Grape Bay — A22

St. David's Lighthouse A23

King George VI A25

Bermudian Water Scene and Yellow-billed Tropic Bird — A24

1938-51   Wmk. 4   Perf. 12
118	A21	1p red & black ('40)	.40	.20
a.		1p rose red & black	12.00	1.00
119	A21	1½p vio brn & bl	3.25	.85
a.		1½p dl vio brn & bl ('43)	2.00	.20
120	A22	2½p blue & lt bl	6.25	.70
120A	A22	2½p ol brn & lt bl ('41)	1.75	.85
b.		2½p dk ol blk & pale blue ('43)	2.00	1.00
121	A23	3p car & blk	10.00	1.40
121A	A23	3p dp ultra & blk ('42)	1.00	.20
c.		3p brt ultra & blk ('41)	.25	.20
121D	A24	7½p yel grn, bl & blk ('41)	3.75	1.40
122	A22	1sh green	1.10	.30

Typo.
Perf. 13
123	A25	2sh ultra & red vio, *bl* ('50)	9.50	8.50
a.		2sh ultra & vio, *bl*, perf. 14	6.75	2.50
b.		2sh ultra & dl vio, *bl* (mottled paper), perf. 14 ('42)	6.75	2.50
124	A25	2sh 6p red & blk, *bl*	10.50	6.25
a.		Perf. 14	20.00	6.50
125	A25	5sh red & grn, *yel*	12.50	11.50
a.		Perf. 14	45.00	15.00
126	A25	10sh red & grn, *grn* ('51)	30.00	24.00
a.		10sh brn lake & grn, *grn*, perf. 14	100.00	75.00
b.		10sh red & grn, *grn*, perf. 14 ('39)	175.00	150.00
127	A25	12sh 6p org & gray blk	65.00	55.00
a.		12sh 6p org & gray, perf. 14	85.00	45.00
b.		12sh 6p yel & gray, perf. 14 ('47)	550.00	450.00
c.		12sh 6p brn org & gray, perf. 14	200.00	80.00

Wmk. 3
128	A25	£1 blk & vio, *red* ('51)	40.00	47.50
a.		£1 blk & pur, *red*, perf. 14	225.00	100.00
b.		£1 blk & dk vio, *salmon*, perf. 14 ('42)	65.00	50.00
		Nos. 118-128 (14)	195.00	158.65
		Set, never hinged	250.00	

No. 127b is the so-called "lemon yellow" shade.
Revenue cancellations are found on Nos. 123-128. Copies with removed revenue cancellations and forged postmarks are abundant.

No. 118a Surcharged in Black

1940, Dec. 20   Wmk. 4   Perf. 12
129	A21	½p on 1p rose red & blk	.30	.30
		Never hinged		.50

> **Catalogue values for unused stamps in this section, from this point to the end of the section, are for Never Hinged items.**

Peace Issue
Common Design Type
Perf. 13½x14
1946, Nov. 6   Engr.   Wmk. 4
131	CD303	1½p brown	.20	.20
132	CD303	3p deep blue	.30	.30

Silver Wedding Issue
Common Design Types
1948, Dec. 1   Photo.   Perf. 14x14½
133	CD304	1½p red brown	.20	.20

Engr.; Name Typo.
Perf. 11½x11
134	CD305	£1 rose carmine	47.50	47.50

Postmaster Stamp of 1848 — A26

1949, Apr. 11   Engr.   Perf. 13x13½
135	A26	2½p dk brown & dp bl	.20	.20
136	A26	3p dp blue & black	.20	.20
137	A26	6p green & rose vio	.45	.45
		Nos. 135-137 (3)	.85	.85

No. 137 shows a different floral arrangement.
Bermuda's first postage stamp, cent.

UPU Issue
Common Design Types
Engr.; Name Typo.
1949, Oct. 10   Perf. 13½, 11x11½
138	CD306	2½p slate	.50	.50
139	CD307	3p indigo	.65	.65
140	CD308	6p rose violet	1.10	1.10
141	CD309	1sh blue green	2.25	2.25
		Nos. 138-141 (4)	4.50	4.50

Coronation Issue
Common Design Type
1953, June 4   Engr.   Perf. 13½x13
142	CD312	1½p dk blue & blk	.40	.20

A27

Easter Lilies — A28

Designs: 1p, 4p, Perot stamp. 2p, Racing dinghy. 2½p, Sir George Somers and "Sea Venture." 3p, 1sh3p, Map. 4½p, 9p, "Sea Venture," boat, hog coin and Perot stamp. 6p, 8p, Yellow-billed tropic bird. 1sh, Hog coins. 2sh, Arms of St. George. 2sh6p, Warwick Fort. 5sh, Hog coin. 10sh, Earliest hog coin. £1, Arms of Bermuda.

1953-58   Perf. 13½x13, 13x13½
143	A27	½p olive green	.40	.20
144	A27	1p rose red & blk	1.00	.20
145	A28	1½p dull green	.20	.20
146	A27	2p red & ultra	.30	.20
147	A27	2½p carmine rose	1.25	.20
148	A27	3p vio (Sandy's)	.20	.20
149	A27	3p violet (Sandys) ('57)	.65	.20
150	A27	4p dp ultra & blk	.20	.20
151	A27	4½p green	.65	.60
152	A27	6p dk bluish grn & blk	3.50	.30
153	A27	8p red & blk ('55)	1.60	.35
154	A27	9p violet ('58)	5.00	.95
155	A27	1sh orange	.30	.20
156	A27	1sh3p blue (Sandy's)	2.25	.35
157	A27	1sh3p blue (Sandys) ('57)	4.50	.50
158	A27	2sh yellow brown	2.50	.65
159	A28	2sh6p scarlet	3.00	1.25
160	A27	5sh dp car rose	12.50	2.00
161	A27	10sh deep ultra	8.50	4.50

Engr. and Typo.
162	A27	£1 dp ol grn & multi	16.00	17.50
		Nos. 143-162 (20)	64.50	30.75

For overprints, see Nos. 164-167.

Type of 1953 Inscribed "ROYAL VISIT 1953"

Design: 6p, Yellow-billed tropic bird.

1953, Nov. 26   Engr.
163	A27	6p dk bluish grn & blk	.40	.35

Visit of Queen Elizabeth II and the Duke of Edinburgh, 1953.

Nos. 148 and 156 Overprinted in Violet Blue or Red

1953, Dec. 8   Perf. 13½x13
164	A27	3p violet	.20	.20
165	A27	1sh3p blue (R)	.45	.40

Three Power Conference, Tucker's Town, December 1953.

Nos. 153 and 156 Overprinted in Black or Red

1956, June 22
166	A27	8p red & black	.25	.30
167	A27	1sh3p blue (R)	.35	.50

Newport-Bermuda Yacht Race, 50th anniv.

Perot Post Office, Hamilton A29

Perf. 13½x13
1959, Jan. 1   Engr.   Wmk. 4
168	A29	6p lilac & black	.50	.30

Restoration and reopening of the post office operated at Hamilton by W. B. Perot in the mid-nineteenth century.

Arms of James I and Elizabeth II — A30

Engr. and Litho.
1959, July 29   Wmk. 314   Perf. 13
Coats of Arms in Blue, Yellow & Red
169	A30	1½p dark blue	.35	.35
170	A30	3p gray	.40	.40
171	A30	4p rose violet	.50	.50
172	A30	8p violet gray	.50	.50
173	A30	9p olive green	.50	.50
174	A30	1sh3p orange brown	.50	.50
		Nos. 169-174 (6)	2.75	2.75

350th anniv. of the shipwreck of the "Sea Venture" which resulted in the first permanent settlement of Bermuda.

The Old Rectory, St. George's, 1730 A31

Designs: 2p, Church of St. Peter. 3p, Government House. 4p, Cathedral, Hamilton. 5p, No. 185A, H.M. Dockyard. 6p, Perot's Post Office, 1848. 8p, General Post Office, 1869. 9p, Library and Historical Society. 1sh, Christ Church, Warwick, 1719. 1sh3p, City Hall, Hamilton. 10p, No. 185, Bermuda Cottage, 1705. 2sh, Town of St. George. 2sh3p, Bermuda House, 1710. 2sh6p, Bermuda House, 18th century. 5sh, Colonial Secretariat, 1833. 10sh, Old Post Office, Somerset, 1890. £1, House of Assembly, 1815.

Wmk. 314 Upright
1962-65   Photo.   Perf. 12½
175	A31	1p org, lil & blk	.20	.45
176	A31	2p sl, lt vio, grn & yel	.25	.20
a.		Light vio omitted	800.00	650.00
b.		Green omitted		2,500.
d.		Imperf., pair	1,250.	
177	A31	3p lt bl & yel brn	.20	.20
a.		Yellow brown omitted	3,750.	
178	A31	4p car rose & red brn	.20	.30
179	A31	5p dk bl & pink	1.25	2.25
180	A31	6p emer, lt & dk bl	.20	.20
181	A31	8p grn, dp org & ultra	.25	.25
182	A31	9p org brn & grnsh bl	.20	.25
182A	A31	10p brt vio & bis ('65)	6.75	1.25
183	A31	1sh multi	.20	.20
184	A31	1sh3p sl, lem & rose car	.65	.25
185	A31	1sh6p brt vio & bis	1.10	1.00
186	A31	2sh brn & org	2.50	1.00

187	A31	2sh3p brn & brt yel grn	1.25	5.00
188	A31	2sh6p grn, yel & sep	.45	.40
189	A31	5sh choc & brt grn	1.10	1.25
190	A31	10sh dl grn, buff & rose car	3.75	4.50
191	A31	£1 cit, bis, blk & org	12.00	11.00
		Nos. 175-191 (18)	32.50	29.95

See #252a. For surcharges see #238-254.

1966-69 Wmk. 314 Sideways
Unnamed Colors as in 1962-65 Issue

176c	A31	2p ('69)	5.00	5.50
181a	A31	8p ('67)	.50	1.40
182b	A31	10p	.70	.55
183a	A31	1sh ('67)	.60	1.25
185A	A31	1sh6p indigo & rose	2.10	.45
186a	A31	2sh ('67)	2.10	.85
		Nos. 176c-186a (6)	11.00	10.00

For surcharges see #239, 245-246, 248-249.

Freedom from Hunger Issue
Common Design Type

1963, June 4			**Perf. 14x14½**	
192	CD314	1sh3p sepia	2.75	2.25

Red Cross Centenary Issue
Common Design Type
Wmk. 314

1963, Sept. 2		**Litho.**	**Perf. 13**	
193	CD315	3p black & red	.50	.30
194	CD315	1sh3p ultra & red	5.50	3.00

Finn Boat — A32

Wmk. 314

1964, Sept. 28		**Photo.**	**Perf. 13½**	
195	A32	3p blue, vio & red	.30	.30

18th Olympic Games, Tokyo, Oct. 10-25.

ITU Issue
Common Design Type
Perf. 11x11½

1965, May 17			**Wmk. 314**	
196	CD317	3p blue & emerald	.40	.30
197	CD317	2sh yel & vio blue	3.50	3.50

Scout Badge and Royal Cipher A33

1965, July 24		**Photo.**	**Perf. 12½**	
198	A33	2sh multicolored		.85 .85

50th anniversary of Scouting in Bermuda.

Intl. Cooperation Year Issue
Common Design Type

1965, Oct. 25		**Litho.**	**Perf. 14½**	
199	CD318	4p blue grn & cl	.30	.30
200	CD318	2sh6p lt violet & grn	2.25	2.25

Churchill Memorial Issue
Common Design Type
1966, Jan. 24 Photo. Perf. 14
Design in Black, Gold and Carmine Rose

201	CD319	3p bright blue	.30	.20
202	CD319	6p green	.65	.45
203	CD319	10p brown	1.25	1.00
204	CD319	1sh3p violet	2.50	2.00
		Nos. 201-204 (4)	4.70	3.65

World Cup Soccer Issue
Common Design Type

1966, July 1		**Litho.**	**Perf. 14**	
205	CD321	10p multicolored	.65	.65
206	CD321	2sh6p multicolored	1.75	1.75

UNESCO Anniversary Issue
Common Design Type

1966, Dec. 1		**Litho.**	**Perf. 14**	
207	CD323	4p "Education"	.40	.40
208	CD323	1sh3p "Science"	1.50	1.50
209	CD323	2sh "Culture"	2.50	2.50
		Nos. 207-209 (3)	4.40	4.40

Post Office, Hamilton A34

Wmk. 314

1967, June 23			**Perf. 14½**	
210	A34	3p vio blue & multi	.20	.20
211	A34	1sh orange & multi	.40	.40
212	A34	1sh6p green & multi	.70	.70
213	A34	2sh6p red & multi	1.10	1.10
		Nos. 210-213 (4)	2.40	2.40

Opening of the new GPO, Hamilton.

Cable Ship Mercury A35

Designs: 1sh, Map of Bermuda and Virgin Islands, telephone and microphone. 1sh6p, Radio tower, television set, telephone and cable. 2sh6p, Cable at sea bottom and ship.

1967, Sept. 14		**Photo.**	**Wmk. 314**	
214	A35	3p multicolored	.20	.20
215	A35	1sh multicolored	.40	.40
216	A35	1sh6p multicolored	.70	.70
217	A35	2sh6p multicolored	1.10	1.10
		Nos. 214-217 (4)	2.40	2.40

Completion of the Bermuda-Tortola, Virgin Islands, telephone link.

Human Rights Flame, Globe and Doves A36

1968, Feb. 1		**Litho.**	**Perf. 14x14½**	
218	A36	3p indigo, lt grn & bl	.20	.20
219	A36	1sh brown, lt bl & bl	.45	.45
220	A36	1sh6p black, pink & blue	.75	.75
221	A36	2sh6p green, yellow & bl	.95	.95
		Nos. 218-221 (4)	2.35	2.35

International Human Rights Year.

Mace A37

#224-225, House of Assembly, Bermuda, Parliament, London & royal cipher.

1968, July 1		**Photo.**	**Perf. 14½**	
222	A37	3p rose red & multi	.20	.20
223	A37	1sh ultra & multi	.45	.45
224	A37	1sh6p yellow & multi	.75	.75
225	A37	2sh6p multicolored	.95	.95
		Nos. 222-225 (4)	2.35	2.35

New constitution.

Olympic Sports and Rings A38

1968, Sept. 24		**Wmk. 314**	**Perf. 12½**	
226	A38	3p lilac & multi	.20	.20
a.		Rose brown omitted ("3d BER-MUDA")	2,500.	
227	A38	1sh multicolored	.40	.35
228	A38	1sh6p multicolored	.60	.60
229	A38	1sh6p multicolored	1.00	1.00
		Nos. 226-229 (4)	2.20	2.15

19th Olympic Games, Mexico City, 10/12-27.

Girl Guides A39

Designs: 1sh, Like 3p. 1sh6p, 2sh6p, Girl Guides and arms of Bermuda.

1969, Feb. 17		**Litho.**	**Perf. 14**	
230	A39	3p lilac & multi	.20	.20
231	A39	1sh green & multi	.35	.35
232	A39	1sh6p gray & multi	.55	.55
233	A39	2sh6p red & multi	1.00	1.00
		Nos. 230-233 (4)	2.10	2.10

Bermuda Girl Guides, 50th anniv.

Gold and Emerald Cross — A40

Design: 4p, 2sh, Different background.

1969, Sept. 29		**Photo.**	**Perf. 14½x14**	
Cross in Yellow, Brown and Emerald				
234	A40	4p violet	.25	.25
235	A40	1sh3p green	.75	.75
236	A40	2sh black	1.10	1.10
237	A40	2sh6p carmine rose	1.40	1.25
		Nos. 234-237 (4)	3.50	3.35

Treasures salvaged off the coast of Bermuda. The cross shown is from the Tucker treasure from the 16th century Spanish galleon San Pedro.

Buildings Issue and Type of 1962-69
Surcharged with New Value and Bar in Black or Brown

1970, Feb. 6		**Wmk. 314**	**Perf. 12½**	
238	A31	1c on 1p multi	.20	1.50
239	A31	2c on 2p multi	.20	.20
a.		Watermark upright	1.00	2.25
b.		Light violet omitted	700.00	
c.		Pair, one without surch.	3,000.	
240	A31	3c on 3p multi	.20	.20
241	A31	4c on 4p multi (Br)	.20	.20
242	A31	5c on 8p multi	.20	1.50

243	A31	6c on 6p multi	.20	.60
244	A31	6c on 9p multi (Br)	.25	1.75
245	A31	10c on 10p multi	.30	.25
246	A31	12c on 1sh multi	.35	.45
247	A31	15c on 1sh3p multi	.70	.85
248	A31	18c on 1sh multi	.70	.55
249	A31	24c on 2sh multi	.85	.75
250	A31	30c on 2sh6p multi	1.00	2.10
251	A31	36c on 2sh3p multi	1.25	5.25
252	A31	60c on 5sh multi	2.00	2.50
a.		Surcharge omitted	700.00	
253	A31	$1.20 on 10sh multi	4.00	13.00
254	A31	$2.40 on £1 multi	8.00	16.00
		Nos. 238-254 (17)	20.60	47.65

Watermark upright on 1c, 3c to 9c and 36c; sideways on others. Watermark is sideways on No. 252a, upright on No. 189.

Spathiphyllum — A41

Flowers: 2c, Bottlebrush. 3c, Oleander, vert. 4c, Bermudiana. 5c, Poinsettia. 6c, Hibiscus. 9c, Cereus. 10c, Bougainvillea, vert. 12c, Jacaranda. 15c, Passion flower. 18c, Coralita. 24c, Morning glory. 30c, Tecoma. 36c, Angel's trumpet. 60c, Plumbago. $1.20, Bird of paradise. $2.40, Chalice cup.

Wmk. 314, Sideways on Horiz. Stamps

1970, July 6			**Perf. 14**	
255	A41	1c lt grn & multi	.20	.20
256	A41	2c pale bl & multi	.25	.20
257	A41	3c yellow & multi	.20	.20
258	A41	4c buff & multi	.20	.20
259	A41	5c pink & multi	.60	.25
a.		Imperf., pair	1,500.	
260	A41	6c org & multi	.60	.30
261	A41	9c lt grn & multi	.35	.20
262	A41	10c pale sal & multi	.35	.20
263	A41	12c pale yel & multi	1.60	.85
264	A41	15c buff & multi	1.40	.70
265	A41	18c pale sal & multi	2.50	1.10
266	A41	24c pink & multi	1.60	.75
267	A41	30c plum & multi	1.60	.75
268	A41	36c dk gray & multi	2.50	1.10
269	A41	60c gray & multi	3.25	1.75
270	A41	$1.20 blue & multi	7.50	3.50
271	A41	$2.40 multicolored	15.00	8.25
		Nos. 255-271 (17)	39.70	20.50

See #322-328. For overprints see #288-291.

1974-76		**Wmk. 314 Upright**		
259b	A41	5c multicolored	1.00	1.00
260a	A41	6c multicolored	2.25	2.25
263a	A41	12c multicolored	1.60	1.60
267a	A41	30c multicolored ('76)	3.00	3.00
		Nos. 259b-267a (4)	7.85	7.85

Issued: 30c, June 11; others, June 13.

1975-76   **Wmk. 373**
256a	A41	2c multicolored	1.00	1.00
260b	A41	6c multicolored	2.00	2.00

Issued: 2c, Dec. 8; 6c, June 11, 1976.

State House, St. George's, 1622-1815 — A42

Designs: 15c, The Sessions House, Hamilton, 1893. 18c, First Assembly House, St. Peter's Church, St. George's. 24c, Temporary Assembly House, Hamilton, 1815-26.

1970, Oct. 12   **Litho.**   **Perf. 14**
272	A42	4c multicolored	.20	.20
273	A42	15c multicolored	.45	.45
274	A42	18c multicolored	.65	.65
275	A42	24c multicolored	1.10	1.10
a.		Souvenir sheet of 4, #272-275	3.75	4.25
		Nos. 272-275 (4)	2.40	2.40

350th anniv. of Bermuda's Parliament.

Street in St. George's A43

"Keep Bermuda Beautiful": 15c, Horseshoe Bay. 18c, Gibb's Hill Lighthouse. 24c, View of Hamilton Harbor.

1971, Feb. 8   **Wmk. 314**   **Perf. 14**
276	A43	4c multicolored	.25	.25
277	A43	15c multicolored	.70	.70
278	A43	18c multicolored	.90	.90
279	A43	24c multicolored	1.50	1.50
		Nos. 276-279 (4)	3.35	3.35

Building of "Deliverance" — A44

Designs: 15c, "Deliverance" and "Patience" arriving in Jamestown, Va., 1610, vert. 18c, Wreck of "Sea Venture," vert. 24c, "Deliverance" and "Patience" under sail, 1610.

1971, May 10   **Litho.**   **Wmk. 314**
280	A44	4c multicolored	.35	.35
281	A44	15c brown & multi	1.40	1.40
282	A44	18c purple & multi	1.75	1.75
283	A44	24c blue & multi	2.50	2.50
		Nos. 280-283 (4)	6.00	6.00

Voyage of Sir George Somers to Jamestown, Va., from Bermuda, 1610.

Ocean View Golf Course A45

Golf Courses: 15c, Port Royal. 18c, Castle Harbour. 24c, Belmont.

1971, Nov. 1   **Perf. 13**
284	A45	4c multicolored	.20	.20
285	A45	15c multicolored	.65	.65
286	A45	18c multicolored	.75	.75
287	A45	24c multicolored	1.10	1.10
		Nos. 284-287 (4)	2.70	2.70

Golfing in Bermuda.

Nos. 258, 264-266 Overprinted: "HEATH-NIXON / DECEMBER 1971"

1971, Dec. 20   **Photo.**   **Perf. 14**
288	A41	4c buff & multi	.20	.20
289	A41	15c buff & multi	.40	.40
290	A41	18c pale sal & multi	.50	.50
291	A41	24c pink & multi	.70	.70
		Nos. 288-291 (4)	1.80	1.80

Meeting of President Richard M. Nixon and Prime Minister Edward Heath of Great Britain, at Hamilton, Dec. 20-21, 1971.

Bonefish A46

1972, Aug. 7   **Litho.**   **Perf. 13½x14**
292	A46	4c shown	.25	.25
293	A46	15c Wahoo	.75	.75
294	A46	18c Yellowfin tuna	.90	.90
295	A46	24c Greater amberjack	1.40	1.40
		Nos. 292-295 (4)	3.30	3.30

World fishing records.

Silver Wedding Issue, 1972
Common Design Type

Design: Queen Elizabeth II, Prince Philip, Admiralty oar and mace.

1972, Nov. 20   **Photo.**   **Perf. 14x14½**
296	CD324	4c violet & multi	.20	.20
297	CD324	15c car rose & multi	.50	.50

Palmettos — A47

1973, Sept. 3   **Wmk. 314**   **Perf. 14**
298	A47	4c shown	.25	.25
299	A47	15c Olivewood	.75	.75
a.		Brown (Queen's head, "15c") omitted	1,400.	
300	A47	18c Bermuda cedar	1.00	1.20
301	A47	24c Mahogany	1.25	1.25
		Nos. 298-301 (4)	3.25	3.45

Bermuda National Trust, and "Plant a Tree" campaign.

Princess Anne's Wedding Issue
Common Design Type

1973, Nov. 21   **Litho.**
302	CD325	15c lilac & multi	.35	.35
303	CD325	18c slate & multi	.45	.45

National Tennis Stadium, Pembroke, 1973 — A48

15c, Bermuda's 1st tennis court, Pembroke, 1873. 18c, Britain's 1st tennis court, Leamington Spa, 1872. 24c, 1t US tennis club, Staten Island, 1874.

1973, Dec. 17   **Wmk. 314**
304	A48	4c black & multi	.20	.20
305	A48	15c black & multi	.65	.65
306	A48	18c black & multi	.90	.90
307	A48	24c black & multi	1.25	1.25
		Nos. 304-307 (4)	3.00	3.00

Centenary of tennis in Bermuda.

Rotary Emblem, Weather Vane, City Hall, Hamilton A49

Rotary Emblem and: 17c, St. Peter's Church, St. George's. 20c, Somerset Drawbridge, Somerset. 25c, Map of Bermuda on globe, 1626.

1974, June 24   **Perf. 14**
308	A49	5c emerald & multi	.25	.25
309	A49	17c blue & multi	.75	.75
310	A49	20c yel org & multi	.90	.90
311	A49	25c lt violet & multi	1.10	1.10
		Nos. 308-311 (4)	3.00	3.00

50th anniv. of Rotary Intl. in Bermuda.

Jack of Clubs and a Good Bridge Hand — A50

Bermuda Bowl and: 17c, Queen of diamonds. 20c, King of hearts. 25c, Ace of spades.

1975, Jan. 27   **Litho.**   **Wmk. 314**
312	A50	5c blue & multi	.25	.25
313	A50	17c dull yel & multi	.75	.75
314	A50	20c ver & multi	.80	.80
315	A50	25c lilac & multi	1.10	1.10
		Nos. 312-315 (4)	2.90	2.90

World Bridge Championship, Bermuda, Jan. 1975.

Queen Elizabeth II and Prince Philip — A51

Perf. 14x14½

1975, Feb. 17   **Photo.**   **Wmk. 373**
316	A51	17c multicolored	.60	.60
317	A51	20c dk blue & multi	.80	.80

Royal Visit, Feb. 16-18, 1975.

British Cavalier Flying Boat, 1937 A52

17c, US Navy airship "Los Angeles," 1925, flying from Lakehurst, NJ to Hamilton, Bermuda. 20c, Constellation over Kindley Field, 1946. 25c, Boeing 747 on tarmac, 1970.

1975, Apr. 28   **Litho.**   **Perf. 14**
318	A52	5c lt green & multi	.40	.40
319	A52	17c lt ultra & multi	1.25	1.25
320	A52	20c multicolored	1.75	1.75
321	A52	25c rose lil & multi	2.00	2.00
a.		Souvenir sheet of 4, #318-321	6.00	7.50
		Nos. 318-321 (4)	5.40	5.40

Airmail service to Bermuda, 50th anniv.

Flower Type of 1970

1975, June 2   **Photo.**   **Wmk. 314**
322	A41	17c Passion flower	1.25	1.25
323	A41	20c Coralita	1.25	1.25
324	A41	25c Morning glory	1.25	1.25
325	A41	40c Angel's trumpet	1.25	1.25
326	A41	$1 Plumbago	2.00	2.00
327	A41	$2 Bird-of-paradise flower	3.50	3.50
328	A41	$3 Chalice cup	6.00	6.00
		Nos. 322-328 (7)	16.50	16.50

Royal Magazine Break-in A54

17c, Sympathizers rowing towards magazine. 20c, Loading gun powder barrels onto ships. 25c, Gun powder barrels on beach.

Perf. 13x13½

1975, Oct. 27   **Litho.**   **Wmk. 373**
329	A54	5c multicolored	.25	.25
330	A54	17c multicolored	.75	.75
331	A54	20c multicolored	.85	.85
332	A54	25c multicolored	1.25	1.25
a.		Souv. sheet, #329-332, perf 14	4.00	5.00
		Nos. 329-332 (4)	3.10	3.10

Gunpowder Plot, 1775, American War of Independence.

Bermuda Biological Station A55

Designs: 5c, Launching of bathysphere from "Ready," vert. 20c, Sailing ship Challenger, 1873. 25c, Descent of Beebe's bathysphere, 1934, and marine life, vert.

1976, Mar. 29   **Litho.**   **Perf. 14**
333	A55	5c multicolored	.30	.30
334	A55	17c multicolored	.70	.70
335	A55	20c multicolored	.85	.85
336	A55	25c multicolored	1.00	1.00
		Nos. 333-336 (4)	2.85	2.85

Bermuda Biological Station, 50th anniv.

Christian Radich, Norway A56

Tall Ships: 12c, Juan Sebastian de Elcano, Spain. 17c, Eagle, US. 20c, Sir Winston Churchill, Great Britain. 40c, Kruzenshtern, USSR. $1, Cutty Sark (silver trophy).

1976, June 15   **Litho.**   **Perf. 13**
337	A56	5c lt green & multi	.30	.30
338	A56	12c violet & multi	.55	.55
339	A56	17c ultra & multi	.75	.75
340	A56	20c blue & multi	1.00	1.00
341	A56	40c yellow & multi	1.50	1.50
342	A56	$1 sl grn & multi	4.50	4.50
		Nos. 337-342 (6)	8.60	8.60

Trans-Atlantic Cutty Sark International Tall Ships Race, Plymouth, England-New York City (Operation Sail '76).

Silver Cup Trophy and Crossed Club Flags A57

Designs: 17c, St. George's Cricket Club and emblem. 20c, Somerset Cricket Club and emblem. 25c, Cricket match.

1976, Aug. 16   **Wmk. 373**   **Perf. 14½**
343	A57	5c multicolored	.25	.25
344	A57	17c multicolored	.85	.85
345	A57	20c multicolored	.95	.95
346	A57	25c multicolored	1.40	1.40
		Nos. 343-346 (4)	3.45	3.45

St. George's and Somerset Cricket Club matches, 75th anniversary.

Queen's Visit to Bermuda, 1975 — A58

Designs: 20c, St. Edward's Crown. $1, Queen seated in Chair of Estate.

1977, Feb. 7   Litho.   Perf. 14x13½
347 A58 5c silver & multi   .20 .20
348 A58 20c silver & multi   .55 .55
349 A58 $1 silver & multi   2.25 2.25
    Nos. 347-349 (3)   3.00 3.00

Reign of Queen Elizabeth II, 25th anniv.

Stockdale House, St. George's A59

UPU Emblem and: 15c, Perot Post Office and Perot Stamp. 17c, St. George's Post Office, c. 1860. 20c, Old GPO, Hamilton, c. 1935. 40c, New GPO, Hamilton, 1967.

1977, June 20   Litho.   Perf. 13x13½
350 A59 5c multicolored   .20 .20
351 A59 15c multicolored   .35 .35
352 A59 17c multicolored   .40 .40
353 A59 20c multicolored   .50 .50
354 A59 40c multicolored   1.00 1.00
    Nos. 350-354 (5)   2.45 2.45

Bermuda's UPU membership, cent.

Sailing Ship, 17th Century, Approaching Castle Island — A60

Designs: 15c, King's pilot leaving 18th century naval ship at Murray's Anchorage. 17c, Pilot gigs racing to meet steamship, early 19th century. 20c, Harvest Queen, late 19th century. 40c, Pilot cutter and Queen Elizabeth II off St. David's Lighthouse.

Perf. 13½x14
1977, Sept. 26   Wmk. 373
355 A60 5c multicolored   .20 .20
356 A60 15c multicolored   .40 .40
357 A60 17c multicolored   .50 .50
358 A60 20c multicolored   .65 .65
359 A60 40c multicolored   1.25 1.25
    Nos. 355-359 (5)   3.00 3.00

Piloting in Bermuda waters.

Elizabeth II A61

Designs: 8c, Great Seal of Elizabeth I. 50c, Great Seal of Elizabeth II.

1978, Aug. 28   Litho.   Perf. 14x13½
360 A61 8c gold & multi   .20 .20
361 A61 50c gold & multi   .85 .85
362 A61 $1 gold & multi   1.60 1.60
    Nos. 360-362 (3)   2.65 2.65

25th anniv. of coronation of Elizabeth II.

White-tailed Tropicbird — A62

Perf. 14; 14x14½ (4c, 5c, $2, $3, $5)
1978-79   Photo.   Wmk. 373
363 A62 3c shown   .20 .20
364 A62 4c White-eyed vireo   .20 .20
365 A62 5c Eastern bluebird   .20 .20
366 A62 7c Whistling tree frog   .20 .20
367 A62 8c Cardinal   .20 .20
368 A62 10c Spiny lobster   .20 .20
369 A62 12c Land crab   .20 .20
370 A62 15c Skink   .25 .25
371 A62 20c Four-eyed butterflyfish   .35 .35
372 A62 25c Red hind   .45 .45
  a.   Greenish blue (background) omitted   450.00
373 A62 30c Monarch butterfly   .50 .50
374 A62 40c Rock beauty   .70 .70
375 A62 50c Banded butterflyfish   1.00 1.00
376 A62 $1 Blue angelfish   2.00 2.00
377 A62 $2 Humpback whale   4.25 4.25
378 A62 $3 Green turtle   6.25 6.25
379 A62 $5 Bermuda Petrel   10.50 10.50
    Nos. 363-379 (17)   27.65 27.65

Issued: 3c, 4c, 5c, 8c, $5, 1978; others, 1979.
For surcharge see No. 509.

Map of Bermuda, by George Somers, 1609 — A63

Old Maps of Bermuda: 15c, by John Seller, 1685. 20c, by Herman Moll, 1729, vert. 25c, by Desbruslins, 1740. 50c, by John Speed, 1626.

1979, May 14   Litho.   Perf. 13½
380 A63 8c multicolored   .20 .20
381 A63 15c multicolored   .30 .30
382 A63 20c multicolored   .40 .40
383 A63 25c multicolored   .45 .45
384 A63 50c multicolored   .95 .95
    Nos. 380-384 (5)   2.30 2.30

Bermuda Police Centenary — A64

20c, Traffic direction, horiz. 25c, Water patrol, horiz. 50c, Motorbike and patrol car.

1979, Nov. 26   Wmk. 373   Perf. 14
385 A64 8c multicolored   .20 .20
386 A64 20c multicolored   .40 .40
387 A64 25c multicolored   .50 .50
388 A64 50c multicolored   1.00 1.00
    Nos. 385-388 (4)   2.10 2.10

Bermuda No. X1, Penny Black — A65

Bermuda #X1 and: 20c, Hill. 25c, "Paid 1" marking on cover. 50c, "Paid 1" marking.

1980, Feb. 25   Litho.   Perf. 13½x14
389 A65 8c multicolored   .20 .20
390 A65 20c multicolored   .40 .40
391 A65 25c multicolored   .50 .50
392 A65 50c multicolored   1.00 1.00
    Nos. 389-392 (4)   2.10 2.10

Sir Rowland Hill (1795-1879), originator of penny postage.

Tristar-500, London 1980 Emblem — A66

1980, May 6   Litho.   Perf. 13x14
393 A66 25c shown   .35 .35
394 A66 50c "Orduna," 1926   .70 .70
395 A66 $1 "Delta," 1856   1.50 1.50
396 A66 $2 "Lord Sidmouth," 1818   3.00 3.00
    Nos. 393-396 (4)   5.55 5.55

London 1980 Intl. Stamp Exhib., May 6-14.

Gina Swainson, Miss World, 1979-80, Arms of Bermuda — A67

1980, May 8   Perf. 14
397 A67 8c shown   .20 .20
398 A67 20c After crowning ceremony   .35 .35
399 A67 50c Welcome home party   .90 .90
400 A67 $1 In carriage   1.75 1.75
    Nos. 397-400 (4)   3.20 3.20

Queen Mother Elizabeth Birthday Issue
Common Design Type
1980, Aug. 4   Wmk. 373   Perf. 14
401 CD330 25c multicolored   .45 .45

Camden, Prime Minister's House A68

1980, Sept. 24   Litho.   Perf. 14
402 A68 8c View from satellite   .20 .20
403 A68 20c shown   .40 .40
404 A68 25c Princess Hotel, Hamilton   .50 .50
405 A68 50c Government House   1.00 1.00
    Nos. 402-405 (4)   2.10 2.10

Commonwealth Finance Ministers Meeting, Bermuda, Sept.

18th Century Kitchen A69

1981, May 21   Wmk. 373   Perf. 14
406 A69 8c shown   .20 .20
407 A69 25c Gathering Easter lilies   .40 .40
408 A69 30c Fisherman   .50 .50
409 A69 40c Stone cutting, 19th cent.   .70 .70
410 A69 50c Onion shipping, 19th cent.   .85 .85
411 A69 $1 Ships, 17th cent.   1.75 1.75
    Nos. 406-411 (6)   4.40 4.40

Royal Wedding Issue
Common Design Type
1981, July 22   Wmk. 373   Perf. 14
412 CD331 30c Bouquet   .50 .50
413 CD331 50c Charles   .90 .90
414 CD331 $1 Couple   1.75 1.75
    Nos. 412-414 (3)   3.15 3.15

Girl Helping Blind Man Cross Street — A70

1981, Sept. 28   Litho.   Perf. 14
415 A70 10c shown   .20 .20
416 A70 25c Kayaking, Paget Island   .50 .50
417 A70 30c Mountain climbing, St. David's Island   .55 .55
418 A70 $1 Duke of Edinburgh   1.90 1.90
    Nos. 415-418 (4)   3.15 3.15

Duke of Edinburgh's Awards, 25th anniv.

Conus Species A71

1982, May 13   Wmk. 373   Perf. 14
419 A71 10c shown   .20 .20
420 A71 25c Bursa finlayi   .50 .50
421 A71 30c Sconsia striata   .60 .60
422 A71 $1 Murex pterynotus lightbourni   1.90 1.90
    Nos. 419-422 (4)   3.20 3.20

Bermuda Regiment A72

1982, June 17   Litho.   Wmk. 373
423 A72 10c Color guard   .20 .20
424 A72 25c Queen's birthday parade   .40 .40
425 A72 30c Governor inspecting honor guard   .60 .60
426 A72 40c Beating the retreat   .80 .80
427 A72 50c Ceremonial gunners   1.00 1.00
428 A72 $1 Royal visit, 1975   2.00 2.00
    Nos. 423-428 (6)   5.00 5.00

Southampton Fort — A73

1982, Nov. 18   Litho.   Wmk. 373
429 A73 10c Charles Fort, vert.   .20 .20
430 A73 25c Pembroks Fort, vert.   .50 .50
431 A73 30c shown   .60 .60
432 A73 $1 Smiths and Pagets Forts   1.90 1.90
    Nos. 429-432 (4)   3.20 3.20

Arms of Sir Edwin Sandys (1561-1629) A74

Coats of Arms: 25c, Bermuda Company. 50c, William Herbert, 3rd Earl of Pembroke (1584-1630). $1, Sir George Somers (1554-1610).

1983, Apr. 14　　Litho.　　Perf. 13½

433	A74	10c multicolored	.20	.20
434	A74	25c multicolored	.45	.45
435	A74	50c multicolored	.90	.90
436	A74	$1 multicolored	1.75	1.75
		Nos. 433-436 (4)	3.30	3.30

See Nos. 457-460, 474-477.

Fitted Dinghies — A75

1983, July 21　　Wmk. 373　　Perf. 14

Old and modern boats.

437	A75	12c multicolored	.25	.25
438	A75	30c multicolored	.55	.55
439	A75	40c multicolored	.70	.70
440	A75	$1 multicolored	1.75	1.75
		Nos. 437-440 (4)	3.25	3.25

Manned Flight Bicentenary — A76

Designs: 12c, Curtiss Jenny, 1919 (first flight over Bermuda). 30c, Stinson Pilot Radio, 1930 (first completed US-Bermuda flight). 40c, Cavalier, 1937 (first scheduled passenger flight). $1, USS Los Angeles airship moored to USS Patoka, 1925.

1983, Oct. 13　　Litho.　　Perf. 14

441	A76	12c multicolored	.30	.30
442	A76	30c multicolored	.65	.65
443	A76	40c multicolored	.90	.90
444	A76	$1 multicolored	1.75	1.75
		Nos. 441-444 (4)	3.60	3.60

Newspaper and Postal Services, 200th Anniv. — A77

1984, Jan. 26　　Litho.　　Perf. 14

445	A77	12c Joseph Stockdale	.25	.25
446	A77	30c First Newspaper	.55	.55
447	A77	40c Stockdale's Postal Service, horiz.	.70	.70
448	A77	$1 "Lady Hammond," horiz.	1.75	1.75
		Nos. 445-448 (4)	3.25	3.25

375th Anniv. of Bermuda Settlement — A78

Designs: 12c, Thomas Gates, George Somers. 30c, Jamestown, Virginia, US. 40c, Sea Venture shipwreck. $1, Fleet leaving Plymouth, England.

1984, May 3　　Litho.　　Wmk. 373

449	A78	12c multicolored	.25	.25
450	A78	30c multicolored	.55	.55
451	A78	40c multicolored	.70	.70

452	A78	$1 multicolored	1.75	1.75
a.		Souv. sheet of 2, #450, 452	5.00	5.00
		Nos. 449-452 (4)	3.25	3.25

1984 Summer Olympics A79

1984, July 19　　Litho.　　Perf. 14

453	A79	12c Swimming, vert.	.20	.20
454	A79	30c Track & field	.50	.50
455	A79	40c Equestrian, vert.	.70	.70
456	A79	$1 Sailing	1.60	1.60
		Nos. 453-456 (4)	3.00	3.00

Arms Type of 1983

1984, Sept. 27　　Litho.　　Perf. 13½

457	A74	12c Southampton	.20	.20
458	A74	30c Smith	.60	.60
459	A74	40c Devonshire	.75	.75
460	A74	$1 St. George	1.60	1.60
		Nos. 457-460 (4)	3.15	3.15

Architecture, Buttery — A80

1985, Jan. 24　　Litho.　　Perf. 13½x13

461	A80	12c shown	.35	.35
462	A80	30c Rooftops	.75	.75
463	A80	40c Chimneys	1.00	1.00
464	A80	$1.50 Archway	3.50	3.50
		Nos. 461-464 (4)	5.60	5.60

Audubon Birth Bicentenary — A81

1985, Mar. 21　　Wmk. 373　　Perf. 14

465	A81	12c Osprey, vert.	.30	.30
466	A81	30c Yellow-crowned night heron, vert.	.75	.75
467	A81	40c Great egret	1.00	1.00
468	A81	$1.50 Bluebird, vert.	3.50	3.50
		Nos. 465-468 (4)	5.55	5.55

Queen Mother 85th Birthday Issue
Common Design Type

Designs: 12c, Queen Consort, 1937. 30c, With grandchildren, 80th birthday. 40c, At Clarence House, 83rd birthday. $1.50, Holding Prince Henry. No. 473, In coach with Prince Charles.

Perf. 14½x14

1985, June 7　　　　　　Wmk. 384

469	CD336	12c gray, bl & blk	.35	.35
470	CD336	30c multicolored	.75	.75
471	CD336	40c multicolored	1.00	1.00
472	CD336	$1.50 multicolored	3.50	3.50
		Nos. 469-472 (4)	5.60	5.60

Souvenir Sheet

473	CD336	$1 multicolored	4.50	4.50

Arms Type of 1983

Coats of Arms: 12c, James Hamilton, 2nd Marquess of Hamilton (1589-1625). 30c, William Paget, 4th Lord Paget (1572-1629). 40c, Robert Rich, 2nd Earl of Warwick (1587-1658). $1.50, Hamilton, 1957.

1985, Sept. 19　　Litho.　　Perf. 13½

474	A74	12c multicolored	.30	.30
475	A74	30c multicolored	.75	.75
476	A74	40c multicolored	1.00	1.00
477	A74	$1.50 multicolored	3.75	3.75
		Nos. 474-477 (4)	5.80	5.80

Halley's Comet A82

1985, Nov. 21　　Wmk. 384　　Perf. 14½

478	A82	15c Bermuda Archipelago	.40	.40
479	A82	40c Nuremberg Chronicles, 1493	1.00	1.00
480	A82	50c Peter Apian woodcut, 1532	1.25	1.25
481	A82	$1.50 Painting by Samuel Scott (c.1702-72)	3.75	3.75
		Nos. 478-481 (4)	6.40	6.40

Shipwrecks — A83

1986　　　　　Wmk. 384　　　Perf. 14

482	A83	3c Constellation, 1943	.20	.20
483	A83	5c Early Riser, 1876	.20	.20
484	A83	7c Madiana, 1903	.20	.20
485	A83	10c Curlew, 1856	.20	.20
486	A83	12c Warwick, 1619	.20	.20
487	A83	15c HMS Vixen, 1890	.30	.30
488	A83	20c San Pedro, 1594	.35	.35
489	A83	25c Alert, 1877	.50	.50
490	A83	40c North Carolina, 1880	.75	.75
491	A83	50c Mark Antonie, 1777	1.00	1.00
492	A83	60c Mary Celestia, 1864	1.10	1.10
493	A83	$1 L'Herminie, 1839	1.75	1.75
494	A83	$1.50 Caesar, 1818	2.75	2.75
495	A83	$2 Lord Amherst, 1778	3.50	3.50
496	A83	$3 Minerva, 1849	5.50	5.50
497	A83	$5 Caraquet, 1923	9.00	9.00
498	A83	$8 HMS Pallas, 1783	14.50	14.50
		Nos. 482-498 (17)	42.00	42.00

Nos. 493, 495-496 exist inscribed "1989." Nos. 482, 488, "1990." See #545-546. For surcharges see #598-600.

Inscribed "1992"

1992　　Litho.　　Wmk. 373　　Perf. 14

485a	A83	10c	.20	.20
487a	A83	15c	.30	.30
488a	A83	20c	.35	.35
489a	A83	25c	.45	.45
492a	A83	60c	1.10	1.10
497a	A83	$5	9.25	9.25
498a	A83	$8	14.75	14.75
		Nos. 485a-498a (7)	26.40	26.40

Queen Elizabeth II 60th Birthday
Common Design Type

15c, Age 3. 40c, With the Earl of Rosebury, Oaks May Meeting, Epsom, 1954. 50c, With Prince Philip, state visit,1979. 60c, At the British embassy in Paris, state visit, 1972. $1.50, Visiting Crown Agents' offices, 1983.

1986, Apr. 21　　Wmk. 384　　Perf. 14½

499	CD337	15c scar, blk & sil	.25	.25
500	CD337	40c ultra & multi	.65	.65
501	CD337	50c green & multi	.80	.80
502	CD337	60c violet & multi	.95	.95
503	CD337	$1.50 rose vio & multi	2.50	2.50
		Nos. 499-503 (5)	5.15	5.15

AMERIPEX '86 — A84

1986, May 22　　　　　　Perf. 14

504	A84	15c No. 452a	.25	.25
505	A84	40c No. 307	.65	.65
506	A84	50c No. 441	.80	.80
507	A84	$1 No. 339	1.60	1.60
		Nos. 504-507 (4)	3.30	3.30

Souvenir Sheet

508	A84	1.50 Statue of Liberty, S.S. Queen of Bermuda	4.50	4.50

Statue of Liberty, cent.

No. 378 Surcharged
Perf. 14x14½

1986, Dec. 4　　Photo.　　Wmk. 373

509	A62	90c on $3 multi	3.00	3.00

Exists with double surcharge.

Transport Railway, c. 1931-1947 — A85

Wmk. 373

1987, Jan. 22　　Litho.　　Perf. 14

510	A85	15c Front Street, c. 1940	.25	.25
511	A85	40c Springfield Trestle	.65	.65
512	A85	50c No. 101, Bailey's Bay Sta.	.80	.80
513	A85	$1.50 No. 31, ship Prince David	2.50	2.50
		Nos. 510-513 (4)	4.20	4.20

Paintings by Winslow Homer (1836-1910) A86

1987, Apr. 30　　　　　　Perf. 14½

514	A86	15c Bermuda Settlers, 1901	.30	.30
515	A86	30c Bermuda, 1900	.55	.55
516	A86	40c Bermuda Landscape, 1901	.75	.75
517	A86	50c Inland Water, 1901	.95	.95
518	A86	$1.50 Salt Kettle, 1899	3.00	3.00
		Nos. 514-518 (5)	5.55	5.55

Booklet Stamps

519	A86	40c like 15c	.65	.65
520	A86	40c like 30c	.65	.65
521	A86	40c like No. 516	.65	.65
522	A86	40c like 50c	.65	.65
523	A86	40c like $1.50	.65	.65
a.		Bklt. pane, 2 each #519-523	6.50	

Nos. 519-523 printed in strips of 5 within pane. "ER" at lower left.

Intl. Flights Inauguration — A87

1987, June 18　　　　　　Perf. 14

524	A87	15c Sikorsky S-42B, 1937	.50	.50
525	A87	40c Shorts S-23 Cavalier	1.40	1.40
526	A87	50c S-42B Bermuda Clipper	1.60	1.60
527	A87	$1.50 Cavalier, Bermuda Clipper	5.00	5.00
		Nos. 524-527 (4)	8.50	8.50

Bermuda Telephone Company, Cent. — A88

1987, Oct. 1   Litho.   Wmk. 384

528	A88	15c Telephone poles on wagon	.25	.25
529	A88	40c Operators	.70	.70
530	A88	50c Telephones	.85	.85
531	A88	$1.50 Satellite, fiber optics, world	2.50	2.50
		Nos. 528-531 (4)	4.30	4.30

Horse-drawn Commercial Vehicles — A89

1988, Mar. 3   Litho.   Perf. 14

532	A89	15c Mail wagon, c. 1869	.30	.30
533	A89	40c Open cart, c. 1823	.75	.75
534	A89	50c Closed cart, c. 1823	.95	.95
535	A89	$1.50 Two-wheel wagon, c. 1930	2.75	2.75
		Nos. 532-535 (4)	4.75	4.75

Old Garden Roses A90

1988, Apr. 21   Wmk. 373

536	A90	15c Old blush	.25	.25
537	A90	30c Anna Olivier	.50	.50
538	A90	40c Rosa chinensis semperflorens, vert.	.70	.70
539	A90	50c Archduke Charles	.90	.90
540	A90	$1.50 Rosa chinensis viridiflora, vert.	2.75	2.75
		Nos. 536-540 (5)	5.10	5.10

See Nos. 561-575.

Lloyds of London, 300th Anniv.
Common Design Type

18c, Loss of the H.M.S. Lutine, 1799. 50c, Cable ship Sentinel. 60c, The Bermuda, Hamilton, 1931. $2, Valerian, lost during a hurricane, 1926.

1988, Oct. 13   Litho.   Wmk. 384

541	CD341	18c multi	.30	.30
542	CD341	50c multi, horiz.	.90	.90
543	CD341	60c multi, horiz.	1.10	1.10
544	CD341	$2 multi	3.50	3.50
		Nos. 541-544 (4)	5.80	5.80

Shipwreck Type of 1986

1988   Litho.   Wmk. 384   Perf. 14

545	A83	18c like 7c	.35	.35
546	A83	70c like $1.50	1.40	1.40

Issue dates: 18c, Sept. 22; 70c, Oct. 27.

Military Uniforms — A91

18c, Devonshire Parish Militia, 1812. 50c, 71st Regiment Highlander, 1831-34. 60c, Cameron Highlander, 1942. $2, Troop of Horse, 1774.

1988, Nov. 10   Wmk. 373   Perf. 14½

547	A91	18c multicolored	.30	.30
548	A91	50c multicolored	.85	.85
549	A91	60c multicolored	1.00	1.00
550	A91	$2 multicolored	3.50	3.50
		Nos. 547-550 (4)	5.65	5.65

Ferry Service A92

1989   Litho.   Wmk. 384   Perf. 14

551	A92	18c Corona	.30	.30
552	A92	50c Rowboat ferry	.85	.85
553	A92	60c St. George's Ferry	1.00	1.00
554	A92	$2 Laconia	3.50	3.50
		Nos. 551-554 (4)	5.65	5.65

Photography, Sesquicent. A93

Perf. 14x14½

1989, May 11   Litho.   Wmk. 373

555	A93	18c Morgan's Is.	.35	.35
556	A93	30c Front Street, Hamilton (cannon in square)	.60	.60
557	A93	50c Front Street (seascape)	1.00	1.00
558	A93	60c Crow Lane, Hamilton Harbor	1.25	1.25
559	A93	70c Hamilton Harbor (shipbuilding)	1.40	1.40
560	A93	$1 Dockyard	2.00	2.00
		Nos. 555-560 (6)	6.60	6.60

Old Garden Roses Type of 1988

1989, July 13   Perf. 14

561	A90	18c Agrippina	.35	.35
562	A90	30c Smith's Parish	.60	.60
563	A90	50c Champney's pink cluster	1.00	1.00
564	A90	60c Rosette delizy	1.25	1.25
565	A90	$1.50 Rosa bracteata	3.00	3.00
		Nos. 561-565 (5)	6.20	6.20

Nos. 561-562 vert.

Old Garden Roses Type of 1988 with Royal Cipher Instead of Queen's Silhouette

1989, July 13   Booklet Stamps

566	A90	50c like No. 562	1.00	1.00
567	A90	50c like No. 540	1.00	1.00
568	A90	50c like No. 561	1.00	1.00
569	A90	50c like No. 538	1.00	1.00
570	A90	50c like No. 563	1.00	1.00
571	A90	50c like No. 536	1.00	1.00
572	A90	50c like No. 564	1.00	1.00
573	A90	50c like No. 537	1.00	1.00
574	A90	50c like No. 565	1.00	1.00
575	A90	50c like No. 539	1.00	1.00
a.		Bklt. pane of 10, #566-575	10.00	

Bermuda Library, 150th Anniv. A94

1989, Sept. 14   Perf. 13½x14

576	A94	18c Hamilton Main Library	.30	.30
577	A94	50c St. George's, The Old Rectory	.85	.85
578	A94	60c Springfield, Sommerset Library	1.00	1.00
579	A94	$2 Cabinet Building	3.50	3.50
		Nos. 576-579 (4)	5.65	5.65

Commonwealth Postal Conference — A95

1989, Nov. 3   Wmk. 384   Perf. 14

580	A95	18c No. 1	.30	.30
581	A95	50c No. 2	.85	.85
582	A95	60c Type A4	1.00	1.00
583	A95	$2 No. 6	3.50	3.50
		Nos. 580-583 (4)	5.65	5.65

For overprints see Nos. 594-597.

Fairylands, Bermuda, c. 1890, by Ross Sterling Turner A96

Paintings: 50c, *Shinebone Alley, c. 1953,* by Ogden M. Pleissner. 60c, *Salt Kettle, 1916,* by Prosper Senate. $2, *St. George's, 1934,* by Jack Bush.

1990, Apr. 19

590	A96	18c multicolored	.30	.30
591	A96	50c multicolored	.85	.85
592	A96	60c multicolored	1.00	1.00
593	A96	$2 multicolored	3.50	3.50
		Nos. 590-593 (4)	5.65	5.65

Nos. 580-583 Overprinted

1990, May 3

594	A95	18c multicolored	.35	.35
595	A95	50c multicolored	1.00	1.00
596	A95	60c multicolored	1.25	1.25
597	A95	$2 multicolored	4.00	4.00
		Nos. 594-597 (4)	6.60	6.60

Stamp World London '90.

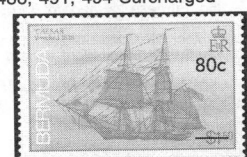

Nos. 486, 491, 494 Surcharged

1990, Aug. 13

598	A83	30c on 12c No. 486	.50	.50
599	A83	55c on 50c No. 491	1.00	1.00
600	A83	80c on $1.50 No. 494	1.50	1.50
		Nos. 598-600 (3)	3.00	3.00

Nova Scotia-Bermuda Cable, Cent. — A97

1990, Oct. 18   Litho.   Unwmk.

601	A97	20c Office	.35	.35
602	A97	55c Cableship SS Westmeath	1.00	1.00
603	A97	70c Radio station, 1928	1.25	1.25
604	A97	$2 Cableship Sir Eric Sharp	3.50	3.50
		Nos. 601-604 (4)	6.10	6.10

Nos. 601-602 with Added Inscription: "BUSH-MAJOR / 16 MARCH 1991"

1991, Mar.   Unwmk.   Perf. 14

605	A97	20c like #601	.40	.40
606	A97	55c like #602	1.10	1.10

Carriages A98

Designs: 20c, Two-seat pony cart, c. 1805. 30c, Varnished rockaway, c. 1830. 55c, Vis-a-Vis Victoria, c. 1895. 70c, Semi-formal phaeton, c. 1900. 80c, Pony runabout, c. 1905. $1, Ladies' phaeton, c. 1910.

Perf. 14x14½

1991, Mar. 21   Litho.   Wmk. 373

607	A98	20c green & multi	.40	.40
608	A98	30c bl gray & multi	.60	.60
609	A98	55c dk car & multi	1.10	1.10
610	A98	70c blue & multi	1.40	1.40
611	A98	80c yel org & multi	1.60	1.60
612	A98	$1 dk gray & multi	2.00	2.00
		Nos. 607-612 (6)	7.10	7.10

Paintings A99

Designs: 20c, Bermuda by Prosper Senat, vert. 55c, Bermuda Cottage by Frank Allison. 70c, Old Maid's Lane by Jack Bush, vert. $2, St. George's by Ogden M. Pleissner.

Perf. 14x13½

1991, May 16   Litho.   Wmk. 373

613	A99	20c multicolored	.40	.40
614	A99	55c multicolored	1.10	1.10
615	A99	70c multicolored	1.40	1.40
616	A99	$2 multicolored	4.00	4.00
		Nos. 613-616 (4)	6.90	6.90

Elizabeth & Philip, Birthdays
Common Design Types

1991, June 20   Wmk. 384   Perf. 14½

617	CD346	55c multicolored	1.10	1.10
618	CD345	70c multicolored	1.40	1.40
a.		Pair, #617-618 + label	2.50	2.50

Bermuda in World War II A100

Designs: 20c, Floating drydock. 55c, Kindley Air Field. 70c, Trans-atlantic air route, Boeing 314. $2, Censored trans-atlantic mail.

1991, Sept. 19   Wmk. 373   Perf. 14

619	A100	20c multicolored	.40	.40
620	A100	55c multicolored	1.10	1.10
621	A100	70c multicolored	1.40	1.40
622	A100	$2 multicolored	4.00	4.00
		Nos. 619-622 (4)	6.90	6.90

Queen Elizabeth II's Accession to the Throne, 40th Anniv.
Common Design Type

1992, Feb. 6

623	CD349	20c multicolored	.40	.40
624	CD349	30c multicolored	.60	.60
625	CD349	55c multicolored	1.10	1.10
626	CD349	70c multicolored	1.40	1.40
627	CD349	$1 multicolored	2.00	2.00
		Nos. 623-627 (5)	5.50	5.50

Age of Exploration — A101

Artifacts: 25c, Rings, medallion. 35c, Ink wells. 60c, Gold pieces. 75c, Bishop button, crucifix. 85c, Pearl earrings and buttons. $1, 8-real coin, jug and measuring cups.

1992, July 23   *Perf. 13½*

628	A101	25c multicolored	.50	.50
629	A101	35c multicolored	.70	.70
630	A101	60c multicolored	1.25	1.25
631	A101	75c multicolored	1.50	1.50
632	A101	85c multicolored	1.75	1.75
633	A101	$1 multicolored	2.00	2.00
		Nos. 628-633 (6)	7.70	7.70

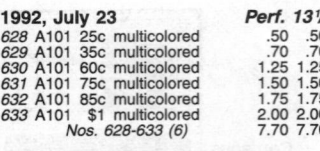

Stained Glass Windows — A102

Designs: 25c, Ship wreck. 60c, Birds in tree. 75c, St. Francis feeding bird. $2, Seashells.

1992, Sept. 24   *Perf. 14*

634	A102	25c multicolored	.50	.50
635	A102	60c multicolored	1.25	1.25
636	A102	75c multicolored	1.50	1.50
637	A102	$2 multicolored	4.00	4.00
		Nos. 634-637 (4)	7.25	7.25

7th World Congress of Kennel Clubs A103

Perf. 13½x14, 14x13½

1992, Nov. 12   Litho.   Wmk. 373

638	A103	25c German shepherd	.50	.50
639	A103	35c Irish setter	.65	.65
640	A103	60c Whippet, vert.	1.10	1.10
641	A103	75c Border terrier, vert.	1.40	1.40
642	A103	85c Pomeranian, vert.	1.60	1.60
643	A103	$1 Schipperke, vert.	1.90	1.90
		Nos. 638-643 (6)	7.15	7.15

A104

Tourist Posters — A105

1993, Feb. 25   Wmk. 373   *Perf. 14*

644	A104	25c Cyclist, carriage, ship	.50	.50
645	A105	60c Golf course	1.10	1.10
646	A105	75c Coastline	1.40	1.40
647	A104	$2 Dancers	3.75	3.75
		Nos. 644-647 (4)	6.75	6.75

Royal Air Force, 75th Anniv.
Common Design Type

Designs: 25c, Consolidated Catalina. 60c, Supermarine Spitfire. 75c, Bristol Beaufighter. $2, Handley Page Halifax.

1993, Apr. 1

648	CD350	25c multicolored	.50	.50
649	CD350	60c multicolored	1.10	1.10
650	CD350	75c multicolored	1.40	1.40
651	CD350	$2 multicolored	3.75	3.75
		Nos. 648-651 (4)	6.75	6.75

Duchesse de Brabant Rose, Bee — A106

1993, Apr. 1   Wmk. 384
Booklet Stamps

652	A106	10c green & multi	.20	.20
653	A106	25c violet & multi	.50	.50
a.		Booklet pane of 5	2.50	
654	A106	50c sepia & multi	1.00	1.00
a.		Booklet pane, 2 #652, 3 #654	3.50	
655	A106	60c vermilion & multi	1.10	1.10
a.		Booklet pane of 5	5.50	
		Nos. 652-655 (4)	2.80	2.80

Hamilton, Bicent. — A107

Designs: 25c, Modern skyline. 60c, Front Street, ships at left. 75c, Front Street, horse carts. $2, Hamilton Harbor, 1823.

Wmk. 373

1993, Sept. 16   Litho.   *Perf. 14½*

656	A107	25c multicolored	.50	.50
657	A107	60c multicolored	1.10	1.10
658	A107	75c multicolored	1.40	1.40
659	A107	$2 multicolored	3.75	3.75
		Nos. 656-659 (4)	6.75	6.75

Furness Lines — A108

25c, Furness Liv-Aboard Bermuda cruises, vert. 60c, SS Queen of Bermuda entering port. 75c, SS Queen of Bermuda, SS Ocean Monarch. $2, Starlit night aboard ship, vert.

Perf. 15x14, 14x15

1994, Jan. 20   Litho.   Wmk. 373

660	A108	25c multicolored	.50	.50
661	A108	60c multicolored	1.10	1.10
662	A108	75c multicolored	1.40	1.40
663	A108	$2 multicolored	3.75	3.75
		Nos. 660-663 (4)	6.75	6.75

Royal Visit — A109

25c, Queen Elizabeth II. 60c, Queen Elizabeth II, Duke of Edinburgh. 75c, Royal yacht Britannia.

Wmk. 373

1994, Mar. 9   Litho.   *Perf. 13½*

664	A109	25c multicolored	.50	.50
665	A109	60c multicolored	1.10	1.10
666	A109	75c multicolored	1.50	1.50
		Nos. 664-666 (3)	3.10	3.10

Flowering Fruits A110

1994-95   Litho.   Wmk. 373   *Perf. 14*

668	A110	5c Peach	.20	.20
669	A110	7c Fig	.20	.20
670	A110	10c Calabash, vert.	.20	.20
671	A110	15c Natal plum	.30	.30

672	A110	18c Locust & wild honey	.35	.35
673	A110	20c Pomegranate	.40	.40
674	A110	25c Mulberry, vert.	.50	.50
675	A110	35c Grape, vert.	.70	.70
676	A110	55c Orange, vert.	1.10	1.10
677	A110	60c Surinam cherry	1.25	1.25
678	A110	75c Loquat	1.50	1.50
679	A110	90c Sugar apple	1.75	1.75
680	A110	$1 Prickly pear, vert.	2.00	2.00
681	A110	$2 Paw paw	4.00	4.00
682	A110	$3 Bay grape	6.00	6.00
683	A110	$5 Banana, vert.	10.00	10.00
684	A110	$8 Lemon	16.00	16.00
		Nos. 668-684 (17)	46.45	46.45

No. 672 exists dated "1996." Nos. 668, 671-674, 678-680 dated "1998."

Issued: 5c, 7c, 15c, 20c, $8, 7/14/94; 10c, 25c, 35c, 55c, $1, $5, 10/6/94; 18c, 60c, 75c, 90c, $2, $3, 3/23/95.

1996-98   Wmk. 384

668a	A110	5c	.20	.20
671a	A110	15c	.30	.30
672a	A110	18c	.35	.35
673a	A110	20c	.40	.40
674a	A110	25c	.50	.50
678a	A110	75c	1.50	1.50
679a	A110	90c	1.75	1.75
680a	A110	$1	2.00	2.00
		Nos. 668a-680a (8)	7.00	7.00

#672a exists dated "1998."

Issued: #668a, 671a, 673a-674a, 678a-680a, 9/1/98; #672a, 9/1/96.

Hospital Care, Cent. — A111

1994, Sept. 15   *Perf. 15x14*

685	A111	25c Child birth	.50	.50
686	A111	60c Dialysis	1.10	1.10
687	A111	75c Emergency	1.50	1.50
688	A111	$2 Therapy	4.00	4.00
		Nos. 685-688 (4)	7.10	7.10

Christmas — A112

1994, Nov. 10   *Perf. 14x15*

689	A112	25c Gombey dancers	.50	.50
690	A112	60c Carollers	1.10	1.10
691	A112	75c Marching band	1.50	1.50
692	A112	$2 Natl. dance group	4.00	4.00
		Nos. 689-692 (4)	7.10	7.10

Decimalization, 25th Anniv. — A113

Stamps, 1970 coins: 25c, #255, one cent. 60c, #259, five cents. 75c, #262, ten cents. $2, #324, twenty-five cents.

Wmk. 373

1995, Feb. 6   Litho.   *Perf. 14*

693	A113	25c multicolored	.50	.50
694	A113	60c multicolored	1.10	1.10
695	A113	75c multicolored	1.50	1.50
696	A113	$2 multicolored	4.00	4.00
		Nos. 693-696 (4)	7.10	7.10

Outdoor Celebrations — A114

Perf. 14x15

1995, May 30   Litho.   Wmk. 373

697	A114	25c Kite flying	.50	.50
698	A114	60c Majorettes	1.10	1.10
699	A114	75c Portuguese dancers	1.50	1.50
700	A114	$2 Floral float	4.00	4.00
		Nos. 697-700 (4)	7.10	7.10

Parliament, 375th Anniv. — A115

Designs: 25c, $1, Bermuda coat of arms.

Perf. 14x13½

1995, Nov. 3   Litho.   Wmk. 373

701	A115	25c blue & multi	.50	.50
702	A115	$1 green & multi	2.00	2.00
		See No. 731.		

Military Bases A116

Force insignia and: 20c, Ordnance Island Submarine Base. 25c, Royal Naval Dockyard. 60c, Fort Bell and Kindley Field. 75c, Darrell's Island. 90c, US Navy Operating Base. $1, Canadian Forces Station, Daniel's Head.

1995, Dec. 4   *Perf. 14*

703	A116	20c multicolored	.40	.40
704	A116	25c multicolored	.50	.50
705	A116	60c multicolored	1.25	1.25
706	A116	75c multicolored	1.50	1.50
707	A116	90c multicolored	1.75	1.75
708	A116	$1 multicolored	2.00	2.00
		Nos. 703-708 (6)	7.40	7.40

Modern Olympic Games, Cent. — A117

Wmk. 384

1996, May 21   Litho.   *Perf. 14*

709	A117	25c Track & field	.50	.50
710	A117	30c Cycling	.65	.65
711	A117	65c Sailing	1.25	1.25
712	A117	80c Equestrian	1.60	1.60
		Nos. 709-712 (4)	4.00	4.00

CAPEX '96 A118

Methods of transportation: 25c, Sommerset Express, c. 1900. 60c, Bermuda Railway, 1930's. 75c, First bus, 1946. $2, Early sightseeing bus, c.1947.

Perf. 13½x14

1996, June 7	Litho.	Wmk. 373	
713 A118	25c multicolored	.50	.50
714 A118	60c multicolored	1.25	1.25
715 A118	75c multicolored	1.50	1.50
716 A118	$2 multicolored	4.00	4.00
Nos. 713-716 (4)		7.25	7.25

Panoramas of Hamilton and St. George's, by E. J. Holland, 1933 — A119

Hamilton, looking across water from Bostock Hill: No. 717, Palm trees, Furness Line ship coming through Two Rock Passage. No. 718, House, buildings on other side. No. 719, Sailboats on water, Princess Hotel. No. 720, Island, Bermudiana Hotel, Cathedral. No. 721, Coral roads on hillside, city of Hamilton.

St. George's, looking across water from St. David's: No. 722, Island, harbor. No. 723, Sailboat, buildings along shore. No. 724, Sailboat, St. George's Hotel, buildings. No. 725, Hillside, ship. No. 726, Homes on hill top, passage out of harbor.

Perf. 14x14½

1996, May 21	Booklet Stamps	Wmk. 373	
717 A119	60c multicolored	1.25	1.25
718 A119	60c multicolored	1.25	1.25
719 A119	60c multicolored	1.25	1.25
720 A119	60c multicolored	1.25	1.25
721 A119	60c multicolored	1.25	1.25
a.	Strip of 5, #717-721	6.25	6.25
722 A119	60c multicolored	1.25	1.25
723 A119	60c multicolored	1.25	1.25
724 A119	60c multicolored	1.25	1.25
725 A119	60c multicolored	1.25	1.25
726 A119	60c multicolored	1.25	1.25
a.	Strip of 5, #722-726	6.25	6.25
b.	Booklet pane, #721a, 726a	12.50	
	Complete booklet, #726b	12.50	

Lighthouses A120

Designs: 30c, Hog Fish Beacon. 65c, Gibbs Hill Lighthouse. 80c, St. David's Lighthouse. $2, North Rock Beacon.

Perf. 14x13½

1996, Aug. 15	Litho.	Wmk. 373	
727 A120	30c multicolored	.60	.60
728 A120	65c multicolored	1.25	1.25
729 A120	80c multicolored	1.60	1.60
730 A120	$2 multicolored	4.00	4.00
Nos. 727-730 (4)		7.45	7.45

See Nos. 737-740.

Bermuda Coat of Arms Type of 1995 Inscribed "Commonwealth Finance Ministers Meeting"

Perf. 14x13½

1996, Sept. 24	Litho.	Wmk. 373	
731 A115	$1 red & multi	2.00	2.00

Queen Elizabeth II — A121

1996, Nov. 7
732 A121	$22 blue & org brn	44.00	44.00

Architectural Heritage — A122

Wmk. 384

1996, Nov. 28	Litho.	Perf. 14	
733 A122	30c Waterville	.60	.60
734 A122	65c Bridge House	1.25	1.25
735 A122	80c Fannie Fox's Cottage	1.60	1.60
736 A122	$2.50 Palmetto House	5.00	5.00
Nos. 733-736 (4)		8.45	8.45

Lighthouse Type of 1996 Redrawn

Wmk. 373

1997, Feb. 12	Litho.	Perf. 14	
737 A120	30c Like #727	.60	.60
738 A120	65c Like #728	1.25	1.25
739 A120	80c Like #729	1.60	1.60
740 A120	$2.50 Like #730	5.00	5.00
Nos. 737-740 (4)		8.45	8.45

Nos. 737-740 each have Hong Kong '97 emblem. No. 738 inscribed "Gibbs Hill Lighthouse c. 1900." No. 739 inscribed "St. David's Lighthouse c. 1900."

Birds A123

Designs: 30c, White-tailed tropicbird. 60c, White-tailed tropicbird, adult, chick, vert. 80c, Cahow, adult, chick, vert. $2.50, Cahow.

Wmk. 384

1997, Apr. 17	Litho.	Perf. 14	
741 A123	30c multicolored	.60	.60
742 A123	60c multicolored	1.25	1.25
743 A123	80c multicolored	1.60	1.60
744 A123	$2.50 multicolored	5.00	5.00
Nos. 741-744 (4)		8.45	8.45

See Nos. 798-801.

Queen Elizabeth II and Prince Philip, 50th Wedding Anniv. A124

Perf. 14x14½

1997, Oct. 9	Litho.	Wmk. 373	
745 A124	30c Queen, crowd	.60	.60
746 A124	$2 Queen, Prince	4.00	4.00
a.	Souvenir sheet of 2, #745-746	4.60	4.60

Education in Bermuda A125

Designs: 30c, Man, children using blocks. 40c, Teacher, students with map. 60c, Boys holding sports trophy. 65c, Students in front of Berkeley Institute. 80c, Students working in lab. 90c, Students in graduation gowns.

Wmk. 384

1997, Dec. 18	Litho.	Perf. 14	
747 A125	30c multicolored	.60	.60
748 A125	40c multicolored	.80	.80
749 A125	60c multicolored	1.25	1.25
750 A125	65c multicolored	1.25	1.25
751 A125	80c multicolored	1.60	1.60
752 A125	90c multicolored	1.75	1.75
Nos. 747-752 (6)		7.25	7.25

Diana, Princess of Wales (1961-97)
Common Design Type

Various portraits: a. 30c. b. 40c. c. 65c. d, 80c.

Perf. 14x14½

1998, Mar. 31	Litho.	Wmk. 373	
753 CD355	Sheet of 4, #a.-d.	4.75	4.75

No. 753 sold for $2.15 + 25c, with surtax from international sales being donated to the Princess Diana Memorial Fund and surtax from national sales being donated to designated local charity.

Paintings of the Islands A126

Designs: 30c, Fox's Cottage, St. David's. 40c, East Side, Somerset. 65c, Long Bay Road, Somerset. $2, Flatts Village.

1998, June 4		Perf. 13½x14	
754 A126	30c multicolored	.60	.60
755 A126	40c multicolored	.80	.80
756 A126	65c multicolored	1.25	1.25
757 A126	$2 multicolored	4.00	4.00
Nos. 754-757 (4)		6.65	6.65

Hospitality for Tourists in Bermuda — A127

Designs: 25c, Carriage ride. 30c, Golfer at registration desk. 65c, Maid leaving flowers on hotel bed. 75c, Chefs preparing food. 80c, Waiter serving couple. 90c, Singer, bartender, guests.

Wmk. 384

1998, Sept. 24	Litho.	Perf. 14½	
758 A127	25c multicolored	.50	.50
759 A127	30c multicolored	.60	.60
760 A127	65c multicolored	1.25	1.25
761 A127	75c multicolored	1.50	1.50
762 A127	80c multicolored	1.60	1.60
763 A127	90c multicolored	1.75	1.75
Nos. 758-763 (6)		7.20	7.20

Bermuda's Botanical Gardens, Cent. — A128

Wmk. 373

1998, Oct. 15	Litho.	Perf. 14	
764 A128	30c Agave attenuata	.60	.60
765 A128	65c Bermuda palmetto tree	1.25	1.25
766 A128	$1 Banyan tree	2.00	2.00
767 A128	$2 Cedar tree	4.00	4.00
Nos. 764-767 (4)		7.85	7.85

Christmas A129

Children's paintings: 25c, Lizard in Santa hat stringing Christmas lights, vert. 40c, Stairway, wreath on door.

Wmk. 373

1998, Nov. 26	Litho.	Perf. 14	
768 A129	25c multicolored	.50	.50
769 A129	40c multicolored	.75	.75

Beaches — A130

Wmk. 373

1999, Apr. 29	Litho.	Perf. 13½	
770 A130	30c Shelly Bay	.60	.60
771 A130	60c Catherine's Bay	1.25	1.25
772 A130	65c Jobson's Cove	1.25	1.25
773 A130	$2 Warwick Long Bay	4.00	4.00
Nos. 770-773 (4)		7.10	7.10

Common Design Type and:

First Manned Moon Landing, 30th Anniv. A131

Wmk. 373

1999, July 20	Litho.	Perf. 13	
774 A131	30c Ground station	.60	.60
775 A131	60c Lift-off, vert.	1.25	1.25
776 A131	75c Aerial view of ground station	1.50	1.50
777 A131	$2 Moon walk, vert.	4.00	4.00
Nos. 774-777 (4)		7.35	7.35

Souvenir Sheet
Wmk. 384
Perf. 14

778 CD357	65c Looking at earth from moon	1.25	1.25

No. 778 contains one 40mm circular stamp.

Mapmaking — A132

Wmk. 373

1999, Aug. 19	Litho.	Perf. 14	
779 A132	30c Somerset Is., theodolite	.60	.60
780 A132	65c 1901 street map	1.25	1.25
781 A132	80c Aerial photo, modern street map	1.60	1.60
782 A132	$1 Satellite, island	2.00	2.00
Nos. 779-782 (4)		5.45	5.45

Mail Boxes and Stamps — A133

Wmk. 373

1999, Oct. 5	Litho.	Perf. 14¼	
783 A133	30c Victoria era, #6	.60	.60
784 A133	75c George V era, #49	1.50	1.50
785 A133	95c George VI era, #121	1.90	1.90
786 A133	$1 Elizabeth II era, #142	2.00	2.00
Nos. 783-786 (4)		6.00	6.00

Pioneers of Progress — A134

No. 787: a, Dr. E. F. Gordon, labor leader. b, Sir Henry Tucker, banker. c, Gladys Morrell, suffragist.
Illustration reduced.

Perf. 13½x13¼
2000, May 1   Litho.   Wmk. 373
787 A134 30c Horiz. strip of 3, #a-c   1.90 1.90

Sailing Ships — A135

Designs: 30c, Amerigo Vespucci. 60c, Europa. 80c Juan Sebastian de Elcano.

2000, May 23   Perf. 14
788 A135 30c multi   .60   .60
789 A135 60c multi   1.25 1.25
790 A135 80c multi   1.60 1.60
Nos. 788-790 (3)   3.45 3.45

Royal Family Birthdays — A136

35c, Prince William, 18th. 40c, Prince Andrew, 40th. 50c, Princess Anne, 50th. 70c, Princess Margaret, 70th. $1, Queen Mother, 100th.

2000, Aug. 7
791 A136 35c multi   .70   .70
792 A136 40c multi   .80   .80
793 A136 50c multi   1.00 1.00
794 A136 70c multi   1.40 1.40
795 A136 $1 multi   2.00 2.00
a.   Souvenir sheet, #791-795   6.00 6.00
Nos. 791-795 (5)   5.90 5.90

Christmas
A137

Children's art: 30c, Santa Claus and Bermuda onion, by Meghan Jones. 45c, Christmas tree, by Carlita Lodge.

Wmk. 384
2000, Sept. 26   Litho.   Perf. 13¾
796-797 A137 Set of 2   1.40 1.40

Bird Type of 1997 Redrawn with WWF Emblem

Designs: No. 798, 15c, White-tailed tropic bird. No. 799, 15c, Cahow. No. 800, 20c, Cahow, vert. No. 801, 20c, White-tailed tropic bird, vert.

Wmk. 373
2001, Feb. 1   Litho.   Perf. 14
798-801 A123 Set of 4   1.40 1.40
801a   Miniature sheet, 4 each
         #798-801   5.75

Hong Kong 2001 Stamp Exhibition (No. 801a).

Historical Tourist Attractions, St. George's A138

Designs: 35c, King's Castle. 50c, Bridge House. 55c, Whitehall. 70c, Fort Cunningham. 85c, St. Peter's Church. 95c, Water Street.

2001, May 1   Perf. 13¾
802-807 A138 Set of 6   7.75 7.75

Boer War, Cent. — A139

Designs: 35c, Crowded boat, plow. 50c, Men, boot last. 70c, Man with children, rings and pin. 95c, Men and women, stamped cover.

2001, June 28   Perf. 14
808-811 A139 Set of 4   5.00 5.00

Aquarium, Museum and Zoo, 75th Anniv. — A140

Designs: 35c, Child, sea urchins, starfish, vert. 50c, Child, museum display. 55c, Child, tortoise. 70c, Aquarium. 80c, Diver in aquarium tank, vert. 95c, Turtle, vert.

Perf. 14¾x14¼, 14¼x14¾
2001, Aug. 9   Litho.   Wmk. 373
812-817 A140 Set of 6   7.75 7.75

Paintings by Charles Lloyd Tucker — A141

Various paintings: 35c, 70c, 85c, $1.

2001, Oct. 9   Perf. 14¼x14¾
818-821 A141 Set of 4   6.00 6.00

POSTAL-FISCAL STAMP

"Revenue Revenue" PF1

1936   Typo.   Wmk. 4   Perf. 14
Chalky Paper
AR1 PF1 12sh6p org & grayish
         blk   1,200. 2,250.
Revenue cancel   75.00

#AR1 was authorized for postal use from Feb. 1 through May, 1937 and during Nov. and Dec. 1937. Used values are for examples with dated postal cancels indicating usage during the authorized periods. Beware of bogus and improperly dated favor cancels

---

WAR TAX STAMPS

No. 42 Overprinted

1918   Wmk. 3   Perf. 14
MR1 A11 1p rose red   .50   .40

No. 42a Overprinted

1920
MR2 A11 1p carmine   .45   .80

BHUTAN
bü-'tän

LOCATION — Eastern Himalayas
GOVT. — Kingdom
AREA — 18,000 sq. mi.
POP. — 1,951,965(?) (1999 est.)
CAPITAL — Thimphu

100 Chetrum = 1 Ngultrum or Rupee

Catalogue values for all unused stamps in this country are for Never Hinged items.

Postal Runner — A1

Designs: 3ch, 70ch, Archer. 5ch, 1.30nu, Yak. 15ch, Map of Bhutan, portrait of Druk Gyalpo (Dragon King) Ugyen Wangchuk (1867-1902) and Paro Dzong (fortress-monastery). 33ch, Postal runner. All horiz. except 2ch and 33ch.

Perf. 14x14½, 14½x14
1962   Litho.   Unwmk.
1 A1 2ch red & gray   .20   .20
2 A1 3ch red & ultra   .20   .20
3 A1 5ch green & brown   .85   .85
4 A1 15ch red, blk & org yel .20 .20
5 A1 33ch blue grn & lil   .20   .20
6 A1 70ch dp ultra & lt blue .50 .50
7 A1 1.30nu blue & black 1.10 1.00
Nos. 1-7 (7)   3.25 3.15

Nos. 1-7 were issued for inland use in April, 1962, and became valid for international mail on Oct. 10, 1962.
For overprint & surcharges see #42, 72-73.

Refugee Year Emblem and Arms of Bhutan A2

1962, Oct. 10   Perf. 14½x14
8 A2 1nu dk blue & dk car rose .75   .75
9 A2 2nu yel grn & red lilac   2.25 2.25

World Refugee Year. For surcharges see #68-69.

Equipment of Ancient Warrior — A3

Boy Filling Grain Box and Wheat Emblem — A4

1963   Unwmk.   Perf. 14x14½
10 A3 33ch multicolored   .20   .20
11 A3 70ch multicolored   .40   .40
12 A3 1.30nu multicolored   .75   .75
Nos. 10-12 (3)   1.35 1.35

Bhutan's membership in Colombo Plan.

1963, July 15   Perf. 13½x14
13 A4 20ch lt blue, yel & red
       brn   .20   .20
14 A4 1.50nu rose lil, bl & red
       brn   .65   .65

FAO "Freedom from Hunger" campaign. For surcharge see No. 117M.

Masked Dancer — A5

Various Bhutanese Dancers (Five Designs; 2ch, 5ch, 20ch, 1nu, 1.30nu vert.)

1964, Apr. 16   Perf. 14½x14, 14x14½
15 A5 2ch multicolored   .20   .20
16 A5 3ch multicolored   .20   .20
17 A5 5ch multicolored   .20   .20
18 A5 20ch multicolored   .20   .20
19 A5 33ch multicolored   .20   .20
20 A5 70ch multicolored   .20   .20
21 A5 1nu multicolored   .35   .35
22 A5 1.30nu multicolored   .40   .40
23 A5 2nu multicolored   .65   .65
Nos. 15-23 (9)   2.60 2.60

For surcharges & overprints see #70-71, 74-75, 129A, 129G, C1-C3, C11-C13.

Stone Throwing A6

Sport: 5ch, 33ch, Boxing. 1nu, 3nu, Archery. 2nu, Soccer.

1964, Oct. 10   Litho.   Perf. 14½
24 A6 2ch emerald & multi   .20   .20
25 A6 5ch orange & multi   .20   .20
26 A6 15ch brt citron & multi .20 .20
27 A6 33ch rose lil & multi .20   .20
28 A6 1nu multicolored   .40   .40
29 A6 2nu rose lilac & multi .60 .60
30 A6 3nu lt blue & multi   .90   .90
Nos. 24-30 (7)   2.70 2.70

18th Olympic Games, Tokyo, Oct. 10-25. See No. B4.
Nos. 24-30 exist imperf. Value $8.

Flags of the World at Half-mast — A7

1964, Nov. 22 Unwmk. Perf. 14½
Flags in Original Colors

31	A7	33ch steel gray	.20 .20
32	A7	1nu silver	.45 .45
33	A7	3nu gold	1.10 1.10
a.		Souv. sheet, perf. 13½ or imperf.	3.50 3.50
		Nos. 31-33 (3)	1.75 1.75

Issued in memory of those who died in the service of their country. Nos. 31-33 exist imperf.

No. 33a contains 2 stamps similar to Nos. 32-33.

For overprints see Nos. 44, 46.

Flowers — A8

1965, Jan. 6 Litho. Perf. 13

34	A8	2ch Primrose	.20 .20
35	A8	5ch Gentian	.20 .20
36	A8	15ch Primrose	.20 .20
37	A8	33ch Gentian	.20 .20
38	A8	50ch Rhododendron	.20 .20
39	A8	75ch Peony	.20 .20
40	A8	1nu Rhododendron	.20 .20
41	A8	2nu Peony	.40 .40
		Nos. 34-41 (8)	1.80 1.80

For overprints see #43, 45, C4-C5, C14-C15.

Nos. 5, 40, 32, 41 and 33 Overprinted: "WINSTON CHURCHILL 1874-1965"

1965, Feb. 27

42	A1	33ch bl grn & lilac	.35 .35
43	A8	1nu pink, grn & dk gray	.60 .60
44	A7	1nu silver & multi	.50 .50
45	A8	2nu sepia, yel & grn	.70 .70
46	A7	3nu gold & multi	.85 .85
		Nos. 42-46 (5)	3.00 3.00

Issued in memory of Sir Winston Churchill (1874-1965), British statesman. The overprint is in three lines on Nos. 42-43 and 45; in two lines on Nos. 43 and 46.

#44, 46 exist imperf. Value, both, $4.50.

Skyscraper, Pagoda and World's Fair Emblem — A9

Designs: 10ch, 2nu, Pieta by Michelangelo and statue of Khmer Buddha. 20ch, Skyline of NYC and Bhutanese village. 33ch, George Washington Bridge, NY, and foot bridge, Bhutan.

1965, Apr. 21 Litho. Perf. 14½

47	A9	1ch blue & multi	.20 .20
48	A9	10ch green & multi	.20 .20
49	A9	20ch rose lilac & multi	.20 .20
50	A9	33ch bister & multi	.20 .20
51	A9	1.50nu bister & multi	.45 .45
52	A9	2nu multicolored	.60 .60
a.		Souv. sheet, perf. 13½ or imperf.	2.75 2.75
		Nos. 47-52 (6)	1.85 1.85

Nos. 47-52 exist imperf.; value $3.50.

No. 52a contains two stamps similar to Nos. 51-52.

For overprints see #87-87B, C6-C10, C16-C20.

Telstar, Short-wave Radio and ITU Emblem — A10

Designs (ITU Emblem and): 2nu, Telstar and Morse key. 3nu, Syncom and ear phones.

1966, Mar. 2 Litho. Perf. 14½

53	A10	35ch multicolored	.20 .20
54	A10	2nu multicolored	.55 .55
55	A10	3nu multicolored	.75 .75
		Nos. 53-55 (3)	1.50 1.50

Cent. (in 1965) of the ITU. Souvenir sheets exist containing two stamps similar to Nos. 54-55, perf. 13½ and imperf. Value, 2 sheets, $5.

Leopard — A11

Animals: 1ch, 4nu, Asiatic black bear. 4ch, 2nu, Pigmy hog. 8ch, 75ch, Tiger. 10ch, 1.50nu, Dhole (Asiatic hunting dog). 1nu, 5nu, Takin (goat).

1966, Mar. 24 Litho. Perf. 13

56	A11	1ch yellow & blk	.20 .20
57	A11	2ch pale grn & blk	.20 .20
58	A11	4ch lt citron & blk	.20 .20
59	A11	8ch lt blue & blk	.20 .20
60	A11	10ch lt lilac & blk	.20 .20
61	A11	75ch lt yel grn & blk	.20 .20
62	A11	1nu lt green & blk	.50 .50
63	A11	1.50nu lt bl grn & blk	.40 .40
64	A11	2nu dull org & blk	.50 .50
65	A11	3nu bluish lil & blk	.75 .75
66	A11	4nu lt green & blk	1.00 1.00
67	A11	5nu pink & black	1.40 1.40
		Nos. 56-67 (12)	5.75 5.75

For surcharges see Nos. 115C, 115E, 115I, 117N, 117P, 129B, 129J.

Nos. 6-9, 20-23 Surcharged

1965(?) Perf. 14½x14, 14x14½

68	A2	5ch on 1nu	26.00 26.00
69	A2	5ch on 2nu	26.00 26.00
70	A5	10ch on 70ch	4.25 4.25
71	A5	10ch on 2nu	4.25 4.25
72	A1	15ch on 70ch	6.25 6.25
73	A1	15ch on 1.30nu	6.25 6.25
74	A5	20ch on 1nu	8.25 8.25
75	A5	20ch on 2nu	8.25 8.25
		Nos. 68-75 (8)	89.50 89.50

The surcharges on Nos. 68-69 contain two bars at left and right obliterating the denomination on both sides of the design. Four bars on Nos. 72-73.

Simtokha Dzong A12

Tashichho Dzong — A13

Daga Dzong A14

Designs: 5ch, Rinpung Dzong. 50ch, Tongsa Dzong. 1nu, Lhuntsi Dzong.

Perf. 14½x14 (A12), 13½ (A13, A14)
1966-70 Photo.

76	A12	5ch orange brn ('67)	.20 .20
77	A13	10ch dk grn & rose vio ('68)	.20 .20
78	A12	15ch brown	.20 .20

79	A12	20ch green	.20 .20
80	A13	50ch blue grn ('68)	.25 .25
81	A14	75ch dk bl & ol gray ('70)	.25 .25
82	A14	1nu dk vio & vio bl ('70)	.40 .40
		Nos. 76-82 (7)	1.70 1.65

Sizes: 5ch, 15ch, 20ch, 37x20½mm. 10ch, 53½x28½mm. 50ch, 35½x25½mm.

King Jigme Wangchuk — A14a

Coins: 1.30nu, 3nu, 5nu, reverse.

Litho. & Embossed on Gold Foil
1966, July 8 Die Cut Imperf.

83	A14a	10ch green	.20 .20
83A	A14a	25ch green	.20 .20
83B	A14a	50ch green	.35 .35
83C	A14a	1nu red	.60 .60
83D	A14a	1.30nu red	.80 .80
83E	A14a	2nu red	1.10 1.10
83F	A14a	3nu red	1.75 1.75
83G	A14a	4nu red	2.50 2.50
83H	A14a	5nu red	3.00 3.00
		Nos. 83-83H (9)	10.50 10.50

See Nos. 98-98B.

Abominable Snowman — A14b

1966 Photo. Perf. 13½

84	A14b	1ch multicolored	.20 .20
84A	A14b	2ch multi, diff.	.20 .20
84B	A14b	3ch multi, diff.	.20 .20
84C	A14b	4ch multi, diff.	.20 .20
84D	A14b	5ch multi, diff.	.20 .20
84E	A14b	15ch like #84	.20 .20
84F	A14b	30ch like #84A	.20 .20
84G	A14b	40ch like #84B	.20 .20
84H	A14b	50ch like #84C	.20 .20
84I	A14b	1.25nu like #84D	.30 .30
84J	A14b	2.50nu like #84	.65 .65
84K	A14b	3nu like #84A	.75 .75
84L	A14b	5nu like #84B	1.25 1.25
84M	A14b	6nu like #84C	1.25 1.25
84N	A14b	7nu like #84D	1.25 1.25
		Nos. 84-84N (15)	7.25 7.25

Issue dates: 1ch, 2ch, 3ch, 4ch, 5ch, 15ch, 30ch, 40ch, 50ch, Oct. 12; others, Nov. 15. Exist imperf.

For overprints see Nos. 93-93G. For surcharges see Nos. 115D, 115K, 115O, 115P, 117I, 117S.

Flowers A14c

Designs: 3ch, 50ch, Lilium sherriffiae. 5ch, 1nu, Meconopsis dhwoju. 7ch, 2.50nu, Rhododendron chaetomallum. 10ch, 4nu, Pleione hookeriana. 5nu, Rhododendron giganteum.

1967, Feb. 9 Litho. Perf. 13

85	A14c	3ch multicolored	.20 .20
85A	A14c	5ch multicolored	.20 .20
85B	A14c	7ch multicolored	.20 .20
85C	A14c	10ch multicolored	.20 .20

Gray Background

85D	A14c	50ch multicolored	.20 .20
85E	A14c	1nu multicolored	.30 .30
85F	A14c	2.50nu multicolored	.75 .75
85G	A14c	4nu multicolored	1.25 1.25
85H	A14c	5nu multicolored	1.50 1.50
		Nos. 85-85H (9)	4.80 4.80

For surcharges see Nos. 115F, 115L.

Boy Scouts — A14d

1967, Mar. 28 Photo. Perf. 13½

86	A14d	5ch Planting tree	.20 .20
86A	A14d	10ch Cooking	.20 .20
86B	A14d	15ch Mountain climbing	.20 .20

Emblem, Border in Gold

86C	A14d	50ch like #86	.20 .20
86D	A14d	1.25nu like #86A	.60 .60
86E	A14d	4nu like #86B	1.75 1.75
f.		Souv. sheet of 2, #86D, 86E	6.00 6.00
		Nos. 86-86E (6)	3.15 3.15

Exist imperf. Value, $6.

See Nos. 89-89E for overprints. For surcharges see Nos. 115G, 117J, 129K.

Nos. 50-52, 52a Ovptd.

Perfs. as Before
1967, May 25 Litho.

87	A9	33ch on #50	.20 .20
87A	A9	1.50nu on #51	.45 .45
87B	A9	2nu on #52	.60 .60
c.		Souv. sheet of 2, on #52a	1.50 1.50
		Nos. 87-87B (3)	1.25 1.25

Nos. 87-87B exist imperf.

Airplanes — A14f

1967, June 26 Litho. Perf. 13½

88	A14f	45ch Lancaster	.20 .20
88A	A14f	2nu Spitfire	.45 .45
88B	A14f	4nu Hurricane	.95 .95
c.		Souv. sheet of 2, #88A, 88B	2.00 2.00
		Nos. 88-88B (3)	1.60 1.60

Churchill and Battle of Britain. Exist imperf. For surcharges see Nos. 117Q, 117T.

Nos. 86-86D, 86e Overprinted "WORLD JAMBOREE / IDAHO, U.S.A. / AUG. 1-9,/67"

1967, Aug. 8 Photo. Perf. 13½

89	A14d	5ch Planting tree	.20 .20
89A	A14d	10ch Cookout	.20 .20
89B	A14d	15ch Mountain climbing	.20 .20
89C	A14d	50ch like #89	.20 .20
89D	A14d	1.25nu like #89A	.55 .55
89E	A14d	4nu like #89B	1.90 1.90
f.		Souv. sheet of 2, #89D, 89E	3.25 3.25
		Nos. 89-89E (6)	3.25 3.25

No. 89Ef sold for 6.25nu. Exist imperf.

Girl Scouts — A14g

1967, Sept. 28 **Photo.** **Perf. 13½**
90	A14g	5ch Painting	.20	.20
90A	A14g	10ch Making music	.20	.20
90B	A14g	15ch Picking fruit	.20	.20

Emblem, Border in Gold
90C	A14g	1.50nu like #90	.50	.50
90D	A14g	2.50nu like #90A	1.00	1.00
90E	A14g	5nu like #90B	2.10	2.10
f.		Souv. sheet of 2, #90A, 90B	5.00	5.00
		Nos. 90-90E (6)	4.20	4.20

Exist imperf. Value, $8.50.
For surcharge see No. 266.

Astronaut, Space Capsule — A14h

Astronaut walking in space and: 5ch, 30ch, 4nu, Orbiter, Lunar modules docked. 7ch, 50ch, 5nu, Lunar module. 10ch, 1.25nu, 9nu, Other astronauts.

1967, Oct. 30 **Litho.** **Imperf.**
91	A14h	3ch multi	.20	.20
91A	A14h	4ch multi	.20	.20
91B	A14h	7ch multi	.20	.20
91C	A14h	10ch multi	.25	.25
m.		Souv. sheet of 4, #91-91C	2.25	2.25
91D	A14h	15ch multi	.35	.35
91E	A14h	30ch multi	.75	.75
91F	A14h	50ch multi	1.25	1.25
91G	A14h	1.25nu multi	3.00	3.00
n.		Souv. sheet of 4, #91D-91G	5.00	5.00
91H	A14h	2.50nu multi	1.75	1.75
91I	A14h	4nu multi	3.00	3.00
91J	A14h	5nu multi	3.75	3.75
91K	A14h	9nu multi	6.50	6.50
o.		Souv. sheet of 4, #91H-91K	15.00	15.00
		Nos. 91-91K (12)	21.20	21.20

Nos. 91H-91K are airmail. Simulated 3-dimensions using a plastic overlay.
For other space issues see designs A15a, A15e.

Pheasants — A14i

Designs: 1ch, 2nu, Tragopan satyra. 2ch, 4nu, Lophophorus sclareti. 4ch, 5nu, Lophophorus impeyanus. 8ch, 7nu, Lophura leucomelana. 15ch, 9nu, Crossoptilon crossoptilon.

1968 **Photo.** **Perf. 13½**
92	A14i	1ch multicolored	.20	.20
92A	A14i	2ch multicolored	.20	.20
92B	A14i	4ch multicolored	.20	.20
92C	A14i	8ch multicolored	.20	.20
92D	A14i	15ch multicolored	.20	.20

Border in Gold
92E	A14i	2nu multicolored	.40	.40
92F	A14i	4nu multicolored	.80	.80
92G	A14i	5nu multicolored	1.00	1.00
92H	A14i	7nu multicolored	1.40	1.40
92I	A14i	9nu multicolored	1.90	1.90
		Nos. 92-92I (10)	6.50	6.50

Issue dates: 1ch, 2ch, 4ch, 8ch, 15ch, 2nu, 4nu, 7nu, Jan 20; 5nu, 9nu, Apr. 23.
Unauthorized imperfs exist. Value, $10.

For surcharges see Nos. 115H, 117R, 117V, 129D, 129L.

Nos. 84G, 84I, 84K, 84M Ovptd. in Black on Silver

a

b

Perfs. as Before
1968, Feb. 16 **Photo.**
Overprint Type "a"
93	A14b	40ch on #84G	.20	.20
93A	A14b	1.25nu on #84I	.20	.20
93B	A14b	3nu on #84K	.50	.50
93C	A14b	6nu on #84M	1.00	1.00

Overprint Type "b"
93D	A14b	40ch on #84G	.20	.20
93E	A14b	1.25nu on #84I	.20	.20
93F	A14b	3nu on #84K	.50	.50
93G	A14b	6nu on #84M	1.00	1.00
		Nos. 93-93G (8)	3.80	3.80

Exist imperf. Value, $20.

Snow Lion — A14j

1968, Mar. 14 **Photo.** **Perf. 12½**
94	A14j	2ch Elephant	.20	.20
94A	A14j	3ch Garuda	.20	.20
94B	A14j	4ch Monastery Tiger	.20	.20
94C	A14j	5ch Wind Horse	.20	.20
94D	A14j	15ch Snow Lion	.20	.20
94E	A14j	20ch like #94	.20	.20
94F	A14j	30ch like #94A	.20	.20
94G	A14j	50ch like #94B	.20	.20
94H	A14j	1.25nu like #94	.20	.20
94I	A14j	1.50nu like #94	.20	.20
94J	A14j	2nu like #94D	.30	.30
94K	A14j	2.50nu like #94A	.30	.30
94L	A14j	4nu like #94B	.55	.55
94M	A14j	5nu like #94C	.75	.75
94N	A14j	10nu like #94D	1.40	1.40
		Nos. 94-94N (15)	5.30	5.30

Nos. 94I, 94K-94N are airmail. All exist imperf.
For surcharges see Nos. 115, 115M, 115Q, 117-117E, 129C, C35-C36.

Butterflies A14k

Designs: 15ch, Catagramma sorana. 50ch, Delias hyparete. 1.25nu, Anteos maerula. Ornithoptera priamus urvilleanus. 3nu, Euploea mulciber. 4nu, Morpho rhetenor. 5nu, Papilio androgeous. 6nu, Troides magellanus.

1968, May 20 **Litho.** **Imperf.**
95	A14k	15ch multi	.45	.45
95A	A14k	50ch multi	.65	.65
95B	A14k	1.25nu multi	1.25	1.25
95C	A14k	2nu multi	1.90	1.90
h.		Souv. sheet of 4, #95-95C	8.00	8.00
95D	A14k	3nu multi	2.00	2.00
95E	A14k	4nu multi	2.75	2.75
95F	A14k	5nu multi	2.00	2.00
95G	A14k	6nu multi	3.00	3.00
i.		Souv. sheet of 4, #95D-95G	11.00	11.00
		Nos. 95-95G (8)	14.00	14.00

Souv. sheets issued Oct. 23. Nos. 95D-95G, 95Gi are airmail. Simulated 3-dimensions using a plastic overlay.

Paintings — A14m

1968 **Litho. & Embossed** **Imperf.**
96	A14m	2ch Van Gogh	.20	.20
96A	A14m	4ch Millet	.20	.20
96B	A14m	5ch Monet	.20	.20
96C	A14m	10ch Corot	.20	.20
p.		Souv. sheet of 4, #96-96C	.80	.80
96D	A14m	45ch like #96	.20	.20
96E	A14m	80ch like #96A	.35	.35
96F	A14m	1.05nu like #96B	.45	.45
96G	A14m	1.40nu like #96C	.60	.60
q.		Souv. sheet of 4, #96D-96G	1.60	1.60
96H	A14m	1.50nu like #96	.65	.65
96I	A14m	2nu like #96A	.85	.85
96J	A14m	2.50nu like #96A	1.10	1.10
96K	A14m	3nu like #96A	1.25	1.25
96L	A14m	4nu like #96B	1.10	1.10
96M	A14m	5nu like #96C	1.40	1.40
r.		Souv. sheet of 4, #96I, 96K-96M	2.50	2.50
96N	A14m	5nu like #96B	1.75	1.75
96O	A14m	8nu like #96C	2.25	2.25
s.		Souv. sheet of 4, #96H, 96J, 96N-96O	5.00	5.00
		Nos. 96-96O (16)	12.75	12.75

Issued: #96-96G, 96I, 96K-96M, 7/8; #96Cp, 96Gq, 96Mr, 8/5; others, 8/28. Nos. 96H, 96J, 96N-96O are airmail.
See Nos. 114-114O, 144-144G.

Summer Olympics, Mexico, 1968 — A14n

1968, Oct. 1 **Photo.** **Perf. 13½**
97	A14n	5ch Discus	.20	.20
97A	A14n	45ch Basketball	.20	.20
97B	A14n	60ch Javelin	.20	.20
97C	A14n	80ch Shooting	.20	.20
97D	A14n	1.05nu like #97	.20	.20
97E	A14n	2nu like #97B	.20	.20
97F	A14n	3nu like #97C	.35	.35
97G	A14n	5nu Soccer	.60	.60
h.		Souv. sheet of 2, #97D, 97G	2.25	2.25
		Nos. 97-97G (8)	2.15	2.15

Exist imperf.
For surcharges see Nos. 129E, B5-B7.

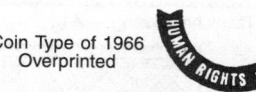

Coin Type of 1966 Overprinted

HUMAN RIGHTS YEAR 1968

Embossed on Gold Foil
1968, Nov. 12 **Die Cut** **Imperf.**
98	A14a	15ch green	.20	.20
98A	A14a	33ch green	.25	.25
98B	A14a	9nu green	4.75	4.75
		Nos. 98-98B (3)	5.20	5.20

Human Rights Year.

Birds A14p

2ch, 20ch, 1.50nu, Crimson-winged laughing thrush. 3ch, 30ch, 2.50nu, Ward's trogon. 4ch, 50ch, 4nu, Grey peacock-pheasant. 5ch, 1.25nu, 5nu, Rufous necked hornbill. 15ch, 2nu, 10nu, Myzornis.

1968-69 **Photo.** **Perf. 12½**
99	A14p	2ch multi	.20	.20
99A	A14p	3ch multi, vert.	.20	.20
99B	A14p	4ch multi, vert.	.20	.20
99C	A14p	5ch multi, vert.	.20	.20
99D	A14p	15ch multi, vert.	.25	.25
99E	A14p	20ch multi	.30	.30
99F	A14p	30ch multi, vert.	.35	.35
99G	A14p	50ch multi	.35	.35
99H	A14p	1.25nu multi, vert.	.50	.50
99I	A14p	1.50nu multi	.60	.60
99J	A14p	2nu multi	.80	.80
99K	A14p	2.50nu multi, vert.	.80	.80
99L	A14p	4nu multi	1.25	1.25
99M	A14p	5nu multi, vert.	1.75	1.75
99N	A14p	10nu multi	3.25	3.25
		Nos. 99-99N (15)	11.00	11.00

Issued: 2c-5ch, 15ch, 30ch, 50ch, 12/7; 20ch, 1.25nu, 2nu, 12/28; others, 1/29/69. 1.50nu, 2.50nu, 4nu, 5nu, 10nu are airmail. Exist imperf.
For surcharges see Nos. 115A-115B, 115I, 115M, 115R, 117F-117G, 117K, 117O, 129H.

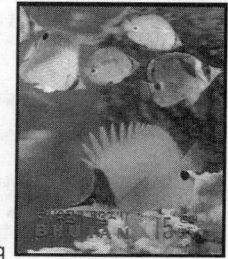

Fish — A14q

1969, Feb. 27 **Litho.** **Imperf.**
100	A14q	15ch multicolored	.75	.75
100A	A14q	20ch multi, diff.	1.00	1.00
100B	A14q	30ch multi, diff.	1.50	1.50
100C	A14q	5nu multi, diff.	2.00	2.00
100D	A14q	6nu multi, diff.	2.50	2.50
100E	A14q	7nu multi, diff.	3.00	3.00
f.		Souv. sheet, #100B-100E	10.75	10.75
		Nos. 100-100E (6)	10.75	10.75

Nos. 100C-100E are airmail. Simulated 3-dimensions using a plastic overlay.

Insects — A14r

1969, Apr. 10 **Litho.** **Imperf.**
101	A14r	10ch multicolored	.55	.55
101A	A14r	75ch multi, diff.	.90	.90
101B	A14r	1.25nu multi, diff.	1.25	1.25
101C	A14r	2nu multi, diff.	2.40	2.40
h.		Souv. sheet, #101-101C	17.50	17.50
101D	A14r	3nu multi, diff.	3.00	3.00
101E	A14r	4nu multi, diff.	1.75	1.75
101F	A14r	5nu multi, diff.	2.40	2.40
101G	A14r	6nu multi, diff.	3.00	3.00
i.		Souv. sheet, #101D-101G	12.50	12.50
		Nos. 101-101G (8)	15.25	15.25

Nos. 101D-101G, 101i are airmail. Stamps from souvenir sheets have inscription at lower right. Simulated 3-dimensions using a plastic overlay.

Admission to UPU — A14s

Illustration reduced.

1969, May 2		Photo.	*Perf. 13*	
102	A14s	5ch multicolored	.20	.20
102A	A14s	10ch multicolored	.20	.20
102B	A14s	15ch multicolored	.20	.20
102C	A14s	45ch multicolored	.20	.20
102D	A14s	60ch multicolored	.20	.20
102E	A14s	1.05nu multicolored	.25	.25
102F	A14s	1.40nu multicolored	.35	.35
102G	A14s	4nu multicolored	1.00	1.00
		Nos. 102-102G (8)	2.60	2.60

Exist imperf.
For surcharges see #117H, 117L, 117U, 129.

History of Steel Making — A14t

Designs: 2ch, Pre-biblical. 5ch, Damascus sword. 15ch, 3nu, Saugus Mill. 45ch, Beehive coke ovens. 75ch, 4nu, Bessemer converter. 1.50nu, 5nu, Rolling mill. 1.75nu, Steel mill. 2nu, 6nu, Future applications.

Litho. on Steel Foil

1969, June 2			*Imperf.*	
103	A14t	2ch multicolored	.20	.20
103A	A14t	5ch multicolored	.20	.20
103B	A14t	15ch multicolored	.20	.20
m.		Souv. sheet, #103A-103B	.60	.60
103C	A14t	45ch multicolored	.20	.20
n.		Souv. sheet, #103, 103C	.60	.60
103D	A14t	75ch multicolored	.20	.20
103E	A14t	1.50nu multicolored	.45	.45
103F	A14t	1.75nu multicolored	.50	.50
o.		Souv. sheet, #103E-103F	.60	.60
103G	A14t	2nu multicolored	.60	.60
p.		Souv. sheet, #103D, 103G	.60	.60
103H	A14t	3nu multicolored	.85	.85
103I	A14t	4nu multicolored	1.10	1.10
103J	A14t	5nu multicolored	1.40	1.40
q.		Souv. sheet, #103I-103J	3.75	3.75
103K	A14t	6nu multicolored	1.60	1.60
r.		Souv. sheet, #103H,103K	3.75	3.75
		Nos. 103-103K (12)	7.50	7.50

Nos. 103H-103K, 103q, 103r are airmail. Souv. sheets issued June 30.

Birds
A14u

1969, Aug. 5		Litho.	*Imperf.*	
104	A14u	15ch Owl	3.50	3.50
104A	A14u	50ch Red birds	3.50	3.50
104B	A14u	1.25nu Hawk	3.50	3.50
104C	A14u	2nu Penguin	3.50	3.50
h.		Souv. sheet, #104-104C	22.50	22.50
104D	A14u	3nu Macaws	3.50	3.50
104E	A14u	4nu Bird of paradise	2.00	2.00
104F	A14u	5nu Duck	2.25	2.25
104G	A14u	6nu Pheasant	3.00	3.00
i.		Souv. sheet, #104D-104G	22.50	22.50
		Nos. 104-104G (8)	24.25	24.25

Nos. 104D-104G, 104Gi are airmail. Simulated 3-dimensions using a plastic overlay. Souv. sheets issued Aug. 28.

Buddhist Prayer Banners — A14v

Litho. on Cloth

1969, Sep. 30			*Imperf.*	

Self-adhesive

Sizes: 15ch, 75ch, 2nu, 57x57mm, 5nu, 6nu, 70x37mm

105	A14v	15ch multicolored	.20	.20
105A	A14v	75ch multi, diff.	.25	.25
105B	A14v	2nu multi, diff.	.70	.70
105C	A14v	5nu multi, diff.	1.75	1.75
105D	A14v	6nu multi, diff.	2.25	2.25
		Nos. 105-105D (5)	5.15	5.15

Souvenir Sheet

105E		Sheet of 3	5.00	5.00

No. 105E shows denominations of 75ch, 5nu, 6nu with design elements of Nos. 105A, 105C, 105D with gray frame. Exists perf. 13½.

Mahatma Gandhi — A15

1969, Oct. 2		Litho.	*Perf. 13x13½*	
106	A15	20ch light blue & brn	.20	.20
107	A15	2nu lemon & brn olive	.75	.75

Mohandas K. Gandhi (1869-1948), leader in India's struggle for independence.

Apollo 11 Moon Landing — A15a

Designs: 3ch, Separation from third stage. 5ch, Entering lunar orbit. 15ch, Lunar module separating from orbiter. 20ch, 3nu, Astronaut standing on lunar module's foot pad. 25ch, Astronaut, lunar module on moon. 45ch, Astronaut, flag. 50ch, 4nu, Setting up experiments. 1.75nu, Lunar module docking with orbiter. 5nu, Lift-off from Cape Canaveral. 6nu, Recovery at sea.

1969		Litho.	*Imperf.*	
108	A15a	3ch multi	.20	.20
108A	A15a	5ch multi	.20	.20
108B	A15a	15ch multi	.20	.20
108C	A15a	20ch multi	.25	.25
m.		Souv. sheet, #108-108C	.60	.60
108D	A15a	25ch multi	.30	.30
108E	A15a	45ch multi	.50	.50
108F	A15a	50ch multi	.55	.55
108G	A15a	1.75nu multi	1.75	1.75
n.		Souv. sheet, #108D-108G	4.00	4.00
108H	A15a	3nu multi	1.50	1.50
108I	A15a	4nu multi	2.00	2.00
108J	A15a	5nu multi	2.50	2.50
108K	A15a	6nu multi	3.00	3.00
o.		Souv. sheet, #108H-108K	21.00	21.00
		Nos. 108-108K (12)	12.95	12.95

Nos. 108H-108K, 108Ko are airmail. Simulated 3-dimensions using a plastic overlay. "Aldrin" misspelled on No. 108o.

Issue dates: Nos. 108-108G, Nov. 3; Nos. 108H-108K, Nov. 20; Souv. sheets, Dec. 20.

Paintings
A15b

1970, Jan. 19		Litho.	*Imperf.*	
109	A15b	5ch Clouet	.20	.20
109A	A15b	10ch van Eyck	.20	.20
109B	A15b	15ch David	.20	.20
109C	A15b	2.75nu Rubens	1.75	1.75
h.		Souv. sheet, #109-109C	2.50	2.50
109D	A15b	3nu Homer	1.10	1.10
109E	A15b	4nu Gentileschi	1.40	1.40
109F	A15b	5nu Raphael	1.75	1.75
109G	A15b	6nu Ghirlandaio	2.25	2.25
i.		Souv. sheet, #109D-109G	7.50	7.50
		Nos. 109-109G (8)	8.85	8.85

Nos. 109D-109G, 109Gi are airmail. Simulated 3-dimensions using a plastic overlay. Souv. sheets issued Feb. 25.

Various Forms of Mail Transport, UPU Headquarters, Bern — A15c

1970, Feb. 27		Photo.	*Perf. 13½*	
110	A15c	3ch ol grn & gold	.20	.20
111	A15c	10ch red brn & gold	.20	.20
112	A15c	20ch Prus bl & gold	.20	.20
113	A15c	2.50nu dp mag & gold	.65	.65
		Nos. 110-113 (4)	1.25	1.25

New Headquarters of Universal Postal Union, Bern, Switzerland.
Exist imperf. Value $5.
For surcharge see No. 129I.

Painting Type of 1968

Paintings of flowers.

Litho. & Embossed

1970, May 6			*Imperf.*	
114	A14m	2ch Van Gogh	.20	.20
114A	A14m	3ch Redon	.20	.20
114B	A14m	5ch Kuroda	.20	.20
114C	A14m	10ch Renoir	.20	.20
p.		Souv. sheet, #114-114C	.20	.20
114D	A14m	15ch Renoir, diff.	.20	.20
114E	A14m	75ch Monet	.30	.30
114F	A14m	80ch like #114	.20	.20
114G	A14m	90ch like #114A	.20	.20
114H	A14m	1nu La Tour	.40	.40
114I	A14m	1.10nu like #114B	.30	.30
114J	A14m	1.40nu Oudot	.60	.60
q.		Souv. sheet, #114D, 114E, 114H, 114J	1.90	1.90
114K	A14m	1.40nu like #114C	.35	.35
r.		Souv. sheet, #114F, 114G, 114I, 114K	1.25	1.25
114L	A14m	1.60nu like #114D	.40	.40
114M	A14m	1.70nu like #114E	.40	.40
114N	A14m	3nu like #114H	.75	.75
114O	A14m	3.50nu like #114J	.85	.85
s.		Souv. sheet, #114L-114O	2.75	2.75
		Nos. 114-114O (16)	5.75	5.75

#114F-114G, 114I, 114K-114O are airmail.

Stamps of 1966-69 Surcharged

1970, June 19				
115	A14j	20ch on 2nu, #94J	2.50	2.50
115A	A14p	20ch on 2nu, #99J	2.50	2.50
115B	A14p	20ch on 2.50nu, #99K	2.50	2.50
115C	A11	20ch on 3nu, #65	2.50	2.50
115D	A14b	20ch on 3nu, #84K	2.50	2.50
115E	A11	20ch on 4nu, #66	2.50	2.50
115F	A14c	20ch on 4nu, #85G	2.50	2.50
115G	A14d	20ch on 4nu, #86E	2.50	2.50
115H	A14i	20ch on 4nu, #92F	2.50	2.50
115I	A14p	20ch on 4nu, #99I	2.50	2.50
115J	A11	20ch on 5nu, #67	2.50	2.50
115K	A14b	20ch on 5nu, #84L	2.50	2.50
115L	A14c	20ch on 5nu, #85H	2.50	2.50
115M	A14j	20ch on 5nu, #94M	2.50	2.50
115N	A14p	20ch on 5nu, #99M	2.50	2.50
115O	A14b	20ch on 6nu, #84M	2.50	2.50
115P	A14b	20ch on 7nu, #84N	2.50	2.50
115Q	A14j	20ch on 10nu, #94N	2.50	2.50
115R	A14p	20ch on 10nu, #99N	2.50	2.50
		Nos. 115-115R (19)	47.50	47.50

Nos. 115B, 115I, 115M-115N, 115Q-115R are airmail.

Animals — A15d

1970, Oct. 15		Litho.	*Imperf.*	
116	A15d	5ch African elephant	.20	.20
116A	A15d	10ch Leopard	.20	.20
116B	A15d	20ch Ibex	.25	.25
116C	A15d	25ch Tiger	.30	.30
116D	A15d	30ch Abominable snowman	.35	.35
116E	A15d	40ch Water buffalo	.50	.50
116F	A15d	65ch Rhinoceros	.80	.80
116G	A15d	75ch Giant pandas	.95	.95
116H	A15d	85ch Snow leopard	1.10	1.10
116I	A15d	2nu Young deer	1.50	1.50
116J	A15d	3nu Wild boar, vert.	2.25	2.25
116K	A15d	4nu Collared bear, vert.	3.00	3.00
116L	A15d	5nu Takin	4.00	4.00
		Nos. 116-116L (13)	15.40	15.40

Nos. 116I-116L are airmail. Simulated 3-dimensions using a plastic overlay.

Stamps of 1963-69 Surcharged

1970, Nov. 2				
117	A14j	5ch on 30ch, #94F	.60	.60
117A	A14j	5ch on 50ch, #94G	.60	.60
117B	A14j	5ch on 1.25nu, #94H	.60	.60
117C	A14j	5ch on 1.50nu, #94I	.60	.60
117D	A14j	5ch on 2nu, #94J	.60	.60
117E	A14j	5ch on 2.50nu, #94K	.60	.60
117F	A14p	20ch on 30ch, #99F	2.50	2.50
117G	A14p	20ch on 50ch, #99G	2.50	2.50
117H	A14s	20ch on 1.05nu, #102E	2.50	2.50
117I	A14b	20ch on 1.25nu, #84I	2.50	2.50
117J	A14d	20ch on 1.25nu, #86D	2.50	2.50
117K	A14p	20ch on 1.25nu, #99H	2.50	2.50
117L	A14s	20ch on 1.40nu, #102F	2.50	2.50
117M	A4	20ch on 1.50nu, #14	2.50	2.50
117N	A11	20ch on 1.50nu, #63	2.50	2.50
117O	A14p	20ch on 1.50nu, #99I	2.50	2.50
117P	A11	20ch on 2nu, #64	2.50	2.50
117Q	A14f	20ch on 2nu, #88A	2.50	2.50
117R	A14i	20ch on 2nu, #92E	2.50	2.50
117S	A14b	20ch on 2.50nu, #84J	2.50	2.50
117T	A14f	20ch on 4nu, #88B	2.50	2.50
117U	A14s	20ch on 4nu, #102G	2.50	2.50
117V	A14i	20ch on 7nu, #92H	2.50	2.50
		Nos. 117-117V (23)	46.10	46.10

Nos. 117C, 117E, 117O are airmail.

Conquest of Space — A15e

Designs: 2ch, Jules Verne's "From the Earth to the Moon." 5ch, V-2 rocket. 15ch, Vostok. 25ch, Mariner 2. 30ch, Gemini 7. 50ch, Lift-off. 75ch, Edward White during space walk. 1.50nu, Apollo 13. 2nu, View of Earth from moon. 3nu, Another galaxy. 6nu, Moon, Earth, Sun, Mars, Jupiter. 7nu, Future space station.

1970		**Litho.**		**Imperf.**
118	A15e	2ch multi	.20	.20
118A	A15e	5ch multi	.20	.20
118B	A15e	15ch multi	.20	.20
118C	A15e	25ch multi	.20	.20
m.		Souv. sheet, #118-118C	.60	.60
118D	A15e	30ch multi	.25	.25
118E	A15e	50ch multi	.35	.35
118F	A15e	75ch multi	.55	.55
118G	A15e	1.50nu multi	1.10	1.10
n.		Souv. sheet, #118D-118G	3.75	3.75
118H	A15e	2nu multi	.65	.65
118I	A15e	3nu multi	1.00	1.00
118J	A15e	6nu multi	2.00	2.00
118K	A15e	7nu multi	2.25	2.25
o.		Souv. sheet, #118H-118K	10.00	10.00
		Nos. 118-118K (12)	8.95	8.95

Issued: #118-118G, 11/9; #118H-118K, 11/30. Souv. sheets, Dec. 18. Nos. 118H-118K are airmail. Simulated 3-dimensions using a plastic overlay.
See #127-127C. For surcharge see #129F.

Wangdiphodrang
Dzong and
Bridge — A15f

1971-72		**Photo.**		**Perf. 13½**
119	A15f	2ch gray	.20	.20
120	A15f	3ch deep red lilac	.20	.20
121	A15f	4ch violet	.20	.20
122	A15f	5ch dark green	.20	.20
123	A15f	10ch orange brown	.20	.20
124	A15f	15ch deep blue	.20	.20
125	A15f	15ch deep plum	.20	.20
		Nos. 119-125 (7)	1.40	1.40

Issued: 5ch-20ch, 2/22; 2ch-4ch, 4/72.

Funeral Mask of King
Tutankhamen — A15g

History of Sculpture: 75ch, Winged Bull. 1.25nu, Head of Zeus. 2nu, She-wolf Suckling Romulus and Remus, horiz. 3nu, Head of Cicero. 4nu, Head of David, by Michaelangelo. 5nu, Age of Bronze, by Rodin. 6nu, Head of Woman, by Modigliani.

1971, Feb. 27		**Litho.**		**Imperf.**
		Self-adhesive		
126	A15g	10ch multicolored	.20	.20
126A	A15g	75ch multicolored	.35	.35
126B	A15g	1.25nu multicolored	.60	.60
126C	A15g	2nu multicolored	1.00	1.00
h.		Souv. sheet, #126-126C	2.50	2.50
126D	A15g	3nu multicolored	.80	.80
126E	A15g	4nu multicolored	1.10	1.10
126F	A15g	5nu multicolored	1.40	1.40

126G	A15g	6nu multicolored	1.60	1.60
i.		Souv. sheet, #126D-126G	5.50	5.50
		Nos. 126-126G (8)	7.05	7.05

Stamps are plastic heat molded into three dimensions. Nos. 126D-126G are airmail.

Conquest of Space Type of 1970

Designs: 10ch, 2.50nu, Lunokhod 1. 1.70nu, 4nu, Apollo 15.

1971, Mar. 20		**Litho.**		**Imperf.**
127	A15e	10ch multicolored	.25	.25
127A	A15e	1.70nu multicolored	1.00	1.00
127B	A15e	2.50nu multicolored	1.50	1.50
127C	A15e	4nu multicolored	2.25	2.25
d.		Souv. sheet of 4, #127-127C	5.00	5.00
		Nos. 127-127C (4)	5.00	5.00

Nos. 127B-127C are airmail. Simulated 3-dimensions using a plastic overlay.

Antique Automobiles — A15h

2ch, Mercedes Benz, Germany. 5ch, Ford, US. 10ch, Alfa Romeo, Italy. 15ch, Cord, US. 20ch, Hispano Suiza, Spain. 30ch, Invicta, Britain. 60ch, Renault, France. 75ch, Talbot, Britain. 85ch, Mercer, US. 1nu, Sunbeam, Britain. 1.20nu, Austrian Daimler. 1.55nu, Bugatti, Italy. 1.80nu, Simplex, US. 2nu, Amilcar, France. 2.50nu, Bentley, Britain. 4nu, Morris Garage, Britain. 6nu, Duesenberg, US. 7nu, Aston Martin, Britain. 9nu, Packard, US. 10nu, Rolls Royce, Britain.

1971		**Litho.**		**Imperf.**
128-128S	A15h	Set of 20	12.00	12.00

Issued: #128-128F, 5/20; #128G-128N, 6/10; #128O-128S, 7/5. Nos. 128O-128S are airmail. Simulated 3-dimensions using a plastic overlay.
"Romeo" misspelled.

Stamps of 1964-71 Surcharged

1971, July 1				
129	A14s	55ch on 60ch, #102D	.75	.75
129A	A5	55ch on 1.30nu, #22	.40	.40
129B	A11	55ch on 3nu, #65	.40	.40
129C	A14j	55ch on 4nu, #94L	.40	.40
129D	A14i	55ch on 5nu, #92G	.40	.40
129E	A14n	90ch on 1.05nu, #97D	1.90	1.90
129F	A15e	90ch on 1.70nu, #127A	4.25	4.25
129G	A5	90ch on 2nu, #23	.40	.40
129H	A14p	90ch on 2nu, #99J	.75	.75
129I	A15c	90ch on 2.50nu, #113	1.10	1.10
129J	A11	90ch on 4nu, #66	.75	.75
129K	A14d	90ch on 4nu, #86E	1.90	1.90
129L	A14i	90ch on 9nu, #92I	.75	.75
		Nos. 129-129L (13)	14.15	14.15

No. 129C is airmail. No. 129F comes with lines 8mm or 18mm long.

UN Emblem and Bhutan Flag — A16

Designs (Bhutan Flag and): 10ch, UN Headquarters, NY. 20ch, Security Council Chamber and mural by Per Krohg. 3nu, General Assembly Hall.

1971, Sept. 21		**Photo.**		**Perf. 13½**
130	A16	5ch gold, bl & multi	.20	.20
131	A16	10ch gold & multi	.20	.20
132	A16	20ch gold & multi	.20	.20
133	A16	3nu gold & multi	.60	.60
		Nos. 130-133,C21-C23 (7)	3.75	3.75

Bhutan's admission to the UN. Exist imperf. For overprints see Nos. 140-143. For surcharge see No. 252.

Boy Scout Crossing Stream in Rope
Sling — A17

Emblem & Boy Scouts: 20ch, 2nu, mountaineering. 50ch, 6nu, reading map. 75ch, as 10ch.

1971, Nov. 30		**Litho.**		**Perf. 13½**
134	A17	10ch gold & multi	.20	.20
135	A17	20ch gold & multi	.20	.20
136	A17	50ch gold & multi	.20	.20
137	A17	75ch silver & multi	.20	.20
138	A17	2nu silver & multi	.40	.40
139	A17	6nu silver & multi	1.00	1.00
a.		Souv. sheet of 2, #138-139 + 2 labels	2.00	2.00
		Nos. 134-139 (6)	2.20	2.20

60th anniv. of the Boy Scouts. Exist imperf. For overprint and surcharge see #253, 383.

Nos. 130-133 Overprinted in Gold

1971, Dec. 23				
140	A16	5ch gold & multi	.20	.20
141	A16	10ch gold & multi	.20	.20
142	A16	20ch gold & multi	.20	.20
143	A16	3nu gold & multi	.85	.85
		Nos. 140-143,C24-C26 (7)	5.45	5.45

World Refugee Year. Exist imperf.

The Bathing
Girl by
Renoir — A17a

Designs: 20ch, A Bar at the Follies, by Monet, horiz. 90ch, Mona Lisa, by da Vinci. 1.70nu, Cart of Father Junier, by Rousseau, horiz. 2.50nu, The Gleaners, by Millet, horiz. 4.60nu, White Horse, by Gaugin. 5.40nu, The Dancing Lesson, by Degas. 6nu, After the Rain, by Gaillauman, horiz.

1972		**Litho. & Embossed**		**Imperf.**
144	A17a	15ch multicolored	.30	.30
144A	A17a	20ch multicolored	.30	.30
144B	A17a	90ch multicolored	.35	.35
144C	A17a	1.70nu multicolored	.50	.50
144D	A17a	2.50nu multicolored	1.00	1.00
h.		Souv. sheet of 4, #144-144B, 144D	3.50	3.50
144E	A17a	4.60nu multicolored	1.40	1.40
144F	A17a	5.40nu multicolored	1.60	1.60

144G	A17a	6nu multicolored	1.90	1.90
i.		Souv. sheet of 4, #144C, 144E-144G	6.00	6.00
		Nos. 144-144G (8)	7.35	7.35

Issued: #144-144B, 144D, 1/29; others, 2/28. Nos. 144C, 144E-144G are airmail.

Famous
Men
A17b

1972, Apr. 17		**Litho.**		**Imperf.**
		Self-adhesive		
145	A17b	10ch John F. Kennedy	.20	.20
145A	A17b	15ch Gandhi	.20	.20
145B	A17b	55ch Churchill	.45	.45
145C	A17b	2nu De Gaulle	.50	.50
145D	A17b	6nu Pope John XVIII	1.50	1.50
145E	A17b	8nu Eisenhower	2.00	2.00
f.		Souv. sheet, #145B-145E	5.00	5.00
		Nos. 145-145E (6)	4.85	4.85

Nos. 145C-145E are airmail. Stamps are plastic heat molded into three dimensions.

Book Year
Emblem
A17c

1972, May 15		**Photo.**		**Perf. 13½x13**
146	A17c	2ch multicolored	.20	.20
146A	A17c	3ch multicolored	.20	.20
146B	A17c	5ch multicolored	.20	.20
146C	A17c	20ch multicolored	.20	.20
		Nos. 146-146C (4)	.80	.80

International Book Year.

1972 Summer Olympics,
Munich — A17d

1972, June 6		**Photo.**		**Perf. 13½**
147	A17d	10ch Handball	.20	.20
147A	A17d	15ch Archery	.20	.20
147B	A17d	20ch Boxing	.20	.20
147C	A17d	30ch Discus	.20	.20
147D	A17d	35ch Javelin	.20	.20
147E	A17d	45ch Shooting	.20	.20
147F	A17d	1.35nu like #147A	.40	.40
147G	A17d	7nu like #147	1.90	1.90
h.		Souv. sheet of 3, #147D, 147F-147G	3.00	3.00
		Nos. 147-147G (8)	3.50	3.50

Nos. 147D, 147F-147G are airmail and have a gold border.
Exist imperf.
For overprint see No. 384.

Apollo 11 Type of 1969

Apollo 16: 15ch, Lift-off, vert. 20ch, Achieving lunar orbit. 90ch, Astronauts Young, Mattingly, Duke, vert. 1.70nu, Lunar module. 2.50nu, Walking on moon. 4.60nu, Gathering rock samples. 5.40nu, Apollo 16 on launch pad, vert. 6nu, Looking at earth, vert.

1972, Sept. 1		**Litho.**		**Imperf.**
148	A15a	15ch multicolored	.20	.20
148A	A15a	20ch multicolored	.20	.20
148B	A15a	90ch multicolored	.20	.20
148C	A15a	1.70nu multicolored	.35	.35
148D	A15a	2.50nu multicolored	.50	.50
h.		Souv. sheet of 4, #148-148B, 148D	3.00	3.00

148E	A15a	4.60nu multicolored	.90	.90
148F	A15a	5.40nu multicolored	1.10	1.10
148G	A15a	6nu multicolored	1.25	1.25
i.		Souv. sheet of 4, #148C, 148E-148G	5.00	5.00
		Nos. 148-148G (8)	4.70	4.70

Nos. 148C, 148E-148G are airmail. Simulated 3-dimensions using a plastic overlay.

Dogs
A17f

1972-73		Photo.	*Perf. 13½*	
149	A17f	2ch Pointer	.20	.20
149A	A17f	3ch Irish Setter	.20	.20
149B	A17f	5ch Lhasa Apso, vert	.20	.20
149C	A17f	10ch Dochi	.20	.20
149D	A17f	15ch Damci	.20	.20
149E	A17f	15ch Collie	.20	.20
149F	A17f	20ch Basset hound	.20	.20
149G	A17f	25ch Damci, diff	.20	.20
149H	A17f	30ch Fox terrier	.20	.20
149I	A17f	55ch Lhasa Apso, diff.	.20	.20
149J	A17f	99ch Boxer	.25	.25
149K	A17f	2.50nu St. Bernard	.55	.55
149L	A17f	4nu Cocker Spaniel	.90	.90
o.		Souv. sheet of 3, #149J-149L, perf. 14	3.00	3.00
149M	A17f	8nu Damci, diff.	1.90	1.90
p.		Souv. sheet of 2, #149I, 149M, perf. 14	3.25	3.25
		Nos. 149-149M (14)	5.60	5.60

Souvenir Sheet
Perf. 14

149N	A17f	18nu Poodle	5.00	5.00

Issued: #149B-149D, 149G, 149I, 149M, 149p, 10/5; #149-149A, 149E-149F, 149H, 149J-149L, 149o, 1/1/73; #149N, 1/15/73. No. 149N is airmail. All exist imperf.
For surcharges & overprints see #268-269, 385.

Roses — A17g

1973, Jan. 30		Photo.	*Perf. 13½*	
		Scented Paper		
150	A17g	15ch Wendy Cussons	.20	.20
150A	A17g	25ch Iceberg	.20	.20
150B	A17g	30ch Marchioness of Urquio	.20	.20
150C	A17g	3nu Pink parfait	.70	.70
150D	A17g	6nu Roslyn	1.40	1.40
150E	A17g	7nu Blue moon	1.60	1.60
f.		Souv. sheet, #150D-150E	2.50	2.50
		Nos. 150-150E (6)	4.30	4.30

#150D-150E are airmail. Exist imperf.

Apollo 11 Type of 1969

Apollo 17: 10ch, Taking photographs on moon. 15ch, Setting up experiments. 55ch, Earth. 2nu, Driving lunar rover. 7nu, Satellite. 9nu, Astronauts Cernan, Evans, Schmitt.

1973, Feb. 28		Litho.	*Imperf.*	
		Size: 50x49mm		
151	A15a	10ch multicolored	.20	.20
151A	A15a	15ch multicolored	.20	.20
151B	A15a	55ch multicolored	.20	.20
151C	A15a	2nu multicolored	.70	.70
f.		Souv. sheet of 4, #151-151C	2.50	2.50

151D	A15a	7nu multicolored	2.25	2.25
151E	A15a	9nu multicolored	3.25	3.25
g.		Souv. sheet of 2, #151D-151E	10.00	10.00
		Nos. 151-151E (6)	6.80	6.80

Simulated 3-dimensions using a plastic overlay. Nos. 151D-151E are airmail. No. 151g is circular, 160mm in diameter.

Phonograph Records

A17h

Recordings: 10ch, Bhutanese History. 25ch, Royal Bhutan Anthem. 1.25nu, Bhutanese History (English). 3nu, Bhutanese History (Bhutanese), Folk Song #1. 7nu, Folk Song #1. 8nu, Folk Song #2. 9nu, History in English, Folk Songs #1 & 2.

1973, Apr. 15

Self-adhesive
Diameter: #152-152B, 152D-152E, 69mm, #152C, 152F, 100mm

152	A17h	10ch yel on red	.70	.70
152A	A17h	25ch gold on grn	1.00	1.00
152B	A17h	1.25nu sil on bl	4.50	4.50
152C	A17h	3nu sil on pur	10.00	10.00
152D	A17h	7nu sil on blk	22.50	22.50
152E	A17h	8nu red on white	30.00	30.00
152F	A17h	9nu blk on yel	32.50	32.50
		Nos. 152-152F (7)	101.20	101.20

Nos. 152C, 152F are airmail.

King Jigme Dorji Wangchuk (d. 1972) — A17i

Embossed on Gold Foil

1973, May 2		Die Cut	*Imperf.*	
153	A17i	10ch orange	.20	.20
153A	A17i	25ch red	.20	.20
153B	A17i	3nu green	.70	.70
153C	A17i	6nu blue	1.40	1.40
153D	A17i	8nu purple	1.90	1.90
e.		Souv. sheet of 2, #153C-153D	4.50	4.50
		Nos. 153-153D (5)	4.40	4.40

Nos. 153C-153D are airmail.

Mushrooms — A17j

Different mushrooms.

1973, Sept. 25		Litho.	*Imperf.*	
154	A17j	15ch multicolored	.20	.20
154A	A17j	25ch multicolored	.20	.20
154B	A17j	30ch multicolored	.25	.25
154C	A17j	3nu multicolored	2.50	2.50
f.		Souv. sheet #154-154C	15.00	15.00
154D	A17j	6nu multicolored	5.75	5.75
154E	A17j	7nu multicolored	6.75	6.75
g.		Souv. sheet #154D-154E	35.00	35.00
		Nos. 154-154E (6)	15.65	15.65

Simulated 3-dimensions using a plastic overlay. Nos. 154D-154E are airmail.

Bhutanese Mail Service — A17k

Designs: 5ch, 6nu, Letter carrier at mail box. 10ch, 5nu, Postmaster, letter carrier. 15ch, Sacking mail. 25ch, Mailtruck. 1.25nu, Sorting mail. 3nu, Hand-delivered mail.

1973, Nov. 14		Photo.	*Perf. 13½*	
155	A17k	5ch multicolored	.20	.20
155A	A17k	10ch multicolored	.20	.20
155B	A17k	15ch multicolored	.20	.20
155C	A17k	25ch multicolored	.20	.20
155D	A17k	1.25nu multicolored	.30	.30
155E	A17k	3nu multicolored	.65	.65
155F	A17k	5nu multicolored	1.10	1.10
155G	A17k	6nu multicolored	1.25	1.25
h.		Souv. sheet, #155F-155G	6.00	6.00
		Nos. 155-155G (8)	4.10	4.10

Indipex '73. Nos. 155F-155G are airmail. All exist imperf.
For surcharges and overprint see Nos. 267, 382, C37-C38.

A set of 15 stamps plus souvenir sheet of 3 showing paintings with reading and writing themes was not authorized.

King Jigme Singye Wangchuk and Royal Crest — A18

Designs (King and): 25ch, 90ch, Flag of Bhutan. 1.25nu, Wheel with 8 good luck signs. 2nu, 4nu, Punakha Dzong, former winter capital. 3nu, 5nu, Crown. 5ch, same as 10ch.

1974, June 2		Litho.	*Perf. 13½*	
157	A18	10ch maroon & multi	.20	.20
158	A18	25ch gold & multi	.20	.20
159	A18	1.25nu multi	.25	.25
160	A18	2nu gold & multi	.50	.50
161	A18	3nu multi	.70	.70
		Nos. 157-161 (5)	1.85	1.85

Souvenir Sheets
Perf. 13½, Imperf.

162		Sheet of 2	2.50	2.50
a.	A18 5ch maroon & multi		.20	
b.	A18 5nu red orange & multi		2.25	

163		Sheet of 2	2.50	2.50
a.	A18 90ch gold & multi		.75	
b.	A18 4nu gold & multi		2.00	

Coronation of King Jigme Singye Wangchuk, June 2, 1974.

Mailman on Horseback
A19

Old and New Locomotives
A20

Designs (UPU Emblem, Carrier Pigeon and): 3ch, Sailing and steam ships. 4ch, Old biplane and jet. 25ch, Mail runner and jeep.

1974, Oct. 9		Litho.	*Perf. 14½*	
164	A19	1ch grn & multi	.20	.20
165	A20	2ch lilac & multi	.20	.20
166	A20	3ch ocher & multi	.20	.20
167	A20	4ch yel grn & multi	.20	.20
168	A20	25ch salmon & multi	.20	.20
		Nos. 164-168,C27-C29 (8)	2.15	2.15

Centenary of Universal Postal Union. Issued in sheets of 50 and sheets of 5 plus label with multicolored margin. Exist imperf.

Family and WPY Emblem — A21

1974, Dec. 17			*Perf. 13½*	
169	A21	25ch bl & multi	.20	.20
170	A21	50ch org & multi	.20	.20
171	A21	90ch ver & multi	.30	.30
172	A21	2.50nu brn & multi	.65	.65
a.		Souvenir sheet, 10nu	2.25	2.25
		Nos. 169-172 (4)	1.35	1.35

For surcharge see No. 254.

Sephisa Chandra — A22

Designs: Indigenous butterflies.

1975, Sept. 15		Litho.	*Perf. 14½*	
173	A22	1ch *shown*	.20	.20
174	A22	2ch *Lethe kansa*	.20	.20
175	A22	3ch *Neope bhadra*	.20	.20
176	A22	4ch *Euthalia duda*	.20	.20
177	A22	5ch *Vindula erota*	.20	.20
178	A22	10ch *Bhutanitis Lidderdale*	.20	.20
179	A22	3nu *Limenitis zayla*	.60	.60
180	A22	5nu *Delis thysbe*	1.40	1.40
		Nos. 173-180 (8)	3.20	3.20

Souvenir Sheet
Perf. 13

181	A22	10nu *Dabasa gyas*	2.50	2.50

For surcharges see Nos. 255-256.

Apollo and Apollo-Soyuz Emblem — A23

Design: No. 183, Soyuz and emblem.

1975, Dec. 1   Litho.   Perf. 14x13½

182	A23	10nu multicolored	2.75	2.75
183	A23	10nu multicolored	2.75	2.75
a.		Souvenir sheet of 2, 15nu	7.00	7.00

Apollo Soyuz link-up in space, July 17. Nos. 182-183 printed se-tenant in sheets of 10. No. 183a contains two 15nu stamps similar to Nos 182-183. Exist imperf.
For surcharges see Nos. 257-258.

Jewelry — A24

Designs: 2ch, Coffee pot, bell and sugar cup. 3ch, Container and drinking horn. 4ch, Pendants and box cover. 5ch, Painter. 15ch, Silversmith. 20ch, Wood carver with tools. 1.50nu, Mat maker. 5nu, 10nu, Printer.

1975, Dec. 17   Perf. 14½

184	A24	1ch multicolored	.20	.20
185	A24	2ch multicolored	.20	.20
186	A24	3ch multicolored	.20	.20
187	A24	4ch multicolored	.20	.20
188	A24	5ch multicolored	.20	.20
189	A24	15ch multicolored	.20	.20
190	A24	20ch multicolored	.20	.20
191	A24	1.50nu multicolored	.40	.40
192	A24	10nu multicolored	2.50	2.50
		Nos. 184-192 (9)	4.30	4.30

Souvenir Sheet
Perf. 13

193	A24	5nu multicolored	1.40	1.40

Handicrafts and craftsmen.
For surcharges sheet see No. 259, 381.

King Jigme Singye Wangchuk A25

Designs: 25ch, 90ch, 1nu, 2nu, 4nu, like 15ch. 1.30nu, 3nu, 5nu, Coat of arms. Sizes (Diameter): 15ch, 1nu, 1.30nu, 38mm. 25ch, 2nu, 3nu, 49mm. 90ch, 4nu, 5nu, 63mm.

Lithographed, Embossed on Gold Foil

1975, Nov. 11   Imperf.

194	A25	15ch emerald	.20	.20
195	A25	25ch emerald	.20	.20
196	A25	90ch emerald	.35	.35
197	A25	1nu bright carmine	.40	.40
198	A25	1.30nu bright carmine	.45	.45
199	A25	2nu bright carmine	.65	.65
200	A25	3nu bright carmine	1.00	1.00
201	A25	4nu bright carmine	1.60	1.60
202	A25	5nu bright carmine	2.00	2.00
		Nos. 194-202 (9)	6.85	6.85

King Jigme Singye Wangchuk's 20th birthday.

Rhododendron Cinnabarinum A28

Rhododendron: 2ch, Campanulatum. 3ch, Fortunei. 4ch, Red arboreum. 5ch, Pink arboreum. 1nu, Falconeri. 3nu, Hodgsonii. 5nu, Keysii. 10nu, Cinnabarinum.

1976, Feb. 15   Litho.   Perf. 15

203	A28	1ch rose & multi	.20	.20
204	A28	2ch lt grn & multi	.20	.20
205	A28	3ch gray & multi	.20	.20
206	A28	4ch lil & multi	.20	.20
207	A28	5ch ol gray & multi	.20	.20

208	A28	1nu brn org & multi	.25	.20
209	A28	3nu ultra & multi	.75	.60
210	A28	5nu gray & multi	1.25	.90
		Nos. 203-210 (8)	3.25	2.70

Souvenir Sheet
Perf. 13½

211	A28	10nu multicolored	2.50	2.50

For surcharge see No. 260.

Slalom and Olympic Games Emblem — A29

Olympic Games Emblem and: 2ch, 4-men bobsled. 3ch, Ice hockey. 4ch, Cross-country skiing. 5ch, Figure skating, women's. 2nu, Downhill skiing. 4nu, Speed skating. 6nu, Ski jump. 10nu, Figure skating, pairs.

1976, Mar. 29   Litho.   Perf. 13½

212	A29	1ch multicolored	.20	.20
213	A29	2ch multicolored	.20	.20
214	A29	3ch multicolored	.20	.20
215	A29	4ch multicolored	.20	.20
216	A29	5ch multicolored	.20	.20
217	A29	2nu multicolored	.40	.35
218	A29	4nu multicolored	.90	.75
219	A29	6nu multicolored	2.50	1.75
		Nos. 212-219 (8)	4.80	3.85

Souvenir Sheet

220	A29	6nu multicolored	1.50	1.50

12th Winter Olympic Games, Innsbruck, Austria, Feb. 4-15.
For surcharges see Nos. 261-262.

Ceremonial Masks A29a

Various masks.

1976, Apr. 23   Litho.   Imperf.

220A	A29a	5ch multicolored	.20	.20
220B	A29a	10ch multicolored	.20	.20
220C	A29a	15ch multicolored	.20	.20
220D	A29a	20ch multicolored	.20	.20
220E	A29a	25ch multi, horiz.	.20	.20
220F	A29a	30ch multi, horiz.	.20	.20
220G	A29a	35ch multi, horiz.	.20	.20
220H	A29a	1nu multi, horiz.	.45	.45
220I	A29a	2nu multi, horiz.	.90	.90
220J	A29a	2.50nu multi, horiz.	1.10	1.10
220K	A29a	3nu multi, horiz.	1.40	1.40
		Nos. 220A-220K (11)	5.25	5.25

Souvenir Sheets

220L	A29a	5nu like #220C	1.60	1.60
220M	A29a	10nu like #220F	3.25	3.25

Simulated 3-dimensions using a plastic overlay. Nos. 220H-220M are airmail.
Sizes of stamps: No. 220L, 59x70mm, No. 220M, 69x57mm.

Double Carp Design A31

Designs: Various symbolic designs and Colombo Plan emblem.

1976, July 1   Litho.   Perf. 14½

230	A31	3ch red & multi	.20	.20
231	A31	4ch ver & multi	.20	.20
232	A31	5ch multicolored	.20	.20
233	A31	25ch bl & multi	.20	.20
234	A31	1.25nu multicolored	.35	.30
235	A31	2nu yel & multi	.60	.50
236	A31	2.50nu vio & multi	.75	.60
237	A31	3nu multicolored	.90	.80
		Nos. 230-237 (8)	3.40	3.00

Colombo Plan, 25th anniversary.
For surcharge see No. 265.

Bandaranaike Conference Hall — A32

1976, Aug. 16   Litho.   Perf. 13½

238	A32	1.25nu multicolored	.35	.25
239	A32	2.50nu multicolored	.65	.45

5th Summit Conference of Non-aligned Countries, Colombo, Sri Lanka, Aug. 9-19.

Elizabeth II — A33

Liberty Bell — A34

Spirit of St. Louis — A35

Souvenir Sheet
Perf. 13½

229	A30	10nu multicolored	2.75	2.50

For surcharges see Nos. 263-264.

Bhutanese Archer, Olympic Rings — A36

Designs: No. 242, Alexander Graham Bell. No. 245, LZ 3 Zeppelin docking, 1907. No. 246, Alfred B. Nobel.

1978, Nov. 15   Litho.   Perf. 14½

240	A33	20nu multicolored	4.00	4.00
241	A34	20nu multicolored	4.00	4.00
242	A33	20nu multicolored	4.00	4.00
243	A35	20nu multicolored	4.00	4.00
244	A36	20nu multicolored	4.00	4.00
245	A35	20nu multicolored	4.00	4.00
246	A33	20nu multicolored	4.00	4.00
		Nos. 240-246 (7)	28.00	28.00

25th anniv. of coronation of Elizabeth II; American Bicentennial; cent. of 1st telephone call by Alexander Graham Bell; Charles A. Lindbergh crossing the Atlantic, 50th anniv.; Olympic Games; 75th anniv. of the Zeppelin; 75th anniv. of Nobel Prize. Seven souvenir sheets exist, each 25nu, commemorating same events with different designs. Size: 103x80mm.

Issues of 1967-1976 Surcharged with New Value and Bars

Perforations and Printing as Before 1978

252	A16	25ch on 3nu	(#133)
253	A17	25ch on 6nu	(#139)
254	A21	25ch on 2.50nu	(#172)
255	A22	25ch on 3nu	(#179)
256	A22	25ch on 5nu	(#180)
257	A23	25ch on 10nu	(#182)
258	A23	25ch on 10nu	(#183)
259	A24	25ch on 10nu	(#192)
260	A28	25ch on 5nu	(#210)
261	A29	25ch on 4nu	(#218)
262	A29	25ch on 10nu	(#219)
263	A30	25ch on 4nu	(#227)
264	A30	25ch on 6nu	(#228)
265	A31	25ch on 2.50nu	(#236)
266	A14g	25ch on 5nu	(#90E)
267	A17k	25ch on 3nu	(#155E)
268	A17f	25ch on 4nu	(#149L)
269	A17f	25ch on 8nu	(#149M)
		Nos. 252-269, C31-C38 (26)	80.00 80.00

Mother and Child, IYC Emblem — A37

IYC Emblem and: 5nu, Mother and two children. 10nu, Boys with blackboards and stylus.

1979, June   Litho.   Perf. 14x13½

289	A37	2nu multicolored	.50	.40
290	A37	5nu multicolored	1.40	1.00
291	A37	10nu multicolored	2.50	2.00
a.		Souv. sheet of 3, #289-291 + label, perf. 15x13½	4.25	3.25
		Nos. 289-291 (3)	4.40	3.40

International Year of the Child.
For overprints see Nos. 761-763.

Conference Emblem and Dove — A38

10nu, Emblem and Bhutanese symbols.

Orchid A30

Designs: Various flowers.

1976, May 29   Litho.   Perf. 14½

221	A30	1ch multicolored	.20	.20
222	A30	2ch multicolored	.20	.20
223	A30	3ch multicolored	.20	.20
224	A30	4ch multicolored	.20	.20
225	A30	5ch multicolored	.20	.20
226	A30	2nu multicolored	.40	.20
227	A30	4nu multicolored	.80	.60
228	A30	6nu multicolored	1.25	1.00
		Nos. 221-228 (8)	3.45	2.90

1979, Sept. 3 Litho. Perf. 14x13½
292 A38 25ch multicolored .20 .20
293 A38 10nu multicolored 3.25 2.50

6th Non-Aligned Summit Conference, Havana, August 1979.

Silver Rattle, Dorji A39

Antiques: 10ch, Silver handell, Dilbu, vert. 15ch, Cylindrical jar, Jadum, vert. 25ch, Ornamental teapot, Jamjee. 1nu, Leather container, Kem, vert. 1.25nu, Brass teapot, Jamjee. 1.70nu, Vessel with elephant-head legs, Sangphor, vert. 2nu, Teapot with ornamental spout, Jamjee, vert. 3nu, Metal pot on claw-shaped feet, Yangtho, vert. 4nu, Dish inlaid with precious stones, Battha. 5nu, Metal circular flask, Chhap, vert.

1979, Dec. 17 Photo. Perf. 14
294 A39 5ch multicolored .20 .20
295 A39 10ch multicolored .20 .20
296 A39 15ch multicolored .20 .20
297 A39 25ch multicolored .20 .20
298 A39 1nu multicolored .45 .40
299 A39 1.25nu multicolored .50 .50
300 A39 1.70nu multicolored .70 .75
301 A39 2nu multicolored .90 .75
302 A39 3nu multicolored 1.25 1.10
303 A39 4nu multicolored 1.60 1.50
304 A39 5nu multicolored 2.25 1.90
Nos. 294-304 (11) 8.45 7.65

Hill, Rinpiang Dzong — A40

Hill Statue, Stamps of Bhutan and: 2nu, Dzong. 5nu, Ounsti Dzong. 10nu, Lingzi Dzong, Gt. Britain Type 81. 20nu, Rope bridge, Penny Black.

1980, May 6 Litho. Perf. 14x13½
305 A40 1nu multicolored .30 .25
306 A40 2nu multicolored .60 .50
307 A40 5nu multicolored 1.60 1.25
308 A40 10nu multicolored 3.00 2.50
Nos. 305-308 (4) 5.50 4.50

Souvenir Sheet
309 A40 5nu multicolored 5.75 4.25

Sir Rowland Hill (1795-1879), originator of penny postage.

Kichu Lhakhang Monastery, Phari — A41

Guru Padma Sambhava's Birthday: Monasteries.

1981, July 11 Litho. Perf. 14
310 A41 1nu Dungtse, Phari, vert .25 .20
311 A41 2nu shown .50 .40
312 A41 2.25nu Kurjey .65 .45
313 A41 3nu Tangu, Thimphu .75 .60
314 A41 4nu Cheri, Thimphu 1.00 .75
315 A41 5nu Chorten, Kora 1.50 1.00
316 A41 7nu Tak-Tsang, Phari, vert 2.00 1.50
Nos. 310-316 (7) 6.65 4.90

Prince Charles and Lady Diana — A42

Orange-bellied Chloropsis — A43

1981, Sept. 10 Litho. Perf. 14½
317 A42 1nu St. Paul's Cathedral .20 .20
318 A42 5nu like #317 1.00 .65
319 A42 20nu shown 4.00 2.50
320 A42 25nu like #319 4.50 3.50
Nos. 317-320 (4) 9.70 6.85

Souvenir Sheet
321 A42 20nu Wedding procession 5.00 4.00

Royal wedding. Nos. 318-319 issued in sheets of 5 plus label.
For surcharges see Nos. 471-475.

1982, Apr. 19 Litho. Perf. 14
322 A43 2nu shown .55 .40
323 A43 3nu Monal pheasant .80 .60
324 A43 5nu Ward's trogon 1.40 1.00
325 A43 10nu Mrs. Gould's sunbird 2.50 2.00
Nos. 322-325 (4) 5.25 4.00

Souvenir Sheet
326 A43 25nu Maroon oriole 7.00 5.00

1982 World Cup — A44

Designs: Various soccer players.

1982, June 25 Litho. Perf. 14½x14
327 A44 1nu multicolored .25 .20
328 A44 2nu multicolored .55 .40
329 A44 3nu multicolored .80 .60
330 A44 20nu multicolored 5.25 4.00
Nos. 327-330 (4) 6.85 5.20

Souvenir Sheets
331 A44 25nu multicolored 12.00 7.50

Nos. 331 have margins continuing design and listing finalists (Algeria, etc. or Hungary, etc.).
For surcharges see Nos. 481-485.

21st Birthday of Princess Diana — A45

1982, Aug.
332 A45 1nu St. James' Palace .25 .20
332A A45 10nu Diana, Charles 2.50 1.75
332B A45 15nu Windsor Castle 4.00 4.50
333 A45 25nu Wedding 6.50 4.50
Nos. 332-333 (4) 13.25 10.95

Souvenir Sheet
334 A45 20nu Diana 5.50 4.00

10nu-15nu issued only in sheets of 5 + label.
For overprints and surcharges see Nos. 361-363, 455-459, 476-480.

Scouting Year A46

1982, Aug. 23 Litho. Perf. 14
335 A46 3nu Baden-Powell, vert. .65 .50
336 A46 5nu Eating around fire 1.10 .85
337 A46 15nu Reading map 3.50 2.50
338 A46 20nu Pitching tents 4.50 3.50
Nos. 335-338 (4) 9.75 7.35

Souvenir Sheet
339 A46 25nu Mountain climbing 6.00 4.50

For surcharges see Nos. 450-454.

Rama and Cubs with Mowgli — A47

Scenes from Disney's The Jungle Book.

1982, Sept. 1 Perf. 11
340 A47 1ch multicolored .20 .20
341 A47 2ch multicolored .20 .20
342 A47 3ch multicolored .20 .20
343 A47 4ch multicolored .20 .20
344 A47 5ch multicolored .20 .20
345 A47 10ch multicolored .20 .20
346 A47 30ch multicolored .20 .20
347 A47 2nu multicolored .50 .35
348 A47 20nu multicolored 5.50 4.25
Nos. 340-348 (9) 7.40 6.00

Souvenir Sheets Perf. 13½
349 A47 20nu Baloo and Mowgli in forest 5.25 4.00
350 A47 20nu Baloo and Mowgli floating 5.25 4.00

George Washington Surveying — A48

1982, Nov. 15 Litho. Perf. 15
351 A48 50ch shown .20 .20
352 A48 1nu FDR, Harvard .20 .20
353 A48 2nu Washington at Valley Forge .30 .25
354 A48 3nu FDR, family .50 .40
355 A48 4nu Washington, Battle of Monmouth .65 .50
356 A48 5nu FDR, White House .85 .65
357 A48 15nu Washington, Mt. Vernon 2.50 2.00
358 A48 20nu FDR, Churchill, Stalin 3.25 2.50
Nos. 351-358 (8) 8.45 6.70

Souvenir Sheets
359 A48 25nu Washington, vert. 4.25 3.25
360 A48 25nu FDR, vert. 4.25 3.25

Washington and Franklin D. Roosevelt.

Nos. 332-334 Overprinted: "ROYAL BABY / 21.6.82"

1982, Nov. 19 Perf. 14½x14
361 A45 1nu multicolored .25 .25
361A A45 10nu multicolored 2.50 1.75
361B A45 15nu multicolored 3.75 3.00
362 A45 25nu multicolored 6.25 4.75
Nos. 361-362 (4) 12.75 9.75

Souvenir Sheet
363 A45 20nu multicolored 5.25 4.25

Birth of Prince William of Wales, June 21.

500th Birth Anniv. of Raphael A51

Portraits.

1983, Mar. 23 Perf. 13½
375 A51 1nu Angelo Doni .25 .20
376 A51 4nu Maddalena Doni 1.00 .75
377 A51 5nu Baldassare Castiglione 1.25 .90
378 A51 20nu La Donna Velata 5.00 3.75
Nos. 375-378 (4) 7.50 5.60

Souvenir Sheets
379 A51 25nu Expulsion of Heliodorus 6.25 4.75
380 A51 25nu Mass of Bolsena 6.25 4.75

Nos. 184, 155F, 139, 184, 147G, 149M Surchd. or Ovptd.: "Druk Air"

1983, Feb. 11
381 A24 30ch on 1ch multi .20 .20
382 A17 5nu multicolored 2.00 1.25
383 A17k 6nu multicolored 2.25 1.50
384 A17d 7nu multicolored 2.50 1.50
385 A17f 8nu multicolored 2.50 1.75
Nos. 381-385 (5) 9.45 6.20

Druk Air Service inauguration. Overprint of 8nu all caps. Nos. 382, 384 air mail.

Manned Flight Bicentenary — A52

1983, Aug. 15 Litho. Perf. 15
386 A52 50ch Dornier Wal .20 .20
387 A52 3nu Savoia-Marchetti S-66 .75 .55
388 A52 10nu Hawker Osprey 2.00 1.75
389 A52 20nu Ville de Paris 4.00 3.75
Nos. 386-389 (4) 6.95 6.25

Souvenir Sheet
390 A52 25nu Balloon Captif 5.00 3.75

Buddhist Symbols — A53

1983, Aug. 11 Litho. Perf. 13½
391 A53 25ch Sacred vase .20 .20
392 A53 50ch Five Sensory Symbols .20 .20
393 A53 2nu Seven Treasures .35 .25
394 A53 3nu Five Sensory Organs .60 .45
395 A53 8nu Five Fleshes 1.50 1.10
396 A53 9nu Sacrificial cake 1.75 1.25
a. Souv. sheet of 6, #391-396 4.50 3.50
Nos. 391-396 (6) 4.60 3.50

Size of Nos. 393, 396: 45x40mm.

World Communications Year
(1983) — A54

Various Disney characters and history of communications.

1984, Apr. 10 Litho. Perf. 14½x14
397	A54	4ch multicolored	.20	.20
398	A54	5ch multicolored	.20	.20
399	A54	10ch multicolored	.20	.20
400	A54	20ch multicolored	.20	.20
401	A54	25ch multicolored	.20	.20
402	A54	50ch multicolored	.20	.20
403	A54	1nu multicolored	.30	.25
404	A54	5nu multicolored	1.10	.95
405	A54	20nu multicolored	4.25	3.75
		Nos. 397-405 (9)	6.85	6.15

Souvenir Sheets
Perf. 14x14½
406	A54	20nu Donald Duck on phone, horiz.	4.75	4.00
407	A54	20nu Mickey Mouse on TV	4.75	4.00

1984 Winter
Olympics — A55

1984, June 16 Perf. 14
408	A55	50ch Skiing	.20	.20
409	A55	1nu Cross-country skiing	.25	.20
410	A55	3nu Speed skating	.60	.45
411	A55	20nu Bobsledding	3.75	3.00
		Nos. 408-411 (4)	4.80	3.85

Souvenir Sheet
412	A55	25nu Hockey	5.00	3.25

Golden Langur   Locomotives
A56   A57

1984, June 10 Litho. Perf. 14½
413	A56	50ch shown	.20	.20
414	A56	1nu Group in tree, horiz.	.20	.20
415	A56	2nu Family, horiz.	.40	.30
416	A56	4nu Group walking	.80	.60
		Nos. 413-416 (4)	1.60	1.30

Souvenir Sheets
417	A56	20nu Snow leopard	4.00	2.00
418	A56	25nu Yak	4.00	2.00
419	A56	25nu Blue sheep, horiz.	4.00	2.00

1984, July 16
420	A57	50ch Sans Pareil, 1829	.20	.20
421	A57	1nu Planet, 1830	.20	.20
422	A57	3nu Experiment, 1832	.60	.45
423	A57	4nu Black Hawk, 1835	.80	.60
424	A57	5.50nu Jenny Lind, 1847	1.10	.85
425	A57	8nu Semmering-Bavaria, 1851	1.60	1.25
426	A57	10nu Great Northern #1, 1870	2.00	1.50

427	A57	25nu German Natl. Tinder, 1880	5.00	3.75
		Nos. 420-427 (8)	11.50	8.80

Souvenir Sheets
428	A57	20nu Darjeeling Himalayan Railway, 1984	4.00	3.00
429	A57	20nu Sondermann Freight, 1896	4.00	3.00
430	A57	20nu Crampton's locomotive, 1846	4.00	3.00
431	A57	20nu Erzsebet, 1870	4.00	3.00
		Nos. 424-427 horiz.		

Classic
Cars
A58

1984, Aug. 29 Litho. Perf. 14
432	A58	50ch Riley Sprite, 1936	.20	.20
433	A58	1nu Lanchester, 1919	.20	.20
434	A58	3nu Itala, 1907	.65	.45
435	A58	4nu Morris Oxford Bullnose, 1913	.90	.60
436	A58	5.50nu Lagonda LG6, 1939	1.25	.85
437	A58	6nu Wolseley, 1903	1.40	.90
438	A58	8nu Buick Super, 1952	1.75	1.25
439	A58	20nu Maybach Zeppelin, 1933	4.50	3.00
		Nos. 432-439 (8)	10.85	7.45

Souvenir Sheets
440	A58	25nu Simplex, 1912	2.50	1.50
441	A58	25nu Renault, 1901	2.50	1.50

For surcharges see Nos. 537-544.

Summer Olympic
Games — A59

1984, Oct. 27   Litho.
442	A59	15ch Women's archery	.20	.20
443	A59	25ch Men's archery	.20	.20
444	A59	2nu Table tennis	.40	.30
445	A59	2.25nu Basketball	.45	.35
446	A59	5.50nu Boxing	1.10	.85
447	A59	6nu Running	1.25	.90
448	A59	8nu Tennis	1.60	1.25
		Nos. 442-448 (7)	5.20	4.05

Souvenir Sheet
449	A59	25nu Archery	5.00	3.50

For overprints see Nos. 537-544.

Nos. 335-339 Surcharged with New Values and Bars in Black or Silver

1985   Litho.   Perf. 14
450	A46	10nu on 3nu multi	2.00	1.50
451	A46	10nu on 5nu multi	2.00	1.50
452	A46	10nu on 15nu multi	2.00	1.50
453	A46	10nu on 20nu multi	2.00	1.50
		Nos. 450-453 (4)	8.00	6.00

Souvenir Sheet
454	A46	20nu on 25nu multi	4.00	3.00

Nos. 332, 332A, 332B, 333-334 Surcharged with New Values and Bars

1985, Feb. 28
455	A45	5nu on 1nu multi	1.00	.70
456	A45	5nu on 10nu multi	1.00	.70
457	A45	5nu on 15nu multi	1.00	.70
458	A45	40nu on 25nu multi	8.00	5.25
		Nos. 455-458 (4)	11.00	7.35

Souvenir Sheet
459	A45	25nu on 20nu multi	5.00	4.00

50th Anniv.
of Donald
Duck — A60

1984, Dec. 10 Litho. Perf. 13½x14
460	A60	4ch Magician Mickey	.20	.20
461	A60	5ch Slide, Donald, Slide	.20	.20
462	A60	10ch Donald's Golf Game	.20	.20
463	A60	20ch Mr. Duck Steps Out	.20	.20
464	A60	25ch Lion Around	.20	.20
465	A60	50ch Alpine Climbers	.20	.20
466	A60	1nu Flying Jalopy	.20	.20
467	A60	5nu Frank Duck	1.10	.95
468	A60	20nu Good Scouts	4.50	3.25
		Nos. 460-468 (9)	7.00	5.40

Souvenir Sheets
469	A60	20nu Three Caballeros	4.50	3.25
470	A60	20nu Sea Scouts	4.50	3.25

Nos. 317-321 Surcharged with New Values and Bars

1985, Feb. 28   Perf. 14½
471	A42	10nu on 1nu multi	2.00	1.50
472	A42	10nu on 5nu multi	2.00	1.50
473	A42	10nu on 20nu multi	2.00	1.50
474	A42	10nu on 25nu multi	2.00	1.50
		Nos. 471-474 (4)	8.00	6.00

Souvenir Sheet
475	A42	30nu on 20nu multi	6.00	5.00

Nos. 361, 361A, 361B, 362-363 Surcharged with New Values and Bars

1985, Feb. 28   Perf. 14½x14
476	A45	5nu on 1nu multi	.75	.75
477	A45	5nu on 10nu multi	.75	.55
478	A45	5nu on 15nu multi	.75	.55
479	A45	40nu on 25nu multi	7.50	5.50
		Nos. 476-479 (4)	9.75	7.35

Souvenir Sheet
480	A45	25nu on 20nu multi	5.00	3.75

Nos. 327-331 Surcharged with New Values and Bars in Black or Silver

1985, June
481	A44	5nu on 1nu multi	1.50	1.10
482	A44	5nu on 2nu multi	1.50	1.10
483	A44	5nu on 3nu multi	1.50	1.10
484	A44	5nu on 20nu multi	1.50	1.10
		Nos. 481-484 (4)	6.00	4.40

Souvenir Sheets
485	A44	20nu on 20nu multi	7.50	5.50

Mask Dance of
the Judgement
of Death — A61

1985, Apr. 27   Perf. 13½
486	A61	5ch Shinje Choegyel	.20	.20
487	A61	35ch Raksh Lango	.20	.20
488	A61	50ch Druelgo	.20	.20
489	A61	2.50nu Pago	.45	.35
490	A61	3nu Telgo	.55	.40
491	A61	4nu Due Nakcung	.75	.60
492	A61	5nu Lha Karpo	.90	.70
a.		Souv. sheet #486-487, 491-492	1.90	1.50
493	A61	5.50nu Nyalbum	1.00	.75
494	A61	6nu Khimda Pelkyi	1.10	.85
		Nos. 486-494 (9)	5.35	4.25

For overprints see Nos. 764-772.

Veteran's
War
Memorial
Building,
San
Francisco
A63

1984, Dec. 1 Litho. Perf. 12
495	A62	10ch Domkhar	.20	.20
496	A62	25ch Shemgang	.20	.20
497	A62	50ch Chapcha	.20	.20
498	A62	1nu Tashigang	.20	.20
499	A62	2nu Pungthang Chhug	.30	.30
500	A62	5nu Dechhenphoda	.70	.70
		Nos. 495-500 (6)	1.80	1.80

1985, Oct. 24 Litho. Perf. 14
502	A63	50ch Flags of Bhutan, UN, vert.	.20	.20
503	A63	15nu Headquarters, NY, vert.	2.75	2.00
504	A63	20nu shown	3.75	2.75
		Nos. 502-504 (3)	6.70	4.95

Souvenir Sheet
505	A63	25nu UN Human Rights Declaration	4.25	3.00

UN, 40th anniv.

Audubon Birth Bicentenary — A64

Illustrations of North American bird species by Audubon.

1985
506	A64	50ch Anas breweri	.20	.20
507	A64	1nu Lagopus lagopus	.20	.20
508	A64	2nu Charadrius montanus	.35	.25
509	A64	3nu Cavia stellata	.50	.40
510	A64	4nu Canachites canadensis	.70	.50
511	A64	5nu Mergus cucullatus	.85	.60
512	A64	15nu Olor buccinator	2.50	1.75
513	A64	20nu Bucephala clangula	3.50	2.50
		Nos. 506-513 (8)	8.80	6.40

Souvenir Sheets
514	A64	25nu Accipiter striatus	3.75	2.25
515	A64	25nu Parus bicolor	3.75	2.25

Issued: #507, 510-511, 514, 11/15; #506, 508-509, 513, 515, 12/6.

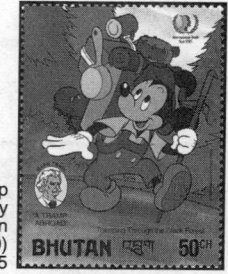

A Tramp
Abroad, by
Mark Twain
(1835-1910)
A65

Walt Disney animated characters.

1985, Nov. 15
516	A65	50ch multicolored	.20	.20
517	A65	2nu multicolored	.35	.25
518	A65	5nu multicolored	.85	.60
519	A65	9nu multicolored	1.50	1.10
520	A65	20nu multicolored	3.50	2.50
		Nos. 516-520 (5)	6.40	4.65

Souvenir Sheet
521	A65	25nu Goofy, Mickey Mouse	5.00	3.50

Intl. Youth Year.
For overprints see Nos. 554, 556-557.

Monasteries
A62

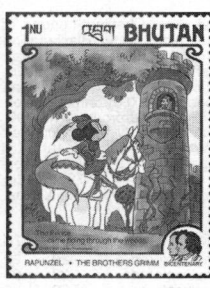

Rapunzel, by Jacob and Wilhelm Grimm
A66

Walt Disney animated characters.

1985, Nov. 15
522	A66	1nu multicolored	.20	.20
523	A66	4nu multicolored	.70	.50
524	A66	7nu multicolored	1.25	.95
525	A66	8nu multicolored	1.40	1.00
526	A66	15nu multicolored	2.50	1.75
		Nos. 522-526 (5)	6.05	4.40

Souvenir Sheet
527	A66	25nu multicolored	5.00	4.00

No. 525 printed in sheets of 8.
For overprints see Nos. 553, 555, 558.

First South Asian Regional Cooperation Summit, Dec. 7-8, Dacca, Bangladesh
A67

1985, Dec. 8   *Perf. 14*
528	A67	50ch multicolored	.20	.20
529	A67	5nu multicolored	.85	.60

Seven Precious Attributes of the Universal King — A68

1986, Feb. 12   Litho.   *Perf. 13x12½*
530	A68	30ch Wheel	.20	.20
531	A68	50ch Gem	.20	.20
532	A68	1.25nu Queen	.20	.20
533	A68	2nu Minister	.30	.30
534	A68	4nu Elephant	.55	.55
535	A68	6nu Horse	.85	.85
536	A68	8nu General	1.10	1.10
		Nos. 530-536 (7)	3.40	3.40

Nos. 442-443, 445-449 Ovptd. with Medal, Winners' Names and Countries. No. 449 Ovptd. for Men's and Women's Events

1986, May 5   Litho.   *Perf. 14*
537	A59	15ch Hyang Soon Seo, So. Korea	.20	.20
538	A59	25ch Darrell Pace, US	.20	.20
539	A59	2.25nu US	.30	.30
540	A59	5.50nu Mark Breland, US	.80	.80
541	A59	6nu Daley Thompson, Britain	.85	.85
542	A59	8nu Stefan Edberg, Sweden	1.10	1.10
		Nos. 537-542 (6)	3.45	3.45

Souvenir Sheets
543	A59	25nu Hyang Soon Seo	3.50	3.50
544	A59	25nu Darrel Pace	3.50	3.50

Kilkhor Mandalas, Deities — A69

Religious art: 10ch, 1nu, Phurpa, ritual dagger. 25ch, 3nu, Amitayus in wrath. 50ch, 5nu, Overpowering Deities. 75ch, 7nu, Great Wrathful One, Guru Rinpoche.

1986, June 17   *Perf. 13½*
545	A69	10ch multicolored	.20	.20
546	A69	25ch multicolored	.20	.20
547	A69	50ch multicolored	.20	.20
548	A69	75ch multicolored	.20	.20
549	A69	1nu multicolored	.20	.20
550	A69	3nu multicolored	.40	.40
551	A69	5nu multicolored	.70	.70
552	A69	7nu multicolored	1.00	1.00
		Nos. 545-552 (8)	3.10	3.10

Nos. 525, 519, 526, 520, 521 and 527 Ovptd. with AMERIPEX '86 Emblem

1986, June 16   Litho.   *Perf. 14*
553	A66	8nu multi	1.40	1.00
554	A65	9nu multi	1.50	1.10
555	A66	15nu multi	2.50	1.75
556	A65	20nu multi	3.50	2.50
		Nos. 553-556 (4)	8.90	6.35

Souvenir Sheets
557	A65	25nu #521	4.25	3.00
558	A66	25nu #527	4.25	3.00

A70

A71

Halley's Comet — A72

Designs: 50ch, Babylonian tablet fragments, 2349 B.C. sighting. 1nu, 17th cent. print, A.D. 66 sighting. 2nu, French silhouette art, 1835 sighting. 3nu, Bayeux Tapestry, 1066 sighting. 4nu, Woodblock, 684 sighting. 5nu, Illustration from Bybel Printen, 1650. 15nu, 1456 Sighting, Cancer constellation. 20nu, Delft plate, 1910 sighting. No. 572, Comet over Himalayas. No. 573, Comet over domed temple Dug-gye Jong.

1986, Nov. 4   Litho.   *Perf. 15*
564	A70	50ch multicolored	.20	.20
565	A70	1nu multicolored	.20	.20
566	A71	2nu multicolored	.35	.30
567	A70	3nu multicolored	.50	.35
568	A70	4nu multicolored	.70	.50
569	A71	5nu multicolored	.85	.65
570	A70	15nu multicolored	2.50	2.00
571	A70	20nu multicolored	3.50	2.50
		Nos. 564-571 (8)	8.80	6.70

Souvenir Sheets
572	A72	25nu multicolored	4.25	3.00
573	A72	25nu multicolored	4.25	3.00

A73

Statue of Liberty, Cent. — A74

Statue and ships: 50ch, Mircea, Romania. 1nu, Shalom, Israel. 2nu, Leonardo da Vinci, Italy. 3nu, Libertad, Argentina. 4nu, France, France. 5nu, SS United States, US. 15nu, Queen Elizabeth II, England. 20nu, Europa, West Germany. No. 582, Statue. No. 583, Statue, World Trade Center.

1986, Nov. 4
574	A73	50ch multicolored	.20	.20
575	A73	1nu multicolored	.20	.20
576	A73	2nu multicolored	.35	.30
577	A73	3nu multicolored	.50	.35
578	A73	4nu multicolored	.65	.50
579	A73	5nu multicolored	.85	.65
580	A73	15nu multicolored	2.50	1.90
581	A73	20nu multicolored	3.50	2.50
		Nos. 574-581 (8)	8.75	6.60

Souvenir Sheets
582	A74	25nu multicolored	4.25	3.00
583	A74	25nu multi, diff.	4.25	3.00

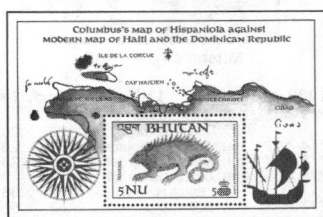

Discovery of America, 500th Anniv. — A75

1987, May 25   Litho.   *Perf. 14*
584	A75	20ch Santa Maria	.40	.40
585	A75	25ch Queen Isabella	.40	.40
586	A75	50ch Ship, flying fish	.40	.40
587	A75	1nu Columbus's coat of arms	.75	.60
588	A75	2nu Christopher Columbus	1.40	1.00
589	A75	3nu Landing in the New World	2.00	2.00
a.		Miniature sheet of 6, #584-589	5.00	5.00
		Nos. 584-589 (6)	5.35	4.80

Souvenir Sheets
590	A75	20ch Pineapple		
591	A75	25ch Indian hammock		
592	A75	50ch Tobacco plant		
593	A75	1nu Flamingo		
594	A75	2nu Navigator, astrolabe, 15th cent.		
595	A75	3nu Lizard		
596	A75	5nu Iguana	1.25	.95

All stamps are vertical except those contained in Nos. 591, 595 and 596. Stamps from No. 589a have white background.

CAPEX '87 — A76

Locomotives.

1987, June 15
597	A76	50ch Canadian Natl. U1-f	.20	.20
598	A76	1nu Via Rail L.R.C.	.20	.20
599	A76	2nu Canadian Natl. GM GF-30t	.35	.25
600	A76	3nu Canadian Natl. 4-8-4	.50	.35

601	A76	8nu Canadian Pacific 4-6-2	1.40	1.00
602	A76	10nu Via Express passenger train	1.75	1.25
603	A76	15nu Canadian Nat. Turbotrain	2.50	1.90
604	A76	20nu Canadian Pacific Diesel-Electric Express	3.25	2.50
		Nos. 597-604 (8)	10.15	7.65

Souvenir Sheet
605	A76	25nu Royal Hudson 4-6-4	4.25	3.00
606	A76	25nu Canadian Natl. 4-8-4, diff.	4.25	3.00

Two Faces, Sculpture by Marc Chagall (1887-1984) A77

Paintings: 1nu, At the Barber's. 2nu, Old Jew with Torah. 3nu, Red Maternity. 4nu, Eve of Yom Kippur. 5nu, The Old Musician. 6nu, The Rabbi of Vitebsk. 7nu, Couple at Dusk. 9nu, The Artistes. 10nu, Moses Breaking the Tablets of the Law. 12nu, Bouquet with Flying Lovers. 20nu, In the Sky of the Opera.

No. 619, Romeo and Juliet. No. 620, Magician of Paris. No. 621, Maternity. No. 622, The Carnival for Aleko: Scene II. No. 623, Visit to the Grandparents. No. 624, The Smolensk Newspaper. No. 625, The Concert. No. 626, Composition with Goat. No. 627, Still Life. No. 628. The Red Gateway. No. 629, Cow with Parasol. No. 630, Russian Village.

1987, Dec. 17   Litho.   *Perf. 14*
607-618	A77	Set of 12	12.75	12.75

Size: 110x95mm

Imperf
619-630	A77	25nu Set of 12	48.00	36.00

1988 Winter Olympics, Calgary — A78

Emblem and Disney animated characters as competitors in Olympic events.

1988, Feb. 15   Litho.   *Perf. 14*
631	A78	50ch Slalom	.20	.20
632	A78	1nu Downhill skiing	.20	.20
633	A78	2nu Ice hockey	.30	.25
634	A78	4nu Biathlon	.65	.50
635	A78	7nu Speed skating	1.10	.85
636	A78	8nu Figure skating	1.25	.95
637	A78	9nu Figure skating, diff.	1.50	1.10
638	A78	20nu Bobsled	3.25	2.50
		Nos. 631-638 (8)	8.45	6.55

Souvenir Sheets
639	A78	25nu Ski jumping	4.00	4.00
640	A78	25nu Ice dancing	4.00	4.00

Transportation Innovations — A79

1988, Mar. 31
641	A79	50ch Pullman Pioneer, 1865	.20	.20
642	A79	1nu Stephenson's Rocket, 1829	.20	.20
643	A79	2nu Pierre L'Allement's Velocipede, 1866	.30	.25
644	A79	3nu Benz Velocipede, 1886	.50	.35
645	A79	4nu Volkswagen Beetle, c. 1960	.65	.50

646	A79	5nu	Natchez Vs. Robert E. Lee, 1870	.80	.60
647	A79	6nu	American La France, 1910	1.00	.75
648	A79	7nu	USS Constitution, 1787, vert.	1.10	.80
649	A79	9nu	Bell Rocket Belt, 1961, vert.	1.50	1.10
650	A79	10nu	Trevithick Locomotive, 1804	1.60	1.25
			Nos. 641-650 (10)	7.85	6.00

Souvenir Sheets

651	A79	25nu	Concorde jet	4.00	4.00
652	A79	25nu	Mallard, 1938, vert.	4.00	4.00
653	A79	25nu	Shinkansen	4.00	4.00
654	A79	25nu	TGV, 1981	4.00	4.00

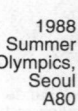

1988 Summer Olympics, Seoul — A80

7nu-20nu vert.

1989, Feb. 15   Litho.

655	A80	50ch	Women's gymnastics	.20	.20
656	A80	1nu	Tae kwon do	.20	.20
657	A80	2nu	Shot put	.30	.25
658	A80	4nu	Women's volleyball	.65	.50
659	A80	7nu	Basketball	1.10	.85
660	A80	8nu	Soccer	1.25	.95
661	A80	9nu	Women's high jump	1.50	1.10
662	A80	20nu	Running	3.25	2.50
			Nos. 655-662 (8)	8.45	6.55

Souvenir Sheets

663	A80	25nu	Archery, vert.	4.00	4.00
664	A80	25nu	Fencing	4.00	4.00

Paintings by Titian — A81

Designs: 50ch, *Gentleman with a Book.* 1nu, *Venus and Cupid, with a Lute Player.* 2nu, *Diana and Actaeon.* 3nu, *Cardinal Ippolito dei Medici.* 4nu, *Sleeping Venus.* 5nu, *Venus Risen from the Waves.* 6nu, *Worship of Venus.* 7nu, *Fête Champetre.* 10nu, *Perseus and Andromeda.* 15nu, *Danae.* 20nu, *Venus at the Mirror.* 25nu, *Venus and the Organ Player.* No. 677, *The Pardo Venus,* horiz. No. 678, *Venus and Cupid, with an Organist.* No. 679, *Miracle of the Irascible Son.* No. 680, *Diana and Callisto.* No. 681, *Saint John the Almsgiver.* No. 682, *Danae with the Shower of Gold,* horiz. No. 683, *Bacchus and Ariadne.* No. 684, *Venus Blindfolding Cupid.* No. 685, *Portrait of Laura Dianti.* No. 686, *Venus of Urbino.* No. 687, *Portrait of Johann Friedrich.* No. 688, *Mater Dolorosa with Raised Hands.*

Perf. 13½x14, 14x13½

1989, Feb. 15   Litho.

665	A81	50ch	multicolored	.20	.20
666	A81	1nu	multicolored	.20	.20
667	A81	2nu	multicolored	.30	.25
668	A81	3nu	multicolored	.50	.35
669	A81	4nu	multicolored	.65	.50
670	A81	5nu	multicolored	.80	.60
671	A81	6nu	multicolored	.90	.75
672	A81	7nu	multicolored	1.10	.85
673	A81	10nu	multicolored	1.60	1.25
674	A81	15nu	multicolored	2.50	1.75
675	A81	20nu	multicolored	3.25	2.50
676	A81	25nu	multicolored	4.00	3.00
			Nos. 665-676 (12)	16.00	12.20

Souvenir Sheets

677-688	A81	25nu	Set of 12	48.00 48.00

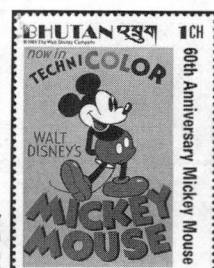

Mickey Mouse, 60th Anniv. (in 1988) — A82

Movie posters: 1ch, Mickey Mouse, 1930s. 2ch, *Barnyard Olympics,* 1932. 3ch, *Society Dog Show,* 1939. 4ch, *Fantasia,* 1980s re-release. 5ch, *The Mad Dog,* 1932. 10ch, *A Gentleman's Gentleman,* 1941. 50ch, *Symphony hour,* 1942. 10nu, *The Moose Hunt,* 1931. 15nu, *Wild Waves,* 1929. 20nu, *Mickey in Arabia,* 1932. 25nu, *Tugboat Mickey,* 1940. 30nu, *Building a Building,* 1933.

#701, *The Mad Doctor,* 1933. #702, *The Meller Drammer,* 1933. #703, *Ye Olden Days,* 1933. #704, *Mickey's Good Deed,* 1932. #705, *Mickey's Pal Pluto,* 1933. #706, *Trader Mickey,* 1932. #707, *Touchdown Mickey,* 1932. #708, *Steamboat Willie,* 1928. #709, *The Whoopee Party,* 1932. #710, *Mickey's Nightmare,* 1932. #711, *The Klondike Kid,* 1932. #712, *The Wayward Canary,* 1932.

1989, June 20   Litho.   **Perf. 13½x14**

689-700	A82	Set of 12	16.00 13.00

Souvenir Sheets

701-712	A82	25nu Set of 12	48.00 48.00

Mushrooms — A83

1989, Aug. 22   Litho.   **Perf. 14**

713	A83	50ch	*Tricholoma pardalotum*	.20	.20
714	A83	1nu	*Suillus placidus*	.20	.20
715	A83	2nu	*Boletus regius*	.30	.25
716	A83	3nu	*Gomphidius glutinosus*	.50	.35
717	A83	4nu	*Boletus calopus*	.65	.50
718	A83	5nu	*Suillus grevillei*	.80	.60
719	A83	6nu	*Boletus appendiculatus*	.90	.70
720	A83	7nu	*Lactarius torminosus*	1.10	.80
721	A83	10nu	*Macrolepiota rhacodes*	1.60	1.25
722	A83	15nu	*Amanita rubescens*	2.50	1.75
723	A83	20nu	*Amanita phalloides*	3.25	2.50
724	A83	25nu	*Amanita citrina*	4.00	3.00
			Nos. 713-724 (12)	16.00	12.10

Souvenir Sheets

725	A83	25nu	*Russula aurata*	4.00	4.00
726	A83	25nu	*Gyroporus castaneus*	4.00	4.00
727	A83	25nu	*Cantharellus cibarius*	4.00	4.00
728	A83	25nu	*Boletus rhodoxanthus*	4.00	4.00
729	A83	25nu	*Paxillus involutus*	4.00	4.00
730	A83	25nu	*Gyroporus cyanescens*	4.00	4.00
731	A83	25nu	*Lepista nuda*	4.00	4.00
732	A83	25nu	*Dentinum repandum*	4.00	4.00
733	A83	25nu	*Lepista saeva*	4.00	4.00
734	A83	25nu	*Hydnum imbricatum*	4.00	4.00
735	A83	25nu	*Xerocomus subtomentosus*	4.00	4.00
736	A83	25nu	*Russula olivacea*	4.00	4.00

Intl. Maritime Organization, 30th Anniv. — A84

Ships: 50ch, Spanish galleon *La Reale,* 1680. 1 nu, Submersible *Turtle,* 1776. 2nu,

Charlote Dundas, 1802. 3nu, *Great Eastern,* c. 1858. 4nu, HMS *Warrior,* 1862. 5nu, Mississippi steamer, 1884. 6nu, *Preussen,* 1902. 7nu, USS *Arizona,* 1915. 10nu, *Bluenose,* 1921. 15nu, Steam trawler, 1925. 20nu, American liberty ship, 1943. No. 748, S.S. *United States,* 1952. No. 749, Moran tug, c. 1950. No. 750, Sinking of the *Titanic,* 1912. No. 751, U-boat, c. 1942. No. 752, Japanese warship *Yamato,* 1944. No. 753, HMS *Dreadnought.* No. 754, S.S. *Normandie,* c. 1933, and a Chinese junk. No. 755, HMS *Victory,* 1805. No. 756, USS *Monitor,* 1862. No. 757, *Cutty Sark,* 1869. No. 758, USS *Constitution.* No. 759, HMS *Resolution.* No. 760, Chinese junk.

1989, Aug. 24   Litho.   **Perf. 14**

737	A84	50ch	multicolored	.20	.20
738	A84	1nu	multicolored	.20	.20
739	A84	2nu	multicolored	.30	.25
740	A84	3nu	multicolored	.50	.35
741	A84	4nu	multicolored	.65	.50
742	A84	5nu	multicolored	.80	.60
743	A84	6nu	multicolored	.90	.70
744	A84	7nu	multicolored	1.10	.80
745	A84	10nu	multicolored	1.60	1.25
746	A84	15nu	multicolored	2.50	1.75
747	A84	20nu	multicolored	3.25	2.50
748	A84	25nu	multicolored	4.00	3.00
			Nos. 737-748 (12)	16.00	12.10

Souvenir Sheets

749-760	A84	25nu each	4.00	4.00

Nos. 289-291 Overprinted:
WORLD / AIDS DAY

1988, Dec. 1   Litho.   **Perf. 14x13½**

761	A37	2nu	multicolored	.45	.35
762	A37	5nu	multicolored	1.10	.90
763	A37	10nu	multicolored	2.25	1.75
			Nos. 761-763 (3)	3.80	3.00

Nos. 486-494 Ovptd. in Silver:
ASIA-PACIFIC EXPOSITION FUKUOKA '89

1989, Mar. 17   **Perf. 13½**

764	A61	5ch	multicolored	.20	.20
765	A61	35ch	multicolored	.20	.20
766	A61	50ch	multicolored	.20	.20
767	A61	2.50nu	multicolored	.40	.30
768	A61	3nu	multicolored	.50	.35
769	A61	4nu	multicolored	.65	.50
770	A61	5nu	multicolored	.80	.60
771	A61	5.50nu	multicolored	.90	.65
772	A61	6nu	multicolored	1.00	.80
			Nos. 764-772 (9)	4.85	3.80

This set exists overprinted in Japanese.

Chhukha Hydroelectric Project — A85

1988, Oct. 21   Litho.   **Perf. 13½**

773	A85	50ch	multicolored	.20	.20

Jawaharlal Nehru (1889-1964), Indian Prime Minister — A85a

1989, Nov. 14   Photo.   **Perf. 14**

773A	A85a	100ch	olive brown	.20	.20

Denomination is shown as 1.00ch in error.

Birds — A86

Designs: 50ch, Larger goldenbacked woodpecker. 1nu, Black-naped monarch. 2nu, White-crested laughing thrush. 3nu, Blood-pheasant. 4nu, Blossom-headed parakeet.

5nu, Rosy minivet. 6nu, Chestnut-headed tit babbler. 7nu, Blue pitta. 10nu, Black-naped oriole. 15nu, Green magpie. 20nu, Indian three-toed kingfisher. No. 785, Ibisbill. No. 786, Great pied hornbill. No. 787, Himalayan redbreasted falconet. No. 788, Lammergeier. No. 789, Large racket-tailed drongo. No. 790, Fire-tailed sunbird. No. 791, Indian crested swift. No. 792, White-eared pheasant. No. 793, Satyr tragopan. No. 794, Wallcreeper. No. 795, Fairy bluebird. No. 796, Little spiderhunter. No. 797, Spotted forktail. Nos. 774-779 vert.

1989, Nov. 22   Litho.   **Perf. 14**

774	A86	50ch	multicolored	.20	.20
775	A86	1nu	multicolored	.20	.20
776	A86	2nu	multicolored	.30	.25
777	A86	3nu	multicolored	.50	.35
778	A86	4nu	multicolored	.65	.50
779	A86	5nu	multicolored	.80	.60
780	A86	6nu	multicolored	.90	.70
781	A86	7nu	multicolored	1.10	.80
782	A86	10nu	multicolored	1.60	1.25
783	A86	15nu	multicolored	2.50	1.75
784	A86	20nu	multicolored	3.25	2.50
785	A86	25nu	multicolored	4.00	3.00
			Nos. 774-785 (12)	16.00	12.10

Souvenir Sheets

786-797	A86	25nu each	4.00	4.00

Steam Locomotives — A87

Designs: 50ch, *Best Friend of Charleston,* 1830, US 1nu, Class U, 1949, France. 2nu, *Consolidation,* 1866, US. 3nu, *Luggage Engine,* 1843, Great Britain. 4nu, Class 60-3 Shay, 1913, US. 5nu, *John Bull,* 1831, US. 6nu, *Hercules,* 1837, US. 7nu, Eight-wheel tank engine, 1874, Great Britain. 10nu, *The Illinois,* 1852, US. 15nu, German State 4-6-4, 1935. 20nu, American Standard, 1865. No. 809, Class Ps-4, 1926, US. No. 810, *Puffing Billy,* 1814, Great Britain. No. 811, Stephenson's *Rocket,* 1829, Great Britain. No. 812, *Cumberland,* 1845, US, vert. No. 813, *John Stevens,* 1849, US, vert. No. 814, No. 22 Baldwin Locomotive Works, 1873, US. No. 815, *Ariel,* 1877, US. No. 816, 1899 *No. 1301* Webb Compound Engine, Great Britain. No. 817, 1893 *No. 999* Empire State Express, US. No. 818, 1923 Class K-36, US. No. 819, 1935 Class A4, Great Britain. No. 820, 1935 Class A, US. No. 821, 1943 Class P-1, US.

1990, Jan. 30

798	A87	50ch	multi	.20	.20
799	A87	1nu	multi	.20	.20
800	A87	2nu	multi	.30	.25
801	A87	3nu	multi	.50	.35
802	A87	4nu	multi	.65	.50
803	A87	5nu	multi	.80	.60
804	A87	6nu	multi	.90	.70
805	A87	7nu	multi	1.10	.80
806	A87	10nu	multi	1.60	1.25
807	A87	15nu	multi	2.50	1.75
808	A87	20nu	multi	3.25	2.50
809	A87	25nu	multi	4.00	3.00
			Nos. 798-809 (12)	16.00	12.10

Souvenir Sheets

810-821	A87	25nu each	4.00	4.00

Butterflies — A88

1990, Jan. 30   Litho.   **Perf. 14**

822	A88	50ch	*Charaxes harmodius*	.20	.20
823	A88	1nu	*Prioneris thestylis*	.20	.20
824	A88	2nu	*Sephisa chandra*	.30	.25
825	A88	3nu	*Penthema usarda*	.50	.35
826	A88	4nu	*Troides aecus*	.65	.50
827	A88	5nu	*Polyura eudamippus*	.80	.60
828	A88	6nu	*Polyura dolon*	.90	.70
829	A88	7nu	*Neope bhadra*	1.10	.80
830	A88	10nu	*Delias descombesi*	1.60	1.25
831	A88	15nu	*Childreni childrena*	2.50	1.75
832	A88	20nu	*Kallima inachus*	3.25	2.50

833	A88	25nu	*Elymnias male-las*	4.00	3.00
			Nos. 822-833 (12)	16.00	12.10

Souvenir Sheets

834	A88	25nu	Red lacewing	4.00	4.00
835	A88	25nu	Bhutan glory	4.00	4.00
836	A88	25nu	Great eggfly	4.00	4.00
837	A88	25nu	Kaiser-I-Hind	4.00	4.00
838	A88	25nu	Chestnut tiger	4.00	4.00
839	A88	25nu	Common map	4.00	4.00
840	A88	25nu	Swallowtail	4.00	4.00
841	A88	25nu	Jungle glory	4.00	4.00
842	A88	25nu	Checkered swal-lowtail	4.00	4.00
843	A88	25nu	Common birdw-ing	4.00	4.00
844	A88	25nu	Blue banded peacock	4.00	4.00
845	A88	25nu	Camberwell beauty	4.00	4.00

Nos. 822-824, 826-827, 830-831, 834-835, 844-845 are vert.

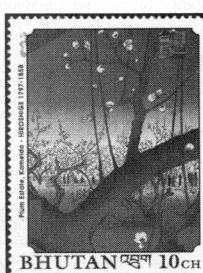

Paintings by
Hiroshige
A89

10ch, Plum Estate, Kameido. 20ch, Yatsumi Bridge. 50ch, Ayase River and Kanegafuchi. 75ch, View of Shiba Coast. 1nu, Grandpa's Teahouse, Meguro. 2nu, Kameido Tenjin Shrine. 6nu, Yoroi Ferry, Koami-cho. 7nu, Sakasai Ferry. 10nu, Fukagawa Lumberyards. 15nu, Suido Bridge & Surugadai. 20nu, Meguro Drum Bridge, Sunset Hill. #857, Atagoshita & Yabu Lane. #858, Towboats Along the Yotsugi-dori Canal. #859, Minowa, Kanasugi, Mikawashima. #860, Horikiri Iris Garden. #861, Fukagawa Susaki & Jumant-subo. #862, Suijin Shrine & Massaki on the Sumida River. #863, New Year's Eve Foxfires at the Changing Tree, Oji. #864, Nihonbashi, Clearing After Snow. #865, View to the North from Asukayama. #866, Komakata Hall & Azuma Bridge. #867, The City Flourishing, Tanabata Festival. #868, Suruga-cho. #869, Sudden Shower over Shin-Ohashi Bridge & Atake.

1990, May 21 Litho. Perf. 13½

846	A89	10ch	multicolored	.20	.20
847	A89	20ch	multicolored	.20	.20
848	A89	50ch	multicolored	.20	.20
849	A89	75ch	multicolored	.20	.20
850	A89	1nu	multicolored	.20	.20
851	A89	2nu	multicolored	.30	.25
852	A89	6nu	multicolored	.95	.70
853	A89	7nu	multicolored	1.10	.85
854	A89	10nu	multicolored	1.60	1.25
855	A89	15nu	multicolored	2.50	1.75
856	A89	20nu	multicolored	3.25	2.50
857	A89	25nu	multicolored	4.00	3.00
			Nos. 846-857 (12)	14.70	11.30

Souvenir Sheets

858-869	A89	25nu	each	4.00	3.00

Hirohito (1901-1989) and enthronement of Akihito as emperor of Japan.

Orchids — A90

1990, Apr. 6 Litho. Perf. 14

870	A90	10ch	*Renanthera monachica*	.20	.20
871	A90	50ch	*Vanda coerulea*	.20	.20
872	A90	1nu	*Phalaenopsis vi-olacea*	.20	.20
873	A90	2nu	*Dendrobium no-bile*	.30	.20
874	A90	5nu	*Vandopsis lis-sochiloides*	.80	.60
875	A90	6nu	*Paphiopedilum rothschildianum*	.95	.70
876	A90	7nu	*Phalaenopsis schilleriana*	1.10	.80

877	A90	9nu	*Paphiopedilum insigne*	1.50	1.10
878	A90	10nu	*Paphiopedilum bellatulum*	1.60	1.25
879	A90	20nu	*Doritis pulcher-rima*	3.25	2.50
880	A90	25nu	*Cymbidium gi-ganteum*	4.00	3.00
881	A90	35nu	*Phalaenopsis mariae*	5.50	4.25
			Nos. 870-881 (12)	19.60	15.00

Souvenir Sheets

882	A90	30nu	*Vanda coerules-cens*	4.75	4.75
883	A90	30nu	*Vandopsis par-ishi*	4.75	4.75
884	A90	30nu	*Dendrobium aphyllum*	4.75	4.75
885	A90	30nu	*Phalaenopsis amabilis*	4.75	4.75
886	A90	30nu	*Paphiopedilum haynaldianum*	4.75	4.75
887	A90	30nu	*Dendrobium lod-digesii*	4.75	4.75
888	A90	30nu	*Vanda alpina*	4.75	4.75
889	A90	30nu	*Phalaenopsis equestris*	4.75	4.75
890	A90	30nu	*Vanda cristata*	4.75	4.75
891	A90	30nu	*Phalaenopsis cornu cervi*	4.75	4.75
892	A90	30nu	*Paphiopedilum niveum*	4.75	4.75
893	A90	30nu	*Dendrobium margaritaceum*	4.75	4.75

EXPO '90 Intl. Garden and Greenery Exposition, Osaka, Apr. 1-Dec. 31.

G.P.O., Thimphu — A90a

1990, May 29 Photo. Perf. 14

893A	A90a	1nu	multicolored	.20	.20

Penny Black, 150th Anniv. A90b

Penny Black and: 50ch, Bhutan #1. 1nu, Oldenburg #1. 2nu, Bergedorf #3. 4nu, German Democratic Republic #48. 5nu, Brunswick #1. 6nu, Basel #3L1. 8nu, Geneva #2L1. 10nu, Zurich #1L1. No. 902, France #3. 20nu, Vatican City #1. 25nu, Israel #1. No. 905, Japan #1.

Penny Black and: No. 906a, Mecklenburg-Schwerin #1. b, Mecklenburg-Strelitz #1. No. 907a, Germany #5, #9. b, Prussia #2. No. 908a, Hamburg #1. b, North German Confederation #1, #7. No. 909a, Baden #1 b, Wurttemberg #1. No. 910a, Heligoland #1. b, Hanover #1. No. 911a, Thurn & Taxis #3. b, Thurn & Taxis #42. No. 912a, Schleswig-Holstein #1. b, Lubeck #5. No. 913, Saxony #1. No. 914, Berlin #9N1. No. 915, No other stamp. No. 916, US #1. No. 917, Bavaria #1.

1990, Oct. 9 Perf. 14

894	A90b	50ch	multicolored	.20	.20
895	A90b	1nu	multicolored	.20	.20
896	A90b	2nu	multicolored	.30	.25
897	A90b	4nu	multicolored	.65	.50
898	A90b	5nu	multicolored	.80	.60
899	A90b	6nu	multicolored	1.00	.75
900	A90b	8nu	multicolored	1.25	1.00
901	A90b	10nu	multicolored	1.60	1.25
902	A90b	15nu	multicolored	2.50	1.75
903	A90b	20nu	multicolored	3.25	2.50
904	A90b	25nu	multicolored	4.00	3.00
905	A90b	30nu	multicolored	4.75	3.50
			Nos. 894-905 (12)	20.50	15.50

Souvenir Sheets
Sheets of 2 (#906-912) or 1

906-912	A90b	15nu	each	4.75	4.75
913-917	A90b	30nu	each	4.75	4.75

Stamp World London '90.

Giant Pandas A91

Tiger A92

Endangered wildlife of Asia.

1990 Perf. 14

918	A91	50ch	multi, diff.	.20	.20
919	A91	1nu	multi, diff.	.20	.20
920	A91	2nu	multi, diff.	.30	.25
921	A91	3nu	shown	.50	.35
922	A91	4nu	multi, diff.	.65	.50
923	A92	5nu	shown	.80	.60
924	A91	6nu	multi, diff.	.90	.70
925	A91	7nu	multi, diff.	1.10	.80
926	A92	10nu	Elephant	1.60	1.25
927	A91	15nu	multi, diff.	2.50	1.75
928	A92	20nu	Barking deer	3.25	2.50
929	A92	25nu	Snow leopard	4.00	3.00
			Nos. 918-929 (12)	16.00	12.10

Souvenir Sheets

930	A92	25nu	Rhinoceros	4.00	4.00
931	A92	25nu	Clouded leopard	4.00	4.00
932	A92	25nu	Asiatic wild dog	4.00	4.00
933	A92	25nu	Himalayan shou	4.00	4.00
934	A92	25nu	Golden cat	4.00	4.00
935	A92	25nu	Himalayan musk deer	4.00	4.00
936	A91	25nu	Panda	4.00	4.00
937	A92	25nu	Asiatic black bear	4.00	4.00
938	A92	25nu	Gaur	4.00	4.00
939	A92	25nu	Pygmy hog	4.00	4.00
940	A92	25nu	Wolf	4.00	4.00
941	A92	25nu	Sloth bear	4.00	4.00

Nos. 919-920 and 927 vert.

Buddhist Musical Instruments — A93

1990, Sept. 29 Litho. Perf. 13½x13

942	A93	10ch	Dungchen	.20	.20
943	A93	20ch	Dungkar	.20	.20
944	A93	30ch	Roim	.20	.20
945	A93	50ch	Tinchag	.20	.20
946	A93	1nu	Dradu & drilbu	.20	.20
947	A93	2nu	Gya-ling	.30	.20
948	A93	2.50nu	Nga	.40	.30
a.			Souv. sheet, #943, 945, 947-948	.85	.65
949	A93	3.50nu	Kang-dung	.55	.45
a.			Souv. sheet, #942, 944, 946, 949	.85	.65
			Nos. 942-949 (8)	2.25	2.00

Year of the Girl Child — A94

1990, Dec. 8

950	A94	50ch	shown	.20	.20
951	A94	20nu	Young girl	3.25	2.50

Wonders of the World — A95

Walt Disney characters viewing: 1ch, Temple of Artemis, Ephesus. 2ch, Statue of Zeus, Olympia. 3ch, Egyptian pyramids. 4ch, Lighthouse, Alexandria. 5ch, Mausoleum at Halicarnassus. 10ch, Colossus of Rhodes. 50ch, Hanging gardens of Babylon. 5nu, Mauna Loa volcano, Hawaii. 6nu, Carlsbad Caverns, New Mexico. 10nu, Rainbow Bridge, Utah. 15nu, Grand Canyon of the Colorado, Arizona. 20nu, Old Faithful geyser, Wyoming. 25nu, Giant sequoias, California. 30nu, Crater Lake and Wizard Island, Oregon. 5nu, 6nu, 10nu, 15nu, 20nu, 25nu, 30nu are horiz.

Walt Disney characters viewing: No. 966, Great Wall of China, horiz. No. 967, Mosque of St. Sophia, Istanbul, Turkey. No. 968, The Leaning Tower of Pisa, Italy. No. 969, Colosseum, Rome. No. 970, Stonehenge, England. No. 971, Catacombs of Alexandria, Egypt. No. 972, Porcelain Tower, Nanking, China, horiz. No. 973, The Panama Canal, horiz. No. 974, Golden Gate Bridge, San Francisco, horiz. No. 975, Sears Tower, Chicago, horiz. No. 976, Gateway Arch, St. Louis. No. 977, Alcan Highway, Alaska and Canada, horiz. No. 978, Hoover Dam, Nevada. No. 979, Empire State Building, New York.

1991, Feb. 2 Litho. Perf. 14

952	A95	1ch	multicolored	.20	.20
953	A95	2ch	multicolored	.20	.20
954	A95	3ch	multicolored	.20	.20
955	A95	4ch	multicolored	.20	.20
956	A95	5ch	multicolored	.20	.20
957	A95	10ch	multicolored	.20	.20
958	A95	50ch	multicolored	.20	.20
959	A95	5nu	multicolored	.80	.60
960	A95	6nu	multicolored	.95	.70
961	A95	10nu	multicolored	1.60	1.25
962	A95	15nu	multicolored	2.50	1.75
963	A95	20nu	multicolored	3.25	2.50
964	A95	25nu	multicolored	4.00	3.00
965	A95	30nu	multicolored	4.75	3.50
			Nos. 952-965 (14)	19.25	14.70

Souvenir Sheets
Perf. 14x13½, 13½x14

966-979	A95	25nu	each	4.00	4.00

Peter Paul Rubens (1577-1640), Painter A96

Entire paintings or different details from: 10ch, 5nu, 6nu, 10nu, No. 992, Atalanta and Meleager. 50ch, Fall of Phaethon. 1nu, No. 993, Feast of Venus Verticordia. 2nu, Achilles Slaying Hector. 3nu, No. 994, Arachne Punished by Minerva. 4nu, No. 995, Jupiter Receives Psyche on Olympus. 7nu, Venus in Vulcan's Furnace. 20nu, No. 996, Briseis Returned to Achilles. 30nu, No. 997, Mars and Rhea Sylvia. No. 998, Venus Shivering. No. 999, Ganymede and the Eagle. No. 1000, Origin of the Milky Way. No. 1001, Adonis and Venus. No. 1002, Hero and Leander. No. 1003, Fall of the Titans.

Nos. 994, 996-997, 1000-1003 are horiz.

1991, Feb. 2

980	A96	10ch	multicolored	.20	.20
981	A96	50ch	multicolored	.20	.20
982	A96	1nu	multicolored	.20	.20
983	A96	2nu	multicolored	.30	.20
984	A96	3nu	multicolored	.50	.20
985	A96	4nu	multicolored	.65	.20
986	A96	5nu	multicolored	.80	.60
987	A96	6nu	multicolored	.95	.70
988	A96	7nu	multicolored	1.10	.85
989	A96	10nu	multicolored	1.60	1.25

990	A96	20nu multicolored	3.25	2.50
991	A96	30nu multicolored	4.75	3.50
		Nos. 980-991 (12)	14.50	10.60

Souvenir Sheets

992-1003	A96	25nu each	4.00	4.00

Vincent Van Gogh (1853-1890),
Painter — A97

Paintings: 10ch, Cottages, Reminiscence of the North. 50ch, Head of a Peasant Woman with Dark Cap. 1nu, Portrait of a Woman in Blue. 2nu, The Midwife. 8nu, Vase with Hollyhocks. 10nu, Portrait of a Man with a Skull Cap. 12nu, Agostina Segatori Sitting in the Cafe du Tambourin. 15nu, Vase with Daisies and Anemones. 18nu, Fritillaries in a Copper Vase. 20nu, Woman Sitting in the Grass. 25nu, On the Outskirts of Paris, horiz. 30nu, Chrysanthemums and Wild Flowers in a Vase. No. 1016, Le Moulin de la Galette. No. 1017, Bowl with Sunflowers, Roses and Other Flowers, horiz. No. 1018, Poppies and Butterflies. No. 1019, Trees in the Garden of Saint-Paul Hospital. No. 1020, Le Moulin de Blute Fin. No. 1021, Le Moulin de la Galette, diff. No. 1022, Vase with Peonies. No. 1023, Vase with Zinnias. No. 1024, Fishing in the Spring, Pont de Clichy, horiz. No. 1025, Village Street in Auvers, horiz. No. 1026, Vase with Zinnias and Other Flowers, horiz. No. 1027, Vase with Red Poppies.

1991, July 22   Litho.   Perf. 13½

1004	A97	10ch multicolored	.20	.20
1005	A97	50ch multicolored	.20	.20
1006	A97	1nu multicolored	.20	.20
1007	A97	2nu multicolored	.30	.20
1008	A97	8nu multicolored	1.25	1.00
1009	A97	10nu multicolored	1.60	1.25
1010	A97	12nu multicolored	2.00	1.50
1011	A97	15nu multicolored	2.50	1.75
1012	A97	18nu multicolored	3.00	2.25
1013	A97	20nu multicolored	3.25	2.50
1014	A97	25nu multicolored	4.00	3.00
1015	A97	30nu multicolored	4.75	3.50
		Nos. 1004-1015 (12)	23.25	17.55

Size: 76x102mm, 102x76mm

Imperf

1016-1027	A97	30nu each	4.75	4.75

History of World Cup Soccer — A98

Winning team pictures, plays or possible future site: 50ch, Uruguay, 1930. 1nu, Italy, 1934. 2nu, Italy, 1938. 3nu, Uruguay, 1950. 5nu, West Germany, 1954. 10nu, Brazil, 1958. 20nu, Brazil, 1962. 25nu, England, 1966. 29nu, Brazil, 1970. 30nu, West Germany, 1974. 31nu, Argentina, 1978. 32nu, Italy, 1982. 33nu, Argentina, 1986. 34nu, West Germany, 1990. 35nu, Los Angeles Coliseum, 1994.

Players: No. 1043, Claudio Caniggia, Argentina, vert. No. 1044, Salvatore Schillaci, Italy, vert. No. 1045, Roberto Baggio, Italy, vert. No. 1046, Peter Shilton, England, vert. No. 1047, Lothar Matthaus, West Germany, vert. No. 1048, Paul Gascoigne, England, vert.

1991, Aug. 1   Litho.   Perf. 13½

1028	A98	50ch multicolored	.20	.20
1029	A98	1nu multicolored	.20	.20
1030	A98	2nu multicolored	.30	.20
1031	A98	3nu multicolored	.50	.20
1032	A98	5nu multicolored	.80	.60
1033	A98	10nu multicolored	1.60	1.25
1034	A98	20nu multicolored	3.25	2.50
1035	A98	25nu multicolored	4.00	3.00
1036	A98	29nu multicolored	4.75	3.50
1037	A98	30nu multicolored	4.75	3.50
1038	A98	31nu multicolored	5.00	3.75
1039	A98	32nu multicolored	5.25	4.00
1040	A98	33nu multicolored	5.50	4.00
1041	A98	34nu multicolored	5.50	4.25
1042	A98	35nu multicolored	5.75	4.25
		Nos. 1028-1042 (15)	47.35	35.40

Souvenir Sheets

1043-1048	A98	30nu each	4.75	4.75

Phila Nippon '91 — A99

1991, Nov. 16   Perf. 13

1049	A99	15nu multicolored	2.50	1.50

Education in Bhutan A100

1992, Mar. 5   Photo.   Perf. 13½

1050	A100	1nu multicolored	.20	.20

A101

1992 Summer Olympics, Barcelona — A102

1992, July 24   Litho.   Perf. 12

1051	A101	25nu Pair, #a.-b.	8.25	8.25

Souvenir Sheet

1052	A102	25nu Archer	4.00	4.00

German Reunification — A103

1992, Oct. 3   Litho.   Perf. 12

1053	A103	25nu multicolored	2.00	2.00

Souvenir Sheet

1054	A103	25nu multicolored	2.00	2.00

Stamp from No. 1054 does not have white inscription or border.

Bhutan Postal Service, 30th Anniv. A104

Designs: 1nu, Mail truck, plane. 3nu, Letter carrier approaching village. 5nu, Letter carrier emptying mail box.

1992, Oct. 9

1055	A104	1nu multicolored	.20	.20
1056	A104	3nu multicolored	.25	.25
1057	A104	5nu multicolored	.40	.40
		Nos. 1055-1057 (3)	.85	.85

Environmental Protection — A105

Designs: a, 7nu, Red panda. b, 20nu, Takin. c, 15nu, Black-necked crane, blue poppy. d, 10nu, One-horned rhinoceros.

1993, July 1   Litho.   Perf. 14

1058	A105	Sheet of 4, #b.-e.

No. 1058 was delayed from its originally scheduled release in 1992, although some copies were made available to the trade at that time.

A106   A107

1992, Sept. 18   Perf. 12

1059	A106	15nu Ship	1.25	1.25
1060	A106	20nu Portrait	1.60	1.60

Souvenir Sheet

1061	A106	25nu like #1060	2.00	2.00

Discovery of America, 500th anniv. Stamp from No. 1061 does not have silver inscription or white border.

1992, Nov. 11   Litho.   Perf. 12

Reign of King Jigme Singye Wangchuk, 20th Anniv.: a, 1nu, Man tilling field, factory. b, 5nu, Airplane. c, 10nu, House, well. d, 15nu, King. 20nu, People, flag, King, horiz.

1062	A107	Block of 4, #a.-d.	2.50	2.50

Souvenir Sheet

1063	A107	20nu multicolored	1.75	1.75

Intl. Volunteer Day — A108

a, 1.50nu, White inscription. b, 9nu, Green inscription. c, 15nu, Red inscription.

1992, Dec. 5   Litho.   Perf. 14

1067	A108	Block of 4, #a.-c. + label	2.00	2.00

Medicinal Plants — A109

1993, Jan. 1   Litho.   Perf. 12

1068	A109	1.50nu Meconopsis grandis prain	.20	.20
1069	A109	7nu Meconopsis sp.	.60	.60
1070	A109	10nu Meconopsis wallichii	.80	.80
1071	A109	12nu Meconopsis horridula	1.00	1.00
1072	A109	20nu Meconopsis discigera	1.75	1.75
		Nos. 1068-1072 (5)	4.35	4.35

Souvenir Sheet

1073	A109	25nu Meconopsis horridula, diff.	2.00	2.00

Miniature Sheet

Lunar New Year — A110

1993, Feb. 22   Litho.   Perf. 14

1074	A110	25nu multicolored	2.00	2.00

No. 1074 Surcharged "TAIPEI '93" in Silver and Black

1993, Aug. 14   Litho.   Perf. 14

1075	A110	30nu on 25nu	2.50	2.50

Door Gods — A112

1993, Dec. 17   Litho.   Perf. 12

1091	A112	1.50nu Namtheo-Say	.20	.20
1092	A112	5nu Pha-Ke-Po	.50	.50
1093	A112	10nu Chen-Mi-Jang	1.00	1.00
1094	A112	15nu Yul-Khor-Sung	1.50	1.50
		Nos. 1091-1094 (4)	3.20	3.20

Flowers — A113

1993, Jan. 1   Perf. 13

Designs: No. 1095a, 1nu, Rhododendron mucronatum. b, 1.50nu, Anemone rupicola. c, 2nu, Polemonium coeruleum. d, 2.5nu, Rosa marophylla. e, 4nu, Paraquilegia microphylla. f, 5nu, Aquilegia nivalis. g, 6nu, Geranium wallichianum. h, 7nu, Rhododendron campanulatum. i, 9nu, Viola suavis. j, 10nu, Cyananthus lobatus.

13nu, Red flower, horiz.

1095	A113	Strip of 10, #a.-j.	4.75 4.75

Souvenir Sheet

1096	A113	13nu multicolored	1.40 1.40

New Year
1994 (Year of
the
Dog) — A114

1994, Feb. 11   **Litho.**   *Perf. 14*

1097	A114	11.50nu multicolored	.80 .80

Souvenir Sheet

1098	A114	20nu like #1097	1.40 1.40

Hong Kong '94.

Stamp Cards — A115

Designs: 16nu, Tagtshang Monastery. 20nu, Map of Bhutan. Illustration reduced.

Rouletted 26 on 2 or 3 Sides

1994, Aug. 15   **Litho.**

Self-Adhesive

Cards of 6 + 6 labels

1099	A115	16nu #a.-f.	6.25 6.25
1100	A115	20nu #a.-f.	7.75 7.75

Individual stamps measure 70x9mm and have a card backing. Se-tenant labels inscribed "AIR MAIL."

Souvenir Sheet

First Manned Moon Landing, 25th
Anniv. — A116

a, 30nu, Astronaut on moon. b, 36nu, Space shuttle, earth, moon. Illustration reduced.

1994, Nov. 11   **Litho.**   *Perf. 14x14½*

1101	A116	Sheet of 2, #a.-b.	4.25 4.25

Nos. 1101a, 1101b have holographic images. Soaking in water may affect the holograms.

Souvenir Sheet

Victory Over
Tibet-Mongol
Army, 350th
Anniv. — A117

Battle scene: a, Mounted officer. b, Hand to hand combat, soldiers in yellow or blue armor. c, Soldier on gray horse. d, Soldiers in red, drummer, horn player.

1994, Dec. 17   **Litho.**   *Perf. 12½*

Granite Paper

1102	A117	15nu Sheet of 4, #a.-d.	4.00 4.00

Souvenir Sheet

Bridges
A118

a, 15nu, Tower Bridge, London, cent. b, 16nu, Wangdue Bridge, Bhutan, 250th anniv.

1994, Nov. 11   *Perf. 12*

1103	A118	Sheet of 2, #a.-b.	2.00 2.00

1994 World Cup Soccer
Championships, US — A119

1994, July 17   **Litho.**   *Perf. 12*

1104	A119	15nu multicolored	1.00 1.00

Souvenir Sheet

World
Tourism
Year
A120

Scenes of Bhutan: a, 1.50nu, Paro Valley. b, 5nu, Chorten Kora. c, 10nu, Thimphu Tshechu. d, 15nu, Wangdue Tshechu.

1995, Apr. 2   **Litho.**   *Perf. 12*

1105	A120	Sheet of 4, #a.-d.	2.00 2.00

Miniature Sheet of 12

New
Year
1995
(Year of
the
Boar)
A121

Symbols of Chinese Lunar New Year: a, 10ch, Rat. b, 20ch, Ox. c, 30ch, Tiger. d, 40ch, Rabbit. e, 1nu, Dragon. f, 2nu, Snake. g, 3nu, Horse. h, 4nu, Sheep. i, 5nu, Monkey. j, 7nu, Rooster. k, 8nu, Dog. l, 9nu, Boar.

10nu, Wood Hog.

1995, Mar. 2

1106	A121	#a.-l.	2.50 2.50

Souvenir Sheet

1107	A121	10nu multicolored	.65 .65

No. 1107 is a continuous design.

A122

Flowers: 9nu, Pleione praecox. 10nu, Primula calderina. 16nu, Primula whitei. 18nu, Notholirion macrophyllum.

1995, May 2   **Litho.**   *Perf. 12*

1108-1111	A122	Set of 4	3.50 3.50

A123

1995, June 26   *Perf. 14*

UN, 50th Anniv.: a, 1.5nu, Human resources development. b, 9nu, Health & population. c, 10nu, Water & sanitation. d, 5nu, Transport & communications. e, 16nu, Forestry & environment. f, 18nu, Peace & security. g, 11.5nu, UN in Bhutan.

1112	A123	Strip of 7	4.75 4.75

Miniature Sheet of 6

Singapore
'95 — A124

Birds - #1113: a, 1nu, Himalayan pied kingfisher. b, 2nu, Blyth's tragopan. c, 3nu, Longtailed minivet. d, 10nu, Red junglefowl. e, 15nu, Black-capped sibia. f, 20nu, Red-billed chough.

No. 1114, Black-neck crane.

1995, June 2   **Litho.**   *Perf. 12*

1113	A124	#a.-f. + 3 labels	3.50 3.50

Souvenir Sheet

1114	A124	20nu multicolored	1.40 1.40

Traditional
Crafts — A125

1nu, Drying parchment. 2nu, Making tapestry. 3nu, Restoring archaeological finds. 10nu, Weaving textiles. 15nu, Sewing garments. No. 1120, 20nu, Carving wooden vessels.

No. 1121, Mosaic.

1995, Aug. 15   **Litho.**   *Perf. 14*

1115-1120	A125	Set of 6	2.50 2.50

Souvenir Sheet

1121	A125	20nu multicolored	1.40 1.40

New Year
1996 (Year of
the
Rat) — A126

Designs: a, Monkey. b, Rat, fire. c, Dragon.

1996, Jan. 1   **Litho.**   *Perf. 14*

1122	A126	10nu Sheet of 3, #a.-c.	2.00 2.00

Butterflies
A127

a, 2nu, Blue pansy. b, 3nu, Blue peacock. c, 5nu, Great Mormon. d, 10nu, Fritillary. e, 15nu, Blue duke. f, 25nu, Brown Gorgon.

No. 1124, Xanthomelas. No. 1124A, Fivebar swordtail.

1996, May 2   **Litho.**   *Perf. 14*

1123	A127	Sheet of 6, #a.-f.	4.00 4.00

Souvenir Sheets

1124-1124A	A127	30nu each	2.00 2.00

1996 Summer
Olympic
Games,
Atlanta
A128

5nu, Silver 300n coin, soccer. 7nu, Silver 300n coin, basketball. 10nu, Gold 5s coin, judo. 15nu, Archery.

1996, June 15   **Litho.**   *Perf. 14*

1125-1127	A128	Set of 3	1.50 1.50

Souvenir Sheet

1128	A128	15nu multicolored	1.00 1.00

Olymphilex '96.

Folktales — A129

Designs: a, 1nu, The White Bird. b, 2nu, Sing Sing Lhamo and the Moon. c, 3nu, The Hoopoe. d, 5nu, The Cloud Fairies. e, 10nu, The Three Wishes. f, 20nu, The Abominable Snowman.

1996, Apr. 15   *Perf. 12*

1129	A129	Sheet of 6, #a.-f.	3.00 3.00

Souvenir Sheet

1130	A129	25nu like #1129d	1.75 1.75

Locomotives — A130

No. 1131: a, 0-6-4 Tank engine (Chile). b, First Pacific locomotive in Europe (France). c, 4-6-0 Passenger engine (Norway). d, Atlantic type express (Germany). e, 4-Cylinder 4-6-0 express (Belgium). f, Standard type "4" diesel-electric (England).

No. 1132: a, Standard 0-6-0 Goods engine (India). b, Main-line 1,900 horsepower diesel-electric (Finland). c, 0-8-0 Shunting tank engine (Russia). d, Alco "PA-1" diesel-electric (US). e, "C11" Class 2-6-4 branch passenger tank engine (Japan). f, "Settebello" deluxe high-speed electric train (Italy).

No. 1133, Class "KD" 0-6-0 Goods locomotive, 1900 (Sweden). No. 1134, Shinkansen "New Railway" series 200 (Japan).

1996, Nov. 25   **Litho.**   *Perf. 14*

Sheets of 6, #a-f

1131-1132	A130	20nu Set of 2	16.00 16.00

Souvenir Sheets

1133-1134	A130	70nu each	4.75 4.75

Penny
Black — A131

Litho. & Embossed
1996, Dec. 17   *Perf. 13½*
1135 A131 140nu black & gold   9.50 9.50

A132

Winter Olympic Medalists: 10nu, Vegard Ulvang, cross-country skiing, 1992. 15nu, Kristi Yamaguchi, figure skating, 1992. 25nu, Markus Wasmeier, giant slalom, 1994. 30nu, Georg Hackl, luge, 1992.
No. 1140: a, Andreas Ostler, 2-man bobsled, 1952. b, Wolfgang Hoppe, 4-man bobsled, 1984. c, Stein Eriksen, giant slalom, 1952. d, Alberto Tomba, giant slalom, 1988.
No. 1141, Henri Oreiller, downhill, 1948. No. 1142, Eduard Scherrer, 4-man bobsled, 1924.

1997, Jan. 1   *Perf. 14*
1136-1139 A132   Set of 4   5.50 5.50
1140 A132 15nu Strip of 4, #a.-d.   4.00 4.00
Souvenir Sheets
1141-1142 A132 70nu each   4.50 4.50
No. 1140 was issued in sheets of 8 stamps.

A133

1997, Jan. 15   *Perf. 13*
Insects and Arachnids: a, 1ch, Apis lobioriosa smith. b, 2ch, Neptunides polychromus. c, 3ch, Conocephalus maculctus. d, 4ch, Blattidae. e, 5ch, Dytiscus marginalis. f, 10ch, Dynastes hercules. g, 15ch, Hippodamia. h, 20ch, Sarcophaga haemorrhoidalis. i, 25ch, Lucanus cervus. j, 30ch, Caterpillar. k, 35ch, Lycia hirtaria. l, 40ch, Clytarlus pennatus. m, 45ch, Ephemera denica. n, 50ch, Gryllus campestris. o, 60ch, Deilephila elpenor. p, 65ch, Gerris. q, 70ch, Agrion splendens. r, 80ch, Tachyta nana. s, 90ch, Eurydema pulchra. t, 1nu, Hadrurus hirsutus. u, 1.50nu, Vespa germanica. v, 2nu, Pyrops. w, 2.50nu, Mantis religiosa. x, 3nu, Araneus diadematus. y, 3.50nu, Atrophaneura.
15nu, Melolontha.

1143 A133   Sheet of 25, #a.-y.   1.40 1.40
Souvenir Sheet
1144 A133 15nu multicolored   1.00 1.00

Hong Kong
'97 — A134

Wildlife: a, Thalarctos maritiumus. b, Phascolarctos cinereus. c, Selenarcios thibelanus. d, Ailurus fulgens.
20nu, Ailuropoda melanoleuca.

1997, Feb. 1   Litho.   *Perf. 14*
1145 A134 10nu Sheet of 4, #a.-
     d.   2.75 2.75
Souvenir Sheet
1146 A134 20nu multicolored   1.40 1.40

Signs of the Chinese Zodiac — A135

No. 1147: a, 1ch, Mouse. b, 2ch, Ox. c, 3ch, Tiger. d, 4ch, Rabbit. e, 5nu, Dragon. f, 6nu, Snake. g, 7nu, Horse. h, 8nu, Sheep. i, 90ch, Monkey. j, 10nu, Rooster. k, 11nu, Dog. l, 12nu, Pig.
20nu, Ox, diff.

1997, Feb. 8   Litho.   *Perf. 14*
1147 A135   Sheet of 12, #a.-l. +
     label   4.00 4.00
Souvenir Sheet
1148 A135 20nu multicolored   1.40 1.40

Fauna
A136

Cuon alpinus: No. 1149: a, Adult, hind legs off ground. b, Adult walking right. c, Mother nursing young. d, Two seated.
Endangered species: No. 1150: a, Lynx. b, Red panda. c, Takin. d, Musk deer. e, Snow leopard. f, Golden langur. g, Tiger. h, Muntjac. i, Marmot.
No. 1151, Pseudois nayaur. No. 1152, Ursus thibetanus.

1997, Apr. 24
1149 A136 10nu Block or strip of
     4, #a.-d.   2.75 2.75
1150 A136 10nu Sheet of 9, #a.-
     i.   6.00 6.00
Souvenir Sheets
1151-1152 A136 70nu each   4.75 4.75
World Wildlife Fund (No. 1149).
No. 1149 issued in sheets of 12 stamps.

UNESCO,
50th Anniv.
A137

No. 1153: a, Mount Hungshan, China. b, Mausoleum of first Qin Emperor, China. c, Imperial Bronze Dragon, China. d, Tikal Natl. Park, Guatemala. e, Evora, Portugal. f, Shirakami-Sanchi, Japan. g, Paris, France. h, Valley Below the Falls, Plitvice Lakes Natl. Park, Croatia.
Sites in Germany: No. 1154: a, Cathedral, Bamberg. b, Bamberg. c, St. Michael's Church, Hildesheim. d, Potsdam Palace. e, Potsdam Church. f, Lubeck. g, Quedlinberg. h, Benedictine Church, Lorsch.
No. 1155, Goslar, Germany, horiz. No. 1156, Cathedral, Comenzada, Portugal, horiz.

1997, May 15
Sheets of 8 + Label
1153 A137 10nu #a.-h.   5.50 5.50

1154 A137 15nu #a.-h.   8.00 8.00
Souvenir Sheets
1155-1156 A137 60nu each   4.00 4.00

Chernobyl
Disaster,
10th Anniv.
A138

1997, May 2   Litho.   *Perf. 13½x14*
1157 A138 35nu UNESCO   2.40 2.40

Dogs — A139   Cats — A140

Designs: 10nu, Dalmatian. 15nu, Siberian husky. 20nu, Saluki. 25nu, Shar pei.
No. 1162: a, Dandie Dinmont terrier. b, Chinese crested. c, Norwich terrier. d, Basset hound. e, Cardigan welsh corgi. f, French bulldog.
60nu, Hovawart.

1997, July 15   *Perf. 14*
1158-1161 A139   Set of 4   4.75 4.75
1162 A139 20nu Sheet of 6, #a.-
     f.   8.00 8.00
Souvenir Sheet
1163 A139 60nu multicolored   4.00 4.00

1997, July 15
Designs: 10nu, Turkish angora. 15nu, Oriental shorthair. 20nu, British shorthair. 25nu, Burmese.
No. 1168: a, Japanese bobtail. b, Ceylon. c, Exotic. d, Rex. e, Ragdoll. f, Russian blue.
60nu, Tonkinese.
1164-1167 A140   Set of 4   4.75 4.75
1168 A140 15nu Sheet of 6, #a.-
     f.   6.00 6.00
Souvenir Sheet
1169 A140 60nu multicolored   4.25 4.25

1998 World
Cup Soccer,
France
A141

English players: 5nu, Pearce. 10nu, Gascoigne. 15nu, Beckham. 20nu, McManaman. 25nu, Adams. 30nu, Ince.
World Cup captains: No. 1176: a, Maradona, Argentina, 1986. b, Alberto, Brazil, 1970. c, Dunga, Brazil, 1994. d, Moore, England, 1966. e, Fritzwalter, Germany, 1954. f, Matthaus, Germany, 1990. g, Beckenbauer, Germany, 1974. h, Passarella, Argentina, 1978.
Winning teams, horiz.: No. 1177: a, Italy, 1938. b, W. Germany, 1954. c, Uruguay, 1958. d, England, 1966. e, Argentina, 1978. f, Brazil, 1962. g, Italy, 1934. h, Brazil, 1970. i, Uruguay, 1930.
No. 1178, Philippe Albert, Belgium, horiz. No. 1179, Salvatore (Toto) Schillaci, Italy, horiz.

     Perf. 13½x14, 14x13½
1997, Oct. 9   Litho.
1170-1175 A141   Set of 6   7.00 7.00

Sheets of 8 or 9
1176 A141 10nu #a.-h. + label   5.50 5.50
1177 A141 10nu #a.-i.   6.00 6.00
Souvenir Sheets
1178-1179 A141 35nu each   3.75 3.75

Friendship
Between India
and Bhutan
A142

3nu, Jawaharlal Nehru, King Jigme Dorji Wangchuk. 10nu, Rajiv Gandhi, King Jigme Singye Wangchuk.
20nu, Indian Pres. R. V. Venkataraman, King Jigme Singye Wangchuk.

1998   Litho.   *Perf. 13x13½*
1180 A142 3nu multicolored   .20 .20
1181 A142 10nu multicolored   .80 .80
Souvenir Sheet
1182 A142 20nu multicolored   1.25 1.25
No. 1182 contains one 76x35mm stamp.

A143

A144

Indepex '97: No. 1183: a, 3nu, Buddha seated with legs crossed. b, 15nu, Buddha seated with legs down. c, 7nu, Gandhi with hands folded. d, 10nu, Gandhi.
No. 1184, Buddha. No. 1185, Gandhi holding staff.

1998   *Perf. 13½x13*
1183 A143   Sheet of 4, #a.-d.   2.10 2.10
Souvenir Sheets
1184-1185 A143 15nu each   1.25 1.25
India's independence, 50th anniv.

1998, Feb. 28   Litho.   *Perf. 14*
New Year 1998 (Year of the Tiger): 3nu, Stylized tiger walking right.
Tigers: No. 1187: a, 5nu, Lying down. b, 15nu, Adult walking forward. c, 17nu, Cub walking over rocks.
20nu, Adult up close.
1186 A144 3nu multicolored   .20 .20
1187 A144   Sheet of 4, #a.-c.,
     #1186   2.40 2.40
Souvenir Sheet
1188 A144 20nu multicolored   1.25 1.25

WHO,
50th
Anniv.
A145

1998, Apr. 7   Litho.   *Perf. 13½*
1189 A145 3nu multicolored   .20 .20
1190 A145 10nu multicolored   .60 .60
Souvenir Sheet
Perf. 14
1191 A145 15nu Mother, child   .90 .90
Safe Motherhood. No. 1191 contains one 35x35mm stamp.

10nu Bhutan

Mother Teresa (1910-97) A146

No. 1191A, Mother Teresa, Princess Diana. No. 1192: a, Portrait (shown). b, Holding child. c, Holding starving infant. d, Seated among nuns. e, Looking down at sick. f, With hands folded in prayer. g, With Pope John Paul II. h, Portrait, diff.
No. 1193: a, like #1191A.b. b, like #1192g.

1998, May 25   Litho.   Perf. 13½
1191A A146 10nu multi   .60 .60
1192 A146 10nu Sheet of 9,
                #a.-h., 1191A 5.50 5.50
Souvenir Sheet of 2
1193 A146 25nu #a.-b.   3.00 3.00
No. 1193 contains two 38x43mm stamps.

Birds — A147

No. 1194: a, 10ch, Red-billed chough. b, 30ch, Great hornbill. c, 50ch, Singing lark. d, 70ch, Chestnut-flanked white-eye. e, 90ch, Magpie-robin. f, 1nu, Mrs. Gould's sunbird. g, 2nu, Tailorbird. h, 3nu, Duck. i, 5nu, Spotted cuckoo. j, 7nu, Gold crest. k, 9nu, Common mynah. l, 10nu, Green cochoa.
15nu, Turtle dove.

1998, July 28   Litho.   Perf. 13
1194 A147 Sheet of 12, #a.-l. 2.50 2.50
Souvenir Sheet
1195 A147 15nu multicolored   .90 .90
No. 1195 contains one 40x30mm stamp.

New Year 1999 (Year of the Rabbit) A148

1999, Jan. 1   Litho.   Perf. 13
1196 A148 4nu White rabbit   .25 .25
1197 A148 15nu Brown rabbit   .90 .90
Souvenir Sheet
Perf. 13½
1198 A148 20nu Rabbit facing
                forward   1.25 1.25
No. 1198 contains one 35x35mm stamp.

King Jigme Singye Wangchuk, 25th Anniv. of Coronation — A149

Various portraits, background color - No. 1199: a, Blue. b, Yellow. c, Orange. d, Green. No. 1200, Bright pink background.

1999, June 2   Litho.   Perf. 12¼
1199 A149 25nu Sheet of 4, #a.-
                d.   5.00 5.00
Souvenir Sheet
1200 A149 25nu multicolored   1.25 1.25

Trains A150

Designs: 5nu, Early German steam. 10nu, EID 711 electric. 20nu, Steam engine. 30nu, Trans Europe Express, Germany.
No. 1205: a, Bullet train, Japan, 1964. b, 2-D-2 Class 26, South Africa, 1953. c, Super Chief, US, 1946. d, Magleus Magnet, Japan, 1991. e, The Flying Scotsman, UK, 1922. f, Kodama Train, Japan, 1958. g, Blue Train, South Africa, 1969. h, Inter-City, Germany, 1960. i, High Speed ET 403, Germany, 1973. j, US Standard 4-4-0, 1855. k, Bayer Garratt, South Africa, 1954. l, Settebello train, Italy, 1953.
No. 1206: a, Diesel-electric, France. b, 6-4-4-6 Pennsylvania RR, US. c, 2-8-2 Steam, Germany. d, Amtrak, US. e, GS&W 2-2-2, Britain. f, Class P steam, Denmark. g, French electric. h, First Japanese locomotive. i, 2-8-2 Germany.
No. 1207: a, Pacific Class 01, Germany. b, Neptune Express, Germany. c, 4-4-0 Steam, Britain. d, Shovelnose streamliner, US. e, German electric. f, Early steam, Germany. g, Union Pacific, US. h, Borsig steam, Germany, 1881. i, Borsig 4-6-4, Germany.
No. 1208, Union Pacific electric locomotive E2 streamliner, US. No. 1209, Great Northern diesel electric streamliner, US.

1999, July 21   Perf. 14
1201-1204 A150 Set of 4   3.25 3.25
Sheets of 12 and 9
1205 A150 10nu Sheet of 12,
                #a.-l.   6.00 6.00
1206-1207 A150 15nu #a.-i.,
                each   6.75 6.75
Souvenir Sheets
1208-1209 A150 80nu each   4.00 4.00

Paintings by Hokusai (1760-1849) A151

Details or entire paintings - No. 1210: a, Suspension Bridge Between Hida and Etchu. b, Drawings of Women (partially nude). c, Exotic Beauty. d, The Poet Nakamaro in China. e, Drawings of Women (clothed). f, Chinese Poet in Snow.
No. 1211: a, Festive Dancers (with umbrella). b, Drawings of Women (holding book). c, Festive Dancers (man wearing checked pattern). d, Festive Dancers (person wearing black outfit). e, Drawings of Women (holding baby). f, Festive Dancers (woman with scarf tied under chin).
No. 1212, horiz.: a, Mount Fuji Seen Above Mist on the Tama River. b, Mount Fuji Seen from Shichirigahama. c, Sea Life (turtle). d, Sea Life (fish). e, Mount Fuji Reflected in a Lake. f, Mount Fuji Seen Through the Piers of Mannenbashi.
No. 1213, The Lotus Pedestal. No. 1214, Kushunoki Masashige. No. 1215, Peasants Leading Oxen.

1999, July 27   Perf. 13½x14, 14x13½
Sheets of 6
1210-1212 A151 15nu #a.-f.,
                each   4.50 4.50
Souvenir Sheet
1213-1215 A151 80nu each   4.00 4.00

Souvenir Sheet

IBRA '99, Nuremberg A152

a, 35nu, City view. b, 40nu, Show emblem.

1999, Apr. 27   Litho.   Perf. 13¾
1216 A152 Sheet of 2, #a.-b.   3.50 3.50

Prehistoric Animals — A153

No. 1217: a, Pterodactylus, Brachiosaurus. b, Pteranodon. c, Anurognathus, Tyrannosaurus. d, Brachiosaurus. e, Corythosaurus. f, Iguanodon. g, Lesothosaurus. h, Allosaurus. i, Velociraptor. j, Triceratops. k, Stegosaurus. l, Compsognatus.
No. 1218: a, Tyrannosaurus, black inscriptions b, Dimorphodon. c, Diplodocus. d, Pterodaustro. e, Tyrannosaurus, white inscriptions. f, Edmontosaurus. g, Apatosaurus. h, Deinonychus. i, Hypsilophodon. j, Oviraptor. k, Stegosaurus, diff. l, Triceratops, diff.
No. 1219: a, Moeritherium. b, Platybelodon. c, Wooly mammoth. d, African elephant. e, Deinonychus, diff. f, Dimorphodon, diff. g, Archaeopteryx. h, Ring-necked pheasant.
No. 1220, Triceratops, vert. No. 1221, Pteranodon. No. 1222, Hoatzin, vert. No. 1223, Ichthyosaur, vert.

1999, Aug. 10   Litho.   Perf. 14
Sheets of 12 and 8
1217-1218 A153 10nu a.-l., each 5.50 5.50
1219 A153 20nu a.-h.   7.50 7.50
Souvenir Sheets
1220-1223 A153 80nu each   3.75 3.75
No. 1221 is incorrectly inscribed "Triceratops" instead of "Pteranodon," and No. 1223 is "Present Day Dolphin" instead of "Ichthysoaur."

Fauna — A154

Designs: a, Musk deer. b, Takin. c, Blue sheep. d, Yak. e, Goral.

1999, Aug. 21   Litho.   Perf. 12¾
1224 A154 20nu Sheet of 5, #a.-
                e. + label   4.75 4.75

Birds A155

No. 1225: a, Chestnut-bellied chlorophonia. b, Yellow-faced Amazon parrot. c, White ibis. d, Caique. e, Green jay. f, Tufted coquette. g, Common troupial. h, Purple gallinule. i, Copper-rumped hummingbird.
No. 1226: a, Common egret. b, Rufous-browed peppershrike. c, Glittering-throated emerald. d, Great kiskadee. e, Cuban green woodpecker. f, Scarlet ibis. g, Belted kingfisher. h, Barred antshrike. i, Caribbean parakeet.
No. 1227, vert.: a, Rufous-tailed jacamar. b, Scarlet macaw. c, Channel-billed toucan. d, Tricolored heron. e, St. Vincent parrot. f, Blue-crowned motmot. g, Horned screamer. h, Black-billed plover. i, Common meadowlark.

No. 1228, Toco toucan. No. 1229, Red-billed scythebill, vert. No. 1230, Military macaws, vert.

1999, Oct. 17   Litho.   Perf. 14
Sheets of 9, #a.-i.
1225-1227 A155 15nu each   6.25 6.25
Souvenir Sheets
1228-1230 A155 80nu each   3.75 3.75

Butterflies A156

Designs: 5nu, Sara orange tip. 10nu, Pipepine swallowtail. 15nu, Longwings. No. 1234, 20nu, Viceroy. 25nu, Silver-spotted skipper, vert. 30nu, Great spangled fritillary, vert. 35nu, Little copper.
No. 1238: a, Frosted skipper. b, Fiery skipper. c, Banded hairstreak. d, Clouded sulphur. e, Milberts tortoise shell. f, Eastern tailed blue.
No. 1239: a, Zebra swallowtail. b, Colorado hairstreak. c, Pink-edged sulphur. d, Fairy yellow. e, Red-spotted purple. f, Aphrodite.
No. 1240, Checkered white. No. 1241, Gray hairstreak, vert. No. 1242, Gulf fritillary, vert. No. 1243, Monarch, vert.

1999, Oct. 4   Litho.   Perf. 14
1231-1237 A156 Set of 7   6.50 6.50
Sheets of 6
1238-1239 A156 20nu #a.-f.,
                each   5.50 5.50
Souvenir Sheets
1240-1243 A156 80nu each   3.75 3.75

First Manned Moon Landing, 30th Anniv. — A157

No. 1244: a, Neil A. Armstrong (with name patch). b, Michael Collins. c, Edwin E. Aldrin, Jr. d, Command and service modules. e, Lunar module. f, Aldrin on Moon.
No. 1245: a, X-15 rocket. b, Gemini 8. c, Apollo 11 Saturn V rocket. d, Command and service modules (docked with lunar module). e, Lunar module (docked with command and service modules). f, Aldrin on lunar module ladder.
No. 1246: a, Yuri Gagarin. b, Alan B. Shepard, Jr. c, John H. Glenn, Jr. d, Valentina Tereshkova. e, Edward H. White II. f, Armstrong (no name patch).
No. 1247, Armstrong, diff. No. 1248, Apollo 11 splashdown. No. 1249, Gemini 8 docked with Agena rocket, horiz.

1999, Nov. 1   Litho.   Perf. 14
Sheets of 6
1244-1246 A157 20nu #a.-f.,
                each   5.50 5.50
Souvenir Sheets
1247-1249 A157 80nu each   3.75 3.75
No. 1249 contains one 57x42mm stamp.

Cats, Horses, Dogs A158

Cats: No. 1250, 5nu, Tortoiseshell. No. 1251, 5nu, Woman and cat. 10nu, Chinchilla Golden Longhair.
No. 1253: a, Russian Blue. b, Birman. c, Devon Rex. d, Pewter Longhair. e, Bombay. f, Sorrel Somali. g, Red Tabby Manx. h, Blue Smoke Longhair. i, Oriental Tabby Shorthair.
70nu, Norwegian Shorthair.

1999, Nov. 15   Litho.   **Perf. 14**
1250-1252 A158   Set of 3   .90   .90
Sheet of 9
1253 A158 12nu #a.-i.   5.00   5.00
Souvenir Sheet
1254 A158 70nu multicolored   3.25   3.25

1999, Nov. 15
Horses: 15nu, Lipizzaner. 20nu, Andalusian. No. 1257: a, Przewalski. b, Shetland. c, Dutch Gelderlander. d, Shire. e, Arabian. f, Boulonnais. g, Falabella. h, Orlov Trotter. i, Suffolk Punch.
70nu, Connemara.
1255-1256 A158   Set of 2   1.60   1.60
Sheet of 9
1257 A158 12nu #a.-i.   5.00   5.00
Souvenir Sheet
1258 A158 70nu multicolored   3.25   3.25

1999, Nov. 15
Dogs: 25nu, Weimaraner. 30nu, German Shepherd.
No. 1261: a, Australian Silky Terrier. b, Samoyed. c, Basset Bleu de Gascogne. d, Bernese Mountain Dog. e, Pug. f, Bergamasco. g, Basenji. h, Wetterhoun. i, Drever.
70nu, Labrador Retriever.
1259-1260 A158   Set of 2   1.60   1.60
Sheet of 9
1261 A158 12nu #a.-i.   5.00   5.00
Souvenir Sheet
1262 A158 70nu multicolored   3.25   3.25

Birds, Mushrooms, Anilmals A159

No. 1263: a, Crested lark. b, Ferruginous duck. c, Blood pheasant. d, Laughing thrush. e, Golden eagle. f, Siberian rubythroat.
No. 1264: a, Red-crested pochard. b, Satyr tragopan. c, Lammergeier vulture. d, Kalij pheasant. e, Great Indian hornbill. f, Stork.
No. 1265, a, Rufous-necked hornbill. b, Drongo. c, Himalayan monal pheasant. d, Black-necked crane. e, Little green bee-eater. f, Ibis.
No. 1266, Siberian rubythroat. No. 1267, Black-naped monarch. No. 1268, Mountain peacock pheasant.

1999, Dec. 17   **Perf. 13¾**
Sheets of 6. #a.-f.
1263-1265 A159 20nu each   5.50   5.50
Souvenir Sheets
1266-1268 A159 100nu each   4.50   4.50

1999, Dec. 17
No. 1269: a, Boletus frostii. b, Morchella estculenta. c, Hypomyces lactifuorum. d, Polyporus auricularius. e, Cantahrellus lateritius. f, Volvariella pusilla.
No. 1270: a, Microglossum rufum. b, Lactarius hygrophoroides. c, Lactarius speciousus complex. d, Calostoma cinnabarina. e, Clitocybe clavipes. f, Microstoma floccosa.
No. 1271: a, Mutinus elegans. b, Pholiota squarrosoides. c, Coprinus quadrifudus. d, Clavulinopsis fusiformis. e, Spathularia velutipes. f, Ganoderma lucidum.
No. 1272, Pholiota aurivella. No. 1273, Ramaria grandis. No. 1274, Oudemansiella lucidum.

Sheets of 6, #a.-f.
1269-1271 A159 20nu each   5.50   5.50
Souvenir Sheets
1272-1274 A159 100nu each   4.50   4.50

1999, Nov. 24   Litho.   **Perf. 13¾**
No. 1275: a, Otter. b, Tibetan wolf. c, Himalayan black bear. d, Snow leopard. e, Flying squirrel. f, Red fox.
No. 1276: a, Bharal. b, Lynx. c, Rat snake. d, Elephant. e, Langur. f, Musk deer.
No. 1277: a, Ibex. b, Takin. c, Agama lizard. d, Marmot. e, Red panda. f, Leopard cat.
No. 1278, Rhinoceros. No. 1279, Cobra. No. 1280, Tiger.

Sheets of 6, #a-f
1275-1277 A159 20nu Set of 3   15.00   15.00
Souvenir Sheets
1278-1280 A159 100nu Set of 3   13.50   13.50

Millennium A160

Frame background color: 10nu, Dark blue green. 20nu, Bright violet.

1999, Dec. 15
1281-1282 A160   Set of 2   1.50   1.50

New Year 2000 (Year of the Dragon) A161

Various dragons. Denominations: 3nu, 5nu, 8nu, 12nu.
15nu, Dragon, vert.

2000
1283-1286 A161   Set of 4   1.25   1.25
Souvenir Sheet
Perf. 12¾
1287 A161 15nu multi   .70   .70
No. 1287 contains one 30x40mm stamp.

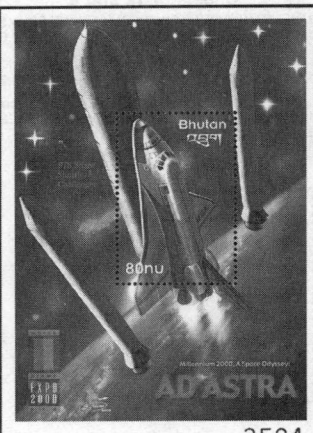

Space — A162

#1288, horiz.: a, Victor Patsayev. b, Vladislav Volkov. c, Georgi Dobrovolski. d, Virgil Grissom. e, Roger Chaffee. f, Edward White.
#1289, horiz.: a, NASA shuttle Challenger. b, X-15. c, Buran. d, Hermes. e, X-33 Venturi Star. f, Hope.
#1290, horiz.: a, Luna 3. b, Ranger 9. c, Lunar Orbiter. d, Lunar Prospector. e, Apollo 11. f, Selene.
#1291, Challenger. #1292, Buran. #1293, Astronaut on moon.
Illustration reduced.

2000, May 15   Litho.   **Perf. 14**
Sheets of 6, #a-f
1288-1290 A162 25nu Set of 3   20.00   20.00
Souvenir Sheets
1291-1293 A162 80nu Set of 3   11.00   11.00
World Stamp Expo 2000, Anaheim.

First Zeppelin Flight, Cent. — A163

#1294, horiz.: a, LZ-1 and hills. b, LZ-9. c, LZ-6 in hangar. d, LZ-10. e, LZ-7. f, LZ-11.
#1295, horiz.: a, LZ-1 and sky. b, LZ-2 and treetops. c, LZ-3 and ground. d, LZ-127. e, LZ-129. f, LZ-130.
#1296, horiz.: a, LZ-1 and treetops. b, LZ-2 and mountains. c, LZ-3 and sky. d, LZ-4. e, LZ-5. f, LZ-6.
#1297, Ferdinand von Zeppelin, without hat. #1298, Zeppelin with white hat. #1299, Zeppelin with black hat.
Illustration reduced.

2000, May 15
Sheets of 6, #a-f
1294-1296 A163 25nu Set of 3   20.00   20.00
Souvenir Sheets
1297-1299 A163 80nu Set of 3   11.00   11.00

Souvenir Sheet

2000 Summer Olympics, Sydney — A164

No. 1300: a, Jesse Owens. b, Kayaking. c, Fulton County Stadium, Atlanta. d, Ancient greek broad jump.
Illustration reduced.

2000, July 24
1300 A164 20nu Sheet of 4, #a-d 3.75   3.75

British Railway System, 175th Anniv. — A165

No. 1301: a, George Stephenson's Rocket. b, London and Birmingham Railway, 1828. c, Northumbrian engine, 1825.
100nu, Stockton and Darlington Railway opening, 1825.
Illustration reduced.

2000, July 31   Litho.   **Perf. 14**
1301 A165   50nu Sheet of 3, #a-c   6.50   6.50
Souvenir Sheet
1302 A165 100nu multi   4.25   4.25

Airplanes — A166

No. 1303, 25nu: a, Laird Commercial. b, Ryan Brougham. c, Cessna AW. d, Travel Air 4000. e, Fairchild F-71. f, Command Aire.
No. 1304, 25nu: a, WACO YMF. b, Piper J4 Cub Coupe. c, Ryan ST-A. d, Spartan Executive. e, Luscombe 8. f, Stinson SR5 Reliant.
No. 1305, 25nu: a, Cessna 195. b, WACO SRE. c, Erco Ercoupe. d, Boeing Stearman. e, Beech Staggerwing. f, Republic Seabee.
No. 1306, 100nu, WACO CSO. No. 1307, 100nu, Curtiss-Wright 19W. No. 1308, 100nu, Grumman G-44 Widgeon.
Illustration reduced.

2000, Aug. 7   **Perf. 13¾**
Sheets of 6, #a-f
1303-1305 A166   Set of 3   20.00   20.00
Souvenir Sheets
1306-1308 A166   Set of 3   13.00   13.00

Berlin Film Festival, 50th Anniv. — A167

No. 1309: a, A Kind of Loving. b, Bushido Zankoku Monogatari. c, Hobson's Choice. d, El Lazarillo de Tormes. e, In the Name of the Father. f, Les Cousins.
100nu, Die Ratten.
Illustration reduced.

2000, Aug. 15   **Perf. 14**
1309 A167   25nu Sheet of 6, #a-f   6.50   6.50
Souvenir Sheet
1310 A167 100nu multi   4.25   4.25

Souvenir Sheet

Albert Einstein (1879-1955) — A168

Illustration reduced.

2000, Sept. 1   **Perf. 12x12¼**
1311 A168 100nu multi   4.25   4.25

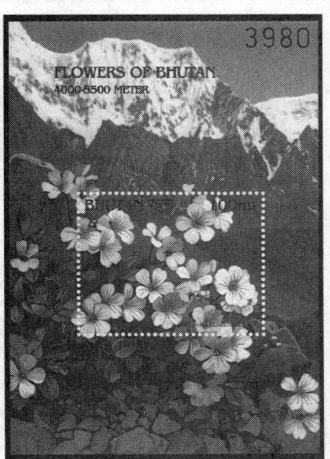

Flowers — A169

No. 1312, 25nu: a, Crinum amoenum. b, Beaumontia grandiflora. c, Trachelospermum lucidum. d, Curcuma aromatica. e, Barleria cristata. f, Holmskioldia sanguinea.
No. 1313, 25nu: a, Meconopsis villosa. b, Salvia hians. c, Caltha palustris. d, Anemone polyanthes. e, Cypripedium cordigerum. f, Cryptochilus luteus.
No. 1314, 25nu: a, Androsace globifera. b, Tanacetum atkinsonii. c, Aster stracheyi. d, Arenaria glanduligera. e, Sibbaldia purpurea. f, Saxifraga parnassifolia.
No. 1315, 100nu, Dendrobium densiflorum, vert. No. 1316, 100nu, Rhododendron arboreum, vert. No. 1317, Gypsophila cerastioides.
Illustration reduced.

Perf. 14¼x14½, 14½x14¼
2000, Sept. 5
Sheets of 6, #a-f

1312-1314	A169	Set of 3	20.00	20.00

Souvenir Sheets

1315-1317	A169	Set of 3	13.00	13.00

St. Thomas Aquinas (1225-1274)
A170

2000, Sept. 18   **Perf. 14x14¾**

1318	A170	25nu multi	1.10	1.10

No. 1318 printed in sheets of 4.

A171

Millennium — A172

Medical pioneers - #1319, 25nu: a, Albert Calmette. b, Camillo Golgi and Santiago Ramón y Cajal. c, Alexander Fleming. d, Jonas Salk. e, Christiaan Barnard. f, Luc Montagnier.

Olympic movement - #1320, 25nu: a, Baron Pierre de Coubertin. b, 1896 Athens Games. c, Jesse Owens. d, 1972 Munich Games. e, 2000 Sydney Games. f, 2004 Athens Games. 100nu, Paro Taktsang.
Illustrations reduced.

2000, Sept. 18   **Perf. 14**

1319-1320	A171	Set of 2	13.00	13.00

Souvenir Sheet

1321	A172	100nu multi	4.25	4.25

Souvenir Sheets

Explorers — A173

No. 1322, Christopher Columbus. No. 1323, Capt. James Cook.
Illustration reduced.

2000, Sept. 18

1322-1323	A173	100nu Set of 2	8.50	8.50

Expo 2000, Hanover — A174

No. 1324 - Dzongs: a, 3nu, Trashigang. b, 4nu, Lhuentse. c, 6nu, Gasa. d, 7nu, Punakha. e, 10nu, Trashichhoe. f, 20nu, Paro.
No. 1325 - Flora and Fauna, 10nu: a, Snow leopard. b, Raven. c, Golden langur. d, Rhododendron. e, Black-necked crane. f, Blue poppy.
Illustration reduced.

Perf. 13x13¼ (#1324), 12¾
2000, June 1   **Litho.**
Sheets of 6, #a-f

1324-1325	A174	Set of 2	4.75	4.75

Souvenir Sheet

1326	A174	15nu Temple	.65	.65

Size of stamps in #1325-1326: 40x31mm.

Paintings from the Prado — A175

No. 1327, 25nu: a, Portrait of an Old man, by Joos van Cleve. b, Mary I, by Anthonis Mor. c, Portrait of a Man, by Jan van Scorel. d, The Court Jester Pejerón, by Mor. e, Elizabeth of France, by Frans Pourbus, the Younger. f, King James I, by Paul van Somer.
No. 1328, 25nu: a, Isabella of Portugal, by Titian. b, Lucrecia di Baccia del Fede, the Painter's Wife, by Andrea del Sarto. c, Self-portrait, by Titian. d, Philip II, by Sofonisba Anguisciola. e, Portrait of a Doctor, by Lucia Anguisciola. f, Anna of Austria, by Sofonisba Anguisciola.
No. 1329, 25nu: a, Duchess. b, Child. c, Duke. d, Isidoro Maiquez, by Goya. e, Doña Juana Galarza de Goicoechea, by Goya. f, Ferdinand VII in an Encampment, by Goya. a-c from #1332.
No. 1330, 100nu, Charles V on Horseback at the Battle of Mühlberg. No. 1331, 100nu, The Relief of Genoa, by Antonio de Pereda y Salgado. No. 1332, 100nu, The Duke and Duchess of Osuna With Their Children, by Goya, horiz.
Illustration reduced.

2000, Oct. 6   **Perf. 12x12¼, 12¼x12**
Sheets of 6, #a-f

1327-1329	A175	Set of 3	19.00	19.00

Souvenir Sheets

1330-1332	A175	Set of 3	13.00	13.00

España 2000 Intl. Philatelic Exhibition.

Indepex 2000 Philatelic Exhibition, India — A176

No. 1333: a, 5nu, Butterfly. b, 8nu, Red jungle fowl. c, 10nu, Zinnia elegans. d, 12nu, Tiger. 15nu, Spotted deer.

2000   **Litho.**   **Perf. 13¾**

1333	A176	Sheet of 4, #a-d	1.50	1.50

Souvenir Sheet
Perf. 13¼x13½

1334	A176	15nu multi	.65	.65

New Year 2001 (Year of the Snake) — A177

Various snakes and flowers with panel colors of: 3nu, Light blue. No. 1337a, 10nu, Dark blue. No. 1337b, 15nu, Green. 20nu, Red.

2001   **Perf. 12¾**

1335-1336	A177	Set of 2	.95	.95

Souvenir Sheet

1337	A177	Sheet, #a-b, 1335-1336	2.00	2.00

Souvenir Sheet

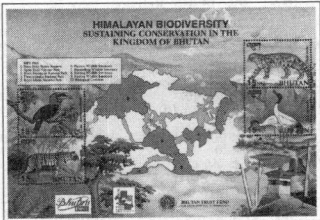

Hong Kong 2001 Stamp Exhibition — A178

No. 1338: a, Uncia uncia. b, Aceros nipalensis. c, Grus nigricollis. d, Panthera tigris.

2001

1338	A178	15nu Sheet of 4, #a-d	2.50	2.50

Intl. Volunteers Year A179

Various children's drawings: 3nu, 4nu, 10nu, 15nu.

2001

1339-1342	A179	Set of 4	1.40	1.40
1342a		Souvenir sheet, #1339-1342	1.40	1.40

SEMI-POSTAL STAMPS

Nos. 10-12 Surcharged

Perf. 14x14½

			Unwmk.	
1964, Mar.		**Litho.**		
B1	A3	33ch + 50ch multi	2.00	2.00
B2	A3	70ch + 50ch multi	2.00	2.00
B3	A3	1.30nu + 50ch multi	2.00	2.00
		Nos. B1-B3 (3)	6.00	6.00

9th Winter Olympic Games, Innsbruck, Jan. 29-Feb. 9, 1964.

Olympic Games Type of Regular Issue, 1964
Souvenir Sheet

1964, Oct. 10   **Perf. 13½, Imperf.**

B4	A6	Sheet of 2	7.50	7.50
a.		1nu + 50ch Archery	.90	.90
b.		2nu + 50ch Soccer	2.00	2.00

18th Olympic Games, Tokyo, Oct. 10-25.

Nos. 97, 97C, 97E Surcharged

1968, Dec. 7	**Photo.**		**Perf. 13½**	
B5	A14n	5ch +5ch	.20	.20
B6	A14n	80ch +25ch	.35	.35
B7	A14n	2nu +50ch	.85	.85
		Nos. B5-B7 (3)	1.40	1.40

AIR POST STAMPS

Nos. 19-21, 38-39, 63-67 Ovptd.

a

Perfs. as Before
1967, Jan. 10   **Litho.**
Overprint "a"

C1	A5	33ch on #19	.20	.20
C2	A5	70ch on #20	.30	.30
C3	A5	1nu on #21	.40	.40

C4	A8	50ch on #38	.20	.20
C5	A8	75ch on #39	.30	.30
C6	A11	1.50nu on #63	.65	.65
C7	A11	2nu on #64	.85	.85
C8	A11	3nu on #65	1.25	1.25
C9	A11	4nu on #66	1.75	1.75
C10	A11	5nu on #67	2.25	2.25

b

Overprint "b"

C11	A5	33ch on #19	.20	.20
C12	A5	70ch on #20	.30	.30
C13	A5	1nu on #21	.40	.40
C14	A8	50ch on #38	.20	.20
C15	A8	75ch on #39	.30	.30
C16	A11	1.50nu on #63	.65	.65
C17	A11	2nu on #64	.85	.85
C18	A11	3nu on #65	1.25	1.25
C19	A11	4nu on #66	1.75	1.75
C20	A11	5nu on #67	2.25	2.25
		Nos. C1-C20 (20)	16.30	16.30

UN Type of Regular Issue

Bhutan Flag and: 2.50nu, UN Headquarters, NYC. 5nu, Security Council Chamber and mural by Per Krohg. 6nu, General Assembly Hall.

1971, Sept. 21   Photo.   Perf. 13½

C21	A16	2.50nu silver & multi	.50	.50
C22	A16	5nu silver & multi	.95	.95
C23	A16	6nu silver & multi	1.10	1.10
		Nos. C21-C23 (3)	2.55	2.55

Bhutan's admission to the United Nations. Exist imperf.

Nos. C21-C23 Overprinted in Gold: "UNHCR / UNRWA / 1971" like Nos. 145-145C

1971, Dec. 23   Litho.   Perf. 13½

C24	A16	2.50nu silver & multi	.70	.70
C25	A16	5nu silver & multi	1.40	1.40
C26	A16	6nu silver & multi	1.90	1.90
		Nos. C24-C26 (3)	4.00	4.00

World Refugee Year. Exist imperf.

UPU Types of 1974

UPU Emblem, Carrier Pigeon and: 1nu, Mail runner and jeep. 1.40nu, 10nu, Old and new locomotives. 2nu, Old biplane and jet.

1974, Oct. 9   Litho.   Perf. 14½

C27	A19	1nu salmon & multi	.25	.25
C28	A20	1.40nu lilac & multi	.40	.40
C29	A20	2nu multicolored	.50	.50
		Nos. C27-C29 (3)	1.15	1.15

Souvenir Sheet
Perf. 13

C30	A20	10nu lilac & multi	2.75	2.75

Cent. of the UPU. Nos. C27-C29 were issued in sheets of 50 and sheets of 5 plus label with multicolored margin. Exist imperf.

Issues of 1968-1974 Surcharged 25ch and Bars

1978   Perf. & Printing as Before

C31	A16	25ch on 5nu, #C22	1.25	1.25
C32	A16	25ch on 6nu, #C23	1.25	1.25
C33	A20	25ch on 1.40nu, #C28	1.25	1.25
C34	A20	25ch on 2nu, #C29	1.25	1.25
C35	A14j	25ch on 4nu, #94L	1.25	1.25
C36	A14j	25ch on 10nu, #94N	1.25	1.25
C37	A17k	25ch on 5nu, #154F	1.25	1.25
C38	A17k	25ch on 6nu, #154G	1.25	1.25
		Nos. C31-C38 (8)	10.00	10.00

BOLIVIA

bə-'li-vē-ə

LOCATION — Central South America, separated from the Pacific Ocean by Chile and Peru.
GOVT. — Republic
AREA — 424,165 sq. mi.
POP. — 7,949,933 (1998 est.)

CAPITAL — Sucre (La Paz is the actual seat of government).

100 Centavos = 1 Boliviano
100 Centavos = 1 Peso Boliviano (1963)
100 Centavos = 1 Boliviano (1987)

> Catalogue values for unused stamps in this country are for Never Hinged items, beginning with Scott 308 in the regular postage section, Scott C112 in the airpost section, Scott RA5 in the postal tax section, and Scott RAC1 in airpost postal tax section.

On Feb. 21, 1863, the Bolivian Government decreed contracts for carrying the mails should be let to the highest bidder, the service to commence on the day the bid was accepted, and stamps used for the payment of postage. On Mar. 18, the contract was awarded to Sr. Justiniano Garcia and was in effect until Apr. 29, 1863, when it was rescinded. Stamps in the form illustrated above were prepared in denominations of ½, 1, 2 and 4 reales. All values exist in black and in blue. The blue are twice as scarce as the black. Value, black, $75 each.

It is said that used copies exist on covers, but the authenticity of these covers remains to be established.

Condor — A1

A2

A3

72 varieties of each of the 5c, 78 varieties of the 10c, 30 varieties of each of the 50c and 100c.

The plate of the 5c stamps was entirely reengraved 4 times and retouched at least 6 times. Various states of the plate have distinguishing characteristics, each of which is typical of most, though not all the stamps in a sheet. These characteristics (usually termed types) are found in the shading lines at the right side of the globe. a, vertical and diagonal lines. b, diagonal lines only. c, diagonal and horizontal with traces of vertical lines. d, diagonal and horizontal lines. e, horizontal lines only. f, no lines except the curved ones forming the outlines of the globe.

1867-68   Unwmk.   Engr.   Imperf.

1	A1	5c yel grn, thin paper (a, b)	5.50	10.00
a.		5c blue green (a)	5.50	14.00
b.		5c deep green (a)	5.50	14.00
c.		5c ol grn, thick paper (a)	35.00	25.00
d.		5c yel grn, thick paper (a)	90.00	90.00
e.		5c yel grn, thick paper (b)	90.00	90.00
f.		5c blue green (b)	5.50	14.00
2	A1	5c green (d)	5.00	10.00
a.		5c green (c)	5.00	10.00
b.		5c green (e)	5.00	10.00
c.		5c green (f)	5.00	10.00
3	A1	5c vio ('68)	175.00	140.00
a.		5c rose lilac ('68)	175.00	140.00
		Revenue cancel		27.50
4	A3	10c brown	225.00	140.00
5	A2	50c orange	20.00	
6	A2	50c blue ('68)	325.00	
a.		50c dark blue ('68)	325.00	
		Revenue cancel		27.50
7	A3	100c blue	60.00	
		Revenue cancel		15.00
8	A3	100c green ('68)	140.00	
a.		100c pale blue grn ('68)	140.00	
		Revenue cancel		27.50

Used values are for postally canceled copies. Pen cancellations usually indicate that the stamps have been used fiscally and such

---

stamps sell for about one-fifth as much as those with postal cancellations.
The 500c is an essay.
Reprints of Nos. 3,4, 6 and 8 are common. Value, $10 each. Reprints of Nos. 2 and 5 are scarcer. Value, $25 each.

Coat of Arms
A4   A5

1868-69   Perf. 12

Nine Stars

10	A4	5c green	17.50	8.75
11	A4	10c vermilion	25.00	8.75
12	A4	50c blue	45.00	25.00
13	A4	100c orange	45.00	27.50
14	A4	500c black	475.00	400.00

Eleven Stars

15	A5	5c green	10.00	6.25
16	A5	10c vermilion	14.00	10.00
a.		Half used as 5c as cover		400.00
17	A5	50c blue	37.50	17.50
18	A5	100c dp orange	35.00	17.50
19	A5	500c black	1,750.	1,750.

See Nos. 26-27, 31-34.

Arms and "The Law" — A6

1878   Various Frames   Perf. 12

20	A6	5c ultra	10.00	2.00
21	A6	10c orange	10.00	2.00
a.		Half used as 5c on cover		50.00
22	A6	20c green	20.00	4.00
a.		Half used as 10c on cover		160.00
23	A6	50c dull carmine	110.00	16.00
		Nos. 20-23 (4)	150.00	24.00

A7   A8
(11 Stars)   (9 Stars)
Numerals Upright

1887   Rouletted

24	A7	1c rose	2.25	1.90
25	A7	2c violet	2.25	1.90
26	A5	5c blue	7.25	3.00
27	A5	10c orange	7.25	3.00
		Nos. 24-27 (4)	19.00	9.80

See No. 37.

1890   Perf. 12

28	A8	1c rose	1.60	.80
29	A8	2c violet	4.25	2.00
30	A4	5c blue	3.00	.80
31	A4	10c orange	6.25	.95
32	A4	20c dk green	12.50	1.60
33	A4	50c red	6.25	1.60
34	A4	100c yellow	12.50	3.25
		Nos. 28-34 (7)	46.35	11.00

See Nos. 35-36, 38-39.

1893   Litho.   Perf. 11

35	A8	1c rose	3.50	2.50
a.		Imperf. pair	35.00	
b.		Horiz. pair, imperf. vert.	20.00	
c.		Horiz. pair, imperf. btwn.	35.00	
36	A8	2c violet	3.50	2.50
a.		Block of 4 imperf. vert. and horiz. through center	50.00	
b.		Horiz. pair, imperf. btwn.	27.50	
37	A7	5c blue	6.00	2.50
a.		Vert. pair, imperf. horiz.	27.50	
b.		Horiz. pair, imperf. btwn.	35.00	
38	A8	10c orange	17.00	4.00
a.		Imperf. pair, vert. or horiz.	140.00	
39	A8	20c dark green	40.00	18.00
a.		Imperf. pair, vert. or horiz.	140.00	
b.		Pair, imperf. btwn., vert. or horiz.	140.00	
		Nos. 35-39 (5)	70.00	29.50

Coat of Arms — A9

1894   Unwmk.   Engr.   Perf. 14, 14½
Thin Paper

40	A9	1c bister	1.00	.60
41	A9	2c red orange	1.00	.60
42	A9	5c green	1.00	.60
43	A9	10c yellow brn	1.00	.60
44	A9	20c dark blue	3.00	1.60
45	A9	50c claret	7.50	1.75
46	A9	100c brown rose	17.50	6.25
		Nos. 40-46 (7)	32.00	11.65

Stamps of type A9 on thick paper were surreptitiously printed in Paris on the order of an official and without government authorization. Some of these stamps were substituted for part of a shipment of stamps on thin paper, which had been printed in London on government order.

When the thick paper stamps reached Bolivia they were at first repudiated but afterwards were allowed to do postal duty. A large quantity of the thick paper stamps were fraudulently canceled in Paris with a cancellation of heavy bars forming an oval.

To be legitimate, copies of the thick paper stamps must have genuine cancellations of Bolivia. Value, on cover, each $125.

The 10c blue on thick paper is not known to have been issued.

Some copies of Nos. 40-46 show part of a papermakers' watermark "1011."

For overprints see Nos. 55-59.

President Tomas Frias — A10   President Jose M. Linares — A11

Pedro Domingo Murillo A12   Bernardo Monteagudo A13

Gen. Jose Ballivian — A14   Gen. Antonio Jose de Sucre — A15

Simon Bolivar — A16   Coat of Arms — A17

1897   Litho.   Perf. 12

47	A10	1c pale yellow grn	1.25	.80
a.		Vert. pair, imperf. horiz.	50.00	
b.		Vert. pair, imperf. btwn.	50.00	
48	A11	2c red	1.75	1.40
49	A12	5c dk green	2.50	.80
a.		Horiz. pair, imperf. btwn.	50.00	

50	A13	10c brown vio	2.50 .80
a.		Vert. pair, imperf. btwn.	50.00
51	A14	20c lake & blk	4.75 .95
a.		Imperf., pair	150.00
52	A15	50c orange	4.75 2.50
53	A16	1b Prus blue	4.75 5.50
54	A17	2b red, yel, grn & blk	37.50 50.00
		Nos. 47-54 (8)	59.75 62.75

Excellent forgeries of No. 54, perf and imperf, exist, some postally used.
Reprint of No. 53 has dot in numeral. Same value.

Nos. 40-44
Handstamped in Violet
or Blue

1899   **Perf. 14½**

55	A9	1c yellow bis	13.00 13.00
56	A9	2c red orange	16.00 16.00
57	A9	5c green	10.50 10.50
58	A9	10c yellow brn	13.00 10.50
59	A9	20c dark blue	21.00 21.00
		Nos. 55-59 (5)	73.50 71.00

The handstamp is found inverted, double, etc. Values twice the listed amounts. Forgeries of this handstamp are plentiful. "E.F." stands for Estado Federal.
The 50c and 100c (Nos. 45-46) were overprinted at a later date in Brazil.

Antonio José de
Sucre — A18

Perf. 11½, 12

1899   **Engr.**   **Thin Paper**

62	A18	1c gray blue	2.50 .75
63	A18	2c brnsh red	1.75 .75
64	A18	5c dk green	6.00 1.50
65	A18	10c yellow org	2.50 1.25
66	A18	20c rose pink	3.00 .80
67	A18	50c bister brn	6.00 2.50
68	A18	1b gray violet	1.75 1.75
		Nos. 62-68 (7)	23.50 9.30

1901

69	A18	5c dark red	1.90 .60

Col. Adolfo
Ballivian
A19

Eliodoro
Camacho
A20

President
Narciso
Campero
A21

Jose Ballivian
A22

Gen. Andres
Santa
Cruz — A23

Coat of
Arms — A24

1901-02   **Engr.**

70	A19	1c claret	.55 .20
71	A20	2c green	.55 .20
73	A21	5c scarlet	.55 .20

74	A22	10c blue	1.40 .20
75	A23	20c violet & blk	.80 .20
76	A24	2b brown	3.75 2.75
		Nos. 70-71,73-76 (6)	7.60 3.75

#73-74 exist imperf. Value, pairs, each $50.
For surcharges see #95-96, 193.

1904   **Litho.**

77	A19	1c claret	2.25 .55

In No. 70 the panel above "CENTAVO" is shaded with continuous lines. In No. 77 the shading is of dots.
See Nos. 103-105, 107, 110.

Coat of Arms
of Dept. of La
Paz — A25

Murillo — A26

Jose Miguel
Lanza — A27

Ismael
Montes — A28

1909   **Litho.**   **Perf. 11**

78	A25	5c blue & blk	9.00 5.00
79	A26	10c green & blk	9.00 5.00
80	A27	20c orange & blk	9.00 5.00
81	A28	2b red & black	9.00 5.00
		Nos. 78-81 (4)	36.00 20.00

Centenary of Revolution of July, 1809.
Nos. 78-81 exist imperf. and tête bêche.
Nos. 79-81 exist with center inverted.

Miguel
Betanzos
A29

Col. Ignacio
Warnes
A30

Murillo
A31

Monteagudo
A32

Esteban
Arce — A33

Antonio Jose
de
Sucre — A34

Simon
Bolivar — A35

Manuel
Belgrano — A36

1909   **Dated 1809-1825**   **Perf. 11½**

82	A29	1c lt brown & blk	.55 .35
83	A30	2c green & blk	.55 .40
84	A31	5c red & blk	.55 .30
85	A32	10c dull bl & blk	.55 .30
86	A33	20c violet & blk	.65 .40
87	A34	50c olive bister & blk	1.00 .55
88	A35	1b gray brn & blk	1.00 .80
89	A36	2b chocolate & blk	1.60 1.10
		Nos. 82-89 (8)	6.45 4.20

War of Independence, 1809-1825.
Exist imperf. For surcharge see #97.

Warnes
A37

Betanzos
A38

Arce — A39

Dated 1910-1825

1910   **Perf. 13x13½**

92	A37	5c green & black	.40 .20
a.		Imperf., pair	5.00
93	A38	10c claret & indigo	.40 .20
a.		Imperf., pair	5.00
94	A39	20c dull blue & indigo	.65 .40
a.		Imperf., pair	5.00
		Nos. 92-94 (3)	1.45 .80

War of Independence.
Nos. 92-94 may be found with parts of a papermaker's watermark: "A I & Co/EXTRA STRONG/9303."
Both perf and imperf exist with inverted centers.

Nos. 71 and 75
Surcharged in Black

1911   **Perf. 11½, 12**

95	A20	5c on 2c green	.45 .20
a.		Inverted surcharge	5.00 5.00
b.		Double surcharge	15.00
c.		Period after "1911"	3.50 .80
d.		Blue surcharge	75.00 60.00
e.		Double dsurch., one invtd.	15.00
96	A23	5c on 20c vio & blk	16.00 16.00
a.		Inverted surcharge	30.00 30.00
b.		Double surch., one invtd.	60.00

No. 83 Handstamp
Surcharged in
Green

97	A30	20c on 2c grn & blk	1,100.

This provisional was issued by local authorities at Villa Bella, a town on the Brazilian border. The 20c surcharge was applied after the stamp had been affixed to the cover. Excellent forgeries of No. 96-97 exist.

"Justice"
A40   A41

1912
**Black or Dark Blue Overprint On
Revenue Stamps**

98	A40	2c green (Bk)	.35 .25
a.		Inverted overprint	
99	A41	10c ver (Bl)	1.10 .40
a.		Inverted overprint	5.00

A42

A43

Red or Black Overprint
Engr.

100	A42	5c orange (R)	.55 .40
a.		Inverted overprint	5.00
b.		Pair, one without overprint	12.50
c.		Black overprint	50.00

Red or Black Surcharge

101	A43	10c on 1c bl (R)	.55 .20
a.		Inverted surcharge	6.00
b.		Double surcharge	6.00
c.		Dbl. surcharge, one invtd.	7.50
d.		Black surcharge	100.00 100.00
e.		As "d," inverted	
f.		As "d," double surcharge	
g.		Pair, one without black surch.	400.00

Fakes of No. 101d are plentiful.

Revenue Stamp Surcharged
"CORREOS / 10 Cts. / - 1917 -" in
Red

1917   **Litho.**

102		10c on 1c blue	6,000. 1,750.

Design similar to type A43.
Excellent forgeries exist.

Types of 1901 and

Frias-A45

Sucre-A46

Bolivar-A47

1913   **Engr.**   **Perf. 12**

103	A19	1c car rose	.40 .25
104	A20	2c vermilion	.40 .20
105	A21	5c green	.45 .20
106	A45	8c yellow	.80 .50
107	A22	10c gray	.80 .25
108	A46	50c dull violet	1.50 .55
109	A47	1b slate blue	2.25 1.40
110	A24	2b black	4.50 2.75
		Nos. 103-110 (8)	11.10 6.10

No. 107, litho., was not regularly issued.

Nine values commemorating the Guiqui-La Paz railroad were printed in 1915 but never issued. Typographed forgeries exist.

Monolith of
Tiahuanacu
A48

Mt. Potosí
A49

Lake
Titicaca — A50

Mt. Illimani — A51

Legislature
Building — A53

FIVE CENTAVOS.
Type I - Numerals have background of vertical lines. Clouds formed of dots.
Type II - Numerals on white background. Clouds near the mountain formed of wavy lines.

1916-17		Litho.	Perf. 11½	
111	A48	½c brown	.20	.20
a.	Horiz. pair, imperf. vert.		5.00	
112	A49	1c gray green	.20	.20
a.	Imperf., pair		2.00	
113	A50	2c car & blk	.25	.20
a.	Imperf., pair		2.00	
b.	Vert. pair, imperf. horiz.			
c.	Center inverted		12.50	11.25
d.	Imperf., center inverted		17.50	
114	A51	5c dk blue (I)	.50	.20
a.	Imperf., pair		2.00	
b.	Vert. pair, imperf. horiz.		3.50	
c.	Horiz. pair, imperf. vert.		3.50	
115	A51	5c dk blue (II)	.50	.20
a.	Imperf., pair		2.50	
116	A53	10c org & bl	1.00	.20
a.	Imperf., pair		3.50	
b.	No period after "Legislativo"		1.00	.20
c.	Center inverted		40.00	40.00
d.	Vertical pair, imperf. between		5.00	
		Nos. 111-116 (6)	2.65	1.20

For surcharges see Nos. 194-196.

Coat of Arms
A54　　　　　A55
Printed by the American Bank Note Co.

1919-20		Engr.	Perf. 12	
118	A54	1c carmine	.25	.20
119	A54	2c dk violet	4.75	3.00
120	A54	5c dk green	.50	.20
121	A54	10c vermilion	.50	.20
122	A54	20c dk blue	1.50	.30
123	A54	22c lt blue	.90	.75
124	A54	24c purple	.60	.50
125	A54	50c orange	4.75	1.75
126	A55	1b red brown	6.00	1.75
127	A55	2b black brn	9.00	4.50
		Nos. 118-127 (10)	28.75	12.00

Printed by Perkins, Bacon & Co., Ltd.

1923-27		Re-engraved	Perf. 13½	
128	A54	1c carmine ('27)	.20	.20
129	A54	2c dk violet	.30	.20
130	A54	5c dp green	.80	.20
131	A54	10c vermilion	14.00	12.00
132	A54	20c slate blue	1.75	.20
135	A54	50c orange	2.75	.60
136	A55	1b red brown	.70	.30
137	A55	2b black brown	.50	.30
		Nos. 128-137 (8)	21.00	14.00

There are many differences in the designs of the two issues but they are too minute to be illustrated or described.
Nos. 128-137 exist imperf.
See #144-146, 173-177. For surcharges see #138-143, 160, 162, 181-186, 236-237.

Stamps of 1919-20
Surcharged in Blue,
Black or Red

1924		A54　5c on 1c car (Bl)	Perf. 12	
138	A54	5c on 1c car (Bl)	.40	.20
a.	Inverted surcharge		5.00	5.00
b.	Double surcharge		5.00	5.00
139	A54	15c on 10c ver (Bk)	.70	.50
a.	Inverted surcharge		6.00	6.00
140	A54	15c on 22c lt bl (Bk)	.70	.30
a.	Inverted surcharge		5.25	5.25
b.	Double surcharge, one inverted			

No. 140 surcharged in red or blue probably are trial impressions. They appear jointly, and with black in blocks.

Same Surcharge on No. 131
Perf. 13½

142	A54	15c on 10c ver (Bk)	.70	.25
a.	Inverted surcharge		6.00	6.00

No. 121 Surcharged

**Habilitada
15 cts.**

Perf. 12

143	A54	15c on 10c ver (Bk)	.90	.30
a.	Inverted surcharge		6.00	6.00
b.	Double surcharge		5.00	5.00
		Nos. 138-143 (5)	3.40	1.55

Type of 1919-20 Issue
Printed by Waterlow & Sons
Second Re-engraving

1925		Unwmk.	Perf. 12½	
144	A54	5c deep green	.80	.25
145	A54	15c ultra	.80	.20
146	A54	20c dark blue	.40	.20
		Nos. 144-146 (3)	2.00	.65

These stamps may be identified by the perforation.

Miner — A56

Condor
Looking
Toward
the Sea
A57

Designs:　2c, Sower. 5c, Torch of Eternal Freedom. 10c, National flower (kantuta). 15c, Pres. Bautista Saavedra. 50c, Liberty head. 1b, Archer on horse. 2b, Mercury. 5b, Gen. A. J. de Sucre.

1925		Engr.	Perf. 14	
150	A56	1c dark green	.75	
151	A56	2c rose	.75	
152	A56	5c red, grn	.75	.35
153	A56	10c car, yel	1.25	.75
154	A56	15c red brown	.50	.25
155	A56	25c ultra	.50	.50
156	A56	50c dp violet	.50	.50
157	A56	1b red	1.25	1.25
158	A57	2b orange	1.75	1.75
159	A56	5b black brn	2.00	2.00
		Nos. 150-159 (10)	10.00	

Cent. of the Republic. The 1c and 2c were not released for general use.
Nos. 150-159 exist imperf. Value, $60 each pair.
For surcharges see Nos. C59-C62.

Stamps of 1919-27
Surcharged in Blue,
Black or Red

1927		A54　5c on 1c car (Bl)		
160	A54	5c on 1c car (Bl)	2.50	.90
a.	Inverted surcharge		6.00	6.00
b.	Black surcharge		22.50	22.50

Perf. 12

162	A54	10c on 24c pur (Bk)	2.50	1.50
a.	Inverted surcharge		30.00	30.00
b.	Red surcharge		22.50	22.50

Coat of Arms — A66

Printed by Waterlow & Sons

1927		Litho.	Perf. 13½	
165	A66	2c yellow	.40	.20
166	A66	3c pink	.50	.50
167	A66	4c red brown	.40	.40
168	A66	20c lt ol grn	.65	.20
169	A66	25c deep blue	.65	.30
170	A66	30c violet	.80	.80
171	A66	40c orange	1.50	1.25
172	A66	50c dp brown	1.50	.50
173	A55	1b red	1.75	1.25
174	A55	2b plum	2.50	2.50
175	A55	3b olive grn	2.50	2.50
176	A55	4b claret	4.00	3.50
177	A55	5b bister brn	4.75	4.00
		Nos. 165-177 (13)	21.90	17.90

For overprints and surcharges see Nos. 178-180, 208, 211-212.

Type of 1927 Issue
Overprinted

1927				
178	A66	5c dark green	.20	.20
179	A66	10c slate	.45	.20
180	A66	15c carmine	.65	.25
		Nos. 178-180 (3)	1.30	.65

Exist with inverted overprint. Value $20 each.

Stamps of 1919-27
Surcharged

1928			Perf. 12, 12½, 13½	
		Red Surcharge		
181	A54	15c on 20c #122	9.00	9.00
182	A54	15c on 20c #132	9.00	9.00
a.	Black surcharge		30.00	
183	A54	15c on 20c #146	160.00	160.00
		Black Surcharge		
184	A54	15c on 24c #124	1.60	.90
a.	Inverted surcharge		5.00	5.00
b.	Blue surcharge		50.00	
185	A54	15c on 50c #125	50.00	42.50
186	A54	15c on 50c #135	1.25	.60
		Nos. 181-186 (6)	230.85	222.00

No. 183 exists with inverted surcharge.

Condor — A67　　Hernando
Siles — A68

Map of Bolivia — A69

Printed by Perkins, Bacon & Co., Ltd.

1928		Engr.	Perf. 13½	
189	A67	5c green	1.50	.20
190	A68	10c slate	.30	.20
191	A69	15c carmine lake	.60	.20
		Nos. 189-191 (3)	2.40	.60

Nos. 104, 111, 113, Surcharged in Various Colors

1930			Perf. 12, 11½	
193	A20	1c on 2c (Bl)	.80	.80
a.	"0.10" for "0.01"		12.50	12.50
194	A50	3c on 2c (Br)	.80	.80
195	A48	25c on ½c (Bk)	.80	.80
196	A50	25c on 2c (V)	.80	.80
		Nos. 193-196 (4)	3.20	3.20

The lines of the surcharges were spaced to fit the various shapes of the stamps. The surcharges exist inverted, double, etc.
Trial printings were made of the surcharges on #193 and 194 in black and on #196 in brown.

Mt.　　　　Mt.
Potosi — A70　Illimani — A71

Eduardo　　　Map of
Abaroa — A72　Bolivia — A73

Sucre — A74　　Bolivar — A75

1931		Engr.	Perf. 14	
197	A70	2c green	1.40	.50
198	A71	5c light brn	1.40	.20
199	A72	10c red orange	1.40	.20
200	A73	15c violet	1.40	.20
201	A73	35c carmine	2.00	.85
202	A73	45c orange	2.00	.75
203	A74	50c gray	.55	.55
204	A75	1b brown	.55	.55
		Nos. 197-204 (8)	10.70	3.80

No. 198 exists imperf.
See #207, 241. For surcharges see #209-210.

Symbols of 1930 Revolution — A76

1931		Litho.	Perf. 11	
205	A76	15c scarlet	2.25	.40
a.	Pair, imperf. between			
206	A76	50c brt violet	.70	.70
a.	Pair, imperf. between		7.50	

Revolution of June 25, 1930.
For surcharges see Nos. 239-240.

Map Type of 1931
Without Imprint

1932			Litho.	
207	A73	15c violet	1.50	.35

Stamps of 1927-31
Surcharged

1933   *Perf. 13½, 14*
208 A66 5c on 1b red   .60 .35
  a. Without period after "Cts" 1.25 1.25
209 A73 15c on 35c car   .35 .35
  a. Inverted surcharge   20.00
210 A73 15c on 45c orange .35 .35
  a. Inverted surcharge   3.00 3.00
211 A66 15c on 50c dp brn 1.50 .30
212 A66 15c on 40c orange .60 .25
  Nos. 208-212 (5)   3.40 1.60

The hyphens in "13-7-33" occur in three positions.

Coat of Arms — A77

1933   *Engr.*   *Perf. 12*
213 A77 2c blue green .25 .20
214 A77 5c blue   .25 .20
215 A77 10c red   .45 .30
216 A77 15c deep violet .35 .20
217 A77 25c dark blue .70 .55
  Nos. 213-217 (5) 2.00 1.45

For surcharges see Nos. 233-235, 238.

Mariano Baptista — A78   Map of Bolivia — A79

1935
218 A78 15c dull violet   .45 .20

1935
219 A79 2c dark blue .20 .20
220 A79 3c yellow   .20 .20
221 A79 5c vermilion .20 .20
222 A79 5c blue grn .35 .20
223 A79 10c black brn .35 .20
224 A79 15c deep rose .35 .20
225 A79 15c ultra   .35 .20
226 A79 20c yellow grn .40 .20
227 A79 25c lt blue .40 .20
228 A79 30c deep rose .80 .55
229 A79 40c orange .80 .55
230 A79 50c gray violet .80 .25
231 A79 1b yellow .55 .35
232 A79 2b olive brown .80 .70
  Nos. 219-232 (14) 6.55 4.20

Regular Stamps of 1925-33 Surcharged in Black

1937   *Perf. 11, 12, 13½*
233 A77 5c on 2c bl grn .25 .25
234 A77 15c on 25c dk bl .30 .30
235 A77 30c on 25c dk bl .50 .50
236 A55 45c on 1b red brn .60 .60
237 A55 1b on 2b plum .75 .75
  a. "1" missing 7.50 7.50
238 A77 2b on 25c dk bl .75 .75

"Comunicaciones" on one line
239 A76 3b on 50c brt vio 1.25 1.25
  a. "3" of value missing 6.00 6.00
240 A76 5b on 50c brt vio 1.25 1.25
  Nos. 233-240 (8) 5.65 5.65

Exist inverted, double, etc.

President Siles — A80

1937   *Unwmk.*   *Perf. 14*
241 A80 1c yellow brown .30 .30

Native School — A81   Oil Wells — A82

Modern Factories A83   Torch of Knowledge A84

Map of the Sucre-Camiri R. R. — A85

Allegory of Free Education — A86   Allegorical Figure of Learning — A87

Symbols of Industry — A88

Modern Agriculture — A89

1938   *Litho.*   *Perf. 10½, 11*
242 A81 2c dull red .40 .40
243 A82 10c pink   .45 .25
244 A83 15c yellow grn .60 .30
245 A84 30c yellow .75 .35
246 A85 45c rose red 1.40 .75
247 A86 60c dk violet 1.10 .35
248 A87 75c dull blue 1.50 .35
249 A88 1b lt brown 2.25 .35
250 A89 2b bister 2.00 .75
  Nos. 242-250 (9) 10.45 3.85

For surcharge see No. 314.

Llamas — A90

Vicuna — A91   Coat of Arms — A92

Cocoi Herons — A93   Chinchilla — A94

Toco Toucan — A95

Condor — A96

Jaguar — A97

1939, Jan. 21 *Perf. 10½, 11½x10½*
251 A90 2c green .40 .30
252 A90 4c fawn .40 .30
253 A90 5c red violet .40 .25
254 A91 10c black .60 .30
255 A91 15c emerald .60 .35
256 A91 20c dk slate grn .60 .25
257 A92 25c lemon .60 .25
258 A92 30c dark blue .60 .30
259 A93 40c vermilion 1.40 .30
260 A93 45c gray 1.40 .30
261 A94 60c rose red 1.40 .55
262 A94 75c slate blue 2.75 .55
263 A93 90c orange 2.00 .55
264 A95 1b blue 2.00 .55
265 A96 2b rose lake 2.75 .55
266 A96 3b dark violet 3.50 .85
267 A97 4b brown org 4.00 1.10
268 A97 5b gray brown 5.00 1.40
  Nos. 251-268 (18) 30.40 9.00

All but 20c exist imperf.
Imperf. counterfeits with altered designs exist of some values.
For surcharges see Nos. 315-317.

Flags of 21 American Republics — A98

1940, Apr. *Litho.* *Perf. 10½*
269 A98 9b multicolored 1.10 1.10

Pan American Union, 150th anniversary.

Statue of Murillo — A99   Urns of Murillo and Sagarnaga — A100

Dream of Murillo — A101   Murillo — A102

1941, Apr. 15
270 A99 10c dull vio brn .20 .20
271 A100 15c lt green .20 .20
  a. Imperf., pair 3.50
  b. Double impression 6.00
272 A101 45c carmine rose .20 .20
  a. Double impression 6.00
273 A102 1.05b dk ultra .40 .20
  Nos. 270-273 (4) 1.00 .80

130th anniv. of the execution of Pedro Domingo Murillo (1759-1810), patriot.
For surcharge see No. 333.

First Stamp of Bolivia and 1941 Airmail Stamp — A103

1942, Oct. *Litho.* *Perf. 13½*
274 A103 5c pink .50 .50
275 A103 10c orange .50 .40
276 A103 20c yellow grn 1.00 .65
277 A103 40c carmine rose 1.25 .80
278 A103 90c ultra 2.50 1.00
279 A103 1b violet 3.00 1.60
280 A103 10b olive bister 10.00 8.25
  Nos. 274-280 (7) 18.75 13.20

1st School Phil. Exposition held in La Paz, Oct., 1941.

Gen. Ballivian Leading Cavalry Charge, Battle of Ingavi — A104

1943   *Photo.*   *Perf. 12½*
281 A104 2c lt blue grn .20 .20
282 A104 3c orange .20 .20
283 A104 25c deep plum .20 .20
284 A104 45c ultra .20 .20
285 A104 3b scarlet .40 .35
286 A104 4b brt rose lilac .55 .45
287 A104 5b black brown .80 .55
  Nos. 281-287 (7) 2.55 2.15

Souvenir Sheets
Perf. 13, Imperf.
288 A104 Sheet of 4 1.50 1.50
289 A104 Sheet of 3 4.50 4.50

Centenary of the Battle of Ingavi, 1841. No. 288 contains 4 stamps similar to Nos. 281-284. No. 289 three stamps similar to Nos. 285-287.

Potosi A107   Quechisla A108

Miner — A109

Dam A110

Mine Interior A111

Chaquiri Dam A112

Entrance to Pulacayo Mine A113

1943   Engr.   Perf. 12½
290 A107	15c red brown	.20	.20
291 A108	45c vio blue	.20	.20
292 A109	1.25b brt rose vio	.25	.30
293 A110	1.50b emerald	.25	.30
294 A111	2b brown blk	.30	.35
295 A112	2.10b lt blue	.40	.45
296 A113	3b red orange	.50	.55
	Nos. 290-296 (7)	2.10	2.35

General José Ballivián and Cathedral at Trinidad A114

1943, Nov. 18
297 A114	5c dk green & brn	.20	.20
298 A114	10c dull pur & brn	.20	.20
299 A114	30c rose red & brn	.20	.20
300 A114	45c brt ultra & brn	.20	.25
301 A114	2.10b dp org & brn	.30	.35
	Nos. 297-301,C91-C95 (10)	2.35	2.30

Department of Beni centenary.

"Honor, Work, Law" — A115   "United for the Country" — A116

1944   Litho.   Perf. 13½
302 A115	20c orange	.20	.20
303 A115	90c ultra	.20	.20
304 A116	1b brt red vio	.20	.20
305 A116	2.40b dull brown	.20	.20

1945
306 A115	20c green	.20	.20
307 A115	90c dp rose	.20	.20
	Nos. 302-307,C96-C99 (10)	2.20	2.00

Nos. 302-307 were issued to commemorate the Revolution of Dec. 20, 1943.

> **Catalogue values for unused stamps in this section, from this point to the end of the section, are for Never Hinged items.**

Leopold Benedetto Vincenti, Joseph Ignacio de Sanjines and Bars of Anthem — A117

1946, Aug. 21   Litho.   Perf. 10½
308 A117	5c rose vio & blk	.20	.20
309 A117	10c ultra & blk	.20	.20
310 A117	15c blue grn & blk	.20	.20
311 A117	30c vermilion & brn	.20	.20
a.	Souv. sheet of 1, imperf.	.65	.65
312 A117	90c dk blue & brn	.20	.20
313 A117	2b black & brn	.30	.20
a.	Souv. sheet of 1, imperf.	1.25	1.25
	Nos. 308-313 (6)	1.30	1.20

Adoption of Bolivia's natl. anthem, cent. Nos. 311a and 313a sold for 4b over face.

Nos. 248 and 262 Surcharged in Carmine, Black or Orange

1947, Mar. 12   Perf. 10½, 11
314 A87	1.40b on 75c (C)	.20	.20
315 A94	1.40b on 75c (Bk)	.20	.20
316 A94	1.40b on 75c (C)	.20	.20
317 A94	1.40b on 75c (O)	.20	.20
	Nos. 314-317,C112 (5)	1.00	1.00

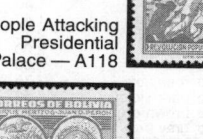

People Attacking Presidential Palace — A118

Arms of Bolivia and Argentina A119

1947, Sept.   Litho.   Perf. 13½
318 A118	20c blue grn	.20	.20
319 A118	50c lilac rose	.20	.20
320 A118	1.40b grnsh bl	.20	.20
321 A118	3.70b dull org	.20	.20
322 A118	4b violet	.20	.20
323 A118	10b olive	.40	.25
	Nos. 318-323,C113-C117 (11)	2.40	2.25

1st anniv. of the Revolution of July 21, 1946. Exist imperf.

1947, Oct. 23
| 324 A119 | 1.40b deep orange | .20 | .20 |

Meeting of Presidents Enrique Hertzog of Bolivia and Juan D. Peron of Argentina at Yacuiba on Oct. 23, 1947. Exist imperf. See No. C118.

Statue of Christ above La Paz — A120

2b, Child kneeling before cross of Golgotha. 3b, St. John Bosco. #328, Virgin of Copacabana. #329, Pope Pius XII blessing University of La Paz.

1948, Sept. 26   Unwmk.   Perf. 11½
325 A120	1.40b blue & yel	.30	.20
326 A120	2b yel grn & sal	.40	.20
327 A120	3b green & gray	.60	.20
328 A120	5b violet & sal	.85	.25
329 A120	5b red brn & lt grn	1.10	.25
	Nos. 325-329,C119-C123 (10)	6.00	2.65

3rd Inter-American Cong. of Catholic Education.

Map and Emblem of Bolivia Auto Club — A125   Pres. Gregorio Pacheco, Map and Post Horn — A126

1948, Oct. 20
| 330 A125 | 5b indigo & salmon | 1.50 | .20 |

Intl. Automobile Races of South America, Sept.-Oct. 1948. See No. C124.

1950, Jan. 2   Litho.   Perf. 11½
331 A126	1.40b violet blue	.20	.20
332 A126	4.20b red	.20	.20
	Nos. 331-332,C125-C127 (5)	1.00	1.00

75th anniv. of the UPU.

No. 273 Surcharged in Black

1950   Perf. 10½
| 333 A102 | 2b on 1.05b dk ultra | .20 | .20 |

Crucifix and View of Potosi — A127   Symbols of United Nations — A128

Perf. 11½
1950, Sept. 14   Litho.   Unwmk.
334 A127	20c violet	.20	.20
335 A127	30c dp orange	.20	.20
336 A127	50c lilac rose	.20	.20
337 A127	1b carmine	.20	.20
338 A127	2b blue	.30	.20
339 A127	6b chocolate	.25	.20
	Nos. 334-339 (6)	1.35	1.20

400th anniv. of the appearance of a crucifix at Potosi. Exist imperf.

1950, Oct. 24
340 A128	60c ultra	1.00	.20
341 A128	2b green	1.40	.22
	Nos. 340-341,C138-C139 (4)	3.55	.82

5th anniv. of the UN, Oct. 24, 1945.

Gate of the Sun and Llama A129

Church of San Francisco — A130

40c, Avenue Camacho. 50c, Consistorial Palace. 1b, Legislative Palace. 1.40b, Communications Bldg. 2b, Arms. 3b, La Gasca ordering Mendoza to found La Paz. 5b, Capt. Alonso de Mendoza founding La Paz. 10b, Arms; portrait of Mendoza.

1951, Mar.   Engr.   Perf. 12½
Center in Black
342 A129	20c green	.20	.20
343 A130	30c dp orange	.20	.20
344 A129	40c bister brn	.20	.20
345 A129	50c dk red	.20	.20
346 A129	1b dp purple	.20	.20
347 A129	1.40b dk vio blue	.20	.20
348 A129	2b dp purple	.20	.20
349 A129	3b red lilac	.20	.20
a.	Sheet, Nos. 345, 346, 348, 349	1.10	1.10
b.	As "a," imperf.	1.10	1.10
350 A129	5b dk red	.25	.20
a.	Sheet, Nos. 344, 347, 350	1.10	1.10
b.	As "a," imperf.	1.10	1.10
351 A129	10b sepia	.50	.25
a.	Sheet, Nos. 342, 343, 351	1.10	1.10
b.	As "a," imperf.	1.10	1.10
	Nos. 342-351,C140-C149 (20)	5.55	5.25

400th anniv. of the founding of La Paz. For surcharges see Nos. 393-402.

Boxing A131

Perf. 12½
1951, July 1   Unwmk.   Engr.
352 A131	20c shown	.20	.20
353 A131	50c Tennis	.20	.20
354 A131	1b Diving	.20	.20
355 A131	1.40b Soccer	.20	.20
356 A131	2b Skiing	.40	.30
357 A131	3b Handball	.80	.80
a.	Sheet, #352-353, 356-357	2.25	1.75
b.	As "a," imperf.	2.25	1.75
358 A131	4b Cycling	1.00	1.00
a.	Sheet, #354-355, 358	2.00	1.50
b.	As "a," imperf.	2.00	1.50
	Nos. 352-358,C150-C156 (14)	8.25	6.25

The stamps were intended to commemorate the 5th athletic championship matches held at La Paz, October 1948.

Eagle and Flag of Bolivia A132

1951, Nov. 5   Litho.   Perf. 11½
Flag in Red, Yellow and Green.
359 A132	2b aqua	.20	.20
360 A132	3.50b ultra	.20	.20
361 A132	5b purple	.20	.20
362 A132	7.50b gray	.20	.20
363 A132	15b dp car	.25	.25
364 A132	30b sepia	.50	.50
	Nos. 359-364 (6)	1.55	1.55

Cent. of the adoption of Bolivia's natl. flag.

Eduardo Abaroa — A133   Queen Isabella I — A134

1952, Mar.   Perf. 11
365 A133	80c dk carmine	.20	.20
366 A133	1b red orange	.20	.20
367 A133	2b emerald	.20	.20

368	A133	5b ultra	.25	.20
369	A133	10b lilac rose	.50	.20
370	A133	20b dk brown	.75	.65

Nos. 365-370,C157-C162 (12) 5.10 4.45

73rd anniv. of the death of Eduardo Abaroa.

1952, July 16 Unwmk. Perf. 13½

371	A134	2b vio bl	.20	.20
372	A134	6.30b carmine	.20	.20

Nos. 371-372,C163-C164 (4) 1.40 1.00

Birth of Isabella I of Spain, 500th anniv.

Columbus Lighthouse — A135

1952, July 16 Litho.

373	A135	2b vio bl, *bl*	.20	.20
374	A135	5b car, *sal*	.50	.40
375	A135	9b emer, *grn*	.85	.60

Nos. 373-375,C165-C168 (7) 2.55 2.00

Miner — A136

1953, Apr. 9

376	A136	2.50b vermilion	.20	.20
377	A136	8b violet	.20	.20

Nationalization of the mines.

Gualberto Villarroel, Victor Paz Estenssoro and Hernan Siles Zuazo
A137

1953, Apr. 9 Perf. 11½

378	A137	50c rose lil	.20	.20
379	A137	1b brt rose	.20	.20
380	A137	2b vio bl	.20	.20
381	A137	3b lt grn	.20	.20
382	A137	4b yel org	.20	.20
383	A137	5b dl vio	.20	.20

Nos. 378-383,C169-C175 (13) 2.85 2.60

Revolution of Apr. 9, 1952, 1st anniv.

Map of Bolivia and Cow's Head — A138

25b, 85b, Map and ear of wheat.

1954, Aug. 2 Perf. 12x11½

384	A138	5b car rose	.20	.20
385	A138	17b aqua	.20	.20
386	A138	25b chalky blue	.20	.20
387	A138	85b blk brn	.20	.20

Nos. 384-387,C176-C181 (10) 2.95 2.10

Nos. 384-385 for the agrarian reform laws of 1953-54. Nos. 386-387 for the 1st National Congress of Agronomy. Exist imperf.

Oil Refinery
A139

1955, Oct. 9 Unwmk. Perf. 12x11½

388	A139	10b ultra & lt ultra	.20	.20
389	A139	35b rose car & rose	.20	.20
390	A139	40b dk & lt yel grn	.20	.20
391	A139	50b red vio & lil rose	.20	.20
392	A139	80b brn & bis brn	.20	.20

Nos. 388-392,C182-C186 (10) 3.50 3.25

Exist imperf.

Nos. 342-351, Surcharged with New Values and Bars in Ultramarine

1957, Feb. 14 Engr. Perf. 12½
Center in Black

393	A129	50b on 3b red lilac	.20	.20
394	A129	100b on 2b dp pur	.20	.20
395	A129	200b on 1b dp pur	.20	.20
396	A129	300b on 1.40b dk vio bl	.20	.20
397	A129	350b on 20c green	.20	.20
398	A129	400b on 40c bis brn	.20	.20
399	A130	600b on 30c dp org	.35	.20
400	A129	800b on 50c dk red	.40	.20
401	A129	1000b on 10b sepia	.40	.20
402	A129	2000b on 3b dk red	.65	.20

Nos. 393-402 (10) 3.00 2.00

See Nos. C187-C196.

CEPAL Building, Santiago de Chile, and Meeting Hall in La Paz — A140

1957, May 15 Litho. Perf. 13

403	A140	150b gray & ultra	.20	.20
404	A140	350b bis brn & gray	.20	.20
405	A140	550b chlky bl & brn	.20	.20
406	A140	750b dp rose & gray	.30	.20
407	A140	900b grn & brn blk	.40	.20

Nos. 403-407,C197-C201 (10) 5.10 3.60

7th session of the C. E. P. A. L. (Comision Economica para la America Latina de las Naciones Unidas), La Paz. Exist imperf.
For surcharges see Nos. 482-484,

Presidents Siles Zuazo and Aramburu
A141

1957, Dec. 15 Unwmk. Perf. 11½

408	A141	50b red org	.20	.20
409	A141	350b blue	.25	.20
410	A141	1000b redsh brn	.45	.20

Nos. 408-410,C202-C204 (6) 2.00 1.20

Opening of the Santa Cruz-Yacuiba Railroad and the meeting of the Presidents of Bolivia and Argentina. Exist imperf.
For surcharge see No. 699.

Flags of Bolivia and Mexico and Presidents Hernan Siles Zuazo and Adolfo Lopez Mateos
A142

1960, Jan. 30 Litho. Perf. 11½

411	A142	350b olive	.20	.20
412	A142	600b red brown	.25	.25
413	A142	1500b black brown	.50	.50

Nos. 411-413,C205-C207 (6) 3.10 2.25

Issued for an expected visit of Mexico's President Adolfo Lopez Mateos. On sale Jan. 30-Feb. 1, 1960.

Indians and Mt. Illimani
A143

1960, Mar. 26 Unwmk.

414	A143	500b olive bister	.50	.20
415	A143	1000b blue	.90	.30
416	A143	2000b brown	2.00	.50
417	A143	4000b green	3.75	2.50

Nos. 414-417,C208-C211 (8) 23.90 12.95

Refugee Children — A144

1960, Apr. 7 Perf. 11½

418	A144	50b brown	.20	.20
419	A144	350b claret	.20	.20
420	A144	400b steel blue	.20	.20
421	A144	1000b gray brown	.50	.50
422	A144	3000b slate green	1.00	1.00

Nos. 418-422,C212-C216 (10) 4.40 4.35

World Refugee Year, 7/1/59-6/30/60.
For surcharges see Nos. 454-458, 529.

Jaime Laredo
A145

1960, Aug. 15 Litho. Perf. 11½

423	A145	100b olive	.20	.20
424	A145	350b deep rose	.30	.25
425	A145	500b Prus green	.40	.20
426	A145	1000b brown	.50	.50
427	A145	1500b violet blue	.85	.90
428	A145	5000b gray	3.00	3.00

Nos. 423-428,C217-C222 (12) 13.00 8.75

Issued to honor violinist Jaime Laredo.
For surcharge see No. 485.

Rotary Emblem and Nurse with Children — A146

1960, Nov. 19 Perf. 11½

429	A146	350b multi	.20	.20
430	A146	500b multi	.25	.20
431	A146	600b multi	.35	.35
432	A146	1000b multi	.40	.20

Nos. 429-432,C223-C226 (8) 6.20 3.70

Issued for the Children's Hospital, sponsored by the Rotary Club of La Paz.
For surcharges see Nos. 486-487.

Designs from Gate of the Sun
A147   A148

Designs: Various prehistoric gods and ornaments from Tiahuanacu excavations.

1960, Dec. 16 Perf. 13x12, 12x13
Gold Background
Surcharge in Black or Dark Red
Sizes: 21x23mm, 23x21mm

433	A147	50b on ½c red	.45	.30
434	A147	100b on 1c red	.35	.20
435	A147	200b on 2c blk	.75	.35

436	A147	300b on 5c grn (DR)	.25	.20
437	A147	350b on 10c grn	.25	.75
438	A148	400b on 15c ind	.35	.20
439	A148	500b on 20c red	.35	.25
440	A148	500b on 50c red	.40	.20
441	A148	600b on 22½c grn	.45	.45
442	A148	600b on 60c vio	.55	.50
443	A148	700b on 25c vio	.70	.20
444	A148	700b on 1b grn	1.00	1.00
445	A148	800b on 30c red	.60	.20
446	A148	900b on 40c grn	.45	.20
447	A148	1000b on 2b bl	.60	.50
448	A148	1800b on 3b gray	5.00	3.50

Perf. 11
Size: 49½x23mm

449	A148	4000b on 4b gray	30.00	25.00

Perf. 11x13½
Size: 49x53mm

450	A147	5000b on 5b gray	7.50	7.00

Nos. 433-450 (18) 50.00 41.00

Nos. 433-450 were not regularly issued without surcharge. Value, set $20.

The decree for Nos. 433-450 stipulated that 7 were for air mail (500b on 50c, 600b on 60c, 700b on 1b, 1000b, 1800b, 4000b and 5000b), but the overprinting failed to include "Aereo."

The 800b surcharge also exists on the 1c red and gold. This was not listed in the decree. For surcharges see Nos. 528, 614.

Miguel de Cervantes
A149

Nuflo de Chaves
A150

1961, Nov. Photo. Perf. 13x12½

451	A149	600b ocher & dl vio	.40	.20

Cervantes' appointment as Chief Magistrate of La Paz. See No. C230.

1961, Nov. Unwmk.

452	A150	1500b dk bl, *buff*	.75	.30

Founding of Santa Cruz de la Sierra, 400th anniv. See #468, C246. For surcharge see #533.

People below Eucharist Symbol — A151

Flowers — A152

1962, Mar. 19 Litho. Perf. 10½

453	A151	1000b gray grn, red & yel	.65	.35

4th Natl. Eucharistic Congress, Santa Cruz, 1961. See No. C231.

Nos. 418-422 Surcharged Horizontally with New Value and Bars or Greek Key Border Segment

1962, June Perf. 11½

454	A144	600b on 50b brown	.20	.20
455	A144	900b on 350b claret	.25	.20
456	A144	1000b on 400b steel blue	.30	.20
457	A144	2000b on 1000b gray brn	.40	.25
458	A144	3500b on 3000b slate grn	.65	.65

Nos. 454-458,C232-C236 (10) 5.20 4.60

Old value obliterated with two short bars on No. 454; four short bars on Nos. 455-456 and Greek key border on Nos. 457-458. The Greek key obliteration comes in two positions: two full "keys" on top, and one full and two half keys on top.

1962, June 28   Litho.   Perf. 10½
459 A152 200b Hibiscus   .30 .20
460 A152 400b Bicolored vanda   .45 .20
461 A152 600b Lily   .75 .20
462 A152 1000b Orchid   1.00 .20
   Nos. 459-462,C237-C240 (8)   7.50 3.45

Bolivia's Armed Forces — A153

Anti-Malaria Emblem — A154

1962, Sept. 5   Perf. 11½
463 A153 400b Infantry   .20 .20
464 A153 500b Cavalry   .20 .20
465 A153 600b Artillery   .20 .20
466 A153 2000b Engineers   .50 .35
   Nos. 463-466,C241-C244 (8)   4.10 2.35

1962, Oct. 4
467 A154 600b dk & lt vio & yel   .25 .25
WHO drive to eradicate malaria. See #C245.

Portrait Type of 1961
Design: 600b, Alonso de Mendoza.

1962   Photo.   Perf. 13x12½
468 A150 600b rose vio, bluish   .25 .20

Soccer and Flags A155

Design: 1b, Goalkeeper catching ball, vert.

1963, Mar. 21   Litho.   Perf. 11½
Flags in National Colors
469 A155 60c gray   .40 .40
470 A155 1b blue   .60 .20
21st South American Soccer Championships. See Nos. C247-C248.

Globe and Wheat Emblem A156

1963, Aug. 1   Unwmk.   Perf. 11½
471 A156 60c dk bl, bl & yel   .25 .25
"Freedom from Hunger" campaign of the FAO. See No. C249.

Oil Derrick and Chart — A157

Designs: 60c, Map of Bolivia. 1b, Students.

1963, Dec. 21   Litho.   Perf. 11½
472 A157 10c green & dk brn   .20 .20
473 A157 60c ocher & dk brn   .25 .20
474 A157 1b dk blue, grn & yel   .30 .20
   Nos. 472-474,C251-C253 (6)   2.65 1.95
Revolution of Apr. 9, 1952, 10th anniv.

Flags of Bolivia and Peru A158

1966, Aug. 10   Wmk. 90   Perf. 13½
Flags in National Colors
475 A158 10c black & tan   .20 .20
476 A158 60c black & lt grn   .20 .20
477 A158 1b black & gray   .40 .35
478 A158 2b black & rose   .50 .50
   Nos. 475-478,C254-C257 (8)   3.00 2.95
Marshal Andrés Santa Cruz (1792-1865), president of Bolivia and of Peru-Bolivian Confederation.

Children — A159

Perf. 13½
1966, Dec. 16   Unwmk.   Litho.
479 A159 30c ocher & sepia   .20 .20
Issued to help poor children. See No. C258.

Map and Flag of Bolivia and Generals Ovando and Barrientos A160

1966, Dec. 16   Litho.   Perf. 13½
Flag in Red, Yellow and Green
480 A160 60c violet brn & tan   .30 .20
481 A160 1b dull grn & tan   .45 .20
Issued to honor Generals Rene Barrientos Ortuno and Alfredo Ovando C., co-Presidents, 1965-66. See Nos. C259-C260.

Various Issues 1957-60 and Type A161 Surcharged with New Values and Bars

A161

1966, Dec. 21
On No. 403: "Centenario de la / Cruz Roja / Internacional"
482 A140 20c on 150b gray
         & ultra   .20 .20
On Nos. 405-406: "Homenaje a la / Generala / J. Azurduy de / Padilla"
483 A140 30c on 550b chlky
         bl & brn   .30 .20
484 A140 2.80b on 750b dp
         rose & grn   .75 .50
On No. 424: "CL Aniversario / Heroinas Coronilla"
485 A145 60c on 350b dp
         rose   .50 .20
Nos. 429-430 Surcharged
486 A146 1.60b on 350b multi   .75 .50
487 A146 2.40b on 500b multi   1.00 .75
Revenue Stamps of 1946 surcharged with New Value, "X" and: "XXV Aniversario / Gobierno Busch"
488 A161 20c on 5b red   .20 .20
Overprinted: "XX Aniversario / Gob. Villaroel"
489 A161 60c on 2b grn   .30 .20
Overprinted: "Centenario do / Rurrenabaque"
490 A161 1b on 10b brn   .50 .20

Overprinted: "XXV Aniversario / Dpto. Pando"
491 A161 1.60b on 50c vio   .50 .20
   Nos. 482-491,C261-C272 (22) 14.50 9.30
For surcharge see No. C272.

Sower A162

"Macheteros" A163

1967, Sept. 20   Litho.   Perf. 13½x13
492 A162 70c multicolored   .35 .20
50th anniv. of Lions Intl. See #C273-C273a.

1968, June 24   Perf. 13½x13
Designs (Folklore characters): 60c, Chunchos. 1b, Wiphala. 2b, Diablada.
493 A163 30c gray & multi   .20 .20
494 A163 60c sky bl & multi   .25 .25
495 A163 1b gray & multi   .40 .20
496 A163 2b gray ol & multi   .65 .20
   Nos. 493-496,C274-C277 (8)   4.00 1.75
Issued to publicize the 9th Congress of the Postal Union of the Americas and Spain.
A souvenir sheet exists containing 4 imperf. stamps similar to #493-496. Size: 131x81 ½mm.

Arms of Tarija — A164

Pres. Gualberto Villaroel — A165

1968, Oct. 29   Litho.   Perf. 13½x13
497 A164 20c pale sal & multi   .20 .20
498 A164 30c gray & multi   .20 .20
499 A164 40c dl yel & multi   .20 .20
500 A164 60c lt yel grn & multi .20 .20
   Nos. 497-500,C278-C281 (8)   3.30 2.60
Battle of Tablada sesquicentennial.

1968, Nov. 6   Unwmk.
501 A165 20c sepia & org   .30 .20
502 A165 30c sepia & dl bl grn   .30 .20
503 A165 40c sepia & dl rose   .30 .20
504 A165 50c sepia & yel grn   .30 .20
505 A165 1b sepia & ol bister   .30 .20
   Nos. 501-505 (5)   1.50 1.00
4th centenary of the founding of Cochabamba. See Nos. C282-C286.

ITU Emblem A166

1968, Dec. 3   Litho.   Perf. 13x13½
506 A166 10c gray, blk & yel   .20 .20
507 A166 60c org, blk & ol   .40 .40
Cent. (in 1965) of the ITU. See Nos. C287-C288.

Polychrome Painted Clay Cup, Inca Period — A167

1968, Nov. 14   Perf. 13½x13
508 A167 20c dk bl grn & multi   .20 .20
509 A167 60c vio bl & multi   .35 .35
20th anniv. (in 1966) of UNESCO. See Nos. C289-C290.

John F. Kennedy A168

1968, Nov. 22   Perf. 13x13½
510 A168 10c yel grn & blk   .20 .20
511 A168 4b vio & blk   1.40 1.40
A souvenir sheet contains one imperf. stamp similar to No. 511. Green marginal inscription. Size: 131x81 ½mm.
See Nos. C291-C292.

Tennis Player — A169

1968, Dec. 10   Perf. 13x13½
512 A169 10c gray, blk & brn   .25 .25
513 A169 20c yel, blk & lt brn   .25 .25
514 A169 30c ultra, blk & lt brn .25 .25
   Nos. 512-514 (3)   .75 .75
32nd South American Tennis Championships, La Paz, 1965. See Nos. C293-C294.
A souvenir sheet exists containing 3 imperf. stamps similar to Nos. 512-514. Size: 131x81 ½mm.

Issue of 1863 — A170

1968, Dec. 23   Litho.   Perf. 13x13½
515 A170 10c yel grn, brn & blk .35 .20
516 A170 30c lt bl, brn & blk   .35 .35
517 A170 2b gray, brn & blk   .35 .35
   Nos. 515-517,C295-C297 (6)   3.55 3.40
Cent. of Bolivian postage stamps. See Nos. C295-C297.
A souvenir sheet exists containing 3 imperf. stamps similar to Nos. 515-517. Yellow green marginal inscription. Size: 131x81 ½mm.

Rifle Shooting A171

Sports: 50c, Equestrian. 60c, Canoeing.

1969, Oct. 29   Litho.   Perf. 13x13½
518 A171 40c red brn, org & blk .40 .40
519 A171 50c emer, red & blk   .40 .40
520 A171 60c bl, emer & blk   .40 .40
   Nos. 518-520,C299-C301 (6)   4.20 3.85
19th Olympic Games, Mexico City, 10/12-27/68.
A souvenir sheet exists containing 3 imperf. stamps similar to #518-520. Size: 130½x81mm.

Temenis Laothoe Violetta A172

Butterflies: 10c, Papilio crassus. 20c, Cat-agramma cynosura. 30c, Eunica eurota flora. 80c, Ituna phenarete.

1970, Apr. 24   Litho.   Perf. 13x13½

521	A172	5c pale lil & multi	.70	.70
522	A172	10c pink & multi	1.40	1.40
523	A172	20c gray & multi	1.40	1.40
524	A172	30c yel & multi	1.40	1.40
525	A172	80c multicolored	1.40	1.40
		Nos. 521-525,C302-C306 (10)	20.20	20.20

A souvenir sheet exists containing 3 imperf. stamps similar to Nos. 521-523. Black marginal inscription. Size: 129½x80mm.

Boy Scout — A173

Design: 10c, Girl Scout planting rose bush.

1970, June 17   Perf. 13½x13

526	A173	5c multicolored	.20	.20
527	A173	10c multicolored	.20	.20
		Nos. 526-527,C307-C308 (4)	1.00	1.00

Honoring the Bolivian Scout movement.

No. 437 Surcharged "EXFILCA 70 / $b. 0.30" and Two Bars in Red

1970, Dec. 6   Litho.   Perf. 13x12

528	A147	30c on 350b on 10c	.25	.25

EXFILCA 70, 2nd Interamerican Philatelic Exhib., Caracas, Venezuela, Nov. 27-Dec. 6.

Nos. 455 and 452 Surcharged in Black or Red

1970, Dec.   Photo.   Perf. 11½

529	A144	60c on 900b on 350b	.25	.20
533	A150	1.20b on 1500b (R)	.50	.20

Amaryllis Yungacensis A174

Bolivian Flowers: 30c, Amaryllis escobar uriae, horiz. 40c, Amaryllis evansae, horiz. 2b, Gymnocalycium chiquitanum.

Perf. 13x13½, 13½x13

1971, Aug. 9   Litho.   Unwmk.

534	A174	30c gray & multi	.30	.30
535	A174	40c multi	.30	.30
536	A174	50c multi	.40	.35
537	A174	2b multi	1.00	.60
		Nos. 534-537,C310-C313 (8)	7.00	4.45

Sica Sica Church, EXFILIMA Emblem — A175

1971, Nov. 6   Perf. 14x13½

538	A175	20c red & multi	.20	.20

EXFILIMA '71, 3rd Inter-American Philatelic Exhibition, Lima, Peru, Nov. 6-14.

A176

Design: Pres. Hugo Banzer Suarez.

1972, Jan. 24   Litho.   Perf. 13½

539	A176	1.20b blk & multi	.50	.20

Bolivia's development, 8/19/71-1/24/72.

A177

1972, Mar. 23   Litho.   Perf. 13½x13

Folk Dances: 20c, Chiriwano de Achocalla. 40c, Rueda Chapaca. 60c, Kena-kena. 1b, Waca Thokori.

540	A177	20c red & multi	.20	.20
541	A177	40c rose lil & multi	.30	.25
542	A177	60c cream & multi	.45	.20
543	A177	1b citron & multi	.55	.25
		Nos. 540-543,C314-C315 (6)	2.65	1.30

Madonna and Child by B. Bitti — A178

Bolivian paintings: 10c, Nativity, by Melchor Perez de Holguin. 50c, Coronation of the Virgin, by G. M. Berrio. 70c, Harquebusier, anonymous. 80c, St. Peter of Alcantara, by Holguin.

1972   Litho.   Perf. 14x13½

544	A178	10c gray & multi	.20	.20
545	A178	50c sal & multi	.25	.20
546	A178	70c lt grn & multi	.35	.20
547	A178	80c buff & multi	.40	.20
548	A178	1b multi	.50	.20
		Nos. 544-548,C316-C319 (9)	3.45	1.80

Issue dates: 1b, Aug. 17; others, Dec. 4.

Tarija Cathedral, EXFILBRA Emblem — A179

1972, Aug. 26

549	A179	30c multi	.20	.20

4th Inter-American Philatelic Exhibition, EXFILBRA, Rio de Janeiro, Brazil, 8/26-9/2.

Echinocactus Notocactus A180

Designs: Various cacti.

1973, Aug. 6   Litho.   Perf. 13½

550	A180	20c crim & multi	.30	.25
551	A180	40c multi	.30	.25
552	A180	50c multi	.30	.20
553	A180	70c multi	.30	.20
		Nos. 550-553,C321-C323 (7)	2.70	1.55

Power Station, Santa Isabel A181

Designs: 20c, Tin industry. 90c, Bismuth industry. 1b, Natural gas plant.

1973, Nov. 26   Litho.   Perf. 13½

554	A181	10c gray & multi	.20	.20
555	A181	20c tan & multi	.20	.20
556	A181	90c lt grn & multi	.25	.20
557	A181	1b yel & multi	.25	.20
		Nos. 554-557,C324-C325 (6)	1.90	1.20

Bolivia's development.

Cattleya Nobilior — A182

Orchids: 50c, Zygopetalum bolivianum. 1b, Huntleya melargis.

1974, May 15   Perf. 13½

558	A182	20c gray & multi	.40	.20
559	A182	50c lt bl & multi	.40	.20
560	A182	1b cit & multi	.40	.20
		Nos. 558-560,C327-C330 (7)	7.70	2.15

For surcharge see No. 704.

UPU and Philatelic Exposition Emblems — A183

1974, Oct. 9

561	A183	3.50b grn, blk & bl	1.00	.40

Centenary of Universal Postal Union: PRENFIL-UPU Philatelic Exhibition, Buenos Aires, Oct. 1-12; EXPO-UPU Philatelic Exhibition, Montevideo, Oct. 20-27.

Gen. Sucre, by I. Wallpher A184

1974, Dec. 9   Litho.   Perf. 13½

562	A184	5b multicolored	1.10	.50

Sesquicentennial of the Battle of Ayacucho.

Lions Emblem and Steles A185

1975, Mar.   Litho.   Perf. 13½

563	A185	30c red & multi	.35	.35

Lions Intl. in Bolivia, 25th anniv.

España 75 Emblem A186

1975, Mar.

564	A186	4.50b yel, red & blk	.80	.35

Espana 75 International Philatelic Exhibition, Madrid, Apr. 4-13.

Emblem A187

1975   Litho.   Perf. 13½

565	A187	2.50b lil, blk & sil	.65	.25

First meeting of Postal Ministers, Quito, Ecuador, March 1974, and for the Cartagena Agreement.

Pando Coat of Arms — A188

Designs: Departmental coats of arms.

1975, July 16   Litho.   Perf. 13½

566	A188	20c shown	.20	.20
567	A188	2b Chuquisaca	.40	.40
568	A188	3b Cochabamba	.50	.50
		Nos. 566-568,C336-C341 (9)	4.25	4.25

Sesquicentennial of Republic of Bolivia.

Simón Bolívar — A189

Presidents and Statesmen of Bolivia: 30c, Victor Paz Estenssoro. 60c, Tomas Frias. 1b, Ismael Montes. 2.50b, Aniceto Arce. 7b, Bautista Saavedra. 10b, Jose Manuel Pando. 15b, Jose Maria Linares. 50b, Simon Bolivar.

1975   Litho.   Perf. 13½
Size: 24x32mm

569	A189	30c multi	.20	.20
569A	A189	60c multi	.20	.20
570	A189	1b multi	.30	.30
571	A189	2.50b multi	.50	.50
572	A189	7b multi	1.40	.50
573	A189	10b multi	2.00	.75
574	A189	15b multi	2.50	2.50

Size: 28x39mm
575 A189   50b multi   10.00 10.00
Nos. 569-575,C346-C353 (16)   36.10 31.20
Sesquicentennial of Republic of Bolivia.

"EXFIVIA
75"
A190

1975, Dec. 1   Litho.   **Perf. 13½**
576 A190   3b multicolored   .75   .60
  a.   Souvenir sheet   1.50 1.50
EXFIVIA 75, 1st Bolivian Philatelic Exposition. #576a contains one stamp similar to #576 with simulated perfs. Sold for 5b.

A191

Chiang Kai-shek, flags of Bolivia and China.

1976, Apr. 4   Litho.   **Perf. 13½**
577 A191   2.50b multi, red circle   1.00 1.00
578 A191   2.50b multi, bl circle   1.00 1.00
Pres. Chiang Kai-shek of China (1887-1975). Erroneous red of sun's circle on Chinese flag of No. 577 was corrected on No. 578 with a dark blue overlay.

A192

1976, Apr.   Litho.   **Perf. 13½**
579 A192   50c Naval insignia   .40   .35
Navy anniversary.

Geological Map, Pickax and
Lamp — A193

1976, May
580 A193   4b multicolored   .80   .60
Bolivian Geological Institute.

Lufthansa Jet, Bolivian and German Colors A194

1976, May
581 A194   3b multicolored   .80   .35
Lufthansa, 50th anniversary.

Boy Scout and
Scout
Emblem — A195

1976, May   Litho.   **Perf. 13½**
582 A195   1b multicolored   .50   .50
Bolivian Boy Scouts, 60th anniversary.

Battle Scene, US Bicentennial
Emblem — A196

1976, May 25
583 A196   4.50b bis & multi   1.40   .65
American Bicentennial.
A souvenir sheet contains one stamp similar to No. 583 with simulated perforations. Size: 130x80mm.

Family, Map of   Vicente
Bolivia — A197   Bernedo — A198

1976   **Perf. 13½**
584 A197   2.50b multicolored   .50   .40
National Census 1976.

1976, Oct.
585 A198   1.50b multicolored   .35   .30
Brother Vicente Bernedo de Potosi (1544-1619), missionary to the Indians.

Policeman
with Dog,
Rainbow over
La
Paz — A199

1976, Oct.
586 A199   2.50b multicolored   .60   .60
Bolivian Police, 150 years of service.

Emblem,
Bolivar
and
Sucre
A200

1976, Nov. 18   Litho.   **Perf. 13½**
587 A200   1.50b multicolored   .60   .60
Intl. Congress of Bolivarian Societies.

Pedro
Poveda, View
of La
Paz — A201

1976, Dec.
588 A201   1.50b multicolored   .35   .25
Pedro Poveda (1874-1936), educator.

A202   Boy and
                       Girl — A203

1976, Dec. 17   **Perf. 10½**
594 A202   20c brown   .30   .20
595 A202   1b ultra   .45   .20
596 A202   1.50b green   .75   .50
   Nos. 594-596 (3)   1.50   .90

1977, Feb. 4   Litho.   **Perf. 13½**
599 A203   50c multicolored   .20   .20
Christmas 1976, and for 50th anniversary of the Inter-American Children's Institute.

Staff of   Supreme Court,
Aesculapius   La Paz
A204   A205

1977, Mar. 18   Litho.   **Perf. 13½x13**
600 A204   3b multicolored   .75   .30
National Seminar on Chagas' disease, Cochabamba, Feb. 21-26.

1977, May 3
Designs: 4b, Manuel Maria Urcullu, first President of Supreme Court.   4.50b, Pantaleon Dalence, President 1883-1889.
601 A205   2.50b multi   .30   .30
602 A205   4b multi   .40   .20
603 A205   4.50b multi   .50   .20
   Nos. 601-603 (3)   1.20   .70
Sesquicentennial of Bolivian Supreme Court.

Newspaper   Map of Bolivia,
Mastheads   Tower and Flag
A206   A207

Designs: 2.50b, Alfredo Alexander and Hoy, horiz. 3b, Jose Carrasco and El Diario, horiz. 4b, Demetrio Canelas and Los Tiempos. 5.50b, Frontpage of Presencia.

1977, June   **Perf. 13½**
604 A206   1.50b multi   .25   .20
605 A206   2.50b multi   .35   .30
606 A206   3b multi   .40   .25

---

607 A206   4b multi   .50   .35
608 A206   5.50b multi   .65   .20
   Nos. 604-608 (5)   2.15 1.30
Bolivian newspapers and their founders.

1977, June
609 A207   3b multi   .50   .20
90th anniversary of Oruro Club.

Games'   Tin Miner and
Poster — A208   Emblem — A209

1977, Oct. 20   Litho.   **Perf. 13½**
610 A208   5b blue & multi   .75   .30
8th Bolivian Games, La Paz, Oct. 1977.

1977, Oct. 31   Litho.   **Perf. 13**
611 A209   3b multicolored   .60   .40
Bolivian Mining Corp., 25th anniv.

Miners, Globe, Tin   Map of Bolivia,
Symbol — A210   Radio
                        Masts — A211

1977, Nov. 3
612 A210   6b silver & multi   .80   .25
Intl. Tin Symposium, La Paz, Nov. 14-21.

1977, Nov. 11
613 A211   2.50b blue & multi   .50   .35
Radio Bolivia, ASBORA, 50th anniversary.

No. 450 Surcharged with New Value, 3
Bars and "EXFIVIA-77"
1977, Nov. 25   Litho.   **Perf. 11x13½**
614 A147   5b on 5000b on 5b   1.00 1.25
EXFIVIA '77 Philatelic Exhibition, Cochabamba.

Eye, Compass,
Book of
Law — A212

1978, May 3   Litho.   **Perf. 13½x13**
615 A212   5b multi   .65   .20
Audit Department, 50th anniversary.

Mt. Illimani   Pre-
A213   Columbian
                        Monolith
                        A214

Design: 1.50b, Mt. Cerro de Potosi.

Perf. 11x10½, 10½x11

1978, June 1   **Litho.**
616 A213   50c bl & Prus bl   .20 .20
617 A214   1b brn & lemon   .20 .20
618 A213   1.50b red & bl gray   .35 .25
    Nos. 616-618 (3)   .75 .65

Andean Countries, Staff of Aesculapius A215

Map of Americas with Bolivia A216

1978, June 1   **Perf. 10½x11**
626 A215   2b org & blk   .35 .20
Health Ministers of Andean Countries, 5th meeting.

1978, June 1
627 A216   2.50b dp ultra & red   .35 .20
World Rheumatism Year.
For surcharges see Nos. 697, 972.

Central Bank Building — A217

Jesus and Children — A218

1978, July 26   **Litho.**   **Perf. 13½**
628 A217   7b multi   1.00 .25
50th anniversary of Bank of Bolivia.

1979, Feb. 20   **Litho.**   **Perf. 13½**
629 A218   8b multicolored   .90 .20
International Year of the Child.

Antofagasta Cancel — A219

Eduardo Abaroa, Chain — A220

Designs: 1b, La Chimba cancel. 1.50b, Mejillones cancel. 5.50b, View of Antofagasta, horiz. 6.50b, Woman in chains, symbolizing captive province. 8b, Map of Antofagasta Province, 1876. 10b, Arms of province.

1979, Mar. 23   **Litho.**   **Perf. 10½**
630 A219   50e buff & blk   .30 .20
631 A219   1b pink & blk   .50 .25
632 A219   1.50b pale grn & blk   .50 .25
    Perf. 13½
633 A220   5.50b multi   .60 .25
634 A220   6.50b multi   .80 .30
635 A220   7b multi   .80 .30
636 A220   8b multi   .90 .35
637 A220   10b multi   1.10 .35
    Nos. 630-637 (8)   5.50 2.25
Loss of Antofagasta coastal area to Chile, cent.
For surcharge see No. 696.

Emblem and Map of Bolivia — A221

Gymnast — A222

1979, Mar. 26   **Perf. 13½x13**
638 A221   3b multicolored   .75 .50
Radio Club of Bolivia.

1979, Mar. 27   **Perf. 13x13½, 13½x13**
6.50b, Runner and Games emblem, horiz.
639 A222   6.50b multi   .80 .50
640 A222   10b multi   1.10 .25
Southern Cross Sports Games, Bolivia, Nov. 3-12, 1978.
A souvenir sheet contains 1 stamp similar to No. 640 with simulated perforations. Sold for 20b. Size: 80x130mm.
For surcharge see No. 965.

Bulgaria No. 1 — A223

1979, Mar. 30   **Perf. 10½**
641 A223   2.50b multi   .35 .25
PHILASERDICA '79 International Philatelic Exhibition, Sofia, Bulgaria, May 18-27.
For surcharge see No. 694.

EXFILMAR Emblem — A224

1979, Apr. 2
642 A224   2b multi   .20 .20
Bolivian Maritime Philatelic Exhibition, La Paz, Nov. 18-28.
For surcharge see No. 698.

OAS Emblem, Map of Bolivia — A226

1979, Oct. 22   **Litho.**   **Perf. 14x13½**
644 A226   6b multi   .75 .25
Organization of American States, 9th Congress, La Paz, Oct.-Nov.

Franz Tamayo — A227

Bolivian and Japanese Flags, Hospital — A228

UN Emblem and Meeting — A229

Radio Tower and Waves — A230

1979, Dec.
645 A227   2.80b blk & gray   .35 .25
646 A228   5b multi   .50 .35
648 A229   5b multi   .50 .35
649 A230   6b multi   .65 .25
    Nos. 645-649 (4)   2.00 1.20
Franz Tamayo, lawyer, birth centenary; Japanese-Bolivian health care cooperation; CEPAL, 18th Congress, La Paz, Sept. 18-26; Bolivian National Radio, 50th anniversary.
For surcharge see No. 695.

Puerto Suarez Iron Ore Deposits A231

1979   **Litho.**   **Perf. 13½x14**
650 A231   9.50b multi   1.10 .50

Bolivia No. 19, EXFILMAR Emblem, Bolivian Flag — A232

1980   **Litho.**   **Perf. 13½**
651 A232   4b multi   .55 .30
EXFILMAR, Bolivian Maritime Philatelic Exhibition, La Paz, Nov. 18-28, 1979.

Juana Azurduy on Horseback A233

1980   **Litho.**   **Perf. 14x13½**
652 A233   4b multi   .55 .30
Juana Azurduy de Padilla, independence fighter, birth bicentenary.

La Salle and World Map A234

1980   **Perf. 13½x14**
653 A234   9b multi   1.10 .60
St. Jean Baptiste de la Salle (1651-1719), educator.
For surcharge see No. 966.

"Victory" in Chariot, Madrid, Exhibition Emblem, Flags of Bolivia and Spain A235

1980, Oct.   **Litho.**   **Perf. 13½x14**
654 A235   14b multi   1.60 .75
ESPAMER '80 Stamp Exhibition, Madrid.

Map of South America, Flags of Argentina, Bolivia and Peru — A236

1980, Oct.   **Perf. 14x13½**
655 A236   2b multi   .25 .20
Ministers of Public Works and Transport of Argentina, Bolivia and Peru meeting.

Santa Cruz-Trinidad Railroad, Inauguration of Third Section — A237

1980, Oct.
656 A237   3b multi   .35 .20

Flag on Provincial Map — A238

Parrots — A239

Perf. 14x13½, 13½x14

1981, May 11			Litho.	
657	A238	1b Soldier, flag, map	.20	.20
658	A238	3b Flag, map	.35	.20
659	A238	40b shown	5.00	1.25
660	A238	50b Soldier, civilians, horiz.	6.00	1.25
	Nos. 657-660 (4)		11.55	2.90

July 17 Revolution memorial.

1981, May 11			Perf. 14x13½	
661	A239	4b Ara macao	.50	.30
662	A239	7b Ara chloroptera	.80	.50
663	A239	8b Ara ararauna	1.00	.60
664	A239	9b Ara rubrogenys	1.10	.65
665	A239	10b Ara auricollis	1.10	.65
666	A239	12b Anodorynchus hyacinthinus	1.50	.75
667	A239	15b Ara militaris	1.75	1.00
668	A239	20b Ara severa	2.25	1.25
	Nos. 661-668 (8)		10.00	5.70

Christmas 1981 — A240

1981, Dec. 7			Litho.	Perf. 10½	
669	A240	1b Virgin and Child, vert.		.20	.20
670	A240	2b Child, star		.25	.20

American Airforces Commanders' 22nd Conference, Buenos Aires — A241

1982, Apr. 12			Litho.	Perf. 13½	
671	A241	14b multi		1.60	.50

75th Anniv. of Cobija — A242

Simon Bolivar Birth Bicentenary (1983) A243

1982, July 8			Litho.	Perf. 13½	
672	A242	28b multi		.40	.25

1982, July 12
| 673 | A243 | 18b multi | | .25 | .20 |

1983 World Telecommunications Day — A244

1982 World Cup — A245

1982, July 15
| 674 | A244 | 26b Receiving station | .40 | .25 |

1982, July 21			Perf. 11	
675	A245	4b shown	.20	.20
676	A245	100b Final Act, by Picasso	1.75	.95

For surcharge see No. 701.

Girl Playing Piano — A246

1982, July 25			Perf. 13½	
677	A246	16b Boy playing soccer, vert.	.25	.20
678	A246	20b shown	.35	.20

Bolivian-Chinese Agricultural Cooperation, 1972-1982 — A247

1982, Aug. 12
| 679 | A247 | 30b multi | .50 | .25 |

First Bolivian-Japanese Gastroenterology Conference, La Paz, Jan. — A248

1982, Aug. 26
| 680 | A248 | 22b multi | | .35 | .25 |

A249

1982, Aug. 31			Litho.	Perf. 14x13½	
681	A249	19b Stamps		.35	.20

10th Anniv. of Bolivian Philatelic Federation.

A250

1982, Sept. 1
| 682 | A250 | 20b tan & dk brown | .30 | .20 |

Pres. Hernando Siles, birth centenary.

Scouting Year — A251   Cochabamba Philatelic Center, 25th Anniv. — A252

1982, Sept. 3			Perf. 11	
683	A251	5b Baden-Powell	.20	.20

For surcharge see No. 703.

1982, Sept. 14
| 684 | A252 | 3b multicolored | .20 | .20 |

For surcharge see No. 700.

Cochabamba Superior Court of Justice Sesquicentennial — A253

1982			Litho.	Perf. 13½	
685	A253	10b multicolored		.20	.20

For surcharge see No. 970.

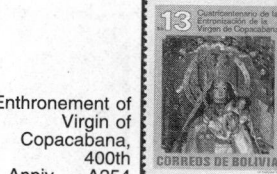

Enthronement of Virgin of Copacabana, 400th Anniv. — A254

1982, Nov. 15			Litho.	Perf. 13½	
686	A254	13b multicolored		.25	.20

For surcharge see No. 971.

Navy Day — A255

1982, Nov. 17
| 687 | A255 | 14b Port Busch Naval Base | .25 | .20 |

A256   A257

1982, Nov. 19			Perf. 11	
688	A256	10b green & gray	.20	.20

Christmas. For surcharge see No. 702.

1983, Feb. 13			Litho.	Perf. 13½	
689	A257	50b multicolored		.80	.40

10th Youth Soccer Championship, Jan. 22-Feb. 13.

EXFIVIA '83 Philatelic Exhibition A258

1983, Nov. 5			Litho.	Perf. 13½	
690	A258	150b brown carmine		1.00	.50

Visit of Brazilian Pres. Joao Figueiredo, Feb. — A259

1984, Feb. 7			Litho.	Perf. 13½x14	
691	A259	150b multicolored		.40	.20

Simon Bolivar Entering La Paz, by Carmen Baptista A260

Paintings of Bolivar: 50b, Riding Horse, by Mulato Gil de Quesada, vert.

Perf. 14x13½, 13½x14
1984, Mar. 30				
692	A260	50b multi	.20	.20
693	A260	200b multi	.55	.25

Types of 1957-79 Surcharged

No. 697

1984, Mar.				
694	A223	40b on 2.50b #641	.20	.20
695	A227	40b on 2.80b #645	.20	.20
696	A219	60b on 1.50b #632	.20	.20
697	A216	60b on 2.50b #627	.20	.20

698 A224 100b on 2b #642 .30 .20
699 A141 200b on 350b #409 .60 .25
Nos. 694-699 (6) 1.70 1.25

See #972 for surcharge similar to #697.

Nos. 675, 683-684, 688, C328
Surcharged

| 1984, June 27 | Litho. | Perf. 11 |
700 A252 500b on 3b #684 .75 .35
701 A245 1000b on 4b #675 1.50 .75
702 A256 2000b on 10b
#688 3.00 1.25
703 A251 5000b on 5b #683 7.50 3.00

Perf. 13½
704 A182 10,000b on 3.80b
#C328 10.00 6.00
Nos. 700-704 (5) 22.75 11.35

Road Safety
Education — A261

Cartoons.

1984, Sept. 7   Litho.   Perf. 11
705 A261 80b Jaywalker .20 .20
706 A261 120b Motorcycle policeman, ambu-
lance .20 .20

Jose Eustaquio
Mendez, 200th
Birth
Anniv. — A262

Perf. 14x13½, 13½x14
1984, Sept. 19
Paintings: 300b, Birthplace, by Jorge Campos. 500b, Mendez Leading the Battle of La
Tablada, by M. Villegas, horiz.
707 A262 300b multi .20 .20
708 A262 500b multi .20 .20

1983 World Cup   Chasqui, Postal
Soccer   Runner — A264
Championships,
Mexico — A263

Sponsoring shoe-manufacturers' trade-
marks on: 100b, 200b, Outline map of
Bolivia, natl. colors. 600b, World map, soccer
ball.

1984, Oct. 26   Perf. 11
709 A263 100b multi .20 .20
710 A263 200b multi .20 .20
711 A263 600b multi, horiz. .20 .20
Nos. 709-711 (3) .60 .60

1985
712 A264 11000b vio bl .25 .20
For surcharge see No. 962.

Intl. Year of   Intl. Anti-Polio
Professional   Campaign
Education   A266
A265

1985, Apr. 25
713 A265 2000b Natl. Manual
Crafts emblem .20 .20
For surcharges see Nos. 721-722, 959.

1985, May 22
714 A266 20000b lt bl & vio .25 .20

Endangered
Wildlife — A267

1985, May 22
715 A267 23000b Altiplano boliviano .20 .20
716 A267 25000b Sarcorhamphus
gryphus .25 .20
717 A267 30000b Blastocaros
dichotomus .30 .20
Nos. 715-717 (3) .75 .60
Nos. 716-717 vert.
For surcharge see No. 963.

Dona Vicenta
Juaristi Eguino (b.
1785),
Independence
Heroine — A268

1985, Oct.   Litho.   Perf. 13½
718 A268 300000b multi .20 .20

UN, 40th
Anniv. — A269

1985, Oct. 24   Perf. 11
719 A269 1000000b bl & gold .65 .30
For surcharge see No. 964.

A270

A271

1985, Nov.
720 A270 200000b multi .20 .20
Soccer Team named "The Strongest," 75th
anniv.

No. 713 Surcharged

1986   Litho.   Perf. 11
721 A265 200000b on 2000b .25 .20
722 A265 5000000b on 2000b 5.25 2.50

1986
723 A271 300000 Emblems,
vert. .30 .20
724 A271 550000 Pique trademark, vert. .60 .25
725 A271 1000000 Azteca Stadium 1.00 .50
726 A271 2500000 World cup,
vert. 2.75 1.25
Nos. 723-726 (4) 4.65 2.20
1986 World Cup Soccer Championships.
For surcharge see No. 961.

Intl. Youth Year
A272   A273

1986
727 A272 150000 brt car rose .20 .20
728 A272 500000 bl grn .55 .30
729 A273 3000000 multi 3.25 1.50
Nos. 727-729 (3) 4.00 2.00
Inscribed 1985.
For surcharge see No. 958.

Alfonso
Sobieta
Viaduct,
Carretera
Quillacollo,
Confital
A274

1986   Perf. 13½
730 A274 400000 int bl & gray .40 .20
Inter-American Development Bank, 25th
anniv.

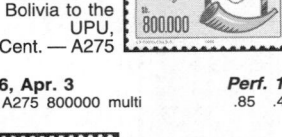

Admission of
Bolivia to the
UPU,
Cent. — A275

1986, Apr. 3   Perf. 11
731 A275 800000 multi .85 .40

Postal Workers
Soc., 50th
Anniv. — A276

1986, Sept. 5
732 A276 2000000 brn & pale
brn 2.10 1.00
For surcharge see No. 967.

Founding
of
Trinidad,
300th
Anniv.
A277

1986, May 25   Perf. 13½x14
733 A277 1400000 Bull and Rider, by Vaca 1.50 .75
For surcharge see No. 960.

Bolivian Philatelic Federation, 15th
Anniv. — A278

1986, Nov. 28
734 A278 600000b No. 19 .60 .30

Death of a Priest,   Intl. Peace
by Jose Antonio   Year — A280
Zampa — A279

1986, Nov. 21   Perf. 14x13½
735 A279 400000b multi .40 .20

1986, Sept. 16   Perf. 11
736 A280 200000 yel grn & pale
grn .25 .20

Natl. Oil Corp.
(YPBF), 50th
Anniv. — A281

1986, Dec. 22   Litho.   Perf. 11
737 A281 1000000b multi 1.50 .50

A282

Photograph of a Devil-mask Dancer, by
Jimenez Cordero.

1987, Feb. 13   Litho.   Perf. 14x13½
738 A282 20c multi .30 .20
February 10th Society, cent. (in 1985).

A283

1987, Mar. 20   Litho.   Perf. 14x13½
739 A283 30c Crossed flags .45 .25
State Visit of Richard von Weizsacker,
Pres. of Germany, Mar. 20.

State
Visit of
King Juan
Carlos of
Spain,
May 20
A284

1987, May 20   Perf. 13½x14
740 A284 60c Natl. arms .90 .40

EXFIVIA
'87 — A285

Mount Potosi, 18th cent. engraving.

1987, Oct.　　Litho.　　Perf. 13½
741 A285 50c multi　　　　.70　.35
See No. 750.

Wildlife
Conservation
A286

1987, Oct.
742 A286 20c Condor　　　.30　.20
743 A286 20c Tapir　　　　.30　.20
744 A286 30c Vicuna　　　.45　.25
745 A286 30c Armadillo　　.45　.25
746 A286 40c Spectacled bears　.60　.30
747 A286 60c Toucans　　　.90　.40
　　Nos. 742-747 (6)　　3.00 1.60
Wildlife in danger of extinction.

ESPAMER '87,
La Coruna
A287

1987, Oct.　　Litho.　　Perf. 14x13½
748 A287 20c Nina, stern of
　　　　　　Santa Maria　.30　.20
749 A287 20c Bow of Santa Ma-
　　　　　　ria, Pinta　　.30　.20
　a.　Pair, #748-749　　　.60　.25
No. 749a has a continuous design.

EXFIVIA Type of 1987
Photograph of Mt. Potosi by Jimenez
Cordero.

1987, Aug. 5　　Litho.　　Perf. 13½
750 A285 40c multi　　　　.60　.30

Musical Instruments — A288

1987, Dec. 3　　Perf. 13½x14, 14x13½
751 A288 50c Zampona and
　　　　　　quena (wind in-
　　　　　　struments)　　.70　.35
752 A288 1b Charango, vert.　1.40　.70

A289

State Visit of
Pope
John Paul II
A290

Pontiff, religious architecture and art: No.
753, Cathedral of Kings, Beni. No. 754,
Carabuco Church. No. 755, Tihuanacu
Church. No. 756, St. Francis's Church, Sucre.
No. 757, St. Joseph's of Chiquitos Church.

40c, Cobija Chapel, vert. No. 759, Jayu Kcota
Church. No. 760, Cochabamba Cathedral,
vert. 60c, St. Francis's Basilica, La Paz, vert.
No. 762, Christ of Machaca Church. No. 763,
St. Lawrence's Church, Potosi, vert. No. 764,
The Holy Family, by Rubens, vert. No. 765,
The Virgin of Copacabana, statue, vert. No.
766, Vallegrande Church. No. 767, Tarija
Cathedral, vert. No. 768, Concepcion Church.

1988　　Litho.　　Perf. 13½x14, 14x13½
753 A289 20c multi　　　　.25　.20
754 A289 20c multi　　　　.25　.20
755 A289 20c multi　　　　.25　.20
756 A289 30c multi　　　　.40　.20
757 A289 30c multi　　　　.40　.20
758 A289 40c multi　　　　.50　.20
759 A289 50c multi　　　　.65　.30
760 A289 50c multi　　　　.65　.30
761 A289 60c multi　　　　.75　.35
762 A289 70c multi　　　　.90　.35
763 A289 70c multi　　　　.90　.35
764 A289 80c multi　　　　1.00　.45
765 A289 80c multi　　　　1.00　.45
766 A289 80c multi　　　　1.00　.45
767 A289 1.30b multi　　　1.60　.75
768 A289 1.30b multi　　　1.60　.75
769 A290 1.50b shown　　　1.90　.90
　　Nos. 753-769 (17)　　14.00 6.65
Issue dates: 1.50b, May 9; others, Mar. 3.

Visit of
Pres.
Jose
Sarney of
Brazil
A291

1988, Aug. 2　　Litho.　　Perf. 13½x14
770 A291 50c multi　　　　.60　.30

St. John Bosco
(1815-1888)
A292

1988, Aug. 16　　　　Perf. 13½
771 A292 30c multi　　　　.40　.20

Bolivian
Railways,
Cent. — A293

Design: 1b, Steam locomotive from the La
Paz-Beni line, made by Marca Shy Ohio, Natl.
Railway Museum, Sucre.

1988, Aug. 29
772 A293 1b multi　　　　1.25　.60

Nataniel Aguirre
(b. 1888),
Author — A294

Department of
Pando, 50th
Anniv. — A295

1988, Sept. 14　　Litho.　　Perf. 13½
773 A294 1b blk & beige　　1.25　.60

1988, Sept. 26　　　　Perf. 13½
Designs: 40c, *Columna Porvenir*, memorial
to the Battle of Bahio. 60c, Siringuero rubber
production (worker sapping latex from *Hevea
brasiliensis*).
774 A295 40c multi　　　　.50　.25
775 A295 60c multi　　　　.70　.35

A296　　　　　　A297

1988, Sept. 27
776 A296 1.50b multi　　　1.90　.90
1988 Summer Olympics, Seoul.

1988
Designs: 70c, Archbishop Bernardino de
Cardenas (1579-1668). 80c, Mother Rosa
Gattorno (1831-1900), founder of the Sisters
of Santa Ana.
777 A297 70c multi　　　　.90　.45
778 A297 80c multi　　　　1.00　.50
　Issue dates: 70c, Oct. 20, 80c, Oct. 14.

Ministry of
Transportation &
Communications
A298

1988, Oct. 24　　Litho.　　Perf. 14x13½
779 A298 2b deep car, blk & pale
　　　　　　olive grn　　2.40 1.00

Army Communications, 50th Anniv. (in
1987) — A299

1988, Nov. 29　　Litho.　　Perf. 13½
780 A299 70c multi　　　　.95　.45

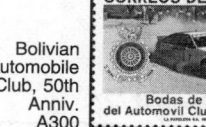

Bolivian
Automobile
Club, 50th
Anniv.
A300

1988, Dec. 29　　Litho.　　Perf. 13½
781 A300 1.50b multi　　　1.50　.70

Flowering
Plants and
Emblems
A301

50c, Orchid, BULGARIA '89 emblem. 60c,
Kantuta blossoms, ITALIA '90 emblem. 70c,
Heliconia humilis, Albertville '86 emblem. 1b,
Hoffmanseggia, Barcelona '92 Games
emblem. 2b, Puya raymondi, Seoul '88 Games
and five-ring emblems.

1989, Feb. 17　　Litho.　　Perf. 13½
782 A301 50c multi, vert.　　.60　.25
783 A301 60c multi　　　　.70　.30
784 A301 70c multi, vert.　　.80　.30
785 A301 1b multi, vert.　　1.10　.45
786 A301 2b multi, vert.　　2.25　.90
　　Nos. 782-786 (5)　　5.45 2.20

Radio FIDES,
50th Anniv.
A302

1989, Feb. 2
787 A302 80c multi　　　　.90　.40

Gold
Quarto of
1852
A303

1989, Feb. 9　　　　Perf. 13½x14
788 A303 1b multi　　　　1.25　.50

French
Revolution,
Bicent. — A304

1989, June 23　　Litho.　　Perf. 14x13½
789 A304 70c red, blk & blue　.90　.35

Uyuni Township,
Cent. — A305

1989, July 9　　Litho.　　Perf. 14x13½
790 A305 30c bl, blk & gray　.40　.20

Noel Kempff
Mercado Natl.
Park, Santa
Cruz — A306

1.50b, Federico Ahlfeld Falls, Pauserna
River. 3b, *Ozotoceros bezcarticus* (deer).

1989, Sept. 24　　Litho.　　Perf. 13½x14
791 A306 1.50b multicolored　2.00　.75
792 A306 3b multicolored　　4.00 1.50

UPAEP
A306a

1989, Oct. 12　　Litho.　　Perf. 13½
792A A306a 50c Metalworking　.50　.20
792B A306a 1b Temple of
　　　　　　Kalasasaya　1.00　.40
See Nos. 808-809.

State Visit by Dr. Carlos Andres Perez, Pres. of Venezuela — A306b

1989, Oct. 14
792C A306b 2b multi 2.00 .80
See Nos. 825-826, 832.

City of Potosi — A306c

1989, Nov. 10 Litho. Perf. 13½
792D A306c 60c Cobija Arch .75 .30
792E A306c 80c Mint .85 .40
f. Pair, #792D-792E 1.60 .70

Christmas — A307

Paintings: 40c, *Andean Stillwaters,* by Arturo Borda. 60c, *The Virgin of the Roses,* anonymous. 80c, *The Conquistador,* by Jorge de la Reza. 1b, *Native Harmony,* by Juan Rimsa. 1.50b, *Woman with Jug,* by Cecilio Guzman de Rojas. 2b, *Bloom of Tenderness,* by Gil Imana. Nos. 794-798 vert.

1989, Dec. 18 Perf. 13½x14, 14x13½
793 A307 40c multicolored .40 .20
794 A307 60c multicolored .60 .25
795 A307 80c multicolored .80 .30
796 A307 1b multicolored 1.00 .40
797 A307 1.50b multicolored 1.50 .60
798 A307 2b multicolored 2.00 .80
Nos. 793-798 (6) 6.30 2.55

A308

1990, Jan. 23 Litho. Perf. 13½
799 A308 80c multicolored .85 .35
Fight against drug abuse.

A309

1990, May 13 Perf. 14x13½
Great Britain #1, Sir Rowland Hill, Bolivia #1
800 A309 4b multicolored 4.00 1.75
Penny Black, 150th anniv.

World Cup Soccer Championships, Italy — A310

1990, June 16 Perf. 13½
801 A310 2b Stadium, Milan 2.00 .80
802 A310 6b Game 6.00 2.40

Organization of American States, Cent. — A311

1990, Apr. 14
803 A311 80c dark bl & brt bl .80 .30

A312

1990, Apr. 16
804 A312 1.20b multi 1.25 .60

A313

1990 Litho. Perf. 14x13½
805 A313 70c Telecommunications .70 .55

National Chamber of Commerce, Cent. — A314

1990, June
806 A314 50c gold, blk & bl .60 .40

Cochabamba Social Club, Cent. — A315

1990, Sept. 14 Litho. Perf. 13½
807 A315 40c multicolored .40 .30

UPAEP Type of 1989
Perf. 13½x14, 14x13½
1990, Oct. 12 Litho.
808 A306a 80c Huts .75 .30
809 A306a 1b Mountains, lake, vert. .95 .40

A317

1990, Oct. 19 Perf. 14x13½
810 A317 1.20b multicolored 1.00 .40
Magistrate's District of Larecaja, 400th Anniv.

A318

1990, Oct. 12 Perf. 14x13½
811 A318 2b multicolored 1.75 .70
Discovery of America, 500th anniv. (in 1992).

German Reunification A319

1990, Nov. 19 Litho. Perf. 14x13½
812 A319 2b multicolored 1.75 .70

Visit of Carlos Salinas de Gortari, Pres. of Mexico A320

Design: 80c, Visit of Rodrigo Borja Cevallos, Pres. of Ecuador.

1990, Dec. 13 Litho. Perf. 13½
813 A320 60c multicolored .75 .30
814 A320 80c multicolored .85 .40

4th Congress of the Andean Presidents — A321

1990, Nov. 29 Perf. 13½x14
815 A321 1.50b multicolored 1.40 .55

Exfivia '90 — A322

Christmas — A323

1990, Dec. 9 Perf. 13½
816 A322 40c dk blue .40 .20

1990, Nov. 20 Perf. 11
817 A323 50c multicolored .45 .20

Express Mail Service A324

1990, Dec. 14 Perf. 13½x14
818 A324 1b multicolored .90 .35

Bolivian Radio Club, 50th Anniv. — A325

1991, Mar. 1 Litho. Perf. 14x13½
819 A325 2.40b multicolored 2.00 .80

End of Chaco War, 56th Anniv. — A326

Map of Heroes of Chaco Highway.

1991, June 14 Litho. Perf. 14x13½
820 A326 60c multicolored .55 .25

National Museums — A327

1991, June 13 Perf. 13½
821 A327 50c Archaeology .40 .20
822 A327 50c Art .40 .20
823 A327 1b Ethnology, Folklore .85 .35
a. Strip of 3, #821-823 1.70 .70
Espamer '91.

A328

Our Lady of Peace, Metropolitan Cathedral.

1991, July 15   Litho.   Perf. 14x13½
824 A328 1.20b multicolored   1.10 .45

Presidential State Visit Type of 1989

Jaime Paz Zamora, Pres. of Bolivia and: No. 825, Dr. Carlos Saul Menem, Pres. of Argentina. No. 826, Dr. Luis Alberto Lacalle, Pres. of Uruguay.

1991   Perf. 13½x14
825 A306b 1b multicolored   .85 .35
826 A306b 1b multicolored   .85 .35
Issue dates: #825, Aug. 5; #826, Aug. 12.

A329

1991, May 31   Perf. 13½
Tremarctos ornatus.
827 A329 30c Adult, 2 cubs   1.10 .20
828 A329 30c Adult's head   1.10 .20
829 A329 30c Adult on tree limb   1.10 .20
830 A329 30c Adult, cubs on tree limb 1.10 .20
Nos. 827-830 (4)   4.40 .80
World Wildlife Fund.

A330

1991, Aug. 21 Litho. Perf. 14x13½
831 A330 70c multicolored   .70 .30
Bolivian Philatelic Federation, 20th anniv.

Presidential State Visit Type of 1989

Design: 50c, Jaime Paz Zamora, Pres. of Bolivia and Alberto Fujimori, Pres. of Peru.

1991, Aug. 29   Perf. 13½x14
832 A306b 50c multicolored   .45 .20

A331

1991, Nov. 19 Litho. Perf. 14x13½
833 A331 50c multicolored   .45 .20
National census.

America Issue — A332

UPAEP emblem and: 60c, First Discovery of Chuquiago, 1535, by Arturo Reque M. 1.20c, Founding of the City of La Paz, 1548, by J. Rimsa, vert.

1991, Oct. 12 Perf. 13½x14, 14x13½
834 A332 60c multicolored   .60 .25
835 A332 1.20b multicolored   1.10 .45

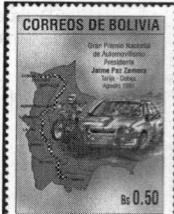
First National Grand Prix Auto and Motorcycle Race — A332a

1991, Sept. 5 Litho. Perf. 14x13½
835A A332a 50c multicolored   .45 .20

ECOBOL, Postal Security System — A333

1991, Sept. 9   Perf. 13½x14
836 A333 1.40b multicolored   1.40 .50

Simon Bolivar — A334

1992, Feb. 15   Litho.   Perf. 13½
837 A334 1.20b buff, brn & org brn   1.10 .45
Exfilbo '92.

Scouting in Bolivia, 75th Anniv. (in 1990) and 1992 Andes Jamboree A335

1992, Jan. 13   Perf. 13½x14
838 A335 1.20b multicolored   1.10 .45
Dated 1991.

Christmas A336

Paintings: 2b, Landscape, by Daniel Pena y Sarmiento. 5b, Woman with Fruit, by Cecilio Guzman de Rojas. 15b, Native Mother, by Crespo Gastelu.

1991, Dec.19   Litho.   Perf. 13½
839 A336 2b multicolored   1.50 .60
840 A336 5b multicolored   3.75 1.50
841 A336 15b multicolored   11.25 4.50
Nos. 839-841 (3)   16.50 6.60

Pacific Ocean Access Pact Between Bolivia and Peru A337

Designs: 1.20b, Pres. Zamora raising flag, vert. 1.50b, Pres. Jaime Paz Zamora of Bolivia and Pres. Alberto Fujimori, Peru. 1.80b, Shoreline of access zone near Ilo, Peru.

1992, Mar. 23 Perf. 14x13½, 13½x14
842 A337 1.20b multicolored   .95 .40
843 A337 1.50b multicolored   1.10 .50
844 A337 1.80b multicolored   1.40 .55
Nos. 842-844 (3)   3.45 1.45

Expo '92, Seville A338

1992, Apr. 15   Perf. 13½x14
845 A338 30c multicolored   .30 .20
846 A338 50c Columbus' ships   .45 .20

Miraflores Rotary Club, District 4690, Mt. Illimani A339

1992, Apr. 30 Litho. Perf. 13½
847 A339 90c multicolored   .70 .45

Prof. Elizardo Perez, Founder of Ayllu of Warisata School, Birth Cent. — A340

1992, June 6   Litho.   Perf. 13½
848 A340 60c multicolored   .50 .25

Government Palace, Sucre — A341

1992, July 10 Litho. Perf. 13½
849 A341 50c multicolored   .40 .20

A342

1992, Sept. 11   Perf. 14x13½
850 A342 50c multicolored   .40 .20
Los Tiempos Newpaper, 25th anniv.

A343

1992, Aug. 9   Perf. 13½
Mario Martinez Guzman, tennis player.
851 A343 1.50b multicolored   1.10 .50
1992 Summer Olympics, Barcelona.

First Intl. Whitewater Canoe Regatta, Bermejo River A343a

1992, Sept. 17 Litho. Perf. 13½
851A A343a 1.20b multicolored   1.10 .50

1994 World Cup Soccer Championships, US — A344

1992, Oct. 2   Litho.   Perf. 13½
852 A344 1.20b multicolored   1.90 .75

Oruro Technical University, Cent. — A345

1992, Oct. 15   Perf. 13½x14
853 A345 50c multicolored   .40 .20

Interamerican Institute for Agricultural Cooperation, 50th Anniv. — A346

1992, Oct. 7   Perf. 13½
854 A346 1.20b Chenopodium quinoa   1.10 .50

Discovery of America, 500th Anniv. A347

Paintings: 60c, Columbus departing from Palos, vert. 2b, Columbus with Caribbean natives.

1992, Oct. 1   Perf. 14x13½, 13½x14
855 A347 60c multicolored   .40 .20
856 A347 2b multicolored   1.40 .60

Battle of Ingavi, 150th Anniv. (in 1991) A348

1992, Nov. 18 Litho. Perf. 13½x14
857 A348 1.20b sepia & black   .95 .40

12th Bolivian Games, Cochabamba and Santa Cruz — A349

1992, Nov. 13
858 A349 2b multicolored   1.50   .60

Fauna, Events A350

Event emblem and fauna: 20c, Beni Dept., sesquicentennial. 50c, caiman. 50c, Polska '93, paca. 1b, Bangkok '93, chinchilla. 2b, 1994 Winter Olympics, Lillehammer, Norway, anteater. 3b, Brandenburg Gate, jaguar. 4b, Brasiliana '93, hummingbird, vert. 5b, 1994 World Cup Soccer Championships, US, piranhas.

1992, Nov. 18   Litho.   Perf. 13½
859 A350 20c multicolored   .20   .20
860 A350 50c multicolored   .35   .20
861 A350 1b multicolored   .75   .35
862 A350 2b multicolored   1.50   .60
863 A350 3b multicolored   2.25   .90
864 A350 4b multicolored   3.00   1.25
865 A350 5b multicolored   3.75   1.50
   Nos. 859-865 (7)   11.80   5.00

Christmas A350a

Designs: 1.20b, Man in canoe, star. 2.50b, Star over churches. 6b, Flowers, church, infant on hay.

1992, Dec. 1   Litho.   Perf. 13½
865A A350a 1.20b multicolored   .90   .35
865B A350a 2.50b multicolored   1.90   .75
865C A350a 6b multicolored   4.50   1.75
   Nos. 865A-865C (3)   7.30   2.85

A351

A352

Nicolaus Copernicus (1473-1543), Polish Astronomer: 50c, Santa Ana Intl. astrometrical observatory, Tarija, horiz.

Perf. 13x13½, 13½x13
1993, Feb. 18   Litho.
866 A351 50c multicolored   .40   .20
867 A351 2b black   1.50   .60

1993, Apr. 14   Litho.   Perf. 13½
868 A352 60c multicolored   .60   .25

Beatification of Mother Nazaria.

12th Bolivar Games A353

1993, Apr. 24   Perf. 13½x14
869 A353 2.30b multicolored   1.60   .65

Bolivia #C240, Brazil #3 A354

1993, May 31
870 A354 2.30b multicolored   1.60   .65

First Brazilian Stamp, 150th anniv.

A355

Eternal Father, by Gaspar de la Cueva.

1993, June 9   Litho.   Perf. 13½
871 A355 1.80b multicolored   1.25   .50

A356

1993, July 31   Litho.   Perf. 14x13½
872 A356 50c Virgin of Urkupina   .35   .20

City of Quillacollo, 400th anniv.

Pedro Domingo Murillo Industrial School A357

1993, Aug. 4   Perf. 13½
873 A357 60c multicolored   .40   .20

Butterflies A358

1993, June 4   Perf. 13½x14
874 A358 60c Archaeoprepona demophon   .55   .20
875 A358 60c Morpho sp.   .55   .20
876 A358 80c Papilio sp.   .70   .25
877 A358 80c Historis odius   .70   .25
878 A358 80c Euptoieta hegesia   .70   .25
879 A358 1.80b Morpho deidamia   1.75   .55
880 A358 1.80b Papilio thoas   1.75   .55
881 A358 1.80b Danaus plexippus   1.75   .55
882 A358 2.30b Caligo sp.   2.00   .60
883 A358 2.30b Anaea marthesia   2.00   .60
884 A358 2.30b Rothschildia sp.   2.00   .60
885 A358 2.70b Heliconius sp.   2.25   .75
886 A358 2.70b Marpesia corinna   2.25   .75
887 A358 2.70b Prepona chromus   2.25   .75
888 A358 3.50b Heliconius sp., diff.   3.00   .95
889 A358 3.50b Siproeta epaphus   3.00   .95
   a.   Sheet of 16, #874-889   30.00   30.00
   Nos. 874-889 (16)   27.20   8.75

Pan-American Health Organization, 90th Anniv. — A359

1993, Oct. 13   Litho.   Perf. 13½
890 A359 80c multicolored   .55   .20

Archaeological Finds — A360

Location of cave paintings: No. 891, Oruro. No. 892, Santa Cruz, vert. No. 893, Beni, vert. No. 894, Chuquisaca, vert. No. 895, Chuquisaca. No. 896, Potosi. No. 897, La Paz, vert. No. 898, Tarija, vert. No. 899, Cochabamba.

1993, Sept. 28
891 A360 80c multicolored   .55   .20
892 A360 80c multicolored   .55   .20
893 A360 80c multicolored   .55   .20
894 A360 80c multicolored   .55   .20
895 A360 80c multicolored   .55   .20
896 A360 80c multicolored   .55   .20
897 A360 80c multicolored   .55   .20
898 A360 80c multicolored   .55   .20
899 A360 80c multicolored   .55   .20
   Nos. 891-899 (9)   4.95   1.80

America Issue — A361

1993, Oct. 9   Litho.   Perf. 13½
900 A361 80c Saimiri sciereus   .55   .20
901 A361 2.30b Felis pordalis   1.50   .60

Famous People — A361a

Designs: 50c, Yolanda Bedregal, poet. 70c, Simon Martinic, President of Cochabamba Philatelic Center. 90c, Eugenio von Boeck, politician, President of Bolivian Philatelic Federation. 1b, Marina Nunez del Prado, sculptor.

1993, Nov. 17   Litho.   Perf. 11
901A A361a 50c sepia   .30   .20
901B A361a 70c sepia   .45   .20
901C A361a 90c sepia   .55   .25
901D A361a 1b sepia   .60   .25
   Nos. 901A-901D (4)   1.90   .90

Christmas A361b

1993, Dec. 8   Perf. 14x13½
Paintings: 2.30b, Adoration of the Shepherds, by Leonardo Flores. 3.50b, Virgin with

Child and Saints, by unknown artist. 6b, Virgin of the Milk, by Melchor Perez de Holguin.
901E A361b 2.30b multicolored   1.40   .55
901F A361b 3.50b multicolored   2.25   .85
901G A361b 6b multicolored   3.75   1.50
   Nos. 901E-901G (3)   7.40   2.90

Town of Riberalta, Cent. — A362

1994, Feb. 3   Litho.   Perf. 13½
902 A362 2b multicolored   1.25   .60

World Population Day — A363

1994, Feb. 17   Litho.   Perf. 13½
903 A363 2.30b multicolored   1.50   .60

A364

1994, Feb. 21   Perf. 13½
904 A364 2b buff & multi   1.25   .60
905 A364 2.30b multi   1.50   .60

Inauguration of Pres. Gonzalo Sanchez de Lozada.

A365

1994, Mar. 22
1994 World Cup Soccer Championships, US: 80c, Mascot. 1.80b, Bolivia, Uruguay. 2.30b, Bolivia, Venezuela. No. 909, Part of Bolivian team, goalies in black. No. 910, Part of Bolivian team, diff. 2.70b, Bolivia, Ecuador. 3.50b, Bolivia, Brazil.
906 A365 80c multicolored   .50   .20
907 A365 1.80b multicolored   1.10   .45
908 A365 2.30b multicolored   1.40   .55
909 A365 2.50b multicolored   1.50   .60
910 A365 2.50b multicolored   1.50   .60
   a.   Pair, #909-910   3.00   1.25
911 A365 2.70b multicolored   1.60   .65
912 A365 3.50b multicolored   2.25   .85
   Nos. 906-912 (7)   9.85   3.90

SOS Children's Village, Bolivia — A366

1994, Apr. 12   Litho.   Perf. 13½
913 A366 2.70b multicolored   1.60   .65

Catholic Archdiocese La Paz, 50th
Anniv. — A367

Churches, priests: 1.80b, Church of San
Pedro, Msgr. Jorge Manrique Hurtado. 2b,
Archbishop Abel I. Antezana y Rojas, Church
of the Sacred Heart of Mary, vert. 3.50b, Msgr.
Luis Sainz Hinojosa, Church of Santo Domingo, vert.

1994, July 12   Litho.   Perf. 13½
914 A367 1.80b multicolored   1.10   .45
915 A367   2b multicolored   1.25   .60
916 A367 3.50b multicolored   2.25   .85
      Nos. 914-916 (3)   4.60   1.90

A368

Design: 2b, Pres. Victor Paz Estenssoro.

1994, Oct. 2   Litho.   Perf. 13½
917 A368 2b multicolored   1.25   .50

A369

1994, Oct. 9
918 A369 1.80b No. 46   1.10   .45

Battle of Ft.
Boqueron
A370

Col. Manuel Marzana Oroza, battle scene.

1994, Oct. 6
919 A370 80c multicolored   .50   .20

San Borja,
300th Anniv.
A371

1994, Oct. 14
920 A371 1.60b Erythrina fusca   1.00   .40

America
Issue — A372

Old, new methods of postal transport: 1b,
Streetcar, van. 5b, Airplane, ox cart.

1994, Oct. 12
921 A372 1b multicolored   .65   .25
922 A372 5b multicolored   3.25   1.25

1994 Solar
Eclipse — A373

1994 Oct. 21
923 A373 3.50b multicolored   2.25   .85

Environmental
Protection — A374

1994, Sept. 21
   Trees: 60c, Buddleja coriacea. 1.80b,
Bertholletia exelsa. 2b, Schinus molle, horiz.
2.70b, Polylepis racemosa. 3, Tabebuia
chrysantha. 3.50b, Erythrina falcata, horiz.

924 A374   60c multicolored   .40   .20
925 A374 1.80b multicolored   1.10   .45
926 A374   2b multicolored   1.25   .50
927 A374 2.70b multicolored   1.60   .65
928 A374   3b multicolored   1.90   .75
929 A374 3.50b multicolored   2.25   .85
      Nos. 924-929 (6)   8.50   3.40

Gen. Antonio
Jose de Sucre
(1795-1830)
A375

1995, Jan. 25   Litho.   Perf. 13½
930 A375 1.80b shown   .75   .30
931 A375 3.50b diff. background   1.50   .60

A377

1994, Nov. 25   Litho.   Perf. 13½
933 A377   2b Tarija girl   1.10   .45
934 A377   5b High plateau
              child   2.75   .45
935 A377 20b Eastern girl   11.00   3.75
      Nos. 933-935 (3)   14.85   4.65
                 Christmas.

A378

1994, Nov. 28   Litho.   Perf. 13½
936 A378 1.80b multicolored   .90   .35
Pan-American   Scout   Jamboree,
Cochabamba

Cathedral of
St.
Anne — A379

1995, Apr. 21   Litho.   Perf. 13½
937 A379 1.90b black & multi   1.25   .60
938 A379 2.90b blue & multi   1.75   .90
      Yacuma-Beni Province, cent.

Franciscans at Copacabana Natl.
Sanctuary, Cent. — A380

1995, May 2
939 A380 60c gray & multi   .40   .20
940 A380 80c bister & multi   .55   .20

A381

1995   Litho.   Perf. 13½
941 A381 2b multicolored   1.00   .40
   Peace Between Bolivia and Paraguay.
Dated 1994.

A382

1995, July 25
942 A382 2.40b multicolored   1.25   .50
   Andes Development Corporation (CAF),
25th anniv.

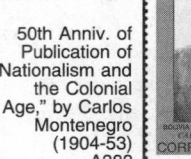

50th Anniv. of
Publication of
"Nationalism and
the Colonial
Age," by Carlos
Montenegro
(1904-53)
A383

1995, Aug. 8
943 A383 1.20b pink & black   .60   .25

A384

1995, Sept. 26
944 A384 1b multicolored   .50   .20
      FAO, 50th anniv.

A385

1995, Oct. 24   Perf. 14½
945 A385 2.90b multicolored   1.50   .60
      UN, 50th anniv.

America
Issue
A386

1995, Nov. 21   Perf. 14
946 A386 5b Condor   2.50   1.00
947 A386 5b Llamas   2.50   1.00
   a.   Pair, #946-947   5.00   2.00

ICAO, 50th
Anniv. — A387

1995, Dec. 4   Perf. 13½x13
948 A387 50c multicolored   .25   .20

Temple of Samaipata — A388

   Archaeological finds and: a, 1.90b, Top of
ruins. b, 1b, Top of ruins, diff. c, 2.40b, Lower
excavation. d, 2b, Floor, tiers.

1995, Dec. 4   Perf. 13x13½
949 A388 Block of 4, #a.-d.   3.75   1.50
   No. 949 is a continuous design.

Taquiña Brewery, Cent. — A389

1995, Dec. 8   *Perf. 14*
950 A389 1b multicolored   .50   .20

Christmas A390

Paintings: 1.20b, The Annunciation, by Cima da Conegliano. 3b, The Nativity, by Hans Baldung. 3.50b, Adoration of the Magi, by Rogier van der Weyden.

1995, Dec. 15   *Perf. 14x13½*
951 A390 1.20b multicolored   .60   .25
952 A390 3b multicolored   1.50   .60
953 A390 3.50b multicolored   1.75   .70
   Nos. 951-953 (3)   3.85   1.55

Natl. Anthem, 150th Anniv. — A391

Designs: 1b, J.I. de Sanjines, lyricist. 2b, B. Vincenti, composer.

1995, Dec. 18   *Litho.*   *Perf. 13½*
954 A391 1b multicolored   .40   .20
955 A391 2b multicolored   .80   .30
  a.   Pair, #954-955   1.20   .45

Decree to Abolish Abuse of Indian Labor, 50th Anniv. — A392

Designs: 1.90b, Modern representations of industry, Gov. Gualberto Villarroel. 2.90, Addressing labor policies, silhouettes of people rejoicing.

1996, Jan. 26   *Perf. 14*
956 A392 1.90b multicolored   .75   .30
957 A392 2.90b multicolored   1.10   .45
  a.   Pair, #956-957   1.90   .75

Nos. 639, 653, 685-686, 712-713, 715, 719, 726, 729, 732-733, C332, C348 Surcharged

Perfs. and Printing Methods as Before

1996
958 A273 50c on 3,000,000b #729   .20   .20
959 A265 60c on 2000b #713   .25   .20
960 A277 60c on 1,400,000b #733   .25   .20
961 A271 1b on 2,500,000b #726   .40   .20
962 A264 1.50b on 11,000b #712   .60   .25
963 A267 2.50b on 23,000b #715   1.00   .40
964 A269 3b on 1,000,000b #719   1.10   .45
965 A222 3.50b on 6.50b #639   1.40   .55
966 A234 3.50b on 9b #653   1.40   .55
967 A276 3.50b on 2,000,000b #732   1.40   .55
968 AP67 3.80b on 3.80b #C332   1.50   .60
969 A189 20b on 3.80b #C348   8.00   3.25
970 A253 20b on 10b #685   8.00   3.25
971 A254 20b on 10b #686   8.00   3.25
   Nos. 958-971 (14)   33.50   13.90
Size and location of surcharge varies.

No. 627 Surcharged

1996   *Litho.*   *Perf. 10½*
972 A216 60c on 2.50b multi   .40   .20
See No. 697 for similar surcharge.

10th Summit of the Chiefs of State and Government(Rio Group), Cochabamba A393

Designs: 2.50b, Stylized person. 3.50b, Stylized globe surrounded by lines.

1996, Sept. 4   *Perf. 14*
973 A393 2.50b multicolored   1.00   .40
974 A393 3.50b multicolored   1.40   .55

Anniversaries A394

50c, Natl. Bank of Bolivia, 125th anniv. 1b, Jose Joaquin de Lemoine (1776-1851), first postal administrator, vert.

1996, Dec. 8   *Litho.*   *Perf. 13½*
975 A394 50c multicolored   .20   .20
976 A394 1b multicolored   .40   .20

Summit of the Americas to Sustain Development A395

1996, Dec. 8   *Perf. 14x13½*
977 A395 2.50b brown & multi   .95   .40
978 A395 5b black & multi   1.90   .75

CARE in Bolivia, 20th Anniv. — A396

1996, Dec. 19   *Perf. 13½*
979 A396 60c Family, horiz.   .25   .20
980 A396 70c shown   .25   .20

Natl. Symphony Orchestra, 50th Anniv. — A397

1996, Dec. 24
981 A397 1.50b shown   .60   .25
982 A397 2b String instruments   .75   .30
  a.   Pair, #981-982   1.40   .55
No. 982a is a continuous design.

Tourism in Oruro A398

Designs: 50c, Miners' Monument, vert. 60c, Folklore costume, vert. 1b, Virgin of Socavon, vert. 1.50b, Sajama mountains. 2.50b, Chipaya child, building, vert. 3b, Raul Shaw, "Moreno."

1997, Feb. 3   *Litho.*   *Perf. 14½*
983 A398 50c multicolored   .20   .20
984 A398 60c multicolored   .25   .20
985 A398 1b multicolored   .40   .20
986 A398 1.50b multicolored   .60   .25
987 A398 2.50b multicolored   .95   .40
988 A398 3b multicolored   1.10   .45
   Nos. 983-988 (6)   3.50   1.70
Dated 1996.

Tourism in Chuquisaca — A399

Designs: 60c, La Glorieta. 1b, Governor's Palace, vert. No. 991, Dinosaur tracks. No. 992, House of Liberty. 2b, Tarabaqueno, vert. 3b, Statue of Juana Azurduy of Padilla, vert.

1997, Jan. 30   *Perf. 13½x14, 14x13½*
989 A399 60c multicolored   .25   .20
990 A399 1b multicolored   .40   .20
991 A399 1.50b multicolored   .60   .25
992 A399 1.50b multicolored   .60   .25
993 A399 2b multicolored   .75   .30
994 A399 3b multicolored   1.10   .45
   Nos. 989-994 (6)   3.70   1.65
Dated 1996.

Tourism in Tarija A400

Designs: 50c, House of Culture, Dorada, vert. 60c, Church of Entre Rios, vert. 80c, San Luis Falls. 1b, Monument to the Chaco War. 3b, Temple, Statue of the Virgin Mary, Chaguay. 20b, Eustaquio Mendez house, monument.

1997, Jan. 24   *Perf. 14x13½, 13½x14*
995 A400 50c multicolored   .20   .20
996 A400 60c multicolored   .25   .20
997 A400 80c multicolored   .30   .20
998 A400 1b multicolored   .40   .20
999 A400 3b multicolored   1.10   .45
1000 A400 20b multicolored   7.75   3.00
   Nos. 995-1000 (6)   10.00   4.25
Dated 1996.

Visit of French Pres. Jacques Chirac A401

Design: Bolivian Pres. Gonzalo Sanchez de Lozada, Chirac.

1997, Mar. 15   *Perf. 14*
1001 A401 4b multicolored   1.50   .60

Salesian Order in Bolivia, Cent. — A402

Designs: 1.50b, St. John Bosco (1815-88), church. 2b, Statue of St. John Bosco talking with boy, church.

1997, Apr. 29   *Litho.*   *Perf. 13½*
1002 A402 1.50b multicolored   .60   .25
1003 A402 2b multicolored   .75   .30

UNICEF, 50th Anniv. A403

Children's drawings: 50c, Houses, children on playground. 90c, Child running, cactus, rock, lake. 1b, Boys, girls arm in arm across globe. 2.50b, Girl on swing, others in background.

1997
1004 A403 50c multicolored   .20   .20
1005 A403 90c multicolored   .35   .20
1006 A403 1b multicolored   .40   .20
1007 A403 2.50b multicolored   .95   .40
   Nos. 1004-1007 (4)   1.90   1.00

Department of La Paz — A404

Tourism: 50c, Mt. Chulumani, Las Yungas, vert. 80c, Inca monolith, vert. 1.50b, City, Mt. Illimani, vert. 2b, Gate of the Sun, Tiwanacu. 2.50b, Traditional dancers, vert. 10b, Virgin of Copacabana, reed boat.

1997, May 28   *Litho.*   *Perf. 13½*
1008 A404 50c multicolored   .20   .20
1009 A404 80c multicolored   .30   .20
1010 A404 1.50b multicolored   .60   .25
1011 A404 2b multicolored   .75   .30
1012 A404 2.50b multicolored   .95   .40
1013 A404 10b multicolored   3.75   1.50
   Nos. 1008-1013 (6)   6.55   2.85

1997 America Cup Soccer Championships, Bolivia — A405

1998 World Cup Soccer Championships, France — A406

1997, June 13
1014 A405 3b multicolored 1.25 .50
1015 A406 5b multicolored 1.90 .75

National Congress A407

1997, July 8 Litho. **Perf. 13½**
1016 A407 1b multicolored .40 .20

America Issue — A408

Women in traditional costumes: 5b, From valley region. 15b, From eastern Bolivia.

1997, July 14 Litho. **Perf. 13½**
1017 A408 5b multicolored 1.90 .75
1018 A408 15b multicolored 5.75 2.25

Mercosur (Common Market of Latin America) A409

1997, Sept. 26
1019 A409 3b multicolored 1.10 .45

See Argentina #1975, Brazil #2646, Paraguay #2565, Uruguay #1681.

Christmas A410

Paintings: 2b, Virgin del Cerro, by unknown artist. 5b, Virgin de la Leche, by unknown artist. 10b, The Holy Family, by Melchor Pérez de Holguin.

1997, Dec. 19 Litho. **Perf. 13½**
1020 A410 2b multicolored .75 .30
1021 A410 5b multicolored 1.75 .75
1022 A410 10b multicolored 3.50 1.50
Nos. 1020-1022 (3) 6.00 2.55

Diana, Princess of Wales (1961-97) A411

1997, Dec. 29
1023 A411 2b Portrait, vert. 1.25 .50
1024 A411 3b In mine field 1.75 .75

Visit of Prime Minister of Spain A412

Hugo Banzer Suarez, Pres. of Bolivia and José Maria Aznar.

1998, Mar. 16
1025 A412 6b multicolored 3.25 1.25

Bolivian Society of Engineers, 75th Anniv. A413

1998, Apr. 28
1026 A413 3.50b multicolored 1.25 .55

A414 A415

1998, Apr. 30 Litho. **Perf. 13½**
1027 A414 5b multicolored 1.75 .75
Rotary Intl. in Bolivia, 70th anniv.

1998, July 9

Letter Carriers, 1942: 3b, Postman delivering mail to woman, vert.
1028 A415 3b multicolored 1.10 .45
1029 A415 4b multicolored 1.40 .60
America Issue.

Famous Men — A416

1.50b, Werner Guttentag Tichauer, bibliographer. 2b, Dr. Martin Cardenas Hermosa, botanist. 3.50b, Adrian Patiño Carpio, composer.

1998, July 10
1030 A416 1.50b brown .55 .20
1031 A416 2b green, vert. .70 .30
1032 A416 3.50b black, vert 1.25 .50
Nos. 1030-1032 (3) 2.50 1.00

Regions in Bolivia A417

Beni: 50c, Victoria regia. 1b, Callandria. 1.50b, White Tajibo tree, vert. 3.50b, Amazon mask. 5b, Nutrea. 7b, Tropical condor.

1998, Oct. 11 Litho. **Perf. 13½**
1033 A417 50c black & multi .20 .20
1034 A417 1b black & multi .35 .20
1035 A417 1.50b black & multi .55 .25
1036 A417 3.50b black & multi 1.25 .55
1037 A417 5b black & multi 1.75 .80
1038 A417 7b black & multi 2.50 1.10
Nos. 1033-1038 (6) 6.60 3.10

Pando: 50c, Acre River. 1b, Sloth climbing bamboo tree, vert. 1.50b, Bahia Arroyo, vert. 4b, Boa. 5b, Family of capybaras. 7b, Houses, palm trees, vert.

1039 A417 50c green & multi .20 .20
1040 A417 1b green & multi .35 .20
1041 A417 1.50b green & multi .55 .25
1042 A417 4b green & multi 1.40 .65
1043 A417 5b green & multi 1.75 .80
1044 A417 7b green & multi 2.50 1.10
Nos. 1039-1044 (6) 6.75 3.20
Nos. 1033-1044 (12) 13.35 6.30

Women of Bolivia — A418

First Lady Yolanda Prada de Banzer and: 1.50b, Women working in fields, making pottery, weaving. 2b, Women working on computer, standing at blackboard.

1998, Oct. 11
1045 A418 1.50b multicolored .55 .25
1046 A418 2b multicolored .70 .30
a. Pair, #1045-1046 1.25 .55
America Issue.

City of La Paz, 450th Anniv. A419

1998, Oct. 14
1047 A419 2b Plaza de Laja Church .70 .30

A420 A422

A421

1998, Nov. 6 Litho. **Perf. 13½x13¾**
1048 A420 3.50b blue & yellow 1.25 .60
Organization of American States, 50th anniv.

1998, Nov. 12 **Perf. 13¼x13½**
1049 A421 2b multicolored .70 .35
Bolivian Philatelic Federation, 25th anniv., Espamer '98, Buenos Aires.

Perf. 13¼x13½, 13½x13¼
1998, Nov. 26

Christmas: 2b, Child's drawing of church. 6b, Pope John Paul II. 7b, John Paul II, Mother Teresa.

1050 A422 2b multi, horiz. .70 .35
1051 A422 6b multi 2.00 .95
1052 A422 7b multi 2.40 1.15
Nos. 1050-1052 (3) 5.10 2.55

UPU, 125th Anniv. A423

1999, Jan. 26 Litho. **Perf. 13½**
1053 A423 3.50b multicolored 1.25 .60

AFC Soccer Club, 75th Anniv. — A424

1999, Apr. 22 Litho. **Perf. 13½**
1054 A424 5b multicolored 4.25 2.25

Geneva Convention and Bolivian Red Cross, 50th Anniv. A425

1999, May 18
1055 A425 5b multicolored 1.90 .95

Bernardo Guarachi, First Bolivian to Reach Summit of Mt. Everest A426

1999, May 25
1056 A426 6b multicolored 2.25 1.10

Special Olympics of Bolivia, 30th Anniv. — A427

Designs: 2b, Medalists on podium. 2.50b, Winners of swimming event, running event.

1999
1057 A427 2b multicolored .75 .35
1058 A427 2.50b multicolored .90 .45

Japanese Immigration to Bolivia, Cent. — A428

Designs: 3b, Golden Pavilion, Kyoto. 6b, Sun setting across water, vert.

1999, June 3
1059 A428 3b multicolored 1.10 .55
1060 A428 6b multicolored 2.25 1.10

Bolivian Cinema, 100th Anniv. A429

1999		Litho.		Perf. 13½	
1061	A429	50c	Hacia la Gloria, 1932-33	.20	.20
1062	A429	50c	Jonas y la Ballena Rosada, 1995	.20	.20
1063	A429	1b	Wara Wara, 1929	.35	.20
1064	A429	1b	Vuelve Sebastiana, 1953	.35	.20
1065	A429	3b	La Campana del Chaco, 1933	.65	.30
1066	A429	3b	La Vertiente, 1958	.65	.30
1067	A429	6b	Yawar Mallku, 1969	2.00	.95
1068	A429	6b	Mi Socio, 1982	2.00	.95
a.		Sheet of 8, #1061-1068		6.50	3.25
		Nos. 1061-1068 (8)		6.40	3.30

SOS Children's Village, 50th Anniv. — A430

1999, July 8
1069 A430 3.50b multicolored   1.25   .60

Intl. Day Against Illegal Drugs A431

Perf. 13¼x13½
1999, June 26   Litho.
1070 A431 3.50b multicolored   1.25   .60

Completion of Bolivian-Brazilian Gas Pipeline — A432

Designs: 3b, Presidents of Bolivia and Brazil, map of pipeline. 6b, Presidents, gas flame.

1999, July 1   Litho.   Perf. 13½
1071 A432 3b multicolored   1.00   .50
1072 A432 6b multicolored   2.00   .95

La Paz Lions Club, 50th Anniv. — A433

1999   Perf. 13½x13¼
1073 A433 3.50b multicolored   1.25   .60

Cochabamba Tourism — A434

50c, Mt. Tunari. 1b, Cochabamba Valley. 2b, Container from Omerque culture, idol from Pachamama culture. 3b, Totora. 5b, Composer Teofilo Vargas Candia. 6b, Statue of Jesus Christ.

1999		Perf. 13½x13¾, 13¾x13½			
1074	A434	50c	multi	.20	.20
1075	A434	1b	multi	.35	.20
1076	A434	2b	multi, vert.	.70	.35
1077	A434	3b	multi	1.10	.55
1078	A434	5b	multi, vert.	1.75	.85
1079	A434	6b	multi, vert.	2.10	1.00
		Nos. 1074-1079 (6)		6.20	3.15

Potosí Tourism A435

50c, Tarapaya Lake. 1b, Obverse and reverse of 1827 Bolivian coin. 2b, Mt. Chorolque. 3b, Lake, llama, birds. 5b, "Mestizo Woman with a Cigaretee Case," by Teofilo Loaiza. 6b, Alfredo Dominguez Romero, musician.

1999		Perf. 13¾x13½, 13½x13¾			Litho.
1080	A435	50c	multi, vert.	.20	.20
1081	A435	1b	multi	.35	.20
1082	A435	2b	multi	.70	.35
1083	A435	3b	multi	1.10	.55
1084	A435	5b	multi	1.75	.90
1085	A435	6b	multi, vert.	2.25	1.10
		Nos. 1080-1085 (6)		6.35	3.30

America Issue, A New Millennium Without Arms — A436

1999   Perf. 13½x13¼
1086 A436 3.50b shown   1.25   .60
1087 A436 3.50b Globe, flower   1.25   .60

Christmas A437

2b, Children, Christmas tree. 6b, The Birth of Jesus, by Gaspar Miguel de Berrios. 7b, Our Families of the World, by Omar Medina.

1999		Perf. 13¼x13½, 13½x13¼			
1088	A437	2b	multi	.70	.35
1089	A437	6b	multi, vert.	2.10	1.00
1090	A437	7b	multi, vert.	2.40	1.25
		Nos. 1088-1090 (3)		5.20	2.60

Discovery of Brazil, 500th Anniv. A438

2000   Litho.   Perf. 13½x13¾
1091 A438 5b multi   1.60   .80

2000 Doble Copacabana Bicycle Race — A439

Various views of racers.

2000					
1092	A439	1b	multi	.35	.20
1093	A439	3b	multi	1.00	.50
1094	A439	5b	multi	1.60	.80
1095	A439	7b	multi	2.40	1.25
		Nos. 1092-1095 (4)		5.35	2.75

Sgt. Maximiliano Paredes Military School, Cent. — A440

2000   Litho.   Perf. 13½x13¾
1096 A440 2.50b multi   .80   .40

Federal Republic of Germany, 50th Anniv. (in 1999) A441

2000
1097 A441 6b multi   2.00   1.00

Paintings of Cecilio Guzmán de Rojas (1900-51) — A442

Designs: 1b, Self-portrait, vert. 2.50b, Triunfo de la Naturaleza. 5b, Andina, vert. 6b, Riña de Estudiantes.

2000   Perf. 13¾x13½, 13½x13¾
1098-1101 A442 Set of 4   4.75   2.40

Artifacts from Natl. Archaeological Museum — A443

Artifacts from: #1102, 50c, Pando. #1103, 50c, Potosí. 70c, Beni. 90c, Tarija. #1106, 1b, Chuquisaca. #1107, 1b, Oruro. 3b, Cochabamba. 5b, Santa Cruz. 20b, La Paz.

2000   Perf. 11¼x11
1102-1110 A443 Set of 9   11.00   5.50

America Issue, Fight Against AIDS — A444

Designs: No. 1111, 3.50b, Symbols for male and female in whirlwind. No. 1112, 3.50b, Man, woman, clouds, brick wall.

2000   Perf. 13¼x13½
1111-1112 A444 Set of 2   2.25   1.10

Victor Agustin Ugarte, Soccer Player — A445

2000, Apr. 24 Litho. Perf. 13½x13¼
1113 A445 3b multi   1.00   .50

Santa Cruz Tourism A446

Designs: 50c, Fountains, Parque el Arenal. 1b, Ox cart. 2b, Writers Raúl Otero Reiche, Gabriel René Moreno, Hernando Sanabria Fernández. 3b, Virgin of Cotoca. 5b, Anthropomorphic vessel, vert. 6b, Speothos venaticus.

Perf. 13½x13¾, 13¾x13½
2000, Apr. 28
1114-1119 A446 Set of 6   6.25   3.25

Millennium — A448

2000   Litho.   Perf. 13½x13¼
1121 A448 5b multi   1.60   .80

Sovereign Military Order of Malta, 900th Anniv. — A449

2000   Perf. 13¾x13½
1122 A449 6b multi   2.00   1.00

Christmas — A450

Angels from Calamarca Church: 3b, Gabriel. 5b, Angel of Virtue. 10b, Angel with spike of grain.

2000
1123-1125 A450 Set of 3   5.75   3.00

Holy Year 2000 — A451

Holy Year emblem and: 4b, Basilica de San Francisco, La Paz. 6b, Wheat stalks, barbed wire.

2000   **Litho.**   **Perf. 13½x13¼**
1126-1127 A451   Set of 2   3.50   1.75

Promotion of Philately A452

National Symbols A453

Designs: 50c, Man carrying first day covers up stairs. 1b, Child, six stamps. 1.50b, Stamp collector. 2b, Child, three stamps. 2.50b, Envelope in bin. 10b, Patuju bandera, current national flower. 20b, La kantuta, previous national flower. 30b, Coat of arms, 1825. 50b, Coat of arms, 1826. 100b, Coat of arms, 1851.

2001   **Litho.**   **Perf. 10½**

1128	A452	50c green	.20	.20
1129	A452	1b green	.30	.20
1130	A452	1.50b green	.50	.25
1131	A452	2b green	.65	.30
1132	A452	2.50b green	.80	.40

Perf. 13¾x13½

1133	A453	10b multi	3.25	1.60
1134	A453	20b multi	6.50	3.25
1135	A453	30b multi	9.75	5.00
1136	A453	50b multi	16.00	8.00
1137	A453	100b multi	32.50	16.00
		Nos. 1128-1137 (10)	70.45	35.20

Issued: 50c, 1b, 1.50b, 2b, 2.50b, 6/12; 10b, 6/29; 20b, 6/8; 30b, 5/16; 50b, 3/16; 100b, 4/16.

Bolivia - European Union Cooperation, 25th Anniv. — A454

2001, May 8   **Litho.**   **Perf. 13½x13¾**
1138 A454 6b multi   2.00   1.00

Law and Political Science Faculty of San Andres University, 171st Anniv. — A455

2001, May 18   **Perf. 13¾x13½**
1139 A455 6b multi   2.00   1.00

Muela del Diablo A457

2001, July 6 Litho.   **Perf. 13½x13¾**
1141 A457 1.50b multi   .50   .25

2001 Census — A458

2001   **Perf. 11**

1142		Horiz. strip of 5	3.00 1.50
a.	A458	1b purple & multi	.30 .20
b.	A458	1.50b red & multi	.50 .25
c.	A458	1.50b green & multi	.50 .25
d.	A458	2.50b blue & multi	.80 .40
e.	A458	3b violet & multi	.90 .45

AIR POST STAMPS

Aviation School
AP1   AP2

1924, Dec. Unwmk. Engr. Perf. 14

C1	AP1	10c ver & blk	.25	.30
a.		Inverted center	800.00	
C2	AP1	15c carmine & blk	1.50	.50
C3	AP1	25c dk bl & blk	.60	.60
C4	AP1	50c orange & blk	1.50	1.25
C5	AP2	1b red brn & blk	.90	.95
C6	AP2	2b blk brn & blk	1.75	1.75
C7	AP2	5b dk vio & blk	5.50	5.50
		Nos. C1-C7 (7)	12.00	10.85

Natl. Aviation School establishment. These stamps were available for ordinary postage. Nos. C1, C3, C5 and C6 exist imperforate. Proofs of the 2b with inverted center exist imperforate and privately perforated.

For overprints and surcharges see Nos. C11-C23, C56-C58.

Emblem of Lloyd Aéreo Boliviano AP3

1928   **Litho.**   **Perf. 11**

C8	AP3	15c green	1.00	1.00
a.		Imperf., pair	50.00	
C9	AP3	20c dark blue	.25	.25
C10	AP3	35c red brown	.60	.60
		Nos. C8-C10 (3)	1.85	1.85

No. C8 exists imperf. between.
For surcharges see #C24-C26, C53-C55.

Graf Zeppelin Issues
Nos. C1-C5 Surcharged or Overprinted in Various Colors:

Nos. C11, C19

Nos. C12-C18, C20-C23

1930, May 6   **Perf. 14**

C11	AP1	5c on 10c ver & blk (G)	9.50	9.50
C12	AP1	10c ver & blk (Bl)	9.50	9.50
C13	AP1	10c ver & blk (Br)	600.00	875.00
C14	AP1	15c car & blk (V)	9.50	9.50
C15	AP1	25c dk bl & blk (R)	9.50	9.50
C16	AP1	50c org & blk (Br)	9.50	9.50
C17	AP1	50c org & blk (R)	475.00	600.00
C18	AP2	1b red brn & blk (gold)	150.00	150.00

Experts consider the 50c with gold or silver overprint and 5c with black to be trial color proofs.

Nos. C11-C18 exist with the surcharges inverted, double, or double with one inverted, but the regularity of these varieties is questioned.

See notes following No. C23.

Surcharged or Overprinted in Bronze Inks of Various Colors

C19	AP1	5c on 10c ver & blk (G)	77.50	80.00
C20	AP1	10c ver & blk (Bl)	67.50	67.50
C21	AP1	15c car & blk (V)	77.50	80.00

C22	AP1	25c dk bl & blk (cop)	77.50	80.00
C23	AP2	1b red brn & blk (gold)	190.00	200.00
		Nos. C19-C23 (5)	490.00	507.50

Flight of the airship Graf Zeppelin from Europe to Brazil and return via Lakehurst, NJ. Nos. C19 to C23 were intended for use on postal matter forwarded by the Graf Zeppelin. No. C18 was overprinted with light gold or gilt bronze ink. No. C23 was overprinted with deep gold bronze ink. Nos. C13 and C17 were overprinted with trial colors but were sold with the regular printings. The 5c on 10c is known surcharged in black and in blue.

No. C8-C10 Surcharged

1930, May 6   **Perf. 11**

C24	AP3	1.50b on 15c	25.00	25.00
a.		Inverted surcharge	57.50	57.50
b.		Comma instead of period after "1"	35.00	35.00
C25	AP3	3b on 20c	25.00	25.00
a.		Inverted surcharge	62.50	62.50
b.		Comma instead of period after "3"	40.00	40.00
C26	AP3	'6b on 35c	37.50	40.00
a.		Inverted surcharge	110.00	110.00
b.		Comma instead of period after "6"	62.50	62.50
		Nos. C24-C26 (3)	87.50	90.00

Airplane and Bullock Cart — AP6

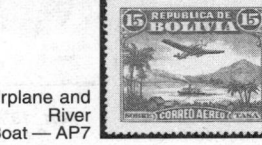

Airplane and River Boat — AP7

1930, July 24   **Litho.**   **Perf. 14**

C27	AP6	5c dp violet	1.25	1.00
C28	AP7	15c red	1.25	1.00
C29	AP7	20c yellow	.50	.45
C30	AP6	35c yellow grn	.40	.25
C31	AP7	50c deep blue	.40	.25
C32	AP6	1b lt brown	.40	.25
C33	AP7	2b deep rose	.40	.40
C34	AP6	3b slate	1.40	1.40
		Nos. C27-C34 (8)	6.00	5.00

Nos. C27 to C34 exist imperforate.
For surcharge see No. C52.

Air Service Emblem AP8

1932, Sept. 16   **Perf. 11**

C35	AP8	5c ultra	.70	.55
C36	AP8	10c gray	.45	.35
C37	AP8	15c dark rose	.70	.55
C38	AP8	25c orange	.70	.55
C39	AP8	30c green	.60	.30
C40	AP8	50c violet	.60	.35
C41	AP8	1b dk brown	.60	.35
		Nos. C35-C41 (7)	4.35	3.00

Map of Bolivia — AP9

1935, Feb. 1   **Engr.**   **Perf. 12**

C42	AP9	5c brown red	.20	.20
C43	AP9	10c dk green	.20	.20
C44	AP9	20c dk violet	.20	.20
C45	AP9	30c ultra	.25	.20
C46	AP9	50c orange	.30	.20
C47	AP9	1b bister brn	.30	.25

C48	AP9	1½b yellow	.60	.20
C49	AP9	2b carmine	.60	.30
C50	AP9	5b green	1.10	.40
C51	AP9	10b dk brown	1.75	.75
		Nos. C42-C51 (10)	5.50	2.90

Nos. C1, C4, C10, C30 Surcharged in Red (#C52-C56) or Green (#C57-C58)

c

1937, Oct. 6   **Perf. 11, 14**

C52	AP6	5c on 35c yel grn	.40	.30
a.		"Carreo"	12.50	
b.		Inverted surcharge		
C53	AP3	20c on 35c red brn	.50	.40
a.		Inverted surcharge	17.50	
C54	AP3	50c on 35c red brn	1.50	1.25
a.		Inverted surcharge	17.50	
C55	AP3	1b on 35c red brn	1.10	.65
a.		Inverted surcharge		
C56	AP1	2b on 50c org & blk	1.60	1.00
a.		Inverted surcharge		
C57	AP1	12b on 10c ver & blk	5.75	4.75
a.		Inverted surcharge	22.50	
C58	AP1	15b on 10c ver & blk	5.75	2.75
a.		Inverted surcharge		

Regular Postage Stamps of 1925 Surcharged in Green or Red -- d

Perf. 14

C59	A56 (d)	3b on 50c dp vio (G)	1.10	1.00
C60	A56 (d)	4b on 1b red (G)	1.40	1.40
C61	A57 (c)	5b on 2b org (G)	1.90	1.60
a.		Double surcharge	90.00	
C62	A56 (d)	10b on 5b blk brn (G)	4.50	3.25
a.		Double surcharge	35.00	
		Nos. C52-C62 (11)	25.50	18.35

No. C59-C62 exist with inverted surcharge, No. C62a with black and black and red surcharges.

Courtyard of Potosi Mint — AP10

Miner — AP11

Emancipated Woman AP12

Pincers, Torch and Good Will Principles AP15

Airplane over Field AP13

Airplanes and Liberty Monument AP14

Airplane over River AP16

Emblem of New Government AP17

Transport Planes over Map of Bolivia AP18

1938, May   Litho.   Perf. 10½

C63 AP10	20c deep rose	.25	.25
C64 AP11	30c gray	.25	.25
C65 AP12	40c yellow	.25	.25
C66 AP13	50c yellow grn	.50	.25
C67 AP14	60c dull blue	.50	.25
C68 AP15	1b dull red	.75	.25
C69 AP16	2b bister	1.25	.25
C70 AP17	3b lt brown	1.25	.25
C71 AP18	5b dk violet	1.90	.25
Nos. C63-C71 (9)		6.90	2.25

40c, 1b, 2b exist imperf.

Chalice — AP19

Virgin of Copacabana AP20

Jesus Christ — AP21

Church of San Francisco, La Paz AP22

St. Anthony of Padua — AP23

1939, July 19 Litho. Perf. 13½, 10½

C72 AP19	5c dull violet	.35	.35
a.	Pair, imperf. between	30.00	
C73 AP20	30c lt bl grn	.30	.20
C74 AP21	45c violet bl	.60	.20
a.	Vertical pair, imperf. between	42.50	
C75 AP22	60c carmine	.40	.35
C76 AP23	75c vermilion	.65	.60
C77 AP23	90c deep blue	.45	.25
C78 AP22	2b dull brown	.75	.25
C79 AP21	4b deep plum	1.00	.40
C80 AP20	5b lt blue	2.50	.25
C81 AP18	10b yellow	5.00	.25
Nos. C72-C81 (10)		12.00	3.10

2nd National Eucharistic Congress.
For surcharge see No. C112.

Plane over Lake Titicaca — AP24

Mt. Illimani and Condor — AP25

1941, Aug. 21   Perf. 13½

C82 AP24	10b dull green	3.25	.40
C83 AP24	20b light ultra	3.75	.60
C84 AP25	50b rose lilac	6.50	1.00
C85 AP25	100b olive bister	16.00	6.00
Nos. C82-C85 (4)		29.50	8.00

Counterfeits exist.

Liberty and Clasped Hands — AP26

1942, Nov. 12

C86 AP26	40c rose lake	.25	.25
C87 AP26	50c ultra	.25	.25
C88 AP26	1b orange brn	1.25	.75
C89 AP26	5b magenta	.75	.25
a.	Double impression		
C90 AP26	10b dull brn vio	2.50	1.25
Nos. C86-C90 (5)		5.00	2.75

Conference of Chancellors, Jan. 15, 1942.

Ballivián Type of Regular Issue

General José Ballivián; old and modern transportation.

1943, Nov. 18   Engr.   Perf. 12½

C91 A114	10c rose vio & brn	.20	.20
C92 A114	20c emerald & brn	.20	.20
C93 A114	30c rose car & brn	.20	.20
C94 A114	3b blue & brn	.25	.20
C95 A114	5b black & brn	.40	.30
Nos. C91-C95 (5)		1.25	1.10

Condor and Sun Rising — AP28

Plane — AP29

1944, Sept. 19   Litho.   Perf. 13½

C96 AP28	40c red violet	.20	.20
C97 AP28	1b blue violet	.20	.20
C98 AP29	1.50b yellow green	.20	.20
C99 AP29	2.50b dk gray blue	.40	.20
Nos. C96-C99 (4)		1.00	.80

Revolution of Dec. 20, 1943.

Map of Natl. Airways — AP30

Map of Bolivian Air Lines — AP31

1945, May 31   Perf. 11

C100 AP30	10c red	.20	.20
a.	Imperf., pair	9.00	
C101 AP30	50c yellow	.20	.20
a.	Imperf., pair	27.50	
C102 AP30	90c lt green	.25	.20
a.	Imperf., pair	30.00	
C103 AP30	5b lt ultra	.35	.20
C104 AP30	20b deep brown	1.00	.45
Nos. C100-C104 (5)		2.00	1.25

10th anniversary of first flight, La Paz to Tacha, Peru, by Panagra Airways.
For surcharges see Nos. C128-C129.

1945, Sept. 15   Perf. 13½
Centers in Red and Blue

C105 AP31	20c violet	.20	.20
C106 AP31	30c orange brn	.20	.20
C107 AP31	50c brt blue grn	.20	.20
C108 AP31	90c brt violet	.20	.20
C109 AP31	2b blue	.20	.20
C110 AP31	3b magenta	.20	.20
C111 AP31	4b olive bister	.35	.20
Nos. C105-C111 (7)		1.55	1.40

Founding of Lloyd Aéreo Boliviano, 20th anniv.

> **Catalogue values for unused stamps in this section, from this point to the end of the section, are for Never Hinged items.**

No. C76 Surcharged in Blue

1947, Mar. 23

C112 AP23	1.40b on 75c ver	.20	.20
Nos. 314-317, C112 (5)		2.15	1.00

Mt. Illimani AP32

L. A. B. Plane AP35

1947, Sept. 15   Litho.   Perf. 11½

C113 AP32	1b rose car	.20	.20
C114 AP32	1.40b emerald	.20	.20
C115 AP32	2.50b blue	.20	.20
C116 AP32	3b dp orange	.20	.20
C117 AP32	4b rose lilac	.20	.20
Nos. C113-C117 (5)		1.00	1.00
Nos. 318-323, C113-C117 (11)		4.85	2.55

1st anniv. of the Revolution of July 21, 1946.
1.40b, 2.50b exist imperf.
For surcharge see No. C137.

Bolivia/Argentina Arms Type

1947, Oct. 23   Perf. 13½

C118 A119	2.90b ultra	.25	.25
a.	Imperf., pair	20.00	
b.	Perf. 10½	5.00	4.00

Statue of Christ Type

Designs: 2.50b, Statue of Christ above La Paz. 3.70b, Child kneeling before cross. No. C121, St. John Bosco. No. C122, Virgin of Copacabana. 13.60b, Pope Plus XII blessing University of La Paz.

1948, Sept. 26   Perf. 11½

C119 A120	2.50b ver & yellow	.45	.35
C120 A120	3.70b rose & cream	.55	.35
C121 A120	4b rose lil & gray	.55	.25
C122 A120	4b lt ultra & sal	.55	.20
C123 A120	13.60b ultra & lt grn	.70	.40
Nos. C119-C123 (5)		2.80	1.55

Bolivia Auto Club Type

1948, Oct.

C124 A125	10b emerald & salmon	1.60	.20

Pacheco Type of Regular Issue

1950, Jan. 2   Unwmk.

C125 A126	1.40b orange brown	.20	.20
C126 A126	2.50b orange	.20	.20
C127 A126	3.30b rose violet	.20	.20
Nos. C125-C127 (3)		.60	.60

75th anniv. of the UPU.

Nos. C100 and C104 Surcharged in Black

1950, May 31   Perf. 11

C128 AP30	4b on 10c red	.20	.20
a.	Inverted surcharge	17.50	17.50
C129 AP30	10b on 20b dp brn	.30	.25
a.	Inverted surcharge	17.50	17.50

Panagra air services in Bolivia, 15th anniv.

1950, Sept. 15   Litho.   Perf. 13½

C130 AP35	20c red orange	.20	.20
C131 AP35	30c purple	.20	.20
C132 AP35	50c green	.20	.20
C133 AP35	1b orange	.20	.20
C134 AP35	3b ultra	.25	.20
C135 AP35	15b carmine	.50	.20
C136 AP35	50b chocolate	1.00	.35
Nos. C130-C136 (7)		2.55	1.55

25th anniv. of the founding of Lloyd Aero Boliviano. 30c, 50c, 15b exist imperforate.
No. C132 exists without imprint at bottom of stamp.

No. C116 Surcharged in Black

1950, Sept. 24   Perf. 11½

C137 AP32	1.40b on 3b dp org	.25	.25

1st anniv. of the ending of the Civil War of Aug. 24-Sept. 24, 1949.
Exists with inverted and double surcharge.

UN Type of Regular Issue

1950, Oct. 24   Unwmk.

C138 A128	3.60b crimson rose	.50	.20
C139 A128	4.70b black brown	.65	.20

La Paz Type of Regular Issue

20c, Gate of the Sun and llama. 30c, Church of Old Ssanfrancisco. 40c, Avenue Camacho. 50c, Consistorial Palace. 1b, Legislative Palace. 2b, Communications Bldg. 3b, Arms. 4b, La Gasca ordering Mendoza to found La Paz. 5b, Capt. Alonso de Mendoza founding La Paz. 10b, Arms; portrait of Mendoza.

1951, Mar. 1   Engr.   Perf. 12½
Center in Black
C140 A129	20c carmine	.20	.20
C141 A130	30c dk vio bl	.20	.20
C142 A129	40c dark blue	.20	.20
C143 A129	50c blue green	.20	.20
C144 A129	1b red	.20	.20
C145 A129	2b red orange	.35	.35
C146 A129	3b deep blue	.35	.35
C147 A129	4b vermilion	.45	.45
a.	Souvenir sheet of 4	1.00	1.00
b.	As "a," imperf.	1.00	1.00
C148 A129	5b dark green	.40	.40
a.	Souvenir sheet of 3	1.00	1.00
b.	As "a," imperf.	1.00	1.00
C149 A129	10b red brown	.65	.65
a.	Souvenir sheet of 3	1.00	1.00
b.	As "a," imperf.	1.00	1.00
	Nos. C140-C149 (10)	3.20	3.20
	Nos. 342-351,C140-C149 (20)	13.20	10.35

#C147a-C147b contain #C143-C145, C147;
#C148a-C148b contain #C142, C146, C148;
#C149a-C149b contain #C140, C141, C149.
For surcharges see Nos. C187-C196.

Athletic Type of Regular Issue
20c, Horsemanship. 30c, Basketball. 50c, Fencing. 1b, Hurdling. 2.50b, Javelin throwing. 3b, Relay race. 5b, La Paz stadium.

1951, Aug. 23   Unwmk.
Center in Black
C150 A131	20c purple	.20	.20
C151 A131	30c rose vio	.30	.20
C152 A131	50c dp red org	.50	.20
C153 A131	1b chocolate	.50	.20
C154 A131	2.50b orange	.75	.30
C155 A131	3b black brn	1.00	.75
a.	Souv. sheet, #C153-C155	4.00	3.50
b.	As "a," imperf.	4.00	4.00
C156 A131	5b red	2.00	1.50
a.	Souv. sheet of 4, #C150-C152, C156	4.50	4.00
b.	As "a," imperf.	4.50	4.50
	Nos. C150-C156 (7)	5.25	3.35
	Nos. 352-358,C150-C156 (10)	19.75	17.85

Eduardo Abaroa Type
1952, Mar. 24   Litho.   Perf. 11
C157 A133	70c rose red	.20	.20
C158 A133	2b orange yel	.20	.20
C159 A133	3b yellow green	.25	.20
C160 A133	5b blue	.25	.20
C161 A133	50b rose lilac	1.00	.90
C162 A133	100b gray black	1.10	1.10
a.	Perf. 14	10.00	
	Nos. C157-C162 (6)	3.00	2.80

Queen Isabella I Type
1952, July 16   Perf. 13½
C163 A134	50b emerald	.35	.25
C164 A134	100b brown	.65	.35

Exist imperforate.

Columbus Lighthouse Type
1952, July 16
C165 A135	2b rose lilac, salmon	.20	.20
C166 A135	3.70b blue grn, bl	.20	.20
C167 A135	4.40b orange, salmon	.20	.20
C168 A135	20b dk brn, cream	.40	.20
	Nos. C165-C168 (4)	1.00	.80

No. C168 exists imperforate.

Revolution Type and:

Soldiers — AP43

Perf. 13½ (AP43), 11½ (A137)
1953, Apr. 9   Litho.
C169 A137	3.70b chocolate	.20	.20
C170 AP43	6b red violet	.20	.20
C171 A137	9b brown rose	.20	.20
C172 A137	10b aqua	.20	.20
C173 A137	16b vermilion	.20	.20
C174 AP43	22.50b dk brown	.25	.20
C175 A137	40b gray	.40	.20
	Nos. C169-C175 (7)	1.65	1.40
	Nos. 378-383,C169-C175 (13)	2.85	2.60

Nos. C169-C170 and C174 exist imperf.

Map and Peasant Type and:

Pres. Victor Paz Estenssoro Embracing Indian — AP45

1954, Aug. 2   Perf. 12x11½
C176 AP45	20b orange brn	.20	.20
C177 A138	27b brt pink	.20	.20
C178 A138	30b red org	.20	.20
C179 A138	45b violet brn	.20	.20
C180 A138	100b blue grn	.35	.20
C181 A138	300b yellow grn	1.00	.30
	Nos. C176-C181 (6)	2.15	1.30
	Nos. C176-C181,384-387 (10)	2.95	2.10

AP45 for 3rd Inter-American Indian Cong.
A138 agrarian reform laws of 1953-54.
Nos. C176-C180 exist imperf.
For surcharge see No. C261.

Oil Derricks — AP47

Map of South America and La Paz Arms — AP48

1955, Oct. 9   Perf. 10½
C182 AP47	55b dk & lt grnsh bl	.20	.20
C183 AP47	70b dk gray & gray	.20	.20
C184 AP47	90b dk & lt grn	.20	.20

Perf. 13
C185 AP47	500b red lilac	.65	.40
C186 AP47	1000b blk brn & fawn	1.25	1.25
	Nos. C182-C186 (5)	2.50	2.25
	Nos. C182-C186,388-392 (10)	3.50	3.25

For surcharge see No. C262.

Nos. C140-C149 Surcharged with New Values and Bars in Black or Carmine
1957   Engr.   Perf. 12½
Center in Black
C187 A129	100b on 3b (C)	.20	.20
C188 A129	200b on 2b	.20	.20
C189 A129	500b on 4b	.20	.20
C190 A129	600b on 1b	.20	.20
C191 A129	700b on 20c	.25	.20
C192 A129	800b on 40c (C)	.35	.20
C193 A130	900b on 30c (C)	.40	.20
C194 A129	1800b on 50c (C)	.60	.25
C195 A129	3000b on 5b (C)	1.00	.45
C196 A129	5000b on 10b (C)	1.60	.75
	Nos. C187-C196 (10)	5.00	2.85

See Nos. 393-402.

Unwmk.
1957, May 25   Litho.   Perf. 12
C197 AP48	700b lilac & vio	.35	.35
C198 AP48	1200b pale brn	.40	.35
C199 AP48	1350b rose car	.55	.50
C200 AP48	2700b blue grn	1.10	.65
C201 AP48	4000b violet bl	1.40	.75
	Nos. C197-C201 (5)	3.80	2.60
	Nos. C197-C201,403-407 (10)	5.10	3.60

Exist imperf.
For surcharges see Nos. C263-C265.

Type of Regular Issue, 1957
1957, Dec. 19   Perf. 11½
C202 A141	600b magenta	.25	.20
C203 A141	700b violet blue	.35	.20
C204 A141	900b pale green	.50	.20
	Nos. C202-C204 (3)	1.10	.60

Type of Regular Issue, 1960
1960, Jan. 30
C205 A142	400b rose claret	.50	.30
C206 A142	800b slate blue	.65	.40
C207 A142	2000b slate	1.00	.60
	Nos. C205-C207 (3)	2.15	1.30

Gate of the Sun, Tiahuanacu AP49
Uprooted Oak Emblem AP50

1960, Mar. 26   Litho.   Perf. 11½
C208 AP49	3000b gray	2.00	1.10
C209 AP49	5000b orange	3.00	1.10
C210 AP49	10,000b rose cl	4.75	2.75
C211 AP49	15,000b blue violet	7.00	4.50
	Nos. C208-C211 (4)	16.75	9.45
	Nos. C208-C211,414-417 (8)	23.90	12.95

1960, Apr. 7   Perf. 11½
C212 AP50	600b ultra	.35	.35
C213 AP50	700b lt red brn	.35	.35
C214 AP50	900b dk bl grn	.35	.35
C215 AP50	1800b violet	.60	.60
C216 AP50	2000b gray	.65	.60
	Nos. C212-C216 (5)	2.30	2.25
	Nos. C212-C216,418-422 (10)	4.40	4.35

WRY, July 1, 1959-June 30, 1960.
No. C215 exists with "1961" overprint in dark carmine, but was not regularly issued in this form.

Jaime Laredo Type
Laredo facing left, Bolivia in color.
Perf. 11½
1960, Aug. 15   Unwmk.   Litho.
C217 A145	600b rose vio	.75	.45
C218 A145	700b ol gray	.75	.25
C219 A145	800b vio brn	.75	.25
C220 A145	900b dk bl	1.00	.25
C221 A145	1800b green	1.50	1.50
C222 A145	4000b dk gray	3.00	1.00
	Nos. C217-C222 (6)	7.75	3.70

Issued to honor the violinist Jaime Laredo.
For surcharges see Nos. C266-C267.

Children's Hospital Type of 1960
1960, Nov. 21   Perf. 11½
C223 A146	600b multi	.40	.25
C224 A146	1000b multi	.60	.25
C225 A146	1800b multi	1.00	1.00
C226 A146	5000b multi	3.00	1.25
	Nos. C223-C226 (4)	5.00	2.75

For surcharges see Nos. C268-C269.

Pres. Paz Estenssoro and Pres. Getulio Vargas of Brazil AP52

1960, Dec. 14   Litho.   Perf. 11½
C227 AP52	1200b on 10b org & blk	.70	.70

Exists with surcharge inverted.
No. C227 without surcharge was not regularly issued, although a decree authorizing its circulation was published. Value, $2.
Postally-used counterfeits of surcharge exist.

Pres. Paz Estenssoro and Pres. Frondizi of Argentina AP53

4000b, Flags of Bolivia and Argentina.

1961, May 23   Perf. 10½
C228 AP53	4000b brn, red, yel, grn & bl	.75	.75
C229 AP53	6000b dk grn & blk	1.50	1.50

Visit of the President of Argentina, Dr. Arturo Frondizi, to Bolivia.
For surcharge see No. C309.

Miguel de Cervantes — AP54

1961, Oct.   Photo.   Perf. 13
C230 AP54	1400b pale grn & dk ol grn	.60	.25

Cervantes' appointment as Chief Magistrate of La Paz. See No. 451.

Virgin of Cotoca and Symbol of Eucharist AP55
Planes and Parachutes AP56

1962, Mar. 19   Litho.   Perf. 10½
C231 AP55	1400b brn, pink & yel	.65	.35

4th Natl. Eucharistic Cong., Santa Cruz, 1961.

Nos. C212-C216 Surcharged Vertically with New Value and Greek Key Border
1962, June   Unwmk.   Perf. 11½
C232 AP50	1200b on 600b	.55	.55
C233 AP50	1300b on 700b	.50	.50
C234 AP50	1400b on 900b	.55	.55
C235 AP50	2800b on 1,800b	.90	.75
C236 AP50	3000b on 2,000b	.90	.75
	Nos. C232-C236 (5)	3.40	3.10

The overprinted segment of Greek key border on Nos. C232-C236 comes in two positions: two full "keys" on top, and one full and two half keys on top.

Flower Type of 1962
Flowers: 100b, 1800b, Cantua buxifolia. 800b, 10,000b, Cantua bicolor.

1962, June 28   Litho.   Perf. 10½
Flowers in Natural Colors
C237 A152	100b dk bl	.25	.20
C238 A152	800b green	.50	.20
C239 A152	1800b violet	1.00	.50
a.	Souvenir sheet of 3	7.50	6.00
C240 A152	10,000b dk bl	3.25	1.75
	Nos. C237-C240 (4)	5.00	2.65

No. C239a contains 3 imperf. stamps similar to Nos. C237-C239, but with the 1,800b background color changed to dark violet blue.
For surcharges see Nos. C270-C271.

1962, Sept. 5   Litho.   Perf. 11½
1200b, 5000b, Plane and oxcart. 2000b, Aerial photography (plane over South America).

Emblem in Red, Yellow & Green
C241 AP56	600b blk & bl	.25	.20
C242 AP56	1200b multi	.50	.20
C243 AP56	2000b multi	.75	.35
C244 AP56	5000b multi	1.50	.65
	Nos. C241-C244 (4)	3.00	1.40

Armed Forces of Bolivia.

Malaria Type of 1962
Design: Inscription around mosquito, laurel around globe.

1962, Oct. 4
C245 A154	2000b ind, grn & yel	.80	.50

Type of Regular Issue, 1961
Design: Pedro de la Gasca (1485-1567).

1962   Unwmk.   Photo.   Perf. 13x12½
C246 A150	1200b brn, yel	.35	.20

Condor, Soccer Ball and Flags — AP57

Alliance for Progress Emblem — AP58

1.80b, Map of Bolivia, soccer ball, goal and flags.

1963, Mar. 21   Litho.   Perf. 11½
C247	AP57	1.40b multi	1.00	.65
C248	AP57	1.80b multi	1.00	1.00

21st South American Soccer Championships.

Freedom from Hunger Type

Design: Wheat, globe and wheat emblem.

1963, Aug. 1   Unwmk.   Perf. 11½
C249	A156	1.20b dk grn, bl & yel	.75	.75

1963, Nov. 15   Perf. 11½
C250	AP58	1.20b dl yel, ultra & grn	.80	.75

2nd anniv. of the Alliance for Progress, which aims to stimulate economic growth and raise living standards in Latin America.

Type of Regular Issue, 1963

1.20b, Ballot box and voters. 1.40b, Map and farmer breaking chain. 2.80b, Miners.

1963, Dec. 21   Perf. 11½
C251	A157	1.20b gray, dk brn & rose	.40	.20
C252	A157	1.40b bister & grn	.50	.25
C253	A157	2.80b slate & buff	1.00	.90
		Nos. C251-C253 (3)	1.90	1.35

Andrés Santa Cruz — AP59

Perf. 13½
1966, Aug. 10   Wmk. 90   Litho.
C254	AP59	20c dp bl	.20	.20
C255	AP59	60c dp grn	.20	.20
C256	AP59	1.20b red brn	.50	.50
C257	AP59	2.80b black	.80	.80
		Nos. C254-C257 (4)	1.70	1.70

Cent. (in 1965) of the death of Marshal Andrés Santa Cruz (1792-1865), pres. of Bolivia and of Peru-Bolivia Confederation.

Children Type of 1966

Design: 1.40b, Mother and children.

1966, Dec. 16   Unwmk.   Perf. 13½
C258	A159	1.40b gray bl & blk	1.00	.40

Co-Presidents Type of Regular Issue

1966, Dec. 16   Litho.   Perf. 12½
Flag in Red, Yellow and Green
C259	A160	2.80b gray & tan	1.40	1.00
C260	A160	10b sep & tan	1.60	.50
a.		Souvenir sheet of 4	6.50	6.50

No. C260a contains 4 imperf. stamps similar to Nos. 480-481 and C259-C260. Dark green marginal inscription. Size: 135x82mm.

Various Issues 1954-62 Surcharged with New Values and Bars

1966, Dec. 21
On No. C177: "XII Aniversario / Reforma / Agraria"
C261	A138	10c on 27b	.20	.20
a.		Agraria/Agraria	10.00	

On No. C182: "XXV / Aniversario Paz / del Chaco"
C262	AP47	10c on 55b	.20	.20

On No. C199: "Centenario de / Tupiza"
C263	AP48	60c on 1350b	.50	

On No. C200: "XXV / Aniversario / Automovil Club / Boliviano"
C264	AP48	2.80b on 2700b	2.00	1.60

On No. C201: "Centenario de la / Cruz Roja / Internacional"
C265	AP48	4b on 4000b	1.40	1.00

On No. C219: "CL Aniversario / Heroinas Coronilla"
C266	A145	1.20b on 800b	.75	.50

On No. C222: "Centenario Himno / Paceño"
C267	A145	1.40b on 4,000b	.75	.50

Nos. C224-C225 Surcharged
C268	A146	1.40b on 1,000b	.60	.60
C269	A146	1.40b on 1,800b	.60	.60

On Nos. C238-C239: "Aniversario / Centro Filatelico / Cochabamba"
C270	A152	1.20b on 800b	1.00	.25
C271	A152	1.20b on 1,800b	1.00	.25

Revenue Stamp of 1946 Surcharged with New Value "X" and: "XXV Aniversario / Dpto. Pando / Aéreo"
C272	A161	1.20b on 1b dk bl	.50	.25
		Nos. C261-C272 (12)	9.50	6.15

Lions Emblem and Prehistoric Sculptures AP60

1967, Sept. 20   Litho.   Perf. 13x13½
C273	AP60	2b red & multi	.80	.65
a.		Souvenir sheet of 2	3.75	3.75

50th anniv. of Lions Intl. No. C273a contains 2 imperf. stamps similar to Nos. 492 and C273.

Folklore Type of Regular Issue

Folklore characters: 1.20p, Pujllay. 1.40p, Ujusiris. 2p, Morenada. 3p, Auki-aukis.

1968, June 24   Perf. 13½x13
C274	A163	1.20b lt yel grn & multi	.35	.20
C275	A163	1.40b gray & multi	.40	.20
C276	A163	2b dk ol bis & multi	.75	.25
C277	A163	3b sky bl & multi	1.00	.25
		Nos. C274-C277 (4)	2.50	.90

A souvenir sheet exists containing 4 imperf. stamps similar to Nos. C274-C277. Size: 131x81½mm.

Moto Mendez — AP61

1968, Oct. 29   Litho.   Perf. 13½x13
C278	AP61	1b multi	.35	.20
C279	AP61	1.40b multi	.40	.35
C280	AP61	2b multi	.75	.50
C281	AP61	4b multi	1.00	.75
		Nos. C278-C281 (4)	2.50	1.80

Battle of Tablada sesquicentennial.

Pres. Gualberto Villaroel AP62

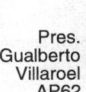

1968, Nov. 6   Perf. 13x13½
C282	AP62	1.40b org & blk	.30	.25
C283	AP62	3b lt bl & blk	.55	.30
C284	AP62	4b rose & blk	.70	.40
C285	AP62	5b gray grn & blk	.85	.55
C286	AP62	10b pale pur & blk	1.60	1.10
		Nos. C282-C286 (5)	4.00	2.60

4th centenary of Cochabamba.

ITU Type of Regular Issue

1968, Dec. 3   Litho.   Perf. 13x13½
C287	A166	1.20b gray, blk & yel	.60	.30
C288	A166	1.40b bl, blk & gray ol	.60	.20

UNESCO Emblem — AP63

1968, Nov. 14   Perf. 13½x13
C289	AP63	1.20b pale vio & blk	.35	.35
C290	AP63	2.80b yel grn & blk	.65	.65

20th anniv. (in 1966) of UNESCO.

Kennedy Type of Regular Issue

1968, Nov. 22   Unwmk.
C291	A168	1b grn & blk	.25	.20
C292	A168	10b scar & blk	2.75	2.75

A souvenir sheet contains one imperf. stamp similar to No. C291. Dark violet marginal inscription. Size: 131x81½mm.

Tennis Type of Regular Issue

1968, Dec. 10   Perf. 13x13½
C293	A169	1.40b org, blk & lt brn	.35	.35
C294	A169	2.80b sky bl, blk & lt brn	.65	.65

A souvenir sheet exists containing one imperf. stamp similar to No. C293. Size: 131x81½mm.

Stamp Centenary Type

Design: 1.40b, 2.80b, 3b, Bolivia No. 1.

1968, Dec. 23   Litho.   Perf. 13x13½
C295	A170	1.40b org, grn & blk	.50	.50
C296	A170	2.80b pale rose, grn & blk	1.00	1.00
C297	A170	3b lt vio, grn & blk	1.00	1.00
		Nos. C295-C297 (3)	2.50	2.50

A souvenir sheet exists containing 3 imperf. stamps similar to Nos. C295-C297. Size: 131x81½mm.

Franklin D. Roosevelt — AP64

1969, Oct. 29   Litho.   Perf. 13½x13
C298	AP64	5b brn, blk & buff	1.75	1.10

Olympic Type of Regular Issue

Sports: 1.20b, Woman runner, vert. 2.80b, Discus thrower, vert. 5b, Hurdler.

Perf. 13½x13, 13x13½
1969, Oct. 29   Litho.
C299	A171	1.20b yel grn, bis & blk	.50	.40
C300	A171	2.80b red, org & blk	1.00	.75
C301	A171	5b bl, lt bl, red & blk	1.50	1.50
		Nos. C299-C301 (3)	3.00	2.65

A souvenir sheet exists containing 3 imperf. stamps similar to Nos. C299-C301. Size: 130½x81mm.

Butterfly Type of Regular Issue

1b, Metamorpha dido wernichei. 1.80b, Heliconius felix. 2.80b, Morpho casica. 3b, Papilio yuracares. 4b, Heliconius melittus.

1970, Apr. 24   Litho.   Perf. 13x13½
C302	A172	1b sal & multi	1.40	1.40
C303	A172	1.80b lt bl & multi	2.00	2.00
C304	A172	2.80b multi	3.25	3.25
C305	A172	3b multi	3.25	3.25
C306	A172	4b multi	4.00	4.00
		Nos. C302-C306 (5)	13.90	13.90

A souvenir sheet exists containing 3 imperf. stamps similar to Nos. C302-C304. Black marginal inscription. Size: 129½x80mm.

Scout Type of Regular Issue

Designs: 50c, Boy Scout building brick wall. 1.20b, Bolivian Boy Scout emblem.

1970, June 17   Litho.   Perf. 13½x13
C307	A173	50c yel & multi	.20	.20
C308	A173	1.20b multi	.40	.40

No. C228 Surcharged

1970, Dec.   Perf. 10½
C309	AP53	1.20b on 4000b multi	.25	.20

Flower Type of Regular Issue

Bolivian Flowers: 1.20b, Amaryllis pseudopardina, horiz. 1.40b, Rebutia kruegeri. 2.80b, Lobivia pentlandii, horiz. 4b, Rebutia tunariensis.

Perf. 13x13½, 13½x13
1971, Aug. 9   Litho.   Unwmk.
C310	A174	1.20b multi	.70	.40
C311	A174	1.40b multi	.80	.50
C312	A174	2.80b multi	1.50	.75
C313	A174	4b multi	2.00	1.25
		Nos. C310-C313 (4)	5.00	2.90

Two souvenir sheets of 4 exist. One contains imperf. stamps similar to Nos. 534-535 and C310, C312. The other contains imperf. stamps similar to Nos. 536-537, C311, C313. Size: 130x80mm.

Folk Dance Type of Regular Issue

1972, Mar. 23   Litho.   Perf. 13½x13
C314	A177	1.20b Kusillo	.50	.20
C315	A177	1.40b Taquirari	.65	.20

Two souvenir sheets of 3 exist. One contains imperf. stamps similar to Nos. 542-543, C314. The other contains imperf. stamps similar to Nos. 540-541, C315. Size: 80x129mm.

Painting Type of Regular Issue

Bolivian Paintings: 1.40b, Portrait of Chola Paceña, by Cecilio Guzman de Rojas. 1.50b, Adoration of the Kings, by G. Gamarra. 1.60b, Adoration of Pachamama (mountain), by A. Borda. 2b, The Kiss of the Idol, by Guzman de Rojas.

1972   Litho.   Perf. 13½
C316	A178	1.40b multi	.40	.20
C317	A178	1.50b multi	.40	.20
C318	A178	1.60b multi	.40	.20
C319	A178	2b multi	.55	.20
		Nos. C316-C319 (4)	1.75	.80

Two souvenir sheets of 2 exist. One contains imperf. stamps similar to Nos. 548 and C318. The other contains imperf. stamps similar to Nos. C317 and C319. Size: 129x80mm. Issued: 1.40b, Dec. 4; others, Aug. 17.

Bolivian Coat of Arms AP65

1972, Dec. 4   Perf. 13½x14
C320	AP65	4b lt bl & multi	1.40	.50

Cactus Type of Regular Issue

Designs: Various cacti.

1973, Aug. 6   Litho.   Perf. 13½
C321	A180	1.20b tan & multi	.35	.20
C322	A180	1.90b org & multi	.50	.20
C323	A180	2b multi	.65	.25
		Nos. C321-C323 (3)	1.50	.65

Development Type of Regular Issue

1.40b, Highway 1Y4. 2b, Rail car on bridge.

1973, Nov. 26   Litho.   Perf. 13½

C324	A181	1.40b salmon & multi	.40	.20
C325	A181	2b multi	.60	.20

Santos-Dumont and 14-Bis Plane — AP66

1973, July 20

C326	AP66	1.40b yel & blk	.65	.35

Alberto Santos-Dumont (1873-1932), Brazilian aviation pioneer.

Orchid Type of 1974

Orchids: 2.50b, Cattleya luteola, horiz. 3.80b, Stanhopaea. 4b, Catasetum, horiz. 5b, Maxillaria.

1974   Litho.   Perf. 13½

C327	A182	2.50b multi	1.00	.25
C328	A182	3.80b rose & multi	1.50	.45
C329	A182	4b multi	1.50	.40
C330	A182	5b sal & multi	2.50	.45
		Nos. C327-C330 (4)	6.50	1.55

Air Force Emblem, Plane over Map of Bolivia AP67

Designs: 3.80b, Plane over Andes. 4.50b, Triple decker and jet. 8b, Rafael Pabon and double decker. 15b, Jet and "50."

1974   Litho.   Perf. 13x13½

C331	AP67	3b multi	.65	.25
C332	AP67	3.80b multi	1.00	.25
C333	AP67	4.50b multi	1.00	.25
C334	AP67	8b multi	1.60	.40
C335	AP67	15b multi	3.50	.50
		Nos. C331-C335 (5)	7.75	1.65

Bolivian Air Force, 50th anniv. Exist imperf. For surcharge see No. 968.

Coat of Arms Type of 1975

Designs: Departmental coats of arms.

1975, July 16   Litho.   Perf. 13½

C336	A188	20c Beni	.20	.20
C337	A188	30c Tarija	.20	.20
C338	A188	50c Potosi	.25	.25
C339	A188	1b Oruro	.50	.50
C340	A188	2.50b Santa Cruz	1.00	1.00
C341	A188	3b La Paz	1.00	1.00
		Nos. C336-C341 (6)	3.15	3.15

LAB Emblem — AP68

Bolivia on Map of Americas AP69

Map of Bolivia, Plane and Kyllmann AP70

1975   Litho.   Perf. 13½

C342	AP68	1b gold, bl & blk	.40	.40
C343	AP69	1.50b multi	.60	.60
C344	AP70	2b multi	.75	.75
		Nos. C342-C344 (3)	1.75	1.75

Lloyd Aereo Boliviano, 50th anniversary, founded by Guillermo Kyllmann.

Bolivar, Presidents Perez and Banzer, and Flags — AP71

1975, Aug. 4   Litho.   Perf. 13½

C345	AP71	3b gold & multi	.75	.65

Visit of Pres. Carlos A. Perez of Venezuela.

Bolivar Type of 1975

Presidents and Statesmen of Bolivia: 50c, Rene Barrientes O. 2b, Francisco B. O'Connor. 3.80b, Gualberto Villarroel. 4.20b, German Busch. 4.50b, Hugo Banzer Suarez. 20b, José Ballivian. 30b, Andres de Santa Cruz. 40b, Antonio Jose de Sucre.

1975   Litho.   Perf. 13½
Size: 24x33mm

C346	A189	50c multi	.25	.25
C347	A189	2b multi	.50	.50
C348	A189	3.80b multi	.75	.75
C349	A189	4.20b multi	1.00	.75

Size: 28x39mm

C350	A189	4.50b multi	1.00	.50

Size: 24x33mm

C351	A189	20b multi	4.00	2.00
C352	A189	30b multi	5.00	5.00
C353	A189	40b multi	6.50	6.50
		Nos. C346-C353 (8)	19.00	16.25

For surcharge see No. 969.

UPU Emblem AP72

1975, Dec. 7   Litho.   Perf. 13½

C358	AP72	25b blue & multi	3.00	3.00

Cent. of UPU (in 1974).

POSTAGE DUE STAMPS

D1

1931   Unwmk.   Engr.   Perf. 14, 14½

J1	D1	5c ultra	1.10	1.25
J2	D1	10c red	1.10	1.25
J3	D1	15c yellow	1.75	2.00
J4	D1	30c deep green	1.75	2.00
J5	D1	40c deep violet	2.75	3.25
J6	D1	50c black brown	4.00	4.50
		Nos. J1-J6 (6)	12.45	14.25

Symbol of Youth — D2

Torch of Knowledge D3

Symbol of the Revolution of May 17, 1936 — D4

1938   Litho.   Perf. 11

J7	D2	5c deep rose	.50	.45
a.		Pair, imperf. between		
J8	D3	10c green	.50	.45
J9	D4	30c gray blue	.50	.45
		Nos. J7-J9 (3)	1.50	1.35

POSTAL TAX STAMPS

Worker — PT1

Imprint: "LITO. UNIDAS LA PAZ."
Perf. 13½x10½, 10½, 13½

1939		**Litho.**	**Unwmk.**	
RA1	PT1	5c dull violet	.70	.20
a.		Double impression		

Redrawn
Imprint: "TALL. OFFSET LA PAZ."

1940			**Perf. 12x11, 11**	
RA2	PT1	5c violet	.60	.20
a.		Horizontal pair, imperf. between	2.00	
b.		Imperf. horiz., pair		

Tax of Nos. RA1-RA2 was for the Workers' Home Building Fund.

Communications Symbols — PT2

Condor, Envelope and Post Horn — PT3

Communication Symbols — PT4

Postman Blowing Horn — PT5

1944-45   Litho.   Perf. 10½

RA3	PT2	10c salmon	.40	.20
RA4	PT2	10c blue ('45)	.40	.20

A 30c orange inscribed "Centenario de la Creacion del Departamento del Beni" was issued in 1946 and required to be affixed to all air and surface mail to and from the Department of Beni in addition to regular postage. Five higher denominations in the same scenic design were used for local revenue purposes.

> **Catalogue values for unused stamps in this section, from this point to the end of the section, are for Never Hinged items.**

Type of 1944 Redrawn

1947-48		**Unwmk.**	**Perf. 10½**	
RA5	PT2	10c carmine	.40	.20
RA6	PT2	10c org yel ('48)	.35	.20
RA7	PT2	10c yel brn ('48)	.35	.20
RA8	PT2	10c emerald ('48)	.35	.20
		Nos. RA5-RA8 (4)	1.45	.80

Post horn and envelope reduced in size.

1951-52

RA9	PT3	20c deep orange	.40	.20
a.		Imperf., pair	20.00	
RA10	PT3	20c green ('52)	.50	.20
a.		Imperf., pair	20.00	
RA11	PT3	20c blue ('52)	.50	.20
a.		Imperf., pair	20.00	
		Nos. RA9-RA11 (3)	1.40	.60

For surcharges see Nos. RA17-RA18.

1952-54   Perf. 13½, 10½, 10½x12

RA12	PT4	50c green	.50	.20
RA13	PT4	50c carmine	.50	.20
RA14	PT4	3b green	.50	.20
RA15	PT4	3b olive bister	.50	.50
RA16	PT4	5b violet ('54)	.50	.50
		Nos. RA12-RA16 (5)	2.50	1.60

For surcharges see Nos. RA21-RA22.

No. RA10 and Type of 1951-52 Surcharged with New Value in Black

1953   Perf. 10½

RA17	PT3	50c on 20c green	.25	.20
RA18	PT3	50c on 20c red vio	.25	.20

1954-55   Unwmk.   Perf. 10½

RA19	PT5	1b brown	.20	.20
RA20	PT5	1b car rose ('55)	.20	.20

Exist imperf.

Nos. RA15 and RA14 Surcharged in Black "Bs. 5.-/D. S./21-IV-55"

1955   Perf. 10½, 10½x12

RA21	PT4	5b on 3b olive bister	.25	.20
RA22	PT4	5b on 3b green	.25	.20

Tax of Nos. RA3-RA22 was for the Communications Employees Fund.

No. RA21 is known with surcharge in thin type of different font and with comma added after "55."

Plane over Airport — PT6

Planes — PT7

Perf. 10½, 12, 13½

1955		**Unwmk.**	**Litho.**	
RA23	PT6	5b dp ultra	.25	.20
a.		Vertical pair imperf. between		

Perf. 11½

RA24	PT7	10b light green	.20	.20

PT8

PT9

1955   **Litho.**   **Perf. 10½**
RA25 PT8 5b red   7.50   7.50
   a.   Imperf., pair   35.00

Perf. 12
RA26 PT9 20b dark brown   .25   .20
   Tax of Nos. RA23-RA26 was for the building of new airports.

General
Alfredo
Ovando and
Three
Men — PT10

1970, Sept. 26   **Litho.**   **Perf. 13x13½**
RA27 PT10 20c black & red   .50   .20
   See No. RAC1.

Pres. German
Busch
PT11

1971, May 13   **Litho.**   **Perf. 13x13½**
RA28 PT11 20c lilac & black   .50   .20

AIR POST POSTAL TAX STAMPS

Catalogue values for unused stamps in this section are for Never Hinged items.

Type of Postal Tax Issue
Design: 30c, General Ovando and oil well.

1970, Sept. 26   **Litho.**   **Perf. 13x13½**
RAC1 PT10 30c blk & grn   .50   .20

Pres.
Gualberto
Villarroel,
Refinery
PTAP1

1971, May 25   **Litho.**   **Perf. 13x13½**
RAC2 PTAP1 30c lt bl & blk   .50   .20

Type of 1971 Inscribed: "XXV ANIVERSARIO DE SU GOBIERNO"
1975   **Litho.**   **Perf. 13x13½**
RAC3 PTAP1 30c lt bl & blk   3.00   3.00

BOSNIA AND HERZEGOVINA

'bäz-nē-ə and ˌhert-sə-gō-'vē-nə

LOCATION — Dalmatia and Serbia
GOVT. — Provinces of Turkey under Austro-Hungarian occupation, 1879-1908; provinces of Austria-Hungary 1908-1918
AREA — 19,768 sq. mi.
POP. — 2,000,000 (approx. 1918)
CAPITAL — Sarajevo

Following World War I Bosnia and Herzegovina united with the kingdoms of Montenegro and Serbia, and Croatia, Dalmatia and Slovenia, to form the

Kingdom of Yugoslavia (See Yugoslavia.)

100 Novcica (Neukreuzer) = 1 Florin (Gulden)
100 Heller = 1 Krone (1900)

Watermark

Wmk. 91- BRIEF-MARKEN or (from 1890) ZEITUNGS-MARKEN in Double-lined Capitals, Across the Sheet

Coat of Arms — A1

Type I - The heraldic eaglets on the right side of the escutcheon are entirely blank. The eye of the lion is indicated by a very small dot, which sometimes fails to print.
Type II - There is a colored line across the lowest eaglet. A similar line sometimes appears on the middle eaglet. The eye of the lion is formed by a large dot which touches the outline of the head above it.
Type III - The eaglets and eye of the lion are similar to type I. Each tail feather of the large eagle has two lines of shading and the lowest feather does not touch the curved line below it. In types I and II there are several shading lines in these feathers, and the lowest feather touches the curved line.

Varieties of the Numerals

2 NOVCICA
A - The "2" has curved tail. All are type I.
B - The "2" has straight tail. All are type II.

15 NOVCICA
C - The serif of the "1" is short and forms a wide angle with the vertical stroke.
D - The serif of the "1" forms an acute angle with the vertical stroke.
The numerals of the 5n were retouched several times and show minor differences, especially in the flag.

Other Varieties

½ NOVCICA:
There is a black dot between the curved ends of the ornaments near the lower spandrels.
G - This dot touches the curve at its right. Stamps of this (1st) printing are litho.
H - This dot stands clear of the curved lines. Stamps of this (2nd) printing are typo.

10 NOVCICA:
Ten stamps in each sheet of type II show a small cross in the upper section of the right side of the escutcheon.

Perf. 9 to 13½ and Compound
1879-94   **Litho.**   **Wmk. 91**
     Type I
1   A1   ½n blk (type II) ('94)   15.00   17.50
2   A1   1n gray   7.50   1.60
  c.   1n gray lilac   1.60
4   A1   2n yellow   11.50   .90
5   A1   3n green   11.00   1.75
6   A1   5n rose red   18.00   .40
7   A1   10n blue   55.00   .85
8   A1   15n brown   57.50   5.50
9   A1   20n gray green ('93)   225.00   8.00
10   A1   25n violet   65.00   6.25
    Nos. 1-10 (9)   465.50   42.75

No. 2c was never issued. It is usually canceled by blue pencil marks and "mint" copies generally have been cleaned.

Perf. 10½ to 13 and Compound
1894-98   **Typo.**
     Type II
1a   A1   ½n black   10.00   15.00
2a   A1   1n gray   3.75   1.00
4a   A1   2n yellow   2.75   .50
5a   A1   3n green   3.75   1.10
6a   A1   5n rose red   72.50   .35
7a   A1   10n blue   5.00   .70
8a   A1   15n brown   4.25   3.25

9a   A1   20n gray green   5.50   3.50
10a   A1   25n violet   6.25   5.75
    Nos. 1a-10a (9)   113.75   31.15

Type III
6b   A1   5n rose red ('98)   3.00   .45

All the preceding stamps exist in various shades.
Nos. 1a to 10a were reprinted in 1911 in lighter colors, on very white paper and perf. 12½. Value, set $25.

A2   A3

Perf. 10½, 12½ and Compound
1900   **Typo.**
11   A2   1h gray black   .25   .20
12   A2   2h gray   .25   .20
13   A2   3h yellow   .25   .20
14   A2   5h green   .20   .20
15   A2   6h brown   .35   .20
16   A2   10h red   .20   .20
17   A2   20h rose   105.00   5.50
18   A2   25h blue   1.00   .30
19   A2   30h bister brown   110.00   6.50
20   A2   40h orange   140.00   10.00
21   A2   50h red lilac   .75   .35
22   A3   1k dark rose   1.00   .50
23   A3   2k ultra   1.40   1.25
24   A3   5k dull blue grn   3.25   4.00
    Nos. 11-24 (14)   363.90   29.60

All values of this issue except the 3h exist on ribbed paper.
Nos. 17, 19 and 20 were reprinted in 1911. The reprints are in lighter colors and on whiter paper than the originals. Reprints of Nos. 17 and 19 are perf. 10½ and those of No. 20 are perf. 12½. Value each $1.50.

Numerals in Black

1901-04   **Perf. 12½**
25   A2   20h pink ('02)   .50   .40
26   A2   30h bister brn ('03)   .50   .40
27   A2   35h blue   .80   .50
  a.   35h ultramarine   110.00   5.50
28   A2   40h orange ('03)   .80   .70
29   A2   45h grnsh blue ('04)   .70   .55
    Nos. 25-29 (5)   3.30   2.55

Nos. 11-16, 18, 21-29 exist imperf. Most of Nos. 11-29 exist perf. 6½; compound with 12½; part perf.; in pairs imperf. between. These were supplied only to some high-ranking officials and never sold at any P.O.

View of
Deboj
A4

The Carsija at
Sarajevo — A5

Designs: 2h, View of Mostar. 3h, Pliva Gate, Jajce. 5h, Narenta Pass and Prenj River. 6h, Rama Valley. 10h, Vrbas Valley. 20h, Old Bridge, Mostar. 25h, Bey's Mosque, Sarajevo. 30h, Donkey post. 35h, Jezero and tourists' pavilion. 40h, Mail wagon. 45h, Bazaar at Sarajevo. 50h, Postal car. 2k, St. Luke's Campanile, Jajce. 5k, Emperor Franz Josef.

Perf. 6½, 9½, 10½ and 12½, also Compounds
1906   **Engr.**   **Unwmk.**
30   A4   1h black   .20   .20
31   A4   2h violet   .20   .20
32   A4   3h olive   .20   .20
33   A4   5h dark green   .30   .20
34   A4   6h brown   .20   .20
  a.   Perf. 13½   13.50   19.00
35   A4   10h carmine   .30   .20
36   A4   20h dark brown   .50   .20
  a.   Perf. 13½   40.00   55.00
37   A4   25h deep blue   1.10   .75
38   A4   30h green   1.25   .30
39   A4   35h myrtle green   1.25   .30
40   A4   40h orange red   1.25   .30
41   A4   45h brown red   1.25   .90

42   A4   50h dull violet   1.50   .65
43   A5   1k maroon   4.00   1.75
44   A5   2k gray green   5.25   7.00
45   A5   5k dull blue   4.25   6.00
    Nos. 30-45 (16)   23.00   19.35

Nos. 30-45 exist imperf. Value, set $50 unused, $37.50 canceled.
For overprint and surcharges see #126, B1-B4.

Birthday Jubilee Issue
Designs of 1906 Issue, with "1830-1910" in Label at Bottom
1910   **Perf. 12½**
46   A4   1h black   .30   .25
47   A4   2h violet   .40   .25
48   A4   3h olive   .40   .25
49   A4   5h dark green   .45   .20
50   A4   6h orange brn   .45   .30
51   A4   10h carmine   .50   .20
52   A4   20h dark brown   1.25   1.50
53   A4   25h deep blue   2.50   2.50
54   A4   30h green   1.75   2.25
55   A4   35h myrtle grn   2.00   2.25
56   A4   40h orange red   2.00   3.00
57   A4   45h brown red   3.75   5.00
58   A4   50h dull violet   4.25   5.00
59   A5   1k maroon   4.25   5.50
60   A5   2k gray green   17.50   20.00
61   A5   5k dull blue   2.25   4.50
    Nos. 46-61 (16)   44.00   52.95

80th birthday of Emperor Franz Josef.

Scenic Type of 1906
Views: 12h, Jaice. 60h, Konjica. 72h, Vishegrad.

1912
62   A4   12h ultra   4.00   4.25
63   A4   60h dull blue   2.50   3.75
64   A4   72h carmine   12.00   14.00
    Nos. 62-64 (3)   18.50   22.00

Value, imperf. set, $75.

See Austria for similar designs inscribed "FELDPOST" instead of "MILITARPOST."

Emperor Franz Josef
A23   A24

A25

A26

1912-14
     Various Frames
65   A23   1h olive green   .35   .20
66   A23   2h brt blue   .35   .20
67   A23   3h claret   .35   .20
68   A23   5h green   .35   .20
69   A23   6h dark gray   .35   .20
70   A23   10h rose car   .40   .20
71   A23   12h dp olive grn   1.10   .30
72   A23   20h orange brn   4.50   .20
73   A23   25h ultra   2.25   .20
74   A23   30h orange red   2.25   .20
75   A23   35h myrtle grn   2.25   .20
76   A24   40h dk violet   6.75   .20
77   A24   45h olive brn   3.00   .20
78   A24   50h slate blue   3.00   .20
79   A24   60h brown vio   2.75   .20
80   A24   72h dark blue   3.25   3.00
81   A25   1k brn vio, straw   12.50   .35
82   A25   2k dk gray, bl   7.25   .25
83   A26   3k carmine, grn   12.00   9.00
84   A26   5k dk vio, gray   22.50   20.00
85   A26   10k dk ultra, gray   82.50   70.00
    ('14)
    Nos. 65-85 (21)   170.00   105.70

Value, imperf. set, $450.

For overprints and surcharges see #127, B5-B8, Austria M1-M21.

A27

A28

1916-17   **Perf. 12½**
86	A27	3h dark gray	.20	.20
87	A27	5h olive green	.25	.35
88	A27	6h violet	.30	.35
89	A27	10h bister	1.40	1.60
90	A27	12h blue gray	.45	.45
91	A27	15h car rose	.20	.20
92	A27	20h brown	.35	.45
93	A27	25h blue	.25	.35
94	A27	30h dark green	.25	.35
95	A27	40h vermilion	.25	.35
96	A27	50h green	.25	.35
97	A27	60h lake	.25	.35
98	A27	80h orange brn	1.25	.40
a.		Perf. 11½	3.50	3.00
99	A27	90h dark violet	.75	.50
a.		Perf. 11½	450.00	675.00
101	A28	2k claret, *straw*	.85	.75
102	A28	3k green, *bl*	2.00	3.25
103	A28	4k carmine, *grn*	5.75	7.25
104	A28	10k dp vio, *gray*	15.00	20.00
		Nos. 86-104 (18)	30.00	37.50

Value, imperf. set, $175.
For overprints see Nos. B11-B12.

Emperor Karl I
A29   A30

1917   **Perf. 12½**
105	A29	3h olive gray	.20	.20
a.		Perf. 11½	75.00	75.00
b.		Perf. 12½x11½	13.00	21.00
106	A29	5h olive green	.20	.20
107	A29	6h violet	.30	.55
108	A29	10h orange brn	.20	.20
a.		Perf. 11½x12½	62.50	95.00
b.		Perf. 11½		
109	A29	12h blue	.50	.75
110	A29	15h brt rose	.20	.20
111	A29	20h red brown	.20	.20
112	A29	25h ultra	1.00	.50
113	A29	30h gray green	.25	.20
114	A29	40h olive bis	.25	.20
115	A29	50h dp green	.85	.50
116	A29	60h car rose	.85	.45
a.		Perf. 11½	15.00	21.00
117	A29	80h steel blue	.25	.25
118	A29	90h dull violet	1.00	1.40
119	A30	2k carmine, *straw*	.50	.45
120	A30	3k green, *bl*	13.00	16.00
121	A30	4k carmine, *grn*	5.25	7.25
122	A30	10k dp vio, *gray*	3.25	5.75
		Nos. 105-122 (18)	28.25	35.25

Value, imperf. set, $85.

Nos. 47 and 66 Overprinted in Red

1918
126	A4	2h violet	.45	.50
b.		Inverted overprint	17.50	
d.		Double overprint	37.50	
f.		Double overprint, one inverted		
127	A23	2h bright blue	.50	.60
a.		Pair, one without overprint		
b.		Inverted overprint	15.00	
c.		Double overprint	15.00	
d.		Double overprint, one inverted		

Emperor Karl I — A31

1918   **Typo.**   **Perf. 12½, Imperf.**
128	A31	2h orange	9.00
129	A31	3h dark green	9.00
130	A31	5h lt green	9.00
131	A31	6h blue green	9.00
132	A31	10h brown	9.00
133	A31	20h brick red	9.00
134	A31	25h ultra	9.00
135	A31	45h dk slate	9.00
136	A31	50h lt bluish grn	9.00
137	A31	60h blue violet	9.00
138	A31	70h ocher	9.00
139	A31	80h rose	9.00
140	A31	90h violet brn	9.00

Engr.
141	A30	1k ol grn, *grnsh*	2,250.
		Nos. 128-140 (13)	117.00

Nos. 128-141 were prepared for use in Bosnia and Herzegovina, but were not issued there. They were sold after the Armistice at the Vienna post office for a few days.

SEMI-POSTAL STAMPS

Nos. 33 and 35 Surcharged in Red

1914   **Unwmk.**   **Perf. 12½**
B1	A4	7h on 5h dk grn	.40	.40
B2	A4	12h on 10h car	.40	.40

Various minor varieties of the surcharge include "4" with open top, narrow "4" and wide "4."
Nos. B1-B2 exist with double and inverted surcharges. Value about $20 each.

#33, 35 Surcharged in Red or Blue

1915   **Perf. 12½**
B3	A4	7h on 5h (R)	9.50	9.00
a.		Perf. 9½	140.00	140.00
B4	A4	12h on 10h (Bl)	.30	.30

Nos. B3-B4 exist with double and inverted surcharges. Value about $18.50 each.

#68, 70 Surcharged in Red or Blue

1915
B5	A23	7h on 5h (R)	.80	.75
a.		"1915" at top and bottom	35.00	37.50
B6	A23	12h on 10h (Bl)	1.40	1.50
a.		Surcharged "7 Heller."	35.00	37.50

Nos. B5-B6 are found in three types differing in length of surcharge lines:
I- date 18mm, denomination 14mm.
II- date 16mm, denomination 14mm.
III- date 18mm, denomination 16mm.
Nos. B5-B6 exist with double and inverted surcharges. Value $25 each.
Nos. B5a and B6a exist double and inverted.

#68, 70 Surcharged in Red or Blue

1916
B7	A23	7h on 5h (R)	.50	.65
B8	A23	12h on 10h (Bl)	.50	.65

Nos. B7-B8 exist with double and inverted surcharges. Value $12.50 each.

Wounded Soldier — SP1   Blind Soldier — SP2

1916   **Engr.**
B9	SP1	5h (+ 2h) green	.65	.60
B10	SP2	10h (+ 2h) magenta	1.00	.90

Nos. B9-B10 exist imperf. Value, set $27.50.

Nos. 89, 91 Overprinted

1917
B11	A27	10h bister	.20	.20
B12	A27	15h carmine rose	.20	.20

Nos. B11-B12 exist imperf. Value set, $16.
Nos. B11-B12 exist with double and inverted overprint. Value $9 each.

Design for Memorial Church at Sarajevo SP3

Archduke Francis Ferdinand — SP4

Duchess Sophia and Archduke Francis Ferdinand SP5

1917   **Typo.**   **Perf. 11½, 12½**
B13	SP3	10h violet black	.20	.20
B14	SP4	15h claret	.20	.20
B15	SP5	40h deep blue	.20	.20
		Nos. B13-B15 (3)	.60	.60

Assassination of Archduke Ferdinand and Archduchess Sophia. Sold at a premium of 2h each which helped build a memorial church at Sarajevo.
Exist imperf. Value, set $2.50.

Blind Soldier — SP6   Emperor Karl I — SP8

Design: 15h, Wounded soldier.

1918   **Engr.**   **Perf. 12½**
B16	SP6	10h (+ 10h) grnsh bl	.60	.55
B17	SP6	15h (+ 10h) red brn	.60	.55

#B16-B17 exist imperf. Value, set $18.50.

1918   **Typo.**   **Perf. 12½x13**
Design: 15h, Empress Zita.
B18	SP8	10h gray green	.35	.45
B19	SP8	15h brown red	.35	.45
B20	SP8	40h violet	.35	.45
		Nos. B18-B20 (3)	1.05	1.35

Sold at a premium of 10h each which went to the "Karl's Fund."
#B18-B20 exist imperf. Value, set $22.50.

POSTAGE DUE STAMPS

D1   D2

Perf. 9½, 10½, 12½ and Compound
1904   **Unwmk.**
J1	D1	1h black, red & yel	.45	.20
J2	D1	2h black, red & yel	.45	.20
J3	D1	3h black, red & yel	.50	.20
J4	D1	4h black, red & yel	.50	.20
J5	D1	5h black, red & yel	.50	.20
J6	D1	6h black, red & yel	.20	.20
J7	D1	7h black, red & yel	2.75	2.50
J8	D1	8h black, red & yel	2.75	.20
J9	D1	10h black, red & yel	.65	.20
J10	D1	15h black, red & yel	.60	.20
J11	D1	20h black, red & yel	3.25	.20
J12	D1	50h black, red & yel	2.25	.20
J13	D1	200h black, red & grn	9.25	.70
		Nos. J1-J13 (13)	24.10	5.70

Value, imperf. set, $150.
For overprints see Western Ukraine Nos. 61-72.

1916-18   **Perf. 12½**
J14	D2	2h red ('18)	.45	.55
J15	D2	4h red ('18)	.35	.40
J16	D2	5h red	.45	.55
J17	D2	6h red ('18)	.35	.40
J18	D2	10h red	.45	.55
J19	D2	15h red	3.25	4.00
J20	D2	20h red	.50	.60
J21	D2	25h red	1.40	1.75
J22	D2	30h red	1.10	1.40
J23	D2	40h red	8.75	10.00
J24	D2	50h red	26.00	32.50
J25	D2	1k dark blue	3.25	4.00
J26	D2	3k dark blue	14.50	17.50
		Nos. J14-J26 (13)	60.80	74.20

Nos. J25-J26 have colored numerals on a white tablet.
Value, imperf. set, $110.
For surcharges see Italy Nos. NJ1-NJ7.

NEWSPAPER STAMPS

Bosnian Girl — N1

1913 Unwmk. Imperf.

P1	N1	2h ultra	.40	.40
P2	N1	6h violet	1.75	1.50
P3	N1	10h rose	1.75	1.50
P4	N1	20h green	2.10	1.90
	Nos. P1-P4 (4)		6.00	5.30

After Bosnia and Herzegovina became part of Yugoslavia stamps of type N1 perf., and imperf. copies surcharged with new values, were used as regular postage stamps. See Yugoslavia Nos. 1L21-1L22, 1L43-1L45.

SPECIAL HANDLING STAMPS

"Lightning" — SH1

1916 Unwmk. Engr. Perf. 12½

QE1	SH1	2h vermilion	.20	.20
a.	Perf. 11½x12½		250.00	250.00
QE2	SH1	5h deep green	.35	.35
a.	Perf. 11½		13.00	13.00

For surcharges see Italy Nos. NE1-NE2.

BOSNIA AND HERZEGOVINA

ˈbäz-nē-ə and ˌhert-sə-gō-ˈvē-nə

LOCATION — Between Croatia and Yugoslavia.
GOVT. — Republic
CAPITAL — Sarajevo

Formerly part of Yugoslavia. Proclamation of independence in 1992 was followed by protracted civil war that was ended by the Dayton Peace Agreement of Nov. 21, 1995.

While Dinars were the official currency until 6/22/98, a currency pegged to the German mark was in use for some time prior to that. Stamps are denominated in pfennigs and marks in 11/97.

100 Paras = 1 Dinar
100 Pfennig = 1 Mark (6/22/98)

Catalogue values for all unused stamps in this country are for Never Hinged items.

Muslim Government in Sarajevo

Natl. Arms — A50

Denominations: 100d, 500d, 1000d, 5000d, 10,000d, 20,000d, 50,000d.

1993, Oct. 27 Litho. Imperf.
Booklet Stamps
200-206 A50 Set of 7   12.50 12.50

Nos. 200-206 each were available in bklts. of 50 (10 strips of 5).

1984 Winter Olympic Games, Sarajevo, 10th Anniv. — A51

#207, Games emblem. #208a, 100,000d, Four man bobsled. #208b, 200,000d, Hockey.

1994, Feb. 8
207 A51 50,000d org & blk   1.00 1.00
Souvenir Sheet
208 A51 Sheet of 2, #a.-b.   8.25 8.25

No. 208 contains 45x27mm stamps.

Souvenir Sheet

Bairam Festival A52

Various illustrations from Koran: a, 400d. b, 600d.

1995, May 12 Perf. 14
209 A52 Sheet of 2, #a.-b.   10.50 10.50

Main Post Office, Sarajevo A53

Designs: 10d, Facade. 20d, 30d, Demolished interior. 35d, 50d, Pre-civil war exterior. 100d, 200d, Post-war exterior.

1995, June 12
210-216 A53 Set of 7   5.00 5.00
216a Pane of 7   6.00 6.00

No. 216a sold unattached in booklet covers.

Bosnian History A54

Designs: 35d, Historical map, 10th-15th cent. 100d, Tomb, vert. 200d, Arms, Kotromanic Dynasty, vert. 300d, Charter by Ban Kulin, 1189.

1995, Aug. 12 Perf. 11½
217-220 A54 Set of 4   7.50 7.50

Peace & Freedom, Europa A55

1995, Sept. 25
221 A55 200d multicolored   2.50 2.50

A56   A57

1995, Sept. 25
222 A56 100d multicolored   1.25 1.25

World Post Day.

1995, Oct. 12
Flowers: No. 223: a, 100d, Simphyandra hofmannii. b, 200d, Lilium bosniacum.
223 A57 Pair, #a.-b.   3.50 3.50

Fish A58

No. 224: a, 100d, Aulopyge hugeli. b, 200d, Paraphoxinus alepidotus.

1995, Oct. 12
224 A58 Pair, #a.-b.   3.50 3.50

Children's Week A59

1995, Oct. 12
225 A59 100d multicolored   1.25 1.25

Electric Tram System, Sarajevo, Cent. A60

1995, Oct. 12
226 A60 200d multicolored   2.50 2.50

Bridges A61

Designs: 20d, Kozija, Sarajevo. 30d, Arslanagica, Trebinje. 35d, Latinska, Sarajevo. 50d, Old Bridge, Mostar. 100d, Visegrad.

1995, Dec. 12
227-231 A61 Set of 5   3.00 3.00

Christmas A62

Designs: 100d, Visiting friends. 200d, Madonna and Child, vert.

1995, Dec. 24
232-233 A62 Set of 2   3.50 3.50

A63   A64

Designs: 30d, Queen Jelena's tomb.

1995, Dec. 31
234 A63 30d multicolored   .35 .35

1995, Dec. 31
Design: Husein Gradascevic (1802-33).
235 A64 35d multicolored   .35 .35

Mirza Safvet Basagic (1870-1934) — A65

1995, Dec. 31
236 A65 100d multicolored   1.10 1.10

Religious Diversity A66

1995, Dec. 31
237 A66 35d multicolored   .50 .50

Destruction of Olympic Stadium, Sarajevo — A67

35d, Stadium, various skaters. 100d, Stadium ablaze, vert.

1995, Dec. 31
238-239 A67 Set of 2   1.60 1.60

Famous Women — A68

Europa: 80d, Bahrija Hadzic (1904-93), opera singer. 120d, Nasiha Hadzic (1932-95), writer.

1996, Apr. 15 Perf. 15
240-241 A68 Set of 2   3.50 3.50

UNICEF, 50th Anniv. — A69

Designs: a, 50d, Child stepping on land mine. b, 150d, Child's handprint.

1996, Apr. 15 Perf. 11½
242 A69 Pair, #a.-b.   3.50 3.50

Bobovac
Castle — A70

Bairam
Festival — A71

1996, May 5   **Perf. 11½**
243 A70 35d multicolored   .50 .50

1996, May 5   **Perf. 14**
244 A71 80d multicolored   1.10 1.10
No. 244 was issued in sheets of 2.

Sarajevo
Town Hall,
Cent.
A72

1996, May 5   **Perf. 11½**
245 A72 80d multicolored   1.10 1.10

Bosnian
Journalists
Assoc.,
Cent.
A73

1996, May 5
246 A73 100d multicolored   1.40 1.40

Essen '96,
Intl.
Philatelic
Expo
A74

1996, May 25   **Perf. 11½**
247 A74 200d multicolored   3.75 3.75

1996 Summer
Olympic Games,
Atlanta — A75

No. 248: a, 120d, Baron de Coubertin. b,
80d, Olympic Torch. c, 30d, Runners. d, 35d,
Atlanta Games emblem.

1996, May 25
248 A75 Block of 4, #a.-d.   4.75 4.75
Background of No. 248 differs with location
on sheet.

Alexander
Graham
Bell's
Telephone,
120th
Anniv.
A76

1996, July 10   **Perf. 11½**
249 A76 80d multicolored   1.40 1.40

Extension of Privleges to Dubrovnik by
Ban Stepan II, 1333
A77

1996, July 10
250 A77 100d multicolored   1.75 1.75

Use of
Mail Vans
in Bosnia,
Cent.
A78

1996, July 10
251 A78 120d multicolored   2.10 2.10

Flowers — A79

No. 252: a, 30d, Campanula hercegovina. b,
35d, Iris bosniaca.

1996, July 10
252 A79 Pair, #a.-b.   1.25 1.25
Printed checkerwise on the sheet.

Dogs
A80

No. 253: a, 35d, Barak. b, 80d, Tornjak.

1996, July 10
253 A80 Pair, #a.-b.   2.00 2.00
Printed checkerwise on the sheet.

SOS Children's
Village,
Sarajevo — A81

1996, Sept. 1
254 A81 100d multicolored   1.75 1.75

A83   A84

Traditional costumes - No. 255: a, 50d, Moslem, Bjelasnice. b, 80d, Croatian. c, 100d,
Moslem, Sarajevo.
Uniforms - No. 256: a, 35d, Bogomil soldier.
b, 80d, Austro-Hungarian rifleman. c, 100d,

Turkish light cavalry. d, 120d, Medieval Bosnian king.

1996, Sept. 20
255 A83 Strip of 3, #a.-c. + label 4.00 4.00
256 A84 Strip of 4, #a.-d.   6.00 6.00

Winter
Festival,
Sarajevo
A85

1996, Nov. 25
257 A85 100d multicolored   1.75 1.75

Bosnia
Day — A86

1996, Nov. 25
258 A86 120d Map, natl. arms   2.10 2.10

Christmas
A87

1996, Dec. 21
259 A87 100d multicolored   1.75 1.75

Visit by Pope John
Paul II — A88

1996, Dec. 21   **Perf. 14**
260 A88 500d multicolored   8.00 8.00

Archaeological
Finds — A89

Designs: 35d, Paleolithic rock carving,
Badanj. 50d, Neolithic ceramic head, Butmir.
80d, Bronze age bird wagon, Glasinac.
Walls of Daorson, Illyria - No. 264: a, 100d,
Walls, rock face at L. b, 120d, Low wall outside
city wall.

1997, Mar. 31   **Perf. 15**
261-263 A89 Set of 3   2.75 2.75
Souvenir Sheet
264 A89 Sheet of 2, #a.-b.   3.50 3.50

Children's
Week — A90

Bairam
Festival — A91

1997, Apr. 15   **Perf. 11½**
265 A90 100d multicolored   1.60 1.60

1997, Apr. 15   **Perf. 11½**
266 A91 200d Ferhad Pasha
Mosque   3.25 3.25

A92

1997, Apr. 25   **Perf. 14**
267 A92 100d multicolored   1.60 1.60
Mujaga Komadina (1839-1925), mayor of
Mostar.

A93

1997, May 3   **Perf. 11½**
Europa (Myths & Legends): 100d, Trojan
warriors, map. 120d, Man on prayer mat, castle from The Miraculous Spring of Ajvatovica.
268-269 A93 Set of 2   3.50 3.50

Greenpeace, 25th Anniv. — A94

Rainbow Warrior, inscribed: a, 35d, Grace.
b, 80d, Dorreboom. c, 100d, Beltra. d, 120d,
Morgan.

1997, May 25
270 A94 Block or strip of 4, #a.-
d.   5.25 5.25

Third Intl.
Film
Festival,
Sarajevo
A95

1997, June 15
271 A95 110d multicolored   1.75 1.75

Mediterranean Games, Bari — A96

Designs: 40d, Games emblem. 130d, Boxing, basketball, kick boxing.

1997, June 15
272-273 A96 Set of 2 .... 2.50 2.50

Discovery of Electrons, Cent. A97

1997, June 25
274 A97 40d multicolored .... .65 .65

Vasco da Gama's Voyage Around Africa, 500th Anniv. — A98

1997, June 25
275 A98 110d multicolored 1.75 1.75

Stamp Day — A99

1997, June 25
276 A99 130d multicolored 2.10 2.10

Railroads in Bosnia & Herzegovina, 125th Anniv. — A100

1997, June 25
277 A100 150d multicolored 2.25 2.25

Fauna — A101 / A102

No. 278: a, 40d, Dinaromys bogdanovi. b, 80d, Triturus alpestris.
No. 279: a, 40d, Oxytropis prenja. b, 110d, Dianthus freynii.

1997, Aug. 25
278 A101 Pair, #a.-b. 1.90 1.90
279 A101 Pair, #a.-b. 2.40 2.40

1997, Aug. 25

World Peace Day: a, 50d, Sweden, Switzerland, Australia & other flags. b, 60d, Flags,

globe showing Europe, Africa. c, 70d, Flags, globe showing North & South America. d, 110d, US, UK, Canadian & other flags.
280 A102 Strip of 4, #a.-d. 4.50 4.50

Great Sarajevo Fire, 300th Anniv. — A103

1997, Sept. 15
281 A103 110d multicolored 1.75 1.75

Architecture — A104

Designs: 40d, House with attic. 50d, Tiled stove, door. 130d, Three-storied house.

1997, Sept. 15
282-284 A104 Set of 3 .... 3.50 3.50

Italian Pioneer Corps Aid in Reconstruction of Sarajevo — A105

1997, Nov. 1   **Perf. 14**
285 A105 1.40m multicolored 2.25 2.25

Famous Men A106

1.30m, Augustin Tin Ujevic (1891-1955), writer. 2m, Zaim Imamovic (1920-94), singer, vert.

1997, Nov. 1   **Perf. 11½**
286-287 A106 Set of 2 .... 5.25 5.25

Diana, Princess of Wales (1961-97) — A107

1997, Nov. 3   **Perf. 14**
288 A107 2.50m multicolored 4.00 4.00

Gnijezdo, by Fikret Libovac A108

globe showing Europe, Africa. c, 70d, Flags, globe showing North & South America. d, 110d, US, UK, Canadian & other flags.

Sarajevo Library, by Nusret Pasic A109

1997, Nov. 6   **Perf. 11½**
289-290 A108-A109 Set of 2 ...... 1.75 1.75

Samac-Sarajevo Railway, 50th Anniv. — A110

1997, Nov. 17   **Perf. 14**
291 A110 35pf multicolored .... .55 .55

A111 / A112

Religious Holidays: 50pf, Nativity Scene, Orthodox Christmas. No. 293, 1.10m, Wreath on door, Christmas. No. 294, 1.10m, Pupils before teacher, Hagada.

1997, Dec. 22   **Perf. 11½**
292-294 A111 Set of 3 .... 4.25 4.25

1998, Jan. 15   **Perf. 14**

Designs: a, 35pf, Sports. b, 1m, Games emblem.
295 A112 Sheet of 2, #a.-b. 2.00 2.00

1998 Winter Olympic Games, Nagano.

Bairam Festival — A113

1998, Jan. 28
296 A113 1m Mosque fountain 1.50 1.50

Ahmed Muradbegovic (1898-1972), Writer — A114

1998, Mar. 20
297 A114 1.50m multicolored 2.25 2.25

Fortified Towns — A115

No. 298: a, 35pf, Zvornik. b, 70pf, Bihac. c, 1m, Pocitelj. d, 1.20m, Gradacac.

1998, Mar. 20
298 A115 Booklet pane of 4, #a.-d. 5.00 5.00
     Complete booklet, #298 .... 5.00

A116 / A117

1998, May 5   **Perf. 11½**
299 A116 1.10m multicolored 1.60 1.60

Intl. Theater Festival, Sarajevo, Europa.

1998, May 5

Former Presidents of Univ. of Arts and Science: 40pf, Branislav Durdev (1908-93). 70pf, Alojz Benac (1914-92). 1.30m, Edhem Camo (1909-96).

300-302 A117 Set of 3 .... 3.50 3.50

A118 / A119

Ciconia Ciconia - No. 303: a, 70pf, Three in water. b, 90pf, Two in flight. c, 1.10m, Two in nest. d, 1.30m, Adult, chicks.

1998, May 5
303 A118 Strip of 4, #a.-d. 4.00 4.00

1998, May 22
304 A119 2m Sheet with 2 labels 3.25 3.25

World Congress of Intl. League of Humanists, Sarajevo.

1998 World Cup Soccer Championships, France — A120

50pf, Soccer balls. 1m, Map, soccer ball. 1.50m, Asim Ferhatovic Hase (1934-87), soccer player.

1998, May 22   **Perf. 14½**
305-307 A120 Set of 3 .... 4.50 4.50

A121   A122

1998, July 20   *Perf. 11½*
308 A121 1.10m multicolored   1.75 1.75
Sarajevo Tunnel, 5th anniv.

1998, July 30
Mushrooms: 50pf, Morchella esculenta. 80pf, Cantharellus cibarius. 1.10m, Boletus edulis. 1.35m, Amanita caesarea.
309-312 A122 Set of 4   6.00 6.00

Paris Subway A123

1998, Aug. 30
313 A123 2m violet blue & green 3.25 3.25

Henri Dunant — A124

1998, Sept. 14   *Perf. 14*
314 A124 50pf multicolored   .75 .75
Intl. Red Cross fight against tuberculosis.

Cities — A125

1998, Sept. 24
315 A125 5pf Travnik   .20 .20
316 A125 38pf Sarajevo   .45 .45

Chess A126

Bosnian players - No. 317: a, 20pf, Woman at chess board. b, 40pf, Silver medal team, 31st Chess Olympiad. c, 60pf, Women's team, 32nd Chess Olympiad. d, 80pf, Men, Women's teams, 11th European Chess Championships.

1998, Sept. 24
317 A126 Sheet of 4, #a.-d.   3.25 3.25

A127   A128

1998, Oct. 9   *Perf. 11½*
318 A127 1m multicolored   1.60 1.60
World Post Day.

1998, Oct. 23
319 A128 80pf Musical instruments   1.40 1.40

Intl. Day of Disabled Persons A129

1998, Dec. 3
320 A129 1m multicolored   1.60 1.60

Mt. Bjelasnica A130

1998, Dec. 3
321 A130 1m multicolored   1.60 1.60

Universal Declaration of Human Rights, 50th Anniv. — A131

1998, Dec. 10   *Perf. 14½*
322 A131 1.35m multicolored   2.25 2.25

New Year A132

Christmas — A133

Designs: 1m, Child's drawing. 1.50m, Fr. Andeo Zvizdovic (1420?-98).

1998, Dec. 18   *Perf. 11½*
323-324 A132-A133 Set of 2   4.25 4.25

School Anniversaries — A134

Designs: No. 325, 40pf, First Sarajevo High School, 120th anniv. No. 326, 40pf, Sarajevo University, 50th anniv., vert.

1999, Apr. 22   *Litho.*   *Perf. 11¾*
325-326 A134 Set of 2   1.10 1.10

Flora and Fauna A135

80pf, Pigeons. 1.10m, Knautia sarajevensis.

1999, Apr. 22   *Litho.*   *Perf. 11¾*
327-328 A135 Set of 2   2.75 2.75

First Manned Moon Landing, 30th Anniv. — A136

1999, May 20   *Litho.*   *Perf. 11¾*
329 A136 2m multicolored   3.00 3.00

Una River - A137

1999, May 20
330 A137 2m multicolored   3.00 3.00

Gorazde A137a

1999, June 9   *Litho.*   *Perf. 14x14¼*
330A A137a 40pf multi   .50 .50

World Environmental Protection Day — A138

1999, June 15   *Litho.*   *Perf. 11¾*
331 A138 80pf Buna River Wellspring   1.10 1.10

Philex France 99 — A139

1999, June 15
332 A139 2m multicolored   2.75 2.75

Special Olympics A140

1999, June 15
333 A140 50pf multicolored   .70 .70

Bosnia & Herzegovina Postage Stamps, 120th Anniv. — A141

1999, July 1
334 A141 1m multicolored   1.00 1.00

UPU, 125th Anniv. — A142

1999, July 1   *Litho.*   *Perf. 11¾*
335 A142 1.50m multi   1.60 1.60

Minerals A143

Designs: 40pf, Tuzlite. 60pf, Siderite. 1.20m, Hijelofan. 1.80m, Quartz, vert.

1999, July 27   *Litho.*   *Perf. 11¾*
336-339 A143 Set of 4   4.25 4.25

Dzuzovi Mehmed Pasha Sokolovic Koran Manuscript A144

1999, Sept. 23
340 A144 1.50m multicolored   1.60 1.60

Kursumli Medresa Library, Founded 1537 — A145

1999, Sept. 23
341 A145 1m multicolored   1.00 1.00

Radiology in Bosnia & Herzegovina, Cent. — A146

1999, Oct. 5
342 A146 90pf multicolored   .95 .95

Handija Kasevljakovic (1888-1959), Historian — A147

1999, Oct. 5
343 A147 1.30m multicolored   1.40 1.40

25th European Chess Club Cup Finals — A148

1999, Oct. 29   Litho.   Perf. 14
344 A148 1.10m multicolored   1.10 1.10

Hvalov Zbornik, Book in Glagolitic Text — A149

1999, Sept. 23   Litho.   Perf. 11¾
345 A149 1.10m multicolored   1.10 1.10

Sarajevo Summit A150

1999, July 29   Litho.   Perf. 14
346 A150 2m multi   2.10 2.10

Expo 2000, Hanover A151

1999, Nov. 9   Litho.   Perf. 11¾
347 A151 1m multi   1.25 1.25

Painting by Afan Ramic A152

1999, Nov. 25
348 A152 1.20m multi   1.50 1.50

Birth of Six Billionth Person A153

1999, Nov. 25   Perf. 14
349 A153 2.50m multi   3.25 3.25

Souvenir Sheet

Bjelasnica Weather Observatory, 105th Anniv. — A154

1999, Dec. 15
350 A154 1.10m multi   1.40 1.40

Sarajevo Philharmonic A155   Sarajevo Intl. Music Festival A156

1999, Dec. 20
351 A155 40pf multi   .50 .50
352 A156 1.10m multi   1.40 1.40

Mehmed Spaho (1883-1939), Politician — A157

2000, Mar. 15   Perf. 11¾
353 A157 1m multi   1.25 1.25

Bairam Festival — A158

2000, Mar. 15
354 A158 1.10m multi   1.40 1.40

Amateur Radio in Bosnia and Herzegovina, 50th Anniv. — A159

2000, Mar. 15
355 A159 1.50m multi   1.90 1.90

Oriental Institute, Sarajevo, 50th Anniv. — A160

2000, Mar. 15
356 A160 2m multi   2.50 2.50

Souvenir Sheet

2000 Summer Olympics, Sydney — A161

Emblem of Sydney Olympics and map of: a, 1.30m, Bosnia & Herzegovina. b, 1.70m, Australia.
Illustration reduced.

2000, Apr. 10   Litho.   Perf. 14¾
357 A161 Sheet of 2, #a-b   3.75 3.75

Europa, 2000
Common Design Type
2000, May 9   Perf. 11¾
358 CD17 2m multi   2.40 2.40

Birds A162

1m, Gyps fulvus. 1.50m, Platalea leucorodia.

2000, May 9   Litho.   Perf. 11¾
359-360 A162 Set of 2   3.00 3.00

Lake Boracko A163

River Una Emeralds — A164

2000, May 9
361 A163 40pf multi   .50 .50
362 A164 1m multi   1.10 1.10
World Environmental Protection Day.

Souvenir Sheet

Greenpeace — A165

a, 50pf, Fish. b, 60pf, Lobster. c, 90pf, Anemones. d, 1.50m, Diver on shipwreck. Illustration reduced.

2000, May 9   Perf. 11¾x11½
363 A165 Sheet of 4, #a-d   4.00 4.00

First Zeppelin Flight, Cent. A166

2000, June 10   Perf. 11¾
364 A166 1.50m multi   1.75 1.75

Animals — A176

No. 383: a, 1.10m, Equus caballus facing right. b, 1.90m, Equus caballus facing left. Illustration reduced.

Perf. 11¾x11½
2001, Mar. 22   Litho.
383 A176 Horiz. pair, #a-b   2.50 2.50
A number has been reserved for an additional item in this set.

Souvenir Sheet

Comic Strips — A179

Inscriptions: a, Ti si moje janje. b, Ti si moj medo. c, Ti si moja maca. d, Ti si moj cvijet. e, Ti si moje pile.

2001, Mar. 22   Litho.   Perf. 11¾
Granite Paper
386 A179 30pf Sheet of 5, #a-e   1.25 1.25

Souvenir Sheet

Europa — A180

2001, Apr. 10   **Perf. 11½x11¾**
387   A180   2m multi   1.75   1.75

BOSNIA AND HERZEGOVINA (CROAT ADMIN.)

Bosnian Croat Administration Located In Mostar
(Herceg Bosna)

100 Paras = 1 Dinar (1993)
100 Lipa = 1 Kuna (1994)
100 pfennig = 1 Mark (6/22/98)

Catalogue values for all unused stamps in this country are for Never Hinged items.

A1

1993, May 12   **Litho.**   **Perf. 14**
1   A1   2000d multicolored   1.60   1.60
Our Lady of Peace Shrine, Medjugorje.

A2

1993
Silvije Kranjcevic (1865-1908), poet: 500d, Waterfall, gate at Jajce. 1000d, Old bridge, Mostar, horiz.

2-4   A2   Set of 3   1.40   1.40
Issued: 200d, 5/20; 500d, 5/18; 1000d, 5/15.

Census in Bosnia & Herzegovina, 250th Anniv. — A3

1993, May 24
5   A3   100d Medieval gravestone   .20   .20

Madonna of the Grand Duke, by Raphael — A4

1993, Dec. 3
6   A4   6000d multicolored   2.75   2.75
Christmas.

Paintings, by Gabrijel Jurkic (1886-1974) — A5

Europa: a, 3500d, Uplands in Bloom. b, 5000d, Wild Poppy.

1993, Dec. 6
7   A5   Pair, #a.-b.   6.75   6.75

Kravica Waterfalls A6

1993, Dec. 7
8   A6   3000d multicolored   1.50   1.50

Grand Duke Hrvoje Vukcic-Hrvatinic (1350-1416) — A7

1993, Dec. 8
9   A7   1500d multicolored   .75   .75

Pleham Monastery A8

1993, Dec. 15
10   A8   2200d multicolored   1.00   1.00

Formation of Bosnian Croat Administration A9

1994, Feb. 10
11   A9   10,000d multicolored   4.25   4.25

Bronze Cross, Rama A10

1994, Nov. 28
12   A10   2.80k multicolored   1.25   1.25

Flora & Fauna — A11

a, 3.80k, Campanula hercegovina. b, 4k, Dog.

1994, Nov. 30
13   A11   Pair, #a.-b.   3.25   3.25

Hutovo Wetlands A12

1994, Dec. 2
14   A12   80 l multicolored   .40   .40

Europa — A13

Transportation: a, 8k, Bicycles, 1885. b, 10k, 1901 Mercedes.

1994, Dec. 5
15   A13   Pair, #a.-b.   7.00   7.00

City of Ljubuski, 550th Anniv. — A14

1994, Dec. 8
16   A14   1k multicolored   .45   .45

Dr. Nikolic Franciscan Hospital, Nova Bila, 2nd Anniv. — A15

1994, Dec. 12
17   A15   5k multicolored   2.25   2.25

UN, 50th Anniv. — A16

1995, Oct. 24   **Rouletted**
Self-Adhesive
18   A16   1.50k Card of 10   6.75   6.75
Color ranges from pale pink at UL of card to dark rose at LR of card. Each stamp is numbered at LR.

Christmas — A17

1995, Dec. 4   **Perf. 14**
19   A17   5.40k multicolored   2.25   2.25

Kraljeva Sutjeska Monastery A18

1995, Dec. 7
20   A18   3k multicolored   1.40   1.40

Cities — A19

Monasteries: 2k, Srebrenica. 4k, Mostar.

1995
21-22   A19   Set of 2   2.50   2.50
Issued: 2k, 12/20; 4k, 12/12.

1995, Dec. 28
23   A20   6.50k multicolored   2.75   2.75

A21   Europa — A22

1996, June 24
24   A21   10k multicolored   4.25   4.25
a.   Booklet pane of 4   17.00
     Complete booklet, #24a   17.00

Apparitions at Medugorje, 15th anniv.

1996, July 20
25   A22   2.40k multicolored   1.00   1.00
Queen Katarina Kosaca Kotromanic.

A23   A24

1996, July 23
26   A23   1.40k multicolored   .60   .60
Franciscan Monastery, Siroki Brijeg, 150th anniv.

1996, Aug. 14   **Rouletted**
Self-Adhesive
Virgin Mary.
27   A24   2k multicolored   .85   .85
a.   Card of 10   8.50
28   A24   9k multicolored   3.75   3.75
a.   Card of 5 + 5 labels   19.00

Nos. 27-28 Surcharged

1.10

1996, Oct. 21   **Rouletted**
Self-Adhesive
29 A24 1.10k on 2k multi
  a.   Card of 10
30 A24 1.10k on 9k multi
  a.   Card of 5 + 5 labels
    Taipei '96 Philatelic Exhibition.

Christmas — A25   Europa — A26

1996, Dec. 8   **Litho.**   **Perf. 14**
31 A25 2.20k multicolored   1.00 1.00

1997, Apr. 4
  Myths & legends: a, 2k, St. George slaying
the dragon. b, 5k, Zeus coming to Europa dis-
guised as a bull.
32 A26 Pair, #a.-b.   2.75 2.75
    No. 32b is 39x34mm.

A27   A28

1997, Apr. 12
33 A27 3.60k multicolored   1.50 1.50
  a.   Pane of 4   6.00
    Visit of Pope John Paul II.

1997, Apr. 20
34 A28 1.40k Samatorje Church   .65 .65

Flora &
Fauna — A29

  Designs: 1k, Ardea purpurea. 2.40k,
Symphyandra hofmannii.

1997
35-36 A29   Set of 2   1.60 1.60
    Issued: 1k, 11/19. 2.40k, 11/17.

Christmas
A30

1997, Dec. 1
37 A30 1.40k multicolored   .65 .65

World
Animated
Film
Festival
A31

1998, Apr. 1
38 A31 6.50k multicolored   2.75 2.75
    Europa.

Hercegovina,
550th
Anniv. — A32

1998, Apr. 8
39 A32 2.30k multicolored   1.00 1.00

City of Livno,
1100th
Anniv. — A33

1998, Apr. 9
40 A33 1.20k multicolored   .50 .50

Sibiraea   Gyps
Croatica — A34   Fulvus — A35

1998, Nov. 9
41 A34 1.40k multicolored   .60 .60

1998, Nov. 16
42 A35 2.40m multicolored   1.00 1.00

A36   A37

1998, Dec. 2
43 A36 5.40k Christmas   2.25 2.25

1999, Mar. 26   **Litho.**   **Perf. 14**
44 A37 40pf Native attire   .65 .65

A. B. Simic (1898-
1925) — A38

1999, Mar. 29
45 A38 30pf multi   .50 .50

Bobovac
Castle — A39

1999, Mar. 30
46 A39 10pf multi   .20 .20

Europa — A40

1999, Mar. 31
47 A40 1.50m Blidinje Park   2.50 2.50

Dianthus
Freynii — A41

1999, Oct. 11   **Litho.**   **Perf. 14**
48 A41 80pf multi   1.00 1.00

Martes
Martes — A42

1999, Oct. 15
49 A42 40pf multi   .50 .50

Stolac
Castle — A43

1999, Nov. 3
50 A43 10pf multi   .20 .20

Christmas — A44

1999, Nov. 22
51 A44 30pf multi   .40 .40

BOSNIA AND
HERZEGOVINA (SERB
ADMIN.)

Bosnian Serb Administra-
tion Located In Banja Luca
(Republika Srpska)

100 Paras = 1 Dinar
100pfennig = 1 mark (6/22/98)

100

Stamps of Yugoslavia
Surcharged   Република
             Српска

1992, Oct. 26   **Litho.**   **Perf. 12½**
1	A559	5d on 10p #2004	.40	.40
2	A559	30d on 3d #2015	125.00	125.00
3	A559	50d on 40p #2007a, perf. 13½	1.00	1.00
a.		Thick bars in obliterator	5.00	5.00
b.		Oon #2007, perf 12½		
4	A559	60d on 20p #2005	1.25	1.25
5	A559	60d on 30p #2006	1.25	1.25
6	A559	100d on 1d #2013	2.00	2.00
7	A559	100d on 2d #2014a, perf. 13½	2.00	2.00
a.		On #2014, perf 12½		
8	A559	100d on 3d #2015	2.00	2.00
9	A621	300d on 5d #2017a, perf. 13½	6.00	6.00
a.		On #2017, perf 12½		
10	A620	500d on 50p #2008	10.00	10.00
11	A619	500d on 60p #2009	10.00	10.00
a.		On #2009 perf. 13½	90.00	90.00
		Nos. 1-11 (11)	160.90	160.90

Obliterator on Nos. 1, 3 and 9 has thin bars.

Musical
Instrument — A1

  Designs: 10d, 20d, 30d, 5000d, 6000d,
10,000d, Stringed instrument. 50d, 100d,
20,000d, 30,000d, Coat of arms, vert. 500d,
50,000d, Monastery.

1993   **Perf. 13¼, 12½ (#19)**
12	A1	10d blk & org yel	.20	.20
13	A1	20d blk & blue	.30	.30
14	A1	30d blk & salmon	.45	.45
15	A1	50d blk & ver	.75	.75
16	A1	100d blk & ver	1.50	1.50
17	A1	500d blk & ver	7.50	7.50
18	A1	5000d blk & lilac	.20	.20
19	A1	6000d blk & yel	.20	.20
20	A1	10,000d blk & vio bl	.30	.30
a.		Perf. 12½		
21	A1	20,000d blk & ver	.60	.60
22	A1	30,000d blk & ver	.90	.90
23	A1	50,000d blk & lilac	1.50	1.50
		Nos. 12-23 (12)	14.40	14.40

Nos. 12-17 dated 1992, others dated 1993.
Issued: Nos. 12-17, 1/11; others 6/8.
  For surcharges see Nos. 24-26, 34-36, 41-
45, F9

Nos. 15-16 Surcharged

1998, June 15
24	A1	7500d on 50d #15	2.00	2.00
25	A1	7500d on 100d #16	2.00	2.00
26	A1	9000d on 50d #15	2.75	2.75
		Nos. 24-26 (3)	6.75	6.75

    Referendum, May 15-16, 1993.

A2

A3

1993, Aug. 16   *Perf. 13¼*
Symbol of St. John, the Evangelist.
27   A2   (A) vermilion   1.00   1.00

1994, Jan. 9   *Perf. 14*
28   A3   1d Icon of St. Stefan   8.00   8.00

King Peter I
Karageorge
A4

1994, May 28
29   A4   80p sepia   5.00   5.00

City of
Banja
Luka,
500th
Anniv.
A5

1994, July 18
30   A5   1.20d multicolored   5.00   5.00

Nos. 31-32 have been reserved for surcharges on Nos. 13, 21. The editors would like to examine these stamps.

Madonna &
Child, Cajnica
Church — A6

1994, Sept. 1
33   A6   1d multicolored   5.00   5.00

Nos. 18, 20, 23
Surcharged

1994, Nov. 1   *Perf. 13¼*
34   A1   (A) on 5000d #18   1.75   1.75
35   A1   40p on 10,000d #20   1.75   1.75
  a.   on #20a
36   A1   2d on 50,000d #23   1.75   1.75
     Nos. 34-36,F9 (4)   7.00   7.00
No. 34 sold for 20p on day of issue.

Mostanica
Monastery
A7

Designs: 60p, Tavna Monastery, vert. 1.20d, Zitomislic Monastery, vert.

1994   *Perf. 14*
37-39   A7   Set of 3   14.50   14.50
Issued: 60p, 11/11; 1d, 12/31; 1.20d, 12/28.

Flora &
Fauna
A8

No. 40: a, Shore lark. b, Dinaromys bogdanovi. c, Edraianthus niveus. d, Aquilegia dinarica.

1996, Mar. 1   *Perf. 13¾*
40   A8   1.20d Block of 4, #a.-d.   7.00   7.00

Nos. 14-16, 19, 22
Surcharged

1996, July 1   *Perf. 13¼*
41   A1   70p on 30d #14   .60   .60
42   A1   1d on 100d #16   .80   .80
43   A1   2d on 30,000d #22   1.60   1.60
44   A1   3d on 50d #15   2.50   2.50
     Perf. 12½
45   A1   5d on 6000d #19   4.50   4.50
     Nos. 41-45 (5)   10.00   10.00

Relay Station, Mt.
Kozara — A9

1.20d, Drina River Bridge, Srbinje, horiz. 2d, Mt. Romanija relay station. 5d, Stolice relay station, Mt. Maljevica. 10d, Visegrad Bridge, horiz.

1996, Sept. 20   *Perf. 14*
46   A9   (A) multicolored   .20   .20
47   A9   1.20d multicolored   .70   .70
48   A9   2d multicolored   1.25   1.25
49   A9   5d multicolored   3.00   3.00
50   A9   10d multicolored   6.00   6.00
     Nos. 46-50,F10 (6)   11.70   11.70
No. 46 sold for 30p on day of issue.

Church,
Bashcharsi
A10

1997, July 7   *Perf. 13¾*
51   A10   2.50d multicolored   1.75   1.75

Mihailo Pupin
(1848-1935),
Electrical
Engineer
A11

1997, July 14
52   A11   2.50d multicolored   1.75   1.75

A12   A13

Flowers: No. 53, Oxytropis compestris. No. 54, Primula kitaibeliana. No. 55, Pedicularis hoermanniana. No. 56, Knautia sarajevensis.

1997, Sept. 12
53-56   A12   3.20d Set of 4   6.50   6.50

1997, Nov. 1   *Perf. 13¾*
Famous Men: A, Branko Copic (1915-85). 1.50d, Mesa Selimovic (1910-82). 3d, Aleksa Santic (1868-1924). 5d, Peter Kocic (1873-1916). 10d, Ivo Andric (1892-1975).
57   A13   A multicolored   .30   .30
58   A13   1.50d multicolored   .70   .70
59   A13   3d multicolored   1.40   1.40
60   A13   5d multicolored   2.25   2.25
61   A13   10d multicolored   4.50   4.50
     Nos. 57-61,F11 (6)   9.60   9.60
No. 57 sold for 60p on day of issue.

A14   Europa — A15

2.50d, Lutra lutra. 4.50d, Capreolus capreolus. 6.50d, Ursus arctos.

1997, Nov. 12
62-64   A14   Set of 3   7.25   7.25

1997, Nov. 12
Stories & legends: 2.50d, Two queens. 6.50d, Prince on horseback.
65-66   A15   Set of 2   6.25   6.25

Diana, Princess of Wales (1961-
97) — A16

"Diana" in: a, Roman letters. b, Cyrillic letters.

1997, Dec. 22
67   A16   3.50d Pair, #a.-b.   13.00   13.00

1998 World Cup
Soccer
Championships,
France — A17

Players, country flags - No. 68: a, Brazil. b, Morocco. c, Norway. d, Scotland. e, Italy. f, Chile. g, Austria. h, Cameroun.
No. 69: a, France. b, Saudi Arabia. c, Denmark. d, South Africa. e, Spain. f, Nigeria. g, Paraguay. h, Bulgaria.
No. 70: a, Netherlands. b, Belgium. c, Mexico. d, South Korea. e, Germany. f, US. g, Yugoslavia. h, Iran.
No. 71: a, Romania. b, England. c, Tunisia. d, Colombia. e, Argentina. f, Jamaica. g, Croatia. h, Japan.

1998, May 5
     Sheets of 8 + label
68-71   A17   90p each   10.00   10.00

Europa — A18

Natl. festivals: No. 72, Instrument at R. No. 73, Instrument at L.

1998, June 9
72-73   A18   7.50d Set of 2   6.25   6.25

Icons,
Chelandari
Monastery
A19

Various icons: 50p, 70p, 1.70d, 2d.

1998
74-77   A19   Set of 4   10.00   10.00

Buildings — A20

Designs: 15pf, Bijelina. 20pf, Sokolac. A, Banja Luca. 75pf, Prijedor. 2m, Brcko, vert. 4.50m, Zvornik, vert. 10m, Doboj.

1999, Mar. 15   *Litho.*   *Perf. 13¾*
78-84   A20   Set of 7   30.00   30.00
No. 80 (A) sold for 50pf on day of issue. See No. F12.

Air Srpska
Airplanes
A21

Airplane: No. 85, 50pf, In clouds. No. 86, 50pf, Over lake. 75pf, Over rocks. 1.50m, Over lake, diff.

1999, Mar. 26   *Litho.*   *Perf. 13¾*
85-88   A21   Set of 4   4.50   4.50

World Table Tennis Championships,
Belgrade — A22

Designs: 1m, Cracked globe as ball. 2m, Table, paddle, ball.

1999, Apr. 19
89-90   A22   Set of 2   5.50   5.50
Issued in sheets of 8 + label.

Europa — A23

Natl. Parks: 1.50m, Kozara. 2m, Peruchitsa.

1999, May 4
91-92   A23   Set of 2   6.00   6.00

Anniversaries — A24

No. 93: a, Gorazde incorporation document. b, Dobrin Monastery (denomination at UL). c, Illuminated letter. d, Zitomislic Monastery. e, Gomionica Monastery (2 steeples). f, Madonna and Child icon. g, St. Nicholas icon. h, Holy trinity icon.
Illustration reduced.

1999, May 26   Litho.   Perf. 13¾
93 A24 50pf Sheet of 8, #a-h, +
        label   6.50 6.50

Dabrobosanska and Zahum-skohercegovacka Archbishopric, 780th anniv., Gorazde Printing Press, 480th anniv.

Fish — A25

No. 94: a, 50pf, Salmo trutta m. fario. b, 50pf, Salmo trutta m. lacustris. c, 75pf, Hucho hucho. d, 1m, Thymallus thymallus.

1999, June 17
94 A25 Horiz. strip of 4, #a-d, +
        central label   5.50 5.50

Issued in sheets of 5 strips with different labels.

Man on the Moon, 30th Anniv. — A26

Designs: 1m, Equipment on moon. 2m, Astronaut, lunar module.

1999, July 21
95-96 A26 Set of 2   5.75 5.75
        Issued in sheets of 8 + 1 label.

UPU, 125th Anniv. — A27

Designs: 75pf, Pencil. 1.25m, Arc and map.

1999, Sept. 9
97-98 A27 Set of 2   4.00 4.00
        Issued in sheets of 8 + 1 label.

Icons — A28

No. 99: a, Madonna and Child (black denomination at UL). b, Madonna and Child (white denomination at UL). c, Madonna and Child (white denomination at LR). d, Saint with cross. e, Pieta. f, Christ enters Jerusalem (on donkey). g, St. Jovan (with scroll). h, Sts. Sava and Simeon.

1999, Oct. 29
99 A28 50pf Sheet of 8, #a-h, +
        label   7.75 7.75

Millennium A29

a, Egyptians, obelisk. b, Hourglass. c, Iron bell. d, Locomotive, steamship. e, Balloon, airplanes, automobiles. f, Man on the moon.

1999, Nov. 22
100   Booklet pane of 6   7.00 7.00
a.-e.   A29 50pf Any single   1.00 1.00
f.   A29 1m multi   2.00 2.00
         Booklet, #100   7.00
        See No. 126.

Postal Services in Serbian Territory, 135th Anniv. — A30

1999, Dec. 23
101 A30 50pf shown   .80 .80
        Souvenir Sheet
102 A30 3m Postriders on
        bridge   40.00 40.00

Prince Stephen Nemanja — A31

2000, Feb. 29
103 A31 1.50m multi   2.50 2.50
        Issued in sheets of 8 + 1 label.

Flora — A32

1m, Prunus domestica. 2m, Corylus avellana.

2000, Mar. 22
104-105 A32 Set of 2   5.00 5.00
        Issued in sheets of 8 + 1 label.

Bridges — A33

#106, Brod (deer at left). #107, Pavlovica (horses and birds). #108, Zepce (bird at right). #109, Zvornik (bird at left).

2000, Apr. 12
106-109 A33 1m Set of 4   6.50 6.50
        Issued in sheets of 8 + 1 label.

Jovan Ducic (1871-1943), Writer — A34

2000, Apr. 26   Litho.   Perf. 13¾
110 A34 20pf multi   .40 .40

Banja Luca Province, Cent. — A36

2000, May 26   Litho.   Perf. 13¾
113 A36 1.50m multi   3.00 3.00

European Soccer Championships A37

Various players. Denominations: 1m, 2m.

2000, June 14
114-115 A37 Set of 2   6.00 6.00
        Souvenir Sheet
116 A37 6m Players, map   15.00 15.00
        No. 116 contains one 35x42mm stamp.

Nevesinje Rebellion, 125th Anniv. — A38

2000, July 12
117 A38 1.50m multi   3.00 3.00

2000 Summer Olympics, Sydney A39

Map of Australia and: No. 118, 50pf, Handball. No. 119, 50pf, Basketball. No. 120, 50pf, Hurdles. No. 121, 50pf, Volleyball.
2m, Emu, kangaroo, Australian arms.

2000, Sept. 6
118-121 A39 Set of 4   4.00 4.00
        Souvenir Sheet
122 A39 2m multi + label   5.00 5.00
        No. 122 contains one 42x35mm stamp.

Locomotives A40

No. 123 - Locomotive from: a, 1848. b, 1865. c, 1930. d, 1990.

2000, Oct. 4   Litho.   Perf. 13¾
123   Horiz. strip of 4 + cen-
         tral label   3.75 3.75
a.-c.   A40 50pf Any single   .75 .75
d.   A40 1m multi   1.50 1.50

Protected Species — A41

Designs: 1m, Leontopodium alpinum. 2m, Proteus anguinus, horiz.

2000, Oct. 31
124-125 A41 Set of 2   4.25 4.25

Millennium Type of 1999

No. 126: a, Ship. b, Glassblowers. c, Blacksmith. d, Printers. e, James Watt, steam engine, steam-powered vehicle. f, Satellites. g, People on shore, ships (105x55mm).

2000, Nov. 22
126   Booklet pane of 7 + la-
         bel   7.50
a.-f.   A29 50pf Any single   .60 .60
g.   A29 3m multi   3.75 3.75
         Booklet, #126   7.50

Icons — A42

Icons from: No. 127, 50pf, 1577-78. No. 128, 50pf, 1607-08. No. 129, 1m, 1577-78. No. 130, 1m, Unknown year.

2000, Dec. 20
127-130 A42 Set of 4   4.25 4.25

Invention of the Telephone, 125th Anniv. — A43

2001, Feb. 27
131 A43 1m multi   1.50 1.50

Manned Space Flight, 40th Anniv.— A44

Designs: 1m, Yuri Gagarin, Vostok 1. 3m, Gagarin, Earth, rocket lift-off.

2001, Mar. 29
132 A44 1m multi   1.40 1.40
Souvenir Sheet
133 A44 3m multi   4.00 4.00
No. 133 contains one 53x35mm stamp.

Vlado
Milosevic,
Composer
A45

Europa
A46

2001, Apr. 11
134 A45 50pf multi   .65 .65

2001, May 4   Perf. 13¾
Designs: Nos. 135, 137a, 1m, Skakavac
Waterfall. No. 136, 137b, 2m, Turjanica River.
White Border
135-136 A46   Set of 2   4.00 4.00
Light Blue Border
Perf. 13¾ Vert.
137 A46   Vert. pair, #a-b   4.00 4.00
No. 137 printed in panes of 3 pairs which
were sold with a booklet cover, but unattached
to it.

Butterflies — A47

Designs: No. 138, 50pf, Maniola jurtina. No.
139, 50pf, Pyrgus malvae. No. 140, 1m,
Papilio machaon. No. 141, 1m, Lycaena
pylaeas.

2001, June   Perf. 13¾
138-141 A47   Set of 4   4.25 4.25

Kostanica
A48

Serbia — A49

2001, Aug.   Litho.   Perf. 13¾
142 A48 25pf multi   .35 .35
143 A49 1m multi   1.40 1.40

Karate
Championships
A50

2001, Aug.
144 A50 1.50m multi   2.10 2.10

REGISTRATION STAMPS

No. 19 Surcharged

1994, Nov. 1   Litho.   Perf. 13¼
F9 A1 (P) on 6,000d #19   1.75 1.75
No. F9 sold for 40p on day of issue.

Relay Station Type of 1996
Kraljica relay station, Mt. Ozren.

1996, Sept. 20   Perf. 14
F10 A9 (R) multicolored   .55 .55
No. F10 sold for 90p on day of issue.

Famous Men Type of 1997
1997, Nov. 1   Perf. 13¾
F11 A13 (R) Jovan Ducic (1871-
            1943)   .45 .45
No. F11 sold for 90p on day of issue.

Building Type of 1999
1999, Mar. 15   Litho.   Perf. 13¾
F12 A20 (R) Trebinje   1.60 1.60
No. F12 sold for 1m on day of issue.

POSTAL TAX STAMPS

Robert Koch
(1843-1910)
PT1

1997, Sept. 14   Litho.   Imperf.
Self-Adhesive
RA1 PT1 15p red & blue   1.25 1.25
Obligatory on mail 9/14-21.

Red
Cross — PT2

1998, May 5
Self-Adhesive
RA2 PT2 90p multicolored   1.50 1.50
Obligatory on mail 5/5-15.

Fight Against
Tuberculosis
PT3

1998, Sept. 14   Perf. 10¾
RA3 PT3 75pf multicolored   1.50 1.50
Obligatory on mail 9/14-21.

Red
Cross — PT4

1999, May 8   Litho.   Perf. 10¾
RA4 PT4 10pf multi   .35 .35
Obligatory on mail 5/8-5/15.

Red Cross — PT5

1999, Sept. 14   Litho.   Perf. 10¾
RA5 PT5 10pf multi   .40 .40
Obligatory on mail 9/14-21.

Red
Cross — PT6

2000, May 8   Litho.   Perf. 10¾
RA6 PT6 10pf multi   .35 .35
Obligatory on mail 5/8-5/15.

Red Cross — PT7

2000, Sept. 14   Litho.   Perf. 10¾
RA7 PT7 10pf multi   .30 .30
Obligatory on mail 9/14-21.

BOTSWANA

bä-'swä-nə

LOCATION — In central South Africa, north of the Republic of South Africa, east of South-West Africa and bounded on the north and east by Angola and Zimbabwe.
GOVT. — Independent republic
AREA — 222,000 sq. mi.
POP. — 1,464,167 (1999 est.)
CAPITAL — Gaborone

The former Bechuanaland Protectorate became an independent republic, September 30, 1966, taking the name Botswana.

100 Cents = 1 Rand
100 Thebe = 1 Pula (1976)

Catalogue values for all unused stamps in this country are for Never Hinged items.

National Assembly Building — A1

Designs: 5c, Abattoir, Lobatsi. 15c, Dakota plane. 35c, State House, Gaborone.

Unwmk.

1966, Sept. 30   Photo.   Perf. 14

1	A1	2½c multicolored	.20	.20
a.		Imperf., pair	225.00	
2	A1	5c multicolored	.30	.20
3	A1	15c multicolored	.90	.25
4	A1	35c multicolored	.60	.50
		Nos. 1-4 (4)	2.00	1.15

Establishment of Republic of Botswana.

Bechuanaland Protectorate Nos. 180-193 Overprinted

Perf. 14x14½, 14½x14

1966, Sept. 30   Wmk. 314

5	A15	1c multicolored	.20	.20
6	A15	2c multicolored	.20	.50
7	A15	2½c multicolored	.20	.20
8	A15	3½c multicolored	.20	.20
9	A15	5c multicolored	.20	.20
10	A15	7½c multicolored	.20	.20
11	A15	10c multicolored	.25	.25
12	A15	12½c multicolored	2.50	2.50
13	A15	20c gray & brown	.75	.40
14	A15	25c yel & dk brn	.55	.55
15	A15	35c dp org & ultra	.70	.70
16	A15	50c lt ol grn & sep	1.50	1.25
17	A15	1r ocher & black	2.50	1.50
18	A15	2r blue & brown	6.00	6.00
		Nos. 5-18 (14)	15.95	14.65

European Golden Oriole — A2

Birds: 2c, African hoopoe. 3c, Ground-scraper thrush. 4c, Blue waxbill. 5c, Secretary bird. 7c, Yellow-billed hornbill. 10c, Crimson-breasted shrike. 15c, Malachite kingfisher. 20c, Fish eagle. 25c, Gray lourie. 35c, Scimitar bill. 50c, Knob-billed duck. 1r, Crested barbet. 2r, Didric cuckoo.

1967, Jan. 3   Photo.   Perf. 14x14½

19	A2	1c gray & multi	.30	.20
20	A2	2c lt blue & multi	.45	.20
21	A2	3c yel green & multi	.60	.20
22	A2	4c salmon & multi	.60	.25
23	A2	5c pink & multi	.60	.30
24	A2	7c slate & multi	.65	.45
25	A2	10c emerald & multi	.65	.55
26	A2	15c lt green & multi	9.25	1.00
27	A2	20c ultra & multi	9.25	1.25
28	A2	25c green & multi	5.50	1.60
29	A2	35c multicolored	7.50	2.00
30	A2	50c dl yel & multi	3.50	3.00
31	A2	1r dl grn & multi	8.50	4.00
32	A2	2r org brn & multi	10.00	12.00
		Nos. 19-32 (14)	57.35	27.00

University Buildings and Graduates — A3

1967, Apr. 7   Perf. 14x14½

33	A3	3c yel, sepia & dp blue	.20	.20
34	A3	7c blue, sepia & dp bl	.20	.20
35	A3	15c dull rose, sepia & dp bl	.20	.20
36	A3	35c lt vio, sepia & dp bl	.30	.30
		Nos. 33-36 (4)	.90	.90

1st conferment of degrees by the University of Botswana, Lesotho and Swaziland at Roma, Lesotho.

Chobe Bush Bucks A4

Designs: 7c, Sable antelopes. 35c, Fishing on the Chobe River.

1967, Oct. 2   Photo.   Perf. 14

37	A4	3c multicolored	.20	.20
38	A4	7c multicolored	.20	.20
39	A4	35c multicolored	.95	.95
		Nos. 37-39 (3)	1.35	1.35

Publicity for Chobe Game Reserve.

Human Rights Flame and Arms of Botswana — A5

Design elements rearranged on 15c, 25c.

1968, Apr. 8   Litho.   Perf. 13½x13

40	A5	3c brown red & multi	.20	.20
41	A5	15c emerald & multi	.25	.35
42	A5	25c yellow & multi	.40	.40
		Nos. 40-42 (3)	.85	.95

International Human Rights Year.

Rock Painting A6

Girl Wearing Ceremonial Beads — A7

Designs: 10c, Baobab Trees, by Thomas Baines (34x25mm). 15c, National Museum and Art Gallery (71½x19mm).

Perf. 13x13½ (3c, 10c); Perf. 12½ (7c); Perf. 12½x13 (15c)

1968, Sept. 30   Litho.

43	A6	3c multicolored	.30	.20
44	A7	7c multicolored	.40	.35
45	A6	10c multicolored	.40	.30
46	A6	15c multicolored	.65	1.40
a.		Souv. sheet of 4, #43-46, perf. 13½	2.00	2.50
		Nos. 43-46 (4)	1.75	2.25

Opening of the National Museum and Art Gallery, Gaborone, Sept. 30, 1968.

African Nativity Scene A8

1968, Nov. 11   Unwmk.   Perf. 13x14

47	A8	1c car & multi	.20	.20
48	A8	2c brown & multi	.20	.20
49	A8	5c green & multi	.20	.20
50	A8	25c dp violet & multi	.25	.50
		Nos. 47-50 (4)	.85	1.10

Christmas.

Boy Scout, Botswana Scout Emblem and Lion — A9

Botswana Boy Scout Emblem, Lion and: 15c, Boy Scouts cooking, vert. 25c, Boy Scouts around campfire.

1969, Aug. 21   Litho.   Perf. 13½

51	A9	3c emerald & multi	.20	.20
52	A9	15c lt brown & multi	.85	.85
53	A9	25c dk brown & multi	1.50	1.50
		Nos. 51-53 (3)	2.55	2.55

22nd World Scouting Conf., Helsinki, Finland, Aug. 21-27.

Mother, Child and Star of Bethlehem — A10

Diamond Treatment Plant, Orapa — A11

1969, Nov. 6   Perf. 14½x14

54	A10	1c dk brn & lt blue	.20	.20
55	A10	2c dk brn & apple grn	.20	.20
56	A10	4c dk brn & dull yel	.20	.20
57	A10	35c dk brn & vio blue	.30	.30
a.		Souv. sheet, #54-57, perf 14½	1.25	1.40
		Nos. 54-57 (4)	.90	.90

Christmas.

1970, Mar. 23   Perf. 14½x14, 14x14½

Designs: 7c, Copper and nickel mining, Selebi-Pikwe. 10c, Copper and nickel mining and metal bars, Selebi-Pikwe, horiz. 35c, Orapa diamond mine and diamonds, horiz.

58	A11	3c multicolored	.50	.30
59	A11	7c multicolored	1.10	.30
60	A11	10c multicolored	2.25	.25
61	A11	35c multicolored	3.50	1.90
		Nos. 58-61 (4)	7.35	2.75

Botswana development program.

Mr. Micawber and Charles Dickens A12

Charles Dickens (1812-70), English novelist and: 7c, Scrooge. 15c, Fagin. 25c, Bill Sykes.

1970, July 7   Litho.   Perf. 11

62	A12	3c gray green & multi	.20	.20
63	A12	7c multicolored	.30	.20
64	A12	15c brown & multi	.60	.50
65	A12	25c dp violet & multi	1.00	.75
a.		Souvenir sheet of 4, #62-65	4.00	4.50
		Nos. 62-65 (4)	2.10	1.65

UN Headquarters, Emblem — A13

1970, Oct. 24   Litho.   Perf. 11

66	A13	15c ultra, red & silver	.70	.40

United Nations' 25th anniversary.

Toys A14

1970, Nov. 3   Litho.   Perf. 14

67	A14	1c Crocodile	.20	.20
68	A14	2c Giraffe	.20	.20
69	A14	7c Elephant	.20	.20
70	A14	25c Rhinoceros	.75	.75
a.		Souvenir sheet of 4, #67-70	2.00	2.00
		Nos. 67-70 (4)	1.35	1.35

Christmas.

Sorghum A15

1971, Apr. 6   Litho.   Perf. 14

71	A15	3c shown	.20	.20
72	A15	7c Millet	.20	.20
73	A15	10c Corn	.25	.20
74	A15	35c Peanuts	1.00	.65
		Nos. 71-74 (4)	1.65	1.25

Ox Head and Botswana Map — A16

Map of Botswana and: 4c, Cogwheels and waves. 7c, Zebra rampant. 10c, Tusk and corn. 20c, Coat of arms of Botswana.

1971, Sept. 30   Perf. 14½x14

75	A16	3c yel grn, blk & brn	.20	.20
76	A16	4c lt blue, blk & bl	.20	.20
77	A16	7c orange & blk	.20	.20

78	A16	10c yellow & multi	.30	.20
79	A16	20c blue & multi	.60	1.75
		Nos. 75-79 (5)	1.50	2.55

5th anniversary of independence.

King Bringing Gift — A17

1971, Nov. 11 *Perf. 14*

Christmas: 2c, King bringing gift. 7c, Kneeling King with gift. 20c, Three Kings and star.

80	A17	2c brt rose & multi	.20	.20
81	A17	3c lt blue & multi	.20	.20
82	A17	7c brt pink & multi	.20	.20
83	A17	20c vio blue & multi	.30	.50
a.		Souvenir sheet of 4, #80-83	1.25	2.00
		Nos. 80-83 (4)	.90	1.10

Constellation Orion — A18

Night Sky over Botswana: 7c, Scorpio. 10c, Centaur. 20c, Southern Cross.

1972, Apr. 24 Litho. *Perf. 14*

84	A18	3c dp org, bl grn & blk	.40	.40
85	A18	7c org, blue & blk	.75	.75
86	A18	10c org, green & blk	1.10	1.10
87	A18	20c emer, vio bl & blk	2.25	2.25
		Nos. 84-87 (4)	4.50	4.50

Gubulawayo Cancel and Map of Trail — A19

Cross, Map of Botswana, Bells — A20

Sections of Mafeking-Gubulawayo Trail and: 4c, Bechuanaland Protectorate No. 65. 7c, Mail runners. 20c, Mafeking 638 killer cancellation.

1972, Aug. 21 *Perf. 13½x13*

88	A19	3c cream & multi	.20	.20
89	A19	4c cream & multi	.20	.20
90	A19	7c cream & multi	.45	.45
91	A19	20c cream & multi	1.50	1.50
a.		Souvenir sheet of 4	12.50	17.50
		Nos. 88-91 (4)	2.35	2.35

84th anniv. of Mafeking to Gubulawayo runner post. No. 91a contains one each of Nos. 88-91, arranged vertically to show map of trail. Compare with design A89.

1972, Nov. 6 Litho. *Perf. 14*

Cross, Map of Botswana and: 3c, Candle. 7c, Christmas tree. 20c, Star and holly.

92	A20	2c yellow & multi	.20	.20
93	A20	3c pale lilac & multi	.20	.20
94	A20	7c yel green & multi	.20	.20
95	A20	20c pink & multi	.50	.50
a.		Souvenir sheet of 4, #92-95	2.00	2.00
		Nos. 92-95 (4)	1.10	1.10

Christmas.

Chariot of the Sun, Trundholm, Denmark — A21

WMO Emblem and: 3c, Thor, Norse thunder god, vert. 7c, Ymir, Icelandic frost giant, vert. 20c, Odin on 8-legged horse Sleipnir.

1973, Mar. 23 Litho. *Perf. 14*

96	A21	3c orange & multi	.20	.20
97	A21	4c yellow & multi	.25	.20
98	A21	7c ultra & multi	.45	.20
99	A21	20c gold & multi	1.25	.90
		Nos. 96-99 (4)	2.15	1.50

Intl. meteorological cooperation, cent.

Livingstone and Boat on Lake Ngwami — A22

Design: 20c, Livingstone and his meeting with Henry Stanley.

1973, Sept. 10 Litho. *Perf. 13½x14*

100	A22	3c gray & multi	.20	.20
101	A22	20c yel green & multi	.95	.80

Dr. David Livingstone (1813-1873), medical missionary and explorer.

Shepherd and Flock — A23

Christmas: 3c, Ass and foal, African huts, vert. 7c, African mother, child and star, vert. 20c, Tribal meeting (kgotla), symbolic of Wise Men.

1973, Nov. 12 Litho. *Perf. 14½*

102	A23	3c multicolored	.20	.20
103	A23	4c multicolored	.20	.20
104	A23	7c multicolored	.20	.20
105	A23	20c multicolored	.30	.40
		Nos. 102-105 (4)	.90	1.00

Gaborone Campus, Botswana — A24

7c, Kwaluseni Campus, Swaziland. 20c, Roma Campus, Lesotho. 35c, Map and flags of Botswana, Swaziland & Lesotho.

1974, May 8 Litho. *Perf. 14*

106	A24	3c lt blue & multi	.20	.20
107	A24	7c yel green & multi	.20	.20
108	A24	20c yel green & multi	.20	.20
109	A24	35c brt blue & multi	.30	.30
		Nos. 106-109 (4)	.90	.90

10th anniversary of the University of Botswana, Lesotho and Swaziland.

UPU Emblem, Mail Vehicles — A25

UPU Cent.: 3c, Post Office, Palapye, c. 1889. 7c, Bechuanaland police camel post, 1900. 20c, 1920 and 1974 planes.

1974, May 22 Litho. *Perf. 13½x14*

110	A25	2c car & multi	.25	.35
111	A25	3c green & multi	.40	.35
112	A25	7c brown & multi	1.00	.70
113	A25	20c blue & multi	3.00	2.50
		Nos. 110-113 (4)	4.65	3.90

Amethyst A26

Minerals, precious and semiprecious stones.

1974, July 1 Photo. *Perf. 14x13*

114	A26	1c shown	.55	.90
115	A26	2c Agate	.55	.90
116	A26	3c Quartz	.60	.70
117	A26	4c Niccolite	.70	.50
118	A26	5c Moss agate	.70	.90
119	A26	7c Agate	.80	.55
120	A26	10c Stilbite	1.60	.55
121	A26	15c Moshaneng banded marble	2.00	2.75
122	A26	20c Gem diamonds	4.00	3.50
123	A26	25c Chrysotile	5.00	2.50
124	A26	35c Jasper	5.25	4.00
125	A26	50c Moss quartz	4.50	6.25
126	A26	1r Citrine	7.75	8.75
127	A26	2r Chalcopyrite	21.00	17.50
		Nos. 114-127 (14)	55.00	50.00

For surcharges see Nos. 155-168.

Stapelia Variegata — A27

1974, Nov. 4 Litho. *Perf. 14*

128	A27	2c multicolored	.20	.45
129	A27	7c multicolored	.55	.20
130	A27	15c multicolored	1.00	1.60
131	A27	20c multicolored	1.50	2.00
a.		Souvenir sheet of 4, #128-131	4.00	4.75
		Nos. 128-131 (4)	3.25	4.25

Pres. Sir Seretse Khama — A28

1975, Mar. 24 Photo. *Perf. 13½x13*

132	A28	4c olive & multi	.20	.20
133	A28	10c yellow & multi	.20	.20
134	A28	20c ultra & multi	.30	.30
135	A28	35c brown & multi	.50	.50
a.		Souvenir sheet of 4, #132-135	1.25	1.75
		Nos. 132-135 (4)	1.20	1.20

10th anniv. of self-government.

Ostrich and Rock Painting A29

Paintings and Animals: 10c, Rhinoceros. 25c, Hyena. 35c, Scorpion.

1975, June 23 Litho. *Perf. 14x14½*

136	A29	4c yel green & multi	.85	.20
137	A29	10c buff & multi	1.40	.20
138	A29	25c blue & multi	2.50	.75

139	A29	35c lilac & multi	2.75	1.50
a.		Souvenir sheet of 4, #136-139	12.50	11.00
		Nos. 136-139 (4)	7.50	2.65

Rock paintings from Tsodilo Hills.

Map of British Bechuanaland — A30

Chiefs Sebele, Bathoen and Khama A31

10c, Khama the Great and antelope.

Perf. 14½x14, 14x14½

1975, Oct. 31 Litho.

140	A30	6c buff & multi	.35	.20
141	A30	10c rose & multi	.45	.20
142	A31	25c lt green & multi	.95	.85
		Nos. 140-142 (3)	1.75	1.25

Establishment of Protectorate, 90th anniv. (6c); Khama the Great (1828-1923), centenary of his accession as chief (10c); visit of the chiefs of the Bakwena, Bangwaketse and Bamangwato tribes to London, 80th anniv. (25c).

Aloe Marlothii — A32

Christmas: 10c, Aloe lutescens. 15c, Aloe zebrina. 25c, Aloe littoralis.

1975, Nov. 3 Litho. *Perf. 14½x14*

143	A32	3c multicolored	.25	.20
144	A32	10c multicolored	.75	.20
145	A32	15c multicolored	1.00	1.75
146	A32	25c multicolored	2.00	3.00
		Nos. 143-146 (4)	4.00	5.15

Drum A33

Traditional Musical Instruments: 10c, Hand piano. 15c, Segankuru (violin). 25c, Kudu signal horn.

1976, Mar. 1 Litho. *Perf. 14*

147	A33	4c yellow & multi	.20	.20
148	A33	10c lilac & multi	.25	.20
149	A33	15c dull yel & multi	.35	.60
150	A33	25c lt blue & multi	.45	1.40
		Nos. 147-150 (4)	1.25	2.40

1-pula Bank Note with Seretse Khama A34

Reverse of Bank Notes: 10c, Farm workers. 15c, Antelopes. 25c, National Assembly building.

1976, June 28 Litho. *Perf. 14*

151	A34	4c rose & multi	.20	.20
152	A34	10c brt green & multi	.20	.20
153	A34	15c yel green & multi	.35	.35

*154 A34 25c blue & multi .50 .50
  a. Souvenir sheet of 4, #151-154 2.00 3.00
  Nos. 151-154 (4) 1.25 1.25

First national currency.

Nos. 114-127 Surcharged in Black or Gold

1976, Aug. 23 Photo. Perf. 14x13
155 A26 1t on 1c multi 1.75 .60
156 A26 2t on 2c multi 1.75 .90
157 A26 3t on 3c multi (G) 1.40 .50
158 A26 4t on 4c multi 2.25 .35
159 A26 5t on 5c multi 2.25 .35
160 A26 7t on 7c multi 1.10 2.10
161 A26 10t on 10c multi 1.25 .65
162 A26 15t on 15c multi (G) 4.00 1.90
163 A26 20t on 20c multi 7.00 .65
164 A26 25t on 25c multi 4.50 1.00
165 A26 35t on 35c multi 4.00 3.75
166 A26 50t on 50c multi 6.50 7.50
167 A26 1p on 1r multi 7.25 8.00
168 A26 2p on 2r multi (G) 10.00 9.25
  Nos. 155-168 (14) 55.00 37.50

Cattle Industry A35

Designs: 10t, Antelope, tourism, vert. 15t, Schoolhouse and children, education. 25t, Rural weaving, vert. 35t, Mining industry, vert.

1976, Sept. 30 Litho. Perf. 14x14½
Textured Paper
169 A35 4t multicolored .20 .20
170 A35 10t multicolored .40 .40
171 A35 15t multicolored .50 .50
172 A35 25t multicolored .75 .75
173 A35 35t multicolored 1.00 1.00
  Nos. 169-173 (5) 2.85 2.85

10th anniversary of independence.

Colophospermum Mopane — A36

Trees: 4t, Baikiaea plurijuga. 10t, Sterculia rogersii. 25t, Acacia nilotica. 40t, Kigelia africana.

1976, Nov. 1 Litho. Perf. 13
174 A36 3t multicolored .20 .20
175 A36 4t multicolored .20 .20
176 A36 10t multicolored .35 .35
177 A36 25t multicolored .75 .75
178 A36 40t multicolored 1.25 1.25
  Nos. 174-178 (5) 2.75 2.75

Christmas.

Pres. Seretse Khama and Elizabeth II — A37

Designs: 25t, Coronation coach in procession. 40t, Recognition scene.

1977, Feb. 7 Litho. Perf. 12
179 A37 4t multicolored .20 .20
180 A37 25t multicolored .25 .30
181 A37 40t multicolored .40 .50
  Nos. 179-181 (3) .85 1.00

Reign of Queen Elizabeth II, 25th anniv.

Clawless Otter — A38

Wildlife Fund Emblem and: 4t, Serval. 10t, Bat-eared foxes. 25t, Pangolins. 40t, Brown hyena.

1977, June 6 Litho. Perf. 14
182 A38 3t multicolored 5.25 .50
183 A38 4t multicolored 5.25 1.00
184 A38 10t multicolored 6.50 1.75
185 A38 25t multicolored 15.00 4.00
186 A38 40t multicolored 18.00 9.00
  Nos. 182-186 (5) 50.00 16.25

Endangered wildlife.

Khama Memorial A39

4t, Cwihaba Caves. 15t, Green's (expedition) tree. 20t, Mmajojo ruins. 25t, Ancient morabaraba board. 35t, Matsieng's footprints.

1977, Aug. 22 Litho. Perf. 14
187 A39 4t multicolored .20 .20
188 A39 15t multicolored .20 .20
189 A39 15t multicolored .45 .45
190 A39 20t multicolored .55 .55
191 A39 25t multicolored .80 .80
192 A39 35t multicolored 1.10 1.10
  a. Souvenir sheet of 6, #187-192 3.50 4.00
  Nos. 187-192 (6) 3.30 3.30

Historical sites and national monuments.

Hypoxis itida — A40

Black Korhaan — A41

Lilies: 5t, Haemanthus magnificus. 10t, Boophane disticha. 25t, Vellozia retinervis. 40t, Ammocharis coranica.

1977, Oct. 31 Litho. Perf. 14
193 A40 3t sepia & multi .20 .20
194 A40 5t gray & multi .20 .20
195 A40 10t multicolored .30 .30
196 A40 25t multicolored .55 .75
197 A40 40t multicolored .75 1.25
  Nos. 193-197 (5) 2.00 2.70

Christmas.

1978, July 3 Photo. Perf. 14
Designs: Birds.
198 A41 1t shown .65 1.00
199 A41 2t Marabou storks .65 1.00
200 A41 3t Red-billed hoopoe .65 .75
201 A41 4t Carmine bee-eaters .65 .65
202 A41 5t African jacana .65 .35
203 A41 7t Paradise flycatcher .65 2.25
204 A41 10t Bennett's woodpecker 1.60 .50
205 A41 15t Red bishop .95 2.25
206 A41 20t Crowned plovers 1.40 1.75
207 A41 25t Giant kingfishers .65 2.25
208 A41 30t White-faced ducks .65 .60
209 A41 35t Green-backed heron .65 2.75
210 A41 45t Black-headed herons .95 2.40
211 A41 50t Spotted eagle owl 6.00 4.00
212 A41 1p Gabar goshawk 3.00 4.00
213 A41 2p Martial eagle 3.75 7.00
214 A41 5p Saddlebill storks 11.50 14.00
  Nos. 198-214 (17) 35.00 47.50

For surcharges see Nos. 289-290.

Tawana Making Kaross (garment) A42

Designs: 5t, Map of Okavango Delta. 15t, Bushman collecting roots. 20t, Herero woman milking cow. 25t, Yei pulling mokoro (boat). 35t, Mbukushu fishing.

1978, Sept. 11 Litho.
Textured Paper Perf. 14
215 A42 4t multicolored .20 .20
216 A42 5t multicolored .20 .20
217 A42 15t multicolored .20 .35
218 A42 20t multicolored .30 .45
219 A42 25t multicolored .40 .50
220 A42 35t multicolored .50 1.25
  a. Souvenir sheet of 6, #215-220 2.50 3.00
  Nos. 215-220 (6) 1.80 2.95

People of the Okavango Delta.

Caralluma Lutea — A43   Boy at Sip Well — A44

Flowers: 10t, Hoodia lugardii. 15t, Ipomoea transvaalensis. 25t, Ansellia gigantea.

1978, Nov. 6
221 A43 5t multicolored .40 .20
222 A43 10t multicolored .60 .30
223 A43 15t multicolored 1.00 .50
224 A43 25t multicolored 1.25 .80
  Nos. 221-224 (4) 3.25 1.80

Christmas.

1979, Feb. 12 Litho. Perf. 14
Water Development: 5t, Watering pit. 10t, Hand-dug well and goats. 25t, Windmill, well and cattle. 40t, Modern drilling rig.

225 A44 3t multicolored .20 .20
226 A44 5t multicolored .20 .20
227 A44 10t multicolored .20 .20
228 A44 25t multicolored .40 .40
229 A44 40t multicolored .65 .65
  Nos. 225-229 (5) 1.65 1.65

Botswana Pot — A45

Handicrafts: 10t, Clay buffalo. 25t, Woven covered basket. 40t, Beaded bag.

1979, June 4 Litho. Perf. 14
230 A45 5t multicolored .20 .20
231 A45 10t multicolored .20 .20
232 A45 25t multicolored .40 .40
233 A45 40t multicolored .65 .65
  a. Souvenir sheet of 4, #230-233 1.60 1.60
  Nos. 230-233 (4) 1.45 1.45

Bechuanaland No. 6, Rowland Hill — A46

Sir Rowland Hill (1795-1879), originator of penny postage, and: 25t, Bechuanaland Protectorate No. 107. 45t, Botswana No. 20.

1979, Aug. 27 Litho. Perf. 13½
234 A46 5t rose & black .20 .20
235 A46 25t multicolored .35 .35
236 A46 45t multicolored .60 .60
  Nos. 234-236 (3) 1.15 1.15

Children Playing A47

Design: 10t, Child playing with rag doll, and IYC emblem, vert.

1979, Sept. 24 Perf. 14
237 A47 5t multicolored .20 .20
238 A47 10t multicolored .25 .25

International Year of the Child.

Ximenia Caffra — A48

Christmas: 10t, Sclerocarya caffra. 15t, Hexalobus monopetalus. 25t, Ficus soldanella.

1979, Nov. 12 Litho. Perf. 14
239 A48 5t multicolored .20 .20
240 A48 10t multicolored .20 .20
241 A48 15t multicolored .30 .30
242 A48 25t multicolored .50 .50
  Nos. 239-242 (4) 1.20 1.20

Flap-Necked Chameleon A49

1980, Mar. 3 Litho. Perf. 14
243 A49 5t shown .20 .20
244 A49 10t Leopard tortoise .20 .20
245 A49 25t Puff adder .45 .45
246 A49 40t White-throated monitor .75 .75
  Nos. 243-246 (4) 1.60 1.60

Rock Breaking (Early Mining) A50

1980, July 7 Litho. Perf. 13½x14
247 A50 5t shown .20 .20
248 A50 10t Ore hoisting .20 .20
249 A50 15t Ore transport .25 .25
250 A50 20t Ore crushing .35 .35
251 A50 25t Smelting .40 .40
252 A50 35t Tools, products .60 .60
  Nos. 247-252 (6) 2.00 2.00

Chiwele and the Giant — A51

Folktales: 10t, Kgori Is Not Deceived. 30t, Nyambi's Wife and Crocodile. 45t, Clever Hare, horiz.

Perf. 14, 14½ (10t, 30t)
1980, Sept. 8
253 A51 5t multicolored .20 .20
  Size: 28x36mm
254 A51 10t multicolored .40 .40
255 A51 30t multicolored .50 .50
  Size: 44x26mm
256 A51 45t multicolored .80 .80
  Nos. 253-256 (4) 1.70 1.70

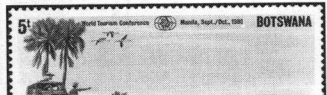

Game Watching — A52

1980, Oct. 6 Litho. Perf. 14
257 A52 5t multicolored .20 .20

World Tourism Conf., Manila, Sept. 27.

Acacia Gerrardii — A53

Christmas: Flowering Trees.

1980, Nov. 3   Litho.   Perf. 14
258 A53 5t shown .20 .20
259 A53 10t Acacia nilotica .20 .20
260 A53 25t Acacia erubescens .30 .30
261 A53 40t Dichrostachys cinerea .45 .45
Nos. 258-261 (4) 1.15 1.15

Heinrich von Stephan, Bechuanaland Protectorate No. 150, Botswana No. 111 — A55

Design: 20t, Von Stephan, Bechuanaland Protectorate No. 151, Botswana No. 112.

1981, Jan. 7   Perf. 14
266 A55 6t multicolored .20 .20
267 A55 20t multicolored .45 .45

Von Stephan (1831-1897), founder of UPU.

Emperor Dragonfly — A56

1981, Feb. 23   Litho.   Perf. 14
268 A56 6t shown .20 .20
269 A56 7t Praying mantis .20 .20
270 A56 10t Elegant grasshopper .20 .20
271 A56 20t Dung beetle .25 .25
272 A56 30t Citrus swallowtail
butterfly .40 .40
273 A56 45t Mopane worm .60 .60
a. Souv. sheet of 6, #268-273 2.00 2.00
Nos. 268-273 (6) 1.85 1.85

Blind Basket Weaver A57

1981, Apr. 4   Litho.   Perf. 14
274 A57 6t Seamstress .20 .20
275 A57 20t shown .30 .30
276 A57 30t Carpenter .40 .40
Nos. 274-276 (3) .90 .90

International Year of the Disabled.

Woman Reading Letter (Literacy Campaign) — A58

1981, June 8
277 A58 6t shown .20 .20
278 A58 7t Man sending telegram .20 .20
279 A58 20t Boy, newspaper .25 .25
280 A58 30t Father and daughter
reading .35 .35
Nos. 277-280 (4) 1.00 1.00

Pres. Seretse Khama and Flag A59

First death anniv. of Pres. Khama: Portrait and local buildings.

1981, July 13
281 A59 6t multicolored .20 .20
282 A59 10t multicolored .20 .20
283 A59 25t multicolored .40 .40
284 A59 45t multicolored .60 .60
Nos. 281-284 (4) 1.40 1.40

Cattle in Agricultural Show — A60

1981, Sept. 21   Litho.   Perf. 14½
285 A60 6t Plowing .20 .20
286 A60 20t shown .20 .20
287 A60 30t Meat Commission .35 .35
288 A60 45t Vaccine Institute .50 .50
Nos. 285-288 (4) 1.25 1.25

Nos. 209, 204 Surcharged in Black

1981, Sept.   Photo.   Perf. 14
289 A41 25t on 35t multicolored .30 .30
290 A41 30t on 10t multicolored .40 .40

Christmas — A61

Designs: Water lilies.

1981, Nov. 2   Litho.
291 A61 6t Nymphaea caerulea .20 .20
292 A61 10t Nymphoides indica .20 .20
293 A61 25t Nymphaea lotus .30 .30
294 A61 40t Ottelia kunenensis .50 .50
Nos. 291-294 (4) 1.20 1.20

Children's Drawings — A62

1982, Feb. 15   Litho.   Perf. 14½x14
295 A62 6t Cattle .20 .20
296 A62 10t Kgotla meeting .20 .20
297 A62 30t Village .40 .40
298 A62 45t Huts .60 .60
Nos. 295-298 (4) 1.40 1.40

Traditional Houses — A63

1982, May 3   Litho.   Perf. 14
299 A63 6t Common type .20 .20
300 A63 10t Kgatleng .20 .20
301 A63 30t Northeastern .40 .40
302 A63 45t Sarwa .60 .60
Nos. 299-302 (4) 1.40 1.40

Red-billed Teals — A64

Perf. 14x14½, 14½x14
1982, July 1   Photo.
303 A64 1t Masked weaver .20 .20
304 A64 2t Lesser double-col-
lared sunbirds .20 .20
305 A64 3t White-fronted
bee-eaters .20 .20
306 A64 4t Ostriches .20 .20
307 A64 5t Grey-headed gulls .30 .30
308 A64 6t Pygmy geese .40 .30
309 A64 7t Cattle egrets .50 .40
310 A64 8t Lanner falcon .60 .45
311 A64 10t Yellow-billed
storks .75 .65
312 A64 15t shown 1.25 1.00
313 A64 20t Barn owls 1.50 1.25
314 A64 25t Hamerkops 2.00 1.40
315 A64 30t Stilts 2.25 1.60
316 A64 35t Blacksmith
plovers 2.75 2.00
317 A64 45t Wattled plover 3.50 2.25
318 A64 50t Crowned guinea-
fowl 3.75 2.75
319 A64 1p Cape vultures 8.00 5.50
320 A64 2p Augur bustards 15.00 11.00
Nos. 303-320 (18) 43.35 31.55

Nos. 303-311 vert.
For surcharges see Nos. 401-403.

Christmas — A65

Endangered Species — A67

A66

Designs: Mushrooms.

1982, Nov. 2   Litho.   Perf. 14½
321 A65 7t Shaggy mane .70 .70
322 A65 15t Orange milk 1.50 1.50
323 A65 35t Panther 3.50 3.50
324 A65 50t King boletus 4.75 4.75
Nos. 321-324 (4) 10.45 10.45

1983, Mar. 14   Litho.   Perf. 14
325 A66 7t Pres. Quett Masire .20 .20
326 A66 15t Dancers .20 .20
327 A66 35t Melbourne Conference Center .50 .50
328 A66 45t Heads of State
meeting .60 .60

Commonwealth Day.

1983, Apr. 19   Litho.   Perf. 14x14½
329 A67 7t Wattle crane .40 .20
330 A67 15t Aloe lutescens 1.10 .70
331 A67 35t Roan antelope 2.75 1.60
332 A67 50t Hyphaene ven-
tricosa 3.50 2.00
Nos. 329-332 (4) 7.75 4.50

Wooden Spoons — A68

1983, July 20   Litho.   Perf. 14
333 A68 7t shown .25 .20
334 A68 15t Jewelry .45 .35
335 A68 35t Ox-hide milk bag 1.10 .85
336 A68 50t Decorated knives 1.25 1.00
a. Souvenir sheet of 4, #333-336 6.00 5.00
Nos. 333-336 (4) 3.05 2.40

Christmas A69

1983, Nov. 7   Litho.   Perf. 14½x14
Designs: Dragonflies.
337 A69 6t Pantala flavescens .20 .20
338 A69 15t Anax imperator .30 .30
339 A69 25t Trithemis arteriosa .50 .50
340 A69 45t Chlorolestes elegans .90 .90
Nos. 337-340 (4) 1.90 1.90

Mining Industry — A70

1984, Mar. 19   Litho.   Perf. 14½
341 A70 7t Diamonds .40 .20
342 A70 15t Lime 1.10 .65
343 A70 25t Copper, nickel, vert. 3.00 2.00
344 A70 50t Coal, vert. 3.50 2.50
Nos. 341-344 (4) 8.00 5.35

Traditional Transport A71

1984, June 16   Litho.   Perf. 14½x14
345 A71 7t Man riding ox .20 .20
346 A71 25t Sled .40 .40
347 A71 35t Wagon .65 .65
348 A71 50t Cart .90 .90
Nos. 345-348 (4) 2.15 2.15

Intl. Civil Aviation Org., 40th Anniv. — A72

1984, Oct. 8   Litho.   Perf. 14x13½
349 A72 7t Avro 504 .20 .20
350 A72 10t Westland Wessex .20 .20
351 A72 15t Junkers 52-3M .25 .25
352 A72 25t Dragon Rapide .40 .40
353 A72 35t DC-3 .60 .60
354 A72 50t F27 Fokker Friendship .80 .80
Nos. 349-354 (6) 2.45 2.45

Christmas A73

Butterflies.

1984, Nov. 5   Litho.   Perf. 14½x14
355 A73 7t Papilio demodocus .40 .30
356 A73 25t Byblia acheloia 1.75 1.00
357 A73 35t Hypolimnas mis-
sipus 2.75 1.50
358 A73 50t Graphium taboranus 3.50 2.00
Nos. 355-358 (4) 8.40 4.80

Traditional & Exotic Foods — A74

Bechuanaland No. 4 — A75

1985, Mar. 18   Litho.   Perf. 14½
359 A74	7t Man preparing seswaa	.20	.20
360 A74	15t Woman preparing bogobe	.20	.20
361 A74	25t Girl eating madilla	.30	.30
362 A74	50t Woman collecting caterpillars	.65	.65
a.	Souvenir sheet of 4, #359-362	1.40	1.40
	Nos. 359-362 (4)	1.35	1.35

Southern African Development Coordination Conference, 5th anniv.

1985, June 24

Postage stamp cent.: 15t, Bechuanaland Protectorate No. 72. 25t, Bechuanaland Protectorate No. 106. 35t, Bechuanaland No. 199, 50t, Botswana No. 1, horiz.

363 A75	7t multicolored	.20	.20
364 A75	15t multicolored	.20	.20
365 A75	25t multicolored	.30	.30
366 A75	35t multicolored	.40	.40
367 A75	50t multicolored	.60	.60
	Nos. 363-367 (5)	1.70	1.70

Police Centenary A76

7t, Bechuanaland Border Police, 1885-95. 10t, Bechuanaland Mounted Police, 1894-1902. 25t, Bechuanaland Protectorate Police, 1903-66. 50t, Botswana Motorcycle Police, 1966-85.

1985, Aug. 5   Perf. 14½x14
368 A76	7t multicolored	.20	.20
369 A76	10t multicolored	.20	.20
370 A76	25t multicolored	.30	.30
371 A76	50t multicolored	.60	.60
	Nos. 368-371 (4)	1.30	1.30

Edible Wild Cucumbers A77

1985, Nov. 4
372 A77	7t Cucumis metuliferus	.20	.20
373 A77	15t Acanthosicyos naudinianus	.20	.20
374 A77	25t Coccinia sessifolia	.30	.30
375 A77	50t Momordica balsamina	.60	.60
	Nos. 372-375 (4)	1.30	1.30

Christmas.

Declaration of Protectorate, Cent. — A78

1985, Dec. 30   Litho.   Perf. 14x14½
376 A78	7t Heads of state meet	.20	.20
377 A78	15t Declaration reading, 1885	.20	.20
378 A78	25t Mackenzie and Khama	.30	.30
379 A78	50t Map	.60	.60
a.	Souvenir sheet of 4, #376-379	1.25	1.25
	Nos. 376-379 (4)	1.30	1.30

Halley's Comet — A79

1986, Mar. 24   Perf. 14½x14
380 A79	7t Comet over Serowe	.20	.20
381 A79	15t Over Bobonong	.20	.20
382 A79	35t Over Gomare swamps	.40	.40
383 A79	50t Over Thamaga, Letlhakeng	.60	.60
	Nos. 380-383 (4)	1.40	1.40

Milk Containers — A80

1986, June 23   Perf. 14½
384 A80	8t Leather bag	.20	.20
385 A80	15t Ceramic pots	.20	.20
386 A80	35t Wood pot	.40	.40
387 A80	50t Woman, pots	.60	.60
	Nos. 384-387 (4)	1.40	1.40

Souvenir Sheet

Natl. Independence, 20th Anniv. — A81

Designs: a, Map of natl. parks and reserves. b, Morupule Power Station. c, Cattle, Kgalagadi. d, Natl. Assembly.

1986, Sept. 30   Litho.   Perf. 14½x14
388	Sheet of 4	.90	.90
a.-d.	A81 20t any single	.25	.25

Flowers of the Okavango Swamps — A82

1986, Nov. 3   Litho.   Perf. 14x14½
389 A82	8t Ludwigia stogonifera	.20	.20
390 A82	15t Sopubia mannii	.20	.20
391 A82	35t Commelina diffusa	.40	.40
392 A82	50t Hibiscus diversifolium	.55	.55
	Nos. 389-392 (4)	1.35	1.35

Christmas.

Traditional Medicine A83

1987, Mar. 2   Litho.   Perf. 14½x14
393 A83	8t Professional diviners	.20	.20
394 A83	15t Lightning prevention	.20	.20
395 A83	35t Rainmaker	.45	.45
396 A83	50t Bloodletting	.65	.65
	Nos. 393-396 (4)	1.50	1.50

UN Child Survival Campaign — A84

1987, June 1
397 A84	8t Oral rehydration therapy	.20	.20
398 A84	15t Growth monitoring	.20	.20
399 A84	35t Immunization	.45	.45
400 A84	50t Breast-feeding	.65	.65
	Nos. 397-400 (4)	1.50	1.50

Nos. 308, 311 and 318 Surcharged
Perf. 14x14½, 14½x14
1987, Apr. 1   Photo.
401 A64	3t on 6t No. 308	.20	.20
402 A64	5t on 10t No. 311	.20	.20
403 A64	20t on 50t No. 318	.30	.30
	Nos. 401-403 (3)	.70	.70

Wildlife Conservation — A85

1987, Aug. 3   Perf. 14
404 A85	1t Cape fox	.20	.20
405 A85	2t Lechwe	.20	.20
406 A85	3t Zebra	.20	.20
407 A85	4t Duiker	.20	.20
408 A85	5t Banded mongoose	.20	.20
409 A85	6t Rusty-spotted genet	.20	.20
410 A85	8t Hedgehog	.20	.20
411 A85	10t Scrub hare	.20	.20
412 A85	12t Hippopotamus	.20	.20
413 A85	15t Suricate	.20	.20
414 A85	20t Caracal	.25	.20
415 A85	25t Steenbok	.35	.30
416 A85	30t Gemsbok	.45	.35
417 A85	35t Square-lipped rhino	.50	.45
418 A85	40t Mountain reedbuck	.60	.50
419 A85	50t Rock dassie	.75	.60
420 A85	1p Giraffe	1.50	1.25
421 A85	2p Tsessebe	3.00	2.50
422 A85	3p Side-striped jackal	4.75	3.75
423 A85	5p Hartebeest	8.00	6.50
	Nos. 404-423 (20)	22.15	18.40

For surcharges see Nos. 480-482, 506-509.

Wetland Grasses — A86

1987, Oct. 26   Perf. 14x14½
424 A86	8t Cyperus articulatus	.20	.20
425 A86	15t Miscanthus junceus	.20	.20
426 A86	30t Cyperus alopecuroides	.35	.35
427 A86	1p Typha latifolia	1.25	1.25
a.	Souvenir sheet of 4, #424-427	1.90	1.90
	Nos. 424-427 (4)	2.00	2.00

Christmas, preservation of the Okavango and Kuando-Chobe River wetlands.

Early Cultivation Techniques A87

1988, Mar. 14   Litho.   Perf. 14½x14
428 A87	8t Digging stick	.20	.20
429 A87	15t Iron hoe	.20	.20
430 A87	35t Wooden plow	.40	.40
431 A87	50t Communal planting, Lesotla	.60	.60
	Nos. 428-431 (4)	1.40	1.40

World Wildlife Fund — A88

Designs: WWF emblem and various red lechwe, Kobus leche.

1988, June 6   Litho.   Perf. 14½x14
432 A88	10t Adult wading	.35	.35
433 A88	15t Adult, sun	.50	.50
434 A88	35t Cow, calf	1.10	1.10
435 A88	75t Herd	2.50	1.75
	Nos. 432-435 (4)	4.45	3.70

Runner Post, Cent. — A89

Routes and: 10t, Gubulawayo, Bechuanaland, cancellation dated Aug. 21 '88. 15t, Bechuanaland Protectorate No. 65. 30t, Pack traders. 60t, Mafeking killer cancel No. 638.

1988, Aug. 22   Litho.   Perf. 14½
436 A89	10t multicolored	.20	.20
437 A89	15t multicolored	.20	.20
438 A89	30t multicolored	.35	.35
439 A89	60t multicolored	.65	.65
a.	Souvenir sheet of 4, #436-439	1.25	1.25
	Nos. 436-439 (4)	1.40	1.40

Printed in a continuous design picturing the Mafeking-Gubulawayo route and part of the Shoshong runner post route.

State Visit of Pope John Paul II, Sept. 13 — A90

Natl. Museum and Art Gallery, Gaborone, 20th Anniv. — A91

1988, Sept. 13   Litho.   Perf. 14x14½
440 A90	10t Map, portrait	.20	.20
441 A90	15t Portrait	.20	.20
442 A90	30t Map, portrait, diff.	.35	.35
443 A90	80t Portrait, diff.	.85	.85
	Nos. 440-443 (4)	1.60	1.60

1988, Sept. 30   Perf. 14½
444 A91	8t Museum	.20	.20
445 A91	15t Pottery, c. 400-1300	.20	.20
446 A91	30t Buffalo bellows	.35	.35
447 A91	60t Children, mobile museum	.70	.70
	Nos. 444-447 (4)	1.45	1.45

A92

Flowering plants of southeastern Botswana.

1988, Oct. 11   Litho.   Perf. 14x14½
448 A92	8t Grewia flava	.20	.20
449 A92	15t Cienfuegosia digitata	.20	.20
450 A92	40t Solanum seaforthianum	.40	.40
451 A92	75t Carissa bispinosa	.80	.80
	Nos. 448-451 (4)	1.60	1.60

Christmas.

A93

1989, Mar. 13 Litho. Perf. 14x14½
Traditional grain storage.
452 A93 8t Sesigo basket granary .20 .20
453 A93 15t Letlole daga granary .20 .20
454 A93 30t Sefalana bisque
granary .30 .30
455 A93 60t Serala granaries .60 .60
Nos. 452-455 (4) 1.30 1.30

Slaty
Egrets
A94

1989, July 5 Perf. 15x14
456 A94 8t Nesting .20 .20
457 A94 15t Young .45 .50
458 A94 30t Adult in flight .75 .60
459 A94 60t Two adults 1.60 1.40
a. Souvenir sheet of 4, #456-459 3.00 2.50
Nos. 456-459 (4) 3.00 2.50

Children's
Drawings
A95

1989, Sept. 4 Perf. 14½x14, 14x14½
460 A95 10t Ephraim Seeletso .20 .20
461 A95 15t Neelma Bhatia,
vert. .20 .20
462 A95 30t Thabo Habana .30 .30
463 A95 1p Thabo Olesitse 1.00 1.00
Nos. 460-463 (4) 1.70 1.70

Star and
Orchids — A96

1989, Oct. 30 Litho. Perf. 14x14½
464 A96 8t Eulophia angolensis .20 .20
465 A96 15t Eulophia hereroen-
sis .25 .25
466 A96 30t Eulophia speciosa .50 .50
467 A96 60t Eulophia petersii 1.10 1.10
Nos. 464-467 (4) 2.05 2.05

Christmas.

Anniversaries — A97

8t, Bechuanaland Protectorate #201. 15t,
Voter at ballot box. 30t, Map & flags of nations
at SADCC conference. 60t, Great Britain #1.

1990, Mar. 5 Perf. 14½
468 A97 8t multicolored .20 .20
469 A97 15t multicolored .20 .20
470 A97 30t multicolored .30 .30
471 A97 60t multicolored .60 .60
Nos. 468-471 (4) 1.30 1.30

25th anniv. of self government (8t); 1st elections, 25th anniv. (15t); Southern African
Development Coordination Conference
(SADCC), 10th anniv. (30t); and Penny Black,
150th anniv. (60t).

Stamp World
London
'90 — A98

Traditional
Dress — A99

Aspects of the telecommunications industry.

1990, May 3
472 A98 8t Training .20 .20
473 A98 15t Transmission .20 .20
474 A98 30t Public telephone .30 .30
475 A98 2p Testing circuitry 2.00 2.00
Nos. 472-475 (4) 2.70 2.70

1990, Aug. 1 Litho. Perf. 14
476 A99 8t Children .20 .20
477 A99 15t Young woman .20 .20
478 A99 30t Man .25 .25
479 A99 2p Adult woman 1.75 1.75
a. Souvenir sheet of 4, #476-479 2.50 2.50
Nos. 476-479 (4) 2.40 2.40

Nos. 404 and 412 Surcharged **10t**

No. 409 Surcharged **20t**

1990
480 A85 10t on 1t No. 404 .20 .20
481 A85 20t on 6t No. 409 .20 .20
482 A85 50t on 12t No. 412 .50 .50
Nos. 480-482 (3) .90 .90

Flowering
Trees — A100

1990, Oct. 30 Litho. Perf. 14
483 A100 8t Acacia nigrescens .20 .20
484 A100 15t Peltophorum africanum .20 .20
485 A100 30t Burkea africana .25 .25
486 A100 2p Pterocarpus
angolensis 1.75 1.75
Nos. 483-486 (4) 2.40 2.40

Christmas.

Natl.
Road
Safety
Day
A101

1990, Dec. 7 Litho. Perf. 14½
487 A101 8t Children playing on
road .20 .20
488 A101 15t Accident .20 .20
489 A101 30t Livestock on road .35 .35
Nos. 487-489 (3) .75 .75

Petroglyphs
A102

Various petroglyphs.

1991, Mar. 4 Litho. Perf. 14x14½
Textured Paper
490 A102 8t multicolored .20 .20
491 A102 15t multicolored .20 .20
492 A102 30t multicolored .30 .30
493 A102 2p multicolored 2.00 2.00
Nos. 490-493 (4) 2.70 2.70

Natl.
Census — A103

1991, June 3 Litho. Perf. 14
494 A103 8t Children playing .20 .20
Perf. 14½
495 A103 15t Houses .20 .20
Perf. 14x14½
496 A103 30t Children in
schoolyard .35 .35
497 A103 2p Children, hospital 2.40 2.40
Nos. 494-497 (4) 3.15 3.15

African
Tourism
Year
A104

1991, Sept. 30 Litho. Perf. 14
498 A104 8t Tourists, elephants .20 .20
499 A104 15t Birds, crocodiles .20 .20
500 A104 35t Airplane, fish eagles .40 .40
Size 26x43mm
501 A104 2p Okavango Delta 2.40 2.40
Nos. 498-501 (4) 3.20 3.20

No. 501 incorporates designs of #498-500.

Christmas — A105

Seed pods: 8t, Harpagophytum procum-
bens. 15t, Tylosema esculentum. 30t, Abrus
precatorius. 2p, Kigelia africana.

1991, Nov. 4 Litho. Perf. 14
502 A105 8t multicolored .20 .20
503 A105 15t multicolored .20 .20
504 A105 30t multicolored .30 .30
505 A105 2p multicolored 2.25 2.25
Nos. 502-505 (4) 2.95 2.95

Nos. 406, 409 & 412
Surcharged   **8t**

1992, Mar. 9 Litho. Perf. 14
506 A85 8t on 12t No. 412 .20 .20
507 A85 10t on 12t No. 412 .20 .20
508 A85 25t on 6t No. 409 .25 .25
509 A85 40t on 3t No. 406 .35 .35
Nos. 506-509 (4) 1.00 1.00

Climbing
Frogs — A106

Designs: 8t, Cacosternum boettgeri, horiz.
10t, Hyperolius marmoratus angolensis. 40t,
Bufo fenoulheti, horiz. 1p, Hyperolius.

1992, Mar. 23 Perf. 14½x14, 14x14½
510 A106 8t multicolored .20 .20
511 A106 10t multicolored .20 .20
512 A106 40t multicolored .40 .40
513 A106 1p multicolored .95 .95
Nos. 510-513 (4) 1.75 1.75

Botswana
Railways
A107

10t, Deluxe air-conditioned coaches. 25t,
BD1 locomotive. 40t, Deluxe coach interio. 2p,
Locomotive pulling air-conditioned coaches.

1992, June 29 Litho. Perf. 14
514 A107 10t multi .20 .20
515 A107 25t multi, vert. .20 .20
516 A107 40t multi, vert. .20 .20
517 A107 2p multi 1.00 1.00
a. Souv. sheet of 4, #514-517 + label 1.40 1.40
Nos. 514-517 (4) 1.60 1.60

Wild Animals
A108

1992, Aug. 3 Litho. Perf. 14½
518 A108 1t Cheetah .20 .20
519 A108 2t Spring hares .20 .20
520 A108 4t Blackfooted cat .20 .20
521 A108 5t Striped mouse .20 .20
522 A108 10t Oribi .20 .20
523 A108 1t Pangolin .20 .20
524 A108 15t Aardwolf .20 .20
525 A108 20t Warthog .20 .20
526 A108 25t Ground squirrels .25 .25
527 A108 35t Honey badger .30 .30
528 A108 40t Common mole
rat .35 .35
529 A108 45t Wild dogs .40 .40
530 A108 50t Water mon-
goose .45 .45
531 A108 80t Klipspringer .70 .70
532 A108 1p Lesser
bushbaby .90 .90
533 A108 2p Bushveld ele-
phant shrew 1.75 1.75
534 A108 5p Zorilla 4.50 4.50
535 A108 10p Vervet monkey 9.00 9.00
Nos. 518-535 (18) 20.20 20.20

For surcharges see Nos. 594A-597.

A109 Ferns — A110

1992, Aug. 7 Perf. 14x15
536 A109 10t Boxer .20 .20
537 A109 50t Four sprinters .45 .45
538 A109 1p Two boxers .95 .95
539 A109 2p Three runners 1.90 1.90
a. Souvenir sheet of 4, #536-539 3.50 3.50
Nos. 536-539 (4) 3.50 3.50

1992 Summer Olympics, Barcelona.

1992, Nov. 23 Litho. Perf. 14½
540 A110 10t Adiantum in-
cisum .20 .20
541 A110 25t Actiniopteris
radiata .25 .25
542 A110 40t Ceratopteris
cornuta .40 .40
543 A110 1.50p Pellaea calome-
lanos 1.40 1.40
Nos. 540-543 (4) 2.25 2.25

Christmas.

Organizations
A111

10t, Lions Intl., conquering blindness. 15t,
Red Cross Society. 25t, Ecumenical Decade,
churches in solidarity with women. 35t, Round

Table supporting the deaf. 40t, Rotary Intl. 50t, Botswana Christian Council.

1993, Mar. 29   Litho.   Perf. 14
544 A111 10t multi, vert. .20 .20
545 A111 15t multi .20 .20
546 A111 25t multi, vert. .20 .20
547 A111 35t multi .30 .30
548 A111 40t multi, vert. .40 .40
549 A111 50t multi .45 .45
    Nos. 544-549 (6) 1.75 1.75

Botswana
Railway,
Cent.
A112

Designs: 10t, Engine No. 1, 6th class 4-6-0, Bechuanaland Railways. 40t, Engine No. 317, 19th class 4-8-2. 50t, Engine No. 256, 12th class 4-8-2. 1.50p, Engine No. 71, 7th class 4-8-0, Rhodesia Railways.

1993, May 24   Litho.   Perf. 15x14
550 A112   10t multicolored .20 .20
551 A112   40t multicolored .40 .40
552 A112   50t multicolored .50 .50
553 A112   1.50p multicolored 1.50 1.50
  a.   Souvenir sheet of 4, #550-553 2.50 2.50
    Nos. 550-553 (4) 2.60 2.60

Eagles — A113

1993, Aug. 30   Litho.   Perf. 14½
554 A113   10t Long crested eagle .20 .20
555 A113   25t Snake eagle .50 .50
556 A113   50t Bateleur eagle 1.00 1.00
557 A113   1.50p Secretary bird 3.00 3.00
    Nos. 554-557 (4) 4.70 4.70

Christmas
A114

1993, Oct. 25   Litho.   Perf. 14x14½
558 A114   12t Aloe zebrina .20 .20
559 A114   25t Croton megalobotrys .20 .20
560 A114   50t Boophane disticha .45 .45
561 A114   1p Euphorbia davyi .90 .90
    Nos. 558-561 (4) 1.75 1.75

Traditional
Children's
Toys
A115

1994, Mar. 28   Litho.   Perf. 14½
562 A115   10t Mantadile .20 .20
563 A115   40t Dikgomo tsa mimopa .30 .30
564 A115   50t Sefuu-fuu .40 .40
565 A115   1p Mantlwane .75 .75
    Nos. 562-565 (4) 1.65 1.65

ICAO,
50th
Anniv.
A116

Perf. 14½x14, 14x14½
1994, June 30   Litho.
566 A116   10t Inside control tower .20 .20
567 A116   25t Fire engine .25 .25
568 A116   40t Baggage carts, vert. .40 .40
569 A116   50t Control tower, vert. .50 .50
    Nos. 566-569 (4) 1.35 1.35

A117

Environmental Protection: 10t, Flamingos, Sua Pan, vert. 35t, Makgadikgadi Pan trees. 50t, Zebra, Makgadikgadi Palm trees, vert. 2p, Map of Makgadikgadi Pans.

1994, Aug. 30   Litho.   Perf. 14
570 A117   10t multicolored .20 .20
571 A117   35t multicolored .45 .45
572 A117   50t multicolored .65 .65
573 A117   2p multicolored 2.50 2.50
    Nos. 570-573 (4) 3.80 3.80

A118

1994, Oct. 24
Edible fruits: 10t, Ziziphus mucronata. 25t, Strychnos cocculoides. 40t, Bauhinia petersiana. 50t, Schinziphyton rautaneii.

574 A118   10t multicolored .20 .20
575 A118   25t multicolored .20 .20
576 A118   40t multicolored .25 .25
577 A118   50t multicolored .35 .35
    Nos. 574-577 (4) 1.00 1.00

Christmas.
See Nos. 587-590.

Traditional
Fishing
A119

1995, Apr. 3   Litho.   Perf. 14
578 A119   15t Spear .20 .20
579 A119   40t Hook .30 .30
580 A119   65t Net .50 .50
581 A119   80t Basket .60 .60
    Nos. 578-581 (4) 1.60 1.60

UN, 50th
Anniv. — A120

1995, Oct. 16   Litho.   Perf. 14
582 A120   20t FAO .20 .20
583 A120   50t World Food Program .35 .35
584 A120   80t Development Plan .60 .60
585 A120   1p UNICEF .70 .70
    Nos. 582-585 (4) 1.85 1.85

World
Wildlife Fund
A121

Hyaena brunnea: a, 20t, Adult walking right. b, 50t, Two young. c, 80t, Adult finding eggs. d, 1p, Two young, adult resting.

1995, Nov. 6
586 A121   Strip of 4, #a.-d. 1.75 1.75

No. 586 was issued in miniature sheets of 4 each.

Christmas Type of 1994

1995, Nov. 27   Litho.   Perf. 14
587 A118   20t Adenia glauca .20 .20
588 A118   50t Pterodiscus ngamicus .35 .35
589 A118   80t Sesamothamnus lugardii .60 .60
590 A118   1p Fockea multiflora .70 .70
    Nos. 587-590 (4) 1.85 1.85

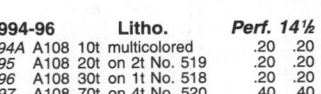

Traditional
Weapons
A122

1996, Mar. 25   Litho.   Perf. 14
591 A122   20t Spears .20 .20
592 A122   50t Axes .30 .30
593 A122   80t Shield, knob-kerries .50 .50
594 A122   1p Knives, cases .60 .60
    Nos. 591-594 (4) 1.60 1.60

No. 523 Surcharged 10t

Nos. 518-520 Surcharged 20t

1994-96   Litho.   Perf. 14½
594A A108   10t multicolored .20 .20
595 A108   20t on 2t No. 519 .20 .20
596 A108   30t on 1t No. 518 .20 .20
597 A108   70t on 4t No. 520 .40 .40
    Nos. 595-597 (3) .80 .80

Issued: #594, 8/1/94; others, 2/12/96.

A123

Radio, Cent.: 20t, Child listening to early radio. 50t, Mobile unit, transmitter. 80t, Local police. 1p, Radio Botswana at the Kgotila.

1996, June 3   Litho.   Perf. 14
598 A123   20t multicolored .20 .20
599 A123   50t multicolored .35 .35
600 A123   80t multicolored .60 .60
601 A123   1p multicolored .75 .75
    Nos. 598-601 (4) 1.90 1.90

A124

1996, July 19   Litho.   Perf. 14
Modern Olympic Games, Cent.: 20t, Hand holding torch, laurel wreath, Olympic rings. 50t, Pierre de Coubertin. 80t, Map, flag of Botswana, athletes. 1p, Ruins of original Olympic Stadium, Olympia.

602 A124   20t multicolored .20 .20
603 A124   50t multicolored .35 .35
604 A124   80t multicolored .60 .60
605 A124   1p multicolored .75 .75
    Nos. 602-605 (4) 1.90 1.90

A125   A126

Worthy Causes: 20t, Family planning education, Welfare Association. 30t, Skills for the blind, Pudulogong Rehabilitation Center. 50t, Collection of seeds, Forestry Association. 70t, Secretarial class, YWCA. 80t, Day care center, Council of Women. 1p, SOS Children's Village, Tlokweng.

1996, Sept. 23   Litho.   Perf. 14
606 A125   20t multicolored .20 .20
607 A125   30t multicolored .25 .25
608 A125   50t multicolored .35 .35
609 A125   70t multicolored .55 .55
610 A125   80t multicolored .60 .60
611 A125   1p multicolored .75 .75
    Nos. 606-611 (6) 2.70 2.70

1996, Nov. 4   Litho.   Perf. 14
Adansonia Digitata
612 A126   20t Leaf, flower .20 .20
613 A126   50t Fruit .35 .35
614 A126   80t Tree in leaf .60 .60
615 A126   1p Tree without leaves .75 .75
    Nos. 612-615 (4) 1.90 1.90

Christmas.

Francistown,
Cent. — A127

20t, Tati Hotel. 50t, Railway station. 80t, Company manager's house. 1p, Monarch Mine.

1997, Apr. 21   Litho.   Perf. 14
616 A127   20t multicolored .20 .20
617 A127   50t multicolored .30 .30
618 A127   80t multicolored .45 .45
619 A127   1p multicolored .55 .55
    Nos. 616-619 (4) 1.50 1.50

Birds — A128

5t, Pel's fishing owl. 10t, Gymnogene. 15t, Meyers parrot. 20t, Harlequin quail. 25t, Marico sunbird. 30t, Kurrichane thrush. 40t, Redheaded finch. 50t, Buffalo weaver. 60t, Sacred ibis. 70t, Cape shoveller. 80t, Greater honeyguide. 1p, Woodland kingfisher. 1.25p, Purple heron. 1.50p, Yellowbilled oxpecker. 2p, Shafttailed whydah. 2.50p, White stork. 5p, Ovambo sparrowhawk. 10p, Spotted crake.

1997, Aug. 4   Litho.   Perf. 13½
620 A128   5t multi, vert. .20 .20
621 A128   10t multi .20 .20
622 A128   15t multi, vert. .20 .20
623 A128   20t multi .20 .20
624 A128   25t multi .20 .20
625 A128   30t multi .20 .20
626 A128   40t multi, vert. .25 .25
627 A128   50t multi, vert. .30 .30
628 A128   60t multi .35 .35
629 A128   70t multi .40 .40
630 A128   80t multi .45 .45
631 A128   1p multi .55 .55
632 A128   1.25p multi, vert. .70 .70
633 A128   1.50p multi .85 .85
634 A128   2p multi, vert. 1.10 1.10
635 A128   2.50p multi, vert. 1.40 1.40
636 A128   5p multi, vert. 2.75 2.75
637 A128   10p multi, vert. 5.50 5.50
    Nos. 620-637 (18) 15.80 15.80

Botswana Railway, Cent. — A129

Designs: 35t, Bechuanaland Rail, 1897. 50t, Elephants on the tracks. 80t, First locomotives in Bechuanaland, Cape of Good Hope 4-6-0. 1p, 4-6-4+4-6-4 Beyer Garratt. 2p, New BD3 locomotive. 2.50p, Fantuzzi Container Stacker.

1997, July 12   Litho.   Perf. 14x14½

638	A129	35t multicolored	.20	.20
639	A129	50t multicolored	.30	.30
640	A129	80t multicolored	.50	.50
641	A129	1p multicolored	.60	.60
642	A129	2p multicolored	1.25	1.25
643	A129	2.50p multicolored	1.50	1.50
		Nos. 638-643 (6)	4.35	4.35

A130　　　　A131

Queen Elizabeth II and Prince Philip, 50th Wedding Anniv.: No. 644, Prince in casual attire. No. 645, Queen wearing white & blue hat. No. 646, Queen with horse. No. 647, Prince with horse. No. 648, Prince, Queen. No. 649, Princess Ann in riding attire.

10p, Queen, Prince riding in open carriage.

1997, Sept. 22   Litho.   Perf. 13

644	A130	35t multicolored	.20	.20
645	A130	35t multicolored	.20	.20
a.		Pair, #644-645	.40	.40
646	A130	2p multicolored	1.25	1.25
647	A130	2p multicolored	1.25	1.25
a.		Pair, #646-647	2.40	2.40
648	A130	2.50p multicolored	1.50	1.50
649	A130	2.50p multicolored	1.50	1.50
a.		Pair, #648-649	3.00	3.00
		Nos. 644-649 (6)	5.90	5.90

Souvenir Sheet

650	A130	10p multicolored	6.00	6.00

1997, Nov. 10   Unwmk.   Perf. 14

Christmas (Combretum):, 35t, Zeyheri. 1p, Apiculatum. 2p, Molle. 2.50p, Imberbe.

651	A131	35t multicolored	.20	.20
652	A131	1p multicolored	.60	.60
653	A131	2p multicolored	1.25	1.25
654	A131	2.50p multicolored	1.50	1.50
		Nos. 651-654 (4)	3.55	3.55

Tourism A132

1998, Mar. 23

655	A132	35t Baobab trees	.20	.20
656	A132	1p Crocodile	.55	.55
657	A132	2p Stalactites, vert.	1.10	1.10
658	A132	2.50p Tourists, vert.	1.40	1.40
		Nos. 655-658 (4)	3.25	3.25

Diana, Princess of Wales (1961-97)
Common Design Type

Portraits: 35t, #663a, Wearing red (without hat). 1p, #663b, Wearing red with hat. 2p, #663c, Wearing white (hand on face). #662, Greeting people.

1998, June 1   Wmk. 373   Perf. 13

659	CD355	35t multicolored	.20	.20
660	CD355	55t multicolored	.55	.55
661	CD355	2p multicolored	1.10	1.10
662	CD355	2.50p multicolored	1.40	1.40
		Nos. 659-662 (4)	3.25	3.25

Sheet of 4

663	CD355	2.50p #a.-c. + #662	5.50	5.50

A133　　　　A134

Textiles: 35t, Tapestry of a village. 55t, Woman arranging materials on ground. 1p, Tapestry of African map, animals, huts, people. 2p, Woman seated at loom. 2.50p, Tapestry of elephants and trees, horiz.

1998, Sept. 28   Litho.   Perf. 14x13½

664	A133	35t multicolored	.20	.20
665	A133	55t multicolored	.30	.30
666	A133	1p multicolored	.55	.55
667	A133	2p multicolored	1.10	1.10
		Nos. 664-667 (4)	2.15	2.15

Souvenir Sheet
Perf. 13½

668	A133	2.50p multicolored	1.40	1.40

1998   Litho.   Perf. 13x13½

Christmas - Berries: 35t, Ficus ingens. 55t, Ficus pygmaea. 1p, Ficus abutilifolia. 2.50p, Ficus sycomorus.

669	A134	35t multicolored	.20	.20
670	A134	55t multicolored	.30	.30
671	A134	1p multicolored	.55	.55
672	A134	2.50p multicolored	1.40	1.40
		Nos. 669-672 (4)	2.45	2.45

Tourism A135

35t, Rock paintings. 55t, Salt pan. 1p, Rock paintings, diff. 2p, Baobab tree.

1999, May 24   Litho.   Perf. 13½x14

673	A135	35t multi	.20	.20
674	A135	55t multi	.25	.25

Perf. 14x13½

675	A135	1p multi, vert.	.45	.45
676	A135	2p multi, vert.	.95	.95
		Nos. 673-676 (4)	1.85	1.85

Souvenir Sheet

Southern African Development Community Day — A136

Illustration reduced.

1999, Aug. 17   Litho.   Perf. 14¼

677	A136	5p multi	2.00	2.00

UPU, 125th Anniv. A137

1999, Oct. 9   Litho.   Perf. 14¼

678	A137	2p multicolored	.85	.85

Mpule Kwelagobe, Miss Universe 1999 — A138

1999, Dec. 1   Perf. 14½

679	A138	35t With crown, vert.	.20	.20
680	A138	1p With headdress	.40	.40
681	A138	2p In swimsuit, vert.	.80	.80
682	A138	2.50p With Botswana sash	1.10	1.10
683	A138	15p With leopard	6.50	6.50
a.		Souvenir sheet of 5, #679-683	9.00	9.00
		Nos. 679-683 (5)	9.00	9.00

River Scenes A139

Designs: 35t, Bird over river. 1p, Hippopotami in river. 2p, Bird, man in canoe. 2.50p, Elephant on shore, vert.

2000, Apr. 5   Litho.   Perf. 14

684	A139	35t multi	.20	.20
685	A139	1p multi	.40	.40
686	A139	2p multi	.80	.80
687	A139	2.50p multi	1.00	1.00
		Nos. 684-687 (4)	2.40	2.40

Moths A140

Designs: 35t, Mopane. 70t, Wild silk. 1p, Crimson-speckled footman. 2p, African lunar. 15p, Speckled emperor.

2000, July 19   Litho.   Perf. 12½

688-692	A140	Set of 5	7.00	7.00
692a		Souvenir sheet, #688-692	7.00	7.00

Literacy Decade A141

Designs: 35t, Mother and child. 70t, Old men learning to read. 2p, Man unaware of fire danger. 2.50p, Man at ATM machine.

2000, Aug. 23   Perf. 12

693-696	A141	Set of 4 + labels	2.10	2.10

Kings and Presidents A142

Designs: 35t, Sebele I of Bakwena, Bathoen I of Bangwaketse, Khama III of Bangwato (60x40mm). 1p, Sir Seretse Khama. 2p, Sir Ketumile J. Masire. 2.50p, Festus G. Mogae.

Litho. & Embossed
2000, Sept. 29   Perf. 14

697-700	A142	Set of 4	2.25	2.25

Botswana Flying Mission — A143

Designs: 35t, Two men, plane with yellow stripes. 1.75p, Plane, nurses, people. 2p, Plane in air, natives in boats. 2.50p, Plane, donkey cart.

2000, Nov. 3   Litho.   Perf. 13½

701-704	A143	Set of 4	2.50	2.50
704a		Horiz. strip of 4, #701-704, + central label	2.50	2.50

Wetlands Fauna A144

Designs: 35t, Hippopotamus. 1p, Tiger fish, tilapia. 1.75p, Wattled crane, painted reed frog, vert. 2p, Vervet monkey, Pels fishing owl, vert. 2.50p, Sitatunga, Nile crocodile, red lechwe.

2000, Dec. 6   Litho.   Perf. 13¾

705-709	A144	Set of 5	3.00	3.00
709a		Souvenir sheet, #705-709, perf. 13½	3.00	3.00
709b		As "a," with emblem of Hong Kong 2001 Stamp Exhibition in margin	3.00	3.00
		Issued: No. 709b, 1/2/01.		

Diamonds — A145

Cut diamond and: 35t, Uncut diamonds. 1.75p, Mine. 2p, Diamond grader. 2.50p, Pendant and ring.
Illustration reduced.

Serpemtine Die Cut 10
2001, Feb. 1   Litho.
Self-Adhesive

710-713	A145	Set of 4	2.50	2.50

Unused value is for stamps with surrounding selvage.

Kgalagadi Transfrontier Park A146

Designs: 35t, Pygmy falcons. 1p, Leopard. 2p, Gemsboks, flags of Botswana and South Africa. 2.50p, Bat-eared fox.

2001, May 12   Litho.   Perf. 13x13¼

714-717	A146	Set of 4	2.25	2.25
717a		Souvenir sheet #715, 717	1.40	1.40

See South Africa Nos. 1252-1255.

Basketry
A147

Designs: 35t, Shown. 1p, Tall basket with triangles and chevrons. 2p, Basket weaver. 2.50p, Spherical basket.

2001, July 30   **Perf. 13¼**
718-721 A147   Set of 4   2.10 2.10
721a   Souvenir sheet, #718-721   2.10 2.10

Sky
Views
A148

Natives and pictures of sun on horizon: 50t, 1p, 2p, 10p.

2001, Sept. 28   **Perf. 13½**
722-725 A148   Set of 4   4.50 4.50

POSTAGE DUE STAMPS

Bechuanaland Protectorate Nos. J10-J12 Overprinted: "REPUBLIC OF / BOTSWANA"

Perf. 14
1967, Mar. 1   **Wmk. 4**   **Typo.**
J1   D2   1c carmine rose   .20   1.00
J2   D2   2c dull violet   .25   1.50
J3   D2   5c olive green   .55   2.00
   Nos. J1-J3 (3)   1.00   4.50

Elephant   Zebra
D1   D2

Perf. 13½
1971, June 9   **Litho.**   **Unwmk.**
J4   D1   1c carmine rose   1.00   2.25
J5   D1   2c violet blue   1.25   3.00
J6   D1   6c sepia   2.00   5.00
J7   D1   14c green   4.00   7.00
   Nos. J4-J7 (4)   8.25   17.25

1978   **Perf. 12½**
J8   D2   1t red orange & black   .70   .70
J9   D2   2t emerald & black   .70   .70
J10   D2   4t red & black   .70   .70
J11   D2   10t dark blue & black   .70   .70
J12   D2   16t brown & black   .70   .70
   Nos. J8-J12 (5)   3.50   3.50

1984   **Perf. 14½x14**
J8a   D2   1t   .60   .60
J9a   D2   2t   .60   .60
J10a   D2   4t   .60   .60
J11a   D2   10t   .60   .60
J12a   D2   16t   .60   .60
   Nos. J8a-J12a (5)   3.00   3.00

1989, Apr. 1   **Perf. 14½**
J8b   D2   1t   .20   .20
J9b   D2   2t   .20   .20
J10b   D2   4t   .20   .20
J11b   D2   10t   .20   .20
J12b   D2   16t   .45   .45
   Nos. J8b-J12b (5)   1.25   1.25

The design is the same size on the 1984 and 1989 issues, but the grass of Nos. J8b-J12b is lower and less defined than on previous issues. The paper is wider on the 1989 issue.

1994, Dec. 1   **Perf. 14**
J8c   D2   1t   .20   .20
J9c   D2   2t   .20   .20
J10c   D2   4t   .20   .20

J11c   D2   10t   .20   .20
J12c   D2   16t   .20   .20
   Nos. J8c-J12c (5)   1.00   1.00
   See note after No. J12b.

BRAZIL

brə-'zil

Brasil (after 1918)

LOCATION — On the north and east coasts of South America, bordering on the Atlantic Ocean.
GOVT. — Republic
AREA — 3,286,000 sq. mi.
POP. — 157,070,163 (1996)
CAPITAL — Brasilia

Brazil was an independent empire from 1822 to 1889, when a constitution was adopted and the country became officially known as The United States of Brazil.

1000 Reis = 1 Milreis
100 Centavos = 1 Cruzeiro (1942)
100 Centavos = 1 Cruzado (1986)
100 Centavos = 1 Cruzeiro (1990)
(Cruzeiro Real 8/2/93-7/1/94)

Catalogue values for unused stamps in this country are for Never Hinged items, beginning with Scott 680 in the regular postage section, Scott B12 in the semipostal section, Scott C66 in the airpost section, Scott RA2 in the postal tax section, and Scott RAB1 in the postal tax semi-postal section.

Values for unused stamps are for examples with original gum as defined in the catalogue introduction except for Nos. 1-38 and 42-52 which are valued without gum.

Watermarks

Wmk. 97-   Wmk. 98-
"CORREIO   "IMPOSTO DE
FEDERAL   CONSUMO
REPUBLICA   REPUBLICA DOS
DOS ESTADOS   ESTADOS
UNIDOS DO   UNIDOS DO
BRAZIL" in Sheet   BRAZIL" in Sheet

Wmk. 99- "CORREIO"

Wmk. 100- "CASA DA MOEDA" in Sheet

Because of the spacing of this watermark, a few stamps in each sheet may show no watermark.

Wmk. 101- Stars and CASA DA MOEDA

Wmk. 193- ESTADOS UNIDOS DO BRASIL

Wmk. 206- Star-framed CM, Multiple

Wmk. 218- E U BRASIL Multiple, Letters 8mm High

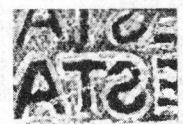

Wmk. 221- ESTADOS UNIDOS DO BRASIL, Multiple, Letters 6mm High

Wmk. 222- CORREIO BRASIL and 5 Stars in Squared Circle

Wmk. 236- Coat of Arms in Sheet

Watermark (reduced illustration) covers 22 stamps in sheet.

Wmk. 245- Multiple "CASA DA MOEDA DO BRASIL" and Small Formee Cross

Wmk. 249- "CORREIO BRASIL" multiple

Wmk. 256- "CASA+DA+MOEDA+DO+BRASIL" in 8mm Letters

Wmk. 264- "*CORREIO*BRASIL*" Multiple, Letters 7mm High

Wmk. 267- "*CORREIO*BRASIL*" Multiple in Small Letters 5mm High

Wmk. 268- "CASA+DA+MOEDA+DO+BRASIL" in 6mm Letters

Wmk. 270- Wavy Lines and Seal

Wmk. 271- Wavy Lines

Wmk. 281- Wavy Lines

Issues of the Empire

A1

Grayish or Yellowish Paper
Fine Impressions
Unwmk.

			Engr.	Imperf.
1843, Aug. 1				
1	A1	30r black	3,000.	550.
c.		Pair, #1-2		300,000.
2	A1	60r black	600.	225.
3	A1	90r black	3,000.	1,200.

Nos. 1-3 were issued with gum, but very few unused examples retain even a trace of their original gum. Copies with original gum command substantial premiums.

Fine impressions are true black and have background lathework complete. Intermediate impressions are grayish black and have weaker lathework in the background. These sell for somewhat less than fine impressions. Worn impressions have white areas in the background surrounding the numerals due to plate wear affecting especially the lathework. These examples sell for somewhat less than intermediate impressions.

Most examples of Nos. 1-3 also exist on white paper, usually thin and somewhat translucent. Such examples are scarce and command premiums.

A2

A3

Grayish or Yellowish Paper

1844-46				
7	A2	10r black	100.00	20.00
8	A2	30r black	125.00	30.00
9	A2	60r black	100.00	20.00
10	A2	90r black	750.00	100.00
11	A2	180r black	3,500.	1,350.
12	A2	300r black	5,250.	1,800.
13	A2	600r black	5,000.	2,000.

Nos. 8, 9 and 10 exist on thick paper and are considerably scarcer.

Grayish or Yellowish Paper

1850, Jan. 1				
21	A3	10r black	25.00	*35.00*
22	A3	20r black	75.00	*100.00*
23	A3	30r black	10.00	3.00
24	A3	60r black	10.00	2.50
25	A3	90r black	80.00	12.00
26	A3	180r black	80.00	55.00
27	A3	300r black	325.00	60.00
28	A3	600r black	375.00	90.00

No. 22 used is generally found precanceled with a single horizontal line in pen or blue crayon. Value precanceled without gum, $75.
All values except the 90r were reprinted in 1910 on very thick paper.

1854				
37	A3	10r blue		12.00 11.50
38	A3	30r blue		32.50 *50.00*

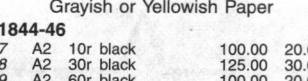

A4

1861				
39	A4	280r red		150.00 100.00
40	A4	430r yellow		225.00 140.00

Nos. 39 and 40 have been reprinted on thick white paper with white gum. They are printed in aniline inks and the colors are brighter than those of the originals.

1866			**Perf. 13½**	
42	A3	10r blue	125.00	*150.00*
43	A3	20r black	900.00	400.00
44	A3	30r black	300.00	150.00
45	A3	30r blue	675.00	*750.00*
46	A3	60r black	125.00	25.00
47	A3	90r black	575.00	275.00
48	A3	180r black	600.00	275.00
49	A4	280r red	650.00	*675.00*
50	A4	300r black	750.00	400.00
51	A4	430r yellow	600.00	350.00
52	A3	600r black	575.00	240.00

Fraudulent perforations abound. Purchases should be accompanied by certificates of authenticity.
A 10r black is questioned.

A5

A6

A7

A8

A8a

A9

Emperor Dom
Pedro — A9a

Thick or Thin White Wove Paper

1866, July 1			**Perf. 12**	
53	A5	10r vermilion	12.00	5.00
54	A6	20r red lilac	20.00	3.00
a.		20r dull violet	65.00	25.00
56	A7	50r blue	30.00	2.50
57	A8	80r slate violet	75.00	5.00
58	A8a	100r blue green	30.00	1.50
a.		100r yellow green	30.00	1.50
59	A9	200r black	100.00	8.00
a.		Half used as 100r on cover		*1,500.*
60	A9a	500r orange	200.00	35.00
		Nos. 53-60 (7)	467.00	60.00

The 10r and 20r exist imperf. on both white and bluish paper. Some authorities consider them proofs.
Nos. 58 and 65 are found in three types.

Bluish Paper

53a	A5	10r	500.00	425.00
54b	A6	20r	160.00	24.00
56a	A7	50r	200.00	25.00
57a	A8	80r	240.00	27.50
58b	A8a	100r	800.00	110.00

1876-77			**Rouletted**	
61	A5	10r vermilion ('77)	60.00	35.00
62	A6	20r red lilac ('77)	70.00	27.50
63	A7	50r blue ('77)	70.00	10.00
64	A8	80r violet ('77)	175.00	20.00
65	A8a	100r green	40.00	1.25
66	A9	200r black ('77)	80.00	7.50
a.		Half used as 100r on cover		*1,100.*
67	A9a	500r orange	190.00	40.00
		Nos. 61-67 (7)	685.00	141.25

A10

A11

A12

A13

A14

A15

A16

A17

A18

A19

A20

1878-79			**Rouletted**	
68	A10	10r vermilion	12.00	3.00
69	A11	20r violet	15.00	2.50
70	A12	50r blue	24.00	2.00
71	A13	80r lake	27.50	10.00
72	A14	100r green	27.50	1.25
73	A15	200r black	140.00	17.50
a.		Half used as 100r on cover		*1,200.*
74	A16	260r dk brown	80.00	22.50
75	A18	300r bister	80.00	6.00
a.		One-third used as 100r on cover		10,000.
76	A19	700r red brown	160.00	85.00
77	A20	1000r gray lilac	190.00	37.50
a.		Half used as 500r on cover		10,000.
		Nos. 68-77 (10)	756.00	187.25

1878, Aug. 21			**Perf. 12**	
78	A17	300r orange & grn	85.00	20.00

Nos. 68-78 exist imperforate.

A21   A22   A23

Small Heads
Laid Paper
Perf. 13, 13½ and Compound

1881, July 15				
79	A21	50r blue	125.00	18.00
80	A22	100r olive green	500.00	30.00
81	A23	200r pale red brn	475.00	110.00
a.		Half used as 100r on cover		*1,750.*

On Nos. 79 and 80 the hair above the ear curves forward. On Nos. 83 and 88 it is drawn backward. On the stamps of the 1881 issue the beard is smaller than in the 1882-85 issues and fills less of the space between the neck and the frame at the left.
See No. 88.

A24

A25

A26

A27

Two types each of the 100 and 200 reis.

100 REIS:
Type I - Groundwork formed of diagonal crossed lines and horizontal lines.
Type II - Groundwork formed of diagonal crossed lines and vertical lines.

200 REIS:
Type I - Groundwork formed of diagonal and horizontal lines.
Type II - Groundwork formed of diagonal crossed lines.

Larger Heads
Laid Paper
Perf. 12½ to 14 and Compound

1882-84				
82	A24	10r black	10.00	*20.00*
83	A25	100r ol grn, type I	37.50	3.00
b.		100r dark green, type II	200.00	12.00
84	A26	200r pale red brn, type I	85.00	22.50
a.		Half used as 100r on cover		*1,100.*
85	A27	200r pale rose, type II	45.00	4.50
a.		Diag. half used as 100r on cover		800.00
		Nos. 82-85 (4)	177.50	50.00

See No. 86.

A28

A29

A30

Three types of A29

Type I - Groundwork of horizontal lines.
Type II - Groundwork of diagonal crossed lines.
Type III - Groundwork solid.

Perf. 13, 13½, 14 and Compound
1884-85

86	A24	10r orange	2.50	2.00
87	A28	20r slate green	30.00	3.00
a.		20r olive green	30.00	3.00
b.		Half used as 10r on newspaper		3,000.
88	A21	50r bl, head larger	30.00	3.00
90	A29	100r lilac, type I	125.00	2.50
a.		100r lilac, type II	450.00	75.00
b.		100r lilac, type III	325.00	55.00
91	A30	100r lilac	175.00	4.00
		Nos. 86-91 (5)	362.50	14.50

A31   A32

Southern Cross A33   Crown A34

Perf. 13, 13½, 14 and Compound
1885

92	A31	100r lilac	100.00	2.50

Compare design A31 with A35.

1887

93	A32	50r chalky blue	27.50	4.00
94	A33	300r gray blue	200.00	25.00
95	A34	500r olive	110.00	12.00
		Nos. 93-95 (3)	337.50	41.00

A35   A36

Entrance to Bay of Rio de Janeiro — A37

1888

96	A35	100r lilac	60.00	1.50
a.		Imperf., pair	125.00	160.00
97	A36	700r violet	65.00	100.00
98	A37	1000r dull blue	250.00	100.00
		Nos. 96-98 (3)	375.00	201.50

Issues of the Republic

Southern Cross — A38

Wove Paper, Thin to Thick
Perf. 12½ to 14, 11 to 11½, and 12½ to 14x11 to 11½, Rough or Clean-Cut
Engraved; Typographed (#102)
1890-91

99	A38	20r gray green	2.00	1.50
a.		20r blue green	2.00	1.50
b.		20r emerald	16.00	6.00
100	A38	50r gray green	5.00	1.50
a.		50r olive green	12.00	6.00
b.		50r yellow green	12.00	6.00
c.		50r dark slate green	7.00	3.50
d.		Horiz. pair, imperf. btwn.		
101	A38	100r lilac rose	350.00	4.50
102	A38	100r red lil, redrawn	25.00	1.50
a.		Tete beche pair	15,000.	16,500.

103	A38	200r purple	8.00	1.50
a.		200r violet	10.00	2.00
b.		200r violet blue	22.50	3.00
104	A38	300r dark violet	75.00	5.00
a.		300r gray	75.00	8.50
b.		300r gray blue	85.00	8.50
c.		300r slate violet	150.00	25.00
105	A38	500r olive bister	17.50	8.00
a.		500r olive gray	17.50	10.00
106	A38	500r slate	17.50	10.00
107	A38	700r fawn	16.00	16.00
a.		700r chocolate	20.00	22.50
108	A38	1000r bister	15.00	3.00
a.		1000r yellow buff	30.00	7.50
		Nos. 99-108 (10)	531.00	54.50

The redrawn 100r may be distinguished by the absence of the curved lines of shading in the left side of the central oval. The pearls in the oval are not well aligned and there is less shading at right and left of "CORREIO" and "100 REIS."

A 100 reis stamp of type A38 but inscribed "BRAZIL" instead of "E. U. DO BRAZIL" was not placed in issue but postmarked copies are known. A reprint on thick paper was made in 1910.

No. 101 exists imperf., not regularly issued. For surcharges see Nos. 151-158.

Liberty Head
A39   A40

Perf. 12½ to 14, 11 to 11½ and 12½ to 14x11 to 11½
1891, May 1   **Typo.**

109	A39	100r blue & red	32.50	1.50
a.		Head inverted	100.00	90.00
b.		Tete beche pair	675.00	750.00
c.		100r ultra & red	32.50	1.50

Perf. 11, 11½, 13, 13½, 14 and Compound
1893, Jan. 18   **Litho.**

111	A40	100r rose	75.00	1.75

Sugarloaf Mountain - A41a
A41

Liberty Head
A42   A42a

Hermes — A43

Perf. 11 to 11½, 12½ to 14 and 12½ to 14x11 to 11½
1894-97   **Unwmk.**

112	A41	10r rose & blue	2.00	.80
113	A41a	10r rose & blue	2.00	.80
114	A41a	20r orange & bl	1.00	.30
115	A41a	50r dk bl & bl	8.00	1.25
116	A42	100r car & blk	4.00	.40
a.		Vert. pair, imperf. btwn.	100.00	
118	A42a	200r orange & blk	1.00	.40
a.		Imperf. horiz., pair	80.00	
b.		Vert. pair, imperf. btwn.	80.00	
119	A42a	300r green & blk	15.00	.60
120	A42a	500r blue & blk	25.00	1.75
121	A42a	700r lilac & blk	16.00	1.75
122	A43	1000r green & vio	55.00	1.75
124	A43	2000r blk & gray lil	60.00	15.00
		Nos. 112-124 (11)	189.00	24.80

The head of No. 116 exists in five types. (See Nos. 140-150A, 159-161, 166-171d.)

Newspaper Stamps Surcharged:

a

b

c

Surcharged on 1889 Issue of type N1
1898   **Rouletted**

Green Surcharge

125	N1 (b)	700r on 500r yel	6.75	10.00
126	N1 (c)	1000r on 700r yel	32.50	27.50
a.		Surcharged "700r"	675.00	775.00
127	N1 (c)	2000r on 1000r yel	27.50	15.00
128	N1 (c)	2000r on 1000r brn	20.00	6.00

Violet Surcharge

129	N1 (a)	100r on 50r brn yel	2.00	45.00
130	N1 (c)	100r on 50r brn yel	65.00	50.00
131	N1 (c)	300r on 200r blk	3.50	1.25
a.		Double surcharge	160.00	275.00

The surcharge on No. 130 is handstamped. The impression is blurred and lighter in color than on No. 129. The two surcharges differ most in the shapes and serifs of the figures "1."

Counterfeits exist of No. 126a.

Black Surcharge

132	N1 (b)	200r on 100r violet	3.50	1.25
a.		Double surcharge	80.00	175.00
b.		Inverted surcharge	80.00	175.00
132C	N1 (b)	500r on 300r car	5.50	3.00
133	N1 (b)	700r on 500r green	8.00	2.00

Blue Surcharge

134	N1 (b)	500r on 300r car	6.50	5.50

Red Surcharge

135	N1 (c)	1000r on 700r ultra	22.50	15.00
a.		Inverted surcharge	200.00	—

Surcharged on 1890-94 Issues:

d   e

Perf. 11 to 14 and Compound
Black Surcharge

136	N3(e)	20r on 10r bl	3.00	6.00
137	N2(d)	200r on 100r red lilac	20.00	15.00
a.		Double surcharge	225.00	250.00

Surcharge on No. 137 comes blue to deep black.

Blue Surcharge

138	N3(e)	50r on 20r grn	8.00	10.00

Red Surcharge

139	N3(e)	100r on 50r grn	18.00	20.00
a.		Blue surcharge	12.50	

The surcharge on Nos. 139 and 139a exists double, inverted, one missing, etc.

Types of 1894-97
1899
Perf. 5½-7 and 11-11½x5½-7

140	A41a	10r rose & bl	4.50	12.00
141	A41a	20r orange & bl	7.50	7.50
142	A41a	50r dk bl & lt bl	9.00	30.00
143	A42	100r car & blk	16.00	4.50
144	A42a	200r org & blk	9.00	3.00
145	A42a	300r green & blk	60.00	7.50
		Nos. 140-145 (6)	106.00	64.50

Perf. 8½-9½, 8½-9½x11-11½

146	A41a	10r rose & bl	4.50	3.00
147	A41a	20r orange & bl	15.00	3.00
147A	A41a	50r dk bl & bl	125.00	30.00
148	A42	100r car & blk	30.00	1.50
149	A42a	200r org & blk	15.00	1.00
150	A42a	300r green & blk	60.00	5.00
150A	A43	1000r green & vio	125.00	12.50
		Nos. 146-150A (7)	374.50	56.00

Nos. 140-150A are valued with perfs just cut into the design on one or two sides. Expect some irregularity of the perforations.

Issue of 1890-93 Surcharged in Violet or Magenta

Perf. 11 to 11½, 12½ to 14 and Compound
1899, June 25

151	A38	50r on 20r gray grn	2.00	3.00
a.		Double surcharge	125.00	125.00
152	A38	100r on 50r gray grn	2.00	3.00
b.		Double surcharge	100.00	100.00
153	A38	300r on 200r pur	7.50	12.00
a.		Double surcharge	250.00	—
b.		Pair, one without surcharge	425.00	—
154	A38	500r on 300r ultra, perf. 13	18.00	7.50
a.		500r on 300r gray lilac	30.00	9.00
b.		Pair, one without surcharge	425.00	500.00
c.		500r on 300r slate violet	37.50	15.00
155	A38	700r on 500r ol bis	24.00	6.00
a.		Pair, one without surcharge	425.00	—
156	A38	1000r on 700r choc	17.50	6.00
157	A38	1000r on 700r fawn	17.50	6.00
a.		Pair, one without surcharge	425.00	500.00
158	A38	2000r on 1000r bister (perf 11-11½	30.00	4.50
a.		2000r on 1000r yel buff (perf 13)	60.00	4.50
b.		Pair, one without surcharge	425.00	500.00
		Nos. 151-158 (8)	118.50	48.00

Types of 1894-97
Perf. 11, 11½, 13 and Compound
1900

159	A41a	50r green	10.00	.60
160	A42	100r rose	20.00	.30
a.		Frame around inner oval	100.00	4.00
161	A42a	200r blue	12.00	.35
		Nos. 159-161 (3)	42.00	1.25

Three types exist of No. 161, all of which have the frame around inner oval.

Cabral Arrives at Brazil — A44

Independence Proclaimed — A45

"Emancipation of Slaves" — A46

Allegory, Republic of Brazil — A47

1900, Jan. 1 **Litho.** **Perf. 12½**
162	A44	100r red	5.50	4.50
a.		Imperf., pair	400.00	500.00
163	A45	200r green & yel	5.50	4.50
164	A46	500r blue	5.50	4.50
165	A47	700r emerald	5.50	4.50
		Nos. 162-165 (4)	22.00	18.00

Discovery of Brazil, 400th anniversary.

Types of 1894-97
Wmk. (97? or 98?)
1905 **Perf. 11, 11½**
166	A41a	10r rose & bl	5.75	4.00
167	A41a	20r org & bl	10.00	2.00
168	A41a	50r green	20.00	3.00
169	A42	100r rose	27.50	1.00
170	A42a	200r dark blue	16.00	1.00
171	A42a	300r grn & blk	55.00	2.00
		Nos. 166-171 (6)	134.25	13.00

Positive identification of Wmk. 97 or 98 places stamp in specific watermark groups below.

Wmk. 97
166b	A41a	10r rose & blue	30.00	16.00
167b	A41a	20r org & blue	30.00	8.00
168b	A41a	50r green	55.00	8.00
169b	A42	100r rose	200.00	30.00
170b	A42a	200r dark blue	125.00	4.00
171b	A42a	300r green & blk	375.00	30.00
171A	A43	1000r grn & vio	290.00	30.00
		Nos. 166b-171A (7)	1,105.	126.00

Wmk. 98
166c	A41a	10r rose & blue	40.00	40.00
167c	A41a	20r org & blue	80.00	20.00
168c	A41a	50r green	160.00	30.00
169c	A42	100r rose	80.00	4.00
170c	A42a	200r dark blue	125.00	4.00
171d	A42a	300r green & blk	290.00	30.00
		Nos. 166c-171d (6)	775.00	128.00

Allegory, Pan-American Congress — A48

1906, July 23 **Litho.** **Unwmk.**
172	A48	100r carmine rose	30.00 30.00
173	A48	200r blue	75.00 10.00

Third Pan-American Congress.

Aristides Lobo
A48a

Benjamin Constant
A49

Pedro Alvares Cabral
A50

Eduardo Wandenkolk
A51

Manuel Deodoro da Fonseca
A52

Floriano Peixoto
A53

Prudente de Moraes
A54

Manuel Ferraz de Campos Salles
A55

Francisco de Paula Rodrigues Alves — A56

Liberty Head — A57

A58

A59

1906-16 **Engr.** **Perf. 12**
174	A48a	10r bluish slate	.90	.20
175	A49	20r aniline vio	.90	.20
176	A50	50r green	.90	.20
a.		Booklet pane of 6 ('08)	40.00	125.00
177	A51	100r anil rose	2.00	.20
a.		Imperf. vert., coil ('16)	4.00	.35
b.		Booklet pane of 6 ('08)	80.00	125.00
178	A52	200r blue	2.00	.20
a.		Booklet pane of 6 ('08)	60.00	125.00
179	A52	200r ultra ('15)	2.00	.35
a.		Imperf. vert., coil ('16)	2.00	.35
180	A53	300r gray blk	3.00	.65
181	A54	400r olive grn	30.00	2.00
182	A55	500r dk violet	6.00	.65
183	A54	600r ol grn ('10)	3.00	1.00
184	A56	700r red brown	6.00	3.00
185	A57	1000r vermilion	32.50	1.00
186	A58	2000r yellow grn	20.00	.65
187	A58	2000r Prus bl ('15)	10.00	1.00
188	A59	5000r car rose	8.00	2.00
		Nos. 174-188 (15)	127.20	13.30

Allegorical Emblems: Liberty, Peace, Industry, etc. — A60

1908, July 14
189	A60	100r carmine	20.00 1.75

National Exhibition, Rio de Janeiro.

Emblems of Peace Between Brazil and Portugal A61

1908, July 14
190	A61	100r red	8.00 1.25

Opening of Brazilian ports to foreign commerce, cent. Medallions picture King Carlos I of Portugal and Pres. Affonso Penna of Brazil.

Bonifacio, Bolivar, Hidalgo, O'Higgins, San Martin, Washington — A62

1909
191	A62	200r deep blue	7.50 1.00

For surcharge see No. E1.

Nilo Peçanha
A63

Baron of Rio Branco
A64

1910, Nov. 15
192	A63	10,000r brown	8.00 2.00

1913-16
193	A64	1000r deep green	3.75 .35
194	A64	1000r slate ('16)	21.00 .65

Cabo Frio — A65

Perf. 11½
1915, Nov. 13 **Litho.** **Wmk. 99**
195	A65	100r dk grn, yelsh	4.00 3.50

Founding of the town of Cabo Frio, 300th anniversary.

Bay of Guajara
A66

1916, Jan. 5
196	A66	100r carmine	7.50 4.00

City of Belem, 300th anniversary.

Revolutionary Flag — A67

1917, Mar. 6
197	A67	100r deep blue	15.00 7.50

Revolution of Pernambuco, Mar. 6, 1817.

Rodrigues Alves — A68

Unwmk.
1917, Aug. 31 **Engr.** **Perf. 12**
198	A68	5000r red brown	60.00 10.00

Liberty Head
A69   A70

Perf. 12½, 13, 13x13½
1918-20 **Typo.**
200	A69	10r orange brn	.50	.25
201	A69	20r slate	.50	.25
202	A69	25r ol gray ('20)	.50	.25
203	A69	50r green	27.50	3.25
204	A70	100r rose	1.75	.25
a.		Imperf., pair		
205	A70	300r red orange	19.00	3.25
206	A70	500r dull violet	19.00	3.25
		Nos. 200-206 (7)	68.75	10.75

1918-20 **Wmk. 100**
207	A69	10r red brown	6.00	1.75
a.		Imperf., pair	—	
207B	A69	20r slate	1.50	1.50
c.		Imperf., pair	—	
208	A69	25r ol gray ('20)	.75	.50
209	A69	50r green	1.50	.50
210	A70	100r rose	47.50	.50
a.		Imperf., pair	—	
211	A70	300r dull blue	6.00	.50
212	A70	300r orange	47.50	3.50
213	A70	500r dull violet	47.50	7.50
214	A70	600r orange	2.50	7.50
		Nos. 207-214 (9)	160.75	23.75

Because of the spacing of this watermark, a few stamps in each sheet may show no watermark.

"Education" — A72

1918 **Engr.** **Perf. 11½**
215	A72	1000r blue	6.00	.25
216	A72	2000r red brown	27.50	6.00
217	A72	5000r dark violet	7.50	6.00
		Nos. 215-217 (3)	41.00	12.25

Watermark note below No. 257 also applies to Nos. 215-217.

See Nos. 233-234, 283-285, 404, 406, 458, 460. For surcharge see No. C30.

Railroad
A73

"Industry"
A74

"Aviation"
A75

Mercury
A76

"Navigation" — A77

Perf. 13½x13, 13x13½
1920-22 **Typo.**
218	A73	10r red violet	.75	.40
219	A73	20r olive green	.75	.40
220	A74	25r brown violet	.60	.40
221	A74	50r blue green	.85	.40
222	A74	50r orange brn ('22)	1.40	.40
223	A75	100r rose red	2.75	.40
224	A75	100r orange ('22)	7.50	.40
225	A75	150r violet ('21)	1.40	.40
226	A75	200r blue	4.50	.40
227	A75	200r rose red ('22)	8.00	.40
228	A76	300r olive gray	12.50	.50
229	A76	400r dull blue ('22)	22.50	3.50
230	A76	500r red brown	17.50	.50
		Nos. 218-230 (13)	81.00	8.50

See Nos. 236-257, 265-266, 268-271, 273-274, 276-281, 302-311, 316-322, 326-340, 357-358, 431-434, 436-441, 461-463B, 467-

470, 472-474, 488-490, 492-494. For surcharges see Nos. 356-358, 376-377.

Perf. 11, 11½
Engr.   Wmk. 100

231	A77	600r red orange	2.00	.35
232	A77	1000r claret	5.00	.25
a.		Perf. 8½	37.50	7.50
233	A72	2000r dull violet	20.00	.75
234	A72	5000r brown	16.00	9.00
		Nos. 231-234 (4)	43.00	10.35

Nos. 233 and 234 are inscribed "BRASIL CORREIO." Watermark note below No. 257 also applies to Nos. 231-234.
See No. 282.

King Albert of Belgium and President Epitacio Pessoa A78

1920, Sept. 19   Engr.   **Perf. 11½x11**
235 A78   100r dull red   .65   .65
Visit of the King and Queen of Belgium.

Types of 1920-22 Issue
Perf. 13x13½, 13x12½
1922-29   Typo.

236	A73	10r red violet	.30	.20
237	A73	20r olive green	.30	.20
238	A74	20r gray vio ('29)	.30	.20
239	A74	25r brown violet	.35	.20
240	A74	50r blue grn	3.25	35.00
241	A74	50r org brn ('23)	.45	.35
a.		Booklet pane of 6		
242	A75	100r rose red	22.50	.40
243	A75	100r orange ('26)	.50	.20
a.		Booklet pane of 6		
244	A75	100r turq grn ('28)	.35	.20
245	A75	150r violet	2.50	.20
246	A75	200r blue	300.00	12.50
247	A76	200r rose red	.40	.20
a.		Booklet pane of 6		
248	A76	200r ol grn ('28)	2.50	3.00
249	A76	300r olive gray	1.90	.25
a.		Booklet pane of 6		
250	A76	300r rose red ('29)	.35	.25
251	A76	400r blue	1.90	.20
252	A76	400r orange ('29)	.75	.60
253	A76	500r red brown	7.50	.50
a.		Booklet pane of 6		
254	A76	500r ultra ('29)	8.50	.20
255	A76	600r brn org ('29)	7.50	3.00
256	A76	700r dull vio ('29)	7.50	1.75
257	A76	1000r turq bl ('29)	9.50	.70
		Nos. 236-257 (22)	379.10	60.30

Because of the spacing of the watermark, a few stamps in each sheet show no watermark.

"Agriculture" — A79

1922   Unwmk.   **Perf. 13x13½**
258 A79   40r orange brown   .50   .35
259 A79   80r grnsh blue   .35   2.50
     See Nos. 263, 267, 275.

Declaration of Ypiranga — A80

Dom Pedro I and Jose Bonifacio — A81

National Exposition and President Pessoa — A82

Unwmk.
1922, Sept. 7   Engr.   **Perf. 14**

260	A80	100r ultra	5.00	.40
261	A81	200r red	6.00	.30
262	A82	300r green	6.00	.30
		Nos. 260-262 (3)	17.00	1.00

Cent. of independence and Natl. Exposition of 1922.

Agriculture Type of 1922
Perf. 13½x12
1923   Wmk. 100   Typo.
263 A79   40r orange brown   .60   .60

Brazilian Army Entering Bahia — A83

1923, July 12   Litho.   **Perf. 13**
264 A83   200r rose   7.50   5.00
Centenary of the taking of Bahia from the Portuguese.

Types of 1920-22 Issues
Perf. 13x13½
1924   Typo.   Wmk. 193

265	A73	10r red violet	5.50	3.75
266	A73	20r olive green	6.00	3.75
267	A79	40r orange brown	4.25	.60
268	A74	50r orange brown	3.75	18.00
269	A75	100r orange	4.25	.35
270	A75	200r rose	6.00	.25
271	A76	400r blue	3.75	3.75
		Nos. 265-271 (7)	33.50	30.45

Arms of Equatorial Confederation, 1824 — A84

1924, July 2   Litho.   **Perf. 11**
272 A84   200r bl, blk, yel, & red   3.00   2.25
a.   Red omitted   275.00   275.00
Centenary of the Equatorial Confederation.

Types of 1920-22 Issues
Perf. 9½ to 13½ and Compound
1924-28   Typo.

273	A73	10r red violet	.45	.30
274	A73	20r olive gray	.45	.30
275	A79	40r orange brn	.45	.30
276	A74	50r orange brn	.75	.30
277	A75	100r red orange	1.50	.30
278	A75	200r rose	.75	.30
279	A76	300r ol gray ('25)	7.00	1.00
280	A76	400r blue	4.00	.35
281	A76	500r red brown	9.00	.45

Engr.

282	A77	600r red orange ('26)	1.00	.30
283	A72	2000r dull vio ('26)	5.00	.30
284	A72	5000r brown ('26)	15.00	.70
285	A72	10,000r rose ('28)	17.50	.90
		Nos. 273-285 (13)	62.85	5.80

Nos. 283-285 are inscribed "BRASIL CORREIO."

Ruy Barbosa — A85

1925   Wmk. 100   **Perf. 11½**
286 A85   1000r claret   4.25   1.50

1926   Wmk. 101
287 A85   1000r claret   1.75   .35

"Justice" — A86

Scales of Justice and Map of Brazil — A87

Perf. 13½x13
1927, Aug. 11   Typo.   Wmk. 206
288 A86   100r deep blue   .90   .50
289 A87   200r rose   .80   .35
Founding of the law courses, cent.

Liberty Holding Coffee Leaves — A88

1928, Mar. 5

290	A88	100r blue green	1.00	.60
291	A88	200r carmine	.65	.60
292	A88	300r olive black	5.00	.40
		Nos. 290-292 (3)	6.65	1.50

Introduction of the coffee tree in Brazil, bicent.

Official Stamps of 1919 Surcharged in Red or Black

Perf. 11, 11½
1928   Wmk. 100   Engr.

293	O3	700r on 500r org	2.25	1.50
a.		Inverted surcharge	175.00	175.00
294	O3	1000r on 100r rose red (Bk)	1.50	.30
295	O3	2000r on 200r dull bl	2.25	.45
296	O3	5000r on 50r grn	2.25	.55
297	O3	10,000r on 10r ol grn	11.00	.90
		Nos. 293-297 (5)	19.25	3.70

#293-297 were used for ordinary postage. Stamps in the outer rows of the sheets are often without watermark.

Ruy Barbosa — A89

Perf. 9, 9½x11, 11, and Compound
1929   Wmk. 101
300 A89   5000r blue violet   12.50   .75
See #405, 459. For surcharge see #C29.

Types of 1920-21 Issue
Perf. 13½x12½
1929   Typo.   Wmk. 218

302	A75	20r gray violet	.25	.20
303	A75	50r red brown	.25	.20
304	A75	100r turq green	.30	.20
305	A75	200r olive green	12.50	2.25
306	A76	300r rose red	.60	.20
307	A76	400r orange	.70	.25
308	A76	500r ultra	7.00	.45
309	A76	600r brown org	8.50	.60
310	A76	700r dp violet	2.25	.20
311	A76	1000r turq blue	4.00	.20
		Nos. 302-311 (10)	36.35	4.75

Wmk. 218 exists both in vertical alignment and in echelon.

Wmk. in echelon

302a	A75	20r	.25	.35
303a	A75	50r	80.00	27.50
306a	A76	300r	.65	.30
308a	A76	500r	110.00	15.00
311a	A76	1000r	6.50	6.50

Architectural Fantasies A90   A91

Architectural Fantasy — A92

Perf. 13x13½
1930, June 20   Wmk. 206

312	A90	100r turq blue	1.25	.80
313	A91	200r olive gray	2.00	.70
314	A92	300r rose red	3.50	.80
		Nos. 312-314 (3)	6.75	2.30

Fourth Pan-American Congress of Architects and Exposition of Architecture.

Types of 1920-21 Issues
1930   Wmk. 221   **Perf. 13x12½**

316	A75	20r gray violet	.20	.20
317	A75	50r red brown	.20	.20
318	A75	100r turq blue	.25	.20
319	A75	200r olive green	3.00	.20
320	A76	300r rose red	.60	.25
321	A76	500r ultra	1.50	.20
322	A76	1000r turq blue	25.00	.65
		Nos. 316-322 (7)	30.75	2.00

Imperforates
Since 1930, imperforate or partly perforated sheets of nearly all commemorative and some definitive issues have become obtainable.

Types of 1920-29 Issue
Perf. 11, 13½x13, 13x12½
1931-34   Typo.

326	A75	10r deep brown	.20	.20
327	A75	20r gray violet	.20	.20
328	A74	25r brn vio ('34)	.20	.60
330	A75	50r blue green	.20	.20
331	A75	50r red brown	.20	.20
332	A75	100r orange	.30	.20
334	A75	200r dp carmine	.45	.20
335	A76	300r olive green	.60	.20
336	A76	400r ultra	.85	.20
337	A76	500r red brown	3.50	.20
338	A76	600r brown org	3.50	.20
339	A76	700r deep violet	3.50	.20
340	A76	1000r turq blue	12.50	.20
		Nos. 326-340 (13)	26.20	3.00

Getulio Vargas and Joao Pessoa A93

Vargas and Pessoa A94

Oswaldo Aranha A95   A96

Antonio
Carlos
A97

Pessoa
A98

Vargas — A99

Unwmk.

1931, Apr. 29   Litho.   Perf. 14

342	A93	10r + 10r lt bl	.20	4.50
343	A93	20r + 20r yel brn	.20	3.25
344	A95	50r + 50r bl grn, red & yel	.20	.20
a.	Red missing at left		.90	.90
345	A93	100r + 50r orange	.30	.30
346	A93	200r + 100r green	.30	.30
347	A94	300r + 150r multi	.30	.30
348	A93	400r + 200r dp rose	1.00	.65
349	A93	500r + 250r dk bl	.70	.55
350	A93	600r + 300r brn vio	.50	6.50
351	A94	700r + 350r multi	.90	.55
352	A96	1000r + 500r brt grn, red & yel	2.00	.25
353	A97	2000r + 1000r gray blk & red	4.00	.55
354	A98	5000r + 2500r blk & red	17.50	4.50
355	A99	10000r + 5000r brt grn & yel	42.50	10.00
		Nos. 342-355 (14)	70.60	32.40

Revolution of Oct. 3, 1930. Prepared as semi-postal stamps, Nos. 342-355 were sold as ordinary postage stamps with stated surtax ignored.

1931

Nos. 306, 320 and 250
Surcharged

200 Réis

Wmk. E U BRASIL Multiple (218)

1931, July 20   Perf. 13½x12½

356	A76	200r on 300r rose red	.90	.90
a.	Wmk. in echelon		17.50	17.50
b.	Inverted surcharge		40.00	

Perf. 13x12½
Wmk. 221

357	A76	200r on 300r rose red	.30	.20
a.	Inverted surcharge		45.00	45.00

Perf. 13½x12½
Wmk. 100

358	A76	200r on 300r rose red	60.00	60.00

Map of South America Showing
Meridian of Tordesillas — A100

Joao
Ramalho
and
Tibiriça
A101

Martim
Affonso
de Souza
A102

King
John III
of
Portugal
A103

Disembarkation of M. A. de Souza at
Sao Vicente — A104

Wmk. 222

1932, June 3   Typo.   Perf. 13

359	A100	20r dk violet	.20	.20
360	A101	100r black	.35	.35
361	A102	200r purple	1.00	.25
362	A103	600r red brown	1.65	1.25

Engr.
Wmk. 101
Perf. 9½, 11, 9½x11

363	A104	700r ultra	2.50	1.75
		Nos. 359-363 (5)	5.70	3.80

1st colonization of Brazil at Sao Vicente, in 1532, under the hereditary captaincy of Martim Affonso de Souza.

Revolutionary Issue

Map of
Brazil — A105

Soldier and
Flag — A106

Allegory:
Freedom,
Justice,
Equality
A107

Soldier's Head
A108

"LEX"
and
Sword
A109

Symbolical of Law and Order — A110

Symbolical of Justice — A111

1932, Sept. 13   Litho.   Perf. 11½

364	A105	100r brown org	.40	2.00
365	A106	200r dk car	.35	.70
366	A107	300r gray green	2.00	3.50
367	A108	400r dark blue	7.25	7.25
368	A105	500r blk brn	7.25	7.25
369	A107	600r red	7.25	7.25
370	A106	700r violet	3.50	7.25
371	A108	1000r orange	1.75	7.25
372	A109	2000r dark brn	14.00	20.00

373	A110	5000r yellow grn	17.50	32.50
374	A111	10000r plum	20.00	37.50
		Nos. 364-374 (11)	81.25	132.45

Issued by the revolutionary forces in the state of Sao Paulo during the revolt of September, 1932. Subsequently the stamps were recognized by the Federal Government and placed in general use.

Excellent counterfeits of Nos. 373 and 374 exist. Counterfeit cancellations abound.

City of Vassouras and Illuminated
Memorial — A112

Wmk. 222

1933, Jan. 15   Typo.   Perf. 12

375	A112	200r rose red	1.00	.90

City of Vassouras founding, cent.

Nos. 306, 320
Surcharged

Perf. 13½x12½

1933, July 28   Wmk. 218

376	A76	200r on 300r rose red	.60	.60
a.	Wmk. 218 in echelon (No. 306a)		12.50	12.50
b.	Wmk. 100 (No. 250)		87.50	87.50

Perf. 13x12½
Wmk. 221

377	A76	200r on 300r rose red	.45	.45
a.	Inverted surcharge		35.00	
b.	Double surcharge		35.00	

Religious Symbols
and
Inscriptions — A113

Wmk. 222

1933, Sept. 3   Typo.   Perf. 13

378	A113	200r dark red	.90	.75

1st Natl. Eucharistic Congress in Brazil.

"Flag of
the Race"
A114

1933, Aug. 18

379	A114	200r deep red	.90	.75

The raising of the "Flag of the Race" and the 441st anniv. of the sailing of Columbus from Palos, Spain, Aug. 3, 1492.

Republic Figure, Flags
of Brazil and
Argentina — A115

Wmk. 101

1933, Oct. 7   Engr.   Perf. 11½

380	A115	200r blue	.35	.25

Thick Laid Paper
Perf. 11, 11½
Wmk. 236

381	A115	400r green	.90	.75
382	A115	600r brt rose	3.00	3.25
383	A115	1000r lt violet	4.50	3.75
		Nos. 380-383 (4)	8.75	8.00

Visit of President Justo of the Argentina to Brazil, Oct. 2-7, 1933.

Allegory: "Faith and
Energy" — A116

Allegory of
Flight — A117

1933   Typo.   Wmk. 222

384	A116	200r dark red	.25	.20
385	A116	200r dark violet	.30	.20

See Nos. 435, 471, 491.

1934, Apr. 15   Engr.   Perf. 12

386	A117	200r blue	.50	.50

1st Natl. Aviation Congress at Sao Paulo.

A118

1934, May 12   Typo.   Perf. 11

387	A118	200r dark olive	.25	.25
388	A118	400r carmine	1.50	1.50
389	A118	700r ultra	1.50	.90
390	A118	1000r orange	3.75	.60
		Nos. 387-390 (4)	7.00	3.25

7th Intl. Fair at Rio de Janeiro.

Christ of
Corcovado
A119

1934, Oct. 20

392	A119	300r dark red	1.90	1.90
a.	Tete beche pair		6.00	7.25
393	A119	700r ultra	8.00	5.00
a.	Tete beche pair		19.00	22.50

Visit of Eugenio Cardinal Pacelli, later Pope Pius XII, to Brazil.

The three printings of Nos. 392-393, distinguishable by shades, sell for different prices.

José de
Anchieta
A120

Thick Laid Paper

1934, Nov. 8   Wmk. 236   Perf. 11, 12

394	A120	200r yellow brown	.55	.20
395	A120	300r violet	.45	.25
396	A120	700r blue	1.75	1.40
397	A120	1000r lt green	3.50	.55
		Nos. 394-397 (4)	6.25	2.40

Jose de Anchieta, S.J. (1534-1597), Portuguese missionary and "father of Brazilian literature."

A121

"Brazil" and "Uruguay" — A122

1935, Jan. 8   Typo.   Perf. 11
398 A121 200r orange   .65 .40
399 A122 300r yellow   .80 .50
400 A122 700r ultra   3.25 3.25
401 A121 1000r dk violet   8.00 4.00
     Nos. 398-401 (4)   12.70 8.15
  Visit of President Terra of Uruguay.

View of Town of Igarassu A123

1935, July 1
402 A123 200r maroon & brn   .85 .45
403 A123 300r vio & olive brn .85 .35
  Captaincy of Pernambuco founding, 400th anniv.

Types of 1918-29
Thick Laid Paper
Perf. 9½, 11, 12, 12x11
1934-36   Engr.
404 A72   2000r violet   3.75 .40
405 A89   5000r blue vio ('36) 11.00 .50
406 A72   10000r claret ('36)   8.75 .75
     Nos. 404-406 (3)   23.50 1.65
  No. 404 is inscribed "BRASIL CORREIO."

Revolutionist A124

Bento Gonçalves da Silva — A125

Duke of Caxias A126

1935, Sept. 20   Perf. 11, 12
407 A124 200r black   .55 .45
408 A124 300r rose lake   .55 .35
409 A125 700r dull blue   2.25 2.25
410 A126 1000r light violet   2.50 1.40
     Nos. 407-410 (4)   5.85 4.45
  Centenary of the "Ragged" Revolution.

Federal District Coat of Arms A127

1935, Oct. 19   Typo.   Perf. 11
411 A127 200r blue   2.25 2.25
  8th Intl. Sample Fair held at Rio de Janeiro.

Coutinho's Ship — A128

Arms of Fernandes Coutinho — A129

1935, Oct. 25
412 A128 300r maroon   2.25 1.00
413 A129 700r turq blue   3.25 2.00
  400th anniversary of the establishment of the first Portuguese colony at Espirito Santo by Vasco Fernandes Coutinho.

Gavea, Rock near Rio de Janeiro A130

1935, Oct. 12   Wmk. 245   Perf. 11
414 A130 300r brown & vio   1.75 1.50
415 A130 300r blk & turq bl   1.75 1.50
416 A130 300r Prus bl & ultra 1.75 1.50
417 A130 300r crimson & blk   1.75 1.50
     Nos. 414-417 (4)   7.00 6.00
  "Child's Day," Oct. 12.

Viscount of Cairu — A131

1936, Jan. 20 Engr. Perf. 11, 12x11
418 A131 1200r violet   6.00 2.75
  Jose da Silva Lisboa, Viscount of Cairu (1756-1835).

View of Cametá A132

1936, Feb. 26   Perf. 11, 12
419 A132 200r brown orange   1.25 1.00
420 A132 300r green   1.25 .80
  300th anniversary of the founding of the city of Cameta, Dec. 24, 1635.

Coining Press A133

Thick Laid Paper
1936, Mar. 24   Perf. 11
421 A133 300r pur brn, *cr*   1.25 .90
  1st Numismatic Cong. at Sao Paulo, Mar., 1936.

Carlos Gomes — A134

"Il Guarany" — A135

Thick Laid Paper
1936, July 11   Perf. 11, 11x12
422 A134 300r dull rose   .50 .35
423 A134 300r black brown   .50 .35
424 A135 700r ocher   2.00 .90
425 A135 700r blue   1.75 .90
     Nos. 422-425 (4)   4.75 2.50
  Birth cent. of Antonio Carlos Gomes, who composed the opera "Il Guarany."

Scales of Justice — A136

1936, July 4   Typo.   Perf. 11
426 A136 300r rose   1.25 .45
  First National Judicial Congress.

Federal District Coat of Arms A137

1936, Nov. 13   Typo.   Wmk. 249
427 A137 200r rose red   .75 .45
  Ninth International Sample Fair held at Rio de Janeiro.

Eucharistic Congress Seal — A138

1936, Dec. 17 Wmk. 245 Perf. 11½
428 A138 300r grn, yel, bl & blk .70 .45
  2nd Natl. Eucharistic Congress in Brazil.

Botafogo Bay A139

Thick Laid Paper
Wmk. 236
1937, Jan. 2   Engr.   Perf. 11
429 A139 700r blue   .75 .45
430 A139 700r black   .75 .45
  Birth cent. of Francisco Pereira Passos, engineer who planned the modern city of Rio de Janeiro.

Types of 1920-21, 1933
Perf. 11, 11½ and Compound
1936-37   Typo.
431 A75   10r deep brown   .20 .20
432 A75   20r dull violet   .20 .20
433 A75   50r blue green   .20 .20
434 A75   100r orange   .25 .20
435 A116 200r dk violet   .45 .20
436 A76   300r olive green   .25 .20
437 A76   400r ultra   .45 .20
438 A76   500r lt brown   .70 .20
439 A76   600r brn org ('37)   1.50 .20
440 A76   700r deep violet   2.75 .20
441 A76   1000r turq blue   3.00 .20
     Nos. 431-441 (11)   9.95 2.20

Massed Flags and Star of Esperanto A140

1937, Jan. 19
442 A140 300r green   1.00 .50
  Ninth Brazilian Esperanto Congress.

Bay of Rio de Janeiro A141

1937, June 9   Unwmk.   Perf. 12½
443 A141 300r orange red & blk .50 .50
444 A141 700r blue & dk brn   1.25 .50
  2nd South American Radio Communication Conf. held in Rio, June 7-19.

Globe — A142

Perf. 11, 12
1937, Sept. 4   Wmk. 249
445 A142 300r green   .85 .50
  50th anniversary of Esperanto.

Monroe Palace, Rio de Janeiro A143

Botanical Garden, Rio
de Janeiro — A144

1937, Sept. 30   Unwmk.   Perf. 12½
446 A143   200r lt brn & bl   .50   .35
447 A144   300r org & ol grn   .50   .35
448 A143   2000r grn & cerise   3.75 5.50
449 A144   10000r lake & indigo 32.50 27.50
      Nos. 446-449 (4)   37.25 33.70

Brig. Gen. Jose
da Silva
Paes — A145

Eagle and
Shield — A146

1937, Oct. 11   Wmk. 249   Perf. 11½
450 A145   300r blue   .75   .30

Bicentenary of Rio Grande do Sul.

1937, Dec. 2   Typo.   Perf. 11
451 A146   400r dark blue   .75   .30

150th anniversary of the US Constitution.

Bags of
Brazilian
Coffee
A147

**Frame Engraved, Center
Typographed**
1938, Jan. 17   Unwmk.   Perf. 12½
452 A147   1200r multicolored   3.00 .40

Arms of
Olinda
A148

Perf. 11, 11x11½
1938, Jan. 24   Engr.
453 A148   400r violet   .50   .25

4th cent. of the founding of the city of Olinda.

Independence
Memorial,
Ypiranga
A149

1938, Jan. 24   Typo.   Perf. 11
454 A149   400r brown olive   .60   .25

Proclamation of Brazil's independence by
Dom Pedro, Sept. 7, 1822.

Iguaçu
Falls — A150

Perf. 12½
1938, Jan. 10   Unwmk.   Engr.
455 A150   1000r sepia & yel
                brn   1.50 .75
456 A150   5000r ol blk & grn   17.00 7.50

Couto de
Magalhaes
A151

Perf. 11, 11x11½
1938, Mar. 17   Wmk. 249
457 A151   400r dull green   .50   .25

General Couto de Magalhaes (1837-1898),
statesman, soldier, explorer, writer, developer.

Types of 1918-38
Perf. 11, 12x11, 12x11½, 12
1938   Engr.
458 A72   2000r blue violet   6.50 .20
459 A89   5000r violet blue   24.00 .20
a.   5000r deep blue   20.00 .50
460 A72   10000r rose lake   27.50 1.00
      Nos. 458-460 (3)   58.00 1.70

No. 458 is inscribed "BRASIL CORREIO."

Types of 1920-22
1938   Wmk. 245   Typo.   Perf. 11
461 A75   50r blue green   .50   .75
462 A75   100r orange   .50   .75
463 A76   300r olive green   .50   .20
463A A76 400r ultra   100.00 35.00
463B A76 500r red brown   .50   10.00
      Nos. 461-463B (5)   102.00 46.70

National
Archives
Building
A152

1938, May 20   Wmk. 249
464 A152   400r brown   .40   .25

Centenary of National Archives.

Souvenir Sheets

Sir Rowland Hill — A153

1938, Oct. 22   Imperf.
465 A153   Sheet of 10   12.50 12.50
a.   400r dull green, single stamp .75   .75

Brazilian Intl. Philatelic Exposition (Brapex).
Issued in sheets measuring 106x118mm. A
few perforated sheets exist.

President Vargas — A154

1938, Nov. 10   Perf. 11
Without Gum
466 A154   Sheet of 10   5.00 8.50
a.   400r slate blue, single stamp .40   .40

Constitution of Brazil, set up by President
Vargas, Nov. 10, 1937. Size: 113x135½mm.

Types of 1920-33
1939   Typo.   Wmk. 256   Perf. 11
467 A75   10r red brown   .30   .25
468 A75   20r dull violet   .30   .20
469 A75   50r blue green   .30   .20
470 A75   100r yellow org   .45   .20
471 A116 200r dk violet   .55   .20
472 A76   400r ultra   1.00 .20
473 A76   600r dull orange   1.00 .20
474 A76   1000r turq blue   7.00 .20
      Nos. 467-474 (8)   10.90 1.65

View of Rio de
Janeiro — A155

View of
Santos — A156

1939, June 14   Engr.   Wmk. 249
475 A155   1200r dull violet   1.25 .25

1939, Aug. 23
476 A156   400r dull blue   .40   .20

Centenary of founding of Santos.

Chalice Vine and
Blossoms — A157

Eucharistic
Congress
Seal — A158

1939, Aug. 23
477 A157   400r green   1.00 .25

1st South American Botanical Congress
held in January, 1938.

1939, Sept. 3
478 A158   400r rose red   .40   .20

Third National Eucharistic Congress.

Duke of Caxias,
Army
Patron — A159

1939, Sept. 12   Photo.   Rouletted
479 A159   400r deep ultra   .40   .25

Issued for Soldiers' Day.

A159a

A159b

A159d

A159c

Designs: 400r, George Washington. 800r,
Emperor Pedro II. 1200r, Grover Cleveland.
1600r, Statue of Friendship, given by US.

Unwmk.
1939, Oct. 7   Engr.   Perf. 12
480 A159a 400r yellow orange .40   .25
481 A159b 800r dark green   .25   .20
482 A159c 1200r rose car   .50   .20
483 A159d 1600r dark blue   .50   .25
      Nos. 480-483 (4)   1.65 .90

New York World's Fair.

Benjamin
Constant — A160

Fonseca on Horseback
- A161

Manuel Deodoro da Fonseca and President Vargas - A162

Wmk. 249

1939, Nov. 15 Photo. *Rouletted*
484	A160	400r deep green	.30	.20
485	A162	1200r chocolate	.75	.30

Engr. Perf. 11
486	A161	800r gray black	.45	.30
		Nos. 484-486 (3)	1.50	.80

Proclamation of the Republic, 50th anniv.

President Roosevelt, President Vargas and Map of the Americas A163

1940, Apr. 14
487	A163	400r slate blue	.70	.40

Pan American Union, 50th anniversary.

Types of 1920-33
1940-41 Typo. **Wmk. 264** *Perf. 11*
488	A75	10r red brown	.20	.25
489	A75	20r dull violet	.25	.25
489A	A75	50r blue grn ('41)	.85	1.25
490	A75	100r yellow org	1.00	.20
491	A116	200r violet	.75	.20
492	A76	400r ultra	4.50	.20
493	A76	600r dull orange	4.50	.20
494	A76	1000r turq blue	11.00	.20
		Nos. 488-494 (8)	23.05	2.75

Map of Brazil — A164

1940, Sept. 7 Engr.
495	A164	400r carmine	.40	.20
a.		Unwmkd.	50.00	30.00

9th Brazilian Congress of Geography held at Florianopolis.

Victoria Regia Water Lily — A165 / President Vargas — A166

Relief Map of Brazil — A167

1940, Oct. 30 **Wmk. 249** *Perf. 11*
Without Gum
496	A165	1000r dull violet	.85	.85
a.		Sheet of 10	8.50	25.00
497	A166	5000r red	6.75	5.00
a.		Sheet of 10	72.50	110.00
498	A167	10,000r slate blue	7.50	2.50
a.		Sheet of 10	100.00	110.00
		Nos. 496-498 (3)	15.10	8.35

New York World's Fair.
All three sheets exist unwatermarked and also with papermaker's watermark of large globe and "AMERICA BANK" in sheet. A few imperforate sheets also exist.

Joaquim Machado de Assis — A168 / Pioneers and Buildings of Porto Alegre — A169

1940, Nov. 1
499	A168	400r black	.50	.20

Birth centenary of Joaquim Maria Machado de Assis, poet and novelist.

1940, Nov. 2 **Wmk. 264**
500	A169	400r green	.40	.20

Colonization of Porto Alegre, bicent.

Proclamation of King John IV of Portugal — A173

1940, Dec. 1 **Wmk. 249**
501	A173	1200r blue black	1.00	.25

800th anniv. of Portuguese independence and 300th anniv. of the restoration of the monarchy.
No. 501 was also printed on paper with papermaker's watermark of large globe and "AMERICA BANK." Unwatermarked copies are from these sheets.

Brazilian Flags and Head of Liberty — A175

Wmk. 256
1940, Dec. 18 Engr. *Perf. 11*
502	A175	400r dull violet	.50	.20
b.		Unwmkd.	40.00	40.00

Wmk. 245
502A	A175	400r dull violet	40.00	40.00

10th anniv. of the inauguration of President Vargas.

Calendar Sheet and Inscription "Day of the Fifth General Census of Brazil" — A176

Wmk. 256
1941, Jan. 14 Typo. *Perf. 11*
503	A176	400r blue & red	.40	.20

Wmk. 245
504	A176	400r blue & red	3.00	.80

Fifth general census of Brazil.

King Alfonso Henriques A177 / Father Antonio Vieira A178

Salvador Corrêia de Sa e Benevides — A179

President Carmona of Portugal and President Vargas A180

Wmk. 264
1940-41 Photo. *Rouletted*
504A	A177	200r pink	.20	.20
505	A178	400r ultra	.20	.20
506	A179	800r brt violet	.25	.20
506A	A180	5400r slate grn	1.65	.70

Wmk. 249
507	A177	200r pink	5.25	3.25
507A	A178	400r ultra	25.00	8.50
508	A180	5400r slate grn	2.50	1.25
		Nos. 504A-508 (7)	35.05	14.30

Portuguese Independence, 800th anniv.
For surcharge & overprint see #C45, C47.

Jose de Anchieta A181 / Amador Bueno A182

Wmk. 264
1941, Aug. 1 Engr. *Perf. 11*
509	A181	1000r gray violet	1.00	.50

Society of Jesus, 400th anniversary.

1941, Oct. 20 *Perf. 11½*
510	A182	400r black	.50	.30

300th anniv. of the acclamation of Amador Bueno (1572-1648) as king of Sao Paulo.

Air Force Emblem A183

1941, Oct. 20 *Perf. 11*
511	A183	5400r slate green	3.00	2.00

Issued in connection with Aviation Week, as propaganda for the Brazilian Air Force.

Petroleum A184 / Agriculture A185

Steel Industry A186 / Commerce A187

Marshal Peixoto A188 / Count of Porto Alegre A189

Admiral J. A. C. Maurity A190 / "Armed Forces" A191

Vargas — A192

1941-42 **Wmk. 264** Typo. *Perf. 11*
512	A184	10r yellow brn	.20	.20
513	A184	20r olive grn	.20	.20
514	A184	50r olive bis	.20	.20
515	A184	100r blue grn	.20	.20
516	A185	200r brown org	.45	.20
517	A185	300r lilac rose	.25	.20
518	A185	400r grnsh blue	.65	.20
519	A185	500r salmon	.30	.20
520	A186	600r violet	.65	.20
521	A186	700r brt rose	.30	.20
522	A186	1000r gray	1.75	.20
523	A186	1200r dl blue	3.00	.20
524	A187	2000r gray vio	2.50	.20

Engr.
525	A188	5000r blue	5.50	.20
526	A189	10,000r rose red	7.00	.20
527	A190	20,000r dp brown	7.00	.35
528	A191	50,000r red ('42)	27.50	21.00
529	A192	100,000r blue ('42)	.60	9.00
		Nos. 512-529 (18)	58.25	33.35

Nos. 512 to 527 and later issues come on thick or thin paper. The stamps on both papers also exist with three vertical green lines printed on the back, a control mark.
See Nos. 541-587, 592-593, 656-670.

Bernardino de Campos A193 / Prudente de Morais A194

1942, May 25
533	A193	1000r red	1.25	.40
534	A194	1200r blue	3.00	.25

100th anniversary of the birth of Bernardino de Campos and Prudente de Morais, lawyers and statesmen of Brazil.

Head of Indo-Brazilian Bull — A195

1942, May 1   Wmk. 264   Perf. 11½
535 A195 200r blue .45 .25
536 A195 400r orange brn .45 .25
  a.   Wmk. 267 45.00 45.00
2nd Agriculture and Livestock Show of Central Brazil held at Uberaba.

Outline of Brazil and Torch of Knowledge A196

Map of Brazil Showing Goiania A197

1942, July 5   Typo.   Perf. 11
537 A196 400r orange brn .30 .25
8th Brazilian Congress of Education.

1942, July 5
538 A197 400r lt violet .40 .30
Founding of Goiania city.

Seal of Congress A198

1942, Sept. 20   Wmk. 264
539 A198 400r olive bister .25 .20
  a.   Wmk. 267 25.00 12.50
4th Natl. Eucharistic Cong. at Sao Paulo.

Types of 1941-42

1942-47   Wmk. 245   Perf. 11
541 A184 20r olive green .20 .40
542 A184 50r olive bister .20 .20
543 A184 100r blue grn .40 .40
544 A185 200r brown org .65 .50
545 A185 400r grnsh blue .40 .20
546 A186 600r lt violet 3.00 .20
547 A186 700r brt rose .35 .80
548 A186 1200r dl blue 1.25 .20
549 A187 2000r gray vio
     ('47) 9.00 9.00

Engr.
550 A188 5000r blue 10.00 .40
551 A189 10,000r rose red 6.00 1.50
552 A190 20,000r dp brn
     ('47) 4.50 .45
553 A192 100,000r blue 3.50 8.00
     Nos. 541-553 (13) 39.45 22.25

Types of 1941-42

1941-47   Typo.   Wmk. 268   Perf. 11
554 A184 20r olive grn .20 .20
555 A184 50r ol bis ('47) .55 .55
556 A184 100r bl grn ('43) .20 .20
557 A185 200r brn org
     ('43) .20 .20
558 A185 300r lilac rose
     ('43) .20 .20
559 A185 400r grnsh bl
     ('42) .30 .20
560 A185 500r sal ('43) .20 .20
561 A186 600r violet .60 .20
562 A186 700r brt rose
     ('45) .35 1.75
563 A186 1000r gray .65 .20
564 A186 1200r dp bl ('44) .85 .20
565 A187 2000r gray vio
     ('43) 3.00 .20

Engr.
566 A188 5000r blue ('43) 4.25 .20
567 A189 10,000r rose red
     ('43) 8.50 .40
568 A190 20,000r dp brn
     ('42) 19.00 .45
569 A191 50,000r red ('42) 21.00 3.00
  a.   50,000r dark brown red ('47) 15.00 8.50
570 A192 100,000r blue .55 .55
     Nos. 554-570 (17) 60.60 8.90

Types of 1941-42

1942-47   Typo.   Wmk. 267
573 A184 20r ol grn ('43) .20 .20
574 A184 50r ol bis ('43) .20 .20
575 A184 100r bl grn ('43) .20 .20
576 A185 200r brn org
     ('43) .25 .25
577 A185 400r grnsh blue .25 .20
578 A185 500r sal ('43) 70.00 10.00

579 A186 600r violet ('43) .45 .30
580 A186 700r brt rose
     ('47) .35 3.50
581 A186 1000r gray ('44) 2.10 .20
582 A186 1200r dl bl 2.50 .20
583 A187 2000r gray vio 2.50 .20

Engr.
584 A188 5000r blue 4.25 .20
585 A189 10,000r rose red
     ('44) 7.00 .60
586 A190 20,000r dp brn
     ('45) 8.50 .45
587 A191 50,000r red ('43) 25.00 5.25
     Nos. 573-587 (15) 123.75 21.95

1942   Typo.   Wmk. 249
592 A184 100r bl grn 4.00 2.50
593 A186 600r violet 4.00 .80

Map Showing Amazon River — A199

1943, Mar. 19   Wmk. 267   Perf. 11
607 A199 40c orange brown .35 .35
Discovery of the Amazon River, 400th anniv.

Reproduction of Brazil Stamp of 1866 — A200

1943, Mar. 28   Wmk. 267
608 A200 40c violet .50 .25
  a.   Wmk. 268 650.00
Centenary of city of Petropolis.

Adaptation of 1843 "Bull's-eye" A201

1943, Aug. 1   Engr.   Imperf.
609 A201 30c black .45 .25
610 A201 60c black .55 .25
611 A201 90c black .45 .25
     Nos. 609-611 (3) 1.45 .75
Cent. of the 1st postage stamp of Brazil. The 30c and 90c exist unwatermarked; values $25 and $65.

Souvenir Sheet

A202

Wmk. 281 Horizontally or Vertically
1943   Engr.   Imperf.
Without Gum
612 A202   Sheet of 3 7.50 6.75
  a.   30c black 1.90 1.90
  b.   60c black 1.90 1.90
  c.   90c black 1.90 1.90

Ubaldino do Amaral — A203

"Justice" — A204

1943, Aug. 27   Typo.   Perf. 11, 12
613 A203 40c dull slate green .40 .20
  a.   Wmk. 267 20.00 15.00
Birth centenary of Ubaldino do Amaral, banker and statesman.

1943, Aug. 30   Wmk. 267
614 A204 2cr bright rose .70 .40
Centenary of Institute of Brazilian Lawyers.

Indo-Brazilian Bull — A205

1943, Aug. 30   Engr.
615 A205 40c dk red brn .70 .40
9th Livestock Show at Bahia.

José Barbosa Rodrigues — A206

1943, Nov. 13   Typo.
616 A206 40c bluish grn .40 .20
Birth cent. of Jose Barbosa Rodrigues, botanist.

Charity Hospital, Santos A207

1943, Nov. 7   Engr.
617 A207 1cr blue .40 .30
400th anniv. of Charity Hospital, Santos.

Pedro Americo de Figueirido e Melo (1843-1905), Artist-hero and Statesman — A208

1943, Dec. 16   Typo.   Perf. 11
618 A208 40c brown orange .20 .20

Gen. A. E. Gomes Carneiro A209

1944, Feb. 9   Engr.
619 A209 1.20cr rose .50 .35
50th anniversary of the Lapa siege.

Statue of Baron of Rio Branco — A210

1944, May 13   Typo.
620 A210 1cr blue .40 .25
Statue of the Baron of Rio Branco unveiling.

Duke of Caxias A211

1944, May 13   Unwmk.   Perf. 12
Granite Paper
621 A211 1.20cr bl grn & pale
     org .50 .30
Centenary of pacification of Sao Paulo and Minas Gerais in an independence movement in 1842.

YMCA Seal — A212

1944, June 7   Litho.   Perf. 11
Granite Paper
622 A212 40c dp bl, car & yel .30 .20
Centenary of Young Men's Christian Assn.

Chamber of Commerce Rio Grande — A213

Wmk. 268
1944, Sept. 25   Engr.   Perf. 12
623 A213 40c lt yellow brn .30 .25
Centenary of the Chamber of Commerce of Rio Grande.

Martim F. R. de Andrada A214

1945, Jan. 30   *Perf. 11*
624 A214 40c blue   .30 .25
Ccentenary of the death of Martim F. R. de Andrada, statesman.

Meeting of Duke of Caxias and David Canabarro A215

1945, Mar. 19   **Photo.**
625 A215 40c ultra   .30 .20
Pacification of Rio Grande do Sul, cent.

Globe and "Esperanto" — A216

1945, Apr. 16
626 A216 40c lt blue grn   .50 .25
10th Esperanto Congress, Rio, Apr. 14-22.

Baron of Rio Branco's Bookplate A217

1945, Apr. 20   Wmk. 268   *Perf. 11*
627 A217 40c violet   .50 .25
Cent. of the birth of Jose Maria da Silva Paranhos, Baron of Rio Branco.

Tranquility A218

Glory — A219

Victory A220

Peace A221

Cooperation — A222

Rouletted 7
1945, May 8   Engr.   Wmk. 268
628 A218 20c dk rose vio   .20 .20
629 A219 40c dk carmine   .20 .20
630 A220 1cr dull orange   .35 .30
631 A221 2cr steel blue   .85 .45
632 A222 5cr green   1.65 .55
   Nos. 628-632 (5)   3.25 1.70
Victory of the Allied Nations in Europe.
Nos. 628-632 exist on thin card, imperf. and unwatermarked.

Francisco Manoel da Silva (1795-1865), Composer (in 1831) of the National Anthem — A223

1945, May 30   Typo.   *Perf. 12*
633 A223 40c brt rose   .45 .30
  a.   Wmk. 268   6.75 6.75

Bahia Institute of Geography and History A224

1945, May 30   Wmk. 268   *Perf. 11*
634 A224 40c lt ultra   .25 .20
50th anniv. of the founding of the Institute of Geography and History at Bahia.

Emblems of 5th Army and B.E.F.
A225   A226

US Flag and Shoulder Patches A227

Brazilian Flag and Shoulder Patches A228

Victory Symbol and Shoulder Patches — A229

1945, July 18   **Litho.**
635 A225 20c multicolored   .20 .20
636 A226 40c multicolored   .20 .20
637 A227 1cr multicolored   .70 .40
638 A228 2cr multicolored   1.00 .60
639 A229 5cr multicolored   3.00 .70
   Nos. 635-639 (5)   5.10 2.10
Honoring the Brazilian Expeditionary Force and the US 5th Army Battle against the Axis in Italy.

Radio Tower and Map — A230

1945, Sept. 3   **Engr.**
640 A230 1.20cr gray   .45 .25
Third Inter-American Conference on Radio Communications.
No. 640 was reproduced on a souvenir card with blue background and inscriptions. Size: 145x161mm.

A 40c lilac stamp, picturing the International Bridge between Argentina and Brazil and portraits of Presidents Justo and Vargas, was prepared late in 1945. It was not issued, but later was sold, without postal value, to collectors. Value, 20 cents.

Admiral Luiz Felipe Saldanha da Gama (1846-1895) — A231

1946, Apr. 7
641 A231 40c gray black   .25 .25

Princess Isabel d'Orleans-Braganca Birth Cent. — A232

1946, July 29   **Unwmk.**
642 A232 40c black   .25 .25

Post Horn, V and Envelope — A233

Post Office, Rio de Janeiro A234

Bay of Rio de Janeiro and Plane A235

1946, Sept. 2   Litho.   *Perf. 11*
643 A233 40c blk & pale org   .20 .20

Perf. 12½
Engr.   Unwmk.
Center in Ultramarine
644 A234 2cr slate   .50 .20
645 A234 5cr orange brn   2.50 .85
646 A234 10cr dk violet   2.75 .50
Center in Brown Orange
647 A235 1.30cr dk green   .30 .35
648 A235 1.70cr car rose   .30 .35
649 A235 2.20cr dp ultra   .50 .50
   Nos. 643-649 (7)   7.05 2.95
5th Postal Union Congress of the Americas and Spain.
No. 643 was reproduced on a souvenir card. Size: 188x239mm. Sold for 10cr.

Liberty — A236

Perf. 11x11½
1946, Sept. 18   **Wmk. 268**
650 A236 40c blk & gray   .25 .20
  a.   Unwmkd.   150.00
Adoption of the Constitution of 1946.

Columbus Lighthouse, Dominican Republic A237

1946, Sept. 14   Litho.   *Perf. 11*
651 A237 5cr Prus grn   4.00 1.50

Orchid — A238

Gen. A. E. Gomes Carneiro — A239

1946, Nov. 8 **Wmk. 268**
652 A238 40c ultra, red & yel .40 .30
a. Unwmkd. 55.00
4th National Exhibition of Orchids, Rio de Janeiro, November, 1946.

1946, Dec. 6 Engr. Perf. 10½x12
653 A239 40c deep green .20 .20
Centenary of the birth of Gen. Antonio Ernesto Gomes Carneiro.

Brazilian Academy of Letters A240

1946, Dec. 14 **Perf. 11**
654 A240 40c blue .25 .20
50th anniv. of the foundation of the Brazilian Academy of Letters, Rio de Janeiro.

Antonio de Castro Alves (1847-1871), Poet — A241

1947, Mar. 14 Litho. Wmk. 267
655 A241 40c bluish green .20 .20

Types of 1941-42, Values in Centavos or Cruzeiros

1947-54 Wmk. 267 Typo. Perf. 11
656 A184 2c olive .20 .20
657 A184 5c yellow brn .20 .20
658 A184 10c green .20 .20
659 A185 20c brown org .20 .20
660 A185 30c dk lil rose .60 .20
661 A185 40c blue .30 .20
b. Wmk. 268 800.00 60.00
661A A185 50c salmon .60 .20
662 A186 60c lt violet 1.00 .20
663 A186 70c brt rose .40 .20
('54)
664 A186 1cr gray 1.00 .20
665 A186 1.20cr dull blue 2.50 .20
a. Wmk. 268 11.00 9.00
666 A187 2cr gray violet 4.00 .20

Engr.
667 A188 5cr blue 7.50 .20
668 A189 10cr rose red 7.50 .20

Perf. 11, 13
669 A190 20cr deep brn 15.00 .75
670 A191 50cr red 30.00 .50
Nos. 656-670 (16) 71.20 4.05
The 5, 20, 50cr also exist with perf. 12-13.

Pres. Gonzalez Videla of Chile A242

1947, June 26 Unwmk. Perf. 12x11
671 A242 40c dk brown orange .20 .20
Visit of President Gabriel Gonzalez Videla of Chile, June 1947.
A souvenir folder contains four impressions of No. 671, and measures 6½x8¼ inches.

"Peace" and Western Hemisphere A243

1947, Aug. 15 **Perf. 11x12**
672 A243 1.20cr blue .20 .20
Inter-American Defense Conference at Rio de Janeiro, August-September, 1947.

Pres. Harry S Truman, Map and Statue of Liberty A244

1947, Sept. 1 Typo. Perf. 12x11
673 A244 40c ultra .20 .20
Visit of US President Harry S Truman to Brazil, Sept. 1947.

Pres. Eurico Gaspar Dutra — A245

Mother and Child — A246

Wmk. 268
1947, Sept. 7 Engr. Perf. 11
674 A245 20c green .20 .20
675 A245 40c rose carmine .20 .20
676 A245 1.20cr deep blue .25 .20
Nos. 674-676 (3) .65 .60
The souvenir sheet containing Nos. 674-676 is listed as No. C73A. See No. 679.

1947, Oct. 10 Typo. Unwmk.
677 A246 40c brt ultra .20 .20
Issued to mark Child Care Week, 1947.

Arms of Belo Horizonte — A247

Globe — A248

1947, Dec. 12 Engr. Wmk. 267
678 A247 1.20cr rose carmine .30 .20
50th anniversary of the founding of the city of Belo Horizonte.

Dutra Type of 1947
1948 Engr. Wmk. 267
679 A245 20c green 1.50 1.50

Catalogue values for unused stamps in this section, from this point to the end of the section, are for Never Hinged items.

1948, July 10 Litho.
680 A248 40c dl grn & pale lil .35 .20
International Exposition of Industry and Commerce, Petropolis, 1948.

Arms of Paranagua A249

Child Reading Book — A250

1948, July 29
681 A249 5cr bister brown 1.75 .50
300th anniversary of the founding of the city of Paranagua, July 29, 1648.

1948, Aug. 1
682 A250 40c green .25 .20
National Education Campaign.
No. 682 was reproduced on a souvenir card. Size: 124x157mm.

Tiradentes A251

Symbolical of Cancer Eradication A252

1948, Nov. 12
683 A251 40c brown orange .25 .20
200th anniversary of the birth of Joaquim José da Silva Xavier (Tiradentes).

1948, Dec. 14
684 A252 40c claret .25 .25
Anti-cancer publicity.

Adult Student A253

1949, Jan. 3 Wmk. 267 Perf. 12x11
685 A253 60c red vio & pink .25 .20
Campaign for adult education.

"Battle of Guararapes," by Vitor Meireles — A254

1949, Feb. 15 **Perf. 11½x12**
686 A254 60c lt blue .95 .60
2nd Battle of Guararapes, 300th anniv.

Church of Sao Francisco de Paula — A255

Manuel de Nobrega — A256

Perf. 11x12
1949, Mar. 8 Unwmk. Engr.
687 A255 60c dark brown .20 .20
a. Souvenir sheet 30.00 30.00
Bicentenary of city of Ouro Fino, state of Minas Gerais.
No. 687a contains one imperf. stamp similar to No. 687, with dates in lower margin. Size: 70x89mm.

1949, Mar. 29 **Imperf.**
688 A256 60c violet .25 .25
Founding of the City of Salvador, 400th anniv.

Emblem of Brazilian Air Force and Plane A257

1949, June 18
689 A257 60c blue violet .25 .25
Issued to honor the Brazilian Air Force.

Star and Angel — A258

1949 Wmk. 267 Litho. Perf. 11x12
690 A258 60c pink .20 .20
1st Ecclesiastical Cong., Salvador, Bahia.

Globe A259

1949, Oct. 31 Typo. Perf. 12x11
691 A259 1.50cr blue .25 .20
75th anniv. of the UPU.

Ruy Barbosa
A260

Unwmk.
1949, Dec. 14   Engr.   Perf. 12
692 A260 1.20cr rose carmine   .65 .30
Centenary of birth of Ruy Barbosa.

Joaquim Cardinal Arcoverde A. Cavalcanti, Birth Centenary — A261

1950, Feb. 27   Litho.   Perf. 11x12
693 A261 60c rose   .25 .20

Grapes and Factory A262

1950, Mar. 15   Perf. 12x11
694 A262 60c rose lake   .25 .20
75th anniversary of Italian immigration to the state of Rio Grande do Sul.

Virgin of the Globe — A263

1950, May 31   Perf. 11x12
695 A263 60c blk & lt bl   .25 .20
Establishment in Brazil of the Daughters of Charity of St. Vincent de Paul, cent.

Globe and Soccer Players — A264

1950, June 24
696 A264 60c ultra, bl & gray   .85 .50
4th World Soccer Championship.

Symbolical of Brazilian Population Growth A265

1950, July 10   Typo.   Perf. 12x11
697 A265 60c rose lake   .25 .20
Issued to publicize the 6th Brazilian census.

Dr. Oswaldo Cruz — A266

1950, Aug. 23   Litho.   Perf. 11x12
698 A266 60c orange brown   .25 .20
5th International Congress of Microbiology.

View of Blumenau and Itajai River A267

Perf. 12x11
1950, Sept. 9   Wmk. 267
699 A267 60c bright pink   .25 .20
Centenary of the founding of Blumenau.

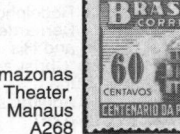

Amazonas Theater, Manaus A268

1950, Sept. 27
700 A268 60c light brn red   .20 .20
Centenary of Amazonas Province.

Arms of Juiz de Fora — A269

1950, Oct. 24   Perf. 11x12
701 A269 60c carmine   .25 .25
Centenary of the founding of Juiz de Fora.

Post Office at Recife A270

1951, Jan. 10   Typo.   Perf. 12x11
702 A270 60c carmine   .20 .20
703 A270 1.20cr carmine   .30 .20
Opening of the new building of the Pernambuco Post Office.

Arms of Joinville — A271

Jean-Baptiste de La Salle — A272

1951, Mar. 9   Perf. 11x12
704 A271 60c orange brown   .25 .20
Centenary of the founding of Joinville.

1951, Apr. 30   Litho.
705 A272 60c blue   .25 .20
Birth of Jean-Baptiste de La Salle, 300th anniv.

Heart and Flowers — A273

Sylvio Romero — A274

1951, May 13   Engr.
706 A273 60c deep plum   .25 .20
Mother's Day, May 14, 1951.

1951, Apr. 21   Litho.
707 A274 60c dl vio brn   .20 .20
Romero (1851-1914), poet and author.

Joao Caetano, Stage and Masks A275

1951, July 9   Perf. 12x11
708 A275 60c lt gray bl   .25 .20
1st Brazilian Theater Cong., Rio, July 9-13, 1951.

Orville A. Derby — A276

First Mass Celebrated in Brazil — A277

1951, July 23   Perf. 11x12
709 A276 2cr slate   .35 .35
Centenary of the birth (in New York State) of Orville A. Derby, geologist.

1951, July 25
710 A277 60c dl brn & buff   .20 .20
4th Inter-American Congress on Catholic Education, Rio de Janeiro, 1951.

Euclides Pinto Martins A278

1951, Aug. 16   Perf. 12x11
711 A278 3.80cr brn & citron   1.50 .35
1st flight from NYC to Rio, 29th anniv.

Monastery of the Rock A279

1951, Sept. 8
712 A279 60c dl brn & cream   .20 .20
Founding of Vitoria, 4th centenary.

Santos-Dumont and Model Plane Contest — A280

Dirigible and Eiffel Tower — A281

Perf. 11x12
1951, Oct. 19   Wmk. 267   Litho.
713 A280 60c salmon & dk brn   .42 .35

Unwmk.   Engr.
714 A281 3.80cr dark purple   1.25 .40
Week of the Wing and 50th anniv. of Santos-Dumont's flight around the Eiffel Tower.
In December 1951, Nos. 713 and 714 were privately overprinted: "Exposicao Filatelica Regional Distrito Federal 15-XII-1951 23-XII-1951." These were attached to souvenir sheets bearing engraved facsimiles of Nos. 38, 49 and 51, which were sold by Clube Filatelico do Brasil to mark its 20th anniversary. The overprinted stamps on the sheets were canceled, but 530 "unused" sets were sold by the club.

Farmers and Ear of Wheat — A282

1951, Nov. 10   Litho.   Wmk. 267
715 A282 60c dp grn & gray   .25   .25
Festival of Grain at Bage, 1951.

Map and Open Bible A283

1951, Dec. 9   Perf. 12x11
716 A283 1.20cr brn org   .50   .35
Issued to publicize the Day of the Bible.

Queen Isabella — A284   Henrique Oswald — A285

1952, Mar. 10   Perf. 11x12
717 A284 3.80cr lt bl   .60   .30
500th anniversary of the birth of Queen Isabella I of Spain.

1952, Apr. 22
718 A285 60c brown   .25   .20
Oswald (1852-1931), composer.

Vicente Licinio Cardoso — A286

Map and Symbol of Labor — A287

1952, May 2
719 A286 60c gray blue   .25   .20
4th Brazilian Homeopathic Congress.

1952, Apr. 30
720 A287 1.50cr brnsh pink   .25   .20
5th International Labor Organization Conference for American Countries.

Gen. Polidoro da Fonseca — A288

Luiz de Albuquerque M. P. Caceres — A289

Portraits: 5cr, Baron de Capanema. 10cr, Minister Eusebio de Queiros.

Unwmk.
1952, May 11   Engr.   Perf. 11
721 A288 2.40cr lt car   .35   .20
722 A288   5cr blue   2.25   .30
723 A288   10cr dk bl grn   2.25   .30
    Nos. 721-723 (3)   4.85   .80
Centenary of telegraph in Brazil.

1952, June 8   Litho.   Perf. 11x12
724 A289 1.20cr vio bl   .25   .20
200th anniversary of the founding of the city of Mato Grosso.

Symbolizing the Glory of Sports — A290

1952, July 21   Perf. 12x11
725 A290 1.20cr dp bl & bl   .60   .40
Fluminense Soccer Club, 50th anniversary.

José Antonio Saraiva — A291

Emperor Dom Pedro — A292

1952, Aug. 16   Perf. 11x12
726 A291 60c lil rose   .25   .20
Centenary of the founding of Terezina, capital of Piaui State.

1952, Sept. 3   Wmk. 267
727 A292 60c lt bl & blk   .25   .20
Issued for Stamp Day and the 2nd Philatelic Exhibition of Sao Paulo.

Flag-encircled Globe — A293

1952, Oct. 24   Perf. 13½
728 A293 3.80cr blue   .85   .50
Issued to publicize United Nations Day.

View of Sao Paulo, Sun and Compasses — A294

1952, Nov. 8   Litho.   Perf. 12x11
729 A294 60c dl bl, yel & gray grn   .25   .20
City Planning Day.

Father Diogo Antonio Feijo — A295

1952, Nov. 9   Perf. 11x12
730 A295 60c fawn   .25   .20

Rodolpho Bernardelli and His "Christ and the Adultress" A297

1952, Dec. 18   Perf. 12x11
732 A297 60c gray blue   .25   .20
Bernardelli, sculptor and painter, birth cent.

Map of Western Hemisphere and View of Rio de Janeiro — A298

1952, Sept. 20
733 A298 3.80cr vio brn & lt grn   .80   .30
2nd Congress of American Industrial Medicine, Rio de Janeiro, 1952.

Arms and Head of Pioneer A299

Coffee, Cotton and Sugar Cane — A300

2.80cr, Jesuit monk planting tree. 3.80cr, 5.80cr, Spiral, symbolizing progress.

1953, Jan. 25   Litho.   Perf. 11
734 A299 1.20cr ol brn & blk brn   .50   .35
735 A300   2cr olive grn & yel   1.75   .35
736 A300 2.80cr red brn & dp org   1.20   .20
737 A300 3.80cr dk brn & yel grn   1.00   .20
738 A300 5.80cr int bl & yel grn   .70   .20
    Nos. 734-738 (5)   5.15   1.30
400th anniversary of Sao Paulo. Used copies of No. 734 exist with design inverted.

Ledger and Winged Cap A301

1953, Feb. 22   Perf. 12x11
739 A301 1.20cr dl brn & fawn   .25   .20
6th Brazilian Accounting Congress.

Joao Ramalho — A302

Wmk. 264
1953, Apr. 8   Engr.   Perf. 11½
740 A302 60c blue   .25   .20
Founding of the city of Santo Andre, 4th cent.

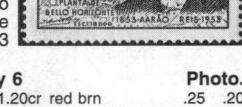

Aarao Reis and Plan of Belo Horizonte A303

1953, May 6   Photo.
741 A303 1.20cr red brn   .25   .20
Aarao Leal de Carvalho Reis (1853-1936), civil engineer.

A304

A305

1953, May 16
742 A304 1.50cr Almirante
Saldanha .40 .25

4th globe-circling voyage of the training ship Almirante Saldanha.

1953, July 5 **Photo.**

Joaquim Jose Rodrigues Torres, Viscount of Itaborai.

743 A305 1.20cr violet .20 .20

Centenary of the Bank of Brazil.

Lamp and Rio-Petropolis
Highway — A306

1953, July 14
744 A306 1.20cr gray .25 .20

10th Intl. Congress of Nursing, Petropolis, 1953.

Bay of Rio
de Janeiro
A307

1953, July 15
745 A307 3.80cr dk bl grn .40 .20

Issued to publicize the fourth World Congress of Baptist Youth, July 1953.

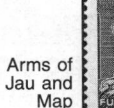

Arms of
Jau and
Map
A308

1953, Aug. 15 **Engr.**
746 A308 1.20cr purple .25 .20

Centenary of the city of Jau.

Ministry of Health
and Education
Building,
Rio — A309

Maria Quiteria de
Jesus
Medeiros — A310

1953, Aug. 1
747 A309 1.20cr dp grn .25 .20

Day of the Stamp and the first Philatelic Exhibition of National Education.

1953, Aug. 21 **Photo.**
748 A310 60c vio bl .25 .20

Centenary of the death of Maria Quiteria de Jesus Medeiros (1792-1848), independence heroine.

Pres. Odria of
Peru — A311

Duke of Caxias
Leading his
Troops — A312

1953, Aug. 25
749 A311 1.40cr rose brn .25 .20

Issued to publicize the visit of Gen. Manuel A. Odria, President of Peru, Aug. 25, 1953.

Engr. (60c, 5.80cr); Photo.
1953, Aug. 25

1.20cr, Caxias' tomb. 1.70cr, 5.80cr, Portrait of Caxias. 3.80cr, Arms of Caxias.

750 A312	60c dp grn	.30	.20
751 A312	1.20cr dp claret	.40	.20
752 A312	1.70cr slate grn	.40	.20
753 A312	3.80cr rose brn	.65	.20
754 A312	5.80cr gray vio	.65	.20
Nos. 750-754 (5)		2.40	1.00

150th anniversary of the birth of Luis Alves de Lima e Silva, Duke of Caxias.

Quill Pen, Map
and Tree — A313

Horacio
Hora — A314

1953, Sept. 12 **Photo.**
755 A313 60c ultra .25 .20

5th National Congress of Journalism.

1953, Sept. 17 Litho. Wmk. 267
756 A314 60c org & dp plum .25 .20

Horacio Pinto de Hora (1853-1890), painter.

Pres. Somoza of
Nicaragua — A315

Auguste de Saint-
Hilaire
A316

1953, Sept. 24 Photo. Wmk. 264
757 A315 1.40cr dk vio brn .25 .20

Issued to publicize the visit of Gen. Anastasio Somoza, president of Nicaragua.

1953, Sept. 30
758 A316 1.20cr dk brn car .25 .25

Centenary of the death of Auguste de Saint-Hilaire, explorer and botanist.

Jose Carlos do
Patrocinio — A317

Clock Tower,
Crato — A318

1953, Oct. 9 **Photo.**
759 A317 60c dk slate gray .25 .20

Jose Carlos do Patrocinio, (1853-1905), journalist and abolitionist.

1953, Oct. 17
760 A318 60c blue green .25 .20

Centenary of the city of Crato.

Joao Capistrano
de Abreu — A319

Allegory:
"Justice" — A320

1953, Oct. 23
761 A319 60c dull blue .20 .20
762 A319 5cr purple .85 .85

Joao Capistrano de Abreu (1853-1927), historian.

1953, Nov. 17
763 A320 60c indigo .25 .20
764 A320 1.20cr dp magenta .25 .20

50th anniv. of the Treaty of Petropolis.

Farm Worker in
Wheat
Field — A321

Teacher and
Pupils — A322

1953, Nov. 29 Photo. Perf. 11½
766 A321 60c dk green .25 .20

3rd Natl. Wheat Festival, Erechim, 1953.

1953, Dec. 14
767 A322 60c red .25 .25

First National Conference of Primary School Teachers, Salvador, 1953.

Zacarias de Gois
e Vasconcellos
A323

Alexandre de
Gusmao — A324

5cr, Porters with trays of coffee beans.

1953-54   **Photo.**
768 A323 2cr org brn & blk, *buff*   .65 .40
   ('54)
a.   White paper   1.75 .40
769 A323 5cr dp org & blk   1.25 .40
Centenary of the state of Parana.

1954, Jan. 13
770 A324 1.20cr brn vio   .25 .20
Gusmao (1695-1753), statesman, diplomat and writer.

Symbolical of Sao Paulo's Growth — A325

Arms and View of Sao Paulo A326

Designs: 2cr, Priest, settler and Indian. 2.80cr, José de Anchieta.

1954, Jan. 25   **Perf. 11½x11**
771 A325 1.20cr dk vio brn   .75 .50
a.   Buff paper   1.75 1.00
    Engr.
772 A325 2cr lilac rose   1.00 .60
773 A325 2.80cr pur gray   1.00 1.00
    Perf. 11x11½
774 A326 3.80cr dl grn   1.25 .50
a.   Buff paper   2.25 2.00
775 A326 5.80cr dl red   1.25 .60
a.   Buff paper   5.00 .75
   Nos. 771-775 (5)   5.25 3.20
400th anniversary of Sao Paulo.

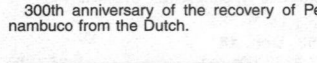

J. Fernandes Vieira, A. Vidal de Negreiros, A. F. Camarao and H. Dias — A327

1954, Feb. 18   **Photo.**   **Perf. 11x11½**
776 A327 1.20cr ultra   .25 .25
300th anniversary of the recovery of Pernambuco from the Dutch.

Sao Paulo and Minerva A328

1954, Feb. 24
777 A328 1.50cr dp plum   .25 .25
10th International Congress of Scientific Organizations, Sao Paulo, 1954.

Stylized Grapes, Jug and Map A329   Monument of the Immigrants A330

1954, Feb. 27   **Photo.**   **Perf. 11½x11**
778 A329 40c dp claret   .25 .20
Grape Festival, Rio Grande do Sul.

1954, Feb. 28
779 A330 60c dp vio bl   .25 .20
Unveiling of the Monument to the Immigrants of Caxias do Sul.

First Brazilian Locomotive — A331

    Perf. 11x11½
1954, Apr. 30   **Unwmk.**
781 A331 40c carmine   .25 .20
Centenary of the first railroad engine built in Brazil.

Pres. Chamoun of Lebanon — A332

1954, May 12   **Photo.**   **Perf. 11½x11**
782 A332 1.50cr maroon   .25 .25
Visit of Pres. Camille Chamoun of Lebanon.

Sao Jose College, Rio de Janeiro A333

J. B. Champagnat Marcelin — A334   Apolonia Pinto — A335

1954, June 6   **Perf. 11x11½, 11½x11**
783 A333 60c purple   .20 .20
784 A334 120cr vio blue   .20 .20
50th anniversary of the founding of the Marist Brothers in Brazil.

1954, June 21   **Photo.**
785 A335 1.20cr bright green   .20 .20
Apolonia Pinto (1854-1937), actress.

Adm. Margues Tamandare — A336

Portraits: 2c, 5c, 10c, Admiral Margues Tamandare. 20c, 30c, 40c, Oswaldo Cruz. 50c, 60c, 90c, Joaquim Murtinho. 1cr, 1.50cr, 2cr, Duke of Caxias. 5cr, 10cr, Ruy Barbosa. 20c, 50c, Jose Bonifacio.

1954-60   **Wmk. 267**   **Perf. 11x11½**
786 A336 2c vio blue   .20 .20
787 A336 5c org red   .20 .20
788 A336 10c brt green   .20 .20
789 A336 20c magenta   .20 .20
790 A336 30c dk gray grn   .20 .20
791 A336 40c rose red   .35 .20
792 A336 50c violet   .25 .20
793 A336 60c gray grn   .20 .20
794 A336 90c orange ('55)   .35 .20
795 A336 1cr brown   .20 .20
796 A336 1.50cr blue   .20 .20
a.   Wmk. 264   16.00 8.00
797 A336 2cr dk bl grn ('56)   .45 .20
798 A336 5cr rose lil ('56)   .35 .20
799 A336 10cr lt grn ('60)   .90 .20
800 A336 20cr crim rose ('59)   .90 .20
801 A336 50cr ultra ('59)   5.50 .20
  Nos. 786-801 (16)   10.65 3.20
See Nos. 890, 930-933.

Boy Scout Waving Flag (Statue) — A337   Baltasar Fernandes, Explorer — A338

1954, Aug. 2   **Unwmk.**   **Perf. 11½x11**
802 A337 1.20cr vio bl   .40 .25
Intl. Boy Scout Encampment, Sao Paulo.

1954, Aug. 15
803 A338 60c dk red   .25 .25
300th anniversary of city of Sorocaba.

Adeodato Giovanni Cardinal Piazza — A339   Our Lady of Aparecida, Map of Brazil — A340

1954, Sept. 2
804 A339 4.20cr red org   .50 .35
Visit of Adeodato Cardinal Piazza, papal legate to Brazil.

1954
Design: 1.20cr, Virgin standing on globe.
805 A340 60c claret   .30 .30
806 A340 1.20cr vio bl   .40 .30
No. 805 was issued for the 1st Cong. of Brazil's Patron Saint (Our Lady of Aparecida); No. 806, the cent. of the proclamation of the dogma of the Immaculate Conception. Both stamps also for the Marian Year.
Issue dates: 60c, Sept. 6; 1.20cr, Sept. 8.

Benjamin Constant and Hand Reading Braille A341

1954, Sept. 27   **Photo.**   **Unwmk.**
807 A341 60c dk grn   .25 .20
Centenary of the founding of the Benjamin Constant Institute.

River Battle of Riachuelo — A342

Admiral F. M. Barroso A343   Dr. Christian F. S. Hahnemann A344

1954, Oct. 6   **Perf. 11½x11, 11½x11**
808 A342 40c redsh brown   .30 .20
809 A343 60c purple   .20 .20
Admiral Francisco Manoel Barroso da Silva (1804-82).

1954, Oct. 8   **Perf. 11½x11**
810 A344 2.70cr dk green   .30 .25
1st World Cong. of Homeopathic Medicine.

Nizia Floresta — A345   Ears of Wheat — A346

1954, Oct. 12
811 A345 60c lilac rose   .25 .20
Reburial of the remains of Nizia Floresta (Dio Nizia Pinto Lisboa), writer and educator.

1954, Oct. 22
812 A346 60c olive green   .20 .20
4th National Wheat Festival, Carazinho.

Basketball Player and Ball-Globe A347   Allegory of the Spring Games A348

1954, Oct. 23   **Photo.**
813 A347 1.40cr orange red   .30 .30
Issued to publicize the second World Basketball Championship Matches, 1954.

1954, Nov. 6   **Wmk. 267**
814 A348 60c red brown   .25 .20

Issued to publicize the 6th Spring Games.

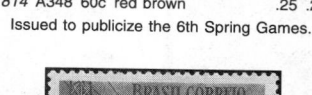

San Francisco Hydroelectric
Plant — A349

1955, Jan. 15   *Perf. 11x11½*
815 A349 60c brown org   .20 .20

Issued to publicize the inauguration of the
San Francisco Hydroelectric Plant.

Itutinga Hydroelectric Plant — A350

1955, Feb. 3
816 A350 40c blue   .20 .20

Issued to publicize the inauguration of the
Itutinga Hydroelectric Plant at Lavras.

Rotary Emblem
and Bay of Rio de
Janeiro — A351

1955, Feb. 23   *Perf. 12x11½*
817 A351 2.70cr slate gray & blk   .85 .25

Rotary International, 50th anniversary.

Fausto
Cardoso
Palace
A352

1955, Mar. 17   *Perf. 11x11½*
818 A352 40c henna brown   .25 .25

Centenary of Aracaju.

Aviation
Symbols
A353

1955, Mar. 13   **Photo.**   *Perf. 11½*
819 A353 60c dark gray green   .20 .20

Issued to publicize the third National Aviation Congress at Sao Paulo, Mar. 6-13.

Arms of
Botucatu
A354

1955, Apr. 14
820 A354   60c orange brn   .20 .20
821 A354 1.20cr brt green   .25 .20

Centenary of Botucatu.

Young
Racers at
Starting
Line
A355

1955, Apr. 30   **Photo.**   *Perf. 11½*
823 A355 60c orange brn   .25 .20

5th Children's Games.

Marshal Hermes
da
Fonseca — A356

Congress Altar,
Sail and Sugarloaf
Mountain — A357

1955, May 12   **Wmk. 267**
824 A356 60c purple   .20 .20

Marshal Hermes da Fonseca, birth cent.

Engraved; Photogravure (2.70cr)
1955, July 17   **Unwmk.**   *Perf. 11½*

Designs: 2.70cr, St. Pascoal. 4.20cr, Aloisi
Benedetto Cardinal Masella.

Granite Paper
825 A357 1.40cr green   .20 .20
826 A357 2.70cr deep claret   .25 .20
827 A357 4.20cr blue   .30 .20
   Nos. 825-827 (3)   .75 .60

36th World Eucharistic Cong. in Rio de
Janeiro.

Girl
Gymnasts
A358

1955, Nov. 12   **Engr.**
Granite Paper
828 A358 60c rose lilac   .20 .20

Issued to publicize the 7th Spring Games.

José B.
Monteiro
Lobato,
Author
A359

1955, Dec. 8
Granite Paper
829 A359 40c dark green   .20 .20

Adolfo
Lutz — A360

Lt. Col. Vilagran
Cabrita — A361

1955, Dec. 18
Granite Paper
830 A360 60c dk green   .20 .20

Centenary of the birth of Adolfo Lutz, public
health pioneer.

1955, Dec. 22   **Photo.**   **Wmk. 267**
831 A361 60c violet blue   .20 .20

First Battalion of Engineers, cent.

Salto
Grande
Hydroelectric
Dam
A362

1956, Jan. 15   **Unwmk.**   *Perf. 11½*
Granite Paper
832 A362 60c brick red   .20 .20

Arms of
Mococa — A363

"G" and
Globe — A364

Wmk. 256
1956, Apr. 17   **Photo.**   *Perf. 11½*
833 A363 60c brick red   .20 .20

Centenary of Mococa, Sao Paulo.

1956, Apr. 14   **Unwmk.**
Granite Paper
834 A364 1.20cr violet blue   .20 .20

18th Intl. Geographic Cong., Rio, Aug. 1956.

Girls' Foot
Race
A365

1956, Apr. 28   **Photo.**
Granite Paper
835 A365 2.50cr brt blue   .30 .20

6th Children's Games.

Plane over Map of
Brazil — A366

1956, June 12   **Wmk. 267**   *Perf. 11½*
836 A366 3.30cr brt vio bl   .40 .20

National Airmail Service, 25th anniv.

Fireman
Rescuing
Child
A367

1956, July 2   **Wmk. 264**
837 A367 2.50cr crimson   .40 .25
   a.   Buff paper   2.25 2.00

Centenary of the Fire Brigade.

Map of
Brazil and
Open Book
A368

1956, Sept. 8   **Wmk. 267**
838 A368 2.50cr brt vio bl   .30 .20

50th anniversary of the arrival of the Marist
Brothers in Northern Brazil.

Church and
Monument,
Franca — A369

1956, Sept. 7   **Engr.**
839 A369 2.50cr dk blue   .30 .20

Centenary of city of Franca, Sao Paulo.

Woman
Hurdler
A370

1956, Sept. 22   **Photo.**   **Unwmk.**
Granite Paper
840 A370 2.50cr dk car   .40 .20

Issued to publicize the 8th Spring Games.

Forest and Map of
Brazil — A371

1956, Sept. 30   **Wmk. 267**   *Perf. 11½*
841 A371 2.50cr dk green   .25 .20

Issued to publicize education in forestry.

Baron da
Bocaina
A372

1956, Oct. 8   Engr.   Wmk. 268
842 A372 2.50cr reddish brown   .25 .20
Centenary of the birth of Baron da Bocaina,
who introduced the special delivery mail system to Brazil.

Marbleized Paper
Paper with a distinct wavy-line or
marbleized watermark (which Brazilians
call *marmorizado* paper) has been
found on many stamps of Brazil, 1956-
68, including Nos. 843-845, 847, 851-
854, 858-858A, 864, 878, 880, 882,
884, 886-887, 896, 909, 918, 920-921,
925-928, 936-939, 949, 955-958, 960,
962-964, 978-979, 983, 985-987, 997-
998, 1002-1003, 1005, 1009-1012,
1017, 1024, 1026, 1055, 1075, 1078,
1082, C82, C82a, C83-C87, C96, C99,
C109.
Quantities are much less than those
of stamps on regular paper.

Panama Stamp
Showing Pres.
Juscelino
Kubitschek
A373

1956, Oct. 12   Photo.   Wmk. 267
843 A373 3.30cr green & blk   .40 .20
Issued on America Day, Oct. 12, to commemorate the meeting of the Presidents and
the Pan-American Conference at Panama
City, July 21-22.

Symbolical
of Steel
Production
A374

Wmk. 267
1957, Jan. 31   Photo.   Perf. 11½
844 A374 2.50cr chocolate   .25 .20
2nd expansion of the National Steel Company at Volta Redonda.

Joaquim E.
Gomes da
Silva — A375

1957, Mar. 1   Photo.   Unwmk.
Granite Paper
845 A375 2.50cr dk bl grn   .25 .20
Centenary of the birth (in 1856) of Joaquim
E. Gomes da Silva.

Allan
Kardec
A376

1957, Apr. 18   Engr.   Perf. 11½
846 A376 2.50cr dk brown   .25 .20
Issued in honor of Allan Kardec, pen name
of Leon Hippolyto Denizard Rivail, and for the
centenary of the publication of his "Codification of Spiritism."

Boy
Gymnast
A377

1957, Apr. 27   Photo.   Unwmk.
Granite Paper
847 A377 2.50cr lake   .50 .25
7th Children's Games.

Pres. Craveiro   Stamp of
Lopes — A378   1932 — A379

1957, June 7   Engr.   Wmk. 267
848 A378 6.50cr blue   .40 .20
Visit of Gen. Francisco Higino Craveiro
Lopes, President of Portugal.

1957, July 9   Photo.
849 A379 2.50cr rose   .25 .20
25th anniv. of the movement for a
constitution.

St. Antonio Monastery,
Pernambuco — A380

1957, Aug. 24   Engr.   Wmk. 267
850 A380 2.50cr deep magenta   .25 .20
300th anniv. of the emancipation of the
Franciscan province of St. Antonio in Pernambuco State.

Volleyball — A381

Basketball — A382

1957, Sept. 28   Photo.   Perf. 11½
851 A381 2.50cr dull org red   .45 .25
Issued for the 9th Spring Games.

1957, Oct. 12
852 A382 3.30cr org & brt grn   .45 .25
2nd Women's International Basketball
Championship, Rio de Janeiro.

Count of
Pinhal and
Sao Carlos
A383

1957, Nov. 4   Wmk. 267   Perf. 11½
853 A383 2.50cr rose   .25 .20
Centenary of the city of Sao Carlos and
honoring the Count of Pinhal, its founder.

Auguste
Comte — A384

1957, Nov. 15
854 A384 2.50cr dk red brn   .25 .20
Centenary of the death of Auguste Comte,
French mathematician and philosopher.

Radio
Station
A385

1957, Dec. 10   Wmk. 268
855 A385 2.50cr dk green   .20 .20
Opening of Sarapui Central Radio Station.

Admiral
Tamandare
and
Warship
A386

Design: 3.30cr, Aircraft carrier.

1957-58   Photo.
856 A386 2.50cr light blue   .25 .20
Engr.
857 A386 3.30cr green ('58)   .30 .20
150th anniversary of the birth of Admiral
Joaquin Marques de Tamandare, founder of
the Brazilian navy.

Coffee Plant and
Symbolic
"R" — A387

Wmk. 267
1957-58   Photo.   Perf. 11½
858 A387 2.50cr magenta   .50 .35
Unwmk.
Granite Paper
858A A387 2.50cr magenta ('58)   .45 .35
Centenary (in 1956) of the city of Ribeirao
Preto in Sao Paulo state.

Dom John
VI — A388

1958, Jan. 28   Engr.   Wmk. 268
859 A388 2.50cr magenta   .35 .25
150th anniversary of the opening of the
ports of Brazil to foreign trade.

Bugler
A389

1958, Mar. 18   Wmk. 267
860 A389 2.50cr red   .35 .25
Brazilian Marine Corps, 150th anniv.

Station at Rio and
Locomotive of
1858 — A390

Court
House — A391

Wmk. 267
1958, Mar. 29   Photo.   Perf. 11½
861 A390 2.50cr red brn   .35 .25
Central Railroad of Brazil, cent.

1958, Apr. 1   Engr.   Wmk. 256
862 A391 2.50cr green   .25 .20
150th anniv. of the Military Superior Court.

Emblem and Brazilian Pavilion A392

1958, Apr. 17　　　　**Wmk. 267**
863 A392 2.50cr dk blue　　.25 .25
　World's Fair, Brussels, Apr. 17-Oct. 19.

High Jump — A393

1958, Apr. 20　**Photo.**　**Unwmk.**
　　　　Granite Paper
864 A393 2.50cr crimson rose　.25 .20
　8th Children's Games.

Marshal Mariano da Silva Rondon A394

1958, Apr. 19　**Engr.**　**Wmk. 267**
865 A394 2.50cr magenta　　.25 .20
　Issued to honor Marshal Mariano da Silva Rondon and the "Day of the Indian."

Hydroelectric Station — A395

1958, Apr. 28　**Wmk. 267**　*Perf. 11½*
866 A395 2.50cr magenta　　.25 .20
　Opening of Sao Paulo State power plant.

National Printing Plant A396

1958, May 22　　　　**Photo.**
867 A396 2.50cr redsh brn　　.20 .20
　150th anniversary of the founding of the National Printing Plant.

Marshal Osorio — A397

1958, May 24
868 A397 2.50cr brt violet　　.20 .20
　150th anniversary of the birth of Marshal Manoel Luiz Osorio.

Pres. Ramon Villeda Morales — A398

Fountain — A399

1958, June 7　**Engr.**　*Perf. 11½*
869 A398 6.50cr dk green　　1.25 .75
　a.　Wmk. 268　　　　5.00 2.00
　Visit of Pres. Ramon Villeda Morales of Honduras.

1958, June 13
870 A399 2.50cr dk green　　.25 .20
　Botanical Garden, Rio de Janeiro, 150th anniv.

Symbols of Agriculture A400

Prophet Joel — A401

1958, June 18　　　　**Photo.**
871 A400 2.50cr rose carmine　.25 .20
　50th anniv. of Japanese immigration to Brazil.

1958, June 21　　　　**Engr.**
872 A401 2.50cr dk blue　　.25 .20
　Bicentenary of the Cathedral of Bom Jesus at Matosinhos.

Stylized Globe A402

1958, July 10　　　　**Photo.**
873 A402 2.50cr dk brown　　.20 .20
　Intl. Investment Conference, Belo Horizonte.

Julio Bueno Brandao — A403

1958, Aug. 1　**Wmk. 268**　*Perf. 11½*
874 A403 2.50cr red brown　　.25 .20
　Centenary of the birth of Julio Bueno Brandao, President of Minas Gerais.

Palacio Tiradentes (House of Congress) A404

1958, July 24　　　　**Engr.**
875 A404 2.50cr sepia　　.25 .20
　47th Interparliamentary Conference, Rio de Janeiro, July 24-Aug. 1.

Presidential Palace, Brasilia — A405

1958, Aug. 8　**Photo.**　**Wmk. 267**
876 A405 2.50cr ultra　　.20 .20
　Issued to publicize the construction of Brazil's new capital, Brasilia.

Freighters A406

1958, Aug. 22
877 A406 2.50cr blue　　.25 .20
　Brazilian merchant marine.

Joaquim Caetano da Silva A407

1958, Sept. 2　　　　**Unwmk.**
　　　　Granite Paper
878 A407 2.50cr redsh brn　　.25 .20
　Joaquim Caetano da Silva, scientist & historian.

Giovanni Gronchi — A408

Archers — A409

1958, Sept. 4　**Engr.**　**Wmk. 268**
879 A408 7cr dk blue　　.50 .20
　Visit of Italy's President Giovanni Gronchi to Brazil.

1958, Sept. 21　**Photo.**　*Perf. 11½*
　　　　Granite Paper
880 A409 2.50cr red org　　.35 .20
　Issued to publicize the 10th Spring Games.

Elderly Couple — A410

Machado de Assis — A411

1958, Sept. 27　　　　**Wmk. 267**
881 A410 2.50cr magenta　　.25 .20
　Day of the Old People, Sept. 27.

1958, Sept. 28　　　　**Unwmk.**
882 A411 2.50cr red brn　　.25 .20
　50th anniversary of the death of Joaquim Maria Machado de Assis, writer.

Pres. Vargas and Oil Derrick A412

1958, Oct. 6　　　　**Wmk. 268**
883 A412 2.50cr blue　　.25 .20
　5th anniv. of Pres. Getulio D. Vargas' oil law.

Globe — A413

Gen. Lauro
Sodré — A414

1958, Nov. 14　　Photo.　　Perf. 11½
884 A413 2.50cr blue　　　　　　.30　.20
　7th Inter-American Congress of
Municipalities.

1958, Nov. 15　　　　　　　Engr.
885 A414 3.30cr green　　　　　　.25　.20
　Cent. of the birth of Gen. Lauro Sodré.

UN
Emblem — A415

Soccer
Player — A416

1958, Dec. 26　　Photo.　　Perf. 11½
886 A415 2.50cr brt blue　　　　.20　.20
　10th anniv. of the signing of the Universal
Declaration of Human Rights.

1959, Jan. 20
887 A416 3.30cr emer & red brn　.40　.20
　World Soccer Championships of 1958.

Railroad Track and
Map — A417

Pres. Sukarno of
Indonesia — A418

1959, Apr.　Wmk. 267　Perf. 11½
888 A417 2.50cr dp orange　　　.25　.20
　Centenary of the linking of Patos and
Campina Grande by railroad.

1959, May 20
889 A418 2.50cr blue　　　　　　.25　.20
　Visit of President Sukarno of Indonesia.

Dom John
VI — A419

Boy Polo
Players — A420

Perf. 10½x11½
1959, June 12　　　　　　Wmk. 267
890 A419 2.50cr crimson　　　　.25　.20

1959, June 13　　　　　　Perf. 11½
891 A420 2.50cr orange brn　　.25　.20
　9th Children's Games.

Loading
Freighter — A421

Organ and
Emblem — A422

1959, July 10
892 A421 2.50cr dk green　　　　.25　.20
　Honoring the merchant marine.

1959, July 16　　　　　　　Photo.
893 A422 3.30cr magenta　　　　.25　.20
　Bicentenary of the Carmelite Order in Brazil.

Joachim Silverio
de Souza — A423

Symbolic
Road — A424

1959, July 20　　　　　　Perf. 11½
894 A423 2.50cr red brown　　　.25　.20
　Birth centenary of Joachim Silverio de
Souza, first bishop of Diamantina, Minas
Gerais.

1959, Sept. 27　　　　　　Wmk. 267
895 A424 3.30cr bl grn & ultra　.25　.20
　11th International Roadbuilding Congress.

Woman
Athlete — A425

1959, Oct. 4
896 A425 2.50cr lilac rose　　　.25　.20
　11th Spring Games.

Map of
Parana
A426

1959, Sept. 27
897 A426 2.50cr dk green　　　.25　.20
　Founding of Londrina, Parana, 25th anniv.

Globe and
Snipes — A427

Cross of
Lusitania — A428

1959, Oct. 22　　　　　　Perf. 11½
898 A427 6.50cr dull grn　　　　.20　.20
　World Championship of Snipe Class Sailboats, Porto Alegre, won by Brazilian
yachtsmen.

1959, Oct. 24　　　　　　　Engr.
899 A428 6.50cr dull blue　　　.20　.20
　4th Intl. Conf. on Brazilian-Portuguese Studies, University of Bahia, Aug. 10-20.

Factory Entrance
and Order of
Southern
Cross — A429

Corcovado Christ,
Globe and
Southern
Cross — A430

1959, Nov. 19　　　　　　　Photo.
900 A429 3.30cr orange red　　.20　.20
　Pres. Vargas Gunpowder Factory, 50th
anniv.

1959, Nov. 26　　　　　　Perf. 11½
901 A430 2.50cr blue　　　　　.20　.20
　Universal Thanksgiving Day.

Burning
Bush
A431

1959, Dec. 24　　　　　　Wmk. 267
902 A431 3.30cr lt grn　　　　　.20　.20
　Centenary of Presbyterian work in Brazil.

Piraja da Silva and Schistosoma
Mansoni — A432

1959, Dec. 28
903 A432 2.50cr rose violet　　.20　.20
　25th anniv. of the discovery and identification of schistosoma mansoni, a parasite of the
fluke family, by Dr. Piraja da Silva.

Luiz de
Matos
A433

1960, Jan. 3　　　　　　　Photo.
904 A433 3.30cr red brown　　.20　.20
　Birth centenary of Luiz de Matos.

Zamenhof — A434

Adél Pinto — A435

1960, Mar. 10   Wmk. 267   Perf. 11½
905 A434 6.50cr emerald   .20 .20
Lazarus Ludwig Zamenhof (1859-1917), Polish oculist who invented Esperanto in 1887.

1960, Mar. 19   Engr.   Wmk. 268
906 A435 11.50cr rose red   .20 .20
Centenary of the birth of Adél Pinto, civil engineer and railroad expert.

Presidential Palace, Colonnade — A436

Design: 27cr, Plan of Brasilia (like #C98).

1960   Photo.   Perf. 11x11½
907 A436 2.50cr brt green   .20 .20
Size: 105x46½mm
908 A436 27cr salmon   .60 .60
    Nos. 907-908,C95-C98 (6)   2.15 1.60
No. 907 for the inauguration of Brazil's new capital, Brasilia, Apr. 21, 1960.
No. 908 for the birthday of Pres. Juscelino Kubitschek and has a 27cr in design of No. C98, flanked by the chief design features of Nos. 907, C95-C97, with Kubitschek signature below. Issued in sheets of 4 with wide horizontal gutter.
Issued: 2.50cr, 4/21; 27cr, 9/12.

Grain, Coffee, Cotton and Cacao — A437

Paulo de Frontin — A438

Perf. 11½x11
1960, July 28   Wmk. 267
909 A437 2.50cr brown   .20 .20
Centenary of Ministry of Agriculture.

1960, Oct. 12   Wmk. 268
910 A438 2.50cr orange red   .20 .20
Cent. of the birth of Paulo de Frontin, engineer.

Woman Athlete Holding Torch — A439

1960, Oct. 18   Perf. 11½x11
911 A439 2.50cr blue grn   .20 .20
12th Spring Games.

Volleyball and Net — A440

Locomotive Wheels — A441

Perf. 11½x11
1960, Nov. 12   Wmk. 268
912 A440 11cr blue   .20 .20
International Volleyball Championships.

1960, Oct. 15   Perf. 11½x11
913 A441 2.50cr ultra   .20 .20
10th Pan-American Railroad Congress.

Symbols of Flight A442

1960, Dec. 16   Photo.   Perf. 11½
914 A442 2.50cr brn & yel   .20 .20
Intl. Fair of Industry and Commerce, Rio.

Emperor Haile Selassie — A443

1961, Jan. 31   Perf. 11½x11
915 A443 2.50cr dk brown   .20 .20
Visit of Emperor Haile Selassie of Ethiopia to Brazil, Dec. 1960.

Map of Brazil, Open Book and Sacred Heart Emblem A444

Perf. 11x11½
1961, Mar. 13   Wmk. 268
916 A444 2.50cr blue   .20 .20
50th anniv. of the operation in Brazil of the Order of the Blessed Heart of Mary.

Map of Guanabara — A445

1961, Mar. 27   Wmk. 267
917 A445 7.50cr org brn   .20 .20
Promulgation of the constitution of the state of Guanabara.

Arms of Agulhas Negras — A446

Brazil and Senegal Linked on Map — A447

Design: 3.30cr, Dress helmet and sword.

Perf. 11½x11
1961, Apr. 23   Wmk. 267
918 A446 2.50cr green   .20 .20
919 A446 3.30cr rose car   .20 .20
Sesquicentennial of the Agulhas Negras Military Academy.

1961, Apr. 28   Photo.
920 A447 27cr ultra   .25 .20
Visit of Afonso Arinos, Brazilian foreign minister, to Senegal to attend its independence ceremonies.

View of Ouro Preto, 1711 A448

1961, June 6   Perf. 11½x11
921 A448 1cr orange   .20 .20
250th anniversary of Ouro Preto.

War Arsenal A449

1961, June 20   Wmk. 256
924 A449 5cr dk red brn   .25 .20
War Arsenal, Rio de Janeiro, 150th anniv.

Coffee Bean and Branch — A450

Rabindranath Tagore — A451

Perf. 11½x11
1961, June 26   Wmk. 267
925 A450 20cr redsh brn   .80 .25
8th Directorial Committee meeting of the Intl. Coffee Convention, Rio, June 26.

1961, July 28   Photo.   Wmk. 267
926 A451 10cr rose car   .20 .20
Rabindranath Tagore, Indian poet, birth cent.

Stamp of 1861 and Map of English Channel A452

Design: 20cr, 430r stamp of 1861 and map of Netherlands.

1961, Aug. 1   Perf. 11x11½
927 A452 10cr rose   .75 .20
928 A452 20cr salmon pink   2.00 .30
Centenary of 1861 stamp issue.

Portrait Type of 1954-60
Designs as Before
1961   Wmk. 268   Perf. 11x11½
930 A336 1cr brown   .80 .50
931 A336 2cr dk bl grn   1.25 .50
932 A336 5cr red lilac   3.75 .30
933 A336 10cr emerald   7.25 .30
    Nos. 930-933 (4)   13.05 1.60
1cr, 5cr, 10cr have patterned background.

Sun, Clouds, Rain and Weather Symbols — A453

Dedo de Deus Peak — A454

1962, Mar. 23   Perf. 11½x11
936 A453 10cr red brown   .75 .30
World Meteorological Day, Mar. 23.

1962, Apr. 14   Photo.   Wmk. 267
937 A454 8cr emerald   .20 .25
50th anniversary of the climbing of Dedo de Deus (Finger of God) peak.

Dr. Gaspar Vianna and Leishmania Protozoa — A455

1962, Apr. 24   Perf. 11x11½
938 A455 8cr blue   .25 .20
Discovery by Gaspar Oliveiro Vianna (1885-1914) of a cure for leishmaniasis, 50th anniv.

Henrique Dias A456

1962, June 18   Wmk. 267
939 A456 10cr dk vio brn   .30 .20
300th anniversary of the death of Henrique Dias, Negro military leader who fought against the Dutch and Spaniards.

Millimeter
Gauge — A457

Sailboats, Snipe
Class — A458

1962, June 26   Perf. 11½x11
940 A457 100cr car rose   .35 .20
Centenary of the introduction of the metric
system in Brazil.

1962, July 21   Photo.   Wmk. 267
941 A458 8cr Prus green   .20 .20
Commemorating the 13th Brazilian championships for Snipe Class sailing.

Julio
Mesquita
A459

1962, Aug. 18   Perf. 11x11½
942 A459 8cr dull brown   .20 .20
Julio Mesquita, journalist and founder of a
Sao Paulo newspaper, birth cent.

Empress
Leopoldina — A460

1962, Sept. 7   Perf. 11½x11
943 A460 8cr rose claret   .20 .20
140th anniversary of independence.

Buildings, Brasilia — A461

**   Perf. 11x11½**
1962, Oct. 24   Wmk. 267
944 A461 10cr orange   .30 .20
51st Interparliamentary Conf., Brasilia.

Pouring
Ladle — A462

1962, Oct. 26   Perf. 11½x11
945 A462 8cr orange   .20 .20
Inauguration of the Usiminas State Iron and
Steel Foundry at Belo Horizonte, Minas
Gerais.

UPAE
Emblem
A463

1962, Nov. 19   Perf. 11x11½
946 A463 8cr bright magenta   .20 .20
Founding of the Postal Union of the Americas and Spain, UPAE, 50th anniv.

Chimney and
Cogwheel Forming
"10" — A464

1962, Nov. 26   Perf. 11½x11
947 A464 10cr lt blue grn   .20 .20
Natl. Economic and Development Bank,
10th anniv.

Quintino
Bocaiuva
A465

Soccer Player
and Globe
A466

1962, Dec. 27   Photo.   Perf. 11½x11
948 A465 8cr brown org   .20 .20
Bocaiuva, journalist, 50th death anniv.

1963, Jan. 14
949 A466 10cr blue grn   .40 .20
World Soccer Championship of 1962.

Carrier Pigeon — A467

1963, Jan. Unwmk. Litho. Perf. 14
950 A467   8cr yel, dk bl, red &
             grn   .20 .20
Souvenir Sheet
Imperf
951 A467 100cr yel, dk bl, red &
             grn   1.25 3.00
300 years of Brazilian postal service.
Issue dates: 8cr, Jan. 25; 100cr, Jan. 31.

Severino
Neiva — A468

**   Perf. 10½x11½**
1963, Jan. 31   Photo.
952 A468 8cr brt vio   .20 .20

Radar Tracking
Station and
Rockets — A469

"Cross of
Unity" — A470

**   Perf. 11½x11**
1963, Mar. 15   Wmk. 268
953 A469 21cr lt ultra   .20 .20
International Aeronautics and Space Exhibition, Sao Paulo.

1963   Wmk. 267   Perf. 11½x11
954 A470 8cr red lilac   .20 .20
Vatican II, the 21st Ecumenical Council of
the Roman Catholic Church.

"ABC" in
Geometric
Form — A471

Basketball
Player — A472

1963, Apr. 22   Photo.   Wmk. 267
955 A471 8cr brt bl & lt bl   .20 .20
Education Week, Apr. 22-27, 3-year alpha-
betization program.

1963, May 15
956 A472 8cr dp lilac rose   .20 .20
4th International Basketball Championships,
Rio de Janeiro, May 10-25, 1963.

Games Emblem
A473

"OEA" and Map
of the Americas
A474

1963, May 22   Perf. 11½x11
957 A473 10cr car rose   .30 .20
4th Pan American Games, Sao Paulo.

1963, June 6
958 A474 10cr org & dp org   .30 .20
15th anniversary of the charter of the
Organization of American States.

José Bonifacio de
Andrada — A475

1963, June 13
959 A475 8cr dk brown   .20 .20
Bicentenary of the birth of José Bonifacio de
Andrada e Silva, statesman.

Wheat
A476

1963, June 19 Photo. Perf. 11x11½
960 A476 10cr blue   .30 .20
FAO "Freedom from Hunger" campaign.

Centenary
Emblem — A477

Joao
Caetano — A478

1963, Aug. 19   Perf. 11½x11
961 A477 8cr yel org & red   .25 .20
Centenary of International Red Cross.

1963, Aug. 24   Perf. 11½x11
962 A478 8cr slate   .20 .20
Death centenary of Joao Caetano, actor.

Symbols of
Agriculture,
Industry and
Atomic
Energy — A479

Hammer
Thrower — A480

1963, Aug. 28
963 A479 10cr car rose   .25 .20
Atomic Development Law, 1st anniv.

1963, Sept. 13
964 A480 10cr gray   .40 .20
Intl. College Students' Games, Porto Alegre.

Marshal Tito — A481

Compass Rose, Map of Brazil and View of Rio — A482

1963, Sept. 19
965 A481 80cr sepia .35 .30
Visit of Marshal Tito of Yugoslavia.

1963, Sept. 20
966 A482 8cr lt blue grn .20 .20
8th International Leprology Congress.

Oil Derrick and Storage Tank A483

1963, Oct. 3 Perf. 11x11½
967 A483 8cr dk slate grn .20 .20
Petrobras, the natl. oil company, 10th anniv.

"Spring Games" A484

1963, Nov. 5 Photo. Wmk. 267
968 A484 8cr yel & org .20 .20
1963 Spring Games.

Dr. Borges de Medeiros (1863-1962), Governor of Rio Grande do Sul — A485

1963, Nov. 29 Perf. 11½x11
969 A485 8cr red brown .20 .20

Sao Joao del Rei A486

1963, Dec. 8 Perf. 11x11½
970 A486 8cr violet blue .20 .20
250th anniversary of Sao Joao del Rei.

Dr. Alvaro Alvim A487

1963, Dec. 19 .20 .20
971 A487 8cr dk gray
Alvaro Alvim (1863-1928), X-ray specialist and martyr of science.

Viscount de Mauá — A488

Mandacaru Cactus and Emblem — A489

1963, Dec. 28 Perf. 11½x11
972 A488 8cr rose car .20 .20
Sesquicentennial of the birth of Viscount de Mauá, founder of first Brazilian railroad.

1964, Jan. 23 Photo. Wmk. 267
973 A489 8cr dull green .20 .20
Bank of Northeast Brazil, 10th anniv.

Coelho Netto — A490

Lauro Müller — A491

1964, Feb. 21 Perf. 11½x11
974 A490 8cr brt violet .20 .20
Birth centenary of Coelho Netto, writer.

1964, Mar. 8 Wmk. 267
975 A491 8cr dp orange .20 .20
Lauro Siverino Müller, politician and member of the Brazilian Academy of Letters, birth cent.

Child Holding Spoon A492

1964, Mar. 25 Perf. 11x11½
976 A492 8cr yel brn & yel .20 .20
Issued for "School Meals Week."

Chalice Rock — A493

Allan Kardec — A494

1964, Apr. 9 Engr. Perf. 11½x11
977 A493 80cr red orange .20 .20
Issued for tourist publicity.

1964, Apr. 18 Photo.
978 A494 30cr slate green .45 .20
Cent. of "O Evangelho" (Gospel) of the codification of Spiritism.

Heinrich Lübke — A495

Pope John XXIII — A496

1964, May 8 Photo. Perf. 11½x11
979 A495 100cr red brown .60 .20
Visit of President Heinrich Lübke of Germany.

1964, June 29 Wmk. 267
980 A496 20cr dk car rose .20 .20
a. Unwmkd. .20 .20
Issued in memory of Pope John XXIII.

Pres. Senghor of Senegal — A497

1964, Sept. 19 Wmk. 267
981 A497 20cr dk brown .25 .20
Visit of Leopold Sedar Senghor, President of Senegal.

Botafogo Bay and Sugarloaf Mountain — A498

Designs: 100cr, Church of Our Lady of the Rock, vert. 200cr, Copacabana beach.

Perf. 11x11½, 11½x11
1964-65 Photo.
983 A498 15cr org & bl .30 .25
984 A498 100cr brt grn & red brn, yel .20 .20
985 A498 200cr black & red 1.75 .30
a. Souvenir sheet of 3 ('65) 4.75 4.00
Nos. 983-985 (3) 2.25 .75
4th cent. of Rio de Janeiro.
No. 985a contains three imperf. stamps similar to Nos. 983-985, but printed in brown. Sold for 320cr. Issued Dec. 30, 1965.
A souvenir card containing one lithographed facsimile of No. 984, imperf., exists, but has no franking value. Size: 100x125mm. Sold by P.O. for 250cr.

Pres. Charles de Gaulle A499

Pres. John F. Kennedy A500

1964, Oct. 13 Perf. 11½x11
986 A499 100cr orange brn .35 .20
Visit of Charles de Gaulle, President of France, Oct. 13-15.

1964, Oct. 24 Photo. Wmk. 267
987 A500 100cr slate .20 .20

"Prophet" by Lisboa — A501

1964, Nov. 18 Perf. 11½x11
988 A501 10cr slate .20 .20
150th death anniv. of the sculptor Antonio Francisco Lisboa, "O Aleijadinho" (The Cripple).

Antonio Goncalves Dias — A502

Designs: 30cr, Euclides da Cunha. 50cr, Prof. Angelo Moreira da Costa Lima. 200cr, Tiradentes. 500cr, Dom Pedro I. 1000cr, Dom Pedro II.

1965-66 Wmk. 267 Perf. 11x11½
989 A502 30cr brt bluish grn ('66) 2.00 .25
989A A502 50cr dull brn ('66) 1.50 .20
990 A502 100cr blue .60 .20
991 A502 200cr brown org 2.00 .20
992 A502 500cr red brown 6.00 .50
992A A502 1000cr sl bl ('66) 10.00 .50
Nos. 989-992A (6) 22.10 1.85

Statue of St. Sebastian, Guanataro Bay — A503

The Arches A504

Design: 35cr, Estacio de Sa (1520-67), founder of Rio de Janeiro.

1965 Photo. Perf. 11½
Size: 24x37mm
993 A503 30cr bl & rose red .30 .20

Lithographed and Engraved
Perf. 11x11½
994 A504 30cr lt bl & blk .30 .20

Photo. Perf. 11½
Size: 21x39mm
995 A503 35cr blk & org .20 .25
a. Souvenir sheet of 3 3.25 4.00
Nos. 993-995 (3) .80 .65
4th cent. of Rio de Janeiro.
No. 995a contains three imperf. stamps similar to Nos. 993-995, but printed in deep orange. Size: 130x79mm. Sold for 100cr.
Issued: #993, 3/5; #994, 11/30; #995, 7/28; #995a, 12/30.

Sword and Cross — A505

1965, Apr. 15 Wmk. 267 Perf. 11½
996 A505 120cr gray .30 .20
1st anniv. of the democratic revolution.

Vital Brazil — A506

Shah of Iran — A507

1965, Apr. 28 Wmk. 267 Perf. 11½
997 A506 120cr deep orange .30 .20
Centenary of birth of Vital Brazil, M.D.
A souvenir card containing one impression similar to No. 997, imperf., exists, printed in dull plum. Sold by P.O. for 250cr. Size: 114x180mm.

1965, May 5 Photo.
998 A507 120cr rose claret .25 .20
Commemorating the visit of Shah Mohammed Riza Pahlavi of Iran.

Marshal Mariano da Silva Rondon — A508

Lions' Emblem — A509

1965, May 7 Engr.
999 A508 30cr claret .25 .20
Marshal Mariano da Silva Rondon (1865-1958), explorer and expert on Indians.

1965, May 14 Photo.
1000 A509 35cr pale vio & blk .20 .20
12th convention of the Lions Clubs of Brazil, Rio de Janeiro, May 11-16.

ITU Emblem, Old and New Communication Equipment — A510

1965, May 21 Perf. 11½
1001 A510 120cr yellow & grn .30 .20
Centenary of the ITU.

Epitácio Pessoa — A511

Statue of Admiral Barroso — A512

1965, May 23 Photo.
1002 A511 35cr blue gray .20 .20
Epitácio da Silva Pessoa (1865-1942), jurist, president of Brazil, 1919-22.

1965, June 11
1003 A512 30cr blue .25 .20
Cent. of the naval battle of Riachuelo.
A souvenir card containing one lithographed facsimile of No. 1003, imperf., exists. Size: 100x139½mm.

José de Alencar and Indian Princess — A513

1965, June 24 Perf. 11½x11
1004 A513 30cr deep plum .25 .20
Centenary of the publication of "Iracema" by Joséde Alencar.
A souvenir card containing one lithographed facsimile of No. 1004, printed in rose red and imperf., exists. Size: 100x141½mm.

Winston Churchill A514

1965, June 25 Perf. 11x11½
1005 A514 200cr slate .50 .25

Scout Jamboree Emblem — A515

1965, July 17 Photo.
1006 A515 30cr dull bl grn .30 .20
1st Pan-American Boy Scout Jamboree, Fundao Island, Rio de Janeiro, July 15-25.

ICY Emblem A516

1965, Aug. 25 Wmk. 267 Perf. 11½
1007 A516 120cr dl bl & blk .25 .20
International Cooperation Year, 1965.

Leoncio Correias — A517

Emblem — A518

1965, Sept. 1 Perf. 11½x11
1008 A517 35cr slate grn .25 .20
Leoncio Correias, poet, birth cent.

1965, Sept. 4
1009 A518 30cr brt rose .20 .20
Eighth Biennial Fine Arts Exhibition, Sao Paulo, Nov.-Dec., 1965.

Pres. Saragat of Italy — A519

1965, Sept. 11 Photo. Wmk. 267
1010 A519 100cr slate grn, *pink* .25 .20
Visit of Pres. Giuseppe Saragat of Italy.

Grand Duke and Duchess of Luxembourg — A520

1965, Sept. 17 Perf. 11x11½
1011 A520 100cr brn olive .25 .20
Visit of Grand Duke Jean and Grand Duchess Josephine Charlotte of Luxembourg.

Biplane — A521

1965, Oct. 8 Photo. Perf. 11½x11
1012 A521 35cr ultra .20 .20
3rd Aviation Week Philatelic Exhibition, Rio.
A souvenir card carries one impression of this 35cr, imperf. Size: 102x140mm. Sold for 100cr.

Flags of OAS Members A522

1965, Nov. 17 Perf. 11x11½
1013 A522 100cr brt bl & blk .25 .20
2nd meeting of OAS Foreign Ministers, Rio.

King Baudouin and Queen Fabiola of Belgium A523

1965, Nov. 18
1014 A523 100cr gray .25 .20
Visit of King and Queen of Belgium.

"Coffee Beans" — A524

1965, Dec. 21 Photo. Perf. 11½x11
1015 A524 30cr brown .30 .20
Brazilian coffee publicity.

Conveyor and Loading Crane A525

1966, Apr. 1 Perf. 11x11½
1016 A525 110cr tan & dk sl grn .25 .20
Opening of the new terminal of the Rio Doce Iron Ore Company at Tubarao.

Pouring Ladle and Steel Beam — A526

Prof. de Rocha Dissecting Cadaver — A527

1966, Apr. 16 Photo. Perf. 11½x11
1017 A526 30cr blk, dp org   .25 .20
25th anniv. of the National Steel Company (nationalization of the steel industry).

1966, Apr. 26
1018 A527 30cr brt bluish grn   .40 .20
50th anniv. of the discovery and description of Rickettsia prowazeki, the cause of typhus fever, by Prof. Henrique de Rocha Lima.

Battle of Tuiuti A528

1966, May 24 Photo. Perf. 11x11½
1019 A528 30cr gray grn   .30 .20
Centenary of the Battle of Tuiuti.

Symbolic Water Cycle — A529

Pres. Shazar of Israel — A530

1966, July 1   Perf. 11½x11
1020 A529 100cr lt brn & bl   .25 .20
Hydrological Decade (UNESCO), 1965-74.

1966, July 18 Photo. Wmk. 267
1021 A530 100cr ultra   .30 .20
Visit of Pres. Zalman Shazar of Israel.

Imperial Academy of Fine Arts A531

1966, Aug. 12 Engr. Perf. 11x11½
1022 A531 100cr red brown   .60 .20
150th anniversary of French art mission.

Military Service Emblem A532

1966, Sept. 6 Photo. Perf. 11x11½
1023 A532 30cr yel, ultra & grn   .25 .20
 a. With commemorative border   3.50 3.00
New Military Service Law.
No. 1023a issued in sheets of 4. It carries at left a 30cr, design A532, in deeper tones of yellow and ultramarine, Wmk. 264. Without gum. Sold for 100cr.

Ruben Dario — A533

1966, Sept. 20 Photo. Perf. 11½x11
1024 A533 100cr brt rose lilac   .25 .20
Ruben Dario (pen name of Felix Ruben Garcia Sarmiento (1867-1916), Nicaraguan poet, newspaper correspondent and diplomat.

Ceramic Candlestick from Santarém — A534

1966, Oct. 6   Perf. 11x11½
1025 A534 30cr dk brn, salmon   .25 .20
Centenary of Goeldi Museum at Belem.

Arms of Santa Cruz — A535

1966, Oct. 15 Photo. Perf. 11½x11
1026 A535 30cr slate grn   .25 .20
1st Natl. Tobacco Exposition, Santa Cruz.

UNESCO Emblem A536

1966, Oct. 24 Engr. Perf. 11½
1027 A536 120cr black   .75 .25
 a. With commemorative border   6.00 6.00
20th anniv. of UNESCO. No. 1027a issued in sheets of 4. It carries at right a design similar to No. 1027. Unwatermarked granite paper, without gum. Sold for 150cr.

Captain Antonio Correia Pinto and Map of Lages — A537

Cross of Lusitania and Southern Cross — A538

1966, Nov. 22 Photo. Perf. 11½x11
1028 A537 30cr salmon pink   .25 .20
Arrival of Capt. Antonio Correia Pinto, cent.

1966, Dec. 4   Perf. 11½
1029 A538 100cr blue green   .30 .20
LUBRAPEX 1966 philatelic exhibition at the National Museum of Fine Arts, Rio.

Madonna and Child — A539

A540

1966, Dec. Photo. Perf. 11½x11
1030 A539 30cr blue green   .25 .20
Perf. 11½
1031 A540 35cr salmon & ultra   .20 .20
 a. 150cr salmon & ultra   2.50 3.00
Christmas 1966.
No. 1031a measures 46x103mm and is printed in sheets of 4. It is inscribed "Pax Hominibus" (but not "Brasil Correio") and carries the Madonna shown on No. 1031. Issued without gum.
Issued: 30cr, 12/8; 35cr, 12/22; 150cr, 12/28.

Arms of Laguna A541

1967, Jan. 4 Engr. Perf. 11x11½
1032 A541 60cr sepia   .20 .20
Centenary of the Post and Telegraph Agency of Laguna, Santa Catarina.

Railroad Bridge A542

1967, Feb. 16 Photo. Wmk. 267
1033 A542 50cr deep orange   .45 .20
Centenary of the Santos-Jundiai railroad.

Black Madonna of Czestochowa, Polish Eagle and Cross — A543

1967, Mar. 12   Perf. 11x11½
1034 A543 50cr yel, bl & rose red   .35 .20
Adoption of Christianity in Poland, 1,000th anniv.

Research Rocket A544

Anita Garibaldi A545

1967, Mar. 23   Perf. 11½x11
1035 A544 50cr blk & brt bl   .60 .30
World Meteorological Day, March 23.

1967-69 Photo. Perf. 11x11½
Portraits: 1c, Mother Joana Angelica. 2c, Marilia de Dirceu. 3c, Dr. Rita Lobato. 6c, Ana Neri. 10c, Darcy Vargas.
1036 A545 1c dp ultra   .20 .20
1037 A545 2c red brn   .20 .20
1038 A545 3c brt grn   .20 .20
1039 A545 5c black   .35 .20
1040 A545 6c brown   .35 .20
1041 A545 10c dk slate grn   1.10 .30
 Nos. 1036-1041 (6)   2.40 1.30
Issued: 1c, 5/3; 2c, 8/14; 3c, 6/7; 5c, 4/14; 6c, 5/14/67; 10c, 6/18/69.

VARIG Airlines — A546

Madonna and Child, by Robert Feruzzi — A548

Lions Emblem and Globes A547

1967, May 8   Perf. 11½x11
1046 A546 6c brt bl & blk   .30 .25
40th anniversary of VARIG Airlines.

1967, May 9   Engr.   Perf. 11x11½
1047 A547 6c green   .30 .25
   a.   Souvenir sheet   2.50 3.00
50th anniv. of Lions Intl. No. 1047a contains one imperf. stamp similar to No. 1047. Sold for 15c.

1967, May 14   Photo.   Perf. 11½x11
1048 A548 5c violet   .25 .20
   a.   15c Souvenir sheet   2.25 2.25
Mother's Day. No. 1048a contains one 15c imperf. stamp in design of No. 1048.

Prince Akihito and Princess Michiko A549

1967, May 25   Perf. 11x11½
1049 A549 10c black & pink   .30 .20
Visit to Brazil of Crown Prince Akihito and Princess Michiko of Japan.

Carrier Pigeon and Radar Screen A550

Brother Vicente do Salvador A551

1967, June 20   Photo.   Perf. 11½x11
1050 A550 10c sl & brt pink   .25 .20
Commemorating the opening of the Communications Ministry in Brasilia.

1967, June 28   Engr.
1051 A551 5c brown   .25 .20
400th birth anniv. of Brother Vicente do Salvador (1564-1636), founder of Franciscan convent in Rio de Janeiro, and historian.

Boy, Girl and 4-S Emblem A552

1967, July 12   Photo.   Perf. 11½
1052 A552 5c green & blk   .25 .20
National 4-S (4-H) Day.

Möbius Strip A553

1967, July 21   Perf. 11x11½
1053 A553 5c brt bl & blk   .25 .20
6th Brazilian Mathematical Congress.

Fish A554

1967, Aug. 1   Perf. 11½
1054 A554 5c slate   .30 .20
Bicentenary of city of Piracicaba.

Golden Rose and Papal Arms — A555

1967, Aug. 15
1055 A555 20c mag & yel   1.00 .40
Offering of a golden rose by Pope Paul VI to the Virgin Mary of Fatima (Our Lady of Peace), Patroness of Brazil.

General Sampaio A556

King Olaf of Norway A557

1967, Aug. 25   Engr.   Perf. 11½x11
1056 A556 5c blue   .25 .20
Honoring General Antonio de Sampaio, hero of the Battle of Tutui.

1967, Sept. 8   Photo.
1057 A557 10c brown org   .25 .20
Visit of King Olaf of Norway.

Sun over Sugar Loaf, Botafogo Bay A558

Nilo Peçanha A559

Photogravure and Embossed
1967, Sept. 25   Wmk. 267   Perf. 11½
1058 A558 10c blk & dp org   .25 .20
22nd meeting of the Intl. Monetary Fund, Intl. Bank for Reconstruction and Development, Intl. Financial Corporation and Intl. Development Assoc.

1967, Oct. 1   Photo.   Perf. 11½x11
1059 A559 5c brown violet   .25 .20
Peçanha (1867-1924), Pres. of Brazil 1909-10.

Virgin of the Apparition and Basilica of Aparecida — A560

Cockerel, Festival Emblem — A561

1967, Oct. 11   Perf. 11½
1060 A560 5c ultra & dl yel   .30 .20
   a.   Souvenir sheet of 2   3.25 3.25
250th anniv. of the discovery of the statue of Our Lady of the Apparition, now in the National Basilica of the Apparition at Aparecida do Norte.
No. 1060a contains imperf. 5c and 10c stamps similar to No. 1060. Issued Dec. 27, 1967, for Christmas.

Engraved and Photogravure
1967, Oct. 16   Perf. 11½x11
1061 A561 20c black & multi   .50 .40
Second International Folksong Festival.

Balloon, Plane and Rocket A562

1967, Oct. 18   Photo.   Perf. 11x11½
1062 A562 10c blue   .50 .30
   a.   15c souvenir sheet   4.50 4.50
Week of the Wing, Oct. 18-23. No. 1062a contains one imperf. 15c stamp similar to No. 1062 and was issued Oct. 23.

Pres. Arthur Bernardes — A563

Portraits of Brazilian Presidents: 20c, Campos Salles. 50c, Wenceslau Pereira Gomes Braz. 1cr, Washington Pereira de Souza Luiz. 2cr, Castello Branco.

1967-68   Photo.   Perf. 11x11½
1063 A563 10c blue   .25 .20
1064 A563 20c dk red brn   .75 .20
            Engr.
1065 A563 50c black ('68)   3.75 .30
1066 A563 1cr lil rose ('68)   6.00 .30
1067 A563 2cr emerald ('68)   1.10 .30
   Nos. 1063-1067 (5)   11.85 1.30

Carnival of Rio — A564

Ships, Anchor and Sailor — A565

1967, Nov. 22   Perf. 11½x11
1070 A564 10c lem, ultra & pink   .30 .20
   a.   15c souvenir sheet   3.50 4.50
Issued for International Tourist Year, 1967. No. 1070a contains a 15c imperf. stamp in design of No. 1070. Issued Nov. 24.

1967, Dec. 6
1071 A565 10c ultra   .30 .25
Issued for Navy Week.

Christmas Decorations A566

1967, Dec. 8   Perf. 11½
1072 A566 5c car, yel & bl   .25 .20
Christmas 1967.

Olavo Bilac, Planes, Tank and Aircraft Carrier A567

1967, Dec. 16   Photo.   Perf. 11x11½
1073 A567 5c brt blue & yel   .30 .20
Issued for Reservists' Day and to honor Olavo Bilac, sponsor of compulsory military service.

Rodrigues de Carvalho — A568

1967, Dec. 18   Engr.   Perf. 11½x11
1074 A568 10c green   .25 .20
Cent. of the birth of Rodrigues de Carvalho, poet and lawyer.

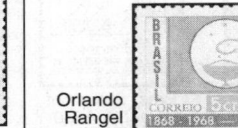

Orlando Rangel A569

1968, Feb. 29   Photo.   Perf. 11x11½
1075 A569 5c lt grnsh bl & blk   .35 .25
Orlando de Fonseca Rangel, pioneer of pharmaceutical industry in Brazil, birth cent.

Virgin of Paranagua and Diver — A570

Map of Brazil Showing Manaus — A571

1968, Mar. 9   Perf. 11½x11
1076 A570 10c dk sl grn & brt yel
    grn   .35 .25
250th anniversary of the first underwater explorations at Paranagua.

1968, Mar. 13   Photo.   Wmk. 267
1077 A571 10c yel, grn & red   .35 .25
Free port of Manaus on the Amazon River.

Human Rights
Flame — A572

Paul Harris and
Rotary
Emblem — A573

1968, Mar. 21   *Perf. 11½x11*
1078 A572 10c blue & salmon   .35   .25
   International Human Rights Year.

1968, Apr. 19   **Litho.**   **Unwmk.**
Without Gum
1079 A573 20c grn & org brn   1.25   .70
   Paul Percy Harris (1868-1947), founder of
Rotary International.

Pedro Alvares Cabral and his
Fleet — A574

Design: 20c, First Mass celebrated in Brazil.

1968   **Without Gum**   *Perf. 11½*
1080 A574 10c multicolored   .55   .45
1081 A574 20c multicolored   .80   .60
   500th anniversary of the birth of Pedro
Alvares Cabral, navigator, who took possession of Brazil for Portugal.
   Issue dates: 10c, Apr. 22; 20c, July 11.

College Arms — A575

1968, Apr. 22   **Photo.**   **Wmk. 267**
1082 A575 10c vio bl, red & gold   .55   .35
   Centenary of St. Luiz College, Sao Paulo.

Motherhood,
by Henrique
Bernardeli
A576

1968, May 12   **Litho.**   **Unwmk.**
Without Gum
1083 A576 5c multicolored   .35   .25
   Issued for Mother's Day.

Harpy Eagle
A577

Photogravure and Engraved
1968, May 28   **Wmk. 267**
1084 A577 20c brt bl & blk   1.50   .50
   Sesquicentennial of National Museum.

Brazilian and Japanese
Women — A578

1968, June 28   **Litho.**   **Unwmk.**
Without Gum
1085 A578 10c yellow & multi   .60   .40
   Commemorating the inauguration of Varig's
direct Brazil-Japan airline.

Horse
Race
A579

1968, July 16   **Litho.**   *Perf. 11x11½*
Without Gum
1086 A579 10c multicolored   .35   .25
   Centenary of the Jockey Club of Brazil.

Musician
Wren
A580

Designs: 10c, Red-crested cardinal, vert.
50c, Royal flycatcher, vert.

Perf. 11½x11, 11x11½
1968-69   **Engr.**
Without Gum
1087 A580 10c multi ('69)   .45   .30
1088 A580 20c multicolored   .75   .30
1089 A580 50c multicolored   1.00   .55
   Nos. 1087-1089 (3)   2.20   1.15
   Some stamps in each sheet of Nos. 1087-
1089 show parts of a two-line papermaker's
watermark: "WESTERPOST / INDUSTRIA
BRASILEIRA" with diamond-shaped emblem
between last two words. Entire watermark
appears in one sheet margin.
   Issued: 10c, 8/20/69; 20c, 7/9/68; 50c,
8/2/68.

Mailbox
and
Envelope
A581

Photogravure and Engraved
1968, Aug. 1   **Wmk. 267**   *Perf. 11*
1091 A581 5c citron, blk & grn   .20   .20
   Stamp Day, 1968 and for 125th anniv. of the
1st Brazilian postage stamps.

Emilio Luiz
Mallet — A582

Map of South
America — A583

1968, Aug. 25   **Engr.**   *Perf. 11½x11*
1092 A582 10c pale purple   .20   .20
   Honoring Marshal Emilio Luiz Mallet, Baron
of Itapevi, patron of the marines.

1968, Sept. 5   **Photo.**
1093 A583 10c deep orange   .20   .20
   Visit of President Eduardo Frei of Chile.

Seal of
Portuguese
Literary
School — A584

Photogravure and Engraved
1968, Sept. 10   *Perf. 11½*
1094 A584 5c pink & grn   .20   .20
   Centenary of Portuguese Literary School.

Map of
Brazil
and Telex
Tape
A585

1968, Sept.   **Photo.**   *Perf. 11x11½*
1095 A585 20c citron & brt grn   .50   .25
   Linking of 25 Brazilian cities by teletype.

Soldiers' Heads on
Medal — A586

1968, Sept. 24   **Litho.**   *Perf. 11½x11*
Without Gum
1096 A586 5c blue & gray   .20   .25
   8th American Armed Forces Conference.

Clef, Notes
and
Sugarloaf
Mountain
A587

1968, Sept. 30   *Perf. 11½*
Without Gum
1097 A587 6c blk, yel & red   .50   .30
   Third International Folksong Festival.

Catalytic
Cracking
Plant
A588

1968, Oct. 4
Without Gum
1098 A588 6c blue & multi   .50   .40
   Petrobras, the natl. oil company, 15th anniv.

Child Protection — A589

Whimsical
Girl — A590

5c, School boy walking toward the sun.

Perf. 11½x11, 11x11½
1968, Oct. 16   **Litho.**
Without Gum
1099 A590 5c gray & lt bl   .30   .30
1100 A589 10c brt bl, dk red &
   blk   .40   .25
1101 A590 20c multicolored   .50   .25
   Nos. 1099-1101 (3)   1.20   .80
   22nd anniv. of UNICEF.

Children
with
Books
A591

1968, Oct. 23   *Perf. 11x11½*
Without Gum
1102 A591 5c multicolored   .25   .25
   Book Week.

UN Emblem and Flags — A592

1968, Oct. 24   *Perf. 11½x11*
Without Gum
1103 A592 20c black & multi   .45   .25
   20th anniv. of WHO.

Jean Baptiste Debret, Self-portrait — A593

1968, Oct. 30   Litho.   Perf. 11x11½
Without Gum
1104 A593 10c dk gray & pale yel   .35 .25
Jean Baptiste Debret, (1768-1848), French painter who worked in Brazil (1816-31). Design includes his "Burden Bearer."

Queen Elizabeth II A594

1968, Nov. 4   Perf. 11½
Without Gum
1105 A594 70c lt bl & multi   1.75 1.00
Visit of Queen Elizabeth II of Great Britain.

Francisco Braga — A595

Perf. 11½x11
1968, Nov. 19   Wmk. 267
1106 A595 5c dull red brn   .40 .25
Cent. of the birth of Antonio Francisco Braga, composer of the Hymn of the Flag.

Brazilian Flag — A596

1968, Nov. 19   Unwmk.   Perf. 11½
Without Gum
1107 A596 10c multicolored   .40 .30
Issued for Flag Day.

Clasped Hands and Globe A597

1968, Nov. 25   Typo.   Perf. 11x11½
Without Gum
1108 A597 5c multicolored   .25 .25
Issued for Voluntary Blood Donor's Day.

Old Locomotive — A598

1968, Nov. 28   Litho.   Perf. 11½
Without Gum
1109 A598 5c multicolored   1.00 .50
Centenary of the Sao Paulo Railroad.

Bell — A599   Francisco Caldas, Jr. — A600

Design: 6c, Santa Claus and boy.

1968   Without Gum   Perf. 11½x11
1110 A599 5c multicolored   .30 .25
1111 A599 6c multicolored   .30 .25
Christmas 1968.
Issue dates: 5c, Dec. 12; 6c, Dec. 20.

1968, Dec. 13
Without Gum
1112 A600 10c crimson & blk   .20 .20
Cent. of the birth of Francisco Caldas, Jr., journalist and founder of Correio de Povo, newspaper.

Map of Brazil, War Memorial and Reservists' Emblem — A601

1968, Dec. 16   Photo.   Perf. 11x11½
1113 A601 5c bl grn & org brn   .30 .20
Issued for Reservists' Day.

Radar Antenna — A602   Viscount of Rio Branco — A603

1969, Feb. 28   Litho.   Perf. 11½x11
Without Gum
1114 A602 30c ultra, lt bl & blk   .70 .55
Inauguration of EMBRATEL, satellite communications ground station bringing US television to Brazil via Telstar.

1969, Mar. 16
Without Gum
1115 A603 5c black & buff   .25 .25
José Maria da Silva Paranhos, Viscount of Rio Branco (1819-1880), statesman.

St. Gabriel — A604

1969, Mar. 24
Without Gum
1116 A604 5c multicolored   .40 .25
Honoring St. Gabriel as patron saint of telecommunications.

Shoemaker's Last and Globe — A605

1969, Mar. 29   Litho.   Perf. 11x11½
Without Gum
1117 A605 5c multicolored   .25 .25
4th Intl. Shoe Fair, Novo Hamburgo.

Allan Kardec A606

1969, Mar. 31   Photo.   Wmk. 267
1118 A606 5c brt grn & org brn   .25 .25
Allan Kardec (pen name of Leon Hippolyto Denizard Rivail, 1803-1869), French physician and spiritist.

Men of 3 Races and Arms of Cuiabá A607

1969, Apr. 8   Litho.   Unwmk.
Without Gum
1119 A607 5c black & multi   .25 .25
250th anniversary of the founding of Cuiabá, capital of Matto Grosso.

State Mint — A608

1969, Apr. 11   Perf. 11½
Without Gum
1120 A608 5c olive bister & org   .45 .35
Opening of the state money printing plant.

Brazilian Stamps and Emblem A609

1969, Apr. 30   Litho.   Perf. 11x11½
Without Gum
1121 A609 5c multicolored   .25 .25
Sao Paulo Philatelic Society, 50th anniv.

St. Anne, Baroque Statue A610

1969, May 8   Perf. 11½
Without Gum
1122 A610 5c lemon & multi   .50 .40
Issued for Mother's Day.

ILO Emblem A611

1969, May 13   Photo.   Perf. 11x11½
1123 A611 5c dp rose red & gold   .25 .25
50th anniv. of the ILO.

Diving Platform and Swimming Pool — A612   Mother and Child at Window — A613

Lithographed and Photogravure
Perf. 11½x11
1969, June 13   Unwmk.
Without Gum
1124 A612 20c bis brn, blk & bl grn   .55 .40
40th anniversary of the Cearense Water Sports Club, Fortaleza.

1969   Litho.   Perf. 11½
Designs: 20c, Modern sculpture by Felicia Leirner. 50c, "The Sun Sets in Brasilia," by Danilo di Prete. 1cr, Angelfish, painting by Aldemir Martins.

Size: 24x36mm
1125 A613 10c orange & multi   .55 .25
Size: 33x34mm
1126 A613 20c red & multi   .55 .50
Size: 33x53mm
1127 A613 50c yellow & multi   1.90 1.25
Without Gum
1128 A613 1cr gray & multi   2.50 1.25
Nos. 1125-1128 (4)   5.50 3.25
10th Biennial Art Exhibition, Sao Paulo, Sept.-Dec. 1969.

Angelfish
A614

Fish — A615

Fish: 10c, Tetra. 15c, Piranha. No. 1130c,
Megalamphodus megalopterus. 30c, Black
tetra.

1969, July 21   Litho.   Perf. 11½
1129 A614 20c multicolored   .70 .40

Souvenir Sheet
1969, July 24   Unwmk.   Imperf.
1130 A615 Sheet of 4   5.00 5.00
  a.   10c yellow & multi   .90 .90
  b.   15c bright blue & multi   .90 .90
  c.   20c green & multi   .90 .90
  d.   30c orange & multi   .90 .90

Issued to publicize the work of ACAPI, an
organization devoted to the preservation and
development of fish in Brazil.

#1130 contains 4 38½x21mm stamps.

L. O. Teles de
Menezes
A616

Mailman
A617

1969, July 26   Photo.   Perf. 11½x11
1131 A616 50c dp org & bl grn   1.25 1.00
Centenary of Spiritism press in Brazil.

1969, Aug. 1
1132 A617 30c blue   1.10 .90
Issued for Stamp Day.

Map of Brazil
A618

Gen. Tasso
Fragoso — A620

Railroad
Bridge
A619

Perf. 11½
1969, Aug. 25   Unwmk.   Litho.
Without Gum
1133 A618 10c lt ultra, grn & yel   .25 .20
Perf. 11x11½
1134 A619 20c multicolored   .80 .40
Engr.   Perf. 11½x11
With Gum
1135 A620 20c green   .80 .50
  Nos. 1133-1135 (3)   1.85 1.10

No. 1133 honors the Army as guardian of
security; No. 1134, as promoter of development. No. 1135 the birth centenary of Gen.
Tasso Fragoso.

Jupia Dam,
Parana River
A621

1969, Sept. 10   Litho.   Perf. 11½
Without Gum
1136 A621 20c lt blue & multi   .35 .35
Inauguration of the Jupia Dam, part of the
Urubupunga hydroelectric system serving Sao
Paulo.

Gandhi
and
Spinning
Wheel
A622

1969, Oct. 2   Perf. 11x11½
1137 A622 20c yellow & blk   .40 .30
Mohandas K. Gandhi (1869-1948), leader in
India's fight for independence.

Santos Dumont, Eiffel Tower and
Module Landing on Moon — A623

1969, Oct. 17   Perf. 11½
Without Gum
1138 A623 50c dk bl & multi   1.75 1.25
Man's first landing on the moon, July 20,
1969. See note after US No. C76.

Smelting
Plant
A624

1969, Oct. 26   Unwmk.   Perf. 11½
Without Gum
1139 A624 20c multicolored   .45 .40
Expansion of Brazil's steel industry.

Steel
Furnace
A625

1969, Oct. 31   Litho.
Without Gum
1140 A625 10c yellow & multi   .45 .40
25th anniversary of Acesita Steel Works.

Water Vendor, by J. B. Debret — A626

Design: 30c, Street Scene, by Debret.

1969-70
Without Gum
1141 A626 20c multicolored   1.25 .50
1141A A626 30c multicolored   1.25 1.00

Jean Baptiste Debret (1768-1848), painter.
Issued: 20c, 11/5/69; 30c, 5/19/70.

Exhibition
Emblem — A627

1969, Nov. 15   Perf. 11½x11
Without Gum
1142 A627 10c multicolored   .35 .20
ABUEXPO 69 Philatelic Exposition, Sao
Paulo, Nov. 15-23.

Plane — A628

1969, Nov. 23
Without Gum
1143 A628 50c multicolored   2.75 1.40
Publicizing the year of the expansion of the
national aviation industry.

Pelé Scoring
A629

1969-70
Without Gum
1144 A629 10c multicolored   .40 .30
Souvenir Sheet
Imperf
1145 A629 75c multi ('70)   4.50 3.50

Commemorating the 1,000th goal scored by
Pele, Brazilian soccer player.
No. 1145 contains one imperf. stamp with
simulated perforations.
Issued: 10c, 11/28/69; 75c, 1/23/70.

Madonna
and Child
from Villa
Velha
Monastery
A630

Perf. 11½
1969, Dec.   Unwmk.   Litho.
Without Gum
1146 A630 10c gold & multi   .35 .20
Souvenir Sheet
Imperf
1147 A630 75c gold & multi   12.00 15.00

Christmas 1969.
No. 1147 has simulated perforations.
Issue dates: 10c, Dec. 8; 75c, Dec. 18.

Destroyer and Submarine — A631

1969, Dec. 9   Engr.   Perf. 11x11½
1148 A631 5c bluish gray   .40 .25
Issued for Navy Day.

Dr. Herman
Blumenau
A632

1969, Dec. 26   *Perf. 11½*
1149 A632 20c gray grn   .85 .40
Dr. Herman Blumenau (1819-1899),
founder of Blumenau, Santa Catarina State.

Carnival Scene — A633

Sugarloaf
Mountain,
Mask,
Confetti and
Streamers
A634

Designs: 5c, Jumping boy and 2 women,
vert. 20c, Clowns. 50c, Drummer.

1969-70   **Litho.**   **Unwmk.**
Without Gum
1150 A633 5c multicolored   .40 .30
1151 A633 10c multicolored   .40 .30
1152 A633 20c multicolored   .50 .40
1153 A634 30c multicolored   3.00 3.00
1154 A634 50c multicolored   2.75 2.50
     Nos. 1150-1154 (5)   7.05 6.50

Carico Carnival, Rio de Janeiro.
Issued: #1150-1152, 12/29; others, 2/5/70.

Opening Bars of "Il Guarani" with
Antonio Carlos Gomes Conducting
A635

1970, Mar. 19   Litho.   Perf. 11½
Without Gum
1155 A635 20c blk, yel, gray & brn .60 .40
Centenary of the opera Il Guarani, by
Antonio Carlos Gomes.

Church of
Penha
A636

1970, Apr. 6   Unwmk.   Perf. 11½
Without Gum
1156 A636 20c black & multi   .30 .20
400th anniversary of the Church of Penha,
State of Espirito Santo.

Assembly
Building
A637

10th anniv. of Brasilia: 50c, Reflecting Pool.
1cr, Presidential Palace.

1970, Apr. 21
Without Gum
1157 A637 20c multicolored   .90 .70
1158 A637 50c multicolored   2.25 1.75
1159 A637 1cr multicolored   2.25 1.75
     Nos. 1157-1159 (3)   5.40 4.20

Symbolic
Water
Design
A638

1970, May 5   Unwmk.   Perf. 11½
Without Gum
1161 A638 50c multicolored   2.50 3.00
Publicizing the Rondon Project for the development of the Amazon River basin.

Marshal Manoel Luiz Osorio and
Osorio Arms — A639

1970, May 8
Without Gum
1162 A639 20c multicolored   1.50 1.00
Commemorating the inauguration of the
Marshal Osorio Historical Park.

Madonna,
from San
Antonio
Monastery,
Rio de
Janeiro
A640

1970, May 10
Without Gum
1163 A640 20c multicolored   .40 .40
Issued for Mother's Day.

Detail from
Brasilia
Cathedral — A641

1970, May 27   Engr.   Wmk. 267
1164 A641 20c lt yellow grn   .25 .25
8th National Eucharistic Congress, Brasilia.

Census
Symbol — A642

Perf. 11½
1970, June 22   Unwmk.   Litho.
Without Gum
1165 A642 20c green & yel   .60 .60
Publicizing the 8th general census.

Soccer Cup,
Maps of
Brazil and
Mexico
A643

Swedish Flag and Player Holding
Rimet Cup — A644

Designs: 2cr, Chilean flag and soccer. 3cr,
Mexican flag and soccer.

1970
Without Gum
1166 A643 50c blk, lt bl & gold   .90 .90
1167 A644 1cr pink & multi   2.75 1.50
1168 A644 2cr gray & multi   5.25 1.50
1169 A644 3cr multicolored   4.50 1.00
     Nos. 1166-1169 (4)   13.40 4.90

9th World Soccer Championships for the
Jules Rimet Cup, Mexico City, May 30-June
21. No. 1166 honors Brazil's victory.
Issued: #1166, 6/24; #1167-1169, 8/4.

Corcovado
Christ and
Map of
South
America
A645

1970, July 18
Without Gum
1170 A645 50c brn, dk red & bl   2.50 2.50
6th World Cong. of Marist Brothers' Alumni.

Pandia Calogeras,
Minister of
War — A646

1970, Aug. 25   Photo.   Perf. 11½x11
1171 A646 20c blue green   .50 .50

Brazilian
Military
Emblems
and Map
A647

1970, Sept. 8   Litho.   Perf. 11x11½
Without Gum
1172 A647 20c gray & multi   .50 .50
25th anniv. of victory in World War II.

Annunciation
(Brazilian
Primitive
Painting)
A648

1970, Sept. 29   *Perf. 11½*
Without Gum
1173 A648 20c multicolored   1.25 1.00
Issued for St. Gabriel's (patron saint of communications) Day.

Boy in
Library — A649

UN
Emblem — A650

1970, Oct. 23
Without Gum
1174 A649 20c multicolored   1.25 1.00
Issued to publicize Book Week.

1970, Oct. 24
Without Gum
1175 A650 50c dk bl, lt bl & sil   1.25 1.25
25th anniversary of the United Nations.

Rio de Janeiro, 1820 — A651

Designs: 50c, LUBRAPEX 70 emblem. 1cr,
Rio de Janeiro with Sugar Loaf Mountain,
1970. No. 1179, like 20c.

1970, Oct.
Without Gum
1176 A651 20c multicolored   1.75 1.00
1177 A651 50c yel brn & blk   3.50 2.00
1178 A651 1cr multicolored   3.50 3.75
     Nos. 1176-1178 (3)   8.75 6.75

Souvenir Sheet
Imperf
1179 A651 1cr multicolored   11.00 17.00
LUBRAPEX 70, 3rd Portuguese-Brazilian
Phil. Exhib., Rio de Janeiro, Oct. 24-31.
Issued: #1176-1178, 10/27; #1179, 10/31.

Holy Family
by Candido
Portinari
A652

1970, Dec.   Litho.   Perf. 11½
Without Gum
1180 A652 50c multicolored   1.50 1.50
Souvenir Sheet
Imperf
1181 A652 1cr multicolored   15.00 24.00
Christmas 1970. No. 1181 contains one
stamp with simulated perforations.
Issue dates: 50c, Dec. 1; 1cr, Dec. 8.

Battleship — A653

CIH
Emblem — A654

1970, Dec. 11   Litho.   Perf. 11½
Without Gum
1182 A653 20c multicolored   1.25 .75
Navy Day.

1971, Mar. 28   Litho.   Perf. 11½
Without Gum
1183 A654 50c black & red   1.50 1.75
3rd Inter-American Housing Cong., 3/27-4/3.

Links Around
Globe — A655

1971, Mar. 31 Litho. Perf. 12½x11
Without Gum
1184 A655 20c grn, yel, blk & red   .65 .50
Intl. year against racial discrimination.

Morpho Melacheilus — A656

Design: 1cr, Papilio thoas brasiliensis.

1971, Apr. 28 Litho.   Perf. 11x11½
Without Gum
1185 A656 20c multicolored   1.25 .60
1186 A656 1cr multicolored   5.50 3.25

Madonna and
Child — A657

1971, May 9   Litho.   Perf. 11½
Without Gum
1187 A657 20c multicolored   .85 .40
Mother's Day, 1971.

Basketball
A658

1971, May 19
Without Gum
1188 A658 70c multicolored   1.50 1.00
6th World Women's Basketball
Championship.

Map of Trans-Amazon
Highway — A659

Perf. 11½
1971, July 1   Unwmk.   Litho.
Without Gum
1189   40c multicolored   5.50 2.75
1190   1cr multicolored   5.50 5.50
  a. 'A659' Pair, #1189-1190 11.00 11.00
Trans-Amazon Highway. No. 1190a printed
in sheets of 28 (4x7). Horizontal rows contain
2 No. 1190a with a label between. Each label
carries different inscription.

Man's Head,
by Victor
Mairelles de
Lima
A661

Stamp Day: 1cr, Arab Violinist, by Pedro
Américo.

1971, Aug. 1
Without Gum
1191 A661 40c pink & multi   1.25 .80
1192 A661 1cr gray & multi   3.25 1.65

Duke of
Caxias and
Map of
Brazil
A662

1971, Aug. 23   Photo.
1193 A662 20c yel grn & red brn   .50 .60
Army Week.

Anita
Garibaldi — A663

1971, Aug. 30   Litho.
Without Gum
1194 A663 20c multicolored   .40 .40
Anita Garibaldi (1821-1849), heroine in liberation of Brazil.

Xavante Jet and Santos Dumont's
Plane, 1910 — A664

1971, Sept. 6
Without Gum
1195 A664 40c yellow & multi   1.40 .75
First flight of Xavante jet plane.

Flags and Map of   "71" in French
Central American   Flag
Nations — A665   Colors — A666

1971, Sept. 15
Without Gum
1196 A665 40c ocher & multi   1.25 .60
Sesquicentennial of the independence of
Central American nations.

1971, Sept. 16
Without Gum
1197 A666 1.30cr ultra & multi 1.25 1.10
French Exhibition.

Black Mother, by   Archangel
Lucilio de   Gabriel
Albuquerque   A668
A667

1971, Sept. 28
Without Gum
1198 A667 40c multicolored   .60 .50
Centenary of law guaranteeing personal
freedom starting at birth.

1971, Sept. 29   Perf. 11½x11
Without Gum
1199 A668 40c multicolored   .75 .65
St. Gabriel's Day.

Bridge over
River
A669

Children's Drawings: 35c, People crossing
bridge. 60c, Woman with hat.

1971, Oct. 25   Perf. 11½
Without Gum
1200 A669 35c pink, bl & blk   .55 .45
1201 A669 45c black & multi   1.40 .45
1202 A669 60c olive & multi   .55 .45
    Nos. 1200-1202 (3)   2.50 1.35
Children's Day.

Werkhäuserii Superba — A670

1971, Nov. 16
Without Gum
1203 A670 40c blue & multi   2.00 1.00
In memory of Carlos Werkhauser, botanist.

Greek Key Pattern
"25" — A671

Design: 40c, like 20c but inscribed "sesc /
servicio social / do comercio."

1971, Dec. 3
Without Gum
1204 A671 20c black & blue   1.25 1.00
1205 A671 40c black & org   1.25 1.00
  a. Pair, #1204-1205   2.50 2.50
25th anniversary of SENAC (national
apprenticeship system) and SESC (commercial social service).

Gunboat
A672

1971, Dec. 8 *Perf. 11*
Without Gum
1206 A672 20c blue & multi .85 .50
Navy Day.

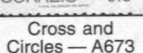

Cross and
Circles — A673

Washing of
Bonfim Church,
Salvador,
Bahia — A674

1971, Dec. 11
1207 A673 20c car & blue .40 .40
1208 A673 75c silver & gray .80 3.00
1209 A673 1.30cr blk, yel, grn &
bl 4.75 2.50
Nos. 1207-1209 (3) 5.95 5.90
Christmas 1971.

1972, Feb. 18 **Litho.** *Perf. 11½x11*
40c, Grape Festival, Rio Grande do Sul.
75c, Festival of the Virgin of Nazareth, Belém.
1.30cr, Winter Arts Festival, Ouro Preto.
Without Gum
1210 A674 20c silver & multi 1.50 .75
1211 A674 40c silver & multi 2.75 .75
1212 A674 75c silver & multi 2.75 3.00
1213 A674 1.30cr silver & multi 6.00 3.00
Nos. 1210-1213 (4) 13.00 7.50

Pres.
Lanusse
and Flag
of
Argentina
A675

1972, Mar. 13 *Perf. 11x11½*
Without Gum
1214 A675 40c blue & multi 2.00 2.50
Visit of Lt. Gen. Alejandro Agustin Lanusse,
president of Argentina.

Presidents Castello Branco, Costa e
Silva and Garrastazu Medici — A676

1972, Mar. 29
Without Gum
1215 A676 20c emerald & multi 1.25 .60
Anniversary of 1964 revolution.

Post Office
Emblem — A677

1972, Apr. 10 **Photo.** *Perf. 11½x11*
1216 A677 20c red brown 2.00 .20
No. 1216 is luminescent.

Pres. Thomas and Portuguese
Flag — A678

1972, Apr. 22 **Litho.** *Perf. 11*
Without Gum
1217 A678 75c ol brn & multi 1.75 1.75
Visit of Pres. Americo Thomas of Portugal to
Brazil, Apr. 22-27.

Soil
Research
(CPRM)
A679

1972, May 3 *Perf. 11½*
Without Gum
1218 A679 20c shown 1.50 .50
1219 A679 40c Offshore oil
rig 3.50 .85
1220 A679 75c Hydroelectric
dam 1.50 1.75
1221 A679 1.30cr Iron ore production 3.50 1.40
Nos. 1218-1221 (4) 10.00 4.50
Industrial development. Stamps are
inscribed with names of industrial firms.
See Nos. 1228-1229.

Souvenir Sheet

Poster for Modern Art Week
1922 — A680

1972, May 5
1222 A680 1cr black & car 26.00 26.00
50th anniversary of Modern Art Week.

Mailman,
Map of
Brazil and
Letters
A681

Designs: 45c, "Telecommunications", vert.
60c, Tropospheric scatter system. 70c, Road
map of Brazil and worker.

1972, May 26
Without Gum
1223 A681 35c blue & multi 1.25 .40
1224 A681 45c silver & multi 1.50 1.50
1225 A681 60c black & multi 1.50 1.25
1226 A681 70c multicolored 1.75 1.25
Nos. 1223-1226 (4) 6.00 4.40
Unification of communications in Brazil.

Development Type and

Automobiles — A682

Perf. 11x11½, 11½x11
1972, June 21 **Photo.**
1227 A682 35c shown 1.00 .50
Litho.
1228 A679 45c Ships 1.00 .60
1229 A679 70c Ingots 1.00 .40
Nos. 1227-1229 (3) 3.00 1.50
Industrial development. The 35c is
luminescent.

Soccer — A683

75c, Folk music. 1.30cr, Plastic arts.

1972, July 7 **Photo.** *Perf. 11½x11*
1230 A683 20c black & yel 1.00 .50
1231 A683 75c black & ver 2.00 3.50
1232 A683 1.30cr black & ultra 4.00 3.50
Nos. 1230-1232 (3) 7.00 7.50
150th anniv. of independence. #1230 pub-
licizes the 1972 sports tournament, a part of
independence celebrations. Luminescent.

Souvenir Sheet

Shout of Independence, by Pedro
Americo de Figueiredo e Melo — A684

1972, July 19 **Litho.** *Perf. 11½*
Without Gum
1233 A684 1cr multicolored 4.00 9.00
4th Interamerican Philatelic Exhibition,
EXFILBRA, Rio de Janeiro, Aug 26-Sept. 2.

Figurehead
A685

Brazilian folklore: 60c, Gauchos dancing
fandango. 75c, Acrobats (capoeira). 1.15cr,
Karajá (ceramic) doll. 1.30cr, Mock bullfight
(bumba meu boi).

1972, Aug. 6
Without Gum
1234 A685 45c multicolored .85 .35
1235 A685 60c org & multi 1.65 1.50
1236 A685 75c gray & multi .30 .30
1237 A685 1.15cr multicolored .55 .55
1238 A685 1.30cr yellow & multi 5.00 2.00
Nos. 1234-1238 (5) 8.35 4.70

Map of
Brazil, by
Diego
Homem,
1568
A686

Designs: 1cr, Map of Americas, by Nicholas
Visscher, 1652. 2cr, Map of Americas, by
Lopo Homem, 1519.

1972, Aug. 26 **Litho.** *Perf. 11½*
Without Gum
1239 A686 70c multicolored .50 .50
1240 A686 1cr multicolored 9.00 1.00
1241 A686 2cr multicolored 4.50 1.50
Nos. 1239-1241 (3) 14.00 3.00
4th Inter-American Philatelic Exhibition,
EXFILBRA, Rio de Janeiro, Aug. 26-Sept. 2.

Dom Pedro Proclaimed Emperor, by
Jean Baptiste Debret — A687

Designs: 30c, Founding of Brazil (people
with imperial flag), vert. 1cr, Coronation of
Emperor Dom Pedro, vert. 2cr, Dom Pedro
commemorative medal. 3.50cr, Independence
Monument, Ipiranga.

1972, Sept. 4 **Litho.** *Perf. 11½x11*
1242 A687 30c yellow & grn 1.25 1.25
1243 A687 70c pink & rose
lil 1.25 .80
1244 A687 1cr buff & red
brn 8.00 1.25
1245 A687 2cr pale yel &
blk 4.00 1.25
1246 A687 3.50cr gray & blk 7.25 4.00
Nos. 1242-1246 (5) 21.75 8.55
Sesquicentennial of independence.

Souvenir Sheet

"Automobile Race" — A688

1972, Nov. 14 *Perf. 11½*
1247 A688 2cr multicolored 10.00 15.00
Emerson Fittipaldi, Brazilian world racing
champion.

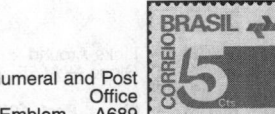

Numeral and Post
Office
Emblem — A689

Möbius
Strip
A689a

Perf. 11½x11
1972-75 **Unwmk.** **Photo.**
1248 A689 5c orange .35 .20
a. Wmk. 267 .20 .20

1249	A689	10c brown ('73)	.20 .20
a.		Wmk. 267	4.00
1250	A689	15c brt blue ('75)	.20 .20
1251	A689	20c ultra	.35 .20
1252	A689	25c sepia ('75)	.25 .20
1253	A689	30c dp carmine	.40 .20
1254	A689	40c dk grn ('73)	.20 .20
1255	A689	50c olive	.30 .20
1256	A689	70c red lilac ('75)	.30 .20

Engr.   **Perf. 11½**

1257	A689a	1cr lilac ('74)	.45 .20
1258	A689a	2cr grnsh bl ('74)	.65 .20
1259	A689a	4cr org & vio ('75)	1.40 .20
1260	A689a	5cr brn, car & buff ('74)	2.00 .20
1261	A689a	10cr grn, blk & buff ('74)	4.50 .30
		Nos. 1248-1261 (14)	11.55 2.90

The 5cr and 10cr have beige lithographed multiple Post Office emblem underprint. Nos. 1248-1261 are luminescent. Nos. 1248a and 1249a are not.

Hand Writing "Mobral" — A690

20c, Multiracial group and population growth curve. 1cr, People and hands holding house. 2cr, People, industrial scene and upward arrow.

1972, Nov. 28   **Litho.**   **Perf. 11½**
Without Gum

1262	A690	10c black & multi	.20 .50
1263	A690	20c black & multi	1.00 .75
1264	A690	1cr black & multi	8.75 .30
1265	A690	2cr black & multi	2.00 .75
		Nos. 1262-1265 (4)	11.95 2.30

Publicity for: "Mobral" literacy campaign (10c); Centenary of census (20c); Housing and retirement fund (1cr); Growth of gross national product (2cr).

Congress Building, Brasilia, by Oscar Niemeyer, and "Os Guerreiros," by Bruno Giorgi — A691

1972, Dec. 4
Without Gum

1266	A691	1cr blue, blk & org	10.00 6.00

Meeting of Natl. Cong., Brasilia, Dec. 4-8.

Holy Family (Clay Figurines) A692   Retirement Plan A693

1972, Dec. 13   **Photo.**   **Perf. 11½x11**

1267	A692	20c ocher & blk	.85 .50

Christmas 1972. Luminescent.

Perf. 11½x11, 11x11½
1972, Dec. 20   **Litho.**

#1269, School children and traffic lights, horiz. 70c, Dr. Oswaldo Cruz with Red Cross, caricature. 2cr, Produce, fish and cattle, horiz.

Without Gum

1268	A693	10c blk, bl & dl org	.50 .50
1269	A693	10c orange & multi	1.00 1.00
1270	A693	70c blk, red & brn	9.00 3.75
1271	A693	2cr green & multi	15.00 6.50
		Nos. 1268-1271 (4)	25.50 11.75

Publicity for: Agricultural workers' assistance program (No. 1268); highway and transportation development (No. 1269); centenary of the birth of Dr. Oswaldo Cruz (1872-1917), Director of Public Health Institute (70c); agricultural and cattle export (2cr). Nos. 1268-1271 are luminescent.

Sailing Ship, Navy A694

Designs: 10c, Monument, Brazilian Expeditionary Force. No. 1274, Plumed helmet, Army. No. 1275, Rocket, Air Force.

Lithographed and Engraved
1972, Dec. 28   **Perf. 11x11½**
Without Gum

1272	A694	10c brn, dk brn & blk	1.50 1.10
1273	A694	30c lt ultra, grn & blk	1.50 1.10
1274	A694	30c yel grn, bl grn & blk	1.50 1.10
1275	A694	30c lilac, mar & blk	1.50 1.10
a.		Block of 4, #1272-1275	6.00 5.00

Armed Forces Day.

Rotary Emblem and Cogwheels A695

1973, Mar. 21   **Litho.**   **Perf. 11½**

1276	A695	1cr ultra, grnsh bl & yel	1.75 1.50

Rotary International serving Brazil 50 years.

Swimming — A696

#1278, Gymnastics. #1279, Volleyball, vert.

1973   **Photo.**   **Perf. 11x11½, 11½x11**

1277	A696	40c brt bl & red brn	.35 .35
1278	A696	40c green & org brn	2.75 .70
1279	A696	40c violet & org brn	.70 .70
		Nos. 1277-1279 (3)	3.80 1.75

Issued: #1277, 4/19; #1278, 5/22; #1279, 10/15.

Flag of Paraguay A697

1973, Apr. 27   **Litho.**   **Perf. 11½**

1280	A697	70c multicolored	1.75 1.25

Visit of Pres. Alfredo Stroessner of Paraguay, Apr. 25-27.

"Communications" — A698

1cr, Neptune, map of South America and Africa.

1973, May 5   **Perf. 11x11½**

1281	A698	70c multicolored	.80 .70
1282	A698	1cr multicolored	4.25 3.00

Inauguration of the Ministry of Communications Building, Brasilia (70c); and of the first underwater telephone cable between South America and Europe, Bracan 1 (1cr).

Congress Emblem — A699

1973, May 19   **Perf. 11½x11**

1283	A699	1cr orange & pur	4.00 3.00

24th Congress of the International Chamber of Commerce, Rio de Janeiro, May 19-26.

Swallowtailed Manakin — A700

Birds: No. 1285, Orange-backed oriole. No. 1286, Brazilian ruby (hummingbird).

1973   **Litho.**   **Perf. 11x11½**

1284	A700	20c multicolored	.50 .20
1285	A700	20c multicolored	.50 .20
1286	A700	20c multicolored	.50 .20
		Nos. 1284-1286 (3)	1.50 .60

Issued: #1284, 5/26; #1285, 6/6; #1286, 6/19.

Tourists A701

1973, June 28   **Litho.**   **Perf. 11x11½**

1287	A701	70c multicolored	.90 .85

National Tourism Year.

Conference at Itu — A702

Satellite and Multi-spectral Image A703

1973   **Perf. 11½x11**

1288	A702	20c shown	.50 .35
1289	A702	20c Decorated wagon	.50 .35
1290	A702	20c Indian	.50 .35
1291	A702	20c Graciosa Road	.50 .35
		Nos. 1288-1291 (4)	2.00 1.40

Centenary of the Itu Convention (1288); sesquicentennial of the July 2 episode (1289); 400th anniversary of the founding of Niterói (1290); centenary of Graciosa Road (1291).
Issue dates: #1291, July 29; others July 2.

1973, July 11   **Perf. 11½**

70c, Official opening of Engineering School, 1913. 1cr, Möbius strips and "IMPA."

1292	A703	20c black & multi	.25 .40
1293	A703	70c dk blue & multi	2.25 1.00
1294	A703	1cr lilac & multi	3.00 1.00
		Nos. 1292-1294 (3)	5.50 2.40

Institute for Space Research (20c); School of Engineering, Itajubá, 60th anniversary (70c); Institute for Pure and Applied Mathematics (1cr).

Santos-Dumont and 14-Bis Plane — A704

Santos-Dumont and: 70c, No. 6 Balloon and Eiffel Tower. 2cr Demoiselle plane.

Lithographed and Engraved
1973, July 20   **Perf. 11x11½**

1295	A704	20c lt grn, brt grn & brn	.75 .25
1296	A704	70c yel, rose red & brn	1.75 1.25
1297	A704	2cr bl, vio bl & brn	1.75 1.25
		Nos. 1295-1297 (3)	4.25 2.75

Centenary of the birth of Alberto Santos-Dumont (1873-1932), aviation pioneer.

Mercator Map A705

#1299, Same, red border on top and at left.

Photogravure and Engraved
1973, Aug. 1   **Wmk. 267**

1298	A705	40c red & black	2.50 1.50
1299	A705	40c red & black	2.10 2.10
a.		Block of 4	21.00 15.00

Stamp Day. Nos. 1298-1299 are printed setenant horizontally and tête bêche vertically in sheets of 55. Blocks of 4 have red border all around.

Gonçalves Dias (1823-1864), Poet — A706

Perf. 11½x11
1973, Aug. 10   **Wmk. 267**

1300	A706	40c violet & blk	.70 .40

Souvenir Sheet

Copernicus and Sun — A707

1973, Aug. 15   Litho.   Perf. 11x11½
1301 A707 1cr multicolored   4.00 5.00

500th anniversary of the birth of Nicolaus Copernicus (1473-1543), Polish astronomer.

Folklore Festival Banner — A708

1973, Aug. 22   Perf. 11½
1302 A708 40c ultra & multi   .75 .50

Folklore Day, Aug. 22.

Masonic Emblem A709

1973, Aug. 24   Photo.   Perf. 11x11½
1303 A709 1cr Prus blue   3.00 2.00

Free Masons of Brazil, 1822-1973.

Nature Protection — A710

#1305, Fire protection. #1306, Aviation safety. #1307, Safeguarding cultural heritage.

1973, Sept. 20   Litho.   Perf. 11x11½
1304 A710 40c brt grn & multi   .75 .40
1305 A710 40c dk blue & multi   .75 .40
1306 A710 40c lt blue & multi   .75 .40
1307 A710 40c pink & multi   .75 .40
    Nos. 1304-1307 (4)   3.00 1.60

Souvenir Sheet

St. Gabriel and Proclamation of Pope Paul VI — A711

Lithographed and Engraved
1973, Sept. 29   Unwmk.   Perf. 11½
1308 A711 1cr bister & blk   7.50 10.00

1st National Exhibition of Religious Philately, Rio de Janeiro, Sept. 29-Oct. 6.

St. Teresa — A712

Photogravure and Engraved
Perf. 11½x11
1973, Sept. 30   Wmk. 267
1309 A712 2cr dk org & brn   3.50 2.50

St. Teresa of Lisieux, the Little Flower (1873-1897), Carmelite nun.

Monteiro Lobato and Emily A713

1973, Oct. 12   Litho.   Perf. 11½
1310 A713 40c shown   .80 .50
1311 A713 40c Aunt Nastacia   .80 .50
1312 A713 40c Snubnose, Peter   .80 .50
        and Rhino
1313 A713 40c Viscount de   .80 .50
        Sabugosa
1314 A713 40c Dona Benta   .80 .50
    a.   Block of 5 + label   4.00 4.00

Monteiro Lobato, author of children's books.

Soapstone Sculpture of Isaiah (detail) A714

Baroque Art in Brazil: No. 1316, Arabesque, gilded wood carving, horiz. 70c, Father José Mauricio Nuñes Garcia and music score. 1cr, Church door, Salvador, Bahia. 2cr, Angels, church ceiling painting by Manoel da Costa Athayde, horiz.

1973, Nov. 5
1315 A714 40c multicolored   .30 .30
1316 A714 40c multicolored   .30 .30
1317 A714 70c multicolored   1.50 1.40
1318 A714 1cr multicolored   9.00 3.00
1319 A714 2cr multicolored   4.00 3.00
    Nos. 1315-1319 (5)   15.10 8.00

Old and New Telephones — A715

1973, Nov. 28   Perf. 11x11½
1320 A715 40c multicolored   .35 .30

50th anniv. of Brazilian Telephone Co.

Symbolic Angel A716

1973, Nov. 30   Perf. 11½
1321 A716 40c ver & multi   .35 .30

Christmas 1973.

River Boats A717

1973, Nov. 30   Litho.   Perf. 11x11½
1322 A717 40c "Gaiola"   .35 .35
1323 A717 70c "Regatao"   1.05 1.05
1324 A717 1cr "Jangada"   4.50 3.00
1325 A717 2cr "Saveiro"   4.25 3.00
    Nos. 1322-1325 (4)   10.15 7.40

Nos. 1322-1325 are luminescent.

Scales of Justice A718

1973, Dec. 5   Perf. 11½
1326 A718 40c magenta & vio   .50 .30

To honor the High Federal Court, created in 1891. Luminescent.

José Placido de Castro — A719

Scarlet Ibis and Victoria Regia — A720

Lithographed and Engraved
Perf. 11½x11
1973, Dec. 12   Wmk. 267
1327 A719 40c lilac rose & blk   .60 .35

Centenary of the birth of Jose Placido de Castro, liberator of the State of Acre.

1973, Dec. 28   Litho.   Perf. 11½x11

Designs: 70c, Jaguar and spathodea campanulata. 1cr, Scarlet macaw and carnauba palm. 2cr, Rhea and coral tree.

1328 A720 40c brown & multi   .80 .50
1329 A720 70c brown & multi   2.25 1.50
1330 A720 1cr bister & multi   3.50 .40
1331 A720 2cr bister & multi   6.25 3.50
    Nos. 1328-1331 (4)   12.80 5.90

Nos. 1328-1331 are luminescent.

Saci Perere, Mocking Goblin — A721

Characters from Brazilian Legends: 80c, Zumbi, last chief of rebellious slaves. 1cr, Chico Rei, African king. 1.30cr, Little Black Boy of the Pasture. 2.50cr, Iara, Queen of the Waters.

1974, Feb. 28   Litho.   Perf. 11½x11
Size: 21x39mm
1332 A721 40c multicolored   .35 .25
1333 A721 80c multicolored   .70 .60
1334 A721 1cr multicolored   1.65 .45

Perf. 11½
Size: 32½x33mm
1335 A721 1.30cr multicolored   2.50 .85
1336 A721 2.50cr multicolored   10.50 2.50
    Nos. 1332-1336 (5)   15.70 4.65

Nos. 1332-1336 are luminescent.

Pres. Costa e Silva Bridge A722

1974, Mar. 11
1337 A722 40c multicolored   .60 .30

Inauguration of the Pres. Costa e Silva Bridge, Rio Niteroi, connecting Rio de Janeiro and Guanabara State.

"The Press" A723

1974, Mar. 25   Perf. 11½
1338 A723 40c shown   .50 .30
1339 A723 40c "Radio"   .25 .25
1340 A723 40c "Television"   .40 .30
    Nos. 1338-1340 (3)   1.15 .85

Communications Commemorations: No. 1338, bicentenary of first Brazilian newspaper, published in London by Hipolito da Costa; No. 1339, founding of the Radio Sociedade do Rio de Janeiro by Roquette Pinto; No. 1340, installation of first Brazilian television station by Assis Chateaubriand. Luminescent.

"Reconstruction" — A724

1974, Mar. 31
1341 A724 40c multicolored   .70 .45

10 years of progress. Luminescent.

Corcovado Christ, Marconi, Colors of Brazil and Italy — A725

1974, Apr. 25   Litho.   Perf. 11½
1342 A725 2.50cr multi   6.00 3.00

Guglielmo Marconi (1874-1937), Italian physicist and inventor. Luminescent.

Stamp Printing Press, Stamp Designing A726

1974, May 6
1343 A726 80c multicolored   1.00 .50

Brazilian mint.

World Map, Indian, Caucasian and Black Men — A727

World Map and: #1345, Brazilians. #1346, Cabin & German horseback rider. #1347, Italian farm wagon. #1348, Japanese woman & torii.

1974, May 3   **Unwmk.**
1344 A727 40c multicolored   .30   .30
1345 A727 40c multicolored   .20   .20
1346 A727 2.50cr multicolored   3.25   1.50
1347 A727 2.50cr multicolored   4.75   1.50
1348 A727 2.50cr multicolored   1.25   .85
    Nos. 1344-1348 (5)   9.75   4.35
Ethnic and migration influences in Brazil.

Sandstone Cliffs, Sete Cidades National Park — A728

Tourist publicity: 80c, Ruins of Cathedral of Sao Miguel das Missões.

Lithographed and Engraved
1974, June 8   **Perf. 11x11½**
1349 A728 40c multicolored   .75   .50
1350 A728 80c multicolored   .75   .50

Souvenir Sheet

Soccer — A729

1974, June 20   **Litho.**   **Perf. 11½**
1351 A729 2.50cr multi   3.50   6.00
World Cup Soccer Championship, Munich, June 13-July 7.

Church and College, Caraça A730

1974, July 6   **Litho.**   **Perf. 11x11½**
1352 A730 40c multicolored   .45   .30
College (Seminary) of Caraça, bicent.

Wave on Television Screen A731

1974, July 15   **Perf. 11½**
1353 A731 40c black & blue   .30   .40
TELEBRAS, Third Brazilian Congress of Telecommunications, Brasilia, July 15-20.

Fernao Dias Paes A732

1974, July 21   **Perf. 11½**
1354 A732 20c green & multi   .30   .30
3rd centenary of the expedition led by Fernao Dias Paes exploring Minas Gerais and the passage from South to North in Brazil.

Mexican Flag — A733

1974, July 24   **Litho.**   **Perf. 11½**
1355 A733 80c multicolored   2.25   1.10
Visit of Pres. Luis Echeverria Alvares of Mexico, July 24-29.

Flags of Brazil and Germany A734

1974, Aug. 5   **Perf. 11x11½**
1356 A734 40c multicolored   .50   .50
World Cup Soccer Championship, 1974, victory of German Federal Republic.

Souvenir Sheet

Congress Emblem — A735

1974, Aug. 7   **Perf. 11½**
1357 A735 1.30cr multi   .85   1.75
5th World Assembly of the World Council for the Welfare of the Blind, Sao Paulo, Aug. 7-16. Stamp and margin inscribed in Braille with name of Assembly.

Raul Pederneiras (1874-1953, Journalist, Professor of Law and Fine Arts), Caricature by J. Carlos — A736

Lithographed and Engraved
1974, Aug. 15   **Perf. 11½x11**
1358 A736 40c buff, blk & ocher   .30   .40

Singer of "Cord" Verses — A742

Society Emblem and Landscape — A737

1974, Aug. 19   **Litho.**   **Perf. 11x11½**
1359 A737 1.30cr multi   1.25   .90
13th Congress of the International Union of Building and Savings Societies.

Souvenir Sheet

Five Women, by Di Cavalcanti — A738

1974, Aug. 26   **Litho.**   **Perf. 11½**
1360 A738 2cr multicolored   2.50   6.00
LUBRAPEX 74, 5th Portuguese-Brazilian Phil. Exhib., Sao Paulo, Nov. 26-Dec. 4.

"UPU" and World Map A739

1974, Oct. 9   **Litho.**   **Perf. 11½**
1361 A739 2.50cr blk & brt bl   4.50   1.75
Centenary of Universal Postal Union.

Hammock (Antillean Arawak Culture) A740

Bilro Lace — A741

Ceramic Figure by Master Vitalino — A743

1974, Oct. 16   **Litho.**   **Perf. 11½**
1362 A740 50c deep rose lilac   2.00   .40
1363 A741 50c lt & dk blue   2.50   .40
1364 A742 50c yel & red brn   .60   .40
1365 A743 50c brt yel & dk brn   .75   .40
   Nos. 1362-1365 (4)   5.85   1.60
Popular Brazilian crafts.

Branch of Coffee A744

1974, Oct. 27   **Unwmk.**   **Perf. 11**
1366 A744 50c multicolored   1.00   .60
Centenary of city of Campinas.

Hornless Tabapua A745

Animals of Brazil: 1.30cr, Creole horse. 2.50cr, Brazilian mastiff.

1974, Nov. 10   **Perf. 11½**
1367 A745 80c multi   1.10   .75
1368 A745 1.30cr multi   1.10   .75
1369 A745 2.50cr multi   7.75   2.50
   Nos. 1367-1369 (3)   9.95   4.00

Christmas — A746

1974, Nov. 18   **Perf. 11½x11**
1370 A746 50c Angel   .70   .30

Solteira Island Hydroelectric Dam — A747

1974, Nov. 11   **Perf. 11½**
1371 A747 50c black & yellow   1.40   .50
Inauguration of the Solteira Island Hydroelectric Dam over Parana River.

The Girls, by
Carlos
Reis — A748

1974, Nov. 26
1372 A748 1.30cr multi   .70 .50
LUBRAPEX 74, 5th Portuguese-Brazilian
Phil. Exhib., Sao Paulo, Nov. 26-Dec. 4.

Youths,
Judge,
Scales
A749

1974, Dec. 20   Litho.   Perf. 11½
1373 A749 90c yel, red & bl   .30 .35
Juvenile Court of Brazil, 50th anniversary.

Long Distance
Runner — A750

1974, Dec. 23
1374 A750 3.30cr multi   .75 .75
Sao Silvestre long distance running, 50th
anniversary.

News
Vendor,
1875,
Masthead,
1975
A751

1975, Jan. 4
1375 A751 50c multicolored   1.25 .75
Newspaper "O Estado de S. Paulo," cent.

Sao
Paulo
Industrial
Park
A752

Designs: 1.40cr, Natural rubber industry,
Acre. 4.50cr, Manganese mining, Amapá.

1975, Jan. 24   Litho.   Perf. 11x11½
1376 A752 50c vio bl & yel   1.25 .40
1377 A752 1.40cr yellow & brn   .60 .40
1378 A752 4.50cr yellow & blk   6.00 .40
     Nos. 1376-1378 (3)   7.85 1.20
     Economic development.

Fort of the
Holy Cross
A753

Colonial forts: No. 1380, Fort of the Three
Kings. No. 1381, Fort of Monteserrat. 90c, Fort
of Our Lady of Help.

Litho. & Engr.
1975, Mar. 14   Perf. 11½
1379 A753 50c yel & red brn   .25 .20
1380 A753 50c yel & red brn   .40 .20
1381 A753 50c yel & red brn   .80 .20
1382 A753 90c yel & red brn   .25 .20
     Nos. 1379-1382 (4)   1.70 .80

House on
Stilts,
Amazon
Region
A754

Designs: 50c, Modern houses and plan of
Brasilia. 1.40cr, Indian hut, Rondonia. 3.30cr,
German-style cottage (Enxaimel), Santa
Catarina.

1975, Apr. 18   Litho.   Perf. 11½
1383 A754 50c yel & multi   1.25 2.25
1384 A754 50c yel & multi   8.50 6.25
   a.   Pair, #1383-1384   10.00 8.50
1385 A754 1cr yel & multi   .85 .25
1386 A754 1.40cr yel & multi   1.75 2.50
1387 A754 1.40cr yel & multi   .50 .85
   a.   Pair, #1386-1387   2.25 3.50
1388 A754 3.30cr yel & multi   .75 1.25
1389 A754 3.30cr yel & multi   3.50 4.00
   a.   Pair, #1388-1380   4.25 5.25
     Nos. 1383-1389 (7)   17.10 17.35
Brazilian architecture. Nos. 1383, 1386,
1388 have yellow strip at right side, others at
left.

Astronotus
Ocellatus
A755

Designs: Brazilian fresh-water fish.

1975, May 2   Litho.   Perf. 11½
1390 A755 50c shown   1.40 .40
1391 A755 50c *Colomesus psitacus*   .25 .25
1392 A755 50c *Phallocerus caudimaculatus*   .25 .40
1393 A755 50c *Symphysodon discus*   .48 .50
     Nos. 1390-1393 (4)   2.38 1.55

Soldier's Head in
Brazil's Colors,
Plane, Rifle and
Ship — A756

Brazilian
Otter — A757

1975, May 8   Perf. 11½x11
1394 A756 50c vio bl & multi   .35 .30
In honor of the veterans of World War II, on
the 30th anniversary of victory.

1975, June 17   Litho.   Perf. 11½
Nature protection: 70c, Brazilian pines,
horiz. 3.30cr, Marsh cayman, horiz.

1395 A757 70c bl, grn & blk   1.05 .50
1396 A757 1cr multi   1.05 1.00
1397 A757 3.30cr multi   .90 .75
     Nos. 1395-1397 (3)   3.00 2.25

Petroglyphs, Stone
of Ingá — A758

Marjoara Vase,
Pará — A759

Vinctifer
Comptoni,
Petrified
Fish
A760

1975, July 8   Litho.   Perf. 11½
1398 A758 70c multicolored   .55 .40
1399 A759 1cr multicolored   .35 .40
1400 A760 1cr multicolored   .35 .40
     Nos. 1398-1400 (3)   1.25 1.20
     Archaeological discoveries.

Immaculate
Conception,
Franciscan
Monastery,
Vitoria — A761

1975, July 15
1401 A761 3.30cr blue & multi   .95 .95
Holy Year 1975 and 300th anniv. of establishment of the Franciscan Province in Southern Brazil.

Post and
Telegraph
Ministry — A762

1975, Aug. 8   Engr.   Perf. 11½
1402 A762 70c dk carmine   .70 .30
     Stamp Day 1975.

Sword
Dance,
Minas Gerais
A763

Folk Dances: No. 1404, Umbrella Dance,
Pernambuco. No. 1405, Warrior's Dance,
Alagoas.

1975, Aug. 22   Litho.   Perf. 11½
1403 A763 70c gray & multi   .35 .35
1404 A763 70c pink & multi   .35 .35
1405 A763 70c yellow & multi   .35 .35
     Nos. 1403-1405 (3)   1.05 1.05

Trees
A764

1975, Sept. 15   Perf. 11x11½
1406 A764 70c multicolored   .30 .25
     Annual Tree Festival.

Globe, Radar and
Satellite — A765

1975, Sept. 16   Perf. 11½
1407 A765 3.30cr multi   .70 .75
Inauguration of 2nd antenna of Tangua
Earth Station, Rio de Janeiro State.

Woman
Holding
Flowers
and Globe
A766

1975, Sept. 23
1408 A766 3.30cr multi   1.00 1.00
International Women's Year 1975.

Tile, Railing
and Column,
Alcantara
A767

Cross and Monastery, Sao
Cristovao — A768

Historic cities: No. 1411, Jug and Clock
Tower, Goiás, vert.

1975, Sept. 27   Litho.   Perf. 11½
1409 A767 70c multicolored   .30 .45
1410 A768 70c multicolored   .60 .45
1411 A768 70c multicolored   .60 .45
     Nos. 1409-1411 (3)   1.50 1.35

"Books
teach how
to live"
A769

1975, Oct. 23   Litho.   Perf. 11½
1412 A769 70c multicolored   .25 .30
     Day of the Book.

ASTA Congress Emblem A770

1975, Oct. 27 *Perf. 11x11½*
1413 A770 70c multicolored .25 .30
American Society of Travel Agents, 45th World Congress, Rio, Oct. 27-Nov. 1.

Angels A771

1975, Nov. 11
1414 A771 70c red & brown .25 .20
Christmas 1975.

Map of Americas, Waves — A772

Dom Pedro II — A773

1975, Nov. 19 *Perf. 11½x12*
1415 A772 5.20cr gray & multi 2.75 2.00
2nd Interamerican Conference of Telecommunications (CITEL), Rio, Nov. 19-27.

1975, Dec. 2 *Engr.* *Perf. 12*
1416 A773 70c violet brown .75 .45
Dom Pedro II (1825-1891), emperor of Brazil, birth sesquicentennial.

People and Cross A774

1975, Nov. 27 *Litho.* *Perf. 11x11½*
1417 A774 70c lt bl & dp bl .50 .65
National Day of Thanksgiving.

Guarapari Beach, Espirito Santo A775

Tourist Publicity: #1419, Salt Stone beach, Piaui. #1420, Cliffs, Rio Grande Do Sul.

1975, Dec. 19 *Litho.* *Perf. 11½*
1418 A775 70c multicolored .30 .30
1419 A775 70c multicolored .30 .30
1420 A775 70c multicolored .30 .30
Nos. 1418-1420 (3) .90 .90

Triple Jump, Games Emblem A776

1975, Dec. 22 *Perf. 11x11½*
1421 A776 1.60cr bl grn & blk .25 .35
Triple jump world record by Joao Carlos de Oliveira in 7th Pan-American Games, Mexico City, Oct. 12-26.

UN Emblem and Headquarters — A777

1975, Dec. 29 *Perf. 11½*
1422 A777 1.30cr dp bl & vio bl .25 .30
United Nations, 30th anniversary.

Light Bulbs, House and Sun A778

Energy conservation: No. 1424, Gasoline drops, car and sun.

1976, Jan. 16
1423 A778 70c multicolored .30 .20
1424 A778 70c multicolored .30 .20

Concorde A779

1976, Jan. 21 *Litho.* *Perf. 11x11½*
1425 A779 5.20cr bluish black .50 .35
First commercial flight of supersonic jet Concorde from Paris to Rio, Jan. 21.

Souvenir Sheet

Nautical Map of South Atlantic, 1776 — A780

1976, Feb. 2 *Perf. 11½*
1426 A780 70c salmon & multi .85 1.50
Centenary of the Naval Hydrographic and Navigation Institute.

Telephone Lines, 1876 Telephone — A781

1976, Mar. 10 *Litho.* *Perf. 11x11½*
1427 A781 5.20cr orange & blue .65 .50
Centenary of first telephone call by Alexander Graham Bell, March 10, 1876.

Eye and Exclamation Point — A782

Kaiapo Body Painting — A783

1976, Apr. 7 *Litho.* *Perf. 11½x11*
1428 A782 1cr vio red brn & brn .50 .75
World Health Day: "Foresight prevents blindness."

1976, Apr. 19 *Litho.* *Perf. 11½*
Designs: No. 1430, Bakairi ceremonial mask. No. 1431, Karajá feather headdress.
1429 A783 1cr light violet & multi .20 .20
1430 A783 1cr light violet & multi .20 .20
1431 A783 1cr light violet & multi .20 .20
Nos. 1429-1431 (3) .60 .60
Preservation of indigenous culture.

Itamaraty Palace, Brasilia A784

1976, Apr. 20
1432 A784 1cr multicolored .60 .60
Diplomats' Day. Itamaraty Palace, designed by Oscar Niemeyer, houses the Ministry of Foreign Affairs.

Watering Can over Stones, by José Tarcisio A785

Fingers and Ribbons, by Pietrina Checcacci A786

1976, May 14 *Litho.* *Perf. 11½*
1433 A785 1cr multi .25 .20
1434 A786 1.60cr multi .25 .20
Modern Brazilian art.

Basketball — A787   Orchid — A788

Designs (Olympic Rings and): 1.40cr, Yachting. 5.20cr, Judo.

1976, May 21 *Litho.* *Perf. 11½*
1435 A787 1cr emerald & blk .20 .20
1436 A787 1.40cr dk blue & blk .20 .20
1437 A787 5.20cr orange & blk .65 .50
Nos. 1435-1437 (3) 1.05 .90
21st Olympic Games, Montreal, Canada, July 17-Aug. 1.

1976, June 4 *Perf. 11½x11*
Nature protection: No. 1439, Golden-faced lion monkey.
1438 A788 1cr multicolored .25 .20
1439 A788 1cr multicolored .25 .20

Film Camera, Brazilian Colors — A789

1976, June 19
1440 A789 1cr vio bl, brt grn & yel .20 .25
Brazilian film industry.

Bahia Woman — A790

Designs: 10c, Oxcart driver, horiz. 20c, Raft fishermen, horiz. 30c, Rubber plantation worker. 40c, Cowboy, horiz. 50c, Gaucho. 80c, Gold panner. 1cr, Banana plantation worker. 1.10cr, Grape harvester. 1.30cr, Coffee picker. 1.80cr, Farmer gathering wax palms. 2cr, Potter. 5cr, Sugar cane cutter. 7cr, Salt mine worker. 10cr, Fisherman. 15cr, Coconut seller. 20cr, Lacemaker.

Perf. 11½x11, 11x11½
1976-78 Photo.
1441 A790 10c red brown ('77) .20 .20
1442 A790 15c brown .25 .30
1443 A790 20c violet blue .20 .20
1444 A790 30c lilac rose .20 .20
1445 A790 40c orange ('77) .20 .20
1446 A790 50c citron .20 .20
1447 A790 80c slate green .40 .20
1448 A790 1cr black .20 .20
1449 A790 1.10cr magenta ('77) .20 .20
1450 A790 1.30cr red ('77) .20 .20
1451 A790 1.80cr dk vio bl ('78) .20 .20
Engr.
1452 A790 2cr brown ('77) .25 .20
1453 A790 5cr dk pur ('77) .50 .20
1454 A790 7cr violet 1.50 .20
1455 A790 10cr yel grn ('77) .55 .20
1456 A790 15cr gray grn ('78) 1.40 .20
1457 A790 20cr blue 1.40 .20
Nos. 1441-1457 (17) 8.05 3.50
See Nos. 1653-1657.

Hyphessobrycon Innesi — A791

Designs: Brazilian fresh-water fish.

1976, July 12		**Litho.**		**Perf. 11x11½**	
1460	A791	1cr shown		.40	.40
1461	A791	1cr Copeina arnoldi		.40	.40
1462	A791	1cr Prochilodus insignis		.40	.40
1463	A791	1cr Crenicichla lepidota		.40	.40
1464	A791	1cr Ageneiosus		.40	.40
1465	A791	1cr Corydoras reticulatus		.40	.40
a.		Block of 6, #1460-1465		2.50	2.50

Santa Marta Lighthouse A792

1976, July 29   **Engr.**   **Perf. 12x11½**
1466 A792 1cr blue   .20   .30

300th anniversary of the city of Laguna.

Children on Magic Carpet A793

1976, Aug. 1   **Litho.**   **Perf. 11½x12**
1467 A793 1cr multicolored   .20   .20

Stamp Day.

Nurse's Lamp and Head A794

1976, Aug. 12   **Litho.**   **Perf. 11½**
1468 A794 1cr multicolored   .20   .20

Brazilian Nurses' Assoc., 50th anniv.

Puppet, Soldier — A795

Winner's Medal — A796

Designs: 1.30cr, Girl's head. 1.60cr, Hand with puppet head on each finger, horiz.

1976, Aug. 20
1469 A795 1cr multi   .20   .20
1470 A795 1.30cr multi   .20   .20
1471 A795 1.60cr multi   .20   .20
   Nos. 1469-1471 (3)   .60   .60

Mamulengo puppet show.

1976, Aug. 21
1472 A796 5.20cr multi   .70   .50

27th International Military Athletic Championships, Rio de Janeiro, Aug. 21-28.

Family Protection — A797

1976, Sept. 12
1473 A797 1cr lt & dk blue   .20   .20

National organizations SENAC and SESC helping commercial employees to improve their living standard, both commercially and socially.

Dying Tree — A798

1976, Sept. 20   **Litho.**   **Perf. 11½**
1474 A798 1cr gray & multi   .20   .20

Protection of the environment.

Atom Symbol, Electron Orbits A799

1976, Sept. 21
1475 A799 5.20cr multi   .70   .50

20th General Conference of the International Atomic Energy Agency, Rio de Janeiro, Sept. 21-29.

Train in Tunnel A800

1976, Sept. 26
1476 A800 1.60cr multi   .25   .25

Sao Paulo subway, 1st in Brazil.

St. Francis and Birds A801

1976, Oct. 4
1477 A801 5.20cr multi   .60   .40

St. Francis of Assisi, 750th death anniv.

Ouro Preto School of Mining — A802

1976, Oct. 12   **Engr.**   **Perf. 12x11½**
1478 A802 1cr dk vio   .40   .50

Ouro Preto School of Mining, centenary.

Three Kings A803

Designs: Children's drawings.

1976, Nov. 4		**Litho.**	**Perf. 11½**	
1479	A803	80c shown	.30	.30
1480	A803	80c Santa Claus on donkey	.30	.30
1481	A803	80c Virgin and Child and Angels	.30	.30
1482	A803	80c Angels with candle	.30	.30
1483	A803	80c Nativity	.30	.30
a.		Strip of 5, #1479-1483	1.40	1.40

Christmas 1976.

Souvenir Sheet

30,000 Reis Banknote — A804

1976, Nov. 5   **Litho.**   **Perf. 11½**
1484 A804 80c multicolored   .40   1.50

Opening of 1000th branch of Bank of Brazil, Barra do Bugres, Mato Grosso.

Virgin of Monte Serrat, by Friar Agostinho A805

St. Joseph, 18th Century Wood Sculpture — A806

5.60cr, The Dance, by Rodolfo Bernadelli, 19th cent. 6.50cr, The Caravel, by Bruno Giorgi, 20th cent. abstract sculpture.

1976, Nov. 5				
1485	A805	80c multi	.20	.20
1486	A806	5cr multi	.65	.40
1487	A805	5.60cr multi	.65	.40
1488	A806	6.50cr multi	.65	.40
		Nos. 1485-1488 (4)	2.15	1.40

Development of Brazilian sculpture.

Praying Hands A807

1976, Nov. 25
1489 A807 80c multicolored   .25   .25

National Day of Thanksgiving.

Sailor, 1840 — A808

Design: 2cr, Marine's uniform, 1808.

1976, Dec. 13   **Litho.**   **Perf. 11½x11**
1490 A808 80c multicolored   .25   .25
1491 A808 2cr multicolored   .30   .25

Brazilian Navy.

"Natural Resources and Development" — A809

1976, Dec. 17   **Perf. 11½**
1492 A809 80c multicolored   .20   .20

Brazilian Bureau of Standards, founded 1940.

Wheel of Life — A810

Designs: 5.60cr, Beggar, sculpture by Agnaldo dos Santos. 6.50cr, Benin mask.

1977, Jan. 14
1493 A810 5cr multi   .55   .35
1494 A810 5.60cr multi   .55   .35
1495 A810 6.50cr multi   1.10   .35
   Nos. 1493-1495 (3)   2.20   1.05

FESTAC '77, 2nd World Black and African Festival, Lagos, Nigeria, Jan. 15-Feb. 12.

A811

1977, Jan. 20   **Litho.**   **Perf. 11½**
1496 A811 6.50cr bl & yel grn   .85   .65

Rio de Janeiro International Airport.

Seminar Emblem with Map of Americas — A812

Salicylate, Microphoto A813

1977, Feb. 6
1497 A812 1.10cr gray, vio bl & bl   .35 .20
  6th Inter-American Budget Seminar.

1977, Apr. 10 Litho. Perf. 11½
1498 A813 1.10cr multi   .20 .20
  International Rheumatism Year.

Lions International Emblem A814

1977, Apr. 16
1499 A814 1.10cr multi   .20 .20
  25th anniv. of Brazilian Lions Intl.

Heitor Villa Lobos A815

1977, Apr. 26   Perf. 11x11½
1500 A815 1.10cr shown   .20 .20
1501 A815 1.10cr Chiquinha Gon-
    zaga   .20 .20
1502 A815 1.10cr Noel Rosa   .20 .20
  Nos. 1500-1502 (3)   .60 .60
  Brazilian composers.

Farmer and Worker — A816

Medicine Bottles and Flask — A817

1977, May 8 Litho. Perf. 11½
1503 A816 1.10cr grn & multi   .20 .20
1504 A817 1.10cr lt & dk grn   .20 .20
  Support and security for rural and urban workers (No. 1503) and establishment in 1971

of Medicine Distribution Center (CEME) for low-cost medicines (No. 1504).

Churchyard Cross, Porto Seguro — A818

  Views, Porto Seguro: 5cr, Beach and boats. 5.60cr, Our Lady of Pena Chapel. 6.50cr, Town Hall.

1977, May 25 Litho. Perf. 11½
1505 A818 1.10cr multi   .20 .20
1506 A818   5cr multi   1.40 .35
1507 A818 5.60cr multi   .55 .45
1508 A818 6.50cr multi   .80 .55
  Nos. 1505-1508 (4)   2.95 1.55
  Cent. of Brazil's membership in UPU.

Diario de Porto Alegre A819

1977, June 1
1509 A819 1.10cr multi   .20 .20
  Diario de Porto Alegre, newspaper, 150th anniv.

Blue Whale A820

1977, June 3
1510 A820 1.30cr multi   .20 .20
  Protection of marine life.

"Life and Development" A821

1977, June 20
1511 A821 1.30cr multi   .20 .20
  National Development Bank, 25th anniv.

Train Leaving Tunnel A822

1977, July 8 Engr. Perf. 11½
1512 A822 1.30cr black   .20 .20
  Centenary of Sao Paulo-Rio de Janeiro railroad.

Vasum Cassiforme A823

Caduceus, Formulas for Water and Fluoride A824

  Sea Shells: No. 1514, Strombus goliath. No. 1515, Murex tenuivaricosus.

1977, July 14   Litho.
1513 A823 1.30cr blue & multi   .20 .20
1514 A823 1.30cr brown & multi   .20 .20
1515 A823 1.30cr green & multi   .20 .20
  Nos. 1513-1515 (3)   .60 .60

1977, July 15   Perf. 11½x11
1516 A824 1.30cr multi   .20 .20
  3rd Intl. Odontology Congress, Rio, 7/15-21.

Masonic Emblem, Map of Brazil — A825

"Stamps Don't Sink or Lose their Way" — A826

1977, July 18   Perf. 11½
1517 A825 1.30cr bl, lt bl & blk   .20 .20
  50th anniversary of the founding of the Brazilian Grand Masonic Lodge.

1977, Aug. 1
1518 A826 1.30cr multi   .20 .20
  Stamp Day 1977.

Dom Pedro's Proclamation A827

Horses and Bulls — A828

1977, Aug. 11 Litho. Perf. 11½
1519 A827 1.30cr multi   .20 .20
  150th anniversary of Brazilian Law School.

Perf. 11½x11, 11x11½
1977, Aug. 20   Litho.
  Brazilian folklore: No. 1521, King on horseback. No. 1522, Joust, horiz.

1520 A828 1.30cr ocher & multi   .20 .20
1521 A828 1.30cr blue & multi   .20 .20
1522 A828 1.30cr yel & multi   .20 .20
  Nos. 1520-1522 (3)   .60 .60

2000-reis Doubloon A829

  Brazilian Colonial Coins: No. 1524, 640r pataca. No. 1525, 20r copper "vintem."

1977, Aug. 31   Perf. 11½
1523 A829 1.30cr vio bl & multi   .20 .20
1524 A829 1.30cr dk red & multi   .20 .20
1525 A829 1.30cr yel & multi   .20 .20
  Nos. 1523-1525 (3)   .60 .60

Pinwheel A830

Neoregelia Carolinae A831

1977, Sept. 1
1526 A830 1.30cr multi   .20 .20
  National Week.

1977, Sept. 21 Litho. Perf. 11½
1527 A831 1.30cr multi   .20 .20
  Nature preservation.

Pen, Pencil, Letters — A832

1977, Oct. 15 Litho. Perf. 11½
1528 A832 1.30cr multi   .20 .20
  Primary education, sesquicentennial.

Dome and Telescope A833

1977, Oct. 15
1529 A833 1.30cr multi   .20 .20
  National Astrophysics Observatory, Brasópolis, sesquicentennial.

"Jahu" Hydroplane (Savoia Marchetti
S-55) — A834

Design: No. 1531, PAX, dirigible.

1977, Oct. 17
1530 A834 1.30cr multi   .25 .25
1531 A834 1.30cr multi   .25 .25
  50th anniv. of crossing of South Atlantic by
Joao Ribeiro de Barros, Genoa-Sao Paulo
(#1530) and 75th anniv. of the PAX airship
(#1531).

A835

A836

1977, Oct. 24
1532 A835 1.30cr Il'Guarani   .20 .20
  Book Day and to honor Jose Martiniano de
Alencar, writer, jurist.

1977, Nov. 5   Litho.   Perf. 11½
1533 A836 1.30cr Waves   .20 .20
  Amateur Radio Operators' Day.

Nativity
A837

  Christmas (folk art): 2cr, Annunciation. 5cr,
Nativity.

1977, Nov. 10
1534 A837 1.30cr bister & multi   .25 .20
1535 A837 2cr bister & multi   .30 .20
1536 A837 5cr bister & multi   .65 .25
    Nos. 1534-1536 (3)   1.20 .65

A838

A839

1977, Nov. 19
1537 A838 1.30cr Emerald   .20 .20
1538 A838 1.30cr Topaz   .20 .20
1539 A838 1.30cr Aquamarine   .20 .20
    Nos. 1537-1539 (3)   .60 .60
  PORTUCALE 77, 2nd International Topical
Exhibition, Porto, Nov. 19-20.

1977, Nov. 24   Litho.   Perf. 11½
1540 A839 1.30cr Angel, cornuco-
           pia   .20 .20
  National Thanksgiving Day.

Army's Railroad Construction
Battalion — A840

  Civilian services of armed forces: No. 1542,
Navy's Amazon flotilla. No. 1543, Air Force's
postal service (plane).

1977, Dec. 5
1541 A840 1.30cr multi   .20 .20
1542 A840 1.30cr multi   .20 .20
1543 A840 1.30cr multi   .20 .20
    Nos. 1541-1543 (3)   .60 .60

Varig
Emblem,
Jet
A841

1977, Dec.   Perf. 11x11½
1544 A841 1.30cr bl & blk   .20 .20
  50th anniversary of Varig Airline.

Sts. Cosme and
Damiao Church,
Igaracu — A842

Woman Holding
Sheaf — A843

  Brazilian Architecture: 7.50cr, St. Bento
Monastery Church, Rio de Janeiro. 8.50cr,
Church of St. Francis of Assisi, Ouro Preto.
9.50cr, St. Anthony Convent Church, Joao
Pessoa.

1977, Dec. 8
1545 A842 2.70cr multi   .30 .20
1546 A842 7.50cr multi   .90 .35
1547 A842 8.50cr multi   .90 .40
1548 A842 9.50cr multi   1.25 .45
    Nos. 1545-1548 (4)   3.35 1.40

1977, Dec. 19   Perf. 11½
1549 A843 1.30cr multi   .20 .20
  Brazilian diplomacy.

Soccer Ball and
Foot — A844

  Designs: No. 1551, Soccer ball in net. No.
1552, Symbolic soccer player.

1978, Mar. 1   Litho.   Perf. 11½
1550 A844 1.80cr multi   .30 .20
1551 A844 1.80cr multi   .30 .20
1552 A844 1.80cr multi   .30 .20
    Nos. 1550-1552 (3)   .90 .60
  11th World Cup Soccer Championship,
Argentina, June 1-25.

"La Fosca"
on La
Scala
Stage and
Carlos
Gomes
A845

1978, Feb. 9
1553 A845 1.80cr multi   .20 .20
  Bicentenary of La Scala in Milan, and to
honor Carlos Gomes (1836-1893), Brazilian
composer.

Symbols of Postal
Mechanization — A846

1978, Mar. 15   Litho.   Perf. 11½
1554 A846 1.80cr multi   .20 .20
  Opening of Postal Staff College.

Hypertension
Chart — A847

Waves from
Antenna Uniting
World — A848

1978, Apr. 4
1555 A847 1.80cr multi   .20 .20
  World Health Day, fight against hypertension.

1978, May 17   Litho.   Perf. 12x11½
1556 A848 1.80cr multi   .20 .20
  10th World Telecommunications Day.

Brazilian
Canary
A849

  Birds: 8.50cr, Cotinga. 9.50cr, Tanager
fastuosa.

1978, June 5   Perf. 11½x12
1557 A849 7.50cr multi   1.00 .75
1558 A849 8.50cr multi   1.00 .80
1559 A849 9.50cr multi   1.00 1.00
    Nos. 1557-1559 (3)   3.00 2.55

Inocencio Serzedelo Correa and
Manuel Francisco Correa,
1893 — A850

1978, June 20   Litho.   Perf. 11x11½
1560 A850 1.80cr multi   .20 .20
  85th anniversary of Union Court of Audit.

Post and
Telegraph
Building
A851

1978, June 22   Perf. 11½
1561 A851 1.80cr multi   .20 .25
    Souvenir Sheet
    Imperf
1562 A851 7.50cr multi   .75 1.50
  Inauguration of Post and Telegraph Building
(ECT), Brasilia, and for BRAPEX, 3rd Brazilian
Philatelic Exhibition, Brasilia, June 23-28 (No.
1562).

Ernesto Geisel,
President of
Brazil — A852

1978, June 22   Engr.   Perf. 11½
1563 A852 1.80cr dull green   .20 .20

Savoia-Marchetti S-64, Map of South Atlantic — A853

1978, July 3   Litho.
1564 A853 1.80cr multi   .20 .20

50th anniv. of 1st crossing of South Atlantic by Carlos del Prete and Arturo Ferrarin.

Symbolic of Smallpox Eradication A854

Brazil No. 68 — A855

1978, July 25
1565 A854 1.80cr multi   .20 .20

Eradication of smallpox.

1978, Aug. 1
1566 A855 1.80cr multi   .20 .20

Stamp Day, centenary of the "Barba Branca" (white beard) issue.

Stormy Sea, by Seelinger A856

1978, Aug. 4
1567 A856 1.80cr multi   .20 .20

Helios Seelinger, painter, birth centenary.

Guitar Players A857

Musicians and Instruments: No. 1569, Flutes. No. 1570, Percussion instruments.

1978, Aug. 22   Litho.   *Perf. 11½*
1568 A857 1.80cr multi   .20 .20
1569 A857 1.80cr multi   .20 .20
1570 A857 1.80cr multi   .20 .20
    Nos. 1568-1570 (3)   .60 .60

Children at Play A858

1978, Sept. 1   Litho.   *Perf. 11½*
1571 A858 1.80cr multi   .20 .20

National Week.

Collegiate Church A859

1978, Sept. 6   Engr.
1572 A859 1.80cr red brn   .20 .20

Restoration of patio of Collegiate Church, Sao Paulo.

Justice by A. Geschiatti A860

1978, Sept. 18   Litho.
1573 A860 1.80cr blk & olive   .20 .20

Federal Supreme Court, sesquicentennial.

Iguacu Falls — A861

Design: No. 1575, Yellow ipecac.

1978, Sept. 21
1574 A861 1.80cr multi   .20 .20
1575 A861 1.80cr multi   .20 .20

Iguacu National Park.

Stages of Intelsat Satellite A862

1978, Oct. 9   Litho.   *Perf. 11½*
1576 A862 1.80cr multi   .20 .20

Flag of Order of Christ A863

Brazilian Flags: No. 1578, Principality of Brazil. No. 1579, United Kingdom. No. 1580, Imperial Brazil. No. 1581, National flag (current).

1978, Oct. 13
1577 A863 1.80cr multi   .65 .55
1578 A863 1.80cr multi   .65 .55
1579 A863 1.80cr multi   .65 .55
1580 A863 8.50cr multi   .65 .55
1581 A863 8.50cr multi   .65 .55
   a.   Block of 5, #1577-1581 + label   4.00 6.50
    Nos. 1577-1581 (5)   3.25 2.75

7th LUBRAPEX Philatelic Exhibition, Porto Alegre.

Mail Street Car A864

Mail Transportation: No. 1583, Overland mail truck. No. 1584, Mail delivery truck. 7.50cr. Railroad mail car. 8.50cr, Mail coach. 9.50cr, Post riders.

1978, Oct. 21   *Perf. 11x11½*
1582 A864 1.80cr multi   .50 .40
1583 A864 1.80cr multi   .50 .40
1584 A864 1.80cr multi   .50 .40
1585 A864 7.50cr multi   .50 .40
1586 A864 8.50cr multi   .50 .40
1587 A864 9.50cr multi   .50 .50
   a.   Block of 6, #1582-1587   3.00 3.00

18th UPU Congress, Rio de Janeiro, 1979.

Gaucho Herding Cattle, and Cactus — A865

1978, Oct. 23   *Perf. 11½x11*
1588 A865 1.80cr multi   .20 .20

Joao Guimaraes Rosa, poet and diplomat, 70th birthday.

St. Anthony's Hill, by Nicholas A. Taunay A866

Landscape Paintings: No. 1590, Castle Hill, by Victor Meirelles. No. 1591, View of Sabara, by Alberto da Veiga Guignard. No. 1592, View of Pernambuco, by Frans Post.

1978, Nov. 6   Litho.   *Perf. 11½*
1589 A866 1.80cr multi   .20 .20
1590 A866 1.80cr multi   .20 .20
1591 A866 1.80cr multi   .20 .20
1592 A866 1.80cr multi   .20 .20
    Nos. 1589-1592 (4)   .80 .80

Angel with Harp — A867

Christmas: No. 1594, Angel with lute. No. 1595, Angel with oboe.

1978, Nov. 10
1593 A867 1.80cr multi   .20 .20
1594 A867 1.80cr multi   .20 .20
1595 A867 1.80cr multi   .20 .20
    Nos. 1593-1595 (3)   .60 .60

Symbolic Candles — A868

1978, Nov. 23
1596 A868 1.80cr blk, gold & car   .20 .20

National Thanksgiving Day.

Red Crosses and Activities A869

1978, Dec. 5   Litho.   *Perf. 11x11½*
1597 A869 1.80cr blk & red   .20 .20

70th anniversary of Brazilian Red Cross.

Paz Theater, Belem A870

12cr, José de Alencar Theater, Portaleza. 12.50cr, Municipal Theater, Rio de Janeiro.

1978, Dec. 6   *Perf. 11½*
1598 A870 10.50cr multi   .70 .25
1599 A870   12cr multi   .70 .25
1600 A870 12.50cr multi   .70 .25
    Nos. 1598-1600 (3)   2.10 .75

Subway Trains — A871

1979, Mar. 5   Litho.   *Perf. 11½*
1601 A871 2.50cr multi   .20 .20

Inauguration of Rio subway system.

Old and New Post Offices A872

Designs: No. 1603, Old and new mail boxes. No. 1604, Manual and automatic mail sorting. No. 1605, Old and new planes. No. 1606, Telegraph and telex machine. No. 1607, Mailmen's uniforms.

1979, Mar. 20   Litho.   *Perf. 11x11½*
1602 A872 2.50cr multi   .25 .20
1603 A872 2.50cr multi   .25 .20
1604 A872 2.50cr multi   .25 .20
1605 A872 2.50cr multi   .25 .20
1606 A872 2.50cr multi   .25 .20
1607 A872 2.50cr multi   .25 .20
   a.   Block of 6, #1602-1607   1.50 1.50

10th anniv. of the new Post and Telegraph Dept., and 18th Universal Postal Union Cong., Rio de Janeiro, Sept.-Oct., 1979.

O'Day 23
Class
Yacht
A873

Yachts and Stamp Outlines: 10.50cr, Penguin Class. 12cr, Hobie Cat Class. 12.50cr, Snipe Class.

1979, Apr. 18   Litho.   Perf. 11x11½
1608 A873   2.50cr multi   .30   .25
1609 A873   10.50cr multi   .55   .45
1610 A873   12cr multi   .55   .35
1611 A873   12.50cr multi   .75   .35
    Nos. 1608-1611 (4)   2.15 1.40
Brasiliana '79, 3rd World Thematic Stamp Exhibition, Sao Conrado, Sept. 15-23.

Children, IYC
Emblem — A874

1979, May 30   Litho.   Perf. 11½
1612 A874   2.50cr multi   .25   .20
Intl. Year of the Child & Children's Book Day.

Giant Water
Lily — A875

12cr, Amazon manatee. 12.50cr, Arrau (turtle).

1979, June 5   Litho.   Perf. 11½
1613 A875   10.50cr multi   .70   .50
1614 A875   12cr multi   .90   .60
1615 A875   12.50cr multi   .90   .60
    Nos. 1613-1615 (3)   2.50 1.70
Amazon National Park, nature conservation.

Bank
Emblem
A876

1979, June 7
1616 A876   2.50cr multi   .20   .20
Northwest Bank of Brazil, 25th anniversary.

Physician
Tending
Patient
15th Cent.
Woodcut
A877

1979, June 30
1617 A877   2.50cr multi   .20   .20
Natl. Academy of Medicine, 50th anniv.

Flower made of
Hearts — A878

1979, July 8   Litho.   Perf. 11½
1618 A878   2.50cr multi   .20   .20
35th Brazilian Cardiology Congress.

Souvenir Sheet

Hotel Nacional, Rio de
Janeiro — A879

1979, July 16
1619 A879   12.50cr multi   .75 1.50
Brasiliana '79 comprising 1st Inter-American Exhibition of Classical Philately and 3rd World Topical Exhibition, Rio de Janeiro, Sept. 15-23.

Cithaerias
Aurora
A880

Moths: 10.50cr, Evenus regalis. 12cr, Caligo eurilochus. 12.50cr, Diaethria clymena janeira.

1979, Aug. 1
1620 A880   2.50cr multi   .20   .20
1621 A880   10.50cr multi   .60   .40
1622 A880   12cr multi   .70   .50
1623 A880   12.50cr multi   .70   .50
    Nos. 1620-1623 (4)   2.20 1.60
Stamp Day 1979.

EMB-121
Xingo
A881

1979, Aug. 19   Litho.   Perf. 11½
1624 A881   2.50cr vio blue   .20   .20
Embraer, Brazilian aircraft comp., 10th anniv.

A882

A883

Natl. emblem over landscape.

1979, Sept. 12
1625 A882   3.20cr multi   .20   .20
National Week.

1979, Sept. 8   Litho.   Perf. 11½
1626 A883   2.50cr multi   .20   .20
Statue of Our Lady of the Apparition, 75th anniversary of coronation.

"UPU,"
Envelope
and Mail
Transport
A884

"UPU" and: No. 1628, Post Office emblems. 10.50cr, Globe. 12cr, Flags of Brazil and UN. 12.50cr, UPU emblem.

1979, Sept. 12   Perf. 11x11½
1627 A884   2.50cr multi   .20   .20
1628 A884   2.50cr multi   .20   .20
1629 A884   10.50cr multi   .50   .50
1630 A884   12cr multi   .70   .70
1631 A884   12.50cr multi   .70   .70
    Nos. 1627-1631 (5)   2.30 2.30
18th UPU Cong., Rio, Sept.-Oct. 1979.

Pyramid Fountain,
Rio de
Janeiro — A885

Fountains: 10.50cr, Facade, Marilia, Ouro Preto, horiz. 12cr, Boa Vista, Recife.

Perf. 12x11½, 11½x12
1979, Sept. 15
1632 A885   2.50cr multi   .20   .20
1633 A885   10.50cr multi   .50   .50
1634 A885   12cr multi   .60   .60
    Nos. 1632-1634 (3)   1.30 1.30
Brasiliana '79, 1st Interamerican Exhibition of Classical Philately.

Church of
the Glory
A886

Landscapes by Leandro Joaquim: 12cr, Fishing on Guanabara Bay. 12.50cr, Boqueirao Lake and Carioca Arches.

1979, Sept. 15   Perf. 11½
1635 A886   2.50cr multi   .20   .20
1636 A886   12cr multi   .60   .60
1637 A886   12.50cr multi   .60   .60
    Nos. 1635-1637 (3)   1.40 1.40
Brasiliana '79, 3rd World Topical Exhibition, Sao Conrado, Sept. 15-23.

World Map
A887

1979, Sept. 20
1638 A887   2.50cr multi   .20   .20
3rd World Telecommunications Exhibition, Geneva, Sept. 20-26.

"UPU" and UPU
Emblem — A888

1979, Oct. 9   Litho.   Perf. 11½x11
1639 A888   2.50cr multi   .20   .20
1640 A888   10.50cr multi   .55   .55
1641 A888   12cr multi   .65   .65
1642 A888   12.50cr multi   .65   .65
    Nos. 1639-1642 (4)   2.05 2.05
Universal Postal Union Day.

IYC
Emblem,
Feather
Toy
A889

IYC Emblem and Toys: No. 1644, Bumble bee, ragdoll. No. 1645, Flower, top. No. 1646, Wooden acrobat.

1979, Oct. 12   Perf. 11½
1643 A889   2.50cr multi   .25   .20
1644 A889   3.20cr multi   .25   .25
1645 A889   3.20cr multi   .25   .25
1646 A889   3.20cr multi   .25   .25
    Nos. 1643-1646 (4)   1.00   .95
International Year of the Child.

Adoration of
the Kings
A890

Christmas 1979: No. 1648, Nativity. No. 1649 Jesus and the Elders in the Temple.

1979, Nov. 12   Litho.   Perf. 11½
1647 A890   3.20cr multi   .20   .20
1648 A890   3.20cr multi   .20   .20
1649 A890   3.20cr multi   .20   .20
    Nos. 1647-1649 (3)   .60   .60

Souvenir Sheet

Hands Reading Braille — A891

Lithographed and Embossed
1979, Nov. 20.   *Perf. 11½*
1650 A891 3.20cr multi   .50 1.25

Publication of Braille script, 150th anniversary. Margin shows extension of stamp design with Braille printed and embossed.

Wheat Harvester — A892

Steel Mill — A893

1979, Nov. 22
1651 A892 3.20cr multi   .20 .20

Thanksgiving 1979.

1979, Nov. 23
1652 A893 3.20cr multi   .20 .20

COSIPA Steelworks, Sao Paulo, 25th anniversary.

Type of 1976

Designs: 70c, Women grinding coconuts. 2.50cr, Basket weaver. 3.20cr, River boatman. 21cr, Harvesting ramie (China grass). 27cr, Man leading pack mule. 3.20cr, 27cr, horiz.

Photogravure, Engraved (21cr)
1979   *Perf. 11x11½, 11½x11*
1653 A790 70c gray green   .20 .20
1654 A790 2.50cr sepia   .20 .20
1655 A790 3.20cr blue   .20 .20
1656 A790 21cr purple   .38 .20
1657 A790 27cr sepia   .45 .20
  Nos. 1653-1657 (5)   1.43 1.00

A894

Designs: 2cr, Coconuts. 3cr, Mangoes. 4cr, Corn. 5cr, Onions. 7cr, Oranges. 10cr, Maracuja. 12cr, Pineapple. 15cr, Bananas. 17cr, Guarana. 20cr, Sugar cane. 24cr, Beekeeping. 30cr, Silkworm. 34cr, Cacao. 38cr, Coffee. 42cr, Soybeans. 45cr, Mandioca. 50cr, Wheat. 57cr, Peanuts. 66cr, Grapes. 100cr, Cashews. 140cr, Tomatoes. 200cr, Mamona. 500cr, Cotton.

1980-83   **Photo.**   *Perf. 11½x11*
1658 A894 2cr yel brn ('82)   .20 .20
1659 A894 3cr red ('82)   .20 .20
1660 A894 4cr orange   .20 .20
1661 A894 5cr dk pur ('82)   .20 .20
1662 A894 7cr org ('81)   .20 .20
1663 A894 10cr bl grn ('82)   .20 .20
1664 A894 12cr dk grn ('81)   .20 .20
1665 A894 15cr gldn brn
                ('83)   .20 .20
1666 A894 17cr brn org ('82)   .25 .20
1667 A894 20cr olive ('82)   .25 .20
1668 A894 24cr bis ('82)   .20 .20

1669 A894 30cr blk ('82)   .20 .20
1670 A894 34cr brown   .35 .20
1671 A894 38cr red ('83)   .20 .20
1672 A894 42cr green   5.75 .50
1673 A894 45cr sepia ('83)   .55 .20
1674 A894 50cr yel org ('82)   .20 .20
1675 A894 57cr brn ('83)   .20 .20
1676 A894 66cr pur ('81)   3.75 .20
1677 A894 100cr dk red brn
                ('81)   2.25 .20
1678 A894 140cr red ('82)   2.75 .20
        Engr.
1678A A894 200cr grn ('82)   2.75 .20
1679 A894 500cr brn ('82)   5.75 .20
  Nos. 1658-1679 (23)   27.00 4.90
        See Nos. 1934-1941.

Plant Inside Raindrop — A896

Light Bulb Containing: 17cr+7cr, Sun. 20cr+8cr, Windmill. 21cr+9cr, Dam.

1980, Jan. 2   **Litho.**   *Perf. 12*
1680 A896 3.20cr multi   .20 .20
1681 A896 24cr (17 + 7)   1.25 .65
1682 A896 28cr (20 + 8)   1.50 .75
1683 A896 30cr (21 + 9)   2.25 .85
  Nos. 1680-1683 (4)   5.20 2.45

Anthracite Industry A897

1980, Mar. 19   **Litho.**   *Perf. 11½*
1684 A897 4cr multi   .20 .20

Map of Americas, Symbols of Development — A898

1980, Apr. 14   **Litho.**   *Perf. 11x11½*
1685 A898 4cr multi   .20 .20

21st Assembly of Inter-American Development Bank Governors, Rio, Apr. 14-16.

Tapirape Mask, Mato Grosso A899

1980, Apr. 18   *Perf. 11½*
1686 A899 4cr shown   .20 .20
1687 A899 4cr Tukuna mask, Amazonas, vert.   .20 .20
1688 A899 4cr Kanela mask, Maranhao, vert.   .20 .20
  Nos. 1686-1688 (3)   .60 .60

Brazilian Television, 30th Anniversary A900

1980, May 5   **Litho.**   *Perf. 11½*
1689 A900 4cr multicolored   .20 .20

Duke of Caxias, by Miranda — A901
The Worker, by Candido Partinari — A902

1980, May 7
1690 A901 4cr multicolored   .20 .20

Duke of Caxias, death centenary.

1980, May 18

Paintings: 28cr, Mademoiselle Pogany, by Constantin Brancusi. 30cr, The Glass of Water, by Francisco Aurelio de Figueiredo.

1691 A902 24cr multi   1.10 .55
1692 A902 28cr multi   1.10 .55
1693 A902 30cr multi   1.65 .55
  Nos. 1691-1693 (3)   3.85 1.65

Graf Zeppelin, 50th Anniversary of Atlantic Crossing A903

1980, June   **Litho.**   *Perf. 11x11½*
1694 A903 4cr multicolored   .20 .20

Pope John Paul II, St. Peter's, Rome, Congress Emblem A904

Pope, Emblem and Brazilian Churches: No. 1696, Fortaleza, vert. 24cr, Apericida 28cr, Rio de Janeiro. 30cr, Brasilia.

1980, June 24   *Perf. 12*
1695 A904 4cr multi   .20 .20
1696 A904 4cr multi   .20 .20
1697 A904 24cr multi   .90 .40
1698 A904 28cr multi   .90 .40
1699 A904 30cr multi   1.75 .40
  Nos. 1695-1699 (5)   3.95 1.60

Visit of Pope John Paul II to Brazil, June 30-July 12; 10th National Eucharistic Congress, Fortaleza, July 9-16.

1st Airmail Flight across the South Atlantic, 50th Anniv. A905

1980, June   **Litho.**   *Perf. 11x11½*
1700 A905 4cr multicolored   .20 .20

Souvenir Sheet

Yacht Sail, Exhibition Emblem — A906

1980, June   *Perf. 11½*
1701 A906 30cr multi   1.00 1.50

Brapex IV Stamp Exhib., Fortaleza, June 13-21.

Rowing, Moscow '80 Emblem A907

1980, June 30
1702 A907 4cr shown   .20 .20
1703 A907 4cr Target shooting   .20 .20
1704 A907 4cr Bicycling   .20 .20
  Nos. 1702-1704 (3)   .60 .60

22nd Summer Olympic Games, Moscow, July 19-Aug. 3.

Rondon Community Works Project A908

1980, July 11
1705 A908 4cr multicolored   .20 .20

Helen Keller and Anne Sullivan A909

1980, July 28
1706 A909 4cr multicolored   .20 .20

Helen Keller (1880-1968), blind deaf writer and lecturer taught by Anne Sullivan (1867-1936).

Souvenir Sheet

Sáo Francisco River Canoe — A910

1980, Aug. 1   **Litho.**   *Perf. 11½*
1707 A910 24cr multi   1.00 1.50

Stamp Day.

Microscope, Red Cross, Insects, Brick and Tile Houses — A911

1980, Aug. 5   **Perf. 11½x11**
1708 A911 4cr multi   .25 .20

National Health Day.

Brazilian Postal Administration, 15th Anniversary — A912

1980, Sept. 16   **Litho.**   **Perf. 12**
1709 A912 5cr multi   .25 .20

Souvenir Sheet

A913

1980, Sept. 29   **Perf. 11½x12**
1710 A913 30cr multi   1.00 1.50

St. Gabriel World Union, 6th congress.

Cattleya Amethystoglossa — A914

1980, Oct. 3   **Perf. 11½**
1711 A914 5cr *shown*   .20 .20
1712 A914 5cr *Laelia cinnabarina*   .20 .20
1713 A914 24cr *Zygopetalum crinitum*   1.10 .60
1714 A914 28cr *Laelia tenebrosa*   1.10 .60
    Nos. 1711-1714 (4)   2.60 1.60

Espamer 80, American-European Philatelic Exhibition, Madrid, Oct. 3-12.

Amazona Braziliensis A915

Captain Rodrigo, Hero of Erico Verissimo's "O Continento" A916

Parrots: #1716, Amazona Vinacea. #1717, Touit melanonota. #1718, Amazona pretrei.

1980, Oct. 18   **Litho.**   **Perf. 12**
1715 A915 5cr multi   .20 .20
1716 A915 5cr multi   .20 .20
1717 A915 28cr multi   1.10 .60
1718 A915 28cr multi   1.10 .60
    Nos. 1715-1718 (4)   2.60 1.60

Lubrapex '80 Stamp Exhib., Lisbon, Oct. 18-26.

1980, Oct. 23
1719 A916 5cr multi   .25 .20

Book Day.

Flight into Egypt A917

1980, Nov. 5
1720 A917 5cr multi   .25 .20

Christmas 1980.

Sound Waves and Oscillator Screen A918

1980, Nov. 7
1721 A918 5cr multi   .25 .20

Telebras Research Center inauguration.

Carvalho Viaduct, Paranagua-Curitiba Railroad — A919

1980, Nov. 10
1722 A919 5cr multi   .25 .20

Engineering Club centenary.

A920

A921

1980, Nov. 18   **Litho.**   **Perf. 11½**
1723 A920 5cr Portable chess board   .25 .50

Postal chess contest.

1980, Nov. 27   **Perf. 11½x11**
1724 A921 5cr Sun, wheat   .25 .40

Thanksgiving 1980

Father Anchieta Writing "Virgin Mary, Mother of God" on Sand of Iperoig Beach — A922

1980, Dec. 8   **Perf. 12**
1725 A922 5cr multi   .25 .20

Christ Carrying Cross, By O Aleijadinho A923

Antonio Francisco Lisboa (O Aleijadinho), 250th Birth Anniv.: Paintings of the life of Christ: a, Mount of Olives. b, Arrest in the Garden. c, Flagellation. d, Crown of Thorns. f, Crucifixion.

1980, Dec. 29
1726   Block of 6   1.60 1.60
a.-f. A923 5cr any single   .25 .20

Agricultural Productivity — A924

1981, Jan. 2   **Litho.**   **Perf. 11x11½**
1727 A924 30cr shown   1.25 .35
1728 A924 35cr Domestic markets   1.10 .30
1729 A924 40cr Exports   1.10 .35
    Nos. 1727-1729 (3)   3.45 1.00

Boy Scout and Campfire A925

1981, Jan. 22   **Litho.**   **Perf. 11x11½**
1730 A925 5cr shown   .25 .20
1731 A925 5cr Scouts cooking   .25 .20
1732 A925 5cr Scout, tents   .25 .20
    Nos. 1730-1732 (3)   .75 .60

4th Pan-American Scout Jamboree.

Souvenir Sheet

Mailman, 1930 — A926

1981, Mar. 11   **Litho.**   **Perf. 11**
1733   Sheet of 3   4.00 4.00
a.   A926 30cr shown   1.00 1.00
b.   A926 35cr Mailman, 1981   1.00 1.00
c.   A926 40cr Telegram messenger, 1930   1.00 1.00

Dept. of Posts & Telegraphs, 50th anniv.

Souvenir Sheet

The Hunter and the Jaguar, by Felix Taunay (1795-1881) — A927

1981, Apr. 10   **Litho.**   **Perf. 11**
1734 A927 30cr multi   1.00 2.00

Lima Barreto and Rio de Janeiro, 1900 A928

1981, May 13   **Litho.**   **Perf. 11½**
1735 A928 7cr multi   .25 .20

Lima Barreto, writer, birth centenary.

Maraca Indian Funerary Urn — A929

1981, May 18
1736 A929 7cr shown   .25 .20
1737 A929 7cr Marajoara triangular jug   .25 .20
1738 A929 7cr Tupi-Guarani bowl   .25 .20
    Nos. 1736-1738 (3)   .75 .60

Lophornis Magnifica A930

Designs: Hummingbirds.

1981, May 22   **Perf. 11½**
1739 A930 7cr shown   .30 .20
1740 A930 7cr Phaethornis pretrei   .30 .20
1741 A930 7cr Chrysolampis mosquitus   .30 .20
1742 A930 7cr Heliactin cornuta   .30 .20
    Nos. 1739-1742 (4)   1.20 .80

Rotary Emblem and Faces A931

1981, May 31
1743 A931 7cr Emblem, hands   .20 .20
1744 A931 35cr shown   1.00 .80

72nd Convention of Rotary Intl., Sao Paulo.

Environmental Protection — A932

1981, June 5 Perf. 12
1745 A932 7cr shown .25 .20
1746 A932 7cr Forest .25 .20
1747 A932 7cr Clouds (air) .25 .20
1748 A932 7cr Village (soil) .25 .20
a. Block of 4, #1745-1748 1.00 1.00

Biplane, 1931 (Airmail Service, 50th Anniv.) A933

1981, June 10 Perf. 11½
1749 A933 7cr multi .25 .20

Madeira-Mamore Railroad, 50th Anniv. of Nationalization — A934

1981, July 10 Litho. Perf. 11x11½
1750 A934 7cr multi .25 .20

66th Intl. Esperanto Congress, Brasilia A935

1981, July 26 Perf. 12
1751 A935 7cr green & blk .25 .20

No. 79 A936

1981, Aug. 1
1752 A936 50cr shown 1.40 .30
1753 A936 55cr No. 80 1.40 .30
1754 A936 60cr No. 81 1.40 .30
Nos. 1752-1754 (3) 4.20 .90
Stamp Day; cent. of "small head" stamps.

Institute of Military Engineering, 50th Anniv. — A937

1981, Aug. 11 Litho. Perf. 11½
1755 A937 12cr multi .25 .20

Reisado Dancers A938

1981, Aug. 22
1756 A938 50cr Dancers, diff. .80 .25
1757 A938 55cr Sailors .80 .25
1758 A938 60cr shown .80 .25
Nos. 1756-1758 (3) 2.40 .70

Intl. Year of the Disabled A939

1981, Sept. 17 Litho. Perf. 11½
1759 A939 12cr multi .25 .20

Flowers of the Central Plateau A940

1981, Sept. 21 Litho. Perf. 12
1760 A940 12cr Palicourea rigida .25 .20
1761 A940 12cr Dalechampia caperonioides .25 .20
1762 A940 12cr Cassia clausseni, vert. .25 .20
1763 A940 12cr Eremanthus sphaerocephalus, vert. .25 .20
Nos. 1760-1763 (4) 1.00 .80

Virgin of Nazareth Statue — A941

Christ the Redeemer Statue, Rio de Janeiro, 50th Anniv. — A942

1981, Oct. 10 Litho. Perf. 12
1764 A941 12cr multi .25 .20
Candle Festival of Nazareth, Belem.

1981, Oct. 12
1765 A942 12cr multi .25 .20

World Food Day A943

1981, Oct. 16
1766 A943 12c multi .25 .20

75th Anniv. of Santos-Dumont's First Flight — A944

1981, Oct. 23 Litho. Perf. 12
1767 A944 60cr multi 1.00 .35

Father José de Santa Rita Durao, Titlepage of his Epic Poem Caramuru, Diego Alvares Correia (Character) — A945

1981, Oct. 29
1768 A945 12cr multi .25 .20
Caramuru publication cent.; World Book Day.

Christmas 1981 A946

Designs: Creches and figurines.

1981, Nov. 10 Litho. Perf. 12
1769 A946 12cr multi .20 .20
1770 A946 50cr multi 1.25 .25
1771 A946 55cr multi, vert. 1.25 .25
1772 A946 60cr multi, vert. 1.25 .30
Nos. 1769-1772 (4) 3.95 1.00

State Flags A947

Designs: a, Alagoas. b, Bahia. c, Federal District. d, Pernambuco. e, Sergipe.

1981, Nov. 19
1773 Block of 5 + label 1.25 1.25
a.-e. A947 12cr, any single .20 .20
Label shows arms of Brazil.
See #1830, 1892, 1962, 2037, 2249, 2726-2727.

Thanksgiving 1981 — A948

1981, Nov. 26 Litho. Perf. 11½
1776 A948 12cr multi .25 .20

Ministry of Labor, 50th Anniv. A949

1981, Nov. 26
1777 A949 12cr multi .20 .20

School of Engineering, Itajuba — A950

1981, Nov. 30 Perf. 11x11½
1778 A950 15cr lt grn & pur .35 .20
Theodomiro C. Santiago, founder, birth centenary.

Sao Paulo State Police Sesquicentennial A951

1981, Dec. 15 Litho. Perf. 12
1779 A951 12cr Policeman with saxophone .20 .20
1780 A951 12cr Mounted policemen .20 .20

Army Library Centenary A952

1981, Dec. 17
1781 A952 12cr multi .20 .20

Souvenir Sheet

A953

1981, Dec. 18 Perf. 11
1782 A953 180cr multi 4.50 4.50
Philatelic Club of Brazil, 50th anniv.

Brigadier Eduardo Gomes A954

1982, Jan. 20 Litho. Perf. 11x11½
1783 A954 12cr blue & blk .30 .20

Birth Centenary of Henrique Lage, Industrialist — A956

1982, Mar. 14 Litho. Perf. 11½
1785 A956 17cr multi .50 .20

1982 World Cup Soccer A957

TB Bacillus
Cent. — A958

Designs: Various soccer players.

1982, Mar. 19
1786	A957	75cr multi	.75	.25
1787	A957	80cr multi	.75	.30
1788	A957	85cr multi	.75	.30
	Nos. 1786-1788 (3)		2.25	.85

Souvenir Sheet
Imperf
1789		Sheet of 3	3.00	6.00
a.	A957	100cr like #1786	1.00	
b.	A957	100cr like #1787	1.00	
c.	A957	100cr like #1788	1.00	

1982, Mar. 24 **Perf. 12**
1790	A958	90cr Microscope, lung	1.25	.80
1791	A958	100cr Lung, pills	1.25	.90
a.		Pair, #1790-1791	2.50	2.00

Souvenir Sheet

BrapexV BLUMENAU - SC

V EXPOSIÇÃO FILATÉLICA BRASILEIRA

A959

1982, Apr. 17 **Litho.** **Perf. 11**
1792	A959	Sheet of 3	3.50	3.25
a.		75cr Laelia Purpurata	1.00	.50
b.		80cr Oncidium flexuosum	1.00	.50
c.		85cr Cleistes revoluta	1.25	.55

BRAPEX V Stamp Exhibition, Blumenau.

Oil Drilling
Centenary
A960

1982, Apr. 18 **Perf. 11½**
1793	A960	17cr multi	.25	.20

400th Birth
Anniv. of
St. Vincent
de Paul
A961

1982, Apr. 24 **Litho.** **Perf. 11½**
1794	A961	17cr multi	.25	.20

Seven
Steps of
Guaira
(Waterfalls)
A962

1982, Apr. 29
1795	A962	17cr Fifth Fall	.20	.20
1796	A962	21cr Seventh Fall	.30	.20

Ministry of Communications, 15th
Anniv. — A963

1982, May 15
1797	A963	21cr multi	.25	.20

Museology
Course,
Natl.
Historical
Museum,
50th Anniv.
A964

1982, May 18
1798	A964	17cr blk & sal pink	.20	.20

Vale de Rio
Doce Mining
Co. — A965

1982, June 1
1799	A965	17cr Gears	.25	.20

Martin
Afonso de
Souza
Reading
Charter to
Settlers
A966

1982, June 3 **Litho.** **Perf. 11½**
1800	A966	17cr multi	.25	.20

Town of Sao Vincente, 450th anniv.

Armadillo
A967

1982, June 4
1801	A967	17cr shown	.55	.20
1802	A967	21cr Wolves	.55	.20
1803	A967	30cr Deer	1.65	.25
	Nos. 1801-1803 (3)		2.75	.65

Film Strip
and Award
A968

1982, June 19
1804	A968	17cr multi	.25	.20

20th anniv. of Golden Palm award for The
Promise Keeper, Cannes Film Festival.

Souvenir Sheet

50th Anniv. of Constitutionalist
Revolution — A969

1982, July 9 **Litho.** **Perf. 11**
1805	A969	140cr multi	1.75	1.75

Church of Our
Lady of
O'Sabara — A970

St. Francis of
Assisi, 800th Birth
Anniv. — A971

Baroque Architecture, Minas Gerais State:
No. 1807, Church of Our Lady of the Rosary,
Diamantina. No. 1808, Town Square, Mariana.

1982, July 16 **Perf. 11½**
1806	A970	17cr multi	.25	.20
1807	A970	17cr multi, horiz.	.25	.20
1808	A970	17cr multi, horiz.	.25	.20
	Nos. 1806-1808 (3)		.75	.60

1982, July 24
1809	A971	21cr multi	.20	.20

Stamp Day
and
Centenary of
Pedro II
"Large
Head"
Stamps
A972

1982, Aug. 1
1810	A972	21cr No. 82	.25	.20

Port of
Manaus
Free
Trade
Zone
A973

1982, Aug. 15 **Perf. 11x11½**
1811	A973	75cr multi	.65	.35

Scouting Year — A974

1982, Aug. 21 **Litho.** **Perf. 11**
1812	A974	Sheet of 2	2.75	3.75
a.		85cr Baden-Powell	1.00	1.10
b.		185cr Scout	1.65	2.00

Orixas Folk
Costumes of
African
Origin
A975

1982, Aug. 21 **Perf. 11½**
1813	A975	20cr Iemanja	.20	.20
1814	A975	20cr Xango	.20	.20
1815	A975	20cr Oxumare	.20	.20
	Nos. 1813-1815 (3)		.60	.60

10th Anniv.
of Central
Bank of
Brazil
Currency
Museum
A976

1982, Aug. 31
1816	A976	25cr 12-florin coin, 1645, obverse and reverse	.25	.20
1817	A976	25cr Emperor Pedro's 6.40-reis coronation coin, 1822	.25	.20

National
Week
A977

1982, Sept. 1
1818	A977	25cr Don Pedro proclaiming independence	.38	.25

A978   A979

1982, Oct. 4
1819	A978	85cr Portrait	1.00	.60

St. Theresa of Avila (1515-1582).

1982, Oct. 15 **Litho.** **Perf. 11½x11**
1820	A979	75cr Instruments	.65	.40
1821	A979	80cr Dancers	.65	.40
1822	A979	85cr Musicians	.70	.40
a.		Souv. sheet, #1820-1822, perf 11	2.75	2.75
	Nos. 1820-1822 (3)		2.00	1.20

Lubrapex '82, 4th Portuguese-Brazilian
Stamp Exhibition. Stamps in No. 1822a are
without "LUBRAPEX 82."

Aviation Industry Day A980

1982, Oct. 17 *Perf. 12*
1823 A980 24cr Embraer EMB-312
trainer plane .25 .20

Bastos Tigre, Poet, Birth Centenary, and "Saudade" Text A981

1982, Oct. 29
1824 A981 24cr multi .25 .20

Book Day.

10th Anniv. of Brazilian Telecommunications Co. — A982

1982, Nov. 9 *Litho.* *Perf. 11½*
1825 A982 24cr multi .25 .20

Christmas 1982 A983

Children's Drawings.

1982, Nov. 10
1826 A983 24cr Nativity .25 .20
1827 A983 24cr Angels .25 .20
1828 A983 30cr Nativity, diff. .30 .45
1829 A983 30cr Flight into Egypt .30 .45
Nos. 1826-1829 (4) 1.10 1.30

State Flags Type of 1981

Designs: a, Ceara. b, Espirito Santo. c, Paraiba. d, Grande de Norte. e, Rondonia.

1982, Nov. 19
1830 Block of 5 + label 5.25 5.25
a.-e. A947 24cr any single 1.00 .20

Thanksgiving 1982 — A985

1982, Nov. 25
1835 A985 24cr multi .25 .20

Homage to the Deaf — A986

1982, Dec. 1
1836 A986 24cr multi .25 .20

Naval Academy Bicentenary A987

Training Ships.

1982, Dec. 14
1837 A987 24cr Brazil .35 .20
1838 A987 24cr Benjamin Constant .35 .20
1839 A987 24cr Almirante Saldanha .35 .20
Nos. 1837-1839 (3) 1.05 .60

Souvenir Sheet

No. 12 — A988

1982, Dec. 18 *Litho.* *Perf. 11*
1840 A988 200cr multi 4.00 5.00

BRASILIANA '83 Intl. Stamp Exhibition, Rio de Janeiro, July 29-Aug. 7.

Brasiliana '83 Carnival A989

1983, Feb. 9 *Litho.* *Perf. 11½*
1841 A989 24cr Samba drummers .20 .20
1842 A989 130cr Street parade 1.40 .50
1843 A989 140cr Dancer 1.40 .50
1844 A989 150cr Male dancer 1.40 .55
Nos. 1841-1844 (4) 4.40 1.75

Antarctic Expedition A990

1983, Feb. 20 *Litho.* *Perf. 11½*
1845 A990 150cr Support ship Barano de Teffe 2.00 .55

50th Anniv. of Women's Rights — A991

1983, Mar. 8
1846 A991 130cr multi 1.25 .50

Itaipu Hydroelectric Power Station Opening — A992

1983, Mar. *Litho.* *Perf. 12*
1847 A992 140cr multi 1.90 .40

Cancer Prevention A993

Martin Luther (1483-1546) A994

30cr, Microscope. 38cr, Antonio Prudente, Paulista Cancer Assoc. founder, Camargo Hospital.

1983, Apr. 18
1848 A993 30cr multi .30 .20
1849 A993 38cr multi .30 .20
a. Pair, #1848-1849 .65 .35

1983, Apr. 18
1850 A994 150cr pale grn & blk 1.25 .50

Agricultural Research A995

1983, Apr. 26 *Litho.* *Perf. 11½*
1851 A995 30cr Chestnut tree .20 .20
1852 A995 30cr Genetic research .20 .20
1853 A995 38cr Tropical soy beans .25 .20
Nos. 1851-1853 (3) .65 .60

Father Rogerio Neuhaus (1863-1934), Centenary of Ordination — A996

1983, May 3 *Perf. 11½x11*
1854 A996 30cr multi .25 .20

30th Anniv. of Customs Cooperation Council — A997

1983, May 5 *Perf. 11x11½*
1855 A997 30cr multi .25 .20

World Communications Year — A998

1983, May 17 *Litho.* *Perf. 11½*
1856 A998 250cr multi 1.50 .45

Toucans A999

1983, May 21
1857 A999 30cr Tucanucu .20 .20
1858 A999 185cr White-breasted 1.25 .40
1859 A999 205cr Green-beaked 1.25 .40
1860 A999 215cr Black-beaked 1.25 .45
Nos. 1857-1860 (4) 3.95 1.45

Souvenir Sheet

Resurrection, by Raphael (1483-1517) — A1000

1983, May 25 *Perf. 11*
1861 A1000 250cr multi 2.50 3.00

Hohenzollern 980 Locomotive,
1875 — A1001

Various locomotives.

1983, June 12　　Litho.　　Perf. 11½
1862 A1001 30cr shown　　　　　.25 .20
1863 A1001 30cr Baldwin #1, 1881 .25 .20
1864 A1001 38cr Fowler #1, 1872 .30 .20
　　Nos. 1862-1864 (3)　　　　.80 .60

9th Women's
Basketball World
Championship
A1002

1983, July 24　　Litho.　　Perf. 11½x11
1865 A1002 30cr Players, front view .20 .20
1866 A1002 30cr Players, rear view .20 .20

Simon Bolivar (1783-1830) — A1003

1983, July 24　　　　　Perf. 12
1867 A1003 30cr multi　　　　　.20 .20

Children's Polio and Measles
Vaccination Campaign — A1004

1983, July 25
1868 A1004 30cr Girl, measles　.20 .20
1869 A1004 30cr Boy, polio　　.20 .20

A1005　　　　　　A1006

1983, July 28　　　　Perf. 11½x11
1870 A1005 30cr Minerva (goddess
　　　　　　of wisdom), com-
　　　　　　puter tape　　.20 .20
　20th Anniv. of Master's program in
engineering.

1983, July 29　　　　　Engr.
Guanabara Bay.
1871 A1006 185cr No. 1　　1.50 .40
1872 A1006 205cr No. 2　　1.50 .40
1873 A1006 215cr No. 3　　1.50 .45
　　Nos. 1871-1873 (3)　　4.50 1.25

Souvenir Sheet
Perf. 11
1874　　　Sheet of 3　　8.00 10.00
　a.　A1006 185cr No. 1　2.00 3.00
　b.　A1006 205cr No. 2　2.00 3.00
　c.　A1006 215cr No. 3　2.00 3.00
　BRASILIANA '83 Intl. Stamp Show, Rio de
Janeiro, July 29-Aug. 7.
　Stamps in No. 1874 have unframed denomination at bottom of the stamps. The background scene is enlarged to cover all 3 stamps
in a continuous design.

Souvenir Sheets
　A set of five 2000cr souvenir sheets
also exist for BRASILIANA '83. These
picture early flying attempts, Ademar
Ferreira da Silva, Olympic gold medal
winner, Soccer, Formula 1 auto racing,
and Gold medal winners in Olympic
sailing.

Souvenir Sheet

The First Mass in Brazil, by Vitor
Meireles (1833-1903) — A1007

1983, Aug. 18　　　　　Perf. 11
1875 A1007 250cr multi　　3.00 1.50

EMB-120
Brasilia
Passenger
Plane
A1008

1983, Aug. 19　　　　　Perf. 12
1876 A1008 30cr multi　　　.25 .20

Vision of
Don Bosco
Centenary
A1009

1983, Aug. 30
1877 A1009 130cr multi　　　.75 .25

Independence Week — A1010

1983, Sept. 1　　Litho.　　Perf. 11½
1878 A1010 50cr multi　　　.25 .20

National
Steel Corp.,
10th Anniv.
A1011

1983, Sept. 17　　Litho.　　Perf. 11½
1879 A1011 45cr multi　　　.25 .20

Cactus
A1012

1983, Sept. 12　　Litho.　　Perf. 11½
1880 A1012 45cr Pilosocereus
　　　　　gounellei　　　　.30 .20
1881 A1012 45cr Melocactus
　　　　　bahiensis　　　.30 .20
1882 A1012 57cr Cereus jamacaru .40 .20
　　Nos. 1880-1882 (3)　　1.00 .60

1st National
Eucharistic
Congress
A1013

1983, Oct. 12　　Litho.　　Perf. 11½
1883 A1013 45cr multi　　　.25 .20

World Food
Program
A1014

1983, Oct. 14　　Litho.　　Perf. 11½
1884 A1014 45cr Mouth, grain　.30 .20
1885 A1014 57cr Fish, sailboat　.40 .20

Souvenir Sheet

Louis Breguet, Death
Centenary — A1015

1983, Oct. 27　　Litho.　　Perf. 11
1886 A1015 376cr Telegraph
　　　　　transmitter　4.25 1.50

Christmas
1983
A1016

　17th-18th Cent. Statues: 45cr, Our Lady of
the Angels. 315cr, Our Lady of the Parturition.
335cr, Our Lady of Joy. 345cr, Our Lady of
the Presentation.

1983, Nov. 10　　Litho.　　Perf. 11½
1887 A1016 45cr multi　　　.25 .20
1888 A1016 315cr multi　　1.65 .60
1889 A1016 335cr multi　　1.65 .65
1890 A1016 345cr multi　　1.65 .70
　　Nos. 1887-1890 (4)　　5.20 2.15

Marshal Mascarenhas Birth
Centenary — A1017

1983, Nov. 13　　Litho.　　Perf. 11½
1891 A1017 45cr Battle sites　.20 .20
　Commander of Brazilian Expeditionary
Force in Italy.

State Flags Type of 1981
　Designs: a, Amazonas. b, Goias. c, Rio. d,
Mato Grosso Do Sol. e, Parana.

1983, Nov. 17　　Litho.　　Perf. 11½
1892　　Block of 5 + label　3.00 3.00
　a.-e.　A947 45cr any single　.50 .20

Thanksgiving — A1018

1983, Nov. 24　　Litho.　　Perf. 12
1896 A1018 45cr Madonna, wheat .35 .20

Manned Flight
Bicentenary
A1019

1983, Dec. 15　　Litho.　　Perf. 12
1897 A1019 345cr Montgolfiere
　　　　balloon, 1783　5.00 .50

Ethnic
Groups
A1020

1984, Jan. 20　　Litho.　　Perf. 12
1898 A1020 45cr multi　　　.20 .20

　50th anniv. of publication of Masters and
Slaves, sociological study by Gilberto Freyre.

Centenary
of Crystal
Palace,
Petropolis
A1021

1984, Feb. 2
1899 A1021 45cr multi　　　.20 .20

Souvenir Sheet

Flags (Sculpture with 40 Figures), by
Victor Brecheret (b. 1894) — A1022

1984, Feb. 22   Litho.   Perf. 11
1900 A1022 805cr multi   1.50 1.00

Naval
Museum
Centenary
A1023

1984, Mar. 23   Litho.   Perf. 11½
1901 A1023 620cr Figurehead,
frigate, 1847   .85 .50

Slavery
Abolition
Centenary
A1024

1984, Mar. 25
1902 A1024 585cr Broken chain,
raft   .85 .55
1903 A1024 610cr Freed slave   .90 .60

Souvenir Sheet

Visit of King Carl XVI Gustaf of
Sweden — A1025

1984, Apr. 2   Perf. 11
1904 A1025 2105cr multi   3.50 2.50

1984
Summer
Olympics
A1026

1984, Apr. 13   Perf. 11½
1905 A1026 65cr Long jump   .20 .20
1906 A1026 65cr 100-meter
race   .20 .20
1907 A1026 65cr Relay race   .20 .20
1908 A1026 585cr Pole vault   .80 .65
1909 A1026 610cr High jump   .85 .70
1910 A1026 620cr Hurdles   .90 .80
   a.   Block of 6, #1905-1910   3.00 3.00

Voters
Casting
Ballots,
Symbols of
Labor
A1027

Pres. Getulio Vargas Birth Centenary: Symbols of Development.

1984, Apr. 19   Litho.   Perf. 11½
1911 A1027 65cr shown   .20 .20
1912 A1027 65cr Oil rig, blast furnace   .20 .20
1913 A1027 65cr High-tension towers   .20 .20
   Nos. 1911-1913 (3)   .60 .60

Columbus, Espana
'84
Emblem — A1028

1984, Apr. 27
1914 A1028   65cr Pedro Cabral   .20 .20
1915 A1028 610cr shown   1.25 .70

Map of Americas,   Lubrapex
Heads — A1029   '84 — A1030

1984, May 7   Litho.   Perf. 11½
1916 A1029 65cr multi   .20 .20

Pan-American Association of Finance and
Guarantees, 8th Assembly.

1984, May 8   Perf. 11½x11
18th Century Paintings, Mariana Cathedral.
1917 A1030   65cr Hunting scene   .20   .20
1918 A1030 585cr Pastoral scene   .75   .40
1919 A1030 610cr People under
umbrellas   .80   .50
1920 A1030 620cr Elephants   .85   .50
   Nos. 1917-1920 (4)   2.60 1.60

Souvenir Sheet

Intl. Fedn. of Soccer Associations,
80th Anniv. — A1031

1984, May 21   Perf. 11
1921 A1031 2115cr Globe   3.50 1.75

Matto
Grosso
Lowland
Fauna
A1032

1984, June 5   Litho.   Perf. 11½
1922   Strip of 3   .60 .30
   a.   A1032 65cr Deer   .20 .20
   b.   A1032 65cr Jaguar   .20 .20
   c.   A1032 80cr Alligator   .20 .20

First Letter Mailed in
Brazil, by Guido
Mondin — A1033

1984, June 8   Perf. 12x11½
1923 A1033 65cr multi   .20 .20
Postal Union of Americas and Spain, first
anniv. of new headquarters.

Brazil-Germany Air Service, 50th
Anniv. — A1034

1984, June 19
1924   610cr Dornier-Wal seaplane   1.00 .70
1925   620cr Steamer Westfalen   1.05 .70
   a. A1034 Pair, #1924-1925   2.05 1.50

Woolly Spider
Monkey, World
Wildlife Fund
Emblem — A1036

1984, July 6   Perf. 11½
1926 A1036 65cr Mother, baby   .50 .20
1927 A1036 80cr Monkey   .30 .20

Agriculture Type of 1980

Designs: 65cr, Rubber tree. 80cr, Brazil
nuts. 120cr, Rice. 150cr, Eucalyptus. 300cr,
Pinha da Parana. 800cr, Carnauba. 1000cr,
Babacu. 2000cr, Sunflower.

**Photogravure (65, 80, 120, 150cr),
Engraved**

1984-85   Perf. 11x11½
1934 A894   65cr lilac   .20   .20
1935 A894   80cr brn red   .25   .20
1936 A894 120cr dk sl bl   .35   .20
1937 A894 150cr green   .20   .20
1938 A894 300cr rose mag   .50   .20
1939 A894 800cr grnsh bl   1.40 .20
1940 A894 1000cr lemon   1.40 .20
1941 A894 2000cr yel org ('85)   .75   .25
   Nos. 1934-1941 (8)   5.05 1.65

Marajo
Isld.
Buffalo
A1037

1984, July 9   Litho.   Perf. 12
1942   Strip of 3   .50 .30
   a.   A1037 65cr Approaching stream .20 .20
   b.   A1037 65cr Standing on bank   .20 .20
   c.   A1037 80cr Drinking   .20 .20

Continuous design.

Banco Economico
Sesquicentenary — A1038

1984, July 13   Perf. 11½
1943 A1038 65cr Bank, coins   .20 .20

Historic
Railway
Stations
A1039

1984, July 23   Litho.   Perf. 11½
1944 A1039 65cr Japeri   .20 .20
1945 A1039 65cr Luz, vert.   .20 .20
1946 A1039 80cr Sao Joao del Rei   .20 .20
   Nos. 1944-1946 (3)   .60 .60

A1040   A1041

1984, Aug. 13   Perf. 11
Souvenir Sheet
1947 A1040 585cr Girl scout   1.40 1.00
Girl Scouts in Brazil, 65th anniv.

1984, Aug. 21   Litho.   Perf. 11½
1948 A1041 65cr Couple sheltered
from rain   .20 .20
Housing project bank, 20th anniv.

Independence Week — A1042

Children's Drawings.

1984, Sept. 3
1949 A1042 100cr Explorer & ship   .20 .20
1950 A1042 100cr Sailing ships   .20 .20
1951 A1042 100cr "BRASIL" mural   .20 .20
1952 A1042 100cr Children under
rainbow   .20 .20
   Nos. 1949-1952 (4)   .80 .80

Rio de Janeiro Chamber of Commerce
Sesquicentenary — A1043

1984, Sept. 10
1953 A1043 100cr Monument,
worker silhou-
ette   .20 .20

Death Sesquicentenary of Don Pedro I
(IV of Portugal) — A1044

1984, Sept. 23   *Perf. 12x11½*
1954 A1044 1000cr Portrait   1.50 1.10

Local Mushrooms
A1045

Book
Day — A1046

1984, Oct. 22   *Perf. 11½*
1955 A1045 120cr Pycnoporus
      sanguineus   .20 .20
1956 A1045 1050cr Calvatia sp   1.10 1.25
1957 A1045 1080cr Pleurotus sp,
      horiz.   1.20 1.30
    Nos. 1955-1957 (3)   2.50 2.75

1984, Oct. 23   *Perf. 11½*
1958 A1046 120cr Girl in open
      book   .20 .20

New State Mint
Opening — A1047

1984, Nov. 1
1959 A1047 120cr multi   .20 .20

Informatics
Fair &
Congress
A1048

1984, Nov. 5   *Litho.*   *Perf. 12*
1960 A1048 120cr Eye, computer
      terminal   .20 .20

Org. of American
States, 14th
Assembly
A1049

1984, Nov. 14
1961 A1049 120cr Emblem, flags   .20 .20

State Flags Type of 1981
Designs: a, Maranhaio. b, Mato Grosso. c,
Minas Gerais. d, Piaui. e, Santa Catarina.

1984, Nov. 19   *Perf. 11½*
1962   Block of 5 + label   1.00 1.00
  a.-e. A947 120cr, any single   .20 .20

Thanksgiving
1984 — A1051

1984, Nov. 22
1963 A1051 120cr Bell tower,
      Brasilia   .20 .20

Christmas
1984
A1052

Paintings: No. 1964, Nativity, by Djanira. No.
1965, Virgin and Child, by Glauco Rodrigues.
No. 1966, Flight into Egypt, by Paul Garfunkel.
No. 1967, Nativity, by Di Cavalcanti.

1984, Dec. 3   *Litho.*   *Perf. 12*
1964 A1052 120cr multi   .20 .20
1965 A1052 120cr multi   .20 .20
1966 A1052 1050cr multi   .85 .40
1967 A1052 1080cr multi   .85 .40
    Nos. 1964-1967 (4)   2.10 1.20

40th Anniv., International Civil Aviation
Organization — A1053

1984, Dec. 7   *Litho.*   *Perf. 12*
1968 A1053 120cr Aircraft, Earth
      globe   .20 .20

25th Anniv., North-Eastern
Development — A1054

1984, Dec. 14   *Litho.*   *Perf. 12*
1969 A1054 120cr Farmer, field   .20 .20

Emilio
Rouede
A1055

Painting: Church of the Virgin of Safe Travels, by Rouede.

1985, Jan. 22   *Litho.*   *Perf. 12*
1970 A1055 120cr multi   .20 .20

BRASILSAT — A1056

1985, Feb. 8   *Litho.*   *Perf. 11½x12*
1971 A1056 150cr Satellite, Brazil   .20 .20

Metropolitan Railways — A1057

1985, Mar. 2   *Litho.*   *Perf. 11x11½*
1972 A1057 200cr Passenger trains   .20 .20

Brasilia
Botanical
Gardens
A1058

1985, Mar. 8   *Litho.*   *Perf. 11½x12*
1973 A1058 200cr Caryocar
      brasiliense   .20 .20

40th Anniv.,
Brazilian
Paratroops
A1059

1985, Mar. 8   *Litho.*   *Perf. 11½x12*
1974 A1059 200cr Parachute drop   .20 .20

Natl. Climate Awareness
Program — A1060

1985, Mar. 18   *Litho.*   *Perf. 11½x12*
1975 A1060 500cr multi   .20 .20

Pure Bred
Horses
A1061

1985, Mar. 19   *Litho.*   *Perf. 12*
1976 A1061 1000cr Campolina   .40 .25
1977 A1061 1500cr Marajoara   .70 .35
1978 A1061 1500cr Mangalarga
      marchador   .70 .35
    Nos. 1976-1978 (3)   1.80 .95

Ouro Preto — A1062

1985, Apr. 18   *Litho.*   *Perf. 11½x12*
1979 A1062 220cr shown   .20 .20
1980 A1062 220cr St. Miguel des
      Missoes   .20 .20
1981 A1062 220cr Olinda   .20 .20
    Nos. 1979-1981 (3)   .60 .60

Polivolume, by Mary
Vieira — A1063

1985, Apr. 20   *Litho.*
1982 A1063 220cr multi   .20 .20
Rio Branco Inst., 40th anniv.

Natl. Capital, Brasilia, 25th
Anniv. — A1064

1985, Apr. 22   *Litho.*
1983 A1064 220cr Natl. Theater,
      acoustic shell   .20 .20
1984 A1064 220cr Catetinho Palace, JK Memorial   .20 .20

A1065

A1065a

1985-86   *Photo.*   *Perf. 11½*
1985 A1065   50cr lake   .20 .20
1986 A1065   100cr dp vio   .20 .20
1987 A1065   150cr violet   .20 .20
1988 A1065   200cr ultra   .20 .20
1989 A1065   220cr green   .20 .20
1990 A1065   300cr royal bl   .20 .20
1991 A1065   500cr olive blk   .30 .25
1992 A1065a 1000cr brn ol ('86)   .20 .20
1993 A1065a 2000cr brt grn ('86)   .30 .25
1994 A1065a 3000cr dl vio   .40 .30
1995 A1065a 5000cr brown   .60 .45
    Nos. 1985-1995 (11)   3.00 2.65

Marshal
Rondon,
120th
Birth
Anniv.
A1066

1985, May 5   *Perf. 11x11½*
1996 A1066 220cr multi   .20 .20
Educator, protector of the Indians, building
superintendent of telegraph lines.

Candido
Fontoura (1885-
1974)
A1067

Brapex VI
A1068

1985, May 14　　　*Perf. 12x11½*
1997 A1067 220cr multi　　　.20 .20
Pioneer of the Brazilian pharmaceutical
industry.

1985, May 18　　　*Perf. 11½x11*
Cave paintings: No. 1998, Deer, Cerca
Grande. No. 1999, Lizards, Lapa do Caboclo.
No. 2000, Running deer, Grande Abrigo de
Santana do Riacho.

1998 A1068　300cr multi　　.20 .20
1999 A1068　300cr multi　　.20 .20
2000 A1068　2000cr multi　　.75 .50
a.　　Souvenir sheet of 3, #1998-
　　　2000, perf. 10½x11　　1.00 1.00
　　Nos. 1998-2000 (3)　　1.15 .90

Wildlife Conservation — A1069

Birds in Marinho dos Abrolhos National
Park.

1985, June 5　　　*Perf. 11½x12*
2001 A1069　220cr Fregata
　　　　　magnificens　　.20 .20
2002 A1069　220cr Sula dactyla-
　　　　　tra　　　.20 .20
2003 A1069　220cr Anous
　　　　　stolidus　　.20 .20
2004 A1069　2000cr Pluvialis
　　　　　squatarola　　.60 .25
　　Nos. 2001-2004 (4)　　1.20 .85

A1070

A1071

1985, June 11　　　*Perf. 12x11½*
2005 A1070　220cr Mother
　　　　breastfeeding
　　　　infant　　　.20 .20
2006 A1070　220cr Hand, eyedrop-
　　　　per, children　.20 .20
a.　　Pair, #2005-2006　　.25 .20
　　UN infant survival campaign.

1985, June 22　Litho.　Perf. 11½x11
Helicopter rescue, search ship, diver.
2007 A1071　220cr multi　　.20 .20
　　Sea Search & Rescue.

Souvenir Sheet

World Cup Soccer, Mexico,
1986 — A1072

1985, June 23　　　*Perf. 11*
2008 A1072　2000cr Player drib-
　　　　bling, World
　　　　Cup　　　4.00 .85

Intl. Youth
Year — A1073

1985, June 28　　　*Perf. 12*
2009 A1073　220cr Circle of children .20 .20

1985, July 16　　　*Perf. 12x11½*
2010 A1074　2000cr Mosaic, Priest
　　　　raising host　　.55 .40

11th Natl.
Eucharistic
Congress
A1074

Director Humberto Mauro, Scene from
Sangue Mineiro, 1929 — A1075

1985, July 27
2011 A1075　300cr multi　　.20 .20
　　Cataguases Studios, 60th anniv.

Escola e Sacro Museum, Convent St.
Anthony, Joao Pessoa, Paraiba
A1076

1985, Aug. 5　　　*Perf. 11½x12*
2012 A1076　330cr multi　　.20 .20
　　Paraiba State 400th anniv.

Inconfidencia
Museum
A1077

Cabanagem
Insurrection,
150th
Anniv. — A1078

1985, Aug. 11　　　*Perf. 12x11½*
2013 A1077　300cr shown　　.20 .20
2014 A1077　300cr Museum of His-
　　　　tory & Diplo-
　　　　macy　　　.20 .20

1985, Aug. 14
Design: Revolutionary, detail from an oil
painting by Guido Mondin.
2015 A1078　330cr multi　　.20 .20

AMX
Subsonic
Air Force
Fighter
Plane
A1079

1985, Aug. 19　　　*Perf. 11½x12*
2016 A1079　330cr multi　　.20 .20
　　AMX Project, joint program with Italy.

16th-17th Century
Military Uniforms
A1080

1985, Aug. 26　　　*Perf. 12x11½*
2017 A1080　300cr Captain, cross-
　　　　bowman　　.20 .20
2018 A1080　300cr Harquebusier,
　　　　sergeant　　.20 .20
2019 A1080　300cr Musketeer, pike-
　　　　man　　　.20 .20
2020 A1080　300cr Fusilier, pikeman　.20 .20
　　Nos. 2017-2020 (4)　　.80 .80

Farrouphilha Insurrection, 150th
Anniv. — A1081

Design: Bento Goncalves and insurrection-
ist cavalry on Southern battlefields, detail of an
oil painting by Guido Mondin.

1985, Sept. 20　　　*Perf. 11½x12*
2021 A1081　330cr multi　　.20 .20

Aparados
da Serra
National
Park
A1082

1985, Sept. 23
2022 A1082　3100cr Ravine　　.65 .50
2023 A1082　3320cr Mountains　.70 .55
2024 A1082　3480cr Forest, wa-
　　　　terfall　　.75 .60
　　Nos. 2022-2024 (3)　　2.10 1.65

President-elect Tancredo
Neves — A1083

Design: Portrait, Natl. Congress, Alvorada
Palace, Federal Supreme Court.

1985, Oct. 10　Litho.　Perf. 11x11½
2025 A1083　330cr multi　　.20 .20

FEB,
Postmark
A1084

1985, Oct. 10　　　*Perf. 11½x12*
2026 A1084　500cr multi　　.20 .20
　　Brazilian Expeditionary Force Postal Service, 41st anniv.

Rio de Janeiro-Niteroi Ferry Service,
150th Anniv. — A1085

1985, Oct. 14　　　*Perf. 11½x12*
2027 A1085　500cr Segunda　　.20 .20
2028 A1085　500cr Terceira　　.20 .20
2029 A1085　500cr Especuladora　.20 .20
2030 A1085　500cr Urca　　.20 .20
　　Nos. 2027-2030 (4)　　.80 .80

Muniz M-7 Inaugural Flight, 50th
Anniv. — A1086

1985, Oct. 22
2031 A1086　500cr multi　　.20 .20

UN 40th Anniv.
A1087

Natl. Press
System
A1088

1985, Oct. 24　　　*Perf. 11½x11*
2032 A1087　500cr multi　　.20 .20

1985, Nov. 7

2033 A1088 500cr Newspaper masthead, reader .20 .20

Diario de Pernambuco, newspaper, 160th anniv.

Christmas 1985 A1089

1985, Nov. 11   *Perf. 11½x12*

2034 A1089 500cr Christ in Manger .20 .20
2035 A1089 500cr Adoration of the Magi .20 .20
2036 A1089 500cr Flight to Egypt .20 .20
    Nos. 2034-2036 (3) .60 .60

State Flags Type of 1981

a, Para. b, Rio Grande do Sul. c, Acre. d, Sao Paulo.

1985, Nov. 19   *Perf. 12*

2037   Block of 4 .80 .60
   a.-d. A947 500cr, any single .20 .20

Thanksgiving Day — A1091

1985, Nov. 28   *Perf. 12x11½*

2038 A1091 500cr Child gathering wheat .20 .20

Economic Development of Serra dos Carajas Region — A1092

1985, Dec. 11   Litho.   *Perf. 11½x12*

2039 A1092 500cr multi .20 .20

Fr. Bartholomeu Lourenco de Gusmao (1685-1724), Inventor, the Aerostat — A1093

1985, Dec. 19   Litho.   *Perf. 11x11½*

2040 A1093 500cr multi .20 .20

A1094

A1095

The Trees, by Da Costa E Silva (b. 1885), poet.

1985, Dec. 20   Litho.   *Perf. 12x11½*

2041 A1094 500cr multi .20 .20

1986, Mar. 3   Litho.   *Perf. 11*
Souvenir Sheet

2042 A1095 10000cr multi 2.25 2.00

1986 World Cup Soccer Championships, Mexico. LUBRAPEX '86, philatelic exhibition.

Halley's Comet — A1096

1986, Apr. 11   Litho.   *Perf. 11½x12*

2043 A1096 50c multi .20 .20

Commander Ferraz Antarctic Station, 2nd Anniv. — A1097

1986, Apr. 25

2044 A1097 50c multi .20 .20

Labor Day — A1098

1986, May 1   Litho.   *Perf. 12x11½*

2045 A1098 50c multi .20 .20

Maternity, by Henrique Bernardelli (1858-1936) A1099

1986, May 8

2046 A1099 50c multi .20 .20

Amnesty Intl., 25th Anniv. A1100

1986, May 28   Litho.   *Perf. 11½x12*

2047 A1100 50c multi .20 .20

Butterflies A1101

1986, June 5   *Perf. 12x11½*

2048 A1101 50c Pyrrhopyge rufi- cauda .20 .20
2049 A1101 50c Prepona eugenes diluta .20 .20
2050 A1101 50c Pierriballia mandel molione .20 .20
    Nos. 2048-2050 (3) .60 .60

Score from Opera "Il Guarani" and Antonio Carlos Gomes (1836-1896), Composer — A1102

1986, July 11   *Perf. 11½x12*

2051 A1102 50c multi .20 .20

Natl. Accident Prevention Campaign — A1103

1986, July 30   Litho.   *Perf. 11½x11*

2052 A1103 50c Lineman .20 .20

Souvenir Sheet

Stamp Day — A1104

1986, Aug. 1   *Perf. 11*

2053 A1104 5cz No. 53 .85 .35

Brazilian Phil. Soc., 75th anniv., and Dom Pedro II issue, Nos. 53-60, 120th anniv.

Architecture A1105   Famous Men A1106

Designs: 10c, House of Garcia D'Avila, Nazare de Mata, Bahia. 20c, Church of Our Lady of the Assumption, Anchieta Village. 50c, Fort Reis Magos, Natal. 1cz, Pilgrim's Column, Alcantara Village, 1648. 2cz, Cloisters, St. Francis Convent, Olinda. 5cz, St. Anthony's Chapel, Sao Roque. 10cz, St. Lawrence of the Indians Church, Niteroi. 20cz, Principe da Beiro Fort, Mato Dentro. 50cz, Jesus of Matozinhos Church, vert. 100cz, Church of our Lady of Sorrow, Campanha. 200cz, Casa dos Contos, Ouro Preto. 500cz, Antiga Alfandega, Belem, Para.

Perf. 11½x11, 11x11½

1986-88			Photo.	
2055 A1105	10c sage grn		.20	.20
2057 A1105	20c brt blue		.20	.20
2059 A1105	50c orange		.20	.20
2064 A1105	1cz golden brn		.20	.20
2065 A1105	2cz dull rose		.25	.20
a.	Litho. perf. 13 ('88)		.20	.20
2067 A1105	5cz lt olive grn		.60	.45
a.	Litho. perf. 13 ('88)		.20	.20
2068 A1105	10cz slate blue		.50	.35
2069 A1105	20cz lt red brn		.75	.60
2070 A1105	50cz brn org		2.25	1.75
2071 A1105	100cz dull grn		2.70	2.00
2072 A1105	200cz deep blue		2.50	1.85
2073 A1105	500cz dull red brn		1.30	1.00
	Nos. 2055-2073 (12)		11.65	9.00

Issued: 10c, 8/11; 20c, 12/8; 50c, 8/19; 1cz, 11/19; 2cz, 11/9; 5cz, 12/30; 10cz, 6/2/87; 20cz, 50cz, 9/18/87; 100cz, 12/21/87; 200cz, 5/9/88; 500cz, 11/22/88.

This is an expanding set. Numbers will change if necessary.

1986   *Perf. 12x11½, 11½x12*

Designs: No. 2074, Juscelino Kubitschek de Oliveira, president 1956-61, and Alvorado Palace, Brasilia. No. 2075, Octavio Mangabeira, statesman, and Itamaraty Palace, Rio de Janeiro, horiz.

2074 A1106 50c multi .20 .20
2075 A1106 50c multi .20 .20

Issued: #2074, Aug. 21; #2075, Aug. 27.

World Gastroenterology Congress, Sao Paulo — A1107

1986, Sept. 7   *Perf. 11½x12*

2076 A1107 50c multi .20 .20

Federal Broadcasting System, 50th Anniv. — A1108   Intl. Peace Year — A1109

1986, Sept. 15   *Perf. 12x11½*

2077 A1108 50c multi .20 .20

1986, Sept. 16
Painting (detail): War and Peace, by Candido Portinari.
2078 A1109 50c multi .20 .20

Ernesto Simoes Filho (b. 1886), Publisher of A Tarde
A1110

1986, Oct. 4   Litho.   Perf. 11½x12
2079 A1110 50c multi .20 .20

Famous Men — A1111

Federal Savings Bank, 125th Anniv. — A1112

Designs: No. 2080, Title page from manuscript, c. 1683-94, by Gregorio Mattose e Guerra (b. 1636), author. No. 2081, Manuel Bandeira (1886-1968), poet, text from I'll Go Back to Pasargada.

1986, Oct. 29   Perf. 11½x11
2080 A1111 50c lake & beige .20 .20
2081 A1111 50c lake & dl grn .20 .20

1986, Nov. 4   Perf. 12x11½
2082 A1112 50c multi .20 .20

Flowering Plants A1113

Glauber Rocha, Film Industry Pioneer A1114

Perf. 12x11½, 11½x12
1986, Sept. 23
2083 A1113 50c Urera mitis .20 .20
2084 A1113 6.50cz Couroupita guyanensis .52 .40
2085 A1113 6.90cz Bauhinia variegata, horiz. .55 .40
Nos. 2083-2085 (3) 1.27 1.00

1986, Nov. 20   Perf. 12x11½
2086 A1114 50c multi .20 .20

LUBRAPEX '86 — A1115

Cordel Folk Tales: No. 2087, Romance of the Mysterious Peacock. No. 2088, History of the Empress Porcina.

1986, Nov. 21   Perf. 11x12
2087 A1115 6.90cz multi .45 .35
2088 A1115 6.90cz multi .45 .35
  a.   Souvenir sheet of 2, #2087-2088, perf. 11 1.10 .85

Christmas A1116

Birds: 50c, And Christ child. 6.50cz, And tree. 7.30cz, Eating fruit.

1986, Nov. 10   Perf. 11½x12
2089 A1116 50c multi .20 .20
2090 A1116 6.50cz multi .65 .50
2091 A1116 7.30cz multi .75 .60
Nos. 2089-2091 (3) 1.60 1.30

Military Uniforms, c. 1930 — A1117

Bartolomeu de Gusmao Airport, 50th Anniv. — A1118

Designs: No. 2092, Navy lieutenant commander, dreadnought Minas Gerais. No. 2093, Army flight lieutenant, WACO S.C.O. biplane, Fortaleza Airport.

1986, Dec. 15   Perf. 12x11½
2092 A1117 50c multi .20 .20
2093 A1117 50c multi .20 .20
Fortaleza Air Base, 50th anniv. (No. 2093).

1986, Dec. 26
2094 A1118 1cz multi .20 .20

Heitor Villa Lobos (1887-1959), Conductor A1119

1987, Mar. 5   Litho.   Perf. 12x11½
2095 A1119 1.50cz multi .20 .20

Natl. Air Force C-130 Transport Plane, Flag, the Antarctic A1120

1987, Mar. 9   Perf. 11x11½
2096 A1120 1cz multi .20 .20
Antarctic Project.

Special Mail Services A1121

1987, Mar. 20   Perf. 12x11½
2097 A1121 1cz Rural delivery .20 .20
2098 A1121 1cz Intl. express .20 .20

TELECOM '87, Geneva A1122

1987, May 5   Perf. 11½x12
2099 A1122 2cz Brazilsat, wave, globe .20 .20

10th Pan American Games, Indianapolis, Aug. 7-25 — A1123

1987, May 20   Perf. 12x11½
2100 A1123 18cz multi 1.00 .75

Natl. Fine Arts Museum, 150th Anniv A1124

1987, Jan. 13   Perf. 11½x12
2101 A1124 1cz multi .20 .20

Marine Conservation — A1125

1987, June 5
2102 A1125 2cz Eubalaena australis .20 .20
2103 A1125 2cz Eretmochelys imbricata .20 .20

Federal Court of Appeal, 40th Anniv. A1126

1987, June 15
2104 A1126 2cz multi .20 .20

Military Club, Cent. — A1127

1987, June 26   Perf. 12x11½
2105 A1127 3cz multi .20 .20

Agriculture Institute of Campinas, Cent. A1128

1987, June 27   Perf. 11½x12
2106 A1128 2cz multi .20 .20

Entomological Society, 50th Anniv. — A1129

1987, July 17
2107 A1129 3cz Zoolea lopiceps .20 .20
2108 A1129 3cz Fulgora servillei .20 .20

Natl. Tourism Year A1130

Designs: No. 2109, Monuments and Sugarloaf Mountain, Rio de Janeiro. No. 2110, Colonial church, sailboats, parrot, cashews.

1987, Aug. 4
2109 A1130 3cz multi .20 .20
2110 A1130 3cz multi .20 .20

Royal Portuguese Cabinet of Literature, 150th Anniv. — A1131

1987, Aug. 27   Perf. 12x11½
2111 A1131 30cz ver & brt grn 1.10 .85

Sport Club Intl. A1132

Championship soccer clubs, Brazil's Gold Cup: b, Sao Paulo. c, Guarani. d, Regatas do Flamengo.

1987, Aug. 29   Perf. 11½x12
2112   Block of 4 .60 .40
  a.-d. A1132 3cz any single .20 .20

St. Francis Convent, 400th Anniv. A1133

1987, Oct. 4
2113 A1133 4cz multi .20 .20

Jose Americo de Almeida, Author A1134

Design: Characters from romance novel, "A Bagaceira," 1928, and portrait of author.

1987, Oct. 23   Litho.   Perf. 11x11½
2114 A1134 4cz multi   .20 .20

Spanish Galleons Anchored in Recife Port, 1537 A1135

1987, Nov. 12   Litho.   Perf. 11½x12
2115 A1135 5cz Harbor entrance   .20 .20
Recife City, 450th anniv.

Thanksgiving A1136

1987, Nov. 26   Perf. 12x11½
2116 A1136 5cz multi   .20 .20

Christmas 1987 A1137

1987, Nov. 30   Perf. 11½x12
2117 A1137 6cz Shepherd and
            flock   .20 .20
2118 A1137 6cz Christmas pag-
            eant   .20 .20
2119 A1137 6cz Six angels   .20 .20
      Nos. 2117-2119 (3)   .60 .60

Pedro II College, 150th Anniv. — A1138

Gold pen Emperor Pedro II used to sign edict establishing the school, and Senator Bernardo Pereira de Vasconcellos, founder.

1987, Dec. 2
2120 A1138 6cz multi   .20 .20

Natl. Orchid Growers' Soc., 50th Anniv. A1139

1987, Dec. 3
2121 A1139 6cz Laelia lobata
            veitch   .20 .20
2122 A1139 6cz Cattleya guttata
            lindley   .20 .20

Marian Year — A1140

Statue of Our Lady and Basilica at Fatima, Portugal.

1987, Dec. 20   Perf. 12x11½
2123 A1140 50cz multi   1.10 .85
Exhibit of the Statue of Our Lady of Fatima in Brazil.

Descriptive Treatise of Brazil, by Gabriel S. de Sousa, 400th Anniv. — A1141

1987, Dec. 21   Litho.   Perf. 11x11½
2124 A1141 7cz multi   .20 .20

Natl. Archives, 150th Anniv. A1142

Design: Text from illuminated Gregorian canticle and computer terminal.

1988, Jan. 5   Perf. 11½x12
2125 A1142 7cz multi   .20 .20

Opening of Brazilian Ports to Ships of Friendly Nations, 180th Anniv. A1143

1988, Jan. 28   Perf. 11x11½
2126 A1143 7cz multi   .25 .20

Souvenir Sheet

Antarctic Research — A1144

1988, Feb. 9   Litho.   Perf. 11
2127 A1144 80cz multi   2.00 2.00

Energy Resources A1145

1988, Mar. 15   Litho.   Perf. 12x11½
2128 A1145 14cz Electricity   .25 .20
2129 A1145 14cz Fossil fuels   .25 .20

Souvenir Sheet

Brazilians as Formula 1 World Champions in 1981, 1983, 1987 — A1146

1988, Mar. 30   Perf. 11
2130 A1146 300cz multi   4.50 4.50

Jose Bonifacio, Armorial and Masonic Emblems A1147

1988, Apr. 6   Perf. 12x11½
2131 A1147 20cz multi   .30 .25
Jose Bonifacio de Andrada e Silva (c. 1763-1838), geologist and prime minister under Pedro I who supported the movement for independence from Portugal and was exiled for opposing the emperor's advisors.

Abolition of Slavery, Cent. — A1148

Telecom '88 — A1149

Designs: 20cz, Declaration and quill pen. 50cz, Slave ship and maps of African coastline and slave trade route between Africa and South America.

1988, May 12   Litho.   Perf. 12x11½
2132 A1148 20cz multi   .25 .20
2133 A1148 50cz multi   .65 .50

1988, May 16   Perf. 11½x11
2134 A1149 50cz multi   .60 .45

Jesus of Matosinhos Sanctuary A1150

1988, May 16   Perf. 11½x12
2135 A1150 20cz shown   .25 .20
2136 A1150 50cz Pilot plan of
            Brazilia   .60 .45
2137 A1150 100cz Salvador his-
            toric district   1.20 .90
      Nos. 2135-2137 (3)   2.05 1.55
LUBRAPEX '88. World heritage list.

Japanese Immigrants in Brazil, 80th Anniv. — A1151

1988, June 18   Litho.   Perf. 11½x11
2138 A1151 100cz multi   .75 .55

A1152   A1153

1988, July 1   Photo.   Perf. 13
2139 A1152 (A) brt blue   .25 .20
No. 2139 met the first class domestic letter postage rate (28cz).
See Nos. 2201, 2218.

1988, July 14   Litho.   Perf. 12x11½
2140 A1153 20cz Judo   .25 .20
1988 Summer Olympics, Seoul.

Wildlife Conservation — A1154

1988, July 24   Perf. 11½x12
2141 A1154 20cz Myrmecopha-
            ga tridactyla   .20 .20
2142 A1154 50cz Chaetomys
            subspinosus   .30 .25
2143 A1154 100cz Speothos
            venaticus   .65 .50
      Nos. 2141-2143 (3)   1.15 .95

Souvenir Sheet

The Motherland, 1919 by Pedro Bruno — A1155

1988, Aug. 1   Litho.   Perf. 11
2144 A1155 250cz multi   1.50 1.50
Stamp Day, BRASILIANA '89.

Natl. Confederation of Industries, 50th Anniv. — A1156

1988, Aug. 12   Perf. 11½x12
2145 A1156 50cz multi   .25 .20

Soccer Clubs A1157

No. 2146, Recife, Pernambuco. No. 2147, Coritiba, Parana. 100cz, Gremio, Porto Alegre, Rio Grando do Sul. 200cz, Fluminense, Rio de Janeiro.

1988, Sept. 29   *Perf. 11½x12*
2146	A1157	50cz multi	.20	.20
2147	A1157	50cz multi	.20	.20
2148	A1157	100cz multi	.30	.25
2149	A1157	200cz multi	.60	.50
a.		Block of 4, #2146-2149	1.25	.95

Poems, 1888 A1158

Portraits and text: 50cz, *O Ateneu*, by Raul Pompeia. 100cz, *Poesias*, by Olavo Bilac.

1988, Oct. 28   *Perf. 11x11½*
2150	A1158	50cz multi	.20	.20
2151	A1158	100cz multi	.25	.20

Souvenir Sheet

1988 Democratic Constitution for the Union of the People and the State — A1159

1988, Oct. 5   **Litho.**   *Perf. 11*
2152	A1159	550cz Government building	2.40	2.40

Origami Art A1160

1988, Nov. 11   **Litho.**   *Perf. 11½x12*
2153	A1160	50cz Abbey, nuns	.20	.20
2154	A1160	100cz Nativity	.25	.20
2155	A1160	200cz Santa Claus, presents	.50	.40
		Nos. 2153-2155 (3)	.95	.80

Christmas.

ARBRAFEX Philatelic Exhibition of Argentina and Brazil — A1161

1988, Nov. 26
2156	A1161	400cz multi	.85	.65

Fresh-water Fish — A1162

Designs: a, *Gasteropelecus*. b, *Osteoglossum ferreirai*. c, *Moenkhausia*. d, *Xavantei*. e, *Ancistrus hoplogenys*. f, *Brochis splendens*. Se-tenant in a continuous design. Illustration reduced.

1988, Nov. 29   **Litho.**   *Perf. 11½x12*
2157		Block of 6	.90	.70
a.-f.	A1162	55cz any single	.20	.20

Souvenir Sheet

BRAPEX '88, Ecological Preservation — A1163

1988, Dec. 10   *Perf. 11*
2158		Sheet of 3	1.80	1.80
a.	A1163	100cz Parrot	.25	.25
b.	A1163	250cz Plant	.60	.60
c.	A1163	400cz Pelican	.95	.95

Satellite Dishes — A1164   Performing Arts — A1165

1988, Dec. 20   *Perf. 12x11½*
2159	A1164	70cz multi	.20	.20

Ansat 10-Earth satellite station communication.

1988, Dec. 21
2160	A1165	70cz multi	.20	.20

Court of Justice, Bahia, 380th Anniv. A1166

1989, Mar. 10   **Litho.**   *Perf. 11½x12*
2161	A1166	25c multi	.40	.30

Public Library Year A1167

1989, Mar. 13   *Perf. 11½*
2162	A1167	25c Library, Bahia, 1811	.40	.30

Brazilian Post & Telegraph Enterprise, 20th Anniv. A1168

Intl. and domestic postal services: a, Facsimile transmission (Post-Grama). b, Express

---

mail (EMS). c, Parcel post (Sedex). d, Postal savings (CEFPostal).

1989, Mar. 20   *Perf. 11½x12*
2163		Block of 4	1.65	1.25
a.-d.	A1168	25c any single	.40	.30

Souvenir Sheet

Ayrton Senna, 1988 Formula 1 World Champion — A1169

1989, Mar. 23
2164	A1169	2cz multi	4.00	4.00

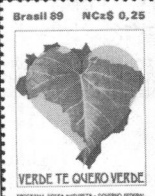

Environmental Conservation A1170

1989, Apr. 6   **Litho.**   *Perf. 12x11½*
2165	A1170	25c multi	.35	.25

Mineira Inconfidencia Independence Movement, Bicent. — A1171

Designs: a, Pyramid, hand. b, Figure of a man, houses. c, Destruction of houses.

1989, Apr. 21   *Perf. 11½x12*
2166		Strip of 3	1.30	.95
a.-b.	A1171	30c any single	.40	.30
c.	A1171	40c multi	.50	.40

First rebellion against Portuguese dominion.

Military School, Rio de Janeiro, Cent. A1172

1989, May 6   **Litho.**   *Perf. 11½x12*
2167	A1172	50c multi	.50	.40

Flowering Plants A1173

1989, June 5   *Perf. 11½x12, 12x11½*
2168	A1173	50c Pavonia alnifolia	.60	.45
2169	A1173	1cz Worsleya rayneri	1.25	.90
2170	A1173	1.50cz Heliconia farinosa	1.75	1.40
		Nos. 2168-2170 (3)	3.60	2.75

Nos. 2169-2170 vert.

Barreto and Recife Law School, Pedro II Square A1174

1989, June 7   *Perf. 11x11½*
2171	A1174	50c multi	.65	.50

Tobias Barreto (b. 1839), advocate of Germanization of Brazil.

Cultura Broadcasting System, 20th Anniv. — A1175

1989, June 27   **Litho.**   *Perf. 11½x12*
2172	A1175	50c multi	.60	.45

Aviation A1176

1989, July 7
2173	A1176	50c Ultra-light aircraft	.50	.40
2174	A1176	1.50cz Eiffel Tower, Demoiselle	1.65	1.10

Flight of Santos-Dumont's *Demoiselle*, 80th anniv (1.50cz).

Indigenous Flora — A1177

1989 Photo.   *Perf. 11x11½, 11½x11*
2176	A1177	10c Dichorisandra, vert.	.20	.20
2177	A1177	20c Quiabentia zehnteri	.25	.20
2178	A1177	50c Bougainvillea glabra	.50	.40
2179	A1177	1cz Impatiens specie	1.00	.80
2180	A1177	2cz Chorisia crispiflora	.25	.20
2181	A1177	5cz Hibiscus trilineatus	.60	.45
		Nos. 2176-2181 (6)	2.80	2.25

Issued: 10c, July 4; 20c, June 21; 50c, June 26; 1cz, June 19; 2cz, 5cz, Dec. 4. No. 2181 vert. See Nos. 2259-2273.

Souvenir Sheet

Largo da Carioca, by Nicolas Antoine Taunay — A1179

1989, July 7   **Litho.**   *Perf. 11*
2197	A1179	3cz multi	3.00	3.00

PHILEXFRANCE '89, French revolution bicent.

Cut and Uncut Gemstones
A1180

1989, July 12 Litho. Perf. 12x11½
2198 A1180 50c Tourmaline .40 .30
2199 A1180 1.50cz Amethyst 1.20 .90

Souvenir Sheet

Paco Imperial, Rio de Janeiro, and Map — A1181

1989, July 28 Perf. 11
2200 A1181 5cz multi 3.75 3.75

BRASILANA '89.

Type of 1988 Redrawn
1989, July 26 Photo. Perf. 13
Size: 17x21mm
2201 A1152 (A) org & brt blue .20 .20

Size of type and postal emblem are smaller on No. 2201; "1e PORTE" is at lower left.
No. 2201 met the first class domestic letter postage rate (cz).

Pernambuco Commercial Assoc., 150th Anniv. — A1182

1989, Aug. 1 Litho. Perf. 11½x12
2202 A1182 50c multi .40 .30

Photography, 150th Anniv. — A1183

1989, Aug. 14
2203 A1183 1.50cz multi 1.10 .85

1st Hydroelecric Power Station in South America, Marmelos-o, Cent. — A1184

1989, Sept. 5 Litho. Perf. 11½x12
2204 A1184 50c multi .35 .25

Conchs Endemic to the Brazilian Coast
A1185

1989, Sept. 8
2205 A1185 50c Voluta ebraea 30 .25
2206 A1185 1cz Morum matthewsi .60 .45
2207 A1185 1.50cz Agaronia travassosi .90 .65
Nos. 2205-2207 (3) 1.80 1.35

Wildlife conservation.

America Issue
A1186

UPAE emblem and pre-Columbian stone carvings: 1cz, Muiraquita ritual statue, vert. 4cz, Ceramic brazier under three-footed votive urn.

Perf. 12x11½, 11½x12
1989, Oct. 12 Litho.
2208 A1186 1cz multicolored .50 .35
2209 A1186 4cz shown 1.85 1.40

Discovery of America 500th anniv. (in 1992).

A1187

Hologram and: a. Lemons, by Danilo di Prete. b. O Indio E A Suacuapara, by sculptor Victor Brecheret. c. Francisco Matarazzo.

1989, Oct. 14 Perf. 11
Souvenir Sheet
2210 A1187 Sheet of 3 3.75 3.75
a. 2cz multicolored .70 .70
b. 3cz multicolored 1.10 1.10
c. 5cz multicolored 1.75 1.75

Sao Paulo 20th intl. art biennial.

A1188

1989, Oct. 26 Perf. 11½x11
Writers, residences and quotes: No. 2211, Casimiro de Abreu (b. 1839). No. 2212, Cora Coralina (b. 1889). No. 2213, Joaquim Machado de Assis (b. 1839).
2211 A1188 1cz shown .55 .40
2212 A1188 1cz multicolored .55 .40
2213 A1188 1cz multicolored .55 .40
Nos. 2211-2213 (3) 1.65 1.20

Federal Police Department, 25th Anniv. — A1189

1989, Nov. 9 Perf. 11½x12
2214 A1189 1cz multicolored .25 .20

Christmas
A1190

Thanksgiving Day — A1191

1989, Nov. 10 Perf. 12x11½
2215 A1190 70c Heralding angel .20 .20
2216 A1190 1cz Holy family .25 .20

1989, Nov. 23
2217 A1191 1cz multicolored .25 .20

Type of 1988 Redrawn
1989, Nov. 6 Photo. Perf. 13x13½
Size: 22x26mm
2218 A1152 (B) org & dark red 2.00 1.50

Size of type and postal emblem are smaller on No. 2218; "1e PORTE" is at lower left.
No. 2218 met the first class intl. letter postage rate, initially at 9cz.

Souvenir Sheet

Proclamation of the Republic, Cent. — A1192

1989, Nov. 19 Litho. Perf. 11
2225 A1192 15cz multicolored 4.50 4.50

Bahia Sports Club, 58th Anniv.
A1193

1989, Nov. 30 Perf. 11½x12
2226 A1193 50c Soccer .20 .20

Yellow Man, by Anita Malfatti (b. 1889)
A1194

1989, Dec. 2 Perf. 12x11½
2227 A1194 1cz multicolored .25 .20

Bahia State Public Archives, Cent. — A1195

1990, Jan. 16 Litho. Perf. 11½x12
2228 A1195 2cz multicolored .30 .20

Brazilian Botanical Soc., 40th Anniv.
A1196

1990, Jan. 21
2229 A1196 2cz Sabia, Caatinga .25 .20
2230 A1196 13cz Pau, Brazil 1.40 1.10

Churches
A1197

Designs: 2cz, St. John the Baptist Cathedral, Santa Cruz do Sul, vert. 3cz, Our Lady of Victory Church, Oeiras. 5cz, Our Lady of the Rosary Church, Ouro Preto, vert.

1990, Feb. 5 Perf. 12x11½, 11½x12
2231 A1197 2cz multicolored .20 .20
2232 A1197 3cz multicolored .25 .20
2233 A1197 5cz multicolored .40 .30
Nos. 2231-2233 (3) .85 .70

Lloyd's of London in Brazil, Cent.
A1198

1990, Feb. 19 Litho. Perf. 11½x12
2234 A1198 3cz multicolored .20 .20

Souvenir Sheet

Antarctic Research Program — A1199

1990, Feb. 22 Litho. Perf. 11
2235 A1199 20cz Fauna, map 1.55 1.55

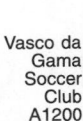

Vasco da Gama Soccer Club A1200

1990, Mar. 5
2236 A1200 10cz multicolored   .50 .40

Lindolfo Collor (b. 1890), Syndicated Columnist, and Labor Monument A1201

1990, Mar. 7
2237 A1201 20cz multicolored   .95 .70

A1202

A1203

Pres. Jose Sarney.

1990, Mar. 8   Perf. 12x11½
2238 A1202 20cz chalky blue   .95 .70

1990, Apr. 6   Perf. 12x11½
2239 A1203 20cz multicolored   .70 .50

AIDS prevention.

Souvenir Sheet

Penny Black, 150th Anniv. — A1204

Designs: 20cr, Dom Pedro, Brazil No. 1. 100cr, Queen Victoria, Great Britain No. 1.

1990, May 3   Perf. 11
2240 A1204 Sheet of 2   2.35 1.75
  a.   20cr multicolored
  b.   100cr multicolored

Central Bank, 25th Anniv. A1205

1990, Mar. 30 Litho. Perf. 11½x12
2241 A1205 20cr multicolored   .70 .50

Amazon River Postal Network, 21st Anniv. A1207

1990, Apr. 20   Perf. 11x11½
2243 A1207 20cr multicolored   .70 .50

Souvenir Sheet

World Cup Soccer Championships, Italy — A1208

1990, May 12 Litho. Perf. 12x11½
2244 A1208 120cr multicolored   3.00 3.00

22nd Congress of the Intl. Union of Highway Transportation — A1209

1990, May 14   Perf. 11½x12
2245 A1209 20cr multicolored   .65 .50
2246 A1209 80cr multicolored   3.00 2.25
  a.   Pair, #2245-2246   3.75 2.75

No. 2246a has a continuous design.

Imperial Crown, 18th Cent. — A1210

Designs: No. 2248, Our Lady of Immaculate Conception, 18th cent.

1990, May 18   Perf. 12x11½
2247 A1210 20cr shown   .70 .50
2248 A1210 20cr multicolored   .70 .50

Imperial Museum, 50th anniv.(No. 2247). Mission Museum, 50th anniv. (No. 2248).

State Flags Type of 1981
1990, May 20   Perf. 11½x12
2249 A947 20cr Tocantins   .70 .50

Army Geographical Service, Cent. — A1212

1990, May 30   Perf. 11x11½
2250 A1212 20cr multicolored   .70 .50

Film Personalities — A1213

1990, June 19   Perf. 11½x12
2251 A1213 25cr Adhemar Gon-
          zaga   .80 .60
2252 A1213 25cr Carmen Miran-
          da   .80 .60
2253 A1213 25cr Carmen Santos   .80 .60
2254 A1213 25cr Oscarito   .80 .60
  a.   Block of 4, #2251-2254   3.20 2.40

France-Brazil House, Rio de Janeiro — A1214

1990, July 14 Litho. Perf. 11½x11
2255 A1214 50cr multicolored   1.50 1.10

See France No. 2226.

World Men's Volleyball Chmpships. A1215

Intl. Literacy Year A1217

CBA 123 A1216

1990, July 28 Litho. Perf. 12x11½
2256 A1215 10cr multicolored   .30 .25

1990, July 30   Perf. 11½x12
2257 A1216 10cr multicolored   .30 .25

1990, Aug. 22   Perf. 12x11½
2258 A1217 10cr multicolored   .30 .25

Flora Type of 1989

1cr, like #2179. 2cr, like #2180. 5cr, like #2181. 10cr, Tibouchina granulosa. 20cr, Cassia macranthera. #2264, Clitoria fairchildiana. #2265, Tibouchina mutabilis. 100cr, Erythrina crista-galli. 200cr, Jacaranda mimosifolia. 500cr, Caesalpinia peltophoroides. 1000, Pachira aquatica. 2000, Hibiscus pernambucensis. 5000, Triplaris surinamensis. 10,000, Tabebuia heptaphylla. 20,000, Erythrina speciosa.

Perf. 11x11½, 11½x11
1989-93   Photo.
Design A1177

2259	A1177	1cr multi	.20 .20
2260	A1177	2cr multi	.20 .20
2261	A1177	5cr multi	.20 .20
2262	A1177	10cr multi	.20 .20
2263	A1177	20cr multi	.20 .20
2264	A1177	50cr multi	.30 .20
2265	A1177	50cr multi	.35 .35
2266	A1177	100cr multi, perf. 13	.55 .30
2267	A1177	200cr multi	1.10 .55
2268	A1177	500cr multi	2.75 1.40
2269	A1177	1000cr multi	.20 .20
2270	A1177	2000cr multi	.20 .20
2271	A1177	5000cr multi	.85 .85
2272	A1177	10,000cr multi	1.65 1.65
2273	A1177	20,000cr multi	2.25 2.25
		Nos. 2259-2273 (15)	11.20 8.95

Issued: 1cr, 11/8/90; 2cr, 11/12/90; 5cr, 11/16/90; #2264, 6/1/89; 10cr, 4/18/90; 20cr, 5/4/90; 100cr, 8/24/90; 200cr, 6/16/91; 500cr, 5/14/91; 1000cr, 9/2/92; 2000cr, 9/8/92; 5000cr, 10/16/92; 10,000cr, 11/16/92; 20,000cr, 4/25/93; #2265, 10/20/93.

Granbery Instutute, Cent. A1218

1990, Sept. 8 Litho. Perf. 11½x12
2279 A1218 13cr multicolored   .40 .30

18th Panamerican Railroad Congress — A1219

1990, Sept. 9
2280 A1219 95cr multicolored   2.00 1.50

Embratel, 25th Anniv. — A1220

1990, Sept. 21
2281 A1220 13cr multicolored   .40 .30

LUBRAPEX '90 A1221

Statues by Ceschiatti and Giorgi (No. 2283).

1990, Sept. 22
2282 A1221 25cr As Banhistas   .60 .45
2283 A1221 25cr Os
          Candangos   .60 .45
2284 A1221 100cr Evangelista
          Sao Joao   1.25 .90
2285 A1221 100cr A Justica   1.25 .90
  a.   Block of 4, #2282-2285   4.00 3.00
  b.   Souv. sheet of 4, #2282-2285 6.00 6.00

Praia Do Sul Wildlife Reserve A1222

1990, Oct. 12

2286	A1222	15cr Flowers	.45	.30
2287	A1222	105cr Shoreline	2.60	1.80
a.		Pair, #2286-2287	3.05	2.10

Discovery of America, 500th anniv. (in 1992).

Natl. Library, 180th Anniv. A1223

Writers: No. 2289, Guilherme de Almeida (1890-1969). No. 2290, Oswald de Andrade (1890-1954).

1990, Oct. 29   Litho.   Perf. 11x11½

2288	A1223	15cr multicolored	.40	.30
2289	A1223	15cr multicolored	.40	.30
2290	A1223	15cr multicolored	.40	.30
		Nos. 2288-2290 (3)	1.20	.90

Natl. Tax Court, Cent. A1224

1990, Nov. 7   Litho.   Perf. 11½x12

2291	A1224	15cr multicolored	.40	.30

Christmas A1225

Architecture of Brasilia: No. 2292, National Congress. No. 2293, Television tower.

1990, Nov. 20

2292	A1225	15cr multicolored	.40	.30
2293	A1225	15cr multicolored	.40	.30

A1226   A1227

1990, Dec. 13   Litho.   Perf. 12x11½

2294	A1226	15cr multicolored	.20	.20

Organization of American States, cent.

1990, Dec. 14

2295	A1227	15cr multicolored	.20	.20

First Flight of Nike Apache Missile, 25th anniv.

Colonization of Sergipe, Founding of Sao Cristovao, 400th Anniv. — A1228

1990, Dec. 18   Litho.   Perf. 11½x12

2296	A1228	15cr multicolored	.20	.20

World Congress of Physical Education A1229

1991, Jan. 7   Perf. 11½x12

2297	A1229	17cr multicolored	.20	.20

Rock in Rio II — A1230

1991, Jan. 9   Perf. 12x11½

2298	A1230	25cr Cazuza	.20	.20
2299	A1230	185cr Raul Seixas	1.65	1.00
a.		Pair, #2298-2299	2.00	1.10

Printed in sheets of 12.

Ministry of Aviation, 50th Anniv. A1231

1991, Jan. 20   Perf. 11x11½

2300	A1231	17cr multicolored	.20	.20

A1232

A1233

Carnivals.

1991, Feb. 8   Litho.   Perf. 12x11½

2301	A1232	25cr Olinda	.25	.20
2302	A1232	30cr Salvador	.25	.20
2303	A1232	280cr Rio de Janeiro	2.50	2.00
		Nos. 2301-2303 (3)	3.00	2.40

1991, Feb. 20

2304	A1233	300cr multicolored	3.00	2.25

Visit by Pres. Collor to Antarctica.

Hang Gliding World Championships — A1234

1991, Feb. 24   Perf. 11½x12

2305	A1234	36cr multicolored	.35	.30

11th Pan American Games, 25th Summer Olympics A1235

1991, Mar. 30   Litho.   Perf. 11½x12

2306	A1235	36cr Sailing	.30	.25
2307	A1235	36cr Rowing	.30	.25
2308	A1235	300cr Swimming	2.50	1.90
a.		Block of 3, #2306-2308 + label	3.25	2.50

Fight Against Drugs — A1236   Yanomami Indian Culture — A1237

1991, Apr. 7   Litho.   Perf. 12x11½

2309	A1236	40cr Drugs	.35	.30
2310	A1236	40cr Alcohol	.35	.30
2311	A1236	40cr Smoking	.35	.30
		Nos. 2309-2311 (3)	1.05	.90

1991, Apr. 19   Perf. 11½x11, 11x11½

2312	A1237	40cr shown	.35	.30
2313	A1237	400cr Indian, horiz.	3.50	2.75

Journal of Brazil, Cent. A1238

1991, Apr. 8   Litho.   Perf. 11x11½

2314	A1238	40cr multicolored	.35	.30

Neochen Jubata (Orinoco Goose) — A1239

1991, June 5   Litho.   Perf. 12x11½

2315	A1239	45cr multi	.30	.25

UN Conference on Development.

Snakes & Dinosaurs A1240

1991, June 6   Perf. 11½x12

2316	A1240	45cr Bothrops jararaca	.30	.25
2317	A1240	45cr Corallus caninus	.30	.25
a.		Pair, #2316-2317	.60	.50
2318	A1240	45cr Teropods	.30	.25
2319	A1240	350cr Sauropods	2.10	1.60
a.		Pair, #2318-2319	2.40	1.85
		Nos. 2316-2319 (4)	3.00	2.35

Flag of Brazil — A1241

1991, June 10   Photo.   Perf. 13x13½

2320	A1241	A multicolored	.25	.20

Valued at domestic letter rate (cr) on day of issue.
Exists with inscription at lower right. Same value.

Fire Pumper A1242

1991, July 2   Litho.   Perf. 11½x12

2321	A1242	45cr multicolored	.30	.25

Tourism A1243

Map location and: 45cr, Painted stones, Roraima. 350cr, Dedo de Deus Mountain, Rio De Janeiro.

1991, July 6   Perf. 11x11½

2322	A1243	45cr multicolored	.28	.20
2323	A1243	350cr multicolored	2.00	1.50

Labor Laws, 50th Anniv. A1244

1991, Aug. 11   Perf. 11½x12

2324	A1244	45cr multicolored	.30	.25

Leonardo Mota, Birth Cent. A1245

1991, Aug. 22

2325	A1245	45cr buff, blk & red	.30	.25

Folklore Festival.

Jose Basilio da Gama (1741-1795), Poet — A1246

#2327, Fagundes Varela (b. 1841), poet. #2328, Jackson de Figueiredo (b. 1891), writer.

1991, Aug. 29

2326	A1246	45cr multicolored	.25	.20
2327	A1246	50cr multicolored	.30	.25
2328	A1246	50cr multicolored	.30	.25
		Nos. 2326-2328 (3)	.85	.70

12th Natl.
Eucharistic
Congress
A1247

1991, Oct. 6   Litho.   Perf. 12x11½
2329 A1247 50cr Pope John
              Paul II   .20   .20
2330 A1247 400cr Map, crosses   1.40 1.05
a.   Pair, #2329-2330   1.60 1.20

    Visit by Pope John Paul II.

First Brazilian Constitution,
Cent. — A1248

1991, Oct. 7   Perf. 11½x12
2331 A1248 50cr multicolored   .20   .20

Telecom
'91 — A1249

1991, Oct. 8   Perf. 12x11½
2332 A1249 50cr multicolored   .20   .20

Sixth World Forum and Exposition on Telecommunications, Geneva, Switzerland.

America
Issue
A1250

UPAEP emblem and explorers: 50cr, Ferdinand Magellan (c. 1480-1521). 400cr, Francisco de Orellana (c. 1490-c. 1546).

1991, Oct. 12   Perf. 11½x12
2333 A1250 50cr multicolored   .20   .20
2334 A1250 400cr multicolored   1.40 1.05

Discovery of America, 500th anniv. (in 1992).

A1251   A1252

BRAPEX VIII (Orchids and Hummingbirds):
50cr, Colibri serrirostris, cattleya warneri. No.
2336, Chlorostilbon aureoventris, rodriguezia
venusta. No. 2337, Clytolaema rubricauda,
zygopetalum intermedium. No. 2338a, 50cr,
Colibri serrirostris. b, 50cr, Chlorostilbon aureoventris. c, 500cr, Clytolaema rubricauda.

1991, Oct. 29   Litho.   Perf. 12x11½
2335 A1251 50cr multicolored   .20   .20
2336 A1251 65cr multicolored   .20   .20
2337 A1251 65cr multicolored   .20   .20
      Nos. 2335-2337 (3)   .60   .60

Souvenir Sheet
2338 A1251   Sheet of 3, #a.-
                  c.   2.20 1.65

1991, Oct. 29   Litho.   Perf. 11½x11
2339 A1252 400cr multicolored   .90   .65

    Lasar Segall, artist, birth cent.

Bureau of
Agriculture and
Provision of Sao
Paulo,
Cent. — A1253

1991, Nov. 11   Perf. 12x11½
2340 A1253 70cr multicolored   .20   .20

First Civilian Presidents, Birth
Sesquicentennials — A1254

1991, Nov. 14   Perf. 11½x12
2341 A1254 70cr Manuel de
                  Campos Sal-
                  les   .20   .20
2342 A1254 90cr Prudente de
                  Moraes Barros   .25   .20
a.   Pair, #2341-2342   .45   .35

Christmas
A1255

Thanksgiving
A1256

1991, Nov. 20   Perf. 12x11½
2343 A1255 70cr multicolored   .20   .20

1991, Nov. 28
2344 A1256 70cr multicolored   .20   .20

Military
Police
A1257

1991, Dec. 1   Perf. 11½x12
2345 A1257 80cr multicolored   .25   .20

Souvenir Sheet

Emperor Dom Pedro (1825-
1891) — A1258

a, 80cr, Older age. b, 800cr, Wearing crown.

Litho. & Engr.
1991, Nov. 29   Perf. 11
2346 A1258 Sheet of 2, #a.-b.   2.50 2.50

    BRASILIANA 93.

Churches
A1259

#2347, Presbyterian Church, Rio de
Janeiro. #2348, First Baptist Church, Niteroi.

1992, Jan. 12   Litho.   Perf. 12x11½
2347 A1259 250cr multicolored   .30   .25
2348 A1259 250cr multicolored   .30   .25

1992
Summer
Olympics,
Barcelona
A1260

Medalists in shooting, Antwerp, 1920:
300cr, Afranio Costa, silver. 2500cr,
Guilherme Paraense, gold.

1992, Jan. 28   Perf. 11½x12
2349 A1260 300cr multicolored   .30   .25
2350 A1260 2500cr multicolored 2.75 2.00

Port of
Santos,
Cent.
A1261

1992, Feb. 3   Litho.   Perf. 11½
2351 A1261 300cr multicolored   .45   .35

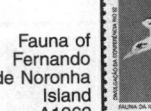

Fauna of
Fernando
de Noronha
Island
A1262

1992, Feb. 25   Litho.   Perf. 11½x12
2352 A1262 400cr White-tailed
                  tropicbirds   .40   .30
2353 A1262 2500cr Dolphins   2.50 1.75

    Earth Summit, Rio de Janeiro.

Yellow
Amaryllis — A1263

1992, Feb. 27   Photo.   Perf. 13½
2354 A1263 (A) multicolored   .25   .20

No. 2354 met the second class domestic
letter postage rate of 265cr on date of issue.

ARBRAFEX '92, Argentina-Brazil
Philatelic Exhibition — A1264

Designs: No. 2355, Gaucho throwing bola at
rhea. No. 2356, Man playing accordion, couple
dancing. No. 2357, Couple in horse-drawn
cart, woman. 1000cr, Gaucho throwing lasso
at steer.
No. 2358c, 250cr, like #2356. d, 500cr, like
#2355. e, 1500cr, like #2358.

1992, Mar. 20   Litho.   Perf. 11½x12
2355 A1264 250cr multicolored   .20   .20
2356 A1264 250cr multicolored   .20   .20
2357 A1264 250cr multicolored   .20   .20
2358 A1264 1000cr multicolored   .60   .60
a.   Block of 4, Nos. 2355-2358 1.05 1.05
Souvenir Sheet
2358B A1264 Sheet of 4,
               #2357, 2358c-
               2358e   1.05 1.05

1992 Summer
Olympics,
Barcelona
A1265

1992, Apr. 3   Perf. 12x11½
2359 A1265 300cr multicolored   .20   .20

Discovery
of America,
500th
Anniv.
A1266

1992, Apr. 24   Perf. 11½x12
2360 A1266 500cr Columbus'
                  fleet   .30   .30
2361 A1266 3500cr Columbus,
                  map   2.10 2.10
a.   Pair, #2360-2361   2.40 2.40

Telebras Telecommunications
System — A1267

1992, May 5   Perf. 11x11½
2362 A1267 350cr multicolored   .20   .20

Installation of 10 million telephones.

Langsdorff Expedition to Brazil, 170th Anniv. A1268

#2363, Aime-Adrien Taunay, natives. #2364, Johann Moritz Rugendas, monkey. #2365, Hercule Florence, flowering plant. 3000cr, Gregory Ivanovitch Langsdorff, map.

1992, June 2   *Perf. 11½x12*
2363	A1268	500cr multicolored	.25	.25
2364	A1268	500cr multicolored	.25	.25
2365	A1268	500cr multicolored	.25	.25
2366	A1268	3000cr multicolored	1.50	1.50
	Nos. 2363-2366 (4)		2.25	2.25

UN Conf. on Environmental Development, Rio.

UN Conference on Environmental Development, Rio de Janeiro — A1269

Globe and: No. 2367, Flags of Sweden and Brazil. No. 2368, City, grain, mountain and tree. 3000cr, Map of Brazil, parrot, orchid.

1992, June 3   *Litho.*   *Perf. 11x11½*
2367	A1269	450cr multicolored	.20	.20
2368	A1269	450cr multicolored	.20	.20
2369	A1269	3000cr multicolored	1.50	1.50
	Nos. 2367-2369 (3)		1.90	1.90

Ecology A1270

Designs: No. 2370, Flowers, waterfall, and butterflies. No. 2371, Butterflies, canoe, and hummingbirds. No. 2372, Boy taking pictures of tropical birds. No. 2373, Armadillo, girl picking fruit.

1992, June 4   *Perf. 11½x12*
2370	A1270	500cr multicolored	.25	.25
2371	A1270	500cr multicolored	.25	.25
2372	A1270	500cr multicolored	.25	.25
2373	A1270	500cr multicolored	.25	.25
a.		Strip of 4, #2370-2373	1.00	1.00

UN Conf. on Environmental Development, Rio.

Floral Paintings by Margaret Mee — A1271

1992, June 5   *Perf. 12x11½*
2374	A1271	600cr Nidularium innocentii	.35	.35
2375	A1271	600cr Canistrum exiguum	.35	.35
2376	A1271	700cr Canistrum cyathiforme	.40	.40
2377	A1271	700cr Nidularium rubens	.40	.40
	Nos. 2374-2377 (4)		1.50	1.50

UN Conf. on Environmental Development, Rio.

Souvenir Sheet

Joaquim Jose da Silva Xavier (1748-1792), Patriot — A1272

Litho. & Engr.
1992, Apr. 21   *Perf. 11*
2378	A1272	3500cr multicolored	2.10	2.10

Souvenir Sheet

A1273

Expedition of Alexandre Rodrigues Ferreira, Bicent.: a, 500cr, Sailing ships, gray and green hulls. b, 1000cr, Sailing ships, red hulls. c, 2500cr, Sailing ship at shore.

1992, May 9   *Litho.*   *Perf. 11½x12*
2379	A1273	Sheet of 3, #a.-c.	2.40	2.40

Lubrapex '92.

A1274   A1275

1992, June 5   *Litho.*   *Perf. 12x11½*
2380	A1274	600cr Hummingbird	.25	.25

Diabetes Day.

1992, July 13   *Litho.*   *Perf. 11½x11*
2381	A1275	550cr multicolored	.25	.25

Volunteer firemen of Joinville.

A1276

A1277

Serra da Capivara National Park: No. 2382, Leopard, animals, map of park. No. 2383, Canyon, map of Brazil.

1992, July 17   *Perf. 12x11½*
2382	A1276	550cr multicolored	.25	.25
2383	A1276	550cr multicolored	.25	.25
a.		Pair, #2382-2383	.45	.45

1992, July 24
2384	A1277	550cr multicolored	.25	.25

Financing for studies and projects.

Natl. Service for Industrial Training, 50th Anniv. — A1278

1992, Aug. 5   *Perf. 11½x12*
2385	A1278	650cr multicolored	.35	.35

Fortresses A1279

1992, Aug. 19   *Litho.*   *Perf. 11½x12*
2386	A1279	650cr Santa Cruz	.30	.30
2387	A1279	3000cr Santo Antonio	1.25	1.25

Masonic Square, Compass and Lodge A1280

1992, Aug. 20
2388	A1280	650cr multicolored	.30	.30

Brazilian Assistance Legion, 50th Anniv. — A1281

1992, Aug. 28   *Perf. 12x11½*
2389	A1281	650cr multicolored	.30	.30

Hospital of Medicine and Orthopedics A1282

1992, Sept. 11
2390	A1282	800cr multicolored	.30	.30

Merry Christmas A1283

1992, Nov. 20   *Perf. 11½*
2391	A1283	(1) multicolored	.25	.25

No. 2391 met the first class domestic letter postage rate of 1090cr on day of issue.

Writers A1284

#2392, Graciliano Ramos (1892-1953). #2393, Menotti del Picchia (1892-1988). 1000cr, Assis Chateaubriand (1892-1968).

Perf. 12x11½, 11½x12
1992, Oct. 29   *Litho.*
2392	A1284	900cr multi, vert.	.25	.25
2393	A1284	900cr multi, vert.	.25	.25
2394	A1284	1000cr multi	.30	.30

Expedition of Luis Cruls, Cent. A1285

1992, Nov. 11   *Perf. 11½x12*
2395	A1285	900cr multicolored	.25	25

Brazillian Program for Quality and Productivity A1286

1992, Nov. 12
2396	A1286	1200cr multicolored	.30	.30

Souvenir Sheet

Tourism Year in the Americas — A1287

a, 1200cr, Mountains, coastline. b, 9000cr, Sugarloaf Mt., aerial tram, Rio de Janeiro.

1992, Nov. 18   *Litho.*   *Perf. 11½x12*
2397	A1287	Sheet of 2, #a.-b.	2.00	2.00

Brasiliana '93.

Sister Irma Dulce A1288

1993, Mar. 13   *Litho.*   *Perf. 11½x12*
2398	A1288	3500cr multicolored	.35	.35

Souvenir Sheet

Water Sports Championships of South America — A1289

Designs: a, 3500cr, Diver. b, 3500cr, Synchronized swimmers. c, 25,000cr, Water polo.

1993, Mar. 21   Litho.   Perf. 11
2399 A1289   Sheet of 3, #a.-c.   2.75   2.75

Curitiba, 300th Anniv. A1290

1993, Mar. 29
2400 A1290 4500cr multicolored   .40   .40

Health and Preservation of Life — A1291

Pedro Americo, 150th Birth Anniv. — A1292

Red Cross emblem and: No. 2401, Bleeding heart, flowers. No. 2402, Cancer symbol, breast. No. 2403, Brain waves, rainbow emerging from head.

1993, Apr. 7   Litho.   Perf. 12x11½
2401 A1291 4500cr multicolored   .30   .30
2402 A1291 4500cr multicolored   .30   .30
2403 A1291 4500cr multicolored   .30   .30
   a.   Strip of 3, #2401-2403   .90   .90

1993, Apr. 29   Perf. 12x11½, 11½x12
Paintings: 5500cr, A Study of Love, 1883. No. 2405, David and Abizag, 1879, horiz. No. 2406, Seated Nude, 1882.

2404 A1292 5500cr multi   .30   .30
2405 A1292 36,000cr multi   1.60 1.60
2406 A1292 36,000cr multi   1.60 1.60
   Nos. 2404-2406 (3)   3.50 3.50

Natl. Flag A1292a

1993, May 26   Litho.   Die Cut
Self-adhesive
2407 A1292a A multicolored   .35   .35
   No. 2407 valued at first class domestic letter rate of 9570cr on day of issue.

Beetles A1293

1993, June 5   Litho.   Perf. 11½x12
2408 A1293 8000cr Dynastes hercules   .35   .35
2409 A1293 55,000cr Batus barbicornis 2.25 2.25

3rd Iberian-American Conference of Chiefs of State and Heads of Government, Salvador — A1294

1993, July 15   Litho.   Perf. 11x11½
2410 A1294 12,000cr multi   .20   .20

1st Brazilian Postage Stamps, 150th Anniv. — A1295

Litho. & Engr.
1993, July 30   Perf. 12x11½
2411 A1295 30,000cr No. 1   .30   .30
2412 A1295 60,000cr No. 2   .60   .60
2413 A1295 90,000cr No. 3   .90   .90
   a.   Souvenir sheet of 3, #2411-2413, wmk. 268   10.00 10.00
   Nos. 2411-2413 (3)   1.80 1.80

No. 2413a sold for 200,000cr and was issued without gum. Stamps in No. 2413a do not have imprint at bottom.

Union of Portuguese Speaking Capitals A1296

a, 15,000cr, Brasilia. b, 71,000cr, Rio de Janeiro.

1993, July 30   Litho.   Perf. 11½x12
2414 A1296 Pair, #a.-b.   .90   .90
   No. 2414 printed in continuous design.

Monica & Friends, by Mauricio de Sousa A1297

Monica, Cebolinha, Cascao, Magali, and Bidu: a, Engraving die. b, Reading proclamation, king, No. 1. c, Writing and sending letter, No. 2. d, Receiving letter, No. 3.

1993, Aug. 1
2415 A1297 (1) Strip of 4, #a.-d.   .85   .85
   First Brazilian postage stamps, 150th anniv. Nos. 2415a-2415d paid the first class rate (9600cr) on day of issue.

Brazilian Post, 330th Anniv. A1298

Postal buildings: a, Imperial Post Office, Rio de Janeiro. b, Petropolis. c, Central office, Rio de Janeiro. d, Niteroi.

1993, Aug. 3   Litho.   Perf. 11½x12
2416 A1298 20,000cr Block of 4, #a.-d.   .45   .45

Brazilian Engineering Schools — A1299

Designs: No. 2417, School of Engineering, Federal University, Rio de Janeiro. No. 2418, Polytechnical School, University of Sao Paulo.

1993, Aug. 24   Litho.   Perf. 11x11½
2417 A1299 17cr multicolored   .30   .30
2418 A1299 17cr multicolored   .30   .30

Preservation of Sambaquis Archaeological Sites — A1300

1993, Sept. 19   Perf. 12x11½
2419 A1300 17cr Two artifacts   .25   .25
2420 A1300 17cr Six artifacts   .25   .25

Ulysses Guimaraes, Natl. Congress — A1301

1993, Oct. 6   Litho.   Perf. 11x11½
2421 A1301 22cr multicolored   .30   .30

A1302   A1303

1993, Oct. 8   Litho.   Perf. 12x11½
2422 A1302 22cr multicolored   .30   .30
   Virgin of Nazare Religious Festival, bicent.

1993, Oct. 13   Litho.   Perf. 11½x11
Endangered birds (America Issue): 22cr, Anodorhynchus hyacinthinus, anodorhynchus glaucus, anodorhynchus leari. 130cr, Cyanopsitta spixii.

2423 A1303 22cr multicolored   .25   .25
2424 A1303 130cr multicolored   1.40 1.40

A1304

A1307

Composers.

1993, Oct. 19   Litho.   Perf. 12x11½
2425 A1304 22cr Vinicius de Moraes   .20   .20
2426 A1304 22cr Pixinguinha   .20   .20

1993, Oct. 29   Litho.   Perf. 12x11½
Poets: No. 2427, Mario de Andrade (1893-1945). No. 2428, Alceu Amoroso Lima (Tristao de Athayde) (1893-1983). No. 2429, Gilka Machado (1893-1980).

2427 A1307 30cr multicolored   .30   .30
2428 A1307 30cr multicolored   .30   .30
2429 A1307 30cr multicolored   .30   .30
   Nos. 2427-2429 (3)   .90   .90
   Natl. Book Day.

Brazil-Portugal Treaty of Consultation and Friendship, 40th Anniv. — A1308

1993, Nov. 3   Litho.   Perf. 11½x12
2430 A1308 30cr multicolored   .30   .30
   See Portugal No. 1980.

Image of the Republic — A1309

Photo. & Engr.

1993, Nov. 3 *Perf. 13*
2431 A1309 (B) multicolored　2.50 2.50
Valued at first class international letter rate (178.70 cr) on day of issue.

2nd Intl. Biennial of Comic Strips A1310

Cartoon drawings: No. 2432, Nho-Quim. No. 2433, Benjamin. No. 2434, Lamparina. No. 2435, Reco-Reco, Bolao, Azeitona.

1993, Nov. 11 **Litho.** *Perf. 11½x12*
2432 A1310 (1) multicolored　.40 .40
2433 A1310 (1) multicolored　.40 .40
2434 A1310 (1) multicolored　.40 .40
2435 A1310 (1) multicolored　.40 .40
　a. Block of 4, #2432-2435　1.75 1.75
Valued at first class domestic letter rate (30.20 cr) on day of issue.

Launching of First Brazilian-Built Submarine — A1311

1993, Nov. 18 *Perf. 11½*
2436 A1311 240cr multicolored　1.75 1.75

Christmas A1312

1993, Nov. 20
2437 A1312 (1) multicolored　.45 .45
Valued at first class domestic letter rate (30.20 cr) on day of issue.

First Fighter Group, 50th Anniv. A1313

1993, Dec. 18 **Litho.** *Perf. 11½*
2438 A1313 42cr multicolored　.35 .35

Convent of Merces, 340th Anniv. A1314

1994, Jan. 31 **Litho.** *Perf. 11½x12*
2439 A1314 58cr multicolored　.30 .30

Mae Menininha of Gantois, Birth Cent. — A1315

1994, Feb. 10 **Litho.** *Perf. 11x11½*
2440 A1315 80cr multicolored　.40 .40

Intl. Olympic Committee, Cent. A1316

1994, Feb. 17 *Perf. 11½x12*
2441 A1316 (1) multicolored　2.25 2.25
No. 2441 valued at first class international letter rate (446.30 cr) on day of issue.

Natl. Flag — A1317

1994, Jan. 31 **Litho.** *Die Cut*
Self-Adhesive
2442 A1317 (1) multicolored　.40 .40
No. 2442 valued at first class domestic letter rate (55.90 cr) on day of issue.

Birds A1318　Image of the Republic A1318a

1994 **Photo.** *Perf. 11x11½*
2443 A1318 10cr Notiochelidon cyanoleuca　.20 .20
2444 A1318 20cr Buteo magnirostris　.20 .20
2445 A1318 50cr Turdus rufiventris　.20 .20
2446 A1318 100cr Columbina talpacoti　.20 .20
2447 A1318 200cr Vanellus chilensis　.20 .20
2448 A1318 500cr Zonotrichia capensis　.50 .50
　Nos. 2443-2448 (6)　1.50 1.50
Issued: 10cr, 3/17; 20cr, 3/9; 50cr, 3/1; 100cr, 200cr, 4/4; 500cr, 4/13. See Nos. 2484-2494.

1994, May 10 **Litho.**
Self-Adhesive
Die Cut
2449 A1318a (1) blue　.25 .25
2450 A1318a (3) claret　.40 .40
Size: 25x35mm
Perf. 12x11½
2451 A1318a (4) green　.85 .85
2452 A1318a (5) henna brown　1.50 1.50
　Nos. 2449-2452 (4)　3.00 3.00
Nos. 2449, 2450, 2451, 2452 valued 131.37cr, 321.14cr, 452.52cr 905.05cr on day of issue.

Prince Henry the Navigator (1394-1460) — A1319

1994, Mar. 4 **Litho.** *Perf. 11½x12*
2463 A1319 635cr multicolored　2.25 2.25
See Macao No. 719, Portugal No. 1987.

America Issue A1320

Postal vehicles: 110cr, Bicycle, country scene. 635cr, Motorcycle, city scene.

1994, Mar. 18
2464 A1320 110cr multicolored　.20 .20
2465 A1320 635cr multicolored　1.10 1.10

Father Cicero Romao Batista, 150th Birth Anniv. A1321

1994, Mar. 24 *Perf. 11x11½*
2466 A1321 (1) multicolored　.35 .35
No. 2466 valued at first class domestic letter rate (98.80 cr) on day of issue.

Albert Sabin, Campaign Against Polio A1322

1994, Apr. 7 *Perf. 11½x12*
2467 A1322 160cr multicolored　.30 .30

Carlos Castello Branco, Journalist A1323

1994, Apr. 14
2468 A1323 160cr multicolored　.30 .30

Karl Friedrich Phillip von Martius, Naturalist A1324

Flowers: No. 2469, Euterpe oleracea. No. 2470, Jacaranda paucifoliolata. No. 2471, Barbacernia tomentosa.

1994, Apr. 24 *Perf. 12x11½*
2469 A1324 (1) multicolored　.35 .35
2470 A1324 (1) multicolored　.35 .35
2471 A1324 (1) multicolored　2.00 2.00
　Nos. 2469-2471 (3)　2.70 2.70
Nos. 2469-2470 were valued at first class domestic letter rate (144 cr) on day of issue. No. 2471 valued at first class intl. letter rate (860 cr) on day of issue.

Monkeys — A1326

No. 2474, Leontopithecus rosalia. No. 2475, Saguinus imperator. No. 2476, Saguinus bicolor.

1994, May 24
2474 A1326 (1) multicolored　.35 .35
2475 A1326 (1) multicolored　.35 .35
2476 A1326 (1) multicolored　.35 .35
　Nos. 2474-2476 (3)　1.05 1.05
Nos. 2474-2476 were valued at first class domestic letter rate (207.03 cr) on day of issue.

1994 World Cup Soccer Championships, US — A1327

1994, May 19 *Perf. 11½x12*
2477 A1327 (1) multicolored　2.00 2.00
No. 2477 was valued at first class intl. rate (1378.32 cr) on day of issue. Soccer in Brazil, cent.

Souvenir Sheet

46th Frankfurt Intl. Book Fair — A1328

Illustration reduced.

1994, May 27
2478 A1328 (1) multicolored　2.00 2.00
No. 2478 was valued at first class intl. rate (1523.83 cr) on day of issue.

Natl. Literacy Program — A1329

#2479, Pencil, buildings. #2480, Pencil, people on television, people watching. #2481, Classroom, pencil. #2482, Pencils crossed over fingerprint, map of Brazil.

1994, June 3 **Litho.** *Perf. 12x11½*
2479 A1329 (1) multicolored　.30 .30
2480 A1329 (1) multicolored　.30 .30
2481 A1329 (1) multicolored　.30 .30
2482 A1329 (1) multicolored　.30 .30
　Nos. 2479-2482 (4)　1.20 1.20
Nos. 2479-2482 were valued at first class domestic letter rate (233.05 cr) on day of issue.

Souvenir Sheet

Treaty of Tordesillas, 500th Anniv. — A1330

1994, June 7
2483 A1330 (1) multicolored 2.25 2.25
No. 2483 was valued at first class intl. letter rate (1689.02 cr) on day of issue.

Bird Type of 1994 and

A1330a

Perf. 11x11½, 13 (15c), 12½13 (22c, (22c)

			Photo.
1994-98			
2484 A1318	1c like No. 2443	.20	.20
2485 A1318	2c like No. 2444	.20	.20
2486 A1318	5c like No. 2445	.20	.20
2487 A1318	10c like No. 2446	.20	.20
2488 A1330a	15c Sicaris flaveola	.35	.35
2489 A1318	20c like No. 2447	.40	.40
2490 A1318	22c Tyrannus savana	.50	.50
2491 A1318	50c like No. 2448	1.00	1.00
2494 A1318	1r Furnarius rufus	2.25	2.25
	Nos. 2484-2494 (9)	5.30	5.30

Size: 21x26mm
Self-Adhesive
Serpentine Die Cut

2498 A1330a 22c Myiozetetes similis .50 .50
2499 A1330a (22c) Volatinia jacarina .50 .50
No. 2499 is inscribed "1o PORTE NATIONAL" and was valued at 22c on day of issue.
Issued: 1c, 2c, 5c, 20c, 20c, 50c, 1r, 7/1/94; 11/16/95; #2490, 10/13/97; #2498, 2/16/98; #2499, 7/22/97.
This is an expanding set. Numbers may change.

Prominent Brazilians A1331

Designs: No. 2504, Edgard Santos (1894-1962), surgeon, educator. No. 2505, Oswaldo Aranha (1894-1960), politician. No. 2507, Otto Lara Resende (1922-92), writer, educator.

1994, July 5 Litho. Perf. 11½x12
2504 A1331 (1) multicolored .30 .30
2505 A1331 (1) multicolored .30 .30
2506 A1331 (1) multicolored .30 .30
Nos. 2504-2506 (3) .90 .90
Nos. 2504-2506 were valued at first class domestic letter rate (12c) on day of issue.

A1332

 A1333

1994, July 15 Perf. 12x11½
2507 A1332 12c multicolored .30 .30
Petrobras, 40th anniv.

Litho. & Engr.
1994, July 26 Perf. 11½
2508 A1333 12c multicolored .30 .30
Brazilian State Mint, 300th anniv.

Campaign Against Famine & Misery A1334

1994, July 27 Litho. Perf. 11½x12
2509 A1334 (1) Fish .30 .30
2510 A1334 (1) Bread .30 .30
Nos. 2509-2510 were valued at first class domestic letter rate (12c) on day of issue.

Institute of Brazilian Lawyers, 150th Anniv. A1335

1994, Aug. 11
2511 A1335 12c multicolored .30 .30

Intl. Year of the Family A1336

1994, Aug. 16 Perf. 11½
2512 A1336 84c multicolored 2.00 2.00

Maternity Hospital of Sao Paulo, Cent. A1337

1994, Aug. 26 Perf. 11½x12
2513 A1337 12c multicolored .30 .30

Vincente Celestino (1894-1968), Singer — A1338

1994, Sept. 12
2514 A1338 12c multicolored .30 .30

"Contos da Carochinha," First Brazilian Children's Book, Cent. — A1339

Fairy tales: a, Joao e Maria (Hansel & Gretel). b, Dona Baratinha. c, Puss 'n Boots. d, Tom Thumb.

1994, Oct. 5 Litho. Perf. 11½x12
2515 Block of 4 4.75 4.75
a.-b. A1339 12c any single .30 .30
c.-d. A1339 84c any single 2.00 2.00

Brazilian Literature A1340

Portraits: No. 2516, Tomas Antonio Gonzaga (1744-1809?), poet. No. 2517, Fernando de Azevedo (1894-1974), author.

1994, Oct. 5 Perf. 11½
2516 A1340 12c multicolored .30 .30
2517 A1340 12c multicolored .30 .30

St. Clare of Assisi (1194-1253) A1341

1994, Oct. 19 Perf. 12x11½
2518 A1341 12c multicolored .30 .30

Ayrton Senna (1960-1994), Race Car Driver — A1342

Designs: a, McClaren Formula 1 race car, Brazilian flag. b, Fans, Senna. c, Flags, race cars, Senna.

1994, Oct. 24 Perf. 11½x12
2519 Triptych 2.75 2.75
a.-b. A1342 12c any single .30 .30
c. A1342 84c multicolored 2.00 2.00

Institute of History & Geography of Sao Paulo, Cent. A1343

1994, Nov. 1
2520 A1343 12c multicolored .30 .30

Popular Music A1344

Designs: No. 2521, Music from "The Sea," by Dorival Caymmi. No. 2522, Adoniran Barbosa (1910-82), samba composer.

1994, Nov. 5 Perf. 11½
2521 A1344 12c multicolored .30 .30
2522 A1344 12c multicolored .30 .30

Christmas A1345

Folk characters: No. 2523: a, Boy wearing Santa coat, pot on head. b, Worm in apple. c, Man, animals singing. d, Shoe on tree stump, man with pipe holding pen.

1994, Dec. 1 Litho. Perf. 11½
2523 Block of 4 2.75 2.75
a. A1345 84c multicolored 1.90 1.90
b.-d. A1345 12c any single .30 .30
e. Booklet pane, #2523 + 4 labels 5.50
Complete booklet, #2523a 5.50

Souvenir Sheet

Brazil, 1994 World Cup Soccer Champions — A1346
Illustration reduced.

1994, Dec. 5 Perf. 12x11½
2524 A1346 2.14r multicolored 5.00 5.00

Louis Pasteur (1822-95) A1347

1995, Feb. 19 Litho. Perf. 11½x12
2525 A1347 84c multicolored 2.00 2.00

Historical Events A1348

Designs: No. 2526, Capture of Monte Castello, 50th anniv. No. 2527, End of the Farroupilha Revolution, 150th anniv.

1995, Feb. 21
2526 A1348 12c multicolored .30 .30
2527 A1348 12c multicolored .30 .30

Pres. Itamar Franco — A1349   **FAO, 50th Anniv. — A1350**

1995, Mar. 22   Litho.   Perf. 12x11½
2528 A1349 12c multicolored .30 .30

1995, Apr. 3   Perf. 11½x11
2529 A1350 84c multicolored 2.00 2.00

Famous Men A1351

#2530, Alexandre de Gusmao (1695-1753), diplomat. #2531, Francisco Brandao, Viscount of Jequitinhonha (1794-1870), lawyer, abolitionist. 15c, Jose da Silva Paranhos, Jr., Baron of Rio Branco (1845-1912), politician, diplomat.

1995, Apr. 28   Perf. 11½x12
2530 A1351 12c multicolored .30 .30
2531 A1351 12c multicolored .30 .30
2532 A1351 15c multicolored .35 .35
  Nos. 2530-2532 (3) .95 .95

Radio, Cent. A1352

Design: Guglielmo Marconi (1874-1937), transmitting equipment.

1995, May 5   Litho.   Perf. 11½x12
2533 A1352 84c multicolored 2.00 2.00

Friendship Between Brazil & Japan A1353

1995, May 29
2534 A1353 84c multicolored 2.00 2.00

Endangered Birds — A1354

1995, June 5   Perf. 12x11½
2535 A1354 12c Tinamus solitarius .30 .30
2536 A1354 12c Mitu mitu .30 .30

June Festivals — A1355

Designs: No. 2537, Couples dancing at Campina Grande, "Greatest St. John's Party of the World." No. 2538, Bride, bridegroom, festivities, Caruaru.

1995, June 11   Perf. 11½x12
2537 A1355 12c multicolored .30 .30
2538 A1355 12c multicolored .30 .30

St. Anthony of Padua (1195-1231) — A1356

1995, June 13
2539 A1356 84c multicolored 2.00 2.00
  See Portugal No. 2054.

Souvenir Sheet

Motion Picture, Cent. — A1357

Louis and Auguste Lumiere, camera.

1995, June 21
2540 A1357 2.14r multicolored 4.75 4.75

New Currency, The Real, 1st Anniv. — A1358

1995, July 1   Litho.   Perf. 12x11½
2541 A1358 12c multicolored .30 .30

Volleyball, Cent. — A1359

1995, July 8
2542 A1359 15c multicolored .35 .35

Dinosaurs A1360

1995, July 23   Perf. 11½x12
2543 A1360 15c Angaturama limai .35 .35
2544 A1360 1.50r Titanosaurus 3.25 3.25

Traffic Safety Program A1361

Designs: 12c, Test dummy without seat belt hitting windshield. 71c, Auto hitting alcoholic beverage glass.

1995, July 25
2545 A1361 12c multicolored .30 .30
2546 A1361 71c multicolored 1.65 1.65

Souvenir Sheet

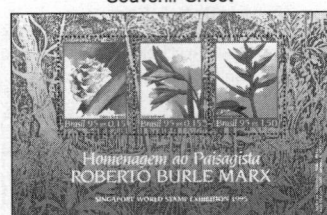

Roberto Burle Marx, Botanist — A1362

Designs: a, 15c, Calathea burle-marxii. b, 15c, Vellozia burle-marxii. c, 1.50r, Heliconia aemygdiana. Illustration reduced.

1995, Aug. 4   Litho.   Perf. 12x11½
2547 A1362 Sheet of 3, #a.-c. 4.50 4.50
  Singapore '95.

Parachute Infantry Brigade, 50th Anniv. — A1363

1995, Aug. 23
2548 A1363 15c multicolored .35 .35

Paulista Museum, Cent. A1364

1995, Sept. 5   Perf. 11½
2549 A1364 15c multicolored .35 .35

Lighthouses A1365

1995, Sept. 28
2550 A1365 15c Olinda .35 .35
2551 A1365 15c Sao Joao .35 .35
2552 A1365 15c Santo Antonio da Barra .35 .35
  Nos. 2550-2552 (3) 1.05 1.05

Wilhelm Röntgen (1845-1923), Discovery of the X-Ray, Cent. A1366

1995, Sept. 30
2553 A1366 84c multicolored 2.00 2.00

Lubrapex '95, 15th Brazilian-Portuguese Philatelic Exhibition — A1367

Wildlife scene along Tiete River: 15c, #2556a, Bird, otter with fish. 84c, #2556b, Birds, river boat.

1995, Sept. 30   Perf. 12x11½
2554 A1367 15c multicolored .35 .35
2555 A1367 84c multicolored 2.00 2.00

Souvenir Sheet
2556 A1367 1.50r Sheet of 2, #a.-b. 6.50 6.50
  No. 2556 is a continuous design.

Flamengo Regatta Soccer Club — A1368

1995, Oct. 6   Perf. 11x11½
2557 A1368 15c multicolored .35 .35

America Issue A1369

Outdoor scenes: 15c, Trees, mushrooms, alligator, lake. 84c, Black-neck swans on lake, false swans in air.

1995, Oct. 12   Litho.   Perf. 11½x12
2558 A1369 15c multicolored .35 .35
2559 A1369 84c multicolored 2.00 2.00
  a. Pair, #2558-2559 2.35 2.35

UN, 50th Anniv. — A1370

1995, Oct. 24   Perf. 12x11½
2560 1.05r multicolored 2.25 2.25
2561 1.05r multicolored 2.25 2.25
  a. A1370 Pair, No. 2560-2561 4.50 4.50

Writers — A1372

Designs: No. 2562, Eca de Queiroz (1845-90), village. No. 2563, Rubem Braga (1913-90), beach, Rio de Janeiro. 23c, Carlos Drummond de Andrade (1902-87), letters.

1995, Oct. 27   *Perf. 12x11*
2562 A1372 15c multicolored   .35 .35
2563 A1372 15c multicolored   .35 .35
2564 A1372 23c multicolored   .50 .50
   Nos. 2562-2564 (3)   1.20 1.20

Souvenir Sheet

Death of Zumbi Dos Palmares, Slave
Resistance Leader, 300th
Anniv. — A1373

Illustration reduced.

1995, Nov. 20   *Perf. 12x11½*
2565 A1373 1.05r multicolored   2.25 2.25

2nd World Short Course Swimming
Championships — A1374

Four swimmers performing different strokes:
a, Freestyle. b, Backstroke. c, Butterfly. d,
Breaststroke.

1995, Nov. 30   *Perf. 11½x12*
2566 A1374 23c Block of 4, #a.-
     d.   2.00 2.00

Christmas
A1375

Designs: a, 23c, Cherub looking right, stars.
b, 15c, Cherub looking left, stars.

1995, Dec. 1   *Perf. 11½*
2567 A1375 Pair, #a.-b.+2 labels   .85 .85

Botafogo
Soccer
and
Regatta
Club
A1376

1995, Dec. 8   *Perf. 11x11½*
2568 A1376 15c multicolored   .35 .35

Diário de
Pernambuco
Newspaper,
170th
Anniv. — A1377

1995, Dec. 14   Litho.   *Perf. 12x11½*
2569 A1377 23c multicolored   .50 .50

Souvenir Sheet

Amazon Theatre, Cent. — A1378

Illustration reduced.

1996, Feb. 27
2570 A1378 1.23r multicolored   2.50 2.50

Francisco
Prestes
Maia,
Politician,
Birth Cent.
A1379

1996, Mar. 19   *Perf. 11½x12*
2571 A1379 18c multicolored   .40 .40

Irineu Bornhausen, Governor of Santa
Catarina, Birth Cent. — A1380

1996, Mar. 25   *Perf. 11x11½*
2572 A1380 27c multicolored   .55 .55

Paintings
A1381

Designs: No. 2573, Boat with Little Flags
and Birds, by Alfredo Volpi. No. 2574, Ouro
Preto Landscape, by Alberto da Veiga
Guignard.

1996, Apr. 15   *Perf. 12x11½*
2573 A1381 15c multicolored   .30 .30
2574 A1381 15c multicolored   .30 .30

UNICEF,
50th Anniv.
A1382

1996, Apr. 16   *Perf. 11½*
2575 A1382 23c multicolored   .50 .50

Portuguese
Discovery of
Brazil, 500th
Anniv. (in
2000) — A1383

1996, Apr. 22   *Perf. 12x11½*
2576 A1383 1.05r multicolored   2.10 2.10
   See No. 2626.

Israel Pinheiro da Silva, Politician,
Business Entrepeneur, Birth
Cent. — A1384

1996, Apr. 23   *Perf. 11½x12*
2577 A1384 18c multicolored   .40 .40

Tourism
A1385

#2578, Amazon River. #2579, Swampland
area. #2580, Sail boat, northeastern states.
#2581, Sugarloaf, Guanabara Bay. #2582,
Iguacu Falls.

1996, Apr. 24   *Die Cut*
     Self-Adhesive
2578 A1385 23c multicolored   .50 .50
2579 A1385 23c multicolored   .50 .50
2580 A1385 23c multicolored   .50 .50
2581 A1385 23c multicolored   .50 .50
2582 A1385 23c multicolored   .50 .50
   a.   Strip of 5, #2578-2582   2.50

Hummingbirds — A1386

Espamer '96: 15c, Topaza pella. 1.05r,
Stephanoxis lalandi. 1.15r, Eupetomena
macroura.

1996, May 4   Litho.   *Perf. 11½*
2583 A1386 15c multicolored   .35 .35
2584 A1386 1.05r multicolored   2.40 2.40
2585 A1386 1.15r multicolored   2.60 2.60
   Nos. 2583-2585 (3)   5.35 5.35

1996
Summer
Olympic
Games,
Atlanta
A1387

1996, May 21
2586 A1387 18c Marathon   .40 .40
2587 A1387 23c Gymnastics   .50 .50
2588 A1387 1.05r Swimming   2.40 2.40
2589 A1387 1.05r Beach volley-
     ball   2.40 2.40
   Nos. 2586-2589 (4)   5.70 5.70

Souvenir Sheet

Brazilian Caverns — A1388

Illustration reduced.

1996, June 5   *Perf. 11½x12*
2590 A1388 2.68r multicolored   6.25 6.25

Americas
Telecom
'96 — A1389

1996, June 10   *Perf. 11½*
2591 A1389 1.05r multicolored   2.40 2.40

Souvenir Sheet

World Day to Fight
Desertification — A1390

Illustration reduced.

1996, June 17   *Perf. 12x11½*
2592 A1390 1.23r multicolored   2.80 2.80

Fight
Against
Drug Abuse
A1391

1996, June 26   *Perf. 11½x12*
2593 A1391 27c multicolored   .65 .65

Year of Education
A1392

1996, July 10   *Perf. 12x11½*
2594 A1392 23c multicolored   .55 .55

Princess Isabel, 150th Birth Anniv. A1393

1996, July 29 *Perf. 11½x12*
2595 A1393 18c multicolored .40 .40

Carlos Gomes (1836-96), Composer A1394

1996, Sept. 16 *Perf. 11½*
2596 A1394 50c multicolored 1.25 1.25

15th World Orchid Conference A1395

#2597, Promenaea stapelioides Lindley. #2598, Cattleya eldorado. #2599, Cattleya loddigesiis.

1996, Sept. 17
2597 A1395 15c multicolored .35 .35
2598 A1395 15c multicolored .35 .35
2599 A1395 15c multicolored .35 .35
Nos. 2597-2599 (3) 1.05 1.05

Apparition of Virgin Mary at La Salette, 150th Anniv. A1396

1996, Sept. 19
2600 A1396 1r multicolored 2.30 2.30

Souvenir Sheet

Popular Legends A1397

Designs: a, 23c, "Cuca" walking from house. b, 1.05r, "Boitatá," snake of life. c, 1.15r, "Caipora," defender of ecology.

1996, Sept. 28 *Perf. 11x10½*
2601 A1397 Sheet of 3, #a.-c. 5.60 5.60
BRAPEX '96.

23rd Sao Paulo Intl. Biennial Exhibition A1398

Designs: a, Marilyn Monroe by Andy Warhol, vert. b, The Scream, by Edvard Munch, vert. c, Abstract, by Louise Bourgeois, vert. d, Woman Drawing, by Pablo Picasso.

1996, Oct. 5 *Perf. 12x11½*
2602 A1398 55c Block of 4, #a.-d. 5.00 5.00

Traditional Costumes A1400

America issue: 50c, Man dressed as cowboy. 1r, Woman dressed in baiana clothes.

1996, Oct. 12 *Litho.* *Perf. 11½*
2604 A1400 50c multicolored 1.15 1.15
2605 A1400 1r multicolored 2.30 2.30

Christmas A1401

José Carlos (1884-1950), Carcicaturist A1402

1996, Nov. 4 *Litho.* *Perf. 12x11½*
2606 A1401 1st multicolored .60 .60
No. 2606 was valued at 23c on day of issue.

1996, Nov. 22
2607 A1402 1st multicolored .60 .60
No. 2607 was valued at 23c on day of issue.

Tourism A1403

#2608, Ipiranga Monument, Sao Paulo. #2607, Hercílio Luz Bridge, Florianópolis. #2608, Natl. Congress Building, Brasília. #2609, Pelourinho, Salvador. #2610, Ver-o-Peso Market, Belém.

Serpentine Die Cut
1996, Dec. 9 *Photo.*
Self-Adhesive
2608 A1403 1st multicolored .75 .75
2609 A1403 1st multicolored .75 .75
2610 A1403 1st multicolored .75 .75
2611 A1403 1st multicolored .75 .75
2612 A1403 1st multicolored .75 .75
a. Strip of 5, #2608-2612 3.75

Nos. 2608-2612 are inscribed "1o PORTE NACIONAL," and were valued at 23c on day of issue. Selvage surrounding each stamp in #2612a is rouletted.

Rio de Janeiro, Candidate for 2004 Summer Olympic Games A1404

1997, Jan. 17 *Litho.* *Perf. 11½*
2613 A1404 1st multicolored 2.25 2.25
No. 2613 is inscribed "1o PORTE INTERNACIONAL" and was valued at 1.05r on day of issue.

The Postman A1405

1997, Jan. 25
2614 A1405 1st multicolored .85 .85
America issue. No. 2614 is inscribed "1o PORTE NACIONAL" and was valued at 23c on day of issue.

Antonio de Castro Alves (1847-71), Poet A1406

1997, Mar. 14
2615 A1406 15c multicolored .35 .35

Marquis of Tamandaré, Naval Officer, Death Cent. — A1407

1997, Mar. 19 *Perf. 11x11½*
2616 A1407 23c multicolored .50 .50

Stamp Design Contest Winner A1408

1997, Mar. 20 *Perf. 11½x12*
2617 A1408 15c "Joy Joy" .35 .35

World Day of Water — A1409

1997, Mar. 22 *Perf. 12x11½*
2618 A1409 1.05r multicolored 2.10 2.10

Brazilian Airplanes A1410

#2619, EMB-145. #2620, AMX. #2621, EMB-312 H Super Tucano. #2622, EMB-120 Brasilia. #2623, EMB-312 Tucano.

1997, Mar. 27 *Litho.* *Die Cut*
Self-Adhesive
2619 A1410 15c multicolored .25 .25
2620 A1410 15c multicolored .25 .25
2621 A1410 15c multicolored .25 .25
2622 A1410 15c multicolored .25 .25
2623 A1410 15c multicolored .25 .25
a. Strip of 5, #2619-2623 1.25

Campaign Against AIDS — A1411

1997, Apr. 7 *Litho.* *Perf. 12x11½*
2624 A1411 23c multicolored .50 .50

Souvenir Sheet

Indian Culture — A1412

Weapons of the Xingu Indians. Illustration reduced.

1997, Apr. 16 *Perf. 11x11½*
2625 A1412 1.15r multicolored 2.25 2.25

Portuguese Discovery of Brazil, 500th Anniv. Type
1997, Apr. 22 *Perf. 12x11½*
2626 A1383 1.05r like #2576 2.10 2.20

No. 2576 has green background and blue in lower right corner. No. 2626 has those colors reversed and is inscribed "BRASIL 97" at top.

Pixinguinha (1897-1973), Composer, Musician — A1413

1997, Apr. 23
2627 A1413 15c multicolored .35 .35

Souvenir Sheet

Brazilian Claim to Trindade Island, Cent. — A1414

Illustration reduced.

1997, May 7 *Perf. 11½x11*
2628 A1414 1.23r multicolored 2.50 2.50

Human Rights — A1415

1997, May 13 **Perf. 12x11½**
2629 A1415 18c multicolored   .45 .45

Souvenir Sheet

Brazilian Antarctic Program — A1416

1997, May 13
2630 A1416 2.68r multicolored   5.50 5.50

Fruits and Nuts — A1417

1c, Oranges. 2c, Bananas. 5c, Papayas. 10c, Pineapple. #2635, 2636L, Cashews. #2636, 2636Q, Sugar apple. #2636A, Grapes. #2636B, 2636M, 2636R, Watermelon. 50c, Surinam cherry (pitanga), 51c, Coconuts. 80c, Apples. 82c, Lemons. 1r, Strawberries.

1997-99 Litho. *Serpentine Die Cut*
Self-Adhesive

2631	A1417	1c multi	.20	.20
2632	A1417	2c multi	.20	.20
2633	A1417	5c multi	.20	.20
2634	A1417	10c multi, vert.	.20	.20
2635	A1417	20c multi, vert.	.40	.40
2636	A1417	20c multi, vert.	.40	.40
2636A	A1417	22c multi	.40	.40
2636B	A1417	(22c) multi	.45	.45
2636C	A1417	50c multi	.55	.55
2636D	A1417	51c multi, vert.	1.00	1.00
2636E	A1417	80c multi, vert.	1.40	1.40
2636F	A1417	82c multi, vert.	1.60	1.60
2636G	A1417	1r multi, vert.	2.00	2.00
		Nos. 2631-2636G (13)	9.00	9.00

Issued: (22c), 5/28; 1c, 6/97; 2c, 10c, #2635, 7/97; 5c, 8/97; 1r, 8/3; 22c, 10/3; #2636, 51c, 80c, 82c, 1/15/98; 50c, 11/26/99.
No. 2636B is inscribed "1o PORTE NATIONAL" and was valued at 22c on day of issue.

Fruits and Nuts Type of 1997-99
1998-99 Litho. *Die Cut*
Self-Adhesive

2636H	A1417	1c multi	.20	.20
2636I	A1417	2c multi	.45	.45
2636J	A1417	5c multi	1.10	1.10
2636K	A1417	10c multi, vert.	2.25	2.25
2636L	A1417	20c multi, vert.	4.25	4.25
2636M	A1417	(22c) multi	4.75	4.75
		Nos. 2636H-2636M (6)	13.00	13.00

Issued: No. 2636M, 1999; others, 1998.

Fruit and Nuts Type of 1997-99
1999 Litho. *Microperfed*
Without Gum

2636N	A1417	1c multi	.25	.25
2636O	A1417	5c multi	1.10	1.10
2636P	A1417	10c multi, vert.	2.25	2.25
2636Q	A1417	20c multi, vert.	4.50	4.50
2636R	A1417	(31c) multi	7.00	7.00
2636S	A1417	51c multi, vert.	11.50	11.50
2636T	A1417	80c multi, vert.	18.00	18.00
2636U	A1417	1r multi, vert.	22.50	22.50
		Nos. 2636N-2636U (8)	67.10	67.10

Issued: Nos. 2636N-2636Q, 9/28/99; No. 2636R, 9/12/99; No. 2636S, 9/22/99; Nos. 2636T, 2636U, 9/15/99.

A1418

Amazon Flora and Fauna — A1419

Designs: No. 2637, Swietenia macropylla. No. 2638, Arapaima gigas.

1997, June 5 Litho. **Perf. 11½x12**
2637 A1418 27c multicolored   .55 .55
2638 A1419 27c multicolored   .55 .55

Fr. José de Anchieta (1534-97), Missionary in Brazil — A1420

Design: No. 2640, Fr. António Vieira (1608-97), missionary in Brazil, diplomat.

1997, June 9 **Perf. 12**
2639 A1420 1.05r multicolored   2.10 2.10
2640 A1420 1.05r multicolored   2.10 2.10

See Portugal Nos. 2168-2169.

Tourism A1421

Designs: No. 2641, Parnaíba River Delta. No. 2642, Lençóis Maranhenses Park.

1997, June 20 **Perf. 11½x12**
2641 A1421 1st multicolored   2.10 2.10
2642 A1421 1st multicolored   2.10 2.10

Nos. 2641-2642 are inscribed "1o PORTE INTERNACIONAL TAXE PERCUE" and were each valued at on day of issue.

Brazilian Academy of Literature, Cent. A1422

1997, July 20
2643 A1422 22c multicolored   .50 .50

Emiliano de Cavalcanti (1897-1976), Painter A1423

1997, Sept. 16 Litho. **Perf. 11½**
2644 A1423 31c multicolored   .65 .65

2nd World Meeting of the Pope with Families, Rio de Janeiro A1424

1997, Sept. 22 **Perf. 11½x12**
2645 A1424 1.20r multicolored   2.50 2.50

A1425

A1426

1997, Sept. 26 **Perf. 12x11½**
2646 A1425 80c multicolored   1.60 1.60

MERCOSUR (Common Market of Latin America). See Argentina #1975, Bolivia #1019, Paraguay #2565, Uruguay #1681.

1997, Sept. 27
2647 A1426 22c multicolored   .45 .45

End of Canudos War, cent.

Integration of MERCOSUR Communications by Telebras, 25th Anniv. — A1427

1997, Oct. 6 **Perf. 11½**
2648 A1427 80c multicolored   1.60 1.60

Composers — A1428

#2649, Oscar Lorenzo Fernandez (1897-1948). #2650, Francisco Mignone (1897-1986).

1997, Oct. 7 **Perf. 11x11½**
2649 A1428 22c multicolored   .45 .45
2650 A1428 22c multicolored   .45 .45

Marist Brothers Presence in Brazil, Cent. A1429

1997, Oct. 22
2651 A1429 22c multicolored   .45 .45

Christmas A1430

1997, Nov. 5 **Perf. 12x11½**
2652 A1430 22c multicolored   .45 .45

Education and Citzenship — A1431

1997, Dec. 10 **Perf. 11x11½**
2653 A1431 31c blue & yellow   .65 .65

City of Belo Horizonte, Cent. A1432

1997, Dec. 12 **Perf. 11½x12**
2654 A1432 31c multicolored   .65 .65

Citzenship A1433

Map of Brazil and: No. 2655, Education, stack of books. No. 2656, Employment, worker's papers. No. 2657, Agriculture, oranges. No. 2658, Health, stethoscope, vert. No. 2659, Culture, clapboard with musical notes, artist's paint brush, vert.

1997, Dec. 20 **Die Cut**
Self-Adhesive
Booklet Stamps

2655	A1433	22c multicolored	.45	.45
2656	A1433	22c multicolored	.45	.45
2657	A1433	22c multicolored	.45	.45
2658	A1433	22c multicolored	.45	.45
2659	A1433	22c multicolored	.45	.45
a.		Bklt. pane, 2 ea #2655-2659	4.50	

The peelable paper backing of No. 2659a serves as a booklet cover.

Gems — A1434

1998, Jan. 22 **Perf. 12x11½**
2660 A1434 22c Alexandrite   .45 .45
2661 A1434 22c Cat's eye chrys-
          oberyl   .45 .45
2662 A1434 22c Indicolite   .45 .45
a.   Strip of 3, #2660-2662   1.40 1.40

Famous Brazilian Women A1435

America Issue: No. 2663, Elis Regina, singer. No. 2664, Clementia de Jesus, singer. No. 2665, Dulcina de Moraes, actress. No. 2666, Clarice Lispector, writer.

1998, Mar. 11 *Perf. 11½*
2663 A1435 22c multicolored .45 .45
2664 A1435 22c multicolored .45 .45
2665 A1435 22c multicolored .45 .45
2666 A1435 22c multicolored .45 .45
a. Block of 4, #2663-2666 1.80 1.80

Education — A1436

1998, Mar. 19 *Perf. 12x11½*
2667 31c Children at desks .65 .65
2668 31c Teacher at blackboard .65 .65
a. A1436 Pair, #2667-2668 1.30 1.30

Cruz e Sousa (1861-98), Poet A1437

1998, Mar. 19 Litho. *Perf. 11½x12*
2669 A1437 36c multicolored .65 .65

Discovery of Brazil, 500th Anniv. — A1438

#2670, 1519 map showing natives, vegetation, fauna. #2671, Caravel from Cabral's fleet.

1998, Apr. 22 *Perf. 12x11½*
2670 1.05r multicolored 1.75 1.75
2671 1.05r multicolored 1.75 1.75
a. A1438 Pair, #2670-2671 3.50 3.50

Volunteer Work A1439

Designs: a, Caring for sick man. b, Caring for sick child. c, Fighting forest fire. d, Child's hand holding adult's finger.

1998, May 5 *Perf. 11½x12*
2672 A1439 31c Block of 4, #a.-d. 2.25 2.25

Brazilian Circus — A1440

Piolin the clown: a, Looking through circle. b, Standing in ring. c, With outside of tent to the left. d, With inside of tent to the right.

1998, May 18 *Perf. 12x11½*
2673 A1440 31c Block of 4, #a.-d. 2.25 2.25

Intl. Year of the Ocean A1441

Pictures, drawings of marine life: a, Turtle. b, Tail fin of whale. c, Barracuda. d, Jellyfish, school of fish. e, School of fish, diver. f, Dolphins. g, Yellow round fish. h, Two whales. i, Two black-striped butterfly fish. j, Orange & yellow fish. k, Manatee. l, Yellow-striped fish. m, Blue & yellow fish. n, Several striped fish. o, Fish with wing-like fins. p, Manta ray. q, Two fish swimming in opposite directions. r, Long, thin fish, coral. s, Moray eel. t, Yellow & black butterfly fish, coral. u, Starfish, fish. v, Crab, coral. w, Black & orange fish, coral. x, Sea horse, coral.

1998, May 22 *Perf. 11½x12*
Sheet of 24
2674 A1441 31c #a.-x. 12.50 12.50
Expo '98.

1998 World Cup Soccer Championships, France — A1442

Stylized paintings, by: a, Gregorio Gruber. b, Mario Gruber. c, Maciej Babinski. d, Cildo Meireles, vert. e, Claudio Tozzi, vert. f, Antonio Henrique Amaral, vert. g, Jose Roberto Aguilar. h, Nelson Leirner. i, Wesley Duke Lee. j, Mauricio Nogueira Lima. k, Zelio Alves Pinto, vert. l, Aldemir Martins, vert. m, Ivald Granato. n, Carlos Vergara. o, Joao Camara, vert. p, Roberto Magalhaes, vert. q, Guto Lacaz, vert. r, Glauco Rodrigues, vert. s, Leda Catunda. t, Tomoshige Kusuno. u, Jose Zaragoza. v, Luiz Zerbine, vert. w, Antonio Peticov, vert. x, Marcia Grostein, vert.

1998, May 28 *Perf. 11½x12, 12x11½*
2675 A1442 22c Sheet of 24, #a.-x. 9.00 9.00

Feijoada, Traditional Cuisine A1443

1998, June 1 *Perf. 11½*
2676 A1443 31c multicolored .55 .55

Preservation of Flora and Fauna — A1444

Designs: No. 2677, Araucaria angustifolia. No. 2678, Cyanocorax caeruleus.

1998, June 5 *Perf. 11½x12*
2677 A1444 22c multicolored .40 .40
2678 A1444 22c multicolored .40 .40
a. Pair, #2677-2678 .80 .80

Launching of Submarine Tapajó A1445

1998, June 5
2679 A1445 51c multicolored .90 .90

Luiz de Queiroz (1849-98), Founder of Agricultural School A1446

1998, June 6 *Perf. 11½*
2680 A1446 36c multicolored .65 .65

Benedictine Monastery, Sao Paulo, 400th Anniv. A1447

1998, July 10 Litho. *Perf. 11½x12*
2681 A1447 22c multicolored .25 .25

Alberto Santos-Dumont (1873-1932), Aviation Pioneer — A1448

#2682, Balloon "Brazil." #2683, Dirigible Nr. 1, Santos-Dumont at controls.

1998, July 18
2682 A1448 31c multicolored .35 .35
2683 A1448 31c multicolored .35 .35
a. Pair, #2682-2683 .70 .70

Brazilian Cinema, Cent. (in 1997) A1449

Designs: a, Guanabara Bay, by Lumière, 1897. b, Taciana Reiss in "Limite," by Mário Peixoto, 1931. c, Actors in (Chanchada)," from "A Dupla do Barulho," by Carlos Manga, 1953. d, Films produced by Vera Cruz pictures, caricature of Mazzaropi from "The Dream Factory." e, Glauber Rocha's "New Cinema". f,

International film festival awards won by Brazilian films.

1998, July 24 *Perf. 11½*
2684 A1449 31c Block of 6, #a.-f. 2.00 2.00

Rodrigo Melo Franco de Andrade (1898-1969) — A1450

Church of Our Lady of the Rosary, Ouro Preto.

1998, Aug. 17 *Perf. 11x11½*
2685 A1450 51c multicolored .60 .60

Luís da Camara Cascudo (1898-1986), Writer — A1451

1998, Aug. 22
2686 A1451 22c multicolored .25 .25

42nd Aeronautical Pentathlon World Championship A1452

Stylized designs: a, Fencing. b, Running. c, Swimming. d, Shooting. e, Basketball.

1998, Aug. 22 *Perf. 12x11½*
2687 A1452 22c Strip of 5, #a.-e. 1.25 1.25

Mercosur — A1453

Design: Missionary Cross, ruins of the Church of Sao Miguel das Missoes.

1998, Sept. 17 *Perf. 11½x12*
2688 A1453 80c multicolored .90 .90

24th Sao Paulo Art Biennial — A1454

a, Biennial emblem, by José Leonilson. b, Tapuia Dance, by Albert von Eckhout. c, The Schoolboy, by Vincent van Gogh. d, Portrait of Michel Leiris, by Francis Bacon. e, The King's Museum, by René Magritte. f, Urutu, by Tarsila do Amaral. g, Facade with Arcs, Circle and Fascia, by Alfredo Volpi. h, The Raft of the Medusa, by Asger Jorn.

1998, Sept. 22
2689 A1454 31c Block of 8, #a.-h. 2.00 2.00

Nos. 2689b, 2689h have horiz. designs placed vert. on stamps.

Child and
Citzenship
Stamp
Design
Contest
Winner
A1455

1998, Oct. 9
2690 A1455 22c multicolored   .25 .25

Reorganization of Maritime Mail from
Portugal to Brazil, Bicent. — A1456

1998, Oct. 9
2691 A1456 1.20r multicolored   1.25 1.25
See Portugal Nos. 2271-2272.

Dom Pedro I
(1798-1834)
A1457

1998, Oct. 13   *Perf. 11½*
2692 A1457 22c multicolored   .25 .25

Frisco's Mango
Refreshment
Promotional
Stamp — A1458

Serpentine Die Cut
1998, Oct. 15   **Photo.**
Self-Adhesive
2693 A1458 36c multicolored   .40 .40
No. 2693 is valid on all mail, but must be
used on mail entries to Frisco on Faustao's
Truck raffle.

Flowers
A1459

Designs: a, Solanum lycocarpum. b, Cattleya walkeriana. c, Kielmeyera coriacea.

1998, Oct. 23   Litho.   Perf. 11½
2694 A1459 31c Strip of 3, #a.-c. 1.00 1.00

Humanitarians — A1460

Designs: a, Mother Teresa (1910-97). b,
Friar Galvao (1739-1822). c, Herbert José de

Souza "Betinho" (b. 1935). d, Friar Damiao
(1898-1997).

1998, Oct. 25
2695 A1460 31c Block of 4, #a.-
       d.   1.40 1.40

Natl. Telecommunications Agency
(ANATEL) — A1461

Design: Sergio Motta, former Minister of
Communications, ANATEL headquarters,
Brasilia.

1998, Nov. 5   Perf. 12x11½
2696 A1461 31c multicolored   .35 .35

Christmas — A1462

Design: Athos Bulcao's tiles, Church of Our
Lady of Fatima, Brasilia, outline of sanctuary.

1998, Nov. 19   Perf. 11½x12
2697 A1462 22c multicolored   .25 .25

Domestic
Animals
A1463

No. 2698, Moxotó goat. No. 2699, Brazilian
donkey. No. 2700, Junqueira ox. No. 2701,
Brazilian terrier. No. 2702, Brazilian shorthair
cat.

1998, Nov. 20   Die Cut
Booklet Stamps
Self-Adhesive
2698 A1463 22c multi   .25 .25
2699 A1463 22c multi   .25 .25
2700 A1463 22c multi   .25 .25
2701 A1463 22c multi, vert.   .25 .25
2702 A1463 22c multi, vert.   .25 .25
 a.   Bklt. pane, 2 ea #2698-2702 2.50
No. 2702a is a complete booklet.

Universal
Declaration of
Human Rights,
50th
Anniv. — A1464

1998, Dec. 9   Perf. 12x11½
2703 A1464 1.20r multicolored 1.25 1.25

Natal,
400th
Anniv.
A1465

Perf. 11x11½, 11½x11
1999, Jan. 6   Litho.
2704 A1465 31c Wise Men's For-
       tress   .35 .35
2705 A1465 31c Mother Luiza
       Lighthouse,
       vert.   .35 .35

Program for
Evaluating
Resources
in Brazil's
Exclusive
Economic
Zone
A1466

No. 2706: a, Satellite, St. Peter and St. Paul
Archpelago. b, Bird on buoy. c, Fishing boat.
d, Sea turtle. e, Dolphin. f, Diver.

1999, Mar. 5   Perf. 11½x12
2706 A1466 31c Block of 6, #a.-f. 2.00 2.00
Australia '99 World Stamp Expo.

UPU, 125th
Anniv.
A1467

No. 2707: a, Stamp vending machines from
1940s and 1998. b, Vending machines, 1906,
1998. c, Collection boxes, 1870, 1973. d, Federal Government's 1998 Quality Award.

1999, Mar. 19   Perf. 11½
2707 A1467 31c Block of 4, #a.-
       d.   1.40 1.40
Reorganization of Brazilian Posts and Telegraphs, 30th anniv.

City of Salvador, 450th
Anniv. — A1468

1999, Mar. 29   Litho.   Perf. 11½x12
2708 A1468 1.05r multi   1.25 1.25

Dinosaurs'
Valley
A1469

1999, Apr. 17   Litho.   Perf. 11½x12
2709 A1469 1.05r multicolored 1.10 1.10

Fort of Santo Amaro da Barra
Grande — A1470

1999, Apr. 21   Litho.   Perf. 11½x12
2710 A1470 22c multicolored   .25 .25

Discovery of Brazil, 500th Anniv. (in
2000) — A1471

Illustration reduced.

1999, Apr. 22   Litho.   Perf. 11½x11
2711 A1471 2.68r multi   3.25 3.25
Lubrapex 2000.

6th Air Transportation Squadron, 30th
Anniv. — A1472

1999, May 12   Litho.   Perf. 11x11½
2712 A1472 51c multicolored   .55 .55

Holy Spirit Feast,
Planaltina — A1473

1999, May 21   Perf. 12x11½
2713 A1473 22c multicolored   .25 .25

Historical
and
Cultural
Heritage
A1474

Views of cities: a, Ouro Preto. b, Olinda. c,
Sao Luís.

1999, June 2   Perf. 11½x11
2714 A1474 1.05r Sheet of 3,
       #a.-c.   3.25 3.25
PhilexFrance '99, World Philatelic Exhibition.

Sao Paolo State Institute for Technological Research, Cent. — A1475

1999, June 24 Litho. Perf. 11½x12
2715 A1475 36c multicolored .40 .40

Flight of Alberto Santos-Dumont's Dirigible No. 3, Cent. — A1476

1999, July 20
2716 A1476 1.20r multicolored 1.40 1.40

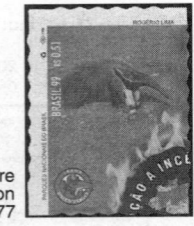

Forest Fire Prevention A1477

a, Anteater. b, Flower. c, Leaf. d, Burnt trunk.

Serpentine Die Cut 6
1999, Aug. 1 Litho.
Self-Adhesive
2717 Block of 4 2.10
a.-d. A1477 51c Any single .50 .50
No. 2717 is printed on recycled paper impregnated with burnt wood odor.

Souvenir Sheet

America Issue, A New Millennium Without Arms — A1478

Designs: a, Hands of adult and child drawing dove. b, Overturned tank.

1999, Aug. 6 Litho. Perf. 12x11½
2718 A1478 90c Sheet of 2, #a.-
b. 1.90 1.90
Issued with rouletted tab at right showing Universal Product Code.

Political Amnesty, 20th Anniv. — A1479

1999, Aug. 18
2719 A1479 22c multicolored .25 .25

Famous Brazilians — A1480

Designs: 22c, Joaquim Nabuco (1849-1910), politician and diplomat. 31c, Ruy Barbosa (1849-1923), politician and justice for International Court.

1999, Aug. 19 Litho. Perf. 11½x12
2720 A1480 22c multicolored .25 .25
2721 A1480 31c multicolored .35 .35

Fish — A1481

Designs: a, 22c, Salminus maxillosus. b, 31c, Brycon microlepsus. c, 36c, Acestrorhynchus pantaneiro. d, 51c, Hyphessobrycon eques. e, 80c, Rineloricaria. f, 90c, Leporinus macrocephalus. g, 1.05r, Abramites. h, 1.20r, Ancistrus.

1999, Aug. 20 Litho. Perf. 11½x12
2722 A1481 Sheet of 8, #a.-h. 5.50 5.50
China 1999 World Philatelic Exhibition. No. 2722h has a holographic image. Soaking in water may affect hologram.

Mercosur Cultural Heritage Day A1482

1999, Sept. 17 Litho. Perf. 11½x12
2723 A1482 80c multi .90 .90

Water Resources A1483

Designs: a, Ecological station, Aguas Emendadas. b, House on water's edge, boat. c, Cedro Dam. d, Orós Dam.

1999, Oct. 21
2724 A1483 31c Block of 4,
#a.-d. 1.40 1.40

National Library of Rio de Janeiro Bookplate A1484

1999, Oct. 29 Litho. Perf. 12x11½
2725 A1484 22c multi .25 .25

State Flag Type of 1981
1999, Nov. 19 Litho. Perf. 11½x12
2726 A947 31c Amapá .35 .35
2727 A947 31c Roraima .35 .35

Antonio Carlos Jobim (1927-94), Composer A1485

1999, Nov. 22
2728 A1485 31c multi .35 .35

Christianity, 2000th Anniv. — A1486

No. 2729: a, The Annunciation. b, Birth of Jesus and adoration of the Magi. c, Presentation of Jesus in the temple. d, Baptism of Jesus by John the Baptist. e, Evangelization of Jesus and Apostles. f, Death of Jesus and resurrection.
Illustration reduced.

1999, Nov. 26 Litho. Perf. 11½
2729 A1486 22c Block of 6, #a-f 1.50 1.50

New Middle School Education System — A1487

1999, Dec. 2 Perf. 11x11½
2730 A1487 31c multi .35 .35

Itamaraty Palace, Rio A1488

Litho. & Engr.
1999, Dec. 6 Perf. 11½x12
2731 A1488 1.05r pale yel & brn 1.25 1.25

New Year 2000 — A1489

Illustration reduced.

2000, Jan. 1 Litho.
2732 A1489 90c multi 1.00 1.00

National School Book Program A1490

2000, Feb. 7 Perf. 11x11½
2733 A1490 31c multi .35 .35

Aviatrixes A1491

No. 2734: a, Ada Rogato (1920-86). b, Thereza de Marzo (1903-86). c, Anésia Pinheiro (1904-99).

2000, Mar. 8 Perf. 11½x12
2734 A1491 22c Horiz. strip of 3,
#a-c .75 .75

Regional Cuisine — A1492

a, Moqueca Capixaba. b, Moqueca Baiana.

2000, Mar. 21
2735 A1492 1.05r Pair, #a-b 2.40 2.40

Gilberto Freyre (1900-87), Sociologist — A1493

Illustration reduced.

2000, Mar. 24
2736 A1493 36c multi .40 .40

UIT Telecom A1494

2000, Apr. 9 Litho. Perf. 11½
2737 A1494 51c multi .55 .55
Discovery of Brazil, 500th anniv.

Discovery of Brazil, 500th Anniv. — A1495

No. 2738: a, Two sailors, three natives, parrot. b, Sailor, ships, four natives. c, Sailors, natives, sails. d, Sailor and natives inspecting tree.
Illustration reduced.

2000, Apr. 11 Litho. Perf. 11½x12
2738 A1495 31c Block of 4, #a-d 1.40 1.40
See Portugal Nos. 2354-2357.

Discovery of Brazil, 500th
Anniv. — A1497

No. 2740: a, Brazilian flag as sails of ship. b,
Man with pineapple, telephone dial, horn. c,
Parrot and ships. d, Ship, map of Brazil, children. e, Race car driver Ayrton Senna. f, Flora
and fauna. g, Map of Brazil, compass roses. h,
Dove. i, Native with decorated face. j, Stylized
"500." k, Native with feathered headdress. l,
Children's drawing. m, Aviator Alberto Santos
Dumont. n, Ship, manuscript. o, World Cup
trophies, soccer player and ball, map. p, Fiber
optic cables, street lights. q, Bull with Brazilian
flag. r, Parrot. s, Native masks. t, Ship, Brazil
highlighted on globe.

2000, Apr. 22   Litho.   Perf. 11½
2740 A1497 45c Sheet of 20,
#a-t, + 4 la-
bels   10.00 10.00

Brazil Trade
Net Website,
2nd Anniv.
A1498

2000, May 11   Litho.   Perf. 11½
2741 A1498 27c multi   .30   .30

National Coastal Management
Program — A1499

2000, May 16   Litho.   Perf. 11½
2742 A1499 40c multi   .40   .40

Souvenir Sheet

Expo 2000, Hanover — A1500

No. 2743: a, Map of Western Brazil. b, Map
of Eastern Brazil. c, Gold and gemstones.
Illustration reduced.

2000, May 19   Litho.   Perf. 10¾x11
2743 A1500 1.30r #a-c   4.00 4.00

Oswaldo Cruz Foundation,
Cent. — A1501

Illustration reduced.

2000, May 25   Perf. 11½x12
2744 A1501 40c multicolored   .40   .40

Africa Day
A1502

2000, May 25   Perf. 11½
2745 A1502 1.10r multi   1.10 1.10

Sailing Feats
of Amyr
Klink
A1503

No. 2746: a, First crossing of South Atlantic
by rowboat, 1984. b, Solo circumnavigation of
Antarctica, 1999.

2000, May 27
2746 A1503 1r Vert. pair, #a-b   2.00 2.00

Juiz de Fora, 150th Anniv. — A1504

Illustration reduced.

2000, May 31   Perf. 11½x12
2747 A1504 60c multi   .60   .60

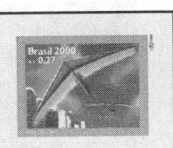

Sports — A1505

Serpentine Die Cut 5¾
2000   Photo.
Self-Adhesive
2748 A1505 27c Hanggliding   .30   .30
2749 A1505 27c Surfing   .30   .30
2750 A1505 40c Mountain climbing   .45   .45
2751 A1505 40c Skateboarding   .45   .45
Nos. 2748-2751 (4)   1.50 1.50
Issued: Nos. 2748, 2750, 6/1; No. 2749,
8/1; No. 2751, 7/1.

Environmental Protection — A1506

No. 2752: a, Trees. b, Trees, Felis tigrina in
background. c, Heads of two Felis tigrina, two
white flowers. d, Felis tigrina, one white flower.
Illustration reduced.

2000, June 5   Perf. 11½
2752 A1506 40c Block of 4, #a-d 1.75 1.75

Ships — A1507

No. 2753: a, Cisne Branco. b, Brasil.
Illustration reduced.

2000, June 11   Litho.   Perf. 11x11½
2753 A1507 27c Pair, #a-b   .60   .60

Souvenir Sheets

Military Presence in
Amazonia — A1508

Illustration reduced.

2000, June 11   Litho.   Perf. 11½x11
2754 A1508 1.50r multi   1.50 1.50
Barcode is separated from the sheet margin
by a row of microperfs.

America Issue — A1509

No. 2755: a, Campaign against AIDS. b,
Natl. anti-drug week.
Illustration reduced.

2000, June 19   Perf. 12x11½
2755 A1509 1.10r Sheet of 2, #a-
b   2.25 2.25
Barcode is separated from the sheet margin
by a row of microperfs.

Anísio Teixeira (1900-71),
Educator — A1510

Illustration reduced.

2000, July 12   Litho.   Perf. 11½x12
2756 A1510 45c multi   .50   .50

Children's and
Teenagers
Statute, 10th
Anniv. — A1511

2000, July 13   Perf. 12x11½
2757 A1511 27c multi   .30   .30

Natl. Movement of
Street Boys and
Girls, 15th
Anniv. — A1512

2000, July 13
2758 A1512 40c multi   .40   .40

Gustavo Capanema (1900-54),
Politician — A1513

Illustration reduced.

2000, Aug. 10   Litho.   Perf. 11½x12
2759 A1513 60c multi   .65   .65

Milton Campos, Politician — A1514

Illustration reduced.

2000, Aug. 16
2760 A1514 1r multi   1.10 1.10

World Ozone
Layer Protection
Day — A1515

2000, Sept. 16   Perf. 12x11½
2761 A1515 1.45r multi   1.60 1.60

Fruit — A1516

Serpentine Die Cut 5¾

2000, Sept. 21 Litho.
Self-Adhesive
2762 A1516 27c Cupuacu .30 .30
2763 A1516 40c Soursop .45 .45

2000 Summer Olympics,
Sydney — A1517

Designs: a, Pommel horse. b, Weight lifting. c, Discus. d, Men's rings. e, Sprinting. f, Javelin. g, Rhythmic gymnastics. h, Field hockey. i, Volleyball. j, Synchronized swimming. k, Judo. l, Wrestling. m, Cycling. n, Rowing. o, Parallel bars. p, Equestrian. q, Pole vault. r, Fencing. s, Shooting. t, Taekwondo.
Illustration reduced.

2000, Sept. 23 Litho. **Perf. 11½x12**
2764 Sheet of 20 + 4 labels 8.75 8.75
a.-t. A1517 40c Any single .40 .40

Olympics Type of 2000
No. 2765: a, Archery. b, Beach volleyball. c, Boxing. d, Soccer. e, Canoeing. f, Handball. g, Diving. h, Rhythmic gymnastics. i, Badminton. j, Swimming. k, Hurdles. l, Pentathlon. m, Basketball. n, Tennis. o, Marathon. p, High jump. q, Long jump. r, Triple jump. s, Triathlon. t, Yachting.

2000, Sept. 23 Litho. **Perf. 11½x12**
2765 Sheet of 20 + 4 labels 8.75 8.75
a.-t. A1517 40c Any single .40 .40

Organ Donation and
Transplantation — A1519

No. 2766: a, Doctor holding heart. b, Heart, hands, body with organs outlined.
Illustration reduced.

2000, Sept. 27
2766 A1519 1.50r Horiz. pair,
#a-b 3.25 3.25

Masks and Puppets A1520

Designs: No. 2767, 27c, Chinese puppet. No. 2768, 27c, Brazilian mask.

2000, Oct. 9
2767-2768 A1520 Set of 2 .60 .60
Brazil-People's Republic of China diplomatic relations, 25th anniv. See People's Republic of China Nos. 3053-3054.

Race Car Drivers A1521

Designs: 1.30r, Francisco "Chico" Landi (1907-89). 1.45r, Ayrton Senna (1960-94).

2000, Oct. 12 **Perf. 11x11½**
2769-2770 A1521 Set of 2 3.00 3.00

Telecourse 2000 Project A1522

2000, Oct. 13 Litho. **Perf. 11½x12**
2771 A1522 27c multi .30 .30

Airplanes A1523

No. 2772: a, EMB 145 AEW. b, Super Tucano. c, AMX-T. d, ERJ 135. e, ERJ 170. f, ERJ 145. g, ERJ 190. h, EMB 145 RS/MP. i, ERJ 140. j, EMB 120.

2000, Oct. 23 Litho. **Die Cut**
Self-Adhesive
2772 Pane of 10 3.00 3.00
a.-j. A1523 27c Any single .30 .30

Christmas A1524

No. 2773: a, Hand of Jesus, star of Bethlehem. b, Mary, baby Jesus. c, Hand of Jesus, fish, boats on Sea of Galilee. d, Jesus, Sea of Galilee. e, Hand of Jesus, mountain, trees, Earth. f, Jesus, Earth.

2000, Nov. 23 **Perf. 11½**
2773 Block of 6 1.80 1.80
a.-f. A1524 27c Any single .30 .30

Light and Sound Project — A1525

2000, Dec. 2 **Perf. 12x11½**
2774 A1525 1.30r multi 1.40 1.40

Settlement of Brazil-French Guiana Border Dispute, Cent. — A1526

2000, Dec. 12 **Perf. 11½x12**
2775 A1526 40c multi .45 .45

Advent of New Millennium — A1527

Designs: Nos. 2776, 2779a, 40c, Chalice and eucharist. Nos. 2777, 2779b, 1.30r, Star of David, menorah, Torah, tablets. Nos. 2778, 2779c, 1.30r, Minaret, dome of mosque, Holy Ka'aba.

2001, Jan. 1 **Perf. 11x11½**
2776-2778 A1527 Set of 3 3.00 3.00
Souvenir Sheet
2779 A1527 Sheet of 3, #a-c 3.00 3.00
Nos. 2779a-2779c lack white border. On No. 2779, barcode is separated from sheet margin by a row of rouletting.

Pan-American Scout Jamboree, Foz do Iguaçu — A1528

No. 2780: a, Flags, map, emblems. b, Scouts in canoe, waterfall.

2001, Jan. 7 **Perf. 12x11½**
2780 A1528 1.10r Horiz. pair,
#a-b 2.25 2.25

New Year 2001 (Year of the Snake) — A1529

Illustration reduced.
Litho. & Embossed
2001, Jan. 24 **Perf. 11½**
2781 A1529 1.45r multi 1.50 1.50
Hong Kong 2001 Stamp Exhibition.

Venomous Animals A1530

No. 2782: a, Dirphya sp. b, Megalopyge sp. c, Phoneutria sp. d, Tityus bahiensis. e, Crotalus durissus. f, Micrurus corallinus. g, Lachesis muta. h, Bothrops jararaca.

2001, Feb. 23 Litho. **Perf. 11½x12**
2782 Sheet of 8 3.25 3.25
a.-h A1530 40c Any single .40 .40
Butantan Institute, cent.

Brazilian Publishing Industry — A1531

2001, Mar. 5 **Perf. 11x11½**
2783 A1531 27c multi .30 .30

Special Exports Program — A1532

Illustration reduced.
2001, Mar. 5 **Perf. 11½x12**
2784 A1532 1.30r multi 1.25 1.25

National Library, 190th Anniv. — A1533

Illustration reduced.
Litho. & Engr.
2001, Mar. 26 **Perf. 11½x12**
2785 A1533 27c multi .25 .25

Council for Scientific and Technical Development — A1534

2001, Apr. 17
2786 A1534 40c blue .35 .35

Soccer Teams — A1535

Designs: No. 2787, Regatas Vasco da Gama. No. 2788, Palmeiras. No. 2789, Gremio. 1r, Santos.

2001 Litho. **Perf. 12x11½**
2787 A1535 70c multi .55 .55
2788 A1535 70c multi .55 .55
2789 A1535 70c multi .55 .55
2790 A1535 1r multi .90 .90
Nos. 2787-2790 (4) 2.55 2.55
Numbers have been reserved for additional stamps in this set. Numbers may change.
Issued: No. 2787, 8/21; No. 2788, 8/26; No. 2789, 9/10; 1r, 4/20.

Intl. Culture of Peace Year — A1536

2001, May 3 Litho. **Perf. 12x11½**
2794 A1536 1.10r multi .95 .95

Murilo Mendes (1901-75), Poet — A1537

2001, May 13 **Perf. 11x11½**
2795 A1537 40c multi .35 .35

Minas Commercial Association, Cent. A1538

2001, May 16   *Perf. 11½*
2796 A1538 40c multi   .35 .35

World Tobacco-free Day — A1539

2001, May 31   *Perf. 12x11½*
2797 A1539 40c multi   .35 .35

José Lins do Rego (1901-87), Writer — A1540

2001, May 31   *Perf. 11x11½*
2798 A1540 60c multi   .50 .50

Souvenir Sheet

Worldwide Fund for Nature (WWF) — A1541

Parrots: a, Anodorhynchus hyacinthinus. b, Aratinga solstitialis auricapilla. c, Pyrrhura cruentata. d, Amazona xanthops.

2001, June 3   *Perf. 11½*
2799 A1541 1.30r Sheet of 4, #a-d   4.50 4.50

Barbosa Lima Sobrinho (1897-2000), Journalist A1542

2001, June 6
2800 A1542 40c multi   .35 .35

Beaches A1543

No. 2801: a, Jericoacoara. b, Ponta Negra. c, Rosa.

2001, June 13   *Perf. 11x11½*
2801   Horiz. strip of 3   1.10 1.10
a.-c.   A1543 40c Any single   .35 .35

Issued in sheets of 25 stamps containing 10 each of Nos. 2801a-2801b and 5 of No. 2801c.

Souvenir Sheet

Automobiles — A1544

No. 2802: a, 1959 Romi Isetta. b, 1965 DKW Vemag. c, 1962 Renault Gordini. d, 1959 Volkswagen 1200. e, 1964 Simca Chambord. f, 1961 Aero-Willys.

2001, June 16   *Perf. 11½x12*
2802 A1544 1.10r Sheet of 6, #a-f   5.75 5.75

Bernardo Sayao (1901-59), Politician A1545

2001, June 18   *Perf. 11½*
2803 A1545 60c multi   .50 .50

Eleazar de Carvalho (1912-96), Composer A1546

2001, July 1
2804 A1546 45c multi   .35 .35

Souvenir Sheet

Third French Tennis Open Victory of Gustavo Kuerten — A1547

2001, July 10
2805 A1547 1.30r multi   1.00 1.00

Academic Qualifications Coordinating Institution, 50th Anniv. — A1548

2001, July 11   *Perf. 11x11½*
2806 A1548 40c multi   .35 .35

Pedro Aleixo, Politician, Cent. of Birth A1549

2001, Aug. 1   *Perf. 11½*
2807 A1549 55c multi   .45 .45

Solidarity Community Programs — A1550

No. 2808: a, Map on man. b, Man on map. Illustration reduced.

2001, Aug. 25
2808 A1550 55c Horiz. pair, #a-b   .85 .85

World Conference Against Racism, Durban, South Africa — A1551

2001, Aug. 30   *Perf. 12x11½*
2809 A1551 1.30r multi   .95 .95

See South Africa No.

SEMI-POSTAL STAMPS

In 1980 three stamps that were intended to be semi-postals were issued as postage stamps at the total combined face value. See Nos. 1681-1683.

National Philatelic Exhibition Issue

SP1

Wmk. Coat of Arms in Sheet (236)
1934, Sept. 16   **Engr.**   *Imperf.*
Thick Paper
B1 SP1 200r + 100r dp cl   1.00 2.00
B2 SP1 300r + 100r ver   1.00 2.00
B3 SP1 700r + 100r brt bl   6.00 17.50
B4 SP1 1000r + 100r blk   6.00 17.50
  Nos. B1-B4 (4)   14.00 39.00

The surtax was to help defray the expenses of the exhibition. Issued in sheets of 60, inscribed "EXPOSICAO FILATELICA NACIONAL."

Red Cross Nurse and Soldier SP2

1935, Sept. 19   **Typo.**   *Perf. 11*
B5 SP2 200r + 100r pur & red   1.25 1.25
B6 SP2 300r + 100r ol brn & red   1.25 .90
B7 SP2 700r + 100r turq bl & red   8.00 7.00
  Nos. B5-B7 (3)   10.50 9.15

3rd Pan-American Red Cross Conf. Exist imperf.

Three Wise Men and Star of Bethlehem — SP3

Angel and Child — SP4

Southern Cross and Child — SP5

Mother and Child — SP6

1939, Dec. 20   **Litho.**   *Perf. 10½*
B8 SP3 100r + 100r chlky bl & bl blk   .75 .75
a.   Horiz. or vert. pair, imperf. between   35.00
B9 SP4 200r + 100r brt grnsh bl   1.00 1.00
a.   Horizontal pair, imperf. between   35.00

B10 SP5 400r + 200r ol grn & ol .80 .50
B11 SP6 1200r + 400r crim & brn red 3.25 1.50
  a. Vertical pair, imperf. between 35.00
  Nos. B8-B11 (4) 5.80 3.75
Surtax for charitable institutions. For surcharges see Nos. C55-C59.

Catalogue values for unused stamps in this section, from this point to the end of the section, are for Never Hinged items.

Children and Citzenship — SP7

Designs: a, Cutouts of children forming pyramid. b, Man and woman's hands holding onto girl. c, Children going into school. d, Pregnant woman in front of house. e, Children flying paper doves. f, Parent working in garden, child writing letters, doves. g, Breastfeeding. h, Father holding birth certificate, mother holding infant. i, Disabled child on wheelchair ramp. j, Mother, father with sick child. k, Stylized child, pencil, letters. l, Hands above and below pregnant woman. m, Two families of different races. n, Small child playing large guitar. o, People looking to baby on pedestal. p, Children, book, "Statute of Children and Adolescent."

1997, Nov. 20 Litho. Perf. 12x11½
B12 Sheet of 16 9.60 9.60
  a.-p. SP7 22c +8c any single .60 .60
Surcharge for Natl. Fund for Children and Adolescents.

Stampin' the Future Children's Stamp Design Contest Winners — SP8

Art by: a, Jonas Sampaio de Freitas. b, Clarissa Cazane. c, Caio Ferreira Guimaraes de Oliveira. d, Milena Karoline Ribeiro Reis. Illustration reduced.

2000, Jan. 1 Litho. Perf. 11½x12
B13 SP8 22c + 8c Block of 4, #a-d 1.40 1.40

AIR POST STAMPS

Nos. O14-O29 Surcharged

1927, Dec. 28 Unwmk. Perf. 12
C1 O2 50r on 10r .35 .35
  a. Inverted surcharge 325.00
  b. Top ornaments missing 75.00
C2 O2 200r on 1000r 2.25 2.75
  a. Double surcharge 325.00
C3 O2 200r on 2000r 1.40 4.75
  a. Double surcharge 750.00
  b. Double surcharge, one inverted 750.00
C4 O2 200r on 5000r 1.50 1.00
  a. Double surcharge 325.00
  b. Double surcharge, one inverted 350.00
  c. Triple surcharge 450.00
C5 O2 300r on 500r 1.50 2.00
C6 O2 300r on 600r .75 .90
  b. Pair, one without surch. —

C6A O2 500r on 10r 325.00 375.00
C7 O2 500r on 50r 1.50 .65
  a. Double surcharge 300.00
C8 O2 1000r on 20r 1.00 .35
  a. Double surcharge 300.00
C9 O2 2000r on 100r 2.25 1.40
  a. Pair, one without surcharge
  b. Double surcharge 300.00
C10 O2 2000r on 200r 2.75 1.40
C11 O2 2000r on 10,000r 2.25 .50
C12 O2 5000r on 20,000r 7.50 3.00
C13 O2 5000r on 50,000r 7.50 3.00
C14 O2 5000r on 100,000r 25.00 30.00
C15 O2 10,000r on 500,000r 27.50 22.50
C16 O2 10,000r on 1,000,000r 25.00 25.00
  Nos. C1-C6,C7-C16 (16) 110.00 99.55
Nos. C1, C1b, C7, C8 and C9 have small diamonds printed over the numerals in the upper corners.

Monument to de Gusmao — AP1

Santos-Dumont's Airship — AP2

Augusto Severo's Airship "Pax" — AP3

Santos-Dumont's Biplane "14 Bis" — AP4

Ribeiro de Barros's Seaplane "Jahu" — AP5

Perf. 11, 12½x13, 13x13½
1929 Typo.
C17 AP1 50r blue grn .35 .20
C18 AP2 200r red 1.40 .20
C19 AP3 300r brt blue 1.75 .20
C20 AP4 500r red violet 2.50 .20
C21 AP5 1000r orange brn 9.00 .40
  Nos. C17-C21 (5) 15.00 1.20
See #C32-C36. For surcharges see #C26-C27.

Bartholomeu de Gusmao AP6

Augusto Severo AP7

Alberto Santos-Dumont — AP8

Perf. 9, 11 and Compound
1929-30 Engr.
C22 AP6 2000r lt green ('30) 7.50 .35
C23 AP7 5000r carmine 7.50 1.25
C24 AP8 10,000r olive grn 7.50 1.40
  Nos. C22-C24 (3) 22.50 3.00
Nos. C23-C24 exist imperf. See Nos. C37, C40.

Allegory: Airmail Service between Brazil and the US — AP9

1929 Typo. Wmk. 206
C25 AP9 3000r violet 10.00 1.75
Exists imperf. See Nos. C38, C41. For surcharge see No. C28.

Nos. C18-C19 Surcharged in Blue or Red

1931, Aug. 16 Perf. 12½x13½
C26 AP2 2500r on 200r (Bl) 25.00 25.00
C27 AP3 5000r on 300r (R) 30.00 30.00

No. C25 Surcharged

1931, Sept. 2 Perf. 11
C28 AP9 2500r on 3000r vio 27.50 27.50
  a. Inverted surcharge 160.00
  b. Surch. on front and back 160.00

Regular Issues of 1928-29 Surcharged

1932, May Wmk. 101 Perf. 11, 11½
C29 A89 3500r on 5000r gray lil 20.00 20.00
C30 A72 7000r on 10,000r rose 20.00 20.00
  b. Horiz. pair, imperf. between 750.00

Imperforates
Since 1933, imperforate or partly perforated sheets of nearly all of the airmail issues have become available.

Flag and Airplane AP10

1933, June 7 Typo. Wmk. 222 Perf. 11
C31 AP10 3500r grn, yel & dk bl 5.00 2.00
See Nos. C39, C42.

1934 Wmk. 222
C32 AP1 50r blue grn 1.75 1.75
C33 AP2 200r red 2.25 .65
C34 AP3 300r brt blue 5.50 1.90

C35 AP4 500r red violet 2.25 .65
C36 AP5 1000r orange brn 7.50 .65
  Nos. C32-C36 (5) 19.25 5.60

1934 Wmk. 236 Engr. Perf. 12x11
Thick Laid Paper
C37 AP6 2000r lt green 4.50 1.50

Types of 1929, 1933
1937-40 Typo. Perf. 11, 11½, 12
C38 AP9 3000r violet 17.50 1.75
C39 AP10 3500r grn, yel & dk bl 3.00 1.50
Engr.
C40 AP7 5000r ver ('40) 4.00 .75
  Nos. C38-C40 (3) 24.50 4.00
Watermark note after #501 also applies to #C40.

Types of 1929-33
1939-40 Typo. Perf. 11, 11½x12
C41 AP9 3000r violet 1.25 .60
C42 AP10 3500r bl, dl grn & yel ('40) .90 .50

Map of the Western Hemisphere Showing Brazil — AP11

1941, Jan. 14 Engr. Perf. 11
C43 AP11 1200r dark brown 2.50 .65
5th general census of Brazil.

No. 506A Overprinted in Carmine

1941, Nov. 10 Wmk. 264 Rouletted
C45 A180 5400r slate grn 2.50 1.25
  a. Overprint inverted 140.00
President Varges' new constitution, 4th anniv.

Nos. 506A and 508 Surcharged in Black

1942, Nov. 10 Wmk. 264
C47 A180 5.40cr on 5400r sl grn 2.50 1.90
  a. Wmk. 249 80.00 80.00
  b. Surcharge inverted 60.00 75.00
President Vargas' new constitution, 5th anniv. The status of No. C47a is questioned.

Southern Cross and Arms of Paraguay AP12

Wmk. 270
1943, May 11 Engr. Perf. 12½
C48 AP12 1.20cr lt gray blue 1.75 1.00
Issued in commemoration of the visit of President Higinio Morinigo of Paraguay.

Map of South
America — AP13

1943, June 30 Wmk. 271 *Perf. 12½*
C49 AP13 1.20cr multi   1.75 .75

Visit of President Penaranda of Bolivia.

Numeral of
Value
AP14

1943, Aug. 7
C50 AP14 1cr blk & dull yel   2.00 1.50
  a. Double impression   30.00
C51 AP14 2cr blk & pale grn   2.75 1.50
  a. Double impression   40.00
C52 AP14 5cr blk & pink   3.25 2.00
   Nos. C50-C52 (3)   8.00 5.00

Centenary of Brazil's first postage stamps.

Souvenir Sheet

AP15

	Without Gum	***Imperf.***
C53 AP15	Sheet of 3	35.00 35.00
a.	1cr black & dull yellow	10.00 10.00
b.	2cr black & pale green	10.00 10.00
c.	5cr black & pink	10.00 10.00

100th anniv. of the 1st postage stamps of
Brazil and the 2nd Phil. Exposition (Brapex).
Printed in panes of 6 sheets, perforated 12½
between. Each sheet is perforated on two or
three sides. Size approximately 155x155mm.

Law
Book — AP16

1943, Aug. 13 *Perf. 12½*
C54 AP16 1.20cr rose & lil rose   .50 .30

2nd Inter-American Conf. of Lawyers.

No. B10
Surcharged in
Red, Carmine or
Black

1944, Jan. 3 Wmk. 249 *Perf. 10½*
C55 SP5   20c on 400r+200r
    (R)   .85 .65
C56 SP5   40c on 400r+200r
    (Bk)   1.25 .65

C57 SP5   60c on 400r+200r
    (C)
C58 SP5   1cr on 400r+200r   1.25 .45
    (Bk)   1.75 .65
C59 SP5   1.20cr on 400r+200r
    (C)   2.25 .45
   Nos. C55-C59 (5)   7.35 2.85

No. C59 is known with surcharge in black
but its status is questioned.

Bartholomeu de
Gusmao and the
"Aerostat" — AP17

Wmk. 268
1944, Oct. 23 Engr. *Perf. 12*
C60 AP17 1.20cr rose carmine   .35 .20

Week of the Wing.

L. L.
Zamenhof
AP18

1945, Apr. 16 Litho. *Perf. 11*
C61 AP18 1.20cr dull brown   .35 .25

Esperanto Congress held in Rio, Apr. 14-22.

Map of South   Baron of Rio
America — AP19   Branco — AP20

1945, Apr. 20
C62 AP19 1.20cr gray brown   .35 .25
C63 AP20 5cr rose lilac   .95 .40

Centenary of the birth of José Maria de
Silva Paranhos, Baron of Rio Branco.

Dove and
Flags of
American
Republics
AP21

1947, Aug. 15 Engr. *Perf. 12x11*
C64 AP21 2.20cr dk blue green   .30 .25

Inter-American Defense Conference at Rio
de Janeiro August-September, 1947.

Santos-Dumont
Monument, St.
Cloud,
France — AP22

Bay of Rio de
Janeiro and
Rotary
Emblem — AP23

1947, Nov. 15 Typo. *Perf. 11x12*
C65 AP22 1.20cr org brn & ol   .30 .25

Issued to commemorate the Week of the
Wing and to honor the Santos-Dumont monument which was destroyed in World War II.

> **Catalogue values for unused
> stamps in this section, from this
> point to the end of the section, are
> for Never Hinged items.**

1948, May 16 Engr. *Perf. 11*
C66 AP23 1.20cr deep claret   .50 .40
C67 AP23 3.80cr dull violet   1.00 .40

39th convention of Rotary Intl., Rio.

Hotel Quitandinha, Petropolis — AP24

1948, July 10 Litho. Wmk. 267
C68 AP24 1.20cr org brn   .25 .25
C69 AP24 3.80cr violet   .50 .30

International Exposition of Industry and
Commerce, Petropolis, 1948.

Musician
and
Singers
AP25

1948, Aug. 13 Engr. Unwmk.
C70 AP25 1.20cr blue   .30 .20

National School of Music, cent.

Luis Batlle
Berres
AP26

1948, Sept. 2 Typo.
C71 AP26 1.70cr blue   .20 .20

Visit of President Luis Batlle Berres of Uruguay, September, 1948.

Merino
Ram
AP27

Perf. 12x11
1948, Oct. 10 Wmk. 267
C72 AP27 1.20cr dp orange   .50 .30

Intl. Livestock Exposition at Bagé.

Eucharistic
Congress
Seal — AP28

Unwmk.
1948, Oct. 23 Engr. *Perf. 11*
C73 AP28 1.20cr dk car rose   .30 .30

5th Natl. Eucharistic Cong., Porto Alegre,
Oct. 24-31.

Souvenir Sheet

AP28a

1948, Dec. 14 Engr. *Imperf.*
Without Gum
C73A AP28a Sheet of 3   50.00 65.00

No. C73A contains one each of Nos. 674-
676. Issued in honor of President Eurico
Gasper Dutra and the armed forces. Exists
both with and without number on back. Measures 130x75mm.

Church of Prazeres,
Guararapes — AP29

1949, Feb. 15 Litho. *Perf. 11½x12*
C74 AP29 1.20cr pink   1.50 .75

Second Battle of Guararapes, 300th anniv.

Thomé de Souza
Meeting
Indians — AP30

1949, Mar. 29 Engr. *Perf. 11x12*
C75 AP30 1.20cr blue   .20 .20

Founding of the City of Salvador, 400th
anniv.

A souvenir folder, issued with No. C75, has
an engraved 20cr red brown postage stamp
portraying John III printed on it, and a copy of
No. C75 affixed to it and postmarked. Paper is
laid, and size of folder front is 100x150mm.
Value, $5.

Franklin D.
Roosevelt
AP31

1949, May 20   Unwmk.   *Imperf.*
C76 AP31 3.80cr deep blue   .60   .60
  a.   Souvenir sheet   12.00 15.00

No. C76a measures 85x110mm, with deep blue inscriptions in upper and lower margins. It also exists with papermaker's watermark.

Joaquim Nabuco
(1849-1910),
Lawyer and
Writer — AP32

1949, Aug. 30   *Perf. 12*
C77 AP32 3.80cr rose lilac   .40   .30
  a.   Wmk. 256, imperf.   25.00

Maracaná
Stadium
AP33

Soccer Player and
Flag — AP34

Perf. 11x12, 12x11
1950, June 24   Litho.
C78 AP33 1.20cr ultra & salmon   .95   .40
C79 AP34 5.80cr bl, yel grn & yel 2.75 .50

4th World Soccer Championship, Rio.

AP35

AP36

Symbolical of Brazilian population growth.

1950, July 10   *Perf. 12x11*
C80 AP35 1.20cr red brown   .30   .20

Issued to publicize the 6th Brazilian census.

1956, Sept. 8   Engr.   *Perf. 11½*
Design: J. B. Marcelino Champagnat.
C81 AP36 3.30cr rose lilac   .30   .20

50th anniversary of the arrival of the Marist Brothers in Northern Brazil.

Santos-Dumont's 1906 Plane — AP37

1956   Photo.
C82 AP37 3cr dk blue grn   .85   .30
C83 AP37 3.30cr brt ultra   .20   .20
C84 AP37 4cr dp claret   .40   .20
C85 AP37 6.50cr red brown   .20   .20
C86 AP37 11.50cr orange red .85   .35
   Nos. C82-C86 (5)   2.50 1.25
Souvenir Sheet
C86A AP37   Sheet of 4   6.00   6.00
  b.   3cr dark carmine   1.50   .90

1st flight by Santos-Dumont, 50th anniv.
Issued: #C86A, 10/14; others 10/16.

Lord Baden-Powell
AP38

1957, Aug. 1   Unwmk.
Granite Paper
C87 AP38 3.30cr deep red lilac   .25   .20

Centenary of the birth of Lord Baden-Powell, founder of the Boy Scouts.

UN
Emblem,
Soldier and
Map of
Suez
Canal Area
AP39

Wmk. 267
1957, Oct. 24   Engr.   *Perf. 11½*
C88 AP39 3.30cr dark blue   .25   .20

Brazilian contingent of the UN Emergency Force.

Basketball
Player — AP40

1959, May 30   Photo.   *Perf. 11½*
C89 AP40 3.30cr brt red brn & bl .25   .20

Brazil's victory in the World Basketball Championships of 1959.

Symbol of
Flight
AP41

1959, Oct. 21   Wmk. 267
C90 AP41 3.30cr deep ultra   .20   .20

Issued to publicize Week of the Wing.

Caravelle
AP42

1959, Dec. 18   *Perf. 11½*
C91 AP42 6.50cr ultra   .20   .20

Inauguration of Brazilian jet flights.

Pres. Adolfo
Lopez
Mateos — AP43

Pres. Dwight D.
Eisenhower
AP44

1960, Jan. 19   Photo.   Wmk. 267
C92 AP43 6.50cr brown   .20   .20

Issued to commemorate the visit of President Adolfo Lopez Mateos of Mexico.

1960, Feb. 23   *Perf. 11½*
C93 AP44 6.50cr deep orange   .20   .20

Visit of Pres. Dwight D. Eisenhower.

World Refugee
Year
Emblem — AP45

Tower at
Brasilia — AP46

1960, Apr. 7   Wmk. 268
C94 AP45 6.50cr blue   .20   .20

WRY, July 1, 1959-June 30, 1960.

Type of Regular Issue and AP46
Designs: 3.30cr, Square of the Three Entities. 4cr, Cathedral. 11.50cr, Plan of Brasilia.

Perf. 11x11½, 11½x11
1960, Apr. 21   Photo.
C95 A436 3.30cr violet   .20   .20
C96 A436 4cr blue   .75   .20
C97 AP46 6.50cr rose carmine .20   .20
C98 A436 11.50cr brown   .20   .20
   Nos. C95-C98 (4)   1.35 .80

Inauguration of Brazil's new capital, Brasilia, Apr. 21, 1960.

Chrismon
and Oil
Lamp
AP47

1960, May 16   *Perf. 11x11½*
C99 AP47 3.30cr lilac rose   .20   .20

7th Natl. Eucharistic Congress at Curitiba.

Cross, Sugarloaf Mountain and
Emblem — AP48

1960, July 1   Wmk. 267
C100 AP48 6.50cr brt blue   .20   .20

10th Cong. of the World Baptist Alliance, Rio.

Boy
Scout — AP49

Caravel — AP50

1960, July 23   *Perf. 11½x11*
C101 AP49 3.30cr orange ver   .20   .20

Boy Scouts of Brazil, 50th anniversary.

1960, Aug. 5   Engr.   Wmk. 268
C102 AP50 6.50cr black   .20   .20

Prince Henry the Navigator, 500th birth anniv.

Maria E.
Bueno
AP51

1960, Dec. 15   Photo.   *Perf. 11x11½*
C103 AP51 60cr pale brown   .20   .20

Victory at Wimbledon of Maria E. Bueno, women's singles tennis champion.

War Memorial, Sugarloaf Mountain
and Allied Flags — AP52

1960, Dec. 22   Wmk. 268
C104 AP52 3.30cr lilac rose   .20   .20

Reburial of Brazilian servicemen of WW II.

Power Line and
Map — AP53

Malaria
Eradication
Emblem — AP54

1961, Jan. 20   *Perf. 11½x11*
C105 AP53 3.30cr lilac rose   .20   .20

Inauguration of Three Marias Dam and hydroelectric station in Minas Gerais.

1962, May 24   Wmk. 267   Engr.
C106 AP54 21cr blue   .20   .20

WHO drive to eradicate malaria.

F. A. de
Varnhagen — AP55

1966, Feb. 17   Photo.   Wmk. 267
C107 AP55 45cr red brown   .20 .20
Francisco Adolfo de Varnhagen, Viscount of Porto Seguro (1816-1878), historian and diplomat.

Map of the Americas and Alliance for Progress Emblem
AP56

1966, Mar. 14   Perf. 11x11½
C108 AP56 120cr grnsh bl & vio bl   .40 .20
5th anniv. of the Alliance for Progress.
A souvenir card contains one impression of No. C108, imperf. Size: 113x160mm.

Nun and Globe — AP57   Face of Jesus from Shroud of Turin — AP58

1966, Mar. 25   Photo.   Perf. 11½x11
C109 AP57 35cr violet   .20 .20
Centenary of the arrival of the teaching Sisters of St. Dorothea.

1966, June 3   Photo.   Wmk. 267
C110 AP58 45cr brown org   .20 .20
Issued to commemorate Vatican II, the 21st Ecumenical Council of the Roman Catholic Church, Oct. 11, 1962-Dec. 8, 1965.
A souvenir card contains one impression of No. C110, imperf. Size: 100x39mm.

Admiral Mariz e Barros — AP59   "Youth" by Eliseu Visconti — AP60

1966, June 13   Photo.   Wmk. 267
C111 AP59 35cr red brown   .20 .20
Death centenary of Admiral Antonio Carlos Mariz e Barros, who died in the Battle of Itaperu.

1966, July 31   Perf. 11½x11
C112 AP60 120cr red brown   .40 .20
Birth centenary of Eliseu Visconti, painter.

SPECIAL DELIVERY STAMPS

No. 191 Surcharged

1930   Unwmk.   Perf. 12
E1 A62 1000r on 200r dp blue   4.00 1.75
a.   Inverted surcharge   500.00

POSTAGE DUE STAMPS

D1   D2

1889   Unwmk.   Typo.   Rouletted
J1 D1 10r carmine   2.00 1.40
J2 D1 20r carmine   2.75 2.00
J3 D1 50r carmine   5.00 4.00
J4 D1 100r carmine   2.00 1.40
J5 D1 200r carmine   55.00 15.00
J6 D1 300r carmine   6.00 8.00
J7 D1 500r carmine   6.00 8.00
J8 D1 700r carmine   10.00 14.00
J9 D1 1000r carmine   10.00 10.00
Nos. J1-J9 (9)   98.75 63.80
Counterfeits are common.

1890
J10 D1 10r orange   .60 .30
J11 D1 20r ultra   .60 .30
J12 D1 50r olive   1.25 .30
J13 D1 200r magenta   6.00 .60
J14 D1 300r blue green   3.00 1.50
J15 D1 500r slate   4.00 3.00
J16 D1 700r purple   4.50 7.50
J17 D1 1000r dk violet   5.50 5.00
Nos. J10-J17 (8)   25.45 18.50

Perf. 11 to 11½, 12½ to 14 and Compound
1895-1901
J18 D2 10r dk blue ('01)   2.00 1.25
J19 D2 20r yellow grn   8.00 3.00
J20 D2 50r yellow grn ('01)   10.00 5.50
J21 D2 100r brick red   6.25 1.25
J22 D2 200r violet   6.00 .60
a.   200r gray lilac ('98)   12.00 2.00
J23 D2 300r dull blue   3.50 2.25
J24 D2 2000r brown   12.00 12.00
Nos. J18-J24 (7)   47.75 25.85

1906   Wmk. 97
J25 D2 10r brick red   8.00 3.00
Wmk. (97? or 98?)
J26 D2 200r violet   7.50 1.25
a.   Wmk. 97   275.00 85.00
b.   Wmk. 98   12.50 50.00

D3   D4

1906-10   Unwmk.   Engr.   Perf. 12
J28 D3 10r slate   .20 .20
J29 D3 20r brt violet   .20 .20
J30 D3 50r dk green   .25 .20
J31 D3 100r carmine   1.75 .60
J32 D3 200r dp blue   1.00 .30
J33 D3 300r gray blk   .40 .60
J34 D3 400r olive grn   1.00 .90
J35 D3 500r dk violet   35.00 35.00
J36 D3 600r violet ('10)   1.25 3.00
J37 D3 700r red brown   30.00 30.00
J38 D3 1000r red   1.50 3.00
J39 D3 2000r brown   4.75 5.50
J40 D3 5000r choc ('10)   1.50 14.00
Nos. J28-J40 (13)   78.80 93.50

Perf. 12½, 11, 11x10½
1919-23   Typo.
J41 D4 5r red brown   .20 .25
J42 D4 10r violet   .25 .25
J43 D4 20r olive gray   .20 .20
J44 D4 50r green ('23)   .20 .20
J45 D4 100r red   1.10 1.00
J46 D4 200r blue   5.25 1.50
J47 D4 400r brown ('23)   1.40 1.25
Nos. J41-J47 (7)   8.60 4.65

Perf. 12½, 12½x13½
1924-35   Wmk. 100
J48 D4 5r red brown   .25 .20
J49 D4 100r red   .75 .30
J50 D4 200r slate bl ('29)   1.00 .50
J51 D4 400r dp brn ('29)   1.50 1.00
J52 D4 600r dk vio ('29)   1.75 1.10
J53 D4 600r orange ('35)   .75 .50
Nos. J48-J53 (6)   6.00 3.60

1924   Wmk. 193   Perf. 11x10½
J54 D4 100r red   45.00 45.00
J55 D4 200r slate blue   5.50 5.50

Perf. 11x10½, 13x13½
1925-27   Wmk. 101
J56 D4 20r olive gray   .20 .20
J57 D4 100r red   1.05 .30
J58 D4 200r slate blue   3.25 .35
J59 D4 400r brown   1.75 1.25
J60 D4 600r dk violet   4.25 2.50
Nos. J56-J60 (5)   10.50 4.60

Wmk. E U BRASIL Multiple (218)
1929-30   Perf. 12½x13½
J61 D4 100r light red   .25 .20
J62 D4 200r blue black   .40 .25
J63 D4 400r brown   .40 .25
J64 D4 1000r myrtle green   .75 .50
Nos. J61-J64 (4)   1.80 1.20

Perf. 11, 12½x13, 13
1931-36   Wmk. 222
J65 D4 10r lt violet ('35)   .20 .20
J66 D4 20r black ('33)   .20 .20
J67 D4 50r blue grn ('35)   .25 .20
J68 D4 100r rose red ('35)   .25 .20
J69 D4 200r sl blue ('35)   .40 .30
J70 D4 400r blk brn ('35)   2.00 2.00
J71 D4 600r dk violet   .35 .20
J72 D4 1000r myrtle grn   .50 .35
J73 D4 2000r brown ('36)   .80 .80
J74 D4 5000r indigo ('36)   1.25 1.00
Nos. J65-J74 (10)   6.20 5.45

1938   Wmk. 249   Perf. 11
J75 D4 200r slate blue   2.00 .75

1940   Typo.   Wmk. 256
J76 D4 10r light violet   .50 .50
J77 D4 20r black   .50 .50
J79 D4 100r rose red   .50 .50
J80 D4 200r myrtle green   .50 .50
Nos. J76-J80 (4)   2.00 2.00

1942   Wmk. 264
J81 D4 10r lt violet   .20 .20
J82 D4 20r olive blk   .20 .20
J83 D4 50r lt blue grn   .20 .20
J84 D4 100r vermilion   .40 .30
J85 D4 200r gray blue   .40 .30
J86 D4 400r claret   .40 .30
J87 D4 600r rose vio   .30 .20
J88 D4 1000r dk bl grn   .30 .20
J89 D4 2000r dp yel brn   .75 .50
J90 D4 5000r indigo   .40 .30
Nos. J81-J90 (10)   3.55 2.70

1949   Wmk. 268
J91 D4 10c pale rose lilac   4.00 3.25
J92 D4 20r black   25.00 25.00
No. J92 exists in shades of gray ranging to gray olive.

OFFICIAL STAMPS

Pres. Affonso Penna   Pres. Hermes da Fonseca
O1   O2

Unwmk.
1906, Nov. 15   Engr.   Perf. 12
O1 O1 10r org & grn   .75 .30
O2 O1 20r org & grn   .90 .30
O3 O1 50r org & grn   1.50 .30
O4 O1 100r org & grn   .75 .30
O5 O1 200r org & grn   .90 .30
O6 O1 300r org & grn   2.75 .50
O7 O1 400r org & grn   6.00 1.75
O8 O1 500r org & grn   3.00 1.25
O9 O1 700r org & grn   4.50 3.00
O10 O1 1000r org & grn   4.50 1.25
O11 O1 2000r org & grn   5.00 2.25
O12 O1 5000r org & grn   10.00 .50
O13 O1 10,000r org & grn   10.00 .50
Nos. O1-O13 (13)   50.55 13.35
The portrait is the same but the frame differs for each denomination of this issue.

1913, Nov. 15   Center in Black
O14 O2 10r gray   .35 .50
O15 O2 20r ol grn   .35 .50
O16 O2 50r gray   .35 .50
O17 O2 100r ver   1.00 .35
O18 O2 200r blue   1.75 .35
O19 O2 500r orange   3.00 .65
O20 O2 600r violet   3.50 2.75
O21 O2 1000r blk brn   4.25 1.25
O22 O2 2000r red brn   6.50 1.25
O23 O2 5000r brown   7.50 3.00
O24 O2 10,000r black   15.00 7.50
O25 O2 20,000r blue   27.50 27.50
O26 O2 50,000r green   50.00 55.00
O27 O2 100,000r org red   175.00 200.00
O28 O2 500,000r brown   300.00 325.00
O29 O2 1,000,000r dk brn   325.00 350.00
Nos. O14-O29 (16)   921.05 976.10
The portrait is the same on all denominations of this series but there are eight types of the frame.

Pres. Wenceslau Braz — O3

Perf. 11, 11½
1919, Apr. 11   Wmk. 100
O30 O3 10r olive green   .40 2.00
O31 O3 50r green   1.00 1.25
O32 O3 100r rose red   2.00 .85
O33 O3 200r dull blue   2.75 .85
O34 O3 500r orange   7.50 14.00
Nos. O30-O34 (5)   13.65 18.95
The official decree called for eleven stamps in this series but only five were issued.
For surcharges see Nos. 293-297.

NEWSPAPER STAMPS

N1

Rouletted
1889, Feb. 1   Unwmk.   Litho.
P1 N1 10r yellow   3.00 3.00
a.   Pair, imperf. between   125.00 140.00
P2 N1 20r yellow   6.00 7.50
P3 N1 50r yellow   10.00 6.00
P4 N1 100r yellow   3.75 3.00
P5 N1 200r yellow   3.00 1.50
P6 N1 300r yellow   3.00 1.50
P7 N1 500r yellow   20.00 8.00
P8 N1 700r yellow   3.00 10.00
P9 N1 1000r yellow   3.00 10.00
Nos. P1-P9 (9)   54.75 50.50
For surcharges see Nos. 125-127.

1889, May 1
P10 N1 10r olive   2.00 .50
P11 N1 20r olive   2.00 .50
P12 N1 50r brn yel   2.75 1.00
P13 N1 100r violet   3.00 2.00
a.   100r deep violet   6.50 15.00
b.   100r lilac   12.00 10.00
P14 N1 200r black   3.00 2.00
P15 N1 300r carmine   12.00 10.00
P16 N1 500r green   50.00 50.00
P17 N1 700r pale blue   25.00 30.00
a.   700r ultramarine   65.00 75.00
b.   700r cobalt   400.00 425.00
P18 N1 1000r brown   12.00 15.00
Nos. P10-P18 (9)   111.75 111.00
For surcharges see Nos. 128-135.

N2　　　　N3

White Wove Paper Thin to Thick
Perf. 11 to 11½, 12½ to 14 and 12½ to 14x11 to 11½

1890			Typo.	
P19	N2	10r blue	14.00	10.00
a.		10r ultramarine	14.00	10.00
P20	N2	20r emerald	40.00	15.00
P21	N2	100r violet	16.00	10.00
		Nos. P19-P21 (3)	70.00	39.00

For surcharge see No. 137.

1890-93				
P22	N3	10r ultramarine	3.00	3.00
a.		10r blue	7.50	4.00
P23	N3	10r ultra, buff	3.00	3.00
P24	N3	20r green	10.00	3.00
a.		20r emerald	10.00	3.00
P25	N3	50r yel grn ('93)	17.50	10.00
		Nos. P22-P25 (4)	33.50	19.00

For surcharges see Nos. 136, 138-139.

POSTAL TAX STAMPS

Icarus from the Santos-Dumont
Monument at St. Cloud, France — PT1

Perf. 13½x12½, 11

1933, Oct. 1			Typo.	
RA1	PT1	100r deep brown	.65	.25

Honoring the Brazilian aviator, Santos-Dumont. Its use was obligatory as a tax on all correspondence sent to countries in South America, the US and Spain. Its use on correspondence to other countries was optional. The funds obtained were used for the construction of airports throughout Brazil.

Catalogue values for unused stamps in this section, from this point to the end of the section, are for Never Hinged items.

Father
Joseph
Damien
and
Children
PT2

1952, Nov. 24		Litho.	Perf. 12x11	
RA2	PT2	10c yellow brown	.25	.20

1953, Nov. 30				
RA3	PT2	10c yellow green	.25	.20

Father
Bento
Dias
Pacheco
PT3

Eunice
Weaver
PT4

1954, Nov. 22		Photo.	Perf. 11½	
RA4	PT3	10c violet blue	.20	.20

1955-69, Nov. 24				
RA5	PT3	10c dk car rose	.20	.20
RA6	PT3	10c org red ('57)	.20	.20
RA7	PT3	10c dp emer ('58)	.20	.20
RA8	PT3	10c red lilac ('61)	.20	.20
RA9	PT3	10c choc ('62)	.20	.20
RA10	PT3	10c slate ('63)	.20	.20
RA11	PT3	2cr dp mag ('64)	.20	.20
RA12	PT3	2cr violet ('65)	.20	.20

RA13	PT3	2cr orange ('66)	.20	.20
RA14	PT3	5c brt yel grn ('68)	1.25	.75
RA15	PT3	5c deep plum ('69)	.50	.25

Issued: 11/25, #RA14; 11/28, #RA15; others, 11/24.

1971-73, Nov. 24				
RA16	PT4	10c slate green	1.00	.40
RA17	PT4	10c brt rose lil ('73)	.20	.20

Father
Nicodemos
PT5

Father
Vicente
Borgard
(1888-1977)
PT6

1975, Nov. 24		Litho.	Unwmk.	
RA18	PT5	10c sepia	.20	.20

1983, Nov. 24		Photo.	Perf. 11½	
RA19	PT6	10cr brown	.60	.60

Father Bento
Dias
Pacheco
PT7

Father
Santiago
Uchoa
PT8

1984, Nov. 24		Photo.	Perf. 11½	
RA20	PT7	30cr deep blue	.20	.20

1985, Nov. 24			Litho.	
RA21	PT7	100cr lake	.20	.20

1986, Nov. 24			Litho.	
RA22	PT7	10c gray brown	.20	.20

1987, Nov. 24			Photo.	
RA23	PT7	30c sage green	.20	.20

1988, Nov. 24			Litho.	
RA24	PT8	1.30cz dull red brn	.20	.20

See Nos. RA29-RA30.

Fr. Joseph
Damien — PT9

1989-92		Photo.	Perf. 11½	
RA25	PT9	2c deep lilac rose	.20	.20
RA26	PT9	50c blue	.20	.20

			Perf. 12½	
RA27	PT9	3cr green	.20	.20
RA28	PT9	30cr brown	.20	.20
		Nos. RA25-RA28 (4)	.80	.80

Issued: 2c, Nov. 24; 50c, Nov. 24, 1990; 3cr, Nov. 24, 1991; 30cr, Nov. 24, 1992.

Father Santiago Uchoa Type of 1988

1993, Nov. 24		Photo.	Perf. 12½	
RA29	PT8	50c blue	.20	.20

1994, Nov. 24				
RA30	PT8	1c dull lake	.20	.20

The tax was for the care and treatment of lepers.
Use of #RA2-RA30 was required for one week.

POSTAL TAX SEMI-POSTAL STAMP

Catalogue values for unused stamps in this section are for Never Hinged items.

Icarus — PTSP1

Wmk. 267

1947, Nov. 15		Typo.	Perf. 11	
RAB1	PTSP1	40c + 10c brt red	.35	.20
a.		Pair, imperf. between	350.00	

Aviation Week, November 15-22, 1947, and compulsory on all domestic correspondence during that week.

BRITISH ANTARCTIC TERRITORY

ˈbri-tish ˌ(ˌ)ant-ˈärk-tik ˈter-ə-ˌtōr-ē

LOCATION — South Atlantic Ocean between 20-80 degrees longitude and south of 60 degrees latitude
GOVT. — British territory
POP. — About 300 scientific staff at research stations.

This territory includes Graham Land (Palmer Peninsula), South Shetland Islands and South Orkney Islands. Formerly part of Falkland Islands Dependency.

12 Pence = 1 Shilling
20 Shillings = 1 Pound
100 Pence = 1 Pound (1971)

Catalogue values for all unused stamps in this country are for Never Hinged items.

M. V. Kista
Dan — A1

1p, Skiers hauling load. 1½p, Muskeg (tractor). 2p, Skiers. 2½p, Beaver seaplane. 3p, R.R.S. John Biscoe. 4p, Camp scene. 6p, H.M.S. Protector. 9p, Dog sled. 1sh, Otter skiplane. 2sh, Huskies & aurora australis. 2sh6p, Helicopter. 5sh, Snocat (truck). 10sh, R.R.S. Shackleton. £1, Map of Antarctica.

1963, Feb. 1		Engr.	Perf. 11x11½	
1	A1	½p dark blue	.75	1.25
2	A1	1p brown	1.00	.75
3	A1	1½p plum & red	1.00	1.25
4	A1	2p rose violet	1.00	.75
5	A1	2½p dull green	1.75	1.25
6	A1	3p Prus blue	3.00	1.25
7	A1	4p sepia	2.25	1.40
8	A1	6p dk blue & olive	3.50	1.90
9	A1	9p olive	2.75	1.90
10	A1	1sh steel blue	3.00	.65
11	A1	2sh dl vio & bis	16.00	6.75
12	A1	2sh6p blue	16.00	7.25
13	A1	5sh rose red & org	17.00	12.50
14	A1	10sh grn & vio bl	35.00	25.00
15	A1	£1 black & blue	45.00	45.00
		Nos. 1-15 (15)	149.00	108.85

See No. 24. For surcharges see Nos. 25-38.

Common Design Types pictured following the introduction.

Churchill Memorial Issue
Common Design Type

1966, Jan. 24		Photo.	Perf. 14	
16	CD319	½p bright blue	.70	4.00
17	CD319	1p green	2.50	4.00
18	CD319	1sh brown	17.50	8.25
19	CD319	2sh violet	20.00	8.75
		Nos. 16-19 (4)	40.70	25.00

Lemaire
Channel,
Iceberg
and
Adelie
Penguins
A2

Designs: 6p, Weather sonde and operator. 1sh, Muskeg (tractor) pulling tent equipment. 2sh, Surveyors with theodolite.

1969, Feb. 6			Litho.	
20	A2	3½p blue, vio bl & blk	3.75	2.50
21	A2	6p emer, blk & dp org	2.00	2.10
22	A2	1sh ultra, blk & ver	2.00	1.75
23	A2	2sh grnsh bl, blk & och	2.00	2.50
		Nos. 20-23 (4)	9.75	8.85

25 years of continuous scientific work in the Antarctic.

Type of 1963
£1, H.M.S. Endurance and helicopter.

1969, Dec. 1		Engr.	Perf. 11x11½	
24	A1	£1 black & rose red	125.00	110.00

Nos. 1-14 Surcharged in Decimal
Currency; Three Bars Overprinted

1971, Feb. 15			Wmk. 314	
25	A1	½p on ½p	.40	2.50
26	A1	1p on 1p	.70	.70
27	A1	1½p on 1½p	.85	.60
28	A1	2p on 2p	.85	.35
29	A1	2½p on 2½p	2.10	1.90
30	A1	3p on 3p	1.75	.60
31	A1	4p on 4p	1.60	.60
32	A1	5p on 6p	3.25	3.00
33	A1	6p on 9p	11.50	7.00
34	A1	7½p on 1sh	12.00	7.25
35	A1	10p on 2sh	14.00	12.00
36	A1	12p on 2sh6p	14.00	13.00
37	A1	25p on 5sh	17.00	14.50
38	A1	50p on 10sh	30.00	26.00
		Nos. 25-38 (14)	110.00	90.00

Map of Antarctica,
Aurora Australis,
Explorers — A3

Capt. Cook and
"Resolution" — A4

Map of Antarctica, Aurora Australis and: 4p, Sea gulls. 5p, Seals. 10p, Penguins.

1971, June 23		Litho. & Engr.	Perf. 14x13	
39	A3	1½p multicolored	4.50	1.25
40	A3	4p multicolored	12.00	4.00
41	A3	5p multicolored	7.00	6.00
42	A3	10p multicolored	16.00	10.00
		Nos. 39-42 (4)	39.50	21.25

10th anniv. of the Antarctic Treaty pledging peaceful uses of and scientific cooperation in Antarctica.

Silver Wedding Issue, 1972
Common Design Type

Design: Queen Elizabeth II, Prince Philip, seals and emperor penguins.

1972, Dec. 13		Photo.	Perf. 14x14½	
43	CD324	5p rose brn & multi	3.00	3.00
44	CD324	10p olive & multi	3.00	3.00

1975-80			Litho.	Perf. 14½

Polar Explorers and their Crafts: 1p, Thaddeus von Bellingshausen and "Vostok." 1½p, James Weddell and "Jane." 2p, John Biscoe and "Tula." 2½p, J. S. C. Dumont d'Urville and "Astrolabe." 3p, James Clark Ross and "Erebus." 4p, C. A. Larsen and "Jason." 5p, Adrien de Gerlache and "Belgica." 6p, Otto Nordenskjöld and "Antarctic." 7½p, W. S. Bruce and "Scotia." 10p, Jean-Baptiste Charcot and "Pourquoi Pas?" 15p, Ernest Shackleton and "Endurance." 25p, Hubert Wilkins and airplane "San Francisco." 50p, Lincoln Ellsworth and airplane "Polar Star." £1, John Rymill and "Penola."

45	A4	½p multi	.20	.20
46	A4	1p multi ('78)	.20	.20
47	A4	1½p multi ('78)	.20	.20

48	A4	2p multi ('79)	.20	.20
49	A4	2½p multi ('79)	.20	.20
50	A4	3p multi ('79)	.20	.20
52	A4	5p multi ('79)	.30	.30
55	A4	10p multi ('79)	.65	.65
56	A4	15p multi ('79)	1.00	1.00
57	A4	25p multi ('79)	1.60	1.60
58	A4	50p multi ('79)	3.25	3.25
59	A4	£1 multi ('78)	5.25	5.25
		Nos. 45-59 (12)	13.25	13.25

1973, Feb. 14   Wmk. 314

45a	A4	½p multi	1.10	2.00
46a	A4	1p multi	2.25	3.25
47a	A4	1½p multi	9.75	4.50
48a	A4	2p multi	2.00	1.75
49a	A4	2½p multi	1.40	1.75
50a	A4	3p multi	.80	1.75
51a	A4	4p multi	.80	1.75
52a	A4	5p multi	.90	1.75
53a	A4	6p multi	1.10	1.75
54a	A4	7½p multi —	1.40	2.25
55a	A4	10p multi	2.50	3.00
56a	A4	15p multi	5.25	4.00
57a	A4	25p multi	3.25	4.00
58a	A4	50p multi	2.25	4.50
59a	A4	£1 multi	2.75	7.75
		Nos. 45a-59a (15)	37.50	46.25

1980   Wmk. 373   Perf. 12

51	A4	4p multi	.30	.30
53	A4	5p multi	.40	.40
54	A4	7½p multi	.50	.50
55b	A4	10p multi	.65	.65
56b	A4	15p multi	.70	.70
57b	A4	25p multi	1.25	1.25
58b	A4	50p multi	2.50	2.50
59b	A4	£1 multi	5.00	5.00
		Nos. 51-59b (8)	11.30	11.30

Princess Anne's Wedding Issue
Common Design Type

1973, Nov. 14   Wmk. 314   Perf. 14

60	CD325	5p ocher & multi	.40	.30
61	CD325	15p blue grn & multi	.85	.80

Wedding of Princess Anne and Capt. Mark Phillips, Nov. 14, 1973.

Churchill and Map of Churchill Peninsula A5

Design: 15p, Churchill and "Trepassey" of Operation Tabarin, 1943.

1974, Nov. 30   Litho.   Perf. 14

62	A5	5p multicolored	1.25	.80
63	A5	15p multicolored	2.50	2.50
a.		Souvenir sheet of 2, #62-63	13.00	13.00

Sir Winston Churchill (1874-1965).

Humpback Whale — A6

1977, Jan. 4   Litho.   Perf. 14

64	A6	2p Sperm whale	5.25	3.50
65	A6	8p Fin whale	6.25	4.00
66	A6	11p shown	6.50	4.00
67	A6	25p Blue whale	7.00	5.50
		Nos. 64-67 (4)	25.00	17.00

Conservation of whales.

Prince Philip in Antarctica, 1956-57 — A7

Designs: 11p, Coronation oath. 33p, Queen before taking oath.

1977, Feb. 7   Perf. 13½x14

68	A7	6p multicolored	.45	.45
69	A7	11p multicolored	.55	.55
70	A7	33p multicolored	2.00	.75
		Nos. 68-70 (3)	3.00	1.75

25th anniv. of the reign of Elizabeth II.

Elizabeth II Coronation Anniversary Issue
Common Design Types
Souvenir Sheet
Unwmk.

1978, June 2   Litho.   Perf. 15

71		Sheet of 6	5.00	5.00
a.	CD326	25p Black bull of Clarence	.75	.75
b.	CD327	25p Elizabeth II	.75	.75
c.	CD328	25p Emperor penguin	.75	.75

No. 71 contains 2 se-tenant strips of Nos. 71a-71c, separated by horizontal gutter with commemorative and descriptive inscriptions and showing central part of coronation procession with coach.

Macaroni Penguins — A8

1979, Jan. 14   Litho.   Perf. 13½x14

72	A8	3p shown	8.75	8.75
73	A8	8p Gentoo	2.50	2.50
74	A8	11p Adelie	2.75	2.75
75	A8	25p Emperor	3.50	3.50
		Nos. 72-75 (4)	17.50	17.50

John Barrow, Tula, Society Emblem A9

Royal Geographical Society Sesquicentennial (Past Presidents and Expedition Scenes): 7p, Clement Markham 11p, Lord Curzon. 15p, William Goodenough. 22p, James Wordie. 30p, Raymond Priestley.

Wmk. 373

1980, Dec. 1   Litho.   Perf. 13½

76	A9	3p multicolored	.20	.20
77	A9	7p multicolored	.20	.20
78	A9	11p multicolored	.30	.30
79	A9	15p multicolored	.50	.50
80	A9	22p multicolored	.75	.75
81	A9	30p multicolored	.95	.95
		Nos. 76-81 (6)	2.90	2.90

20th Anniv. of Antarctic Treaty — A10

1981, Dec. 1   Perf. 13½x14

82	A10	10p Map	.25	.65
83	A10	13p Conservation research	.40	.75
84	A10	25p Satellite image mapping	.70	.80
85	A10	26p Global geophysics	.75	.80
		Nos. 82-85 (4)	2.10	3.00

Continental Drift and Climatic Change — A11

1982, Mar. 8   Litho.   Perf. 13½x14

86	A11	3p Land, water	.25	.35
87	A11	6p Shrubs	.30	.45
88	A11	10p Dinosaur	.30	.55
89	A11	13p Volcano	.40	.60
90	A11	25p Trees	.50	.65
91	A11	26p Penguins	.50	.65
		Nos. 86-91 (6)	2.25	3.25

Princess Diana Issue
Common Design Type

1982, July 1   Litho.   Perf. 14½x14

92	CD333	5p Arms	.20	.20
93	CD333	17p Diana, by Bryan Organ	.55	.55
94	CD333	37p Wedding	1.25	1.25
95	CD333	50p Portrait	1.60	1.60
		Nos. 92-95 (4)	3.60	3.60

10th Anniv. of Convention for Conservation of Antarctic Seals — A12

1982, Nov.   Litho.

96	A12	5p shown	.20	.20
97	A12	10p Weddell seals	.30	.30
98	A12	13p Elephant seals	.40	.40
99	A12	17p Fur seals	.55	.55
100	A12	27p Ross seal	.55	.55
101	A12	34p Crabeater seals	1.10	1.10
		Nos. 96-101 (6)	3.10	3.10

Corethron Criophilum — A13

1p, shown. 2p, Desmonema gaudichaudi. 3p, Tomopteris carpenteri. 4p, Pareuchaeta antarctica. 5p, Antarctomysis maxima. 6p, Antarcturus signiensis. 7p, Serolis cornuta. 8p, Parathemisto gaudichaudii. 9p, Bovallia gigantea. 10p (#110A), Euphausia superba. 15p, Colossendeis australis. 20p, Todarodes sagittatus. 25p, Notothenia neglecta. 50p, Chaenocephalus aceratus. £1, Lobodon carcinophagus. £3, Antarctic marine food chain.

1984, Mar. 15   Litho.   Perf. 14

102-116	A13	Set of 16	17.00	30.00

Manned Flight Bicentenary — A14

1983, Dec. 17   Wmk. 373

117	A14	5p De Havilland Twin Otter	.20	.20
118	A14	13p De Havilland Single Otter	.35	.35
119	A14	17p Consolidated Canso	.55	.55
120	A14	50p Lockheed Vega	1.60	1.60
		Nos. 117-120 (4)	2.70	2.70

British-Graham Land Expedition, 1934-1937 — A15

Designs: 7p, M. Y. Penola in Stella Creek. 22p, Northern base, Winter Island. 27p, D. H. Fox Moth at southern base, Barry Island. 54p, Dog team near Ablation Point, George VI Sound.

1985, Mar. 23   Litho.   Perf. 14½

121	A15	7p multicolored	.20	.20
122	A15	22p multicolored	.55	.55
123	A15	27p multicolored	.65	.65
124	A15	54p multicolored	1.40	1.40
		Nos. 121-124 (4)	2.80	2.80

A16

Naturalists, fauna and flora: 7p, Robert McCormick (1800-1890), Catharacta Skua Maccormicki. 22p, Sir Joseph Dalton Hooker (1817-1911), Deschampsea antarctica. 27p, Jean Rene C. Quoy (1790-1869), Lagenorhynchus cruciger. 54p, James Weddell (1787-1834), Leptonychotes weddelli.

1985, Nov. 4   Litho.   Perf. 14½

125	A16	7p multicolored	.25	.25
126	A16	22p multicolored	.85	.85
127	A16	27p multicolored	1.00	1.00
128	A16	54p multicolored	2.00	2.00
		Nos. 125-128 (4)	4.10	4.10

A17

1986, Jan. 6   Wmk. 373   Perf. 14

Halley's comet.

129	A17	7p Edmond Halley	.30	.30
130	A17	22p Halley Station	.95	.95
131	A17	27p Trajectory, 1531	1.25	1.25
132	A17	54p Giotto space probe	2.50	2.50
		Nos. 129-132 (4)	5.00	5.00

Intl. Glaciological Society, 50th Anniv. — A18

Different snowflakes.

1986, Dec. 6   Wmk. 384   Perf. 14½

133	A18	10p dp blue & lt bl	.30	.30
134	A18	24p blue grn & lt bl grn	.70	.70
135	A18	29p dp rose lil & lt lil	.85	.85
136	A18	58p dp vio & pale vio blue	1.75	1.75
		Nos. 133-136 (4)	3.60	3.60

Capt. Robert Falcon Scott, CVO RN (1868-1912) A19

Designs: 24p, The Discovery at Hut Point, 1902-1904. 29p, Cape Evans Hut, 1911-1913. 58p, South Pole, 1912.

1987, Mar. 19   Litho.   Wmk. 373

137	A19	10p multicolored	.30	.30
138	A19	24p multicolored	.70	.70
139	A19	29p multicolored	.85	.85
140	A19	58p multicolored	1.75	1.75
		Nos. 137-140 (4)	3.60	3.60

Intl. Geophysical Year, 30th Anniv. — A20

1987, Dec. 25   **Wmk. 384**
141 A20 10p Emblem   .40   .40
142 A20 24p Port Lockroy   .90   .90
143 A20 29p Argentine Islands   1.10 1.10
144 A20 58p Halley Bay   2.25 2.25
     Nos. 141-144 (4)   4.65 4.65

Commonwealth
Trans-Antarctic
Expedition] — A21

1988, Mar. 19   **Perf. 14**
145 A21 10p Aurora over South
     Ice   .35   .35
146 A21 24p Otter aircraft   .80   .80
147 A21 29p Seismic ice-depth
     sounding   .95   .95
148 A21 58p Sno-cat over
     crevasse   1.90 1.90
     Nos. 145-148 (4)   4.00 4.00

Lichens
A22

1989, Mar. 25   **Wmk. 373**
149 A22 10p Xanthoria elegans   .40   .40
150 A22 24p Usnea aurantiaco-
     atra   1.00 1.00
151 A22 29p Cladonia
     chlorophaea   1.25 1.25
152 A22 58p Umbilicaria antarcti-
     ca   2.50 2.50
     Nos. 149-152 (4)   5.15 5.15

Fossils
A23

1990, Apr. 2   **Litho.**   **Wmk. 384**
153 A23 1p Archaeocyath   .20   .20
154 A23 2p Brachiopod   .20   .20
155 A23 3p Trilobite
     (Triplagnostus)   .20   .20
156 A23 4p Trilobite (Lyrias-
     pis)   .20   .20
157 A23 5p Gymnosperm   .20   .20
158 A23 6p Fern   .20   .20
159 A23 7p Belemnite   .20   .20
160 A23 8p Ammonite
     (Sanmartinocer-
     as)   .20   .20
161 A23 9p Bivalve (Pinna)   .25   .25
162 A23 10p Bivalve (Aucel-
     lina)   .30   .30
163 A23 20p Bivalve (Trigonia)   .60   .60
164 A23 25p Gastropod   .70   .70
165 A23 50p Ammonite (Ai-
     noceras)   1.40 1.40
166 A23 £1 Ammonite (Gun-
     narites)   2.75 2.75
167 A23 £3 Crayfish   8.00 8.00
     Nos. 153-167 (15)   15.60 15.60

Queen Mother, 90th Birthday
Common Design Types
1990, Aug. 4   **Wmk. 384**   **Perf. 14x15**
170 CD343 26p Wedding portrait,
     1923   .90   .90

      Perf. 14½
171 CD344 £1 Family portrait,
     1940   3.25 3.25

Age of
Dinosaurs
A24

1991, Mar. 27   **Wmk. 373**   *Perf. 14*
172 A24 12p Late Cretaceous
     forest   .75   .75
173 A24 26p Hypsilophodont di-
     nosaur   1.50 1.50
174 A24 31p Frilled shark   1.90 1.90
175 A24 62p Mosasaur, plesio-
     saur   3.50 3.50
     Nos. 172-175 (4)   7.65 7.65

Antarctic
Ozone
Hole — A25

1991, Mar. 30   *Perf. 14½x14*
176 A25 12p Launching weather
     balloon   .40   .40
177 A25 26p Measuring ozone   .95   .95
178 A25 31p Ozone hole over
     Antarctica   1.25 1.25
179 A25 62p Airplane, chemical
     studies   2.40 2.40
     Nos. 176-179 (4)   5.00 5.00

Antarctic Treaty,
30th
Anniv. — A26

1991, June 24   *Perf. 14½*
180 A26 12p Dry valley   .40   .40
181 A26 26p Mapping ice sheet   .95   .95
182 A26 31p BIOMASS emblem   1.25 1.25
183 A26 62p Ross seal   2.40 2.40
     Nos. 180-183 (4)   5.00 5.00

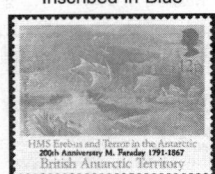

Royal
Research
Ship James
Clark
Ross — A27

Designs: 12p, HMS Erebus and Terror in
Antarctic by John W. Carmichael. 26p, Launch
of RRS James Clark Ross. 62p, Scientific
research.

1991, Dec. 10   *Perf. 14x14½*
184 A27 12p multicolored   .40   .40
185 A27 26p multicolored   .95   .95
186 A27 31p shown   1.25 1.25
187 A27 62p multicolored   2.40 2.40
     Nos. 184-187 (4)   5.00 5.00

Inscribed in Blue

1991, Dec. 24
188 A27 12p like #184   .40   .40
189 A27 26p like #185   .95   .95
190 A27 31p like #186   1.25 1.25
191 A27 62p like #187   2.40 2.40
     Nos. 188-191 (4)   5.00 5.00

Seals
and
Penguins
A28

1992, Oct. 20   *Perf. 13½*
192 A28 4p Ross seal   .20   .20
193 A28 5p Adelie penguin   .20   .20
194 A28 7p Weddell seal   .30   .30

---

195 A28 29p Emperor penguin   1.25 1.25
196 A28 34p Crabeater seal   1.50 1.50
197 A28 68p Chinstrap penguin   3.00 3.00
     Nos. 192-197 (6)   6.45 6.45
     World Wildlife Fund.

Lower
Atmospheric
Phenomena
A29

1992, Dec. 22   **Litho.**   **Perf. 14x14½**
198 A29 14p Sun pillar at Fara-
     day   .50   .50
199 A29 29p Halo with iceberg   1.10 1.10
200 A29 34p Lee wave cloud   1.25 1.25
201 A29 68p Nacreous clouds   2.50 2.50
     Nos. 198-201 (4)   5.35 5.35

Research
Ships
A30

1993, Dec. 13   **Litho.**   **Perf. 14**
202 A30 1p SS Fitzroy   .20   .20
203 A30 2p HMS William
     Scoresby   .20   .20
204 A30 3p SS Eagle   .20   .20
205 A30 4p MV Trepassey   .20   .20
206 A30 5p RRS John Bis-
     coe (I)   .20   .20
207 A30 10p MV Norsel   .30   .30
208 A30 29p HMS Protector   .55   .55
209 A30 30p MV Oluf Sven   .85   .85
210 A30 62p RRS John Bis-
     coe (II), RRS
     Shackleton   1.40 1.40
   a.   Souvenir sheet of 1   1.75 1.75
211 A30 £1 MV Tottan   2.75 2.75
   a.   Souvenir sheet of 1   3.50 3.50
212 A30 £3 MV Perla Dan   8.50 8.50
213 A30 £5 HMS Endurance
     (I)   14.00 14.00
     Nos. 202-213 (12)   29.35 29.35

No. 210a for Hong Kong '97. Issued 2/3/97.
No. 211a for return of Hong Kong to China.
Issued 7/1/97.

Operation
Taberin, 50th
Anniv. — A31

Designs: 15p, Bransfield House and Post
Office, Port Lockroy. 31p, Survey team, Hope
Bay. 36p, Dog team, Hope Bay. 72p, SS Fitz-
roy, HMS William Scoresby at sea.

1994, Mar. 19   **Litho.**   **Perf. 14**
214 A31 15p multicolored   .45   .45
215 A31 31p multicolored   .90   .90
216 A31 36p multicolored   1.10 1.10
217 A31 72p multicolored   2.25 2.25
     Nos. 214-217 (4)   4.70 4.70

Old and New Transportation — A32

Designs: 15p, Huskies. 24p, DeHavilland
DHC-2 Turbo Beaver, British Antarctic Survey.
31p, Dogs, cargo being taken from aircraft.
36p, DHC-6 Twin Otter, sled team. 62p, DHC-
6 in flight. 72p, DHC-6 taxiing down runway.

1994, Mar. 21
218 A32 15p multicolored   .45   .45
219 A32 24p multicolored   .70   .70
220 A32 31p multicolored   .90   .90
221 A32 36p multicolored   1.10 1.10
222 A32 62p multicolored   1.75 1.75
223 A32 72p multicolored   2.25 2.25
     Nos. 218-223 (6)   7.15 7.15

Ovptd. with Hong Kong '94 Emblem
1994, Feb. 18
224 A32 15p on #218   .45   .45
225 A32 24p on #219   .70   .70
226 A32 31p on #220   .90   .90
227 A32 36p on #221   1.10 1.10
228 A32 62p on #222   1.75 1.75
229 A32 72p on #223   2.25 2.25
     Nos. 224-229 (6)   7.15 7.15

Antarctic
Food
Chain — A33

a, Crabeater seals. b, Blue whale. c, Wandering albatross. d, Mackeral icefish. e, Krill. f,
Squid.

1994, Nov. 29
230 A33 35p Sheet of 6, #a-f   6.50 6.50

Geological
Structures
A34

Designs: 17p, Hauberg Mountains, folded
sedimentary rocks. 35p, Arrowsmith Peninsula, dikes cross-cutting granite. 40p, Colbert
Mountains, columnar jointing in volcanic rocks.
76p, Succession Cliffs, flat-lying sedimentary
rocks.

1995, Nov. 28   **Litho.**   **Perf. 14x14½**
231 A34 17p multicolored   .55   .55
232 A34 35p multicolored   1.10 1.10
233 A34 40p multicolored   1.25 1.25
234 A34 76p multicolored   2.50 2.50
     Nos. 231-234 (4)   5.40 5.40

Scientific Committee on Antarctic
Research (SCAR) — A35

Designs: 17p, World map showing SCAR
member countries. 35p, Earth sciences. 40p,
Atmospheric sciences. 76p, Life sciences.
£1, Cambridge, August 1996.

1996, Mar. 23   **Litho.**   **Perf. 14**
235 A35 17p multicolored   .55   .55
236 A35 35p multicolored   1.10 1.10
237 A35 40p multicolored   1.25 1.25
238 A35 76p multicolored   2.50 2.50
     Nos. 235-238 (4)   5.40 5.40

Souvenir Sheet
239 A35 £1 multicolored   3.25 3.25

Queen Elizabeth II, 70th Birthday
Common Design Type

Various portraits of Queen: 17p, Pink outfit.
35p, In formal dress, tiara. 40p, Blue outfit.
76p, Red coat.

1996, Nov. 25   **Litho.**   **Perf. 14½**
240 CD354 17p multicolored   .60   .60
241 CD354 35p multicolored   1.10 1.10
242 CD354 40p multicolored   1.40 1.40
243 CD354 76p multicolored   2.50 2.50
     Nos. 240-243 (4)   5.60 5.60

Whales
A36

1996, Nov. 25   Litho.   Perf. 14

244	A36	17p Killer whale	.60	.60
245	A36	35p Sperm whale	1.10	1.10
246	A36	40p Minke whale	1.40	1.40
247	A36	76p Blue whale	2.50	2.50
		Nos. 244-247 (4)	5.60	5.60

Souvenir Sheet

248	A36	£1 Humpback whale	3.50	3.50

Christmas — A37

Penguins in snow: 17p, Sledding. 35p, Caroling. 40p, Throwing snowballs. 76p, Ice skating.

1997, Dec. 22   Litho.   Perf. 14½

249	A37	17p multicolored	.55	.55
250	A37	35p multicolored	1.10	1.10
251	A37	40p multicolored	1.40	1.40
252	A37	76p multicolored	2.40	2.40
		Nos. 249-252 (4)	5.45	5.45

History of Mapping — A38

Maps of Antarctic: on 16p, Surveyor looking through theodolite, 1902-03. 30p, Cartographer, 1949. 35p, Man using radar rangefinder, 1964. 40p, Satellite, 1981. 65p, Tripod, hand held remote control device, 1993.

1998, Mar. 19   Litho.   Perf. 14

253	A38	16p multicolored	.55	.55
254	A38	30p multicolored	1.00	1.00
255	A38	35p multicolored	1.25	1.25
256	A38	40p multicolored	1.40	1.40
257	A38	65p multicolored	2.25	2.25
		Nos. 253-257 (5)	6.45	6.45

Diana, Princess of Wales (1961-97)
Common Design Type

a, Wearing sun glasses. b, In white top. c, Up close. d, Wearing blue-green blazer.

1998, Mar. 31   Perf. 14½x14

258	CD355	35p Sheet of 4, #a-d	5.25	5.25

No. 258 sold for £1.40 + 20p, with surtax and 50% of profit from total sales being donated to the Princess Diana Memorial Fund.

Antarctic Clothing Through the Ages — A39

Man outfitted for cold weather: 30p, Holding shovel, sailing ship, 1843. 35p, With dog, sailing ship, 1900. 40p, With sketch pad, tripod, dog, steamer ship, 1943. 65p, Wearing red suit, penguins, ship, 1998.

1998, Nov. 30   Litho.   Perf. 14½x14

259	A39	30p multicolored	1.00	1.00
260	A39	35p multicolored	1.10	1.10
261	A39	40p multicolored	1.25	1.25
262	A39	65p multicolored	2.10	2.10
		Nos. 259-262 (4)	5.45	5.45

Birds A40

Designs: 1p, Sheathbill. 2p, Antarctic prion. 5p, Adelie penguin. 10p, Emperor penguin. 20p, Antarctic tern. 30p, Black bellied storm petrel. 35p, Antarctic fulmar. 40p, Blue eyed shag. 50p, McCormick's skua. £1, Kelp gull. £3, Wilson's storm petrel. £5, Brown skua.

1998   Perf. 14

263	A40	1p multicolored	.20	.20
264	A40	2p multicolored	.20	.20
265	A40	5p multicolored	.20	.20
266	A40	10p multicolored	.35	.35
267	A40	20p multicolored	.65	.65
268	A40	30p multicolored	1.00	1.00
269	A40	35p multicolored	1.10	1.10
270	A40	40p multicolored	1.25	1.25
271	A40	50p multicolored	1.60	1.60
272	A40	£1 multicolored	3.25	3.25
273	A40	£3 multicolored	10.00	10.00
274	A40	£5 multicolored	16.00	16.00
		Nos. 263-274 (12)	35.80	35.80

Fish — A41

Wmk. 373

1999, Nov. 14   Litho.   Perf. 13½

275	A41	10p Mackerel icefish	.35	.35
276	A41	20p Toothfish	.65	.65
277	A41	25p Borch	.80	.80
278	A41	50p Marbled notothen	1.60	1.60
279	A41	80p Bernach	2.60	2.60
		Nos. 275-279 (5)	6.00	6.00

Survey Discoveries — A42

15p, Map of crustal microplates of West Antarctica. 30p, Lead levels in ice. 35p, Gigantism in marine invertebrates. 40p, Ozone hole. 70p, Electric field associated with aurora.

Wmk. 373

1999, Dec. 18   Litho.   Perf. 14

280	A42	15p multi, vert.	.45	.45
281	A42	30p multi, vert.	.95	.95
282	A42	35p multi	1.10	1.10
283	A42	40p multi	1.25	1.25
284	A42	70p multi	2.25	2.25
		Nos. 280-284 (5)	6.00	6.00

Sir Ernest Shackleton (1874-1922), Polar Explorer — A43

Designs: 35p, Wreck of the Endurance. 40p, Ocean Camp on ice floe. 65p, Launching the James Caird from Elephant Island.

2000, Feb. 10   Wmk. 373

285	A43	35p multi	1.10	1.10
286	A43	40p multi	1.25	1.25
287	A43	65p multi	2.10	2.10
		Nos. 285-287 (3)	4.45	4.45

See Falkland Islands Nos. 758-760, South Georgia and South Sandwich Islands Nos. 254-256.

The Stamp Show 2000, London — A44

Commonwealth Trans-Antarctic Exhibition of 1955-58: a, Map of route. b, Expedition at South Pole, 1958. c, MV Magga Dan. d, Sno-cat repair camp. e, Sno-cat over crevasse. f, Seismic explosion.
Illustration reduced.

Perf. 13¼x13¾

2000, May 22   Litho.   Wmk. 373

288	A44	37p Sheet of 6, #a-f	6.75	6.75

Survey Ships A45

Designs: 20p, RRS Bransfield unloading near Halley, vert. 33p, Supply boat Tula and RRS Ernest Shackleton, vert. 37p, RRS Bransfield. 43p, RRS Ernest Shackleton.

Wmk. 373

2000, Nov. 30   Litho.   Perf. 14

289-292	A45	Set of 4	4.00	4.00

Composing of Antarctic Symphony, by Sir Peter Maxwell Davies — A46

Designs: No. 293, 37p, RRS James Clark Ross and track cut through ice. No. 294, 37p, Iceberg. No. 295, 43p, Camp on Jones Ice Shelf. No. 296, 43p, Iceberg, diff.

2000, Dec. 4

293-296	A46	Set of 4	4.75	4.75

SEMI-POSTAL STAMPS

Antarctic Heritage SP1

Designs: 17p+3p, Capt. James Cook, HMS Resolution. 35p+15p, Sir James Clark Ross, HMS Erebus, HMS Terror. 40p+10p, Capt. Robert Falcon Scott. 76p+4p, Sir Ernest Shackleton, HMS Endurance trapped in ice.

Wmk. 384

1994, Nov. 23   Litho.   Perf. 14½

B1	SP1	17p + 3p multi	.65	.65
B2	SP1	35p + 15p multi	1.50	1.50
B3	SP1	40p + 10p multi	1.50	1.50
B4	SP1	76p + 4p multi	2.50	2.50
		Nos. B1-B4 (4)	6.15	6.15

Surtax for United Kingdom Antarctic Heritage Trust.

BRITISH CENTRAL AFRICA

ˈbri-tish ˈsen-trəl ˈa-fri-kə

LOCATION — Central Africa, on the west shore of Lake Nyassa

GOVT. — British territory, under charter to the British South Africa Company
AREA — 37,800 sq. mi.
POP. — 1,639,329
CAPITAL — Zomba

In 1907 the name was changed to Nyasaland Protectorate, and stamps so inscribed replaced those of British Central Africa.

12 Pence = 1 Shilling
20 Shillings = 1 Pound

Rhodesia Nos. 2, 4-19 Overprinted in Black   **B.C.A.**

1891-95   Unwmk.   Perf. 14

1	A1	1p black	3.25	3.50
2	A2	2p gray green & ver	3.25	3.50
3	A2	4p red brn & blk	3.50	4.50
4	A1	6p ultramarine	45.00	24.00
5	A1	6p dark blue	5.00	7.50
6	A2	8p rose & blue	12.00	27.50
7	A1	1sh bis brown	12.00	10.00
8	A1	2sh vermilion	22.50	45.00
9	A1	2sh6p gray lilac	55.00	70.00
10	A2	3sh brn & grn ('95)	50.00	55.00
11	A2	4sh gray & ver ('93)	55.00	75.00
12	A1	5sh yellow	55.00	67.50
13	A1	10sh green	110.00	160.00
14	A3	£1 blue	600.00	650.00
15	A3	£2 rose red	800.00	900.00
16	A3	£5 yel green	1,600.	1,700.
17	A3	£10 red brown	3,250.	3,500.
		Nos. 1-13 (13)	431.50	553.00

High values with fiscal cancellation are fairly common and can be purchased at a small fraction of the above values. This applies to subsequent issues also.
For surcharge see No. 20.

Rhodesia Nos. 13-14 Surcharged in Black   **B.C.A. THREE SHILLINGS.**

1892-93

18	A2	3sh on 4sh gray & ver ('93)	300.00	300.00
19	A1	4sh on 5sh yellow	75.00	75.00

No. 2 Surcharged in Black, with Bar   **B.C.A. ONE PENNY.**

1895

20	A2	1p on 2p	7.50	25.00
	a.	Double surcharge	3,000.	2,400.

A double surcharge, without period after "Penny," and measuring 16mm instead of 18mm, is from a trial printing.

A4

Coat of Arms of the Protectorate — A5

1895   Unwmk.   Typo.   Perf. 14

21	A4	1p black	11.00	6.50
22	A4	2p green & black	17.50	11.00
23	A4	4p org & black	32.50	26.00
24	A4	6p ultra & black	50.00	7.50
25	A4	1sh rose & black	55.00	22.50
26	A5	2sh6p vio & black	150.00	225.00
27	A5	3sh yel & black	85.00	45.00
28	A5	5sh olive & blk	125.00	150.00
29	A5	£1 org & black	800.00	375.00

30	A5	£10 ver & black	3,750.	3,250.
31	A5	£25 bl grn & blk	6,500.	6,500.
		Nos. 21-28 (8)	526.00	493.50

1896   **Wmk. 2**

32	A4	1p black	4.00	4.50
33	A4	2p green & black	12.50	5.75
34	A4	4p org brown & blk	19.00	16.00
35	A4	6p ultra & black	19.00	10.00
36	A4	1sh rose & black	19.00	12.00

Wmk. 1 Sideways

37	A5	2sh6p vio rose & blk	100.00	100.00
38	A5	3sh yel & black	75.00	45.00
39	A5	5sh olive & blk	110.00	140.00
40	A5	£1 blue & blk	800.00	475.00
41	A5	£10 ver & blk	4,250.	3,250.
42	A5	£25 bl grn & blk	9,500.	9,500.
		Nos. 32-39 (8)	358.50	333.25

A6   A7

1897-1901   **Wmk. 2**

43	A6	1p ultra & black	2.25	.80
44	A6	1p rose & violet ('01)	1.75	.80
45	A6	2p yel & black	1.75	1.60
46	A6	4p car rose & blk	5.00	2.25
47	A6	4p ol grn & vio ('01)	7.00	10.00
48	A6	6p green & black	37.50	4.00
49	A6	6p red brn & vio ('01)	4.00	2.75
50	A6	1sh gray lilac & blk	8.50	6.25

Wmk. 1

51	A7	2sh6p ultra & blk	40.00	37.50
52	A7	3sh gray grn & blk	175.00	200.00
53	A7	4sh car rose & blk	62.50	70.00
54	A7	10sh olive & blk	100.00	110.00
55	A7	£1 dp vio & blk	240.00	150.00
56	A7	£10 orange & black	4,000.	1,700.
		Nos. 43-54 (12)	445.25	445.95

No. 52 Surcharged in Red

1897

57	A7	1p on 3s	5.00	8.00
a.		"PNNEY"	1,700.	1,700.
b.		"PENN"	1,150.	900.00
c.		Double surcharge	675.00	

A8

Type I - The vertical framelines are not continuous between stamps.
Type II - The vertical framelines are continuous between stamps.

1898, Mar. 11   **Unwmk.**   *Imperf.*

Type I
Control on Reverse

58	A8	1p ver & ultra	—	75.00
a.		1p ver & deep ultra	—	75.00
b.		No control on reverse	1,750.	125.00
c.		Control double		375.00
d.		Control on front	3,000.	
e.		Pair, one without oval	10,000.	

Type II
Control on Reverse

f.		1p ver & ultra	—	350.00

No Control on Reverse

i.		Oval inverted	9,500.	
j.		Oval double		
k.		Pair, with 3 ovals		

Perf. 12
Type I
Control on Reverse

59	A8	1p ver & ultra	1,750.	15.00
a.		1p ver & deep ultra	—	27.50
b.		Two diff. controls on reverse		550.00

No Control on Reverse

d.		1p ver & ultra	1,800.	75.00

There are 30 types of each setting of Nos. 58-59.
No. 58 issued without gum.
Control consists of figures or letters.
See the *Scott Classic Catalogue* for additional varieties.

A9   King Edward VII — A'10

1903-04   **Wmk. 2**

60	A9	1p car & black	4.25	1.60
61	A9	2p vio & dull vio	3.00	2.25
62	A9	4p blk & gray green	2.25	8.00
63	A9	6p org brn & blk	2.25	4.00
64	A9	1sh pale blue & blk ('04)	2.50	8.75

Wmk. 1

65	A10	2sh6p gray green	35.00	57.50
66	A10	4sh vio & dl vio	55.00	67.50
67	A10	10sh blk & gray green	80.00	160.00
68	A10	£1 scar & blk	200.00	150.00
69	A10	£10 ultra & blk	3,750.	3,000.
		Nos. 60-68 (9)	384.25	459.60

1907   **Wmk. 3**

70	A9	1p car & black	4.00	2.25
71	A9	2p vio & dull vio	8,250.	
72	A9	4p blk & gray grn	8,250.	
73	A9	6p org brn & blk	25.00	40.00

Nos. 71-72 were not issued.
British Central Africa stamps were replaced by those of Nyasaland Protectorate in 1908.

BRITISH EAST AFRICA

'bri-tish 'ēst 'a-fri-kə

LOCATION — Included all of the territory in East Africa under British control.

Postage stamps were issued by the British East Africa Company in 1896. Later the territory administered by this company was incorporated in the East Africa and Uganda Protectorate which, together with Kenya, became officially designated Kenya Colony.

16 Annas = 1 Rupee

Queen Victoria

A1   A2   A3

1890   **Wmk. 30**   *Perf. 14*

1	A1	½a on 1p lilac	300.00	200.00
2	A2	1a on 2p grn & car rose	400.00	275.00
3	A3	4a on 5p lilac & bl	400.00	275.00

Sun and Crown Symbolical of "Light and Liberty"
A4   A5

1890-94   **Unwmk.**   **Litho.**   *Perf. 14*

14	A4	½a bister brown	1.00	4.50
b.		½a deep brown	1.00	3.00
d.		As "b," horiz. pair, imperf. btwn.	1,500.	750.00
15	A4	1a blue green	3.00	4.25
16	A4	2a vermilion	2.50	3.50
17	A4	2½a black, *yel* ('91)	4.00	5.00
b.		Vert. pair, imperf. btwn.	1,200.	400.00
c.		Horiz. pair, imperf. btwn.	1,200.	525.00
18	A4	3a black, *red* ('91)	1.60	4.50
b.		Horiz. pair, imperf. btwn.	700.00	400.00
c.		Vert. pair, imperf. btwn.	550.00	375.00
19	A4	4a yellow brown	2.50	5.00
20	A4	4½a brown vio ('91)	2.50	12.50
b.		4½a gray violet ('91)	32.50	12.50
c.		Horiz. pair, imperf. btwn.	1,250.	1,250.
d.		Vert. pair, imperf. btwn.	850.00	450.00
21	A4	4a black, *blue* ('94)	1.25	10.00
22	A4	7½a black ('94)	1.25	12.00
23	A4	8a blue	5.50	8.00
24	A4	8a gray	275.00	325.00
25	A4	1r rose	6.00	8.50
26	A4	1r gray	225.00	225.00
27	A5	2r brick red	12.50	24.00
28	A5	3r gray violet	7.50	27.50
29	A5	4r ultra	12.00	30.00
30	A5	5r gray green	35.00	60.00
		Nos. 14-30 (17)	598.10	769.25

Some of the paper used for this issue had a papermaker's watermark and parts of it often can be seen on the stamps.
Values for Nos. 14c, 14d, 17b, 17c, 18b, 18c, 20c, 20d, unused, are for copies with little or no original gum. Stamps with natural straight edges are almost as common as fully perforated stamps from the early printings of Nos. 14-30, and for all printings of the rupee values. Values about the same.
For surcharges and overprints see #31-53.

1890-91   *Imperf.*
Values for Pairs except No. 19b.

14a	A4	½a bister brown	800.	375.
14e	A4	½a deep brown	900.	500.
15a	A4	1a blue green	1,000.	500.
16a	A4	2a vermilion	1,350.	550.
17a	A4	2½a black, *yellow*	900.	400.
18a	A4	3a black, *red*	850.	600.
19a	A4	4a yel brown	1,500.	700.
19b	A4	4a gray	1,400.	1,400.
20a	A4	4½a dull violet	1,300.	525.
23a	A4	8a blue	2,250.	650.
25a	A4	1r rose	2,750.	700.

A6   A7

Handstamped Surcharges

1891   *Perf. 14*

31	A6	½a on 2a ver ("A.D.")	3,750.	900.00
a.		Double surcharge		3,750.
32	A6	1a on 4a yel brn ("A.B.")	6,500.	1,500.

Nos. 31-32 are initialed in manuscript "A.D." or "A.B." See note below No. 35.

Manuscript Surcharges

1891-95

33	A6	½a on 2a ver ("A.B.")	3,500.	725.00
a.		"½ Annas" ("A.B.")		1,200.
b.		Initialed "A.D."		1,750.
c.		"½ Annas" ("A.D.")		2,000.
34	A6	½a on 3a blk, *red* ("T.E.C.R.")	350.00	50.00
b.		Initialed "A.B."	4,750.	1,375.
34A	A6	1a on 3a blk, *red* ("V.H.M.")	4,750.	1,200.
c.		Initialed "T.E.C.R."	3,750.	1,800.
35	A6	1a on 4a yel brn ("A.B.")	3,500.	1,275.

The manuscript initials on Nos. 31-35, given in parentheses, stand for Andrew Dick, Archibald Brown, Victor H. Mackenzie (1891) and T. E. C. Remington (1895).

Printed Surcharges

1894

36	A7	5a on 8a blue	52.50	75.00
37	A7	7½a on 1r rose	52.50	75.00

Stamps of 1890-94
Handstamped in Black

1895

38	A4	½a deep brown	60.00	24.00
39	A4	1a blue green	70.00	65.00
40	A4	2a vermilion	140.00	125.00
41	A4	2½a black, *yellow*	110.00	45.00
42	A4	3a black, *red*	50.00	37.50
43	A4	4a yel brown	37.50	37.50
44	A4	4½a gray violet	125.00	85.00
a.		4½a brown violet	750.00	650.00
45	A4	4½a black, *blue*	150.00	90.00
b.		Inverted overprint		2,000.
46	A4	7½a black	87.50	80.00
47	A4	8a blue	80.00	75.00
b.		Inverted overprint		2,000.
48	A4	1r rose	47.50	47.50
49	A5	2r brick red	250.00	175.00
50	A5	3r gray violet	140.00	125.00
b.		Inverted overprint		
51	A4	4r ultra	125.00	125.00
52	A5	5r gray green	325.00	350.00
		Nos. 38-52 (15)	1,797.	1,486.

Double Overprints

38a	A4	½a	350.	350.
39a	A4	1a	350.	350.
40a	A4	2a	400.	400.
41a	A4	2½a	400.	350.
43a	A4	4a	375.	375.
44a	A4	4½a gray violet	475.	450.
44c	A4	4½a brown violet	1,500.	1,400.
45a	A4	5a	700.	650.
46a	A4	7½a	450.	450.
47a	A4	8a	475.	475.
48a	A5	1r	425.	425.
50a	A5	3r	750.	750.
51a	A5	4r	750.	750.
52a	A5	5r	1,100.	1,100.

2½

Surcharged in Red

1895

53	A4	2½a on 4½a gray vio	90.00	60.00
a.		Double overprint (#44b)	700.00	700.00

Stamps of India 1874-95 Overprinted or Surcharged

British East Africa

2½ 2½ 2½
a   b   c

1895   **Wmk. Star (39)**

54	A17	½a green	4.25	4.50
55	A19	1a maroon	3.50	4.25
56	A20	1a6p bister brn	3.50	4.00
57	A21	2a ultra	4.25	2.50
58	A28	2a6p green	5.00	2.75
59	A20(a)	2½a on 1a6p bis brown	60.00	35.00
a.		"½" without fraction line	70.00	
d.		As "a," "1" of "½" invtd.	775.00	600.00
62	A22	3a orange	7.00	8.50
63	A23	4a olive green	27.50	22.50
64	A25	8a red violet	27.50	45.00
a.		8a red lilac	50.00	57.50
65	A26	12a vio, *red*	20.00	25.00
66	A27	1r gray	60.00	60.00
67	A29	1r car & grn	40.00	75.00
a.		Dbl. ovpt., one sideways	400.00	675.00
68	A30	2r bis & rose	60.00	90.00
69	A30	3r grn & brn	65.00	110.00
70	A30	5r vio & ultra	85.00	125.00
a.		Double overprint	1,800.	

Wmk. Elephant's Head (38)

71	A14	6a bister	25.00	40.00
		Nos. 54-59,62-71 (16)	497.50	654.00

Varieties of the overprint include: "British," "Brltish," "Bpitish" and "Biitish"; "Africa," "Eas" and "Easa."
No. 59 is surcharged in bright red; surcharges in brown red were prepared for the UPU, but not regularly issued as stamps. See note following No. 93.

Queen Victoria and British Lions — A8

1896-1903   **Engr.**   **Wmk. 2**   *Perf. 14*

72	A8	½a yel green	1.25	.70
73	A8	1a carmine	3.00	.40
a.		1a red	3.00	.40

74	A8	1a dp rose ('03)	27.50	3.75
75	A8	2a chocolate	3.75	4.00
76	A8	2½a dark blue	5.00	1.40
77	A8	3a gray	2.50	5.50
78	A8	4a deep green	6.00	3.25
79	A8	4½a orange	4.50	12.50
80	A8	5a dk ocher	7.00	4.00
81	A8	7½a lilac	5.00	20.00
82	A8	8a olive gray	2.50	5.50
83	A8	1r ultra	45.00	42.50
a.		1r pale blue	35.00	22.50
84	A8	2r red orange	47.50	24.00
85	A8	3r deep violet	55.00	27.50
86	A8	4r lake	55.00	55.00
87	A8	5r dark brown	50.00	40.00
		Nos. 72-87 (16)	320.50	250.00

Zanzibar Nos. 38-40,
44-46 Overprinted in
Black

1897   Wmk. Rosette (71)

88	A2	½a yel grn & red	45.00	45.00
89	A2	1a indigo & red	80.00	80.00
90	A2	2a red brn & red	27.50	22.50
91	A2	4½a org & red	42.50	25.00
92	A2	5a bister & red	42.50	30.00
93	A2	7½a lilac & red	42.50	35.00
a.		Ovptd. on front and back		
		Nos. 88-93 (6)	280.00	237.50

The 1a red overprint, which includes a period after "Africa", was sent to the UPU, but never placed in use. Nos. 88, 90-93 and 95-100 also exist with period (in black) in sets sent to the UPU. Some experts consider these essays.

**Black Ovpt. on Zanzibar #39, 42
New Value Surcharged in Red**

1897

95	A2(a)	2½a on 1a	75.00	50.00
a.		Black overprint double	6,500.	
96	A2(b)	2½a on 1a	160.00	90.00
97	A2(c)	2½a on 1a	85.00	55.00
a.		Black overprint double	6,500.	
98	A2(a)	2½a on 3a	75.00	45.00
99	A2(b)	2½a on 3a	160.00	85.00
100	A2(c)	2½a on 3a	80.00	50.00
		Nos. 95-100 (6)	635.00	375.00

A special printing of the 2½a surcharge on the 1a and 3a stamps was made for submission to the U.P.U. Stamps have a period after "Africa" in the overprint, and the surcharges included a "2" over "1" error in the fraction of the surcharge. These stamps were never placed in use. The fraction error appears on both the 1a and 3a stamps. Value, each, $1,200.

A10

1898   Wmk. 1   Engr.

102	A10	1r gray blue	40.00	22.50
a.		1r ultramarine	160.00	125.00
103	A10	2r orange	60.00	60.00
104	A10	3r dk violet	65.00	80.00
105	A10	4r carmine	175.00	225.00
106	A10	5r black brown	140.00	190.00
107	A10	10r bister	160.00	200.00
108	A10	20r yel green	575.00	1,250.
109	A10	50r lilac	1,900.	3,500.
		Nos. 102-107 (6)	640.00	802.50

The stamps of this country were superseded in 1904 by the stamps of East Africa and Uganda Protectorate.

BRITISH GUIANA

ˈbri-tish gē-ˈa-nə, -ˈä-nə

LOCATION — On the northeast coast of South America
GOVT. — British Crown Colony
AREA — 83,000 sq. mi.
POP. — 628,000 (estimated 1964)
CAPITAL — Georgetown

British Guiana became the independent state of Guyana May 26, 1966.

100 Cents = 1 Dollar

> **Catalogue values for unused stamps in this country are for Never Hinged items, beginning with Scott 242 in the regular postage section and Scott J1 in the postage due section.**

> Values for unused stamps are for copies with original gum except for Nos. 6-12 and 35-53, which are valued without gum. Very fine examples of all stamps from No. 6 on will have four clear margins. Inferior copies sell at much reduced prices, depending on the condition of the individual specimen.

A1

Typeset 1850-51   Typeset
Unwmk.   Imperf.

1	A1	2c blk, *pale rose,* cut to shape ('51)	70,000.
2	A1	4c black, *orange*	24,000.
		Cut to shape	3,750.
a.		4c black, *yellow*	35,000.
		Cut to shape	4,250.
3	A1	4c blk, *yellow* (pelure)	42,500.
		Cut to shape	4,750.
4	A1	8c black, *green*	14,000.
		Cut to shape	3,000.
5	A1	12c black, *blue*	5,250.
		Cut to shape	2,000.
a.		12c black, *pale blue*	11,000.
		Cut to shape	3,000.
b.		12c black, *indigo*	13,000.
		Cut to shape	3,000.
c.		"1" of "12" omitted	35,000.

These stamps were initialed before use by the Deputy Postmaster General or by one of the clerks of the Colonial Postoffice at Georgetown. The following initials are found:—E. T. E. D(alton); E. D. W(ight); G. B. S(mith); H. A. K(illikelley); W. H. L(ortimer). As these stamps are type-set there are several types of each value.

Ship and Motto of Colony A2	Seal of the Colony A3

1852   Litho.

6	A2	1c black, *magenta*	10,000.	5,250.
7	A2	4c black, *blue*	15,000.	5,750.

Both 1c and 4c are found in two types. Copies with paper cracked or rubbed sell for much less.
Some copies are initialed E. D. W(ight).
The reprints are on thicker paper and the colors are brighter. They are perforated 12½ and imperforate. Value $15 each.

1853-59   Imperf.
Without Line above Value

8	A3	1c vermilion	4,500.	1,150.

Copies in reddish brown probably are proofs.

Full or Partial White Line Above Value

9	A3	1c red	2,750.	950.
10	A3	4c blue	1,100.	450.
a.		4c dark blue	2,000.	600.
b.		4c pale blue	1,000.	375.

On No. 9, "ONE CENT" varies from 11 to 13mm in width.

No. 10 Retouched; White Line above Value Removed

11	A3	4c blue	1,650.	600.
a.		4c dark blue	2,400.	850.
b.		4c pale blue	1,600.	650.

Reprints of Nos. 8 and 10 are on thin paper, perf. 12½ or imperf. The 1c is orange red, the 4c sky blue.

1860
Numerals in Corners Framed

12	A3	4c blue	3,250.	450.

A4

1856	**Typeset**		**Imperf.**
13	A4	1c black, *magenta*	
14	A4	4c black, *magenta*	7,500.
a.		4c black, *rose carmine*	20,000. 10,500.
15	A4	4c black, *blue*	45,000.
16	A4	4c black, *blue, paper colored through*	60,000.

These stamps were initialed before being issued and the following initials are found:—E. T. E. D.; E. D. W.; W. H. L.; C. A. W. No. 13 is unique.

A5

Wide space between value and "Cents"

1860-61   Litho.   Perf. 12
Thick Paper

17	A5	1c brown red ('61)	350.00	100.00
18	A5	1c pink	1,100.	200.00
19	A5	2c orange	160.00	37.50
20	A5	8c orange	325.00	60.00
21	A5	12c gray	375.00	35.00
a.		12c lilac	450.00	40.00
22	A5	24c green	950.00	75.00

All denominations of type A5 above four cents are expressed in Roman numerals.
Bisects and trisects are found on covers. These were not officially authorized.
The reprints of the 1c pink are perforated 12½; the other values have not been reprinted.

Thin Paper

1862-65

23	A5	1c brown	400.00	175.00
24	A5	1c black	100.00	45.00
25	A5	2c orange	80.00	32.50
26	A5	8c rose	110.00	45.00
27	A5	12c lilac	150.00	32.50
28	A5	24c green	700.00	85.00

Perf. 12½ and 13

29	A5	1c black	60.00	25.00
30	A5	2c orange	80.00	22.50
31	A5	8c rose	225.00	75.00
32	A5	12c lilac	475.00	110.00
33	A5	24c green	550.00	75.00

Medium Paper

33A	A5	1c black	50.00	27.50
33B	A5	2c orange	52.50	17.00
33C	A5	8c pink	150.00	50.00
33D	A5	12c lilac ('65)	425.00	95.00
33E	A5	24c green	160.00	65.00
f.		24c deep green	325.00	85.00

Perf. 10

34	A5	12c gray lilac	400.00	65.00

Imperfs. are proofs. See Nos. 44-62.

A6	A7

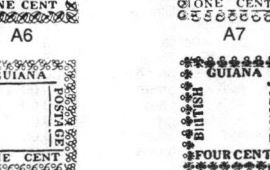

A8	A9

A10	A11

Typeset 1862   Typeset   Rouletted

35	A6	1c black, *rose*	2,000.	450.
		Unsigned	225.	
36	A7	1c black, *rose*	2,750.	575.
		Unsigned	275.	
37	A8	1c black, *rose*	4,000.	750.
		Unsigned	450.	
38	A6	2c black, *yellow*	2,000.	300.
		Unsigned	700.	
39	A7	2c black, *yellow*	2,750.	375.
		Unsigned	750.	
40	A8	2c black, *yellow*	4,000.	600.
		Unsigned	900.	
41	A9	4c black, *blue*	3,000.	600.
		Unsigned	475.	
42	A10	4c black, *blue*	4,000.	1,450.
a.		Without inner lines	3,000.	600.
		As "a," unsigned		475.
43	A11	4c black, *blue*	2,250.	450.
		Unsigned	475.	

Nos. 35-43 were typeset, there being 24 types of each value. They were initialed before use "R. M. Ac. R. G.," being the initials of Robert Mather, Acting Receiver General.
The initials are in black on the 1c and in red on the 2c. An alkali was used on the 4c stamps, which, destroying the color of the paper, caused the initials to appear to be written in white.
Uninitialed stamps are remainders, few sheets having been found.
Specimens with roulette on all sides are valued higher.

Narrow space between value and "Cents"

1860   Thick Paper   Litho.   Perf. 12

44	A5	4c blue	275.00	60.00
c.		4c deep blue	375.00	75.00

Thin Paper

44A	A5	4c blue	77.50	25.00

Perf. 12½ and 13

44B	A5	4c blue	75.00	22.50

Medium Paper

1863-68   Perf. 12½ and 13

45	A5	1c black ('66)	32.50	20.00
46	A5	2c orange	35.00	5.00
47	A5	4c blue ('64)	65.00	12.50
48	A5	8c rose ('68)	150.00	15.00
49	A5	12c lilac ('67)	375.00	22.50
		Nos. 45-49 (5)	657.50	75.00

1866   Perf. 10

50	A5	1c black	8.00	4.00
51	A5	2c orange	20.00	3.00
52	A5	4c blue	75.00	7.50
a.		Half used as 2c on cover		4,000.
53	A5	8c rose	110.00	17.50
a.		Diagonal half used as 4c on cover		
54	A5	12c lilac	125.00	17.50
a.		Third used as 4c on cover		
		Nos. 50-54 (5)	338.00	49.50

1875   Perf. 15

58	A5	1c black	40.00	7.50
59	A5	2c orange	125.00	8.00
60	A5	4c blue	250.00	85.00
61	A5	8c rose	250.00	80.00
62	A5	12c lilac	550.00	50.00
		Nos. 58-62 (5)	1,215.	230.50

Seal of Colony

A12	A13

1863   Perf. 12

63	A12	24c yellow green	125.00	12.50
a.		24c green	250.00	22.50

Perf. 12½ to 13

64	A12	6c blue	85.00	40.00
65	A12	24c green	125.00	10.00
66	A12	48c deep red	200.00	45.00
a.		48c rose	250.00	45.00
		Nos. 63-66 (4)	535.00	107.50

1866   Perf. 10

67	A12	6c blue	100.00	27.50
a.		6c ultramarine	125.00	37.50

68	A12	24c yellow green	150.00	8.00
69	A12	24c green	190.00	10.00
	a.	24c green	275.00	27.50
		Nos. 67-69 (3)	525.00	63.00

For surcharges see Nos. 83-92.

1875 **Perf. 15**

70	A12	6c ultra	400.00	80.00
71	A12	24c yellow green	525.00	35.00
	a.	24c deep green	675.00	65.00

1876 Typo. Wmk. 1 Perf. 14

72	A13	1c slate	3.00	1.50
	a.	Perf. 14x12½		200.00
73	A13	2c orange	37.50	2.00
74	A13	4c ultra	110.00	8.00
	a.	Perf. 12½	1,350.	200.00
75	A13	6c chocolate	70.00	7.50
76	A13	8c rose	100.00	1.00
77	A13	12c lilac	55.00	2.50
78	A13	24c green	65.00	4.00
79	A13	48c red brown	125.00	22.50
80	A13	96c bister	475.00	275.00
		Nos. 72-80 (9)	1,040.	324.00

See Nos. 107-111. For surcharges see Nos. 93-95, 98-101.

Stamps Surcharged by Brush-like Pen Lines

Surcharge Types:
Type a - Two horiz. lines.
Type b - Two lines, one horiz., one vert.
Type c - Three lines, two horiz., one vert.
Type d - One horiz. line.

On Nos. 75 and 67

1878 **Perf. 10, 14**

82	A13(a)	(1c) on 6c choc	37.50	90.00
83	A12(b)	(1c) on 6c blue	140.00	65.00
84	A13(b)	(1c) on 6c choc	225.00	85.00

On Nos. O3, O8-O10

85	A13(c)	(1c) on 4c ultra	175.00	85.00
	a.	Type b		2,500.
86	A13(c)	(1c) on 6c choc	250.00	85.00
87	A5(c)	(2c) on 8c rose	1,000.	225.00
88A	A13(b)	(2c) on 8c rose	250.00	90.00

On Nos. O1, O3, O6-O7

89	A5(d)	(1c) on 1c blk	160.00	75.00
89A	A5(d)	(2c) on 8c rose		
90	A13(d)	(1c) on 1c sl	140.00	50.00
91	A13(d)	(2c) on 2c org	250.00	85.00

The provisional values of Nos. 82 to 91 were established by various official decrees. The horizontal lines crossed out the old value, "OFFICIAL," or both.

Nos. 69 and 80 Surcharged with New Values in Black

No. 92   No. 93

No. 94   No. 95

1881

92	A12	1c on 48c red	35.00	5.00
93	A13	1c on 96c bister	4.50	5.50
94	A13	2c on 96c bister	4.50	10.00
95	A13	2c on 96c bister	45.00	70.00
		Nos. 92-95 (4)	89.00	90.50

Unissued Official Stamps Surcharged with New Values

No. 96

No. 97   Nos. 99, 101

No. 102

1881

96	A13	1c on 12c lilac	110.00	65.00
97	A13	1c on 48c red brn	125.00	90.00
98	A24	2c on 12c lilac	350.00	250.00
99	A13	2c on 12c lilac	60.00	25.00
	a.	"2" inverted		
	b.	"2" double	750.00	475.00
100	A24	2c on 24c green	575.00	575.00
101	A13	2c on 24c green	75.00	40.00
	a.	"2" inverted		
	d.	Double surcharge	800.00	
102	A13	2c on 24c green	200.00	125.00

A27

Typeset

ONE AND TWO CENTS.
Type I - Ship with three masts.
Type II - Brig with two masts.

"SPECIMEN"
Perforated Diagonally across Stamp

1882 **Unwmk.** **Perf. 12**

103	A27	1c black, lil rose, I	35.00	30.00
	a.	Without "Specimen"	400.00	290.00
104	A27	1c black, lil rose, II	35.00	30.00
	a.	Without "Specimen"	400.00	300.00
105	A27	2c black, yel, I	55.00	40.00
	a.	Without "Specimen"	350.00	325.00
	b.	Diagonal half used as 1c on cover		
106	A27	2c black, yel, II	60.00	45.00
	a.	Without "Specimen"	350.00	325.00
		Nos. 103-106 (4)	185.00	145.00

Nos. 103-106 were typeset, 12 to a sheet, and, to prevent fraud on the government, the word "Specimen" was perforated across them before they were issued. There were 2 settings of the 1c and 3 settings of the 2c, thus there are 24 types of the former and 36 of the latter.

Type of 1876

1882 Typo. Wmk. 2 Perf. 14

107	A13	1c slate	7.50	.35
108	A13	2c orange	20.00	.35
	a.	"2 CENTS" double		
109	A13	4c ultra	80.00	6.50
110	A13	6c brown	6.00	7.50
111	A13	8c rose	85.00	1.00
		Nos. 107-111 (5)	198.50	15.70

A28   A29

4 CENTS and $4
Type I - Figure "4" is 3mm high.
Type II - Figure "4" is 3½mm high.
6 CENTS
Type I - Top of "6" is flat.
Type II - Top of "6" turns downward.

"INLAND REVENUE" Overprint and Surcharged in Black

1889

112	A28	1c lilac	1.75	.55
113	A28	2c lilac	1.50	.40
114	A28	3c lilac	1.00	.40
115	A28	4c lilac, I	5.00	.40
116	A28	4c lilac, II	21.00	12.50
117	A28	6c lilac, I	18.00	4.50
118	A28	6c lilac, II	5.50	3.00
119	A28	8c lilac	1.75	.65
120	A28	10c lilac	6.00	2.50
121	A28	20c lilac	17.50	10.00
122	A28	40c lilac	20.00	15.00
123	A28	72c lilac	35.00	40.00
124	A28	$1 green	400.00	400.00
125	A28	$2 green	175.00	175.00
126	A28	$3 green	110.00	110.00
127	A28	$4 green, I	350.00	350.00
127A	A28	$4 green, II	950.00	975.00
128	A28	$5 green	225.00	200.00
		Nos. 112-128 (18)	2,344.	2,299.

For surcharges see Nos. 129, 148-151B.

No. 113 Surcharged "2" in Red

1889

129	A29	2c on 2c lilac	1.10	.40

Inverted and double surcharges of "2" were privately made.

A30   A31

1889-1903 **Typo.**

130	A30	1c lilac & gray	2.50	1.60
131	A30	1c green ('90)	.50	.20
131A	A30	1c gray grn ('00)	3.00	3.00
132	A30	2c lilac & org	1.50	.20
133	A30	2c lil & rose ('00)	3.50	.25
134	A30	2c vio & blk, red ('01)	1.25	.20
135	A30	4c lilac & ultra	4.00	1.50
	a.	4c lilac & blue	19.00	2.25
136	A30	5c ultra ('91)	3.00	.25
137	A30	6c lilac & mar	6.00	10.00
	a.	6c lilac & brown	32.50	11.00
138	A30	6c gray blk & ultra ('02)	6.50	10.00
139	A30	8c lilac & rose	11.00	.75
140	A30	8c lil & blk ('90)	3.00	2.00
141	A30	12c lilac & vio	8.00	2.00
142	A30	24c lilac & grn	7.50	2.50
143	A30	48c lilac & ver	15.00	8.50
144	A30	48c dk gray & lil brn ('01)	27.50	27.50
	a.	48c gray & purple brown	50.00	35.00
145	A30	60c gray grn & car ('03)	60.00	160.00
146	A30	72c lil & org brn	27.50	35.00
	a.	72c lilac & yellow brown	70.00	75.00
147	A30	96c lilac & car	70.00	75.00
	a.	96c lilac & rose	75.00	80.00
		Nos. 130-147 (19)	261.25	340.45

Stamps of the 1889-1903 issue with pen or revenue cancellation sell for a small fraction of the above quotations.
See Nos. 160-177.

Red Surcharge

1890

148	A31	1c on $1 grn & blk	1.25	.50
	a.	Double surcharge		80.00
149	A31	1c on $2 grn & blk	.90	.60
	a.	Double surcharge	80.00	
150	A31	1c on $3 grn & blk	1.50	1.25
	a.	Double surcharge	90.00	
151	A31	1c on $4 grn & blk, type I	2.00	6.00
	a.	Double surcharge	80.00	
151B	A31	1c on $4 grn & blk, type II	10.00	25.00
	c.	Double surcharge		
		Nos. 148-151B (5)	15.65	33.35

Mt. Roraima A32

Kaieteur (Old Man's) Falls — A33

1898 **Wmk. 1** **Engr.**

152	A32	1c car & gray blk	3.50	.90
153	A33	2c indigo & brn	12.50	1.60
	a.	Horiz. pair, imperf. between	16.00	
	b.	2c blue & brown	2.00	
154	A32	5c brown & grn	3.50	4.50
155	A33	10c red & blue blk	16.00	20.00
156	A32	15c blue & red brn	24.00	15.00
		Nos. 152-156 (5)	91.00	42.00

60th anniv. of Queen Victoria's accession to the throne.

Nos. 154-156 Surcharged in Black

1899

157	A32	2c on 5c brn & grn	2.25	1.75
158	A33	2c on 10c red & bl black	1.75	1.75
	a.	"GENTS"	55.00	75.00
	b.	Inverted surcharge	325.00	375.00
	c.	Without period	25.00	50.00
159	A32	2c on 15c bl & red brown	1.50	1.50
	a.	Without period	57.50	57.50
	b.	Double surcharge	475.00	650.00
	c.	Inverted surcharge	350.00	425.00
		Nos. 157-159 (3)	5.50	5.00

There are many slight errors in the setting of this surcharge, such as: small "E" in "CENTS"; no period and narrow "C"; comma between "T" and "S"; dash between "TWO" and "CENTS"; comma between "N" and "T."

Ship Type of 1889-1903

1905-10 **Wmk. 3**

Chalky Paper

160	A30	1c gray green	3.50	3.00
	a.	1c blue green, ordinary paper ('10)	13.50	2.50
	b.	Booklet pane of 6		
161	A30	2c vio & blk, red	3.25	.20
162	A30	4c lilac & ultra	10.00	11.00
163	A30	5c lil & blue, bl	7.00	6.00
164	A30	6c gray black & ultra	14.00	37.50
165	A30	12c lilac & vio	20.00	37.50
166	A30	24c lil & grn ('06)	3.50	4.25
167	A30	48c gray & vio brn	12.50	17.50
168	A30	60c gray grn & car rose	12.50	75.00
169	A30	72c lil & org brn ('07)	32.50	60.00
170	A30	96c blk & red, yel ('06)	35.00	42.50
		Nos. 160-170 (11)	153.75	294.45

The 2c-60c exist on ordinary paper.

A34

George V — A35

Black Overprint

171	A34	$2.40 grn & vio	190.00	190.00

Ship Type of 1889-1903
Ordinary Paper

TWO CENTS
Type I - Only the upper right corner of the flag touches the mast.
Type II - The entire right side of the flag touches the mast.

1907

172	A30	2c red, type I	3.75	.30
	b.	2c red, type II	1.00	.30
174	A30	4c brown & vio	3.25	1.60
175	A30	5c blue	5.00	.70
176	A30	6c gray & black	12.50	5.00
177	A30	12c orange & vio	5.50	5.00
		Nos. 172-177 (5)	30.00	12.60

1913-16 **Perf. 14**

178	A35	1c green	1.75	.20
179	A35	2c scarlet	.85	.20
	a.	2c carmine	.65	.20
180	A35	4c brn & red vio	1.10	.40
181	A35	5c ultra	1.10	.45
182	A35	6c gray & black	1.10	.95
183	A35	12c org & vio	1.50	1.50

Chalky Paper

184	A35	24c dl vio & grn	2.50	2.50
185	A35	48c blk & vio brn	6.00	6.00
186	A35	60c grn & car	13.00	19.00
187	A35	72c dl vio & org brn	24.00	30.00

Surface Colored Paper

188	A35	96c blk & red, yel	24.00	30.00

Paper Colored Through

189	A35	96c blk & red, yel ('16)	17.00	21.00
		Nos. 178-189 (12)	93.90	112.20

The 72c and late printings of the 2c and 5c are from redrawn dies. The ruled lines behind the value are thin and faint, making the tablet appear lighter than before. The shading lines in other parts of the stamps are also lighter.

1921-27   **Wmk. 4**

191	A35	1c green	3.00	.20
192	A35	2c rose red	2.50	.20
193	A35	2c dp vio ('23)	1.75	.20
194	A35	4c brn & vio	3.25	.20
195	A35	6c ultra	1.90	.20
196	A35	12c org & vio	1.90	1.00

Chalky Paper

197	A35	24c dl vio & grn	1.40	3.00
198	A35	48c blk & vio brn ('26)	6.50	2.25
199	A35	60c grn & car ('26)	7.00	30.00
200	A35	72c dl vio & brn org	14.00	32.50
201	A35	96c blk & red, *yel* ('27)	12.50	29.00
		Nos. 191-201 (11)	55.70	98.75

Plowing a Rice Field — A36

Indian Shooting Fish — A37

Kaieteur Falls — A38

Georgetown, Public Buildings A39

1931, July 21   **Engr.**   **Perf. 12½**

205	A36	1c blue green	1.25	.50
206	A37	2c dk brown	1.25	.45
207	A38	4c car rose	2.75	1.75
208	A39	6c ultra	2.25	2.50
209	A38	$1 violet	24.00	30.00
		Nos. 205-209 (5)	31.50	35.20

Cent. of the union of Berbice, Demerara and Essequibo to form the Colony of British Guiana.

A40

A41

Gold Mining — A42

Shooting Logs over Falls — A44

Kaieteur Falls — A43

Stabroek Market — A45

Sugar Cane in Punts — A46

Forest Road — A47

Victoria Regia Lilies — A48

Mt. Roraima — A49

Sir Walter Raleigh and Son — A50

Botanical Gardens A51

1934, Oct. 1   **Perf. 12½**

210	A40	1c green	.40	.25
211	A41	2c brown	.75	.20
212	A42	3c carmine	.30	.20
b.		Perf. 12½x13½ ('43)	.50	.75
c.		Perf. 13x13½ ('49)	.50	.20
213	A43	4c vio black	1.50	.50
a.		Vert. pair, imperf. horiz.	—	7,500.
214	A44	6c dp ultra	2.00	1.75
215	A45	12c orange	.20	.20
a.		Perf. 13½x13 ('51)	.20	.40
216	A46	24c rose violet	3.00	1.75
217	A47	48c black	10.50	9.25
218	A43	50c green	12.00	15.00
219	A48	60c brown	21.00	24.00
220	A49	72c rose violet	1.25	1.00
221	A50	96c black	20.00	25.00
222	A51	$1 violet	25.00	22.50
		Nos. 210-222 (13)	97.90	101.60

See Nos. 236, 238, 240.

Common Design Types pictured following the introduction.

Silver Jubilee Issue
Common Design Type

1935, May 6   **Perf. 13½x14**

223	CD301	2c gray blk & ultra	.25	.20
224	CD301	6c blue & brown	.75	.80
225	CD301	12c indigo & grn	2.50	4.50
226	CD301	24c brt vio & ind	3.50	4.50
		Nos. 223-226 (4)	7.00	10.00
		Set, Never Hinged	11.00	

Coronation Issue
Common Design Type

1937, May 12   **Perf. 13½x14**

227	CD302	2c brown	.20	.20
228	CD302	4c gray black	.40	.40
229	CD302	6c bright ultra	.45	.45
		Nos. 227-229 (3)	1.05	1.05
		Set, Never Hinged	1.25	

A52

A53   A54

A56

A55

A57

A58

Victoria Regia Lilies and Jacanas — A59

1938-52   **Engr.**   **Perf. 12½**

230	A52	1c green	.20	.20
b.		Perf. 14x13 ('49)	.20	.65

Perf. 13x14

231	A53	2c violet blk ('49)	.20	.20
b.		Perf. 12½	.45	.20
232	A54	4c black & rose ('52)	.35	.20
a.		Perf. 12½	.55	.20
c.		Vert. pair, imperf. between	11,000.	7,500.
233	A55	6c dp ultra ('49)	.20	.20
a.		Perf. 12½	.30	.20

Perf. 12½

234	A56	24c deep green	.95	.20
a.		Wmk. upright	20.00	8.75
235	A53	36c purple	1.40	.20
a.		Perf. 13x14 ('51)	2.50	.25
236	A47	48c orange yel	.45	.35
a.		Perf. 14x13 ('51)	1.25	1.10
237	A57	60c brown	8.50	3.00
238	A50	96c brown vio	1.90	2.25
a.		Perf. 12½x13½ ('44)	4.00	5.00
239	A58	$1 deep violet	7.75	.30
a.		Perf. 14x13 ('51)	225.00	300.00
240	A49	$2 rose vio ('45)	3.25	11.00
a.		Perf. 14x13 ('50)	10.00	12.50

241	A59	$3 org brn ('45)	19.00	21.00
a.		Perf. 14x13 ('52)	20.00	37.50
		Nos. 230-241 (12)	44.15	39.10
		Set, Never Hinged	65.00	

The watermark on No. 234 is sideways.

> **Catalogue values for unused stamps in this section, from this point to the end of the section, are for Never Hinged items.**

Peace Issue
Common Design Type

1946, Oct. 21   **Perf. 13½x14**

242	CD303	3c carmine	.20	.20
243	CD303	6c deep blue	.20	.20

Silver Wedding Issue
Common Design Types

1948, Dec. 20 Photo.   **Perf. 14x14½**

244	CD304	3c scarlet	.20	.20

Engr.

Perf. 11½x11

245	CD305	$3 orange brown	11.00	17.00

UPU Issue
Common Design Types
Engr.; Name Typo. on 6c and 12c
Perf. 13½, 11x11½

1949, Oct. 10   **Wmk. 4**

246	CD306	4c rose carmine	.35	.20
247	CD307	6c indigo	.55	.55
248	CD308	12c orange	.70	.70
249	CD309	24c blue green	1.40	1.40
		Nos. 246-249 (4)	3.00	2.85

University Issue
Common Design Types

1951, Feb. 16 Engr.   **Perf. 14x14½**

250	CD310	3c carmine & black	.30	.20
251	CD311	6c dp ultra & black	.40	.40

Coronation Issue
Common Design Type

1953, June 2   **Perf. 13½x13**

252	CD312	4c carmine & black	.20	.20

G. P. O., Georgetown A60

Indian Shooting Fish — A61

Designs: 2c, Botanical gardens. 3c, Victoria regia lilies and jacanas. 5c, Map. 6c, Rice combine. 8c, Sugar cane entering factory. 12c, Felling greenheart tree. 24c, Bauxite mining. 36c, Mt. Roraima. 48c, Kaieteur Falls. 72c, Arapaima (fish). $1, Toucan. $2, Dredging gold. $5, Coat of Arms.

Engr., Center Litho. on $1
Perf. 12½x13, 13

1954, Dec. 1   **Wmk. 4**

253	A60	1c black	.20	.20
254	A60	2c dark green	.20	.20
255	A60	3c red brn & ol	2.50	.20
256	A61	4c violet	.20	.20
257	A60	5c black & red	.25	.20
258	A60	6c yellow green	.20	.20
259	A60	8c ultramarine	.20	.20
260	A61	12c brown & black	.50	.30
261	A60	24c orange & black	3.50	.20
262	A60	36c black & rose	1.25	.45
263	A61	48c red brn & ultra	.60	.35
264	A61	72c emerald & rose	9.50	2.00
265	A60	$1 blk, yel, grn & sal	10.00	1.90
266	A60	$2 magenta	10.00	3.25
267	A61	$5 black & ultra	10.50	12.00
		Nos. 253-267 (15)	49.60	21.85

See Nos. 279-287.

Clasped Hands — A62

1961, Oct. 23   Photo.   *Perf. 14½x14*
268	A62	5c sal pink & brown	.20	.20
269	A62	6c lt blue grn & brown	.20	.20
270	A62	30c lt orange & brown	.40	.40
		Nos. 268-270 (3)	.80	.80

Fourth annual History and Culture Week.

Freedom from Hunger Issue
Common Design Type

1963, June 4   *Perf. 14x14½*
271	CD314	20c lilac	.45	.45

Red Cross Centenary Issue
Common Design Type

1963, Sept. 2   Litho.   *Wmk. 314*   *Perf. 13*
272	CD315	5c black & red	.20	.20
273	CD315	20c ultra & red	.65	.65

Queen Types of 1954
Engr.; Center Litho. on $1
Perf. 12½x13, 13

1963-65   *Wmk. 314*
279	A60	3c red brn & ol ('65)	4.75	4.75
280	A60	5c black & red ('64)	.20	.20
281	A61	12c brown & blk ('64)	.20	.20
282	A61	24c orange & black	1.50	.20
283	A61	36c black & rose	.50	.20
284	A61	48c red brn & ultra	1.00	2.00
285	A61	72c emerald & rose	3.25	16.00
286	A60	$1 blk, yel, grn & sal	5.75	.75
287	A60	$2 magenta	6.25	12.50
		Nos. 279-287 (9)	23.40	36.80

Weight Lifter A63

1964, Oct. 1   Photo.   *Perf. 13x13½*
290	A63	5c orange	.20	.20
291	A63	8c blue	.20	.20
292	A63	12c carmine rose	.40	.40
		Nos. 290-292 (3)	.80	.80

18th Olympic Games, Tokyo, Oct. 10-25.

ITU Issue
Common Design Type

1965, May 17   Litho.   *Perf. 11x11½*
293	CD317	5c emerald & olive	.20	.20
294	CD317	25c lt blue & brt pink	.45	.45

Intl. Cooperation Year Issue
Common Design Type

1965, Oct. 25   *Wmk. 314*   *Perf. 14½*
295	CD318	5c blue grn & claret	.20	.20
296	CD318	25c lt vio & green	.50	.50

Winston Churchill and St. George's Cathedral, Georgetown — A64

1966, Jan. 24   Photo.   *Perf. 14x14½*
297	A64	5c multicolored	.20	.20
298	A64	25c dp blue, blk & gold	.60	.50

Sir Winston Leonard Spencer Churchill (1874-1965), statesman and WWII leader.

Royal Visit Issue
Common Design Type

1966, Feb. 4   Litho.   *Perf. 11x12*
299	CD320	3c violet blue	.25	.20
300	CD320	25c dark car rose	1.40	1.10

POSTAGE DUE STAMPS

> Catalogue values for unused stamps in this section are for Never Hinged items.

D1

		Perf. 13½x14		
1940-52		Typo.	**Wmk. 4**	
J1	D1	1c green	1.10	7.50
a.		Wmk. 4a (error)	45.00	
J2	D1	2c black	1.10	3.25
a.		Wmk. 4a (error)	37.50	
J3	D1	4c ultra ('52)	.25	7.50
a.		Wmk. 4a (error)	37.50	
J4	D1	12c carmine	5.00	20.00
		Nos. J1-J4 (4)	7.45	38.25

The 2c and 12c are on chalky paper as well as ordinary paper.

WAR TAX STAMP

Regular Issue No. 179 Overprinted

1918, Jan. 4   *Wmk. 3*   *Perf. 14*
MR1	A35	2c scarlet	.20	.20

OFFICIAL STAMPS

> Counterfeit overprints exist.

No. 50 Overprinted in Red   **OFFICIAL**

1875   Unwmk.   *Perf. 10*
O1	A5	1c black	40.00	17.50
a.		Horiz. pair, imperf btwn.		4,250.

Nos. 51, 53-54, 68 Overprinted in Black   **OFFICIAL**
O2	A5	2c orange	150.00	17.50
O3	A5	8c rose	375.00	150.00
O4	A5	12c lilac	1,450.	575.00
O5	A12	24c green	875.00	275.00

For surcharges see Nos. 87, 89, 89A, 96, 102.

Nos. 72-76 Overprinted "OFFICIAL" Similar to #O2-O5

1877   *Wmk. 1*   *Perf. 14*
O6	A13	1c slate	250.00	95.00
a.		Vert. pair, imperf btwn.		6,500.
O7	A13	2c orange	95.00	17.50
O8	A13	4c ultramarine	100.00	35.00
O9	A13	4c chocolate	3,750.	625.00
O10	A13	8c rose	2,250.	525.00

The type A13 12c lilac, 24c green and 48c red brown overprinted "OFFICIAL" were never placed in use. A few copies of the 12c and 24c have been seen but the 48c is only known surcharged with new value for provisional use in 1881.
See #97-101. For surcharges see #85-86, 88A, 90-91.

BRITISH HONDURAS

'bri-tish hän-'dur-əs

LOCATION — Central America bordering on Caribbean on east, Mexico on north and Guatemala on west.
GOVT. — British Crown Colony
AREA — 8,867 sq. mi.
POP. — 130,000 (est. 1972)
CAPITAL — Belmopan

Before British Honduras became a colony (subordinate to Jamaica) in 1862, it was a settlement under British influence. In 1884 it became an independent colony. In 1973 the colony changed its name to Belize.

12 Pence = 1 Shilling
100 Cents = 1 Dollar (1888)

> Catalogue values for unused stamps in this country are for Never Hinged items, beginning with Scott 127 in the regular postage section, Scott J1 in the postage due section.

Values for unused stamps are for examples with original gum as defined in the catalogue introduction. Very fine examples of Nos. 1-37 will have perforations touching the design on at least one side due to the narrow spacing of the stamps on the plates. Stamps with perfs clear of the design on all four sides are extremely scarce and will command higher prices.

Queen Victoria — A1

1866   Unwmk.   Typo.   *Perf. 14*
1	A1	1p pale blue	60.00	50.00
a.		Horiz. pair, imperf. btwn.		
2	A1	6p rose	250.00	110.00
3	A1	1sh green	275.00	100.00
		Nos. 1-3 (3)	585.00	260.00

The 6p and 1sh were printed only in a sheet with the 1p. The 1sh is known in se-tenant gutter pairs with the 1p and the 6p.

1872   *Wmk. 1*   *Perf. 12½*
4	A1	1p blue	60.00	17.00
5	A1	3p brown	100.00	65.00
6	A1	6p rose	190.00	30.00
7	A1	1sh green	300.00	27.50
a.		Horiz. pair, imperf. btwn.		12,500.
		Nos. 4-7 (4)	650.00	139.50

For surcharges see Nos. 18-19.
No. 7a is unique and has faults.

1877-79   *Perf. 14*
8	A1	1p blue	50.00	14.00
a.		Horiz. strip of 3, imperf. btwn.		4,500.
9	A1	3p brown	90.00	17.50
10	A1	4p violet ('79)	140.00	10.00
11	A1	6p rose ('78)	275.00	175.00
12	A1	1sh green	175.00	12.50
		Nos. 8-12 (5)	730.00	229.00

For surcharges see Nos. 20-21, 29.

1882-87   *Wmk. 2*
13	A1	1p blue ('84)	40.00	18.00
14	A1	1p rose ('84)	20.00	12.50
a.		Diag. half used as ½p on cover		
15	A1	4p violet	70.00	4.25
16	A1	6p yellow ('85)	250.00	175.00
17	A1	1sh gray ('87)	250.00	150.00
		Nos. 13-17 (5)	630.00	359.75

For surcharges see Nos. 22-26, 28-35.

Stamps of 1872-87 Surcharged in Black

1888   *Wmk. 1*   *Perf. 12½*
18	A1	2c on 6p rose	140.00	100.00
19	A1	3c on 3p brown	10,000.	5,250.

Perf. 14
20	A1	2c on 6p rose	80.00	70.00
a.		Diagonal half used as 1c on cover		210.00
b.		Double surcharge	1,350.	
c.		"2" with curved tail	900.00	—
21	A1	3c on 3p brown	55.00	55.00

Wmk. 2
22	A1	2c on 1p rose	9.00	17.50
a.		Diagonal half used as 1c on cover		225.00
b.		Double surcharge	1,000.	950.00
c.		Inverted surcharge	1,500.	1,400.
23	A1	10c on 4p violet	40.00	15.00
a.		Inverted surcharge		
24	A1	20c on 6p yellow	27.50	30.00
25	A1	50c on 1sh gray	350.00	500.00

No. 25 with Additional Surcharge in Red or Black
26	A1	2c (R) on 50c on 1sh gray	40.00	75.00
a.		"TWO" in black	8,750.	8,500.
b.		"TWO" double (Blk + R)	8,750.	8,000.
c.		Diagonal half used as 1c on cover		275.00

Stamps of 1872-87 Surcharged in Black

c

1888-89
28	A1	2c on 1p rose	.45	1.60
a.		Diagonal half used as 1c on cover		100.00
29	A1	3c on 3p brown	2.25	1.40
30	A1	10c on 4p violet	5.50	1.50
a.		Double surcharge	1,400.	
31	A1	20c on 6p yel ('89)	11.00	15.00
32	A1	50c on 1sh gray	25.00	65.00
		Nos. 28-32 (5)	44.20	84.50

For other examples of this surcharge see Nos. 36, 47. For overprint see No. 51.

No. 30 with Additional Surcharge in Black or Red

1891
33	A1	6c (Blk) on 10c on 4p	.90	3.25
a.		"6" and bar inverted	2,750.	825.
b.		"6" only inverted		2,750.
34	A1	6c (R) on 10c on 4p	.90	2.25
a.		"6" and bar inverted	450.	450.
b.		"6" only inverted		2,750.

Stamps similar to No. 33 but with "SIX" instead of "6," both with and without bar, were prepared but not regularly issued.
See No. 37.

No. 29 with Additional Surcharge in Black

1891
35	A1	5c on 3c on 3p brown	1.40	3.00
a.		Double surcharge of "Five" and bar	240.00	275.00

Black Surcharge, Type "c"
36	A1	6c on 3p blue	2.25	10.00

No. 36 with Additional Surcharge like Nos. 33-34 in Red

1891
37	A1	15c (R) on 6c on 3p blue	10.00	21.00
a.		Double surcharge		

A8   A9

1891-98   Wmk. 2   Perf. 14

38	A8	1c green	1.75	1.10
39	A8	2c carmine rose	1.60	.25
40	A8	3c brown	5.00	3.00
41	A8	5c ultra ('95)	11.00	.80
42	A8	6c ultramarine	4.75	1.75
43	A8	10c vio & grn ('95)	8.00	8.00
44	A8	12c vio & green	3.50	2.50
45	A8	24c yellow & blue	5.50	12.50
46	A8	25c red brn & grn ('98)	47.50	85.00
		Nos. 38-46 (9)	88.60	114.90

Numeral tablet on Nos. 43-46 has lined background with colorless value and "c."
For overprints see Nos. 48-50.

Type of 1866 Surcharged Type "c"

1892
47	A1	1c on 1p green	.55	1.40

Regular Issue
Overprinted in Black

1899
48	A8	5c ultramarine	8.00	2.25
a.		"BEVENUE"	70.00	80.00
49	A8	10c lilac & green	3.50	11.50
a.		"BEVENUE"	175.00	225.00
50	A8	25c red brn & grn	2.75	27.50
a.		"BEVENUE"	125.00	
51	A1	50c on 1sh gray (No. 32)	125.00	250.00
a.		"BEVENUE"	2,750.	
		Nos. 48-51 (4)	139.25	291.25

The overprint is found in two lengths: 12mm (43 to the pane) and 11mm (17 to the pane). The "U" is found in both a tall, narrow type and the more common small type.

1899-1901
52	A9	5c gray blk & ultra, bl ('00)	12.50	2.25
53	A9	10c vio & grn ('01)	8.00	7.00
54	A9	50c grn & car rose	20.00	50.00
55	A9	$1 grn & car rose	55.00	90.00
56	A9	$2 green & ultra	75.00	110.00
57	A9	$5 green & black	240.00	275.00
		Nos. 52-57 (6)	410.50	534.25

Numeral tablet on Nos. 53-54 has lined background with colorless value and "c."

King Edward VII — A10

1902-04   Typo.   Wmk. 2

58	A10	1c gray grn & grn ('04)	3.50	19.00
59	A10	2c vio & blk, red	1.75	.30
60	A10	5c gray blk & ultra, blue	4.50	.70
61	A10	20c dl vio & vio ('04)	4.50	15.00
		Nos. 58-61 (4)	14.25	35.00

1904-06   Chalky Paper   Wmk. 3

62	A10	1c green	.60	1.60
63	A10	2c vio & blk, red	.60	.60
64	A10	5c blk & ultra, bl ('05)	1.60	.20
65	A10	10c vio & grn ('06)	4.50	10.00
67	A10	25c vio & org ('06)	6.25	37.50
68	A10	50c grn & car rose ('06)	13.50	62.50
69	A10	$1 grn & car rose ('06)	42.50	62.50
70	A10	$2 grn & ultra ('06)	75.00	140.00
71	A10	$5 grn & blk ('06)	160.00	225.00
		Nos. 62-71 (9)	304.55	539.50

The 1c and 2c exist also on ordinary paper.

1909
Ordinary Paper
72	A10	2c carmine	8.50	.20
73	A10	5c ultramarine	1.60	.20

1911
74	A10	25c black, green	5.50	40.00

Numeral tablet on #61, 65-68, 74 has lined background with colorless value and "c."

King George V
A11   A12

1913-17   Wmk. 3   Perf. 14

75	A11	1c green	1.00	.40
76	A11	2c scarlet	1.10	.30
a.		2c carmine	.90	.95
77	A11	3c orange ('17)	.45	.20
78	A11	5c ultra	2.25	1.25

Chalky Paper
79	A12	10c dl vio & ol grn	2.50	5.00
80	A12	25c blk, gray grn	3.75	7.50
a.		25c black, emerald	2.50	12.50
b.		25c blk, bl grn, olive back	3.25	13.00
81	A12	50c vio & ultra, bl	4.50	9.00
82	A11	$1 black & scar	8.00	17.50
83	A11	$2 grn & dull vio	32.50	37.50
84	A11	$5 vio & blk, red	225.00	250.00
		Nos. 75-84 (10)	281.05	328.65

See #91. For overprints see #MR2-MR5.

With Moire Overprint in Violet

1915
85	A11	1c green	2.00	12.50
86	A11	2c carmine	2.25	.40
87	A11	5c ultramarine	.25	4.50
		Nos. 85-87 (3)	4.50	17.40

For overprint see No. MR1.

Peace Commemorative Issue

Seal of Colony
and George V
A13

1921, Apr. 28   Engr.
89	A13	2c carmine	2.50	1.00

Similar to A13 but without "Peace Peace"

1922   Wmk. 4
90	A13	4c dark gray	4.50	.95

Type of 1913-17

1921   Typo.   Wmk. 4
91	A11	1c green	3.50	7.50

A14

1922-33   Typo.   Wmk. 4

92	A14	1c green ('29)	.80	1.10
93	A14	2c dark brown	.35	.20
94	A14	2c rose red ('27)	.85	.70
95	A14	3c orange ('33)	3.50	1.00
96	A14	4c gray ('29)	1.25	.25
97	A14	5c ultramarine	1.00	.20

Chalky Paper
98	A14	10c olive grn & lil	1.25	.35
99	A14	25c black, emerald	1.50	4.00
100	A14	50c ultra & vio, bl	4.00	9.00
101	A14	$1 scarlet & blk	6.50	12.50
102	A14	$2 red vio & grn	22.50	50.00

Wmk. 3
103	A14	25c black, emerald	4.25	17.50
104	A14	$5 blk & vio, red	200.00	190.00
		Nos. 92-104 (13)	247.75	286.80

For surcharges see Nos. B1-B5.

Common Design Types pictured following the introduction.

Silver Jubilee Issue
Common Design Type

1935, May 6   Engr.   Perf. 11x12

108	CD301	3c black & ultra	.65	.45
109	CD301	4c indigo & grn	1.10	3.25
110	CD301	5c ultra & brn	2.00	.75
111	CD301	25c brn vio & ind	4.00	3.75
		Nos. 108-111 (4)	7.75	8.20
		Set, never hinged		12.00

Coronation Issue
Common Design Type

1937, May 12   Perf. 13½x14

112	CD302	3c deep orange	.20	.25
113	CD302	4c gray black	.30	.25
114	CD302	5c bright ultra	.50	1.00
		Nos. 112-114 (3)	1.00	1.50
		Set, never hinged	1.60	

 Mayan Figures A15

Chicle Tapping — A16   Cohune Palm — A17

Local Products A18

Grapefruit Industry A19

Mahogany Logs in River — A20

Sergeant's Cay — A21

Dory — A22

Chicle Industry A23

Court House, Belize — A24   Mahogany Cutting — A25

Seal of Colony — A26

1938   Perf. 11x11½, 11½x11

115	A15	1c green & violet	.20	.70
116	A16	2c car & black	.20	.70
a.		Perf. 12 ('47)	1.10	.75
117	A17	3c brown & dk vio	.20	.50
118	A18	4c green & black	.20	.50
119	A19	5c slate bl & red vio	.40	.30
120	A20	10c brown & yel grn	.50	.50
121	A21	15c blue & brown	.70	.50
122	A22	25c green & ultra	1.10	.85
123	A23	50c dk vio & blk	7.00	2.50
124	A24	$1 ol green & car	12.50	5.25
125	A25	$2 rose lake & ind	14.00	13.00
126	A26	$5 brn & carmine	13.00	19.00
		Nos. 115-126 (12)	50.00	44.30
		Set, never hinged	80.00	

Issued: 3c-5c, 1/10; 1c, 2c, 10c-50c, 2/14; $1-$5, 2/28.

> Catalogue values for unused stamps in this section, from this point to the end of the section, are for Never Hinged items.

Peace Issue
Common Design Type

1946, Sept. 9   Engr.   Perf. 13½x14
127	CD303	3c brown	.20	.20
128	CD303	5c deep blue	.20	.20

Silver Wedding Issue
Common Design Types

1948, Oct. 1   Photo.   Perf. 14x14½
129	CD304	4c dark green	.20	.20

Engraved; Name Typographed
Perf. 11½x11
130	CD305	$5 light brown	20.00	30.00

St. George's Cay — A27

H.M.S. Merlin — A28

1949, Jan. 10   Engr.   Perf. 12½

131	A27	1c green & ultra	.20	.20
132	A27	3c yel brn & dp blue	.20	.20
133	A27	4c purple & brn ol	.30	.30
134	A28	5c dk blue & brown	.30	.30
135	A28	10c vio brn & blue grn	.50	.50
136	A28	15c ultra & emerald	.90	.90
		Nos. 131-136 (6)	2.40	2.40

Battle of St. George's Cay, 150th anniv.

UPU Issue
Common Design Types
Perf. 13½, 11x11½

1949, Oct. 10   Engr.

137	CD306	4c blue green	.35	.35
138	CD307	5c indigo	.55	.55
139	CD308	10c chocolate	.90	.90
140	CD309	25c blue	1.50	1.50
		Nos. 137-140 (4)	3.30	3.30

University Issue
Common Design Types

1951, Feb. 16   Engr.   Perf. 14x14½

141	CD310	3c choc & purple	.35	.35
142	CD311	10c choc & green	.65	.65

Coronation Issue
Common Design Type

1953, June 2   Perf. 13½x13
143	CD312	4c dk green & black	.40	.40

Arms — A29

Maya — A30

Designs: 2c, Tapir. 3c, Legislative Council Chamber and mace. 4c, Pine industry. 5c, Spiny lobster. 10c, Stanley Field Airport. 15c, Mayan frieze. 25c, Blue butterfly. $1, Armadillo. $2, Hawkesworth Bridge. $5, Pine Ridge orchid.

1953-57		Engr.		Perf. 13½	
144	A29	1c gray blk & green		.20	.20
145	A29	2c gray blk & brn, perf. 14 ('57)		.20	.20
a.		Perf. 13½		.35	.30
146	A29	3c mag & rose lil, perf. 14 ('57)		.20	.20
a.		Perf. 13½		.25	.20
147	A29	4c grn & dk brn		.30	.20
148	A29	5c car & ol brn, perf. 14 ('57)		.20	.20
a.		Perf. 13½		.50	.45
149	A29	10c ultra & bl gray		.20	.20
150	A29	15c vio & yel grn		.20	.35
151	A29	25c brown & ultra		4.25	1.75
152	A30	50c purple & brown		5.00	1.60
153	A30	$1 red brn & sl bl		3.75	3.50
154	A30	$2 gray & car		4.50	4.00
155	A30	$5 blue gray & pur		32.50	15.00
		Nos. 144-155 (12)		51.50	27.40

Issued: 5c, 5/15; 2c, 3c, 9/18, perf. 13½, 9/2.
For overprints see Nos. 159-166.

View of Belize, 1842 — A31

Designs: 10c, Public seals, 1860 and 1960. 15c, Tamarind Tree, Newtown Barracks.

Perf. 11½x11

1960, July 1			Wmk. 314	
156	A31	2c green	.20	.20
157	A31	10c carmine	.25	.25
158	A31	15c blue	.45	.45
		Nos. 156-158 (3)	.90	.90

Cent. of the establishment of a local PO.

Nos. 145-146 and 149-150
Overprinted: "NEW CONSTITUTION/1960"

1961, Mar. 1		Wmk. 4	Perf. 14, 13	
159	A29	2c gray black & brn	.20	.20
160	A29	3c mag & rose lilac	.20	.20
161	A29	10c ultra & blue gray	.35	.25
162	A29	15c violet & yel green	.50	.35
		Nos. 159-162 (4)	1.25	1.00

Nos. 144, 149, 151 and 152
Overprinted: "HURRICANE/HATTIE"

1962, Jan. 15			Perf. 13	
163	A29	1c gray black & green	.20	.20
164	A29	10c ultra & blue gray	.20	.20
165	A29	25c brown & ultra	.30	.30
166	A30	50c purple & brown	.70	.70
		Nos. 163-166 (4)	1.40	1.40

Hurricane Hattie struck Belize, Oct. 31, 1961.

Great Curassow A32

Birds: 2c, Red-legged honeycreeper. 3c, American jacana. 4c, Great kiskadee. 5c, Scarlet-rumped tanager. 10c, Scarlet macaw. 15c, Massena trogon. 25c, Redfooted booby. 50c, Keel-billed toucan. $1, Magnificent frigate

bird. $2, Rufoustailed jacamar. $5, Montezuma oropendola.

1962, Apr. 2 Photo. Perf. 14x14½
Birds in Natural Colors; Black Inscriptions

167	A32	1c yellow	.90	.70
168	A32	2c gray	1.40	.20
a.		Green omitted	200.00	
169	A32	3c lt yel green	1.40	.85
a.		Dark grn (legs) omitted	300.00	
170	A32	4c lt gray	2.75	1.25
171	A32	5c buff	1.60	.20
172	A32	10c beige	1.90	.20
a.		Blue omitted	225.00	
173	A32	15c pale lemon	.90	.30
174	A32	25c bluish gray & pink	3.50	.25
175	A32	50c pale blue	5.00	.35
b.		Blue (beak & claw) omitted	—	
176	A32	$1 blue	7.75	.70
177	A32	$2 pale gray	8.25	2.50
178	A32	$5 light blue	24.00	12.50
		Nos. 167-178 (12)	59.35	20.00

For overprints see Nos. 182-186, 195-199.

1967		Wmk. 314 Sideways		
		Colors as 1962 Issue		
167a	A32	1c	.20	.20
168b	A32	2c	.20	.20
170a	A32	4c	.30	.25
171a	A32	5c	.55	.30
172b	A32	10c	.80	.65
173a	A32	15c	1.10	.90
175a	A32	50c	4.25	3.50
		Nos. 167a-175a (7)	7.40	6.00

Issued: 1, 4, 5, 50c, 2/16; 2, 10, 15c, 11/28.

Freedom from Hunger Issue
Common Design Type

1963, June 4		Perf. 14x14½	
179	CD314 22c green	.85	.85

Red Cross Centenary Issue
Common Design Type
Wmk. 314

1963, Sept. 2		Litho.	Perf. 13	
180	CD315	4c black & red	.20	.20
181	CD315	22c ultra & red	1.40	1.40

Nos. 167, 169, 170, 172 and 174
Overprinted: "SELF GOVERNMENT / 1964"

1964		Photo.	Perf. 14x14½	
182	A32	1c multicolored	.20	.20
a.		Yellow omitted	125.00	
183	A32	3c multicolored	.20	.20
184	A32	4c multicolored	.20	.20
185	A32	10c multicolored	.35	.30
186	A32	25c multicolored	.65	.55
		Nos. 182-186 (5)	1.60	1.45

Attainment of self-government.

ITU Issue
Common Design Type

1965, May 17		Litho.	Perf. 11x11½	
187	CD317	2c ver & green	.20	.20
188	CD317	50c yel & red lilac	1.00	1.00

Intl. Cooperation Year Issue
Common Design Type

1965, Oct. 25			Perf. 14½	
189	CD318	1c bl grn & claret	.20	.20
190	CD318	22c lt violet & green	.75	.75

Churchill Memorial Issue
Common Design Type

1966, Jan. 24		Photo.	Perf. 14	
Design in Black, Gold and Carmine Rose				
191	CD319	1c bright blue	.20	.20
192	CD319	4c green	.20	.20
193	CD319	22c brown	.70	.70
194	CD319	25c violet	.90	.90
		Nos. 191-194 (4)	2.00	2.00

Bird Type of 1962 Overprinted:
"DEDICATION OF SITE / NEW CAPITAL / 9th OCTOBER 1965"
Wmk. 314 Sideways

1966, July 1			Perf. 14x14½	
195	A32	1c multicolored	.20	.20
196	A32	3c multicolored	.25	.20
197	A32	4c multicolored	.20	.20
198	A32	10c multicolored	.30	.25
199	A32	25c multicolored	.50	.50
		Nos. 195-199 (5)	1.50	1.35

Citrus Grove — A33

10c, Half Moon Cay & Lighthouse Reef. 22c, Hidden Valley Falls & Mountain Pine Ridge. 25c, Xunantunich Mayan ruins in Cayo district.

1966, Oct. 1		Photo.	Perf. 14x14½	
200	A33	5c multicolored	.20	.20
201	A33	10c multicolored	.20	.20
202	A33	22c multicolored	.25	.25
203	A33	25c multicolored	.35	.35
		Nos. 200-203 (4)	1.00	1.00

1st British Honduras stamp issue, cent.

International Tourist Year — A34

1967, Dec. 4			Perf. 12½	
204	A34	5c Sailfish	.20	.20
205	A34	10c Deer	.20	.20
206	A34	22c Jaguar	.35	.35
207	A34	25c Tarpon	.45	.45
		Nos. 204-207 (4)	1.20	1.20

Schomburgkia Tibicinis — A35

Belizean Patriots' Memorial, Belize City, and Human Rights Flame — A36

Orchids: 10c, Maxillaria tenuifolia. 22c, Bletia purpurea. 25c, Sobralia macrantha.

Inscribed: "20th Anniversary of E.C.L.A."

1968, Apr. 16		Photo.	Perf. 14½x14	
208	A35	5c violet & multi	.20	.20
209	A35	10c green & multi	.20	.20
210	A35	22c multicolored	.35	.35
211	A35	25c olive & multi	.50	.50
		Nos. 208-211 (4)	1.25	1.25

20th anniv. of the Economic Commission for Latin America. See #226-229, 255-258.

1968, July 15		Litho.	Perf. 13x13½	

Design: 50c, Mayan motif stele, monument at new capital site and Human Rights flame.

| 212 | A36 | 22c multicolored | .30 | .30 |
| 213 | A36 | 50c multicolored | .70 | .70 |

International Human Rights Year.

Jewfish A37

Designs: 2c, White-lipped peccary. 3c, Grouper (sea bass). 4c, Collared anteater. 5c, Bonefish. 10c, Paca. 15c, Dolphinfish. 25c, Kinkajou. 50c, Yellow-and-green-banded muttonfish. $1, Tayra. $2, Great barracudas. $5, Mountain lion.

1968, Oct. 15		Litho.	Perf. 13x12½	
214	A37	1c yellow & multi	.20	.20
215	A37	2c brt yel & multi	.20	.20
216	A37	3c pink & multi	.20	.20
217	A37	4c brt grn & multi	.20	.20
218	A37	5c brick red & multi	.20	.20
219	A37	10c lilac & multi	.20	.20
220	A37	15c org yel & multi	.25	.20
221	A37	25c multicolored	.45	.40
222	A37	50c bl grn & multi	.95	.85
223	A37	$1 ocher & multi	1.90	1.75

224	A37	$2 violet & multi	3.75	3.50
225	A37	$5 ultra & multi	8.25	7.50
		Nos. 214-225 (12)	16.75	15.40

See Nos. 234-240, Belize 327-339.
For overprints see Nos. 251-254, 281-282.

Orchid Type of 1968
Inscribed "Orchids of Belize"

Designs: 5c, Rhyncholaetia digbyana. 10c, Cattleya bowringiana. 22c, Lycaste cochleatum. 25c, Coryanthes speciosum.

1969, Apr. 9		Photo.	Perf. 14½x14	
226	A35	5c Prus blue & multi	.20	.20
227	A35	10c olive bis & multi	.30	.30
228	A35	22c yellow grn & multi	.70	.70
229	A35	25c violet blue & multi	.80	.80
		Nos. 226-229 (4)	2.00	2.00

Hardwood Trees — A38

Virgin and Child, by Giovanni Bellini — A39

1969, Sept. 1		Litho.	Perf. 14	
230	A38	5c Ziricote	.20	.20
231	A38	10c Rosewood	.20	.20
232	A38	22c Mayflower	.30	.30
233	A38	25c Mahogany	.40	.40
		Nos. 230-233 (4)	1.10	1.10

Timber industry of British Honduras. Issued in sheets of 9 (3x3) on simulated wood background.

Fish-Animal Type of 1968

Designs: ½c, Crana (fish). Others as before.

1969-72		Litho.	Perf. 13x12½	
234	A37	½c vio bl, yel & blk	.20	.20
235	A37	½c citron, blk & bl ('71)	.70	1.00
236	A37	2c brt yel, blk & grn ('72)	3.00	3.00
237	A37	3c pink & multi ('72)	1.00	1.60
a.		Wmk. sideways ('72)	3.00	3.00
238	A37	5c brick red & multi ('72)	1.00	1.60
239	A37	10c lilac & multi ('72)	1.00	1.60
a.		Wmk. sideways ('72)	3.50	3.50
240	A37	$5 ultra & multi ('70)	9.00	9.00
		Nos. 234-240 (7)	15.90	18.00

For overprints see Nos. 251-252.

1969, Oct. 1		Litho.	Perf. 14	

Christmas: 22c, 25c, Adoration of the Kings, by Veronese.

247	A39	5c multicolored	.20	.20
248	A39	15c dp orange & multi	.20	.20
249	A39	22c lilac rose & multi	.40	.40
250	A39	25c emerald & multi	.50	.50
		Nos. 247-250 (4)	1.30	1.30

Nos. 238-239 and Type of 1968
Overprinted "POPULATION/ CENSUS 1970"
Wmk. 314 Sideways

1970, Feb. 2		Photo.	Perf. 13x12½	
251	A37	5c brick red & multi	.20	.20
252	A37	10c lilac & multi	.20	.20
253	A37	15c org yel & multi	.25	.25
254	A37	25c multicolored	.35	.35
		Nos. 251-254 (4)	1.00	1.00

Orchid Type of 1968
Inscribed: "Orchids of Belize"

1970, Apr. 2	Litho.	Perf. 14	
255 A35	5c Black	.20	.20
256 A35	15c White butterfly	.35	.35
257 A35	22c Swan	.50	.50
258 A35	25c Butterfly	.60	.60
	Nos. 255-258 (4)	1.65	1.65

Santa Maria Tree and Wood (Calophyllum Brasiliense) A40

Nativity, by Arthur Hughes A41

Hardwood Trees and Woods: 15c, Nargusta (terminalia amazonia). 22c, Cedar (cedrela mexicana). 25c, Sapodilla (achras sapota).

1970, Sept. 7		Perf. 14	
259 A40	5c multicolored	.20	.20
260 A40	15c multicolored	.30	.30
261 A40	22c multicolored	.45	.45
262 A40	25c multicolored	.45	.45
	Nos. 259-262 (4)	1.40	1.40

1970, Nov. 2		Perf. 14	
263 A41	½c black & multi	.20	.20
264 A41	5c brown & multi	.20	.20
265 A41	10c multicolored	.20	.20
266 A41	15c slate bl & multi	.25	.25
267 A41	22c dk green & multi	.40	.40
268 A41	50c black & multi	.85	.85
	Nos. 263-268 (6)	2.10	2.10

Christmas: 5c, 15c, 50c, Mystic Nativity, by Botticelli.

Legislative Assembly House A42

Designs: 5c, View of South Side of Belize. 10c, Government Plaza, Belmopan. 22c, Magistrates' Court. 25c, Police Headquarters. 50c, New General Post Office.

1971, Jan. 30 Litho.	Perf. 13½x14		
Size: 59x22mm			
269 A42	5c multicolored	.20	.20
270 A42	10c multicolored	.20	.20
Size: 37x21½mm			
271 A42	15c multicolored	.20	.20
272 A42	22c multicolored	.30	.30
273 A42	26c multicolored	.40	.40
274 A42	50c multicolored	.70	.70
	Nos. 269-274 (6)	2.00	2.00

New capital at Belmopan.

Tabebuia Chrysantha — A43

Flowers: 5c, 22c, Hymenocallis littoralis. 10c, 25c, Hippeastrum equestre. 15c, like ½c.

1971, Mar. 27	Litho.	Perf. 14	
275 A43	½c vio blue & multi	.20	.20
276 A43	5c olive & multi	.20	.20
277 A43	10c violet & multi	.20	.20
278 A43	15c multicolored	.30	.30
279 A43	22c multicolored	.45	.45
280 A43	25c lt brown & multi	.55	.55
	Nos. 275-280 (6)	1.90	1.90

Easter.

Type of 1968 Overprinted: "RACIAL EQUALITY / YEAR—1971"

1971, June 14	Litho.	Perf. 13x12½	
281 A37	10c lilac & multi	.20	.20
282 A37	50c blue green & multi	.70	.70

Intl. year against racial discrimination.

Tubroos (Enterolobium Cyclocarpum) A44

Hardwood Trees of Belize: 15c, Yemeri (Vochysia hondurensis). 26c, Billyweb (Sweetia panamensis). 50c, Logwood (Haematoxylum campechiaum).

1971, Aug. 16		Perf. 14	
Queen's Head in Silver			
283 A44	5c green, brn & blk	.20	.20
284 A44	15c multicolored	.50	.50
285 A44	26c multicolored	.80	.80
286 A44	50c multicolored	1.50	1.50
a.	Souvenir sheet of 4, #283-286	5.25	5.25
	Nos. 283-286 (4)	3.00	3.00

Verrazano-Narrows Bridge, New York, and Quebec Bridge, Canada — A45

Bridges of the World: ½c, Hawksworth Bridge connecting San Ignacio and Santa Helena and Belcan Bridge, Belize, Br. Honduras. 26c, London Bridge in 1871, and at Lake Havasu City, Ariz., in 1971. 50c, Belize-Mexico Bridge and Belize Swing Bridge.

1971, Sept. 23		Litho.	
287 A45	½c multicolored	.20	.20
288 A45	5c multicolored	.20	.20
289 A45	26c multicolored	.50	.50
290 A45	50c multicolored	1.10	1.10
	Nos. 287-290 (4)	2.00	2.00

Petrae Volubis — A46

Seated Jade Figure — A47

Wild Flowers: 15c, Vochysia hondurensis. 26c, Tabebuia pentaphylla. 50c, Erythrina americana.

1972, Feb. 28			
Flowers in Natural Colors; Black Inscriptions			
292 A46	6c lilac & yellow	.20	.20
293 A46	15c lt blue & pale grn	.35	.35
294 A46	26c pink & lt blue	.65	.65
295 A46	50c orange & lt grn	1.25	1.25
	Nos. 292-295 (4)	2.45	2.45

Easter.

Perf. 14x13½, 13½x14			
1972, May 22		Unwmk.	

Mayan Carved Jade, 4th-8th centuries: 6c, Dancing priest. 16c, Sun god's head, horiz.

26c, Priest on throne and sun god's head. 50c, Figure and mask.

296 A47	3c rose red & multi	.20	.20
297 A47	6c vio bl & multi	.20	.20
298 A47	16c brown & multi	.25	.25
299 A47	26c ol grn & multi	.40	.40
300 A47	50c purple & multi	.85	.85
	Nos. 296-300 (5)	1.90	1.90

Black inscription with details of designs on back of stamps.

Banak (Virola Koschnyi) — A48

Hardwood Trees of Belize: 5c, Quamwood (Schizolobium parahybum). 16c, Waika chewstick (Symphonia globulifera). 26c, Mammeeapple (Mammea americana). 50c, My lady (Aspidosperma megalocarpon).

1972, Aug. 21	Wmk. 314	Perf. 14	
Queen's Head in Gold			
301 A48	3c brt pink & multi	.20	.20
302 A48	5c gray & multi	.20	.20
303 A48	16c green & multi	.30	.30
304 A48	26c lemon & multi	.50	.50
305 A48	50c lt violet & multi	.90	.90
	Nos. 301-305 (5)	2.10	2.10

Silver Wedding Issue, 1972
Common Design Type

Design: Queen Elizabeth II, Prince Philip and Belize orchids.

1972, Nov. 20	Photo.	Perf. 14x14½	
306 CD324	26c slate grn & multi	.40	.40
307 CD324	50c violet & multi	.75	.75

Baron Bliss Day A49

Festivals of Belize: 10c, Labor Day boat race. 26c, Carib Settlement Day dance. 50c, Pan American Day parade.

1973, Mar. 9	Litho.	Perf. 14½	
308 A49	3c dull blue & black	.20	.20
309 A49	10c red & multi	.20	.20
310 A49	26c ver & multi	.40	.40
311 A49	50c black & multi	.75	.75
	Nos. 308-311 (4)	1.55	1.55

SEMI-POSTAL STAMPS

Regular Issue of 1921-29 Surcharged in Black or Red	BELIZE RELIEF FUND PLUS 3 CENTS	

1932	Wmk. 4	Perf. 14	
B1 A14	1c + 1c green	1.50	5.00
B2 A14	2c + 2c rose red	1.50	4.75
B3 A14	3c + 3c orange	2.50	11.00
B4 A14	4c + 4c gray (R)	3.25	14.50
B5 A14	5c + 5c ultra	5.00	10.00
	Nos. B1-B5 (5)	13.75	45.25

The surtax was for a fund to aid sufferers from the destruction of the city of Belize by a hurricane in Sept. 1931.

POSTAGE DUE STAMPS

Catalogue values for unused stamps in this section are for Never Hinged items.

D1

1923-64	Typo.	Wmk. 4	Perf. 14	
J1 D1	1c black		.35	15.00
J2 D1	2c black		.35	15.00
J3 D1	4c black		.60	10.00
	Nos. J1-J3 (3)		1.30	40.00

Nos. J1-J3 were re-issued on chalky paper in 1956. Values shown are for the 1956 issue. The 1923 issue, on yellowish thin ordinary paper, sells for $5 unused, $25 used. The 1c was reprinted in 1964 on white, ordinary paper, value $8.50 unused, $25 used.

Perf. 13½x13, 13½x14			
1965-72		Wmk. 314	
J4 D1	2c black ('72)	1.50	3.00
J5 D1	4c black	1.00	3.50

WAR TAX STAMPS

Nos. 85, 75 and 77 Overprinted

1916-17	Wmk. 3	Perf. 14	
With Moire Overprint			
MR1 A11	1c green	.20	.35
a.	"WAR" inverted	250.00	250.00
Without Moire Overprint			
MR2 A11	1c green ('17)	.25	.75
MR3 A11	3c orange ('17)	.75	.75
a.	Double overprint	450.00	450.00
	Nos. MR1-MR3 (3)	1.20	1.85

Nos. 75 and 77 Overprinted

1918			
MR4 A11	1c green	.20	.25
MR5 A11	3c orange	.20	.50

BRITISH INDIAN OCEAN TERRITORY

'bri-tish 'in-dēən 'ō-chən 'ter-ə-ˌtōr-ē

LOCATION — Indian Ocean
GOVT. — British Dependency
POP. — 0

B.I.O.T. was established Nov. 8, 1965. This island group lies 1,180 miles north of Mauritius. It consisted of Chagos Archipelago (chief island: Diego Garcia), Aldabra, Farquhar and Des Roches Islands until June 23, 1976, when the last three named islands were returned to Seychelles.

There is no permanent population on the islands. There are military personel located there.

100 Cents = 1 Rupee
100 Pence = 1 Pound (1990)

Catalogue values for all unused stamps in this country are for Never Hinged items.

Seychelles Nos. 198-202, 204-212
Overprinted

Perf. 14½x14, 14x14½

			Photo.
1968, Jan. 17			
Size: 24x31, 31x24mm			
1	A17	5c multicolored	.20	.55
2	A17	10c multicolored	.20	.20
3	A17	15c multicolored	.20	.20
4	A17	20c multicolored	.20	.20
5	A17	25c multicolored	.20	.20
6	A18	40c multicolored	.20	.20
7	A18	45c multicolored	.20	.25
8	A17	50c multicolored	.20	.25
9	A17	75c multicolored	.20	.30
10	A18	1r multicolored	.40	.30
11	A18	1.50r multicolored	1.75	1.40
12	A18	2.25r multicolored	3.00	3.25
13	A18	3.50r multicolored	3.00	4.00
14	A18	5r multicolored	8.75	6.75

Perf. 13x14

Size: 22½x39mm

15	A17	10r multicolored	18.50	18.00
		Nos. 1-15 (15)	37.20	36.05

Lascar
A1

Marine Fauna: 10c, Hammerhead shark, vert. 15c, Tiger shark. 20c, Sooty eagle ray. 25c, Butterflyfish, vert. 30c, Robber crab. 40c, Green carangue. 45c, Needlefish, vert. 50c, Barracuda. 60c, Spotted pebble crab. 75c, Parrotfish. 85c, Rainbow runner (fish). 1r, Giant hermit crab. 1.50r, Humphead. 2.25r, Rock cod. 3.50r, Black marlin. 5r, Whale shark, vert. 10r, Lionfish.

Perf. 14x13½, 13½x14; 14 (30c, 60c, 85c)

			Litho.
1968-73			
16	A1	5c multicolored	.40	.40
a.	Wmk. upright ('73)		.65	.65
17	A1	10c multicolored	.20	.20
18	A1	15c multicolored	.20	.20
19	A1	20c multicolored	.20	.20
20	A1	25c multicolored	.35	.35
21	A1	30c multi ('70)	.40	.40
22	A1	40c multicolored	.35	.35
23	A1	45c multicolored	2.75	2.75
24	A1	50c multicolored	.35	.35
25	A1	60c multi ('70)	.90	.90
26	A1	75c multicolored	4.00	4.00
27	A1	85c multi ('70)	1.75	1.75
28	A1	1r multicolored	1.40	1.40
29	A1	1.50r multicolored	1.75	1.75
30	A1	2.25r multicolored	14.00	14.00
31	A1	3.50r multicolored	4.00	4.00
32	A1	5r multicolored	6.00	6.00
33	A1	10r multicolored	17.00	17.00
		Nos. 16-33 (18)	56.00	56.00

No. 16 has watermark sideways.

Aldabra Atoll and Sacred Ibis — A2

			Litho.	**Perf. 13½x13**
1969, July 10				
34	A2	2.25r vio blue & multi	2.00	1.50

Outrigger Canoe — A3

75c, Beaching canoe. 1r, Merchant ship Nordvaer. 1.50r, Yacht, Isle of Farquhar.

			Litho.	**Perf. 13½x14**
1969, Dec. 15				
35	A3	45c multicolored	.45	.40
36	A3	75c multicolored	.85	.75
37	A3	1r multicolored	1.25	1.10
38	A3	1.50r multicolored	2.25	1.75
		Nos. 35-38 (4)	4.80	4.00

Giant Land Tortoise — A4

Designs: 75c, Aldabra lily. 1r, Aldabra tree snail. 1.50r, Dimorphic egrets.

			Litho.	**Wmk. 314**
1971, Feb. 1				
39	A4	45c multicolored	2.00	2.00
40	A4	75c multicolored	2.50	2.00
41	A4	1r multicolored	5.00	2.25
42	A4	1.50r multicolored	6.50	7.75
		Nos. 39-42 (4)	16.00	14.00

Aldabra Nature Reserve.

Society Coat of Arms and Flightless
Rail — A5

			Litho.	**Perf. 13½**
1971, June 30				
43	A5	3.50r multicolored	12.00	8.50

Opening of Royal Society Research Station at Aldabra.

Acropora
Formosa
A6

Corals: 60c, Goniastrea pectinata. 1r, Fungia fungites. 1.75r, Tubipora musica.

1972, Mar. 1				
44	A6	40c blue & multi	3.25	3.25
45	A6	60c brt pink & multi	3.75	3.75
46	A6	1r blue & multi	3.75	3.75
47	A6	1.75r brt pink & multi	4.50	4.50
		Nos. 44-47 (4)	15.25	15.25

Common Design Types
pictured following the introduction.

Silver Wedding Issue, 1972
Common Design Type

Design: Queen Elizabeth II, Prince Philip, flightless rail and sacred ibis.

			Photo.	**Perf. 14x14½**
1972, Nov. 20				
48	CD324	95c multicolored	1.00	.50
49	CD324	1.50r violet & multi	1.00	.50

Crucifixion, 17th   Upsidedown
Century — A7   Jellyfish — A8

Paintings, Ethiopian Manuscripts, 17th Century: 75c, 1.50r, Joseph and Nicodemus burying Jesus. 1r, Like 45c.

			Litho.	**Perf. 14**
1973, Apr. 9				
50	A7	45c buff & multi	.30	.40
51	A7	75c buff & multi	.45	.55
52	A7	1r buff & multi	.65	.40
53	A7	1.50r buff & multi	1.10	.70
a.	Souvenir sheet of 4, #50-53		3.00	3.50
		Nos. 50-53 (4)	2.50	2.05

Easter.

			Litho.	**Wmk. 314**
1973, Nov. 12				
54	A8	50c shown	3.25	2.75
55	A8	1r Butterflies	3.50	2.75
56	A8	1.50r Spider	3.75	2.75
		Nos. 54-56 (3)	10.50	8.25

Nordvaer and July
14, 1969
Cancel — A9

2.50r, Nordvaer offshore and cancel.

1974, July 14			
57	A9	85c multicolored	.85	.50
58	A9	2.50r multicolored	1.40	1.50

Nordvaer traveling post office, 5th anniv.

Terebra Maculata and Terebra
Subulata — A10

Sea Shells: 75c, Turbo marmoratus. 1r, Drupa rubusidaeus. 1.50r, Cassis rufa.

			Litho.	**Perf. 13½x14**
1974, Nov. 12				
59	A10	45c multicolored	2.10	.70
60	A10	75c multicolored	2.40	1.25
61	A10	1r multicolored	2.50	1.75
62	A10	1.50r multicolored	3.00	3.00
		Nos. 59-62 (4)	10.00	6.70

Aldabra   Grewia
Drongo — A11   Salicifolia — A12

Birds: 10c, Malagasy coucal. 20c, Red-headed forest fody. 25c, Fairy tern. 30c, Crested tern. 40c, Brown booby. 50c, Noddy tern. 60c, Gray heron. 65c, Blue-faced booby. 95c, Malagasy white-eye. 1r, Green-backed heron. 1.75r, Lesser frigate bird. 3.50r, White-tailed tropic bird. 5r, Souimanga sunbird. 10r, Malagasy turtledove. Nos. 69, 71-77 horiz.

			Litho.	**Wmk. 314**	**Perf. 14**
1975, Feb. 28					
63	A11	5c buff & multi	.20	2.40
64	A11	10c lt ultra & multi	.20	2.40
65	A11	20c dp yel & multi	.20	2.40
66	A11	25c ultra & multi	.25	2.40
67	A11	30c dl yel & multi	.35	2.40
68	A11	40c bis & multi	.45	2.50
69	A11	50c lt blue & multi	.50	2.50
70	A11	60c yel & multi	.55	2.50
71	A11	65c yel grn & multi	.65	2.50
72	A11	95c citron & multi	.80	2.50
73	A11	1r bister & multi	1.00	2.50
74	A11	1.75r yel & multi	2.00	4.25
75	A11	3.50r blue & multi	4.00	4.25
76	A11	5r pale sal & multi	6.50	4.25
77	A11	10r brt yel & multi	10.00	7.75
		Nos. 63-77 (15)	27.65	47.50

		Litho.	**Wmk. 314**
1975, July 10			

Native Plants: 65c, Cassia aldabrensis. 1r, Hypoestes aldabrensis. 1.60r, Euphorbia pyrifolia.

78	A12	50c multicolored	.35	1.10
79	A12	65c multicolored	.50	1.25
80	A12	1r multicolored	.75	1.25
81	A12	1.60r multicolored	1.25	1.40
		Nos. 78-81 (4)	2.85	5.00

Nature protection.

Aldabra and Compass Rose — A13

Maps of Islands: 1r, Desroches. 1.50r, Farquhar. 2r, Diego Garcia.

			Litho.	**Perf. 13½x14**
1975, Nov. 8				
82	A13	50c blk, blue & grn	.80	.80
83	A13	1r green & multi	.95	.95
84	A13	1.50r blk, ultra & grn	1.10	1.10
85	A13	2r blk, lilac & grn	1.25	1.25
a.	Souvenir sheet of 4, #82-85		7.50	7.50
		Nos. 82-85 (4)	4.10	4.10

British Indian Ocean Territory, 10th anniv.

Crimson Speckled Moth — A14

Insects: 1.20r, Dysdercus fasciatus. 1.50r, Sphex torridus. 2r, Oryctes rhinoceros.

			Litho.	**Wmk. 373**
1976, Mar. 22				
86	A14	65c multicolored	.45	.40
87	A14	1.20r multicolored	.70	.65
88	A14	1.50r multicolored	1.00	.90
89	A14	2r multicolored	1.50	1.40
		Nos. 86-89 (4)	3.65	3.35

Exhibition
Emblem
and No.
37 — A15

			Wmk. 373	**Perf. 14**
1990, May 3				
90	A15	15p No. 62	2.50	2.00
91	A15	20p No. 89	2.75	2.25
92	A15	34p No. 85	4.00	3.25
93	A15	54p shown	5.75	5.00
		Nos. 90-93 (4)	15.00	12.50

Stamp World London '90.

Birds — A16

1990, May 3   Wmk. 384   Perf. 14
94	A16	15p	White-tailed tropic birds	1.10 1.75
95	A16	20p	Turtle doves	1.25 1.75
96	A16	24p	Greater frigate birds	1.40 1.75
97	A16	30p	Little green herons	1.50 2.00
98	A16	34p	Greater sand plovers	1.75 2.00
99	A16	41p	Crab plovers	1.75 2.25
100	A16	45p	Crested terns	2.00 2.25
101	A16	54p	Lesser crested terns	2.25 2.50
102	A16	62p	Fairy terns	2.25 2.50
103	A16	71p	Red-footed boobies	2.25 2.75
104	A16	80p	Indian mynahs	2.50 3.00
105	A16	£1	Madagascar fodies	2.50 3.00
			Nos. 94-105 (12)	22.50 27.50

For overprints see Nos. 145-146.

Queen Mother, 90th Birthday
Common Design Types

Designs: 24p, Lady Elizabeth Bowes-Lyon, 1923. £1, Queen, Princesses Elizabeth & Margaret, 1940.

1990, Aug. 4   Wmk. 384   Perf. 14x15
106	CD343	24p	multicolored	1.25 1.10

Perf. 14½
107	CD344	£1	brown & black	5.00 4.50

British Indian Ocean Territory, 25th Anniv. — A17

1990, Nov. 8   Litho.   Perf. 14
108	A17	20p	Flag	.90 .80
109	A17	24p	Coat of arms	1.25 1.10

Souvenir Sheet
110	A17	£1	Map	5.00 5.00

Govt. Services A18

1991, June 3   Litho.   Perf. 14
111	A18	20p	Postal service	.70 .70
112	A18	24p	Royal Marines	.85 .85
113	A18	34p	Police station, officers	1.25 1.25
114	A18	54p	Customs service	1.90 1.90
			Nos. 111-114 (4)	4.70 4.70

Visiting Ships A19

1991, Nov. 8
115	A19	20p	Survey ship Experiment, 1786	.70 .70
116	A19	24p	US Brig Pickering, 1819	.90 .90
117	A19	34p	SMS Emden, 1914	1.25 1.25

118	A19	54p	HMS Edinburgh, 1988	1.90 1.90
			Nos. 115-118 (4)	4.75 4.75

Queen Elizabeth II's Accession to the Throne, 40th Anniv.
Common Design Type

1992, Feb. 6   Litho.   Perf. 14
119	CD349	15p	multicolored	.50 .50
120	CD349	20p	multicolored	.75 .70
121	CD349	24p	multicolored	1.00 .90
122	CD349	34p	multicolored	1.50 1.25
123	CD349	54p	multicolored	2.25 2.00
			Nos. 119-123 (5)	6.00 5.35

Aircraft A20

1992, Oct. 23   Litho.   Perf. 14
124	A20	20p	Catalina	.90 .80
125	A20	24p	Nimrod	1.25 1.00
126	A20	34p	P-3 Orion	1.75 1.50
127	A20	54p	B-52	3.00 2.50
			Nos. 124-127 (4)	6.90 5.80

Christmas — A21

Paintings: 5p, The Mystical Marriage of St. Cathrin, by Correggio. 24p, Madonna and Child by unknown artist. 34p, Madonna and Child by unknown artist, diff. 54p, The Birth of Jesus, by Kaspar Jele.

1992, Nov. 27   Perf. 14½
128	A21	5p	multicolored	.25 .20
129	A21	24p	multicolored	.90 .80
130	A21	34p	multicolored	1.25 1.10
131	A21	54p	multicolored	2.00 1.90
			Nos. 128-131 (4)	4.40 4.00

Coconut Crab A22

1993, Mar. 3   Litho.   Perf. 14
132	A22	10p	Crab, coconut	1.10 1.10
133	A22	10p	Large crab	1.10 1.10
134	A22	10p	Two crabs	1.10 1.10
135	A22	15p	Crab on tree trunk	1.50 1.50
			Nos. 132-135 (4)	4.80 4.80

World Wildlife Fund.

Royal Air Force, 75th Anniv.
Common Design Type

#136, Vickers Virginia. 24p, Bristol Bulldog. 34p, Short Sunderland. 54p, Bristol Blenheim IV.

#140: a, Douglas Dakota. b, Gloster Javelin. c, Blackburn Beverley. d, Vickers VC10.

1993, Apr. 1   Wmk. 373
136	CD350	20p	multicolored	.75 .65
137	CD350	24p	multicolored	.85 .75
138	CD350	34p	multicolored	1.25 1.10
139	CD350	54p	multicolored	1.75 1.50
			Nos. 136-139 (4)	4.60 4.00

Souvenir Sheet of 4
140	CD350	20p	#a.-d.	3.00 2.75

Flowers — A23

Christmas: 20p, Stachytarpheta urticifolia. 24p, Ipomea pes-caprae. 34p, Sida pusilla. 54p, Catharanthus roseus.

1993, Nov. 22   Litho.   Perf. 14½
141-144	A23	Set of 4		3.75 3.75

Nos. 96, 105 Ovptd. with Hong Kong '94 Emblem

1994, Feb. 18   Litho.   Perf. 14
145	A16	24p	multicolored	.65 .65
146	A16	£1	multicolored	2.75 2.75

A24

18th Cent. Maps and Charts: a, 20p, Sketch of Diego Garcia. b, 24p, Plan of harbor, Chagos Island or Diego Garcia, by Lt. Archibald Blair. c, 34p, Chart of Chagos Archipelago, by Lt. Blair. d, 44p, Plan of part of Chagos Island or Diego Garcia, from survey made by the Drake. e, 54p, Plan of Chagos Island or Diego Garcia, by M. Aa Fontaine.

1994, June 1   Wmk. 373
147	A24	Strip of 5, #a.-e.		5.25 5.25

Butterflies — A25

1994, Aug. 16   Wmk. 384
148	A25	24p	Junonia villida	1.10 1.10
149	A25	30p	Petrelaea dana	1.40 1.40
150	A25	56p	Hypolimnas misippus	2.50 2.50
			Nos. 148-150 (3)	5.00 5.00

Sharks A26

1994, Nov. 1   Wmk. 373
151	A26	15p	Nurse	.45 .45
152	A26	20p	Silver tip	.60 .60
153	A26	24p	Black tip reef	.75 .75
154	A26	30p	Oceanic white tip	.95 .95
155	A26	35p	Black tip	1.10 1.10
156	A26	41p	Smooth hammerhead	1.25 1.25
157	A26	46p	Lemon	1.40 1.40
158	A26	55p	White tip reef	1.75 1.75
159	A26	65p	Tiger	2.00 2.00
a.			Souvenir sheet of 1	2.00 2.00
160	A26	74p	Indian sand tiger	2.25 2.25
a.			Souvenir sheet of 1	2.25 2.25
161	A26	80p	Great hammerhead	2.50 2.50
162	A26	£1	Great white	3.00 3.00
			Nos. 151-162 (12)	18.00 18.00

No. 159a for Hong Kong '97. Issued 2/3/97.
No. 160a for return of Hong Kong to China. Issued 7/1/97.

End of World War II, 50th Anniv.
Common Design Types

20p, War graves, memorial cross, Diego Garcia. 24p, 6-inch naval gun, Cannon Point. 30p, Sunderland flying boat, 230 Squadron. 56p, HMIS Clive.
£1, Reverse of War Medal 1939-45.

1995, May 8   Litho.   Perf. 14
163	CD351	20p	multicolored	.50 .50
164	CD351	24p	multicolored	.65 .65
165	CD351	30p	multicolored	.80 .80
166	CD351	56p	multicolored	1.50 1.50
			Nos. 163-166 (4)	3.45 3.45

Souvenir Sheet
167	CD352	£1	multicolored	2.75 2.75

Game Fish A27

1995, Oct. 6   Wmk. 384
168	A27	20p	Dolphinfish	.60 .60
169	A27	24p	Sailfish	.75 .75
170	A27	30p	Wahoo	.90 .90
171	A27	56p	Striped marlin	1.75 1.75
			Nos. 168-171 (4)	4.00 4.00

Sea Shells A28

20p, Terebra crenulata. 24p, Bursa bufonia. 30p, Nassarius papillosus. 56p, Lopha cristagalli.

1996, Jan. 8   Wmk. 373   Perf. 14
172	A28	20p	multicolored	.60 .60
173	A28	24p	multicolored	.75 .75
174	A28	30p	multicolored	.90 .90
175	A28	56p	multicolored	1.75 1.75
			Nos. 172-175 (4)	4.00 4.00

Queen Elizabeth II, 70th Birthday
Common Design Type

Various portraits of Queen, scenes of British Indian Ocean Territory: 20p, View to north from south end of lagoon. 24p, Manager's House, Peros Banhos. 30p, Wireless station, Peros Banhos. 56p, Sunset scene.
£1, Wearing crown, formal dress.

Perf. 14x14½
1996, Apr. 22   Wmk. 384
176	CD354	20p	multicolored	.65 .65
177	CD354	24p	multicolored	.80 .80
178	CD354	30p	multicolored	1.00 1.00
179	CD354	56p	multicolored	1.75 1.75
			Nos. 176-179 (4)	4.20 4.20

Souvenir Sheet
180	CD354	£1	multicolored	3.25 3.25

Turtles A29

1996, Sept. 2   Wmk. 373
181	A29	20p	Loggerhead	.60 .60
182	A29	24p	Leatherback	.75 .75
183	A29	30p	Hawksbill	.90 .90
184	A29	56p	Green	1.75 1.75
			Nos. 181-184 (4)	4.00 4.00

Uniforms — A30

Designs: 20p, British representative. 24p, Royal Marine officer. 30p, Royal Marine in camouflage. 56p, Police dog handler, female police officer.

1996, Dec. — Perf. 14

185	A30	20p multicolored	.65 .65
186	A30	24p multicolored	.80 .80
187	A30	30p multicolored	1.00 1.00
188	A30	56p multicolored	1.90 1.90
		Nos. 185-188 (4)	4.35 4.35

Queen Elizabeth II and Prince Philip, 50th Wedding Anniv. — A31

#189, Queen up close. #190, 4-horse team fording river. #191, Queen riding in open carriage. #192, Prince Philip up close. #193, Prince driving 4-horse team, Prince, Queen near jeep. #194, Queen on horseback, castle in distance.

£1.50, Queen, Prince riding in open carriage.

1997, July 10 — Perf. 14½x14

189	A31	20p multicolored	.65 .65
190	A31	20p multicolored	.65 .65
a.		Pair, #189-190	1.30 1.30
191	A31	24p multicolored	.80 .80
192	A31	24p multicolored	.80 .80
a.		Pair, #191-192	1.60 1.60
193	A31	30p multicolored	1.00 1.00
194	A31	30p multicolored	1.00 1.00
a.		Pair, #193-194	2.00 2.00
		Nos. 189-194 (6)	4.90 4.90

Souvenir Sheet

195	A31	£1.50 multicolored	5.00 5.00

Ocean Wave '97, Naval Exercise A32

Designs: a, HMS Richmond, HMS Beaver. b, HMS Illustrious. c, HMS Beaver. d, RFA Sir Percivale. HMY Britannia, HMS Beaver. e, HMY Britannia. f, HMS Richmond, HMS Beaver, HMS Gloucester. g, HMS Richmond. h, HMS Illustrious (aerial view). i, HMS Sheffield. j, RFA Diligence, HMS Trenchant. k, HMS Illustrious, RFA Fort George, HMS Gloucester. l, HMS Richmond, HMS Beaver, HMS Gloucester.

1997, Dec. 1 — Litho. — Perf. 14x14½

196	A32	24p Sheet of 12, #a.-l.	9.25 9.25

Diana, Princess of Wales (1961-97)
Common Design Type

Various portraits: a, 26p, shown. b, 26p, Close-up. c, 34p. d, 60p.

1998, Mar. 31 — Perf. 14½x14

197	CD355	Sheet of 4, #a.-d.	5.50 5.50

No. 197 sold for £1.46 + 20p, with surtax and 50% of profits from total sale being donated to the Princess Diana Memorial Fund.

Royal Air Force, 80th Anniv.
Common Design Type of 1993
Re-inscribed

Designs: 26p, Blackburn Iris, 1930-34. 34p, Gloster Gamecock, 1926-33. 60p, North American Sabre F86, 1953-56. 80p, Avro Lincoln, 1945-55.

No. 202: a, Sopwith Baby, 1915-19. b, Martinsyde Elephant, 1916-19. c, De Havilland Tiger Moth, 1932-55. d, North American Mustang III, 1943-47.

1998, Apr. 1 — Wmk. 384 — Perf. 14

198	CD350	26p multicolored	.85 .85
199	CD350	34p multicolored	1.10 1.10
200	CD350	60p multicolored	2.00 2.00
201	CD350	80p multicolored	2.75 2.75
		Nos. 198-201 (4)	6.70 6.70

Souvenir Sheet

202	CD350	34p Sheet of 4, #a.-d.	4.50 4.50

Intl. Year of the Ocean A33

Dolphins and whales: No. 203, Striped dolphin. No. 204, Bryde's whale. No. 205, Pilot whale. No. 206, Spinner dolphin.

1998, Dec. 7 — Litho. — Perf. 14

203	A33	26p multicolored	.85 .85
204	A33	26p multicolored	.85 .85
205	A33	34p multicolored	1.10 1.10
206	A33	34p multicolored	1.10 1.10
		Nos. 203-206 (4)	3.90 3.90

Sailing Ships — A34

2p, Bark "Westminster," 1837. 15p, "Sao Cristovao," Spain, 1589. 20p, Clipper ship "Sea Witch," US, 1849. 26p, HMS "Royal George," 1778. 34p, Clipper ship "Cutty Sark," 1883. 60p, British East India Co. ship "Mentor," 1789. 80p, HM brig "Trinculo," 1809. £1, Paddle steamer "Enterprise," 1825. £1.15, Privateer "Confiance," France, 1800. £2, British East India Co. ship "Kent," 1820.

1999, Feb. 1 — Litho. — Perf. 14

207	A34	2p multicolored	.20 .20
208	A34	15p multicolored	.50 .50
209	A34	20p multicolored	.65 .65
210	A34	26p multicolored	.85 .85
211	A34	34p multicolored	1.10 1.10
212	A34	60p multicolored	1.90 1.90
213	A34	80p multicolored	2.50 2.50
214	A34	£1 multicolored	3.25 3.25
215	A34	£1.15 multicolored	3.75 3.75
216	A34	£2 multicolored	6.50 6.50
		Nos. 207-216 (10)	21.20 21.20

Tea Race, 1872 A35

a, Cutty Sark (up close). b, Thermopylae (in distance).

1999, Mar. 19 — Litho. — Perf. 14

217	A35	60p Sheet of 2, #a.-b.	3.75 3.75

Australia '99 World Stamp Expo.

The Stamp Show 2000, London — A36

Winning photos in photography contest: a, 26p, Field vole by Colin Sargent. b, 34p, Puffin, by P. J. Royal. c, 55p, Red fox, by Jim Wilson. d, £1, Robin, by Harry Smith. Illustration reduced.

Perf. 14½x14¼
2000, May 22 — Litho. — Wmk. 373

218	A36	Sheet of 4, #a-d	6.50 6.50

Satellite Images A37

Designs: 15p, Salomon Atoll. 20p, Egmont Atoll. 60p, Blenheim Reef. 80p, Diego Garcia.

Wmk. 373
2000, July 3 — Litho. — Perf. 14

219-222	A37	Set of 4	5.00 5.00

Queen Mother, 100th Birthday — A38

Designs: 26p, Blue hat. 34p, Blue green hat. No. 225: a, 55p, Blue hat. £1, Yellow hat.

2000, Aug. 4 — Wmk. 373 — Perf. 13¾

223-224	A38	Set of 2	1.75 1.75

Souvenir Sheet

225	A38	Sheet of 2, #a-b	4.50 4.50

Flowers — A39

Designs: 26p, Delonix regia. 34p, Barringtonia asiatica. 60p, Zephyranthes rosea.

2000, Dec. 4 — Perf. 14½x14¼

226-228	A39	Set of 3	3.75 3.75

Souvenir Sheet

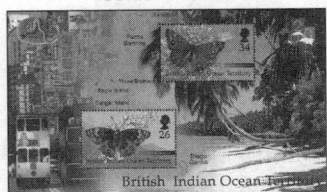

New Year 2001 (Year of the Snake) — A40

Butterflies: a, 26p, Precis orithya. b, 34p, Junonia villida chagoensis. Illustration reduced.

Perf. 14 ¼
2001, Feb. 1 — Litho. — Wmk. 373

229	A40	Sheet of 2, #a-b	1.75 1.75

Hong Kong 2001 Stamp Exhibition.

Souvenir Sheet

Royal Navy Submarines, Cent. — A41

No. 230: a, 26p, HMS Turbulent. b, 26p, HMS Churchill. c, 34p, HMS Resolution. d, 34p, HMS Vanguard. e, 60p, HMS Otter. f, 60p, HMS Oberon. Size of Nos. 230e-230f: 75x30mm.

Perf. 14¼x14½
2001, May 28 — Litho. — Wmk. 373

230	A41	Sheet of 6, #a-f	6.75 6.75

Worldwide Fund for Nature (WWF) A42

Starfish: 15p, Cushion star. 26p, Azure sea star. 34p, Crown-of-thorns. 56p, Banded bubble star.

Wmk. 373
2001, Aug. 1 — Litho. — Perf. 13¾

231-234	A42	Set of 4	3.75 3.75
234a		Strip, #231-234	3.75 3.75

Plants — A43

Designs: 10p, Catharanthus roseus, horiz. 26p, Scadoxus multiflora. 34p, Striga asiatica. 60p, Argusia argentia, horiz. 70p, Euphorbia cyathophora, horiz.

2001, Sept. 24 — Perf. 13¾x14¼

235	A43	26p multi	.75 .75
a.		Perf. 14½	.75 .75
236	A43	34p multi	1.00 1.00
a.		Perf. 14½	1.00 1.00

Souvenir Sheet
Perf. 14½

237		Sheet, #a-c, 235a, 236a	5.75 5.75
a.	A43	10p multi	.25 .25
b.	A43	60p multi	1.75 1.75
c.	A43	70p multi	2.00 2.00

Souvenir Sheet

Birdlife International World Bird Festival — A44

Crab plover: a, Resting. b, Eating crab, vert. c, Close-up of head, vert. d, In flight. e, Standing on one leg.

2001, Oct. 1 — Perf. 14½

238	A44	50p Sheet of 5, #a-e	7.25 7.25

BRUNEI

'brü-,nī

LOCATION — On the northwest coast of Borneo
GOVT. — Independent state
AREA — 2,226 sq. mi.
POP. — 322,982 (1999 est.)
CAPITAL — Bandar Seri Begawan

Brunei became a British protectorate in 1888. A treaty between the sultan and the British Government in 1979 provided for independence in 1983.

100 Cents (Sen) = 1 Dollar

Catalogue values for unused stamps in this country are for Never Hinged items, beginning with Scott 62.

Watermarks

Wmk. 385 - CARTOR

Wmk. 388- Multiple "SPM"

Syncopated Perforation

Type A (first stamp #555): On 2 longer sides, oval holes equal in width to 3 holes which are the 11th hole from the top and 10th hole from the bottom.

Labuan Stamps of 1902-03
Overprinted or Surcharged in Red:

		1906 Unwmk.	Perf. 12 to 16	
1	A38	1c violet & blk	22.50	45.00
a.		Black overprint	2,000.	2,750.
2	A38	2c on 3c brn & blk	1.50	7.50
a.		"BRUNEI." double	4,250.	3,000.
b.		"TWO CENTS." double	9,500.	
3	A38	2c on 8c org & blk	25.00	70.00
a.		"TWO CENTS." double	8,250.	
b.		"TWO CENTS." omitted, in pair with normal	9,250.	
4	A38	3c brown & blk	25.00	70.00
5	A38	4c on 12c yel & black	2.00	5.00
6	A38	5c on 16c org brn & green	37.50	60.00
7	A38	8c orange & blk	8.00	25.00
8	A38	10c on 16c org brn & green	6.50	18.00
9	A38	25c on 16c org brn & green	90.00	125.00
10	A38	30c on 16c org brn & green	85.00	125.00
11	A38	50c on 16c org brn & black	85.00	125.00
12	A38	$1 on 8c org & blk	85.00	125.00
		Nos. 1-12 (12)	473.00	800.50

The 25c surcharge reads: "25 CENTS."

Scene on Brunei River — A1

Two Types of 1908 1c, 3c:
Type I - Dots form bottom line of water shading. (Double plate.)
Type II - Dots removed. (Single plate.)

		1907-21 Engr. Wmk. 3	Perf. 14	
13	A1	1c yel green & blk	2.00	9.00
14	A1	1c green (II) ('08)	.55	1.60
a.		Type I ('19)	.75	2.10
15	A1	2c red & black	2.40	4.00
16	A1	2c brn & blk ('11)	2.25	1.50
17	A1	3c red brn & blk	12.50	18.00
18	A1	3c car (I) ('08)	2.25	1.50
a.		Type II ('17)	60.00	32.50
19	A1	4c lilac & blk	7.00	9.00
20	A1	4c claret ('12)	3.50	.70
21	A1	5c ultra & blk	45.00	85.00
22	A1	5c org & blk ('08)	6.50	6.50
23	A1	5c orange ('16)	12.00	12.00
24	A1	8c orange & blk	7.00	20.00
25	A1	8c blue ('08)	6.50	10.00
26	A1	8c ultra ('16)	4.50	20.00
27	A1	10c dk green & blk	4.00	13.50
28	A1	10c violet, yel ('12)	1.40	1.25
29	A1	25c yel brn & blue	27.50	45.00
30	A1	25c violet ('12)	3.25	12.00
31	A1	30c black & pur	19.00	27.50
32	A1	30c org & red vio ('12)	8.00	12.50
33	A1	50c brown & grn	17.50	27.50
34	A1	50c blk, grn ('12)	25.00	60.00
35	A1	50c blk, grnsh bl ('21)	8.00	30.00
36	A1	$1 slate & red	62.50	85.00
37	A1	$1 red & blk, bl ('12)	22.50	50.00
38	A1	$5 lake, grn ('08)	85.00	140.00
39	A1	$25 blk, red ('08)	450.00	800.00
		Nos. 13-38 (26)	397.60	703.05

Used value for No. 39 is for a CTO example dated before December 1941. CTOs dated later are worth about half the value given.

Stamps of 1908-21 Overprinted in Black: "MALAYA-BORNEO EXHIBITION, 1922" in Four Lines

		1922		
14b	A1	1c green	2.25	17.00
16a	A1	2c brown & black	5.00	21.00
18b	A1	3c claret	6.75	30.00
20a	A1	4c claret	5.25	35.00
23a	A1	5c orange	10.00	45.00
28a	A1	10c violet, yellow	8.75	45.00
30a	A1	25c violet	19.00	67.50
35a	A1	50c greenish blue	60.00	125.00
37a	A1	$1 red & black, blue	92.50	160.00
		Nos. 14b-37a (9)	209.50	545.50

Industrial fair, Singapore, Mar. 31-Apr. 15.

Type of 1907 Issue

		1924-37	Wmk. 4	
43	A1	1c black ('26)	.55	.35
44	A1	2c deep brown	.90	3.75
45	A1	2c green ('33)	.55	.35
46	A1	3c green	.80	4.00
47	A1	4c claret brown	1.60	.80
48	A1	4c orange ('29)	1.10	.50
49	A1	5c orange	3.50	.95
50	A1	5c lt gray ('31)	9.25	7.50
51	A1	5c brown ('33)	6.75	.30
52	A1	8c ultra ('27)	6.25	4.50
53	A1	8c gray ('33)	6.50	.50
54	A1	10c violet, yel ('37)	12.00	20.00
55	A1	25c dk violet ('31)	5.25	9.50
56	A1	30c org & red vio ('31)	7.50	13.50
57	A1	50c black, grn ('31)	7.50	12.50
58	A1	$1 red & blk, bl ('31)	25.00	60.00
		Nos. 43-58 (16)	95.00	139.00

For overprints see Nos. N1-N20.

Dwellings in Town of Brunei A2

		1924-31		
59	A2	6c black	10.50	9.25
60	A2	6c red ('31)	3.00	10.00
61	A2	12c blue	4.00	8.25
		Nos. 59-61 (3)	17.50	27.50

See note after Nos. N1-N19.

Catalogue values for unused stamps in this section, from this point to the end of the section, are for Never Hinged items.

Types of 1907-24

		1947-51 Engr.	Perf. 14	
62	A1	1c brown	.45	1.10
63	A1	2c gray	.85	1.50
a.		Perf. 14½x13½ ('50)	1.75	4.00
64	A2	3c dark green	1.00	3.00
65	A1	5c deep orange	.80	1.25
a.		Perf. 14½x13½ ('50)	4.00	12.50
66	A2	6c gray black	1.00	3.00
67	A1	8c scarlet	.45	.80
a.		Perf. 13 ('51)	.60	8.00
68	A1	10c violet	.70	.25
a.		Perf. 14½x13½ ('50)	2.25	5.00
69	A1	15c brt ultra	.45	.60
70	A1	25c red violet	1.00	.70
a.		Perf. 14½x13½ ('51)	1.75	7.50
71	A1	30c dp org & gray blk	.95	1.00
a.		Perf. 14½x13½ ('51)	1.75	11.00
72	A1	50c black	1.60	.90
a.		Perf. 13 ('50)	3.50	14.00
73	A1	$1 scar & gray blk	3.75	.90
74	A1	$5 red org & grn ('48)	15.00	15.00
75	A1	$10 dp claret & gray blk ('48)	40.00	30.00
		Nos. 62-75 (14)	68.00	60.00

Sultan Ahmed and Pile Dwellings A3

		1949, Sept. 22 Wmk. 4	Perf. 13	
76	A3	8c car & black	1.60	1.60
77	A3	25c red orange & pur	1.60	1.60
78	A3	50c blue & black	2.00	2.00
		Nos. 76-78 (3)	5.20	5.20

25th anniv. of the reign of Sultan Ahmed Tajudin Akhazul Khair Wad-din.

Common Design Types pictured following the introduction.

UPU Issue
Common Design Types
Engr.; Name Typo. on 15c and 25c

		1949, Oct. 10	Perf. 13½, 11x11½	
79	CD306	8c rose car	.50	.50
80	CD307	15c indigo	.75	.75
81	CD308	25c red lilac	1.25	1.25
82	CD309	50c slate	2.50	2.50
		Nos. 79-82 (4)	5.00	5.00

Sultan Omar Ali Saifuddin — A4

River Kampong A5

		1952, Mar. 1 Engr.	Perf. 13½x13	
		Center in Black		
83	A4	1c black	.20	.20
84	A4	2c red orange	.20	.20
85	A4	3c red brown	.20	.20
86	A4	4c green	.20	.20
87	A4	6c gray	.25	.20
88	A4	8c carmine	.30	.20
89	A4	10c olive brown	.30	.20
90	A4	12c violet	.35	.20
91	A4	15c blue	.50	.20
92	A4	25c purple	.75	.25
93	A4	50c ultramarine	1.10	.30

		Perf. 13		
94	A5	$1 dull green	3.00	.60
95	A5	$2 red	4.50	1.50
96	A5	$5 deep plum	15.00	5.00
		Nos. 83-96 (14)	26.85	9.45

See Nos. 101-114.

Mosque and Sultan Omar A6

		1958, Sept. 24 Wmk. 314	Perf. 13	
		Center in Black		
97	A6	8c dull green	.25	.30
98	A6	15c carmine rose	.30	.25
99	A6	35c rose violet	.45	.75
		Nos. 97-99 (3)	1.00	1.30

Opening of the Brunei Mosque.

Freedom from Hunger Issue
Common Design Type with Portrait of Sultan Omar

		1963, June 4 Photo.	Perf. 14x14½	
100	CD314	12c sepia	1.50	1.50

Types of 1952

		1964-70 Engr.	Perf. 13½x13	
		Center in Black		
101	A4	1c black	.20	.20
102	A4	2c red orange	.20	.20
103	A4	3c red brown	.20	.20
104	A4	4c green	.20	.20
105	A4	6c black	.25	.20
106	A4	8c dk carmine	.45	.20
107	A4	10c olive brown	.35	.25
108	A4	12c violet	.55	.30
109	A4	15c blue	.60	.35
110	A4	25c purple	1.25	.40
111	A4	50c ultramarine	2.50	1.50
		Perf. 13		
112	A5	$1 dull green ('68)	4.75	3.00
113	A5	$2 red ('70)	16.00	10.00
114	A5	$5 deep plum ('70)	32.50	25.00
		Nos. 101-114 (14)	60.00	42.00

Nos. 101-112 were reissued in 1968-70 on whiter, glazed paper; the $2 and $5 are only on this paper.

		Wmk. 314 Sideways		
		1972-73	Perf. 13½x13	
		Center in Black		
102a	A4	2c red orange	.35	.35
103a	A4	3c red brown	.40	.40
104a	A4	4c green	.50	.50
105a	A4	6c black	.85	.85
106a	A4	8c dark carmine	1.10	1.10
107a	A4	10c olive brown	1.50	1.50
108a	A4	12c violet	1.75	1.75
109a	A4	15c blue	3.00	3.00
		Nos. 102a-109a (8)	9.45	9.45

The stamps with watermark sideways are on the whiter, glazed paper.
Issue dates: 2c, 8c, May 9, 1973, others, Nov. 17, 1972.

The following six sets are Common Design Types but with the portrait of Sultan Omar.

ITU Issue

		1965, May 17 Litho.	Perf. 11x11½	
116	CD317	4c red lil & org brn	.20	.20
117	CD317	75c orange & emer	1.40	1.40

Intl. Cooperation Year Issue

		1965, Oct. 25	Perf. 14½	
118	CD318	4c blue grn & claret	.20	.20
119	CD318	15c lt violet & grn	.70	.70

Churchill Memorial Issue

		1966, Jan. 24 Photo.	Perf. 14	
120	CD319	3c multicolored	.25	.20
121	CD319	6c multicolored	.65	.35
122	CD319	15c multicolored	1.00	.60
123	CD319	75c multicolored	3.50	2.50
		Nos. 120-123 (4)	5.40	3.65

World Cup Soccer Issue

		1966, July 4 Litho.	Perf. 14	
124	CD321	4c multicolored	.20	.20
125	CD321	75c multicolored	1.25	1.25

WHO Headquarters Issue

1966, Sept. 20		**Litho.**	*Perf. 14*	
126	CD322	12c multicolored	.25	.20
127	CD322	25c multicolored	.75	.75

UNESCO Anniversary Issue

1966, Dec. 1		**Litho.**	**Wmk. 314**	
128	CD323	4c "Education"	.20	.20
129	CD323	15c "Science"	.45	.45
130	CD323	75c "Culture"	2.25	2.25
		Nos. 128-130 (3)	2.90	2.90

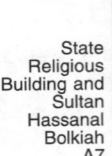

State
Religious
Building and
Sultan
Hassanal
Bolkiah
A7

1967, Dec. 19		**Photo.**	*Perf. 12½*	
131	A7	4c violet & multi	.20	.20
132	A7	10c red & multi	.20	.20
133	A7	25c orange & multi	.35	.35
134	A7	50c lt violet & multi	.65	.65
		Nos. 131-134 (4)	1.40	1.40

A three-stamp set (12c, 25c, 50c) showing views of the new Language and Communications Headquarters was prepared and announced for release in April, 1968. The Crown Agents distributed sample sets, but the stamps were not issued. Later, Nos. 144-146 were issued instead.

Sultan
Hassanal
Bolkiah,
Brunei
Mosque
and Flags
A8

Sultan Hassanal Bolkiah Installation: 12c, Sultan, Mosque and flags, horiz.

Perf. 13x14, 14x13				
1968, July 9			**Photo.**	
135	A8	4c green & multi	.20	.20
136	A8	12c dp bister & multi	.30	.30
137	A8	25c violet & multi	.75	.75
		Nos. 135-137 (3)	1.25	1.25

Sultan
Hassanal
Bolkiah
A9

		Wmk. 314		
1968, July 15		**Litho.**	*Perf. 12*	
138	A9	4c multicolored	.20	.20
139	A9	12c multicolored	.20	.20
140	A9	25c multicolored	.40	.50
		Nos. 138-140 (3)	.80	.90

Sultan Hassanal Bolkiah's birthday.

Coronation of
Sultan Hassanal
Bolkiah, Aug. 1,
1968 — A10

1968, Aug. 1		**Photo.**	*Perf. 14½x14*	
141	A10	4c Prus blue & multi	.20	.20
142	A10	12c rose lilac & multi	.25	.25
143	A10	25c multicolored	.55	.55
		Nos. 141-143 (3)	1.00	1.00

A11

Hall of Language and Culture — A12

Perf. 13½, 12½x13½ (A12)				
1968, Sept. 29			**Photo.**	
144	A11	10c blue grn & multi	.20	.25
145	A12	15c ocher & multi	.20	.30
146	A12	30c ultra & multi	.45	.75
		Nos. 144-146 (3)	.85	1.30

Opening of the Hall of Language and Culture and of the Broadcasting and Information Department Building. Nos. 144-146 are overprinted "1968" and 4 bars over the 1967 date. They were not issued without this overprint.

Human Rights
Flame and
Struggling
Man — A13

		Unwmk.		
1968, Dec. 16		**Litho.**	*Perf. 14*	
147	A13	12c green, yel & blk	.20	.20
148	A13	25c ultra, yel & blk	.35	.35
149	A13	75c dk plum, yel & blk	.90	.90
		Nos. 147-149 (3)	1.45	1.45

International Human Rights Year.

Sultan
and WHO
Emblem
A14

1968, Dec. 19		**Litho.**	*Perf. 14*	
150	A14	4c lt blue, org & blk	.20	.20
151	A14	15c brt purple, org & blk	.25	.25
152	A14	25c olive, org & blk	.40	.40
		Nos. 150-152 (3)	.85	.85

20th anniv. of the WHO.

Sultan Hassanal Bolkiah, Pengiran
Shahbandar and Oil Rig — A15

1969, July 10		**Photo.**	*Perf. 14x13*	
153	A15	12c green & multi	.20	.20
154	A15	40c dk rose brn & multi	.60	.60
155	A15	50c violet & multi	.75	.75
		Nos. 153-155 (3)	1.55	1.55

Installation of Pengiran Shahbandar as Second Minister (Di-Galong Sahibol Mal).

Royal Assembly Hall and Council
Chamber — A16

Design: 50c, Front view of buildings.

		Unwmk.		
1969, Sept. 23		**Litho.**	*Perf. 15*	
156	A16	12c multicolored	.20	.20
157	A16	25c multicolored	.35	.35
158	A16	50c violet & pink	.65	.65
		Nos. 156-158 (3)	1.20	1.20

Opening of the Royal Assembly Hall and Council Chamber.

Youth Center — A17

1969, Dec. 20		**Litho.**	**Wmk. 314**	
159	A17	6c lt org, blk & dull vio	.20	.20
160	A17	10c cit, blk & dl Prus grn	.20	.20
161	A17	30c yel green, blk & brn	.45	.45
		Nos. 159-161 (3)	.85	.85

Opening of Youth Center, Mar. 15, 1969.

Helicopter and Emblem — A18

Designs: 10c, Soldier and emblem, vert. 75c, Patrol boat and emblem.

1971, May 31		**Litho.**	*Perf. 14*	
162	A18	10c green & multi	.40	.20
163	A18	15c Prus blue & multi	.45	.25
164	A18	75c lt ultra & multi	2.75	1.75
		Nos. 162-164 (3)	3.60	2.20

10th anniv. of Royal Brunei Malay Reg.

50th Anniv. of
the Royal Brunei
Police
Force — A19

1971, Aug. 14			*Perf. 14½*	
165	A19	10c Superintendent	.40	.25
166	A19	15c Constable	.50	.30
167	A19	50c Traffic policeman	2.25	1.60
		Nos. 165-167 (3)	3.15	2.15

Sultan, Heir Apparent and View of
Brunei — A20

Portraits and: 25c, View of Brunei with Mosque. 50c, Mosque and banner.

1971, Aug. 27		**Litho.**	**Wmk. 314**	
168	A20	15c multicolored	.40	.25
169	A20	25c multicolored	.75	.55
170	A20	50c multicolored	1.40	1.10
		Nos. 168-170 (3)	2.55	1.90

Installation of Sultan Hassanal Bolkiah's brother Muda Omar Ali Saifuddin as heir apparent (Perdana Wazir).

Brass and
Copper
Goods
A21

Designs: 12c, Basketware. 15c, Leather goods. 25c, Silverware. 50c, Brunei Museum.

1972, Feb. 29			*Perf. 13½x14*	
Size: 37x21mm				
171	A21	10c brn, sal & yel grn	.20	.20
172	A21	12c org, yel & green	.20	.20
173	A21	15c dk grn, emer & org	.25	.25
174	A21	25c brown, org & slate	.70	.60
Size: 58x21mm				
175	A21	50c dull blue & multi	1.50	1.10
		Nos. 171-175 (5)	2.85	2.35

Opening of Brunei Museum.

Queen Elizabeth II, Sultan and
View — A22

Queen Elizabeth II, Sultan Hassanal Bolkiah and: 15c, View of Brunei. 25c, Mosque and barge. 50c, Royal Assembly Hall.

1972, Feb. 29		**Photo.**	*Perf. 13x13½*	
176	A22	10c lt brown & multi	.25	.20
177	A22	15c lt blue & multi	.35	.30
178	A22	25c lt green & multi	.70	.60
179	A22	50c dull purple & multi	2.00	2.00
		Nos. 176-179 (4)	3.30	3.10

Visit of Queen Elizabeth II, Feb. 29.

Bangunan Secretariat (Government
Buildings) — A23

Sultans Omar Ali Saifuddin and Hassanal Bolkiah: 15c, Istana Darul Hana (Sultan's residence). 25c, View of capital. 50c, View of new Mosque.

1972, Oct. 4   Litho.   Perf. 13½
180 A23 10c org, blk & green   .20 .20
181 A23 15c green & multi   .30 .30
182 A23 25c ultra & multi   .50 .50
183 A23 50c rose red & multi   1.00 1.00
Nos. 180-183 (4)   2.00 2.00

Change of capital's name from Brunei to Bandar Seri Begawan, Oct. 4, 1970.

Beverley Plane Landing — A24

Design: 25c, Blackburn Beverley plane dropping supplies by parachute, vert.

Perf. 14x13½, 13½x14
1972, Nov. 15   Litho.
184 A24 25c blue & multi   1.60 1.60
185 A24 75c ultra & multi   4.00 4.00

Opening of Royal Air Force Museum, Hendon, London.

Silver Wedding Issue, 1972
Common Design Type
Design: Queen Elizabeth II, Prince Philip; girl and boy with traditional gifts.

1972, Nov. 20   Photo.   Perf. 14x14½
186 CD324 12c multi   .40 .20
187 CD324 75c multi   1.25 1.25

INTERPOL Emblem and Headquarters, Paris — A25

Design: 50c, similar to 25c.

1973, Sept. 7   Litho.   Perf. 14x14½
188 A25 25c emerald & multi   .75 .75
189 A25 50c multicolored   1.50 1.50

50th anniv. of Intl. Criminal Police Org. (INTERPOL).

Princess Anne and Mark Phillips — A26

1973, Nov. 14   Litho.   Perf. 13½
190 A26 25c vio blue & multi   .20 .20
191 A26 50c red lilac & multi   .40 .40

Wedding of Princess Anne and Capt. Mark Phillips, Nov. 14, 1973.

Churchill Painting Outdoors A27

Sultan Hassanal Bolkiah A28

Design: 50c, Churchill making "V" sign.

1973, Dec. 31   Litho.   Perf. 14x13½
192 A27 12c car rose & multi   .20 .20
193 A27 50c dk green & multi   .55 .55

Winston Churchill Memorial Exhibition.

1974, July 15   Photo.   Perf. 13x15
194 A28 4c blue grn & multi   .20 .20
195 A28 5c dull blue & multi   .20 .20
196 A28 6c olive grn & multi   .20 .20
197 A28 10c lt violet & multi   .20 .20
 b. Watermark upright ('76)   .20 .20
198 A28 15c brown & multi   .20 .20
199 A28 20c buff & multi   .20 .20
 b. Watermark upright ('76)   .20 .20
200 A28 25c olive & multi   .20 .20
 b. Watermark upright ('76)   .20 .20
201 A28 30c multicolored   .25 .20
202 A28 35c gray & multi   .25 .25
203 A28 40c multicolored   .30 .30
204 A28 50c yel brn & multi   .40 .35
205 A28 75c multicolored   .60 .50
206 A28 $1 dull org & multi   .75 .65
207 A28 $2 multicolored   1.60 1.40
208 A28 $5 silver & multi   3.50 3.25
209 A28 $10 gold & multi   8.25 8.25
Nos. 194-209 (16)   17.30 16.55

Issue date: Nos. 197b-200b, Apr. 12.

1975, Aug. 13   Wmk. 373
194a A28 4c   .20 .20
195a A28 5c   .20 .20
196a A28 6c   .20 .20
197a A28 10c   .20 .20
198a A28 15c   .20 .20
199a A28 20c   .20 .20
200a A28 25c   .20 .20
201a A28 30c   .25 .25
202a A28 35c   .30 .30
203a A28 40c   .35 .35
204a A28 50c   .40 .40
205a A28 75c   .60 .60
206a A28 $1   .80 .80
207a A28 $2   1.60 1.60
208a A28 $5   4.00 4.00
209a A28 $10   8.00 8.00
Nos. 194a-209a (16)   17.70 17.70

For surcharge see No. 225.

Brunei Airport A29

Design: 75c, Sultan Hassanal Bolkiah in uniform and jet over airport.

Perf. 14x14½, 12½x13 (75c)
1974, July 18   Litho.
Size: 44x28mm
215 A29 50c multicolored   1.00 1.00
Size: 47x36mm
216 A29 75c multicolored   1.40 1.40

Opening of Brunei Airport.

UPU Emblem A30

1974, Oct. 28   Perf. 14½
217 A30 12c orange & multi   .20 .20
218 A30 50c blue & multi   .50 .50
219 A30 75c emerald & multi   .75 .75
Nos. 217-219 (3)   1.45 1.45

Centenary of Universal Postal Union.

Winston Churchill A31

Design: 75c, Churchill smoking cigar.

1974, Nov. 30   Wmk. 373   Perf. 14
220 A31 12c vio blue, blue & gold   .20 .20
221 A31 75c dk green, black & gold   .90 .90

Sir Winston Churchill (1874-1965).

Boeing 737 Planes at Airport A32

Designs: 35c, Boeing 737 over Bandar Seri Begawan Mosque. 75c, Boeing 737 in flight. All planes with crest of Royal Brunei Airlines.

Perf. 12½x12
1975, May 14   Unwmk.
222 A32 12c multicolored   .30 .25
223 A32 35c multicolored   1.00 .75
224 A32 75c multicolored   2.00 2.00
Nos. 222-224 (3)   3.30 3.00

Inauguration of Royal Brunei Airlines.

No. 196a Surcharged in Silver

1976, Aug. 16   Photo.   Perf. 13x15
225 A28 10c on 6c multicolored   .25 .25

British Royal Coat of Arms — A33

20c, Imperial State Crown. 75c, Elizabeth II.

1977, June 7   Litho.   Perf. 14
226 A33 10c dk blue & multi   .20 .20
227 A33 20c purple & multi   .20 .20
228 A33 75c yellow & multi   .60 .60
Nos. 226-228 (3)   1.00 1.00

25th anniv. of the reign of Elizabeth II.

Coronation of Elizabeth II A34

20c, Elizabeth II with coronation regalia. 75c, Departure from Westminster Abbey (coach).

1978, June 2   Litho.   Perf. 13½x13
229 A34 10c multicolored   .20 .20
230 A34 20c multicolored   .20 .20
231 A34 75c multicolored   .60 .60
Nos. 229-231 (3)   1.00 1.00

25th anniv. of coronation of Elizabeth II.

Sultan's Coat of Arms — A35

Struggling Man, Human Rights Flame — A36

Coronation of Sultan Hassanal Bolkiah, 10th Anniv.: 20c, Ceremony. 75c, Royal crown.

1978, Aug. 1   Wmk. 373   Perf. 12
232 A35 10c multicolored   .20 .20
233 A35 20c multicolored   .25 .20
234 A35 75c multicolored   .90 .75
 a. Souvenir sheet of 3, #232-234   8.50 6.00
Nos. 232-234 (3)   1.35 1.15

1978, Dec. 10   Litho.   Perf. 14
235 A36 10c red, black & multi   .20 .20
236 A36 20c violet, black & yel   .20 .20
237 A36 75c olive, black & yel   .60 .60
Nos. 235-237 (3)   1.00 1.00

Universal Declaration of Human Rights, 30th anniversary.

Children and IYC Emblem A37

1979, June 30   Wmk. 373   Perf. 14
238 A37 10c shown   .20 .20
239 A37 $1 IYC emblem   .90 .90

Telisai Earth Satellite Station A38

Designs: 20c, Radar screen and satellite. 75c, Cameraman, telex operator, telephone.

1979, Sept. 23   Litho.   Perf. 14½x14
240 A38 10c multicolored   .20 .20
241 A38 20c multicolored   .20 .20
242 A38 75c multicolored   .75 .75
Nos. 240-242 (3)   1.15 1.15

Hajeer Emblem — A39

1979, Nov. 21
243 A39 10c multicolored   .20 .20
244 A39 20c multicolored   .20 .20
245 A39 75c multicolored   .75 .75
 a. Souvenir sheet of 3, #243-245   2.50 2.50
Nos. 243-245 (3)   1.15 1.15

Hegira, 1400th anniversary.

A40

A41

1980   Litho.   Perf. 14
246 A40 10c Installation ceremony   .20   .20
247 A40 10c Ceremony, diff.   .20   .20
248 A40 75c Jefri Bolkiah   .60   .60
249 A40 75c Sufri Bolkiah   .60   .60
    Nos. 246-249 (4)   1.60   1.60

Installation of Jefri Bolkiah and Sufri Bolkiah as Wizars (Ministers of State for Royalty) 1st anniv. Issued: #246, 248, 11/8; others, 12/6.

1981, Jan. 19   Litho.   Perf. 12x11½
255 A41 10c Umbrella   .20   .20
256 A41 15c Dagger, shield   .20   .20
257 A41 20c Spears   .25   .25
258 A41 30c Gold pouch   .35   .35

Size: 22½x40mm
Perf. 14x13½
259 A41 50c Headdress   .60   .60
    a. Souvenir sheet of 5, #255-259   2.25   2.25
        Nos. 255-259 (5)   1.60   1.60

A42   A43

1981, May 17   Litho.   Perf. 13x13½
260 A42 10c car rose & black   .20   .20
261 A42 75c dp violet & black   .75   .75
13th World Telecommunications Day.

Perf. 12½x12, 12 (75c)
1981, July 15   Litho.
Deep Rose Lilac Background
262 A43 10c Dagger, case   .20   .20
263 A43 15c Rifle, powder pouch   .20   .20
264 A43 20c Spears   .20   .20
265 A43 30c Sword, tunic, shield   .30   .30
266 A43 50c Horns   .50   .50

Size: 28½x45mm
267 A43 75c Gold bowl, table   .75   .75
    Nos. 262-267 (6)   2.15   2.15

See Nos. 278-289.

Royal Wedding Issue
Common Design Type

1981, July 29   Perf. 14
268 CD331 10c Bouquet   .20   .20
269 CD331 $1 Charles   .65   .65
270 CD331 $2 Couple   1.25   1.25
    Nos. 268-270 (3)   2.10   2.10

World Food   Intl. Year of the
Day — A44   Disabled — A45

1981, Oct. 16   Litho.   Perf. 12
271 A44 10c Fishermen   .20   .20
272 A44 $1 Produce   .80   .80

1981, Dec. 16   Wmk. 373   Perf. 12
273 A45 10c Blind man   .20   .20
274 A45 20c Sign language   .20   .20
275 A45 75c Man in wheelchair   .60   .60
    Nos. 273-275 (3)   1.00   1.00

TB Bacillus Centenary — A46

1982, Mar. 24   Perf. 12, 13½ (75c)
276 A46 10c Lungs   .20   .20
277 A46 75c Bacillus, microscope   .60   .60

Type of 1981

1982, May 31   Litho.   Perf. 12½x12
Deep Magenta Background
278 A43 10c shown   .20   .20
279 A43 15c Pedestal urn   .20   .20
280 A43 20c Silver bowl   .20   .20
281 A43 30c Candle   .30   .30
282 A43 50c Gold pipe   .50   .50

Size: 28x44mm
Perf. 13½
283 A43 75c Silver pointer   .75   .75
    Nos. 278-283 (6)   2.15   2.15

1982, July 15   Litho.   Perf. 12½x12
Violet Background
284 A43 10c Urn   .20   .20
285 A43 15c Crossed banners   .20   .20
286 A43 20c Golden fan   .20   .20
287 A43 30c Lid   .30   .30
288 A43 50c Sword, sheath   .50   .50

Size: 28x44mm
Perf. 12
289 A43 75c Golden chalice pole   .75   .75
    Nos. 284-289 (6)   2.15   2.15

A47

1983, Mar. 14   Litho.   Perf. 13½
290 A47 10c Flag   .20   .20
291 A47 20c Natl. palace   .20   .20
292 A47 75c Oil drilling   .75   .75
293 A47 $2 Sultan Bolkiah   2.00   2.00
    a. Block of 4, #290-293   3.00   3.00

Commonwealth Day.

World Communications Year — A48

1983, July 15   Litho.   Perf. 13½
294 A48 10c Mail delivery   .20   .20
295 A48 75c Typewriter, phone   .80   .80
296 A48 $2 Dish antenna, satellite, TV   2.00   2.00
    Nos. 294-296 (3)   3.00   3.00

Opening of Hassanal Bolkiah National
Stadium — A49

1983, Sept. 23   Litho.   Perf. 12
297 A49 10c Soccer, vert.   .20   .20
298 A49 75c Runners, vert.   1.00   1.00
299 A49 $1 shown   1.25   1.25
    Nos. 297-299 (3)   2.45   2.45

Size, Nos. 297-298: 26x33mm.

Fishing Industry — A50

1983, Sept. 23   Litho.   Perf. 13½
300 A50 10c Shrimp, lobster   .20   .20
301 A50 50c Pacific jacks   .65   .65
302 A50 75c Parrotfish, flatfish   .90   .90
303 A50 $1 Tuna   1.25   1.25
    Nos. 300-303 (4)   3.00   3.00

State
Assembly
Building — A51

Map of Southeast Asia, Flag — A52

Sultan Hassanal
Bolkiah — A53

1984, Jan. 1   Litho.   Perf. 13
304 A51 10c shown   .20   .20
305 A51 20c State Secretariat building   .25   .25
306 A51 35c New Law Court   .40   .40
307 A51 50c Liquid natural gas well   .60   .60
308 A51 75c Omar Ali Saifuddin Mosque   .90   .90
309 A51 $1 Sultan's Palace   1.25   1.25
310 A52 $3 shown   3.75   3.75
    a. Souvenir sheet of 7, #304-310   7.25   7.25
        Nos. 304-310 (7)   7.35   7.35

Souvenir Sheets
311   Sheet of 4, Constitution signing, 1959   1.25   1.25
    a.-d. A53 25c any single   .25   .25
312   Sheet of 4, Brunei U.K. Friendship Agreement, 1979   1.25   1.25
    a.-d. A53 25c any single   .25   .25

Forestry Resources — A54

1984, Apr. 21   Litho.   Perf. 13½
313 A54 10c Forests, enrichment planting   .20   .20
314 A54 50c Irrigation canal   .65   .65
315 A54 75c Recreation forest   .90   .90
316 A54 $1 Wildlife   1.25   1.25
    Nos. 313-316 (4)   3.00   3.00

Philakorea
1984 — A55

Litho. & Engr.
1984, Oct. 22   Perf. 13
317 A55 10c No. 93   .20   .20
    a. Souvenir sheet of 1   .20   .20
318 A55 75c No. 27   .90   .90
    a. Souvenir sheet of 1   .90   .90
319 A55 $2 1895 local stamp   2.50   2.50
    a. Souvenir sheet of 1   2.50   2.50
        Nos. 317-319 (3)   3.60   3.60

Brunei
Admission to
Intl.
Organizations
A56

1985, Sept. 23   Litho.   Perf. 13
320 A56 50c UN   .45   .45
321 A56 50c Commonwealth   .45   .45
322 A56 50c ASEAN   .45   .45
323 A56 50c OIC   .45   .45
    a. Souv. sheet, #320-323 + label   2.00   2.00
        Nos. 320-323 (4)   1.80   1.80

Intl. Youth
Year
A57

1985, Oct. 17   Perf. 12
324 A57 10c shown   .20   .20
325 A57 75c Industry, education   .55   .55
326 A57 $1 Public Service   .70   .70
    Nos. 324-326 (3)   1.45   1.45

Intl. Day of
Solidarity
with the
Palestinian
People
A58

1985, Nov. 29   Perf. 12x12½
327 A58 10c lt blue & multi   .20   .20
328 A58 50c pink & multi   .55   .55
329 A58 $1 lt green & multi   1.10   1.10
    Nos. 327-329 (3)   1.85   1.85

Natl. Scout   Sultan Hassanal
Jamboree, Dec.   Bolkiah — A60
14-20 — A59

1985, Dec. 14   Perf. 13½
330 A59 10c Scout handshake   .20   .20
331 A59 20c Semaphore   .20   .20
332 A59 $2 Jamboree emblem   1.75   1.75
    Nos. 330-332 (3)   2.15   2.15

1985-86   Wmk. 233   Perf. 13½x14½
333 A60 10c multi   .20   .20
334 A60 15c multi   .20   .20
335 A60 20c multi   .20   .20
336 A60 25c multi   .25   .25
337 A60 35c multi ('86)   .30   .30
338 A60 40c multi ('86)   .35   .35
339 A60 50c multi ('86)   .45   .45
340 A60 75c multi ('86)   .70   .70

Size: 35x42mm
Perf. 14
341 A60 $1 multi ('86)   .90   .90
342 A60 $2 multi ('86)   1.75   1.75
343 A60 $5 multi ('86)   4.50   4.50
344 A60 $10 multi ('86)   9.00   9.00
    Nos. 333-344 (12)   18.80 18.80

Issued: #333-336, Dec. 23; #337-340, Jan. 15; #341-343, Feb. 23; #344, Mar. 29.

Admission to
Intl.
Organizations
A61

Wmk. Cartor (385)

1986, Apr. 30   Litho.   Perf. 13
345 A61 50c WMO .50 .60
346 A61 50c ITU .50 .60
347 A61 50c UPU .50 .60
348 A61 50c ICAO .50 .60
  a. Souv. sheet of #345-348 + label 2.25 2.50
    Nos. 345-348 (4) 2.00 2.40

Royal
Brunei
Armed
Forces,
25th
Anniv.
A62

1986, May 31   Unwmk.   Perf. 13½
349 Strip of 4 1.40 1.40
  a. A62 10c In combat .20 .20
  b. A62 20c Communications .20 .20
  c. A62 50c Air and sea defense .45 .45
  d. A62 75c On parade, Royal Palace .70 .70

Royal
Ensigns — A63

#350, Tunggul charok buritan, Pisang-pisang, Alam bernaga, Sandaran. #351, Dadap, Tunggul kawan, Ambal, Payong ubor-ubor, Sapu-sapu ayeng and Rawai lidah. #352, Ula-ula besar, Payong haram, Sumbu layang. #353, Payong ubor-ubor tiga ringkat and Payong tinggi. #354, Panji-panji, Chogan istiadat, Chogan ugama. #355, Lambang duli yang maha mulia and Mahligai.

1986   Litho.   Perf. 12½
350 A63 10c multicolored .20 .20
351 A63 10c multicolored .20 .20
352 A63 75c multicolored .70 .70
353 A63 75c multicolored .70 .70
354 A63 $2 multicolored 1.75 1.75
355 A63 $2 multicolored 1.75 1.75
    Nos. 350-355 (6) 5.30 5.30

Intl. Peace
Year — A64

1986, Oct. 24   Litho.   Perf. 12
356 A64 50c Peace doves .50 .50
357 A64 75c Hands .70 .70
358 A64 $1 Peace symbols .90 .90
    Nos. 356-358 (3) 2.10 2.10

Natl. Anti-Drug
Campaign
Posters — A65

Brass
Artifacts — A66

1987, Mar. 15   Litho.   Perf. 12
359 A65 10c Jail .20 .20
360 A65 75c Noose .65 .65
361 A65 $1 Execution .90 .90
    Nos. 359-361 (3) 1.75 1.75

1987, July 15
362 A66 50c Kiri (kettle) .45 .45
363 A66 50c Langguai (bowl) .45 .45
364 A66 50c Badil (cannon) .45 .45
365 A66 50c Pelita (lamp) .45 .45
    Nos. 362-365 (4) 1.80 1.80
    See Nos. 388-391.

Dewan Bahasa Dan Pustaka, 25th
Anniv. — A67

Illustration reduced.

1987, Sept. 29   Perf. 13½x13
366 A67 Strip of 3 1.75 1.75
  a. 10c multicolored .20 .20
  b. 50c multicolored .30 .30
  c. $2 multicolored 1.25 1.25
    Language and Literature Bureau.

ASEAN, 20th
Anniv. — A68

1987, Aug. 8   Litho.   Perf. 14x13½
367 A68 20c Map .20 .20
368 A68 50c Year dates .45 .45
369 A68 $1 Flags, emblem .90 .90
    Nos. 367-369 (3) 1.55 1.55

World
Food
Day
A70

Fruit: a, Artocarpus odoratissima. b, Canarium odontophyllum mig. c, Litsea garciae. d, Mangifera foetida lour.

1987, Oct. 31   Perf. 12½
370 Strip of 4 1.90 1.90
  a.-d. A70 50c any single .45 .45
    See Nos. 374, 405, 423, 457-460.

Intl. Year of
Shelter for
the
Homeless
A71

Various houses.

1987, Nov. 28   Litho.   Perf. 13
371 A71 50c multi .50 .50
372 A71 75c multi, diff. .70 .70
373 A71 $1 multi, diff. .95 .95
    Nos. 371-373 (3) 2.15 2.15

Fruit Type of 1987
Without FAO Emblem, Dated 1988

Fruit: a, Durio. b, Durio oxleyanus. c, Durio graveolens (cross section at L). d, Durio graveolens (cross section at R).

1988, Jan. 30   Litho.   Perf. 12
374 Strip of 4 2.00 2.00
  a.-d. A70 50c, any single .50 .50

Opening of Malay
Technology
Museum — A72

1988, Feb. 29   Perf. 12½x12
375 A72 10c Wooden lathe .20 .20
376 A72 75c Water wheel, buffalo .80 .80
377 A72 $1 Bird caller in blind 1.00 1.00
    Nos. 375-377 (3) 2.00 2.00

Handwoven Cloth — A73

Designs: 10c, Kain Beragi Bunga Sakah-Sakah Dan Bunga Cengkih. 20c, Kain Jong Sarat. 25c, Kain Si Pugut. 40c, Kain Si Pugut Bunga Berlapis. 75c, Kain Si Lobang Bangsi Bunga Belitang Kipas.

1988, Apr. 30   Litho.   Perf. 12
378 A73 10c multicolored .20 .20
379 A73 20c org brown & blk .20 .20
380 A73 25c multicolored .25 .25
381 A73 40c multicolored .40 .40
382 A73 75c multicolored .75 .75
  a. Souvenir sheet of 5, #378-382 + label 2.00 2.00
    Nos. 378-382 (5) 1.80 1.80

1988, Sept. 29   Litho.   Perf. 12
Designs: 10c, Kain Beragi. 20c, Kain Bertabur. 25c, Kain Sukma Indra. 40c, Kain Si Pugut Bunga Bersusup. 75c, Kain Beragi Si Lobang Bangsi Bunga Cendera Kesuma.

383 A73 10c multicolored .20 .20
384 A73 20c multicolored .20 .20
385 A73 25c multicolored .25 .25
386 A73 40c multicolored .40 .40
387 A73 75c multicolored .75 .75
  a. Souvenir sheet of 5, #383-387 2.00 2.00
    Nos. 383-387 (5) 1.80 1.80

Brass Artifacts Type of 1987

1988, June 30   Litho.   Perf. 12
388 A66 50c Celapa (repousse box) .50 .50
389 A66 50c Gangsa (footed plate) .50 .50
390 A66 50c Periok (lidded pot) .50 .50
391 A66 50c Lampong (candle-stick) .50 .50
    Nos. 388-391 (4) 2.00 2.00

Coronation of
Sultan Hassanal
Bolkiah, 20th
Anniv. — A74

1988, Aug. 1   Litho.   Perf. 14
392 A74 20c shown .25 .25
393 A74 75c Reading from the Koran .75 .75

Size: 26x62mm
Perf. 12½x13
394 A74 $2 In full regalia 2.00 2.00
  a. Souvenir sheet of 3, #392-394 3.00 3.00
    Nos. 392-394 (3) 3.00 3.00

Eradicate Malaria, WHO 40th
Anniv. — A75

1988, Dec. 17   Litho.   Perf. 14x13½
395 A75 25c Mosquito .25 .25
396 A75 35c Extermination .35 .35
397 A75 $2 Microscope, infected blood cells 2.10 2.10
    Nos. 395-397 (3) 2.70 2.70

Natl. Day
A76

1989, Feb. 23   Litho.   Perf. 12
Size of 60c: 22x54½mm
398 A76 20c Sultan Bolkiah, officials .20 .20
399 A76 30c Honor guard .30 .30
400 A76 60c Fireworks, palace, vert. .60 .60
401 A76 $2 Religious ceremony 2.00 2.00
  a. Souvenir sheet of 4, #398-401 3.25 3.25
    Nos. 398-401 (4) 3.10 3.10

Independence from Britain, 5th anniv.

Solidarity with the Palestinians — A77

1989, Apr. 1   Litho.   Perf. 13½
402 A77 20c shown .25 .25
403 A77 75c Map, flag .75 .75
404 A77 $1 Dome of the Rock 1.00 1.00
    Nos. 402-404 (3) 2.00 2.00

Fruit Type of 1987
Without FAO Emblem, Dated 1989

Designs: a, Daemonorops fissa. b, Eleiodoxa conferia. c, Salacca zalacca. d, Calamus ornatus.

1989, Oct. 31   Litho.   Perf. 12
405 Strip of 4 2.50 2.50
  a.-d. A70 60c any single .80 .80

Oil and
Gas
Industry,
60th Anniv.
A79

1989, Dec. 28   Perf. 13½
406 A79 20c Drill .25 .25
407 A79 60c Tanker .65 .65
408 A79 90c Refinery 1.00 1.00
409 A79 $1 Rail transport 1.10 1.10
410 A79 $2 Offshore rig 2.25 2.25
    Nos. 406-410 (5) 5.25 5.25

Brunei
Museum,
25th
Anniv.
A80

1990, Jan. 1   Litho.   Perf. 12x12½
411 A80 30c Exhibits .30 .30
412 A80 60c Official opening, 1965 .60 .60
413 A80 $1 Museum exterior 1.00 1.00
    Nos. 411-413 (3) 1.90 1.90

Intl.
Literacy
Year
A81

1990, July 15   Litho.   Perf. 12x12½
414 A81 15c multicolored .20 .20
415 A81 90c multicolored .95 .95
416 A81 $1 multicolored 1.10 1.10
    Nos. 414-416 (3) 2.25 2.25

Tarsier — A82

Fight Against
AIDS — A83

1990, Sept. 29   Litho.   Perf. 12
417 A82 20c shown   .25   .25
418 A82 60c Eating leaves   .75   .75
419 A82 90c Climbing tree   1.00 1.00
      Nos. 417-419 (3)   2.00 2.00

1990, Dec. 1   Litho.   Perf. 13
420 A83 20c shown   .25   .25
421 A83 30c AIDS transmission   .35   .35
422 A83 90c Tombstone, skulls   1.00 1.00
      Nos. 420-422 (3)   1.60 1.60

Fruit Type of 1987
Without FAO Emblem, Dated 1990
Fruit: a, Willoughbea (uncut core). b, Willoughbea (core cut in half). c, Willoughbea angustifolia.

1990, Dec. 31   Perf. 12½
423   Strip of 3   2.10 2.10
  a.-c. A70 60c any single   .70   .70

Proboscis
Monkey — A84

1991, Mar. 30   Litho.   Perf. 13½x14
424 A84 15c shown   .20   .20
425 A84 20c Head, facing   .25   .25
426 A84 50c Sitting on branch   .60   .60
427 A84 60c Adult with young   .70   .70
      Nos. 424-427 (4)   1.75 1.75

Teacher's
Day
A85

Design: 90c, Teacher at blackboard.

1991, Sept. 23   Litho.   Perf. 13½x14
428 A85 60c multicolored   .70   .70
429 A85 90c multicolored   1.10 1.10

Brunei
Beauty
A86

1991, Oct. 1   Litho.   Perf. 13
430 A86 30c Three immature   .35   .35
431 A86 60c Female   .70   .70
432 A86 $1 Adult male   1.25 1.25
      Nos. 430-432 (3)   2.30 2.30

Happy Family
Campaign — A87

1991, Nov. 30   Litho.   Perf. 13
433 A87 20c Family, graduating
           son   .25   .25
434 A87 60c Mothers, children   .65   .65
435 A87 90c Adults, children,
           heart   1.10 1.10
      Nos. 433-435 (3)   2.00 2.00

World Health
Day — A88

1992, Apr. 7   Litho.   Perf. 13
436 A88 20c multicolored   .25   .25
437 A88 50c multi, diff.   .60   .60
Size: 48x28mm
438 A88 75c multi, diff.   .90   .90
      Nos. 436-438 (3)   1.75 1.75

Brunei-Singapore and Brunei-
Malaysia-Philippines Fiber Optic
Submarine Cables — A89

1992, Apr. 28   Litho.   Perf. 12
439 A89 20c Map   .25   .25
440 A89 30c Diagram   .35   .35
441 A89 90c Submarine cable   1.10 1.10
      Nos. 439-441 (3)   1.70 1.70

Visit
ASEAN
Year — A90

Designs: a, 20c, Sculptures. b, 60c, Judo exhibition. c, $1, Sculptures, diff.

1992, June 30   Litho.   Perf. 13½x14
442 A90   Strip of 3, #a.-c.   2.00 2.00

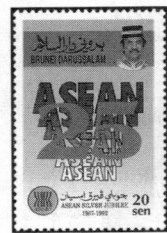

ASEAN, 25th
Anniv. — A91   A92

1992, Aug. 8   Litho.   Perf. 14
443 A91 20c shown   .25   .25
444 A91 60c Building   .65   .65
445 A91 90c Views of member
           states   1.10 1.10
      Nos. 443-445 (3)   2.00 2.00

1992, Oct. 5   Perf. 14x13½
Sultan in various forms of dress and: No. 446a, Coronation procession. b, Airport. c,

New Law Court, Sultan's Palace. d, Ship and Brunei University. e, Mosque, buildings.
446 A92 25c Strip of 5, #a.-e.   1.50 1.50

Sultan Hassanal Bolkiah's Accession to the Throne, 25th Anniv.

Birds
A93

Designs: No. 447, Crested wood partridge, vert. No. 448, Long-tailed parakeet, vert. No. 449, Chestnut-breasted malkoha. No. 450, Asian paradise flycatcher, vert. No. 451, Magpie robin, vert. No. 452, White-rumped shama. No. 453, Great argus pheasant, vert. No. 454, Malay lorikeet, vert. No. 455, Black and red broadbill, vert.

Perf. 14x13½, 13½x14
1992-93   Litho.
447 A93 30c multicolored   .40   .40
448 A93 30c multicolored   .40   .40
449 A93 30c multicolored   .40   .40
450 A93 60c multicolored   .75   .75
451 A93 60c multicolored   .75   .75
452 A93 60c multicolored   .75   .75
453 A93 $1 multicolored   1.25 1.25
454 A93 $1 multicolored   1.25 1.25
455 A93 $1 multicolored   1.25 1.25
      Nos. 447-455 (9)   7.20 7.20

Issued: #447, 450, 453, 12/30/92; #448, 451, 454, 1/27/93; others, 5/3/93.

Natl. Day, 10th
Anniv. — A94

10th anniv. emblem and: a, 10c, Natl. flag. b, 20c, Hands supporting inscription. c, 30c, Natl. day emblems, 1985-93. d, 60c, Emblem with star, crossed swords.

1994, June 16   Litho.   Perf. 13
456 A94   Strip of 4, #a.-d.   1.50 1.50

Fruit Type of 1987
Without FAO Emblem, Dated 1994
#457, Nephelium mutabile. #458, Nephelium xerospermoides. #459, Nephelium spp. #460, Nephelium macrophyllum.

1994, Aug. 8   Litho.   Perf. 13½x13
457 A70 60c multicolored   .75   .75
458 A70 60c multicolored   .75   .75
459 A70 60c multicolored   .75   .75
460 A70 60c multicolored   .75   .75
      Nos. 457-460 (4)   3.00 3.00

A95

A96

World Stop Smoking Day: 10c, Cigarette, lung, fetus over human figure. 15c, People throwing away tobacco, cigarettes, pipe. $2, Arms around world crushing out cigarettes.

1994, Sept. 1   Litho.   Perf. 13½x13
461 A95 10c multicolored   .20   .20
462 A95 15c multicolored   .20   .20
463 A95 $2 multicolored   2.50 2.50
      Nos. 461-463 (3)   2.90 2.90

1994, Oct. 7   Perf. 13½
Girl Guides in Brunei, 40th anniv.: a, Leader. b, Girl receiving award. c, Girl reading. d, Girls in various costumes. e, Girls camping out.
464 A96 40c Strip of 5, #a.-e.   2.50 2.50

Royal
Brunei
Airlines,
20th Anniv.
A97

Airplanes: 10c, Twin-engine propeller. 20c, Passenger jet attached to tow bar. $1, Passenger jet in air.

1994, Nov. 18   Litho.   Perf. 13½
465 A97 10c multicolored   .20   .20
466 A97 20c multicolored   .30   .30
467 A97 $1 multicolored   1.25 1.25
      Nos. 465-467 (3)   1.75 1.75

Intl. Day Against
Drug Abuse — A98

Healthy people wearing traditional costumes: 20c, 60c, $1.

1994, Dec. 30   Litho.   Perf. 13½
468 A98   Strip of 3, #a.-c.   2.25 2.25
No. 468 is a continuous design.

City of
Bandar
Seri
Begawan,
25th Anniv.
A100

Aerial view of city: 30c, In 1970. 50c, In 1980, with details of significant buildings. $1, In 1990.

1995, Oct. 4   Litho.   Perf. 13½
481 A100 30c multicolored   .40   .40
482 A100 50c multicolored   .70   .70
483 A100 $1 multicolored   1.40 1.40
      Nos. 481-483 (3)   2.50 2.50

A101

A102

UN headquarters: 20c, Delegates in General Assembly. 60c, Security Council. 90c, Exterior.

1995, Oct. 24   *Perf. 14½x14*
484	A101	20c multicolored	.30	.30
485	A101	60c multicolored	.85	.85

Size: 27x44mm
486	A101	90c multicolored	1.25	1.25
		Nos. 484-486 (3)	2.40	2.40

UN, 50th anniv.

1995, Oct. 28   *Perf. 13x13½*

University of Brunei, 10th Anniv.: 30c, Students in classroom. 50c, Campus buildings. 90c, Sultan in procession.
487	A102	30c multicolored	.40	.40
488	A102	50c multicolored	.70	.70
489	A102	90c multicolored	1.25	1.25
		Nos. 487-489 (3)	2.35	2.35

A103

A104

Royal Brunei Police, 75th Anniv.: 25c, Policemen in various uniforms. 50c, Various tasks performed by police. 75c, Sultan reviewing police.

1996, Feb. 10   **Litho.**   *Perf. 13½x13*
490	A103	25c multicolored	.35	.35
491	A103	50c multicolored	.75	.75
492	A103	75c multicolored	1.10	1.10
		Nos. 490-492 (3)	2.20	2.20

1996, May 17   **Litho.**   *Perf. 13½*

World Telecommunications Day: 20c, Cartoon telephone, cordless telephone. 35c, Globe, telephone dial surrounded by communication devices. $1, Signals transmitting from earth, people communicating.
493	A104	20c multicolored	.30	.30
494	A104	35c multicolored	.50	.50
495	A104	$1 multicolored	1.40	1.40
		Nos. 493-495 (3)	2.20	2.20

A105

A106

Sultan: No. 496, Among people, in black attire. No. 497, Waving, in yellow attire. No. 498, In blue shirt. No. 499, Among people, wearing cream-colored robe. $1, Hand raised in yellow attire.

1996, July 15   **Litho.**   *Perf. 13*
496	A105	50c multicolored	.75	.75
497	A105	50c multicolored	.75	.75
498	A105	50c multicolored	.75	.75
499	A105	50c multicolored	.75	.75
		Nos. 496-499 (4)	3.00	3.00

Souvenir Sheet
500	A105	$1 multicolored	1.40	1.40

Sultan Paduka Seri Baginda, 50th birthday. A souvenir sheet of five $50 stamps exists.

1996, Nov. 11   **Litho.**   *Perf. 13½*

Terns.
501	A106	20c Black-naped tern	.30	.30
502	A106	30c Roseate tern	.45	.45
503	A106	$1 Bridle tern	1.40	1.40
		Nos. 501-503 (3)	2.15	2.15

No. 502 is spelled "Roslate" on stamp.

Sultan Hassanal Bolkiah
A107   A108

1996, Oct. 9   **Litho.**   *Perf. 14x13½*
Background Color
504	A107	10c yellow green	.20	.20
505	A107	15c pale pink	.20	.20
506	A107	20c lilac pink	.30	.30
507	A107	30c salmon	.45	.45
508	A107	50c yellow	.75	.75
509	A107	60c pale green	.85	.85
510	A107	75c blue	1.10	1.10
511	A107	90c lilac	1.25	1.25
512	A108	$1 pink	1.40	1.40
513	A108	$2 orange yellow	3.00	3.00
514	A108	$5 light blue	7.25	7.25
515	A108	$10 bright yellow	14.50	14.50
		Nos. 504-515 (12)	31.25	31.25

Flowers
A109

1997, May 29   **Litho.**   *Perf. 12*
516	A109	20c Acanthus ebracteatus	.30	.30
517	A109	30c Lumnitzera littorea	.45	.45
518	A109	$1 Nypa fruticans	1.40	1.40
		Nos. 516-518 (3)	2.15	2.15

Marine Life
A110

Designs: No. 519, Bohadschia argus. No. 520, Oxycomanthus bennetti. No. 521, Heterocentrotus mammillatus. No. 522, Linckia laevigata.

1997, Dec. 15   **Litho.**   *Perf. 12*
519	A110	60c multicolored	.85	.85
520	A110	60c multicolored	.85	.85
521	A110	60c multicolored	.85	.85
522	A110	60c multicolored	.85	.85
		Nos. 519-522 (4)	3.40	3.40

Asian and Pacific Decade of Disabled Persons (1993-2002) — A111

Designs: 20c, Silhouettes of people, hands finger spelling "Brunei," children. 50c, Fireworks over city, blind people participating in arts, crafts, music. $1, Handicapped people playing sports.

1998, Mar. 31   **Litho.**   *Perf. 13x13½*
523	A111	20c multicolored	.25	.25
524	A111	50c multicolored	.65	.65
525	A111	$1 multicolored	1.25	1.25
		Nos. 523-525 (3)	2.15	2.15

ASEAN, 30th Anniv. — A112

Designs: No. 526, Night scene of Sultan's Palace, buildings, map of Brunei. No. 527, Flags of ASEAN nations. No. 528, Daytime scenes of Sultan's Palace, transportation methods, buildings in Brunei.

1998, Aug. 8   **Litho.**   *Perf. 13½*
526	A112	30c multicolored	.40	.40
527	A112	30c multicolored	.40	.40
528	A112	30c multicolored	.40	.40
		Nos. 526-528 (3)	1.20	1.20

Sultan Hassanal Bolkiah, 30th Anniv. of Coronation — A113

Designs: 60c, In procession, saluting, on throne. 90c, Sultan Omar Ali Saifuddin standing, Sultan Hassanal Bolkiah on throne. $1, Procession.

1998, Aug. 1   **Litho.**   *Perf. 12*
529	A113	60c multicolored	.65	.65
530	A113	90c multicolored	1.10	1.10
531	A113	$1 multicolored	1.25	1.25
a.		Souvenir sheet, #529-531	3.00	3.00
		Nos. 529-531 (3)	3.00	3.00

A114   A115

Investiture of Crown Prince Al-Muhtadee Billah: $1, Signing document. $2, Formal portrait. $3, Arms of the Crown Prince.

1998, Aug. 10
532	A114	$1 multicolored	1.25	1.25
533	A114	$2 multicolored	2.50	2.50
534	A114	$3 multicolored	3.50	3.50
a.		Souvenir sheet, #532-534	7.25	7.25
		Nos. 532-534 (3)	7.25	7.25

1998, Sept. 29   *Perf. 13x13½*

30c, Hands clasped, woman, man. 60c, Dollar sign over book, arrows, "7.45AM." 90c, Silhouettes of people seated at table, standing, scales.
535	A115	30c multicolored	.35	.35
536	A115	60c multicolored	.70	.70
537	A115	90c multicolored	1.10	1.10
		Nos. 535-537 (3)	2.15	2.15

Civil Sevice Day, 5th anniv.

A116

A117

Kingfishers.

1998, Nov. 11   **Litho.**   *Perf. 13½x13*
538	A116	20c Blue-eared	.25	.25
539	A116	30c Common	.35	.35
540	A116	60c White-collared	.75	.75
541	A116	$1 Stork-billed	1.25	1.25
		Nos. 538-541 (4)	2.60	2.60

1999, Feb. 23   **Litho.**   *Perf. 13*

National Day, 15th Anniv.: 20c, Boat docks, residential area. 60c, Methods of communications. 90c, Buildings, roadways, tower, oil rig.
542	A117	20c multicolored	.25	.25
543	A117	60c multicolored	.75	.75
544	A117	90c multicolored	1.10	1.10
a.		Souvenir sheet, #542-544	2.25	2.25
		Nos. 542-544 (3)	2.10	2.10

20th Sea Games, 1999 — A119

No. 549: a, Field hockey, cycling. b, Basketball, soccer. c, Tennis, track and field. d, Billiards. e, Bowling.
No. 550: a, Shooting. b, Golf, squash. c, Boxing. d, Kick fighting, badminton, ping pong. e, Swimming, rowing.
$1, Shooting, tennis, running, soccer, cycling, basketball.

1999, Aug. 7   **Litho.**   *Perf. 14¼*
Strips of 5, #a.-e.
549-550	A119	20c each	2.40	2.40

Souvenir Sheet
551	A119	$1 multicolored	1.25	1.25

No. 551 contains one 35x35mm stamp.

UPU, 125th Anniv. — A120

20c, Handshake, globe, letters. 30c, Emblems of UPU, Brunei Post. 75c, Postal workers & services.

1999, Oct. 9   **Litho.**   *Perf. 14*
552	A120	20c multicolored	.25	.25
553	A120	30c multicolored	.35	.35
554	A120	75c multicolored	.90	.90
		Nos. 552-554 (3)	1.50	1.50

Millennium
A121

No. 555: a, Building with clock, children at computer. b, Building with red roof, man and woman at computer. c, Building with gray roof, mosque. d, Map of park. e, Airplane and ships. f, Satellite dishes.

Perf. 13¾x13½ Syncopated Type A
2000, Feb. 1   **Litho.**
555 A121 20c Strip of 6, #a-f   1.40 1.40
   g.   Souvenir sheet, #555   1.40 1.40

Flowers
A122

Designs: 30c, Rafflesia pricei. 50c, Rhizanthes lowi. 60c, Nepenthes rafflesiana.

2000, Oct. 2   **Litho.**   **Perf. 14¼x14**
556-558 A122   Set of 3   1.60 1.60

Asia-Pacific Economic Cooperation A123

Designs: 20c, Satellite dish, people at computers. 30c, Food processing enterprises. 60c, Eco-tourism (flower and bridge).

2000, Nov. 15   **Perf. 13½x13**
559 A123 20c multi   .20 .20
   a.   Booklet pane of 1   .20
560 A123 30c multi   .35 .35
   a.   Booklet pane of 1   .35
561 A123 60c multi   .70 .70
   a.   Booklet pane of 1   .70
     Booklet #559a-561a   1.25
   b.   Souvenir sheet, #559-561   1.25 1.25

The 20th Century — A124

No. 562 - Scenes from: a, 1901-20. b, 1921-40. c, 1941-60. d, 1961-80. e, 1981-99.

Perf. 13¾x13½ Syncopated Type A
2000, Feb. 23   **Litho.**
562   Strip of 5   1.75 1.75
   a.-e.   A124 30c Any single   .35 .35

Turtles
A125

No. 563: a, Green turtle. b, Hawksbill turtle. c, Olive Ridley turtle.

2000, Nov. 16   **Perf. 13¼x13**
563   Strip of 3   1.10 1.10
   a.-c.   A125 30c Any single   .35 .35

Sultans — A126

No. 564: a, Hashim Jalilul Alam. b, Muhammad Jamalul Alam II. c, Ahmed Tajudin. d, Haji Omar Ali Saifuddin. e, Haji Hassanal Bolkiah.

2000, July 15   **Litho.**   **Perf. 13¾**
564   Horiz. strip of 5   3.50 3.50
   a.-e.   A126 60c Any single   .70 .70
   f.   Souvenir sheet, #564, perf. 14¼x14   3.50 3.50
   g.   Booklet pane of 1, #564a   .70
   h.   Booklet pane of 1, #564b   .70
   i.   Booklet pane of 1, #564c   .70
   j.   Booklet pane of 1, #564d   .70
   k.   Booklet pane of 1, #564e   .70
     Booklet, #564g-564k   3.50

Visit Brunei Year — A127

Designs: 20c, People in boat. 30c, Houses on pilings. 60c, Shown.

2001, Mar. 14   **Perf. 14¼x13¾**
565-567 A127   Set of 3   1.25 1.25

Sultan Hassanal Bolkiah, 55th Birthday — A128

No. 568: a, Navy blue uniform. b, Light blue uniform. c, Robes. d, Camouflage uniform. e, White uniform.
No. 569, Casual shirt.

Perf. 12¼
2001, July 15   **Litho.**   **Unwmk.**
568   Horiz. strip of 5   3.25 3.25
   a.-e.   A128 55c Any single   .65 .65
Souvenir Sheet
Perf. 12
569 A128 55c multi   .65 .65
No. 569 contains one 40x70mm stamp.

International Youth Camp 2001 — A129

No. 570: a, Scout, administering first aid. b, Girls, tents. c, Scouts and leader.

2001, Aug. 5   **Wmk. 388**   **Perf. 12¼**
570   Horiz. strip of 3   1.00 1.00
   a.-c.   A129 30c Any single   .30 .30
   d.   Souvenir sheet, #570   1.00 1.00

First Intl. Islamic Expo A130

No. 571: a, Jewelry, cane. b, Mosque exterior. c, Computer, satellite dishes. d, Mosque interior.

2001, Aug. 18   **Wmk. 388**   **Perf. 12**
571   Horiz. strip of 4   1.00 1.00
   a.-d.   A130 20c Any single   .25 .25

Visit Brunei Year A131

No. 572: a, Bridge. b, Waterfall. c, Aerial view of city. d, Dock.

Perf. 13¼x13½
2001, Sept. 1   **Unwmk.**
572   Horiz. strip of 4   1.00 1.00
   a.-d.   A131 20c Any single   .25 .25

Year of Dialogue Among Civilizations A132

No. 573: a, Emblem. b, Two abstract heads. c, Cubist-style head, native. d, Multicolored leaves.

2001, Oct. 9   **Unwmk.**   **Perf. 12**
573   Horiz. strip of 4   1.25 1.25
   a.-d.   A132 30c Any single   .30 .30

Worldwide Fund for Nature (WWF) — A133

No. 574 - Bulwer's pheasant: a, Male and female. b, Male. c, Female and chicks. d, Female.

2001, Nov. 1   **Wmk. 388**   **Perf. 12**
574   Horiz. strip of 4   1.25 1.25
   a.-d.   A133 30c Any single   .30 .30

OCCUPATION STAMPS

Issued under Japanese Occupation
Stamps and Types of 1908-37 Handstamped in Violet, Red Violet, Blue or Red

Perf. 14, 14x11½ (#N7)
1942-44   **Wmk. 4**

N1	A1	1c black	6.50	24.00
N2	A1	2c green	57.50	110.00
N3	A1	2c dull orange	3.00	8.00
N4	A1	3c green	30.00	75.00
N5	A1	4c orange	4.00	14.00
N6	A1	5c brown	4.00	14.00
N7	A2	6c slate gray	60.00	200.00
N8	A2	6c red	575.00	575.00
N9	A1	8c gray (RV)	700.00	850.00
N10	A2	8c carmine	5.00	12.00
N11	A1	10c violet, *yel*	11.00	26.00
N12	A2	12c blue	24.00	26.00
N13	A2	15c ultra	13.00	26.00
N14	A1	25c dk violet	24.00	65.00
N15	A1	30c org & red vio	100.00	190.00
N16	A1	50c blk, *green*	45.00	80.00
N17	A1	$1 red & blk, *bl*	60.00	100.00

Wmk. 3

N18	A1	$5 lake, *green*	900.00	1,750.
N19	A1	$25 black, *red*	1,000.	1,750.

Overprints vary in shade. Nos. N3, N7, N10 and N13 without overprint are not believed to have been regularly issued.

No. 43 Surcharged in Red

1944   **Wmk. 4**   **Perf. 14**
N20 A1 $3 on 1c black   6,000. 5,500.
   a.   On No. N1   3,250. 3,250.

BULGARIA
ˌbəl-'gar-ē-ə

LOCATION — Southeastern Europe bordering on the Black Sea on the east and the Danube River on the north
GOVT. — Republic
AREA — 42,855 sq. mi.
POP. — 8,194,772 (1999 est.)
CAPITAL — Sofia

In 1885 Bulgaria, then a principality under the suzerainty of the Sultan of Turkey, was joined by Eastern Rumelia. Independence from Turkey was obtained in 1908.

100 Centimes = 1 Franc
100 Stotinki = 1 Lev (1881)

Catalogue values for unused stamps in this country are for Never Hinged items, beginning with Scott 293 in the regular postage section, Scott B1 in the semipostal section, Scott C15 in the airpost section, Scott CB1 in the airpost semi-postal section, Scott E1 in the special delivery section, Scott J47 in the postage due section, Scott O1 in the officials section, and Scott Q1 in the parcel post section.

Watermarks

Wmk. 145- Wavy Lines

Wmk. 168- Wavy Lines and EZGV in Cyrillic

Wmk. 275- Entwined Curved Lines

Lion of Bulgaria
A1   A2   A3

Perf. 14½x15
1879, May 1   Wmk. 168   Typo.
Laid Paper

1	A1	5c black & orange	65.00	18.00
2	A1	10c black & green	325.00	60.00
3	A1	25c black & violet	175.00	15.00
a.		Imperf.		
4	A1	50c black & blue	325.00	50.00
5	A2	1fr black & red	50.00	17.50

1881, Apr. 10

6	A3	3s red & silver	12.50	2.50
7	A3	5s black & orange	15.00	2.50
a.		Background inverted		1,750.
8	A3	10s black & green	65.00	6.50
9	A3	15s dp car red & green	60.00	6.50
10	A3	25s black & violet	325.00	30.00
11	A3	30s blue & fawn	17.50	6.50

1882, Dec. 4

12	A3	3s orange & yellow	1.00	.50
a.		Background inverted	2,750.	1,400.
13	A3	5s green & pale green	6.00	.50
a.		5s rose & pale rose (error)	1,600.	1,300.
14	A3	10s rose & pale rose	8.00	.75
15	A3	15s red vio & pale lil	6.00	.40
16	A3	25s blue & pale blue	6.00	.50
17	A3	30s violet & green	6.00	.75
18	A3	50s blue & pink	6.00	.75
		Nos. 12-18 (7)	39.00	4.15

See Nos. 207-210, 286.

A4   A5

Surcharged in Black, Carmine or Vermilion

1884, May 1
Typo. Surcharge

19	A4	3s on 10s rose (Bk)	95.00	30.00
20	A4	5s on 30s blue & fawn (C)	95.00	45.00
20A	A4	5s on 30s bl & fawn (Bk)	1,750.	1,750.
21	A5	15s on 25s blue (C)	140.00	40.00

On some values the surcharge may be found inverted or double.

1885, Apr. 5
Litho. Surcharge

21B	A4	3s on 10s rose (Bk)	45.00	27.50
21C	A4	5s on 30s bl & fawn (V)	50.00	35.00
21D	A5	15s on 25s blue (V)	70.00	45.00
22	A5	50s on 1fr blk & red (Bk)	190.00	125.00

Forgeries of Nos. 19-22 are plentiful.

Word below left star in oval has 5 letters
A6

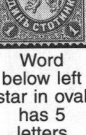

Third letter below left star is "A"
A7

1885, May 25

23	A6	1s gray vio & pale gray	12.00	5.00
24	A7	2s sl grn & pale gray	12.00	4.00

Word below left star has 4 letters
A8

Third letter below left star is "b" with cross-bar in upper half
A9

A10

1886-87

25	A8	1s gray vio & pale gray	1.00	.20
26	A9	2s sl grn & pale gray	1.00	.20
27	A10	1 l black & red ('87)	27.50	3.00
		Nos. 25-27 (3)	29.50	3.40

For surcharge see No. 40.

A11

Perf. 10½, 11, 11½, 13, 13½
1889   Wove Paper   Unwmk.

28	A11	1s lilac	.20	.20
29	A11	2s gray	.60	.20
30	A11	3s bister brown	.40	.20
31	A11	5s yellow green	.25	.20
a.		Vert. pair, imperf. btwn.		
32	A11	10s rose	1.10	.20
33	A11	15s orange	.60	.20
34	A11	25s blue	1.00	.20
35	A11	30s dk brown	9.00	.20
36	A11	50s green	.60	.30
37	A11	1 l orange red	.50	.40
		Nos. 28-37 (10)	14.25	2.30

The 10s orange is a proof.
Nos. 28-34 exist imperforate. Value, set $225.
See Nos. 39, 41-42. For overprints and surcharges see Nos. 38, 55-56, 77-81, 113.

No. 35 Surcharged in Black

1892, Jan. 26

38	A11	15s on 30s brn	10.00	1.00
a.		Inverted surcharge	70.00	52.50

1894   Perf. 10½, 11, 11½
Pelure Paper

39	A11	10s red	7.00	.50
a.		Imperf.	57.50	

No. 26 Surcharged in Red

Wmk. Wavy Lines (168)
1895, Oct. 25   Perf. 14½x15
Laid Paper

40	A9	1s on 2s	.75	.20
a.		Inverted surcharge	6.00	5.00
b.		Double surcharge	62.50	62.50
c.		Pair, one without surcharge	125.00	125.00

This surcharge on No. 24 is a proof.

Wmk. Coat of Arms in the Sheet
1896, Apr. 30   Perf. 11½, 13
Wove Paper

41	A11	2 l rose & pale rose	2.00	1.50
42	A11	3 l black & buff	3.50	3.00

Coat of Arms
A14

Cherry Wood Cannon
A15

1896, Feb. 2   Perf. 13

43	A14	1s blue green	.30	.20
44	A14	5s dark blue	.30	.20
45	A14	15s purple	.50	.20
46	A14	25s red	4.75	.85
		Nos. 43-46 (4)	5.85	1.45

Baptism of Prince Boris.
Examples of Nos. 41-46 from sheet edges show no watermark.
Nos. 43, 45-46 were also printed on rough unwatermarked paper.

1901, Apr. 20   Litho.   Unwmk.

53	A15	5s carmine	1.25	.90
54	A15	15s yellow green	1.25	.90

Insurrection of Independence in April, 1876, 25th anniversary.
Exist imperf. Forgeries exist.

Nos. 30 and 36 Surcharged in Black

1901, Mar. 24   Typo.

55	A11	5s on 3s bister brn	1.75	.75
a.		Inverted surcharge	42.50	42.50
b.		Pair, one without surcharge	70.00	70.00
56	A11	10s on 50s green	2.25	.75
a.		Inverted surcharge	50.00	50.00
b.		Pair, one without surcharge	70.00	70.00

Tsar Ferdinand
A17

Fighting at Shipka Pass
A18

ONE LEV:
Type I - The numerals in the upper corners have, at the top, a sloping serif on the left side and a short straight serif on the right.
Type II - The numerals in the upper corners are of ordinary shape without the serif at the right.

1901, Oct. 1-05   Typo.   Perf. 12½

57	A17	1s vio & gray blk	.20	.20
58	A17	2s brnz grn & ind	.20	.20
a.		Imperf.		
59	A17	3s orange & ind	.20	.20
60	A17	5s emerald & brn	2.25	.20
61	A17	10s rose & blk	1.50	.20
62	A17	15s claret & gray blk	.65	.20
63	A17	25s blue & blk	.65	.20
64	A17	30s bis & gray blk	15.00	.20
65	A17	50s dk blue & brn	.80	.20
66	A17	1 l red org & brnz grn, type I	45.00	4.75
67	A17	1 l brn red & brnz grn, II ('05)	2.00	1.25
68	A17	2 l carmine & blk	4.00	.85
69	A17	2 l slate & red brn	5.00	1.90
		Nos. 57-69 (13)	77.45	10.55

For surcharges see Nos. 73, 83-85, 87-88.

1902, Aug. 29   Litho.   Perf. 11½

70	A18	5s lake	1.00	.35
71	A18	10s blue green	1.00	.35
72	A18	15s blue	5.25	1.60
		Nos. 70-72 (3)	7.25	2.30

Battle of Shipka Pass, 1877.
Imperf. copies are proofs.
Excellent forgeries of Nos. 70 to 72 exist.

No. 62 Surcharged in Black

1903, Oct. 1   Perf. 12½

73	A17	10s on 15s	5.00	.35
a.		Inverted surcharge	57.50	50.00
b.		Double surcharge	57.50	50.00
c.		Pair, one without surcharge	100.00	100.00
d.		10s on 10s rose & black	275.00	275.00

Ferdinand in 1887 and 1907 A19

1907, Aug. 12   Litho.   Perf. 11½
74	A19	5s deep green	6.50	.90
75	A19	10s red brown	11.50	.90
76	A19	25s deep blue	17.00	1.75
		Nos. 74-76 (3)	35.00	3.55

Accession to the throne of Ferdinand I, 20th anniversary.
Nos. 74-76 imperf. are proofs. Nos. 74-76 exist in pairs imperforate between.

Stamps of 1889 Overprinted

1909
77	A11	1s lilac	1.00	.50
a.		Inverted overprint	21.00	17.50
b.		Double overprint, one inverted	24.00	24.00
78	A11	5s yellow green	1.00	.50
a.		Inverted overprint	25.00	25.00
b.		Double overprint	25.00	25.00

With Additional Surcharge

1909
79	A11	5s on 30s brown (Bk)	1.50	.20
a.		"5" double	700.00	550.00
b.		"1990" for "1909"		
80	A11	10s on 15s org (Bk)	1.50	.40
a.		Inverted surcharge	17.50	17.50
b.		"1909" omitted	27.50	27.50
81	A11	10s on 50s dk grn (R)	1.50	.40
a.		"1990" for "1909"	100.00	100.00
b.		Black surcharge	52.50	52.50

Nos. 62 & 64
Surcharged with Value Only
83	A17	5s on 15s (Bl)	1.75	.60
a.		Inverted surcharge	21.00	21.00
84	A17	10s on 15s (Bl)	4.50	.40
a.		Inverted surcharge	21.00	21.00
85	A17	25s on 30s (R)	5.75	.90
a.		Double surcharge	70.00	70.00
b.		"2" of "25" omitted	87.50	87.50
c.		Blue surcharge	275.00	175.00

Nos. 59 and 62
Surcharged in Blue

1910, Oct.
87	A17	1s on 3s	3.50	.75
a.		"1910" omitted	21.00	
88	A17	5s on 15s	1.50	.50

Tsar Assen's Tower (Crown over lion) A20

Tsar Ferdinand A21

City of Trnovo A22

Tsar Ferdinand A23

Ferdinand A24

Isker River A25

Ferdinand A26

Rila Monastery (Crown at UR) A27

Tsar and Princes — A28

Ferdinand in Robes of Ancient Tsars — A29

Monastery of Holy Trinity — A30

View of Varna — A31

1911, Feb. 14   Engr.   Perf. 12
89	A20	1s myrtle green	.20	.20
90	A21	2s car & blk	.20	.20
91	A22	3s lake & blk	.40	.20
92	A23	5s green & blk	1.00	.20
93	A24	10s dp red & blk	1.40	.20
94	A25	15s brown bister	2.50	.20
95	A26	25s ultra & blk	.50	.20
96	A27	30s blue & blk	6.75	.20
97	A28	50s ocher & blk	16.00	.25
a.		Center inverted		2,250.
98	A29	1 l chocolate	6.00	1.25
99	A30	2 l dull pur & blk	1.60	1.90
100	A31	3 l blue vio & blk	6.75	3.00
		Nos. 89-100 (12)	43.30	8.00

See Nos. 114-120, 161-162. For overprints and surcharges see Nos. 104-112, 188, B8, Greece N167-N178, N182-N187, Thrace 16-21, Romania 2N1-2N4.

Tsar Ferdinand — A32

1912, Aug. 2   Typo.   Perf. 12½
101	A32	5s olive green	2.25	.70
a.		5s pale green	275.00	125.00

102	A32	10s claret	3.50	1.50
103	A32	25s slate	5.25	1.75
		Nos. 101-103 (3)	11.00	3.95

25th year of reign of Tsar Ferdinand.

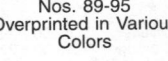

Nos. 89-95 Overprinted in Various Colors

1913, Aug. 6   Engr.
104	A20	1s myrtle grn (C)	.20	.20
105	A21	2s car & blk (Bl)	.20	.20
107	A22	3s lake & blk (Bl Bk)	.20	.20
108	A23	5s grn & blk (R)	.20	.20
109	A24	10s dp red & blk (Bk)	.30	.20
110	A25	15s brown bis (G)	.55	.25
111	A26	25s ultra & blk (R)	2.75	.40
		Nos. 104-111 (7)	4.40	1.65

Victory over the Turks in Balkan War of 1912-1913.

No. 95 Surcharged in Red

1915, July 6
112	A26	10s on 25s	.50	.20

No. 28 Surcharged in Green

113	A11	3s on 1s lilac	3.50	4.50

Types of 1911 Re-engraved
1915, Nov. 7   Perf. 11½, 14
114	A20	1s dk bl grn	.20	.20
115	A21	5s grn & brn vio	1.40	.20
116	A24	10s red brn & brnsh blk	.25	.20
117	A25	15s olive green	.25	.20
118	A26	25s indigo & blk	.25	.20
119	A27	30s ol grn & red brn	.25	.20
120	A29	1 l dark brown	.30	.30
		Nos. 114-120 (7)	2.90	1.50

Widths: No. 114 is 19½mm; No. 89, 18½mm. No. 118 is 19¼mm; No. 95, 18¼mm. No. 120 is 20mm; No. 98, 19mm. The re-engraved stamps also differ from the 1911 issue in many details of design. Nos. 114-120 exist imperforate.
The 5s and 10s exist perf. 14x11½.
For Nos. 114-116 and 118 overprinted with Cyrillic characters and "1916-1917," see Romania Nos. 2N1-2N4.

Coat of Arms — A33

Peasant and Bullock — A34

Soldier and Mt. Sonichka — A35

View of Nish — A36

Town and Lake Okhrida - A37

Demir-Kapiya (Iron Gate) — A37a

View of Gevgeli — A38

Perf. 11½, 12½x13, 13x12½
1917-19   Typo.
122	A33	5s green	.30	.20
123	A34	15s slate	.20	.20
124	A35	25s blue	.20	.20
125	A36	30s orange	.20	.20
126	A37	50s violet	.50	.30
126A	A37a	2 l brn org ('19)	.50	.35
127	A38	3 l claret	1.75	1.75
		Nos. 122-127 (7)	3.65	3.20

Liberation of Macedonia. A 1 l dark green was prepared but not issued. Value $1.65.
For surcharges see Nos. B9-B10, B12.

View of Veles — A39

Monastery of St. Clement at Okhrida — A40

1918   Perf. 13x14
128	A39	1s gray	.20	.20
129	A40	5s green	.20	.20

Tsar Ferdinand A41

Plowing with Oxen A42

1918, July 1   Perf. 12½x13
130	A41	1s dark green	.20	.20
131	A41	2s dark brown	.20	.20
132	A41	3s indigo	.30	.20
133	A41	10s brown red	.30	.20
		Nos. 130-133 (4)	1.00	.80

Ferdinand's accession to the throne, 30th anniv.

1919   Perf. 13½x13
134	A42	1s gray	.20	.20

Sobranye Palace — A43

Tsar Boris III — A44

1919   Perf. 11½x12, 12x11½
135	A43	1s black	.20	.20
137	A43	2s olive green	.20	.20

For surcharges see Nos. 186, B1.

1919, Oct. 3

138	A44	3s orange brn	.20	.20
139	A44	5s green	.20	.20
140	A44	10s rose red	.20	.20
141	A44	15s violet	.20	.20
142	A44	25s deep blue	.20	.20
143	A44	30s chocolate	.20	.20
144	A44	50s yellow brn	.20	.20
		Nos. 138-144 (7)	1.40	1.40

1st anniv. of enthronement of Tsar Boris III.
Nos. 135-144 exist imperforate.
For surcharges see Nos. 187, B2-B7.

Birthplace of Vazov at Sopot and Cherrywood Cannon — A47

"The Bear Fighter"-a Character from "Under the Yoke" — A48

Ivan Vazov in 1870 and 1920 — A49

Vazov — A50

The Monk Paisii — A52

Homes of Vazov at Plovdiv and Sofia A51

1920, Oct. 20   Photo.   Perf. 11½

147	A47	30s brown red	.20	.20
148	A48	50s dark green	.20	.20
149	A49	1 l drab	.25	.30
150	A50	2 l light brown	.60	.60
151	A51	3 l black violet	.95	.65
152	A52	5 l deep blue	1.10	.80
		Nos. 147-152 (6)	3.30	2.75

70th birthday of Ivan Vazov (1850-1921), Bulgarian poet and novelist.
Several values of this series exist imperforate and in pairs imperforate between.

Tsar Ferdinand
A53   A54

Mt. Shar — A55

Bridge over Vardar River — A56

View of Ohrid — A57

Perf. 13x14, 14x13

1921, June 11   Typo.

153	A53	10s claret	.20	.20
154	A54	10s claret	.20	.20
155	A55	10s claret	.20	.20
156	A56	10s rose lilac	.20	.20
157	A57	20s blue	.20	.20
		Nos. 153-157 (5)	1.10	1.00

Nos. 153-157 were intended to be issued in 1915 to commemorate the liberation of Macedonia. They were not put in use until 1921. A 50s violet was prepared but never placed in use. Value $1.75.

View of Sofia — A58

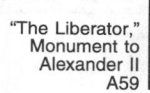

"The Liberator," Monument to Alexander II A59

Monastery at Shipka Pass — A62

Tsar Boris III — A63

Harvesting Grain — A64

Tsar Assen's Tower (No crown over lion) — A65

Rila Monastery (Rosette at upper right) — A66

1921-23   Engr.   Perf. 12

158	A58	10s blue gray	.20	.20
159	A59	20s deep green	.20	.20
160	A63	25s blue grn ('22)	.20	.20
161	A22	50s orange	.20	.20
162	A22	50s dk blue ('23)	2.50	2.50
163	A62	75s dull vio	.20	.20
164	A62	75s dp blue ('23)	.30	.20
165	A63	1 l carmine	.30	.20
166	A63	1 l dp blue ('22)	.30	.20
167	A64	1 l brown	.30	.10
168	A65	3 l brown vio	1.40	1.10
169	A68	5 l lt blue	2.50	1.25
170	A63	10 l violet brn	6.75	2.10
		Nos. 158-170 (13)	15.35	9.55

For surcharge see No. 189.

Bourchier in Bulgarian Costume A67

James David Bourchier A68

View of Rila Monastery A69

1921, Dec. 31

171	A67	10s red orange	.20	.20
172	A67	20s orange	.20	.20
173	A68	30s dp gray	.20	.20
174	A68	50s bluish gray	.20	.20
175	A68	1 l dull vio	.20	.20
176	A69	1½ l olive grn	.20	.20
177	A69	2 l deep green	.20	.20
178	A69	3 l Prus blue	.45	.20
179	A69	5 l red brown	.85	.35
		Nos. 171-179 (9)	2.70	1.95

Death of James D. Bourchier, Balkan correspondent of the London Times.
For surcharges see Nos. B13-B16.

Postage Due Stamps of 1919-22 Surcharged

a

1924

182	D6	10s on 20s yellow	.20	.20
183	D6	20s on 5s gray grn	.20	.20
a.		20s on 5s emerald	7.00	7.00
184	D6	20s on 10s violet	.20	.20
185	D6	20s on 30s blue	.20	.20
		Nos. 182-185 (4)	.80	.80

Nos. 182 to 185 were used for ordinary postage.

Regular Issues of 1919-23 Surcharged in Blue or Red:

1 ЛЕВЪ

b   c

186	A43 (a)	10s on 1s black (R)	.20	.20
187	A44 (b)	1 l on 5s emer (Bl)	.20	.20
188	A22 (c)	3 l on 50s dk bl (R)	.20	.20
189	A63 (b)	6 l on 1 l car (Bl)	.60	.20
		Nos. 186-189 (4)	1.20	.80

The surcharge of No. 188 comes in three types: normal, thick and thin.
#182, 184-189 exist with inverted surcharge.

A70

Lion of Bulgaria — A71

Tsar Boris III — A72

New Sofia Cathedral — A73

Harvesting A74

1925   Typo.   Perf. 13, 11½

191	A70	10s red & bl, pink	.20	.20
192	A70	15s car & org, blue	.20	.20
193	A70	30s blk & buff	.20	.20
a.		Cliche of 15s in plate of 30s		
194	A71	50s choc, green	.20	.20
195	A72	1 l dull green	.50	
196	A73	2 l dk grn & buff	1.10	.20
197	A74	4 l lake & yellow	1.10	.20
		Nos. 191-197 (7)	3.50	1.40

Several values of this series exist imperforate and in pairs imperforate between.
See #199, 201. For overprint see #C2.

Cathedral of Sveta Nedelya, Sofia, Ruined by Bomb — A75

1926   Perf. 11½

198	A75	50s gray black	.20	.20

A76   A77

Type A72 Re-engraved. (Shoulder at left does not touch frame)

1926

199	A76	1 l gray	.45	.20
a.		1 l green	.45	.20
201	A76	2 l olive brown	.50	.20

Center Embossed

202	A77	6 l dp bl & pale lemon	1.10	.20
203	A77	10 l brn blk & brn org	4.00	.75
		Nos. 199-203 (3)	6.05	1.35

For overprints see Nos. C1, C3-C4.

Christo Botev — A78

Tsar Boris III — A79

1926, June 2

204	A78	1 l olive green	.30	.20
205	A78	2 l slate violet	.90	.20
206	A78	4 l red brown	.90	.35
		Nos. 204-206 (3)	2.10	.75

Botev (1847-76), Bulgarian revolutionary, poet.

Lion Type of 1881

1927-29   *Perf. 13*
207 A3   10s dk red & drab   .20 .20
208 A3   15s blk & org ('29)   .20 .20
209 A3   30s dk bl & bis brn ('28)   .20 .20
   a.   30s indigo & buff
210 A3   50s blk & rose red ('28)   .20 .20
     Nos. 207-210 (4)   .80 .80

1928, Oct. 3   *Perf. 11½*
211 A79   1 l olive green   .90 .20
212 A79   2 l deep brown   1.00 .20

St. Clement
A80

Konstantin
Miladinov
A81

George S.
Rakovski
A82

Drenovo
Monastery
A83

Paisii — A84

Tsar
Simeon — A85

Lyuben
Karavelov
A86

Vassil Levski
A87

Georgi
Benkovski
A88

Tsar Alexander II
A89

1929, May 12
213 A80   10s dk violet   .20 .20
214 A81   15s violet brn   .40 .40
215 A82   30s red   .20 .20
216 A83   50s olive grn   .25 .20
217 A84   1 l orange brn   .60 .20
218 A85   2 l dk blue   .70 .20
219 A86   3 l dull green   1.50 .45
220 A87   4 l olive brown   2.50 .25
221 A88   5 l brown   1.50 .35
222 A89   6 l Prus green   2.25 .90
     Nos. 213-222 (10)   10.10 3.35

Millenary of Tsar Simeon and 50th anniv. of the liberation of Bulgaria from the Turks.

Royal Wedding Issue

Tsar Boris
and Fiancee,
Princess
Giovanna
A90

Queen Ioanna and Tsar Boris — A91

1930, Nov. 12   *Perf. 11½*
223 A90   1 l green   .25 .25
224 A91   2 l dull violet   .25 .30
225 A90   4 l rose red   .25 .30
226 A91   6 l dark blue   .25 .40
     Nos. 223-226 (4)   1.00 1.25

Fifty-five copies of a miniature sheet incorporating one each of Nos. 223-226 were printed and given to royal, governmental and diplomatic personages.

Tsar Boris III
A92   A93
Perf. 11½, 12x11½, 13

1931-37   **Unwmk.**
227 A92   1 l blue green   .25 .20
228 A92   2 l carmine   .40 .20
229 A92   4 l red org ('34)   .75 .20
230 A92   4 l yel org ('37)   .20 .20
231 A92   6 l deep blue   .70 .20
232 A92   7 l dp bl ('37)   .20 .20
233 A92   10 l slate blk   8.75 .70
234 A92   12 l lt brown   .40 .20
235 A92   14 l lt brn ('37)   .30 .25
236 A93   20 l claret & org brn   1.00 .45
     Nos. 227-236 (10)   12.95 2.80

Nos. 230-233 and 235 have outer bars at top and bottom as shown on cut A92; Nos. 227-229 and 234 are without outer bars.
See Nos. 251, 279-280, 287. For surcharge see No. 252.

Balkan Games Issues

Gymnast
A95

Soccer — A96

Riding — A97

Swimmer
A100

"Victory"
A101

Designs: 6 l, Fencing. 10 l, Bicycle race.

1931, Sept. 18   *Perf. 11½*
237 A95   1 l lt green   1.75 .50
238 A95   2 l garnet   1.75 .50
239 A97   4 l carmine   4.00 .75
240 A95   6 l Prus blue   7.50 1.25

241 A95   10 l red org   20.00 3.75
242 A100   12 l dk blue   65.00 7.50
243 A101   50 l olive brn   60.00 22.50
     Nos. 237-243 (7)   160.00 36.75

1933, Jan. 5
244 A95   1 l blue grn   1.25 .95
245 A96   2 l blue   2.00 .95
246 A97   4 l brn vio   2.75 1.10
247 A95   6 l brt rose   5.00 1.60
248 A95   10 l olive brn   40.00 9.00
249 A100   12 l orange   65.00 18.00
250 A101   50 l red brown   175.00 82.50
     Nos. 244-250 (7)   291.00 114.10

Nos. 244-250 were sold only at the philatelic agency.

Boris Type of 1931
Outer Bars at Top and Bottom Removed

1933   *Perf. 13*
251 A92   6 l deep blue   .80 .20

Type of 1931 Surcharged in Blue **2**

1934
252 A92   2 (l) on 3 l ol brn   4.00 .25

Soldier
Defending
Shipka Pass
A102

Shipka Battle
Memorial
A103

Color-Bearer
A104

Veteran of the
War of
Liberation,
1878 — A105

Widow and
Orphans — A106

Perf. 10½, 11½

1934, Aug. 26   **Wmk. 145**
253 A102   1 l green   .45 .40
254 A103   2 l pale red   .45 .25
255 A104   3 l bister brn   1.50 1.25
256 A105   4 l dk carmine   1.25 .60
257 A104   7 l dk blue   2.25 2.00
258 A106   14 l plum   6.00 5.75
     Nos. 253-258 (6)   11.90 10.25

Shipka Pass Battle memorial unveiling.
An unwatermarked miniature sheet incorporating one each of Nos. 253-258 was put on sale in 1938 in five cities at a price of 8,000 leva. Printing: 100 sheets.

1934, Sept. 21
259 A102   1 l bright green   .45 .40
260 A103   2 l dull orange   .45 .25
261 A104   3 l yellow   1.40 1.25
262 A105   4 l rose   1.25 .60
263 A104   7 l blue   2.25 2.00
264 A106   14 l olive bister   6.00 5.75
     Nos. 259-264 (6)   11.80 10.25

An unwatermarked miniature sheet incorporating one each of Nos. 259-263 was issued.

Velcho A.
Djamjiyata
A108

Capt. G. S.
Mamarchev
A109

1935, May 5   *Perf. 11½*
265 A108   1 l deep blue   .95 .25
266 A109   2 l maroon   .95 .30

Bulgarian uprising against the Turks, cent.

Soccer Game
A110

Cathedral of
Alexander
Nevski
A111

Soccer Team
A112

Symbolical of
Victory
A113

Player and
Trophy
A114

The Trophy
A115

1935, June 14
267 A110   1 l green   2.25 .90
268 A111   2 l blue gray   3.50 1.40
269 A112   4 l crimson   4.50 2.00
270 A113   7 l brt blue   11.00 2.50
271 A114   14 l orange   11.00 3.50
272 A115   50 l lilac brn   95.00 52.50
     Nos. 267-272 (6)   127.25 62.55

5th Balkan Soccer Tournament.

Gymnast on
Parallel Bars
A116

Youth in
"Yunak"
Costume
A117

Girl in "Yunak"
Costume
A118

Pole Vaulting
A119

Stadium, Sofia
A120

Yunak Emblem
A121

1935, July 10

273	A116	1 l	green	2.00	1.10
274	A117	2 l	lt blue	2.75	1.10
275	A118	4 l	carmine	5.50	2.25
276	A119	7 l	dk blue	5.50	3.00
277	A120	14 l	dk brown	5.50	3.00
278	A121	50 l	red	65.00	42.50
	Nos. 273-278 (6)			86.25	52.95

8th tournament of the Yunak Gymnastic Organization at Sofia, July 12-14.

Boris Type of 1931

1935   Wmk. 145   Perf. 12½, 13

279	A92	1 l	green	.30	.20
280	A92	2 l	carmine	20.00	.20

Janos Hunyadi
A122

King Ladislas Varnenchik
A123

Varna Memorial
A124

King Ladislas III — A125

Battle of Varna, 1444 — A126

1935, Aug. 4   Perf. 10½, 11½

281	A122	1 l	brown org	1.10	.75
282	A123	2 l	maroon	1.10	.75
283	A124	4 l	vermilion	5.50	3.75
284	A125	7 l	dull blue	2.50	1.25
285	A126	14 l	green	2.50	1.25
	Nos. 281-285 (5)			12.70	7.75

Battle of Varna, and the death of the Polish King, Ladislas Varnenchik (1424-44).

Lion Type of 1881

1935   Wmk. 145   Perf. 13

286	A3	10s	dk red & drab	.70	.20

Boris Type of 1933
Outer Bars at Top and Bottom Removed

1935

287	A92	6 l	gray blue	.60	.20

Dimitr Monument
A127

Haji Dimitr — A128

Haji Dimitr and Stefan Karaja
A129

Taking the Oath — A130

Birthplace of Dimitr
A131

1935, Oct. 1   Unwmk.   Perf. 11½

288	A127	1 l	green	1.25	.35
289	A128	2 l	brown	1.75	.70
290	A129	4 l	car rose	3.50	2.50
291	A130	7 l	blue	4.50	3.50
292	A131	14 l	orange	4.50	3.50
	Nos. 288-292 (5)			15.50	10.55

67th anniv. of the death of the Bulgarian patriots, Haji Dimitr and Stefan Karaja.

> **Catalogue values for unused stamps in this section, from this point to the end of the section, are for Never Hinged items.**

A132

A133

1936-39   Perf. 13x12½, 13

293	A132	10s	red org ('37)	.20	.20
294	A132	15s	emerald	.20	.20
295	A133	30s	maroon	.20	.20
296	A133	30s	yel brn ('37)	.20	.20
297	A133	30s	Prus bl ('37)	.20	.20
298	A133	50s	ultra	.20	.20
299	A133	50s	dk car ('37)	.20	.20
300	A133	50s	slate grn ('39)	.20	.20
	Nos. 293-300 (8)			1.60	1.60

Meteorological Station, Mt. Moussalla
A134

Peasant Girl
A135

Town of Nessebr
A136

1936, Aug. 16   Photo.   Perf. 11½

301	A134	1 l	purple	1.40	.65
302	A135	2 l	ultra	1.40	.60
303	A136	7 l	dark blue	3.75	1.50
	Nos. 301-303 (3)			6.55	2.75

4th Geographical & Ethnographical Cong., Sofia, Aug. 1936.

Sts. Cyril and Methodius
A137

Displaying the Bible to the People
A138

1937, June 2

304	A137	1 l	dk green	.25	.20
305	A137	2 l	dk plum	.25	.20
306	A138	4 l	vermilion	.45	.25
307	A137	7 l	dk blue	1.75	1.10
308	A138	14 l	rose red	1.75	1.10
	Nos. 304-308 (5)			4.45	2.85

Millennium of Cyrillic alphabet.

Princess Marie Louise
A139

Tsar Boris III
A140

1937, Oct. 3

310	A139	1 l	yellow green	.35	.20
311	A139	2 l	brown red	.25	.20
312	A139	4 l	scarlet	.35	.20
	Nos. 310-312 (3)			.95	.60

Issued in honor of Princess Marie Louise.

1937, Oct. 3

313	A140	2 l	brown red	.35	.20

19th anniv. of the accession of Tsar Boris III to the throne. See No. B11.

National Products Issue

Peasants Bundling Wheat
A141

Sunflower
A142

Wheat — A143

Chickens and Eggs — A144

Cluster of Grapes — A145

Rose and Perfume Flask — A146

Strawberries
A147

Girl Carrying Grape Clusters
A148

Rose — A149

Tobacco Leaves — A150

1938   Perf. 13

316	A141	10s	orange	.20	.20
317	A141	10s	red org	.20	.20
318	A142	15s	brt rose	.30	.20
319	A142	15s	deep plum	.20	.20
320	A143	30s	golden brn	.20	.20
321	A143	30s	copper brn	.20	.20
322	A144	50s	black	.20	.20
323	A144	50s	indigo	.20	.20
324	A145	1 l	yel grn	.65	.20
325	A145	1 l	green	.65	.20
326	A146	2 l	rose pink	.60	.20
327	A146	2 l	rose brn	.60	.20
328	A147	3 l	dp red lil	1.25	.20
329	A147	3 l	brn lake	1.25	.20
330	A148	4 l	plum	.80	.20
331	A148	4 l	golden brn	.80	.20
332	A149	7 l	vio blue	1.50	1.50
333	A149	7 l	dp blue	1.50	1.50
334	A150	14 l	dk brown	2.25	1.90
335	A150	14 l	red brn	2.25	1.90
	Nos. 316-335 (20)			15.90	10.00

Several values of this series exist imperforate.

Crown Prince Simeon
A151   A153

Designs: 2 l, Same portrait as 1 l, value at lower left. 14 l, similar to 4 l, but no wreath.

1938, June 16

336	A151	1 l	brt green	.20	.20
337	A151	2 l	rose pink	.20	.20
338	A153	4 l	dp orange	.20	.20

339	A151	7 l	ultra	.80	.40
340	A153	14 l	dp brown	.80	.40
			Nos. 336-340 (5)	2.20	1.40

First birthday of Prince Simeon.

Tsar Boris III
A155   A156

Various Portraits of Tsar.

1938, Oct. 3

341	A155	1 l	lt green	.20	.20
342	A156	2 l	rose brown	.60	.20
343	A156	4 l	golden brn	.20	.20
344	A156	7 l	brt ultra	1.00	1.00
345	A156	14 l	deep red lilac	.35	.25
			Nos. 341-345 (5)	2.35	1.85

Reign of Tsar Boris III, 20th anniv.

Early Locomotive A160

Designs: 2 l, Modern locomotive. 4 l, Train crossing bridge. 7 l, Tsar Boris in cab.

1939, Apr. 26

346	A160	1 l	yel green	.25	.20
347	A160	2 l	copper brn	.25	.20
348	A160	4 l	red orange	1.50	.20
349	A160	7 l	dark blue	3.50	.85
			Nos. 346-349 (4)	5.50	1.45

50th anniv. of Bulgarian State Railways.

Post Horns and Arrows — A164

Central Post Office, Sofia — A165

1939, May 14   **Typo.**

350	A164	1 l	yellow grn	.25	.20
351	A165	2 l	brt carmine	.30	.20

Establishment of the postal system, 60th anniv.

Gymnast on Bar — A166

Yunak Emblem — A167

Discus Thrower — A168

Athletic Dancer — A169

Weight Lifter — A170

1939, July 7   **Photo.**

352	A166	1 l	yel grn & pale grn	.35	.20
353	A167	2 l	brt rose	.35	.20
354	A168	4 l	brn & gldn brn	.50	.25
355	A169	7 l	dk bl & bl	1.25	.60
356	A170	14 l	plum & rose vio	5.50	2.75
			Nos. 352-356 (5)	7.95	4.00

9th tournament of the Yunak Gymnastic Organization at Sofia, July 4-8.

Tsar Boris III — A171

Bulgaria's First Stamp — A172

1940-41   **Typo.**

356A	A171	1 l	dl grn ('41)	.80	.20
357	A171	2 l	brt crimson	.20	.20

1940, May 19   **Photo.**   **Perf. 13**

20 l, Similar design, scroll dated "1840-1940."

358	A172	10 l	olive black	1.25	.85
359	A172	20 l	indigo	1.25	.85

Cent. of 1st postage stamp. Exist imperf.

Peasant Couple and Tsar Boris — A174

Flags over Wheat Field and Tsar Boris — A175

Tsar Boris and Map of Dobrudja A176

1940, Sept. 20

360	A174	1 l	slate green	.20	.20
361	A175	2 l	rose red	.20	.20
362	A176	4 l	dark brown	.20	.20
363	A176	7 l	dark blue	1.60	1.25
			Nos. 360-363 (4)	2.20	1.85

Return of Dobrudja from Romania.

Fruit A177

Bees and Flowers A178

Plowing A179

Shepherd and Sheep A180

Tsar Boris III — A181

Perf. 10, 10½x11½, 11½, 13

1940-44   **Typo.**   **Unwmk.**

364	A177	10s	red orange	.20	.20
365	A178	15s	blue	.20	.20
366	A179	30s	olive brn ('41)	.20	.20
367	A180	50s	violet	.20	.20
368	A181	1 l	brt green	.20	.20
369	A181	2 l	rose car	.20	.20
370	A181	4 l	red orange	.20	.20
371	A181	6 l	red vio ('44)	.30	.20
372	A181	7 l	blue	.30	.20
373	A181	10 l	blue grn ('41)	.30	.20
			Nos. 364-373 (10)	2.30	2.00

See Nos. 373A-377, 440. For overprints see Nos. 455-463, C31-C32.

1940-41   **Wmk. 145**   **Perf. 13**

373A	A180	50s	violet ('41)	.20	.20
374	A181	1 l	brt grn	.20	.20
375	A181	2 l	rose car	.20	.20
376	A181	7 l	dull blue	.45	.20
377	A181	10 l	blue green	.65	.20
			Nos. 373A-377 (5)	1.70	1.00

Watermarked vertically or horizontally.

P. R. Slaveikov A182

Sofronii, Bishop of Vratza A183

Saint Ivan Rilski — A184

Martin S. Drinov — A185

Monk Khrabr — A186

Kolio Ficheto — A187

1940, Sept. 23   **Photo.**   **Unwmk.**

378	A182	1 l	brt bl grn	.20	.20
379	A183	2 l	brt carmine	.20	.20
380	A184	3 l	dp red brn	.20	.20
381	A185	4 l	red orange	.20	.20
382	A186	7 l	deep blue	1.00	.60
383	A187	10 l	dp red brn	1.50	.85
			Nos. 378-383 (6)	3.30	2.25

Liberation of Bulgaria from the Turks in 1878.

Johannes Gutenberg A188

N. Karastoyanov, 1st Bulgarian Printer A189

1940, Dec. 16

384	A188	1 l	slate green	.20	.20
385	A189	2 l	orange brown	.20	.20

500th anniv. of the invention of the printing press and 100th anniv. of the 1st Bulgarian printing press.

Christo Botev — A190

Monument to Botev — A192

Botev with his Insurgent Band — A191

1941, May 3

386	A190	1 l	dark blue green	.20	.20
387	A191	2 l	crimson rose	.20	.20
388	A192	3 l	dark brown	.65	.30
			Nos. 386-388 (3)	1.05	.70

Christo Botev, patriot and poet.

Palace of Justice, Sofia — A193

20 l, Workers' hospital. 50 l, National Bank.

1941-43   **Engr.**   **Perf. 11½**

389	A193	14 l	lt gray brn ('43)	.20	.20
390	A193	20 l	gray grn ('43)	.40	.20
391	A193	50 l	lt bl gray	1.90	1.25
			Nos. 389-391 (3)	2.50	1.65

Macedonian Woman — A196

City of Okhrida — A200

Outline of Macedonia and Tsar Boris III A197

View of Aegean Sea — A198

Poganovski Monastery A199

1941, Oct. 3   **Photo.**   **Perf. 13**

392	A196	1 l	slate grn	.20	.20
393	A197	2 l	crimson	.20	.20
394	A198	2 l	red org	.20	.20

395 A199   4 l org brn   .20 .20
396 A200   7 l dp gray bl   1.40 1.25
  Nos. 392-396 (5)   2.20 2.05

Issued to commemorate the acquisition of Macedonian territory from neighboring countries.

Peasant Working in a Field — A201

Designs: 15s, Plowing. 30s, Apiary. 50s, Women harvesting fruit. 3 l, Shepherd and sheep. 5 l, Inspecting cattle.

1941-44
397 A201 10s dk violet   .20 .20
398 A201 10s dk blue   .20 .20
399 A201 15s Prus blue   .20 .20
400 A201 15s dk ol brn   .20 .20
401 A201 30s red orange   .20 .20
402 A201 30s dk slate grn   .20 .20
403 A201 50s blue vio   .20 .20
404 A201 50s red lilac   .20 .20
405 A201   3 l henna brn   .40 .25
406 A201   3 l dk brn ('44) 1.40 1.10
407 A201   5 l sepia   .50 .50
408 A201   5 l vio bl ('44) 1.40 1.10
  Nos. 397-408 (12)   5.30 4.55

Girls Singing — A207

Boys in Camp — A208

Raising Flag — A209

Folk Dancers — A211

Camp Scene A210

1942, June 1   Photo.
409 A207   1 l dk bl grn   .20 .20
410 A208   2 l scarlet   .20 .20
411 A209   4 l olive gray   .20 .20
412 A210   7 l deep blue   .20 .20
413 A211 14 l fawn   .30 .25
  Nos. 409-413 (5)   1.10 1.05

National "Work and Joy" movement.

Wounded Soldier — A212

Soldier's Farewell A213

4 l, Aiding wounded soldier. 7 l, Widow & orphans at grave. 14 l, Tomb of Unknown Soldier. 20 l, Queen Ioanna visiting wounded.

1942, Sept. 7
414 A212   1 l slate grn   .20 .20
415 A213   2 l brt rose   .20 .20
416 A213   4 l yel org   .20 .20
417 A213   7 l dark blue   .20 .20
418 A213 14 l brown   .20 .20
419 A213 20 l olive blk   .25 .20
  Nos. 414-419 (6)   1.25 1.20

Issued to aid war victims. No. 419 was printed in sheets of 50, alternating with 50 labels.

Legend of Kubrat — A218

Cavalry Charge — A219

Designs: 30s, Rider of Madara. 50s, Christening of Boris I. 1 l, School, St. Naum. 2 l, Crowning of Tsar Simeon by Boris I. 3 l, Golden era of Bulgarian literature. 4 l, Sentencing of the Bogomil Basil. 5 l, Proclamation of 2nd Bulgarian Empire. 7 l, Ivan Assen II at Trebizond. 10 l, Deporting the Patriarch Jeftimi. 14 l, Wandering minstrel. 20 l, Monk Paisii. 30 l, Monument, Shipka Pass.

1942, Oct. 12
420 A218 10s bluish blk   .20 .20
421 A219 15s Prus grn   .20 .20
422 A219 30s dk rose vio   .20 .20
423 A219 50s indigo   .20 .20
424 A219   1 l slate grn   .20 .20
425 A219   2 l crimson   .20 .20
426 A219   3 l brown   .20 .20
427 A219   4 l orange   .20 .20
428 A219   5 l grnsh blk   .20 .20
429 A219   7 l dk blue   .20 .20
430 A219 10 l brown blk   .20 .20
431 A219 14 l olive blk   .20 .20
432 A219 20 l henna brn   .40 .30
433 A219 30 l black   .70 .40
  Nos. 420-433 (14)   3.50 3.10

Tsar Boris III A234

Designs: Various portraits of Tsar.

Perf. 13, Imperf.
1944, Feb. 28 Photo.   Wmk. 275
Frames in Black
434 A234   1 l olive grn   .20 .20
435 A234   2 l red brown   .20 .20
436 A234   4 l brown   .20 .20
437 A234   7 l gray vio   .30 .20
438 A234   7 l slate blue   .30 .20
  Nos. 434-438 (5)   1.20 1.00

Tsar Boris III (1894-1943).

Tsar Simeon II — A239

Perf. 11½, 13
1944, June 12 Typo.   Unwmk.
439 A239   3 l red orange   .30 .20

Shepherd Type of 1940
1944
440 A180 50s yellow green   .20 .20

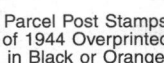

Parcel Post Stamps of 1944 Overprinted in Black or Orange

1945, Jan. 25   Perf. 11½
448 PP5   1 l dk carmine   .20 .20
449 PP5   7 l rose lilac   .20 .20
450 PP5   20 l org brn   .20 .20
451 PP5   30 l dk brn car   .20 .20
452 PP5   50 l red orange   .25 .20
453 PP5 100 l blue (O)   .60 .20

Overprint reads: "Everything for the Front."

No. 448 with Additional Surcharge of New Value in Black
454 PP5 4 l on 1 l dk car .20 .20
  Nos. 448-454 (7)   1.85 1.40

Nos. 368 to 370 Overprinted in Black

1945, Mar. 15   Perf. 11½, 13
455 A181   1 l brt green   .25 .20
456 A181   2 l rose carmine .40 .20
457 A181   4 l red orange   .60 .20

Overprint reads: "Collect old iron."

Overprinted in Black
458 A181   1 l brt green   .25 .20
459 A181   2 l rose carmine .40 .20
460 A181   4 l red orange   .60 .20

Overprint reads: "Collect discarded paper."

Overprinted in Black
461 A181   1 l brt green   .25 .20
462 A181   2 l rose carmine .40 .20
463 A181   4 l red orange   .60 .20
  Nos. 455-463 (9)   3.75 1.80

Overprint reads: "Collect all kinds of rags."

Oak Tree — A245

Imperf., Perf. 11½.
1945   Litho.   Unwmk.
464 A245   4 l vermilion   .20 .20
465 A245 10 l blue   .20 .20

Imperf
466 A245 50 l brown lake   .20 .20
  Nos. 464-466 (3)   .60 .60

Slav Congress, Sofia, March, 1945.

A246

A247

A248

A249

A251

A252

A253

A254

2 l and 4 l:
Type I. Large crown close to coat of arms.
Type II. Smaller crown standing high.

1945-46   Photo.   Perf. 13
469 A246 30s yellow grn   .20 .20
470 A247 50s peacock grn   .20 .20
471 A248   1 l dk green   .20 .20
472 A249   2 l choc (l)   .20 .20
 a.   Type II   —   —
473 A249   4 l dk blue (l) .20 .20
 a.   Type II   —   —
475 A251   5 l red violet   .20 .20
476 A251   9 l slate gray   .20 .20
477 A252 10 l Prus blue   .20 .20
478 A253 15 l brown   .20 .20
479 A254 20 l carmine   .20 .20
480 A254 20 l gray blk   .20 .20
  Nos. 469-480 (11)   2.20 2.20

Breaking Chain — A255

1 Lev Coin — A256

Water Wheel — A257

Coin and Symbols of Agriculture and Industry — A258

Unwmk.
1945, June 4　　Litho.　　*Imperf.*
Laid Paper

481	A255	50 l brn red, *pink*	.20	.20
482	A255	50 l org, *pink*	.20	.20
483	A256	100 l gray bl, *pink*	.20	.20
484	A256	100 l brn, *pink*	.20	.20
485	A257	150 l dk ol gray, *pink*	.35	.20
486	A257	150 l dl car, *pink*	.35	.20
487	A258	200 l dp bl, *pink*	.50	.30
488	A258	200 l ol grn, *pink*	.50	.30

Nos. 481-488 (8)　2.50　1.80

Souvenir Sheets

489		Sheet of 4	3.00 1.75
a.	A255	50 l violet blue	.30 .20
b.	A256	100 l violet blue	.30 .20
c.	A257	150 l violet blue	.30 .20
d.	A258	200 l violet blue	.30 .20
490		Sheet of 4	3.00 1.75
a.	A255	50 l brown orange	.30 .20
b.	A256	100 l brown orange	.30 .20
c.	A257	150 l brown orange	.30 .20
d.	A258	200 l brown orange	.30 .20

Publicizing Bulgaria's Liberty Loan.

Olive Branch — A260

1945, Sept. 1　Typo.　Perf. 13

491	A260	10 l org brn & yel grn	.20	.20
492	A260	50 l dull red & dp grn	.25	.20

Victory of Allied Nations, World War II.

September 9, 1944 — A261　　Numeral, Broken Chain — A262

1945, Sept. 7

493	A261	1 l gray green	.20	.20
494	A261	4 l deep blue	.20	.20
495	A261	5 l rose lilac	.20	.20
496	A262	10 l lt blue	.20	.20
497	A262	20 l brt car	.20	.20
498	A261	50 l brt bl grn	.40	.20
499	A261	100 l orange brn	.50	.35

Nos. 493-499 (7)　1.90　1.55

1st anniv. of Bulgaria's liberation.

Old Postal Savings Emblem — A263　　Child Putting Coin in Bank — A265

First Bulgarian Postal Savings Stamp A264

Postal Savings Building, Sofia — A266

1946, Apr. 12

500	A263	4 l brown org	.20	.20
501	A264	10 l dk olive	.20	.20
502	A265	20 l ultra	.20	.20
503	A266	50 l slate gray	.50	.50

Nos. 500-503 (4)　1.10　1.10

50th anniv. of Bulgarian Postal Savings.

Refugee Children A267　　Nurse Assisting Wounded Soldier A269

Wounded Soldier A268

35 l, 100 l, Red Cross hospital train.

1946, Apr. 4
Cross in Carmine

504	A267	2 l dk olive	.20	.20
505	A268	4 l violet	.20	.20
506	A267	10 l plum	.20	.20
507	A268	20 l ultra	.20	.20
508	A269	30 l brown org	.20	.20
509	A268	35 l gray blk	.20	.20
510	A269	50 l violet brn	.25	.20
511	A268	100 l gray brn	.70	.60

Nos. 504-511 (8)　2.15　2.00

See Nos. 553-560.

Advancing Troops A271

Grenade Thrower — A272　　Attacking Planes — A274

Designs: 5 l, Horse-drawn cannon. 9 l, Engineers building pontoon bridge. 10 l, 30 l, Cavalry charge. 40 l, Horse-drawn supply column. 50 l, Motor transport column. 60 l, Infantry, tanks and planes.

1946, Aug. 9　Typo.　Unwmk.

512	A271	2 l dk red vio	.20	.20
513	A272	4 l dk gray	.20	.20
514	A271	5 l dk org red	.20	.20
515	A274	6 l black brn	.20	.20
516	A271	9 l rose lilac	.20	.20
517	A271	10 l dp violet	.20	.20
518	A271	20 l dp blue	.25	.20
519	A271	30 l red org	.25	.20
520	A271	40 l dk ol bis	.30	.20
521	A271	50 l dk green	.30	.20
522	A271	60 l red brown	.40	.30

Nos. 512-522 (11)　2.70　2.30

Bulgaria's participation in World War II.

Arms of Russia and Bulgaria A279　　Lion Rampant A280

1946, May 23

523	A279	4 l red orange	.20	.20
525	A279	20 l turq green	.25	.20

Congress of the Bulgarian-Soviet Association, May 1946. The 4 l exists in dk car rose and 20 l in blue, value, set $7.

1946, May 25　　*Imperf.*

526	A280	20 l blue	.30 .25

Day of the Postage Stamp, May 26, 1946.

Alekandr Stamboliski A281　　Flags of Albania, Romania, Bulgaria and Yugoslavia A282

1946, June 13　　Perf. 12

527	A281	100 l red orange	4.25 2.75

23rd anniversary of the death of Alekandr Stamboliski, agrarian leader.

1946, July 6　　Perf. 11½

528	A282	100 l black brown	.75 .50

1946 Balkan Games.

Sheet of 100 arranged so that all stamps are tete beche vert. and horiz., except 2 center rows in left pane which provide 10 vert. pairs that are not tete beche vert.

St. Ivan Rilski — A283　　A286

A284

A285

Views of Rila Monastery A287

1946, Aug. 26

529	A283	1 l red brown	.20	.20
530	A284	4 l black brn	.20	.20
531	A285	10 l dk green	.20	.20
532	A286	20 l dp blue	.20	.20
533	A287	50 l dk red	.80	.50

Nos. 529-533 (5)　1.60　1.30

Millenary of Rila Monastery.

People's Republic

A288

1946, Sept. 15　　Typo.

534	A288	4 l brown lake	.20	.20
535	A288	20 l dull blue	.20	.20
536	A288	50 l olive bister	.20	.20

Nos. 534-536 (3)　.60　.60

No. 535 is inscribed "BULGARIA" in Latin characters.

Referendum of Sept. 8, 1946, resulting in the establishment of the Bulgarian People's Republic.

Partisan Army — A289

Snipers — A290　　Soldiers: Past and Present — A291

Design: 30 l, Partisans advancing.

1946, Dec. 2

537	A289	1 l violet brn	.20	.20
538	A290	4 l dull grn	.20	.20
539	A290	5 l chocolate	.20	.20
540	A290	10 l crimson	.20	.20
541	A289	20 l ultra	.25	.20
542	A290	30 l olive bister	.25	.20
543	A291	50 l black	.30	.25

Nos. 537-543 (7)　1.60　1.45

Relief Worker and Children — A294　　Child with Gift Parcels — A295

Waiting for Food Distribution A296　　Mother and Child A297

1946, Dec. 30

545	A294	1 l dk vio brn	.20	.20
546	A295	4 l brt red	.20	.20
547	A295	9 l olive bis	.20	.20
548	A294	10 l slate gray	.20	.20
549	A296	20 l ultra	.20	.20
550	A297	30 l dp brn org	.20	.20
551	A296	40 l maroon	.20	.20
552	A294	50 l peacock grn	.30	.30

Nos. 545-552 (8)　1.70　1.70

"Bulgaria" is in Latin characters on No. 548.

Red Cross Types of 1946

1947, Jan. 31

Cross in Carmine

553	A267	2 l olive bister	.20	.20
554	A268	4 l olive black	.20	.20
555	A267	10 l blue grn	.20	.20
556	A268	20 l brt blue	.20	.20
557	A269	30 l yellow grn	.30	.25
558	A268	35 l grnsh gray	.30	.25
559	A269	50 l henna brn	.50	.35
560	A268	100 l dark blue	.70	.50
		Nos. 553-560 (8)	2.60	2.15

Laurel Branch, Allied and Bulgarian Emblems
A298

Dove of Peace
A299

1947, Feb. 28

561	A298	4 l olive	.20	.20
562	A299	10 l brown red	.20	.20
563	A299	20 l deep blue	.20	.20
		Nos. 561-563 (3)	.60	.60

Return to peace at the close of World War II. "Bulgaria" in Latin characters on No. 563.

A302

Guerrilla Fighters
A303   A304

1947, Jan. 21   **Perf. 11½**

567	A302	10 l choc & brn org	.30	.30
568	A303	20 l dk bl & bl	.30	.20
569	A304	70 l dp claret & rose	18.00	18.00
		Nos. 567-569 (3)	18.60	18.40

Issued to honor the anti-fascists.

Hydroelectric Station
A305

Miner — A306

Symbols of Industry — A307

Tractor
A308

1947, Aug. 6

570	A305	4 l olive green	.20	.20
571	A306	9 l red brown	.20	.20
572	A307	20 l deep blue	.20	.20
573	A308	40 l olive brown	.40	.30
		Nos. 570-573 (4)	1.00	.90

Exhibition Building
A309

Former Home of Alphonse de Lamartine
A310

Symbols of Agriculture and Horticulture
A311

Perf. 11x11½, 11½x11

1947, Aug. 31   Litho.   Unwmk.

574	A309	4 l scarlet	.20	.20
575	A310	9 l brown lake	.20	.20
576	A311	20 l brt ultra	.20	.20
		Nos. 574-576 (3)	.60	.60

Plovdiv Intl. Fair, 1947. See No. C54.

Basil Evstatiev Aprilov — A312

1947, Oct. 19   Photo.   Perf. 11

577	A312	40 l brt ultra	.35	.20

Cent. of the death of Basil Evstatiev Aprilov, educator and historian. See No. 603.

Bicycle Race — A313

Basketball
A314

Chess
A315

Balkan Games: 20 l, Soccer players. 60 l, Four flags of participating nations.

1947, Sept. 29   Typo.   Perf. 11½

578	A313	2 l plum	.20	.20
579	A314	4 l dk olive grn	.20	.20
580	A315	9 l orange brn	.40	.20
581	A315	20 l brt ultra	.80	.20
582	A315	60 l violet brn	1.60	.75
		Nos. 578-582 (5)	3.20	1.55

People's Theater, Sofia
A316

National Assembly
A317

Central Post Office, Sofia
A318

Presidential Mansion
A319

1947-48   Typo.   Perf. 12½

583	A316	50s yellow grn	.20	.20
584	A317	50s yellow grn	.20	.20
585	A318	1 l green	.20	.20
586	A319	1 l green	.20	.20
587	A316	2 l brown lake	.20	.20
588	A317	2 l lt brown	.20	.20
589	A316	4 l deep blue	.20	.20
590	A316	4 l deep blue	.20	.20
591	A316	4 l carmine	.35	.20
592	A317	20 l deep blue	.75	.30
		Nos. 583-592 (10)	2.70	2.10

On Nos. 583-592 inscription reads "Bulgarian Republic." No. 592 is inscribed in Latin characters.

Redrawn

added to inscription

593	A318	1 l green	.20	.20
594	A318	2 l brown lake	.20	.20
595	A318	4 l deep blue	.20	.20
		Nos. 593-595 (3)	.60	.60

Cyrillic inscription beneath design on Nos. 593-595 reads "Bulgarian People's Republic."

Geno Kirov — A320

Actors' Portraits: 1 l, Zlatina Nedeva. 2 l, Ivan Popov. 3 l, Athanas Kirchev. 4 l, Elena Snejina. 5 l, Stoyan Bachvarov.

Perf. 10½

1947, Dec. 8   Unwmk.   Litho.

596	A320	50s bister brn	.20	.20
597	A320	1 l lt blue grn	.20	.20
598	A320	2 l slate green	.20	.20
599	A320	3 l dp blue	.20	.20
600	A320	4 l scarlet	.20	.20
601	A320	5 l red brown	.20	.20
		Nos. 596-601,B22-B26 (11)	2.50	2.30

National Theater, 50th anniversary.

Merchant Ship "Fatherland" — A321

1947, Dec. 19

602	A321	50 l Prus bl, *cream*	.45	.20

B. E. Aprilov — A322

Worker — A323

1948, Feb. 19   Perf. 11

603	A322	4 l brn car, *cream*	.20	.20

Centenary of the death of Basil Evstatiev Aprilov, educator and historian.

1948, Feb. 29 Photo.   Perf. 11½x12

604	A323	4 l dp blue, *cream*	.20	.20

2nd Bulgarian Workers' Congress.

Self-education
A324

Accordion Player — A325

Factory Recess — A326

Girl Throwing Basketball — A327

1948, Mar. 31   Photo.

605	A324	4 l red	.20	.20
606	A325	20 l deep blue	.20	.20
607	A326	40 l dull green	.20	.20
608	A327	60 l brown	.60	.35
		Nos. 605-608 (4)	1.20	.95

Nicholas Vaptzarov — A328

Portraits: 9 l, P. K. Iavorov. 15 l, Christo Smirnenski. 20 l, Ivan Vazov. 45 l, P. R. Slaveikov.

1948, May 18   Litho.   Perf. 11

Cream Paper

611	A328	4 l brt ver	.20	.20
612	A328	9 l lt brown	.20	.20
613	A328	15 l claret	.20	.20
614	A328	20 l deep blue	.20	.20
615	A328	45 l green	.30	.30
		Nos. 611-615 (5)	1.10	1.10

Soviet Soldier — A329

Civilians
Offering Gifts
to Soldiers
A330

Designs: 20 l, Soldiers, 1878 and 1944. 60 l,
Stalin and Spasski Tower.

1948, July 5   **Photo.**
    Cream Paper
616 A329   4 l   brown org   .20   .20
617 A330 10 l   olive grn   .20   .20
618 A330 20 l   dp blue   .20   .20
619 A329 60 l   olive brn   .40   .35
        Nos. 616-619 (4)   1.00 .95
The Soviet Army.

Demeter
Blagoev — A331

Monument to
Bishop Andrey
A332

9 l, Gabriel Genov. 60 l, Marching youths.

1948, Sept. 6   **Litho.**
    Cream Paper
620 A331   4 l   dk brown   .20   .20
621 A331   9 l   brown org   .20   .20
622 A332 20 l   dp blue   .20   .20
623 A332 60 l   brown   .50   .40
        Nos. 620-623 (4)   1.10 1.00
No. 623 is inscribed in Cyrillic characters.
Natl. Insurrection of 1923, 25th anniv.

Christo   Battle of
Smirnenski   Grivitza, 1877
A333   A334

1948, Oct. 2   Photo.   Perf. 11½
    Cream Paper
624 A333   4 l   blue   .20   .20
625 A333 16 l   red brown   .20   .20
Christo Smirnenski, poet, 1898-1923.

1948, Nov. 1
626 A334 20 l   blue   .20   .20
        Nos. 626,C56-C57 (3)   .95   .70
Romanian-Bulgarian friendship.

Bath, Gorna   Bath,
Banya — A335   Bankya — A336

Mineral Bath,   Maliovitza
Sofia   A338
A337

1948-49   Typo.   Perf. 12½
627 A335   2 l   red brown   .20   .20
628 A336   3 l   red orange   .20   .20
629 A337   4 l   deep blue   .20   .20
630 A338   5 l   violet brown   .20   .20
631 A336 10 l   red violet   .20   .20
632 A338 15 l   olive grn ('49)   .20   .20
633 A335 20 l   deep blue   .75   .20
        Nos. 627-633 (7)   1.95 1.40
Latin characters on No. 633. See No. 653.

Emblem of the
Republic — A339

1948-50
634   A339 50s red orange   .20   .20
634A A339 50s org brn ('50)   .20   .20
635   A339   1 l green   .20   .20
636   A339   9 l black   .20   .20
        Nos. 634-636 (4)   .80   .80

Botev's
Birthplace,
Kalofer
A340

Christo
Botev — A341

Designs: 9 l, Steamer "Radetzky." 15 l,
Kalofer village. 20 l, Botev in uniform. 40 l,
Botev's mother. 50 l, Pen, pistol and wreath.

Perf. 11x11½, 11½
1948, Dec. 21   **Photo.**
    Cream Paper
638 A340   1 l   dk green   .20   .20
639 A341   4 l   violet brn   .20   .20
640 A340   9 l   violet   .20   .20
641 A340 15 l   brown   .20   .20
642 A341 20 l   blue   .20   .20
643 A340 40 l   red brown   .25   .20
644 A341 50 l   olive blk   .35   .25
        Nos. 638-644 (7)   1.60 1.45
Botev, Bulgarian natl. poet, birth cent.

Lenin — A342   Lenin
                   Speaking — A343

1949, Jan. 24   Unwmk.   Perf. 11½
    Cream Paper
645 A342   4 l   brown   .25   .20
646 A343 20 l   brown red   .35   .20
25th anniversary of the death of Lenin.

Road
Construction
A344

Designs: 5 l, Tunnel construction. 9 l, Locomotive. 10 l, Textile worker. 20 l, Female tractor driver. 40 l, Workers in truck.

1949, Apr. 6   **Perf. 10½**
    Inscribed: "CHM"
    Cream Paper
647 A344   4 l   dark red   .20   .20
648 A344   5 l   dark brown   .20   .20
649 A344   9 l   dk slate grn   .25   .20
650 A344 10 l   violet   .25   .20
651 A344 20 l   dull blue   .60   .40
652 A344 40 l   brown   .95   .55
        Nos. 647-652 (6)   2.45 1.75
Honoring the Workers' Cultural Brigade.

Type of 1948
Redrawn
Country Name and "POSTA" in Latin
Characters
1949   Typo.   Perf. 12½
653 A337 20 l   deep blue   .55   .20

Miner — A345

1949   **Perf. 11x11½**
654 A345   4 l   dark blue   .20   .20

A347

Prime Minister
George
Dimitrov, 1882-
1949
A348

1949, July 10   **Photo.**
656 A347   4 l   red brown   .25   .20
657 A348 20 l   dark blue   .50   .20

Power   Grain
Station — A349   Towers — A350

Farm
Machinery — A351

Tractor Parade
A352

Agriculture
and Industry
A353

1949, Aug. 5   Perf. 11½x11, 11x11½
658 A349   4 l   olive green   .20   .20
659 A350   9 l   dark red   .20   .20
660 A351 15 l   purple   .20   .20
661 A352 20 l   blue   .55   .40
662 A353 50 l   orange brn   1.75 .85
        Nos. 658-662 (5)   2.90 1.85
Bulgaria's Five Year Plan.

Grenade and Javelin
Throwers — A354

Hurdlers
A355

Motorcycle
and Tractor
A356

Boy and Girl
Athletes — A357

1949, Sept. 5
663 A354   4 l   brown orange   .30   .20
664 A355   9 l   olive green   .60   .25
665 A356 20 l   violet blue   1.25 .65
666 A357 50 l   red brown   3.00 1.25
        Nos. 663-666 (4)   5.15 2.35

A358

Frontier
Guards — A359

1949, Oct. 31
667 A358   4 l   chestnut brn   .20   .20
668 A359 20 l   gray blue   .60   .25
        See No. C60.

George
Dimitrov — A360

Allegory of
Labor — A361

Laborers of Both
Sexes — A362

Workers and
Flags of Bulgaria
and
Russia — A363

Perf. 11½

1949, Dec. 13   Photo.   Unwmk.

669	A360	4 l	orange brn	.20	.20
670	A361	9 l	purple	.20	.20
671	A362	20 l	dull blue	.30	.25
672	A363	50 l	red	.65	.45
	Nos. 669-672 (4)			1.35	1.10

Joseph V.
Stalin — A364

Stalin and
Dove — A365

1949, Dec. 21

673	A364	4 l	deep orange	.25	.20
674	A365	40 l	rose brown	.65	.30

70th anniv. of the birth of Joseph V. Stalin.

Kharalamby
Stoyanov — A366

Communications
Strikers — A368

Railway
Strikers
A367

1950, Feb. 15

675	A366	4 l	yellow brown	.20	.20
676	A367	20 l	violet blue	.25	.20
677	A368	60 l	brown olive	.60	.40
	Nos. 675-677 (3)			1.05	.80

30th anniv. (in 1949) of the General Railway and Postal Employees' Strike of 1919.

Miner — A369

Locomotive
A370

Shipbuilding — A371

Tractor
A372

Stalin Central
Heating
Plant — A374

Textile
Worker — A375

Farm Machinery
A373

1950-51   Perf. 11½, 13

678	A369	1 l	olive	.20	.20
679	A370	2 l	gray blk	.20	.20
680	A371	3 l	gray blue	.20	.20
681	A372	4 l	dk blue grn	1.75	.50
682	A373	5 l	henna brn	.40	.20
682A	A373	9 l	gray blk ('51)	.20	.20
683	A374	10 l	dp plum ('51)	.30	.20
684	A375	15 l	dk car ('51)	.40	.20
685	A375	20 l	dk blue ('51)	.70	.40
	Nos. 678-685 (9)			4.35	2.30

No. 685 is inscribed in Latin characters.
See Nos. 750-751A.

Vassil Kolarov
(1877-1950) — A377

1950, Mar. 6   Perf. 11½
Size: 21½x31½mm

686	A377	4 l	red brown	.20	.20

Size: 27x39½mm

687	A377	20 l	violet blue	.25	.25

No. 687 has altered frame and is inscribed in Latin characters.

Stanislav
Dospevski, Self-
portrait
A378

King Kaloyan
and Desislava
A379

Plowman
Resting, by
Christo
Stanchev
A380

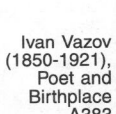

Statue of
Dimtcho
Debelianov, by
Ivan
Lazarov — A381

"Harvest," by V.
Dimitrov — A382

Design: 9 l, Nikolai Pavlovich, self-portrait.

1950, Apr. 15   Perf. 11½

688	A378	1 l	dk olive grn	.30	.20
689	A379	4 l	dk red	.90	.25
690	A378	9 l	chocolate	.90	.25
691	A380	15 l	brown	1.50	.25
692	A380	20 l	deep blue	2.00	.80
693	A381	40 l	red brown	2.75	1.25
694	A382	60 l	deep orange	4.00	1.60
	Nos. 688-694 (7)			12.35	4.60

Latin characters on No. 692.

Ivan Vazov
(1850-1921),
Poet and
Birthplace
A383

1950, June 26

695	A383	4 l	olive green	.20	.20

Road
Building
A384

Men of Three Races
and "Stalin"
Flag — A385

Perf. 11½x11, 11x11½
1950, Sept. 19

696	A384	4 l	brown red	.20	.20
697	A385	20 l	violet blue	.30	.20

2nd National Peace Conference.

Molotov,
Kolarov,
Stalin and
Dimitrov
A386

Spasski Tower
and
Flags — A387

Russian and
Bulgarian
Women — A388

Loading Russian
Ship — A389

Perf. 11½

1950, Oct. 10   Unwmk.   Photo.

698	A386	4 l	brown	.20	.20
699	A387	9 l	rose carmine	.20	.20
700	A388	20 l	gray blue	.20	.20
701	A389	50 l	dk grnsh blue	1.10	.45
	Nos. 698-701 (4)			1.70	1.05

2nd anniversary of the Soviet-Bulgarian treaty of mutual assistance.

St. Constantine
Sanatorium — A390

2 l, 10 l, Children at seashore. 5 l, Rest home.

1950   Typo.

702	A390	1 l	dark green	.20	.20
703	A390	2 l	carmine	.20	.20
704	A390	5 l	deep orange	.20	.20
705	A390	10 l	deep blue	.40	.25
	Nos. 702-705 (4)			1.00	.85

Originally prepared in 1945 as "Sunday Delivery Stamps," this issue was released for ordinary postage in 1950.

Runners — A393

1950, Aug. 21   Photo.   Perf. 11

706	A393	4 l	shown	.20	.20
707	A393	9 l	Cycling	.20	.20
708	A393	20 l	Shot put	.20	.20
709	A393	40 l	Volleyball	.40	.40
	Nos. 706-709 (4)			1.00	1.00

Marshal Fedor I.
Tolbukhin — A394

Natives Greeting Tolbukhin A395

Perf. 11½x11, 11x11½
1950, Dec. 10   Photo.   Unwmk.
710 A394 4 l claret   .20 .20
711 A395 20 l dk blue   .35 .20

The return of Dobrich and part of the province of Dobruja from Romania to Bulgaria.

Dimitrov's Birthplace A396

George Dimitrov
A397   A398
Various Portraits, Inscribed:

Design: 2 l, Dimitrov Museum, Sofia.

1950, July 2   Perf. 10½
712 A396 50s olive grn   .20 .20
713 A397 50s brown   .20 .20
714 A397 1 l redsh brn   .25 .20
715 A396 2 l gray   .25 .20
716 A397 4 l claret   .45 .20
717 A397 9 l red brown   .65 .25
718 A396 10 l brown red   .70 .35
719 A396 15 l olive gray   .70 .35
720 A396 20 l dark blue   1.75 .55
    Nos. 712-720,C61 (10)   8.15 3.60

1st anniversary of the death of George Dimitrov, statesman. No. 720 is inscribed in Latin characters.

A. S. Popov — A400

1951, Feb. 10
722 A400 4 l red brown   .20 .20
723 A400 20 l dark blue   .55 .20

No. 723 is inscribed in Latin characters.

Arms of Bulgaria
A401   A402

1950   Unwmk.   Typo.   Perf. 13
724 A401 2 l dk brown   .20 .20
725 A401 3 l rose   .20 .20
726 A402 5 l carmine   .20 .20
727 A402 9 l aqua   .20 .20
    Nos. 724-727 (4)   .80 .80

Nos. 724-727 were prepared in 1947 for official use but were issued as regular postage stamps Oct. 1, 1950.

Heroes Chankova, Antonov-Malchik, Dimitrov and Dimitrova — A403

Stanke Dimitrov-Marek   George Kirkov
A404   A405

George Dimitrov at Leipzig   Natcho Ivanov and Avr. Stoyanov
A406   A407

9 l, Anton Ivanov. 15 l, Christo Michailov.

1951, Mar. 25   Photo.   Perf. 11½
728 A403 1 l red violet   .20 .20
729 A404 2 l dk red brn   .20 .20
730 A405 4 l car rose   .20 .20
731 A405 9 l orange brn   .45 .20
732 A405 15 l olive brn   .80 .25
733 A406 20 l dark blue   1.10 .55
734 A407 50 l olive gray   2.50 .90
    Nos. 728-734 (7)   5.45 2.50

First Bulgarian Tractor A408

First Steam Roller — A409

First Truck — A410

Bulgarian Embroidery — A411

15 l, Carpet. 20 l, Tobacco & roses. 40 l, Fruits.

Perf. 11x10½
1951, Mar. 30   Photo.   Unwmk.
735 A408 1 l olive brn   .20 .20
736 A409 2 l violet   .30 .20
737 A410 4 l red brown   .50 .20
738 A411 9 l purple   .70 .20
739 A409 15 l deep plum   1.00 .30
740 A411 20 l violet blue   1.50 .30
741 A410 40 l deep green   2.50 .65

Perf. 13
Size: 23x18½mm
742 A408 1 l purple   .20 .20
743 A409 2 l Prus green   .28 .20
744 A410 4 l red brown   .28 .20
    Nos. 735-744 (10)   7.46 2.65

See #894, 973. For surcharge see #973.

Turkish Attack on Mt. Zlee Dol A412

Designs: 4 l, Georgi Benkovski speaking to rebels. 9 l, Cherrywood cannon of 1876 and Russian cavalry, 1945. 20 l, Rebel, 1876 and partisan, 1944. 40 l, Benkovski and Dimitrov.

1951, May 3   Perf. 10½
Cream Paper
745 A412 1 l redsh brown   .20 .20
746 A412 4 l dark green   .20 .20
747 A412 9 l violet brown   .50 .30
748 A412 20 l deep blue   .65 .50
749 A412 40 l dark red   1.00 .70
    Nos. 745-749 (5)   2.55 1.90

75th anniv. of the "April" revolution.

Industrial Types of 1950
1951   Perf. 13
750 A369 1 l violet   .20 .20
751 A370 2 l dk brown   .20 .20
751A A372 4 l dk yel grn   .75 .20
    Nos. 750-751A (3)   1.15 .60

Demeter Blagoev Addressing 1891 Congress at Busludja — A413

1951   Photo.   Perf. 11
752 A413 1 l purple   .25 .20
753 A413 4 l dark green   .35 .20
754 A413 9 l deep claret   .65 .30
    Nos. 752-754 (3)   1.25 .70

60th anniversary of the first Congress of the Bulgarian Social-Democratic Party.
See Nos. 1174-1176.

Day Nursery A414

Designs: 4 l, Model building construction. 9 l, Playground. 20 l, Children's town.

1951, Oct. 10   Unwmk.
755 A414 1 l brown   .20 .20
756 A414 4 l deep plum   .20 .20
757 A414 9 l blue green   .60 .25
758 A414 20 l deep blue   1.00 .55
    Nos. 755-758 (4)   2.00 1.20

Children's Day, Sept. 25, 1951.

Order of Labor
A415   A416

1952, Feb. 1   Perf. 13
Reverse of Medal
759 A415 1 l red brown   .20 .20
760 A415 4 l blue green   .20 .20
761 A415 9 l dark blue   .30 .20

Obverse of Medal
762 A416 1 l carmine   .20 .20
763 A416 4 l green   .20 .20
764 A416 9 l purple   .30 .20
    Nos. 759-764 (6)   1.40 1.20

No. 764 has numeral at lower left and different background.

Workers and Symbols of Industry — A417

Design: 4 l, Flags, Dimitrov, Chervenkov.

1951, Dec. 29   Perf. 11
Inscribed: "16 XII 1951"
765 A417 1 l olive black   .20 .20
766 A417 4 l chocolate   .20 .20

Third Congress of Bulgarian General Workers' Professional Union.

Dimitrov and Chemical Works — A418

George Dimitrov and V. Chervenkov — A419

Portrait: 80s, Dimitrov.

Unwmk.
1952, June 18   Photo.   Perf. 11
767 A418 16s brown   .35 .25
768 A419 44s brown carmine   .55 .25
769 A418 80s brt blue   1.10 .50
    Nos. 767-769 (3)   2.00 1.00

70th anniv. of the birth of George Dimitrov.

Vassil Kolarov Dam — A420

Republika Power Station — A421

1952, May 16   Perf. 13
770 A420 4s dark green   .20 .20
771 A420 12s purple   .20 .20
772 A420 16s red brown   .20 .20
773 A420 44s rose brown   .50 .20
774 A420 80s brt blue   1.60 .20
    Nos. 770-774 (5)   2.70 1.00

No. 774 is inscribed in Latin characters.

1952, June 30   Perf. 13, Pin Perf.
775 A421 16s dark brown   .20 .20
776 A421 44s magenta   .75 .20

Nikolai I.
Vapzarov
A422

Designs: Various portraits.

1952, July 23   *Perf. 10½*
777 A422 16s rose brown .20 .20
778 A422 44s dk red brn .65 .20
779 A422 80s dk olive brn 1.40 .50
    Nos. 777-779 (3) 2.25 .90

10th anniversary of the death of Nikolai I. Vapzarov, poet and revolutionary.

Dimitrov and Youth
Conference — A423

16s, Resistance movement incident. 44s, Frontier guards & industrial scene. 80s, George Dimitrov & young workers.

1952, Sept. 1   *Perf. 11x11½*
780 A423 2s brown carmine .20 .20
781 A423 16s purple .20 .20
782 A423 44s dark green .50 .30
783 A423 80s dark brown 1.10 .60
    Nos. 780-783 (4) 2.00 1.30

40th anniv. of the founding conference of the Union of Social Democratic Youth.

Assault on the
Winter
Palace — A424

Designs: 8s, Volga-Don Canal. 16s, Symbols of world peace. 44s, Lenin and Stalin. 80s, Himlay hydroelectric station.

     Perf. 11½
1952, Nov. 6   **Unwmk.**   **Photo.**
     Dated: "1917-1952"
784 A424 4s red brown .20 .20
785 A424 8s dark green .20 .20
786 A424 16s dark blue .20 .20
787 A424 44s brown .30 .20
788 A424 80s olive brown .75 .35
    Nos. 784-788 (5) 1.65 1.15

35th anniv. of the Russian revolution.

Vassil
Levski — A425

Design: 44s, Levski and comrades.

1953, Feb. 19   *Perf. 11*
     Cream Paper
789 A425 16s brown .20 .20
790 A425 44s brown blk .25 .20

80th anniv. of the death of Levski, patriot.

Ferrying
Artillery
and
Troops
into
Battle
A426

Soldier
A427

Mother and
Children
A428

Designs: 44s, Victorious soldiers. 80s, Soldier welcomed. 1 l, Monuments.

1953, Mar. 3   *Perf. 10½*
791 A426 8s Prus green .20 .20
792 A427 16s dp brown .25 .20
793 A426 44s dk slate grn .40 .20
794 A426 80s dull red brn .85 .20
795 A426 1 l black 1.10 .30
    Nos. 791-795 (5) 2.80 1.10

Bulgaria's independence from Turkey, 75th anniv.

1953, Mar. 9
796 A428 16s slate green .20 .20
797 A428 16s bright blue .20 .20

Women's Day.

Woodcarvings at Rila Monastery
A429   A430

Designs: 12s, 16s, 28s, Woodcarvings, Rila Monastery. 44s, Carved Ceilings, Trnovo. 80s, 1 l, 4 l, Carvings, Pasardjik.

1953   **Unwmk.**   **Photo.**   *Perf. 13*
798 A429 2s gray brown .20 .20
799 A430 8s dk slate grn .20 .20
800 A430 12s brown .20 .20
801 A430 16s rose lake .25 .20
802 A429 28s dk olive grn .30 .20
803 A430 44s dk brown .50 .20
804 A430 80s ultra .85 .20
805 A430 1 l violet blue 1.75 .25
806 A430 4 l rose lake 3.50 .90
    Nos. 798-806 (9) 7.75 2.55

For surcharge see No. 1204.

Karl
Marx — A431

"Das
Kapital" — A432

1953, Apr. 30   *Perf. 10½*
807 A431 16s bright blue .20 .20
808 A432 44s deep brown .30 .20

70th anniversary of the death of Karl Marx.

Labor Day
Parade — A433

Joseph V.
Stalin — A434

1953, Apr. 30   *Perf. 13*
809 A433 16s brown red .20 .20
    Labor Day, May 1, 1953.

1953, May 23   *Perf. 13x13½*
810 A434 16s dark gray .25 .20
811 A434 16s dark brown .25 .20

Death of Joseph V. Stalin, Mar. 5, 1953.

Georgi
Delchev — A435

Battle
Scene — A436

Peasants
Attacking
Turkish Troops
A437

1953, Aug. 8   *Perf. 13*
812 A435 16s dark brown .20 .20
813 A436 44s purple .30 .20
814 A437 1 l deep claret .45 .20
    Nos. 812-814 (3) .95 .60

50th anniv. of the Ilinden Revolt (#812, 814) and the Preobrazhene Revolt (#813).

Soldier and
Rebels
A438

44s, Soldier guarding industrial construction.

1953, Sept. 18
815 A438 16s deep claret .20 .20
816 A438 44s greenish blue .35 .20

Army Day.

George
Dimitrov and
Vassil Kolarov
A439

Demeter
Blagoev — A440

Designs: 16s, Citizens in revolt. 44s, Attack.

1953, Sept. 22
817 A439 8s olive gray .20 .20
818 A439 16s dk red brn .20 .20
819 A439 44s cerise .45 .20
    Nos. 817-819 (3) .85 .60

September Revolution, 30th anniversary.

1953, Sept. 21
   Portraits: 44s, G. Dimitrov and D. Blagoev.
820 A440 16s brown .25 .20
821 A440 44s red brown .40 .20

50th anniversary of the formation of the Social Democratic Party.

Railway
Viaduct
A441

Pouring Molten
Metal — A442

Designs: 16s, Welder and storage tanks. 80s, Harvesting machine.

1953, Oct. 17
826 A441 8s brt blue .20 .20
827 A441 16s grnsh blk .20 .20
828 A442 44s brown red .30 .20
829 A441 80s orange .45 .30
    Nos. 826-829 (4) 1.15 .90

Month of Bulgarian-Russian friendship.

Belladonna
A443

Kolarov Library, Sofia
A444

Medicinal Flowers: 4s, Jimson weed. 8s, Sage. 12s, Dog rose. 16s, Gentian. 20s, Poppy. 28s, Peppermint. 40s, Bear grass. 44s, Coltsfoot. 80s, Cowslip. 1 l, Dandelion. 2 l, Foxglove.

1953   **Unwmk.**   **Photo.**   *Perf. 13*
     White or Cream Paper
830 A443 2s dull blue .20 .20
831 A443 4s brown org .20 .20
832 A443 8s blue grn .20 .20
833 A443 12s brown org .20 .20
834 A443 12s blue grn .20 .20
835 A443 16s violet blue .20 .20
836 A443 16s dp red brn .20 .20
837 A443 20s car rose .20 .20
838 A443 28s dk gray grn .30 .20
839 A443 40s dark blue .35 .20
840 A443 44s brown .35 .20
841 A443 80s yellow brn .60 .35
842 A443 1 l henna brn 2.00 .50
843 A443 2 l purple 3.50 1.25
a.   Souvenir sheet 27.50 20.00
    Nos. 830-843 (14) 8.70 4.30

No. 843a contains 12 stamps, one of each denomination above, printed in dark green. Size: 161x172mm. Sold for 6 leva.

1953, Dec. 16
854 A444 44s brown .25 .20

75th anniversary of the founding of the Kolarov Library, Sofia.

Singer and
Accordionist
A445

Lenin and Stalin
A446

1953, Dec. 26
855 A445 16s shown .20 .20
856 A445 44s Dancers .20 .20

1954, Mar. 13

Designs: 44s, Lenin statue. 80s, Lenin mausoleum, Moscow. 1 l, Lenin.

Cream Paper

857	A446	16s brown	.20	.20
858	A446	44s rose brown	.25	.20
859	A446	80s blue	.40	.20
860	A446	1 l dp olive grn	.60	.25
		Nos. 857-860 (4)	1.45	.85

30th anniversary of the death of Lenin.

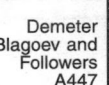

Demeter Blagoev and Followers
A447

Design: 44s, Blagoev at desk.

1954, Apr. 28

Cream Paper

861	A447	16s dp red brn	.20	.20
862	A447	44s black brn	.30	.20

30th anniv. of the death of Demeter Blagoev.

George Dimitrov — A448

Dimitrov and Refinery
A449

1954, June 11

863	A448	44s lake, cream	.25	.20
864	A449	80s brown, cream	.65	.20

5th anniv. of the death of George Dimitrov.

Train Leaving Tunnel — A450

1954, July 30

865	A450	44s dk grn, cream	.60	.20
866	A450	44s blk brn, cream	.60	.20

Day of the Railroads, Aug. 1, 1954.

Miner at Work — A451

1954, Aug. 19

867	A451	44s grnsh blk, cream	.20	.20

Miners' Day.

Academy of Science
A452

1954, Oct. 27

868	A452	80s black, cream	.55	.20

85th anniversary of the foundation of the Bulgarian Academy of Science.

Horsemanship — A454

16s, 44s, 2 l, vert.

1954, Dec. 21

869	A454	16s Gymnastics	.50	.20
870	A454	44s Wrestling	.60	.20
871	A454	80s shown	1.25	.55
872	A454	2 l Skiing	3.00	1.60
		Nos. 869-872 (4)	5.35	2.55

Welcoming Liberators
A455

Soldier's Return — A456

28s, Refinery. 44s, Dimitrov & Workers. 80s, Girl & boy. 1 l, George Dimitrov.

1954, Oct. 4

Cream Paper

873	A455	12s brown car	.20	.20
874	A456	16s dp carmine	.20	.20
875	A455	28s indigo	.20	.20
876	A455	44s redsh brn	.20	.20
877	A456	80s deep blue	.55	.25
878	A456	1 l dark green	.55	.25
		Nos. 873-878 (6)	1.90	1.30

10th anniversary of Bulgaria's liberation.

Recreation at Workers' Rest Home — A457

Metal Worker and Furnace — A458

80s, Dimitrov, Blagoev, Kirkov.

Unwmk.

1954, Dec. 28 Photo. Perf. 13

Cream Paper

879	A457	16s dark green	.20	.20
880	A458	44s brown orange	.20	.20
881	A457	80s dp violet blue	.40	.20
		Nos. 879-881 (3)	.80	.60

50th anniversary of Bulgaria's trade union movement.

Geese — A459

Designs: 4s, Chickens. 12s, Hogs. 16s, Sheep. 28s, Telephone building. 44s, Communist party headquarters. 80s, Apartment buildings. 1 l, St. Kiradgieff Mills.

1955-56

882	A459	2s dk blue grn	.20	.20
883	A459	4s olive green	.30	.20
884	A459	12s dk red brn	.40	.20
885	A459	16s brown orange	.65	.20
886	A459	28s violet blue	.30	.20
887	A459	44s lil red, cream	.60	.20
a.		44s brown red	4.50	
888	A459	80s dk red brown	.75	.20
889	A459	1 l dk blue green	1.50	.20
		Nos. 882-889 (8)	4.70	1.60

Issued: #887, 4/20/56; others, 2/19/55.

Textile Worker
A460

Mother and Child — A461

Design: 16s, Woman feeding calf.

1955, Mar. 5

890	A460	12s dark brown	.20	.20
891	A460	16s dark green	.20	.20
892	A461	44s dk car rose	.50	.20
893	A461	44s blue	.50	.20
		Nos. 890-893 (4)	1.40	.80

Women's Day, Mar. 8, 1955.

No. 744 Surcharged in Blue

1955, Mar. 8 Perf. 13

894	A410	16s on 4 l red brown	.45	.20

May Day Demonstration of Workers — A462

Sts. Cyril and Methodius
A463

Design: 44s, Three workers and globe.

1955, Apr. 23 Photo.

895	A462	16s car rose	.20	.20
896	A462	44s blue	.30	.20

Labor Day, May 1, 1955.

1955, May 21

Designs: 8s, Paisii Hilendarski. 16s, Nicolas Karastoyanov's printing press. 28s, Christo Botev. 44s, Ivan Vazov. 80s, Demeter Blagoev and socialist papers. 2 l, Blagoev printing plant, Sofia.

Cream Paper

897	A463	4s deep blue	.20	.20
898	A463	8s olive	.20	.20
899	A463	16s black	.20	.20
900	A463	28s henna brn	.20	.20
901	A463	44s brown	.30	.20
902	A463	80s rose red	.50	.20
903	A463	2 l black	1.50	.40
		Nos. 897-903 (7)	3.10	1.60

Creation of the Cyrillic alphabet, 1100th anniv. Latin lettering at bottom on #901-903.

Sergei Rumyantzev
A464

Mother and Children
A465

16s, Christo Jassenov. 44s, Geo Milev.

1955, June 30 Unwmk. Perf. 13

Cream Paper

904	A464	12s orange brn	.20	.20
905	A464	16s lt brown	.20	.20
906	A464	44s grnsh blk	.40	.20
		Nos. 904-906 (3)	.80	.60

30th anniv. of the deaths of Sergei Rumyanchev, Christo Jassenov and Geo Milev. Latin lettering at bottom of No. 906.

1955, July 30

907	A465	44s brn car, cream	.30	.20

World Congress of Mothers in Lausanne, 1955.

Young People of Three Races — A466

Friedrich Engels and Book — A467

1955, July 30

908	A466	44s blue, cream	.30	.20

5th World Festival of Youth in Warsaw, July 31-Aug. 14.

1955, July 30

909	A467	44s brown	.30	.20

60th anniv. of the death of Friedrich Engels.

Entrance to Fair, 1892 — A468

Statuary Group at Fair, 1955 — A469

Designs: 44s, "Fruit of our Land." 80s, Woman holding Fair emblem.

1955, Aug. 31

Cream Paper

910	A468	4s deep brown	.20	.20
911	A469	16s dk car rose	.20	.20
912	A468	44s olive blk	.20	.20
913	A469	80s deep blue	.45	.20
		Nos. 910-913 (4)	1.05	.80

16th International Plovdiv Fair. Latin lettering on Nos. 912-913.

Friedrich von Schiller — A470

44s, Adam Mickiewicz. 60s, Hans Christian Andersen. 80s, Baron de Montesquieu. 1 l, Miguel de Cervantes. 2 l, Walt Whitman.

1955, Oct. 31
Cream Paper

914	A470	16s brown	.20	.20
915	A470	44s brown red	.40	.20
916	A470	60s Prus blue	.60	.20
917	A470	80s black	.60	.20
918	A470	1 l rose violet	1.40	.30
919	A470	2 l olive green	1.90	.50
		Nos. 914-919 (6)	5.10	1.60

Various anniversaries of famous writers. Nos. 918 and 919 are issued in sheets alternating with labels without franking value. The labels show title pages for Leaves of Grass and Don Quixote in English and Spanish, respectively. Latin lettering on #915-919.

A471

A472

A473

2s, Karl Marx Industrial Plant. 4s, Alexandr Stamboliski Dam. 16s, Bridge over Danube. 44s, Friendship Monument. 80s, I. V. Michurin. 1 l, Vladimir V. Mayakovsky.

1955, Dec. 1   **Unwmk.**

920	A471	2s slate blk	.20	.20
921	A471	4s deep blue	.20	.20
922	A471	16s dk blue grn	.20	.20
923	A472	44s red brown	.20	.20
924	A473	80s dark green	.25	.20
925	A473	1 l gray blk	.40	.20
		Nos. 920-925 (6)	1.45	1.20

Russian-Bulgarian friendship.

Library Seal — A474

Krusto Pishurka A475

Portrait: 44s, Bacho Kiro.

1956, Feb. 10   **Perf. 11x10½**

926	A474	12s car lake, cream	.20	.20
927	A475	16s dp brn, cream	.20	.20
928	A475	44s slate blk, cream	.25	.20
		Nos. 926-928 (3)	.65	.60

100th anniversary of the National Library. Latin lettering at bottom of No. 928.

Canceled to Order
Beginning about 1956, some issues were sold in sheets canceled to order. Values in second column when much less than unused are for "CTO" copies. Postally used stamps are valued at slightly less than, or the same as, unused.

Quinces — A476

Cherrywood Cannon A477

8s, Pears. 16s, Apples. 44s, Grapes.

1956   **Photo.**   **Perf. 13**

929	A476	4s carmine	.75	.20
930	A476	8s blue green	.30	.20
931	A476	16s lilac rose	.80	.20
932	A476	44s deep violet	.80	.20
		Nos. 929-932 (4)	2.65	.80

Latin lettering on #932. See #964-967. For surcharge see #1364.

1956, Apr. 28   **Perf. 11x10½**

933	A477	16s shown	.20	.20
934	A477	44s Cavalry attack	.25	.20

April Uprising against Turkish rule, 80th anniv.

Demeter Blagoev (1856-1924), Writer, Birthplace A478

Cherries — A479

1956, May 30   **Perf. 11**

935	A478	44s Prus blue	.25	.20

1956   **Unwmk.**   **Perf. 13**

936	A479	2s shown	.20	.20
937	A479	12s Plums	.20	.20
938	A479	28s Peaches	.20	.20
939	A479	80s Strawberries	.55	.20
		Nos. 936-939 (4)	1.15	.80

Latin lettering on No. 939.

Gymnastics A480

Pole Vaulting A481

Designs: 12s, Discus throw. 44s, Soccer. 80s, Basketball. 1 l, Boxing.

Perf. 11x10½, 10½x11

1956, Aug. 29

940	A480	4s brt ultra	.20	.20
941	A480	12s brick red	.20	.20
942	A481	16s yellow brn	.30	.20
943	A480	44s dark green	.50	.25
944	A480	80s dark red brn	1.00	.50
945	A481	1 l deep magenta	1.60	.65
		Nos. 940-945 (6)	3.80	2.00

Latin lettering on Nos. 943-945. 16th Olympic Games at Melbourne, Nov. 22-Dec. 8, 1956.

Tobacco, Rose and Distillery — A482

People's Theater A483

1956, Sept. 1   **Perf. 13**

946	A482	44s deep carmine	.40	.20
947	A482	44s olive green	.40	.20

17th International Plovdiv Fair.

1956, Nov. 16   **Unwmk.**

Design: 44s, Dobri Woinikoff and Sawa Dobroplodni, dramatists.

948	A483	16s dull red brown	.20	.20
949	A483	44s dark blue green	.25	.20

Bulgarian Theater centenary.

Benjamin Franklin — A484

Cyclists, Palms and Pyramids — A485

Portraits: 20s, Rembrandt. 40s, Mozart. 44s, Heinrich Heine. 60s, Shaw. 80s, Dostoevski. 1 l, Ibsen. 2 l, Pierre Curie.

1956, Dec. 29

950	A484	16s dark olive grn	.20	.20
951	A484	20s brown	.20	.20
952	A484	40s dark car rose	.20	.20
953	A484	44s dark violet brn	.25	.20
954	A484	60s dark slate	.30	.20
955	A484	80s dark brown	.45	.20
956	A484	1 l bluish grn	.80	.30
957	A484	2 l Prus green	1.75	.50
		Nos. 950-957 (8)	4.15	2.00

Great personalities of the world.

1957, Mar. 6   **Photo.**   **Perf. 10½**

958	A485	80s henna brown	.50	.25
959	A485	80s Prus green	.50	.25

Fourth Egyptian bicycle race.

Woman Technician A486

"New Times" Review — A487

Designs: 16s, Woman and children. 44s, Woman feeding chickens.

1957, Mar. 8

960	A486	12s deep blue	.20	.20
961	A486	16s henna brown	.20	.20
962	A486	44s slate green	.30	.20
		Nos. 960-962 (3)	.70	.60

Women's Day. Latin lettering on 44s.

1957, Mar. 8   **Unwmk.**

963	A487	16s deep carmine	.20	.20

60th anniversary of the founding of the "New Times" review.

Fruit Type of 1956.

4s, Quinces. 8s, Pears. 16s, Apples. 44s, Grapes.

1957   **Photo.**   **Perf. 13**

964	A476	4s yellow green	.20	.20
965	A476	8s brown orange	.20	.20
966	A476	16s rose red	.20	.20
967	A476	44s orange yellow	.40	.20
		Nos. 964-967 (4)	1.00	.80

Latin lettering on #967. For surcharge see #1364.

Sts. Cyril and Methodius — A488

Basketball A489

1957, May 22   **Perf. 11**

968	A488	44s olive grn & buff	.50	.20

Centenary of the first public veneration of Sts. Cyril and Methodius, inventors of the Cyrillic alphabet.

1957, June 20 **Photo.** **Perf. 10½x11**

969	A489	44s dark green	.95	.30

10th European Basketball Championship at Sofia.

Dancer and Spasski Tower, Moscow — A490

1957, July 18   **Perf. 13**

970	A490	44s blue	.30	.20

Sixth World Youth Festival in Moscow.

George Dimitrov (1882-1949) — A491

1957, July 18
971 A491 44s deep carmine   .50   .20

Vassil Levski — A492

1957, July 18   *Perf. 11*
972 A492 44s grnsh black   .30   .20

120th anniversary of the birth of Vassil Levski, patriot and national hero.

No. 742 Surcharged in Carmine
1957   *Unwmk.*   *Perf. 13*
973 A408 16s on 1 l purple   .20   .20

Trnovo and Lazarus L. Zamenhof A493

1957, July 27
974 A493 44s slate green   .50   .20

50th anniv. of the Bulgarian Esperanto Society and the 70th anniv. of Esperanto. For surcharge see No. 1235.

Bulgarian Veteran of 1877 War and Russian Soldier — A494

Design: 44s, Battle of Shipka Pass.

1957, Aug. 13
975 A494 16s dk blue grn   .20   .20
976 A494 44s brown   .30   .20

80th anniversary of Bulgaria's liberation from the Turks. Latin lettering on No. 976.

Woman Planting Tree — A495

Red Deer in Forest — A496

16s, Dam, lake and forest. 44s, Plane over forest. 80s, Fields on edge of forest.

1957, Sept. 16   *Photo.*   *Perf. 13*
977 A495 2s deep green   .20   .20
978 A496 12s dark brown   .20   .20
979 A496 16s Prus blue   .20   .20
980 A496 44s Prus green   .25   .20
981 A496 80s yellow green   .40   .20
    Nos. 977-981 (5)   1.25 1.00

Latin lettering on Nos. 980 and 981.

Lenin — A497

Designs: 16s, Cruiser "Aurora." 44s, Dove over map of communist area. 60s, Revolutionaries and banners. 80s, Oil refinery.

1957, Oct. 29   *Perf. 11*
982 A497 12s chocolate   .20   .20
983 A497 16s Prus green   .30   .20
984 A497 44s deep blue   .65   .20
985 A497 60s dk car rose   .75   .20
986 A497 80s dark green   1.25   .25
    Nos. 982-986 (5)   3.15 1.05

40th anniv. of the Communist Revolution. Latin lettering on Nos. 984-985.

Globes A498

1957, Oct. 4   *Perf. 13*
987 A498 44s Prus blue   .30   .20

4th Intl. Trade Union Cong., Leipzig, 10/4-15.

Vassil Kolarov Hotel A499

Bulgarian Health Resorts: 4s, Skis and Pirin Mountains. 8s, Old house at Koprivspitsa. 12s, Rest home at Velingrad. 44s, Momin-Prochod Hotel. 60s, Nesebr Hotel, shoreline and peninsula. 80s, Varna beach scene. 1 l, Hotel at Varna.

1958   *Photo.*   *Perf. 13*
988 A499 4s blue   .20   .20
989 A499 8s orange brn   .20   .20
990 A499 12s dk green   .20   .20
991 A499 16s green   .20   .20
992 A499 44s dk blue grn   .20   .20
993 A499 60s deep blue   .20   .20
994 A499 80s fawn   .30   .20
995 A499 1 l dk red brn   .35   .20
    Nos. 988-995 (8)   1.85 1.60

Latin lettering on 44s, 60s, 80s, and 1 l. Issue dates: #991-994, 1/20; others, 7/5. For surcharges see Nos. 1200, 1436.

Mikhail I. Glinka — A500

Portraits: 16s, Jan A. Komensky (Comenius). 40s, Carl von Linné. 44s, William Blake. 60s, Carlo Goldoni. 80s, Auguste Comte.

1957, Dec. 30
996 A500 12s dark brown   .20   .20
997 A500 16s dark green   .20   .20
998 A500 40s Prus blue   .20   .20
999 A500 44s maroon   .20   .20
1000 A500 60s orange brown   .75   .20
1001 A500 80s deep plum   2.50   .90
    Nos. 996-1001 (6)   4.05 1.90

Famous men of other countries. Latin lettering on Nos. 999-1001.

Young Couple, Flag, Dimitrov — A501   People's Front Salute — A502

1957, Dec. 28   *Perf. 11*
1002 A501 16s carmine rose   .20   .20

10th anniversary of Dimitrov's Union of the People's Youth.

1957, Dec. 28
1003 A502 16s dk violet brn   .20   .20

15th anniversary of the People's Front.

Hare A503

12s, Red deer (doe), vert. 16s, Red deer (stag). 44s, Chamois. 80s, Brown bear. 1 l, Wild boar.

      Perf. 10½
1958, Apr. 5   *Unwmk.*   *Photo.*
1004 A503 2s lt & dk ol grn   .20   .20
1005 A503 12s sl grn & red brn   .20   .20
1006 A503 16s bluish grn & dk red brn   .20   .20
1007 A503 44s blue & brown   .25   .20
1008 A503 80s bis & dk brn   .75   .25
1009 A503 1 l stl bl & dk brn   1.00   .25
    Nos. 1004-1009 (6)   2.60 1.30

Value, imperf. set $4.

Marx and Lenin A504

Designs: 16s, Marchers and flags. 44s, Lenin blast furnaces.

1958, July 2   *Perf. 11*
1010 A504 12s dark brown   .20   .20
1011 A504 16s dark carmine   .20   .20
1012 A504 44s dark blue   .85   .20
    Nos. 1010-1012 (3)   1.25   .60

Bulgarian Communist Party, 7th Congress.

Wrestlers — A505

1958, June 20   *Perf. 10½*
1013 A505 60s dk carmine rose   .65   .35
1014 A505 80s deep brown   1.10   .55

World Wrestling Championship, Sofia.

Chessmen and Globe A506

      Perf. 10½
1958, July 18   *Unwmk.*   *Photo.*
1015 A506 80s grn & yel grn   2.50   .80

5th World Students' Chess Games, Varna.

Conference Emblem A507

1958, Sept. 24
1016 A507 44s blue   .40   .20

World Trade Union Conference of Working Youth, Prague, July 14-20.

Swimmer A508

1958 Students' Games: 28s, Dancer, vert. 44s, Volleyball, vert.

1958, Sept. 19   *Perf. 11x10½*
1017 A508 16s bright blue   .20   .20
1018 A508 28s brown orange   .25   .20
1019 A508 44s bright green   .30   .20
    Nos. 1017-1019 (3)   .75   .60

Onions — A509

Vegetables: 12s, Garlic. 16s, Peppers. 44s, Tomatoes. 80s, Cucumbers. 1 l, Eggplant.

1958, Sept. 20   *Perf. 13*
1020 A509 2s orange brown   .20   .20
1021 A509 12s Prus blue   .20   .20
1022 A509 16s dark green   .20   .20
1023 A509 44s deep carmine   .20   .20
1024 A509 80s deep green   .40   .20
1025 A509 1 l brt purple   .60   .20
    Nos. 1020-1025 (6)   1.80 1.20

Value, imperf. set $4.
See No. 1072. For surcharge see No. 1201.

Plovdiv Fair Building A510

1958, Sept. 14   *Unwmk.*   *Perf. 11*
1026 A510 44s deep carmine   .40   .20

18th International Plovdiv Fair.

Attack — A511

44s, Fighter dragging wounded man.

1958, Sept. 23   *Photo.*   *Perf. 11*
1027 A511 16s orange ver   .20   .20
1028 A511 44s lake   .35   .20

35th anniv. of the September Revolution.

Emblem, Brussels Fair — A512

1958, Oct. 13   *Perf. 11*
1029 A512 1 l blk & brt blue   5.00 1.25
Brussels World's Fair, Apr. 17-Oct. 19.
Exists imperf.

Runner at Finish Line — A513

Woman Throwing Javelin A514

60s, High jumper. 80s, Hurdler. 4 l, Shot putter.

1958, Nov. 30
1030 A513 16s red brn, *pnksh*   .35 .20
1031 A514 44s olive, *yelsh*   .35 .20
1032 A514 60s dk bl, *bluish*   .65 .20
1033 A514 80s dp grn, *grnsh*   .90 .20
1034 A513 4 l dp rose cl, *pnksh*   5.75 1.40
   Nos. 1030-1034 (5)   8.00 2.20
1958 Balkan Games.
Latin lettering on Nos. 1032-1033.

Christo Smirnenski A515

1958, Dec. 22
1035 A515 16s dark carmine   .20 .20
Christo Smirnenski (1898-1923), poet.

Girls Harvesting — A516

Girl Tending Calves A517

16s, Boy & girl laborers. 40s, Boy pushing wheelbarrow. 44s, Headquarters building.

1959, Nov. 29   **Photo.**
1036 A516 8s dk olive green   .20 .20
1037 A517 12s redsh brown   .20 .20
1038 A516 16s violet brown   .20 .20

1039 A517 40s Prus blue   .20 .20
1040 A516 44s deep carmine   .60 .20
   Nos. 1036-1040 (5)   1.40 1.00
4th Congress of Dimitrov's Union of People's Youth.

UNESCO Building, Paris A518

1959, Mar. 28   **Unwmk.**   *Perf. 11*
1041 A518 2 l dp red lilac, *cream*   1.25 1.00
Opening of UNESCO Headquarters, Paris, Nov. 3, 1958. Value imperf. $2.50.

Skier — A519

Soccer Players — A520

1959, Mar. 28   *Perf. 11*
1042 A519 1 l blue, *cream*   .90 .50
Forty years of skiing in Bulgaria.

1959, Mar. 25
1043 A520 2 l chestnut, *cream*   1.25 .65
1959 European Youth Soccer Championship.

Russian Soldiers Installing Telegraph Wires — A521

First Bulgarian Postal Coach A522

Designs: 60s, Stamp of 1879. 80s, First Bulgarian automobile. 1 l, Television tower. 2 l, Strike of railroad and postal workers, 1919.

1959, May 4
1044 A521 12s dk grn & cit   .20 .20
1045 A522 16s deep plum   .20 .20
1046 A521 60s dk brn & yel   .30 .20
1047 A522 80s hn brn & sal   .45 .20
1048 A521 1 l blue   .60 .20
1049 A522 2 l dk red brown   1.60 .80
   Nos. 1044-1049 (6)   3.35 1.80
80th anniv. of the Bulgarian post. Latin lettering on Nos. 1046-1049.
Two imperf. souvenir sheets exist with olive borders and inscriptions. One contains one copy of No. 1046 in black & ocher, and measures 92x121mm. The other sheet contains one copy each of Nos. 1044-1045 and 1047-1048 in changed colors: 12s, olive green & ocher; 16s, deep claret & ocher; 80s, dark red & ocher; 1 l, olive & ocher. Each sheet sold for 5 leva. Value, each $24.

Great Tits A523

Birds: 8s, Hoopoe. 16s, Great spotted woodpecker, vert. 45s, Gray partridge, vert. 60s, Rock partridge, vert. 80s, European cuckoo.

1959, June 30   **Photo.**
1050 A523 2s olive & sl grn   .20 .20
1051 A523 8s dp orange & blk   .20 .20
1052 A523 16s chestnut & dk brn   .25 .20
1053 A523 45s brown & blk   .30 .20
1054 A523 60s dp blue & gray   .65 .20
1055 A523 80s dp bl grn & gray   1.10 .20
   Nos. 1050-1055 (6)   2.70 1.20

Bagpiper — A524

12s, Acrobats. 16s, Girls exercising with hoops. 20s, Male dancers. 80s, Ballet dancers. 1 l, Ceramic pitcher. 16s, 20s, 80s are horiz.

1959, Aug. 29   **Unwmk.**   *Perf. 11*
   Surface-colored Paper
1056 A524 4s dk olive   .20 .20
1057 A524 12s scarlet   .20 .20
1058 A524 16s maroon   .20 .20
1059 A524 20s dk blue   .25 .20
1060 A524 80s brt green   .50 .25
1061 A524 1 l brown org   .95 .40
   Nos. 1056-1061 (6)   2.30 1.45
7th International Youth Festival, Vienna. Latin inscriptions on Nos. 1060-1061.

Partisans in Truck A525

Designs: 16s, Partisans and soldiers shaking hands. 45s, Refinery. 60s, Tanks. 80s, Harvester. 1.25 l, Children with flag, vert.

1959, Sept. 8
1062 A525 12s red & Prus grn   .20 .20
1063 A525 16s red & dk pur   .20 .20
1064 A525 45s red & int bl   .20 .20
1065 A525 60s red & ol grn   .20 .20
1066 A525 80s red & brn   .25 .20
1067 A525 1.25 l red & dp brn   .65 .40
   Nos. 1062-1067 (6)   1.70 1.40
15th anniversary of Bulgarian liberation.

Soccer A526

1959, Oct. 10   **Unwmk.**   *Perf. 11*
1068 A526 1.25 l dp green, *yel*   3.50 2.00
50 years of Bulgarian soccer.
Set exists imperf. in changed colors. Value $7.50 unused, $4 canceled.

Batak Defenders A527

1959, Aug. 8
1069 A527 16s deep claret   .20 .20
300th anniv. of the settlement of Batak.

Post Horn and Letter — A528

Bird-shaped Lyre — A529

Design: 1.25 l, Dove and letter.

1959, Nov. 23
1070 A528 45s emerald & blk   .30 .20
1071 A528 1.25 l lt blue, red & blk   .50 .20
Intl. Letter Writing Week Oct. 5-11.

Type of 1958 Surcharged "45 CT." in Dark Blue
Design: Tomatoes.

1959   **Photo.**   *Perf. 13*
1072 A509 45s on 44s scarlet   .55 .20

1960, Feb. 23   **Unwmk.**   *Perf. 10½*
1073 A529 80s shown   .40 .20
1074 A529 1.25 l Lyre   .70 .20
50th anniv. of Bulgaria's State Opera.

N. I. Vapzarov — A530

Parachute and Radio Tower — A531

1959, Dec. 14   *Perf. 11*
1075 A530 80s yel grn & red brn   .35 .20
Vapzarov, poet and patriot, 50th birth anniv.

1959, Dec. 3   **Photo.**
1076 A531 1.25 l dp grnsh bl & yel   1.25 .45
3rd Cong. of Voluntary Participants in Defense.

Cotton Picker — A532

Harvester Combine A533

Designs: 2s, Kindergarten. 4s, Woman doctor and child. 10s, Woman milking cow. 12s, Woman holding tobacco leaves. 15s, Woman working loom. 16s, Stalin textile mill, Dimitrovgrad. 25s, Rural electrification. 28s, Woman picking sunflowers. 40s, "Cold-well" hydroelectric dam. 45s, Miner. 60s, Foundry worker. 80s, Woman harvesting grapes. 1 l, Worker and peasant with cogwheel. 1.25 l, Industrial worker. 2 l, Party leader.

1959-61   Photo.   Perf. 13

1077	A533	2s brn org ('60)	.20	.20
1077A	A532	4s gldn brn ('61)	.20	.20
1078	A532	5s dk green	.20	.20
1079	A533	10s red brn ('61)	.20	.20
1080	A532	12s red brown	.20	.20
1081	A532	15s red lil ('60)	.20	.20
1082	A533	16s dp vio ('60)	.20	.20
1083	A532	20s orange	.20	.20
1084	A532	25s brt blue ('60)	.20	.20
1085	A532	28s brt green	.20	.20
1086	A533	40s brt grnsh bl	.30	.20
1087	A532	45s choc ('60)	.25	.20
1088	A533	60s scarlet	.40	.20
1089	A532	80s olive ('60)	.50	.20
1090	A532	1 l maroon	.50	.20
1090A	A533	1.25 l dull bl ('61)	1.75	.30
1091	A532	2 l dp car ('60)	1.10	.25
	Nos. 1077-1091 (17)		6.80	3.55

Early completion of the 5-year plan (in 1959).
For surcharges see Nos. 1192-1199, 1202-1203.

L. L. Zamenhof
A534

Path of Lunik 3 — A535

1959, Dec. 5   Unwmk.   Perf. 11

1092	A534	1.25 l dk grn & yel grn	.80	.40

Lazarus Ludwig Zamenhof (1859-1917), inventor of Esperanto.

1960, Mar. 28   Perf. 11

1093	A535	1.25 l Prus bl & brt yel	3.50	1.90

Flight of Lunik 3 around moon. Value, imperf. $5

Skier
A536

1960, Apr. 15   Litho.

1094	A536	2 l ultra, blk & brn	.95	.35

8th Winter Olympics, Squaw Valley, CA, Feb. 18-29. Value, imperf. $2 unused, $1 canceled.

Vela Blagoeva
A537

Portraits: 28s, Anna Maimunkova. 45s, Vela Piskova. 60s, Rosa Luxemburg. 80s, Klara Zetkin. 1.25 l, N. K. Krupskaya.

1960, Apr. 27   Photo.   Perf. 11

1095	A537	16s rose & red brn	.20	.20
1096	A537	28s citron & olive	.20	.20
1097	A537	45s ol grn & sl grn	.20	.20
1098	A537	60s lt bl & Prus bl	.20	.20
1099	A537	80s red org & dp brn	.35	.20
1100	A537	1.25 l dull yel & olive	.60	.20
	Nos. 1095-1100 (6)		1.75	1.20

International Women's Day, Mar. 8, 1960.

Lenin — A538

1960, May 12

1101	A538	16s shown	.50	.20
1102	A538	45s Lenin sitting	1.10	.20

90th anniversary of the birth of Lenin.

A539

1960, June 3   Perf. 11

1103	A539	1.25 l yel & slate grn	.85	.35

Seventh European Women's Basketball championships.

A541

1960, June 29   Litho.

1105	A541	16s Parachutist	.55	.30
1106	A541	1.25 l Parachutes	1.50	.45

5th International Parachute Championships.

Yellow Gentian — A542

5s, Tulips. 25s, Turk's-cap lily. 45s, Rhododendron. 60s, Lady's-slipper. 80s, Violets.

1960, July 27   Photo.   Perf. 11

1107	A542	2s beige, grn & yel	.20	.20
1108	A542	5s yel grn, grn & car rose	.20	.20
1109	A542	25s pink, grn & org	.20	.20
1110	A542	45s pale lil, grn & rose lil	.35	.20
1111	A542	60s yel, grn & org	.75	.20
1112	A542	80s gray, grn & vio bl	.90	.25
	Nos. 1107-1112 (6)		2.60	1.25

Soccer
A543

12s, Wrestling. 16s, Weight lifting. 45s, Woman gymnast. 80s, Canoeing. 2 l, Runner.

1960, Aug. 29   Unwmk.   Perf. 11
Athletes' Figures in Pink

1113	A543	8s brown	.25	.20
1114	A543	12s violet	.25	.20
1115	A543	16s Prus blue	.25	.20
1116	A543	45s deep plum	.25	.20
1117	A543	80s blue	.50	.20
1118	A543	2 l deep green	1.75	.35
	Nos. 1113-1118 (6)		3.25	1.35

17th Olympic Games, Rome, 8/25-9/11. Value, set imperf. in changed colors, $3.50.

Globes — A544

Unwmk.

1125	A544	1.25 l blue & ultra	.50	.20

1960, Oct. 12   Photo.   Perf. 11

15th anniversary of the World Federation of Trade Unions.

Alexander Popov
A545

1960, Oct. 12

1126	A545	90s blue & blk	.75	.20

Centenary of the birth of Alexander Popov, radio pioneer.

Bicyclists
A546

1960, Sept. 22

1127	A546	1 l yel, red org & blk	.90	.45

The 10th Tour of Bulgaria Bicycle Race.

Jaroslav Vésin
A547

1960, Nov. 22   Unwmk.   Perf. 11

1128	A547	1 l brt citron & ol grn	2.75	.65

Birth centenary of Jaroslav Vesin, painter.

UN Headquarters
A548

Costume of Kyustendil
A549

1961, Jan. 14   Photo.   Perf. 11

1129	A548	1 l brown & yel	1.00	.45
a.		Souvenir sheet	4.00	2.75

15th anniv. of the UN. #1129 sold for 2 l. Value, imperf. $3.50.
No. 1129a sold for 2.50 l and contains one copy of No. 1129, imperf, in dark olive and pink.

1961, Jan. 28

Regional Costumes: 16s, Pleven. 28s, Sliven. 45s, Sofia. 60s, Rhodope. 80s, Karnobat.

1130	A549	12s sal, sl grn & yel	.20	.20
1131	A549	16s pale lil, brn vio & buff	.20	.20
1132	A549	28s pale grn, sl grn & rose	.20	.20
1133	A549	45s blue & red	.30	.20
1134	A549	60s grnsh bl, Prus bl & yel	.50	.20
1135	A549	80s yel, sl grn & pink	.60	.25
	Nos. 1130-1135 (6)		2.00	1.25

Theodor Tiro (Fresco)
A550

Designs: 60s, Boyana Church. 1.25 l, Duchess of Dessislava (fresco).

1961, Jan. 28   Photo.

1136	A550	60s yel grn, blk & grn	.50	.20
1137	A550	80s yel, sl grn & org	.50	.20
1138	A550	1.25 l yel grn, hn brn & buff	1.00	.25
	Nos. 1136-1138 (3)		2.00	.65

700th anniv. of murals in Boyana Church.

Clock Tower, Vratsa — A551

Wooden Jug — A552

Designs: 12s, Clock tower, Bansko. 20s, Anguchev House, Mogilitsa. 28s, Oslekov House, Koprivspitsa, horiz. 40s, Pasha's house. Melnik, horiz. 45s, Lion sculpture. 60s, Man on horseback, Madara. 80s, Fresco, Bratchkovo monastery. 1 l, Tsar Assen coin.

1961, Feb. 25   Unwmk.   Perf. 11
Denomination and Stars in Vermilion

1139	A551	8s olive grn	.20	.20
1140	A551	12s lt violet	.20	.20
1141	A551	16s dk red brn	.20	.20
1142	A551	20s brt blue	.20	.20
1143	A551	28s grnsh blue	.20	.20
1144	A551	40s red brown	.20	.20
1145	A552	45s olive gray	.20	.20
1146	A552	60s slate	.30	.20
1147	A552	80s dk olive gray	.55	.20
1148	A552	1 l green	.70	.20
	Nos. 1139-1148 (10)		2.95	2.00

Capercaillie
A553

Birds: 4s, Dalmatian pelican. 16s, Ring-necked pheasant. 80s, Great bustard. 1 l, Lammergeier. 2 l, Hazel hen.

1961, Mar. 31

1149	A553	2s blk, sal & Prus grn	.20	.20
1150	A553	4s blk, yel grn & org	.20	.20
1151	A553	16s brn, lt grn & org	.20	.20

1152	A553	80s brn, bluish grn & yel	.35	.20
1153	A553	1 l blk, lt bl & yel	.65	.20
1154	A553	2 l brn, bl & yel	1.60	.55
		Nos. 1149-1153 (5)	1.60	1.00

Radio Tower and Winged Anchor
A554

1961, Apr. 1   Unwmk.   Perf. 11
1155 A554 80s brt green & blk   .45 .20
50th anniv. of the Transport Workers' Union.

T. G. Shevchenko
A555

Water Polo — A556

1961, Apr. 27
1156 A555 1 l olive & blk   2.50 .65
Centenary of the death of Taras G. Shevchenko, Ukrainian poet.

1961, May 15
Designs: 5s, Tennis. 16s, Fencing. 45s, Throwing the discus. 1.25 l, Sports Palace. 2 l, Basketball. 5 l, Sports Palace, different view. 5s, 16s, 45s and 1.25 l, are horizontal.

Black Inscriptions
1157	A556	4s lt ultra	.20	.20
1158	A556	5s orange ver	.20	.20
1159	A556	16s olive grn	.20	.20
1160	A556	45s dull blue	.20	.20
1161	A556	1.25 l yellow brn	.60	.20
1162	A556	2 l lilac	.85	.40
		Nos. 1157-1162 (6)	2.25	1.40

Souvenir Sheet
Imperf
1163 A556 5 l yel grn, dl bl & yel   7.50 6.50
1961 World University Games, Sofia, Aug. 26-Sept. 3.
Value, Nos. 1157-1162 in changed colors, imperf. $4.50.

Monk Seal A557

Black Sea Fauna: 12s, Jellyfish. 16s, Dolphin. 45s, Black Sea sea horse, vert. 1 l, Starred sturgeon. 1.25 l, Thornback ray.

1961, June 19   Perf. 11
1164	A557	2s green & blk	.20	.20
1165	A557	12s Prus grn & pink	.20	.20
1166	A557	16s ultra & vio bl	.20	.20
1167	A557	45s lt blue & brn	.30	.20
1168	A557	1 l yel grn & Prus grn	.65	.20
1169	A557	1.25 l lt vio bl & red brn	1.10	.35
		Nos. 1164-1169 (6)	2.65	1.35

Hikers — A558

Designs: 4s, "Sredetz" hostel, horiz. 16s, Tents. 1.25 l, Mountain climber.

1961, Aug. 25   Litho.   Perf. 11
1170	A558	4s yel grn, yel & blk	.20	.20
1171	A558	12s lt bl, cr & blk	.20	.20
1172	A558	16s green, cr & blk	.20	.20
1173	A558	1.25 l bister, cr & blk	.45	.20
		Nos. 1170-1173 (4)	1.05	.80
"Know Your Country" campaign.

Demeter Blagoev Addressing 1891 Congress at Busludja — A559

1961, Aug. 5   Photo.
1174	A559	45s dk red & buff	.20	.20
1175	A559	80s blue & pink	.30	.20
1176	A559	2 l dk brn & pale cit	.75	.25
		Nos. 1174-1176 (3)	1.25	.65
70th anniversary of the first Congress of the Bulgarian Social-Democratic Party.

The Golden Girl A560

Fairy Tales: 8s, The Living Water. 12s, The Golden Apple. 16s, Krali-Marko, hero. 45s, Samovila-Vila, Witch. 80s, Tom Thumb.

1961, Oct. 10   Unwmk.   Perf. 11
1177	A560	2s blue, blk & org	.20	.20
1178	A560	8s rose lil, blk & gray	.25	.20
1179	A560	12s bl grn, blk & pink	.25	.20
1180	A560	16s red, blk, bl & gray	.40	.20
1181	A560	45s ol grn, blk & pink	.75	.25
1182	A560	80s ocher, blk & dk car	1.10	.30
		Nos. 1177-1182 (6)	2.95	1.35

Caesar's Mushroom A561

Miladinov Brothers and Title Page — A562

Designs: Various mushrooms.

1961, Dec. 20   Photo.   Perf. 11
Denominations in Black
1183	A561	2s lemon & red	.20	.20
1184	A561	4s ol grn & red brn	.20	.20
1185	A561	12s bister & red brn	.20	.20
1186	A561	16s lilac & red brn	.20	.20
1187	A561	45s car rose & yel	.20	.20
1188	A561	80s brn org & sepia	.20	.20
1189	A561	1.25 l vio & dk brn	.40	.20
1190	A561	2 l org brn & brn	.70	.40
		Nos. 1183-1190 (8)	2.30	1.80
Value, denomination in dark grn, imperf. set $5 unused, $1.75 canceled.

1961, Dec. 21   Unwmk.   Perf. 10½
1191 A562 1.25 l olive & blk   .60 .20
Publication of "Collected Folksongs" by the Brothers Miladinov, Dimitri and Konstantin, cent.

Nos. 1079-1085, 1087, 992, 1023, 1090-1091 and 806 Surcharged with New Value in Black, Red or Violet

1962, Jan. 1
1192	A533	1s on 10s red brown	.20	.20
1193	A532	1s on 12s red brown	.20	.20
1194	A532	2s on 15s red lilac	.20	.20
1195	A533	2s on 16s dp vio (R)	.20	.20
1196	A533	2s on 20s orange	.20	.20
a.		"2 CT." on 2 lines	.20	.20
1197	A532	3s on 25s brt bl (R)	.20	.20
a.		Black surcharge	6.00	4.00
1198	A532	3s on 28s brt grn (R)	.20	.20
1199	A532	5s on 45s chocolate	.20	.20
1200	A499	5s on 44s dk bl grn (R)	.20	.20
1201	A509	5s on 44s dp car (V)	.20	.20
1202	A532	10s on 1 l maroon	.25	.20
1203	A532	20s on 2 l dp car	.70	.25
1204	A430	40s on 4 l rose lake (V)	1.50	.50
		Nos. 1192-1204 (13)	4.45	2.95

Freighter "Varna" A563

Designs: 5s, Tanker "Komsomoletz." 20s, Liner "G. Dimitrov."

1962, Mar. 1   Photo.   Perf. 10½
1205	A563	1s lt grn & brt bl	.20	.20
1206	A563	5s lt blue & grn	.20	.20
1207	A563	20s gray bl & grnsh bl	.70	.20
		Nos. 1205-1207 (3)	1.10	.60

Dimitrov Working as Printer — A564

Roses — A565

13s, Griffin, emblem of state printing works.

1962, Mar. 19   Unwmk.
1208 A564 2s ver, blk & yel   .20 .20
1209 A564 13s red org, blk & yel .40 .20
80th anniversary (in 1961) of the George Dimitrov state printing works.

1962, Mar. 28
Various Roses in Natural Colors
1210	A565	1s deep violet	.20	.20
1211	A565	2s salmon & dk car	.20	.20
1212	A565	3s gray & car	.20	.20
1213	A565	4s dark green	.20	.20
1214	A565	5s ultra	.25	.20
1215	A565	6s bluish grn & dk car	.50	.20
1216	A565	8s citron & car	1.10	.20
1217	A565	13s blue	2.25	.60
		Nos. 1210-1217 (8)	4.90	2.00
For overprint and surcharges see Nos. 1281-1283.

Malaria Eradication Emblem and Mosquito A566

Design: 20s, Malaria eradication emblem.

1962, Apr. 19
1218 A566 5s org brn, yel & blk .40 .20
1219 A566 20s emerald, yel & blk .85 .35
WHO drive to eradicate malaria.
Value, imperf. $2.50 unused, $1.50 canceled.

Lenin and First Issue of Pravda A567

1962, May 4   Unwmk.   Perf. 10
1220 A567 5s deep rose & slate .25 .20
50th anniversary of Pravda, Russian newspaper founded by Lenin.

Blackboard and Book — A568

1962, May 21   Photo.
1221 A568 5s Prus bl, blk & yel .25 .20
The 1962 Teachers' Congress.

Soccer Player and Globe A569

1962, May 26   Perf. 10½
1222 A569 13s brt grn, blk & lt brn .65 .25
World Soccer Championship, Chile, May 30-June 17. Value, imperf. in changed colors, $2.50 unused, $1.65 canceled.

George Dimitrov A570

1962, June 18   Photo.
1223 A570 2s dark green .20 .20
1224 A570 5s turq blue .40 .20
80th anniv. of the birth of George Dimitrov (1882-1949), communist leader and premier of the Bulgarian Peoples' Republic.

Bishop — A571

1962, July 7   Unwmk.   Perf. 10½
1225	A571	1s shown	.20	.20
1226	A571	2s Rook	.20	.20
1227	A571	3s Queen	.20	.20
1228	A571	13s Knight	.65	.25
1229	A571	20s Pawn	1.10	.40
		Nos. 1225-1229 (5)	2.35	1.25

15th Chess Olympics, Varna. Nos. 1225-1229 were also issued imperf. in changed colors.

An imperf. souvenir sheet contains one 20s horizontal stamp showing five chessmen. Size: 75x66mm.

Rila Mountain
A572

Designs: 2s, Pirin mountain. 6s, Nesebr, Black Sea. 8s, Danube. 13s, Vidin Castle. 1 l, Rhodope mountain.

1962-63   Perf. 13
1230	A572	1s dk blue grn	.20	.20
1231	A572	2s blue	.20	.20
1232	A572	6s grnsh blue	.20	.20
1233	A572	8c lilac	.20	.20
1234	A572	13s yellow grn	.40	.20
1234A	A572	1 l dp green ('63)	3.25	.30
		Nos. 1230-1234A (6)	4.45	1.30

No. 974 Surcharged in Red

1962, July 14   Perf. 13
1235	A493	13s on 44s slate grn	2.25	.80

25th Bulgarian Esperanto Congress, Burgas, July 14-16.

Girl and Festival Emblem A573

Design: 5s, Festival emblem.

1962, Aug. 18   Photo.   Perf. 10½
1236	A573	5s green, lt bl & pink	.20	.20
1237	A573	13s lilac, lt bl & gray	.35	.20

8th Youth Festival for Peace and Friendship, Helsinki, July 28-Aug. 6, 1962.

Parnassius Apollo — A574

1962, Sept. 13
Various Butterflies in Natural Colors
1238	A574	1s pale cit & dk grn	.20	.20
1239	A574	2s rose & brown	.20	.20
1240	A574	3s buff & red brn	.20	.20
1241	A574	4s gray & brown	.20	.20
1242	A574	5s lt gray & brn	.20	.20
1243	A574	6s gray & black	.20	.20
1244	A574	10s pale grn & blk	1.25	.25
1245	A574	13s buff & red brn	1.90	.40
		Nos. 1238-1245 (8)	4.35	1.85

Planting Machine — A575

2s, Electric locomotive. 3s, Blast furnace. 13s, Blagoev, Dimitrov & Communist flag.

1962, Nov. 1   Perf. 11½
1246	A575	1s bl grn & dk ol grn	.20	.20
1247	A575	2s bl & Prus bl	.20	.20
1248	A575	3s carmine & brn	.20	.20
1249	A575	13s plum, red & blk	.55	.20
		Nos. 1246-1249 (4)	1.15	.80

Bulgarian Communist Party, 8th Congress.

Title Page of "Slav-Bulgarian History" — A576

Paisii Hilendarski Writing History A577

1962, Dec. 8   Unwmk.   Perf. 10½
1250	A576	2s olive grn & blk	.20	.20
1251	A577	5s brown org & blk	.20	.20

200th anniv. of "Slav-Bulgarian History."

Aleco Konstantinov (1863-1897), Writer A578

1963, Mar. 5   Photo.   Perf. 11½
1252	A578	5s red, grn & blk	.25	.20

Printed with alternating red brown and black label showing Bai Ganu, hero from Konstantinov's books.

A579

Sofia University — A580

#1255, Levski Stadium, Sofia. #1256, Arch, Nissaria. #1257, Parachutist.

1963, Feb. 20   Unwmk.   Perf. 10
1253	A579	1s brown red	.20	.20
1254	A580	1s red brown	.20	.20
1255	A580	1s blue green	.20	.20
1256	A580	1s dark green	.20	.20
1257	A580	1s brt blue	.20	.20
		Nos. 1253-1257 (5)	1.00	1.00

Vassil Levski
A581

Boy, Girl and Dimitrov — A582

1963, Apr. 11   Photo.
1258	A581	13s grnsh blue & buff	.75	.25

90th anniversary of the death of Vassil Levski, revolutionary leader in the fight for liberation from the Turks.

1963, Apr. 25   Unwmk.   Perf. 11½
13s, Girl with book & boy with hammer.
1259	A582	2s org, ver, red brn & blk	.20	.20
1260	A582	13s bluish grn, brn & blk	.40	.20

10th Congress of Dimitrov's Union of the People's Youth.

Red Squirrel — A583

Sun Coast Promenade A584

2s, Hedgehog. 3s, European polecat. 5s, Pine marten. 13s, Badger. 20s, Otter. 2s, 3s, 13s, horiz.

1963, Apr. 30
Red Numerals
1261	A583	1s grn & brn, grnsh	.20	.20
1262	A583	2s grn & blk, yel	.20	.20
1263	A583	3s grn & brn, bis	.20	.20
1264	A583	5s vio & red brn, lil	.20	.20
1265	A583	13s red brn & blk, pink	.80	.20
1266	A583	20s blk & brn, blue	1.25	.20
		Nos. 1261-1266 (6)	2.85	1.20

1963, Mar. 12   Unwmk.   Perf. 13
Black Sea Resorts: 2s, 3s, 13s, Views of Gold Sand. 5s, 20s, Sun Coast.
1267	A584	1s blue	.20	.20
1268	A584	2s vermilion	.25	.20
1269	A584	2s car rose	.40	.20
1270	A584	3s ocher	.20	.20
1271	A584	5s lilac	.20	.20
1272	A584	13s blue green	.50	.20
1273	A584	20s green	.95	.20
		Nos. 1267-1273 (7)	2.70	1.40

Freestyle Wrestling A585

Design: 20s, Freestyle wrestling, horiz.

1963, May 31   Perf. 11½
1274	A585	5s yel bister & blk	.20	.20
1275	A585	20s org brn & blk	.80	.20

15th International Freestyle Wrestling Competitions, Sofia.

"Women for Peace" A586

1963, June 24   Unwmk.   Perf. 11½
1276	A586	20s blue & blk	.60	.20

World Congress of Women, Moscow, June 24-29.

Esperanto Emblem and Arms of Sofia — A587

Moon, Earth and Lunik 4 — A588

1963, June 29   Photo.
1277	A587	13s multicolored	.65	.20

48th World Esperanto Congress, Sofia, Aug. 3-10.

1963, July 22
2s, Radar equipment. 3s, Satellites and moon.
1278	A588	1s ultra	.20	.20
1279	A588	2s red lilac	.20	.20
1280	A588	3s greenish blue	.20	.20
		Nos. 1278-1280 (3)	.60	.60

Russia's rocket to the moon, Apr. 2, 1963.

Nos. 1211-1212 and 1215 Overprinted or Surcharged in Green, Ultramarine or Black

1963, Aug. 31   Perf. 10½
1281	A565	2s (G)	.25	.20
1282	A565	5s on 3s (U)	.40	.20
1283	A565	13s on 6s	.70	.25
		Nos. 1281-1283 (3)	1.35	.65

Intl. Stamp Fair, Riccione, Aug. 31.

Women's Relay Race — A589

2s, Hammer thrower. 3s, Women's long jump. 5s, Men's high jump. 13s, Discus thrower.

1963, Sept. 13 Photo. Unwmk.
Flags in National Colors
1284	A589	1s slate green	.20 .20
1285	A589	2s purple	.20 .20
1286	A589	3s Prus blue	.20 .20
1287	A589	5s maroon	.45 .30
1288	A589	13s chestnut brn	1.60 1.25
		Nos. 1284-1288 (5)	2.65 2.15

Perf. 11½

Balkan Games. A multicolored, 50s, imperf. souvenir sheet shows design of women's relay race. Size: 74x70mm.

"Slav-Bulgarian History" — A590

1963, Sept. 19 *Perf. 10½*
1289	A590	5s sal pink, slate & yel	.20 .20

5th International Slavic Congress.

Revolutionists
A591

Christo
Smirnenski
A592

1963, Sept. 22 *Perf. 11½*
1290	A591	2s brt red & blk	.20 .20

40th anniv. of the September Revolution.

1963, Oct. 28 *Perf. 10½*
1291	A592	13s pale lilac & indigo	.45 .20

Christo Smirnenski, poet, 65th birth anniv.

Columbine
A593

Horses — A594

1963, Oct. 9 Photo. *Perf. 11½*
1292	A593	1s shown	.20 .20
1293	A593	2s Edelweiss	.20 .20
1294	A593	3s Primrose	.20 .20
1295	A593	5s Water lily	.20 .20
1296	A593	6s Tulips	.20 .20
1297	A593	8s Larkspur	.30 .20
1298	A593	10s Alpine clematis	.70 .20
1299	A593	13s Anemone	1.25 .25
		Nos. 1292-1299 (8)	3.25 1.65

1963, Dec. 28 Unwmk. *Perf. 10½*
Designs: 2s, Charioteer and chariot. 3s, Trumpeters. 5s, Woman carrying tray with food. 13s, Man holding bowl. 20s, Woman in armchair. Designs are from a Thracian tomb at Kazanlik.

1300	A594	1s gray, org & dk red	.20 .20
1301	A594	2s gray, ocher & pur	.20 .20
1302	A594	3s gray, dl yel & sl grn	.20 .20
1303	A594	5s pale grn, ocher & brn	.20 .20
1304	A594	13s pale grn, bis & blk	.40 .20
1305	A594	20s pale grn, org & dk car	.75 .30
		Nos. 1300-1305 (6)	1.95 1.30

World Map
and
Emblem
A595

Designs: 2s, Blood transfusion. 3s, Nurse bandaging injured wrist. 5s, Red Cross nurse. 13s, Henri Dunant.

1964, Jan. 27 *Perf. 10½*
1306	A595	1s lem, blk & red	.20 .20
1307	A595	2s ultra, blk & red	.20 .20
1308	A595	3s gray, sl, blk & red	.20 .20
1309	A595	5s brt bl, blk & red	.20 .20
1310	A595	13s org yel, blk & red	.40 .20
		Nos. 1306-1310 (5)	1.20 1.00

Centenary of International Red Cross.

Speed
Skating
A596

Sports: 2s, 50s, Women's figure skating. 3s, Cross-country skiing. 5s, Ski jump. 10s, Ice hockey goalkeeper. 13s, Ice hockey players.

1964, Feb. 21 Unwmk. *Perf. 10½*
1311	A596	1s grnsh bl, ind & ocher	.20 .20
1312	A596	2s brt pink, ol grn & dk sl grn	.20 .20
1313	A596	3s dl grn, dk grn & brn	.20 .20
1314	A596	5s bl, blk & yel brn	.20 .20
1315	A596	10s gray, org & blk	.40 .20
1316	A596	13s lil, blk & lil rose	.70 .30
		Nos. 1311-1316 (6)	1.90 1.30

Miniature Sheet
Imperf
1317	A596	50s gray, Prus grn & pink	4.00 3.00

9th Winter Olympic Games, Innsbruck, Jan. 29-Feb. 9, 1964.

Mask of
Nobleman,
2nd Century
A597

2s, Thracian horseman. 3s, Ceramic jug. 5s, Clasp & belt. 6s, Copper kettle. 8s, Angel. 10s, Lioness. 13s, Scrub woman, contemporary sculpture.

1964, Mar. 14 Photo. *Perf. 10½*
Gray Frame
1318	A597	1s dp green & red	.20 .20
1319	A597	2s ol gray & red	.20 .20
1320	A597	3s bister & red	.20 .20
1321	A597	5s indigo & red	.20 .20
1322	A597	6s org brn & red	.25 .20
1323	A597	8s brn red & red	.40 .20
1324	A597	10s olive & red	.40 .20
1325	A597	13s gray ol & red	.65 .25
		Nos. 1318-1325 (8)	2.50 1.65

2,500 years of Bulgarian art.

"The
Unborn
Maid"
A598

Fairy Tales: 2s, Grandfather's Glove. 3s, The Big Turnip. 5s, The Wolf and the Seven Kids. 8s, Cunning Peter. 13s, The Wheat Cake.

1964, Apr. 17 Unwmk. *Perf. 10½*
1326	A598	1s bl grn, red & org brn	.20 .20
1327	A598	2s ultra, ocher & blk	.20 .20
1328	A598	3s cit, red & blk	.20 .20
1329	A598	5s dp rose, brn & blk	.20 .20
1330	A598	8s yel grn, red & blk	.20 .20
1331	A598	13s lt vio bl, grn & blk	.70 .20
		Nos. 1326-1331 (6)	1.70 1.20

Ascalaphus
Otomanus
A599

Insects: 2s, Nemoptera coa., vert. 3s, Saga natalia (grasshopper). 5s, Rosalia alpina, vert. 13s, Anisoplia austriaca, vert. 20s, Scolia flavitrons.

1964, May 16 Photo. *Perf. 11½*
1332	A599	1s brn org, yel & blk	.20 .20
1333	A599	2s dl bl grn, bis & blk	.20 .20
1334	A599	3s gray, grn & blk	.20 .20
1335	A599	5s lt ol grn, blk & vio	.20 .20
1336	A599	13s vio, bis & blk	.55 .20
1337	A599	20s gray bl, yel & blk	.85 .30
		Nos. 1332-1337 (6)	2.20 1.30

Soccer — A600

Designs: 13s, Women's volleyball. 60s, Map of Europe and European Women's Volleyball Championship Cup (rectangular, size: 60x69mm).

1964, June 8 Unwmk. *Perf. 11½*
1338	A600	2s bl, dk bl, ocher & red	.20 .20
1339	A600	13s bl, dk bl, ocher & red	.50 .25

Miniature Sheet
Imperf
1340	A600	60s ultra, ocher, red & gray	3.00 2.25

Levski Physical Culture Assoc., 50th anniv.

Peter Beron and Title Page of
Primer — A601

1964, June 22 *Perf. 11½*
1341	A601	20s red brn & dk brn, *grysh*	1.00 .60

140th anniversary of the publication of the first Bulgarian primer.

Robert Stephenson's "Rocket"
Locomotive, 1825 — A602

Designs: 2s, Modern steam locomotive. 3s, Diesel locomotive. 5s, Electric locomotive. 8s, Freight train on bridge. 13s, Diesel locomotive and tunnel.

1964, July 1 Photo. *Perf. 11½*
1342	A602	1s multicolored	.20 .20
1343	A602	2s multicolored	.20 .20
1344	A602	3s multicolored	.20 .20
1345	A602	5s multicolored	.20 .20
1346	A602	8s multicolored	.30 .20
1347	A602	13s multicolored	.80 .20
		Nos. 1342-1347 (6)	1.90 1.20

German Shepherd — A603

1964, Aug. 22 Photo.
1348	A603	1s shown	.20 .20
1349	A603	2s Setter	.20 .20
1350	A603	3s Poodle	.20 .20
1351	A603	4s Pomeranian	.20 .20
1352	A603	5s St. Bernard	.20 .20
1353	A603	6s Terrier	.25 .20
1354	A603	10s Pointer	1.40 .25
1355	A603	13s Dachshund	2.75 .40
		Nos. 1348-1355 (8)	5.40 1.85

Partisans — A604

Designs: 2s, People welcoming Soviet army. 3s, Russian aid to Bulgaria. 4s, Blast furnace, Kremikovski. 5s, Combine. 6s, Peace demonstration. 8s, Sentry. 13s, Demeter Blagoev and George Dimitrov.

1964, Sept. 9 Unwmk. *Perf. 11½*
Flag in Red
1356	A604	1s lt & dp ultra	.20 .20
1357	A604	2s ol bis & dp ol	.20 .20
1358	A604	3s rose lil & mar	.20 .20
1359	A604	4s lt vio & vio	.20 .20
1360	A604	5s org & red brn	.20 .20
1361	A604	6s bl & dp bl	.20 .20
1362	A604	8s lt grn & grn	.20 .20
1363	A604	13s fawn & red brn	.40 .20
		Nos. 1356-1363 (8)	1.80 1.60

20th anniv. of People's Government of Bulgaria.

No. 967 Surcharged

1964, Sept. 13 *Perf. 13*
1364	A476	20s on 44s org yel	1.00 .35

International Plovdiv Fair.

Gymnast on Parallel Bars — A606

Vratcata Mountain Road — A607

Sports: 2s, Long jump. 3s, Woman diver. 5s, Soccer. 13s, Women's volleyball. 20s, Wrestling.

1964, Oct. 10　　　　　　Perf. 11½
1366　A606　1s pale grn, grn & red　.20　.20
1367　A606　2s pale vio, vio bl & red　.20　.20
1368　A606　3s bl grn, brn & red　.20　.20
1369　A606　5s pink, pur & red　.20　.20
1370　A606　13s bl, Prus grn & red　.50　.20
1371　A606　20s yel, grn & red　.90　.25
　　Nos. 1366-1371 (6)　2.20　1.25

18th Olympic Games, Tokyo. Oct. 10-25. See No. B27.

1964, Oct. 26　Photo.　Perf. 12½x13
Bulgarian Views: 2s, Ritlite mountain road. 3s, Pines, Malovica peak. 4s, Pobitite rocks. 5s, Erkupria. 6s, Rhodope mountain road.

1372　A607　1s dk slate grn　.20　.20
1373　A607　2s brown　.20　.20
1374　A607　3s grnsh blue　.20　.20
1375　A607　4s dk red brn　.20　.20
1376　A607　5s deep green　.20　.20
1377　A607　6s blue violet　.30　.20
　　Nos. 1372-1377 (6)　1.30　1.20

Mail Coach, Plane and Rocket A608

1964, Oct. 3　Unwmk.　Perf. 11½
1378　A608　20s greenish blue　1.25　.50

First national stamp exhibition, Sofia, Oct. 3-18. Issued in sheets of 12 stamps and 12 labels (woman's head and inscription, 5x5) arranged around one central label showing stylized bird design.
Exists imperf.

Students Holding Book — A609

1964, Dec. 30　　　　　　Photo.
1379　A609　13s lt blue & blk　.45　.20

8th Intl. Students' Congress, Sofia.

500-Year-Old Walnut Tree at Golemo Drenovo — A610

Designs: Various old trees.

1964, Dec. 28
1380　A610　1s blk, buff & cl brn　.20　.20
1381　A610　2s blk, pink & dp cl　.20　.20
1382　A610　3s blk, yel & dk brn　.20　.20
1383　A610　4s blk, lt bl & Prus bl　.20　.20
1384　A610　10s blk, pale grn & grn　.25　.20
1385　A610　13s blk, pale bis & dk ol grn　.40　.20
　　Nos. 1380-1385 (6)　1.45　1.20

Soldiers' Monument A611

1965, Jan. 1　　　　　　Unwmk.
1386　A611　2s red & black　.20　.20

Bulgarian-Soviet friendship.

Olympic Medal Inscribed "Olympic Glory" A612

1965, Jan. 27　Photo.　Perf. 11½
1387　A612　20s org brn, gold & blk　.60　.20

Bulgarian victories in the 1964 Olympic Games.

"Victory Over Fascism" A613

13s, "Fight for Peace" (dove and globe).

1965, Apr. 16　　　　　　Perf. 11½
1388　A613　5s gray, blk & ol bis　.20　.20
1389　A613　13s gray, blk & blue　.25　.20

Victory over Fascism, 5/9/45, 20th anniv.

Vladimir M. Komarov and Section of Globe — A614

Designs: 2s, Konstantin Feoktistov. 5s, Boris B. Yegorov. 13s, Komarov, Feoktistov and Yegorov. 20s, Spaceship Voskhod.

1965, Feb. 15　　　　　　Photo.
1390　A614　1s pale lil & dk bl　.20　.20
1391　A614　2s lt bl, ind & dl vio　.20　.20
1392　A614　5s pale grn, grn & ol grn　.20　.20
1393　A614　13s pale pink, dp rose & mar　.40　.20
1394　A614　20s lt bl, vio bl, grnsh bl & yel　.75　.20
　　Nos. 1390-1394 (5)　1.75　1.00

Russian 3-man space flight, Oct. 12-13, 1964.
Imperfs in changed colors. Four low values se-tenant. Value, set $2 unused, $1 canceled.

Bullfinch — A615

Birds: 2s, European golden oriole. 3s, Common rock thrush. 5s, Barn swallow. 8s, European roller. 10s, European goldfinch. 13s, Rosy pastor starling. 20s, Nightingale.

1965, Apr. 20　Unwmk.　Perf. 11½
Birds in Natural Colors
1395　A615　1s blue green　.20　.20
1396　A615　2s rose lilac　.20　.20
1397　A615　3s rose　.20　.20
1398　A615　5s brt blue　.20　.20
1399　A615　8s citron　.30　.20
1400　A615　10s gray　1.10　.20
1401　A615　13s lt vio blue　1.10　.20
1402　A615　20s emerald　2.25　.35
　　Nos. 1395-1402 (8)　5.55　1.75

Black Sea Fish A616

1965, June 10　Photo.　Perf. 11½
Gray Frames
1403　A616　1s Sting ray　.20　.20
1404　A616　2s Belted bonito　.20　.20
1405　A616　3s Hogfish　.20　.20
1406　A616　5s Gurnard　.20　.20
1407　A616　10s Scad　.75　.20
1408　A616　13s Turbot　1.10　.25
　　Nos. 1403-1408 (6)　2.65　1.25

Plane, Bus, Train, Ship and Whale A617

1965, Apr. 30
1409　A617　13s multicolored　.45　.20

4th Intl. Conf. of Transport, Dock and Fishery Workers, Sofia, May 10-14.

ITU Emblem and Communications Symbols — A618

1965, May 17
1410　A618　20s multicolored　.65　.30

Centenary of the ITU.

Col. Pavel Belyayev and Lt. Col. Alexei Leonov — A619

Design: 20s, Leonov floating in space.

1965, May 20　　　　　　Unwmk.
1411　A619　2s gray, dull bl & dk brn　.20　.20
1412　A619　20s multicolored　1.00　.45

Space flight of Voskhod 2 and the first man floating in space, Lt. Col. Alexei Leonov.

ICY Emblem A620

1965, May 15　　　　　　Photo.
1413　A620　20s orange, olive & blk　.65　.20

International Cooperation Year, 1965.

Corn — A621　　　Marx and Lenin — A622

1965, Apr. 1　　　　　　Perf. 12½x13
1414　A621　1s shown　.20　.20
1415　A621　2s Wheat　.20　.20
1416　A621　3s Sunflowers　.20　.20
1417　A621　4s Sugar beet　.20　.20
1418　A621　5s Clover　.20　.20
1419　A621　10s Cotton　.40　.20
1420　A621　13s Tobacco　.60　.20
　　Nos. 1414-1420 (7)　2.00　1.40

1965, June　　　　　　Perf. 10½
1421　A622　13s red & dk brn　.65　.20

6th Conference of Postal Ministers of Communist Countries, Peking, June 21-July 15.

Film and UNESCO Emblem A623

1965, June 30
1422　A623　13s dp bl, blk & lt gray　.50　.20

Balkan Film Festival, Varna.

Ballerina — A624

1965, July 10　　　　　　Photo.
1423　A624　5s dp lil rose & blk　.60　.25

2nd Intl. Ballet Competition, Varna.

Map of Balkan Peninsula and Dove with Letter
A625

Col. Pavel Belyayev and Lt. Col. Alexei Leonov — A626

2s, Sailboat and modern buildings. 3s, Fish and plants. 13s, Symbolic sun and rocket. 40s, Map of Balkan Peninsula and dove with letter (like 1s).

1965		Perf. 10½	
1424 A625	1s sil, dp ultra & yel	.20	.20
1425 A625	2s sil, pur & yel	.20	.20
1426 A625	3s gold, grn & yel	.20	.20
1427 A625	13s gold, hn brn & yel	.55	.55
1428 A626	20s sil, bl & brn	.70	.55
	Nos. 1424-1428 (5)	1.85	1.65

Miniature Sheet
Imperf

1429 A625	40s gold & brt bl	1.75	1.00

Balkanphila 1965 Philatelic Exhibition, Varna, Aug. 7-15, and visit of Russian astronauts Belyayev and Leonov.
Value, No. 1428 imperf. in changed colors, 90 cents.
Issued: 20s, 40s, 8/7; others, 7/23.

Woman Gymnast — A627

Designs: 2s, Woman gymnast on parallel bars. 3s, Weight lifter. 5s, Automobile and chart. 10s, Women basketball players. 13s, Automobile and map of rally.

1965, Aug. 14		Perf. 10½	
1430 A627	1s crim, brn & blk	.20	.20
1431 A627	2s rose vio, dp cl & blk	.20	.20
1432 A627	3s dp car, brn & blk	.20	.20
1433 A627	5s fawn, red brn & blk	.25	.20
1434 A627	10s dp lil rose, dp cl & blk	.50	.20
1435 A627	13s lilac, claret & blk	.65	.20
	Nos. 1430-1435 (6)	2.00	1.20

Sports events in Bulgaria during May-June, 1965.

No. 989 Surcharged

1965, Aug. 12		Perf. 13	
1436 A499	2s on 8s orange brn	.75	.25

1st Natl. Folklore Competition, Aug. 12-15.

Escaping Prisoners — A628   Fruit — A629

1965, July 23		Perf. 10½	
1437 A628	2s slate	.20	.20

40th anniversary of the escape of political prisoners from Bolshevik Island.

1965, July 1		Perf. 13	
1438 A629	1s Apples	.20	.20
1439 A629	2s Grapes	.20	.20
1440 A629	3s Pears	.20	.20
1441 A629	4s Peaches	.20	.20
1442 A629	5s Strawberries	.30	.20
1443 A629	6s Walnuts	1.30	1.20
	Nos. 1438-1443 (6)		

Horsemanship — A630

1965, Sept. 30	Unwmk.	Perf. 10½	
1444 A630	1s Dressage	.20	.20
1445 A630	2s Three-day test	.20	.20
1446 A630	3s Jumping	.20	.20
1447 A630	5s Race	.20	.20
1448 A630	10s Steeplechase	.75	.20
1449 A630	13s Hurdle race	1.40	.30
	Nos. 1444-1449 (6)	2.95	1.30

See No. B28.

Smiling Children — A631

Designs: 2s, Two girl Pioneers. 3s, Bugler. 5s, Pioneer with model plane. 8s, Two singing girls in national costume. 13s, Running boy.

1965, Oct. 24		Photo.	
1450 A631	1s dk bl grn & yel grn	.20	.20
1451 A631	2s vio & deep rose	.20	.20
1452 A631	3s olive & lemon	.20	.20
1453 A631	5s dp blue & bister	.20	.20
1454 A631	8s olive bister & org	.30	.20
1455 A631	13s rose car & vio	.65	.25
	Nos. 1450-1455 (6)	1.75	1.25

Dimitrov Pioneer Organization.

U-52 Plane over Trnovo A632

2s, 1L-14 over Plovdiv. 3s, Mi-4 Helicopter over Dimitrovgrad. 5s, Tu-104 over Ruse. 13s, IL-18 over Varna. 20s, Tu-114 over Sofia.

1965, Nov. 25		Perf. 10½	
1456 A632	1s gray, blue & red	.20	.20
1457 A632	2s gray, lilac & red	.20	.20
1458 A632	3s gray, grnsh bl & red	.20	.20
1459 A632	5s gray, orange & red	.20	.20
1460 A632	13s gray, bister & red	.70	.20
1461 A632	20s gray, lt grn & red	1.00	.30
	Nos. 1456-1461 (6)	2.50	1.30

Development of Bulgarian Civil Air Transport.

IQSY Emblem, and Earth Radiation Zones A633

Designs (IQSY Emblem and): 2s, Sun with corona. 13s, Solar eclipse.

1965, Dec. 15	Photo.	Perf. 10½	
1462 A633	1s grn, yel & ultra	.20	.20
1463 A633	2s yel, red lil & red	.20	.20
1464 A633	13s bl, yel & blk	.30	.20
	Nos. 1462-1464 (3)	.70	.60

International Quiet Sun Year, 1964-65.

"North and South Bulgaria" A634

"Martenitsa" Emblem — A635

1965, Dec. 6			
1465 A634	13s brt yel grn & blk	.50	.25

Union of North and South Bulgaria, cent.

1966, Jan. 10	Photo.	Perf. 10½	

"Spring" in Folklore: 2s, Drummer. 3s, Bird ornaments. 5s, Dancer "Lazarka." 8s, Vase with flowers. 13s, Bagpiper.

1466 A635	1s rose lil, vio bl & gray	.20	.20
1467 A635	2s gray, blk & crim	.20	.20
1468 A635	3s red, vio & gray	.20	.20
1469 A635	5s lil, blk & crimson	.20	.20
1470 A635	8s rose lil, brn & pur	.25	.20
1471 A635	13s bl, blk & rose lilac	.50	.20
	Nos. 1466-1471 (6)	1.55	1.20

Church of St. John the Baptist, Nessebr A636

Designs: 1s, Christ, fresco from Bojana Church. 2s, Ikon "Destruction of Idols," horiz. 3s, Bratchkovo Monastery. 4s, Zemen Monastery, horiz. 13s, Nativity, ikon from Arbanassi. 20s, Ikon "Virgin and Child," 1342.

1966, Feb. 25	Litho.	Perf. 11½	
1472 A636	1s gray & multi	3.50	1.25
1473 A636	2s gray & multi	.25	.20
1474 A636	3s multicolored	.25	.20
1475 A636	4s multicolored	.25	.20
1476 A636	5s multicolored	.25	.20
1477 A636	13s gray & multi	.50	.20
1478 A636	20s multicolored	.95	.35
	Nos. 1472-1478 (7)	5.95	2.60

2,500 years of art in Bulgaria.

Georgi Benkovski and T. Kableshkov — A637

1s, Proclamation of April Uprising, Koprivstitsa. 3s, Dedication of flag, Panaguriste. 5s, V. Petleshkov, Z. Dyustabanov. 10s, Botev landing at Kozlodui. 13s, P. Volov, Ilarion Dragostinov.

1966, Mar. 3	Photo.	Perf. 10½	
	Center in Black		
1479 A637	1s red brn & gold	.20	.20
1480 A637	2s brt red & gold	.20	.20
1481 A637	3s ol grn & gold	.20	.20
1482 A637	5s steel bl & gold	.20	.20
1483 A637	10s brt rose lil & gold	.20	.20
1484 A637	13s lt vio & gold	.50	.20
	Nos. 1479-1484 (6)	1.50	1.20

April Uprising against the Turks, 90th anniv.

Sofia Zoo Animals A638

1966, May 23		Litho.	
1485 A638	1s Elephant	.20	.20
1486 A638	2s Tiger	.20	.20
1487 A638	3s Chimpanzee	.20	.20
1488 A638	4s Siberian ibex	.20	.20
1489 A638	5s Polar bear	.25	.20
1490 A638	8s Lion	.25	.20
1491 A638	13s Bison	.80	.20
1492 A638	20s Kangaroo	1.50	.30
	Nos. 1485-1492 (8)	3.60	1.70

WHO Headquarters, Geneva — A639

1966, May 3		Photo.	
1493 A639	13s deep blue & silver	.60	.25

Inauguration of the WHO Headquarters, Geneva.

Worker A640

1966, May 9	Photo.	Perf. 10½	
1494 A640	20s gray & rose	.65	.20

Sixth Trade Union Congress.

Yantra River Bridge, Biela — A641

#1496, Maritsa River Bridge, Svilengrad. #1497, Fountain, Samokov. #1498, Ruins of Fort, Kaskovo. 8s, Old Fort, Ruse. 13s, House, Gabrovo.

1966, Feb. 10	Photo.	Perf. 13	
1495 A641	1s Prus blue	.20	.20
1496 A641	1s brt green	.20	.20
1497 A641	2s olive green	.20	.20
1498 A641	2s dk red brown	.20	.20

1499	A641	8s red brown	.25	.20
1500	A641	13s dark blue	.40	.20
		Nos. 1495-1500 (6)	1.45	1.20

Souvenir Sheet

Moon Allegory — A642

1966, Apr. 29   *Imperf.*
1501 A642 60s blk, plum & sil   2.50 1.25

1st Russian soft landing on the moon by Luna 9, Feb. 3, 1966.

Steamer Radetzky and Bugler — A643

1966, May 28   *Perf. 10½*
1502 A643 2s multicolored   .20 .20

90th anniv. of the participation of the Danube steamer Radetzky in the uprising against the Turks.

Standard Bearer Nicola Simov-Kuruto A644

1966, May 30
1503 A644 5s bister, green & olive   .25 .20

Hero of the Turkish War.

UNESCO Emblem A645

1966, June 8
1504 A645 20s gold, blk & ver   .60 .20

20th anniv. of UNESCO.

Youth Federation Badge — A646

1966, June 6   **Photo.**   *Perf. 10½*
1505 A646 13s silver, bl & blk   .40 .20

7th Assembly of the Intl. Youth Federation.

Soccer — A647

Various soccer scenes. 50s, Jules Rimet Cup.

1966, June 27
1506	A647	1s gray, yel brn & blk	.20	.20
1507	A647	2s gray, crim & blk	.20	.20
1508	A647	5s gray, ol bis & blk	.20	.20
1509	A647	13s gray, ultra & blk	.35	.20
1510	A647	20s gray, Prus bl & blk	.60	.20
		Nos. 1506-1510 (5)	1.55	1.00

Miniature Sheet
Imperf
1511 A647 50s gray, dp lil rose & gold   2.25 1.50

World Soccer Cup Championship, Wembley, England, July 11-30. Size of No. 1511: 60x64mm.

Woman Javelin Thrower — A648

No. 1513, Runner. No. 1514, Young man and woman carrying banners, vert.

1966   **Photo.**   *Perf. 10½*
1512	A648	2s grn, yel & ver	.20	.20
1513	A648	13s dp grn, yel & sal pink	.40	.20
1514	A648	13s bl, lt bl & salmon	.40	.20
		Nos. 1512-1514 (3)	1.00	.60

Nos. 1512-1513: 3rd Spartacist Games; issued Aug. 10. No. 1514: 3rd congress of the Bulgarian Youth Federation; issued May 25.

Wrestlers Nicolas Petrov and Dan Kolov — A649

1966, July 29
1515 A649 13s bis brn, dk brn & lt ol grn   .40 .20

3rd International Wrestling Championships.

Map of Balkan Countries, Globe and UNESCO Emblem — A650

1966, Aug. 26   *Perf. 10½x11½*
1516 A650 13s ultra, lt grn & pink   .40 .20

First Congress of Balkanologists.

Children with Building Blocks A651

2s, Bunny & teddy bear with book. 3s, Children as astronauts. 13s, Children with pails & shovel.

1966, Sept. 1   *Perf. 10½*
1517	A651	1s dk car, org & blk	.20	.20
1518	A651	2s emerald, blk & red brn	.20	.20
1519	A651	3s ultra, org & blk	.20	.20
1520	A651	13s blue, rose & blk	.60	.20
		Nos. 1517-1520 (4)	1.20	.80

Children's Day.

Yuri A. Gagarin and Vostok 1 — A652

Designs: 2s, Gherman S. Titov, Vostok 2. 3s, Andrian G. Nikolayev, Pavel R. Popovich, Vostoks 3 & 4. 5s, Valentina Tereshkova, Valeri Bykovski, Vostoks 5 & 6. 8s, Vladimir M. Komarov, Boris B. Yegorov, Konstantin Feoktistov, Voskhod 1. 13s, Pavel Belyayev, Alexei Leonov, Voskhod 2.

1966, Sept. 29   **Photo.**   *Perf. 11½x11*
1521	A652	1s slate & gray	.20	.20
1522	A652	2s plum & gray	.20	.20
1523	A652	3s yel brn & gray	.20	.20
1524	A652	5s brn red & gray	.20	.20
1525	A652	8s ultra & gray	.20	.20
1526	A652	13s Prus bl & gray	.50	.20
		Nos. 1521-1526,B29 (7)	2.50	1.55

Russian space explorations.

St. Clement, 14th Century Wood Sculpture A653

1966, Oct. 27   **Photo.**   *Perf. 11½x11*
1527 A653 5s red, buff & brown   .20 .20

1050th anniversary of the birth of St. Clement of Ochrida.

Metodi Shatorov A654

Portraits: 3s, Vladimir Trichkov. 5s, Valcho Ivanov. 10s, Raiko Daskalov. 13s, General Vladimir Zaimov.

1966, Nov. 8   *Perf. 11x11½*
Gold Frame, Black Denomination
1528	A654	2s crimson & bl vio	.20	.20
1529	A654	3s magenta & blk	.20	.20
1530	A654	5s car rose & dk bl	.20	.20
1531	A654	10s orange & olive	.30	.20
1532	A654	13s red & brown	.40	.20
		Nos. 1529-1532 (4)	1.10	.80

Fighters against fascism.

George Dimitrov — A655

Steel Worker — A656

1966, Nov. 14   **Photo.**   *Perf. 11½x11*
| 1533 | A655 | 2s magenta & blk | .20 | .20 |
| 1534 | A656 | 20s fawn, gray & blk | .70 | .20 |

Bulgarian Communist Party, 9th Congress.

Deer's Head Drinking Cup A667

Gold Treasure: 2s, 6s, 10s, Various Amazon's head jugs. 3s, Ram's head cup. 5s, Circular plate. 8s, Deer's head cup. 13s, Amphora. 20s, Ram drinking horn.

1966, Nov. 28   *Perf. 12x11½*
Vessels in Gold and Brown; Black Inscriptions
1535	A667	1s gray & violet	.20	.20
1536	A667	2s gray & green	.20	.20
1537	A667	3s gray & dk bl	.20	.20
1538	A667	5s gray & red brn	.20	.20
1539	A667	6s gray & Prus bl	.20	.20
1540	A667	8s gray & brn ol	.85	.20
1541	A667	10s gray & sepia	.85	.20
1542	A667	13s gray & dk vio bl	.85	.30
1543	A667	20s gray & vio brn	.95	.30
		Nos. 1535-1543 (9)	4.50	2.00

The gold treasure from the 4th century B.C. was found near Panagyurishte in 1949.

Tourist House, Bansko — A668

Tourist Houses: No. 1545, Belogradchik. No. 1546, Triavna. 20s, Rila.

1966, Nov. 29   **Photo.**   *Perf. 11x11½*
1544	A668	1s dark blue	.20	.20
1545	A668	2s dark green	.20	.20
1546	A668	2s brown red	.20	.20
1547	A668	20s lilac	.40	.20
		Nos. 1544-1547 (4)	1.00	.80

Decorated Tree A669

Design: 13s, Jug with bird design.

1966, Dec. 12   *Perf. 11*
| 1548 | A669 | 2s grn, pink & gold | .20 | .20 |
| 1549 | A669 | 13s brn lake, rose, emer & gold | .40 | .20 |

New Year, 1967.

Pencho Slavikov, Author — A670

Dahlia — A671

Portraits: 2s, Dimcho Debeljanov, author. 3s, P. H. Todorov, author. 5s, Dimitri Dobrovich, painter. 8s, Ivan Markvichka, painter. 13s, Ilya Bezhkov, painter.

1966, Dec. 15   *Perf. 10½x11*
1550	A670	1s blue, olive & org	.20	.20
1551	A670	2s org, brn & gray	.20	.20
1552	A670	3s olive, bl & org	.20	.20
1553	A670	5s gray, red brn & org	.20	.20

1554 A670 8s lilac, dk gray & bl .30 .20
1555 A670 13s blue, vio & lil .40 .20
Nos. 1550-1555 (6) 1.50 1.20

1966, Dec. 29

Flowers: No. 1557, Clematis. No. 1558, Foxglove. No. 1559, Narcissus. 5s, Snowdrop. 3s, Petunia. 13s, Tiger lily. 20s, Bellflower.

Flowers in Natural Colors

1556 A671 1s gray & lt brn .20 .20
1557 A671 1s gray & dull bl .20 .20
1558 A671 2s gray & dull lil .20 .20
1559 A671 2s gray & brown .20 .20
1560 A671 3s gray & dk grn .20 .20
1561 A671 5s gray & dp ultra .25 .20
1562 A671 13s gray & brown .60 .20
1563 A671 20s gray & ultra .95 .20
Nos. 1556-1563 (8) 2.80 1.60

Ringnecked Pheasant — A672

Game: 2s, Rock partridge. 3s, Gray partridge. 5s, Hare. 8s, Roe deer. 13s, Red deer.

1967, Jan. 28 **Perf. 11x10½**

1564 A672 1s lt ultra, dk brn & ocher .20 .20
1565 A672 2s pale yel grn & dk grn .20 .20
1566 A672 3s lt bl, blk & cr .20 .20
1567 A672 5s lt grn & blk .20 .20
1568 A672 8s pale bl, dk brn & ocher .70 .20
1569 A672 13s bl & dk brn 1.25 .25
Nos. 1564-1569 (6) 2.75 1.25

Bulgaria No. 1, 1879 — A673

Thracian Coin, 6th Century, B.C. — A674

1967, Feb. 4 **Photo.** **Perf. 10½**

1570 A673 10s emerald, blk & yel .75 .25
Bulgarian Philatelic Union, 10th Congress.

1967, Mar. 30 **Perf. 11½x11**

Coins: 2s, Macedonian tetradrachma, 2nd cent. B.C. 3s, Tetradrachma of Odessus, 2nd cent. B.C. 5s, Philip II of Macedonia, 4th cent., B.C. 13s, Thracian King Seuthus VII, 4th cent., B.C., obverse and reverse. 20s, Apollonian coin, 5th cent., B.C., obverse and reverse.

Size: 25x25mm

1571 A674 1s brn, blk & sil .20 .20
1572 A674 2s red lil, blk & sil .20 .20
1573 A674 3s grn, blk & sil .20 .20
1574 A674 5s brn org, blk & sil .20 .20

Size: 37½x25mm

1575 A674 13s brt bl, blk & brnz .70 .25
1576 A674 20s vio, blk & sil 1.25 .45
Nos. 1571-1576 (6) 2.75 1.50

Partisans Listening to Radio — A675

Design: 20s, George Dimitrov addressing crowd and Bulgarian flag.

1967, Apr. 20 **Perf. 11x11½**

1577 A675 1s red, gold, buff & sl grn .20 .20
1578 A675 20s red, gold, dl red, grn & blk .55 .20
25th anniversary of the Union of Patriotic Front Organizations.

Nikolas Kofardjiev A676

2s, Petko Napetov. 5s, Petko D. Petkov. 10s, Emil Markov. 13s, Traitcho Kostov.

1967, Apr. 24 **Perf. 11½x11**

1579 A676 1s brn red, gray & blk .20 .20
1580 A676 2s ol grn, gray & blk .20 .20
1581 A676 5s brn, gray & blk .20 .20
1582 A676 10s dp bl, gray & blk .20 .20
1583 A676 13s mag, gray & blk .20 .20
Nos. 1579-1583 (5) 1.20 1.00
Fighters against fascism.

Symbolic Flower and Flame — A677

1967, May 18 **Photo.** **Perf. 11x11½**

1584 A677 13s gold, yel & lt grn .45 .20
First Cultural Congress, May 18-19.

Gold Sand Beach and ITY Emblem A678

20s, Hotel, Pamporovo. 40s, Nessebr Church.

1967, June 12 **Photo.** **Perf. 11x11½**

1585 A678 13s ultra, yel & blk .30 .20
1586 A678 20s Prus bl, blk & buff .40 .20
1587 A678 40s brt grn, blk & ocher 1.00 .30
Nos. 1585-1587 (3) 1.70 .70
International Tourist Year, 1967.

Angora Cat — A679

Cats: 2s, Siamese, horiz. 3s, Abyssinian. 5s, Black European. 13s, Persian, horiz. 20s, Striped domestic.

Perf. 11½x11, 11x11½

1967, June 19

1588 A679 1s dl vio, dk brn & buff .20 .20
1589 A679 2s ol, sl & brt bl .20 .20
1590 A679 3s dull blue & brn .20 .20
1591 A679 5s grn, blk & yel .20 .20
1592 A679 13s dl red brn, sl & org .90 .20
1593 A679 20s gray grn, brn & buff 1.60 .25
Nos. 1588-1593 (6) 3.30 1.25

Scene from Opera "The Master of Boyana" by K. Iliev A680

Songbird on Keyboard — A681

1967, June 19

1594 A680 5s gray, vio bl & dp car .40 .20
1595 A681 13s gray, dp car & dk bl 1.10 .20
3rd Intl. Competition for Young Opera Singers.

George Kirkov (1867-1919), Revolutionist — A682

1967, June 24 **Perf. 11x11½**

1596 A682 2s rose red & dk brn .20 .20

Symbolic Tree and Stars — A683

1967, July 28 **Photo.** **Perf. 11½x11**

1597 A683 13s dp bl, car & blk .30 .20
11th Congress of Dimitrov's Union of the People's Youth.

Roses and Distillery A684

Designs: No. 1599, Chick and incubator. No. 1600, Cucumbers and hothouse. No. 1601, Lamb and sheep farm. 3s, Sunflower and oil mill. 4s, Pigs and pig farm. 5s, Hops and hop farm. 6s, Corn and irrigation system. 8s, Grapes and Bolgar tractor. 10s, Apples and cultivated tree. 13s, Bees and honey. 20s, Bee, blossoms and beehives.

1967 **Perf. 11x11½**

1598 A684 1s multicolored .20 .20
1599 A684 1s dk car, yel & blk .20 .20
1600 A684 2s vio, lt grn & blk .20 .20
1601 A684 2s brt grn, gray & blk .20 .20
1602 A684 3s yel grn, yel & blk .20 .20
1603 A684 4s brt pur, yel & blk .20 .20
1604 A684 5s ol bis, yel grn & blk .20 .20
1605 A684 6s ol, brt grn & blk .20 .20
1606 A684 8s grn, bis & blk .20 .20
1607 A684 10s multicolored .25 .20
1608 A684 13s grn, bis brn & blk .40 .20
1609 A684 20s grnsh bl, brt pink & blk .55 .20
Nos. 1598-1609 (12) 3.00 2.40

Issue dates: Nos. 1598-1601, 1607, 1609, July 15; Nos. 1602-1606, 1608, July 24.

Map of Communist Countries, Spasski Tower A685

2s, Lenin speaking to soldiers. 3s, Fighting at Wlodaja, 1918. 5s, Marx, Engels & Lenin. 13s, Oil refinery. 20s, Molniya communication satellite.

1967, Aug. 25 **Perf. 11**

1610 A685 1s multicolored .20 .20
1611 A685 2s magenta & olive .20 .20
1612 A685 3s mag & dull vio .20 .20
1613 A685 5s magenta & red .20 .20
1614 A685 13s mag & ultra .25 .20
1615 A685 20s magenta & blue .45 .20
Nos. 1610-1615 (6) 1.50 1.20
Russian October Revolution, 50th anniv.

Rod, "Fish" and Varna A686

1967, Aug. 29 **Photo.** **Perf. 11**

1616 A686 10s multicolored .35 .20
7th World Angling Championships, Varna.

Skiers and Winter Olympics' Emblem — A687

Sports and Emblem: 2s, Ski jump. 3s, Biathlon. 5s, Ice hockey. 13s, Figure skating couple.

1967, Sept. 20 **Photo.** **Perf. 11**

1617 A687 1s dk bl grn, red & blk .20 .20
1618 A687 2s ultra, blk & ol .20 .20
1619 A687 3s vio brn, bl & blk .20 .20
1620 A687 5s green, yel & blk .20 .20
1621 A687 13s vio bl, blk & buff .20 .20
Nos. 1617-1621,B31 (6) 2.25 1.30
10th Winter Olympic Games, Grenoble, France, Feb. 6-18, 1968.

Mountain Peaks — A688

1967, Sept. 25 **Engr.** **Perf. 11½**

1622 A688 1s Bogdan .20 .20
1623 A688 2s Czerny .20 .20
1624 A688 3s Ruen, vert. .20 .20
1625 A688 5s Persenk .20 .20
1626 A688 10s Botev .20 .20
1627 A688 13s Rila, vert. .25 .20
1628 A688 20s Vihren .55 .20
Nos. 1622-1628 (7) 1.80 1.40

George
Rakovski
A689

1967, Oct. 20   Photo.   Perf. 11
1629 A689 13s yellow grn & blk   .40 .20
Centenary of the death of George Rakovski, revolutionary against Turkish rule.

Yuri A. Gagarin, Valentina Tereshkova
and Alexei Leonov — A690

Designs: 2s, Lt. Col. John H. Glenn, Jr., and Maj. Edward H. White. 5s, Earth and Molniya 1. 10s, Gemini 6 and 7. 13s, Luna 13 moon probe. 20s, Gemini 10 and Agena rocket.

1967, Nov. 25
1630 A690   1s Prus bl, blk & yel   .20 .20
1631 A690   2s dl bl, blk & dl yel   .20 .20
1632 A690   5s vio bl, grnsh bl &
                     blk   .20 .20
1633 A690 10s dk bl, blk & red   .35 .20
1634 A690 13s grnsh bl, brt yel &
                     blk   .55 .20
1635 A690 20s dl bl, blk & red   .75 .20
       Nos. 1630-1635 (6)   2.25 1.20
Achievements in space exploration.

Various Views
of Trnovo
A691

1967, Dec. 5   Photo.   Perf. 11
1636 A691   1s multicolored   .20 .20
1637 A691   2s multicolored   .20 .20
1638 A691   3s multicolored   .20 .20
1639 A691   5s multicolored   .20 .20
1640 A691 13s multicolored   .30 .20
1641 A691 20s multicolored   .50 .20
       Nos. 1636-1641 (6)   1.60 1.20
Restoration of the ancient capital Veliko Trnovo.

Ratchenitza Folk Dance, by Ivan
Markvichka — A692

1967, Dec. 9
1642 A692 20s gold & gray grn   1.00 .80
Belgo-Bulgarian Philatelic Exposition, Brussels, Dec. 9-10. Printed in sheets of 8 stamps and 8 labels.

Cosmos 186
and 188
Docking — A693

40s, Venus 4 and orbits around Venus.

1968, Jan.
1643 A693 20s multi   .55 .20
1644 A693 40s multi, horiz.   1.00 .25
Docking maneuvers of the Russian spaceships Cosmos 186 and Cosmos 188, Nov. 1, 1967, and the flight to Venus of Venus 4, June 12-Nov. 18, 1967.

Crossing the Danube, by
Orenburgski — A694

Paintings: 2s, Flag of Samara, by J. Veschin, vert. 3s, Battle of Pleven by Orenburgski. 13s, Battle of Orlovo Gnezdo, by N. Popov, vert. 20s, Welcome for Russian Soldiers, by D. Gudienov.

1968, Jan. 25   Photo.   Perf. 11
1645 A694   1s gold & dk green   .20 .20
1646 A694   2s gold & dk blue   .20 .20
1647 A694   3s gold & chocolate   .20 .20
1648 A694 13s gold & dk vio   .30 .20
1649 A694 20s gold & Prus grn   .50 .20
       Nos. 1645-1649 (5)   1.40 1.00
90th anniv. of the liberation from Turkey.

Shepherds, by Zlatyn
Boyadjiev — A695

Paintings: 2s, Wedding dance, by V. Dimitrov, vert. 3s, Partisans' Song, by Ilya Petrov. 5s, Portrait of Anna Penchovich, by Nikolai Pavlovich, vert. 13s, Self-portrait, by Zachary Zograf, vert. 20s, View of Old Plovdiv, by T. Lavrenov. 60s, St. Clement of Ochrida, by A. Mitov.

1967, Dec.   Litho.   Perf. 11½
Size: 45x38mm, 38x45mm
1650 A695   1s gray & multi   .20 .20
1651 A695   2s gray & multi   .20 .20
       Size: 55x35mm
1652 A695   3s gray & multi   .25 .20
       Size: 38x45mm, 45x38mm
1653 A695   5s gray & multi   .40 .20
1654 A695 13s gray & multi   .90 .25
1655 A695 20s gray & multi   1.25 .40
       Nos. 1650-1655 (6)   3.20 1.45
       Miniature Sheet
       Size: 65x84mm
       Imperf
1656 A695 60s multicolored   3.25 1.90

Marx Statue,
Sofia — A696

Maxim
Gorky — A697

1968, Feb. 20   Photo.   Perf. 11
1657 A696 13s black & red   .35 .20
150th anniversary of birth of Karl Marx.

1968, Feb. 20
1658 A697 13s ver & grnsh blk   .40 .20
Maxim Gorky (1868-1936), Russian writer.

Folk Dancers — A698

5s, Runners. 13s, Doves. 20s, Festival poster, (head, flowers, birds). 40s, Globe & Bulgaria No. 1 under magnifying glass.

1968, Mar. 20
1659 A698   2s multicolored   .20 .20
1660 A698   5s multicolored   .20 .20
1661 A698 13s multicolored   .25 .20
1662 A698 20s multicolored   .50 .20
1663 A698 40s multicolored   1.10 .40
       Nos. 1659-1663 (5)   2.25 1.20
9th Youth Festival for Peace and Friendship, Sofia, July 28-Aug. 6.

Bellflower — A699

1968, Apr. 25   Perf. 11
1664 A699   1s shown   .20 .20
1665 A699   2s Gentian   .20 .20
1666 A699   3s Crocus   .20 .20
1667 A699   5s Iris   .20 .20
1668 A699 10s Dog-tooth violet .20 .20
1669 A699 13s Sempervivum   .70 .20
1670 A699 20s Dictamnus   .95 .25
       Nos. 1664-1670 (7)   2.65 1.45

"The
Unknown
Hero," Tale
by Ran
Bosilek
A700

Design: 20s, The Witch and the Young Man (Hans Christian Andersen fairy tale.)

1968, Apr. 25   Photo.   Perf. 10½
1671 A700 13s black & multi   .35 .20
1672 A700 20s black & multi   .50 .20
Bulgarian-Danish Philatelic Exhibition.

Memorial Church, Shipka — A701

1968, May 3
1673 A701 13s multi + label   .60 .20
Bulgarian Stamp Exhibition in Berlin.

Show Jumping
A702

Olympic Rings and: 1s, Gymnast on bar. 3s, Fencer. 10s, Boxer. 13s, Woman discus thrower.

1968, June 24   Photo.   Perf. 10½
1674 A702   1s red & black   .20 .20
1675 A702   2s gray, blk & rose
                     brn   .20 .20
1676 A702   3s mag, gray & blk   .20 .20
1677 A702 10s grnsh bl, blk &
                     lem   .20 .20
1678 A702 13s vio bl, gray & pink .55 .20
       Nos. 1674-1678,B33 (6)   2.35 1.30
19th Olympic Games, Mexico City, 10/12-27.

Battle of
Buzluja
A703

Design: 13s, Haji Dimitr and Stefan Karaja.

1968, July 1
1679 A703   2s silver & red brn .20 .20
1680 A703 13s gold & sl grn   .30 .20
Centenary of the death of the patriots Haji Dimitr and Stefan Karaja.

Lakes of   Sofia Zoo,
Smolian — A704   Cent. — A705

Bulgarian Scenes: 2s, Ropotamo Lake. 3s, Erma-Idreloto mountain pass. 8s, Isker River dam. 10s, Slanchev Breg (sailing ship). 13s, Cape Caliacra. 40s, Old houses, Sozopol. 2 l, Chudnite Skali ("Strange Mountains").

1968   Photo.   Perf. 13
1681 A704   1s Prus green   .20 .20
1682 A704   2s dark green   .20 .20
1683 A704   3s dark brown   .20 .20
1684 A704   8s olive green   .20 .20
1685 A704 10s redsh brown   .20 .20
1686 A704 13s dk olive grn   .25 .20
1687 A704 40s Prus blue   .60 .25
1688 A704   2 l sepia   3.75 .85
       Nos. 1681-1688 (8)   5.60 2.30

1968, July 29 — Perf. 10½
1689	A705	1s Cinereous vulture	.20	.20
1690	A705	2s Crowned crane	.20	.20
1691	A705	3s Zebra	.25	.20
1692	A705	5s Cheetah	.40	.20
1693	A705	13s Indian python	.70	.20
1694	A705	20s African crocodile	1.25	.30
		Nos. 1689-1694 (6)	3.00	1.30

Human Rights
Flame — A706

1968, July 8
1695	A706	20s dp blue & gold	.60	.20

International Human Rights Year, 1968.

Congress Hall, Varna, and Emblem A707

1968, Sept. 17 — Photo. Perf. 10½
1696	A707	20s bister, grn & red	.50	.20

56th International Dental Congress, Varna.

Flying Swans
A708

Rose
A709

Stag Beetle — A710

Designs: 2s, Jug. 20s, Five Viking ships.

1968 — Photo. Perf. 10½
1697	A709	2s green & ocher	.75	.50
1698	A708	5s dp blue & gray	.75	.50
1699	A708	13s dp plum & lil rose	.75	.50
a.		Pair, #1698, 1699 + label	1.50	1.00
1700	A708	20s dp vio & gray	.75	.50
a.		Pair, #1697, 1700 + label	1.50	1.00
		Nos. 1697-1700 (4)	3.00	2.00

Cooperation with the Scandinavian countries.
Issued: 5s, 13s, Sept. 12; 2s, 20s, Nov. 22.

Perf. 12½x13, 13x12½
1968, Aug. 26
#1702, Ground beetle (Procerus scabrosus). #1703, Ground beetle (Calosoma sycophania). #1704, Scarab beetle, horiz. #1705, Saturnid moth, horiz.

1701	A710	1s brown olive	.20	.20
1702	A710	1s dark blue	.20	.20
1703	A710	1s dark green	.20	.20
1704	A710	1s orange brown	.20	.20
1705	A710	1s magenta	.20	.20
		Nos. 1701-1705 (5)	1.00	1.00

Turks Fighting Insurgents, 1688 — A711

1968, Aug. 22 — Perf. 10½
1706	A711	13s multicolored	.45	.20

280th anniversary of the Tchiprovtzi insurrection.

Christo Smirnenski (1898-1923), Poet — A712

1968, Sept. 28 — Litho. Perf. 10½
1707	A712	13s gold, red org & blk	.40	.20

Dalmatian Pelican — A713

Birds: 2s, Little egret. 3s, Crested grebe. 5s, Common tern. 13s, European spoonbill. 20s, Glossy ibis.

1968, Oct. 28 — Photo.
1708	A713	1s silver & multi	.20	.20
1709	A713	2s silver & multi	.20	.20
1710	A713	3s silver & multi	.20	.20
1711	A713	5s silver & multi	.20	.20
1712	A713	13s silver & multi	.50	.20
1713	A713	20s silver & multi	1.10	.30
		Nos. 1708-1713 (6)	2.40	1.30

Srebrina wild life reservation.

Carrier Pigeon A714

1968, Oct. 19
1714	A714	20s emerald	.70	.25
a.		Sheet of 4 + labels	5.00	1.60

2nd Natl. Stamp Exhib. in Sofia, Oct. 25-Nov. 15. No. 1714a contains 4 No. 1714 and 5 labels.

Man and Woman from Lovech A715

Regional Costumes: 1s, Silistra. 3s, Yambol. 13s, Chirpan. 20s, Razgrad. 40s, Ihtiman.

1968, Nov. 20 — Litho. Perf. 13½
1715	A715	1s dp org & multi	.20	.20
1716	A715	2s Prus bl & multi	.20	.20
1717	A715	3s multicolored	.20	.20
1718	A715	13s multicolored	.30	.20
1719	A715	20s multicolored	.55	.25
1720	A715	40s green & multi	1.40	.45
		Nos. 1715-1720 (6)	2.85	1.50

St. Arsenius
A716

10th cent. Murals & Icons: 2s, Procession with relics of St. Ivan Rilsky, horiz. 3s, St. Michael Torturing the Soul of the Rich Man. 13s, St. Ivan Rilski. 20s, St. John. 40s, St. George. 1 l, Procession meeting relics of St. Ivan Rilsky, horiz.

Perf. 11½x12½, 12½x11½
1968, Nov. 25 — Photo.
1721	A716	1s gold & multi	.20	.20
1722	A716	2s gold & multi	.20	.20
1723	A716	3s gold & multi	.20	.20
1724	A716	13s gold & multi	.40	.20
1725	A716	20s gold & multi	.95	.30
1726	A716	40s gold & multi	1.40	.60
		Nos. 1721-1726 (6)	3.35	1.70

Souvenir Sheet
Imperf
1727	A716	1 l gold & multi	3.75	2.75

Millenium of Rila Monastery. No. 1727 also: Sofia 1969 Intl. Phil. Exhib., May 31-June 8, 1969. No. 1727 contains one stamp, size: 57x51mm.

Medlar
A717

Herbs: No. 1729, Camomile. 2s, Lily-of-the-valley. 3s, Belladonna. 5s, Mallow. 10s, Buttercup. 13s, Poppies. 20s, Thyme.

1969, Jan. 2 — Litho. Perf. 10½
1728	A717	1s blk, grn & org red	.20	.20
1729	A717	1s black, grn & yel	.20	.20
1730	A717	2s blk, emer & grn	.20	.20
1731	A717	3s black & multi	.20	.20
1732	A717	5s black & multi	.20	.20
1733	A717	10s black, grn & yel	.20	.20
1734	A717	13s black & multi	.30	.20
1735	A717	20s black, lil & grn	.65	.20
		Nos. 1728-1735 (8)	2.15	1.60

Silkworms and Spindles A718

Designs: 2s, Silkworm, cocoons and pattern. 3s, Cocoons and spinning wheel. 5s, Cocoons, woof-and-warp diagram. 13s, Silk moth, Cocoon and spinning frame. 20s, Silk moth, eggs and shuttle.

1969, Jan. 30 — Photo. Perf. 10½
1736	A718	1s bl, grn, sl & blk	.20	.20
1737	A718	2s dp car, sil & blk	.20	.20
1738	A718	3s Prus bl, sil & blk	.20	.20
1739	A718	5s pur, ver, sil & blk	.20	.20
1740	A718	13s red lil, ocher, sil & blk	.25	.20
1741	A718	20s grn, org, sil & blk	.45	.20
		Nos. 1736-1741 (6)	1.50	1.20

Bulgarian silk industry.

Attack and Capture of Emperor Nicephorus A719

Sts. Cyril and Methodius, Mural, Troian Monastery A720

Designs (Manasses Chronicle): No. 1742, Death of Ivan Asen. 3s, Khan Kroum feasting after victory. No. 1748, Invasion of Bulgaria by Prince Sviatoslav of Kiev. No. 1750, Russian invasion and campaigns of Emperor John I Zimisces, c. 972 A.D. 40s, Tsar Ivan Alexander, Jesus and Constantine Manasses.

Horizontal designs: No. 1743, Kings Nebuchadnezzar, Balthazar, Darius and Cyrus. No. 1745, Kings Cambyses, Gyges and Darius. 5s, King David and Tsar Ivan Alexander. No. 1749, Persecution of Byzantine army after battle of July 26, 811. No. 1751, Christening of Bulgarian Tsar Boris, 865. 60s, Arrival of Tsar Simeon in Constantinople and his succeeding surprise attack on that city.

1969 — Photo. Perf. 14x13½, 13½x14
1742	A719	1s multicolored	.20	.20
1743	A719	1s multicolored	.20	.20
1744	A719	2s multicolored	.20	.20
1745	A719	2s multicolored	.20	.20
1746	A719	3s multicolored	.20	.20
1747	A719	5s multicolored	.20	.20
1748	A719	13s multicolored	.40	.20
1749	A719	13s multicolored	.40	.20
1750	A719	20s multicolored	.80	.20
1751	A719	20s multicolored	.80	.20
1752	A719	40s multicolored	1.25	.40
1753	A719	60s multicolored	2.25	.40
		Nos. 1742-1753 (12)	7.10	2.80

1969, Mar. 23
1754	A720	28s gold & multi	.75	.45

Post
Horn — A721

Designs: 13s, Bulgaria Nos. 1 and 534. 20s, Street fighting at Stackata, 1919.

1969, Apr. 15 — Photo. Perf. 10½
1755	A721	2s green & yel	.20	.20
1756	A721	13s multicolored	.40	.20
1757	A721	20s dk bl & lt bl	.50	.20
		Nos. 1755-1757 (3)	1.10	.60

Bulgarian postal administration, 90th anniv.

The Fox and the Rabbit A722

Children's Drawings: 2s, Boy reading to wolf and fox. 13s, Two birds and cat singing together.

1969, Apr. 21
1758 A722 1s emer, org & blk   .20 .20
1759 A722 2s org, lt bl & blk   .20 .20
1760 A722 13s lt bl, ol & blk   .40 .20
       Nos. 1758-1760 (3)   .80 .60
       Issued for Children's Week.

ILO
Emblem — A723

1969, Apr. 28
1761 A723 13s dull grn & blk   .30 .20
       50th anniv. of the ILO.

St. George
and SOFIA
69 Emblem
A724

Designs: 2s, Virgin Mary and St. John Bogoslov. 3s, Archangel Michael. 5s, Three Saints. 8s, Jesus Christ. 13s, Sts. George and Dimitrie. 20s, Christ, the Almighty. 40s, St. Dimitrie. 60s, The 40 Martyrs. 80s, The Transfiguration.

1969, Apr. 30   Perf. 11x12
1762 A724 1s gold & multi   .20 .20
1763 A724 2s gold & multi   .20 .20
1764 A724 3s gold & multi   .20 .20
1765 A724 5s gold & multi   .20 .20
1766 A724 8s gold & multi   .20 .20
1767 A724 13s gold & multi   .30 .20
1768 A724 20s gold & multi   .65 .25
1769 A724 40s gold & multi   1.40 .40
   a.   Sheet of 4   5.75 5.00
1770 A724 60s gold & multi   1.75 .85
1771 A724 80s gold & multi   2.75 1.00
       Nos. 1762-1771 (10)   7.85 3.70

Old Bulgarian art from the National Art Gallery. No. 1769a contains 4 of No. 1769 with center gutter showing Alexander Nevski Shrine. See note on SOFIA 69 after Nos. C112-C120.

St. Cyril
Preaching
A725

Design: 28s, St. Cyril and followers.

1969, June 20   Litho.   Perf. 10½
1772 A725 2s sil, grn & red   .20 .20
1773 A725 28s sil, dk bl & red   .75 .25

St. Cyril (827-869), apostle to the Slavs, inventor of Cyrillic alphabet. Issued in sheets of 25 with se-tenant labels; Cyrillic inscription on label of 2s, Glagolitic inscription on label of 28s.

St. Sophia
Church — A726

Sofia Through the Ages: 1s, Roman coin with inscription "Ulpia Serdica." 2s, Roman coin with Aesculapius Temple. 4s, Bojana Church. 5s, Sobranic Parliament. 13s, Vasov National Theater. 20s, Alexander Nevski Shrine. 40s, Clement Ochrida University. 1 l, Coat of arms.

1969, May 25   Perf. 13x12½
1774 A726 1s gold & blue   .20 .20
1775 A726 2s gold & ol grn   .20 .20
1776 A726 3s gold & red brn   .20 .20
1777 A726 4s gold & purple   .20 .20
1778 A726 5s gold & plum   .20 .20
1779 A726 13s gold & brt grn   .30 .20
1780 A726 20s gold & vio bl   .45 .20
1781 A726 40s gold & dp car   1.10 .25
       Nos. 1774-1781 (8)   2.85 1.65

Souvenir Sheet
Imperf
1782 A726 1 l grn, gold & red   2.25 2.00

Historic Sofia in connection with the International Philatelic Exhibition, Sofia, 5/31-6/8. #1782 contains one 43½x43½mm stamp. Emblems of 8 preceding philatelic exhibitions in metallic ink in margin; gold inscription. No. 1782 was overprinted in green "IBRA 73" and various symbols, and released May 4, 1973, for the Munich Philatelic Exhibition. The overprint also exists in gray.

St. George
A727

1969, June 9   Litho.   Perf. 11½
1783 A727 40s sil, blk & pale rose 1.25 .50
       38th FIP Congress, June 9-11.

Hand
Planting
Sapling
A728

1969, Apr. 28   Photo.   Perf. 11
1784 A728 2s ol grn, blk & lilac   .20 .20
       25 years of the reforestation campaign.

Partisans — A729

Designs: 2s, Combine harvester. 3s, Dam. 5s, Flutist and singers. 13s, Factory. 20s, Lenin, Dimitrov, Russian and Bulgarian flags.

1969, Sept. 9
1785 A729 1s blk, pur & org   .20 .20
1786 A729 2s blk, ol bis & org   .20 .20
1787 A729 3s blk, bl grn & org   .20 .20
1788 A729 5s blk, brn red & org   .20 .20
1789 A729 13s blk, bl & org   .30 .20
1790 A729 20s blk, brn & org   .50 .20
       Nos. 1785-1790 (6)   1.60 1.20
       25th anniversary of People's Republic.

Women Gymnasts — A730

1969, Sept.   Photo.   Perf. 11
1791 A730 2s shown   .20 .20
1792 A730 20s Wrestlers   .40 .25
       Third National Spartakiad.

Tchanko Bakalov
Tcherkovski,
Poet. Birth
Cent. — A731

1969, Sept. 6
1793 A731 13s multicolored   .35 .20

Woman
Gymnast
A732

2s, Two women with hoops. 3s, Woman with hoop. 5s, Two women with spheres.

1969, Oct.
Gymnasts in Light Gray
1794 A732 1s green & dk blue   .20 .20
1795 A732 2s blue & dk blue   .20 .20
1796 A732 3s emer & sl grn   .20 .20
1797 A732 5s orange & pur   .20 .20
       Nos. 1794-1797,B35-B36 (6) 1.90 1.30
       World Championships for Artistic Gymnastics, Varna.

The Priest
Rilski, by
Zachary
Zograf
A733

Paintings from the National Art Gallery. 2s, Woman at Window, by Vasil Stoilov. 3s, Workers at Rest, by Nenko Balkanski, horiz. 4s, Woman Dressing (Nude), by Ivan Nenov. 5s, Portrait of a Woman, by N. Pavlovich. 13s, Falstaff, by Duzunov Kr. Sarafov. No. 1804, Portrait of a Woman, by N. Mihajlov, horiz. No. 1805, Workers at Mealtime, by Stojan Sotirov, horiz. 40s, Self-portrait, by Tcheno Togorov.

Perf. 11½x12, 12x11½
1969, Nov. 10
1798 A733 1s gold & multi   .20 .20
1799 A733 2s gold & multi   .20 .20
1800 A733 3s gold & multi   .20 .20
1801 A733 4s gold & multi   .20 .20
1802 A733 5s gold & multi   .20 .20
1803 A733 13s gold & multi   .30 .20
1804 A733 20s gold & multi   .70 .25
1805 A733 20s gold & multi   .70 .25
1806 A733 40s gold & multi   1.40 .60
       Nos. 1798-1806 (9)   4.10 2.30

Roman Bronze Wolf — A734

Design: 2s, Roman statue of woman, found at Silistra, vert.

1969, Oct.   Photo.   Perf. 11
1807 A734 2s sil, ultra & gray   .20 .20
1808 A734 13s sil, dk grn & gray .40 .20
       City of Silistra's 1,800th anniversary.

Worker and
Factory
A735

1969   Perf. 13
1809 A735 6s ultra & blk   .20 .20
       25th anniversary of the factory militia.

European Hake — A736

Designs: No. 1811, Deep-sea fishing trawler. Fish: 2s, Atlantic horse mackerel. 3s, Pilchard. 5s, Dentex macrophthalmus. 10s, Chub mackerel. 13s, Otolithes macrognathus. 20s, Lichia vadigo.

1969   Perf. 11
1810 A736 1s ol grn & blk   .20 .20
1811 A736 1s ultra, ind & gray   .20 .20
1812 A736 2s lilac & blk   .20 .20
1813 A736 3s vio bl & blk   .20 .20
1814 A736 5s rose cl, pink & blk .25 .24
1815 A736 10s gray & blk   .50 .20
1816 A736 13s ver, sal & blk   .70 .20
1817 A736 20s ocher & black   1.25 .20
       Nos. 1810-1817 (8)   3.50 1.60

Marin
Drinov
A737

1969, Nov. 10   Litho.   Perf. 11
1818 A737 20s black & red org   .35 .20
       Centenary of the Bulgarian Academy of Science, founded by Marin Drinov.

Trapeze
Artists — A738

Pavel Bania
Sanatorium
A739

Circus Performers: 2s, Jugglers. 3s, Jugglers with loops. 5s, Juggler and bear on bicycle. 13s, Woman and performing horse. 20s, Musical clowns.

1969   **Photo.**   **Perf. 11**

1819	A738	1s dk blue & multi	.20	.20
1820	A738	2s dk green & multi	.20	.20
1821	A738	3s dk violet & multi	.20	.20
1822	A738	5s multicolored	.20	.20
1823	A738	13s multicolored	.30	.20
1824	A738	55s multicolored	.55	.20
		Nos. 1819-1824 (6)	1.65	1.20

1969, Dec.   **Photo.**   **Perf. 10½-14**

Health Resorts: 5s, Chisar Sanatorium. 6s, Kotel Children's Sanatorium. 20s, Narechen Polyclinic.

1825	A739	2s blue	.20	.20
1826	A739	5s ultra	.20	.20
1827	A739	6s green	.20	.20
1828	A739	20s emerald	.30	.20
		Nos. 1825-1828 (4)	.90	.80

G. S. Shonin, V. N. Kubasov and Spacecraft
A740

Designs: 2s, A. V. Filipchenko, V. N. Volkov, V. V. Gorbatko and spacecraft. 3s, Vladimir A. Shatalov, Alexei S. Yeliseyev and spacecraft. 28s, Three spacecraft in orbit.

1970, Jan.   **Photo.**   **Perf. 11**

1829	A740	1s rose car, ol grn & blk	.20	.20
1830	A740	2s bl, dl cl & blk	.20	.20
1831	A740	3s grnsh bl, vio & blk	.20	.20
1832	A740	28s vio bl, lil rose & lt bl	.70	.20
		Nos. 1829-1832 (4)	1.30	.80

Russian space flights of Soyuz 6, 7 and 8, Oct. 11-13, 1969.

Khan Krum and Defeat of Emperor Nicephorus, 811 — A741

Bulgarian History: 1s, Khan Asparuch and Bulgars crossing the Danube (679). 3s, Conversion of Prince Boris to Christianity, 865. 5s, Tsar Simeon and battle of Akhelo, 917. 8s, Tsar Samuel defeating the Byzantines, 976. 10s, Tsar Kaloyan defeating Emperor Baldwin, 1205. 13s, Tsar Ivan Assen II defeating Greek King Theodore Komnine, 1230. 20s, Coronation of Tsar Ivailo, 1277.

1970, Feb.   **Perf. 10½**

1833	A741	1s gold & multi	.20	.20
1834	A741	2s gold & multi	.20	.20
1835	A741	3s gold & multi	.20	.20
1836	A741	5s gold & multi	.20	.20
1837	A741	8s gold & multi	.20	.20
1838	A741	10s gold & multi	.30	.20
1839	A741	13s gold & multi	.40	.20
1840	A741	20s gold & multi	.70	.20
		Nos. 1833-1840 (8)	2.40	1.60

See Nos. 2126-2133.

Bulgarian Pavilion, EXPO '70 — A742

1970   **Perf. 12½**

1841	A742	20s brown, sil & org	.75	.50

EXPO '70 International Exposition, Osaka, Japan, Mar. 15-Sept. 13, 1970.

Soccer — A743

Designs: Various views of soccer game.

1970, Mar. 4   **Photo.**   **Perf. 12½**

1842	A743	1s blue & multi	.20	.20
1843	A743	2s rose car & multi	.20	.20
1844	A743	3s ultra & multi	.20	.20
1845	A743	5s green & multi	.20	.20
1846	A743	20s emerald & multi	.55	.20
1847	A743	40s red & multi	1.25	.30
		Nos. 1842-1847 (6)	2.60	1.30

9th World Soccer Championships for the Jules Rimet Cup, Mexico City, May 30-June 21, 1970. See No. B37.

Lenin (1870-1924) — A744

1970, Apr. 22

1848	A744	2s shown	.20	.20
1849	A744	13s Portrait	.30	.20
1850	A744	20s Writing	.70	.20
		Nos. 1848-1850 (3)	1.20	.60

Tephrocactus Alexanderi V. Bruchii — A745

Cacti: 2s, Opuntia drummondii. 3s, Hatiora cilindrica. 5s, Gymnocalycium vatteri. 8s, Heliantho cereus grandiflorus. 10s, Neochilenia andreaeana. 13s, Peireskia vargasii v. longispina. 20s, Neobesseya rosiflora.

1970   **Photo.**   **Perf. 12½**

1851	A745	1s multicolored	.20	.20
1852	A745	2s dk green & multi	.20	.20
1853	A745	3s multicolored	.20	.20
1854	A745	5s blue & multi	.20	.20
1855	A745	8s brown & multi	.30	.20
1856	A745	10s vio bl & multi	1.00	.20
1857	A745	13s brn red & multi	1.00	.20
1858	A745	20s purple & multi	1.40	.30
		Nos. 1851-1858 (8)	4.50	1.70

Rose — A746

Designs: Various Roses.

1970, June 5   **Litho.**   **Perf. 13½**

1859	A746	1s gray & multi	.20	.20
1860	A746	2s gray & multi	.20	.20
1861	A746	3s gray & multi	.20	.20
1862	A746	4s gray & multi	.20	.20
1863	A746	5s gray & multi	.20	.20
1864	A746	13s gray & multi	.20	.20
1865	A746	20s gray & multi	1.10	.20
1866	A746	28s gray & multi	1.90	.40
		Nos. 1859-1866 (8)	4.20	1.85

Gold Bowl
A747

Designs: Various bowls and art objects from Gold Treasure of Thrace.

1970, June 15   **Photo.**   **Perf. 12½**

1867	A747	1s blk, bl & gold	.20	.20
1868	A747	2s blk, lt vio & gold	.20	.20
1869	A747	3s blk, ver & gold	.20	.20
1870	A747	5s blk, yel grn & gold	.20	.20
1871	A747	13s blk, org & gold	.70	.20
1872	A747	20s blk, lil & gold	.85	.20
		Nos. 1867-1872 (6)	2.35	1.20

EXPO Emblem, Rose and Bulgarian Woman — A748

Designs (EXPO Emblem and): 2s, Three women. 3s, Woman and fruit. 28s, Dancers. 40s, Mt. Fuji and pavilions.

1970, June 20

1873	A748	1s gold & multi	.20	.20
1874	A748	2s gold & multi	.20	.20
1875	A748	3s gold & multi	.20	.20
1876	A748	28s gold & multi	.70	.25
		Nos. 1873-1876 (4)	1.30	.85

Miniature Sheet
Imperf

1877	A748	40s gold & multi	1.25	.60

EXPO '70 International Exposition, Osaka, Japan, Mar. 15-Sept. 13. No. 1877 contains one stamp with simulated perforations.

Ivan Vasov
A749

1970, Aug. 1   **Photo.**   **Perf. 12½**

1878	A749	13s violet blue	.40	.20

Ivan Vasov, author, 120th birth anniv.

UN Emblem — A750

1970, Aug. 1

1879	A750	20s Prus bl & gold	.50	.20

25th anniversary of the United Nations.

George Dimitrov — A751

Retriever
A752

1970, June 8

1880	A751	20s blk, gold & org	.60	.20

BZNC (Bulgarian Communist Party), 70th anniv.

1970   **Photo.**   **Perf. 12½**

Dogs: 1s, Golden retriever, horiz. 3s, Great Dane. 4s, Boxer. 5s, Cocker spaniel. 13s, Doberman pinscher. 20s, Scottish terrier. 28s, Russian greyhound, horiz.

1881	A752	1s multicolored	.20	.20
1882	A752	2s multicolored	.20	.20
1883	A752	3s multicolored	.20	.20
1884	A752	4s multicolored	.20	.20
1885	A752	5s multicolored	.20	.20
1886	A752	13s multicolored	.50	.20
1887	A752	20s multicolored	1.10	.20
1888	A752	28s multicolored	1.60	.30
		Nos. 1881-1888 (8)	4.20	1.75

Volleyball
A753

#1890, Two women players. #1891, Woman player. #1892, Man player.

1970, Sept.   **Photo.**   **Perf. 12½**

1889	A753	2s dk red brn, bl & blk	.20	.20
1890	A753	2s ultra, org & blk	.20	.20
1891	A753	20s Prus bl, yel & blk	.50	.20
1892	A753	20s grn, yel & blk	.50	.20
		Nos. 1889-1892 (4)	1.40	.80

World Volleyball Championships.

Enrico Caruso and "I Pagliacci" by Ruggiero Leoncavallo — A754

Opera Singers and Operas: 2s, Christina Morfova and "The Bartered Bride" by Bedrich Smetana. 3s, Peter Reitchev and "Tosca" by Giacomo Puccini. 10s, Svetana Tabakova and "The Flying Dutchman" by Richard Wagner. 13s, Katia Popova and "The Masters" by Paroshkev Hadjev. 20s, Feodor Chaliapin and "Boris Godunov" by Modest Musorgski.

1970, Oct. 15   **Photo.**   **Perf. 14**

1893	A754	1s black & multi	.20	.20
1894	A754	2s black & multi	.20	.20
1895	A754	3s black & multi	.20	.20
1896	A754	10s black & multi	.20	.20
1897	A754	13s black & multi	.30	.20
1898	A754	20s black & multi	1.00	.25
		Nos. 1893-1898 (6)	2.10	1.25

Honoring opera singers in their best roles.

Ivan Assen II Coin — A755

Coins from 14th Century with Ruler's Portrait: 2s, Theodor Svetoslav. 3s, Mikhail Chichman. 13s, Ivan Alexander and Mikhail Assen. 20s, Ivan Sratsimir. 28s, Ivan Chichman (initials).

1970, Nov.			Perf. 12½	
1899	A755	1s buff & multi	.20	.20
1900	A755	2s gray & multi	.20	.20
1901	A755	3s multicolored	.20	.20
1902	A755	13s multicolored	.25	.20
1903	A755	20s lt blue & multi	.60	.20
1904	A755	28s multicolored	.85	.25
		Nos. 1899-1904 (6)	2.30	1.25

Fire Protection A756

1970		Litho.	Perf. 12½	
1905	A756	1s Fireman	.20	.20
1906	A756	3s Fire engine	.20	.20

Bicyclists A757

Congress Emblem — A758

1970			Photo.	
1907	A757	20s grn, yel & pink	.50	.20

20th Bulgarian bicycle race.

1970				
1908	A758	13s gold & multi	.35	.20

7th World Congress of Sociology, Varna, Sept. 14-19.

Ludwig van Beethoven A759

Friedrich Engels — A760

1970				
1909	A759	28s lil rose & dk bl	.90	.40

Beethoven (1770-1827), composer.

1970		Photo.	Perf. 12½	
1910	A760	13s ver, tan & brn	.30	.20

Friedrich Engels (1820-1895), German socialist, collaborator of Karl Marx.

Miniature Sheets

Luna 16 A761

Russian moon mission: 80s, Lunokhod 1, unmanned vehicle on moon, horiz.

1970		Photo.	Imperf.	
1911	A761	80s plum, sil, blk & bl	2.00	2.00
1912	A761	1 l vio bl, sil & red	4.00	2.75

No. 1911, Lunokhod 1, Nov. 10-17. No. 1912, Luna 16 mission, Sept. 12-24.
Issue dates: 80s, Dec. 18; 1 l, Nov. 10.

Snowflake — A762

1970, Dec. 15		Photo.	Perf. 12½x13	
1913	A762	2s ultra & multi	.20	.20

New Year 1971.

Birds and Flowers A763

Folk Art: 2s, Bird and flowers. 3s, Flying birds. 5s, Birds and flowers. 13s, Sun. 20s, Tulips and pansies.

1971, Jan. 25			Perf. 12½x13½	
1914	A763	1s multicolored	.20	.20
1915	A763	2s multicolored	.20	.20
1916	A763	3s multicolored	.20	.20
1917	A763	5s multicolored	.20	.20
1918	A763	13s multicolored	.20	.20
1919	A763	20s multicolored	.55	.20
		Nos. 1914-1919 (6)	1.55	1.20

Spring 1971.

Girl, by Zeko Spiridonov A764

Modern Bulgarian Sculpture: 2s, Third Class (people looking through train window), by Ivan Funev. 3s, Bust of Elin Pelin, by Marko Markov. 13s, Bust of Nina, by Andrej Nikolov. 20s, Monument to P. K. Yavorov (kneeling woman), by Ivan Lazarov. 28s, Engineer, by Ivan Funev. 1 l, Refugees, by Sekul Krimov, horiz.

1970, Dec. 28			Perf. 12½	
1920	A764	1s gold & vio	.20	.20
1921	A764	2s gold & dk ol grn	.20	.20
1922	A764	3s gold & rose brn	.20	.20
1923	A764	13s gold & dk grn	.30	.20
1924	A764	20s gold & red brn	.50	.20
1925	A764	28s gold & dk brn	.80	.20
		Nos. 1920-1925 (6)	2.20	1.20

Souvenir Sheet
Imperf

1926	A764	1 l gold, dk brn & buff	2.00	1.75

Runner A765

Design: 20s, Woman putting the shot.

1971, Mar. 13		Photo.	Perf. 12½x13	
1927	A765	2s brown & multi	.20	.20
1928	A765	20s dp grn, org & blk	.90	.25

2nd European Indoor Track and Field Championships.

Bulgarian Secondary School, Bolgrad — A766

Educators: 20s, Dimiter Mitev, Prince Bogoridi and Sava Radoulov.

1971, Mar. 16			Perf. 12½	
1929	A766	2s silver, brn & grn	.20	.20
1930	A766	20s silver, brn & vio	.50	.20

First Bulgarian secondary school, 1858, in Bolgrad, USSR.

Communards — A767

1971, Mar. 18		Photo.	Perf. 12½x13	
1931	A767	20s rose magenta & blk	.50	.20

Centenary of the Paris Commune.

Dimitrov Facing Goering, Quotation, FIR Emblem — A768

1971, Apr. 11			Perf. 12½	
1932	A768	2s grn, gold, blk & red	.20	.20
1933	A768	13s plum, gold, blk & red	.70	.20

Intl. Fed. of Resistance Fighters (FIR), 20th anniv.

George S. Rakovski (1821-1867), Revolutionary Against Turkish Rule — A769

1971, Apr. 14				
1934	A769	13s olive & blk brn	.30	.20

Edelweiss Hotel, Borovets A770

2s, Panorama Hotel, Pamporovo. 4s, Boats at Albena, Black Sea. 8s, Boats at Rousalka. 10s, Shtastlivetsa Hotel, Mt. Vitosha.

1971			Perf. 13	
1935	A770	1s brt green	.20	.20
1936	A770	2s olive gray	.20	.20
1937	A770	4s brt blue	.20	.20
1938	A770	8s blue	.20	.20
1939	A770	10s bluish green	.25	.20
		Nos. 1935-1939 (5)	1.05	1.00

Technological Progress — A771

Designs: 1s, Mason with banner, vert. 13s, Two men and doves, vert.

1971, Apr. 20		Photo.	Perf. 12½	
1940	A771	1s gold & multi	.20	.20
1941	A771	2s gray blue & multi	.20	.20
1942	A771	13s lt green & multi	.50	.20
		Nos. 1940-1942 (3)	.90	.60

10th Cong. of Bulgarian Communist Party.

Panayot Pipkov and Anthem A772

1971, May 20				
1943	A772	13s sil, blk & brt grn	.45	.20

Panayot Pipkov, composer, birth cent.

Mammoth A773

Prehistoric Animals: 2s, Bear, vert. 3s, Hipparion (horse). 13s, Platybelodon. 20s, Dinotherium, vert. 28s, Saber-tooth tiger.

1971, May 29			Perf. 12½	
1944	A773	1s dull bl & multi	.20	.20
1945	A773	2s lilac & multi	.20	.20
1946	A773	3s multicolored	.20	.20
1947	A773	13s multicolored	.50	.20
1948	A773	20s dp grn & multi	.80	.20
1949	A773	28s multicolored	1.40	.30
		Nos. 1944-1949 (6)	3.30	1.30

Khan Asparuch Crossing Danube, 679 A.D., by Boris Angelushev — A774

Historical Paintings: 3s, Reception at Trnovo, by Ilya Petrov. 5s, Chevartov's Troops at Benkovsky, by P. Morozov. 8s, Russian Gen. Gurko and People in Sofia, 1878, by D. Gudjenko. 28s, People Greeting Red Army, by S. Venov.

1971, Mar. 6   *Perf. 13½x14*
1950	A774	2s gold & multi	.20	.20
1951	A774	3s gold & multi	.20	.20
1952	A774	5s gold & multi	.20	.20
1953	A774	8s gold & multi	.30	.20
	a.	Souv. sheet of 4, #1950-1953	1.00	.50
1954	A774	28s gold & multi	2.75	.85
		Nos. 1950-1954 (5)	3.65	1.65

In 1973, No. 1953a was surcharged 1 lev and overprinted "Visitez la Bulgarie," airline initials and emblems, and, on the 5s stamp, "Par Avion."

Freed Black, White and Yellow Men — A775

1971, May 20   **Photo.**   *Perf. 12½*
1955	A775	13s blue, blk & yel	.35	.20

Intl. Year against Racial Discrimination.

Map of Europe, Championship Emblem — A776

"XXX" Supporting Barbell — A777

1971, June 19
1956	A776	2s lt blue & multi	.20	.20
1957	A777	13s yellow & multi	.60	.20

30th European Weight Lifting Championships, Sofia, June 19-27.

Facade, Old House, Koprivnica — A778

Designs: Decorated facades of various old houses in Koprivnica.

1971, July 10   **Photo.**   *Perf. 12½*
1958	A778	1s green & multi	.20	.20
1959	A778	2s brown & multi	.20	.20
1960	A778	6s violet & multi	.20	.20
1961	A778	13s dk red & multi	.40	.20
		Nos. 1958-1961 (4)	1.00	.80

Frontier Guard and German Shepherd A779

1971, July 31   *Perf. 13*
1962	A779	2s green & ol grn	.20	.20

25th anniversary of the Frontier Guards.

Congress of Busludja, Basrelief — A780

1971, July 31   *Perf. 12½*
1963	A780	2s dk red & ol grn	.20	.20

80th anniversary of the first Congress of the Bulgarian Social Democratic party.

Young Woman, by Ivan Nenov — A781

Paintings: 2s, Lazarova in Evening Gown, by Stefan Ivanov. 3s, Performer in Dress Suit, by Kyril Zonev. 13s, Portrait of a Woman, by Detchko Uzunov. 20s, Woman from Kalotina, by Vladimir Dimitrov. 40s, Gorjanin (Mountain Man), by Stoyan Venev.

1971, Aug. 2   *Perf. 14x13½*
1964	A781	1s green & multi	.20	.20
1965	A781	2s green & multi	.20	.20
1966	A781	3s green & multi	.20	.20
1967	A781	13s green & multi	.40	.20
1968	A781	20s green & multi	.75	.30
1969	A781	40s green & multi	1.60	.45
		Nos. 1964-1969 (6)	3.35	1.55

National Art Gallery.

Wrestlers A782

Designs: 13s, Wrestlers.

1971, Aug. 27   *Perf. 12½*
1970	A782	2s green, blk & bl	.20	.20
1971	A782	13s red org, blk & bl	.50	.20

European Wrestling Championships.

Young Workers — A783

Industrial Buildings: 2s, Petro-chemical works, Pleven, vert. 10s, Chemical works,

Post Horn Emblem A784

1971   **Photo.**   *Perf. 13*
1972	A783	2s dark blue	.20	.20

25th anniv. of the Young People's Brigade.

1971, Sept. 15   *Perf. 12½*
1973	A784	20s dp green & gold	.45	.20

8th meeting of postal administrations of socialist countries, Varna.

FEBS Waves Emblem — A785

1971, Sept. 20
1974	A785	13s black, red & mar	.50	.20

7th Congress of European Biochemical Association (FEBS), Varna.

Statue of Republic — A786

Design: 13s, Bulgarian flag.

1971, Sept. 20   *Perf. 13x12½*
1975	A786	2s gold, yel & dk red	.20	.20
1976	A786	13s gold, grn & red	.40	.20

Bulgarian People's Republic, 25th anniv.

Cross Country Skiing and Winter Olympics Emblem A787

Sport and Winter Olympics Emblem: 2s, Downhill skiing. 3s, Ski jump and skiing. 4s, Women's figure skating. 13s, Ice hockey. 28s, Slalom skiing. 1 l, Torch and stadium.

1971, Sept. 25   *Perf. 12½*
1977	A787	1s dk green & multi	.20	.20
1978	A787	2s vio blue & multi	.20	.20
1979	A787	3s ultra & multi	.20	.20
1980	A787	4s dp plum & multi	.20	.20
1981	A787	13s dk blue & multi	.40	.20
1982	A787	28s multicolored	.90	.35
		Nos. 1977-1982 (6)	2.10	1.35

Miniature Sheet

Imperf
1983	A787	1 l multicolored	3.50	1.60

11th Winter Olympic Games, Sapporo, Japan, Feb. 3-13, 1972.

Factory, Botevgrad A788

Vratsa. 13s, Maritsa-Istok Power Station, Dimitrovgrad. 40s, Electronics works, Sofia.

1971   **Photo.**   *Perf. 13*
1984	A788	1s violet	.20	.20
1985	A788	2s orange	.20	.20
1986	A788	10s deep purple	.20	.20
1987	A788	13s lilac rose	.25	.20
1988	A788	40s deep brown	.70	.20
		Nos. 1984-1988 (5)	1.55	1.00

UNESCO Emblem A789

1971, Nov. 4   *Perf. 12½*
1989	A789	20s lt bl, blk, gold & red	.45	.20

25th anniv. of UNESCO.

Soccer Player, by Kyril Zonev (1896-1971) A790

Paintings by Kyril Zonev: 2s, Landscape, horiz. 3s, Self-portrait. 13s, Lilies. 20s, Landscape, horiz. 40s, Portrait of a Young Woman.

1971, Nov. 10   *Perf. 11x12*
1990	A790	1s gold & multi	.20	.20
1991	A790	2s gold & multi	.20	.20
1992	A790	3s gold & multi	.20	.20
1993	A790	13s gold & multi	.25	.20
1994	A790	20s gold & multi	.85	.25
1995	A790	40s gold & multi	1.25	.35
		Nos. 1990-1995 (6)	2.95	1.40

Salyut Space Station — A791

Astronauts Dobrovolsky, Volkov and Patsayev — A792

Designs: 13s, Soyuz 11 space transport. 40s, Salyut and Soyuz 11 joined.

1971, Dec. 20   *Perf. 12½*
1996	A791	2s dk grn, yel & red	.20	.20
1997	A791	13s multicolored	.25	.20
1998	A791	40s dk blue & multi	1.25	.40
		Nos. 1996-1998 (3)	1.70	.80

Souvenir Sheet

Imperf
1999	A792	80s multicolored	2.00	1.50

Salyut-Soyuz 11 space mission, and in memory of the Russian astronauts Lt. Col. Georgi T. Dobrovolsky, Vladislav N. Volkov and Victor I. Patsayev, who died during the Soyuz 11 space mission, June 6-30, 1971.

Oil Tanker Vihren — A793

1972, Jan. 8　　Photo.　　*Perf. 12½*
2000 A793　18s lil rose, vio & blk　.75　.25
Bulgarian shipbuilding industry.

Goce Delchev A794

5s, Jan Sandanski. 13s, Damjan Gruev.

1972, Jan. 21　　Photo.　　*Perf. 12½*
2001 A794　2s brick red & blk　.20　.20
2002 A794　5s green & blk　.20　.20
2003 A794　13s lemon & blk　.35　.20
　　Nos. 2001-2003 (3)　.75　.60
Centenary of the births of Bulgarian patriots Delchev (1872-1903) and Sandanski, and of Macedonian Gruev (1871-1906).

Gymnast with Hoop, Medals — A795

13s, Gymnast with ball, medals. 70s, Gymnasts with hoops, medals.

1972, Feb. 10
2004 A795　13s multicolored　.40　.20
2005 A795　18s multicolored　.55　.20

Miniature Sheet
Imperf
2006 A795　70s multicolored　2.50　2.00
5th World Women's Gymnastic Championships, Havana, Cuba.

View of Melnik, by Petar Mladenov — A796

Paintings from National Art Gallery: 2s, Plower, by Pencho Georgiev. 3s, Funeral, by Alexander Djendov. 13s, Husband and Wife, by Vladimir Dimitrov. 20s, Nursing Mother, by Nenko Balkanski. 40s, Paisii Hilendarski Writing History, by Koio Denchev.

1972, Feb. 20　　　*Perf. 13½x14*
2007 A796　1s green & multi　.20　.20
2008 A796　2s green & multi　.20　.20
2009 A796　3s green & multi　.20　.20
2010 A796　13s green & multi　.40　.20
2011 A796　20s green & multi　.75　.20
2012 A796　40s green & multi　1.25　.35
　　Nos. 2007-2012 (6)　3.00　1.35
Paintings from National Art Gallery.

Worker — A797

1972, Mar. 7　　　*Perf. 12½*
2013 A797　13s silver & multi　.20　.20
7th Bulgarian Trade Union Congress.

Singing Harvesters A798

Designs: Paintings by Vladimir Dimitrov.

1972, Mar. 31　*Perf. 11½x12, 12x11½*
2014 A798　1s shown　.20　.20
2015 A798　2s Harvester　.20　.20
2016 A798　3s Women Diggers　.20　.20
2017 A798　13s Fabric Dyers　.35　.20
2018 A798　20s "My Mother"　.70　.20
2019 A798　40s Self-portrait　1.40　.30
　　Nos. 2014-2019 (6)　3.05　1.30
Vladimir Dimitrov, painter, 90th birth anniv.

"Your Heart is your Health" — A799

1972, Apr. 30　　　*Perf. 12½*
2020 A799　13s red, blk & grn　.70　.30
World Health Day.

St. Mark's Basilica and Wave — A800

1972, May 6　　　*Perf. 13x12½*
Design: 13s, Ca' D'Oro and wave.
2021 A800　2s ol grn, bl grn & lt bl　.20　.20
2022 A800　13s red brn, vio & lt grn　.50　.20
UNESCO campaign to save Venice.

Dimitrov in Print Shop, 1901 — A801

Designs: Life of George Dimitrov.

1972, May 8　　Photo.　　*Perf. 12½*
2023 A801　1s shown　.20　.20
2024 A801　2s Dimitrov as leader of 1923 uprising　.20　.20
2025 A801　3s Leipzig trial, 1933　.20　.20
2026 A801　5s As Communist functionary, 1935　.20　.20
2027 A801　13s As leader and teacher, 1948　.20　.20
2028 A801　18s Addressing youth rally, 1948　.40　.20
2029 A801　28s With Pioneers, 1948　.65　.20
2030 A801　40s Mausoleum　1.00　.30
2031 A801　80s Portrait　2.75　.45
　a.　Souvenir sheet　4.25　2.50
　　Nos. 2023-2031 (9)　5.80　2.15
90th anniversary of the birth of George Dimitrov (1882-1949), communist leader.
No. 2031a contains one imperf. stamp similar to No. 2031, but in different colors.
Value, No. 2031 imperf. in slightly changed colors, $5.

Paisii Hilendarski A802

Design: 2s, Flame and quotation.

1972, May 12
2032 A802　2s gold, grn & brn　.20　.20
2033 A802　13s gold, grn & brn　.50　.20
Paisii Hilendarski (1722-1798), monk, writer of Bulgarian-Slavic history.

Canoeing, Motion and Olympic Emblems — A803

Designs (Motion and Olympic emblems and): 2s, Gymnastics. 3s, Swimming, women's. 13s, Volleyball. 18s, Jumping. 40s, Wrestling. 80s, Stadium and sports.

1972, June 25
Figures of Athletes in Silver & Black
2034 A803　1s lt blue & multi　.20　.20
2035 A803　2s orange & multi　.20　.20
2036 A803　3s multicolored　.20　.20
2037 A803　13s yellow & multi　.20　.20
2038 A803　18s multicolored　.40　.20
2039 A803　40s pink & multi　1.25　.30
　　Nos. 2034-2039 (6)　2.45　1.30

Miniature Sheet
Imperf
Size: 62x60mm
2040 A803　80s gold, ver & yel　1.75　1.00
20th Olympic Games, Munich, 8/26-9/11.

Angel Kunchev A804

1972, June 30　　Photo.　　*Perf. 12½*
2041 A804　2s mag, dk pur & gold　.20　.20
Centenary of the death of Angel Kunchev, patriot and revolutionist.

Zlatni Pyassatsi A805

1972, Sept. 16
2042 A805　1s shown　.20　.20
2043 A805　2s Drouzhba　.20　.20
2044 A805　3s Slunchev Bryag　.20　.20
2045 A805　15s Primorsko　.20　.20
2046 A805　28s Roussalka　.60　.25
2047 A805　40s Albena　.85　.30
　　Nos. 2042-2047 (6)　2.25　1.35
Bulgarian Black Sea resorts.

Bronze Medal, Olympic Emblems, Canoeing — A806

Olympic Emblems and: 2s, Silver medal, broad jump. 3s, Gold medal, boxing. 18s, Gold medal, wrestling. 40s, Gold medal, weight lifting.

1972, Sept. 29
2048 A806　1s Prus bl & multi　.20　.20
2049 A806　2s dk green & multi　.20　.20
2050 A806　3s orange brn & multi　.20　.20
2051 A806　18s olive & multi　.50　.20
2052 A806　40s multicolored　1.00　.40
　　Nos. 2048-2052 (5)　2.10　1.20
Bulgarian victories in 20th Olympic Games. For overprint see No. 2066.

Stoj Dimitrov — A807

Resistance Fighters: 2s, Cvetko Radoinov. 3s, Bogdan Stivrodski. 5s, Mirko Laiev. 13s, Nedelyo Nikolov.

1972, Oct. 30　　Photo.　　*Perf. 12½x13*
2053 A807　1s olive & multi　.20　.20
2054 A807　2s multicolored　.20　.20
2055 A807　3s multicolored　.20　.20
2056 A807　5s multicolored　.20　.20
2057 A807　13s multicolored　.30　.20
　　Nos. 2053-2057 (5)　1.10　1.00

"50 Years USSR" A808

1972, Nov. 3　　Photo.　　*Perf. 12½x13*
2058 A808　13s gold, red & yel　.25　.20
50th anniversary of Soviet Union.

Turk's-cap Lily — A809

Protected Plants: 2s, Gentian. 3s, Sea daffodil. 4s, Globe flower. 18s, Primrose. 23s, Pulsatilla vernalis. 40s, Snake's-head.

1972, Nov. 25   **Perf. 12½**

Flowers in Natural Colors

2059	A809	1s olive bister	.20	.20
2060	A809	2s olive bister	.20	.20
2061	A809	3s olive bister	.20	.20
2062	A809	4s olive bister	.20	.20
2063	A809	18s olive bister	.30	.20
2064	A809	23s olive bister	.75	.20
2065	A809	40s olive bister	1.40	.35
		Nos. 2059-2065 (7)	3.25	1.55

No. 2052 Overprinted in Red

1972, Nov. 27
2066 A806 40s multicolored   .95 .25

Bulgarian weight lifting Olympic gold medalists.

Dobri Chintulov
A810

1972, Nov. 28   **Photo.**   **Perf. 12½**
2067 A810 2s gray, dk & lt grn   .20 .20

Chintulov, writer, 150th birth anniv.

Forehead Band — A811

Designs (14th-19th Century Jewelry): 2s, Belt buckles. 3s, Amulet. 8s, Pendant. 23s, Earrings. 40s, Necklace.

1972, Dec. 27   **Engr.**   **Perf. 14x13½**

2068	A811	1s red brn & blk	.20	.20
2069	A811	2s emerald & blk	.20	.20
2070	A811	3s Prus bl & blk	.20	.20
2071	A811	8s dk red & blk	.20	.20
2072	A811	23s red org & multi	.50	.20
2073	A811	40s violet & blk	1.10	.40
		Nos. 2068-2073 (6)	2.40	1.40

Skin Divers
A812

Designs: 2s, Shelf-1 underwater house and divers. 18s, Diving bell and diver, vert. 40s, Elevation balloon and divers, vert.

1973, Jan. 24   **Photo.**   **Perf. 12½**

2074	A812	1s lt bl, blk & yel	.20	.20
2075	A812	2s blk, bl & org yel	.20	.20
2076	A812	18s blk, Prus bl & dl org	.40	.20
2077	A812	40s blk, ultra & bister	.95	.30
		Nos. 2074-2077 (4)	1.75	.90

Bulgarian deep-sea research in the Black Sea.

A souvenir sheet of four contains imperf. 20s stamps in designs of Nos. 2074-2077 with colors changed. Sold for 1 l. Value $3.50 unused, $3 canceled.

Execution of Levski, by Boris Angelushev
A813

20s, Vassil Levski, by Georgi Danchev.

1973, Feb. 19   **Perf. 13x12½**

2078	A813	2s dull rose & Prus grn	.20	.20
2079	A813	20s dull grn & brn	.90	.20

Centenary of the death of Vassil Levski (1837-1873), patriot, executed by the Turks.

Kukersky Mask, Elhovo Region
A814

Nicolaus Copernicus
A815

Kukersky Masks at pre-Spring Festival: 2s, Breznik. 3s, Hissar. 13s, Radomir. 20s, Karnobat. 40s, Pernik.

1973, Feb. 26   **Perf. 12½**

2080	A814	1s dp rose & multi	.20	.20
2081	A814	2s emerald & multi	.20	.20
2082	A814	3s violet & multi	.20	.20
2083	A814	13s multicolored	.35	.20
2084	A814	20s multicolored	.40	.20
2085	A814	40s multicolored	2.25	1.10
		Nos. 2080-2085 (6)	3.60	2.10

1973, Mar. 21   **Photo.**   **Perf. 12½**
2086 A815 28s ocher, blk & claret   1.25 .60

500th anniversary of the birth of Nicolaus Copernicus (1473-1543), Polish astronomer.

Vietnamese Worker and Rainbow — A816

1973, Apr. 16
2087 A816 18s lt blue & multi   .35 .20

Peace in Viet Nam.

A817   A818

Wild flowers.

1973, May   **Photo.**   **Perf. 13**

2088	A817	1s Poppy	.20	.20
2089	A817	2s Daisy	.20	.20
2090	A817	3s Peony	.20	.20
2091	A817	13s Centaury	.25	.20
2092	A817	18s Corn cockle	2.75	1.10
2093	A817	28s Ranunculus	.60	.25
		Nos. 2088-2093 (6)	4.20	2.15

1973, June 2

2094	A818	2s pale grn, buff & brn	.20	.20
2095	A818	18s pale brn, gray & grn	.65	.40

Christo Botev (1848-1876), poet.

"Suffering Worker" — A819

1s, Asen Halachev and revolutionists.

1973, June 6   **Photo.**   **Perf. 13**
2096	A819	1s gold, red & blk	.20	.20
2097	A819	2s gold, org & dk brn	.20	.20

50th anniversary of Pleven uprising.

Muskrat
A820

Perf. 12½x13, 13x12½

1973, June 29   **Litho.**

2098	A820	1s shown	.20	.20
2099	A820	2s Racoon	.20	.20
2100	A820	3s Mouflon, vert.	.20	.20
2101	A820	12s Fallow deer, vert.	.25	.20
2102	A820	18s European bison	.50	.20
2103	A820	40s Elk	2.50	1.00
		Nos. 2098-2103 (6)	3.85	2.00

Aleksandr Stamboliski
A821

1973, June 14   **Photo.**   **Perf. 12½**
2104	A821	18s dp brown & org	.35	.20
a.		18s orange	2.50	.75

Aleksandr Stamboliski (1879-1923), leader of Peasants' Party and premier.

Trade Union Emblem — A822

Stylized Sun, Olympic Rings — A823

1973, Aug. 27   **Photo.**   **Perf. 12½**
2105 A822 2s yellow & multi   .20 .20

8th Congress of World Federation of Trade Unions, Varna, Oct. 15-22.

1973, Aug. 29   **Perf. 13**

28s, Emblem of Bulgarian Olympic Committee & Olympic rings. 80s, Soccer, emblems of Innsbruck & Montreal 1976 Games, horiz.

2106	A823	13s multicolored	.70	.30
2107	A823	18s multicolored	1.25	.40

Souvenir Sheet

2108 A823 80s multicolored   3.25 1.75

Olympic Congress, Varna. No. 2108 contains one stamp. It also exists imperf.; also with violet margin, imperf.

Revolutionists with Communist Flag — A824

Designs: 5s, Revolutionists on flatcar blocking train. 13s, Raising Communist flag, vert. 18s, George Dimitrov and Vassil Kolarov.

1973, Sept. 22   **Photo.**   **Perf. 12½**

2109	A824	2s magenta & multi	.20	.20
2110	A824	5s magenta & multi	.20	.20
2111	A824	13s magenta & multi	.30	.20
2112	A824	18s magenta & multi	.85	.30
		Nos. 2109-2112 (4)	1.55	.90

50th anniv. of the September Revolution.

Warrior Saint
A825

Murals from Boyana Church: 1s, Tsar Kaloyan and 2s, his wife Dessislava. 5s, "St. Wystratti." 10s, Tsar Constantine Assen. 13s, Deacon Laurentius. 18s, Virgin Mary. 20s, St. Ephraim. 28s, Jesus. 80s, Jesus in the Temple, horiz.

1973, Sept. 24

2113	A825	1s gold & multi	.20	.20
2114	A825	2s gold & multi	.20	.20
2115	A825	3s gold & multi	.20	.20
2116	A825	5s gold & multi	.20	.20
2117	A825	10s gold & multi	.35	.20
2118	A825	13s gold & multi	.45	.20
2119	A825	18s gold & multi	.70	.20
2120	A825	20s gold & multi	.95	.20
2121	A825	28s gold & multi	3.50	.35
		Nos. 2113-2121 (9)	6.75	1.95

Miniature Sheet
Imperf

2122 A825 80s gold & multi   3.75 2.25

No. 2122 contains one stamp with simulated perforations.

Christo Smirnenski — A826

1973, Sept. 29   **Photo.**   **Perf. 12½**
2123	A826	1s multicolored	.20	.20
2124	A826	2s vio blue & multi	.20	.20

Christo Smirnenski (1898-1923), poet.

Human Rights Flame — A827

1973, Oct. 10
2125 A827 13s dk bl, red & gold   .30 .20

Universal Declaration of Human Rights, 25th anniv.

Bulgarian History Type

1s, Tsar Theodor Svetoslav receiving Byzantine envoys. 2s, Tsar Mihail Shishman's army in battle with Byzantines. 3s, Tsar Ivan

Alexander's victory at Russocastro. 4s, Patriarch Euthimius at the defense of Turnovo. 5s, Tsar Ivan Shishman leading horsemen against the Turks. 13s, Momchil attacking Turks at Umour. 18s, Tsar Ivan Stratsimir meeting King Sigismund's crusaders. 28s, The Boyars Balik, Theodor & Dobrotitsa, meeting ship bringing envoys from Anne of Savoy.

1973, Oct. 23   *Perf. 13*
Silver and Black Vignettes

2126	A741	1s olive bister	.20	.20
2127	A741	2s Prus blue	.20	.20
2128	A741	3s lilac	.20	.20
2129	A741	4s green	.20	.20
2130	A741	5s violet	.20	.20
2131	A741	13s orange & brn	.25	.20
2132	A741	18s olive green	.40	.20
2133	A741	28s yel brn & brn	1.10	.50
		Nos. 2126-2133 (8)	2.75	1.90

Finn Class — A828

Sailboats: 2s, Flying Dutchman. 3s, Soling class. 13s, Tempest class. 20s, Class 470. 40s, Tornado class.

1973, Oct. 29   **Litho.**   *Perf. 13*

2134	A828	1s ultra & multi	.20	.20
2135	A828	2s green & multi	.20	.20
2136	A828	3s dk blue & multi	.20	.20
2137	A828	13s dull vio & multi	.30	.20
2138	A828	20s gray bl & multi	.60	.30
2139	A828	40s dk blue & multi	2.50	2.00
		Nos. 2134-2139 (6)	4.00	3.10

Value, set imperf. in changed colors, $10.

Village, by Bencho Obreshkov — A829

Paintings: 2s, Mother and Child, by Stoyan Venev. 3s, Rest (woman), by Tsenko Boyadjiev. 13s, Flowers in Vase, by Sirak Skitnik. 18s, Meri Kuneva (portrait), by Ilya Petrov. 40s, Winter in Plovdiv, by Zlatyu Boyadjiev. 13s, 18s, 40s, vert.

Perf. 12½x12, 12x12½

1973, Nov. 10

2140	A829	1s gold & multi	.20	.20
2141	A829	2s gold & multi	.20	.20
2142	A829	3s gold & multi	.20	.20
2143	A829	13s gold & multi	.25	.20
2144	A829	18s gold & multi	.40	.20
2145	A829	40s gold & multi	2.25	.75
		Nos. 2140-2145 (6)	3.50	1.75

Souvenir Sheet

Paintings by Stanislav Dospevski: a, Domnica Lambreva. b, Self-portrait. Both vert.

2146	Sheet of 2	2.75	1.75
a.	A829 50s gold & multi	.70	.50
b.	A829 50s gold & multi	.70	.50

Bulgarian paintings. No. 2146 commemorates the 150th birth anniv. of Stanislav Dospevski.

Souvenir Sheet

Soccer — A830

1973, Dec. 10   **Photo.**   *Perf. 13*

2147	A830	28s multicolored	4.00	3.50

No. 2147 sold for 1 l. Exists overprinted for Argentina 78.

Angel and Ornaments A831

1s, Attendant facing right. 2s, Passover table and lamb. 3s, Attendant facing left. 8s, Abraham and ornaments. 13s, Adam and Eve. 28s, Expulsion from Garden of Eden.

1974, Jan. 21   **Photo.**   *Perf. 13*

2148	A831	1s fawn, yel & brn	.20	.20
2149	A831	2s fawn, yel & brn	.20	.20
2150	A831	3s fawn, yel & brn	.20	.20
a.	Strip of 3, #2148-2150	.25	.20
2151	A831	5s slate grn & yel	.20	.20
2152	A831	8s slate grn & yel	.20	.20
a.	Pair, #2151-2152	.30	.25
2153	A831	13s lt brown, yel & ol	.30	.25
2154	A831	28s lt brown, yel & ol	.50	.30
a.	Pair, #2153-2154	.80	.35
		Nos. 2148-2154 (7)	1.80	1.55

Woodcarvings from Rozhen Monastery, 19th century.

Lenin, by N. Mirtchev — A832

18s, Lenin visiting Workers, by W. A. Serov.

1974, Jan. 28   **Litho.**   *Perf. 12½x12*

2155	A832	2s ocher & multi	.20	.20
2156	A832	18s ocher & multi	.50	.25

50th anniversary of the death of Lenin.

1974, Jan. 28

Demeter Blagoev at Rally, by G. Kowachev.

2157	A832	2s multicolored	.20	.20

50th anniversary of the death of Demeter Blagoev, founder of Bulgarian Communist Party.

Domestic Animals A833

1974, Feb. 1   **Photo.**   *Perf. 13*

2158	A833	1s Sheep	.20	.20
2159	A833	2s Goat	.20	.20
2160	A833	3s Pig	.20	.20
2161	A833	5s Cow	.20	.20
2162	A833	13s Buffalo cow	.30	.20
2163	A833	20s Horse	.80	.30
		Nos. 2158-2163 (6)	1.90	1.30

Comecon Emblem A834

1974, Feb. 11   **Photo.**   *Perf. 13*

2164	A834	13s silver & multi	.40	.20

25th anniversary of the Council of Mutual Economic Assistance.

Soccer — A835

Designs: Various soccer action scenes.

1974, Mar.   **Photo.**   *Perf. 13*

2165	A835	1s dull green & multi	.20	.20
2166	A835	2s brt green & multi	.20	.20
2167	A835	3s slate grn & multi	.20	.20
2168	A835	13s olive & multi	.20	.20
2169	A835	28s blue grn & multi	.65	.40
2170	A835	40s emerald & multi	1.50	.70
		Nos. 2165-2170 (6)	2.95	1.90

Souvenir Sheet

2171	A835	1 l green & multi	3.00	1.60

World Soccer Championship, Munich, June 13-July 7. No. 2171 exists imperf.

Salt Production A836

Children's Paintings: 1s, Cosmic Research for Peaceful Purposes. 3s, Fire Dancers. 28s, Russian-Bulgarian Friendship (train and children). 60s, Spring (birds).

1974, Apr. 15   **Photo.**   *Perf. 13*

2172	A836	1s lilac & multi	.20	.20
2173	A836	2s lt green & multi	.20	.20
2174	A836	3s blue & multi	.20	.20
2175	A836	28s slate & multi	1.75	.95
		Nos. 2172-2175 (4)	2.35	1.55

Souvenir Sheet
Imperf

2176	A836	60s blue & multi	2.25	1.75

Third World Youth Philatelic Exhibition, Sofia, May 23-30. No. 2176 contains one stamp with simulated perforations.

Folk Singers — A837

Designs: 2s, Folk dancers (men). 3s, Bagpiper and drummer. 5s, Wrestlers. 13s, Runners (women). 18s, Gymnast.

1974, Apr. 25   *Perf. 13*

2178	A837	1s vermilion & multi	.20	.20
2179	A837	2s org brn & multi	.20	.20
2180	A837	3s brn red & multi	.20	.20
2181	A837	5s blue & multi	.20	.20
2182	A837	13s ultra & multi	.75	.25
2183	A837	18s violet bl & multi	.40	.20
		Nos. 2178-2183 (6)	1.95	1.25

4th Amateur Arts and Sports Festival

Flowers A838

1974, May   **Photo.**   *Perf. 13*

2184	A838	1s Aster	.20	.20
2185	A838	2s Petunia	.20	.20
2186	A838	3s Fuchsia	.20	.20
2187	A838	18s Tulip	.30	.20
2188	A838	28s Carnation	.60	.25
2189	A838	28s Pansy	1.60	.55
		Nos. 2184-2189 (6)	3.10	1.60

Souvenir Sheet

2190	A838	80s Sunflower	1.75	.85

Automobiles and Emblems — A839

1974, May 15   **Photo.**   *Perf. 13*

2191	A839	13s multicolored	.30	.20

International Automobile Federation (FIA) Spring Congress, Sofia, May 20-24.

Old and New Buildings, UNESCO Emblem A840

1974, June 15

2192	A840	18s multicolored	.30	.20

UNESCO Executive Council, 94th Session, Varna.

Postrider A841

Designs: 18s, First Bulgarian mail coach. 28s, UPU Monument, Bern.

1974, Aug. 5

2193	A841	2s ocher, blk & vio	.20	.20
2194	A841	18s ocher, blk & grn	.40	.20

Souvenir Sheet

2195	A841	28s ocher, blk & bl	2.00	1.50

UPU cent. No. 2195 exists imperf.

Pioneer and
Komsomol
Girl — A842

Designs: 2s, Pioneer and birds. 60s,
Emblem with portrait of George Dimitrov.

1974, Aug. 12

2196	A842	1s green & multi	.20	.20
2197	A842	2s blue & multi	.20	.20

Souvenir Sheet

2198	A842	60s red & multi	1.00	1.00

30th anniversary of Dimitrov Pioneer Organization, Septemvrilche.

"Bulgarian
Communist
Party" — A843

Symbolic Designs: 2s, Russian liberators.
5s, Industrialization. 13s, Advanced agriculture and husbandry. 18s, Scientific and technical progress.

1974, Aug. 20

2199	A843	1s blue gray & multi	.20	.20
2200	A843	2s blue gray & multi	.20	.20
2201	A843	5s gray & multi	.20	.20
2202	A843	13s gray & multi	.25	.20
2203	A843	18s gray & multi	.35	.20
		Nos. 2199-2203 (5)	1.20	1.00

30th anniversary of the People's Republic.

Gymnast on
Parallel
Bars — A844

Design: 13s, Gymnast on vaulting horse.

1974, Oct. 18   Photo.   Perf. 13

2204	A844	2s multicolored	.20	.20
2205	A844	13s multicolored	.30	.20

18th Gymnastic Championships, Varna.

Souvenir Sheet

Symbols of Peace — A845

1974, Oct. 29   Photo.   Perf. 13

2206	A845	Sheet of 4	2.50	1.10
a.		13s Doves	.20	.20
b.		13s Map of Europe	.20	.20
c.		13s Olive Branch	.20	.20
d.		13s Inscription	.20	.20

1974 European Peace Conference. "Peace" in various languages written on Nos. 2206a-2206c. Sold for 60s. Exists imperf.

Nib and
Envelope — A846

1974, Nov. 20

2207	A846	2s yellow, blk & grn	.20	.20

Introduction of postal zone numbers.

Flowers
A847

1974, Dec. 5

2208	A847	2s emerald & multi	.20	.20

St. Todor, Ceramic
Icon — A848

Fruit Tree
Blossoms — A849

Designs: 2s, Medallion, Veliko Turnovo. 3s, Carved capital. 5s, Silver bowl. 8s, Goblet. 13s, Lion's head finial. 18s, Gold plate with Cross. 28s, Breastplate with eagle.

1974, Dec. 18   Photo.   Perf. 13

2209	A848	1s orange & multi	.20	.20
2210	A848	2s pink & multi	.20	.20
2211	A848	3s blue & multi	.20	.20
2212	A848	5s lt vio & multi	.20	.20
2213	A848	8s brown & multi	.20	.20
2214	A848	13s multicolored	.25	.20
2215	A848	18s red & multi	.30	.20
2216	A848	28s ultra & multi	1.00	.60
		Nos. 2209-2216 (8)	2.55	2.00

Art works from 9th-12th centuries.

1975, Jan.   Photo.   Perf. 13

2217	A849	1s Apricot	.20	.20
2218	A849	2s Apple	.20	.20
2219	A849	3s Cherry	.20	.20
2220	A849	19s Pear	.30	.20
2221	A849	28s Peach	.70	.20
		Nos. 2217-2221 (5)	1.60	1.00

Tree and
Book
A850

1975, Mar. 25   Photo.   Perf. 13

2222	A850	2s gold & multi	.20	.20

Forestry High School, 50th anniversary.

Souvenir Sheet

Farmers' Activities (Woodcuts) — A851

1975, Mar. 25

2223	A851	Sheet of 4	.80	.50
a.		2s Farmer with ax and flag		
b.		5s Farmers on guard		
c.		13s Dancing couple		
d.		18s Woman picking fruit		

Bulgarian Agrarian Peoples Union, 75th anniv.

Michelangelo,
Self-portrait
A852

13s, Night, horiz. 18s, Day, horiz. Both designs after sculptures from Medici Tomb, Florence.

1975

2224	A852	2s plum & dk blue	.20	.20
2225	A852	13s vio bl & plum	.25	.20
2226	A852	18s brown & green	.50	.20
		Nos. 2224-2226 (3)	.95	.60

Souvenir Sheet

2227	A852	2s olive & red	1.25	1.25

Michelangelo Buonarotti (1475-1564), Italian sculptor, painter and architect. No. 2227 issued to publicize ARPHILA 75 Intl. Phil. Exhib., Paris, June 6-16. Sheet sold for 60s. Issued: #2224-2226, 3/28; #2227, 3/31.

Souvenir Sheet

Spain No. 1 and España 75
Emblem — A853

1975, Apr. 4

2228	A853	40s multicolored	3.75	3.00

Espana 75 International Philatelic Exhibition, Madrid, Apr. 4-13.

Gabrov
Costume
A854

Regional Costumes: 3s, Trnsk. 5s, Vidin. 13s, Gocedelchev. 18s, Risen.

1975, Apr.   Photo.   Perf. 13

2229	A854	2s blue & multi	.20	.20
2230	A854	3s emerald & multi	.20	.20
2231	A854	5s orange & multi	.20	.20
2232	A854	13s olive & multi	.35	.20
2233	A854	18s multicolored	.80	.25
		Nos. 2229-2233 (5)	1.75	1.05

Red Star and
Arrow — A855

Design: 13s, Dove and broken sword.

1975, May 9

2234	A855	2s red, blk & gold	.20	.20
2235	A855	13s blue, blk & gold	.30	.20

Victory over Fascism, 30th anniversary.

Standard Kilogram
and Meter — A856

1975, May 9   Perf. 13x13½

2236	A856	13s silver, lil & blk	.35	.20

Cent. of Intl. Meter Convention, Paris, 1875.

IWY Emblem, Woman's Head — A857

Ivan Vasov — A858

1975, May 20   Photo.   Perf. 13
2237 A857 13s multicolored   .35   .20
International Women's Year 1975.

1975, May
Design: 13s, Ivan Vasov, seated.
2238 A858 2s buff & multi   .20   .20
2239 A858 13s gray & multi   .30   .20
125th birth anniversary of Ivan Vasov.

Nikolov and Sava Kokarechkov — A859

2s, Mitko Palaouzov, Ivan Vassilev. 5s, Nicolas Nakev, Stevtcho Kraychev. 13s, Ivanka Pachkoulova, Detelina Mintcheva.

1975, May 30
2240 A859 1s multicolored   .20   .20
2241 A859 2s multicolored   .20   .20
2242 A859 5s multicolored   .20   .20
2243 A859 13s multicolored   .28   .20
    Nos. 2240-2243 (4)   .88   .80
Teen-age resistance fighters, killed during World War II.

Mother Feeding Child, by John E. Millais A861

Etchings: 2s, The Dead Daughter, by Goya. 3s, Reunion, by Beshkov. 13s, Seated Nude, by Renoir. 20s, Man in a Fur Hat, by Rembrandt. 40s, The Dream, by Daumier, horiz. 1 l, Temptation, by Dürer.

Photogravure and Engraved
1975, Aug.   Perf. 12x11½, 11½x12
2248 A861 1s yel grn & multi   .20   .20
2249 A861 2s orange & multi   .20   .20
2250 A861 3s lilac & multi   .20   .20
2251 A861 13s lt blue & multi   .25   .20
2252 A861 20s ocher & multi   .40   .20
2253 A861 40s rose & multi   1.10   .30
    Nos. 2248-2253 (6)   2.35   1.30

Souvenir Sheet
2254 A861 1 l emerald & multi   2.00   1.25
World Graphics Exhibition.

Letter "Z" from 12th Century Manuscript A862

Initials from Illuminated Manuscripts: 2s, "B" from 17th cent. prayerbook. 3s, "V" from 16th cent. Bouhovo Gospel. 8s, "B" from 14th cent. Turnovo collection. 13s, "V" from Dobreisho's Gospel, 13th cent. 18s, "E" from 11th cent. Enina book of the Apostles.

1975, Aug.   Litho.   Perf. 11½
2255 A862 1s multicolored   .20   .20
2256 A862 2s multicolored   .20   .20
2257 A862 3s multicolored   .20   .20
2258 A862 8s multicolored   .20   .20
2259 A862 13s multicolored   .25   .20
2260 A862 18s multicolored   .65   .20
    Nos. 2255-2260 (6)   1.70   1.20
Bulgarian art.

Whimsical Globe — A863

1975, Aug.   Photo.   Perf. 13
2261 A863 2s multicolored   .20   .20
Festival of Humor and Satire.

Lifeboat Dju IV and Gibraltar-Cuba Route — A864

1975, Aug. 5   Photo.   Perf. 13
2262 A864 13s multicolored   .25   .20
Oceanexpo 75, 1st Intl. Ocean Exhib., Okinawa, July 20, 1975-Jan. 18, 1976.

Sts. Cyril and Methodius — A865

Sts. Constantine and Helena — A866

St. Sophia Church, Sofia, Woodcut by V. Zahriev — A867

1975, Aug. 21
2263 A865 2s ver, yel & brn   .20   .20
2264 A866 13s green, yel & brn   .25   .20

Souvenir Sheet
2265 A867 50s orange & multi   1.25   .80
Balkanphila V, philatelic exhibition, Sofia, Sept. 27-Oct. 5.

Peace Dove and Map of Europe — A868

1975, Nov.   Photo.   Perf. 13
2266 A868 18s ultra, rose & yel   .45   .25
European Security and Cooperation Conference, Helsinki, Finland, July 30-Aug. 1. No. 2266 printed in sheets of 5 stamps and 4 labels, arranged checkerwise.

Acherontia Atropos — A869

Designs: Moths.

1975   Photo.   Perf. 13
2267 A869 1s *shown*   .20   .20
2268 A869 2s *Daphnis nerii*   .20   .20
2269 A869 3s *Smerinthus ocellata*   .20   .20
2270 A869 10s *Deilephila nicea*   .20   .20
2271 A869 13s *Choerocampa elpenor*   .25   .20
2272 A869 18s *Macroglossum fuciformis*   .90   .25
    Nos. 2267-2272 (6)   1.95   1.25

Soccer Player — A870

1975, Sept. 21
2273 A870 2s multicolored   .20   .20
8th Inter-Toto (soccer pool) Soccer Championships, Varna.

Constantine's Rebellion Against the Turks, 1403 — A871

Designs (Woodcuts): 2s, Campaign of Vladislav III, 1443-1444. 3s, Battles of Turnovo, 1598 and 1686. 10s, Battle of Liprovsko, 1688. 13s, Guerrillas, 17th century. 18s, Return of exiled peasants.

1975, Nov. 27   Photo.   Perf. 13
2274 A871 1s bister, grn & blk   .20   .20
2275 A871 2s blue, car & blk   .20   .20
2276 A871 3s yellow, lil & blk   .20   .20
2277 A871 10s orange, grn & blk   .20   .20
2278 A871 13s green, lil & blk   .25   .20
2279 A871 18s pink, grn & blk   .45   .20
    Nos. 2274-2279 (6)   1.50   1.20
Bulgarian history.

Red Cross and First Aid — A872

Design: 13s, Red Cross and dove.

1975, Dec. 1
2280 A872 2s red brn, red & blk   .20   .20
2281 A872 13s bl grn, red & blk   .25   .20
90th anniversary of Bulgarian Red Cross.

Egyptian Galley A873

Historic Ships: 2s, Phoenician galley. 3s, Greek trireme. 5s, Roman galley. 13s, Viking longship. 18s, Venetian galley.

1975, Dec. 15   Photo.   Perf. 13
2282 A873 1s multicolored   .20   .20
2283 A873 2s multicolored   .20   .20
2284 A873 3s multicolored   .20   .20
2285 A873 5s multicolored   .20   .20
2286 A873 13s multicolored   .30   .20
2287 A873 18s multicolored   .60   .20
    Nos. 2282-2287 (6)   1.70   1.20
See Nos. 2431-2436, 2700-2705.

Souvenir Sheet

Ethnographical Museum, Plovdiv — A874

1975, Dec. 17
2288   Sheet of 3   4.50   2.50
    a. A874 80s grn, yel & dark brn   1.25   .65
European Architectural Heritage Year. No. 2288 contains 3 stamps and 3 labels showing stylized bird.

Dobri
Hristov — A875

1975, Dec.   *Perf. 13*
2289 A875 5s brt green, yel & brn   .20   .20
Dobri Hristov, musician, birth centenary.

United Nations
Emblem — A876

1975, Dec.
2290 A876 13s gold, blk & mag   .20   .20
United Nations, 30th anniversary.

Glass Ornaments — A877

13s, Peace dove, decorated ornament.

1975, Dec. 22   **Photo.**   *Perf. 13*
2291 A877 2s brt violet & multi   .20   .20
2292 A877 13s gray & multi   .20   .20
New Year 1976.

Downhill Skiing — A878

Designs (Winter Olympic Games Emblem and): 2s, Cross country skier, vert. 3s, Ski jump. 13s, Biathlon, vert. 18s, Ice hockey, vert. 23s, Speed skating, vert. 80s, Figure skating, pair, vert.

1976, Jan. 30   *Perf. 13½*
2293 A878 1s silver & multi   .20   .20
2294 A878 2s silver & multi   .20   .20
2295 A878 3s silver & multi   .20   .20
2296 A878 13s silver & multi   .25   .20
2297 A878 18s silver & multi   .30   .20
2298 A878 23s silver & multi   .80   .30
     Nos. 2293-2298 (6)   1.95 1.30
      Souvenir Sheet
2299 A878 80s silver & multi   1.75 1.10
12th Winter Olympic Games, Innsbruck, Austria, Feb. 4-15.

Electric Streetcar, Sofia, 1976 — A879

Design: 13s, Streetcar and trailer, 1901.

1976, Jan. 12   **Photo.**   *Perf. 13½x13*
2300 A879 2s gray & multi   .20   .20
2301 A879 13s gray & multi   .40   .20
75th anniversary of Sofia streetcars.

Stylized
Bird — A880

5s, Dates "1976," "1956" & star. 13s, Hammer & sickle. 50s, George Dimitrov.

1976, Mar. 1   *Perf. 13*
2302 A880 2s gold & multi   .20   .20
2303 A880 5s gold & multi   .20   .20
2304 A880 13s gold & multi   .25   .20
     Nos. 2302-2304 (3)   .65   .60
      Souvenir Sheet
2305 A880 50s gold & multi   .25   .45
11th Bulgarian Communist Party Congress.

A. G. Bell and Telephone,
1876 — A881

1976, Mar. 10
2306 A881 18s dk brn, yel & ocher   .25   .20
Centenary of first telephone call by Alexander Graham Bell, Mar. 10, 1876.

Mute Swan — A882

Waterfowl: 2s, Ruddy shelduck. 3s, Common shelduck. 5s, Garganey teal. 13s, Mallard. 18s, Red-crested pochard.

1976, Mar. 27   **Litho.**   *Perf. 11½*
2307 A882 1s vio bl & multi   .20   .20
2308 A882 2s yel grn & multi   .20   .20
2309 A882 3s blue & multi   .20   .20
2310 A882 5s multicolored   .25   .20
2311 A882 13s purple & multi   .65   .20
2312 A882 18s green & multi   .90   .20
     Nos. 2307-2312 (6)   2.40 1.20

Guerrillas — A883

Designs (Woodcuts by Stoev): 2s, Peasants with rifle and proclamation. 5s, Raina Knaginia with horse and guerrilla. 13s, Insurgents with cherrywood cannon.

1976, Apr. 5   **Photo.**   *Perf. 13*
2313 A883 1s multicolored   .20   .20
2314 A883 2s multicolored   .20   .20
2315 A883 5s multicolored   .25   .20
2316 A883 13s multicolored   .25   .20
     Nos. 2313-2316 (4)   .85   .80
Centenary of uprising against Turkey.

Guard
and Dog
A884

13s, Men on horseback, observation tower.

1976, May 15
2317 A884 2s multicolored   .20   .20
2318 A884 13s multicolored   .20   .20
30th anniversary of Border Guards.

Construction
Worker — A885

1976, May 20
2319 A885 2s multicolored   .20   .20
Young Workers Brigade, 30th anniversary.

Busludja, Bas-
relief
A886

AES
Complex — A887

Design: 5s, Memorial building.

1976, May 28   **Photo.**   *Perf. 13*
2320 A886 2s green & multi   .20   .20
2321 A886 5s violet bl & multi   .20   .20
First Congress of Bulgarian Social Democratic Party, 85th anniversary.

1976, Apr. 7
8s, Factory. 10s, Apartment houses. 13s, Refinery. 20s, Hydroelectric station.
2322 A887 5s green   .20   .20
2323 A887 8s maroon   .20   .20
2324 A887 10s green   .20   .20
2325 A887 13s violet   .30   .20
2326 A887 20s brt green   .40   .20
     Nos. 2322-2326 (5)   1.30 1.00
Five-year plan accomplishments.

Children Playing Around Table — A888

Kindergarten Children: 2s, with doll carriage & hobby horse. 5s, playing ball. 23s, in costume.

1976, June 15
2327 A888 1s green & multi   .20   .20
2328 A888 2s yellow & multi   .20   .20
2329 A888 5s lilac & multi   .20   .20
2330 A888 23s rose & multi   .40   .20
     Nos. 2327-2330 (4)   1.00   .80

Demeter
Blagoev — A889

1976, May 28
2331 A889 13s bluish blk, red &
            gold   .25   .20
Demeter Blagoev (1856-1924), writer, political leader, 120th birth anniversary.

Christo Botev — A890

1976, May 25
2332 A890 13s ocher & slate grn   .25   .20
Christo Botev (1848-1876), poet, death centenary. Printed se-tenant with yellow green and ocher label, inscribed with poem.

Boxing, Montreal
Olympic
Emblem — A891

Belt
Buckle — A892

Designs (Montreal Olympic Emblem): 1s, Wrestling, horiz. 3s, 1 l, Weight lifting. 13s, One-man kayak. 18s, Woman gymnast. 28s, Woman diver. 40s, Woman runner.

1976, June 25
2333 A891 1s orange & multi   .20   .20
2334 A891 2s multicolored   .20   .20
2335 A891 3s lilac & multi   .20   .20
2336 A891 13s multicolored   .20   .20
2337 A891 18s multicolored   .30   .20
2338 A891 28s blue & multi   .40   .20
2339 A891 40s lemon & multi   .75   .30
     Nos. 2333-2339 (7)   2.25 1.50
      Souvenir Sheet
2340 A891 1 l orange & multi   1.60 1.10
21st Olympic Games, Montreal, Canada, July 17-Aug. 1.

1976, July 30   **Photo.**   *Perf. 13*
Thracian Art (8th-4th Centuries): 2s, Brooch. 3s, Mirror handle. 5s, Helmet cheek

cover. 13s, Gold ornament. 18s, Lion's head (harness decoration). 20s, Knee guard. 28s, Jeweled pendant.

2341	A892	1s brown & multi	.20	.20
2342	A892	2s blue & multi	.20	.20
2343	A892	3s multicolored	.20	.20
2344	A892	5s claret & multi	.20	.20
2345	A892	13s purple & multi	.25	.20
2346	A892	18s multicolored	.30	.20
2347	A892	20s multicolored	.40	.20
2348	A892	28s multicolored	.60	.20
		Nos. 2341-2348 (8)	2.35	1.60

Souvenir Sheet

Composite of Bulgarian Stamp Designs — A893

1976, June 5
2349 A893 50s red & multi   1.60 .65
International Federation of Philately (F.I.P.), 50th anniversary and 12th Congress.

Partisans at Night, by Ilya Petrov — A894

Paintings: 5s, Old Town, by Tsanko Lavenov. 13s, Seated Woman, by Petrov, vert. 18s, Seated Boy, by Petrov, vert. 28s, Old Plovdiv, by Lavenov, vert. 80s, Ilya Petrov, self-portrait, vert.

1976, Aug. 11   Photo.   Perf. 14
2350	A894	2s multicolored	.20	.20
2351	A894	5s multicolored	.20	.20
2352	A894	13s ultra & multi	.30	.20
2353	A894	18s multicolored	.45	.20
2354	A894	28s multicolored	.65	.20
		Nos. 2350-2354 (5)	1.80	1.00

Souvenir Sheet
2354A A894 80s multicolored   1.25 .95

Souvenir Sheet

Olympic Sports and Emblems — A895

1976, Sept. 6   Photo.   Perf. 13
2355 A895   Sheet of 4   1.60 1.00
a.	25s Weight Lifting	.35	.20
b.	25s Rowing	.35	.20
c.	25s Running	.35	.20
d.	25s Wrestling	.35	.20
Medalists, 21st Olympic Games, Montreal.

Souvenir Sheet

Fresco and UNESCO Emblem — A896

1976, Dec. 3
2356 A896 50s red & multi   1.25 .55
UNESCO, 30th anniv.

"The Pianist" by Jendov — A897

Fish and Hook — A898

Designs (Caricatures by Jendov): 5s, Imperialist "Trick or Treat." 13s, The Leader, 1931.

1976, Sept. 30   Photo.   Perf. 13
2357	A897	2s green & multi	.20	.20
2358	A897	5s purple & multi	.20	.20
2359	A897	13s magenta & multi	.30	.20
		Nos. 2357-2359 (3)	.70	.60
Alex Jendov (1901-1953), caricaturist.

1976, Sept. 21   Photo.   Perf. 13
2360 A898 5s multicolored   .20 .20
World Sport Fishing Congress, Varna.

St. Theodore A899

Frescoes: 3s, St. Paul. 5s, St. Joachim. 13s, Melchizedek. 19s, St. Porphyrius. 28s, Queen. 1 l, The Last Supper.

1976, Oct. 4   Litho.   Perf. 12x12½
2361	A899	2s gold & multi	.20	.20
2362	A899	3s gold & multi	.20	.20
2363	A899	5s gold & multi	.20	.20
2364	A899	13s gold & multi	.30	.20
2365	A899	19s gold & multi	.35	.20
2366	A899	28s gold & multi	.65	.20
		Nos. 2361-2366 (6)	1.90	1.20

Miniature Sheet
Perf. 12
2367 A899 1 l gold & multi   1.50 .95
Zemen Monastery frescoes, 14th cent.

Document A900

1976, Oct. 5
2368 A900 5s multicolored   .20 .20
State Archives, 25th anniversary.

Cinquefoil A901

1976, Oct. 14   Photo.   Perf. 13
2369	A901	1s Chestnut	.20	.20
2370	A901	2s shown	.20	.20
2371	A901	5s Holly	.20	.20
2372	A901	8s Yew	.20	.20
2373	A901	13s Daphne	.30	.20
2374	A901	23s Judas tree	.60	.20
		Nos. 2369-2374 (6)	1.70	1.20

Dimitri Polianov — A902

1976, Nov. 19
2375 A902 2s dk purple & ocher   .20 .20
Dimitri Polianov (1876-1953), poet.

Christo Botev, by Zlatyu Boyadjiev A903

Paintings: 2s, Partisan Carrying Cherrywood Cannon, by Ilya Petrov. 3s, "Necklace of Immortality" (man's portrait), by Detchko Uzunov. 13s, "April 1876," by Georgi Popoff. 18s, Partisans, by Stoyan Venev. 60s, The Oath, by Svetlin Ruseff.

1976, Dec. 8
2376	A903	1s bister & multi	.20	.20
2377	A903	2s bister & multi	.20	.20
2378	A903	3s bister & multi	.20	.20
2379	A903	13s bister & multi	.25	.20
2380	A903	18s bister & multi	.35	.20
		Nos. 2376-2380 (5)	1.20	1.00

Souvenir Sheet
Imperf
2381 A903 60s gold & multi   .95 .55
Uprising against Turkish rule, centenary.

"Pollution" and Tree A904

Design: 18s, "Pollution" obscuring sun.

1976, Nov. 10   Perf. 13
2382 A904 2s ultra & multi   .20 .20
2383 A904 18s blue & multi   .30 .20
Protection of the environment.

Congress Emblem A904a

Flags — A904b

1976, Nov. 28   Photo.   Perf. 13
2384 A904a 2s multicolored   .20 .20
2384A A904b 13s multicolored   .25 .20
33rd BSIS Cong. (Bulgarian Socialist Party).

Tobacco Workers, by Stajkov A905

Paintings by Stajkov: 2s, View of Melnik. 13s, Shipbuilder.

1976, Dec. 16   Photo.   Perf. 13
2385	A905	1s multicolored	.20	.20
2386	A905	2s multicolored	.20	.20
2387	A905	13s multicolored	.30	.20
		Nos. 2385-2387 (3)	.70	.60
Veselin Stajkov (1906-1970), painter.

Snowflake A906

1976, Dec. 20
2388 A906 2s silver & multi   .20 .20
New Year 1977.

Zachary Stoyanov (1851-1889), Historian — A907

1976, Dec. 30
2389 A907 2s multicolored   .20 .20

Bronze Coin of Septimus Severus — A908

Roman Coins: 2s, 13s, 18s, Bronze coins of Caracalla, diff. 23s, Copper coin of Diocletian.

1977, Jan. 28 Photo.   Perf. 13½x13
2390 A908 1s gold & multi   .20 .20
2391 A908 2s gold & multi   .20 .20
2392 A908 13s gold & multi   .20 .20
2393 A908 18s gold & multi   .25 .20
2394 A908 23s gold & multi   .45 .20
    Nos. 2390-2394 (5)   1.30 1.00
Coins struck in Serdica (modern Sofia).

Skis and Compass — A909

1977, Feb. 14   Perf. 13
2395 A909 13s ultra, red & lt bl   .25 .20
2nd World Ski Orienteering Championships.

1977, Feb. 24   Photo.   Perf. 13
2396 A910 2s multicolored   .20 .20
5th Congress of Bulgarian Tourist Organization.

Tourist Congress Emblem — A910

Bellflower A911

Designs: Various bellflowers.

1977, Mar. 2
2397 A911 1s yellow & multi   .20 .20
2398 A911 2s rose & multi   .20 .20
2399 A911 3s lt blue & multi   .20 .20

2400 A911 13s multicolored   .30 .20
2401 A911 43s yellow & multi   1.10 .30
    Nos. 2397-2401 (5)   2.00 1.10

Vasil Kolarov — A912

Union Congress Emblem — A913

1977, Mar. 21   Photo.   Perf. 13
2402 A912 2s blue & black   .20 .20
Vasil Kolarov (1877-1950), politician.

1977, Mar. 25
2403 A913 2s multicolored   .20 .20
8th Bulgarian Trade Union Cong., Apr. 4-7.

Wolf A914

Wild Animals: 2s, Red fox. 10s, Weasel. 13s, European wildcat. 23s, Jackal.

1977, May 16   Litho.   Perf. 12½x12
2404 A914 1s multicolored   .20 .20
2405 A914 2s multicolored   .20 .20
2406 A914 10s multicolored   .20 .20
2407 A914 13s multicolored   .35 .20
2408 A914 23s multicolored   .60 .20
    Nos. 2404-2408 (5)   1.55 1.00

Diseased Knee — A915

1977, Mar. 31   Photo.   Perf. 13
2409 A915 23s multicolored   .40 .15
World Rheumatism Year.

Writers' Congress Emblem A916

1977, June 7
2410 A916 23s lt bl & yel grn   .65 .20
International Writers Congress: "Peace, the Hope of the Planet." No. 2410 printed in sheets of 8 stamps and 4 labels with signatures of participating writers.

Old Testament Trinity, Sofia, 16th Century A917

Icons: 1s, St. Nicholas, Nessebur, 13th cent. 3s, Annunciation, Royal Gates, Veliko Turnovo, 16th cent. 5s, Christ Enthroned, Nessebur, 17th cent. 13s, St. Nicholas, Elena, 18th cent. 23s, Presentation of the Virgin, Rila Monastery, 18th cent. 35s, Virgin and Child, Tryavna, 19th cent. 40s, St. Demetrius on Horseback, Provadia, 19th cent. 1 l, The 12 Holidays, Rila Monastery, 18th cent.

1977, May 10   Photo.   Perf. 13
2411 A917 1s black & multi   .20 .20
2412 A917 2s green & multi   .20 .20
2413 A917 3s brown & multi   .20 .20
2414 A917 5s blue & multi   .20 .20
2415 A917 13s olive & multi   .30 .20
2416 A917 23s maroon & multi   .50 .20
2417 A917 35s green & multi   .80 .25
2418 A917 40s dp ultra & multi   1.10 .40
    Nos. 2411-2418 (8)   3.50 1.85
Miniature Sheet
Imperf
2419 A917 1 l gold & multi   2.25 1.10
Bulgarian icons. See Nos. 2615-2619.

Souvenir Sheet

St. Cyril — A918

1977, June 7   Photo.   Perf. 13
2420 A918 1 l gold & multi   1.75 .90
St. Cyril (827-869), reputed inventor of Cyrillic alphabet.

Congress Emblem — A919

1977, May 9
2421 A919 2s red, gold & grn   .20 .20
13th Komsomol Congress.

Newspaper Masthead — A920

1977, June 3   Photo.   Perf. 13
2422 A920 2s multicolored   .20 .20
Cent. of Bulgarian daily press and 50th anniv. of Rabotnichesko Delo newspaper.

Patriotic Front Emblem — A921

Weight Lifting — A922

1977, May 26
2423 A921 2s gold & multi   .20 .20
8th Congress of Patriotic Front.

1977, June 15
2424 A922 13s dp brown & multi   .25 .20
European Youth Weight Lifting Championships, Sofia, June.

Women Basketball Players — A923

1977, June 15   Perf. 13
2425 A923 23s multicolored   .50 .20
7th European Women's Basketball Championships.

Wrestling — A924

Games Emblem and: 13s, Running. 23s, Basketball. 43s, Women's gymnastics.

1977, Apr. 15
2426 A924 2s multicolored   .20 .20
2427 A924 13s multicolored   .20 .20
2428 A924 23s multicolored   .40 .20
2429 A924 43s multicolored   .70 .25
    Nos. 2426-2429 (4)   1.50 .85
UNIVERSIADE '77, University Games, Sofia, Aug. 18-27.

TV Tower,
Berlin — A925

1977, Aug. 12   Litho.   *Perf. 13*
2430 A925 25s blue & dk blue   .50 .20
SOZPHILEX 77 Philatelic Exhibition, Berlin,
Aug. 19-28.

Ship Type of 1975

Historic Ships: 1s, Hansa cog. 2s, Santa
Maria, caravelle. 3s, Golden Hind, frigate. 12s,
Santa Catherina, carrack. 13s, La Corone, gal-
leon. 43s, Mediterranean galleass.

1977, Aug. 29   Photo.   *Perf. 13*
2431 A873 1s multicolored   .20 .20
2432 A873 2s multicolored   .20 .20
2433 A873 3s multicolored   .20 .20
2434 A873 12s multicolored   .25 .20
2435 A873 13s multicolored   .25 .20
2436 A873 43s multicolored   1.00 .25
       Nos. 2431-2436 (6)   2.10 1.25

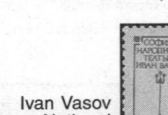

Ivan Vasov
National
Theater
A926

Buildings, Sofia: 13s, Party Headquarters.
23s, House of the People's Army. 30s, Clement Ochrida University. 80s, National Gallery.
1 l, National Assembly.

1977, Aug. 30   Photo.   *Perf. 13*
2437 A926 12s red, *gray*   .20 .20
2438 A926 13s red brn, *gray*   .20 .20
2439 A926 23s blue, *gray*   .30 .20
2440 A926 30s olive, *gray*   .40 .20
2441 A926 80s violet, *gray*   1.10 .40
2442 A926 1 l claret, *gray*   1.40 .50
       Nos. 2437-2442 (6)   3.60 1.70

Map of
Europe
A927

1977, June 10
2443 A927 23s brown, bl & grn   .40 .20
21st Congress of the European Organization for Quality Control, Varna.

Union of
Earth and
Water, by
Rubens
A928

Rubens Paintings: 23s, Venus and Adonis.
40s, Pastoral Scene (man and woman). 1 l,
Portrait of a Lady in Waiting.

1977, Sept. 23   Litho.   *Perf. 12*
2444 A928 13s gold & multi   .50 .20
2445 A928 23s gold & multi   .70 .20
2446 A928 40s gold & multi   1.10 .25
       Nos. 2444-2446 (3)   2.30 .65
             Souvenir Sheet
2447 A928 1 l gold & multi   2.75 1.60
Peter Paul Rubens (1577-1640).

George
Dimitrov
A929

1977, June 17   Photo.   *Perf. 13*
2448 A929 13s red & deep claret   .35 .20
George Dimitrov (1882-1947).

Flame with
Star — A930

Smart Pete on
Donkey, by Ilya
Beshkov — A931

1977, May 17
2449 A930 13s gold & multi   .25 .20
3rd Bulgarian Culture Congress.

1977, May 19
2450 A931 2s multicolored   .20 .20
11th National Festival of Humor and Satire
Gabrovo.

Elin Pelin — A932

Writers: 2s, Pelin (Dimitur Ivanov Stojanov,
(1877-1949). 5s, Peju K. Jaworov (1878-
1914).
Artists: 13s, Boris Angelushev (1902-1966),
23s, Ceno Todorov (Ceno Todorov Dikov,
1877-1953). Each printed with label showing
scenes from authors' works or illustrations by
the artists.

1977, Aug. 26   Photo.   *Perf. 13*
2451 A932 2s gold & brown   .20 .20
2452 A932 5s gold & gray grn   .20 .20
2453 A932 13s gold & claret   .25 .20
2454 A932 23s gold & blue   .45 .20
       Nos. 2451-2454 (4)   1.10 .80

13th Canoe World
Championships — A933

1977, Sept. 1   Photo.   *Perf. 13*
2455 A933 2s shown   .20 .20
2456 A933 23s 2-man canoe   .40 .20

Albena,
Black
Sea
A933a

1977, Oct. 5   Photo.   *Perf. 13*
2456A A933a 35s shown   .65 .25
2456B A933a 43s Rila Monastery   .80 .30
Sheet contains 4 each plus label.

Dr.
Pirogov — A934

1977, Oct. 14   Photo.   *Perf. 13*
2457 A934 13s olive, ocher & brn   .25 .20
Centenary of visit by Russian physician N.
J. Pirogov during war of liberation from Turkey.

Peace Decree,
1917 — A935

Old Soldier with
Grandchild
A936

13s, Lenin, 1917. 23s, "1917" as a flame.

1977, Oct. 21
2458 A935 2s black, buff & red   .20 .20
2459 A935 13s multicolored   .25 .20
2460 A935 23s multicolored   .45 .20
       Nos. 2458-2460 (3)   .90 .60
60th anniv. of Russian October Revolution.

1977, Sept. 30

Designs (Festival Posters): 13s, "The
Bugler." 23s, Liberation Monument, Sofia
(detail). 25s, Samara flag.

2461 A936 2s multicolored   .20 .20
2462 A936 13s multicolored   .25 .20
2463 A936 23s multicolored   .40 .20
2464 A936 25s multicolored   .50 .25
       Nos. 2461-2464 (4)   1.35 .85
Liberation from Turkish rule, centenary.

Souvenir Sheet

Games' and Sports Emblems — A937

1977, Aug. 10   Photo.   *Perf. 13½x13*
2465 A937 1 l multicolored   1.50 1.25
University Games '77, Sofia.

Conference Building — A938

1977, Sept. 12   *Perf. 13½*
2466 A938 23s multicolored   .40 .20
64th Interparliamentary Union Conf., Sofia.

Bulgarian
Worker's
Newspaper,
Anniversaries
A939

1977, Sept. 12   Photo.   *Perf. 13*
2467 A939 2s yel grn, blk & red   .20 .20

Ornament
A940

New Year 1978: 13s, Different ornament.

1977, Dec. 1
2468 A940 2s gold & multi   .20 .20
2469 A940 13s silver & multi   .25 .20

Railroad Bridge — A941

1977, Nov. 9
2470 A941 13s green, yel & gray   .30 .20
Transport Organization, 50th anniversary.

A942

1977, Nov. 15
2471 A942 8s gold & vio brn .20 .20

Petko Ratchev Slaveikov (1827-95), poet, birth sesquicentennial. No. 2471 printed in sheets of 8 stamps and 8 labels in 4 alternating vertical rows.

A943

Designs: 23s, Soccer player and Games' emblem. 50s, Soccer players.

1978, Jan. 30   Photo.   Perf. 13
2472 A943 13s multicolored .25 .20
2473 A943 23s multicolored .45 .20

Souvenir Sheet
2474 A943 50s ultra & multi 1.00 .85

11th World Cup Soccer Championship, Argentina, June 1-25.

Todor Zhivkov and Leonid I. Brezhnev — A944

Ostankino Tower, Moscow, Bulgarian Post Emblem — A945

1977, Sept. 7   Photo.   Perf. 13
2475 A944 18s gold, car & brn .30 .20

Bulgarian-Soviet Friendship. No. 2475 issued in sheets of 3 stamps and 3 labels.

1978, Mar. 1
2476 A945 13s multicolored .25 .20

Comecon Postal Organization (Council of Mutual Economic Assistance), 20th anniv.

Leo Tolstoy — A946

Shipka Pass Monument — A947

5s, Fedor Dostoevski. 13s, Ivan Sergeevich Turgenev. 23s, Vasili Vasilievich Vershchagin. 25s, Giuseppe Garibaldi. 35s, Victor Hugo.

1978, Mar. 28   Photo.   Perf. 13
2477 A946 2s yellow & dk grn .20 .20
2478 A946 5s lemon & brown .20 .20
2479 A946 13s tan & sl grn .25 .20
2480 A946 23s gray & vio brn .35 .20
2481 A946 25s yel grn & blk .40 .20
2482 A946 35s lt bl & vio bl .80 .40
Nos. 2477-2482 (6) 2.20 1.40

Souvenir Sheet
2483 A947 50s multicolored .80 .60

Bulgaria's liberation from Ottoman rule, cent.

Bulgarian and Russian Colors A948

1978, Mar. 18
2484 A948 2s multicolored .20 .20

30th anniv. of Russo-Bulgarian co-operation.

Heart and WHO Emblem A949

1978, May 12
2485 A949 23s gray, red & org .30 .20

World Health Day, fight against hypertension.

Goddess A950

Ceramics (2nd-4th Cent.) & Exhibition Emblem: 5s, Mask of bearded man. 13s, Vase. 23s, Vase. 35s, Head of Silenus. 53s, Cock.

1978, Apr. 26
2486 A950 2s green & multi .20 .20
2487 A950 5s multicolored .20 .20
2488 A950 13s multicolored .25 .20
2489 A950 23s multicolored .50 .20
2490 A950 35s multicolored .75 .25
2491 A950 53s carmine & multi 1.25 .30
Nos. 2486-2491 (6) 3.15 1.35

Philaserdica Philatelic Exhibition.

Nikolai Roerich, by Svyatoslav Roerich — A951

"Mind and Matter," by Andrei Nikolov — A952

1978, Apr. 5
2492 A951 8s multicolored .20 .20
2493 A952 13s multicolored .30 .20

Nikolai K. Roerich (1874-1947) and Andrei Nikolov (1878-1959), artists.

Bulgarian Flag and Red Star — A953

1978, Apr. 18
2494 A953 2s vio blue & multi .20 .20

Bulgarian Communist Party Congress.

Young Man, by Albrecht Dürer A954

Paintings: 23s, Bathsheba at Fountain, by Rubens. 25s, Portrait of a Man, by Hans Holbein the Younger. 35s, Rembrandt and Saskia, by Rembrandt. 43s, Lady in Mourning, by Tintoretto. 60s, Old Man with Beard, by Rembrandt. 80s, Knight in Armor, by Van Dyck.

1978, June 19   Photo.   Perf. 13
2495 A954 13s multicolored .20 .20
2496 A954 23s multicolored .30 .20
2497 A954 25s multicolored .30 .20
2498 A954 35s multicolored .45 .20
2499 A954 43s multicolored .55 .20
2500 A954 60s multicolored .85 .25
2501 A954 80s multicolored 1.10 .40
Nos. 2495-2501 (7) 3.75 1.65

Dresden Art Gallery paintings.

Doves and Festival Emblem — A955

1978, May 31
2502 A955 13s multicolored .25 .20

11th World Youth Festival, Havana, 7/28-8/5.

Fritillaria Stribrnyi — A956

Rare Flowers: 2s, Fritillaria drenovskyi. 3s, Lilium rhodopaeum. 13s, Tulipa urumoffii. 23s, Lilium jankae. 43s, Tulipa rhodopaea.

1978, June 27
2503 A956 1s multicolored .20 .20
2504 A956 2s multicolored .20 .20
2505 A956 3s multicolored .20 .20
2506 A956 13s multicolored .25 .20
2507 A956 23s multicolored .45 .20
2508 A956 43s multicolored .90 .30
Nos. 2503-2508 (6) 2.20 1.30

Yacht Cor Caroli and Map of Voyage A957

1978, May 19   Photo.   Perf. 13
2509 A957 23s multicolored .50 .20

First Bulgarian around-the-world voyage, Capt. Georgi Georgiev, 12/20/76-12/20/77.

Market, by Naiden Petkov — A958

Views of Sofia: 5s, Street, by Emil Stoichev. 13s, Street, by Boris Ivanov. 23s, Tolbukhin Boulevard, by Nikola Tanev. 35s, National Theater, by Nikola Petrov. 53s, Market, by Anton Mitov.

1978, Aug. 28   Litho.   Perf. 12½x12
2510 A958 2s multicolored .20 .20
2511 A958 5s multicolored .20 .20
2512 A958 13s multicolored .20 .20
2513 A958 23s multicolored .30 .20
2514 A958 35s multicolored .50 .20
2515 A958 53s multicolored .85 .30
Nos. 2510-2515 (6) 2.25 1.30

Miniature Sheet

Sleeping Venus, by Giorgione — A959

1978, Aug. 7   Photo.   Imperf.
2516 A959 1 l multicolored 2.25 .85

View of Varna — A960

1978, July 13   Photo.   *Perf. 13*
2517 A960 13s multicolored   .25 .20
63rd Esperanto Cong., Varna, 7/29-8/5.

Black Woodpecker
A961

Woodpeckers: 2s, Syrian. 3s, Three-toed. 13s, Middle spotted. 23s, Lesser spotted. 43s, Green.

1978, Sept. 1
2518 A961 1s multicolored   .25 .20
2519 A961 2s multicolored   .25 .20
2520 A961 3s multicolored   .25 .20
2521 A961 13s multicolored   .30 .20
2522 A961 23s multicolored   .45 .20
2523 A961 43s multicolored   1.10 .25
    Nos. 2518-2523 (6)   2.60 1.25

"September 1923" — A962

1978, Sept. 5
2524 A962 2s red & brn   .25 .20
55th anniversary of September uprising.

Souvenir Sheet

National Theater, Sofia A963

Photogravure and Engraved
1978, Sept. 1   *Perf. 12x11½*
2525   Sheet of 4   2.50 1.00
  a. A963 40s shown   .60 .20
  b. A963 40s Festival Hall, Sofia .60 .20
  c. A963 40s Charles Bridge, Prague .60 .20
  d. A963 40s Belvedere Palace,
           Prague   .60 .20
PRAGA '78 and PHILASERDICA '79 Philatelic Exhibitions.

Black and White Hands, Human Rights Emblem — A964

1978, Oct. 3   Photo.   *Perf. 13x13½*
2526 A964 13s multicolored   .25 .20
Anti-Apartheid Year.

Gotse Deltchev — A965

Bulgarian Calculator — A966

1978, Aug. 1   Photo.   *Perf. 13*
2527 A965 13s multicolored   .25 .20
Gotse Deltchev (1872-1903), patriot.

1978, Sept. 3
2528 A966 2s multicolored   .20 .20
International Sample Fair, Plovdiv.

Guerrillas — A967

1978, Aug. 1
2529 A967 5s blk & rose red   .20 .20
Ilinden and Preobrazhene revolts, 75th anniv.

"Pipe Line" and Flags A968

1978, Oct. 3
2530 A968 13s multicolored   .25 .20
Construction of gas pipe line from Orenburg to Russian border.

A969

1978, Oct. 4   *Perf. 13x13½*
2531 A969 13s Three acrobats   .25 .20
3rd World Acrobatic Championships, Sofia, Oct. 6-8.

A970

1978, Sept. 18   Photo.   *Perf. 13*
2532 A970 2s dp claret & ocher   .20 .20
Christo G. Danov (1828-1911), 1st Bulgarian publisher. No. 2532 printed with se-tenant label showing early printing press.

Insurgents, by Todor Panajotov — A971

1978, Sept. 20
2533 A971 2s multicolored   .20 .20
Vladaja mutiny, 60th anniversary.

A972

A973

1978, Oct. 11   Photo.   *Perf. 13*
2534 A972 13s dk brn & org red   .25 .20
Salvador Allende (1908-1973), president of Chile.

1978, Oct. 18
2535 A973 23s Human Rights flame   .50 .20
Universal Declaration of Human Rights, 30th anniversary.

A974

A975

Bulgarian Paintings: 1s, Levski and Matei Mitkaloto, by Kalina Tasseva. 2s, "Strength for my Arm" by Zlatyu Boyadjiev. 3s, Rumena, woman military leader, by Nikola Mirchev, horiz. 13s, Kolju Ficeto, by Elza Goeva. 23s, Family, National Revival Period, by Naiden Petkov.

Perf. 12x12½, 12½x12
1978, Oct. 25   Litho.
2536 A974 1s multicolored   .20 .20
2537 A974 2s multicolored   .20 .20
2538 A974 3s multicolored   .20 .20
2539 A974 13s multicolored   .25 .20
2540 A974 23s multicolored   .40 .20
    Nos. 2536-2540 (5)   1.25 1.00
1300th anniversary of Bulgaria (in 1981).

1978, Nov. 1   Photo.   *Perf. 13*
Designs: a, Tourism building, Plovdiv. b, Chrelo Tower, Rila Cloister.

Souvenir Sheet
2541   Sheet of 5 + label   4.00 2.00
  a. A975 43s multicolored   .70 .30
  b. A975 43s multicolored   .70 .30
Conservation of European architectural heritage. No. 2541 contains 3 No. 2541a & 2 No. 2541b.

Ferry, Map of Black Sea with Route A976

1978, Nov. 1   Photo.   *Perf. 13*
2542 A976 13s multicolored   .25 .20
Opening of Ilychovsk-Varna Ferry.

Bird, from Marble Floor, St. Sofia Church — A977

1978, Nov. 20
2543 A977 5s multicolored   .20 .20
3rd Bulgaria '78, National Philatelic Exhibition, Sofia. Printed se-tenant with label showing emblems of Bulgaria '78 and Philaserdica '79.

Initial, 13th Century Gospel — A978

Designs: 13s, St. Cyril, miniature, 1567. 23s, Book cover, 16th century. 80s, St. Methodius, miniature, 13th century.

1978, Dec. 15   Photo.   *Perf. 13*
2544 A978 2s multicolored   .20 .20
2545 A978 13s multicolored   .20 .20
2546 A978 23s multicolored   .35 .20
    Nos. 2544-2546 (3)   .75 .60

Souvenir Sheet
2547 A978 80s multicolored   1.25 1.00
Cent. of the Cyril and Methodius Natl. Library.

Bulgaria No. 53 A979

Bulgarian Stamps: 13s, #534. 23s, #968. 35s, #1176, vert. 53s, #1223, vert. 1 l, #1.

1978, Dec. 30

2548	A979	2s ol grn & red	.20	.20
2549	A979	13s ultra & rose car	.20	.20
2550	A979	23s rose lil & ol grn	.30	.20
2551	A979	35s brt bl & blk	.50	.20
2552	A979	53s ver & sl grn	.90	.30
		Nos. 2548-2552 (5)	2.10	1.10

Souvenir Sheet

2553	A979	1 l multicolored	1.75	1.25

Philaserdica '79, International Philatelic Exhibition, Sofia, May 18-27, 1979, and centenary of Bulgarian stamps. No. 2553 exists imperf. See Nos. 2560-2564.

St. Clement of Ochrida — A980

1978, Dec. 8

2554	A980	2s multicolored	.20	.20

Clement of Ochrida University, 90th anniv.

Ballet Dancers A981

1978, Dec. 22

2555	A981	13s multicolored	.30	.20

Bulgarian ballet, 50th anniversary.

Nikola Karastojanov — A982

1978, Dec. 12

2556	A982	2s multicolored	.20	.20

Nikola Karastojanov (1778-1874), printer. No. 2556 printed se-tenant with label showing printing press.

Christmas Tree Made of Birds — A983

1978, Dec. 22

2557	A983	2s shown	.20	.20
2558	A983	13s Post horn	.20	.20
		New Year 1979.		

COMECON Building, Moscow, Members' Flags — A984

1979, Jan. 25   Photo.   Perf. 13

2559	A984	13s multicolored	.25	.20

Council for Mutual Economic Aid (COMECON), 30th anniversary.

**Philaserdica Type of 1978
Designs as Before**

1979, Jan. 30

2560	A979	2s brt bl & red	.20	.20
2561	A979	13s grn & dk car	.20	.20
2562	A979	23s org brn & multi	.30	.20
2563	A979	35s dl red & blk	.50	.25
2564	A979	53s vio & dk ol	.90	.35
		Nos. 2560-2564 (5)	2.10	1.20

Philaserdica '79.

Bank Building, Commemorative Coin — A985

1979, Feb. 13

2565	A985	2s yel, gray & silver	.20	.20

Centenary of Bulgarian People's Bank.

Aleksandr Stamboliski A986

1979, Feb. 28

2566	A986	2s orange & dk brn	.20	.20

Aleksandr Stamboliski (1879-1923), leader of peasant's party and premier.

Flower with Child's Face, IYC Emblem — A987

1979, Mar. 8

2568	A987	23s multicolored	.40	.20

International Year of the Child.

Stylized Heads, World Association Emblem — A988

1979, Mar. 20

2569	A988	13s multicolored	.25	.20

8th World Cong. for the Deaf, Varna, June 20-27.

"75" and Trade Union Emblem — A989

1979, Mar. 20

2570	A989	2s slate grn & org	.20	.20

75th anniversary of Bulgarian Trade Unions.

Souvenir Sheet

Sculptures in Sofia — A990

Designs: 2s, Soviet Army Monument (detail). 5s, Mother and Child, Central Railroad Station. 13s, 23s, 25s, Bas-relief from Monument of the Liberators.

1979, Apr. 2   Photo.   Perf. 13

2571	A990	Sheet of 5 + label	1.40	.60
a.		2s multicolored		.20
b.		5s multicolored		.20
c.		13s multicolored		.25
d.		23s multicolored		.40
e.		25s multicolored		.50

Centenary of Sofia as capital.

Rocket Launch, Space Flight Emblems A991

Intercosmos & Bulgarian-USSR Flight Emblems and: 25s, Link-up, horiz. 35s, Parachute descent. 1 l, Globe, emblems & orbit, horiz.

1979, Apr. 11

2572	A991	12s multicolored	.20	.20
2573	A991	25s multicolored	.45	.20
2574	A991	35s multicolored	.60	.25
		Nos. 2572-2574 (3)	1.25	.65

Souvenir Sheet

2575	A991	1 l multicolored	1.60	.75

1st Bulgarian cosmonaut on Russian space flight.
A slightly larger imperf. sheet similar to No. 2575 with control numbers at bottom and rockets at sides exists.

Nicolai Rukavishnikov — A992

Design: 13s, Rukavishnikov and Soviet cosmonaut Georgi Ivanov.

1979, May 14   Photo.   Perf. 13

2576	A992	2s multicolored	.20	.20
2577	A992	13s multicolored	.30	.20

Col. Rukavishnikov, 1st Bulgarian astronaut.

Souvenir Sheet

Thracian Gold-leaf Collar — A993

1979, May 16

2578	A993	1 l multicolored	2.25	1.50

48th International Philatelic Federation Congress, Sofia, May 16-17.

Post Horn, Carrier Pigeon, Jet, Globes and UPU Emblem — A994

Designs (Post Horn, Globes and ITU Emblem): 5s, 1st Bulgarian and modern telephones. 13s, Morse key and teleprinter. 23s, Old radio transmitter and radio towers. 35s, Bulgarian TV tower and satellite. 50s, Ground receiving station

1979, May 8   Perf. 13½x13

2579	A994	2s multicolored	.20	.20
2580	A994	5s multicolored	.20	.20
2581	A994	13s multicolored	.20	.20
2582	A994	23s multicolored	.40	.20
2583	A994	35s multicolored	.60	.25
		Nos. 2579-2583 (5)	1.60	1.05

**Souvenir Sheet
Perf. 13**

2584	A994	50s vio, blk & gray	1.10	.65

Intl. Telecommunications Day and cent. of Bulgarian Postal & Telegraph Services. Size of stamp in #2584: 39x28mm. #2584 exists imperf.

Hotel Vitosha-New Otani — A996

1979, May 20

2586	A996	2s ultra & pink	.20	.20

Philaserdica '79 Day.

Horseman Receiving Gifts, by Karellia and Boris Kuklievi — A997

1979, May 23
2587 A997 2s multicolored .20 .20
Bulgarian-Russian Friendship Day.

A998

A999

Man on Donkey, by Boris Angeloushev.

1979, May 23 Photo. Perf. 13½
2588 A998 2s multicolored .20 .20
12th National Festival of Humor and Satire, Gabrovo.

Lithographed and Engraved
1979, May 31 Perf. 14x13½
Durer Engravings: 13s, Four Women. 23s, Three Peasants. 25s, The Cook and his Wife. 35s, Portrait of Helius Eobanus Hessus. 80s, Rhinoceros, horiz.

2589 A999 13s multicolored .25 .20
2590 A999 23s multicolored .40 .20
2591 A999 25s multicolored .45 .20
2592 A999 35s multicolored .65 .20
Nos. 2589-2592 (4) 1.75 .80

Souvenir Sheet
Imperf
2593 A999 80s multicolored 2.00 1.25
Albrecht Durer (1471-1528), German engraver and painter.

R. Todorov (1879-1916) — A1000

Bulgarian Writers: #2595, Dimitri Dymov (1909-66). #2596, S. A. Kostov (1879-1939).

1979, June 26 Photo. Perf. 13
2594 A1000 2s multicolored .20 .20
2595 A1000 2s slate grn & yel grn .20 .20
2596 A1000 2s dp claret & yel .20 .20
Nos. 2594-2596 (3) .60 .60

Nos. 2594-2596 each printed se-tenant with label showing title page or character from writer's work.

Moscow '80 Emblem, Runners A1001

Moscow '80 Emblem and: 13s, Pole vault, horiz. 25s, Discus. 35s, Hurdles, horiz. 43s, High jump, horiz. 1 l, Long jump.

1979, May 15 Perf. 13
2597 A1001 2s multicolored .20 .20
2598 A1001 13s multicolored .20 .20
2599 A1001 25s multicolored .40 .20
2600 A1001 35s multicolored .80 .25
2601 A1001 43s multicolored 1.00 .30
2602 A1001 1 l multicolored 2.25 .65
Nos. 2597-2602 (6) 4.85 1.80

Souvenir Sheet
2602A A1001 2 l multicolored 6.00 3.25
22nd Summer Olympic Games, Moscow, July 19-Aug. 3, 1980.

Rocket — A1002

5s, Flags of USSR and Bulgaria. 13s, "35."

1979, Sept. 4 Photo.
2603 A1002 2s multicolored .20 .20
2604 A1002 5s multicolored .20 .20
2605 A1002 13s multicolored .20 .20
Nos. 2603-2605 (3) .60 .60
35th anniversary of liberation.

Moscow '80 Emblem, Gymnast A1003

Moscow '80 Emblem & gymnasts.

1979, July 31 Photo. Perf. 13
2606 A1003 2s multi .20 .20
2607 A1003 13s multi, horiz. .20 .20
2608 A1003 25s multi .50 .20
2609 A1003 35s multi .75 .25
2610 A1003 43s multi 1.00 .25
2611 A1003 1 l multi 2.25 .80
Nos. 2606-2611 (6) 4.90 1.90

Souvenir Sheet
2612 A1003 2 l multicolored 6.00 3.25
22nd Summer Olympic Games, Moscow, July 19-Aug. 3, 1980.

A1004

A1005

1979, July 8 Photo. Perf. 13
2613 A1004 13s ultra & blk .20 .20
Theater Institute, 18th Congress.

1979, July 17
2614 A1005 8s multicolored .20 .20
Journalists' Vacation House, Varna, 20th Anniv.

Icon Type of 1977

Virgin and Child from: 13s, 23s, Nesebar, 16th cent., diff. 35s, 43s, Sozopol, 16th cent., diff. 53s, Samokov, 19th cent. Inscribed 1979.

1979, Aug. 7 Litho. Perf. 12½
2615 A917 13s multicolored .20 .20
2616 A917 23s multicolored .35 .20
2617 A917 35s multicolored .50 .20
2618 A917 43s multicolored .60 .20
2619 A917 53s multicolored .85 .25
Nos. 2615-2619 (5) 2.50 1.05

A1006

A1007

1979, Aug. 9 Photo. Perf. 13x13½
2620 A1006 2s Anton Besenschek .20 .20
Bulgarian stenography centenary.

1979, Aug. 28 Perf. 13
2621 A1007 2s multicolored .20 .20
Bulgarian Alpine Club, 50th anniv.

Public Health Ordinance — A1008

1979, Aug. 31 Perf. 13½
2622 A1008 2s multicolored .20 .20
Public Health Service centenary. No. 2622 printed with label showing Dimitar Mollov, founder.

Isotope Measuring Device — A1009

1979, Sept. 8 Perf. 13½x13
2623 A1009 2s multicolored .20 .20
International Sample Fair, Plovdiv.

Games' Emblem A1010

1979, Sept. 20 Perf. 13
2624 A1010 5s multicolored .20 .20
Universiada '79, World University Games, Mexico City, Sept.

Sofia Locomotive Sports Club, 50th Anniversary — A1011

1979, Oct. 2
2625 A1011 2s blue & org red .20 .20

Ljuben Karavelov (1837-1879), Poet and Freedom Fighter — A1012

1979, Oct. 4 Photo. Perf. 13
2626 A1012 2s blue & slate grn .20 .20

A1013

A1014

1979, Oct. 20

2627	A1013	2s Biathlon	.20	.20
2628	A1013	13s Speed skating	.25	.20
2629	A1013	23s Downhill skiing	.40	.20
2630	A1013	43s Luge	.75	.25
	Nos. 2627-2630 (4)		1.60	.85

Souvenir Sheet

Imperf

2631	A1013	1 l Slalom	1.75	1.10

13th Winter Olympic Games, Lake Placid, NY, Feb. 12-24.

1979, Oct. 31   *Perf. 14*

Decko Uzunov, 80th Birthday: 12s, Apparition in Red. 13s, Woman from Thrace. 23s, Composition.

2632	A1014	12s multicolored	.25	.20
2633	A1014	13s multicolored	.25	.20
2634	A1014	23s multicolored	.40	.20
	Nos. 2632-2634 (3)		.90	.60

Swimming, Moscow '80
Emblem — A1016

1979, Nov. 30   **Photo.**   *Perf. 13*

2636	A1016	2s Two-man kayak, vert.	.20	.20
2637	A1016	13s Swimming, vert.	.20	.20
2638	A1016	25s shown	.40	.20
2639	A1016	35s One-man kayak	.80	.20
2640	A1016	43s Diving, vert	1.00	.40
2641	A1016	1 l Diving, vert., diff.	2.25	.70
	Nos. 2636-2641 (6)		4.85	1.90

Souvenir Sheet

2642	A1016	2 l Water polo, vert.	6.00	3.25

22nd Summer Olympic Games, Moscow, July 19-Aug. 3, 1980.

Nikola Vapzarov — A1017

1979, Dec. 7   **Photo.**   *Perf. 13*

2643	A1017	2s claret & rose	.20	.20

Vapzarov (1909-1942), poet and freedom fighter. No. 2643 printed with label showing smokestacks.

The First Socialists, by Bojan Petrov — A1018

Paintings: 13s, Demeter Blagoev Reading Newspaper, by Demeter Gjudshenov, 1892. 25s, Workers' Party March, by Sotir Sotirov, 1917. 35s, Dawn in Plovdiv, by Johann Leviev, vert.

Perf. 12½x12, 12x12½

1979, Dec. 10   **Litho.**

2644	A1018	2s multicolored	.20	.20
2645	A1018	13s multicolored	.25	.20
2646	A1018	25s multicolored	.40	.20
2647	A1018	35s multicolored	.55	.20
	Nos. 2644-2647 (4)		1.40	.80

Sharpshooting, Moscow '80 Emblem A1019

1979, Dec. 22   **Photo.**   *Perf. 13*

2648	A1019	2s shown	.20	.20
2649	A1019	13s Judo, horiz.	.20	.20
2650	A1019	25s Wrestling, horiz.	.40	.20
2651	A1019	35s Archery	.80	.25
2652	A1019	43s Fencing, horiz.	1.00	.50
2653	A1019	1 l Fencing	2.25	.90
	Nos. 2648-2653 (6)		4.85	2.25

Souvenir Sheet

2654	A1019	2 l Boxing	6.00	4.00

Procession with Relics, 11th Century Fresco A1020

Frescoes of Sts. Cyril and Methodius, St. Clement's Basilica, Rome: 13s, Reception by Pope Hadrian II. 23s, Burial of Cyril the Philosopher, 18th century. 25s, St. Cyril. 35s, St. Methodius.

1979, Dec. 25

2655	A1020	2s multicolored	.20	.20
2656	A1020	13s multicolored	.25	.20
2657	A1020	23s multicolored	.40	.20
2658	A1020	25s multicolored	.45	.20
2659	A1020	35s multicolored	.65	.20
	Nos. 2655-2659 (5)		1.95	1.00

Bulgarian Television Emblem — A1021

1979, Dec. 29   *Perf. 13½*

2660	A1021	5s violet bl & lt bl	.20	.20

Bulgarian television, 25th anniversary. No. 2660 printed with label showing Sofia television tower.

Doves in Girl's Hair A1022

Design: 2s, Children's heads, mosaic, vert.

1979   *Perf. 13*

2661	A1022	2s multicolored	.20	.20
2662	A1022	13s multicolored	.20	.20

International Year of the Child. Issue dates: 2s, July 17; 13s, Dec. 14.

Puppet on Horseback, IYC Emblem — A1023

Thracian Rider, Votive Tablet, 3rd Century — A1024

1980, Jan. 22   **Photo.**   *Perf. 13*

2663	A1023	2s multicolored	.20	.20

UNIMA, Intl. Puppet Theater Organization, 50th anniv. (1979); Intl. Year of the Child (1979).

1980, Jan. 29   **Photo.**   *Perf. 13x13½*

National Archaeological Museum Centenary; 13s, Deines stele, 5th century B.C.

2664	A1024	2s brown & gold	.20	.20
2665	A1024	13s multicolored	.20	.20

Dimitrov Meeting Lenin in Moscow, by Alexander Poplilov A1026

1980, Mar. 28   *Perf. 12x12½*

2667	A1026	13s multicolored	.20	.20

Lenin, 110th birth anniversary.

A1027

A1027a

Circulatory system, lungs enveloped in smoke.

1980, Apr. 7   *Perf. 13*

2668	A1027	5s multicolored	.20	.20

World Health Day fight against cigarette smoking.

1980, Apr. 10   **Photo.**   *Perf. 13*

2669	A1027a	2s Basketball	.20	.20
2670	A1027a	13s Soccer	.20	.20
2671	A1027a	25s Hockey	.40	.20
2672	A1027a	35s Cycling	.80	.20
2673	A1027a	43s Handball	1.00	.40
2674	A1027a	1 l Volleyball	2.25	.70
	Nos. 2669-2674 (6)		4.85	1.90

Souvenir Sheet

2675	A1027a	2 l Weightlifting	6.50	4.25

Souvenir Sheet

Intercosmos Emblem, Cosmonauts — A1028

1980, Apr. 22   *Perf. 12*

2676	A1028	50s multicolored	1.00	.45

Intercosmos cooperative space program.

Penio Penev (1930-1959), Poet — A1029

1980, Apr. 22   **Photo.**   *Perf. 13*

2677	A1029	5s multicolored	.20	.20

Se-tenant with label showing quote from author's work.

Penny Black — A1030

1980, Apr. 24   *Perf. 13*

2678	A1030	25s dark red & sepia	.60	.45

London 1980 International Stamp Exhibition, May 6-14; printed se-tenant with label showing Rowland Hill between every two stamps.

Demeter H. Tchorbadjiiski, Self-portrait — A1031

1980, Apr. 29

2679	A1031	5s shown	.20	.20
2680	A1031	13s "Our People"	.20	.20

Nikolai Giaurov — A1032

1980, Apr. 30
2681 A1032 5s multicolored   .20 .20
  Nikolai Giaurov (b. 1930), opera singer; printed se-tenant with label showing Boris Godunov.

Raising Red Flag Reichstag Building, Berlin — A1033

  Armistice, 35th Anniversary: 13s, Soviet Army memorial, Berlin-Treptow.

1980, May 6   **Perf. 13x13½**
2682 A1033 5s multicolored   .20 .20
2683 A1033 13s multicolored   .20 .20

Numeral — A1034

1979   **Perf. 14**
2684 A1034 2s ultra   .20 .20
2685 A1034 5s rose car   .20 .20

A1034a

A1035

1980, May 12   Photo.   Perf. 13
2685A A1034a 5s multicolored   .20 .20
  75th Anniv. of Teachers' Union.

1980, May 14   Photo.   Perf. 13
2686 A1035 13s multicolored   .20 .20
  Warsaw Pact, 25th anniv.

A1036

A1037

Statues.

1980, June 10
2687 A1036 2s multicolored   .20 .20
2688 A1036 13s multicolored   .20 .20
2689 A1036 25s multicolored   .40 .20
2690 A1036 35s multicolored   .80 .30
2691 A1036 43s multicolored   1.00 .60
2692 A1036 1 l multicolored   2.25 1.10
  Nos. 2687-2692 (6)   4.85 2.60

Souvenir Sheet
2693 A1036 2 l multicolored   6.00 3.25
  22nd Summer Olympic Games, Moscow, July 19-Aug. 3.

1980, Sept.   Photo.   Perf. 13
2694 A1037 13s multicolored   .25 .20
  10th Intl. Ballet Competition, Varna.

Hotel Europa, Sofia A1038

  Hotels: No. 2696, Bulgaria, Burgas, vert. No. 2697, Plovdiv, Plovdiv. No. 2698, Riga, Russe, vert. No. 2699, Varna, Djuba.

1980, July 11
2695 A1038 23s lt ultra & multi   .30 .20
2696 A1038 23s orange & multi   .30 .20
2697 A1038 23s gray & multi   .30 .20
2698 A1038 23s blue & multi   .30 .20
2699 A1038 23s yellow & multi   .30 .20
  Nos. 2695-2699 (5)   1.50 1.00
        See No. 2766.

Ship Type of 1975

  Ships of 16th, 17th Centuries: 5s, Christ of Lubeck, galleon. 8s, Roman galley. 13s, Eagle, Russian galleon. 23s, Mayflower. 35s, Maltese galley. 53s, Royal Louis, galleon.

1980, July 14
2700 A873 5s multicolored   .20 .20
2701 A873 8s multicolored   .20 .20
2702 A873 13s multicolored   .25 .20
2703 A873 23s multicolored   .45 .20
2704 A873 35s multicolored   .70 .20
2705 A873 53s multicolored   1.10 .35
  Nos. 2700-2705 (6)   2.90 1.35

Int'l Year of the Child, 1979 — A1040

  Designs: Children's drawings and IYC emblem. 43s, Tower. 5s, 25s, 43s, vert.

1980   Litho.   Perf. 12½x12, 12x12½
2708 A1040 3s multicolored   .20 .20
2709 A1040 5s multicolored   .20 .20
2710 A1040 8s multicolored   .20 .20
2711 A1040 13s multicolored   .20 .20
2712 A1040 25s multicolored   .40 .20
2713 A1040 35s multicolored   .50 .20
2714 A1040 43s multicolored   .65 .20
  Nos. 2708-2714 (7)   2.35 1.40

Helicopter, Missile Transport, Tank — A1041

1980, Sept. 23   Photo.   Perf. 13
2715 A1041 3s shown   .20 .20
2716 A1041 5s Jet, radar, rocket .20 .20
2717 A1041 8s Helicopter, ships   .20 .20
  Nos. 2715-2717 (3)   .60 .60
  Bulgarian People's Army, 35th anniversary.

St. Anne, by Leonardo da Vinci A1042

  Da Vinci Paintings: 8s, 13s, Annunciation (diff.). 25s, Adoration of the Kings. 35s, Lady with the Ermine. 50s, Mona Lisa.

1980, Nov.
2718 A1042 5s multicolored   .20 .20
2719 A1042 8s multicolored   .20 .20
2720 A1042 13s multicolored   .20 .20
2721 A1042 25s multicolored   .40 .20
2722 A1042 35s multicolored   .55 .20
  Nos. 2718-2722 (5)   1.55 1.00

Souvenir Sheet
Imperf
2723 A1042 50s multicolored   1.10 .35

International Peace Conference, Sofia — A1043

1980, Sept. 4   Photo.   Perf. 13
2724 A1043 25s multicolored   .35 .20

Yordan Yovkov (1880-1937), Writer — A1044

1980, Sept. 19
2725 A1044 5s multicolored   .20 .20
  Se-tenant with label showing scene from Yovkov's work.

International Samples Fair, Plovdiv — A1045

1980, Sept. 24   Perf. 13½x13
2726 A1045 5s multicolored   .20 .20

Blooming Cacti — A1045a

1980, Nov. 4   Photo.   Perf. 13
2726A A1045a 5s multicolored   .20 .20
2726B A1045a 13s multicolored   .20 .20
2726C A1045a 25s multicolored   .40 .20
2726D A1045a 35s multicolored   .60 .25
2726E A1045a 53s multicolored   1.00 .30
  Nos. 2726A-2726E (5)   2.40 1.15

Souvenir Sheet

03728

25th Anniv. of Bulgarian UN Membership — A1045b

1980, Nov. 25
2726F A1045b 60s multicolored   2.25 2.00

World Ski Racing Championship, Velingrad — A1046

1981, Jan. 17   Photo.   Perf. 13
2727 A1046 43s multicolored   .60 .20

Hawthorn A1047

Slalom — A1048

Designs: Medicinal herbs.

1981, Jan.

2728	A1047	3s shown	.20	.20
2729	A1047	5s St. John's wort	.20	.20
2730	A1047	13s Common elder	.20	.20
2731	A1047	25s Blackberries	.40	.20
2732	A1047	35s Lime	.55	.20
2733	A1047	43s Wild briar	.65	.25
	Nos. 2728-2733 (6)		2.20	1.25

1981, Feb. 27   **Photo.**   **Perf. 13**

2734	A1048	43s multicolored	.60	.25

Evian Alpine World Ski Cup Championship, Borovets.

Nuclear Traces, Research
Institute — A1049

1981, Mar. 10   **Perf. 13½x13**

2735	A1049	13s gray & blk	.20	.20

Nuclear Research Institute, Dubna, USSR,
25th anniversary.

Congress Emblem — A1050

1981, Mar. 12   **Perf. 13½**

2736	A1050	5s shown	.20	.20
2737	A1050	13s Stars	.20	.20
2738	A1050	23s Teletape	.35	.20
	Nos. 2736-2738 (3)		.75	.60

Souvenir Sheet

2739	A1050	50s Demeter Blagoev, George Dimitrov	.80	.50

12th Bulgarian Communist Party Congress.
Nos. 2736-2738 each printed se-tenant with
label.

Paintings by Zachary
Zograf — A1050a

1981, Mar. 23   **Photo.**   **Perf. 12x12½**

2739A	A1050a	5s multicolored	.20	.20
2739B	A1050a	13s multicolored	.25	.20
2739C	A1050a	23s multicolored	.40	.20
2739D	A1050a	25s multicolored	.50	.20
2739E	A1050a	35s multicolored	.70	.20
	Nos. 2739A-2739E (5)		2.05	1.00

Nos. 2739A-2739C are vert.

EXPO '81,
Plovdiv
A1050b

1981, Apr. 7

2739F	A1050b	5s multicolored	.20	.20
2739G	A1050b	8s multicolored	.20	.20
2739H	A1050b	13s multicolored	.25	.20
2739J	A1050b	25s multicolored	.45	.20
2739K	A1050b	53s multicolored	1.00	.25
	Nos. 2739F-2739K (5)		2.10	1.05

Centenary of Bulgarian
Shipbuilding — A1050c

1981, Apr. 15   **Photo.**   **Perf. 13**

2739L	A1050c	35s Georgi Dimitrov, liner	.55	.20
2739M	A1050c	43s 5th from RMS, freighter	.65	.25
2739N	A1050c	53s Khan Asparuch, tanker	.80	.30
	Nos. 2739L-2739N (3)		2.00	.75

Arabian
Horse
A1051

1980, Nov. 27   **Litho.**   **Perf. 12½x12**

2740	A1051	3s multicolored	.20	.20
2741	A1051	5s multicolored	.20	.20
2742	A1051	13s multicolored	.30	.20
2743	A1051	23s multicolored	.45	.20
2744	A1051	35s multicolored	.75	.20
	Nos. 2740-2744 (5)		1.90	1.00

Vassil Stoin, Ethnologist, Birth
Centenary — A1052

1980, Dec. 5   **Photo.**   **Perf. 13½x13**

2745	A1052	5s multicolored	.20	.20

12th Bulgarian
Communist Party
Congress — A1052a

1980, Dec. 26   **Photo.**   **Perf. 13x13½**

2745A	A1052a	5s Party symbols	.20	.20

New Year
A1053

1980, Dec. 8   **Perf. 13**

2746	A1053	5s shown	.20	.20
2747	A1053	13s Cup, date	.20	.20

Culture
Palace,
Sofia
A1053a

1981, Mar. 13   **Photo.**   **Perf. 13**

2747A	A1053a	5s multicolored	.20	.20

Vienna
Hofburg
Palace
A1054

1981, May 15   **Photo.**   **Perf. 13**

2748	A1054	35s multicolored	.45	.20

WIPA 1981 Intl. Philatelic Exhibition,
Vienna, May 22-31.

34th Farmers' Union
Congress — A1055

1981, May 18   **Perf. 13½**

2749	A1055	5s shown	.20	.20
2750	A1055	8s Flags	.20	.20
2751	A1055	13s Flags, diff.	.20	.20
	Nos. 2749-2751 (3)		.60	.60

Wild Cat — A1056

1981, May 27

2752	A1056	5s shown	.20	.20
2753	A1056	13s Boar	.25	.20
2754	A1056	23s Mouflon	.40	.20
2755	A1056	25s Mountain goat	.45	.20
2756	A1056	35s Stag	.60	.20
2757	A1056	53s Roe deer	1.00	.25
	Nos. 2752-2757 (6)		2.90	1.25

Souvenir Sheet

Perf. 13½x13

2758	A1056	1 l Stag, diff.	1.75	.85

EXPO '81 Intl. Hunting Exhibition, Plovdiv.
Nos. 2752-2757 each se-tenant with labels
showing various hunting rifles. No. 2758 contains one stamp, size: 48½x39mm.

25th Anniv. of
UNESCO
Membership
A1057

1981, June 11   **Perf. 13**

2759	A1057	13s multicolored	.20	.20

Hotel Type of 1980

1981, July 13   **Photo.**   **Perf. 13**

2766	A1038	23s Veliko Tirnovo Hotel	.35	.20

Flying Figure, Sculpture by Velichko
Minekov — A1059

Bulgarian Social Democratic Party Buzludja
Congress, 90th Anniv. (Minkov Sculpture):
13s, Advancing Female Figure.

1981, July 16   **Perf. 13½**

2767	A1059	5s multicolored	.20	.20
2768	A1059	13s multicolored	.20	.20

Kukeri, by Georg
Tschapkanov
A1060

Statistics Office
Centenary
A1061

1981, May 28   **Photo.**   **Perf. 13**

2769	A1060	5s multicolored	.20	.20

13th Natl. Festival of Humor and Satire.

1981, June 9

2770	A1061	5s multicolored	.20	.20

Gold Dish
A1063

Designs: Goldsmiths' works, 7th-9th cent.

1981, July 21

2772	A1063	5s multicolored	.20	.20
2773	A1063	13s multicolored	.20	.20
2774	A1063	23s multicolored	.35	.25
2775	A1063	25s multicolored	.40	.25
2776	A1063	35s multicolored	.55	.35
2777	A1063	53s multicolored	.90	.40
	Nos. 2772-2777 (6)		2.60	1.65

35th Anniv. of Frontier Force — A1064

1981, July 28 Perf. 13½x13
2778 A1064 5s multicolored .20 .20

1300th Anniv. of First Bulgarian
State — A1065

Designs: No. 2779, Sts. Cyril and
Methodius. No. 2780, 9th cent. bas-relief. 8s,
Floor plan, Round Church, Preslav, 10th cent.
12s, Four Evangelists of King Ivan Alexander,
miniature, 1356. No. 2783, King Ivan Asen II
memorial column. No. 2784, Warriors on
horseback. 16s, April uprising, 1876. 23s,
Russian liberators, Tirnovo. 25s, Social Democratic Party founding, 1891. 35s, September
uprising, 1923. 41s, Fatherland Front. 43s,
Prime Minister George Dimitrov, 5th Communist Party Congress, 1948. 50s, Lion, 10th
cent. bas-relief. 53s, 10th Communist Party
Congress. 55s, Kremikovski Metalurgical
Plant. 1 l, Brezhnev, Gen. Todor Zhivkov.

1981, Aug. 10
2779 A1065 5s multicolored .20 .20
2780 A1065 5s multicolored .20 .20
2781 A1065 8s multicolored .20 .20
2782 A1065 12s multicolored .20 .20
2783 A1065 13s multicolored .20 .20
2784 A1065 13s multicolored .20 .20
2785 A1065 16s multicolored .25 .20
2786 A1065 23s multicolored .30 .20
2787 A1065 25s multicolored .35 .20
2788 A1065 35s multicolored .50 .20
2789 A1065 41s multicolored .55 .25
2790 A1065 43s multicolored .60 .25
2791 A1065 53s multicolored .75 .30
2792 A1065 55s multicolored .75 .30
   Nos. 2779-2792 (14) 5.25 3.10

Souvenir Sheets
2793 A1065 50s multicolored .90 .55
2794 A1065 1 l multicolored 1.90 1.10

European
Volleyball
Championship
A1066

1981, Sept. 16 Perf. 13
2795 A1066 13s multicolored .20 .20

Pegasus, Bronze
Sculpture (Word
Day) — A1067

World Food
Day — A1068

1981, Oct. 2
2796 A1067 5s olive & cream .20 .20

1981, Oct. 16
2797 A1068 13s multicolored .20 .20

Professional
Theater
Centenary
A1069

1981, Oct. 30
2798 A1069 5s multicolored .20 .20

Anti-Apartheid Year — A1070

1981, Dec. 2
2799 A1070 5s multicolored .20 .20

Espana '82
World Cup
Soccer — A1071

Designs: Various soccer players.

1981, Dec.
2800 A1071 5s multicolored .20 .20
2801 A1071 13s multicolored .25 .20
2802 A1071 43s multicolored .70 .25
2803 A1071 53s multicolored .95 .35
   Nos. 2800-2803 (4) 2.10 1.00

Heritage
Day
A1072

1981, Nov. 21 Photo. Perf. 13
2804 A1072 13s multicolored .20 .20
   Souvenir Sheet
2804A A1072 60s multicolored 5.00 1.10

Bagpipe — A1073

Public Libraries
and Reading
Rooms, 125th
Anniv — A1074

1982, Jan. 14
2805 A1073 13s shown .20 .20
2806 A1073 25s Flutes .40 .20
2807 A1073 30s Rebec .50 .20
2808 A1073 35s Flute, recorder .55 .25
2809 A1073 44s Mandolin .75 .30
   Nos. 2805-2809 (5) 2.40 1.15

1982, Jan. 20
2810 A1074 5s dk grn .20 .20

Souvenir Sheet

Intl. Decade for Women (1975-
1985) — A1075

1982, Mar. 8
2811 A1075 1 l multicolored 1.75 1.00

New Year
1982
A1076

1981, Dec. 22 Photo. Perf. 13
2812 A1076 5s Ornament .20 .20
2813 A1076 13s Ornament, diff. .20 .20

The Sofia Plains, by Nicolas Petrov
(1881-1916) — A1077

1982, Feb. 10 Perf. 12½
2814 A1077 5s shown .20 .20
2815 A1077 13s Girl Embroidering .20 .20
2816 A1077 30s Fields of Peshtera .50 .20
   Nos. 2814-2816 (3) .90 .60

35th Anniv. of
UNICEF
(1981) — A1078

Mother and Child Paintings.

1982, Feb. 25 Perf. 14
2817 A1078 53s Vladimir Dimi-
         trov .80 .30
2818 A1078 53s Basil Stoilov .80 .30
2819 A1078 53s Ivan Milev .80 .30
2820 A1078 53s Liliana Russeva .80 .30
   Nos. 2817-2820 (4) 3.20 1.20

Figures, by Vladamir Dimitrov (1882-
1961) — A1079

1982, Mar. 8 Litho.
2821 A1079 5s shown .20 .20
2822 A1079 8s Landscape .20 .20
2823 A1079 13s View of Istanbul .25 .20
2824 A1079 25s Harvesters, vert. .40 .20
2825 A1079 30s Woman in a
         Landscape,
         vert. .50 .20
2826 A1079 35s Peasant Wo-
         man, vert. .60 .25
   Nos. 2821-2826 (6) 2.15 1.25
   Souvenir Sheet
2827 A1079 50s Self-portrait .85 .65

   No. 2827 contains one stamp, size:
54x32mm.

Trade Union Congress — A1080

1982, Apr. 8 Photo. Perf. 13½
2828 A1080 5s Dimitrov reading
         union paper .20 .20
2829 A1080 5s Culture Palace .20 .20

   #2828-2829 se-tenant with label showing
text.

Marsh Snowdrop
A1081

Designs: Medicinal plants.

1982, Apr. 10   **Photo.**   *Perf. 13*
2830 A1081 3s shown .20 .20
2831 A1081 5s Chicory .20 .20
2832 A1081 8s Chamaenerium
      angustifolium .20 .20
2833 A1081 13s Solomon's seal .25 .20
2834 A1081 25s Violets .50 .20
2835 A1081 35s Centaury .70 .25
    Nos. 2830-2835 (6) 2.05 1.25

Cosmonauts' Day — A1082

1982, Apr. 12   *Perf. 13½*
2836 A1082 13s Salyut-Soyuz link-
      up .20 .20

Se-tenant with label showing K.E. Tsiolkov-sky (space pioneer).

Souvenir Sheet

SOZFILEX Stamp Exhibition — A1083

1982, May 7   *Perf. 13*
2837 A1083 50s Dimitrov, em-
      blems 1.00 .45

14th Komsomol Congress (Youth Communists) — A1084

1982, May 25
2838 A1084 5s multicolored .20 .20

PHILEXFRANCE '82 Intl. Stamp Exhibition, Paris, June 11-21 — A1085

1982, May 28
2839 A1085 42s France #1, Bulga-
      ria #1 .70 .25

19th Cent. Fresco A1086

Designs: Various floral pattern frescoes.

1982, June 8   *Perf. 11½*
2840 A1086 5s red & multi .20 .20
2841 A1086 13s green & multi .25 .20
2842 A1086 25s violet & multi .40 .20
2843 A1086 30s ol grn & multi .50 .20
2844 A1086 42s blue & multi .75 .25
2845 A1086 60s brown & multi 1.00 .40
    Nos. 2840-2845 (6) 3.10 1.45

Souvenir Sheet

George Dimitrov (1882-1949), First Prime Minister — A1087

1982, June 15   *Perf. 13*
2846 A1087 50s multicolored 1.10 .45

9th Congress of the National Front — A1088

1982, June 21   **Photo.**   *Perf. 13*
2847 A1088 5s Dimitrov .20 .20

35th Anniv. of Balkan Bulgarian Airline — A1089

1982, June 28   *Perf. 13½x13*
2848 A1089 42s multicolored .65 .25

A1090

A1091

1982, July 15   *Perf. 13*
2849 A1090 13s multicolored .25 .20

Nuclear disarmament.

1982, July   **Photo.**   *Perf. 13*
2850 A1091 5s multicolored .20 .20
2851 A1091 5s multicolored .20 .20

Souvenir Sheet
2852 A1091 1 l multicolored 1.25 .75

Ludmila Zhivkova (b. 1942), artist.

5th Congress of Bulgarian Painters — A1092

1982, July 27   *Perf. 13½*
2853 A1092 5s multicolored .20 .20

Se-tenant with label showing text.

Flag of Peace Youth Assembly — A1093

Various children's drawings.

1982, Aug. 10   *Perf. 14*
2853A A1093 3s multicolored .20 .20
2853B A1093 5s multicolored .20 .20
2853C A1093 8s multicolored .20 .20
2853D A1093 13s multicolored .25 .20
    Nos. 2853A-2853D (4) .85 .80

Souvenir Sheet
    Perf. 14, Imperf.
2853E A1093 50s In balloon 3.25 .35
See Nos. 2864-2870, 3052-3058, 3321-3327.

10th Anniv. of UN Conference on Human Environment, Stockholm — A1093a

1982, Nov. 10   *Perf. 13*
2854 A1093a 13s dk blue & grn .20 .20

A1094

A1095

Designs: No. 2855, Park Hotel Moskva, Sofia. No. 2856, Tchernomore, Varna.

1982, Oct. 20   **Photo.**   *Perf. 13*
2855 A1094 32s lt blue & multi .40 .20
2856 A1094 32s pink & multi .40 .20

1982, Nov. 4
2857 A1095 13s Cruiser Aurora,
      Sputnik II .20 .20

October Revolution, 65th anniv.

60th Anniv. of Institute of Communications A1096

1982, Dec. 9
2858 A1096 5s ultra .20 .20

60th Anniv. of USSR A1097

1982, Dec. 9
2859 A1097 13s multicolored .20 .20

The Piano, by Pablo Picasso (1881-1973) A1098

    Perf. 11½x12½
1982, Dec. 24   *Litho.*
2860 A1098 13s shown .20 .20
2861 A1098 30s Portrait of Jac-
      queline .40 .20
2862 A1098 42s Maternity .60 .25
    Nos. 2860-2862 (3) 1.20 .65

Souvenir Sheet
2863 A1098 1 l Self-portrait 2.75 .75

Children's Drawings Type of 1982
Various children's drawings. 8s, 13s, 50s vert.

1982, Dec. 28   *Perf. 14*
2864 A1093 3s multicolored .20 .20
2865 A1093 5s multicolored .20 .20
2866 A1093 8s multicolored .20 .20
2867 A1093 13s multicolored .20 .20
2868 A1093 25s multicolored .35 .20
2869 A1093 30s multicolored .40 .20
    Nos. 2864-2869 (6) 1.55 1.20

Souvenir Sheet
    Perf. 14, Imperf.
2870 A1093 50s Shaking hands 2.75 .35

New Year
A1100

1982, Dec. 28   Photo.   Perf. 13
2872 A1100   5s multicolored   .20   .20
2873 A1100   13s multicolored   .20   .20

A1101

1982, Dec. 28
2874 A1101   25s Robert Koch   .40   .20
2875 A1101   30s Simon Bolivar   .40   .20
2876 A1101   30s Rabindranath
      Tagore (1861-
      1941)   .40   .20
    Nos. 2874-2876 (3)   1.20   .60
    No. 2874 also for TB bacillus cent.

A1102

1983, Jan. 10   Photo.   Perf. 13x13½
2877 A1102   5s olive & brown   .25   .20
    Vassil Levski (1837-73), revolutionary.

Universiade Games — A1103

1983, Feb. 15   Perf. 13
2878 A1103   30s Downhill skiing   .35   .20

Fresh-water Fish — A1104

1983, Mar. 24   Photo.   Perf. 13½x13
2879 A1104   3s Pike   .20   .20
2880 A1104   5s Sturgeon   .20   .20
2881 A1104   13s Chub   .20   .20
2882 A1104   25s Perch   .40   .20
2883 A1104   30s Catfish   .40   .20
2884 A1104   42s Trout   .55   .25
    Nos. 2879-2884 (6)   1.95   1.25

Karl Marx (1818-
1883)
A1105

1983, Apr. 5   Perf. 13x13½
2885 A1105   13s multicolored   .20   .20

Jaroslav Hasek (1883-1923) — A1106

1983, Apr. 20   Photo.   Perf. 13
2886 A1106   13s multicolored   .20   .20

Martin
Luther
(1483-1546)
A1107

1983, May 10
2887 A1107   13s multicolored   .20   .20

55th Anniv. of Komsomol Youth
Movement — A1108

1983, May 13
2888 A1108   5s "PMC"   .20   .20

A1109

A1111

National costumes.

1983, May 17   Litho.   Perf. 14
2889 A1109   5s Khaskovo   .20   .20
2890 A1109   8s Pernik   .20   .20
2891 A1109   13s Burgas   .20   .20
2892 A1109   25s Tolbukhin   .35   .20
2893 A1109   30s Blagoevgrad   .40   .20
2894 A1109   42s Topolovgrad   .50   .20
    Nos. 2889-2894 (6)   1.85   1.20

1983, May 20
    6th Intl. Satire and Humor Biennial,
Gabrovo: Old Man Feeding Chickens.
2900 A1111   5s multicolored   .20   .20

Christo Smirnensky (1898-1983),
Poet — A1112

1983, May 25
2901 A1112   5s multicolored   .20   .20

17th Intl.
Geodesists'
Congress
A1113

1983, May 27
2902 A1113   30s Emblem   .45   .20

Interarch '83 Architecture Exhibition,
Sofia — A1114

1983, June 6
2903 A1114   30s multicolored   .45   .20

8th European
Chess
Championships,
Plovdiv
A1115

1983, June 20   Photo.   Perf. 13
2904 A1115   13s Chess pieces, map
          of Europe   .20   .20

Souvenir Sheet

BRASILIANA '83 Philatelic
Exhibition — A1116

1983, June 24
2905 A1116   1 l Brazilian and
          Bulgarian
          stamps   1.50   .95

Social Democratic Party Congress of
Russia, 80th Anniv. — A1118

    Design: Lenin addressing congress.

1983, July 29   Photo.   Perf. 13
2907 A1118   5s multicolored   .25   .20

Ilinden-Preobrazhensky Insurrection,
80th Anniv. — A1119

1983, July 29
2908 A1119   5s Gun, dagger, book   .20   .20

Institute of
Mining and
Geology, Sofia,
30th
Anniv. — A1120

1983, Aug. 10
2909 A1120   5s multicolored   .20   .20

60th Anniv. of September 1923
Uprising — A1121

1983, Aug. 19
2910 A1121   5s multicolored   .20   .20
2911 A1121   13s multicolored   .20   .20

Angora
Cat
A1123

1983, Sept. 26   Perf. 13
2917 A1123   5s shown   .20   .20
2918 A1123   13s Siamese   .25   .20
2919 A1123   20s Abyssinian, vert.   .40   .20
2920 A1123   25s Persian   .45   .20
2921 A1123   30s European, vert.   .55   .25
2922 A1123   42s Indochinese   .75   .30
    Nos. 2917-2922 (6)   2.60   1.35

Animated Film Festival — A1124

1983, Sept. 15 Photo. Perf. 14x13½
2923 A1124 5s Articulation layout .20 .20

Trevethick's Engine, 1804 — A1125

Locomotives: 13s, Blenkinsop's Prince Royal, 1810. 42s, Hedley's Puffing Billy, 1812. 60s, Adler (first German locomotive), 1835.

1983, Oct. 20 Perf. 13
2924	A1125	5s multicolored	.20	.20
2925	A1125	13s multicolored	.30	.20
2926	A1125	42s multicolored	.95	.30
2927	A1125	60s multicolored	1.40	.40
	Nos. 2924-2927 (4)		2.85	1.10

See Nos. 2983-2987.

Souvenir Sheet

Liberation Monument, Plovdiv — A1126

1983, Nov. 4
2928 A1126 50s multicolored 1.00 .60
Philatelic Federation, 90th anniv.

Sofia Opera, 75th Anniv. — A1127

1983, Dec. 2 Perf. 13x13½
2929 A1127 5s Mask, lyre, laurel .20 .20

Composers' Assoc., 50th Anniv. — A1128

Composers: 5s, Ioan Kukuzel (14th cent.) 8s, Atanasov. 13s, Petko Stainov. 20s, Veselin Stodiov. 25s, Liubomir Pipkov. 30s, Pancho Vladigerov. Se-tenant with labels showing compositions.

1983, Dec. 5
2930	A1128	5s multicolored	.20	.20
2931	A1128	8s multicolored	.20	.20
2932	A1128	13s multicolored	.20	.20
2933	A1128	20s multicolored	.30	.20
2934	A1128	25s multicolored	.40	.20
2935	A1128	30s multicolored	.50	.20
	Nos. 2930-2935 (6)		1.80	1.20

New Year 1984 A1129

1983, Dec. 10 Perf. 13
2936 A1129 5s multicolored .20 .20

Angelo Donni, by Raphael A1130

1983, Dec. 22 Perf. 14
2937	A1130	5s shown	.20	.20
2938	A1130	13s Cardinal	.20	.20
2939	A1130	30s Baldassare Castiglioni	.45	.20
2940	A1130	42s Donna Belata	.70	.30
	Nos. 2937-2940 (4)		1.55	.90

Souvenir Sheet
2941 A1130 1 l Sistine Madonna 1.75 1.25

Bat, World Wildlife Emblem — A1131

Various bats and rodents.

1983, Dec. 30 Perf. 13
2942	A1131	12s multicolored	.25	.20
2943	A1131	13s multicolored	.25	.20
2944	A1131	20s multicolored	.40	.20
2945	A1131	30s multicolored	.50	.25
2946	A1131	42s multicolored	.70	.30
	Nos. 2942-2946 (5)		2.10	1.15

Dmitri Mendeleev (1834-1907), Russian Chemist — A1132

1984, Mar. 14
2947 A1132 13s multicolored .25 .20

Ljuben Karavelov, Poet and Freedom Fighter, Birth Sesquicentenary A1133

1984, Jan. 31 Perf. 13x13½
2948 A1133 5s multicolored .20 .20

Tanker Gen. V.I. Zaimov A1137

1984, Mar. 22 Perf. 13½
2959	A1137	5s shown	.20	.20
2960	A1137	13s Mesta	.20	.20
2961	A1137	25s Veleka	.40	.20
2962	A1137	32s Ferry	.50	.20
2963	A1137	42s Cargo ship Rossen	.70	.30
	Nos. 2959-2963 (5)		2.00	1.10

Souvenir Sheet

18246

World Cup Soccer Commemorative of 1982, Spain No. 2281 — A1137a

1984, Apr. 18 Photo. Perf. 13x13½
2963A A1137a 2 l multicolored 3.25 2.50
ESPANA '84.

Dove with Letter over Globe — A1138

1984, Apr. 24 Perf. 13
2964 A1138 5s multicolored .20 .20
World Youth Stamp Exhibition, Pleven, Oct. 5-11.

Berries — A1139

1984, May 5
2965	A1139	5s Cherries	.20	.20
2966	A1139	8s Strawberries	.20	.20
2967	A1139	13s Blackberries	.20	.20

2968	A1139	20s Raspberries	.35	.20
2969	A1139	42s Currants	.70	.30
	Nos. 2965-2969 (5)		1.65	1.10

A1140

A1142

1984, May 23
2970 A1140 13s Athlete, doves .20 .20
6th Republican Spartikiade games,

1984, June 12
2972 A1142 5s Folk singer, drum .20 .20
6th amateur art festival.

Bulgarian-Soviet Relations, 50th Anniv. — A1143

1984, June 27
2973 A1143 13s Initialed seal .20 .20

Doves and Pigeons A1144

1984, July 6 Litho. Perf. 14
2974	A1144	5s Rock dove	.20	.20
2975	A1144	13s Stock dove	.20	.20
2976	A1144	20s Wood pigeon	.35	.20
2977	A1144	30s Turtle dove	.50	.20
2978	A1144	42s Domestic pigeon	.70	.30
	Nos. 2974-2978 (5)		1.95	1.10

1st Natl. Communist Party Congress, 60th Anniv. — A1145

1984, May 18 Photo. Perf. 13½x13
2979 A1145 5s multicolored .20 .20

Souvenir Sheet

Intl. Stamp Exhibition, Essen, May 26-31 — A1146

Europa Conf. stamps: a, 1980. b, 1981.

1984, May 22   **Perf. 13x13½**
2980 A1146   Sheet of 2   12.50   10.00
  a.-b.   1.50 l multi   6.00   5.00

Mount Everest
A1147

1984, May 31   **Perf. 13**
2981 A1147 5s multicolored   .20   .20
   1st Bulgarian Everest climbing expedition, Apr. 20-May 9.

Souvenir Sheet

UPU Congress, Hamburg — A1148

1984, June 11   **Perf. 13½x13**
2982 A1148   3 l   Sailing ship   12.50   10.00

Locomotives Type of 1983

1984, July 31   **Perf. 13**
2983 A1125 13s Best Friend of
        Charleston,
        1830, US   .25   .20
2984 A1125 25s Saxonia, 1836,
        Dresden   .40   .25
2985 A1125 30s Lafayette, 1837,
        US   .50   .30
2986 A1125 42s Borsig, 1841,
        Germany   .75   .40
2987 A1125 60s Philadelphia,
        1843, Austria   1.10   .65
    Nos. 2983-2987 (5)   3.00   1.80

September 9
Revolution, 40th
Anniv. — A1149

1984, Aug. 4
2988 A1149   5s K, production
        quality emblem   .20   .20
2989 A1149 20s Victory Monu-
        ment, Sofia   .30   .20
2990 A1149 30s Star, "9"   .40   .30
    Nos. 2988-2990 (3)   .90   .70

Paintings by Nenko Balkanski (1907-1977) — A1150

1984, Sept. 17   **Perf. 14**
2991 A1150   5s Boy Playing
        Harmonica,
        vert.   .20   .20
2992 A1150 30s A Paris Win-
        dow, vert.   .55   .30
2993 A1150 42s Double Portrait   .80   .40
    Nos. 2991-2993 (3)   1.55   .90

Souvenir Sheet
2994 A1150   1 l Self-portrait,
        vert.   1.90   1.25

MLADPOST '84
International
Youth Stamp
Exhibition,
Pleven — A1151

Buildings in Pleven: 5s, Mausoleum to Russian soldiers, 1877-78 Russo-Turkish War. 13s, Panorama Building.

1984, Sept. 20   **Perf. 13**
2995 A1151   5s multicolored   .20   .20
2996 A1151 13s multicolored   .30   .20

Septembrist Young Pioneers Org., 40th Anniv. — A1152

1984, Sept. 21   **Photo.**   **Perf. 13**
2997 A1152 5s multicolored   .20   .20

Nikola
Vapzarov
A1153

1984, Oct. 2
2998 A1153 5s maroon & pale yel   .20   .20

Natl.
Soccer,
75th
Anniv.
A1154

1984, Oct. 3
2999 A1154 42s multicolored   .75   .40

Souvenir Sheet

MLADPOST '84 — A1155

1984, Oct. 5   **Photo.**   **Perf. 13**
3000 A1155 50s multicolored   1.10   .50

Bridges and Maps — A1156

1984, Oct. 5   **Photo.**   **Perf. 13½x13**
3001 A1156   5s Devil's Bridge,
        Arda River   .20   .20
3002 A1156 13s Koljo-Fitscheto,
        Bjala   .25   .20
3003 A1156 30s Asparuchow,
        Warna   .60   .30
3004 A1156 42s Bebresch High-
        way Bridge,
        Botevgrad   .75   .40
    Nos. 3001-3004 (4)   1.80   1.10

Intl. Olympic Committee, 90th
Anniv. — A1158

1984, Oct. 24   **Photo.**   **Perf. 13**
3007 A1158 13s multicolored   .25   .20

A1159

A1160

Pelecanus crispus.

1984, Nov. 2
3008 A1159   5s Adult, young   .25   .20
3009 A1159 13s Two adults   .35   .20
3010 A1159 20s Adult in water   .45   .20
3011 A1159 32s In flight   .70   .30
    Nos. 3008-3011 (4)   1.75   .90
    World Wildlife Fund.

1984, Nov. 2
3012 A1160 5s multicolored   .20   .20
    Anton Ivanov (1884-1942), labor leader.

Women's Socialist Movement, 70th
Anniv. — A1161

1984, Nov. 9
3013 A1161 5s multicolored   .20   .20

Telecommunication Towers — A1162

1984, Nov. 23
3014 A1162   5s Snezhanka   .20   .20
3015 A1162   1 l Orelek   1.90   1.00

Snowflakes, New Year 1985 — A1163

1984, Dec. 5
3016 A1163   5s Doves, posthorns   .20   .20
3017 A1163 13s Doves, blossom   .25   .20

Paintings by
Stoyan Venev
(b.
1904) — A1164

1984, Dec. 10   **Litho.**
3018 A1164   5s September Nights   .20   .20
3019 A1164 30s Man with Three
        Medals   .50   .30
3020 A1164 42s The Best   .70   .40
    Nos. 3018-3020 (3)   1.40   .90

Butterflies
A1165

1984, Dec. 14 *Perf. 11½*
3021 A1165 13s Inachis io .25 .20
3022 A1165 25s Papilio
machaon .45 .25
3023 A1165 35s Brintesia circe .55 .30
3024 A1165 42s Anthocaris
cardamines .80 .40
3025 A1165 60s Vanessa atalanta 1.10 .60
Nos. 3021-3025 (5) 3.15 1.75
Souvenir Sheet
3026 A1165 1 l Limenitis populi 2.25 1.00

A1166

A1167

1984, Dec. 18 Photo. *Perf. 13x13½*
3027 A1166 13s multicolored .25 .20
Cesar Augusto Sandino (1895-1934), Nicaraguan freedom fighter.

1984, Dec. 28 Litho. *Perf. 14*
3028 A1167 5s The Three
Graces .20 .20
3029 A1167 13s Cupid and the
Graces .30 .20
3030 A1167 30s Original Sin .55 .30
3031 A1167 42s La Fornarina .80 .40
Nos. 3028-3031 (4) 1.85 1.10
Souvenir Sheet
3032 A1167 1 l Galatea 2.25 1.00
Raphael, 500th birth anniv. (1983).

Cruise Ship Sofia, Maiden
Voyage — A1168

1984, Dec. 29 Photo. *Perf. 13*
3033 A1168 13s blue, dk bl & yel .25 .20

Predators
A1170

1985, Jan. 17
3035 A1170 13s Conepatus
leuconotus .25 .20
3036 A1170 25s Prionodon lin-
sang .40 .25
3037 A1170 30s Ictonix striatus .50 .30

3038 A1170 42s Hemigalus
derbyanus .75 .40
3039 A1170 60s Galidictis fas-
ciata 1.00 .60
Nos. 3035-3039 (5) 2.90 1.75

Nikolai Liliev (1885-1960), Poet,
UNESCO Emblem — A1171

1985, Jan. 25
3040 A1171 30s multicolored .50 .30

Zviatko Radojnov (1895-1942), Labor
Leader — A1172

1985, Jan. 29
3041 A1172 5s dk red & dk brn .20 .20

Dr. Assen
Zlatarov (1885-
1936), Chemist
A1173

1985, Feb. 14
3042 A1173 5s multicolored .20 .20

Souvenir Sheet

Akademik, Research Vessel — A1174

1985, Mar. 1
3043 A1174 80s multicolored 1.40 .80
UNESCO Intl. Oceanographic Commission,
25th anniv.

Souvenir Sheet

Lenin — A1175

1985, Mar. 12
3044 A1175 50s multicolored .75 .50

A1176

A1177

1985, Mar. 19
3045 A1176 13s multicolored .25 .20
Warsaw Treaty Org., 30th anniv.

1985, Mar. 25

Composers.

3046 A1177 42s Bach .50 .30
3047 A1177 42s Mozart .50 .30
3048 A1177 42s Tchaikovsky .50 .30
3049 A1177 42s Mussorgsky .50 .30
3050 A1177 42s Verdi .50 .30
3051 A1177 42s Tenev .50 .30
Nos. 3046-3051 (6) 3.00 1.80

Children's Drawings Type of 1982

Inscribed 1985. Various children's
drawings.

1985, Mar. 26 Litho. *Perf. 14*
3052 A1093 5s multicolored .20 .20
3053 A1093 8s multicolored .20 .20
3054 A1093 13s multicolored .20 .20
3055 A1093 20s multicolored .30 .20
3056 A1093 25s multicolored .40 .25
3057 A1093 30s multicolored .50 .30
Nos. 3052-3057 (6) 1.80 1.35
Souvenir Sheet
3058 A1093 50s Children dancing, vert. 1.10 .50
3rd Flag of Peace Intl. Assembly, Sofia. No.
3058 exists imperf. with blue control number,
same value.

St. Methodius,
1100th Death
Anniv. — A1179

1985, Apr. 6 Photo. *Perf. 13*
3059 A1179 13s multicolored .25 .20

Victory Parade, Moscow,
1945 — A1180

13s, 11th Infantry on parade, Sofia. 30s,
Soviet soldier, orphan. 50s, Soviet flag-raising,
Berlin.

1985, Apr. 30 *Perf. 13½*
3060 A1180 5s multicolored .20 .20
3061 A1180 13s multicolored .25 .20
3062 A1180 30s multicolored .50 .30
Nos. 3060-3062 (3) .95 .70
Souvenir Sheet
Perf. 13
3063 A1180 50s multicolored 1.10 .50
Defeat of Nazi Germany, end of World War
II, 40th anniv. Nos. 3060-3062 printed se-ten-
ant with labels picturing Soviet (5s, 30s) and
Bulgarian medals of honor.

7th Intl. Humor and Satire
Biennial — A1181

1985, Apr. 30 *Perf. 13½*
3064 A1181 13s yel, sage grn &
red .25 .20
No. 3064 printed se-tenant with label picturing Gabrovo Cat emblem.

Intl. Youth Year — A1182

1985, May 21 *Perf. 13*
3065 A1182 13s multicolored .25 .20

Ivan Vasov
(1850-1921),
Poet — A1183

1985, May 30   *Perf. 13½*
3066 A1183 5s tan & sepia   .20 .20
No. 3066 printed se-tenant with label picturing Vasov's birthplace in Sopot.

Soviet
War
Memorial,
Haskovo
City Arms
A1184

1985, June 1   *Perf. 13*
3067 A1184 5s multicolored   .20 .20
Haskovo millennium.

12th World Youth
Festival,
Moscow — A1185

1985, June 25
3068 A1185 13s multicolored   .20 .20

Indira Gandhi (1917-1984), Prime
Minister of India — A1186

1985, June 26
3069 A1186 30s org yel, sep & ver   .60 .30

Vasil Aprilov,
Founder — A1187

1985, June 30
3070 A1187 5s multicolored   .20 .20
1st secular school, Gabrovo, 150th anniv.

INTERSTENO '85 — A1188

1985, June 30
3071 A1188 13s multicolored   .25 .20
Congress for the Intl. Union of Stenographers and Typists, Sofia.

Alexander
Nevski
Cathedral
A1189

1985, July 9
3072 A1189 42s multicolored   .80 .40
World Tourism Org., general assembly, Sofia.

UN, 40th
Anniv.
A1190

1985, July 16
3073 A1190 13s multicolored   .25 .20

A1191

Roses — A1192

1985, July 16
3074 A1191 13s multicolored   .25 .20
Admission of Bulgaria to UN, 30th anniv.

1985, July 20   *Litho.*
3075 A1192 5s Rosa damascena   .20 .20
3076 A1192 13s Rosa trakijka   .25 .20
3077 A1192 20s Rosa radiman   .35 .20
3078 A1192 30s Rosa marista   .50 .30
3079 A1192 42s Rosa valentina   .75 .40
3080 A1192 60s Rosa maria   1.00 .60
   a.   Min. sheet of 6, #3075-3080   3.50 2.00
    Nos. 3075-3080 (6)   3.05 1.90

Helsinki Conference, 10th
Anniv. — A1193

1985, Aug. 1   *Photo.*
3081 A1193 13s multicolored   .25 .20

European Swimming Championships,
Sofia — A1194

1985, Aug. 2   *Litho.*   *Perf. 12½*
3082 A1194 5s Butterfly stroke   .20 .20
3083 A1194 13s Water polo, vert.   .20 .20
3084 A1194 42s Diving, vert.   .60 .35
3085 A1194 60s Synchronized swimming   .75 .40
    Nos. 3082-3085 (4)   1.75 1.15
The 60s exists with central design inverted.

Natl.
Tourism
Assoc.,
90th
Anniv.
A1195

1985, Aug. 15   *Photo.*   *Perf. 13*
3086 A1195 5s multicolored   .20 .20

1986 World Cup
Soccer
Championships,
Mexico
A1196

Various soccer plays.

1985, Aug. 29   *Perf. 13*
3087 A1196 5s multicolored   .20 .20
3088 A1196 13s multicolored   .20 .20
3089 A1196 30s multicolored   .40 .20
3090 A1196 42s multicolored   .50 .25
    Nos. 3087-3090 (4)   1.30 .85
    Souvenir Sheet
3091 A1196 1 l multi, horiz.   1.25 .75

Union of Eastern
Rumelia and
Bulgaria,
1885 — A1197

1985, Aug. 29   *Perf. 14x13½*
3092 A1197 5s multicolored   .20 .20

Computer Design Portraits — A1198

1985, Sept. 23   *Perf. 13*
3093 A1198 5s Boy   .20 .20
3094 A1198 13s Youth   .25 .20
3095 A1198 30s Cosmonaut   .50 .30
    Nos. 3093-3095 (3)   .95 .70
Intl. Exhibition of the Works of Youth Inventors, Plovdiv.

St. John the
Baptist Church,
Nessebar
A1199

Natl. restoration projects: 13s, Tyrant Hreljo Tower, Rila Monastery. 35s, Soldier, fresco, Ivanovo Rock Church. 42s, Archangel Gabriel, fresco, Bojana Church. 60s, Thracian Woman, fresco, Tomb of Kasanlak, 3rd century B.C. 1 l, The Horseman of Madara, bas-relief.

1985, Sept. 25   *Litho.*   *Perf. 12½*
3096 A1199 5s multicolored   .20 .20
3097 A1199 13s multicolored   .25 .20
3098 A1199 35s multicolored   .60 .30
3099 A1199 42s multicolored   .75 .40
3100 A1199 60s multicolored   1.10 .60
    Nos. 3096-3100 (5)   2.90 1.70
    Souvenir Sheet
    Imperf
3101 A1199 1 l multicolored   1.90 1.00
UNESCO, 40th anniv.

Souvenir Sheet

Ludmila Zhishkova Cultural Palace,
Sofia — A1200

1985, Oct. 8   *Perf. 13*
3102 A1200 1 l multicolored   1.60 1.00
UNESCO 23rd General Assembly, Sofia.

Colosseum, Rome — A1201

1985, Oct. 15   **Photo.**   *Perf. 13½*
3103 A1201 42s multicolored   .75 .40
ITALIA '85. No. 3103 printed se-tenant with label picturing the exhibition emblem.

Souvenir Sheet

Cultural Congress, Budapest — A1202

Designs: No. 3104a, St. Cyril, patron saint of Europe. No. 3104b, Map of Europe. No. 3104c, St. Methodius, patron saint of Europe.

Perf. 13, 13 Vert. (#3104b)
1985, Oct. 22   **Photo.**
3104 A1202   Sheet of 3   3.00 1.50
a.-c.   50s, any single   .90 .50
Helsinki Congress, 10th anniv.

Flowers — A1203

1985, Oct. 22   **Photo.**   *Perf. 13x13½*
3105 A1203 5s Gladiolus hybridy   .20 .20
3106 A1203 5s Iris germanica   .20 .20
3107 A1203 5s Convolvulus tricolor   .20 .20
   Nos. 3105-3107 (3)   .60 .60
See Nos. 3184-3186.

Historic Sailing Ships A1204

1985, Oct. 28   **Photo.**   *Perf. 13*
3108 A1204 5s Dutch   .20 .20
3109 A1204 12s Sea Sovereign, Britain   .20 .20
3110 A1204 20s Mediterranean   .20 .20
3111 A1204 25s Royal Prince, Britain   .25 .20
3112 A1204 42s Mediterranean   .50 .30
3113 A1204 60s British battleship   .85 .35
   Nos. 3108-3113 (6)   2.20 1.45

Souvenir Sheet

PHILATELIA '85, Cologne — A1205

Designs: a, Cologne Cathedral. b, Alexander Nevski Cathedral, Sofia.

1985, Nov. 4   *Imperf.*
3114 A1205   Sheet of 2   1.40 .65
a.-b.   30s, any single   .60 .30

Conspiracy to Liberate Bulgaria from Turkish Rule, 150th Anniv. — A1206

Freedom fighters and symbols: #3115, Georgi Stojkov Rakowski (1820-76). #3116, Batscho Kiro (1835-76). #3117, Sword, Bible & hands.

1985, Nov. 6   *Perf. 13*
3115 A1206   5s multicolored   .20 .20
3116 A1206   5s multicolored   .20 .20
3117 A1206   13s multicolored   .25 .20
   Nos. 3115-3117 (3)   .65 .60

Liberation from Byzantine Rule, 800th Anniv. — A1207

Paintings: 5s, The Revolt 1185, by G. Bogdanov. 13s, The Revolt 1185, by Alexander Tersiev. 30s, Battle Near Klokotnitza, by B. Grigorov and M. Ganowski. 42s, Velika Tarnovo Town Wall, by Zanko Lawrenov. 1 l, St. Dimitriev Church, 12th cent.

1985, Nov. 15   *Litho.*
3118 A1207   5s multicolored   .20 .20
3119 A1207   13s multicolored   .25 .20
3120 A1207   30s multicolored   .50 .30
3121 A1207   42s multicolored   .75 .40
   Nos. 3118-3121 (4)   1.70 1.10

Souvenir Sheet
Imperf
3122 A1207   1 l multicolored   2.00 1.00

Souvenir Sheet

BALKANPHILA '85 — A1208

1985, Nov. 29   **Photo.**   *Perf. 13*
3123 A1208 40s Dove, posthorn   .50 .40

Intl. Post and Telecommunications Development Program — A1209

1985, Dec. 2
3124 A1209 13s multicolored   .25 .20

Anton Popov (1915-1942), Freedom Fighter — A1210

1985, Dec. 11   **Photo.**   *Perf. 13*
3125 A1210 5s lake   .20 .20

New Year 1986 A1211

1985, Dec. 11   **Photo.**   *Perf. 13*
3126 A1211 5s Doves, snowflake   .20 .20
3127 A1211 13s Doves   .25 .20

Hunting Dogs and Prey — A1212

5s, Pointer, partridge. 8s, Irish setter, pochard. 13s, English setter, mallard. 20s, Cocker spaniel, woodcock. 25s, German pointer, rabbit. 30s, Balkan hound, boar. 42s, Shorthaired dachshund, fox.

1985, Dec. 27   **Litho.**   *Perf. 13x12½*
3128 A1212   5s multicolored   .20 .20
3129 A1212   8s multicolored   .20 .20
3130 A1212   13s multicolored   .20 .20
3131 A1212   20s multicolored   .20 .20
3132 A1212   25s multicolored   .30 .20
3133 A1212   30s multicolored   .40 .20
3134 A1212   42s multicolored   .80 .30
   Nos. 3128-3134 (7)   2.30 1.50

Intl. Year of the Handicapped — A1213

1985, Dec. 30   **Photo.**   *Perf. 13*
3135 A1213 5s multicolored   .20 .20

George Dimitrov (1882-1949) — A1214

1985, Dec. 30   **Photo.**   *Perf. 13*
3136 A1214 13s brn lake   .25 .20
7th Intl. Communist Congress, Moscow.

UN Child Survival Campaign — A1215

1986, Jan. 21   **Photo.**   *Perf. 13*
3137 A1215 13s multicolored   .25 .20
UNICEF, 40th anniv.

Demeter Blagoev (1856-1924) A1216

1986, Jan. 28   **Photo.**   *Perf. 13*
3138 A1216 5s dk lake, car & dk red   .20 .20

Intl. Peace Year A1217

1986, Jan. 31   *Perf. 13½*
3139 A1217 5s multicolored   .20 .20

Orchids — A1218

1986, Feb. 12   **Litho.**   *Perf. 13x12½*
3140 A1218 5s Dactylorhiza romana   .20 .20
3141 A1218 13s Epipactis palustris   .20 .20
3142 A1218 30s Ophrys cornuta   .40 .30
3143 A1218 32s Limodorum abortivum   .40 .30
3144 A1218 42s Cypripedium calceolus   .50 .40
3145 A1218 60s Orchis papilionacea   1.00 .50
a.   Min. sheet of 6, #3140-3145   3.25 1.50
   Nos. 3140-3145 (6)   2.70 1.90

Hares and
Rabbits
A1219

1986, Feb. 24   **Perf. 12½x12**
3146 A1219   5s multicolored   .20   .20
3147 A1219   25s multicolored   .45   .25
3148 A1219   30s multicolored   .55   .30
3149 A1219   32s multicolored   .60   .30
3150 A1219   42s multicolored   .75   .40
3151 A1219   60s multicolored   1.00   .60
    Nos. 3146-3151 (6)   3.55   2.05

Bulgarian Eagle, Newspaper, 140th
Anniv. — A1220

Front page of 1st issue & Ivan Bogorov,
journalist.

1986, Feb. 2   **Photo.**   **Perf. 13**
3152 A1220 5s multicolored   .20   .20

Souvenir Sheet

Halley's
Comet
A1221

Comet's orbit in the Solar System: a, 1980.
b, 1910-86. c, 1916-70. d, 1911.

1986, Mar. 7   **Perf. 13½x13**
3153   Sheet of 4   1.90   1.25
a.-d. A1221 25s, any single   .40   .30

A1222

A1223

1986, Mar. 12   **Perf. 13x13½**
3154 A1222 5s dp bl & bl   .20   .20
Vladimir Bachev (1935-1967), poet.

1986, Mar. 17   **Perf. 13**
3155 A1223   5s Wavy lines   .20   .20
3156 A1223   8s Star   .20   .20
3157 A1223   13s Worker   .25   .20
    Nos. 3155-3157 (3)   .65   .60
Souvenir Sheet
Imperf
3158 A1223 50s Scaffold, flags   .70   .50
13th Natl. Communist Party Congress.

Souvenir Sheet

1st Manned Space Flight, 25th
Anniv. — A1224

Designs: a, Vostok I, 1961. b, Yuri Gagarin
(1934-68), Russian cosmonaut.

1986, Mar. 28   **Perf. 13½x13**
3159   Sheet of 2   1.90   1.00
a.-b. A1224 50s, any single   1.00   .50

April Uprising
against the Turks,
110th
Anniv. — A1225

Monuments: 5s, 1876 Uprising monument,
Panagjuriste. 13s, Christo Botev, Vraca.

1986, Mar. 30   **Perf. 13**
3160 A1225 5s multicolored   .20   .20
3161 A1225 13s multicolored   .25   .20

A1225a

Levsky-Spartak Sports Club, 75th
Anniv. — A1226

1986   **Perf. 13**
3161A A1225a 5s multicolored   .20   .20
Souvenir Sheet
Imperf
3162   A1226   50s Rhythmic gym-
              nastics   .90   .50
Issue dates: 5s, Dec. 50s, May 12.

A1227

A1228

1986, May 19   **Perf. 13**
3163 A1227   5s Congress emblem   .20   .20
3164 A1227   8s Emblem on globe   .20   .20
3165 A1227   13s Flags   .25   .20
    Nos. 3163-3165 (3)   .65   .60
35th Congress of Bulgarian farmers, Sofia.

1986, May 27   **Perf. 13x13½**
3166 A1228 13s multicolored   .25   .20
Conference of Transport Ministers from
Socialist Countries.

17th Intl. Book
Fair,
Sofia — A1229

1986, May 28
3167 A1229 13s blk, brt red &
            grysh blk   .25   .20

1986 World Cup Soccer
Championships, Mexico — A1230

Various soccer plays; attached labels picture Mexican landmarks.

1986, May 30   **Perf. 13½**
3168 A1230   5s multi, vert.   .20   .20
3169 A1230   13s multicolored   .25   .20
3170 A1230   20s multicolored   .35   .20
3171 A1230   30s multicolored   .55   .30
3172 A1230   42s multicolored   .75   .40
3173 A1230   60s multi, vert.   1.10   .60
    Nos. 3168-3173 (6)   3.20   1.90
Souvenir Sheet
Perf. 13
3174 A1230   1 l Azteca Stadium   2.00   1.00

Treasures of Preslav — A1231

Gold artifacts: 5s, Embossed brooch. 13s,
Pendant with pearl cross, vert. 20s, Crystal
and pearl pendant. 30s, Embossed shield.
42s, Pearl and enamel pendant, vert. 60s,
Enamel shield.

1986, June 7   **Perf. 13½x13, 13x13½**
3175 A1231   5s multicolored   .20   .20
3176 A1231   13s multicolored   .25   .20
3177 A1231   20s multicolored   .35   .20
3178 A1231   30s multicolored   .55   .30
3179 A1231   42s multicolored   .75   .40
3180 A1231   60s multicolored   1.00   .60
    Nos. 3175-3180 (6)   3.10   1.90

World Fencing Championships, Sofia,
July 25-Aug. 3 — A1232

1986, July 25   **Photo.**   **Perf. 13**
3181 A1232   5s Head cut, lunge   .20   .20
3182 A1232   13s Touche   .25   .20
3183 A1232   25s Lunge, parry   .45   .25
    Nos. 3181-3183 (3)   .90   .65

Flower Type of 1985

1986, July 29   **Perf. 13x13½**
3184 A1203   8s Ipomoea tricolor   .20   .20
3185 A1203   8s Anemone
            coronaria   .20   .20
3186 A1203   32s Lilium auratum   .55   .30
    Nos. 3184-3186 (3)   .95   .70

A1233

A1234

1986, Aug. 25
3187 A1233 42s sepia, sal brn &
            lake   .75   .40
STOCKHOLMIA '86. No. 3187 printed in
sheets of 3 + 3 labels picturing folk art.

Miniature Sheet

Environmental Conservation: a, Ciconia
ciconia. b, Nuphar lutea. c, Salamandra salamandra. d, Nymphaea alba.

1986, Aug. 25   **Litho.**   **Perf. 14**
3188   Sheet of 4 + label   3.25   1.00
a.-d. A1234 30s any single   .50   .25

No. 3188 contains center label picturing the
oldest oak tree in Bulgaria, Granit Village.

Natl. Arms, Building of the
Sobranie — A1235

1986, Sept. 13   **Photo.**   **Perf. 13**
3189 A1235 5s Prus grn, yel grn &
            red   .20   .20
People's Republic of Bulgaria, 40th anniv.

15th Postal Union Congress — A1236

1986, Sept. 24
3190 A1236 13s multicolored   .25   .20

Natl. Youth Brigade Movement, 40th Anniv. — A1237

Intl. Organization of Journalists, 10th Congress A1238

1986, Oct. 4
3191 A1237 5s multicolored ... .20 .20

1986, Oct. 13
3192 A1238 13s blue & dark blue ... .25 .20

Sts. Cyril and Methodius, Disciples — A1239

1986, Oct. 23   *Perf. 13½*
3193 A1239 13s dark brown & buff ... .25 .20
Sts. Cyril and Methodius in Bulgaria, 1100th anniv. No. 3193 se-tenant with inscribed label.

Telephones in Bulgaria, Cent. — A1240

1986, Nov. 5   *Perf. 13*
3194 A1240 5s multicolored ... .20 .20

World Weight Lifting Championships — A1241

1986, Nov. 6
3195 A1241 13s multicolored ... .25 .20

Ships A1242

1986, Nov. 20
3196 A1242 5s King of Prussia ... .20 .20
3197 A1242 13s East Indiaman, 18th cent. ... .25 .20

3198 A1242 25s Shebek, 18th cent. ... .45 .25
3199 A1242 30s St Paul ... .55 .30
3200 A1242 32s Topsail schooner, 18th cent. ... .60 .30
3201 A1242 42s Victory ... .80 .40
    Nos. 3196-3201 (6) ... 2.85 1.65

Souvenir Sheet

European Security and Cooperation Congress, Vienna — A1243

Various buildings and emblems: a, Bulgaria. b, Austria. c, Donau Park, UN.

Perf. 13, Imperf. x13 (#3202b)
1986, Nov. 27
3202   Sheet of 3 ... 3.25 1.50
a.-c. A1243 50s any single ... 1.00 .50
Exists imperf. bearing control number.

Rogozen Thracian Pitchers A1244

1986, Dec. 5   *Perf. 13*
3203 A1244 10s Facing left ... .20 .20
3204 A1244 10s Facing right ... .20 .20
a.   Block, #3203-3204 + 2 labels ... .40 .40
Union of Bulgarian Philatelists, 14th Congress.

New Year 1987 A1245

1986, Dec. 9
3205 A1245 5s shown ... .20 .20
3206 A1245 13s Snow flakes ... .25 .20

Home Amateur Radio Operators in Bulgaria, 60th Anniv. — A1246

1986, Dec. 10
3207 A1246 13s multicolored ... .25 .20

Miniature Sheet

Paintings by Bulgarian Artists — A1247

a, Red Tree, by Danail Dechev (1891-1962). b, Troopers Confront Two Men, by Ilya

Beshkov (1901-58). c, View of Melnik, by Veselin Stajkov (1906-70). d, View of Houses through Trees, by Kyril Zonev (1896-1961).

1986, Dec. 10   Litho.   *Perf. 14*
3208 A1247 Sheet of 4 ... 2.25 1.10
a.-b.   25s any single ... .50 .25
c.-d.   30s any single ... .60 .30
Sofia Academy of Art, 90th anniv.

Augusto Cesar Sandino (1893-1934), Nicaraguan Revolutionary, and Flag — A1248

1986, Dec. 16   Photo.   *Perf. 13*
3209 A1248 13s multicolored ... .20 .20
Sandinista movement in Nicaragua, 25th anniv.

Smoyan Mihylovsky (b. 1856), Writer — A1249

Ran Bossilek (b. 1886) A1250

Title Page from Bulgarian Folk Songs of the Miladinov Brothers — A1251

Annivs. and events: No. 3211, Pentcho Slaveyckov (b. 1861), writer. No. 3212, Nickola Atanassov (b. 1886), musician.

1986, Dec. 17
3210 A1249 5s multicolored ... .20 .20
3211 A1249 5s multicolored ... .20 .20
3212 A1249 8s multicolored ... .20 .20
3213 A1250 8s multicolored ... .20 .20
3214 A1251 10s multicolored ... .20 .20
    Nos. 3210-3214 (5) ... 1.00 1.00

Paintings by Titian — A1252

A1253

Various portraits.

1986, Dec. 23   Litho.   *Perf. 14*
3215 A1252 5s multicolored ... .20 .20
3216 A1252 13s multicolored ... .35 .20
3217 A1252 20s multicolored ... .45 .20
3218 A1252 30s multicolored ... .65 .30
3219 A1252 32s multicolored ... .75 .30
3220 A1252 42s multicolored ... .90 .40
a.   Min. sheet of 6, #3215-3220 ... 3.00 1.50
    Nos. 3215-3220 (6) ... 3.30 1.60

Souvenir Sheet
3221 A1253 1 l multicolored ... 2.75 1.00

Rayko Daskalov (b. 1886), Politician — A1254

1986, Dec. 23   Photo.   *Perf. 13*
3222 A1254 5s deep claret ... .20 .20

Sports Cars — A1255

1986, Dec. 30   Litho.   *Perf. 13½*
3223 A1255 5s 1905 Fiat ... .20 .20
3224 A1255 10s 1928 Bugatti ... .20 .25
3225 A1255 25s 1936 Mercedes ... .40 .25
3226 A1255 32s 1952 Ferrari ... .50 .30
3227 A1255 40s 1985 Lotus ... .60 .40
3228 A1255 42s 1986 McLaren ... .65 .40
    Nos. 3223-3228 (6) ... 2.55 1.75

Varna Railway Inauguration, 120th Anniv. — A1257

1987, Jan. 19   Photo.   *Perf. 13½*
3229 A1257 5s multicolored ... .20 .20
a.   Perf. 11 ... .40 .40

Dimcho Debelianov (1887-1916), Poet — A1258

1987, Jan. 20   Photo.   *Perf. 13*
3230 A1258 5s blue, dull yel & dp blue ... .20 .20

L.L. Zamenhof, Creator of
Esperanto — A1259

1987, Feb. 12
3231　A1259　13s multicolored　　　.25　.20

Mushrooms
A1260

10th Natl. Trade
Unions
Congress
A1261

1987, Feb. 6　Litho.　Perf. 11½
3232　A1260　5s Amanita
　　　　　rubescens　　　　.20　.20
3233　A1260　20s Boletus regius　.35　.25
3234　A1260　30s Leccinum auran-
　　　　　tiacum　　　　　　.50　.35
3235　A1260　32s Coprinus co-
　　　　　matus　　　　　　.55　.40
3236　A1260　40s Russula vesca　.75　.50
3237　A1260　42s Cantharellus
　　　　　cibarius　　　　　1.00　.60
　a.　　Min. sheet of 6, #3232-3237　5.25
　　　Nos. 3232-3237 (6)　　3.35　2.30

1987, Mar. 20　Photo.　Perf. 13
3238　A1261　5s dark red & violet　.20　.20

Rogozen
Thracian
Treasure
A1262

Embossed and gilded silver artifacts: 5s,
Plate, Priestess Auge approaching Heracles.
8s, Pitcher, lioness attacking stag. 20s, Plate,
floral pattern. 30s, Pitcher, warriors on horseback dueling. 32s, Urn, decorative pattern.
42s, Pitcher (not gilded), winged horses.

1987, Mar. 31
3239　A1262　5s multicolored　.20　.20
3240　A1262　8s multicolored　.20　.20
3241　A1262　20s multicolored　.45　.30
3242　A1262　30s multicolored　.70　.45
3243　A1262　32s multicolored　.75　.50
3244　A1262　42s multicolored　.90　.60
　　　Nos. 3239-3244 (6)　　3.20　2.25

Miniature Sheet

Modern Architecture — A1263

Designs: a, Ludmila Zhivkova conf. center,
Varna. b, Ministry of Foreign Affairs, Sofia. c,
Interpred Building, Sofia. d, Hotel, Sandanski.

1987, Apr. 7　　Perf. 13½x13
3245　　Sheet of 4　　3.25　1.90
　a.-d.　A1263 30s any single　.75　.45
Exists imperf. with black control number.

European
Freestyle
Wrestling
Championships
A1264

1987, Apr. 22　　Perf. 13
3246　A1264　5s multicolored　.20　.20
3247　A1264　13s multi, diff.　.40　.20

CAPEX
'87,
Toronto
A1265

1987, Apr. 24
3248　A1265　42s multicolored　1.00　.40

10th Congress
of the Natl.
Front — A1266

1987, May 11
3249　A1266　5s multicolored　.20　.20

15th Communist Youth
Congress — A1267

1987, May 13
3250　A1267　5s George Dimitrov　.20　.20

8th Intl. Humor
and Satire
Biennial,
Gabrovo — A1268

1987, May 15　　Perf. 13x13½
3251　A1268　13s multicolored　.35　.20

13th World
Rhythmic
Gymnastics
Championships,
Varna — A1269

Gymnasts.

1987, Aug. 5　Photo.　Perf. 13
3252　A1269　5s Maria Gigova　.20　.20
3252A　A1269　8s Iliana Raeva　.20　.20
3252B　A1269　13s Anelia
　　　　　Ralenkova　.30　.20
3252C　A1269　25s Pilyana Ge-
　　　　　orgieva　.55　.30
3252D　A1269　30s Lilia Ignatova　.65　.40
3252E　A1269　42s Bianca Pa-
　　　　　nova　.90　.50
　　　Nos. 3252-3252E (6)　2.80　1.80

Souvenir Sheet
Perf. 13x13½
3252F　A1269　1 l Neshka
　　　　　Robeva,
　　　　　coach　2.50　1.50
Exists imperf. with black control number.

Vassil Kolarov — A1270

1987, June 3　　Perf. 13
3253　A1270　5s dk red, yel & dk
　　　　　bl　.20　.20

Stela Blagoeva
(b.
1887) — A1271

1987, June 4
3254　A1271　5s pink & sepia　.20　.20

Rabotnichesko Delo Newspaper, 60th
Anniv. — A1272

1987, May 28
3255　A1272　5s black & lake　.20　.20

Deer
A1273

1987, June 23　　Litho.
3256　A1273　5s Capreolus
　　　　　capreolus, vert.　.20　.20
3257　A1273　10s Alces alces　.25　.20
3258　A1273　32s Dama dama,
　　　　　vert.　.75　.25
3259　A1273　40s Cervus nippon,
　　　　　vert.　1.10　.30
3260　A1273　42s Cervus elaphus　1.10　.30
3261　A1273　60s Rangifer
　　　　　tarandus, vert.　1.40　.45
　a.　　Min. sheet, #3256-3261, im-
　　　perf　6.25　2.75
　　　Nos. 3256-3261 (6)　4.80　1.70

Vassil
Levski
(1837-73)
A1274

Various portraits.

1987, June 19　　Photo.
3262　A1274　5s red brn & dark grn　.20　.20
3263　A1274　13s dark grn & red brn　.35　.20

Namibia
Day
A1275

1987, July 8
3264　A1275　13s org, blk & dark red　.30　.20

Georgi Kirkov
(1867-1919),
Revolutionary
A1276

1987, July 17　　Perf. 13x13½
3265　A1276　5s claret & dp claret　.20　.20

Bees and
Plants — A1277

1987, July 29　　Litho.　Perf. 13
3266　A1277　5s Phacelia tanace-
　　　　　tifolia　.20　.20
3267　A1277　10s Helianthus an-
　　　　　nuus　.20　.20
3268　A1277　30s Robinia
　　　　　pseudoacacia　.60　.35
3269　A1277　32s Lavandula vera　.65　.40
3270　A1277　42s Tilia parvifolia　.90　.50
3271　A1277　60s Onobrychis sa-
　　　　　tiva　1.10　.70
　a.　　Min. sheet of 6, #3266-3271　4.75　2.75
　　　Nos. 3266-3271 (6)　3.65　2.35

BULGARIA '89 — A1278

1987, Sept. 3   ***Perf. 13½x13***
3272 A1278 13s No. 1   .45 .20

HAFNIA '87 — A1279

1987, Sept. 8   ***Perf. 13***
3273 A1279 42s multicolored   1.00 .60

No. 3273 issued in sheets of 3 plus 2 labels picturing emblems of the HAFNIA '87 and BULGARIA '89 exhibitions, and 1 label with background similar to Denmark Type A32 with castle instead of denomination.

Portrait of a Girl, by Stefan Ivanov — A1280

Paintings in the Sofia City Art Galler: 8s, Grape-gatherer, by Bencho Obreshkov. 20s, Portrait of a Lady with a Hat, by David Perets. 25s, Listeners of Marimba, by Kiril Tsonev. 32s, Boy with an Harmonica, by Nenko Balkanski. 60s, Rumyana, by Vasil Stoilov.

1987, Sept. 15 **Litho.** ***Perf. 14***
3274 A1280 5s shown   .20 .20
3275 A1280 8s multicolored   .20 .20
3276 A1280 20s multicolored   .50 .30
3277 A1280 25s multicolored   .60 .35
3278 A1280 32s multicolored   .75 .45
3279 A1280 60s multicolored   1.25 .80
    Nos. 3274-3279 (6)   3.50 2.30

Intl. Atomic Energy Agency, 30th Anniv. A1281

1987, Sept. 15 **Photo.** ***Perf. 13½x13***
3280 A1281 13s red, lt blue & emer   .35 .20

Songbirds A1282

1987, Oct. 12 **Litho.** ***Perf. 12½x12***
3281 A1282 5s Troglodytes troglodytes   .20 .20
3282 A1282 13s Emberiza citrinella   .20 .20
3283 A1282 20s Sitta europaea   .30 .20
3284 A1282 30s Turdus merula   .45 .30

3285 A1282 42s Coccothraustes coccothraustes   .70 .35
3286 A1282 60s Cinclus cinclus   1.00 .45
  a. Min. sheet of 6, #3281-3286   2.75 2.25
    Nos. 3281-3286 (6)   2.85 1.70

Balkan War, 75th Anniv. A1283

1987, Sept. 15 **Photo.** ***Perf. 13½***
3287 A1283 5s buff, blk & brt org   .20 .20

Newspaper Anniversaries — A1283a

1987, Sept. 24 **Photo.** ***Perf. 13***
3287A A1283a 5s multicolored   .20 .20

Rabotnik, 95th anniv., *Rabotnicheski Vstnik*, 90th anniv. and *Rabotnichesko Delo*, 60th anniv.

October Revolution, Russia, 70th Anniv. — A1284

Lenin and: 5s, Revolutionary. 13s, Cosmonaut.

1987, Oct. 27 **Photo.** ***Perf. 13***
3288 A1284 5s rose brn & red org   .20 .20
3289 A1284 13s brt ultra & red org   .20 .20

1988 Winter Olympics, Calgary A1285

1987, Oct. 27 **Litho.** ***Perf. 13x13½***
3290 A1285 5s Biathlon   .20 .20
3291 A1285 13s Slalom   .40 .20
3292 A1285 30s Women's figure skating   .85 .45
3293 A1285 42s 4-Man bobsled   1.10 .60
    Nos. 3290-3293 (4)   2.55 1.45

Souvenir Sheet
3294 A1285 1 l Ice hockey   2.75 1.50

No. 3294 exists imperf. Same value.

Souvenir Sheet

Soviet Space Achievements, 1937-87 — A1286

Designs: No. 3295a, Vega probe. No. 3295b, Mir-Soyuz Space Station.

1987, Dec. 24 **Photo.** ***Perf. 13½x13***
3295 A1286 Sheet of 2   3.00 1.50
  a.-b. 50s any single   1.25 .75

Exists imperf.

New Year 1988 A1287

Sofia stamp exhibition emblem within folklore patterns.

1987, Dec. 25   ***Perf. 13***
3296 A1287 5s multicolored   .20 .20
3297 A1287 13s multi, diff.   .35 .20

Souvenir Sheet

European Security Conferences — A1288

Conferences held in Helsinki, 1973, and Vienna, 1987: a, Helsinki Conf. Center. b, Map of Europe. c, Vienna Conf. Center.

Perf. 13x13½ on 2 or 4 Sides
1987, Dec. 30
3298 A1288 Sheet of 3   4.25 3.00
  a.-c. 50s any single   1.50 .75

Exists imperf.

A1289

A1290

1988, Jan. 20
3299 A1289 5s multicolored   .20 .20

Christo Kabaktchiev (b. 1878), party leader.

1988, Jan. 25 **Litho.** ***Perf. 12***
Marine flowers.
3300 A1290 5s Scilla bythynica   .20 .20
3301 A1290 10s Geum rhodopaeum   .20 .20
3302 A1290 13s Caltha polypetala   .20 .20
3303 A1290 25s Nymphoides peltata   .30 .20
3304 A1290 30s Cortusa matthioli   .40 .20
3305 A1290 42s Stratiotes aloides   .60 .45
  a. Min. sheet of 6, #3300-3305   1.75 1.50
    Nos. 3300-3305 (6)   1.90 1.45

Liberation of Bulgaria, 110th Anniv. A1291

1988, Feb. 15 **Photo.** ***Perf. 13***
3306 A1291 5s Officer, horse   .20 .20
3307 A1291 13s Soldiers   .35 .20

8th Intl. Civil Servants Congress, Sofia — A1292

1988, Mar. 22 **Photo.** ***Perf. 13***
3308 A1292 13s multicolored   .30 .20

State Railways, Cent. — A1293

Locomotives: 5s, Jantra, 1888. 13s, Christo Botev, 1905. 25s, 0-10-1, 1918. 32s, 4-12-1 heavy duty, 1943. 42s, Diesel, 1964. 60s, Electric, 1979.

1988, Mar. 25 **Litho.** ***Perf. 11***
3309 A1293 5s multicolored   .20 .20
3310 A1293 13s multicolored   .25 .20
3311 A1293 25s multicolored   .50 .30
3312 A1293 32s multicolored   .65 .35
3313 A1293 42s multicolored   .80 .45
3314 A1293 60s multicolored   1.00 .60
  a. Min. sheet of 6, #3309-3314   3.50 2.00
    Nos. 3309-3314 (6)   3.40 2.10

Ivan Nedyalkov (1880-1925) A1294

Postal workers, heroes of socialism: 8s, Delcho Spasov (1918-43). 10s, Nikola

Ganchev (1915-43). 13s, Ganka Stoyanova Rasheva (1921-44).

1988, Mar. 31   Photo.   Perf. 13½x13
3315	A1294	5s buff & dark rose brn	.20	.20
3316	A1294	8s pale ultra & violet blue	.20	.20
3317	A1294	10s pale olive grn & olive grn	.25	.20
3318	A1294	13s pale pink & lake	.25	.20
		Nos. 3315-3318 (4)	.90	.80

Georgi Traikov (b. 1898), Statesman — A1295

Intl. Red Cross and Red Crescent Organizations, 125th Annivs. — A1296

1988, Apr. 8   Litho.   Perf. 13x13½
3319	A1295	5s orange & brn	.20	.20

1988, Apr. 26   Photo.   Perf. 13
3320	A1296	13s multicolored	.25	.20

Children's Drawings Type of 1982

Designs: 5s, Girl wearing a folk costume, vert. 8s, Painter at easel, vert. 13s, Children playing. 20s, Ringing bells for peace. 32s, Accordion player, vert. 42s, Cosmonaut, vert. 50s, Assembly emblem.

1988, Apr. 28   Litho.   Perf. 14
3321	A1093	5s multicolored	.20	.20
3322	A1093	8s multicolored	.20	.20
3323	A1093	13s multicolored	.30	.20
3324	A1093	20s multicolored	.40	.25
3325	A1093	32s multicolored	.65	.40
3326	A1093	42s multicolored	.90	.50
		Nos. 3321-3326 (6)	2.65	1.75

Souvenir Sheet
3327	A1093	50s multicolored	1.10	.60

4th Intl. Children's Assembly, Sofia. No. 3327 exists imperf.

Karl Marx — A1297

1988, May 5   Perf. 13
3328	A1297	13s multicolored	.30	.20

Birds — A1297a

1988, May 6   Litho.   Perf. 13x13½
3328A	A1297a	5s Ciconia ciconia	.25	
3328B	A1297a	5s Larus argentatus	.25	
3328C	A1297a	8s Ardea cinerea	.25	
3328D	A1297a	8s Corvus corone cornix	.25	.20
3328E	A1297a	10s Accipiter gentillis	.30	.20
3328F	A1297a	42s Bubo bubo	1.00	.50
		Nos. 3328A-3328F (6)	2.30	1.50

Dated 1987.

Sofia Zoo — A1298

1988, May 20
3329	A1298	5s Loxodonta africana	.20	.20
3330	A1298	13s Ceratotherium simum	.25	.20
3331	A1298	25s Lycaon pictus	.50	.30
3332	A1298	30s Pelecanus onocrotalus	.65	.35
3333	A1298	32s Bucorvus abissinicus	.70	.40
3334	A1298	42s Nyctea scandiaca	.90	.55
a.		Min. sheet of 6, #3329-3334	3.75	1.75
		Nos. 3329-3334 (6)	3.20	2.00

FINLANDIA '88 — A1299

1988, June 7
3335	A1299	30s Finland No. 1	.70	.35

No. 3335 printed in miniature sheets of 3 plus 3 labels picturing skyline, SOFIA '89 and FINLANDIA '88 exhibition emblems. Exists imperf.

2nd Joint USSR-Bulgaria Space Flight — A1300

1988, June 7
3336	A1300	5s shown	.20	.20
3337	A1300	13s Rocket, globe	.30	.20

EXPO '91, Plovdiv — A1301

1988, June 7   Perf. 13½x13
3338	A1301	13s multicolored	.30	.20

1988 European Soccer Championships — A1302

1988, June 10   Perf. 13
3339	A1302	5s Corner kick	.20	.20
3340	A1302	13s Heading the ball	.25	.20
3341	A1302	30s Referee, player	.55	.35
3342	A1302	42s Player holding trophy	.85	.55
		Nos. 3339-3342 (4)	1.85	1.30

Souvenir Sheet
3343	A1302	1 l Stadium	2.25	1.25

Paintings by Dechko Usunov (1899-1986) — A1303

Designs: 5s, Portrait of a Young Girl. 13s, Portrait of Maria Wassilewa. 30s, Self-portrait.

1988, June 14   Perf. 13x13½
3344	A1303	5s multicolored	.20	.20
3345	A1303	13s multicolored	.30	.20
3346	A1303	30s multicolored	.70	.35
		Nos. 3344-3346 (3)	1.20	.75

Souvenir Sheet

1st Woman in Space, 25th Anniv. — A1304

1988, June 16   Perf. 13½x13
3347	A1304	1 l multicolored	2.75	1.50

Valentina Tereshkova's flight, June 16-19, 1963.

Kurdzhali Region Religious Art — A1305

Designs: 5s, St. John the Baptist, 1592. 8s, St. George Slaying the Dragon, 1841.

1988, June 27   Perf. 13½x13½
3348	A1305	5s multicolored	.20	.20
3349	A1305	8s multicolored	.20	.20

1988 Summer Olympics, Seoul — A1306

1988, July 25   Litho.   Perf. 13
3350	A1306	5s High jump	.20	.20
3351	A1306	13s Weight lifting	.30	.20
3352	A1306	30s Greco-Roman wrestling	.60	.40
3353	A1306	42s Rhythmic gymnastics	.90	.50
		Nos. 3350-3353 (4)	2.00	1.30

Souvenir Sheet
3354	A1306	1 l Volleyball	2.75	1.25

No. 3354 exists imperf.

Dimitr and Karaja — A1307

1988, July 25   Litho.   Perf. 13
3355	A1307	5s blk, dark olive bister & grn	.20	.20

120th anniv. of the deaths of Haji Dimitr and Stefan Karaja, patriots killed during the Balkan Wars.

Problems of Peace and Socialism, 30th Anniv. — A1308

1988, July 26   Photo.
3356	A1308	13s multicolored	.20	.20

Paintings in the Ludmila Zhivkova Art Gallery — A1309

Paintings: No. 3357, Harbor, Algiers, by Albermarke (1875-1947). No. 3358, Portrait of Ermin David in the Studio, by Jul Pasken (1885-1930). No. 3359, Madonna with Child and Sts. Sebastian and Roko, by Giovanni Rosso (1494-1540). No. 3360, The Barren Tree, by Roland Udo (1879-1982).

1988, July 27   Litho.   Perf. 14
3357	A1309	30s multicolored	.65	.40
3358	A1309	30s multicolored	.65	.40
3359	A1309	30s multicolored	.65	.40
3360	A1309	30s multicolored	.65	.40
		Nos. 3357-3360 (4)	2.60	1.60

St. Clement of Ohrid University, Sofia,
100th Anniv. — A1310

1988, Aug. 22   *Perf. 13*
3361 A1310 5s blk & pale yel   .20   .20

PRAGA
'88
A1311

1988, Aug. 22
3362 A1311 25s Czechoslovakia #2
in vermilion   .60   .30
Printed in miniature sheets of 3 plus 3 labels
picturing skyline, PRAGA '88 and SOFIA '89
exhibition emblems.
Exists imperf.

OLYMPHILEX '88 — A1312

1988, Sept. 1
3363 A1312 62s Korea No. 1   1.25 .75
Printed in miniature sheets of 3 plus 3 labels
picturing skyline, OLYMPHILEX '88 and
SOFIA '89 exhibition emblems.
Exists imperf.

A1313

A1314

1988, Sept. 15
3364 A1313 5s dp bl, lt bl & red   .20   .20
Kremikovtsi steel mill, 25th anniv.

1988, Sept. 16   *Perf. 13½x13*
3365 A1314 13s dark red & ultra   .25   .20
80th Interparliamentary Conference.

Transportation Commission 80th
Congress — A1315

1988, Oct. 17
3366 A1315 13s deep lil rose &
blk   .25   .20

Kurdzhali
Region
Artifacts
A1316

5s, Earthenware bowl, 13th-14th cent. 8s,
Medieval fortification, Gorna Krepost Village,
vert.

1988, Sept. 20   *Perf. 13*
3367 A1316 5s multicolored   .20   .20
3368 A1316 8s multicolored   .20   .20

Chiprovo Uprising, 300th
Anniv. — A1317

1988, Sept. 23
3369 A1317 5s multicolored   .20   .20

Bears
A1318

1988, Sept. 26   *Perf. 12½*
3370 A1318 5s *Ursus arctos*   .20   .20
3371 A1318 8s *Thalassarctos
maritimus*   .20   .20
3372 A1318 13s *Melursus ur-
sinus*   .30   .20
3373 A1318 20s *Helarctos
malayanus*   .45   .25
3374 A1318 32s *Selenarctos
thibetanus*   .70   .40
3375 A1318 42s *Tremarctos
ornatus*   .95   .50
    a.   Min. sheet of 6, #3370-3375 3.25 1.50
         Nos. 3370-3375 (6)   2.80 1.75

ECOFORUM for Peace — A1319

1988, Oct. 29   *Perf. 13*
3376 A1319 20s multicolored   .50   .25

PLOVDIV '88 — A1320

Design: Amphitheater ruins, PRAGA '88
and PLOVDIV '88 emblems.

1988, Nov. 2
3377 A1320 5s multicolored   .20   .20
Exists in imperf. sheet of six.

Radio & Television
Authority, 25th
Anniv. — A1321

1988, Nov. 17   *Litho.*   *Perf. 13*
3378 A1321 5s multicolored   .20   .20

BULGARIA '89 — A1321a

1988, Nov. 22   *Litho.*   *Perf. 13*
3379 A1321a 42s No. 1   1.10 .60
Printed in miniature sheets of 3+3 labels
picturing exhib. emblem and conf. center.
Exists imperf.

Souvenir Sheet

Danube Cruise Excursion Industry,
40th Anniv. — A1321b

1988, Nov. 25   *Perf. 13½x13*
3380   Sheet of 2   5.00 2.75
    a. A1321b 1 l *Russia*   2.50 1.40
    b. A1321b 1 l *Aleksandr Stamboliski* 2.50 1.40

Traffic
Safety
A1321c

1988, Nov. 28
3381 A1321c 5s multicolored   .20   .20

New Year
1989 — A1321d

1988, Dec. 20   *Perf. 13*
3382 A1321d 5s shown   .20   .20
3383 A1321d 13s multi, diff.   .35   .25

Hotels in
Winter
A1322

1988, Dec. 19   *Litho.*   *Perf. 13½x13*
3384 A1322 5s shown   .20   .20
3385 A1322 8s multi, diff.   .20   .20
3386 A1322 13s multi, diff.   .30   .20
3387 A1322 30s multi, diff.   .70   .40
    Nos. 3384-3387 (4)   1.40 1.00

Souvenir Sheet

Soviet Space Shuttle *Energija-
Buran* — A1322a

1988, Dec. 28   *Perf. 13½x13*
3387A A1322a 1 l dark blue   3.00 1.50

BULGARIA '89 — A1322b

Traditional modes of postal conveyance.

1988, Dec. 29   *Perf. 13½x13*
3387B A1322b 25s Mail coach   .50   .30
3387C A1322b 25s Biplane   .50   .30
3387D A1322b 25s Truck   .50   .30
3387E A1322b 25s Steam packet   .50   .30
    Nos. 3387B-3387E (4)   2.00 1.20

Philatelic Exhibitions — A1323

1989   *Litho.*   *Perf. 13*
3388 A1323 42s France No. 1   1.00 .50
3389 A1323 62s India No. 200   1.50 .80
    BULGARIA '89 and PHILEXFRANCE '89
(42s) or INDIA '89 (62s).
    Nos. 3388-3389 each printed in sheets of 3
+ 3 labels picturing skylines, BULGARIA '89

and PHILEXFRANCE or INDIA exhibition labels. Exist in sheets of 4 also. Exist imperf. Issue dates: 42s, Feb. 23; 62s, Jan. 14.

Souvenir Sheet

Universiade Winter Games, Sofia — A1324

Designs: a, Downhill skiing. b, Ice hockey. c, Cross-country skiing. d, Speed skating.

1989, Jan. 30   **Litho.**   *Imperf.*
Simulated Perforations
3390   Sheet of 4   2.40   1.25
   a.-d.   A1324 25s multicolored   .55   .30

No. 3390 exists imperf. without simulated perforations and containing black control number.

Humor and Satire Festival, Gabrovo A1325

1989, Feb. 7   *Perf. 13½x13*
3391   A1325   13s Don Quixote   .30   .20

Endangered Plant Species — A1326

1989, Feb. 22   *Perf. 13x13½*
3392   A1326   5s *Ramonda serbi-*
           ca   .20   .20
3393   A1326   10s *Paeonia masku-*
           la   .20   .20
3394   A1326   25s *Viola perinensis*   .50   .30
3395   A1326   30s *Dracunculus vul-*
           garis   .60   .35
3396   A1326   42s *Tulipa splendens*   .85   .50
3397   A1326   60s *Rindera umbel-*
           lata   1.25   .70
   a.   Min. sheet of 6, #3392-3397   4.25   2.50
     Nos. 3392-3397 (6)   3.60   2.25

World Wildlife Fund A1327

Bats.

1989, Feb. 27   *Perf. 13*
3398   A1327   5s *Nyctalus noctula*   .25   .20
3399   A1327   13s *Rhinolophus fer-*
           rumequinum   .35   .20
3400   A1327   30s *Myotis myotis*   .75   .35
3401   A1327   42s *Vespertilio*
           murinus   1.10   .50
   a.   Min. sheet of 4, #3398-3401   2.50   1.25
     Nos. 3398-3401 (4)   2.45   1.25

Aleksandr Stamboliski (1879-1923), Premier — A1328

1989, Mar. 1   *Perf. 13½x13*
3402   A1328   5s brt org & blk   .20   .20

Souvenir Sheet

Soviet-Bulgarian Joint Space Flight, 10th Anniv. — A1329

Designs: a, Liftoff. b, Crew.

1989, Apr. 10   *Perf. 13*
3403   A1329   Sheet of 2   2.40   1.25
   a.-b.   50s any single   1.10   .60
        Exists imperf.

EXPO '91 Young Inventors Exhibition, Plovdiv — A1330

1989, Apr. 20   *Perf. 13½x13*
3404   A1330   5s multicolored   .20   .20

Petko Enev (b. 1889) A1331

Stanke Dimitrov Marek (b. 1889) — A1332

1989, Apr. 28   *Perf. 13½x13, 13x13½*
3405   A1331   5s scarlet & black   .20   .20
3406   A1332   5s scarlet & black   .20   .20

Icons — A1333

Photocopier A1334

Paintings by Bulgarian artists: No. 3407, Archangel Michael, by Dimiter Molerov. No. 3408, Mother and Child, by Toma Vishanov. No. 3409, St. John, by Vishanov. No. 3410, St. Dimitri, by Ivan Terziev.

1989, Apr. 28   *Perf. 13x13½*
3407   A1333   30s multicolored   .65   .35
3408   A1333   30s multicolored   .65   .35
3409   A1333   30s multicolored   .65   .35
3410   A1333   30s multicolored   .65   .35
     Nos. 3407-3410 (4)   2.60   1.40

Nos. 3408, 3410 exist in sheets of four. Nos. 3407-3410 exist in souvenir sheets of four and together in one sheet of four, imperf.

1989, May 5
3411   A1334   5s shown   .20   .20
3412   A1334   8s Computer   .20   .20
3413   A1334   35s Telephone   .80   .45
3414   A1334   42s Dish receiver   .90   .50
     Nos. 3411-3414 (4)   2.10   1.35

Bulgarian Communications, 110th anniv. Nos. 3411-3413 exist in imperf. sheets of six.

Souvenir Sheet

58th FIP Congress — A1335

1989, May 22
3415   A1335   1 l Charioteer   2.25   1.00
        Exists imperf.

1st Communist Party Congress in Bulgaria, 70th Anniv. — A1336

Famous Men — A1337

1989, June 15
3416   A1336   5s mar, blk & dk red   .20   .20

1989

#3417, Ilya Blaskov. #3418, Sofronii, Bishop of Vratza. #3419, Vassil Aprilov (b. 1789), educator, historian. #3420, Christo Jassenov (1889-1925). 10s, Stoyan Zagorchinov (1889-1969).

3417   A1337   5s black & gray ol   .20   .20
3418   A1337   5s blk, brn blk &
           pale green   .20   .20
3419   A1337   8s lt blue, blk & vio
           blk   .30   .20
3420   A1337   8s tan, blk & dark
           red brown   .25   .20
3421   A1337   10s blk, pale pink &
           gray blue   .30   .20
     Nos. 3417-3421 (5)   1.25   1.00

Issued: #3417-3418, June 15; #3419, Aug. 1; #3420, Sept. 25; 10s, Aug. 5.

French Revolution, Bicent. — A1338

1989, June 26   *Perf. 13½x13*
3422   A1338   13s Anniv. emblem   .25   .20
3423   A1338   30s Jean-Paul Marat   .60   .35
3424   A1338   42s Robespierre   .85   .50
     Nos. 3422-3424 (3)   1.70   1.05

7th Army Games — A1339

1989, June 30   *Perf. 13*
3425   A1339   5s Gymnast   .20   .20
3426   A1339   13s Equestrian   .30   .20
3427   A1339   30s Running   .65   .40
3428   A1339   42s Shooting   .95   .50
     Nos. 3425-3428 (4)   2.10   1.30

22nd World Canoe and Kayak Championships, Plovdiv — A1340

1989, Aug. 11   **Litho.**   *Perf. 13*
3429   A1340   13s Woman paddling   .30   .20
3430   A1340   30s Man rowing   .60   .25

Photography, 150th Anniv. — A1341

1989, Aug. 29   *Perf. 13½x13*
3431   A1341   42s blk, buff & yel   .95   .45

September 9 Revolution, 45th Anniv. — A1342

1989, Aug. 30   *Perf. 13*

3432	A1342	5s Revolutionaries	.20 .20
3433	A1342	8s Couple embracing	.20 .20
3434	A1342	13s Faces in a crowd	.20 .20
	Nos. 3432-3434 (3)		.60 .60

Natural History Museum, Cent. A1343

1989, Aug. 31

3435	A1343	13s multicolored	.30 .20

Postal Workers Killed in World War II — A1343a

Designs: 5s, L.D. Dardjikov. 8s, I.B. Dobrev. 10s, N.P. Antonov.

1989, Sept. 22   *Litho.*   *Perf. 13*

3436	A1343a	5s multicolored	.20 .20
3437	A1343a	8s multicolored	.20 .20
3438	A1343a	13s multicolored	.30 .20
	Nos. 3436-3438 (3)		.70 .60

12th Shipping Unions Congress (FIATA) — A1344

1989, Sept. 25   *Litho.*   *Perf. 13½x13*

3439	A1344	42s light bl & dark bl	.85 .45

Jawaharlal Nehru, 1st Prime Minister of Independent India — A1346

1989, Oct. 10

3440	A1346	13s blk, pale yel & brn	.30 .20

Souvenir Sheet

European Ecology Congress — A1347

1989, Oct. 12   *Perf. 13*

3441	A1347	Sheet of 2	3.75 1.75
a.		50s multicolored	1.25 .60
b.		1 l multicolored	2.25 1.10

Snakes A1368

1989, Oct. 20   *Litho.*   *Perf. 13*

3491	A1368	5s *Eryx jaculus turcicus*	.20 .20
3492	A1368	10s *Elaphe longissima*	.25 .20
3493	A1368	25s *Elaphe situla*	.55 .30
3494	A1368	30s *Elaphe quatuorlineata*	.65 .35
3495	A1368	42s *Telescopus fallax*	.90 .50
3496	A1368	60s *Coluber rubriceps*	1.25 .70
a.		Min. sheet of 6, #3491-3496	4.25 2.00
	Nos. 3491-3496 (6)		3.80 2.25

Intl. Youth Science Fair, Plovdiv, 1989 — A1369

1989, Nov. 4

3497	A1369	13s multicolored	.25 .20

1990 World Soccer Championships, Italy — A1370

Various athletes: No. 3502a, Athletes facing right. No. 3502b, Athletes facing left.

1989, Dec. 1

3498	A1370	5s shown	.20 .20
3499	A1370	13s multi, diff.	.30 .20
3500	A1370	30s multi, diff.	.70 .35
3501	A1370	42s multi, diff.	1.00 .50
	Nos. 3498-3501 (4)		2.20 1.25

Souvenir Sheet

3502		Sheet of 2	2.40 1.10
a.-b.		A1370 50s any single	1.10 .55

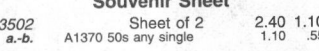

Air Sports A1371

1989, Dec. 8

3503	A1371	5s Glider planes	.20 .20
3504	A1371	13s Hang glider	.30 .20
3505	A1371	30s Sky diving	.70 .35
3506	A1371	42s Three sky divers	1.00 .50
	Nos. 3503-3506 (4)		2.20 1.25

82nd General conference of the FAI, Varna.

Traffic Safety A1372

1989, Dec. 12

3507	A1372	5s multicolored	.20 .20

New Year 1990 — A1373

1989, Dec. 25   *Litho.*   *Perf. 13*

3508	A1373	5s Santa's sleigh	.20 .20
3509	A1373	13s Snowman	.30 .20

Cats A1374

#3510, Persian. #3511, Tiger. 8s, Tabby. #3513, Himalayan. #3511, Persian, diff. 13s, Siamese. #3511, 3514-3515 vert.

Perf. 13½x13, 13x13½

1989, Dec. 26   **Background Color**

3510	A1374	5s gray	.20 .20
3511	A1374	5s yellow	.20 .20
3512	A1374	8s orange	.20 .20
3513	A1374	10s blue	.25 .20
3514	A1374	10s brown orange	.25 .20
3515	A1374	13s red	.30 .20
	Nos. 3510-3515 (6)		1.40 1.20

Explorers and Their Ships — A1375

1990, Jan. 17   *Perf. 13*

3516	A1375	5s Columbus	.20 .20
3517	A1375	8s da Gama	.20 .20
3518	A1375	13s Magellan	.25 .20
3519	A1375	32s Drake	.60 .35
3520	A1375	42s Hudson	.75 .50
3521	A1375	60s Cook	1.00 .70
a.		Min. sheet of 6, #3516-3521	3.75 1.75
	Nos. 3516-3521 (6)		3.00 2.15

Natl. Esperanto Movement, Cent. — A1376

1990, Feb. 23   *Litho.*   *Perf. 13*

3522	A1376	10s multicolored	.30 .20

Paintings by Foreign Artists in the Natl. Museum A1377

Artists: No. 3523, Suzanna Valadon (1867-1938). No. 3524, Maurice Brianchon (1899-1978). No. 3525, Moise Kisling (1891-1953). No. 3526, Giovanni Beltraffio (1467-1516).

1990, Mar. 23   *Perf. 14*

3523	A1377	30s multicolored	.65 .40
3524	A1377	30s multicolored	.65 .40
3525	A1377	30s multicolored	.65 .40
3526	A1377	30s multicolored	.65 .40
	Nos. 3523-3526 (4)		2.60 1.60

1990 World Soccer Championships, Italy — A1378

Various athletes.

1990, Mar. 26   *Perf. 13*

3527	A1378	5s multicolored	.20 .20
3528	A1378	13s multi, diff.	.30 .20
3529	A1378	30s multi, diff.	.70 .40
3530	A1378	42s multi, diff.	.95 .50
	Nos. 3527-3530 (4)		2.15 1.30

Souvenir Sheet

3531		Sheet of 2	2.40 1.25
a.		A1378 50s Three players	1.10 .60
b.		A1378 50s Two players	1.10 .60

Bavaria No. 1 A1379

1990, Apr. 6   *Litho.*   *Perf. 13*

3532	A1379	42s vermilion & blk	1.00 .50

ESSEN '90, Germany, Apr. 12-22. No. 3532 printed in sheets of 3 + 3 labels.

Souvenir Sheet

Penny Black, 150th Anniv. A1380

1990, Apr. 10

3533		Sheet of 2	2.25 1.25
a.		A1380 50s Great Britain #1	1.10 .60
b.		A1380 50s Sir Rowland Hill	1.10 .60

Cooperative Farming in Bulgaria, Cent. — A1381

1990, Apr. 17

3534	A1381	5s multicolored	.20 .20

Dimitar Chorbadjiski-Chudomir (1890-1967) — A1382

1990, Apr. 24
3535 A1382 5s multicolored   .20   .20

Labor Day, Cent. — A1383

1990, May 1   **Perf. 13x13½**
3536 A1383 10s multicolored   .25   .20

ITU, 125th Anniv. — A1384

1990, May 13 Litho.   Perf. 13½x13
3537 A1384 20s bl, red & blk   .50   .25

Belgium No. 1 A1385

1990, May 23   **Perf. 13**
3538 A1385 30s multicolored   .75   .40
Belgica '90. No. 3538 printed in sheets of 3 + 3 labels.

Lamartine (1790-1869), French Poet — A1386

1990, June 15   **Perf. 13½x13**
3539 A1386 20s multicolored   .45   .25

Dinosaurs — A1387

1990, June 19   **Perf. 12½**
3540 A1387 5s Brontosaurus   .20   .20
3541 A1387 8s Stegosaurus   .20   .20
3542 A1387 13s Edaphosaurus   .30   .20

3543 A1387 25s Rhamphorhynchus .60   .30
3544 A1387 32s Protoceratops   .80   .40
3545 A1387 42s Triceratops   1.10 .55
  a.   Min. sheet of 6, #3540-3545   3.50 1.60
      Nos. 3540-3545 (6)   3.20 1.85

1992 Summer Olympic Games, Barcelona — A1388

1990, July 13   **Perf. 13½x13**
3546 A1388 5s Swimming   .20   .20
3547 A1388 13s Handball   .30   .20
3548 A1388 30s Hurdling   .75   .40
3549 A1388 42s Cycling   1.10 .55
      Nos. 3546-3549 (4)   2.35 1.35

Souvenir Sheet
3550   Sheet of 2   2.75 1.25
  a. A1388 50s Tennis, forehand   1.25 .60
  b. A1388 50s Tennis, backhand   1.25 .60

Butterflies A1389

1990, Aug. 8 Litho.   Perf. 13
3551 A1389 5s Zerynthia Polyx-
              ena   .20   .20
3552 A1389 10s Panaxia
              quadripunctaria   .20   .20
3553 A1389 20s Proserpinus pro-
              serpina   .20   .20
3554 A1389 25s Hyles lineata   .25   .20
3555 A1389 42s Thecla betulae   .30   .20
3556 A1389 60s Euphydryas
              cynthia   1.75 .60
  a.   Min. sheet of 6, #3551-3556   3.00 1.75
      Nos. 3551-3556 (6)   2.90 1.60

Airplanes — A1390

1990, Aug. 30 Litho.   Perf. 13½x13
3557 A1390 5s Airbus A-300   .20   .20
3558 A1390 10s Tu-204   .20   .20
3559 A1390 25s Concorde   .30   .25
3560 A1390 30s DC-9   .40   .30
3561 A1390 42s Il-86   .55   .40
3562 A1390 60s Boeing 747   .75   .55
  a.   Min. sheet of 6, #3557-3562   3.25 2.00
      Nos. 3557-3562 (6)   2.40 1.90

Exarch Joseph I (1840-1915), Religious Leader — A1391

1990, Sept. 27   **Perf. 13**
3563 A1391 5s blk, pur & grn   .20   .20

Intl. Traffic Safety Year A1392

1990, Oct. 9   Litho.   Perf. 13
3564 A1392 5s multicolored   .20   .20

Olymphilex '90, Varna — A1393

1990, Oct. 16   Perf. 13x13½
3565 A1393 5s Shot put   .20   .20
3566 A1393 13s Discus   .25   .20
3567 A1393 42s Hammer throw   .90   .55
3568 A1393 60s Javelin   1.25 .70
  a.   Souv. sheet of 4, #3565-
        3568, imperf.   13.00 7.50
      Nos. 3565-3568 (4)   2.60 1.65

Space Exploration — A1394

Designs: 5s, Sputnik, 1957, USSR. 8s, Vostok, 1961, USSR. 10s, Voshkod 2, 1965, USSR. 20s, Apollo-Soyuz, 1975, US-USSR. 42s, Space Shuttle Columbia, 1981, US. 60s, Galileo, 1989-1996, US. 1 l, Apollo 11 Moon landing, 1969, US.

1990, Oct. 22   Perf. 13½x13
3569 A1394 5s multicolored   .20   .20
3570 A1394 8s multicolored   .20   .20
3571 A1394 10s multicolored   .20   .20
3572 A1394 20s multicolored   .40   .25
3573 A1394 42s multicolored   .90   .55
3574 A1394 60s multicolored   1.25 .70
      Nos. 3569-3574 (6)   3.15 2.10

Souvenir Sheet
3575 A1394 1 l multicolored   2.75 1.50

St. Clement of Ohrid — A1395

1990, Nov. 29   Litho.   Perf. 13
3576 A1395 5s multicolored   .20   .20

Christmas A1396

1990, Dec. 25   Litho.   Perf. 13
3577 A1396 5s Christmas tree   .20   .20
3578 A1396 20s Santa Claus   .40   .25

European Figure Skating Championships, Sofia — A1397

1991, Jan. 18   Perf. 13½x13
3579 A1397 15s multicolored   .35   .20

Farm Animals A1398

1991-92   **Perf. 14x13½**
3581 A1398 20s Sheep   .20   .20
3582 A1398 25s Goose   .20   .20
3583 A1398 30s Hen, chicks   .30   .20
3584 A1398 40s Horse   .30   .25
3585 A1398 62s Goat   .50   .30
3586 A1398 86s Sow   .70   .50
3587 A1398 95s Goat   .50   .30
3588 A1398 1 l Donkey   .80   .40
3589 A1398 2 l Bull   1.75 .50
3590 A1398 5 l Turkey   2.75 1.25
3591 A1398 10 l Cow   4.75 1.75
      Nos. 3581-3591 (11)   12.75 5.85

Issued: 20s, 25s, 40s, 86s, 1 l, 8/21; 10 l, 2/22; 95s, 5/5/92; others, 2/11/91.

Mushrooms A1399

1991, Mar. 19   Perf. 12½x13
3597 A1399 5s Amanita phal-
              loides   .20   .20
3598 A1399 10s Amanita verna   .20   .20
3599 A1399 20s Amanita
              pantherina   .20   .20
3600 A1399 32s Amanita mus-
              caria   .40   .30
3601 A1399 42s Gyromitra es-
              culenta   .45   .35
3602 A1399 60s Boletus satanas   .70   .50
  a.   Min. sheet of 6, #3597-3602   3.25 1.50
      Nos. 3597-3602 (6)   2.15 1.75

French Impressionists A1400

Designs: 20s, Good Morning, by Gauguin. 43s, Madame Dobini, by Degas. 62s, Peasant Woman, by Pissarro. 67s, Woman with Black Hair, by Manet. 80s, Blue Vase, by Cezanne. 2 l, Jeanny Samari, by Renoir. 3 l, Self portrait, by Van Gogh.

1991, Apr. 1   **Perf. 13**
3603 A1400 20s multicolored   .25   .20
3604 A1400 43s multicolored   .50   .40
3605 A1400 62s multicolored   .70   .55
3606 A1400 67s multicolored   .80   .60
3607 A1400 80s multicolored   1.00 .75
3608 A1400 2 l multicolored   2.25 1.75
      Nos. 3603-3608 (6)   5.50 4.25

Miniature Sheet
3609 A1400 3 l multicolored   4.75 2.75

Swiss Confederation, 700th Anniv. — A1401

1991, Apr. 11
3610 A1401 62s multicolored .90 .55

Philatelic Review, Cent. — A1402

1991, May 7 **Litho.** **Perf. 13**
3611 A1402 30s multicolored .45 .25

Europa — A1403

1991, May 10 **Perf. 13x13½**
3612 A1403 43s Meteosat .70 .40
3613 A1403 62s Ariane rocket 1.00 .55

Horses — A1404

1991, May 21 **Perf. 13x12½**
3614 A1404 5s Przewalski's horse .20 .20
3615 A1404 10s Tarpan .20 .20
3616 A1404 25s Arabian .35 .20
3617 A1404 35s Arabian .45 .30
3618 A1404 42s Shetland pony .55 .35
3619 A1404 60s Draft horse .80 .50
  a. Min. sheet of 6, #3614-3619 3.25 1.50
    Nos. 3614-3619 (6) 2.55 1.75

EXPO 91, Plovdiv — A1405

1991, June 6 **Litho.** **Perf. 13½x13**
3620 A1405 30s multicolored .45 .30

Wolfgang Amadeus Mozart A1406

1991, July 2 **Perf. 13**
3621 A1406 62s multicolored 1.00 .55

Space Shuttle Missions, 10th Anniv. A1407

1991, July 23 **Litho.** **Perf. 13**
3622 A1407 12s Columbia .20 .20
3623 A1407 32s Challenger .30 .20
3624 A1407 50s Discovery .40 .20
3625 A1407 86s Atlantis, vert. .75 .40
3626 A1407 1.50 l Buran, vert. 1.25 .60
3627 A1407 2 l Atlantis, diff., vert. 1.50 .75
    Nos. 3622-3627 (6) 4.40 2.35

Souvenir Sheet
3628 A1407 3 l US shuttle, earth 4.25 2.00

1992 Winter Olympics, Albertville A1408

1991, Aug. 7 **Litho.** **Perf. 13x13½**
3629 A1408 30s Luge .40 .30
3630 A1408 43s Slalom skiing .50 .40
3631 A1408 67s Ski jumping .85 .60
3632 A1408 2 l Biathlon 2.50 1.75
    Nos. 3629-3632 (4) 4.25 3.05

Souvenir Sheet
3633 A1408 3 l Two-man bob-sled 4.75 2.75

Sheraton Sofia Hotel Balkan A1409

1991, Sept. 6 **Litho.** **Perf. 13**
3634 A1409 62s multicolored 1.25 .55
Printed in sheets of 3 + 3 labels.

Dogs — A1410

1991, Oct. 11 **Perf. 13x13½**
3635 A1410 30s Japanese .25 .20
3636 A1410 43s Chihuahua .40 .20
3637 A1410 62s Pinscher .55 .30
3638 A1410 80s Yorkshire terrier .70 .35
3639 A1410 1 l Chinese .90 .45
3640 A1410 3 l Pug 2.50 1.25
  a. Min. sheet of 6, #3635-3640 5.75 2.75
    Nos. 3635-3640 (6) 5.30 2.75

Cologne '91, Intl. Philatelic Exhibition A1411

1991, Oct. 21 **Perf. 13**
3641 A1411 86s multicolored 1.60 .75
Printed in sheets of 3 + 3 labels.

Souvenir Sheet

Brandenburg Gate, Bicent. — A1412

1991, Oct. 23
3642 A1412 4 l multicolored 7.50 3.50
Exists imperf.

Phila Nippon '91 A1413

1991, Nov. 11
3643 A1413 62s Japan #1 1.10 .55
Printed in sheets of 3 + 3 labels.

Bulgarian Railroad, 125th Anniv. — A1414

1991, Nov. 30
3644 A1414 30s Locomotive .55 .30
3645 A1414 30s Passenger car .55 .30

Medicinal Plants — A1415

Designs: 30s, Pulsatilla vernalis. 40s, Pulsatilla pratensis. 55s, Pulsatilla halleri. 60s, Aquilegia nigricans. 1 l, Hippophae rhamnoides. 2 l, Ribes nigrum.

1991, Nov. 20 **Litho.** **Perf. 13**
3646 A1415 30s +15s label .40 .20
3647 A1415 40s multicolored .35 .20
3648 A1415 55s multicolored .50 .25
3649 A1415 60s multicolored .55 .30
3650 A1415 1 l multicolored .90 .45
3651 A1415 2 l multicolored 1.75 .90
  a. Min. sheet of 6, #3646-3651 4.75 2.50
    Nos. 3646-3651 (6) 4.45 2.30

No. 3646 printed se-tenant with label. No. 3651a sold for 5 l, but does not contain the 15s label printed with No. 3646.

Basketball, Cent. A1416

1991, Dec. 6 **Perf. 13½x13**
3652 A1416 43s Ball below rim .50 .25
3653 A1416 62s Ball at rim .75 .40
3654 A1416 90s Ball in cylinder 1.10 .55
3655 A1416 1 l Ball in basket 1.25 .65
    Nos. 3652-3655 (4) 3.60 1.85

El Greco, 450th Birth Anniv. — A1417

Paintings: 43s, Christ Carrying the Cross. 50s, Holy Family with St. Anne. 60s, St. John the Evangelist and St. John the Baptist. 62s, St. Andrew and St. Francis. 1 l, Holy Family with St. Mary Magdalene. 2 l, Cardinal Nino de Guevara. 3 l, Holy Family with St. Anne (detail).

1991, Dec. 13 **Perf. 13**
3656 A1417 43s multicolored .45 .25
3657 A1417 50s multicolored .55 .30
3658 A1417 60s multicolored .65 .35
3659 A1417 62s multicolored .70 .40
3660 A1417 1 l multicolored 1.10 .55
3661 A1417 2 l multicolored 2.00 1.00
    Nos. 3656-3661 (6) 5.45 2.85

Souvenir Sheet
3662 A1417 3 l multicolored 4.25 2.00
No. 3662 contains one 43x53mm stamp.

Christmas — A1418

1991, Dec. 18
3663 A1418 30s Snowman, candle, bell, heart .55 .30
3664 A1418 62s Star, angel, flower, house, tree 1.10 .55

Marine Mammals — A1419

Designs: 30s, Phogophoca graenlandica. 43s, Orcinus orca. 62s, Odobenus rosmarus. 68s, Tursiops truncatus. 1 l, Monachus monachus. 2 l, Phocaena phocaena.

1991, Dec. 24
3665 A1419 30s multicolored .35 .20
3666 A1419 43s multicolored .50 .25
3667 A1419 62s multicolored .75 .40
3668 A1419 68s multicolored .80 .40
3669 A1419 1 l multicolored 1.25 .65
3670 A1419 2 l multicolored 2.50 1.25
  a. Min. sheet of 6, #3665-3670 6.50 3.25
    Nos. 3665-3670 (6) 6.15 3.15

Settlement of Jews in Bulgaria, 500th Anniv. — A1420

1992, Mar. 5   Litho.   *Perf. 13*
3671 A1420 1 l multicolored   1.75   .90

Gioacchino Rossini (1792-1868), Composer — A1421

1992, Mar. 11
3672 A1421 50s multicolored   .90   .45

Plovdiv Fair, Cent. A1422

1992, Mar. 25
3673 A1422 1 l buff & black   1.75   .90

Fiat Croma — A1423

Automobiles.

1992, Mar. 26   *Perf. 13½x13*
3674 A1423 30s Volvo 740   .25   .20
3675 A1423 45s Ford Escort   .45   .30
3676 A1423 50s shown   .50   .30
3677 A1423 50s Mercedes 600   .50   .30
3678 A1423 1 l Peugeot 605   1.00   .55
3679 A1423 2 l BMW 316   1.50   .90
     Nos. 3674-3679 (6)   4.20   2.55

Francisco de Orellana A1424

Explorers: No. 3681, Vespucci. No. 3682, Magellan. No. 3683, Gonzalo Jimenez de Quesada (1500-1579). 2 l, Drake. 3 l, Pedro de Valdivia (1500-1553). 4 l, Columbus.

1992, Apr. 22   Litho.   *Perf. 13*
3680 A1424 50s multicolored   .45   .25
3681 A1424 50s multicolored   .45   .25
3682 A1424 1 l multicolored   .90   .45
3683 A1424 1 l multicolored   .90   .45
3684 A1424 2 l multicolored   1.75   .90
3685 A1424 3 l multicolored   2.70   1.40
     Nos. 3680-3685 (6)   7.15   3.70
     Souvenir Sheet
3686 A1424 4 l multicolored   3.75   1.75

Granada '92 A1425

1992, Apr. 23
3687 A1425 62s multicolored   .55   .30
No. 3687 printed in sheets of 3 + 3 labels.

Discovery of America, 500th Anniv. — A1426

1992, Apr. 24
3688 1 l Ships, map   .90   .45
3689 2 l Columbus, ship   1.75   .90
   a. A1426 Pair, #3688-3689   2.75   1.40
Europa.

SOS Children's Village A1427

1992, June 15   Litho.   *Perf. 13*
3690 A1427 1 l multicolored   .90   .45

1992 Summer Olympics, Barcelona — A1428

1992, July 15   *Perf. 13½x13*
3691 A1428 50s Swimming   .45   .25
3692 A1428 50s Long jump   .45   .25
3693 A1428 1 l High jump   .90   .45
3694 A1428 3 l Gymnastics   2.70   1.40
     Nos. 3691-3694 (4)   4.50   2.35
     Souvenir Sheet
     Perf. 13x13½
3695 A1428 4 l Torch, vert.   4.00   1.75

Motorcycles — A1429

Designs: 30s, 1902 Laurin & Klement. No. 3697, 1928 Puch 200 Luxus. No. 3698, 1931 Norton CS1. 70s, 1950 Harley Davidson. 1 l, 1986 Gilera SP 01. 2 l, 1990 BMW K1.

1992, July 30   *Perf. 13*
3696 A1429 30s multicolored   .20   .20
3697 A1429 50s multicolored   .30   .20
3698 A1429 50s multicolored   .30   .20
3699 A1429 70s multicolored   .40   .20
3700 A1429 1 l multicolored   .60   .30
3701 A1429 2 l multicolored   1.25   .65
     Nos. 3696-3701 (6)   3.05   1.75

Genoa '92 Intl. Philatelic Exhibition A1430

1992, Sept. 18   *Perf. 13*
3702 A1430 1 l multicolored   .90   .45
   This is a developing set. Numbers may change.

Insects A1431

1992   Litho.   *Perf. 14x13½*
3710 A1431 1 l Dragonfly   .20
3711 A1431 2 l Mayfly   .25
3712 A1431 3 l Locust   .30
3713 A1431 4 l Stag beetle   .45
3714 A1431 5 l Carrion bee-tle   .55
3715 A1431 7 l Ant   .75
3716 A1431 20 l Bee   2.25
3717 A1431 50 l Praying mantis   5.75
     Nos. 3710-3717 (8)   10.50

   Issued: 7, 20 l, 9/25; 3, 50 l, 11/30; 1, 2, 4, 5 l, 12/15/93.

A1432

1992, Sept. 30   *Perf. 13*
3719 A1432 1 l blk, pink & rose   .90   .45
   Higher Institute of Architecture and Building, 50th anniv.

1992, Oct. 16   Litho.   *Perf. 13*
   Trees: No. 3720, Quercus mestensis. No. 3721, Aesculus hippocastanum. No. 3722, Quercus thracica. No. 3723, Pinus peuce. 2 l, Acer heldreichii. 3 l, Pyrus bulgarica.

A1433

3720 A1433 50s multicolored   .30   .20
3721 A1433 50s multicolored   .30   .20
3722 A1433 1 l multicolored   .60   .30
3723 A1433 1 l multicolored   .60   .30
3724 A1433 2 l multicolored   1.25   .65
3725 A1433 3 l multicolored   2.00   1.00
     Nos. 3720-3725 (6)   5.05   2.65

Ethnographical Museum, Cent. — A1434

1992, Oct. 23
3726 A1434 1 l multicolored   .90   .45

Tanker Bulgaria — A1435

1992, Oct. 30   Litho.   *Perf. 13*
3727 A1435 30s Freighter Bulga-ria   .20   .20
3728 A1435 50s Castor   .30   .20
3729 A1435 1 l Hero of Sevas-topol   .60   .30
3730 A1435 2 l shown   1.25   .65
3731 A1435 2 l Aleko Constanti-nov   1.25   .65
3732 A1435 3 l Varna   2.00   1.00
     Nos. 3727-3732 (6)   5.60   3.00
   Bulgarian Merchant Fleet, Cent.

Bulgaria, Member of the Council of Europe — A1436

1992, Nov. 6   Litho.   *Perf. 13*
3733 A1436 7 l multicolored   6.25   3.00

     Souvenir Sheet

4th World Congress of Popular Sports, Varna — A1437

1992, Nov. 17   Litho.   *Perf. 13*
3734 A1437 4 l multicolored   3.50

Christmas A1438

1992, Dec. 1   *Perf. 13½x13*
3735 A1438 1 l Santa Claus   .75
3736 A1438 7 l Madonna & Child   5.25

Wild Cats — A1439

1992, Dec. 18   Litho.   *Perf. 13*
3737 A1439 50s Panthera pardus   .25
3738 A1439 50s Acinonyx jubatus   .25
3739 A1439 1 l Panthera onca   .50
3740 A1439 2 l Panthera tigris   1.00

3741 A1439 2 l Felis concolor 1.00
3742 A1439 3 l Panthera leo 1.50
Nos. 3737-3742 (6) 4.50

Sports
A1440

1992, Dec. 18
3743 A1440 50s Baseball .35
3744 A1440 50s Cricket .35
3745 A1440 1 l Polo .75
3746 A1440 1 l Harness racing .75
3747 A1440 2 l Field hockey 1.50
3748 A1440 3 l Football 2.25
Nos. 3743-3748 (6) 5.95

Owls
A1441

1992, Dec. 23
3749 A1441 30s Aegolius funer-
eus .20
3750 A1441 50s Strix aluco .25
3751 A1441 1 l Asio otus .50
3752 A1441 2 l Otus scops 1.00
3753 A1441 2 l Asio flammeus 1.00
3754 A1441 3 l Tyto alba 1.50
Nos. 3749-3754 (6) 4.45

Nos. 3749, 3751, 3753-3754 are vert.

Paintings
Depicting
History of
Bulgaria
A1442

Artists: 50s, Dimiter Gyudzhenov. 1 l, 3 l,
Nikolai Pavlovich. 2 l, Dimiter Panchev. 4 l,
Mito Ganovski.

1992, Dec. 28
3755 A1442 50s multicolored .40
3756 A1442 1 l multicolored .75
3757 A1442 2 l multicolored 1.50
3758 A1442 3 l multicolored 2.25
Nos. 3755-3758 (4) 4.90
Souvenir Sheet
3759 A1442 4 l multicolored,
vert. 3.25

Archeological
Museum,
Cent. — A1443

1993 World
Biathlon
Championships,
Borovetz — A1444

1993, Jan. 1 Litho. Perf. 13x13½
3760 A1443 1 l multicolored .75

1993, Feb. 5
3761 A1444 1 l Woman aiming
rifle .75
3762 A1444 7 l Skiing 5.25

Neophit
Rilski, Birth
Bicent.
A1445

1993, Apr. 22 Litho. Perf. 13½x13
3763 A1445 1 l henna brn & ol bis .75

Contemporary
Art — A1446

Europa: 3 l, Sculpture of centaur, by Georgi
Chapkinov. 8 l, Painting of geometric forms, by
D. Bujukliski.

1993, Apr. 29 Perf. 13x13½
3764 A1446 3 l multicolored 2.25
3765 A1446 8 l multicolored 6.00

Fish
A1447

1993, June 29 Litho. Perf. 13
3766 A1447 1 l C.a.j. bi-
caudatus .75
3767 A1447 2 l Mollienesia ve-
lifera 1.50
3768 A1447 3 l Aphyosemion
bivittatum 2.25
3769 A1447 3 l Pterophyllum
eimekei 2.25
3770 A1447 4 l Symphysodon
discus 3.00
3771 A1447 8 l Trichogaster
leeri 6.00
Nos. 3766-3771 (6) 15.75

Fruit — A1448

1993, July 8 Perf. 13x13½
3772 A1448 1 l Malus domestica .20
3773 A1448 2 l Pyrus sativa .30
3774 A1448 2 l Persica vulgaris .30
3775 A1448 3 l Cydonia oblonga .45
3776 A1448 5 l Punica
granatum .90
3777 A1448 7 l Ficus carica 1.40
Nos. 3772-3777 (6) 3.55

Claudio Monteverdi (1567-1643),
Composer — A1449

1993, July 20 Litho. Perf. 13½x13
3778 A1449 1 l multicolored .75

17th
World
Summer
Games
for the
Deaf
A1450

1993, July 20 Perf. 13
3779 A1450 1 l shown .75
3780 A1450 2 l Swimming 1.50
3781 A1450 3 l Cycling 2.25
3782 A1450 4 l Tennis 3.00
Nos. 3779-3782 (4) 7.50
Souvenir Sheet
3783 A1450 5 l Soccer

Miniature Sheet

A1451

Council of Preslav, Cyrillic Alphabet in Bulgaria, 1100th Anniv.: a, Baptism of Christian
convert. b, Tsar Boris I (852-889). c, Tsar
Simeon (893-927). d, Battle between Bulgari-
ans and Byzantians.

1993, Sept. 16 Litho. Perf. 13½x13
3784 A1451 5 l Sheet of 4, #a.-d. 3.75

Alexander of
Battenberg (1857-
93), Prince of
Bulgaria — A1452

1993, Sept. 23 Perf. 13x13½
3785 A1452 3 l multicolored .50

Peter I.
Tchaikovsky
(1840-93)
A1453

1993, Sept. 30 Perf. 13½x13
3786 A1453 3 l multicolored .50

Small Arms — A1454

Isaac
Newton
(1643-1725)
A1455

1993, Oct. 22 Litho. Perf. 13½x14
3787 A1454 1 l Crossbow, 16th
cent. .20
3788 A1454 2 l Pistol, 18th cent. .35
3789 A1454 3 l Luger, 1908 .50
3790 A1454 3 l Pistol, 1873 .50
3791 A1454 5 l Rifle, 1938 .85
3792 A1454 7 l Kalashnikov,
1947 1.25
Nos. 3787-3792 (6) 3.65

1993, Oct. 29 Perf. 13½x13
3793 A1455 1 l multicolored .20

Organized
Philately in
Bulgaria,
Cent.
A1456

1993, Nov. 16
3794 A1456 1 l multicolored .20

Ecology
A1457

1993, Nov. 17
3795 A1457 1 l shown .20
3796 A1457 7 l Ecology 1.25

Game
Animals
A1458

1993, Nov. 25
3797 A1458 1 l Anas
platrhynchos .20
3798 A1458 1 l Phasianus
colchicus .20
3799 A1458 2 l Vulpes vulpes .35
3800 A1458 3 l Capreolus capreolus .50
3801 A1458 6 l Lepus europaeus 1.00
3802 A1458 8 l Sus scrofa 1.40
Nos. 3797-3802 (6) 3.65

Christmas
A1459

Signs of Zodiac on sundial: No. 3803a, Taurus, Gemini, Cancer. b, Libra, Virgo, Leo.
No. 3804a, Aquarius, Pisces, Aries. b, Capricorn, Sagittarius, Scorpio.

1993, Dec. 1
3803 A1459 1 l Pair, #a.-b. .35
3804 A1459 7 l Pair, #a.-b. 2.50

When placed together, Nos. 3803-3804
form a complete sundial.

Regional Folk Costumes for
Men
A1460 A1461

1993, Dec. 16 Litho. Perf. 13½x14
3805 A1460 1 l Sofia .20
3806 A1461 1 l Plovdiv .20
3807 A1460 2 l Belogradchik .25
3808 A1460 3 l Shumen .30
3809 A1461 3 l Oryakhovitsa .30
3810 A1461 8 l Kurdzhali .90
Nos. 3805-3810 (6) 2.15

1994 Winter
Olympics,
Lillehammer
A1462

1994, Feb. 8   *Perf. 13*
3811 A1462   1 l   Freestlye skiing   .20
3812 A1462·2 l   Speed skating   .25
3813 A1462   3 l   2-Man luge   .30
3814 A1462   4 l   Hockey   .45
    Nos. 3811-3814 (4)   1.20
Souvenir Sheet
3815 A1462   5 l   Downhill skiing   .60

Nikolai
Pavlovich
(1835-94)
A1463

1994, Feb. 16   *Perf. 13½x13*
3816 A1463   3 l   multicolored   .30

Dinosaurs — A1464

1994, Apr. 27   Litho.   *Perf. 13*
3817 A1464   2 l   Plesiosaurus   .20
3818 A1464   3 l   Iguanodon   .20
3819 A1464   3 l   Archaeopteryx   .20
3820 A1464   4 l   Edmontonia   .20
3821 A1464   5 l   Styracosaurus   .20
3822 A1464   7 l   Tyrannosaurus
                Rex   .30
    Nos. 3817-3822 (6)   1.30

1994 World Cup Soccer
Championships, US — A1465

Players in championships of : 3 l, Chile, 1962. 6 l, England, 1966. 7 l, Mexico, 1970. 9 l, West Germany, 1974. No. 3827a, Mexico, 1986, vert. b, US, 1994.

1994, Apr. 28
3823 A1465   3 l   multicolored   .20
3824 A1465   6 l   multicolored   .25
3825 A1465   7 l   multicolored   .30
3826 A1465   9 l   multicolored   .35
    Nos. 3823-3826 (4)   1.10
Souvenir Sheet
3827 A1465   5 l   Sheet of 2, #a.-b.   .50

For No. 3827 with inscription reading up along the left margin, see No. 3851.

Europa
A1466

European Discoveries: 3 l, Axis of symmetry. 15 l, Electrocardiogram.

1994, Apr. 29   Litho.   *Perf. 13½*
3828 A1466   3 l   multicolored   .20
3829 A1466   15 l   multicolored   .60

Boris Hristov (1914-93) — A1467

1994, May 18   Litho.   *Perf. 13*
3830 A1467   3 l   brown & bister   .20

Cricetus
Cricetus
A1468

Designs: 3 l, In nest. 7 l, Emerging from burrow. 10 l, Standing on hind legs. 15 l, Finding berry.

1994, Sept. 23   Litho.   *Perf. 13*
3831 A1468   3 l   multicolored   .25
3832 A1468   7 l   multicolored   .35
3833 A1468   10 l   multicolored   .45
3834 A1468   15 l   multicolored   .65
    Nos. 3831-3834 (4)   1.70

World Wildlife Fund.

Space
Program — A1469

1994, Nov. 4   Litho.   *Perf. 13*
3835 A1469   3 l   multicolored   .20

Intl. Olympic
Committee,
Cent. — A1470

1994, Nov. 7
3836 A1470   3 l   multicolored   .20

Icons — A1471

Christmas
A1472

1994, Nov. 24   Litho.   *Perf. 13x13½*
3837 A1471   2 l   Christ   .20
3838 A1471   3 l   Christ, the healer   .20

3839 A1471   5 l   Crucifixion   .20
3840 A1471   7 l   Archangel
                Michael   .25
3841 A1471   8 l   Sts. Cyril,
                Methodius   .25
3842 A1471   15 l   Madonna &
                Child   .45
    Nos. 3837-3842 (6)   1.55

1994, Dec. 1
3843 A1472   3 l   Ancient coin   .20
3844 A1472   15 l   Coin, diff.   1.00

Roses
A1473

1994, Dec. 12   *Perf. 13*
Color of Rose
3845 A1473   2 l   yellow   .20
3846 A1473   3 l   rose red   .20
3847 A1473   5 l   white   .20
3848 A1473   7 l   salmon   .20
3849 A1473   10 l   carmine   .30
3850 A1473   15 l   orange & yellow   .40
    Nos. 3845-3850 (6)   1.50
Souvenir Sheet
No. 3827 with Additional Inscription in
Left Sheet Margin
1994, Dec. 15   Litho.   *Perf. 13*
3851 A1465   5 l   Sheet of 2, #a.-b.   .55

Trams — A1474

1994, Dec. 29
3852 A1474   1 l   Model 1912   .20
3853 A1474   2 l   Model 1928   .20
3854 A1474   3 l   Model 1931   .20
3855 A1474   5 l   Model 1942   .20
3856 A1474   8 l   Model 1951   .25
3857 A1474   10 l   Model 1961   .30
    Nos. 3852-3857 (6)   1.35

Vassil Petleshkov (1845-76),
Revolutionary — A1475

1995, Feb. 27   Litho.   *Perf. 13½x13*
3858 A1475   3 l   multicolored   .20

End of World War
II, 50th
Anniv. — A1476

Europa: 15 l, Dove holding olive branch standing on gun barrel.

1995, May 3   Litho.   *Perf. 13*
3859 A1476   3 l   multicolored   .20
3860 A1476   15 l   multicolored   .45

Souvenir Sheet

Men's
World
Volleyball
League,
Cent.
A1477

Designs: a, 10 l, Player digging ball. b, 15 l, Player spiking ball, vert.

1995, May 25   Litho.   *Perf. 13*
3861 A1477   Sheet of 2, #a.-b.   .80

Souvenir Sheet

European Nature Conservation
Year — A1478

Designs: a, 10 l, Pancratium maritimum. b, 15 l, Aquila heliaca. Illustration reduced.

1995, June 23   Litho.   *Perf. 13*
3862 A1478   Sheet of 2, #a.-b.   2.00

Antarctic Wildlife — A1479

1 l, Euphausia superba. 2 l, Chaenocephalus. 3 l, Physeter catodon. 5 l, Leptonychotes weddelli. 8 l, Stercorarius skua. 10 l, Aptenodytes forsteri, vert.

1995, June 29
3863 A1479   1 l   multicolored   .20
3864 A1479   2 l   multicolored   .20
3865 A1479   3 l   multicolored   .20
3866 A1479   5 l   multicolored   .20
3867 A1479   8 l   multicolored   .25
3868 A1479   10 l   multicolored   .30
    Nos. 3863-3868 (6)   1.35

Stephan Stambolov (1854-95),
Revolutionary Leader,
Politician — A1480

1995, July 6   Litho.   *Perf. 13*
3869 A1480   3 l   multicolored   .20

1996 Summer Olympics, Atlanta A1481

Designs: 3 l, Pole vault. 7 l, High jump. 10 l, Women's long jump. 15 l, Track.

1995, July 17
3870	A1481	3 l multicolored	.20
3871	A1481	7 l multicolored	.20
3872	A1481	10 l multicolored	.30
3873	A1481	15 l multicolored	.45
	Nos. 3870-3873 (4)		1.15

Legumes — A1482

1995, July 31
3874	A1482	2 l	Pisum sativum	.20
3875	A1482	3 l	Glicine	.20
3876	A1482	3 l	Cicer arietinum	.20
3877	A1482	4 l	Spinacia oler-acea	.20
3878	A1482	5 l	Arachis hypogaea	.20
3879	A1482	15 l	Lens esculenta	.45
	Nos. 3874-3879 (6)			1.45

Organized Tourism in Bulgaria, Cent. — A1483

1995, Aug. 21   Litho.   Perf. 13
3880	A1483	3 l multicolored	.20

Vassil Zahariev (1895-1971), Graphic Artist — A1484

Designs: 2 l, Woodcut of a man. 3 l, Woodcut of building in valley. 5 l, Self-portrait. 10 l, Carving of two women.

1995, Sept. 4   Litho.   Perf. 13
3881	A1484	2 l multicolored	.20
3882	A1484	3 l multicolored	.20
3883	A1484	5 l multicolored	.20
3884	A1484	10 l multicolored	.30
	Nos. 3881-3884 (4)		.90

UN, 50th Anniv. A1485

1995, Sept. 12
3885	A1485	3 l multicolored	.20

Airplanes — A1486

1995, Sept. 26   Litho.   Perf. 13
3886	A1486	3 l	PO-2	.20
3887	A1486	5 l	Li-2	.20
3888	A1486	7 l	JU52-3M	.20
3889	A1486	10 l	FV-58	.30
	Nos. 3886-3889 (4)			.90

Motion Pictures, Cent. — A1487

Designs: 2 l, Charlie Chaplin, Mickey Mouse. 3 l, Marilyn Monroe, Marlene Dietrich. 5 l, Humphrey Bogart. 8 l, Sophia Loren, Liza Minnelli. 10 l, Toshiro Mifune. 15 l, Katya Paskaleva.

1995, Oct. 16
3890	A1487	2 l multicolored	.20
3891	A1487	3 l multicolored	.20
3892	A1487	5 l multicolored	.20
3893	A1487	8 l multicolored	.25
3894	A1487	10 l multicolored	.30
3895	A1487	15 l multicolored	.45
	Nos. 3890-3895 (6)		1.60

Minerals A1488

1995, Nov. 20   Litho.   Perf. 13
3896	A1488	1 l	Agate	.20
3897	A1488	2 l	Sphalerite	.20
3898	A1488	5 l	Calcite	.20
3899	A1488	7 l	Quartz	.20
3900	A1488	8 l	Pyromorphite	.25
3901	A1488	10 l	Almandine	.30
	Nos. 3896-3901 (6)			1.35

Christmas A1489

1995, Dec. 8   Litho.   Perf. 13
3902	A1489	3 l	shown	.20
3903	A1489	15 l	Magi	.45

Southern Fruit, by Cyril Tsonev (1896-1961) — A1490

1996, Jan. 25   Litho.   Perf. 13
3904	A1490	3 l multicolored	.20

Martin Luther (1483-1546) — A1491

1996, Feb. 5
3905	A1491	3 l multicolored	.20

Historic Buildings A1492

Monasteries: 3 l, Preobragenie. 5 l, Arapovsky. 10 l, Drianovo. 20 l, Bachkovo. 25 l, Troyan. 40 l, Zografski.

1996, Feb. 28   Perf. 14x13½
3906	A1492	3 l	green	.20
3907	A1492	5 l	red	.20
3908	A1492	10 l	blue	.30
3909	A1492	20 l	yellow orange	.60
3910	A1492	25 l	brown	.75
3911	A1492	40 l	purple	1.25
	Nos. 3906-3911 (6)			3.30

5th Meeting of European Bank for Reconstruction and Development A1493

1996, Apr. 15   Litho.   Perf. 13
3912	A1493	7 l	shown	.20
3913	A1493	30 l	Building, diff.	.50

Conifers A1494

Designs: 5 l, Taxus baccata. 8 l, Abies alba. 10 l, Picea abies. 20 l, Pinus silvestris. 25 l, Pinus heldreichii. 40 l, Juniperus excelsa.

1996, Apr. 23   Perf. 13½x13
3914	A1494	5 l multicolored	.20
3915	A1494	8 l multicolored	.20
3916	A1494	10 l multicolored	.20
3917	A1494	20 l multicolored	.30
3918	A1494	25 l multicolored	.45
3919	A1494	40 l multicolored	.65
	Nos. 3914-3919 (6)		2.00

A1495

A1496

10 l, People in distress. 40 l, Khristo Botev (1848-1876), poet, patriot, horiz.

1996, May 1   Perf. 13
3920	A1495	10 l multicolored	.20
3921	A1495	40 l multicolored	.65

April Uprising, death of Khristo Botev, 120th anniv.

1996, May 6
Uniforms: 5 l, Light brown dress uniform. 8 l, Brown combat, helmet. 10 l, Brown uniform, holding gun with fixed bayonet. 20 l, Early red, blue dress uniform. 25 l, Officer's early green dress uniform. 40 l, Soldier's green uniform.

1996, May 6
3922	A1496	5 l multicolored	.20
3923	A1496	8 l multicolored	.20
3924	A1496	10 l multicolored	.20
3925	A1496	20 l multicolored	.30
3926	A1496	25 l multicolored	.45
3927	A1496	40 l multicolored	.65
	Nos. 3922-3927 (6)		2.00

Republic of Bulgaria, 50th Anniv. — A1497

1996, May 13   Litho.   Perf. 13½
3928	A1497	10 l multicolored	.20

Famous Women A1498

Europa: 10 l, Elisaveta Bagriana (1893-1990), poet. 40 l, Katia Popova (1924-66), opera singer.

1996, May 29   Litho.   Perf. 13
3929	A1498	10 l multicolored	.25
	Complete booklet, 5 #3929		1.40
3930	A1498	40 l multicolored	.95
	Complete booklet, 5 #3930		5.00

A1499

A1500

10 l, Soccer player. 15 l, Soccer player, diff.

1996, June 4
Souvenir Sheet
3931	A1499	Sheet of 2, #a.-b.	.60

Euro '96, European Soccer Championships, Great Britain.

1996, July 4
3932	A1500	5 l	Wrestling	.20
3933	A1500	8 l	Boxing	.20
3934	A1500	10 l	Women's shot put	.25
3935	A1500	25 l	Women sculling	.60
	Nos. 3932-3935 (4)			1.25

Souvenir Sheet

3936 A1500 15 l Pierre de Coubertin   .40

1996 Summer Olympic Games, Atlanta. Olymphilex '96 (#3936).

Crabs
A1501

Designs: 5 l, Gammarus arduus. 10 l, Asellus aquaticus. 12 l, Astacus astacus. 25 l, Palaemon serratus. 30 l, Cumella limicola. 40 l, Carcinus mediterraneus.

1996, July 30

3937	A1501	5 l	multicolored	.20
3938	A1501	10 l	multicolored	.25
3939	A1501	12 l	multicolored	.30
3940	A1501	25 l	multicolored	.60
3941	A1501	30 l	multicolored	.70
3942	A1501	40 l	multicolored	.95
		Nos. 3937-3942 (6)		3.00

Francisco Goya (1746-1828)
A1502

Entire paintings or details: 8 l, Young Woman with a Letter. 26 l, The Second of May, 1808. 40 l, Neighboring Women on a Balcony.

No. 3947: a, 10 l, The Clothed Maja. b, 15 l, The Naked Maja.

1996, July 9   Litho.   Perf. 13

3943	A1502	5 l	multicolored	.20
3944	A1502	8 l	multicolored	.20
3945	A1502	26 l	multicolored	.60
3946	A1502	40 l	multicolored	1.00
		Nos. 3943-3946 (4)		2.00

Souvenir Sheet
Perf. 13½x13

3947 A1502 Sheet of 2, #a.-b.   .65

No. 3947 contains two 54x29mm stamps.

Souvenir Sheet

St. John of Rila (876-946), Founder of Rila Monastery — A1503

1996, Sept. 3

3948 A1503 10 l multicolored   .25

Bulgarian Renaissance Houses
A1504

Various multi-level houses.

1996, Sept. 12   Litho.   Perf. 14x13½
Background Color

3949	A1504	10 l	buff	.20
3950	A1504	15 l	orange yellow	.20
3951	A1504	30 l	yellow green	.30
3952	A1504	50 l	red lilac	.45
3953	A1504	60 l	apple green	.55
3954	A1504	100 l	green blue	.95
		Nos. 3949-3954 (6)		2.65

Steam Locomotives — A1505

1996, Sept. 24   Perf. 13

3955	A1505	5 l	1836	.20
3956	A1505	10 l	1847	.20
3957	A1505	12 l	1848	.20
3958	A1505	26 l	1876	.25
		Nos. 3955-3958 (4)		.85

Natl. Gallery of Art, Cent.
A1506

1996, Oct. 14   Litho.   Perf. 13

3959 A1506 15 l multicolored   .20

Defeat of Byzantine Army by Tsar Simeon, 1100th Anniv. — A1507

10 l, Sword hilt, soldiers on horseback. 40 l, Sword blade, dagger, fallen soldiers.

1996, Oct. 21

3960	A1507	10 l	multicolored	.20
3961	A1507	40 l	multicolored	.35
a.		Pair, #3960-3961		.55

No. 3961 is a continuous design.

UNICEF, 50th Anniv. — A1508

Children's drawings: 7 l, Diver, fish. 15 l, Circus performers. 20 l, Boy, artist's pallete. 60 l, Women seated at table.

1996, Nov. 18   Litho.   Perf. 13

3962	A1508	7 l	multicolored	.20
3963	A1508	15 l	multicolored	.30
3964	A1508	20 l	multicolored	.40
3965	A1508	60 l	multicolored	1.25
		Nos. 3962-3965 (4)		2.15

A1509

A1510

1996, Nov. 26

| 3966 | A1509 | 15 l | Candles on tree | .30 |
| 3967 | A1509 | 60 l | Church | 1.25 |

Christmas.

1996, Dec. 11   Litho.   Perf. 13

Painting of Old Bulgarian Town, by Tsanko Lavrenov (1896-1978).

3968 A1510 15 l multicolored   .30

Puppies
A1511

1997, Feb. 25   Litho.   Perf. 13

3969	A1511	5 l	Pointer	.20
3970	A1511	7 l	Chow chow	.20
3971	A1511	25 l	Carakachan dog	.30
3972	A1511	50 l	Basset hound	.60
		Nos. 3969-3972 (4)		1.30

Alexander Graham Bell (1847-1922) — A1512

1997, Mar. 10

3973 A1512 30 l multicolored   .40

Ivan Milev (1897-1927), Painter — A1513

Stories and Legends — A1514

Paintings: 5 l, Boy drinking from jar. 15 l, Person with head bowed holding up hand. 30 l, Woman. 60 l, Woman carrying child.

1997, Mar. 20

3974	A1513	5 l	multicolored	.20
3975	A1513	15 l	multicolored	.20
3976	A1513	30 l	multicolored	.50
3977	A1513	60 l	multicolored	1.00
		Nos. 3974-3977 (4)		1.90

1997, Apr. 14

Europa: 120 l, "March" lady in folk costume, symbol of spring. 600 l, St. George.

| 3978 | A1514 | 120 l | multicolored | .20 |
| 3979 | A1514 | 600 l | multicolored | 1.00 |

Konstantin Kissimov (1897-1965), Actor — A1515

1997, Apr. 16

3980 A1515 120 l multicolored   .20

1997, Apr. 21

A1516   A1517

3981 A1516 60 l multicolored   .20

Heinrich von Stephan (1831-97).

1997, May 2   Perf. 13½

Historical Landmarks: 80 l, Nessebar. 200 l, Ivanovo Rock Churches. 300 l, Boyana Church. 500 l, Madara horseman. 600 l, Tomb of Sveshtari. 1000 l, Tomb of Kazanlak.

3982	A1517	80 l	brn & multi	.20
3983	A1517	200 l	pur & multi	.20
3984	A1517	300 l	bis & multi	.30
3985	A1517	500 l	grn & multi	.45
3986	A1517	600 l	yel & multi	.55
3987	A1517	1000 l	org & multi	1.00
		Nos. 3982-3987 (6)		2.70

Composers
A1518

Designs: a, Gaetano Donizetti (1797-1848). b, Franz Schubert (1797-1828). c, Felix Mendelssohn (1809-1847). d, Johannes Brahms (1833-1897).

1997, May 29   Litho.   Perf. 13½x13

3988 A1518 120 l Sheet of 4, #a.-d.   1.10

Plants in Bulgaria's Red Book — A1519

Designs: 80 l, Trifolium rubens. 100 l, Tulipa hageri. 120 l, Inula spiraeifolia. 200 l, Paeonia tenuifolia.

1997, June 24   Perf. 13

3989	A1519	80 l	multicolored	.20
3990	A1519	100 l	multicolored	.20
3991	A1519	120 l	multicolored	.20
3992	A1519	200 l	multicolored	.25
		Nos. 3989-3992 (4)		.85

A1520

A1521

1997, June 29 Litho. Perf. 13
3993 A1520 120 l multicolored .20
Civil aviation in Bulgaria, 50th anniv.

1997, July 3
3994 A1521 120 l multicolored .20
Evlogy Georgiev (1819-97), banker, philanthopist.

Sofia '97, Modern Pentathlon World Championship — A1522

60 l, Equestrian cross-country, running. 80 l, Fencing, swimming. 100 l, Running, women's fencing. 120 l, Men's shooting, diving. 200 l, Equestrian jumping, women's shooting.

1997, July 25
3995 A1522 60 l multicolored .20
3996 A1522 80 l multicolored .20
3997 A1522 100 l multicolored .20
3998 A1522 120 l multicolored .20
3999 A1522 200 l multicolored .20
      Nos. 3995-3999 (5) 1.00

City of Moscow, 850th Anniv. — A1523

1997, July 30
4000 A1523 120 l multicolored .20
No. 4000 is printed se-tenant with label for Moscow '97 Intl. Philatelic Exhibition.

Diesel Engine, Cent. A1524

1997, Sept. 8 Litho. Perf. 13½x13
4001 A1524 80 l Boat .20
4002 A1524 100 l Tractor .20
4003 A1524 120 l Truck .20
4004 A1524 200 l Forklift .30
      Nos. 4001-4004 (4) .90

43rd General Assembly of Atlantic Club of Bulgaria — A1525

Designs: a, Goddess Tyche. b, Eagle on sphere. c, Building, lion statue, denomination UL. d, Building, denomination UR.

1997, Oct. 2 Perf. 13
4005 A1525 120 l Sheet of 4, #a.-d. .55

Miguel de Cervantes (1547-1616) — A1526

1997, Oct. 15
4006 A1526 120 l multicolored .20

Asen Raztsvetnikov (1897-1951), Poet, Writer — A1527

1997, Nov. 5
4007 A1527 120 l multicolored .20

Tsar Samuel (d. 1014), Ascension to Throne, 1000th Anniv. A1528

1997, Nov. 18 Perf. 13½x13
4008 A1528 120 l Inscription .20
4009 A1528 600 l Tsar, soldiers .85
  a. Pair, #4008-4009 1.00

Christmas A1529

Designs: 120 l, Snow-covered houses, stars inside shape of Christmas tree, animals. 600 l, Nativity scene.

1997, Dec. 8 Perf. 13x13½
4010 A1529 120 l multicolored .20
4011 A1529 600 l multicolored .85

1998 Winter Olympic Games, Nagano A1530

Designs: 60 l, Speed skating. 80 l, Skiing. 120 l, Biathlon. 600 l, Pairs figure skating.

1997, Dec. 17 Perf. 13½x13
4012 A1530 60 l multicolored .20
4013 A1530 80 l multicolored .20
4014 A1530 120 l multicolored .20
4015 A1530 600 l multicolored .85
      Nos. 4012-4015 (4) 1.45
For overprint see No. 4029.

Coat of Arms of Bulgaria A1531

1997, Dec. 22 Litho. Perf. 13½x13
4016 A1531 120 l multicolored .35

Souvenir Sheet

Bulgarian Space Program, 25th Anniv. — A1532

Illustration reduced.

1997, Dec. 22 Perf. 13
4017 A1532 120 l multicolored .35

Christo Botev (1848-76), Revolutionary, Poet — A1533

Bertolt Brecht (1898-1956), Playwright A1534

1998, Jan. 6 Litho. Perf. 13
4018 A1533 120 l multicolored .20

1998, Feb. 10
4019 A1534 120 l multicolored .20

Bulgarian Telegraph Agency, Cent. A1535

1998, Feb. 13
4020 A1535 120 l multicolored .20

Illustrations by Alexander Bozhinov (1878-1968) A1536

Designs: a, Bird wearing bonnet. b, Black bird wearing hat. c, Grandfather Frost, children. d, Girl among flowers looking upward at rain.

1998, Feb. 24 Perf. 13½x13
4021 A1536 120 l Sheet of 4, #a.-d. .60

A1537

Easter — A1538

1998, Feb. 27 Perf. 13
4022 A1537 120 l Prince Alexander .20
4023 A1537 600 l Monument .65
  a. Pair, #4022-4023 .80
Bulgarian independence from Turkey, 120th anniv.

1998, Mar. 27 Litho. Perf. 13
4024 A1538 120 l multicolored .20

Bulgarian Olympic Committee, 75th Anniv. — A1539

1998, Mar. 30
4025 A1539 120 l multicolored .20

PHARE (Intl. Post and Telecommunications Program) — A1540

1998, Apr. 24 Litho. Perf. 13
4026 A1540 120 l multicolored .35

National Days and Festivals — A1541

Europa: 120 l, Girls with flowers, "Enyovden." 600 l, Masked men with bells, "Kukery."

1998, Apr. 27
4027 A1541 120 l multicolored .35
4028 A1541 600 l multicolored 1.60

No. 4014 Overprinted

1998, Apr. 29   *Perf. 13½x13*
4029 A1530 120 l multicolored   2.50

Dante and Virgil in Hell, by Eugene Delacroix (1798-1863) A1542

1998, Apr. 30
4030 A1542 120 l multicolored   .35

A1543

1998, May 15   *Perf. 13*
4031 A1543 120 l multicolored   .20
Soccer Team of Central Sports Club of the Army, 50th anniv.

1998, May 25
Cats: 60 l, European tabby. 80 l, Siamese. 120 l, Exotic shorthair. 600 l, Birman.
4032 A1544   60 l multicolored   .20
4033 A1544   80 l multicolored   .20
4034 A1544 120 l multicolored   .20
4035 A1544 600 l multicolored   1.10
   Nos. 4032-4035 (4)   1.70

A1544

Are You Jealous?, by Paul Gauguin (1848-1903) — A1545

1998, June 4
4036 A1545 120 l multicolored   .30

Neophit Hylendarsky-Bozvely (1745-1848), Priest, Author — A1546

1998, June 4
4037 A1546 120 l multicolored   .35

1998 World Cup Soccer Championships, France — A1547

Lion mascot with soccer ball, various stylized soccer plays.

1998, June 10
4038 A1547   60 l multicolored   .20
4039 A1547   80 l multicolored   .20
4040 A1547 120 l multicolored   .35
4041 A1547 600 l multicolored   1.60
   Nos. 4038-4041 (4)   2.35
     Souvenir Sheet
4042 A1547 120 l Mascot, Eiffel Tower   .35

A. Aleksandrov's Flight on Mir, 10th Anniv. — A1548

1998, June 17   *Litho.*   *Perf. 13*
4043 A1548 120 l multicolored   .20

Lisbon '98 — A1549

Designs: a, Map showing route around Cape of Good Hope, Vasco da Gama (1460-1524). b, Sailing ship, map of Africa.

1998, June 23
4044 A1549 600 l Sheet of 2, #a.-b. + 2 labels   1.40

Helicopters — A1550

80 l, Focke Wulf FW61, 1937. 100 l, Sikorsky R-4, 1943. 120 l, Mil Mi-12 (V-12), 1970. 200 l, McDonnell-Douglas MD-900, 1995.

1998, July 7   *Litho.*   *Perf. 13*
4045 A1550   80 l multicolored   .20   .20
4046 A1550 100 l multicolored   .25   .25
4047 A1550 120 l multicolored   .30   .30
4048 A1550 200 l multicolored   .45   .45
   Nos. 4045-4048 (4)   1.20   1.20

     Souvenir Sheet

Intl. Year of the Ocean — A1551

Monachus monachus. Illustration reduced.

1998, July 14   *Litho.*   *Perf. 13*
4049 A1551 120 l multicolored   .35   .30

Dimitr Talev (1898-1966), Writer — A1552

1998, Sept. 14
4050 A1552 180 l multicolored   .20   .20

A1553

1998, Sept. 22
4051 A1553 180 l multicolored   .20   .20
Declaration of Bulgarian Independence, 90th anniv.

1998, Sept. 24
Butterflies, flowers: 60 l, Limenitis redukta, ligularia sibirica. 180 l, Vanessa cardui, anthemis macrantha. 200 l, Vanessa atalanta, trachelium jacquinii. 600 l, Anthocharis gruneri, geranium tuberosum.
4052 A1554   60 l multicolored   .20   .20
4053 A1554 180 l multicolored   .20   .20
4054 A1554 200 l multicolored   .25   .25
4055 A1554 600 l multicolored   .75   .75
   Nos. 4052-4055 (4)   1.40   1.40

A1554

Christo Smirnenski (1898-1923), Poet — A1555

1998, Sept. 29
4056 A1555 180 l multicolored   .20   .20

Universal Declaration of Human Rights, 50th Anniv. — A1556

1998, Oct. 26   *Litho.*   *Perf. 13*
4057 A1556 180 l multicolored   .20   .20

Giordano Bruno (1548-1600), Philosopher — A1557

1998, Oct. 26
4058 A1557 180 l multicolored   .20   .20

Greetings Stamps A1558

#4059, Man diving through flaming heart, "I Love You." #4060, Baby emerging from chalice, "Happy Birthday." #4061, Grape vine, bird, wine coming from vat, "Happy Holiday." #4062, Waiter carrying tray with glass & ttle of wine, "Happy Name Day."

1998, Nov. 11
4059 A1558 180 l multi   .20   .20
4060 A1558 180 l multi, vert.   .20   .20
4061 A1558 180 l multi, vert.   .20   .20
4062 A1558 180 l multi, vert.   .20   .20
   Nos. 4059-4062 (4)   .80   .80

Christmas A1559

1998, Dec. 2   *Litho.*   *Perf. 13½x13*
4063 A1559 180 l multicolored   .20   .20

Ivan Geshov (1849-1924), Finance Minister — A1560

1999, Feb. 8   *Litho.*   *Perf. 13*
4064 A1560 180 l multicolored   .20   .20

Third Bulgarian State, 120th
Anniv. — A1561

Designs: a, Reflection of National Assembly. b, Men, paper, Council of Ministers. c, Scales of Justice, Supreme Court of Appeal. d, Coins, Bulgarian Natl. Bank. e, Soldiers, Bulgarian Army. f, Lion, lightpost, Sofia, capital of Bulgaria.

1999, Feb. 10
4065 A1561 180 l Sheet of 6,
    #a.-f.   1.25 1.25

Bulgarian Culture and Art — A1562

180 l, Georgy Karakashev (1899-1970), set designer. 200 l, Bencho Obreshkov (1899-1970), artist. 300 l, Assen Naydenov (1899-1995), conductor. 600 l, Pancho Vladiguerov (1899-1978), composer.

1999, Mar. 12   Litho.   **Perf. 13**
4066 A1562 180 l multicolored   .20 .20
4067 A1562 200 l multicolored   .20 .20
4068 A1562 300 l multicolored   .30 .30
4069 A1562 600 l multicolored   .50 .35
    Nos. 4066-4069 (4)   1.20 1.05

Bulgaria
'99 — 4069A

Parrots: a, Trichoglossus haematodus. b, Platycercus eximius. c, Melopsittacus undulatus. d, Ara chloroptera.

1999, Mar. 15   Litho.   **Perf. 13x13¼**
    Sheet of 4
4069A A1562a 600 l #a.-d.   18.00 15.00

NATO, 50th Anniv. — A1563

1999, Mar. 29   Litho.   **Perf. 13**
4070 A1563 180 l multicolored   .20 .20

Easter
A1564

1999, Apr. 1
4071 A1564 180 l multicolored   .20 .20

National Parks and Nature
Preserves — A1565

Europa: 180 l, Duck, pond, Ropotamo Preserve. 600 l, Ibex, waterfall, Central Balkan Natl. Park.

1999, Apr. 13   Litho.   **Perf. 13**
4072 A1565 180 l multicolored   .20 .20
4073 A1565 600 l multicolored   .65 .65

IBRA '99, Intl. Philatelic Exhibition,
Nuremberg — A1566

1999, Apr. 15
4074 A1566 600 l multicolored   .65 .65
No. 4074 is divided in half by vert. simulated perfs. and was issued in sheets of 3 + 3 labels.

Council of Europe, 50th
Anniv. — A1567

1999, May 5   Litho.   **Perf. 13**
4075 A1567 180 l multicolored   .20 .20

Foreign Culture and Art — A1567a

Designs: 180 l, Honoré de Balzac (1799-1850), novelist. 200 l, Johann Wolfgang von Goethe (1749-1832), poet. 250 l, Aleksandr Pushkin (1799-1837), poet. 600 l, Diego Velázquez (1599-1660), painter.

1999, May 18
4076   A1567a 180 l multi   .20 .20
4077   A1567a 200 l multi   .20 .20
4078   A1567a 300 l multi   .30 .30
4078A A1567a 600 l multi   .65 .65
    Nos. 4076-4078A (4)   1.35 1.35

Bicycles — A1568

Designs: 180 l, Large front-wheeled bicycle, 1867. 200 l, Multi-gear bicycle. 300 l, BMX racing bike. 600 l, Mountain racing bike.

1999, June 1   Litho.   **Perf. 13¼**
4079 A1568 180 l multicolored   .20 .20
4080 A1568 200 l multicolored   .20 .20
4081 A1568 300 l multicolored   .35 .35
4082 A1568 600 l multicolored   .65 .65
    Nos. 4079-4082 (4)   1.40 1.40

Sts. Cyril and
Methodius
A1569

Various paintings of Sts. Cyril and Methodius standing side by side with denomination at: a, UL. b, UR. c, LL. d, LR.

1999, June 15   Litho.   **Perf. 13¼**
4083 A1569 600 l Sheet of 4,
    #a.-d.   12.50 10.00
Bulgaria '99, European Philatelic Exhibition.

Flowers
A1570

a, Oxytropis urumovii. b, Campanula transsilvanica. c, Iris reichenbachii. d, Gentiana punctata.

1999, July 20
4084 A1570 60s Sheet of 4,
    #a.-d.   10.00 10.00
Bulgaria '99, European Philatelic Exhibition.

Mushrooms
A1571

Designs: a, 10s, Russula virescens. b, 18s, Agaricus campestris. c, 20s, Hygrophorus russula. d, 60s, Lepista nuda.

1999, July 27
4085 A1571   Sheet of 4, #a.-d.   2.75 2.75

Souvenir Sheet

Total Solar Eclipse, Aug. 11,
1999 — A1572

Illustration reduced.

1999, Aug. 10   **Perf. 13**
4086 A1572 20s multicolored   .50 .50

A1573

A1574

1999, Sept. 23   Litho.   **Perf. 13**
4087 A1573 18s multicolored   .20 .20
Organized agrarian movement in Bulgaria, 100th anniv.

  Souvenir Sheet of 4
1999, Oct. 5   **Perf. 13x13½**
Lion (portion) and: a, No. J2. b, Dove and letter. c, Eastern hemisphere. d, Western hemisphere.
4088 A1574 60s #a.-d.   8.00 7.00
Bulgaria '99, UPU 125th anniv.

Birds, Eggs and
Nests — A1575

8s, Lanius minor. 18s, Turdus viscivorus. 20s, Prunella modularis. 60s, Emberiza hortulana.

1999, Oct. 6   **Perf. 13**
4089 A1575 8s multicolored   .20 .20
4090 A1575 18s multicolored   .20 .20
4091 A1575 20s multicolored   .20 .20
4092 A1575 60s multicolored   .70 .70
    Nos. 4089-4092 (4)   1.30 1.30

Endangered Turtles — A1576

10s, Testudo graeca. 18s, Emys orbicularis. 30s, Testudo hermanni. 60s, Mauremys caspica.

1999, Oct. 8   **Perf. 13**
4093 A1576 10s multicolored   .20 .20
4094 A1576 18s multicolored   .20 .20
4095 A1576 30s multicolored   .40 .40
4096 A1576 60s multicolored   .75 .75
    Nos. 4093-4096 (4)   1.55 1.55

Olympic
Sports
A1577

1999, Oct. 10
4097 A1577 10s Boxing   .20 .20
4098 A1577 20s High jump   .20 .20
4099 A1577 30s Weight lifting   .35 .35
4100 A1577 60s Wrestling   .65 .65
    Nos. 4097-4100 (4)   1.40 1.40

Fountains — A1578

Fountains from: 1s, Sopotski Monastery. 8s, Karlovo. 10s, Koprivshchitsa. 18s, Sandanski. 20s, Karlovo. 60s, Sokolski Monastery.

1999   **Litho.**   **Perf. 13½x14**
Fountain Color
4101 A1578 1s bister   .20   .20
4102 A1578 8s green   .20   .20
4103 A1578 10s brown   .20   .20
4104 A1578 18s light blue   .30   .30
4105 A1578 20s dark blue   .35   .35
4109 A1578 60s brown   1.00 1.00
       Nos. 4101-4109 (6)   2.25 2.25

Issued: 8s, 60s, 11/22/99; others, 1999. This is an expanding set. Numbers may change.

Police Trade Unions' European Council, 10th Anniv. — A1579

1999, Nov. 8   **Litho.**   **Perf. 13**
4113 A1579 18s multi   .30   .30

A1580   A1581

Various gold artifacts from Panagyurishte.

1999, Nov. 15   **Perf. 13½x14**
4114 A1580 2s multi   .20   .20
4115 A1580 3s multi   .20   .20
4116 A1580 5s multi   .20   .20
4117 A1580 30s multi   .50   .50
4118 A1580 1 l multi   1.60 1.60
       Nos. 4114-4118 (5)   2.70 2.70

1999, Nov. 22   **Perf. 13**
4119 A1581 18s Icon, 1600   .30   .30
4120 A1581 60s Icon, 1607   1.00 1.00

Scouting A1582

10s, Scout, campfire. 18s, Scout assisting another. 30s, Salute. 60s, Scouts, cross.

1999, Dec. 6
4121 A1582 10s multi   .20   .20
4122 A1582 18s multi   .30   .30
4123 A1582 30s multi   .50   .50
4124 A1582 60s multi   1.00 1.00
       Nos. 4121-4124 (4)   2.00 2.00

Expo 2005, Japan — A1583

1999, Dec. 21   **Perf. 13**
4125 A1583 18s multi   .30   .30

Start of Negotiations for Bulgaria's Entry into European Community — A1584

2000, Feb. 15   **Litho.**   **Perf. 13**
4126 A1584 18s multi   .30   .30

Souvenir Sheet

Ciconia Ciconia — A1585

Illustration reduced.

2000, Mar. 22
4127 A1585 60s multi   2.50 1.50

Petar Beron (1800-71), Scientist — A1586

Zakhari Stoyanov (1850-89), Writer — A1586a

Kolyo Ficheto (1800-81), Architect — A1586b

2000, Mar. 30   **Litho.**   **Perf. 13¼**
4128 A1586   10s multi   .20   .20
4129 A1586a 20s multi   .30   .30
4130 A1586b 50s multi   .75   .75
       Nos. 4128-4130 (3)   1.25 1.25

Europa A1587

2000, Apr. 26   **Litho.**   **Perf. 13**
4131 A1587 18s shown   .30   .30
4132 A1587 60s Madonna and 1.00 1.00
             child at R

2000 Summer Olympics, Sydney — A1588

2000, Apr. 28   **Perf. 13¼x13**
4133 A1588 10s Judo   .20   .20
4134 A1588 18s Tennis   .30   .30
4135 A1588 20s Shooting   .35   .35
4136 A1588 60s Long jump   1.00 1.00
       Nos. 4133-4136 (4)   1.85 1.85

Bulgarian Art A1589

Designs: No. 4137, Friends, by Assen Vassilev (1900-81). No. 4138, Landscape from Veliko Turnovo, by Ivan Hristov (1900-87). No. 4139, At the Fountain, sculpture by Ivan Funev (1900-83). No. 4140, All Souls' Day, by Pencho Georgiev (1900-40).

2000, May 23   **Perf. 13**
4137 A1589 18s multi   .30   .30
4138 A1589 18s multi   .30   .30
4139 A1589 18s multi   .30   .30
4140 A1589 18s multi   .30   .30
       Nos. 4137-4140 (4)   1.20 1.20

Souvenir Sheet

Fairy Tales — A1590

Designs: a, Puss in Boots, by Charles Perrault. b, Little Red Riding Hood, by the Brothers Grimm. c, Thumbelina, by Hans Christian Andersen.
Illustration reduced.

2000, May 23   **Perf. 13¼x13**
4141 A1590 18s Sheet of 3, #a-c   .90   .90
             + 3 labels

Expo 2000, Hanover — A1591

Illustration reduced.

2000, May 31   **Perf. 13**
4142 A1591 60s multi + label 1.00 1.00

Birth and Death Anniversaries — A1592

Designs: 10s, Johann Gutenberg, inventor of movable type (c. 1400-68). 18s, Johann Sebastian Bach, composer (1685-1750). 20s, Guy de Maupassant, writer (1850-93). 60s, Antoine de Saint-Exupéry, writer (1900-44).

2000, June 20
4143 A1592 10s multi   .20   .20
4144 A1592 18s multi   .30   .30
4145 A1592 20s multi   .35   .35
4146 A1592 60s multi   1.00 1.00
       Nos. 4143-4146 (4)   1.85 1.85

Airships — A1593

Designs: 10s, Le Jaune over Paris. 18s, LZ-13 Hansa over Cologne. 20s, N-1 Norge over Rome. 60s, Graf Zeppelin over Sofia.

2000, July 3   **Litho.**   **Perf. 13¼**
4147 A1593 10s multi   .20   .20
4148 A1593 18s multi   .25   .25
4149 A1593 20s multi   .30   .30
4150 A1593 60s multi   .85   .85
       Nos. 4147-4150 (4)   1.60 1.60

Ivan Vazov (1850-1921), Writer — A1594

2000, July 9
4151 A1594 18s multi   .25   .25

Souvenir Sheet

European Security and Cooperation Conference, Helsinki, 25th Anniv. — A1595

No. 4152: a, Hands. b, Three "e's." Illustration reduced.

2000, July 19   **Litho.**   **Perf. 13**
4152 A1595 20s Sheet of 2, #a-b   .60   .60

Churches
A1596

Panel colors: 22s, Blue. 24s, Red violet.
50s, Bister. 65s, Bright green. 3 l, Brown. 5 l,
Red.

2000, Sept. 1   **Perf. 14x13¾**
4153-4158 A1596 Set of 6   8.75 8.75

Animals
A1597

Designs: 10s, Capra ibex. 22s, Ovis
ammon. 30s, Bison bonasus. 65s, Bos
grunniens.

2000, Sept. 25   **Perf. 13**
4159-4162 A1597 Set of 4   1.10 .75

Flowers — A1598

Designs: 10s, Gladiolus segetum. 22s,
Hepatica nobilis. 30s, Adonis vernalis. 65s,
Anemone pavonina.

2000, Oct. 17   **Perf. 13x13¼**
4163-4166 A1598 Set of 4   1.10 .75

European
Convention
on Human
Rights,
50th Anniv.
A1599

2000, Nov. 3   **Litho.**   **Perf. 13¼x13**
4167 A1599 65s multi   .65 .65

Bulgarian
Orders — A1600

Designs: 12s, Bravery. 22s, St. Alexander.
30s, Citizen's merit. 65s, Sts. Cyril and
Methodius.

2000, Nov. 28   **Perf. 13**
4168-4171 A1600 Set of 4   1.25 1.25

Souvenir Sheet

Christianity, 2000th Anniv. — A1601

No. 4172: a, 22s, St. Boris Michael (2000 at
UL). b, 22s, St. Sofroni Vrachanski (2000 at
LL). c, 65s, Madonna and Child (2000 at UL).
d, 65s, Exarch Antim I (2000 at LL).

2000, Nov. 28   **Perf. 13¼x13**
4172 A1601 Sheet of 4, #a-d   1.75 1.75

First Bulgarian
Law, 120th
Anniv. — A1602

2000, Dec. 8   **Perf. 13x13¼**
4173 A1602 22s multi   .20 .20

Advent of New Millennium — A1603

2001, Jan. 8   **Perf. 13x12¾**
4174 A1603 22s multi   .20 .20

Souvenir Sheet

Electrified City Transport in Bulgaria,
Cent. — A1604

No. 4175: a, 22s, Streetcar. b, 65s, Two
streetcars.

2001, Jan. 12   **Perf. 13**
4175 A1604   Sheet, 2 each
       #4175a-4175b   1.75 1.75

Viticulture
A1605

Wine glass, wine grapes and buildings: 12s,
Muscat, Evxinograd Palace. 22s, Gumza,
Baba Vida Fortress. 30s, Wide Melnik, houses
in Melnik. 65s, Mavroud, Assenova Fortress.

2001, Feb. 7
4176-4179 A1605   Set of 4   1.25 1.25

Souvenir Sheet

Bulgaria and the Information
Society — A1606

No. 4180: a, 22s, Circuits, "@" character. b,
65s, Letters, Dr. John Atanasov (1903-95),
computer pioneer.

2001, Mar. 1   **Perf. 13¼x13**
4180 A1606   Sheet, #a-b   .85 .85

Souvenir Sheet

"Atlantic" Values, 10th Anniv. — A1607

2001, Apr. 4   **Perf. 13x12¾**
4181 A1607 65s multi   .60 .60

Europa
A1608

Designs: 22s, Aerial view of Rila Lakes. 65s,
Rock bridges, Rhodope Mountains.

2001, Apr. 18   **Perf. 12¾x13**
4182-4183 A1608   Set of 2   .80 .80

Todor Kableshkov (1851-1876),
Organizer of 1876 April
Uprising — A1609

2001, May 1   **Perf. 13**
4184 A1609 22s multi   .20 .20

Protected Species Neophron
Percnopterus — A1610

Designs: 12s, Juvenile in flight. 22s, Juvenile with mouth open. 30s, Adult and chick.
65s, Adult and eggs.

2001, May 21   **Litho.**   **Perf. 13**
4185-4188 A1610 Set of 4   1.25 1.25

Souvenir Sheet

Athletes — A1611

No. 4189: a, 22s, Georgi Asparuchov (1943-
71), soccer player. b, 30s, Dan Kolov (1892-
1940), wrestler. c, 65s, Krum Lekarski (1898-
1981), equestrian.

2001, June 29
4189 A1611   Sheet of 3, #a-c, +
       3 labels   1.25 1.25

UN High
Commissioner
for Refugees,
50th
Anniv. — A1612

2001, July 11
4190 A1612 65s multi   .60 .60

Writers
A1613

Designs: 22s, Aleksandr Zhendov (1901-53). 65s, Ilya Beshkov (1901-58).

2001, July 24
4191-4192 A1613   Set of 2   .85   .85

Constitutional Court, 10th
Anniv. — A1614

2001, Oct. 3
4193 A1614   25s multi   .25   .25

Souvenir Sheet

Sofia Summit 2001 — A1615

Flags of various countries: a, 12s. b, 24s. c, 25s. d, 65s.

2001, Oct. 5   **Perf. 13¼x13**
4194 A1615   Sheet of 4, #a-d   1.25   1.25

Year of Dialogue
Among
Civilizations
A1616

2001, Oct. 9   **Perf. 13**
4195 A1616   65s multi   .60   .60

Souvenir Sheet

Intl. Black Sea Preservation
Day — A1617

2001, Oct. 31
4196 A1617   65s multi   .60   .60

Christmas
A1618

2001, Nov. 19
4197 A1618   25s multi   .25   .25

Lighthouses
A1619

Designs: 25s, Shabla. 32s, Kaliakra.

2001, Nov. 19   **Perf. 14x13½**
4198-4199 A1619   Set of 2   .55   .55

Souvenir Sheet

Zograf Monastery, Mount Athos,
Greece — A1620

No. 4200: a, 25s, Monastery. b, 65s, Icon of St, George.

2001, Nov. 27
4200 A1620   Sheet of 2, #a-b   .85   .85

SEMI-POSTAL STAMPS

> **Catalogue values for unused stamps in this section are for Never Hinged items.**

Regular Issues of 1911-20 Surcharged:

a   b

c

Perf. 11½x12, 12x11½

1920, June 20   **Unwmk.**
B1	A43 (a)	2s + 1s ol grn	.20	.20
B2	A44 (b)	5s + 2½s grn	.20	.20
B3	A44 (b)	10s + 5s rose	.20	.20
B4	A44 (b)	15s + 7½s vio	.20	.20
B5	A44 (b)	25s + 12½s dp bl	.20	.20
B6	A44 (b)	30s + 15s choc	.20	.20
B7	A44 (b)	50s + 25s yel brn	.20	.20
B8	A29 (c)	1 l + 50s dk brn	.20	.20

B9	A37a (a)	2 l + 1 l brn org	.25	.25
B10	A38 (a)	3 l + 1½ l claret	.55	.45
	Nos. B1-B10 (10)		2.40	2.30

Surtax aided ex-prisoners of war. Value, Nos. B1-B7 imperf., $7.75.

Tsar Boris Type of 1937
Souvenir Sheet

1937, Nov. 22   **Photo.**   **Imperf.**
B11 A140   2 l + 18 l ultra   6.00   4.00

19th anniv. of the accession of Tsar Boris III to the throne.

Stamps of
1917-21
Surcharged in
Black

1939, Oct. 22   **Perf. 12½, 12**
B12	A34	1 l + 1 l on 15s slate	.20	.20
B13	A69	2 l + 1 l on 1½ l ol grn	.20	.20
B14	A69	4 l + 2 l on 2 l dp grn	.20	.20
B15	A69	7 l + 4 l on 3 l Prus bl	.50	.30
B16	A69	14 l + 7 l on 5 l red brn	.85	.50
	Nos. B12-B16 (5)		1.95	1.40

Surtax aided victims of the Sevlievo flood. The surcharge on #B13-B16 omits "leva."

Map of
Bulgaria
SP2

1947, June 6   **Typo.**   **Perf. 11½**
B17 SP2   20 l + 10 l dk brn red & grn   .45   .30

30th Jubilee Esperanto Cong., Sofia, 1947.

Postman — SP3   Radio
                  Towers — SP6

#B19, Lineman. #B20, Telephone operators.

1947, Nov. 5
B18	SP3	4 l + 2 l ol brn	.20	.20
B19	SP3	10 l + 5 l brt red	.20	.20
B20	SP3	20 l + 10 l dp ultra	.20	.20
B21	SP6	40 l + 20 l choc	.70	.55
	Nos. B18-B21 (4)		1.30	1.15

Christo
Ganchev — SP7

Actors' Portraits: 10 l+6 l, Adriana Budevska. 15 l+7 l, Vasil Kirkov. 20 l+15 l, Sava Ognianov. 30 l+20 l, Krostyu Sarafov.

1947, Dec. 8   **Litho.**   **Perf. 10½**
B22	SP7	9 l + 5 l Prus grn	.20	.20
B23	SP7	10 l + 6 l car lake	.20	.20
B24	SP7	15 l + 7 l rose vio	.20	.20
B25	SP7	20 l + 15 l ultra	.20	.20
B26	SP7	30 l + 20 l vio brn	.50	.30
	Nos. B22-B26 (5)		1.30	1.10

National Theater, 50th anniversary.

Souvenir Sheet

Olympic Emblem — SP8

1964, Oct. 10   **Litho.**   **Imperf.**
B27 SP8   40s + 20s bis, red & bl   2.50   1.40

18th Olympic Games, Tokyo, Oct. 10-25.

Horsemanship Type of 1965
Miniature Sheet

1965, Sept. 30   **Photo.**   **Imperf.**
B28 A630   40s + 20s Hurdle race   2.00   1.00

Space Exploration Type of 1966

Designs: 20s+10s, Yuri A. Gagarin, Alexei Leonov and Valentina Tereshkova. 30s+10s, Rocket and globe.

1966, Sept. 29   **Photo.**   **Perf. 11½x11**
B29 A652   20s + 10s pur & gray   1.00   .35

Miniature Sheet
B30 A652   30s + 10s gray, fawn & blk   2.00   .95

Winter Olympic Games Type of 1967

Sports and Emblem: 20s+10s, Slalom. 40s+10s, Figure skating couple.

1967, Sept.   **Photo.**   **Perf. 11**
B31 A687   20s + 10s multi   1.10   .30

Souvenir Sheet
Imperf
B32 A687   40s + 10s multi   2.25   .85

Type of Olympic Games Issue, 1968

Designs: 20s+10s, Rowing. 50s+10s, Stadium, Mexico City, and communications satellite.

1968, June 24   **Photo.**   **Perf. 10½**
B33 A702   20s + 10s vio bl, gray & pink   1.00   .30

Miniature Sheet
Imperf
B34 A702   50s + 10s gray, blk & Prus bl   2.25   1.50

Sports Type of Regular Issue, 1969

Designs: 13s+5s, Woman with ball. 20s+10s, Acrobatic jump.

1969, Oct.   **Photo.**   **Perf. 11**
Gymnasts in Light Gray
B35	A732	13s + 5s brt rose & vio	.40	.20
B36	A732	20s + 10s citron & bl grn	.70	.30

Miniature Sheet

Soccer Ball — SP9

1970, Mar. 4   Photo.   Imperf.
B37 SP9 80s + 20s multi   2.25 1.40

9th World Soccer Championships for the Jules Rimet Cup, Mexico City, May 30-June 21, 1970.

Souvenir Sheet

Yuri A. Gagarin — SP10

1971, Apr. 12   Photo.   Imperf.
B38 SP10 40s + 20s multi   2.25 1.10

10th anniversary of the first man in space.

SP11

SP12

Bulgarian lion, magnifying glass, stamp tongs

1971, July 10   Photo.   Perf. 12½
B39 SP11 20s + 10s brn org, blk & gold   .90 .40

11th Congress of Bulgarian Philatelists, Sofia, July, 1971.

1989, Nov. 10   Litho.   Perf. 13x13½

Toys: a, Skateboarding. b, Doll. c, Rope. d, Train set.

Souvenir Sheet

B40   Sheet of 4   3.00 1.40
a.-d. SP12 30s +15s any single   .65 .35

For the benefit of the Children's Foundation.

AIR POST STAMPS

Regular Issues of 1925-26 Overprinted in Various Colors

1927-28   Unwmk.   Perf. 11½
C1 A76 2 l ol (R) ('28)   1.10 .70
C2 A74 4 l lake & yel (Bl)   1.10 .70
C3 A77 10 l brn blk & brn org (G) ('28)   17.00 13.00

Overprinted Vertically and Surcharged with New Value

C4 A77 1 l on 6 l dp bl & pale lem (C)   1.10 .70
a.   Inverted surcharge   325.00 275.00
b.   Pair, one without surcharge   425.00
      Nos. C1-C4 (4)   20.30 15.10

Nos. C2-C4 overprinted in changed colors were not issued, value set $10.50.

Dove Delivering Message AP1

Junkers Plane, Rila Monastery AP2

1931, Oct. 28   Typo.
C5 AP1 1 l dk green   .20 .20
C6 AP1 2 l maroon   .20 .20
C7 AP1 6 l dp blue   .30 .20
C8 AP1 12 l carmine   .30 .30
C9 AP1 20 l dk violet   .65 .55
C10 AP1 30 l dp orange   1.00 1.00
C11 AP1 50 l orange brn   2.25 1.40
      Nos. C5-C11 (7)   4.90 4.10

Counterfeits exist. See Nos. C15-C18.

1932, May 9
C12 AP2 18 l blue grn   14.00 11.00
C13 AP2 24 l dp red   14.00 11.00
C14 AP2 28 l ultra   14.00 11.00
      Nos. C12-C14 (3)   42.00 33.00

> **Catalogue values for unused stamps in this section, from this point to the end of the section, are for Never Hinged items.**

1938, Dec. 27
C15 AP1 1 l violet brown   .25 .20
C16 AP1 2 l green   .20 .20
C17 AP1 6 l deep rose   .70 .30
C18 AP1 12 l peacock blue   .85 .30
      Nos. C15-C18 (4)   2.00 1.00

Counterfeits exist.

Mail Plane — AP3

Plane over Tsar Assen's Tower — AP4

Designs: 4 l, Plane over Bachkovski Monastery. 6 l, Bojurishte Airport, Sofia. 10 l, Plane, train and motorcycle. 12 l, Planes over Sofia Palace. 16 l, Plane over Pirin Valley. 19 l, Plane over Rila Monastery. 30 l, Plane and Swallow. 45 l, Plane over Sofia Cathedral. 70 l,

---

Plane over Shipka Monument. 100 l, Plane and Royal Cipher.

1940, Jan. 15   Photo.   Perf. 13
C19 AP3 1 l dk green   .20 .20
C20 AP4 2 l crimson   1.10 .20
C21 AP4 4 l red orange   .20 .20
C22 AP3 6 l dp blue   .20 .20
C23 AP4 10 l dk brown   .30 .20
C24 AP3 12 l dull brown   .50 .20
C25 AP3 16 l brt bl vio   .55 .25
C26 AP3 19 l sapphire   .75 .30
C27 AP4 30 l rose lake   1.10 .50
C28 AP4 45 l gray violet   2.75 .95
C29 AP4 70 l rose pink   2.75 1.25
C30 AP4 100 l dp slate bl   9.00 3.75
      Nos. C19-C30 (12)   19.40 8.20

Nos. 368 and 370 Overprinted in Black

1945, Jan. 26
C31 A181 1 l bright green   .20 .20
C32 A181 4 l red orange   .20 .20

A similar overprint on Nos. O4, O5, O7 and O8 was privately applied.

Type of Parcel Post Stamps of 1944 Surcharged or Overprinted in Various Colors

Imperf

C37 PP5 10 l on 100 l dl yel (Bl)   .20 .20
C38 PP5 45 l on 100 l dl yel (C)   .30 .20
C39 PP5 75 l on 100 l dl yel (G)   .40 .25
C40 PP5 100 l dl yel (V)   .70 .35
      Nos. C37-C40 (4)   1.60 1.00

Plane and Sun — AP16

Pigeon with Letter — AP17

Plane, Letter AP18

Wings, Posthorn AP19

Winged Letter — AP20

Plane, Sun — AP21

Pigeon, Posthorn AP22

Mail Plane AP23

Conventionalized Figure Holding Pigeon — AP24

1946, July 15   Litho.   Perf. 13
C41 AP16 1 l dull lilac   .20 .20
C42 AP16 1 l slate gray   .20 .20
C43 AP17 4 l violet blk   .20 .20
C44 AP18 6 l blue   .20 .20
C45 AP19 10 l turq green   .20 .20
C46 AP20 12 l yellow brn   .20 .20
C47 AP20 16 l rose violet   .20 .20
C48 AP19 19 l carmine   .20 .20
C49 AP21 30 l orange   .20 .20
C50 AP22 45 l lt ol grn   .20 .20
C51 AP22 75 l red brown   .25 .20
C52 AP23 100 l slate blk   .65 .25
C53 AP24 100 l red   .65 .25
      Nos. C41-C53 (13)   3.55 2.70

No. C47 exists imperf. Value $90.

People's Republic

Plane over Plovdiv AP25

1947, Aug. 31   Photo.   Imperf.
C54 AP25 40 l dull olive grn   .60 .50

Plovdiv International Fair, 1947.

Baldwin's Tower — AP26

1948, May 23   Litho.   Perf. 11½
C55 AP26 50 l ol brn, *cr*   .75 .60

Stamp Day and the 10th Congress of Bulgarian Philatelic Societies, June 1948.

Romanian and Bulgarian Parliament Buildings AP27

Romanian and Bulgarian Flags, Bridge over Danube AP28

1948, Nov. 3   Photo.
C56 AP27 40 l ol gray, *cr*   .25 .20
C57 AP28 100 l red vio, *cr*   .50 .30

Romanian-Bulgarian friendship.

Mausoleum of Pleven — AP29

1949, June 26
C58 AP29 50 l brown   2.00 1.25

7th Congress of Bulgarian Philatelic Associations, June 26-27, 1949.

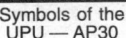

Symbols of the
UPU — AP30

Frontier Guard
and
Dog — AP31

1949, Oct. 10   **Perf. 11½**
C59 AP30 50 l violet blue   1.75 .75
75th anniv. of the UPU.

1949, Oct. 31
C60 AP31 60 l olive black   1.25 .90

Dimitrov
Mausoleum
AP32

1950, July 3   **Perf. 10½**
C61 AP32 40 l olive brown   3.00 1.10
1st anniv. of the death of George Dimitrov.

Belogradchic
Rocks — AP33

Air View of Plovdiv
Fair — AP34

Designs: 16s, Beach, Varna. 20s, Harvesting grain. 28s, Rila monastery. 44s, Studena dam. 60s, View of Dimitrovgrad. 80s, View of Trnovo. 1 l, University building, Sofia. 4 l, Partisans' Monument.

1954, Apr. 1   **Unwmk.**   **Perf. 13**
C62 AP33	8s olive black	.20	.20
C63 AP34	12s rose brown	.20	.20
C64 AP33	16s brown	.20	.20
C65 AP33	20s brn red, *cream*	.20	.20
C66 AP33	28s dp bl, *cream*	.20	.20
C67 AP33	44s vio brn, *cream*	.20	.20
C68 AP33	60s red brn, *cream*	.25	.20
C69 AP34	80s dk grn, *cream*	.30	.20
C70 AP33	1 l dk bl grn, *cream*	1.25	.35
C71 AP34	4 l deep blue	3.00	.80
	Nos. C62-C71 (10)	6.00	2.75

Glider on
Mountainside
AP35

60s, Glider over airport. 80s, Three gliders.

1956, Oct. 15   **Photo.**
C72 AP35	44s brt blue	.20	.20
C73 AP35	60s purple	.30	.20
C74 AP35	80s dk blue grn	.50	.20
	Nos. C72-C74 (3)	1.00	.60

30th anniv. of glider flights in Bulgaria.

Passenger Plane — AP36

1957, May 21   **Unwmk.**   **Perf. 13**
C75 AP36 80s deep blue   .65 .30
10th anniv. of civil aviation in Bulgaria.

Sputnik 3
over Earth
AP37

1958, Nov. 28   **Perf. 11**
C76 AP37 80s brt grnsh blue   3.00 2.25
International Geophysical Year, 1957-58. Value, imperf. $7.50.

Lunik 1 Leaving
Earth for
Moon — AP38

1959, Feb. 28   **Perf. 10½**
C77 AP38 2 l brt blue & ocher   3.00 2.75
Launching of 1st man-made satellite to orbit moon. Value, imperf. in slightly different colors, $7.50 unused, $5.25 canceled.

Statue of
Liberty
and Tu-
110
Airliner
AP39

         Perf. 10½
1959, Nov. 11   **Photo.**   **Unwmk.**
C78 AP39 1 l violet bl & pink   1.75 1.50
Visit of Khrushchev to US. Value, imperf. $5.

Lunik 2 and
Moon — AP40

1960, June 23   **Litho.**   **Perf. 11**
C79 AP40 1.25 l blue, blk & yel   3.50 1.60
Russian rocket to the Moon, Sept. 12, 1959.

Sputnik 5 and Dogs Belka and
Strelka — AP41

1961, Jan. 14   **Photo.**   **Perf. 11**
C80 AP41 1.25 l brt grnsh bl &
       org   4.00 2.50
Russian rocket flight of Aug. 19, 1970.

Maj. Yuri
A.
Gagarin
and
Vostok 1
AP42

1961, Apr. 26   **Unwmk.**
C81 AP42 4 l grnsh bl, blk &
       red   2.50 1.50
First manned space flight, Apr. 12, 1961.

Soviet
Space
Dogs
AP43

1961, June 28   **Perf. 11**
C82 AP43 2 l slate & dk car   2.00 1.00

Venus-bound
Rocket — AP44

1961, June 28
C83 AP44 2 l brt bl, yel & org   4.00 2.50
Soviet launching of the Venus space probe, 2/12/61.

Maj.
Gherman
Titov
AP45

Design: 1.25 l, Spaceship Vostok 2.

1961, Nov. 20   **Photo.**   **Perf. 11x10½**
C84 AP45 75s dk ol grn & gray
       grn   1.75 1.00
C85 AP45 1.25 l vio bl, lt bl &
       pink   2.25 1.00
1st manned space flight around the world, Maj. Gherman Titov of Russia, 8/6-7/61.

Iskar River
Narrows
AP46

Designs: 2s, Varna and sailboat. 3s, Melnik. 10s, Trnovo. 40s, Pirin mountains.

1962, Feb. 3   **Unwmk.**   **Perf. 13**
C86 AP46	1s bl grn & gray bl	.20	.20
C87 AP46	2s blue & pink	.20	.20
C88 AP46	3s brown & ocher	.25	.20
C89 AP46	10s black & lemon	.45	.20
C90 AP46	40s dk green & green	1.10	.30
	Nos. C86-C90 (5)	2.20	1.10

Ilyushin
Turboprop
Airliner
AP47

1962, Aug. 18   **Perf. 1**
C91 AP47 13s blue & black   .60 .2
15th anniversary of TABSO airline.

Konstantin E. Tsiolkovsky and Rocket
Launching — AP48

Design: 13s, Earth, moon and rocket on future flight to the moon.

1962, Sept. 24   **Perf. 1**
C92 AP48 5s dp green & gray   1.90 .85
C93 AP48 13s ultra & yellow   1.10 .35
13th meeting of the International Astronautical Federation.

Maj. Andrian G. Nikolayev — AP49

Designs: 2s, Lt. Col. Pavel R. Popovich 40s, Vostoks 3 and 4 in orbit.

1962, Dec. 9   **Photo.**   **Unwmk.**
C94 AP49	1s bl, sl grn & blk	.20	.20
C95 AP49	2s bl grn, grn & blk	.25	.20
C96 AP49	40s dk bl grn, pink &		
	blk	1.60	.85
	Nos. C94-C96 (3)	2.05	1.25

First Russian group space flight of Vostoks 3 and 4, Aug. 12-15, 1962.

Spacecraft "Mars 1" Approaching
Mars — AP50

Design: 13s, Rocket launching spacecraft, Earth, Moon and Mars.

1963, Feb. 25   **Unwmk.**   **Perf. 11**
C97 AP50 3s multicolored   .50 .30
C98 AP50 13s multicolored   1.00 .45
Launching of the Russian spacecraft "Mars 1," Nov. 1, 1962.

Lt. Col.
Valeri F.
Bykovski
AP51

Designs: 2s, Lt. Valentina Tereshkova. 5s, Globe and trajectories.

1963, Aug. 26   **Unwmk.**   **Perf. 11½**
C99 AP51	1s pale vio & Prus bl	.20	.20
C100 AP51	2s citron & red brn	.20	.20
C101 AP51	5s rose & dk red	.20	.20
	Nos. C99-C101 (3)	.60	.60

The space flights of Valeri Bykovski, June 14-19, and Valentina Tereshkova, first woman cosmonaut, June 16-19, 1963. An imperf. souvenir sheet contains one 50s stamp showing Spasski tower and globe in lilac and red brown. Light blue border with red brown inscription. Size: 77x67mm. Value $2.50. See No. CB3.

Nos. C99-C100 Surcharged in Magenta or Green

1964, Aug. 22

| C102 | AP51 | 10s on 1s (M) | .30 | .20 |
| C103 | AP51 | 20s on 2s | .65 | .25 |

International Space Exhibition in Riccione, Italy. Overprint in Italian on No. C103.

St. John's Monastery, Rila — AP52

13s, Notre Dame, Paris; French inscription.

1964, Dec. 22   Photo.   Perf. 11½

| C104 | AP52 | 5s pale brn & blk | .20 | .20 |
| C105 | AP52 | 13s lt ultra & sl bl | .65 | .20 |

The philatelic exhibition at St. Ouen (Seine) organized by the Franco-Russian Philatelic Circle and philatelic organizations in various People's Democracies.

Paper Mill, Bukijovtz AP53

10s, Metal works, Plovdiv. 13s, Metal works, Kremikovtsi. 20s, Oil refinery, Stara-Zagora. 40s, Fertilizer plant, Stara-Zagora. 1 l, Rest home, Meded.

1964-68   Unwmk.   Perf. 13

C106	AP53	8s grnsh blue	.20	.20
C107	AP53	10s red lilac	.20	.20
C108	AP53	13s brt violet	.25	.20
C109	AP53	20s slate blue	.75	.20
C110	AP53	40s dk olive grn	1.10	.20
C111	AP53	1 l red ('68)	1.90	.20
		Nos. C106-C111 (6)	4.40	1.30

Issue dates: 1 l, May 6. Others, Dec. 7.

Three-master AP54

Veliko Turnovo — AP55

Means of Communication: 2s, Postal coach. 3s, Old steam locomotive. 5s, Early cars. 10s, Montgolfier balloon. 13s, Early plane. 20s, Jet planes. 40s, Rocket and satellites. 1 l, Postrider.

1969, Mar. 31   Photo.   Perf. 13x12½

C112	AP54	1s gray & multi	.20	.20
C113	AP54	2s gray & multi	.20	.20
C114	AP54	3s gray & multi	.20	.20
C115	AP54	5s gray & multi	.20	.20
C116	AP54	10s gray & multi	.20	.20
C117	AP54	13s gray & multi	.25	.20
C118	AP54	20s gray & multi	.50	.20
C119	AP54	40s gray & multi	.90	.40
		Nos. C112-C119 (8)	2.65	1.85

Miniature Sheet
Imperf

| C120 | AP54 | 1 l gold & org | 2.25 | 1.50 |

SOFIA 1969 Philatelic Exhibition, Sofia, May 31-June 8.

1973, July 30   Photo.   Perf. 13

Designs: Historic buildings in various cities.

C121	AP55	2s shown	.20	.20
C122	AP55	13s Roussalka	.25	.20
C123	AP55	20s Plovdiv	1.50	.80
C124	AP55	28s Sofia	.65	.20
		Nos. C121-C124 (4)	2.60	1.40

Aleksei A. Leonov and Soyuz AP56

Designs: 18s, Thomas P. Stafford and Apollo. 28s, Apollo and Soyuz over earth. 1 l, Apollo Soyuz link-up.

1975, July 15

C125	AP56	13s blue & multi	.30	.20
C126	AP56	18s purple & multi	.40	.20
C127	AP56	28s multicolored	1.00	.30
		Nos. C125-C127 (3)	1.70	.70

Souvenir Sheet

| C128 | AP56 | 1 l violet & multi | 2.00 | 1.25 |

Apollo Soyuz space test project (Russo-American cooperation), launching July 15; link-up July 17.

Balloon Over Plovdiv — AP57

1977, Sept. 3

| C129 | AP57 | 25s yellow, brn & red | .50 | .20 |

Alexei Leonov Floating in Space — AP58

Designs: 25s, Mariner 6, US spacecraft. 35s, Venera 4, USSR Venus probe.

1977, Oct. 14   Photo.   Perf. 13½

C130	AP58	12s multicolored	.20	.20
C131	AP58	25s multicolored	.40	.20
C132	AP58	35s multicolored	.60	.25
		Nos. C130-C132 (3)	1.20	.65

Space era, 20 years.

TU-154, Balkanair Emblem AP59

1977   Perf. 13

| C133 | AP59 | 35s ultra & multi | .75 | .35 |

30th anniv. of Bulgarian airline, Balkanair. Issued in sheets of 6 stamps + 3 labels (in lilac) with inscription and Balkanair emblem.

Baba Vida Fortress AP60

Design: 35s, Peace Bridge, connecting Rousse, Bulgaria, with Giurgiu, Romania.

1978   Photo.   Perf. 13

| C134 | AP60 | 25s multicolored | .40 | .40 |
| C135 | AP60 | 35s multicolored | .55 | .55 |

The Danube, European Intercontinental Waterway. Issued in sheets containing 5 each of Nos. C134-C135 and 2 labels, one showing course of Danube, the other hydrofoil and fish.

Red Cross AP61

1978, Mar.   Photo.   Perf. 13

| C136 | AP61 | 25s multicolored | .50 | .20 |

Centenary of Bulgarian Red Cross.

AP62

1979, June 5   Litho.   Perf. 12x12½

C137	AP62	13s Byalla Cherkva	.20	.20
C138	AP62	23s Botevgrad	.30	.20
C139	AP62	25s Pazardgick	.30	.20
C140	AP62	35s Grabovo	.40	.20
C141	AP62	53s Tryavna	.75	.30
		Nos. C137-C141 (5)	1.95	1.10

AP63

1980, Oct. 22   Photo.   Perf. 12x12½

C142	AP62	13s Bjala	.20	.20
C143	AP62	23s Rasgrad	.35	.25
C144	AP62	25s Karnabat	.40	.20
C145	AP62	35s Serlievo	.50	.25
C146	AP62	53s Berkovitza	.80	.35
		Nos. C142-C146 (5)	2.25	1.25

1980

| C147 | AP63 | 13s shown | .20 | .20 |
| C148 | AP63 | 25s Parachutist | .40 | .20 |

15th World Parachute Championships, Kazanluk.

DWVY-1 Aircraft — AP64

1981, June 27   Litho.   Perf. 12½

C149	AP64	5s shown	.20	.20
C150	AP64	12s LAS-7	.20	.20
C151	AP64	25s LAS-8	.40	.20
C152	AP64	35s DAR-1	.50	.20
C153	AP64	45s DAR-3	.70	.25
C154	AP64	55s DAR-9	.90	.30
		Nos. C149-C154 (6)	2.90	1.35

AP65

AP66

1983, June 28

C155		Sheet of 2	1.50	1.00
a.		AP65 50s Valentina Tereshkova	.75	.50
b.		AP65 50s Svetlana Savitskaya	.75	.50

Women in space, 20th anniv.

1983, July 20   Photo.   Perf. 13

C156	AP66	5s TV tower, Tolbukhin	.20	.20
C157	AP66	13s Postwoman	.25	.20
C158	AP66	30s TV tower, Mt. Botev	.60	.30
a.		Strip of 3, #C156-C158	.95	.50

World Communications Year. Emblems of World Communications Year, Bulgarian Post, UPU and ITU on attached margins.

Souvenir Sheet

Geophysical Map of the Moon, Russia's Luna I, II and III Satellites — AP67

1984, Oct. 24   Photo.   Perf. 13

| C159 | AP67 | 1 l multicolored | 1.75 | 1.00 |

Conquest of Space.

Intl. Civil Aviation Org., 40th
Anniv. — AP68

1984, Dec. 21　Photo.　*Perf. 13*
C160 AP68 42s Balkan Airlines jet　.85　.40

Balkan Airlines — AP69

Design: Helicopter MU-8, passenger jet TU-154 and AN-21 transport plane.

1987, Aug. 25　　　　　Photo.
C161 AP69 25s multicolored　　　.75　.35

2nd Joint Soviet-Bulgarian Space
Flight — AP70

Cosmonauts: A. Aleksandrov, A. Solovov and V. Savinich.

1989, June 7　Litho.　*Perf. 13½x13*
C162 AP70 13s multicolored　　　.35　.20

AIR POST SEMI-POSTAL STAMPS

Catalogue values for unused stamps in this section are for Never Hinged items.

Statue of
Liberty, Plane
and Bridge
SPAP1

Perf. 11½.
1947, May 24　Unwmk.　Litho.
CB1 SPAP1 70 l + 30 l red brn　.95　.95

5th Philatelic Congress, Trnovo, and CIPEX, NYC, May, 1947.

Bulgarian
Worker
SPAP2

1948, Feb. 28　Photo.　*Perf. 12x11½.*
CB2 SPAP2 60 l henna brn, *cream*　.45　.35

2nd Bulgarian Workers' Congress, and sold by subscription only, at a premium of 16 l over face value.

Type of Air Post Stamps, 1963
Valeri Bykovski & Valentina Tereshkova.

1963, Aug. 26　Unwmk.　*Perf. 11½*
CB3 AP51 20s + 10s pale bluish
　　　　grn & dk grn　　　　1.25　.45
　　See note after No. C101.

SPECIAL DELIVERY STAMPS

Catalogue values for unused stamps in this section are for Never Hinged items.

Postman on
Bicycle — SD1

Mail Car — SD2

Postman on
Motorcycle — SD3

1939　Unwmk.　Photo.　*Perf. 13*
E1 SD1　5 l deep blue　　.60　.20
E2 SD2　6 l copper brn　　.25　.20
E3 SD3　7 l golden brn　　.35　.20
E4 SD2　10 l red orange　.65　.20
E5 SD1　20 l bright rose　1.25　.40
　　Nos. E1-E5 (5)　　　3.10　1.20

POSTAGE DUE STAMPS

D1　　　　　　D2

Large Lozenge Perf. 5½ to 6½
1884　D1　Typo.　Unwmk.
J1 D1　5s orange　　150.00　15.00
J2 D1　25s lake　　　75.00　10.00
J3 D1　50s blue　　　12.00　5.00
　Nos. J1-J3 (3)　　237.00　30.00

1886　　　　　　　*Imperf.*
J4 D1　5s orange　　75.00　2.50
J5 D1　25s lake　　125.00　2.50
J6 D1　50s blue　　　5.00　2.75
　Nos. J4-J6 (3)　　205.00　7.75

1887　　　　　*Perf. 11½*
J7 D1　5s orange　　9.50　1.00
J8 D1　25s lake　　　9.50　1.00
J9 D1　50s blue　　　3.50　1.00
　Nos. J7-J9 (3)　　22.50　3.00

Same, Redrawn
24 horizontal lines of shading in upper part instead of 30 lines

1892　　　　*Perf. 10½, 11½*
J10 D1　5s orange　　7.50　1.25
J11 D1　25s lake　　　7.50　1.25

1893
Pelure Paper
J12 D2　5s orange　　10.00　3.50

D3　　　　　　D4

1895　　　　　　*Imperf.*
J13 D3　30s on 50s blue　7.00　2.00
**　　*Perf. 10½, 11½***
J14 D3　30s on 50s blue　7.00　2.00

Wmk. Coat of Arms in the Sheet
1896　　　　　　*Perf. 13*
J15 D4　5s orange　　3.00　.75
J16 D4　10s purple　2.00　.75
J17 D4　30s green　1.40　.45
　Nos. J15-J17 (3)　6.40　1.95

Nos. J15-J17 are also known on unwatermarked paper from the edges of sheets.

In 1901 a cancellation, "T" in circle, was applied to Nos. 60-65 and used provisionally as postage dues.

D5　　　　　　D6

1901-04　Unwmk.　*Perf. 11½*
J19 D5　5s dl rose　　.20　.20
J20 D5　10s yel grn　　.40　.20
J21 D5　20s dl bl ('04)　3.25　.20
J22 D5　30s vio brn　　.35　.20
J23 D5　50s org ('02)　5.50　4.00
　Nos. J19-J23 (5)　9.70　4.80

Nos. J19-J23 exist imperf. and in pairs imperf. between. Value, imperf., $250.

1915　　Unwmk.　*Perf. 11½*
Thin Semi-Transparent Paper
J24 D6　5s green　　.20　.20
J25 D6　10s purple　.20　.20
J26 D6　20s dl rose　.20　.20
J27 D6　30s dp org　1.10　.20
J28 D6　50s dp bl　　.35　.20
　Nos. J24-J28 (5)　2.05　1.00

1919-21　　　*Perf. 11½, 12x11½*
J29 D6　5s emerald　　.20　.20
a.　5s gray green ('21)　.30　.20
J30 D6　10s violet　　.20　.20
J31 D6　20s salmon　.20　.20
a.　20s yellow　　.20　.20
J32 D6　30s orange　.20　.20
a.　30s red orange ('21)　.65　.65
J33 D6　50s blue　　.20　.20
J34 D6　1 l emerald ('21)　.20　.20
J35 D6　2 l rose ('21)　.20　.20
J36 D6　3 l brown org ('21)　.35　.20
　Nos. J29-J36 (8)　1.75　1.60

Stotinki values of the above series surcharged 10s or 20s were used as ordinary postage stamps. See Nos. 182-185.

The 1919 printings are on thicker white paper with clean-cut perforations, the 1921 printings on thicker grayish paper with rough perforations.

Most of this series exist imperforate and in pairs imperforate between.

Heraldic Lion — D7

1932, Aug. 15
Thin Paper
J37 D7　1 l olive bister　.25　.20
J38 D7　2 l rose brown　.25　.20
J39 D7　6 l brown violet　.75　.35
　Nos. J37-J39 (3)　1.25　.75

Lion of
Trnovo — D8　　　National
　　　　　　　Arms — D9

1933, Apr. 10
J40 D8　20s dk brn　　.20　.20
J41 D8　40s dp bl　　.20　.20
J42 D8　80s car rose　.20　.20
J43 D9　1 l org brn　　.25　.20
J44 D9　2 l olive　　.30　.25

J45 D9　6 l dl vio　　.20　.20
J46 D9　14 l ultra　　.25　.20
　Nos. J40-J46 (7)　1.60　1.45

Catalogue values for unused stamps in this section, from this point to the end of the section, are for Never Hinged items.

National Arms — D10

1947, June　Typo.　*Perf. 10½*
J47 D10　1 l chocolate　.20　.20
J48 D10　2 l deep claret　.20　.20
J49 D10　8 l deep orange　.20　.20
J50 D10　20 l blue　　.25　.20
　Nos. J47-J50 (4)　.85　.80

Arms of the People's
Republic — D11

1951　　　　*Perf. 11½x10½*
J51 D11　1 l chocolate　.20　.20
J52 D11　2 l claret　　.20　.20
J53 D11　8 l red orange　.25　.20
J54 D11　20 l deep blue　.60　.30
　Nos. J51-J54 (4)　1.25　.90

OFFICIAL STAMPS

Catalogue values for unused stamps in this section are for Never Hinged items.

Bulgarian Coat of Arms
O1　　　　　　O2

1942　Unwmk.　Typo.　*Perf. 13*
O1 O1　10s yel grn　.20　.20
O2 O1　30s red　　.20　.20
O3 O1　50s bister　.20　.20
O4 O2　1 l vio bl　　.20　.20
O5 O2　2 l dk grn　.20　.20
O6 O2　3 l lilac　　.20　.20
O7 O2　4 l rose　　.20　.20
O8 O2　5 l carmine　.20　.20
　Nos. O1-O8 (8)　1.60　1.60

1944　　　　*Perf. 10½x11½*
O9 O2　1 l blue　　.20　.20
O10 O2　2 l brt red　.20　.20

Lion Rampant
O3　　　　　　O4

O5

1945　　　　　　*Imperf.*
O11 O5　1 l pink　　.20　.20

Perf. 10½x11½, Imperf.

O12	O3	2 l	blue green		.20	.20
O13	O4	3 l	bister brown		.20	.20
O14	O4	4 l	light ultra		.20	.20
O15	O5	5 l	brown lake		.20	.20
		Nos. O11-O15 (5)			1.00	1.00

In 1950, four stamps prepared for official use were issued as regular postage stamps. See Nos. 724-727.

PARCEL POST STAMPS

Catalogue values for unused stamps in this section are for Never Hinged items.

Weighing Packages — PP1

Parcel Post — PP2

Designs: 3 l, 8 l, 20 l, Parcel post truck. 4 l, 6 l, 10 l, Motorcycle.

Perf. 12½x13½, 13½x12½

1941-42			Photo.	Unwmk.	
Q1	PP1	1 l	slate grn	.20	.20
Q2	PP2	2 l	crimson	.20	.20
Q3	PP2	3 l	dull brn	.20	.20
Q4	PP2	4 l	red org	.20	.20
Q5	PP2	5 l	deep blue	.20	.20
Q6	PP1	5 l	slate grn ('42)	.20	.20
Q7	PP2	6 l	red vio	.20	.20
Q8	PP2	6 l	henna brn ('42)	.20	.20
Q9	PP2	7 l	dark blue	.20	.20
Q10	PP1	7 l	dk brn ('42)	.20	.20
Q11	PP2	8 l	brt bl grn	.20	.20
Q12	PP2	8 l	green ('42)	.25	.20
Q13	PP2	9 l	olive gray	.20	.20
Q14	PP2	9 l	dp olive ('42)	.20	.20
Q15	PP2	10 l	orange	.20	.20
Q16	PP2	20 l	gray vio	.40	.20
Q17	PP2	30 l	dull blk	.55	.20
Q18	PP2	30 l	sepia ('42)	.50	.20
		Nos. Q1-Q18 (18)		4.50	3.60

Arms of Bulgaria — PP5

1944			Litho.	Imperf.	
Q21	PP5	1 l	dk carmine	.20	.20
Q22	PP5	3 l	blue grn	.20	.20
Q23	PP5	5 l	dull bl grn	.20	.20
Q24	PP5	7 l	rose lilac	.20	.20
Q25	PP5	10 l	deep blue	.20	.20
Q26	PP5	20 l	orange brn	.20	.20
Q27	PP5	30 l	dk brn car	.20	.20
Q28	PP5	50 l	red orange	.30	.20
Q29	PP5	100 l	blue	.50	.25
		Nos. Q21-Q29 (9)		2.20	1.85

For overprints and surcharges see Nos. 448-454, C37-C40.

POSTAL TAX STAMPS

The use of stamps Nos. RA1 to RA18 was compulsory on letters, etc., to be delivered on Sundays and holidays. The money received from their sale was used toward maintaining a sanatorium for employees of the post, telegraph and telephone services.

View of Sanatorium PT1

Sanatorium, Peshtera PT2

1925-29			Unwmk. Typo.	Perf. 11½	
RA1	PT1	1 l	blk, grnsh bl	2.75	.20
RA2	PT1	1 l	chocolate ('26)	2.75	.20
RA3	PT1	1 l	orange ('27)	3.00	.20
RA4	PT1	1 l	pink ('28)	4.50	.20
RA5	PT1	1 l	vio, pnksh ('29)	4.25	.20
RA6	PT2	2 l	blue green	.35	.20
RA7	PT2	2 l	violet ('27)	.35	.20
RA8	PT2	5 l	deep blue	3.00	.80
RA9	PT2	5 l	rose ('27)	3.75	.40
		Nos. RA1-RA9 (9)		24.70	2.60

St. Constantine Sanatorium PT3

1930-33					
RA10	PT3	1 l	red brn & ol grn	4.00	.20
RA11	PT3	1 l	ol grn & yel ('31)	.50	.20
RA12	PT3	1 l	red vio & ol brn ('33)	.50	.20
		Nos. RA10-RA12 (3)		5.00	.60

Trojan Rest Home — PT4

Sanatorium PT5

1935			Wmk. 145	Perf. 11, 11½	
RA13	PT4	1 l	choc & red org	.30	.20
RA14	PT4	1 l	emer & indigo	.30	.20
RA15	PT5	5 l	red brn & indigo	1.40	.35
		Nos. RA13-RA15 (3)		2.00	.75

St. Constantine Sanatorium PT6

2 l, Children at seashore. 5 l, Rest home.

1941			Unwmk. Photo.	Perf. 13	
RA16	PT6	1 l	dark olive green	.20	.20
RA17	PT6	2 l	red orange	.20	.20
RA18	PT6	5 l	deep blue	.30	.20
		Nos. RA16-RA18 (3)		.70	.60

See Nos. 702-705 for same designs in smaller size issued as regular postage.

BURKINA FASO

bur-'kē-nə-'fä-sō

Upper Volta

LOCATION — Northwestern Africa, north of Ghana
GOVT. — Republic
AREA — 105,869 sq. mi.
POP. — 11,575,898 (1999 est.)
CAPITAL — Ouagadougou

In 1919 the French territory of Upper Volta was detached from the southern section of Upper Senegal and Niger and made a separate colony. In 1933 the colony was divided among its neighbors: French Sudan, Ivory Coast, and Niger Territory. The Republic of Upper Volta was proclaimed December 11, 1958; the name was changed to Burkina Faso on August 4, 1984.

100 Centimes = 1 Franc

> Catalogue values for unused stamps in this country are for Never Hinged items, beginning with Scott 70 in the regular postage section, Scott B1 in the semipostal section, Scott C1 in the airpost section, Scott J21 in the postage due section, and Scott O1 in the official section.

See French West Africa Nos. 67, 84 for additional stamps inscribed "Haute Volta" and "Afrique Occidentale Francaise."

Stamps and Types of Upper Senegal and Niger, 1914-17, Overprinted in Black or Red

		1920-28	Unwmk.	Perf. 13½x14	
1	A4	1c brn vio & vio		.20	.20
2	A4	2c gray & brn vio (R)		.20	.20
3	A4	4c blk & bl		.20	.20
4	A4	5c yel grn & bl grn		.60	.25
5	A4	5c ol brn & dk brn ('22)		.20	.20
6	A4	10c red org & rose		1.00	.50
7	A4	10c yel grn & bl grn ('22)		.20	.20
8	A4	10c claret & bl ('25)		.25	.25
a.		Overprint omitted		80.00	
9	A4	15c choc & org		.40	.30
10	A4	20c brn vio & blk (R)		.65	.55
11	A4	25c ultra & bl		.80	.50
12	A4	25c blk & bl grn ('22)		.45	.40
a.		Overprint omitted		65.00	
13	A4	30c ol brn & brn (R)		1.50	1.25
14	A4	30c red org & rose ('22)		.40	.35
15	A4	30c vio & brn red ('25)		.40	.35
16	A4	30c dl grn & bl grn ('27)		.70	.60
17	A4	35c car rose & vio		.45	.30
18	A4	40c gray & car rose		.45	.35
19	A4	45c bl & brn (R)		.35	.20
20	A4	50c blk & grn		1.75	1.25
21	A4	50c ultra & bl ('22)		.50	.50
22	A4	50c red org & bl ('25)		.60	.60
23	A4	60c org red ('26)		.20	.20
24	A4	65c bis & pale bl ('28)		.80	.60
25	A4	75c org & brn		.30	.30
26	A4	1fr brn & brn vio		.80	.70
27	A4	2fr grn & bl		1.25	.80
28	A4	5fr vio & blk (R)		2.50	2.25
		Nos. 1-28 (28)		18.10	14.35

No. 9 Surcharged in Various Colors

		1922			
29	A4	0,01c on 15c (Bk)		.40	.40
a.		Double surcharge		65.00	65.00
30	A4	0,02c on 15c (Bl)		.40	.40
31	A4	0,05c on 15c (R)		.40	.40
		Nos. 29-31 (3)		1.20	1.20

Type of 1920 Surcharged

		1922			
32	A4	60c on 75c vio, pnksh		.35	.35

Stamps and Types of 1920 Surcharged with New Value and Bars

		1924-27			
33	A4	25c on 2fr grn & bl		.45	.45
34	A4	25c on 5fr vio & blk		.45	.45
35	A4	65c on 45c bl & brn ('25)		.50	.50
36	A4	85c on 75c org & brn ('25)		.70	.70
37	A4	90c on 75c brn red & sal pink ('27)		.70	.70
38	A4	1.25fr on 1fr dp bl & lt bl (R) ('26)		.45	.45
39	A4	1.50fr on 1fr dp bl & ultra ('27)		1.25	1.25
40	A4	3fr on 5fr dl red & brn org ('27)		1.60	1.60
41	A4	10fr on 5fr ol grn & lil rose ('27)		7.25	7.25
42	A4	20fr on 5fr org brn & vio ('27)		10.00	10.00
		Nos. 33-42 (10)		23.35	23.35

Hausa Chief — A5

Hausa Woman — A6

Hausa Warrior A7

		1928	Typo.	Perf. 13½x14	
43	A5	1c indigo & grn		.20	.20
44	A5	2c brn & lil		.20	.20
45	A5	4c blk & yel		.20	.20
46	A5	5c indigo & gray bl		.20	.20
47	A5	10c indigo & pink		.55	.55
48	A5	15c brn & bl		1.00	1.00
49	A5	20c brn & grn		1.00	1.00
50	A5	25c brn & yel		1.50	1.50
51	A6	30c dp grn & grn		1.40	1.40
52	A6	40c blk & pink		1.40	1.40
53	A6	45c brn & blue		2.00	2.00
54	A6	50c blk & grn		1.60	1.60
55	A6	65c indigo & bl		2.00	2.00
56	A6	75c blk & lil		1.75	1.75
57	A6	90c brn red & lil		1.75	1.75

			Perf. 14x13½		
58	A7	1fr brn & grn		1.50	1.50
59	A7	1.10fr indigo & lil		1.50	1.50
60	A7	1.50fr ultra & grysh		2.50	2.50
61	A7	2fr blk & bl		2.25	2.25
62	A7	3fr brn & yel		2.50	2.50
63	A7	5fr brn & lil		2.50	2.50

64	A7	10fr blk & grn		13.00	13.00
65	A7	20fr blk & pink		17.50	17.50
		Nos. 43-65 (23)		60.00	60.00

> Common Design Types pictured following the introduction.

Colonial Exposition Issue
Common Design Types

		1931	Engr.	Perf. 12½	
		Country Name Typo. in Black			
66	CD70	40c dp grn		2.00	2.00
67	CD71	50c violet		2.25	2.25
68	CD72	90c red org		2.25	2.25
69	CD73	1.50fr dull blue		2.75	2.75
		Nos. 66-69 (4)		9.25	9.25

> Catalogue values for unused stamps in this section, from this point to the end of the section, are for Never Hinged items.

Republic

President Ouezzin Coulibaly — A8

Deer Mask and Deer — A9

		1959	Unwmk.	Engr.	Perf. 13	
70	A8	25fr black & magenta			.45	.40

1st anniv. of the proclamation of the Republic; Ouezzin Coulibaly, Council President, who died in December, 1958.

> ### Imperforates
> Most Upper Volta stamps from 1959 onward exist imperforate in issued and trial colors, and also in small presentation sheets in issued colors.

1960

Animal Masks: 1fr, 2fr, 4fr, Wart hog. 5fr, 6fr, 8fr, Monkey. 10fr, 15fr, 20fr, Buffalo. 25fr, Coba (antelope). 30fr, 40fr, 50fr, Elephant. 60fr, 85fr, Secretary bird.

71	A9	30c rose & violet		.20	.20
72	A9	40c buff & dp claret		.20	.20
73	A9	50c bl grn & gray ol		.20	.20
74	A9	1fr red, blk & red brn		.20	.20
75	A9	2fr emer, yel grn & dk grn		.20	.20
76	A9	4fr bl, vio & ind		.20	.20
77	A9	5fr ol bis, red & brn		.20	.20
78	A9	6fr grnsh bl & vio brn		.20	.20
79	A9	8fr org & red brn		.20	.20
80	A9	10fr lt yel grn & plum		.20	.20
81	A9	15fr org, ultra & brn		.20	.20
82	A9	20fr green & ultra		.25	.20
83	A9	25fr bl, emer & dp claret		.25	.20
84	A9	30fr dk bl grn, blk & brn		.30	.20
85	A9	40fr ultra, ind & dk car		.40	.20
86	A9	50fr brt pink, brn & grn		.45	.20
87	A9	60fr org brn & bl		.55	.25
88	A9	85fr gray ol & dk bl		.80	.30
		Nos. 71-88 (18)		5.20	3.75

C.C.T.A. Issue
Common Design Type

		1960	Engr.	Perf. 13	
89	CD106	25fr vio bl & slate		.40	.25

Emblem of the Entente — A9a

Pres. Maurice Yameogo — A10

		1960	Photo.	Perf. 13x13½	
90	A9a	25fr multicolored		.40	.30

Council of the Entente.

		1960, May 1	Engr.	Perf. 13	
91	A10	25fr dk vio brn & slate		.25	.20

Flag, Village and Couple — A11

		1960, Aug. 5	Unwmk.	Perf. 13	
92	A11	25fr red brn, blk & red		.40	.25

Proclamation of independence, Aug. 5, 1960.

World Meteorological Organization Emblem — A12

		1961, May 4			
93	A12	25fr blk, bl & red		.30	.25

First World Meteorological Day.

Arms of Republic — A13

		1961, Dec. 8	Photo.	Perf. 12x12½	
94	A13	25fr multicolored		.25	.20

The 1961 independence celebrations.

WMO Emblem, Weather Station and Sorghum Grain — A14

		1962, Mar. 23	Unwmk.	Perf. 13	
95	A14	25fr dk bl, emer & brn		.40	.35

UN 2nd World Meteorological Day, Mar. 23.

Hospital and Nurse — A15

1962, June 23   *Perf. 13x12*
96 A15 25fr multicolored   .45 .35
Founding of Upper Volta Red Cross.

Buffalos at Water
Hole — A16

Designs: 10fr, Lions, horiz. 15fr, Defassa
waterbuck. 25fr, Arly reservation, horiz. 50fr,
Diapaga reservation, horiz. 85fr, Buffon's kob.

Perf. 12½x12, 12x12½
1962, June 30   *Engr.*
97 A16 5fr sepia, bl & grn   .20 .20
98 A16 10fr red brn, grn & yel   .25 .20
99 A16 15fr sepia, grn & yel   .60 .30
100 A16 25fr vio brn, bl & grn   .60 .35
101 A16 50fr vio brn, bl & grn   .85 .70
102 A16 85fr red brn, bl & grn   2.00 1.25
    Nos. 97-102 (6)   4.50 3.00

Abidjan Games Issue
Common Design Type
Designs: 20fr, Soccer. 25fr, Bicycling. 85fr,
Boxing. All horiz.

1962, July 21   *Photo.*   *Perf. 12½x12*
103 CD109 20fr multicolored   .30 .20
104 CD109 25fr multicolored   .50 .25
105 CD109 85fr multicolored   .95 .40
    Nos. 103-105 (3)   1.75 .85

African-Malgache Union Issue
Common Design Type
1962, Sept. 8   *Unwmk.*
106 CD110 30fr red, bluish grn &
       gold   .70 .50

Weather
Map and
UN
Emblem
A17

1963, Mar. 23   *Perf. 12x12½*
107 A17 70fr multicolored   .85 .45
3rd World Meteorological Day, Mar. 23.

Friendship Games,
Dakar, Apr. 11-
21 — A18

1963, Apr. 11   *Engr.*   *Perf. 13*
108 A18 20fr Basketball   .30 .20
109 A18 25fr Discus   .30 .20
110 A18 50fr Judo   .65 .25
    Nos. 108-110 (3)   1.25 .65

Amaryllis
A19

Flowers: 50c, Hibiscus. 1fr, Oldenlandia
grandiflora. 1.50fr, Rose moss (portulaca). 2fr,
Tobacco. 4fr, Morning glory. 5fr, Striga senegalensis. 6fr, Cowpea. 8fr, Lepidagathis
heudelotiana. 10fr, Spurge. 25fr, Argyreia
nervosa. 30fr, Rangoon creeper. 40fr, Water
lily. 50fr, White plumeria. 60fr, Crotalaria
retusa. 85fr, Hibiscus.

1963   *Photo.*
111 A19 50c multi, vert.   .20 .20
112 A19 1fr multi, vert.   .20 .20
113 A19 1.50fr multi, vert.   .20 .20
114 A19 2fr multi, vert.   .20 .20
115 A19 4fr multi, vert.   .20 .20
116 A19 5fr multi, vert.   .20 .20
117 A19 6fr multi, vert.   .20 .20
118 A19 8fr multi, vert.   .20 .20
119 A19 10fr multi, vert.   .20 .20
120 A19 15fr multi   .20 .20
121 A19 25fr multi   .30 .20
122 A19 30fr multi   .35 .20
123 A19 40fr multi   .40 .30
124 A19 50fr multi   .55 .40
125 A19 60fr multi   .65 .45
126 A19 85fr multi   .90 .55
    Nos. 111-126 (16)   5.15 4.10

Centenary
Emblem and
Globe — A20

Scroll — A21

1963, Oct. 21   *Unwmk.*   *Perf. 12*
127 A20 25fr multicolored   .60 .40
Centenary of International Red Cross.

1963, Dec. 10   *Photo.*   *Perf. 13x12½*
128 A21 25fr dp claret, gold & bl   .45 .25
15th anniv. of the Universal Declaration of
Human Rights.

Sound
Wave
Patterns
A22

1964, Jan. 16   *Perf. 12½x13*
129 A22 25fr multicolored   .25 .20
Upper Volta's admission to the ITU.

Barograph
and WMO
Emblem
A23

1964, Mar. 23   *Engr.*   *Perf. 13*
130 A23 50fr dk car rose, grn & bl   .55 .40
4th World Meteorological Day, Mar. 23.

World Connected by Letters and
Carrier Pigeon — A24

60fr, World connected by letters and jet
plane.

1964, Mar. 29   *Photo.*   *Perf. 13x12*
131 A24 25fr gray brn & ultra   .25 .20
132 A24 60fr gray brn & org   .60 .40
Upper Volta's admission to the UPU.

IQSY Emblem and
Seasonal
Allegories — A25

1964, Aug. 17   *Engr.*   *Perf. 13*
133 A25 30fr grn, ocher & car   .50 .25
International Quiet Sun Year.

Cooperation Issue
Common Design Type
1964, Nov. 7   *Unwmk.*   *Perf. 13*
134 CD119 70fr dl bl grn, dk brn &
       car   .65 .40

Hotel Independance,
Ouagadougou — A26

1964, Dec. 11   *Litho.*   *Perf. 12½x13*
135 A26 25fr multicolored   1.10 .45

Pigmy Long-
tailed
Sunbird — A27

Comoe
Waterfall — A28

1965, Mar. 1   *Photo.*   *Perf. 13x12½*
        Size: 22x36mm
136 A27 10fr shown   .35 .20
137 A27 15fr Olive-bellied Sun-
       bird   .50 .25
138 A27 25fr Splendid Sunbird   .80 .45
    Nos. 136-138,C20 (4)   10.65 4.40

1965   *Engr.*   *Perf. 13*
25fr, Great Waterfall of Banfora, horiz.
139 A28 5fr yel grn, bl & red brn   .30 .20
140 A28 25fr dk red, brt bl & grn   .40 .20
    Nos. 139-140 (2)   .70 .40

Soccer — A29

Abraham
Lincoln — A30

Designs: 25fr, Boxing gloves and ring. 70fr,
Tennis rackets, ball and net.

1965, July 15   *Unwmk.*   *Perf. 13*
141 A29 15fr brn, red & dk grn   .20 .20
142 A29 25fr pale org, bl & brn   .30 .20
143 A29 70fr dk car & brt grn   .60 .30
    Nos. 141-143 (3)   1.10 .70
1st African Games, Brazzaville, July 18-25.

1965, Nov. 3   *Photo.*   *Perf. 13x12½*
144 A30 50fr green & multi   .50 .40
Centenary of death of Abraham Lincoln.

Pres. Maurice Yameogo — A31

1965, Dec. 11   *Photo.*   *Perf. 13x12½*
145 A31 25fr multicolored   .25 .20

Mantis
A32

Wart Hog
A33

Headdress
A34

1966   *Perf. 13x12½, 12½x13*
146 A33 1fr Nemopistha impera-
       trix   .20 .20
147 A33 2fr Ball python   .20 .20
148 A32 3fr shown   .20 .20
149 A32 4fr Grasshopper   .20 .20
150 A32 5fr shown   .20 .20
151 A32 6fr Scorpion   .20 .20
152 A32 8fr Green monkey   .20 .20
153 A32 10fr Dromedary   .40 .20
154 A33 15fr Leopard   .20 .20
155 A32 20fr Cape buffalo   .55 .20
156 A33 25fr Hippopotamus   .60 .20
157 A32 30fr Agama lizard   .45 .20
158 A33 45fr Common puff adder   .90 .25
159 A33 50fr Chameleon   1.10 .35
160 A33 60fr Ugada limbata   1.40 .40
161 A33 85fr Elephant   1.50 .50
    Nos. 146-161 (16)   8.50 3.90

1966, Apr. 9   *Photo.*   *Perf. 13x12½*
25fr, Plumed headdress. 60fr, Male dancer.
162 A34 20fr yel grn, choc & red   .20 .20
163 A34 25fr multicolored   .25 .20
164 A34 60fr org, dk brn & red   .55 .35
    Nos. 162-164 (3)   1.00 .75
Intl. Negro Arts Festival, Dakar, Senegal,
4/1-24.

Pô Church
A35

Design: No. 166, Bobo-Dioulasso Mosque.

1966, Apr. 15   *Perf. 12½x13*
165 A35 25fr multicolored   .25 .20
166 A35 25fr bl, cream & red brn   .25 .20

The Red Cross
Helping the
World — A36

1966, June   *Photo.*   *Perf. 13x12½*
167 A36 25fr lemon, blk & car   .25 .20
Issued to honor the Red Cross.

Boy Scouts in Camp A37

15fr, Two Scouts on a cliff exploring the country.

1966, June 15   **Perf. 12½x13**
168 A37 10fr multicolored   .20 .20
169 A37 15fr blk, bis brn, & dl yel   .20 .20
Issued to honor the Boy Scouts.

Cow Receiving Injection A38

1966, Aug. 16   Photo.   Perf. 12½x13
170 A38 25fr yel, blk & blue   .25 .20
Campaign against cattle plague.

Plowing with Donkey A39

Design: 30fr, Crop rotation, Kamboince Experimental Station.

1966, Sept. 15   Photo.   Perf. 12½x13
171 A39 25fr multicolored   .25 .20
172 A39 30fr multicolored   .25 .20
Natl. and rural education; 3rd anniv. of the Kamboince Experimental Station (No. 172).

UNESCO Emblem and Map of Africa A40

UNICEF Emblem and Children A41

1966, Dec. 10   Engr.   Perf. 13
173 A40 50fr brt bl, blk & red   .50 .25
174 A41 50fr dk vio, dp lil & dk red   .50 .25
20th anniv. of UNESCO and of UNICEF.

Arms of Upper Volta — A42

Symbols of Agriculture, Industry, Men and Women — A43

1967, Jan. 2   Photo.   Perf. 12½x13
175 A42 30fr multicolored   .25 .20

Europafrica Issue
1967, Feb. 4   Photo.   Perf. 12½
176 A43 60fr multicolored   .50 .30

Scout Handclasp and Jamboree Emblem A44

5fr, Jamboree emblem, Scout holding hat.

1967, June 8   Photo.   Perf. 12½x13
177 A44 5fr multicolored   .20 .20
178 A44 20fr multicolored   .55 .40
12th Boy Scout World Jamboree, Farragut State Park, Idaho, Aug. 1-9. See No. C41.

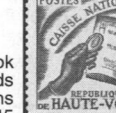

Bank Book and Hands with Coins A45

1967, Aug. 22   Engr.   Perf. 13
179 A45 30fr slate grn, ocher & olive   .25 .20
National Savings Bank.

Mailman on Bicycle — A46

1967, Oct. 15   Engr.   Perf. 13
180 A46 30fr dk bl, emer & brn   .30 .20
Stamp Day.

Monetary Union Issue
Common Design Type
1967, Nov. 4   Engr.   Perf. 13
181 CD125 30fr dk vio & dl bl   .25 .20

View of Nizier A47

Olympic Emblem and: 50fr, Les Deux-Alps, vert. 100fr, Ski lift and view of Villard-de-Lans.

1967, Nov. 28
182 A47 15fr brt bl, grn & brn   .20 .20
183 A47 50fr brt bl & slate grn   .45 .20
184 A47 100fr brt bl, grn & red   .90 .45
Nos. 182-184 (3)   1.55 .85
10th Winter Olympic Games, Grenoble, France, Feb. 6-18, 1968.

White and Black Men Holding Human Rights Emblem A48

1968, Jan. 2   Photo.   Perf. 12½x13
185 A48 20fr brt bl, gold & dp car   .20 .20
186 A48 30fr grn, gold & dp car   .30 .20
International Human Rights Year.

Administration School and Student — A49

1968, Feb. 2   Engr.   Perf. 13
187 A49 30fr ol bis, Prus bl & brt grn   .25 .20
National School of Administration.

WHO Emblem and Sick People A50

1968, Apr. 7   Engr.   Perf. 13
188 A50 30fr ind, brt bl & car rose   .30 .20
189 A50 50fr brt bl, sl grn & lt brn   .45 .25
WHO, 20th anniversary.

Telephone Office, Bobo-Dioulasso — A51

1968, Sept. 30   Photo.   Perf. 12½x12
190 A51 30fr multicolored   .30 .20
Opening of the automatic telephone office in Bobo-Dioulasso.

Weaver A52

1968, Oct. 30   Engr.   Perf. 13
Size: 36x22mm
191 A52 30fr magenta, brn & ocher   .30 .20
See No. C58.

Grain Pouring over World, Plower and FAO Emblem — A53

1969, Jan. 7   Engr.   Perf. 13
192 A53 30fr slate, vio bl & maroon   .25 .20
UNFAO world food program.

Automatic Looms and ILO Emblem A54

1969, Mar. 15   Engr.   Perf. 13
193 A54 30fr brt grn, mar & indigo   .25 .20
ILO, 50th anniversary.

Smith A55

1969, Apr. 3   Engr.   Perf. 13
Size: 36x22mm
194 A55 5fr magenta & blk   .20 .20
See No. C64.

Blood Donor — A56

1969, May 15   Engr.   Perf. 13
195 A56 30fr blk, bl & car   .25 .20
League of Red Cross Societies, 50th anniv.

Nile Pike — A57

Fish: 20fr, Nannocharax gobioides. 25fr, Hemigrammocharax polli. 55fr, Alestes luteus. 85fr, Micralestes voltae.

1969   Engr.   Perf. 13
Size: 36x22mm
196 A57 20fr brt bl, brn & yel   .30 .20
197 A57 25fr slate, brn & dk brn   .30 .20
198 A57 30fr dk olive & blk   .45 .25
199 A57 55fr dk grn, yel & ol   .60 .40
200 A57 85fr slate brn & pink   1.25 .90
Nos. 196-200,C66-C67 (7)   5.20 2.95

Development Bank Issue
Common Design Type
1969, Sept. 10   Engr.   Perf. 13
201 CD130 30fr sl grn, grn & ocher   .25 .20

Millet A58

Design: 30fr, Cotton.

1969, Oct. 30   Photo.   Perf. 12½x13
202 A58 15fr dk brn, grn & brt bl   .20 .20
203 A58 30fr dp claret & brt bl   .30 .20
Nos. 202-203,C73-C74 (4)   2.85 1.20

ASECNA Issue
Common Design Type
1969, Dec. 12   Engr.   Perf. 13
204 CD132 100fr brown   .80 .50

Niadale Mask — A59

Carvings from National Museum: 30fr, Niaga. 45fr, Man and woman, Iliu Bara. 80fr, Karan Weeba figurine.

1970, Mar. 5   Engr.   Perf. 13
207 A59 10fr dk car rose, org & dk brn   .20 .20
209 A59 30fr dk brn, brt vio & grnsh bl   .25 .20
211 A59 45fr yel grn, brn & bl   .30 .20
212 A59 80fr pur, rose lil & brn   .60 .25
Nos. 207-212 (4)   1.35 .85

African Huts and European City — A60

1970, Apr. 25   Engr.   Perf. 13
213 A60 30fr dk brn, red & bl   .25 .20
Issued for Linked Cities' Day.

Mask for Nebwa Gnomo Dance A61

Designs: 8fr, Cauris dancers, vert. 20fr, Gourmantchés dancers, vert. 30fr, Larllé dancers.

1970, May 7   Photo.   Perf. 13
214 A61 5fr lt brn, vio bl & blk   .20 .20
215 A61 8fr org brn, car & blk   .20 .20
216 A61 20fr dk brn, sl grn & ocher   .20 .20
217 A61 30fr dp car, dk gray & brn   .25 .20
    Nos. 214-217 (4)   .85 .80

Education Year Emblem, Open Book and Pupils A62

Design: 90fr, Education Year emblem, telecommunication and education symbols.

1970, May 14   Perf. 12½x12
218 A62 40fr black & multi   .35 .20
219 A62 65fr olive & multi   .65 .35

International Education Year.

UPU Headquarters Issue

Abraham Lincoln, UPU Headquarters and Emblem — A63

1970, May 20   Engr.   Perf. 13
220 A63 30fr dk car rose, ind & red brn   .30 .20
221 A63 60fr dk brn grn, vio & red brn   .50 .25

See note after CD133, Common Design section.

Ship-building Industry — A64

45fr, Chemical industry. 80fr, Electrical industry.

1970, June 15
222 A64 15fr brt pink, red brn & blk   .20 .20
223 A64 45fr emerald, dp bl & blk   .35 .20
224 A64 80fr red brn, claret & blk   .65 .35
    Nos. 222-224 (3)   1.20 .75

Hanover Fair.

Cattle Vaccination A65

1970, June 30   Photo.   Perf. 13
225 A65 30fr Prus bl, yel & sepia   .30 .20

National Veterinary College.

Vaccination and Red Cross — A66

1970, Aug. 28   Engr.   Perf. 12½x13
226 A66 30fr chocolate & car   .25 .20

Issued for the Upper Volta Red Cross. For surcharge see No. 252.

Europafrica Issue

Nurse with Child, by Frans Hals — A67

Paintings: 30fr, Courtyard of a House in Delft, by Pieter de Hooch. 150fr, Christina of Denmark, by Hans Holbein. 250fr, Courtyard of the Royal Palace at Innsbruck, Austria, by Albrecht Dürer.

1970, Sept. 25   Litho.   Perf. 13x14
227 A67 25fr multicolored   .25 .20
228 A67 30fr multicolored   .35 .20
229 A67 150fr multicolored   1.40 .60
230 A67 250fr multicolored   2.00 1.00
    Nos. 227-230 (4)   4.00 2.00

Citroen A68

Design: 40fr, Old and new Citroen cars.

1970, Oct. 16   Engr.   Perf. 13
231 A68 25fr ol brn, mar & sl grn   .25 .20
232 A68 40fr brt grn, plum & sl   .40 .20

57th Paris Automobile Salon.

Professional Training Center A69

1970, Dec. 10   Engr.   Perf. 13
233 A69 50fr grn, bis & brn   .40 .20

Opening of Professional Training Center under joint sponsorship of Austria and Upper Volta.

Upper Volta Arms and Soaring Bird — A70

1970, Dec. 10   Photo.
234 A70 30fr lt blue & multi   .25 .20

Tenth anniversary of independence, Dec. 11.

Political Maps of Africa — A71

1970, Dec. 14   Litho.   Perf. 13½
235 A71 50fr multicolored   .40 .20

10th anniv. of the declaration granting independence to colonial territories and countries.

Beingolo Hunting Horn — A72

Musical Instruments: 15fr, Mossi guitar, vert. 20fr, Gourounsi flutes, vert. 25fr, Lunga drums.

1971, Mar. 1   Engr.   Perf. 13
236 A72 5fr blue, brn & car   .20 .20
237 A72 15fr grn, crim rose & brn   .20 .20
238 A72 20fr car rose, bl & gray   .20 .20
239 A72 25fr brt grn, red brn & ol gray   .20 .20
    Nos. 236-239 (4)   .80 .80

Voltaphilex I, National Phil. Exhibition.

Four Races — A73

1971, Mar. 21   Engr.   Perf. 13
240 A73 50fr rose cl, lt grn & dk brn   .40 .25

Intl. year against racial discrimination.

Telephone and Globes A74

1971, May 17   Engr.   Perf. 13
241 A74 50fr brn, gray & dk pur   .40 .20

3rd World Telecommunications Day.

Cane Field Worker, Banfora Sugar Mill — A75

Cotton and Voltex Mill Emblem — A76

1971, June 24   Photo.   Perf. 13
242 A75 10fr multicolored   .20 .20
243 A76 35fr multicolored   .25 .20

Industrial development.

Gonimbrasia Hecate — A77

Butterflies and Moths: 2fr, Hamanumida daedalus. 3fr, Ophideres materna. 5fr, Danaus chrysippus. 40fr, Hypolimnas misippus. 45fr, Danaus petiverana.

1971, June 30
244 A77 1fr blue & multi   .20 .20
245 A77 2fr lt lilac & multi   .20 .20
246 A77 3fr multicolored   .20 .20
247 A77 5fr gray & multi   .20 .20
248 A77 40fr ocher & multi   .60 .35
249 A77 45fr multicolored   .80 .50
    Nos. 244-249 (6)   2.20 1.65

Kabuki Actor — A78

40fr, African mask and Kabuki actor.

1971, Aug. 12   Photo.   Perf. 13
250 A78 25fr multicolored   .20 .20
251 A78 40fr multicolored   .30 .20

Philatokyo 71, Philatelic Exposition, Tokyo, Apr. 19-29.

No. 226 Surcharged

1971   Engr.   Perf. 12½x13
252 A66 100fr on 30fr choc & car   .65 .40

10th anniversary of Upper Volta Red Cross.

Seed Preparation A79

Designs: 75fr, Old farmer with seed packet, vert. 100fr, Farmer in rice field.

1971, Sept. 30   Photo.   Perf. 13
253 A79 35fr ocher & multi   .25 .20
254 A79 75fr lt blue & multi   .50 .20
255 A79 100fr brown & multi   .65 .35
    Nos. 253-255 (3)   1.40 .75

National campaign for seed protection.

Outdoor Classroom A80

Design: 50fr, Mother learning to read.

1971, Oct. 14
256 A80 35fr multicolored   .25 .20
257 A80 50fr multicolored   .40 .20

Women's education.

Joseph Dakiri, Soldiers Driving Tractors — A81

Children and UNICEF Emblem — A84

Spraying Lake, Fly, Man Leading Blind Women A82

40fr, Dakiri & soldiers gathering harvest.

1971, Oct. 13 *Perf. 12x12½*
258 A81 15fr blk, yel & red brn .20 .20
259 A81 40fr blue & multi .20 .20
Joseph Dakiri (1938-1971), inaugurator of the Army-Aid-to-Agriculture Program.

1971, Nov. 26 **Photo.** *Perf. 13*
260 A82 40fr dk brn, yel & bl .25 .20
Drive against onchocerciasis, roundworm infestation.
For surcharge see No. 295.

1971, Dec. 11 *Perf. 13*
262 A84 45fr red, bister & blk .35 .20
UNICEF, 25th anniv.

Peulh House A85

Upper Volta Houses: 20fr, Gourounsi house. 35fr, Mossi houses. 45fr, Bobo house, vert. 50fr, Dagari house, vert. 90fr, Bango house, interior.

Perf. 13x13½, 13½x13
1971-72 **Photo.**
263 A85 10fr ver & multi .20 .20
264 A85 20fr multicolored .20 .20
265 A85 35fr brt grn & multi .25 .20
266 A85 45fr multi ('72) .35 .20
267 A85 50fr multi ('72) .40 .20
268 A85 90fr multi ('72) .60 .35
Nos. 263-268 (6) 2.00 1.35

Town Halls of Bobo-Dioulasso and Chalons-sur-Marne — A86

1971, Dec. 23 *Perf. 13x12½*
269 A86 40fr yellow & multi .25 .20
Kinship between the cities of Bobo-Dioulasso, Upper Volta, and Chalons-sur-Marne, France.

Louis Armstrong — A87

1972, May 17 *Perf. 14x13*
270 A87 45fr multicolored .45 .25
Black musician. See No. C104.

Red Crescent, Cross and Lion Emblems A88

1972, June 23 *Perf. 13x14*
271 A88 40fr yellow & multi .35 .20
World Red Cross Day. See No. C105.

Coiffure of Peulh Woman — A89

Designs: Various hair styles.

1972, July 23 **Litho.** *Perf. 13*
272 A89 25fr blue & multi .20 .20
273 A89 35fr emerald & multi .25 .20
274 A89 75fr yellow & multi .45 .20
Nos. 272-274 (3) .90 .60

Classroom A90

15fr, Clinic. 20fr, Factory. 35fr, Cattle. 40fr, Flowers. 85fr, Road building machinery.

1972, Oct. 30 **Engr.** *Perf. 13*
275 A90 10fr sl grn, lt grn & choc .20 .20
276 A90 15fr brt grn, brn org & brn .20 .20
277 A90 20fr bl, lt brn & grn .20 .20
278 A90 35fr grn, brn & brt bl .20 .20
279 A90 40fr choc, pink & sl grn .25 .20
Nos. 275-279,C106 (6) 1.50 1.25
2nd Five-Year Plan.

West African Monetary Union Issue
Common Design Type
1972, Nov. 2
280 CD136 40fr brn, bl & gray .25 .20

Lottery Office and Emblem A91

1972, Nov. 6 **Litho.**
281 A91 35fr multicolored .25 .20
5th anniversary of National Lottery.

Domestic Animals — A92

1972, Dec. 4 **Litho.** *Perf. 13½x12½*
282 A92 5fr Donkeys .20 .20
283 A92 10fr Geese .20 .20
284 A92 30fr Goats .20 .20
285 A92 50fr Cow .35 .20
286 A92 65fr Dromedaries .40 .20
Nos. 282-286 (5) 1.35 1.00

Mossi Woman's Hair Style, and Village — A93

1973, Jan. 24 **Engr.** *Perf. 13*
287 A93 5fr slate grn, org & choc .20 .20
288 A93 40fr bl, org & chocolate .25 .20

Eugene A. Cernan and Lunar Module A94

65fr, Ronald E. Evans & splashdown. 100fr, Capsule, in orbit & interior, horiz. 150fr, Harrison H. Schmitt & lift-off. 200fr, Conference & moon-buggy. 500fr, Moon-buggy & capsule, horiz.

Perf. 12½x13½, 13½x12½
1973, Mar. 29 **Litho.**
289 A94 50fr multi .30 .20
290 A94 65fr multi .40 .20
291 A94 100fr multi .60 .30
292 A94 150fr multi .90 .45
293 A94 200fr multi 1.25 .60
Nos. 289-293 (5) 3.45 1.75
Souvenir Sheet
294 A94 500fr multi 3.50 1.60
Apollo 17 moon mission.

No. 260 Surcharged in Red

1973, Apr. 7 **Photo.** *Perf. 13*
295 A82 45fr on 40fr multi .25 .20
WHO, 25th anniversary.

Scout Bugler A95

1973, July 18 **Litho.** *Perf. 12½x13*
296 A95 20fr multicolored .20 .20
Nos. 296,C160-C163 (5) 3.35 1.80

African Postal Union Issue
Common Design Type
1973, Sept. 12 **Engr.** *Perf. 13*
297 CD137 100fr brt red, mag & dl yel .65 .25

Pres. Kennedy, Saturn 5 on Assembly Trailer A96

Pres. John F. Kennedy (1917-1963) and: 10fr, Atlas rocket carrying John H. Glenn. 30fr, Titan 2 rocket and Gemini 3 capsule.

1973, Sept. 12 **Litho.** *Perf. 12½x13*
298 A96 5fr multicolored .20 .20
299 A96 10fr multicolored .20 .20
300 A96 30fr multicolored .20 .20
Nos. 298-300,C167-C168 (5) 4.00 2.25

Cross-examination — A97

Designs: 65fr, "Diamond Ede." 70fr, Forensic Institute. 150fr, Robbery scene.

1973, Sept. 15 *Perf. 13x12½*
301 A97 50fr multicolored .30 .20
302 A97 65fr multicolored .40 .20
303 A97 70fr multicolored .40 .20
304 A97 150fr multicolored .90 .40
Nos. 301-304 (4) 2.00 1.00
Interpol, 50th anniversary. See No. C170.

Market Place, Ouagadougou — A98

40fr, Swimming pool, Hotel Independence.

1973, Sept. 30
305 A98 35fr multicolored .25 .20
306 A98 40fr multicolored .25 .20
Nos. 305-306,C171 (3) 1.15 .75
Tourism. See No. C172.

Protestant Church — A99

Design: 40fr, Ouahigouya Mosque.

1973, Sept. 28 *Perf. 13x12½*
307 A99 35fr multicolored .25 .20
308 A99 40fr multicolored .25 .20
Nos. 307-308,C173 (3) 1.90 1.05
Houses of worship.

Kiembara
Dancers
A100

Folklore: 40fr, Dancers.

1973, Nov. 30   Litho.   Perf. 12½x13

309	A100	35fr multicolored	.25	.20
310	A100	40fr multicolored	.25	.20
		Nos. 309-310,C174-C175 (4)	2.65	1.45

Yuri Gagarin and Aries — A101

Famous Men and their Zodiac Signs: 10fr, Lenin and Taurus. 20fr, John F. Kennedy, rocket and Gemini. 25fr, John H. Glenn, orbiting capsule and Cancer. 30fr, Napoleon and Leo. 50fr, Goethe and Virgo. 60fr, Pelé and Libra. 75fr, Charles de Gaulle and Scorpio. 100fr, Beethoven and Sagittarius. 175fr, Conrad Adenauer and Capricorn. 200fr, Edwin E. Aldrin, Jr. (Apollo XI) and Aquarius. 250fr, Lord Baden-Powell and Pisces.

1973, Dec. 15   Litho.   Perf. 13x14

311	A101	5fr multicolored	.20	.20
312	A101	10fr multicolored	.20	.20
313	A101	20fr multicolored	.20	.20
314	A101	25fr multicolored	.20	.20
315	A101	30fr multicolored	.20	.20
316	A101	50fr multicolored	.30	.20
317	A101	60fr multicolored	.40	.20
318	A101	75fr multicolored	.45	.20
319	A101	100fr multicolored	.60	.30
320	A101	175fr multicolored	1.10	.55
321	A101	200fr multicolored	1.25	.55
322	A101	250fr multicolored	1.50	.70
		Nos. 311-322 (12)	6.60	3.70

See Nos. C176-C178.

Rivera with Italian Flag and
Championship '74 Emblem — A102

40fr, World Cup, soccer ball, World Championship '74 emblem & Pelé with Brazilian flag.

1974, Jan. 15   Perf. 13x12½

323	A102	5fr multicolored	.20	.20
324	A102	40fr multicolored	.20	.20
		Nos. 323-324,C179-C181 (5)	3.20	1.80

10th World Cup Soccer Championship, Munich, June 13-July 7.

Charles de
Gaulle
A103

40fr, De Gaulle memorial. 60fr, Pres. de Gaulle.

1974, Feb. 4   Litho.   Perf. 12½x13

325	A103	35fr multicolored	.20	.20
326	A103	40fr multicolored	.20	.20
327	A103	60fr multicolored	.35	.20
a.		Strip of 3, Nos. 325-327	.75	.45
		Nos. 325-327,C183 (4)	2.75	1.60

Gen. Charles de Gaulle (1890-1970), president of France. See #C184.

N'Dongo
and
Cameroun
Flag
A104

World Cup, Emblems and: 20fr, Kolev and Bulgarian flag. 50fr, Keita and Mali flag.

1974, Mar. 19

328	A104	10fr multicolored	.20	.20
329	A104	20fr multicolored	.20	.20
330	A104	30fr multicolored	.35	.20
		Nos. 328-330,C185-C186 (5)	3.00	1.75

10th World Cup Soccer Championship, Munich, June 13-July 7.

Map and
Flags of
Members
A105

1974, May 29   Photo.   Perf. 13x12½

331	A105	40fr blue & multi	.25	.20

15th anniversary of the Council of Accord.

UPU Emblem and Mail Coach — A106

1974, July 23   Litho.   Perf. 13½

332	A106	35fr shown	.25	.20
333	A106	40fr Steamship	.25	.20
334	A106	85fr Mailman	.50	.30
		Nos. 332-334,C189-C191 (6)	4.00	2.20

Universal Postal Union centenary.
For overprints see #339-341, C197-C200.

Soccer Game, Winner Italy, in France,
1938 — A107

World Cup, Game and Flags: 25fr, Uruguay, in Brazil, 1950. 50fr, East Germany, in Switzerland, 1954.

1974, Sept. 2   Litho.   Perf. 13½

335	A107	10fr multicolored	.20	.20
336	A107	25fr multicolored	.20	.20
337	A107	50fr multicolored	.35	.20
		Nos. 335-337,C193-C195 (6)	4.75	2.60

World Cup Soccer winners.

Map and Farm Woman — A108

1974, Oct. 2   Litho.   Perf. 13x12½

338	A108	35fr yellow & multi	.20	.20

Kou Valley Development.

Nos. 332-334 Overprinted in Red
"100e ANNIVERSAIRE DE L'UNION
POSTALE UNIVERSELLE / 9
OCTOBRE 1974"

1974, Oct. 9

339	A106	35fr multicolored	.25	.20
340	A106	40fr multicolored	.25	.20
341	A106	85fr multicolored	.50	.30
		Nos. 339-341,C197-C199 (6)	5.00	2.70

Universal Postal Union centenary.

Flowers, by
Pierre
Bonnard
A109

Flower Paintings by: 10fr, Jan Brueghel. 30fr, Jean van Os. 50fr, Van Brussel.

1974, Oct. 31   Litho.   Perf. 12½x13

342	A109	5fr multicolored	.20	.20
343	A109	10fr multicolored	.20	.20
344	A109	30fr multicolored	.20	.20
345	A109	50fr multicolored	.25	.20
		Nos. 342-345,C201 (5)	2.85	1.80

Churchill as Officer of India
Hussars — A110

Churchill: 75fr, As Secretary of State for Interior. 100fr, As pilot. 125fr, meeting with Roosevelt, 1941. 300fr, As painter. 450fr, and "HMS Resolution."

1975, Jan. 11   Perf. 13½

346	A110	50fr multicolored	.30	.20
347	A110	75fr multicolored	.45	.20
348	A110	100fr multicolored	.55	.30
349	A110	125fr multicolored	.70	.40
350	A110	300fr multicolored	1.60	.80
		Nos. 346-350 (5)	3.60	1.90

Souvenir Sheet

351	A110	450fr multicolored	2.50	1.25

Sir Winston Churchill, birth centenary.

US No. 619 and Minutemen — A111

US Stamps: 40fr, #118 and Proclamation of Independence. 75fr, #798 and Signing the Constitution. 100fr, #703 and Surrender at Yorktown. 200fr, #1003 and George Washington. 300fr, #644 and Surrender of Burgoyne at Saratoga. 500fr, #63, 68, 73, 157, 179, 228 and 1483a.

1975, Feb. 17   Litho.   Perf. 11

352	A111	35fr multicolored	.20	.20
353	A111	40fr multicolored	.25	.20
354	A111	75fr multicolored	.40	.20
355	A111	100fr multicolored	.55	.30
356	A111	200fr multicolored	1.25	.55
357	A111	300fr multicolored	1.60	.80
		Nos. 352-357 (6)	4.25	2.25

Souvenir Sheet
Imperf

358	A111	500fr multicolored	3.00	1.50

American Bicentennial.

"Atlantic" No. 2670, 1904-12 — A112

Locomotives from Mulhouse, France, Railroad Museum: 25fr, No. 2029, 1882. 50fr, No. 2129, 1882.

1975, Feb. 28   Litho.   Perf. 13x12½

359	A112	15fr multicolored	.20	.20
360	A112	25fr multicolored	.20	.20
361	A112	50fr multicolored	.35	.20
		Nos. 359-361,C203-C204 (5)	2.80	1.60

French Flag and Renault Petit Duc,
1910 — A113

Flags and Old Cars: 30fr, US and Ford Model T, 1909. 35fr, Italy and Alfa Romeo "Le Mans," 1931.

1975, Apr. 6   Perf. 14x13½

362	A113	10fr multicolored	.20	.20
363	A113	30fr multicolored	.20	.20
364	A113	35fr multicolored	.20	.20
		Nos. 362-364,C206-C207 (5)	3.00	1.75

Washington and Lafayette — A114

American Bicentennial: 40fr, Washington reviewing troops at Valley Forge. 50fr, Washington taking oath of office.

1975, May 6   Litho.   Perf. 14
365   A114 30fr multicolored   .20   .20
366   A114 40fr multicolored   .25   .20
367   A114 50fr multicolored   .35   .20
      Nos. 365-367,C209-C210 (5)   4.20 2.25
Souvenir Sheet
367A A114 500fr multicolored   3.50 1.60

Schweitzer and Pelicans — A115

15fr, Albert Schweitzer and bateleur eagle.

1975, May 25   Litho.   Perf. 13½
368   A115 5fr multicolored   .20   .20
369   A115 15fr multicolored   .20   .20
      Nos. 368-369,C212-C214 (5)   4.00 2.10
Albert Schweitzer, birth centenary.

Apollo and Soyuz Orbiting Earth — A116

Design: 50fr, Apollo and Soyuz near link-up.

1975, July 18
370   A116 40fr multicolored   .25   .20
371   A116 50fr multicolored   .35   .20
      Nos. 370-371,C216-C218 (5)   4.60 2.40
Apollo-Soyuz space test project, Russo-American cooperation, launched July 15, link-up July 17.

Maria Picasso Lopez, Artist's Mother A117

Paintings by Pablo Picasso (1881-1973): 60fr, Self-portrait. 90fr, First Communion.

1975, Aug. 7
372   A117 50fr multicolored   .35   .20
373   A117 60fr multicolored   .40   .20
374   A117 90fr multicolored   .60   .30
      Nos. 372-374,C220-C221 (5)   4.60 2.45

Expo '75 Emblem and Tanker, Idemitsu Maru — A118

Oceanographic Exposition, Okinawa: 25fr, Training ship, Kaio Maru. 45fr, Firefighting ship, Hiryu. 50fr, Battleship, Yamato. 60fr, Container ship, Kamakura Maru.

1975, Sept. 26   Litho.   Perf. 11
375   A118 15fr multicolored   .20   .20
376   A118 25fr multicolored   .20   .20
377   A118 45fr multicolored   .30   .20
377A A118 50fr multicolored   .35   .20
378   A118 60fr multicolored   .40   .20
      Nos. 375-378,C223 (6)   2.20 1.40

Woman, Globe and IWY Emblem — A119

1975, Nov. 20   Photo.   Perf. 13
379   A119 65fr multicolored   .40   .25
International Women's Year.

Msgr. Joanny Thevenoud and Cathedral — A120

65fr, Father Guillaume Templier & Cathedral.

1975, Nov. 20   Engr.   Perf. 13x12½
380   A120 55fr grn, blk & dl red   .20   .20
381   A120 65fr blk, org & dl red   .25   .20
75th anniv. of the Evangelization of Upper Volta.

Farmer's Hat, Hoe and Emblem A121

1975, Dec. 10   Photo.   Perf. 13x13½
382   A121 15fr buff & multi   .20   .20
383   A121 50fr lt green & multi   .20   .20
Development of the Volta valleys.

Sledding and Olympic Emblem — A122

Innsbruck Background, Olympic Emblem and: 45fr, Figure skating. 85fr, Skiing.

1975, Dec. 16   Litho.   Perf. 13½
384   A122 35fr multicolored   .20   .20
385   A122 45fr multicolored   .25   .20
386   A122 85fr multicolored   .50   .25
      Nos. 384-386,C225-C226 (5)   3.00 1.65
12th Winter Olympic Games, Innsbruck, Austria, Feb. 4-15, 1976.

Gymnast and Olympic Emblem — A123

1976, Mar. 17
387   A123 40fr shown   .20   .20
388   A123 50fr Sailing   .25   .20
389   A123 100fr Soccer   .55   .30
      Nos. 387-389,C228-C229 (5)   2.40 1.40
21st Olympic Games, Montreal, Canada, July 17-Aug. 1.

Olympic Emblem and Sprinters A124

Olympic Emblem and: 55fr, Equestrian. 75fr, Hurdles.

1976, Mar. 25   Litho.   Perf. 11
390   A124 30fr multicolored   .20   .20
391   A124 55fr multicolored   .30   .20
392   A124 75fr multicolored   .40   .20
      Nos. 390-392,C231-C232 (5)   2.65 1.50
21st Olympic Games, Montreal.
For overprints see #420-422, C245-C247.

Blind Woman and Man — A125

1976, Apr. 7   Engr.   Perf. 13
393   A125 75fr dk brn, grn & org   .40   .25
394   A125 250fr dk brn, ocher & brn   1.40   .80
Drive against onchocerciasis, roundworm infestation.

"Deutschland" over Friedrichshafen — A126

Airships: 40fr, "Victoria Louise" over sailing ships. 50fr, "Sachsen" over German countryside.

1976, May 11   Litho.   Perf. 11
395   A126 10fr multicolored   .70   .20
396   A126 25fr multicolored   .25   .20
397   A126 50fr multicolored   .35   .20
      Nos. 395-397,C234-C236 (6)   5.30 2.60
75th anniversary of the Zeppelin.

Viking Lander and Probe on Mars — A127

Viking Mars project: 55fr, Viking orbiter in flight. 75fr, Titan rocket start for Mars, vert.

1976, June 24   Perf. 13½
398   A127 30fr multicolored   .20   .20
399   A127 55fr multicolored   .25   .20
400   A127 75fr multicolored   .30   .20
      Nos. 398-400,C238-C239 (5)   3.25 1.80

World Map, Arms of Upper Volta A128

Design: 100fr, World map, arms and dove.

1976, Aug. 19   Litho.   Perf. 12½
401   A128 55fr brown & multi   .25   .20
402   A128 100fr blue & multi   .40   .30
5th Summit Conference of Non-aligned Countries, Colombo, Sri Lanka, Aug. 9-19.

Bicentennial, Interphil 76 Emblems and Washington at Battle of Trenton — A129

90fr, Bicentennial, Interphil 76 emblems, Seat of Government, Pennsylvania.

1976, Sept. 30   Perf. 13½
403   A129 60fr multicolored   .40   .20
404   A129 90fr multicolored   .60   .25
      Nos. 403-404,C241-C243 (5)   5.00 2.45
American Bicentennial, Interphil 76, Philadelphia, Pa., May 29-June 6.

UPU and UN Emblems — A130

1976, Dec. 8   Engr.   Perf. 13
405   A130 200fr red, olive & blue   1.00   .60
UN Postal Administration, 25th anniv.

Arms of Tenkodogo A131

Bronze Statuette A132

Coats of Arms: 20fr, 100fr, Ouagadougou.

1977, May 2　Litho.　Perf. 13
406	A131	10fr multicolored	.20	.20
407	A131	20fr multicolored	.20	.20
408	A131	65fr multicolored	.35	.25
409	A131	100fr multicolored	.55	.35
		Nos. 406-409 (4)	1.30	1.00

1977, June 13　Photo.　Perf. 13

Design: 65fr, Woman with bowl, bronze.

410	A132	55fr multicolored	.30	.20
411	A132	65fr multicolored	.35	.20

#410-411 issued in sheets and coils with black control number on every 5th stamp.

Granaries
A133

Handbags
A134

1977, June 20　Photo.　Perf. 13½x13
412	A133	5fr Samo	.20	.20
413	A133	35fr Boromo	.20	.20
414	A133	45fr Banfora	.25	.20
415	A133	55fr Mossi	.30	.20
		Nos. 412-415 (4)	.95	.80

1977, June 20
416	A134	30fr Gouin	.20	.20
417	A134	40fr Bissa	.20	.20
418	A134	60fr Lobi	.35	.20
419	A134	70fr Mossi	.40	.25
		Nos. 416-419 (4)	1.15	.85

Nos. 390-392 Overprinted in Gold:
a. VAINQUEUR 1976 / LASSE VIREN / FINLANDE
b. VAINQUEUR 1976 / ALWIN SCHOCKEMOHLE / R.F.A.
c. VAINQUEUR 1976 / JOHANNA SCHALLER / R.D.A.

1977, July 4　Litho.　Perf. 11
420	A124 (a)	30fr multicolored	.20	.20
421	A124 (b)	55fr multicolored	.30	.20
422	A124 (c)	75fr multicolored	.20	.20
		Nos. 420-422,C245-C246 (5)	3.30	1.75

Winners, 21st Olympic Games.

Crinum
Ornatum — A135

Haemanthus
Multiflorus
A136

Hannoa
Undulata
A137

Designs: Flowers, flowering branches and wild fruits. 175fr, 300fr, horiz.

1977　Litho.　Perf. 12½
423	A137	2fr Cordia myxa	.20	.20
424	A137	3fr Opilia celtidifolia	.20	.20
425	A135	15fr shown	.20	.20
426	A136	25fr shown	.20	.20
427	A137	50fr shown	.25	.20
428	A135	90fr Cochlospermum planchonii	.45	.35
429	A135	125fr Clitoria ternatea	.65	.50
430	A136	150fr Cassia alata	.80	.60
431	A136	175fr Nauclea latifolia	.90	.70
432	A136	300fr Bombax costatum	1.60	1.25
433	A135	400fr Eulophia cuculata	2.00	1.60
		Nos. 423-433 (11)	7.45	6.00

Issued: 25fr, 150fr, 175fr, 300fr, 8/1; 2fr, 3fr, 50fr, 8/8; 15fr, 90fr, 125fr, 400fr, 8/23.

De Gaulle
and Cross of
Lorraine
A138

Designs: 200fr, King Baudouin of Belgium.

1977, Aug. 16　Perf. 13½x14
434	A138	100fr multicolored	.55	.25
435	A138	200fr multicolored	1.10	.40

Elizabeth II
A139

Designs: 300fr, Elizabeth II taking salute. 500fr, Elizabeth II after Coronation.

1977, Aug. 16
436	A139	200fr multicolored	.80	.30
437	A139	300fr multicolored	1.25	.50

Souvenir Sheet
438	A139	500fr multicolored	2.00	.90

25th anniv. of reign of Queen Elizabeth II. For overprints see Nos. 478-480.

Lottery Tickets, Cars and Map of
Upper Volta in Flag Colors — A140

1977, Sept. 16　Photo.　Perf. 13
439	A140	55fr multicolored	.30	.25

10th anniversary of National Lottery.

Selma Lagerlof, Literature — A141

Nobel Prize Winners: 65fr, Guglielmo Marconi, physics. 125fr, Bertrand Russell, literature. 200fr, Linus C. Pauling, chemistry. 300fr, Robert Koch, medicine. 500fr, Albert Schweitzer, peace.

1977, Sept. 22　Litho.　Perf. 13½
440	A141	55fr multicolored	.30	.20
441	A141	65fr multicolored	.40	.20
442	A141	125fr multicolored	.60	.25
443	A141	200fr multicolored	1.10	.40
444	A141	500fr multicolored	1.60	.60
		Nos. 440-444 (5)	4.00	1.70

Souvenir Sheet
445	A141	500fr multicolored	2.50	1.20

The Three
Graces, by
Rubens
A142

Paintings by Peter Paul Rubens (1577-1640): 55fr, Heads of Black Men, horiz. 85fr, Bathsheba at the Fountain. 150fr, The Drunken Silenus. 200fr, 300fr, Life of Maria de Medicis, diff.

1977, Oct. 19　Litho.　Perf. 14
446	A142	55fr multicolored	.30	.20
447	A142	65fr multicolored	.40	.20
448	A142	85fr multicolored	.45	.25
449	A142	150fr multicolored	.80	.40
450	A142	200fr multicolored	1.10	.45
451	A142	300fr multicolored	1.60	.60
		Nos. 446-451 (6)	4.65	2.10

Lenin in His
Office
A143

85fr, Lenin Monument, Kremlin. 200fr, Lenin with youth. 500fr, Lenin & Leonid Brezhnev.

1977, Oct. 28　Litho.　Perf. 12
452	A143	10fr multicolored	.20	.20
453	A143	85fr multicolored	.45	.25
454	A143	200fr multicolored	1.10	.65
455	A143	500fr multicolored	2.50	1.60
		Nos. 452-455 (4)	4.25	2.70

Russian October Revolution, 60th anniv.

Stadium and Brazil No. C79 — A144

Stadium and: 65fr, Brazil #1144. 125fr, Gt. Britain #458. 200fr, Chile #340. 300fr, Switzerland #350. 500fr, Germany #1147.

1977, Dec. 30　Litho.　Perf. 13½
456	A144	55fr multicolored	.30	.20
457	A144	65fr multicolored	.40	.20
458	A144	125fr multicolored	.60	.25
459	A144	200fr multicolored	1.10	.40
460	A144	300fr multicolored	1.60	.65
		Nos. 456-460 (5)	4.00	1.70

Souvenir Sheet
461	A144	500fr multicolored	2.50	1.25

11th World Cup Soccer Championship, Argentina. For overprints see Nos. 486-491.

Jean Mermoz and Seaplane — A145

History of Aviation: 75fr, Anthony H. G. Fokker. 85fr, Wiley Post. 90fr, Otto Lilienthal, vert. 100fr, Concorde. 500fr, Charles Lindbergh and "Spirit of St. Louis."

1978, Jan. 2　Litho.　Perf. 13½
462	A145	65fr multicolored	.35	.20
463	A145	75fr multicolored	.40	.20
464	A145	85fr multicolored	.45	.20
465	A145	90fr multicolored	.50	.20
466	A145	100fr multicolored	.55	.20
		Nos. 462-466 (5)	2.25	1.00

Souvenir Sheet
467	A145	500fr multicolored	2.50	1.25

Crataeva
Religiosa — A146

1978, Feb. 28　Litho.　Perf. 12½
468	A146	55fr shown	.30	.25
469	A146	75fr Fig tree	.40	.30

Souvenir Sheet

Virgin and Child, by Rubens — A147

1978, May 24　Litho.　Perf. 13½x14
470	A147	500fr multicolored	2.50	1.25

Peter Paul Rubens (1577-1640).

Antenna
and ITU
Emblem
A148

1978, May 30　Perf. 13
471	A148	65fr silver & multi	.40	.20

10th World Telecommunications Day.

Fetish Gate of
Bobo — A149

1978, July 10   Litho.   **Perf. 13½**
472 A149 55fr shown   .30 .20
473 A149 65fr Mossi fetish   .40 .20

Capt. Cook and "Endeavour" — A150

Capt. James Cook (1728-1779) and: 85fr, Death on Hawaiian beach. 250fr, Navigational instruments. 350fr, "Resolution."

1978, Sept. 1   Litho.   **Perf. 14½**
474 A150 65fr multicolored   .40 .20
475 A150 85fr multicolored   .45 .20
476 A150 250fr multicolored   1.40 .65
477 A150 350fr multicolored   1.90 .80
    Nos. 474-477 (4)   4.15 1.85

Nos. 436-438 Overprinted Vertically in Silver: "ANNIVERSAIRE DU COURONNEMENT 1953-1978"

1978, Oct. 24   Litho.   **Perf. 13½x14**
478 A139 200fr multicolored   1.10 .40
479 A139 300fr multicolored   1.60 .65

Souvenir Sheet
480 A139 500fr multicolored   2.50 1.25

25th anniversary of Coronation of Queen Elizabeth II. Overprint in 3 lines on 200fr, in 2 lines on 300fr and 500fr.
#478-480 exist with overprint in metallic red.

Trent Castle, by Dürer — A151

Paintings by Albrecht Durer (1471-1528): 150fr, Virgin and Child with St. Anne, vert. 250fr, Sts. George and Eustachius, vert. 350fr, Hans Holzschuher, vert.

Perf. 14x13½, 13½x14
1978, Nov. 20   Litho.
481 A151 65fr multicolored   .40 .20
482 A151 150fr multicolored   .80 .40
483 A151 250fr multicolored   1.40 .65
484 A151 350fr multicolored   1.90 .65
    Nos. 481-484 (4)   4.50 1.90

Human Rights Emblem A152

1978, Dec. 10   Litho.   **Perf. 12½**
485 A152 55fr multicolored   .30 .20

Universal Declaration of Human Rights, 30th anniv.

Nos. 456-461 Overprinted in Silver
a, VAINQUEURS 1950 URUGUAY / 1978 / ARGENTINE
b, VAINQUEURS 1970 BRESIL / 1978 ARGENTINE
c, VAINQUEURS 1966 GRANDE BRETAGNE / 1978 ARGENTINE
d, VAINQUEURS / 1962 BRESIL / 1978 ARGENTINE
e, VAINQUEURS 1954 ALLEMAGNE (RFA) / 1978 ARGENTINE
f, VAINQUEURS 1974 ALLEMAGNE (RFA) / 1978 ARGENTINE

1979, Jan. 4   Litho.   **Perf. 13½**
486 A144(a) 55fr multicolored   .30 .20
487 A144(b) 65fr multicolored   .40 .20
488 A144(c) 125fr multicolored   .60 .25

489 A144(d) 200fr multicolored   1.10 .40
490 A144(e) 300fr multicolored   1.60 .65
    Nos. 486-490 (5)   4.00 1.70

Souvenir Sheet
491 A144(f) 500fr multicolored   2.50 1.25

Winners, World Soccer Cup Championships 1950-1978.

Radio Station A153

Design: 65fr, Mail plane at airport.

1979, Mar. 30   Litho.   **Perf. 12½**
492 A153 55fr multicolored   .30 .20
493 A153 65fr multicolored   .40 .20

Post and Telecommunications Org., 10th anniv.

Teacher and Pupils, IYC Emblem — A154

1979, Apr. 9   **Perf. 13½**
494 A154 75fr multicolored   .40 .20

International Year of the Child.

Telecommunications — A155

1979, May 17   Litho.   **Perf. 13**
495 A155 70fr multicolored   .45 .20

11th Telecommunications Day.

Basketmaker and Upper Volta No. 111 — A156

Design: No. 497, May of Upper Volta, Concorde, truck and UPU emblem.

1979, June 8   Photo.
496 A156 100fr multicolored   .65 .35
497 A156 100fr multicolored   .65 .35

Philexafrique II, Libreville, Gabon, June 8-17. Nos. 496, 497 each printed in sheets of 10 and 5 labels showing exhibition emblem.

Synodontis Voltae A157

Fresh-water Fish: 50fr, Micralestes comoensis. 85fr, Silurus.

1979, June 10   Litho.   **Perf. 12½**
498 A157 20fr multicolored   .20 .20
499 A157 50fr multicolored   .35 .20
500 A157 85fr multicolored   .55 .30
    Nos. 498-500 (3)   1.10 .70

Rowland Hill, Train and Upper Volta No. 60 — A158

Sir Rowland Hill (1795-1879), originator of penny postage, Trains and Upper Volta Stamps: 165fr, #59. 200fr, #57. 300fr, #56. 300fr, #55.

1979, June   Litho.   **Perf. 13½**
501 A158 65fr multicolored   .40 .20
502 A158 165fr multicolored   1.10 .55
503 A158 200fr multicolored   1.40 .65
504 A158 300fr multicolored   2.00 1.00
    Nos. 501-504 (4)   4.90 2.40

Souvenir Sheet
505 A158 500fr multicolored   3.50 1.60

Wildlife Fund Emblem and Protected Animals — A159

1979, Aug. 30   Litho.   **Perf. 14½**
506 A159 30fr Waterbuck   .30 .20
507 A159 40fr Roan antelope   .40 .20
508 A159 60fr Caracal   .85 .20
509 A159 100fr African bush elephant   1.25 .35
510 A159 175fr Hartebeest   2.10 .55
511 A159 250fr Leopard   3.50 .80
    Nos. 506-511 (6)   8.40 2.30

Adult Students and Teacher — A160

Design: 55fr, Man reading book, vert.

1979, Sept. 8   **Perf. 12½x13, 13x12½**
512 A160 55fr multicolored   .40 .20
513 A160 250fr multicolored   1.60 .85

World Literacy Day.

Map of Upper Volta, Telephone Receiver and Lines, Telecom Emblem — A161

1979, Sept. 20   **Perf. 13x12½**
514 A161 200fr multicolored   1.40 .65

3rd World Telecommunications Exhibition, Geneva, Sept. 20-26.

King Vulture — A162

1979, Oct. 26   Litho.   **Perf. 13**
515 A162 5fr shown   .20 .20
516 A162 10fr Hoopoe   .20 .20
517 A162 15fr Bald vulture   .20 .20
518 A162 25fr Herons   .20 .20
519 A162 35fr Ostrich   .25 .20
520 A162 45fr Crowned crane   .30 .20
521 A162 125fr Eagle   .80 .40
    Nos. 515-521 (7)   2.15 1.60

Control Tower, Emblem, Jet — A163

1979, Dec. 12   Photo.   **Perf. 13x12½**
522 A163 65fr multicolored   .45 .20

ASECNA (Air Safety Board), 20th anniv.

Central Bank of West African States — A164

1979, Dec. 28   Litho.   **Perf. 12½**
523 A164 55fr multicolored   .40 .20

Eugene Jamot, Map of Upper Volta, Tsetse Fly — A165

1979, Dec. 28   **Perf. 13x13½**
524 A165 55fr multicolored   .40 .20

Eugene Jamot (1879-1937), discoverer of sleeping sickness cure.

UPU Emblem, Upper Volta Type D4 under Magnifier A166

1980, Feb. 26   Litho.   Perf. 12½x13
525 A166 55fr multicolored   .40 .20
Stamp Day.

World Locomotive Speed Record, 25th Anniversary A167

1980, Mar. 30   Litho.   Perf. 12½
526 A167 75fr multicolored   .50 .25
527 A167 100fr multicolored   .65 .35

Pres. Sangoule Lamizana, Pope John Paul II, Cardinal Pau Zoungrana, Map of Upper Volta — A168

1980, May 10   Litho.   Perf. 12½
528 A168 65fr shown   .45 .20
Size: 21x36mm
529 A168 100fr Pope John Paul II   .65 .35
Visit of Pope John Paul II to Upper Volta.

A169   A170

1980, May 17   Perf. 13x12½
530 A169 50fr multicolored   .35 .20
12th World Telecommunications Day.

1980, June 12   Litho.   Perf. 13
531 A170 65fr Sun and earth   .45 .20
532 A170 100fr Solar energy   .65 .35

Downhill Skiing, Lake Placid '80 Emblem — A171

1980, June 26   Perf. 14½
533 A171 65fr shown   .35 .20
534 A171 100fr Women's down-
             hill   .50 .30

---

535 A171 200fr Figure skating   1.25 .50
536 A171 350fr Slalom, vert.   1.90 1.00
   Nos. 533-536 (4)   4.00 2.00
Souvenir Sheet
537 A171 500fr Speed skating   3.50 1.60
12th Winter Olympic Game Winners, Lake Placid, NY, Feb. 12-24.

Map of Europe and Africa, Jet — A172

Hand Holding Back Sand Dune — A173

Europafrica Issue
1980, July 14   Litho.   Perf. 13
538 A172 100fr multicolored   .65 .35

1980, July 18
Operation Green Sahel: 55fr, Hands holding seedlings.
539 A173 50fr multicolored   .35 .20
540 A173 55fr multicolored   .40 .20

Gourmantche Chief Initiation — A174

1980, Sept. 12   Litho.   Perf. 14
541 A174 30fr shown   .20 .20
542 A174 55fr Moro Naba, Mossi
             Emperor   .35 .20
543 A174 65fr Princess Guimbe
             Quattara, vert.   .45 .20
   Nos. 541-543 (3)   1.00 .60

A175

A176

Gourounsi mask, conference emblem.
1980, Oct. 6   Perf. 13½x13
544 A175 65fr multicolored   .45 .20
World Tourism Conf., Manila, Sept. 27.

1980, Nov. 5   Litho.   Perf. 12½
545 A176 55fr Agriculture   .40 .20
546 A176 65fr Transportation   .45 .20
547 A176 75fr Dam, highway   .50 .25
548 A176 100fr Industry   .65 .35
   Nos. 545-548 (4)   2.00 1.00
West African Economic Council, 5th anniv.

20th Anniv. of Independence — A177

1980, Dec. 11   Perf. 13
549 A177 500fr multicolored   3.50 1.60

Madonna and Child, by Raphael — A178

West African Postal Union, 5th Anniv. — A179

Christmas: Paintings of Madonna and Child, by Raphael.
1980, Dec. 22   Perf. 12½
550 A178 60fr multicolored   .40 .20
551 A178 150fr multicolored   1.00 .50
552 A178 250fr multicolored   1.60 .80
   Nos. 550-552 (3)   3.00 1.50

1980, Dec. 24   Photo.   Perf. 13½
553 A179 55fr multicolored   .40 .20

Dung Beetle A180

Perf. 13x13½, 13½x13
1981, Mar. 10   Litho.
554 A180 5fr shown   .20 .20
555 A180 10fr Crickets   .20 .20
556 A180 15fr Termites   .20 .20
557 A180 20fr Praying mantis,
             vert.   .20 .20
558 A180 55fr Emperor moth   .40 .25
559 A180 65fr Locust, vert.   .45 .25
   Nos. 554-559 (6)   1.65 1.30

Antelope Mask, Kouroumba A181

Designs: Various ceremonial masks.

1981, Mar. 20   Litho.   Perf. 13
560 A181 45fr multicolored   .25 .20
561 A181 55fr multicolored   .30 .20
562 A181 85fr multicolored   .50 .25
563 A181 105fr multicolored   .60 .35
   Nos. 560-563 (4)   1.65 1.00

Notre Dame of Kologh' Naba College, 25th Anniv. A182

1981, Mar. 30
564 A182 55fr multicolored   .30 .20

Heinrich von Stephan, UPU Founder, Birth Sesquicentennial — A183

1981, May 4   Litho.   Perf. 13
565 A183 65fr multicolored   .35 .20

13th World Telecommunications Day — A184

1981, May 17   Perf. 13½x13
566 A184 90fr multicolored   .50 .25

Diesel Train, Abidjan-Niger Railroad — A185

Designs: Trains.

1981, July 6   Litho.   Perf. 13
567 A185 25fr shown   .20 .20
568 A185 30fr Gazelle   .20 .20
569 A185 40fr Belier   .25 .20
   Nos. 567-569 (3)   .65 .60

Tree Planting Month A186

1981, July 15
570 A186 70fr multicolored   .45 .25

Natl. Red Cross, 20th Anniv. A187

1981, July 31   Perf. 12½x13
571 A187 70fr multicolored   .45 .25

Intl. Year of the
Disabled — A188

1981, Aug. 20   Litho.   Perf. 13x12½
572 A188 70fr multicolored   .45 .25

View of
Koudougou
A189

1981, Sept. 3   Litho.   Perf. 12½
573 A189 35fr shown   .25 .20
574 A189 45fr Toma   .30 .20
575 A189 85fr Volta Noire   .55 .30
     Nos. 573-575 (3)   1.10 .70

World Food Day — A190

1981, Oct. 16   Perf. 13
576 A190 90fr multicolored   .60 .30

Elephant
A191

Designs: Various protected species.

1981, Oct. 21   Photo.   Perf. 14
577 A191 5fr multicolored   .20 .20
578 A191 15fr multicolored   .20 .20
579 A191 40fr multicolored   .25 .20
580 A191 60fr multicolored   .40 .20
581 A191 70fr multicolored   .45 .20
     Nos. 577-581 (5)   1.50 1.00

Fight Against
Apartheid — A192

1981, Dec. 9   Litho.   Perf. 12½
582 A192 90fr red orange   .60 .30

Mangoes — A193

1981, Dec. 15   Perf. 13x13½, 13½x13
583 A193 20fr Papayas, horiz.   .20 .20
584 A193 35fr Fruits, vegetables,
                horiz.   .25 .20
585 A193 75fr shown   .50 .25
586 A193 90fr Melons, horiz.   .60 .35
     Nos. 583-586 (4)   1.55 1.00

Guinea
Hen — A194

West African Rice
Development
Assoc., 10th
Anniv. — A195

Designs: Breeding animals. 10fr, 25fr, 70fr,
250fr, 300fr horiz.

1981, Dec. 22   Perf. 13
587 A194 10fr Donkey   .20 .20
588 A194 25fr Pig   .20 .20
589 A194 70fr Cow   .45 .25
590 A194 90fr shown   .55 .30
591 A194 250fr Rabbit   1.60 .80
     Nos. 587-591 (5)   3.00 1.75

Souvenir Sheet
592 A194 300fr Sheep   2.00 1.00

1981, Dec. 29
593 A195 90fr multicolored   .60 .30

20th Anniv. of
World Food
Program — A196

1982, Jan. 18
594 A196 50fr multicolored   .35 .20

Traditional Houses — A197

1982, Apr. 23   Litho.   Perf. 12½
595 A197 30fr Morhonaba Pal-
               ace, vert.   .20 .20
596 A197 70fr Bobo   .45 .25
597 A197 100fr Gourounsi   .65 .35
598 A197 200fr Peulh   1.40 .65
599 A197 250fr Dagari   1.60 .80
     Nos. 595-599 (5)   4.30 2.25

14th World Telecommunications
Day — A198

1982, May 17
600 A198 125fr multicolored   .85 .40

Water
Lily — A199

25th Anniv. of
Cultural Aid
Fund — A201

African
Postal
Union
A200

1982, Sept. 22   Perf. 13x12½
601 A199 25fr shown   .20 .20
602 A199 40fr Kapoks   .20 .20
603 A199 70fr Frangipani   .35 .20
604 A199 90fr Cochlospermum
               planchonii   .60 .25
605 A199 100fr Cotton   .50 .25
     Nos. 601-605 (5)   1.85 1.10

1982, Oct. 7
606 A200 70fr multicolored   .45 .25
607 A200 90fr multicolored   .60 .30

1982, Nov. 10   Perf. 12½x13
608 A201 70fr multicolored   .45 .25

Map, Hand
Holding
Grain,
Steer Head
A202

1982   Perf. 12½
609 A202 90fr multicolored   .60 .30

Traditional
Hairstyle
A203

1983, Jan.   Litho.   Perf. 12½
610 A203 90fr lt green & multi .50 .25
611 A203 120fr lt blue & multi .70 .35
612 A203 170fr pink & multi   .95 .50
     Nos. 610-612 (3)   2.15 1.10

For overprints see Nos. 884-886.

8th Film Festival,
Ouagadougou — A204

1983, Feb. 10   Litho.   Perf. 13x12½
613 A204 90fr Scene   .60 .30
614 A204 500fr Filmmaker
               Dumarou Ganda   3.50 1.60

UN Intl. Drinking
Water and
Sanitation
Decade, 1981-
90 — A205

1983, Apr. 21   Litho.   Perf. 13½x13
615 A205 60fr Water drops   .40 .20
616 A205 70fr Carrying water   .45 .25

Manned Flight
Bicentenary
A206

Portraits and Balloons: 15fr, J.M.
Montgolfier, 1783. 25fr, Etienne Montgolfier's
balloon, 1783, Pilatre de Rozier. 70fr, Charles
& Roberts flight, 1783, Jacques Charles. 90fr,
Flight over English Channel, John Jeffries.
100fr, Testu-Brissy's horseback flight,
Wilhemine Reichardt. 250fr, Andree's Spitz-
bergen flight, 1897, S.A. Andree. 300fr, Pic-
card's stratosphere flight, 1931, August
Piccard.

1983, Apr. 15   Litho.   Perf. 13½
617 A206 15fr multicolored   .20 .20
618 A206 25fr multicolored   .20 .20
619 A206 70fr multicolored   .45 .25
620 A206 90fr multicolored   .60 .30
621 A206 100fr multicolored   .65 .35
622 A206 250fr multicolored   1.60 .80
     Nos. 617-622 (6)   3.70 2.10

Souvenir Sheet
623 A206 300fr multicolored   2.00 1.00

No. 623 contains one stamp 38x47mm.
Nos. 621-623 airmail.

World
Communications
Year — A207

1983, May 26   Litho.   Perf. 12½
624 A207 30fr Man reading letter .20 .20
625 A207 35fr Like No. 624   .20 .20
626 A207 45fr Aircraft over stream .25 .20
627 A207 90fr Girl on telephone .50 .25
     Nos. 624-627 (4)   1.15 .85

Fishing
Resources
A208

1983, July 28   Litho.   Perf. 13
628 A208 20fr Synadontis
               gambiensis   .20 .20
629 A208 30fr Palmotochromis   .20 .20
630 A208 40fr Boy fishing, vert. .20 .20
631 A208 50fr Fishing with net .20 .20
632 A208 75fr Fishing with bas-
               ket   .20 .20
     Nos. 628-632 (5)   1.00 1.00

Anti-deforestation — A209

1983, Sept. 13   Litho.   Perf. 13
633 A209 10fr Planting saplings .20 .20
634 A209 50fr Tree nursery   .20 .20
635 A209 100fr Prevent forest
               fires   .35 .20
636 A209 150fr Woman cooking   .50 .25
637 A209 200fr Prevent felling,
               vert.   .65 .35
     Nos. 633-637 (5)   1.90 1.20

Fresco Detail, by Raphael — A210

Paintings: 120fr, Self-portrait, by Pablo Picasso, 1901, vert. 185fr, Self-portrait at the palette, by Manet, 1878, vert. 350fr, Fresco Detail, diff., by Raphael. 500fr, Goethe, by George Oswald May, 1779, vert.

1983, Nov.   Litho.   Perf. 13
638 A210 120fr multicolored   .40   .20
639 A210 185fr multicolored   .60   .30
640 A210 300fr multicolored   1.00   .50
641 A210 350fr multicolored   1.25   .60
642 A210 500fr multicolored   1.60   .80
  Nos. 638-642 (5)   4.85 2.40

25th Anniv. of the Republic A211

1983, Dec. 9   Litho.   Perf. 14
643 A211 90fr Arms   .30   .20
644 A211 500fr Family, flag   1.60   .80

A212

Scouting — A213

1984, May 29   Litho.   Perf. 12½
645 A212 90fr multicolored   .30   .20
646 A212 100fr multicolored   .35   .20
  Council of Unity, 25th anniv.

1984, June 15   Litho.   Perf. 13½
647 A213 25fr Polystictus le-
         oninus   .20   .20
648 A213 185fr Pterocarpus
         Lucens   .85   .45
649 A213 200fr Phlebopus co-
         lossus
         sudanicus   1.10   .50
650 A213 250fr Cosmos
         sulphureus   1.25   .60
651 A213 300fr Trametes versi-
         color   1.50   .80
652 A213 400fr Ganoderma
         lucidum   2.00 1.10
  Nos. 647-652 (6)   6.90 3.65

Souvenir Sheet
653 A213 600fr Leucocoprinus
         cepaestipes   3.25 1.60
  Nos. 651-653 are airmail. For overprints see Nos. 669-674.

Wildlife A214

Wildlife — A215

1984, July 19
654 A214 15fr Cheetah, four
         cubs   .20   .20
655 A214 35fr Two adults   .35   .20
656 A214 90fr One adult   .85   .20
657 A214 120fr Cheetah, two
         cubs   1.10   .25
658 A214 300fr Baboons   1.25   .55
659 A214 400fr Vultures   1.50   .80
  Nos. 654-659 (6)   5.25 2.20

Souvenir Sheet
660 A215 1000fr Antelopes   4.00 1.90
  World Wildlife Fund (Nos. 654-567); Rotary Intl. (Nos. 658, 660); Natl. Boy Scouts (No. 659). Nos. 658-660 are airmail.

Sailing Ships and Locomotives — A216

1984, Aug. 14   Perf. 12½
661 A216 20fr Maiden Queen   .20   .20
662 A216 40fr CC 2400 ch   .20   .20
663 A216 60fr Scawfell   .25   .20
664 A216 100fr PO 1806   .40   .20
665 A216 120fr Harbinger   .45   .25
666 A216 145fr Livingstone   .55   .30
667 A216 400fr True Briton   1.50   .80
668 A216 450fr Pacific C51   1.60   .85
  Nos. 661-668 (8)   5.15 3.00

Natl. Defense — A216a

Design: 120fr, Capt. Sankara, crowd, horiz.

1984, Nov. 21   Litho.   Perf. 13½
668A A216a 90fr multicolored
668B A216a 120fr multicolored

Nos. 647-652 Ovptd. with Two Bars and "BURKINA FASO"

1985, Mar. 5   Litho.   Perf. 13½
669 A213 25fr multicolored   .20   .20
670 A213 185fr multicolored   .55   .25
671 A213 200fr multicolored   .60   .30
672 A213 250fr multicolored   .75   .40
673 A213 300fr multicolored   .90   .45
674 A213 400fr multicolored   1.25   .60
  Nos. 669-674 (6)   4.25 2.20

A217

Designs: 5fr, 120fr, Flag. 15fr, 150fr, Natl. Arms, vert. 90fr, 185fr, Map.

1985, Mar. 8   Litho.   Perf. 12½
675 A217 5fr multicolored
676 A217 15fr multicolored
677 A217 90fr multicolored
678 A217 120fr multicolored
679 A217 150fr multicolored
680 A217 185fr multicolored
  Nos. 678-680 are airmail.

1986 World Cup Soccer Championships, Mexico — A218

Various soccer plays and Aztec artifacts.

1985, Apr. 20   Litho.   Perf. 13
681 A218 25fr multicolored   .20   .20
682 A218 45fr multicolored   .20   .20
683 A218 90fr multicolored   .35   .20
684 A218 100fr multicolored   .40   .20
685 A218 150fr multicolored   .55   .25
686 A218 200fr multicolored   .70   .40
687 A218 250fr multicolored   .90   .45
  Nos. 681-687 (7)   3.30 1.90

Souvenir Sheet
688 A218 500fr multicolored   1.90 1.25
  Nos. 681-685 vert. No. 684-688 are airmail. No. 688 contains one 40x32mm stamp.

Motorcycle, Cent. — A220

1985, May 26
689 A220 50fr Steam tricycle,
         G.A. Long   .20   .20
690 A220 75fr Pope   .25   .20
691 A220 80fr Manet-90   .30   .20
692 A220 100fr Ducati   .40   .20
693 A220 150fr Jawa   .55   .30
694 A220 200fr Honda   .70   .40
695 A220 250fr B.M.W.   .90   .50
  Nos. 689-695 (7)   3.30 2.00
  Nos. 692-695 are airmail.

Reptiles A221

1985, June 20
696 A221 5fr Chamaeleon
         dilepis   .20   .20
697 A221 15fr Agama stellio   .20   .20
698 A221 35fr Lacerta Lepida   .20   .20
699 A221 85fr Hiperolius
         marmoratus   .30   .20
700 A221 100fr Echis leucogaster .40   .20
701 A221 150fr Kinixys erosa   .55   .30
702 A221 250fr Python regius   .90   .45
  Nos. 696-702 (7)   2.75 1.75
  #696-697 vert. #700-702 are airmail.

A222

Queen Mother, 85th Birthday A222a

75fr, On pony bobs. 85fr, Wedding, 1923. 500fr, Holding infant Elizabeth, 1926. 600fr, Coronation of King George VI, 1937. 1000fr, Christening of Prince William, 1982. #707A, Christening of Prince Harry, 1985.

1985, June 21   Perf. 13½
703 A222 75fr multicolored   .25   .20
704 A222 85fr multicolored   .25   .20
705 A222 500fr multicolored   1.60   .80
706 A222 600fr multicolored   1.90   .90
  Nos. 703-706 (4)   4.00 2.10

Litho. & Embossed
Perf. 13¼
706A A222a 1500fr gold & multi

Souvenir Sheets
Litho.
707 A222 1000fr multicolored 3.25 1.60

Litho. & Embossed
707A A222a 1500fr gold & multi
  Nos. 705-707A are airmail.

Vintage Autos and Aircraft — A223

1985, June 21
708 A223 5fr Benz Victoria,
         1893   .20   .20
709 A223 25fr Peugeot 174,
         1927   .20   .20
710 A223 45fr Louis Bleriot   .20   .20
711 A223 50fr Breguet 14   .20   .20
712 A223 500fr Bugatti Coupe
         Napoleon T41
         Royale   1.90   .90
713 A223 500fr Airbus A300-
         P4   1.90   .90
714 A223 600fr Mercedes-
         Benz 540K,
         1938   2.25 1.25
715 A223 600fr Airbus A300B   2.25 1.25
  Nos. 708-715 (8)   9.10 5.10

Souvenir Sheet
716 A223 1000fr Louis Bleriot,
         Karl Benz   4.00 1.90
  Automobile, cent. Nos. 712-716 are airmail.

Audubon Birth Bicent. A224

Illustrations of No. American bird species by Audubon and scouting trefoil.

1985, June 21
717	A224	60fr Aix sponsa	.25	.20
718	A224	100fr Mimus polyglotos	.40	.20
719	A224	300fr Icterus galbula	1.25	.60
720	A224	400fr Sitta carolinensis	1.50	.80
721	A224	500fr Asyndesmus lewis	1.50	.90
722	A224	600fr Buteo cagopus	2.25	1.10
		Nos. 717-722 (6)	7.15	3.80

Souvenir Sheet
723	A224	1000fr Columba leucocephala	4.00	1.90

Nos. 721-723 are airmail.

ARGENTINA '85, Buenos Aires — A225

Various equestrians.

1985, July 5   **Perf. 13**
724	A225	25fr Gaucho, piebald	.20	.20
725	A225	45fr Horse and rider, Andes Mountains	.20	.20
726	A225	90fr Rodeo	.30	.20
727	A225	100fr Hunting gazelle	.40	.20
728	A225	150fr Gauchos, 3 horses	.55	.25
729	A225	200fr Rider beside mount	.70	.35
730	A225	250fr Contest	.90	.40
		Nos. 724-730 (7)	3.25	1.80

Souvenir Sheet
731	A225	500fr Foal	1.90	.70

Nos. 727-731 are airmail.

Locomotives — A226

1985, July 23
732	A226	50fr 105-30 electric, tank wagon	.20	.20
733	A226	75fr Diesel shunting locomotive	.25	.20
734	A226	80fr Diesel locomotive	.25	.20
735	A226	100fr Diesel railcar	.35	.20
736	A226	150fr No. 6093	.50	.25
737	A226	200fr No. 105 diesel railcar	.60	.35
738	A226	250fr Diesel, passenger car	.75	.40
		Nos. 732-738 (7)	2.90	1.80

Nos. 735-738 are airmail.

Artifacts — A227

Fungi — A228

10fr, 4-legged jar, Tikare. 40fr, Lidded pot with bird handles, P. Bazega. 90fr, Mother and child, bronze statue, Ouagadougou. 120fr, Drummer, bronze statue, Ouagadougou.

1985, July 27   **Perf. 13x12½**
739-742	A227		1.10	.55

No. 742 is airmail.

1985, Aug. 8   **Perf. 13**
743	A228	15fr Philiota mutabilis	.20	.20
744	A228	20fr Hypholoma (nematoloma) fasciculare	.20	.20
745	A228	30fr Ixocomus granulatus	.20	.20
746	A228	60fr Agaricus campestris	.20	.20
747	A228	80fr Trachypus scaber	.30	.20
748	A228	150fr Armillaria mellea	.50	.25
749	A228	250fr Marasmius scorodonius	.75	.40
		Nos. 743-749 (7)	2.35	1.65

Nos. 748 is airmail.

ITALIA '85 A228a

Paintings by Botticelli: 25fr, Virgin and Child. 45fr, Portrait of a Man. 90fr, Mars and Venus. 100fr, Birth of Venus. 150fr, Allegory of the Calumny. 200fr, Pallas and the Centaur. 250fr, Allegory of Spring. 500fr, The Virgin of Melagrana.

1985, Oct. 25   **Litho.**   **Perf. 12½x13**
749A	A228a	25fr multicolored	.20	.20
749B	A228a	45fr multicolored	.25	.20
749C	A228a	90fr multicolored	.45	.25
749D	A228a	100fr multicolored	.50	.25
749E	A228a	150fr multicolored	.70	.40
749F	A228a	200fr multicolored	1.00	.50
749G	A228a	250fr multicolored	1.25	.60
		Nos. 749A-749G (7)	4.35	2.40

Souvenir Sheet
749H	A228a	500fr multicolored	2.50	1.25

No. 749D-749H are airmail.

Intl. Red Cross in Burkina Faso, 75th Anniv. A229

1985, Nov. 10
750	A229	40f Helicopter	.20	.20
751	A229	85fr Ambulance	.30	.20
752	A229	150fr Henri Dunant	.60	.25
753	A229	250fr Physician, patient	.90	.35
		Nos. 750-753 (4)	2.00	1.00

Nos. 752-753 are vert. and airmail.

Child Survival A230

1986, Jan. 6
754	A230	90fr Breast-feeding	.50	.25

Dated 1985.

Dodo Carnival — A231

1986, Jan. 6   **Perf. 12½**
755	A231	20fr Three children, drummer	.20	.20
756	A231	25fr Lion, 4 dancers	.20	.20
757	A231	40fr Two dancers, two drummers	.25	.20
758	A231	45fr Three dancers	.25	.20
759	A231	90fr Zebra, ostrich, dancers	.50	.25
760	A231	90fr Elephant, dancer	.50	.25
		Nos. 755-760 (6)	1.90	1.30

Dated 1985.

Christopher Columbus (1451-1506) — A232

Columbus: 250fr, At Court of King of Portugal, the Nina. 300fr, Using astrolabe, the Santa Maria. 400fr, Imprisonment at Hispanola, 1500, the Santa Maria. 450fr, At San Salvador, 1492, the Pinta. 1000fr, Fleet departing Palos harbor, 1492.

1986, Feb. 10   **Perf. 13½**
761	A232	250fr multicolored	1.40	.70
762	A232	300fr multicolored	1.60	.80
763	A232	400fr multicolored	2.25	1.10
764	A232	450fr multicolored	2.50	1.25
		Nos. 761-764 (4)	7.75	3.85

Souvenir Sheet
765	A232	1000fr multicolored	5.50	2.75

Nos. 764-765 are airmail. Dated 1985.

Railroad Construction — A233

1986, Feb. 10
766	A233	90fr Man, woman carrying rail	.50	.25
767	A233	120fr Laying rails	.65	.30
768	A233	185fr Diesel train on new tracks	1.00	.50
769	A233	500fr Adler locomotive, 1835	2.75	1.40
		Nos. 766-769 (4)	4.90	2.45

Souvenir Sheet
770	A233	1000fr Electric train, Series 290 diesel	5.00	2.75

German Railways, sesquicentennial. Nos. 769-770 are airmail. Dated 1985.

Intl. Peace Year — A234

World Health by the Year 2000 — A235

1986, Oct. 10   **Photo.**   **Perf. 12½x13**
771	A234	90fr blue	1.10	.55

1986, Aug. 8   **Litho.**   **Perf. 13**

Designs: 100fr, Primary care medicine. 150fr, Mass inoculations.
772	A235	90fr multicolored	.65	.30

Size: 26x30mm
Perf. 12½x13
773	A235	100fr multicolored	.70	.30
774	A235	120fr multicolored	.85	.40
		Nos. 772-774 (3)	2.20	1.00

Insects — A236

World Post Day — A237

1986, Sept. 10   **Litho.**   **Perf. 12½x13**
775	A236	15fr Phryneta aurocinta	.20	.20
776	A236	20fr Sternocera interrupta	.20	.20
777	A236	40fr Prosoprocera lactator	.35	.20
778	A236	45fr Gonimbrasia hecate	.40	.20
778A	A236	85fr Charaxes epijasius	.85	.35
		Nos. 775-778A (5)	2.00	1.15

1986, Oct. 9   **Perf. 13**
779	A237	120fr multicolored	.70	.35

UN Child Survival Campaign — A238

Designs: 30fr, Mother feeding child. 60fr, Adding medicines to food. 90fr, Nurse vaccinating child.

1986, Oct. 8   **Litho.**   **Perf. 11½x12**
780	A238	30fr multicolored	
781	A238	60fr multicolored	
782	A238	90fr multicolored	

No. 783 has been reserved for a 120fr stamp.

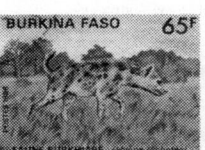

Mammals A239

Designs: 50fr, Warthog. 65fr, Hyena. 90fr, Antelope. 100fr, Gazelle. 120fr, Bushbuck. 145fr, Kudu. 500fr, Gazelle, diff.

1986, Nov. 3   **Litho.**   **Perf. 13x12½**
784	A239	50fr multicolored	
784A	A239	65fr multicolored	
784B	A239	90fr multicolored	
784C	A239	100fr multicolored	
784D	A239	120fr multicolored	
784E	A239	145fr multicolored	
784F	A239	500fr multicolored	

Traditional Dances — A240

Designs: 10fr, Namende. 25fr, Mouhoun. 90fr, Houet. 105fr, Seno. 120fr, Ganzourgou.

1986, Nov. 3   Litho.   Perf. 12½x13
785	A240	10fr multicolored	
785A	A240	25fr multicolored	
785B	A240	90fr multicolored	
785C	A240	105fr multicolored	
785D	A240	120fr multicolored	

Hairstyles A241

1986, Nov. 4   Litho.   Perf. 12½x13
788	A241	35fr Peul	.30	.20
789	A241	75fr Dafing	.55	.30
790	A241	90fr Peul, diff.	.70	.35
791	A241	120fr Mossi	.95	.50
792	A241	185fr Peul, diff.	1.50	.75
	Nos. 788-792 (5)		4.00	2.10

10th African Film Festival — A242

Intl Women's Day — A243

1987, Feb. 21   Litho.   Perf. 12x12½
793	A242	90fr Maps, cameras		
794	A242	120fr Jolson, camer- amen		
795	A242	185fr Charlie Chaplin		

60th Anniv. of the film *The Jazz Singer* (120fr); 10th anniv. of the death of Charlie Chaplin (185fr).

1987, Mar. 8   Perf. 13½
796 A243 90fr multicolored

Flora — A244

Fight Against Leprosy — A245

1987, June 6   Litho.   Perf. 12½x13
797	A244	70fr Calotropis procera	.50	.25
798	A244	75fr Acacia seyal	.55	.25
799	A244	85fr Parkia biglobosa	.60	.30
800	A244	90fr Sterospernum kunthianum	.65	.30
801	A244	100fr Dichrostachys cinerea	.70	.35
802	A244	300fr Combretum paniculatum	2.10	1.00
	Nos. 797-802 (6)		5.10	2.45

1987, Aug. 6   Perf. 13

Raoul Follereau (1903-1977) and: 90fr, Doctors examining African youth. 100fr, Laboratory research. 120fr, Gerhard Hansen (1841-1912), microscope, bacillus under magnification. 300fr, Follereau embracing cured leper.

803	A245	90fr multicolored	.60	.25
804	A245	100fr multicolored	.70	.35
805	A245	120fr multicolored	.85	.40
806	A245	300fr multicolored	2.10	1.00
	Nos. 803-806 (4)		4.25	2.00

World Environment Day — A246

1987, Aug. 18   Litho.   Perf. 13x12½
807	A246	90fr shown	.70	.35
808	A246	145fr Emblem, huts	1.10	.55

Pre-Olympic Year — A247

1987, Aug. 31   Perf. 12½
809	A247	75fr High jump	.55	.30
810	A247	85fr Tennis, vert.	.60	.35
811	A247	90fr Ski jumping	.70	.35
812	A247	100fr Soccer	.75	.40
813	A247	145fr Running	1.10	.55
814	A247	350fr Pierre de Coubertin, tennis, vert.	2.60	1.25
	Nos. 809-814 (6)		6.30	3.15

Pierre de Coubertin (1863-1937).

World Post Day — A248

1987, Oct. 5   Litho.   Perf. 12½x13
815 A248 90fr multicolored

Fight Against Apartheid — A249

1987, Nov. 11   Litho.   Perf. 13
816	A249	90fr shown	1.00	.50
817	A249	100fr Luthuli, book, 1962	1.10	.55

Albert John Luthuli (1898-1967), South African reformer, author and 1960 Nobel Peace Prize winner. No. 817 incorrectly inscribed "1899-1967."

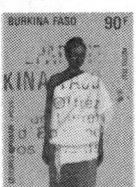

Traditional Costumes — A250

1987, Dec. 4   Litho.   Perf. 11½x12
818	A250	10fr Dagari	
819	A250	30fr Peul	
820	A250	90fr Mossi	
821	A250	200fr Senoufo	

No. 822 has been reserved for a 500fr stamp.

Traditional Musical Instruments A251

Perf. 12x11½, 11½x12

1987, Dec. 4   Litho.
823	A251	20fr Xylophone	.20	.20
824	A251	25fr 3-Stringed lute, vert.	.25	.20
825	A251	35fr Zither	.30	.20
826	A251	90fr Conical drum	.75	.40
827	A251	1000fr Calabash drum, vert.	7.50	3.75
	Nos. 823-827 (5)		9.00	4.75

Intl. Year of Shelter for the Homeless — A252

1987, Dec. 4   Litho.   Perf. 13
828 A252 90fr multicolored   .65   .30

Five-year Natl. Development Plan — A253

1987, Dec. 15   Perf. 13½
829	A253	40fr Small businesses	.30	.20
830	A253	55fr Agriculture	.40	.20
831	A253	60fr Constructing schools	.45	.25
832	A253	90fr Transportation and communications	.65	.30
833	A253	100fr Literacy	.75	.35
834	A253	120fr Animal husbandry	.90	.45
	Nos. 829-834 (6)		3.45	1.75

World Health Organization, 40th Anniv. — A254

1988, Mar. 31   Litho.   Perf. 12½x13
835 A254 120fr multicolored   .80   .40

1988 Summer Olympics, Seoul A255

1988, May 5   Perf. 13x12½
836	A255	30fr shown	.25	.20
837	A255	160fr Torch, vert.	1.10	.50
838	A255	175fr Soccer	1.25	.60
839	A255	235fr Volleyball, vert.	1.50	.75
840	A255	450fr Basketball, vert.	2.90	1.50
	Nos. 836-840 (5)		7.00	3.55

Souvenir Sheet
Perf. 12½x13
841 A255 500fr Runners   3.25   1.60

No. 841 contains one stamp, size: 40x52mm plus two labels.

Ritual Masks A256

1988, May 30   Litho.   Perf. 13
842	A256	10fr Epervier, Houet	.20	.20
843	A256	20fr Jeunes Filles, Oullo	.20	.20
844	A256	30fr Bubale, Houet	.20	.20
845	A256	40fr Forgeron, Mouhoun	.35	.20
846	A256	120fr Nounouma, Ouri	.80	.40
847	A256	175fr Chauve-souris, Ouri	1.25	.60
	Nos. 842-847 (6)		3.00	1.80

Nos. 842-846 vert.

Handicrafts A257

1988, Aug. 22   Litho.   Perf. 13½
848	A257	5fr Kieriebe ceramic pitcher, vert.	.20	.20
849	A257	15fr Mossi basket	.20	.20
850	A257	25fr Gurunsi chair	.20	.20
851	A257	30fr Bissa basket	.20	.20
852	A257	45fr Ougadougou leather box	.35	.20
853	A257	85fr Ougadougou bronze statue, vert.	.70	.35
854	A257	120fr Ougadougou leather valise	.80	.40
	Nos. 848-854 (7)		2.65	1.75

World Post Day — A258

1988, Oct. 9   Litho.   Perf. 13
855 A258 120fr multicolored   .80   .40

Aquatic Fauna A259

1988, Oct. 31   **Perf. 12**
856	A259	70fr	Angler martin	.50	.25
857	A259	100fr	Mormyrus rume	.70	.35
858	A259	120fr	Frog	.80	.40
859	A259	160fr	Duck	1.10	.55
		Nos. 856-859 (4)		3.10	1.55

Civil Rights and Political Activists A260

Designs: 80fr, Mohammed Ali Jinnah (1876-1948), 1st Governor General of Pakistan. 120fr, Mahatma Gandhi (1869-1948), India. 160fr, John F. Kennedy. 235fr, Martin Luther King, Jr.

1988, Nov. 22   **Litho.**   **Perf. 14**
860	A260	80fr	multicolored	.50	.25
861	A260	120fr	multicolored	.80	.40
862	A260	160fr	multicolored	1.00	.50
863	A260	235fr	multicolored	1.50	.75
		Nos. 860-863 (4)		3.80	1.90

A261   A262

Christmas: Stained-glass windows.

1988, Dec. 2   **Perf. 12**
864	A261	120fr	Adoration of the shepherds	.85	.40
865	A261	160fr	Adoration of the Magi	1.00	.50
866	A261	450fr	Madonna and child	2.90	1.50
867	A261	1000fr	Flight into Egypt	6.25	3.25
		Nos. 864-867 (4)		11.00	5.65

1989, Feb. 25   **Litho.**   **Perf. 14**
868	A262	75fr	shown	.20	.20
869	A262	500fr	Ababacar Makharam	1.60	.80
870	A262	500fr	Jean Tchissoukou	1.60	.80
871	A262	500fr	Paulin Vieyra	1.60	.80
		Nos. 868-871 (4)		5.00	2.60

Souvenir Sheet
872		Sheet of 3	9.00	4.50
a.-c.		A262 500fr like #869-871, inscribed in gold	3.00	1.50

Panafrican Film Festival (FESPACO), 20th anniv. Nos. 869-872 are airmail.

World Fight Against AIDS A263

1989, Apr. 7   **Litho.**   **Perf. 13**
873	A263	120fr	multicolored	.80	.40

Council for Rural Development, 30th Anniv. — A264

1989, May 3   **Litho.**   **Perf. 15x14**
874	A264	75fr	multicolored	.50	.25

Parasitic Plants — A265

Legumes and cereals.

1989, Oct. 9   **Litho.**   **Perf. 11½**
Granite Paper
875	A265	20fr	Striga generiodes	.20	.20
876	A265	50fr	Striga hermonthica	.30	.20
877	A265	235fr	Striga aspera	1.50	.80
878	A265	450fr	Alectra vogelii	3.00	1.50
		Nos. 875-878 (4)		5.00	2.70

Dogs A266

1989, Oct. 9   **Perf. 15x14½**
879	A266	35fr	Sahel	.25	.20
880	A266	50fr	Puppy	.35	.20
881	A266	60fr	Hunting dog	.40	.20
882	A266	350fr	Guard dog	2.25	1.10
		Nos. 879-882 (4)		3.25	1.70

Solidarity with the Palestinian People — A267

1989, Nov. 15   **Perf. 13**
883	A267	120fr	Monument, Place de la Palestine	.80	.40

Nos. 610-612 Overprinted

1988, Dec. 21   **Litho.**   **Perf. 12½**
884	A203	90fr	multicolored	.60	.30
885	A203	120fr	multicolored	.85	.40
886	A203	170fr	multicolored	1.25	.60
		Nos. 884-886 (3)		2.70	1.30

Visit of Pope John Paul II A268

1990, Jan. 1   **Litho.**   **Perf. 15x14**
887	A268	120fr	Our Lady of Yagma	.85	.40
888	A269	160fr	Pope, crowd	1.25	.60

150th Anniv. of the Postage Stamp A269

1990, Mar. 20   **Litho.**   **Perf. 15x14**
889	A269	120fr	multicolored	1.00	.50

Souvenir Sheet
Perf. 14x15
890	A269	500fr	Penny Black, ship	4.00	2.00

Stamp World London '90.

World Cup Soccer Championships, Italy — A270

1990, Apr. 26   **Litho.**   **Perf. 11½**
891	A270	30fr	multicolored	.25	.20
892	A270	150fr	multi, diff.	1.10	.55

Souvenir Sheet
893	A270	1000fr	multi, horiz.	7.25	3.75

Intl. Literacy Year A271

1990, July 10   **Litho.**   **Perf. 13**
894	A271	40fr	multicolored	.30	.20
895	A271	130fr	multicolored	.90	.45

Mushrooms — A272

1990, May 17   **Litho.**   **Perf. 11½**
896	A272	10fr	Cantharellus cibarius	.20	.20
897	A272	15fr	Psalliota bispora	.20	.20
898	A272	60fr	Amanita caesarea	.50	.25
899	A272	190fr	Boletus badius	1.50	.75
a.		Souv. sheet of 4, #896-899	2.25	1.10
		Nos. 896-899 (4)		2.40	1.40

Intl. Exposition of Handicrafts — A273

1990, Sept. 25   **Litho.**   **Perf. 13**
900	A273	35fr	Masks, fans, vert.	.30	.20
901	A273	45fr	shown	.40	.20
902	A273	270fr	Rattan chair, vert.	2.50	1.25
		Nos. 900-902 (3)		3.20	1.65

Gen. Charles de Gaulle (1890-1970) A274

1990, Nov. 22   **Litho.**   **Perf. 13**
903	A274	200fr	multicolored	1.75	.90

Minerals A275

1991, Feb. 4   **Litho.**   **Perf. 15x14**
904	A275	20fr	Quartz	.20	.20
905	A275	50fr	Granite	.40	.20
906	A275	280fr	Amphibolite	2.25	1.10
		Nos. 904-906 (3)		2.85	1.50

African Film Festival — A276   Fight Against Drugs — A277

1991, Feb. 20   **Perf. 11½**
907	A276	150fr	multicolored	1.25	.60

Souvenir Sheet
908	A276	1000fr	Award	8.00	4.00

1991, Feb. 20
909	A277	130fr	multicolored	1.00	.55

Samuel F.B. Morse (1791-1872), Inventor — A278

1991, May 17   **Litho.**   **Perf. 13**
910	A278	200fr	multicolored	1.60	.80

Native Girl — A279

Flowers A280

1991-93   **Litho.**   **Perf. 14½x15**
911	A279	5fr	gray & multi	.20	.20
912	A279	10fr	yellow & multi	.20	.20
913	A279	25fr	lilac rose & multi	.20	.20
914	A279	50fr	red lilac & multi	.30	.20
915	A279	130fr	blue & multi	1.10	.55
916	A279	150fr	multicolored	1.25	.60

920 A279 200fr multicolored 1.60 .80
922 A279 330fr orange & multi 2.75 1.40
Nos. 911-922 (8) 7.60 4.15

Issued: 150fr, 200fr, 6/20/91; 130fr, 330fr, 1/15/93; 5-50fr, 5/3/94. This is an expanding set. Numbers may change.

1991, July 31 Litho. Perf. 11½
926 A280 5fr Grewia tenax .20 .20
927 A280 15fr Hymenocardia acide .20 .20
928 A280 60fr Cassia sieberiana, vert. .50 .25
929 A280 100fr Adenium obesum .80 .40
930 A280 300fr Mitragyna inermis 2.40 1.25
Nos. 926-930 (5) 4.10 2.30

Traditional Dance Costumes A281

World Post Day — A282

1991, Aug. 20 Perf. 12½
931 A281 75fr Warba .60 .30
932 A281 130fr Wiskamba 1.00 .50
933 A281 280fr Pa-zenin 2.25 1.10
Nos. 931-933 (3) 3.85 1.90

1991, Oct. 9 Perf. 13½
934 A282 130fr multicolored 1.00 .50

Cooking Utensils A283

1992, Jan. 8 Litho. Perf. 11½
935 A283 45fr Pancake fryer .35 .20
936 A283 130fr Cooking pot, vert. 1.00 .55
937 A283 310fr Mortar & pestle, vert. 2.40 1.25
938 A283 500fr Ladle, calabash 4.00 2.00
Nos. 935-938 (4) 7.75 4.00

1992 African Soccer Championships, Senegal — A284

1992, Jan. 17 Perf. 13½
939 A284 50fr Yousouf Fofana .40 .20
940 A284 100fr Francois-Jules Bocande .80 .40
Souvenir Sheet
Perf. 13x12½
941 A284 500fr Trophy 4.00 2.00

UN Decade For the Handicapped — A285

1992, Mar. 31 Litho. Perf. 12½
942 A285 100fr multicolored .85 .40

World Health Day — A286

1992, Apr. 7 Perf. 13
943 A286 330fr multicolored 2.75 1.40

Discovery of America, 500th Anniv. A287

1992, Aug. 12 Litho. Perf. 12½
944 A287 50fr Columbus, Santa Maria .40 .25
945 A287 150fr Ships, natives 1.25 .65
Souvenir Sheet
946 A287 350fr Map 3.00 1.50

Genoa '92. No. 946 contains one 52x31mm stamp.

A288

A289

Insects.

1992, Aug. 17 Perf. 15x14
947 A288 20fr Dysdercus voelkeri .20 .20
948 A288 40fr Rhizopertha dominica .35 .20
949 A288 85fr Orthetrum microstigma .75 .35
950 A288 500fr Apis mellifera 4.25 2.25
Nos. 947-950 (4) 5.55 3.00

1992, Dec. 21 Perf. 11½
Christmas: 10fr, Boy, creche. 130fr, Children decorating creche. 1000fr, Boy holding painting of Madonna and Child.
951 A289 10fr multicolored .20 .20
952 A289 130fr multicolored 1.00 .50
953 A289 1000fr multicolored 8.00 4.00
Nos. 951-953 (3) 9.20 4.70

Invention of the Diesel Engine, Cent. A290

1993, Jan. 25 Litho. Perf. 11½
954 A290 1000fr multicolored 8.00 4.00

The date of issue is in question.

Paris '94, Philatelic Exhibition A291

1993, July 15
955 A291 400fr multicolored 3.50 1.75
956 A291 650fr multi, diff. 5.50 2.75

African Film Festival — A292   Birds — A293

Designs: 250fr, Monument to the cinema. 750fr, M. Douta (1919-1991), comedian, horiz.

Perf. 11½x12, 12x11½
1993, Feb. 16 Litho.
957 A292 250fr multicolored 2.00 1.00
958 A292 750fr multicolored 6.00 3.00

1993, Mar. 31 Perf. 11½x12
100fr, Mycteria ibis. 200fr, Leptoptilos crumeniferus. 500fr, Ephippiorhynchus senegalensis.
959 A293 100fr multicolored .80 .40
960 A293 200fr multicolored 1.60 .80
961 A293 500fr multicolored 4.00 2.00
a. Souvenir sheet of 3, #959-961 9.50 4.75
Nos. 959-961 (3) 6.40 3.20

No. 961a sold for 1200fr.

1994 World Cup Soccer Championships, US — A294

1993, Apr. 8 Perf. 15
962 A294 500fr shown 4.00 2.00
963 A294 1000fr Players, US flag 8.00 4.00

Fruit Trees — A295

150fr, Saba senegalensis, vert. 300fr, Butyrospermum parkii. 600fr, Adansonia digitata, vert.

1993, June 2 Litho. Perf. 11½
964 A295 150fr multicolored 1.25 .65
965 A295 300fr multicolored 2.50 1.25
966 A295 600fr multicolored 5.00 2.50
Nos. 964-966 (3) 8.75 4.40

Traditional Jewelry A296

1993, Sept. 25 Litho. Perf. 11½
967 A296 200fr Ring for hair 1.60 .85
968 A296 250fr Agate necklace, vert. 2.00 1.00
969 A296 500fr Bracelet 4.00 2.00
Nos. 967-969 (3) 7.60 3.85

Gazella Rufifrons A297

1993, Dec. 10 Litho. Perf. 14½
970 A297 30fr shown .55 .25
971 A297 40fr Two facing left .60 .25
972 A297 60fr Two standing 1.25 .65
973 A297 100fr Young gazelle 2.10 1.10
a. Souvenir sheet, #970-973 3.25 3.25
Nos. 970-973 (4) 4.50 2.25

World Wildlife Fund (#970-973). No. 973a sold for 400fr.

Kingfishers — A298

1994, Mar. 8 Litho. Perf. 11½
974 A298 600fr Halcyon senegalensis 2.00 1.00
975 A298 1200fr Halcyon chelicuti 4.25 2.25
Souvenir Sheet
976 A298 2000fr Ceyx picta 7.00 3.50

1994 World Cup Soccer Championships, US — A299

1994, Mar. 28
977 A299 1000fr Players, US map 3.50 1.75
978 A299 1800fr Soccer ball, players 6.50 3.25
a. Souvenir sheet of 1 7.00 3.50

No. 978a sold for 2000fr.

First Manned Moon Landing, 25th Anniv. — A300

1994, July 15 Litho. Perf. 11½
979 A300 750fr Astronaut, flag 3.75 1.90
980 A300 750fr Lunar module, earth 3.75 1.90
a. Pair, #979-980 7.50 3.75

No. 980a is a continuous design.

First Stamp
Exhibition,
Paris, 1994
A301

1994, Apr. 28
981　A301　1500fr Dogs　　　　　7.75　3.75
　a.　Souvenir sheet of 1　　　　7.75　3.75

Legumes — A302

40fr, Hibiscus sabdariffa. 45fr, Solanum
aethiopicum. 75fr, Solanum melongena. 100fr,
Hibiscus esculentus.

1994　　　　Litho.　　　Perf. 11½
982　A302　40fr multicolored　　　.20　.20
983　A302　45fr multicolored　　　.25　.20
984　A302　75fr multicolored　　　.40　.20
985　A302　100fr multicolored　　.50　.25
　　　Nos. 982-985 (4)　　　　　1.35　.85

Intl. Olympic
Committee,
Cent. — A303

Domestic
Animals — A304

1994, Oct. 10　　　　　　Perf. 15
986　A303　320fr multicolored　　1.60　.80

1994, Oct. 10　　　　　　Perf. 11½
987　A304　150fr Pig, horiz.　　　.75　.35
988　A304　1000fr Capra hircus　4.75　2.50
989　A304　1500fr Ovis aries,
　　　　　　horiz.　　　　　7.25　3.75
　　　Nos. 987-989 (3)　　　12.75　6.60

Elvis Presley
(1935-77)
A305

A305a

Portraits in feature films: 300fr, Loving You.
500fr, Jailhouse Rock. 1000fr, Blue Hawaii.
1500fr, Marilyn Monroe, Presley. 0

1995　　　　　　　Perf. 13½
990-992　A305　Set of 3　　　7.50　3.75
Souvenir Sheets
993　A305　1500fr multicolored　6.00　3.00
Litho. & Embossed
993A　A305a　3000fr gold & multi

Nos. 990-992 exist in souvenir sheets of
one. No. 993 contains one 51x42mm stamp

with continuous design. No. 993A, exists in
souvenir sheets of silver & multi with different
designs in sheet margin.
　Issued: No. 993A, 2/24/95.
　See Nos. 1012-1015A.

Crocodile — A306

1995, Feb. 6　　Litho.　　Perf. 15x14½
994　A306　10fr brown & multi　　.20　.20
995　A306　20fr lilac & multi　　　.20　.20
996　A306　25fr olive brn & multi　.20　.20
997　A306　30fr green & multi　　.20　.20
998　A306　40fr red brn & multi　.20　.20
999　A306　50fr gray & multi　　.25　.20
1000　A306　75fr gray vio & multi　.35　.20
1001　A306　100fr gray brn & multi　.50　.25
1002　A306　150fr olive & multi　　.75　.40
1003　A306　175fr gray bl & multi　.90　.45
1004　A306　250fr brn lake & multi　1.25　.65
1005　A306　400fr bl grn & multi　2.00　1.00
　　　Nos. 994-1005 (12)　　　7.00　4.15

World Tourism
Organization,
20th Anniv.
A307

Designs: 150fr, Man riding donkey, vert.
350fr, Bobo-Dioulasso railroad station. 450fr,
Grand Mosque, Bani. 650fr, Gazelle, map.

1995, Jan. 26　　Litho.　　Perf. 11½
1006　A307　150fr multicolored　.75　.40
1007　A307　350fr multicolored　1.75　.90
1008　A307　450fr multicolored　2.25　1.10
1009　A307　650fr multicolored　3.25　1.60
　　　Nos. 1006-1009 (4)　　8.00　4.00

FESPACO
'95 — 1010

Motion pictures: 150fr, "Rabi," Gaston
Kabore. 250fr, "Tilai," Idrissa Ouedraogo.

1995　　　　　　　Perf. 13½
1010　A308　150fr multicolored　.80　.40
1011　A308　250fr multicolored　1.40　.70
　　Nos. 1010-1011 exist in souvenir sheets of
one. Motion pictures, cent.

Traditional
Houses
A308a

1995　　　　Litho.　　Perf. 13½
1011A　A308a　70fr Mossi
1011B　A308a　100fr Kassena
1011C　A308a　200fr Bobo

An additional stamp was issued in this set.
The editors would like to examine it.

Stars of Motion Pictures Type of 1995
　Marilyn Monroe in feature films: 400fr, The
Joyful Parade. 650fr, The Village Tramp. 750fr,
Niagara.
　1500fr, The Seven Year Itch. 3000fr, Marilyn
Monroe (1926-62).

1995　　　　Litho.　　Perf. 13½
1012-1014　A305　Set of 3　　7.50　3.75

Souvenir Sheets
1015　A305　1500fr multicolored　6.00　3.00
Litho. & Embossed
1015A　A305a　3000fr gold & multi

　#1012-1014 exist in souvenir sheets of 1.
#1015 contains one 42x51mm stamp with
continuous design. #1015A exists in souvenir
sheets of silver & multi with different designs in
sheet margin.

Birds — A309

Designs: 450fr, Laniarius barbarus. 600fr,
Estrilda bengala. 750fr, Euplectes afer.

1995, Apr. 5　　Litho.　　Perf. 11½
1016　A309　450fr multicolored　2.00　1.00
1017　A309　600fr multicolored　2.75　1.40
1018　A309　750fr multicolored　3.50　1.75
　a.　Souv. sheet, #1016-1018　9.00　4.50
　　　Nos. 1016-1018 (3)　　8.25　4.15
　　No. 1018a sold for 2000fr.

Reptiles
A310

Designs: 450fr, Psammophis sibilans. 500fr,
Eryx muelleri. 1500fr, Turtle.

1995, Dec. 31
1019　A310　450fr multicolored　2.00　1.00
1020　A310　500fr multicolored　2.25　1.10
1021　A310　1500fr multicolored　6.75　3.50
　　　Nos. 1019-1021 (3)　　11.00　5.60

1996 Summer
Olympics,
Atlanta
A311

Design: 3000fr, Tennis, diff.

1995, Sept. 20　Litho.　Perf. 13½
1022　A311　150fr Basketball　.70　.35
1023　A311　250fr Baseball　1.25　.60
1024　A311　650fr Tennis　　3.00　1.50
1025　A311　750fr Table tennis　3.50　1.75
　a.　Souv. sheet, #1022-1025　8.50　4.25
　　　Nos. 1022-1025 (4)　　8.45　4.20

Souvenir Sheets
1026　A311　1500fr Equestrian
　　　　　event　　　7.00　7.00
Litho. & Embossed
1026A　A311　3000fr gold & multi

　No. 1026A also exists as a silver & multi
souvenir sheet with different design in sheet
margin. Both the gold & silver stamps also
exist together in a souvenir sheet of 2.

Sports
Figures
A312

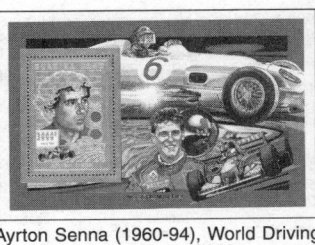

Ayrton Senna (1960-94), World Driving
Champion — A313

　Designs: 300fr, Juan Manuel Fangio, race
car driver, 1955 Mercedes W 196. 400fr,
Andre Agassi, US tennis player. 500fr, Ayrton
Senna (1960-94), race car driver, McLaren MP
4/6 Honda. 1000fr, Michael Schumacher, race
car driver, 1995 Benetton B 195.
　1500fr, Enzo Ferrari, 412 TR, F40.

1995, Sept. 20
1027　A312　300fr multi　　2.25　1.10
1028　A312　400fr multi　　3.25　1.60
1029　A312　500fr multi　　4.00　2.00
1030　A312　1000fr multi　　8.00　4.00
　a.　Souvenir sheet of 3, #1027,
　　　1029-1030　　　14.50　7.25
　　　Nos. 1027-1030 (4)　　17.50　8.70

Souvenir Sheets
1031　A312　1500fr multicolored　7.00　3.50
Litho. & Embossed
1032　A313　3000fr gold & multi

　#1027-1030 exist in souvenir sheets of 1.
#1031 contains one 55x48mm stamp.
　No. 1032 also exists as a silver & multi souvenir sheet with different design in sheet margin. Both the gold and silver stamps also exist
together in a souvenir sheet of 2.
　For surcharge see No. 1078.

Souvenir Sheets

John Lennon (1940-1980) — A314

　Designs: No. 1033, With guitar, circular pattern with name "LENNON," portrait. No. 1034,
With guitar, emblem, portrait.

1995　Litho. & Embossed　Perf. 13½
1033　A314　3000fr gold & multi
1034　A314　3000fr gold & multi

　Nos. 1033-1034 each exist in souvenir
sheets of silver & multi. Souvenir sheets of one
gold and one silver exist in same designs and
one of each design.

1995 Boy
Scout
Jamboree,
Holland
A315

Mushrooms: 150fr, Russula nigricans.
250fr, Lepiota rhacodes. 300fr, Xerocomus
subtomentos. 400fr, Boletus erythropus. 500fr,
Russula sanguinea. 650fr, Amanita
rubescens. 750fr, Amanita vaginata. 1000fr,
Geastrum sessil.
　No. 1043, Amanita muscaria. No. 1044,
Morchella esculenta.

1996, Feb. 20　Litho.　Perf. 13½
1035-1042　A315　Set of 8　16.00　8.00
1041a　　Sheet of 4, #1035, 1037,
　　　　1040-1041　　　7.50　3.75
1042a　　Sheet of 4, #1036, 1038-
　　　　1039, 1042　　　8.50　4.25
Souvenir Sheets
1043-1044　A315　1500fr each　6.00　3.00

Mushrooms — A316

Designs: 175fr, Hygrophore perroquet. 250fr, Pleurote en huitre. 300fr, Pezize (oreille d'ane). 450fr, Clavaire jolie.

1996, Jan. 24
1045-1048	A316	Set of 4	4.50	2.25
1048a		Souv. sheet, #1045-1048	4.50	2.25

#1045-1048 each exist in souv. sheets of 1.

UN, 50th Anniv. A317

Designs: 500fr, UN headquarters, New York. 1000fr, UN emblem, people, vert.

1995, Dec. 20 — **Perf. 11½**
1049	A317	500fr multicolored	2.75	1.25
1050	A317	1000fr multicolored	5.25	2.75

Christmas A318

Designs: 150fr, Christmas tree, children pointing to picture of nativity scene. 450fr, Yagma Grotto. 500fr, Flight into Egypt. 1000fr, Adoration of the Magi.

1995, Dec. 18
1051	A318	150fr multicolored	.80	.40
1052	A318	450fr multicolored	2.40	1.25
1053	A318	500fr multicolored	2.75	1.40
1054	A318	1000fr multicolored	5.25	2.75
		Nos. 1051-1054 (4)	11.20	5.80

Entertainers — A319

Portraits: No. 1062, Elvis Presley, smiling. No. 1063, Presley, hand under chin. No. 1064, Stevie Wonder.

1996, May 14 — **Litho.** — **Perf. 13½**
Souvenir Sheets
1062-1064	A319	1500fr each	5.25	2.50

Numbers have been reserved for a set of 8 individual stamps released with these souvenir sheets.
Dated 1995.

Butterflies and Insects A320

100fr, Epiphora bauhiniae. 150fr, Kraussella amabile. 175fr, Charaxes epijasius. 250fr, Locusta migratoria.

1996 — **Litho.** — **Perf. 13½**
1065	A320	100fr multi, vert.	.40	.20
1066	A320	150fr multi, vert.	.70	.35
1067	A320	175fr multi, vert.	.80	.40
1068	A320	250fr multi	1.10	.60
		Nos. 1065-1068 (4)	3.00	1.55

Two souvenir sheets containing Nos. 1065, 1067 and Nos. 1066, 1068, respectively, exist.

Butterflies A321

Designs: 150fr, Morpho rega. 250fr, Hypolymnas misippus. 450fr, Pseudacraea boisduvali. 600fr, Charaxes castor. 1500fr, Antanartia delius.

1996, June 28 — **Litho.** — **Perf. 13½**
1069	A321	150fr multicolored	.70	.35
1070	A321	250fr multicolored	1.10	.55
1071	A321	450fr multicolored	2.00	1.00
1072	A321	600fr multicolored	2.75	2.75
		Nos. 1069-1072 (4)	6.55	4.65

Souvenir Sheet
1073	A321	1500fr multicolored	6.75	6.75
a.		Ovptd. in sheet margin	6.25	6.25

Overprint in silver in sheet margin of No. 1073a contains Hong Kong '97 Exhibition emblem and two line inscription in Chinese. Issued in 1997.

Insects — A321a

c, 25fr, Sauterelle. d, 75fr, Schistocerca gregaria. e, 300fr, Pardolata haasi. f, 400fr, Psammomys obesus.

1996, June 28 — **Litho.** — **Perf. 13½**
1073B	A321a	Strip of 4, #c.-f.	2.75	1.40

1998 World Cup Soccer Championships, France — A322

Various soccer plays.

1996 — **Litho.** — **Perf. 13**
1074	A322	50fr multi	.20	.20
1075	A322	150fr multi, vert.	.65	.25
1076	A322	250fr multi, vert.	1.10	.55
1077	A322	450fr multi, vert.	1.90	1.00
		Nos. 1074-1077 (4)	3.85	2.00

No. 1028 Ovptd. in Metallic Red

1996 — **Litho.** — **Perf. 13½**
1078	A312	400fr multicolored	1.60	.80

No. 1078 exists in souvenir sheet of 1.

Wild Cats — A323

Designs: 100fr, Panthera leo. 150fr, Acinonyx jubatus. 175fr, Lynx caracal. 250fr, Panthera pardus.
Illustration reduced.

1996 — **Perf. 12½x12**
1079	A323	100fr multicolored	.40	.20
1080	A323	150fr multicolored	.55	.30
1081	A323	175fr multicolored	.65	.35
1082	A323	250fr multicolored	.95	.45
		Nos. 1079-1082 (4)	2.55	1.30

Orchids — A324

Various orchids.

1996, Aug. 30 — **Litho.** — **Perf. 12½x13**
1083	A324	100fr blue & multi	1.10	.55
1084	A324	175fr lilac & multi	1.90	.95
1085	A324	250fr orange & multi	2.75	1.25
1086	A324	300fr olive & multi	3.25	1.60
		Nos. 1083-1086 (4)	9.00	4.35

UNICEF, 50th Anniv. — A324a

Design: 250fr, Vaccination of child.

1996 (?) — **Litho.** — **Perf. 11¾**
1086A	A324a	250fr multi		

The editors suspect that more stamps were issued in this set, and would like to examine any examples.

Birds — A325

Designs: 500fr, Falco peregrinus. 750fr, Crossoptilon mantchuricum. 1000fr, Branta canadensis. 1500fr, Pelecanus crispus.

1996, June 25 — **Perf. 12½x12**
1087	A325	500fr multicolored	2.00	1.00
1088	A325	750fr multicolored	2.50	1.25
1089	A325	1000fr multicolored	3.75	1.90
1090	A325	1500fr multicolored	5.75	2.75
		Nos. 1087-1090 (4)	14.00	6.90

#1087-1090 each printed se-tenant with labels.

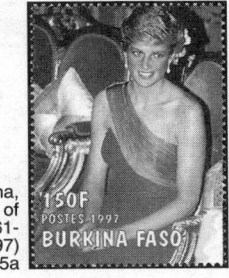

Diana, Princess of Wales (1961-97) A325a

Various portraits, color of sheet margin: #1090A, blue. #1090K, deep pink. #1090U, In yellow. #1090V, Wearing tiara.

1997 — **Litho.** — **Perf. 13½**
Sheets of 9
1090A	A325a	150fr #Ab-Aj	4.75	2.40
1090K	A325a	180fr #Kl-Kti	5.75	3.00

Souvenir Sheets
1090U-1090V	A325a	2000fr each	7.25	3.50

#1090U-1090V each contain one 41x46mm stamp.
See Nos. 1126-1128.

Flowers A325b

Design: 175fr, Costus pectabilis.

1997 (?) — **Litho.** — **Perf. 13¼x13½**
1090W	A325b	175fr multi		

The editors suspect that more stamps were issued in this set, and would like to examine any examples.

A326 A327

Various portraits, color of sheet margin: No. 1091, Pale pink. No. 1092, Pale blue. No. 1093, Pale yellow.
No. 1094, In white dress, serving food to child (in sheet margin). No. 1095, Wearing wide-brimmed hat.

1998 — **Litho.** — **Perf. 14**
Sheets of 6
1091	A326	425fr #a.-f.	8.75	4.50
1092	A326	530fr #a.-f.	11.00	5.50
1093	A326	590fr #a.-f.	12.00	6.00

Souvenir Sheets
1094-1095	A326	1500fr each	5.00	2.50

Diana, Princess of Wales (1961-97).

1998 — **Litho.** — **Perf. 14**
1096	A327	260fr shown	.60	.30

Souvenir Sheet
1097	A327	1500fr Portrait, diff.	5.00	2.50

Mother Teresa (1910-97). No. 1096 was issued in sheets of 6. Nos. 1096-1097 have birth date inscribed "1907."

Birds — A328

5fr, White-winged triller. 10fr, Golden sparrow. 100fr, American goldfinch. 170fr, Red-legged thrush. 260fr, Willow warbler. 425fr, Blue grosbeak.
No. 1104: a, Bank swallow. b, Kirtland's warbler. c, Long-tailed minivet. d, Blue-gray gnatcatcher. e, Reed-bunting. f, Black-collared apalis. g, American robin. h, Cape long-claw. i, Wood thrush.
No. 1105: a, Song sparrow. b, Dartford warbler. c, Eastern bluebird. d, Rock thrush. e, Northern mockingbird. f, Northern cardinal. g, Eurasian goldfinch. h, Varied thrush. i, Northern oriole.
No. 1106, Golden whistler. No. 1107, Barn swallow, horiz.

1998, Oct. 1   Litho.   Perf. 13½
1098-1103 A328 Set of 6   3.50 1.75

Sheets of 9
1104 A328 260fr #a.-i.   8.25 4.00
1105 A328 425fr #a.-i.   14.00 7.00

Souvenir Sheets
1106-1107 A328 1500fr each   5.50 2.75

Butterflies and Moths A329

No. 1108: a, Arctia caja. b, Nymphalis antiopa. c, Brahmaea wallichii. d, Issoria lathonia. e, Speyeria cybele. f, Vanessa virginiensis. g, Rothchildia orizaba. h, Cethosia hypsea. i, Marpesia petreus.
No. 1109: a, Agraulis vanillae. b, Junonia coenia. c, Danaus gilippus. d, Polygonia comma. e, Anthocharis cardamines. f, Heliconius aoede. g, Atlides halesus. h, Mesosemia croseus. i, Automeris io.
No. 1110, Papilio xuthus. No. 1111, Pterourus multicaudatus. No. 1112, Pterourus troilus. No. 1113, Papilio machaon.

1998, Oct. 25
Sheets of 9
1108 A329 170fr #a.-i.   5.25 2.75
1109 A329 530fr #a.-i.   16.00 8.00

Souvenir Sheets
1110-1113 A329 1500fr each   5.50 2.75
#1110-1113 contain one 56x42mm stamp.

Christmas 1114

Fauna, flora with Christmas items: 100fr, Tersina viridis, holly, vert. 170fr, Citherias menander, present, vert. 260fr, Chrysanthemum, reindeer, sleigh, vert. 425fr, Swallowtail butterfly, greeting card. 530fr, European bee eater, Santa Claus, snowman.
No. 1119, Anthemis tinctoria, sleigh. No. 1120, Papilio ulysses, greeting card.

1998, Dec. 1   Litho.   Perf. 14
1114-1118 A330 Set of 5   5.50 2.75

Souvenir Sheets
1119-1120 A330 1500fr each   5.50 2.75

Handicrafts A330a

Design: 25f, Stool with carved heads. 100fr, Dagari stool. 150fr, Basket. 170f, Wooden statue, Wooden statue, Pasoré region, vert.

1996-98 (?)   Litho.   Perf. 11¾
1120B A330a 25fr multi
1120G A330a 100fr multi
1120H A330a 150fr multi
1120I A330a 170fr multi
1120J A330a 260fr multi

Issued: No. 1120B, 170fr, 260f, 6/20/98. Six additional stamps were issued in this set. The editors would like to examine them.

34th Organization for African Unity Summit, Ouagadougou — A330b

Design: 170fr, OAU emblem, horses.

1998, May 20   Litho.   Perf. 13x13¼
1120K A330b 170fr multi

An additional stamp was issued in this set. The editors would like to examine them.

Protected Wildlife — A330c

Designs: 170fr, Leptoptilos crumeniferus. 200fr, Acionyx jubatus. 260fr, Orycteropus afer. 530fr, Struthio camulus. 590fr, Hippopotamus amphibius, horiz.

Perf. 13¼x13, 13x13¼
1998, May 20   Litho.
1120M A330c 170fr multi
1120N A330c 200fr multi
1120O A330c 260fr multi
1120P A330c 530fr multi
1120Q A330c 590fr multi

15th FESPACO Film Festival — A330d

Film: 150fr, Enfance et Jeunesse.

1997, Feb. 5   Litho.   Perf. 11½x11¾
1120R A330d 150fr multi

An additional stamp was released in this set. The editors would like to examine it.

Wild Animals — A330e

Design: 150fr, Bubale.

Perf. 11½x11¾
1997, Mar. 20   Litho.
1120V A330e 150fr multi

Three additional stamps were issued in this set. The editors would like to examine them.

Trains - A331

No. 1121: a, CDR No. 19, Ireland. b, EMD "F" Series Bo-Bo, US. c, Class 72000, France. d, Class AE 4/4 Bo-Bo, Switzerland. e, Class 277, Spain. f, ET 403 four car train, West Germany. g, Class EM2 Co-Co, UK. h, Europe Dutch Swiss Tee.
No. 1122: a, DF 4 East Wind IV Co-Co, China. b, Union Pacific Railroad, US. c, No. 3.641, Norway. d, Class GE 4/4 Bo-bo, Switzerland. e, Class GE Bo-Co, South Africa. f, WDM-2 Co-Co, India. g, Kraus Mafeei Co-Co, US. h, RTG Four-car transit, France.
No. 1123, ETR 401 Pendolino, Italy. No. 1124, No. 12 Sarah Siddons, UK.

1998, Nov. 10
Sheets of 8
1121 A331 170fr #a.-h.   5.00 2.50
1122 A331 425fr #a.-h.   12.50 6.25

Souvenir Sheets
1123-1124 A331 1500fr each   5.50 2.75

Intl. Fund for Agricultural Development Type of 1998
150fr, Restoration of degraded soils.

1998, Mar. 20   Litho.   Perf. 13½
1124A A331a 150fr multi

Intl. Fund for Agricultural Development, 20th Anniv. — A331a

Design: 400fr, "20," wheat stalk.

1998 (?)   Litho.   Perf. 13½x13¼
1125 A331a 400fr multi

The editors suspect that more stamps were issued in this set, and would like to examine any examples.

Ceramics — A331b

Design: 450fr, Vase.

Perf. 11½x11¾
1997, Sept. 11   Litho.
1125H A331b 450fr multi

Three additional stamps were released in this set. The editors would like to examine them.

Fish A331c

Design: 100fr, Aplocheilichthys pfaffi.

1997, Nov. 20   Litho.   Perf. 13¼
1125I A331c 100fr multi

Three additional stamps were issued in this set. The editors would like to examine them.

African Soccer Championships — A331d

Design: 175fr, Goalie making save.

1998, Jan. 20   Litho.   Perf. 13x13¼
1125N A331d 175fr multi

Three additional stamps were issued in this set. The editors would like to examine them.

Traditional Costumes A331e

Design: 250fr, Peulh (Boodi). 450fr, Bissa (Gangadruku).

1998, Feb. 20   Litho.   Perf. 13½x13
1125S A331e 250fr multi
1125T A331e 450fr multi

Two additional stamps were released in this set. The editors would like to examine them.

Diana, Princess of Wales Type
425fr, Diana in white blouse. 590fr, Diana with Pope John Paul II. #1127A: various portraits, color of sheet margin is violet.
1500fr, Diana speaking, American Red Cross emblem in sheet margin. 2000fr, Diana wearing Japanese kimono.

1997   Litho.   Perf. 13½
1126 A325a 425fr multi   1.60 1.60
1127 A325a 590fr multi   2.25 1.10

Sheet of 9
1127A A325a 180fr #b-j   6.00 3.00

Souvenir Sheets
1127K A325a 1500fr multi   5.50 2.75
1128 A325a 2000fr multi   7.50 3.75

No. 1127 was issued in sheets of 9. #1127K contains one 41x46mm stamp.

Airplanes A332

No. 1129: a, Sukhoi Su-24. b, Yakovlev Yak-38. c, Tupolev Blackjack. d, Antonov An-26. e, Antonov An-22 Anteus. f, Antonov An-124. 1000fr, Ilyushin Il-76T.

1999, Sept. 8   Litho.   Perf. 14
1129 A332 425fr Sheet of 6,
          #a.-f.   8.50 8.50

Souvenir Sheet
1130 A332 1000fr multicolored 3.25 3.25

No. 1130 contains one 57x43mm stamp.

Ships A333

No. 1131: a, Portland. b, Goethe. c, Fulton.
No. 1132: a, CSS Nashville. b, Cutty Sark. c, Brilliant. d, Eagle. e, Red Jacket. f, USS Columbia. g, HMS Rose. h, Resolution. i, 1000-ton paquebot. j, Mayflower.
No. 1133: a, USS Tennessee. b, HMS Alacrity. c, Bismarck. d, Yamoto. e, Aurora. f, Iowa class battleship. g, Liberty Ship. h, F209. i, Star. j, Big Eagle.
No. 1134, Batavia. No. 1135, Grand Voilier.

1999, Sept. 8
Sheets of 3 and 10

1131	A333 170fr #a.-c.	1.75	1.75
1132	A333 100fr #a.-j.	3.25	3.25
1133	A333 200fr #a.-j.	6.50	6.50

Souvenir Sheets

1134-1135	A333 1000fr each	3.25	3.25

Domesticated Animals — A334

5fr, Tabby cat, vert. 10fr, Chinchilla. 20fr, Yorkshire terriers. 25fr, Cocker spaniels. No. 1140, vert.: a, Afghan hound. b, Fox terrier. c, Pug. d, Dalmatian. e, Boston terrier. f, Cocker spaniel.
No. 1141: a, American wirehaired. b, Tabby. c, Blue Burmese. d, Abyssinian. e, Lilac Burmese. f, Siamese.
No. 1142, Persian. No. 1143, Japanese bobtail, vert. No. 1144, Labrador retriever, vert. No. 1145, Labrador retrievers, vert.

1999, Oct. 4

1136-1139	A334 Set of 4	.20	.20

Sheets of 6

1140	A334 260fr #a.-f.	5.25	5.25
1141	A334 530fr #a.-f.	10.50	10.50

Souvenir Sheets

1142-1145	A334 1000fr each	3.25	3.25

Domesticated Animals — A335

No. 1146 - Horses: a, Gelderlander. b, Trait lourd. c, Vladimir. d, Percheron. e, Sumba. f, Dartmoor.
No. 1147 - Dogs: a, French bulldog. b, Bernese. c, Griffon. d, King Charles spaniel. e, Spitz. f, Yorkshire terrier.
No. 1148 - Cats: a, American wirehaired. b, Japanese bobtail. c, Himalayan. d, LaPerm. e, Lilac Siamese colorpoint. f, Norwegian forest cat.
No. 1149, Shetland pony, vert. No. 1150, Basset hound, vert. No. 1151, Japanese bobtail, diff., vert.

1999, Oct. 4   **Sheets of 6**

1146	A335 170fr #a.-f.	3.50	3.50
1147	A335 425fr #a.-f.	8.50	8.50
1148	A335 590fr #a.-f.	11.50	11.50

Souvenir Sheets

1149-1151	A335 1000fr each	3.25	3.25

Fight Against Hunger — A337

1999, Dec.   Litho.   Perf. 14

1157	A337 350fr multi	1.00	1.00

Issued in sheets of 5.

FESPACO '99 Film Festival - A338

Award winning film: 170fr, Tilai, by Idrissa Ouédraogo. 260fr, Map of Africa, camera, clapper board, vert.

1999   Litho.   Perf. 13x13¼, 13¼x13

1158	A338 170fr multi	
1159	A338 260fr multi	
1159A	A338 425fr multi	

Issued: 1159A, 2/22/99. The editors suspect other stamps with this theme may have been issued, and would like to examine examples. Numbers have been reserved for these possible additions.

Council of the Entente, 40th Anniv. A338a

Denomination color: 170fr, Black. 260fr, Green.

1999, May 5   Litho.   Perf. 13x13¼

1160-1161	A338a Set of 2	

Lions A338b

1999, May 26   Litho.   Perf. 13x13¼
Panel Colors

1161A	A338b 170fr blue		
1161B	A338b 260fr red	—	—
1161C	A338b 425fr green	—	—
1161D	A338b 530fr orange		
1161E	A338b 590fr purple		

Philex France 99.

Orchids — A339

No. 1162: a, Angraecum orchid cape. b, Disa kirstenbossck pride. c, Disa blackii. d, Angraecum long icalear. e, Bulbophyllum falcatum. f, Phragmipedium schlimii (two flowers). g, Polystachya affinis. h, Jumellea sagittata (with leaves).
No. 1163: a, Angraecum sesquipedale. b, Oeceoclades maculata. c, Ancistrochilus childianus. d, Polystachyabella. e, Bulbophyllum lepidum. f, Vanilla imperialis. g, Tridactyle tridactylites. h, Eulophia guineensis.
No. 1164: a, Ansellia africana. b, Aerangis luteo-alba. c, Disa uniflora. d, Angraecum distichum. e, Bulbophyllum falcatum. f, Phragmepedium schlimii (pink flower). g, Polystachya affinis. h, Jumellea sagittata (without leaves).
No. 1165, Disa tripetaloides, horiz. No. 1166, Liparis guineensis, horiz. No. 1167, Bolusiella talbotii, horiz.

2000, Jan. 10   Litho.   Perf. 14
Sheets of 8, #a.-h.

1162-1164	A339 425fr each	7.25	7.25

Souvenir Sheets

1165-1167	A339 1500fr each	5.25	5.25

Space Exploration A340

No. 1168: a, Robert H. Goddard and 1926 rocket. b, Sputnik 1. c, X-15. d, Chinese, inventors of rockets. e, V-2. f, Explorer 1.

No. 1169: a, Vostok 1. b, Friendship 7. c, Soyuz 1. d, Freedom 7. e, Gemini 4. f, Apollo 7.
No. 1170, horiz.: a, Gemini 8. b, Agena target vehicle. c, Soyuz 11. d, Salyut 1. e, Apollo 18. f, Soyuz 19.
No. 1171, Tacsat satellite. No. 1172, Hubble Space Telescope. No. 1173, Viking Lander, horiz.

2000, Jan. 10
Sheets of 6

1168	A340 350fr #a.-f.	7.50	7.50
1169	A340 425fr #a.-f.	9.00	9.00
1170	A340 530fr #a.-f.	11.00	11.00

Souvenir Sheets

1171-1173	A340 1500fr each	5.50	5.50

No. 1173 contains one 57x42mm stamp.

Peter Pan — A341

Designs: a, 75fr, Fairy, red flowers. b, 75fr, Parrot. c, 75fr, Moon, Wendy, Michael, John. d, 75fr, White flower. e, 80fr, Fairy, pink flower. f, 80fr, Butterflies. g, 80fr, Peter Pan. h, 80fr, Fairy. i, 90fr, Red flower. j, 90fr, Butterflies. k, 90fr, Egret. l, 90fr, White flower. m, 100fr, Mermaid. n, 100fr, Pirate ship, crocodile's tail. o, 100fr, Crocodile's head. p, 100fr, Captain Hook.

2000, Jan. 10   Perf. 12¼

1174	A341 Sheet of 16, #a.-p.	4.25	4.25

2000 Summer Olympics, Sydney — A343

No. 1191: a, Hannes Kohlemainen. b, Runner. c, US flag, Fulton County Stadium, Atlanta. d, Discus thrower.
Illustration reduced.

2000, Nov. 12   Litho.   Perf. 14

1191	A343 350fr Sheet of 4, #a-d	3.75	3.75

First Zeppelin Flight, Cent. — A344

No. 1192, 350fr: a, LZ-1, b, LZ-2 (dark gray at left). c, LZ-2 (white at left) d, LZ-5. e, LZ-8. f, LZ-7.
No. 1193, 350fr: a, LZ-9. b, LZ-10. c, LZ-11. d, LZ-127. e, LZ-129. f, LZ-130.
No. 1194, 1500fr: LZ-1. No. 1195, 1500fr, LZ-4.

Illustration reduced.

2000, Nov. 12
Sheets of 6, #a-f

1192-1193	A344 Set of 2	11.00	11.00

Souvenir Sheets

1194-1195	A344 Set of 2	8.00	8.00

Berlin Film Festival, 50th Anniv. — A345

No. 1196: a, Le Grand Blond Avec Une Chaussure Noire. b Ruy Guerra. c, Mario Monicelli. d, Mudhur Jaffrey. e, Orökbefogadás. f, Palermo Oder Wolfsburg.
Illustration reduced.

2000, Nov. 12   Litho.   Perf. 14
Sheet of 6

1196	A345 420fr #a-f	7.25	7.25

Souvenir Sheet

1197	A345 1500fr Platoon	4.50	4.50

Souvenir Sheets

Public Railways, 175th Anniv. — A346

No. 1198: a, George Stephenson, Locomotion No. 1. b, Stourbridge Lion.
No. 1199: a, George Stephenson, Brusselton inclined plane. b, Robert Stephenson, turnpike crossing near Darlington. c, Locomotive built by George Stephenson. d, Experiment passenger coach built by Robert Stephenson.
Illustration reduced.

2000, Nov. 12
Sheets of 2 and 4

1198	A346 550fr #a-b	3.25	3.25
1199	A346 800fr #a-d	9.25	9.25

Fruits — A347

2000   Litho.   Perf. 14¾

1200	A347 100fr Baobab	

The editors suspect that other stamps of this type were issued and would like to examine any examples.

Fruit Type of 2000

2000, Feb. 23   Litho.   *Perf. 14¾*
1201 A347 170fr Tamarind, horiz.

Two additional stamps were released in this set. The editors would like to examine them.

Elephants
A348

2000, Mar. 22   Litho.   *Perf. 14¾*
1204 A348 200fr Facing left

Two additional stamps were released in this set. The editors would like to examine them.

National
Culture
Week
A349

2000   Litho.   *Perf. 13x13½*
1210 A349 590fr Dancers

The editors suspect that additional stamps were issued in this set and would like to examine any examples.

SEMI-POSTAL STAMPS

Catalogue values for unused stamps in this section are for Never Hinged items.

Anti-Malaria Issue
Common Design Type

1962, Apr. 7   Engr.   *Perf. 12½x12*
B1 CD108 25fr + 5fr red org   .50 .50

Freedom from Hunger Issue
Common Design Type

1963, Mar. 21   *Perf. 13*
B2 CD112 25fr + 5fr dk grn, bl & brn   .50 .50

CAN '96 (African Nations) Soccer
Championships — SP1

Designs: 150fr+25fr, Stallions, soccer ball. 250fr+25fr, Map of Africa, soccer player.

1996, Jan. 2   Litho.   *Perf. 11½*
B3 SP1 150fr +25fr multi   .95 .45
   a.   Souvenir sheet of 1   2.75 1.40
B4 SP1 250fr +25fr multi   1.50 .75

No. B3a sold for 500fr.

AIR POST STAMPS

Catalogue values for unused stamps in this section are for Never Hinged items.

Plane over Map Showing Air
Routes — AP1

200fr, Plane at airport, Ouagadougou.
500fr, Champs Elysees, Ouagadougou.

Unwmk.
1961, Mar. 4   Engr.   *Perf. 13*
C1 AP1 100fr multicolored   .90 .40
C2 AP1 200fr multicolored   2.25 .70
C3 AP1 500fr multicolored   5.25 2.40
   Nos. C1-C3 (3)   8.40 3.50

Air Afrique Issue
Common Design Type

1962, Feb. 17
C4 CD107 25fr brt pink, dk pur & lt grn   .30 .20

UN Emblem and Upper Volta
Flag — AP2

**   *Perf. 13½x12½***
1962, Sept. 22   Photo.
C5 AP2 50fr multicolored   .50 .25
C6 AP2 100fr multicolored   1.00 .50

Admission to UN, second anniversary.

Post Office, Ouagadougou — AP3

1962, Dec. 11   *Perf. 13x12*
C7 AP3 100fr multicolored   1.00 .40

Jet
Over
Map
AP4

1963, June 24
C8 AP4 200fr multicolored   3.50 1.50

First jet flight, Ouagadougou to Paris.
For surcharge see No. C10.

African Postal Union Issue
Common Design Type

1963, Sept. 8   Unwmk.   *Perf. 12½*
C9 CD114 85fr dp vio, ocher & red   .90 .50

No. C8 Surcharged in Red

1963, Nov. 19   *Perf. 13x12*
C10 AP4 50fr on 200fr multi   .90 .40

See note after Mauritania No. C26.

Europafrica Issue
Common Design Type

50fr, Sunburst & Europe linked with Africa.

1964, Jan. 6   *Perf. 12x13*
C11 CD116 50fr multicolored   .85 .50

Ramses II, Abu
Simbel — AP5

Greek Sculptures
AP6

1964, Mar. 8   Engr.   *Perf. 13*
C12 AP5 25fr dp green & choc   .35 .30
C13 AP5 100fr brt bl & brn   1.40 1.25

UNESCO world campaign to save historic monuments of Nubia.

1964, July 1   Unwmk.   *Perf. 13*
C14 AP6 15fr Greek Portrait Head   .35 .20
C15 AP6 25fr Seated boxer   .45 .20
C16 AP6 85fr Victorious athlete   .95 .60
C17 AP6 100fr Venus of Milo   1.50 .70
   a.   Min. sheet of 4, #C14-C17   6.00 6.00
     Nos. C14-C17 (4)   3.25 1.70

18th Olympic Games, Tokyo, Oct. 10-25.

West African
Gray
Woodpecker
AP7

President John F.
Kennedy (1917-
1963)
AP8

1964, Oct. 1   Engr.   *Perf. 13*
C18 AP7 250fr multicolored   6.00 2.25

1964, Nov. 25   Photo.   *Perf. 12½*
C19 AP8 100fr orange, brn & lil   1.50 .80
   a.   Souvenir sheet of 4   4.50 4.50

Bird Type of Regular Issue, 1965

1965, Mar. 1   Photo.   *Perf. 13*
Size: 27x48mm
C20 A27 500fr Abyssinian roller   9.00 3.50

Earth and Sun — AP9

1965, Mar. 23   Engr.
C21 AP9 50fr multicolored   .45 .20

5th World Meteorological Day.

Hughes Telegraph, ITU Emblem and
Dial Telephone — AP10

1965, May 17   Unwmk.   *Perf. 13*
C22 AP10 100fr red, sl grn & bl grn   .80 .40

ITU, centenary.

Intl. Cooperation Year — AP10a

1965, June 21   Photo.   *Perf. 13*
C23 AP10a 25fr multicolored   .20 .20
C24 AP10a 100fr multicolored   .55 .25
   a.   Min. sheet, 2 each #C23-C24   1.90 1.90

Sacred Sabou Crocodile — AP11

1965, Aug. 9   Engr.   *Perf. 13*
C25 AP11 60fr shown   .60 .30
C26 AP11 85fr Lion, vert.   .80 .40

Early Bird
Satellite over
Globe — AP12

Tiros Satellite
and Weather
Map — AP13

1965, Sept. 15   Unwmk.   *Perf. 13*
C27 AP12 30fr brt bl, brn & brn red   .30 .20
Space communications.

1966, Mar. 23   Engr.   *Perf. 13*
C28 AP13 50fr dk car, brt bl & blk   .40 .30
6th World Meteorological Day.

FR-1 Satellite over Ouagadougou
Space Tracking Station — AP14

1966, Apr. 28   *Perf. 13*
C29 AP14 250fr mag, ind & org
brn   2.00 .90

Inauguration of WHO Headquarters,
Geneva — AP15

1966, May 3   Photo.
C30 AP15 100fr yel, blk & bl   .80 .45

Air Afrique Issue
Common Design Type
1966, Aug. 31   Photo.   *Perf. 13*
C31 CD123 25fr tan, blk & yel grn   .30 .20

Sir Winston Churchill, British Lion and
"V" Sign — AP16

1966, Nov. 5   Engr.   *Perf. 13*
C32 AP16 100fr slate grn & car
rose   1.00 .55
Sir Winston Spencer Churchill (1874-1965),
statesman and WWII leader.

Pope Paul VI, Peace Dove, UN
General Assembly and
Emblem — AP17

1966, Nov. 5   Engr.   *Perf. 13*
C33 AP17 100fr dk blue & pur   1.00 .55
Pope Paul's appeal for peace before the UN
General Assembly, Oct. 4, 1965.

Blind Man and Lions Emblem — AP18

1967, Feb. 28   Engr.   *Perf. 13*
C34 AP18 100fr dk vio bl, brt bl &
dk brn   1.40 .55
50th anniversary of Lions Intl.

UN Emblem and
Rain over
Landscape
AP19

Diamant
Rocket — AP20

1967, Mar. 23   Engr.   *Perf. 13*
C35 AP19 50fr ultra, dk grn & bl grn .50 .25
7th World Meteorological Day.

1967, Apr. 18   Engr.   *Perf. 13*
French Spacecraft: 20fr, FR-1 satellite,
horiz. 30fr, D1-C satellite. 100fr, D1-D satel-
lite, horiz.
C36 AP20   5fr brt bl, sl grn &
org   .20 .20
C37 AP20   20fr lilac & slate blue   .20 .20
C38 AP20   30fr red brn, brt bl &
emer   .30 .20
C39 AP20 100fr emer & dp claret   .90 .40
Nos. C36-C39 (4)   1.60 1.00
For overprint see No. C69.

Albert Schweitzer
(1875-1965),
Medical
Missionary and
Organ
Pipes — AP21

1967, May 12   Engr.   *Perf. 13*
C40 AP21 250fr claret & blk   1.75 .95

World Map and 1967 Jamboree
Emblem — AP22

1967, June 8   Photo.
C41 AP22 100fr multicolored   1.00 .55
12th Boy Scout World Jamboree, Farragut
State Park, Idaho, Aug. 1-9.

Madonna
and Child,
15th
Century
AP23

Paintings: 20fr, Still life by Paul Gauguin.
50fr, Pietà, by Dick Bouts. 60fr, Anne of
Cleves, by Hans Holbein the Younger. 90fr,
The Money Lender and his Wife, by Quentin
Massys (38x40mm). 100fr, Blessing of the
Risen Christ, by Giovanni Bellini. 200fr, The
Handcart, by Louis Le Nain, horiz. 250fr, The
Four Evangelists, by Jacob Jordaens.

Perf. 12½x12, 12x12½, 13½ (90fr)
1967-68   Photo.
C42 AP23   20fr multi ('68)   .25 .20
C43 AP23   30fr multi   .30 .20
C44 AP23   50fr multi   .50 .25
C45 AP23   60fr multi ('68)   .60 .25
C46 AP23   90fr multi ('68)   .85 .40
C47 AP23 100fr multi   1.00 .40
C48 AP23 200fr multi ('68)   2.00 .70
C49 AP23 250fr multi   2.75 1.00
Nos. C42-C49 (8)   8.25 3.40
See Nos. C70-C72.

African Postal Union Issue, 1967
Common Design Type
1967, Sept. 9   Engr.   *Perf. 13*
C50 CD124 100fr multicolored   .80 .35

Caravelle "Ouagadougou" — AP24

1968, Feb. 29   Engr.   *Perf. 13*
C51 AP24 500fr bl, dp cl & blk   3.75 1.40

WMO Emblem, Sun, Rain,
Wheat — AP25

1968, Mar. 23   Engr.   *Perf. 13*
C52 AP25 50fr dk red, ultra & gray
grn   .45 .25
8th World Meteorological Day.

Europafrica Issue

Clove Hitch — AP25a

1968, July 20   Photo.   *Perf. 13*
C53 AP25a 50fr yel bis, blk & dk
red   .40 .20
See note after Niger No. C89.

Vessel in Form of Acrobat with Bells,
Colima Culture — AP26

Mexican Sculptures: 30fr, Ballplayer, Vera-
cruz, vert. 60fr, Javelin thrower, Colima, vert.
100fr, Seated athlete with cape, Jalisco.

1968, Oct. 14   Engr.   *Perf. 13*
C54 AP26   10fr dk red, ocher &
choc   .20 .20
C55 AP26   30fr bl grn, brt grn &
dk brn   .25 .20
C56 AP26   60fr ultra, ol & mar   .45 .25
C57 AP26 100fr brt grn, bl & mar   .65 .35
Nos. C54-C57 (4)   1.55 1.00
19th Olympic Games, Mexico City, 10/12-27.

Artisan Type of Regular Issue
1968, Oct. 30   Engr.   *Perf. 13*
Size: 48x27mm
C58 A52 100fr Potter   .70 .30

PHILEXAFRIQUE Issue

Too Late or
The Letter,
by Armand
Cambon
AP27

1968, Nov. 22   Photo.   *Perf. 12½*
C59 AP27 100fr multicolored   1.00 .75
PHILEXAFRIQUE, Phil. Exhib., Abidjan,
Feb. 14-23, 1969. Printed with alternating rose
claret label.

Albert John
Luthuli — AP28

Design: No. C61, Mahatma Gandhi.

1968, Dec. 16   Photo.   Perf. 12½
C60 AP28 100fr dk grn, yel grn &
                blk   .75 .40
C61 AP28 100fr dk grn, yel & blk   .75 .40
  a. Min. sheet, 2 each #C60-C61   3.00 3.00
        Exponents of non-violence.

2nd PHILEXAFRIQUE Issue
Common Design Type
50fr, Upper Volta #59, dancers & musicians.

1969, Feb. 14   Engr.   Perf. 13
C62 CD128 50fr pur, bl car & brn   .55 .55

Weather Sonde, WMO Emblem, Mule
and Cattle in Irrigated Field — AP29

1969, Mar. 24   Engr.   Perf. 13
C63 AP29 100fr dk brn, brt bl &
                grn   .90 .50
        9th World Meteorological Day.

Artisan Type of Regular Issue
Design: 150fr, Basket weaver.

1969, Apr. 3   Engr.   Perf. 13
        Size: 48x27mm
C64 A55 150fr brn, bl & blk   1.25 .60

Lions Emblem, Eye and Blind
Man — AP30

1969, Apr. 30   Photo.
C65 AP30 250fr red & multi   2.50 1.00
  12th Congress of District 403 of Lions Intl.,
Ouagadougou, May 2-3.

Fish Type of Regular Issue
Designs: 100fr, Phenacogrammus pabrensis. 150fr, Upside-down catfish.

1969   Engr.   Perf. 13
                Size: 48x27mm
C66 A57 100fr slate, pur & yel   .90 .40
C67 A57 150fr org brn, gray &
                slate   1.40 .60

Earth and Astronaut — AP31

Embossed on Gold Foil
1969   Die-cut Perf. 10½x10
C68 AP31 1000fr gold   8.25 8.25
  Apollo 8 mission, which put the first man
into orbit around the moon, Dec. 21-27, 1968.

No. C39 Overprinted in red with Lunar
Landing Module and: "L'HOMME SUR
LA LUNE / JUILLET 1969 / APOLLO
11"

1969, July 25   Engr.   Perf. 13
C69 AP20 100fr emer & dp claret 2.25 1.90
        See note after Mali No. C80.

Painting Type of 1967-68
Paintings: 50fr, Napoleon Crossing Great
St. Bernard Pass, by Jacques Louis David.
150fr, Napoleon Awarding the First Cross of
the Legion of Honor, by Jean-Baptiste Debret.
250fr, Napoleon Before Madrid, by Carle
Vernet.

1969, Aug. 18   Photo.   Perf. 12½x12
C70 AP23 50fr carmine & multi   .45 .35
C71 AP23 150fr violet & multi   1.10 .80
C72 AP23 250fr green & multi   2.25 1.40
        Nos. C70-C72 (3)   3.80 2.55
    Napoleon Bonaparte (1769-1821).

Agriculture Type of Regular Issue
1969, Oct. 30   Photo.   Perf. 12½x13
                Size: 47½x27mm
C73 A58 100fr Peanuts   .75 .25
C74 A58 200fr Rice   1.60 .55

AP32

AP33

Tree of Life, symbols of science, agriculture
and industry.

1969, Nov. 21   Photo.   Perf. 12x13
C75 AP32 100fr multicolored   .65 .35
        See note after Mauritania No. C28.

1970, Apr. 22   Photo.   Perf. 12½
Designs: 20fr, Lenin. 100fr, Lenin Addressing Revolutionaries in Petrograd, by V. A.
Serov, horiz.

C76 AP33 20fr ocher & brn   .20 .20
C77 AP33 100fr blk, lt grn & red   .65 .40
    Lenin (1870-1924), Russian communist
leader.

Pres. Roosevelt with Stamp
Collection — AP34

10fr, Franklin Delano Roosevelt, vert.

1970, June 4   Photo.   Perf. 12½
C78 AP34 10fr dk brn, emer &
                red brn   .20 .20
C79 AP34 200fr vio bl, gray & dk
                car   1.40 .45

Soccer Game and Jules Rimet
Cup — AP35

100fr, Goalkeeper catching ball, globe.

1970, June 4   Engr.   Perf. 13
C80 AP35 40fr olive, brt grn &
                brn   .40 .20
C81 AP35 100fr blk, lil, brn & grn .90 .40
  9th World Soccer Championships for the
Jules Rimet Cup, Mexico City, 5/30-6/21/70.

EXPO Emblem,
Monorail and
"Cranes at the
Seashore"
AP36

UN Emblem,
Dove and
Star — AP37

Design: 150fr, EXPO emblem, rocket, satellites and "Geisha."

1970, Aug. 7   Photo.   Perf. 12½
C82 AP36 50fr multicolored   .35 .20
C83 AP36 150fr green & multi   1.00 .60
  Issued to publicize EXPO '70 International
Exhibition, Osaka, Japan, Mar. 15-Sept. 13.

1970, Oct. 2   Engr.   Perf. 13
  250fr, UN emblem and doves, horiz.
C84 AP37 60fr dk bl, bl & grn   .40 .20
C85 AP37 250fr dk red brn, vio bl
                & ol   1.60 .65
    25th anniversary of the United Nations.

Holy Family — AP38

Silver Embossed
1970, Nov. 27   Die-Cut Perf. 10
C86 AP38 300fr silver   2.50 2.50
Gold Embossed
C87 AP38 1000fr gold   9.00 9.00
        Christmas.

Family and Upper
Volta
Flag — AP39

Gamal Abdel
Nasser — AP41

UN "Key to a Free World" — AP40

Litho.; Gold Embossed
1970, Dec. 10   Perf. 12½
C88 AP39 500fr gold, blk & red   2.50 1.50
    10th anniversary of independence, Dec. 11.

1970, Dec. 14   Engr.   Perf. 13
C89 AP40 40fr red, bister & blue   .35 .20
  UN Declaration of Independence for Colonial Peoples, 10th anniv.

1971, Jan. 30   Photo.   Perf. 12½
C90 AP41 100fr green & multi   .65 .30
    Nasser (1918-1970), president of Egypt.

Herons, Egyptian Art, 1354 — AP42

250fr, Page from Koran, Egypt, 1368-1388.

1971, May 13   Photo.   Perf. 13
C91 AP42 100fr multi   .55 .25
C92 AP42 250fr multi, vert.   1.40 .70

Olympic Rings and Various
Sports — AP43

1971, June 10   Engr.   Perf. 13
C93 AP43 150fr vio bl & red   1.00 .60
        Pre-Olympic Year.

Boy Scout and Buildings — AP44

1971, Aug. 12   Photo.   Perf. 12½
C94 AP44 45fr multicolored   .35 .20
13th Boy Scout World Jamboree, Asagiri Plain, Japan, Aug. 2-10.

De Gaulle, Map of Upper Volta, Cross of Lorraine — AP45

Charles de Gaulle — AP46

1971, Nov. 9   Photo.   Perf. 13x12
C95 AP45 40fr lt brn, grn & blk   .40 .35
Lithographed; Gold Embossed Perf. 12½
C96 AP46 500fr gold & grn   4.00 3.75
Gen. Charles de Gaulle (1890-1970), president of France.

African Postal Union Issue, 1971
Common Design Type
Design: 100fr, Mossi dancer and UAMPT building, Brazzaville, Congo.

1971, Nov. 13   Photo.   Perf. 13x13½
C97 CD135 100fr bl & multi   .65 .35

Gen. Sangoule Lamizana AP47

Kabuki Actor and Ice Hockey AP48

1971, Dec. 11   Perf. 12½
C98 AP47 35fr sep, blk, gold & ultra .25 .20
Inauguration of 2nd Republic of Upper Volta.

1972, Feb. 15   Engr.   Perf. 13
C99 AP48 150fr red, bl & pur   1.00 .60
11th Winter Olympic Games, Sapporo, Japan, Feb. 3-13.

Music, by Pietro Longhi AP49

Design: 150fr, Gondolas and general view, by Ippolito Caffi, horiz.

1972, Feb. 28   Photo.   Perf. 13
C100 AP49 100fr gold & multi   .65 .35
C101 AP49 150fr gold & multi   1.10 .40
UNESCO campaign to save Venice.

Running and Olympic Rings — AP50

Design: 200fr, Discus and Olympic rings.

1972, May 5   Engr.   Perf. 13
C102 AP50 65fr dp bl, brn & grn .35 .20
C103 AP50 200fr dp bl & brn   1.10 .35
a.   Min. sheet of 2, #C102-C103   1.60 1.60
20th Olympic Games, Munich, 8/26-9/10.

Musician Type of Regular Issue
Design: 500fr, Jimmy Smith and keyboard.

1972, May 17   Photo.   Perf. 14x13
C104 A87 500fr green & multi   4.00 1.90

Red Crescent Type of Regular Issue
1972, June 23   Perf. 13x14
C105 A88 100fr yellow & multi   .65 .25

2nd Plan Type of Regular Issue
Design: 85fr, Road building machinery.

1972, Oct. 30   Engr.   Perf. 13
C106 A90 85fr brick red, bl & blk   .45 .25

Presidents Pompidou and Lamizana — AP51

Design: 250fr, Presidents Pompidou and Lamizana, different design.

1972, Nov. 20   Photo.   Perf. 13
Size: 48x37mm
C107 AP51 40fr gold & multi   .45 .35
Photogravure; Gold Embossed
Size: 56x36mm
C108 AP51 250fr yel grn, dk grn & gold   2.50 2.50
Visit of Pres. Georges Pompidou of France, Nov. 1972.

Skeet-shooting, Scalzone, Italy — AP52

Gold-medal Winners: 40fr, Pentathlon, Peters, Great Britain. 45fr, Dressage, Meade, Great Britain. 50fr, Weight lifting, Talts, USSR. 60fr, Boxing, light-weight, Seales, US. 65fr, Fencing, Ragno-Lonzi, Italy. 75fr, Gymnastics, rings, Nakayama, Japan. 85fr, Gymnastics, Touritcheva, USSR. 90fr, 110m high hurdles, Milburn, US. 150fr, Judo, Kawaguchi, Japan. 200fr, Sailing, Finn class, Maury, France. 250fr, Swimming, Spitz, US (7 gold). 300fr, Women's high jump, Meyfarth, West Germany. 350fr, Field Hockey, West Germany. 400fr, Javelin, Wolfermann, West Germany. No. C124, Women's diving, King, US. No. C125, Cycling, Morelon, France. No. C126, Individual dressage, Linsenhoff, West Germany.

1972-73   Litho.   Perf. 12½
C109 AP52 35fr multi ('73)   .20 .20
C110 AP52 40fr multi   .20 .20
C111 AP52 45fr multi ('73)   .25 .20
C112 AP52 50fr multi   .25 .20
C113 AP52 60fr multi ('73)   .30 .20
C114 AP52 65fr multi   .35 .20
C115 AP52 75fr multi ('73)   .40 .20
C116 AP52 85fr multi   .40 .20
C117 AP52 90fr multi   .45 .25
C118 AP52 150fr multi ('73)   .80 .40
C119 AP52 200fr multi   1.10 .50
C120 AP52 250fr multi ('73)   1.40 .65
C121 AP52 300fr multi   1.60 .80
C122 AP52 350fr multi ('73)   1.90 .90
C123 AP52 400fr multi ('73)   2.00 1.10
Nos. C109-C123 (15)   11.60 6.20
Souvenir Sheets
C124 AP52 500fr multi   2.25 1.60
C125 AP52 500fr multi ('73)   2.25 1.60
C126 AP52 500fr multi ('73)   2.25 1.60
20th Olympic Games, Munich.

Nativity, by Della Notte — AP53

Christmas: 200fr, Adoration of the Kings, by Albrecht Dürer.

1972, Dec. 23   Photo.   Perf. 13
C127 AP53 100fr gold & multi   .50 .25
C128 AP53 200fr gold & multi   1.10 .65

Madonna and Child, by Albrecht Dürer AP54

Christmas: 75fr, Virgin Mary, Child and St. John, by Joseph von Führich. 100fr, The Virgin of Grand Duc, by Raphael. 125fr, Holy Family, by David. 150fr, Madonna and Child, artist unknown. 400fr, Flight into Egypt, by Gentile da Fabriano, horiz.

1973, Mar. 22   Litho.   Perf. 12½x13
C129 AP54 50fr multi   .35 .20
C130 AP54 75fr multi   .50 .25
C131 AP54 100fr multi   .65 .35
C132 AP54 125fr multi   .80 .40
C133 AP54 150fr multi   1.00 .50
Nos. C129-C133 (5)   3.30 1.70
Souvenir Sheet
C134 AP54 400fr multi   2.50 1.40

Manned Lunar Buggy on Moon — AP55

Moon Exploration: 65fr, Lunakhod, Russian unmanned vehicle on moon. 100fr, Lunar module returning to orbiting Apollo capsule. 150fr, Apollo capsule in moon orbit. 200fr, Space walk. 250fr, Walk in Sea of Tranquillity.

1973, Apr. 30   Litho.   Perf. 13x12½
C135 AP55 50fr multi   .35 .20
C136 AP55 65fr multi   .40 .20
C137 AP55 100fr multi   .65 .35
C138 AP55 150fr multi   1.00 .50
C139 AP55 200fr multi   1.40 .65
Nos. C135-C139 (5)   3.80 1.90
Souvenir Sheet
C140 AP55 250fr multi   1.60 .80

Giraffes AP56

African Wild Animals: 150fr, Elephants. 200fr, Leopard, horiz. 250fr, Lion, horiz. 300fr, Rhinoceros, horiz. 500fr, Crocodile, horiz.

Perf. 12½x13, 13x12½
1973, May 3   Litho.
C141 AP56 100fr multi   65 .35
C142 AP56 150fr multi   1.00 .50
C143 AP56 200fr multi   1.40 .65
C144 AP56 250fr multi   1.60 .80
C145 AP56 500fr multi   3.50 1.60
Nos. C141-C145 (5)   8.15 3.90
Souvenir Sheet
C146 AP56 300fr multi   2.00 1.00

Europafrica Issue

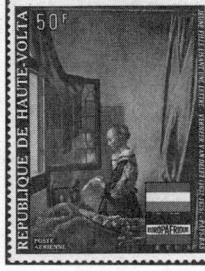

Girl Reading Letter, by Jan Vermeer AP57

Paintings: 65fr, Portrait of a Lady, by Roger van der Weyden. 100fr, Young Lady at her Toilette, by Titian. 150fr, Jane Seymour, by Hans Holbein. 200fr, Mrs. Williams, by John Hoppner. 250fr, Milkmaid, by Jean-Baptiste Greuze.

1973, June 7   Litho.   Perf. 12½x13
C147 AP57 50fr multi   .35 .20
C148 AP57 65fr multi   .40 .20
C149 AP57 100fr multi   .65 .35

C150	AP57	150fr multi	1.00	.50
C151	AP57	200fr multi	1.40	.65
	Nos. C147-C151 (5)		3.80	1.90

Souvenir Sheet

C152	AP57		1.60	.80

For overprint see No. C165-C166.

Africa
Encircled by
OAU Flags
AP58

1973, June 7

C153	AP58	45fr multi	.30	.20

10th anniv. of Org. for African Unity.

Locomotive "Pacific" 4546,
1908 — AP59

Locomotives from Railroad Museum, Mulhouse, France: 40fr, No. 242, 1927. 50fr, No. 2029, 1882. 150fr, No. 701, 1885-92. 250fr, "Coupe-Vent" No. C145, 1900. 350fr, Buddicomb No. 33, Paris to Rouen, 1884.

1973, June 30   Perf. 13x12½

C154	AP59	10fr multi	.20	.20
C155	AP59	40fr multi	.25	.20
C156	AP59	50fr multi	.35	.20
C157	AP59	150fr multi	1.00	.50
C158	AP59	250fr multi	1.60	.80
	Nos. C154-C158 (5)		3.40	1.90

Souvenir Sheet

C159	AP59	350fr multi	2.25	1.25

Boy Scout Type of 1973

40fr, Flag signaling. 75fr, Skiing. 150fr, Cooking. 200fr, Hiking. 250fr, Studying stars.

1973, July 18   Litho.   Perf. 12½x13

C160	A95	40fr multi	.25	.20
C161	A95	75fr multi	.50	.25
C162	A95	150fr multi	1.00	.50
C163	A95	200fr multi	1.40	.65
	Nos. C160-C163 (4)		3.15	1.60

Souvenir Sheet

C164	A95	250fr multi	1.60	.80

Nos. C148 and C150 Surcharged in Silver New Value and "SECHERESSE / SOLIDARITE AFRICAINE / ET INTERNATIONALE"

1973, Aug. 16

C165	AP57	100fr on 65fr multi	.65	.35
C166	AP57	200fr on 150fr multi	1.40	.65

Drought relief.

Kennedy Type, 1973

John F. Kennedy and: 200fr, Firing Saturn 1 rocket, Apollo program. 300fr, First NASA manned space capsule. 400fr, Saturn 5 countdown.

1973, Sept. 12   Litho.   Perf. 12½x13

C167	A96	200fr multi	1.40	.65
C168	A96	300fr multi	2.00	1.00

Souvenir Sheet

C169	A96	400fr multi	2.50	1.40

10th death anniv. of Pres John F. Kennedy.

Interpol Type of 1973
Souvenir Sheet

Design: Victim in city street.

1973, Sept. 15   Perf. 13x12½

C170	A97	300fr multi	2.00	1.00

Tourism Type of 1973
1973, Sept. 30

C171	A98	100fr Waterfalls	.65	.35

Souvenir Sheet

C172	A98	275fr Elephant	1.90	.90

House of Worship Type of 1973

Cathedral of the Immaculate Conception.

1973, Sept. 28

C173	A99	200fr multi	1.40	.65

Folklore Type of 1973

100fr, 225fr, Bobo masked dancers, diff.

1973, Nov. 30   Litho.   Perf. 12½x13

C174	A100	100fr multi	.65	.35
C175	A100	225fr multi	1.50	.70

Zodiac Type of 1973
Souvenir Sheets

Zodiacal Light and: #C176, 1st 4 signs of Zodiac. #C177, 2nd 4 signs. #C178, Last 4 signs.

1973, Dec. 15   Perf. 13x14

C176	A101	250fr multi	1.60	.80
C177	A101	250fr multi	1.60	.80
C178	A101	250fr multi	1.60	.80

Nos. C176-C178 have multicolored margin showing night sky and portraits: No. C176, Louis Armstrong; No. C177, Mahatma Gandhi; No. C178, Martin Luther King.

Soccer Championship Type, 1974

Championship '74 emblem and: 75fr, Gento, Spanish flag. 100fr, Bereta, French flag. 250fr, Best, British flag. 400fr, Beckenbauer, West German flag.

1974, Jan. 15   Litho.   Perf. 13x12½

C179	A102	75fr multi	.50	.25
C180	A102	100fr multi	.65	.35
C181	A102	250fr multi	1.60	.80
	Nos. C179-C181 (3)		2.75	1.40

Souvenir Sheet

C182	A102	400fr multi	2.50	1.40

De Gaulle Type, 1974

300fr, De Gaulle, Concorde, horiz. 400fr, De Gaulle, French space shot.

Perf. 13x12½, 12½x13
1974, Feb. 4   Litho.

C183	A103	300fr multi	2.00	1.00

Souvenir Sheet

C184	A103	400fr multi	2.50	1.40

Soccer Cup Championship Type, 1974

World Cup, Emblems and: 150fr, Brindisis, Argentinian flag. No. C186, Kenko, Zaire flag. No. C187, Streich, East German flag. 400fr, Cruyff, Netherlands flag.

1974, Mar. 19   Perf. 12½x13

C185	A104	150fr multi	.75	.40
C186	A104	300fr multi	1.50	.75

Souvenir Sheets

C187	A104	300fr multi	1.50	.75
C188	A104	400fr multi	2.00	1.00

UPU Type, 1974

UPU Emblem and: 100fr, Dove carrying mail. 200fr, Air Afrique 707. 300fr, Dish antenna. 500fr, Telstar satellite.

1974, July 23   Perf. 13½

C189	A106	100fr multi	.50	.25
C190	A106	200fr multi	1.00	.50
C191	A106	300fr multi	1.50	.75
	Nos. C189-C191 (3)		3.00	1.50

Souvenir Sheet

C192	A106	500fr multi	2.50	1.25

For overprint see No. C197-C200.

Soccer Cup Winners Type, 1974

World Cup, Game and Flags: 150fr, Brazil, in Sweden, 1958. 200fr, Brazil, in Chile, 1962. 250fr, Brazil, in Mexico, 1970. 450fr, England, in England, 1966.

1974, Sept. 2

C193	A107	150fr multi	1.00	.50
C194	A107	200fr multi	1.40	.70
C195	A107	250fr multi	1.60	.80
	Nos. C193-C195 (3)		4.00	2.00

Souvenir Sheet

C196	A107	450fr multi	3.00	1.50

Nos. C189-C192 Overprinted in Red "100e ANNIVERSAIRE DE L'UNION POSTALE UNIVERSELLE / 9 OCTOBRE 1974"

1974, Oct. 9

C197	A106	100fr multi	.60	.35
C198	A106	200fr multi	1.40	.65
C199	A106	300fr multi	2.00	1.00
	Nos. C197-C199 (3)		4.00	2.00

Souvenir Sheet

C200	A106	500fr multi	3.00	1.40

Universal Postal Union, centenary.

Flower Type of 1974

Flower Paintings by: 300fr, Auguste Renoir. 400fr, Carl Brendt.

1974, Oct. 31   Litho.   Perf. 12½x13

C201	A109	300fr multi	2.00	1.00

Souvenir Sheet

C202	A109	400fr multi	2.50	1.40

Locomotive Type of 1975

Locomotives from Railroad Museum. Mulhouse, France: 100fr, Crampton No. 80, 1852. 200fr, No. 701, 1885-92. 300fr, "Forquenot," 1882.

1975, Feb. 28   Litho.   Perf. 13x12½

C203	A112	100fr multi	.65	.35
C204	A112	200fr multi	1.40	.65

Souvenir Sheet

C205	A112	300fr multi	2.00	1.00

Old Cars Type, 1975

Flags and Old Cars: 150fr, Germany and Mercedes-Benz, 1929. 200fr, Germany and Maybach, 1936. 400fr, Great Britain and Rolls Royce Silver Ghost, 1910.

1975, Apr. 6   Perf. 14x13½

C206	A113	150fr multi	1.00	.50
C207	A113	200fr multi	1.40	.65

Souvenir Sheet

C208	A113	400fr multi	2.50	1.40

American Bicentennial Type

200fr, Washington crossing Delaware. 300fr, Hessians Captured at Trenton.

1975, May 6   Perf. 14

C209	A114	200fr multi	1.40	.65
C210	A114	300fr multi	2.00	1.00

Schweitzer Type of 1975

Albert Schweitzer and: 150fr, Toucan. 175fr, Vulturine guinea fowl. 200fr, King vulture. 450fr, Crested corythornis.

1975, May 25   Litho.   Perf. 13½

C212	A115	150fr multi	.95	.50
C213	A115	175fr multi	1.25	.55
C214	A115	200fr multi	1.40	.65
	Nos. C212-C214 (3)		3.60	1.70

Souvenir Sheet

C215	A115	450fr multi	3.00	1.50

Apollo Soyuz Type of 1975

100fr, Apollo, Soyuz near link-up. 200fr, Cosmonauts Alexei Leonov, Valeri Kubasov. 300fr, Astronauts Donald K. Slayton, Vance Brand, Thomas P. Stafford. 500fr, Apollo Soyuz emblem, US, USSR flags.

1975, July 18   Litho.   Perf. 13½

C216	A116	100fr multi	.60	.35
C217	A116	200fr multi	1.40	.65
C218	A116	300fr multi	2.00	1.00
	Nos. C216-C218 (3)		4.00	2.00

Souvenir Sheet

C219	A116	500fr multi	3.50	1.60

Picasso Type of 1975

Picasso Paintings: 150fr, El Prado, horiz. 350fr, Couple in Patio. 400fr, Science and Charity.

1975, Aug. 7

C220	A117	150fr multi	1.00	.50
C221	A117	350fr multi	2.25	1.25

Souvenir Sheet

C222	A117	400fr multi	2.50	1.40

EXPO '75 Type of 1975

Expo '75 emblem and: 150fr, Passenger liner Asama Maru. 300fr, Future floating city Aquapolis.

1975, Sept. 26   Litho.   Perf. 11

C223	A118	150fr multi	.75	.40

Souvenir Sheet
Perf. 13½

C224	A118	300fr multi	1.50	.75

Winter Olympic Games Type of 1975

Innsbruck Background, Olympic Emblem and: 100fr, Ice hockey. 200fr, Ski jump. 300fr, Speed skating.

1975, Dec. 15   Perf. 13½

C225	A122	100fr multi	.65	.35
C226	A122	200fr multi	1.40	.65

Souvenir Sheet

C227	A122	300fr multi	2.00	1.00

Olympic Games Type of 1976

Olympic Emblem and: 125fr, Heavyweight judo. 150fr, Weight lifting. 500fr, Sprint.

1976, Mar. 17   Litho.   Perf. 13½

C228	A123	125fr multi	.65	.30
C229	A123	150fr multi	.75	.40

Souvenir Sheet

C230	A123	500fr multi	2.50	1.25

Summer Olympic Games Type of 1976

Olympic emblem and: 150fr, Pole vault. 200fr, Gymnast on balance beam. 500fr, Two-man sculls.

1976, Mar. 25   Perf. 11

C231	A124	150fr multi	.75	.40
C232	A124	200fr multi	1.00	.50

Souvenir Sheet

C233	A124	500fr multi	2.50	1.25

For overprint see No. C245-C247.

Zeppelin Type of 1976

Airships: 100fr, Graf Zeppelin over Swiss Alps. 200fr, LZ-129 over city. 300fr, Graf Zeppelin. 500fr, Zeppelin over Bodensee.

1976, May 11

C234	A126	100fr multi	.60	.35
C235	A126	200fr multi	1.40	.65
C236	A126	300fr multi	2.00	1.00
	Nos. C234-C236 (3)		4.00	2.00

Souvenir Sheet

C237	A126	500fr multi	3.50	1.60

Viking Mars Type of 1976

Designs: 200fr, Viking lander assembly. 300fr, Viking orbiter in descent on Mars. 450fr, Viking in Mars orbit.

1976, June 24   Litho.   Perf. 13½

C238	A127	200fr multi	1.00	.50
C239	A127	300fr multi	1.50	.75

Souvenir Sheet

C240	A127	450fr multi	2.25	1.10

American Bicentennial Type

Bicentennial and Interphil '76 Emblems and: 100fr, Siege of Yorktown. 200fr, Battle of Cape St. Vincent. 300fr, Peter Francisco's bravery. 500fr, Surrender of the Hessians.

1976, Sept. 30   Litho.   Perf. 13½

C241	A129	100fr multi	.60	.35
C242	A129	200fr multi	1.40	.65
C243	A129	300fr multi	2.00	1.00
	Nos. C241-C243 (3)		4.00	2.00

Souvenir Sheet

C244	A129	500fr multi	3.50	1.60

Nos. C231-C233 Overprinted in Gold:
  a. VAINQUEUR 1976 / TADEUSZ SLUSARSKI / POLOGNE
  b. VAINQUEUR 1976 / NADIA COMANECI / ROUMANIE
  c. VAINQUEUR 1976 / FRANK ET ALF HANSEN / NORVEGE

1976, July 4   Litho.   Perf. 11

C245	A124(a)	150fr multi	1.00	.50
C246	A124(b)	200fr multi	1.40	.65

Souvenir Sheet

C247	A124(c)	500fr multi	3.50	1.60

Winners, 21st Olympic Games.

UPU Emblem over Globe — AP60

1978, Aug. 8   Litho.   Perf. 13
C248 AP60 350fr multi   2.25 1.50
Congress of Paris, establishing UPU, cent.

Jules Verne, Apollo 11 Emblem,
Footprint on Moon, Neil
Armstrong — AP61

Space Conquest: 50fr, Yuri Gagarin and
moon landing. 100fr, Montgolfier hot air balloon and memorial medal, 1783; Bleriot's
monoplane, 1909.

1978, Sept. 27   Litho.   Perf. 13x12½
C249 AP61 50fr multi   .35 .20
C250 AP61 60fr multi   .40 .20
C251 AP61 100fr multi   .65 .35
    Nos. C249-C251 (3)   1.40 .75

Anti-Apartheid
Year — AP62

1978, Oct. 12   Litho.   Perf. 13
C252 AP62 100fr blue & multi   .65 .35

Philexafrique II-Essen Issue
Common Design Types

#C253, Hippopotamus, Upper Volta #C18.
#C254, Hummingbird, Hanover #1.

1978, Nov. 1   Litho.   Perf. 12½
C253 CD138 100fr multi   .65 .35
C254 CD139 100fr multi   .65 .35

Nos. C253-C254 printed se-tenant.

Sun God Horus
with Sun — AP63

Jules Verne and
Balloon — AP64

300fr, Falcon with cartouches, UNESCO
emblem.

1978, Dec. 4
C255 AP63 200fr multi   1.40 .65
C256 AP63 300fr multi   2.00 1.00

UNESCO Campaign to safeguard monuments at Philae.

1978, Dec. 10   Engr.   Perf. 13
C257 AP64 200fr multi   1.40 .65

Verne (1828-1905), science fiction writer.

Bicycling, Olympic Rings — AP65

Designs: Bicycling scenes.

1980   Perf. 14½
C258 AP65 65fr multi   .65 .30
C259 AP65 150fr multi, vert.   1.00 .50
C260 AP65 250fr multi   1.60 .80
C261 AP65 350fr multi   2.25 1.25
    Nos. C258-C261 (4)   5.50 2.85
Souvenir Sheet
C262 AP65 500fr multi   3.50 1.60

22nd Summer Olympic Games, Moscow,
July 19-Aug. 3.

Nos. C258-C262 Overprinted with
Name of Winner and Country

1980, Nov. 22   Litho.   Perf. 14½
C263 AP65 65fr multi   .40 .20
C264 AP65 150fr multi   1.00 .50
C265 AP65 250fr multi   1.60 .80
C266 AP65 350fr multi   2.25 1.25
    Nos. C263-C266 (4)   5.25 2.75
Souvenir Sheet
C267 AP65 500fr multi   3.50 1.60

1982 World
Cup — AP66

Designs: Various soccer players.

1982, June 22   Litho.   Perf. 13½
C268 AP66 70fr multi   .45 .25
C269 AP66 90fr multi   .60 .30
C270 AP66 150fr multi   1.00 .45
C271 AP66 300fr multi   2.00 1.00
    Nos. C268-C271 (4)   4.05 2.00
Souvenir Sheet
C272 AP66 500fr multi   3.50 1.60

Anniversaries and Events — AP67

1983, June   Litho.   Perf. 13½
C273 AP67 90fr Space Shuttle   .30 .20
C274 AP67 120fr World Soccer
            Cup   .40 .20
C275 AP67 300fr Cup, diff.   1.00 .50
C276 AP67 450fr Royal Wedding   1.50 .70
    Nos. C273-C276 (4)   3.20 1.60
Souvenir Sheet
C277 AP67 500fr Prince Charles,
            Lady Diana   1.60 1.60

Pre-Olympics, 1984 Los
Angeles — AP68

1983, Aug. 1   Litho.   Perf. 13
C278 AP68 90fr Sailing   .30 .20
C279 AP68 120fr Type 470   .40 .20
C280 AP68 300fr Wind surfing   1.00 .50
C281 AP68 400fr Wind surfing,
            diff.   1.40 .65
    Nos. C278-C281 (4)   3.10 1.55
Souvenir Sheet
C282 AP68 500fr Soling Class,
            Wind surfing   1.60 1.60

Christmas
AP69

Rubens Paintings.

1983   Litho.   Perf. 13
C283 AP69 120fr Adoration of
            the Shepherds   .40 .20
C284 AP69 350fr Virgin of the
            Garland   1.25 .60
C285 AP69 500fr Adoration of
            the Kings   1.60 .80
    Nos. C283-C285 (3)   3.25 1.60

1984 Summer Olympics — AP70

1984, Mar. 26   Litho.   Perf. 12½
C286 AP70 90fr Handball, vert.   .30 .20
C287 AP70 120fr Volleyball, vert.   .40 .20
C288 AP70 150fr Handball, diff.   .50 .25
C289 AP70 250fr Basketball   .80 .40
C290 AP70 300fr Soccer   1.00 .50
    Nos. C286-C290 (5)   3.00 1.55
Souvenir Sheet
C291 AP70 500fr Volleyball, diff.   1.60 .80

Local Birds — AP71

1984, May 14   Litho.   Perf. 12½
C292 AP71 90fr Phoenicopterus
            roseus   .30 .20
C293 AP71 185fr Choriotis kori,
            vert.   .60 .30
C294 AP71 200fr Buphagus ery-
            throrhynchus,
            vert.   .65 .35
C295 AP71 300fr Bucorvus
            leadbeateri   1.00 .50
    Nos. C292-C295 (4)   2.55 1.35

AP72

Famous Men — AP73

Designs: 5fr, Houari Boumediene (1927-
1978), president of Algeria 1965-78. 125fr,
Gottlieb Daimler (1834-1900), German auto-
motive pioneer, and 1886 Daimler. 250fr,
Louis Bleriot (1872-1936), French aviator, first
to fly the English Channel in a heavier-than-air
craft. 300fr, Abraham Lincoln. 400fr, Henri
Dunant (1828-1910), founder of the Red
Cross. 450fr, Auguste Piccard (1884-1962),
Swiss physicist, inventor of the bathyscaphe
Trieste, 1948. 500fr, Robert Baden-Powell
(1856-1941), founder of Boy Scouts. 600fr,
Anatoli Karpov, Russian chess champion.
1000fr, Paul Harris (1868-1947), founder of
Rotary Intl.

1984, May 21   Litho.   Perf. 13½
C296 AP72 5fr multi   .20 .20
C297 AP72 125fr multi   .50 .25
C298 AP72 250fr multi   1.00 .50
C299 AP72 300fr multi   1.25 .60
C300 AP72 400fr multi   1.60 .80
C301 AP72 450fr multi   1.90 .90
C302 AP72 500fr multi   2.00 1.00
C303 AP72 600fr multi   2.25 1.25
    Nos. C296-C303 (8)   10.70 5.50
Souvenir Sheet
C304 AP73 1000fr multi   4.00 2.00

No. C304 contains one 51x30mm stamp.

Burkina Faso

Butterflies — AP73a

1984, May 23   Perf. 13½
C305 AP73a 10fr Graphium pyl-
            ades   .20 .20
C306 AP73a 120fr Hypolimnas
            misippus   .50 .25

C307	AP73a	400fr Danaus chrysippus	1.60	.80
C308	AP73a	450fr Papilio demodocus	1.90	.90
		Nos. C305-C308 (4)	4.20	2.15

Philexafrica '85, Lome — AP74

1985, May 20   **Litho.**   **Perf. 13**

C309	AP74	200fr Solar & wind energy	.55	.25
C310	AP74	200fr Children	.55	.25
a.		Pair, #C309-C310 + label	1.10	.75

PHILEXAFRICA '85, Lome — AP75

National development: No. C311, Youth. No. C312, Communications and transportation.

1985, Nov. 16   **Litho.**   **Perf. 13**

C311	AP75	250fr multi	.90	.45
C312	AP75	250fr multi	.90	.45
a.		Pair, #C311-C312 + label	1.80	1.25

Intl. Youth Year (No. C311).

French Revolution, Bicent. — AP76

Designs: 150fr, *Oath of the Tennis Court*, by David. 200fr, *Storming of the Bastille*, by Thevenin. 600fr, *Rouget de Lisle Singing La Marseillaise*, by Pils. Illustration reduced.

1989, May 3   **Litho.**   **Perf. 13**

C313	AP76	150fr multi	.90	.45
C314	AP76	200fr multi	1.25	.60
C315	AP76	600fr multi	3.50	1.75
		Nos. C313-C315 (3)	5.65	2.80

PHILEXFRANCE '89.

POSTAGE DUE STAMPS

Postage Due Stamps of Upper Senegal and Niger, 1914, Overprinted in Black or Red

1920   **Unwmk.**   **Perf. 14x13½**

J1	D2	5c green	.30	.30
J2	D2	10c rose	.30	.30
J3	D2	15c gray	.30	.30
J4	D2	20c brown (R)	.40	.40
J5	D2	30c blue	.45	.45
J6	D2	50c black (R)	.65	.65
J7	D2	60c orange	.65	.65
J8	D2	1fr violet	.95	.95
		Nos. J1-J8 (8)	4.00	4.00

Type of 1914 Issue Surcharged

1927

J9	D2	2fr on 1fr lilac rose	2.25	2.25
J10	D2	3fr on 1fr orange brn	2.50	2.50

Red-fronted Gazelle
D3   D4

1928   **Typo.**

J11	D3	5c green	.30	.30
J12	D3	10c rose	.30	.30
J13	D3	15c dark gray	.40	.40
J14	D3	20c dark brown	.40	.40
J15	D3	30c dark blue	.50	.50
J16	D3	50c black	1.75	1.75
J17	D3	60c orange	2.00	2.00
J18	D3	1fr dull violet	3.50	3.50
J19	D3	2fr lilac rose	6.00	6.00
J20	D3	3fr orange brn	6.50	6.50
		Nos. J11-J20 (10)	21.65	21.65

Catalogue values for unused stamps in this section, from this point to the end of the section, are for Never Hinged items.

Republic

1962, Jan. 31   **Perf. 14x13½**
Denomination in Black

J21	D4	1fr bright blue	.20	.20
J22	D4	2fr orange	.20	.20
J23	D4	5fr brt vio blue	.20	.20
J24	D4	10fr red lilac	.20	.20
J25	D4	20fr emerald	.45	.45
J26	D4	50fr rose red	1.10	1.10
		Nos. J21-J26 (6)	2.35	2.35

OFFICIAL STAMPS

Catalogue values for unused stamps in this section are for Never Hinged items.

Elephant — O1

Perf. 12½

1963, Feb. 1   **Unwmk.**   **Photo.**
Center in Sepia

O1	O1	1fr red brown	.20	.20
O2	O1	5fr yel green	.20	.20
O3	O1	10fr deep vio	.20	.20
O4	O1	15fr red org	.25	.25
O5	O1	25fr brt rose lilac	.35	.35
O6	O1	50fr brt green	.55	.55
O7	O1	60fr brt red	.70	.70
O8	O1	85fr dk slate grn	1.10	1.10
O9	O1	100fr brt blue	1.75	1.75
O10	O1	200fr bright rose	3.00	3.00
		Nos. O1-O10 (10)	8.30	8.30

BURMA
ˈbər-mə

Myanmar

LOCATION — Bounded on the north by China; east by China, Laos and Thailand; south and west by the Bay of Bengal, Bangladesh and India.
GOVT. — Republic
AREA — 261,228 sq. mi.
POP. — 48,081,302 (1999 est.)
CAPITAL — Yangon (Rangoon)

Burma was part of India from 1826 until April 1, 1937, when it became a self-governing unit of the British Commonwealth and received a constitution. On January 4, 1948, Burma became an independent nation. In 1990 they became the Union of Myanmar.

12 Pies = 1 Anna
16 Annas = 1 Rupee
100 Pyas = 1 Kyat (1953)

Catalogue values for unused stamps in this country are for Never Hinged items, beginning with Scott 35 in the regular postage section and Scott O28 in the official section.

Watermarks

Wmk. 254-   Wmk. 257-
Elephant Heads   Curved Wavy Lines

Stamps of India 1926-36 Overprinted

1937, Apr. 1   **Wmk. 196**   **Perf. 14**

1	A46	3p slate	.25	.20
2	A71	½a green	.65	.20
3	A68	9p dark green	.65	.20
4	A72	1a dark brown	.35	.20
5	A49	2a ver (small die)	.35	.20
6	A57	2a6p buff	.30	.20
7	A51	3a carmine rose	.65	.25
8	A70	3a6p deep blue	.55	.20
9	A52	4a olive green	.60	.20
10	A53	6a bister	.50	.25
11	A54	8a red violet	1.25	.20
12	A55	12a claret	2.40	.70

Overprinted

13	A56	1r green & brown	14.00	2.25
14	A56	2r brn org & car rose	22.50	7.25
15	A56	5r dk violet & ultra	30.00	12.50
16	A56	10r car & green	65.00	45.00
17	A56	15r ol green & ultra	210.00	80.00
18	A56	25r blue & ocher	400.00	200.00
		Nos. 1-18 (18)	750.00	350.00

For overprints see #1N1-1N3, 1N25-1N26, 1N47.

King George VI
A1   A2

Royal Barge — A3

Elephant Moving Teak Log — A4

Farmer Plowing Rice Field — A5

Sailboat on Irrawaddy River — A6

Peacock — A7   George VI — A8

Perf. 13½x14

1938-40   **Litho.**   **Wmk. 254**

18A	A1	1p red org ('40)	.85	.30
19	A1	3p violet	.20	.20
20	A1	6p ultramarine	.20	.20
21	A1	9p yel green	.55	.35
22	A2	1a brown violet	.20	.20
23	A2	1½a turquoise grn	.20	.20
24	A2	2a carmine	.30	.20

Perf. 13

25	A3	2a6p rose lake	.80	.45
26	A4	3a dk violet	2.50	.50
27	A5	3a6p dp bl & brt bl	1.50	*2.75*
28	A2	4a slate blue, perf. 13½x14	.20	.20
29	A6	8a slate green	1.50	.20

Perf. 13½

30	A7	1r brt ultra & dk violet	2.25	.30
31	A7	2r dk vio & red brown	5.50	1.50
32	A8	5r car & dull vio	22.50	9.00
33	A8	10r gray grn & brn	45.00	35.00
		Nos. 18A-33 (16)	84.25	51.55
		Set, never hinged	110.00	

See Nos. 51-65. For overprints and surcharges see Nos. 34-50, O15-O27, 1N4-1N11, 1N28-1N30, 1N37-1N46, 1N48-1N49.

No. 25 Surcharged in Black

1940, May 6   **Perf. 13**

34	A3	1a on 2a6p rose lake	1.00	.80
		Never hinged	4.00	

Centenary of first postage stamp.

Catalogue values for unused stamps in this section, from this point to the end of the section, are for Never Hinged items.

Nos. 18A to 33 Overprinted in Black:

a

b

MILY ADMN

1945

35	A1(a)	1p red orange	.20	.20
36	A1(a)	3p violet	.20	.20
37	A1(a)	6p ultramarine	.20	.20
38	A1(a)	9p yel green	.20	.20
39	A2(a)	1a brown violet	.20	.20
40	A2(a)	1½a turq green	.20	.20
41	A2(a)	2a carmine	.20	.20
42	A3(b)	2a6p rose lake	.45	.45
43	A4(b)	3a dk violet	.75	.20
44	A5(b)	3a6p dp bl & brt bl	.20	.20
45	A2(a)	4a slate blue	.20	.20
46	A6(b)	8a slate green	.20	.20
47	A7(b)	1r brt ultra & dk vio	.30	.40
48	A7(b)	2r dk vio & red brn	.30	.75
49	A8(b)	5r car & dull vio	.70	.80
50	A8(b)	10r gray grn & brn	1.50	1.50
		Nos. 35-50 (16)	6.00	6.10

Types of 1938

1946, Jan. 1 Litho. Perf. 13½x14

51	A1	3p brown	.20	.20
52	A1	6p violet	.20	.20
53	A1	9p dull green	.20	.20
54	A2	1a deep blue	.20	.20
55	A2	1½a salmon	.20	.20
56	A2	2a rose lake	.20	.20

Perf. 13

57	A3	2a6p greenish blue	.25	.20
58	A4	3a blue violet	6.75	1.50
59	A5	3a6p ultra & gray blk	.20	.20
60	A2	4a rose lil, perf. 13½x14	.20	.20
61	A6	8a deep magenta	2.25	.20

Perf. 13½

62	A7	1r dp mag & dk vio	1.25	.25
63	A7	2r sal & red brn	7.50	1.75
64	A8	5r red brn & dk grn	7.50	7.50
65	A8	10r dk vio & car	7.50	7.50
		Nos. 51-65 (15)	34.60	20.50

For overprints see Nos. 70-84, O28-O42.

Burmese Man — A9

Burmese Woman — A10

Mythological Chinze — A11

Elephant Hauling Teak — A12

1946, May 2 Perf. 13

66	A9	9p peacock green	.20	.20
67	A10	1½a brt violet	.20	.20
68	A11	2a carmine	.20	.20
69	A12	3a6p ultramarine	.20	.20
		Nos. 66-69 (4)	.80	.80

Victory of the Allied Nations in WWII.

Nos. 51-65 Overprinted in Black

1947, Oct. 1 Perf. 13½x14, 13, 13½

70	A1	3p brown	.45	.45
71	A1	6p violet	.20	.25
72	A1	9p dull green	.20	.20
a.		Inverted overprint	12.50	12.50
73	A2	1a deep blue	.20	.25
74	A2	1½a salmon	1.25	.20
75	A2	2a rose lake	.35	.20
76	A3	2a6p greenish bl	1.40	.75
77	A4	3a blue violet	2.50	1.25
78	A5	3a6p ultra & gray blk	.50	.75
79	A2	4a rose lilac	1.60	.25
80	A6	8a dp magenta	1.60	.70
81	A7	1r dp mag & dk vio	2.25	.30
82	A7	2r sal & red brn	2.50	2.50
83	A8	5r red brn & dk grn	3.50	3.75
84	A8	10r dk vio & car	3.50	3.75
		Nos. 70-84 (15)	22.00	15.60

The overprint is slightly larger on #76-78, 80-84. The Burmese characters read "Interim Government."

Other denominations are known with the overprint inverted or double.

Issues of the Republic

U Aung San Map and Chinze — A13

Martyrs' Memorial — A14

1948, Jan. 6 Litho. Perf. 12½x12

85	A13	½a emerald	.20	.20
86	A13	1a deep rose	.20	.20
87	A13	2a carmine	.20	.20
88	A13	3½a blue	.20	.20
89	A13	8a lt chocolate	.20	.20
		Nos. 85-89 (5)	1.00	1.00

Attainment of independence, Jan. 4, 1948.

1948, July 19 Engr. Perf. 14x13½

90	A14	3p ultramarine	.20	.20
91	A14	6p green	.20	.20
92	A14	9p dp carmine	.20	.20
93	A14	1a purple	.20	.20
94	A14	2a lilac rose	.20	.20
95	A14	3½a dk slate green	.20	.20
96	A14	4a yel brown	.20	.20
97	A14	8a orange red	.20	.20
98	A14	12a claret	.20	.20
99	A14	1r blue green	.20	.20
100	A14	2r deep blue	.50	.35
101	A14	5r chocolate	1.25	.80
		Nos. 90-101 (12)	3.75	3.15

1st anniv. of the assassination of Burma's leaders in the fight for independence.

Ball Game (Chinlon) A15

Bell A16

Mythical Bird — A17

Rice Planting A18

Throne — A19

Designs: 6p, Dancer. 9p, Musician. 3a, Spinning. 3a6p, Royal Palace. 4a, Cutting teak. 8a, Plowing rice field.

Perf. 12½ (A15-A17), 12x12½ (A18), 13 (A19)

1949, Jan. 4

102	A15	3p ultramarine	.20	.20
103	A15	6p green	.20	.20
104	A15	9p carmine	.20	.20
105	A16	1a red orange	.20	.20
106	A17	2a orange	.20	.20
107	A18	2a6p lilac rose	.20	.20
108	A18	3a purple	.20	.20
109	A18	3a6p dk slate grn	.20	.20
110	A18	4a chocolate	.20	.20
111	A18	8a carmine	.25	.20
112	A19	1r blue green	.40	.20
a.		Perf. 14		2.50
113	A19	2r deep blue	.90	.30
114	A19	5r chocolate	1.75	.70
115	A19	10r orange red	4.00	1.00
		Nos. 102-115 (14)	9.10	4.20

See Nos. 122-135, 139-152, O56-O67.

UPU Monument, Bern — A20

1949, Oct. 9 Unwmk. Perf. 13

116	A20	2a orange	.20	.20
117	A20	3½a olive grn	.20	.20
118	A20	6a lilac	.30	.20
119	A20	8a crimson	.40	.20
120	A20	12½a ultra	.50	.20
121	A20	1r blue green	.75	.50
		Nos. 116-121 (6)	2.35	1.50

75th anniv. of the UPU.

Types of 1949

Designs as before.

Perf. 13½x14, 14x13½, 13

1952-53 Litho.

122	A15	3p brown orange	.20	.20
123	A15	6p deep plum	.20	.20
124	A15	9p blue	.20	.20
125	A16	1a violet bl	.20	.20
126	A17	2a green ('52)	.20	.20
127	A18	2a6p green	.20	.20
128	A18	3a sal pink ('52)	.20	.20
129	A18	3a6p brown orange	.20	.20
130	A16	4a vermilion	.20	.30
131	A18	8a lt blue ('52)	.20	.20
132	A19	1r rose violet	.25	.20
133	A19	2r yel green	.55	.25
134	A19	5r ultramarine	1.75	.85
135	A19	10r aquamarine	3.25	1.60
		Nos. 122-135 (14)	7.80	4.90

Map of Burma and Monument — A21

1953, Jan. 4 Perf. 14

136	A21	14p green	.20	.20

Perf. 13

Size: 36½x26mm

137	A21	20p salmon pink	.20	.20
138	A21	25p ultramarine	.20	.20

Fifth anniversary of independence. For surcharge see No. 166.

Types of 1949

Designs: 2p, Dancer. 3p, Musician. 20p, Spinning. 25p, Royal Palace. 30p, Cutting teak. 50p, Plowing rice field.

1954, Jan. 4 Perf. 14x13½, 13, 14

139	A15	1p brown orange	.20	.20
140	A15	2p plum	.20	.20
141	A15	3p blue	.20	.20
142	A16	5p ultramarine	.20	.20
143	A18	10p yel green	.20	.20
144	A17	15p green	.20	.20
145	A18	20p vermilion	.20	.20
146	A18	25p lt red org	.20	.20
147	A18	30p vermilion	.20	.20
148	A18	50p blue	.25	.20
149	A19	1k rose violet	.50	.20
150	A19	2k green	1.00	.20
151	A19	5k ultramarine	2.75	.20
152	A19	10k light blue	5.00	.25
		Nos. 139-152 (14)	11.30	2.85

For overprints and surcharges see Nos. 163-165, 173-175, O68-O79, O80-O81, O83, O85, O87.

Peace Pagoda, Monks' Hostels and Meeting-cave — A22

Designs: 10p, Sangha (community) of Cambodia. 15p, Council meeting. 50p, Sangha of Thailand. 1k, Sangha of Ceylon. 2k, Sangha of Laos.

1954 Typo. Perf. 13

153	A22	10p deep blue	.20	.20
154	A22	15p deep claret	.20	.20
155	A22	35p dark brown	.20	.20
156	A22	50p green	.20	.20
157	A22	1k carmine	.30	.20
158	A22	2k violet	.60	.40
		Nos. 153-158 (6)	1.70	1.40

6th Buddhist Council, Rangoon, 1954-56.

Marble Markers of 5th Buddhist Council A23

Designs: 40p, Thatbyinnyu Pagoda. 60p, Shwedagon Pagoda, Rangoon. 1.25k, Aerial View of 6th Buddhist Council, Yegu.

1956, May 24 Litho. Perf. 11x11½

159	A23	20p blue & gray olive	.20	.20
160	A23	40p blue & brt yel grn	.20	.20
161	A23	60p green & lemon	.20	.20
162	A23	1.25k gray blue & yel	.30	.20
		Nos. 159-162 (4)	.90	.80

2500th anniv. of the Buddhist Era.

Nos. 146, 149-150 Surcharged or Overprinted

1959, Nov. 9 Wmk. 254 Perf. 13, 14

163	A18	15p on 25p lt red org	.20	.20
164	A19	1k rose violet	.25	.20
165	A19	2k green	.55	.45
		Nos. 163-165 (3)	1.00	.85

Centenary of Mandalay, former capital. The two lines of overprint are 4mm apart on No. 163; 7mm on Nos. 164-165.

No. 136 Surcharged:

1961, June   **Perf. 14**
166 A21 15p on 14p green   .30 .20

Children
A24

Unwmk.
1961, Dec. 11 Litho. Perf. 13
167 A24 15p claret & rose claret .20 .20
15th anniversary of UNICEF.

Runner with
Torch — A25

Soccer, Pole Vault
and Shot Put — A26

Designs: 50p, Women runners. 1k, Hurdling, weight lifting, boxing, bicycling and swimming.

1961, Dec. 11 Photo. Perf. 14x13
168 A25 15p red & ultra   .20 .20
169 A26 25p dk green & ocher   .20 .20
170 A26 50p vio blue & pink   .20 .20
171 A25 1k brt green & yel   .40 .25
    Nos. 168-171 (4)   1.00 .85
2nd South East Asia Peninsular Games, Rangoon.

Map and Flag of
Burma — A27

Wmk. 254
1963, Mar. 2 Engr. Perf. 13
172 A27 15p red   .20 .20
First anniversary of new government.

Nos. 143 and 148 Overprinted in
Violet or Red: "FREEDOM FROM
HUNGER"

1963, Mar. 21   Litho.
173 A18 10p yel green (V)   .20 .20
174 A18 50p blue (R)   .20 .20
FAO "Freedom from Hunger" campaign.

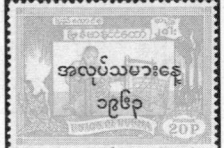

No. 145
Overprinted

1963, May 1
175 A18 20p vermilion   .20 .20
Issued for May Day.

White-browed
Fantail — A28

Indian
Roller — A29

Birds: 20p, Red-whiskered bulbul. 25p, Crested serpent eagle. 50p, Sarus crane. 1k, Malabar pied hornbill. 2k, Lineated kalij pheasant. 5k, Green peafowl.

Unwmk.
1964, Apr. 16 Photo. Perf. 13
Size: 25x21mm
176 A28 1p gray   .20 .20
177 A28 2p carmine rose   .20 .20
178 A28 3p blue green   .20 .20
Size: 22x26½mm
179 A29 5p violet blue   .20 .20
180 A29 10p orange brn   .20 .20
181 A29 15p olive   .20 .20
Size: 35x25mm
182 A28 20p rose & brn   .20 .20
Size: 27x36½mm, 36½x27mm
183 A29 25p yel & brown   .20 .20
184 A29 50p red, blk & gray   .50 .20
185 A29 1k gray, ind & yel   1.00 .20
186 A29 2k pale ol, ind & red   2.00 .30
187 A29 5k citron, dk bl & red 4.75 .70
    Nos. 176-187 (12)   9.85 3.00

See Nos. 197-208. For overprints see Nos.
O82, O84, O86, O88-O93, O94-O115.

ITU Emblem, Old and New
Communication Equipment — A30

1965, May 17 Litho. Perf. 15
Size: 32x22mm
188 A30 20p bright pink   .20 .20
Perf. 13
Size: 34x24½mm
189 A30 50p dull green   .25 .25
Centenary of the ITU.

ICY
Emblem
A31

1965, July 1 Unwmk. Perf. 13
190 A31 5p violet blue   .20 .20
191 A31 10p brown orange   .20 .20
192 A31 15p olive   .20 .20
    Nos. 190-192 (3)   .60 .60
International Cooperation Year.

Rice
Farmer — A32

Cogwheel and
Hammer — A33

1966, Mar. 2
193 A32 15p multicolored   .20 .20
Issued for Farmers' Day.

1967, May 1 Litho. Unwmk.
194 A33 15p lt blue, yel & black .20 .20
Issued for Labor Day, May 1.

Aung
San,
Tractor
and
Farmers
A34

1968, Jan. 4   Unwmk.   Perf. 13
195 A34 15p sky bl, blk & ocher   .20 .20
20th anniversary of independence.

Largest
Burmese
Pearl — A35

1968, Mar. 4 Litho. Perf. 13½x13
196 A35 15p blue, ultra, gray & yel .20 .20
Burmese pearl industry.

Bird Types of 1964 in Changed Sizes;
Designs as Before

Unwmk.
1968, July 1 Photo. Perf. 14
Size: 21x17mm
197 A28 1p gray   .20 .20
198 A28 2p carmine rose   .20 .20
199 A28 3p blue green   .20 .20
Size: 23½x28mm
200 A29 5p violet blue   .20 .20
201 A29 10p orange brown   .20 .20
202 A29 15p olive   .20 .20
Size: 38½x21, 21x38½mm
203 A28 20p rose & brown   .20 .20
204 A28 25p yel & brown   .20 .20
205 A29 50p ver, blk & gray   .30 .20
206 A29 1k gray, ind & yel   .65 .20
207 A28 2k dull cit, ind & red 1.40 .25
208 A29 5k yel, dk blue & red   3.25 .55
    Nos. 197-208 (12)   7.20 2.80

For overprints see Nos. O92-O102.

Wheat — A36

1969, Mar. 2 Litho. Perf. 13
209 A36 15p blue, emerald & yel   .20 .20
Issued for Peasant's Day.

ILO
Emblem
A37

1969, Oct. 29 Photo. Wmk. 254
210 A37 15p dk blue grn & gold   .20 .20
211 A37 50p dp carmine & gold   .20 .20
50th anniv. of the ILO.

Soccer — A38

Designs: 25p, Runner, horiz. 50p, Weight lifter. 1k, Women's volleyball.

Perf. 12½x13, 13x12½
1969, Dec. 1   Litho.
212 A38 15p brt olive & multi   .20 .20
213 A38 25p brown & multi   .20 .20
214 A38 50p brt green & multi   .25 .20
215 A38 1k blue, yel grn & blk   .45 .30
    Nos. 212-215 (4)   1.10 .90
5th South East Asia Peninsular Games,
Rangoon.

Burmese Flags and Marching
Soldiers — A39

1970, Mar. 27   Perf. 13
216 A39 15p multicolored   .20 .20
Issued for Armed Forces Day.

Solar
System
and UN
Emblem
A40

1970, June 26 Photo. Unwmk.
217 A40 15p lt ultra & multi   .20 .20
25th anniversary of the United Nations.

Scroll, Marchers, Peacock
Emblem — A41

Designs: 25p, Students' boycott demonstration. 50p, Banner and marchers at Shwedagon Camp.

1970, Nov. 23 Litho. Perf. 13x13½
218 A41 15p ultra & multi   .20 .20
219 A41 25p multicolored   .20 .20
220 A41 50p lt blue & multi   .25 .20
    Nos. 218-220 (3)   .65 .60
50th National Day (Students' 1920 uprising).

Workers, Farmers, Technicians — A42

15p, Burmese of various races, & flags. 25p, Hands holding document. 50p, Red party flag.

1971, June 28   Litho.   Perf. 13½

221	A42	5p blue & multi	.20	.20
222	A42	15p blue & multi	.20	.20
223	A42	25p blue & multi	.20	.20
224	A42	50p blue & multi	.25	.20
a.		Souvenir sheet of 4, #221-224	.45	.45
		Nos. 221-224 (4)	.85	.80

1st Congress of Burmese Socialist Program Party.

Child Drinking Milk — A43

UNICEF, 25th Anniv.: 50p, Marionettes.

1971, Dec. 11   Perf. 14½

225	A43	15p lt ultra & multi	.20	.20
226	A43	50p emerald & multi	.30	.20

Aung San, Independence Monument, Pinlon — A44

Union Day, 25th Anniv.: 50p, Bogyoke Aung San and people in front of Independence Monument. 1k, Map of Burma with flag pointing to Pinlon, vert.

1972, Feb. 12   Perf. 14

227	A44	15p ocher & multi	.20	.20
228	A44	50p blue & multi	.25	.20
229	A44	1k green, ultra & red	.40	.20
		Nos. 227-229 (3)	.85	.60

Burmese and Double Star A45

1972   Litho.   Perf. 14

230	A45	15p bister & multi	.20	.20

Revolutionary Council, 10th anniversary.

"Your Heart is your Health" — A46

1972, Apr. 7   Perf. 14x14½

231	A46	15p yellow, red & black	.20	.20

World Health Day.

Burmese of Various Ethnic Groups A47

1973, Feb. 12   Litho.   Perf. 14

232	A47	15p multicolored	.20	.20

1973 census.

Casting Vote — A48

Natl. Referendum: 10p, Voters holding map of Burma. 15p, Farmer & soldier holding ballots.

Perf. 14x14½, 14½x14

1973, Dec. 15   Litho.

233	A48	5p deep org & black	.20	.20
234	A48	10p blue & multi	.20	.20
235	A48	15p blue & multi, vert.	.20	.20
		Nos. 233-235 (3)	.60	.60

Open-air Meeting A49

Designs: 15p, Regional flags. 1k, Scales of justice and Burmese emblem.

1974, Mar. 2   Photo.   Perf. 13
Size: 80x26mm

236	A49	15p blue & multi	.20	.20

Size: 37x25mm

237	A49	50p blue & multi	.20	.20
238	A49	1k lt blue, bis & blk	.40	.25
		Nos. 236-238 (3)	.80	.65

First meeting of People's Parliament.

Messenger Bird and UPU Emblem — A50

UPU Cent.: 20p, Mother reading letter to child, vert. 50p, Simulated block of stamps, vert. 1k, Burmese doll, vert. 2k, Mailman delivering letter to family.

1974, May 22

239	A50	15p grn, lt grn & org	.20	.20
240	A50	20p multicolored	.20	.20
241	A50	50p green & multi	.25	.20
242	A50	1k ultra & multi	.50	.25
243	A50	2k blue & multi	.95	.50
		Nos. 239-243 (5)	2.10	1.35

Children A51   Man and Woman A52

Designs: 3p, Girl. 5p, 15p, Man and woman. 10p, Children (like 1p). 50p, Woman with fan. 1k, Seated woman. 5k, Drummer.

Perf. 13, 13x13½ (#248-251)
1974-78   Photo.

244	A51	1p rose & lilac rose	.20	.20
245	A51	3p dk brown & pink	.20	.20
246	A51	5p pink & violet	.20	.20
246A	A51	10p Prus blue ('76)	.20	.20
247	A51	15p lt grn & ol ('75)	.20	.20
248	A52	20p lt blue & multi	.20	.20
249	A52	50p ocher & multi	.25	.20
250	A52	1k brt rose & multi	.55	.30
251	A52	5k ol green & multi	2.00	1.40
		Nos. 244-251 (9)	4.00	3.10

For different country names see Nos. 298-303.

IWY Emblem, Woman and Globe A53

IWY: 2k, Symbolic flower, globe and IWY emblem, vert.

1975, Dec. 15   Photo.   Perf. 13½

252	A53	50p green & black	.20	.20
253	A53	2k black & blue	.70	.50

Burmese with Raised Fists A54

Constitution Day: 50p, Demonstrators with banners and emblem. 1k, People and map of Burma, emblem.

1976, Jan. 3   Perf. 14

254	A54	20p blue & black	.20	.20
255	A54	50p blue, blk & brn	.25	.20

Size: 56x20mm

256	A54	1k blue & multi	.45	.20
		Nos. 254-256 (3)	.90	.60

Students, Campaign Emblem — A55

Abacus A56

Intl. Literacy Year: 50p, Campaign emblem. 1k, Emblem, book and globe.

1976, Sept. 8   Photo.   Perf. 14

257	A55	10p salmon & black	.20	.20
258	A56	15p blue grn & multi	.20	.20
259	A56	50p ultra, org & blk	.25	.20
260	A55	1k multicolored	.60	.30
		Nos. 257-260 (4)	1.25	.90

Steam Locomotive A57

Diesel Train Emerging from Tunnel — A58

Cent. of Burma's Railroad: 20p, Early train and oxcart. 25p, Old and new trains approaching station. 50p, Railroad bridge.

1977, May 1   Perf. 13½

261	A57	15p multicolored	.20	.20

Size: 38x26, 26x38mm

262	A57	20p multicolored	.20	.20
263	A57	20p multicolored	.20	.20
264	A57	50p multicolored	.25	.20
265	A58	1k multicolored	.50	.20
		Nos. 261-265 (5)	1.35	1.00

Karaweik Pagoda A59

Design: 1k, Karaweik Pagoda, front view.

1977

266	A59	50p light brown	.20	.20

Size: 78x25mm

267	A59	1k multicolored	.35	.25

Jade Dragon — A60

Precious Jewelry: 20p, Gold bird with large pearl. 50p, Hand holding pearl necklace with pendant. 1k, Gold dragon, horiz.

1978   Photo.   Perf. 13

268	A60	15p green & yel grn	.20	.20
269	A60	20p multicolored	.20	.20
270	A60	50p multicolored	.30	.20

Size: 55x20mm
Perf. 14

271	A60	1k multicolored	.50	.30
		Nos. 268-271 (4)	1.20	.90

Satellite over Map of Asia A61

1979, Feb., 12   Photo.   Perf. 13

272	A61	25p multicolored	.20	.20

IYC Emblem in Map of Burma — A62   Weather Balloon, WMO Emblem — A63

1979, Dec.   Photo.   Perf. 13½

273	A62	25p multicolored	.20	.20
274	A62	50p multicolored	.30	.20

International Year of the Child.

1980, Mar. 23   Photo.   Perf. 13½

275	A63	25p shown	.20	.20
276	A63	50p Weather satellite, cloud	.30	.20

World Meteorological Day.

Weight Lifting, Olympic Rings A64

1980, Dec.   Litho.   Perf. 14

277	A64	20p shown	.20	.20
278	A64	50p Boxing	.20	.20
279	A64	1k Soccer	.40	.25
		Nos. 277-279 (3)	.80	.65

22nd Summer Olympic Games, Moscow, July 19-Aug. 3.

13th World Telecommunications
Day — A65

1981, May 17   Photo.   Perf. 13½
280 A65 25p orange & black   .20   .20

World Food
Day — A66

1981, Oct. 16   Photo.   Perf. 13½
281 A66 25p Livestock, produce   .20   .20
282 A66 50p Farmer, rice, pro-
                  duce   .20   .20
283 A66 1k Emblems   .40   .25
       Nos. 281-283 (3)   .80   .65

Intl. Year
of the
Disabled
A67

1981, Dec. 12
284 A67 25p multicolored   .20   .20

World Communications Year — A68

1983, Sept. 15   Litho.   Perf. 14½x14
285 A68 15p pale blue & black   .20   .20
286 A68 25p dull lake & black   .20   .20
287 A68 50p pale brn, blk & lake .30   .20
288 A68 1k buff, blk, beige &
                  yel grn   .60   .40
       Nos. 285-288 (4)   1.30 1.00

Fish, Ship, Globe,
FAO
Emblem — A69

1983, Oct. 16   Photo.   Perf. 14x14½
289 A69 15p brt blue, bister & blk .20   .20
290 A69 25p yel grn, pale org &
                  blk   .20   .20
291 A69 50p org, pale grn & blk   .30   .20
292 A69 1k yel, ultra & black   .60   .40
       Nos. 289-292 (4)   1.30 1.00
                World Food Day.

Stylized Trees, Hemispheres and
Log — A70

1984, Oct. 16   Perf. 14½x14
293 A70 15p org, black & blue   .20   .20
294 A70 25p pale yel, blk & lt vio .20   .20
295 A70 50p pale pink, blk & lt
                  grn   .30   .20
296 A70 1k yel, blk & lt rose vio .60   .40
       Nos. 293-296 (4)   1.30 1.00

            World Food Day.

Intl. Youth
Year — A71

1985, Oct. 15   Perf. 14x14½
297 A71 15p multicolored   .20   .20

            Types of 1974
      Inscribed: Union of Burma
1989   Photo.   Perf. 13½
298 A51 15p olive & lt green   .20   .20
299 A52 50p violet & brown   .25   .25
300 A52 1k multicolored   .55   .55
       Nos. 298-300 (3)   1.00 1.00

   Issued: 15p, 6/26; 50p, 6/12; 1k, 9/6.

        UNION OF MYANMAR
     Inscribed: Union of Myanmar
1990-91   Photo.   Perf. 13½
301 A51 15p olive & lt green   .20   .20
301A A51 20p brown, greenish
                  blue & black ('91) —   —
302 A52 50p violet & brown   .25   .25
303 A52 1k multicolored   .50   .50

     Issued: 15p, May 26; 50p, May 12.

Fountain, Natl. Assembly Park — A74

Illustration reduced.

1990, May 27   Litho.   Perf. 14½x14
304 A74 1k multicolored   1.00   .50
   State Law and Order Restoration Council.

A75

1990, Dec. 20   Litho.   Perf. 14x14½
305 A75 2k multicolored   1.75 1.10
      UN Development Program, 40th anniv.

1991, Jan. 26

A76

306 A76 50p Nawata ruby   1.00   .65

Painting of
Freedom
Fighters — A77

Bronze
Statue — A78

1992, Jan. 4   Litho.   Perf. 14x14½
307 A77 50p multicolored   .40   .40
308 A78 2k multicolored   1.60 1.60

A79

A80

1992, Apr. 10   Litho.   Perf. 14x14½
309 A79 50p multicolored   .50   .50
         National Sports Festival.

1992, Dec. 1   Litho.   Perf. 14x14½
310 A80 50p red   .60   .35
       World Campaign Against AIDS.

A81

Artifacts — A82

1992, Dec. 5   Litho.   Perf. 14x14½
         Background Color
311 A81 50p pink   .20   .20
312 A81 1k yellow   .40   .40
313 A81 3k orange   1.25 1.25
314 A81 5k green   2.00 2.00
       Nos. 311-314 (4)   3.85 3.85

   Intl. Conference on Nutrition, Rome.

1993, Sept. 1   Litho.   Perf. 14x14½
315 A82 5k Bird   1.60 1.60
316 A82 10k shown   3.25 3.25

Natl.
Assembly — A83

1993, Jan. 1   Litho.   Perf. 14x14½
317 A83 50p multicolored   .25   .25
318 A83 3k multicolored   1.25 1.25

Equestrian Festival — A84

1993, Oct. 23   Litho.   Perf. 14½x14
319 A84 3k multicolored   1.50 1.00

A85

A86

1994, June 5   Litho.   Perf. 14
320 A85 4k multicolored   1.75 1.50
            Environment day.

1994, Sept. 15   Litho.   Perf. 14
321 A86 3k multicolored   1.25 1.25
Union of Solidarity & Development, 1st anniv.

Armed
Forces,
50th
Anniv.
A87

1995, Mar. 27   Litho.   Perf. 14½x14
322 A87 50p multicolored   .25   .25

A88

A89

1995, June 26   Litho.   Perf. 14
323 A88 2k multicolored   .80 .80
Prevent drug abuse.

1995, Oct. 17   Litho.   Perf. 14x14½
324 A89 50p multicolored   .40 .40
Myanmar motion pictures, 60th anniv.

A90

A91

1995, Oct. 24
325 A90 4k UN, 50th Anniv.   2.00 2.00

1995, Nov. 1
326 A91 50p pink & multi   .25 .25
327 A91 2k green & multi   1.00 1.00
University of Yangon (Rangoon), 75th anniv.

Visit
Myanmar
Year
A92

Designs: 50p, Couple in boat on Inlay Lake
with food bowl for Buddha, Buddhist monks.
4k, Decorated royal barge on Kandawgyi
(Royal Lake), Yangoon. 5k, Royal moat,
entrance of Yadanabon (Mandalay), vert.

Perf. 14½x14, 14x14½
1996, Mar. 1   Litho.
328 A92 50p multicolored   .20 .20
329 A92 4k multicolored   1.75 1.75
330 A92 5k multicolored   2.25 2.25
    Nos. 328-330 (3)   4.20 4.20

UNICEF, 50th
Anniv. — A93

Stylized designs: 1k, Mother breastfeeding.
2k, Vaccinating child. 4k, Girls going to school.

1996, Dec. 11   Litho.   Perf. 14x14½
331 A93 1k multicolored   .40 .40
332 A93 2k multicolored   .85 .85
333 A93 4k multicolored   1.75 1.75
    Nos. 331-333 (3)   3.00 3.00

Intl. Letter
Writing
Week
A94

Designs: 2k, Men in canoe. 5k, Stylized
figures forming pyramid, flag, map, vert.

1996, Oct. 7   Perf. 14½x14, 14x14½
334 A94 2k multicolored   .85 .85
335 A94 5k multicolored   2.00 2.00

A95

A96

1997, July 24   Litho.   Perf. 14x14½
336 A95 1k blue & multi   .40 .40
337 A95 2k yellow & multi   .85 .85
    Assoc. of Southeast Asian Nations
(ASEAN), 30th anniv.

1998, Jan. 4   Litho.   Perf. 14x14½
338 A96 2k multicolored   .90 .90
    Independence, 50th anniv.

Musical
Instruments
A97

1998   Photo.   Perf. 13¼
339 A97 5k Xylophone   2.00 2.00
340 A97 10k Mon brass
                gongs   3.75 3.75
341 A97 20k Rakhine (drum)   7.75 7.75
342 A97 30k Harp   11.50 11.50
343 A97 50k Shan pot drum   18.00 18.00
344 A97 100k Kachin brass
                gong   37.50 37.50
    Nos. 339-344 (6)   80.50 80.50
    Issued: 5k, 8/28/98.

Decade of
Disabled Persons
(1993-2002)
A98

1998   Litho.   Perf. 14
345 A98 2k yellow & multi   .75 .75
346 A98 5k apple green & multi   1.90 1.90

UPU, 125th
Anniv. — A99

1999   Litho.   Perf. 14x14¼
347 A99 2k blue & multi   .75 .75
348 A99 5k purple & multi   1.90 1.90

Independence,
52nd
Anniv. — A100

2000
349 A100 2k multi   .70 .70

World Meteorological Day — A101

2000 Photo.   Perf. 14x14¼, 14¼x14
350 A101 2k Anemometer, vert.   .65 .65
351 A101 5k shown   1.75 1.75
352 A101 10k Cloud, sun   3.25 3.25
    Nos. 350-352 (3)   5.65 5.65

Diplomatic Relations with People's
Republic of China, 50th Anniv. — A102

2000   Litho.   Perf. 14¼x14
353 A102 5k multi   1.90 1.90

OFFICIAL STAMPS

Stamps of India, 1926-
34, Overprinted in Black

1937   Wmk. 196   Perf. 14
O1 A46 3p gray   .40 .20
O2 A71 ½a green   2.25 .20
O3 A68 9p dark green   1.50 .40
O4 A72 1a dark brown   1.50 .25
O5 A49 2a vermilion   2.25 .55
O6 A57 2a6p buff   2.25 .90
O7 A52 4a olive grn   1.50 .90
O8 A53 6a bister   2.25 3.50
O9 A54 8a red violet   1.40 1.00
O10 A55 12a claret   1.40 1.75

Overprinted

O11 A56 1r green & brown   11.00 3.25
O12 A56 2r buff & car rose   20.00 17.50
O13 A56 5r dk vio & ultra   47.50 32.50
O14 A56 10r car & green   140.00 85.00
    Nos. O1-O14 (14)   235.20 147.90
    For overprint see No. 1N27.

Regular Issue of 1938
Overprinted in Black

Perf. 13½x14, 13, 13½
1939   Wmk. 254
O15 A1 3p violet   .20 .20
O16 A1 6p ultramarine   .20 .20
O17 A1 9p yel green   3.25 .20
O18 A2 1a brown violet   .20 .20
O19 A2 1½a turquoise green   3.00 .20
O20 A2 2a carmine   .80 .20
O21 A2 4a slate blue   3.50 .40

Overprinted

O22 A3 2a6p rose lake   16.00 2.40
O23 A6 8a slate green   16.00 3.00
O24 A7 1r brt ultra & dk
              vio   25.00 3.00
O25 A7 2r dk vio & red
              brn   30.00 5.00
O26 A8 5r car & dull vio   27.50 32.50
O27 A8 10r gray grn & brn   80.00 42.50
    Nos. O15-O27 (13)   205.65 90.00
    For overprints see Nos. 1N12-1N16, 1N31-
1N36, 1NO1.

> **Catalogue values for unused
> stamps in this section, from this
> point to the end of the section, are
> for Never Hinged items.**

**Nos. 51-56, 60 Overprinted Like Nos.
O15-O21**
1946   Perf. 13½x14
O28 A1 3p brown   1.40 2.25
O29 A1 6p violet   1.40 1.75
O30 A1 9p dull green   .20 2.40
O31 A2 1a deep blue   .20 1.60
O32 A2 1½a salmon   .20   .20
O33 A2 2a rose lake   .20 1.75
O34 A2 4a rose lilac   1.50   .55

**Nos. 57, 61-65 Ovptd.
Like Nos. O22-O27**
Perf. 13, 13½
O35 A3 2a6p greenish blue   .20 4.00
O38 A6 8a deep magenta   2.00 2.75
O39 A7 1r dp mag & dk vio   .70 2.75
O40 A7 2r salmon & red
              brn   8.00 30.00
O41 A8 5r red brn & dk grn   10.00 35.00
O42 A8 10r dk violet & car   19.00 40.00
    Nos. O28-O42 (13)   45.00 125.00

Nos. O28 to
O42
Overprinted
in Black

1947
O43 A1 3p brown   .20   .35
O44 A1 6p violet   .70   .10
O45 A1 9p dull green   1.10   .75
O46 A2 1a deep blue   1.50   .70
O47 A2 1½a salmon   3.00   .25
O48 A2 2a rose lake   1.50   .20
O49 A3 2a6p greenish bl   21.00 7.75

O50	A2	4a rose lilac	7.00	.35
O51	A6	8a dp magenta	6.00	3.50
O52	A7	1r dp mag & dk vio	12.00	1.90
O53	A7	2r sal & red brn	12.00	16.00
O54	A8	5r red brn & dk grn	12.00	17.50
O55	A8	10r dk vio & car	12.00	26.00
		Nos. O43-O55 (13)	90.00	75.35

The overprint is slightly larger on Nos. O49 and O51 to O55. The Burmese characters read "Interim Government."

Issues of the Republic

Nos. 102-106, 109-115
Overprinted in Carmine
or Black

a. Overprint 13mm long.
b. Overprint 15mm long.

1949		**Unwmk.**	**Perf. 12½, 13**	
O56	A15(a)	3p ultra (C)	.20	.20
O57	A15(a)	6p green (C)	.20	.20
O58	A15(a)	9p carmine	.20	.20
O59	A16(a)	1a red orange	.20	.20
O60	A17(a)	2a orange	.20	.20
O61	A18(b)	3a6p dk sl grn (C)	.20	.20
O62	A16(a)	4a chocolate	.20	.20
O63	A18(b)	8a carmine	.20	.20
O64	A19(b)	1r blue green (C)	.35	.20
O65	A19(b)	2r dp blue (C)	.65	.40
O66	A19(b)	5r chocolate	1.60	1.25
O67	A19(b)	10r orange red	3.25	2.50
		Nos. O56-O67 (12)	7.45	6.00

Same Overprint in Black on Nos. 139-142, 144-152

1954-57		**Perf. 14x13½, 13, 14**	**Wmk. 254**	
O68	A15(a)	1p brown org	.20	.20
O69	A15(a)	2p plum	.20	.20
O70	A15(a)	3p blue	.20	.20
O71	A16(a)	5p ultra	.20	.20
O72	A17(a)	15p green	.20	.20
O72A	A18(b)	20p ver ('57)	.20	.20
O73	A18(b)	25p lt red org	.20	.20
O74	A16(a)	30p vermilion	.20	.20
O75	A18(b)	50p blue	.20	.20
O76	A19(b)	1k rose violet	.50	.20
O77	A19(b)	2k green	.85	.20
O78	A19(b)	5k ultra	1.60	.35
O79	A19(b)	10k light blue	3.25	.45
		Nos. O68-O79 (13)	8.00	3.00

No. 141 Ovptd.   **Service**

1964		**Litho.**	**Perf. 14**	
O80	A15	3p blue	10.00	7.00

Nos. 139, 141-142, 144,
177-179, 181, 183
Ovptd.

1964-65		**Overprint: 11½mm**		
O81	A15	1p brown orange	3.00	.75
O82	A28	2p carmine rose ('65)	2.50	.60
O83	A15	3p blue	3.00	.75
O84	A28	3p blue green ('65)	2.50	.60
O85	A16	5p ultramarine	3.00	.75
O86	A28	5p violet blue ('65)	2.50	.60
O87	A17	15p green	3.00	.75
O88	A28	15p olive ('65)	2.50	.60
O89	A29	25p yel & brn ('65)	2.60	.60
		Nos. O81-O89 (9)	24.60	6.00

အစိုးရတိစ္စ   အစိုးရကစ္စ
#176-178   #181
Ovptd.   Ovptd.

1966		**Overprint: 15mm**		
O90	A28	1p black		
O91	A28	2p carmine rose		
O92	A28	3p blue green		
		Overprint: 12mm		
O93	A28	15p olive		

Nos. 176-179, 181-
187 Overprinted in
Black or Red

1967		**Unwmk.**	**Photo.**	**Perf. 13**
		Overprint: 15mm		
		Size: 25x21mm		
O94	A28	1p gray	.20	.20
O95	A28	2p carmine rose	.20	.20
O96	A28	3p blue green	.20	.20
		Size: 22x26½mm		
O97	A29	5p violet blue	.20	.20
O98	A29	15p olive	.20	.20
		Size: 35x25mm		
O99	A28	20p rose & brown	.20	.20
		Size: 27x36½mm, 36½x27mm		
O100	A29	25p yel & brown (R)	.20	.20
O101	A29	50p red, blk & gray	.25	.20
O102	A29	1k gray, ind & yel (R)	.50	.20
O103	A28	2k pale ol, ind & red (R)	1.10	.30
O104	A29	5k cit, dk bl & red (R)	2.75	.65
		Nos. O94-O104 (11)	6.00	2.75

Similar Overprint on Nos. 197-200,
202-208 in Black or Red

1968		**Unwmk.**		**Perf. 14**
		Size: 21x17mm		
		Overprint: 13mm		
O105	A28	1p gray	.20	.20
O106	A28	2p carmine rose	.20	.20
O107	A28	3p blue green	.20	.20
		Size: 23½x28mm		
		Overprint: 15mm		
O108	A29	5p violet blue	.20	.20
O109	A29	15p olive	.20	.20
		Size: 38½x21mm, 21x38½mm		
		Overprint: 14mm		
O110	A28	20p rose & brn	.20	.20
O111	A29	25p yel & brown (R)	.20	.20
O112	A29	50p ver, blk & gray	.25	.20
O113	A29	1k gray, ind & yel (R)	.50	.20
O114	A28	2k dl cit, ind & red (R)	1.10	.25
O115	A29	5k yel, dk bl & red (R)	2.75	.55
		Nos. O105-O115 (11)	6.00	2.60

OCCUPATION STAMPS

Issued by Burma Independence Army (in conjunction with Japanese occupation officials)

Stamps of Burma, 1937-40, Overprinted in Blue, Black Blue, Black or Red

Henzada Issue
#1, 3, 5 Overprinted in Blue or Black

Henzada Type I

1942, May		**Wmk. 196**	**Perf. 14**	
1N1	A46	3p slate	5.00	7.50
1N2	A68	9p dark green	17.50	25.00
1N3	A49	2a vermilion	50.00	75.00
		On 1938-40 George VI Issue		
		Perf. 13½x14		
		Wmk. 254		
1N4	A1	1p red orange	150.00	87.50
1N5	A1	3p violet	17.50	35.00
1N6	A1	6p ultra	15.00	30.00
1N7	A1	9p yel green	200.00	
1N8	A2	1a brown violet	5.00	7.50
1N9	A2	1½a turq green	12.50	17.50
1N10	A2	2a carmine	15.00	17.50
1N11	A2	4a slate blue	30.00	37.50
		On Official Stamps of 1939		
1N12	A1	3p violet	50.00	62.50
1N13	A1	6p ultra	45.00	62.50
1N14	A2	1½a turq green	65.00	87.50
1N15	A2	2a carmine	150.00	150.00
1N16	A2	4a slate blue	200.00	250.00

Authorities believe this overprint was officially applied only to postal

---

stationery and that the adhesive stamps existing with it were not regularly issued. It has been called "Henzada Type II."

Myaungmya Issue
1937 George V Issue Overprinted in Black

Myaungmya Type I

1942, May		**Wmk. 196**	**Perf. 14**	
1N25	A68	9p dk green	50.00	62.50
1N26	A70	3a6p deep blue	25.00	32.50
		On Official Stamp of 1937, No. O8		
1N27	A53	6a bister	50.00	62.50
		On 1938-40 George VI Issue		
		Perf. 13½x14		
		Wmk. 254		
1N28	A1	9p yel green	100.00	125.00
1N29	A2	1a brown vio	175.00	225.00
1N30	A2	4a sl blue (blk ovpt. over red)	100.00	125.00
		On Official Stamps of 1939		
1N31	A1	3p violet	15.00	15.00
1N32	A1	6p ultra	7.50	10.00
1N33	A2	1a brown vio	7.50	10.00
1N34	A2	1½a turq green	400.00	
1N35	A2	2a carmine	15.00	20.00
1N36	A2	4a slate blue	12.50	17.50

1938-40 George VI Issue Overprinted

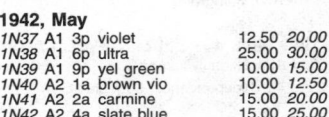

Myaungmya Type II

1942, May				
1N37	A1	3p violet	12.50	20.00
1N38	A1	6p ultra	25.00	30.00
1N39	A1	9p yel green	10.00	15.00
1N40	A2	1a brown vio	10.00	12.50
1N41	A2	2a carmine	15.00	20.00
1N42	A2	4a slate blue	15.00	25.00

Nos. 30-31 Overprinted

Myaungmya Type III

1N43	A7	1r brt ultra & dk vio	150.00	
1N44	A7	2r dk vio & red brn	110.00	

Pyapon Issue

No. 5 and 1938-40
George VI Issue
Overprinted

1942, May				
1N45	A1	6p ultra	75.00	
1N46	A2	1a brown vio	65.00	50.00
1N47	A49	2a vermilion	75.00	
1N48	A2	2a carmine	45.00	62.50
1N49	A2	4a slate blue	50.00	200.00
		Nos. 1N45-1N49 (5)	410.00	

Counterfeits of the peacock overprints exist.

OCCUPATION OFFICIAL STAMP

Myaungmya Issue
Burma No. O23 Overprinted in Black

1942, May		**Wmk. 254**	**Perf. 13**	
1NO1	A6	8a slate green	50.00	62.50

Overprint characters translate: "Office use." Two types of overprint differ mainly in base of peacock which is either 5mm or 8mm.

ISSUED UNDER JAPANESE OCCUPATION

Yano Seal — OS1

Handstamped Wmk. ABSORBO DUPLICATOR and Outline of Elephant in Center of Sheet
Handstamped

1942, June 1			**Perf. 12x11**	
		Without Gum		
2N1	OS1	1(a) vermilion	30.00	37.50

This stamp is the handstamped impression of the personal chop or seal of Shizuo Yano, chairman of the committee appointed to re-establish the Burmese postal system. It was prepared in Rangoon on paper captured from the Burma Government Offices. Not every stamp shows a portion of the watermark.

Farmer
Plowing — OS2

Vertically Laid Paper
Without Gum
Wmk. ELEPHANT BRAND and Outline of Trumpeting Elephant Covering Several Stamps

1942, June 15		**Litho.**	**Perf. 11x12**	
2N2	OS2	1a scarlet	20.00	25.00

See illustration OS4.

Same, Surcharged with New Value

1942, Oct. 15				
2N3	OS2	5c on 1a scarlet	12.50	10.50

Rice
Harvest -
A83

General
Nogi - A84

Power Plant
- A85

Admiral
Togo - A86

Diamond Mountains, Korea - A89

Meiji Shrine, Tokyo - A90

Yomei Gate, Nikko - A91

Mount Fuji and Cherry Blossoms - A94

Torii of Miyajima Shrine - A96

Stamps of Japan, 1937-42, Handstamp Surcharged with New Value in Black

1942, Sept.   Wmk. 257   Perf. 13

2N4	A83	¼a on 1s fawn	12.50	15.00
2N5	A84	½a on 2s crim	12.50	15.00
2N6	A85	¾a on 3s green	20.00	20.00
2N7	A86	1a on 5s brn lake	17.50	20.00
2N8	A89	3a on 7s dp green	30.00	32.50
2N9	A86	4a on 4s dk green	22.50	27.50
a.		4a on 4s + 2s dk green (#B5)	75.00	87.50
2N10	A90	4a on 8s dk pur & pale vio	100.00	100.00
a.		Red surcharge	140.00	150.00
2N11	A91	1r on 10s lake	12.50	15.00
2N12	A94	2r on 20s lake	30.00	35.00
a.		Red surcharge	37.50	37.50
2N13	A96	5r on 30s pck bl	10.00	10.00
a.		Red surcharge	15.00	15.00
		Nos. 2N4-2N13 (10)	267.50	290.00

Numerous double, inverted, etc., surcharges exist.

Re-surcharged in Black

1942, Oct. 15

2N14	A83	1c on ¼a on 1s	25.00	25.00
2N15	A84	2c on ½a on 2s	25.00	25.00
2N16	A85	3c on ¾a on 3s	30.00	32.50
a.		"3C." in blue	75.00	100.00
2N17	A86	5c on 1a on 5s	40.00	40.00
a.		"3C." in black	125.00	
2N18	A89	10c on 3a on 7s	45.00	45.00
2N19	A86	15c on 4a on 4s	10.50	10.50
2N20	A90	20c on 8a on 8s (#2N10)	110.00	90.00
a.		On #2N10a	125.00	
		Nos. 2N14-2N20 (7)	285.50	268.00

No. 2N16a was issued in the Shan States. Done locally, numerous different handstamps of each denomination can exist.

Stamps of Japan, 1937-42, Handstamp Surcharged with New Value in Black

1942, Oct. 15

2N21	A83	1c on 1s fawn	10.00	12.50
2N22	A84	2c on 2s crim	17.50	20.00
2N23	A85	3c on 3s green	20.00	25.00
a.		"3C." in blue	75.00	87.50
2N24	A86	5c on 5s brn lake	20.00	25.00
a.		"5C." in violet	87.50	100.00
2N25	A89	10c on 7s dp grn	25.00	30.00
2N26	A86	15c on 4s dk grn	10.00	12.50
2N27	A90	20c on 8s dk pur & pale vio	70.00	60.00
		Nos. 2N21-2N27 (7)	172.50	185.00

Nos. 2N23a and 2N24a were issued in the Shan States.

Burma State Government Crest — OS3

Unwmk.

1943, Feb. 15   Litho.   Perf. 12

2N29	OS3	5c carmine	10.00	12.50
a.		Imperf.	12.50	13.50

This stamp was intended to be used to cover the embossed George VI envelope stamp and generally was sold affixed to such envelopes. It is also known used on private envelopes.

Farmer Plowing — OS4

1943, Mar.   Without Gum   Typo.

2N30	OS4	1c deep orange	1.00	1.00
2N31	OS4	2c yel green	1.00	1.50
2N32	OS4	3c blue	1.00	1.00
a.		Laid paper	10.00	10.00
2N33	OS4	5c carmine	.50	.65
a.		Small "5c"	3.00	4.00
b.		Imperf.		
2N34	OS4	10c violet brown	.75	.90
2N35	OS4	15c red violet	.25	.25
a.		Laid paper	10.00	
2N36	OS4	20c dull purple	.25	.75
2N37	OS4	30c blue green	.25	.75
		Nos. 2N30-2N37 (8)	5.00	6.80

Small "c" in Nos. 2N34 to 2N37.

Burmese Soldier Carving "Independence" OS5

Farmer Rejoicing OS6

Boy with Burmese Flag — OS7

Hyphen-hole Perf., Pin-Perf. x Hyphen-hole Perf.

1943, Aug. 1   Typo.

2N38	OS5	1c orange	1.00	2.00
a.		Perf. 11	3.50	4.00
2N39	OS6	3c blue	1.00	2.00
a.		Perf. 11	3.50	4.00
2N40	OS7	5c rose	1.00	2.00
a.		Perf. 11	3.50	4.00
		Nos. 2N38-2N40 (3)	3.00	6.00

Declaration of the independence of Burma by the Ba Maw government, Aug. 1, 1943.

Burmese Girl Carrying Water Jar — OS8

Elephant Carrying Teak Log — OS9

Watch Tower of Mandalay Palace — OS10

1943, Oct. 1   Litho.   Perf. 12½

2N41	OS8	1c dp salmon	17.00	10.00
2N42	OS8	2c yel green	.60	1.25
2N43	OS8	3c violet	.60	1.00
2N44	OS9	5c rose	.65	1.00
2N45	OS9	10c blue	.80	.60
2N46	OS9	15c vermilion	.80	1.00
2N47	OS9	20c yel green	.80	1.25
2N48	OS9	30c brown	.80	1.25
2N49	OS10	1r vermilion	.35	3.00
2N50	OS10	2r violet	.35	5.00
		Nos. 2N41-2N50 (10)		

No. 2N49 exists imperforate. Canceled to order copies of Nos. 2N42-2N50 same values as unused.

Bullock Cart OS11

Shan Woman OS12

1943, Oct. 1   Perf. 12½

2N51	OS11	1c brown	22.50	35.00
2N52	OS11	2c yel green	22.50	35.00
2N53	OS11	3c violet	20.00	30.00
2N54	OS11	5c ultra	4.50	12.00
2N55	OS12	10c blue	20.00	35.00
2N56	OS12	20c rose	22.50	35.00
2N57	OS12	30c brown	22.50	35.00
		Nos. 2N51-2N57 (7)	134.50	217.00

For use only in the Shan States. Perak No. N34 also used in Shan States. CTO's ½ used value.

Surcharged in Black

1944, Nov. 1

2N58	OS11	1c brown	4.00	5.00
2N59	OS11	2c yel green	.20	1.25
a.		Inverted surcharge	150.00	200.00
2N60	OS11	3c ultra	2.50	4.00
2N61	OS11	5c ultra	1.25	1.50
2N62	OS12	10c blue	2.50	3.50
2N63	OS12	20c rose	.60	1.50
2N64	OS12	30c brown	.75	1.50
		Nos. 2N58-2N64 (7)	11.80	18.25

Top line of surcharge reads: "Bama naing ngan daw" (Burma State). Bottom line repeats denomination in Burmese. Surcharge applied when the Shan States came under Burmese government administration, Dec. 24, 1943. CTO's same value as unused.

BURUNDI

bu-'rün-dē

LOCATION — Central Africa, adjoining the ex-Belgian Congo Republic, Rwanda and Tanzania
GOVT. — Republic
AREA — 10,759 sq. mi.
POP. — 5,735,937 (1999 est.)
CAPITAL — Bujumbura

Burundi was established as an independent country on July 1, 1962. With Rwanda, it had been a UN trusteeship territory (Ruanda-Urundi) administered by Belgium. A military coup overthrew the monarchy November 28, 1966.

100 Centimes = 1 Franc

Catalogue values for all unused stamps in this country are for Never Hinged items.

Flower Issue of Ruanda-Urundi, 1953 Overprinted:

Perf. 11½

1962, July 1   Unwmk.   Photo.
Flowers in Natural Colors

1	A27	25c dk grn & dull org	.20	.20
2	A27	40c grn & salmon	.20	.20
3	A27	60c blue grn & pink	.20	.20
4	A27	1.25fr dk grn & blue	9.75	9.75
5	A27	1.50fr vio & apple grn	.30	.25
6	A27	5fr dp plum & lt bl grn	.40	.30
7	A27	7fr dk grn & fawn	.85	.55
8	A27	10fr dp plum & pale ol	1.25	.80
		Nos. 1-8 (8)	13.15	12.25

Animal Issue of Ruanda-Urundi, 1959-61 with Similar Overprint or Surcharge in Black or Violet Blue
Size: 23x33mm, 33x23mm

9	A29	10c multicolored	.20	.20
10	A30	20c multicolored	.20	.20
11	A29	40c multicolored	.20	.20
12	A30	50c multicolored	.20	.20
a.		Larger overprint and bar	.20	.20
13	A29	1fr multicolored	.20	.20
14	A30	1.50fr multi (VB)	.20	.20
15	A29	2fr multicolored	.20	.20
16	A30	3fr multicolored	.20	.20
17	A30	3.50fr on 3fr multi	.20	.20
18	A30	4fr on 10fr multi ("XX" 6mm wide)	.20	.20
a.		"XX" 4mm wide	.45	.45
19	A30	5fr multicolored	.20	.20
20	A30	6.50fr multicolored	.25	.25
21	A30	8fr multicolored	.30	.25
a.		Violet blue overprint	.65	.65
22	A30	10fr multicolored	.35	.30
		Size: 45x26½mm		
23	A30	20fr multicolored	.65	.65
24	A30	50fr multi (ovpt. bars 2mm wide)	1.25	1.10
a.		Overprint bars 4mm wide	1.90	1.10
		Nos. 9-24 (16)	5.00	4.70

On #12a, "Burundi" is 13mm long; bar is continuous line across sheet. On #12, "Burundi" is 10mm; bar is 29mm. #12a was issued in 1963.

Two types of overprint exist on 10c, 40c, 1fr and 2fr: I, "du" is below "me"; bar 22½mm. II, "du" below "oy"; bar 20mm.

The 50c and 3fr exist in two types, besides the larger 50c overprint listed as No. 12: I, "du" is closer to "Royaume" than to "Burundi"; bar is less than 29mm; wording is centered above bar. II, "du" is closer to "Burundi"; bar is more than 30mm; wording is off-center leftward.

King Mwami Mwambutsa IV and Royal Drummers — A1

Flag and Arms of Burundi — A2

2fr, 8fr, 50fr, Map of Burundi and King.

Unwmk.

1962, Sept. 27   Photo.   Perf. 14

25	A1	50c dull rose car & dk brn	.20	.20
26	A2	1fr dk grn, red & emer	.20	.20
27	A1	2fr brown ol & dk brn	.20	.20
28	A1	3fr vermilion & dk brn	.20	.20
29	A2	4fr Prus bl, red & emer	.20	.20
30	A1	8fr violet & dk brn	.20	.20
31	A1	10fr brt green & dk brn	.20	.20
32	A2	20fr brown, red & emer	.35	.20
33	A1	50fr brt pink & dk brn	1.00	.40
		Nos. 25-33 (9)	2.75	2.00

Burundi's independence, July 1, 1962.
See #47-50. For overprints see #45-46, 51-52.

Ruanda-Urundi Nos. 151-152
Surcharged:

Photogravure, Surcharge Engraved
1962, Oct. 31   **Perf. 11½**
Inscription in French

34	A31	3.50fr on 3fr ultra & red	.20	.20
35	A31	6.50fr on 3fr ultra & red	.20	.20
36	A31	10fr on 3fr ultra & red	.30	.25

Inscription in Flemish

37	A31	3.50fr on 3fr ultra & red	.20	.20
38	A31	6.50fr on 3fr ultra & red	.20	.20
39	A31	10fr on 3fr ultra & red	.30	.25
		Nos. 34-39 (6)	1.40	1.30

Dag Hammarskjold, Secretary General of the United Nations, 1953-61.

King Mwami Mwambutsa IV, Map of
Burundi and Emblem — A3

1962, Dec. 10   **Photo.**   **Perf. 14**

40	A3	8fr yel, bl grn & blk brn	.30	.20
41	A3	50fr gray grn, bl grn & blk brn	1.10	.30

WHO drive to eradicate malaria.
Stamps of type A3 without anti-malaria emblem are listed as Nos. 27, 30 and 33.

Sowing Seed over
Africa — A4

1963, Mar. 21   **Perf. 14x13**

42	A4	4fr olive & dull pur	.20	.20
43	A4	8fr dp org & dull pur	.20	.20
44	A4	15fr emerald & dull pur	.20	.20
		Nos. 42-44 (3)	.60	.60

FAO "Freedom from Hunger" campaign.

Nos. 27 and 33 Overprinted in Dark
Green

1963, June 19   **Unwmk.**   **Perf. 14**

45	A1	2fr brn olive & dk brn	1.60	1.25
46	A1	50fr brt pink & dk brn	1.90	1.25

Conquest and peaceful use of outer space.

Types of 1962 Inscribed: "Premier
Anniversaire" in Red or Magenta

1963, July 1   **Photo.**

47	A2	4fr olive, red & emer (R)	.20	.20
48	A1	8fr orange & dk brn (M)	.20	.20
49	A1	10fr lilac & dk brn (M)	.20	.20
50	A2	20fr gray, red & emer (R)	.40	.25
		Nos. 47-50 (4)	1.00	.85

First anniversary of independence.

Nos. 26 and 32 Surcharged in Brown
1963, Sept. 24   **Unwmk.**   **Perf. 14**

51	A2	6.50fr on 1fr multi	.30	.20
52	A2	15fr on 20fr multi	.55	.25

Red Cross Flag over
Globe with Map of
Africa — A5

1963, Sept. 26   **Perf. 14x13**

53	A5	4fr emer, car & gray	.20	.20
54	A5	8fr brn ol, car & gray	.25	.20
55	A5	10fr blue, car & gray	.35	.20
56	A5	20fr lilac, car & gray	.70	.30
		Nos. 53-56 (4)	1.50	.90

Centenary of International Red Cross.
See No. B7.

"1962", Arms of Burundi, UN and
UNESCO Emblems — A6

UN Agency Emblems: 8fr, ITU. 10fr, World Meteorological Organization. 20fr, UPU. 50fr, FAO.

1963, Nov. 4   **Unwmk.**   **Perf. 14**

57	A6	4fr yel, ol grn & blk	.20	.20
58	A6	8fr pale lil, Prus bl & blk	.20	.20
59	A6	10fr blue, lil & blk	.20	.20
60	A6	20fr yel grn, grn & blk	.35	.20
61	A6	50fr yel, red brn & blk	.90	.30
a.		Souvenir sheet of 2	3.00	3.00
		Nos. 57-61 (5)	1.85	1.10

1st anniv. of Burundi's admission to the UN. No. 61a contains two imperf. stamps with simulated perforations similar to Nos. 60-61. The 20fr stamp shows the FAO and the 50fr the WMO emblems.

UNESCO Emblem, Scales and
Map — A7

Designs: 3.50fr, 6.50fr, Scroll, scales and "UNESCO." 10fr, 20fr, Abraham Lincoln, broken chain and scales.

1963, Dec. 10   **Litho.**   **Perf. 14x13½**

62	A7	50c pink, lt bl & blk	.20	.20
63	A7	1.50fr org, lt bl & blk	.20	.20
64	A7	3.50fr fawn, lt grn & blk	.20	.20
65	A7	6.50fr lt vio, lt grn & blk	.20	.20
66	A7	10fr blue, bis & blk	.25	.20
67	A7	20fr pale brn, ocher, bl & blk	.45	.20
		Nos. 62-67 (6)	1.50	1.20

15th anniv. of the Universal Declaration of Human Rights and the cent. of the American Emancipation Proclamation (Nos. 66-67).

Ice Hockey — A8   Impala — A9

3.50fr, Women's figure skating. 6.50fr, Torch. 10fr, Men's speed skating. 20fr, Slalom.

Unwmk.
1964, Jan. 25   **Photo.**   **Perf. 14**

68	A8	50c olive, blk & gold	.20	.20
69	A8	3.50fr lt brown, blk & gold	.20	.20
70	A8	6.50fr pale gray, blk & gold	.40	.20
71	A8	10fr gray, blk & gold	.20	.20
72	A8	20fr tan, blk & gold	1.00	.30
		Nos. 68-72 (5)	2.30	1.10

Issued to publicize the 9th Winter Olympic Games, Innsbruck, Jan. 29-Feb. 9, 1964.
A souvenir sheet contains two stamps (10fr+5fr and 20fr+5fr) in tan, black and gold.

Canceled to Order
Starting about 1964, values in the used column are for "canceled to order" stamps. Postally used copies sell for much more.

Perf. 14x13, 13x14
1964, Feb. 10   **Litho.**

Animals: 1fr, 5fr, Hippopotamus, horiz. 1.50fr, 10fr, Giraffe. 2fr, 8fr, Cape buffalo, horiz. 3fr, 6.50fr, Zebra, horiz. 3.50fr, 15fr, Defassa waterbuck. 20fr, Cheetah. 50fr, Elephant. 100fr, Lion.

Size: 21½x35mm, 35x21½mm

73	A9	50c multi	.20	.20
74	A9	1fr multi	.20	.20
75	A9	1.50fr multi	.20	.20
76	A9	2fr multi	.20	.20
77	A9	3fr multi	.20	.20
78	A9	3.50fr multi	.20	.20

Size: 26x42mm, 42x26mm

79	A9	4fr multi	.25	.20
80	A9	5fr multi	.30	.20
81	A9	6.50fr multi	.35	.20
82	A9	8fr multi	.40	.20
83	A9	10fr multi	.50	.20
84	A9	15fr multi	.65	.20

Perf. 14
Size: 53x33mm

85	A9	20fr multi	.85	.20
86	A9	50fr multi	2.25	.30
87	A9	100fr multi	4.00	.65
		Nos. 73-87,C1-C7 (22)	14.50	5.15

Burundi
Dancer — A10

Designs: Various Dancers and Drummers.

Unwmk.
1964, Aug. 21   **Litho.**   **Perf. 14**
Dancers Multicolored

88	A10	50c gold & emerald	.20	.20
89	A10	1fr gold & vio blue	.20	.20
90	A10	4fr gold & brt blue	.20	.20
91	A10	6.50fr gold & red	.20	.20
92	A10	10fr gold & brt blue	.30	.20
93	A10	15fr gold & emerald	.45	.20

94	A10	20fr gold & red	.65	.25
a.		Souvenir sheet of 3, #92-94	2.75	2.75
		Nos. 88-94 (7)	2.20	1.45

1965, Sept. 10
Dancers Multicolored

88a	A10	50c silver & emerald	.20	.20
89a	A10	1fr silver & violet blue	.20	.20
90a	A10	4fr silver & bright blue	.20	.20
91a	A10	6.50fr silver & red	.20	.20
92a	A10	10fr silver & bright blue	.20	.20
93a	A10	15fr silver & emerald	.20	.20
94b	A10	20fr silver & red	.30	.20
c.		Souvenir sheet of 3, #92a-94b	2.00	2.00
		Nos. 88a-94b (7)	1.50	1.50

New York World's Fair, 1964-65.

Pope Paul VI and King Mwami
Mwambutsa IV — A11

22 Sainted
Martyrs — A12

4fr, 14fr, Pope John XXIII and King Mwami.

1964, Nov. 12   **Photo.**   **Perf. 12**

95	A11	50c brt bl, gold & red brn	.20	.20
96	A12	1fr mag, gold & slate	.20	.20
97	A11	4fr pale rose lil, gold & brn	.20	.20
98	A12	8fr red, gold & brn	.20	.20
99	A11	14fr lt grn, gold & brn	.40	.20
100	A11	20fr red brn, gold & grn	.65	.30
		Nos. 95-100 (6)	1.85	1.30

Canonization of 22 African martyrs, 10/18/64.

Shot
Put — A13

African Purple
Gallinule — A14

Sports: 1fr, Discus. 3fr, Swimming. 4fr, Running. 6.50fr, Javelin, woman. 8fr, Hurdling. 10fr, Broad jump. 14fr, Diving, woman. 18fr, High jump. 20fr, Vaulting.
3fr, 8fr, 10fr, 18fr, 20fr are horiz.

1964, Nov. 18   **Litho.**   **Perf. 14**

101	A13	50c olive & multi	.20	.20
102	A13	1fr brt pink & multi	.20	.20
103	A13	3fr multi	.20	.20
104	A13	4fr multi	.20	.20
105	A13	6.50fr multi	.20	.20
106	A13	8fr lt bl & multi	.20	.20
107	A13	10fr multi	.20	.20
108	A13	14fr multi	.25	.20

109	A13	18fr bister & multi	.30 .20
110	A13	20fr gray & multi	.35 .20
		Nos. 101-110 (10)	2.30 2.00

18th Olympic Games, Tokyo, Oct. 10-25, 1964. See No. B8.

1965   Unwmk.   Perf. 14

Birds: 1fr, 5fr, Little bee eater. 1.50fr, 6.50fr, Secretary bird. 2fr, 8fr, Yellow-billed stork. 3fr, 10fr, Congo peacock. 3.50fr, 15fr, African anhinga. 20fr, Saddle-billed stork. 50fr, Abyssinian ground hornbill. 100fr, Crowned crane.

Birds in Natural Colors

Size: 21x35mm

111	A14	50c tan, grn & blk	.20 .20
112	A14	1fr pink, mag & blk	.20 .20
113	A14	1.50fr blue & blk	.20 .20
114	A14	2fr yel grn, dk grn & blk	.20 .20
115	A14	3fr yellow, brn & blk	.20 .20
116	A14	3.50fr yel grn, dk grn & blk	.20 .20

Size: 26x43mm

117	A14	4fr tan, grn & blk	.20 .20
118	A14	5fr pink, mag & blk	.20 .20
119	A14	6.50fr blue & blk	.20 .20
120	A14	8fr yel grn, dk grn & blk	.20 .20
121	A14	10fr yel, brn & blk	.20 .20
122	A14	15fr yel grn, dk grn & blk	.35 .20

Size: 33x53mm

123	A14	20fr rose lilac & blk	.45 .30
124	A14	50fr yellow, brn & blk	1.25 .30
125	A14	100fr green, yel & blk	2.75 .40
		Nos. 111-125 (15)	7.00 3.30

Issue dates: Nos. 111-116, Mar. 31. Nos. 117-122, Apr. 16. Nos. 123-125, Apr. 30.
For overprints see #174-184, C35A-C35I.

Relay Satellite and Morse Key — A15

3fr, Telstar & old telephone handpiece. 4fr, Relay satellite & old wall telephone. 6.50fr, Orbiting Geophysical Observatory & radar screen. 8fr, Telstar II & headphones. 10fr, Sputnik II & radar aerial. 14fr, Syncom & transmission aerial. 20fr, Interplanetary Explorer & tracking aerial.

1965, July 3   Litho.   Perf. 13

126	A15	1fr multi	.20 .20
127	A15	3fr multi	.20 .20
128	A15	4fr multi	.20 .20
129	A15	6.50fr multi	.20 .20
130	A15	8fr multi	.20 .20
131	A15	10fr multi	.20 .20
132	A15	14fr multi	.25 .20
133	A15	20fr multi	.30 .20
		Nos. 126-133 (8)	1.75 1.60

Cent. of the ITU. Perf. and imperf. souv. sheets of 2 contain Nos. 131, 133. Size: 120x86mm. Value, both sheets, $7.50.

Globe and ICY Emblem — A16

Designs: 4fr, Map of Africa and UN development emblem. 8fr, Map of Asia and Colombo Plan emblem. 10fr, Globe and UN emblem. 18fr, Map of the Americas and Alliance for Progress emblem. 25fr, Map of Europe and

EUROPA emblems. 40fr, Map of Outer Space and satellite with UN wreath.

1965, Oct. 1   Litho.   Perf. 13

134	A16	1fr ol green & multi	.20 .20
135	A16	4fr dull blue & multi	.20 .20
136	A16	8fr pale yellow & multi	.20 .20
137	A16	10fr lilac & multi	.20 .20
138	A16	18fr salmon & multi	.25 .20
139	A16	25fr gray & multi	.40 .20
140	A16	40fr blue & multi	.60 .20
a.		Souvenir sheet of 3, #138-140	2.25 2.25
		Nos. 134-140 (7)	2.05 1.40

International Cooperation Year.

Protea A17

Flowers: 1fr, 5fr, Crossandra. 1.50fr, 6.50fr, Ansellia. 2fr, 8fr, Thunbergia. 3fr, 10fr, Schizoglossum. 3.50fr, 15fr, Dissotis. 4fr, 20fr, Protea. 50fr, Gazania. 100fr, Hibiscus. 150fr, Markhamia.

1966   Unwmk.   Perf. 13½

Size: 26x26mm

141	A17	50c multi	.20 .20
142	A17	1fr multi	.20 .20
143	A17	1.50fr multi	.20 .20
144	A17	2fr multi	.20 .20
145	A17	3fr multi	.20 .20
146	A17	3.50fr multi	.20 .20

Size: 31x31mm

147	A17	4fr multi	.20 .20
148	A17	5fr multi	.20 .20
149	A17	6.50fr multi	.20 .20
150	A17	8fr multi	.20 .20
151	A17	10fr multi	.20 .20
152	A17	15fr multi	.30 .20

Size: 39x39mm

153	A17	20fr multi	.40 .20
154	A17	50fr multi	1.00 .25
155	A17	100fr multi	1.90 .40
156	A17	150fr multi	2.75 .55
		Nos. 141-156,C17-C25 (25)	15.55 5.75

Issue dates: Nos. 141-147, Feb. 28; Nos. 148-153, May 18; Nos. 154-156, June 15.
For overprints see Nos. 159-173, C27-C35.

Souvenir Sheets

Allegory of Prosperity and Equality Tapestry by Peter Colfs — A18

1966, Nov. 4   Litho.   Perf. 13½

157	A18	Sheet of 7 (1.50fr)	.65 .25
158	A18	Sheet of 7 (4fr)	1.10 .50

20th anniv. of UNESCO. Each sheet contains 6 stamps showing a reproduction of the Colfs tapestry from the lobby of the General Assembly Building, NYC, and one stamp with the UNESCO emblem plus a label. The labels on Nos. 157-158 and C26 are inscribed in French or English. The 3 sheets with French inscription have light blue marginal border. The 3 sheets with English inscription have pink border. See No. C26.

Republic

Nos. 141-152, 154-156 Overprinted

1967   Litho.   Perf. 13½

Size: 26x26mm

159	A17	50c multi	.20 .20
160	A17	1fr multi	.20 .20
161	A17	1.50fr multi	.20 .20
162	A17	2fr multi	.20 .20
163	A17	3fr multi	.20 .20
164	A17	3.50fr multi	.20 .20

Size: 31x31mm

165	A17	4fr multi	.80 .30
166	A17	5fr multi	.20 .20
167	A17	6.50fr multi	.20 .20
168	A17	8fr multi	.25 .20
169	A17	10fr multi	.30 .20
170	A17	15fr multi	.40 .20

Size: 39x39mm

171	A17	50fr multi	3.75 1.25
172	A17	100fr multi	6.25 2.50
173	A17	150fr multi	5.00 2.25
		Nos. 159-173,C27-C35 (24)	29.65 11.80

Nos. 111, 113, 116, 118-125 Overprinted "REPUBLIQUE DU BURUNDI" and Horizontal Bar

1967   Litho.   Perf. 14

Birds in Natural Colors

Size: 21x35mm

174	A14	50c multi	1.25 .65
175	A14	1.50fr blue & black	.20 .20
176	A14	3.50fr multi	.20 .20

Size: 26x43mm

177	A14	5fr multi	.20 .20
178	A14	6.50fr blue & black	.20 .20
179	A14	8fr multi	.20 .20
180	A14	10fr yel, brn & blk	.30 .20
181	A14	15fr multi	.65 .20

Size: 33x53mm

182	A14	20fr multi	2.00 .40
183	A14	50fr multi	4.00 1.40
184	A14	100fr multi	6.00 2.75
		Nos. 174-184 (11)	15.20 6.60

Haplochromis Multicolor — A19

Various Tropical Fish.

1967   Photo.   Perf. 13½

Size: 42x19mm

186	A19	50c multi	.20 .20
187	A19	1fr multi	.20 .20
188	A19	1.50fr multi	.20 .20
189	A19	2fr multi	.20 .20
190	A19	3fr multi	.20 .20
191	A19	3.50fr multi	.20 .20

Size: 50x25mm

192	A19	4fr multi	.20 .20
193	A19	5fr multi	.20 .20
194	A19	6.50fr multi	.25 .20
195	A19	8fr multi	.30 .20
196	A19	10fr multi	.35 .20
197	A19	15fr multi	.50 .20

Size: 59x30mm

198	A19	20fr multi	.75 .20
199	A19	50fr multi	1.50 .20
200	A19	100fr multi	3.00 .30
201	A19	150fr multi	4.25 .45
		Nos. 186-201,C46-C54 (25)	21.00 5.40

Issue Dates: Nos. 186-191, Apr. 4; Nos. 192-197, Apr. 28; Nos. 198-201, May 18.

Ancestor Figures, Ivory Coast — A20

African Art: 1fr, Seat of Honor, Southeast Congo. 1.50fr, Antelope head, Aribinda Region. 2fr, Buffalo mask, Upper Volta. 4fr, Funeral figures, Southwest Ethiopia.

1967, June 5   Photo.   Perf. 13½

202	A20	50c silver & multi	.20 .20
203	A20	1fr silver & multi	.20 .20
204	A20	1.50fr silver & multi	.20 .20

205	A20	2fr silver & multi	.20 .20
206	A20	4fr silver & multi	.20 .20
		Nos. 202-206,C36-C40 (10)	2.25 2.00

Scouts on Hiking Trip — A21

Designs: 1fr, Cooking at campfire. 1.50fr, Lord Baden-Powell. 2fr, Boy Scout and Cub Scout giving Scout sign. 4fr, First aid.

1967, Aug. 9   Photo.   Perf. 13½

207	A21	50c silver & multi	.20 .20
208	A21	1fr silver & multi	.20 .20
209	A21	1.50fr silver & multi	.20 .20
210	A21	2fr silver & multi	.20 .20
211	A21	4fr silver & multi	.20 .20
		Nos. 207-211,C41-C45 (10)	2.85 2.00

60th anniv. of the Boy Scouts and the 12th Boy Scout World Jamboree, Farragut State Park, Idaho, Aug. 1-9.

The Gleaners, by Francois Millet A22

Paintings Exhibited at EXPO '67: 8fr, The Water Carrier of Seville, by Velazquez. 14fr, The Triumph of Neptune and Amphitrite, by Nicolas Poussin. 18fr, Acrobat Standing on a Ball, by Picasso. 25fr, Marguerite van Eyck, by Jan van Eyck. 40fr, St. Peter Denying Christ, by Rembrandt.

1967, Oct. 12   Photo.   Perf. 13½

212	A22	4fr multi	.20 .20
213	A22	8fr multi	.20 .20
214	A22	14fr multi	.25 .20
215	A22	18fr multi	.30 .20
216	A22	25fr multi	.50 .20
217	A22	40fr multi	.75 .25
a.		Souvenir sheet of 2, #216-217	1.25 1.00
		Nos. 212-217 (6)	2.20 1.25

EXPO '67 International Exhibition, Montreal, Apr. 28-Oct. 27. Printed in sheets of 10 stamps and 2 labels inscribed in French or English. No. 217a exists imperf.

Place de la Revolution and Pres. Michel Micombero — A23

Designs: 5fr, President Michel Micombero and flag. 14fr, Formal garden and coat of arms. 20fr, Modern building and coat of arms.

1967, Nov. 23   Perf. 13½

218	A23	5fr multi	.20 .20
219	A23	14fr multi	.20 .20
220	A23	20fr multi	.30 .20
221	A23	30fr multi	.45 .25
		Nos. 218-221 (4)	1.15 .85

First anniversary of the Republic.

Madonna by Carlo Crivelli — A24

Designs: 1fr, Adoration of the Shepherds by Juan Bautista Mayno. 4fr, Holy Family by Anthony Van Dyck. 14fr, Nativity by Maitre de Moulins.

1967, Dec. 7   Photo.   Perf. 13½

222	A24	1fr multi	.20	.20
223	A24	4fr multi	.20	.20
224	A24	14fr multi	.25	.20
225	A24	26fr multi	.60	.25
	Nos. 222-225 (4)		1.25	.85

Christmas 1967. Printed in sheets of 25 and one corner label inscribed "Noel 1967" and giving name of painting and painter.

Slalom — A25

10fr, Ice hockey. 14fr, Women's skating. 17fr, Bobsled. 26fr, Ski jump. 40fr, Speed skating. 60fr, Hand holding torch, and Winter Olympics emblem.

1968, Feb. 16   Photo.   Perf. 13½

226	A25	5fr silver & multi	.20	.20
227	A25	10fr silver & multi	.20	.20
228	A25	14fr silver & multi	.25	.20
229	A25	17fr silver & multi	.30	.20
230	A25	26fr silver & multi	.50	.20
231	A25	40fr silver & multi	.75	.20
232	A25	60fr silver & multi	1.25	.20
	Nos. 226-232 (7)		3.45	1.40

Issued to publicize the 10th Winter Olympic Games, Grenoble, France, Feb. 6-18. Issued in sheets of 10 stamps and label.

The Lacemaker, by Vermeer A26

Paintings: 1.50fr, Portrait of a Young Man, by Botticelli. 2fr, Maja Vestida, by Goya, horiz.

1968, Mar. 29   Photo.   Perf. 13½

233	A26	1.50fr gold & multi	.20	.20
234	A26	2fr gold & multi	.20	.20
235	A26	4fr gold & multi	.20	.20
	Nos. 233-235,C59-C61 (6)		2.00	1.20

Issued in sheets of 6.

Moon Probe A27

Designs: 6fr, Russian astronaut walking in space. 8fr, Weather satellite. 10fr, American astronaut walking in space.

1968, May 15   Photo.   Perf. 13½
Size: 35x35mm

236	A27	4fr silver & multi	.20	.20
237	A27	6fr silver & multi	.20	.20
238	A27	8fr silver & multi	.20	.20
239	A27	10fr silver & multi	.25	.20
	Nos. 236-239,C62-C65 (8)		2.55	1.60

Issued to publicize peaceful space explorations.

A souvenir sheet contains one 25fr stamp in Moon Probe design and one 40fr in Weather Satellite design. Stamp size: 41x41mm. Value $2. Sheet exists imperf. Price $3.

Salamis Aethiops A28

Butterflies: 1fr, 5fr, Graphium ridleyanus. 1.50fr, 6.50fr, Cymothoe. 2fr, 8fr, Charaxes eupale. 3fr, 10fr, Papilio bromius. 3.50fr, 15fr, Teracolus annae. 20fr, Salamis aethiops. 50fr, Papilio zonobia. 100fr, Danais chrysippus. 150fr, Salamis temora.

1968

		Size: 30x33½mm		
240	A28	50c gold & multi	.20	.20
241	A28	1fr gold & multi	.20	.20
242	A28	1.50fr gold & multi	.20	.20
243	A28	2fr gold & multi	.20	.20
244	A28	3fr gold & multi	.20	.20
245	A28	3.50fr gold & multi	.20	.20
		Size: 33½x37½mm		
246	A28	4fr gold & multi	.20	.20
247	A28	5fr gold & multi	.20	.20
248	A28	6.50fr gold & multi	.55	.20
249	A28	8fr gold & multi	.65	.20
250	A28	10fr gold & multi	.75	.20
251	A28	15fr gold & multi	.90	.20
		Size: 41x46mm		
252	A28	20fr gold & multi	1.50	.20
253	A28	50fr gold & multi	3.00	.20
254	A28	100fr gold & multi	5.00	.30
255	A28	150fr gold & multi	7.50	.50
	Nos. 240-255,C66-C74 (25)		31.45	5.40

Issue dates: Nos. 240-245, June 7; Nos. 246-251, June 28; Nos. 252-255, July 19.

Women, Along the Manzanares, by Goya — A29

Paintings: 7fr, The Letter, by Pieter de Hooch. 11fr, Woman Reading a Letter, by Gerard Terborch. 14fr, Man Writing a Letter, by Gabriel Metsu.

Soccer — A30

1968, Sept. 30   Photo.   Perf. 13½

256	A29	4fr multi	.20	.20
257	A29	7fr multi	.20	.20
258	A29	11fr multi	.20	.20
259	A29	14fr multi	.30	.20
	Nos. 256-259,C84-C87 (8)		2.90	1.60

International Letter Writing Week.

1968, Oct. 24

260	A30	4fr shown	.20	.20
261	A30	7fr Basketball	.20	.20
262	A30	13fr High jump	.20	.20
263	A30	24fr Relay race	.35	.20
264	A30	40fr Javelin	.60	.30
	Nos. 260-264,C88-C92 (10)		4.20	2.20

19th Olympic Games, Mexico City, Oct. 12-27. Printed in sheets of 8.

Virgin and Child, by Fra Filippo Lippi — A31

Paintings: 5fr, The Magnificat, by Sandro Botticelli. 6fr, Virgin and Child, by Albrecht Durer. 11fr, Madonna del Gran Duca, by Raphael.

1968, Nov. 26   Photo.   Perf. 13½

265	A31	3fr multi	.20	.20
266	A31	5fr multi	.20	.20
267	A31	6fr multi	.20	.20
268	A31	11fr multi	.25	.20
a.	Souvenir sheet of 4, #265-268		1.00	1.00
	Nos. 265-268,C93-C96 (8)		2.00	1.60

Christmas 1968. For overprints see Nos. 272-275, C100-C103.

WHO Emblem and Map of Africa — A32

1969, Jan. 22

269	A32	5fr gold, dk grn & yel	.20	.20
270	A32	6fr gold, vio & ver	.20	.20
271	A32	11fr gold, pur & red lil	.25	.20
	Nos. 269-271 (3)		.65	.60

20th anniv. of WHO in Africa.

Nos. 265-268 Overprinted in Silver

1969, Feb. 17   Photo.   Perf. 13½

272	A31	3fr multi	.20	.20
273	A31	5fr multi	.20	.20
274	A31	6fr multi	.25	.20
275	A31	11fr multi	.25	.20
	Nos. 272-275,C100-C103 (8)		2.20	1.65

Man's 1st flight around the moon by the US spacecraft Apollo 8, Dec. 21-27, 1968.

Map of Africa, and CEPT Emblem A33

Designs: 14fr, Plowing with tractor. 17fr, Teacher and pupil. 26fr, Maps of Europe and Africa and CEPT (Conference of European Postal and Telecommunications Administrations) emblem, horiz.

1969, Mar. 12   Photo.   Perf. 13

276	A33	5fr multi	.20	.20
277	A33	14fr multi	.20	.20
278	A33	17fr multi	.25	.20
279	A33	26fr multi	.35	.20
	Nos. 276-279 (4)		1.00	.80

5th anniv. of the Yaounde (Cameroun) Agreement, creating the European and African-Malgache Economic Community.

Resurrection, by Gaspard Isenmann — A34

Paintings: 14fr, Resurrection by Antoine Caron. 17fr, Noli me Tangere, by Martin Schongauer. 26fr, Resurrection, by El Greco.

1969, Mar. 24

280	A34	11fr gold & multi	.20	.20
281	A34	14fr gold & multi	.20	.20
282	A34	17fr gold & multi	.25	.20
283	A34	26fr gold & multi	.35	.20
a.	Souvenir sheet of 4, #280-283		1.50	1.50
	Nos. 280-283 (4)		1.00	.80

Easter 1969.

Potter — A35

ITU Emblem and: 5fr, Farm workers. 7fr, Foundry worker. 10fr, Woman testing corn crop.

1969, May 17   Photo.   Perf. 13½

284	A35	3fr multicolored	.20	.20
285	A35	5fr multicolored	.20	.20
286	A35	7fr multicolored	.20	.20
287	A35	10fr multicolored	.20	.20
	Nos. 284-287 (4)		.80	.80

50th anniv. of the ILO.

Industry and Bank's Emblem A36

African Development Bank Emblem and: 17fr, Communications. 30fr, Education. 50fr, Agriculture.

1969, July 29		Photo.	Perf. 13½	
288 A36	10fr gold & multi		.20	.20
289 A36	17fr gold & multi		.30	.20
290 A36	30fr gold & multi		.50	.20
291 A36	50fr gold & multi		.80	.25
a.	Souvenir sheet of 4, #288-291		1.90	1.90
	Nos. 288-291 (4)		1.80	.85

African Development Bank, 5th anniv.

Girl Reading Letter, by Vermeer A37

Paintings: 7fr, Graziella (young woman), by Auguste Renoir. 14fr, Woman writing a letter, by Gerard Terborch. 26fr, Galileo Galilei, painter unknown. 40fr, Ludwig van Beethoven, painter unknown.

1969, Oct. 24		Photo.	Perf. 13½	
292 A37	4fr multicolored		.20	.20
293 A37	7fr multicolored		.20	.20
294 A37	14fr multicolored		.30	.20
295 A37	26fr multicolored		.55	.20
296 A37	40fr multicolored		.75	.20
a.	Souvenir sheet of 2, #295-296		1.75	1.75
	Nos. 292-296 (5)		2.00	1.00

Intl. Letter Writing Week, Oct. 7-13.

Rocket Launching A38

Moon Landing: 6.50fr, Rocket in space. 7fr, Separation of landing module from capsule. 14fr, 26fr, Landing module landing on moon. 7fr, Capsule in space. 40fr, Neil A. Armstrong leaving landing module. 50fr, Astronaut on moon.

1969, Nov. 6		Photo.	Perf. 13½	
297 A38	4fr blue & multi		.20	.20
298 A38	6.50fr vio blue & multi		.25	.20
299 A38	7fr vio blue & multi		.25	.20
300 A38	14fr black & multi		.35	.20
301 A38	17fr vio blue & multi		.55	.25
	Nos. 297-301,C104-C106 (8)		3.75	2.15

Souvenir Sheet

302	Sheet of 3	3.00	3.00
a.	A38 26fr multicolored	.50	.50
b.	A38 40fr multicolored	.75	.75
c.	A38 50fr multicolored	1.00	1.00

See note after Algeria No. 427.

Madonna and Child, by Rubens — A39

Paintings: 6fr, Madonna and Child with St. John, by Giulio Romano. 10fr, Magnificat Madonna, by Botticelli.

1969, Dec. 2		Photo.	
303 A39	5fr gold & multi	.20	.20
304 A39	6fr gold & multi	.20	.20
305 A39	10fr gold & multi	.25	.20
a.	Souvenir sheet of 3, #303-305	.75	.75
	Nos. 303-305,C107-C109 (6)	2.45	1.30

Christmas 1969.

Sternotomis Bohemani — A40

Designs: Various Beetles and Weevils.

1970		Perf. 13½	
	Size: 39x28mm		
306 A40	50c multicolored	.20	.20
307 A40	1fr multicolored	.20	.20
308 A40	1.50fr multicolored	.20	.20
309 A40	2fr multicolored	.20	.20
310 A40	3fr multicolored	.20	.20
311 A40	3.50fr multicolored	.20	.20
	Size: 46x32mm		
312 A40	4fr multicolored	.20	.20
313 A40	5fr multicolored	.20	.20
314 A40	6.50fr multicolored	.20	.20
315 A40	8fr multicolored	.20	.20
316 A40	10fr multicolored	.25	.20
317 A40	15fr multicolored	.40	.20
	Size: 52x36mm		
318 A40	20fr multicolored	.50	.20
319 A40	50fr multicolored	1.00	.20
320 A40	100fr multicolored	1.90	.35
321 A40	150fr multicolored	2.75	.20
	Nos. 306-321,C110-C118 (25)	19.80	5.75

Issue dates: Nos. 306-313, Jan. 20; Nos. 314-318, Feb. 17; Nos. 319-321, Apr. 3.

Jesus Condemned to Death — A41

Stations of the Cross, by Juan de Aranoa y Carredano: 1.50fr, Jesus carries His Cross. 2fr, Jesus falls the first time. 3fr, Jesus meets His mother. 3.50fr, Simon of Cyrene helps carry the cross. 4fr, Veronica wipes the face of Jesus. 5fr, Jesus falls the second time.

1970, Mar. 16		Photo.	Perf. 13½	
322 A41	1fr gold & multi		.20	.20
323 A41	1.50fr gold & multi		.20	.20
324 A41	2fr gold & multi		.20	.20
325 A41	3fr gold & multi		.20	.20
326 A41	3.50fr gold & multi		.20	.20
327 A41	4fr gold & multi		.20	.20
328 A41	5fr gold & multi		.20	.20
a.	Souv. sheet, #322-328 + label		.60	.60
	Nos. 322-328,C119-C125 (14)		3.60	2.90

Easter 1970.

Parade and EXPO '70 Emblem — A42

Designs (EXPO '70 Emblem and): 6.50fr, Aerial view. 7fr, African pavilions. 14fr, Pagoda, vert. 26fr, Recording pavilion and pool. 40fr, Tower of the Sun, vert. 50fr, Flags of participating nations.

1970, May 5		Photo.	Perf. 13½	
329 A42	4fr gold & multi		.20	.20
330 A42	6.50fr gold & multi		.20	.20
331 A42	7fr gold & multi		.20	.20
332 A42	14fr gold & multi		.25	.20
333 A42	26fr gold & multi		.40	.20
334 A42	40fr gold & multi		.55	.20
335 A42	50fr gold & multi		.80	.20
	Nos. 329-335 (7)		2.60	1.40

EXPO '70 Intl. Exhibition, Osaka, Japan, Mar. 15-Sept. 13, 1970. See No. C126.

White Rhinoceros — A43

Fauna: a, i, Camel. c, d, Dromedary. g, r, Okapi. f, m, Addax. j, o, Rhinoceros. l, p, Burundi cow (each animal in 2 different poses).
Map of the Nile: b, Delta and pyramids. e, dhow. h, Falls. k, Blue Nile and crowned crane. n, Victoria Nile and secretary bird. q, Lake Victoria and source of Nile on Mt. Gikizi. Continuous design.

1970, July 8		Photo.	Perf. 13½	
336		Sheet of 18	7.00	1.50
a.-r.	A43 7fr any single		.40	.20

Publicizing the southernmost source of the Nile on Mt. Gikizi in Burundi. See No. C127.

Winter Wren, Firecrest, Skylark and Crested Lark — A44

Birds: 2fr, 3.50fr, 5fr, vert.; others horiz.

1970, Sept. 30		Photo.	Perf. 13½	
	Stamp Size: 44x33mm			
337 A44	Block of 4		.60	.20
a.	2fr Northern shrike		.20	
b.	2fr European starling		.20	
c.	2fr Yellow wagtail		.20	
d.	2fr Bank swallow		.20	
338 A44	Block of 4		.90	.20
a.	3fr Winter wren		.20	
b.	3fr Firecrest		.20	
c.	3fr Skylark		.20	
d.	3fr Crested lark		.20	
339 A44	Block of 4		1.25	.20
a.	3.50fr Woodchat shrike		.30	
b.	3.50fr Common rock thrush		.30	
c.	3.50fr Black redstart		.30	
d.	3.50fr Ring ouzel		.30	
340 A44	Block of 4		1.50	.20
a.	4fr European Redstart		.35	
b.	4fr Hedge sparrow		.35	
c.	4fr Gray wagtail		.35	
d.	4fr Meadow pipit		.35	
341 A44	Block of 4		1.75	.20
a.	5fr Eurasian hoopoe		.40	
b.	5fr Pied flycatcher		.40	
c.	5fr Great reed warbler		.40	
d.	5fr Eurasian kingfisher		.40	
342 A44	Block of 4		2.00	.20
a.	6.50fr House martin		.50	
b.	6.50fr Sedge warbler		.50	
c.	6.50fr Fieldfare		.50	
d.	6.50fr European Golden oriole		.50	
	Nos. 337-342,C132-C137 (12)		38.50	3.65

Nos. 337-342 are printed in sheets of 16.

Library, UN Emblem — A45

Designs: 5fr, Students taking test, and emblem of University of Bujumbura. 7fr, Students in laboratory and emblem of Ecole Normale Superieure of Burundi. 10fr, Students with electron-microscope and Education Year emblem.

1970, Oct. 23				
343 A45	3fr gold & multi		.20	.20
344 A45	5fr gold & multi		.20	.20
345 A45	7fr gold & multi		.20	.20
346 A45	10fr gold & multi		.20	.20
	Nos. 343-346 (4)		.80	.80

Issued for International Education Year.

Pres. and Mrs. Michel Micombero — A46

Designs: 7fr, Pres. Michel Micombero and Burundi flag. 11fr, Pres. Micombero and Revolution Memorial.

1970, Nov. 28		Photo.	Perf. 13½	
347 A46	4fr gold & multi		.20	.20
348 A46	7fr gold & multi		.20	.20
349 A46	11fr gold & multi		.20	.20
a.	Souvenir sheet of 3		.50	.50
	Nos. 347-349 (3)		.60	.60

4th anniv. of independence. No. 349a contains 3 stamps similar to Nos. 347-349, but inscribed "Poste Aerienne." Exists imperf. See Nos. C140-C142.

Lenin with Delegates A47

Designs (Lenin, Paintings): 5fr, addressing crowd. 6.50fr, with soldier and sailor. 15fr, speaking from balcony. 50fr, Portrait.

1970, Dec. 31		Photo.	Perf. 13½	
350 A47	3.50fr dk red brown		.20	.20
351 A47	5fr dk red brown		.20	.20
352 A47	6.50fr dk red brown		.20	.20
353 A47	15fr dk red brown		.30	.20
354 A47	50fr dk red brown		1.10	.20
	Nos. 350-354 (5)		2.00	1.00

Lenin's birth centenary (1870-1924).

Lion — A48

1971, Mar. 19   Photo.   Perf. 13½
Size: 38x38mm

355	Strip of 4	.35	.20
a.	A48 1fr Lion	.20	
b.	A48 1fr Cape buffalo	.20	
c.	A48 1fr Hippopotamus	.20	
d.	A48 1fr Giraffe	.20	
356	Strip of 4	.40	.20
a.	A48 2fr Hartebeest	.20	
b.	A48 2fr Black rhinoceros	.20	
c.	A48 2fr Zebra	.20	
d.	A48 2fr Leopard	.20	
357	Strip of 4	.50	.20
a.	A48 3fr Grant's gazelles	.20	
b.	A48 3fr Cheetah	.20	
c.	A48 3fr African white-backed vultures	.20	
d.	A48 3fr Johnston's okapi	.20	
358	Strip of 4	.75	.20
a.	A48 5fr Chimpanzee	.20	
b.	A48 5fr Elephant	.20	
c.	A48 5fr Spotted hyenas	.20	
d.	A48 5fr Beisa	.20	
359	Strip of 4	1.00	.40
a.	A48 6fr Gorilla	.25	
b.	A48 6fr Gnu	.25	
c.	A48 6fr Wart hog	.25	
d.	A48 6fr Cape hunting dog	.25	
360	Strip of 4	2.00	.45
a.	A48 11fr Sable antelope	.50	
b.	A48 11fr Caracal lynx	.50	
c.	A48 11fr Ostriches	.50	
d.	A48 11fr Bongo	.50	
	Nos. 355-360,C146-C151 (12)	24.25	3.65

For overprints and surcharges see Nos. C152, CB15-CB18.

The Resurrection, by Il Sodoma — A49

Paintings: 6fr, Resurrection, by Andrea del Castagno. 11fr, Noli me Tangere, by Correggio.

1971, Apr. 2

361	A49 3fr gold & multi	.20	.20
362	A49 6fr gold & multi	.20	.20
363	A49 11fr gold & multi	.30	.20
a.	Souvenir sheet of 3, #361-363	.60	.60
	Nos. 361-363,C143-C145 (6)	1.45	1.20

Easter 1971. No. 363a exists imperf.

Young Venetian Woman, by Dürer — A50

Dürer Paintings: 11fr, Hieronymus Holzschuher. 14fr, Emperor Maximilian I. 17fr, Holy Family, from Paumgartner Altar. 26fr, Haller Madonna. 31fr, Self-portrait, 1498.

1971, Sept. 20

364	A50 6fr multicolored	.20	.20
365	A50 11fr multicolored	.25	.20
366	A50 14fr multicolored	.40	.20
367	A50 17fr multicolored	.45	.25
368	A50 26fr multicolored	.65	.35
369	A50 31fr multicolored	.80	.40
a.	Souvenir sheet of 2, #368-369	1.60	1.60
	Nos. 364-369 (6)	2.75	1.60

International Letter Writing Week. Albrecht Dürer (1471-1528), German painter and engraver. No. 369a exists imperf.

Nos. 364-369, 369a Overprinted in Black and Gold: "VIème CONGRES / DE L'INSTITUT INTERNATIONAL / DE DROIT D'EXPRESSION FRANCAISE"

1971, Oct. 8

370	A50 6fr multicolored	.20	.20
371	A50 11fr multicolored	.25	.20
372	A50 14fr multicolored	.30	.20
373	A50 17fr multicolored	.35	.20

374	A50 26fr multicolored	.50	.20
375	A50 31fr multicolored	.65	.20
a.	Souvenir sheet of 2	1.25	1.25
	Nos. 370-375 (6)	2.25	1.20

6th Cong. of the Intl. Legal Institute of the French-speaking Area, Bujumbura, 8/10-19.

Madonna and Child, by Il Perugino — A51

Paintings of the Madonna and Child by: 5fr, Andrea del Sarto. 6fr, Luis de Morales.

1971, Nov. 2   Photo.   Perf. 13½

376	A51 3fr dk green & multi	.20	.20
377	A51 5fr dk green & multi	.20	.20
378	A51 6fr dk green & multi	.20	.20
a.	Souvenir sheet of 3, #376-378	.40	.40
	Nos. 376-378,C153-C155 (6)	1.75	1.20

Christmas 1971. No. 378a exists imperf.
For surcharges see Nos. B49-B51, CB19-CB21.

Lunar Orbiter A52

Designs: 11fr, Vostok. 14fr, Luna 1. 17fr, Apollo 11 astronaut on moon. 26fr, Soyuz 11. 40fr, Lunar Rover (Apollo 15).

1972, Jan. 15

379	A52 6fr gold & multi	.20	.20
380	A52 11fr gold & multi	.25	.20
381	A52 14fr gold & multi	.30	.20
382	A52 17fr gold & multi	.40	.20
383	A52 26fr gold & multi	.40	.30
384	A52 40fr gold & multi	.60	.30
a.	Souvenir sheet of 6	2.25	2.25
	Nos. 379-384 (6)	2.15	1.40

Conquest of space. See No. C156.
No. 384a contains one each of Nos. 379-384 inscribed "APOLLO 16."

Slalom and Sapporo '72 Emblem — A53

Sapporo '72 Emblem and: 6fr, Figure skating, pairs. 11fr, Figure skating, women's. 14fr, Ski jump. 17fr, Ice hockey. 24fr, Speed skating, men's. 26fr, Snow scooter. 31fr, Downhill skiing. 50fr, Bobsledding.

1972, Feb. 3

385	A53 5fr silver & multi	.20	.20
386	A53 6fr silver & multi	.20	.20
387	A53 11fr silver & multi	.20	.20
388	A53 14fr silver & multi	.25	.20
389	A53 17fr silver & multi	.30	.20
390	A53 24fr silver & multi	.35	.20
391	A53 26fr silver & multi	.40	.20
392	A53 31fr silver & multi	.50	.20
393	A53 50fr silver & multi	.80	.20
	Nos. 385-393 (9)	3.20	1.80

11th Winter Olympic Games, Sapporo, Japan, Feb. 3-13. Printed in sheets of 12. See No. C157.
Issued: #385-390, 2/1; #391-393, 2/21.

Ecce Homo, by Quentin Massys — A54

Paintings: 6.50fr, Crucifixion, by Rubens. 10fr, Descent from the Cross, by Jacopo da Pontormo. 18fr, Pieta, by Ferdinand Gallegos. 27fr, Trinity, by El Greco.

1972, Mar. 20   Photo.   Perf. 13½

394	A54 3.50fr gold & multi	.20	.20
395	A54 6.50fr gold & multi	.20	.20
396	A54 10fr gold & multi	.20	.20
397	A54 18fr gold & multi	.25	.20
398	A54 27fr gold & multi	.65	.20
a.	Souv. sheet, #394-398 + label	1.50	1.25
	Nos. 394-398 (5)	1.50	1.00

Easter 1972. Printed in sheets of 8 with label. No. 398a exists imperf.

Gymnastics, Olympic Rings and "Motion" A55

1972, May 19

399	A55 5fr shown	.20	.20
400	A55 6fr Javelin	.20	.20
401	A55 11fr Fencing	.25	.20
402	A55 14fr Bicycling	.25	.20
403	A55 17fr Pole vault	.30	.20
	Nos. 399-403,C158-C161 (9)	3.05	1.80

Souvenir Sheet

404	Sheet of 2	1.75	1.25
a.	A55 31fr Discus	.45	.45
b.	A55 40fr Soccer	.60	.60

20th Olympic Games, Munich, 8/26-9/11.

Prince Rwagasore, Pres. Micombero, Burundi Flag, Drummers A56

7fr, Rwagasore, Micombero, flag, map of Africa, globe. 13fr, Micombero, flag, globe.

1972, Aug. 24   Photo.   Perf. 13½

405	A56 5fr silver & multi	.20	.20
406	A56 7fr silver & multi	.20	.20
407	A56 13fr silver & multi	.25	.20
a.	Souvenir sheet of 3, #405-407	.50	
	Nos. 405-407,C162-C164 (6)	1.65	1.20

10th anniversary of independence.

Madonna and Child, by Andrea Solario — A57

Paintings of the Madonna and Child by: 10fr, Raphael. 15fr, Botticelli.

1972, Nov. 2

408	A57 5fr lt blue & multi	.20	.20
409	A57 10fr lt blue & multi	.20	.20
410	A57 15fr lt blue & multi	.25	.20
a.	Souvenir sheet of 3, #408-410	.50	
	Nos. 408-410,C165-C167 (6)	1.95	1.20

Christmas 1972. Sheets of 20 stamps + label.
For surcharges see #B56-B58, CB26-CB28.

Platycoryne Crocea — A58

1972
Size: 33x33mm

411	A58 50c shown	.20	.20
412	A58 1fr Cattleya trianaei	.20	.20
413	A58 2fr Eulophia cucullata	.20	.20
414	A58 3fr Cymbidium hamsey	.20	.20
415	A58 4fr Thelymitra pauciflora	.20	.20
416	A58 5fr Miltassia	.20	.20
417	A58 6fr Miltonia	.20	.20

Size: 38x38mm

418	A58 7fr Like 50c	.20	.20
419	A58 8fr Like 1fr	.20	.20
420	A58 9fr Like 2fr	.20	.20
421	A58 10fr Like 3fr	.25	.20
	Nos. 411-421,C168-C174 (18)	11.00	3.60

Orchids. Issued: #411-417, 11/6; #418-421, 11/29.

Henry Morton Stanley — A59

Designs: 7fr, Porters, Stanley's expedition. 13fr, Stanley entering Ujiji.

1973, Mar. 19   Photo.   Perf. 13½

422	A59 5fr gold & multi	.20	.20
423	A59 7fr gold & multi	.20	.20
424	A59 13fr gold & multi	.20	.20
	Nos. 422-424,C175-C177 (6)	1.60	1.20

Exploration of Africa by David Livingstone (1813-1873) and Henry Morton Stanley (John Rowlands; 1841-1904).

Crucifixion, by
Roger van der
Weyden — A60

Easter (Paintings): 5fr, Flagellation of Christ,
by Caravaggio. 13fr, The Burial of Christ, by
Raphael.

1973, Apr. 10
425	A60	5fr gold & multi	.20	.20
426	A60	7fr gold & multi	.20	.20
427	A60	13fr gold & multi	.20	.20
a.		Souvenir sheet of 3, #425-427	.60	.60
		Nos. 425-427,C178-C180 (6)	1.75	1.20

INTERPOL Emblem, Flag — A61

Design: 10fr, INTERPOL flag and emblem.
18fr, INTERPOL Headquarters and emblem.

1973, May 19   Photo.   Perf. 13½
428	A61	5fr silver & multi	.20	.20
429	A61	10fr silver & multi	.20	.20
430	A61	18fr silver & multi	.30	.20
		Nos. 428-430,C181-C182 (5)	1.60	1.00

Intl. Criminal Police Organization, 50th anniv.

Signs of the Zodiac, Babylon — A62

Designs: 5fr, Greek and Roman gods representing planets. 7fr, Ptolemy (No. 433a) and
Ptolemaic solar system. 13fr, Copernicus (No.
434a) and heliocentric system.
a, UL. b, UR. c, LL. d, LR.

1973, July 27   Photo.   Perf. 13½
431	A62	3fr Block of 4, #a.-d.	.20	.20
432	A62	5fr Block of 4, #a.-d.	.25	.20
433	A62	7fr Block of 4, #a.-d.	.30	.20
434	A62	13fr Block of 4, #a.-d.	.75	.20
a.		Souvenir sheet of 4, #431-434	2.75	1.40
		Nos. 431-434,C183-C186 (8)	9.25	2.65

500th anniversary of the birth of Nicolaus
Copernicus (1473-1543), Polish astronomer.

Flowers and Butterflies — A63

Block of 4 containing 2 flower & 2 butterfly
designs. The 1fr, 2fr, 5fr and 11fr have flower
designs listed as "a" and "d" numbers, butterflies as "b" and "c" numbers; the arrangement
is reversed for the 3fr and 6fr.

1973, Sept. 3   Photo.   Perf. 13
Stamp Size: 34x41½mm
435	A63	Block of 4	.35	.20
a.		1fr Protea cynaroides	.20	.20
b.		1fr Precis octavia	.20	.20
c.		1fr Epiphora bauhiniae	.20	.20
d.		1fr Gazania longiscapa	.20	.20
436	A63	Block of 4	.35	.20
a.		2fr Kniphofia	.20	.20
b.		2fr Cymothoe coccinata	.20	.20
c.		2fr Nudaurelia zambesina	.20	.20
d.		2fr Freesia refracta	.20	.20
437	A63	Block of 4	.40	.20
a.		3fr Calotis eupompe	.20	.20
b.		3fr Narcissus	.20	.20
c.		3fr Cineraria hybrida	.20	.20
d.		3fr Cyrestis camillus	.20	.20
438	A63	Block of 4	.65	.20
a.		5fr Iris tingitana	.20	.20
b.		5fr Papilio demodocus	.20	.20
c.		5fr Catopsilia avelaneda	.20	.20
d.		5fr Nerine sarniensis	.20	.20
439	A63	Block of 4	.80	.20
a.		6fr Hypolimnas dexithea	.20	.20
b.		6fr Zantedeschia tropicalis	.20	.20
c.		6fr Sandersonia aurantiaca	.20	.20
d.		6fr Drurya antimachus	.20	.20
440	A63	Block of 4	1.75	.25
a.		11fr Nymphaea capensis	.40	.20
b.		11fr Pandoriana pandora	.40	.20
c.		11fr Precis orythia	.40	.20
d.		11fr Pelargonium domestica	.40	.20
		Nos. 435-440,C187-C192 (12)	34.80	4.45

Virgin and
Child, by
Giovanni
Bellini — A64

Virgin and Child by: 10fr, Jan van Eyck. 15fr,
Giovanni Boltraffio.

1973, Nov. 13   Photo.   Perf. 13
441	A64	5fr gold & multi	.20	.20
442	A64	10fr gold & multi	.20	.20
443	A64	15fr gold & multi	.20	.20
a.		Souvenir sheet of 3, #441-443	.50	.50
		Nos. 441-443,C193-C195 (6)	1.90	1.20

Christmas 1973.
For surcharges see #B59-B61, CB29-CB31.

Pietá, by Paolo
Veronese — A65

Paintings: 10fr, Virgin and St. John, by van
der Weyden. 18fr, Crucifixion, by van der
Weyden. 27fr, Burial of Christ, by Titian. 40fr,
Pietá, by El Greco.

1974, Apr. 19   Photo.   Perf. 14x13½
444	A65	5fr gold & multi	.20	.20
445	A65	10fr gold & multi	.20	.20
446	A65	18fr gold & multi	.30	.20
447	A65	27fr gold & multi	.40	.20
448	A65	40fr gold & multi	.65	.20
a.		Souvenir sheet of 5, #444-448	1.60	1.60
		Nos. 444-448 (5)	1.75	1.00

Easter 1974.

Fish — A66

1974, May 30   Photo.   Perf. 13
Stamp Size: 35x35mm
449	A66	Block of 4	.30	.20
a.		1fr Haplochromis multicolor	.20	.20
b.		1fr Pantodon buchholzi	.20	.20
c.		1fr Tropheus duboisi	.20	.20
d.		1fr Distichodus sexfasciatus	.20	.20
450	A66	Block of 4	.30	.20
a.		2fr Pelmatochromis kribensis	.20	.20
b.		2fr Nannaethiops tritaeniatus	.20	.20
c.		2fr Polycentropsis abbreviata	.20	.20
d.		2fr Hemichromis bimaculatus	.20	.20
451	A66	Block of 4	.30	.20
a.		3fr Ctenopoma acutirostre	.20	.20
b.		3fr Synodontis angelicus	.20	.20
c.		3fr Tilapia melanopleura	.20	.20
d.		3fr Aphyosemion bivittatum	.20	.20
452	A66	Block of 4	.50	.20
a.		5fr Monodactylus argenteus	.20	.20
b.		5fr Zanclus canescens	.20	.20
c.		5fr Pygoplites diacanthus	.20	.20
d.		5fr Cephalopholis argus	.20	.20
453	A66	Block of 4	.60	.20
a.		6fr Priacanthus arenatus	.20	.20
b.		6fr Pomacanthus arcuatus	.20	.20
c.		6fr Scarus guacamaia	.20	.20
d.		6fr Zeus faber	.20	.20
454	A66	Block of 4	1.00	.20
a.		11fr Lactophrys quadricornis	.20	.20
b.		11fr Balistes vetula	.20	.20
c.		11fr Acanthurus bahianus	.20	.20
d.		11fr Holocanthus ciliaris	.20	.20
		Nos. 449-454,C207-C212 (12)	18.75	2.85

Soccer
and Cup
A67

Designs: Various soccer scenes and cup.

1974, July 4   Photo.   Perf. 13
455	A67	5fr gold & multi		.20
456	A67	6fr gold & multi		.20
457	A67	11fr gold & multi		.20
458	A67	14fr gold & multi		.25
459	A67	17fr gold & multi		.25
a.		Souvenir sheet of 3	1.40	
		Nos. 455-459,C196-C198 (8)	2.40	

World Soccer Championship, Munich, June
13-July 7. No. 459a contains 3 stamps similar
to Nos. C196-C198 without "Poste Aerienne."
Nos. 455-459 and 459a exist imperf.

Flags over UPU Headquarters,
Bern — A68

#460b, G.P.O., Bujumbura. #461a, Mailmen
("11F" in UR). #461b, Mailmen ("11F" in UL).
#462a, UPU emblem. #462b, Means of trans-
portation. #463a, Pigeon over globe showing
Burundi. #463b, Swiss flag, pigeon over map
showing Bern. Pairs are continuous designs.

1974, July 23
460	A68	6fr Pair, #a.-b.		.35
461	A68	11fr Pair, #a.-b.		.60
462	A68	14fr Pair, #a.-b.		.80
463	A68	17fr Pair, #a.-b.		.90
c.		Souvenir sheet of 8, #460-463	2.75	
		Nos. 460-463,C199-C202 (8)	9.90	
		Set, used		1.00

Cent. of UPU.

St. Ildefonso
Writing
Letter, by El
Greco
A69

Paintings: 11fr, Lady Sealing Letter, by
Chardin. 14fr, Titus at Desk, by Rembrandt.
17fr, The Love Letter, by Vermeer. 26fr, The
Merchant G. Gisze, by Holbein. 31fr, Portrait
of Alexandre Lenoir, by David.

1974, Oct. 1   Photo.   Perf. 13
468	A69	6fr gold & multi		.20
469	A69	11fr gold & multi		.20
470	A69	14fr gold & multi		.25
471	A69	17fr gold & multi		.25
472	A69	26fr gold & multi		.40
473	A69	31fr gold & multi		.45
a.		Souvenir sheet of 2, #472-473	1.10	
		Nos. 468-473 (6)	1.75	

International Letter Writing Week, Oct. 6-12.
No. 473a exists imperf.

Virgin and
Child, by
Bernaert van
Orley — A70

Paintings of the Virgin and Child: 10fr, by
Hans Memling. 15fr, by Botticelli.

1974, Nov. 7   Photo.   Perf. 13
474	A70	5fr gold & multi		.20
475	A70	10fr gold & multi		.20
476	A70	15fr gold & multi		.25
a.		Souvenir sheet of 3, #474-476	.50	
		Nos. 474-476,C213-C215 (6)	1.95	

Christmas 1974. Sheets of 20 stamps and
one label. No. 476a exists imperf.

Apollo-Soyuz Space Mission and
Emblem — A71

1975, July 10   Photo.   Perf. 13
477	A71	Block of 4	.80	
a.		26fr A.A. Leonov, V.N. Kubasov, Soviet flag	.20	
b.		26fr Soyuz and Soviet flag	.20	
c.		26fr Apollo and American flag	.20	
d.		26fr D.K. Slayton, V.D. Brand, T.P. Stafford, American flag	.20	
478	A71	Block of 4	1.25	
a.		31fr Apollo-Soyuz link-up	.30	
b.		31fr Apollo, blast-off	.30	
c.		31fr Soyuz, blast-off	.30	
d.		31fr Kubasov, Leonov, Slayton, Brand, Stafford	.30	
		Nos. 477-478,C216-C217 (4)	4.30	

Apollo Soyuz space test project (Russo-
American cooperation), launching July 15;
link-up, July 17.

Addax — A72

1975, July 31   Photo.   Perf. 13½

479	Strip of 4	.20
a.	A72 1fr shown	.20
b.	A72 1fr Roan antelope	.20
c.	A72 1fr Nyala	.20
d.	A72 1fr White rhinoceros	.20
480	Strip of 4	.20
a.	A72 2fr Mandrill	.20
b.	A72 2fr Eland	.20
c.	A72 2fr Salt's dik-dik	.20
d.	A72 2fr Thomson's gazelles	.20
481	Strip of 4	.20
a.	A72 3fr African small-clawed otter	.20
b.	A72 3fr Reed buck	.20
c.	A72 3fr Indian civet	.20
d.	A72 3fr Cape buffalo	.20
482	Strip of 4	.35
a.	A72 5fr White-tailed gnu	.20
b.	A72 5fr African wild asses	.20
c.	A72 5fr Black-and-white colobus monkey	.20
d.	A72 5fr Gerenuk	.20
483	Strip of 4	.35
a.	A72 6fr Dama gazelle	.20
b.	A72 6fr Black-backed jackal	.20
c.	A72 6fr Sitatungas	.20
d.	A72 6fr Zebra antelope	.20
484	Strip of 4	.65
a.	A72 11fr Fennec	.20
b.	A72 11fr Lesser kudus	.20
c.	A72 11fr Blesbok	.20
d.	A72 11fr Serval	.20
	Nos. 479-484,C218-C223 (12)	12.70

For overprints see Nos. C224-C227.

Jonah, by Michelangelo — A73

Paintings from Sistine Chapel: #485b, Libyan Sybil. #486a, Prophet Isaiah. #486b, Delphic Sybil. #487a, Daniel. #487b, Cumaean Sybil.

1975, Dec. 3   Photo.   Perf. 13

485	A73 5fr Pair, #a.-b.	.20
486	A73 13fr Pair, #a.-b.	.40
487	A73 13fr Pair, #a.-b.	.75
c.	Souvenir sheet of 6, #485-487	2.00
	Nos. 485-487,C228-C230 (6)	4.90

Michelangelo Buonarotti (1475-1564), Italian sculptor, painter and architect. Printed in sheets of 18 stamps + 2 labels.
For surcharges see Nos. B65-B67, CB35-CB37.

Speed Skating — A74

Basketball — A75

Designs (Innsbruck Games Emblem and): 24fr, Figure skating, women's. 26fr, Two-man bobsled. 31fr, Cross-country skiing.

1976, Jan. 23   Photo.   Perf. 14x13½

491	A74 17fr dp bl & multi	.30
492	A74 24fr multi	.45
493	A74 26fr multi	.50
494	A74 31fr plum & multi	.55
a.	Souvenir sheet of 4, perf. 13½	2.25
	Nos. 491-494,C234-C236 (7)	3.70

12th Winter Olympic Games, Innsbruck, Austria, Feb. 4-15.
No. 494a contains stamps similar to #C234-C236, without "POSTE AERIENNE."

1976, May 3   Litho.   Perf. 13½

Montreal Games Emblem and: #495b, 497a, 499b, Pole vault. #496a, 497b, 499d, Running. #496b, 498a, 499a, Soccer. #498b, 499c, Basketball.

495	A75 14fr Pair, #a.-b.	.50
496	A75 17fr Pair, #a.-b.	.60
497	A75 28fr Pair, #a.-b.	1.00
498	A75 40fr Pair, #a.-b.	1.40
	Nos. 495-498,C237-C239 (7)	7.15

Souvenir Sheet

499	Sheet of 4	1.60
a.	A75 14fr red & multi	.25
b.	A75 17fr olive & multi	.25
c.	A75 28fr blue & multi	.40
d.	A75 40fr magenta & multi	.60

21st Olympic Games, Montreal, Canada, July 17-Aug. 1.

Virgin and Child, by Dirk Bouts — A76

Virgin and Child by: 13fr, Giovanni Bellini. 27fr, Carlo Crivelli.

1976, Oct. 18   Photo.   Perf. 13½

504	A76 5fr gold & multi	.20
505	A76 13fr gold & multi	.20
506	A76 27fr gold & multi	.40
a.	Souvenir sheet of 3, #504-506	2.10
	Nos. 504-506,C250-C252 (6)	2.10

Christmas 1976. Sheets of 20 stamps and descriptive label.
For surcharges see #B71-B73, CB41-CB43.

St. Veronica, by Rubens A77

Paintings by Rubens: 21fr, Christ on the Cross. 27fr, Descent from the Cross. 35fr, The Deposition.

1977, Apr. 5   Photo.   Perf. 13

507	A77 10fr gold & multi	.20
508	A77 21fr gold & multi	.30
509	A77 27fr gold & multi	.40
510	A77 35fr gold & multi	.55
a.	Souvenir sheet of 4	1.50
	Nos. 507-510 (4)	1.45

Easter 1977. Sheets of 30 stamps and descriptive label. No. 510a contains 4 stamps similar to Nos. 507-510 inscribed "POSTE AERIENNE."

A78

#511a, Alexander Graham Bell. #511b, Intelsat Satellite, Modern & Old Telephones. #512a, Switchboard operator, c. 1910, wall telephone. #512b, Intelsat, radar. #513a, A.G. Bell, 1st telephone. #513b, Satellites around globe, videophone.

1977, May 17   Photo.   Perf. 13

511	A78 10fr Pair, #a.-b.	.20
512	A78 17fr Pair, #a.-b.	.30
513	A78 26fr Pair, #a.-b.	.50
	Nos. 511-513,C253-C254 (5)	1.75

Centenary of first telephone call by Alexander Graham Bell, Mar. 10, 1876.

Buffon's Kob — A80

1977, Aug. 22   Photo.   Perf. 14x14½

517	Strip of 4	.40
a.	A80 2fr shown	.20
b.	A80 2fr Marabous	.20
c.	A80 2fr Brindled gnu	.20
d.	A80 2fr River hog	.20
518	Strip of 4	.60
a.	A80 5fr Zebras	.20
b.	A80 5fr Shoebill	.20
c.	A80 5fr Striped hyenas	.20
d.	A80 5fr Chimpanzee	.20
519	Strip of 4	1.00
a.	A80 8fr Flamingos	.25
b.	A80 8fr Nile crocodiles	.25
c.	A80 8fr Green mamba	.25
d.	A80 8fr Greater kudus	.25
520	Strip of 4	1.25
a.	A80 11fr Hyrax	.30
b.	A80 11fr Cobra	.30
c.	A80 11fr Jackals	.30
d.	A80 11fr Verreaux's eagles	.30
521	Strip of 4	2.50
a.	A80 21fr Honey badger	.60
b.	A80 21fr Harnessed antelopes	.60
c.	A80 21fr Secretary bird	.60
d.	A80 21fr Klipspringer	.60
522	Strip of 4	2.50
a.	A80 27fr African big-eared fox	.60
b.	A80 27fr Elephants	.60
c.	A80 27fr Vulturine guineafowl	.60
d.	A80 27fr Impalas	.60
	Nos. 517-522,C258-C263 (12)	28.25

The Goose Girl, by Grimm — A81

Fairy Tales: 5fr, by Grimm Brothers. 11fr, by Aesop. 14fr, by Hans Christian Andersen. 17fr, by Jean de La Fontaine. 26fr, English fairy tales.

1977, Sept. 14   Perf. 14

523	Block of 4	.40
a.	A81 5fr shown	.20
b.	A81 5fr The Two Wanderers	.20
c.	A81 5fr The Man of Iron	.20
d.	A81 5fr Snow White and Rose Red	.20
524	Block of 4	.85
a.	A81 11fr The Quarreling Cats	.20
b.	A81 11fr The Blind and the Lame	.20
c.	A81 11fr The Hermit and the Bear	.20
d.	A81 11fr The Fox and the Stork	.20
525	Block of 4	1.00
a.	A81 14fr The Princess and the Pea	.25
b.	A81 14fr The Old Tree Mother	.25
c.	A81 14fr The Ice Maiden	.25
d.	A81 14fr The Old House	.25
526	Block of 4	1.25
a.	A81 17fr The Oyster and the Suitors	.30
b.	A81 17fr The Wolf and the Lamb	.30
c.	A81 17fr Hen with the Golden Egg	.30
d.	A81 17fr The Wolf as Shepherd	.30
527	Block of 4	2.00
a.	A81 26fr Three Heads in the Well	.50
b.	A81 26fr Mother Goose	.50
c.	A81 26fr Jack and the Beanstalk	.50
d.	A81 26fr Alice in Wonderland	.50
	Nos. 523-527 (5)	5.50

Security Council Chamber, UN Nos. 28, 46, 37, C7 — A82

UN Stamps and: 8fr, UN General Assembly, interior. 21fr, UN Meeting Hall.

1977, Oct. 10   Photo.   Perf. 13½

528	A82 Block of 4	.65
a.	8fr No. 25	.20
b.	8fr No. C5	.20
c.	8fr No. 23	.20
d.	8fr No. 2	.20
529	A82 Block of 4	.75
a.	10fr No. 28	.20
b.	10fr No. 46	.20
c.	10fr No. 37	.20
d.	10fr No. C7	.20
530	A82 Block of 4	1.50
a.	21fr No. 45	.35
b.	21fr No. 42	.35
c.	21fr No. 17	.35
d.	21fr No. 13	.35
e.	Souvenir sheet of 3	.35
	Nos. 528-530,C264-C266 (6)	10.05

25th anniv. (in 1976) of the UN Postal Administration. No. 530e contains 8fr in design of No. 529d, 10fr in design of No. 530b, 21fr in design of No. 528c.

Virgin and Child — A83

Designs: Paintings of the Virgin and Child.

1977, Oct. 31   Photo.   Perf. 14x13

531	A83 5fr By Meliore Toscano	.20
532	A83 13fr By J. Lombardos	.20
533	A83 27fr By Emmanuel Tzanes, 1610-1680	.40
a.	Souvenir sheet of 3, #531-533	.75
	Nos. 531-533,C267-C269 (6)	2.20

Christmas 1977. Sheets of 24 stamps with descriptive label.
For surcharges see #B74-B76, CB44-CB46.

Cruiser Aurora, Russia Nos. 211, 303, 1252, 187 — A84

Russian Stamps and: 8fr, Kremlin, Moscow. 11fr, Pokrovski Cathedral, Moscow. 13fr, Labor Day parade, 1977 and 1980 Olympic Games emblem.

1977, Nov. 14   Photo.   Perf. 13

534	A84 Block of 4	.40
a.	5fr No. 211	.20
b.	5fr No. 303	.20
c.	5fr No. 1252	.20
d.	5fr No. 187	.20
535	A84 Block of 4	.65
a.	8fr No. 856	.20
b.	8fr No. 1986	.20
c.	8fr No. 908	.20
d.	8fr No. 2551	.20
536	A84 Block of 4	.85
a.	11fr No. 3844b	.20
b.	11fr No. 3452	.20
c.	11fr No. 3382	.20
d.	11fr No. 3837	.20
537	A84 Block of 4	1.00
a.	13fr No. 4446	.25
b.	13fr No. 3844	.25
c.	13fr No. 2926	.25
d.	13fr No. 2365	.25
	Nos. 534-537 (4)	2.90

60th anniv. of Russian October Revolution.

Ship at Dock, Arms and Flag — A85

Burundi Arms and Flag and: 5fr, Men at lathes. 11fr, Male leopard dance. 14fr, Coffee harvest. 17fr, Government Palace.

1977, Nov. 25   Photo.   Perf. 13½
538 A85 1fr sil & multi	.20
539 A85 5fr sil & multi	.20
540 A85 11fr sil & multi	.20
541 A85 14fr sil & multi	.20
542 A85 17fr sil & multi	.20
Nos. 538-542 (5)	1.00

15th anniversary of independence.

A86

Paintings of the Virgin and Child by: 13fr, Rubens. 17fr, Solario. 27fr, Tiepolo. 31fr, Gerard David. 40fr, Bellini.

1979, Feb.   Photo.   Perf. 14x13
543 A86 13fr multi	.20
544 A86 17fr multi	.25
545 A86 27fr multi	.40
546 A86 31fr multi	.50
547 A86 40fr multi	.65
Nos. 543-547 (5)	2.00

Christmas 1978. See No. C270.

A87

1979   Photo.   Perf. 13½x13
548 A87 1fr Abyssinian hornbill	.20
549 A87 2fr Snakebird	.20
550 A87 3fr Melittophagus pusillus	.20
551 A87 5fr Flamingo	.20
552 A87 8fr Afropavo congenis	.20
553 A87 10fr Gallinule	.35
554 A87 20fr Martial eagle	.65
555 A87 27fr Ibis	.85
556 A87 50fr Saddle-billed stork	1.75
Nos. 548-556,C273-C281 (18)	13.45

Mother and Infant, IYC Emblem A88

IYC Emblem and: 20fr, Infant. 27fr, Girl with doll. 50fr, Children in Children's Village.

1979, July 19   Photo.   Perf. 14
557 A88 10fr multi	.20
558 A88 20fr multi	.25
559 A88 27fr multi	.30
560 A88 50fr multi	.55
Nos. 557-560 (4)	1.30

Intl. Year of the Child. See No. B82.

A89

A90

Virgin and Child by: 20fr, del Garbo. 27fr, Giovanni Penni. 31fr, G. Romano. 50fr, Jacopo Bassano.

1979, Oct. 12
561 A89 20fr multi	.30
562 A89 27fr multi	.40
563 A89 31fr multi	.55
564 A89 50fr multi	.75
Nos. 561-564,B83-B86 (8)	4.00

Christmas 1979. See Nos. C271, CB48.

1979, Nov. 6

Designs: 20fr, Rowland Hill, Penny Black. Stamps of Burundi: 27fr, German East Africa Nos. 17, N17. 31fr, Nos. 4, 24. 40fr, Nos. 29, 294. 60fr, Heinrich von Stephan, Nos. 464-465.

565 A90 20fr multi	.30
566 A90 27fr multi	.40
567 A90 31fr multi	.50
568 A90 40fr multi	.60
569 A90 60fr multi	.90
Nos. 565-569 (5)	2.70

Sir Rowland Hill (1795-1879), originator of penny postage. See No. C272.

A91

#570a, 110-meter hurdles. #570b, Hurdles, Thomas Munkelt. A#570c, Hurdles, R.D.A. #571a, Discus. #571b, Discus, V. Rassh-chupkin. #571c, Discus, U.R.S.S. #572a, shown. #572b, "Football." #572c, Soccer, Tchecoslovaquie.

1980, Oct. 24   Photo.   Perf. 13x13½
570 A91 20fr Strip of 3, #a.-c.	1.25
571 A91 30fr Strip of 3, #a.-c.	1.60
572 A91 40fr Strip of 3, #a.-c.	2.25
Nos. 570-572 (3)	5.10

22nd Summer Olympic Games, Moscow, July 19-Aug. 3. See No. C282.

Virgin and Child, by Mainardi A92

Christmas 1980 (Paintings): 30fr, Holy Family, by Michelangelo. 40fr, Virgin and Child, by di Cosimo. 45fr, Holy Family, by Fra Bartolomeo.

1980, Dec. 12   Photo.   Perf. 13½x13
579 A92 10fr multi	.20
580 A92 30fr multi	.30
581 A92 40fr multi	.40
582 A92 45fr multi	.45
Nos. 579-582,B87-B90 (8)	2.75

UPRONA Party National Congress, 1979 — A93

1980, Dec. 29   Perf. 14x13½
583 A93 10fr multi	.20
584 A93 40fr multi	.60
585 A93 45fr multi	.65
Nos. 583-585 (3)	1.45

Johannes Kepler, Dish Antenna A94

1981, Feb. 12   Perf. 14
586 A94 10fr shown	.20
587 A94 40fr Satellite	.60
588 A94 45fr Satellite, diff.	.65
a. Souvenir sheet of 3, #586-588	1.50
Nos. 586-588 (3)	1.45

350th death anniv. of Johannes Kepler and 1st earth satellite station in Burundi.

Lion A95

1983, Apr. 22   Photo.   Perf. 13
|589 A95 2fr shown|
|590 A95 3fr Giraffes|
|591 A95 5fr Rhinoceros|
|592 A95 10fr Cape buffalo|
|593 A95 20fr Elephant|
|594 A95 25fr Hippopotamus|
|595 A95 30fr Zebra|
|596 A95 50fr Warthog|
|597 A95 60fr Oryx|
|598 A95 65fr Wild dog|
|599 A95 70fr Cheetah|
|600 A95 75fr Wildebeest|
|601 A95 85fr Hyena|
|Nos. 589-601 (13)|50.00|

Nos. 589-601 Overprinted in Silver with World Wildlife Fund Emblem

1983   Photo.   Perf. 13
|589a A95 2fr multi|
|590a A95 3fr multi|
|591a A95 5fr multi|
|592a A95 10fr multi|
|593a A95 20fr multi|
|594a A95 25fr multi|
|595a A95 30fr multi|
|596a A95 50fr multi|
|597a A95 60fr multi|
|598a A95 65fr multi|
|599a A95 70fr multi|
|600a A95 75fr multi|
|601a A95 85fr multi|
|Nos. 589a-601a (13)|600.00|

Apparently there is speculation in these two sets.

20th Anniv. of Independence, July 1, 1982 — A96

Flags, various arms, map or portrait.

1983   Perf. 14
602 A96 10fr multi	.20
603 A96 25fr multi	.40
604 A96 30fr multi	.45

605 A96 50fr multi	.75
606 A96 65fr multi	1.00
Nos. 602-606 (5)	2.80

Christmas 1983 — A97

Virgin and Child paintings: 10fr, by Luca Signorelli (1450-1523). 25fr, by Esteban Murillo (1617-1682). 30fr, by Carlo Crivelli (1430-1495). 50fr, by Nicolas Poussin (1594-1665).

1983, Oct. 3   Litho.   Perf. 14½x13½
607 A97 10fr multi	.20
608 A97 25fr multi	.40
609 A97 30fr multi	.45
610 A97 50fr multi	.75
Nos. 607-610,B91-B94 (8)	3.65

See Nos. C285, CB50.

Butterflies — A98

#611a, Cymothoe coccinata. #611b, Papilio zalmoxis. #612a, Asterope pechueli. #612b, Papilio antimachus. #613a, Papilio hesperus. #613b, Bebearia mardania. #614a, Euphaedra neophron. #614b, Euphaedra perseis. #615a, Euphaedra imperialis. #615b, Pseudocraea striata.

1984, June 29   Photo.   Perf. 13
611 A98 5fr Pair, #a.-b.	.40
612 A98 10fr Pair, #a.-b.	.80
613 A98 30fr Pair, #a.-b.	2.00
614 A98 35fr Pair, #a.-b.	2.50
615 A98 65fr Pair, #a.-b.	4.50
Nos. 611-615 (5)	10.20

For surcharges see No. 654D.

19th UPU Congress, Hamburg A99

UPU emblem and: 10fr, German East Africa, #17, N17. 30fr, #4, 24. 35fr, Discus, #294, 595. 65fr, Dr. Heinrich von Stephan, #464-465.

1984, July 14   Litho.   Perf. 13x13½
621 A99 10fr multi	.20
622 A99 30fr multi	.45
623 A99 35fr multi	.50
624 A99 65fr multi	1.00
Nos. 621-624 (4)	2.15

See No. C286.

1984 Summer Olympics — A100

Gold medalists: 10fr, Jesse Owens, US, track and field, Berlin, 1936. 30fr, Rafer Johnson, US, decathlon, 1960. 35fr, Bob Beamon, US, long jump, 1968. 65fr, Kipchoge Keino, Kenya, 3000-meter steeplechase, 1972.

1984, Aug. 6   *Perf. 13½x13*
625	A100	10fr multi	.25
626	A100	30fr multi	.70
627	A100	35fr multi	.85
628	A100	65fr multi	1.50
		Nos. 625-628 (4)	3.30

See No. C287.

Christmas 1984 — A101

Paintings: 10fr, Rest During the Flight into Egypt, by Murillo (1617-1682). 25fr, Virgin and Child, by R. del Garbo. 30fr, Virgin and Child, by Botticelli (1445-1510). 50fr, The Adoration of the Shepherds, by Giacomo da Bassano (1517-1592).

1984, Dec. 15   *Perf. 13½*
629	A101	10fr multi	.20
630	A101	25fr multi	.40
631	A101	30fr multi	.45
632	A101	50fr multi	.75
		Nos. 629-632,B95-B98 (8)	3.65

See Nos. C288, CB51.

Flowers — A102

1986, July 31   Photo.   *Perf. 13x13½*
633	A102	2fr Thunbergia	.20
634	A102	3fr Saintpaulia	.20
635	A102	5fr Clivia	.20
636	A102	10fr Cassia	.20
637	A102	20fr Strelitzia	.25
638	A102	35fr Gloriosa	.55
		Nos. 633-638,C289-C294 (12)	8.40

Intl. Peace Year — A103

1986, May 1   Litho.   *Perf. 14*
639	A103	10fr Rockets as housing	.20
640	A103	20fr Atom as flower	.20
641	A103	30fr Handshake	.25
642	A103	40fr Globe, chicks	.35
a.		Souvenir sheet of 4, #639-642	.90
		Nos. 639-642 (4)	1.00

No. 642a exists imperf.

Great Lake Nations Economic Community (CEPGI), 10th Anniv. — A104

Outline maps of Lake Tanganyika, CEPGI emblem and: 5fr, Aviation. 10fr, Agriculture. 15fr, Industry. 25fr, Electrification. 35fr, Flags of Burundi, Rwanda and Zaire.

1986, May 1   Photo.   *Perf. 13½x14½*
643	A104	5fr multi	.20
644	A104	10fr multi	.20
645	A104	15fr multi	.20
646	A104	25fr multi	.30
647	A104	35fr multi	.45
a.		Souv. sheet, #643-647 + label	1.25
		Nos. 643-647 (5)	1.35

Intl. Year of Shelter for the Homeless A105

1987, June   Litho.   *Perf. 14*
648	A105	10fr Hovel	.30
649	A105	20fr Drain pipe shelter	.55
650	A105	80fr Shoveling sand	2.15
651	A105	150fr Children, house model	4.00
a.		Souvenir sheet of 4, #648-651	7.00
		Nos. 648-651 (4)	7.00

A106

A107

1987(?)   Litho.   *Perf. 14*
652	A106	5fr shown	.20
653	A106	20fr Skull, lungs	.30
654	A106	80fr Cigarette, face	1.25
		Nos. 652-654 (3)	1.75

WHO Anti-smoking campaign.

No. 613 Surcharged

1989   Photo.   *Perf. 13*
654D	A98	80fr on 30fr, pair #e.-f.	

Numbers have been reserved for additional values in this set.

1990   Litho.   *Perf. 14*
655	A107	5fr red lil & multi	.20
656	A107	10fr blue & multi	.25
657	A107	20fr gray & multi	.50
658	A107	30fr ol grn & multi	.70
659	A107	50fr brt blue & multi	1.25
660	A107	80fr grn bl & multi	2.00
a.		Souv. sheet of 6, #655-660, perf. 13½	4.75
		Nos. 655-660 (6)	4.90

Visit of Pope John Paul II.

Animals A108

1991, Oct. 4   Litho.   *Perf. 14*
661	A108	5fr Hippopotamus	.20
662	A108	10fr Chickens	.20
663	A108	20fr Lion	.30
664	A108	20fr Elephant	.50
665	A108	50fr Guinea fowl	.80
666	A108	80fr Crocodile	1.25
a.		Souv. sheet of 6, #661-666, perf. 13½	3.25
		Nos. 661-666 (6)	3.25

No. 666a exists imperf.

Flowers — A108a

1992, June 2   Litho.   *Perf. 14*
666B	A108a	15fr Impatiens petersiana	.40
666C	A108a	20fr Lachenalia aloides	.50
666D	A108a	30fr Nymphaea lotus	.85
666E	A108a	50fr Clivia miniata	1.25
f.		Souvenir sheet of 4, #666B-666E, perf. 13½	3.00
		Nos. 666B-666E (4)	3.00

A109

Native Music and Dancing A110

15fr, Native drummer. 30fr, Two dancers. 115fr, Drummers. 200fr, Five dancers.

1992, Apr. 2   Litho.   *Perf. 14*
667	A109	15fr multicolored	.25
668	A109	30fr multicolored	.50
669	A110	115fr multicolored	1.75
670	A110	200fr multicolored	3.00
a.		Souvenir sheet	5.75
		Nos. 667-670 (4)	5.50

No. 670a contains one each of Nos. 667-668, perf. 13x13½, and Nos. 669-670, perf. 13½x13.

Independence, 30th Anniv. — A111

30fr, 140fr, People with flag. 85fr, 115fr, Natl. flag. 110fr, 200fr, Monument. 120fr, 250fr, Map.

1992, June 30   Litho.   *Perf. 15*
671	A111	30fr multi	.35
672	A111	85fr multi	1.00
673	A111	110fr multi, vert.	1.25
674	A111	115fr multi	1.25
675	A111	120fr multi, vert.	1.40
676	A111	140fr multi	1.60
677	A111	200fr multi, vert.	2.25
678	A111	250fr multi, vert.	3.00
		Nos. 671-678 (8)	12.10

Discovery of America, 500th Anniv. A112

Columbus' fleet, globe and: 200fr, Pre-Columbian artifacts. 400fr, Fruits and vegetables.

1992, Oct. 12   Litho.   *Perf. 15*
679	A112	200fr multicolored	3.00
680	A112	400fr multicolored	6.25

Felis Serval A113

1992, Oct. 16
681	A113	30fr shown	.40
682	A113	130fr multi	1.60
683	A113	200fr One standing, one lying	2.50
684	A113	220fr Two faces	3.00
		Nos. 681-684 (4)	7.50

World Wildlife Fund.

Mushrooms A114

1992 Summer Olympics, Barcelona A115

Designs: 10fr, Russula ingens. 15fr, Russula brunneorigida. 20fr, Amanita zambiana. 30fr, Russula subfistulosa. 75fr, 85fr, Russula meleagris. 100fr, Russula immaculata. 110fr, like #685. 115fr, like #686. 120fr, 130fr, Russula sejuncta. 250fr, Afroboletus luteolus.

1992-93   *Perf. 11½x12*
Granite Paper
685	A114	10fr multicolored	.20
686	A114	15fr multicolored	.25
687	A114	20fr multicolored	.30
688	A114	30fr multicolored	.50
689	A114	75fr multicolored	1.10
690	A114	85fr multicolored	1.40
691	A114	100fr multicolored	1.50
691A	A114	110fr multicolored	1.60
691B	A114	115fr multicolored	1.75
692	A114	120fr multicolored	1.90
693	A114	130fr multicolored	2.00
694	A114	250fr multicolored	3.75
		Nos. 685-694 (12)	16.25

Issued: 110fr, 115fr, 1993; others, 9/30/92.

1992, Nov. 6   *Perf. 15*
695	A115	130fr Runners	2.00
696	A115	500fr Hurdler	7.75

A116   A116a

Christmas (Details of Adoration of the Kings, by Gentile da Fabriano): a, 100fr, Crowd, horses. b, 130fr, Kings. c, 250fr, Nativity scene.

1992, Dec. 7   Litho.   Perf. 11½
697 A116 Strip of 3, #a.-c.   5.25
d.   Souvenir sheet of 3, #697a-697c   6.50

Nos. 697a-697c have white border. No. 697d has continuous design and sold for 580fr.

1992, Dec. 5   Litho.   Perf. 15

Designs: 200fr, Emblems. 220fr, Profile of person made from fruits and vegetables.

697E A116a 200fr multicolored   5.25
697F A116a 220fr multicolored   5.75

Intl. Conference on Nutrition, Rome.

European Common Market A117

Designs: 130fr, Flags, stars. 500fr, Europe, Africa, clasped hands, stars.

1993, Mar. 29   Litho.   Perf. 15
698 A117 130fr multicolored   1.50
699 A117 500fr multicolored   5.75

1994 World Cup Soccer Championships, US — A118

Players, stadium, US flag and: 130fr, Statue of Liberty. 200fr, Golden Gate Bridge.

1993, July 5   Litho.   Perf. 15
700 A118 130fr multicolored   1.50
701 A118 200fr multicolored   2.25

Traditional Musical Instruments — A119

1993, Apr. 30   Litho.   Perf. 15
702 A119 200fr Indonongo   2.25
703 A119 220fr Ingoma   2.50
704 A119 250fr Ikembe   2.75
705 A119 300fr Umuduri   3.50
       Nos. 702-705 (4)   11.00

A120   A121

1993, June 4   Litho.   Perf. 11½
706 A120 130fr Papilio bromius   1.50
707 A120 200fr Charaxes eupale   2.25
708 A120 250fr Cymothoe caenis   2.75
709 A120 300fr Graphium ridleyanus 3.50
a.   Souvenir sheet of 4, #706-709 11.50
       Nos. 706-709 (4)   10.00

No. 709a sold for 980fr.

1993, Dec. 9   Perf. 14
710 A121 100fr Cattle   1.10
711 A121 120fr Sheep   1.40
712 A121 130fr Pigs   1.50
713 A121 250fr Goats   2.75
       Nos. 710-713 (4) 6.75

Christmas — A122

Rock Stars — A123

Natives adoring Christ Child: a, 100fr, Woman carrying baby, two people kneeling. b, 130fr, With Christ Child. 250fr, c, Woman carrying baby, three other people.

1993, Dec. 10   Perf. 11½
714 A122 Strip of 3, #a.-c.   5.00
d.   Souvenir sheet of 3, #714a-714c   6.00

#714a-714c have white border. #714d has continuous design and sold for 580fr.

1994   Litho.   Perf. 15
715 A123 60fr Elvis Presley   .65
716 A123 115fr Mick Jagger   1.25
717 A123 120fr John Lennon   1.25
718 A123 200fr Michael Jackson 2.25
a.   Souvenir sheet, #715-718   6.50
       Nos. 715-718 (4)   5.40

No. 718a sold for 600fr.

A124

A125

1994, Oct. 10   Litho.   Perf. 15
719 A124 150fr multicolored   1.10

Intl. Olympic Committee, cent.

1994, Dec. 14   Photo.   Perf. 15

Christmas (Madonna and Child): a, 115fr, Chinese. b, 120fr, Japanese. c, 250fr, Polish.

720 A125 Strip of 3, #a.-c.   5.00
d.   Souvenir sheet of 1, #720c   2.75

A126   A127

115fr, FAO, 50th anniv. 120fr, UN, 50th anniv.

1995, Feb. 21   Litho.   Perf. 11½
721 A126 115fr multicolored   1.25
722 A126 120fr multicolored   1.25

1995   Litho.   Perf. 11½

Flowers: 15fr, Cassia didymobotrya. 20fr, Mitragyna rubrostipulosa. 30fr, Phytolacca dodecandra. 85fr, Acanthus pubescens. 100fr, Bulbophyllum comatum. 110fr, Angraecum evradianum. 115fr, Eulophia burundiensis. 120fr, Habenaria adolphii.

Granite Paper
723 A127 15fr multicolored   .20
724 A127 20fr multicolored   .20
725 A127 30fr multicolored   .30
726 A127 85fr multicolored   .80
727 A127 100fr multicolored   .90
728 A127 110fr multicolored   1.00
729 A127 115fr multicolored   1.00
730 A127 120fr multicolored   1.10
       Nos. 723-730 (8)   5.50

Transportation Methods — A128

30fr, Otraco bus. 115fr, Transintra semi truck. 120fr, Arnolac tugboat. 250fr, Air Burundi airplane.

1995, Nov. 16   Litho.   Perf. 11½
731 A128 30fr multicolored   .45
732 A128 115fr multicolored   1.75
733 A128 120fr multicolored   1.75
734 A128 250fr multicolored   3.50
       Nos. 731-734 (4)   7.45

A129

A130

Christmas (African sculpture): a, 100fr, Boy with panga, basket on head. b, 130fr, Boy carrying sheaf of wheat. c, 250fr, Mother, children.

1995, Dec. 26   Litho.   Perf. 11½x12
735 A129 Strip of 3, #a.-c.   2.25
d.   Souvenir sheet of 3, #735a-735c   2.25

1996, June 28   Litho.   Perf. 14

Athlete, national flag: 130fr, Venuste Niyongabo. 500fr, Arthemon Hatungimana.

736 A130 130fr multicolored   .65
737 A130 500fr multicolored   2.50

1996 Summer Olympic Games, Atlanta.

Birds A131

Designs: 15fr, Hagedashia hagedash. 20fr, Alopochen aegyptiacus. 30fr, Haliaeetus vocifer. 120fr, Ardea goliath. 165fr, Balearica regulorum. 220fr, Actophilornis africana.

1996   Perf. 14
740 A131 15fr multicolored   .20
741 A131 20fr multicolored   .20
742 A131 30fr multicolored   .30
743 A131 120fr multicolored   1.10
744 A131 165fr multicolored   1.60
745 A131 220fr multicolored   2.00
       Nos. 740-745 (6)   5.40

Fish of Lake Tanganyika A132

Designs: 30fr, Julidochromis malieri. 115fr, Cyphotilapia frontosa. 120fr, Lamprologus brichardi. 250fr, Synodonis petricola.

1996, June 4   Litho.   Perf. 11¾x11½
746 A132 30fr multicolored   .20 .20
747 A132 115fr multicolored   .40 .40
748 A132 120fr multicolored   .40 .40
749 A132 250fr multicolored   .85 .85
a.   Souv. sheet, #746-749, perf 11¾   2.10 2.10
       Nos. 746-749 (4)   1.85 1.85

No. 749a sold for 615fr.
Although ostensibly issued in 1996, this set was not available in the philatelic marketplace until 1999.

SOS Children's Village, 50th Anniv. A133

100fr, Children in Village. 250fr, Children, flags. 270fr, Children around flagpole.

1998, Dec. 26   Litho.   Perf. 14
750 A133 100fr multicolored   .35 .35
751 A133 250fr multicolored   .85 .85
752 A133 270fr multicolored   .90 .90
       Nos. 750-752 (3)   2.10 2.10

Christmas — A134

Various paintings of Madonna and Child.

1999, Jan. 19   Perf. 11¾
Frame color
753 A134 100fr green   .35 .35
754 A134 130fr yellow brown   .45 .45
755 A134 250fr rose   .85 .85
a.   Souvenir sheet of 3, #753-755   2.00 2.00
       Nos. 753-755 (3)   1.65 1.65

Nos. 753-755 are dated "1996," "1997," and "1998," respectively.
No. 755a sold for 580fr.

Diana, Princess of Wales (1961-97) A135

Denominations: a, 100fr. b, 250fr. c, 300fr.

1999, Sept. 30   Perf. 13¾
756 A135 Sheet of 6, 2 each #a.-c.   4.50 4.50

Fight Against Hunger — A136

2000, Feb. 28   Litho.   *Perf. 14*
757   A136   350fr   Danny Kaye   1.10   1.10

Issued in sheets of 5.

Space — A137

No. 758, horiz.: a, Space plane (2003). b, Reuseable space plane. c, Future space ship. d, Galileo. e, Space telescope. f, Space platform. g, Satellite launched Feb. 17, 1996. h, Cassini. i, Solar probe. j, Vehicle without fenders. k, Vehicle with fenders. l, Spacecraft for Mars.

Illustration reduced.

2000, July 24   Litho.   *Perf. 14*
758   A137   165fr   Sheet of 12, #a-l   5.25   5.25

Souvenir Sheet

759   A137   1500fr   Newton's telescope   4.00   4.00

SEMI-POSTAL STAMPS

Prince Louis Rwagasore — SP1

Prince and Stadium SP2

#B3, B6, Prince, memorial monument.

Perf. 14x13, 13x14

1963, Feb. 15   Photo.
B1   SP1   50c + 25c brt vio   .20   .20
B2   SP2   1fr + 50c red org & dk bl   .20   .20
B3   SP2   1.50fr + 75c lem & dk vio   .20   .20
B4   SP1   3.50fr + 1.50fr lil rose   .20   .20
B5   SP2   5fr + 2fr rose pink & dk bl   .20   .20
B6   SP2   6.50fr + 3fr gray ol & dk vio   .20   .20
    Nos. B1-B6 (6)   1.20   1.20

Issued in memory of Prince Louis Rwagasore (1932-61), son of King Mwami

---

Mwambutsa IV and Prime Minister. The surtax was for the stadium and monument in his honor.

Red Cross Type of Regular Issue
Souvenir Sheet

1963, Sept. 26   Litho.   *Imperf.*
B7   Sheet of 4   2.00   2.00
  a.   A5 4fr + 2fr fawn, red & black   .30   .30
  b.   A5 8fr + 2fr green, red & black   .40   .40
  c.   A5 10fr + 2fr gray, red & black   .45   .45
  d.   A5 20fr + 2fr ultra, red & black   .65   .65

Surtax for Red Cross work in Burundi.

Olympic Type of Regular Issue
Souvenir Sheet

Designs: 18fr+2fr, Hurdling, horiz. 20fr+5fr, Vaulting, horiz.

1964, Nov. 18   *Perf. 13½*
B8   Sheet of 2   3.00   2.75
  a.   A13 18fr + 2fr yel grn & multi   1.25   1.00
  b.   A13 20fr + 5fr brt pink & multi   1.25   1.00

Scientist with Microscope and Map of Burundi — SP3

Lithographed and Photogravure

1965, Jan. 28   Unwmk.   *Perf. 14½*
B9   SP3   2fr + 50c multi   .20   .20
B10   SP3   4fr + 1.50fr multi   .20   .20
B11   SP3   5fr + 2.50fr multi   .20   .20
B12   SP3   8fr + 3fr multi   .25   .20
B13   SP3   10fr + 5fr multi   .40   .20
    Nos. B9-B13 (5)   1.25   1.00

Souvenir Sheet
Perf. 13x13½

B14   SP3   10fr + 10fr multi   .85   .85

Issued for the fight against tuberculosis.

Coat of Arms, 10fr Coin, Reverse SP4

Designs (Coins of Various Denominations): 4fr+50c, 8fr+50c, 15fr+50c, 40fr+50c, King Mwambutsa IV, obverse.

Lithographed; Embossed on Gilt Foil

1965, Aug. 9   *Imperf.*
     Diameter: 39mm
B15   SP4   2fr + 50c crim & org   .20   .20
B16   SP4   4fr + 50c ultra & ver   .20   .20
     Diameter: 45mm
B17   SP4   6fr + 50c org & gray   .20   .20
B18   SP4   8fr + 50c bl & mag   .20   .20
     Diameter: 56mm
B19   SP4   12fr + 50c lt grn & red lil   .25   .25
B20   SP4   15fr + 50c yel grn & lt lil   .30   .30
     Diameter: 67mm
B21   SP4   25fr + 50c vio bl & buff   .50   .50
B22   SP4   40fr + 50c brt pink & red brn   .75   .75
    Nos. B15-B22 (8)   2.60   2.60

Stamps are backed with patterned paper in blue, orange and pink engine-turned design.

Prince Louis Rwagasore and Pres. John F. Kennedy SP5

4fr+1fr, 20fr+5fr, Prince Louis, memorial. 20fr+2fr, 40fr+5fr, Pres. John F. Kennedy, library shelves. 40fr+2fr, King Mwambutsa IV at Kennedy grave, Arlington, vert.

1966, Jan. 21   Photo.   *Perf. 13½*
B23   SP5   4fr + 1fr gray bl & dk brn   .20   .20
B24   SP5   10fr + 1fr pale grn, ind & brn   .20   .20
B25   SP5   20fr + 2fr lil & dp grn   .40   .20
B26   SP5   40fr + 2fr gray grn & dk brn   .65   .20
    Nos. B23-B26 (4)   1.45   .80

Souvenir Sheet
B27   Sheet of 2   1.50   1.00
  a.   SP5 20fr + 5fr gray bl & dk brn   .50   .45
  b.   SP5 40fr + 5fr gray grn & dk brn   .75   .50

Issued in memory of Prince Louis Rwagasore and President John F. Kennedy.

Republic

Winston Churchill and St. Paul's, London SP6

Designs: 15fr+2fr, Tower of London and Churchill. 20fr+3fr, Big Ben and Churchill.

1967, Mar. 23   Photo.   *Perf. 13½*
B28   SP6   4fr + 1fr multi   .20   .20
B29   SP6   15fr + 2fr multi   .35   .20
B30   SP6   20fr + 3fr multi   .45   .20
    Nos. B28-B30 (3)   1.00   .60

Issued in memory of Sir Winston Churchill (1874-1965), statesman and World War II leader.

A souvenir sheet contains one airmail stamp, 50fr+5fr, with Churchill portrait centered. Size: 80x80mm. Exists perf. and imperf. Value, each sheet, $3.50.

Nos. B28-B30 Overprinted

1967, July 14   Photo.   *Perf. 13½*
B31   SP6   4fr + 1fr multi   .20   .20
B32   SP6   15fr + 2fr multi   .40   .20
B33   SP6   20fr + 3fr multi   .65   .30
    Nos. B31-B33 (3)   1.25   .70

50th anniversary of Lions International. Exist with dates transposed.
The souvenir sheets described below No. B30 also received this Lions overprint. Value, each $3.50.

Blood Transfusion and Red Cross — SP7

Designs: 7fr+1fr, Stretcher bearers and wounded man. 11fr+1fr, Surgical team. 17fr+1fr, Nurses tending blood bank.

1969, June 26   Photo.   *Perf. 13½*
B34   SP7   4fr + 1fr multi   .20   .20
B35   SP7   7fr + 1fr multi   .20   .20
B36   SP7   11fr + 1fr multi   .30   .20
B37   SP7   17fr + 1fr multi   .30   .20
    Nos. B34-B37,CB9-CB11 (7)   2.60   1.40

League of Red Cross Societies, 50th anniv.

Pope Paul VI and Map of Africa — SP8

3fr+2fr, 17fr+2fr, Pope Paul VI. 10fr+2fr, Flag made of flags of African Nations. 14fr+2fr, View of St. Peter's, Rome. 40fr+2fr, 40fr+5fr, Martyrs of Uganda. 50fr+2fr, 50fr+5fr, Pope on Throne.

1969, Sept. 12   Photo.   *Perf. 13½*
B38   SP8   3fr + 2fr multi, vert.   .20   .20
B39   SP8   5fr + 2fr multi   .20   .20
B40   SP8   10fr + 2fr multi   .30   .20
B41   SP8   14fr + 2fr multi   .40   .20
B42   SP8   17fr + 2fr multi, vert.   .50   .20
B43   SP8   40fr + 2fr multi   1.00   .20
B44   SP8   50fr + 2fr multi   1.10   .20
    Nos. B38-B44 (7)   3.70   1.40

Souvenir Sheet
B45   Sheet of 2   2.00   1.75
  a.   SP8 40fr + 5fr multi   .90   .75
  b.   SP8 50fr + 5fr multi   1.00   .90

Visit of Pope Paul VI to Uganda, 7/31-8/2.

Virgin and Child, by Albrecht Dürer — SP9

Christmas (Paintings): 11fr+1fr, Madonna of the Eucharist, by Sandro Botticelli. 20fr+1fr, Holy Family, by El Greco.

1970, Dec. 14   Photo.   *Perf. 13½*
Gold Frame
B46   SP9   6.50fr + 1fr multi   .20   .20
B47   SP9   11fr + 1fr multi   .25   .20
B48   SP9   20fr + 1fr multi   .40   .20
  a.   Souv. sheet of 3, #B46-B48   .90   .90
    Nos. B46-B48,CB12-CB14 (6)   2.20   1.20

Nos. 376-378 Surcharged in Gold and Black

1971, Nov. 27
B49   A51   3fr + 1fr multi   .20   .20
B50   A51   5fr + 1fr multi   .20   .20
B51   A51   6fr + 1fr multi   .20   .20
  a.   Souvenir sheet of 3   .55   .55
    Nos. B49-B51,CB19-CB21 (6)   1.90   1.20

UNICEF, 25th anniv. #B51a contains 3 stamps similar to #B49-B51 with 2fr surtax each.

"La Polenta," by Pietro Longhi SP10

Designs: 3fr+1fr, Archangel Michael, Byzantine icon from St. Mark's 6fr+1fr, "Gossip," by Pietro Longhi. 11fr+1fr, "Diana's Bath," by Giovanni Batista Pittoni. All stamps inscribed UNESCO.

1971, Dec. 27

B52	SP10	3fr + 1fr gold & multi	.20	.20
B53	SP10	5fr + 1fr gold & multi	.20	.20
B54	SP10	6fr + 1fr gold & multi	.20	.20
B55	SP10	11fr + 1fr gold & multi	.30	.20
a.		Souvenir sheet of 4	.75	.50
		Nos. B52-B55,CB22-CB25 (8)	2.40	1.60

The surtax was for the UNESCO campaign to save the treasures of Venice. No. B55a contains 4 stamps similar to Nos. B52-B55, but with 2fr surtax. Sheet exists imperf.

Nos. 408-410 Surcharged "+1F" in Silver

1972, Dec. 12   **Photo.**   *Perf. 13½*

B56	A57	5fr + 1fr multi	.20	.20
B57	A57	10fr + 1fr multi	.25	.20
B58	A57	15fr + 1fr multi	.30	.20
a.		Souvenir sheet of 3	.75	.70
		Nos. B56-B58,CB26-CB28 (6)	2.10	1.20

Christmas 1972. No. B58a contains 3 stamps similar to Nos. B56-B58, but with 2fr surtax.

Nos. 441-443 Surcharged "+1F" in Silver

1973, Dec. 14   **Photo.**   *Perf. 13*

B59	A64	5fr + 1fr multi	.20	.20
B60	A64	10fr + 1fr multi	.20	.20
B61	A64	15fr + 1fr multi	.30	.20
a.		Souvenir sheet of 3	.65	.65
		Nos. B59-B61,CB29-CB31 (6)	2.00	1.20

Christmas 1973. No. B61a contains 3 stamps similar to Nos. B59-B61 with 2fr surtax each.

Christmas Type of 1974

1974, Dec. 2   **Photo.**   *Perf. 13*

B62	A70	5fr + 1fr multi	.20	.20
B63	A70	10fr + 1fr multi	.20	.20
B64	A70	15fr + 1fr multi	.30	.20
a.		Souvenir sheet of 3	.75	.50
		Nos. B62-B64,CB32-CB34 (6)	2.20	1.50

No. B64a contains 3 stamps similar to Nos. B62-B64 with 2fr surtax each.

Nos. 485-487 Surcharged "+ 1F" in Silver and Black

1975, Dec. 22   **Photo.**   *Perf. 13*
Pairs, #a.-b.

B65	A73	5fr + 1fr #485		.25
B66	A73	13fr + 1fr #486		.60
B67	A73	27fr + 1fr #487		1.00
c.		Souvenir sheet of 6		2.50
		Nos. B65-B67,CB35-CB37 (6)		5.15

Michelangelo Buonarroti (1475-1564), 500th birth anniversary. No. B67c contains 6 stamps similar to Nos. B65a-B67b with 2fr surcharge each.

Nos. 504-506 Surcharged "+1f" in Silver and Black

1976, Nov. 25   **Photo.**   *Perf. 13½*

B71	A76	5fr + 1fr multi		.20
B72	A76	13fr + 1fr multi		.25
B73	A76	27fr + 1fr multi		.40
a.		Souvenir sheet of 3		.85
		Nos. B71-B73,CB41-CB43 (6)		2.25

Christmas 1976. No. B73a contains 3 stamps similar to Nos. B71-B73 with 2fr surtax each.

Nos. 531-533 Surcharged "+1fr" in Silver and Black

1977   **Photo.**   *Perf. 14x13*

B74	A83	5fr + 1fr multi		.20
B75	A83	13fr + 1fr multi		.25
B76	A83	27fr + 1fr multi		.40
a.		Souvenir sheet of 3		.85
		Nos. B74-B76,CB44-CB46 (6)		2.25

Christmas 1977. No. B76a contains 3 stamps similar to Nos. B74-B76 with 2fr surtax each.

Christmas Type of 1979

1979, Feb.   **Photo.**   *Perf. 14x13*

B77	A86	13fr + 1fr multi	.25
B78	A86	17fr + 1fr multi	.30
B79	A86	27fr + 1fr multi	.40
B80	A86	31fr + 1fr multi	.50
B81	A86	40fr + 1fr multi	.60
		Nos. B77-B81 (5)	2.05

IYC Type of 1979

1979, July 19   **Photo.**   *Perf. 14*

B82		Sheet of 4	1.25 1.00
a.	A88	10fr + 2fr like #557	.20 .20
b.	A88	20fr + 2fr like #558	.25 .20
c.	A88	27fr + 2fr like #559	.30 .20
d.	A88	50fr + 2fr like #560	.55 .30

Christmas Type of 1979

1979, Dec. 10   **Photo.**   *Perf. 13½*

B83	A89	20fr + 1fr like #561	.30
B84	A89	27fr + 1fr like #562	.40
B85	A89	31fr + 1fr like #563	.50
B86	A89	40fr + 2fr like #564	.80
		Nos. B83-B86 (4)	2.00

Christmas Type of 1980

1981, Jan. 16   **Photo.**   *Perf. 13½x13*

B87	A92	10fr + 1fr like #579	.20
B88	A92	30fr + 1fr like #580	.30
B89	A92	40fr + 1fr like #581	.40
B90	A92	50fr + 1fr like #582	.50
		Nos. B87-B90 (4)	1.40

Christmas Type of 1983

1983, Nov. 2   **Litho.**   *Perf. 14½x13½*

B91	A97	10fr + 1fr like #607	.20
B92	A97	25fr + 1fr like #608	.40
B93	A97	30fr + 1fr like #609	.50
B94	A97	50fr + 1fr like #610	.75
		Nos. B91-B94 (4)	1.85

Christmas Type of 1984

1984, Dec. 15   *Perf. 13½*

B95	A101	10fr + 1fr like #629	.20
B96	A101	25fr + 1fr like #630	.40
B97	A101	30fr + 1fr like #631	.50
B98	A101	50fr + 1fr like #632	.75
		Nos. B95-B98 (4)	1.85

Multi-party Elections, 1st Anniv.
SP11   SP12

30fr+10fr, Pres. Buyoya handing Baton of Power to Pres. Ndadaye. 110fr+10fr, Pres. Ndadaye giving inauguration speech. 115fr+10fr, Arms, map of Burundi. 120fr+10fr, Warrior, flag of Burundi, trees, map of Burundi.

1994, Oct. 20   **Litho.**   *Perf. 15*

B99	SP11	30fr +10fr multi	.30
B100	SP11	110fr +10fr multi	.90
B101	SP12	115fr +10fr multi	.95
B102	SP12	120fr +10fr multi	1.00
		Nos. B99-B102 (4)	3.15

AIR POST STAMPS

Animal Type of Regular Issue

6fr, Zebra. 8fr, Cape buffalo (bubalis). 10fr, Impala. 14fr, Hippopotamus. 15fr, Defassa waterbuck. 20fr, Cheetah. 50fr, Elephant.

Unwmk.

1964, July 2   **Litho.**   *Perf. 14*
Size: 42x21mm, 21x42mm

C1	A9	6fr multi	.20	.20
C2	A9	8fr multi	.20	.20
C3	A9	10fr multi, vert.	.25	.20
C4	A9	14fr multi	.35	.20
C5	A9	15fr multi, vert.	.40	.20

Size: 53x32½mm

C6	A9	20fr multi	.60	.20
C7	A9	50fr multi	1.75	.40
		Nos. C1-C7 (7)	3.75	1.60

Bird Type of Regular Issue

Birds: 6fr, Secretary bird. 8fr, African anhinga. 10fr, African peacock. 14fr, Bee eater. 15fr, Yellow-billed stork. 20fr, Saddle-billed stork. 50fr, Abyssinian ground hornbill. 75fr, Martial eagle. 130fr, Lesser flamingo.

1965, June 10   **Litho.**   *Perf. 14*
Size: 26x43mm

C8	A14	6fr multi	.20	.20
C9	A14	8fr multi	.20	.20
C10	A14	10fr multi	.30	.20
C11	A14	14fr multi	.30	.20
C12	A14	15fr multi	.40	.20

Size: 33x53mm

C13	A14	20fr multi	.60	.20
C14	A14	50fr multi	1.25	.20
C15	A14	75fr multi	1.75	.25
C16	A14	130fr multi	3.00	.35
		Nos. C8-C16 (9)	8.00	2.00

For overprints see Nos. C35A-C35I.

Flower Type of Regular Issue

Flowers: 6fr, Dissotis. 8fr, Crossandra. 10fr, Ansellia. 14fr, Thunbergia. 15fr, Schizoglossum. 20fr, Gazania. 50fr, Protea. 75fr, Hibiscus. 130fr, Markhamia.

1966, Oct. 10   **Unwmk.**   *Perf. 13½*
Size: 31x31mm

C17	A17	6fr multi	.20	.20
C18	A17	8fr multi	.20	.20
C19	A17	10fr multi	.25	.20
C20	A17	14fr multi	.30	.20
C21	A17	15fr multi	.40	.20

Size: 39x39mm

C22	A17	20fr multi	.45	.20
C23	A17	50fr multi	1.10	.20
C24	A17	75fr multi	1.60	.20
C25	A17	130fr multi	2.50	.30
		Nos. C17-C25 (9)	7.00	1.95

For overprints see Nos. C27-C35.

Tapestry Type of Regular Issue
Souvenir Sheet

1966, Nov. 4   **Unwmk.**   *Perf. 13½*

C26	A18	Sheet of 7 (14fr)	1.50	1.00

See note after No. 158.

REPUBLIC
Nos. C17-C25 Overprinted

REPUBLIQUE DU BURUNDI

1967   **Litho.**   *Perf. 13½*
Size: 31x31mm

C27	A17	6fr multi	.20	.20
C28	A17	8fr multi	.25	.20
C29	A17	10fr multi	.25	.20
C30	A17	14fr multi	.50	.20
C31	A17	15fr multi	.50	.20

Size: 39x39mm

C32	A17	20fr multi	.70	.20
C33	A17	50fr multi	1.90	.50
C34	A17	75fr multi	3.00	.50
C35	A17	130fr multi	4.00	1.10
		Nos. C27-C35 (9)	11.30	3.30

Nos. C8-C16 Overprinted
"REPUBLIQUE / DU / BURUNDI" and Horizontal Bar

1967   **Litho.**   *Perf. 14*
Size: 26x43mm

C35A	A14	6fr multi	.20
C35B	A14	8fr multi	.20
C35C	A14	10fr multi	.20
C35D	A14	14fr multi	.30
C35E	A14	15fr multi	.50

Size: 33x53mm

C35F	A14	20fr multi	.75
C35G	A14	50fr multi	1.90
C35H	A14	75fr multi	3.00
C35I	A14	130fr multi	3.50
		Nos. C35A-C35I (9)	10.55

African Art Type of Regular Issue

10fr, Spirit of Bakutu figurine, Equatorial Africa. 14fr, Pearl throne of Sultan of the Bamum, Cameroun. 17fr, Bronze head of Mother Queen of Benin, Nigeria. 24fr, Statue of 109th Bakouba king, Kata-Mbula, Central Congo. 26fr, Baskets and lances, Burundi.

1967, June 5   **Photo.**   *Perf. 13½*

C36	A20	10fr gold & multi	.20	.20
C37	A20	14fr gold & multi	.20	.20
C38	A20	17fr gold & multi	.20	.20
C39	A20	24fr gold & multi	.25	.20
C40	A20	26fr gold & multi	.40	.20
		Nos. C36-C40 (5)	1.25	1.00

Boy Scout Type of Regular Issue

10fr, Scouts on hiking trip. 14fr, Cooking at campfire. 17fr, Lord Baden-Powell. 24fr, Boy Scout & Cub Scout giving Scout sign. 26fr, First aid.

1967, Aug. 9   *Perf. 13½*

C41	A21	10fr gold & multi	.20	.20
C42	A21	14fr gold & multi	.25	.20
C43	A21	17fr gold & multi	.30	.20
C44	A21	24fr gold & multi	.40	.20
C45	A21	26fr gold & multi	.70	.20
		Nos. C41-C45 (5)	1.85	1.00

A souvenir sheet of 2 contains one each of #C44-C45 and 2 labels in the designs of #208-209 with commemorative inscriptions was issued 1/8/68. Size: 100x100mm

Fish Type of Regular Issue

Designs: Various Tropical Fish

1967, Sept. 8   **Photo.**   *Perf. 13½*
Size: 50x23mm

C46	A19	6fr multi	.20	.20
C47	A19	8fr multi	.20	.20
C48	A19	10fr multi	.30	.20
C49	A19	14fr multi	.40	.20
C50	A19	15fr multi	.40	.20

Size: 58x27mm

C51	A19	20fr multi	.50	.20
C52	A19	50fr multi	1.25	.20
C53	A19	75fr multi	2.00	.20
C54	A19	130fr multi	3.25	.25
		Nos. C46-C54 (9)	8.50	1.85

Boeing 707 of Air Congo and ITY Emblem — AP1

Designs: 14fr, Boeing 727 of Sabena over lake. 17fr, Vickers VC10 of East African Airways over lake. 26fr, Boeing 727 of Sabena over airport.

1967, Nov. 3   **Photo.**   *Perf. 13*

C55	AP1	10fr blk, yel brn & sil	.20	.20
C56	AP1	14fr blk, org & sil	.20	.20
C57	AP1	17fr blk, brt bl & sil	.25	.20
C58	AP1	26fr blk, brt rose lil & sil	.35	.20
		Nos. C55-C58 (4)	1.00	.80

Opening of the jet airport at Bujumbura and for International Tourist Year, 1967.

Paintings Type of Regular Issue

Paintings: 17fr, Woman with Cat, by Renoir. 24fr, The Jewish Bride, by Rembrandt, horiz. 26fr, Pope Innocent X, by Velazquez.

1968, Mar. 29   **Photo.**   *Perf. 13½*

C59	A26	17fr multi	.35	.20
C60	A26	24fr multi	.45	.20
C61	A26	26fr multi	.60	.20
		Nos. C59-C61 (3)	1.40	.60

Issued in sheets of 6.

Space Type of Regular Issue

14fr, Moon Probe. 18fr, Russian astronaut walking in space. 25fr, Weather satellite. 40fr, American astronaut walking in space.

1968, May 15   **Photo.**   *Perf. 13½*
Size: 41x41mm

C62	A27	14fr sil & multi	.25	.20
C63	A27	18fr sil & multi	.30	.20
C64	A27	25fr sil & multi	.45	.20
C65	A27	40fr sil & multi	.70	.20
		Nos. C62-C65 (4)	1.70	.80

Butterfly Type of Regular Issue

Butterflies: 6fr, Teracolus annae. 8fr, Graphium ridleyanus. 10fr, Cymothoe. 14fr, Charaxes eupale. 15fr, Papilio bromius. 20fr, Papilio zenobia. 50fr, Salamis aethiops. 75fr, Danais chrysippus. 130fr, Salamis temora.

1968, Sept. 9   Photo.   Perf. 13½
Size: 38x42mm

C66	A28	6fr gold & multi	.20	.20
C67	A28	8fr gold & multi	.20	.20
C68	A28	10fr gold & multi	.35	.20
C69	A28	14fr gold & multi	.40	.20
C70	A28	15fr gold & multi	.50	.20

Size: 44x49mm

C71	A28	20fr gold & multi	.60	.20
C72	A28	50fr gold & multi	1.25	.20
C73	A28	75fr gold & multi	2.50	.20
C74	A28	130fr gold & multi	4.00	.20
		Nos. C66-C74 (9)	10.00	1.80

Painting Type of Regular Issue

Paintings: 17fr, The Letter, by Jean H. Fragonard. 26fr, Young Woman Reading Letter, by Jan Vermeer. 40fr, Lady Folding Letter, by Elisabeth Vigée-Lebrun. 50fr, Mademoiselle Lavergne, by Jean Etienne Liotard.

1968, Sept. 30   Photo.   Perf. 13½

C84	A29	17fr multi	.25	.20
C85	A29	26fr multi	.45	.20
C86	A29	40fr multi	.60	.20
C87	A29	50fr multi	.70	.20
		Nos. C84-C87 (4)	2.00	.80

Olympic Games Type

1968, Oct. 24

C88	A30	10fr Shot put	.20	.20
C89	A30	17fr Running	.25	.20
C90	A30	26fr Hammer throw	.40	.20
C91	A30	50fr Hurdling	.70	.20
C92	A30	75fr Broad jump	1.10	.30
		Nos. C88-C92 (5)	2.65	1.10

Christmas Type of 1968

Paintings: 10fr, Virgin and Child, by Correggio. 14fr, Nativity, by Federigo Baroccio. 17fr, Holy Family, by El Greco. 26fr, Adoration of the Magi, by Maino.

1968, Nov. 26   Photo.   Perf. 13½

C93	A31	10fr multi	.20	.20
C94	A31	14fr multi	.25	.20
C95	A31	17fr multi	.30	.20
C96	A31	26fr multi	.40	.20
a.		Souv. sheet of 4, #C93-C96	1.10	
		Nos. C93-C96 (4)	1.15	.80

For overprints see Nos. C100-C103.

Human Rights Flame, Hand and Globe — AP2

1969, Jan. 22

C97	AP2	10fr multi	.20	.20
C98	AP2	14fr multi	.25	.20
C99	AP2	26fr lil & multi	.40	.20
		Nos. C97-C99 (3)	.85	.60

International Human Rights Year, 1968.

Nos. C93-C96 Overprinted in Silver

1969, Feb. 17   Photo.

C100	A31	10fr multi	.20	.20
C101	A31	14fr multi	.30	.20
C102	A31	17fr multi	.35	.20
C103	A31	26fr multi	.50	.25
		Nos. C100-C103 (4)	1.35	.85

Man's 1st flight around the moon by the US spacecraft Apollo 8, Dec. 21-27, 1968.

Moon Landing Type of 1969

Designs: 26fr, Neil A. Armstrong leaving landing module. 40fr, Astronaut on moon. 50fr, Splashdown in the Pacific.

1969, Nov. 6   Photo.   Perf. 13½

C104	A38	26fr gold & multi	.50	.25
C105	A38	40fr gold & multi	.75	.40
C106	A38	50fr gold & multi	.90	.45
		Nos. C104-C106 (3)	2.15	1.10

Christmas Type of 1969

Paintings: 17fr, Madonna and Child, by Benvenuto da Garofalo. 26fr, Madonna and Child, by Jacopo Negretti. 50fr, Madonna and Child, by Il Giorgione. All horizontal.

1969, Dec. 2   Photo.

C107	A39	17fr gold & multi	.40	.20
C108	A39	26fr gold & multi	.50	.20
C109	A39	50fr gold & multi	.90	.30
a.		Souv. sheet of 3, #C107-C109	1.90	1.50
		Nos. C107-C109 (3)	1.80	.70

Insect Type of Regular Issue

Designs: Various Beetles and Weevils.

1970   Perf. 13½
Size: 46x32mm

C110	A40	6fr gold & multi	.20	.20
C111	A40	8fr gold & multi	.20	.20
C112	A40	10fr gold & multi	.20	.20
C113	A40	14fr gold & multi	.30	.20
C114	A40	15fr gold & multi	.35	.20

Size: 52x36mm

C115	A40	20fr gold & multi	1.00	.20
C116	A40	50fr gold & multi	2.00	.25
C117	A40	75fr gold & multi	3.00	.25
C118	A40	130fr gold & multi	3.75	.40
		Nos. C110-C118 (9)	11.00	2.10

Issued: #C110-C115, 1/20; $C116-C118, 2/27.

Easter Type of 1970

Stations of the Cross, by Juan de Aranoa y Carredano: 8fr, Jesus meets the women of Jerusalem. 10fr, Jesus falls a third time. 14fr, Jesus stripped. 15fr, Jesus nailed to the cross. 18fr, Jesus dies on the cross. 20fr, Descent from the cross. 50fr, Jesus laid in the tomb.

1970, Mar. 16   Photo.   Perf. 13½

C119	A41	8fr gold & multi	.20	.20
C120	A41	10fr gold & multi	.20	.20
C121	A41	14fr gold & multi	.25	.20
C122	A41	15fr gold & multi	.25	.20
C123	A41	18fr gold & multi	.30	.20
C124	A41	20fr gold & multi	.30	.20
C125	A41	50fr gold & multi	.70	.30
a.		Souv. sheet of 7, #C119-C125 + label	2.25	1.75
		Nos. C119-C125 (7)	2.20	1.50

EXPO '70 Type of Regular Issue
Souvenir Sheet

Designs: 40fr, Tower of the Sun, vert. 50fr, Flags of participating nations, vert.

1970, May 5   Photo.   Perf. 13½

C126		Sheet of 2	1.40	1.40
a.		A42 40fr multi	.50	.50
b.		A42 50fr multi	.60	.60

Rhinoceros Type of Regular Issue

Fauna: a, i, Camel. c, d, Dromedary. g, r, Okapi. f, m, Addax. j, o, Rhinoceros. l, p, Burundi cow (each animal in 2 different poses).

Map of the Nile: b, Delta and pyramids. e, dhow. h, Falls. k, Blue Nile and crowned crane. n, Victoria Nile and secretary bird. q, Lake Victoria and source of Nile on Mt. Gikizi. Continuous design.

1970, July 8   Photo.   Perf. 13½

C127		Sheet of 18	5.25	
a.-r.		A43 14fr any single	.30	.20

Publicizing the southernmost source of the Nile on Mt. Gikizi in Burundi.

UN Emblem and Headquarters, NYC — AP3

25th Anniv. of the UN (UN Emblem and): 11fr, Security Council and mural by Per Krohg. 26fr, Pope Paul VI and U Thant. 40fr, Flags in front of UN Headquarters, NYC.

1970, Oct. 23   Photo.   Perf. 13½

C128	AP3	7fr gold & multi	.20	.20
C129	AP3	11fr gold & multi	.20	.20
C130	AP3	26fr gold & multi	.40	.20
C131	AP3	40fr gold & multi	.60	.20
a.		Souvenir sheet of 2	1.10	.90
		Nos. C128-C131 (4)	1.40	.80

No. C131a contains 2 stamps similar to Nos. C130-C131 but without "Poste Aerienne." Exists imperf.

Bird Type of Regular Issue

8fr, 14fr, 30fr, vert.; 10fr, 20fr, 50fr, horiz.

1970   Photo.   Perf. 13½
Stamp size: 52x44mm

C132	A44	Block of 4	2.00	.20
a.		8fr Northern shrike	.50	.20
b.		8fr European starling	.50	.20
c.		8fr Yellow wagtail	.50	.20
d.		8fr Bank swallow	.50	.20
C133	A44	Block of 4	2.50	.20
a.		10fr Winter wren	.60	.20
b.		10fr Firecrest	.60	.20
c.		10fr Skylark	.60	.20
d.		10fr Crested lark	.60	.20
C134	A44	Block of 4	3.00	.25
a.		14fr Woodchat shrike	.75	.20
b.		14fr Common rock thrush	.75	.20
c.		14fr Black redstart	.75	.20
d.		14fr Ring ouzel	.75	.20
C135	A44	Block of 4	5.00	.35
a.		20fr European redstart	1.25	.20
b.		20fr Hedge sparrow	1.25	.20
c.		20fr Gray wagtail	1.25	.20
d.		20fr Meadow pipit	1.25	.20
C136	A44	Block of 4	7.00	.55
a.		30fr Eurasian hoopoe	1.75	.20
b.		30fr Pied flycatcher	1.75	.20
c.		30fr Great reed warbler	1.75	.20
d.		30fr Eurasian kingfisher	1.75	.20
C137	A44	Block of 4	11.00	.90
a.		50fr House martin	2.75	.20
b.		50fr Sedge warbler	2.75	.20
c.		50fr Fieldfare	2.75	.20
d.		50fr European Golden oriole	2.75	.20
		Nos. C132-C137 (6)	30.50	2.45

Queen Fabiola and King Baudouin of Belgium AP4

Designs: 20fr, Pres. Michel Micombero and King Baudouin. 40fr, Pres. Micombero and coats of arms of Burundi and Belgium.

1970, Nov. 28   Photo.   Perf. 13½

C140	AP4	6fr multicolored	.20	.20
C141	AP4	20fr multicolored	.45	.20
C142	AP4	40fr multicolored	.90	.30
a.		Souvenir sheet of 3	1.50	1.50
		Nos. C140-C142 (3)	1.55	.70

Visit of the King and Queen of Belgium. No. C142a contains 3 stamps similar to Nos. C140-C142, but without "Poste Aerienne." No. C142a exists imperf.

Easter Type of Regular Issue

Paintings of the Resurrection: 14fr, by Louis Borrassá. 17fr, Piero della Francesca. 26fr, Michel Wohlgemuth.

1971, Apr. 2   Photo.   Perf. 13½

C143	A49	14fr gold & multi	.20	.20
C144	A49	17fr gold & multi	.25	.20
C145	A49	26fr gold & multi	.30	.20
a.		Souv. sheet of 3, #C143-C145	.75	.75
		Nos. C143-C145 (3)	.75	.60

Easter 1971. No. C145a sheet exists imperf.

Animal Type of Regular Issue

1971   Photo.   Perf. 13½
Size: 44x44mm

C146		Strip of 4	1.50	.20
a.	A48	10fr Lion	.35	.20
b.	A48	10fr Cape buffalo	.35	.20
c.	A48	10fr Hippopotamus	.35	.20
d.	A48	10fr Giraffe	.35	.20
C147		Strip of 4	2.25	.25
a.	A48	14fr Hartebeest	.55	.20
b.	A48	14fr Black rhinoceros	.55	.20
c.	A48	14fr Zebra	.55	.20
d.	A48	14fr Leopard	.55	.20
C148		Strip of 4	3.00	.25
a.	A48	17fr Grant's gazelles	.75	.20
b.	A48	17fr Cheetah	.75	.20
c.	A48	17fr African white-backed vultures	.75	.20
d.	A48	17fr Johnston's okapi	.75	.20
C149		Strip of 4	3.50	.35
a.	A48	24fr Chimpanzee	.85	.20
b.	A48	24fr Elephant	.85	.20
c.	A48	24fr Spotted Hyenas	.85	.20
d.	A48	24fr Beisa	.85	.20
C150		Strip of 4	4.00	.40
a.	A48	26fr Gorilla	1.00	.20
b.	A48	26fr Gnu	1.00	.20
c.	A48	26fr Warthog	1.00	.20
d.	A48	26fr Cape hunting dog	1.00	.20
C151		Strip of 4	5.00	.55
a.	A48	31fr Sable antelope	1.25	.20
b.	A48	31fr Caracal lynx	1.25	.20
c.	A48	31fr Ostriches	1.25	.20
d.	A48	31fr Bongo	1.25	.20
		Nos. C146-C151 (6)	19.25	2.00

For overprint and surcharges see Nos. C152, CB15-C18.

No. C146 Overprinted in Gold and Black

1971, July 20   Photo.   Perf. 13½

C152		Strip of 4	.60	.20
a.	A48	10fr Lion	.20	.20
b.	A48	10fr Cape buffalo	.20	.20
c.	A48	10fr Hippopotamus	.20	.20
d.	A48	10fr Giraffe	.20	.20

Intl. Year Against Racial Discrimination.

Christmas Type of Regular Issue

Paintings of the Madonna and Child by: 14fr, Cima de Conegliano. 17fr, Fra Filippo Lippi. 31fr, Leonardo da Vinci.

1971, Nov. 2   Photo.   Perf. 13½

C153	A51	14fr red & multi	.30	.20
C154	A51	17fr red & multi	.35	.20
C155	A51	31fr red & multi	.50	.20
a.		Souv. sheet of 3, #C153-C155	1.10	1.10
		Nos. C153-C155 (3)	1.15	.60

Christmas 1971. No. C155a exists imperf. For surcharges see Nos. CB19-CB21.

Spacecraft Type of Regular Issue
Souvenir Sheet

1972, Jan. 15   Photo.   Perf. 13½

C156		Sheet of 6	1.50	1.00
a.	A52	6fr Lunar Orbiter	.20	.20
b.	A52	11fr Vostok	.20	.20
c.	A52	14fr Luna I	.20	.20
d.	A52	17fr Apollo 11 astronaut on moon	.25	.20
e.	A52	26fr Soyuz 11	.35	.20
f.	A52	40fr Lunar rover (Apollo 15)	.50	.25

Sapporo '72 Type of Regular Issue
Souvenir Sheet

Emblem and: 26fr, Snow scooter. 31fr, Downhill skiing. 50fr, Bobsledding.

1972, Feb. 3

C157		Sheet of 3	1.50	1.25
a.	A53	26fr silver & multi	.35	.25
b.	A53	31fr silver & multi	.40	.30
c.	A53	50fr silver & multi	.65	.40

Olympic Games Type of 1972

1972, July 24   Photo.   *Perf. 13½*

C158	A55	24fr Weight lifting	.35 .20
C159	A55	26fr Hurdles	.40 .20
C160	A55	31fr Discus	.50 .20
C161	A55	40fr Soccer	.60 .20
		Nos. C158-C161 (4)	1.85 .80

Independence Type of 1972

Designs: 15fr, Prince Rwagasore, Pres. Micombero, Burundi flag, drummers. 18fr, Rwagasore, Micombero, flag, map of Africa, globe. 27fr, Micombero, flag, globe.

1972, Aug. 24   Photo.   *Perf. 13½*

C162	A56	15fr gold & multi	.25 .20
C163	A56	18fr gold & multi	.30 .20
C164	A56	27fr gold & multi	.45 .20
a.		Souv. sheet of 3, #C162-C164	1.10 1.10
		Nos. C162-C164 (3)	1.00 .60

Christmas Type of 1972

Paintings of the Madonna and Child by: 18fr, Sebastiano Mainardi. 27fr, Hans Memling. 40fr, Lorenzo Lotto.

1972, Nov. 2   Photo.   *Perf. 13½*

C165	A57	18fr dk car & multi	.30 .20
C166	A57	27fr gold & multi	.40 .20
C167	A57	40fr gold & multi	.60 .20
a.		Souv. sheet of 3, #C165-C167	1.40 1.40
		Nos. C165-C167 (3)	1.30 .60

For surcharges see Nos. CB26-CB28.

Orchid Type of Regular Issue

1973, Jan. 18   Photo.   *Perf. 13½*
Size: 38x38mm

C168	A58	13fr Thelymitra pauciflora	.80 .20
C169	A58	14fr Miltassia	.80 .20
C170	A58	15fr Miltonia	.90 .20
C171	A58	18fr Platycoryne crocea	1.00 .20
C172	A58	20fr Cattleya trinaei	1.25 .20
C173	A58	27fr Eulophia cucullata	1.75 .20
C174	A58	36fr Cymbidium hamsey	2.25 .20
		Nos. C168-C174 (7)	8.75 1.40

African Exploration Type of 1973

Designs: 15fr, Livingstone writing his diary. 18fr, "Dr. Livingstone, I presume." 27fr, Livingstone and Stanley discussing expedition.

1973, Mar. 19   Photo.   *Perf. 13½*

C175	A59	15fr gold & multi	.25 .20
C176	A59	18fr gold & multi	.30 .20
C177	A59	27fr gold & multi	.45 .20
a.		Souv. sheet of 3	1.10 1.10
		Nos. C175-C177 (3)	1.00 .60

#C177a contains 3 stamps similar to #C175-C177, but without "Poste Aerienne."

Easter Type of 1973

Paintings: 15fr, Christ at the Pillar, by Guido Reni. 18fr, Crucifixion, by Mathias Grunewald. 27fr, Descent from the Cross, by Caravaggio.

1973, Apr. 10

C178	A60	15fr gold & multi	.30 .20
C179	A60	18fr gold & multi	.35 .20
C180	A60	27fr gold & multi	.50 .20
a.		Souv. sheet of 3, #C178-C180	1.25 1.25
		Nos. C178-C180 (3)	1.15 .60

INTERPOL Type of Regular Issue

Designs: 27fr, INTERPOL emblem and flag. 40fr, INTERPOL flag and emblem.

1973, May 19   Photo.   *Perf. 13½*

C181	A61	27fr gold & multi	.40 .20
C182	A61	40fr gold & multi	.50 .20

Copernicus Type of Regular Issue

Designs: 15fr, Copernicus (C183a), Earth, Pluto, and Jupiter. 18fr, Copernicus (No. C184a), Venus, Saturn, Mars. 27fr, Copernicus (No. C185a), Uranus, Neptune, Mercury. 36fr, Earth and various spacecraft.
a, UL. b, UR. c, LL. d, LR.

1973, July 27   Photo.   *Perf. 13½*

C183	A62	15fr Block of 4, #a.-d.	1.40 .30
C184	A62	18fr Block of 4, #a.-d.	1.60 .35
C185	A62	27fr Block of 4, #a.-d.	2.00 .50
C186	A62	36fr Block of 4, #a.-d.	2.75 .70
e.		Souv. sheet #C183-C186	7.00 7.00
		Nos. C183-C186 (4)	7.75 1.85

Flower-Butterfly Type of 1973

Designs: Each block of 4 contains 2 flower and 2 butterfly designs. The 10fr, 15fr, 24fr and 31fr have flower designs listed as "a" and "d" numbers, butterflies as "b" and "c" numbers; the arrangement is reversed for the 17fr and 26fr.

1973, Sept. 28   Photo.   *Perf. 13*
Stamp Size: 35x45mm

C187	A63	Block of 4	3.00 .40
a.		10fr Protea cynaroides	.75 .20
b.		10fr Precis octavia	.75 .20
c.		10fr Epiphora bauhiniae	.75 .20
d.		10fr Gazania longiscapa	.75 .20
C188	A63	Block of 4	4.00 .50
a.		14fr Kniphofia	1.00
b.		14fr Cymothoe coccinata	1.00
c.		14fr Nudaurelia zambesina	1.00
d.		14fr Freesia refracta	1.00
C189	A63	Block of 4	5.00 .60
a.		17fr Calotis eupompe	1.25
b.		17fr Narcissus	1.25
c.		17fr Cineraria hybrida	1.25
d.		17fr Cyrestis camillus	1.25
C190	A63	Block of 4	5.50 .50
a.		24fr Iris tingitana	1.25
b.		24fr Papilio demodocus	1.25
c.		24fr Catopsilia avelanda	1.25
d.		24fr Nerine sarniensis	1.25
C191	A63	Block of 4	6.00 .55
a.		26fr Hypolimnas dexithea	1.50
b.		26fr Zantedeschia tropicalis	1.50
c.		26fr Sandersonia aurantiaca	1.50
d.		26fr Drurya antimachus	1.50
C192	A63	Block of 4	7.00 .65
a.		31fr Nymphaea capensis	1.75
b.		31fr Pandoriana parisatis	1.75
c.		31fr Precis orythia	1.75
d.		31fr Pelargonium domestica	1.75
		Nos. C187-C192 (6)	30.50 3.20

Christmas Type of 1973

Virgin and Child by: 18fr, Raphael. 27fr, Pietro Perugino. 40fr, Titian.

1973, Nov. 19

C193	A64	18fr gold & multi	.30 .20
C194	A64	27fr gold & multi	.40 .20
C195	A64	40fr gold & multi	.60 .20
a.		Souv. sheet of 3, #C193-C195	1.40 1.40
		Nos. C193-C195 (3)	1.30 .60

For surcharges see Nos. CB239-CB31.

Soccer Type of Regular Issue

Designs: Various soccer scenes and cup.

1974, July 4   Photo.   *Perf. 13*

C196	A67	20fr gold & multi	.30
C197	A67	26fr gold & multi	.40
C198	A67	40fr gold & multi	.60
		Nos. C196-C198 (3)	1.30

For souvenir sheet see No. 459a.

UPU Type of 1974

#C199a, Flags over UPU Headquarters, Bern. #C199b, G.P.O., Usumbura. #C200a, Mailmen ("26F" in UR). #C200b, Mailmen ("26F" in UL). #C201a, UPU emblem. #C201b, Means of transportation. #C202a, Pigeon over globe showing Burundi. #C202b, Swiss flag, pigeon over map showing Bern.

1974, July 23

C199	A68	24fr Pair, #a.-b.	1.25
C200	A68	26fr Pair, #a.-b.	1.50
C201	A68	31fr Pair, #a.-b.	2.00
C202	A68	40fr Pair, #a.-b.	2.50
c.		Souv. sheet of #C199-C202	7.50
		Nos. C199-C202 (4)	7.25

Fish Type of 1974

1974, Sept. 9   Photo.   *Perf. 13*
Size: 35x35mm

C207	A66	Block of 4	1.50 .20
a.		10fr Haplochromis multicolor	.35 .20
b.		10fr Pantodon buchholzi	.35 .20
c.		10fr Tropheus duboisi	.35 .20
d.		10fr Distichodus sexfasciatus	.35 .20
C208	A66	Block of 4	1.75 .20
a.		14fr Pelmatochromis kribensis	.40 .20
b.		14fr Nannaethiops tritaeniatus	.40 .20
c.		14fr Polycentropsis abbreviata	.40 .20
d.		14fr Hemichromis bimaculatus	.40 .20
C209	A66	Block of 4	2.50 .20
a.		17fr Ctenopoma acutirostre	.60 .20
b.		17fr Synodontis angelicus	.60 .20
c.		17fr Tilapia melanopleura	.60 .20
d.		17frAphyosemion bivittatum	.60 .20
C210	A66	Block of 4	3.00 .30
a.		24fr Monodactylus argenteus	.75 .20
b.		24fr Zancius canescens	.75 .20
c.		24fr Pygoplites diacanthus	.75 .20
d.		24fr Cephalopholis argus	.75 .20
C211	A66	Block of 4	3.00 .35
a.		26fr Priacanthus arenatus	.75
b.		26fr Pomacanthus arcutus	.75
c.		26fr Scarus guacamaia	.75
d.		26fr Zeus faber	.75
C212	A66	Block of 4	4.00 .40
a.		31fr Lactophrys quadricornis	1.00
b.		31fr Balistes vetula	1.00
c.		31fr Acanthurus bahianus	1.00
d.		31fr Holocanthus ciliaris	1.00
		Nos. C207-C212 (6)	15.75 1.65

Christmas Type of 1974

Paintings of the Virgin and Child: 18fr, by Hans Memling. 27fr, by Filippino Lippi. 40fr, by Lorenzo di Gredi.

1974, Nov. 7   Photo.   *Perf. 13*

C213	A70	18fr gold & multi	.30 .25
C214	A70	27fr gold & multi	.40 .30
C215	A70	40fr gold & multi	.60 .50
a.		Souv. sheet of 3, #C213-C215	1.50 1.50
		Nos. C213-C215 (3)	1.30 1.00

Christmas 1974. Sheets of 20 stamps and one label. No. C215a exists imperf.

Apollo-Soyuz Type of 1975

1975, July 10   Photo.   *Perf. 13*

C216	A71	Block of 4	1.00
a.		27fr A.A. Leonov, V.N. Kubasov, Soviet flag	.25
b.		27fr Soyuz and Soviet flag	.25
c.		27fr Apollo and American flag	.25
d.		27fr Slayton, Brand, Stafford, American flag	.25
C217	A71	Block of 4	1.25
a.		40fr Apollo-Soyuz link-up	.30
b.		40fr Apollo, blast-off	.30
c.		40fr Soyuz, blast-off	.30
d.		40fr Kubasov, Leonov, Slayton, Brand, Stafford	.30

Nos. C216-C217 are printed in sheets of 32 containing 8 blocks of 4.

Animal Type of 1975

1975, Sept. 17   Photo.   *Perf. 13½*

C218		Strip of 4	1.00
a.	A72	10fr Addax	.25
b.	A72	10fr Roan antelope	.25
c.	A72	10fr Nyala	.25
d.	A72	10fr White rhinoceros	.25
C219		Strip of 4	1.25
a.	A72	14fr Mandrill	.30
b.	A72	14fr Eland	.30
c.	A72	14fr Salt's dik-dik	.30
d.	A72	14fr Thomson's gazelles	.30
C220		Strip of 4	1.50
a.	A72	17fr African small-clawed otter	.35
b.	A72	17fr Reed buck	.35
c.	A72	17fr Indian civet	.35
d.	A72	17fr Cape buffalo	.35
C221		Strip of 4	2.00
a.	A72	24fr White-tailed gnu	.50
b.	A72	24fr African wild asses	.50
c.	A72	24fr Black-and-white colobus monkey	.50
d.	A72	24fr Gerenuk	.50
C222		Strip of 4	2.25
a.	A72	26fr Dama gazelle	.55
b.	A72	26fr Black-backed jackal	.55
c.	A72	26fr Sitatungas	.55
d.	A72	26fr Zebra antelope	.55
C223		Strip of 4	2.75
a.	A72	31fr Fennec	.65
b.	A72	31fr Lesser kudus	.65
c.	A72	31fr Blesbok	.65
d.	A72	31fr Serval	.65
		Nos. C218-C223 (6)	10.75

Nos. C218-C219 Overprinted in Black and Silver with IWY Emblem and: "ANNEE INTERNATIONALE / DE LA FEMME"

1975, Nov. 19   Photo.   *Perf. 13½*

C224		Strip of 4	.60 .20
a.	A72	10fr Addax	.20 .20
b.	A72	10fr Roan antelope	.20 .20
c.	A72	10fr Nyala	.20 .20
d.	A72	10fr White rhinoceros	.20 .20
C225		Strip of 4	.80 .20
a.	A72	14fr Mandrill	.20 .20
b.	A72	14fr Eland	.20 .20
c.	A72	14fr Dik-dik	.20 .20
d.	A72	14fr Thomson's gazelles	.20 .20

International Women's Year 1975.

Nos. C222-C223 Overprinted in Black and Silver with UN Emblem and: "30ème ANNIVERSAIRE DES/ NATIONS UNIES"

1975, Nov. 19

C226		Strip of 4	1.60 .30
a.	A72	26fr Dama gazelle	.40 .20
b.	A72	26fr Wild dog	.40 .20
c.	A72	26fr Sitatungas	.40 .20
d.	A72	26fr Striped duiker	.40 .20
C227		Strip of 4	1.90 .30
a.	A72	31fr Fennec	.45 .20
b.	A72	31fr Lesser kudus	.45 .20
c.	A72	31fr Blesbok	.45 .20
d.	A72	31fr Serval	.45 .20

United Nations, 30th anniversary.

Michelangelo Type of 1975

Paintings from Sistine Chapel: #C228a, Zachariah. #C228b, Joel. #C229a, Erythrean Sybil. #C229b, Prophet Ezekiel. #C230a, Persian Sybil. #C230b, Prophet Jeremiah.

1975, Dec. 3   Photo.   *Perf. 13*

C228	A73	18fr Pair, #a.-b.	.70
C229	A73	31fr Pair, #a.-b.	1.25
C230	A73	40fr Pair, #a.-b.	1.60
c.		Souv. sheet of 6, #C228-C230	3.75
		Nos. C228-C230 (3)	3.55

Printed in sheets of 18 stamps + 2 labels. For surcharges see Nos. CB35-CB37.

Olympic Games Type, 1976

Designs (Olympic Games Emblem and): 18fr, Ski jump. 36fr, Slalom. 50fr, Ice hockey.

1976, Jan. 23   Photo.   *Perf. 14x13½*

C234	A74	18fr ol brn & multi	.30
C235	A74	36fr grn & multi	.70
C236	A74	50fr pur & multi	.90
a.		Souvenir sheet of 4	2.00
		Nos. C234-C236 (3)	1.90

No. C236a contains 4 stamps similar to Nos. 491-494, perf. 13½, inscribed "POSTE AERIENNE."

21st Olympic Games, Montreal, Canada, July 17-Aug. 1 — AP5

Montreal Games Emblem and: #C237a, C239a, C240b, High jump. #C238a, C239b, C240a, Athlete on rings. #C237a, C238b, C240c, Hurdles.

1976, May 3   Litho.   *Perf. 13½*

C237	AP5	27fr Pair, #a.-b.	.80
C238	AP5	31fr Pair, #a.-b.	1.10
C239	AP5	50fr Pair, #a.-b.	1.75
		Nos. C237-C239 (3)	3.65

Souvenir Sheet

C240	AP5	Sheet of 3, #a.-c.	1.75

Battle of Bunker Hill, by John Trumbull — AP6

Paintings: 26fr, Franklin, Jefferson and John Adams. 36fr, Declaration of Independence, by John Trumbull.

1976, July 16   Photo.   *Perf. 13*

C244	AP6	18fr Pair, #a.-b.	.70
C245	AP6	27fr Pair, #a.-b.	.90
C246	AP6	36fr Pair, #a.-b.	1.50
		Souv. sheet of 6, #C244-C246	3.25
		Nos. C244-C246 (3)	3.10

American Bicentennial.

Christmas Type of 1976

Paintings: 18fr, Virgin and Child with St. Anne, by Leonardo da Vinci. 31fr, Holy Family with Lamb, by Raphael. 40fr, Madonna of the Basket, by Correggio.

1976, Oct. 18   Photo.   *Perf. 13½*

C250	A76	18fr gold & multi	.25
C251	A76	31fr gold & multi	.45
C252	A76	40fr gold & multi	.60
a.		Souv. sheet of 3, #C250-C252	1.40
		Nos. C250-C252 (3)	1.30

Christmas 1976. Sheets of 20 stamps and descriptive label.
For surcharges see Nos. CB41-CB43.

A.G. Bell Type of 1977

10fr, A.G. Bell and 1st telephone. #C253a, 17fr, A.G. Bell speaking into microphone. #C253a, C255e, Satellites around globe, videophone. #C254a, Switchboard operator, c.1910, wall telephone. #C254b, 26fr, Intelsat satellite, modern & old telephones. #C255c, Intelsat, radar.

1977, May 17   Photo.   *Perf. 13*

C253	A78	18fr Pair, #a.-b.	.25
C254	A78	36fr Pair, #a.-b.	.50
C255		Sheet of 5	1.75 1.00
a.	A78	10fr multi	.20 .20
b.	A78	17fr multi	.25 .20
c.	A79	18fr multi	.25 .20
d.	A79	26fr multi	.40 .20
e.	A79	36fr multi	.50 .25

#C255c, C255e are air post stamps.

Animal Type of 1977

1977, Aug. 22   Photo.   *Perf. 14x14½*

C258		Strip of 4	1.00
a.	A80	9fr Buffon's kob	.25
b.	A80	9fr Marabous	.25
c.	A80	9fr Brindled gnu	.25
d.	A80	9fr River hog	.25
C259		Strip of 4	1.25
a.	A80	13fr Zebras	.30
b.	A80	13fr Shoebill	.30
c.	A80	13fr Striped hyenas	.30
d.	A80	13fr Chimpanzee	.30

C260	Strip of 4	2.75	
a.	A80 30fr Flamingos	.70	
b.	A80 30fr Nile Crocodiles	.70	
c.	A80 30fr Green mamba	.70	
d.	A80 30fr Greater kudus	.70	
C261	Strip of 4	3.50	
a.	A80 35fr Hyrax	.85	
b.	A80 35fr Cobra	.85	
c.	A80 35fr Jackals	.85	
d.	A80 35fr Verreaux's eagles	.85	
C262	Strip of 4	5.25	
a.	A80 54fr Honey badger	1.25	
b.	A80 54fr Harnessed antelopes	1.25	
c.	A80 54fr Secretary bird	1.25	
d.	A80 54fr Klipspringer	1.25	
C263	Strip of 4	6.25	
a.	A80 70fr African big-eared fox	1.50	
b.	A80 70fr Elephants	1.50	
c.	A80 70fr Vulturine guineafowl	1.50	
d.	A80 70fr Impalas	1.50	
	Nos. C258-C263 (6)	20.00	

UN Type of 1977

Designs (UN Stamps and): 24fr, UN buildings by night. 27fr, UN buildings and view of Manhattan. 35fr, UN buildings by day.

1977, Oct. 10   Photo.   Perf. 13½

C264	A82 Block of 4	1.90	
a.	24fr No. 77	.45	
b.	24fr No. 78	.45	
c.	24fr No. 40	.45	
d.	24fr No. 32	.45	
C265	A82 Block of 4	2.00	
a.	27fr No. 50	.50	
b.	27fr No. 21	.50	
c.	27fr No. 30	.50	
d.	27fr No. 44	.50	
C266	A82 Block of 4	3.25	
a.	35fr No. C6	.75	
b.	35fr No. 105	.75	
c.	35fr No. 4	.75	
d.	35fr No. 1	.75	
e.	Souvenir sheet of 3	1.40	
	Nos. C264-C266 (3)	7.15	

No. C266e contains 24fr in design of No. C265b, 27fr in design of No. C266a, 35fr in design of No. C264c.

Christmas Type of 1977

Designs: Paintings of the Virgin and Child.

1977, Oct. 31   Photo.   Perf. 14x13

C267	A83 18fr Master of Moulins	.30	
C268	A83 31fr Workshop of Lorenzo de Credi	.50	
C269	A83 40fr Palma Vecchio	.60	
a.	Souv. sheet of 3, #C267-C269	1.50	
	Nos. C267-C269 (3)	1.40	

Sheets of 24 stamps and descriptive label. For surcharges see Nos. CB44-CB46.

Christmas 1978 Type of 1979
Souvenir Sheet

1979, Feb.   Photo.   Perf. 14x13½

C270	Sheet of 5	2.00	
a.	A86 13fr like #543	.20	
b.	A86 17fr like #544	.25	
c.	A86 27fr like #545	.40	
d.	A86 31fr like #546	.50	
e.	A86 40fr like #547	.60	

Christmas Type of 1979
Souvenir Sheet

1979, Oct. 12   Perf. 13½

C271	Sheet of 4	2.00	1.25
a.	A89 20fr like #561	.30	.20
b.	A89 27fr like #562	.40	.25
c.	A89 31fr like #563	.50	.30
d.	A89 50fr like #564	.75	.40

Hill Type of 1979
Souvenir Sheet

1979, Nov. 6

C272	Sheet of 5	3.50	1.75
a.	A90 20fr like #565	.40	.20
b.	A90 27fr like #566	.55	.25
c.	A90 31fr like #567	.60	.30
d.	A90 40fr like #568	.80	.35
e.	A90 50fr like #569	1.00	.50

Bird Type of 1979

1979   Photo.   Perf. 13½x3

C273	A87 6fr like #548	.20	
C274	A87 13fr like #549	.40	
C275	A87 18fr like #550	.55	
C276	A87 26fr like #551	.75	
C277	A87 31fr like #552	1.00	
C278	A87 36fr like #553	1.10	
C279	A87 40fr like #554	1.25	
C280	A87 54fr like #555	1.60	
C281	A87 70fr like #556	2.00	
	Nos. C273-C281 (9)	8.85	

Olympic Type of 1980
Souvenir Sheet

1980, Oct. 24   Photo.   Perf. 13½

C282	Sheet of 9	4.25	
a.	A91 20fr like #570	.30	
b.	A91 20fr like #571	.30	
c.	A91 20fr like #572	.30	
d.	A91 30fr like #573	.45	
e.	A91 30fr like #574	.45	
f.	A91 30fr like #575	.45	
g.	A91 40fr like #576	.60	
h.	A91 40fr like #577	.60	
i.	A91 40fr like #578	.60	

Christmas Type of 1980
Souvenir Sheet

1980, Dec. 12   Photo.   Perf. 13½x13

C283	Sheet of 4	1.90	1.40
a.	A92 10fr like #579	.20	.20
b.	A92 30fr like #580	.45	.30
c.	A92 40fr like #581	.60	.40
d.	A92 45fr like #582	.65	.45

UPRONA Type of 1980
Souvenir Sheet

1980, Dec. 29   Perf. 14½x13½

C284	Sheet of 3	1.50	
a.	A93 10fr like #583	.20	
b.	A93 40fr like #584	.60	
c.	A93 45fr like #585	.65	

Christmas Type of 1983
Souvenir Sheet

1983, Oct. 3   Litho.   Perf. 14½x13½

C285	Sheet of 4	1.75	
a.	A97 10fr like #607	.20	
b.	A97 25fr like #608	.40	
c.	A97 30fr like #609	.45	
d.	A97 50fr like #610	.75	

UPU Congress Type of 1984
Souvenir Sheet

1984, July 14   Perf. 13x13½

C286	Sheet of 4	2.25	
a.	A99 10fr like #621	.20	
b.	A99 30fr like #622	.45	
c.	A99 35fr like #623	.50	
d.	A99 65fr like #624	1.00	

Summer Olympics Type of 1984
Souvenir Sheet

1984, Aug. 6   Perf. 13½x13

C287	Sheet of 4	2.25	
a.	A100 10fr like #625	.20	
b.	A100 30fr like #626	.45	
c.	A100 35fr like #627	.50	
d.	A100 65fr like #628	1.00	

Christmas Type of 1984
Souvenir Sheet

1984, Dec. 15   Perf. 13½

C288	Sheet of 4	1.75	
a.	A101 10fr like #629	.20	
b.	A101 25fr like #630	.40	
c.	A101 30fr like #631	.45	
d.	A101 50fr like #632	.75	

Flower Type of 1986 with Dull Lilac Border

1986, July 31   Photo.   Perf. 13x13½

C289	A102 70fr like #633	.80	
C290	A102 75fr like #634	.90	
C291	A102 80fr like #635	1.00	
C292	A102 85fr like #636	1.10	
C293	A102 100fr like #637	1.25	
C294	A102 150fr like #638	1.75	
	Nos. C289-C294 (6)	6.80	

Animals AP8

1992, June 2   Litho.   Perf. 14

C298	AP8 100fr M. nemestrina	1.50	
C299	AP8 115fr Equus grevyi	1.75	
C300	AP8 200fr Long horn cattle	3.00	
C301	AP8 220fr Pelecanus onocrotalus	3.50	
a.	Souvenir sheet of 4, #C298-C301, perf. 13½	10.00	
	Nos. C298-C301 (4)	9.75	

AIR POST SEMI-POSTAL STAMPS

Coin Type of Semi-Postal Issue

Designs (Coins of Various Denominations): 3fr+1fr, 11fr+1fr, 20fr+1fr, 50fr+1fr, Coat of Arms, reverse. 5fr+1fr, 14fr+1fr, 30fr+1fr, 100fr+1fr, King Mwambutsa IV, obverse.

Lithographed; Embossed on Gilt Foil

1965, Nov. 15   Imperf.

Diameter: 39mm

CB1	SP4 3fr + 1fr lt & dk vio	.20	.20
CB2	SP4 5fr + 1fr pale grn & red	.20	.20

Diameter: 45mm

CB3	SP4 11fr + 1fr org & lilac	.25	.25
CB4	SP4 14fr + 1fr red & emer	.30	.30

Diameter: 56mm

CB5	SP4 20fr + 1fr ultra & blk	.40	.40
CB6	SP4 30fr + 1fr dp org & mar	.60	.60

Diameter: 67mm

CB7	SP4 50fr + 1fr bl & vio bl	1.00	1.00
CB8	SP4 100fr + 1fr rose & dp cl	2.25	2.25
	Nos. CB1-CB8 (8)	5.20	5.20

Stamps are backed with patterned paper in blue, orange, and pink engine-turned design.

Red Cross Type of Semi-Postal Issue

Designs: 26fr+3fr, Laboratory. 40fr+3fr, Ambulance and thatched huts. 50fr+3fr, Red Cross nurse with patient.

1969, June 26   Photo.   Perf. 13½

CB9	SP7 26fr + 3fr multi	.40	.20
CB10	SP7 40fr + 3fr multi	.55	.20
CB11	SP7 50fr + 3fr multi	.65	.20
	Nos. CB9-CB11 (3)	1.60	.60

Perf. and imperf. souvenir sheets exist containing 3 stamps similar to Nos. CB9-CB11, but without "Poste Aerienne." Size: 90½x97mm.

Christmas Type of Semi-Postal Issue

Paintings: 14fr+3fr, Virgin and Child, by Velázquez. 26fr+3fr, Holy Family, by Joos van Cleve. 40fr+3fr, Virgin and Child, by Rogier van der Weyden.

1970, Dec. 14   Photo.   Perf. 13½

CB12	SP9 14fr + 3fr multi	.25	.20
CB13	SP9 26fr + 3fr multi	.45	.20
CB14	SP9 40fr + 3fr multi	.65	.20
a.	Souv. sheet of 3, #CB12-CB14	1.50	1.50
	Nos. CB12-CB14 (3)	1.35	.60

No. C147 Surcharged in Gold and Black

1971, Aug. 9   Photo.   Perf. 13½

CB15	Strip of 4	.80	.20
a.	A48 14fr+2fr Hartebeest	.20	.20
b.	A48 14fr+2fr Black rhinoceros	.20	.20
c.	A48 14fr+2fr Zebra	.20	.20
d.	A48 14fr+2fr Leopard	.20	.20

UNESCO campaign against illiteracy.

No. C148 Surcharged in Gold and Black

1971, Aug. 9

CB16	Strip of 4	1.00	.20
a.	A48 17fr+1fr Grant's gazelles	.25	.20
b.	A48 17fr+1fr Cheetah	.25	.20
c.	A48 17fr+1fr African white-backed vultures	.25	.20
d.	A48 17fr+1fr Johnston's okapi	.25	.20

International help for refugees.

Nos. C150-C151 Surcharged in Black and Gold

a

b

1971, Aug. 16

CB17	Strip of 4	2.25	.45
a.	A48(a) 26fr+1fr Gorilla	.55	.20
b.	A48(a) 26fr+1fr Gnu	.55	.20
c.	A48(a) 26fr+1fr Warthog	.55	.20
d.	A48(a) 26fr+1fr Cape hunting dog	.55	.20
CB18	Strip of 4	3.00	.60
a.	A48(b) 31fr+1fr Sable antelope	.75	.20
b.	A48(b) 31fr+1fr Caracal lynx	.75	.20
c.	A48(b) 31fr+1fr Ostriches	.75	.20
d.	A48(b) 31fr+1fr Bongo	.75	.20

75th anniv. of modern Olympic Games (#CB17); Olympic Games, Munich, 1972 (#CB18).

Nos. C153-C155 Surcharged

1971, Nov. 27   Photo.   Perf. 13½

CB19	A51 14fr + 1fr multi	.30	.20
CB20	A51 24fr + 1fr multi	.40	.20
CB21	A51 31fr + 1fr multi	.60	.20
	Nos. CB19-CB21 (3)	1.30	.60

25th anniv. of UNICEF.

Casa D'Oro, Venice SPAP1

Views in Venice: 17fr+1fr, Doge's Palace. 24fr+1fr, Church of Sts. John and Paul. 31fr+1fr, Doge's Palace and Piazzetta at Feast of Ascension, by Canaletto.

1971, Dec. 27

CB22	SPAP1 10fr + 1fr multi	.20	.20
CB23	SPAP1 17fr + 1fr multi	.30	.20
CB24	SPAP1 24fr + 1fr multi	.45	.20
CB25	SPAP1 31fr + 1fr multi	.55	.20
a.	Souvenir sheet of 4	1.50	1.50
	Nos. CB22-CB25 (4)	1.50	.80

Surtax for the UNESCO campaign to save the treasures of Venice. No. CB25a contains 4 stamps similar to Nos. CB22-CB25, but with 2fr surtax.

Nos. C165-C167, C193-C195
Surcharged "+1F" in Silver

1972, Dec. 12   Photo.   Perf. 13½

CB26	A57 18fr + 1fr multi	.30	.20
CB27	A57 27fr + 1fr multi	.45	.20
CB28	A57 40fr + 1fr multi	.60	.20
a.	Souvenir sheet of 3	1.50	1.50
	Nos. CB26-CB28 (3)	1.35	.60

Christmas 1972. No. CB28a contains 3 stamps similar to Nos. CB26-CB28 but with 2fr surtax.

1973, Dec. 14   Photo.   Perf. 13

CB29	A64 18fr + 1fr multi	.30	.20
CB30	A64 27fr + 1fr multi	.40	.20
CB31	A64 40fr + 1fr multi	.60	.20
a.	Souvenir sheet of 3	1.50	1.50
	Nos. CB29-CB31 (3)	1.30	.60

Christmas 1973. No. CB31 contains 3 stamps similar to Nos. CB29-CB31 with 2fr surtax each.

Christmas Type of 1974

1974, Dec. 2   Photo.   Perf. 13

CB32	A70 18fr + 1fr multi	.30	.20
CB33	A70 27fr + 1fr multi	.50	.30
CB34	A70 40fr + 1fr multi	.70	.40
a.	Souvenir sheet of 3	1.75	1.75
	Nos. CB32-CB34 (3)	1.50	.90

Christmas 1974. No. CB34a contains 3 stamps similar to Nos. CB32-CB34 with 2fr surtax.

Nos. C228-C230 Surcharged "+ 1F" in Silver and Black

1975, Dec. 22   Photo.   Perf. 13

CB35	A73 18fr +1fr Pair, #a-b	.70	
CB36	A73 31fr +1fr Pair, #a-b	1.10	
CB37	A73 40fr +1fr Pair, #a-b	1.50	
c.	Souvenir sheet of 6	4.25	
	Nos. CB35-CB37 (3)	3.30	

Michelangelo Buonarroti (1475-1564). No. CB37c contains 6 stamps similar to Nos. CB35-CB37 with 2fr surtax each.

Nos. C250-C252 Surcharged "+1f" in Silver and Black

1976, Nov. 25   Photo.   Perf. 13½

CB41	A76 18fr + 1fr multi	.30	
CB42	A76 31fr + 1fr multi	.50	
CB43	A76 40fr + 1fr multi	.60	
a.	Souvenir sheet of 3	1.50	
	Nos. CB41-CB43 (3)	1.40	

Christmas 1976. No. CB43a contains 3 stamps similar to Nos. CB41-CB43 with 2fr surtax each.

Nos. C267-C269 Surcharged "+1fr" in Silver and Black

1977   Photo.   Perf. 14x13

CB44	A83 18fr + 1fr multi	.30	
CB45	A83 31fr + 1fr multi	.50	
CB46	A83 40fr + 1fr multi	.60	
a.	Souvenir sheet of 3	1.50	
	Nos. CB44-CB46 (3)	1.40	

Christmas 1977. No. CB46a contains 3 stamps similar to Nos. CB44-CB46 with 2fr surtax each.

Christmas 1978 Type
Souvenir Sheet

1979, Feb.   Photo.   Perf. 14x13

CB47	Sheet of 5	3.00	
a.	A86 13fr + 2fr multi	.30	
b.	A86 17fr + 2fr multi	.35	
c.	A86 27fr + 2fr multi	.55	
d.	A86 31fr + 2fr multi	.70	
e.	A86 40fr + 2fr multi	.85	

Christmas Type of 1979
Souvenir Sheet

1979, Dec. 10   Photo.   Perf. 13½

CB48	Sheet of 4	2.75	
a.	A89 20fr + 2fr like #561	.45	
b.	A89 27fr + 2fr like #562	.55	
c.	A89 31fr + 2fr like #563	.70	
d.	A89 50fr + 2fr like #564	1.00	

Christmas Type of 1980
Souvenir Sheet

1981, Jan. 16   Photo.   Perf. 13½x13

CB49	Sheet of 4	2.50	
a.	A92 10fr + 2fr like #579	.20	
b.	A92 20fr + 2fr like #580	.55	
c.	A92 40fr + 2fr like #581	.75	
d.	A92 50fr + 2fr like #582	.90	

Christmas Type of 1983
Souvenir Sheet

1983, Nov. 2   Litho.   Perf. 14½x13½

CB50	Sheet of 4	1.90	
a.	A97 10fr + 2fr like #607	.20	
b.	A97 25fr + 2fr like #608	.40	
c.	A97 30fr + 2fr like #609	.50	
d.	A97 50fr + 2fr like #610	.75	

Christmas Type of 1984
Souvenir Sheet

1984, Dec. 15   Perf. 13½

CB51	Sheet of 4	1.90	
a.	A101 10fr + 2fr like #629	.20	
b.	A101 25fr + 2fr like #630	.40	
c.	A101 30fr + 2fr like #631	.50	
d.	A101 50fr + 2fr like #632	.75	

BUSHIRE

bü-'shir

LOCATION — On Persian Gulf

Bushire is a Persian port which British troops occupied Aug. 8, 1915.

20 Chahis (or Shahis) = 1 Kran
10 Krans = 1 Toman

Watermark

Wmk. 161 - Lion

ISSUED UNDER BRITISH OCCUPATION

Basic Iranian Designs

Shah Ahmed — A32

Imperial Crown — A33

King Darius, Ahura-Mazda Overhead A34

Ruins of Persepolis A35

Iranian Stamps of 1911-13 Overprinted in Black

Perf. 11½, 11½x11

1915, Aug. 15   Typo. & Engr.

N1	A32	1c green & org	27.50	30.00
N2	A32	2c red & sepia	27.50	27.50
N3	A32	3c gray brn & grn	32.50	40.00
N4	A32	5c brown & car	300.00	300.00
N5	A32	6c green & red brn	26.00	22.50
N6	A32	9c yel brn & vio	27.50	30.00
a.		Double overprint		
N7	A32	10c red & org brn	30.00	32.50
N8	A32	12c grn & ultra	37.50	40.00
N9	A32	1k ultra & car	52.50	27.50
a.		Double overprint	5,250.	
N10	A32	24c vio & grn	52.50	40.00
N11	A32	2k grn & red vio	175.00	140.00
N12	A32	3k vio & blk	150.00	160.00

N13	A32	5k red & ultra	82.50	75.00
N14	A32	10k ol bis & cl	75.00	75.00
		Nos. N1-N14 (14)	1,096.	1,040.

Nos. N1-N14, except No. N4, exist without period after "Occupation." This variety sells for more.
Forged overprints exist of Nos. N1-N29.
The Bushire overprint exists on Iran No. 537 but is considered a forgery.

On Iranian Stamps of 1915
Perf. 11, 11½

1915, Sept.   Wmk. 161

N15	A33	1c car & indigo	350.	350.
N16	A33	2c blue & car	5,250.	8,500.
N17	A33	3c dk grn	375.	400.
N18	A33	5c red	4,500.	4,750.
N19	A33	6c ol grn & car	3,500.	4,000.
N20	A33	9c yel brn & vio	500.	525.
N21	A33	10c bl grn & yel brn	800.	900.
N22	A33	12c ultra	950.	1,250.
N23	A34	1k sil, yel brn & gray	350.	375.
N24	A33	24c yel brn & dk brn	450.	400.
N25	A34	2k sil, bl & rose	300.	350.
N26	A34	3k sil, vio & brn	450.	475.
N27	A34	5k sil, brn & grn	425.	450.
a.		Inverted overprint		10,000.
N28	A35	1t gold, pur & blk	350.	400.
N29	A35	3t gold, cl & red brn	2,500.	2,750.

Persia resumed administration of Bushire post office Oct. 16, 1915.

. . . .

Hagner Style Stock Pages

Stock pages to accommodate every size stamp safely and give you all kinds of flexibility. Use them to store stamps before you put them in your album. Ideal for the topical or specialist collector who requires various page styles to store a complete collection.

- Flexible storage system meets highest philatelic standards.
- Black background makes for beautiful stamp presentation.
- Quick and easy. No need to cut mounts.
- Clamping strips use pull away/snap back principle.
- Three-hole punch fits all standard three ring binders.
- Safe, philatelically sound materials are distortion free and are 100% free of plasticizers.
- 9 different 8 1/2 by 11 inch page formats hold every size stamp safely.

. . . .

Scott Blank Specialty and National Pages with Printed Borders

- Special high-quality paper developed exclusively for Scott.
- Eliminates feathering and bleed-through when you use India ink to make your own write-ups.
- Use your favorite Rapidograph®-type pens and inks or typewriter.

Vol. 1 Number Additions, Deletions & Changes

United States

Number in 2002 Catalogue	Number in 2003 Catalogue
new	73e
73e	73f
73f	73g
new	146c
146c	146d
new	444a
new	504b
new	530c
new	911a
new	912a
new	917a
new	918a
new	921a
1361a	1361b
new	1394b
new	1394c
new	1424a
new	1433b
new	1478a
new	1525b
new	1570d
new	1689t
new	1716a
new	1816a
new	1869f
new	2004a
new	2019b
new	2020a
new	2145d
new	2177d
new	2219l
new	2224a
new	2343b
new	2478a
new	2484c
2485c	deleted
new	2485c
new	2489b
new	2500b
new	2618f
new	2630a
new	2636b
new	2636c
new	2721a
new	2818a
new	2872d
new	2877b
new	2911a
new	2915Aj
new	2920i
new	3052i
new	3052Eg
new	3052Eh
new	3058a
new	3127c
new	3228a
new	3259a
new	3280a
new	3280b
new	3411c
new	3412b
new	3412c
new	3413c
new	3413d
new	3451d
new	3453a
new	3483d
new	3492c
new	3496b
new	3523a
C74a	deleted
new	C81b
new	C135a
new	4LB7a
new	6LB6
new	U312a
new	W480a
new	U502c
new	U502d
new	U520D
new	U595c
new	U642b
new	U642c
new	UC1a
new	R54f
new	R286a

United States

Number in 2002 Catalogue	Number in 2003 Catalogue
new	RW29a

Hawaii

31	31a
31a	31

Philippines

new	240c
new	245a
new	267a

Afghanistan

new	196b
new	203a

Albania

1899	1901
1900	1902
1901	1903
1902	1899
1903	1904
1904	1900
new	J39a

Andorra (Spanish)

new	28a
new	34A

Angola

4a	deleted

Anguilla

1005	1010a
1005a	1005
1005b	1006
1005c	1007
1005d	1008
1005e	1009
1005f	1010
1006	1011
1007	1012
1008	1013
1009	1014
1010	1015
1011	1016

Antigua

2493 (Oct. Update)	2492
2494 (Oct. Update)	2493

Argentina

7Fk	7Fq
45	45a
45a	45
54	54a
54a	54
footnoted	1027a
footnoted	1029a
footnoted	1108a
footnoted	1109a
footnoted	1179a

Australian States

Queensland

new	5a
new	8a
new	38a
46a	deleted
new	49G
new	49H
84a	90a

Australia

new	147a
new	151a
1198	1183b
1406	Deleted
1407	Deleted
1408	Deleted
1409	Deleted
1410	Deleted
1411	Deleted
1412	Deleted
1413	Deleted
1414	Deleted

Australia

Number in 2002 Catalogue	Number in 2003 Catalogue
1415	Deleted
1416	Deleted
1417	Deleted
1418	Deleted
new	J10b
new	J11a
new	J11b
new	J12a
new	J13a
new	J14b
new	J17a
new	J18b
new	J19a
new	J40a
new	J41a
new	J44a
new	M3a

Austria

new	J35d
new	J36c
new	J38c
new	J40c

Azores

new	24b

Barbados

new	12B

Belgium

Q7a	deleted
Q7b	deleted
Q9a	deleted
Q9b	deleted
Q10a	deleted
Q11a	deleted
Q11b	deleted
Q12a	deleted
Q14a	deleted
Q14b	deleted

Benin

C408	deleted
C448	deleted

Brazil

83a	deleted
104	104c
104c	104
158	158a
158a	158

British East Africa

95b	deleted
new	97a
98a	deleted

British Honduras

new	30a

Burkina Faso

1120A	1120G
1120B	1120H

scott**mounts**

For stamp presentation unequaled in beauty and clarity, insist on ScottMounts. Made of 100% inert poly-styrol foil, ScottMounts protect your stamps from the harmful effects of dust and moisture. Available in your choice of clear or black backs, ScottMounts are center-split across the back for easy insertion of stamps and feature crystal clear mount faces. Double layers of gum assure stay-put bonding on the album page. Discover the quality and value ScottMounts have to offer. ScottMounts are available from your favorite stamp dealer or direct from:

Discover the quality and value ScottMounts have to offer.
For a complete list of ScottMount sizes or a free sample pack call or write Scott Publishing Co.

Dies of British Colonial Stamps

DIE A

DIE B

DIE I

DIE II

DIE A:
1. The lines in the groundwork vary in thickness and are not uniformly straight.
2. The seventh and eighth lines from the top, in the groundwork, converge where they meet the head.
3. There is a small dash in the upper part of the second jewel in the band of the crown.
4. The vertical color line in front of the throat stops at the sixth line of shading on the neck.

DIE B:
1. The lines in the groundwork are all thin and straight.
2. All the lines of the background are parallel.
3. There is no dash in the upper part of the second jewel in the band of the crown.
4. The vertical color line in front of the throat stops at the eighth line of shading on the neck.

DIE I:
1. The base of the crown is well below the level of the inner white line around the vignette.
2. The labels inscribed "POSTAGE" and "REVENUE" are cut square at the top.
3. There is a white "bud" on the outer side of the main stem of the curved ornaments in each lower corner.
4. The second (thick) line below the country name has the ends next to the crown cut diagonally.

DIE Ia.	DIE Ib.
1 as die II.	1 and 3 as die II.
2 and 3 as die I.	2 as die I.

DIE II:
1. The base of the crown is aligned with the underside of the white line around the vignette.
2. The labels curve inward at the top inner corners.
3. The "bud" has been removed from the outer curve of the ornaments in each corner.
4. The second line below the country name has the ends next to the crown cut vertically.

Wmk. 1
Crown and C C

Wmk. 2
Crown and C A

Wmk. 3
Multiple Crown and C A

Wmk. 4
Multiple Crown and Script C A

Wmk. 4a

Wmk. 314
St. Edward's Crown and C A Multiple

Wmk. 373

Wmk. 384

British Colonial and Crown Agents Watermarks

Watermarks 1 to 4, 314, 373, and 384, common to many British territories, are illustrated here to avoid duplication.

The letters "CC" of Wmk. 1 identify the paper as having been made for the use of the Crown Colonies, while the letters "CA" of the others stand for "Crown Agents." Both Wmks. 1 and 2 were used on stamps printed by De La Rue & Co.

Wmk. 3 was adopted in 1904; Wmk. 4 in 1921; Wmk. 314 in 1957; Wmk. 373 in 1974; and Wmk. 384 in 1985.

In Wmk. 4a, a non-matching crown of the general St. Edwards type (bulging on both sides at top) was substituted for one of the Wmk. 4 crowns which fell off the dandy roll. The non-matching crown occurs in 1950-52 printings in a horizontal row of crowns on certain regular stamps of Johore and Seychelles, and on various postage due stamps of Barbados, Basutoland, British Guiana, Gold Coast, Grenada, Northern Rhodesia, St. Lucia, Swaziland and Trinidad and Tobago. A variation of Wmk. 4a, with the non-matching crown in a horizontal row of crown-CA-crown, occurs on regular stamps of Bahamas, St. Kitts-Nevis and Singapore.

Wmk. 314 was intentionally used sideways, starting in 1966. When a stamp was issued with Wmk. 314 both upright and sideways, the sideways varieties usually are listed also — with minor numbers. In many of the later issues, Wmk. 314 is slightly visible.

Wmk. 373 is usually only faintly visible.

Illustrated Identifier

This section pictures stamps or parts of stamp designs that will help identify postage stamps that do not have English words on them.

Many of the symbols that identify stamps of countries are shown here as well as typical examples of their stamps.

See the Index and Identifier on the previous pages for stamps with inscriptions such as "sen," "posta," "Baja Porto," "Helvetia," "K.S.A.," etc.

Linn's Stamp Identifier is now available. The 144 pages include more 2,000 inscriptions and over 500 large stamp illustrations. Available from Linn's Stamp News, P.O. Box 29, Sidney, OH 45365-0029.

1. HEADS, PICTURES AND NUMERALS

GREAT BRITAIN

Great Britain stamps never show the country name, but, except for postage dues, show a picture of the reigning monarch.

Victoria

Edward VII   George V   Edward VIII

George VI

Elizabeth II

Some George VI and Elizabeth II stamps are surcharged in annas, new paisa or rupees. These are listed under Oman.

Silhouette (sometimes facing right, generally at the top of stamp)

The silhouette indicates this is a British stamp. It is not a U.S. stamp.

VICTORIA

Queen Victoria

INDIA
Other stamps of India show this portrait of Queen Victoria and the words "Service" and "Annas."

AUSTRIA

YUGOSLAVIA

(Also BOSNIA & HERZEGOVINA if imperf.)

BOSNIA & HERZEGOVINA

Denominations also appear in top corners instead of bottom corners.

HUNGARY

Another stamp has posthorn facing left

BRAZIL

AUSTRALIA

Kangaroo and Emu

GERMANY
Mecklenburg-Vorpommern

SWITZERLAND

2. ORIENTAL INSCRIPTIONS

CHINA

Any stamp with this one character is from China (Imperial, Republic or People's Republic). This character appears in a four-character overprint on stamps of Manchukuo. These stamps are local provisionals, which are unlisted. Other overprinted Manchukuo stamps show this character, but have more than four characters in the overprints. These are listed in People's Republic of China.

Some Chinese stamps show the Sun.

Most stamps of Republic of China show this series of characters.

Stamps with the China character and this character are from People's Republic of China.

Calligraphic form of People's Republic of China

Chinese stamps without China character

REPUBLIC OF CHINA

PEOPLE'S REPUBLIC OF CHINA

Mao Tse-tung

MANCHUKUO

Temple   Emperor Pu-Yi

The first 3 characters are common to many Manchukuo stamps.

The last 3 characters are common to other Manchukuo stamps.

Orchid Crest

Manchukuo stamp without these elements

JAPAN

Chrysanthemum Crest   Country Name

Japanese stamps without these elements

The number of characters in the center and the design of dragons on the sides will vary.

RYUKYU ISLANDS

Country Name

PHILIPPINES
(Japanese Occupation)

Country Name

NORTH BORNEO
(Japanese Occupation)

Indicates Japanese   Country
Occupation   Name

MALAYA
(Japanese Occupation)

Indicates Japanese Occupation   Country Name

BURMA
(Japanese Occupation)

Indicates Japanese Occupation   Country Name

Other Burma Japanese Occupation stamps without these elements

Burmese Script

KOREA

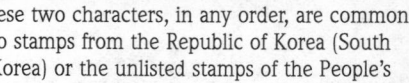

These two characters, in any order, are common to stamps from the Republic of Korea (South Korea) or the unlisted stamps of the People's Democratic Republic of Korea (North Korea).

This series of four characters can be found on the stamps of both Koreas.

Yin Yang appears on some stamps.

Indicates Republic of Korea (South Korea)

South Korean postage stamps issed after 1952 do not show currency expressed in Latin letters. Stamps wiith "HW," "HWAN," "WON," "WN," "W" or "W" with two lines through it, if not illustrated in listings of stamps before this date, are revenues. North Korean postage stamps do not have currency expressed in Latin letters.

THAILAND

Country Name

King Chulalongkorn

King Prajadhipok and
Chao P'ya Chakri

3. CENTRAL AND EASTERN ASIAN INSCRIPTIONS

INDIA - FEUDATORY STATES

Alwar   Bhor

Bundi

Similar stamps come with
different designs in corners
and differently drawn daggers
(at center of circle).

Dhar   Faridkot

Hyderabad

Similar stamps exist with straight line frame around stamp, and also with different central design which is inscribed "Postage" or "Post & Receipt."

Indore   Jhalawar

A similar stamp has
the central figure in
an oval.

Nandgaon

Nowanuggur

Poonch

Similar stamps exist
in various sizes

Rajpeepla   Soruth

BANGLADESH

Country Name

NEPAL

Similar stamps are smaller, have squares in upper corners and have five or nine characters in central bottom panel.

TANNU TUVA   **ISRAEL**

GEORGIA

This inscription is found on other pictorial stamps.

Country Name

ARMENIA

The four characters are found somewhere on pictorial stamps. On some stamps only the middle two are found.

4. AFRICAN INSCRIPTIONS

ETHIOPIA

5. ARABIC INSCRIPTIONS

AFGHANISTAN

Many early Afghanistan stamps show Tiger's head, many of these have ornaments protruding from outer ring, others show inscriptions in black.

Arabic Script

Mosque Gate & Crossed Cannons
The four characters are found somewhere
on pictorial stamps. On some stamps only
the middle two are found.

BAHRAIN

EGYPT

Postage

INDIA - FEUDATORY STATES

Jammu & Kashmir

Text and thickness of
ovals vary. Some stamps
have flower devices
in corners.

India-Hyderabad

IRAN

Country Name

Royal Crown

Lion with Sword

Symbol

IRAQ

JORDAN

LEBANON

Similar types have
denominations at top and
slightly different design.

LIBYA

Country Name in various styles

Other Libya stamps show Eagle and Shield (head
facing either direction) or Red, White and Black
Shield (with or without eagle in center).

SAUDI ARABIA

Tughra (Central design)

Palm Tree and Swords

SYRIA

THRACE	YEMEN

PAKISTAN

PAKISTAN - BAHAWALPUR

Country Name in top panel, star and crescent

TURKEY

Star & Crescent is a device found on many Turkish stamps, but is also found on stamps from other Arabic areas (see Pakistan-Bahawalpur)

Tughra (similar tughras can be found on stamps of Turkey in Asia, Afghanistan and Saudi Arabia)

Mohammed V

Mustafa Kemal

Plane, Star and Crescent

TURKEY IN ASIA

Other Turkey in Asia pictorials show star & crescent.
Other stamps show tughra shown under Turkey.

6. GREEK INSCRIPTIONS

GREECE

Country Name in various styles
(Some Crete stamps overprinted with the Greece country name are listed in Crete.)

Lepta

Drachma   Drachmas   Lepton

Abbreviated Country Name

Other forms of Country Name

No country name

CRETE

Country Name

These words are on other stamps

Grosion

Crete stamps with a surcharge that have the year "1922" are listed under Greece.

EPIRUS   IONIAN IS.

Country Name

---

7. CYRILLIC INSCRIPTIONS

RUSSIA

Postage Stamp

Imperial Eagle

Postage in various styles

Abbreviation   Abbreviation   Russia
for Kopeck   for Ruble

Abbreviation for Russian Soviet Federated Socialist Republic
RSFSR stamps were overprinted (see below)

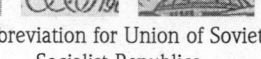

Abbreviation for Union of Soviet Socialist Republics

This item is footnoted in Latvia

RUSSIA - Army of the North

"OKCA"

RUSSIA - Wenden

RUSSIAN OFFICES IN THE TURKISH EMPIRE

These letters appear on other stamps of the Russian offices.

The unoverprinted version of this stamp and a similar stamp were overprinted by various countries (see below).

ARMENIA

BELARUS

FAR EASTERN REPUBLIC

Country Name

SOUTH RUSSIA

Country Name

FINLAND

Circles and Dots on stamps similar to Imperial Russia issues

BATUM

Forms of Country Name

TRANSCAUCASIAN FEDERATED REPUBLICS

Abbreviation for Country Name

KAZAKHSTAN

Country Name

KYRGYZSTAN

Country Name

ROMANIA

TADJIKISTAN

Country Name & Abbreviation

UKRAINE

Country Name in various forms

The trident appears on many stamps, usually as an overprint.

Abbreviation for Ukrainian Soviet Socialist Republic

WESTERN UKRAINE

Abbreviation for Country Name

AZERBAIJAN

AZƏRBAYCAN

Country Name

Abbreviation for Azerbaijan Soviet Socialist Republic

MONTENEGRO

ЦРНА ГОРА

Country Name in various forms

Abbreviation for country name

No country name (A similar Montenegro stamp without country name has same vignette.)

SERBIA

СРБИЈА

Country Name in various forms

Abbreviation for country name

No country name

YUGOSLAVIA

Showing country name

No Country Name

MACEDONIA

МАКЕДОНИЈА

МАКЕДОНИЈА

Country Name

МАКЕДОНСКИ

Different form of Country Name

BULGARIA

Country Name   Postage

Stotinka

Stotinki (plural)   Abbreviation for
                    Stotinki

Country Name in various forms and styles

No country name

 Abbreviation for
Lev, leva

MONGOLIA

ШУУДАН   ТӨГРӨГ

Country name in   Tugrik in Cyrillic
one word

МОНГОЛ   МӨНГӨ
ШУУДАН

Country name in   Mung in Cyrillic
two words

Mung
in Mongolian

Tugrik
in Mongolian

Arms

No Country Name

value priced **stockbooks**

Stockbooks are a classic and convenient storage alternative for many collectors. These German-made stockbooks feature heavyweight archival quality paper with 9 pockets on each page. The 8½" x 11⅝" pages are bound inside a handsome leatherette grain cover and include glassine interleaving between the pages for added protection. The Value Priced Stockbooks are available in two page styles, the white page stockbooks feature glassine pockets while the black page variety includes clear acetate pockets

WHITE PAGE STOCKBOOKS GLASSINE POCKETS

BLACK PAGE STOCKBOOKS ACETATE POCKETS

ITEM	COLOR	PAGES	RETAIL
ST16RD	Red	16 pages	$9.95
ST16GR	Green	16 pages	$9.95
ST16BL	Blue	16 pages	$9.95
ST16BK	Black	16 pages	$9.95
ST32RD	Red	32 pages	$14.95
ST32GR	Green	32 pages	$14.95
ST32BL	Blue	32 pages	$14.95
ST32BK	Black	32 pages	$14.95
ST64RD	Red	64 pages	$27.95
ST64GR	Green	64 pages	$27.95
ST64BL	Blue	64 pages	$27.95
ST64BK	Black	64 pages	$27.95

ITEM	DESCRIPTION		RETAIL
SW16BL	Blue	16 pages	$5.95
SW16GR	Green	16 pages	$5.95
SW16RD	Red	16 pages	$5.95

Scott Value Priced Stockbooks are available from your favorite dealer or direct from:

SCOTT
P.O. Box 828
Sidney OH 45365-0828
www.amosadvantage.com
1-800-572-6885

AMOS
HOBBY PUBLISHING

*The black page stockbook is available in three sizes:
16 pages
32 pages
64 pages.*

Index and Identifier

Pronunciation Symbols

ə .... banana, collide, abut

ˈə, ˌə .... humdrum, abut

ə .... immediately preceding \l\, \n\, \m\, \ŋ\, as in battle, mitten, eaten, and sometimes open \ˈō-pᵊm\, lock and key \-ᵊŋ-\; immediately following \l\, \m\, \r\, as often in French table, prisme, titre

ər .... further, merger, bird

ˈər-
ˈə-r } .... as in two different pronunciations of hurry \ˈhər-ē, ˈhə-rē\

a .... mat, map, mad, gag, snap, patch

ā .... day, fade, date, aorta, drape, cape

ä .... bother, cot, and, with most American speakers, father, cart

à .... father as pronounced by speakers who do not rhyme it with bother; French patte

au̇ .... now, loud, out

b .... baby, rib

ch .... chin, nature \ˈnā-chər\

d .... did, adder

e .... bet, bed, peck

ˈē, ˌē .... beat, nosebleed, evenly, easy

ē .... easy, mealy

f .... fifty, cuff

g .... go, big, gift

h .... hat, ahead

hw .... whale as pronounced by those who do not have the same pronunciation for both whale and wail

i .... tip, banish, active

ī .... site, side, buy, tripe

j .... job, gem, edge, join, judge

k .... kin, cook, ache

k̲ .... German ich, Buch; one pronunciation of loch

l .... lily, pool

m .... murmur, dim, nymph

n .... no, own

ⁿ .... indicates that a preceding vowel or diphthong is pronounced with the nasal passages open, as in French un bon vin blanc \œ̃ⁿ-bōⁿ-vaⁿ-bläⁿ\

ŋ .... sing \ˈsiŋ\, singer \ˈsiŋ-ər\, finger \ˈfiŋ-gər\, ink \ˈiŋk\

ō .... bone, know, beau

ȯ .... saw, all, gnaw, caught

œ .... French boeuf, German Hölle

œ̄ .... French feu, German Höhle

ȯi .... coin, destroy

p .... pepper, lip

r .... red, car, rarity

s .... source, less

sh .... as in shy, mission, machine, special (actually, this is a single sound, not two); with a hyphen between, two sounds as in grasshopper \ˈgras-ˌhä-pər\

t .... tie, attack, late, later, latter

th .... as in thin, ether (actually, this is a single sound, not two); with a hyphen between, two sounds as in knighthood \ˈnīt-ˌhu̇d\

t̲h̲ .... then, either, this (actually, this is a single sound, not two)

ü .... rule, youth, union \ˈyün-yən\, few \ˈfyü\

u̇ .... pull, wood, book, curable \ˈkyu̇r-ə-bəl\, fury \ˈfyu̇r-ē\

ue .... German füllen, hübsch

ūe .... French rue, German fühlen

v .... vivid, give

w .... we, away

y .... yard, young, cue \ˈkyü\, mute \ˈmyüt\, union \ˈyün-yən\

ʸ .... indicates that during the articulation of the sound represented by the preceding character the front of the tongue has substantially the position it has for the articulation of the first sound of yard, as in French digne \dēnʸ\

z .... zone, raise

zh .... as in vision, azure \ˈa-zhər\ (actually, this is a single sound, not two); with a hyphen between, two sounds as in hogshead \ˈhȯgz-ˌhed, ˈhägz-\

\ .... slant line used in pairs to mark the beginning and end of a transcription: \ˈpen\

ˈ .... mark preceding a syllable with primary (strongest) stress: \ˈpen-mən-ˌship\

ˌ .... mark preceding a syllable with secondary (medium) stress: \ˈpen-mən-ˌship\

- .... mark of syllable division

( ) .... indicate that what is symbolized between is present in some utterances but not in others: factory \ˈfak-t(ə-)rē\

÷ .... indicates that many regard as unacceptable the pronunciation variant immediately following: cupola \ˈkyü-pə-lə, ÷-ˌlō\

2003
VOLUME 1
DEALER DIRECTORY
YELLOW PAGE LISTINGS

This section of your Scott Catalogue contains advertisements to help you conveniently find what you need, when you need it...!

Accessories

**BROOKLYN GALLERY COIN &
STAMP**
8725 4th Avenue
Brooklyn, NY 11209
718-745-5701
718-745-2775 Fax
Email: info@brooklyngallery.com
Web: www.brooklyngallery.com

Appraisals

CONNEXUS
P.O. Box 819
Snow Camp, NC 27349
336-376-8207 Phone/Fax
Email: Connexus1@world.att.net

RANDY SCHOLL STAMP CO.
Southhampton Square
7460 Jager Court
Cincinnati, OH 45230-4344
513-624-6800
Email: randyscholl@fuse.net

Approvals-Personalized
WW & U.S.

THE KEEPING ROOM
P.O. Box 257
Trumbull, CT 06611
203-372-8436

Asia

**HENRY GITNER PHILATELISTS,
INC.**
P.O. Box 3077-S
Middletown, NY 10940
845-343-5151 or 800-947-8267
845-343-0068 Fax
Email: hgitner@hgitner.com
Web: www.hgitner.com

MICHAEL ROGERS, INC.
199 E. Welbourne Ave.
Suite 3
Winter Park, FL 32789
407-644-2290 or 800-843-3751
407-645-4434 Fax
Email: mrogersinc@aol.com
Web: www.michaelrogersinc.com

Auctions

DANIEL F. KELLEHER CO., INC.
24 Farnsworth Street
Suite 605
Boston, MA 02210
617-443-0033
617-443-0789 Fax

JACQUES C. SCHIFF, JR., INC.
195 Main Street
Ridgefield Park, NJ 07660
201-641-5566
From NYC: 662-2777
201-641-5705 Fax

SAM HOUSTON PHILATELICS
13310 Westheimer #150
Houston, TX 77077
281-493-6386 or 800-231-5926
281-496-1445 Fax
Email: shduck@aol.com
Web: www.shduck.com

**STAMP CENTER/DUTCH
COUNTRY AUCTIONS**
4115 Concord Pike
Wilmington, DE 19803
302-478-8740
302-478-8779 Fax
Email: scdca@dol.net
Web: www.thestampcenter.com

SUBURBAN STAMP INC.
176 Worthington Street
Springfield, MA 01103
413-785-5348
413-746-3788 Fax
Email:
suburbanstamp@earthlink.net

Auctions - Mail Bid

DALE ENTERPRISES INC.
P.O. Box 539-C
Emmaus, PA 18049
610-433-3303
610-965-6089 Fax
Email: daleent@fast.net
Web: www.dalestamps.com

SUBURBAN STAMP INC.
176 Worthington Street
Springfield, MA 01103
413-785-5348
413-746-3788 Fax
Email:
suburbanstamp@earthlink.net

Auctions-Public

ALAN BLAIR STAMPS/AUCTIONS
5407 Lakeside Ave.
Suite 4
Richmond, VA 23228
800-689-5602 Phone/Fax
Email: alanblair@prodigy.net

Auctions-Public

SUBURBAN STAMP INC.
176 Worthington Street
Springfield, MA 01103
413-785-5348
413-746-3788 Fax
Email:
suburbanstamp@earthlink.net

Australia

COLONIAL STAMP COMPANY
5757 Wilshire Blvd. PH #8
Los Angeles, CA 90036
323-933-9435
323-939-9930 Fax
Email: gwh225@aol.com
Web: www.colonialstamps.com

Austria

AMEEN STAMPS
8831 Long Point Road, Suite 204
Houston, TX 77055
713-468-0644
713-468-2420 Fax
Email: rameen@ev1.net

**HENRY GITNER PHILATELISTS,
INC.**
P.O. Box 3077-S
Middletown, NY 10940
845-343-5151 or 800-947-8267
845-343-0068 Fax
Email: hgitner@hgitner.com
Web: www.hgitner.com

Austria

JOSEPH EDER
P.O. Box 185529
Hamden, CT 06518
203-281-0742
203-230-2410 Fax
Email: j.eder@worldnet.att.net
Web: www.ederstamps.com

Bahamas

COLONIAL STAMP COMPANY
5757 Wilshire Blvd. PH #8
Los Angeles, CA 90036
323-933-9435
323-939-9930 Fax
Email: gwh225@aol.com
Web: www.colonialstamps.com

Bangkok

COLONIAL STAMP COMPANY
5757 Wilshire Blvd. PH #8
Los Angeles, CA 90036
323-933-9435
323-939-9930 Fax
Email: gwh225@aol.com
Web: www.colonialstamps.com

Barbados

COLONIAL STAMP COMPANY
5757 Wilshire Blvd. PH #8
Los Angeles, CA 90036
323-933-9435
323-939-9930 Fax
Email: gwh225@aol.com
Web: www.colonialstamps.com

China

MICHAEL ROGERS, INC.
199 E. Welbourne Ave.
Suite 3
Winter Park, FL 32789
407-644-2290 or 800-843-3751
407-645-4434 Fax
Email: mrogersinc@aol.com
Web: www.michaelrogersinc.com

China - Expertising

EXPERTS & CONSULTANTS LTD.
Dr. Shiu - Hon Chan & Mr. K.L.
Poon
P.O. Box 9840
General Post Office
HONG KONG
852-2519-6510 Fax
Email: poonchan@netvigator.com

China - Imperial

TREASURE-HUNTERS LTD.
G.P.O. Box 11446
HONG KONG
+852-2507-3773 or +852-2507-
5770
+852-2519-6820 Fax
Email: thunters@netvigator.com
Web: www.treasure-hunters.com.hk

Conservation Stamps

SAM HOUSTON DUCK CO.
P.O. Box 820087
Houston, TX 77282
281-493-6386 or 800-231-5926
281-496-1445 Fax
Email: shduck@aol.com
Web: www.shduck.com

Ducks

MICHAEL JAFFE
P.O. Box 61484
Vancouver, WA 98666
360-695-6161 or 800-782-6770
360-695-1616 Fax
Email:
mjaffe@brookmanstamps.com
Web: www.brookmanstamps.com

SAM HOUSTON DUCK CO.
P.O. Box 820087
Houston, TX 77282
281-493-6386 or 800-231-5926
281-496-1445 Fax
Email: shduck@aol.com
Web: www.shduck.com

Ducks - Foreign

METROPOLITAN STAMP CO., INC.
P.O. Box 1133
Chicago, IL 60690-1133
815-439-0142
815-439-0143 Fax

Errors, Freaks & Oddities

SAM HOUSTON PHILATELICS
13310 Westheimer #150
Houston, TX 77077
281-493-6386 or 800-231-5926
281-496-1445
Email: shduck@aol.com
Web: www.shduck.com

France

JOSEPH EDER
P.O. Box 185529
Hamden, CT 06518
203-281-0742
203-230-2410 Fax
Email: j.eder@worldnet.att.net
Web: www.ederstamps.com

German Colonies

COLONIAL STAMP COMPANY
$1 million - photo price list,
$5.00
(refundable against purchase)
5757 Wilshire Blvd. PH #8
Los Angeles, CA 90036
323-933-9435
323-939-9930 Fax
Email: gwh225@aol.com
Web: www.colonialstamps.com

JOSEPH EDER
P.O. Box 185529
Hamden, CT 06518
203-281-0742
203-230-2410 Fax
Email: j.eder@worldnet.att.net
Web: www.ederstamps.com

German Occupation

JOSEPH EDER
P.O. Box 185529
Hamden, CT 06518
203-281-0742
203-230-2410 Fax
Email: j.eder@worldnet.att.net
Web: www.ederstamps.com

Germany

JOSEPH EDER
P.O. Box 185529
Hamden, CT 06518
203-281-0742
203-230-2410 Fax
Email: j.eder@worldnet.att.net
Web: www.ederstamps.com

Germany- Third Reich

JOSEPH EDER
P.O. Box 185529
Hamden, CT 06518
203-281-0742
203-230-2410 Fax
Email: j.eder@worldnet.att.net
Web: www.ederstamps.com

Great Britain

COLONIAL STAMP COMPANY
5757 Wilshire Blvd. PH #8
Los Angeles, CA 90036
323-933-9435
323-939-9930 Fax
Email: gwh225@aol.com
Web: www.colonialstamps.com

Insurance

COLLECTIBLES INSURANCE AGENCY
P.O. Box 1200 SSC
Westminster, MD 21158
888-837-9537
410-876-9233 Fax
Email:
info@insurecollectibles.com
Web: www.collectinsure.com

Japan

MICHAEL ROGERS, INC.
199 E. Welbourne Ave.
Suite 3
Winter Park, FL 32789
407-644-2290 or 800-843-3751
407-645-4434 Fax
Email: mrogersinc@aol.com
Web: www.michaelrogersinc.com

Korea

MICHAEL ROGERS, INC.
199 E. Welbourne Ave.
Suite 3
Winter Park, FL 32789
407-644-2290 or 800-843-3751
407-645-4434 Fax
Email: mrogersinc@aol.com
Web: www.michaelrogersinc.com

Latin America

GUY SHAW
P.O. Box 10025
Bakersfield, CA 93389
661-834-7135 Phone/Fax
Email: guyshaw@guyshaw.com
Web: www.guyshaw.com

Lots & Collections

DR. ROBERT FRIEDMAN & SONS
2029 West 75th Street
Woodridge, IL 60517
630-985-1515
630-985-1588 Fax

Mail Order

ALMAZ STAMP CO., DEPT. VY
P.O. Box 100-812
Vanderveer Station
Brooklyn, NY 11210
718-241-6360 Phone/Fax

Manchukuo

MICHAEL ROGERS, INC.
199 E. Welbourne Ave.
Suite 3
Winter Park, FL 32789
407-644-2290 or 800-843-3751
407-645-4434 Fax
Email: mrogersinc@aol.com
Web: www.michaelrogersinc.com

New Issues

DALE ENTERPRISES INC.
P.O. Box 539-C
Emmaus, PA 18049
610-433-3303
610-965-6089 Fax
Email: daleent@fast.net
Web: www.dalestamps.com

DAVIDSON'S STAMP SERVICE
P.O. Box 36355
Indianapolis, IN 46236-0355
317-826-2620
Email: davidson@in.net
Web: www.newstampissues.com

New Issues- Retail

BOMBAY PHILATELIC INC.
P.O. Box 480009
Delray Beach, FL 33448
561-499-7990
561-499-7553 Fax
Email: sales@bombaystamps.com
Web: www.bombaystamps.com

New Issues- Wholesale

BOMBAY PHILATELIC INC.
P.O. Box 480009
Delray Beach, FL 33448
561-499-7990
561-499-7553 Fax
Email: sales@bombaystamps.com
Web: www.bombaystamps.com

Philatelic Literature

LEWIS KAUFMAN
P.O. Box 255
Kiamesha Lake, NY 12751
845-794-8013 Phone/Fax
800-491-5453 Phone/Fax
Email: mamet1@aol.com

Publications - Collector

AMERICAN PHILATELIC SOCIETY
Dept. TZ
P.O. Box 8000
State College, PA 16803
814-237-3803
814-237-6128 Fax
Email: flsente@stamps.org
Web: www.stamps.org

South America

GUY SHAW
P.O. Box 10025
Bakersfield, CA 93389
661-834-7135 Phone/Fax
Email: guyshaw@guyshaw.com
Web: www.guyshaw.com

Stamp Shows

ATLANTIC COAST EXHIBITIONS
Division of Beach Philatelics
42 Baltimore Lane
Palm Coast, FL 32137-8850
386-445-4550
386-447-0811 Fax
Email: mrstamp2@aol.com
Web: www.beachphilatelics.com

STAMP STORES

Arizona

B.J.'S STAMPS
Barbara J. Johnson
6342 W. Bell Road
Glendale, AZ 85308
623-878-2080
623-412-3456 Fax
Email: info@bjstamps.com
Web: www.bjstamps.com

California

ASHTREE STAMP & COIN
2410 N. Blackstone
Fresno, CA 93703
559-227-7167

BROSIUS STAMP & COIN
2105 Main Street
Santa Monica, CA 90405
310-396-7480
310-396-7455 Fax

COLONIAL STAMP CO./BRITISH EMPIRE SPECIALIST
5757 Wilshire Blvd. PH #8 (by appt.)
Los Angeles, CA 90036
323-933-9435
323-939-9930 Fax
Email: gwh225@aol.com
Web: www.colonialstamps.com

California

NATICK STAMPS & HOBBIES
405 S. Myrtle Avenue
Monrovia, CA 91016
626-305-7333
626-305-7335 Fax
Email: natickco@earthlink.net
Web: www.natickco.com

STANLEY M. PILLER
3351 Grand Avenue
Oakland, CA 94610
510-465-8290
510-465-7121 Fax
Email: stmpdlr@aol.com

Colorado

ACKLEY'S STAMPS
3230 N. Stone Avenue
Colorado Springs, CO 80907
719-633-1153

SHOWCASE STAMPS
3865 Wadsworth
Wheat Ridge, CO 80033
303-425-9252
Email: kbeiner@colbi.net

STAMP STORES

Connecticut

MILLER'S STAMP SHOP
41 New London Turnpike
Uncasville, CT 06382
860-848-0468
860-848-1926 Fax
Email: millstamps@aol.com
Web: www.millerstamps.com

SILVER CITY COIN & STAMP
41 Colony Street
Meriden, CT 06451
203-235-7634
203-237-4915 Fax

Florida

BEACH PHILATELICS
Daytona Flea Market (Fri-Sun)
I 95 Exit 87 (Tamoka Farms Rd.)
Corner Shoppes Bldg. - Booths 70-72
Daytona Beach, FL 32119
386-503-6598

CORBIN STAMP & COIN, INC.
108 West Robertson Street
Brandon, FL 33511
813-651-3266

Florida

R.D.C. STAMPS
7381 SW 24th Street
Miami, FL 33155-1402
305-264-4213
305-262-2919 Fax
Email: rdcstamps@aol.com

SUN COAST STAMP CO.
3231 Gulf Gate Drive
Suite 102
Sarasota, FL 34231
941-921-9761 or 800-927-3351
941-921-1762 Fax
Email: suncoaststamp@aol.com

WINTER PARK STAMP SHOP
Ranch Mall (17-92)
325 S. Orlando Ave.
Suite 1-2
Winter Park, FL 32789-3608
407-628-1120 or 800-845-1819
407-628-0091 Fax
Email: jim@winterparkstampshop.com
Web: www.winterparkstampshop.com

Georgia

STAMPS UNLIMITED OF GEORGIA
133 Carnegie Way
Room 250
Atlanta, GA 30303
404-688-9161

Illinois

DON CLARK'S STAMPS & COINS
937 1/2 W. Galena Blvd.
Aurora, IL 60506
630-896-4606

DR. ROBERT FRIEDMAN & SONS
2029 West 75th Street
Woodridge, IL 60517
630-985-1515
630-985-1588 Fax

STAMP STORES

Indiana

KNIGHT STAMP & COIN CO.
237 Main Street
Hobart, IN 46342
219-942-4341 or 800-634-2646
Email: knight@knightcoin.com
Web: www.knightcoin.com

Kentucky

COLLECTORS STAMPS LTD.
4012 Dupont Circle #313
Louisville, KY 40207
502-897-9045
Email: csl@aye.net

Maryland

BALTIMORE COIN & STAMP EXCHANGE
10194 Baltimore National Pike
Unit 104
Ellicott City, MD 21042
410-418-8282
410-418-4813 Fax

BULLDOG STAMP COMPANY
4641 Montgomery Avenue
Bethesda, MD 20814
301-654-1138

Massachusetts

KAPPY'S COINS & STAMPS
534 Washington Street
Norwood, MA 02062
781-762-5552
781-762-3292 Fax
Email: kappyscoins@aol.com

SUBURBAN STAMP INC.
176 Worthington Street
Springfield, MA 01103
413-785-5348
413-746-3788 Fax
Email: suburbanstamp@earthlink.net

Michigan

THE MOUSE AND SUCH
696 N. Mill Street
Plymouth, MI 48170
734-454-1515

STAMP STORES

New Jersey

AALLSTAMPS
38 N. Main Street
P.O. Box 249
Milltown, NJ 08850
732-247-1093
732-247-1094 Fax
Email: mail@aallstamps.com
Web: www.aallstamps.com

BERGEN STAMPS & COLLECTIBLES
717 American Legion Drive
Teaneck, NJ 07666
201-836-8987

RON RITZER STAMPS INC.
Millburn Mall
2933 Vauxhall Road
Vauxhall, NJ 07088
908-687-0007
908-687-0795 Fax
Email: ritzerstamps@earthlink.net

TRENTON STAMP & COIN CO.
Thomas DeLuca
Store: Forest Glen Plaza
1804 Route 33
Hamilton Square, NJ 08690
Mail: P.O. Box 8574
Trenton, NJ 08650
800-446-8664
609-587-8664 Fax

New York

CHAMPION STAMP CO., INC.
432 West 54th Street
New York, NY 10019
212-489-8130
212-581-8130 Fax
Email: championstamp@aol.com
Web: www.championstamp.com

Ohio

FEDERAL COIN & STAMP EXCHANGE
P.O. Box 14579
401 Euclid Ave.
Suite 45
Cleveland, OH 44114
216-861-1160
216-861-5960 Fax

STAMP STORES

Ohio

HILLTOP STAMP SERVICE
Richard A. Peterson
P.O. Box 626
Wooster, OH 44691
330-262-8907 or 330-262-5378
Email: hilltop@bright.net

THE LINK STAMP CO.
3461 E. Livingston Ave.
Columbus, OH 43227
614-237-4125 Phone/Fax
800-546-5726 Phone/Fax

Pennsylvania

LARRY LEE STAMPS
322 S. Front Street
Greater Harrisburg Area
Wormleysburg, PA 17043
717-763-7605
Email: llstamps1@aol.com

PHILLY STAMP & COIN CO., INC.
1804 Chestnut Street
Philadelphia, PA 19103
215-563-7341
215-563-7382 Fax
Email: phillysc@netreach.net
Web:
www.phillystampandcoin.com

Tennessee

HERRON HILL, INC.
5007 Black Road
Suite 140
Memphis, TN 38117
901-683-9644

Texas

SAM HOUSTON PHILATELICS
13310 Westheimer #150
Houston, TX 77077
281-493-6386 or 800-231-5926
281-496-1445
Email: shduck@aol.com
Web: www.shduck.com

Virginia

KENNEDY'S STAMPS & COINS
7059 Brookfield Plaza
Springfield, VA 22150
703-569-7300
703-569-7644 Fax
Email: kennedy@patriot.net

LATHEROW & CO., INC.
5054 Lee Hwy.
Arlington, VA 22207
703-538-2727 or 800-647-4624
703-538-5210 Fax

Washington

TACOMA MALL BLVD. COIN & STAMP
5225 Tacoma Mall Blvd. E101
Tacoma, WA 98409
253-472-9632
253-472-8948 Fax
Email: kfeldman01@sprynet.com
Web: www.tmbcoinandstamp.com

Wisconsin

JIM LUKES' STAMP & COIN
815 Jay Street
P.O. Box 1780
Manitowoc, WI 54221
920-682-2324 Phone/Fax

Supplies

GOPHER SUPPLY
2525 Nevada Ave. N
Suite 102
Minneapolis, MN 55427
800-815-3868 or 763-525-1750
763-544-4683 Fax
Web: www.gophersupply.com

Topicals

MINI-ARTS
P.O. Box 457
Estherville, IA 51334
712-362-4710
Email: pmga@rconnect.com
Web:
www.ebaystores.com/miniarts

Topicals - Columbus

MR. COLUMBUS
Box 1492
Fennville, MI 49408
616-543-4755
616-543-3507 Fax
Email: columbus@accn.org

Topicals - Miscellaneous

BOMBAY PHILATELIC INC.
P.O. Box 480009
Delray Beach, FL 33448
561-499-7990
561-499-7553 Fax
Email: sales@bombaystamps.com
Web: www.bombaystamps.com

Ukraine

MR. VAL ZABIJAKA
P.O. Box 3711
Silver Spring, MD 20918
301-593-5316 Phone/Fax
Email: bnm123@erols.com

United States

BROOKMAN STAMP CO.
P.O. Box 90
Vancouver, WA 98666
360-695-1391 or 800-545-4871
360-695-1616 Fax
Email:
dave@brookmanstamps.com
Web: www.brookmanstamps.com

United States

DALE ENTERPRISES INC.
P.O. Box 539-C
Emmaus, PA 18049
610-433-3303
610-965-6089 Fax
Email: daleent@fast.net
Web: www.dalestamps.com

DR. ROBERT FRIEDMAN & SONS
2029 West 75th Street
Woodridge, IL 60517
630-985-1515
630-985-1588 Fax

GARY POSNER
1407 Avenue Z, PMB #535
Brooklyn, NY 11235
800-323-4279
718-241-2801 Fax
Email: garyposnerinc@aol.com
Web: www.garyposnerinc.com
    www.gemstamps.com

HENRY GITNER PHILATELISTS, INC.
P.O. Box 3077-S
Middletown, NY 10940
845-343-5151 or 800-947-8267
845-343-0068 Fax
Email: hgitner@hgitner.com
Web: www.hgitner.com

WULFF'S STAMPS
P.O. Box 661746
Sacramento, CA 95866
800-884-0656 Phone/Fax
916-489-0656 Phone/Fax
Email: service@wulffstamps.com
Web: www.wulffstamps.com

U.S. - Booklets

DALE ENTERPRISES INC.
P.O. Box 539-C
Emmaus, PA 18049
610-433-3303
610-965-6089 Fax
Email: daleent@fast.net
Web: www.dalestamps.com

LEWIS KAUFMAN
P.O. Box 255
Kiamesha Lake, NY 12751
845-794-8013 Phone/Fax
800-491-5453 Phone/Fax
Email: mamet1@aol.com

U.S. - Classics

DALE ENTERPRISES INC.
P.O. Box 539-C
Emmaus, PA 18049
610-433-3303
610-965-6089 Fax
Email: daleent@fast.net
Web: dalestamps.com

GARY POSNER
1407 Avenue Z, PMB #535
Brooklyn, NY 11235
800-323-4279
718-241-2801 Fax
Email: garyposnerinc@aol.com
Web: www.garyposnerinc.com
    www.gemstamps.com

SUBURBAN STAMP INC.
176 Worthington Street
Springfield, MA 01103
413-785-5348
413-746-3788 Fax
Email:
suburbanstamp@earthlink.net

U.S. - Collections Wanted

SUBURBAN STAMP INC.
176 Worthington Street
Springfield, MA 01103
413-785-5348
413-746-3788 Fax
Email:
suburbanstamp@earthlink.net

U.S. - Errors, Freaks & Oddities

GARY POSNER
1407 Avenue Z, PMB #535
Brooklyn, NY 11235
800-323-4279
718-241-2801 Fax
Email: garyposnerinc@aol.com
Web: www.garyposnerinc.com
    www.gemstamps.com

SUBURBAN STAMP INC.
176 Worthington Street
Springfield, MA 01103
413-785-5348
413-746-3788 Fax
Email:
suburbanstamp@earthlink.net

U.S. - Federal Duck Stamps

METROPOLITAN STAMP CO., INC.
P.O. Box 1133
Chicago, IL 60690-1133
815-439-0142
815-439-0143 Fax

SAM HOUSTON DUCK CO.
P.O. Box 820087
Houston, TX 77282
281-493-6386 or 800-231-5926
281-496-1445 Fax
Email: shduck@aol.com
Web: www.shduck.com

U.S. - Plate Blocks

GARY POSNER
1407 Avenue Z, PMB #535
Brooklyn, NY 11235
800-323-4279
718-241-2801 Fax
Email: garyposnerinc@aol.com
Web: www.garyposnerinc.com
    www.gemstamps.com

LEWIS KAUFMAN
P.O. Box 255
Kiamesha Lake, NY 12751
845-794-8013 Phone/Fax
800-491-5453 Phone/Fax
Email: mamet1@aol.com

U.S. - Postal History

LEWIS KAUFMAN
P.O. Box 255
Kiamesha Lake, NY 12751
845-794-8013 Phone/Fax
800-491-5453 Phone/Fax
Email: mamet1@aol.com

U.S. - Postal Stationery

LEWIS KAUFMAN
P.O. Box 255
Kiamesha Lake, NY 12751
845-794-8013 Phone/Fax
800-491-5453 Phone/Fax
Email: mamet1@aol.com

U.S. - Price Lists

DALE ENTERPRISES INC.
P.O. Box 539-C
Emmaus, PA 18049
610-433-3303
610-965-6089 Fax
Email: daleent@fast.net
Web: www.dalestamps.com

U.S. - Price Lists

ROBERT E. BARKER
P.O. Box 1100
Warren, ME 04864
207-273-6200 or 800-833-0217
207-273-4254 or 888-325-5158
Email: rebarker@rebarker.com
Web: www.rebarker.com

U.S. - Proofs & Essays

LEWIS KAUFMAN
P.O. Box 255
Kiamesha Lake, NY 12751
845-794-8013 Phone/Fax
800-491-5453 Phone/Fax
Email: mamet1@aol.com

U.S. - Proofs & Essays

SUBURBAN STAMP INC.
176 Worthington Street
Springfield, MA 01103
413-785-5348
413-746-3788 Fax
Email:
suburbanstamp@earthlink.net

U.S. - Rare Stamps

GARY POSNER
1407 Avenue Z, PMB #535
Brooklyn, NY 11235
800-323-4279
718-241-2801 Fax
Email: garyposnerinc@aol.com
Web: www.garyposnerinc.com
www.gemstamps.com

SUBURBAN STAMP INC.
176 Worthington Street
Springfield, MA 01103
413-785-5348
413-746-3788 Fax
Email:
suburbanstamp@earthlink.net

U.S. - Souvenir Cards

LEWIS KAUFMAN
P.O. Box 255
Kiamesha Lake, NY 12751
845-794-8013 Phone/Fax
800-491-5453 Phone/Fax
Email: mamet1@aol.com

U.S. - Souvenir Pages/Panels

LEWIS KAUFMAN
P.O. Box 255
Kiamesha Lake, NY 12751
845-794-8013 Phone/Fax
800-491-5453 Phone/Fax
Email: mamet1@aol.com

U.S. - State Duck Stamps

SAM HOUSTON DUCK CO.
P.O. Box 820087
Houston, TX 77282
281-493-6386 or 800-231-5926
281-496-1445 Fax
Email: shduck@aol.com
Web: www.shduck.com

U.S. - Transportation Coils

DALE ENTERPRISES INC.
P.O. Box 539-C
Emmaus, PA 18049
610-433-3303
610-965-6089 Fax
Email: daleent@fast.net
Web: www.dalestamps.com

U.S. - Used

LEWIS KAUFMAN
P.O. Box 255
Kiamesha Lake, NY 12751
845-794-8013 Phone/Fax
800-491-5453 Phone/Fax
Email: mamet1@aol.com

Want Lists

BROOKMAN INTERNATIONAL
P.O. Box 450
Vancouver, WA 98666
360-695-1391 or 800-545-4871
360-695-1616 Fax
Email:
dave@brookmanstamps.com

CHARLES P. SCHWARTZ
P.O. Box 165
Mora, MN 55051
320-679-4705
Email: charlesp@ecenet.com

Want Lists- British Empire 1840-1935 German Col./Offices

COLONIAL STAMP COMPANY
5757 Wilshire Blvd. PH #8
Los Angeles, CA 90036
323-933-9435
323-939-9930 Fax
Email: gwh225@aol.com
Web: www.colonialstamps.com

Want Lists - U.S.

GARY POSNER
1407 Avenue Z, PMB #535
Brooklyn, NY 11235
800-323-4279
718-241-2801 Fax
Email: garyposnerinc@aol.com
Web: www.garyposnerinc.com
www.gemstamps.com

Wanted – U.S. Collections

SUBURBAN STAMP INC.
176 Worthington Street
Springfield, MA 01103
413-785-5348
413-746-3788 Fax
Email:
suburbanstamp@earthlink.net

Wanted - Estates

DALE ENTERPRISES INC.
P.O. Box 539-C
Emmaus, PA 18049
610-433-3303
610-965-6089 Fax
Email: daleent@fast.net
Web: www.dalestamps.com

SUBURBAN STAMP INC.
176 Worthington Street
Springfield, MA 01103
413-785-5348
413-746-3788 Fax
Email:
suburbanstamp@earthlink.net

Wanted - Worldwide Collections

DR. ROBERT FRIEDMAN & SONS
2029 West 75th Street
Woodridge, IL 60517
630-985-1515
630-985-1588 Fax

Wanted - Worldwide Collections

SUBURBAN STAMP INC.
176 Worthington Street
Springfield, MA 01103
413-785-5348
413-746-3788 Fax
Email:
suburbanstamp@earthlink.net

Wanted - U.S.

GARY POSNER
1407 Avenue Z, PMB #535
Brooklyn, NY 11235
800-323-4279
718-241-2801 Fax
Email: garyposnerinc@aol.com
Web: www.garyposnerinc.com
www.gemstamps.com

JAMES J. REEVES, INC.
P.O. Box 219
Huntingdon, PA 16652
800-364-2948 Ext. 302
814-641-2600 Fax
Email: Reeves5@vicon.net
Web: www.jamesjreeves.com
For Supplies: 888-574-6229 or
www.supplies.fromjjr.com

SUBURBAN STAMP INC.
176 Worthington Street
Springfield, MA 01103
413-785-5348
413-746-3788 Fax
Email:
suburbanstamp@earthlink.net

Wholesale -U.S.

GARY POSNER
1407 Avenue Z, PMB #535
Brooklyn, NY 11235
800-323-4279
718-241-2801 Fax
Email: garyposnerinc@aol.com
Web: www.garyposnerinc.com
www.gemstamps.com

Worldwide-Collections

BOB & MARTHA FRIEDMAN
624 Homestead Place
Joliet, IL 60435
815-725-6666
815-725-4134 Fax

DR. ROBERT FRIEDMAN & SONS
2029 West 75th Street
Woodridge, IL 60517
630-985-1515
630-985-1588 Fax

Worldwide-Year Sets

BOMBAY PHILATELIC INC.
P.O. Box 480009
Delray Beach, FL 33448
561-499-7990
561-499-7553 Fax
Email: sales@bombaystamps.com
Web: www.bombaystamps.com

WALLACE STAMPS
Box 82
Port Washington, NY 11050
516-883-5578